YEARBOOK OF THE UNITED NATIONS 2006

Volume 60

YEARBOOK OF THE UNITED NATIONS, 2006

Volume 60 Sales No. E.08.I.1 H

Prepared by the Yearbook Unit of the Publications and Editorial Cluster of the Department of Public Information, United Nations, New York. Although the *Yearbook* is based on official sources, it is not an official record.

Chief Editor: Peter Jackson

Senior Editors: Edoardo Bellando, Federigo Magherini, Jullyette Ukabiala

Editors/Writers: Ehud Bell, Judith Gehler, Lawri Moore, John R. Sebesta

Contributing Editor: Kathryn Gordon

Contributing Writers: Luisa Balacco, Jessamy Garver-Affeldt, Maria Carlino, Melisssa Gorelick, Namrita Talwar

Copy Editors: Sunita Chabra, Charlotte Maitre, Herminia Roque, Karen Sholto

Senior Typesetter: Laura Frischeisen

Typesetter: Galina Brazhnikova

Copy Coordinators: Jennifer Payulert, Rodney Pascual, Norma Ibrahim

Administrative Assistant: Carmelita Aquilizan

Editorial Assistant: Beata Gloza

Indexer: David Golante

Jacket Design: Graphic Design Unit

YEARBOOK OF THE UNITED NATIONS 2006

Volume 60

Department of Public Information
United Nations, New York

Yearbook of the United Nations, 2006
Vol. 60
ISBN: 978-92-1-101168-5
ISSN: 0082-8521

UNITED NATIONS PUBLICATIONS
SALES NO. E.08.I.1 H

Printed in the United States

FOREWORD

The United Nations strived throughout 2006 to fulfil its traditional mission of promoting peace, development and human rights. Those efforts spanned a broad spectrum of global concerns, from development to disaster protection, from peace-keeping to humanitarian assistance, from safeguarding the environment to protecting human dignity.

The final year of Secretary-General Kofi Annan's tenure was also one in which the imperative for UN reform remained high on the agenda. The General Assembly undertook a comprehensive review of governance and oversight within the United Nations system, including the funds, programmes and specialized agencies. Two new intergovernmental bodies began work: the Human Rights Council and the Peacebuilding Commission—the former with the aim of strengthening our ability to review the situation of all human rights in all countries, the latter to draw much-needed attention to the critical challenges facing societies recovering from armed conflict. My predecessor, for his part, issued two reports—"Investing in the United Nations" and "Delivering as One"—that sought to provide a blueprint for better managing the Secretariat in carrying out the mandates given to it by the Member States.

This volume chronicles these wide-ranging activities. It depicts an Organization committed to keeping pace with changing times and an evolving global environment. It highlights not only the progress achieved, but also the obstacles that arose. Like previous volumes of the *Yearbook*, this sixtieth volume is a comprehensive and authoritative work of reference. I commend it to scholars, policy-makers and anyone else around the world interested in learning more about the abiding efforts of the United Nations to build a safer, better world for all.

Ban Ki-moon

Secretary-General of the United Nations

New York, May 2009

Contents

FOREWORD by SECRETARY-GENERAL BAN KI-MOON v

ABOUT THE 2006 EDITION OF THE *YEARBOOK* xvi

ABBREVIATIONS COMMONLY USED IN THE *YEARBOOK* xvii

EXPLANATORY NOTE ON DOCUMENTS xviii

REPORT OF THE SECRETARY-GENERAL ON THE WORK OF THE ORGANIZATION 3

Part One: *Political and security questions*

I. INTERNATIONAL PEACE AND SECURITY 45

PROMOTION OF INTERNATIONAL PEACE AND SECURITY, 45: Conflict prevention, 48; Peacemaking and peacebuilding, 53; Special political missions and offices, 63; Roster of special political missions and offices in 2006, 64. THREATS TO INTERNATIONAL PEACE AND SECURITY, 65: International terrorism, 65. PEACEKEEPING OPERATIONS, 77: General aspects of UN peacekeeping, 77; Comprehensive review of peacekeeping, 85; Operations in 2006, 86; Roster of 2006 operations, 87; Financial and administrative aspects of peacekeeping operations, 89.

II. AFRICA 112

PROMOTION OF PEACE IN AFRICA, 114. CENTRAL AFRICA AND GREAT LAKES REGION, 120: Democratic Republic of the Congo, 126; Burundi, 148; Central African Republic, 162; Chad and Central African Republic, 166; Uganda, 168; Rwanda, 171. WEST AFRICA, 172: Regional issues, 173; Côte d'Ivoire, 176; Liberia, 211; Sierra Leone, 230; Guinea-Bissau, 244; Cameroon-Nigeria, 251; Guinea, 253. HORN OF AFRICA, 254: Sudan, 256; Somalia, 301; Eritrea-Ethiopia, 315. NORTH AFRICA, 329: Western Sahara, 329. OTHER ISSUES, 339: Libyan Arab Jamahiriya, 339; Mauritius-United Kingdom/France, 339. Cooperation between the AU and the UN system, 339.

III. AMERICAS 341

CENTRAL AMERICA, 341. HAITI, 342: Political and security situation, 342. OTHER QUESTIONS, 357: Cuba-United States, 357; Cooperation between the United Nations and regional organizations, 359.

IV. ASIA AND THE PACIFIC 361

AFGHANISTAN, 362: Situation in Afghanistan, 362; Sanctions, 381. IRAQ, 389: Situation in Iraq, 389; UN Assistance Mission for Iraq, 394; Multinational force, 402; International Advisory and Monitoring Board, 405; UN Monitoring, Verification and Inspection Commission and IAEA activities, 406. IRAQ-KUWAIT, 409: Oil-for-food programme: high-level Independent Inquiry Committee, 409; POWS, Kuwaiti property and missing persons, 410; UN Iraq-Kuwait Observation Mission, 411. TIMOR-LESTE, 412: United Nations Office in Timor-Leste, 412; Financing of UN operations, 428. IRAN, 431. DEMOCRATIC PEOPLE'S REPUBLIC OF KOREA, 441. OTHER MATTERS, 447: Cambodia, 447; Fiji, 447; India-Pakistan, 447; Myanmar, 448; Nepal, 449; Tajikistan, 450; United Arab Emirates-Iran, 451; Regional meetings, 451.

V. EUROPE AND THE MEDITERRANEAN 452

BOSNIA AND HERZEGOVINA, 453: Implementation of Peace Agreement, 453; European Union missions in Bosnia and Herzegovina, 460. SERBIA AND MONTENEGRO, 461: Situation in Kosovo, 462; Montenegro independence, 472. GEORGIA, 472: UN Observer Mission in Georgia, 473. ARMENIA AND AZERBAIJAN, 483. REPUBLIC OF MOLDOVA, 485. ESTABLISHMENT OF GUAM, 486. CYPRUS, 486: Good offices mission, 487; UNFICYP, 487. OTHER ISSUES, 493: Strengthening of security and cooperation in the Mediterranean, 493; Stability and development in South-Eastern Europe, 494; Cooperation with the Council of Europe, 496; Cooperation with the Organization for Security and Cooperation in Europe, 497.

VI. MIDDLE EAST 498

PEACE PROCESS, 499: Overall situation, 499; Occupied Palestinian Territory, 501. ISSUES RELATED TO PALESTINE, 547: General aspects, 547; Assistance to Palestinians, 554; UNRWA, 557. PEACEKEEPING OPERATIONS, 565: Lebanon, 566; Syrian Arab Republic, 603.

VII. DISARMAMENT 609

UN ROLE IN DISARMAMENT, 610: UN machinery, 610. NUCLEAR DISARMAMENT, 616: Conference on Disarmament, 617; Disarmament Commission, 619; START and other bilateral agreements and unilateral measures, 619; Comprehensive Nuclear-Test-Ban Treaty, 628; Prohibition of the use of nuclear weapons, 631; Advisory opinion of the International Court of Justice, 632. NON-PROLIFERATION ISSUES, 633: Non-Proliferation Treaty, 633; Non-proliferation of weapons of mass destruction, 634; Multilateralism in disarmament and non-proliferation, 637; International Atomic Energy Agency, 639; Radioactive waste, 643; Nuclear-weapon-free zones, 644. BACTERIOLOGICAL (BIOLOGICAL) AND CHEMICAL WEAPONS, 650: Bacteriological (biological) weapons, 650; 1925 Geneva Protocol, 652; Chemical weapons, 653. CONVENTIONAL

WEAPONS, 655: Towards an arms trade treaty, 655; Small arms, 656; Convention on excessively injurious conventional weapons and Protocols, 663; Practical disarmament, 665; Transparency, 667; Anti-personnel mines, 670. OTHER DISARMAMENT ISSUES, 672: Prevention of an arms race in outer space, 672; Disarmament and development, 674; Human rights, human security and disarmament, 676; Arms limitation and disarmament agreements, 676. STUDIES, INFORMATION AND TRAINING, 677: Disarmament studies programme, 677. REGIONAL DISARMAMENT, 681: Africa, 684; Asia and the Pacific, 688; Europe, 690; Latin America and the Caribbean, 692.

VIII. OTHER POLITICAL AND SECURITY QUESTIONS 695

GENERAL ASPECTS OF INTERNATIONAL SECURITY, 696: Support for democracies, 696. REGIONAL ASPECTS OF INTERNATIONAL PEACE AND SECURITY, 699: South Atlantic, 699. DECOLONIZATION, 699: Decade for the Eradication of Colonialism, 699; Puerto Rico, 712; Territories under review, 713. INFORMATION, 726: UN public information, 726; Information and telecommunications in the context of international security, 738. SCIENCE AND TECHNOLOGY IN INTERNATIONAL SECURITY AND DISARMAMENT, 740. PEACEFUL USES OF OUTER SPACE, 741: Implementation of UNISPACE III recommendations, 745; Scientific and Technical Subcommittee, 746; Legal Subcommittee, 750. EFFECTS OF ATOMIC RADIATION, 751.

Part Two: Human Rights

I. PROMOTION OF HUMAN RIGHTS 755

UN MACHINERY, 755: Commission on Human Rights, 755; Human Rights Council, 756; Subcommission on the Promotion and Protection of Human Rights, 762; Office of the High Commissioner for Human Rights, 762. HUMAN RIGHTS INSTRUMENTS, 768: General aspects, 768; Covenant on Civil and Political Rights and Optional Protocols, 771; Covenant on Economic, Social and Cultural Rights, 772; Convention against racial discrimination, 773; Convention against torture, 776; Convention on elimination of discrimination against women and Optional Protocol, 777; Convention on the Rights of the Child, 777; Convention on migrant workers, 784; Convention on genocide, 784; Convention on rights of persons with disabilities, 785; International Convention for protection from enforced disappearance, 800. OTHER ACTIVITIES, 808: Follow-up to 1993 World Conference, 808; Human rights education, 809; Strengthening action to protect human rights, 815.

II. PROTECTION OF HUMAN RIGHTS 819

CIVIL AND POLITICAL RIGHTS, 820: Racism and racial discrimination, 820; Right to nationality, 834; Protection of migrants, 835; Other forms of intolerance, 839; Right to self-determination, 851; Right of Palestinians to self-determination, 852; Administration of justice, 855; Other issues, 868. ECONOMIC, SOCIAL AND CULTURAL RIGHTS, 885; Right to development, 885; Corruption, 899; Extreme poverty, 899; Right to food, 902; Right to adequate housing, 905; Right to education, 908; Environmental and scientific concerns, 909; Right to physical and mental health, 910; Slavery and related issues, 912; Vulnerable groups, 913.

III. HUMAN RIGHTS COUNTRY SITUATIONS 937

GENERAL ASPECTS, 937: Strengthening country engagements, 937. AFRICA, 938: Burundi, 938; Democratic Republic of the Congo, 938; Liberia, 939; Sierra Leone, 940; Somalia, 941; Sudan, 941; Uganda, 943. AMERICAS, 944: Colombia, 944; Cuba, 945; Guatemala, 946; Haiti, 947. ASIA, 948: Afghanistan, 948; Cambodia, 948; Democratic People's Republic of Korea, 949; Iran, 952; Myanmar, 954; Nepal, 958; Sri Lanka, 960; Timor-Leste, 960; Turkmenistan, 960; Uzbekistan, 960. EUROPE AND THE MEDITERRANEAN, 961: Belarus, 961; Cyprus, 963. MIDDLE EAST, 964: Lebanon, 964; Territories occupied by Israel, 967.

Part Three: *Economic and social questions*

I. DEVELOPMENT POLICY AND INTERNATIONAL ECONOMIC COOPERATION 975

INTERNATIONAL ECONOMIC RELATIONS, 976: Development and international economic cooperation, 976; Sustainable development, 981; Follow-up to 2005 World Summit, MDGS, internationally agreed development goals, 986; Eradication of poverty, 992; Science and technology for development, 997. ECONOMIC AND SOCIAL TRENDS, 1004. DEVELOPMENT POLICY AND PUBLIC ADMINISTRATION, 1007: Committee for Development Policy, 1007; Public administration, 1008. GROUPS OF COUNTRIES IN SPECIAL SITUATIONS, 1010: Least developed countries, 1010; Island developing States, 1016; Landlocked developing countries, 1018; Economies in transition, 1020; Poor mountain countries, 1022.

II. OPERATIONAL ACTIVITIES FOR DEVELOPMENT 1023

SYSTEM-WIDE ACTIVITIES, 1023. TECHNICAL COOPERATION THROUGH UNDP, 1030: UNDP/UNFPA Executive Board, 1031; UNDP operational activities, 1032; Programme planning and management, 1035; Financing, 1040. OTHER TECHNICAL COOPERATION, 1044: Development Account,

1044; UN activities, 1045; UN Office for Partnerships, 1046; UN Office for Project Services, 1046; UN Volunteers, 1049; Economic and technical cooperation among developing countries, 1050; UN Capital Development Fund, 1050.

III. HUMANITARIAN AND SPECIAL ECONOMIC ASSISTANCE 1053

HUMANITARIAN ASSISTANCE, 1053: Coordination, 1053; Resource mobilization, 1061; White Helmets, 1061; New international humanitarian order, 1063; Humanitarian activities, 1063. SPECIAL ECONOMIC ASSISTANCE, 1071: African economic recovery and development, 1071; Other economic assistance, 1086. DISASTER RESPONSE, 1089: International cooperation, 1090; Disaster reduction, 1093; Disaster assistance, 1100.

IV. INTERNATIONAL TRADE, FINANCE AND TRANSPORT 1108

UNCTAD XI Follow-up, 1109. INTERNATIONAL TRADE, 1110: Trade policy, 1115; Trade promotion and facilitation, 1118; Commodities, 1121. FINANCE, 1125: Financial policy, 1125; Financing for development, 1133; Investment, technology and related financial issues, 1136. TRANSPORT, 1141: Maritime transport, 1141; Transport of dangerous goods, 1141. UNCTAD INSTITUTIONAL AND ORGANIZATIONAL QUESTIONS, 1141.

V. REGIONAL ECONOMIC AND SOCIAL ACTIVITIES 1145

REGIONAL COOPERATION, 1145. AFRICA, 1146: Economic trends, 1147; Activities in 2006, 1148; Regional cooperation, 1153. ASIA AND THE PACIFIC, 1155: Economic trends, 1155; Activities in 2006, 1157; Programme and organizational questions, 1165; UN-Economic Cooperation Organization relations, 1166. EUROPE, 1171: Economic trends, 1171; Activities in 2006, 1172; Programme and organizational questions, 1175. LATIN AMERICA AND THE CARIBBEAN, 1187: Economic trends, 1188; Activities in 2006, 1188; Programme and organizational questions, 1194. WESTERN ASIA, 1195: Activities in 2006, 1196; Programme and organizational questions, 1199.

VI. ENERGY, NATURAL RESOURCES AND CARTOGRAPHY 1201

ENERGY AND NATURAL RESOURCES, 1201: Energy, 1202; Natural resources, 1203. CARTOGRAPHY, 1204.

VII. ENVIRONMENT AND HUMAN SETTLEMENTS 1206

ENVIRONMENT, 1206: UN Environment Programme, 1206; International conventions and mechanisms, 1219; Environmental activities, 1227. HUMAN SETTLEMENTS, 1249: Follow-up to the 1996 UN Conference on Human Settlements (Habitat II) and the 2001 General Assembly special session, 1249; UN Human Settlements Programme, 1254.

VIII. POPULATION 1257

FOLLOW-UP TO THE 1994 CONFERENCE ON POPULATION AND DEVELOPMENT, 1257: Implementation of Programme of Action, 1257; International migration and development, 1259. UN POPULATION FUND, 1263. OTHER POPULATION ACTIVITIES, 1269.

IX. SOCIAL POLICY, CRIME PREVENTION AND HUMAN RESOURCES DEVELOPMENT 1272

SOCIAL POLICY AND CULTURAL ISSUES, 1272: Social development, 1272; Persons with disabilities, 1278; Cultural development, 1279. CRIME PREVENTION AND CRIMINAL JUSTICE, 1287: Follow-up to Eleventh UN Crime Congress, 1287; Commission on Crime Prevention and Criminal Justice, 1289; Crime prevention programme, 1291; Transnational organized crime, 1296; Strategies for crime prevention, 1301; UN standards and guidelines, 1306; Other crime prevention and criminal justice issues, 1322. HUMAN RESOURCES DEVELOPMENT, 1322: UN research and training institutes, 1322.

X. WOMEN 1328

FOLLOW-UP TO THE FOURTH WORLD CONFERENCE ON WOMEN AND BEIJING+5, 1328: Critical areas of concern, 1333. UN MACHINERY, 1354: Convention on the elimination of discrimination against women, 1354; Commission on the Status of Women, 1355; UN Development Fund for Women (UNIFEM), 1359; International Research and Training Institute (INSTRAW), 1359.

XI. CHILDREN, YOUTH AND AGEING PERSONS 1361

CHILDREN, 1361: Follow-up to the 2002 General Assembly special session on children, 1361; United Nations Children's Fund, 1362. YOUTH, 1379. AGEING PERSONS, 1381: Follow-up to the Second World Assembly on Ageing (2002), 1381.

XII. REFUGEES AND DISPLACED PERSONS 1385

OFFICE OF THE UNITED NATIONS HIGH COMMISSIONER FOR REFUGEES, 1385: Programme policy, 1385; Financial and administrative questions, 1391. REFUGEE PROTECTION AND ASSISTANCE, 1394: Protection issues, 1394; Assistance measures, 1395; Regional activities, 1397.

XIII. HEALTH, FOOD AND NUTRITION 1409

HEALTH, 1409: Follow-up to 2005 World Summit, 1409; AIDS prevention and control, 1410; International Year of Sanitation, 1419; World Diabetes Day, 1420; Tobacco, 1420; Roll Back Malaria initiative, 1421; Global public health, 1425; Road safety, 1426. FOOD AND AGRICULTURE, 1426: Food aid, 1426; Food security, 1428. NUTRITION, 1428.

XIV. INTERNATIONAL DRUG CONTROL 1430

FOLLOW-UP TO THE TWENTIETH SPECIAL SESSION, 1430. CONVENTIONS, 1436: International Narcotics Control Board, 1438. WORLD DRUG SITUATION, 1440. UN ACTION TO COMBAT DRUG ABUSE, 1453: UN Office on Drugs and Crime, 1453; Commission on Narcotic Drugs, 1455; Strengthening UN mechanisms, 1464.

XV. STATISTICS 1465

WORK OF STATISTICAL COMMISSION, 1465: Economic statistics, 1466; Demographic and social statistics, 1470; Other statistical activities, 1472.

Part Four: *Legal questions*

I. INTERNATIONAL COURT OF JUSTICE 1477

Judicial work of the Court, 1477; Other questions, 1482.

II. INTERNATIONAL TRIBUNALS AND COURT 1484

INTERNATIONAL TRIBUNAL FOR THE FORMER YUGOSLAVIA, 1484: The Chambers, 1485; Office of the Prosecutor, 1492; The Registry, 1492; Financing, 1493. INTERNATIONAL TRIBUNAL FOR RWANDA, 1494: The Chambers, 1494; Office of the Prosecutor, 1500; The Registry, 1500; Financing, 1500. FUNCTIONING OF THE TRIBUNALS, 1501: Implementation of completion strategies, 1502. INTERNATIONAL CRIMINAL COURT, 1503. The Chambers, 1505.

III. INTERNATIONAL LEGAL QUESTIONS 1508

LEGAL ASPECTS OF INTERNATIONAL POLITICAL RELATIONS, 1508; International Law Commission, 1508; International State relations and international law, 1515; Diplomatic Relations, 1520; Treaties and agreements, 1523. OTHER INTERNATIONAL LEGAL QUESTIONS, 1524; Rule of law at national and international levels, 1524; International economic law, 1525; International organizations and international law, 1531; Host country relations, 1537.

IV. LAW OF THE SEA 1540

UN CONVENTION ON THE LAW OF THE SEA, 1540: Institutions created by the Convention, 1554; Other developments related to the Convention, 1555; Division for Ocean Affairs and the Law of the Sea, 1568.

Part Five: *Institutional, administrative and budgetary questions*

I. UN RESTRUCTURING AND INSTITUTIONAL MATTERS 1571

RESTRUCTURING ISSUES, 1571: Programme of reform, 1571. INSTITUTIONAL MATTERS, 1586: Intergovernmental machinery, 1586. INSTITUTIONAL MACHINERY, 1592: Admission of new Member: Montenegro, 1592; General Assembly, 1592; Security Council, 1594; Economic and Social Council, 1594. COORDINATION, MONITORING AND COOPERATION, 1595; Institutional mechanisms, 1595; Other coordination matters, 1596; UN AND OTHER ORGANIZATIONS: 1597; Cooperation with organizations, 1597; Participation in UN work, 1605.

II. UNITED NATIONS FINANCING AND PROGRAMMING 1609

FINANCIAL SITUATION, 1609. UN BUDGET, 1610: Reform of budget process and financial management, 1610; Budget for 2006-2007, 1611; Programme budget outline for 2008-2009, 1622. CONTRIBUTIONS, 1624: Assessments, 1624. ACCOUNTS AND AUDITING, 1631: Review of UN administrative and financial functioning, 1633. PROGRAMME PLANNING, 1635: Strategic framework for 2008-2009, 1635; Programme performance, 1638.

III. ADMINISTRATIVE AND STAFF MATTERS 1642

ADMINISTRATIVE MATTERS, 1643: Managerial reform and oversight, 1643. OTHER ADMINISTRATIVE MATTERS, 1654: Conference management, 1654; UN information systems, 1664; UN premises and property, 1666; Security issues, 1673. STAFF MATTERS, 1676; Appointment of Secretary-General, 1676; Conditions of service, 1677; Staff safety and security, 1684; Other staff matters, 1687; UN Joint Staff Pension Fund, 1703; Travel-related matters, 1707; Administration of justice, 1707.

Appendices

I. ROSTER OF THE UNITED NATIONS 1713

II. CHARTER OF THE UNITED NATIONS AND STATUTE OF THE INTERNATIONAL COURT OF JUSTICE 1715

III. STRUCTURE OF THE UNITED NATIONS 1730

IV. AGENDAS OF UNITED NATIONS PRINCIPAL ORGANS IN 2006 1743

V. UNITED NATIONS INFORMATION CENTRES 1755

VI. INTERGOVERMENTAL ORGANIZATIONS RELATED TO THE UNITED NATIONS 1758

Indexes

USING THE SUBJECT INDEX 1762
SUBJECT INDEX 1763
INDEX OF RESOLUTIONS AND DECISIONS 1790
INDEX OF 2006 SECURITY COUNCIL PRESIDENTIAL STATEMENTS 1793
HOW TO OBTAIN VOLUMES OF THE *YEARBOOK* 1795

About the 2006 edition of the *Yearbook*

This volume of the *YEARBOOK OF THE UNITED NATIONS* continues the tradition of providing the most comprehensive coverage of the activities of the United Nations. It is an indispensable reference tool for the research community, diplomats, government officials and the general public seeking readily available information on the UN system and its related organizations.

Structure and scope of articles

The *Yearbook* is subject-oriented and divided into five parts covering political and security questions; human rights issues; economic and social questions; legal questions; and institutional, administrative and budgetary questions. Chapters and topical headings present summaries of pertinent UN activities, including those of intergovernmental and expert bodies, major reports, Secretariat activities and, in selected cases, the views of States in written communications.

Activities of United Nations bodies. All resolutions, decisions and other major activities of the principal organs and, on a selective basis, those of subsidiary bodies are either reproduced or summarized in the appropriate chapter. The texts of all resolutions and decisions of substantive nature adopted in 2006 by the General Assembly, the Security Council and the Economic and Social Council are reproduced or summarized under the relevant topic. These texts are preceded by procedural details giving date of adoption, meeting number and vote totals (in favour–against–abstaining) if any; and an indication of their approval by a sessional or subsidiary body prior to final adoption. The texts are followed by details of any recorded or roll-call vote on the resolution/decision as a whole.

Major reports. Most reports of the Secretary-General, in 2006, along with selected reports from other UN sources, such as seminars and working groups, are summarized briefly.

Secretariat activities. The operational activities of the United Nations for development and humanitarian assistance are described under the relevant topics. For major activities financed outside the UN regular budget, selected information is given on contributions and expenditures.

Views of States. Written communications sent to the United Nations by Member States and circulated as documents of the principal organs have been summarized in selected cases, under the relevant topics. Substantive actions by the Security Council have been analysed and brief reviews of the Council's deliberations given, particularly in cases where an issue was taken up but no resolution was adopted.

Multilateral treaties. Information on signatories and parties to multilateral treaties and conventions is taken from Multilateral Treaties Deposited with the Secretary-General: Status as at 31 December 2006.

Terminology

Formal titles of bodies, organizational units, conventions, declarations and officials are given in full on first mention in an article or sequence of articles. They are also used in resolution/decision texts, and in the SUBJECT INDEX under the key word of the title. Short titles may be used in subsequent references.

How to find information in the *Yearbook*

The user may locate information on the United Nations activities contained in this volume by the use of the Table of Contents, the Subject Index, the Index of Resolutions and Decisions and the Index of Security Council presidential statements. The volume also has six appendices: Appendix I comprises a roster of Member States; Appendix II reproduces the Charter of the United Nations, including the Statute of the International Court of Justice; Appendix III gives the structure of the principal organs of the United Nations; Appendix IV provides the agenda for each session of the principal organs in 2006; Appendix V gives the addresses of the United Nations information centres and services worldwide; and Appendix VI gives the names and addressed of the specialized agencies and other related organizations of the UN system.

For more information on the United Nations and its activities, visit our Internet site at:

www.un.org

ABBREVIATIONS COMMONLY USED IN THE *YEARBOOK*

ACABQ	Advisory Committee on Administrative and Budgetary Questions
AU	African Union
CARICOM	Caribbean Community
CEB	United Nations System Chief Executives Board for Coordination
CIS	Commonwealth of Independent States
CPC	Committee for Programme and Coordination
DPKO	Department of Peacekeeping Operations
DPRK	Democratic People's Republic of Korea
DRC	Democratic Republic of the Congo
ECA	Economic Commission for Africa
ECE	Economic Commission for Europe
ECLAC	Economic Commission for Latin America and the Caribbean
ECOWAS	Economic Community of West African States
ESCAP	Economic and Social Commission for Asia and the Pacific
ESCWA	Economic and Social Commission for Western Asia
EU	European Union
FAO	Food and Agriculture Organization of the United Nations
FYROM	The former Yugoslav Republic of Macedonia
GDP	gross domestic product
GNP	gross national product
HIV/AIDS	human immunodeficiency virus/acquired immuno-deficiency syndrome
HIPC	Highly-indebted Poor Countries
IAEA	International Atomic Energy Agency
ICAO	International Civil Aviation Organization
ICC	International Criminal Court
ICJ	International Court of Justice
ICRC	International Committee of the Red Cross
ICT	information and communication technology
ICTR	International Criminal Tribunal for Rwanda
ICTY	International Tribunal for the Former Yugoslavia
IDA	International Development Association
IDPs	Internally displaced persons
IFAD	International Fund for Agricultural Development
IFC	International Finance Corporation
ILO	International Labour Organization
IMF	International Monetary Fund
IMO	International Maritime Organization
ITU	International Telecommunication Union
JIU	Joint Inspection Unit
LDC	least developed country
MDGs	Millennium Development Goals
MINURSO	United Nations Mission for the Referendum in Western Sahara
MINUSTAH	United Nations Stabilization Force in Haiti
MONUC	United Nations Organization Mission in the Democratic Republic of the Congo
MYFF	multi-year Funding Framework
NATO	North Atlantic Treaty Organization
NGO	non-governmental organization
NPT	Treaty on the Non-Proliferation of Nuclear Weapons
NSGT	Non-Self-Governing Territory
OAS	Organization of American States
OCHA	Office for the Coordination of Humanitarian Affairs
ODA	official development assistance
OECD	Organisation for Economic Co-operation and Development
OHCHR	Office of the United Nations High Commissioner for Human Rights
OIOS	Office of Internal Oversight Services
ONUB	United Nations Operation in Burundi
OSCE	Organization for Security and Cooperation in Europe
PA	Palestinian Authority
PRSPs	poverty-reduction strategy papers
UNAIDS	Joint United Nations Programme on HIV/AIDS
UNAMA	United Nations Assistance Mission in Afghanistan
UNAMI	United Nations Assistance Mission for Iraq
UNCTAD	United Nations Conference on Trade and Development
UNDOF	United Nations Disengagement Observer Force (Golan Heights)
UNDP	United Nations Development Programme
UNEP	United Nations Environment Programme
UNESCO	United Nations Educational, Scientific and Cultural Organization
UNFICYP	United Nations Peacekeeping Force in Cyprus
UNFPA	United Nations Population Fund
UN-Habitat	United Nations Human Settlements Programme
UNHCR	Office of the United Nations High Commissioner for Refugees
UNIC	United Nations Information Centre
UNICEF	United Nations Children's Fund
UNIDO	United Nations Industrial Development Organization
UNIFIL	United Nations Interim Force in Lebanon
UNMEE	United Nations Mission in Ethiopia and Eritrea
UNMIK	United Nations Interim Administration Mission in Kosovo
UNMOGIP	United Nations Military Observer Group in India and Pakistan
UNOCI	United Nations Operation in Côte d'Ivoire
UNODC	United Nations Office on Drugs and Crime
UNOMIG	United Nations Observer Mission in Georgia
UNOPS	United Nations Office for Project Services
UNRWA	United Nations Relief and Works Agency for Palestine Refugees in the Near East
UNTSO	United Nations Truce Supervision Organization
UNWTO	World Tourism Organization
WFP	World Food Programme
WHO	World Health Organization
WIPO	World Intellectual Property Organization
WMDs	weapons of mass destruction
WMO	World Meteorological Organization
WTO	World Trade Organization
YUN	Yearbook of the United Nations

EXPLANATORY NOTE ON DOCUMENTS

References in square brackets in each chapter of Parts One to Five of this volume give the symbols of the main documents issued in 2006 on the topic. The following is a guide to the principal document symbols:

A/- refers to documents of the General Assembly, numbered in separate series by session. Thus, A/61/- refers to documents issued for consideration at the sixty-first session, beginning with A/61/1. Documents of special and emergency special sessions are identified as A/S- and A/ES-, followed by the session number.

A/C.- refers to documents of the Assembly's Main Committees, e.g. A/C.1/- is a document of the First Committee, A/C.6/-, a document of the Sixth Committee. A/BUR/- refers to documents of the General Committee. A/AC.- documents are those of the Assembly's ad hoc bodies and A/CN.-, of its commissions; e.g. A/AC.105/- identifies documents of the Assembly's Committee on the Peaceful Uses of Outer Space, A/CN.4/-, of its International Law Commission. Assembly resolutions and decisions since the thirty-first (1976) session have been identified by two arabic numerals; the first indicates the session of adoption; the second, the sequential number in the series. Resolutions are numbered consecutively from 1 at each session. Decisions since the fifty-seventh session are numbered consecutively, from 401 for those concerned with elections and appointments, and from 501 for all other decisions. Decisions of special and emergency special sessions are numbered consecutively, from 11 for those concerned with elections and appointments, and from 21 for all other decisions.

E/- refers to documents of the Economic and Social Council, numbered in separate series by year. Thus, E/2006/- refers to documents issued for consideration by the Council at its 2006 sessions, beginning with E/2006/1. E/AC.-, E/C.- and E/CN.-, followed by identifying numbers, refer to documents of the Council's subsidiary ad hoc bodies, committees and commissions. For example, E/CN.5/- refers to documents of the Council's Commission for Social Development, E/C.2/-, to documents of its Committee on Non-Governmental Organizations. E/ICEF/- documents are those of the United Nations Children's Fund (UNICEF). Symbols for the Council's resolutions and decisions, since 1978, consist of two arabic numerals: the first indicates the year of adoption and the second, the sequential number in the series. There are two series: one for resolutions, beginning with 1 (resolution 2006/1); and one for decisions, beginning with 201 (decision 2006/201).

S/- refers to documents of the Security Council. Its resolutions are identified by consecutive numbers followed by the year of adoption in parentheses, beginning with resolution 1(1946).

ST/-, followed by symbols representing the issuing department or office, refers to documents of the United Nations Secretariat.

Documents of certain bodies bear special symbols, including the following:

CD/-	Conference on Disarmament
CERD/-	Committee on the Elimination of Racial Discrimination
DC/-	Disarmament Commission
DP/-	United Nations Development Programme
HS/-	Commission on Human Settlements
ITC/-	International Trade Centre
TD/-	United Nations Conference on Trade and Development
UNEP/-	United Nations Environment Programme

Many documents of the regional commissions bear special symbols, which are sometimes preceded by the following:

E/ECA/-	Economic Commission for Africa
E/ECE/-	Economic Commission for Europe
E/ECLAC/-	Economic Commission for Latin America and the Caribbean
E/ESCAP/-	Economic and Social Commission for Asia and the Pacific
E/ESCWA/-	Economic and Social Commission for Western Asia

"L" in a symbol refers to documents of limited distribution, such as draft resolutions; "CONF." to documents of a conference; "INF." to those of general information. Summary records are designated by "SR.", verbatim records by "PV.", each followed by the meeting number.

United Nations sales publications each carry a sales number with the following components separated by periods: a capital letter indicating the language(s) of the publication; two arabic numerals indicating the year; a Roman numeral indicating the subject category; a capital letter indicating a subdivision of the category, if any; and an arabic numeral indicating the number of the publication within the category. Examples: E.06.II.A.2; E/F/R.05.II.E.8; E.05.X.1.

Documents cited in the text in square brackets may be obtained through the UN Official Document System by logging on to: http://documents.un.org.

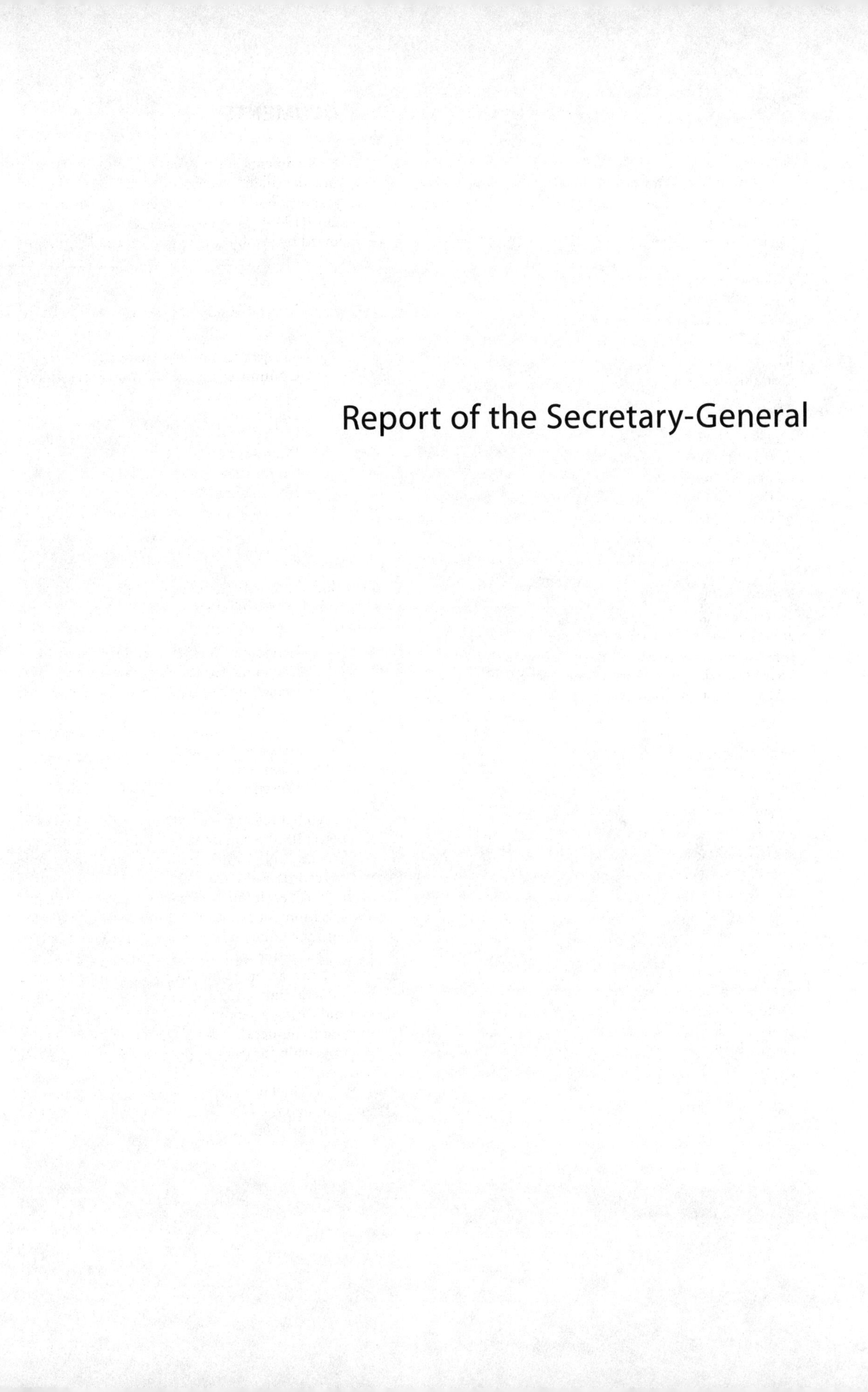

Report of the Secretary-General

Report of the Secretary-General on the work of the Organization

Following is the Secretary-General's report on the work of the Organization [A/61/1 & Corr.1], *dated 10 August 2006, submitted to the sixty-first session of the General Assembly. The Assembly took note of it on 2 October* (**decision 61/504**).

Chapter I

Introduction

1. In this, my tenth and last annual report, I have sought to provide an overview of the Organization's main achievements and challenges during the past 12 months in the light of the critical developments in the decade since I took office at the beginning of 1997. I have also subsumed in a single report both the work of the Organization as such and the progress made in implementing the Millennium Declaration, which in previous years has been the subject of a separate report.

2. The report is arranged under headings that readers will recognize as corresponding to the four main sections of the outcome document of the 2005 World Summit of September 2005, which in turn followed the structure of my "In larger freedom" report: development; peace and security; human rights, rule of law and humanitarian affairs; and strengthening the United Nations. To these I have added a fifth, "global constituencies", to cover an area that has not previously been classified as central to the Organization's work but has become increasingly important—and will, I believe, become even more so as the new century advances.

3. Over its lifetime the United Nations has changed from being principally a conference-servicing Organization to become a truly global service provider working on the ground in virtually every corner of the world to improve the lives of people who need help. This transformation has occurred in a dramatic way during the past decade. More than 70 per cent of our $10 billion annual budget now relates to peacekeeping and other field operations, compared to about 50 per cent of a budget less than half that size 10 years ago. Over 50 per cent of our 30,000 civilian staff now serve in the field. The number of humanitarian offices increased from 12 offices with 114 staff members in 1997 to 43 offices with 815 staff members in 2005. Human rights work at the country level has grown significantly; in 1996 the Office of the United Nations High Commissioner for Human Rights (OHCHR) was present in 14 countries, and currently OHCHR-supported human rights personnel are deployed in over 40 countries. We have been called upon to support over 100 national elections. In addition, the Millennium Development Goals have become an operational template for use by Governments and peoples around the world to advance the well-being of all. The Joint United Nations Programme on HIV/AIDS (UNAIDS) is leading the charge to combat existential threats such as HIV/AIDS by bringing together the efforts and resources of 10 United Nations system organizations to the global AIDS response, and the UNAIDS secretariat works on the ground in more than 75 countries.

4. If any one phenomenon can be said to have dominated the decade we have just lived through, it must surely be globalization. This term has been variously defined, but to me it conveys above all an era in which international relations are no longer almost exclusively about relations between nation-States, but also relations among people of different nationalities who interact with each other in a whole host of ways as individuals or as members of self-constituted groups across national boundaries, indeed across continents and oceans, often without needing to refer to the State at all. While the United Nations is constituted by Member States, these "non-State actors" on the international stage form new global constituencies with which the United Nations is increasingly called upon to interact.

5. The United Nations is having to learn how to work with global business and global civil society in all their manifold forms. The Organization must encourage partnerships with these vital actors to promote desirable changes and deliver growth, security and services, especially in the field.

6. But while nation-States are no longer the sole players in international relations, they are still the most important. And they face collective challenges that no single State can solve by itself.

7. Certainly, the State has not withered away or become redundant. On the contrary, the role of the State as regulator (though not administrator) of economic activity and mediator between different interest groups becomes all the more important as society becomes more complex. The more deadly weapons proliferate, the more essential is the State's monopoly on the means of coercion. To convince oneself of this, one has only to look at those unhappy countries where States are weak or are said to have failed. Many of them are countries that the United Nations knows all too well, since it is often where States are weak or have failed that we are summoned to assist.

8. That, too, is an important change. Our founders conceived of the Organization as working mainly to preserve the peace *between* States. They even forbade the Organization, in Article 2.7 of its Charter, a living document that remains vitally relevant today, to intervene "in matters which are essentially within the domestic jurisdiction of any state", though with the sensible reservation that this principle should not prejudice the application of enforcement measures under Chapter VII when the Security Council takes action with respect to threats to the peace, breaches of the peace or acts of aggression.

9. In recent years the Council has made use of this reservation many times, because it has found that breaches of the peace and acts of aggression most often begin *within* States, yet swiftly develop into threats to the peace of a whole region, if not the whole world. Thus the United Nations comes increasingly to see the security of its Member States as inseparable from that of the populations who inhabit them and are represented by them. That is why the world's heads of State and Government felt it necessary, at last year's historic summit, to reaffirm that "each individual State has the responsibility to protect its populations from genocide, war crimes, ethnic cleansing and crimes against humanity", and to affirm that the international community also has the responsibility to take timely and decisive action for this purpose, through the Security Council, when peaceful means prove inadequate and national authorities are manifestly failing to do it.

10. States, in short, are the servants and instruments of human beings, and not the other way round. Once this fundamental principle is understood and accepted, it becomes easy to see why the three cardinal purposes of the Organization—development, security and human rights—are so indissolubly interconnected.

11. In order to develop and prosper, human beings must be able to look to the State for security and protection and be able to exercise their individual rights—not only civil and political but also economic, social and cultural—under the rule of law.

12. Likewise, human beings can feel truly secure only if they enjoy economic as well as political or military security and if they can be confident that their basic rights and human dignity will not be violated.

13. Human beings will enjoy meaningful human rights only if they can escape from grinding and degrading poverty and if they can rely on a strong and just State—one in which their views and interests are truly represented—to protect them from violence and crime.

14. In carrying out its mission on all three fronts, one of the Organization's greatest assets is its idealistic and courageous staff, many of whom serve in situations of hardship and danger. During the past decade United Nations personnel have been increasingly targeted in places of strife and conflict. Our mission to build a safer, better world for all people is no longer a guarantee of protection. The United Nations has suffered a real loss of innocence in recent years. Consequently, we have had to learn how best to advance our mission to help others without excessively endangering our own.

15. But our commitment must never change. The United Nations, founded in the name of "We the peoples", must be able to advance their interests effectively in all three areas—development, security and human rights. Indeed, my millennium report "We the peoples" and my 2005 report "In larger freedom" reflect my own vision of this global responsibility, which has underpinned my tenure as Secretary-General. This report shows how the Organization has sought to do so in the past year and in the light of the past 10 years. I believe there is much in it that we can be proud of. But I am also fully conscious of the alarming extent to which, on all three fronts, our capacities fall short of the challenges we face. That is why I am convinced that the task of strengthening the United Nations is no mere bookkeeping exercise, but an imperative that

directly concerns the interests of all Member States and should, much more than it appears to do at present, engage their urgent attention.

Chapter II
Development

Internationally agreed development goals and the Millennium Development Goals

To spare no effort: the millennium promise

16. In the Millennium Declaration of 2000 (General Assembly resolution 55/2), world leaders set forth a bold and inclusive new vision for humanity. Pledging to channel the fruits of globalization to benefit all people, leaders committed themselves "to spare no effort to free our fellow men, women and children from the abject and dehumanizing conditions of extreme poverty". Since 2000, the United Nations, together with eminent voices from Government, civil society, business and science, has given spirit to this commitment in a manner that many would have deemed impossible only a few years ago. The result has been dramatically increased global attention for the full one sixth of humanity who still live in the most extreme form of poverty, measured as income of less than one dollar per day.

17. Such political momentum offers the opportunity to build on the world's considerable recent development successes. As highlighted in the statistical annex to the present report, from 1990 to 2002, the developing world's proportion of people living in extreme poverty dropped from 28 per cent to 19 per cent, driven mostly by gains in eastern and southern Asia. Average child mortality rates in developing countries fell from 95 deaths per 1,000 live births in 1990 to 79 in 2004. More than 1.2 billion people gained access to improved sanitation over the same period. From 1991 to 2004, average net primary enrolment ratios in developing regions increased from 79 per cent to 86 per cent.

18. But progress has been uneven and the ongoing levels of human deprivation remain staggering. Each year, more than 10 million children die before their fifth birthday, mostly from preventable causes. Women in the developing world are more than 45 times more likely, on average, to die during pregnancy and childbirth than women in the developed world. More than 800 million people remain chronically undernourished. Half the developing world still lacks access to sanitation, a fifth has no access to safe water, and slum populations are growing steadily. The environment on which livelihoods depend is suffering degradation in all developing regions. The world missed the international goal for gender parity in education by 2005, and the epidemic of violence against women remains a scourge on humanity.

19. Prior to the Millennium Declaration, the foundations for tackling these challenges were consolidated through the major conferences and summits of the 1990s. At the 2002 International Conference on Financing for Development, held in Monterrey, Mexico, world leaders committed themselves to a new global partnership to achieve the internationally agreed development goals, including the Millennium Development Goals. The Monterrey Consensus reasserted each country's primary responsibility for its own economic and social development through sound governance and policies to fully mobilize domestic resources. These national efforts were to be supplemented by the commitment from developed countries to provide improved access to international markets, more and more effective, stable and predictable official development assistance and private capital flows and a better international architecture to prevent and manage financial crises. As an essential contribution to this process, developed countries also pledged to make concrete efforts towards the target of 0.7 per cent of gross national income as official development assistance and to pursue innovative sources of financing for development. Increased national responsibility was also to be accompanied by a greater voice and greater representation for developing countries in international economic decision-making. In the same year, at the World Summit on Sustainable Development, held in Johannesburg, South Africa, Member States focused on the implementation of sustainable development goals and added partnerships as a major new dimension to achieving those goals. The Summit reinforced the Millennium Development Goals by agreeing to specific, time-bound sustainable development targets, including particular targets for Africa.

20. In implementing this vision of global partnership, many developing and developed countries are leading by inspirational example. But many of them, despite their best efforts, simply remain too poor to make the investments needed to escape the trap of extreme poverty. It is these countries that require the most urgent international support if we are to fulfil the promises of the Millennium Declaration.

21. Recent global political debates have rightly shifted the emphasis from principles to practicalities. In January 2005, the Millennium Project presented to me its report entitled *Investing in Development: A*

Practical Plan to Achieve the Millennium Development Goals, stressing the need for practical measures and the feasibility of major success. I welcomed the analysis and the recommendations of the Millennium Project. In March of the same year, I submitted to the General Assembly my report entitled "In larger freedom: towards development, security and human rights for all", which set out a strategic vision for collective action to achieve universal freedom from want, as well as freedom from fear and the realization of dignity for all. Both reports stressed that breakthrough action was required at all levels if implementation were to proceed at a scale commensurate with countries' development needs. Other Secretariat reports, such as the *Report on the World Social Situation 2005* and the *World Economic and Social Survey 2006*, have focused on the growing inequalities that are emerging both within and among countries and that make it challenging, but all the more imperative, to reach the Millennium Development Goals.

2005—a year of commitments

22. As the first major checkpoint since the Millennium Summit, 2005 saw a number of important commitments to a global development agenda, culminating at the 2005 World Summit. All Member States emphasized the vital role played by the major United Nations conferences and summits in shaping a broad development vision and in identifying commonly agreed objectives, and strongly reaffirmed the Millennium Development Goals as the shared, time-bound, integrated and measurable framework for development cooperation. For the United Nations system, it has been extremely encouraging to see the Goals gain political momentum with each passing year. Citizens around the world are rightfully calling upon their Governments to be ever bolder in following through on the Goals. As a result, international development efforts have regained ambition, fusing the possibility for success with a heightened sense of urgency.

23. At the 2005 World Summit (see General Assembly resolution 60/1), Member States agreed to a practical framework for decade-long action when they committed to embedding the global goals into the country-level processes where operational and budgetary decisions are made. In particular, Member States agreed to adopt, by the end of 2006, comprehensive national strategies to achieve the internationally agreed development goals and objectives, including the Millennium Development Goals, supported by the global partnership for development agreed in Monterrey. Member States also committed to launching "quick-impact initiatives", immediate steps that can save and improve millions of lives within the span of only a few years. These include actions to distribute anti-malaria bed nets, free of charge, to eliminate user fees in basic education and health and to expand school meal programmes using locally produced food.

24. World leaders further agreed to several other important targets at the 2005 World Summit. I am therefore recommending the incorporation of these commitments into the set of targets used to follow up on the Millennium Declaration. This includes: a new target under Millennium Development Goal 1: to make the goals of full and productive employment and decent work for all, including for women and young people, a central objective of our relevant national and international policies and our national development strategies; a new target under Goal 5: to achieve universal access to reproductive health by 2015; a new target under Goal 6: to come as close as possible to universal access to treatment for HIV/AIDS by 2010 for all those who need it; and a new target under Goal 7: to significantly reduce the rate of loss of biodiversity by 2010. The existing target on developing decent and productive work for youth, now under Millennium Development Goal 8, would be encompassed by the new target (under Goal 1). Technical work to select the appropriate indicators would be undertaken by the Inter-agency and Expert Group on Millennium Development Goal Indicators. In this work, the system will be able to build on the Ministerial Declaration on Employment Generation and Decent Work adopted at the 2006 session of the Economic and Social Council, which calls for the development of 10-year action plans and assigns the Council a clear role in monitoring progress in its implementation.

25. As emphasized in Monterrey, commitments can be implemented only if backed by adequate international financing, another realm of significant breakthroughs in 2005. The Multilateral Debt Relief Initiative endorsed the cancellation of debts to the African Development Bank, the International Monetary Fund and the World Bank for those countries that completed the enhanced Heavily Indebted Poor Countries Initiative. Worth approximately $50 billion in face value, this debt relief is projected to save qualifying countries more than $1 billion per year in debt-servicing payments over the coming decade. This agreement marks unambiguous progress and highlights the need for relief for other deserving countries too.

26. Of much greater quantitative importance for development finance, 16 of 22 members of the Organization for Economic Cooperation and

Development (OECD) Development Assistance Committee have now either met the official development assistance target of 0.7 per cent of gross national income or set timetables for doing so by 2015. In May 2005, the 15 Development Assistance Committee members that are members of the European Union each agreed to meet a minimum target of 0.51 per cent of gross national income by 2010, en route to 0.7 per cent by 2015. Admirably, Member States that joined the European Union after 2002 set a development assistance target of 0.33 per cent of gross national income by 2015. The Group of Eight summit held in Gleneagles, United Kingdom of Great Britain and Northern Ireland, built on this momentum with an agreement to augment total annual development assistance by $50 billion by 2010, with half of the increase directed to Africa. An increasing number of donors are meeting the target to provide at least 0.15 to 0.20 per cent of their gross national income to assist the least developed countries, and official development assistance to least developed countries has thus increased sharply in recent years. Innovative sources of financing have also been explored and various initiatives are being implemented.

2006—translating commitments into action

27. If history judges 2005 for its promises, then 2006 must be judged on implementation. Are we on course to look back, in 2015, and say that no effort was spared? So far the record is mixed. The words of 2005 have yet to have a direct impact on the lives of the poor people they are meant to help. Nor have they produced the implementation breakthroughs required to achieve the Millennium Development Goals. The challenges remain most pressing in Africa, particularly sub-Saharan Africa, where the proportion of people living in extreme poverty is essentially unchanged since 1990 and the absolute number has increased dramatically.

28. There has been progress, however. For example, the Multilateral Debt Relief Initiative has followed a prompt timetable towards completion; international malaria control efforts are gathering speed, backed by increased donor assistance; momentum is under way to launch the African Green Revolution agreed upon at the 2005 World Summit; and recent global commitments have also prompted new notions of investment scale-up to tackle broader development priorities. To ensure that Member States can respond to their countries' development priorities, last year I personally wrote to all Heads of State and Government offering United Nations assistance and support. I am heartened to note that the United Nations country teams are currently helping many countries to prepare and implement Millennium Development Goal-based national development strategies.

29. Putting the Millennium Development Goals into action, the United Nations has collaborated with Governments and other stakeholders to support so-called millennium villages throughout Africa. The project began with a single village in Sauri, Kenya, in August 2004 and has expanded to 12 sites in Ethiopia, Ghana, Kenya, Malawi, Mali, Nigeria, Rwanda, Senegal, Uganda and the United Republic of Tanzania. Among other successes, the villages are transforming themselves from areas of chronic hunger, tripling their crop production in a short time. Using scientific technology and understanding the agro-ecological zones of the areas, villagers are now able to sell their produce in nearby markets.

30. Thanks to efforts by the World Health Organization (WHO), the United Nations Children's Fund (UNICEF) and others, progress is being made to slow the spread of infectious diseases and provide assistance to those suffering from them. Aid is increasing throughout Africa and other areas to provide insecticide-treated mosquito nets, which can save as many as 20 per cent of children who would otherwise die from malaria. Policies regarding artemisinin-based combination therapy for malaria are now in place, helping to stem the burden of resistance to former malaria treatments and helping many to overcome the disease. A large campaign to eradicate polio over the past decade has nearly been completed, with only four polio-endemic countries left. It is suspected that transmission of the disease could be halted throughout the world by the end of 2006, with the possibility of the world being certified polio-free by the end of 2010.

31. From the work of the Permanent Forum on Indigenous Issues to ensure that policies to attain the Millennium Development Goals reach out to indigenous people to the likely conclusion of the first ever convention on protection and promotion of the rights and dignity of persons with disabilities this year, progress towards policy implementation is evident. Another key issue from the 2005 World Summit—how to realize the great potential of migration to advance worldwide development—will be addressed at the forthcoming high-level dialogue in the General Assembly. This offers a unique opportunity for the Organization to move policies towards economic and social progress for migrants and their countries of origin and destination.

32. The Economic and Social Council has been called upon to play a critical role in the systematic follow-up and monitoring of progress of various

programmes. The annual ministerial reviews can become the major mechanism for strengthening accountability for international commitments to the Millennium Development Goals and the other agreed development goals. The Council's high-level development cooperation forum will provide a global platform where all will be able to discuss key policy issues that affect development cooperation in all its forms. I trust that the Council will rise to this major challenge.

33. In spite of these advances, progress remains much too incomplete. Most fundamentally, international financial commitments remain inadequate in terms of timing, volume and quality for achieving the internationally agreed development goals, including the Millennium Development Goals. Many of the new promises will take years to materialize, so it is difficult for low-income countries to begin real investment scale-up. Aggregate official development assistance reached a record high of $106 billion in 2005, up from $69 billion in 2003, but only a small fraction of this nominal increase actually represented additional finance to support real ground-level investments in the countries that need them most. Even multilateral debt relief yields little immediate gain for qualifying countries, since benefits are backloaded and additional financing is still necessary to ensure that multilateral development banks are adequately resourced to finance scale-up programmes. It therefore remains as important as ever for developed countries without timetables for achieving the 0.7 per cent aid target to set them as soon as possible. Moreover, aid delivery mechanisms require dramatic improvement, building on the 2005 Paris Declaration on Aid Effectiveness.

34. Another cause for concern is the suspension of negotiations of the World Trade Organization's Doha Development Round. Developing countries require greater market access and support for capacity development in order to develop the long-term competitiveness that sustains economic development. Following the Ministerial Conference held in Hong Kong, China, in December 2005, which produced few areas of agreement and little momentum, the talks were stalled in July 2006. In the coming months, leadership will be required from all sides, particularly the developed countries, if negotiations are to be saved. It is also important that the Aid for Trade Initiative endorsed at Hong Kong be pursued.

35. The costs of delay and inaction are borne globally, not just locally. One need only consider the challenges posed by emerging diseases such as avian influenza to understand the shared and urgent global interest in supporting practical development steps in all countries. We must recognize the nature of global trust at stake and the danger that many developing countries' hopes could be irredeemably pierced if even the greatest anti-poverty movement in history is insufficient to break from "business as usual". As we move towards implementation in 2006 and beyond, we still must spare no effort.

HIV/AIDS

36. In the 25 years since the first cases of AIDS were reported, AIDS has killed more than 25 million people, orphaned 15 million children and exacerbated hunger and poverty. It has become the leading cause of death among both men and women aged 15 to 59, and women now represent 50 per cent of people living with HIV worldwide. After a tragically late and slow start, the world's response has gathered strength. The adoption of the Declaration of Commitment on HIV/AIDS in June 2001 marked a watershed moment when the world recognized the challenge posed by AIDS and pledged to take action.

37. A great deal of progress has been achieved since then. The Global Fund to Fight AIDS, Tuberculosis and Malaria was established in 2002 to provide low- and middle-income countries with additional financing. More domestic and international resources have been mobilized. The prices of some AIDS medicines have been greatly reduced and the "3 by 5 Initiative", launched by UNAIDS and WHO, has helped to generate a substantial increase in the number of people receiving antiretroviral treatment. Yet, the pace of the epidemic continues to outstrip current efforts. An estimated 38.6 million people worldwide were living with HIV in 2005. An estimated 4.1 million people became infected with HIV and an estimated 2.8 million lost their lives to AIDS. The global impact of AIDS has already been so devastating that the *Human Development Report 2005* of the United Nations Development Programme (UNDP) concluded that the HIV/AIDS pandemic had inflicted the single greatest reversal in human development.

38. In the 2005 World Summit Outcome, world leaders committed to a massive scaling up of HIV prevention, treatment and care with the aim of coming as close as possible to the goal of universal access to treatment by 2010 for all who need it. The impact is starting to be seen in some areas, with trends in national HIV prevalence showing recent declines in two sub-Saharan African countries, namely Kenya and Zimbabwe, in urban areas in Burkina Faso and Haiti, nationally in Cambodia and Thailand and in four states in India. More than 1.3 million people were receiving antiretroviral therapy in low- and

middle-income countries by December 2005, and in sub-Saharan Africa the number of people receiving treatment increased more than eightfold (from 100,000 to 810,000) between 2003 and 2005 and more than doubled in 2005 alone. The number of people receiving antiretroviral therapy in Asia increased almost threefold, to 180,000, in 2005.

39. In response to the request of the General Assembly contained in its resolution 60/224, UNAIDS and its co-sponsors helped to facilitate inclusive country-driven processes to develop practical strategies for moving towards universal access. The report entitled "Towards universal access: assessment by the Joint United Nations Programme on HIV/AIDS on scaling up HIV prevention, treatment, care and support", provides a summary of these country-driven processes and contains practical recommendations on setting and supporting national priorities; ensuring predictable and sustainable financing; strengthening human resources and systems; removing the barriers to ensure affordable commodities; protecting the AIDS-related human rights of people living with HIV, women and children and people in vulnerable groups; and setting targets and accountability mechanisms.

40. The high-level meeting and review of progress on HIV/AIDS, which was held in New York from 31 May to 2 June 2006, provided world leaders with an opportunity to assess progress made in achieving the targets set out in the Declaration of Commitment on HIV/AIDS and to strengthen the global response against the epidemic. In the Declaration of Commitment on HIV/AIDS: five years later, Member States: *(a)* committed to taking specific actions to scale up nationally driven, sustainable and comprehensive AIDS responses—including the full and active participation of civil society—towards the goal of universal access to HIV prevention, treatment, care and support by 2010; *(b)* recognized the UNAIDS estimate that $20 billion to $23 billion would be required annually by 2010 to fund sufficiently scaled-up responses; *(c)* committed to setting up ambitious national targets and costed national plans; and *(d)* agreed to focus on the key drivers of the epidemic, in particular gender disparity, challenges for young people and stigma and discrimination.

41. The HIV/AIDS epidemic demands an exceptional response. Among the main challenges ahead are the need to work more closely and openly with populations most affected by HIV and AIDS, such as men who have sex with men, sex workers and injecting drug users, and moving from short-term emergency response to a longer-term response that recognizes the exceptionality of AIDS and is integrated with national development planning and implementation. We need an ambitious and balanced strategy of both prevention and treatment and adequate urgent funding. A real difference can be made in a very short time.

The special needs of Africa

42. World leaders made an unprecedented commitment in the Millennium Declaration to recognize and provide for the special needs of Africa. The need for urgent and concerted action was compelling, as Africa continues to suffer more than its share of the hardships caused by violent conflict, poverty and disease.

43. It must be recognized, however, that encouraging developments have taken place in Africa during the past 10 years. The number of democratically elected national Governments in Africa has increased significantly, and economic growth in some African countries is relatively strong and sustained. There has been a marked resolve by African leaders to take control of the continent's destiny. The Organization of African Unity has been transformed into the African Union, which continues to strengthen its peacekeeping and mediation capacities and its peer-review mechanism, and implementation of the New Partnership for Africa's Development (NEPAD) is moving ahead.

44. Yet major challenges remain. Sub-Saharan Africa lags behind the rest of the developing world in achieving the Millennium Development Goals. About half of the world's armed conflicts, and the vast majority of United Nations peacekeepers, are in Africa. There is a high prevalence of HIV/AIDS in many countries.

45. Providing support for the development of Africa has become a top priority of the United Nations. Regional actions and international initiatives have further strengthened impetus for progress in conflict resolution, economic growth, consolidation of democracy and implementation of NEPAD. With a recent agreement, the Multilateral Debt Relief Initiative has helped Nigeria to shift approximately $1 billion a year from debt servicing to poverty-reduction programmes. Ghana and the Netherlands recently launched a partnership to support Ghana's nationwide school meals programme using locally produced food. Many African countries are preparing 10-year education plans, while Kenya, Malawi, Uganda and the United Republic of Tanzania continue to show the benefits for primary-school enrolment of abolishing user fees for education. Earlier this year Zambia cancelled fees for basic rural health services and Burundi introduced free medical care for mothers and children.

46. The Africa Fertilizer Summit held in June 2006 in Abuja mapped out a common strategy for the continent to achieve food self-sufficiency and launch the rural economic transformation required to overcome extreme poverty. African leaders set targets for 2007 and 2008 en route to a 2015-based plan of action to help farmers move to higher-yielding land practices, with increased use of improved seeds, fertilizers and irrigation.

47. Meanwhile, the Millennium Project launched the Millennium Villages initiative, which aims to identify how recent global commitments can be translated to Government- and community-led development efforts to further the Millennium Development Goals. Ten countries so far are partnering with UNDP in the initiative.

48. The United Nations system offered further assistance in a wide range of areas. The independent panel of experts that I established two years ago has submitted its second report on the theme "From commitments to results: moving forward NEPAD implementation". The report includes a number of proposals for advancing the NEPAD agenda.

49. In 2005, the Office of the Special Adviser on Africa released a report entitled "Resource flows to Africa: an update on statistical trends". The report found that while official development assistance remained the main external resource flow to Africa, remittances from Africans working abroad had overtaken foreign direct investment in the period 2000-2003. Consequently, public policy should aim to facilitate an increase in remittances, in particular by reducing the cost of transfers so as to achieve the key objective of greater resource flows to households in Africa.

50. Other contributions of the Office of the Special Adviser on Africa include a conference organized in collaboration with the Government of Sierra Leone on disarmament, demobilization, reintegration and stability in Africa in Freetown, in June 2005. It brought together African practitioners and their international partners to share experiences and ideas about ways to improve the design, operation and implementation of disarmament, demobilization and reintegration programmes to better promote sustainable peace on the continent. A similar round table of experts was convened in Cairo in June 2006 on the theme "Natural resources and conflict in Africa: transforming a peace liability into a peace asset" in an effort to promote socially responsible and economically sound resource management in post-conflict countries in Africa.

51. In the years ahead, the United Nations must respond even better to Africa's needs and aspirations. This is consistent with the Organization's ideals, and the people of Africa deserve nothing less.

Ensuring environmental sustainability

52. In 1992 the United Nations Conference on Environment and Development was held in Rio de Janeiro, Brazil, to address pressing issues regarding environmental protection and socio-economic development. Over 100 world leaders signed the United Nations Framework Convention on Climate Change and the Convention on Biological Diversity, endorsed the Rio Declaration and adopted a strategic plan for preventing environmental degradation and achieving environmental sustainability in the twenty-first century, the so-called Agenda 21. The Commission on Sustainable Development was created to monitor and report on implementation of the Earth Summit agreements. Five years later, in 1997, the General Assembly met in special session in New York to reaffirm the Earth Summit compact and review the implementation of Agenda 21 by countries, international organizations and civil society.

53. During my tenure, I have seen a greater understanding among Governments that human security is also threatened by environmental degradation. The continuing increase in the number of ratifications of major multilateral environmental agreements shows the growing commitment of countries to address global environmental issues. Ensuring environmental sustainability is one of the main pillars of the global fight against poverty, and it is essential for achieving the Millennium Development Goals. The United Nations has been active in seeking ways to improve and sustain the environment.

54. The Millennium Ecosystem Assessment, which I launched in 2001 and a report on which was released in March 2005, highlighted the urgency of making more progress towards environmental sustainability. It found that 60 per cent of the world's ecosystems, such as drylands, forests, fisheries and even the air we breathe, are being degraded or used unsustainably. The United Nations system must continue to help countries to integrate environmental concerns effectively into national policy frameworks for development and poverty reduction. The Bali Strategic Plan for Technology Support and Capacity-building, adopted by the Governing Council of the United Nations Environment Programme (UNEP), is aimed at strengthening the capacity of Governments of developing countries and countries with economies in transition to achieve their environmental goals and targets, as well as the environment-related development goals agreed internationally, thus enhancing the environmental sustainability of their countries' develop-

ment. UNEP, UNDP and their relevant partners are intensifying their activities as envisaged in the Bali Strategic Plan.

55. At the 2005 World Summit, world leaders decided on a number of measures aimed at protecting our common environment, including a call for a more coherent institutional framework to address the environmental challenges of today. While the General Assembly has started its consideration of these matters, I have established the High-level Panel on United Nations System-wide Coherence that will present its proposals on how to ensure and enhance coordination of United Nations activities in the areas of development, humanitarian affairs and the environment. In the meantime, UNEP and UNDP, two of the main implementing agencies of the Global Environment Facility, have integrated their respective poverty and environmental projects into the Poverty and Environment Initiative, which was announced at the "Environment for the Millennium Development Goals" high-level event during the Summit in September.

56. Action on climate change is particularly urgent, and implementing a global response to it is a priority of the United Nations. The entry into force of the Kyoto Protocol in February 2005 represented a historic moment in the international response to climate change. Yet this is just one step. There is a need to build a stronger international consensus for setting goals beyond the first Kyoto commitment period of 2008-2012. As at July 2006, 164 countries had ratified the Protocol, representing over 60 per cent of emissions from industrial countries. The wider United Nations Framework Convention on Climate Change remains the multilateral framework for action.

57. A major challenge for all countries in the years ahead is the development of new and sustainable energy sources. Governments, businesses and communities around the world have an important role to play in this endeavour and in the broader effort, in the words of the Millennium Declaration, to free all of humanity from the threat of living on a planet irredeemably spoiled by human activities, and whose resources would no longer be sufficient for human needs.

Chapter III
Peace and security

Conflict prevention and peacemaking

58. The United Nations was founded on a commitment to prevent war and to strengthen means for conflict resolution. The Millennium Declaration reaffirmed that preventing deadly conflicts and protecting people from violence is a priority of the Organization. We continue to be reminded of the importance of peacemaking and attempting to prevent conflict before it develops. Early action to address the root causes of potentially violent conflict, as well as diplomatic initiatives to bring parties together to bridge their differences, are less costly than waiting until conflicts erupt or run their destructive course.

59. During the past decade, the Organization has begun taking prevention more seriously. Efforts to live up to the Charter and the Millennium Declaration have brought improvements around the world. In Africa, the United Nations has been instrumental in peacemaking, as well as in peacekeeping and peacebuilding, in Sierra Leone, Liberia, Angola, Mozambique, Cameroon, Nigeria and elsewhere. In Europe, United Nations-mediated final status talks on Kosovo are under way, and in Cyprus United Nations efforts have been aimed at encouraging a resumption of negotiations for a comprehensive settlement. In Asia, the United Nations has been lending support to reconciliation efforts in Iraq and peace processes in Nepal. In Central Asia I initiated the establishment of a regional United Nations centre for preventive diplomacy, an initiative that enjoys the support of five countries in the region. In the Americas, the General Assembly discontinued its annual review of Central America in 2005, marking the end of over 20 years of successful United Nations peacemaking efforts in the region. Meanwhile, conflict-prevention activities are under way in the Andean region and in Guyana. In countless other cases, through development programming, good offices and other means, United Nations officials shore up fragile situations and help national counterparts to avoid the scourge of war.

60. The Organization has seen institutional progress in peacemaking over the past decade. I warmly welcomed the decisions of the 2005 World Summit with respect to conflict prevention and mediation and can report several steps towards implementation of those decisions. A dedicated mediation support capacity is being established within the Department of Political Affairs, which will serve as a repository of lessons and experiences and will offer more systematic support to United Nations mediators and to mediation partners outside of the United Nations. There has also been important normative, political and institutional progress in the area of conflict prevention. Unfortunately, however, we still have a long way to go to ensure that effective preventive action is taken when the opportunity arises. At the systemic, structural and operational

levels, more understanding, resources, cooperation and will are needed to make armed conflict less viable and less likely.

Peacekeeping

61. Over the past decade, we have been reminded that United Nations peacekeeping plays a crucial role in securing States and individual political freedoms. Missions such as those in Sierra Leone, Timor-Leste, the Democratic Republic of the Congo and the Balkans have been central to my tenure. When I became Secretary-General, the United Nations had fewer than 13,000 troops deployed worldwide and was recovering from the setbacks of the early 1990s. Today 65,500 troops and military observers, 7,500 police and more than 15,000 international and local civilian personnel serve in 15 peacekeeping operations and 3 special political or peacebuilding missions, in Afghanistan, Sierra Leone and Timor-Leste. The annual budget for United Nations peacekeeping has increased from approximately $1 billion in 1997 to approximately $5 billion today—totaling 0.5 per cent of global military spending. In 1997 military and police personnel were drawn from about 70 countries versus over 100 countries currently. In 1998 4 out of the top 10 contributors of troops were developing countries, whereas today all 10 are developing countries.

62. The past year has witnessed the successful transition from peacekeeping to peacebuilding in Sierra Leone and support for the organization of fair and largely calm elections from the Democratic Republic of the Congo, Liberia, Burundi and Haiti. In the particularly challenging environments of Afghanistan and the Democratic Republic of the Congo, peacekeeping operations have facilitated complex transitional political processes.

63. But the year has also brought harsh reminders that the risk of failure is high. We withdrew our peacekeepers from Sierra Leone in December 2005. However, while we pulled our last soldiers from Timor-Leste in May 2005, within just one year an international force had returned to the country as it slipped back towards violence. Meanwhile, progress in the Democratic Republic of the Congo was tempered by violent incidents in the eastern part of the country, which highlighted the challenging and often hostile environment in which our peacekeeping operations take place.

64. The transformation of United Nations peacekeeping is not only numerical. Our traditional role of monitoring ceasefires remains very important, but we have become deeply engaged in facilitating political processes to give countries and territories emerging from conflict the opportunity for legitimate Government. This has been particularly important in, for example, Kosovo, where the United Nations has served as the interim administration and is now leading the political process to determine Kosovo's future status. In addition, in 2005 alone, over 50 million registered voters had the chance to participate in elections and referendums overseen by United Nations peacekeeping missions. Because we recognize that voting alone does not bring stable politics, we are increasingly engaged in helping Governments to reform their security sectors and in providing social services to all. In Liberia and Haiti, our missions are also paying particular attention to the way in which State services are provided and, together with partners, assisting national authorities to enhance the accountability of Government finances.

65. Building these capacities requires significant resources. Over the past year I have been grateful to the Security Council for strengthening the mandates of our missions in Burundi, the Democratic Republic of the Congo and Haiti and for permitting the transfer of personnel from Liberia to Côte d'Ivoire and from Burundi to the Democratic Republic of the Congo. I recall my earlier statements that fulfilling complex mandates requires the highest-calibre civilian staff, drawn from across the United Nations system, other multilateral organizations and Member States. This year, we made important progress in approving and staffing the initial operating capability for a standing police capacity. We must continue to work to get the best professionals, civilian and uniformed, in the field on the shortest possible notice.

66. But building peace takes not only strong personnel but time. Observing the setback in Timor-Leste, we have been reminded that, while the concerns of the Organization's financial and personnel contributors must always be taken into account, it is important that the international community does not withdraw too hastily from conflict-scarred countries. I am hopeful that the new Peacebuilding Commission, which has, with the support of the two Governments, identified Burundi and Sierra Leone for attention, will play an important role in coordinating the rebuilding of post-conflict societies.

67. We also need strong partners. This year we have continued to develop our relationships with other international organizations. I welcome the European Union's decision to provide a standby force to support the United Nations Operation in the Congo during national elections in the Democratic Republic of the Congo, and am grateful to the North Atlantic Treaty Organization, the European Union

and the Organization for Security and Cooperation in Europe for their continued collaboration in ensuring stability and political progress in Kosovo. Meanwhile, the United Nations has made marked progress in cooperating with the African Union, as demonstrated by the joint United Nations-African Union assessment mission to Darfur, Sudan, in June. This allowed the two organizations to develop a consolidated plan for strengthening the current African Union Mission in the Sudan and to provide recommendations for the transfer from that mission to a United Nations peacekeeping operation in the region.

68. Yet we must also recognize that, in spite of this cooperation and considerable effort by the international community, the Government of the Sudan has yet to approve a United Nations peacekeeping operation in Darfur. Alongside the constraints placed on the operations of the United Nations Mission in Ethiopia and Eritrea by the Government of Eritrea and the request of the Government of Burundi that the United Nations Operation in Burundi withdraw, this is a potent reminder that we can build peace and stability only where there is sustained local political support and raises very hard questions about why we sometimes fail to win that support from parties when we need it most. The answers are primarily political. The parties to a conflict may not always perceive an effective peacekeeping operation as being in their interest. There are also often misperceptions about the agenda of our peacekeeping operations. However, once the parties have recognized that United Nations peacekeeping has no other goal than that of promoting international peace and security, we must ensure that our peacekeepers meet the highest standards and that the necessary resources are made available.

69. We have recognized that we sometimes lose local support because of our operational failings, most obviously in the case of sexual exploitation and abuse, which we have worked hard to eradicate in recent years. We also accept that we lose credibility when we lack the full range of resources necessary to address multiple challenges, such as localized violence by politically motivated spoilers and organized crime. Too often, our stature is eroded by disenchantment with the often slow processes of development or institution-building. Our own morale also suffers badly in these circumstances.

70. But we must understand above all that the deployment of peacekeepers, under direct United Nations command or otherwise, will bring real peace only where the international community maintains close involvement in finding political solutions with local actors and in creating conditions for effective reconstruction and development. At a time when our peacekeeping forces are so overextended, and often taking significant risks, it must be remembered that their presence can ease dialogue and succeed only where there is political will, and cannot act as an easy long-term alternative to it.

71. As we approach the end of my term of office and as we continue to search for a settlement to the great crises of our time, such as those in the Middle East and the Sudan, it is crucial that we continue to muster the political will that can translate our investment of financial and human resources into peace.

Peacebuilding

72. In the course of the past decade, ever more focus at the United Nations has been devoted to post-conflict peacebuilding—that is, in the aftermath of conflict, the restoration of State authority, the revitalization of State-society relations and of civil society and the reconstruction of the institutional foundations of economic and social development.

73. The track record of peacebuilding efforts is decidedly mixed. By some counts between a third and half of those countries that emerge from war relapse into it within five years. This phenomenon was illustrated in recent years by the relapse into violence in Haiti and a resurgence of tension in Timor-Leste, in both cases requiring the return of international peacekeepers. In these and similar cases, too little had been done to re-establish the institutional and economic conditions that can sustain political competition within a framework of constitutional order and law.

74. That peacebuilding often fails is not a source of surprise. The political fractures, social and economic inequalities, resource scarcities and other tensions that generate conflict are exacerbated, not diminished, by war. The mere fact of the signing of a peace agreement does not signify an end to these sources of conflict; peace agreements are at best merely a long-term road map for overcoming them. Implementation of those agreements and the wider process of restoring political and economic relationships is the harder part of the battle.

75. A source of surprise, no; but a source of deep concern, certainly. For not only does relapse into war squander national and international investments in peacemaking and recovery, the fighting that occurs after the collapse of a peace agreement is sometimes far more deadly than in earlier rounds, as parties' belief in the prospects of reconciliation is shattered, the possibility of power-sharing seems more remote, and thus a winner-take-all mentality

pervades. In such circumstances parties often commit to total war and the mass killing it can entail.

76. Parties themselves are often conscious of this risk, and thus sometimes take the necessary tough decisions to forge the necessary political compromises, build the necessary institutional restraints and make the necessary sacrifices to restore the populations' faith in the prospects of recovery and lead people away from war. Where peacebuilding succeeds it is always the leadership of domestic actors that is the essential ingredient of success. No amount of international engagement can substitute for domestic political leaders shouldering their responsibilities and leading their people towards peace and development.

77. Domestic leadership is the essential condition of peacebuilding, but it is rarely a sufficient condition. Rather, substantial international support has often made a crucial difference. Indeed, notwithstanding important failures, the fact is that over the past decade international assistance for the implementation of peace agreements and for wider peacebuilding processes has made a critical contribution to an overall decline in the level of civil war in the world—an achievement of historic significance.

78. And when peacebuilding efforts have succeeded—as they have in El Salvador, Guatemala, Mozambique, Cambodia, Rwanda and Eastern Slavonia and show every sign of doing in Burundi, Sierra Leone and Liberia—they show the United Nations system at its best and in all of its facets.

79. The United Nations is first and foremost, of course, a membership organization. And peacebuilding highlights this not only because of the irreducible role of national leadership, but also in that the major contributors to peacebuilding efforts are Member States—both regional Governments that can vitally help to stabilize emergent national authorities and donor Governments that provide the bulk of financial resources to the reconstruction process and an additional layer of political support.

80. The United Nations is also a network of capacities. Some of these, such as the World Bank, the International Monetary Fund and UNDP, play central roles in economic and institutional reconstruction, while others, such as the Office of the United Nations High Commissioner for Refugees (UNHCR), OHCHR, the World Food Programme and UNICEF play vital roles in humanitarian and social recovery.

81. The United Nations is also a source of operational capacity. The deployment of such capacities—particularly in the form of peacekeeping operations, which are now routinely structured to integrate within them all of the various aspects of United Nations operational engagement—has proved vital to helping parties overcome their divisions, provide a secure space within which they can resolve tensions and serve as a channel for resources for the rehabilitation of State and social infrastructure.

82. Bringing all of these roles together has been a major challenge in the past decade. But it is precisely this role that the Peacebuilding Commission was established to play. By creating a forum that links the General Assembly, the Economic and Social Council and the Security Council; by bringing a wider range of States, especially regional actors and the major financial and troop contributors, into the deliberations of the Security Council; by creating a body with an interest in long-term, sustained engagement beyond the normal period of a peacekeeping operation; by creating a forum in which the United Nations system as a whole, including the international financial institutions, can meet with a core set of the most engaged Member States; and, most importantly, by creating a platform for national authorities to set out their own vision and their own priorities for reconstruction—in all of these ways, the establishment of the Peacebuilding Commission holds the promise of more effective, more reliable peacebuilding results.

83. The Peacebuilding Commission has been slow to start and has yet to show its full promise. But good things take time, and we should not be discouraged by the fact that this new body is still trying to find effective ways of working. The creation of a Peacebuilding Support Office and the establishment of a Peacebuilding Fund will add critical tools to its repertoire. Over the next decade, I anticipate that the Peacebuilding Commission will be at the core of the work of the United Nations and the international community in peacebuilding—rightly recognized by the 2005 World Summit as a vital role for the Organization.

Combating terrorism

84. The threat of terrorism to international peace, security and development has taken on new importance during the past 10 years. Consequently, the international community has taken a number of important steps to provide a solid legal basis for common actions against terrorism, including the adoption of 13 universal instruments and their protocols and amendments, the latest of which—the Convention for the Suppression of Acts of Nuclear Terrorism—was opened for signature during the World Summit in September 2005. In the Millennium Declaration world leaders resolved

to take concerted action against international terrorism. At the World Summit they strongly condemned, for the first time, terrorism in all its forms and manifestations, committed by whomever, wherever and for whatever purposes. I trust that the conclusion of a comprehensive convention on international terrorism will be forthcoming.

85. United Nations counter-terrorism activities have expanded dramatically in order to address the growing challenge of terrorism. The milestone Security Council resolutions, 1267(1999), 1373(2001), 1540(2004) and 1624(2005), and expert groups that support the three counter-terrorism subsidiary bodies have made States more responsible for taking practical steps to prevent terrorist financing, travel and access to weapons of mass destruction, as well as the incitement of terrorism. A remarkably wide array of organizations, departments and agencies in the United Nations system, including the International Atomic Energy Agency (IAEA), the United Nations Office on Drugs and Crime, Interpol, the United Nations Educational, Scientific and Cultural Organization, the International Civil Aviation Organization, the International Maritime Organization, WHO and many others, are actively involved in different aspects of preventing and combating terrorism.

86. However, the increasing demand by Member States for technical assistance in implementing universal instruments and the corresponding need for coordination among the growing number of United Nations entities involved in countering terrorism have demonstrated the need for a comprehensive, coherent and consistent counter-terrorism strategy.

87. At the 2005 World Summit, world leaders welcomed my identification of the five elements of a counter-terrorism strategy that I set out in Madrid in March 2005 and agreed to develop them further to fashion a strategy that makes the international community stronger and terrorists weaker. In addition, they requested that I submit proposals to strengthen the capacity of the United Nations system to assist States in combating terrorism and to enhance the coordination of United Nations activities in this regard.

88. In April 2006 I submitted my report entitled "Uniting against terrorism: recommendations for a global counter-terrorism strategy". My proposals stem from the fundamental conviction that no cause, no matter how just, can excuse terrorism. These proposals are focused around five main elements: dissuading groups from resorting to terrorism or supporting it; denying terrorists the means to carry out an attack; deterring States from supporting terrorist groups; developing State capacity to prevent terrorism; and defending human rights in the context of terrorism and counter-terrorism.

89. Throughout the report I have highlighted operational actions to enable Governments, the United Nations and other international organizations, civil society and the private sector—all using their comparative advantages—to work together to counter terrorism while respecting the rule of law and human rights. Over the years, the international community has come to realize that effective counter-terrorism measures and the protection of human rights are not conflicting goals, but complementary and mutually reinforcing ones. The importance of a culture of peace and the fact that terrorism does not emanate from any particular region, ideology or religion—nor is it directed only at certain groups of countries or people—have also become increasingly clear. In this regard, efforts to promote a dialogue among civilizations serve an increasingly useful purpose.

90. I am confident that the United Nations system has vital contributions to make in many aspects of counter-terrorism—from promoting the rule of law and effective criminal justice systems to ensuring that countries have the means to counter the financing of terrorism to strengthening capacity to prevent terrorists from acquiring nuclear, biological, chemical or radiological materials. Biological terrorism in particular poses a formidable challenge and acutely requires new thinking on the part of the international community. For this reason I proposed in my report the need for a multi-stakeholder dialogue in order to ensure that advances in biotechnology are not used for nefarious purposes. We must also never forget that victims are the true face of terrorism: protecting their rights, ensuring that their voices are heard and providing assistance to facilitate their reintegration are of utmost importance. While the primary responsibility for this lies with individual States, the relevant United Nations entities can help.

91. To achieve these goals, I am taking steps to institutionalize the Counter-Terrorism Implementation Task Force that I created one year ago, which brings together 23 United Nations system entities that address different aspects of terrorism, to ensure overall coordination and coherence in United Nations counter-terrorism efforts. I am also establishing a focal point in the Secretariat to help coordinate a civil society campaign to counter terrorism, and I have suggested the creation of an informal group of United Nations technical assistance providers, donors and recipients to exchange information and coordinate efforts.

92. I am pleased that the General Assembly has used my recommendations to foster discussions on a global counter-terrorism strategy. The adoption of such a strategy will enhance operational measures to counter terrorism and will mark a historic step, bringing together all 192 Member States to demonstrate their resolve—and ability—to defeat this scourge. I trust that agreement on a strategy will be forthcoming without delay. All States—large or small, strong or weak—are vulnerable to terrorism and its consequences. They all stand to benefit from a strategy to counter it.

Disarmament and non-proliferation of weapons of mass destruction

93. The elimination of weapons "adaptable to mass destruction" has been on the United Nations agenda since 1946. Over the past decade, we have witnessed at first rising and then diminishing expectations concerning weapons of mass destruction. In 1995, parties to the Treaty on the Non-Proliferation of Nuclear Weapons agreed to extend the treaty indefinitely. A year later, the Comprehensive Nuclear-Test-Ban Treaty was signed. In 2000 the Review Conference of the Parties to the Non-Proliferation Treaty adopted new political commitments to advance the treaty's aims. In 2005 Member States had two opportunities to strengthen the foundations of the treaty, first at the Review Conference in May and then at the World Summit in September. On both occasions, failure to reach consensus on non-proliferation and disarmament sent a terrible signal of a growing international rift on what is potentially the most dangerous threat to international peace and prosperity. At the same time, the world has made remarkable progress in forging a global taboo against chemical weapons. Since its entry into force in 1997, membership in the Chemical Weapons Convention has grown to 178. The treaty is the first to provide for a robust international system to verify the destruction of an entire class of weapons of mass destruction. Since 1995, membership in the Biological Weapons Convention has grown to 155 with the addition of 21 parties. However, concerns persist over the lack of means to verify compliance and the need to expand membership even further.

94. Today the United Nations continues to play an active and influential role in efforts to stem the proliferation of lethal weaponry. In several major speeches this year, I have drawn attention to my overriding concern that the international community is presently facing two very divergent courses. One path, that of active engagement by all Member States, can take us to a world in which the proliferation of nuclear weapons is restricted and reversed through trust, dialogue and negotiated agreement. The other more dangerous course could lead to a world of fearful instability where such weapons are the currency of international relations and in which non-State actors acquire the means to carry out terrorism with potentially catastrophic consequences.

95. If ever there was a time to break the deadlock in multilateral negotiations and bring disarmament back into the limelight of the international agenda, I believe that it is now. At such a moment, we should remember what the Treaty on the Non-Proliferation of Nuclear Weapons has achieved. With near-universal membership, it has entrenched a norm against nuclear proliferation. The success of the treaty, the global support it enjoys and its resilience too often pass unacknowledged.

96. I have also drawn attention to the need to resolve two specific issues of concern. The continuing impasse on the Korean peninsula is especially disappointing given the agreement reached in September 2005 in the Six-Party Talks, which included a set of principles for a verifiable denuclearization of the peninsula. The Islamic Republic of Iran, for its part, needs to enable IAEA to assure the world that its nuclear activities are exclusively peaceful in nature. In both cases, there is a need for solutions that are not only peaceful, but that buttress the integrity of the Treaty on the Non-Proliferation of Nuclear Weapons.

97. While there has been some progress towards disarmament, nuclear weapons worldwide still number in the thousands, many of them on hair-trigger alert. Moreover, new missile testing in 2006 underscores the absence of a multilateral instrument regulating missiles. If we want to avoid a cascade of nuclear proliferation, then there must be a more concerted international effort to build a common understanding of the most immediate nuclear threats. The debate between those who insist on disarmament before taking further non-proliferation measures and those who argue the opposite is in my view self-defeating. Both are essential for security.

98. During a visit to Geneva in June 2006, I was heartened by the fact that the Conference on Disarmament appeared much readier than it has been in recent years to move forward on a programme of work. For the first time in a decade, the Conference is working to an agreed schedule, with particular efforts to reflect the security concerns of all States. In Geneva, I acknowledged the importance of proposals from China and the Russian Federation on preventing the weaponization of outer space and called attention to the elements of a ground-breaking instrument for halting the pro-

duction of fissile materials for weapons purposes proposed by the United States of America. I hope that these steps represent the beginnings of a new period of productivity.

99. IAEA continues its outstanding work of verifying and assuring compliance with the practical aspects of implementing the Treaty on the Non-Proliferation of Nuclear Weapons. The award of the Nobel Peace Prize to the Director General, Mohamed El Baradei, on behalf of the Agency was further evidence of the indispensable role that he and the Organization currently play.

100. I am also pleased to report that in April 2006 the Security Council renewed its resolution 1540(2004), requiring all Member States to enact and enforce effective national legal and regulatory measures, inter alia to prevent non-State actors from acquiring weapons of mass destruction.

101. In my April 2006 report "Uniting against terrorism", I emphasized the likely devastating impact of a nuclear, biological, chemical or radiological terrorist attack. In that report I suggested that bioterrorism—the misuse of biological agents and toxins by non-State actors—was one of the most important under-addressed threats relating to peace and security. I therefore proposed a forum that would bring together key biotechnology stakeholders to provide momentum for a global initiative to minimize the dangers of misuse of biotechnology.

102. The proliferation of small arms continues to pose a serious threat to peace and security in many regions of the world. These weapons may be small, but they cause massive destruction. In 2001 Member States made a commitment to urgently address the illicit trade in small arms and light weapons. I am encouraged by the General Assembly's adoption in December 2005 of an international tracing instrument to identify and trace illicit small arms. However, I am disappointed that the 2006 United Nations conference to review progress made in the implementation of the Programme of Action on Small Arms ended without agreement on further measures. Still, it did succeed in drawing the issue to the attention of the international community, which clearly remains committed to the Programme of Action as the main framework for measures to curtail the illegal trade in those weapons.

103. The various challenges we presently face have never been greater, more varied or, in many respects, more dangerous. They will demand a shared level of commitment, innovative thinking and practical action on the part of all Member States if we are to prove ourselves equal to the challenge. My vision for the United Nations of the twenty-first century is one in which we are increasingly determined to move forward on three fronts—security, development and human rights—simultaneously. These issues are all inextricably linked precisely because they depend upon and reinforce one another. We cannot afford to fail.

Chapter IV
Human rights, rule of law and humanitarian affairs

Rule of law

104. The United Nations was established in the aftermath of a terrible war to ensure that relations among nations would be grounded in international law, including human rights and the dignity of the human person. "Rule of law" is the core concept at the heart of the Organization's work and mission. Those principles apply at the international level as well as within States. Indeed, the Millennium Declaration reaffirmed the commitment of all nations to the rule of law as the all-important framework for advancing human security and prosperity.

105. At the international level, the most striking development over the past decade has occurred in the area of international criminal justice. The International Tribunals for the former Yugoslavia and Rwanda established by the Security Council in 1993 and 1994 respectively marked the first generation of tribunals since the International Military Tribunal established in Nuremberg. They demonstrated the collective will not to allow grave violations of international law to go unpunished. It will be important to continue to ensure that the two tribunals work effectively and efficiently to complete their work. I encourage Member States to cooperate fully with them and to surrender indictees to them upon request.

106. One of the greatest and possibly most lasting achievements of the tribunals was to make the vigorous prosecution of such crimes an accepted practice. Indeed, those groundbreaking efforts contributed to the establishment of the Special Court for Sierra Leone and the Extraordinary Chambers in the courts of Cambodia. In the development of the new tribunals, the Organization applied important lessons learned from the experiences of the first two. Both of the second-generation tribunals, unlike their predecessors, provide for the participation of national judges and prosecutors and the application of national as well as international law.

107. As 2005 came to a close, the Security Council, in its resolution 1644(2005), requested me to begin a process aimed at the establishment of a

tribunal of an international character for Lebanon as a result of the bombing on 14 February 2005 that killed former Lebanese Prime Minister Rafik Hariri and other persons. As we move towards the establishment of this tribunal, the Secretariat will ensure that it applies the highest standards of international justice as it carries out its work. In addition, in Burundi, pursuant to Security Council resolution 1606(2005), the Secretariat is undertaking an approach that combines judicial and non-judicial accountability mechanisms through discussions with the Burundian authorities regarding the legal framework for both a truth and reconciliation commission and a tribunal. In these efforts, the Secretariat will seek to build on the lessons learned from the previous tribunals.

108. The establishment of the International Criminal Court in 2002 was the realization of a long effort to end impunity and undertake through the rule of law that those who commit the crime of genocide, crimes against humanity and war crimes will no longer be beyond the reach of justice. This important step demonstrated the international community's commitment to a permanent and universal mechanism to ensure that as regards those most serious of crimes, impunity will not be tolerated. One hundred Member States have become parties to the Rome Statute of the International Criminal Court. Importantly, the Statute provides for action by national legal authorities before the exercise of international jurisdiction. Since 2004, the Court has opened investigations into situations in the Democratic Republic of the Congo, Uganda and Darfur, the latter being referred to the Court by the Security Council. One suspect alleged to have committed war crimes, a Congolese national, was arrested and transferred to the Court in March 2006. In October 2005, the Court's pre-trial chamber unsealed arrest warrants for five senior leaders of the Lord's Resistance Army for crimes against humanity and war crimes committed in Uganda since July 2002. Extending the participation of Member States in the International Criminal Court will be a further challenge in the area of international justice.

109. Justice, especially transitional justice in conflict and post-conflict societies, is a fundamental building block of peace. In the face of pressures to the contrary, the international community should ensure that justice and peace are considered to be complementary requirements. Indeed, we must never choose between justice and peace, even if it is not possible to pursue both goals in parallel. This is particularly important because it remains our firm position that there should be no amnesty for international crimes.

110. As I pointed out in my report of 23 August 2004 to the Security Council on the rule of law and transitional justice in conflict and post-conflict societies, the rule of law, in this context, refers to a principle of governance in which all persons, institutions and entities, public and private, including the State itself, are accountable to laws that are consistent with international human rights norms and standards. Many parts of the United Nations system work to varying extents on expanding the rule of law, including transitional justice. We have tried, at least in the area of peacebuilding, to ensure coherence and effectiveness in our efforts. As a result, I am encouraged by the recent establishment of the Peacebuilding Commission, which will assist States to ensure that in troubled areas of the world the rule of law is upheld.

111. The rule of law should also apply in the work of the organs of the United Nations. I am pleased that the Security Council has recently renewed its commitment to ensure that fair and clear procedures exist for placing individuals and entities on sanctions lists, for removing them and for granting humanitarian exceptions.

112. In 2004 I spoke to the General Assembly about the need to restore and extend the rule of law throughout the world. I characterized it as a framework in which rather than might making right, right would make might. I warned that the rule of law was at risk around the world, with laws being disregarded in too many quarters. The United Nations as a collective, and each of its Member States individually, must commit to ensuring that at all levels and in all situations we adhere to and promote those legal principles that constitute our Organization's foundation.

Human rights

113. Over the past decade, we have seen a significant and welcome elevation of the importance of human rights in the work of the Organization. The Millennium Declaration and the 2005 World Summit Outcome reaffirmed the basic premise that human rights formed a central pillar and were the shared responsibility of the United Nations system as a whole.

114. Mainstreaming all human rights, including the right to development, has been central to the series of United Nations reform efforts I have initiated since 1997. It has been an important focus of the work of OHCHR in strengthening the linkages between the normative and operational work of the United Nations system. Progress has been made in

this regard across the system in many areas. Building on this progress, I argued in my 2002 and 2005 reports on United Nations reform that more focused attention was needed to support Member States in their efforts to build stronger national systems for the promotion and protection of human rights. The 2005 World Summit gave unprecedented political backing to strengthening the capacity of the High Commissioner and her office to integrate the promotion and protection of human rights into national policies.

115. At the World Summit, Member States accepted my suggestion that, in order to establish human rights at its proper level within the system, they should create a Human Rights Council, directly elected by the General Assembly, to work alongside the Security Council and the Economic and Social Council. In March 2006 the General Assembly adopted a resolution establishing the Council to replace the Commission on Human Rights. One of the features of the Council is that it will review, on a periodic basis, the fulfilment of the human rights obligations of all countries through a universal periodic review mechanism. On 9 May 2006, the 47 members of the Council were elected, and they committed to fully cooperating with the Council and to upholding the highest standards in the promotion and protection of human rights. Together with many other dignitaries, I addressed the opening of the first session on 19 June 2006. Among the important actions taken, the Council adopted the International Convention for the Protection of All Persons from Enforced Disappearances and the United Nations Declaration on the Rights of Indigenous Peoples. It also decided to establish two intersessional open-ended intergovernmental working groups: one to develop the modalities of the universal periodic review mechanism and the other to formulate concrete recommendations on the issue of reviewing and, where necessary, improving and rationalizing all mandates, mechanisms, functions and responsibilities in order to maintain a system of special procedures, expert advice and a complaint procedure.

116. The 2005 World Summit Outcome represented a clear and unambiguous acceptance by all Governments of the collective international responsibility to protect populations from genocide, war crimes, ethnic cleansing and crimes against humanity. For the first time ever, Member States expressed a willingness to take timely and decisive collective action for that purpose, through the Security Council, when peaceful means prove inadequate and national authorities are manifestly failing to do it. The decision represents a renewal of the United Nations promise of "never again", but we must match our rhetoric with a real willingness to take action.

117. Following my report "In larger freedom", the High Commissioner for Human Rights released her plan of action (May 2005), presenting an overall vision for the future direction of OHCHR. In early 2006, she launched her first biennial strategic management plan, which articulates how OHCHR aims to implement the vision in the plan of action and provides a comprehensive overview of the areas of work on which OHCHR will focus and the resources that will be required. In the autumn of 2005, the General Assembly supported the implementation of the new plan by resolving to double the regular budget of the Office over five years. In the biennium 2006-2007, this means an additional 91 posts and a further $20 million in available funding.

118. The plan of action calls for attention to be paid to a range of implementation gaps on the ground and points to the need for concerted action by OHCHR and the United Nations system to work with countries to close those gaps for the effective protection and realization of human rights. The "action 2 programme" I established as a follow-up to my 2002 report "Strengthening of the United Nations: an agenda for further change", is led by OHCHR with participation by the United Nations Development Group and Executive Committee on Humanitarian Affairs agencies. As country-level implementation of action 2 intensifies, increased attention will be needed to direct the wider efforts of the United Nations system at the country level to ensure that they effectively contribute to greater development of national capacity for more effective and sustainable protection of human rights.

119. The treaty bodies made progress in harmonizing their working methods and considering means to assist States parties to fulfil their substantive commitments and meet their reporting obligations. Guidelines for a common core document now exist and are available for States parties to use. In March 2006, the High Commissioner prepared a concept paper that elaborated on the proposal in the plan of action for a unified standing treaty body. It provides a basis on which options for reform could be explored.

120. Special procedures mechanisms fulfilled an important role in the protection of human rights. In the period from September 2005 to June 2006 they undertook fact-finding missions to over 40 countries. During the same period they sent over 900 communications to 125 countries in all regions of the world, covering almost 2,500 individuals.

They also undertook a number of ground-breaking studies in thematic areas related to their mandates.

121. In line with my reform programme and the High Commissioner's plan of action, OHCHR is enhancing its country engagement efforts and increasing its field operations. In 2005, OHCHR opened three new offices, in Nepal, Guatemala and Uganda.

122. The OHCHR office in Nepal has a broad mandate to protect and promote human rights, including by conducting monitoring activities throughout the country. During the demonstrations and protests in April 2006, OHCHR monitoring teams throughout the country documented events, helped deter violence and visited over a thousand people who were detained. With regional offices around the country and monitoring on the street, OHCHR was uniquely placed to contribute to the protection of human rights on the ground.

123. Against the background of violent incidents that took place in Timor-Leste in April and May 2006, the Government of Timor-Leste requested the United Nations to establish an independent commission to review the incidents. I then asked the High Commissioner to establish and support an independent special commission of inquiry for Timor-Leste. The commissioners began their work in Timor-Leste in July 2006 and will report to me by October 2006.

124. In my 2005 report "In larger freedom", I argued that together with development and security, human rights formed the third pillar of the Organization's work. The cause of human rights has entered a new era—an era of implementation. The reforms adopted in the past year, as well as those still under way, reflect this evolution and will better equip the United Nations to fulfil the promise of the Charter.

Democracy and good governance

125. The last decade has witnessed substantial progress for democratic governance. Today more Governments have been chosen by competitive elections than at any time in history. This symbolizes important gains in human rights, freedom and choice. Inclusive public participation and competitive multi-party elections are essential for empowering the poor and for building lasting peace settlements, although they are not sufficient by themselves.

126. The past year witnessed several landmark elections in countries emerging from conflict. The United Nations played a key role in providing assistance with elections in Afghanistan, Burundi, Côte d'Ivoire, the Democratic Republic of the Congo, Haiti, Iraq, Liberia and Palestine—registering voters, administering polling places, facilitating the establishment of electoral laws and strengthening independent electoral commissions. One important outcome of the first legislative elections for the 249-seat Wolesi Jirga ("House of the People") in Afghanistan in September 2005 was the election of 68 women. The United Nations mounted its most ambitious programme ever when aiding elections in the Democratic Republic of the Congo, costing an estimated $432 million. The Democratic Republic of the Congo had not held a multi-party election since 1965 and the country was emerging from an extended period of crisis. The complicated political and electoral situation in Côte d'Ivoire led to a new form of United Nations electoral support: the appointment of a High Representative for Elections to facilitate solutions to electoral disagreements.

127. The United Nations has also assisted dozens of countries that have requested advice or support with more routine electoral administration processes, such as training of professional electoral officials, assisting with electoral dispute resolution, advising on electoral system design, supporting voter education programmes, training journalists in campaign coverage and assessing the costs of registration and balloting.

128. Despite these positive developments, many important challenges remain. Organizing inclusive and competitive elections is only one step—though a necessary one—in building democracy. Elections raise expectations that governing institutions and processes will be responsive to the needs and concerns of all citizens, including the poor and marginalized. To fulfil these hopes, work at the United Nations has gradually shifted during the past decade from a traditional emphasis on public administration towards challenging new issues in democratic governance.

129. To strengthen the efforts of Governments, civil society and non-governmental actors and regional and international organizations that are striving to build and consolidate the pillars of democracy, the World Summit decided in September 2005 to establish the United Nations Democracy Fund. The Fund has attracted $49 million in pledged or contributed funds. The Fund will finance projects designed to empower civil society, strengthen the rule of law, increase popular participation and ensure that people are able to exercise their democratic rights.

130. The United Nations works today with countries to ensure that parliaments are effective and representative, human rights are respected, judges are fair and impartial, the media are inde-

pendent and free and decision-making is responsive to local concerns. Democratic participation and Government capacity-building need to go hand-in-hand. If people vote but experience no real improvement in their daily lives, then they may become disillusioned. If Governments are strengthened but are not accountable to the people, then this process may benefit the few and not the many. This long-term twin challenge lies at the heart of the work of the United Nations on strengthening democratic governance.

131. To achieve these ends, the United Nations provides a wide range of services, policy advice and technical assistance designed to strengthen justice systems and human rights, parliamentary representation, local governance and decentralization, public administration reform and anti-corruption efforts, gender equality, e-governance and access to information, civil society and public opinion. In these programmes, the United Nations collaborates closely with many partners and donor organizations, as well as with parliamentary networks, civil society organizations and other entities.

132. Parliaments can play a critical role by linking citizens and the State, as well as by reducing conflict. The United Nations has worked to strengthen these institutions in more than 50 countries, especially in West African and Arab States. Decentralizing governance is also important for delivering services and achieving the Millennium Development Goals. Improving communities and reducing poverty requires public sector management to be efficient and responsive and for corruption to be eradicated.

133. The International Conference of New or Restored Democracies, working with the United Nations, is a forum especially suited to supporting democracy among approximately 120 countries from the developing and developed world. The sixth conference will take place in Doha in October 2006, the first time it will have been held in the Arab world. Together with the Conference, the Community of Democracies also works with the United Nations to widen acceptance of democratic governance within the international community.

134. The last decade has seen important advances in building effective democratic institutions in many countries, including in some of the poorest nations in the world. The United Nations has contributed substantially towards those developments. Yet in many places the quality of democratic governance continues to need further strengthening and in some, democratic progress has stalled and even moved backwards. Unless international commitment and support is maintained well after polling day, elections may generate empty promises and democratic governance and human development may fail to be sustained.

Humanitarian affairs

135. Humanitarian assistance serves as a tangible demonstration of the United Nations commitment to save lives and alleviate suffering by providing urgently needed help to communities devastated by violent conflict or natural disaster. Emergency relief aid serves as the first rung on the ladder of development, helping vulnerable populations survive catastrophes as they move towards ever-greater self-reliance. In the past 10 years, the humanitarian community has provided assistance and protection to tens of millions of civilians, who tragically continue to be the primary victims of conflict and civil strife. Multiple crises now occur simultaneously across the globe, with humanitarian access and insecurity a growing challenge, especially in fragile or failing States. In 1996 the United Nations issued 13 consolidated appeals totalling $1.8 billion to assist 17 million people in crises around the world. Ten years later, consolidated appeals sought $4.7 billion to fund 18 humanitarian programmes serving 31 million people in 26 countries.

136. As part of my reform programme in 1998, the Department of Humanitarian Affairs was reorganized into the Office for the Coordination of Humanitarian Affairs in an effort to strengthen the coherence and overall effectiveness of humanitarian action. The mandate was expanded to include the coordination of humanitarian response, policy development and humanitarian advocacy. In the past decade, the United Nations has intensified inter-agency coordination, improved field-level coordination and bolstered resource mobilization efforts.

137. As I noted in my report "In larger freedom", no country, weak or strong, can remain isolated from or immune to threats of man or nature that transcend borders. Now more than ever we need a revitalized, effective and accountable United Nations that is capable of meeting the humanitarian challenges ahead. To that end, in 2005 the United Nations launched a comprehensive reform of the global humanitarian system that is already demonstrating life-saving results for some of the world's most desperate and destitute communities.

Humanitarian achievements

138. In 2005 the United Nations embarked on a series of reforms aimed at strengthening the global humanitarian system to ensure a more predictable, coordinated, efficient and effective response.

In March 2006 I launched the Central Emergency Response Fund, one of the first reform proposals announced at the 2005 World Summit, marking a critical improvement of the capacity for humanitarian response by the United Nations. To date, more than 40 donors have pledged $264 million to the new Fund, which upgrades the former Central Emergency Revolving Fund with a grant facility of up to $450 million added to the $50 million loan component already in place.

139. Using the Fund, United Nations agencies can now jump start relief operations in the earliest days of a crisis when most lives are on the line and timely resources are most needed. The Fund also redresses some of the current inequities in humanitarian funding by dedicating one third of its resources to core, life-saving activities in chronically neglected crises. Launched five months ago, the Fund has provided more than $100 million to 10 organizations for more than 150 projects in 20 countries, the majority of them in Africa. Most importantly, the Fund has helped save lives and alleviate the suffering of millions.

140. The second element of reform addresses the need for improved accountability and predictability of response. With humanitarian resources stretched; multiple, simultaneous crises on several continents; and ever-more aid actors in the field, response coordination is not a luxury but a necessity. The newly launched "cluster leadership" provides more systematic predictability by clearly identifying roles and responsibilities within United Nations agencies in nine key areas of response, from relief to early recovery, to help fill gaps in assistance needs.

141. The third element of humanitarian reform underscores the need for strengthened United Nations country-level representation, as endorsed by the Economic and Social Council and reaffirmed in the 2005 World Summit Outcome.

Humanitarian response: results

142. In 2005, the world saw the number of natural disasters increase in frequency and severity. Bracketed by the Indian Ocean tsunami in late 2004 and the South Asian earthquake in October, United Nations humanitarian agencies were stretched to their limits in providing emergency assistance to all those in need.

143. To meet global relief and protection requirements, in 2006 the United Nations issued a consolidated humanitarian appeal for $4.7 billion to fund 18 programmes serving 31 million people in 26 countries. By mid-year, the appeal was 35 per cent funded. The 2005 consolidated appeal sought nearly $6 billion to assist 30 million people in 29 countries, and 67 per cent was funded by year's end.

144. Last year, United Nations humanitarian agencies provided food aid to 97 million people in 82 countries, including 6.5 million in the Sudan; vaccinated over 30 million children in emergency situations against measles; supported hundreds of health facilities; provided access to shelter, suitable land, safe drinking water and sanitation to hundreds of thousands of people; created hundreds of emergency education facilities; provided protection and assistance to some 20 million refugees and displaced persons; and supported child protection activities in some 150 countries.

Natural disasters

145. While recovery from the tsunami tragedy and efforts to "build back better" proceeded apace, humanitarian actors struggled to cope with an 18 per cent increase in the number of large-scale natural disasters in 2005; 157 million people were affected and 92,000 killed in those disasters. As always, poor communities were at greatest risk—and least able to withstand—nature's destructive potential.

146. Floods, droughts and windstorms accounted for more than 96 per cent of those affected by natural disasters in 2005. Twenty-seven tropical storms, thirteen of which became hurricanes, devastated populations in twelve countries, killing more than 1,000 people and displacing hundreds of thousands.

147. Earthquakes, volcanoes and tsunamis were the deadliest natural hazards last year. The worst of these tragedies occurred in October 2005 when a massive earthquake in South Asia killed more than 73,000 people, injured 69,400 and left 3.3 million homeless. Despite unprecedented logistical challenges and harsh Himalayan weather, relief efforts assisted upward of 3 million people with winterized shelter, medical care, food, water and sanitation.

148. In the Horn of Africa, recurring cycles of drought have exacerbated food insecurity and affected 15 million people. In April 2006, I launched a regional appeal for the Horn of Africa addressing both immediate needs for more than 8 million people as well as underlying causes of vulnerability. Of the $855 million requested, less than 40 per cent of this emergency appeal has been met.

Refugees and displaced persons

149. As 2005 drew to a close, the world saw the number of refugees decline for the fifth straight year, while the number of new refugees was the low-

est in nearly 30 years. Globally, there are now 12.7 million refugees registered by the United Nations (of whom 4.3 million are Palestine refugees in the Occupied Palestinian Territory, Jordan, Lebanon and the Syrian Arab Republic). In Afghanistan, Burundi and Liberia, hundreds of thousands of people who had been forced from their homes have been able to return to their countries.

150. Sadly, however, there has been a significant rise in the number of internally displaced persons. Worldwide some 23 million people remain displaced as a result of violence and armed conflict. Millions more have been displaced by natural disasters.

Complex emergencies

151. Conflicts in the Democratic Republic of the Congo, the Sudan and northern Uganda, among others, continue to claim hundreds of thousands of lives, deprive people of land and property, destroy livelihoods, and foment instability. Regional spillover of localized conflicts in Chad and northern Uganda pose challenges to humanitarian operations, as do the issues of access and security.

152. In Darfur, currently the world's largest relief operation, some 13,000 aid workers are struggling to assist 3 million destitute people—half of Darfur's population—despite daily acts of hideous violence and harassment. In large pockets of Western and Northern Darfur, limited access threatens to sever the humanitarian lifeline for hundreds of thousands of civilians. Overall funding is insufficient to the region's massive humanitarian needs.

153. Humanitarian needs are also acute in the Democratic Republic of the Congo, where 3.9 million people have perished from hunger and disease during the country's civil war. Some 1,200 people continue to die each day—a silent tsunami death toll every six months. Despite these grim statistics, only 51 per cent of the country's $212 million humanitarian appeal was funded in 2005.

154. As we see all too plainly in Darfur, aid cannot be a substitute for political solutions or remain an excuse for political inaction. We must address both symptoms and causes of crises if we are to staunch the world's haemorrhage of human suffering.

The road ahead: humanitarian challenges

155. Significant progress has been made in strengthening our global humanitarian system. However, we need to focus more attention on protecting civilians and establishing safe access to asylum. Thousands of women are still raped and violated as a matter of course, and defenceless civilians continue to be killed. We need earlier conflict mediation efforts, increased access for humanitarian workers and, most importantly, well-trained and -financed peacekeepers with strong mandates to protect civilians.

156. Funding inequities remain as persistent as they are pervasive; some neglected crises receive barely 20 per cent of funds required. We also need to improve the speed of humanitarian funding so that monies arrive when they can do the most good. Currently, United Nations emergency "flash appeals" receive on average only 16 per cent of funds during the critical first month of a crisis.

157. Humanitarian crises exact a terrible toll on children, who are at grave risk of violence, exploitation, abuse and recruitment into fighting forces. Each year hundreds of thousands of children die from malnutrition, hunger and preventable disease.

158. In the last decade, the number of people affected by disasters was three times higher than in the 1970s. As our climate changes we need to strengthen our disaster risk reduction and preparedness measures, drawing on inter-agency early warning and contingency planning efforts.

159. The need for a reformed, strengthened global humanitarian system has never been more apparent or necessary. We need to work together, harnessing the world's generosity, strength and attention, to tackle the most pressing humanitarian challenges of our day. The Millennium Development Goals represent a shared vision of how to tackle some of these challenges. Our generation has no more worthy goal and no more important aspiration. Let us seize this opportunity. Lives depend on it.

Chapter V

Strengthening the United Nations

The intergovernmental machinery

160. As I have said on several occasions, as the world changes, the United Nations must continue the process of renewal and adaptation. The effort to make the United Nations a more effective instrument of its members' collective will is one that is of vital importance for people around the world who look to the Organization for help in defeating poverty, preserving peace, easing humanitarian emergencies and protecting human rights. At the Millennium Summit in 2000, Member States clearly recognized that all the principal organs of the United Nations were in need of reform. At the

2005 World Summit they reaffirmed their commitment to a more efficient and effective United Nations, including with a call for a strengthened intergovernmental machinery.

Security Council

161. I have always maintained that no reform of the United Nations will be complete without the reform of the Security Council. The Council should be more representative of today's geopolitical realities and more efficient and transparent in its working methods. The Millennium Declaration called for an intensification of Member States' efforts "to achieve a comprehensive reform of the Security Council in all its aspects". At the 2005 World Summit, world leaders stated that Security Council reform was "an essential element of our overall effort to reform the United Nations". Enhancing the Council's legitimacy through such reform will enable it to better fulfil its primary responsibility for the maintenance of peace and security in the world.

162. The High-level Panel on Threats, Challenges and Change, which I commissioned to recommend practical measures for ensuring effective collective responses to global security challenges, proposed two models for an equitable enlargement of the Security Council. In my report "In larger freedom", I urged the membership to consider the options and reiterated the need for reform of the Council's working methods. Member States responded actively, by taking initiatives and engaging in debate on both the expansion of the Council and on possible ways to improve the Council's methods of work.

163. There is broad support within the membership on the need for reform of the Security Council. It is important to find common ground for action on this fundamental piece of overall United Nations reform. Indeed, decisions on such reform, taken sooner rather than later, will ensure that the United Nations machinery to promote the establishment and maintenance of peace and security will remain relevant and credible to meet today's and tomorrow's challenges.

General Assembly

164. The Millennium Declaration and the 2005 World Summit Outcome reaffirmed the General Assembly's central position as the chief deliberative, policymaking and representative organ of the United Nations. In recent years much has been achieved on improvement of the Assembly's working methods. For example, presidents of the Assembly are now elected several months in advance of the opening of the session, as are the Main Committee chairs and bureaux, thereby dovetailing the transitions between sessions and ensuring the maximum passage and retention of institutional memory. Progress also continues to be made on shortening the agenda, on institutionalizing interactive discussions and question periods with senior Secretariat officials on specific programmes, mandates and activities and on working to ensure maximum coordination and minimum duplication in the subjects and areas covered by different bodies.

165. However, much remains to be done to increase the Assembly's effectiveness and its contribution to the Organization's activities. I am encouraged to see that the Ad Hoc Working Group on the Revitalization of the General Assembly has devoted a number of general debates and thematic meetings to these issues during the current session.

166. While everyone agrees on the need for General Assembly revitalization, there remain contending views on the ways in which this goal might best be achieved. Some Member States focus on the rationalization of the Assembly's working methods, while others advocate a more substantive reinforcement of its role and authority, I continue to believe that many of the elements of these approaches and others could contribute to the greater effectiveness and efficiency that so many Member States wish to see the General Assembly regain.

Economic and Social Council

167. In my report "In larger freedom", I called for a revived role for the Economic and Social Council in shaping, implementing and coordinating the development agenda. During the course of its work, the Council has initiated various relevant initiatives to promote coherence and harmonization, however more could be done to enhance its functions of coordination, policy review and policy dialogue in the economic and social areas mandated by the Charter.

168. At the 2005 World Summit, world leaders recognized the need for a more effective and efficient Economic and Social Council. In response to my proposals to revamp the unique functions of the Council, they agreed to strengthen it by reconceiving its function of serving as a platform for high-level dialogue on global economic and social affairs but also assigning some new functions. In particular, Member States decided to establish a high-level development cooperation forum, to be held every two years, for the purpose of reviewing trends in development cooperation, promoting greater coherence in the various development interventions and better linking the normative and operational

work of the Organization. Member States further agreed to hold every year an assessment of progress in the achievement of the internationally agreed development goals, including the Millennium Development Goals, at the ministerial level. I am confident that these functions will contribute to our efforts to strengthen the role of the United Nations in the area of development. In order to allow the Council to respond effectively and efficiently, world leaders also agreed to review and adapt its methods of work.

169. In the follow-up to the World Summit, the President of the General Assembly launched a negotiating process to define the details of the decisions made by world leaders. A draft resolution was tabled by the co-chairs and informal consultations have been held. Member States will resume consultations at the end of August, and I am confident that a final agreement can be reached expeditiously. The strengthening of the Economic and Social Council has long been needed. It is my hope that a strengthened Council will be able to assert its leadership in driving a global development agenda and providing direction to the efforts of the intergovernmental bodies of the Organization working in this field.

The Secretariat

170. Reforming the United Nations has been a priority of mine since I assumed office in 1997. In the past 10 years I have proposed and implemented numerous ideas and changes to bring the United Nations up to best international practices. This has included changes to work programmes, structures and systems, at headquarters locations and in the field. Much of my reform agenda has been implemented, however, not all the reforms were accepted by Member States. Understanding that the Organization needs to continue to improve, in March 2006 I released a final reform package in my report "Investing in the United Nations: for a stronger Organization worldwide". Much of the agenda contained in the report will be for my successor to implement over the coming years. It is my hope that the Organization will continue to move towards enhanced efficiency and effectiveness.

171. The 1997 reform package included a number of changes to the Secretariat structure, most notably the creation of the Department of Economic and Social Affairs from three existing departments and the consolidation of two programmes into the Office for Drug Control and Crime Prevention (now the United Nations Office on Drugs and Crime). The Centre for Human Rights was also merged into the Office of the United Nations High Commissioner for Human Rights. Three important new structures were introduced to improve United Nations management: the post of Deputy Secretary-General was created, a cabinet in the form of the Senior Management Group was established and four sectoral committees were formed to bring coherence to the work of the United Nations on peace and security, humanitarian affairs, development and economic and social affairs. In 2002 I proposed a second major reform package, which contained proposals for a major overhaul of the Department of Public Information and the Department of General Assembly Affairs and Conference Services (now the Department for General Assembly and Conference Management). In 2005, two senior management committees were created to improve executive decision-making and a Management Performance Board was established to improve senior managerial accountability.

172. Efforts to improve the overall efficiency of the Organization also moved on several other fronts. Approximately 1,000 staff posts were permanently eliminated in the 1998-1999 budget. In the 2004-2005 budget cycle, nearly 1,000 reports and activities were consolidated or discontinued and resources were redeployed to higher-priority areas of work. Asked to do more with less, the Organization has had in fact only very limited real growth in its regular budget. Much has been invested in information technologies since the late 1990s. One visible benefit is that all United Nations official reports and publications can now be retrieved for free through the Official Document System, which is available over the Internet. The United Nations website provides extensive materials in multiple languages, making up-to-date information and images available through multimedia sources. Open debates of the Security Council are now webcast along with other important meetings.

173. More broadly, following the findings of an internal staff survey and in response to reported shortcomings in the management of the oil-for-food programme, I introduced at the beginning of 2005 a series of measures to strengthen accountability and improve ethical conduct. In particular, an Ethics Office was established in December 2005, which is now administering new policies of protection for reporting of misconduct and financial disclosure. The Ombudsman, whose office was established in 2002, has been facilitating the informal resolution of disputes between United Nations staff and management. At the request of the General Assembly, I have also commissioned a multidisciplinary panel to analyse and review all aspects of the existing internal justice system. The panel will report to the Assembly at its sixty-first session.

174. Reforms on procurement were initiated in 1999, and the United Nations has undergone significant transformation since then. To ensure more effectiveness, annual procurement plans now are posted on the United Nations website, which, in addition to providing advance information, allows vendors not registered with the Procurement Division to register and participate. Furthermore, all purchasing requirements are now posted on the website, progress on a transaction can be traced and details of the awards are posted in accordance with international standards. These and other procurement reform efforts were validated by an independent review conducted by the United States National Institute of Government Purchasing in mid-2005. Following a revelation of criminal misconduct concerning a United Nations procurement official, later that year I ordered a comprehensive review of internal and financial controls. The General Assembly approved emergency funding in July 2006 to increase the professional capacity in this area. Further reforms are to be discussed by Member States at the sixty-first session of the Assembly.

175. The budgeting system has been transformed from one focusing on a detailed description of inputs and resources to one that identifies intended outcomes and measurable indicators of achievement. The long-range planning cycle has been reduced from four years to two and a duplicative intergovernmental review eliminated. In addition, the Financial Regulations and Rules of the United Nations have been updated and consolidated to delegate more authority but make managers more accountable. In the reform package set out in "Investing in the United Nations", I propose more comprehensive strengthening of the financial management and budgetary processes.

176. My latest reform proposals recognize the need for an integrated and mobile global workforce that draws on and develops the experience and talent existing both at Headquarters and in the field. A host of improvements to the United Nations system of managing its people has been introduced in recent years. First, a new web-based recruitment system for hiring, reassigning and promoting staff to ensure greater transparency in advertising vacancies was put in place in 2002. Managers are now empowered to select their own staff, subject to appropriate checks and balances. Second, incentives to encourage staff mobility between duty stations and functions were introduced. Training and learning programmes for all staff are now more widely available. Third, a new performance appraisal system was introduced. Finally, a number of "staff-friendly" benefits were introduced to bring the United Nations in line with major corporations offering similar incentives, including the introduction of flexible working hours, telecommuting possibilities and paternity leave entitlements. However, more can and should be done, and I have appealed to Member States for a significant infusion of resources for this purpose.

177. Facing a sharp escalation in threats against United Nations personnel, the staff security procedures were reviewed, first in 2000 and again in 2003, following the tragic loss of 22 United Nations staff in Baghdad. In late 2004 I recommended a major overhaul of the United Nations security system. This included a request for a sizeable increase in resources allocated for protection of staff and proposals to strengthen and clarify the chain of command. A new Department of Safety and Security was subsequently created, consolidating functions previously performed by separate offices. It now provides timely, professional advice on security-related matters, including through more thorough threat and risk assessment. The new department is responsible for the security of some 100,000 United Nations staff and 300,000 dependants in 150 duty stations throughout the United Nations system, many of which are in crisis and post-conflict risk situations.

The mandates of the Organization

178. In 1954, Dag Hammarskjöld conducted the first review of mandates, at the request of the membership. Since then there has been no other attempt to review the mandates adopted by Member States to guide the work of the Organization. I therefore proposed in my report "In larger freedom" that Member States undertake a review of all mandates older than five years to see whether activities concerned were still genuinely needed or whether the resources assigned to them could be reallocated in response to new and emerging challenges. I stressed the need for "a capable and effective" Secretariat that could change in response to changing needs of the Organization. I underlined that Member States had a central role to play in ensuring that the Organization's mandates stayed current.

179. In September 2005 at the World Summit, world leaders responded by requesting the General Assembly and other relevant organs to review all mandates older than five years originating from resolutions of the General Assembly and other organs in order "to strengthen and update the programme of work of the United Nations". They further requested me to facilitate this process with analysis and recommendations. In response to that request, I provided an analytical framework for review of the

Organization's mandates in my report "Mandating and delivering: analysis and recommendations to facilitate the review of mandates". That report addressed key challenges in the mandate generation cycle, including the lack of evaluative information on the effectiveness of mandates, burdensome reporting requirements, overlap between and within organs and the gap between mandates and resources. The report also made recommendations in relation to each of the Organization's programme priorities. It was supplemented by an online inventory of mandates, designed to facilitate Member States' review.

180. The General Assembly began reviewing its mandates through a series of informal consultations, which also saw the participation of senior programme managers. Member States responded to the recommendations in my report and provided additional proposals of their own aimed at strengthening the programme of work of the Organization. The Assembly also authorized an ad hoc working group to review in the first stage of the exercise mandates older than five years that have not been renewed. Work is ongoing, and the Secretariat will continue to assist and facilitate the exercise throughout the process.

181. Concurrently with the consultations in the General Assembly, the Economic and Social Council and the Security Council have begun the process of reviewing their own mandates. The review of the Economic and Social Council has been following a process similar to that in the Assembly. The Security Council has focused on an initial set of mandates for its first phase. As I have mentioned on several occasions, the review of mandates is a historic opportunity to renew and strengthen the work of the Organization. Member States should seize this opportunity to ensure that our Organization can respond effectively to today's needs.

Cooperating with regional organizations

182. Over the past decade there has been a significant increase in the range of partnerships between the United Nations and regional organizations in such areas as peacekeeping and peacemaking, strengthening good governance and the rule of law, promoting respect for human rights and responding to humanitarian emergencies. I have stressed the importance of a new vision of global security that draws upon the resources and legitimacy of effective regional and global institutions that are both flexible and responsive to the complex challenges of today's world.

183. To support those efforts, I have engaged the heads of regional organizations in regular exchanges of views on issues of common concern. The high-level meetings with the heads of regional organizations and other intergovernmental organizations have now been made an annual event so that we can focus on practical cooperation on key issues and follow up more effectively. At the sixth high-level meeting, which I convened in July 2005, we established a standing committee to provide overall guidance to the process of creating a more structured relationship between the United Nations and regional organizations so a genuine agreement based on comparative advantages can be realized.

184. At the World Summit last September, world leaders supported a stronger relationship between the United Nations and regional and subregional organizations, as envisaged in Chapter VIII of the Charter, and resolved to expand cooperation with such organizations through practical means, such as formalized agreements between their respective secretariats. The implementation process will be reported to the seventh high-level meeting, which I will convene in September 2006. Also, a report capturing the past, present and future of our evolving joint work is being submitted to the Security Council for its meeting on 20 September under the presidency of Greece. This is an important opportunity to consolidate institutional relationships and look to the future.

185. Our joint working groups have also decided to enlist the support of the United Nations University's comparative regional integration studies programme to study the organizational, operational and resource capacities of partner organizations in the maintenance of peace and security. Meanwhile, I have moved to ensure that the Secretariat itself is adequately resourced to service the strengthening partnership.

System-wide coherence

186. The fragmentation of the United Nations system and the consequent inability of United Nations support to generate maximum impact at the country level has been an issue of concern to Member States for many years.

187. In response to this concern, I have introduced several important initiatives, which together have made a significant difference in the way the United Nations works, especially at the country level. Four Executive Committees were established in 1997—on development, humanitarian affairs, peace and security, and economic and social affairs—to provide a forum where United Nations departments and programmes could discuss specific issues on a regular basis and plan more coherent ap-

proaches to each issue. As they began to be effective, most of the specialized agencies asked to join, resulting in greatly increased communication and understanding among the various entities working on those issues.

188. At the same time, as I noted earlier, I established a cabinet structure, the Senior Management Group, wherein the heads of the key departments of the Secretariat could interact and, by inviting the chairs of the four Executive Committees, provided a link to the wider United Nations system. The Policy and Management Committees are enhancing decision-making at the most senior level.

189. These Headquarters coordination and decision-making mechanisms have complemented the pre-existing United Nations System Chief Executives Board for Coordination, which I chair twice a year, bringing together the heads of all United Nations entities to further cooperation on a range of substantive and management issues.

190. While addressing the need for better coordination at Headquarters, I have also focused most of my efforts on country-level coordination. The resident coordinator system has been improved, including through an expanded United Nations Development Group and a toolkit that includes operational tools and procedures agreed upon across the development agencies, thus providing for much more coherent action at the country level. Furthermore, the humanitarian coordinators can count on strong technical support and guidance, an emergency fund at his or her disposal and agreed leadership roles to play to ensure a fast and effective humanitarian response. Progress has also been made in ensuring synergy and coherence between the activities of peacekeeping operations and country teams, both during and after the mission period, through the establishment of a post under the Special Representative of the Secretary-General charged with bridging the two United Nations presences in the field and leading joint planning at the country level.

191. At the 2005 World Summit, leaders called for stronger system-wide coherence across the United Nations system and in particular across development-related organizations, agencies, funds and programmes of the United Nations system. To this end, the Summit Outcome specifically invited me "to launch work to further strengthen the management and coordination of United Nations operational activities", while continuing ongoing efforts to strengthen the governance, management and coordination of the Organization.

192. In February 2006, I created a High-level Panel on United Nations System-wide Coherence. The Panel brings together 15 eminent persons, whose extraordinary experience and authority are a measure of the importance that I attach to the Panel's work and are a reflection of the wish of all Member States to create a more coherent and effective Organization.

193. The objective of the Panel is to propose recommendations that will lead to a revitalized United Nations system that is better equipped to help achieve the internationally agreed development goals, including the Millennium Development Goals. In particular, the Panel's aim is to help create a United Nations system that provides more effective support for plans and priorities defined at the country level to address development, humanitarian, environmental and other critical challenges, including gender issues, human rights and sustainable development. The Panel is expected to deliver its recommendations to me by September 2006 to allow for a formal presentation to the General Assembly at its sixty-first session and possible implementation in 2007.

194. In order to ensure the engagement and commitment of all key stakeholders, the Panel has undertaken a broad consultative process including country, regional and thematic consultations, as well as meetings with Member States and United Nations organizations and hearings with civil society organizations. Moreover, the work of the Panel is enriched by research, analysis and insights from inside and outside the Organization, and takes into account other complementary United Nations reform efforts.

Chapter VI
Global constituencies

Strengthening ties to civil society

195. Since the early 1990s, and particularly during my term as Secretary-General, the relationship of the United Nations with civil society has greatly deepened and expanded. This has been the case even though the United Nations is and will remain an intergovernmental organization, where decisions are taken by its Member States. This process of increasing engagement with civil society and other non-State actors has strengthened both the institution and the intergovernmental debate and has been part of the ongoing process of modernization and institutional change that the Organization has undergone in the past decade. As I wrote in "In larger freedom: towards development, security and human rights for all", the goals of the United

Nations can be achieved only if civil society and Governments are fully engaged.

196. Civil society has been a key partner of the United Nations since its inception, whether at the country level delivering humanitarian assistance or at the global level participating in debates in the Economic and Social Council. But in the past two decades or so, there has been an enormous transformation in the nature and importance of the role of civil society, at the national level and in the international arena, including at the United Nations. The growth of civil society at the international level has paralleled the globalization process. Globalization, and the technologies that partly propelled it, has led to a broadening of horizons, the multiplication of global issues, a widening of interests and increased opportunities for participatory democracy.

197. Where once representative democracy was at the core of democratic forms of governance, today participatory democracy is increasingly important. Representative democracy is under stress in many countries, as demonstrated by low turnouts for elections and disillusioned citizens. The ability of civil society organizations to represent the interests of citizens, to interact directly with Governments and to participate directly in policy debates at the national and international levels contributes to the legitimacy of democratic ideals.

198. Where once large intergovernmental meetings and conferences were mainly the realm of Governments, today it would be unthinkable to stage such events without the policy perspectives, unique advocacy and mobilization of civil society. The engagement of civil society has clearly enhanced the legitimacy, accountability and transparency of intergovernmental decision-making. A recent example is the global mobilization of civil society around debt, trade and aid issues and the Millennium Development Goals by the Global Call to Action against Poverty in 2005.

199. Where once agendas were set by Governments, today civil society has brought new issues to the table and has been instrumental in, for instance, the establishment of the International Criminal Court and the adoption of the Convention on the Prohibition of the Use, Stockpiling, Production and Transfer of Anti-personnel Mines and on Their Destruction.

200. Where once governance was limited to Governments, today various non-State actors, including civil society, are part of various governance structures. Recent examples are the Programme Coordinating Board of UNAIDS and the Internet Governance Forum, which will have its first meeting from 30 October to 2 November 2006 in Athens.

201. Where once monitoring and enforcement were largely the role of Governments, today civil society has an important role in making sure that commitments are implemented, for example in timber certification, the fight against child labour, corporate social responsibility and human rights.

202. Where once checks and balances in democratic societies were largely the domain of national parliaments, today civil society plays its part.

203. Given the increasing importance of civil society, the United Nations has found several ways to engage with it. Many United Nations entities, including funds, programmes and specialized agencies, consult with civil society on a regular basis through various mechanisms, such as forums, hearings, consultations, advisory committees and the like. This is, of course, critical given the fact that civil society has become an essential partner for different kinds of humanitarian, development and peacebuilding operations of the United Nations. The number of operational activities of the United Nations where civil society has played an increasingly important role has expanded, and now also includes such areas as electoral support and conflict prevention.

204. In July, the High-level Panel on United Nations System-wide Coherence in the areas of development, humanitarian assistance and the environment that I appointed in February and the High-level Group for the Alliance of Civilizations held hearings with civil society in Geneva.

205. Throughout my term as Secretary-General, I have consistently encouraged a deeper relationship between the United Nations and civil society. I have myself actively engaged with civil society on many occasions—including at the major United Nations conferences and summits, during my travels and at Headquarters. One recent example is my visit to Darfur in March 2005, where I met with representatives of non-governmental organizations, who work in Darfur under very dangerous circumstances, to underline the crucial role of non-governmental organizations in the international community's efforts there.

206. The exponential growth in both numbers and influence prompted me to establish a Panel of Eminent Persons on United Nations-Civil Society Relations, chaired by the former president of Brazil, Fernando Henrique Cardoso, to assess and draw lessons from interactions between the United Nations and civil society and recommend ways to improve them. The Panel submitted its report in June 2004 and I presented my response to it in September of the same year.

207. The Panel argued very convincingly that the United Nations must become an even more

outward-looking organization. That means using its unique convening power to reach out to diverse constituencies, especially where such actors command great expertise or resources relevant to a particular issue. Facilitating the participation of different stakeholders in relevant debates of global significance can only enhance the quality and depth of policy analysis and implementable outcomes, including in the form of partnerships. In that way, the United Nations will expand its global reach and influence, ensuring that its decisions will be better understood and supported by a broad and diverse public.

208. Unfortunately, the Member States have not taken any formal action on the Cardoso Panel's recommendations and my response to them. Nevertheless, a number of actions have been taken. For example, the United Nations Development Group is strengthening the capacity of United Nations resident coordinators to engage with civil society at the country level. A number of country offices have appointed a civil society focal point in the United Nations country team to strengthen engagement of the United Nations system with civil society, pursuant to my recommendations. Work is also under way to establish a trust fund to support the country teams in their work with civil society.

209. In addition, at the intergovernmental level, the General Assembly has held four informal interactive hearings with representatives of non-governmental organizations, civil society organizations and the private sector. The first one was held during the lead-up to the 2005 World Summit, and three additional ones were held in 2006 as inputs to the high-level meetings to review the Declaration of Commitment on HIV/AIDS, on the midterm comprehensive global review of the implementation of the Programme of Action for the Least Developed Countries for the Decade 2001-2010 and on international migration and development. These hearings have been an important innovation for interaction between civil society and the Assembly.

210. The President of the sixtieth session of the General Assembly appointed in May 2006 the Permanent Representatives of Indonesia and Norway as his personal advisers on the relationship between Member States and civil society, including non-governmental organizations. The advisers conducted a series of consultations with non-governmental organizations, Member States and United Nations staff. The President sent their report to all Member States on 7 July 2006.

211. The report acknowledges that there are clear differences in expectations between Member States and civil society on the relationship between them. Yet, it suggests that there is sufficient ground to explore better interaction and more meaningful inclusiveness, for example, through meetings between the President of the General Assembly and civil society at the beginning of his or her term or at other key moments, and between the chairs of the Main Committees of the Assembly and civil society.

212. Civil society is now such a powerful force in the world that the United Nations will have to continue exploring new mechanisms and formats for engaging with it. As we move forward on this together, it is important that we collectively address some Member States' lingering concerns about, and sometimes mistrust of, civil society. Our civil society partners must ensure that they comply scrupulously with the responsibilities and obligations that accompany their rights at the United Nations and continue to improve their overall transparency and accountability to others. I am aware that many civil society organizations, associations, networks and bodies are rising to these challenges in a variety of creative ways, and this bodes well for the future.

213. One other area that requires attention is the frequent underrepresentation of civil society from developing countries at United Nations meetings. Establishing a better regional balance would require changes both within civil society and by Member States. International civil society organizations, for example, could make more of an effort to include organizations from developing countries in their networks, choose citizens from developing countries as their representatives at the United Nations and base their headquarters more often in developing countries. Member States could help by generously supporting travel and related expenses of participants from developing countries in United Nations events. At the same time, we should use modern communication technologies to explore how civil society organizations from different regions can make contributions to global policy debates and discussions without having to be physically present.

Engaging the business community

214. For the first time in over 60 years of United Nations history, we are making business and other social actors vital partners in pursuit of our goals. This new relationship has had two fundamental implications for the work of the Organization.

215. First, it has furthered progress in achieving the Millennium Development Goals, ultimately improving the lives of the poor by facilitating support in critical areas, ranging from simple advocacy of United Nations goals to the

provision of humanitarian assistance and the formation of partnerships in information technology, microcredit and health. Hundreds of projects in support of the Millennium Development Goals have resulted from this engagement, including those initiated under the Growing Sustainable Business for Poverty Reduction initiative, which aims to stimulate profitable foreign investment in the world's poorest countries to foster sustainable economic opportunities on the ground.

216. Second, new forms of engagement with businesses also advance United Nations reform by providing the Organization with exposure to improved management practices and better ways of leveraging its moral authority and convening power, thus becoming a powerful catalyst for institutional innovation across the system.

217. At the centre of these efforts is the Global Compact, which I launched in July 2000. It is the world's largest corporate citizenship initiative today, with over 3,000 participants from more than 100 countries, over half from the developing world. Through learning, dialogue and partnership projects, the Global Compact has brought about far-reaching changes. The alignment of corporate activities with broader United Nations goals has also brought about significant improvements in governance and capacity-building for suppliers and small enterprises. By advocating universal principles as an integral part of business strategies and operations, global markets have become more robust and inclusive.

218. Through the Global Compact Office, many United Nations organizations have found a new entry point for engaging businesses and improving their own ability to work with the private sector. The Organization itself, through the United Nations Joint Staff Pension Fund and the procurement process, is internalizing the Global Compact's principles, thus gaining credibility and ethical strength. Overall, these changes are bringing greater efficiency and innovative ways of leveraging institutional advantages throughout the Organization.

219. The other main entry point for the business community is the United Nations Fund for International Partnerships (UNFIP), which has provided vital support to a wide array of United Nations programmes, generated nearly $1 billion in new resources for United Nations causes, and has evolved into the United Nations Office for Partnerships. While our engagement of businesses is firmly rooted in the understanding that the goals of business and the United Nations are very distinct, there are increasingly overlapping objectives. Nonetheless, this cooperation requires clear rules of engagement in order to protect the United Nations while forging partnerships that advance practical implementation. Today, the Organization has in place integrity measures and policy frameworks to define the rules of engagement. The Global Compact Office has spearheaded many of these developments, and I am confident that it will continue to lead this promising reform from within the Organization. It is my hope that Member States will continue to support these efforts and that engagement with the business community and other societal actors will continue to evolve as an integral part of organizational change to make the United Nations fit for the twenty-first century.

Chapter VII

Conclusion

220. The themes of good governance and accountability run through this report like golden threads. The Member States need to be well governed and accountable to their citizens if they are to nourish economic and social development, if they are to achieve lasting security and if they are to uphold human rights under the rule of law. The Organization, for its part, can become stronger and more effective only if it is better managed and more clearly accountable to the Member States.

221. Let me conclude by observing that these principles are also valid for the global order. The United Nations is not a world government, and therefore ensuring good governance and accountability at the global level is not simply a matter of improving the efficiency of the United Nations. It goes far beyond that. It is a matter of ensuring that governors are responsible to the governed and that world Powers remember their responsibility to those whose lives may be transformed, for better or worse, by their decisions.

222. That implies a need for greater accountability and transparency, and fairer representation, in all global institutions. More than that, it implies that all global institutions need to be transformed into an effective expression of an emerging global community, underpinned by shared values, held together by bonds of human solidarity and inspired by mutual respect and understanding among people of different cultures and traditions. If we continue to move in this direction, the human species will not simply survive on this small planet but will in fact thrive. The fact that the destinies of all the world's inhabitants are so closely interlinked will no longer be simply a reality, but indeed a source of hope.

Statistical annex

Millennium Development Goals, targets and indicators, 2006

	World	Developing regions	Africa		Latin America & Caribbean	Asia				Oceania	CIS			Developed regions	T.C. of South-Eastern Europe	LDC	LLDC	SIDS
			Northern	Sub-Saharan		Eastern	Southern	South-Eastern	Western		All	Europe	Asia					
GOAL 1 | Eradicate extreme poverty and hunger																		
TARGET 1 - Halve, between 1990 and 2015, the proportion of people whose income is less than one dollar a day																		
Indicator 1. Population below $1 purchasing power parity per day (percentage)[a]																		
1990		27.9	2.2[b]	44.6	11.3	33.0	39.4	19.6	2.2[b]	19.6	0.4				0.4			
2002		19.4	2.4[b]	44.0	14.1	14.1	31.2	7.3	2.4[b]	7.3	2.5				1.8			
TARGET 2 - Halve, between 1990 and 2015, the proportion of people who suffer from hunger																		
Indicator 4. Prevalence of underweight children under five years of age (percentage)																		
1990		33	10	32	11	19	53	39	11									
2004		28	9	30	7	8	47	28	8									
Indicator 5. Proportion of population below minimum level of dietary energy consumption (percentage)																		
1990-1992		20	4	33	13	16	25	18	6	15	7[c]	4[c]	16[c]	<2.5[c]		22	38	23
2001-2003		17	4	31	10	12	21	12	9	12	7	3	20	<2.5		19	36	19
GOAL 2 | Achieve universal primary education																		
TARGET 3 - Ensure that, by 2015, children everywhere, boys and girls alike, will be able to complete a full course of primary schooling																		
Indicator 6. Net enrolment ratio in primary education (primary-level enrolees per 100 children of enrolment age)[d]																		
1991	81.2	78.8	80.6	53.0	85.8	97.7	72.2	92.3	79.7	74.4	88.8	91.0	84.1	96.4		52.1	51.7	66.5
2004	87.0	85.8	94.0	64.2	94.9	94.1	89.3	92.9	82.9	79.6	90.9	90.1	91.8	95.6		69.0	69.4	82.8
Indicator 8. Literacy rate of 15-24 year-olds (percentage)																		
1990	84.3	80.9	66.3	67.4	92.7	95.5	61.5	94.3	80.1	73.5	99.2	99.8	97.7	99.7		56.3	65.0	84.8
2000-2004[e]	87.2	85.0	84.3	73.1	96.0	98.9	72.2	96.2	91.3	72.8	99.7	99.7	99.8	99.3		63.7	70.3	85.3
GOAL 3 | Promote gender equality and empower women																		
TARGET 4 - Eliminate gender disparity in primary and secondary education, preferably by 2005, and to all levels of education no later than 2015																		
Indicator 9a. Ratio of girls' gross enrolment ratios to boys' gross enrolment ratios in primary education																		
1991	0.89	0.87	0.82	0.84	0.97	0.93	0.76	0.96	0.83	0.92	0.99	1.00	0.99	0.99		0.79	0.82	0.96
2004	0.94	0.94	0.94	0.89	0.97	1.00	0.91	0.97	0.89	0.91	0.99	0.99	0.98	0.99		0.88	0.86	0.95

				Africa			Asia					CIS							
		World	Developing regions	Northern	Sub-Saharan	Latin America & Caribbean	Eastern	Southern	South-Eastern	Western	Oceania	All	Europe	Asia	Developed regions	T.C. of South-Eastern Europe	LDC	LLDC	SIDS
Indicator 9b. Ratio of girls' gross enrolment ratios to boys' gross enrolment ratios in secondary education																			
	1999	0.92	0.88	0.93	0.82	1.07	0.95	0.74	0.97	0.79	0.93	1.03	1.05	0.96	1.01		0.77	0.81	1.05
	2004	0.94	0.92	0.97	0.79	1.08	1.00	0.83	1.00	0.80	0.93	0.98	0.99	0.96	1.01		0.81	0.81	1.04
Indicator 9c. Ratio of girls' gross enrolment ratios to boys' gross enrolment ratios in tertiary education																			
	1999	0.97	0.78	0.69	0.69	1.12	0.55	0.63	0.99	0.82	0.67	1.20	1.27	0.89	1.19		0.57	0.73	1.15
	2004	1.03	0.87	0.93	0.63	1.17	0.81	0.70	1.04	0.89	0.90	1.28	1.32	1.02	1.27		0.63	0.83	1.25
Indicator 10. Ratio of literate women to men, 15-24 years old																			
	1990	0.91	0.88	0.73	0.80	1.00	0.96	0.72	0.97	0.81	0.87	1.00	1.00	1.00	1.00		0.72	0.80	0.97
	2000-2004[e]	0.93	0.91	0.87	0.88	1.01	0.99	0.79	0.99	0.92	0.94	1.00	1.00	1.00	1.00		0.80	0.86	1.00
Indicator 11. Share of women in wage employment in the non-agricultural sector																			
	1990	35.9		20.1	32.4	38.3	37.9	13.1	37.3	16.6	28.4	48.5			43.4				
	2004	39.1		20.3	35.0	43.2	41.2	17.3	38.3	20.1	37.3	51.1			46.4				
Indicator 12. Proportion of seats held by women in national parliament (single or lower house only, percentage)																			
	1990	12.4	10.4	2.6	7.2	11.9	20.2	5.7	10.4	4.6	1.2				15.4		7.3	14.0	14.4
	2006[f]	16.6	15.3	7.0	16.2	20.4	19.5	12.8	15.8	7.6	3.2	10.8	11.0	10.6	21.1		15.6	16.3	17.8
GOAL 4 | Reduce child mortality																			
TARGET 5 - Reduce by two thirds, between 1990 and 2015, the under-5 mortality rate																			
Indicator 13. Under-5 mortality rate (deaths per 1,000 live births)																			
	1990	95	106	88	185	54	48	126	78	69	87	50	28	83	12	29			
	2004	79	87	37	168	31	31	90	43	58	80	44	20	78	7	17			
Indicator 15. Proportion of 1-year old children immunized against measles (percentage of children aged 12-23 months who received at least one dose of measles vaccine)																			
	1990	73	71	85	56	76	98	58	71	80	70	85			84	93			
	2004	76	73	94	65	92	85	62	81	88	48	98			92	96			
GOAL 5 | Improve maternal health																			
TARGET 6 - Reduce by three quarters, between 1990 and 2015, the maternal mortality ratio																			
Indicator 17. Proportion of births attended by skilled health personnel																			
	1990	47	43	40	42	72	51	30	38	60		99	99	97		96			
	2004	58	56	71	46	88	79	36	68	66		99	99	99		96			

	World	Developing regions	Africa: Northern	Africa: Sub-Saharan	Latin America & Caribbean	Asia: Eastern	Asia: Southern	Asia: South-Eastern	Asia: Western	Oceania	CIS: All	CIS: Europe	CIS: Asia	Developed regions	T.C. of South-Eastern Europe	LDC	LLDC	SIDS
GOAL 6 | Combat HIV/AIDS, malaria and other diseases																		
TARGET 7 - Have halted by 2015 and begun to reverse the spread of HIV/AIDS																		
Indicator 18a. HIV prevalence (estimated adult, 15-49, percentage)																		
1990		0.37	<0.1	2.7	0.3	<0.1	0.1	0.1	<0.1	<0.1		<0.1	<0.1	0.2				
2005		1.1	0.1	5.8	0.6	0.1	0.7	0.5	<0.1	1.5		1.1	0.2	0.5				
Indicator 18b. HIV prevalence (percentage of adults living with HIV who are women)																		
1990			<20	54	33	<20	<20	<20	<20	<20		<20	<20	<20				
2005			22	59	34	27	28	33	<20	59		31	27	28				
Indicator 19a. Condom use at last high-risk sex (percentage of population 15-24 that used a condom during last high-risk sex,[g] 1998-2004; number of countries covered by the surveys provided in parentheses)																		
Women				27 (26)			51 (1)											
Men				43 (25)			59 (1)						54 (3)					
Indicator 19b. Percentage of population aged 15-24 with comprehensive correct knowledge[h] of HIV/AIDS (percentage, 1998-2004; number of countries covered by the surveys provided in parentheses)																		
Women				24 (34)			21 (1)	18 (3)					6 (5)					
Men				31 (18)			17 (1)											
Indicator 20. Ratio of school attendance of orphans to school attendance of non-orphans aged 10-14[i] (number of countries covered by the surveys provided in parentheses)																		
1998-2004				0.85 (39)														
TARGET 8 - Have halted by 2015 and begun to reverse the incidence of malaria and other major diseases																		
Indicator 22a. Population in malaria-risk areas using effective malaria prevention measures (percentage of children under 5 who sleep under insecticide-treated bed nets)																		
1999-2004				4														
Indicator 22b. Population in malaria-risk areas using effective malaria treatment measures (percentage of children under 5 with fever who are appropriately treated)																		
1999-2004				37				3										
Indicator 23a. Incidence and death rates associated with tuberculosis (number of cases per 100,000 population, excluding HIV infected)																		
1990	122	149	59	148	98	116	173	272	68	203	51	48	60	28				
2004	128	151	49	281	59	102	166	217	50	166	108	104	117	16				
Indicator 23b. Prevalence and death rates associated with tuberculosis (number of deaths per 100,000 population, excluding HIV infected)																		
1990	28	35	5	38	14	25	45	67	11	53	9	9	9	3				
2004	23	27	4	56	8	16	31	36	8	29	17	17	17	2				
Indicator 24a. Proportion of tuberculosis cases detected under DOTS (percentage)																		
2000	28	29	82	36	43	30	15	39	27	13	11	3	36	22				
2004	53	54	83	47	58	63	51	65	26	26	22	13	46	44				

	World	Developing regions	Africa: Northern	Africa: Sub-Saharan	Latin America & Caribbean	Asia: Eastern	Asia: Southern	Asia: South-Eastern	Asia: Western	Oceania	CIS: All	CIS: Europe	CIS: Asia	Developed regions	T.C. of South-Eastern Europe	LDC	LLDC	SIDS
Indicator 24b. Proportion of tuberculosis cases cured under DOTS (percentage)																		
2000	82	82	88	72	81	94	83	86	81	76	76	68	78	77				
2003	82	83	86	72	83	93	86	86	83	67	72	62	76	76				
GOAL 7 | Ensure environmental sustainability																		
TARGET 9 – Integrate the principles of sustainable development into country policies and programmes and reverse the loss of environmental resources																		
Indicator 25. Proportion of land area covered by forest (percentage)																		
1990	31.3		1.3	29.2	49.9	16.5	14.0	56.3	3.3	68.3	38.6	46.6	3.9	30.4				
2005	30.3		1.5	26.5	46.0	19.8	14.2	46.8	3.5	63.4	38.6	46.7	3.9	30.8				
Indicator 26. Area protected to maintain biological diversity (percentage of total territorial area, including terrestrial and marine)																		
1990	8.7	9.0	3.5	10.5	12.8	10.4	4.8	6.1	4.0[j]	1.2	6.5	7.3	3.0	12.4		8.5	9.0	2.0
2005	11.6	12.2	4.7	11.2	17.7	14.4	6.0	9.5	18.7[j]	1.6	7.7	8.6	3.9	16.3		9.5	11.6	3.4
Indicator 27. Energy use per $1,000 GDP (consumption of kg oil equivalent)[k]																		
1990	235	266	164	360	167	419	245	203	250		658[l]	625[l]	985[l]	216	415	258		
2003	212	218	165	363	162	219	201	211	287		531	519	627	189	261	260		
Indicator 28. Carbon dioxide emissions (per capita, in metric tons)[m]																		
1990	4.0	1.6[n]	1.9[n]	0.8[n]	2.4[n]	2.4[n]	0.8[n]	1.0[n]	4.7[n]	1.4[n]	13.2[n]	12.6[o]	7.2[o]	12.6[p]				
2003	4.0	2.2[n]	2.8[n]	0.7[n]	2.4[n]	3.4[n]	1.2[n]	1.7[n]	5.8[n]	1.4[n]	8.1[n]	9.1[n]	5.1[n]	12.9[p]				
Indicator 28b. Consumption of ozone-depleting substances (CFC in millions of ODP tonnes)																		
1990		113.4	9.1	8.9	32.6	41.8	2.5	16.1	6.1	0.04	105.9	104.5	1.4	514.7	3.5	1.0	1.5	
2004		63.4	4.3	3.9	13.6	22.9	7.1	8.2	4.2	0.02	0.7	0.5	0.2	1.9	0.6	2.7	0.9	
TARGET 10 - Halve, by 2015, the proportion of people without sustainable access to safe drinking water and basic sanitation																		
Indicator 30. Proportion of population with sustainable access to an improved water source, urban and rural (percentage)																		
1990 Total	78	71	89	49	83	71	72	76	85	51	92			100				
Urban	95	93	95	82	93	99	90	93	94	92	97			100				
Rural	64	60	82	36	60	59	66	68	70	39	84			99				
2004 Total	83	80	91	56	91	78	85	82	91	51	92			99				
Urban	95	92	96	80	96	93	94	89	97	80	99			100				

				Africa			Asia					CIS							
		World	Developing regions	Northern	Sub-Saharan	Latin America & Caribbean	Eastern	Southern	South-Eastern	Western	Oceania	All	Europe	Asia	Developed regions	T.C. of South-Eastern Europe	LDC	LLDC	SIDS
	Rural	73	70	86	42	73	67	81	77	79	40	80			95				
Indicator 31. Proportion of population with access to improved sanitation, urban and rural (percentage)																			
1990	Total	49	35	65	32	68	24	20	49	81	54	82			100				
	Urban	79	68	84	52	81	64	54	70	97	80	92			100				
	Rural	26	17	47	24	36	7	8	40	55	46	63			99				
2004	Total	59	50	77	37	77	45	38	67	84	53	83			99				
	Urban	80	73	91	53	86	69	63	81	96	80	92			100				
	Rural	39	33	62	28	49	28	27	56	59	43	67			98				
TARGET 11 - By 2020, to have achieved a significant improvement in the lives of at least 100 million slum dwellers																			
Indicator 32a. Access to secure tenure (slum population in millions)																			
	1990	721.6	660.9	21.7	101.0	110.8	150.8	198.7	49.0	28.6	0.4		9.2	9.7	41.8		81.9	46.5	5.7
	2001	924.0	860.1	21.4	166.2	127.6	193.8	253.1	56.8	40.7	0.5		8.9	9.8	45.2		140.1	47.3	7.3
Indicator 32b. Access to secure tenure (percentage of urban population living in slums)																			
	1990	31.6	47.0	37.7	72.3	35.4	41.1	63.7	36.8	34.4	24.5		6.0	30.3	6.0		76.3	48.4	24.0
	2001	31.6	43.3	28.2	71.9	31.9	36.4	59.0	28.0	35.3	24.1		6.0	29.4	6.0		78.2	56.5	24.4
GOAL 8 | Develop a global partnership for development																			
TARGET 12 - Develop further an open, rule-based, predictable, non-discriminatory trading and financial system																			
TARGET 13 - Address the special needs of the least developed countries																			
TARGET 14 - Address the special needs of landlocked countries and small island developing States																			
TARGET 15 - Deal comprehensively with the debt problems of developing countries through national and international measures in order to make debt sustainable in the long term																			
Indicator 33a. Net ODA to all developing and least developed countries (annual total assistance in billions of United States dollars)																			
	1990		52.7														15.2		
	2004		106.5[q]														23.5		
Indicator 33b. Net ODA, to all developing and least developed countries (percentage of OECD/DAC donors' gross national income)																			
	1990		0.33														0.09		
	2004		0.33[q]														0.08		
Indicator 34. Proportion of bilateral, sector allocable ODA of OECD/DAC donors to basic social services - basic education, primary health care, nutrition, safe water and sanitation (percentage)																			
	1995-1996	8.1																	

	World	Developing regions	Africa: Northern	Africa: Sub-Saharan	Latin America & Caribbean	Asia: Eastern	Asia: Southern	Asia: South-Eastern	Asia: Western	Oceania	CIS: All	CIS: Europe	CIS: Asia	Developed regions	T.C. of South-Eastern Europe	LDC	LLDC	SIDS
2003-2004	16.0																	
Indicator 35. Proportion of bilateral official development assistance of OECD/DAC donors[r] that is untied (percentage)																		
1990	67.6																	
2004	91.3																	
Indicator 36. ODA received in landlocked developing countries as a proportion of their gross national incomes (percentage)																		
1990																	6.5	
2004																	7.3	
Indicator 37. ODA received in small island developing states as a proportion of their gross national incomes (percentage)																		
1990																		2.8
2004																		1.1
Indicator 38a. Proportion of total developed country imports (by value, excluding arms) from developing countries and least developed countries, admitted free of duty (percentage)																		
1996		52														67		
2004		75														81		
Indicator 38b. Proportion of total developed country imports (by value, excluding arms and oil) from developing countries and least developed countries, admitted free of duty (percentage)																		
1996		53														77		
2004		75														79		
Indicator 39a. Average tariffs imposed by developed countries on agricultural products from developing countries (percentage)																		
1996		9.8														4.3		
2004		8.4														3.4		
Indicator 39b. Average tariffs imposed by developed countries on textiles from developing countries (percentage)																		
1996		8.1														5.7		
2004		5.7														1.5		
Indicator 39c. Average tariffs imposed by developed countries on clothing from developing countries (percentage)																		
1996		14.5														11.4		
2004		10.4														2.5		
Indicator 40. Agricultural support estimate for OECD countries as a percentage of their gross domestic product																		
1990														1.90				

	World	Developing regions	Africa: Northern	Africa: Sub-Saharan	Latin America & Caribbean	Asia: Eastern	Asia: Southern	Asia: South-Eastern	Asia: Western	Oceania	CIS: All	CIS: Europe	CIS: Asia	Developed regions	T.C. of South-Eastern Europe	LDC	LLDC	SIDS
2004[s]														1.16				
Indicator 41. Proportion of ODA provided to help build trade capacity (trade-related technical assistance/capacity-building as a percentage of total sector allocable ODA)																		
2001	4.0																	
2004	3.6																	
Indicator 42a. Total number of countries that have reached their HIPC completion points																		
2000	1			1														
2006	18			14	4													
Indicator 42b. Total number of countries that have reached their HIPC decision points (but not completion point)																		
2000	21			17	4													
2006	11			11														
Indicator 42c. Total number of countries that have yet to be considered for HIPC decision points																		
2000	16																	
2006	9			7				2										
Indicator 42d. Total number of countries eligible for HIPC																		
2000	38																	
2006	38																	
Indicator 43. Debt relief committed under HIPC (to countries that have reached their decision or completion point, in billions of United States dollars, cumulative)																		
2000	34																	
2006[t]	59																	
Indicator 44. Debt service as a percentage of exports of goods and services																		
1990		16.4	39.8	11.5	20.5	4.7	17.7	16.7		14	3.9[u]	3.9[u]	3.5[u]		9.4	16.8		
2004		7	10.9	5.8	14.6	0.9	14.7	9.2		1.2[v]	5.5	5.6	4.4		8.9	8.2		
TARGET 16 - In cooperation with developing countries, develop and implement strategies for decent and productive work for youth																		
Indicator 45. Unemployment rate of young people aged 15-24 years																		
1995	12.1		33.9	18.0	14.2	7.2	9.4	9.7	20.8	7.9	19.4			15.8				
2005	13.7		34.5	18.3	15.2	7.8	11.3	17.0	23.6	6.6	18.1			13.8				
TARGET 17 - In cooperation with pharmaceutical companies, provide access to affordable, essential drugs in developing countries																		
TARGET 18 - In cooperation with the private sector, make available the benefits of new technologies, especially information and communications																		
Indicator 47. Telephone lines and cellular subscribers (number of telephone lines and cellular subscribers per 100 population)																		
1990	10.1	2.3	2.9	1.0	6.4	2.4	0.7	1.4	10.0	3.4	12.5			45.4	13.8	0.3	2.3	7.3

				Africa			Asia					CIS							
		World	Developing regions	Northern	Sub-Saharan	Latin America & Caribbean	Eastern	Southern	South-Eastern	Western	Oceania	All	Europe	Asia	Developed regions	T.C. of South-Eastern Europe	LDC	LLDC	SIDS
	2004	46.4	31.7	27.6	8.2	50.0	54.1	8.4	27.4	52.5	10.1	57.1			130.1	73.8	3.2	7.4	37.8
Indicator 48a. Personal computers and Internet users (number of personal computers per 100 population)																			
	1990	2.5	0.3	0.1	0.3	0.6	0.3	0.0	0.3	1.2	0.0	0.3			11.1	0.2	0.1	0.0	3.9
	2004	13.0	4.9	2.6	1.6	9.0	6.9	1.7	3.5	10.8	6.5	9.6			55.9	8.1	0.8	1.3	13.3
Indicator 48b. Personal computers and Internet users (number of Internet users per 100 population)																			
	1990	0.3	0.0	0.0	0.0	0.0	0.0	0.0	0.0	0.0	0.0	0.0			0.3	0.0	0.0	0.0	0.0
	2004	13.7	7.0	6.3	1.8	11.9	10.3	3.4	7.4	10.5	4.7	8.9			51.4	16.5	0.7	1.4	12.9

Source: United Nations Inter-Agency and Expert Group on the Millennium Development Goal Indicators and Millennium Development Goal indicators database (http://mdgs.un.org).

Abbreviations: CDIAC, Carbon Dioxide Information Analysis Center (United States of America); CFC, chlorofluorocarbons; CIS, Commonwealth of Independent States; DOTS, directly observed treatment strategy; GDP, gross domestic product; HIPC, heavily indebted poor countries initiative; LDC, least developed countries; LLDC, landlocked developing countries; ODA, official development assistance; ODP, ozone-depletion potential; OECD/DAC, Organization for Economic Cooperation and Development/Development Assistance Committee; SIDS, small island developing States; TC, transitional countries.

Notes

Given the limited space available, indicators for which no new data are available are not presented here, with the exception of indicator 32, Proportion of households with access to secure tenure, which is the only indicator to monitor the target. Also, indicator 14, Infant mortality rate, is not presented because trends can be assessed by the indicator on child mortality. The complete statistical annex, including all indicators used in monitoring progress towards the Millennium Development Goals, is available at http://mdgs.un.org.

Except where indicated, regional groupings are based on United Nations geographical regions with some modifications to create to the extent possible homogenous groups of countries for analysis and presentation. The regional composition adopted for the 2006 reporting of Millennium Development Goal indicators is available at http://mdgs.un.org under "Data".

The Commonwealth of Independent States (CIS) comprises Belarus, the Republic of Moldova, the Russian Federation and Ukraine in Europe, and Armenia, Azerbaijan, Georgia, Kazakhstan, Kyrgyzstan, Tajikistan, Turkmenistan and Uzbekistan in Asia. "Developed regions" comprises Europe (except CIS countries), Australia, Canada, Japan, New Zealand and the United States of America. Developed regions always include transition countries in Europe unless the latter are presented separately as "transition countries of south-eastern Europe".

Indicator 1

[a]Estimates by the World Bank in May 2006. High-income economies, as defined by the World Bank, are excluded.

[b]Combined estimates for North Africa and Western Asia.

Indicator 5

[c]Data refer to the period 1993-1995.

Indicator 6

[d]The net enrolment ratios in primary education correspond to school years ending in the years displayed.

Indicators 8 and 10

[e]Data refer to the latest literacy estimates and projections released by the United Nations Educational, Scientific and Cultural Organization Institute for Statistics for the period 2000-2004.

Indicator 12

[f]As at 1 January 2006.

Indicator 19a

[g]Percentage of young women and men aged 15-24 reporting the use of a condom during sexual intercourse with a non-regular sexual partner in the past 12 months among those who had such a partner in the past 12 months.

Indicator 19b

[h]Percentage of young women and men aged 15-24 correctly identifying the two major ways of preventing the sexual transmission of HIV (using condoms and limiting sex to one faithful, uninfected partner) who reject two common local misconceptions and who know that a healthy-looking person can transmit the AIDS virus.

Indicator 20

[i]Ratio of the current school attendance rate of children aged 10-14 both of whose biological parents have died to the current school attendance rate of children aged 10-14 both of whose parents are still alive and who currently live with at least one biological parent.

Indicator 26

[j]The figures from 1995 to 2005 are due to the establishment of a new large protected area in Saudi Arabia.

Indicator 27

[k]Data are not directly comparable with earlier series because constant price GDP has been rescaled to year 2000 international (purchasing power parity) dollars.

[l]Figures are for years other than that specified.

Indicator 28

[m]Total CO_2 emissions from fossil fuels (expressed in millions of metric tons of CO_2) includes CO_2 emissions from: solid fuel consumption, liquid fuel consumption, gas fuel consumption, cement production and gas flaring (CDIAC).

[n]Based on data provided by CDIAC.

[o]Based on data provided by CDIAC. The 1990 rows show 1992 data for CIS countries.

[p]Based on the annual national emission inventories of annex I countries (with the exception of Belarus, the Russian Federation and Ukraine, which are included under CIS) that report to the United Nations Framework Convention on Climate Change; non-annex I countries do not have annual reporting obligations. In order to assess trends for annex I countries as a group, the aggregate figures for 2003 include data referring to a previous year for countries where 2003 data were not available. Data refer to 2002 for Poland. Emissions/sinks from land-use change and forestry are excluded.

Indicators 33a and 33b

[q]Data are preliminary and are for 2005.

Indicator 35

[r]Based on only some 40 per cent of total ODA commitments from OECD/DAC member countries, as it excludes technical cooperation and administrative costs, as well as all ODA from Austria, Luxembourg, New Zealand and the United States that do not report the tying status of their official development assistance.

Indicator 40

[s]Preliminary data.

Indicator 43

[t]As at March 2006.

Indicator 44

[u]Data are for 1994.

[v]Data are for 2003.

PART ONE

Political and security questions

Chapter I

International peace and security

The United Nations continued to strengthen its efforts to promote and maintain international peace and security. The Peacebuilding Commission, established in 2005 to improve the management of UN peace operations worldwide, was inaugurated in June 2006 and convened country-specific meetings on the situations in Sierra Leone and Burundi in October and December. The Secretary-General took steps to establish the Peacebuilding Support Office to assist and support the Commission, as well as the Peacebuilding Fund to support peacebuilding activities that directly contributed to the stabilization of countries emerging from conflict.

The General Assembly proclaimed 2009 the International Year of Reconciliation and invited Governments and international and non-governmental organizations (NGOs) to support reconciliation processes among societies affected and/or divided by conflicts.

Acts of international terrorism continued unabated in 2006, including deadly attacks in Egypt, India and Iraq. In a series of statements, the Security Council condemned those attacks, underlined the need to bring the planners and perpetrators to justice, and urged States to fulfil their obligation to combat terrorism. In other action, the Council adopted further measures against Al-Qaida, the Taliban and their associates, and the General Assembly called on Member States to support international efforts to prevent terrorists from acquiring weapons of mass destruction and their means of delivery. In April, the Secretary-General, acting in response to the 2005 World Summit Outcome, submitted recommendations for the United Nations Global Counter-Terrorism Strategy to strengthen the capacity of the UN system to assist States in combating terrorism and enhance the coordination of UN counter-terrorism activities. The Assembly adopted the Strategy in September.

The United Nations continued to improve the management and operation of its peacekeeping missions. Following up on the recommendations contained in the 2005 report of the Secretary-General's Adviser on Sexual Exploitation and Abuse by United Nations Peacekeepers, the Department of Peacekeeping Operations (DPKO) developed a comprehensive strategy on sexual exploitation and abuse by UN peacekeeping personnel aimed at preventing misconduct, enforcing UN standards of conduct and taking remedial action. DPKO also created a multidisciplinary conduct and discipline team at DPKO headquarters, in addition to teams established in Burundi, Côte d'Ivoire, the Democratic Republic of the Congo (DRC), Haiti, Liberia, Sierra Leone, the Sudan and Timor-Leste, to develop policy, provide oversight of disciplinary issues and ensure the coherent application of UN standards of conduct. In May, the Secretary-General submitted to the Assembly President a draft policy statement and draft comprehensive strategy on assistance and support to victims of sexual exploitation and abuse by UN staff and related personnel. In December, the High-level Conference on Eliminating Sexual Exploitation and Abuse by UN and NGO Personnel issued the Statement of Commitment on Eliminating Sexual Exploitation, by which senior leaders of UN and non-UN entities reaffirmed their determination to prevent and respond to acts of sexual exploitation and abuse by their personnel.

The Organization maintained 12 political and peacebuilding missions and offices and 15 peacekeeping operations in 2006. At year's end, a record 99,355 uniformed and civilian personnel were serving in the field, compared to 85,000 in 2005.

The financial position of UN peacekeeping operations improved in 2006; expenditures increased to $4,582.8 million, compared to $4,074.3 million in 2005, a 12.5 per cent increase, mainly attributable to the full-year impact of the United Nations Mission in the Sudan and the expansion of operations in Côte d'Ivoire, the DRC, and Haiti. Unpaid assessed contributions amounted to $1.3 billion, compared to $1.7 billion the previous year.

Promotion of international peace and security

Rule of law and maintenance of international peace and security

On 22 June [meeting 5474], the Security Council held a debate on the Council's role in strengthening international law: rule of law and maintenance of international peace and security. Denmark, in a

7 June discussion paper on the topic [S/2006/367], said that the debate would consider the Council's role in promoting international law and identify current challenges in promoting the international legal order. The Council, operating within the purposes and principles of the Charter, had continuously developed and expanded its approach to maintaining international peace and security in the light of changing global threats and challenges, and increasingly resorted to legal mechanisms in fulfilling its responsibilities. The paper outlined issues meriting special attention, including the promotion of rule of law in conflict and post-conflict situations, ending impunity for international crimes, and enhancing the efficiency and credibility of UN sanctions regimes. In opening the debate, Denmark identified the peaceful settlement of disputes, including through the International Court of Justice, as an issue meriting attention.

The UN Legal Counsel, Nicolas Michel, addressing the Council on those issues, said that the promotion of the rule of law in conflict and post-conflict situations, including the promotion of human rights, could not be limited to those situations only. In recent years, the Council's decisions had reflected its resolve to end impunity for perpetrators of international crimes, thereby keeping pace with one of the major evolutions of the culture of the international community and international law. Within that evolution, justice and peace had to be regarded as complementary requirements and there could be no lasting peace without justice; amnesty for international crimes was unacceptable in international practice and should be enshrined as a standard to be enforced; and the system of international penal jurisdictions was a primary responsibility of States and a complementary responsibility of the International Criminal Court, within the constraints of the 1998 Rome Statute establishing it [YUN 1998, p. 1209].

The Legal Counsel said that the Secretary-General had set out minimum standards required to ensure that the procedures for the listing and de-listing of individuals and entities on sanctions lists were fair and transparent. The Legal Counsel identified the four basic elements of those standards: a person against whom measures had been taken by the Council had the right to be informed of those measures and to know the case against him or her; to be heard, via written submissions, within a reasonable time by the relevant decision-making body and to be subject to review by an effective mechanism; and the Security Council should, possibly through its Committees, periodically review targeted individual sanctions, especially the freezing of assets, in order to mitigate the risk of violating the right to property and human rights. Those elements would apply mutatis mutandis in respect of entities.

The President of the International Court of Justice (ICJ), Judge Rosalyn Higgins, told the Council that strengthening international law meant widening and deepening its content and fortifying mechanisms for securing compliance or enforcement. The reach of international law had expanded to an extraordinary extent, and was generally complied with in everyday life. However, the challenges for the Council in fulfilling its functions under the Charter and international law, such as the problem of a lack of rule of law matched with the collapse of communal justice systems, and the place of law vis-à-vis non-State actors, were interrelated. The United Nations therefore had to have as its prime objective the prevention of those conflicts and post-conflict situations that raised key rule of law questions. The Court was always prepared to deal with legal issues within the wider context of political controversy, and could, in providing impartial pronouncement on underlying claims, stop high tensions from developing into military action. As a principal UN organ, it was at the center of the general system for the maintenance of international peace and security through its contribution to the peaceful settlement of disputes. However, the challenge was mobilizing that potential. The Council should develop a policy whereby, in all political disputes that threatened peace and security and where claims of legal entitlement were made, it could strongly indicate to the parties that they should have recourse to the Court, as provided for under Article 36 of the Charter. Unfortunately, the Council had failed to make use of the provision contained in that Article. That tool should be made a central Council policy. The Court stood ready to work alongside the Council in the fulfilment of the goals of the Charter.

SECURITY COUNCIL ACTION

On 22 June [meeting 5474], following consultations among Security Council members, the President made statement **S/PRST/2006/28** on behalf of the Council:

> The Security Council reaffirms its commitment to the Charter of the United Nations and international law, which are indispensable foundations of a more peaceful, prosperous and just world. The Council underscores its conviction that international law plays a critical role in fostering stability and order in international relations and in providing a framework for cooperation among States in addressing common challenges, thus contributing to the maintenance of international peace and security.
>
> The Council is committed to and actively supports the peaceful settlement of disputes and reiterates its

call upon the Member States to settle their disputes by peaceful means as set forth in Chapter VI of the Charter, including by use of regional preventive mechanisms and the International Court of Justice. The Council emphasizes the important role of the Court, the principal judicial organ of the United Nations, in adjudicating disputes among States.

The Council attaches vital importance to promoting justice and the rule of law, including respect for human rights, as an indispensable element for lasting peace. The Council considers the enhancement of rule of law activities as crucial in peacebuilding strategies in post-conflict societies and emphasizes the role of the Peacebuilding Commission in this regard. The Council supports the idea of establishing a rule of law assistance unit within the Secretariat and looks forward to receiving the proposals of the Secretariat for implementation of the recommendations set out in paragraph 65 of the report of the Secretary-General on the rule of law and transitional justice in conflict and post-conflict societies. The Council urges Member States which are interested in doing so to contribute national expertise and materials to these developments within their means, and to improve their capacities in these areas.

The Council emphasizes the responsibility of States to comply with their obligations to end impunity and to prosecute those responsible for genocide, crimes against humanity and serious violations of international humanitarian law. The Council reaffirms that ending impunity is essential if a society in conflict or recovering from conflict is to come to terms with past abuses committed against civilians and to prevent future abuses. The Council intends to continue forcefully to fight impunity with appropriate means and draws attention to the full range of justice and reconciliation mechanisms to be considered, including national, international and "mixed" criminal courts and tribunals and truth and reconciliation commissions.

The Council considers sanctions an important tool in the maintenance and restoration of international peace and security. The Council resolves to ensure that sanctions are carefully targeted in support of clear objectives and are implemented in ways that balance effectiveness against possible adverse consequences. The Council is committed to ensuring that fair and clear procedures exist for placing individuals and entities on sanctions lists and for removing them, as well as for granting humanitarian exemptions. The Council reiterates its request to the Security Council Committee established pursuant to resolution 1267(1999) to continue its work on the Committee's guidelines, including on listing and de-listing procedures, and on the implementation of its exemption procedures contained in resolution 1452(2002) of 20 December 2002.

Enhancing UN support for the rule of law

Report of Secretary-General. In follow-up to his 2004 report on the rule of law and transitional justice in conflict and post-conflict situations [YUN 2004, p. 65], the General Assembly's request in resolution 60/1 [YUN 2005, p. 48] on the 2005 World Summit Outcome for the establishment of a rule of law unit within the Secretariat, supported by the Security Council in presidential statement S/PRST/2006/28 (see above) and reiterated by the Assembly in **resolution 61/39** of 4 December (see p. 1524), the Secretary-General submitted a December report [A/61/636-S/2006/980], which set out practical measures the UN system should take to enhance its arrangements for supporting the rule of law and transitional justice activities. It also identified priority areas in which the United Nations would provide advice and assistance to Member States, in partnership with other non-UN actors.

The Secretary-General said that rule of law and transitional justice issues were being integrated into the strategic and operational planning of new peace operations, and Member States almost universally had recognized the establishment of the rule of law as an important aspect of peace missions. The guidelines, manuals and tools developed by the Task Force for the Development of Comprehensive Rule of Law Strategies for Peace Operations of the Executive Committee on Peace and Security had been updated and several UN departments, agencies, funds and programmes continued to develop lessons-learned studies and guidance materials in the areas of police, prison systems, legal and judicial systems and transitional justice, while incorporating gender considerations. Despite those steps, much remained to be done with regard to the Organization's capacity, coherence and coordination efforts. While supporting Member States in strengthening the rule of law was central to the work of the UN system, dedicated UN capacities for doing so were modest, both at Headquarters and in the field. The Organization needed to deepen and rationalize its rule of law work, strengthen its capacities, enhance its institutional memory and coordinate more effectively within the United Nations and with outside actors. Accordingly, in July, the Secretary-General asked the Working Group on Rule of Law and Justice to prepare options on how best to structure UN rule of law capacity at Headquarters and in the field, and make recommendations for strengthening that capacity. Following the Working Group's recommendations, the Secretary-General decided that the primary objectives for the Secretariat and other key UN actors should be to significantly enhance coherence and coordination across the Organization and with non-UN actors, at the global and country levels, and to increase and deepen capacity in priority areas of the three main categories of rule of law activity: rule of law at the international level; in the context of conflict and post-conflict situations, including transitional justice and strengthening national justice systems and institutions; and in the context of long-term development. Lead entities would assume clearly defined responsibilities for specific areas of UN rule of law activity. At the global level, those entities would support Member States; collaborate with non-UN actors; assess capacity and ensure that required capacities and mechanisms existed; coordinate activities; develop policy; and provide training and substantive guidance. At the country level, they would act as the primary counterpart to national authorities; identify key partners; coordinate planning and strategy development; coordinate programme implementation; ensure relevant standards were made known; provide training; and mobilize resources. The aim of the proposed approach was to increase predictability, while preserving sufficient flexibility to take into account country-level circumstances.

The Secretary-General decided to create a Rule of Law Coordination and Resource Group consisting of key UN actors and chaired by the Deputy Secretary-General, which would act as Headquarters focal point for coordinating system-wide attention on the rule of law to ensure policy coherence and coordination. It would identify priority gaps in UN rule of law capacity and recommend where and when capacities should be established. Supported by a Secretariat unit, the Group would coordinate the preparation of an inventory of UN activities devoted to the promotion of the rule of law, as requested in resolution 61/39.

The Secretary-General reaffirmed the commitment of the United Nations to support Member States in ensuring that fair and effective national legal, judicial, prison and police institutions were in place so that societies could emerge from a violent past. He believed that his decision to ensure that the Organization had a core cadre of rule of law expertise, coupled with meaningful and robust coordination, could only benefit Member States in their recommitment to an international order based on the rule of law. The Secretary-General was also convinced that the investment by Member States in increasing UN capacity to support their efforts to uphold the rule of law would contribute significantly to peace and security and sustainable development.

Conflict prevention

Prevention of armed conflict

In response to General Assembly resolutions 55/281 [YUN 2001, p. 50] and 57/337 [YUN 2003, p. 50] and Security Council resolution 1366(2001) [YUN 2001, p. 50], the Secretary-General, in July [A/60/891], submitted his second progress report on the prevention of armed conflict; his first report on the subject was submitted in 2001 [YUN 2001, p. 48]. The report described ways to address the sources of tension within and between societies, States and regions that made them vulnerable to conflict; how norms and institutions that made conflicts less viable or likely could be strengthened; mechanisms for resolving inter-State disputes; the contribution of national and international actors in conflict prevention; and the role of the UN system.

The Secretary-General noted that a culture of prevention was beginning to take hold at the United Nations, with progress at the normative, political and institutional levels having been made since 2001, most notably in the adoption of the above-mentioned resolutions, as well as Council resolution 1625(2005) [YUN 2005, p. 86] on strengthening the effectiveness of the Council's role in conflict prevention, particularly in Africa. In the 2005 World Summit Outcome, set out in Assembly resolution 60/1 [YUN 2005, p. 48], Member States renewed their commitment to promote a culture of prevention of armed conflicts as a means of addressing interconnected security and development challenges, and there was evidence that the overall trend in the number and severity of armed conflicts worldwide was decreasing, due largely to an upsurge in international activism in conflict prevention, peacekeeping and peacebuilding. The United Nations had developed important tools and mechanisms for working cooperatively in conflict prevention. However, an unacceptable gap remained between rhetoric and reality with regard to conflict prevention. Over the previous five years, $18 billion had been spent on UN peacekeeping, partly because of inadequate preventive measures. The dual challenge was to address or diminish the sources of tension in society and strengthen those institutions that enabled it to channel conflict non-violently and allow for dialogue. Going to war had to be made as unattractive an option as possible, while peaceful dispute resolution and dialogue mechanisms had to be made more appealing and accessible. Efforts to address the root causes of conflict therefore had to shift from reactive, external interventions to internally driven initiatives, which would foster home-grown, self-sustaining infrastructures for peace.

The Secretary-General, referring to the distinction he had made between structural and operational prevention in his 2001 report, introduced a third sphere of preventive action, systematic prevention, to describe measures for addressing the global risk of conflict that transcended particular States.

In discussing the UN contribution in advancing elements of the prevention agenda, the Secretary-General reported that, in response to resolution 57/337, he had conducted a detailed review of UN system conflict-prevention capacity, assessing the strengths and weaknesses of the Secretariat, agencies, funds and programmes. The review showed that the UN system had made significant progress in the prevention of armed conflict, but a number of gaps remained. Some targeted capacity-building would therefore be required, along with a number of structural adjustments, to further advance the implementation of the prevention agenda. The review also found that, while most UN system entities understood conflict prevention as a core activity of their work and had integrated it into their mandates and programme activities, system-wide strategic leadership in prevention was still weak. Moreover, existing coordination mechanisms for addressing specific sectors related to conflict prevention had fallen short of providing a coherent, overarching strategy in the field and at Headquarters. No significant progress had been made in strengthening UN early warning capacity, or information collection and analysis, as called for in resolution 57/337, and the Organization still lacked the capability to analyse and integrate data from different parts of the system into comprehensive early warning reports and strategies on conflict prevention. The Organization's capacity to use its leverage to prevent armed conflict in conjunction with other actors was not being fully harnessed. Funding for prevention activities, in addition to being insufficient, was insecure, thus preventing long-term prevention activities and urgent ad hoc interventions.

The Secretary-General urged Member States to more comprehensively address the primary sources of tension for conflict-vulnerable regions and countries, including through increased regulation of trade in natural resources that often fuelled conflict; offering more support to private sector initiatives on conflict-sensitive business practices; reducing illicit flows of small arms and light weapons; finding common ground on preventing the use of nuclear, chemical and biological weapons; fighting the spread of HIV/AIDS; addressing environmental degradation; paying more attention to the nexus of prevention and migration; redoubling efforts for the attainment of the Millennium Development Goals (MDGS) [YUN 2000, p. 51]; and strengthening respect for human rights. He called on Member States to fulfil Assembly resolution 57/337 by acceding to, ratifying and complying with international human rights, humanitarian and other legal instruments relevant to the prevention of armed conflict. Individual Governments should strengthen their national capacities for addressing structural risk factors, with UN support. A more robust and strategic approach to assistance in democracy-building, elections and constitutional capacity should be developed, and Member States should continue to support the United Nations Democracy Fund [YUN 2005, p. 655], as a tool for strengthening democratic institutions and practices.

The Secretary-General encouraged more creative and constructive use of sanctions as a conflict prevention tool, with due attention to fair and clear procedures. Parties to disputes should make active and early use of the means outlined in Article 33, paragraph 1, of the Charter, namely, to engage in negotiation, enquiry, mediation, and conciliation, and resort to regional agencies or arrangements, or other peaceful means that the parties might choose, to prevent the escalation of conflict. All actors, including civil society and individual Governments, regional organizations and the UN system, should accept and act on the principles of shared vulnerability and mutual responsibility so that effective preventive action could be taken at all the levels outlined in the report. Member States should consider innovative means to intensify dialogue with civil society, including by inviting their representatives to provide regular briefings to pertinent bodies. The Secretary-General reiterated his call for the speedy implementation of the UN System-wide Action Plan on women, peace and security [YUN 2005, p. 1255] for implementation of Security Council resolution 1325(2000) [YUN 2000, p. 1113], and urged Member States and the UN system to pay more attention to preventing gender-based violence.

The Secretary-General requested the Human Rights Council to recommend specific conflict-prevention measures to Member States, the UN system and other actors in the implementation of its mandate, and the Peacebuilding Commission to provide recommendations on the prevention of the recurrence of conflict. He asked Member States to support the strengthening of UN capacity to analyse conflicts, and the joint efforts of the wider UN system, especially those based on collaboration among its development, humanitarian, human rights and political arms, for the prevention of violent conflict. In particular, he called for greater support of Member States' efforts in building their own capacities for the prevention of armed conflict and for mediating conflicts. The Secretary-General called upon Member States to consider the deployment of the United Nations Integrated Office in Sierra Leone and a similar office requested by Burundi, following the winding down of peacekeeping operations in those countries, and with relevant parts of the UN system, to launch a dialogue on conflict prevention, and to consider dedicating 2 per cent of the annual peacekeeping budget to the prevention of armed conflict.

GENERAL ASSEMBLY ACTION

On 7 September [meeting 98], the General Assembly adopted **resolution 60/284** [draft: A/60/L.61] without vote [agenda item 12].

Prevention of armed conflict

The General Assembly,

Recalling its resolution 57/337 of 3 July 2003,

Bearing in mind its responsibilities, functions and powers under the Charter of the United Nations, in particular with respect to matters related to the prevention of armed conflict,

Taking note of the statements made during the consideration of the agenda item entitled "Prevention of armed conflict" at its sixtieth session,

1. *Takes note* of the report of the Secretary-General on the prevention of armed conflict;
2. *Decides* to continue its consideration of the report of the Secretary-General and the recommendations contained therein at its sixty-first session.

The Assembly, by **decision 61/552** of 22 December, decided that the agenda item on the prevention of armed conflict would remain for consideration during its resumed sixty-first (2007) session.

Conflict diamonds

Report of Group of Experts on Côte d'Ivoire. In accordance with Security Council resolution 1643(2005) [YUN 2005, p. 251], the Chairman of the Security Council Committee established pursuant to Council resolution 1572(2004) [YUN 2004, p. 187] transmitted, in September [S/2006/735], the final report of the Group of Experts on the situation in Côte d'Ivoire, which included information on the embargo, imposed by the Council in resolution 1643(2005), on the export of diamonds from Côte d'Ivoire.

The Group concluded that Ivorian rough diamonds were being exported in violation of the embargo, transiting Ghana and Mali, prior to entering international markets. It recommended that Ghana create a credible system of internal controls for rough diamonds; Mali take measures to prevent illegal smuggling of diamonds into its territory from Côte d'Ivoire; the issue of internal controls as a regional problem be made a key agenda item at the November meeting of the Kimberley Process (see below); and international trading centres introduce a better system for identifying suspicious shipments of rough diamonds. The Group investigated the production of Ivorian rough diamonds and recommended that the United Nations Operation in Côte d'Ivoire conduct regular inspections of Bobi dyke and its vicinity to verify if heavy machinery was employed to exploit the diamond mines.

(For more information on the situation in Côte d'Ivoire, see p. 176.)

Kimberley Process. At its 2006 regular session, the plenary meeting of the Kimberley Process (Gaborone, Botswana, 6-9 November) reviewed the implementation of the Kimberley Process Certification Scheme (KPCS), established in 2003 [YUN 2003, p. 55] to stop the use of conflict diamonds in fuelling armed conflict, protect the legitimate diamond industry and ensure implementation of resolutions on trade in conflict diamonds. In accordance with General Assembly resolution 60/182 [YUN 2005, p. 89], the report of the plenary meeting was transmitted to the Secretary-General in November [A/61/589] by Botswana, in its capacity as Chair of the Kimberley Process.

The plenary approved a plan to help Ghana, which faced a possible loss of Kimberley Process status, to strengthen its internal diamond controls. It addressed the findings of the Kimberley Process review visit to Ghana (30 October–1 November) and reports from the United Nations Group of Experts on Côte d'Ivoire (see above) that diamonds mined in the rebel-held territory were entering markets through Ghana. The plenary concluded that there might be credible indications that Ghana had not complied with its Kimberley Process obligations. It decided that Ghana had to take immediate steps to ensure that it exported only Ghanaian diamonds, and agreed to send a review mission to the country by February 2007 to verify compliance.

The plenary considered the report of the third-year review of KPCS, which focused on the impact of the Scheme on the international trade in rough diamonds and the extent to which KPCS had been effective in preventing the flow of conflict diamonds into the legitimate trade; the functioning of KPCS technical provisions; and the effectiveness and efficiency of KPCS operations. According to the report, available data suggested that the majority of the international trade in rough diamonds was carried on within KPCS, and all significant diamond producing and trading centres, with the exception of Liberia, which remained under UN diamond sanctions, were implementing the Scheme. However, conflict diamonds were still being mined by rebel groups in Côte d'Ivoire and were reportedly entering the legitimate trade. There were also reports of illicit diamond extraction and trading by rebel factions and militias in the Democratic Republic of the Congo (DRC). KPCS was operating well and the statistics and peer review monitoring systems were proving to be essential tools, but they could be improved. Participants and observers made recommendations in the areas of statistical requirements and the peer review monitoring system that were included in the review's recommendations. The plenary endorsed the conclusions of the review, adopting 46 recommendations to strengthen the Kimberly Process.

The plenary agreed to publish the names of participants that habitually failed to submit statistics; highlight requirements related to illegal shipments; develop proposals related to interim measures, including possible suspension in cases of significant non-compliance; and to create the Working Group on Artisanal-Alluvial Production. It also agreed to give priority attention to: funding and resource requirements; improving statistical data gathering and analysis; effective and credible government oversight; and the treatment of illegal shipments. The plenary agreed on stronger internal controls standards for participants that produced, traded, cut and polished diamonds.

Noting the information by the Working Group on Statistics that participants were providing data regularly and the quality of the data and the analysis had improved, the plenary endorsed the concept of transparency in statistical reporting by approving the immediate release of KPCS summary data on trade and production.

The European Community would assume the Chair of the Kimberly Process for one year, beginning on 1 January 2007; India was elected Vice-Chair for 2007.

GENERAL ASSEMBLY ACTION

On 4 December [meeting 64], the General Assembly adopted **resolution 61/28** [draft: A/61/L.27 & Add.1] without vote [agenda item 10].

The role of diamonds in fuelling conflict: breaking the link between the illicit transaction of rough diamonds and armed conflict as a contribution to prevention and settlement of conflicts

The General Assembly,

Recognizing that the trade in conflict diamonds continues to be a matter of serious international concern, which can be directly linked to the fuelling of armed conflict, the activities of rebel movements aimed at undermining or overthrowing legitimate Governments and the illicit traffic in and proliferation of armaments, especially small arms and light weapons,

Recognizing also the devastating impact of conflicts fuelled by the trade in conflict diamonds on the peace, safety and security of people in affected countries, and the systematic and gross human rights violations that have been perpetrated in such conflicts,

Noting the negative impact of such conflicts on regional stability and the obligations placed upon States by the Charter of the United Nations regarding the maintenance of international peace and security,

Recognizing, therefore, that continued action to curb the trade in conflict diamonds is imperative,

Recalling that the elimination of illicit diamonds from legitimate trade is the primary objective of the Kimberley Process,

Bearing in mind the positive benefits of the legitimate diamond trade to producing countries, and underlining the need for continued international action to prevent the problem of conflict diamonds from negatively affecting the trade in legitimate diamonds, which makes a critical contribution to the economies of many of the producing, exporting and importing States, especially developing States,

Noting that the vast majority of rough diamonds produced in the world are from legitimate sources,

Recalling the Charter and all the relevant resolutions of the Security Council related to conflict diamonds, and determined to contribute to and support the implementation of the measures provided for in those resolutions,

Recalling also Security Council resolution 1459(2003) of 28 January 2003, in which the Council strongly supported the Kimberley Process Certification Scheme as a valuable contribution against trafficking in conflict diamonds,

Welcoming the important contribution of the Kimberley Process, which was initiated by African diamond-producing countries,

Noting with satisfaction that the implementation of the Kimberley Process Certification Scheme continues to have a positive impact in reducing the opportunity for conflict diamonds to play a role in fuelling armed conflict and would help to protect legitimate trade and ensure the effective implementation of the relevant resolutions on trade in conflict diamonds,

Recalling its resolutions 55/56 of 1 December 2000, 56/263 of 13 March 2002, 57/302 of 15 April 2003, 58/290 of 14 April 2004, 59/144 of 15 December 2004 and 60/182 of 20 December 2005, in which it called for the development and implementation as well as a periodic review of proposals for a simple, effective and pragmatic international certification scheme for rough diamonds,

Welcoming, in this regard, the implementation of the Kimberley Process Certification Scheme in such a way as not to impede the legitimate trade in diamonds or impose an undue burden on Governments or industry, particularly smaller producers, nor hinder the development of the diamond industry,

Welcoming also the decision of forty-seven Kimberley Process participants, representing seventy-one countries, including the twenty-five members of the European Union represented by the European Commission, to address the problem of conflict diamonds by participating in the Process and implementing the Kimberley Process Certification Scheme,

Welcoming further the important contributions made and that continue to be made by the diamond industry, in particular the World Diamond Council, as well as civil society, to assist international efforts to stop the trade in conflict diamonds,

Welcoming the voluntary self-regulation initiatives for the diamond industry announced by the World Diamond Council, and recognizing that a system of such voluntary self-regulation will contribute, as described in the Interlaken Declaration of 5 November 2002 on the Kimberley Process Certification Scheme for Rough Diamonds, to ensuring the effectiveness of national systems of internal control for rough diamonds,

Appreciating in this regard the decision taken by the plenary meeting of the Kimberley Process, held in Gaborone from 6 to 9 November 2006, based on calls from participants, civil society and the World Diamond Council urging stronger internal control standards for participants, together with measures offering clearer guidance on implementing effective controls from mine to export, stronger government oversight of the diamond industry, and spot checks of industry compliance,

Noting with appreciation that the Kimberley Process has pursued its deliberations on an inclusive basis, involving concerned stakeholders, including producing, exporting and importing States, the diamond industry and civil society, as well as applicants,

Recognizing that State sovereignty should be fully respected and that the principles of equality, mutual benefits and consensus should be adhered to,

Recognizing also that the Kimberley Process Certification Scheme, which came into effect on 1 January 2003, will be credible only if all participants have requisite national legislation coupled with effective and credible internal systems of control designed to eliminate the presence of conflict diamonds in the chain of producing, exporting and importing rough diamonds within their own territories, while taking into account that differences in production methods and trading practices, as well as differences in institutional controls thereof, may require different approaches to meeting minimum standards,

1. *Reaffirms its strong and continuing support* for the Kimberley Process Certification Scheme and the Kimberley Process as a whole;

2. *Recognizes* that the Kimberley Process Certification Scheme can help to ensure the effective implementation of relevant resolutions of the Security Council containing sanctions on the trade in conflict diamonds and act as a mechanism for the prevention of future conflicts, and calls for the full implementation of existing Council measures targeting the illicit trade in rough diamonds, particularly conflict diamonds which play a role in fuelling conflict;

3. *Also recognizes* the important contributions that the international efforts to address the problem of conflict diamonds, including the Kimberley Process Certification Scheme, have made to the settlement of conflicts and the consolidation of peace in Angola, the Democratic Republic of the Congo, Liberia and Sierra Leone;

4. *Takes note* of Security Council resolution 1643(2005) of 15 December 2005 which calls upon the States in the West Africa region that are not participants in the Kimberley Process to intensify their efforts to join the Process, stresses that the widest possible participation in the Kimberley Process Certification Scheme is essential, and encourages all Member States to contribute to the work of the Process by seeking membership, participating actively in the Certification Scheme and complying with its undertakings;

5. *Takes note with appreciation* of the report of the Chair of the Kimberley Process submitted pursuant to resolution 60/182, and congratulates the Governments, the regional economic integration organization, the diamond industry and civil society participating in the Process for contributing to the development, implementation and monitoring of the Kimberley Process Certification Scheme;

6. *Notes* the decision of the General Council of the World Trade Organization of 15 May 2003 granting a waiver with respect to the measures taken to implement the Kimberley Process Certification Scheme, effective from 1 January 2003 to 31 December 2006, and the decision of the General Council of 17 November 2006 granting an extension of the waiver until 31 December 2012;

7. *Notes with satisfaction* that in line with paragraph 7 of its resolution 60/182, the preliminary development of "footprints" that characterize diamond production from Côte d'Ivoire has been undertaken, and encourages expeditious commencement of further work to develop similar footprints for other diamond producers;

8. *Notes with appreciation* the contribution of the Kimberley Process in preparing a detailed assessment of the volume of rough diamonds produced in and exported from Côte d'Ivoire as requested by Security Council resolution 1643(2005) and, recognizing the cooperation between the Process and the United Nations Operation in Côte d'Ivoire, calls for the full implementation of the resolution on the subject of illicit diamond production in Côte d'Ivoire adopted by the plenary meeting of the Process held in Moscow from 15 to 17 November 2005, and encourages continued cooperation between the Process and the United Nations in tackling this issue;

9. *Also notes with appreciation* the action taken by the Kimberley Process to address concerns raised in the context of the report of the Group of Experts on Côte d'Ivoire submitted to the Security Council involving allegations that Ivorian diamonds were entering legitimate trade through third countries;

10. *Welcomes* the establishment of a new Working Group of the Kimberley Process on Artisanal Alluvial Production under the chairmanship of Angola, which will address issues of particular concern to artisanal alluvial producers and further contribute to the implementation of the existing declaration on improving internal controls over alluvial diamond production, and encourages potential donors to provide capacity-building assistance to further the effective implementation of the Kimberley Process Certification Scheme;

11. *Notes with appreciation* the contribution of the Kimberley Process and of its Chair to the work of the Security Council Committee established pursuant to resolution 1521(2003) concerning Liberia, including the submission of a report on the results of the Kimberley Process expert mission to Liberia, as well as the progress made by Liberia towards putting in place the necessary internal controls and other requirements in order to satisfy the minimum requirements of the Process pursuant to Council resolution 1521(2003), welcomes the contributions of the United Nations Mission in Liberia, the United States of America and other donors to these efforts, and encourages all those in a position to assist Liberia, to do so;

12. *Also notes with appreciation* the conclusions of the three-year review of the Kimberley Process Certification Scheme and the recommendations adopted by the plenary meeting of the Kimberley Process held in Gaborone and notes that the timely implementation of these recommendations will strengthen and consolidate the Process, and therefore encourages the timely implementation of those recommendations;

13. *Recognizes* that the peer review mechanism and the collection and submission of statistical data are critical monitoring tools, essential for effective implementation of the Kimberley Process Certification Scheme, and in this respect:

(a) Welcomes the important progress made in the implementation of the peer review mechanism in the Kimberley Process Certification Scheme, encourages all remaining participants to receive voluntary review visits, and notes with appreciation the intention of the Kimberley Process to commence a second round of review visits in 2007;

(b) Also welcomes the progress made towards the collection and submission of statistical reports on the production of and trade in rough diamonds, encourages all of the Kimberley Process participants to enhance the quality of data, and to this end applauds the decision of the plenary meeting held in Gaborone to release Kimberley Process summary data on trade and production, by value and volume, and certificate counts for 2004 and 2005 data;

14. *Notes with appreciation* the assistance and capacity-building efforts extended by various donors, and encourages other donors to provide financial and technical expertise to Kimberley Process participants to help them to develop tighter monitoring and control measures;

15. *Acknowledges with great appreciation* the important contribution that Botswana, as Chair of the Kimberley Process in 2006, has made to the efforts to curb the trade in conflict diamonds, and welcomes the succession of the European Community as Chair and India as Vice-Chair of the Process for 2007;

16. *Requests* the Chair of the Kimberley Process to submit a report on the implementation of the Process to the General Assembly at its sixty-second session;

17. *Decides* to include in the provisional agenda of its sixty-second session the item entitled "The role of diamonds in fuelling conflict".

Peacemaking and peacebuilding

Post-conflict peacebuilding

International Year of Reconciliation (2009)

On 20 November [meeting 56], the General Assembly adopted **resolution 61/17** [draft: A/61/L.22 & Add.1] without vote [agenda item 150].

International Year of Reconciliation, 2009

The General Assembly,

Bearing in mind the Charter of the United Nations, including the purposes and principles contained therein, and in particular those of saving succeeding generations from the scourge of war, bringing about by peaceful means, and in conformity with the principles of justice and international law, adjustment or settlement of international disputes or situations which might lead to a breach of the peace, and practising tolerance and living together in peace with one another as good neighbours, thus developing friendly relations among nations and promoting international cooperation to resolve international economic, social, cultural and humanitarian issues,

Recognizing that reconciliation processes are particularly necessary and urgent in countries and regions of the world which have suffered or are suffering situations of conflict that have affected and divided societies in their various internal, national and international facets,

Recognizing also that many of the activities of the United Nations system in general and the international community as a whole to support peacekeeping and peacebuilding, conflict prevention, disarmament, sustainable development, the promotion and protection of human rights and dignity, democracy, the rule of law and governance, inter alia, lead to the initiation and development of reconciliation processes,

Aware that dialogue among opponents from positions of respect and tolerance is an essential element of peace and reconciliation,

Aware also that truth and justice are indispensable elements for the attainment of reconciliation and lasting peace,

Bearing in mind the role of the media in reporting on reconciliation processes,

Convinced that the declaration of an international year of reconciliation at the end of the first decade of the new millennium will provide the international community with the opportunity to pursue, with the active involvement of all stakeholders, efforts to develop reconciliation processes, which are necessary to and a condition for the establishment of firm and lasting peace,

1. *Expresses its steadfast determination* to pursue reconciliation processes in those societies that are affected and/or divided by conflicts;

2. *Decides* to proclaim 2009 the International Year of Reconciliation;

3. *Invites* concerned Governments and international and non-governmental organizations to support

reconciliation processes among affected and/or divided societies and to plan and implement adequate cultural, educational and social programmes to promote the concept of reconciliation, including by holding conferences and seminars and disseminating information about the issue.

Disarmament, demobilization and reintegration

In response to General Assembly resolution 59/296 [YUN 2005, p. 133], the Secretary-General submitted a March report [A/60/705] on UN engagement in disarmament, demobilization and reintegration processes in complex peacekeeping and non-peacekeeping operations. The report discussed the increased engagement in such processes over the previous five years, including lessons learned and the development of a new integrated approach within the UN system. The report described the concept, definitions, and principles underpinning the integrated approach to disarmament, demobilization and reintegration, as well as its implementation.

Since the Secretary-General's report on the role of UN peacekeeping in disarmament, demobilization and reintegration, issued in 2000 [YUN 2000, p. 78], six UN peacekeeping missions had included those elements as part of their mandates: the United Nations Organization Mission in the Democratic Republic of the Congo (MONUC) (see p. 145); the United Nations Mission in Liberia (UNMIL) (see p. 221); the United Nations Operation in Côte d'Ivoire (UNOCI) (see p. 207); the United Nations Operation in Burundi (ONUB) (see p. 158); the United Nations Stabilization Mission in Haiti (MINUSTAH) (see p. 353); and the United Nations Mission in the Sudan (UNMIS) (see p. 265). The Organization had become increasingly engaged in countries where peacekeeping operations had not been deployed. The United Nations Development Programme (UNDP) and other UN agencies, departments, funds and programmes supported the development of disarmament, demobilization and reintegration strategies and implementation of a variety of activities, such as counselling and referral services to ex-combatants, ensuring the availability of reintegration options and meeting the specific needs of women. The Organization was particularly committed to demobilizing and removing children used by armed forces and groups in situations of ongoing conflict, in conformity with international norms and standards. While the scale, complexity and type of the UN work in disarmament, demobilization and reintegration had changed, the means of planning and implementing such operations had not. The operations were often conducted in a fractured way, resulting in poor coordination and sometimes competition between and among peacekeeping operations, agencies, funds and programmes. The narrow focus on short-term security goals often led to the exclusion of key target groups, including women combatants, supporters and dependents, leading to disjointed programmes and disillusioned ex-combatants returning to arms, as in Haiti and Sierra Leone.

To reverse that situation, the Organization had embarked on a new system-wide approach to improving performance through the establishment by the Executive Committee on Peace and Security of the Inter-Agency Working Group on Disarmament, Demobilization and Reintegration, comprising 15 departments, agencies, funds and programmes. The Working Group developed new policies and concepts for planning and implementing disarmament, demobilization and reintegration operations in a peacekeeping context, known as the integrated disarmament, demobilization and reintegration standards, and was working on a training and capacity-building strategy and the piloting of integrated programmes in Haiti and the Sudan. The new standards provided a comprehensive set of policies, guidelines and standard operating procedures on all aspects of disarmament, demobilization and reintegration, emphasizing: a people-centred approach; a flexible, transparent and accountable approach; an integrated approach centred on the principles of integration, especially in planning and integration; and a national ownership-centred approach, encouraging Governments and citizens in post-conflict countries to take responsibility for disarmament, demobilization and reintegration programming. They identified five phases of internal UN planning, including pre-planning and preparatory assistance; initial technical assessments; development of a strategic and policy framework; a programme and operational framework; and a post-mission plan. The standards would be supported by an operational handbook, and a note for senior managers engaged in peace negotiations and in planning, implementing and managing peace operations with a disarmament, demobilization and reintegration component, complemented by a web-based resource centre. The standards constituted a common UN approach to disarmament, demobilization and reintegration in a peacekeeping environment and favoured the development of a streamlined means of supporting national needs, as opposed to proposing blueprint solutions. The comprehensive approach should be adopted as a means to underpin all future UN efforts; however, the Working Group would continue if possible and reflect on lessons learned from the new and increasingly complex situations in which disarmament, demobilization and reintegration were taking place.

The Secretary-General concluded that the Inter-Agency Working Group would continue to strengthen and consolidate the partnership it had built up over the previous two years. He identified the need for an integrated, inter-agency UN disarmament, demobilization and reintegration capacity to provide ongoing policy development, strategic advice, support and training to country programmes. That body would engage with partners outside the United Nations; assist with training, resource mobilization and planning; and support disarmament, demobilization and reintegration programmes. The secretariat should be expanded and mandated to provide wider support to disarmament, demobilization and reintegration. A key priority would be to implement the integrated disarmament, demobilization and reintegration standards at the country level. The United Nations had begun to pilot the standards through the formation of integrated disarmament, demobilization and reintegration units in MINUSTAH and UNMIS and the joint training of their military, police and civilian personnel. The UN system would test the new approach in Haiti and the Sudan, implement it in other disarmament, demobilization and reintegration programmes, and ensure that new programmes were developed in line with the standards. Implementation of an integrated approach would require new coordination mechanisms, which could include integrated disarmament, demobilization and reintegration teams staffed jointly by personnel from UNDP, DPKO and other agencies, and/or a UN country team disarmament, demobilization and reintegration steering group to facilitate the exchange of information, joint planning and operations within the peacekeeping mission and with the country team. The report contained recommendations for addressing institutional constraints; developing policies and tools; maintaining and developing an online resource centre; training and developing capacity within the United Nations; and strengthening partnerships with international and national actors.

Special Committee on Peacekeeping Operations consideration. The Special Committee on Peacekeeping Operations, at its 2006 substantive session (New York, 27 February–17 March) [A/60/19] (see p. 85), called for long-term commitment by the donor community in support of disarmament, demobilization and reintegration programmes and requested the Secretary-General to identify the additional resources needed. It recommended that the Secretary-General's report on the subject (see above) be considered at the Committee's next session and called on the Secretariat to use an inter-agency forum to bolster Headquarters support to disarmament, demobilization and reintegration programmes. The Special Committee stressed the importance of ensuring that all women and children associated with armed forces and groups were systematically included in every disarmament, demobilization and reintegration process, with a particular emphasis on reintegration and education.

ACABQ report. The Advisory Committee on Administrative and Budgetary Questions (ACABQ), in its July report [A/60/929], noted the Secretary-General's intention to provide additional support to disarmament, demobilization and reintegration programmes in the field and to create an integrated, inter-agency UN capacity, building on the existing Secretariat. It also pointed to the necessity of defining the relationship between the Inter-Agency Working Group and the Peacebuilding Commission (see below).

Peacebuilding Commission

The Peacebuilding Commission, established concurrently in 2005 by Security Council resolution 1645(2005) [YUN 2005, p. 94] and General Assembly resolution 60/180 [ibid.] as an intergovernmental advisory body to provide an overall strategic approach and coherence for international peacebuilding efforts, serve as a dedicated institutional mechanism to address the special needs of countries emerging from conflict, and assist those countries in laying the foundations for sustainable peace and development, was inaugurated on 23 June 2006. The Commission's standing Organizational Committee, comprising seven members each from the Security Council and the Economic and Social Council and the five top providers of assessed contributions and military personnel, was also established (see p. 56). Both the Commission and its Organizational Committee were supported by the Peacebuilding Support Office. The Commission held country-specific meetings on 12 and 13 October and 12 and 13 December. The Organizational Committee met on 23 June, 13 July, 9 October, and 7 and 12 December. On 20 December, the Commission Chairman submitted to the Security Council President a report [S/2006/1050] on the Commission's country-specific meetings on Burundi and Sierra Leone. The Commission identified the critical challenges that needed to be addressed in those countries to lay the foundation for sustainable peace and create the enabling environment for development and reconstruction.

On 22 December, the Assembly decided that the agenda item on the report of the Peacebuilding Commission would remain for consideration during its resumed sixty-first (2007) session (**decision 61/552**).

Organizational Committee

Membership

On 17 January [S/2006/25], the Security Council President informed the Secretary-General of the selection of Denmark and the United Republic of Tanzania, following informal consultations, as members of the Council's elected member category for the Peacebuilding Commission's Organizational Committee for a term of one year, until the end of 2006. The Council also noted Argentina's position, supported by Peru, that a member of the Latin American and Caribbean States Group be considered for selection when the terms of Denmark and the United Republic of Tanzania expired.

On 5 May [A/60/847], Jordan informed the Secretary-General that, in accordance with resolution 60/180, the 10 top providers of military personnel and civilian police to UN missions had selected Bangladesh, Ghana, India, Nigeria and Pakistan to serve on the Organizational Committee for the first two-year term.

GENERAL ASSEMBLY ACTION

On 8 May [meeting 79], the General Assembly adopted **resolution 60/261** [draft: A/60/L.52] without vote [agenda item 112 (*f*)].

Election of seven members of the Organizational Committee of the Peacebuilding Commission

The General Assembly,

Recalling its resolution 60/180 and Security Council resolution 1645(2005), both of 20 December 2005, in which the Assembly and the Council concurrently operationalized the decision by the 2005 World Summit to establish the Peacebuilding Commission as an intergovernmental advisory body,

Recalling in particular paragraphs 4 (*a*) to (*e*) and 5 of the above-mentioned resolutions setting out the arrangements for the composition of the Organizational Committee of the Commission,

Bearing in mind that, in accordance with paragraph 4 (*e*) of the above-mentioned resolutions, seven additional members of the Organizational Committee shall be elected according to rules and procedures decided by the General Assembly,

Emphasizing that, in electing members of the Organizational Committee, the General Assembly should give due consideration to representation from all regional groups in the overall composition of the Committee and to representation from countries that have experienced post-conflict recovery,

Emphasizing also that Member States from all regional groups should have the possibility of presenting candidatures for election in the General Assembly, in accordance with paragraph 4 (*e*) of the above-mentioned resolutions,

1. *Notes* that the elections and/or selections that have taken place, in accordance with the provisions of paragraphs 4 (*a*) to (*d*) of General Assembly resolution 60/180 and Security Council resolution 1645(2005), have resulted in the following distribution of seats for this year among the five regional groups in the Organizational Committee of the Peacebuilding Commission:

(*a*) Five members from African States;

(*b*) Seven members from Asian States;

(*c*) Two members from Eastern European States;

(*d*) One member from Latin American and Caribbean States;

(*e*) Nine members from Western European and other States;

2. *Decides* that the seven seats for election by the General Assembly for membership in the Organizational Committee for this year shall be distributed among the five regional groups as follows:

(*a*) Two seats for African States;

(*b*) One seat for Asian States;

(*c*) One seat for Eastern European States;

(*d*) Three seats for Latin American and Caribbean States;

(*e*) No seats for Western European and other States;

3. *Also decides* that the rules of procedure and established practice of the General Assembly for the election of members of its subsidiary bodies shall apply to its election of members of the Organizational Committee;

4. *Reiterates* that the members of the Organizational Committee shall serve for renewable terms of two years, as applicable, beginning on the day of the first meeting of the Committee;

5. *Calls upon* Member States to give due consideration to representation from countries that have experienced post-conflict recovery when electing members of the Organizational Committee in the General Assembly;

6. *Decides* that the term of membership shall be staggered, and that two members from different regional groups, to be drawn by lots in the first election, shall serve for an initial period of one year;

7. *Also decides* that each of the five regional groups shall have no less than three seats in the overall composition of the Organizational Committee;

8. *Further decides* that the elections to be held by the General Assembly this year will set no precedent for future elections and that the distribution of seats as set out in paragraph 2 above will be reviewed annually, on the basis of changes in the membership in other categories established in paragraphs 4 (*a*) to (*d*) of the above-mentioned resolutions, in order to give due consideration to representation of all regional groups in the overall composition of the Organizational Committee.

On 8 May [A/60/839], Egypt reconfirmed, in the light of the adoption of resolution 60/261 (above), its candidature for one of the two seats on the Organizational Committee allocated to African States.

On the same date [A/60/848], the United States, as facilitator of the group of 10 leading contributors to the United Nations, conveyed to the Secretary-General the five top contributors—Germany, Italy, Japan, the Netherlands and Norway—to serve for the first term on the Organizational Committee. The 10 contributors agreed that Canada and Sweden would be provided the opportunity to serve in the second term.

ECONOMIC AND SOCIAL COUNCIL ACTION

On 8 May [meeting 8], the Economic and Social Council adopted **resolution 2006/3** [draft: E/2006/L.2/Rev.1] without vote [agenda item 2].

Membership of the Economic and Social Council on the Organizational Committee of the Peacebuilding Commission pursuant to paragraph 4 *(b)* of General Assembly resolution 60/180 and of Security Council resolution 1645(2005)

The Economic and Social Council,

Recalling General Assembly resolution 60/180 of 20 December 2005 and Security Council resolution 1645(2005) of 20 December 2005 concurrently establishing the Peacebuilding Commission,

Recalling also, in particular, paragraphs 12 (*b*), 13 and 17 of General Assembly resolution 60/180 and Security Council resolution 1645(2005), establishing the institutional relationship between the Economic and Social Council and the Peacebuilding Commission,

Recognizing the important role to be performed by the Peacebuilding Commission towards recovery, reintegration and reconstruction in countries emerging from conflict, particularly in Africa,

Recalling that due consideration is to be given to countries that have experienced post-conflict recovery in the composition of the Organizational Committee of the Peacebuilding Commission,

1. *Decides* that the distribution of the seven seats allocated to the Economic and Social Council on the Organizational Committee of the Peacebuilding Commission shall be as follows:

(a) One seat for each of the five regional groups, namely, African States, Asian States, Eastern European States, Latin American and Caribbean States and Western European and other States;

(b) For the purpose of the first election, the two remaining seats shall be allocated to the regional groups of African States and Asian States;

2. *Also decides* that members of the Council shall be elected to the Organizational Committee for a two-year term with the possibility, as applicable, of sharing the term within the concerned regional group for the seats allocated to it, subject to the concurrence of the Council;

3. *Further decides* that elections from among its members to the Organizational Committee shall be held every other year;

4. *Decides* that the rules of procedure and established practice of the Council for the election of members of its subsidiary bodies shall apply to the election of members of the Organizational Committee by the Council;

5. *Also decides* to hold the first election at a meeting of its organizational session for 2006.

Meetings

The Organizational Committee met on 23 June [PBC/OC/1/SR.1], 13 July [PBC/OC/1/SR.2], 9 October [PBC/1/OC/SR.3], 7 December [PBC/1/OC/SR.4], and 12 December [PBC/1/OC/SR.5], all in New York. The Committee discussed, among other matters, selection of participants in, and the process and schedule of, country-specific meetings; requests submitted to the Committee; membership of the Committee; and the Peacebuilding Commission's reporting requirements to the Security Council and General Assembly. At its first meeting in June, the Committee considered a 21 June request of the Security Council [PBC/1/OC/2 & Corr.1] for the Commission's advice on the situations in Burundi and Sierra Leone; at its July meeting, the Committee decided that the Commission's first two country-specific meetings would address the situations in those countries.

At its June meeting, the Committee adopted the Commission's provisional rules of procedure [PBC/1/OC/1] through a consultative process among Member States. At its 12 December meeting, it agreed to review those rules in 2007, and established an expert group for that purpose.

At its October meeting, the Committee established an ad hoc working group on pending issues to address those aspects that needed further elaboration in the provisional rules of procedure, especially the implementation of Assembly resolution 60/180 and Council resolution 1645(2005) [YUN 2005, p. 94] concerning the participation of the World Bank, the International Monetary Fund and other international donors, as well as the modalities for civil society participation in Commission meetings.

Establishment of Peacebuilding Fund

In response to General Assembly resolution 60/180 and Security Council resolution 1645(2005) [YUN 2005, p. 94], the Secretary-General submitted an August report [A/60/984] on arrangements for establishing the Peacebuilding Fund, which was designed to support interventions considered critical to the peacebuilding process, and pave the way for the sustained support and engagement of other key stakeholders. The Fund would support peacebuilding activities that directly contributed to the stabilization of countries emerging from conflict, facilitate the implementation of peace agreements, strengthen country capacities to promote peaceful resolution of conflicts and respond to threats that might lead to the recurrence of conflict.

The terms of reference for the Fund, which were annexed to the report, focused on allocation and disbursement modalities, including eligibility for funding and the role of the Peacebuilding Commission in advising the Secretary-General on the selection of countries eligible for consideration for funding. Funding would be informed by an analysis of critical gaps in peacebuilding, which would be conducted by national authorities and the United Nations. Management of the Fund would be assumed by UNDP. Both the Assembly and the Peacebuilding Commission would have a role in the Fund's governance arrangements. An independent advisory group of eminent personalities with peacebuilding experience would be appointed to advise the Secretary-General on strengthening the functioning and use of the Fund. The initial funding target of the Fund was set at $250 million.

The Secretary-General concluded that resources from the Fund, combined with the efforts of the Peacebuilding Commission, would help ensure that post-conflict countries continued to benefit from the sustained attention and support of the international community. Member States were invited to support the Fund by providing regular voluntary contributions to ensure that it effectively addressed the critical peacebuilding activities of countries emerging from conflict.

GENERAL ASSEMBLY ACTION

On 8 September [meeting 99], the General Assembly adopted **resolution 60/287** [draft: A/60/L.63 & Add.1] without vote [agenda items 46 & 120].

The Peacebuilding Fund

The General Assembly,

Recalling the 2005 World Summit Outcome,

Recalling also its resolution 60/180 and Security Council resolution 1645(2005) of 20 December 2005 on the operationalization of the Peacebuilding Commission, in particular paragraphs 24 and 25 thereof,

1. *Takes note* of the arrangements for establishing the Peacebuilding Fund as contained in the report of the Secretary-General and the terms of reference for the Fund contained in the annex thereto;

2. *Affirms* its role to provide overall policy guidance on the use of the Fund to maximize its impact and improve its functioning;

3. *Welcomes* the contributions and financial pledges already made to the Fund, and emphasizes the necessity of sustained contributions in order to enhance the capacity of the Fund to immediately release the resources needed to launch post-conflict peacebuilding activities;

4. *Urges* all Member States to consider making voluntary contributions to the Fund;

5. *Requests* the Secretary-General to submit an annual report to the General Assembly on the operation and activities of the Fund;

6. *Decides* to include in the draft agenda of its sixty-first session an item entitled "Report of the Secretary-General on the Peacebuilding Fund".

The Fund was officially launched by the Secretary-General on 11 October.

On 22 December, the Assembly decided that the agenda item on the report of the Secretary-General on the Peacebuilding Fund would remain for consideration during the resumed sixty-first (2007) session (**decision 61/552**).

Establishment of Peacebuilding Support Office

The Peacebuilding Support Office, established in accordance with General Assembly resolutions 60/1 [YUN 2005, p. 48] and 60/180 [ibid., p. 94], was intended to assist the Peacebuilding Commission in addressing the fragmentation and lack of coherence in UN peacebuilding capacities; provide the Commission with analytical and technical support to help it undertake its advisory role and make informed decisions regarding the development and implementation of integrated peace strategies for countries emerging from conflict; and facilitate the development of strategies and options by the actors on the ground, especially transitional authorities and resident UN leadership. The assistance provided by the Support Office could include both facilitation and technical support. Neither the Commission, nor the Support Office would possess direct operational capacity in countries, but would count on and complement the capacities of existing actors, including Secretariat offices and departments, specialized agencies, and UN funds and programmes. The Office would support the Commission in financing for peacebuilding, planning, policy and analysis, and other support; oversee the management, coordination and decision-making aspects of the Peacebuilding Fund, as specified in the terms of reference of that facility (see above); and ensure that the Commission's oversight and reporting needs were met. The Support Office would draw on the best expertise in the UN system and outside networks on country-specific and thematic peacebuilding issues in order to provide the Commission with sound analysis and information to enable it to make informed decisions and to perform its advisory role.

Financing

The Secretary-General, in revised estimates to the proposed 2006-2007 programme budget [A/60/537] submitted in 2005, had proposed an amount of $4,175,200, under section 3, Political affairs, and section 35, Staff assessment, later revised further to $7,002,400, to take account of additional requirements under section 2, General Assembly and Economic and Social Council affairs and conference management [A/C.5/60/22].

ACABQ, in December 2005 [A/60/7/Add.25], recommended that the Assembly decide that, in view of the requirement that the Support Office be staffed from existing resources, there should be no additional appropriation under section 3 of the proposed 2006-2007 programme budget. The Secretary-General should be requested to revisit the matter and submit a proposal consistent with the Assembly's intent.

The Fifth (Administrative and Budgetary) Committee, having considered the Secretary-General's statement and the related ACABQ report [A/60/598], informed the Assembly that the adoption of resolution 60/180 would not give rise to any additional requirements under the proposed 2006-2007 programme budget at that stage, nor any additional appropriation under section 3 of the proposed budget. The Assembly requested the Secretary-General to report back to it pursuant to the ACABQ report.

In response to the Committee's decision, the Secretary-General submitted a February 2006 report [A/60/694] updating information on the status of the establishment of the Peacebuilding Support Office, including information on resource requirements and the proposed arrangements to meet them.

The total requirements of the Peacebuilding Support Office for the 2006-2007 biennium amounted to $5,595,400, of which $2,790,000, corresponding to eight posts, would be met through redeployment or secondment of staff from other UN system organizations. The remaining requirements would be accommodated within the overall resources approved for 2006-2007, through the utilization of the provision for special political missions appropriated under section 3, Political affairs, of the 2006-2007 programme budget.

The Assembly was requested to approve the 2006-2007 budget for the Peacebuilding Support Office, as well as a charge of $2,805,400 corresponding to the remaining requirements of the Office against the provision for special political missions already approved under section 3 of the 2006-2007 programme budget.

ACABQ, in a March report [A/60/7/Add.36], said that the Secretary-General's proposal did not comply with the Assembly's request that the cost associated with the establishment of the Office be accommodated from within existing resources in the sense that a balance of $52.6 million would remain available from within the appropriation of $356 million for special political missions, if current proposals before the Assembly were approved. It was of the opinion that the staffing needs of the Support Office, including grade levels, should be reviewed within one year after the Peacebuilding Commission started its work. The results of the review should be submitted as a separate analysis during the consideration of the proposed 2008-2009 programme budget. ACABQ recommended that the use of in-house capacity for the work of the Support Office be maximized and that requirements for consultants be requested and fully justified in the review.

ACABQ recommended that the Assembly note that 5 of the 15 posts requested for the Support Office would be accommodated through redeployment and that a further 3 posts would be provided through non-reimbursable secondment by other UN system organizations. It further recommended that the proposed charge against the provision for special political missions of $2,805,400 under section 3 of the programme budget for the 2006-2007 biennium be reduced by $1,234,100. The total charge against the provision for special political missions would thus amount to $1,571,300.

The Assembly took action with regard to the Secretary-General's proposals and ACABQ recommendations in section II of **resolution 60/255** of 8 May (see p. 1618).

Cooperation with regional organizations

In response to Security Council resolution 1631(2005) [YUN 2005, p. 97], the Secretary-General submitted a July report [A/61/204-S/2006/590] on a regional-global security partnership: challenges and opportunities. The report described the development of that partnership between 1994 and 2006, the challenges facing cooperation between the United Nations and regional and subregional organizations in maintaining international peace and security, including the need to clarify roles and build capacity, and identified opportunities for cooperation.

The Secretary-General said that it had long been recognized that the United Nations could not handle every crisis on its own and that partnerships with other intergovernmental organizations should be developed. That had materialized over the years, especially through six high-level meetings convened between the United Nations and regional and other intergovernmental organizations and thematic meetings of the Security Council. As a result of guidance given by those meetings, significant operational cooperation in peace and security had developed between the United Nations and partner organizations, especially in the areas of conflict prevention, peacemaking, peacekeeping, peacebuilding and special areas of disarmament and non-proliferation, the protection of civilians and natural disasters. In describing current operational cooperation in those areas, the Secretary-General said that respect for human rights, which was central to conflict prevention and building regional capacity for protection of human rights had become one of the strategic goals of UN partnership with subregional organizations. That partnership was sustained through the establishment of regional offices around the world and a subregional centre for human rights and democracy based in Yaoundé, Cameroon. The United Nations was willing to engage in dialogue with partner organizations on how to advance the process of building a global-regional mechanism in conflict prevention. UN system work in conflict prevention had evolved to include an integrated, multisectoral approach, and the Organization was exploring new ways to partner with the development sectors of regional and subregional organizations.

To strengthen cooperation in peacemaking, the UN Department of Political Affairs would launch a systematic, region-by-region analysis of mediation experiences in order to draw practical conclusions and develop useful tools, and a web-based peacemaking databank for international peacemaking professionals. Regional organizations had become important contributors to international efforts to assist States in the transition from armed conflict to sustainable peace, and there had been dramatic growth in partner engagement in peacekeeping, particularly in Africa and Europe. In the coming years, the United Nations should promote capacity in peacekeeping, target capacity-building efforts, and reinforce a collective approach to security. The United Nations would work closely with partner organizations in the protection of civilians, with the objective of establishing a consultative network with interested partner organizations to identify options for a common framework on protection of civilians in armed conflict, based on agreed core policies and legal elements.

With regard to natural disaster relief, the Secretary-General requested regional organizations to coordinate closely with the United Nations Emergency Relief Coordinator to ensure that collective efforts met internationally agreed guidelines and methodologies, benefited from lessons learned and best practices, avoided competition for resources or collision of mandates and built effective partnerships.

The report outlined progress in realizing the goals of Council resolution 1631(2005) [YUN 2005, p. 97], in which the Council expressed its determination to further develop cooperation between the United Nations and partner organizations in maintaining peace and security, including in the areas of standby arrangements, rapid deployment, small arms and light weapons, counter-terrorism and capacity-building assistance.

Challenges to be addressed with regard to the partnership between the United Nations and regional and subregional organizations in the maintenance of international peace and security included clarification of the identity and role of each member of the partnership and the establishment of a programme of action for capacity-building to ensure more equal ability among the partners. With regard to opportunities for cooperation, the Secretary-General said that the global security mechanism of the future rested on a balanced distribution of capacity and resources across all regions. The Security Council had to retain primary responsibility for maintaining international peace and security, but it should seek a willing and capable subsidiary role for regional and other intergovernmental organizations.

To address the challenges described in the report, the Secretary-General recommended that the United Nations should strengthen its capacity to develop a global-regional conflict prevention mechanism with which comparable regional and subregional mechanisms could interact, and establish a databank on conflict prevention capacities of partner organizations and the UN system as a foundation for such a mechanism. The United Nations and partner organizations should host jointly a series of workshops on lessons learned in conflict prevention and in building the global-regional mechanism. A dedicated research capacity should be established, to be shared by partner organizations and the United Nations, to advance joint lessons-learned capacity in the field. Partner organizations should become active users of, and contributors to, the Department for Political Affairs peacemaking databank.

To improve the effectiveness and ensure greater impact of disarmament and non-proliferation activities at the regional and subregional levels, the United Nations should: strengthen its cooperation with regional and other intergovernmental organizations to further implement the 2001 Programme of Action to Prevent, Combat and Eradicate the Illicit Trade in Small Arms and Light Weapons in

All Its Aspects [YUN 2001, p. 499], in particular to facilitate and promote programmes of technical assistance and international cooperation; strengthen its efforts to promote the universalization and full implementation of multilateral disarmament and non-proliferation treaties and other politically binding instruments through the establishment of regional integrated databases; and hold a series of workshops, in collaboration with regional and other intergovernmental organizations, with a view to raising awareness and facilitating the provision of assistance and cooperation to strengthen States' capacity to implement their obligations under Security Council resolutions 1540(2004) [YUN 2004, p. 544] and 1673(2006) (see p. 635) on non-proliferation of weapons of mass destruction. Other recommendations dealt with peacekeeping, peacebuilding, clarification of the roles of the partners, and the formalization of the partnership.

Security Council consideration. On 20 September [meeting 5529], the Security Council met with representatives of the Association of Southeast Asian Nations, the Collective Security Treaty Organization, the Commonwealth of Independent States, the Council of Europe, the European Union (EU), the League of Arab States, the North Atlantic Treaty Organization (NATO), the Organization of American States (OAS), the Organization of the Islamic Conference, and the Organization for Security and Cooperation in Europe to consider cooperation in maintaining international peace and security. The Council had before it the Secretary-General's report on a regional-global partnership and a 6 September letter [S/2006/719] from Greece to the Secretary-General, transmitting a paper on the challenges of cooperation between the United Nations and regional organizations to help guide discussion on the subject.

Greece, in its capacity as Council President, noted that, while Chapter VIII of the UN Charter referred to regional agencies and arrangements and set out their functional relationship with the Council, it was silent on their constitutional relationship. The time had come for greater clarity on issues that would facilitate the shaping of the vision of a global-regional mechanism for peace and security, including clarifying the criteria for distinguishing those agencies from other international organizations, for the purposes of applying Chapter VIII, and thus give the Council greater reliance on constitutionally delegated executive functions to genuine regional agencies.

In his statement to the meeting, the Secretary-General said that the security partnership between the United Nations and regional organizations was stronger than in the previous decade; many of the regional and subregional partners were stronger; and the interaction was more intense, substantial and meaningful. In 2006, political and operational collaboration included: cooperation with the African Union (AU) peacekeeping operation in the Sudan; cooperation with the EU in support of the peace process in the DRC; and ongoing partnerships with the Economic Community of West African States (ECOWAS), NATO in Afghanistan and the Kosovo province of Serbia, and OAS in support of Haiti's electoral process. The political engagement of regional actors was improving the Organization's knowledge of specific situations and the military and peacekeeping capacities of those actors had made it possible to respond more quickly at the outset of crisis. In the next decade, the demand for peacekeeping and related services would continue to grow, and the time had come to take the regional-global partnership to a new level of clarity, practicality and seriousness. The Secretary-General urged that efforts continue to find new ways to cooperate and create a global collective security mechanism that protected people and laid the groundwork for lasting peace.

SECURITY COUNCIL ACTION

On 20 September [meeting 5529], following consultations among Security Council members, the President made statement **S/PRST/2006/39** on behalf of the Council:

The Security Council recalls its previous relevant resolutions and the statements by its President on cooperation with regional and subregional organizations and its three previous meetings on this subject, held on 11 April 2003 under the presidency of Mexico, and on 20 July 2004 and 17 October 2005 under the presidency of Romania.

Member States emphasized that the Council has primary responsibility for the maintenance of international peace and security and that the establishment of a more effective partnership between the United Nations and regional and other intergovernmental organizations, consistent with Chapter VIII of the Charter of the United Nations, would contribute to the maintenance of peace and security.

The Council notes the start of the practice of annual Secretary-General's high-level meetings, their high-level attendance and their broadening substantive agenda. The Council notes that the seventh high-level meeting takes place immediately after its meeting of 20 September 2006, and the President of the Security Council has been invited to report the results of that meeting to the seventh high-level meeting.

The Council welcomes the progress made in realizing the goals of resolution 1631(2005), as elaborated by the Secretary-General in his report, and commends the efforts of the Secretary-General in strengthening partnerships with regional, subregional and other intergovernmental organizations on peace and security, thereby contributing to the realization of the recommendations of the 2005 World Summit Outcome for a stronger relationship between such organizations and the United Nations. The Council calls upon the next Secretary-General to continue and strengthen these efforts.

The Council notes that a working-level meeting was organized by the United Nations Secretariat with regional and other intergovernmental organizations in early July 2006 to review the progress in implementing resolution 1631(2005) and calls for this practice to continue in 2007.

The Council stresses the benefits of closer cooperation with regional and subregional organizations in the maintenance of international peace and security, including the brokering of peace agreements in conflict situations. In this regard, the Council agreed, in the recently adopted note by the President of the Security Council on the work of the Informal Working Group on Documentation and Other Procedural Questions, to expand consultation and cooperation with regional and subregional organizations by:

—Inviting relevant regional and subregional organizations to participate in the public and private meetings of the Council, when appropriate;

—Continuing to consult informally with regional and subregional organizations when drafting, inter alia, resolutions, presidential statements and press statements, as appropriate;

—Drawing the attention of representatives of regional and subregional organizations, where appropriate, to relevant resolutions, presidential statements and press statements.

The Council encourages regional and subregional organizations to convey their perspectives and analysis to the Council prior to its examination of regionally relevant agenda items.

The Council invites all regional and subregional organizations that have a capacity for peacekeeping or rapid response in crisis situations to enhance their working relations with the Secretariat and cooperate with the Secretariat to determine the conditions in which this capacity could contribute to the fulfilment of United Nations mandates and goals.

The Council invites the Secretariat and regional and subregional organizations to explore further information-sharing on respective capabilities and lessons learned in peacekeeping by expanding the scope of the website of the Peacekeeping Best Practices Section of the Department of Peacekeeping Operations of the Secretariat to cover the deployment experiences of all regional and subregional organizations and all experiences of cooperation in peacekeeping between the United Nations and these organizations.

The Council takes note of the progress report of the Secretary-General on the prevention of armed conflict, including the recognition therein of the role played by regional and subregional organizations. The Council urges the Secretariat and United Nations agencies, as well as all States and other relevant international organizations to continue their efforts to contribute to the capacity-building of regional and subregional organizations, in particular of the African Union and African subregional organizations, which play a useful role in brokering peace agreements, conflict prevention, crisis management and post-conflict stabilization.

The Council welcomes the intent of many regional and subregional organizations to be closely associated with the work of the Peacebuilding Commission and commits to facilitating their participation, as relevant, in the country-specific activities of the Commission.

The Council equally welcomes efforts under way to enhance cooperation between the Secretariat and regional and subregional organizations in mediation and peacemaking, and invites the Secretariat to expand without delay its Peacemaking databank to regional and subregional organizations so as to facilitate mutual information and exchanges of experience.

The Council notes with appreciation the efforts of an increasing number of regional and subregional organizations, working with the subsidiary bodies of the Council, to address the threats to international peace and security posed by acts of terrorism, and calls upon them to intensify their activity to develop the counter-terrorism capacity of their member States.

The Council urges regional and subregional organizations to assist States, as appropriate, in implementing existing agreements and enhance efforts to eradicate the illicit trade in small arms and light weapons, including via more effective regional mechanisms. The Council also urges regional and subregional organizations to encourage their member States to strengthen their legislations in this field.

The Council recalls the relevant paragraphs of the 2005 World Summit Outcome and notes with gratitude the many steps that the Secretary-General has undertaken to strengthen the relationship between the United Nations and regional and subregional and other intergovernmental organizations. In this context, the Council intends to consider further steps to promote closer and more operational cooperation between the United Nations and regional, subregional and other intergovernmental organizations participating in the high-level meetings convened by the Secretary-General, in particular in the field of conflict prevention, peacebuilding and peacekeeping.

On 16 November [A/61/630], the Secretary-General and the Chairperson of the AU Commission signed in Addis Ababa, Ethiopia, a declaration entitled "Enhancing UN-AU Cooperation: Framework for the Ten-Year Capacity-Building Programme for the African Union" (see p. 340), which was considered at the seventh high-level meeting between the United Nations and regional organizations on 22 September.

Special political missions and offices

OIOS audit of management of special political missions

In response to section I of General Assembly **resolution 60/255** of 8 May (see p. 1618), the Office of Internal Oversight Services (OIOS) submitted a September report [A/61/357] on its audit of the management of special political missions by the UN Department of Political Affairs (DPA). The audit assessed DPA's ability to guide and manage special political missions; reviewed the appropriateness of related policies and procedures; and determined the sufficiency of internal controls.

According to the audit, while DPA's ability to backstop the missions appeared to be satisfactory, and the timely recruitment of qualified mission personnel was improving, as evidenced by the drop in vacancy rates from 43 to 35 per cent between June 2005 and May 2006, its ability to provide political and substantive policy guidance to the missions and to equip its desk officers with management tools needed significant improvement. In addition, budget controls were inadequate, since they were not formalized or comprehensively reviewed at the departmental level. The number of complaints raised by special political missions about the effectiveness of DPA support was the only indicator for measuring managerial performance in the Department's results-based budget framework, which OIOS considered to be insufficient. DPA's mandate, as the UN focal point for post-conflict peacebuilding, needed to reflect the recent inauguration of the Peacebuilding Commission (see p. 55) and the Peacebuilding Support Office (see p. 58), as well the expansion of its responsibilities for directing special political missions, in addition to peacekeeping field missions.

The decision to assign to a UN department lead responsibility for special political missions was taken by the Policy Committee, a body established by the Secretary-General in 2005 to focus on strategic decisions. However, there were no clear criteria or transparent decision-making mechanisms in place for making that determination, thereby increasing the risk of misunderstandings among the parties involved about their roles and responsibilities.

OIOS said that there was potential for duplication and overlap between the Peacebuilding Support Office and DPA, which needed to clarify its working relationship with the Office to maximize synergies and coordination, and between the functions of DPA regional divisions and DPKO, as both Departments could be assigned the lead role for directing the substantive political operations of field missions. There was also potential for duplication in countries with peacekeeping missions and special political missions/special envoys of the Secretary-General, as in Cyprus and Western Sahara. Therefore the Secretary-General issued a lead-department policy, with measures for minimizing its occurrence. However, measures such as the creation of an interdepartmental task force and the development of a coordination methodology by the lead department, had not been sufficiently implemented.

OIOS recommended that DPA's mandate, as the UN focal point for post-conflict peacebuilding, be updated to reflect the establishment of the Peacebuilding Commission and the Peacebuilding Support Office, and clarify its responsibilities for managing and directing special political missions, as well as to reflect DPKO's responsibilities for directing the substantive operations of the special political missions, in addition to peacekeeping operations. The Secretary-General should develop and disseminate clear criteria for assigning the lead responsibility for managing field missions to ensure transparency; include reference to the lead-department policy in the official mandates of DPA and DPKO to enhance its visibility and transparency and ensure that his strategy of forming interdepartmental task forces, as provided for in the lead-department policy, was being implemented effectively.

The Department of Management should revise the current budget presentation by categorizing the entities funded under section 3B in order to clearly indicate the lead-department responsibility for each operation. DPA should establish a monitoring and oversight mechanism in the form of an operational agreement with DPKO to address accountability for the budget resources of field missions; establish a formal working group for budget review; request resources in the context of the 2008-2009 programme budget to appoint a staff member with budget expertise as the Department's overall focal point for overseeing and monitoring the budgets of the special political missions; and enhance budgetary controls by issuing performance reports of expenditures for the special political missions annually rather than biennially.

DPA should develop standard operating procedures that would provide desk officers with better management tools and increase the quality and consistency of the Department's support for special political missions, and strengthen its performance evaluation of the management of those missions. It should develop and propose to the Assembly and the Security Council exit strategies for all special political missions, and a working-level methodology for establishing interdepartmental task forces, with relevant terms of reference. DPA should develop, with the Peacebuilding Support Office, terms of reference specifying their respective roles and responsibilities in peacebuilding activities, and formulate a coordination strategy to prevent possible duplication and overlap.

Roster of special political missions and offices in 2006

During 2006, 12 UN political missions and offices were in operation: 6 in Africa, 4 in Asia and the Pacific, and 2 in the Middle East.

With regard to Africa, the mandates of the United Nations Peacebuilding Support Office in the Central African Republic and the United Nations Peacebuilding Support Office in Guinea-Bissau were extended until 31 December 2007; the United Nations Integrated Office in Sierra Leone until 31 December 2007; and that of the Special Representative of the Secretary-General for the Great Lakes Region for a final period of three months, until 31 March 2007.

In Asia and the Pacific, the Council extended the mandate of the United Nations Office in Timor-Leste until 25 August 2006, when the mission was terminated. On the same date, the Council established, as a follow-on mission, the United Nations Integrated Mission in Timor-Leste, for an initial period of six months. The activities of the United Nations Tajikistan Office of Peacebuilding were extended until 1 June 2007. The Council extended the mandate of the United Nations Assistance Mission in Afghanistan until 23 March 2007, and that of the United Nations Assistance Mission for Iraq until 10 August 2007. In the Democratic People's Republic of Korea, the United Nations Command continued to implement the maintenance of the 1953 Armistice Agreement [YUN 1953, p. 136].

UNPOS

United Nations Political Office for Somalia

Established: 15 April 1995.

Mandate: To monitor the situation in Somalia and keep the Security Council informed, particularly about developments affecting the humanitarian and security situation, repatriation of refugees and impacts on neighbouring countries.

Special Representative of the Secretary-General: François Lonseny Fall (Guinea).

Strength: 17 international civilian staff, 9 local civilian staff.

Great Lakes Region

Office of the Special Representative of the Secretary-General for the Great Lakes Region

Established: 19 December 1997.

Mandate: To monitor developments in the region and their implications for peace and security and to contribute to regional efforts in the prevention or peaceful settlement of conflicts.

Special Representative of the Secretary-General: Ibrahima Fall (Senegal).

Strength: 9 international civilian staff, 7 local civilian staff.

UNOGBIS

United Nations Peacebuilding Support Office in Guinea-Bissau

Established: 3 March 1999.

Mandate: To support efforts to consolidate constitutional rule, enhance political dialogue and promote national reconciliation, respect for the rule of law and human rights; assist in strengthening the capacity of national institutions; and to support security sector reform.

Representative of the Secretary-General: Shola Omoregie (Nigeria).

Strength: 9 international civilian staff, 2 military advisers, 1 police adviser, 10 local civilian staff, 1 UN volunteer.

UNSCO

Office of the United Nations Special Coordinator for the Middle East Peace Process

Established: 1 October 1999.

Mandate: To act as the focal point for the United Nations contribution to the implementation of the peace agreements and to enhance UN assistance.

Special Coordinator for the Middle East Peace Process and Personal Representative of the Secretary-General to the Palestine Liberation Organization and the Palestinian Authority: Alvaro de Soto (Peru).

Strength: 27 international civilian staff, 23 local civilian staff.

BONUCA

United Nations Peacebuilding Support Office in the Central African Republic

Established: 15 February 2000.

Mandate: To support efforts to consolidate peace and promote national reconstruction and economic recovery.

Representative of the Secretary-General: General Lamine Cissé (Senegal).

Strength: 26 international civilian staff, 5 military advisers, 6 police, 51 local civilian staff, 3 UN volunteers.

UNTOP

United Nations Tajikistan Office of Peacebuilding

Established: 1 June 2000.

Mandate: To provide a political framework and leadership for post-conflict peacebuilding.

Representative of the Secretary-General: Vladimir Sotirov (Bulgaria).

Strength: 8 international civilian staff, 1 police adviser, 20 local civilian staff.

Lebanon

Office of the Personal Representative of the Secretary-General for Lebanon

Established: 4 August 2000.

Mandate: To help coordinate UN activities with regard to southern Lebanon.

Personal Representative of the Secretary-General for southern Lebanon: Geir O. Pedersen (Norway).

Strength: 6 international civilian staff, 6 local civilian staff.

UNOWA

Office of the Special Representative of the Secretary-General for West Africa

Established: March 2002.

Mandate: To ensure the strengthening of harmonization and coordination of UN system activities in an integrated regional perspective and the development of a partnership with the Economic Community of West African States, other subregional organizations and international and national actors, including civil society.

Special Representative of the Secretary-General: Ahmedou Ould-Abdallah (Mauritania).

Strength: 7 international civilian staff, 9 local civilian staff.

UNAMA

United Nations Assistance Mission in Afghanistan

Established: 28 March 2002.

Mandate: To fulfil the tasks and responsibilities entrusted to the United Nations in the Bonn Agreement; promote national reconciliation and rapprochement; manage all UN humanitarian relief, recovery and reconstruction activities; and assist in the promotion of the political process.

Special Representative of the Secretary-General: Tom Koenigs (Germany).

Strength: 206 international civilian staff, 848 local civilian staff, 11 military observers, 3 civilian police, 34 UN volunteers.

UNAMI

United Nations Assistance Mission for Iraq

Established: 14 August 2003.

Mandate: To support the Secretary-General in the fulfilment of his mandate under Security Council resolution 1483(2003).

Special Representative of the Secretary-General: Ashraf Jehangir Qazi (Pakistan).

Strength: 228 international civilian staff, 352 local civilian staff, 223 troops, 11 military observers.

UNOTIL

United Nations Office in Timor-Leste

Established: 28 April 2005.

Ended: 25 August 2006.

Mandate: To support the development of critical State institutions, support the further development of the police and provide training in the observance of democratic governance and human rights.

Special Representative of the Secretary-General: Sukehiro Hasegawa (Japan).

UNIOSIL

United Nations Integrated Office in Sierra Leone

Established: 1 January 2006.

Mandate: To assist in building the capacity of State institutions; developing a national action plan for human rights; enhancing good governance, transparency and accountability; strengthening the rule of law and the security sector; and promoting a culture of peace, dialogue and participation.

Executive Representative for UNIOSIL*:* Victor da Silva Angelo (Portugal).

Strength: 71 international civilian staff, 176 local civilian staff, 9 military observers, 17 police, 29 UN volunteers.

Threats to international peace and security

International terrorism

Global counter-terrorism strategy

In response to the General Assembly's request, contained in resolution 60/1 on the 2005 World Summit Outcome [YUN 2005, p. 48], that he submit proposals for strengthening UN system capacity to assist States in combating terrorism and enhancing the coordination of UN activities in that regard, the Secretary-General submitted an April report [A/60/825] on uniting against terrorism: recommendations for a global counter-terrorism strategy. The Secretary-General was assisted in formulating the recommendations by the Counter-Terrorism Implementation Task Force, which he had created in 2005 to bring together key UN system actors and their partners dealing with counter-terrorism issues. The recommendations for the counter-terrorism strategy laid out in the report were based on the five pillar elements identified by the Secretary-General in 2005 [YUN 2005, p. 101]: dissuading groups from resorting to terrorism or supporting it; denying terrorists the means to carry out an attack; deterring States from supporting terrorist groups; developing State capacity to prevent terrorism; and defending human rights in the context of terrorism and counter-terrorism.

The Secretary-General said that universal agreement on a counter-terrorism strategy would demonstrate the resolve of the international community to deal definitively with the scourge of terrorism and create the basis for a truly global response. Member States would need to ensure that it was regularly updated to respond to evolving challenges and, more importantly, was fully implemented; and agree to review it regularly and ensure accountability through follow-up. UN system institutions would play an important role in that follow-up, and the Secretary-General would ask the Counter-Terrorism Implementation Task Force to support and facilitate coordination in that regard.

The United Nations Global Counter-Terrorism Strategy was adopted by the Assembly in September (see below).

GENERAL ASSEMBLY ACTION

On 8 September [meeting 99], the General Assembly adopted **resolution 60/288** [draft: A/60/L.62] without vote [agenda items 46 & 120].

The United Nations Global Counter-Terrorism Strategy

The General Assembly,

Guided by the purposes and principles of the Charter of the United Nations, and reaffirming its role under the Charter, including on questions related to international peace and security,

Reiterating its strong condemnation of terrorism in all its forms and manifestations, committed by whomever, wherever and for whatever purposes, as it constitutes one of the most serious threats to international peace and security,

Reaffirming the Declaration on Measures to Eliminate International Terrorism, contained in the annex to General Assembly resolution 49/60 of 9 December 1994, the Declaration to Supplement the 1994 Declaration on Measures to Eliminate International Terrorism, contained in the annex to General Assembly resolution 51/210 of 17 December 1996, and the 2005 World Summit Outcome, in particular its section on terrorism,

Recalling all General Assembly resolutions on measures to eliminate international terrorism, including resolution 46/51 of 9 December 1991, and Security Council resolutions on threats to international peace and security caused by terrorist acts, as well as relevant resolutions of the General Assembly on the protection of human rights and fundamental freedoms while countering terrorism,

Recalling also that, in the 2005 World Summit Outcome, world leaders rededicated themselves to support all efforts to uphold the sovereign equality of all States, respect their territorial integrity and political independence, to refrain in their international relations from the threat or use of force in any manner inconsistent with the purposes and principles of the United Nations, to uphold the resolution of disputes by peaceful means and in conformity with the principles of justice and international law, the right to self-determination of peoples which remain under colonial domination or foreign occupation, non-interference in the internal affairs of States, respect for human rights and fundamental freedoms, respect for the equal rights of all without distinction as to race, sex, language or religion, international cooperation in solving international problems of an economic, social, cultural or humanitarian character, and the fulfilment in good faith of the obligations assumed in accordance with the Charter,

Recalling further the mandate contained in the 2005 World Summit Outcome that the General Assembly should develop without delay the elements identified by the Secretary-General for a counter-terrorism strategy, with a view to adopting and implementing a strategy to promote comprehensive, coordinated and consistent responses, at the national, regional and international levels, to counter terrorism, which also takes into account the conditions conducive to the spread of terrorism,

Reaffirming that acts, methods and practices of terrorism in all its forms and manifestations are activities aimed at the destruction of human rights, fundamental freedoms and democracy, threatening territorial integrity, security of States and destabilizing legitimately constituted Governments, and that the international community should take the necessary steps to enhance cooperation to prevent and combat terrorism,

Reaffirming also that terrorism cannot and should not be associated with any religion, nationality, civilization or ethnic group,

Reaffirming further Member States determination to make every effort to reach an agreement on and conclude a comprehensive convention on international terrorism, including by resolving the outstanding issues related to the legal definition and scope of the acts covered by the convention, so that it can serve as an effective instrument to counter terrorism,

Continuing to acknowledge that the question of convening a high-level conference under the auspices of the United Nations to formulate an international response to terrorism in all its forms and manifestations could be considered,

Recognizing that development, peace and security, and human rights are interlinked and mutually reinforcing,

Bearing in mind the need to address the conditions conducive to the spread of terrorism,

Affirming Member States' determination to continue to do all they can to resolve conflict, end foreign occupation, confront oppression, eradicate poverty, promote sustained economic growth, sustainable development, global prosperity, good governance, human rights for all and rule of law, improve intercultural understanding and ensure respect for all religions, religious values, beliefs or cultures,

1. *Expresses its appreciation* for the report entitled "Uniting against terrorism: recommendations for a global counter-terrorism strategy" submitted by the Secretary-General to the General Assembly;

2. *Adopts* the present resolution and its annex as the United Nations Global Counter-Terrorism Strategy ("the Strategy");

3. *Decides*, without prejudice to the continuation of the discussion in its relevant committees of all their agenda items related to terrorism and counter-terrorism, to undertake the following steps for the effective follow-up of the Strategy:

(a) To launch the Strategy at a high-level segment of its sixty-first session;

(b) To examine in two years progress made in the implementation of the Strategy, and to consider updating it to respond to changes, recognizing that many of the measures contained in the Strategy can be achieved immediately, some will require sustained work through the coming few years and some should be treated as long-term objectives;

(c) To invite the Secretary-General to contribute to the future deliberations of the General Assembly on the review of the implementation and updating of the Strategy;

(d) To encourage Member States, the United Nations and other appropriate international, regional and subregional organizations to support the implementation of the Strategy, including through mobilizing resources and expertise;

(e) To further encourage non-governmental organizations and civil society to engage, as appropriate, on how to enhance efforts to implement the Strategy;

4. *Decides* to include in the provisional agenda of its sixty-second session an item entitled "The United Nations Global Counter-Terrorism Strategy".

ANNEX

Plan of action

We, the States Members of the United Nations, resolve:

1. To consistently, unequivocally and strongly condemn terrorism in all its forms and manifestations, committed by whomever, wherever and for whatever purposes, as it constitutes one of the most serious threats to international peace and security;

2. To take urgent action to prevent and combat terrorism in all its forms and manifestations and, in particular:

(a) To consider becoming parties without delay to the existing international conventions and protocols against terrorism, and implementing them, and to make every effort to reach an agreement on and conclude a comprehensive convention on international terrorism;

(b) To implement all General Assembly resolutions on measures to eliminate international terrorism and relevant General Assembly resolutions on the protection of human rights and fundamental freedoms while countering terrorism;

(c) To implement all Security Council resolutions related to international terrorism and to cooperate fully with the counter-terrorism subsidiary bodies of the Security Council in the fulfilment of their tasks, recognizing that many States continue to require assistance in implementing these resolutions;

3. To recognize that international cooperation and any measures that we undertake to prevent and combat terrorism must comply with our obligations under international law, including the Charter of the United Nations and relevant international conventions and protocols, in particular human rights law, refugee law and international humanitarian law.

I. Measures to address the conditions conducive to the spread of terrorism

We resolve to undertake the following measures aimed at addressing the conditions conducive to the spread of terrorism, including but not limited to prolonged unresolved conflicts, dehumanization of victims of terrorism in all its forms and manifestations, lack of the rule of law and violations of human rights, ethnic, national and religious discrimination, political exclusion, socio-economic marginalization and lack of good governance, while recognizing that none of these conditions can excuse or justify acts of terrorism:

1. To continue to strengthen and make best possible use of the capacities of the United Nations in areas such as conflict prevention, negotiation, mediation, conciliation, judicial settlement, rule of law, peacekeeping and peacebuilding, in order to contribute to the successful prevention and peaceful resolution of prolonged unresolved conflicts. We recognize that the peaceful resolution of such conflicts would contribute to strengthening the global fight against terrorism;

2. To continue to arrange under the auspices of the United Nations initiatives and programmes to promote dialogue, tolerance and understanding among civilizations, cultures, peoples and religions, and to promote mutual respect for and prevent the defamation of religions, religious values, beliefs and cultures. In this regard, we welcome the launching by the Secretary-General of the initiative on the Alliance of Civilizations. We also welcome similar initiatives that have been taken in other parts of the world;

3. To promote a culture of peace, justice and human development, ethnic, national and religious tolerance

and respect for all religions, religious values, beliefs or cultures by establishing and encouraging, as appropriate, education and public awareness programmes involving all sectors of society. In this regard, we encourage the United Nations Educational, Scientific and Cultural Organization to play a key role, including through interfaith and intra-faith dialogue and dialogue among civilizations;

4. To continue to work to adopt such measures as may be necessary and appropriate and in accordance with our respective obligations under international law to prohibit by law incitement to commit a terrorist act or acts and prevent such conduct;

5. To reiterate our determination to ensure the timely and full realization of the development goals and objectives agreed at the major United Nations conferences and summits, including the Millennium Development Goals. We reaffirm our commitment to eradicate poverty and promote sustained economic growth, sustainable development and global prosperity for all;

6. To pursue and reinforce development and social inclusion agendas at every level as goals in themselves, recognizing that success in this area, especially on youth unemployment, could reduce marginalization and the subsequent sense of victimization that propels extremism and the recruitment of terrorists;

7. To encourage the United Nations system as a whole to scale up the cooperation and assistance it is already conducting in the fields of rule of law, human rights and good governance to support sustained economic and social development;

8. To consider putting in place, on a voluntary basis, national systems of assistance that would promote the needs of victims of terrorism and their families and facilitate the normalization of their lives. In this regard, we encourage States to request the relevant United Nations entities to help them to develop such national systems. We will also strive to promote international solidarity in support of victims and foster the involvement of civil society in a global campaign against terrorism and for its condemnation. This could include exploring at the General Assembly the possibility of developing practical mechanisms to provide assistance to victims.

II. Measures to prevent and combat terrorism

We resolve to undertake the following measures to prevent and combat terrorism, in particular by denying terrorists access to the means to carry out their attacks, to their targets and to the desired impact of their attacks:

1. To refrain from organizing, instigating, facilitating, participating in, financing, encouraging or tolerating terrorist activities and to take appropriate practical measures to ensure that our respective territories are not used for terrorist installations or training camps, or for the preparation or organization of terrorist acts intended to be committed against other States or their citizens;

2. To cooperate fully in the fight against terrorism, in accordance with our obligations under international law, in order to find, deny safe haven and bring to justice, on the basis of the principle of extradite or prosecute, any person who supports, facilitates, participates or attempts to participate in the financing, planning, preparation or perpetration of terrorist acts or provides safe havens;

3. To ensure the apprehension and prosecution or extradition of perpetrators of terrorist acts, in accordance with the relevant provisions of national and international law, in particular human rights law, refugee law and international humanitarian law. We will endeavour to conclude and implement to that effect mutual judicial assistance and extradition agreements and to strengthen cooperation between law enforcement agencies;

4. To intensify cooperation, as appropriate, in exchanging timely and accurate information concerning the prevention and combating of terrorism;

5. To strengthen coordination and cooperation among States in combating crimes that might be connected with terrorism, including drug trafficking in all its aspects, illicit arms trade, in particular of small arms and light weapons, including man-portable air defence systems, money-laundering and smuggling of nuclear, chemical, biological, radiological and other potentially deadly materials;

6. To consider becoming parties without delay to the United Nations Convention against Transnational Organized Crime and to the three protocols supplementing it, and implementing them;

7. To take appropriate measures, before granting asylum, for the purpose of ensuring that the asylum-seeker has not engaged in terrorist activities and, after granting asylum, for the purpose of ensuring that the refugee status is not used in a manner contrary to the provisions set out in section II, paragraph 1, above;

8. To encourage relevant regional and subregional organizations to create or strengthen counter-terrorism mechanisms or centres. Should they require cooperation and assistance to this end, we encourage the Counter-Terrorism Committee and its Executive Directorate and, where consistent with their existing mandates, the United Nations Office on Drugs and Crime and the International Criminal Police Organization, to facilitate its provision;

9. To acknowledge that the question of creating an international centre to fight terrorism could be considered, as part of international efforts to enhance the fight against terrorism;

10. To encourage States to implement the comprehensive international standards embodied in the Forty Recommendations on Money-Laundering and Nine Special Recommendations on Terrorist Financing of the Financial Action Task Force, recognizing that States may require assistance in implementing them;

11. To invite the United Nations system to develop, together with Member States, a single comprehensive database on biological incidents, ensuring that it is complementary to the biocrimes database contemplated by the International Criminal Police Organization. We also encourage the Secretary-General to update the roster of experts and laboratories, as well as the technical guide-

lines and procedures, available to him for the timely and efficient investigation of alleged use. In addition, we note the importance of the proposal of the Secretary-General to bring together, within the framework of the United Nations, the major biotechnology stakeholders, including industry, the scientific community, civil society and Governments, into a common programme aimed at ensuring that biotechnology advances are not used for terrorist or other criminal purposes but for the public good, with due respect for the basic international norms on intellectual property rights;

12. To work with the United Nations with due regard to confidentiality, respecting human rights and in compliance with other obligations under international law, to explore ways and means to:

(*a*) Coordinate efforts at the international and regional levels to counter terrorism in all its forms and manifestations on the Internet;

(*b*) Use the Internet as a tool for countering the spread of terrorism, while recognizing that States may require assistance in this regard;

13. To step up national efforts and bilateral, subregional, regional and international cooperation, as appropriate, to improve border and customs controls in order to prevent and detect the movement of terrorists and prevent and detect the illicit traffic in, inter alia, small arms and light weapons, conventional ammunition and explosives, and nuclear, chemical, biological or radiological weapons and materials, while recognizing that States may require assistance to that effect;

14. To encourage the Counter-Terrorism Committee and its Executive Directorate to continue to work with States, at their request, to facilitate the adoption of legislation and administrative measures to implement the terrorist travEl-related obligations and to identify best practices in this area, drawing whenever possible on those developed by technical international organizations, such as the International Civil Aviation Organization, the World Customs Organization and the International Criminal Police Organization;

15. To encourage the Committee established pursuant to Security Council resolution 1267(1999) to continue to work to strengthen the effectiveness of the travel ban under the United Nations sanctions regime against Al-Qaida and the Taliban and associated individuals and entities, as well as to ensure, as a matter of priority, that fair and transparent procedures exist for placing individuals and entities on its lists, for removing them and for granting humanitarian exceptions. In this regard, we encourage States to share information, including by widely distributing the International Criminal Police Organization/United Nations special notices concerning people subject to this sanctions regime;

16. To step up efforts and cooperation at every level, as appropriate, to improve the security of manufacturing and issuing identity and travel documents and to prevent and detect their alteration or fraudulent use, while recognizing that States may require assistance in doing so. In this regard, we invite the International Criminal Police Organization to enhance its database on stolen and lost travel documents, and we will endeavour to make full use of this tool, as appropriate, in particular by sharing relevant information;

17. To invite the United Nations to improve coordination in planning a response to a terrorist attack using nuclear, chemical, biological or radiological weapons or materials, in particular by reviewing and improving the effectiveness of the existing inter-agency coordination mechanisms for assistance delivery, relief operations and victim support, so that all States can receive adequate assistance. In this regard, we invite the General Assembly and the Security Council to develop guidelines for the necessary cooperation and assistance in the event of a terrorist attack using weapons of mass destruction;

18. To step up all efforts to improve the security and protection of particularly vulnerable targets, such as infrastructure and public places, as well as the response to terrorist attacks and other disasters, in particular in the area of civil protection, while recognizing that States may require assistance to this effect.

III. Measures to build States' capacity to prevent and combat terrorism and to strengthen the role of the United Nations system in this regard

We recognize that capacity-building in all States is a core element of the global counter-terrorism effort, and resolve to undertake the following measures to develop State capacity to prevent and combat terrorism and enhance coordination and coherence within the United Nations system in promoting international cooperation in countering terrorism:

1. To encourage Member States to consider making voluntary contributions to United Nations counter-terrorism cooperation and technical assistance projects, and to explore additional sources of funding in this regard. We also encourage the United Nations to consider reaching out to the private sector for contributions to capacity-building programmes, in particular in the areas of port, maritime and civil aviation security;

2. To take advantage of the framework provided by relevant international, regional and subregional organizations to share best practices in counter-terrorism capacity-building, and to facilitate their contributions to the international community's efforts in this area;

3. To consider establishing appropriate mechanisms to rationalize States' reporting requirements in the field of counter-terrorism and eliminate duplication of reporting requests, taking into account and respecting the different mandates of the General Assembly, the Security Council and its subsidiary bodies that deal with counter-terrorism;

4. To encourage measures, including regular informal meetings, to enhance, as appropriate, more frequent exchanges of information on cooperation and technical assistance among Member States, United Nations bodies dealing with counter-terrorism, relevant specialized agencies, relevant international, regional and subregional organizations and the donor community, to develop States' capacities to implement relevant United Nations resolutions;

5. To welcome the intention of the Secretary-General to institutionalize, within existing resources, the Counter-Terrorism Implementation Task Force within the Secretariat in order to ensure overall coordination and coherence in the counter-terrorism efforts of the United Nations system;

6. To encourage the Counter-Terrorism Committee and its Executive Directorate to continue to improve the coherence and efficiency of technical assistance delivery in the field of counter-terrorism, in particular by strengthening its dialogue with States and relevant international, regional and subregional organizations and working closely, including by sharing information, with all bilateral and multilateral technical assistance providers;

7. To encourage the United Nations Office on Drugs and Crime, including its Terrorism Prevention Branch, to enhance, in close consultation with the Counter-Terrorism Committee and its Executive Directorate, its provision of technical assistance to States, upon request, to facilitate the implementation of the international conventions and protocols related to the prevention and suppression of terrorism and relevant United Nations resolutions;

8. To encourage the International Monetary Fund, the World Bank, the United Nations Office on Drugs and Crime and the International Criminal Police Organization to enhance cooperation with States to help them to comply fully with international norms and obligations to combat money-laundering and the financing of terrorism;

9. To encourage the International Atomic Energy Agency and the Organization for the Prohibition of Chemical Weapons to continue their efforts, within their respective mandates, in helping States to build capacity to prevent terrorists from accessing nuclear, chemical or radiological materials, to ensure security at related facilities and to respond effectively in the event of an attack using such materials;

10. To encourage the World Health Organization to step up its technical assistance to help States to improve their public health systems to prevent and prepare for biological attacks by terrorists;

11. To continue to work within the United Nations system to support the reform and modernization of border management systems, facilities and institutions at the national, regional and international levels;

12. To encourage the International Maritime Organization, the World Customs Organization and the International Civil Aviation Organization to strengthen their cooperation, work with States to identify any national shortfalls in areas of transport security and provide assistance, upon request, to address them;

13. To encourage the United Nations to work with Member States and relevant international, regional and subregional organizations to identify and share best practices to prevent terrorist attacks on particularly vulnerable targets. We invite the International Criminal Police Organization to work with the Secretary-General so that he can submit proposals to this effect. We also recognize the importance of developing public-private partnerships in this area.

IV. Measures to ensure respect for human rights for all and the rule of law as the fundamental basis of the fight against terrorism

We resolve to undertake the following measures, reaffirming that the promotion and protection of human rights for all and the rule of law is essential to all components of the Strategy, recognizing that effective counter-terrorism measures and the protection of human rights are not conflicting goals, but complementary and mutually reinforcing, and stressing the need to promote and protect the rights of victims of terrorism:

1. To reaffirm that General Assembly resolution 60/158 of 16 December 2005 provides the fundamental framework for the "Protection of human rights and fundamental freedoms while countering terrorism";

2. To reaffirm that States must ensure that any measures taken to combat terrorism comply with their obligations under international law, in particular human rights law, refugee law and international humanitarian law;

3. To consider becoming parties without delay to the core international instruments on human rights law, refugee law and international humanitarian law, and implementing them, as well as to consider accepting the competence of international and relevant regional human rights monitoring bodies;

4. To make every effort to develop and maintain an effective and rule of law-based national criminal justice system that can ensure, in accordance with our obligations under international law, that any person who participates in the financing, planning, preparation or perpetration of terrorist acts or in support of terrorist acts is brought to justice, on the basis of the principle to extradite or prosecute, with due respect for human rights and fundamental freedoms, and that such terrorist acts are established as serious criminal offences in domestic laws and regulations. We recognize that States may require assistance in developing and maintaining such effective and rule of law-based criminal justice systems, and we encourage them to resort to the technical assistance delivered, inter alia, by the United Nations Office on Drugs and Crime;

5. To reaffirm the important role of the United Nations system in strengthening the international legal architecture by promoting the rule of law, respect for human rights and effective criminal justice systems, which constitute the fundamental basis of our common fight against terrorism;

6. To support the Human Rights Council and to contribute, as it takes shape, to its work on the question of the promotion and protection of human rights for all in the fight against terrorism;

7. To support the strengthening of the operational capacity of the Office of the United Nations High Commissioner for Human Rights, with a particular emphasis on increasing field operations and presences. The Office should continue to play a lead role in examining the question of protecting human rights while countering terrorism, by making general recommendations on the human rights obligations of States and providing them with assistance and advice, in particular in the area of

raising awareness of international human rights law among national law-enforcement agencies, at the request of States;

8. To support the role of the Special Rapporteur on the promotion and protection of human rights and fundamental freedoms while countering terrorism. The Special Rapporteur should continue to support the efforts of States and offer concrete advice by corresponding with Governments, making country visits, liaising with the United Nations and regional organizations and reporting on these issues.

Terrorist attacks in 2006

Egypt

On 24 April, a series of bombs exploded in the Egyptian resort town of Dahab, located on the Gulf of Aqaba coast of the Sinai Peninsula. At least 23 people, mostly Egyptians, were killed, along with German, Hungarian, Lebanese, Russian and Swiss nationals. Around 80 people were wounded, including tourists from Australia, Denmark, France, Germany, Israel, South Korea, Lebanon, the Palestinian Territories, the United Kingdom and the United States.

SECURITY COUNCIL ACTION

On 25 April [meeting 5424], following consultations among Security Council members, the President made statement **S/PRST/2006/18** on behalf of the Council:

> The Security Council condemns in the strongest terms the terrorist bombings that took place in Dahab, Egypt, on 24 April 2006.
>
> The Council expresses its deepest sympathy and condolences to the victims of these attacks and their families, and to the people and the Government of Egypt, as well as to all other countries whose citizens have been killed or injured in these bombings.
>
> The Council underlines the need to bring the perpetrators, organizers, financers and sponsors of these intolerable acts to justice, and urges all States, in accordance with their obligations under international law and resolutions 1373(2001) and 1624(2005), to cooperate with and provide support and assistance, as appropriate, to the Government of Egypt in this regard.
>
> The Council reaffirms that terrorism in all its forms and manifestations constitutes one of the most serious threats to international peace and security, and that any acts of terrorism are criminal and unjustifiable, regardless of their motivation, wherever, whenever and by whomsoever committed.
>
> The Council further reaffirms the need to combat by all means, in accordance with the Charter of the United Nations, threats to international peace and security caused by terrorist acts.
>
> The Council reiterates its determination to combat all forms of terrorism, in accordance with its responsibilities under the Charter.

Iraq

On 3 June, militants in Baghdad, Iraq, ambushed an automobile carrying five diplomatic staff of the embassy of the Russian Federation, killing one official and abducting the other four. On 19 June, the Mujahedeen Shura Council, a group affiliated with the Al-Qaida terrorist organization, claimed responsibility for the attack and issued an ultimatum to the Russian Federation to withdraw from Chechnya and release all Muslim prisoners within 48 hours. On 25 June, the group issued a statement saying that it had beheaded three of the hostages and shot to death the fourth; the statement was accompanied by a video showing the bodies of two of the deceased and the killings of the other two.

The Secretary-General, in a 26 June press statement [SG/SM/10540], condemned, in the strongest possible terms, the abduction and killings which, he said, no cause could justify. He urged the Iraqi authorities to do everything possible to bring those responsible to justice, and reiterated his call for the immediate and unconditional release of all hostages in Iraq.

SECURITY COUNCIL ACTION

On 29 June [meeting 5477], following consultations among Security Council members, the President made statement **S/PRST/2006/29** on behalf of the Council:

> The Security Council is appalled by the horrific death of members of the Russian diplomatic mission in Iraq who had been kidnapped by a terrorist group and later ruthlessly and in cold blood executed by their captors.
>
> The Council condemns in the strongest possible terms this crime committed by the terrorists and conveys its deepest sympathy and condolences to the families of the deceased, and the people and the Government of the Russian Federation.
>
> The Council confirms that no cause can justify such acts of terror as this crime and previous attacks on foreign diplomats committed by the terrorists, and reaffirms its utmost determination to combat terrorism, in accordance with its responsibilities under the Charter of the United Nations.
>
> The Council urges all States, in accordance with their obligation under resolution 1373(2001), to cooperate actively in efforts to find and bring to justice the perpetrators, organizers and sponsors of these barbaric acts.
>
> The Council also calls upon the international community to support the Government of Iraq in exercising its responsibility to provide protection to the

diplomatic community in Iraq, United Nations staff and other foreign civilian personnel working in Iraq.

The Council also underlines the importance of continuing the efforts of the Government of Iraq and the multinational force in combating terrorism and improving security in Iraq in line with resolutions 1546(2004) and 1637(2005). The Council reiterates the importance of efforts to promote national reconciliation, dialogue and inclusion in ensuring peace, security and stability in Iraq, and in that context commends the Government of Iraq for initiating the Reconciliation and National Dialogue Plan.

The Council reaffirms the independence, sovereignty, unity and territorial integrity of Iraq.

An 11 July letter from the Russian Federation to the Secretary-General [S/2006/512] contained the decision and statement of the State Duma of the Federal Assembly of the Russian Federation in connection with the killings of the Russian citizens in Iraq. The State Duma insisted that there should be an urgent, comprehensive examination of the circumstances of the tragedy and an analysis of measures to ensure security for staff of the Russian Federation, especially in areas where there was a continued danger of terrorist acts and where military activity was conducted. The deputies demanded that the Iraqi authorities and occupying powers investigate thoroughly the killings of the Russian citizens in Iraq and insisted that all possible steps should be taken to apprehend and punish the criminals. (For more information on the situation in Iraq, see p. 389.)

Sri Lanka

On 15 June, a mine attack on a bus in Sri Lanka killed at least 64 people, including many children, and wounded 80. The Government blamed the Liberation Tigers of Tamil Eelam for the attack, which took place in the Sinhalese town of Kabithigollewa, located about 200 kilometres north of Colombo.

In a 16 June statement [S/2006/452], the European Union condemned the most recent incidents of violence in Sri Lanka, particularly the bus bombing, and called upon all parties to put an end to the violence and return to the negotiating table.

India

On 11 July, seven bombs exploded over an 11-minute period on the Suburban Railway in Mumbai, India, killing 209 people and injuring over 700. The bombings came hours after a series of grenade attacks in the city of Srinagar, in the Indian state of Jammu and Kashmir; however, the Indian Home Secretary said there was no link between the attacks. On 14 July, the terrorist group Lashkar-e-Qahhar claimed responsibility for the Mumbai bombings.

The Secretary-General, on 11 July [SG/SM/10562], said that he was appalled by the attacks in Mumbai and Srinagar. He believed that such acts only served to reaffirm that terrorism constituted one of the most serious threats to international peace and security, and to increase the urgency of coordinated action by all countries to defeat it in all forms and manifestations.

SECURITY COUNCIL ACTION

On 12 July [meeting 5484], following consultations among Security Council members, the President made statement **S/PRST/2006/30** on behalf of the Council:

The Security Council condemns in the strongest terms the series of bomb attacks that occurred in different parts of India, including Mumbai, on 11 July 2006, causing numerous deaths and injuries, and expresses its deepest sympathy and condolences to the victims of these heinous acts of terrorism and their families, and to the people and the Government of India.

The Council underlines the need to bring the perpetrators, organizers, financers and sponsors of these reprehensible acts of terrorism to justice, and urges all States, in accordance with their obligations under international law and resolutions 1373(2001) and 1624(2005), to cooperate actively with the Indian authorities in this regard.

The Council reaffirms that terrorism in all its forms and manifestations constitutes one of the most serious threats to international peace and security, and that any acts of terrorism are criminal and unjustifiable, regardless of their motivation, wherever, whenever and by whomsoever committed.

The Council further reaffirms the need to combat by all means, in accordance with the Charter of the United Nations, threats to international peace and security caused by terrorist acts. The Council reminds States that they must ensure that any measures taken to combat terrorism comply with all their obligations under international law, in particular international human rights, refugee and humanitarian law.

The Council reiterates its determination to combat all forms of terrorism, in accordance with its responsibilities under the Charter.

Measures to eliminate international terrorism

During 2006, the United Nations pursued actions on several fronts to combat and eliminate terrorism. The Security Council, by **resolution 1735(2006)** (see p. 384) adopted further measures against Al-Qaida, the Taliban and their associates.

The General Assembly, having considered the Secretary-General's report on measures to eliminate terrorism [A/61/210], in **resolution 61/40** of 4 December (see p. 1516), called on all States to cooperate to prevent and suppress terrorist acts and asked the Terrorism Prevention Branch of the United Nations Office on Drugs and Crime to continue its efforts to enhance UN capabilities in the prevention of terrorism. In **resolution 61/86** of 6 December (see p. 637), the Assembly called on Member States to support international efforts to prevent terrorists from acquiring weapons of mass destruction and their means of delivery.

Communications. In a 31 May statement [S/2006/371], the Council of the European Union decided to include the Liberation Tigers of Tamil Eelam in the EU list for the application of specific measures to combat terrorism.

On 24 April [A/60/820-S/2006/265], Panama transmitted to the Secretary-General the Panama Declaration on International Cooperation against Terrorism and Transnational Organized Crime, adopted at the Ministerial Conference on the subject (Panama City, Panama, 4-7 April).

On 1 August [A/60/965-S/2006/600], Iran protested against France's 16 June decision to lift restrictions on a number of the leading members of the Mujahedeen Khalq Organization (MKO), which Iran called a well-known terrorist group, and cautioned France about the possible negative consequences of its decision. On 3 August [S/2006/617], Iran, noting that MKO, on 11 February, had marched in a military parade in Iraq, with air cover provided by United States helicopters, protested against United States support for Iraq-based terrorist groups hostile to Iran and condemned the double standard approach of the United States in dealing with terrorists in Iraq. On 11 August [S/2006/649], it also protested the invitation extended by the European Parliament to MKO head Maryam Rajavi, the presence of MKO elements in the EU Parliament on 5 July, and the use of Parliament facilities to hold a press conference, underlining that such actions ran counter to the will of the international community to fight terrorism, and contravened Security Council resolution 1373(2001) [YUN 2001, p. 61] and the decisions of the European Community. On 22 October [A/61/570-S/2006/883], Iran condemned the invitation extended to Mrs. Rajavi to address the Belgian Senate on 24 October, and called upon Belgium to prevent her from entering the country and to cancel all the programmes planned for her.

On 30 November [A/61/606-S/2006/936], the Russian Federation transmitted to the Secretary-General the Strategy for Partnerships between States and Businesses to Counter Terrorism, adopted at the Global Forum for such partnerships (Moscow, 28-30 November).

Follow-up to 2005 Security Council summit-level meeting

CTC report on implementation of resolution 1624(2005). In September [S/2006/737], the Counter-Terrorism Committee (CTC) (see below) submitted to the Security Council its report on the implementation of Council resolution 1624(2005) [YUN 2005, p. 102], which called on all States to take steps to combat terrorism, including prohibiting by law and preventing incitement to commit terrorist acts. As at 7 September, only 69 States had reported to CTC on their implementation of resolution 1624(2005), thus limiting the scope of CTC's implementation report. The report contained information provided by States on their efforts to: prohibit and prevent incitement; deny safe haven to persons suspected of incitement; strengthen the security of international borders; enhance dialogue and understanding among civilizations; counter incitement motivated by extremism and intolerance; and comply with their obligations under international law.

Of the 69 reporting States, 21 informed CTC that they had expressly prohibited incitement in their criminal laws, and 13 were considering doing so. Other States provided CTC with information on other kinds of measures they had taken or were considering taking. Concerning denial of safe haven, information was provided on areas such as the processing of claims for refugee status and the handling of extradition requests. States described various forms of international cooperation on strengthening the security of international borders and provided information on new procedures and technologies that had been adopted in order to prevent document fraud and enhance the effectiveness of passenger screening. Steps taken at national and international levels to enhance dialogue and broaden understanding among civilizations were also reported, including countering incitement motivated by extremism and intolerance. States also described their international law obligations and the specific ways those obligations were upheld in their counter-terrorism programmes.

Counter-Terrorism Committee

In 2006, the Chairperson of the Counter-Terrorism Committee (CTC), established by Security Council resolution 1373(2001) [YUN 2001, p. 61], submitted CTC work programmes for the periods from 1 January to 31 March [S/2006/107], 1 April to 30 June [S/2006/276] and 1 July to 31 December [S/2006/607]. The Council considered those work programmes at meetings held on 21 February, 30 May and 28 September.

Security Council consideration (February). The CTC Chairperson, reporting to the Council on 21 February [meeting 5375] on the Committee's work, said that, with CTC's Executive Directorate (CTED) fully staffed as from September 2005 [YUN 2005, p. 111], the backlog of reports from States on the implementation of resolution 1373(2001) had been cleared. CTC agreed on policy guidelines for fulfilling its mandate to facilitate technical assistance to States that lacked the capacity to implement fully the provisions of resolution 1373(2001), and discussed a CTED proposal on how to put those guidelines into action. Since the Chairperson's previous report to the Council in 2005 [ibid.], CTED staff had visited Algeria and the United Republic of Tanzania, and were preparing to visit the former Yugoslav Republic of Macedonia (FYROM). CTC would make a special effort to ensure appropriate follow-up to enhance the results of its 2005 visit to Morocco [ibid., p. 109], and to other States, with their consent.

CTC, in revising its reporting procedures, focused on analysing States' individual accomplishments in implementing resolution 1373(2001); that analysis, prepared by CTED, would guide the Committee in determining how to engage better with the States concerned in furthering their implementation efforts. The Chairperson hoped that streamlining the reporting procedures would encourage States to cooperate more fully with the Committee, and that requests for further reporting would be based on very thorough considerations, taking into account the resources required to prepare those reports. States that had fallen behind on reporting were invited to re-engage with the Committee. CTC hoped that the revised approach would allow it to engage more substantially with States that sought assistance, and allow those States that had already put in place the basic tools to implement resolution 1373(2001) to keep the Committee informed of developments in strengthening their systems.

CTC would focus especially on States that had requested capacity-building assistance, to help them identify priority needs, and to disseminate that information to organizations that might be in a position to meet them. It was updating its list of best practices to assist States in implementing resolution 1373(2001), and was reviewing its cooperation with international, regional and subregional organizations, with the aim of developing closer working relationships. CTC would remain committed to previously established cooperative arrangements with regional organizations, while reaching out to other regional groupings that were developing their own counter-terrorism agenda.

Report of CTC Chairperson (May). Reporting to the Security Council in May [meeting 5446], the CTC Chairperson said that, based on the recommendations from the Council's comprehensive review of CTED, the Committee decided to focus on revising the reporting regime, enhancing dialogue with Member States in need of technical assistance, and deepening CTC relations with international, regional and subregional organizations. With regard to reporting, the Chairperson pointed out that, while she understood the concerns of many States regarding the issue of "reporting fatigue", many of the reports that CTC received had created a solid foundation for the Committee to advise and assist States in implementing resolution 1373(2001). As part of its efforts to revise the reporting regime, the Committee developed and was testing the preliminary implementation assessment, an analytical tool for monitoring the extent to which States had implemented the obligations and provisions of resolution 1373(2001). The introduction of the tool was expected to ease the reporting burden on States. CTC would seek further ways of easing that burden and allow more resources to go towards enhancing implementation. It had again contacted all States that were behind in reporting, in the hope that they would re-establish dialogue with the Committee, in the light of its updated working methods. She also urged States that might need assistance in preparing the report to inform the Committee of that need.

Since the Chairperson's February report (see above), CTED had visited FRYOM, and CTC had approved more country visits. The Committee would continue to discuss how the visits could be more results-oriented, including through the design of a thorough follow-up process, and further measures to strengthen cooperation with donors. It agreed on guidance for CTED on how to ensure that any measure taken by States to combat terrorism complied with all their obligations under international law, in particular human rights law, refugee law and humanitarian law.

Report of CTC Chairperson (September). In her September report to the Security Council [meeting 5538], the CTC Chairperson discussed the conclusions of CTC's report on the implementation of Council resolution 1624(2005) (see p. 173) and said that CTC and CTED would continue to engage actively and constructively with Member States. The Committee continued to focus on enhancing its tools, including by revising the reporting regime; enhancing the facilitation of technical assistance for States in need; and deepening relations with the international, regional and subregional organizations. CTC had updated its website to include best practices, which the Chairperson encouraged States to use to implement the provisions of resolution 1373(2001). CTC had visited 10 States to date, and was working to ensure that the necessary follow-up to those visits took place, and led to as many concrete, measurable results as possible. It continued the coordination of its activities with the Committees established pursuant to Council resolutions 1267(1999) [YUN 1999, p. 265] concerning Al-Qaida, the Taliban and associated individuals and entities, and 1540(2004) [YUN 2004, p. 544] concerning the implementation of measures to combat the proliferation of weapons of mass destruction and their means of delivery.

The Chairperson said that the implementation of resolution 1373(2001) remained as crucial as ever in the international community's fight against terrorism, and CTC's main task remained vital and urgent.

Comprehensive review of CTC Executive Directorate

Communication. On 15 December [S/2006/1002], the Secretary-General drew the attention of the Security Council President to his intention, expressed in a December 2005 letter to the Council [S/2005/817], to review CTED reporting lines. Since the Council was about to complete its comprehensive review of CTED by 31 December 2006 (see below), he wanted to address the process for submitting CTED semi-annual reports and programmes of work to CTC. As CTED activities had to reflect the policy guidance provided by CTC, the Council might wish to consider allowing CTED to submit those documents directly to CTC.

CTC report on CTED comprehensive review. On 18 December [S/2006/989], the CTC Chairperson submitted the Committee's report for consideration by the Security Council, as part of its comprehensive review of CTED. The report was prepared in response to the Council's request in presidential statement S/PRST/2005/64 that CTC prepare another review before 31 December 2006, as it was only able to draw limited conclusions in the first review [ibid.]. The report examined clear directions for CTED future work; efforts to promote and monitor implementation of resolution 1373(2001) [YUN 2001, p. 61] through dialogue; strengthening technical assistance and contacts and coordination with other UN bodies; enhancing cooperation and coordination among international, regional and subregional organizations; improving the collection of information for monitoring purposes and facilitating technical assistance; improving CTC capacity to make recommendations to the Council related to implementation of resolution 1373(2001); expediting work and streamlining procedures; implementing resolution 1624(2005); adopting a proactive communication strategy; and developing and maintaining expertise.

Based on the priorities set in the 2005 comprehensive review, CTC had discussed and provided guidance to CTED on a number of issues, including an implementation plan on technical assistance; human rights policy; the use of statistics; the development of best practices; cooperation with international, regional and subregional organizations; the contribution of CTC and CTED to the implementation of the United Nations Counter-Terrorism Strategy, adopted by the General Assembly in resolution 60/288 (see p. 66); country visits; and communications. CTC encouraged CTED to strengthen its focus on concrete outcomes and its core mandates and to prioritize its activities. It stressed that an action-oriented approach, overall consistency and transparency were essential for the efficiency of CTED work. The Committee recommended that the Council consider positively the amendments to CTED reporting lines suggested by the Secretary-General (see above) and allow it to present its draft work programmes and semi-annual reports directly to the Committee. Appended to the CTC report were semi-annual reports on CTED work for the periods 1 January–30 June and 1 July–31 December.

CTED work programmes for the April-June and July-December periods indicated that CTED would complete 100 new preliminary implementation assessments and preliminary implementation for 130 Member States. It had provided CTC with 42 preliminary implementation assessments, and 46 had been prepared but not yet presented. CTC stressed the importance of enhancing efforts to monitor and promote implementation of resolution 1373(2001) and looked forward to receiving a comprehensive analysis of the status of implementation of the resolution based on the preliminary assessment of all States' implementation in time for the Committee's next briefing to the Council.

CTC encouraged CTED to continue its work on the implementation of Council resolution 1624(2005) [YUN 2005, p. 102] on the prohibition and prevention of incitement to commit terrorist acts. It looked forward to more concrete results against agreed targets with regard to visits, technical assistance and increased work with international, regional and subregional organizations, and encouraged CTED to maintain and deepen its dialogue with States on their implementation of resolution 1373(2001).

The Committee continued to regard as key its work on the facilitation of technical assistance related to States' implementation of their obligations under resolution 1373(2001), and encouraged CTED to strengthen its role in that regard, in accordance with the policy guidance and the related implementation plan, with a view to ensuring that more States received the required assistance. CTED should focus on identifying and meeting priority needs and proposals on how to get more States and organizations to become assistance providers.

SECURITY COUNCIL ACTION

On 20 December [meeting 5600], following consultations among Security Council members, the President made statement **S/PRST/2006/56** on behalf of the Council:

The Security Council reaffirms that terrorism constitutes one of the most serious threats to international peace and security, and that any acts of terrorism are criminal and unjustifiable, regardless of their motivation, wherever, whenever and by whomsoever committed.

The Council reiterates its determination to combat all forms of terrorism, in accordance with its responsibilities under the Charter of the United Nations.

The Council reaffirms the importance of resolution 1373(2001) as well as its other resolutions concerning threats to international peace and security caused by terrorist acts, and calls upon States to implement their obligations under those resolutions as a matter of priority.

The Council reiterates its call upon States to become parties to all relevant international conventions and protocols relating to terrorism, and to make full use of the sources of assistance and guidance which are available.

The Council further reaffirms the need to combat by all means, in accordance with the Charter, threats to international peace and security caused by terrorist acts.

The Council reminds States that they must ensure that any measures taken to combat terrorism comply with all their obligations under international law, in particular international human rights, refugee and humanitarian law.

The Council recognizes the importance of cross-United Nations cooperation on counter-terrorism issues, and confirms that it stands ready to play its part in the implementation of the United Nations Global Counter-Terrorism Strategy.

The Council calls upon the relevant United Nations departments, programmes and specialized agencies, as appropriate, to consider, within their existing mandates, how to pursue counter-terrorism objectives.

The Council welcomes the renewed focus of the Security Council Committee established pursuant to resolution 1373(2001) concerning counter-terrorism (the Counter-Terrorism Committee) on enhancing the implementation of resolution 1373(2001) through a proactive fulfilment of its mandate to promote and monitor implementation by States.

The Council recalls its resolution 1624(2005) and encourages the Counter-Terrorism Committee to continue its work on the implementation of that resolution.

The Council calls upon the Counter-Terrorism Committee to report on the status of the implementation of resolution 1373(2001). In particular, the Council encourages the Counter-Terrorism Committee to report to the Council on any outstanding issues, when necessary and on a regular basis, in order to receive strategic guidance from the Council.

The Council recalls its resolution 1535(2004), by which it decided to establish the Counter-Terrorism Committee Executive Directorate (hereinafter CTED) as a special political mission under the policy guidance of the Counter-Terrorism Committee, to enhance the ability of the Committee to monitor the implementation of resolution 1373(2001) and effectively continue the capacity-building work in which it is engaged. The Council stresses that the mandate of the Counter-Terrorism Committee Executive Directorate flows from that of the Counter-Terrorism Committee.

The Council further recalls the statement by its President of 21 December 2005, which included the conclusions of the comprehensive review of CTED by the Council in 2005, and in which the Council decided to carry out another comprehensive review of CTED by 31 December 2006, prepared by the Counter-Terrorism Committee. During today's consultations, the Council endorsed the report prepared by the Committee and forwarded to the Council, and agreed with the recommendations and conclusions contained therein.

The Council welcomes the letter dated 15 December 2006 from the Secretary-General to the President of the Council regarding CTED reporting lines. The Council has considered this matter and endorses the recommendation of the Counter-Terrorism Committee with regard to CTED reporting lines so that CTED would henceforth present its draft work programmes and its semi-annual reports directly to the Committee.

The Council notes with appreciation the enhanced cooperation among its three Committees (the 1267 Committee, the Counter-Terrorism Committee and the 1540 Committee) that deal with counter-terrorism and their expert teams. It encourages the three Committees to ensure that, in their dialogue with States, they present a consolidated message from the Council on its efforts to fight terrorism. Also, it encourages the three Committees and their expert teams to avoid duplication, including in their requests for information from Member States about their implementation. In this regard, it encourages the three Committees and their expert teams to continue to strengthen the sharing of information among themselves, specifically information reported by States regarding implementation. The Council will continue to evaluate how its counter-terrorism efforts can be organized most efficiently.

On the same date [S/2006/932], Cuba submitted a statement its Permanent Representative had planned to deliver before the Council but was unable to do so due to a change in the Council's procedure.

Reports of States. Between January and December, the CTC Chairperson transmitted to the Council President reports submitted by Member States on action they had taken or planned to implement resolutions 1373(2001) and 1624(2005) and letters from the Committee requesting follow-up information: [S/2005/265/Add.1 & Corr.1, S/2005/442/Add.1, S/2006/34-35, S/2006/68-70, S/2006/86-88, S/2006/98, S/2006/119-121, S/2006/147, S/2006/149 & Add.1, S/2006/152, S/2006/171-172 & Add.1, S/2006/174, S/2006/183, S/2006/185, S/2006/211-212, S/2006/215, S/2006/254, S/2006/280-284, S/2006/299, S/2006/309, S/2006/311-312, S/2006/329, S/2006/350 & Add.1, S/2006/351-352, S/2006/384-387 & Corr.1, S/2006/395-401 & Add.1, S/2006/402-404, S/2006/415, S/2006/421-424, S/2006/431, S/2006/445-447, S/2006/470-473, S/2006/477, S/2006/503-504, S/2006/506, S/2006/523, S/2006/527, S/2006/544-545, S/2006/547, S/2006/551-552, S/2006/566-568, S/2006/604, S/2006/611-612, S/2006/620, S/2006/627, S/2006/633-634, S/2006/680-682, S/2006/703, S/2006/717, S/2006/757, S/2006/762, S/2006/768, S/2006/784, S/2006/802, S/2006/836-837, S/2006/856-857, S/2006/902-903, S/2006/918, S/2006/970, S/2006/1028, S/2006/1038-1039].

IAEA action

The General Conference of the International Atomic Energy Agency (IAEA), at its fiftieth session (Vienna, Austria, 18-22 September), adopted resolution GC(50)/RES/11 on measures to protect against nuclear terrorism, in which it called upon its member States to provide political, financial and technical support, including in-kind contributions, to improve nuclear and radiological security and prevent nuclear and radiological terrorism. It also called upon all States not to provide any form of support to non-State actors that committed or intended to commit acts of nuclear or radiological terrorism, and to take all steps required by Security Council resolution 1540(2004) [YUN 2004, p. 544] to, among other things, prevent illicit trafficking of nuclear and other radioactive materials.

Peacekeeping operations

In 2006, the General Assembly and the Security Council continued to oversee the management and operation of UN peacekeeping missions. The Council addressed key issues pertaining to the overall conduct of those operations, including the problem of sexual exploitation and abuse by UN peacekeeping personnel in the field. It also reviewed the mandates of several ongoing operations and created new ones to deal with new security concerns. The Assembly took action on a number financial and administrative matters.

The Department of Peacekeeping Operations (DPKO) continued to implement the recommendations of the Special Committee on Peacekeeping Operations, whose mandate was to review the whole question of peacekeeping operations in all their aspects, as well as those of the Assembly.

General aspects of UN peacekeeping

Sexual exploitation and abuse in UN peacekeeping operations

On 23 February [meeting 5379], the Security Council considered the issue of sexual exploitation and abuse by UN peacekeeping personnel. In his briefing to the Council, the Under-Secretary-General for Peacekeeping Operations, Jean-Marie Guéhenno, said that concrete and meaningful progress had been made to implement the comprehensive strategy developed by DPKO to address the issue based on the recommendations contained in the 2005 report of the Special Committee on Peacekeeping Operations [YUN 2005, p. 120] and endorsed by the General Assembly in resolution 59/300 [ibid., p. 122]. All UN civilian staff, military personnel, contingents, UN volunteers and contractors were bound by the strict standards outlined in the Secretary-General's bulletin [ST/SGB/2003/13] on sexual exploitation and abuse [YUN 2004, p. 107]. Between 79 and 90 per cent of civilian police and military personnel had received mandatory training, for which tools and training materials had been developed. Missions addressed the welfare of their staff as a high priority, creating recreation outlets, and establishing multipurpose sporting, socializing and dining facilities. Managers and commanders were made aware that they would be held accountable for those under their chain of command, and DPKO had received the cooperation of two Member States in repatriating entire units for misconduct, which was in part related to sexual exploitation and abuse.

As recommended in the 2005 report of the Secretary-General's Adviser on Sexual Exploitation and Abuse by United Nations Peacekeeping Personnel [YUN 2005, p. 119] and endorsed by the Assembly in resolution 59/300, DPKO had designed, recruited and staffed a multidisciplinary conduct and discipline team at Headquarters, in addition to eight teams established in peacekeeping operations in Burundi, Côte d'Ivoire, the Democratic Republic of the Congo, Haiti, Liberia, Sierra Leone, the Sudan and Timor-Leste. The teams developed policy, provided oversight of disciplinary issues and ensured the coherent application of UN standards of conduct. They also provided policy advice to mission heads, received allegations from complainants, collaborated with the Integrated Mission Training Centres, and helped mission leadership oversee all related conduct and discipline issues. The teams were making communities aware of the various methods through which complaints could be made. A public information strategy and implementing procedure were developed to guide missions in responding transparently to local media and host populations on sexual exploitation and abuse issues.

The Under-Secretary-General said that the measures described in his briefing were the beginning of a programme of systematic and sustained change, but there was a great deal left to be done. Despite negative publicity and attention, not all troop contingents or staff on the ground fully supported aspects of the zero-tolerance policy with regard to sexual exploitation and abuse, particularly as it pertained to prostitution. The capacity of peacekeeping operations and of the Office of Internal Oversight Services (OIOS) to investigate violations, while respecting due process, needed to be strengthened markedly.

The Secretary-General's Special Adviser on Sexual Exploitation and Abuse by United Nations Peacekeeping Personnel, Prince Zeid Ra'ad Zeid Al-Hussein (Jordan), told the Council that the Secretariat and Member States had largely completed the changes called for by the Special Committee, following its review of his 2005 report on the subject [ibid.]. What remained was to finalize the revisions to the 1997 model memorandum of understanding [YUN 1997, p. 55] between the United Nations and troop-contributing countries (see p. 181); reach an agreement between Member States on the national investigations officer concept, which was being refined by OIOS; and receive the report of the group of legal experts relating to the de facto impunity enjoyed by some civilian staff members, and the UN policy statement and comprehensive strategy on assistance and support to victims (see p. 180). The Special Committee, in revisiting the issue of troop-contributing countries conducting their courts martial in the mission area, should, through the Assembly, invite all countries possessing that capacity to do so and to establish modalities for that purpose.

The Special Adviser said that the number of allegations of sexual exploitation and abuse by UN peacekeeping personnel in some locations was still a cause of concern, and Member States, together with all personnel serving in the field, had to exert even greater efforts to reduce that number. More resources needed to be provided to OIOS so that it could carry out its preliminary investigations efficiently, in conjunction with troop contributors.

Special Committee consideration (February/March). The Special Committee on Peacekeeping Operations (New York, 27 February–17 March) [A/60/19], while commending the Secretary-General's efforts to address conduct and discipline issues in the light of the report of his Special Adviser and its own recommendations, remained concerned by the large number of allegations of sexual misconduct by UN peacekeeping personnel. It emphasized that due process and national legal requirements had to be observed during investigations and requested the United Nations to take steps to restore the image and credibility of any UN peacekeeping mission, troop-contributing country or UN peacekeeping personnel, when allegations of misconduct were ultimately found to be legally unproven. The Special Committee reiterated that the responsibility for creating and maintaining an environment that prevented sexual exploitation and abuse should be part of the performance objectives of managers and commanders involved in UN peacekeeping operations, and that those who failed to meet such objectives should be held accountable.

The Special Committee recommended that DPKO improve living conditions and welfare and recreation facilities for all categories of personnel. It reiterated its recommendation that the Secretary-General carry out a comprehensive review, including a cost-benefit analysis, of the welfare and recreation needs for all categories of UN peacekeeping personnel, and make proposals on the issue to the Assembly. The Special Committee endorsed the development of a Secretariat database to track allegations of sexual exploitation and abuse and the follow-up given to those allegations. It stressed that the database had to be employed to ensure that persons against whom an allegation of misconduct had been proved after due process were not rehired.

The Special Committee was concerned with the number of outstanding allegations of sexual exploitation and abuse awaiting investigation and encouraged further cooperation between the United Nations and troop-contributing countries in the investigations, without prejudice to the exclusive jurisdiction of those countries over their contingents. It remained committed to implementing fundamental, systemic changes as a matter of urgency, drawing on the recommendations in the Committee's 2005 report, and decided to consider, during the Assembly's resumed sixtieth (2006) session, the Secretary-General's strategy for victim assistance and the revised draft model memorandum of understanding (see p. 181), which should be made available to Member States no later than the end of April 2006. The Special Committee established an open-ended ad hoc working group of experts to consider those documents and other questions, whose findings would be considered by a reconvened session of the Special Committee, which would make recommendations on a way forward.

The Special Committee encouraged troop-contributing countries to utilize in-mission courts martial and other disciplinary and judicial procedures where national legislation permitted, and requested the United Nations and host countries to facilitate procedures for doing so. It recommended that the Secretariat ensure that the group of legal experts, appointed in 2005 [YUN 2005, p. 121] to examine issues related to impunity of UN staff and experts on mission, report before the end of the Assembly's resumed sixtieth (2006) session. The Special Committee looked forward to incorporating the group's findings in its future deliberations and urged the Secretariat to appoint a further group of legal experts to take up the remaining elements identified by the Special Committee in its 2005 report.

Reports of Secretary-General. In May [A/60/862], the Secretary-General submitted a comprehensive report, prepared pursuant to Assembly resolution 59/296 [YUN 2005, p. 133], on sexual exploitation and abuse, including policy development, implementation and full justification of proposed capacity on personnel conduct issues. DPKO developed a comprehensive strategy on sexual exploitation and abuse by UN peacekeeping personnel, based primarily on the reforms endorsed by the Assembly in resolution 59/300 [ibid., p. 122]. The strategy's three-pronged approach comprised measures for preventing misconduct, enforcing UN standards of conduct and taking remedial action. DPKO also developed generic training materials on UN standards of conduct relating to sexual exploitation and abuse, called Module 1: Prevention of sexual exploitation and abuse, which was mandatory for all peacekeeping personnel as of July 2005; a number of missions reported high coverage of trained personnel. In February 2006, DPKO conducted capacity-building workshops on policy issues for eight newly established conduct and discipline teams from field missions. In May, it launched a Community of Practice network, which facilitated information exchange and the development and dissemination of guidance and best practices to all participants.

In accordance with Assembly resolution 59/287 [ibid., p. 1474], DPKO transferred sexual exploitation and abuse investigations to OIOS, for which joint interim cooperation procedures were developed on the handling of allegations and investigations of misconduct allegations.

Standard operating procedures and guidelines on public information activities relating to sexual exploitation and abuse were finalized, providing guidance in terms of explaining the Secretary-General's zero-tolerance policy on sexual exploitation and abuse to the media, UN personnel and host populations; reporting complaints; and providing information to victims on the status of misconduct allegations. Pending the finalization of an organizational policy statement and strategy on victim assistance, DPKO instructed its missions to refer any person alleging to have been sexually exploited or abused by UN peacekeeping personnel to medical and psychosocial services available in the host country, with costs to be covered from existing mission budgets.

DPKO was developing a mission directive on sexual exploitation and abuse for senior mission leadership. Following discussions with Member States, the Secretary-General prepared further revisions to the draft 1997 model memorandum of understanding between the United Nations and troop-contributing countries to reflect the reforms proposed by his Special Adviser on Sexual Exploitation and Abuse by United Nations Peacekeeping Personnel in 2005 [ibid., p. 119]. The revisions included a new clause and annex relating to UN standards of conduct and an article on the conduct of investigations by a national investigations officer into allegations of criminal offences committed by military contingent members serving in UN peacekeeping operations.

The Secretary-General concluded that significant progress had been made in implementing the reforms endorsed by the Assembly in resolution 59/300, but dedicated resources were required to complete them and continue to provide oversight and guidance on conduct and discipline issues. A longer-term, dedicated capacity to address conduct and discipline issues at DPKO Headquarters and in all field missions was key to an efficient and professional approach to peacekeeping. Proposed conduct and discipline teams would provide the head of mission with strategic guidance and an overview of the state of discipline in the mission and ensure that a systematic and consistent approach was taken to conduct and discipline issues in peacekeeping operations. The Secretary-General requested the Assembly to approve posts for a conduct and discipline unit at DPKO in the support account for peacekeeping operations for the 2006-2007 budget.

Annexed to the report were the terms of reference of the DPKO Headquarters Conduct and Discipline Team; model terms of reference for a Conduct and Discipline Team in a DPKO-led peace operation; and proposed staffing tables for the teams in peacekeeping operations and special political missions for 2006-2007.

The Secretary-General, in his May report [A/60/861] on special measures for protection from sexual exploitation and sexual abuse, submitted in response to Assembly resolution 57/306 [YUN 2003, p. 1237], presented data on allegations of sexual exploitation and abuse in DPKO, as well as other UN entities, as at 31 December 2005. DPKO reported 340 new allegations, 193 of which were brought against military personnel, 24 related to civilian police, 80 against UN staff and 42 related to other personnel, such as consultants and individual contractors. Among the 193 allegations brought against uniformed personnel, 50 were deemed to have required no further action, 3 were pending preliminary investigation, 7 were deemed to be unsubstantiated, 3 were substantiated and 15 submitted to Headquarters for disciplinary action as at 31 December 2005. Seventy-six allegations were under investigation by OIOS.

Policy statement and strategy on victim assistance. In May [A/60/877], the Secretary-General submitted to the Assembly President a draft policy statement and draft comprehensive strategy on assistance and support to victims of sexual exploitation and abuse by UN staff and related personnel, as requested by the Special Committee on Peacekeeping Operations in 2005 [YUN 2005, p. 120] and endorsed by the General Assembly in resolution 59/300 [ibid., p. 122]. In the World Summit Outcome, adopted by the General Assembly in resolution 60/1 [ibid., p. 48], Member States also encouraged the Secretary-General to submit proposals leading to a comprehensive approach to victim's assistance. The strategy represented more than 12 months of internal and external consultation with UN departments, agencies, funds and programmes, Member States, non-governmental organizations (NGOs) and other specialists and interested parties, both at Headquarters and in the field. The strategy identified the categories of persons who should receive assistance and support, the nature of assistance and support and how it should be provided. It noted that gender-based violence, including sexual exploitation and abuse, was endemic in the environments where the United Nations worked and that the resources for responding to it needed to be increased. That assistance should be provided in a manner that was appropriate to the community context, did not further isolate the victims, and improved the response capacity of service providers. The strategy also proposed that, to facilitate access to such services, the United Nations engage implementing partners to provide victim advocate services.

Special Committee consideration (July). The Special Committee on Peacekeeping Operations and its Working Group reported in August [A/60/19/Add.1] on its first resumed session in 2006 (New York, 27 July). The Ad Hoc Working Group of Experts met on 26 and 27 June to consider the draft strategy for victim assistance (see above) and the draft revision to the 1997 model memorandum of understanding between the United Nations and Member States contributing resources to UN peacekeeping operations; a proposal on national investigations officers concept (see p. 179); and the proposed unification of standards of conduct for UN peacekeeping contingents. The Special Committee, having considered the Working Group's recommendations, requested that the Secretariat submit the revised draft model memorandum of understanding to Member States as a General Assembly document by September. It decided to continue consideration of the draft policy statement and strategy and the revised draft model memorandum of understanding, and intended to reconvene the Ad Hoc Working Group to consider them from 11 to 15 December. It requested that the revised draft model memorandum of understanding take into consideration views expressed by Member States in 2005 and 2006.

GENERAL ASSEMBLY ACTION

On 8 September [meeting 99], the General Assembly, on the recommendation of the Fourth (Special Political and Decolonization) Committee [A/60/478/Add.2 & Corr.1], adopted **resolution 60/289** without vote [agenda item 32].

Comprehensive review of a strategy to eliminate future sexual exploitation and abuse in United Nations peacekeeping operations

The General Assembly,

Recalling its resolution 2006(XIX) of 18 February 1965 and all other relevant resolutions,

Recalling in particular its resolution 60/1, paragraph 165, of 16 September 2005, and its resolutions 59/281 of 29 March 2005 and 59/300 of 22 June 2005,

Recalling its resolution 60/263 of 6 June 2006, in which it endorsed the decision of the Special Committee on Peacekeeping Operations, contained in paragraph 74 of its report, to consider, during the sixtieth session of the General Assembly, the Secretary-General's strategy for victim assistance and the revised draft model memorandum of understanding, including a proposal on national investigations officers,

Reaffirming its resolution 59/296 of 22 June 2005, as well as resolutions 59/300 and 60/263, and the need for the United Nations to implement its policy of zero tolerance of sexual exploitation and abuse in its peacekeeping operations as recommended by the Special Committee,

Affirming the need for a comprehensive strategy of assistance to victims of sexual exploitation and abuse by United Nations staff or related personnel,

Convinced of the need for the United Nations to take strong and effective steps in this regard,

1. *Welcomes* the report of the Special Committee on Peacekeeping Operations on its 2006 resumed session;

2. *Endorses* the proposals, recommendations and conclusions of the Special Committee contained in paragraphs 5 to 10 of the report on its 2006 resumed session;

3. *Urges* Member States, the Secretariat and the relevant organs of the United Nations to take all necessary steps to implement the aforementioned proposals, recommendations and conclusions of the Special Committee, and supports the request of the Special Committee to the Secretary-General that he provide a progress report on the implementation of its recommendations at its next regular session;

4. *Requests* the Special Committee to include this issue in its report to the General Assembly at its sixty-first session.

Revised draft model memorandum of understanding. In response to General Assembly resolutions 59/300 [YUN 2005, p. 122], 60/263 (see p. 185) and 60/289 (see above), the Secretary-General, in a 3 October note [A/61/494], submitted the revised draft model memorandum of understanding between the United Nations and troop-contributing countries for consideration by the open-ended Ad Hoc Working Group of Experts, scheduled to convene in December. An earlier draft model memorandum was submitted in 1997 [YUN 1997, p. 55].

Special Committee consideration (December). At its second 2006 resumed session (New York, 18 December) [A/61/19 (Part I)], the Special Committee on Peacekeeping Operations requested the open-ended Ad Hoc Working Group of Experts to continue consideration of the revised draft model memorandum of understanding at a resumed session in 2007. It reiterated its belief that a strategy for victim assistance was an important element of a comprehensive response to the problem of sexual exploitation and abuse and requested the Chairperson of the Special Committee to consult with the Fourth Committee Chairman and the General Assembly President on the modalities for further consideration of the draft strategy, and to report to the Special Committee at its next substantive session. Until a comprehensive strategy for assistance to victims of sexual exploitation and abuse was implemented, missions should continue to provide emergency assistance to such victims within current mission budgets.

Strengthening operational capacity

The Special Committee on Peacekeeping Operations, at its 2006 substantive session (New York, 27 February–17 March) [A/60/19], recognized that the current level of resources limited the scope and number of missions that DPKO could effectively undertake and manage. It shared the Secretary-General's assessment that UN peacekeeping continued to face significant gaps, in particular in enabling and niche capabilities, rapid reaction in crisis situations, and strategic lift capabilities. The Special Committee requested the Secretariat to continue to provide it with information on how to address those issues.

Concerning rapid deployment, the Special Committee recommended that DPKO continue to facilitate enabling arrangements, including through Member States and bilateral arrangements, for overcoming the shortfall in contingent-owned equipment and sustainability faced by some troop-contributing countries. The Secretariat should continue to explore options for enhanced rapidly deployable capacities, in consultation with Member States, reinforce UN peacekeeping operations in crises, and report to the Special Committee at its next session; and refine existing UN Standby Arrangements System mechanisms. DPKO should produce a generic reinforcement policy for field missions, and conduct a reinforcement needs assessment for each mission, which should be revised periodically. While supporting the call for rapid deployment, the Special Committee urged the Secretariat to optimize pre-mandate operational preparedness and deployment. It called for more efficient management of the financial and logistical aspects of UN peacekeeping operations, both at Headquarters and in the field, to make deployment both rapid and effective.

The Special Committee requested that, within the integrated mission planning process, the practice of sharing the operational concept and plan early in the mission planning stage with relevant stakeholders, in particular troop-contributing countries, should be formalized, thus facilitating national planning, further enhancing DPKO planning, enhancing transparency prior to submitting recommendations to the Security Council, and adding impetus to force generation. It recognized that an integrated mission planning process training course and handbook would be crucial to improving the planning process and should eventually be made available to relevant stakeholders, in particular the troop-contributing countries, as well as to all UN agencies.

The Special Committee recommended the early selection of Force Commanders, Police Commissioners and key mission headquarters staff, as well as joint training, before deployment. Key mission staff should be provided with induction and orientation training and the appropriate integrated planning tools. It stressed the need for the Secretariat to identify qualified candidates from troop-contributing countries for senior mission leadership posts and fully supported the UN Senior Mission Leaders Course and Senior Leadership Induction Programme, both of which should be mandatory for all senior mission leaders. It also emphasized the necessity for common guidelines and training for joint operation and joint mission analysis centres across all missions to maximize their potential.

The Special Committee welcomed the creation of an initial operating capability for the Standing Police Capacity and requested the Secretariat to review it at the end of its first year of operation and report to the Special Committee in 2007. The Secretariat should propose, for the Special Committee's consideration, a UN formed police unit policy and doctrine on roles, responsibilities and anticipated tasks.

The Special Committee noted the definition of doctrine in the context of UN peacekeeping as the evolving body of institutional guidance that provided support and direction to personnel preparing for, planning and implementing UN peacekeeping operations, and which included guiding principles and concepts, as well as the policies, standard operating procedures, guidelines and manuals that support practitioners. It requested the Secretariat to provide an interim glossary of terminology for approval by the Special Committee that would be used during the further development of doctrine. It welcomed the proposal by DPKO to prepare a report articulating guiding principles, clarifying core tasks and encompassing major lessons learned, and expected an initial briefing in mid-2006 in order to elaborate the operational guidance framework and materials available.

Guidance on Integrated Missions. On 9 February, the Secretary-General issued a revised Note of Guidance on Integrated Missions, clarifying further the role, responsibility and authority of the Special Representative, Deputy Special Representative and the Resident Coordinator/Humanitarian Coordinator.

Strategies for complex peacekeeping operations

The Special Committee on Peacekeeping Operations, at its 2006 substantive session (New York, 27 February–17 March) [A/60/19], reaffirmed the need for DPKO to plan and conduct UN peacekeeping activities in such a manner as to facilitate post-conflict peacebuilding and long-term prevention of the recurrence of armed conflict. It should develop, together with the UN system and other relevant actors, coherent operational strategies and early integrated mission planning based on lessons learned in the areas of disarmament, demobilization and reintegration; strengthening the rule of law; justice and reconciliation; security sector reform; quick-impact projects; and mine action. Cooperation and coordination for ensuring common needs assessments, operational clarity and policy coherence on the ground during implementation of the comprehensive strategies in the post-conflict peacebuilding phases should be strengthened, so as to ensure a smooth transition to long-term development activities. The Special Committee underscored the need for a coordinated, coherent and integrated approach at all phases and levels of UN peacekeeping and peacebuilding at Headquarters and in the field; noted efforts to improve UN system coherence in countries emerging from conflict; welcomed the current review of the integrated mission planning process; and requested the Secretariat to continue to report on efforts to improve coordination in existing operations.

The Special Committee decided to develop appropriate forms of interaction for consultation and coordination with the Peacebuilding Commission, and encouraged DPKO to collaborate closely with the Peacebuilding Support Office. It was of the view that a framework for coordination among those entities should be developed as early as possible.

The Special Committee requested that the Secretariat assess lessons learned regarding the rule of law, options for rule of law strategies for ongoing and future UN peacekeeping operations, the potential need for human and material resources to support UN peacekeeping activities in the judicial, legal and prison spheres. It urged DPKO to elaborate a comprehensive policy on gender mainstreaming in UN peacekeeping operations, including systematic reporting about the nature and impact of gender-mainstreaming activities, building on the Gender Mainstreaming Policy Statement of the Under-Secretary-General issued in March 2005. The Special Committee commended DPKO for engaging staff members in workshops to design an action plan for the implementation of Security Council resolution 1325(2000) on women and peacekeeping [YUN 2000, p. 1113], and recommended that similar workshops be held in field operations. It supported the development of a roster of qualified female candidates from different geographical regions for senior appointments in UN peacekeeping operations. It urged Member States to include HIV/AIDS awareness training as part of predeployment preparation, and urged DPKO to ensure that all missions had sufficient HIV voluntary counselling and testing capacity for all UN peacekeeping personnel.

Safety and security

The Special Committee on Peacekeeping Operations, at its 2006 substantive session [A/60/19], expressed concern about the precarious security environment in many field missions and called upon the Secretariat to give the utmost priority to enhancing the safety and security of United Nations and associated personnel in the field. It condemned the killing of UN peacekeeping personnel in several missions and recognized that the continued attacks and other acts of violence against them constituted a major challenge to the Organization's field operations.

The Special Committee agreed with the assessment of the Secretary-General's 2005 report [YUN 2005, p. 128] that the actors outside of a peace process posed serious risks for the safety and security of UN peacekeeping personnel, and although the new risk assessment process and better capacity for the collection, analysis and dissemination of field information reduced risks, it continued to advocate that the best assurance against such risks was a properly planned and mandated mission.

The Special Committee welcomed the Secretary-General's report on a strengthened and unified security management system for the United Nations [ibid., p. 1558], in particular the progress made in improving coordination between the Department of Safety and Security and DPKO, and stressed the need for a clear and concise policy in that regard. Concerned that the Secretariat had not developed an accountability framework, it stressed the need for immediate action towards that end. The Special Committee requested the development of clear guidelines and procedures for information-sharing between the Secretariat and troop-contributing countries on safety and security issues and security management in peacekeeping operations. Constant communication with concerned Member States should be initiated and maintained throughout the investigation process whenever an incident in a field mission negatively impacted operational effectiveness and/or resulted in the serious injury or death of UN peacekeeping personnel. The findings of the Board of Inquiries on serious injury or death and lessons learned from such incidents should be shared with the Member States concerned, including troop-contributing countries in the field. It requested, as an urgent priority, that DPKO provide field missions with the capacity for improved use of information technology to ensure that information was disseminated to commanders and leaders in field missions, as underscored in the 2005 OIOS report on the effectiveness of military information management in UN peacekeeping operations [ibid., p. 113].

The Special Committee recommended that the Security Council, together with the countries hosting UN peacekeeping operations, continue to ensure that those operations implemented their mandates fully and effectively, and called on DPKO to ensure that UN peacekeeping personnel were deployed in accordance with agreed concepts of operation. It stressed the need for accountability at all levels for the employment of UN peacekeeping personnel and their effective and efficient deployment, particularly in hostile and hazardous conditions. Welcoming the proposed establishment of joint operational and mission analysis centres, the Special Committee urged the Secretariat to provide a policy paper on the structure, functions and role of those centres, as requested in its 2005 report [ibid., p. 126].

The Special Committee stressed the need for priority action by DPKO to examine how all forms of technical monitoring and surveillance, in particular aerial monitoring, could be used by the United Nations to ensure the safety and security of UN peacekeeping personnel, particularly in volatile and dangerous conditions, and in situations too dangerous for ground-based monitoring. It recommended that DPKO discuss that issue with troop-contributing countries, and reiterated its request to the Secretary-General to provide the Special Committee with a comprehensive assessment in that regard in his next report. The Secretariat should undertake a comprehensive analysis of the factors and circumstances that contributed to all types of fatalities of UN peacekeeping personnel in the field, and report its findings to the Special Committee at its next session, including the mechanism for addressing that issue.

By **decision 60/551 B** of 8 May, the General Assembly deferred until its sixty-first (2006) session consideration of the 2005 OIOS report [ibid., p. 126] on the global audit of field security management.

Cooperation with regional organizations

The Special Committee on Peacekeeping Operations [A/60/19] recognized that regional arrangements had unique and complementary capacities to offer, in cooperation with UN peacekeeping operations, and urged the United Nations to strengthen its operational linkages and partnership with such arrangements. It recommended that DPKO develop modalities for the use of regional capacities for enhanced, rapidly deployable capacities with regional arrangements; such modalities should also include provision for early warning and a smooth transition from one operation to another. The Special Committee welcomed the EU ongoing dialogue with the United Nations to define modalities and practical arrangements for enhancing cooperation.

Women in peacekeeping

On 26 October [meeting 5556], the Security Council discussed the question of women and peace and security. It had before it the Secretary-General's September report [S/2006/770] (see p. 1339) reviewing implementation of the 2005 System-wide Action Plan [YUN 2005, p. 1255] for the implementation of Council resolution 1325(2000) on women, peace and security [YUN 2000, p. 1113].

The Under-Secretary-General for Peacekeeping Operations, reporting on DPKO efforts to implement resolution 1325(2000), said that assaults on women's rights and gender equality continued in every post-conflict situation. He highlighted three priority issues facing peacekeeping missions in supporting women's participation in transitional processes and beyond, which required the Council's urgent attention. Those priorities were: the continuing problem of insecurity, even after fighting had stopped; beyond the initial step of supporting the participation of women in electoral processes, ensuring sustained support for women in the political arena so that they might be part of the decision-making process; and amending and reforming discriminatory laws that undermined equality of rights, so as to enable the effective participation of women in the peacebuilding process.

DPKO had developed a comprehensive action plan to support implementation of resolution 1325(2000), which was being monitored by a senior management team. The team provided policy guidance and training tools to peacekeepers and Member States; developed operational guidelines for DPKO mission personnel to enable them to translate resolution 1325(2000) into practice; and established gender components in missions and at Headquarters to oversee that work.

Although progress had been made, real gaps remained in the implementation of resolution 1325(2000), including pockets of resistance in seeking to transform the working culture. Some personnel had yet to understand their own responsibility for the implementation of resolution 1325(2000), and that it was not the sole responsibility of gender advisers, nor could it be outsourced to DPKO UN partners. In addition, a critical mass of male champions to advocate and support the translation of the commitments to gender equality into practice had to be built, and DPKO needed a senior male envoy to support its political advocacy efforts. Besides the action plan, the Under-Secretary-General planned to issue a policy directive to guide efforts to implement resolution 1325(2000).

Beyond DPKO actions, some of the outstanding challenges could best be addressed through partnerships with Member States and the broader UN system. Member States needed to nominate more women candidates for senior civilian positions in missions. As an operational imperative, a greater number of women peacekeepers had to be deployed in order to engage more effectively with the local population, and stronger partnership with UN agencies was needed to sustain the investments of peacekeeping missions during the transitional period. DPKO experiences in Sierra Leone and Timor-Leste highlighted the need for a smooth transitioning of gender-related programmes to the UN country team, following the completion of a peacekeeping mandate to avoid creating a programmatic gap that could unravel the gains made by peacekeeping missions. DPKO UN partners needed to be on the ground from the very beginning with the capacities and resources required to support women in the wide range of areas that fell beyond the scope and mandate of peacekeeping missions.

The Under-Secretary-General said that the United Nations had to continue to invest resources in creating a stable and secure environment that would allow women to restore dignity, normalcy and hope to their lives in the post-conflict period. Programmes for women's economic and political empowerment and to support the education of girls could be sustained only under conditions of security. Therefore, Member States had to meet their obligations to contribute sufficient troops to enable peacekeeping operations to deliver that security.

The Council President, in statement **S/PRST/2006/42** of 26 October (see p. 1340), emphasized the need for the inclusion of gender components in peacekeeping operations and encouraged Member States and the Secretary-General to increase the participation of women in all areas and levels of peacekeeping operations, including civilian, police and military aspects.

Comprehensive review of peacekeeping

Special Committee on Peacekeeping Operations

As requested by the General Assembly in resolution 59/281 [YUN 2005, p. 129], the Special Committee on Peacekeeping Operations and its Working Group continued their comprehensive review of the whole question of peacekeeping operations in all their aspects [A/60/19 & Add.1; A/61/19 (Part I)]. In response to the Committee's request, the Secretary-General submitted a report on the implementation of the Committee's 2006 [A/61/668 & Add.1 & Corr.1] recommendations.

The Special Committee held three sessions in 2006, its substantive session (27 February–17 March) and two resumed sessions (27 July and 18 December, respectively), all in New York. During its substantive session, the Special Committee discussed safety and security, conduct and discipline, the agenda for reform of UN peacekeeping, strengthening operational capacity, strategies for complex peacekeeping operations, cooperation with troop-contributing countries, enhancement of African peacekeeping capabilities, cooperation with regional arrangements, best practices, training, and personnel and financial matters (for details, see respective sections above). It continued to consider the recommendations contained in the 2005 report of the Secretary-General's Special Adviser on Sexual Exploitation and Abuse on a comprehensive strategy to eliminate future sexual exploitation and abuse in UN peacekeeping operations [YUN 2005, p. 119].

Communications. In separate letters of 20 February, Sierra Leone, in its capacity as Chairman of the African Group, informed the Presidents of the General Assembly [A/60/688] and the Security Council [S/2006/117] that the Group had noted with concern the Council's decision to hold separate open debates on the themes "Peacekeeping operations management (procurement)" and "Sexual exploitation in United Nations peacekeeping missions", on 22 and 23 February, respectively. The Group viewed the decision as an encroachment on the Assembly's responsibilities and functions and incompatible with the current spirit of the ongoing discussions aimed at revitalizing the Assembly. In its letter to the Assembly, the Group stated that it wished to rely on the Assembly President's leadership to safeguard the Assembly's primacy and authority as the deliberative, policy-making and representative organ of the United Nations. The execution of the Assembly's mandate without hindrances from organs such as the Security Council was indispensable to its revitalization.

GENERAL ASSEMBLY ACTION

On 6 June [meeting 88], the General Assembly, on the recommendation of the Fourth Committee [A/60/478/Add.1], adopted **resolution 60/263** without vote [agenda item 32].

Comprehensive review of the whole question of peacekeeping operations in all their aspects

The General Assembly,

Recalling its resolution 2006(XIX) of 18 February 1965 and all other relevant resolutions,

Recalling in particular its resolutions 59/281 of 29 March 2005 and 59/300 of 22 June 2005,

Affirming that the efforts of the United Nations in the peaceful settlement of disputes, including through its peacekeeping operations, are indispensable,

Convinced of the need for the United Nations to continue to improve its capabilities in the field of peacekeeping and to enhance the effective and efficient deployment of its peacekeeping operations,

Considering the contribution that all States Members of the United Nations make to peacekeeping,

Noting the widespread interest in contributing to the work of the Special Committee on Peacekeeping Operations expressed by Member States, in particular troop-contributing countries,

Bearing in mind the continuous necessity of preserving the efficiency and strengthening the effectiveness of the work of the Special Committee,

1. *Welcomes* the report of the Special Committee on Peacekeeping Operations;
2. *Endorses* the proposals, recommendations and conclusions of the Special Committee, contained in paragraphs 28 to 188 of its report;
3. *Urges* Member States, the Secretariat and relevant organs of the United Nations to take all necessary steps to implement the proposals, recommendations and conclusions of the Special Committee;
4. *Reiterates* that those Member States that become personnel contributors to the United Nations peacekeeping operations in years to come or participate in the future in the Special Committee for three consecutive years as observers shall, upon request in writing to the Chair-

man of the Special Committee, become members at the following session of the Special Committee;

5. *Decides* that the Special Committee, in accordance with its mandate, shall continue its efforts for a comprehensive review of the whole question of peacekeeping operations in all their aspects and shall review the implementation of its previous proposals and consider any new proposals so as to enhance the capacity of the United Nations to fulfil its responsibilities in this field;

6. *Requests* the Special Committee to submit a report on its work to the General Assembly at its sixty-first session;

7. *Decides* to include in the provisional agenda of its sixty-first session the item entitled "Comprehensive review of the whole question of peacekeeping operations in all their aspects".

On 12 December [S/2006/972], Japan, in its capacity as Chairman of the Security Council Working Group on Peacekeeping Operations, submitted the Working Group's report, covering its meetings and activities from 1 January 2005 to 6 November 2006.

By **decision 61/520** of 14 December, the Assembly took note of the report of the Fourth Committee [A/61/409] on its consideration of the agenda item "Comprehensive review of the whole question of peacekeeping operations in all their aspects". On 22 December, the Assembly decided that the agenda item would remain for consideration during its resumed sixty-first (2007) session (**decision 61/552**).

Operations in 2006

As at 1 January 2006, there were 15 peacekeeping missions in operation—7 in Africa, 1 in the Americas, 1 in Asia, 3 in Europe and the Mediterranean and 3 in the Middle East. During the year, one mission was closed (in Burundi) and a new one launched (in Timor-Leste); thus, the total number of missions in operation at the end of the year remained at 15.

Africa

In Africa, the mandate of the United Nations Operation in Burundi (ONUB) was extended for a final period of six months, until 31 December. The Security Council also extended the mandates of the United Nations Organization Mission in the Democratic Republic of the Congo (MONUC) until 15 February 2007; the United Nations Mission for the Referendum in Western Sahara (MINURSO) until 30 April 2007; the United Nations Mission in Ethiopia and Eritrea (UNMEE) until 31 January 2007; the United Nations Operation in Côte d'Ivoire (UNOCI) until 10 January 2007; and the United Nations Mission in Liberia (UNMIL) until 31 March 2007. The Council expanded the mandate of the United Nations Mission in the Sudan (UNMIS) to include support for the implementation of the 2006 Darfur Peace Agreement (see p. 274) and the 2004 N'Djamena Humanitarian Ceasefire Agreement [YUN 2004, p. 235]; authorized an increase in the Mission's strength by up to 17,300 military personnel and 3,300 civilian police; and extended its mandate until 30 April 2007.

Americas

In the Americas, the Security Council extended the mandate of the United Nations Stabilization Mission in Haiti (MINUSTAH) until 15 February 2007.

Asia

In Asia, the United Nations Military Observer Group in India and Pakistan (UNMOGIP), established in 1949, continued to monitor the ceasefire in Jammu and Kashmir.

On 25 August, the Security Council established the United Nations Integrated Mission in Timor-Leste (UNMIT) as a follow-on mission to the United Nations Mission of Support in East Timor (UNMISET), which ended in 2005 [YUN 2005, p. 131]. The mission's broad mandate included supporting the Government of Timor-Leste and relevant institutions with a view to consolidating stability, enhancing a culture of democratic governance and facilitating political dialogue among Timorese stakeholders. UNMIT had an authorized strength of 1,608 police personnel and 34 military liaison and staff officers.

The Council extended, in September, the authorization of the International Security Assistance Force in Afghanistan for a further period of 12 months beyond 13 October 2006 (**resolution 1707(2006)**) (see p. 381), and in November, the authorization for the multinational force in Iraq until 31 December 2007 (**resolution 1723(2006)**) (see p. 403).

Europe and the Mediterranean

In Europe and the Mediterranean, the Security Council extended the mandates of the United Nations Observer Mission in Georgia (UNOMIG) until 15 April 2007 and of the United Nations Peacekeeping Force in Cyprus (UNFICYP) until 15 June 2007. The United Nations Interim Administration Mission in Kosovo (UNMIK), Serbia (formerly Serbia and Montenegro), remained in place. On 21 November 2006, the Council authorized the Member States, acting through or in cooperation with the EU, to establish for a further period of 12 months a multinational stabilization force

(EUFOR) in Bosnia and Herzegovina (**resolution 1722(2006)**) (see p.458).

Middle East

Three long-standing operations continued in the Middle East. The United Nations Truce Supervision Organization (UNTSO) continued to observe the truce in Palestine. The mandate of the United Nations Disengagement Observer Force (UNDOF) was renewed until 30 June 2007. Consequent upon the escalation of hostilities in Lebanon and Israel, the Security Council, in **resolution 1701(2006)** of 11 August (see p. 583), authorized an increase in the strength of the United Nations Interim Force in Lebanon (UNIFIL) to a maximum of 15,000 troops and extended its mandate until 31 August 2007.

Roster of 2006 operations

UNTSO

United Nations Truce Supervision Organization

Established: June 1948.

Mandate: To assist in supervising the observance of the truce in Palestine.

Strength as at December 2006: 150 military observers.

UNMOGIP

United Nations Military Observer Group in India and Pakistan

Established: January 1949.

Mandate: To supervise the ceasefire between India and Pakistan in Jammu and Kashmir.

Strength as at December 2006: 41 military observers.

UNFICYP

United Nations Peacekeeping Force in Cyprus

Established: March 1964.

Mandate: To prevent the recurrence of fighting between the two Cypriot communities.

Strength as at December 2006: 853 troops, 64 civilian police.

UNDOF

United Nations Disengagement Observer Force

Established: June 1974.

Mandate: To supervise the ceasefire between Israel and the Syrian Arab Republic and the disengagement of Israeli and Syrian forces in the Golan Heights.

Strength as at December 2006: 1,048 troops.

UNIFIL

United Nations Interim Force in Lebanon

Established: March 1978.

Mandate: To restore peace and security and assist the Lebanese Government in ensuring the return of its effective authority in the area; expanded in 2006 to include monitoring the cessation of hostilities in Lebanon and Israel (see p. 583), supporting the deployment of the Lebanese Armed Forces throughout southern Lebanon, helping to ensure humanitarian access to civilian populations and the safe return of displaced persons, and assisting the Lebanese Armed Forces in establishing a permanent ceasefire and long-term solution to the situation between the two countries.

Strength as at December 2006: 11,563 troops.

MINURSO

United Nations Mission for the Referendum in Western Sahara

Established: April 1991.

Mandate: To monitor and verify the implementation of a settlement plan for Western Sahara and assist in the holding of a referendum in the Territory.

Strength as at December 2006: 31 troops, 183 military observers, 4 civilian police.

UNOMIG

United Nations Observer Mission in Georgia

Established: August 1993.

Mandate: To verify compliance with a ceasefire agreement between the parties to the conflict in Georgia and investigate ceasefire violations; expanded in 1994 to include monitoring the implementation of an agreement on a ceasefire and separation of forces and observing the operation of a multinational peacekeeping force.

Strength as at December 2006: 127 military observers, 12 civilian police.

UNMIK

United Nations Interim Administration Mission in Kosovo

Established: June 1999.

Mandate: To promote, among other things, the establishment of substantial autonomy and self-government in Kosovo, perform basic civilian administrative functions, organize and oversee the development of provisional institutions, facilitate a political process to determine Kosovo's future status, support the reconstruction of key infrastructure, maintain civil law and order, protect human rights and assure the return of refugees and displaced persons.

Strength as at December 2006: 1,960 civilian police, 37 military observers.

MONUC

United Nations Organization Mission in the Democratic Republic of the Congo

Established: November 1999.

Mandate: To establish contacts with the signatories to the Ceasefire Agreement, provide technical assistance in the implementation of the Agreement, provide information on security conditions, plan for the observation of the ceasefire, facilitate the delivery of humanitarian assistance and assist in the protection of human rights.

Strength as at December 2006: 16,487 troops, 734 military observers, 1,075 civilian police.

UNMEE

United Nations Mission in Ethiopia and Eritrea

Established: July 2000.

Mandate: To establish and put into operation the mechanism for verifying the cessation of hostilities and to assist the Military Coordination Commission in tasks related to demining and in administrative support to its field offices.

Strength as at December 2006: 2,063 troops, 222 military observers.

UNMIL

United Nations Mission in Liberia

Established: 19 September 2003.

Mandate: To support the implementation of the ceasefire agreement and the peace process; protect UN staff, facilities and civilians; support humanitarian and human rights activities; and assist in national security reform, including national police training and formation of a new, restructured military.

Strength as at December 2006: 13,613 troops, 188 military observers, 1,097 civilian police.

UNOCI

United Nations Operation in Côte d'Ivoire

Established: April 2004.

Mandate: To monitor the implementation of the 3 May 2003 comprehensive ceasefire agreement and the movement of armed groups; assist in disarmament, demobilization, reintegration, repatriation and resettlement; protect UN personnel, institutions and civilians; support humanitarian assistance; support implementation of the peace process; assist in the promotion of human rights, public information, and law and order.

Strength as at December 2006: 7,847 troops, 190 military observers, 992 civilian police.

MINUSTAH

United Nations Stabilization Mission in Haiti

Established: 1 June 2004.

Mandate: To ensure a secure and stable environment in support of the Transitional Government; to support the constitutional and political process, and the Transitional Government in bringing about national dialogue, conducting free and fair elections, and extending State authority throughout the country; to promote and protect human rights and coordinate with the Government in the provision of humanitarian assistance.

Strength as at December 2006: 6,684 troops, 1,692 civilian police.

ONUB

United Nations Operation in Burundi

Established: 1 June 2004.

Ended: 31 December 2006.

Mandate: To monitor the implementation of ceasefire agreements; promote the re-establishment of confidence between Burundian forces; assist in disarmament and demobilization; monitor the quartering of the Armed Forces of Burundi and their heavy weapons; create security conditions for the provision of humanitarian assistance and the voluntary return of refugees; assist in the electoral process; protect civilians under threat, as well as UN personnel and facilities.

UNMIS

United Nations Mission in the Sudan

Established: 24 March 2005.

Mandate: To support the implementation of the Comprehensive Peace Agreement signed between the Government of the Sudan and the Sudan People's Liberation Movement/Army on 9 January 2005; facilitate and coordinate the voluntary return of refugees and internally displaced persons, and humanitarian assistance; assist with humanitarian demining; and protect and promote human rights. The mandate was expanded in 2006 to support implementation of the May 2006 Darfur Peace Agreement (see p. 274) and the 2004 N'Djamena Humanitarian Ceasefire Agreement on the Conflict in Darfur [YUN 2004, p. 235].

Strength as at December 2006: 8,734 troops, 592 military observers, 680 civilian police.

UNMIT

United Nations Integrated Mission in Timor-Leste

Established: August 2006.

Mandate: To support the Government of Timor-Leste in: consolidating stability; enhancing a culture of democratic governance; facilitating political dialogue among stakeholders; the 2007 electoral process; establishing a continuous presence in the three border districts, alongside UN police officers; reviewing the future role and needs of the security sector; building the capacity of State and Government institutions and strengthening capacity and mechanisms for monitoring, promoting and protecting human rights; and promoting justice and reconciliation.

Strength as at December 2006: 32 military observers, 1,099 civilian police.

Financial and administrative aspects of peacekeeping operations

The General Assembly considered a number of issues related to the financial and administrative aspects of UN peacekeeping operations, including budget presentation; the use of consultants; vacancy rates; staffing of field missions; accountability, fraud, corruption, mismanagement, misconduct and conflict of interest; integrated missions; procurement; quick-impact projects; regional cooperation; fuel management; cost structure for air operations; spare parts; better use of technology; disaster recovery; and strategic deployment stocks. It also considered issues related to the peacekeeping support accounts; the consolidation of peacekeeping accounts; commitment authority; accounts and auditing; reimbursement issues, including the UN Logistics Base; and restructuring issues and personnel matters. (These issues are considered in their respective sections below.)

GENERAL ASSEMBLY ACTION

On 30 June [meeting 92], the General Assembly, on the recommendation of the Fifth Committee [A/60/916], adopted **resolution 60/266** without vote [agenda item 136].

Administrative and budgetary aspects of the financing of the United Nations peacekeeping operations: cross-cutting issues

The General Assembly,

Recalling its resolutions 49/233 A of 23 December 1994, 49/233 B of 31 March 1995, 51/218 E of 17 June 1997, 57/290 B of 18 June 2003, 58/315 of 1 July 2004 and 59/296 of 22 June 2005,

Having considered the interim report of the Advisory Committee on Administrative and Budgetary Questions on the administrative and budgetary aspects of the financing of the United Nations peacekeeping operations,

I

1. *Reaffirms* its resolution 59/296, and requests full implementation of its relevant provisions;
2. *Appreciates* the efforts of all peacekeeping personnel in the field and at Headquarters;
3. *Decides* to consider the report of the Secretary-General on the overview of the financing of the United Nations peacekeeping operations and other relevant reports on the administrative and budgetary aspects of the financing of the United Nations peacekeeping operations at the main part of its sixty-first session;
4. *Requests* the Secretary-General to report to the General Assembly at its sixty-first session on progress in training in peacekeeping;

II

Budget presentation

1. *Recalls* the unique nature and mandate of each operation, and stresses that the resource requirements should respond to the mandates and circumstances of each operation;
2. *Requests* the Secretary-General to continue to undertake the review of staffing requirements, function and level of posts that would reflect evolving mandates, changing operational requirements, actual responsibilities and functions performed, with a view to ensuring the most cost-effective use of resources;
3. *Recalls* section I, paragraph 6, of its resolution 49/233 A, and requests the Secretary-General to include in all performance reports in respect of peacekeeping operations, the United Nations Logistics Base at Brindisi, Italy, and the support account, details of monthly expenditure patterns, as well as to provide, in the context of the consideration of the budget submission, to the extent possible, supplementary information on the most up-to-date financial data available on actual expenditures for the current period;
4. *Regrets* the late issuance and receipt of budgets of some peacekeeping operations, which has placed some considerable strain on the ability of the General Assembly to engage in a detailed consideration of the requirements, and requests the Secretary-General to make every effort to improve the timely submission of peacekeeping budgets;
5. *Notes* the practice of allowing peacekeeping staff to take up temporary duty positions in other peacekeeping missions, and requests the Secretary-General to review this practice, including for staff currently seconded on temporary duty, to consider ways to limit the length of temporary duty secondments as well as to elaborate on the exceptions and ensure that such secondments do not impact adversely on the operational activities of the parent mission, in particular when the parent mission has existing vacancies;

III

Use of consultants

1. *Requests* the Secretary-General to ensure full utilization of synergies present in the United Nations system and to develop an effective evaluation mechanism for the use of outside expertise;

2. *Also requests* the Secretary-General to ensure that the commissioning of external consultants in the Organization by senior management and programme managers is conducted according to established administrative procedures and financial regulations and rules, with full respect for the mandates of internal and external oversight bodies and the oversight role of the General Assembly, and to report thereon;

IV

High vacancy rates

1. *Requests* the Secretary-General to intensify his ongoing efforts, including through innovative approaches, to ensure the expeditious filling of all vacant posts;

2. *Also requests* the Secretary-General to continue to ensure greater use of national staff in peacekeeping operations;

3. *Further requests* the Secretary-General, cognizant of the continuously high international staff vacancy rates in many missions, to consider, when formulating budget submissions, greater utilization of national staff, as appropriate, commensurate with the requirements of the mission and its mandate;

4. *Requests* the Secretary-General to strengthen coordination between the Department of Peacekeeping Operations of the Secretariat and the United Nations Volunteers programme for the use of volunteers in peacekeeping operations and to evaluate the contribution of United Nations Volunteers as a component of peacekeeping operations;

V

Accountability, fraud, corruption, mismanagement, misconduct and conflict of interest

1. *Notes with concern* the observations contained in the reports of the Advisory Committee on Administrative and Budgetary Questions, the Board of Auditors and the Office of Internal Oversight Services, concerning instances of non-compliance with established guidelines, rules, regulations and procedures;

2. *Regrets* any incidence of fraud, corruption, mismanagement and misconduct;

3. *Requests* the Secretary-General, within his purview, to address all cases of fraud, corruption, mismanagement and misconduct and to ensure that United Nations staff are held accountable for any proven wrongdoings;

4. *Also requests* the Secretary-General to entrust the Office of Internal Oversight Services with ensuring that all current and future investigations by the Office are conducted impartially, thoroughly, expeditiously, taking into account current capacity, and with full respect for due process, and that they are not subject to any unnecessary delays;

5. *Further requests* the Secretary-General to take all necessary steps to recover financial and other losses and to take appropriate measures to prevent fraud, corruption, mismanagement and misconduct;

6. *Requests* the Secretary-General to ensure that the application and enforcement of accountability in the United Nations system is carried out impartially at all levels and without exception;

7. *Notes with concern* the increase in the level of fraud and presumptive fraud in respect of fuel abuse within some peacekeeping operations, and requests the Secretary-General to ensure that lessons learned from addressing these cases are shared systematically with all missions;

8. *Requests* the Secretary-General to report to the General Assembly at its sixty-first session on the implementation of paragraphs 1 to 7 above;

9. *Reiterates* paragraph 28 of its resolution 52/226 A of 31 March 1998 and paragraph 30 of its resolution 54/14 of 29 October 1999, related to the issue of conflict of interest, and requests the Secretary-General to ensure their expeditious implementation and to submit the proposals requested in the aforementioned paragraphs to the General Assembly at the main part of its sixty-first session;

VI

Integrated missions

1. *Requests* the Secretary-General to continue to refine the concept and functioning of integrated missions, strengthening the mission planning process, and to clearly detail lines of responsibility and accountability within integrated missions as well as the interaction between such missions and the different partners;

2. *Also requests* the Secretary-General to ensure that the utilization of mission assets by United Nations agencies is fully justified and reimbursed and that such utilization is duly recorded and reported properly;

VII

Procurement opportunities

1. *Requests* the Secretary-General, taking fully into account the observations of the Board of Auditors, in paragraphs 71 to 74 of its report, to increase efforts to improve procurement opportunities for vendors from developing countries and countries with economies in transition, in accordance with the relevant resolutions of the General Assembly, and to report to the Assembly at its sixty-first session on the implementation thereof;

2. *Recalls* section XVI, paragraph 4, of its resolution 59/296, and requests the Secretary-General to continue to ensure that information on procurement opportunities in peacekeeping operations is made available to business communities, in particular in developing countries and countries with economies in transition, through, inter alia, continued cooperation between the Department of

Public Information of the Secretariat and the Procurement Service of the Department of Management of the Secretariat, utilizing the United Nations information centres and offices, as appropriate;

3. *Requests* the Secretary-General to make the *United Nations Procurement Manual* available to Member States through the website of the Procurement Service no later than August 2006;

VIII

Quick-impact projects

1. *Welcomes* the inclusion of quick-impact projects in the budgets of peacekeeping operations, and recognizes the important contribution that they make towards the successful implementation of the mandates of peacekeeping operations;

2. *Stresses* that quick-impact projects are an integral part of mission planning and development, as well as of the implementation of comprehensive strategies to meet the challenges facing complex peacekeeping operations;

3. *Emphasizes* the need for a comprehensive policy, including on resource allocations, for quick-impact projects, and, bearing in mind the unique nature and mandate of each operation, requests the Secretary-General to report thereon to the General Assembly at its sixty-first session, addressing, inter alia: the definition of quick-impact projects and the selection processes; the duration of such projects; how, and if, quick-impact projects complement the activities of other United Nations bodies on the ground; the role of the Mission, other United Nations bodies and implementing partners in managing and implementing quick-impact projects in the short and longer term; and how administrative costs can be minimized;

IX

Regional cooperation

1. *Welcomes* the efforts to increase collaboration between missions, in particular those in the same region, and emphasizes the importance of further enhancing collaboration, to the extent possible, with a view to achieving greater synergy in the effective and efficient use of the resources of the United Nations and the implementation of missions' mandates, bearing in mind that individual missions bear a responsibility for the preparation and for overseeing their own budgets and for controlling their own assets and logistical operations;

2. *Requests* the Secretary-General to develop and implement regional coordination plans aligned to the missions' objectives, while mindful of the specific mandate of each mission, and to report on the progress achieved in the context of his next overview report;

X

Fuel management

Requests the Secretary-General to review all aspects of fuel management, including the preparation of a comprehensive fuel management manual, implementation of the electronic fuel accounting system, development of standard operating procedures on fuel management and preparation of an annual fuel procurement plan, and to report on the status of implementation;

XI

Costing structure for air operations

1. *Welcomes* the efforts to enhance the optimal use of air assets, and requests the Secretary-General to ensure that operations share best practices in order to increase utilization of air assets;

2. *Requests* the Secretary-General to undertake an analysis of the impact of the new costing structure relating to air operations, bearing in mind the relevant observations and recommendations of the Advisory Committee on Administrative and Budgetary Questions and the Board of Auditors, to determine whether the application of the new costing structure for air operations contracts has resulted in savings or brought about other benefits and to report thereon to the General Assembly at the sixty-second session in the context of his overview report;

3. *Also requests* the Secretary-General, mindful of the importance of air services to the effective operational activities of peacekeeping operations, to review, in all peacekeeping operations, the ongoing necessity and current frequency of flights, to ensure the optimal use of air assets, to reconfigure them to respond to changing circumstances, to increase the utilization of air assets, inter alia, by continuing to review flight schedules to accommodate more passengers and cargo and to report thereon to the General Assembly at its sixty-first session;

4. *Further requests* the Secretary-General to continue to explore ways to increase regional management of air assets and further strengthen the coordination between the Department of Peacekeeping Operations and relevant United Nations departments and entities, with a view to sharing air assets, when feasible;

XII

Spare parts

1. *Encourages* the Secretary-General to continue his efforts to limit the acquisition of new spare parts in the light of the current high level of holdings, requests the Secretary-General to report to the General Assembly at its sixty-first session on optimal levels for spare parts in all missions, and also requests that the budget proposals for the period from 1 July 2007 to 30 June 2008 not exceed those levels;

2. *Requests* the Secretary-General to report to the General Assembly at its sixty-first session on the possible establishment of a mechanism for global management of spare parts at United Nations Headquarters, including the ongoing identification of spare parts requirements, the capacity to redeploy them from other missions and any efficiencies to be achieved from such a mechanism;

XIII

Better use of technology

Requests the Secretary-General to make greater use of videoconferencing facilities and e-learning programmes for training and other purposes and to report to the General Assembly at its sixty-first session on improvements and efficiencies made through greater utilization of those tools;

XIV

Staffing of field missions, including the use of 300-series and 100-series appointments

Having considered the report of the Secretary-General on the staffing of field missions, including the use of 300-series and 100-series appointments and the related report of the Advisory Committee on Administrative and Budgetary Questions,

1. *Takes note* of the report of the Secretary-General on the staffing of field missions, including the use of 300-series and 100-series appointments;
2. *Recalls* section VIII of its resolution 59/296;
3. *Decides* to continue to suspend the application of the four-year maximum limit for appointments of limited duration until 31 December 2006;
4. *Authorizes* the Secretary-General, bearing in mind paragraph 3 above, to reappoint, under the 100 series of the Staff Rules, those mission staff whose service under 300-series contracts has reached the four-year limit by 31 December 2006, provided that their functions have been reviewed and found necessary and their performance has been confirmed as fully satisfactory, and requests the Secretary-General to report thereon to the General Assembly at its sixty-first session;
5. *Requests* the Secretary-General to continue the practice of using 300-series contracts as the primary instrument for the appointment of new staff;

XV

Disaster recovery

Requests the Secretary-General to submit to the General Assembly at its resumed sixty-first session a comprehensive report on the proposed establishment of and justification for mission onsite, mission in theatre and off site, and off site and out-of-theatre redundant data centres for disaster recovery and business continuity in peacekeeping missions, as well as on a secondary active communications facility and a disaster recovery and business continuity centre for information technology;

XVI

Strategic deployment stocks

Requests the Secretary-General to submit to the General Assembly at its sixty-first session a comprehensive report on the implementation of strategic deployment stocks and the use of logistics base and installations, as well as all mechanisms for rapid deployment, including on the evolving concepts used in this regard, taking fully into account the surge in peacekeeping operations, the location, operational and strategic requirements of peacekeeping operations and the need to ensure the utmost efficiencies in the use of resources.

By **decision 60/551 C** of 7 July, the Assembly deferred until its sixty-first (2006) session consideration of the Secretary-General's 2005 report on the updated financial position of closed peacekeeping missions as at 30 June 2005 and the related ACABQ report [YUN 2005, p. 142].

On 22 December, the Assembly decided that the agenda item "Administrative and budgetary aspects of the financing of the United Nations peacekeeping operations" would remain for consideration during its resumed sixty-first (2007) session (**decision 61/552**).

Financing

Expenditures for United Nations peacekeeping operations for the period 1 July 2005 to 30 June 2006 totalled $4,582.8 million, compared to $4,074.3 million for the previous twelve-month period. The 12.5 per cent increase in expenditure was mainly attributable to the full-year impact of UNMIS and the expansion of MINUSTAH, MONUC and UNOCI, which was offset by the closure of the United Nations Mission in Sierra Leone (UNAMSIL) and the United Nations Mission of Support in East Timor (UNMISET) in 2005 [YUN 2005, p. 131], as well as scaled-down operations in ONUB, UNMEE, UNMIK and UNMIL.

Overall liquidity improved markedly, as assessments and expenditures for active missions increased, while unpaid assessments decreased by $375.3 million or 34 per cent. There was no significant change with respect to unpaid assessments of closed missions. As at 30 June 2006, total unpaid assessments amounted to $1.3 billion, compared to $1.7 billion in the previous financial period.

Available cash for active missions totalled $1,642 million, while liabilities dropped to $1,419 million. For closed missions, available cash totalled $341.2 million, while liabilities came to $362.2 million. Closed missions with cash surpluses continued to be the only available source for lending to active peacekeeping missions. During the reporting period, new loans totalling $44.5 million were made. Total loans outstanding as at 30 June 2006, amounted to $23.6 million.

Notes of Secretary-General. In January [A/C.5/60/27], the Secretary-General, in accordance with General Assembly resolution 49/233 A [YUN 1994, p. 1338], submitted to the Assembly's Fifth Committee information on the approved resources for peacekeeping operations for the period 1 July

2005 to 30 June 2006, including requirements for the United Nations Logistics Base (UNLB) at Brindisi, Italy, and the support account for peacekeeping operations, amounting to $5,025,238,400. That figure took into account 2005 Assembly decisions in respect of MINUSTAH, MONUC, UNMIS and UNOCI.

In May [A/C.5/60/30], the Secretary-General submitted proposed budgetary requirements for peacekeeping operations, UNLB and the support account for peacekeeping operations for the period 1 July 2006 to 30 June 2007, amounting to $4,768,987,500; and in July [A/C.5/60/32], information on the approved resources for them for the same period, amounting to $4,747,282,700.

Financial performance

In February [A/60/696], the Secretary-General submitted an overview report on the financing of UN peacekeeping operations: budget performance for the period from 1 July 2004 to 30 June 2005 and the budget for the period from 1 July 2006 to 30 June 2007.

In April [A/60/784], the Advisory Committee on Administrative and Budgetary Questions (ACABQ), in its comments and observations on the report of the Board of Auditors on the accounts of UN peacekeeping operations for the period from 1 July 2004 to 30 June 2005 [A/60/5 (vol. II) & Corr.1] and the Secretary-General's report on the implementation of the Board's recommendations for the period ended 30 June 2005 [A/60/691], noted the Board of Auditors' concern over the increase in the cancellation of prior-period obligations from $73.6 million to $167.8 million in 2004-2005, indicating either a need to improve budget planning and monitoring or invalid obligations had initially been raised, and urged the Administration to take prompt action to address any shortcomings in that regard. As to the registration of prospective local vendors, ACABQ said that a common framework or guidance was needed for ensuring consistency in the relevant procedures for evaluating those vendors. The Committee, noting that non-compliance with procurement directives had resulted in the failure to obtain performance bonds, supported the Board's recommendation that they should be obtained in a timely manner. It urged the Administration to re-examine the contract approval process, including the delegation of authority, giving due account to the need for strong accountability measures.

ACABQ shared the Board's view that the Administration should formalize the concept of integrated mission partnerships, determine their function, structure and role, and finalize principles, policies and guidelines for governing them, paying careful attention to establishing clear lines of accountability.

ACABQ shared the Board's concern over the increase in the cases of fraud and presumptive fraud and encouraged the Administration to be proactive in its dealings with missions to ensure that cases were reported in a timely and accurate manner. The Committee requested the Administration to confirm the final list of fraud and presumptive fraud cases to the Board.

In June [A/60/880], ACABQ submitted an interim report on a number of cross-cutting issues in peacekeeping operations due to the late submission of Secretariat documentation and the subsequent delay in convening its winter session. Those issues related to: the assignment of staff to temporary duty in other missions; the use of general temporary assistance; air operations; quick-impact projects; fraud; the use of consultants; high vacancy rates in missions; and integrated and complex missions. The Committee recommended that any current consideration of cross-cutting issues should be preliminary in nature, pending a broader, definitive exposition of those matters after the relevant documentation had been received and considered.

Peacekeeping support account

In February [A/60/681 & Corr.1 & Add.1], the Secretary-General submitted the financial performance report on the budget of the support account for peacekeeping operations for the period from 1 July 2004 to 30 June 2005. Expenditure for the period totalled $118,025,500 against approved resources of $121,610,300, resulting in an unencumbered balance of $3,584,800, attributable mainly to underexpenditure in respect of post resources, as well as unspent balances under official travel, facilities and infrastructure, communications, information technology, medical and other supplies, services and equipment. The Secretary-General recommended that Member States waive their respective shares in other income and from the unencumbered balance, to be applied to meeting current and future UN after-service health insurance liabilities, and that the remaining unencumbered balance of $2,719,100 be applied to the 2006/2007 support account budget.

In March [A/60/727], the Secretary-General submitted the budget for the support account for the period from 1 July 2006 to 30 June 2007 in the amount of $189,538,800, which provided for 831 continuing posts and a net increase of 142 posts, representing 146 new posts, the transfer of five existing resident auditor posts from UNMIS to the support account budget, the abolishment of four resident auditor posts in UNAMSIL and the transfer of five posts from the support account to UNLB.

In April [A/60/807], ACABQ, while noting that peacekeeping missions had evolved into complex, multidimensional operations, emphasized that additional functions or tasks to be performed should not necessarily lead to a requirement for additional posts, nor should the creation of new units be proposed as a means to justify new or higher-level posts. The Committee reiterated that an analysis of the support account, as described in its 2005 report [YUN 2005, p. 140], be conducted by the Board of Auditors, which should also determine whether posts approved by the General Assembly in the years following the 2000 report of the Panel on United Nations Peace Operations [YUN 2000, p. 83] had been and continued to be used for the intended purposes. It should also analyse the ability of the relevant departments to manage senior staff flexibility so as to respond to new responsibilities and challenges without creating new structures and senior-level posts. An analysis should also be conducted of whether funds expended on consultancy represented the best use of financial resources, and on how the support account related to the regular budget.

ACABQ recommended approval of 55 posts of the 142 net additional posts proposed by the Secretary-General; that 45 posts not be approved; and that action on 42 be deferred. Of the posts recommended for deferral, 22 would be considered in the context of the Secretary-General's forthcoming report on the evaluation on governance and oversight, which would include a detailed review of OIOS. It also recommended reductions amounting to $31,663,500 gross ($28,786,100 net) in the proposed 2006-2007 support account budget. Should the Assembly not be able to take action on the report to be submitted in follow-up to the Secretary-General's report "Investing in the United Nations: for a stronger Organization worldwide" [A/60/692 & Corr.1] (see p. 1575), which included proposals related to peacekeeping (see p. 96), it might wish to consider approving general temporary assistance equivalent to 50 per cent of the posts deferred, amounting to an additional $2,425,800, including non-post resources.

With regard to the Secretary-General's recommendation that Member States waive their respective shares in other income and from the unencumbered balance, to be applied for meeting current and future after-service health insurance liabilities, ACABQ said that those amounts would be dealt with in a manner to be decided by the Assembly. The Committee recommended approval of the Secretary-General's proposal that the remaining unencumbered balance of $2,719,100 be applied to the 2006-2007 budget, and that the amount of $15,804,000 in excess of the authorized level of the Peacekeeping Reserve Fund, related to the period 1 July 2004 to 30 June 2005, be applied to the resources required for the period from 1 July 2006 to 30 June 2007.

OIOS support account resource requirements

The Secretary-General, in a June note [A/60/898] on resource requirements for the Office of Internal Oversight Services (OIOS) under the support account for peacekeeping operations for the period from 1 July 2006 to 30 June 2007, proposed that the General Assembly approve resources in the amount of $21,847,300 as an interim measure for OIOS in the support account for the 2006-2007 period, including $2,128,900 for general temporary assistance. The Secretary-General also proposed that the Assembly include the total amount in the resources for the support account for peacekeeping operations, to be prorated among the budgets of the active operations for the year ending 30 June 2007.

In June [A/60/900], ACABQ recommended maintenance of the resource level for the period from 1 July 2005 to 30 June 2006 and continuation of general temporary assistance approved in the 2005-2006 period, recosted using the budget parameters for the period 1 July 2006 to 30 June 2007, amounting to $18,799,600, on the understanding that the required level of resources for OIOS would be revisited following the Assembly's consideration of relevant forthcoming reports, including the Secretary-General's report on governance and oversight. It also recommended approval of 50 per cent of the $2,128,900 in additional resources proposed by the Secretary-General. ACABQ intended to revisit the question of resources required for OIOS under the support account once the relevant decisions had been taken by the Assembly. In that connection, the Secretary-General should prepare revised estimates, including for the support account, that would reflect such decisions.

GENERAL ASSEMBLY ACTION

On 30 June [meeting 92], the General Assembly, on the recommendation of the Fifth Committee [A/60/916], adopted **resolution 60/268** without vote [agenda item 136].

Support account for peacekeeping operations

The General Assembly,

Recalling its resolutions 45/258 of 3 May 1991, 47/218 A of 23 December 1992, 48/226 A of 23 December 1993, 56/241 of 24 December 2001, 56/293 of 27 June 2002, 57/318 of 18 June 2003, 58/298 of 18 June

2004 and 59/301 of 22 June 2005, its decisions 48/489 of 8 July 1994, 49/469 of 23 December 1994 and 50/473 of 23 December 1995 and other relevant resolutions of the General Assembly,

Having considered the reports of the Secretary-General on the financing of the support account for peacekeeping operations, the note by the Secretary-General on the resource requirements for the Office of Internal Oversight Services under the support account for peacekeeping operations for the financial period from 1 July 2006 to 30 June 2007 and the related reports of the Advisory Committee on Administrative and Budgetary Questions,

Recognizing the importance for the United Nations to be able to respond and deploy rapidly to a peacekeeping operation upon adoption of a relevant resolution of the Security Council, within thirty days for traditional peacekeeping operations and ninety days for complex peacekeeping operations,

Recognizing also the need for adequate support during all phases of peacekeeping operations, including the liquidation and termination phases,

Mindful that the level of the support account should broadly correspond to the mandate, number, size and complexity of peacekeeping missions,

1. *Takes note* of the reports of the Secretary-General on the financing of the support account for peacekeeping operations and the note by the Secretary-General on the resource requirements for the Office of Internal Oversight Services under the support account for peacekeeping operations for the financial period from 1 July 2006 to 30 June 2007;

2. *Reaffirms* the need for effective and efficient administration and financial management of peacekeeping operations, and urges the Secretary-General to continue to identify measures to increase the productivity and efficiency of the support account;

3. *Also reaffirms* the need for adequate funding for the backstopping of peacekeeping operations, as well as the need for full justification for that funding in support account budget submissions;

4. *Requests* the Secretary-General to ensure the full implementation of the relevant provisions of its resolutions 59/296 of 22 June 2005 and 60/266 of 30 June 2006 as well as other relevant resolutions;

5. *Endorses* the conclusions and recommendations contained in the reports of the Advisory Committee on Administrative and Budgetary Questions, subject to the provisions of the present resolution;

6. *Decides* to establish the following posts:

(a) Senior Political Affairs Officer (P-5) for the United Nations Stabilization Mission in Haiti team in the Office of Operations of the Department of Peacekeeping Operations of the Secretariat;

(b) Policy Coordinator (P-4) in the Peacekeeping Best Practices Section of the Department of Peacekeeping Operations;

(c) Secretariat Services Officer (P-3) in the Fifth Committee secretariat;

(d) Information/communications expert (P-3) in support of the African Peacekeeping Capacity in the Department of Peacekeeping Operations in Addis Ababa;

(e) Administration/finance analyst (P-3) in support of the African Peacekeeping Capacity in the Department of Peacekeeping Operations in Addis Ababa;

7. *Also decides* to approve the establishment of the post of Chief of the Integrated Training Service (D-1) in the Department of Peacekeeping Operations, and requests the Secretary-General to evaluate the functioning of this post and to report thereon within the context of the support account budget for the financial period from 1 July 2007 to 30 June 2008;

8. *Further decides* to approve the establishment of the post of Chief of the Transport and Movement Service (D-1) of the Department of Peacekeeping Operations, to be funded from the abolishment of one existing P-4 post, with the balance of the requirements to be funded from within the approved level of the support account for the financial period from 1 July 2006 to 30 June 2007;

9. *Decides* to approve the establishment of the post of Environmental Engineer (P-3) in the Department of Peacekeeping Operations and requests the Secretary-General to rejustify the requirement for this post in the support account budget for the financial period from 1 July 2007 to 30 June 2008;

10. *Decides* not to approve the post of Security Coordinator Officer (P-4) in the Department of Safety and Security, and requests the Secretary-General to rejustify the requirement for this post in the support account budget for the financial period from 1 July 2007 to 30 June 2008;

11. *Decides* to approve an amount of 23,265,700 United States dollars in general temporary assistance and an amount of 4,417,900 dollars in non-post resources in the financial period from 1 July 2006 to 30 June 2007 in respect of the African Peacekeeping Capacity in the Department of Peacekeeping Operations, the Office of Internal Oversight Services, the Procurement Service and the Headquarters Committee on Contracts in the Department of Management of the Secretariat, procurement-related functions in the Office of Legal Affairs of the Secretariat and in the Department of Peacekeeping Operations, and conduct and discipline capacity in the Department of Peacekeeping Operations;

12. *Decides* not to approve an amount of 154,200 dollars under consultancy;

13. *Notes* the request of the Advisory Committee on Administrative and Budgetary Questions and requests the Secretary-General to undertake a comprehensive analysis of the evolution of the support account, on the basis of the recommendation of the Advisory Committee and in close consultation with the Office of Internal Oversight Services, bearing in mind section IV, paragraph 5, of General Assembly resolution 59/296, and to share the analysis with the Board of Auditors, and to report thereon to the Assembly at the second part of its resumed sixty-first session within the context of his next budget proposal for the support account;

14. *Reaffirms* section VIII of General Assembly resolution 53/221 of 7 April 1999, section IX of resolution 55/258 of 14 June 2001, section V of resolution 57/305 of 15 April 2003 and section XI of resolution 59/266 of 23 December 2004;

15. *Notes with concern* that the financial provision for consultants has steadily increased in recent years despite the parallel provision of additional posts for the support account, while bearing in mind that the provisions were needed, inter alia, to enhance the quality of work, management efficiencies and skills of staff;

16. *Requests* the Secretary-General, when proposing resources for consultancies in subsequent support account budgets, to include a trend-analysis comparing the requested level of resources with the approved resource levels in the previous five financial years and to provide supplementary information with full justification for all consultancies including, inter alia, information on why the expertise is not available within the Organization;

17. *Also requests* the Secretary-General to entrust to the Office of Internal Oversight Services the task of refining the methodology for allocating resident auditors, taking also into account the risks and complexity of the operation of individual peacekeeping operations, and to report thereon to the General Assembly;

18. *Further requests* the Secretary-General to report to the General Assembly at its sixty-first session, within the appropriate context, on the efforts made in support of African Union capacity-building, taking into account the functions and contributions to be provided by the United Nations, its funds, programmes and agencies and all external partners, including the efforts made to avoid duplication and overlap;

19. *Requests* the Secretary-General to elaborate, at the sixty-first session of the General Assembly, on the relationship between the Senior Review Group and the proposed senior leadership review group in the Department of Peacekeeping Operations within the context of human resources management;

20. *Decides* to maintain, for the financial period from 1 July 2006 to 30 June 2007, the funding mechanism for the support account used in the current period, from 1 July 2005 to 30 June 2006, as approved in paragraph 3 of its resolution 50/221 B of 7 June 1996;

21. *Reaffirms* the need for the Secretary-General to ensure that the delegation of authority to the Department of Peacekeeping Operations and field missions is in strict compliance with relevant resolutions and decisions and the relevant rules and procedures of the General Assembly on this matter;

Financial performance report for the period from 1 July 2004 to 30 June 2005

22. *Takes note* of the report of the Secretary-General on the financial performance of the support account for peacekeeping operations for the period from 1 July 2004 to 30 June 2005;

Budget estimates for the financial period from 1 July 2006 to 30 June 2007

23. *Approves* the support account requirements in the amount of 183,187,000 dollars for the financial period from 1 July 2006 to 30 June 2007, including 734 continuing and 56 new temporary posts and their related post and non-post requirements;

Financing of the budget estimates

24. *Decides* that the requirements for the support account for peacekeeping operations for the financial period from 1 July 2006 to 30 June 2007 shall be financed as follows:

(a) The unencumbered balance of 3,584,800 dollars and other income of 2,121,900 dollars in respect of the financial period ended 30 June 2005, to be applied to the resources required for the financial period from 1 July 2006 to 30 June 2007;

(b) The amount of 15,804,000 dollars in excess of the authorized level of the Peacekeeping Reserve Fund in respect of the financial period ended 30 June 2005, to be applied to the resources required for the financial period from 1 July 2006 to 30 June 2007;

(c) The balance of 161,676,300 dollars to be prorated among the budgets of the active peacekeeping operations for the financial period from 1 July 2006 to 30 June 2007;

(d) The net estimated staff assessment income of 18,186,100 dollars, comprising the amount of 18,804,200 dollars for the financial period from 1 July 2006 to 30 June 2007 and the decrease of 618,100 dollars in respect of the financial period ended 30 June 2005, to be set off against the balance referred to in subparagraph *(c)* above, to be prorated among the budgets of the individual active peacekeeping operations.

Consolidation of peacekeeping accounts

The Secretary-General, among the reform measures contained in his report "Investing in the United Nations: for a stronger Organization worldwide" [A/60/692 & Corr.1], made a number of proposals for improving financial management, including consolidating peacekeeping accounts (see below) and increasing the ceiling for commitment authority (see p. 97).

In the report, the Secretary-General again proposed that peacekeeping accounts for separate field missions be consolidated into a single set of accounts and reports, starting in 2007, to improve cash management and operational flexibility. The issue was last raised in 2003, when the General Assembly requested, in resolution 57/319 [YUN 2003, p. 90], that the Secretary-General submit a comprehensive report on the subject.

In response to the Secretary-General's report, the Assembly's 2003 request and its **resolution 60/260** of 8 May 2006 (see p. 1576), the Secretary-General, in a 12 May report [A/60/846], elaborated on the proposals put forward in his March report, taking into consideration guidance provided by ACABQ on 24 March [A/60/735]. Under the proposal related to financial management practices, the Assembly was requested to consolidate the various peacekeeping accounts retroactively, excluding those of the United Nations Emergency Force (UNEF), the United Nations Operation in the Congo (ONUC), the Peacekeeping Reserve Fund and the strategic deployment stocks, effective 1 July 2007. It was also asked to consolidate the individual resolutions on the financing of peacekeeping operations into a single resolution beginning with the 2007-2008 fiscal period, and the various peacekeeping assessments on Member States into two assessments at the beginning and at the halfway point of the peacekeeping fiscal period, also starting with the 2007-2008 period; and approve the de-linking of assessments for peacekeeping operations from the duration of the mandates approved by the Security Council and issue assessments in two separate components, and the consolidation of individual performance reports into a single report that would provide the overall peacekeeping budget level, as well as performance data identifying the budget provisions and expenditures for each individual mission. The Assembly was further asked to apply to the consolidated account the standard practice of utilizing unencumbered balances, interest income and other miscellaneous income to provide the first element of financing of appropriations for the subsequent fiscal period; return to Member States credits available in the accounts of closed missions with cash surpluses; and settle outstanding liabilities in the accounts of closed missions with cash deficits, except for ONUC and UNEF, on the date of consolidation.

An addendum to the report [A/60/846/Add.3] provided further details concerning the Secretary-General's proposals in terms of the implications, benefits and specific issues to be considered. The proposed consolidation of the separate peacekeeping accounts into a single set of accounts and reports would allow a more consistent and timely reimbursement to troop- and formed police-contributing countries by improving cash management and operational flexibility, and would simplify the legislative and administrative processes for the financing of peacekeeping operations. It would result in the combined recording and accounting for income, expenditure, assets and liabilities for all peacekeeping operations in a single fund, while preserving the substantive identity of the budgeted provisions for, and expenditures of, individual missions. The consolidation should also assist the Assembly in better fulfilling its financial management functions, facilitate planning by Member States and the review of the financing of peacekeeping operations by legislative bodies, allow greater flexibility in the use of peacekeeping resources.

It was proposed that the consolidation should be effective no later than 1 July 2007 for the 2007-2008 financial period. The current overall level of the Peacekeeping Reserve Fund at $150 million was, based on past experience, considered adequate to cover requirements for start-up or expansion of peacekeeping operations. The consolidation of peacekeeping accounts would strengthen liquidity and working capital further and permit repayment of the outstanding loan of $12.8 million by the United Nations Mission in the Central African Republic.

Annexed to the addendum were mock-ups of a financing resolution, an assessment note and financial statements; an outline of the proposed consolidated performance report; a summary of the changes proposed to the current practice; and a table illustrating the effect of consolidation on the reimbursement to troop- and formed police-contributing countries for 2004 and 2005.

In June [A/60/870], ACABQ said that it was for Member States to decide whether or not the managerial advantages of the consolidation of peacekeeping accounts outweighed the fact that the overall availability of cash would continue to depend on the prompt payment of assessments by Member States. Consideration of the related proposals depended on the decisions the Assembly might take with regard to the consolidation of peacekeeping accounts.

The General Assembly, in section VII of **resolution 60/283** of 7 July (see p. 1580), deferred consideration of the consolidation of peacekeeping accounts until the second part of its resumed sixty-first (2007) session.

Commitment authority

The Secretary-General, in his March report "Investing in the United Nations: for a stronger Organization worldwide" [A/60/692 & Corr.1], proposed that the ceiling of the commitment authority granted by the General Assembly for peacekeeping operations be increased from $50 million to $150 million and de-linked from a specified number of Security Council decisions.

ACABQ, in its comments and observations on the Secretary-General's proposals contained in its March report [A/60/735], said that clear and convincing justification was needed before the ceiling of the commitment authority for peacekeeping operations could be considered.

In his May report [A/60/846] elaborating further those proposals, the Secretary-General said that the scope of the commitment authority granted him by resolution 49/233 A [YUN 1994, p. 1338] was expanded when the Assembly approved, in resolution 59/299 [YUN 2005, p. 145], the inclusion of strategic deployment stocks replenishment within that authority.

In view of the increasing size of new and expanding peacekeeping operations, including complex integrated structures and large military components, and the current practice of including projected expenditures for the replenishment of strategic deployment stocks in the overall estimate of requirements based on a decision of the Security Council relating to the start-up phase or expansion of peacekeeping operations, it was necessary to review the level of commitment authority currently established at a ceiling of $50 million per decision of the Security Council, not to exceed three such decisions. The Secretary-General outlined a proposed model for planning and start-up, including strategic deployment concept and replenishment, including estimated costs of $7.2 million for six months for a dedicated integrated planning team. Details on the composition of the planning team and related costing parameters were provided in an annex to the addendum. The model showed that for a complex mission, the current pre-mandated commitment authority of $50 million was inadequate to cover not only mission planning and start-up as originally conceived, but also complete strategic deployment stocks replenishment, which was critical in ensuring that adequate stocks were available to enable rapid deployment of peacekeeping operations. Under the Secretary-General's proposal (see above), the pre-mandate commitment authority would be requested based on the individual mission planning requirements, including replenishment of the strategic deployment stocks, up to but not to exceed the level of the Peacekeeping Reserve Fund of $150 million. If the Fund was fully committed and the establishment of a new peacekeeping mission was anticipated, the matter would be brought to the General Assembly for a decision on commitment authority and assessment, in accordance with resolution 49/233 A. The proposal would not require additional funding from Member States, since the existing limit of the Peacekeeping Reserve Fund would be maintained. Governance and oversight arrangements would also remain unchanged.

The Secretary-General requested that the Assembly authorize him, with the prior concurrence of ACABQ, to enter into commitments not to exceed the current authorized level of the Peacekeeping Reserve Fund of $150 million, regardless of the number of Security Council decisions; increase the current delegation of commitment authority to ACABQ to the current authorized level of the Fund; and amend financial regulations 4.6 and 4.8 by replacing in each case the figure of $50 million with $150 million.

In a June report [A/60/870], ACABQ pointed out that the current level of commitment authority was set in 1994 in response to a sharp increase in peacekeeping activities, and it was not clear that the current heightened level of activity would continue. Moreover, commitment authority was decided on an urgent basis for the start-up phase of a mission, and ACABQ did not want to be in a position in which it would agree to a budget and related decisions without the necessary time for proper elaboration and consideration. For those reasons, ACABQ recommended that the current procedures for granting commitment authority be maintained.

The General Assembly, in section VII of **resolution 60/283** of 7 July (see p. 1580), deferred consideration of increases in the Peacekeeping Reserve Fund and commitment authority until the second part of its resumed sixty-first (2007) session.

Accounts and auditing

At its resumed sixtieth (2006) session, the General Assembly considered the financial report and audited financial statements for UN peacekeeping operations for 1 July 2004 to 30 June 2005 [A/60/5 (vol. II) & Corr.1], the Secretary-General's report on the implementation of the recommendations of the Board of Auditors [A/60/691] and the related ACABQ report [A/60/784].

GENERAL ASSEMBLY ACTION

On 30 June [meeting 92], the General Assembly, on the recommendation of the Fifth Committee [A/60/561/Add.1], adopted **resolution 60/234 B** without vote [agenda item 121].

Financial reports and audited financial statements, and reports of the Board of Auditors

The General Assembly,

Recalling its resolutions 58/249 B of 18 June 2004, 59/264 B of 22 June 2005 and 60/234 A of 23 December 2005,

Having considered the financial report and audited financial statements for the twelve-month period from 1 July 2004 to 30 June 2005 and the report of the Board of Auditors on the United Nations peacekeeping operations, the report of the Advisory Committee on Administrative and Budgetary Questions on the report of the Board of Auditors on the accounts of the United Nations peacekeeping operations for the financial period ended 30 June 2005 and the report of the Secretary-General on the implementation of the recommendations of the Board of Auditors concerning the United Nations peacekeeping operations for the period ended 30 June 2005,

1. *Accepts* the audited financial statements on the United Nations peacekeeping operations for the period from 1 July 2004 to 30 June 2005;

2. *Takes note* of the observations and endorses the recommendations contained in the report of the Board of Auditors;

3. *Also takes note* of the observations and endorses the recommendations contained in the report of the Advisory Committee on Administrative and Budgetary Questions related to the report of the Board of Auditors;

4. *Commends* the Board of Auditors for the quality of its report and the streamlined format thereof;

5. *Takes note* of the report of the Secretary-General on the implementation of the recommendations of the Board of Auditors concerning the United Nations peacekeeping operations in respect of the financial period ended 30 June 2005;

6. *Requests* the Secretary-General to ensure full implementation of the recommendations of the Board of Auditors and the related recommendations of the Advisory Committee in a prompt and timely manner;

7. *Also requests* the Secretary-General to indicate an expected time frame for the implementation of the recommendations of the Board of Auditors as well as the priorities for their implementation, including the office-holders to be held accountable;

8. *Further requests* the Secretary-General to provide, in the next report on the implementation of the recommendations of the Board of Auditors concerning the United Nations peacekeeping operations, full explanation for the delays in implementation of the recommendations of the Board for the period ended 30 June 2005 or the prior periods.

OIOS audit of standard costs applied to Headquarters overhead

In February [A/60/682], OIOS reported on its audit of the standard costs applied to Headquarters overhead. The audit, conducted pursuant to General Assembly resolution 59/301 [YUN 2005, p. 140], assessed whether the standard cost guidelines for estimating common service costs in New York were applied consistently during budget preparation. The audit covered estimates for facilities and infrastructure, communications, and information technology, totalling $18.3 million, which were included in the budget for the support account for peacekeeping operations for the period from 1 July 2005 to 30 June 2006.

OIOS found that the Department of Peacekeeping Operations (DPKO) had not established a policy for maintaining and updating the guidelines, which, in the past, had been adjusted only to reflect cost escalations based on an annual inflation rate of 2.2 per cent; some of the documentation for substantiating the cost structure of the guidelines was not available from the Department; and the guidelines were not applicable to all objects of expenditure. There were also instances in which the guidelines could have been applied but were not. In some of those cases, OIOS noted that the unit costs used by the Peacekeeping Financing Division were more appropriate, as they reflected current actual costs of goods and services.

With respect to costs for facilities and infrastructure, OIOS found that standard costs included in the guidelines needed to be aligned with the corresponding actual costs, and UN space standards were not applied consistently in estimating the costs of renting premises or making alterations and improvements. The Peacekeeping Financing Division did not apply the guidelines with regard to communications costs, establishing the budget instead on the basis of actual departmental expenditures, which, in the view of OIOS, was an effective practice that should be included in the guidelines. With respect to the budget for information technology, OIOS found that the actual cost structure for service-level agreements needed to be aligned with the current costs of services.

OIOS issued 12 recommendations for improving the use of standard costs in preparing the support account for the peacekeeping operations budget and for budget adjustments. It recommended that the Department of Management reassess the relevance of the standard cost guidelines every biennium or when major changes occurred in the way departments operated, and that it formalize its procedures for reviewing the standard cost guidelines. To facilitate budgetary control, the Department should improve its monitoring of the application of standard cost guidelines to the support account for peacekeeping operations. It should ensure that the Office of Central Support Services identified the most efficient space criterion for estimating rental costs, using the average market price, and align the standard costs for utilities, management and other rent-related costs with actual costs. In view of the significant variance between the standard cost per square foot and actual costs of alteration and improvement projects, the Department should revise the standard cost guidelines to include estimates based on justifiable historical expenditures.

OIOS recommended that the Department of Management update the standard cost guidelines to reflect the most current costs paid to the United Nations for furniture and the rental of office equipment and supplies. In updating the guidelines, the Department should estimate the communication costs for each department on the basis of historical expenditures and any other pertinent assumptions, instead of adopting a flat rate for all departments. The Information Technology Services Division should review the cost structure of service-level agreements to reflect actual costs, and the revised agreements should be included in the guidelines. It should develop a clear policy for determining an efficient printer/desktop ratio; update the costs of acquiring desktop computers, printers and laptop computers set out in the standard cost guidelines whenever new contractual agreements or market conditions required such a change; and estimate and include in the guidelines a provision for spare parts and supplies.

OIOS also recommended that the Department of Management revise the current estimates for the support account to reflect the cost estimates made by OIOS for each category of expenditure reviewed by the audit. The adjustments should result in a net reduction of $970,000 in the proposed support account budget for the period from 1 July 2005 to 30 June 2006.

The Department of Management generally accepted the recommendations issued by OIOS and would implement them by reviewing and updating the standard costs in the context of preparing the 2006-2007 support account budget.

By **decision 60/551 C** of 7 July, the Assembly deferred until its sixty-first (2006) session consideration of the OIOS report.

Results-based budgeting

In response to General Assembly resolution 57/290 B [YUN 2003, p. 83], the Secretary-General, in a March note [A/60/709], transmitted the Joint Inspection Unit (JIU) report entitled "Evaluation of results-based budgeting in peacekeeping operations". The evaluation was intended to identify and evaluate the critical factors for the successful implementation of results-based management, as a basis for developing a broad management strategy for UN peacekeeping operations, and provide a benchmarking framework for that implementation. The analysis was based on relevant elements of JIU's results-based management benchmarking framework, which covered the comprehensive implementation of results-based management. Since peacekeeping operations applied results-based budgeting and not results-based management, only some elements of the framework were included in the analysis. As results-based budgeting was a planning process for achieving results through improved strategic management, increased administrative and programme effectiveness and enhanced accountability of programme managers, there was an urgent need to develop further the results approach within peacekeeping operations. Therefore, the current implementation of results-based budgeting should be further developed towards a full implementation of results-based management, which should be applied with flexibility, taking into consideration the uniqueness and specific environment of each peacekeeping operation. The report also analysed the current peacekeeping planning process, and discussed aspects of the human resource management required for a sound implementation of any results-based approach, including accountability, delegation of authority, managerial flexibility and performance management, and all of which needed further development if full implementation were to be achieved.

The report set out nine benchmarks for achieving results-based management in peacekeeping operations. Those benchmarks related to a results-based management conceptual framework as a broad management strategy; the definition of the responsibilities of the main parties of the United Nations; the formulation of long-term objectives for the United Nations and the alignment of UN programmes with long-term objectives and resources; an effective performance monitoring system; the effective use of evaluation findings; the internalization of results-based management throughout the Organization; and the development of a knowledge-management strategy to support results-based management.

JIU recommended that the Assembly, in keeping with resolution 55/231 [YUN 2000, p. 1295], request the Secretary-General to develop feasible measures for implementing results-based management and apply them gradually and fully in peacekeeping operations. He should submit to the relevant organs for consideration and approval a proposal for assisting the Security Council in the adoption of coherent and consistent mandates and objectives for peacekeeping operations and the provision of related resources for their implementation. The Secretary-General's reports to the Council and Assembly on peacekeeping operations should conform with the principles, methodology and benchmarks of results-based management, in particular with regard to the need for proposing specific, measurable, attainable, relevant and time-bound mandates and objectives. The Assembly should re-examine the recommendation contained in the 2000 report of the Chairman of the Panel on United Nations Peace Operations [YUN 2000, p. 83] and request the Secretary-General to establish the Executive Committee on Peace and Security Information and Strategic Analysis secretariat [ibid., p. 84]. The Secretary-General, as the Chairman of the UN System Chief Executives Board for Coordination (CEB), should lead the preparation of an institutional framework within CEB for UN system involvement in integrated peace missions and submit it for approval by UN system organizations. He should enforce full integration and coordination within the Secretariat and UN funds and programmes throughout the planning, programming, budgeting, monitoring, evaluation and reporting cycle of the integrated missions by formulating a clear instruction in that regard and designating a leading coordinator department.

JIU further recommended that the Secretary-General review all aspects of human resources management in peacekeeping operations, with a view to realigning policies, regulations, rules, procedures and practices to the specific needs of the operations in a results-based management framework, and present a revised human resources management policy framework for the Assembly's consideration and approval at its resumed sixty-first (2007) session. He should review the disparity between the financial and human resources management cycles and recommend ways to harmonize them; and streamline the process of preparation, submission and approval of peacekeeping budgets. The Assembly should call upon internal and external oversight and control bodies to adhere to their advisory and mutually complementary functions in relation to the Assembly and the Secretary-General, and not interfere in the management of peacekeeping operations, and coordinate their oversight and control activities with a view to avoiding overlapping, duplications and potentially contradictory guidance in their coverage of operations.

Further recommendations dealt with the Secretary-General's report to the Security Council for new integrated missions and the consolidation of progress and performance reports related to results-based budgeting; the procedure for approving future peacekeeping operations; the development of the enterprise budget application by DPKO and the Office of Programme Planning, Budget and Accounts (OPPBA); and the development of a results-based management training module.

In March [A/60/709/Add.1], the Secretary-General, in transmitting his comments on the JIU report, noted that the application of results-based budgeting in peacekeeping operations had facilitated a greater understanding of the need to focus on the achievement of results.

Reimbursement issues

Methodology for rates of reimbursement to troop-contributing countries

The General Assembly, in resolution 59/298 [YUN 2005, p. 144], requested the Secretary-General to submit a comprehensive report on the rates used to reimburse troop-contributing countries to compensate for the pay and allowances of troops and for supplementary payments for specialists contributing to UN peacekeeping. Based on the information provided, it would also review the daily allowance for troops. The Secretary-General, in a March report on the review of the methodology for rates of reimbursement [A/60/725 & Add.1], proposed a methodology for determining those rates, as well as for adjusting the daily allowance for troops.

Since the establishment of the standard rates of reimbursement for troop-contributing countries by the Assembly in 1974 [YUN 1974, p. 215], they had been reviewed by the Secretariat nine times, and five surveys had been conducted. In 2001 and 2002, the Assembly had approved a 2 per cent increase on an interim and ad hoc basis because of problems with the reliability and validity of the data collected for review. The new methodology for determining the rates proposed by the Secretary-General, which took into account the guidance provided by the Assembly, consisted of four phases that would define the survey process, including survey design, data collection, data analysis and reporting. The survey design phase would cover periodicity, population and modes of dissemination of the survey. The data collection phase would determine the cost components of the survey and the actual questionnaire to be sent to the population, and cover the design of the portfolio of evidence for the collected data. The data analysis phase would define the response rate that would yield representative data on costs of countries contributing troops to peacekeeping, technical details on the calculation of the absorption factor used to analyse the cost data and the presentation (level of aggregation) of the actual rates of reimbursement. The reporting phase would describe how the outcomes of the data analysis would be conveyed to the Assembly, to enable fully informed decisions concerning rates of reimbursement.

Previous reviews had not considered the daily allowance for troops, which was originally intended to cover incidental personal requirements, and which had remained unchanged at the rate of $1.28 since 1974. In the absence of a methodology for conducting a review, the Secretary-General proposed a three-tiered approach. Data and views on the rate would be collected through separate questionnaires to force commanders and randomly selected peacekeepers, and the Secretariat would summarize the data from the surveys and report its findings to the Assembly for further consideration. The proposed questionnaires were contained in the addendum to the report.

The Secretary-General recommended that the Assembly approve: the proposed methodology for the rates of reimbursement, including the proposed questionnaire; the proposed rate of exchange reference for conversion of collected cost data from national currencies to United States dollars; the conduct of the first survey in 2006 and the proposed periodicity of every three years thereafter; and the proposed field questionnaires for collecting data on the daily allowance for troops.

Contingent-owned equipment

On 11 January [A/C.5/60/26], the Chairman of the 2004 Working Group on Contingent-Owned Equipment transmitted to the General Assembly the Contingent-Owned Equipment Manual. The Manual, which was distributed in the six official UN languages, would allow Member States to become fully conversant with contingent-owned equipment policy, processes and procedures, ensure a common understanding of those procedures, and improve their effective application.

Management of peacekeeping assets

UN Logistics Base

The General Assembly, at its resumed sixtieth (2006) session, considered the performance report on the budget of the United Nations Logistics Base (UNLB) at Brindisi, Italy, for the period from 1 July 2004 to 30 June 2005 and implementation of the strategic deployment stocks, including the award of contracts for procurement [A/60/700]. Expenditure for the period totalled $28,184,700 gross ($26,580,000 net) against total apportions of $28,422,000 gross ($26,861,400 net), resulting in an unencumbered balance of $237,300. The Assembly was asked to decide that Member States would waive their respective shares in other income for the period ended 30 June 2005 and from the unencumbered balance, to be applied to meeting current and future UN after-service health insurance liabilities. It was also asked to decide on the treatment of the remaining unencumbered balance.

As recommended by ACABQ in 2004 [YUN 2004, p. 100] and endorsed by the Assembly in resolution 58/297 [ibid., p. 99], the report also contained information on the implementation of the strategic deployment stocks and a summary of the award of strategic deployment stocks procurement contracts for the period from 1 July 2004 to 30 June 2005, during which the strategic deployment stock replenishment expenditure totalled $89,400,800 and assets valued at $106,657,000 were issued to missions.

The Assembly also had before it the proposed budget for UNLB for the period from 1 July 2006 to 30 June 2007 [A/60/711] in the amount of $35,621,200, an increase of $4,108,100, or 13 per cent in total resources over the previous twelve-month period, and provided for the deployment of 47 international and 169 national staff. It also included an initiative to relocate the Training Delivery Cell of DPKO's Integrated Training Service from Headquarters to UNLB and a pilot project to establish a regional aviation safety office at the Base.

In April [A/60/787], ACABQ recommended that the unencumbered balance and other income/adjustments for the period ended 30 June 2005 be credited to Member States in a manner to be determined by the Assembly, and that the Secretary-General's proposal on the financing of UNLB during the financial period ending 30 June 2007 be approved.

In June [A/C.5/60/31], the Secretary-General submitted to the Fifth Committee a note on the amounts to be appropriated in respect of each peacekeeping mission, including the prorated share of UNLB for the period from 1 July 2006 to 30 June 2007.

GENERAL ASSEMBLY ACTION

On 30 June [meeting 92], the General Assembly, on the recommendation of the Fifth Committee [A/60/916], adopted **resolution 60/267** without vote [agenda item 136].

Financing of the United Nations Logistics Base at Brindisi, Italy

The General Assembly,

Recalling section XIV of its resolution 49/233 A of 23 December 1994,

Recalling also its decision 50/500 of 17 September 1996 on the financing of the United Nations Logistics Base at Brindisi, Italy, and its subsequent resolutions and decisions thereon, the latest of which was resolution 59/299 of 22 June 2005,

Recalling further its resolution 56/292 of 27 June 2002 concerning the establishment of the strategic deployment stocks and its subsequent resolutions 57/315 of 18 June 2003, 58/297 of 18 June 2004 and 59/299 on the status of the implementation of the strategic deployment stocks,

Having considered the reports of the Secretary-General on the financing of the United Nations Logistics Base and implementation of the strategic deployment stocks, including the award of contracts for procurement, the report of the Secretary-General on the use of the United Nations Logistics Base to provide efficient and economical communications and information technology services, as well as other services, for United Nations peacekeeping and Headquarters clients, the report of the Secretary-General on the cost-benefit analysis on the issue of the transfer of vehicles with high mileage to the United Nations Logistics Base, to other missions and to upcoming

United Nations peacekeeping operations, and the related report of the Advisory Committee on Administrative and Budgetary Questions,

Reiterating the importance of establishing an accurate inventory of assets,

1. *Notes with appreciation* the facilities provided by the Government of Italy to the United Nations Logistics Base at Brindisi, Italy;

2. *Takes note* of the report of the Secretary-General on the use of the United Nations Logistics Base to provide efficient and economical communications and information technology services, as well as other services, for United Nations peacekeeping and Headquarters clients, and the report of the Secretary-General on the cost-benefit analysis on the issue of the transfer of vehicles with high mileage to the United Nations Logistics Base, to other missions and to upcoming United Nations peacekeeping operations;

3. *Also takes note* of the proposals of the Secretary-General for the establishment at the United Nations Logistics Base during the fiscal year 2007/08 of a strategic air operations centre, an aviation quality assurance programme, a central design unit and a geographical information system centre;

4. *Endorses* the conclusions and recommendations contained in the report of the Advisory Committee on Administrative and Budgetary Questions, and requests the Secretary-General to ensure their full implementation;

5. *Recalls* paragraph 3 of its resolution 59/299, in which it took note of the proposal to expand the United Nations Logistics Base, and requests the Secretary-General that detailed information on the concept of operations, financial and legal implications and expected benefits that may arise from the expansion be submitted with the budget for 2007/08 to the General Assembly for its decision;

6. *Requests* the Secretary-General to provide to the General Assembly at its sixty-first session, in the context of the reporting on the Training Delivery Cell, detailed information on the efficiency and effectiveness of all Department of Peacekeeping Operations training programmes to be implemented at the United Nations Logistics Base, drawing a comparison with training programmes provided at other facilities and United Nations offices;

7. *Welcomes* the establishment of a pilot project for the regional aviation safety office at the United Nations Logistics Base, and requests the Secretary-General to provide, to the extent possible, a preliminary assessment of the pilot project in the next presentation of the budget, and notes that if the concept is applicable it will consider proposals to establish regional aviation safety offices for other peacekeeping missions;

8. *Encourages* the Secretary-General to ensure the active participation of the Department of Peacekeeping Operations of the Secretariat in the negotiations with the Government of Italy concerning the possible extensions of the facilities at Brindisi;

9. *Requests* the Secretary-General, in future budget submissions, to report on any proposals to extend the facilities at Brindisi;

10. *Also requests* the Secretary-General to continue to analyse how the Logistics Base could best be utilized to provide efficient and economical communications and information technology services, as well as other services for United Nations peacekeeping and Headquarters clients, and to ensure that any related proposals contain full justification and detailed cost-benefit analyses;

11. *Further requests* the Secretary-General to ensure the full implementation of the relevant provisions of General Assembly resolutions 59/296 of 22 June 2005 and 60/266 of 30 June 2006;

12. *Reiterates* the need to implement, as a matter of priority, an effective inventory management standard, especially in respect of peacekeeping operations involving high inventory value;

Financial performance report for the period from 1 July 2004 to 30 June 2005

13. *Takes note* of the report of the Secretary-General on the financial performance of the United Nations Logistics Base for the period from 1 July 2004 to 30 June 2005 and implementation of the strategic deployment stocks, including the award of contracts for procurement;

Budget estimates for the period from 1 July 2006 to 30 June 2007

14. *Approves* the cost estimates for the United Nations Logistics Base amounting to 35,478,700 United States dollars for the period from 1 July 2006 to 30 June 2007;

Financing of the budget estimates

15. *Decides* that the requirements for the United Nations Logistics Base for the period from 1 July 2006 to 30 June 2007 shall be financed as follows:

(a) The unencumbered balance and other income in the total amount of 1,399,200 dollars in respect of the financial period ended 30 June 2005 to be applied against the resources required for the period from 1 July 2006 to 30 June 2007;

(b) The balance of 34,079,500 dollars to be prorated among the budgets of the active peacekeeping operations for the period from 1 July 2006 to 30 June 2007;

(c) The net estimated staff assessment income of 2,579,300 dollars, comprising the amount of 2,535,200 dollars for the period from 1 July 2006 to 30 June 2007 and the increase of 44,100 dollars in respect of the financial period ended 30 June 2005, to be set off against the balance referred to in subparagraph *(b)* above, to be prorated among the budgets of the individual active peacekeeping operations;

16. *Also decides* to consider at its sixty-first session the question of the financing of the United Nations Logistics Base at Brindisi, Italy.

In December [A/61/679], the Secretary-General submitted the financial performance report on the UNLB budget for the period from 1 July 2005 to 30 June 2006 and implementation of the strategic deployment stocks, including the award of contracts for procurement. Expenditure for the period totalled $27,527,400 gross ($25,678,300 net) against total apportionments of $31,513,100 gross ($29,280,000 net), resulting in a total unencumbered balance of $3,985,700. Strategic deployment stocks replenishment expenditure totalled $47,831,100, and assets valued at $30,625,600 were issued to missions.

Communications and information technology services

In March [A/60/715], the Secretary-General reported on the use of UNLB to provide efficient and economical communications and information technology services, and other services, for UN peacekeeping and Headquarters clients. In response to General Assembly resolution 59/299 [YUN 2005, p. 145], the Secretariat conducted a review of its peacekeeping operations and identified services that could be provided by UNLB.

The report discussed functions proposed for establishment at UNLB for the fiscal years 2006-2007 and 2007-2008. In 2006-2007, a Regional Aviation Safety Office and a Training Delivery Cell were to be established. In the 2007-2008 fiscal year, the significant increase in DPKO's aviation fleet would necessitate the strengthening of the Department's aviation programme for commercially contracted and Government-provided air assets by establishing a Strategic Operations Centre, which would consist of the Strategic Air Operations Centre and the Aviation Quality Assurance Programme. DPKO would establish a Central Design Unit at UNLB to reduce or eliminate the requirement for engineering skills in missions and standardize designs and drafting of accommodation and other engineering work. The establishment of a Geographical Information System Centre at UNLB would support rapid mission start-up and improve field mission readiness by, among other functions, acquiring/producing base geographical data for mission start-up and planning; providing on-demand geographical analysis and maps, Geographical Information System (GIS) application services and logistics and requisitions support for start-up missions; and deploying a GIS start-up team to provide on-site assistance.

The Secretariat continued to expand its operations at UNLB to meet the increasingly complex information needs of field missions and satisfy disaster recovery and business continuity requirements within infrastructure limitations. A centralized data backup system between field missions and UNLB, between UNLB and Headquarters, and vice versa, was in place. Other expansion projects included the centralization of information systems utilizing web technologies, the transfer of critical information and communications technology infrastructure and equipment to a secure and fault-tolerant facility, and an expansion of the video bridge to facilitate secure videoconferencing. DPKO would also establish a secondary active communications facility and a disaster recovery and business continuity centre for information and communications technology.

The report also cited major improvements in the composition of strategic deployment stocks, including increased capacities to support the material requirements of new minimum operating safety standards; increased variety and quantities of fuel equipment to support the rapid deployment of aircraft in remote locations; and the creation of a second fly-away kit to provide the capacity to support multiple rapid deployments of new or expanding peacekeeping operations.

Vehicles and other equipment

In response to General Assembly resolution 59/296 [YUN 2005, p. 133], the Secretary-General, in February [A/60/699], submitted a cost-benefit analysis on the issue of the transfer of high mileage vehicles to UNLB, other missions and upcoming UN peacekeeping operations. DPKO would continue to review the transfer of such vehicles to new and expanding missions, as exceptions and on a case-by-case basis, keeping in view operational needs, the condition of vehicles and the cost-effectiveness of such shipments.

In May [A/60/842], responding to Assembly resolution 59/270 [YUN 2004, 1368], the Secretary-General reported on the procedures implemented for the purchase and utilization of vehicles and other equipment by UN field missions. DPKO had greatly enhanced the level of standardization of its vehicle fleet by establishing system contracts for almost all of its vehicle requirements. As a result, about 90 per cent of the vehicle fleet would be sourced from six major manufacturers, with the remaining 10 per cent, including specialized equipment, from 70 different manufacturers. It also established system contracts for spare parts, as well as focal points in each mission to improve information-sharing and inter-mission cooperation on the use and transfer to other missions of excess spare parts.

DPKO reviewed the mission budgets to ensure that mission vehicle holdings were within the established standard ratios, and developed a policy setting limits on the number and price of vehicles for senior mission personnel. It took steps to help minimize vehicle accidents in missions, including the appointment of dangerous goods safety advisers in each mission, and established a system of vehicle rotation to ensure optimal use and maintenance of vehicles.

Air operations

In April [A/60/784], ACABQ, having considered the report of the Board of Auditors on the accounts of UN peacekeeping operations for the period from 1 July 2004 to 30 June 2005 [A/60/5 (Vol. II) & Corr.1], noted that DPKO had moved from the commercial industry approach of block-hours costing for air operations contracts to a costing structure whereby a basic monthly fee was paid, as well as a fee for every hour flown. ACABQ believed that DPKO had sufficient experience with implementing the new costing structure for air operations contracts to be able to undertake a meaningful analysis of its impact, and joined the Board in recommending that the Administration determine whether the change to the new costing structure had resulted in savings or other benefits. It reiterated its recommendation that DPKO continue to explore ways to increase regional management of air assets and recommended that DPKO coordinate with the UN Department of Political Affairs with a view to sharing assets between peacekeeping operations and special political missions.

Improvement of internal controls

In response to General Assembly resolution 59/270 [YUN 2004, p. 1368], the Secretary-General, in May [A/60/843], reported on the improvement of internal controls in management, accounting and reporting of assets of all UN field missions. DPKO prepared a comprehensive Property Management Manual, to be promulgated to all field missions in 2006, standardizing property management practices and providing guidance on day-to-day operational matters. It also issued related policies for standardizing the management, accounting and reporting of UN assets in field missions and annual guidelines for the preparation of financial year-end inventory reports, and monitored their submission from the field. Peacekeeping missions provided a monthly status report on the level of assets pending write-offs and disposal. DPKO completed the implementation of the Galileo Inventory Management System in peacekeeping missions in 2005 to facilitate the management and recording of United Nations–owned property. A Galileo asset disposal module was developed to enhance the utility of the system in the field, which was expected to be fully implemented by the second half of 2006. DPKO conducted training courses on property management for staff at UNLB and at Headquarters. It launched a one-year codification and data integrity project in 2005, which, on its completion in 2006, would improve the global oversight of assets. In response to a request by legislative bodies for a comprehensive review of property management, DPKO was constituting a Property Management Steering Group, which would review cross-cutting property management issues continuously and provide authoritative guidance on those issues.

Restructuring issues

Management audit

In response to General Assembly resolution 59/296 [YUN 2005, p. 133], the Secretary-General, in March [A/60/717], transmitted the OIOS report on the comprehensive management audit of DPKO. The main objectives of the audit were to identify and report on risks and exposures to duplication, fraud and abuse of authority in finance and budgeting; procurement; human resources, including recruitment and training; and information technology.

OIOS concluded that DPKO had made some progress in improving the management of peacekeeping operations. Recent initiatives included the introduction of the integrated mission planning process for new missions; the establishment of strategic deployment stocks, which reduced the time frame for mission start-up; the design and delivery of training programmes for peacekeeping personnel; and a robust response to allegations of sexual exploitation and abuse in field missions. However, those achievements had not kept pace with the challenges of the rapid increase in field operations. DPKO, in cooperation with the UN Department of Management, needed to do more to strengthen internal controls and ensure their enforcement. Inadequate emphasis on establishing a high level of ethical behaviour and accountability had led to a culture of impunity.

In the opinion of OIOS, the control environment in DPKO and the Department of Management was inadequate. OIOS was particularly concerned about the risks and exposures in the area of procurement, where it found a number of cases indicating systematic breaches of UN regulations and rules. One of the root causes of that situation was management's reluctance to hold staff members accountable for violations of rules and regulations and poor management, which led to an unacceptably high exposure to the risk of fraud and abuse. Appropriate mechanisms needed to be established to ensure managerial accountability at all levels, both at Headquarters and in field missions. OIOS noted that management had initiated an inquiry into the specific cases highlighted in the report to address the issue of accountability.

OIOS identified the scope for improving the management of peacekeeping operations, including reorganizing the budget process for efficiency and to eliminate duplication; delegating recruitment authority to field missions concomitant with effective monitoring at Headquarters; optimizing the use of information and communication technology; strengthening the capacity for mission planning and the provision of strategic guidance and direction; improving coordination between DPKO and other UN departments and agencies; and placing greater emphasis on the identification and dissemination of best practices from lessons learned.

The report summarized some of the critical recommendations relating to OIOS major findings in the areas of procurement, financial management and budgeting, human resources management, information and communication technology, mission planning, substantive operations and best practices.

In the area of procurement, OIOS recommended that the Secretary-General hold senior management and staff in DPKO and the Department of Management accountable for lapses in internal controls and failure to establish a high level of ethical integrity. Both Departments should jointly review the appointments of chief/director of administration and section chief with fiduciary responsibility to ensure that they had the requisite qualifications and experience. They should address managerial responsibility for the specific instances of waste of resources, poor planning, inflated requirements and losses identified by OIOS; and reorganize the budget process for peacekeeping operations to eliminating specifically duplication of tasks between the Finance Management and Support Service and the Office of Programme Planning, Budget and Accounts (OPPBA).

Regarding financial management and budgeting, the two Departments should revise the procedures for reviewing the monthly and annual financial statements of missions, so as to eliminate duplication, and assess the resource requirements resulting from such elimination. DPKO should revise the Secretary-General's bulletin [ST/SGB/2000/9] on the functions and organization of the Department to establish clear lines of authority, responsibility and accountability for the peacekeeping budget process and develop a template for strategic mission planning. The Department of Management should seek the approval of legislative bodies to develop a shorter budgeting model when mission mandates changed or when operational requirements necessitated substantial revision of the budget and study the feasibility of implementing an enterprise resource planning application, which would include a budgeting module.

As to human resources management, OIOS recommended that the Department of Management conduct an objective assessment of the success of the delegation of authority of human resources management to DPKO. OHRM should establish a human resources action plan with each field mission to better manage the missions' human resources. DPKO should complete its succession planning strategy to fill vacancies in a timely manner and ensure that the appointment of field staff adhered to the principles in Article 101 of the Charter; reassign roster management responsibilities to a team independent of recruitment and placement functions; and develop separate training programmes for its core functions and for staff development.

In the area of information and communication technology (ICT), DPKO should finalize its information management strategy; establish a function dedicated to the development and enforcement of ICT security standards and procedures and the monitoring of compliance therewith; and develop standard telephone billing and accounting procedures.

Regarding mission planning, OIOS recommended that DPKO expedite the development of strategic guidance, policies and standard operating procedures for the system-wide implementation of the integrated mission planning process; establish a dedicated planning cell with staff at Headquarters to lead, coordinate and monitor the process; appoint senior leaders of a new mission early to ensure their involvement at the initial stage of planning; and integrate the results-based budgeting requirements into the process.

OIOS also recommended that DPKO should develop a framework for cooperation and a clear division of labour with UN departments and agencies on substantive programmes. It should develop adequate institutional capacity at Headquarters for policy advice and the monitoring and evaluation of human rights, the rule of law, civil affairs and protection of civilians in peacekeeping missions; strengthen coordination between the Peacekeeping Best Practices Section and the Office of Operations for monitoring the implementation of disarmament, demobilization and reintegration programme plans; and institutionalize compliance with the International Mine Action Standards by troop-contributing countries. OIOS further recommended that DPKO ensure that the Peacekeeping Best Practices Section focused its activities on its core functions, and review the responsibilities of the Director of Change Management to address overlap in that Section.

In all, OIOS made 158 recommendations, including 105 considered to be critical, in the seven audit reports that were issued to DPKO and the Departments of Management and Political Affairs. Of those, 133 recommendations were accepted by the departments concerned, most of which were being implemented. OIOS reiterated 25 unaccepted recommendations for reconsideration by those departments.

By **decision 60/551 C** of 7 July, the Assembly deferred until its sixty-first (2006) session consideration of the OIOS report.

Review of management structure

In response to General Assembly decision 59/507 [YUN 2004, p. 94], the Secretary-General submitted a May note [A/60/856] on the review of the management structure of all peacekeeping operations. The management structure and the levels of posts were reviewed in the context of the preparation of the 2006-2007 budget submissions of individual missions. In addition, an extensive external management review was conducted of the United Nations Organization Mission in the Democratic Republic of the Congo (MONUC). The results of the reviews were reflected in the 2006-2007 budget proposals.

The mission reviews yielded two significant findings. Firstly, while the mandate, complexity and operational environment of individual missions were unique, the types of activities performed were fairly consistent across multidimensional missions, suggesting that there were basic building blocks from which missions were constructed and models and standards could be created. Secondly, existing organizational design tools for stable headquarters operations were dated. The development and implementation of field-relevant model mission structures, benchmarks and standards would build on the ongoing analysis of existing structures and identified norms.

Work on the review continued as part of a broader DPKO initiative to better position itself, both at Headquarters and in the field, to meet future peacekeeping challenges. The initiative comprised two parallel exercises: to benchmark the functions performed in, and post requirements for, multidimensional peacekeeping operations; and to develop standard organizational models that would enable senior leadership to focus on achieving mandates, ensure manageable spans of control, clarify reporting lines and promote coordination and communication. As the review was still in progress, the Secretariat was unable to submit the completed report on the review for consideration at the second part of the resumed sixtieth (2006) session. It was expected that the report would be submitted for consideration by the Assembly at its sixty-first (2006) session.

Personnel matters

Discipline in field missions

In March [A/60/713], OIOS reported on its global review of discipline in field missions led by DPKO. The objective of the review, which was conducted at the request of the Under-Secretary-General for Peacekeeping Operations, was to assist DPKO senior management in strengthening UN standards of conduct and ensuring full compliance. Towards that end, OIOS assessed the state of discipline in field missions, identified gaps in relevant policies and procedures, and identified tools the missions needed to maintain good order and adherence to the UN standards of conduct. Based on the reviews, OIOS issued 19 individual reports to management in the field recommending corrective actions.

In recent years, a sharp increase in the number of reported cases of serious misconduct, especially sexual exploitation and abuse, highlighted the overall issue of discipline in peacekeeping and other field missions. In 2003 and 2004, the OIOS Investigations Division received 1,182 cases of various types of misconduct and violations of UN rules and regulations, including sexual exploitation and abuse. OIOS findings with regard to the general subject of discipline were generally in line with those contained in the 2005 report of the Secretary-General's Adviser on Sexual Exploitation and Abuse by United Nations Peacekeeping Personnel [YUN 2005, p. 119]. (For further information on sexual exploitation and abuse in UN peacekeeping operations, see p. 77.)

OIOS found that indiscipline existed to varying degrees in all missions, but the inadequacy of records and their inconsistency with Headquarters data made it impossible to determine precisely the extent of the problem. Headquarters guidance was inadequate in terms of policies, procedures and guidelines; enforcement of policies and procedures at Headquarters and in the field was poor; and resources and skills were insufficient to prevent misconduct and to enforce the Organization's standards of conduct. Management efforts to address the problem were made mainly in reaction to events and negative publicity, were inconsistent across missions, and had only recently been undertaken. Accordingly, deep-rooted and long-standing indiscipline issues had not been addressed adequately. Overall, the review showed that monitoring the conduct of peacekeepers could no longer be addressed in an ad hoc manner, and peacekeepers clearly required sustained, methodical vigilance, through an institutionalized, full-time professional capacity at Headquarters and in the field.

The report discussed major findings related to management responsibilities, duties and accountability; policies, directives and guidelines; the handling and recording of complaints; coordination and information-sharing; and misconduct prevention programmes.

OIOS issued 28 recommendations to address the issues discussed in the report and to improve the state of discipline in field missions. It recommended that DPKO establish a full-time capacity at Headquarters and in the missions to address misconduct issues; establish procedures and guidelines and ensure their consistent application; and develop and implement prevention programmes and data tracking to ensure that personnel acted under the highest standards of efficiency, competence and integrity, as required by the Charter of the United Nations. DPKO should create, under the aegis of the Special Committee on Peacekeeping Operations, a joint committee or working group to monitor the conduct of peacekeepers and the enforcement of disciplinary mechanisms and accountability in the field; and ensure that senior managers and commanders led by example. The Department should ensure the consistent and fair application of the Organization's disciplinary mechanism across all categories and levels of peacekeeping personnel; establish procedures to include the implementation of measures to address misconduct in the field, especially sexual exploitation and abuse, in the performance goals of civilian managers and civilian police managers in their performance evaluations; and establish criteria to evaluate the performance of uniformed managers and contingent commanders in preventing sexual exploitation and abuse. It should also prepare a report for the General Assembly recommending the mandatory adoption of the standards of conduct contained in the Secretary-General's 2003 bulletin [ST/SGB/2003/13] [YUN 2004, p. 107] and the DPKO publications "Ten Rules: Code of Personal Conduct for Blue Helmets" and "We Are United Nations Peacekeepers". DPKO should also establish a policy on the maintenance and retention of records concerning misconduct cases; develop a comprehensive code of ethics specific to procurement staff, and require all Headquarters and field procurement staff, and members of the Headquarters Committee on Contracts and the local Committee on Contracts to acknowledge in writing annually that they had read and understood the code; include a provision on preventing sexual exploitation and abuse cases in new contracts; and require existing and new contractors to certify in writing that they would comply with the provisions of the Secretary-General's bulletin. DPKO should develop a standardized, comprehensive data tracking system to enable senior management to obtain information on the number and type of allegations and the status of follow-up action or investigations, and ensure that those found culpable of serious misconduct were not rehired; develop formal procedures for receiving, handling and monitoring complaints; and establish formal coordination mechanisms for improving information-sharing and coordination of misconduct investigations.

OIOS recommended that DPKO ensure that training programmes on the UN standards of conduct for all categories and levels of peacekeeping personnel were instituted prior to deployment and during the mission assignment, and provide additional training to senior managers in the missions, up to the level of head of mission. It should include the discipline risk assessment in the pre-mandate assessment for each mission, pre-deployment assessments of uniformed personnel and any ongoing evaluations during the life of the mission, and direct the missions to conduct an ongoing, regular risk assessment exercise. It should provide guidance to missions on enforcing UN standards of conduct; be more proactive in instituting measures to ease living conditions in the missions; and ensure that missions identified the reasons for the dissatisfaction of UN staff members and volunteers, particularly women, along with the state of discipline in the field and the missions' ability to address conduct and discipline issues.

OIOS recommended that the UN Office of Human Resources Management compile existing policies, regulations and rules on misconduct in a more user-friendly form, and assist DPKO in providing guidelines to managers in the field on how to address misconduct based on lessons learned and frequently asked questions. It should develop practical guidance on how to implement the Secretary-General's 2003 bulletin [ST/SGB/2003/13], expedite the finalization and implementation of policies and procedures dealing with the protection of whistle-blowers among UN staff members and develop consistent policies for their protection. In consultation with the UN Office of Legal Affairs, DPKO should determine what disciplinary regime applied to formed police units and whether they should be accorded a status similar to that of troops deployed under the memorandum of understanding with troop-contributing countries or regular civilian police officers hired under individual secondment contracts.

DPKO and OHRM accepted the recommendations and had started to implement most of them.

By **decision 60/551 C** of 7 July, the Assembly deferred until its sixty-first (2006) session consideration of the OIOS report.

Criminal accountability of UN staff and experts on mission

In response to General Assembly resolution 59/300 [YUN 2005, p. 122], the Secretary-General established a Group of Legal Experts to prepare a report on how to ensure that UN staff and experts on mission would never be effectively exempt from the consequences of criminal acts committed at their duty station, nor unjustly penalized. In August [A/60/980], the Secretary-General transmitted the Group's report, which discussed accountability with regard to criminal conduct and misconduct; the jurisdiction of the host State, of States other than the host State, and of an international court or tribunal; and investigations. Annexed to the report were the Group's terms of reference and a draft convention on the criminal accountability of UN officials and experts on mission.

Among its recommendations for overcoming the obstacles in holding UN peacekeeping personnel accountable for crimes committed during peacekeeping operations, the Group proposed that the United Nations give priority to facilitating the exercise of jurisdiction by the host State, and should not assume that the host State was unable to exercise jurisdiction merely because a peacekeeping operation was conducted in a post-conflict area. If the host State was unable, even with UN assistance, to exercise all aspects of criminal jurisdiction, other States would need to be relied on to do so. However, even in those circumstances, the host State might be able to provide some assistance to enable the exercise of criminal jurisdiction by another State, including by gathering evidence or arresting alleged offenders. Jurisdiction was not an indivisible concept and the host State and other States might be involved in different but mutually supportive aspects of the overall exercise of criminal jurisdiction.

Nevertheless, the exercise of jurisdiction by States other than the host State presented many challenges that were not unique to the peacekeeping environment, including the extradition of persons and securing admissible evidence for use in another jurisdiction. To provide a sound legal basis for the exercise of jurisdiction by States other than the host State, the Group recommended the development of a new international convention to address jurisdiction and related issues. Administrative investigations conducted by the United Nations for disciplinary purposes might be relevant to holding a person criminally accountable, as they might be the only means of gathering evidence of an alleged crime; therefore, UN administrative investigators needed to be cognizant of the fact that the material they collected might be used to support not only disciplinary action but also criminal proceedings. The Group also made recommendations for ensuring that administrative investigations were carried out to the highest possible standard.

The Group, in acknowledging the steps taken by the United Nations to ensure that departments adopted a cooperative and coordinated approach to dealing with misconduct issues, said there needed to be clearer guidelines about the role of OIOS and its relationship with other departments, in particular DPKO and peacekeeping missions.

By **decision 60/563** of 8 September, the General Assembly postponed consideration of the Group's report until the Assembly's sixty-first (2006) session to avail the Sixth (Legal) Committee of the opportunity to consider the report at that session.

GENERAL ASSEMBLY ACTION

On 4 December [meeting 64], the General Assembly, on the recommendation of the Sixth (Legal) Committee [A/61/450], adopted **resolution 61/29** without vote [agenda item 33].

Criminal accountability of United Nations officials and experts on mission

The General Assembly,

Recalling its resolution 59/281 of 29 March 2005, in which it endorsed the recommendation in paragraph 56 of the report of the Special Committee on Peacekeeping Operations that the Secretary-General make available to the United Nations membership a comprehensive report on the issue of sexual exploitation and abuse in United Nations peacekeeping operations,

Noting that the Secretary-General, on 24 March 2005, transmitted to the President of the General Assembly a report of his Adviser concerning sexual exploitation and abuse by United Nations peacekeeping personnel,

Recalling its resolution 59/300 of 22 June 2005 endorsing the recommendation of the Special Committee on Peacekeeping Operations that a group of legal experts be established to provide advice on the best way to proceed so as to ensure that the original intent of the Charter of the United Nations can be achieved, namely that United Nations staff and experts on mission would never be effectively exempt from the consequences of criminal acts committed at their duty station, nor unjustly penalized, in accordance with due process,

Noting the report of the Group of Legal Experts established by the Secretary-General pursuant to resolution 59/300,

Convinced of the need for the United Nations to take strong and effective steps in this regard,

1. *Decides* to establish an Ad Hoc Committee, open to all States Members of the United Nations or members of specialized agencies or of the International Atomic Energy Agency, for the purpose of considering the report of the Group of Legal Experts, in particular its legal aspects;

2. *Decides also* that the Ad Hoc Committee shall meet from 9 to 13 April 2007;

3. *Requests* the Secretary-General to provide the Ad Hoc Committee with the necessary facilities for the performance of its work;

4. *Requests* the Ad Hoc Committee to report on its work to the General Assembly at its sixty-second session;

5. *Decides* to include in the provisional agenda of its sixty-second session the item entitled "Criminal accountability of United Nations officials and experts on mission".

Peacekeeping standards and norms of conduct

In response to General Assembly resolution 59/300 [YUN 2005, p. 122], the Secretary-General established a Group of Legal Experts with two distinct terms of reference. Under the first term of reference, the Group was tasked with providing advice on how the standards contained in the Secretary-General's 2003 bulletin [YUN 2004, p. 107] on special measures for protection from sexual exploitation and sexual abuse [ST/SGB/2003/13] could bind contingent members in the period prior to the conclusion of a memorandum of understanding or other agreement or action by a troop-contributing country that incorporated those standards in a legally effective way under its national laws. Under the second term of reference, the Group was to propose ways of standardizing the norms of conduct applicable to all categories of peacekeeping personnel, paying particular attention to sexual exploitation and abuse. The Secretary-General transmitted the Group's report on 18 December [A/61/645].

The Group considered the process for deploying personnel from a troop-contributing country and identified a number of ways by which such a country could be obliged in international law to ensure that allegations of sexual exploitation and abuse by members of its contingent could be investigated properly and, if substantiated, punished. The Group also considered the roles of heads of mission, Force Commanders, Security Council resolutions and troop-contributing countries themselves. It noted that, even if a troop-contributing country was under an international law obligation, the United Nations might still be unable to compel it to take the necessary action under its domestic law to ensure that members of its national contingent were bound by the 2003 bulletin. It was for each troop-contributing country to act in accordance with its national legal system to ensure that the conduct proscribed by that bulletin was punishable in accordance with its laws.

Since a formal invitation was usually sent by the United Nations to potential troop-contributing countries in the form of a note, following the adoption of the Security Council resolution authorizing the peacekeeping operation, the Group recommended that DPKO consider including in the note a statement that the contribution of a national contingent was based on the understanding that the country would take action to ensure that its members observed the standards contained in the 2003 bulletin and take measures under its national law to ensure that allegations against its personnel of sexual exploitation and abuse were properly investigated and, if substantiated, punished; or that the general administrative arrangements applicable to the contribution were those set out in the guidelines for the peacekeeping operation, which should require troop-contributing countries to prohibit sexual exploitation and abuse. The pre-deployment visit should be used to ascertain whether and how the troop-contributing country intended to ensure that its members observed the standards of conduct set out in the 2003 bulletin, and the practice of including in Security Council resolutions authorizing or extending peacekeeping mandates a call on the Secretary-General to take all necessary action to give effect to the bulletin should be retained. To reinforce the importance of the UN zero-tolerance policy on sexual exploitation and abuse, the Directive to the Force Commander should include a specific reference to the need to ensure compliance with the bulletin, and heads of mission and/or Force Commanders should issue directives prohibiting the conduct set out in the bulletin and requiring contingent commanders to disseminate them and ensure compliance. Troop-contributing countries should consider taking formal legislative action to ensure that, where acts prohibited by the 2003 bulletin amounted to crimes under their national law, those laws were applied to crimes committed abroad by members of their national contingent. DPKO should reinstate the practice of receiving assurances from participating States on the exercise of criminal jurisdiction in accordance with the status-of-forces agreement, and from troop-contributing countries that commands were issued in a manner binding under their military and/or criminal justice system either proscribing the conduct set out in the 2003 bulletin and/or giving effect to the Force Commander's directives that related to the bulletin.

Under its second term of reference, the Group reviewed instruments that set out the norms of conduct for peacekeeping personnel, and found that the same basic norms were generally applicable to all categories of peacekeeping personnel. Differences resulted largely from mission-specific rules and rules for different categories of peacekeeping personnel that could not apply readily to other categories. The analysis also showed that different categories of peacekeeping personnel were subject to different consequences for failure to comply with the norms of conduct. As the different categories of peacekeeping personnel served the United Nations under different terms and conditions and performed different functions, having a single set of norms was neither practical nor necessary; however, there might be specific issues that were of significance to the United Nations, including that of sexual exploitation and abuse, where a common set of norms were justified. The Group recommended that consideration should continue to be given to applying the same norms of conduct to all categories of peacekeeping personnel in relation to such issues.

Some basic norms of conduct were set out in two pocket guides: "We Are United Nations Peacekeepers" and "Ten Rules: Code of Personal Conduct for Blue Helmets". However, there was no convenient guide that summarized the basic norms for all categories of peacekeeping personnel. The Group considered that there was merit in having such a guide and identified two options for doing so. The first and simplest option was to amend "We Are United Nations Peacekeepers" to make it applicable to all categories of peacekeeping personnel; a draft of the amended document, entitled "We Are United Nations Peacekeeping Personnel", was annexed to the report. The second option was to replace both of the pocket guides with a new one setting out the basic norms of conduct that were common to all categories of peacekeeping personnel; a draft of such a guide, drawn from instruments that already applied and bound peacekeeping personnel, was also annexed to the report. Each option standardized the conduct proscribed by the 2003 bulletin. The decision as to whether either option was pursued and what should be included in such a document were matters of policy to be addressed by DPKO in consultation with relevant stakeholders.

Staffing of field missions

As requested by the General Assembly in resolution 59/296 [YUN 2005, p. 133], the Secretary-General reported in February [A/60/698 & Corr. 1, 2] on the staffing of field missions, including the use of 300- and 100-series appointments. As a follow-up to his 2005 report on the subject [YUN 2005, p. 150], the February report provided information on the reappointment of mission staff under 300- to 100-series contracts after reaching the four-year limit of their 300-series contracts.

As at 30 June, 482 international staff would have reached four years of service under 300-series appointments of limited duration and were considered for reappointment under a 100-series contract, in accordance with the criteria set out in section VIII of resolution 59/296 [Ibid., p. 135]. As a result of the review, 403 staff members met the criteria set out in resolution 59/296, and 21 did not. The reappointment of 58 staff members was still being reviewed.

As part of his effort to standardize contractual arrangements, the Secretary-General noted that, given the growth in demand in peacekeeping, with mission staff accounting for over half of the total staff of the global secretariat at the end of 2005, some 45 per cent of which served under appointments of limited duration in difficult and often dangerous duty stations with inferior conditions of service, the concept of the appointment of limited duration no longer met peacekeeping needs. It did not provide competitive compensation or job security to attract and retain the skilled experts, or the leaders and managers needed in larger, multidimensional missions, nor did it allow the Organization to develop and capitalize on the talents of mission staff. Pending the Assembly's consideration of the Secretary-General's proposals on human resources management reform at its sixty-first (2006) session (see p. 1689), the Secretariat sought approval to continue the practice of reappointing serving staff under 100-series contracts on a case-by-case basis, provided the criteria set out in section VIII of resolution 59/296 were met.

In May [A/60/851], ACABQ reported that following an in-depth discussion with the representatives of the Secretary-General on the status of the various reports related to the staffing of field missions, the Secretariat modified the proposal contained in the Secretary-General's February report, requesting instead that consideration of the recommendation to use the 100-series contract for the appointment of all mission staff be deferred, and as an interim measure, the Secretary-General be authorized to continue the practice of reappointing staff under a 100-series appointment after completing four years on a 300-series contract, subject to the conditions specified in section X of Assembly resolution 59/266 [YUN 2004, p. 1418], and section VIII of resolution 59/296. ACABQ was informed that the International Civil Service Commission (ICSC), at its sixty-second session (Vienna, 13-31 March), took up the question of contractual instruments available to common system field staff, pursuant to section X of resolution 59/266, and that the Secretary-General intended to provide further views on the subject to ICSC at its sixty-third session (New York, 10-28 July). Pending the outcome of those deliberations and consideration of the relevant reports of the Secretary-General, ACABQ recommended that the modified measures requested by the Secretariat be authorized.

Chapter II

Africa

During 2006, the United Nations maintained its strong commitment to promoting peace, stability and development in Africa through six UN political missions and offices and seven peacekeeping missions, supported by some 60,000 military personnel. The Organization faced tremendous challenges in helping the countries in conflict situations and those in transition to post-conflict peacebuilding in Central Africa and the Great Lakes region, West Africa and the Horn of Africa to return to peace, stability and prosperity. The Office of the Special Adviser on Africa and the United Nations Office for West Africa continued to bring a regional perspective to issues facing the continent, promote conflict prevention and raise awareness about subregional problems, in particular, youth unemployment and migration. The United Nations worked closely with the African Union (AU), the Economic Community of West African States, the Economic Community of Central African States and the Intergovernmental Authority for Development to assist African Governments in improving security, ensuring humanitarian access, energizing peace processes and promoting economic and social development.

Central Africa and the Great Lakes region continued to be affected by the activities of militias, local warlords and international companies illegally exploiting the region's natural resources, in violation of UN sanctions. In January, the Security Council, in a ministerial-level debate on the Great Lakes region, discussed improving cooperation between the United Nations and African organizations, such as the AU, particularly in peacekeeping and conflict prevention. At the International Conference on Peace, Security, Democracy and Development in the Great Lakes Region (Nairobi, Kenya, 14-15 December), the region's Heads of State and Government signed the Pact on Security, Stability and Development in the Great Lakes Region. Meanwhile, in the Democratic Republic of the Congo, the four-year transitional process concluded with the successful holding of elections that led to the installation of the National Assembly and the inauguration of Joseph Kabila as President. The Security Council, in January, re-established the Group of Experts monitoring the embargo on the illegal exploitation of resources, as numerous violations of the embargo had been uncovered. The peace process continued in Burundi, where the Government and the last major rebel group, the Palipehutu-National Liberation Forces, concluded a peace agreement in June, and a ceasefire agreement in September. Burundi, in view of significant improvements in the security situation, requested the United Nations to establish an integrated peacebuilding office, which the Council endorsed. One of the region's most devastating conflicts, opposing Uganda and the Lord's Resistance Army, came closer to a solution, with the signing on 26 August, in Juba, the Sudan, of the Agreement on Cessation of Hostilities. To help the parties reach a comprehensive political solution to the conflict, the Secretary-General named former Mozambican President Joaquim Chissano as his Special Envoy to help deal with the issue. The Central African Republic was increasingly drawn into the crisis affecting Chad and the Darfur region of the Sudan. Forces opposed to Central African Republic President François Bozizé appeared to have forged links with rebels fighting against Chad's President Idriss Déby Itno. At the same time, the crisis in Darfur had spilled over into Chad and the Central African Republic, with both countries accusing the Sudan of supporting armed groups increasingly active in their territories. The Tripoli Agreement signed on 8 February and the 26 July N'Djamena Agreement between the two countries did not defuse the crisis. The Security Council, in August, requested the United Nations Mission in the Sudan to establish a political and military presence in Chad and, if necessary, in the Central African Republic.

In West Africa, while progress was made in the transition from peacekeeping to peacebuilding in Liberia and Sierra Leone, the region faced other significant challenges, such as illicit cross-border trafficking, institutional weaknesses, slow economic recovery, difficulties in security sector reform, demilitarization, demobilization and rehabilitation of ex-combatants and the return of refugees and internally displaced persons. The peace process in Côte d'Ivoire was impeded by political stalemates, disagreements and missed deadlines for the completion of crucial tasks, as well as violent demonstrations and inflammatory statements. Having missed the 31 October deadline for the holding of presidential elections, regional leaders extended the political transition period for another year and addressed the ambiguities that had plagued the previous transition period. In Liberia, the inauguration of Ellen Johnson-Sirleaf, Africa's first elected woman Head of State, and the installation of a new Government marked the completion of that country's two-year transitional process. The new Government tackled the issues of corruption and governance reform and took measures to enhance transparency and accountability. With the assistance of the United Nations Mission in Liberia and other regional and international actors, the country made substantial progress in restoring its administrative authority over the entire country and in controlling all areas of economic activity. Similarly, events in Sierra Leone were dominated by efforts to further consolidate peace and stability and prepare for elections in 2007. The transition from the United Nations Mission in Sierra Leone to the United Nations Integrated Office in Sierra Leone, established to support the Government in consolidating peace, building national capacity and preparing for those elections, was successfully completed. However, youth unemployment, rampant corruption, dire economic conditions and tension along the borders, especially with Guinea, were potential threats to stability. A significant development during the year was the apprehension and transfer of former Liberian President Charles Taylor into the custody of the Special Court for Sierra Leone in Freetown, and later to The Hague, the Netherlands, to stand trial. Guinea-Bissau continued to be polarized by political tensions, especially in the new National Popular Assembly. Dialogue initiatives aimed at reconciling the different factions and political groupings were launched, with the support of the Community of Portuguese-Speaking Countries. The strained political situation even risked jeopardizing the disbursement of funds pledged by donors, as political stability was a precondition for such disbursement. The mandate of the United Nations Peacebuilding Support Office in Guinea-Bissau, which assisted in consolidating peace and promoting national reconciliation, was streamlined to highlight its mediation and good offices functions. Cameroon and Nigeria continued to cooperate peacefully to advance progress in implementing, through the Cameroon-Nigeria Mixed Commission, the 2002 International Court of Justice ruling on the land and maritime boundaries between them.

However, the political landscape in the Horn of Africa was not so encouraging, as the region continued to be affected by complex, interlocking conflicts. While the Sudan took positive steps to implement the 2005 Comprehensive Peace Agreement, areas of the country were still plagued by armed militias, disagreements over borders, disputed oil revenues and the escalating crisis in the Darfur states. The crisis in the Darfur region continued to deteriorate, and although AU-mediated talks in Abuja, Nigeria, culminated in the signing of the Darfur Peace Agreement on 5 May, only the Government and one of the Darfur rebel groups signed the pact. The AU, in January, endorsed a transition from its Mission in the Sudan (AMIS) to a UN peacekeeping operation, which the Security Council approved in resolution 1663(2006) of 24 March. However, the Sudan did not support the idea, citing threats to its sovereignty. On 31 August, the Council expanded the mandate and increased the troop strength of the United Nations Mission in the Sudan by up to 17,300 international military personnel, to be deployed to Darfur. That was also rejected by the Sudan. On 16 November, agreement was reached on the deployment of a hybrid AU-UN force in Darfur. That was endorsed by the AU, Sudan's Council of Ministers and the Security Council. In Somalia, the year opened on a promising note, with the January signing of the Aden Declaration, brokered by Yemen, to end differences between the President and the Speaker of the Transitional Federal Parliament. The Transitional Federal Government and Parliament relocated to Baidoa, 140 miles northwest of Mogadishu, and the Parliament held its first session in February. That same month, however, there was a dramatic shift in Somalia's complicated clan-based balance of power, with the emergence of the Alliance for the Restoration of Peace and Counter-Terrorism (ARPCT), whose aim was to combat the rapid advance of the Union of Islamic Courts, accused of supporting and harbouring foreign terrorism suspects. ARPCT and Islamic Courts fighters engaged in fierce battles in Mogadishu, and by June, the Courts had routed ARPCT and established their authority in central and southern Somalia. A sense of law and order returned to Mogadishu for the first time in 15 years. By contrast, the Transitional Federal Government barely held control of Baidoa. The Courts expanded the territory under their control, taking the strategically important port city of Kismayo and had flanked Baidoa by late October. The Security Council, on 6 December, endorsed the request for a joint peace operation to be deployed by the Intergovernmental Authority for Development and the AU. However, the military build-up by both sides came to a head on 24 December, when skirmishes threatened the Transitional Government seat in Baidoa and provoked the full force of the Government, backed by Ethiopian troops. The

Courts militia retreated to Mogadishu, which fell to the Transitional Government/Ethiopian coalition on 28 December, and then to Kismayo, which fell soon after. Despite diplomatic initiatives by the United States and the Ethiopia-Eritrea Boundary Commission, the Ethiopia and Eritrea stalemate in the demarcation of the border between them remained. The situation in the buffer zone, the Temporary Security Zone, and adjacent areas turned tense in mid-October, when Eritrean defence forces entered the Zone in Sector West. The situation was exacerbated by Eritrean restrictions on the United Nations Mission in Ethiopia and Eritrea, including a continued flight ban on the Mission's helicopters, which greatly curtailed its capacity to monitor the Zone. The Eritrea-Ethiopia Boundary Commission, which failed to advance its demarcation activities, announced, on 27 November, that, because of impediments in fulfilling its mandate, it planned to demarcate the border on maps, leaving the two countries to establish the physical boundary and to reach agreement on border demarcation within one year. If no agreement was reached, the locations established in its 2002 delimitation decision would take effect. Both countries rejected the Commission's proposal.

The deadlock in the search for an agreed political solution to the long-standing conflict concerning the governance of the Territory of Western Sahara continued, with no hope of an early breakthrough. The Secretary-General's Special Envoy intensified his efforts in exploring with the parties, Morocco and the Frente Popular para La Liberación de Saguía el-Hamra de Río de Oro (Frente Polisario), the best way to achieve a mutually acceptable solution. The Secretary-General recommended that the Security Council call upon the parties to enter into open-ended negotiations without preconditions, rather than just extending the mandate of the United Nations Mission for the Referendum in Western Sahara.

In other matters, Mauritius complained that, 38 years after its independence, it still was not able to exercise its sovereignty over the Chagos Archipelago, including Diego Garcia. The United Kingdom, maintaining that the Territory was British, reiterated the undertaking that the Territory would be ceded when no longer required for defence purposes and it would liaise closely with Mauritius at that time.

Both the Security Council and the General Assembly discussed the issue of cooperation between the United Nations and the AU. The two organizations signed a declaration entitled "Enhancing UN-AU Cooperation: Framework for the ten-year Capacity-Building Programme for the African Union".

Promotion of peace in Africa

In 2006, the United Nations continued to identify and address the root causes of conflict in Africa and consider ways to promote sustainable peace and development on the continent. The Security Council held debates on the situation in the Great Lakes Region (27 January) and the consolidation of peace in West Africa (9 August). It heard briefings by the African Union (AU) Chairman (31 May) and the Under-Secretary-General for Humanitarian Affairs on the situations in the Democratic Republic of the Congo (DRC) (15 September), the Darfur region of the Sudan and northern Uganda (22 November).

The Ad Hoc Working Group on Conflict Prevention and Resolution in Africa, established in 2002 [YUN 2002, p. 93] to monitor the implementation of Council recommendations relating to its role in conflict prevention and resolution in Africa, continued to contribute to the Council's work by promoting a better understanding of ways to address crises on the continent.

The New York-based Office of the Special Adviser on Africa (OSAA), headed by Legwaila Joseph Legwaila (Botswana), continued to facilitate global intergovernmental deliberations on Africa, in particular on the New Partnership for Africa's Development (NEPAD) [YUN 2001, p. 900], and to assist the Secretary-General in improving the coordination of UN system support to Africa. The Geneva-based Special Adviser to the Secretary-General on Africa, Mohamed Sahnoun (Algeria), continued to contribute, as part of the Secretary-General's good offices function, to the promotion of peace and security in the Horn of Africa, closely monitoring the situation there and striving to resolve conflicts in the region.

On 15 November [A/61/580-S/2006/897], China, the Congo and Ethiopia transmitted to the Secretary-General the Declaration of the Beijing Summit of the Forum on China-Africa Cooperation (Beijing, 4-5 November), as well as the speeches made on 4 November at the Summit's opening ceremony by China's President, Hu Jintao, Congo's President Denis Sassou-Nguesso and Ethiopia's Prime Minister, Meles Zenawi. The meeting, which brought together representatives from 48 African countries, adopted the Beijing Action Plan of the Forum on China-Africa Cooperation (2007-2009).

Security Council consideration. On 27 January, the Security Council held an open meeting on the situation in the Great Lakes Region (see p. 121) and on 9 August an open debate on the consolidation of peace in West Africa (see p. 173).

On 31 May [meeting 5548], AU Chairman, President Denis Sassou-Nguesso of the Congo, briefing the Security Council on armed conflict in Africa, expressed his organization's gratitude to the Council for its tireless efforts and determination in supporting peace and security on the continent. He said that the Secretary-General's 1998 report on the causes of conflict and the promotion of durable peace and sustainable development in Africa [YUN 1998, p. 66] remained relevant, providing a broad strategy of prevention, and taking into account all the dimensions of the violent crises on the African continent. Most of the current conflicts were at least three years old. However, the tragic case of Somalia, the situation between Eritrea and Ethiopia, the crisis in northern Uganda and the situation in Western Sahara, had unfortunately lasted because they had not been dealt with appropriately, nor had there been commitment or mutual confidence on the part of the principal protagonists. On the other hand, conflicts that had been among the worst on the continent, such as in Angola, Liberia and Sierra Leone, had been settled in an encouraging way. However, to manage some post-conflict situations, sustained international support was needed to prevent a relapse into conflict.

As to current conflicts, scenarios developed by the international community should make it possible to end them, such as those in Côte d'Ivoire, the DRC and the Darfur region of the Sudan. In Darfur, there was a framework for a transition towards a UN operation, with a strong African component, following the accord reached in Abuja on 5 May. The partnership between the United Nations and the AU should be strengthened. In implementing that partnership, Africa had the tools in the area of conflict prevention, in particular the AU Peace and Security Council and the Non-Aggression and Common Defence Pact. The common will was to put an end to those intolerable situations by making the best use of all the means that the partnership between the two organizations provided.

On 15 September [meeting 5525], Under-Secretary-General for Humanitarian Affairs, Jan Egeland, briefed the Council on his trip to assess the humanitarian situation in the DRC and northern Uganda. He called on the Council to bolster its commitment to ending two of the worst conflicts. The United Nations and the Congolese Transitional Government had made much progress in increasing security and holding successful elections, but not enough on the issue of impunity. Sexual abuse had become a cancer, while military and civilian authorities were still not accountable for crimes against civilians. More than 1,000 raped women had been treated so far that year in South Kivu alone, and it was not known how many more had suffered in inaccessible parts of the province. Expressing concern about the impact of operations by the armed forces on civilians, he said more than 500,000 people had been newly displaced in eastern DRC, following Government operations against militia groups. Too often, civilians who had fled the fighting were then victimized by the armed forces, accusing them of supporting the militias. The only long-term solution was to form one competent national army with the exclusive right to bear arms. While the humanitarian situation had improved, there were still insufficient resources to meet the country's overwhelming needs, including the some 1.6 million internally displaced persons who had returned home the previous year. The Council had to show its commitment to the country by maintaining the strength of the United Nations Organization Mission in the Democratic Republic of the Congo (MONUC) and keeping pressure on the Government to end impunity and promote the rule of law.

Turning to northern Uganda, he said that the picture there was more promising than it had been in years. Security had increased dramatically since the start of negotiations between Uganda and the Lord's Resistance Army (LRA) in Juba, southern Sudan, earlier in the year. The improved security would allow conditions in the camps for internally displaced persons to improve and preparations to be made for the return of more than 1.5 million people. On 26 August, the two sides signed a Cessation of Hostilities Agreement, and the Government of South Sudan asked for UN assistance, including the provision of monitors. The question of impunity and International Criminal Court indictments against LRA leaders were discussed with internally displaced persons in Uganda and the parties in Juba, who all expressed concern that the indictments could threaten progress in the talks that were going on. However, there could be no impunity for mass murder and crimes against humanity, he said, and the parties should look at different solutions for meeting local needs for reconciliation, as well as universal standards of justice and accountability.

Briefing the Council on 22 November [meeting 5571] on his visit to Darfur and northern Uganda, Mr. Egeland said that Government forces, militias, rebels groups and Chadian armed opposition groups continued to spread fear and terror throughout much of that region. The Government's failure to protect its citizens, even in areas where there were no rebels, had been shameful. The United Nations had also failed to live up to its pledge to protect civilians where Governments manifestly failed to do so. The rampant insecurity, proliferation of arms and banditry on roads had taken their toll on the delivery capacity of an increasingly beleaguered humanitarian community. Humanitarian workers were being harassed, attacked and killed. If that trend continued, there would be a dramatic escalation of human suffering and loss of life beyond anything had been witnessed so far. Referring to an agreement reached in Addis Ababa regarding the deployment of a hybrid United Nations/African Union peacekeeping mission (see p. 290), he said that the agreement could mark a historic turning point, but he feared that time was being lost in talks on the intricacies of the accord, rather than on the immediate deployment of a more effective force with a more proactive mandate.

As to the Juba peace talks between Uganda and LRA, he said that, except for small incidents, the cessation of hostilities had been respected, allowing hundreds of thousands of internally displaced persons to start returning to northern Uganda. He had met with LRA leader Joseph Kony and had urged him to move towards a speedy end to the conflict, ensure the assembly of the LRA forces in the agreed areas and release abducted women and children. The mediation efforts by the Government of Southern Sudan should be supported by continued funding. Continued UN political assistance to the mediation was also necessary.

Office of the Special Adviser on Africa

In 2006, the Office of the Special Adviser on Africa (OSAA), established by General Assembly resolution 57/7 [YUN 2002, p. 910], continued to enhance international support for Africa's development and security through its advocacy and analytical work, assist the Secretary-General in improving coherence and coordination of UN system support to Africa, and facilitate global inter-governmental deliberations on Africa, in particular relating to NEPAD [YUN 2001, p. 900]. Analytical work undertaken by OSAA during the year focused on the contribution of the private sector to the implementation of NEPAD, assessing, among other things, ongoing private-sector participation by both African and non-African firms and constraints to such participation. The Office provided research, logistical and administrative support for the second report of the Secretary-General's Advisory Panel on International Support for NEPAD [A/61/138].

The Office convened an expert group meeting on natural resources and conflict in Africa (Cairo, Egypt, 17-19 June), which focused on improving natural resources management in post-conflict countries in Africa, and another on the participation of Africa's youth as partners in peace and development in post-conflict countries (Windhoek, Namibia, 14-16 November), which devised strategies and mechanisms to include youth as key actors in rehabilitation, reconciliation and rebuilding of war-torn communities. It organized a panel discussion on institutional challenges in implementing NEPAD (New York, 12 October), coinciding with the General Assembly debate on NEPAD, at which experts presented policies and strategies that had been successful in addressing such challenges.

Implementation of Secretary-General 1998 recommendations on promotion of peace

Report of Secretary-General. In response to General Assembly resolution 60/223 [YUN 2005, p. 158], the Secretary-General submitted an August report [A/61/213] on the implementation of the recommendations contained in his 1998 report on the causes of conflict and promotion of durable peace and sustainable development in Africa [YUN 1998, p. 66]. The report examined conflict prevention and peacemaking, progress in countries with UN peacekeeping missions, post-conflict peacebuilding, cross-cutting issues, building African capacity and enhancing cooperation. Updating developments since his follow-up report on the subject [YUN 2005, p. 157], he said that, while prospects for peace in a number of African countries had improved during the year, the root causes, such as extreme poverty, gross inequalities and weak State capacity continued to cause conflict. They were exacerbated by other factors, such as external support for repressive regimes, exclusionary Government policies and small-arms proliferation. Religion, ethnicity and economic conditions also mobilized people to engage in violent action, while forsaking civil responsibility.

Increased and concerted action was needed to prevent simmering crises from escalating and ensure that the hard-won peace in countries emerging from conflict was irreversible. Greater efforts were required to address youth unemployment, the impact of HIV/AIDS, the illicit exploitation of natural resources and the illegal flows of small arms. Cooperation between the United Nations and African regional organizations was vital to strengthen African peace support and early-warning capacity.

Of concern were several developments that could undermine the achievements and investments made, such as unconstitutional takeovers, efforts to prolong terms in public office, attempts to disqualify opposition members, incitement to hatred and attacks for political and electoral gain. African States and regional organizations should be alert to those problems and send a clear message that they would not be tolerated.

Progress was made in several countries with UN peacekeeping missions. As at 31 May, Africa hosted 75 per cent of total UN peacekeeping forces. Over 63,000 troops, police and civilian personnel were deployed in seven peacekeeping missions, which had expanded their operations to include peacebuilding activities. To support the transition from conflict to peace, the World Bank was engaged in 17 conflict-affected African countries, providing some $3.1 billion in grants and loans for 64 projects and raising over $1 billion through multi-donor trust funds.

The Secretary-General stated that peace would remain fragile if the living conditions of ordinary people, particularly the youth, were not improved. Peace consolidation strategies should involve realistic plans for economic recovery, appropriate policies, such as preferential trade, aid agreements and debt relief, as well as measures to promote land reform, reduce massive unemployment and better manage natural resources.

The Secretary-General called upon African Member States to assist those African countries emerging from conflict in devising natural resource and public revenue-management structures to transform those resources from a peace liability to a peace asset, and the international community to assist them by providing adequate financial and technical assistance. He urged African leaders to continue to spearhead normative and regulatory innovations and enact policies providing incentives to domestic and international investors. The role of the media was critical, and better training for journalists, the promotion of ethical standards and adequate pay should discourage hate media and promote responsible journalism. He called for regional alertness, and urged States, African regional organizations, the Bretton Woods institutions (the World Bank Group and the International Monetary Fund) and development partners to assist African countries emerging from conflict to introduce better economic and employment opportunities to prevent a relapse into conflict.

GENERAL ASSEMBLY ACTION

On 22 December [meeting 84], the General Assembly adopted **resolution 61/230** [draft: A/61/L.41/Rev.1 & Add.1] without vote [agenda item 62 *(b)*].

Implementation of the recommendations contained in the report of the Secretary-General on the causes of conflict and the promotion of durable peace and sustainable development in Africa

The General Assembly,

Recalling the report of the Open-ended Ad Hoc Working Group on the Causes of Conflict and the Promotion of Durable Peace and Sustainable Development in Africa, and its resolutions 53/92 of 7 December 1998, 54/234 of 22 December 1999, 55/217 of 21 December 2000, 56/37 of 4 December 2001, 57/296 of 20 December 2002, 57/337 of 3 July 2003, 58/235 of 23 December 2003, 59/255 of 23 December 2004 and 60/223 of 23 December 2005, as well as resolution 59/213 of 20 December 2004 on cooperation between the United Nations and the African Union,

Recalling also, in this context, Security Council resolutions 1325(2000) of 31 October 2000 on women and peace and security, 1366(2001) of 30 August 2001 on the role of the Council in the prevention of armed conflicts, 1612(2005) of 26 July 2005 on the plight of children in armed conflict, 1625(2005) of 14 September 2005 on strengthening the effectiveness of the Council's role in conflict prevention, particularly in Africa, and 1631(2005) of 17 October 2005 on cooperation between the United Nations and regional and subregional organizations in maintaining international peace and security,

Recalling further the 2005 World Summit Outcome, through which world leaders reaffirmed their commitment to addressing the special needs of Africa,

Recalling the creation by the Economic and Social Council, by its resolution 2002/1 of 15 July 2002, of ad hoc advisory groups on African countries emerging from conflict,

Recognizing that development, peace and security and human rights are interlinked and mutually reinforcing,

Stressing that the responsibility for peace and security in Africa, including the capacity to address the root causes of conflict and to resolve conflicts in a peaceful manner, lies primarily with African countries, while recognizing the need for support from the international community,

Recognizing, in particular, the importance of strengthening the capacity of African regional and subregional organizations to address the causes of conflict in Africa,

Noting that despite the positive trends and advances in Africa, the conditions required for sustained peace and development have yet to be consolidated throughout the continent,

Noting also that conflict prevention and the consolidation of peace would benefit from the coordinated, sustained and integrated efforts of the United Nations system and Member States, and regional and subregional organizations, as well as international and regional financial institutions,

Reaffirming the need to strengthen the synergy between Africa's economic and social development programmes and its peace and security agenda,

Recognizing the importance of the Peacebuilding Commission as a dedicated mechanism to address the special needs of countries emerging from conflict towards recovery, reintegration and reconstruction and to assist them in laying the foundation for peace and sustainable development,

Underlining the need to address the negative implications of the illegal exploitation of natural resources in all its aspects on peace, security and development in Africa, and underlining also that the illicit trade in natural resources is a matter of serious international concern, which can be directly linked to the fuelling of armed conflicts and the illicit trade in and proliferation of arms, especially small arms and light weapons,

1. *Takes note* of the progress report of the Secretary-General on the implementation of the recommendations contained in his report on the causes of conflict and the promotion of durable peace and sustainable development in Africa, including recent efforts in conflict prevention, peacemaking, peacekeeping and peacebuilding undertaken by African countries, African regional organizations and the United Nations system;

2. *Welcomes* the progress made in the prevention, management and resolution of conflict and in post-conflict peacebuilding in a number of African countries;

3. *Also welcomes* the determination of the African Union to strengthen its peacekeeping capacity and to take the lead in peacekeeping operations in the continent, in accordance with Chapter VIII of the Charter of the United Nations and in close coordination with the United Nations, through the Peace and Security Council, as well as ongoing efforts to develop a continental early warning system, enhanced mediation capacity, including through the establishment of the Panel of the Wise, and the African Standby Force;

4. *Urges* the United Nations and invites other development partners to increase their support for the African Union in order to enhance its capacity and effectiveness in the planning, deployment and management of peacekeeping operations and the advanced training to African peacekeepers, and urges the donor community to replenish the Peace Fund of the African Union;

5. *Welcomes* the commitment of international partners to support and strengthen African capabilities in the prevention, management and resolution of conflicts in Africa, including through financial and technical support for further development of the African Peace and Security Architecture, and in this regard welcomes the continued support of the European Union to the African Peace Facility, initiatives by members of the Group of Eight, such as the Reinforcement of African Peacekeeping Capacities programme of France, the new initiative for consolidating peace in Africa under the Tokyo International Conference on African Development framework by Japan and the Global Peace Operations Initiative of the United States of America, and also welcomes the successful convening of the first Beijing Summit of the Forum on China-Africa Cooperation, which resulted in the adoption of the Declaration of the Beijing Summit and the Beijing Action Plan;

6. *Encourages* further contributions by the partners, including through the existing forums of cooperation with Africa, to the promotion of durable peace and sustainable development in Africa by strengthening the capacity of African regional and subregional organizations to address the causes of conflict in Africa and the capacity for the prevention and resolution of armed conflicts, peacekeeping operations and peacebuilding;

7. *Calls for* a holistic and coordinated approach at the national, regional and international levels to identify causes of each conflict situation as a means to improve the effectiveness of conflict prevention and resolution, crisis management, peacemaking, peacekeeping and post-conflict peacebuilding efforts in Africa;

8. *Stresses* the critical importance of a regional approach to conflict prevention, particularly with respect to cross-border issues such as disarmament, demobilization and reintegration programmes, the prevention of illegal exploitation of natural resources and trafficking in high-value commodities and the illicit trade in small arms and light weapons in all its aspects, and emphasizes the central role of the African Union and subregional organizations in addressing such issues;

9. *Welcomes* efforts to enhance practical cooperation, within the framework of an effective partnership, between the United Nations and the African Union in the realm of conflict prevention and resolution, crisis management, peacemaking, peacekeeping and post-conflict peacebuilding in Africa, and in this context urges the United Nations system and the international community to increase, coordinate and sustain their efforts aimed at assisting African countries in addressing the full range of causes of conflict in Africa;

10. *Stresses* the importance of effectively addressing challenges which continue to hamper the achievement of peace and stability on the continent, inter alia, youth unemployment, the devastating social, economic and political impact of the HIV/AIDS crisis, the illegal exploitation of natural resources and the illicit trade in small arms and light weapons;

11. *Notes with concern* that violence against women everywhere continues and often increases, even as armed conflicts draw to an end, and urges further progress in the implementation of policies and guidelines relating to protection of and assistance to women in conflict and post-conflict situations;

12. *Calls for* the enhancement of the role of women in conflict prevention, conflict resolution and post-conflict peacebuilding;

13. *Notes with concern* the tragic plight of children in conflict situations in Africa, particularly the phenomenon of child soldiers, and stresses the need for the protection of children in armed conflicts, post-conflict counselling, rehabilitation and education;

14. *Recognizes* the important role of the good offices of the Secretary-General in Africa, and encourages the Secretary-General to use mediation as often as possible

to help to solve conflicts peacefully, taking due consideration of the work performed by the African Union and other subregional organizations in that regard;

15. *Welcomes* the strengthening of the United Nations peacemaking support capacity through the establishment of the Mediation Support Unit within the Department of Political Affairs of the Secretariat as well as the launch of United Nations Peacemaker, a Web-based knowledge-sharing and operational tool;

16. *Invites* the United Nations and the donor community to increase efforts to support ongoing regional efforts to build African mediation and negotiation capacity;

17. *Welcomes* African-led initiatives to strengthen political, economic and corporate governance, such as the African Peer Review Mechanism, encourages more African countries to join this Mechanism process as soon as possible, and calls upon the United Nations system and Member States to assist African Member States and regional and subregional organizations in their efforts to improve good governance, including the rule of law and the holding of free and fair elections;

18. *Recognizes* the role that the Peacebuilding Commission can perform to ensure the national ownership of the peacebuilding process in countries emerging from conflict and that nationally evolved priorities are at the core of international and regional efforts in addressing the root causes of the conflicts in the countries under consideration, and calls for the full engagement and commitment of all relevant actors to the work of the Peacebuilding Commission with a view to addressing identified critical peacebuilding priorities and issues through a coherent, holistic and inclusive peacebuilding process;

19. *Calls upon* the United Nations system and invites Member States to assist African countries emerging from conflict in their efforts to build national capacities of governance, including the rehabilitation of the security sector, disarmament, demobilization and the reintegration of ex-combatants, provision for the safe return of internally displaced persons and refugees, the launch of income-generation activities, particularly for youth and women, and the delivery of basic public services;

20. *Stresses* the importance of creating an environment conducive to national reconciliation and social and economic recovery in countries emerging from conflict;

21. *Takes note* of the conclusions of the Expert Group Meeting on "Natural Resources and Conflict in Africa: Transforming a Peace Liability into a Peace Asset", held in Cairo from 17 to 19 June 2006, calls upon African Member States and regional and subregional organizations to assist African countries emerging from conflict in devising national natural resources and public revenue management structures, and urges the international community to assist in this process by providing adequate financial and technical assistance, as well as by renewing commitment to efforts aimed at combating the illegal exploitation of the natural resources of those countries;

22. *Notes* the positive role the media can play in conflict prevention and resolution, welcomes decision EX.CL/Dec.215 (VII) of the seventh ordinary session of the Executive Council of the African Union, held from 28 June to 2 July 2005, as adopted by the Assembly of Heads of State and Government in Sirte, Libyan Arab Jamahiriya, to establish the Pan-African Television Channel as a vehicle to mitigate the sociocultural causes of conflict in Africa, and calls upon the international community to increase efforts to support the establishment of such a channel and to discourage hate media and promote responsible journalism;

23. *Decides* to continue to monitor the implementation of the recommendations contained in the report of the Secretary-General on the causes of conflict and the promotion of durable peace and sustainable development in Africa;

24. *Requests* the Secretary-General to submit to the General Assembly at its sixty-second session a progress report on the implementation of the present resolution;

25. *Also requests* the Secretary-General to include in the aforementioned progress report concrete proposals for possible United Nations actions and plans in support of the goal of achieving a conflict-free Africa by 2010.

African peacekeeping capacity

The Special Committee on Peacekeeping Operations, at its 2006 substantive session (New York, 27 February–17 March [A/60/19], continued discussion on the enhancement of African peacekeeping capacities. The Special Committee reiterated its support for the development of a joint action plan for addressing the systemic constraints identified by African Member States, including in the areas of common doctrine and training standards, logistical support, funding, and institutional capacity for planning and managing peacekeeping operations within the AU and subregional organizations. The Special Committee called for better coordination among donors, the matching of expectations in partnerships and a deeper understanding of African needs. Given the multiplicity of stakeholders involved in African capacity-building, there was a need for effective coordination of support to the AU. The Special Committee stressed the importance of the AU lead and ownership of its 10-year capacity-building plan, including donor coordination. Noting that the 2005 World Summit [YUN 2005, p. 47] had supported the development and implementation of a 10-year plan for capacity-building with the AU, the Special Committee expressed support for that effort as it related to African peacekeeping capacities and welcomed the proposal for a new organizational entity in the Department of Peacekeeping Operations as the focal point for all contacts between the Department and other regional arrangements.

Central Africa and Great Lakes region

In 2006, Central Africa and the Great Lakes region continued to be affected by the activities of militia groups. The Central African Republic witnessed the strengthening of rebel movements in the north, and in Chad, rebel groups launched increasingly coordinated attacks against the army. Meanwhile, local warlords and international companies continued the illegal exploitation of the region's natural resources, particularly in the Democratic Republic of the Congo (DRC), in violation of a UN embargo.

However, the region also made noticeable steps towards the resolution of long-standing conflicts. Uganda and the Lord's Resistance Army (LRA) signed, in August, an Agreement on Cessation of Hostilities. In Burundi, the Government and the last major rebel group, the Palipehutu-National Liberation Forces (FNL), signed a peace agreement in June, and a ceasefire agreement in September.

In January, the Security Council held an all-day ministerial-level debate on the Great Lakes region. It discussed, among other topics, improving cooperation between the United Nations and African organizations, such as the AU, particularly in peacekeeping and conflict prevention, and preparations for the second summit of the International Conference on Peace, Security, Democracy and Development in the Great Lakes Region.

The four-year transitional process in the DRC concluded with elections that led to the installation of the National Assembly on 22 September, and the inauguration of President Joseph Kabila on 6 December. The United Nations Mission in the Democratic Republic of the Congo was instrumental in ensuring a peaceful electoral process, with the assistance of a European Union (EU) special force. The Council continued to address problems affecting the DRC, including activities of irregular fighters, particularly the Forces démocratiques pour la libération du Rwanda, as well as the connection between neighbouring countries' concerns and interests in the DRC and violations of the arms embargo. In January, the Council re-established the Group of Experts to monitor the embargo, and, in July, extended by another year its arms embargo against militia groups in the DRC.

In Burundi, negotiations between the Government and FNL, the last major rebel group, hosted by the United Republic of Tanzania and facilitated by South Africa, resulted in the conclusion of a peace agreement in June, and a ceasefire agreement in September. In view of significant improvements in the security situation, Burundi requested the United Nations, in May, to establish an integrated peacebuilding office. The mandate of the United Nations Operation in Burundi expired on 31 December, and the United Nations Integrated Office in Burundi was to be launched on 1 January 2007.

One of the region's most devastating conflicts, opposing Uganda and LRA, came closer to a solution, with the signing on 26 August, in Juba, the Sudan, of the Agreement on Cessation of Hostilities. The brutal insurgency waged by LRA since 1987, had caused the deaths of some 100,000 people in northern Uganda and the displacement of up to 2 million more. In an effort to bring about a comprehensive political solution to the conflict, the Secretary-General, in December, named former Mozambican President, Joaquim Chissano, as his Special Envoy to help deal with the LRA issue.

The Central African Republic was increasingly drawn into the crisis affecting Chad and the Darfur region of the Sudan. Forces opposed to Central African Republic President François Bozizé appeared to have forged links with rebels fighting against Chad's President Idriss Déby Itno. Attacks by those forces in the north increased in intensity and became an armed rebellion against the Government. In October-November, members of a coalition of three rebel movements took control of four northern cities, but were later expelled by a Government counter-offensive. The Central African Republic accused the Sudan of supporting the rebellion, an accusation the Sudan denied. The conflict created a humanitarian crisis, with thousands of displaced people crossing into Chad and Cameroon to flee the violence. At the request of the Government, the Security Council extended the mandate of the United Nations Peacebuilding Office in the Central African Republic (BONUCA) for another year.

The crisis in the Darfur region of the Sudan spilled over into Chad and the Central African Republic, with the two countries accusing the Sudan of supporting armed groups increasingly active in their territories. The Tripoli Agreement signed on 8 February by Chadian President Idriss Déby Itno and Sudanese President Omar Hassan al-Bashir, and the 26 July N'Djamena Agreement between Chad and the Sudan did not defuse the crisis. The Security Council, in August, requested the United Nations Mission in Sudan to establish a political and military presence in Chad and, if necessary, in the Central African Republic. The Secretary-General dispatched an assessment mission to the two countries, and, in December, reported to the

Council that conditions on the ground did not permit the deployment of a peacekeeping operation, but only of a robust monitoring and protection mission.

At the International Conference on Peace, Security, Democracy and Development in the Great Lakes Region (Nairobi, Kenya, 14-15 December), Heads of State and Government signed the Pact on Security, Stability and Development in the Great Lakes Region. The 11 countries committed themselves to cooperating in the areas of security, democracy and governance, economic development and humanitarian and social welfare.

Security Council ministerial meeting

On 4 January the United Republic of Tanzania, in its capacity as Security Council President, announced the holding of an open debate on peace, security and development in the Great Lakes region. On 18 January [S/2006/27], it submitted to the Secretary-General a concept paper on the subject as a basis for discussion during the debate, scheduled for 27 January. According to the paper, the debate would focus on finding ways of implementing and coordinating the various regional and international initiatives for peace and stability in the region. It would highlight the search for effective means of applying broader UN peace and security initiatives for Africa to the Great Lakes region; identifying strategies for linking UN initiatives on conflict prevention, resolution and peacebuilding with those of the Great Lakes region; and implementing resolutions 1625(2005) [YUN 2005, p. 155], 1631(2005) [ibid., p. 97], 1649(2005) [ibid., p. 187], as well as the mandate of the Peacebuilding Commission [ibid., p. 94]. Topics should also include ways to strengthen democracy, good governance and the rule of law and provide protection and humanitarian assistance to civilians, including refugees, internally displaced persons and returnees. The outcome should, among other things, lead to the creation of a mechanism for enhancing cooperation between the UN Security Council and the AU Peace and Security Council.

On 27 January [meeting 5359], during the Security Council's consideration of the subject, Council President Asha-Rose Migiro said that the Great Lakes peace initiative was embodied in the Dar es Salaam Declaration adopted in November 2004 at the first International Conference on Peace, Security, Democracy and Development in the Great Lakes Region [YUN 2004, p. 116] and was the foundation for building a framework for realizing enduring peace, democratic governance and respect for human rights, economic cooperation and sustainable development. Collective political will was needed to prevent and resolve conflicts, consolidate peace and build democratic governance institutions. The region faced residual and new challenges and needed to consolidate its achievements and mobilize international community support to accomplish its objectives. The countries of the region were working to create mechanisms to strengthen mutual confidence and trust as a basis for peace and stability and were committed to developing arrangements to deepen cooperation and sustain peace and security. They had embraced democracy and good governance, not only as intrinsic values, but as necessary for their peaceful coexistence and development. The desirability of a regional approach in that endeavour could not be overemphasized.

Congo's Foreign Affairs Minister said that recent developments indicated that progress was being made in terms of peace and security in the region. In Burundi, the transition had led to democratic, free and transparent elections. The political transition in the DRC was proceeding favourably, and everything should be done to stop the armed groups in the east of the country from jeopardizing the process. The DRC, Rwanda and Uganda should pursue efforts to ease tension and establish relations of trust, which would in turn help resolve the problems of the illicit circulation of small arms and light weapons, alleviate the plight of refugees and displaced persons, eliminate the presence of armed groups in neighbouring States and curb the illegal exploitation of natural resources. In that spirit of mutual trust, his Government was facilitating the voluntary repatriation of Rwandan refugees and members of the former armed forces of Zaire to their countries of origin.

The DRC said that, in December 2005, the Congolese people had voted overwhelmingly for a draft constitution. The electoral law had been discussed and would soon be adopted by Parliament, and efforts were under way to bring together troops from various warring factions to create an integrated army. Unfortunately, on 23 January 2006, eight Guatemalan members of the United Nations Organization Mission in the Democratic Republic of the Congo (MONUC) were killed in Garamba National Park, while pursuing armed groups. That tragedy strengthened the DRC determination to eliminate all armed groups creating insecurity along the eastern border. Although relations with neighbouring States had improved, some of them continued to harbour criminals, and the DRC had requested their extradition, in accordance with Council resolutions. The Council should exert pressure on such countries to cease their support of the militias. As the country prepared to elect the future leaders of its institutions, it expected of all neighbouring States an attitude of solidarity so that no outside threat would disrupt the process.

Rwanda said that the prospects for peace, stability and prosperity were better than at any other moment since the 1994 genocide [YUN 1994, p. 282]. However, the unimplemented aspects of the Lusaka Ceasefire Agreement [YUN 1999, p. 87] should be addressed. One key impediment to peace still remained: the presence of genocidal forces and other armed groups in the region, whose sole purpose was destabilization. Until the people of the region were free of the fear, tyranny and attacks of the Forces démocratiques de libération du Rwanda (FDLR), LRA, FNL and other armed groups sowing desolation in eastern DRC and the rest of the region, the emerging peace would continue to be fragile. Rwandans wished to know why the Security Council had not ended the threat posed by those forces, and why the Council Committee established pursuant to resolution 1533(2004) [YUN 2004, p. 138] and the Group of Experts established under resolution 1596(2005) [YUN 2005, p. 142] had not yet seriously tackled the flow of arms and supplies to those groups.

Uganda said that progress in peace initiatives indicated that the prospects were greater than ever for transforming the Great Lakes into a region of peace, prosperity and cooperation. However, the biggest obstacle remained the problem of the negative forces, especially the Allied Democratic Forces (ADF), FDLR, the People's Redemption Army (PRA) and LRA, which continued to cause untold suffering to civilian populations. The LRA, based in southern Sudan and the Garamba National Park in the DRC, had caused thousands of deaths and tremendous suffering to people in northern Uganda and southern Sudan. For too long, the Ugandan defence force had single-handedly fought against the LRA in a two-track policy combining military pressure and political negotiations. Although the military campaign had not completely eliminated the LRA threat, it had severely weakened it by reducing its ranks from 3,000 to between 500 and 600 through defections and capture. The Government had also embarked on peace initiatives to resolve the conflict through a negotiated political settlement. The 2000 Amnesty Act and its implementing Amnesty Commission had sought to accommodate those who renounced rebellion and promote reconciliation. More than 2,000 LRA rebels had taken advantage of the amnesty. The Government had initiated or supported major efforts for a negotiated peace settlement since 1994, but the lack of a political agenda by LRA and pressure from its external backers had made such efforts fruitless.

South Africa lauded the progress made, including the recent agreement between the DRC and Uganda to manage LRA activity in Haut-Uele, Orientale Province, and the subsequent elimination of LRA activity in the DRC; the agreement between the two countries to create a Ugandan Amnesty Commission Office in North Kivu to help disarm and repatriate Ugandan combatants; and the success of the DRC and MONUC in dealing with Congolese Revolutionary Movement (MRC) elements active in Kilo and Mongwalu, as well as the efforts of the DRC and Uganda to disarm and repatriate those MRC elements that had relocated in Uganda. Nevertheless, several issues of concern remained, such as the presence of FDLR and Mai-Mai forces in Kivu, which was a serious threat to regional stability, the integrity of the DRC transition to peace and the regional demobilization, disarmament and rehabilitation process.

SECURITY COUNCIL ACTION

On 27 January [meeting 5359], the Security Council unanimously adopted **resolution 1653(2006)**. The draft [S/2006/51] was prepared in consultations among Council members.

The Security Council,

Recalling its resolutions and the statements by its President on the Great Lakes region of Africa and concerning the situation in the Democratic Republic of the Congo and in Burundi, in particular resolutions 1649(2005) and 1650(2005) of 21 December 2005,

Recalling also its resolution 1625(2005) of 14 September 2005 on strengthening the effectiveness of the Security Council and the role of civil society in the prevention and resolution of armed conflict, particularly in Africa,

Recalling further its resolution 1631(2005) of 17 October 2005 on cooperation between the United Nations and regional organizations and General Assembly resolution 59/213 of 20 December 2004 on cooperation between the United Nations and the African Union,

Reaffirming its respect for the sovereignty, territorial integrity, unity and political independence of all States in the region, and recalling the importance of the principles of good-neighbourliness, non-interference and cooperation in the relations among States in the region,

Reiterating its condemnation of the genocide in Rwanda of 1994 and the armed conflicts which have plagued the Great Lakes region in the past decade, and expressing its profound concern at the violations of human rights and international humanitarian law resulting in widescale loss of life, human suffering and destruction of property,

Aware that the link between the illegal exploitation of natural resources, the illicit trade in those resources and the proliferation of and trafficking in arms is one of the factors fuelling and exacerbating conflicts in the Great

Lakes region, and especially in the Democratic Republic of the Congo,

Expressing its deep concern at the devastating impact of conflict and insecurity on the humanitarian situation throughout the Great Lakes region and their implications for regional peace and security, especially where arms and armed groups move across borders, such as the long-running and brutal insurgency by the Lord's Resistance Army in northern Uganda, which has caused the death, abduction and displacement of thousands of innocent civilians in Uganda, the Sudan and the Democratic Republic of the Congo,

Welcoming the efforts undertaken by the Tripartite Plus Joint Commission comprising Burundi, the Democratic Republic of the Congo, Rwanda and Uganda as a significant contribution to heightened dialogue between the countries of the Great Lakes region,

Recalling its previous resolutions that reaffirmed the importance of holding an international conference on peace, security and stability in the Great Lakes region, and recognizing the continued ownership of the process by the countries of the region with the facilitation of the United Nations, the African Union, the Group of Friends of the Great lakes Region and all others concerned,

Taking note with satisfaction of the holding of the first International Conference on Peace, Security, Democracy and Development in the Great Lakes Region, in Dar es Salaam, United Republic of Tanzania, on 19 and 20 November 2004,

Recognizing the "Good-Neighbourly Declaration" adopted on 25 September 2003 by the representatives of Burundi, the Democratic Republic of the Congo, Rwanda and Uganda and the Dar es Salaam Declaration on Peace, Security, Democracy and Development in the Great Lakes Region adopted on 20 November 2004 by the first summit of the International Conference on the Great Lakes Region,

Recognizing also the significant achievements and progress in the peace processes in the Great Lakes region, the recent installation of a democratically elected Government in Burundi and progress in the transition to democratic institutions in the Democratic Republic of the Congo,

Expressing its gratitude to the United Nations Organization Mission in the Democratic Republic of the Congo and to the United Nations Operation in Burundi for their significant contribution to peace in the region,

Paying tribute to the donor community for the assistance it is providing to the countries in the region, and encouraging it to maintain that assistance,

Welcoming General Assembly resolution 60/1 of 16 September 2005 on the 2005 World Summit Outcome and, in particular, the commitment to address the special needs of Africa,

1. *Commends* the positive role played by the Secretary-General, the African Union, the Group of Friends of the Great Lakes Region and other stakeholders in organizing and participating in the first summit of the International Conference on Peace, Security, Democracy and Development in the Great Lakes Region;

2. *Urges* the countries of the Great Lakes region to continue their collective efforts to develop a subregional approach for promoting good relations, peaceful coexistence and peaceful resolution of disputes as envisaged in the Dar es Salaam Declaration on Peace, Security, Democracy and Development in the Great Lakes Region, and encourages them, in partnership with the Special Representative of the Secretary-General for the Great Lakes Region and other stakeholders, to finalize the preparations for the second summit, to be held in Nairobi, including a clear focus on peace and security issues, with a view to adopting a security, stability and development pact for the countries of the Great Lakes region;

3. *Calls upon* the countries of the region to agree on confidence-building measures based on effective and concrete actions;

4. *Encourages and supports* the countries of the Great Lakes region, individually and collectively, in strengthening and institutionalizing respect for human rights and humanitarian law, including respect for women's rights and protection of children affected by armed conflict, good governance, rule of law, democratic practices as well as development cooperation;

5. *Encourages* the development of the prevailing goodwill and relations among the countries of the region which have positively influenced the successful transition in Burundi and the course of the ongoing democratic transition in the Democratic Republic of the Congo;

6. *Urges* all States concerned to take action to bring to justice perpetrators of grave violations of human rights and international humanitarian law and to take appropriate measures of international cooperation and judicial assistance in this regard;

7. *Expresses its support* for the efforts of States in the region to build independent and reliable national judicial institutions in order to put an end to impunity;

8. *Strongly condemns* the activities of militias and armed groups operating in the Great Lakes region, such as the Forces démocratiques de libération du Rwanda, the Parti pour la libération du peuple hutu-Forces nationales de libération and the Lord's Resistance Army, which continue to attack civilians and United Nations and humanitarian personnel and commit human rights abuses against local populations and threaten the stability of individual States and the region as a whole, and reiterates its demand that all such armed groups lay down their arms and engage voluntarily and without any delay or preconditions in their disarmament and in their repatriation and resettlement;

9. *Stresses* the need for the States in the region, within their respective territories, to disarm, demobilize and cooperate in the repatriation or resettlement, as appropriate, of foreign armed groups and local militias, and commends in this regard the robust action of the United Nations Organization Mission in the Democratic Republic of the Congo, acting in accordance with its mandate, in support of the Armed Forces of the Democratic Republic of the Congo in the eastern part of the country;

10. *Underscores* the fact that the Governments in the region have a primary responsibility to protect their populations, including from attacks by militias and armed groups, and stresses the importance of ensuring the full, safe and unhindered access of humanitarian workers to people in need in accordance with international law;

11. *Calls upon* all States in the region to deepen their cooperation with a view to putting an end to the activities of illegal armed groups, and underlines the fact that these States must abide by their obligations under the Charter of the United Nations to refrain from the threat or use of force against the territorial integrity or political independence of their neighbours;

12. *Urges* the international community, non-governmental organizations and civil society to increase humanitarian assistance to civilians affected by displacements and violence from years of protracted conflicts in the Great Lakes region;

13. *Commends* the efforts of the United Nations missions in the region, in accordance with their respective mandates, to protect civilians, including humanitarian personnel, to enable delivery of humanitarian aid and to create the necessary conditions for the voluntary return of refugees and internally displaced persons;

14. *Requests* the Secretary-General to make recommendations to the Security Council, as appropriate, on how best to support efforts by States in the region to put an end to the activities of illegal armed groups, and to recommend how United Nations agencies and missions—the United Nations Mission in the Sudan, the United Nations Organization Mission in the Democratic Republic of the Congo and the United Nations Operation in Burundi—can help, including through further support for the efforts of the Governments concerned to ensure the protection of, and humanitarian assistance to, civilians in need;

15. *Calls upon* the countries of the region to continue their efforts to create conditions conducive to voluntary repatriation and safe and durable integration of refugees and former combatants in their respective countries of origin, and in this regard, calls for commensurate international support for refugees and reintegration and reinsertion of returnees, internally displaced persons and former combatants;

16. *Also calls upon* the countries of the region to reinforce their cooperation with the Security Council Committee and the Group of Experts established pursuant to resolution 1533(2004) in enforcing the arms embargo in the Democratic Republic of the Congo and to combat cross-border trafficking in illicit small arms, light weapons and illicit natural resources as well as the movement of combatants, and reiterates its demand that the Governments of Uganda, Rwanda, the Democratic Republic of the Congo and Burundi take measures to prevent the use of their respective territories in support of the activities of armed groups present in the region;

17. *Urges* the Governments concerned in the region to enhance their cooperation to promote lawful and transparent exploitation of natural resources among themselves and in the region;

18. *Welcomes* the establishment of the Peacebuilding Commission, and underlines its potential importance to the work of the Council in this region;

19. *Invites* the international community, including regional organizations, international financial institutions and relevant bodies of the United Nations system, to support and complement the peacebuilding and development initiatives required to sustain peace, security and stability in the countries of the Great Lakes region;

20. *Decides* to remain seized of the matter.

Second International Conference on Great Lakes Region

The second International Conference on the Great Lakes Region was held on 14 and 15 December, in Nairobi, Kenya. Organized under the auspices of the United Nations and the AU, the summit meeting was preceded by meetings of the Regional Inter-Ministerial Committee (February, Central African Republic; 22 September, New York; 11 December, Nairobi, Kenya). In January [S/2006/46], the Secretary-General had submitted to the Security Council a report on the preparations for holding the Conference.

The Conference was attended by the Heads of State and Government of the 11 countries comprising the region (Angola, Burundi, the Central African Republic, Congo, DRC, Kenya, Rwanda, the Sudan, the United Republic of Tanzania, Uganda, Zambia). The Conference adopted the Pact on Security, Stability and Development in the Great Lakes Region, by which the leaders pledged to translate into reality the priority political options and guiding principles of the Dar es Salaam Declaration, adopted at the first Conference in 2004 [YUN 2004, p. 116]. The objectives of the Pact were to provide a legal framework governing relations among States of the region, implement the Dar es Salaam Declaration and the mechanisms of the Pact and create conditions for security, stability and sustainable development among the States. It contained protocols on non-aggression and mutual defence; democracy and good governance; judicial cooperation, prevention and punishment of the crime of genocide, war crimes and crimes against humanity and all forms of discrimination; illegal exploitation of natural resources; the specific reconstruction and development zone; prevention and suppression of sexual violence against women and children; protection and assistance to internally displaced persons; property rights of returning persons; and management of information and communication. The Pact also contained a Programme of Action and established a Special Fund for Reconstruction and Development and a Regional Follow-up Mechanism, which would include a Conference secretariat to be headed by an Executive Secretary. Liberata Mulamula (United Republic of Tanzania) was nominated to the post of Executive Secretary.

Security Council consideration. The Security Council, on 20 December [meeting 5603], was briefed by the Secretary-General's Special Representative for the Great Lakes Region, Ibrahima Fall, who heralded the pact as substantive and forward-looking. The region, he said, had turned a page of despair and opened a new chapter of regional and national destiny, managed by Governments and non-governmental actors. There was a commitment to ratify the Pact speedily and respect its spirit and letter, reflected in the decision to immediately establish the political follow-up mechanisms and the Conference secretariat. It was also reflected in the decision to establish the secretariat headquarters in Burundi, with Liberata Mulamula as the first Executive Secretary, and to institutionalize the special fund for reconstruction and development, to which the United Republic of Tanzania had pledged $500,000 and the DRC $1 million. The collective political will had been evident both in the outcome and the preparatory process, through the inclusion of non-governmental actors, including young people, women, civil society, the private sector and religious organizations.

He said that development partners welcomed the signing of the Pact and believed that the Conference had the potential to promote peace, security and development in the region. Canada, the co-chair of the Group of Friends of the Great Lakes Region, reaffirmed the Group's support for the establishment of the Regional Follow-up Mechanism and funding for it until June 2007. Other partners pledged financial and other support.

The Executive Secretary designate, in his address to the Council, appealed for the extension of the Office of the Special Representative of the Secretary-General for the Great Lakes until March 2007, as requested by the Regional Inter-Ministerial Committee at their February meeting in Bangui, in order to provide the new Conference secretariat with technical support and allow a smooth transition of responsibilities.

SECURITY COUNCIL ACTION

On 20 December [meeting 5603], following consultations among Security Council members, the President made statement **S/PRST/2006/57** on behalf of the Council:

> The Security Council commends the countries of the Great Lakes region for the successful conclusion of the Second Summit of the International Conference on the Great Lakes Region in Nairobi on 15 December 2006.
>
> The Council congratulates regional leaders on the signing of the Pact on Security, Stability and Development in the Great Lakes Region and welcomes their commitment to its implementation.
>
> The Council further welcomes the decision to establish a Regional Follow-up Mechanism, to include a Conference Secretariat headed by the first Executive Secretary, Ms. Liberata Mulamula, of the United Republic of Tanzania, as well as the decision to establish the offices of the Conference Secretariat in Bujumbura.
>
> The Council pays tribute to the joint African Union/United Nations Secretariat, the Group of Friends of the Great Lakes Region co-chaired by Canada and the Netherlands, the United Nations lead agencies, the African Union, the European Union, the African Development Bank and the international community for their support and assistance to the International Conference process.
>
> The Council also pays tribute to the Secretary-General and his Special Representative, Mr. Ibrahima Fall, for their support, commitment and effective facilitation of the process leading to the convening of the Second Summit and the signing of the Pact on Security, Stability and Development.
>
> The Council supports the request of the Regional Inter-Ministerial Committee to extend the mandate of the Office of the Special Representative of the Secretary-General for a final period of three months, until 31 March 2007, with a view to ensuring regional ownership of the Follow-up Mechanism and completing successfully the transition to the Conference Secretariat.
>
> The Council appeals to the countries of the region, the Group of Friends, the United Nations agencies, funds and programmes and the international community to consider providing assistance to the Conference Secretariat and the Special Fund for Reconstruction and Development in the Great Lakes Region to support implementation by the parties of the Pact on Security, Stability and Development.

Office of the Special Representative for Great Lakes Region

On 15 March [S/2006/192], the Secretary-General notified the Security Council that the mandate of his Special Representative for the Great Lakes Region, Ibrahima Fall, would expire on 31 March, but given his involvement with preparations for the second International Conference on the Great Lakes Region (see p. 124), he intended to extend the Special Representative's mandate until 30 September.

On 29 March [S/2006/193], the Council took note of that intention, and encouraged the Special Representative to focus on three priorities—assist the countries of the region to convene the Summit and include a clear focus on peace and security; facilitate adoption of a security, stability and development pact; support the core countries so that the planned, regionally-led follow-up mechanism was fully operational by the time of the Summit; and transfer residual UN responsibilities to the core countries.

On 4 October [S/2006/811], the Secretary-General notified the Council of his intention to extend further the mandate of the Office of the Special Representative until 31 December to finalize preparations for the Summit. That extension had been requested by the International Conference's Regional inter-Ministerial Committee, meeting in New York on 22 September. On 13 October [S/2006/812], the Council took note of the Secretary-General's intention.

On 31 January [A/60/585/Add.1], the Secretary-General had informed the General Assembly that the estimated requirements for the Office of the Special Representative for the period 1 January to 31 December would amount to $2,151,200.

In its March report [A/60/7/Add.37], the Advisory Committee on Administrative and Budgetary Questions (ACABQ) recommended acceptance of the Secretary-General's proposal, which the General Assembly approved in section I of **resolution 60/255** of 8 May (see p. 1618).

In November [A/61/525/Add.3 & Corr.1], the Secretary-General proposed resource requirements in the amount of $2,064,200 (net) for the period 1 January to 31 December 2007. ACABQ, in its December report [A/61/640 & Corr.1], recommended a 10 per cent reduction in resource requirement for all special political missions, good offices and other political initiatives authorized by the General Assembly or the Security Council, which the Assembly approved in section VII of **resolution 61/252** of 22 December (see p. 1614).

Standing Advisory Committee on Security Questions

The United Nations Standing Advisory Committee on Security Questions in Central Africa held its twenty-fourth ministerial meeting in Kigali, Rwanda, from 25 to 29 September [A/61/502-S/2006/796], with all Committee members (Angola, Burundi, Cameroon, Central African Republic, Chad, Congo, DRC, Equatorial Guinea, Gabon, Rwanda, Sao Tome and Principe) participating. The Committee, reviewing the geopolitical and security situation in Burundi, the Central African Republic, the DRC and Chad, noted that overall developments in those countries continued to be positive. Despite a few armed confrontations and a worrying humanitarian and human rights situation, steady progress was achieved in the peace processes, with multiparty elections held in Sao Tome and Principe, the DRC, Chad and Gabon. However, the fragility of those processes, as seen once again in the DRC, required that the parties, the other countries of the subregion and the international community redouble their efforts to usher in a new era of development.

The Committee also considered the impact of the crisis in the Darfur region of the Sudan on member countries of the Committee and appealed to the international community to ensure that the borders between Chad, the Central African Republic and the Sudan were properly secured and that assistance to refugees and displaced persons was increased. It encouraged the steps taken to deploy a UN peacekeeping operation in the Darfur region of the Sudan, and acknowledged the necessity of the subregional approach to stabilize the area. It called for the early convening of a subregional conference to examine ways of solving cross-border problems.

Concerned by the aggravation of trans-border crime, the Committee encouraged member countries to continue to tackle such crime and develop a concerted subregional approach.

The Committee welcomed progress made in programmes for disarming, demobilizing and reintegrating former combatants, including child soldiers, particularly through the collection and destruction of arms. It expressed concern over the lack of funds for launching and executing those programmes in the countries that were emerging from conflict and urged donors to provide substantial support. The Committee urged member countries to redouble their efforts in combating the illicit trade in small arms and light weapons and appealed for more international support to combat the phenomenon.

The Secretary-General, in response to General Assembly resolution 60/87 [YUN 2005, p. 645], submitted a September report [A/61/365] on the Committee's activities since the submission of the previous report in July 2005 [ibid., p. 164]. He noted that, in recent years, financial support for the Committee, most of which was voluntary, seemed to be waning, resulting in its inability to fully implement its programme of work. However, the Committee continued to play an important role in promoting peace and security in the region. Committee member States needed to assume full ownership of its activities. In that regard, it was critical that the Council for Peace and Security in Central Africa of the Economic Community of Central African States and its structures, in particular its early-warning mechanism, became operational, and that the capacity of the Community's secretariat be strengthened, so that it could spearhead implementation of the Committee's declarations, decisions and recommendations.

Democratic Republic of the Congo

The transitional process in the DRC, in the context of the 2002 Global and All Inclusive Agreement on the Transition in the Democratic Republic of the Congo [YUN 2002, p. 125], came to a close with the holding of elections that led to the installation of the National Assembly on 22 September and the inauguration of President Joseph Kabila on 6 December. The transition and election preparations were supported by the International Committee in Support of the Transition, composed of the five permanent members of the Security Council, as well as Angola, Belgium, Canada, Gabon, South Africa and Zambia, the EU and the AU, and the United Nations Organization Mission in the Democratic Republic of the Congo.

A Security Council mission visited the country ahead of the elections. MONUC was instrumental in ensuring a peaceful election process, supported by a 1,000-strong European reserve force. Throughout the year, MONUC backed efforts by the Congolese army to bring rebel forces under control.

The Council re-established the Group of Experts monitoring the embargo against militia groups in the DRC. It extended the embargo by another year, and expanded the sanctions to political and military leaders recruiting children, and directed attention to the militias' illegal exploitation of natural resources to fund their activities. The Council extended MONUC mandate until 15 February 2007, which was instrumental in ensuring peaceful elections and bringing a measure of stability to the country. Tragically, eight Mission peacekeepers were killed on 23 January in combat with the Ugandan rebel group Lord's Resistance Army (LRA), and another on 28 May during a confrontation between militias and UN-backed soldiers from the national army.

In May, as requested by the Council, the Secretary-General submitted his proposals on disarming foreign combatants in the DRC. Thousands of foreign combatants still plagued the eastern part of the country, particularly the Rwandan Hutu rebel Forces démocratiques de libération du Rwanda (FDLR), the Burundian rebel Forces nationales de liberation (FNL), and the Ugandan rebel groups, LRA and the Allied Democratic Forces/National Army for the Liberation of Uganda (ADF/NALU).

In March, in Kinshasa, DRC authorities arrested and transferred to the International Criminal Court (ICC) militia leader Thomas Lubanga Dyilo, after the ICC Prosecutor issued an arrest warrant. Mr. Lubanga, the first person to be tried by the Court, was commander-in-chief of the Forces patriotiques pour la libération du Congo (FPLC) in 2002-2003 in the Ituri district in the north-eastern DRC. The ICC Prosecutor, on 28 August, formally charged him with recruiting child soldiers. Hearings began on 9 November.

Political developments and MONUC activities

Attack on peacekeepers

In his March report on MONUC [S/2006/390], the Secretary-General said that the United Nations Organization Mission in the Democratic Republic of the Congo (MONUC), on 18 January, had deployed its Guatemalan special forces unit to the Garamba National Park, after it received information about the alleged presence there of elements of the Lord's Resistance Army (LRA), including the militia leader, Vincent Otti, for whom the International Criminal Court had issued an arrest warrant. On 23 January, while approaching a militia camp, the unit came under heavy fire by suspected LRA elements. Eight troops were killed and five injured.

SECURITY COUNCIL ACTION

On 25 January [meeting 5356], following consultations among Security Council members, the President made statement **S/PRST/2006/4** on behalf of the Council:

> The Security Council condemns with the utmost firmness the attack against a detachment of the United Nations Organization Mission in the Democratic Republic of the Congo, which occurred on 23 January 2006 in the national park of Garamba, resulting in the death of eight Guatemalan peacekeepers and the severe wounding of five others. It offers its condolences to the families of the victims and to the authorities of Guatemala. It commends the dedication of the personnel of the Mission, who operate in particularly hazardous conditions.
>
> The Council considers this aggression to be an unacceptable outrage. The peacekeepers were involved in an operation against suspected elements of the Lord Resistance Army reported to be present in the park of Garamba. The Lord Resistance Army has conducted a long-running and vicious insurgency in northern Uganda which has caused the death, abduction and displacement of thousands of innocent civilians in Uganda, the Sudan and the Democratic Republic of the Congo. The Council calls upon the Government of National Unity and Transition immediately to take all necessary measures to bring to justice those responsible for this attack.
>
> The Council also condemns with the utmost firmness the recent seizure of villages in the area of Rutshuru, North Kivu province, by insurgent elements. It expresses its concern at atrocities and human rights abuses which have been reported in this context. It considers all such actions to be a serious threat to the peace process and to the transition, and demands that they cease immediately. It stresses the need for unreserved commitment to the integration process of the armed forces, in the spirit of the Global and All-Inclusive Agreement on the Transition in the Democratic Republic of the Congo, signed at Pretoria on 17 December 2002.
>
> The Council underlines the importance of the electoral process not being disturbed and in this regard encourages ongoing efforts for community reconciliation. It also stresses in this context the importance of early adoption of the electoral law under discussion in the Parliament, and of respect

for the timetable drawn up by the Independent Electoral Commission.

The Council reaffirms its commitment to respect the national sovereignty, political independence, territorial integrity and unity of the Democratic Republic of the Congo. It expresses its solidarity with the Congolese people and its support for the Government of National Unity and Transition. It calls for the prompt extension of State authority throughout the Congolese territory.

The Council reiterates its call upon States in the region to deepen their cooperation with a view to putting an end to the activities of illegal armed groups, and reaffirms that any recourse to the threat or use of force against the territorial integrity of a State is contrary to the Charter of the United Nations.

The Council reaffirms its full support for the Mission, and urges the Mission to continue to fulfil its mandate with determination.

Electoral preparations

Report of Secretary-General. The Secretary-General reported [S/2006/390] that the constitutional referendum in December 2005 [YUN 2005, p. 190] and the promulgation of the electoral law on 9 March 2006 were important steps towards the holding of democratic elections. The electoral law established 169 electoral constituencies, a two-round system of presidential elections and a mixed system of simple majority and proportional representation for the election of the 500 National Assembly deputies. Registration of candidates began on 10 March, and some 213 parties and coalitions presented candidates, with some 24 of them having a nationwide base. On 16 April, the Independent Electoral Commission published the final list of candidates for the presidential elections, 33 of whom were cleared by the Commission and the Supreme Court, and the provisional list of 9,406 candidates for the legislative elections, 1,305 of whom were women. Some 10,500 candidates would run in the Provincial Assembly elections, on the basis of which the Senate and the provincial governors would be chosen. On 30 April, the Commission set 30 July as the date for the first round of presidential and legislative elections.

The elections, in which 25.5 million voters would cast their ballot for the first time in 45 years, were the largest and most challenging electoral processes ever conducted with UN support. The Secretary-General expressed concern at reports regarding limitations on civil liberties, widespread misuse of public funds, endemic corruption, arbitrary detention of political party members and increasing intimidation of the media, which threatened to undermine the transparency of the elections.

In view of the importance of the electoral process to peace and stability, the Secretary-General visited the country from 21 to 24 March, the Under-Secretary-General for Peacekeeping Operations from 4 to 17 March and the Assistant Secretary-General for Peacekeeping Operations from 18 to 28 March. The Secretary-General urged the Congolese leaders to rise above short-term interests and work for the unity and stability of the country.

The Independent Electoral Commission and MONUC prepared an integrated operational plan for the elections, highlighting the need to spread the UN presence to the 166 territorial capitals and cities and requiring the deployment of additional MONUC staff. The Commission planned to open some 50,000 polling stations to ensure that voting was completed in one day. MONUC continued to enhance the population's understanding of the electoral process through its public information outlets, including Radio Okapi, and by targeting women and youth. The Mission planned to deter armed challenges to the electoral process and provide a safe environment for the vote. A United Nations Development Programme (UNDP) project provided support to the electoral process, and as at 29 March, had spent or committed $219,250,770 for election-related activities.

Authorization of EU force

On 12 April [S/2006/219], the Secretary-General informed the Security Council that the United Nations remained concerned about the possibility of violence during and after the electoral period. On 27 December 2005, Under-Secretary-General for Peacekeeping Operations Jean-Marie Guéhenno had requested the European Union (EU) to consider making available a force reserve that could be deployed, if necessary, to support MONUC during the electoral process. On 28 March, the EU Council conveyed that organization's willingness to provide such support, subject to Security Council authorization under Chapter VII of the UN Charter. The Secretary-General felt that deploying such a force would contribute to the DRC efforts in ensuring the successful holding of elections.

The DRC had informed the Security Council, on 30 March [S/2006/203], that the country's Supreme Defence Council had endorsed the establishment of an EU force, known as EUFOR R.D. Congo.

SECURITY COUNCIL ACTION

On 25 April [meeting 5421], the Security Council unanimously adopted **resolution 1671(2006)**. The draft [S/2006/2531] was prepared in consultations among Council members.

The Security Council,

Recalling its previous resolutions and the statements by its President on the Democratic Republic of the Congo, in particular resolutions 1565(2004) of 1 October 2004, 1592(2005) of 30 March 2005, 1621(2005) of 6 September 2005 and 1635(2005) of 28 October 2005, and the statement by its President of 21 December 2005,

Commending the people of the Democratic Republic of the Congo on the successful holding of a referendum on the Constitution that entered into force on 18 February 2006,

Underlining the importance of elections as the foundation for the longer-term restoration of peace and stability, national reconciliation and the establishment of the rule of law in the Democratic Republic of the Congo,

Commending the efforts of the Independent Electoral Commission to prepare for the holding of the elections, and expressing its appreciation for the unprecedented and outstanding logistical support provided to the Commission by the United Nations Organization Mission in the Democratic Republic of the Congo,

Stressing the primary responsibility of the Government of the Democratic Republic of the Congo for ensuring security during the period encompassing the elections,

Commending the donor community, in particular the European Union, for the assistance that it is providing to the electoral process and in the interest of a successful outcome to the transition in the Democratic Republic of the Congo, and encouraging it to continue its support,

Welcoming the additional assistance that the European Union is providing in the context of the forthcoming elections by temporarily reinforcing its European Union Police Mission in Kinshasa to support the coordination of relevant units of the police forces of the Democratic Republic of the Congo,

Taking note of the request expressed in the letter dated 27 December 2005 from the Under-Secretary-General for Peacekeeping Operations to the Presidency of the European Union,

Taking note also of the response to that letter by the Minister for Foreign Affairs of Austria on behalf of the Council of the European Union, dated 28 March 2006,

Welcoming the intention of the European Union to deploy a force to support the United Nations Organization Mission in the Democratic Republic of the Congo during the electoral period in the Democratic Republic of the Congo as expressed in the above-mentioned letter dated 28 March 2006, which stated, inter alia, that this force would not substitute for the Mission or the armed forces of the Democratic Republic of the Congo in their tasks, and which noted the assessment that the capabilities of the Mission in certain parts of the territory of the Democratic Republic of the Congo should enable it to address possible difficulties without support from the European Union,

Considering that the current mandate of the Mission will be subject to renewal by 30 September 2006, and expressing its intention to extend it for a further period beyond this date,

Determining that the situation in the Democratic Republic of the Congo continues to constitute a threat to international peace and security in the region,

Acting under Chapter VII of the Charter of the United Nations,

1. *Takes note* of the letter dated 30 March 2006 from the Permanent Representative of the Democratic Republic of the Congo to the United Nations addressed to the President of the Security Council and of the support of the Government of the Democratic Republic of the Congo for the temporary deployment of a European Union force ("EUFOR R.D. Congo") to support the United Nations Organization Mission in the Democratic Republic of the Congo during the period encompassing the elections in the Democratic Republic of the Congo;

2. *Authorizes*, for a period ending four months after the date of the first round of the presidential and parliamentary elections, the deployment of EUFOR R.D. Congo in the Democratic Republic of the Congo;

3. *Notes* that EUFOR R.D. Congo will comprise advance elements concentrated in Kinshasa and other elements held outside the Democratic Republic of the Congo (an "over-the-horizon" force) with the appropriate capacity;

4. *Decides* that the authorization for the deployment mentioned in paragraph 2 above shall not exceed the term of the mandate of the Mission and will be subject, beyond 30 September 2006, to the extension of the mandate of the Mission;

5. *Requests* the Secretary-General to inform the Council of the decision to be taken by the Congolese authorities on the definitive timetable for the holding of the elections;

6. *Stresses* that EUFOR R.D. Congo is authorized immediately to take all appropriate steps, including the deployment of advance elements in the Democratic Republic of the Congo, in order to prepare its full operational capability;

7. *Invites* the European Union to take all appropriate steps with a view to the well-coordinated disengagement of its force following the completion of its mandate;

8. *Decides* that EUFOR R.D. Congo is authorized to take all necessary measures, within its means and capabilities, to carry out the following tasks, in accordance with the agreement to be reached between the European Union and the United Nations:

(a) To support the Mission to stabilize a situation, in case the Mission faces serious difficulties in fulfilling its mandate within its existing capabilities;

(b) To contribute to the protection of civilians under imminent threat of physical violence in the areas of its deployment, and without prejudice to the responsibility of the Government of the Democratic Republic of the Congo;

(c) To contribute to airport protection in Kinshasa;

(d) To ensure the security and freedom of movement of the personnel as well as the protection of the installations of EUFOR R.D. Congo;

(e) To execute operations of limited character in order to extract individuals in danger;

9. *Notes* that decisions to engage EUFOR R.D. Congo on the tasks mentioned in paragraph 8 above will be taken by the European Union upon request by the Secretary-

General, or, in emergency cases, in close consultation with the Mission, to fulfil tasks mentioned in paragraphs 8 *(b)*, *(c)*, *(d)* and *(e)* above;

10. *Decides* that the measures imposed by paragraph 20 of resolution 1493(2003) of 28 July 2003 and paragraph 1 of resolution 1596(2005) of 18 April 2005 shall not apply to supplies of arms and related materiel as well as technical training and assistance intended solely for the support of or use by EUFOR R.D. Congo;

11. *Requests* the European Union and the Secretary-General to ensure close cooperation during the preparation of the establishment of EUFOR R.D. Congo and for the duration of its mandate, and until its full disengagement;

12. *Urges* the Government of the Democratic Republic of the Congo and the European Union to conclude a status-of-forces agreement before the deployment of advance elements of EUFOR R.D. Congo as referred to in paragraph 6 above, and decides that, until such an agreement is concluded, the terms of the status-of-forces agreement for the Mission dated 4 May 2000 shall apply mutatis mutandis between the European Union and the Government of the Democratic Republic of the Congo in respect of EUFOR R.D. Congo, including possible third-country contributors;

13. *Requests* all Member States, in particular those in the vicinity of the Democratic Republic of the Congo, to provide all necessary support to facilitate the swift deployment of EUFOR R.D. Congo, and in particular to ensure the free, unhindered and expeditious movement to the Democratic Republic of the Congo of its personnel, as well as equipment, provisions, supplies and other goods, including vehicles and spare parts, which are for its exclusive and official use;

14. *Authorizes* the Mission, within the limit of its capacities, to provide all necessary logistical support to EUFOR R.D. Congo, on a cost-reimbursement basis;

15. *Requests* the European Union to report regularly to the Government of the Democratic Republic of the Congo and to the Council on the implementation of the mandate of EUFOR R.D. Congo;

16. *Calls upon* all Congolese parties to demonstrate their full commitment to a democratic process by ensuring that the upcoming presidential and legislative elections are free, fair, peaceful and transparent;

17. *Calls upon* the Government of the Democratic Republic of the Congo to do its utmost to ensure that the presidential and parliamentary elections are held in accordance with the timetable of the Independent Electoral Commission;

18. *Decides* to remain actively seized of the matter.

Temporary ONUB redeployment

On 30 March [S/2006/206], the Secretary-General informed the Security Council that, after consulting with the DRC, MONUC and the United Nations Operation in Burundi (ONUB), he intended to temporarily redeploy to the DRC, one ONUB infantry battalion, a military hospital and up to 50 military observers until 31 December 2006. The battalion, which would operate in the central area of Katanga Province, would carry out the mandate entrusted to MONUC by the Council in resolution 1291(2000) [YUN 2000, p. 123] and subsequent resolutions on the DRC. The military observers would be deployed in teams to various areas of the DRC in the context of the increased military observer capacity required during the election period. Related costs would be covered from within the ONUB and MONUC budgets.

SECURITY COUNCIL ACTION

On 10 April [meeting 5408], the Security Council unanimously adopted **resolution 1669(2006)**. The draft [S/2006/224] was prepared in consultations among Council members.

The Security Council,

Recalling its previous resolutions and the statements by its President relating to the situation in Burundi and in the Great Lakes region, in particular resolution 1650(2005) of 21 December 2005,

Reaffirming its strong commitment to the sovereignty, independence, territorial integrity and unity of Burundi, and recalling the importance of the principles of good-neighbourliness, non-interference and cooperation in the relations among States in the region,

Congratulating the people of Burundi for the successful conclusion of the transitional period and the peaceful transfer of authority to representative and democratically elected government and institutions,

Taking note of the letter dated 30 March 2006 from the Secretary-General addressed to the President of the Security Council,

Recalling that the current mandates of the United Nations Operation in Burundi and the United Nations Organization Mission in the Democratic Republic of the Congo will expire on 1 July 2006 and 30 September 2006, respectively,

Noting that, although there has been an improvement in the security situation since the completion of the transitional period, factors of instability remain in Burundi and in the Great Lakes region of Africa, which continue to constitute a threat to international peace and security in the region,

Acting under Chapter VII of the Charter of the United Nations,

1. *Decides* to authorize the Secretary-General to redeploy temporarily a maximum of one infantry battalion, a military hospital and up to 50 military observers from the United Nations Operation in Burundi to the United Nations Organization Mission in the Democratic Republic of the Congo, until 1 July 2006, in accordance with resolution 1650(2005), and with the intention to renew such authorization according to future decisions by the Security Council concerning the renewal of the mandates of the United Nations Operation in Burundi and the United Nations Organization Mission in the Democratic Republic of the Congo;

2. *Decides also* to remain actively seized of the matter.

Role of foreign combatants

On 1 May [S/2006/274], the DRC transmitted to the Security Council a 27 April communiqué from its Ministry of Foreign Affairs and International Cooperation on a skirmish that took place that day between elements of the Second Commando Battalion of the DRC Armed Forces (FARDC) and suspected elements of the Uganda People's Defence Forces (UPDF). MONUC had dispatched military observers to the site and opened an inquiry, the DRC said, adding that, according to the MONUC spokesperson, "Following verification, MONUC believes that reports that Ugandan troops had entered the DRC appear credible".

The confrontation took place near Adau, 17 kilometres south-west of Aba, in the Haut-Uélé, in Orientale Province. For some time there had been reports of a concentration of Ugandan Army forces along the common frontier to augment surveillance on the movements of LRA groups in the Garamba National Park.

The DRC stated that LRA elements were just as much of a threat to the DRC as to Uganda. FARDC and MONUC were working to track those armed gangs. The DRC would not allow foreign troops to cross its borders for any reason whatsoever and, while it deplored the loss of human life, it could not tolerate the violation of its borders. A protest note had been delivered to the Ugandan Embassy in Kinshasa.

Report on foreign combatants (May). The Secretary-General, in a May report [S/2006/310], submitted pursuant to resolution 1649(2005) [YUN 2005, p. 187], presented to the Council a comprehensive and integrated strategy for disarming, repatriating and resettling foreign combatants operating in the DRC. In 2002 [YUN 2002, p. 105], MONUC estimated the likely maximum number of foreign combatants in the DRC at approximately 17,500. Following UN-led repatriation operations, more than 13,000 combatants and their dependants were repatriated to their countries of origin—Uganda, Rwanda and Burundi. The current number of foreign combatants was estimated at between 8,000 and 9,000, with about 5,000 in North Kivu and 3,000 to 3,500 in South Kivu. Of those, most belonged to the Forces démocratiques de libération du Rwanda (FDLR), with perhaps as few as 600 to the Ugandan Allied Democratic Forces/National Army for the Liberation of Uganda (ADF/NALU) and a small handful to the Burundian Forces nationales de libération (FLN). In the absence of political or ceasefire agreements with the foreign armed groups, nearly all the combatants and their dependants who had left the DRC were repatriated by MONUC.

As part of its strategy towards foreign armed groups, MONUC continued to conduct joint operations with FARDC against them, and strengthened the capacity of FARDC and the police to provide security. It had also put in place political, military, socio-economic and justice-related incentives. MONUC believed that the way to resolve the foreign armed group problem was to support and sustain a long-term coordinated and comprehensive effort by the DRC to extend State authority to the entire territory of the country as early as possible and enforce law and order, as well as establish good relations with its neighbours. The Secretary-General strongly encouraged closer cooperation between Burundi, the DRC, Rwanda, Uganda and MONUC to resolve the problem, in particular the FDLR issue. To do so, FDLR hard-line political and military leaders, including rank-and-file elements, would have to be isolated. Other elements of the proposed strategy included strengthening the exchange of information on FDLR, and targeting their supply/resource lines through local and international mechanisms; establishing and publishing a list of FDLR members accused of serious crimes; broadening Security Council sanctions; and strengthening border control and immigration mechanisms. The robust but voluntary MONUC approach to disarmament, demobilization, repatriation, resettlement and reintegration was dictated in part by its desire to minimize further bloodshed in the DRC, where an estimated 4 million people had died because of the armed conflict. Following recent consultations, it had become generally accepted that implementation of a comprehensive and integrated strategy for addressing the issue depended primarily on the Governments of the DRC, Rwanda, Uganda and Burundi taking full responsibility, with the assistance of the international community. The Secretary-General urged Member States to encourage their mining and trading companies to abide by transparent business practices, and to take action to prevent arms embargo violations and the illegal exploitation of DRC natural resources.

Report of Secretary-General (June). In his June [S/2006/390] report on MONUC, submitted pursuant to Security Council resolution 1635(2005) [YUN 2005, p. 186], the Secretary-General said that tensions with Uganda increased following the incursion of LRA elements into the DRC. On 25 April, MONUC reported an incursion into the country by elements of the Ugandan People's Defence Force.

Meanwhile, the security situation in Ituri remained generally stable, despite continued militia activity. Between March and May, joint FARDC and MONUC operations were conducted to contain militias and force them to disarm. MONUC, in consultation with the transitional Government, developed an overall political-military strategy to address the activities of militias remaining in Ituri. With UNDP, it developed an action plan to facilitate the extension of State authority there and alleviate the immediate economic and social needs of the population. In North Kivu, MONUC launched operations that successfully cleared Rwindi and Kibrizi of rebel elements. It also engaged local communities in conflict resolution and reconciliation efforts. In South Kivu, a joint FARDC-MONUC operation in late February against FDLR elements in Bunyakiri territory caused the splintering of their hierarchy. Some 1,000 Rwandan combatants migrated from South Kivu to North Kivu, reducing the number of FDLR forces in South Kivu to some 2,500. In Katanga, following MONUC sensitization efforts in March, and agreement with the FARDC regional command, elements from the main Mayi-Mayi group led by Kyungu Mutanga, known as Gédéon, surrendered to MONUC in April and began disarming in May. Gédéon himself surrendered on 12 May.

Serious human rights violations by FARDC against civilians continued to be reported, particularly following military operations in Ituri and Katanga. While steps were taken to fight impunity, including the sentencing by a military court in Equateur of seven FARDC officers to life imprisonment for committing mass rapes, concerns persisted as to the capacity of the military and judiciary authorities, in view of interference from politicians and military officers, to address impunity and hold trials for serious human rights violations. While the authorities cooperated with the International Criminal Court in arresting former Ituri militia leader, Thomas Lubanga, and transferring him to the Court's headquarters in The Hague, several dangerous Ituri militia leaders were released. Efforts of military judicial authorities to investigate alleged crimes remain blocked by the lack of resources and political will. Progress on human rights promotion and protection was mixed. While the amnesty law was promulgated in January, only 58 convicted prisoners had been granted amnesty for war crimes. No political prisoner had been released.

Security Council mission to DRC

On 30 May [S/20060344], the Security Council President informed the Secretary-General that the Council had decided to send a mission to the DRC from 10 to 12 June, headed by Jean-Marc de La Sablière (France).

The mission's report [S/2006/434] summarized its findings in relation to the political and electoral process, security issues and governance and made a number of recommendations. Regarding the elections, the mission encouraged the Congolese authorities and stakeholders to ensure that the announced date of 30 July was respected. Any dialogue among the parties aimed at defusing the tense political atmosphere should not lead to further delays in implementing the electoral calendar. Political parties should carry out the electoral campaign in an atmosphere of calm and tolerance, focusing on programmes addressing the interest of the population and avoiding hate language, incitement to ethnic hatred and exclusion. The transitional authorities should ensure equitable access for all parties and candidates to the media, which should remain impartial. The security services should guarantee the independence of journalists and the security of the electorate and candidates, curbing acts of intimidation and violence.

Regarding security sector reform, the mission recommended that efforts aimed at reforming and restructuring the army, including the integration of coherent units and the administrative reform of the military command structure, should be pursued urgently. More systematic efforts were needed to put an end to impunity within the military and police by bringing to justice alleged human rights violators and relieving high-ranking officers showing leadership deficiencies of their duties. The international community should increase its support for security sector reform.

Regarding governance, the mission recommended that the authorities should strive to meet International Monetary Fund and World Bank requirements for resuming assistance to them. The continuing functioning of the State and its institutions, including transparent and responsible economic management, in the period between the holding of the first polls and the establishment of the elected Government, was critical. The Government should address the prevalence of sexual violence, including by ending impunity within the armed forces.

Security Council consideration. The Security Council considered the mission's report on 16 June [meeting 5466] and 6 July [meeting 5482]. The head of the mission, Ambassador de La Sablière, in his briefing to the Council on 16 June, said that the mission, the seventh to the DRC, which took place just prior to the 30 June elections, had shown the

Council's resolve to give the Congolese people its fullest support for truly successful elections. Their success would affect the stability of the whole region and possibly the continent, owing to that country's location, size, population and natural resources.

Although violence persisted in the east, in Ituri, with armed groups in Kivu still not fully controlled, it was not likely to significantly disrupt the elections. The police training programmes for the elections, involving some 50,000 police officers, had been well run, making it possible to keep the army's role to a minimum and only in some unstable areas. Moreover, the EU standby reserve force was ready to intervene in support of MONUC. The Congolese people, who had registered to vote in a great national movement, had considerable expectations, and it was important for them to see a lasting change. The mission stressed the need to ensure that the gains achieved be built upon by the legitimacy provided by the elections. Winners should be generous and losers should accept the choice of the voters. The main priorities were the swift establishment of an integrated and professional army, properly equipped and paid; the settlement of the vexing problem of armed groups in the east; and the improvement of the country's administration.

During the 6 July briefing, Ambassador de La Sablière told the Council that the mission had come away with the understanding that conditions had been met to allow for the holding of the elections. Nevertheless, members of the mission were concerned about the deterioration of the political atmosphere, particularly regarding messages of division and exclusion being broadcast by the media. The elections were not an end in themselves and the mission underlined the importance of the period to follow.

The DRC said it agreed with all of the mission's recommendations. Mission members undoubtedly understood that an unequivocal consensus was emerging in favour of concluding the peace process as soon as possible. The elections were the right path towards resolving the country's eternal problem of government legitimacy. Messages of hate and exclusion should be expunged from the electoral campaign. The Congolese people had clearly expressed their wish to see an end to the transition through the selection of leaders of their choice. The security situation, particularly in the east of the country, remained disturbing, and the decision of the Council and the EU to substantially increase their presence was a welcome development. The DRC would do everything possible to ensure that the elections took place in a calm atmosphere.

SECURITY COUNCIL ACTION

On 30 June [meeting 5480], the Security Council unanimously adopted **resolution 1693(2006)**. The draft [S/2006/457] was prepared in consultations among Council members.

The Security Council,

Recalling its resolutions and the statements by its President concerning the Democratic Republic of the Congo, in particular resolutions 1565(2004) of 1 October 2004, 1592(2005) of 30 March 2005, 1596(2005) of 18 April 2005, 1621(2005) of 6 September 2005, 1628(2005) of 30 September 2005, 1635(2005) of 28 October 2005 and 1671(2006) of 25 April 2006,

Reaffirming its commitment to respect the sovereignty, territorial integrity and political independence of the Democratic Republic of the Congo and its support for the process of the Global and All-Inclusive Agreement on the Transition in the Democratic Republic of the Congo, signed at Pretoria on 17 December 2002,

Underlining the importance of elections as the foundation for the longer-term restoration of peace and stability, national reconciliation and establishment of the rule of law in the Democratic Republic of the Congo,

Taking note of the fact that the election of members of the National Assembly and the first round of the election of the President of the Republic are scheduled for 30 July 2006,

Paying tribute to the donor community for the assistance they provide to the Democratic Republic of the Congo, in particular to the electoral process, and encouraging them to maintain it,

Recalling the importance of the security sector reform for the long-term stabilization of the Democratic Republic of the Congo, and the contribution brought by the United Nations Organization Mission in the Democratic Republic of the Congo, the European Union Mission of Assistance for Security Sector Reform and other international partners in this field,

Reiterating its serious concern regarding the continuation of hostilities by militias and foreign armed groups in the eastern part of the Democratic Republic of the Congo, and at the threat they pose to the holding of elections,

Taking note of the report of the Secretary-General of 13 June 2006 and the recommendations contained therein,

Noting that the situation in the Democratic Republic of the Congo continues to constitute a threat to international peace and security in the region,

Acting under Chapter VII of the Charter of the United Nations,

1. *Decides* to extend until 30 September 2006 the increase in the military and civilian police strength of the United Nations Organization Mission in the Democratic Republic of the Congo authorized by resolutions 1621(2005) and 1635(2005);

2. *Underlines* the temporary character of the increase referred to in paragraph 1 above, and requests the Secretary-General to take the necessary steps with a view to downsizing or repatriating this additional strength

by 30 September 2006, as long as their presence in the Democratic Republic of the Congo would no longer be vital to the successful conduct of the electoral process;

3. *Calls once again upon* the transitional institutions and all Congolese parties to ensure that free, fair and peaceful elections take place, that the timetable for polls developed by the Independent Electoral Commission is scrupulously respected and that security forces exercise restraint and remain impartial while providing security for the electoral process, and to respect the right of every candidate to conduct a campaign;

4. *Calls upon* all Congolese parties to refrain from incitement to hatred and violence;

5. *Recalls* that the Mission has the mandate, as set out in paragraph 7 of resolution 1565(2004), within its capacity and without prejudice to carrying out tasks stipulated in paragraphs 4 and 5 of resolution 1565(2004), inter alia, to provide assistance to the transitional government and authorities in order to contribute to their efforts, including those carried out with the support of the European Union Mission of Assistance for Security Sector Reform, with a view to taking forward the security sector reform;

6. *Decides* to remain actively seized of the matter.

July elections and their aftermath

Report of Secretary-General (September). In his September report on MONUC [S/2006/759], the Secretary-General said that the first democratic elections in more than 40 years in the DRC were held on 30 July. During the preceding weeks, political and civil society leaders raised concerns about the conduct and organization of the elections, especially the concern expressed on 30 June by the main political parties about an alleged lack of impartiality and transparency, particularly regarding the number of supplementary ballot papers and the publication of the voters list. To strengthen confidence in the electoral process, MONUC facilitated the establishment of an International Committee of Eminent Persons, chaired by former Mozambican President Joachim Chissano, which met for the first time on 28 July.

The electoral campaign, launched on 29 June, took place in a generally peaceful atmosphere. However, it was marked by clashes between supporters of candidates in Kinshasa, Kindu and Mbandaka, misconduct by national and local authorities, unequal access to the media by some candidates, politically biased coverage and intimidation of journalists. On 27 July, a confrontation at a political rally between the security guards of Vice-President Jean-Pierre Bemba and the police resulted in four people reportedly being killed and 17 injured.

The 30 July elections took place in a generally peaceful and orderly manner. Some 70.5 per cent of the more than 25 million registered voters participated. The polls were observed by some 47,500 national observers, 466,000 political party witnesses and 1,773 international observers, including from the AU, the Association of European Parliamentarians for Africa, the Carter Center, the Electoral Institute of Southern Africa, the EU, the International Organization de la Francophonie, the Electoral Commissions Forum of the Southern African Development Community (SADC) and the SADC Parliamentary Forum.

MONUC deployed electoral, police, military observer and security officers to 78 locations across the country, including to all 64 Commission Liaison Offices. On polling day, UN teams visited polling centres to help the Commission staff identify and quickly resolve problems. Problems were experienced at polling stations, especially in Mbuji Mayi in Kasaï Oriental, where delays were experienced following the burning of trucks delivering electoral material and the destruction of 58 polling stations. Several donors provided funds for the elections, including through the UNDP-managed project in support of the elections, which had a 2006 budget of $144 million. South Africa provided substantial in-kind contributions for producing and transporting ballot papers. On 1 August, the international electoral observer missions, in a joint statement, acknowledged some shortcomings, but noted the strong turnout and high level of participation.

SECURITY COUNCIL ACTION

On 3 August [meeting 5504], following consultations among Security Council members, the President made statement **S/PRST/2006/36** on behalf of the Council:

The Security Council pays tribute to the citizens of the Democratic Republic of the Congo who, on 30 July 2006, took part in great numbers, freely and peacefully, in democratic elections of historic importance for their nation. It appeals to them to receive the results with the same spirit of civic responsibility, and to display the same commitment in the subsequent polls, with a view to ensuring the success of the democratic process.

The Council expresses its appreciation to the Independent Electoral Commission for the untiring efforts they made to ensure that the polls could take place in the best possible conditions, and looks forward to the official announcement of the results by the Commission. It expresses its support to the Committee of the Wise [also known as the International Committee of Eminent Persons] chaired by President Joachim Chissano, whose role contributes greatly to the serenity and fairness of the electoral process.

The Council expresses its gratitude to the United Nations Organization Mission in the Democratic Republic of the Congo as well as to all the international partners of the Democratic Republic of the Congo that provided support to the electoral process, in particular its African partners, especially South Africa, as well as the European Union and the force it has temporarily deployed during this period.

The Council notes that the electoral campaign and the voting process took place largely in a calm environment. It deplores the incidents which occurred in recent days, in particular in Kinshasa, Mbuji Mayi and Mweka. It endorses the opinion of the International Committee in Support of the Transition, which welcomed, in this context, the work of the National Police forces.

The Council urges all political actors in the Democratic Republic of the Congo to continue to work to ensure that the electoral process proceeds in a free, transparent and peaceful manner, in accordance with the agreed timetable. The Council calls upon political leaders to refrain from making inflammatory speeches.

The Council underlines that those elections will mark the completion of a long period of rule by transitional institutions and the start of democratic rule. The people who will be destined to lead the country will bear the important responsibility to provide long-term foundations for the restoration of peace and stability, national reconciliation and the establishment of the rule of law in the Democratic Republic of the Congo.

Election results. Provisional results of the elections were announced on 20 August, said the Secretary-General in his September report [S/2006/759]. President Kabila won 44.8 per cent of the votes, followed by Vice-President Bemba (20.3 per cent), Antoine Gizenga (13.6 per cent) and Nzanga Mobutu (4.8 per cent). As no candidate won an absolute majority, the two candidates with the highest vote percentage would contest a run-off presidential election.

President Kabila and his Alliance pour la majorité présidentielle (AMP) called for the holding of the run-off elections 15 days after the announcement of the first round, as provided for in article 71 of the Constitution, and for the separation of the second presidential round from that of the Provincial Assembly elections. The Secretary-General's Special Representative, William Lacy Swing, and the International Committee in Support of the Transition (CIAT) interpreted the wording of article 71 to mean that the Independent Electoral Commission would "proceed" to the second round within 15 days and first steps should be taken to organize the elections. On 21 August, at Mr. Swing's request, CIAT met to discuss the high level of tension between the supporters of the President and the Vice-President, and the call for holding the run-off elections 15 days after the announcement of the results of the first. Shortly after the meeting began at the residence of the Vice-President, shots were heard around the house, making it impossible for CIAT members to leave. MONUC and EU troops and the MONUC Chief of Security immediately moved to the area. Mr. Swing contacted the President and his advisers, while the Force Commander established contact with the FARDC Chief of Staff. After discussions, two MONUC companies and one EUFOR R.D. Congo company extracted CIAT members and stabilized the situation. EUFOR R.D. Congo took action within its mandate and deployed along a key section of the main boulevard in central Kinshasa.

MONUC and EUFOR R.D. troops in the vicinity reported that a company of the President's Republican Guard was assembled at a strategic junction, apparently ready to advance towards the Vice-President's residence. Meanwhile, small groups of the Republican Guard were seen in the area exchanging fire with a group of some 200 of the Vice-President's guards, who were positioned among the houses around his residence. During the fighting, the Vice-President's personal helicopter was destroyed. Mr. Swing sought to end hostilities and restore calm, including by arranging a telephone conversation between the President and the Vice-President. The Secretary-General warned both parties that the fighting was jeopardizing the achievements of the transitional process. Calm was restored by early evening, and MONUC and EUFOR units deployed at key road junctions.

Following interventions by Mr. Swing and other members of the international community, MONUC facilitated the establishment of a working group, comprising the Ministers of Defence and the Interior, the FARDC Chief of Staff, the police Inspector General, representatives of the Vice-President's guards, the commander of the Republican Guard, as well as the EUFOR and MONUC Force Commanders, to establish confidence-building measures, encourage dialogue and resolve security disputes. The President and Vice-President also agreed to establish a joint commission, facilitated by MONUC, to conduct an impartial inquiry into the events of 20 to 22 August and to foster agreement on rules of conduct for the upcoming run-off and provincial elections. They also agreed, in principle, to a weapon-free zone in Kinshasa. On 13 September, the President and Vice-President met to discuss the violence. On 26 August, representatives of several media outlets had signed an agreement committing themselves to respecting journalistic ethics during the electoral period.

The Supreme Court reviewed the provisional results, examined the electoral complaints, and on 14 September, confirmed that the President and Vice-President would contest a second round of presidential elections.

On 7 September, the Independent Electoral Commission announced the provisional results for the National Assembly elections, which indicated that AMP, the platform of parties supporting President Kabila, had won 224 of the 500 seats, followed by the Regroupement des nationalistes congolais

(RENACO), the parties supporting Vice-President Bemba, 116 seats, and the Coalition des démocrates congolais (CODECO) supporting Pierre Pay-Pay, 25 seats. Individually, Vice-President Ruberwa's Rassemblement congolais pour la démocratie (RCD) won 15 seats, President Kabila's own party, PPRD, won 111 seats, and Vice-President Bemba's party, Mouvement de libération du Congo (MLC), 64 seats.

In rulings issued on 13 and 15 September, the Supreme Court of Justice reaffirmed the requirement under article 71 of the Constitution that the run-off elections be held within 15 days but acknowledged that that was not possible. It therefore granted an extension of up to 50 days after the announcement of the final results of the first round.

SECURITY COUNCIL ACTION

On 22 September [meeting 5533], following consultations among Security Council members, the President made statement **S/PRST/2006/40** on behalf of the Council:

The Security Council pays tribute once again to the extraordinary commitment of the citizens of the Democratic Republic of the Congo demonstrated by their peaceful participation in the first stage of democratic elections of historic importance to their nation.

The Council commends the substantial efforts being made by the United Nations Organization Mission in the Democratic Republic of the Congo, and the international community as a whole in support of peace and democratic elections in the Democratic Republic of the Congo. It stresses its commitment to the peaceful conduct of the second round of the presidential election and of the provincial elections scheduled for 29 October 2006, and its determination to ensure that the peace process in the Democratic Republic of the Congo succeeds, in the interests of the Congolese people, as well as central Africa and the Great Lakes region.

The Council deplores the violence that erupted in Kinshasa from 20 to 22 August 2006 between security forces loyal to President Kabila and Vice-President Bemba, and commends the effective action of the European Union force, EUFOR R.D. Congo, in support of the Mission.

The Council shares the serious concern expressed by the International Committee in Support of the Transition, in its statement of 11 September 2006, regarding the unchecked circulation of weapons and armed individuals in Kinshasa. It endorses the call by the International Committee for a cantonment of the security forces of both candidates and of troops of the Armed Forces of the Democratic Republic of the Congo in the province of Kinshasa, and for a ban on the circulation of armed individuals in this province.

The Council calls upon all political parties and in particular President Kabila and Vice-President Bemba to restate their commitment to the peace process and to work within the framework they have agreed to establish with the facilitation of the Mission as a means of peacefully resolving political differences. It welcomes the meeting that took place between President Kabila and Vice-President Bemba as a first step in this direction and encourages them to continue to seek a peaceful resolution of their differences.

The Council reiterates its support to the Independent Electoral Commission and to the High Media Authority. It urges all candidates and all parties in the Democratic Republic of the Congo to banish any message that could incite hatred and violence and to comply with the codes of conduct that those institutions have respectively elaborated for the conduct of free, fair and transparent elections in a peaceful climate. It commends the role of the International Committee of Eminent Persons and reiterates its support for it. It emphasizes again the importance of respecting the electoral calendar.

The Council invites the Security Council Committee established pursuant to resolution 1533(2004) to examine the situation in Kinshasa, if appropriate, in the context of the arms embargo imposed by resolutions 1493(2003) and 1596(2005) and renewed by resolution 1698(2006). It also expresses its readiness to consider possible measures against individuals and entities who would further threaten the conduct of free and fair elections, in particular through the use of hate media, preventing equal and responsible access to media, inciting violence and recourse to violence to prevent elections, dispute their outcome or subvert the peace process.

The Council emphasizes the need for all political parties to act responsibly within the framework of democratic institutions after the elections.

The Council underscores to the Congolese parties the importance of preventing impunity for those responsible for violations of human rights and international humanitarian law that constitute crimes.

Further developments. On the security front, said the Secretary-General in his September report, there were positive developments in the Ituri District, where armed groups continued to operate. MONUC and FARDC continued joint operations to protect civilians and compel militia groups to disarm. A joint MONUC-FARDC operation in Djugu territory was launched on 20 May to dislodge and capture elements of the Front des nationalistes et integrationistes (FNI), led by Peter Karim. On 28 May, a MONUC unit was attacked by FNI during a cordon and search operation. One MONUC soldier was killed, three injured and seven captured and held by FNI. Two of the soldiers were safely released to MONUC on 27 June and the remaining five on 28 July. On 5 June, the Government reopened the disarmament and demobilization process in Ituri and, as at 8 September, 4,758 militia elements had surrendered, with 2,332 weapons.

In North Kivu, where the situation remained stable but fragile, standoffs and tension between the integrated brigades and the militias continued to be problematic. In South Kivu, MONUC patrols enhanced security for the population and deterred the militias. Katanga remained relatively calm, with the exception of the northern and central area, where Mayi-Mayi groups remained reluctant to demobilize. Although the Mayi-Mayi leader Gédéon had surrendered (see p. 132), splinter factions continued to commit atrocities. MONUC deployed an additional battalion of four companies, a level 2 hospital and an aviation unit in Kamina.

The security situation in Kinshasa was tense following the August clashes between the guards of the Vice-President and the Republican Guard. The situation required the redeployment of Western Brigade troops to the capital, reinforced by a special forces company stationed in Lumubashi. EUFOR, on 29 July, reached its full operational capacity, with 1,100 troops stationed in the DRC and 1,307 troops stationed in Gabon, capable of responding to a MONUC request for assistance.

The Secretary-General recommended extending MONUC mandate for four and a half months, from 1 October 2006 to 15 February 2007, to allow time for consultations with the new Government on the Mission's future role. He also recommended that the Security Council extend until 15 February 2007, the authorization to redeploy troops from ONUB to MONUC and the increase in the military and civilian police strength.

SECURITY COUNCIL ACTION

On 29 September [meeting 5541], the Security Council unanimously adopted **resolution 1711(2006)**. The draft [S/2006/759] was prepared in consultations among Council members.

The Security Council,

Recalling its resolutions and the statements by its President concerning the Democratic Republic of the Congo, in particular resolutions 1565(2004) of 1 October 2004, 1592(2005) of 30 March 2005, 1596(2005) of 18 April 2005, 1621(2005) of 6 September 2005, 1628(2005) of 30 September 2005, 1635(2005) of 28 October 2005, 1671(2006) of 25 April 2006 and 1693(2006) of 30 June 2006, and its resolutions 1650(2005) of 21 December 2005, 1669(2006) of 10 April 2006 and 1692(2006) of 30 June 2006 relating to the situation in Burundi and in the Great Lakes region,

Paying tribute again to the citizens of the Democratic Republic of the Congo who, on 30 July 2006, demonstrated their extraordinary commitment to the democratic process by taking part in great numbers, freely and peacefully, in the first stage of democratic elections of historic importance to their nation,

Reaffirming its commitment to respect the sovereignty, territorial integrity and political independence of the Democratic Republic of the Congo as well as all States in the region, and its support for the process of the Global and All-Inclusive Agreement on the Transition in the Democratic Republic of the Congo, signed at Pretoria on 17 December 2002,

Underlining the importance of elections as the foundation for longer-term restoration of peace and stability, national reconciliation and establishment of the rule of law in the Democratic Republic of the Congo,

Commending the role in support of the electoral process played by the United Nations Organization Mission in the Democratic Republic of the Congo, the United Nations Development Programme and other international partners of the Democratic Republic of the Congo that provided support to the electoral process, in particular its African partners, especially South Africa, as well as the European Union and the force it has temporarily deployed during this period ("EUFOR R.D. Congo"),

Taking note of the fact that the second round of the presidential elections, as well as the provincial elections, are scheduled for 29 October 2006,

Stressing the primary responsibility of the Government of the Democratic Republic of the Congo for ensuring security during the period encompassing the elections,

Paying tribute to the donor community for the assistance it provides to the Democratic Republic of the Congo, in particular to the electoral process, and encouraging it to maintain that assistance,

Deploring again the violence that erupted in Kinshasa from 20 to 22 August 2006 between security forces loyal to the two remaining presidential candidates,

Condemning the continuation of hostilities by militias and foreign armed groups in the eastern part of the Democratic Republic of the Congo, and the threat it poses to the holding of elections,

Deploring the persistence of violations of human rights and international humanitarian law in the Democratic Republic of the Congo, in particular those carried out by these militias and foreign armed groups and by elements of the Armed Forces of the Democratic Republic of the Congo, and stressing the urgent need for those responsible for these crimes to be brought to justice,

Condemning the continuing illicit flow of weapons within and into the Democratic Republic of the Congo, and declaring its determination to continue close monitoring of the implementation of the arms embargo imposed by resolution 1493(2003) of 28 July 2003 and expanded by resolution 1596(2005), and to enforce the measures provided for in paragraphs 13 and 15 of resolution 1596(2005) against persons and entities acting in violation of this embargo,

Bearing in mind that the mandate of the United Nations Operation in Burundi will expire on 31 December 2006,

Taking note of the report of the Secretary-General of 21 September 2006, and of the recommendations contained therein,

Noting that the situation in the Democratic Republic of the Congo continues to constitute a threat to international peace and security in the region,

Acting under Chapter VII of the Charter of the United Nations,

1. *Decides* to extend the mandate of the United Nations Organization Mission in the Democratic Republic of the Congo, as contained in resolutions 1565(2004), 1592(2005), 1596(2005), 1621(2005) and 1635(2005), until 15 February 2007;

2. *Decides also* to extend until 15 February 2007 the increase in the military and civilian police strength of

the Mission authorized by resolutions 1621(2005) and 1635(2005);

3. *Decides further* to extend until 31 December 2006 the authorization contained in resolutions 1669(2006) and 1692(2006) for the Secretary-General to redeploy temporarily a maximum of one infantry battalion, a military hospital and 50 military observers from the United Nations Operation in Burundi to the Mission;

4. *Takes note* of the recommendation of the Secretary-General to temporarily maintain until 15 February 2007 the capabilities referred to in paragraph 3 above, and expresses its intention to re-examine this issue before 31 December 2006 with a view to ensuring that the Mission has adequate capabilities to perform its mandate fully until the date referred to in paragraph 1 above;

5. *Underlines* the temporary character of the provisions of paragraphs 2 and 3 above, and requests the Secretary-General to take the necessary steps with a view to downsizing or repatriating this additional strength by 15 February 2007, as long as their presence in the Democratic Republic of the Congo would no longer be vital to the successful completion of the electoral process;

6. *Calls once again upon* the transitional institutions and all Congolese parties to ensure that free, fair and peaceful elections take place and that the next steps of the timetable for polls developed by the Independent Electoral Commission are scrupulously respected, and calls upon all candidates, in particular the two remaining presidential candidates, to restate their commitment to the democratic process;

7. *Reiterates* the importance of a cantonment of non-police security forces in the province of Kinshasa and its support for the International Committee in Support of the Transition in this regard, and takes note of the Commitment for a weapons-free city-province of Kinshasa signed on 23 September 2006;

8. *Calls upon* the transitional institutions and all Congolese parties to ensure that the security forces exercise restraint and remain impartial while providing security to the electoral process, and to respect the right of every candidate to conduct a campaign;

9. *Calls upon* all Congolese parties to refrain from incitement to hatred and violence and from any threat or use of force to prevent elections, dispute their outcome or subvert the peace process, and to resolve political differences by peaceful means, including through the framework established with the facilitation of the Mission, and within the framework of democratic institutions and the rule of law;

10. *Welcomes* the intention expressed by the Secretary-General to consult closely with the new Congolese authorities on an adjustment of the mandate and capacities of the Mission after the completion of the electoral process, requests the Secretary-General to submit recommendations to the Security Council in this regard by the end of January 2007, and expresses its commitment to continue to contribute to the consolidation of peace and stability in the Democratic Republic of the Congo in the post-transitional period;

11. *Decides* to remain actively seized of the matter.

Elections (October). In a later report [S/2007/156], the Secretary-General said that the second round of the presidential and Provincial Assembly elections took place on 29 October, in a generally peaceful environment. The Independent Electoral Commission improved its performance in the conduct of the polls, the vote count and the compilation of results. Voter turnout was lower than in the first presidential round, with 65 per cent of the electorate casting votes. National and international observer missions, including those of the AU, the EU, South Africa and the Carter Center, regarded the elections as technically sound, transparent and credible.

SECURITY COUNCIL ACTION

On 7 November [meeting 5562], following consultations among Security Council members, the President made statement **S/PRST/2006/44** on behalf of the Council:

The Security Council pays tribute to the sense of civic responsibility once again demonstrated by the people of the Democratic Republic of the Congo, who participated peacefully and in large numbers in the provincial elections and the second round of the presidential election held on 29 October 2006.

The Council expresses its gratitude to the Independent Electoral Commission and the Congolese National Police, which played a central role in, respectively, organizing the elections and providing security for them. It underlines the role of the High Media Authority, the International Committee of Eminent Persons and the International Committee in Support of the Transition in promoting a smooth conduct of the electoral process and a calm political climate and reaffirms its support for them. It also welcomes the support provided for the holding of the elections by the United Nations Organization Mission in the Democratic Republic of the Congo, the European Union operation in the Democratic Republic of the Congo, EUFORD R.D. Congo, and the country's other international and regional partners, in particular South Africa and the European Union.

The Council takes note of the fact that voting generally took place in an orderly and safe atmosphere. It deplores the isolated incidents that occurred, notably in Bumba and Bikoro in Equateur province and in Fataki in Ituri district.

The Council recalls that the Independent Electoral Commission is responsible for announcing the election results. It calls upon all political actors and the Congolese people to await and receive these results calmly and responsibly, refraining from any incitement to hatred or recourse to violence and respecting democratic institutions and the rule of law.

The Council attaches great importance to the signing of a declaration of post-electoral intent by the representatives of the two candidates in the second round of the presidential election at Kinshasa on 29 October 2006. It emphasizes that political differences must be settled by peaceful means only and calls upon the parties to comply with all the confidence-building measures to which they agreed after the incidents of 20 to 22 August 2006.

The Council recalls that these elections are historic for the Democratic Republic of the Congo and looks forward to the installation of a democratically elected government.

It stresses that the new authorities and all Congolese political actors will be responsible for ensuring the long-term sustainability of the restoration of peace and stability and for continuing to promote national reconciliation and the establishment of democratic institutions and the rule of law in the country.

The Secretary-General reported on 15 November that the President of the Independent Electoral Commission announced the provisional results of the second round of presidential elections, declaring President Kabila the winner with 58.5 per cent of the vote. On 18 November, Vice-President Bemba appealed to the Supreme Court, alleging electoral irregularities. On 21 November, violent demonstrations outside the Supreme Court building caused a temporary suspension of the Court's review of the provisional results. Order was quickly restored with MONUC assistance, and on 27 November, the Supreme Court ruled that the complaints of irregularities were unfounded and officially declared Joseph Kabila President-elect. On 28 November, Vice-President Bemba stated that, in the interest of maintaining peace, he had accepted the results and would lead a strong opposition.

Two broad alliances emerged in the 500-seat National Assembly: AMP, the Parti lumumbiste unifié and the Union des démocrates mobutistes, having more than 300 seats, formed a bloc supporting President Kabila, while parties supporting Mr. Bemba's presidential bid, including the Mouvement de libération du Congo (MLC) and a number of former presidential candidates, formed a political opposition, Union pour la nation (UPN), with some 116 seats. Vital Kamerhe was elected Assembly President.

With the installation of the National Assembly and the inauguration of President Kabila on 6 December, the transition process envisaged by the 2002 Global and All-Inclusive Agreement [YUN 2002, p. 125] was brought to a formal conclusion. President Kabila, in his inaugural speech on 6 December, outlined an agenda of reform to end the cycle of crises and improve living conditions. On 30 December, the President appointed Antoine Gizenga as Prime Minister.

SECURITY COUNCIL ACTION

On 6 December [meeting 5580], following consultations among Security Council members, the President made statement **S/PRST/2006/50** on behalf of the Council:

The Security Council welcomes the announcement by the Supreme Court of Justice on 27 November 2006 of the formal results of the second round of the presidential election in the Democratic Republic of the Congo.

The Council congratulates President Joseph Kabila on his election and once again commends the Congolese people, whose determination and sense of civic responsibility enabled the first democratic elections to be held in the Democratic Republic of the Congo in more than 40 years.

The Council welcomes the commitment by Mr. Jean-Pierre Bemba, in his statement of 28 November 2006, to continue to participate actively in Congolese politics within the framework of the institutions of the Republic.

The Council looks forward to the completion of the electoral process, and reiterates the need for all political parties to act responsibly after the elections within the framework of democratic institutions and the rule of law. The Council attaches great importance to the fact that the democratically elected government should work side by side with all Congolese people and political actors to address the many reconstruction and security challenges facing the country and ensure long-term peace and stability in the Democratic Republic of the Congo.

The Council expresses its sincere appreciation for the central role played by the Independent Electoral Commission and the Congolese National Police in, respectively, organizing the elections and providing security during the electoral process. It commends the invaluable support provided for the holding of the elections by the United Nations Organization Mission in the Democratic Republic of the Congo, the European Union operation in the Democratic Republic of the Congo, EUFORD R.D. Congo, and all the regional and international partners, in particular the African Union, South Africa and the European Union. The Council also recalls the vital roles that the International Committee of Eminent Persons and the International Committee in Support of the Transition have been playing throughout the electoral process.

The Council pays tribute to the donor community for the assistance it has provided to the Democratic Republic of the Congo, in particular to the electoral process, and encourages the international community as a whole to continue to assist the Democratic Republic of the Congo during the process of peace consolidation, reconstruction and recovery.

The Council expresses its serious concern at the recent hostilities launched by non-integrated army units in Sake, in North Kivu province, and at the impact that these actions have had on the civilian population, including women, children and the elderly. It calls upon these units to cease their hostilities, return without delay to their initial positions and submit themselves to the army integration or demobilization process.

The Council encourages the Mission, in accordance with its mandate, to continue to address with determination such security challenges, and supports the steps it has taken recently in this regard, particularly in Ituri district and North Kivu province.

Temporary increase of MONUC strength. On 15 November [S/2006/892], the Secretary-General requested the Security Council to consider a temporary increase in MONUC authorized military strength to accommodate the 916 ONUB troops the Council had authorized on 10 April (see p. 130).

The Secretary-General, in support of his request, recalled that the Council, by resolution 1711(2006) (see p. 137), had taken note of his recommendation to temporarily maintain ONUB forces in the DRC until 15 February 2007, and the Council's intention to re-examine the issue by 31 December.

The redeployed forces, stationed in northern and central Katanga since July, had helped to stabilize the situation and build an atmosphere of security, where uncontrolled Mayi-Mayi groups, which had resisted demobilization, had been preying on the population. The brigade utilized mobile operating base operations, compelling the Mayi-Mayi groups to disarm and engage in the disarmament, demobilization and reintegration process. Some 787 of an estimated 3,500 armed Mayi-Mayi elements in the area had disarmed, and some 132,703 internally displaced persons, out of an estimated 239,520, had returned to their communities.

However, northern and central Katanga continued to face serious security challenges. As a result of the financial crisis faced by the Government's disarmament, demobilization and reintegration structures, the programme for the Mayi-Mayi in Katanga was brought to a virtual standstill. Unpaid brigades of the armed forces continued to harass the population. The Secretary-General warned that, should the 916 troops be withdrawn on 31 December, the security situation could worsen, with a negative impact on stability and reductions in the return of internally displaced persons in the province.

SECURITY COUNCIL ACTION

On 22 December [meeting 5610], the Security Council unanimously adopted **resolution 1736(2006)**. The draft [S/2006/1014] was submitted by France.

The Security Council,

Recalling its resolutions and the statements by its President concerning the situation in the Democratic Republic of the Congo, Burundi and the Great Lakes region,

Paying tribute again to the citizens of the Democratic Republic of the Congo for the remarkable commitment they have demonstrated to the democratic process,

Taking note of the letter dated 15 November 2006 from the Secretary-General to the President of the Security Council, and of the recommendation it contains,

Noting that the 50 military observers deployed in the Democratic Republic of the Congo under the authorized military strength of the United Nations Operation in Burundi pursuant to resolutions 1669(2006) of 10 April 2006 and 1692(2006) of 30 June 2006 have successfully performed observation tasks related to the electoral process and will be repatriated by 31 December 2006,

Condemning the continuation of hostilities by militias and foreign armed groups in the eastern part of the Democratic Republic of the Congo, and the threat it poses to the security of civilians and to the stability of the region,

Deploring the persistence of violations of human rights and international humanitarian law in the Democratic Republic of the Congo, in particular those carried out by these militias and foreign armed groups and by elements of the Armed Forces of the Democratic Republic of the Congo, and stressing the urgent need for those responsible for these crimes to be brought to justice,

Bearing in mind that the mandates of the United Nations Operation in Burundi and the United Nations Organization Mission in the Democratic Republic of the Congo will expire on 31 December 2006 and 15 February 2007 respectively,

Looking forward to the proposals of the Secretary-General, after close consultations with the new Congolese authorities, regarding the future mandate of the Mission, including a review of its military strength,

Noting that the situation in the Democratic Republic of the Congo continues to constitute a threat to international peace and security in the region,

Acting under Chapter VII of the Charter of the United Nations,

1. *Authorizes*, from 1 January 2007 until the expiry of the current mandate of the United Nations Organization Mission in the Democratic Republic of the Congo on 15 February 2007, an increase in the military strength of the Mission of up to 916 military personnel, to allow for the continued deployment to the Mission of the infantry battalion and the military hospital currently authorized under the mandate of the United Nations Operation in Burundi, and expresses its intention to examine this issue further before 15 February, in the context of the forthcoming proposals of the Secretary-General, with a view to ensuring that the Mission has adequate capabilities to perform its mandate;
2. *Decides* to remain actively seized of the matter.

General Assembly decision. On 22 December, by **decision 61/552**, the Assembly decided that agenda item "Armed Aggression against the Democratic Republic of the Congo" would remain for consideration during its resumed sixty-first (2007) session.

Arms embargo

The Security Council Committee established pursuant to resolution 1533(2004) [YUN 2004, p. 137] (Security Council Committee on the DRC) to review and monitor the arms embargo imposed by resolution 1493(2003) [YUN 2003, p. 130] reported [S/2006/1048] on its activities from 1 January to 31 December 2006, during which it held 11 informal consultations. The Committee received replies from 19 States to the request contained in resolution 1596(2005) [YUN 2005, p. 192] that all States inform the Committee of measures they had taken to comply with the arms embargo.

Group of Experts

The Group of Experts established pursuant to Security Council resolution 1533(2004) (Group of

Experts on the DRC) to gather and analyse information on the flow of arms and related materiel, as well as networks, in violation of the measures imposed by paragraph 20 of resolution 1493(2003) submitted two reports during the year [S/2006/53 and S/2006/525] (see below).

On 7 March [S/2006/139], the Secretary-General, as requested by resolution 1654(2006) (see below), re-established the Group of Expert for a period expiring on 31 July 2006, and appointed five experts to constitute the Group. On 7 August [S/2006/624], as requested in resolution 1698(2006) (see p. 143) that he take measures to extend the Group's mandate until 31 July 2007, the Secretary-General reappointed four experts until 31 December 2006. On 28 August [S/2006/693], he appointed an additional arms expert to the Group for that period. On 15 December [S/2006/984], he reappointed four experts until 31 July 2007.

Report of Group of Experts (January). In January [S/2006/53 & Add.1], the Security Council Committee on the DRC submitted the report of the Group of Experts on the DRC, as requested in resolution 1616(2005) [YUN 2005, p. 196].

The Group had requested, but not obtained, from the DRC, Rwanda and Uganda, documents identifying the exact nature of arms shipments imported since the beginning of the embargo. Elements of the DRC military had illegally flown within the country five cargo planes with weapons and ammunition, in violation of the embargo. One country that had produced weapons collected in a demobilization exercise stated it was not able to trace the weapons because of the date of manufacture. At Lumumbashi, a designated DRC site for legally importing military supplies, records were not kept on any of the firearms imported. Deficiencies in record keeping and firearms identification by many of those involved made distinguishing between legally and illegally held firearms difficult.

On the financing of arms embargo violations, the Group revealed abuses in the industrial extraction of precious minerals by DRC companies, as well as continued avoidance of full disclosure and transparency of gold imports by Uganda and cassiterite imports by Rwanda. Armed groups employed sophisticated means to entrench themselves and exploit their regional dominance. Through the parastatal goldmining company, OKIMO, the armed group FNI, had set up a parallel quasi-governmental structure, featuring a "Presidency" supported by an administration modeled on a conventional civil service and whose largest income came from taxation of the mining sector. Many financial aspects of the embargo violations could be prevented if neighbouring States imposed more scrupulous controls over the mainly illegal imports of natural resources. Instead of cooperating with the Group, some States preferred to frustrate each inquiry with deceptive information. Responses by Uganda in respect to its gold trading industry, and by Rwanda in respect to cassiterite and tin ore transactions were erroneous and unreliable. Low technology exploitation of the Shinkolobwe uranium mining site continued unabated, despite the prohibition of such activities. When Labo Laboratories, a local assayer from Lubumbashi, was authorized to apply some export controls, a number of States in southern and eastern Africa discovered smuggled quantities of minerals with intolerably high levels of radioactivity, forcing them to request the assistance of the International Atomic Energy Agency (IAEA) to secure and safely store those materials. Regarding the Ituri gold trade, there was evidence that sanctionable activities were being carried out by the Argor-Heraeus group and other companies, with all the parties involved in gold transactions, including entities and individuals based in Ituri, Uganda, Switzerland and the United Kingdom, acting against the embargo. An enhanced traceability system was therefore needed for all precious minerals, including through a certification of origin system that would support fair and profitable trading relationships among all countries of the region.

With respect to civil aviation, the Group reported many cases of non-compliance. Considerable quantities of firearms and ammunition entered the region by air, and the documents on board some aircraft did not always include an authorization to ship dangerous materials. To overcome those problems, while rebuilding the capacity of its air traffic control authority, the DRC should make MONUC responsible for air traffic services in the eastern part of the country.

SECURITY COUNCIL ACTION

On 31 January [meeting 5360], the Security Council unanimously adopted **resolution 1654(2006)**. The draft [S/2006/56] was prepared in consultations among Council members.

The Security Council,

Recalling its previous resolutions concerning the Democratic Republic of the Congo, in particular resolutions 1616(2005) of 29 July 2005 and 1649(2005) of 21 December 2005,

Declaring its determination to closely monitor compliance with the arms embargo imposed by resolution 1493(2003) of 28 July 2003 and expanded by resolution 1596(2005) of 18 April 2005, and to enforce the measures provided for in paragraphs 13 and 15 of resolution 1596(2005) against persons and entities acting in violation of this embargo,

Noting that the situation in the Democratic Republic of the Congo continues to constitute a threat to international peace and security in the region,

Acting under Chapter VII of the Charter of the United Nations,

1. *Requests* the Secretary-General, in consultation with the Security Council Committee established pursuant to paragraph 8 of resolution 1533(2004), to re-establish the Group of Experts referred to in paragraph 10 of resolution 1533(2004) and paragraph 21 of resolution 1596(2005), within thirty days of the date of adoption of the present resolution and for a period expiring on 31 July 2006;

2. *Requests* the Group of Experts to continue fulfilling its mandate as defined in resolutions 1533(2004), 1596(2005) and 1649(2005), to update the Committee on its work by 10 April 2006, and to report to the Council in writing, through the Committee, before 10 July 2006;

3. *Reaffirms its demand* that all parties and all States cooperate fully with the work of the Group of Experts, and that they ensure:

(a) The safety of its members;

(b) Unhindered and immediate access, in particular to persons, documents and sites that the Group of Experts deems relevant to the execution of its mandate;

4. *Decides* to remain seized of the matter.

Communication. On 10 April [S/2006/264], Uganda, in its response to the Group of Experts' report, expressed concern about omissions and attempts to obscure vital issues. Pointing out that it had a deep interest in the success of the arms embargo and the stabilization of the DRC, Uganda said it was dismayed by the report's attempts to implicate it in embargo violations and the Group's confrontational approach. In fact, Uganda had undertaken several measures to strengthen the embargo, including the creation of a joint Uganda-DRC-MONUC verification mechanism to carry out surprise inspections, and establishment of a regional intelligence fusion cell and a joint DRC-Uganda security liaison office monitoring the border.

Uganda had provided the Group with all available information regarding air traffic, provided responses on precious minerals, and shared information and statistics. No arms transfer had taken place from Uganda to the DRC, and to allege otherwise was to engage in falsehood. Uganda had been the lead advocate for establishing an embargo over the whole territory of the DRC, not just the eastern part, and was ready to strengthen the embargo and make it more effective. The embargo had not been as effective as originally hoped for, and the task at hand was to address its weaknesses, which the Group of Experts had glossed over.

Report of Group of Experts (July). On 18 July [S/2006/525], the Security Council Committee on the DRC submitted to the Council the report of the Group of Experts on the DRC, as requested in resolution 1654(2006) (see above).

The report reviewed illegal movements of firearms and contraband across borders; the reluctance by FDLR to join the disarmament and demobilization process; civil aviation, including identification of suspicious flights, and air transport of arms and ammunition; responses by States to the embargo measures; the financing of arms embargo violations, including diversions of natural resources and reported incidents of smuggling of radioactive materials; customs and migratory flows, including efforts by the Congolese authorities to re-establish its control; cooperation between Member States and the Group of Experts; and compliance with financial sanctions and travel bans. The Group stated that persistent problems with border porosity, continued lack of air space surveillance and poor monitoring of financial flows had created a permissive environment for embargo violations.

To counter the illegal movements of firearms, the Group recommended that all arms held or imported by the DRC, including those of the armed forces and those collected in disarmament programmes, be separately registered and marked on the basis of a dedicated system, which should be supported by the international community. FARDC should establish an accurate database of its military materiel and those responsible for maintaining it be held accountable for any loss or theft.

The Group listed air transport operators based in Kazakhstan, Kyrgyzstan, Rwanda and Serbia, which had flown arms and ammunition from Bulgaria to Rwanda, and from which it had been difficult to obtain information for verification purposes. Since most arms and ammunition were shipped by air into the Great Lakes countries, the Group recommended that States identify and keep up-to-date lists of airlines authorized to transport arms, approved arms brokers and companies suspected of arms smuggling; ensure that requests by airlines for authorization to fly over or land specified what was being transported; and enact laws to prevent the smuggling of arms and ammunition

To address the illegal exploitation of natural resources for funding embargo violations, the Group recommended that the DRC develop, with international assistance, a natural resources control system, and that the Security Council make, for a period of one year, all illegal exploration, exploitation and commerce of DRC resources a sanctionable act.

In the area of customs, extensive fraud and the porosity of the DRC eastern borders facilitated cross-border movements of weapons by networks that illegally exploited natural resources in collusion with militia groups and administrative and military authorities. Armed groups profited from export fraud, and many reports showed that the Mayi-Mayi militia drew substantial income from the illegal tapping of Katanga's mineral resources to purchase arms. In the Ituri district, customs frauds perpetrated by rebel forces continued, with the complicity of the political, military and administrative authorities and national and foreign economic operators. Since the DRC General Directorate for Immigration had stated that the central authority was not responsible for any of the immigration agents unlawfully serving on the eastern borders, the rebel leaders enjoyed complete freedom of movement between the DRC and Uganda. The Group recommended reinforcing border controls and strengthening the capacities of customs and immigration services.

Cooperation with the Group by most Great Lakes region States continued to improve, with the exception of Uganda. As the Group felt that Uganda had ignored the Council's specific demands, it recommended that the Council consider imposing restrictive measures, should Uganda continue to withhold its cooperation.

SECURITY COUNCIL ACTION

On 31 July [meeting 5502], the Security Council unanimously adopted **resolution 1698(2006)**. The draft [S/2006/585] was prepared in consultations among Council members.

The Security Council,

Recalling its previous resolutions and the statements by its President concerning the Democratic Republic of the Congo, in particular resolutions 1493(2003) of 28 July 2003, 1533(2004) of 12 March 2004, 1552(2004) of 27 July 2004, 1565(2004) of 1 October 2004, 1592(2005) of 30 March 2005, 1596(2005) of 18 April 2005, 1616(2005) of 29 July 2005, 1649(2005) of 21 December 2005 and 1654(2006) of 31 January 2006,

Reaffirming its commitment to respect the sovereignty, territorial integrity and political independence of the Democratic Republic of the Congo as well as all States in the region,

Condemning the continuing illicit flow of weapons within and into the Democratic Republic of the Congo, and declaring its determination to continue close monitoring of the implementation of the arms embargo imposed by resolution 1493(2003) and expanded by resolution 1596(2005), and to enforce the measures provided for in paragraphs 13 and 15 of resolution 1596(2005) against persons and entities acting in violation of the embargo,

Reiterating its serious concern regarding the presence of armed groups and militias in the eastern part of the Democratic Republic of the Congo, particularly in the provinces of Ituri, North Kivu and South Kivu, which perpetuate a climate of insecurity in the whole region,

Recognizing the linkage between the illegal exploitation of natural resources, illicit trade in such resources and the proliferation of and trafficking in arms as one of the factors fuelling and exacerbating conflicts in the Great Lakes region of Africa,

Encouraging the authorities of the Democratic Republic of the Congo to continue their efforts with a view to promoting good governance and transparent economic management, and welcoming in this regard the work of the Special Commission of the National Assembly charged with evaluating the validity of the economic and financial contracts concluded during the 1996-1997 and 1998 conflicts,

Taking note of the reports of the Group of Experts referred to in paragraph 10 of resolution 1533(2004) and paragraph 21 of resolution 1596(2005) (hereinafter the Group of Experts), transmitted on 26 January and 18 July 2006 by the Security Council Committee established pursuant to paragraph 8 of resolution 1533(2004) (hereinafter the Committee),

Recalling its resolution 1612(2005) of 26 July 2005 and its previous resolutions on children and armed conflict,

Taking note of the report of the Secretary-General of 13 June 2006 on children and armed conflict in the Democratic Republic of the Congo, and of the recommendations contained therein,

Taking note also of the report of the Security Council mission on the electoral process in the Democratic Republic of the Congo which visited Kinshasa from 10 to 12 June 2006, and endorsing the recommendations contained therein,

Noting that the situation in the Democratic Republic of the Congo continues to constitute a threat to international peace and security in the region,

Acting under Chapter VII of the Charter of the United Nations,

1. *Reaffirms* the demands made in paragraphs 15, 18 and 19 of resolution 1493(2003), paragraph 5 of resolution 1596(2005) and paragraphs 15 and 16 of resolution 1649(2005);

2. *Decides*, in the light of the failure by the parties to comply with the demands of the Security Council, to renew until 31 July 2007 the provisions of paragraphs 20 to 22 of resolution 1493(2003), as amended and expanded by paragraph 1 of resolution 1596(2005) and by paragraph 2 of resolution 1649(2005), and reaffirms paragraphs 2, 6, 10 and 13 to 16 of resolution 1596(2005), as well as paragraphs 3 to 5 of resolution 1649(2005) and paragraph 10 of resolution 1671(2006) of 25 April 2006;

3. *Requests* the Secretary-General to take the necessary administrative measures as expeditiously as possible with a view to extending the mandate of the Group of Experts for a period expiring on 31 July 2007, drawing, as appropriate, on the expertise of the members of the Group of Experts established pursuant to resolution 1654(2006) and appointing new members as necessary in consultation with the Committee;

4. *Requests* the Group of Experts to continue fulfilling its mandate as defined in resolutions 1533(2004), 1596(2005) and 1649(2005), to update regularly the Committee on its work, and to report to the Council in writing, through the Committee, by 20 December 2006, and again before 10 July 2007;

5. *Recalls* that, by its resolutions 1533(2004), 1596(2005), 1616(2005) and 1649(2005), the Council has mandated the Group of Experts:

(a) To examine and analyse information gathered by the United Nations Organization Mission in the Democratic Republic of the Congo in the context of its monitoring mandate;

(b) To gather and analyse all relevant information in the Democratic Republic of the Congo, in countries of the region and, as necessary, in other countries, in cooperation with the Governments of those countries, on flows of arms and related materiel, as well as networks operating in violation of the measures imposed by paragraph 20 of resolution 1493(2003);

(c) To consider and recommend, where appropriate, ways of improving the capabilities of interested States, in particular those of the region, to ensure that the measures imposed by paragraph 20 of resolution 1493(2003) are effectively implemented;

(d) To report to the Council in writing, through the Committee, on the implementation of the measures imposed by paragraph 20 of resolution 1493(2003) and on the implementation of the measures set forth in paragraphs 1, 6, 10, 13 and 15 of resolution 1596(2005), with recommendations in this regard, including information on the sources of financing, such as from natural resources, which are funding the illicit trade in arms;

(e) To keep the Committee frequently updated on its activities;

(f) To exchange with the Mission, as appropriate, information that might be of use in the fulfilment of its monitoring mandate as described in paragraphs 3 and 4 of resolution 1533(2004);

(g) To provide the Committee, in its reports, with a list, with supporting evidence, of those found to have violated the measures imposed by paragraph 20 of resolution 1493(2003), and those found to have supported them in such activities, for possible future measures by the Council;

(h) Within its capabilities and without prejudice to the execution of the other tasks in its mandate, to assist the Committee in the designation of the leaders referred to in paragraph 2 of resolution 1649(2005);

6. *Requests* the Group of Experts, in close consultation with all relevant stakeholders, including the Governments of the Democratic Republic of the Congo and of the neighbouring States, the World Bank, the Mission and private sector actors:

— To include in its report to be submitted by 20 December 2006 further recommendations based on paragraphs 158 and 159 of its report transmitted on 18 July 2006, on feasible and effective measures that the Council might impose to prevent the illegal exploitation of natural resources financing armed groups and militias in the eastern part of the Democratic Republic of the Congo, including through a certificate of origin regime;

— To include in the above-mentioned report an assessment of the relative importance of the exploitation of natural resources to the armed groups as compared to other sources of income;

7. *Requests* the Secretary-General to enable the Group of Experts to perform the tasks set out in paragraph 6 above without prejudice to the execution of the other tasks in its mandate, by providing it with the necessary additional resources;

8. *Also requests* the Secretary-General to submit before 15 February 2007, in close consultation with the Group of Experts, a report comprising an assessment of the potential economic, humanitarian and social impact on the population of the Democratic Republic of the Congo of implementation of the recommendations and possible measures referred to in paragraph 6 above;

9. *Expresses its intention* to consider, after it reviews the reports referred to in paragraphs 6 and 8 above, possible measures to stem the sources of financing of armed groups and militias, including the illegal exploitation of categories of natural resources, in the eastern part of the Democratic Republic of the Congo;

10. *Urges* the Government of the Democratic Republic of the Congo to strengthen its efforts, with the support of the international community, including specialized international organizations, with a view to effectively extending State authority throughout its territory, to establishing its control over the exploitation and export of natural resources, and to improving the transparency of export revenue from those natural resources;

11. *Welcomes* the recommendations of the Group of Experts aimed at improving the tracking of ore and precious metals within a regional framework, and encourages States in the Great Lakes region of Africa to agree on ways to act upon those recommendations;

12. *Recalls* the terms of paragraph 13 of resolution 1493(2003), and once again strongly condemns the continued use and recruitment of children in the hostilities in the Democratic Republic of the Congo;

13. *Decides* that, for a period expiring on 31 July 2007, the provisions of paragraphs 13 to 16 of resolution 1596(2005) shall extend to the following individuals, operating in the Democratic Republic of the Congo and designated by the Committee:

— Political and military leaders recruiting or using children in armed conflict in violation of applicable international law;

— Individuals committing serious violations of international law involving the targeting of children in situations of armed conflict, including killing and maiming, sexual violence, abduction and forced displacement;

14. *Decides also* that the tasks of the Committee set out in paragraph 18 of resolution 1596(2005) shall extend to the provisions set out in paragraph 13 above;

15. *Expresses its intention* to modify or to remove the provisions set out above if it determines that the demands reaffirmed in paragraph 1 above have been satisfied;

16. *Recalls* that, by its resolution 1565(2004), the Council has mandated the Mission:

— To monitor the implementation of the measures imposed by paragraph 20 of resolution 1493(2003), including on the lakes, in cooperation with the United Nations Operation in Burundi and, as appropriate, with the Governments concerned and with the Group of Experts, including by inspecting, as it deems it necessary and without notice, the cargo of aircraft and of any transport vehicle using the ports, airports, airfields, military bases and border crossings in North Kivu, in South Kivu and in Ituri;

— To seize or collect, as appropriate, arms and any related materiel whose presence in the territory of the Democratic Republic of the Congo violates the measures imposed by paragraph 20 of resolution 1493(2003), and dispose of such arms and related materiel as appropriate;

17. *Requests* the Working Group of the Security Council on Children and Armed Conflict, the Secretary-General and his Special Representative for Children and Armed Conflict, as well as the Group of Experts, within its capabilities and without prejudice to the execution of the other tasks in its mandate, to assist the Committee in the designation of the individuals referred to in paragraph 13 above, by making known to the Committee without delay any useful information;

18. *Reaffirms its demand*, expressed in paragraph 19 of resolution 1596(2005), that all parties and all States cooperate fully with the work of the Group of Experts, and that they ensure:

— The safety of its members;

— Unhindered and immediate access, in particular to persons, documents and sites that the Group of Experts deems relevant to the execution of its mandate;

19. *Demands* that all parties and all States ensure the cooperation with the Group of Experts of individuals and entities within their jurisdiction or under their control, and calls upon all States in the region to implement fully their obligations under paragraph 18 above;

20. *Acknowledges* the assurances given by the Government of Uganda to the Committee on 23 May 2006 in relation to its commitment to fulfil its obligations under paragraph 19 of resolution 1596(2005), and calls upon the Government of Uganda to demonstrate this commitment fully;

21. *Expresses its intention* to consider extending the application of the individual measures provided for in paragraphs 13 and 15 of resolution 1596(2005) to individuals obstructing the action of the Mission or of the Group of Experts, and requests the Secretary-General to present to the Council his observations in this regard;

22. *Recalls* that, in accordance with paragraphs 2 *(c)* and 4 of resolution 1596(2005), States have an obligation to notify in advance to the Committee supplies to the Democratic Republic of the Congo of non-lethal military equipment intended solely for humanitarian or protective use, and related technical assistance and training, as well as authorized shipments of arms and related materiel to the Democratic Republic of the Congo consistent with such exemptions noted in paragraph 2 *(a)* of resolution 1596(2005);

23. *Decides* to remain actively seized of the matter.

Communications. On 5 September [S/2006/722], Uganda, responding to the 18 July report of the Group of Experts, stated that it had provided the Group with air traffic records, had always provided prompt, accurate and substantive responses to the questions posed by the Group, and remained available to provide further information. Uganda also addressed specific points raised in the report.

As required by resolution 1596(2005), Argentina [S/AC.43/2006/3], Brazil [S/AC.43/2006/1] and Ukraine [S/AC.43/2006/2] informed the Security Council Committee on the DRC of measures they had taken to comply with the arms embargo.

Children and armed conflict. In June, as requested by resolution 1612(2005) [YUN 2005, p. 863], the Secretary-General submitted to the Council and its Working Group on children and armed conflict a report [S/2006/389] on children and armed conflict in the DRC, which provided information on progress in ending the recruitment and use of children and other grave violations being committed against war-affected children in the DRC. The report contained recommendations for securing strengthened action for the protection of affected children in the DRC. (For more information see p. 895.)

MONUC

The United Nations Organization Mission in the Democratic Republic of the Congo (MONUC), established by Security Council resolution 1279(1999) [YUN 1999, p. 92], continued to discharge its mandate, as enhanced by Council resolution 1565(2004) [YUN 2004, p. 129], to provide operational and security support to guarantee the advancement of the transitional processes in the DRC. MONUC, headquartered in the DRC capital, Kinshasa, was headed by William Lacy Swing (United States), the Secretary-General's Special Representative for the Democratic Republic of the Congo.

On 30 March [S/2006/206], the Secretary-General informed the Security Council that, after consulting with the DRC, MONUC and the United Nations Operation in Burundi (ONUB), he intended to temporarily redeploy one ONUB infantry battalion, a military hospital and up to 50 military observers to MONUC until 31 December 2006. The battalion, which would operate in the central area of the DRC Katanga Province, would carry out the mandate entrusted to MONUC by the Council in resolution 1291(2000) [YUN 2000, p. 123] and subsequent resolutions on the DRC. The military observers would be deployed in teams to various areas of the country in the context of the increased military observer capacity required during the election period. Related costs would be covered within the ONUB and MONUC budgets.

Sexual exploitation and abuse

Following allegations of sexual exploitation and misconduct by MONUC personnel [YUN 2005, p. 165], the Mission put in place a strategy for reporting and tracking allegations; enhancing sensitization and training; and identifying responsibility and accountability of the chain of command. Thousands of UN personnel were briefed and trained on the code of conduct for UN personnel [ibid. p. 119] through numerous briefing sessions, including train-the-trainer workshops for military personnel. During 2006, 176 allegations of sexual exploitation and abuse were reported to the Office of Internal Oversight Services. Investigations were completed against 49 personnel, as a result of which, three military contingent members were repatriated on disciplinary grounds. The remaining allegations were still under investigation. The head of Mission reaffirmed the accountability of all managers and their responsibility to ensure adherence to the code of conduct by all personnel, which were reiterated on numerous occasions in writing to all heads of regional offices and during briefing sessions for military and civilian senior staff.

Financing

In February [A/60/669], the Secretary-General submitted the performance report on the MONUC budget for the period 1 July 2004 to 30 June 2005, amounting to $937,242,800, with expenditures amounting to $866,001,800, the proposed MONUC budget for the period 1 July 2006 to 30 June 2007, amounting to $1,100,299,500 [A/60/840], and the related ACABQ report [A/60/888].

GENERAL ASSEMBLY ACTION

On 30 June [meeting 92], the General Assembly, on the recommendation of the Fifth (Administrative and Budgetary) Committee [A/60/574/Add.1], adopted **resolution 60/121 B** without vote [agenda item 140].

Financing of the United Nations Organization Mission in the Democratic Republic of the Congo

The General Assembly,

Having considered the reports of the Secretary-General on the financing of the United Nations Organization Mission in the Democratic Republic of the Congo and the related report of the Advisory Committee on Administrative and Budgetary Questions,

Recalling Security Council resolutions 1258(1999) of 6 August 1999 and 1279(1999) of 30 November 1999 regarding, respectively, the deployment to the region of the Democratic Republic of the Congo of military liaison personnel and the establishment of the United Nations Organization Mission in the Democratic Republic of the Congo, and the subsequent resolutions by which the Council extended the mandate of the Mission, the latest of which was resolution 1635(2005) of 28 October 2005, by which the Council extended the mandate of the mission until 30 September 2006,

Recalling also its resolution 54/260 A of 7 April 2000 on the financing of the Mission, and its subsequent resolutions thereon, the latest of which was resolution 60/121 A of 8 December 2005,

Recalling further its resolution 58/315 of 1 July 2004,

Reaffirming the general principles underlying the financing of United Nations peacekeeping operations, as stated in General Assembly resolutions 1874 (S-IV) of 27 June 1963, 3101 (XXVIII) of 11 December 1973 and 55/235 of 23 December 2000,

Noting with appreciation that voluntary contributions have been made to the Mission,

Mindful of the fact that it is essential to provide the Mission with the necessary financial resources to enable it to fulfil its responsibilities under the relevant resolutions of the Security Council,

1. *Requests* the Secretary-General to entrust the Head of Mission with the task of formulating future budget proposals in full accordance with the provisions of General Assembly resolutions 59/296 of 22 June 2005 and 60/266 of 30 June 2006, as well as other relevant resolutions;

2. *Takes note* of the status of contributions to the United Nations Organization Mission in the Democratic Republic of the Congo as at 30 April 2006, including the contributions outstanding in the amount of 172.1 million United States dollars, representing some 5 per cent of the total assessed contributions, notes with concern that only fifty-seven Member States have paid their assessed contributions in full, and urges all other Member States, in particular those in arrears, to ensure payment of their outstanding assessed contributions;

3. *Expresses its appreciation* to those Member States which have paid their assessed contributions in full, and urges all other Member States to make every possible effort to ensure payment of their assessed contributions to the Mission in full;

4. *Expresses concern* at the financial situation with regard to peacekeeping activities, in particular as regards the reimbursements to troop contributors that bear additional burdens owing to overdue payments by Member States of their assessments;

5. *Also expresses concern* at the delay experienced by the Secretary-General in deploying and providing adequate resources to some recent peacekeeping missions, in particular those in Africa;

6. *Emphasizes* that all future and existing peacekeeping missions shall be given equal and non-discriminatory

treatment in respect of financial and administrative arrangements;

7. *Also emphasizes* that all peacekeeping missions shall be provided with adequate resources for the effective and efficient discharge of their respective mandates;

8. *Reiterates its request* to the Secretary-General to make the fullest possible use of facilities and equipment at the United Nations Logistics Base at Brindisi, Italy, in order to minimize the costs of procurement for the Mission;

9. *Welcomes* the establishment and development of the logistics base for the Mission at Entebbe, Uganda, as a regional hub for common use by missions in the region to enhance the efficiency and responsiveness of logistical support operations, and requests the Secretary-General to report to the General Assembly in the context of his overview report, to be submitted during the second part of its resumed sixty-first session, on economies and efficiencies realized through its utilization and on the increased effectiveness of regional support for peacekeeping operations;

10. *Notes with concern* the late submission to the General Assembly of the reports related to the financing of the Mission;

11. *Endorses* the conclusions and recommendations contained in the report of the Advisory Committee on Administrative and Budgetary Questions, and requests the Secretary-General to ensure their full implementation;

12. *Requests* the Secretary-General to ensure the full implementation of the relevant provisions of its resolutions 59/296 and 60/266;

13. *Emphasizes* the importance of ensuring coordination and collaboration of efforts with the United Nations agencies and programmes, and requests the Secretary-General to report to the General Assembly on measures taken, including on the progress made in the development of an integrated work plan and the coordination network referred to in paragraph 54 of the report of the Advisory Committee on Administrative and Budgetary Questions;

14. *Requests* the Secretary-General to ensure that the recommendations in the consultants' report on the comprehensive review of staffing and structure of the Mission are fully analysed by the Mission and that the results of the analysis are reflected in the budget for the Mission for the period from 1 July 2007 to 30 June 2008;

15. *Looks forward* to the consideration of the comprehensive report requested in section VIII, paragraph 3, of its resolution 60/266;

16. *Requests* the Secretary-General to ensure that quick-impact projects are implemented in compliance with the original intent of such projects and relevant General Assembly resolutions;

17. *Decides* to approve the resources requested for quick-impact projects in the proposed budget for the Mission for the period from 1 July 2006 to 30 June 2007, in the interim;

18. *Requests* the Secretary-General to ensure full implementation of the quick-impact projects in the financial period from 1 July 2006 to 30 June 2007;

19. *Also requests* the Secretary-General to review the administrative support structure of quick-impact projects with a view to minimizing overhead costs for their implementation;

20. *Further requests* the Secretary-General to take all necessary action to ensure that the Mission is administered with a maximum of efficiency and economy;

21. *Requests* the Secretary-General, in order to reduce the cost of employing General Service staff, to continue efforts to recruit local staff for the Mission against General Service posts, commensurate with the requirements of the Mission;

Financial performance report for the period from 1 July 2004 to 30 June 2005

22. *Takes note* of the report of the Secretary-General on the financial performance of the Mission for the period from 1 July 2004 to 30 June 2005;

Budget estimates for the period from 1 July 2006 to 30 June 2007

23. *Decides* to appropriate to the Special Account for the United Nations Organization Mission in the Democratic Republic of the Congo the amount of 1,138,533,000 dollars for the period from 1 July 2006 to 30 June 2007, inclusive of 1,091,242,800 dollars for the maintenance of the Mission, 39,060,000 dollars for the support account for peacekeeping operations and 8,230,200 dollars for the United Nations Logistics Base;

Financing of the appropriation

24. *Decides also* to apportion among Member States the amount of 284,633,250 dollars for the period from 1 July to 30 September 2006, in accordance with the levels updated in General Assembly resolution 58/256 of 23 December 2003, and taking into account the scale of assessments for 2006, as set out in its resolution 58/1 B of 23 December 2003;

25. *Decides further* that, in accordance with the provisions of its resolution 973(X) of 15 December 1955, there shall be set off against the apportionment among Member States, as provided for in paragraph 24 above, their respective share in the Tax Equalization Fund of the amount of 5,944,125 dollars, comprising the estimated staff assessment income of 4,690,000 dollars approved for the Mission, the prorated share of 1,098,375 dollars of the estimated staff assessment income approved for the support account and the prorated share of 155,750 dollars of the estimated staff assessment income approved for the Untied Nations Logistics Base;

26. *Decides* to apportion among Member States the amount of 853,899,750 dollars for the period from 1 October 2006 to 30 June 2007 at a monthly rate of 94,877,750 dollars, in accordance with the levels updated in General Assembly resolution 58/256, and taking into account the scale of assessments for 2006, as set out in its resolution 58/1 B, and the scale of assessments for 2007, subject to a decision of the Security Council to extend the mandate of the Mission;

27. *Decides also* that, in accordance with the provisions of its resolution 973(X), there shall be set off against the apportionment among Member States, as provided for in paragraph 26 above, their respective share in the Tax Equalization Fund of the amount of 17,832,375 dollars, comprising the estimated staff assessment income of 14,070,000 dollars approved for the Mission, the prorated share of 3,295,125 dollars of the estimated staff assessment income approved for the support account and the prorated share of 467,250 dollars of the estimated staff assessment income approved for the United Nations Logistics Base;

28. *Decides further* that, for Member States that have fulfilled their financial obligations to the Mission, there shall be set off against their apportionment, as provided for in paragraph 24 above, their respective share of the unencumbered balance and other income in the total amount of 68,769,500 dollars in respect of the financial period ended 30 June 2005, in accordance with the levels updated in its resolution 58/256, and taking into account the scale of assessments for 2005, as set out in its resolution 58/1 B;

29. *Decides* that, for Member States that have not fulfilled their financial obligations to the Mission, there shall be set off against their outstanding obligations their respective share of the unencumbered balance and other income in the total amount of 68,769,500 dollars in respect of the financial period ended 30 June 2005, in accordance with the scheme set out in paragraph 28 above;

30. *Decides also* that the decrease of 2,640,600 dollars in the estimated staff assessment income in respect of the financial period ended 30 June 2005 shall be set off against the credits from the amount of 68,769,500 dollars referred to in paragraphs 28 and 29 above;

31. *Emphasizes* that no peacekeeping mission shall be financed by borrowing funds from other active peacekeeping missions;

32. *Encourages* the Secretary-General to continue to take additional measures to ensure the safety and security of all personnel under the auspices of the United Nations participating in the Mission, bearing in mind paragraphs 5 and 6 of Security Council resolution 1502(2003) of 26 August 2003;

33. *Invites* voluntary contributions to the Mission in cash and in the form of services and supplies acceptable to the Secretary-General, to be administered, as appropriate, in accordance with the procedure and practices established by the General Assembly;

34. *Decides* to include in the provisional agenda of its sixty-first session the item entitled "Financing of the United Nations Organization Mission in the Democratic Republic of the Congo".

On 22 December [A/61/672], the Secretary-General submitted to the Assembly a performance report on the MONUC budget for the period 1 July 2005 to 30 June 2006, which showed expenditures amounting to $1,055,040,300 ($1,038,004,800 net).

Also on 22 December, by **decision 61/552**, the Assembly decided that the agenda item "Financing of the United Nations Organization Mission in the Democratic Republic of the Congo" would remain for consideration during its resumed sixty-first (2007) session.

Burundi

Significant Progress was made in restoring Burundi to peace and stability in 2006. The Government and the last major rebel group outside the country's peace process, the Palipehutu-National Liberation Forces (Palipehutu-FNL), signed, on 18 June, the Agreement on Principles towards Lasting Peace, Security and Stability in Burundi, and on 7 September, the Comprehensive Ceasefire Agreement, intended to put an end to all hostilities.

The withdrawal of the United Nations Operation in Burundi (ONUB), requested by Burundi in 2005, in the light of significant improvements in the security situation, continued through 2006. On 30 June, the Security Council extended ONUB mandate for the last time until 31 December. Meanwhile, Burundi requested the United Nations to establish an integrated office to assist in reform, reconstruction and development. On 25 October, emphasizing the need for the UN system and the international community to maintain their support for the country, the Security Council set up the United Nations Integrated Office in Burundi.

Political developments and ONUB activities

Report of Secretary-General (March). In his March report on ONUB [S/2006/163] updating developments in Burundi since his November 2005 report [YUN 2005, p. 211], the Secretary-General stated that the Government had taken further steps to consolidate its authority. All key executive appointments were made and key legislation was adopted. Disarmament and demobilization proceeded broadly on schedule, and progress was made in disbanding militias. Although the Government addressed the country's daunting socio-economic problems, significant challenges remained, making the situation fragile. No progress was made in reaching a negotiated solution with the Palipehutu-Forces nationales de libération (FNL), and an intensification of the confrontation with that group led to a further deterioration of the human rights and humanitarian situations. Advances towards the much-needed security sector reform and reintegration of former combatants were slow. The provision of public services continued to be impeded by a weak public administration and budgetary constraints. Food shortages and the movement of refugees worsened, with over 6,000 Burundian refugees seeking shelter in the United Republic of Tanzania.

At the institutional level, over 60 presidential decrees were issued appointing senior Government officials and constitutionally mandated ethnic and gender quotas were generally respected. To expedite the processing of key legislation, President Pierre Nkurunziza convened an extraordinary parliamentary session in January, during which bills on the status of National Defence Force and Burundi National Police personnel, the intelligence services, and anti-corruption were adopted.

At a donors conference held in the capital Bujumbura on 28 February, the Government presented its emergency programme for 2006, which focused on the needs of the drought-affected population, education and health services, return and settlement of refugees and displaced persons, governance, rule of law and budget support. Donors pledged $170 million during the conference, $50 million of which was committed by the EU. The Burundi Partners' Forum, meeting on 2 and 10 February, agreed that it would be transformed into a flexible framework for the exchange of views among international partners on issues related to peacebuilding, development and the consolidation of peace.

The security situation improved in most provinces, except the three affected by military confrontation with FNL. Criminality rose throughout the country, causing the midnight curfews to remain in force and movement on major routes restricted. Cross-border illicit activities reportedly committed by FNL, the Forces démocratique de libération du Rwanda and other groups included looting and arms smuggling. However, increased coordination between Burundi and DRC armed forces led to the handover of several FNL combatants to Burundi, and one Forces démocratique de libération du Rwanda element to the DRC. FNL remained militarily active and outside the peace process, and despite efforts by the United Republic of Tanzania to facilitate negotiations, no progress was achieved in that regard. In the meantime, the Government intensified its military campaign against FNL, which continued its military attacks and acts of violence. The volatile situation along the borders with the DRC remained a threat to stability, with reports of continued collaboration between FNL and Congolese and foreign armed groups and the illicit cross-border movement of arms and combatants.

The disarmament and demobilization of former combatants proceeded with support from international partners and ONUB. As at 22 February, 16,724 adult combatants, including 482 women, and 3,015 child-soldiers had been demobilized. With the demobilization of 7,332 members of the National Defence Force, the Government achieved the target of a 30,000-member force, thus securing the disbursement of funds pledged by the European Commission and France. With support from the World Bank, 96 per cent of former combatants received reinsertion allowances for the first 18 months following their demobilization. Despite delays, the dismantling of militias proceeded satisfactorily, with 15,088 militia members having been disbanded.

Security sector reform saw scant progress. Two presidential decrees issued in January addressed the restructuring of the Ministry of Defence and the establishment of a single military court, and legislation was adopted on the status of security services personnel. A task force was established to address the remaining ethnic imbalances within the National Defence Force. However, the development of a framework for security sector reform did not advance. Both the Defence Force and the police continued to suffer from operational weaknesses due to lack of training, as well as essential equipment, logistics and infrastructure. The many human rights violations and common crimes committed by the Defence Force, the police and the intelligence services also affected operational effectiveness and credibility.

The rate of return of Burundian refugees from the United Republic of Tanzania decreased significantly. From a high of 68,000 in December 2005, only 1,747 returns were registered in January and February 2006. The decline was attributed to the precarious security situation, food insecurity in the north and east, increased human rights abuses, inadequate infrastructure and public services, as well as conflicts over access to land. Those problems led to an outflow of more than 6,000 Burundians to the United Republic of Tanzania since November 2005, including many new returnees. The return of displaced persons to their places of origin had also been minimal.

The human rights situation deteriorated noticeably in the western provinces as a result of the Government's intensified military campaign against FNL. ONUB documented serious abuses, principally implicating the security forces, including summary executions, arbitrary arrests and detentions, torture and ill-treatment, mainly of individuals suspected of supporting FNL. Hundreds of suspected FNL combatants or supporters remained detained, many arbitrarily, and credible testimonies indicated that they were tortured during interrogation. Following complaints by human rights organizations, human rights monitors were given access to most detainees, and the police expedited their investigation of cases to facilitate legal proceedings. ONUB intensified its campaign against sexual violence, which remained prevalent. On the humanitarian side, an estimated 68 per cent of the population suffered from food insecurity. Food shortages increased due to the security situation, poor rainfall, crop diseases and rural poverty. According to the World Food Programme (WFP), 2.2 million Burundians needed food aid in 2006.

Although ONUB started in December 2005 [YUN 2005, p. 216], the drawdown of 40 per cent of its military force, the precarious security situation in the western provinces forced it to reinforce its military observer teams in Bubanza, Bujumbura Rural and Cibitoke. Following consultations with the Burundian authorities, ONUB submitted, on 27 January, proposals for the second phase of the withdrawal, which envisaged complete disengagement of the Mission by 31 December 2006, and for the completion of the liquidation phase by mid-2007. The proposals provided for a full withdrawal from Cibitoke by the end of September, from Bubanza in November, and from Bujumbura Marie in December. The proposals were approved on 15 February and the Government requested that a joint evaluation of the situation and the ONUB drawdown be carried out in May.

The Secretary-General observed that the Government had focused its initial steps on enhancing longer-term prospects for peace, putting forward an ambitious legislative programme, with an emphasis on enhancing security and combating corruption, supported by a budget focused on improving the delivery of social services and basic human needs. At the same time, the country faced a daunting combination of immediate and longer-term security, humanitarian, development and social challenges. Burundi's security and economic situations remained extremely fragile. Continued fighting with FNL posed a long-term threat to Burundi and the region, impeded economic development and imposed enormous human suffering.

While strides towards building peace were made, peace remained fragile in view of the complex and deep-seated origins of the conflict, the scale of the changes required and the enormity of the challenges in all spheres. The peace process needed continual consultations and consensus-building among the various political and ethnic groups.

As to the plan to withdraw ONUB from Burundi by 31 December, given the severity of the challenges and the lessons learned by the United Nations in similar post-conflict situations, the risks involved should not be underestimated. In the absence of solid progress in addressing the root causes of conflict, the possibility of a relapse remained strong.

SECURITY COUNCIL ACTION

On 23 March [meeting 5394], following consultations among Security Council members, the President made statement **S/PRST/2006/12** on behalf of the Council:

> The Security Council has taken note of the sixth report of the Secretary-General on the United Nations Operation in Burundi, and approves his recommendations.
>
> The Council is deeply concerned by the continuing violence carried out by the Forces nationales de libération and fighting between them and the Burundian army, by the human rights abuses committed by both sides, as well as by factors of instability remaining in the region. It calls for the immediate cessation of hostilities and human rights abuses. It welcomes President Nkurunziza's commitment to bring to justice those responsible for such abuses and encourages the Government of Burundi to work closely with the United Nations human rights monitors to this end.
>
> The Council welcomes the statements recently made by the leader of the Forces nationales de libération, Mr. Agathon Rwasa, in Dar es Salaam, United Republic of Tanzania, expressing his readiness to negotiate with a view to putting a final end to violence. The Council urges both parties to seize this opportunity for negotiations with a view to bringing peace to the whole country.
>
> The Council requests, in this context, the Secretary-General to keep it regularly informed of developments in the situation and, in consultation with the Government of Burundi, the disengagement plan for the United Nations Operation in Burundi.
>
> The Council welcomes the progress made by the Government of Burundi since the completion of the transition, in particular its efforts to reduce poverty.
>
> The Council encourages the Burundian parties to continue on the course of the reforms agreed in Arusha, United Republic of Tanzania, while maintaining the spirit of dialogue, consensus and inclusion which made possible the success of the transition in their country.
>
> The Council invites the States of the Regional Peace Initiative on Burundi to continue to work with the Burundian authorities on the consolidation of peace in the country and in the region. It encourages the international community, including the relevant United Nations agencies, to continue to support the Burundian authorities following the disengagement of the United Nations Operation in Burundi in the long term.

Report of Secretary-General (June). In his June report [S/2006/429] on ONUB, the Secretary-General said that the Government continued to implement governance reforms and institution-building. The Parliament worked towards the adoption of new legislation related to good governance and democratic reform, and took further measures to combat corruption. Despite the emergence of internal differences within the two largest parties, Conseil national pour la défense de la démocracie-Forces pour la défense de la démocracie (CNDD-FDD) and Front pour la démocracie au Burundi (FRODEBU), political stability was maintained and overall consensus sustained within the Government regarding its priorities. The Parliament adopted legislation establishing the framework for the creation of the National Commission on Land and Property and two laws on the privatization of public enterprises and community public services. The Commission on Political Prisoners completed its work by issuing a third decree releasing 1,846 prisoners, bringing the total to 4,330 since January.

Prospects for ending the armed conflict through a negotiated settlement between the Government and FNL gained momentum with the announcement by the FNL leader, Agathon Rwasa, on 11 March, of his movement's willingness to negotiate with the Government without preconditions and to cease hostilities. The United Republic of Tanzania subsequently invited the Government of Burundi to undertake discussions with FNL in Dar es Salaam. Negotiations between the Government and FNL (Rwasa) began on 2 June, hosted by the United Republic of Tanzania and facilitated by South Africa's Safety and Security Minister Charles Nqakula. The discussions took place in a Military Commission, to address the disarmament and demobilization of FNL elements or their integration into the security services, and in a Political Commission, to address provisional immunity for FNL leadership, refugee returns, resettlement of displaced persons and FNL participation in national politics. In the presence of South African President Thabo Mbeki, and Tanzanian President Jakaya Kikwete, the Government and FNL signed, on 18 June, in Dar es Salaam, an Agreement on Principles towards Lasting Peace, Security and Stability in Burundi. The Agreement outlined agreed principles on political and military aspects. Detailed technical negotiations were to continue towards a comprehensive ceasefire agreement.

Further progress was made in disarmament and demobilization. In April, 588 National Defence Force members were demobilized, reducing its strength to less than 28,000 personnel, which was within reach of the Government's target of 25,000. The disbanding of militias also progressed. By 1 June, 26,041 militia elements, or 87 per cent of the caseload, had received their "recognition of service" benefits. The National Programme for Demobilization, Reinsertion and Reintegration continued to provide support to demobilized ex-combatants, reaching 99 per cent of the intended beneficiaries. However, the quality of services varied among the 11 national implementation partners.

The rate of Burundian refugee returns from the United Republic of Tanzania remained significantly below expectations. From January to June, the Office of the United Nations High Commissioner for Refugees (UNHCR) assisted 4,840 returnees, including 161 spontaneous returnees. The security situation and poor socio-economic conditions continued to dissuade refugees from returning. By mid-May, UNHCR and its partners had facilitated also the return of 1,805 Rwandans, leaving an estimated 19,311 Rwandan asylum-seekers still in Burundi.

The number of reported human rights abuses declined, but serious violations continued, mainly in the western provinces. ONUB continued to combat impunity and called upon the authorities to fully investigate allegations and to sanction perpetrators. On 29 March, the President met with National Intelligence Service personnel and reprimanded those responsible for the ill-treatment and torture of detainees. The meeting led to several positive developments, including a commitment to stop the use of an intelligence facility as a detention centre. The Administrator of the Service requested that ONUB provide human rights training for intelligence officers, which began in May. In March, a UN mission visited Burundi to consult with the Government, and other stakeholders on the establishment of a Truth and Reconciliation Commission and a Special Tribunal. Subsequently, the UN Legal Counsel wrote to the Government setting out the key issues arising from the consultations, including the principle of no immunity or amnesty for genocide, crimes against humanity and war crimes, and the need for neutrality and independence of the two bodies.

The ONUB military drawdown continued, and as at 15 June, its military strength stood at 3,516. In a 13 April letter addressed to the Secretary-General, the President requested that the UN system in Burundi be restructured by January 2007 to support the country's reconstruction and development priorities. Following a visit to Burundi of a UN needs-assessment mission, the Government, on 24 May, confirmed its request for the establishment of a United Nations integrated office in Burundi, following the termination of ONUB mandate. As agreed with the Government, the priority areas of UN assistance identified were: peace consolidation and democratic governance; security sector reform and civilian disarmament; human rights, judicial reform and transitional justice; information and communications; and reconstruction and socio-economic development. The UN system was developing a common action plan to ensure a streamlined, coherent and integrated approach to UN activities in Burundi, with benchmarks for the achievement and completion of tasks (see p. 152). The Secretary-General would submit to the Council the details of the structure and resource requirements of the office. He therefore recommended the establishment of the office for an initial 12-month period, beginning 1 January 2007 and a final extension of ONUB mandate until 31 December 2006.

SECURITY COUNCIL ACTION

On 30 June [meeting 5479], the Security Council unanimously adopted **resolution 1692(2006)**. The draft [S/2006/456] was prepared in consultations among Council members.

The Security Council,

Recalling its previous resolutions and the statements by its President relating to the situation in Burundi and in the Great Lakes region of Africa, in particular resolutions 1650(2005) of 21 December 2005 and 1669(2006) of 10 April 2006,

Reaffirming its strong commitment to the sovereignty, independence, territorial integrity and unity of Burundi, and recalling the importance of the principles of good-neighbourliness, non-interference and cooperation in the relations among States in the region,

Congratulating again the people of Burundi on the successful conclusion of the transitional period and the peaceful transfer of authority to a representative and democratically elected government and institutions,

Welcoming the ongoing negotiations between the Government of Burundi and the Parti pour la libération du peuple hutu-Forces nationales de libération which have been facilitated by South Africa and the Regional Peace Initiative on Burundi, and looking forward to the early conclusion of a comprehensive ceasefire agreement,

Bearing in mind that the current mandates of the United Nations Operation in Burundi and the United Nations Organization Mission in the Democratic Republic of the Congo will expire on 1 July 2006 and 30 September 2006, respectively,

Taking note of the report of the Secretary-General of 21 June 2006 on the United Nations Operation in Burundi,

Noting that, although there has been an improvement in the security situation since the completion of the transitional period, factors of instability remain in Burundi and in the Great Lakes region of Africa, which continue to constitute a threat to international peace and security in the region,

Acting under Chapter VII of the Charter of the United Nations,

1. *Decides* to extend the mandate of the United Nations Operation in Burundi until 31 December 2006;

2. *Decides also* to extend until 30 September 2006 the authorization contained in paragraph 1 of resolution 1669(2006) for the Secretary-General to redeploy temporarily a maximum of one infantry battalion, a military hospital and 50 military observers from the United Nations Operation in Burundi to the United Nations Organization Mission in the Democratic Republic of the Congo, in accordance with resolution 1669(2006), with the intention of renewing such authorization according to future decisions by the Security Council concerning the renewal of the mandate of the Mission;

3. *Welcomes* the intention of the Secretary-General to establish at the end of the period mentioned in paragraph 1 above an integrated office of the United Nations in Burundi, and looks forward with interest, with a view to further consideration, to his proposals on structure, tasking and requisite resources in an addendum to his report of 21 June 2006 as mentioned in paragraph 79 of the report, as well as benchmarks referred to in paragraph 66 of the report;

4. *Decides* to remain actively seized of the matter.

UN Integrated Office in Burundi. In an August addendum [S/2006/429/Add.1], the Secretary-General outlined the proposed structure, mandate and requisite resources for the United Nations Integrated Office in Burundi (BINUB), as well as benchmarks and proposed time frames for completing its tasks. The benchmarks for achieving the tasks in the UN common plan during BINUB mandate, after which UN agencies, funds and programmes would continue to provide assistance under a country team configuration, included cessation of armed conflict between the two sides and implementation of both political and military aspects of a possible comprehensive agreement between them, along with full respect for constitutional provisions, such as power-sharing arrangements; the adoption of a national plan for reform of the security sector; notable improvements in the human rights situation and implementation of measures to deal with impunity; development and launching of a comprehensive legal and judicial reform strategy; a strengthened national council for monitoring the media and communications; qualitative improvement in the provision of basic services; and the successful reintegration of refuges and other war-affected population groups. Taking into consideration the need to ensure a seamless transition in UN support to Burundi following ONUB departure, the Secretary-General noted that the successful implementation of BINUB proposed mandate ultimately depended on the Government's full support and engagement, as well as significantly enhanced donor assistance. Substantial financial support was required to address the immediate and longer-term reconstruction and development requirements. He recommended that the Council approve the proposed structure for an initial period of one year.

Security Council statement (August). On 25 August, following a briefing by the Secretary-General's acting Special Representative, Nureldin Satti, on the situation in Burundi and on the setting up of BINUB, Council members, in a press statement [SC/8818], expressed concerns about reports of a possible coup attempt and the subsequent arrests of political leaders (see p. 155); encouraged the Government to follow due process in its investigations; and called upon the Government and all parties to preserve peace and national reconciliation and to promote social cohesion in the country.

Peacebuilding Commission. On 13 October, the Peacebuilding Commission [S/2006/1050] discussed Burundi and recommended it for assistance from the Peacebuilding Fund. On 13 December, the Commission announced that it would allocate $25 million to Burundi from the Peacebuilding Fund.

Comprehensive ceasefire agreement

On 7 September, a Comprehensive Ceasefire Agreement was signed by the Government and FNL, marking a milestone in the peace process, the Secretary-General reported [S/2006/842]. It was endorsed by regional leaders and signed by President Nkurunziza, on behalf of the Government of Burundi, and by Agathon Rwasa, on behalf of FNL, at a summit of the Regional Peace Initiative for Burundi, held in Dar es Salaam, United Republic of Tanzania. The Agreement, which entered into force on 10 September, provided for a cessation of hostilities, as well as the integration of FNL combatants into the national security forces or their disarmament, demobilization and reintegration. Its implementation would be coordinated by a joint verification and monitoring mechanism and subsidiary bodies comprising representatives from the Government, FNL, the AU and the United Nations, with the Regional Peace Initiative for Burundi as guarantor. The Agreement provided also for the deployment of an AU special task force to protect FNL leaders and combatants, while moving to designated assembly areas during the disarmament, demobilization and reintegration process. ONUB would provide security at the assembly areas. On 28 September, the Government expressed its commitment to the comprehensive ceasefire agreement and reaffirmed its adherence to the provisions granting provisional immunity to FNL members. The joint verification and monitoring mechanism was launched on 11 October.

SECURITY COUNCIL ACTION

On 25 October [meeting 5554], the Security Council unanimously adopted **resolution 1719(2006)**. The draft [S/2006/839] was prepared in consultations among Council members.

The Security Council,

Recalling its resolutions and the statements by its President on Burundi, in particular resolutions 1545(2004) of 21 May 2004, 1577(2004) of 1 December 2004, 1602(2005) of 31 May 2005, 1606(2005) of 20 June 2005, 1650(2005) of 21 December 2005 and 1692(2006) of 30 June 2006,

Reaffirming its strong commitment to the sovereignty, independence, territorial integrity and unity of Burundi, and emphasizing the importance of national ownership by Burundi of peacebuilding, security and long-term development,

Congratulating again the people of Burundi on the successful conclusion of the transitional period and the peaceful transfer of authority to a representative and democratically elected Government and institutions,

Welcoming the signing, on 7 September 2006 at Dar es Salaam, United Republic of Tanzania, of the Comprehensive Ceasefire Agreement between the Government of Burundi and the Parti pour la libération du peuple hutu-Forces nationales de libération,

Paying tribute to the efforts made by the States of the Regional Peace Initiative on Burundi, in particular Uganda and the United Republic of Tanzania, and the facilitation efforts of South Africa in the service of peace in Burundi, welcoming the continued commitment and engagement of these States, and recalling the role played by the Burundi Partners' Forum established at the summit meeting on Burundi, held in New York on 13 September 2005,

Taking note with concern of reports of a possible attempt to perpetrate a coup d'état in Burundi and of the subsequent arrest of a number of political figures,

Reaffirming its support for legitimately elected institutions, and stressing that any attempt to seize power by force or derail the democratic process would be deemed unacceptable,

Calling upon the authorities and all political actors in Burundi to persevere in their dialogue on achieving stability and national reconciliation and to promote social harmony in their country, and underscoring the importance of successfully completing the reforms provided for in the Peace and Reconciliation Agreement for Burundi, signed at Arusha, United Republic of Tanzania, on 28 August 2000, in the Global Ceasefire Agreement signed at Dar-es-Salaam on 16 November 2003 and in the Comprehensive Ceasefire Agreement signed at Dar-es-Salaam on 7 September 2006,

Calling upon the authorities to persevere in their efforts to promote good governance, including through continued measures to combat corruption,

Emphasizing the need for the United Nations system and the international community to maintain their support for the security and long-term development of Burundi, inter alia, by strengthening the capacity of the Government of Burundi,

Expressing once again its gratitude to the United Nations Operation in Burundi, as well as to the African Mission in Burundi previously deployed by the African Union, for their important contribution to the successful completion of the transition process in Burundi and to peace in the region,

Welcoming the holding on 13 October 2006 of the first country-specific meeting of the Peacebuilding Commission on Burundi, and taking note of the Chairman's summary of that meeting,

Having considered the seventh report of the Secretary-General on the United Nations Operation in Burundi, of 21 June 2006, and the addendum thereto, of 14 August 2006, and welcoming his recommendation on the establishment of a United Nations integrated office in Burundi following the withdrawal of the United Nations Operation in Burundi, with a view to providing continued peacebuilding assistance to the Government of Burundi by strengthening national capacity to address the root causes of conflict,

Underscoring the need for a smooth transition from the United Nations Operation in Burundi to the United Nations integrated office in Burundi and to ensure the proper functioning of that entity,

1. *Requests* the Secretary-General to establish the United Nations Integrated Office in Burundi as recommended in the addendum to his report, of 14 August 2006, for an initial period of twelve months, commencing on 1 January 2007, to support the Government of Burundi in its effort towards long-term peace and stability throughout the peace consolidation phase in Burundi, including by ensuring coherence and coordination of the United Nations agencies in Burundi, under the leadership of the Executive Representative of the Secretary-General for Burundi;

2. *Requests* that, once established, the United Nations Integrated Office in Burundi focus on and support the Government of Burundi in the following areas, in coordination with donors and taking account of the agreement concluded on 24 May 2006 by the Government and the Secretary-General and the role of the Peacebuilding Commission:

Peace consolidation and democratic governance

(*a*) Strengthening the capacity of national institutions and civil society to address the root causes of conflict and to prevent, manage and resolve internal conflicts, particularly through reforms in the political and administrative spheres;

(*b*) Strengthening good governance and the transparency and accountability of public institutions;

(*c*) Promotion of freedom of the press and strengthening the legal and regulatory framework for the media and communications, and enhancing the professionalization of the media;

(*d*) Consolidation of the rule of law, in particular by strengthening the justice and corrections system, including independence and capacity of the judiciary;

Disarmament, demobilization and reintegration and reform of the security sector

(*e*) Support for the implementation of the Comprehensive Ceasefire Agreement signed at Dar es Salaam on 7 September 2006;

(*f*) Support for the development of a national plan for reform of the security sector, including human rights training, and the provision of technical assistance for its implementation, including training and capacity-building for the Burundi National Police, and technical assistance to enhance the professionalization of the National Defence Force of Burundi;

(*g*) Support for the completion of the national programme for the demobilization and reintegration of former combatants;

(*h*) Support for efforts to combat the proliferation of small arms and light weapons;

Promotion and protection of human rights and measures to end impunity

(*i*) Promotion and protection of human rights, including by building national institutional capacity in that area, particularly with regard to the rights of women, children and other vulnerable groups, by assisting with the design and implementation of a national human rights action plan, including the establishment of an independent national human rights commission;

(*j*) Support for efforts to combat impunity, particularly through the establishment of transitional justice mechanisms, including a truth and reconciliation commission and a special tribunal;

Donor and United Nations agency coordination

(*k*) Strengthening the partnership between the Government and donors for the implementation of priority, emergency and longer-term activities, within the framework of the Government's Emergency Programme and the Poverty Reduction Strategy Paper, which is being finalized;

(*l*) Strengthening the Government's capacity for donor coordination, effective communication with donors and mobilization of resources in line with the Poverty Reduction Strategy Paper, when finalized;

(*m*) Ensuring effective coordination among the strategies and programmes of the various United Nations agencies, funds and programmes in Burundi;

3. *Urges* the United Nations Integrated Office in Burundi to take account of the rights of women and gender considerations, as set out in resolution 1325(2000) of 31 October 2000, as cross-cutting issues in all the areas outlined in paragraph 2 above, including through consultation with local and international women's groups, and requests the Secretary-General, where appropriate, to include in his reporting to the Security Council progress on gender mainstreaming throughout the Integrated Office and all other aspects relating to the situation of women and girls, especially in relation to the need to protect them from gender-based violence;

4. *Stresses* the need for cooperation, within the limits of their respective capacities and current mandates, between the United Nations Integrated Office in Burundi and the United Nations Organization Mission in the Democratic Republic of the Congo;

5. *Welcomes* the recommendation, contained in the addendum to the report of the Secretary-General, that the United Nations Integrated Office in Burundi should be headed by an Executive Representative of the Secretary-General for Burundi and that the latter should also serve as the Resident Representative of the United Nations Development Programme and as the United Nations Resident Coordinator and Humanitarian Coordinator;

6. *Takes note* of the benchmarks outlined in the addendum to the report of the Secretary-General for gauging progress made by the United Nations Integrated Office in Burundi during its mandate, in particular as they relate to the priorities mentioned in paragraph 2 above, and of the proposed time frame for the eventual transition to a primarily development-focused engagement, and reaffirms its willingness to adjust, as appropriate, the United Nations presence in Burundi during the peace consolidation phase, taking all circumstances into account;

7. *Emphasizes* that the Government of Burundi bears the primary responsibility for peacebuilding, security and long-term development in the country, and urges international donors to continue to support the efforts of the Government in those areas;

8. *Urges* the authorities and all political actors in Burundi to pursue the reforms agreed upon at Arusha and Dar es Salaam and to maintain the spirit of dialogue, consensus-building and inclusiveness that enabled them to achieve a successful transition in their country;

9. *Encourages* the Burundian authorities to continue to cooperate with the Secretary-General, including for the establishment of the mechanisms referred to in resolution 1606(2005);

10. *Calls upon* the Burundian authorities, in their investigations into the alleged attempt to perpetrate a coup d'état, to follow due process and to respect the guarantees provided for by law and international obligations;

11. *Expresses its deep concern* at reports of continuing human rights violations, and urges the Government of Burundi to investigate all such reports, take the necessary steps to prevent further violations and ensure that those responsible for such violations are brought to justice;

12. *Calls upon* the Government of Burundi and the Parti pour la libération du peuple hutu-Forces nationales de libération to expeditiously implement in good faith the Comprehensive Ceasefire Agreement which they signed at Dar es Salaam on 7 September 2006 and to pursue their efforts to resolve outstanding issues in a spirit of cooperation;

13. *Encourages* the States of the Regional Peace Initiative on Burundi and the South African Facilitation to continue to work with the Burundian authorities to consolidate peace in their country and in the region;

14. *Requests* the Secretary-General to keep the Council regularly informed of the progress made in establishing the United Nations Integrated Office in Burundi and, subsequently, to report regularly to the Council on the implementation of the present resolution, including with respect to the security situation and the human rights situation;

15. *Decides* to remain actively seized of the matter.

Further developments

Report of Secretary-General (October). In his October report [S/2006/842] on ONUB, the Secretary-General said that the signing on 7 September of a Comprehensive Ceasefire Agreement (see p. 153) contributed to an overall improvement in the security situation and appeared to spur refugee returns. However, there were continuing tensions between the Government and some political parties, the media and civil society, including allegations of a coup plot, associated arrests, and accusations by opposition parties of Government violations of the Constitution. Serious human rights abuses by national security elements were reported before the signing of the Agreement. At the same time, steps were taken to prosecute security service personnel responsible for abuses. The completion of the poverty reduction strategy paper was an important step towards addressing socio-economic challenges.

FNL did not participate in the first meeting of the joint verification and monitoring mechanism, stating that the Government should release their prisoners beforehand. On 12 October, FNL President Rwasa, in letters to the Chairman of the Regional Peace Initiative for Burundi and Ugandan President Yoweri Museveni, accused the Burundi Government of violating the Ceasefire Agreement by breaching provisions granting provisional immunity to FNL members, as well as by its continued detention of FNL members. In the meantime, groups of FNL elements, mostly of the Jean-Bosco Sindayigaya faction, began to assemble in the western provinces in anticipation of the disarmament, demobilization and reintegration process. On 28 September, the Government requested ONUB support for protecting assembly areas for FNL combatants, as stipulated in the Ceasefire Agreement.

Attempted coup plot. Political tensions heightened, following the Government's allegation of a coup plot in August and the resignation of Second Vice-President Alice Nzomukunda. On 3 August, at a meeting with diplomats, UN representatives and the media, the Ministers of Information and of Interior and Public Security announced that an attempt to destabilize the Government had been foiled. Eight individuals were arrested by the security services between 31 July and 3 August, including former transitional Vice-President Alphonse-Marie Kadege and other political and military figures. Former transitional President Domitien Ndayizeye was also arrested on 21 August. On 22 August, two of the nine detainees accused of involvement in the alleged coup were released without charge, including a National Defence Force officer who had confessed to involvement prior to his detention. On 24 August, one of the detainees stated that he had falsely confessed to participation, in response to threats against his family. That fuelled media speculation that the alleged coup plot was fabricated. The Government denied such allegations, and on 16 September, the President stated that there was irrefutable proof of the detainees' involvement. Reports that several of them had been tortured caused concern. When interviewed by ONUB human rights officers, three of the detainees, including former Vice-President Kadege, showed visible signs of torture. Political parties, civil society groups and human rights organizations denounced the arrests of the alleged plotters and their treatment. As at 20 October, seven detainees, including Mr. Ndayizeye, were still in custody, after the Attorney-General overruled the Supreme Court's decision ordering their release on bail.

Meanwhile, second Vice-President Nzomukunda resigned on 5 September, citing among other reasons, the Government's gross violation of human rights and the lack of respect for the rule of law. The confirmation by the National Assembly of Marina Barampama to replace her sparked public debate. FRODEBU and Union pour le progrès national (UPRONA) challenged the legality of the appointment through the Constitutional Court. FRODEBU also boycotted Parliament. There was also tension at the local government level, with communal administrators accused of mismanagement and embezzlement being suspended from duty.

Request for ONUB assistance. On 1 November [S/2006/866], the Secretary-General informed the Security Council that the South African Facilitation of the Burundi peace process had requested ONUB to carry out until the end of December some of the tasks envisaged for the AU special task force under the 7 September Ceasefire Agreement (see p. 153). Those tasks included providing escorts to returning FNL leaders and combatants, as they moved to designated assembly areas. The Facilitation also requested ONUB logistical support during the deployment of the AU Force, expected to start in November. The Secretary-General agreed to those requests, which would not affect the expiration of ONUB mandate of 31 December. On 6 November [S/2006/867], the Council took note of the Secretary-General's intention.

AU communiqué. On 9 November [S/2006/889], the AU Peace and Security Council, meeting in Addis Ababa, Ethiopia, approved the establishment of the Special Task Force for protecting FNL leaders and combatants in fulfillment of the September Ceasefire Agreement. It mandated the Chairperson of the Commission on the implementation of the Agreement to seek the support of member States and to submit proposals on the modalities for establishing the Task Force.

Report of Secretary-General (December). In his December report [S/2006/994] on ONUB, submitted pursuant to resolution 1692(2006) (see p. 152), the Secretary-General said that implementation of the Ceasefire Agreement remained stalled. The FNL leadership continued to demand the release of all FNL prisoners and provisional immunity for FNL elements, as conditions for their leaders' return to Burundi. In the absence of FNL representatives, the Joint Verification and Monitoring Mechanism provided for in the Agreement did not convene. On 3 November, FNL accused the Government of violating the Agreement in various ways, including the continued detention of FNL members and supporters. FNL also alleged that the Government was conducting hostile military manoeuvres in areas where its combatants were located. On 14 November, FNL blamed the Government for the delay in the implementation of the Agreement and accused the South African Facilitation of bias in favour of the Government. On 27 November, President Nkurunziza promulgated a law providing provisional immunity to FNL members.

The demobilization, reinsertion and reintegration programme continued to make progress. Some 390 National Defence Force personnel were demobilized, bringing the total number of former combatants and soldiers demobilized to 21,769, as at 14 November. The National Commission for Demobilization, Reinsertion and Reintegration continued to support the reintegration of former combatants. As at 14 November, 18,642 adult former combatants had received cash reinsertion benefits, while 5,412 had received other forms of reintegration assistance. Of the 3,015 demobilized children, 599 were in school and 896 were receiving vocational training. On 1 November, presidential decrees were issued establishing a mechanism for the verification of combat status, eligibility criteria for the programme, and criteria and modalities for the attribution of ranks during demobilization, including for FNL combatants. ONUB continued to work with the Government in destroying unserviceable weapons and ammunition, destroying 17,880 rounds of munitions collected during the demobilization, disarmament and reintegration process.

The absence of major confrontations between the security forces and FNL continued to have a positive impact on the human rights situation in the north-western provinces, where FNL had been most active. Nevertheless, impunity continued to prevail and, despite some arrests, the Government had yet to prosecute the security forces' personnel implicated in serious violations. In some instances, there was political interference in the judicial process, including the prevention of the execution of arrest warrants by senior Government officials. Reporting to the Human Rights Council [A/HCR/4/5], following his 7-14 October assessment visit to Burundi, the independent expert on the situation of human rights in Burundi, Akich Okola, highlighted the systematic human rights violations, the threats to freedom of expression and opinion, the tensions between the Government and political parties and civil society and the ineffectiveness of the judicial and administrative systems. In other developments, the national criminal code was revised to bring it into line with international human rights treaties. Important changes proposed included the abolition of the death penalty and the criminalization of torture, and new provisions for the protection of women against sexual violence and for the protection of children.

The United Nations continued to develop a common understanding of its support to the national peace consolidation efforts and modalities for enhancing UN coordination and integration at the programmatic and operational levels. In addition to the 2007-2008 UN common action plan, the overall UN approach to peace consolidation would be articulated through the reformulation of the United Nations Development Assistance Framework, renamed the United Nations Integrated Peace Consolidation Assistance Framework. To ensure that BINUB was fully operational by January 2007, a number of joint programmes in the areas of governance, security sector reform, disarmament, demobilization and reintegration were developed in close coordination with the Framework process. Reflecting on the significant contribution of the United Nations, and particularly ONUB, to the Burundi peace process, the Secretary-General said that the Mission had been instrumental in creating the conditions that allowed Burundi to complete the process started by the 2000 Arusha Agreement on Peace and Reconciliation in Burundi [YUN 2000, p. 146]. The Organization had played a critical mediation role, provided extensive support to the electoral process, actively supported the disarmament and demobilization of former combatants, provided for a thorough and systematic monitoring of the country's human rights situation, had a positive impact in monitoring the borders and providing military escorts, and supported negotiations between the Government and FNL. With the departure of ONUB, the United Nations intended to continue to help Burundi to address the root causes and immediate consequences of the conflict, help develop the capacity to sustain peace and create a propitious environment for economic recovery and development.

End-of-year developments. In a later report [S/2007/287], the Secretary-General said that the South African Facilitation organized a meeting in Dar es Salaam in December, at which the Government and FNL reached agreement on the issue of provisional immunity for FNL members and the release of detained FNL members who were nominated to participate in the Joint Verification and Monitoring Mechanism. Also in December, the AU Special Task Force became operational and the Chairman of the Joint Verification and Monitoring Mechanism, Brigadier-General M. E. Phako (South Africa), arrived in Burundi.

On 21 December [meeting 5604], the Security Council held a private meeting with ONUB troop-contributing countries and was briefed by the Secretary-General's acting Special Representative, Nureldin Satti. After the meeting, the Council President, in a press statement [SC/8921], called upon the authorities and all political actors to persevere in their dialogue on achieving stability and national reconciliation; urged all parties to promote social harmony, the rule of law and respect for human rights; and called upon the authorities to investigate human rights violations and ensure those responsible were brought to justice. He reiterated the need for the parties to the Comprehensive Ceasefire Agreement, in particular FNL, to proceed with its implementation without delay.

On 27 December [S/2006/1031], the Council noted the Secretary-General's intention, set out in his 22 December letter [S/2006/1030], to seek the General Assembly's approval of his decision to provide limited logistical assistance to the AU Special Task Force, following the conclusion of ONUB mandate on 31 December. ONUB last military contingent, the South African battalion, was re-hatted on 29 December to form the core of the AU Special Task Force supporting the implementation of the Ceasefire Agreement. That had become necessary as no progress was made in the implementation of the Agreement.

Head of BINUB. In an exchange of letters of 18 [S/2006/1020] and 22 [S/2006/1021] December between the Secretary-General and the Security Council President, Deputy Special Representative for Burundi, Youssef Mahmoud (Tunisia), was appointed the Executive Representative of the Secretary-General for Burundi and Head of BINUB as of 1 January 2007.

Report on children and armed conflict. The Secretary-General, in October [S/2006/851], presented to the Security Council and its Working Group on children and armed conflict a report on children and armed conflict in Burundi. The report, prepared in accordance with Security Council resolution 1612(2005) [YUN 2005, p. 863] and covering the period August 2005 to September 2006, provided information on progress in ending the recruitment of children into armed groups and other grave violations against war-affected children.

(For action by the Economic and Social Council on the reports of its Ad Hoc Advisory Group on the humanitarian and economic needs of Burundi, see p. 1084.)

ONUB

The United Nations Operation in Burundi, established in 2004 by Security Council resolution 1545(2004) [YUN 2004, p. 145] and extended until 1 July 2006 by resolution 1650(2005) [YUN 2005, p. 214], continued to carry out its mandate, which included ensuring respect of the ceasefire agreements; promoting the re-establishment of confidence between the Burundian forces; carrying out the disarmament and demobilization portions of the national programme of disarmament, demobilization and reintegration of combatants; monitoring the quartering of the Armed Forces of Burundi and their heavy weapons, and the illegal flow of arms and movement of combatants across Burundi's borders; contributing to the completion of the electoral process and to the creation of security conditions for providing humanitarian assistance; facilitating the return of refugees and internally displaced persons; protecting civilians under imminent threat of violence; and ensuring the protection of UN personnel, facilities and equipment.

Headquartered in the capital, Bujumbura, ONUB was headed until 31 March by the Secretary-General's Special Representative for Burundi, Carolyn McAskie (Canada). Her deputy, Nureldin Satti (Sudan), served as Acting Special Representative of the Secretary-General and Acting Head of Mission of ONUB for the rest of the year.

ONUB Financing

In June, the General Assembly considered the Secretary-General's March report on ONUB financing [A/60/731 & Add.1], in which he requested commitment authority in the amount of $79,179,200 for the period from 1 July to 31 October 2006, as well as the related ACABQ report [A/60/893], pending submission of a full budget for the period 1 July 2006 to 30 June 2007.

GENERAL ASSEMBLY ACTION

On 30 June [meeting 92], the General Assembly, on the recommendation of the Fifth Committee [A/60/917], adopted **resolution 60/269** without vote [agenda item 137].

Financing of the United Nations Operation in Burundi

The General Assembly,

Having considered the report of the Secretary-General on the financing of the United Nations Operation in Burundi and the related report of the Advisory Committee on Administrative and Budgetary Questions,

Recalling Security Council resolution 1545(2004) of 21 May 2004, by which the Council authorized, for an initial period of six months as from 1 June 2004, with the intention to renew it for further periods, the deployment of a peacekeeping operation called the United Nations Operation in Burundi, and the subsequent resolutions by which the Council extended the mandate of the Operation, the latest of which was resolution 1650(2005) of 21 December 2005,

Recalling also its resolution 58/312 of 18 June 2004 on the financing of the Operation and its subsequent resolutions thereon, the latest of which was resolution 59/15 B of 22 June 2005,

Reaffirming the general principles underlying the financing of United Nations peacekeeping operations, as stated in General Assembly resolutions 1874(S-IV) of 27 June 1963, 3101(XXVIII) of 11 December 1973 and 55/235 of 23 December 2000,

Mindful of the fact that it is essential to provide the Operation with the necessary financial resources to enable it to fulfil its responsibilities under the relevant resolutions of the Security Council,

1. *Requests* the Secretary-General to entrust the Head of Mission with the task of formulating future budget proposals in full accordance with the provisions of General Assembly resolutions 59/296 of 22 June 2005 and 60/266 of 30 June 2006, as well as other relevant resolutions;

2. *Takes note* of the status of contributions to the United Nations Operation in Burundi as at 30 April 2006, including the contributions outstanding in the amount of 47.3 million United States dollars, representing some 7 per cent of the total assessed contributions, notes with concern that only thirty-nine Member States have paid their assessed contributions in full, and urges all other Member States, in particular those in arrears, to ensure payment of their outstanding assessed contributions;

3. *Expresses its appreciation* to those Member States which have paid their assessed contributions in full, and urges all other Member States to make every possible effort to ensure payment of their assessed contributions to the Operation in full;

4. *Expresses concern* at the financial situation with regard to peacekeeping activities, in particular as regards the reimbursements to troop contributors that bear additional burdens owing to overdue payments by Member States of their assessments;

5. *Also expresses concern* at the delay experienced by the Secretary-General in deploying and providing

adequate resources to some recent peacekeeping missions, in particular those in Africa;

6. *Emphasizes* that all future and existing peacekeeping missions shall be given equal and non-discriminatory treatment in respect of financial and administrative arrangements;

7. *Also emphasizes* that all peacekeeping missions shall be provided with adequate resources for the effective and efficient discharge of their respective mandates;

8. *Reiterates its request* to the Secretary-General to make the fullest possible use of facilities and equipment at the United Nations Logistics Base at Brindisi, Italy, in order to minimize the costs of procurement for the Operation;

9. *Welcomes* the use of the Entebbe installation to enhance the efficiency and responsiveness of its logistical support operations for peacekeeping missions in the region;

10. *Endorses* the conclusions and recommendations contained in the report of the Advisory Committee on Administrative and Budgetary Questions, and requests the Secretary-General to ensure their full implementation;

11. *Requests* the Secretary-General to ensure the full implementation of the relevant provisions of its resolutions 59/296 and 60/266;

12. *Also requests* the Secretary-General to take all necessary action to ensure that the Operation is administered with a maximum of efficiency and economy;

13. *Further requests* the Secretary-General, in order to reduce the cost of employing General Service staff, to continue efforts to recruit local staff for the Operation against General Service posts, commensurate with the requirements of the Operation;

Budget estimates for the period from 1 July to 31 October 2006

14. *Authorizes* the Secretary-General to enter into commitments for the Operation for the period from 1 July to 31 October 2006 for the maintenance of the Operation in a total amount not exceeding 78,959,200 dollars;

Financing of the commitment authority

15. *Decides* to apportion among Member States the amount of 40 million dollars at a monthly rate of 10 million dollars, in accordance with the levels updated in General Assembly resolution 58/256 of 23 December 2003 and taking into account the scale of assessments for 2006, as set out in its resolution 58/1 B of 23 December 2003, subject to a decision of the Security Council to extend the mandate of the Operation;

16. *Decides also* that, in accordance with the provisions of its resolution 973(X) of 15 December 1955, there shall be set off against the apportionment among Member States, as provided for in paragraph 15 above, their respective share in the Tax Equalization Fund of 2,092,500 dollars, representing the estimated staff assessment income approved for the Operation for the period from 1 July to 31 October 2006;

Estimates for the support account for peacekeeping operations and the United Nations Logistics Base for the period from 1 July 2006 to 30 June 2007

17. *Decides further* to appropriate to the Special Account for the United Nations Operation in Burundi the amount of 3,426,800 dollars for the period from 1 July 2006 to 30 June 2007, comprising 2,830,400 dollars for the support account for peacekeeping operations and 596,400 dollars for the United Nations Logistics Base;

Financing of the appropriation

18. *Decides* to apportion among Member States the amount of 3,426,800 dollars, in accordance with the levels updated in its resolution 58/256 and taking into account the scale of assessments for 2006, as set out in its resolution 58/1 B, and the scale of assessments for 2007;

19. *Decides also* that, in accordance with the provisions of its resolution 973(X), there shall be set off against the apportionment among Member States, as provided for in paragraph 18 above, their respective share in the Tax Equalization Fund of 363,400 dollars, comprising the prorated share of 318,300 dollars of the estimated staff assessment income approved for the support account and the prorated share of 45,100 dollars of the estimated staff assessment income approved for the United Nations Logistics Base;

20. *Emphasizes* that no peacekeeping mission shall be financed by borrowing funds from other active peacekeeping missions;

21. *Encourages* the Secretary-General to continue to take additional measures to ensure the safety and security of all personnel under the auspices of the United Nations participating in the Operation, bearing in mind paragraphs 5 and 6 of Security Council resolution 1502(2003) of 26 August 2003;

22. *Invites* voluntary contributions to the Operation in cash and in the form of services and supplies acceptable to the Secretary-General, to be administered, as appropriate, in accordance with the procedure and practices established by the General Assembly;

23. *Decides* to include in the provisional agenda of its sixty-first session the item entitled "Financing of the United Nations Operation in Burundi".

In September [A/61/309], the Secretary-General submitted to the Assembly the ONUB budget for the period from 1 July 2006 to 30 June 2007, in the amount of $144,621,800, inclusive of the commitment authority approved in resolution 60/269 (above). ACABQ [A/61/485] recommended the appropriation of an amount of $115,221,800, a reduction of $29.4 million.

Also before the Assembly were the financial performance report for the period 1 July 2004 to 30 June 2005 [A/60/612 & Corr.1] and ACABQ comments and recommendations thereon [A/61/485].

GENERAL ASSEMBLY ACTION

On 31 October [meeting 44], the General Assembly, on the recommendation of the Fifth Committee [A/61/547], adopted **resolution 61/9** without vote [agenda item 133].

Financing of the United Nations Operation in Burundi

The General Assembly,

Having considered the reports of the Secretary-General on the financing of the United Nations Operation in Burundi and the related report of the Advisory Committee on Administrative and Budgetary Questions,

Recalling Security Council resolution 1545(2004) of 21 May 2004, by which the Council authorized, for an initial period of six months as from 1 June 2004, with the intention to renew it for further periods, the deployment of a peacekeeping operation called the United Nations Operation in Burundi, and the subsequent resolutions by which the Council extended the mandate of the Operation, the latest of which was resolution 1692(2006) of 30 June 2006, by which the Council extended the mandate of the Operation until 31 December 2006,

Recalling also its resolution 58/312 of 18 June 2004 on the financing of the Operation and its subsequent resolutions thereon, the latest of which was resolution 60/269 of 30 June 2006,

Reaffirming the general principles underlying the financing of United Nations peacekeeping operations, as stated in General Assembly resolutions 1874 (S-IV) of 27 June 1963, 3101(XXVIII) of 11 December 1973 and 55/235 of 23 December 2000,

Mindful of the fact that it is essential to provide the Operation with the necessary financial resources to enable it to fulfil its responsibilities under the relevant resolutions of the Security Council,

1. *Takes note* of the status of contributions to the United Nations Operation in Burundi as at 30 June 2006, including the contributions outstanding in the amount of 31.1 million United States dollars, representing some 5 per cent of the total assessed contributions, notes with concern that only forty-nine Member States have paid their assessed contributions in full, and urges all other Member States, in particular those in arrears, to ensure payment of their outstanding assessed contributions;

2. *Expresses its appreciation* to those Member States which have paid their assessed contributions in full, and urges all other Member States to make every possible effort to ensure payment of their assessed contributions to the Operation in full;

3. *Expresses concern* at the financial situation with regard to peacekeeping activities, in particular as regards the reimbursements to troop contributors that bear additional burdens owing to overdue payments by Member States of their assessments;

4. *Also expresses concern* at the delay experienced by the Secretary-General in deploying and providing adequate resources to some recent peacekeeping missions, in particular those in Africa;

5. *Emphasizes* that all future and existing peacekeeping missions shall be given equal and non-discriminatory treatment in respect of financial and administrative arrangements;

6. *Also emphasizes* that all peacekeeping missions shall be provided with adequate resources for the effective and efficient discharge of their respective mandates;

7. *Reiterates its request* to the Secretary-General to make the fullest possible use of facilities and equipment at the United Nations Logistics Base at Brindisi, Italy, in order to minimize the costs of procurement for the Operation;

8. *Welcomes* the use of the installation at Entebbe, Uganda, to enhance the efficiency and responsiveness of its logistical support operations for peacekeeping missions in the region;

9. *Endorses* the conclusions and recommendations contained in the report of the Advisory Committee on Administrative and Budgetary Questions, and requests the Secretary-General to ensure their full implementation, subject to the provisions of the present resolution;

10. *Takes note* of the recommendations contained in paragraphs 21, 25 and 27 of the report of the Advisory Committee;

11. *Decides* to establish two National Officer posts for the Human Rights Office and one National Officer post for the Office of the Chief of Administrative Services through redeployment of posts;

12. *Also decides* to establish four general temporary assistance positions (one P-4, one P-2 and two national staff, including one National Officer) for the Conduct and Discipline Team;

13. *Re-emphasizes* the need to refine budgetary assumptions through closer scrutiny of expenditure patterns of the Operation;

14. *Reaffirms* its resolution 59/296 of 22 June 2005, and requests the Secretary-General to ensure the full implementation of its relevant provisions and the relevant provisions of its resolution 60/266 of 30 June 2006;

15. *Requests* the Secretary-General to take all necessary action to ensure that the Operation is administered with a maximum of efficiency and economy;

16. *Also requests* the Secretary-General, in order to reduce the cost of employing General Service staff, to continue efforts to recruit local staff for the Operation against General Service posts, commensurate with the requirements of the Operation;

17. *Welcomes* the efforts of the Operation and its personnel, and looks forward to the successful completion of the mandate of the Operation;

18. *Requests* the Secretary-General to ensure an orderly transition, including the transfer of assets, to the planned follow-on mission—the United Nations Integrated Office in Burundi—and the efficient liquidation of the Operation's assets in accordance with the Operation's exit strategy and liquidation timetables;

19. *Also requests* the Secretary-General to encourage strong coordination between the Operation, the planned follow-on mission and the United Nations country team with a view to ensuring a smooth transition to the

planned follow-on mission and to reducing the potential duplication of activities among members of the United Nations country team;

20. *Further requests* the Secretary-General to ensure that the lessons learned from other peacekeeping missions are applied during the Operation's drawdown, liquidation and transition to the planned follow-on mission;

21. *Notes* the additional information on projected expenditure for the Operation for the period from 1 July 2006 to 30 June 2007, amounting to 128,536,700 dollars, provided by the Secretary-General;

Financial performance report for the period from 1 July 2004 to 30 June 2005

22. *Takes note* of the report of the Secretary-General on the financial performance of the Operation for the period from 1 July 2004 to 30 June 2005;

Budget estimates for the period from 1 July 2006 to 30 June 2007

23. *Decides* to appropriate to the Special Account for the United Nations Operation in Burundi the amount of 128,536,700 dollars for the maintenance and administrative liquidation of the Operation for the period from 1 July 2006 to 30 June 2007, inclusive of the amount of 78,959,200 dollars previously authorized by the General Assembly under the terms of its resolution 60/269 for the maintenance of the Operation for the period from 1 July to 31 October 2006, and in addition to the amount of 3,426,800 dollars already appropriated under the terms of the same resolution for the support account for peacekeeping operations and the United Nations Logistics Base at Brindisi, Italy, for the period from 1 July 2006 to 30 June 2007;

Financing of the appropriation for the period from 1 July 2006 to 30 June 2007

24. *Also decides*, taking into account the amount of 40 million dollars already apportioned under the terms of its resolution 60/269 for the maintenance of the Operation for the period from 1 July to 31 October 2006, to apportion among Member States the additional amount of 88,536,700 dollars for the maintenance and administrative liquidation of the Operation for the period from 1 July 2006 to 30 June 2007, in accordance with the levels updated in its resolution 58/256 of 23 December 2003, and taking into account the scale of assessments for 2006, as set out in its resolution 58/1 B of 23 December 2003, and the scale of assessments for 2007;

25. *Further decides* that, in accordance with the provisions of its resolution 973(X) of 15 December 1955, there shall be set off against the apportionment among Member States, as provided for in paragraph 24 above, their respective share in the Tax Equalization Fund of the amount of 1,774,600 dollars, representing the estimated additional staff assessment income approved for the Operation for the period from 1 July 2006 to 30 June 2007;

26. *Decides* that, for Member States that have fulfilled their financial obligations to the Operation, there shall be set off against their apportionment, as provided for in paragraph 24 above, their respective share of the additional unencumbered balance in the amount of 115,500 dollars in respect of the financial period ended 30 June 2004, in accordance with the levels updated in its resolution 58/256, and taking into account the scale of assessments for 2004, as set out in its resolution 58/1 B;

27. *Also decides* that, for Member States that have not fulfilled their financial obligations to the Operation, there shall be set off against their outstanding obligations their respective share of the additional unencumbered balance in the amount of 115,500 dollars in respect of the financial period ended 30 June 2004, in accordance with the scheme set out in paragraph 26 above;

28. *Further decides* that, for Member States that have fulfilled their financial obligations to the Operation, there shall be set off against their apportionment, as provided for in paragraph 24 above, their respective share of the unencumbered balance and other income in the total amount of 31,523,100 dollars in respect of the financial period ended 30 June 2005, in accordance with the levels updated in its resolution 58/256, and taking into account the scale of assessments for 2005, as set out in its resolution 58/1 B;

29. *Decides* that, for Member States that have not fulfilled their financial obligations to the Operation, there shall be set off against their outstanding obligations their respective share of the unencumbered balance and other income in the total amount of 31,523,100 dollars in respect of the financial period ended 30 June 2005, in accordance with the scheme set out in paragraph 28 above;

30. *Also decides* that the decrease in the estimated staff assessment income in the amount of 583,800 dollars in respect of the financial period ended 30 June 2005 shall be set off against the credits from the amount of 31,523,100 dollars referred to in paragraphs 28 and 29 above;

31. *Emphasizes* that no peacekeeping mission shall be financed by borrowing funds from other active peacekeeping missions;

32. *Encourages* the Secretary-General to continue to take additional measures to ensure the safety and security of all personnel under the auspices of the United Nations participating in the Operation, bearing in mind paragraphs 5 and 6 of Security Council resolution 1502(2003) of 26 August 2003;

33. *Invites* voluntary contributions to the Operation in cash and in the form of services and supplies acceptable to the Secretary-General, to be administered, as appropriate, in accordance with the procedure and practices established by the General Assembly;

34. *Decides* to keep under review during its sixty-first session the item entitled "Financing of the United Nations Operation in Burundi".

On 22 December, by **decision 61/552**, the Assembly decided that the agenda item "Financing of the United Nations Operation in Burundi" would remain for consideration during its resumed sixty-first (2007) session.

Central African Republic

Despite hopes for peace following successful presidential elections, the Central African Republic, in 2006, was increasingly drawn into the crisis affecting Chad and the Darfur region of the Sudan. In January, Government troops clashed with local insurgents near the border with Chad. Rebel attacks in the north increased during the year, becoming a rebellion aimed at toppling the Government.

As the conflict continued to affect the civilian population, some 5,000 refugees fled to southern Chad from attacks by Government forces, rebel groups and bandits, increasing the number of Central African refugees in that country to more than 48,000. In June, rebel groups attacked an army outpost in the north-western town of Gordil, near the Chad-Sudan border. Three rebel movements active in the north formed a coalition, and took the city of Birao and two other cities on 30 October. On 27 November, one of the rebel movements attacked the city of Ndélé. The Central African Republic accused the Sudan of supporting the rebellion, an accusation the Sudan denied. A Government counter offensive in November-December resulted in it retaking the city. Various diplomatic efforts by countries in the region did not defuse tensions between the Central African Republic and Chad, and the Sudan.

Established in 2000 [YUN 2000, p. 162], the United Nations Peacebuilding Office in the Central African Republic continued to support Government efforts to return the country to stability and achieve reconciliation and reconstruction. On 22 November, the Security Council extended its mandate for another year. The multinational force of the Central African Economic and Monetary Community continued to assist in stabilization efforts.

Political and security developments

AU communiqué. The AU Peace and Security Council, in a 30 March declaration on the situation in the Central African Republic [S/2006/216], noted with concern the insecurity in the north of the country and its consequences on the political situation and the life of the population there, with several thousands of people already having sought refuge in Chad. The AU Council welcomed the decision of the AU Commission Chairperson to dispatch a multidisciplinary expert mission to the country to evaluate its needs and make recommendations on the assistance that member States and the AU could provide. The Council called on the AU Commission, the Central African Government, the United Nations Nations Peacebuilding Office in the Central African Republic (BONUCA) and the Central African Economic and Monetary Authority (CEMAC) to work together to find a lasting solution.

Report of Secretary-General (June). In a report [S/2006/441] on BONUCA activities from January to June, submitted in response to Security Council presidential statement S/PRST/2001/25 [YUN 2001, p. 156], the Secretary-General said that the security situation remained volatile and dependent on the situation in neighbouring Chad and the Sudan. The country was a victim of the tension between Chad and the Sudan, which had accused each other of supporting rebels hostile to their respective regimes, even though providing such support was prohibited under the Tripoli Agreement signed on 8 February by Chadian President Idriss Déby Itno and Sudanese President Omar Hassan al-Bashir (see p. 297).

Since April, rebels hostile to the regime of Chad's President had crossed through the north-eastern part of the Central African Republic to attack the Chadian army. On 25 and 26 April, an Antonov 35 aircraft unloaded armed men and military equipment in the north-eastern locality of Tiringoulou, violating the country's territorial integrity. The Government objected to those repeated incursions and closed its border with the Sudan. However, armed individuals appeared to have established a foothold in the north-east, and the Central African Armed Forces were unable to control the situation for lack of adequate manpower and logistics. The Government, concerned about the situation, requested support from bilateral and multilateral partners.

Bangui, the capital, recorded a lull in the violence, thanks to the Central African Armed Forces patrols, supported by the CEMAC multinational force (FOMUC). In more remote areas, particularly in the north, security was undermined by abuses committed by armed gangs, "roadblockers" and rebels seeking to destabilize the country. The Government was faced with an armed rebellion, based in the north, aimed at overthrowing the regime of President François Bozizé. The rebellion included four armed groups: the Union des forces républicaines (UFR), the Armée pour la restauration de la république et la démocratie (APRD), the Mouvement patriotique pour la restauration de la république centrafricaine (MPRC) and the front démocratique du peuple centrafricain (FDPC). The armed forces, which were slowly being restructured, were not in a position to secure the national territory, even with FOMUC support.

The political situation was marked by the emergence of internal crises in several major political parties, the work of the National Assembly's first regular session of 2006 and a number of peace and security initiatives. The National Assembly adopted several draft laws, including on the establishment, organization and operation of the country's High Council for Communication and on the organization and operation of the National Mediation Council.

The humanitarian situation deteriorated sharply, particularly in the north-west, where civilian populations had left their villages and taken refuge in the fields or forests or across the border in Chad, as a result of the insecurity created by the rebels, attacks by robbers and reprisals by the Armed Forces. An estimated 30,000 people were in need of emergency assistance. Despite the prevailing insecurity, UN agencies provided basic health care and food and non-food assistance through international NGOs operating in areas bordering Chad.

The Office of the United Nations High Commissioner for Refugees (UNHCR) continued to register urban refugees in Bangui. On 1 February, the Central African Republic, the Sudan and UNHCR signed a tripartite agreement on the repatriation of Sudanese refugees. Some 2,115 refugees, out of 12,000 living in the south-eastern part of the country, were repatriated. On 15 April, UNHCR suspended its operations because of the Government's decision to close the border with the Sudan.

The human rights situation also deteriorated, with many reports of arbitrary or summary execution, torture, cruel, inhuman or degrading treatment, arbitrary arrest and detention, violation of time limits on police custody and restriction of the freedom of movement. The execution of a Staff Sergeant by members of the Presidential Guard, the assassination of the mayor of Bossangoa, for which rebels had claimed responsibility, the killing of the mayor of Koron-Mpoko municipality and his son by unidentified armed individuals, and the murder of two local physicians on official mission in the north were examples of the violations perpetrated in the country.

The emergence of rebel movements in the north, the situation in Chad and tension between that country and the Sudan seriously threatened the relative stability that had prevailed, the Secretary-General said. As a subregional force, FOMUC continued to play a key role in efforts to make the country more secure. The international community should intensify efforts to make the borders between Chad, the Central African Republic and the Sudan more secure, in order to discourage armed movements from taking root. For its part, the Government should engage in a dialogue with all national actors. The President should work towards promoting justice and respect for the rule of law, shed light on the serious human rights violations committed in recent months and put an end to impunity by bringing those responsible to justice.

Press statement (July). On 7 July, Security Council members [SC/8771], after a briefing on the situation in the country by the Secretary-General's Special Representative and Head of BONUCA, General Lamine Cissé, and by a representative of the Department of Peacekeeping Operations, expressed, in a press statement, their concern at the increase in poverty, the fragility of the country's economic recovery and the deterioration of the humanitarian situation. They invited the Central African authorities to continue to improve public finances and governance, and urged bilateral partners and international institutions to increase their support of those efforts and provide the necessary humanitarian assistance.

Council members called on the authorities and all political parties to settle their disputes through peaceful means and dialogue, and to work for peace and national cohesion in full respect of human rights and the rule of law. They urged the authorities to put an end to impunity by bringing to justice those responsible for human rights violations.

Council members, concerned that the persisting violence in the Darfur region of the Sudan and the deterioration of relations between Chad and the Sudan might further negatively affect the security and stability of the country, condemned the attack perpetrated by armed groups in Gordil on 26 June (see p. 164). They stressed the importance of implementing the 8 February Tripoli Agreement ending the Chadian-Sudanese conflict (see p. 297), reiterated their respect of the territorial integrity of the Central African Republic and called upon all States in the region to cooperate in ensuring regional stability.

Council members invited the authorities to expedite the restructuring of the National Armed Forces, commended FOMUC efforts in support of the Armed Forces and welcomed the financial and material assistance provided to FOMUC by the EU, France and Germany.

Report of Secretary-General (October). As requested by the Council on 7 July, the Secretary-General, in October, submitted an interim report [S/2006/828] on the situation in the country. The lack of security continued to be a major concern, the Secretary-General said. While the situation had somewhat stabilized in the capital, it was precarious in the interior, particularly in the north and centre, where "roadblockers", armed bands and rebels continued to prey on civilians, kidnapping the children of herdsmen for ransom and attacking traders on the main highways. The 26 June attack by armed groups against an outpost of the Armed Forces and FOMUC in the north-western town of Gordil, near the Central African Republic/Chad/Sudan border triangle, resulted in deaths and injuries on both sides. The attack confirmed that rebel groups were operating in the north, and that insecurity was gradually expanding to the north-east, towards the Vakaga region bordering on Darfur region of the Sudan. The armed forces would continue to be supported by FOMUC, whose mandate had been extended until June 2007.

The security situation was made worse by the situation in neighbouring countries, particularly Chad and the Sudan. The Government was threatened by rebels and armed bands established along the border with Chad and the Sudan. President Bozizé had stated that security was seriously threatened in the northern part of the country, which was virtually living under occupation, posing a grave threat to the integrity of the national territory. The President appealed to the international community to help the Central African Republic find a solution to that situation. The rapprochement between the Sudan and Chad, as evidenced by the 26 July N'Djamena agreement (see p. 299) signed by both Heads of State was encouraging, but renewed hostilities in eastern Chad in September, and in Darfur, together with the presence of rebels and armed groups on Central African territory, were discouraging hopes for a lull in the conflict. The special summit meeting of CEMAC, held in N'Djamena, Chad, on 7 August, mandated President Omar Bongo Ondimba of Gabon, Chairman of the Ad Hoc Committee on the Central African Republic, and AU Chairman, President Denis Sassou Nguesso of the Congo to study ways of addressing the security problem in the country. A subregional approach to resolving the crisis should continue to be given preference, the Secretary-General said.

Roadblocks and confrontations between the army and rebel groups had a negative impact on the humanitarian situation and development activities, especially in the north-west and north-east, where UN humanitarian missions were unable to operate outside the urban centres. The human rights situation was marked by a resurgence of violence by "roadblockers", unidentified armed gangs and regular soldiers, particularly in the north.

The Secretary-General observed that, although the defence and security forces were newly organized, with the support of France, they were still unable to repel the armed groups. Therefore, the Government, with subregional support, had requested the international community to provide additional resources to help the armed forces enhance their operational capabilities.

On the political front, President Bozizé, on 28 July, issued an invitation to all political groups and social strata to take part in a dialogue on peace and security. Participants unanimously agreed that the lack of security was the chief cause of the slowdown in economic activity and trade and was holding back development. Meanwhile, disagreements persisted within many of the political parties, chiefly as a result of crises in leadership and reorganization efforts. The Minister of the Interior, on 3 August, issued a circular prohibiting access to the media for political parties plagued by internal division, because of the risk to public order arising from statements made by the various camps. He set a three-month deadline for political organizations to resolve their leadership divisions or risk suspension. Politicians saw the Minister's injunction as interference in their internal affairs. BONUCA, at the Minister's request, organized a meeting, on 21 August, to clarify the terms of the circular. The discussions, also attended by the Chairperson of the committee responsible for monitoring the outcome of the national dialogue, and by journalists and diplomats, helped to dispel tension. Participants agreed to prepare a text to put into effect the order relating to political parties and the status of the opposition, to refrain from inciting hatred through the media, and to observe discipline in their parties. Participants were satisfied with the outcome and asked BONUCA to organize similar meetings on a regular basis.

A joint International Monetary Fund (IMF)/World Bank/African Development Bank (ADB) mission to Bangui (12-19 August) assessed the execution of the second post-conflict programme adopted in January, and recommended that the Government continue to improve the management of the national treasury. The IMF invited the authorities to meet all quantitative targets so that discussions could begin on preparing a programme under the Poverty Reduction and Growth Facility, an essential condition for reaching the decision point of the Heavily Indebted Poor Countries Initiative. The World Bank and the ADB pursued dialogue with the Government on clearing the country's arrears to multilateral financial institutions—a precondition for their re-engagement.

In the light of the Central African Government's request for the renewal of BONUCA mandate for another year, the Secretary-General said that discussions were ongoing to determine the priority areas of further UN commitment.

Security Council consideration (October). On 30 October [meeting 5558], the Security Council held a private meeting on the situation in the Central African Republic, during which Council members, Central African Republic Prime Minister Elie Doté and the Secretary-General's Special Representative exchanged views on the situation in the country.

SECURITY COUNCIL ACTION.

On 22 November [meeting 5572], following consultations among Security Council members, the President made statement **S/PRST/2006/47** on behalf of the Council:

In October 2006, the Security Council heard Mr. Elie Doté, Prime Minister of the Central African Republic, as well as General Lamine Cissé, Special Representative of the Secretary-General for the Central African Republic. It reiterated its full support for the United Nations Peacebuilding Support Office in the Central African Republic and for the United Nations staff in the Central African Republic.

The Council welcomes the efforts of the Government of the Central African Republic to revive dialogue through meetings with political stakeholders and representatives of civil society. It calls upon the Secretary-General to encourage, through the United Nations Peacebuilding Support Office in the Central African Republic, the holding on a regular basis of such meetings, which are vital to restoring trust among Central Africans and promoting lasting reconciliation.

The Council also welcomes the courageous efforts of the Government of the Central African Republic to implement the reforms advocated by the bilateral partners and international financial institutions aimed at improving the management of the national treasury, ensuring transparency in economic activities and good governance. In that regard, it calls upon the Government to continue the reforms and dialogue with its international partners with a view to restoring economic growth and reducing poverty in the country.

The Council is deeply concerned about the deterioration of the security situation in the Central African Republic, especially in the wake of the attacks on the towns of Birao, Ouanda-Djalle and Sam Ouandja. It expresses serious concern that instability along the border areas of Chad, the Sudan and the Central African Republic represents a threat to security and stability in the Central African Republic and its neighbours, while noting that Central African defence and security forces are still unable to repel the armed groups in the northern and north-eastern parts of the country.

The Council reaffirms its commitment to the territorial integrity of the Central African Republic. It calls for the adoption of a subregional approach to stabilize the borders of the Central African Republic. It urges the Central African authorities to expedite their efforts to restructure the armed forces and enhance their operational capabilities, and encourages the Multinational Force of the Central African Economic and Monetary Community to continue supporting the Central African armed forces beyond 30 June 2007. It notes that the Department of Peacekeeping Operations of the Secretariat has dispatched a fact-finding mission to Chad and the Central African Republic to assess how the United Nations might help those countries to address the current instability. The Council looks forward to the findings and recommendations of the mission.

The Council requests the Secretary-General to reinforce cooperation between the United Nations and member States of the Central African Economic and Monetary Community with a view to facilitating and strengthening initiatives aimed at addressing trans-border insecurity in the subregion and bringing to an end the violations by armed groups of the territorial integrity of the Central African Republic. It also requests the Secretary-General to provide to it a report on the situation in the Central African Republic by 31 December 2006.

The Council decides to renew the mandate of the United Nations Peacebuilding Support Office in the Central African Republic for a period of one year, until 31 December 2007, and invites the Secretary-General to submit to it the new modalities of the mission of the Office for the new period, no later than 30 November 2006.

Following the Security Council's request for the submission of new modalities for BONUCA mission, the Secretary-General, on 30 November [S/2006/934], said that the Office, in 2007, would focus on: supporting national reconciliation and dialogue; assisting efforts to strengthen democratic institutions; facilitating the mobilization of resources for national reconstruction, economic recovery, poverty alleviation and good governance; mainstreaming a gender perspective into peacebuilding, in line with Council resolution 1325(2000) [YUN 2000, p. 1113]; and reinforcing cooperation between the United Nations and CEMAC member States and other regional entities to facilitate and strengthen initiatives aimed at addressing transborder insecurity in the subregion.

Report of Secretary-General (December). In his December report [S/2006/1034] on the situation in the country and the activities of BONUCA, the Secretary-General said that the political situation had been marked by the rebellion in the north, led by the Armée pour la restauration de la république et la démocratie, the Front démocratique du peuple centrafricain and the Union des forces républicaines. The Government believed former President Ange-Félix Patassé to be complicit with those insurgents. The rebel movements had formed a coalition, the Union de forces démocratiques pour le rassemblement, whose members, on 30 October, attacked and occupied the northern city of Birao, capital of Vakaga prefecture, and the neighbouring cities of Ouanda-Djallé and Sam Ouandja. The Sudan denied accusations by the Central African Republic that it was supporting the rebellion. A high-level Sudanese mission visiting Bangui on 11 November reiterated that the Sudan wished to maintain good-neighbourly relations with the Central African Republic.

In their southward advance, the Union des forces républicaines rebels attacked the north-eastern city of Ndélé on 27 November. A Government-led counter-offensive, supported by French and FOMUC contingents, retook Birao and Ndélé on 27 November and Sam-Ouandja and Ouanda-Djallé in December. To find a solution to the crisis, on 7 November, the President exchanged views with Bangui municipal, neighbourhood and group leaders on ways of avoiding a military escalation. On 8 November, he addressed the people of Bangui, following a peaceful protest march organized by civil society organizations. Several national consultations were also held from 14 to 18 November, involving all political parties, trade unions and civil society organizations. The AU Special Envoy for the Central African Republic visited Bangui from 15 to 18 November, and the AU Peace and Security Council met on 7 December to raise awareness of the urgency of assisting the country. President Muammar Gaddafi of the Libyan Arab Jamahiriya organized a mini-summit in Tripoli on 22 November, attended by the Presidents of Chad, the Sudan and the Central African Republic, as well as by Egyptian President Mohamed Hosni Mubarak, to discuss the tensions between Chad, the Central African Republic and the Sudan, but to no avail.

Confrontations between rebel groups and Government forces in the north and north-west led to the displacement of some 15,000 to 20,000 people, making it harder for them to receive humanitarian assistance. However, collaboration among UN agencies and international non-governmental organizations (NGOs) operating in the field facilitated the delivery of emergency assistance, with the World Food Programme reaching some 50,000 displaced persons. On 12 December, UN agencies and NGOs launched a joint appeal for $50 million to meet the immediate needs of the internally displaced.

The restructuring of the defence and security forces moved forward and continued to benefit from BONUCA technical support. The same was true of the ex-combatant reintegration and community support project, which entered its final phase. BONUCA continued to strengthen the capacity of the police and gendarmerie, while its military team helped to train many contingents of the armed forces, thereby building their professional capacity.

The year was marked by further growth in the country's gross domestic product (GDP). Experts estimated that overall GDP should reach 3 per cent. In July, the African Development Bank approved a $4.9 million grant for a national economic management capacity recovery programme, and in November, the World Bank approved a transaction of nearly $82 million, allowing the country to clear its arrears.

Financing of BONUCA

On 31 January [A/60/585/Add.1], the Secretary-General submitted a budget in the amount of $6,467,400 for financing BONUCA throughout the year. The General Assembly, on 22 December, in section VII of **resolution 61/252** (see p. 1614), approved that amount as part of the $326,500,000 approved for special political missions, good offices and other political initiatives authorized by the General Assembly and/or the Security Council.

Chad and Central African Republic

During 2006, the conflict in the Darfur region of Sudan spilled over into Chad and the Central African Republic. Following attacks by armed groups in the eastern part of the country, Chad declared a state of emergency in the east and accused the Sudan of supporting the rebels. Likewise, after armed groups in the north-eastern Central African Republic mounted a rebellion against the Government, the Central African authorities accused the Sudan of backing the rebels. In August, the Security Council requested the United Nations Mission in the Sudan to establish a political and military presence in Chad and, if necessary, in the Central African Republic. The Secretary-General dispatched an assessment mission to the two countries, and in December, reported to the Council that conditions on the ground did not permit the deployment of a full-fledged peacekeeping operation, but only a robust monitoring and protection mission.

Security Council request (August). On 31 August the Security Council, by resolution 1706(2006) (see p. 282), decided that the United Nations Mission in the Sudan (UNMIS) should deploy to Darfur to assist in addressing regional security issues, in liaison with international efforts to improve the security situation along the borders of the Sudan with Chad and the Central African Republic, including by establishing a presence in key locations in Chad, including in the internally displaced persons and refugee camps, and if necessary, in the Central African Republic. The Council also requested UNMIS to contribute to the implementation of the 26 July N'Djamena Agreement between the Sudan and Chad (see p. 299).

On 20 September, the AU Peace and Security Council, in a communiqué, encouraged any steps that could be taken, including by the United Nations, to enhance security along the Sudan/Chad and Sudan/Central African Republic borders, as well as to ensure the protection of refugees in Chad.

Security Council mission. The Secretary-General, in response to the Security Council request in resolution 1706(2006) that he make recommendations for a UN presence along the borders of Chad, the Central African Republic and the Sudan, sent a technical assessment mission to Chad and the Central African Republic from 21 November to 3 December. The mission met with President Déby of Chad and President Bozizé of the Central African Republic, senior Government officials, political leaders from both majority and opposition parties, and civil society, humanitarian and human rights representatives. In the Central African Republic, the team met with the commander of the FOMUC multinational force, as well as with a joint EU-AU mission, which was in the country to conduct a midterm review of FOMUC.

Due to the security situation, the mission was not able to visit the north-eastern region of the Central African Republic and eastern Chad, both of which bordered the Darfur region of the Sudan. The visit to Chad was also curtailed, as the team was held up in Bangui for two days due to security concerns, following a major rebel attack on Abéché and other areas in eastern Chad at the end of November. Only a part of the team subsequently travelled to N'Djamena, as it became clear that a field visit to eastern Chad would not be possible.

Report of Secretary-General (December). In a December report [S/2006/1019] on Chad and the Central African Republic, based on the mission's findings, the Secretary-General outlined some preliminary options for the mandate, structure and operations of a possible UN presence in both countries. According to the report, the Darfur conflict had clearly spilled over into Chad and the conflict there, and those in Chad and the Central African Republic, were increasingly interlinked. The situation in the border areas had deteriorated considerably and was threatening peace and security in the whole region. The humanitarian and human rights situations had also worsened and had a serious impact on the civilian populations in eastern Chad and north-eastern Central African Republic.

In Chad, rebel groups had exploited the volatile situation in the border areas to launch increasingly coordinated attacks against the national army. The rebel groups reportedly comprised significant numbers of former army officers, as well as non-Chadians, including Sudanese nationals. In addition, some Sudanese armed elements appeared to be present in north-eastern Chad. Following the 8 February Tripoli Agreement between Chad and the Sudan ending the conflict between them (see p. 297) and the 26 July N'Djamena Agreement (see p. 299), Chad and the Sudan agreed to establish a joint mechanism to monitor the border situation. However, the Agreements had not been implemented and relations between the two countries deteriorated considerably, with both parties accusing each other of supporting rebel groups and mercenaries to destabilize their respective Governments. Rebel and criminal activities, as well as inter-ethnic clashes, increased in eastern Chad, while Janjaweed militias based in the Sudan launched raids into Chad, looting and pillaging. On 13 November, Chad declared a state of emergency in the eastern part of the country. Following a brief occupation of Abéché, in eastern Chad, by rebels on 25 November, the upsurge of rebel activities in the Abéché area and threats to attack N'Djamena, the Government, on 28 November, declared that it was in a state of war with the Sudan.

The conflict in Darfur and the instability in northern Central African Republic created a humanitarian crisis in Chad. As at 30 November, Chad was hosting approximately 232,000 refugees from Darfur, and an additional 48,000 from the Central African Republic. Altogether, some 92,000 Chadians had been displaced in the eastern part of the country as a consequence of the upsurge in fighting, out of a total population of about 1.1 million.

The technical assessments mission confirmed that the Darfur conflict had spilled over into Chad, with serious consequences for the country and beyond, while, in the Central African Republic, the Government asserted that the Sudan was backing the rebels in the northeast. At the same time, the north-east of the Central African Republic had been used by Chadian rebel groups to bypass the Darfur-Chad border, thereby destabilizing the north-eastern Central African prefecture of Vakaga.

The deployment of the UN presence envisaged in resolution 1706(2006) had been discussed with the Presidents of both countries. President Bozizé called for the deployment of UN troops as soon as possible, while President Déby indicated his acceptance, in principle, but wanted the nature, strength and composition to be further discussed.

The Secretary-General observed that the situation in eastern Chad and the north-eastern Central African Republic was extremely fluid, with ongoing hostilities between the respective Governments and rebel groups, especially in Chad. There were limited prospects for dialogue and reconciliation between the Governments and the rebels. Similarly, there were no signs of a credible and inclusive political process in Darfur. The deployment of a UN peacekeeping force in eastern Chad and the north-eastern Central African Republic would face considerable risks, and its safe entry would depend on the consent of the parties. Otherwise, any UN presence could become the target of attacks by rebel groups, if they were to perceive it as interfering with their cross-border activities. Unless all the parties concerned were to agree to a ceasefire and engage in an intra- and inter-State dialogue aimed at a political solution, a UN force would be operating in the midst of continuing hostilities and would have no clear exit strategy. The Secretary-General held the view that the conditions for an effective peacekeeping operation did not seem to be in place.

However, should the Council decide to pursue the idea, it should authorize the deployment of a robust monitoring and protection mission to facilitate the political process, protect civilians, monitor the human rights situation and strengthen the local judicial, police and correctional system. In addition to monitoring and reporting on the cross-border activities of armed groups along the border with Darfur, such a force would provide protection to civilians under imminent threat in its deployment areas, deter attacks by armed groups and react preemptively to protect civilians, including refugees and internally displaced persons.

Meanwhile, the Secretary-General recommended that the Council consider dispatching an advance team to the two countries to collect more information on the situation in the border areas, explore the possibilities of a political agreement and conduct detailed planning and logistical preparation.

Uganda

Communications. On 5 January [S/2006/13], Canada asked the Security Council to place the situation in northern Uganda on its agenda for immediate consideration. The humanitarian situation there, Canada said, was nothing short of catastrophic, with 1.7 million displaced persons confined to over 200 squalid and unsafe camps, and over 90 per cent of the rural population enduring those conditions. The main cause of the displacement was the conflict that had plagued northern Uganda for almost 20 years, and in which the insurgent group, the Lord's Resistance Army (LRA), had attacked the population, raided the camps and abducted over 25,000 children, who had been forced into fighting or sexual slavery. There was a serious and growing threat to regional peace and security, as the LRA was bringing its violence into neighbouring countries. LRA had long taken refuge in the south of the Sudan, and its violence during recent months had interrupted the return of refugees and displaced persons to that country, following the signing of the Comprehensive Peace Agreement [YUN 2005, p. 301] that had ended the north-south conflict in the Sudan. More recently, the LRA had entered the eastern part of the DRC.

Canada outlined a number of steps the Council could take to address the situation, including calling upon all parties to ensure safe access to civilian populations for aid agencies, and for LRA to hand over those individuals indicted by the International Criminal Court (ICC). The Council should insist that all States in the region cease their support for LRA; call upon all parties to pursue a negotiated settlement to the conflict; and call for tripartite talks between Uganda, the DRC and the Sudan to ensure a coordinated response to LRA activity in the region.

On 16 January [S/2006/29], Uganda transmitted to the Council its position paper on the humanitarian situation in northern Uganda, which gave a factual account of the situation and of the Government's efforts to address it. Any call for putting the situation on the Council's agenda was therefore unjustified, Uganda said. The paper outlined the Government's policy recommendations for resolving the LRA problem and the humanitarian situation.

Uganda said that the LRA, a renegade faction of the defeated Uganda National Liberation Army, which had re-organized under the Holy Spirit Movement of Alice Lakwena, had opted to continue fighting, despite the peace treaty signed in 1988. After their defeat, Joseph Kony emerged to take over the reigns of those forces under the new name "the Lord's Resistance Army" and by March 2002, had some 3000 armed fighters. The LRA operated in northern Uganda until 1994, when it started operating out of southern Sudan. Since 1998, the Uganda Peoples Defence Force had undertaken a number of military campaigns to dislodge the LRA. As a result, only a few remnants were located in South Gulu, Pader, Kitgum, Apach and Lira districts and some areas of southern Sudan and the DRC/Uganda border in the Garamba National Park. Several peace initiatives had been undertaken over the years, the latest in 2004, when contact was initiated between the Government and the LRA. The Government responded positively and declared a ceasefire and a safe zone for conducting the talks, but as at 31 December 2004, the Government team was still waiting for the LRA team to turn up. Due to the neutralization of its various fighters and their commanders, the LRA structure had broken down, reducing their capacity to plan. The losses incurred had also reduced their manpower, and defections of its senior commanders had further demoralized the force. Cooperation with the Government of the Sudan since 2000 enabled Uganda to dislodge the LRA from its major bases. Between 2002 and 2005, 17,779 abductees were rescued and handed over to various reception centres. The Uganda Peoples Defence Force continued to rescue those remaining in captivity, and had retrained and absorbed into its ranks LRA defectors. The ICC had indicted

Mr. Kony and four other LRA leaders for war crimes and crimes against humanity.

As a way forward, Uganda recommended that sustained political and diplomatic pressure be put on the DRC and the Sudan to disarm and arrest or neutralize the remaining LRA elements in their territories and arrest and hand over those indicted; the AU efforts to disarm all groups in eastern DRC, including LRA elements in Garamba National Park be fully supported; increase support be provided to Uganda to modernize and equip its army; and humanitarian support increased, including financing for the National Resettlement Strategic Plan for internally displaced persons.

Security Council meeting on the Great Lakes Region (January). During the Security Council's 27 January meeting [meeting 5359] on the situation in the Great Lakes region (see p. 121), Uganda's Minister for Foreign Affairs said that his country wanted to engage the Council on the question of the LRA, a terrorist group that had inflected tremendous suffering on the people of northern Uganda and southern Sudan, as well as the DRC. The Uganda People's Defence Force had single-handedly fought against the LRA. Uganda was committed to working with the Secretary-General, the core partner countries (Norway, the Netherlands, the United States, the United Kingdom), as well as with the EU and NGOs in addressing the humanitarian challenges of the situation in northern Uganda. Although the military campaign had not been completely eliminated, the LRA threat had been weakened, as it was reduced from a force of 3,000 to about 500-600 through defections and capture. Uganda was convinced that the LRA leadership would be captured and handed over to the ICC if it crossed back into the country. The Government had embarked on a number of peace initiatives to resolve the conflict. The 2000 Amnesty Act, and its implementing Amnesty Commission, were in place and some 2000 LRA rebels had taken advantage of it.

Uganda said that it had circulated to the Council a document detailing the Government's commitment to effective interventions, in cooperation with UN agencies and NGOs, to deal with the humanitarian situation in northern Uganda. It called upon the Council to urge those countries and groups that provided financial, material and logistical support to the LRA to cease such support; and the DRC and the Sudan to disarm the LRA and cooperate with ICC in arresting and handing over LRA terrorist leaders.

Security Council consideration (April). Briefing the Security Council on 19 April [meeting 5415], Uganda's Ministers of Defence and Foreign Affairs asked the Council to support strong measures to disarm the LRA. Defence Minister Amama Mbabazi called for combined regional efforts to disarm, capture or arrest the indicted LRA terrorist leaders and hand them over to ICC. He also proposed an arrangement with the DRC, similar to the one between Uganda and the Sudan, by which the Ugandan defence force would be allowed to enter Congolese territory and hand over LRA terrorists, under close supervision of the United Nations organization Mission in the DRC (MONUC). He also urged that MONUC and the United Nations Mission in the Sudan (UNMIS) be mandated to forcefully disarm the LRA operating in the countries of their responsibility. Foreign Minister Sam Kutesa also informed the Council of the Joint Monitoring Committee and an emergency action plan for humanitarian intervention to be launched by President Musevini on 26 April.

On 28 April [S/2006/271], Uganda submitted a draft concept paper on the proposed regional mechanism to deal with the LRA as a threat to regional peace and security.

Report of Secretary-General report (June). In a June report [S/2006/478] submitted pursuant to Security Council resolution 1663(2006) (see p. 259), the Secretary-General said that for two decades the LRA had inflicted enormous suffering on the Acholi, the very ethnic group on whose behalf it claimed to be fighting. The conflict had claimed an estimated 100,000 victims. Throughout the two-decade insurgency, LRA had made the civilian population the target of most of its activity, carrying out abductions of children and adults, extrajudicial killings and sexual and gender-based violence, mostly rape and torture.

Although LRA forces were believed to have diminished over the past years, it remained active in the border regions between the DRC, Uganda and southern Sudan, and despite its reduced numbers, it presented a real threat and added to the security problems in the Great Lakes region. While it seemed to consist of no more than several hundred combatants, it had a proven ability to regroup and continue committing atrocities.

The Secretary-General observed that implementation of the Comprehensive Peace Agreement [YUN 2005, p. 301] in southern Sudan had enhanced the opportunity for peace in northern Uganda. However, the challenges created by two decades of conflict required greater effort by all concerned, including building mutual trust between the Government and the Acholi community, as immediate prospects for a political settlement remained uncertain. The regional impact of the insurgency was a cause for further concern, which was underscored by the clash in

January between MONUC peacekeepers and the LRA in Garamba National Park. The crisis in northern Uganda went beyond the confrontation between the Ugandan Government and the LRA. It was fuelled, in part, by the general resentment of the population in that region against perceived economic, political and social exclusion.

The Secretary-General, noting the call for the establishment of a panel of experts to expose the sources of material and financial support for LRA, recommended that Member States examine what possible action they could take in respect of LRA sources of funding and, in that regard, the Security Council should decide on the advisability of establishing a new sanctions mechanism. He also urged the Council to endorse and support the implementation of the national peace, recovery and development plan for northern Uganda, which would provide a framework for international involvement in efforts to address the root causes and implications of the LRA insurgency. He urged the Core Group to work with the Government on the issues of socio-economic reintegration of former LRA combatants and assistance to internally displaced persons and other affected groups, and donors to support the efforts of the Amnesty Commission. Dealing with the regional implications of LRA activities remained the responsibility of the regional Governments, and while UNMIS and MONUC could provide assistance, they should not be seen as an alternative to the authorities in the LRA-affected region in the maintenance of law and order. Governments of the region had the capacity to address the LRA threat, if they could find a way to strengthen cooperation among their security forces to deal more effectively with it. However, UN agencies needed to work closer with Member States in gathering and sharing information about the LRA. The disarmament, demobilization, repatriation and reintegration of LRA elements should be encouraged through the establishment of a formal mechanism, and a focused and comprehensive approach should be taken to help Uganda address the challenges of recovery, rehabilitation and sustained development. The Secretary-General urged the international community to support Uganda during the development and implementation of its peace, recovery and development plan. He noted the proposal by some Member States for the appointment of a special envoy to help Uganda deal with the situation created by LRA activities. However, while President Museveni had agreed in principle with the idea, the mandate still had to be agreed upon, as the Government was reluctant to accept a special envoy to deal with what it considered domestic issues.

Commenting on the report in a 20 July letter [S/2006/558] to the Council President, Uganda said that the humanitarian situation had changed dramatically. Congestion in the internally displaced persons camps had been addressed, many people were returning to their villages and the Government was providing people with tools to farm and build houses. The Joint Monitoring Committee, to which the Government was fully committed, was adequate to address the humanitarian situation and foster reconciliation, rehabilitation and reintegration. Uganda reiterated its position on the appointment of a special envoy, whose mandate should be limited to coordinating regional efforts to arrest and disarm LRA fighters, especially the indicted leaders. It did not see the need for a group of experts to trace the sources of LRA funding and arms. Instead, all efforts should be directed at arresting LRA leaders, and UNMIS and MONUC should have a robust mandate to disarm them. Noting that the task of dealing with LRA was being left largely to the Governments of the region, Uganda was of the view that the Security Council, with the primary responsibility of maintaining international peace and security, had to be a key player in arresting LRA members.

Uganda-LRA agreement. On 26 August, Uganda and the LRA signed, in Juba, the Sudan, an Agreement on Cessation of Hostilities between the Government of Uganda and the Lord's Resistance Army/Movement, which Uganda transmitted [S/2006/861] to the Security Council on 3 November. By the Agreement, the parties agreed to cease all hostile military action, as well as media and propaganda campaigns; identify the places of assembly of LRA forces; and guarantee safe passage to LRA forces moving to the assembly points, which should be completed in three weeks. They also agreed to the creation of a Cessation of Hostilities Monitoring Team. An addendum to the Agreement [S/2006/944], signed in Juba on 1 November, addressed issues such as violations, the determination of hostile propaganda, monitoring, additional obligations of the Government of Southern Sudan, and mechanisms to review implementation of the Agreement.

SECURITY COUNCIL ACTION

On 16 November [meeting 5566], following consultations among Security Council members, the President made statement **S/PRST/2006/45** on behalf of the Council:

> The Security Council welcomes efforts aimed at bringing to an end the long-running conflict in northern Uganda, and is following closely the Juba talks process between the Government of the Uganda and the Lord's Resistance Army.

The conflict with the Lord's Resistance Army has caused the displacement of up to 2 million people and the death of about 100,000 people in the region, as well as leading to the death of 8 United Nations peacekeepers.

The Council welcomes the cessation of hostilities which took effect on 29 August 2006, and was renewed on 1 November 2006, and stresses the importance, for peace and stability in the region, of both parties respecting that cessation of hostilities. The Council commends the Government of Southern Sudan for facilitating this agreement and for its efforts to further a long-term and peaceful solution to the conflict, and calls upon all parties to commit themselves fully to this end.

The Council demands that the Lord's Resistance Army immediately release all women, children and other noncombatants, in accordance with Council resolution 1612(2005) on children and armed conflict, and that the peace process be concluded expeditiously.

The Council will continue to monitor developments closely. It invites Member States to support efforts to bring this conflict to an end so that peace and security can be restored to the region and the rule of law re-established, and to ensure that those responsible for serious violations of human rights and international humanitarian law are brought to justice.

The Council welcomes the briefing provided by the Secretariat on 7 November 2006, which it will consider further, in particular in the light of progress in the Juba talks process. It recalls the briefing provided on 19 April 2006 by the Ministers for Foreign Affairs and Defence of Uganda, the visit to Uganda by the Special Representative of the Secretary-General for Children and Armed Conflict in June 2006 and the briefings provided by the Under-Secretary-General for Humanitarian Affairs on northern Uganda on 20 April and 15 September 2006.

The Council welcomes the announcement by the Government of Uganda of the establishment of a Joint Monitoring Committee to oversee the delivery of a prioritized Emergency Action Plan to tackle the humanitarian issues in northern Uganda, looks forward to further progress on improving the living conditions for civilians in northern Uganda, measurable against clear benchmarks, and urges Member States to maintain their support to these efforts. It also welcomes the work done by the Government of Uganda so far on its Peace, Recovery and Development Plan to address the long-term needs of the region.

Appointment of Special Envoy. On 30 November [S/2006/930], the Secretary-General informed the Security Council of his intention to appoint former Mozambican President Joaquim Chissano as his Special Envoy for the LRA-affected areas. The regional dimensions of LRA activities, the Secretary-General said, required a comprehensive and sustained approach pursuant to Security Council resolutions 1653(2006) and 1663(2006) (see p. 122 & 259), which called for his recommendations on how the United Nations could address the problem. He had decided to offer his good offices to the countries of the region and, following consultations with Uganda and other countries in the region, to appoint a Special Envoy, who would facilitate the search for a comprehensive political solution to address the root causes of the conflict, develop a comprehensive and forward-looking policy approach and liaise with ICC, UN missions in the Great Lakes Region and other actors.

Rwanda

Arms embargo

On 9 March [S/2006/164], the Security Council Committee established pursuant to resolution 918(1994) [YUN 1994, p. 285] concerning the arms embargo against non-governmental forces in Rwanda issued a report on its activities from 1 January to 31 December 2005. During the reporting period, no violations were brought to the Committee's attention.

On 28 December [S/2006/1049], the Committee reported to the Council on its activities from 1 January to 31 December 2006, which included three informal consultations on 25 April, 10 August and 3 November. On 10 March, the Security Council Committee established pursuant to resolution 1533(2004) [YUN 2004, p. 138] (the DRC Committee) observed that an arms export/import transaction between Bulgaria and the Government of Rwanda, referred to in the report of the Group of Experts on the DRC (see p. 142), might fall under the Council's request that States notify the Committee of such imports/exports. In a 10 November reply, the Committee stated that Bulgaria and Rwanda had acted in accordance with previous Committee judgements; however, the Committee was reviewing the notification requirement mechanism for any future arms transfer to the Government of Rwanda.

The Committee informed the Council that, due to differing views among its members, it was unable to reach agreement on future notification requirements, and asked the Council to decide on that issue.

Information and outreach programme

In June [A/60/863], the Secretary-General issued a report on the information and outreach programme entitled "The Rwanda Genocide and the United Nations". The General Assembly had requested that programme, in resolution 60/225 [YUN 2005, p. 216], to mobilize civil society for Rwanda genocide victim remembrance and education, in order to help prevent future acts of genocide. The responsibility for developing the information and outreach campaign was assigned to the Department of Public Information, which in addition to its partnerships with civil society and NGOs, forged new relationships with groups working on human rights, genocide and women's development issues, particularly those in the Great Lakes Region and Rwanda. The report outlined action taken by the Department to establish the programme in the first six months of its mandate.

The programme, which was being implemented in consultation with interested Member States, including Rwanda, focused on two key themes: the prevention of genocide, especially the responsibility to protect; and genocide victim remembrance, with an emphasis on the impact of genocide on women, including victims of sexual violence. The two-year information and outreach programme, launched at UN Headquarters (5-7 April) and simultaneously in 11 other countries, coincided with the twelfth anniversary of the Rwanda genocide. The programme aimed to raise the awareness of civil society and the public at large on the need to recognize, at the earliest possible stages, the danger signs associated with genocide, and to seek help early to prevent its further development.

West Africa

In 2006, despite progress achieved in the transition from peacekeeping to peacebuilding in West Africa, the region still faced significant challenges, such as illicit cross-border issues, institutional weaknesses, slow economic recovery, difficulties in security sector reform, the demilitarization, demobilization and rehabilitation of ex-combatants, and the return of refugees and internally displaced persons. The United Nations Office for West Africa (UNOWA) continued to bring a regional perspective to issues, promote conflict prevention and raise awareness about subregional problems, in particular, youth unemployment and migration. It worked in close collaboration with the Economic Community of West African States (ECOWAS) and the African Union to assist governments in improving security, ensuring humanitarian access and energizing peace processes.

In Côte d'Ivoire, efforts continued to move the peace process forward through the implementation of the 2005 Pretoria Agreement on the peace process in that country, and Security Council resolution 1633(2005), which provided a road map to guide the country towards the achievement of the Agreement. The ceasefire, monitored by the United Nations Operation in Côte d'Ivoire and the French Licorne forces, continued to hold, with no major violations of the UN imposed arms embargo. However, the peace process was impeded by political stalemates, disagreements over procedures for the preparation of voter lists and identification processes, and missed deadlines for the completion of crucial tasks in the peace process, such as dismantling of militias and identification of the population. Violent demonstrations, inflammatory statements and deliberate acts to obstruct the implementation of those processes further impeded progress. As the 31 October deadline for the holding of presidential elections was not met, regional leaders established new arrangements and guidelines for another twelve-month transition period, allowing President Gbagbo to remain as Head of State, and clarifying the role and authority of Prime Minister Banny, in order to address ambiguities that had arisen in the previous transition period.

In Liberia, the January inauguration of Ellen Johnson-Sirleaf as President of Liberia and Africa's first elected woman Head of State, and the installment of a new Government signaled the completion of the two-year transitional process stipulated in the 2003 Comprehensive Peace Agreement. President Johnson-Sirleaf addressed issues of corruption and governance reform and enacted measures to enhance transparency and accountability in the Government, which led to the lifting of UN sanctions. With the assistance of the United Nations Mission in Liberia, ECOWAS and other regional and international actors, Liberia made progress in several areas, including the resettlement of refugees and internally displaced persons; the launching of the Truth and Reconciliation Commission; and the establishment of the Governance and Economic Management Assistance Programme. In the light of that progress, the United Nations set benchmarks for the drawdown of its Mission in the country.

Meanwhile, events in Sierra Leone were dominated by efforts to further consolidate the peace and stability achieved in previous years. Preparations for the 2007 elections progressed, with the establishment of regional offices by the National Electoral Commission and completion of the boundary delimitation process, which would enable the elections to be constituency-based for the first time in two decades. Other developments included the signing by eight registered parties of a Political Parties Code of Conduct for the elections, the selection of Sierra Leone as one of the first countries to be considered by the Peacebuilding Commission and its eligibility to benefit from the Peacekeeping Fund. The transition from the United Nations Mission in Sierra Leone to the United Nations Integrated Office in Sierra Leone, established to support the Government in consolidating peace, building national capacity and preparing for the 2007 elections, was successfully completed. However, youth unemployment, rampant corruption, dire economic conditions and tension along the borders, especially with Guinea, were potential threats to stability.

The Special Court for Sierra Leone continued to try those bearing the greatest responsibility for serious violations of international humanitarian and Sierra Leonean laws committed in the territory of Sierra Leone. The apprehension and transfer of the former President of Liberia, Charles Taylor, into the Court's custody in Freetown, and then later to The Hague, Netherlands, where he would stand trial, was a major achievement towards the completion of the Court's mandate.

In Guinea-Bissau, political tensions, which had surfaced following the 2005 presidential elections, polarized the new National Popular Assembly. Dialogue initiatives among the different factions and political groupings, such as the "Estados Gerais", were launched, with the support of the Community of Portuguese-Speaking Countries and ECOWAS, which established an International Contact Group on Guinea-Bissau. The United Nations Peacebuilding Support Office in Guinea-Bissau (UNOGBIS) continued to assist the country in further consolidating peace and promoting national reconciliation. It used its good offices to build on the progress already achieved and played a critical advisory role in supporting national efforts towards security sector reform. In view of those developments, the Secretary-General streamlined UNOGBIS mandate to highlight its mediation and good offices functions.

Cameroon and Nigeria continued to cooperate peacefully to advance progress in implementing the 2002 ruling of the International Court of Justice on the land and maritime boundary between them, through the Cameroon-Nigeria Mixed Commission.

The worsening economic and social conditions in Guinea led to unprecedented national strikes and demonstrations over low wages, soaring prices and government inefficiency, some of which escalated into violence. The Secretary-General expressed his concern over the killing of some 10 students during the demonstrations and appealed to all social and political circles in the country to pursue constructive dialogue.

Regional issues

Peace consolidation in West Africa

Security Council consideration. The Security Council held an open debate on 9 August [meeting 5509] on peace consolidation in West Africa. To guide its deliberations, the Council had before it a concept paper [S/2006/610] on the subject, submitted by Ghana. Ghana noted that the political instability that had afflicted West Africa as a result of violent internal conflicts in Côte d'Ivoire, Guinea-Bissau, Liberia and Sierra Leone had for the most part subsided, creating a unique opportunity for nation-building and the promotion of sustainable development. Over the years, the Economic Community of West African States (ECOWAS) and the Security Council had been actively engaged in addressing the question of peace and security in the region, both through separate initiatives and collaboratively. The Council's debate, which was being held at the ministerial level, was therefore an opportunity for UN members to propose concrete and realistic recommendations to enable the Council to formulate definitive measures spanning the peace consolidation spectrum of conflict prevention, peacekeeping and peacebuilding. The themes to be discussed included conflict prevention; human security and economic development to achieve sustainable peace; and the development of more complementary relationships between ECOWAS/African Union(AU)/ United Nations and other regional organizations. Issues underpinning those themes related to the strengthening of national institutional capacity; promotion of health and education; transparent management of natural resources and the economy; disarmament, demobilization and reintegration; post-conflict recovery and reconstruction; mobilization of resources; establishment of monitoring and evaluation systems to assess local and external actors' performance; strengthening of international cooperation between the UN/ECOWAS/AU and other regional organizations; and the role of the Peacebuilding Commission.

In his statement to the Council, the Secretary-General said that political stability and prosperity continued to elude most West African countries. The region remained plagued by widespread shortcomings in governance, hampering progress in social and economic development. As conflicts in one country often spread and created problems in neighbouring countries, he stressed the need to focus on ending conflicts in the region and developing meaningful peacebuilding initiatives, including reconciliation and confidence-building processes, as well as mechanisms for strengthening the rule of law, especially in the fragile post-conflict countries of Liberia, Guinea-Bissau and Sierra Leone.

Building on themes proposed in the concept paper (see above), the Council President said that the peace consolidation strategy should focus on six broad objectives: resolving ongoing conflicts or at least preventing their escalation; preventing a relapse in countries emerging from war, and new outbreaks of conflict; developing institutional frameworks and capacities for peace initiatives; mobilizing the required resources for peace initiatives; and addressing the underlying causes of conflict in a comprehensive manner. Those objectives should translate into programmes and plans of action, the details of which could be elaborated during the Council's debate. Issues posing clear and immediate danger to security in West Africa should be immediately addressed, namely: the completion of the disarmament, demobilization and reintegration process for ex-combatants, particularly for child soldiers and mercenaries; cross-border issues, such as the illicit trade in small arms and light weapons; illegal dealings in natural resources; narcotics smuggling; human trafficking; repatriation of refugees; and resettlement of internally displaced persons.

The Special Representative for West Africa and Head of the United Nations Office for West Africa, Mr. Ould-Abdallah, said that the region was in transition from the era of single parties to one of multiparty democracy and from State-run to private sector-led economies. Moreover, changing demographics, which indicated that 60 percent of the ECOWAS population of 270 million inhabitants was under 30 years old and mostly unemployed, represented a further threat to stability. For two decades, war had been the primary employer, and legitimate employment alternatives were essential to move forward. The informal migration of young people, sometimes referred to as "clandestine migration" was also emerging as a major political challenge for Governments of the sub-region. He cited other destabilizing factors, such as the vulnerability of border zones as shelters to criminal activity, the lessening visibility of well-established religious groups carrying out social functions formerly performed by the State and the development of piracy on the high seas. Despite those challenges, he said, West Africa was making progress and was more integrated politically and economically than it had been in the past. The Special Representative credited the work of ECOWAS as contributing to that progress. He identified youth unemployment, unauthorized immigration and conflict prevention as areas requiring immediate attention.

SECURITY COUNCIL ACTION

On 9 August [meeting 5509], following consultations among Security Council members, the President made statement **S/PRST/2006/38** on behalf of the Council:

The Security Council, recalling its relevant resolutions and the statements by its President, stresses the importance of addressing the issue of peace consolidation in West Africa in a comprehensive and coordinated manner. It recognizes the need for such an approach for durable solutions to the conflicts in West Africa and to explore ways and means to promote sustainable peace, security and development.

The Council welcomes the transition from war to democratic rule in Sierra Leone, Guinea-Bissau and Liberia, as well as current efforts aimed at implementing measures leading to free and fair elections in Côte d'Ivoire. It also notes that the security situation in those countries remains generally stable but fragile.

The Council stresses the need to build the capacity of national institutions to address the root causes of conflict as an essential part of peace consolidation, especially in the areas of political and economic governance as well as the rule of law and the fight against impunity.

The Council recalls the measures it has implemented on the illegal exploitation of natural resources in the region and encourages member States of the Economic Community of West African States to promote transparent and sustainable exploitation of such resources.

The Council stresses the primary role of each West African Government in peace consolidation for the benefit of all citizens and reiterates the importance of all leaders working together for peace and security in the region.

The Council considers that illicit trafficking in small arms and light weapons still poses a threat to peace and security in the region. In this connection, it welcomes the decision of member States of the Economic Community of West African States to transform the moratorium on the importation, exportation and manufacture of small arms and light weapons in West Africa into a binding Convention on Small Arms and Light Weapons, Their Ammunition and Other Related Materials. It further urges all States, both within and outside the region, to ensure compliance with its existing arms embargoes in West Africa, and States within the Economic Community to ratify the Convention as soon as possible to enable it to come into effect promptly.

The Council considers that civil society, including women's organizations, has a role to play in supporting peace consolidation initiatives in the region and that their efforts in this regard deserve to be supported as appropriate.

The Council underlines the crucial importance of the disarmament, demobilization and reintegration of ex-combatants, taking into account the special needs of child soldiers and women, and encourages the international community to work in close partnership with the countries concerned. It further affirms the need to find lasting solutions to the problem of youth unemployment in order to prevent the recruitment of such youth by illegal armed groups.

The Council considers reform of the security sector an essential element for sustainable peace and stability in West Africa and urgently calls upon the donor community and the international financial institutions to coordinate their efforts to support the States concerned.

The Council stresses the continued need for assisting West African States and the Economic Community of West African States to curb illicit cross-border activities.

The Council reiterates the importance of finding effective solutions to the problem of refugees and internally displaced persons in the region and urges the States in the region, in collaboration with relevant international organizations and donor countries, to create the necessary conditions for their voluntary and safe return.

The Council welcomes the positive role played by the international community and civil society in addressing the humanitarian situation in many parts of the region and urges them to provide adequate resources as part of a coordinated humanitarian response strategy to improve the human security of the people of West Africa in need of such protection.

The Council stresses the need to ensure improved coordination of donor initiatives in order to make the best use of available resources, and encourages donor partners to redeem their pledges in a timely manner.

The Council further stresses the need for continued and enhanced cooperation between the United Nations, the Economic Community of West African States and the African Union in peace consolidation initiatives, based on an integrated approach and with the aim of maximizing the use of available resources. In this connection, it commends the role of the United Nations Office for West Africa, as well as other United Nations offices, missions and agencies in the region in facilitating, in close cooperation with the Executive Secretariat and member States of the Economic Community, the achievement of peace and security priorities of the region. It further encourages the Special Representative of the Secretary-General for West Africa and the United Nations missions in the region to continue their efforts in coordinating United Nations activities to ensure their improved cohesion and maximum efficiency.

The Council underscores the importance and the role of the Peacebuilding Commission in assisting countries emerging from conflict to achieve sustainable peace and stability.

The Council emphasizes the regional dimension of peace and security in West Africa and requests the Secretary-General, in consultation with the secretariat of the Economic Community of West African States, to submit to it by the end of the year a report with recommendations on the cooperation between the United Nations missions deployed in the region and on the cross-border issues in West Africa.

UNOWA

The United Nations Office for West Africa (UNOWA), established by the Secretary-General in 2001 [YUN 2001, p. 162], and extended for three years from 1 January 2005 to 31 December 2007 on the recommendation of the Secretary-General [YUN 2004, p. 170] and the concurrence of the Security Council [YUN 2005, p. 224], continued to support the Organization's peacekeeping and peacebuilding efforts. UNOWA continued to be headed by the Secretary-General's Special Representative for West Africa, Ahmedou Ould-Abdallah (Mauritania) and maintained its headquarters in Dakar, Senegal.

A midterm review of UNOWA was conducted by an independent consultant from 22 September to 30 November 2006, encompassing visits to UN Headquarters in New York and UNOWA premises in Dakar, to assess progress made in carrying out its mandate, including the enhanced functions assigned to it in 2005 [ibid.]; explore its strengths and constraints and the risks and opportunities it faced; highlight good practices and lessons learned; and offer recommendations for future policy and practice. Feedback on the work of UNOWA obtained from UN entities with regional offices in West Africa, ECOWAS and other key international partners of the region was also incorporated into the review.

UNOWA activities

During the year, UNOWA held regular meetings with the heads of UN operations and regional offices in West Africa to develop an integrated approach to conflict prevention and management, and to promote peace, security and development in the region. It continued to monitor the crisis in Côte d'Ivoire; promoted the electoral processes in Benin and Mauritania; convened regional meetings to consolidate peace in West Africa; and addressed the avian flu epidemic in Nigeria and its impact on the sub-region. In April, UNOWA warned that increasing levels of youth unemployment in West Africa—with almost three quarters of the population under 30 years of age—posed a serious threat to security and stability in the region. A second edition of UNOWA "Youth Unemployment and Regional Insecurity in West Africa" study was published in August, which highlighted, among other measures, the need to increase regional economic integration and address the issue of illegal checkpoints, as they represented a significant impediment to free circulation and trade. UNOWA also issued a study entitled "Life after State House: Addressing Unconstitutional Changes in West Africa", which focused on military coups in West Africa and their impact.

UNOWA financing

In a January report [A/60/585/Add.1] on estimates in respect of special political missions, good offices and other political initiatives authorized by the General Assembly and/or the Security Council, the Secretary-General submitted the proposed budget for UNOWA, which amounted to $4,150,400 for the period from 1 January to 31 December 2006. The estimated requirements would provide for a new military adviser; a civilian staffing component; services of experts and consultants; official travel; and other operational requirements.

In March [A/60/7/Add.37], the Advisory Committee on Administrative and Budgetary Questions (ACABQ) recommended acceptance of the Secretary-General's recommendations. The Committee also looked forward to the results of the mid-term review of UNOWA scheduled for July 2006 (see above).

On 8 May, in Section I of **resolution 60/255**, the Assembly endorsed ACABQ conclusions and recommendations (see p. 1618).

Other regional developments

Throughout the year ECOWAS continued efforts to realize its peace consolidation strategy, particularly in the area of security sector reform and the on-going process of articulating an ECOWAS conflict prevention framework, as envisaged during the 2004 Security Council mission to region [YUN 2004, p. 169]. On 14 June 2006, ECOWAS Heads of State and Government signed the ECOWAS Convention on Small Arms and Light Weapons, Their Ammunition and Other Related Materials, to replace the 1998 moratorium on the importation, exportation and manufacture of light weapons [YUN 1998, p. 537]. The Convention would provide a legal basis for the control of small arms in West Africa and address the issue of their illicit trafficking and proliferation (see p. 684). The second and third memoranda on the ECOWAS Cross-Border Initiatives Programme, aimed at compiling, coordinating and formalizing West African cross-border initiatives to increase cooperation frameworks on intra-community borders, were issued in January and December, respectively.

During the year, ECOWAS also restructured its Executive Secretariat into a nine-member Commission to enable the institution to be more effective and allow ECOWAS parliamentarians to fully play their role in the integration process. The Commission, which would be composed of the President, Vice-President and seven Commissioners, would start functioning from January 2007.

Côte d'Ivoire

In 2006, concerted efforts by the United Nations, ECOWAS, the AU and the international community helped to move the Côte d'Ivoire peace process forward. Further progress was made in the implementation of the 2005 Pretoria Agreement on the Peace Process in Côte d'Ivoire [YUN 2005, p. 232] and Security Council resolution 1633(2005) [ibid., p. 243], which provided a road map for the transition period. A Zone of Confidence separated troops belonging to the National Armed Forces of Côte d'Ivoire (FANCI), deployed in the Government-controlled south of the country, from those of the rebel movement, Forces nouvelles, deployed in the north. The main responsibility for peacekeeping rested with the Licorne (French forces), whose deployment was endorsed by the Security Council in resolution 1464(2003) [YUN 2003, p. 168]. Those efforts were supported by the United Nations Operation in Côte d'Ivoire (UNOCI), established by the Council in resolution 1528(2004) [YUN 2004, p. 173] to, among other things, monitor the May 2003 ceasefire and movements of armed groups, assist in the disarmament, demobilization, reintegration, repatriation and resettlement of ex-combatants and support humanitarian assistance and implementation of the peace process. The Mission was headed by the Special Representative of the Secretary-General. In February, the Council authorized the redeployment of one infantry battalion from the United Nations Mission in Liberia (UNMIL) to UNOCI, and in June, it authorized an increase in UNOCI military strength by 1,500 troops, bringing the Mission's total military strength to 8,115 personnel. The Council also increased the number of UN police officers to 1,200.

During the year, the ceasefire monitored by UNOCI and the French Licorne forces continued to hold, and there were no major violations of the UN imposed arms embargo. However, the target dates for disarmament processes, including the pre-cantonment of combatants, the dismantling of militias and the identification of the population, were not met; nor was the 31 October deadline for the holding of presidential elections. In an effort to break the political stalemate, the Secretary-General convened a high-level meeting in Yamoussoukro, in July, where the Ivorian parties reaffirmed their commitment to implement the disarmament, identification and electoral processes outlined in the road map for peace in resolution 1633(2005) and set deadlines for the completion of specific crucial tasks. Nevertheless, disagreements over voters' lists and the identification of the population, in particular the issuance of certificates of nationality by mobile courts, impeded the peace process. Demonstrations and violent protests by militia groups intent on disrupting the identification process and inflammatory statements by political leaders escalated tensions. A toxic waste dumping incident in late July, which became a major humanitarian and security crisis, leading to the dissolution of the Government in September, further complicated the situation.

Meanwhile, new disagreements emerged over the responsibilities of the Independent Electoral Commission and the National Institute of Statistics with regard to the preparation of the voter lists and the electoral process. ECOWAS convened an extraordinary summit on the situation in Côte d'Ivoire and submitted its recommendations on the way forward to the AU. New arrangements and guidelines were established for another twelve-month transition period, in which President Gbagbo would remain as Head of State; the role and authority of Prime Minister Banny were more clearly delineated to address ambiguities that had arisen in the previous transition period; and elections would be held in October 2007. The Security Council endorsed the new arrangements in November.

In the latter months of 2006, the political atmosphere deteriorated further, with deepening disagreements between the President and the Prime Minister, one of which resulted in the dismissal by Presidential decree of the Director General and management board of Radio Télévision Ivorienne. The incident prompted renewed hostilities and demonstrations to protest the President's decisions. Despite the setbacks, optimism remained that the new transition period, drawing upon lessons learned and building on progress achieved, would move the country out of the current impasse and relaunch the key processes of the road map, including the dismantling and disarming of militias, security sector reform, restoration of State authority throughout the country, and, ultimately, the holding of national elections by October 2007.

Political and security developments

Report of Secretary-General (January). In his January progress report on UNOCI [S/2006/2], the Secretary-General said that the October 2005 decision of the AU Peace and Security Council [YUN 2005, p. 241], followed by the adoption of Security Council resolution 1633(2005) [ibid., p. 243] and the efforts of regional leaders [ibid., p. 246], played a crucial role in preventing a dangerous political and security crisis from developing in Côte d'Ivoire and gave the peace process a new lease on life. Going forward, all Ivorian parties would therefore have to extend full cooperation to the new Prime Minister and his Government and move expeditiously to implement the outstanding tasks under the peace agreements, including the dismantling of militias, the redeployment of State administration; the identification of nationals, the registration of voters and the organization of elections. They also had to work with the Prime Minister and the High Representative for the elections to resolve the bickering within the Independent Electoral Commission, respect the interim arrangement decided by the International Working Group concerning the enactment of legislation in the interim period [ibid.], respect the human rights of the Ivorian people, guarantee the free movement of the impartial forces throughout the country and create an enabling environment for the holding of the elections. The Secretary-General urged the Prime Minister to work with the AU International Working Group and the Mediation Group to finalize the road map for the transition period and convene the Forum for National Dialogue to ensure full implementation of the outstanding tasks under the peace agreements. He urged the Security Council to consider imposing targeted measures against individuals and groups obstructing the peace process, including incitement to violence, human rights violations and violations of the arms embargo.

However, the challenges ahead were formidable and urgent. The potential for violent disturbances remained very high throughout the country. Despite the semblance of calm following the appointment of the Prime Minister, there was concern over underlying tensions caused by such factors as combatants yet to be disarmed; ethnic and urban militias; extremist groups, such as the Young Patriots; elements who felt disempowered by the post-30 October governance arrangements; the soaring crime rate; and continuing human rights abuses. UNOCI reported an increase in violent acts against opposition political party leaders and some members of the armed forces, as well as extortion and racketeering activities. In the western part of the country, where reports of targeted ethnic killings by militia groups persisted, UNOCI and the impartial forces were obstructed from gaining access to areas dominated by such groups and the Young Patriots. Moreover, militia groups targeted UNOCI equipment for attack, notably in Gagnoa and San Pédro and incited anti-UN sentiment. On a positive note, the overall security assessment indicated that, despite rumors of attacks, the probability of renewed direct conflict between the National Armed Forces of Côte d'Ivoire (FANCI) and the Forces nouvelles remained relatively low.

In anticipation of the review by the Security Council of UNOCI troop strength, which had been requested by the AU Peace and Security Council in October 2005, the Secretariat sent a technical team to Côte d'Ivoire to assess the Mission's troop and police strength, taking into consideration the new circumstances since the adoption of resolution 1633(2005). The technical team confirmed that UNOCI troops were stretched thinly throughout the country. Moreover, concurrent implementation of the outstanding tasks under the peace agreements, as stipulated in resolution 1633(2005), would create such a surge in the military, police and civilian support personnel required on the ground that would be difficult, if not impossible, to manage within existing UNOCI resources. It therefore recommended that UNOCI troop strength be increased by four battalions (3,400 troops), including the battalion requested by the Secretary-General in his previous reports, to relieve infantry companies redeployed to reinforce security in Abidjan, and provide a secure environment for the concomitant implementation of the outstanding tasks of the peace agreements.

The team ascertained that no additional support to UNOCI could be expected from the Licorne forces beyond the current arrangements, particularly in the event of a violent crisis. In exploring options for generating the proposed additional troops, the team considered the arrangements under Security Council resolution 1609(2005) [YUN 2005, p. 236], which authorized the temporary redeployment of troops from the United Nations Mission in Liberia (UNMIL) to strengthen UNOCI, and concluded that, in the event of a crisis in Côte d'Ivoire, a short notice reinforcement of UNOCI from UNMIL would not be feasible. However, reinforcement from UNMIL for pre-planned tasks, such as the identification process, voter registration and the elections, might be possible. The team also recommended that three additional formed police units (375 officers) and 100 civilian police officers be deployed to the Mission immediately. That would allow the 533 security auxiliaries trained by UN police to be deployed to 54 locations in the northern part of the country, which had been left without any law enforcement since the displacement of 4,000 police and gendarmes by the conflict.

The Secretary-General urged the Council to approve his recommendations for reinforcing the Mission's strength, as a number of key tasks mandated to UNOCI were scheduled to start in early 2006. He also recommended the extension of UNOCI mandate for 12 months, until 24 January 2007, to adequately cover the post-election period.

Transitional Government. On 11 January [S/2006/21], Côte d'Ivoire transmitted to the Security Council President the list of members of the Transitional Government, which was announced on 28 December 2005 [YUN 2005, p. 246] by Prime Minister Charles Konan Banny. The 32-member cabinet, consisting of all parties that were signatories to the Linas-Marcoussis Agreement [YUN 2003, p. 166], included two senior Ministers, Guillaume Soros, the Secretary-General of the Forces nouvelles as Minister of State, Minister responsible for the reconstruction and reintegration programme, and Antoine Bouabré of the ruling Front populaire ivoirien, as Minister of State, Minister of planning and development; and two independent Ministers, René Kouassi, Minister of Defence and Joseph Dja Blé, Minister of Internal Affairs. Prime Minister Banny also assumed the functions of Minister of Economy and Finance, as well as Communication.

SECURITY COUNCIL ACTION

On 24 January [meeting 5354], the Security Council unanimously adopted **resolution 1652(2006)**. The draft [S/2006/41] was prepared in consultations among Council members.

The Security Council,

Recalling its previous resolutions and the statements by its President relating to the situation in Côte d'Ivoire and in the subregion,

Reaffirming its strong commitment to the sovereignty, independence, territorial integrity and unity of Côte d'Ivoire, and recalling the importance of the principles of good-neighbourliness, non-interference and regional cooperation,

Recalling that it endorsed the final communiqué of the International Working Group of 15 January 2006, and reaffirming the mandate of the International Working Group to assist the Prime Minister and his Government in the implementation of the road map it has established, and to evaluate, monitor and follow up closely the implementation of the peace process, in accordance with resolution 1633(2005) of 21 October 2005,

Taking note of the report of the Secretary-General of 3 January 2006,

Expressing its serious concern at the persistence of the crisis in Côte d'Ivoire and of obstacles to the peace and national reconciliation process from all sides,

Determining that the situation in Côte d'Ivoire continues to pose a threat to international peace and security in the region,

Acting under Chapter VII of the Charter of the United Nations,

1. *Decides* to extend the respective mandates of the United Nations Operation in Côte d'Ivoire and of the French forces supporting it until 15 December 2006;

2. *Decides also* to extend the provisions of paragraph 3 of resolution 1609(2005) of 24 June 2005 for the period specified in paragraph 1 above;

3. *Expresses its intention* to keep under review the tasks and the troop level of the United Nations Operation in Côte d'Ivoire, and specifically to review these when the Security Council considers the forthcoming report of the Secretary-General on the United Nations Mission in Liberia, taking into account the situation in both Côte d'Ivoire and Liberia, in the light of progress in the implementation of the road map established by the International Working Group, leading to the organization of free, fair, open and transparent elections no later than 31 October 2006;

4. *Decides* to remain actively seized of the matter.

International Working Group meeting (January)

The International Working Group, created by the AU Peace and Security Council in 2005, and supported by the UN Security Council in resolution 1633(2005) [YUN 2005, p. 243], to evaluate, monitor and follow up the peace process, held its third ministerial meeting on 15 January in Abidjan. In a communiqué issued on the same date, and transmitted by the Secretary-General on 2 February [S/2006/79], the Group, comprising Ministers from

Benin, France, Ghana, Guinea, the Niger, South Africa, the United Kingdom and the United States, congratulated Prime Minister Banny on the formation of the new Government. However, the Group indicated that, after holding extensive consultations with the Ivorian parties on the functioning of State institutions, it had concluded that the mandate of the National Assembly, which ended on 16 December 2005, should not be extended. The Group recommended that, during the transitional period, the Prime Minister, in consultation with the Head of State, should entrust specific tasks to experienced former parliamentarians, with a view to promoting peace and national reconciliation. It condemned the 2 January attack on the military barracks in the Akouédo district of Abidjan and the resulting gross violations of the human rights of innocent civilians; encouraged the Government and the impartial forces to create a secure environment for the smooth implementation of the road map; and expressed concern over the inflammatory tone used by some political actors and the media, which ran counter to the spirit of peace and reconciliation. To assure an atmosphere of stability and security for the implementation of the key tasks of the peace process, the Group recommended that the Security Council review the personnel levels of UNOCI military and the police force.

The Security Council, in its Presidential statement S/PRST/2006/2 of 19 January (see p. 180), endorsed the Group's 15 January communiqué.

However, in a communiqué issued the previous day [S/2006/50] following a meeting held the same day between the AU Chairman, Nigerian President Olusegun Obasanjo and Ivorian President Laurent Gbagbo, in the presence of Prime Minister Banny, the Special Representatives of the Secretary-General, the AU Mediator and the Representative of the ECOWAS Executive Secretary, the leaders took the position that, as it did not have the authority to do so, the International Working Group did not dissolve the National Assembly at the end of its 15 January meeting (see above). They invited the Ivorian President and Prime Minister to continue consultations on a political solution, which would be communicated to the nation by the International Working Group, and to urge the population to return to their homes, as well as to work the next day.

In a further letter dated 20 January [S/2006/43], Côte d'Ivoire drew the Security Council's attention to "misunderstandings" regarding the implementation of resolution 1633(2005), which could seriously endanger the peace process. It stated that the International Working Group had deviated from its defined mandate "to monitor the implementation process", by reinterpreting the provisions of the aforementioned resolution, particularly when the Group stated at its first meeting on 8 November 2005 [YUN 2005, p. 245] that the Prime Minister had to have "independent executive powers", which was contrary to the resolution's terms. Côte d'Ivoire accused the Group of continuing the same approach in its 15 January 2006 communiqué relating to the National Assembly, which had led to protests in Abidjan and a number of towns in the interior of the country. Its decision to oppose the extension of the National Assembly's mandate not only adversely impacted the functioning of an Ivorian institution, but disregarded the views of the Constitutional Council. Côte d'Ivoire was also concerned that the UN Security Council had endorsed the Group's final communiqué. While the Government would respect the outcome of the negotiations undertaken by the AU Chairperson, it hoped that the Group would, in future, abide strictly by the terms of its clearly defined mandate, pursuant to resolution 1633(2005).

Outbreak of violence and National Assembly mandate

An outbreak of violence early in the year presented a setback in the peace process. The Secretary-General reported [S/2006/222] that from 15 to 20 January, the Young Patriots organized violent demonstrations in Abidjan and in the western areas of the country to protest against the decisions of the International Working Group contained in its 15 January communiqué (see above). The well-orchestrated demonstrations stemmed from the deliberate falsification of the aforementioned communiqué to the effect that the Group had "decided to dissolve the National Assembly in contravention of the country's sovereignty". The virulent anti-UN propaganda and incitement of violence, especially on Ivorian Radio and Television and local radio networks, resulted in looting and destruction of assets and property of the United Nations and humanitarian agencies and non-governmental organizations in the western towns of Daloa, San Pédro and Guiglo. UNOCI headquarters in Abidjan, the French Embassy and the 43rd French marine infantry battalion were repeatedly attacked for several days by crowds of the Young Patriots, resulting in extensive damage. The situation was exacerbated by serious inflammatory statements.

On 18 January, the AU Chairman, Nigerian President Obasanjo, visited Abidjan to help defuse the situation. Presidents Obasanjo and Gbagbo issued a joint communiqué (see above) stating that the International Working Group neither had the authority nor had it dissolved the National Assembly, and calling for the cessation of violence. Following the intervention by President Obasanjo, demonstrations by the Young Patriots ceased.

EU statement. The European Union (EU) Presidency, in a 19 January statement [S/2006/44], condemned the orchestrated acts of violence that had taken place in Côte d'Ivoire, particularly in Abidjan, since 16 January, as well as the attacks on the UNOCI contingent. It called upon all political players to bring an end immediately to such unacceptable acts and requested that all necessary measures be taken to ensure the safety of the international and diplomatic presence in the country.

SECURITY COUNCIL ACTION

On 19 January [meeting 5350], following consultations among Security Council members, the President made statement **S/PRST/2006/2** on behalf of the Council:

> The Security Council strongly condemns the recent violent attacks against the United Nations Operation in Côte d'Ivoire and international non-governmental organization facilities in Côte d'Ivoire by street militias and other groups associated with the 'Young Patriots', as well as their instigators. The Council also expresses its deep concern at the violent and orchestrated street protests led by the Young Patriots, in particular in Abidjan and in several cities in the west.
>
> The Council regards these particularly serious and unacceptable incidents as endangering the process of national reconciliation enshrined in resolution 1633(2005) and as contrary to that resolution. It calls upon all Ivorians to refrain from any hostile action, and demands the immediate end of this violence and of all hate messages in the media, in particular the attacks against the United Nations. The Council welcomes the urgent mission to Abidjan led by President Obasanjo. It pays tribute to his efforts and hopes that they will lead to a rapid decrease in the current tensions on the ground.
>
> The Council also underlines the fact that the occupation of the facilities of Ivorian Radio and Television constitutes an attack against freedom and neutrality of information as well as a breach of the principles of the process of national reconciliation, of previous Council resolutions and of the peace agreements. It demands that effective control by the Board and the General Director over Ivorian Radio and Television be re-established immediately.
>
> The Council reiterates its full support for the Prime Minister, Mr. Charles Konan Banny, and invites the United Nations Operation in Côte d'Ivoire, in accordance with its mandate, to provide him with all the necessary support. It also reiterates its full support for the International Working Group, the Special Representative of the Secretary-General for Côte d'Ivoire and the High Representative for the elections in Côte d'Ivoire. It endorses the final communiqué of the International Working Group of 15 January 2006.
>
> The Council firmly calls upon all the Ivorian parties to cooperate with the Prime Minister, the International Working Group, the Mediation Group, the Special Representative and the High Representative in implementing the road map.
>
> It underlines the fact that targeted measures will be imposed against persons to be designated by the Security Council Committee established pursuant to paragraph 14 of resolution 1572(2004) who, among other things, block the implementation of the peace process, including by attacking or obstructing the action of the United Nations Operation in Côte d'Ivoire, of the French forces, of the High Representative or of the International Working Group, or who publicly incite hatred and violence, as provided for in resolutions 1572(2004) and 1643(2005).

Presidential decree on National Assembly mandate. On 27 January, based on the December 2005 recommendations of the Constitutional Council, President Gbagbo signed a decree extending the National Assembly's mandate. However, opposition parties and the Forces nouvelles rejected the extension, indicating that it was a flagrant violation of Côte d'Ivoire's Constitution, as well as Security Council resolution 1633(2005).

On 29 January [SG/SM/10328], the Secretary-General issued a statement expressing concern that the Presidential decree on the National Assembly did not appear to be in conformity with the information received from Nigerian President Obasanjo on his visit to Abidjan.

Further developments. In the light of the continuing incitement to violence, the Secretary-General issued a further statement, on 1 February, reminding the highest civilian and military authorities of Côte d'Ivoire, including President Gbagbo and the Chief of Staff, General Mangou, of their personal responsibility to prevent violence in the country, such as attacks perpetrated against UN personnel and installations and against ethnic groups.

An extraordinary session of the Parliament from 9 to 16 February, called for by the former Speaker of the National Assembly to review the extension of the mandate of mayors, was attended by 102 of 202 parliamentarians, primarily from the ruling party, the Front populaire ivoirien (FPI), while most of the representatives of the opposition boycotted the meeting. The matter of the extention of the Assembly's mandate remained unresolved and concerns were raised when reports emerged that another extraordinary session of the National Assembly would be convened, as it might undermine the progress achieved and jeopardize the implementation of the next phases of the peace process.

Security and humanitarian crisis

As a result of the violent demonstrations organized by the Young Patriots (see p. 179), without any resistance on the part of the authorities and often with silent abetting, the security situation deteriorated sharply. There were serious obstructions to the freedom of movement of the impartial forces, interruption of social activities and rampant insecurity in Abidjan, as well as in various parts of Government-controlled areas, particularly Daloa, Guiglo, San Pédro and Yamoussoukro. Violent attacks against United Nations and humanitarian personnel led to the relocation of UNOCI camps to the Zone of Confidence. The growing insecurity and temporary departure of UNOCI troops from the western part of the country forced UN agencies to relocate their personnel, causing a dangerous security and humanitarian vacuum in those areas, leaving nearly 14,000 internally displaced persons, refugees and ethnic minorities unprotected. Humanitarian activities came to a standstill, owing to the destruction by protesters of the offices of the United Nations and other humanitarian agencies, their relief supplies, warehouses, and communications and other equipment. UNOCI relocated 382 staff to the designated safe haven in the region to minimize high security threats against UNOCI personnel.

On 1 February [S/2006/71], the Secretary-General, pending further consideration by the Security Council of the recommendations in his January report for strengthening UNOCI (see p. 177), and considering the situation in Côte d'Ivoire, sought the Council's consent for his proposal, under the arrangements provided in Security Council resolution 1609(2005), to temporarily redeploy up to one mechanized infantry battalion and one formed police unit from UNMIL to UNOCI for an initial period of three months. The battalion, which would be deployed to Abidjan in phases, would provide extra security coverage for UN personnel and property and perform other tasks entrusted to UNOCI by the Council.

SECURITY COUNCIL ACTION

On 6 February [meeting 5366], the Security Council unanimously adopted **resolution 1657(2006)**. The draft [S/2006/73] was submitted by France.

The Security Council,

Recalling its previous resolutions and the statements by its President relating to the situation in Côte d'Ivoire and in the subregion, in particular resolutions 1609(2005) of 24 June 2005, 1626(2005) of 19 September 2005 and 1652(2006) of 24 January 2006,

Reaffirming its strong commitment to the sovereignty, independence, territorial integrity and unity of Côte d'Ivoire, and recalling the importance of the principles of good-neighbourliness, non-interference and regional cooperation,

Taking note of the letter dated 1 February 2006 from the Secretary-General addressed to the President of the Security Council,

Recalling that the current mandate of the United Nations Mission in Liberia will expire on 31 March 2006,

Expressing its serious concern at the persistence of the crisis in Côte d'Ivoire and of obstacles to the peace and national reconciliation process from all sides,

Determining that the situation in Côte d'Ivoire continues to pose a threat to international peace and security in the region,

Acting under Chapter VII of the Charter of the United Nations,

1. *Decides* to authorize the Secretary-General to redeploy immediately a maximum of one infantry company from the United Nations Mission in Liberia to the United Nations Operation in Côte d'Ivoire, until 31 March 2006, in order to provide extra security coverage for United Nations personnel and property, and to perform other tasks mandated to the United Nations Operation in Côte d'Ivoire, without prejudice to any future decision by the Security Council concerning the renewal of the mandate and the level of troops of the United Nations Mission in Liberia and a further extension of the redeployment mentioned above;
2. *Expresses its intention* to review the provisions of paragraph 1 above in thirty days, and by 31 March 2006, in the light of the situation in Côte d'Ivoire and in Liberia;
3. *Also expresses its intention* to keep under review possible additional redeployments of troops between the United Nations Mission in Liberia and the United Nations Operation in Côte d'Ivoire;
4. *Decides* to remain actively seized of the matter.

Further political and security developments

International Working Group meeting (February). The International Working Group held its fourth ministerial meeting on 17 February, in Abidjan. In the final communiqué issued the same day [S/2006/131], the Group congratulated the Prime Minister on his efforts to implement the road map for peace drawn up by the Group, in particular, his initiative to convene a Government seminar (Yamoussoukro, 9-11 February), which was attended by most Cabinet Ministers, including the Secretary-General of Forces nouvelles, Guillaume Soro, and where it was agreed to establish monitoring mechanisms for the implementation of key aspects of the road map. The Group called upon the Ivorian parties to proceed with the disarmament and identification processes, commit to strictly comply with the ban on public demonstrations and refrain from inflammatory statements or actions likely to exacerbate tensions. It also underscored the need to enhance the security of the personnel and equipment of Ivorian Radio and Television and to ensure its independence and the equitable access of all Ivorian parties to its broadcasts.

The Group endorsed the arbitration by the High Representative for the elections issued in his 16 February communiqué, according to which the election of the Independent Electoral Commission was in compliance with the Pretoria Agreement; and his recommendation to invite the Head of State, the Prime Minister and the political parties to reach, as soon as possible, a political understanding to ensure the effective functioning of the Independent Electoral Commission, before the beginning of March.

SECURITY COUNCIL ACTION

On 23 February [meeting 5378], following consultations among Security Council members, the President made statement **S/PRST/2006/9** on behalf of the Council:

> The Security Council reiterates its full support for the International Working Group and endorses its fourth final communiqué, of 17 February 2006. It commends Prime Minister Charles Konan Banny for his efforts to implement the road map established by the International Working Group in accordance with resolution 1633(2005). The Council reiterates its full support for him. It also welcomes the cooperation between the Prime Minister and the President.
>
> The Council also endorses the arbitration by the High Representative for the elections in Côte d'Ivoire, according to which the election of the Bureau of the Independent Electoral Commission is in compliance with the Pretoria Agreement. It urges the Ivorian parties to ensure the effective functioning of the Commission as soon as possible.
>
> The Council also underscores the imperative to guarantee the independence and neutrality of Ivorian Radio and Television.
>
> The Council urges the Ivorian State authorities to facilitate, notably in the west, the return of humanitarian agencies and organizations.
>
> The Council will review at the beginning of March 2006 the progress made in the implementation of resolution 1633(2005) and the decisions of the International Working Group. It will pay special attention to the functioning of the Independent Electoral Commission, the steps taken in order to guarantee unhindered and equitable access to Ivorian Radio and Television, and the launch of disarmament operations and the identification process.

Yamoussoukro meetings of Ivoirian leaders. Pursuant to a recommendation made at the 17 February Government seminar (see above), Prime Minister Banny convened a summit meeting (Yamoussoukro, 28 February) of the main Ivorian political leaders, which included President Gbagbo, former President, Henri Konan Bédié, former Prime Minister, Alassane Ouattara, and the Secretary-General of the Forces nouvelles, Guillaume Soro. In a communiqué issued at the conclusion of the meeting, their first such gathering since the crisis began in September 2002, Ivorian leaders reiterated their readiness to engage in constructive dialogue and reaffirmed that Security Council resolution 1633(2005) did not contradict the Ivorian Constitution and should be complied with in a constructive, consensual and coherent manner. The leaders also agreed that the disarmament, demobilization and reintegration process should commence without further delay; the identification process and preparations for the elections should be conducted simultaneously; and the Independent Electoral Commission Bureau should be reconstituted, based on a balanced representation of political forces. Emphasis was also placed on the central role of Ivorian Radio and Television in the reconciliation process, as well as the need to ensure that all parties had equitable access to its broadcasting facilities.

International Working Group meeting (March). On 17 March, in the final communiqué issued following its fifth ministerial meeting held in Abidjan [S/2006/190], the International Working Group commended the political leaders for the 28 February meeting in Yamoussoukro (see above), welcomed the new spirit of political dialogue among the Ivorian political class and called upon leaders to promote that spirit among their followers to ensure that everyone contributed positively to the peace and reconciliation process and desisted from any incitement to hatred or violence. The Group noted the establishment of the Bureau of the Independent Electoral Commission and urged the Commission to ensure that the elections were held no later than 31 October 2006. With regard to the repeated obstructions to the freedom of movement of the impartial forces, the Group underscored the imperative of facilitating the immediate redeployment of UNOCI troops to the western part of the country to pursue their peace and security mission, as well as the return of humanitarian agencies to facilitate the resumption of assistance to vulnerable groups.The Group called for the return of that region to civilian authority. It condemned the persistent human rights violations, particularly the attacks against Government Ministers, and called upon the Ivorian parties to combat the growing impunity in the country.

Communication. On 22 March [S/2006/184], the Secretary-General, in follow up to his January request to the Security Council to increase UNOCI strength by four battalions (see p. 178), updated the Council on recent developments in the political process in Côte d'Ivoire, which in his view, called for the reinforcement of UNOCI beyond the interim arrangements under which the Council had approved the transfer of one infantry company from UNMIL to UNOCI in February. He cited steps taken by Ivorian leaders to move the peace process forward, such as the seminar and round-table meeting, held respectively from 9 to 11 and 28 February in Yamoussoukro; the swearing-in of the members of the Independent Electoral Commission on 7 March and the subsequent submission to the cabinet of a framework for conducting the identification and voter registration processes, thereby setting the stage for those crucial aspects of the process to begin; the conduct of school examinations in the northern part of Côte d'Ivoire, the first time since the outbreak of the conflict, and the 14 March arrival of the leader of the Forces nouvelles, Guillaume Soro, in Abidjan, to take up his post in the Government of Prime Minister Banny.

The Secretary-General stressed that the recent progress achieved had set in motion a fledgling process, which, if sustained, could put the peace process on track. It was therefore crucial to adequately reinforce UNOCI to enable it to support the full implementation of the road map and the organization of elections by October. Adding that UNOCI should be prepared to support the process, including in the area of security, he appealed to the Council to approve the recommendations contained in his January report.

Security Council consideration (March). In a 29 March [meeting 5399] briefing to the Security Council, the Ivorian Minister for Foreign Affairs, Youssouf Bakayoko, said that Côte d'Ivoire had entered a new era, which allowed the peace and reconciliation process to develop significantly. He summarized positive developments that had taken place since the adoption of Security Council resolution 1633(2005), including, among others, the February Yamoussoukro meeting (see p. 182), during which a fourth vice-president post for the ruling Front populaire ivoirienne was established to enable balanced representation of the political forces; the creation of the climate for the implementation of resolution 1633(2005) and the road map; the installation of the Independent Electoral Commission; and the return of the Forces nouvelles Secretary-General Soro after 17 months of absence from Abidjan. Moreover, the University of Bouaké, the headquarters of the Forces nouvelles, had been officially reopened on 28 March.

In the light of the events that created the humanitarian crisis in January, an interministerial commission, including humanitarian agencies, was set up, as a coordination framework for humanitarian action on a national scale, and a Special Counsellor for Humanitarian Action appointed by the Prime Minister. He identified the areas in which further work was required: financing of the electoral process; disarmament, demobilization and reintegration; strengthening security throughout the territory to guarantee voter safety; resolving humanitarian problems; supporting human rights; strengthening the capacity of judicial institutions; providing support for the State's economy and finances to reduce high youth unemployment; and facilitating the return of refugees and displaced persons.

The Foreign Minister remarked that the progress attained had to be irreversible and security matters accorded the utmost attention. In an effort to create a more disciplined and professional army, the Government launched, on 21 February, a programme to restore the military barracks. The Minister, in recognition of the need to organize undisputed general elections as the only way out of the crisis, called upon the Secretary-General to appoint as soon as possible a new UN High Representative for the elections, to succeed Antonio Monteiro. Noting that strengthening security throughout the entire national territory was the greatest concern of all Ivorians, he appealed to the Council to support the Secretary-General's proposal for strengthening UNOCI.

SECURITY COUNCIL ACTION

On 29 March [meeting 5400], following consultations among Security Council members, the President made statement **S/PRST/2006/14** on behalf of the Council:

The Security Council expresses its full support for the International Working Group and endorses its fifth final communiqué, of 17 March 2006. It commends Prime Minister Charles Konan Banny for his initiatives, taken in cooperation with President Laurent Gbagbo, which gave a new momentum to the peace process, and reiterates its full support for him. It also welcomes the efforts of Mr. António Monteiro and encourages the Secretary-General to appoint a new High Representative for the elections in Côte d'Ivoire, as soon as possible.

The Council welcomes the progress achieved in recent weeks, in particular the meeting of the entire Cabinet, the establishment of the Independent Electoral Commission, the organization of examinations in the north, and the preparation of operations of identification of the populations and disarmament.

The Council urges Ivorian leaders to fulfil all their commitments, in particular those made at Yamoussoukro on 28 February 2006, and to rapidly implement the road map, in good faith and in a spirit of trust, in order to organize free, fair, open and transparent elections by 31 October 2006. It underlines the urgency of progress in the identification process, the establishment of the electoral registers and the commencement of the disarmament, demobilization and reintegration programme.

The Council calls upon donor countries to provide the Prime Minister with all the necessary support for the full and immediate implementation of the road map.

The Council nevertheless reiterates its grave concern at the situation in the west. It urges the United Nations Operation in Côte d'Ivoire to continue its redeployment in this region. It also calls for the return of this region to civilian authority.

The Council strongly condemns the persistence of violations of human rights, the attacks against members of the Government, the obstacles to the freedom of movement of impartial forces, and the incitements to hatred and violence in the media. In this regard, it requests the Ivorian authorities to guarantee, in close liaison with the United Nations Operation in Côte d'Ivoire, that all steps are taken to preserve the independence of Ivorian Radio and Television.

Appointment of new High Representative. In an exchange of letters on 11 [S/2006/242] and 13 April [S/2006/243] between the Secretary-General and the Security Council President, Gérard Stoudmann (Switzerland) was appointed High Representative for the elections in Côte d'Ivoire, replacing Antonio Monteiro.

Report of Secretary-General (April). In his April report [S/2006/222] on UNOCI, the Secretary-General said that the formation of the new Government, the resumption of dialogue among the parties, the end of the protracted stalemate over the Independent Election Commission and the return of the Forces nouvelles Secretary-General to the Government were encouraging developments. The positive steps taken by the parties had eased tensions and improved the overall political atmosphere, thereby permitting the redeployment of UNOCI.

Despite those positive developments, the security situation continued to present obstacles in the peace process. The failed attack on the military barracks in the Akouédo district of Abidjan on 2 January had heightened the feeling of insecurity among the population and further undermined confidence among the parties. The Government's investigation of the matter was inconclusive. The violent demonstrations conducted by the Young Patriots from 15 to 20 January (see p. 179) had also created a security and humanitarian crisis, impacting some 14,000 persons. On 7 February, the Security Council Committee established pursuant to resolution 1572(2004) [YUN 2004, p. 187] imposed targeted sanctions on two leaders of the Young Patriots. In contrast to earlier threats to unleash a new wave of violence against UN personnel and property, the leaders of the Young Patriots called upon their followers not to react. Nevertheless, the security situation in the western part of the country remained highly volatile and was marred by several incidents. From 26 February to 2 March, confrontations between Licorne and the National Armed Forces of Côte d'Ivoire (FANCI) occurred around the villages of Bouenneu and Zouan Hounien, in what appeared to be deliberate attempts to obstruct Licorne's freedom of movement. On two occasions, armed FANCI soldiers infiltrated the Zone of Confidence at Bouenneu and harassed French soldiers maintaining the integrity of the Zone. In the meantime, UNOCI developed plans to return to its former locations in the west. On 19 March, an advanced UNOCI joint military/police group was successfully deployed in Toulépleu and an infantry company in Bloléquin on 28 March. Formed police units were deployed alongside UN troops returning to the west. The redeployment, however, was hampered by local authorities and radical groups opposed to it.

Overall, UNOCI continued to carry out its Security Council-mandated tasks, including mobile patrolling of the Zone of Confidence; arms embargo inspections in both the Government and rebel-held areas; and improving its state of preparedness to prevent and address future disturbances. UNOCI also established a security sub-office at Duékoué to monitor the activities of UN agencies in the Guiglo sector and serve as a liaison with the local military administrations of the Moyen Cavally region. As at 31 March, UNOCI strength stood at 6,893 military and 696 police personnel. The Secretary-General said that the arrival of the one infantry battalion from UNMIL, authorized by Security Council resolution 1657(2006), served as a timely deterrent, and enhanced UNOCI's response preparedness. However, as that reinforcement was limited and temporary, an urgent decision on the reinforcements proposed in his January report was needed. He added that the security situation could still deteriorate suddenly, triggered by the lack of progress in the peace process. It was therefore essential that UNOCI credibility and its role in the peace process were not challenged again.

With regard to implementation of the disarmament, demobilization and reintegration process, on 24 March, President Gbagbo appointed General Gaston Koné as Coordinator of the National Programme for Demilitarization, Demobilization and Reintegration. Although the Programme was still undergoing some restructuring, the sequencing of the exercise was expected to remain as foreseen in the Yamoussoukro timetable signed on 9 July 2005 [YUN 2005, p. 240] by FANCI and the Forces nouvelles. The Chiefs of Staff of both forces met on 1 April to agree on the modalities for the commencement of the disarmament, demobilization and reintegration process. UNOCI support of the Programme would include, securing disarmament and cantonment sites; assuming security functions previously undertaken by the disarmed troops in the north, alongside 600 Ivorian security auxiliaries trained by UNOCI; escorting and/or providing transportation to former combatants; responding to any disturbances around the camps; providing weapons control and destruction facilities; and ensuring a secure environment. UNOCI also provided technical assistance to the Office of the Prime Minister in formulating a comprehensive approach to disarmament, which would include the disarmament and dismantling of militias and the restructuring of the army.

Progress continued with the redeployment of State administration. Of the estimated 24,400 civil servants displaced during the conflict, some 6,000 had been redeployed, mainly in the southern and western areas of the country under Government control. Some 20,000 needed to be redeployed in areas under the control of the Forces nouvelles. UNOCI would be required to provide a secure environment for that process, which was expected to run parallel with the identification process and electoral registration.

In March, the working group on identification and elections made a number of recommendations for facilitating the identification process and voter registration. Although the cabinet endorsed its recommendation to conduct both processes simultaneously, there was fear that a considerable number of potential voters might not be able to obtain the necessary documentation for those purposes, as no appropriate judicial mechanisms existed in the north and in the Zone of Confidence, and many civil register records were missing. Modalities for the creation of mobile courts to facilitate the issuance of new national identity cards or other forms of legal identification to potential voters were under consideration. A divergence of ideas among the parties on the modalities for implementing the identification process also hampered progress.

Following the resolution of the stalemate that had prevented the Independent Electoral Commission from becoming operational, the High Representative for the elections, in a 16 February communiqué, confirmed that the October 2005 election of the Bureau of the Independent Electoral Commission, which had been contested by President Gbagbo's supporters, was in conformity with the Pretoria Agreement. The Commission was formally inaugurated on 9 March and focused on a number of priority issues. UNOCI would provide support for the organization of the elections, and if strengthened, contribute to general security in main voting areas. The Mission, which would ensure security for 11,000 voter registration sites, the distribution and storage of electoral materials, and 18,000 polling stations, had already deployed electoral advisers to prepare for the establishment of the local branches of the Electoral Commission.

With regard to the Forum for National Dialogue, the Prime Minister initiated consultations with all political leaders to secure their agreement for the holding of such a dialogue. The Prime Minister's Office also agreed with UNOCI to establish a joint mechanism to prepare for a donor conference, following which a standing resource mobilization committee would be established to secure funds for the implementation of the road map.

The Secretary-General observed that, despite the January violence in Abidjan and the west of the country, the peace process was advancing. Urging the parties to agree on the modalities for implementing the identification process, he indicated the UN willingness to assist in that regard. He emphasized that the window of opportunity was very narrow and further delays or disruptions would hinder the completion of the critical tasks necessary for elections to be held by October. If that deadline was not met, the international community might not again agree to extend the current governance arrangements. He again appealed to the Security Council to consider his recommendations on strengthening UNOCI, as the risk remained that any unraveling of the security situation in Côte d'Ivoire could spill over into the subregion, particularly to Liberia. The Secretary-General reminded the national authorities of their responsibility to ensure the security and freedom of movement of UNOCI, Licorne and the humanitarian and non-governmental agencies in the country. He said that those committing attacks against the United Nations should be held accountable for their actions, and underscored the urgent need to put an end to the culture of impunity in the country.

International Working Group meeting (April). On 20 April, in the final communiqué issued following its sixth ministerial meeting [S/2006/260] in Abidjan, the International Working Group expressed concern over delays in commencing activities for effectively implementing the road map. The Group called on the Government of National Reconciliation to accelerate the simultaneous implementation of the identification and the disarmament, demobilization and reintegration processes; encouraged the Chiefs of staff of FANCI and the Forces nouvelles to restore, under the leadership of the Government, conditions for the smooth continuation of their dialogue, with a view to ensuring the commencement of the disarmament, demobilization and reintegration process; and urged them to sensitize their followers to the need to abide by all commitments made during the Yamoussoukro meetings. The Group invited all Ivorian parties to cooperate with the new High Representative for the elections, in order to accelerate preparations for holding the elections. It also invited the Security Council Committee established pursuant to resolution 1572(2004), in the light of persistent violations of resolutions 1633(2005) and 1643(2005) [YUN 2005, p. 251], to identify the perpetrators and take appropriate measures. It also recommended that the Security Council provide UNOCI with the additional means to achieve its mandate.

Security Council consideration (April). On 27 April [meeting 5426], the Council heard a briefing by Prime Minister Banny, who said that, although events were not proceeding as quickly as the majority of observers and Ivorians would wish, the general situation in Côte d'Ivoire was satisfactory. He said that the momentum lost in the military staff-level contact was not a definitive breakdown, as everything pointed towards an early resumption of the talks. He pointed out that some resistance still existed, which prevented swifter progress in accordance with the timetable established by the International Working Group. However, the Government was working to resolve the basic problems resulting from the crisis. To help consolidate the progress made by the Ivorian Government, the Prime Minister shared the Secretary-General's desire to see UNOCI further strengthened, particularly as various elements of the process of emerging from the crisis, such as the disarmament, demobilization and disarmament programme, the security of the electoral operations and safety of people during the elections, required an atmosphere of safety and confidence, which could only be assured by a more significant military presence that would also act as a deterrent. He appealed to the Council to increase the number of UNOCI troops as close as possible to that requested by the Secretary-General.

On the same date, the Council further met in private with Prime Minister Banny on the situation in Côte d'Ivoire [meeting 5427].

SECURITY COUNCIL ACTION

On 27 April [meeting 5428], following consultations among Security Council members, the President made statement **S/PRST/2006/20** on behalf of the Council:

The Security Council commends Prime Minister Charles Konan Banny for his initiatives, taken in cooperation with President Laurent Gbagbo, which have injected a new momentum into the peace process as defined by resolution 1633(2005) and the road map established by the International Working Group, and which must lead to the organization of free, open, fair and transparent elections by 31 October 2006. It reiterates to him its full support.

The Council expresses its full support for the International Working Group and endorses its sixth final communiqué of 20 April 2006.

The Council welcomes the appointment of Mr. Gérard Stoudmann as High Representative for the elections in Côte d'Ivoire. It encourages him to take all necessary measures, in accordance with his mandate, to expedite the preparation of the electoral process. It calls upon all Ivorian parties to cooperate fully with him.

The Council, while taking note of the progress achieved, expresses its grave concern at the serious delay in the implementation of the disarmament, demobilization and reintegration programme and of the identification operations. It recalls the commitments made by the main Ivorian political leaders in this regard at their meeting held in Abidjan on 8 April 2006 (Yamoussoukro II), under the auspices of the Chair of the African Union. It urges them to fulfil those commitments without delay.

The Council shares the concern, expressed by the Secretary-General in paragraph 74 of his report of 11 April 2006, over the consequences of any additional delays in the implementation of the key deadlines of the road map.

The Council therefore invites the Prime Minister and the Government of National Reconciliation that he leads to take immediately all the measures necessary for the simultaneous implementation of the disarmament, demobilization and reintegration and identification operations. It also invites the International Working Group, in accordance with paragraph 10 of resolution 1633(2005), to report to it any hindrance or difficulty which the Prime Minister may face in implementing his tasks.

The Council will continue to evaluate and monitor closely the implementation of the road map, in particular the disarmament, demobilization and reintegration and identification operations. It continues to underline the fact that targeted measures are to be imposed against persons to be designated by the Security Council Committee established pursuant to paragraph 14 of resolution 1572(2004) who, among other things, block the implementation of the peace process, including by attacking or obstructing the action of the United Nations Operation in Côte d'Ivoire, of the French forces, of the High Representative for the elections or of the International Working Group, or who publicly incite hatred and violence, as provided for in resolutions 1572(2004) and 1643(2005).

Incident between Ivorian and French Licorne forces

In a letter dated 2 May [S/2006/294], Côte d'Ivoire drew the attention of the Security Council to alleged human rights violations committed by French Licorne troops against members of the Ivorian Defence and Security Forces, on 26 February, in Zouan-Hounien. It had reported the incident, on 12 April, to the Security Council Committee established pursuant to resolution 1572(2004). He described the treatment inflicted on seven soldiers for allegedly entering the Zone of Confidence as cruel and degrading, and indicated that, if there was no reaction from the Security Council, it was likely to encourage further such incidents. Moreover, silence could give the impression that the condemnation of human rights violations depended on the nationality of the perpetrators. Annexed to the letter was a copy of Côte d'Ivoire's 12 April statement to the Committee established pursuant to resolution 1572(2004), as well as the map that the Secretary-General had annexed to his April report on UNOCI (see above), which he said, clearly showed that Zouan-Hounien was within the area under

Government control and fell outside the Zone of Confidence.

Renewed political tension and hostilities

The renewal of political tension and hostilities in April and early May further impeded progress in the peace process. The Secretary-General reported [S/2006/532] that the Young Patriots, leading members of the ruling party, and the Speaker of the former National Assembly led a campaign against the planned simultaneous implementation of the disarmament and identification processes. The campaign consisted of strident public statements aimed at discrediting UNOCI and the Prime Minister; threats against UN personnel; the announcement of plans to organize violent demonstrations; and an attack on a bus carrying UNOCI staff in the Yopougon area of Abidjan on 28 April. Following a discussion between the Secretary-General's Special Representative and President Gbagbo on the negative impact of the hostile campaign on the political and security situation, the President's spokesman issued a statement condemning the attack on the UNOCI bus, disavowed the Young Patriots' plans to organize violent demonstrations and called upon all Ivorians to allow UNOCI to perform its mission. On 9 May, President Gbagbo and Prime Minister Banny held a joint press conference, during which the President urged all Ivorians to allow the Prime Minister to do his work.

Meanwhile, the overall security situation in Côte d'Ivoire remained fragile and volatile. Between 27 April and 3 May, five persons were killed, at least 15 were injured, and some 4,000 people fled from their villages around Bangolo, in the western part of the Zone of Confidence. In addition, the lack of agreement on specific issues concerning the disarmament, demobilization and reintegration process and the planned reintegration of Forces nouvelles military personnel into the Iviorian Defence and Security Forces, the delay in the implementation of that programme, as well as the postponement of the dismantling of the militias, had affected military dialogue between FANCI and the Forces nouvelles, giving rise to the potential threat of extremist groups and militias undermining the peace process.

Attempts by the Young Patriots to disrupt, between 18 and 26 May, the pilot project to test the procedures for the identification of the population through the deployment of mobile courts in seven locations failed. Some 3,907 persons, out of 5,003 applicants, received certificates of nationality through the project. In the meantime, the pre-cantonment of FANCI and Forces nouvelles troops was launched on 22 May.

International Working Group meeting (May). On 19 May, in the final communiqué issued following its seventh ministerial meeting [S/2006/332] in Abidjan, the International Working Group welcomed the launch of the mobile court pilot project and the arrangements being made by the Chiefs of Staff of the Defence and Security Forces and the Forces nouvelles for the pre-cantonment of combatants. Concerned by persisting delays in the implementation of tasks, it called on both Chiefs of Staff to set new dates for implementing the timetable for the disarmament, demobilization and reintegration process.

The Group also expressed concern over the persistent culture of impunity and intensification of incitement to hatred and violence and condemned the acts of violence committed against the population, political leaders and the impartial forces, as well as the systemic denigration of representatives of the international community by certain organs of the media and political figures. The Group urged the national authorities to speed up the investigations into those acts of violence and identify and punish the perpetrators. It also warned those who were obstructing the implementation of the road map, that such activities would invite the Security Council Committee established pursuant to resolution 1572(2004) to take appropriate measures against them.

SECURITY COUNCIL ACTION

On 24 May [meeting 5442], following consultations among Security Council members, the President made statement **S/PRST/2006/23** on behalf of the Council:

> The Security Council expresses its full support for the International Working Group and endorses its seventh final communiqué, of 19 May 2006.
>
> The Council welcomes the launching of the first pilot operations of public hearings in seven locations, in particular in Abidjan, in the south and in the north of the country. It welcomes also the discussions engaged by the Chiefs of Staff of the National Armed Forces of Côte d'Ivoire and the Armed Forces of the Forces nouvelles to initiate without delay the disarmament, demobilization and reintegration programme.
>
> The Council commends Prime Minister Charles Konan Banny for having taken, in cooperation with President Laurent Gbagbo, these concrete initiatives which constitute a first step towards the implementation of the peace process that he leads. It reiterates to him its full support.
>
> The Council calls upon the community of donors to provide all the necessary financial resources to the High Representative for the elections in Côte d'Ivoire to support the full implementation of his mission.

The Council underlines the fact that many of the essential tasks envisaged in the road map established by the International Working Group remain to be executed. It reiterates its grave concern at the serious delay in the implementation of the road map, as well as the concern expressed by the Secretary-General in paragraph 74 of his report of 11 April 2006.

The Council strongly condemns the acts of violence against civilians, political leaders and impartial forces. It demands that all Ivorian parties refrain from making any public messages that incite hatred and violence. It warns all Ivorian parties in that regard.

The Council invites the Prime Minister and the Government of National Reconciliation that he leads to take immediately, with the support of the United Nations Operation in Côte d'Ivoire in accordance with its mandate, all the necessary measures to accelerate the implementation of the road map, in particular the disarmament, demobilization and reintegration and identification operations, the redeployment of the administration throughout the territory and the reunification of the country.

The Council calls upon the Ivorian authorities to take without delay all the necessary steps so that those responsible for acts of violence are identified and punished, to keep the International Working Group and the Secretary-General informed in this regard, and, in close liaison with the United Nations Operation in Côte d'Ivoire, to ensure the full independence and neutrality of Ivorian Radio and Television.

The Council urges all Ivorian parties, including the Chiefs of Staff of the National Armed Forces of Côte d'Ivoire and the Armed Forces of the Forces nouvelles, to closely cooperate with the Prime Minister in order to create the conditions indispensable for the holding of free, open, fair and transparent elections by 31 October 2006.

The Council invites the International Working Group to report to it as soon as possible on its assessment of the implementation of the road map.

The Council underlines the fact that targeted measures are to be imposed against persons to be designated by the Security Council Committee established pursuant to paragraph 14 of resolution 1572(2004) who, among other things, block the implementation of the peace process, including by attacking or obstructing the action of the United Nations Operation in Côte d'Ivoire, of the French forces supporting it, of the High Representative for the elections in Côte d'Ivoire or of the International Working Group, or who publicly incite hatred and violence, as provided for in resolutions 1572(2004) and 1643(2005).

Strengthening of UNOCI

Communications. On 22 May [S/2006/345], the Security Council President informed the Secretary-General that the Council had taken note of his recommendations concerning the reinforcement of UNOCI. As the members were planning to consider a resolution on the strengthening of the Operation, the Council requested that he begin, without delay, planning for the possible deployment of additional troops to reinforce UNOCI.

On 25 May [S/2006/334], the Secretary-General, drawing the Security Council's attention to the latest developments in Côte d'Ivoire, called for the urgent reinforcement of UNOCI to the levels indicated in his previous reports and for the Council to expedite its decision thereon. He said that the pilot project for determining the identification of citizens, launched by Prime Minister Banny on 18 May, would lead to the implementation of the disarmament, demobilization and reintegration programme throughout Côte d'Ivoire, as well as the identification of populations and preparation of electoral lists. It was anticipated that the arrangements for the pre-regroupment of the Forces nouvelles and FANCI troops would be finalized in a short period of time. It was therefore crucial for UNOCI to be adequately reinforced to fulfil its mandate to support the delicate identification and disarmament processes.

SECURITY COUNCIL ACTION

On 2 June [meeting 5451], the Security Council unanimously adopted **resolution 1682(2006).** The draft [S/2006/357] was prepared in consultations among Council members.

The Security Council,

Recalling its previous resolutions and the statements by its President relating to the situation in Côte d'Ivoire and in the subregion, in particular resolutions 1652(2006) of 24 January 2006 and 1667(2006) of 31 March 2006, and reaffirming in particular the provisions of paragraph 3 of resolution 1667(2006),

Reaffirming its strong commitment to the sovereignty, independence, territorial integrity and unity of Côte d'Ivoire, and recalling the importance of the principles of good-neighbourliness, non-interference and regional cooperation,

Taking note of the reports of the Secretary-General of 3 January and 11 April 2006 and of the letters dated 1 February, 22 March and 25 May 2006 from the Secretary-General to the President of the Security Council,

Expressing its serious concern at the persistence of the crisis in Côte d'Ivoire and of obstacles to the peace and national reconciliation process from all sides,

Determining that the situation in Côte d'Ivoire continues to pose a threat to international peace and security in the region,

Acting under Chapter VII of the Charter of the United Nations,

1. *Takes note* of the recommendations of the Secretary-General contained in his report of 3 January 2006, in particular paragraphs 48 and 52 thereof, and notes that those recommendations have been reiterated in his report of 11 April 2006;
2. *Authorizes*, until 15 December 2006, an increase in the strength of the United Nations Operation in Côte d'Ivoire of up to 1,500 additional personnel, including a maximum of 1,025 military personnel and 475 civilian police personnel;
3. *Expresses its intention* to keep under review the appropriate personnel levels for the United Nations Operation in Côte d'Ivoire, in the light of the situation in Côte d'Ivoire and in the subregion;
4. *Decides* to remain actively seized of the matter.

Implementation of resolution 1633(2005)

International Working Group meeting (June). On 23 June, at its eighth ministerial meeting [S/2006/455], the International Working Group commended the Prime Minister's 22 June initiative launching peace and reconciliation missions entrusted to former parliamentarians, whose emoluments, the Group demanded, should be paid in full and without discrimination so that they could devote themselves exclusively to that task. The Group called upon the Prime Minister to ensure the speedy resumption of the mobile court hearings and their completion within the established deadlines, and upon the competent national authorities to set a definitive date for the commencement of the dismantling and disarming of militias. While welcoming the resumption of dialogue between the Chiefs of Staff of FANCI and the Armed Forces of Forces nouvelles, the Group stressed that the tasks should not be used as a pretext to reopen the debate on questions already agreed upon between the parties and urged both Chiefs of Staff to involve the impartial forces in their discussions, with a view to finalizing the calendar for the disarmament, demobilization and reintegration process. Concerned at the slow pace of the Independent Electoral Commission activities throughout the national territory, the Group requested the Prime Minister to earmark appropriate budgetary resources to give impetus to the electoral process. The Group also appealed to all parties to refrain from any action that would jeopardize the Commission's independence or threaten the security of its members.

Yamoussoukro high-level meeting and establishment of benchmarks

Following consultations conducted with various African Heads of State in the margins of the AU Summit (1-2 July, Banjul, the Gambia), the Secretary-General convened a high-level meeting in Yamoussoukro, Côte d'Ivoire, on 5 July, to discuss the situation in the country and implementation of the road map for the peace process. The meeting was attended by the Presidents of Nigeria and South Africa, the Ministers for Foreign Affairs of the Congo, Burkina Faso and Ghana, representatives of ECOWAS, the Under-Secretary-General for Peacekeeping Operations, the Secretary-General's Special Representative for West Africa, the co-chairs of the International Working Group and Ivorian authorities and leaders.

Reporting on the outcome of the meeting to the Security Council President on 12 July [S/2006/516], the Secretary-General said that participants reaffirmed their commitment to the peace process and the need to continue all efforts to implement Security Council resolution 1633(2005). They reaffirmed the commitments made at the 28 February Yamoussoukro meeting of Ivorian political leaders (see p. 182), in particular, that the media, and especially the written press, should embrace the peace process and refrain from printing articles that could jeopardize the process, and that political leaders should prevail on journalists close to them to join the peace process, and create an environment conducive to the conduct of political activities. The meeting agreed that a compulsory code of conduct should be established for members of the media. The Ivorian parties recommitted themselves to doing everything possible to accelerate the disarmament, demobilization and reintegration, identification and electoral processes. Recognizing that the freedom of movement and involvement of the impartial forces in the military dialogue were crucial to the credibility and transparency of the process, the meeting decided to establish a Monitoring Committee for disarmament, demobilization and reintegration. The Secretary-General said that he intended to convene a meeting in mid-September, in New York, to take stock of the situation and make any further determinations as might be necessary.

The meeting established a timetable for the completion of tasks related to the electoral process, disarmament, demobilization and reintegration, and the media, which included: the deployment of 50 mobile courts by 15 July; issuance of a Presidential decree by 15 July to allow the Independent Electoral Commission to make adjustments to the electoral code; deployment of the Independent Electoral Commission's countrywide structure by 31 July; reaffirmation of the validity of the July 2005 Pretoria Declaration [YUN 2005, p. 239]; convening of a donors' conference to seek funds for closing the budgetary gap of the electoral process; establishment of the disarmament, demobilization and reintegration monitoring group by 15 July; immediate resumption of the quadripartite control of the pre-cantonment process to facilitate its completion by 31 July; the dismantling and disarmament of the militias by 31 July; and respect for the Pretoria and Yamoussoukro agreements on the media, which called for responsible behaviour by journalists, particularly during the elections. The Ivorian parties agreed to take action on those decisions.

SECURITY COUNCIL ACTION

On 19 July [meeting 5491], following consultations among Security Council members, the President made statement **S/PRST/2006/32** on behalf of the Council:

The Security Council welcomes the initiative of the Secretary-General, who organized the high-level meeting held in Yamoussoukro on 5 July 2006. It urges all Ivorian parties to implement, in close liaison with the impartial forces, all their commitments made on this occasion concerning the identification operations, the establishment of a monitoring group for the disarmament, demobilization and reintegration programme, the completion of the pre-cantonment process, the adjustment to the electoral code, the dismantling of militias and the establishment of a code of conduct for the media, and urges them in particular to meet the agreed deadlines.

The Council also urges all Ivorian parties to accelerate the implementation of the road map in order to create the conditions indispensable for the holding of free, open, fair and transparent elections by 31 October 2006.

The Council calls upon the International Working Group to monitor the full implementation of the decisions taken by all Ivorian parties in Yamoussoukro on 5 July 2006 and to report to the Council on its assessment in that regard.

The Council underlines the fact that it is fully prepared to impose targeted measures against persons to be designated by the Security Council Committee established pursuant to paragraph 14 of resolution 1572(2004) who are determined to be, among other things, blocking the implementation of the peace process, including by attacking or obstructing the action of the United Nations Operation in Côte d'Ivoire, of the French forces supporting it, of the High Representative for the elections in Côte d'Ivoire or of the International Working Group, responsible for serious violations of human rights and international law committed in Côte d'Ivoire since 19 September 2002, publicly inciting hatred and violence or in violation of the arms embargo, as provided for in resolutions 1572(2004) and 1643(2005).

The Council welcomes the intention of the Secretary-General to call a meeting on the situation in Côte d'Ivoire in September 2006 to take stock of the situation regarding the implementation of the road map defined by resolution 1633(2005) and the International Working Group and to make any further determinations as may be needed. In this regard, it requests the Secretary-General to report to it before the September meeting on the obstacles encountered in the implementation of the road map and on those responsible.

The Council expresses its full support for the International Working Group and endorses its eighth final communiqué, of 23 June 2006. It reiterates its full support for the Special Representative of the Secretary-General for Côte d'Ivoire and the High Representative.

Report of Secretary-General (July). In his ninth report [S/2006/532] on UNOCI, the Secretary-General said that the political atmosphere remained generally calm, underpinned by the working relationship between President Gbagbo and Prime Minister Banny, assisted by periodic consultations within the framework of the "quintet", comprising the five Ivorian political leaders: the President; the Prime Minister; the President of the Parti démocratique de Côte d'Ivoire, Henri Konan Bédié; the President of the Rassemblement des Républicains, Alassane Ouattara; and the Secretary-General of the Forces nouvelles, Guillaume Soro. During the visit to Côte d'Ivoire of the AU Chairman, President Denis Sassou-Nguesso (Congo), from 6 to 8 April, the quintet reconfirmed its commitment expressed at the 28 February Yamoussoukro meeting to work together to launch simultaneously the disarmament and identification processes. However, renewed political tension in April and May (see p. 187) impeded progress. The expected simultaneous pre-cantonment of the forces, which represented the first phase of the disarmament, demobilization and reintegration programme, could not begin as the Forces nouvelles and FANCI disagreed on the modalities of the process. The identification process, initially scheduled to begin on 15 June, was delayed, owing to logistical reasons. The deployment of 50 mobile courts was expected to begin by mid-July, followed by an additional 100 teams. Thus, 150 mobile court teams would be deployed throughout the country to identify approximately 3.5 million people, including 1.8 million persons of voting age. Prime Minister Banny estimated that the operation would take two months to complete and would be followed by the issuance of national identity cards. The cost of the identification process countrywide was estimated at $55 million, of which $32 million was still needed.

Pre-cantonment of FANCI and Forces nouvelles troops was launched on 22 May, and by 18 June, some 12,547 elements of FANCI had been pre-cantoned at the 35 sites designated in their areas of control, and 12,885 elements of the Forces nouvelles at 31 of their 50 designated sites. Controversy arose over the next step in the process, the cantonment and collection of weapons, with the Forces nouvelles insisting that identification of the entire population, including combatants, should take place prior to the collection of weapons, while FANCI maintained that identification of combatants should be conducted during the pre-cantonment stage, as agreed by the parties. Moreover, the Chiefs of Staff of FANCI and Forces nouvelles were unable to agree on Forces nouvelles demands for the retention of current military ranks, the establishment of an integrated military command and the payment of salary arrears. Limited progress was made toward the dismantling and disarming of militias, due to postponements, demands of militia leaders to include more individuals in the programme and lack of agreed modalities for dismantling militias in parts of the country, including Abidjan. The cost of the disarmament, demobilization and reintegration programme was estimated at $150 million, of which $140 million had been pledged. No pledges had been made for meeting the cost of dismantling and disarming of militias, estimated at $2.5 million.

With regard to election preparations, the High Representative for the elections in Côte d'Ivoire worked with national and international actors to press for the launching of the electoral process. The Institute of National Statistics continued to assert that it was responsible for preparing the register of voters and initiated unilateral preparations for doing so. At its June meeting, the International Working Group recalled the exclusive responsibility of the Independent Electoral Commission for the entire electoral process (see p. 189). The Commission Chairman submitted an electoral budget of $74 million, for which there was shortfall of $34 million.

In other political developments, on 26 April, the Speaker of the National Assembly convened an ordinary session of the Assembly and introduced new rules of procedure suspending the indemnities of the opposition parliamentarians who had not attended Assembly sessions since the expiration of its mandate in December 2005. On 19 June, following a request by the Mediation Group, President Gbagbo and the Prime Minister met with all members of the former National Assembly and set up a committee to formulate recommendations. On 22 June, the committee recommended that: parliamentarians return to the Assembly and carry out their duties; the National Assembly carry out its functions in conformity with the Constitution and Security Council resolution 1633(2005) until the next parliamentary elections; Assembly members undertake peace missions to be assigned by the Prime Minister in consultation with the President; legislators count on the President to resolve the issue of their unpaid salaries; and amendments made to the Assembly's internal procedures in the absence of the opposition members should be rescinded. On 23 June, the opposition accepted the recommendations. On the same date, at its eighth ministerial meeting, the International Working Group demanded the payment of emoluments of former parliamentarians in their entirety and without discrimination.

The Secretary-General observed that the peace process in Côte d'Ivoire was again at the crossroads. The consolidation of the fragile gains achieved since the beginning of the year would need the sustained political will and efforts of all Ivorian parties. It was also critical that, in addition to the timely implementation of all components of the road map for peace, the conditions of a lasting peace be rapidly established throughout the country, including the promotion and protection of human rights, respect for the rule of law and assistance to the most vulnerable.

He also noted that, while much still remained to be done to prepare and conduct free and fair elections, the process of fostering national reconciliation and unity should not end with the completion of the transition period. In order to build lasting peace and stability, it was essential for all Ivorian parties to pursue dialogue on how to carry forward the efforts to foster unity and national reconciliation beyond the elections.

Implementation of Yamoussoukro benchmarks

Reporting on the implementation of the benchmarks established at the 5 July Yamoussoukro high-level meeting (see p. 189), the Secretary-General said that of the 50 mobile courts agreed to be deployed by 15 July to conduct public hearings for the issuance of birth certificates and certificates of nationality to those eligible, only about 25 had become operational. In the southern part of the country, the courts were disrupted by supporters of the ruling Front populaire ivoirien (FPI) party. The party's President, Affi N'Guessan, urged its followers to oppose the operation of the courts "by all means", claiming that the issuance of certificates of nationality by such courts was inconsistent with the law. In addition, despite the joint monitoring mechanism put in place by UNOCI and the High Representative for the elections, Gérard Stoudmann, President Laurent Gbagbo and his party warned that the mobile courts could be used fraudulently to grant Ivorian citizenship to those who were not eligible. The attempts by FPI supporters, in particular the Young Patriots, to disrupt the operations of the courts, led to violent clashes with the opposition parties. In Divo and Grand-Bassam, the clashes resulted in the death of at least eight Ivorians on 22 and 23 July. The violent disruption campaign continued until early August, when the Prime Minister announced new guidelines, based on a strict interpretation of the nationality law, which prohibited the mobile courts from issuing certificates of nationality. The opposition parties rejected the new guidelines, arguing that the public hearings conducted by mobile courts had been legally used to issue certificates of nationality prior to the conflict and that no law expressly prohibited the practice. After the proclamation of the new guidelines, the number of persons appearing before the mobile courts dropped precipitously. By mid-September, the operations of the mobile courts, which were initially scheduled to run for two months, had completely stopped in all areas. Between 17 July and 15 September, only 933 mobile court hearings were held (327 in the southern part of the country, 583 in the north, and 23 in the Zone of Confidence), issuing some 74,000 birth certificates and 70,000 certificates of nationality. UNOCI provided logistical support for the operation, including transporting préfets and sous-préfets to the areas controlled by the Forces nouvelles.

With regard to disarmament, demobilization and integration, the monitoring group was established on 13 July, but the Forces nouvelles suspended its participation in the group and in the dialogue on military issues in reaction to the proclamation of the new guidelines on the operations of the mobile courts. The monitoring group was therefore unable to verify the claims by the Forces nouvelles and FANCI that they had completed the pre-cantonment of their respective combatants (24,000 FANCI personnel and 13,000 Forces nouvelles elements). With the breakdown of the military dialogue, many combatants reportedly left the pre-cantonment sites and returned to their deployment areas, and the two sides had not yet submitted the lists of their combatants and weapons. The Forces nouvelles insisted that the restructuring of the national army should proceed immediately, as part of the disarmament, demobilization and reintegration process, and in that regard, called for the establishment of an integrated command under the authority of the Prime Minister.

The dismantling and disarming of the militias started in the western part of the country on 26 July. However, the process was suspended on 4 August on account of the low number and poor quality of the surrendered weapons. Efforts to resume the process in a more credible fashion had not yet succeeded, and militia leaders were demanding that an additional 3,000 individuals be allowed to join the programme.

Concerning the preparation of elections, on 29 July, the President signed a decision empowering the Independent Electoral Commission to submit its proposed amendments to the electoral code to the Prime Minister, who would, in turn, assess them and refer them to the President for promulgation.

The leaders of the Parti démocratique de Côte d'Ivoire, Henri Konan Bédié, and the Rassemblement des républicains, Alassane Ouattara, conveyed to the Secretary-General, on 17 August, their concern that President Gbagbo had not been following the AU consultative process for issuing such decisions, which had crucial implications for the electoral process. They also contended that the decision gave the President the final say on matters governing an election in which he would be a candidate.

As to the decision for the Independent Electoral Commission to establish countrywide structures by 31 July, only 19 regional commissions were established out of the 24 envisaged under its operational plan. The deployment was hampered by inadequate funding and organizational capacity, security concerns and the provision in the electoral law that each subnational commission should have the same membership composition as the central commission. That would require a total of some 33,000 commissioners, which made it impracticable. The High Representative for the elections suggested that the extraordinary procedures for changing the electoral law should be used to reduce the size of the local commissions.

Meanwhile, President Gbagbo and his supporters adamantly opposed the preparation of a new voters' roll, maintaining that the 2000 voters' list should be updated by the National Institute of Statistics. The opposition parties, for their part, rejected that list, insisting that a new voters' roll should be prepared by the Independent Electoral Commission, and not the Institute, on the basis of the identification process. On 19 July, in response to a formal request from President Gbagbo, the AU Mediator, South African President Mbeki, clarified the disputed roles of the two institutions, reaffirming the exclusive responsibility of the Independent Electoral Commission for organizing the elections and indicating that the National Institute of Statistics should report directly to the Commission. The opposition parties were, however, concerned that the top posts at the Institute were dominated by officials with ties to the leadership of the ruling party. To resolve the stalemate, the Secretary-General proposed that identified FPI-affiliated officers should be replaced with non-partisan individuals. With regard to the re-establishment of State administration in the northern part of the country, the Prime Minister reported on 8 September to the International Working Group that 92 mayors' offices had been reopened, as of 24 August, and 61 officials redeployed to their prefectures by 31 August. To date, some 12,000 displaced civil servants were yet to return to the areas controlled by the Forces nouvelles. UNOCI assisted the media regulatory bodies in preparing a draft code of conduct, but it had not yet been implemented.

Political stalemate and impasse in peace process

Despite the gains achieved, major disagreements among the Ivorian parties on fundamental issues relating to the disarmament, demobilization and reintegration and identification processes, resulted in a political stalemate and impeded further progress in the peace process, especially regarding the implementation of mobile courts to conduct the identification process, which started on 17 July, the Secretary-General reported [S/2006/821].

International Working Group meeting (July). On 20 July, at its ninth ministerial meeting [S/2006/584], the International Working Group requested that the mobile court hearings, whose operation had been disrupted by FPI supporters and had led to violent clashes, should no longer be impeded and should proceed under the best possible conditions of security and transparency. The Group condemned the serious disturbances in July that were provoked by organized groups impeding the smooth conduct of mobile court hearings and the call made by certain political leaders to oppose the operations. It called on national authorities to take urgent steps to put an end to the interference with the free movement of the population and of the impartial forces. It also condemned the incidents that took place on 15 July and called for strengthened security at Radio and Television Ivorien in order to preserve its independence. The Group expressed its wish to submit those elements for consideration by the Security Council Committee established pursuant to resolution 1572(2004) so that it could take appropriate measures against the perpetrators of those incidents and those behind them.

Press statements. In a 25 July press statement [SG/SM/10576], the Secretary-General expressed deep concern about inflammatory statements by the FPI leadership, which had incited the Young Patriots to resort to violent acts aimed at disrupting the ongoing identification process in Côte d'Ivoire, and resulted in the loss of human lives and an attack on the vehicle of the High Representative for the elections, Gérard Stoudmann. He strongly condemned those acts, which, he said, were in breach of the agreements reached among Ivorian parties at the 5 July High-level meeting at Yamoussoukro, and urged all Ivorian parties to extend their full cooperation to the Prime Minister.

On 26 July [SC/8786], the Security Council condemned the obstruction to the normal functioning of the mobile courts, as well as the violence committed, and stated its intention to inform the sanctions committee. The Council also indicated that it would work on a presidential statement in order, in particular, to take stock of the implementation of the road map and the Yamoussoukro III agreemen [see p. 189], and of the responsibilities of those who blocked the process, including the Ivorian defence and security forces.

SECURITY COUNCIL ACTION

On 7 August [meeting 5505], following consultations among Security Council members, the President made statement **S/PRST/2006/37** on behalf of the Council:

The Security Council affirms its commitment to the implementation of the peace process and of the road map established by the International Working Group. It welcomes the initiatives of the Prime Minister, Mr. Charles Konan Banny, and the ongoing dialogue among President Laurent Gbagbo, the Prime Minister and all other Ivorian parties.

The Council reiterates its full support for the Prime Minister. It welcomes his determination to implement the decisions taken by all Ivorian parties at the high-level meeting held in Yamoussoukro on 5 July 2006. It strongly encourages him to continue his efforts and demands that all Ivorian parties cooperate with him fully and in good faith.

The Council welcomes the launch of the mobile courts throughout Côte d'Ivoire and the announcement by the Prime Minister of the completion of the pre-cantonment of the Defence and Security Forces of Côte d'Ivoire and of the Armed Forces of the Forces nouvelles. The Council also welcomes the establishment of the disarmament, demobilization and reintegration monitoring group, the measures taken to implement the quadripartite control of pre-cantonment operations and the beginning of operations to dismantle and disarm the militias. It takes note of the signing of a presidential decree allowing the Independent Electoral Commission to propose any technical adjustments to the electoral code for the transitional elections.

The Council expresses its concern that the structures of the Independent Electoral Commission as well as the local offices of the National Commission of Supervision of Identification have not been deployed throughout the country. It urges the Ivorian parties to settle these issues without delay.

The Council strongly condemns the obstructions to the normal functioning of the mobile courts which followed the calls for such action made by political leaders, in particular the Chairman of the Front populaire ivoirien and the President of the former National Assembly. It notes that the procedures of the mobile courts were decided in consultation with President Laurent Gbagbo. It urges all parties to ensure that the mobile courts function without further hindrance.

The Council expresses its utmost concern and condemns the acts of violence committed by organized groups, in particular the Young Patriots, which led to the deaths of civilians, and further condemns the attack of 24 July 2006 against the High Representative for the elections in Côte d'Ivoire, despite the presence of the Republican Guard at the scene.

The Council condemns also the incidents of 15 July 2006 at the premises of Radio Télévision Ivoirienne. It calls upon the Ivorian authorities to strengthen security measures at Radio Télévision Ivoirienne. It underlines the importance of guaranteeing the independence and neutrality of the media in Côte d'Ivoire.

The Council reaffirms its support for the implementation of measures against those responsible, as provided for in paragraphs 9 and 11 of resolution 1572(2004), and underlines that the reports of the events described above will be examined by the sanctions committee established pursuant to paragraph 14 of resolution 1572(2004).

The Council demands that the Defence and Security Forces of Côte d'Ivoire, including the Republican Guard, act within the law of the land at all times to ensure full security of the population, including foreigners, and support the implementation of the road map led by the Prime Minister. It reaffirms in this regard paragraphs 8 and 9 of resolution 1633(2005). It recalls that the Defence and Security Forces and the Forces nouvelles must ensure the security of the mobile court hearings in the areas under their control.

The Council demands also that all Ivorian parties cooperate fully in the operations of the impartial forces, in particular by guaranteeing the safety, security and freedom of movement of their personnel, as well as associated personnel, throughout the territory of Côte d'Ivoire, and affirms that any obstacle to their freedom of movement or to the full implementation of their mandates will not be tolerated. It recalls paragraph 4 of resolution 1643(2005) in this regard.

The Council reaffirms the importance of the concomitant implementation of the identification and disarmament, demobilization and reintegration operations and of the acceleration by all Ivorian parties of the implementation of the road map in order to create the conditions indispensable for the holding of free, open, fair and transparent elections within the agreed timetable.

The Council therefore considers that it is necessary to deploy throughout the territory of Côte d'Ivoire as many mobile courts as possible towards the objective of 150 mobile courts called for in the Prime Minister's plan and to complete the second phase of the disarmament, demobilization and reintegration programme, the cantonment of combatants, before the next meeting of the International Working Group. It encourages the Prime Minister to take all the necessary actions to this end, with the agreement of all Ivorian parties, as well as for the organization of the elections. It calls upon the Working Group to monitor such progress and to report to it on its assessment of the progress made.

The Council expresses its full support for the International Working Group and endorses its ninth communiqué of 20 July 2006. It reiterates its full support for the Special Representative of the Secretary-General for Côte d'Ivoire and the High Representative for the elections.

Yamoussoukro meeting (5 September). On 5 September, Prime Minister Banny convened, in Yamoussoukro, a further meeting of the main Ivorian political leaders, President Gbagbo, former President Bédié, former Prime Minister Ouattara and the Forces nouvelles Secretary-General Guillaume Soro, to work out an agreement on measures to break the stalemate in the peace process. Their discussions focused on proposals by Prime Minister Banny for the adoption of extraordinary measures to allow the issuance of certificates of nationality to eligible Ivorians. As no agreement could be reached on the issue, the leaders requested the Prime Minister to continue his search for alternative solutions.

Toxic waste crisis. The impasse in the peace process was further compounded by the dissolution of the transitional Government by Prime Minister Banny on 6 September, following a scandal created in late August by the dumping of over 580 cubic metres of toxic petrochemical waste from a foreign cargo ship at 18 sites in Abidjan. The resulting contamination caused the death of eight people, while some 100,000 others received medical treatment. The UN system assisted the Government in providing an emergency response to the environmental and public health crisis. Although the Prime Minister announced the formation of a new Government on 16 September, in which he replaced the Ministers of Transport and Environment, the toxic waste crisis sidetracked efforts to break the impasse in the peace process. For several weeks, Ivorian youth held demonstrations against the dumping of toxic waste, which at times turned violent.

International Working Group meeting (September). On 8 September, at its tenth ministerial meeting [S/2006/738], the International Working Group condemned the dumping of toxic waste in various sites in the district of Abidjan and the culture of impunity that made it possible. It urged the Government to accelerate the investigations in order to identify and punish those responsible for such criminal acts and appealed to international partners to assist the Government in remedying the health and environmental disaster. The Group took note of the reasons mentioned by the Prime Minister for the resignation of his Government and called upon Ivorian political forces to support his efforts to promptly form a new Government. It cited the main obstacles to the peace process, such as the lack of political will by main actors; disagreement on the establishment of credible voters' lists; halting of the dismantling of the militias; interruption of the military dialogue; institutional duality and legal interpretation conflicts; and the impossibility of the Prime Minister to exercise the powers conferred upon him by resolution 1633(2005). It urged the adoption of exceptional measures to relaunch the mobile court operations and to allow the issuance of duplicate birth certificates and certificates of nationality in an equitable manner. Concluding that it would be impossible to meet the deadline for the holding of the elections, the Group recommended that the Security Council define a new transitional framework that would address the blockages identified, including the adoption of a resolution, which would eliminate the ambiguities in the current transition arrangements and reinforce the powers of the Prime Minister. It also recommended individual sanctions against those responsible for obstructing the peace and reconciliation process.

Report of Secretary-General (October). In his tenth report [S/2006/821] on UNOCI, the Secretary-General said that, in further efforts to break the political stalemate, on 11 and 12 September, the AU Chairman, President Denis Sassou-Nguesso of the Congo, visited Côte d'Ivoire and met with the five main Ivorian leaders to help resolve the issue of the procedures for issuing certificates of nationality, but his compromise solution was not accepted by one of the parties.

On 20 September, the Secretary-General, as indicated at the 5 July High-level Yamoussoukro meeting (see p. 189), convened a follow-up meeting of the Ivorian and regional leaders during the sixty-first session of the General Assembly. A week before the meeting, President Gbagbo, who had made public statements rejecting the International Working Group's 8 September communiqué (see p. 194), informed the Secretary-General that he would not be attending the meeting, as he intended to present his own proposals on the Ivorian peace process to the AU. In his reply, the Secretary-General pointed out that the outcome and views emerging from the follow-up meeting in New York would be conveyed to the AU, ECOWAS and the Security Council, and, as such, the planned meeting was not intended to replace the meetings of those bodies.

At the 20 September meeting, the Secretary-General proposed that, in addition to taking stock of progress towards meeting the Yamoussoukro benchmarks and discussing measures needed to break the political stalemate, the meeting should also discuss the way forward after the 31 October elections and measures to ensure that the new transition period did not end again without the holding of those elections. The participants agreed that it was not technically feasible to organize and conduct elections in Côte d'Ivoire by 31 October, and an extension of the transition period was therefore necessary. Prime Minister Banny stressed the need to resolve the impasse regarding procedures for issuing certificates of nationality. However, President Mbeki said that it would be inappropriate to decide on those crucial issues in the absence of President Gbagbo. The participants agreed that it was important for the AU, ECOWAS and the Security Council to decide without delay on measures to break the impasse and on the extension of the transition period. In that connection, ECOWAS proposed convening an extraordinary summit to consider the situation (see below).

ECOWAS summit. The Economic Community of West African States (ECOWAS) convened an extraordinary summit (6 October, Abuja) to discuss the crisis in Côte d'Ivoire and measures to address the political stalemate in the country. The summit reaffirmed that Security Council resolution 1633(2005) remained an ideal framework for resolving the Ivorian crisis and recommended that the Council take all necessary measures to address the obstacles to its implementation. In a closed session, the ECOWAS leaders agreed on specific recommendations that were not made public, and which were to be considered at the meeting of the AU Peace and Security Council (17 October, Addis Ababa) (see p. 196). On 27 October [S/2006/855], Côte d'Ivoire transmitted to the Council President the text of President Gbagbo's statement delivered at the ECOWAS summit.

Further developments. The Secretary-General reported [S/2006/821] that the security situation remained unpredictable and volatile owing to tension created by the disruption of the mobile court hearings; the poor living conditions of combatants who had assembled at pre-cantonment sites; disagreements over implementation of the disarmament, demobilization and reintegration programme; the toxic waste scandal; inflammatory statements by political leaders; and strikes and protests by public servants and personnel from the gendarmerie. There were concerns that inflammatory statements by the President of the ruling party, calling for the departure of the French Licorne force, as well as public calls by President Gbagbo for the lifting of the Zone of Confidence, could exacerbate tensions and further obstruct the freedom of movement of the two forces. On 2 October, inflammatory statements were issued also threatening violence against ECOWAS nationals living in Côte d'Ivoire, should the 6 October ECOWAS summit fail to take a decision to force the Forces nouvelles to disarm. UNOCI continued to monitor and report on hate media. In August, President Gbagbo signed two decrees related to the mandates and powers of the National Press Council and the National Council on Audio-Visual media. Meanwhile, UNOCI and the High Representative for the elections elaborated, for adoption, a compulsory code of conduct for the media during the electoral period.

The Secretary-General expressed his disappointment that events in Côte d'Ivoire had taken a negative turn, with the main Ivorian political leaders unwilling to transcend bias and place the national interest first. Although the second transition period was coming also to a close without elections having taken place, the Secretary-General urged the international community to remain engaged in Côte d'Ivoire. He welcomed ECOWAS' recommendations on the way forward after the expiration of the current transition period on 31 October, and encouraged the AU and the Security Council to build upon those proposals so as to accelerate the peace process and guarantee the success of the new transition arrangements. The duration of the new transition period should be determined by the time required to complete the disarmament, demobilization and reintegration process; conduct effective identification; dismantle the militias; re-establish State authority; and finalize the technical preparations for the elections. It should be made clear to the Ivorian leaders that the proposed extension of the transition period should be the last, and if they again failed to move towards elections, the AU, ECOWAS and the Security Council should consider putting in place transitional governance arrangements, comprising eminent, non-partisan personalities from civil society to complete the remaining processes. However, the Council also needed to give specific guidance on the core issues concerning the conflict; if not, the anticipated new transition period would end up like the first.

To eliminate loopholes and avoid previous obstacles in the transitional arrangements, the Secretary-General proposed ground rules and safeguards: international instruments setting out the special arrangements for the transition period should take precedence where there might be a divergence with the Constitution and national laws; the Prime Minister should have authority over all relevant public offices pertaining to the implementation of the road map, as well as the Defence and Security Forces; Defense and Security Forces commanders and political leaders should be held accountable for activities disrupting implementation of the road map, and should be subject to the imposition of individual sanctions by the Security Council or referral to the International Criminal Court for more serious cases; the Ivorian population and the impartial forces should be allowed freedom of movement; and the Prime Minister should have full and unfettered authority to implement the disarmament programme, the identification process, the dismantling of the militia and the re-establishment of State authority throughout the country, and to commit the necessary funds to ensure the implementation of those processes. The Secretary-General further proposed the establishment of two task forces under the Prime Minister's authority, one on restructuring of the defense and security force, and the other on the identification process.

On the role of the international community, the Secretary-General said that, in anticipation of the UN enhanced role, the UNOCI mandate should be reviewed by the Council and its resources augmented. As AU and ECOWAS support would be critical during the transition process, he called upon the two regional bodies to forge unity among the regional actors and mediators and urged the AU and ECOWAS Chairpersons to ensure that all mediation efforts were harmonized and properly coordinated. He hoped that the AU Peace and Security Council would come up with clear decisions for effective and expeditious implementation of the peace process at its upcoming summit.

Communication. On 16 November [S/2006/820], the Secretary-General informed the Security Council that voluntary contributions received to support the activities of the High Representative for the elections in Côte d'Ivoire were insufficient to maintain the functions entrusted to him by Security Council resolution 1603(2005) [YUN 2005, p. 233]. The UNDP special project for supporting the High Representative had not generated enough funds to enable the office to become operational, nor effective to deal with the important aspects of his work. The Secretary-General therefore informed the Council of his intention to seek General Assembly approval for the use of assessed contributions to fund the office of the High Representative.

Decision of AU Peace and Security Council (October). The AU Peace and Security Council, meeting in Addis Ababa, Ethiopia, at the level of Heads of State and Government on 17 October, issued a communiqué [S/2006/829] endorsing the observations of the 6 October ECOWAS extraordinary summit (see p. 195) on the expiration of the twelve-month transition period and the impossibility of organizing presidential elections on the scheduled date. Taking note of the ECOWAS recommendations on the management of the post-31 October period, it decided that a new twelve-month transition period should be established, commencing on 1 November 2006, to complete the identification and registration of voters, disarmament, demobilization and reintegration and restructuring of the defence forces, dismantling of the militias, restoration of State authority throughout the country, and technical preparations for the elections. President Gbagbo would continue as Head of State and Prime Minister Banny would have necessary powers and means to implement those key activities, as well as authority over all of the integrated Ivorian defense and security forces. Ministers would be accountable to the Prime Minister, who should have full authority over his Cabinet; and the Council of Ministers could, in all matters, take decisions by ordinances and decrees within the spirit of the law to speed up the issuing of duplicates of birth certificates and certificates of nationality. The Prime Minister would not be eligible to stand for election, to be organized on 31 October 2007.

The Peace and Security Council accepted President Thabo Mbeki's request for South Africa to hand over the mediation role, following its election to the UN Security Council, and decided to entrust that role to President Denis Sassou Nguesso of the Congo, in his capacity as AU Chairperson, with his representative leading the day-to-day mediation in Côte d'Ivoire. It urged the Government to ensure the speedy adoption and implementation of the code of conduct for the media. The Peace and Security Council called on the UN Security Council to take measures, including sanctions, against individuals or groups impeding or disrupting implementation of the peace process and relevant Council resolutions on Côte d'Ivoire, and to take appropriate measures for the effective implementation of the arms embargo. It requested the AU Chairperson to submit its decision to the UN Security Council.

Security Council consideration. On 25 October [meeting 5555], the Security Council met in private on the situation in Côte d'Ivoire and heard a briefing by Said Djinnit, the AU Commissioner for Peace and Security and a statement by Youssouf Bakayoko, the Foreign Affairs Minister for Côte d'Ivoire.

SECURITY COUNCIL ACTION

On 1 November [meeting 5561], the Security Council unanimously adopted **resolution 1721(2006).** The draft [S/2006/854] was prepared in consultations among Council members.

The Security Council,

Recalling its previous resolutions and the statements by its President relating to the situation in Côte d'Ivoire,

Reaffirming its strong commitment to respect for the sovereignty, independence, territorial integrity and unity of Côte d'Ivoire, and recalling the importance of the principles of good-neighbourliness, non-interference and regional cooperation,

Recalling that it endorsed the agreement signed by the Ivorian political forces at Linas-Marcoussis, France, on 23 January 2003 (the Linas-Marcoussis Agreement) and approved by the Conference of Heads of State on Côte d'Ivoire, held in Paris on 25 and 26 January 2003, the agreement signed at Accra on 30 July 2004 (the Accra III Agreement) and the agreement signed at Pretoria on 6 April 2005 (the Pretoria Agreement),

Commending the continued efforts of the African Union, the Economic Community of West African States and the leaders of the region to promote peace and stability in Côte d'Ivoire, and reiterating its full support for them,

Paying tribute to President Thabo Mbeki of South Africa for the untiring efforts he has deployed in the service of peace and reconciliation in Côte d'Ivoire, as well as the numerous initiatives he has taken to move forward the peace process, in his capacity as African Union Mediator, driven by his deep commitment to finding African solutions to African problems,

Commending the constant efforts of the Special Representative of the Secretary-General for Côte d'Ivoire, Mr. Pierre Schori, the High Representative for the elections in Côte d'Ivoire, Mr. Gerard Stoudmann, and the International Working Group, and reiterating its full support for them,

Reaffirming its support to the impartial forces, namely the United Nations Operation in Côte d'Ivoire and the French forces supporting it,

Having taken note of the decision of the Peace and Security Council of the African Union adopted at its sixty-fourth meeting, held at the level of Heads of State and Government in Addis Ababa on 17 October 2006 ("the decision of the Peace and Security Council"),

Having heard on 25 October 2006 the report by Mr. Said Djinnit, Commissioner of the African Union,

Having taken note of the report of the Secretary-General of 17 October 2006, in particular paragraphs 68 to 80 thereof,

Bearing in mind that the constitutional mandate of President Laurent Gbagbo expired on 30 October 2005 and the mandate of the former National Assembly expired on 16 December 2005,

Expressing its serious concern at the persistence of the crisis and the deterioration of the situation in Côte d'Ivoire, including its grave humanitarian consequences causing large-scale civilian suffering and displacement,

Reiterating its firm condemnation of all violations of human rights and international humanitarian law in Côte d'Ivoire,

Determining that the situation in Côte d'Ivoire continues to pose a threat to international peace and security in the region,

Acting under Chapter VII of the Charter of the United Nations,

1. *Endorses* the decision of the Peace and Security Council of the African Union, underlines that its unfettered implementation requires the full support of the Security Council, considers, therefore, that the following provisions of the present resolution, based on the decision of the Peace and Security Council, aim at implementing fully the peace process in Côte d'Ivoire and at organizing free, open, fair and transparent elections in the country by 31 October 2007, and affirms that such provisions are intended to be applicable during the transition period until a newly elected President takes up his duties and a new National Assembly is elected;

2. *Takes note* of the tenth final communiqué of the International Working Group, of 8 September 2006;

3. *Takes note also* of the impossibility of organizing elections, presidential and legislative, on the scheduled date and of the expiry, on 31 October 2006, of the transition period and of the mandates of President Laurent Gbagbo and Prime Minister Charles Konan Banny;

4. *Recalls* paragraphs 5 and 8 of the tenth final communiqué of the International Working Group, paragraph 10 of the decision of the Peace and Security Council and paragraph 75 *(a)* of the report of the Secretary-General of 17 October 2006, and therefore declares that the full implementation of the present resolution, consistent with paragraphs 13 and 14 of the decision of the Peace and Security Council, and of the peace process led by the Prime Minister requires full compliance by all Ivorian parties and that no legal provisions should be invoked by them to obstruct the process;

5. *Endorses* the decision of the Peace and Security Council that President Laurent Gbagbo shall remain Head of State as from 1 November 2006 for a new and final transition period not exceeding twelve months;

6. *Endorses also* the decision of the Peace and Security Council to renew the mandate of the Prime Minister, Mr. Charles Konan Banny, as from 1 November 2006 for

a new and final transition period not exceeding twelve months, and endorses further the decision of the Peace and Security Council that the Prime Minister shall not be eligible to stand for the presidential elections to be organized by 31 October 2007;

7. *Stresses* that the Prime Minister shall have a mandate to implement all the provisions of the road map drawn up by the International Working Group and of the agreements concluded between the Ivorian parties with a view to holding free, open, fair and transparent elections by 31 October 2007 at the latest, with support from the United Nations and potential donors, and to carry out, in particular:

— The disarmament, demobilization and reintegration programme;

— The identification of the population and registration of voters in order to compile credible electoral rolls;

— The operations of disarmament and dismantling of militias;

— The restoration of State authority and the redeployment of the administration and public services throughout the territory of Côte d'Ivoire;

— The technical preparations for the elections;

— The restructuring of the armed forces, in accordance with paragraph 17 of the decision of the Peace and Security Council and paragraph 3*(f)* of the Linas-Marcoussis Agreement;

8. *Stresses also* that the Prime Minister, for the implementation of the mandate set out in paragraph 7 above, must have all the necessary powers, and all appropriate financial, material and human resources, as well as full and unfettered authority, consistent with the recommendations of the Economic Community of West African States of 6 October 2006, and must be empowered to take all necessary decisions, in all matters, within the Council of Ministers or the Council of Government, by ordinances or decree-laws;

9. *Stresses further* that the Prime Minister, for the implementation of the mandate set out in paragraph 7 above, must also have the necessary authority over the Defence and Security Forces of Côte d'Ivoire;

10. *Recalls* paragraph 10 (iii) of the decision of the Peace and Security Council of 6 October 2005 and the statement by the President of the Security Council of 9 December 2005, reaffirms the provisions of paragraphs 6 and 7 of resolution 1633(2005) of 21 October 2005, and recalls that the Prime Minister shall have full authority over the Government that he will establish;

11. *Reaffirms* that the disarmament, demobilization and reintegration and identification processes should be carried out concomitantly, stresses the centrality of both processes to the peace process, urges the Prime Minister to implement them without delay, and calls upon all the Ivorian parties to cooperate fully with him in this regard;

12. *Demands* the immediate resumption of the programme for the disarmament and dismantling of militias throughout the national territory, stresses that this programme is a key element of the peace process, and underlines the individual responsibility of the leaders of the militias in the full implementation of this process;

13. *Urges* the Prime Minister to take immediately all appropriate measures, through the signing of the relevant ordinances in the conditions set out in paragraph 8 above, to expedite the issuance of birth and nationality certificates in the context of the identification process, in a spirit of equity and transparency;

14. *Demands* that all the Ivorian parties concerned, in particular the Armed Forces of the Forces nouvelles and the Armed Forces of Côte d'Ivoire, participate fully and in good faith in the work of the quadripartite commission responsible for overseeing the implementation of the disarmament, demobilization and reintegration programme and the operations for the disarmament and dismantling of militias;

15. *Invites* the Prime Minister to establish immediately, in liaison with all the Ivorian parties, the United Nations Operation in Côte d'Ivoire and the French forces supporting it, a working group responsible for submitting to him a plan on the restructuring of the defence and security forces and preparing possible seminars on security sector reform to be organized by the African Union and the Economic Community of West African States, with a view to rebuilding defence and security forces committed to the values of integrity and republican morality;

16. *Encourages* the African Union and the Economic Community of West African States to organize seminars on security sector reform, in collaboration with partners and with the participation of commanding and senior officers from West African countries emerging from conflict, to examine, among other issues, the principles of civilian control of armed forces and personal and individual responsibility for acts of impunity or violation of human rights;

17. *Invites* the Prime Minister to establish immediately, in liaison with all the Ivorian parties concerned and the High Representative for the elections in Côte d'Ivoire, a working group responsible for helping him to implement the identification of the population and the registration of voters, in order to ensure their credibility and transparency;

18. *Encourages* the Prime Minister to seek, as appropriate, the active involvement of civil society in moving the peace process forward, and urges the Ivorian parties, the High Representative for the elections and the United Nations Operation in Côte d'Ivoire to take account of the rights and resources of women and of gender considerations as set out in resolution 1325(2000) of 31 October 2000 as cross-cutting issues in the implementation of the peace process, including through consultations with local and international women's groups;

19. *Demands* that all Ivorian parties end all incitement to hatred and violence, in radio and television broadcasting as well as in any other media, and urges the Prime Minister to establish and implement without delay a code of conduct for the media, in conformity with the decisions taken at Yamoussoukro on 5 July 2006 and the decision of the Peace and Security Council;

20. *Endorses* the decision of the Peace and Security Council that, to avoid multiple and conflicting mediation efforts, President Denis Sassou Nguesso of the Congo ("the Mediator"), in his capacity as Chairperson of the African Union, shall lead the mediation efforts, in liaison with the Chairmen of the African Union Commission and the Economic Community of West African States and, as the need may arise, in liaison with any other African leader willing to make a contribution to the search for peace in Côte d'Ivoire, and underlines that the representative of the Mediator in Côte d'Ivoire will lead, in liaison with the Special Representative of the Secretary-General for Côte d'Ivoire, the day-to-day mediation;

21. *Requests* the African Union and the Economic Community of West African States to continue to monitor and follow up closely the implementation of the peace process, and invites them to review before 1 February 2007 the progress achieved and, should they deem it appropriate, to review the situation again between that date and 31 October 2007, and requests them to report to the Security Council, through the Secretary-General, on their assessment and, if necessary, to submit to the Council any new recommendations;

22. *Renews* for a period of twelve months the mandate of the High Representative for the elections laid down in paragraph 7 of resolution 1603(2005) of 3 June 2005, underscores that the Peace and Security Council has encouraged the High Representative to play a greater role in the resolution of disputes linked to the electoral process, or issues arising out of the procedures and processes to be adopted to ensure open, free, fair and transparent elections, and decides, therefore, that, in addition to that mandate, the High Representative, with the full support of and in consultation with the Prime Minister:

— Shall be the sole authority authorized to arbitrate with a view to preventing or resolving any problems or disputes related to the electoral process, in liaison with the Mediator;
— Shall certify that all stages of the electoral process, including the process of identification of the population, the establishment of a register of voters and the issuance of voters' cards, provide all the necessary guarantees for the holding of open, free, fair and transparent presidential and legislative elections in accordance with international standards;

23. *Requests* the United Nations Operation in Côte d'Ivoire, consistent with its mandate in resolution 1609(2005) of 24 June 2005 to protect United Nations personnel, to provide security to the High Representative for the elections, within its capabilities and its areas of deployment;

24. *Recalls* paragraph 9 above, and stresses, therefore, that the Prime Minister must have authority over the personnel of the Defence and Security Forces of Côte d'Ivoire who ensure his close protection and provide the security of his offices, including by designating them, without prejudice to the provisions of paragraph *2(l)* of resolution 1609(2005);

25. *Recalls also* the International Working Group's role of guarantor and impartial arbitrator of the peace process, and requests the Working Group:

— To establish as soon as possible, in liaison with the Prime Minister, a precise timetable for the implementation of the main components of the road map;
— To evaluate, monitor and follow up closely the progress achieved in implementing the road map on a monthly basis;
— To report to the Security Council, through the Secretary-General, on its assessment of the progress achieved and on any obstacles encountered by the Prime Minister in carrying out his mandate set out in paragraph 7 above;
— To submit, as appropriate, to all the Ivorian parties concerned and to the Council any recommendations it deems necessary;

26. *Demands* that all Ivorian parties refrain from any use of force and violence, including against civilians and foreigners, and from all kinds of disruptive street protests;

27. *Demands also* that all Ivorian parties guarantee the security and freedom of movement of all Ivorian nationals throughout the territory of Côte d'Ivoire;

28. *Demands further* that all Ivorian parties cooperate fully with the operations of the United Nations Operation in Côte d'Ivoire and the French forces supporting it, as well as United Nations agencies and associated personnel, in particular by guaranteeing the safety, security and freedom of movement of their personnel, as well as associated personnel, throughout the territory of Côte d'Ivoire, and reaffirms that any obstacle to their freedom of movement or to the full implementation of their mandates would not be tolerated;

29. *Urges* countries neighbouring Côte d'Ivoire to prevent any cross-border movement of combatants or arms into Côte d'Ivoire;

30. *Reiterates its serious concern* at all violations of human rights and international humanitarian law in Côte d'Ivoire, and urges the Ivorian authorities to investigate these violations without delay in order to put an end to impunity;

31. *Recalls* the individual responsibility of all Ivorian parties, including members of the Defence and Security Forces of Côte d'Ivoire and of the Armed Forces of the Forces nouvelles, whatever their rank, in the implementation of the peace process;

32. *Underlines* that it is fully prepared to impose targeted measures against persons to be designated by the Security Council Committee established pursuant to paragraph 14 of resolution 1572(2004) who are determined to be, among other things, blocking the implementation of the peace process, including by attacking or obstructing the action of the United Nations Operation in Côte d'Ivoire, of the French forces supporting it, of the High Representative for the elections, of the International Working Group, of the Mediator or of his representative in Côte d'Ivoire, responsible for serious violations of human rights and international humanitar-

ian law committed in Côte d'Ivoire since 19 September 2002, publicly inciting hatred and violence or in violation of the arms embargo, as provided for in resolutions 1572(2004) of 15 November 2004 and 1643(2005) of 15 December 2005;

33. *Decides* to remain actively seized of the matter.

EU statement. In a 10 November statement [S/2006/954], the EU urged all Ivorian parties to give Prime Minister Banny the support he needed to bring the peace and reconciliation process to a successful conclusion and condemned the declarations opposing the framework outlined by the Security Council. The EU called on the United Nations to impose targeted sanctions against anyone who obstructed, by whatever means, the implementation of the peace process.

Implementation of resolution 1721(2006)

Report of Secretary-General (December). In his eleventh report on UNOCI [S/2006/939], the Secretary-General said that, while Security Council resolution 1721(2006) was perceived in the subregion as a major step forward, it received mixed reactions from the Ivorian parties. In his 2 November address to the nation, President Gbagbo welcomed the resolution, but added that those of its provisions that were inconsistent with Côte d'Ivoire's Constitution would not be implemented. He subsequently announced a series of consultations with various segments of Ivorian society to develop an alternative framework for solving the Ivorian crisis, since, in his view, the peace plans devised by the international community since the conflict started had failed and Ivorians had the responsibility to find their own solution. The FANCI Chief of Staff, General Philippe Mangou, supported the President's position in a 3 November radio/television broadcast, in which he assured the President of the Defence and Security Forces support. On 18 November, supporters of President Gbagbo, united under the umbrella group, the National Resistance Council for Democracy (CNRD), issued a statement calling for the appointment of a new Prime Minister; separation of the identification process from the preparation of the electoral rolls; the lifting of the Zone of Confidence; and the withdrawal of the French Licorne force. For its part, the Forces nouvelles had issued a 2 November statement in support of resolution 1721(2006), as it addressed their major concerns. The coalition of opposition parties, the Rassemblement des Houphouëtistes pour la démocratie at la paix, also welcomed the resolution and called on its supporters to boycott the consultations initiated by President Gbagbo. Addressing the nation on 8 November, Prime Minister Banny expressed his determination to implement the resolution and saw no need for another framework to resolve the crisis. He announced his intention to focus on the outstanding tasks assigned to him, to relaunch the disarmament programme and establish a new structure for the military dialogue between the Forces nouvelles and FANCI. The Prime Minister was supported by the Forces nouvelles, opposition parties and several civil society groups.

The Secretary-General called upon the AU Chairmen and ECOWAS to intervene to secure acceptance of the resolution by all parties and avert the new developing stalemate. His Special Representative, along with the High Representative for the elections and the Special Representative of the AU Mediator, General Jean-Marie Mokoko, engaged in extensive consultations with the main Ivorian parties and the local media to impress upon them the need to implement the resolution in good faith. On 23 November, President Gbagbo and Prime Minister Banny held a private meeting, facilitated by the Special Representative of the International Organization of la Francophonie, Lansana Kouyaté, to discuss the way forward in setting the new transition period in motion.

Despite those efforts to encourage the Ivorian leaders to open a constructive dialogue and work together to relaunch the implementation of key tasks of the peace process, the political atmosphere deteriorated, with deepening disagreements between the President and the Prime Minister. On 23 November, the national commission of inquiry into the toxic waste scandal submitted its final report, in which it confirmed that the four officials (the Minister of Transport, the General Manager of the Port of Abidjan, the Director General of Customs and the Governor of the District of Abidjan) who had been suspended by the Prime Minister should be held accountable for the dumping of toxic waste. However, on 26 November, President Gbagbo issued presidential decrees limiting their suspension to three months. The next day, the Office of the Prime Minister broadcast a statement on national television stating that the Prime Minister had not been consulted on the decrees and that the President's decisions were contrary to the principles of good governance, transparency and justice. On 28 November, the Defence and Security Forces entered the premises of the State-owned Ivorian Radio and Television by force and prevented a repeat broadcast of the Prime Minister's statement; later the same day, President Gbagbo issued a decree dismissing its Director General and the management board. The President had, on 26 November, also dismissed the Director General and the board of the newspaper

Fraternité Matin, after it had published an article expressing the view that resolution 1721(2006) was the only way out of the crisis. The situation deteriorated, with demonstrations organized in several towns to protest against the President's decisions. In addition, on 1 December, the Republican Guard blocked the UNOCI unit in charge of the Prime Minister's security from access to the Prime Minister's compound.

Violent clashes, unrelated to the resolution, occurred in Yopougon, near Abidjan, on 1 and 3 November, when the local population reacted to criminal harassment by the Groupement des patriotes pour la paix militia and the support that militia was receiving from the Defence and Security Forces. At least five people were killed during the clashes, including two militiamen who were burned alive by Yopougon residents. Other incidents involved demonstrations or protests. In the north, a significant rise in crime was reported, while ethnic tensions rose in the Zone of Confidence and in the south-west of the country, leading to the killing of five persons around the village of Blodi. To minimize the risk of escalation of the prevailing tensions in the country, particularly in Abidjan, UNOCI conducted extensive operational activities, in close cooperation with the French Licorne force. The Secretary-General said that, during the new transition period, UNOCI would adjust the overall posture of its military component, gradually reducing its presence in the Zone of Confidence, and shifting its emphasis from separating the armed groups to increasing its presence and mobility throughout the country, with a view to enhancing its role in providing security for the resumption of the mobile courts and for the cantonment, demobilization and disarmament sites, as well as securing the electoral process. It would provide technical assistance for the restructuring of the armed forces, strengthening the protection of civilians, and facilitating the freedom of movement, especially between the north and the south.

The report included steps to be undertaken to relaunch the key processes under the road map, and provided lessons learned and recommendations on the concomitant resumption of identification and disarmament processes; dismantling and disarming of militias; restructuring of the Defence and Security Forces; redeployment of the State administration; and technical preparations for the elections.

The humanitarian situation continued to be a source of concern, with new reports of cholera and yellow fever outbreaks, as well as continued shortages of water and sanitation facilities in the northern part of the country. UNOCI continued to assist the Government in mitigating the consequences of the dumping of toxic waste from foreign ship in Abidjan in August. As at 23 October, 10 people had died, 64 had been hospitalized and some 104,000 had sought health consultations.

The Secretary-General observed that Security Council resolution 1721(2006) provided tools and safeguards to overcome obstacles that had impeded progress in previous transition periods. However, complementary efforts from both Ivorian and international stakeholders were required to nurture a political environment in which trust could take root among the main political leaders. He called on President Gbagbo, Prime Minister Banny and international mediators to provide the leadership for sustained dialogue and the maintenance of constructive working relationships among all stakeholders. Ivorian civil society, which had also been marginalized, should be included in the peace process. Together, Ivorian political leaders and civil society should address the factors underlying the inclination to maintain the status quo. Moreover, in order to emerge from conflict, all Ivorian stakeholders had to recognize and accept the need for exceptional measures during and immediately following the transition period, including the possibility of power-sharing arrangements. The Secretary-General called upon the international community to support the peace process and to offer incentives to the parties, while being prepared to act against those who deliberately obstructed it or committed crimes against the civilian population.

With regard to UNOCI, he urged the Security Council to approve his recommendations on the Mission's role in the transition process and to extend its mandate to 15 December 2007. He also appealed for the Council's support for an expanded presence of UNOCI civil affairs, political affairs, human rights and rule of law components in the northern and western parts of the country to support the restoration of State administration. UNOCI public information component would develop a sensitization campaign, in collaboration with relevant counterparts and the High Representative for the elections, to combat hate media and sensitize the population to key processes, including the elections. It would also expand its radio coverage to remote areas, such as Aboisso, Bouna, Korhogo and Odienné.

On security aspects, the Secretary-General said that the conduct of the process for the identification of the population and preparations for the elections would require effective security from the impartial forces. With the need to adjust the posture of the UNOCI military component and enhance its role in facilitating freedom of movement and protecting civilians, he again appealed to the Council to approve the remaining three battalions for UNOCI, out of the four recommended in his January progress report. In that connection, and pursuant to resolution 1609(2005) [YUN 2005, p. 236], he proposed that the Council take advantage of the envisaged departure of one UNMIL battalion at the end of 2006 to reinforce UNOCI. As funding from voluntary contributions for the activities of the High Representative for the elections continued to pose significant challenges, he appealed to potential donors to urgently provide resources to sustain the work of that office.

International Working Group meeting (December). On 1 December, at its eleventh ministerial meeting [S/2006/950], the first meeting following the adoption of Security Council resolution 1721(2006), the International Working Group clarified, at Prime Minister Banny's request, the authority vested in him by that resolution over the Defence and Security Forces and the Forces nouvelles. The Group noted with concern the delay in the implementation of the resolution, as well as the deterioration of the political climate, particularly with regard to the recommendations of the National Commission of Inquiry into the toxic waste dumping crisis and the reinstatement of those officials suspended by the Prime Minister. The Group, condemning the dismissal of the Directors General of Ivorian Radio and Television and the newspaper *Fraternité Matin*, and the dissolution of their respective Boards of Directors, called for their reinstatement. Bearing in mind the assessment of the peace process scheduled to be conducted by 1 February 2007, the Group invited the Prime Minister to take or initiate the following measures: relaunch the pre-identification process for issuing substitute birth certificates and certificates of nationality, and by 10 December 2006, adopt regulatory texts to make that process more efficient, and assign new judges to the new jurisdictions so that registration could be completed by 1 February 2007; establish the working group on identification by 5 December 2006; ensure the nomination by political actors of their representatives on the local structures of the Independent Electoral Commission before 15 December, which should also publish an electoral timetable, including the date of the first round of presidential elections; ensure full participation of parties controlling the militias and ex-combatants in the disarmament, demobilization and reintegration process and the dismantling of the militias, with rehabilitation sites being completed by 15 January 2007; establish the working group on security sector reform by 5 December 2006, with the dates of the national seminar announced at the same time; and publish the Code of Conduct for the media by 15 December 2006.

The Group recommended that the impartial forces should help ensure the security of the electoral process, particularly in its pre-identification and identification phases, as well as the disarmament, demobilization and reintegration process. It also reminded Ivorian parties that it would recommend to the UN Security Council appropriate sanctions against any person obstructing the effective start-up of the implementation of resolution 1721(2006), including through incitements to hatred and violence.

Security Council consideration. On 12 December [meeting 5585], the Security Council met in private with the troop-contributing countries to UNOCI and heard a briefing by Pierre Schori, the Special Representative of the Secretary-General for UNOCI.

SECURITY COUNCIL ACTION

On 15 December [meeting 5591], the Security Council unanimously adopted **resolution 1726(2006)**. The draft [S/2006/981] was prepared in consultations among Council members.

The Security Council,

Recalling its previous resolutions and the statements by its President relating to the situation in Côte d'Ivoire,

Reaffirming its strong commitment to respect for the sovereignty, independence, territorial integrity and unity of Côte d'Ivoire, and recalling the importance of the principles of good-neighbourliness, non-interference and regional cooperation,

Having taken note of the report of the Secretary-General of 4 December 2006,

Reaffirming its support to the impartial forces, namely the United Nations Operation in Côte d'Ivoire and the French forces supporting it,

Expressing its serious concern at the persistence of the crisis and the deterioration of the situation in Côte d'Ivoire, including its grave humanitarian consequences causing large-scale civilian suffering and displacement,

Determining that the situation in Côte d'Ivoire continues to pose a threat to international peace and security in the region,

Acting under Chapter VII of the Charter of the United Nations,

1. *Decides* that the mandate of the United Nations Operation in Côte d'Ivoire and of the French forces supporting it shall be extended until 10 January 2007;

2. *Decides also* to remain actively seized of the matter.

On 21 December [meeting 5606], following consultations among Security Council members on the 1 December communiqué issued by the International Working Group (see p. 202), the President made statement **S/PRST/2006/58** on behalf of the Council:

> The Security Council reiterates its full support for the International Working Group, recalls its role as guarantor and impartial arbiter of the peace process, and endorses its final communiqué of 1 December 2006. It also encourages the Working Group to promote enhanced dialogue with all Ivorian parties. It insists that all Ivorian parties apply, under the direction of the Prime Minister, the implementation timeline for the road map drawn up by the Working Group.
>
> The Council shares the grave concern expressed by the International Working Group at delays in the implementation of resolution 1721(2006), and urges all Ivorian parties to cooperate fully with the Prime Minister in order to implement all the provisions of the road map drawn up by the Working Group and referred to in resolution 1721(2006), including the identification of the population and the registration of voters, and the disarmament, demobilization and reintegration programme, which are central to the peace process in Côte d'Ivoire.
>
> The Council, bearing in mind the provisions of resolution 1572(2004), recalls that the neutrality and impartiality of the public media are essential to the peace process, and supports the International Working Group, which considered that it is indispensable to reinstate the dismissed officials of Radio Télévision Ivoirienne and *Fraternité Matin*. It recalls also that obstacles to the freedom of movement of the impartial forces, in particular those put up by the Republican Guard, are unacceptable.
>
> The Council reiterates its full support for the Prime Minister, Mr. Charles Konan Banny. It strongly encourages him to continue his endeavours, in consultation with President Laurent Gbagbo, including his efforts to fight impunity and promote good governance, and to utilize all the powers referred to in resolution 1721(2006) to prepare for elections, which must be held by 31 October 2007 at the latest. The Council welcomes in this regard the announcement by the Prime Minister of immediate measures to relaunch the identification process, and expects more concrete measures in place to implement the disarmament, demobilization and reintegration programme. The Council reaffirms that the Prime Minister must exercise his powers without hindrance, including his authority over the Defence and Security Forces referred to in resolution 1721(2006), and calls upon all Ivorian parties to support his efforts.
>
> The Council invites the African Union Mediator to visit Côte d'Ivoire to relaunch the peace process as soon as possible, if necessary in cooperation with all other African leaders.
>
> The Council requests the International Working Group, in preparation for its next meeting on 12 January 2007, to provide a detailed update on the timeline for the implementation of the peace process, and all the recommendations needed for the consideration of the situation by the Economic Community of West African States and the African Union by 1 February 2007 at the latest.
>
> The Council reiterates its full support for the Special Representative of the Secretary-General for Côte d'Ivoire, Mr. Pierre Schori, the High Representative for the elections in Côte d'Ivoire, Mr. Gerard Stoudmann, and the United Nations Operation in Côte d'Ivoire, as well as the French forces supporting it.

Later developments. In a later report [S/2007/133], the Secretary-General said that at year's end, the political stalemate in the peace process remained unresolved, with no significant progress towards implementing Security Council resolution 1721(2006). In a 19 December radio address, with the aim of finding a "home-grown" solution to the crisis, President Gbagbo announced a new initiative, offering to open direct dialogue with the Forces nouvelles under the auspices of the President of Burkina Faso, Blaise Compaoré. He also called for the removal of the Zone of Confidence dividing the country; proposed the enactment of a new amnesty law; indicated his intention to launch a national civilian service for young people and an assistance programme for resettling displaced persons; and proposed that the elections be held by July 2007.

Prime Minister Banny made efforts to reinvigorate the peace process by implementing the schedule proposed by the International Working Group at its 1 December meeting, but the results achieved were limited. The working groups on identification of the population and on security sector reform were established on 5 and 12 December, respectively. However, the 15 December deadline for nominating political party representatives on the Independent Electoral Commission's local structures, which was to be followed by the opening of those structures and the announcement of an electoral timetable by the Commission, was not met.

Sanctions

The Security Council Committee established pursuant to resolution 1572(2004) [YUN 2004, p. 187] concerning Côte d'Ivoire continued to monitor implementation of the arms embargo, travel restrictions and assets freeze on designated individuals and entities imposed by that resolution, as renewed and expanded by resolution 1643(2005) [YUN 2005, p. 251] banning the importation of all rough diamonds from Côte d'Ivoire. In 2006, the Committee held two formal meetings and nine informal consultations.

The Committee considered reports by Member States, submitted in accordance with their obligations under resolution 1643(2005), containing information on measures taken to implement the resolution [S/AC.45/2006/1-23]. In a report on its 2006 activities [S/2006/1017], the Committee Chairman indicated that, on 23 January, the Committee considered the implementation of targeted measures, and adopted, on 7 February, the list of individuals and entities subject to measures imposed by Council resolution 1572(2004). On 25 January, it adopted the annual report on its 2005 activities [YUN 2005, p. 248].

On 14 March 2006, the Committee received a briefing from the Under-Secretary-General for Humanitarian Affairs and Emergency Relief Coordinator on his visit to Côte d'Ivoire. The Committee took note of the climate of impunity and the continuing incitement to violence by local media, and issued a 16 March press statement [SC/8665] expressing concern at the situation in the western part of the country. The Committee also sought explanations from the Ivorian authorities on incidents that had occurred between FANCI and Licorne forces.

On 17 May, the Committee considered the report by Côte d'Ivoire on the February incidents between FANCI and the French forces. The Committee was also briefed by the Department of Peacekeeping Operations on the same incidents, as well as on instances of incitement to hatred by the local media. The Committee agreed to seek information from Côte d'Ivoire on the measures the Government intended to adopt to prevent further dissemination by local media of messages inciting violence. The Committee also considered UNOCI monthly arms embargo and media monitoring reports, the mid-term and final reports of the Group of Experts established by Council resolution 1643(2005) to assess compliance with the sanctions, and the Group's updated report, in accordance with resolution 1632(2005) [YUN 2005, p. 249]. On 18 December, the Committee approved an updated list of individuals and entities subject to the measures imposed by resolutions 1572(2004) and 1643(2005).

Appointment. In letters of 27 February [S/2006/135] and 20 September [S/2006/755], the Secretary-General, as requested in resolutions 1643(2005) and 1708(2006), informed the Council of the appointment of Agim de Bruycker (Belgium), Christian Dietrich (United States), Oumar Dièye Sidi (Niger), Nawa Raj Silwal (Nepal) and Alex Vines (United Kingdom) to the Group of Experts concerning Côte d'Ivoire.

Report of Group of Experts (March). In accordance with resolutions 1572(2004) and 1632(2005), the Group of Experts issued an update [S/2006/204] to its November 2005 report [YUN 2005, p. 250] on the situation in Côte d'Ivoire. The Committee considered the updated report at informal consultations on 14 March.

Communication. On 2 May [S/2006/294], Côte d'Ivoire informed the Security Council President of alleged human rights violations committed by French Licorne troops against members of the Ivorian Defence and Security Forces, and transmitted his 12 April statement to the Security Council Committee established pursuant to resolution 1572(2004) on the matter. The Committee considered the report on 12 April.

Report of Group of Experts (September). In September [S/2006/735], the Chairman of the Security Council Committee established pursuant to resolution 1572(2004) transmitted to the Council President the final report of the Group of Experts on the situation in Côte d'Ivoire, in accordance with resolution 1643(2005). The report examined political developments; arms and disarmament; provision of military assistance, advice and training; maintaining airpower; embargo inspections; defence expenditure and natural resources; diamond embargo; and targeted measures on three Ivorian individuals.

The Group found no evidence of gross violations of Security Council measures. However, there were a number of incidents that the Group believed were cause for concern. It recommended that the Security Council Committee urgently address them, including concerns about the authenticity of Burkina Faso end-user certificate 732 that could be used to violate the sanctions; missing ammunition from the Bangladesh Battalion 2 and the need for UNOCI to mark its ammunition to avoid future unaccounted losses, and review its inspection process; limited feedback from and direction by the Security Council Committee on the monthly embargo reports, which had contributed to a sense within UNOCI that all was fine; and the potential danger of maintaining the status quo, as it undermined the Council's reputation and could lead to the monitoring system being easily circumvented in the event of a serious deterioration of the peace process.

On the provision of military assistance, advice and training, the Group recommended that the Committee should urgently request details from UNOCI and the Government about the pro-Government militia group, LIMA FS, and its leadership, which appeared to still maintain Liberians among its ranks. Other concerns included the need for increased patrolling of the Ivorian-Liberian border; the continued provision by nationals of Belarus, the Russian Federation and possibly Ukraine of assistance, advice and training to the Force aérienne de Côte d'Ivoire, and the continued maintenance and testing of a Mil Mi-24 Hind attack helicopter.

The Group believed that financial disclosure and expenditure transparency had improved under Prime Minister Banny, but the investigation of reports that quasi-fiscal coffee and cocoa agencies had been used to channel funds for off-budget security expenditures made little progress. The Group concluded that Ivorian rough diamonds were being exported in violation of the Security Council embargo, via Ghana and Mali, prior to entering the international trade markets, and recommended that Ghana create a credible system of internal controls for rough diamonds and take effective measures to prevent illegal smuggling. International trading centres also needed to introduce a better system of identifying suspicious shipments of rough diamonds.

The Group said that, while the targeted measures imposed on three Ivorian individuals in February appeared to have had a calming affect, further targeting of individuals by the Committee without effective monitoring and compliance systems in place by States neighbouring Côte d'Ivoire could be counter productive.

SECURITY COUNCIL ACTION

On 14 September [meeting 5524], the Security Council unanimously adopted **resolution 1708(2006)**. The draft [S/2006/736] was prepared in consultations among Council members.

The Security Council,

Recalling its previous resolutions concerning the situation in Côte d'Ivoire, in particular resolutions 1572(2004) of 15 November 2004, 1584(2005) of 1 February 2005, 1633(2005) of 21 October 2005 and 1643(2005) of 15 December 2005, and the relevant statements by its President,

Welcoming the ongoing efforts of the Secretary-General, the African Union and the Economic Community of West African States towards re-establishing peace and stability in Côte d'Ivoire,

Recalling the final report of the Group of Experts created by the Secretary-General pursuant to paragraph 9 of resolution 1643(2005),

Determining that the situation in Côte d'Ivoire continues to constitute a threat to international peace and security in the region,

Acting under Chapter VII of the Charter of the United Nations,

1. *Decides* to extend the mandate of the Group of Experts until 15 December 2006, and requests the Secretary-General to take the necessary administrative measures;

2. *Requests* the Group of Experts to submit a brief written update to the Security Council, through the Security Council Committee established pursuant to paragraph 14 of resolution 1572(2004), before 1 December 2006, on the implementation of the measures imposed by paragraphs 7, 9 and 11 of resolution 1572(2004) and paragraphs 4 and 6 of resolution 1643(2005), with recommendations in this regard;

3. *Decides* to remain actively seized of the matter.

Report of Group of Experts (December). In December [S/2006/964], the Chairman of the Security Council Committee established pursuant to resolution 1572(2004) transmitted to the Council President an update by the Group of Experts on the situation in Côte d'Ivoire, in accordance with resolution 1708(2006). The report examined arms; provision of military assistance; embargo inspections; diamonds; and targeted measures on three Ivorians. With regard to arms, in October, the Group intervened before the National Police could import ammunition and tear gas from Iran. The transaction would be placed before the Security Council Committee for exemption. The Group investigated the importation of small-arms ammunition into Côte d'Ivoire by a criminal network, using international courier firms. Yssouf Diabaté was arrested in September, in San Diego, California, and the ammunition was seized by United States agents. The ammunition already sent by Mr. Diabaté to Abidjan was also seized by customs in Abidjan. Noting the Ivorian Government admission that it had hired three foreign technicians for its Mi-24 helicopter, the Group recommended minimum requirements under an exemption system approved by the Security Council to permit test flights and technical assistance, including full disclosure of the identities of foreign or dual-nationality Mi-24 technicians.

An embargo cell was created by UNOCI in August, to mainstream embargo monitoring. The cell would benefit from the services of a short-time maritime customs consultant to assist UNOCI in monitoring shipping activities, given that Côte d'Ivoire's ports were open to abuse and UNOCI had not conducted a port inspection since August.

The Group found continued evidence of production and illicit exportation of diamonds in Côte d'Ivoire, especially to Mali. The Group welcomed the efforts of the participants of the Kimberley Process Certification Scheme for controlling the production of rough diamonds (see p. 50) in assisting Ghana to reform its internal diamond controls so as to ensure that it did not receive conflict diamonds from Côte d'Ivoire. The Group also highlighted that Dubai had released a package of suspect "Ghanaian" diamonds to its importer without conducting a proper investigation.

SECURITY COUNCIL ACTION

On 15 December [meeting 5592], the Security Council unanimously adopted **resolution 1727(2006)**. The draft [S/2006/982] was prepared in consultations among Council members.

The Security Council,

Recalling its previous resolutions and the statements by its President relating to the situation in Côte d'Ivoire,

Reaffirming its strong commitment to respect for the sovereignty, independence, territorial integrity and unity of Côte d'Ivoire, and recalling the importance of the principles of good-neighbourliness, non-interference and regional cooperation,

Taking note of the reports of the Group of Experts on Côte d'Ivoire issued on 5 October and 12 December 2006,

Expressing its serious concern at the persistence of the crisis and the deterioration of the situation in Côte d'Ivoire, including its grave humanitarian consequences causing large-scale civilian suffering and displacement,

Determining that the situation in Côte d'Ivoire continues to pose a threat to international peace and security in the region,

Acting under Chapter VII of the Charter of the United Nations,

1. *Decides* to renew until 31 October 2007 the provisions of paragraphs 7 to 12 of resolution 1572(2004) of 15 November 2004 and paragraph 6 of resolution 1643(2005) of 15 December 2005;

2. *Demands* that all Ivorian parties, including the transitional Government and the Forces nouvelles, provide unhindered access, particularly to the Group of Experts established pursuant to paragraph 9 of resolution 1643(2005), to equipment, sites and installations referred to in paragraph 2 *(a)* of resolution 1584(2005) of 1 February 2005, and to the United Nations Operation in Côte d'Ivoire and French forces supporting it to enable them to carry out the tasks set out in paragraphs 2 and 12 of resolution 1609(2005) of 24 June 2005;

3. *Reiterates* that any serious obstacle to the freedom of movement of the United Nations Operation in Côte d'Ivoire and of the French forces supporting it, or any attack or obstruction to the action of the United Nations Operation in Côte d'Ivoire, of the French forces, of the High Representative for the elections in Côte d'Ivoire, of the International Working Group, of the Mediator mentioned in paragraph 20 of resolution 1721(2006) of 1 November 2006 or of his representative in Côte d'Ivoire constitutes a threat to the peace and national reconciliation process for purposes of paragraphs 9 and 11 of resolution 1572(2004);

4. *Requests* the Secretary-General and the Government of France to report to it immediately, through the Security Council Committee established pursuant to paragraph 14 of resolution 1572(2004) (the Committee), of any serious obstacle to the freedom of movement of the United Nations Operation in Côte d'Ivoire and of the French forces supporting it, including the names of those responsible, and requests the High Representative for the elections, the International Working Group, the Mediator mentioned in paragraph 20 of resolution 1721(2006) or his representative in Côte d'Ivoire to report to it immediately, through the Committee, any attack or obstruction to their action;

5. *Requests* all States concerned, in particular those in the region, to report to the Committee, within ninety days of the date of adoption of the present resolution, on the practical steps they have taken to implement the measures imposed by paragraphs 7, 9 and 11 of resolution 1572(2004) and paragraph 6 of resolution 1643(2005), and authorizes the Committee to request whatever further information it may consider necessary;

6. *Decides* that at the end of the period mentioned in paragraph 1 above, the Council shall review the measures imposed by paragraphs 7, 9 and 11 of resolution 1572(2004) and paragraph 6 of resolution 1643(2005) and reiterated in paragraph 3 above, in the light of progress accomplished in the peace and national reconciliation process in Côte d'Ivoire as referred to in resolution 1721(2006), and expresses its readiness to consider the modification or termination of those measures before the aforesaid period only if the provisions of resolution 1721(2006) have been fully implemented;

7. *Decides also* to extend the mandate of the Group of Experts for a further six months, and requests the Secretary-General to take the necessary administrative measures as expeditiously as possible, drawing, as appropriate, on the expertise of the members of the Group of Experts and appointing new members as necessary, in consultation with the Committee, the mandate to be as follows:

(a) To exchange information with the United Nations Operation in Côte d'Ivoire and the French forces in the context of their monitoring mandate set out in paragraphs 2 and 12 of resolution 1609(2005);

(b) To gather and analyse all relevant information in Côte d'Ivoire and elsewhere, in cooperation with the Governments of those countries, on flows of arms and related materiel, on provision of assistance, advice or training related to military activities, on networks operating in violation of the measures imposed by paragraph 7 of resolution 1572(2004), and on the sources of financing, including from the exploitation of natural resources in Côte d'Ivoire, for purchases of arms and related materiel and activities;

(c) To consider and recommend, where appropriate, ways of improving the capabilities of States, in particular those in the region, to ensure the effective implementation of the measures imposed by paragraph 7 of resolution 1572(2004) and paragraph 6 of resolution 1643(2005);

(d) To seek further information regarding the action taken by States with a view to implementing effectively the measures imposed by paragraph 6 of resolution 1643(2005);

(e) To report to the Council in writing before 15 June 2007, through the Committee, on the implementation of the measures imposed by paragraphs 7, 9 and 11 of resolution 1572(2004) and paragraph 6 of resolution 1643(2005), with recommendations in this regard;

(f) To keep the Committee regularly updated on its activities;

(g) To provide the Committee in its reports with evidence of any violations of the measures imposed by paragraph 7 of resolution 1572(2004) and paragraph 6 of resolution 1643(2005);

(h) To cooperate with other relevant groups of experts, in particular the group of experts on Liberia established pursuant to resolutions 1521(2003) of 22 December 2003 and 1579(2004) of 21 December 2004;

(i) To monitor the implementation of the individual measures set out in paragraphs 9 and 11 of resolution 1572(2004);

8. *Requests* the Secretary-General to communicate, as appropriate, to the Council, through the Committee, information gathered by the United Nations Operation in Côte d'Ivoire and, when possible, reviewed by the Group of Experts, about the supply of arms and related materiel to Côte d'Ivoire;

9. *Requests* the Government of France to communicate, as appropriate, to the Council, through the Committee, information gathered by the French forces and, when possible, reviewed by the Group of Experts, about the supply of arms and related materiel to Côte d'Ivoire;

10. *Requests* the Kimberley Process to communicate, as appropriate, to the Council, through the Committee, information, when possible, reviewed by the Group of Experts, about the production and illicit export of diamonds;

11. *Urges* all States, relevant United Nations bodies and other organizations and interested parties, including the Kimberley Process, to cooperate fully with the Committee, the Group of Experts, the United Nations Operation in Côte d'Ivoire and the French forces, in particular by supplying any information at their disposal on possible violations of the measures imposed by paragraphs 7, 9 and 11 of resolution 1572(2004) and paragraph 6 of resolution 1643(2005) and reiterated in paragraph 3 above;

12. *Underlines* that it is fully prepared to impose targeted measures against persons to be designated by the Committee who are determined to be, among other things:

(a) A threat to the peace and national reconciliation process in Côte d'Ivoire, in particular by blocking the implementation of the peace process as referred to in resolution 1721(2006);

(b) Attacking or obstructing the action of the United Nations Operation in Côte d'Ivoire, of the French forces supporting it, of the High Representative for the elections, of the International Working Group, of the Mediator or of his representative in Côte d'Ivoire;

(c) Responsible for obstacles to the freedom of movement of the United Nations Operation in Côte d'Ivoire and of the French forces supporting it;

(d) Responsible for serious violations of human rights and international humanitarian law committed in Côte d'Ivoire;

(e) Publicly inciting hatred and violence;

(f) Acting in violation of the measures imposed by paragraph 7 of resolution 1572(2004);

13. *Decides* to remain actively seized of the matter.

UNOCI

The United Nations Operation in Côte d'Ivoire (UNOCI) was established in 2004 by Security Council resolution 1528(2004) [YUN 2004, p. 173] to replace the United Nations Mission in Côte d'Ivoire and ECOWAS forces. Its mandate was to monitor the ceasefire and the movement of armed groups; assist in disarmament, demobilization, reintegration, repatriation and resettlement; protect UN personnel and civilians; support implementation of the peace process; and provide assistance in the monitoring of human rights, public information and law and order. The Mission comprised a civilian, judiciary and corrections components, and was supported by the French Licorne forces. Headquartered in Abidjan, it was headed by the Special Representative of the Secretary-General, Pierre Schori. The Security Council extended the Mission's mandate until 10 January 2007.

Appointment. In an exchange of letters with the Security Council President on 30 August [S/2006/715] and 6 September [S/2006/716], the Secretary-General appointed Major General Fernand Marcel Amoussou (Benin) as Force Commander, to replace Major Gereral Abdoulaye Fall, who left the Mission in April.

UNOCI financing

In June, at its resumed sixtieth (2006) session, the General Assembly considered the performance report on the UNOCI budget for the period from 1 July 2004 to 30 June 2005 [A/60/630], showing actual expenditures of $336,890,500 against a total appropriation of $378,472,800, and the proposed budget for UNOCI for the period from 1 July 2006 to 30 June 2007 [A/60/753 & Corr.1] in the amount of $420,175,200, gross, together with the related ACABQ report [A/60/896]. The budget provided for the deployment of 200 military observers, 6,890 contingent personnel, including 120 force headquarters staff officers, 350 UN police officers, 375 formed police personnel, 467 international and 575 national staff, including 36 national officers, as well as 277 United Nations Volunteers and 8 government-provided personnel. ACABQ recommended approval of the full amount proposed by the Secretary-General for the period from 1 July 2006 to 30 June 2007.

GENERAL ASSEMBLY ACTION

On 30 June [meeting 92], the General Assembly, on the recommendation of the Fifth Committee [A/60/540/Add.1], adopted **resolution 60/17 B** without vote [agenda item 138].

Financing of the United Nations Operation in Côte d'Ivoire

The General Assembly,

Having considered the reports of the Secretary-General on the financing of the United Nations Operation in Côte d'Ivoire and the related report of the Advisory Committee on Administrative and Budgetary Questions,

Recalling Security Council resolution 1528(2004) of 27 February 2004, by which the Council established the United Nations Operation in Côte d'Ivoire for an initial period of twelve months as from 4 April 2004, and the subsequent resolutions by which the Council extended the mandate of the Operation, the latest of which was resolution 1652(2006) of 24 January 2006, by which the Council extended the mandate of the Operation until 15 December 2006,

Recalling also its resolution 58/310 of 18 June 2004 on the financing of the Operation and its subsequent resolutions thereon, the latest of which was resolution 60/17 A of 23 November 2005,

Recalling further its resolution 58/315 of 1 July 2004,

Reaffirming the general principles underlying the financing of United Nations peacekeeping operations, as stated in its resolutions 1874(S-IV) of 27 June 1963, 3101(XXVIII) of 11 December 1973 and 55/235 of 23 December 2000,

Mindful of the fact that it is essential to provide the Operation with the necessary financial resources to enable it to fulfil its responsibilities under the relevant resolutions of the Security Council,

1. *Requests* the Secretary-General to entrust the Head of Mission with the task of formulating future budget proposals in full accordance with the provisions of its resolutions 59/296 of 22 June 2005 and 60/266 of 30 June 2006, as well as other relevant resolutions;

2. *Takes note* of the status of contributions to the United Nations Operation in Côte d'Ivoire as at 30 April 2006, including the contributions outstanding in the amount of 80.7 million United States dollars, representing some 9 per cent of the total assessed contributions, notes with concern that only twenty-eight Member States have paid their assessed contributions in full, and urges all other Member States, in particular those in arrears, to ensure payment of their outstanding assessed contributions;

3. *Expresses its appreciation* to those Member States which have paid their assessed contributions in full, and urges all other Member States to make every possible effort to ensure payment of their assessed contributions to the Operation in full;

4. *Expresses concern* at the financial situation with regard to peacekeeping activities, in particular as regards the reimbursements to troop contributors that bear additional burdens owing to overdue payments by Member States of their assessments;

5. *Also expresses concern* at the delay experienced by the Secretary-General in deploying and providing adequate resources to some recent peacekeeping missions, in particular those in Africa;

6. *Emphasizes* that all future and existing peacekeeping missions shall be given equal and non-discriminatory treatment in respect of financial and administrative arrangements;

7. *Also emphasizes* that all peacekeeping missions shall be provided with adequate resources for the effective and efficient discharge of their respective mandates;

8. *Reiterates its request* to the Secretary-General to make the fullest possible use of facilities and equipment at the United Nations Logistics Base at Brindisi, Italy, in order to minimize the costs of procurement for the Operation;

9. *Endorses* the conclusions and recommendations contained in the report of the Advisory Committee on Administrative and Budgetary Questions, and requests the Secretary-General to ensure their full implementation;

10. *Requests* the Secretary-General to ensure the full implementation of the relevant provisions of its resolutions 59/296 and 60/266;

11. *Looks forward* to the consideration of the comprehensive report requested in section VIII, paragraph 3, of its resolution 60/266;

12. *Requests* the Secretary-General to ensure that quick-impact projects are implemented in compliance with the original intent of such projects and relevant General Assembly resolutions;

13. *Decides* to approve the resources requested for quick-impact projects in the proposed budget for the Operation for the period from 1 July 2006 to 30 June 2007, in the interim;

14. *Requests* the Secretary-General to ensure the full implementation of the quick-impact projects in the financial period from 1 July 2006 to 30 June 2007;

15. *Also requests* the Secretary-General to take all necessary action to ensure that the Operation is administered with a maximum of efficiency and economy;

16. *Further requests* the Secretary-General, in order to reduce the cost of employing General Service staff, to continue efforts to recruit local staff for the Operation against General Service posts, commensurate with the requirements of the Operation;

Financial performance report for the period from 1 July 2004 to 30 June 2005

17. *Takes note* of the report of the Secretary-General on the financial performance of the Operation for the period from 1 July 2004 to 30 June 2005;

Budget estimates for the period from 1 July 2006 to 30 June 2007

18. *Decides* to appropriate to the Special Account for the United Nations Operation in Côte d'Ivoire the amount of 438,366,800 dollars for the period from 1 July 2006 to 30 June 2007, inclusive of 420,175,200 dollars for the maintenance of the Operation, 15,025,600 dollars for the support account for peacekeeping operations and 3,166,000 dollars for the United Nations Logistics Base;

Financing of the appropriation

19. *Decides also* to apportion among Member States the amount of 200,328,914 dollars for the period from 1 July to 15 December 2006, in accordance with the levels updated in General Assembly resolution 58/256 of 23 December 2003, and taking into account the scale of assessments for 2006, as set out in its resolution 58/1 B of 23 December 2003;

20. *Decides further* that, in accordance with the provisions of its resolution 973(X) of 15 December 1955, there shall be set off against the apportionment among Member States, as provided for in paragraph 19 above, their respective share in the Tax Equalization Fund of 4,483,156 dollars, comprising the estimated staff assessment income of 3,601,258 dollars approved for the Operation, the prorated share of 772,403 dollars of the estimated staff assessment income approved for the support account and the prorated share of 109,495 dollars of the estimated staff assessment income approved for the United Nations Logistics Base;

21. *Decides* to apportion among Member States the amount of 238,037,886 dollars at a monthly rate of 36,530,566 dollars for the period from 16 December 2006 to 30 June 2007, in accordance with the levels updated in its resolution 58/256, and taking into account the scale of assessments for 2006, as set out in its resolution 58/1 B, and the scale of assessments for 2007, subject to a decision of the Security Council to extend the mandate of the Operation;

22. *Decides also* that, in accordance with the provisions of its resolution 973 (X), there shall be set off against the apportionment among Member States, as provided for in paragraph 21 above, their respective share in the Tax Equalization Fund of 5,327,044 dollars, comprising the estimated staff assessment income of 4,279,142 dollars approved for the Operation, the prorated share of 917,797 dollars of the estimated staff assessment income approved for the support account and the prorated share of 130,105 dollars of the estimated staff assessment income approved for the United Nations Logistics Base;

23. *Decides further* that, for Member States that have fulfilled their financial obligations to the Operation, there shall be set off against their apportionment, as provided for in paragraph 19 above, their respective share of the unencumbered balance and other income in the total amount of 57,385,300 dollars in respect of the financial period ended 30 June 2005, in accordance with the levels updated in its resolution 58/256, and taking into account the scale of assessments for 2005, as set out in its resolution 58/1 B;

24. *Decides* that, for Member States that have not fulfilled their financial obligations to the Operation, there shall be set off against their outstanding obligations their respective share of the unencumbered balance and other income in the total amount of 57,385,300 dollars in respect of the financial period ended 30 June 2005, in accordance with the scheme set out in paragraph 23 above;

25. *Decides also* that the decrease of 1,436,900 dollars in the estimated staff assessment income in respect of the financial period ended 30 June 2005 shall be set off against the credits from the amount of 57,385,300 dollars referred to in paragraphs 23 and 24 above;

26. *Emphasizes* that no peacekeeping mission shall be financed by borrowing funds from other active peacekeeping missions;

27. *Encourages* the Secretary-General to continue to take additional measures to ensure the safety and security of all personnel under the auspices of the United Nations participating in the Operation, bearing in mind paragraphs 5 and 6 of Security Council resolution 1502(2003) of 26 August 2003;

28. *Invites* voluntary contributions to the Operation in cash and in the form of services and supplies acceptable to the Secretary-General, to be administered, as appropriate, in accordance with the procedure and practices established by the General Assembly;

29. *Decides* to include in the provisional agenda of its sixty-first session the item entitled "Financing of the United Nations Operation in Côte d'Ivoire".

On 26 September [A/61/468], the Secretary-General submitted a revised budget amounting to $472,889,300, including an increase of $52,714,100 to accommodate the increase in UNOCI strength, authorized by the Security Council in resolution 1682(2006) (see p. 188). In its October report [A/61/551], ACABQ recommended approval of the full amount proposed by the Secretary-General for the period from 1 July 2006 to 30 June 2007.

On 22 December [meeting 84], the General Assembly, on the recommendation of the Fifth Committee [A/61/621], adopted **resolution 61/247 A** without vote [agenda item 134].

Financing of the United Nations Operation in Côte d'Ivoire

The General Assembly,

Having considered the report of the Secretary-General on the financing of the United Nations Operation in Côte d'Ivoire and the related report of the Advisory Committee on Administrative and Budgetary Questions,

Recalling Security Council resolution 1528(2004) of 27 February 2004, by which the Council established the United Nations Operation in Côte d'Ivoire for an initial period of twelve months as from 4 April 2004, the subsequent resolutions by which the Council extended the mandate of the Operation, the latest of which was resolution 1652(2006) of 24 January 2006, and resolution 1682(2006) of 2 June 2006, in which the Council authorized an increase in the strength of the Operation of up to 1,500 additional personnel, by a maximum of 1,025 military and 475 civilian police personnel,

Recalling also its resolution 58/310 of 18 June 2004 on the financing of the Operation and its subsequent resolutions thereon, the latest of which was resolution 60/17 B of 30 June 2006,

Reaffirming the general principles underlying the financing of United Nations peacekeeping operations, as stated in its resolutions 1874 (S-IV) of 27 June 1963, 3101(XXVIII) of 11 December 1973 and 55/235 of 23 December 2000,

Mindful of the fact that it is essential to provide the Operation with the necessary financial resources to enable it to fulfil its responsibilities under the relevant resolutions of the Security Council,

1. *Requests* the Secretary-General to entrust the Head of Mission with the task of formulating future budget proposals in full accordance with the provisions of its resolutions 59/296 of 22 June 2005 and 60/266 of 30 June 2006, as well as other relevant resolutions;

2. *Takes note* of the status of contributions to the United Nations Operation in Côte d'Ivoire as at 30 September 2006, including the contributions outstanding in the amount of 186.6 million United States dollars, representing some 17 per cent of the total assessed contributions, notes with concern that only thirty Member States have paid their assessed contributions in full, and urges all other Member States, in particular those in arrears, to ensure payment of their outstanding assessed contributions;

3. *Expresses its appreciation* to those Member States which have paid their assessed contributions in full, and urges all other Member States to make every possible effort to ensure payment of their assessed contributions to the Operation in full;

4. *Expresses concern* at the financial situation with regard to peacekeeping activities, in particular as regards the reimbursements to troop contributors that bear additional burdens owing to overdue payments by Member States of their assessments;

5. *Also expresses concern* at the delay experienced by the Secretary-General in deploying and providing adequate resources to some recent peacekeeping missions, in particular those in Africa;

6. *Emphasizes* that all future and existing peacekeeping missions shall be given equal and non-discriminatory treatment in respect of financial and administrative arrangements;

7. *Also emphasizes* that all peacekeeping missions shall be provided with adequate resources for the effective and efficient discharge of their respective mandates;

8. *Reiterates its request* to the Secretary-General to make the fullest possible use of facilities and equipment at the United Nations Logistics Base at Brindisi, Italy, in order to minimize the costs of procurement for the Operation;

9. *Endorses* the conclusions and recommendations contained in the report of the Advisory Committee on Administrative and Budgetary Questions, and requests the Secretary-General to ensure their full implementation;

10. *Reaffirms* its resolution 59/296, and requests the Secretary-General to ensure the full implementation of its relevant provisions and the relevant provisions of its resolution 60/266;

11. *Requests* the Secretary-General to take all necessary action to ensure that the Operation is administered with a maximum of efficiency and economy;

12. *Also requests* the Secretary-General, in order to reduce the cost of employing General Service staff, to continue efforts to recruit local staff for the Operation against General Service posts, commensurate with the requirements of the Operation;

Revised budget estimates for the period from 1 July 2006 to 30 June 2007

13. *Decides* to appropriate to the Special Account for the United Nations Operation in Côte d'Ivoire the amount of 52,714,100 dollars for the maintenance of the Operation for the period from 1 July 2006 to 30 June 2007, in addition to the amount of 438,366,800 dollars already appropriated for the same period under the terms of its resolution 60/17 B;

Financing of the appropriation

14. *Decides also*, taking into account the amount of 438,366,800 dollars previously apportioned for the period from 1 July 2006 to 30 June 2007 under the terms of its resolution 60/17 B, to apportion among Member States the additional amount of 24,089,777 dollars for the period from 1 July to 15 December 2006, in accordance with the levels updated in its resolution 58/256 of 23 December 2003, and taking into account the scale of assessments for 2006, as set out in its resolution 58/1 B of 23 December 2003;

15. *Decides further* that, in accordance with the provisions of its resolution 973 (X) of 15 December 1955, there shall be set off against the apportionment among Member States, as provided for in paragraph 14 above, their respective share in the Tax Equalization Fund of 63,842 dollars, representing the estimated increase in staff assessment income approved for the Operation for the period from 1 July to 15 December 2006;

16. *Decides* to apportion among Member States the additional amount of 28,624,323 dollars at a monthly rate of 4,403,742 dollars for the period from 16 December 2006 to 30 June 2007, in accordance with the levels updated in its resolutions 58/256 of 23 December 2003 and 61/243 of 22 December 2006, and taking into account the scale of assessments for 2006, as set out in its resolution 58/1 B, and the scale of assessments for 2007, as set out in its resolution 61/237 of 22 December 2006, subject to a decision of the Security Council to extend the mandate of the Operation;

17. *Decides also* that, in accordance with the provisions of its resolution 973 (X), there shall be set off against the apportionment among Member States, as provided for in paragraph 16 above, their respective share in the Tax Equalization Fund of the amount of 75,858 dollars, representing the estimated increase in staff assessment income approved for the Operation for the period from 16 December 2006 to 30 June 2007;

18. *Emphasizes* that no peacekeeping mission shall be financed by borrowing funds from other active peacekeeping missions;

19. *Encourages* the Secretary-General to continue to take additional measures to ensure the safety and security of all personnel under the auspices of the United Nations participating in the Operation, bearing in mind paragraphs 5 and 6 of Security Council resolution 1502(2003) of 26 August 2003;

20. *Invites* voluntary contributions to the Operation in cash and in the form of services and supplies acceptable to the Secretary-General, to be administered, as appro-

priate, in accordance with the procedure and practices established by the General Assembly;

21. *Decides* to keep under review during its sixty-first session the item entitled "Financing of the United Nations Operation in Côte d'Ivoire".

On 22 December, by **decision 61/552**, the General Assembly deferred consideration of the item on "Financing of the United Nations Operation in Côte d'Ivoire" until its resumed sixty-first (2007) session.

Liberia

In 2006, Liberia's return to political stability and democratic governance was marked by two significant events— the inauguration of Ellen Johnson-Sirleaf as President, and the installation of a new Government, thereby completing the two-year transitional process stipulated in the 2003 Comprehensive Peace Agreement. Nevertheless, Liberia still faced significant challenges in laying the foundation for a future built on sustainable peace, stability, democracy and rule of law. President Johnson-Sirleaf immediately began addressing issues of corruption and governance reform and enacted measures to enhance transparency and accountability in the Government, including the passage of forestry reform legislation, which led to the lifting of timber sanctions. With the assistance of the United Nations Mission in Liberia (UNMIL), the Economic Community of West African States and other regional and international actors, Liberia made progress in several areas, including the consolidation of peace and promotion of national reconciliation; the resettlement of refugees and internally displaced persons; security sector reform; the launch of the Truth and Reconciliation Commission; the fight against corruption; and the launch of the Governance and Economic Management Assistance Programme.

The Panel of Experts established to assess the implementation, impact and effectiveness of the arms, travel, diamond and timber sanctions imposed on Liberia, indicated that the assets freeze had not been implemented and that it was not aware of any travel ban violations in Liberia. Timber sanctions had been effective, but the illegal domestic industry continued. While considerable progress was made in meeting the requirements for lifting diamond sanctions, several important steps still needed to be taken. The Panel found that financial administration in Liberia had improved since the installation of the new Government and recommended continued vigilance to ensure that revenues directly benefited Liberians and would not be used to support conflict. In June, the Security Council lifted the sanctions on timber and adjusted the arms embargo to allow for the equipping and training of Liberia's police and security officers. In December, the Council renewed the travel ban and extended the arms sanctions for a further 12 months and the diamond measures for six months.

Former President Charles Taylor was apprehended by UNMIL, while making his escape from Nigeria, where he had been in exile, and handed over to the Special Court for Sierra Leone and transferred to The Hague, where he would stand trial for war crimes and other serious violations of humanitarian law.

An interdepartmental mission, led by the United Nations Department of Peacekeeping Operations, reviewed UNMIL mandate in the light of developments in Liberia and concluded that, although UNMIL had completed its initial core responsibilities, critical tasks remained in order to safeguard the progress already achieved. The mission proposed that there be a two-year consolidation phase, during which UNMIL would continue to support the Government. It established benchmarks for the future drawdown of the UNMIL military personnel. In September, the Security Council extended UNMIL mandate until 31 March 2007.

Implementation of Comprehensive Peace Agreement and UNMIL activities

On 16 January [SG/SM/10302], the Secretary-General congratulated Ellen Johnson-Sirleaf on her inauguration as the President of the Republic of Liberia, and Africa's first elected woman Head of State. He acknowledged that, while the establishment of a democratically elected Government in the country marked the successful completion of the two-year transitional period stipulated in the 2003 Accra Comprehensive Peace Agreement [YUN 2003, p. 192], several challenges faced the new Government, including restructuring the security sector; stimulating economic growth; consolidating State authority throughout the country; re-establishing basic services; and strengthening economic governance, the rule of law and the protection of human rights. Assuring the Government of the continued support of the United Nations, he called on the international community to assist Liberia as it laid the foundation for a better future.

Report of Secretary-General (March). In his March progress report on the United Nations Mission in Liberia (UNMIL) [S/2006/159], the Secretary-General provided recommendations on a drawdown plan for the Mission and an update on developments since his 2005 December report

[YUN 2005, p. 267]. He said that completion of the transitional process and the handover of power to the new Government dominated political activity in Liberia. On 16 January, Ellen Johnson-Sirleaf, who was sworn into office as President, identified, in her inaugural address, national reconciliation, political inclusion, sustainable development and economic governance reforms as the key priorities of her administration. Promising to address corruption, she announced that all persons appointed to high office would be required to declare their personal assets. On 28 January, she ordered all National Transitional Government political appointees to resign. Two days later, she ordered an audit of the Transitional Government and requested transitional officials to seek permission before travelling overseas, pending the outcome of the audit. In other initiatives to enhance transparency, the President declared null and void a contract between the Liberian National Port Authority and Global Seals System, as well as all forestry concessions granted to timber companies under the former administration. Under the Governance and Economic Management Assistance Programme, an international financial expert assumed the post of Chief Administrator at the Central Bank of Liberia on 5 February, while international financial controllers for Liberia's state-owned enterprises, as well as international concessions and budget experts for the Ministry of Lands, Mines and Energy and the Bureau of the Budget were being recruited. In welcoming the Programme, the President called upon donors to develop integrated capacity-building mechanisms to facilitate eventual Liberian ownership of it. The dividends from tighter control of Government revenue were becoming evident, as revenue inflow to the Ministry of Finance was higher in January 2006 than at the same time a year earlier.

On 17 January, the President began announcing nominees to Cabinet, Supreme Court and other key positions. As at 1 March, the Senate had confirmed 47 of the 200 nominees. Nominations to Cabinet posts were not without controversy. On 12 February, the opposition Congress for Democratic Change challenged the President's nominations for the positions of Minister of Justice and Chairperson of the National Elections Commission. Those nominations were reviewed by the Senate.

The security situation in Liberia remained fragile. Disgruntled former armed forces personnel continued to challenge the restructuring of the armed forces. On 14 January, after repeated orders from the Transitional Government, former soldiers finally vacated Camp Shiefflin, the proposed training site for the new army, but left several buildings stripped and roofless. Meanwhile, widows of former soldiers protested the non-payment of allowances and pensions, and members of the disbanded Anti-Terrorist Unit—a militia group established by former President Charles Taylor—protested their exclusion from the security sector reform programme, as well as the unpaid salary arrears. Moreover, various groups and human rights organizations continued to call on President Johnson-Sirleaf to request the Government of Nigeria to transfer former President Charles Taylor, who was in exile there, to the Special Court for Sierra Leone where he was under indictment for war crimes.

The volatile conflict situation in neighbouring Côte d'Ivoire remained a security concern due to the movement of armed groups across the border; the recruitment of former Liberian combatants, including children; and the risk of a surge of Ivorians seeking refuge in Liberia due to escalating violence in their country. UNMIL conducted air and ground patrols in border areas and the Government established a joint task force with UNMIL to investigate cases of recruitment of Liberians. One individual was arrested in January on suspicion of recruiting Liberians to fight in Côte d'Ivoire.

Assessment mission. In the light of developments in Liberia, a UN Secretariat interdepartmental mission, led by the Department of Peacekeeping Operations (DPKO), conducted a comprehensive review of UNMIL (3-15 February) to assess the status of implementation of all aspects of its mandate, with a view to making recommendations for the Mission's future direction. It also analysed the security situation in the country, reviewed the Government's priorities and action plan, surveyed views on UNMIL future role and determined the required adjustments to UNMIL mandate, size and configuration for the post-transition phase.

The assessment mission concluded that UNMIL had completed many aspects of its initial mandate and made substantial progress in implementing several remaining key tasks. However, while the overwhelming presence of 15,000 UN military personnel and 1,115 police personnel had provided the security environment for the successful implementation of the Comprehensive Peace Agreement, the security situation in Liberia and neighbouring countries remained fragile and key unfinished tasks needed to be urgently completed in order to ensure sustainable peace and stability. UNMIL had disarmed 101,495 combatants, of which approximately 65,000 had benefited from reintegration and rehabilitation opportunities and 37,000 were awaiting placement in reintegration programmes. The Mission collected and destroyed some 28,000 weapons, 34,000 unexploded ordnance and 6.5 million rounds of small arms ammunition. Progress was made in police reform, with UNMIL having trained 1,442 of the 3,500 Liberian National Police required, as well as 513 police in specialty areas. Shortfalls in funding, however, impeded the restructuring process and the Police still needed basic equipment, uniforms, arms, ammunition, vehicles and communication equipment. Reform of the armed forces continued, with the launch of a joint Government/United States recruitment and restructuring programme on 18 January. The new army would be made up of 2,000 military personnel.

UNMIL also facilitated the return of over 2,200 Government officials to the counties, but the poor condition of Government structures, lack of basic services and irregular payment of civil servant salaries had slowed progress in the extension of State authority, which remained limited in most parts of the country. In the area of human rights, national conciliation and justice, progress was made with the launch of the Truth and Reconciliation Commission on 20 February. New laws were enacted, including on rape. The lack of State control over Liberia's natural resources continued to be a source of instability, with the illegal occupation and exploitation of rubber plantations, and a large number of ex-combatants and unemployed youth engaged in illegal diamond and gold mining. Progress was made toward meeting the conditions to join the Kimberley Process Certification Scheme [YUN 2003, p. 55], but funds to support those efforts were lacking. With the support of UNMIL and the Liberia Forestry Initiative, advances were achieved by the Forestry Development Authority in meeting conditions for the lifting of timber sanctions. The President ordered the establishment of a Forestry Reform Monitoring Committee.

The Government informed the assessment mission of its agenda for the reconstruction of Liberia, which encompassed both a short-term (150 days) and long-term (1,000 days) plan, based on four priority areas: security; economic revitalization; basic services and infrastructure; and the rule of law and good governance. The proposed 150-day action plan focused on "quick win" projects, such as partial restoration of electricity, the repair of roads and the rehabilitation of Government infrastructure. The Liberia Reconstruction and Development Committee, chaired by the President, was established to coordinate those activities.

The assessment mission observed that several critical tasks urgently needed to be completed to sustain peace and stability in the country. The assessment mission, the Government, UNMIL, the UN country team and international partners agreed that a two-year consolidation phase was required, during which UNMIL would focus on an adjusted mandate. UNMIL priority tasks would include: maintaining a secure environment, facilitating the return and resettlement of refugees and internally displaced persons, accelerating the training and development of the Liberian National Police and demobilizing the former police, supporting the Government in building the capacity of State institutions, completing the reintegration programme for ex-combatants, restructuring the armed forces, consolidating State authority country-wide, meeting the conditions for lifting the diamond and timber sanctions, rebuilding the culture of human rights and respect for the rule of law, strengthening the capacity of judicial institutions and implementing the Governance and Economic Management Assistance Programme and other initiatives to ensure the collection and utilization of national revenues for the public good.

There was a consensus that a significant UN presence was needed to guarantee peace and stability during the consolidation period, and therefore, it was too early for a major drawdown of UNMIL. After conducting a troop-to-task analysis, the assessment mission recommended reducing UNMIL military component by two infantry battalions, one in mid-2006 and another in early 2007. Troop strength would be reduced by 250 troops by 31 March 2006. The assessment mission also recommended the deployment of an additional formed police unit for UNMIL, so as to give the Liberian Police Support Unit more time to develop the experience required to eventually assume those responsibilities currently performed by UNMIL. Following those adjustments to its military and police strength, UNMIL would commence its drawdown, beginning in early 2007, security conditions permitting.

The Secretary-General recommended the extension of UNMIL mandate for one year until 31 March 2007, and the approval of the proposed adjustments to UNMIL military troop capacity, police strength and revised mandate. He would submit a timetable for a calibrated drawdown of UNMIL, with specific benchmarks and timelines.

Security Council consideration (March). On 17 March [meeting 5389], President Johnson-Sirleaf presented the Government's strategy for peacebuilding to the Security Council and indicated that she would personally lead the Liberia Reconstruction and Development Committee, established to coordinate the reconstruction effort. She cited reform mechanisms that had been enacted in the diamond and timber sectors to enable the lifting of sanctions and to enhance transparency in governance. In addition to the establishment of the Truth and Reconciliation Commission to address issues such as impunity and national reconciliation, the Supreme Court had been reconstituted to start the reform of the judiciary. Concerning former President Charles Taylor, who was in exile in Nigeria, President Johnson-Sirleaf said that she had asked President Obasanjo of Nigeria to consult with colleagues in the subregion and the international community on the resolution of the matter. In closing, she emphasized that Liberia was a fragile State, and as security sector reform was not complete, she urged the Council to maintain its support for UNMIL. She also appealed for urgent donor contributions for Liberia's recovery and development agenda, including debt relief.

On 24 March [meeting 5395], the Council met in private with UNMIL troop-contributing countries and heard a briefing by the Special Representative of the Secretary-General for Liberia, Alan Doss (United Kingdom).

Arrest and transfer of Charles Taylor. On 25 March, Nigerian President Obasanjo officially informed President Johnson-Sirleaf that, pursuant to her request, and following consultations with African leaders, the Government of Nigeria would release Charles Taylor to the custody of the Government of Liberia. On 28 March, the Nigerian Government announced that Mr. Taylor had absconded from his official residence, but was subsequently apprehended the following day and flown to the Liberian capital, Monrovia. In accordance with Security Council resolution 1638(2005) [YUN 2005, p. 267], Mr. Taylor was promptly apprehended and detained by UNMIL and handed over to the Special Court for Sierra Leone in Freetown to be tried for war crimes, crimes against humanity and other serious violations of international humanitarian law in Sierra Leone.

On 16 June, the Security Council, determining that ex-President Taylor's presence in the West African subregion was an impediment to stability and a threat to peace in Liberia and Sierra Leone, took note, in **resolution 1688(2006)**, (see p. 242) of the intention of the Freetown-based Special Court for Sierra Leone to move Mr. Taylor's trial to The Hague, at the premises of the International Criminal Court.

Mr Taylor was transferred to The Hague on 20 June.

SECURITY COUNCIL ACTION

On 31 March [meeting 5406], the Security Council unanimously adopted **resolution 1667(2006)**. The draft [S/2006/202] was prepared in consultations among Council members.

The Security Council,

Recalling its previous resolutions and the statements by its President concerning the situation in Liberia and the subregion, in particular resolutions 1626(2005) of 19 September 2005 and 1638(2005) of 11 November 2005,

Welcoming the report of the Secretary-General of 14 March 2006,

Welcoming also the inauguration of President Ellen Johnson-Sirleaf and the installation of the newly elected Government of Liberia,

Emphasizing that significant challenges remain in completing the reintegration and repatriation of ex-combatants and the restructuring of the Liberian security sector, as well as maintaining stability in Liberia and the subregion,

Expressing its appreciation for the continuing support of the Economic Community of West African States and the African Union for the Liberian peace process, as well as for financial and other assistance provided by the international community,

Welcoming the transfer of former President Charles Taylor to the custody of the Special Court for Sierra Leone, and renewing its expression of appreciation to Nigeria and its President, Mr. Olusegun Obasanjo, for providing for the temporary stay in Nigeria of former President Taylor,

Determining that the situation in Liberia continues to constitute a threat to international peace and security in the region,

Acting under Chapter VII of the Charter of the United Nations,

1. *Decides* that the mandate of the United Nations Mission in Liberia shall be extended until 30 September 2006;
2. *Decides also* to extend the provisions of paragraph 6 of resolution 1626(2005) for the period specified in paragraph 1 above;
3. *Reaffirms its intention* to authorize the Secretary-General to redeploy troops between the Mission and the United Nations Operation in Côte d'Ivoire on a temporary basis in accordance with the provisions of resolution 1609(2005) of 24 June 2005, as may be needed;
4. *Takes note* of the letter dated 22 March 2006 from the Secretary-General addressed to the President of the Security Council, and expresses its determination to review the tasks and the troop level of the United Nations Operation in Côte d'Ivoire by the end of April 2006, with a view to a decision on its reinforcement;
5. *Requests* the Secretary-General to review his recommendations for a drawdown plan for the Mission and to present further recommendations in his next regular report to the Security Council on the progress of the Mission in the implementation of its mandate;
6. *Decides* to remain actively seized of the matter.

Report of Secretary-General (June). In his June progress report on UNMIL [S/2006/376], the Secretary-General said that the transfer of former Liberian

President Charles Taylor to the Special Court for Sierra Leone had elicited mixed reactions from the Liberian public. Some believed that he should be tried immediately to demonstrate that impunity would not be tolerated, while others argued that he should have been left in Nigeria, as his trial could disrupt the Liberian national reconciliation process and destabilize the country and the subregion. On 30 March, President Johnson-Sirleaf urged the Security Council to adopt a resolution that would allow Mr. Taylor's trial before the Special Court for Sierra Leone to take place in The Hague, Netherlands.

In other political developments, the Liberian President undertook assessment visits to all 15 counties in Liberia from February to May and consulted with county officials and leaders on the challenges facing their communities, including poor roads, inadequate health and education facilities and the lack of office and residential accommodation for Government officials. Meanwhile, Senate confirmation hearings for high level officials continued. On 30 March, 21 cabinet ministers, along with their deputy and assistant ministers, the chairman and the commissioners of the National Elections Commission and the President's nominees to several Government agencies and parastatals were sworn into office, rendering the three branches of Government fully functioning. In addition, as at 1 June, all 15 county superintendents had been confirmed by the Senate.

However, several issues, such as the payment of benefits for legislators, the release by a Supreme Court associate justice of two imprisoned ministers the day after their sentencing by the Senate for contempt of the Legislature, and claims that the President had failed to consult with the Legislature on the transfer of Mr. Taylor to the Special Court for Sierra Leone, created tensions between the executive and legislative branches of the Government. To improve relations, the President appointed a senior Government official to act as liaison between the two branches. As part of efforts to address the issues of governance and corruption, President Johnson-Sirleaf, by executive order, extended the life of the Governance Reform Commission and redefined its mandate to include preparation of an anti-corruption strategy and a code of conduct for public servants.

With regard to security matters, UNMIL launched Operation Kilbride to address the security concerns raised by Mr. Taylor's transfer to the Special Court for Sierra Leone. The security measures introduced, including robust patrolling within Monrovia, deployment of the UNMIL Quick Reaction Force in border areas not covered by the Mission and an increase of UNMIL troop presence in Mr. Taylor's former strongholds, were intended to reassure the populace, send a message of the Mission's resolve to maintain peace and stability in the country and deter potential spoilers. Nevertheless, the security situation was marred by various incidents. Demobilized armed forces personnel staged several violent street demonstrations, the most serious occurring on 25 April, when approximately 400 ex-army personnel blockaded three roads leading to the Ministry of National Defense. Tires and military checkpoints were set on fire and UNMIL troops were attacked, as well as personnel of the Liberian Police Support Unit who were protecting the Ministry. In response to the incident, the Government made arrangements for the payment of severance pay and other arrears, and announced measures to deal with public disorder, which included the arrest and prosecution of the instigators or leaders of the attack, as well as those who had destroyed property; a ban against a demonstration by civil servants scheduled for the following day, 26 April; a temporary ban on the sale of petroleum in glass bottles; and a ban on the carrying of cutlasses and machetes during the night, as those weapons were usually used to attack citizens in their homes. The illegal occupation by former combatants of rubber plantations remained a threat to stability, as some former commanders of the disbanded warring factions continued to organize the illegal exploitation of the plantations and operate criminal groups there. Other security risks included disputes over land and other property, as refugees, internally displaced persons and ex-combatants returned to their communities, and the unstable situation in neighbouring Côte d'Ivoire.

UNMIL continued to assist Liberia in its recovery, rehabilitation and development efforts. In the area of security sector reform, progress was made in restructuring the Liberian National Police. The target of 3,500 fully trained police personnel was expected to be completed by July 2007. The Government appointed a new Director of Police and several deputy and assistant directors. Nonetheless, basic and specialized training programmes for the police were still inadequately funded, with a shortfall of some $1.6 million, and operations continued to be hampered by the lack of equipment, uniforms, weapons and vehicles.

The recruitment drive for the armed forces was ongoing, with 1,776 of 4,265 applicants having passed the initial screening as at 1 June. The report of a United States-funded security sector review, conducted by the RAND Corporation, was presented to the Government and would form the basis of a national dialogue on security sector reform.

The Government intensified efforts to regain control over the exploitation of the country's natural resources. On 23 May, a joint Government/UN task force established to assess Liberia's rubber plantations submitted its report to the President, which contained recommendations for ending the use of forced and child labour and for halting the illegal trafficking of raw rubber, including the repossession of illegally occupied plantations, review of concession and management agreements and the establishment of interim management teams. The Forestry Reform Management Monitoring Committee, established in February, reviewed new proposals for the allocation of forestry concessions and contracts and the establishment of a forestry strategic management plan.

Other UNMIL activities included facilitating the return of Government officials to their duty stations; providing transportation to customs, excise, immigration and naturalization officers to enable them to monitor revenue collection points and border crossings; assisting the Government in deploying mineral inspectors to diamond-mining areas, setting up Kimberley Process Certification Scheme offices and carrying out diamond-mining area surveillance and inspections; operating joint UNMIL/Forestry Development Authority checkpoints to ensure adherence to new pit-sawing policy; supporting the Truth and Reconciliation Commission's public outreach programme; advising the Government on engaging national prosecutorial consultants to reduce the backlog of pending criminal cases; rehabilitating or repairing more than 2,500 kilometres of unpaved roads; carrying out community-level broadcasts and increasing its programming on Government activities; and assisting the Government in the implementation of its 150-day action plan to address the most basic needs of the population.

The resettlement of internally displaced persons was completed, with some 312,015 persons having been assisted. As at 18 May, a total of 266,059 refugees had returned to Liberia, with another 169,525 registered refugees remaining in other West African countries.

On the drawdown of UNMIL, the Secretary-General indicated that progress made in security sector reform and restructuring should constitute the key security benchmark to determine the pace of that process. Given the relative stability in the country and based on the detailed assessment in his March report (see p. 212), he recommended that the first military component infantry battalion be withdrawn during the latter part of 2006, subject to the continued stability of the security situation. Details of the adjustment would be provided in his next report and further adjustments, including the withdrawal of the second infantry battalion in early 2007, would be considered as the situation permitted.

In view of the ongoing police reform and restructuring programme and the critical role of UNMIL formed police units in supporting the Liberian National Police in addressing recurrent violent demonstrations, the Secretary-General concluded that the security situation did not permit a drawdown of the UNMIL police component. He reiterated his March recommendation for the deployment of an additional formed police unit to enhance UNMIL capacity to respond effectively to public unrest and other security threats that could arise.

SECURITY COUNCIL ACTION

On 13 July [meeting 5487], the Security Council unanimously adopted **resolution 1694(2006)**. The draft [S/2006/509] was submitted by the United States.

The Security Council,

Recalling its previous resolutions and the statements by its President, including resolution 1667(2006) of 31 March 2006,

Noting that, in his report of 14 March 2006 the Secretary-General recommended, inter alia, changes to the configuration of the United Nations Mission in Liberia, in view of the completion by the Mission of a number of tasks, and in the context of a review of the appropriate mandates for and composition of the Mission, and that, in his report of 9 June 2006, he reiterated his recommendation for the addition of a formed police unit,

Determining that the situation in Liberia continues to constitute a threat to international peace and security,

Acting under Chapter VII of the Charter of the United Nations,

1. *Decides* to increase the authorized size of the civilian police component of the United Nations Mission in Liberia by 125 and to decrease the authorized size of the military component of the Mission by 125, from the current authorized levels;

2. *Decides also* to remain actively seized of the matter.

Further peace process developments

Report of Secretary-General (September). In his September report on UNMIL [S/2006/743], the Secretary-General said that he had visited Liberia from 3 to 5 July and was reassured by the progress made, notwithstanding the country's economic and financial limitations. In August, the Legislature passed and President Johnson-Sirleaf signed into law the Government's first national budget for the fiscal period 2006-2007, based on revenue projections of $129.9 million. The President continued the anti-corruption campaign, dismissing a number of senior Government officials for corruption and terminating the appointments of three revenue collectors, a senior economist and a supervisor of the foreign travel section for financial improprieties. She reconstituted the task force on recovery of public assets, and instructed the Ministry of Justice to conclude action on the audit reports of different Government entities and identify, for the purpose of prosecution, individuals who had abused the public trust. In July, the Government released the long-awaited ECOWAS report on economic crime in Liberia, prepared during the tenure of the National Transitional Government [YUN 2005, p. 262]. In the report, recommendations were made for the immediate dismissal of four former senior officials of that Government for misappropriation and mismanagement of public funds. Civil society groups called for the prosecution of the individuals so named. On 20 August, the Cabinet approved a draft anti-corruption policy paper prepared by the Governance Reform Commission, which set out a framework for tackling impunity and promoting a system of accountability and public integrity. The Commission also submitted a draft code of conduct and declaration of income, assets and liabilities form for public servants.

The overall security situation remained calm but fragile. While the transfer of Mr. Taylor's trial from the region had reduced tensions considerably, the activities of his associates and supporters remained a concern. Demobilized personnel from the former armed forces, national police and special security services staged demonstrations to demand severance payments and other benefits. Some of the demands were met, but many of them had limited access to employment opportunities and were susceptible to manipulation by various interest groups. Incidents of armed robbery within Monrovia and its environs increased, leading to calls by the public for arming the Liberian National Police and adopting more extensive security measures. Armed robberies and killings were reported also at the Cocopa and Guthrie rubber plantations. UNMIL police, in cooperation with the Liberian National Police, increased their patrol in high crime areas in Monrovia, including night patrols, as well as in Cocopa and other rubber plantations. On 15 August, with UNMIL assistance, the Government officially re-established control over the Guthrie rubber plantation and efforts instituted interim management teams at abandoned or contested plantations, as recommended by the joint Government/UNMIL task force on rubber plantations. Concerns over the security of President Johnson-Sirleaf arose on 26 July, when a fire broke out in the Executive Mansion, causing extensive damage, as well as in August, when shooting incidents occurred in Monrovia involving officials of the Special Security Service, which provided close protection to the President. No one was injured in the fire and an investigation, conducted with the assistance of UNMIL and South African forensic experts, attributed its cause to an electrical fault. Three separate shootings on 3, 5 and 8 August took place at the residence of the Director of the Special Security Service, with one resulting in the death of the Director's personal bodyguard.

The programme for the establishment of a new police service was on course, with 2,073 Liberian National Police, 392 Special Security Services and 155 Seaport Police officers having been trained and deployed as at 1 September. To achieve the target of 3,500 fully trained National Police personnel by July 2007, the field training programme was compressed from 26 weeks to 16 weeks. UNMIL developed a basic management course and a senior leadership qualification programme to address the shortfall in the mid-level ranks of the police service. The presence of National Police in the interior of the country remained far below acceptable levels, with only 454 officers deployed throughout Liberia's 15 counties.

To assist in the restoration and consolidation of State authority throughout Liberia, UNMIL facilitated the return of government officials to their duty stations. Three additional Central Bank payment centres were constructed, with UNMIL assistance, in Kakata, Gbarnga and Buchanan for the payment of salaries to officials stationed in remote locations. Other progress included the election of a new nine-member National Traditional Council of Paramount Chiefs and Elders and preparation by the National Elections Commission for municipal and chieftaincy elections in October 2007.

To regain control over the country's natural resources, the Government, with UNMIL assistance, enacted a national forestry reform law, implemented its policy on the movement of timber within the country at joint UNMIL/Forestry Development Authority checkpoints and developed an environmentally sustainable pit-sawing policy. The mandate of the joint Government/UNMIL task force was extended to oversee the implementation of the recommendations contained in its May assessment report on Liberia's rubber plantations. The Government accepted the recommendations of the Kimberley Process assessment team, including the need to establish a task force on Kimberley process compliance and to suspend all large-scale mining activities. As illegal artisanal mining continued to be reported in the western part of the country and in Nimba and Sinoe counties, UNMIL assisted the Government with its surveillance, mapping and inspection activities.

Judicial system reform progressed, with the completion of six court construction and renovation projects, with another seven in progress, all of which were funded by UNMIL quick-impact project scheme. UNMIL assisted with the hiring of 12 national prosecutorial and 11 public defense consultants for an initial six-month period, resulting in more cases being heard by the courts, and provided advice and assistance to legal and judicial officers in the counties. The Mission assisted the Bureau of Corrections in improving conditions at correctional facilities, with work being completed at Kakata prison, while rehabilitation at the Buchanan, Gbarnga, Harper and Monrovia prisons and the Zwedru Palace of Corrections were at varying stages of completion.

Further progress was made with the implementation of the Governance and Economic Management Assistance Programme. On 16 June, the Government signed a memorandum of understanding for the consolidation of operational bank accounts for State-owned enterprises. The Economic Governance Steering Committee technical team worked with the internationally recruited experts to improve financial management and transparency and build the capacity of Government institutions through the transfer of skills. At the partner's review meeting to assess the Government's performance during its first six months in office (Monrovia, 12-13 July) and to agree on the way forward for Liberia's national recovery, reconstruction and development, the Government highlighted the capacity and implementation constraints it faced in achieving its objectives and presented a case for targeted budgetary support and early debt relief. The World Bank signed an agreement with the Government for the first part of a $68 million grant to conduct emergency rehabilitation and repair of critical infrastructure, including rehabilitation of the Monrovia-Buchanan and Monrovia-Ganta highways, repairs of 65 bridges and the construction of six more. The second part of the grant would be used to increase Government capacity to carry out road maintenance functions, build the Liberia Water and Sewer Corporation's capacity and to construct ports, airports, schools and health clinics.

The Secretary-General observed that Liberia continued to make tangible progress in a number of areas and served as an example of what could be achieved when leaders and citizens worked together and were committed to peace. Nevertheless, the country still faced enormous challenges. He emphasized that the Government and UNMIL would need to remain vigilant and carefully manage the internal threats to stability, as well as closely monitor Liberia's borders in the light of the volatile situation in the subregion, particularly in Côte d'Ivoire. The Government should also work expeditiously to develop its national security policy, which would enable it to set out a road map for assuming security responsibility for the entire country. He called on donors to support judicial sector reform, the enhancement of the rule of law and the work of the Independent National Human Rights Commission and the Truth and Reconciliation Commission. In the light of the security issues outlined in the report, and the planned drawdown of UNMIL, the Secretary-General recommended the extension of the Mission's mandate until 30 September 2007. Benchmarks for phase I of UNMIL consolidation, drawdown and withdrawal were annexed to the report.

Security Council consideration. On 25 September [meeting 5534], the Council met in private with UNMIL troop-contributing countries and heard a briefing by the Special Representative of the Secretary-General for Liberia.

SECURITY COUNCIL ACTION

On 29 September [meeting 5542], the Security Council unanimously adopted **resolution 1712(2006)**. The draft [S/2006/773] was prepared in consultations among Council members.

The Security Council,

Recalling its previous resolutions and the statements by its President concerning the situation in Liberia and the subregion, in particular resolutions 1509(2003) of 19 September 2003, 1667(2006) of 31 March 2006 and 1694(2006) of 13 July 2006,

Welcoming the report of the Secretary-General of 12 September 2006,

Welcoming also the steps taken by the Government of Liberia to combat corruption,

Expressing its appreciation for the continuing support of the Economic Community of West African States and the African Union for the Liberian peace process, as well as for financial and other assistance provided by the international community,

Commending the United Nations Mission in Liberia, under the leadership of the Special Representative of the Secretary-General for Liberia, for the significant part its support has played in restoring peace and stability to Liberia,

Emphasizing that significant challenges remain in completing the reintegration and repatriation of ex-combatants and the urgent restructuring of the Liberian security sector, as well as maintaining stability in Liberia and the subregion,

Welcoming deployments of the Mission in vulnerable areas at Liberia's borders,

Reiterating the continuing need for support by the Mission for the security of the Special Court for Sierra Leone,

Determining that the situation in Liberia continues to constitute a threat to international peace and security in the region,

Acting under Chapter VII of the Charter of the United Nations,

1. *Decides* that the mandate of the United Nations Mission in Liberia shall be extended until 31 March 2007;

2. *Reaffirms its intention* to authorize the Secretary-General to redeploy troops between the Mission and the United Nations Operation in Côte d'Ivoire on a temporary basis in accordance with the provisions of resolution 1609(2005) of 24 June 2005, as may be needed;

3. *Endorses* the recommendations of the Secretary-General for a phased, gradual consolidation, drawdown and withdrawal of the troop contingent of the Mission, as the situation permits and without compromising the security of Liberia;

4. *Requests* the Secretary-General to monitor progress on the stabilization of Liberia and to continue to keep the Security Council informed, with particular reference to the broad benchmarks laid down in paragraphs 71 and 72 of his report of 12 September 2006 and in annex I thereto, in particular the restructuring of the security sector, the reintegration of former combatants, the facilitation of political and ethnic reconciliation, the consolidation of State authority throughout the country, judicial reform, the restoration of effective Government control over the country's natural and mineral resources, and the establishment of a stable and secure environment necessary to foster economic growth;

5. *Calls upon* the Government of Liberia, in close coordination with the Mission, to take the necessary steps on its part towards achieving the benchmarks laid down in paragraph 4 above, including ensuring the effective implementation of the National Forestry Reform Law, the continuing commitment to the Government and Economic Management Assistance Programme, and the rapid development of a national security policy and architecture, and encourages the international community to support those efforts;

6. *Welcomes* the efforts undertaken by the Mission to implement the Secretary-General's zero-tolerance policy on sexual exploitation and abuse and to ensure full compliance of its personnel with the United Nations code of conduct, and requests the Secretary-General to take all necessary action in this regard and to keep the Council informed, and urges troop-contributing countries to take appropriate preventive action, including conducting predeployment awareness training, and to take disciplinary and other action to ensure that allegations of sexual exploitation or abuse against their personnel are properly investigated and, if substantiated, punished;

7. *Decides* to remain actively seized of the matter.

Report of Secretary-General (December). In his December report [S/2006/958], the Secretary-General said that the relationship between the legislative and executive branches of the Government improved, allowing the national forestry reform law to be passed. To further national reconciliation, President Johnson-Sirleaf reaffirmed her Government's commitment to religious freedom and tolerance, and on 21 November, convened a meeting of the leaders of registered political parties, including those who had contested the 2005 presidential elections. The party leaders exchanged views on several issues of national importance, such as national security and the country's draft interim poverty reduction strategy. The Presidential Commission established to investigate inter-ethnic land and property disputes in Nimba County completed its work. UNMIL worked closely also with the Government and civil society organizations to address other inter-ethnic, religious, community and property disputes in various parts of the country.

The President, in continuing efforts to combat corruption, signed into law two acts ratifying the African Union Convention on Preventing and Combatting Corruption and the United Nations Convention against Corruption [YUN 2003, p. 112]. The Government also approved the Governance Reform Commission's anti-corruption policy statement and considered a draft national anti-corruption strategy. Improvements by the Ministry of Finance in the process for the payment of civil servant salaries resulted in the removal of over 4,700 "ghost" workers from the Government's payroll.

Disturbances by deactivated security service personnel demanding outstanding benefits and salary arrears prompted President Johnson-Sirleaf to direct her Cabinet, the Inspector General of the Liberian National Police and the Director of the Special Security Services to carry out a comprehensive assessment of the remaining salary arrears and pensions and develop a plan for their liquidation and payment. On 8 September, in response to the increase in reported criminal activities, especially armed robberies and rapes, the President launched a joint Liberian National Police/UNMIL operation, which resulted in a significant reduction in violent crime in Monrovia and its environs. UNMIL conducted successful operational readiness exercises to respond to a possible major deterioration of the security situation in Monrovia and closely monitored the security situation along Liberia's borders with Côte d'Ivoire, Guinea and Sierra Leone.

Although efforts to rehabilitate and reintegrate ex-combatants continued, as at 15 November, some 39,000 of them had not yet been absorbed into reintegration programmes. The Joint Implementation Unit approved 10 new vocational skills training projects, which would absorb 8,000 ex-combatants, 3,000 of whom had so far registered for the projects. Ex-combatants also had the option of enrolling in several formal education schemes. Further progress was made in the training and restructuring of the Liberian National Police. As at 1 December, 2,214 police officers had been trained and deployed, and some 358 Special Security Service personnel and 155 Seaport Police officers had graduated from the National Police Academy. An intensified countrywide recruitment drive was launched, targeting civil society leaders and educational institutions in an effort to identify and attract young recruits. Training of the new armed forces continued with the assistance of the United States. On 4 November, the first group of 106 recruits for the new army graduated from basic training and 500 recruits were selected for the next basic training class scheduled to commence in early 2007.

UNMIL continued its promotion, protection and monitoring of the human rights situation in Liberia. An UNMIL consultant conducted an audit of key Liberian legislation and concluded that several laws, including some provisions of the Constitution, were not in compliance with international human rights standards and instruments, and recommended that the applicable laws be amended to comply with those standards. On 10 October, the Truth and Reconciliation Commission commenced taking statements in the counties. UNMIL assisted in training more than 200 statement-takers on the promotion and protection of human rights, but the programme had to be suspended on 28 November, due to insufficient funds to pay their salaries. The Secretary-General appealed to the international community to support the work of the Commission. In the area of judicial reform, with UNMIL support in the engagement of national lawyers, court activities increased throughout the country, particularly trials for serious offences. Significant progress was also made in the establishment of the Law Reform Commission.

The Government achieved steady progress in gaining control over the exploitation of the country's natural resources. Following the full lifting of the sanctions on timber exports on 20 October (see p. 226), the Government finalized regulations for the effective management of the timber industry. Between April and November, with UNMIL assistance, the Forestry Development Authority issued 1,873 permits for the transportation of 695,480 pieces of timber, which resulted in public revenue of $423,321, compared to $62,262 for the same period in 2005. President Johnson-Sirleaf established a National Diamond Task Force to work on implementing the Kimberley Process Certification Scheme, with a view to ensuring that conditions for lifting Security Council sanctions on diamonds were met. The Government also convened a stakeholders' forum to prepare a national mineral policy for Liberia. UNMIL continued to support the Government in re-establishing its authority over the Guthrie Rubber Plantation. The interim management team appointed by the Government began commercial operations and provided employment for more than 1,500 workers on the plantation. In addition, some 200 registered ex-combatants and residents at the plantation had signed up to participate in reintegration and rehabilitation programmes.

The Secretary-General reported that progress was made in meeting the broad benchmarks outlined in his September report for the drawdowm of UNMIL personnel (see p. 218). Progress in meeting those benchmarks included the likelihood of reaching the recruitment target of 3,500 trained police officers by July 2007; marked improvement in financial management and revenue administration in the public sector; and the restoration of street lighting and piped water in parts of Monrovia. On the other hand, the new army would not be fully operational until 2008; deployment of police officers remained hampered by logistical and management constraints; some 39,000 ex-combatants had yet to access reintegration programmes; corrections facilities had been established in only seven of the 15 counties; extension of public health services to the counties remained limited; and the country was heavily dependent on non-governmental organizations, which provided 90 per cent of primary health care and hospital services. He said that a full update on progress made in meeting the benchmarks would be provided in his next progress report on UNMIL, and subsequently on a six-monthly basis at the time of each mandate renewal.

The Secretary-General encouraged President Johnson-Sirleaf to continue involving Liberians in the country's recovery process and appealed to all political and civil society leaders to continue their engagement in the reconstruction and reform processes. He called upon the Government to finalize its national security strategy and prepare a comprehensive architecture to enable Liberian security agencies to sustain a stable security environment, which was a crucial element in the planning and management of the drawdown of UNMIL forces. As a review team from DPKO would travel to Liberia in early 2007 to assess the impact of the work of UNMIL police component on the capacity of the National Police, the Secretary-General stressed that everything possible should be done to operationalize the force and expedite its deployment to the countryside. Deeply concerned by the high incidence of sexual violence, in particular rape committed against women and girl children, the Secretary-General further emphasized that every effort should be made to ensure that criminal justice was fairly addressed and widespread violence against women and children brought to an end.

On 20 December, by **resolution 61/218** on humanitarian assistance and reconstruction, the General Assembly appealed to donors and the international community to provide assistance to Liberia, including financial and technical support for the Government's national reconstruction and development agenda (see p. 1081).

UNMIL

The United Nations Mission in Liberia (UNMIL), established by Security Council resolution 1509(2003) [YUN 2003, p. 194], was mandated to support the implementation of the 2003 Agreement on Ceasefire and Cessation of Hostilities [ibid., p. 189] and of the peace process; protect UN staff, facilities and civilians; support humanitarian and human rights activities; and assist in national security reform, including national police training and the formation of a new, restructured military. By resolution 1638(2005) [YUN 2005, p. 267], the Council enhanced the mandate to include the apprehension and detention of former President Charles Taylor, as well as his transfer to the Special Court for Sierra Leone.

By resolution 1694(2006) (see p. 216), the Council supported the Secretary-General's recommendation to increase the civilian police component by 125 personnel and decrease the military troop strength by the same number. By resolutions 1667(2006) (see p. 214) and 1712(2006) (see p. 218), it extended UNMIL mandate until 30 September 2006, and 31 March 2007, respectively, and endorsed the Secretary-General's recommendation for a phased consolidation, drawdown and withdrawal of the troop contingent, as the situation permitted. The Council, by **resolution 1657(2006)** (see p. 181), authorized the transfer of one military company from UNMIL to the United Nations Operation in Côte d'Ivoire, until 31 March 2006.

During 2006, the Secretary-General submitted reports to the Security Council on developments in Liberia and the activities of UNMIL in March [S/2006/159] (see p. 211); June [S/2006/376] (see p. 214); September [S/2006/743] (see p. 216); and December [S/2006/958] (see p. 219). In addition to political and security aspects, the reports summarized UNMIL activities to address the humanitarian and human rights situation in the country, as well as efforts to assist in national recovery, reconstruction and development. Throughout the year, the Mission also provided HIV/AIDS awareness training and sensitization to its personnel and promoted gender mainstreaming in its activities.

UNMIL continued to be headed by the Special Representative of the Secretary-General for Liberia, Alan Doss (United Kingdom) and maintained its headquarters in the Liberian capital, Monrovia. Lieutenant General Chikadibia Isaac Obiakor (Nigeria) continued as the Force Commander of UNMIL.

UNMIL financing

In June, at its resumed sixtieth (2006) session, the General Assembly considered the performance report on the UNMIL budget for 1 July 2004 to 30 June 2005 [A/60/645], showing actual expenditures of $740,964,800, against a total appropriation of $821,986,000. It also considered the proposed budget for UNMIL for 1 July 2006 to 30 June 2007 [A/60/653 & Corr.1,2] of $716,855,700, gross, and the related ACABQ report [A/60/852]. The budget provided for the deployment of 215 military observers, 14,785 military contingents, 1,115 civilian police officers, including formed units, 599 international staff, 957 national staff and 278 United Nations Volunteers. ACABQ recommended a reduction of $138,000 in the proposed UNMIL budget for the period from 1 July 2006 to 30 June 2007.

GENERAL ASSEMBLY ACTION

On 30 June [meeting 92], the General Assembly, on the recommendation of the Fifth Committee [A/60/924], adopted **resolution 60/276** without vote [agenda item 148].

Financing of the United Nations Mission in Liberia

The General Assembly,

Having considered the reports of the Secretary-General on the financing of the United Nations Mission in Liberia and the related report of the Advisory Committee on Administrative and Budgetary Questions,

Recalling Security Council resolution 1497(2003) of 1 August 2003, by which the Council declared its readiness to establish a United Nations stabilization force to support the transitional government and to assist in the implementation of a comprehensive peace agreement in Liberia,

Recalling also Security Council resolution 1509(2003) of 19 September 2003, by which the Council decided to establish the United Nations Mission in Liberia for a period of twelve months, and the subsequent resolutions by which the Council extended the mandate of the Mission, the latest of which was resolution 1667(2006) of 31 March 2006, by which the Council extended the mandate of the Mission until 30 September 2006,

Recalling further its resolution 58/315 of 1 July 2004,

Recalling its resolution 58/261 A of 23 December 2003 on the financing of the Mission and its subsequent resolutions thereon, the latest of which was resolution 59/305 of 22 June 2005,

Reaffirming the general principles underlying the financing of United Nations peacekeeping operations, as stated in General Assembly resolutions 1874(S-IV) of 27 June 1963, 3101(XXVIII) of 11 December 1973 and 55/235 of 23 December 2000,

Noting with appreciation that voluntary contributions have been made to the Mission,

Mindful of the fact that it is essential to provide the Mission with the necessary financial resources to enable it to fulfil its responsibilities under the relevant resolutions of the Security Council,

1. *Requests* the Secretary-General to entrust the Head of Mission with the task of formulating future budget proposals in full accordance with the provisions of General Assembly resolutions 59/296 of 22 June 2005 and 60/266 of 30 June 2006, as well as other relevant resolutions;

2. *Takes note* of the status of contributions to the United Nations Mission in Liberia as at 30 April 2006, including the contributions outstanding in the amount of 212.9 million United States dollars, representing some 8.9 per cent of the total assessed contributions, notes with concern that only six Member States have paid their assessed contributions in full, and urges all other Member States, in particular those in arrears, to ensure payment of their outstanding assessed contributions;

3. *Expresses its appreciation* to those Member States which have paid their assessed contributions in full, and urges all other Member States to make every possible effort to ensure payment of their assessed contributions to the Mission in full;

4. *Expresses concern* at the financial situation with regard to peacekeeping activities, in particular as regards the reimbursements to troop contributors that bear additional burdens owing to overdue payments by Member States of their assessments;

5. *Also expresses concern* at the delay experienced by the Secretary-General in deploying and providing adequate resources to some recent peacekeeping missions, in particular those in Africa;

6. *Emphasizes* that all future and existing peacekeeping missions shall be given equal and non-discriminatory treatment in respect of financial and administrative arrangements;

7. *Also emphasizes* that all peacekeeping missions shall be provided with adequate resources for the effective and efficient discharge of their respective mandates;

8. *Reiterates its request* to the Secretary-General to make the fullest possible use of facilities and equipment at the United Nations Logistics Base at Brindisi, Italy, in order to minimize the costs of procurement for the Mission;

9. *Endorses* the conclusions and recommendations contained in the report of the Advisory Committee on Administrative and Budgetary Questions, subject to the provisions of the present resolution, and requests the Secretary-General to ensure their full implementation;

10. *Emphasizes* the importance of ensuring coordination and collaboration of efforts with the United Nations agencies and programmes and implementation of a unified workplan, and requests the Secretary-General to report to the General Assembly on measures taken, as well as progress made and to provide clear descriptions of respective roles and responsibilities in its future budget submissions;

11. *Looks forward* to the consideration of the comprehensive report requested in section VIII, paragraph 3, of its resolution 60/266;

12. *Requests* the Secretary-General to ensure that quick impact projects are implemented in compliance with the original intent of such projects and relevant resolutions of the General Assembly;

13. *Decides* to provide 1 million dollars for quick impact projects for the period 2006/07, in the interim, and requests the Secretary-General to utilize resources in strict compliance with the original intent of this type of project;

14. *Requests* the Secretary-General to review the administrative support structure for the quick impact projects with a view to minimizing overhead costs for their implementation;

15. *Decides* to reduce operational costs by 1 million dollars;

16. *Requests* the Secretary-General to ensure the full implementation of the relevant provisions of its resolutions 59/296 and 60/266;

17. *Also requests* the Secretary-General to take all necessary action to ensure that the Mission is administered with a maximum of efficiency and economy;

18. *Further requests* the Secretary-General, in order to reduce the cost of employing General Service staff, to continue efforts to recruit local staff for the Mission against General Service posts, commensurate with the requirements of the Mission;

Financial performance report for the period from 1 July 2004 to 30 June 2005

19. *Takes note* of the report of the Secretary-General on the financial performance of the Mission for the period from 1 July 2004 to 30 June 2005;

Budget estimates for the period from 1 July 2006 to 30 June 2007

20. *Decides* to appropriate to the Special Account for the United Nations Mission in Liberia the amount of 745,572,300 dollars for the period from 1 July 2006 to 30 June 2007, inclusive of 714,613,300 dollars for the maintenance of the Mission, 25,571,000 dollars for the sup-

port account for peacekeeping operations and 5,388,000 dollars for the United Nations Logistics Base;

Financing of the appropriation

21. *Also decides* to apportion among Member States the amount of 186,393,100 dollars for the period from 1 July to 30 September 2006, in accordance with the levels updated in General Assembly resolution 58/256 of 23 December 2003, and taking into account the scale of assessments for 2006, as set out in its resolution 58/1 B of 23 December 2003;

22. *Further decides* that, in accordance with the provisions of its resolution 973 (X) of 15 December 1955, there shall be set off against the apportionment among Member States, as provided for in paragraph 21 above, their respective share in the Tax Equalization Fund of 3,394,000 dollars, comprising the estimated staff assessment income of 2,573,000 dollars approved for the Mission, the prorated share of 719,100 dollars of the estimated staff assessment income approved for the support account and the prorated share of 101,900 dollars of the estimated staff assessment income approved for the United Nations Logistics Base;

23. *Decides* to apportion among Member States the amount of 559,179,200 dollars for the period from 1 October 2006 to 30 June 2007 at a monthly rate of 62,131,022 dollars, in accordance with the levels updated in General Assembly resolution 58/256, and taking into account the scale of assessments for 2006, as set out in its resolution 58/1 B, and the scale of assessments for 2007, subject to a decision of the Security Council to extend the mandate of the Mission;

24. *Also decides* that, in accordance with the provisions of its resolution 973 (X), there shall be set off against the apportionment among Member States, as provided for in paragraph 23 above, their respective share in the Tax Equalization Fund of 10,182,100 dollars, comprising the estimated staff assessment income of 7,718,900 dollars approved for the Mission, the prorated share of 2,157,300 dollars of the estimated staff assessment income approved for the support account and the prorated share of 305,900 dollars of the estimated staff assessment income approved for the United Nations Logistics Base;

25. *Further decides* that, for Member States that have fulfilled their financial obligations to the Mission, there shall be set off against their apportionment, as provided for in paragraph 21 above, their respective share of the unencumbered balance and other income in the total amount of 108,308,700 dollars in respect of the financial period ended 30 June 2005, in accordance with the levels updated in General Assembly resolution 58/256, and taking into account the scale of assessments for 2005 as set out in its resolution 58/1 B;

26. *Decides* that, for Member States that have not fulfilled their financial obligations to the Mission, there shall be set off against their outstanding obligations their respective share of the unencumbered balance and other income in the total amount of 108,308,700 dollars in respect of the financial period ended 30 June 2005, in accordance with the scheme set out in paragraph 25 above;

27. *Also decides* that the decrease of 316,800 dollars in the estimated staff assessment income in respect of the financial period ended 30 June 2005 shall be set off against the credits from the amount of 108,308,700 dollars referred to in paragraphs 25 and 26 above;

28. *Emphasizes* that no peacekeeping mission shall be financed by borrowing funds from other active peacekeeping missions;

29. *Encourages* the Secretary-General to continue to take additional measures to ensure the safety and security of all personnel under the auspices of the United Nations participating in the Mission, bearing in mind paragraphs 5 and 6 of Security Council resolution 1502(2003) of 26 August 2003;

30. *Invites* voluntary contributions to the Mission in cash and in the form of services and supplies acceptable to the Secretary-General, to be administered, as appropriate, in accordance with the procedure and practices established by the General Assembly;

31. *Decides* to include in the provisional agenda of its sixty-first session the item entitled "Financing of the United Nations Mission in Liberia".

On 22 December, by **decision 61/552**, the General Assembly deferred consideration of the item "Financing of the United Nations Mission in Liberia" until its resumed sixty-first (2007) session.

Sanctions

The Security Council received several reports on the implementation of sanctions imposed on Liberia, pursuant to Council resolutions 1521(2003) [YUN 2003, p. 208] and 1647(2005) [YUN 2005, p. 274]. Those sanctions banned the importation of arms and related materiel, military training, the export of Liberian timber products and rough diamonds, and international travel by individuals constituting a threat to the peace process in Liberia and the subregion. Financial sanctions had also been imposed on Mr. Charles Taylor and his immediate family by resolution 1532(2004) [YUN 2004, p. 204].

Appointment of Panel. On 23 January [S/2006/36], the Secretary-General informed the Council of his appointment of five members of the Panel of Experts established pursuant to resolution 1647(2005), which was mandated to conduct an assessment mission to Liberia and neighbouring States in order to report on the implementation of resolution 1521(2003) and any violations of the sanctions imposed by that resolution and by resolution 1532(2004); the impact and effectiveness of the measures imposed; progress made towards meeting the conditions for lifting the sanctions; and the humanitarian and socio-economic impact of the measures imposed by resolution 1521(2003). The Secretary-General, on 23 June [S/2006/438], informed the Security Council of the names of the five experts he had re-appointed to the Panel of Experts pursuant to resolution 1689(2006) (see p. 226).

Implementation of sanctions regime

Communication. On 6 June [S/2006/365], Liberia transmitted the text of a 24 May letter from President Johnson-Sirleaf requesting that the Security Council consider the lifting of sanctions imposed on Liberia under resolution 1521(2003), as the country had complied with the demands of the relevant paragraphs of the resolution and had taken additional measures to satisfy the Council's demands for the lifting of the sanctions. She noted that Liberia, Sierra Leone and the subregion were at peace; former Liberian President Charles Taylor was in the custody of the Special Court for Sierra Leone; and most of the individuals considered to be a threat to peace in the subregion were positively engaged in the country, either in private business or public office. In addition, the war in Liberia had ended, a democratic government had been elected, all combatants had been disarmed and demobilized, and in keeping with the terms of the 2003 Comprehensive Peace Accord, the military and security sectors were being reformed and restructured.

President Johnson-Sirleaf outlined 14 specific measures, eight related to the diamond industry and six pertaining to the timber industry, which the Government of Liberia had taken to meet the conditions for lifting the sanctions. She stated that the Panel of Experts established pursuant to resolutions 1521(2003) had documented the severe socio-economic effects of the sanctions on the Government and the population and emphasized that Liberia could not make any significant stride in poverty reduction or the provision of social services with the diamond and timber industry—two significant life wires in the country's economy—under UN sanctions. The Government also requested a review of the travel ban, taking into account that those sanctions were imposed because of the relationship with or involvement in the activities of former President Taylor. Where no relationship continued to exist or where there was no threat to the security of Liberia by the activities of those individuals, the Government wanted to have those sanctions lifted to send a message to law-abiding citizens that they could enjoy the rights granted them by the Liberian constitution.

She reiterated the call by ECOWAS at its Ministerial Conference (Monrovia, 15 May) for the United Nations to lift the sanctions to enable the new Government to have access to needed resources to execute its programmes and improve the standard of living of the people.

SECURITY COUNCIL ACTION

On 13 June [meeting 5454], the Security Council unanimously adopted **resolution 1683(2006)**. The draft [S/2006/370] was prepared in consultations among Council members.

The Security Council,

Recalling its previous resolutions and the statements by its President on the situation in Liberia and West Africa,

Welcoming the leadership of newly elected President Mrs. Ellen Johnson-Sirleaf and her efforts to restore peace, security and harmony throughout Liberia,

Underscoring the continuing need for the United Nations Mission in Liberia to support the Government of Liberia in building a stable environment that will allow democracy to flourish,

Recognizing the need for newly vetted and trained Liberian security forces to assume greater responsibility for national security, including policing, intelligence-gathering and executive protection,

Determining that, despite significant progress having been made in Liberia, the situation there continues to constitute a threat to international peace and security in the region,

Acting under Chapter VII of the Charter of the United Nations,

1. *Decides* that the measures imposed by paragraphs 2 *(a)* and *(b)* of resolution 1521(2003) of 22 December 2003 shall not apply to the weapons and ammunition already provided to members of the Special Security Service for training purposes pursuant to advance approval, under paragraph 2 *(e)* of that resolution, by the Security Council Committee established pursuant to paragraph 21 of that resolution, and that those weapons and ammunition may remain in the custody of the Special Security Service for unencumbered operational use;

2. *Decides also* that the measures imposed by paragraphs 2 *(a)* and *(b)* of resolution 1521(2003) shall not apply to limited supplies of weapons and ammunition, as approved in advance on a case-by-case basis by the Committee, intended for use by members of the Government of Liberia police and security forces who have been vetted and trained since the inception of the United Nations Mission in Liberia in October 2003;

3. *Decides further* that a request made in accordance with paragraph 2 above shall be submitted to the Committee by the Government of Liberia and the exporting State, and, in case of approval, the Government of Liberia shall subsequently mark the weapons and ammunition, maintain a registry of them and formally notify the Committee that these steps have been taken;

4. *Reiterates* the importance of continuing assistance by the Mission to the Government of Liberia, the Committee and the Panel of Experts on Liberia, within its capabilities and areas of deployment, and without prejudice to its mandate, including in monitoring the implementation of the measures in paragraphs 2, 4, 6 and 10 of resolution 1521(2003), and in this regard requests the Mission to inspect inventories of weapons and ammu-

nition obtained in accordance with paragraphs 1 and 2 above to ensure that all such weapons and ammunition are accounted for, and to make periodic reports to the Committee on its findings;

5. *Decides* to remain seized of the matter.

Report of Expert Panel (June). The Panel of Experts established pursuant to Security Council resolutions 1521(2003) and 1647(2005) concerning Liberia transmitted a June report [S/2006/379] to the Council, which contained an assessment of all sanctions. While the Panel indicated that there had been no evidence of timber exports or detection of industrial logging, pitsawing—using chainsaws to process logs into planks—remained widespread, with approximately 1,000 pitsawyers, many of whom were ex-combatants. The Panel concluded that, although the export sanctions were effective, the domestic industry continued illegally and the necessary reforms, including laws and regulations, had not been completed and enacted. In addition to its previous recommendations, the Panel proposed further Forestry Development Authority (FDA) collaboration with UNMIL military observers in conducting joint patrols; continued FDA cooperation with the Liberia Forestry Initiative (LFI) and the newly established Forest Reform Monitoring Committee (FRMC) to implement the agreed reform package; and codification by the European Commission and China of a voluntary partnership agreement with Liberia to ensure that only legal wood entered international trade.

The Panel continued to work with the Ministry of Lands, Mines and Energy towards meeting the Security Council requirements, especially with the disbursement by the United States of a $1.4 million funding package for achieving Kimberley Process compliance. However, illegal mining activity continued unabated, with one large, foreign-owned operation being of particular concern. Surveys of mining areas conducted by the Panel in Nimba County, Sinoe County and the Lofa River regions from March to May, revealed that activity had steadily increased during the dry season. Illicit diamond-buying offices continued to operate in Monrovia and provincial towns and Liberian diamonds were being trafficked through Guinea and Sierra Leone. The Panel estimated Liberian diamond production to be worth some $1.2 to $1.5 million per month.

While most of the components for a credible, internationally accredited certification scheme were available, harmonization into a functioning mechanism had yet to be completed. The Panel recommended that the international community continue to support the Liberian Government in its efforts to meet the requirements of the Security Council and the Kimberley Process and that UNMIL be given a robust mandate to assist the Government to regularize and control the diamond sector.

The Panel determined that financial administration in Liberia was improving, but continued vigilance was needed to improve the overall transparency of all financial activities and ensure that revenues went directly to the Government. The Panel recommended that all donations and contributions made by State-owned enterprises to functionaries of the former National Transitional Government of Liberia be investigated to confirm that they had been used appropriately and that all balance amounts, vehicles and equipment were properly transferred to the new Government. It advised that the Liberia Petroleum Refining Corporation (LPRC) should reconcile actual quarterly payments made by importers, so that they could be reflected in the determination of the prices of petroleum products. The General Auditing Office (GAO) should be strengthened and provided with adequate infrastructure and qualified manpower to perform its responsibilities, which should include, among other functions, auditing of the payment of import duties by rice importers, as well as the conduct of a new audit of the Liberian Mining Company (LIMINCO). The Panel also proposed that the Government should discuss with the Liberian International Ship and Corporate Registry ways to restore revenues back to the 1997-2000 level.

Two years after the Security Council passed resolution 1532(2004) concerning the assets freeze [YUN 2004, p. 204], the Government still had not frozen anyone's assets. The Panel recommended that all efforts be made to speed up the legislation process to enable the Government to implement the Council's resolution. Indicating that the lack of infrastructure and information about the travel ban, combined with corruption and the porosity of the borders constituted serious obstacles to controlling travel, the Panel concluded that it was likely that the travel ban had been violated by more individuals than those identified in its report. Moreover, it was not clear if countries had monitoring systems in place to detect violations. The Panel advised countries to report at least once a year to the Committee, describing their investigations and any travel ban violations.

Concerned that an undetermined number of ex-combatants had kept weapons, even if only for protection, the Panel recommended that the arms embargo remain in place until the end of the training of the Liberian Army, and if it were lifted, the lifting should not extend to non-State actors.

The Panel found that the socio-economic impact of the sanctions had changed little. The commodity sanctions had resulted in a loss of jobs and revenue and poor road maintenance. The Panel recommended that Liberia and its international partners create opportunities for Liberians to have greater access to markets and other social services in the larger population centres around the country; give priority to the development of Liberia's human capital; and adopt a proactive stance in ensuring the sustainable management of its natural resources, particularly the forests.

SECURITY COUNCIL ACTION

On 20 June [meeting 5468], the Security Council unanimously adopted **resolution 1689(2006)**. The draft [S/2006/413] was prepared in consultations among Council members.

The Security Council,

Recalling its previous resolutions and the statements by its President on the situation in Liberia and West Africa,

Welcoming the rapid progress made by President Ellen Johnson-Sirleaf since January 2006 in rebuilding Liberia for the benefit of all Liberians, with the support of the international community,

Applauding the actions of President Johnson-Sirleaf, President Olusegun Obasanjo of the Federal Republic of Nigeria, and others in the international community for their roles in transferring Mr. Charles Taylor to the Special Court for Sierra Leone,

Welcoming the progress made by the Government of Liberia in implementing the Governance and Economic Management Assistance Program, designed to ensure prompt implementation of the Comprehensive Peace Agreement signed at Accra on 18 August 2003 and to expedite the lifting of the measures imposed by resolution 1521(2003) of 22 December 2003,

Applauding the commitment of the Government of Liberia to transparent management of the country's forestry resources for the benefit of Liberians and its reforms in the timber sector, including promulgating Executive Order No. 1 of 2 February 2006, which declared all purported forest concessions null and void; creating a Forest Reform Monitoring Committee; placing an internationally recruited financial controller in the Forestry Development Authority, making progress towards implementing a management contract to ensure transparency in timber operations; establishing a mechanism for civil society to monitor the forestry sector; and drafting new forestry laws and regulations,

Stressing that Liberia's progress in the timber sector is held back by the absence of appropriate forestry legislation, and urging speedy adoption of the necessary laws,

Taking note of the announcement by President Johnson-Sirleaf on 10 June 2006 of a moratorium on timber exports and new timber concessions pending the passage by the Liberian legislature of forestry legislation that respects Executive Order No. 1 and that is consistent with the recommendations of the Forest Reform Monitoring Committee,

Welcoming the continuing cooperation by the Government of Liberia with the Kimberley Process Certification Scheme, and noting Liberia's progress towards compliance with the Kimberley Process,

Stressing the continuing importance of the United Nations Mission in Liberia in improving security throughout Liberia and helping the new Government to establish its authority throughout the country, particularly in the diamond- and timber-producing regions and border areas,

Taking note of the report of the Panel of Experts on Liberia submitted on 7 June 2006,

Having reviewed the measures imposed and conditions set out by paragraphs 6 to 9 of resolution 1521(2003), and concluding that insufficient progress has been made towards meeting those conditions,

Having reviewed also the measures imposed and conditions set out by paragraphs 10 and 11 of resolution 1521(2003), and concluding that sufficient progress has been made towards meeting those conditions,

Underlining its determination to support the Government of Liberia, and encouraging donors to do likewise,

Determining that the situation in Liberia continues to constitute a threat to international peace and security in the region,

Acting under Chapter VII of the Charter of the United Nations,

1. *Decides* not to renew the measure in paragraph 10 of resolution 1521(2003) that obligates Member States to prevent the import into their territories of all round logs and timber products originating in Liberia;

2. *Decides also* to review the decision in paragraph 1 above after a period of ninety days, and expresses its determination to reinstate the measure in paragraph 10 of resolution 1521(2003) unless the Security Council is informed by that time that the forestry legislation proposed by the Forest Reform Monitoring Committee has been passed;

3. *Urges* the speedy adoption of the forestry legislation proposed by the Forest Reform Monitoring Committee;

4. *Decides* that the measures imposed by paragraph 6 of resolution 1521(2003) shall be renewed for an additional six months with a review by the Council after four months, to allow the Government of Liberia sufficient time to establish an effective certificate of origin regime for trade in Liberian rough diamonds that is transparent and internationally verifiable, with a view to joining the Kimberley Process, and calls upon the Government of Liberia to provide the Security Council Committee established pursuant to paragraph 21 of resolution 1521(2003) with a detailed description of the proposed regime;

5. *Requests* that the Secretary-General renew for an additional six months the mandate of the Panel of Experts re-established pursuant to paragraph 9 of resolution 1647(2005) of 20 December 2005, and requests that

the Panel of Experts report to the Council through the Committee no later than 15 December 2006 its observations and recommendations;

6. *Decides* to remain actively seized of the matter.

Security Council press statement. The Security Council, in a 20 October press statement [SC/8856], stated that after having been briefed by the Sanctions Committee, and pursuant to resolution 1689(2006) (see above), it had reviewed the Council's decisions not to renew the ban on the import of round logs and timber products from Liberia and had decided to renew the ban on imports of rough diamonds from Liberia until 20 December.

The Council commended the Liberian legislature for passing the National Forestry Reform Law, within the 90-day deadline set by resolution 1689(2006), which would ensure a transparent, accountable and Government-controlled forestry sector and that revenues from the timber industry would not again fuel conflict. Noting that the law was signed by President Johnson-Sirleaf on 5 October, it urged the Government to bring the law into effect as soon as possible. The Council concluded that there was no basis for reinstating the measures on timber. However, as the Panel of Experts had determined that more needed to be done to meet the requirements for lifting the measures on diamonds, the Council urged the Government to accelerate implementation of the necessary reforms, including stronger management and effective verification and accountability mechanisms, so that Liberia could join the Kimberley Process.

Report of Expert Panel (November). The 27 November report of the Panel of Experts was transmitted by the Chairman of the Sanctions Committee to the Security Council President [S/2006/976]. The Panel reported that, while the January 2005 moratorium on diamond mining imposed by the Ministry of Lands, Mines and Energy continued, the Government had been unable to fully enforce the measure. The Panel commended the Ministry for successfully stopping all class A industrial and class B semi-industrial activity in the interior. However, it remained concerned by illegal artisanal digging in Sinoe County, especially at the Butaw Oil Palm Corporation site, where another substantial satellite mining camp had opened. The Panel estimated that some of the 130,000 to 150,000 carats of Liberia's annual diamond production might have been smuggled through Côte d'Ivoire to Ghana, where it was exported through legitimate channels to the international market. A United States-based company, Futures Group, was contracted to assist the Government in diamond sector reform and in applying for participation in the Kimberley Process Certification Scheme. Following the second Kimberley Process expert mission to Liberia, from 22 to 27 May, the Ministry and the Futures Group agreed to modify the proposed system of internal controls to include the issuance of sales vouchers or vendor forms that would record the seller, buyer, volume and value of the transaction and the registration of all actors in a national computerized, relational database to enable effective and accurate cross-checking. The Panel concluded that, while most of the components of an internal control system were in place, the country was still not in a position to demonstrate the functioning of such a system necessary for participation in the Kimberley Process Certification Scheme. It emphasized that stronger leadership and ownership by relevant stakeholders, especially by the Ministry of Lands, Mines and Energy, were needed, as well as effective, ongoing management of human, financial and material resources.

Sanctions on timber continued to effectively reduce the timber trade. However, concerns were raised over the forthcoming three-year phase-out of UNMIL peacekeepers, who were controlling forest areas in Liberia, and the limited capacity of Forestry Development Authority (FDA) regional offices to control illegal pit-sawing. In addition, the dramatic increase in revenue since January, suggested that the previous National Transitional Government managers, who belonged to the rebel group MODEL, had profited from logging. Evidence also indicated that logging was being directed by ex-combatants. The Panel recommended that the FDA should accept UNMIL offer to provide joint patrols in order to establish control over pit-sawing.The results of a financial audit conducted by the European Commission (EC) and the FDA, covering the period from 1 October 2003 to 31 January 2006, validated concerns of corruption and incompetence during the National Transitional Government period. The Panel recommended that the Government should hold accountable those who had committed crimes, including fraud and misappropriation of timber revenues, especially those identified in the EC audit report. To make international buyers accept responsibility, the EC should sign a voluntary partnership agreement with Liberia to ensure that only legal timber was exported and that trade did not fund conflict.

On economic and financial matters, the Panel received positive feedback on the effectiveness of the Governance and Economic Management Assistance Programme in increasing revenue from State-owned enterprises. The Panel recommended that the Government and its international partners speed up the construction and rehabilitation of the country's infrastructure, which would provide employment opportunities and facilitate the delivery of development aid and social services to rural Liberia and increase access to markets by rural farmers. The Panel indicated that the Government's financial management had improved owing to higher revenues, stricter enforcement of tax regulations and tighter expenditure control. However, concerns remained over the lack of internal control systems and external oversight. The Panel recommended annual audits of ministries, departments and agencies going back to 2003, with legal action pursued against corrupt officials; an audit of the payment of import duties and taxes; immediate commencement of pre-shipment inspection of petroleum imports; establishment by the Government of a collections department to pursue outstanding arrears; disallowance of contracts or concessions to anyone in arrears; and annual audits of ministries, departments and major revenue-generating parastatals.

Two and a half years after its imposition, the assets freeze had not been implemented, and there was no chance that the required legislation could be passed by the Legislature. The Panel recommended that the Government institute measures, whether through legislation or executive order, to implement the related Security Council resolutions without delay. The Panel documented travel ban violations in Côte d'Ivoire, Ghana, the Netherlands and Togo, as well as two waivers granted by the Council. It was not aware of any violations in Liberia and indicated that facilities to obtain fraudulent passports, the lack of political will, and poorly equipped and trained law enforcement staff combined to make the travel ban difficult to enforce.

SECURITY COUNCIL ACTION

On 20 December [meeting 5602], the Security Council unanimously adopted **resolution 1731(2006)**. The draft [S/2006/1001] was prepared in consultations among Council members.

The Security Council,

Recalling its previous resolutions and the statements by its President on the situation in Liberia and West Africa,

Welcoming the sustained progress made by the Government of Liberia since January 2006 in rebuilding Liberia for the benefit of all Liberians, with the support of the international community,

Recalling its decision not to renew the measures in paragraph 10 of resolution 1521(2003) of 22 December 2003 regarding round logs and timber products originating in Liberia, and stressing that Liberia's progress in the timber sector must continue with the effective implementation and enforcement of the National Forestry Reform Law signed into law on 5 October 2006, including the resolution of land and tenure rights,

Welcoming the Government of Liberia's continuing cooperation with the Kimberley Process Certification Scheme, and noting Liberia's progress towards putting in place the necessary internal controls and other requirements in order to satisfy the minimum requirements of the Kimberley Process,

Stressing the continuing importance of the United Nations Mission in Liberia in improving security throughout Liberia and helping the new Government to establish its authority throughout the country, particularly in the diamond- and timber-producing regions and border areas,

Recognizing the need for newly vetted and trained Liberian security forces to assume greater responsibility for national security, and taking note of the need for Liberian armed forces to procure humanitarian, medical and/or training equipment,

Taking note of the report of the Panel of Experts on Liberia of 27 November 2006, including on the issues of diamonds, timber, rubber and arms,

Having reviewed the measures imposed by paragraphs 2, 4, and 6 of resolution 1521(2003) and paragraph 1 of resolution 1532(2004) of 12 March 2004 and the progress towards meeting the conditions set out in paragraphs 5 and 7 of resolution 1521(2003), and concluding that insufficient progress has been made towards that end,

Underlining its determination to support the Government of Liberia in its efforts to meet those conditions, and encouraging donors to do likewise,

Determining that, despite significant progress having been made in Liberia, the situation there continues to constitute a threat to international peace and security in the region,

Acting under Chapter VII of the Charter of the United Nations,

1. *Decides*, on the basis of its assessment of progress made to date towards meeting the conditions for lifting the measures imposed by resolution 1521(2003):

(a) To renew the measures on arms imposed by paragraph 2 of resolution 1521(2003) and modified by paragraphs 1 and 2 of resolution 1683(2006) of 13 June 2006 and to renew the measures on travel imposed by paragraph 4 of resolution 1521(2003) for a further period of twelve months from the date of adoption of the present resolution;

(b) That the measures on arms imposed by paragraphs 2 *(a)* and *(b)* of resolution 1521(2003) shall not apply to supplies of non-lethal military equipment, excluding non-lethal weapons and ammunition, as notified in advance to the Security Council Committee established pursuant to paragraph 21 of resolution 1521(2003), intended solely for use by members of the Government of Liberia police and security forces who have been vetted and trained since the inception of the United Nations Mission in Liberia in October 2003;

(c) To renew the measures on diamonds imposed by paragraph 6 of resolution 1521(2003) and renewed by

paragraph 4 of resolution 1689(2006) of 20 June 2006 for an additional six months, with a review by the Council after four months, to allow the Government of Liberia sufficient time to establish an effective certificate of origin regime for trade in Liberian rough diamonds that is transparent and internationally verifiable, with a view to joining the Kimberley Process, and calls upon the Government of Liberia to provide the Committee with a detailed description of the proposed regime;

(d) To review any of the above measures at the request of the Government of Liberia, once the Government reports to the Council that the conditions set out in resolution 1521(2003) for terminating the measures have been met, and provides the Council with information to justify its assessment;

2. *Notes* that the measures imposed by paragraph 1 of resolution 1532(2004) remain in force, and reconfirms its intention to review those measures at least once a year;

3. *Encourages* the Government of Liberia to benefit from the Mission's offer to provide joint patrols with the Forestry Development Authority with a view to strengthening Government control in forestry areas;

4. *Decides* to extend the mandate of the current Panel of Experts appointed pursuant to paragraph 5 of resolution 1689(2006) for a further period until 20 June 2007 to undertake the following tasks:

(a) To conduct a follow-up assessment mission to Liberia and neighbouring States in order to investigate and compile a report on the implementation, and any violations, of the measures imposed by resolution 1521(2003) and renewed in paragraphs 1 and 2 above, including any information relevant to the designation by the Committee of the individuals described in paragraph 4 *(a)* of resolution 1521(2003) and paragraph 1 of resolution 1532(2004), and including the various sources of financing, such as from natural resources, for the illicit trade in arms;

(b) To assess the impact and effectiveness of the measures imposed by paragraph 1 of resolution 1532(2004), including, in particular, with respect to the assets of former President Charles Taylor;

(c) To assess the implementation of forestry legislation passed by the Liberian Congress on 19 September 2006 and signed into law by President Johnson-Sirleaf on 5 October 2006 and the progress and humanitarian and socio-economic impact of the measures imposed by paragraphs 2, 4 and 6 of resolution 1521(2003) and renewed in paragraph 1 of resolution 1647(2005) of 20 December 2005;

(d) To report to the Council, through the Committee, by 6 June 2007 on all the issues listed in the present paragraph, and to provide informal updates to the Committee, as appropriate, before that date, especially on progress towards meeting the conditions for lifting the measures imposed by paragraph 6 of resolution 1521(2003) and on progress in the timber sector since the lifting in June 2006 of the measures imposed by paragraph 10 of resolution 1521(2003);

(e) To cooperate with other relevant groups of experts, in particular the group of experts on Côte d'Ivoire established pursuant to resolution 1708(2006) of 14 September 2006, and with the Kimberley Process Certification Scheme;

(f) To identify and make recommendations regarding areas in which the capacity of States in the region can be strengthened to facilitate the implementation of the measures imposed by paragraph 4 of resolution 1521(2003) and paragraph 1 of resolution 1532(2004);

5. *Requests* the Secretary-General to take the necessary measures, in this exceptional instance, to reappoint the current members of the Panel of Experts as referred to in his letter dated 23 June 2006 to the President of the Security Council and to make the necessary financial and security arrangements to support the work of the Panel;

6. *Calls upon* all States and the Government of Liberia to cooperate fully with the Panel of Experts in all the aspects of its mandate;

7. *Encourages* the Kimberley Process to inform, as appropriate, the Council, through the Committee, about any possible follow-up visit to Liberia and its assessment of progress made by the Government of Liberia towards joining the Kimberley Process Certification Scheme;

8. *Decides* to remain actively seized of the matter.

Security Council Committee. The Security Council Committee established pursuant to resolution 1521(2003) concerning Liberia submitted a report [S/2006/1044] on its activities for the period 1 January to 31 December 2006. During the reporting period, the Committee held three formal and 10 informal meetings.

The Committee received four requests for exemptions to the arms embargo. It approved requests for an exemption to ship weapons and ammunitions for training the Liberian Special Security Service, to import material for the training of Liberian police officers, as well as the armed forces of Liberia. The fourth request concerned the import of sidearms and related material for use by the Liberian National Police, which had been petitioned in 2005 [YUN 2005, p. 275], but had remained in limbo at the end of the year. The Committee also received and approved a request for the import of dummy weapons and special effects equipment for a company shooting a feature film on location in the country. Following the adoption of resolution 1683(2006), which modified the arms embargo on Liberia to allow for exceptions for the Government (see p. 224), the Committee agreed on procedures to facilitate its consideration of those requests and ensure, with UNMIL assistance, that any arms exported to Liberia were accounted for, as called for in the resolution.

The Committee considered 14 requests for travel ban waivers, three of which were granted. It held quarterly reviews of the travel ban list, initially issued on 16 March 2004 [YUN 2004, p. 211], retaining the names of 58 of the 59 persons listed as at 31 December 2005, having removed one individual from the list during the reporting period [SC/8909]. The Committee conducted three six-month reviews of the assets freeze list in January, June and December. It considered four de-listing requests, but did not remove any names from the assets-freeze list in 2006.

The Committee did not receive any additional replies from States on actions taken to implement resolution 1521(2003); thus, the total number of replies received remained at 17. It received one reply from a State on action taken to trace and freeze the funds, other financial assets and economic resources described in resolution 1532(2004), bringing the total number of replies received to 15.

Sierra Leone

Sierra Leone made further efforts to consolidate peace and stability by strict adherence to the 2000 Agreement on the Ceasefire and Cessation of Hostilities [YUN 2000, p. 210]. To assist in that process, the United Nations Mission in Sierra Leone (UNAMSIL) successfully transitioned to the United Nations Integrated Office in Sierra Leone (UNIOSIL), which was established to support the Government in consolidating peace, building national capacity and in preparing for the 2007 elections. The Office became operational on 1 January 2006. During the year, UNIOSIL, the UN country team and the Government of Sierra Leone developed a peace consolidation strategy, which identified challenges and set out programme interventions to address them. In anticipation of the increased workload of the Office in 2007, particularly with regard to the elections, the Security Council authorized an increase in UNIOSIL strength and extended its mandate to 31 December 2007.

Preparations by the Government of Sierra Leone for the 2007 elections progressed with the establishment of regional offices by the National Electoral Commission, the allocation of seats to the 14 electoral districts and completion of the electoral boundary delimitation process. Some 28 parties registered with the Political Parties Registration Commission and a turnout of 4 million voters was expected. However, a number of challenges emerged, such as signs of political intolerance among political party leaders and their supporters; perceptions that the ruling party was using its incumbency to its advantage; and persistent funding shortfalls. A UN-led electoral assessment mission visited the country in October to determine in what ways the United Nations could assist in facilitating the electoral process. The leaders of eight registered parties signed a Political Parties Code of Conduct for the elections.

Other developments included the selection of Sierra Leone as one of the first countries to be considered by the Peacebuilding Commission; its eligibility to benefit from the Peacekeeping Fund; and the conclusion of investigations into several high-profile cases by the Anti-Corruption Commission.

Although the security situation in the country remained calm, following the departure of UNAMSIL, youth unemployment, rampant corruption, dire economic conditions and tension along the borders, especially with Guinea, were potential threats to stability. The security sector reform programme passed a milestone when it reached its targeted goal of 9,500 fully-trained police.

The Special Court for Sierra Leone continued to try those bearing the greatest responsibility for serious violations of international humanitarian and Sierra Leonean laws committed in the territory of Sierra Leone since 1996. The trial stages of two cases were completed, with judgments expected to be delivered in 2007. The apprehension and transfer of the former President of Liberia, Charles Taylor, into the Court's custody in Freetown, and then later to The Hague, Netherlands, where he would stand trial, was a major achievement towards the completion of the Court's mandate.

In the light of the progress made in peacebuilding efforts during 2006, the Chairman of the Sanctions Committee encouraged the Security Council to determine the appropriate time to streamline the legal basis for sanctions in Sierra Leone.

Peacebuilding efforts

Peace consolidation process and UNIOSIL activities

Report of Secretary-General (April). In his first report on the United Nations Integrated Office in Sierra Leone (UNIOSIL) [S/2006/269], the Secretary-General said that the Office was the first of its kind established to support the peace-consolidation process after completion of a peacekeeping operation. The transition from the United Nations Mission in Sierra Leone (UNAMSIL) to the Office, which became operational on 1 January, was well planned and executed. UNIOSIL comprised a small office to support the Secretary-General's Special Representative, Victor Angelo (Portugal), and five components focusing on the key areas of its mandate: peace and governance; human rights and the rule of law; civilian police; UNIOSIL military cell; and public information. The UN country team constituted the development component, and an administrative/logistical component supported the UNAMSIL liquidation team. In addition to its headquarters in Freetown, field offices were co-located with other UN entities in all 12 of the country's administrative districts.

UNIOSIL, the UN country team and the Government jointly developed a peace consolidation strategy to address a broad category of challenges, such as minimizing internal and external security threats; ensuring accountability in governance; promoting and monitoring respect for human rights and access to justice; promoting national reconciliation; promoting economic recovery; and installing a national infrastructure for peace. The strategy also set out specific programme interventions for addressing those issues. UNIOSIL and the UN country team developed an integrated workplan for 2006, which designated priority activities to be carried out by UNIOSIL individual components, in collaboration with the relevant UN agencies. The peace consolidation strategy complemented the national poverty reduction strategy and the UN development assistance framework. UNIOSIL and the UN country team also agreed on a joint public information strategy to promote national cohesion, political tolerance and partnership in the development process.

In political developments, concern increased over what was perceived as the Government's heavy-handed approach in dealing with the political opposition. The ongoing trial of Chales Margai, who had left the ruling Sierra Leone People's Party (SLPP) and formed the People's Movement for Democratic Change (PMDC), was seen by some as politically motivated. Opposition political parties complained about the Government's use of the police to break up their political meetings and allegations emerged about the politicization of the paramount chieftancy system and its use to deny the opposition access to their supporters, particularly in the Eastern and Southern Provinces.

While progress was made in streamlining the operations of the Anti-Corruption Commission by adopting performance benchmarks for 2006, no high-profile case had been fully prosecuted and there was a general feeling that the Commission was unable or unwilling to achieve tangible results. Slow, but encouraging progress was made in Sierra Leone's decentralization process, especially through implementation of the World Bank-funded capacity-building programme, and the UNDP-supported agriculture sector decentralization initiatives. Efforts were made to strengthen the capacity of the local councils to address the pressing needs of their communities.

Progress was also made in the trial of members of the former Revolutionary United Front (RUF) and the "Westside Boys" militia, arrested and detained without trial since 2000. Of the 57 RUF members charged with conspiracy to murder and shooting with intent to kill, 42 had been acquitted and discharged; three sentenced to ten years' imprisonment each, and 12 were awaiting a final ruling. With respect to the "Westside Boys", 26 were acquitted and discharged, and six sentenced to long prison terms.

The security situation remained calm since the departure of UNAMSIL, although the worsening youth employment situation threatened stability. Violent student and labour protests, as well as an upsurge in criminality throughout the country, were consequences of the dire economic conditions in Sierra Leone. The lack of improvement in water and power supplies, the high cost of basic commodities, the persistent fuel shortages and the general perception that the Government's inability to deliver was due to corruption and mismanagement had become a source of tension. Illegal diamond mining and trading, the ongoing trials of the former armed groups at the Special Court for Sierra Leone, and the transfer of the former President of Liberia, Charles Taylor to the Court (see p. 214) also posed serious challenges to efforts to consolidate peace and stability. An increase in incidents of encroachment by the armed forces of Guinea on Sierra Leonean territory in the Eastern and Northern provinces further exacerbated the fragile security situation. It was reported that Guinean troops were still occupying border-disputed areas and harassing the local Sierra Leonean population. Dialogue between the two countries to resolve the dispute over the Makona/Moa River, in the Yenga village area, had stalled. A study of the 1912 Franco-British Protocols regarding the exact boundary line between Guinea and Sierra Leone conducted by cartographical experts from France and the United Kingdom, produced conflicting reports and further compounded the stalemate. Boundary problems developed also in the Kambia District, where Guinean troops encroached on Sierra Leonean territory and ordered a bauxite mining company licensed by the Government of Sierra Leone to stop prospecting activities. On 19 April, the Secretary-General expressed his concern to Sierra Leonian President Ahmad Tejan Kabbah and Guinean President Lansana Conté over reports of mounting border tension between the two countries and informed them of the UN readiness to assist in their efforts to resolve the dispute.

The reform and training of the Sierra Leone police and armed forces, which had taken over responsibility for security following the departure of UNAMSIL, continued to make satisfactory progress. The graduation of 405 more recruits in February from the Police Training School brought the overall strength of the police to 9,267 personnel. Although the police force was well-equipped and maintained high mobility and visibility throughout the country, it was still plagued by corruption, inexperience, and a shortage of accommodation, vehicles and communications equipment. The reform and restructuring of the armed forces by the International Military Advisory and Training Team continued, with a focus on low-level training and reducing troop strength to 10,500, as initially approved by the Government. As at February, troop strength stood at 10,600 military personnel and the Government was considering a further reduction to 8,500. However, increasing disaffection within the armed forces with regard to the demobilization of personnel, including more than 70 senior officers, was an issue, as was the serious decline in the operation of the District and Provincial Security Committees, following the departure of UNAMSIL. UNIOSIL and the Office of National Security discussed ways to improve the work of those Committees.

The Secretary-General said that, although the security situation remained calm since the departure of UNAMSIL, he was concerned by the dire economic situation, increasing youth unemployment, rampant corruption and mismanagement, as well as the growing tension along border areas, particularly with Guinea. He urged the Government to focus on those issues and take corrective measures expeditiously, especially against the corrupt elements of the police. He appealed to Member States to provide logistical assistance to the Sierra Leone police and armed forces to support the security sector reform programme.

Report of Secretary-General (August). In his August report [S/2006/695] on UNIOSIL, the Secretary-General said that he had visited Sierra Leone on 1 and 2 July and consulted with the President, Vice-President and other senior Government officials, as well as UNIOSIL personnel and the UN country team, on the situation in the country. Representatives of both the Government and the UN system expressed satisfaction with the progress made in the peace consolidation process, particularly with the finalization of the peace consolidation strategy. They also reported on gains made in security sector and governance reforms and on the support provided by the UN system and other partners to improve the socio-economic situation. Illustrations of the strengthening democracy, which were highlighted in the President's 23 June address to Parliament, included the increase in the number of political parties to 28, the expansion of political discourse throughout the country and the proliferation of local media outlets. There were 49 daily newspapers and 39 radio stations operating in Sierra Leone. On the other hand, the Government and UNIOSIL cited youth unemployment as the most immediate potential threat to stability and said that slow economic recovery hindered efforts to create economic opportunities. The need to intensify anti-corruption efforts and accelerate reform of the judiciary was stressed. They underlined the challenges that the 2007 elections posed for the limited capacity of the national security sector and the National Electoral Commission, and in that regard, agreed on the need for substantial technical, logistical and financial support from the international community to ensure the success and credibility of the elections.

In June, President Kabbah's Office issued a statement expressing the Government's determination to address emerging negative trends in the country, including corruption within the police and the lack of respect shown by personnel in some Government ministries. Concerned also by increasing lawlessness and indiscipline across the spectrum of political and civil society, the President called upon political parties and their members to respect the Constitution and the law, and urged Government officials to conduct themselves in a professional manner. The fragility of the political stability in Sierra Leone was underscored by a controversial election on 12 August to fill the vacancy of the Biriwa-Limba Chiefdom in the Northern Province, which divided the population of the fiefdom along ethnic lines. Ignoring the National Electoral Commission's rejection of its request to conduct the election on account of the insecurity in the chiefdom and procedural problems, the Government proceeded to hold the election, contending that the Commission did not have the mandate to do so. The six Limba candidates boycotted the election, and the seat, which had been vacant since 2002, was won by the sole candidate of the Mandingo ethnic group. The prolonged period of heightened tension between the Limba ethnic group, which traditionally held the chieftancy and was challenging the election, and the minority Mandingo ethnic group continued to simmer and created security concerns in the area. Other developments during the period included the consultations held in July by civil society groups to identify possible areas of support by the United Nations Peacebuilding Commission and the President's announcement, on 17 August, of the Government's intention to initiate amendments to the Constitution, which would be included on the ballot for a referendum during the 2007 elections. The Law Reform Commission reviewed the 1991 Constitution to ensure that it reflected the country's new political, social and economic reality. The Government emphasized that, notwithstanding that review, the Constitution would remain in force during and after the 2007 elections.

In the area of governance reform, progress was made in the decentralization of responsibilities, which led to improved participation in local governance, although local councils still suffered from lack of funding. However, some ministries were reluctant to devolve their authority to local councils, and overlapping roles and functions of traditional leaders in the new local government structure had not been rationalized. As its effectiveness was hampered by its limited capacity to detect, investigate and document corrupt practices, the Anti-Corruption Commission developed a strategic plan of action, which would include benchmarks, focusing on improving its investigation, detection and prosecutoral capabilities. It also worked to sensitize the general public to the social and economic consequences of corruption.

A major potential source of instability in the country was removed on 20 June, when former Liberian President Charles Taylor was transferred by the Special Court for Sierra Leone in Freetown to the Hague for trial (see p. 214). The continuing border dispute between Guinea and Sierra Leone remained a concern. The technical committees of Guinea and Sierra Leone met in Conakry in May, and follow-up consultations between the Minister of Territorial Affairs of Guinea and the Sierra Leone Government were held on 25 August. The Secretary-General appealed to Presidents Conté and Kabbah to expedite the peaceful and mutually acceptable resolution of the matter.

Progress in security sector reform continued, with the troop strength of the police and the armed forces standing at 8,900 and 10,300, respectively. Still short of the target strength of 9,500 police set by the Government, a six-month training course for a new group of police recruits was held, and the police developed a comprehensive strategic plan for 2006-2008 to enhance professionalism in the force, particularly in middle management. While UNIOSIL continued to support the police in key areas, given the wide range of areas requiring support and capacity-building, the small team of 20 UNIOSIL police advisers was overstretched. With regard to the armed forces, the Ministry of Defence reviewed their overall structures, with a view to achieving cost effectiveness and sustainability, without compromising their capacity to carry out their constitutionally mandated tasks and responsibilities. The international community contributed significantly to strengthening the capacity of the armed forces, including the provision of patrol boats, which had enhanced the capability of the maritime wing. The conditions of service for the armed services continued to improve, especially medical care, rations and the payment of salaries. However, a lack of adequate housing for soldiers, mainly in the outlying areas of the country, continued to negatively impact their morale. UNIOSIL continued to assist in security sector reform, with a focus on planning guidance at all levels and information-gathering to help in the Government's decision-making process. The Office of National Security continued to enhance its role of coordinating security agencies and other government departments on security-related matters, as well as to establish liaison with its counterpart in Liberia for the purpose of sharing information.

UNIOSIL continued to coordinate UN system support to the Government's peace consolidation efforts. It held an international workshop (30 June–1 July, Freetown) to discuss ways of implementing the peace consolidation strategy jointly prepared by UNIOSIL, the Government and the UN country team; co-organized a number of workshops to strengthen the capacity of Parliament to conduct informed debates and provided training for its staff; and proposed, along with other partners, an early review of the implementation of the National Anti-Corruption Strategy launched in 2005.

The Secretary-General concluded that overall, the Government had made considerable progress towards consolidating peace in Sierra Leone. He was optimistic about its prospects for long-term peace, stability and economic recovery, yet remained concerned about potentially destabilizing factors, such as youth unemployment, pervasive poverty, as well persistent mismanagement. He considered the inclusion of Sierra Leone on the Peacebuilding Commission's agenda as an opportunity to benefit from the goodwill of the international community and recommended that the Government, Commission members, UNIOSIL and other international partners agree on the specific priorities and modalities of the Commission's engagement at its next meeting in October (see p. 237). The Secretary-General also urged the Government and all national stakeholders to implement the recommendations of the Truth and Reconciliation Commission and to exercise tolerance as the country moved toward the elections.

Report of Secretary-General (November). In his third report on UNIOSIL [S/2006/922], the Secretary-General said that further gains were made in reforming the security sector and in building the capacity of the national institutions responsible for conducting the 2007 elections. On 24 October, the Government announced the establishment of the Constitutional Review Commission, which was mandated to bring the 1991 Constitution into conformity with the new political, social and economic realities of the county. The participation of paramount chiefs in partisan politics was the subject of national debate, with the citizenry supporting the role of the traditional leaders. However, there were reports that opposition parties were being prevented from conducting electoral activities in some chiefdoms and concerns raised that the existing legislation prohibiting meetings without prior approval from the relevant paramount chiefs and the police might be abused during the pre-electoral period. With regard to the August election of the paramount chief in the Biriwa Chiefdom (see p. 232), on 10 November, the Supreme Court ruled against the petition of the Limba ethnic group contesting it, on the grounds that the election was not a public election and therefore, did not require the involvement of the National Electoral Commission.

Parliament continued to improve its oversight functions, with ministers and Heads of Government agencies being invited to brief Parliament on the implementation of their respective mandates. Three new bills were prepared to address practices affecting women's rights, including the Devolution of Estates Act 2006, the Registration of Customary Marriage and Divorce Act 2006, and the Domestic Violence Act 2006. The Anti-Corruption Commission concluded investigations into several high-profile cases involving senior civil servants and parliamentarians and forwarded them to the Attorney General for prosecution. The Secretary-General said that prompt action taken on the cases would attest to the Government's political will to deal resolutely with corruption and dispel the perception that the anti-corruption drive might have stalled. Following a discussion of the national anti-corruption strategy at a conference of the main stakeholders (16 November, Freetown), participants established a review mechanism to remedy identified flaws and ensure that the strategy was consistent with the priorities and actions of the Improved Governance and Accountability Pact, agreed by the Government in July 2006, with the United Kingdom Department for International Development, the World Bank and the European Commission. Other progress included the establishment of the National Human Rights Commission in October, with the nomination by President Kabbah and approval by Parliament of five commissioners to serve as its members.

The capacity of the police to maintain law and order and discharge its security responsibilities continuing to develop. At a national conference (30-31 August), organized by UNIOSIL and UNDP, on the role of the police in the 2007 elections, participants expressed confidence in the police force's ability to maintain law and order during the electoral process. However, stability remained threatened by the high level of youth unemployment, the poor social and economic conditions and the public perception of the Government's mismanagement of public funds. Student demonstrations and industrial action by employees in schools increased, with riotous and sometimes destructive behaviour spilling into the streets and straining the limited resources of the police. Many of the incidents were related to the deplorable conditions in the schools and colleges, and the poor conditions of service of teachers. The situation was further exacerbated by the activities of the three major political parties on college campuses.

Further steps were taken to resolve the border dispute between Guinea and Sierra Leone. The Ministers of Interior for both countries met on 18 and 19 September and decided to request that the Economic Community of West African States (ECOWAS) provide boundary demarcation experts to work with the technical committees of both countries. UNIOSIL continued to play a facilitating role in the conduct of border patrols between Liberia and Sierra Leone, and discussed modalities of joint border patrols between the Guinean and Sierra Leonean security agencies.

The programme for security sector reform passed a major milestone when the full strength of 9,500 trained police personnel was achieved during the reporting period. A recruitment programme for 2007 was developed for a further 250 officers, and key updates on basic crowd control and maintenance of public order were added to the training curriculum to ensure that it remained operationally relevant. UNIOSIL and international partners also developed a special training programme to further enhance the ability of the police to respond to possible civil unrest during the electoral period. The planned downsizing of the armed forces was completed and its strength stood at some 10,300 personnel. However, as Sierra Leone was unlikely to be able to sustain an armed force of that size, the Government discussed the appropriate size of the army in the medium-term, being mindful of the socio-economic situation in considering further retrenchments of the armed forces. A survey of morale within the armed forces conducted by UNIOSIL indicated that recent improvements in the training and welfare of army personnel had resulted in a corresponding improvement in morale.

Strengthening UNIOSIL. The UNIOSIL police personnel increased considerably its focus to training Sierra Leone police officers to perform election-related tasks. It was envisaged that during 2007, UNIOSIL police personnel would continue to coordinate the development of a Sierra Leone training task force; support the capacity-building of the police by training an additional 25 officers to become part of the Force's newly formed Evaluation Team; and increase support for the improvement of corrections facilities and the training of management personnel. As a result, the Secretary-General proposed temporarily increasing UNIOSIL police personnel by 10, to bring their total strength to 30, and the UNIOSIL Military Liaison Team by an additional five military advisers, both of which would to be withdrawn during the second half of 2007 after the elections.

The Secretary-General concluded that Sierra Leone would need the sustained support of the international community in its future peacebuilding efforts and urged the Government to work closely with the Peacebuilding Commission to make further progress in consolidating peace in the country. He said that the security architecture needed to be further strengthened so that both the police and the armed forces could carry out their tasks effectively and be sustainable in the long term. He recommended that the Security Council approve the proposed increases in the strength of the UNIOSIL Military Liaison Team and Police Section. Highlighting the significant contribution UNIOSIL had made during the previous 12 months in assisting the Government to consolidate peace and address the root causes of the conflict, the Secretary-General stated that the upcoming July 2007 elections would be a major milestone, which would help define an exit strategy for UNIOSIL. In that respect, he indicated that a comprehensive assessment of the role of the Office should be conducted—closer to the election date—with a view to determining its exit point after the elections. In the meantime, he recommended the extension of UNIOSIL mandate for an additional 12 months, until 31 December 2007.

On 22 December, by resolution 1734(2006), the Security Council endorsed the Secretary-General's recommendations (see p. 238).

Preparations for 2007 elections

In April [S/2006/269], the Secretary-General reported that national elections in Sierra Leone were scheduled to be held between February and May 2007. The allocation of seats to the 14 electoral districts were announced on 23 March, and the boundary delimitation process was expected to start in July, and voter registration in September. The National Electoral Commission, which had already established 14 regional offices, faced a number of remaining challenges, including the shortage of vehicles, overall logistics support for the elections, recruitment and training of 800 Commission staff, and the conduct of civic and voter education. The Political Parties Registration Commission formulated its 2006 action plan, emphasizing inter-party conflict management and the monitoring of party activities. There were 28 registered political parties in Sierra Leone, with only four being active between elections: the ruling Sierra Leone People's Party (SLPP), the All People's Congress (APC), the People's Movement for Democratic Change (PMDC) and the Peace and Liberation Party. Following allegations by opposition political parties that the ruling party was campaigning ahead of schedule and denying its opponents access to the State radio, the National Electoral Commission broadcast a statement explaining what constituted electoral activities and calling on all parties to abide by the rules.

Election costs were estimated at $26 million, of which the Government would contribute one-third and donors the balance. UNIOSIL, with funding from UNDP, provided technical assistance to the National Electoral Commission and the Political Parties Registration Commission, and helped to mobilize donor support for political party capacity-building and the promotion of inter-party dialogue. As the Sierra Leone Police was expected to provide overall security for the 2007 elections, a committee was set up to continuously review police preparedness for that task. The National Electoral Commission signed a memorandum of understanding with the police and was consulting on the preparation of a police operational plan for the elections.

In August [S/2006/695], the Secretary-General reported that there were worrisome signs of growing intolerance among political party leaders and their supporters, some of whom had reportedly declared certain areas "off-limits" to their opponents. The Government's 21 June directive requiring political parties to obtain police permission to hold political meetings created concern that it had the potential for abuse and could limit legitimate political activities. In July, a UN-sponsored consultant reviewed the country's electoral legal framework and recommended revisions for bringing it into conformity with international electoral and human rights standards, minimizing the potential for abuse, establishing a credible electoral dispute process and guaranteeing the freedoms of association, speech and assembly.

On 3 August, President Kabbah announced that presidential and parliamentary elections would be held on 28 July 2007. The National Electoral Commission completed the delimitation of the 112 boundaries in the country's 14 districts, which would be submitted to Parliament for approval, and was developing a detailed workplan, with timelines. The Political Parties Registration Commission, in addition to registering political parties, focused its activities on monitoring their conduct and mediating disputes. It also collaborated with UNIOSIL to finalize a political parties' code of conduct. UNIOSIL and UNDP worked jointly with the Commission to host conflict-prevention workshops for Sierra Leonean political parties.

With the announcement of the date for the elections, the Secretary-General indicated his intention to dispatch an electoral needs assessment mission to discuss with the Government the nature and scope of assistance the UN system could provide.

In November [S/2006/922], the Secretary-General reported that the National Electoral Commission, with UN assistance, continued to prepare for the voter registration exercise, which was expected to commence between late February and early March 2007. The Commission recruited its core personnel, and four UN technical advisers were assigned to support its work. A voter registration operational task force was established, specifications for voter registration equipment and personnel finalized, and a database of estimated voter population per constituency developed. Preparations for the Commission's public information and voter education campaign were under way, including a civic education programme targeting youths. The UN electoral advisory team was strengthened, with the number of international advisers and UN volunteers expected to reach 44 by the end of January 2007.

All political parties, including the ruling SLPP, APC and PMDC, intensified their election-related activities. However, the Secretary-General noted that the general culture of political intolerance in the country and the perception among opposition parties that the ruling party might be using its incumbency to its advantage, while denying the opposition a level playing field, were potential sources of heightened tensions. Furthermore, the socio-economic marginalization of a large segment of society, particularly young people, rendered them susceptible to political manipulation. A polarized atmosphere had emerged, in which the three main parties displayed a "winner takes all" attitude, even though none of them had articulated a clear political platform.

The Political Parties Registration Commission continued to face serious staffing and resource shortages, as well as a leadership problems. President Kabbah appointed a new Chairman on 2 November, which required confirmation by the Parliament. In a positive development, on 23 November, the leaders of eight registered political parties signed the Political Parties Code of Conduct for the elections, which had been developed by the Commission with UNIOSIL support. The Code provided for a monitoring and enforcement mechanism to address irregularities and complaints. The Commission would also play a key role in ensuring compliance with the Code.

Electoral assessment mission. An interdisciplinary electoral assessment mission, led by the Electoral Assistance Division of the UN Department of Political Affairs visited Sierra Leone (15-23 October) to conduct a comprehensive review of electoral preparations and consult with the Government on assistance the UN system could provide to support the process. The mission identified serious challenges to the successful conduct of the 2007 elections, including the delay in parliamentary approval of the draft law on boundary delimitation prepared by the National Electoral Commission, finalization of the amendments to the legal framework for the elections, and the failure to establish the mechanism for resolving electoral disputes.

The mission concluded that the elections could be conducted in a timely and credible manner, if the national electoral institutions received financial and technical support from the Government and donors on time; outstanding laws, including on boundary delimitations, were passed expeditiously by Parliament; overall security remained stable and national security agencies met their obligations to secure the electoral process; measures were taken to strengthen the electoral dispute mechanisms; and an electoral offences court—broadly accepted and credible across the political spectrum—was established quickly.

The mission recommended that the Government should avoid creating a perception that State resources were being used to promote the interests of one party; all parties should have equitable access to the State media; and paramount chiefs should be encouraged to allow free campaigning and political expression in their areas of control. The UN system should provide substantial technical support to the voter registration exercise and identify the technical challenges that could arise due to the inclusion of the constitutional referendum on the ballot. The UN system and the international community, particularly African organizations, should also consider providing long-term observers to the electoral process. Observing that Sierra Leone needed considerable technical and material support from its international partners to ensure the success of the elections, the Secretary-General reiterated his appeal to Member States to close the funding gap.

Other electoral developments. In later developments [S/2007/257], the Secretary-General reported that, on 30 November, the Sierra Leone Parliament approved the constituency boundary delimitation proposal prepared by the National Electoral Commission, which established new boundaries and took into account the population's considerable movement throughout the country since the end of the conflict. Since the general elections held in 2002 [YUN 2002, p. 153] were based on proportional representation, the July 2007 voting process would be the first constituency-based elections to be held in more than two decades. With regard to security matters, UNIOSIL and other major stakeholders were jointly developing a national security plan for voter registration. Donor contributions of £2.5 million received in November and a grant of € 8 million, in December, helped to alleviate the shortfall in electoral funding.

Peacebuilding Commission consideration

The Peacebuilding Commission, established by Security Council resolution 1646(2005) and General Assembly resolution 60/180 [YUN 2005, p. 94], at the first meeting of its Organizational Committee on 23 June, selected Sierra Leone as one of the first countries to be considered by the Commission (see p. 55). The Commission held an informal country-specific meeting on Sierra Leone on 19 July, and its first (12 October) and second (13 December) country-specific meetings, all in New York, in response to a 21 June request [PBC/OC/1/2] of the Council President for the Commission's advice on the situation in Sierra Leone. The Commission Chairman, responding to that request, submitted to the Council President, on 20 December [S/2006/1050], his summary of those meetings.

At the Commission's informal meeting on 19 July, the Foreign Minister of Sierra Leone stressed that the problem of youth unemployment in the country was compounded by the large number of ex-combatants and school dropouts, who could be a source of threat to the country's security. He acknowledged that there was a persistent public perception of corruption within the Government and State institutions, and identified Sierra Leone's weak infrastructure as a major constraint to stimulating economic recovery. Civil society groups in the country also held consultations (19-20 July, Freetown) to identify possible areas where the Commission could support Sierra Leone.

At the Commission's first country-specific meeting, participants reinforced the Government's view of the specific critical challenges that were impeding the consolidation of peace, and which needed to be addressed urgently. Those challenges included social and youth empowerment and employment, consolidating democracy and good governance, justice and security sector reform and capacity building, and ensuring community recovery. Taking note of the poverty reduction strategy and the peace consolidation strategy developed by the Government and its partners, the Commission asked the international community to remain engaged in Sierra Leone, and requested donors to increase their support. The Commission declared Sierra Leone eligible to benefit from the Peacebuilding Fund and invited it to consult with the UN country team on accessing those funds. The Commission called upon the international community to sustain its political and financial support to Sierra Leone and encouraged the United Nations, the World Bank, the International Monetary Fund and other donors to ensure the allocation of resources and activities to reflect the Government's peacebuilding priorities.

At its second country-specific meeting, the Commission assessed progress achieved and identified gaps, with regard to the four critical challenges highlighted at the October meeting: social and youth empowerment and employment; consolidating democracy and governance; justice and security sector reform; and capacity-building. While it emphasized the importance of mapping the identification of further gaps, the Commission recommended that completion of the mapping process should be carried out in parallel with the provision of support for immediate, short-term, quick-impact priorities. It requested the Peacebuilding Support Office to present a calendar of ongoing and planned peacebuilding-related activities in Sierra Leone, and the Chair of the country-specific meeting for Sierra Leone to develop a workplan with a clear timelines and division of responsibilities for actions to be undertaken by the Government, the UN system and other stakeholders in preparation for the Commission's next country-specific meeting.

Security Council consideration (December). On 22 December [meeting 5608], the Security Council heard a briefing by the Commission Chairman (the Netherlands), who highlighted some of the key outcomes of the country-specific meetings on Sierra Leone. He announced that approximately $25 million could be made available, as an initial contribution from the Peacebuilding Fund, and that the next follow-up meeting of the Commission on Sierra Leone would be held in March 2007. The United Kingdom representative identified three priority areas for 2007: the fight against corruption, civil service reform and the development of clear policies and strategies, particularly to address youth unemployment, poverty and economic development. He cited the work of the Special Court for Sierra Leone as crucial to reconciliation and the establishment of the rule of law and stressed the need for further work on implementing resolution 1325(2000), as gender inequality remained a serious problem in the country.

SECURITY COUNCIL ACTION

On 22 December [meeting 5608], the Security Council unanimously adopted **resolution 1734(2006)**. The draft [S/2006/1012] was prepared in consultations among Council members.

The Security Council,

Recalling its previous resolutions and the statements by its President concerning the situation in Sierra Leone, in particular resolutions 1620(2005) of 31 August 2005 and 1688(2006) of 16 June 2006,

Commending the valuable contribution that the United Nations Integrated Office in Sierra Leone has made to the recovery of Sierra Leone from conflict and to the country's peace, security and development,

Having considered the report of the Secretary-General of 28 November 2006, and welcoming his recommendation that the mandate of the United Nations Integrated Office in Sierra Leone be extended for a further twelve months, until 31 December 2007, with a view to providing continued peacebuilding assistance to the Government of Sierra Leone and preparing for the general elections in July 2007,

Taking note of the letter dated 27 November 2006 from the President of Sierra Leone to the Secretary-General that likewise emphasizes the need for the mandate of the United Nations Integrated Office in Sierra Leone to be extended for a further twelve months,

Stressing that the July 2007 elections and the wide acceptance of their outcome will be a major milestone indicating the sustainability of peace and security in Sierra Leone, which should also help to define an exit strategy for the United Nations Integrated Office in Sierra Leone,

Emphasizing the importance of the continued support of the United Nations system and the international community for the long-term peace, security and development of Sierra Leone, particularly through the strengthening of the capacity of the Government of Sierra Leone,

Taking note of the country-specific meetings of the Peacebuilding Commission held on 12 October and 13 December 2006, at which the Commission discussed four priority areas for peacebuilding efforts in Sierra Leone as well as gaps in those areas, recommended next steps for peacebuilding and noted the determination of the Government of Sierra Leone to coordinate and prioritize work in the country, working with the United Nations Integrated Office in Sierra Leone, donors, international institutions, civil society and the private sector to take forward these priorities in order to help to bring about a sustainable peace,

Welcoming the progress made in reforming the security sector in Sierra Leone and, in particular, the developing professionalism of the Sierra Leone armed forces and police, and urging further strengthening and rationalizing of the security architecture so that the police and armed forces are sustainable in the long term and able to carry out their tasks effectively, in particular in connection with the elections in July 2007,

Welcoming also the launch in July 2006 of the Improved Governance and Accountability Pact agreed between main donors and the Government of Sierra Leone, which sets out ten critical governance commitments, including on anti-corruption, public procurement, civil service reform and democracy, and a further ten donor principles of engagement to improve aid effectiveness,

Reiterating its appreciation for the work of the Special Court for Sierra Leone and its vital contribution to reconciliation and the rule of law in Sierra Leone and the subregion, stressing the importance of the forthcoming trial of former Liberian President Charles Taylor by the Special Court and the progress being made in other trials, reiterating its expectation that the Special Court will finish its work expeditiously, noting in this regard the Secretary-General's letter of 27 November 2006, and calling upon Member States to contribute generously to the Special Court,

Encouraging the member States of the Mano River Union and other regional organizations to continue their dialogue aimed at building regional peace and security,

1. *Decides* to extend the mandate of the United Nations Integrated Office in Sierra Leone, as outlined in resolution 1620(2005), until 31 December 2007;

2. *Endorses* the increase in the number of personnel of the United Nations Integrated Office in Sierra Leone recommended in paragraph 70 of the report of the Secretary-General of 28 November 2006 for the period from 1 January to 31 October 2007 in order to enhance the support provided by the Office for the elections and its ability to carry out its functions elsewhere in Sierra Leone;

3. *Calls upon* the Secretary-General to conduct a comprehensive assessment of the role of the United Na-

tions Integrated Office in Sierra Leone, closer to the election date, with a view to developing its exit strategy;

4. *Calls upon* all parties in Sierra Leone to demonstrate their full commitment to the democratic process and to ensure that the 2007 presidential and parliamentary elections are peaceful, transparent, free and fair;

5. *Calls upon* the Government of Sierra Leone to provide the necessary support for the electoral institutions, and urges Member States to provide technical and material support, including to address the shortfall in the electoral budget;

6. *Emphasizes* that the Government of Sierra Leone bears the primary responsibility for peacebuilding, security and long-term development in the country, and encourages the Government to continue its close engagement with the Peacebuilding Commission and international donors to continue to provide support to the Government;

7. *Calls upon* the Government of Sierra Leone, the United Nations Integrated Office in Sierra Leone and all other stakeholders in the country to increase their efforts to promote good governance, including through continued measures to combat corruption, improve accountability, promote the development of the private sector to generate wealth and employment opportunities, strengthen the judiciary and promote human rights;

8. *Calls upon* the Government of Sierra Leone to expedite the implementation of the recommendations of the Truth and Reconciliation Commission, and calls upon Member States to assist the Government in funding the activities of the National Human Rights Commission;

9. *Emphasizes* the important role of women in the prevention and resolution of conflicts and in peacebuilding, as recognized in resolution 1325(2000) of 31 October 2000, underlines that a gender perspective should be taken into account in implementing all aspects of the mandate of the United Nations Integrated Office in Sierra Leone, welcomes in this regard the action plan developed by the Office, encourages the Office to work with the Government of Sierra Leone in this area, and requests the Secretary-General to ensure that there is adequate capacity, expertise and resources within the Office to carry out this work;

10. *Requests* the Secretary-General, where appropriate, to include in his reporting to the Security Council progress on gender mainstreaming throughout the United Nations Integrated Office in Sierra Leone and all other aspects relating to the situation of women and girls, especially in relation to the need to protect them from gender-based violence;

11. *Welcomes* the efforts undertaken by the United Nations Integrated Office in Sierra Leone to implement the Secretary-General's zero-tolerance policy on sexual exploitation and abuse to ensure full compliance of its personnel with the United Nations code of conduct;

12. *Requests* the Secretary-General to keep the Council regularly informed of progress made in the implementation of the mandate of the United Nations Integrated Office in Sierra Leone and the present resolution;

13. *Decides* to remain actively seized of the matter.

UNIOSIL

The United Nations Integrated Office in Sierra Leone (UNIOSIL), established by Security Council resolution 1620(2005) [YUN 2005, p. 282], was mandated to assist the Government of Sierra Leone in strengthening the capacity of State institutions, rule of law, human rights and the security sector; developing economic empowerment initiatives for youth; improving transparency and good governance; building capacity to hold free and fair elections in 2007; as well as liaising with the Sierra Leonean security sector; coordinating with UN missions and regional organizations in West Africa to address cross-border issues; and coordinating with the Special Court for Sierra Leone.

In 2006, the Secretary-General submitted reports to the Security Council on developments in Sierra Leone and the activities of UNIOSIL in April [S/2006/269]; August [S/2006/695]; and November [S/2006/922]; with a later report covering the remainder of the year [S/2007/257]. In addition to political and security aspects, the reports summarized UNIOSIL activities relating to humanitarian issues, human rights and the rule of law, public information, as well as its efforts to assist in the country's recovery, reconstruction and development.

Financing of missions

UNIOSIL

In a January report [A/60/585/Add.1] on estimates in respect of 26 special political missions, good offices and other political initiatives authorized by the General Assembly and/or the Security Council, the Secretary-General proposed requirements for UNIOSIL amounting to $23,298,600 for the period from 1 January to 31 December 2006.

On 8 May, in section I of **resolution 60/255** (see p. 1618), the General Assembly approved, as recommended by ACABQ [A/60/7/Add.37], for UNIOSIL a prorated amount out of the additional charges of $202,469,500 approved for the special political missions under Section 3, Political affairs, of the 2006-2007 programme budget.

In his November report [A/61/525/Add.3] on estimates for special political missions, including ten in Thematic cluster III, the Secretary-General submitted proposed requirements for UNIOSIL in the amount of $30,564,000 for the period 1 January to

31 December 2007, which ACABQ recommended for approval in December [A/61/640 & Corr.1].

On 22 December, in section VII of **resolution 61/252** (see p. 1615), the Assembly endorsed ACABQ recommendations on UNIOSIL budget for the period 1 January to 31 December 2007.

UNAMSIL

In June, the General Assembly considered the performance report on the UNAMSIL budget for the period from 1 July 2004 to 30 June 2005 [A/60/631], which showed expenditures of $264,525,800 against a total appropriation of $291,603,600, leaving an unencumbered balance of $27,077,800.

ACABQ [A/60/786] recommended that the unencumbered balance, as well as income and adjustments of $72,209,800 be credited to the Member States in a manner to be determined by the General Assembly.

GENERAL ASSEMBLY ACTION

On 22 June [meeting 92], the General Assembly, on the recommendation of the Fifth Committee [A/60/926], adopted **resolution 60/279** without vote [agenda item 150].

Financing of the United Nations Mission in Sierra Leone

The General Assembly,

Having considered the report of the Secretary-General on the financing of the United Nations Mission in Sierra Leone and the related report of the Advisory Committee on Administrative and Budgetary Questions,

Bearing in mind Security Council resolution 1270(1999) of 22 October 1999, by which the Council established the United Nations Mission in Sierra Leone, and the subsequent resolutions by which the Council revised and extended the mandate of the Mission, the latest of which was resolution 1610(2005) of 30 June 2005, by which the Council extended the mandate of the Mission for a final period of six months until 31 December 2005,

Recalling its resolution 53/29 of 20 November 1998 on the financing of the United Nations Observer Mission in Sierra Leone and subsequent resolutions on the financing of the United Nations Mission in Sierra Leone, the latest of which was resolution 59/14 B of 22 June 2005,

Reaffirming the general principles underlying the financing of United Nations peacekeeping operations, as stated in General Assembly resolutions 1874(S-IV) of 27 June 1963, 3101(XXVIII) of 11 December 1973 and 55/235 of 23 December 2000,

Noting with appreciation that voluntary contributions have been made to the Mission,

Mindful of the fact that it is essential to provide the Mission with the necessary financial resources to enable it to meet its outstanding liabilities,

1. *Takes note* of the status of contributions to the United Nations Observer Mission in Sierra Leone and the United Nations Mission in Sierra Leone as at 30 April 2006, including the contributions outstanding in the amount of 42.6 million United States dollars, representing some 2 per cent of the total assessed contributions, notes with concern that only eighty-three Member States have paid their assessed contributions in full, and urges all other Member States, in particular those in arrears, to ensure payment of their outstanding assessed contributions;

2. *Expresses its appreciation* to those Member States which have paid their assessed contributions in full, and urges all other Member States to make every possible effort to ensure payment of their assessed contributions to the Mission in full;

3. *Welcomes* the great efforts of the Mission and its personnel in the successful completion of the mandate of the Mission;

4. *Also welcomes* the structured, carefully planned and executed drawdown that allowed the established benchmarks to be achieved as scheduled;

5. *Requests* the Secretary-General to ensure that the lessons learned from the Mission, including its drawdown stages, are applied, as best practices, in other missions as appropriate, and to report thereon in the context of the final performance report;

6. *Notes with concern* the cases of fraud and presumptive fraud identified by the Mission, and requests the Secretary-General to report to the General Assembly at its sixty-first session on the matters, including investigations undertaken in this regard and actions taken regarding proven cases, in accordance with established procedures, as well as efforts to recover any lost funds;

7. *Endorses* the conclusions and recommendations contained in the report of the Advisory Committee on Administrative and Budgetary Questions, and requests the Secretary-General to ensure their full implementation;

Financial performance report for the period from 1 July 2004 to 30 June 2005

8. *Takes note* of the report of the Secretary-General on the financial performance of the Mission for the period from 1 July 2004 to 30 June 2005;

9. *Decides* that Member States that have fulfilled their financial obligations to the Mission shall be credited with their respective share of the unencumbered balance and other income in the amount of 99,287,600 dollars in respect of the financial period ended 30 June 2005, in accordance with the levels updated in its resolution 58/256 of 23 December 2003, and taking into account the scale of assessments for 2005, as set out in its resolution 58/1 B of 23 December 2003;

10. *Decides also* that, for Member States that have not fulfilled their financial obligations to the Mission, their share of the unencumbered balance and other income in the amount of 99,287,600 dollars in respect of the financial period ended 30 June 2005 shall be set off against their outstanding obligations in accordance with the scheme set out in paragraph 9 above;

11. *Decides further* that, the decrease of 1,339,800 dollars in the estimated staff assessment income in respect of the financial period ended 30 June 2005 shall be set off against the credits from the amount of 99,287,600 dollars referred to in paragraphs 9 and 10 above;

12. *Encourages* Member States that are owed credits for the closed peacekeeping mission accounts to apply those credits to any accounts where the Member State concerned has outstanding assessed contributions;

13. *Decides* to include in the provisional agenda of its sixty-first session the item entitled "Financing of the United Nations Mission in Sierra Leone".

In December [A/61/682], the Secretary-General submitted the performance report on the UNAMSIL budget for the period from 1 July 2005 to 30 June 2006, which showed expenditures of $86,137,300, against a total appropriation of $107,539,300, leaving an unencumbered balance of $21,402,000.

By **decision 61/552** of 22 December, the General Assembly deferred consideration of the item on "Financing the United Nations Mission in Sierra Leone" to its resumed sixty-first (2007) session.

Special Court for Sierra Leone

The Special Court for Sierra Leone, jointly established by the Government of Sierra Leone and the United Nations in 2002 [YUN 2002, p. 164], pursuant to Security Council resolution 1315(2000) [YUN 2000, p. 205], continued, in 2006, to try those bearing the greatest responsibility for violations of international humanitarian and Sierra Leonean laws committed in the territory of Sierra Leone since November 1996. The trial stages of two cases were completed: the Civil Defence Forces trial closed in November and the Armed Forces Revolutionary Council trial closed in December, with the judgements expected to be delivered in June and July 2007, respectively. The apprehension and transfer of former Liberian President Charles Taylor to the Special Court for Sierra Leone in Freetown, and later to The Hague, Netherlands, where he would stand trial, was another milestone achieved in the completion of the Court's mandate (see below). The indictment against him was amended in March, and he made his initial appearance before the Court on 3 April, during which he pleaded not guilty to all counts. On 20 June, Mr. Taylor was transferred to the Hague, where the Special Court would retain full legal control and authority over him and assume full legal responsibility for his custody.

In October, the UN Office for Legal Affairs appointed an independent expert to assess the Court's operations. On 8 December, the Secretary-General appointed Stephen Rapp (United States) as Prosecutor for the Special Court, succeeding Desmond de Silva.

Transfer of trial and former President of Liberia to The Hague

On 29 March, following consultations between President Johnson-Sirleaf of Liberia and President Olusegun Obasanjo of Nigeria, former Liberian President Charles Taylor, who was in exile in Nigeria, was flown to Monrovia and apprehended by the United Nations Mission in Liberia (UNMIL), which transferred him to Freetown to be tried by the Special Court for Sierra Leone for war crimes and other violations of Sierra Leonean humanitarian law. However, as regional leaders and the wider international community considered his continued presence in the country an immediate threat to regional security, concerns arose over the feasibility of holding the trial in Sierra Leone. On 30 March, President Johnson-Sirleaf urged the Security Council to allow Mr. Taylor's trial to take place in The Hague, Netherlands, before the Special Court.

Communications. On 31 March [S/2006/207], the Netherlands informed the Security Council that, in response to the request of the Special Court for Sierra Leone seeking its consent to hold Mr. Taylor's trial and facilitate its conduct in the Netherlands, the Government had indicated its willingness to host the Special Court for the trial, provided that conditions outlined in an annex to the letter were met. The conditions related to the establishment of the legal basis for the Special Court to detain and conduct the trial in the Netherlands; the arrangement for the immediate transfer of Mr. Taylor outside of the Netherlands after the final judgment of the Special Court; and the ascertainment by the Special Court that one or more existing international criminal courts in the Netherlands would provide appropriate facilities, including a courtroom and detention cell, for the purpose of the trial. Costs resulting from the trial would be expenses of the Special Court for Sierra Leone, and no additional costs would be incurred by the Netherlands without its consent.

In a 3 April statement [S/2006/237], the EU commended the courage of President Johnson-Sirleaf in facilitating Mr. Taylor's extradition and the important role played by President Obasanjo and the Nigerian authorities in securing his arrest. In addition, it expressed its support for the Special Court for Sierra Leone.

In his initial appearance before the Court, also on 3 April, Mr. Taylor pleaded not guilty to all counts in the indictment, which, as amended on 16

March, alleged that he was at the head of a joint criminal enterprise responsible for war crimes, crimes against humanity and other serious violations of humanitarian law. On 13 April, the Registry of the Special Court concluded a memorandum of understanding with the International Criminal Court (ICC) allowing the Special Court to use its courtroom and detention facilities for the purposes of Mr. Taylor's trial.

On 15 June [S/2006/406], the United Kingdom indicated that it would allow former President Taylor, if convicted, to enter the country to serve any sentence imposed by the Special Court, without prejudice to the eventual location or outcome of the trial. It also stressed that Mr. Taylor's right to a fair trial had to be respected. However, should the Court acquit Mr. Taylor, the United Kingdom would not be required to allow him to come to the country. Furthermore, upon his subsequent release after serving a sentence, Mr. Taylor would be required to leave or face removal from the United Kingdom.

SECURITY COUNCIL ACTION

On 16 June [meeting 5467], the Security Council unanimously adopted **resolution 1688(2006)**. The draft [S/2006/405] was submitted by the United Kingdom.

The Security Council,

Recalling its previous resolutions and the statements by its President concerning Liberia, Sierra Leone and West Africa, in particular resolutions 1470(2003) of 28 March 2003, 1508(2003) of 19 September 2003, 1537(2004) of 30 March 2004 and 1638(2005) of 11 November 2005,

Recalling also that the Special Court for Sierra Leone ("the Special Court") was established by the Agreement between the United Nations and the Government of Sierra Leone on 16 January 2002 ("the Agreement") pursuant to Security Council resolution 1315(2000) of 14 August 2000,

Recalling further article 10 of the Agreement, pursuant to which the Special Court may meet away from its seat if it considers it necessary for the efficient exercise of its functions, and recalling rule 4 of the Rules of Procedure and Evidence of the Special Court, pursuant to which the President of the Special Court may authorize a Chamber or a Judge to exercise their functions away from the seat of the Special Court,

Recalling the determination of the Council to end impunity, establish the rule of law and promote respect for human rights and to restore and maintain international peace and security, in accordance with international law and the purposes and principles of the Charter of the United Nations,

Expressing its appreciation to President Johnson-Sirleaf of the Republic of Liberia for her courageous decision to request the transfer of former President Taylor in order that he may be tried at the Special Court,

Expressing its appreciation also to President Obasanjo of the Federal Republic of Nigeria for his decision to facilitate the transfer of former President Taylor, and noting the role that Nigeria has played in securing and promoting peace in Liberia and the wider subregion, including President Obasanjo's decision in 2003 to facilitate the removal of former President Taylor from Liberia, which allowed the Comprehensive Peace Agreement to take effect, and recognizing the contribution made by the Economic Community of West African States in this regard,

Recognizing that the proceedings in the Special Court in the case against former President Taylor will contribute to achieving truth and reconciliation in Liberia and the wider subregion,

Expressing that it remains committed to assisting the Governments of Liberia and Sierra Leone in their efforts to a more stable, prosperous and just society,

Reiterating its appreciation for the essential work of the Special Court and its vital contribution to the establishment of the rule of law in Sierra Leone and the subregion,

Welcoming the transfer of former President Taylor to the Special Court on 29 March 2006, and noting that, at present, the trial of former President Taylor cannot be conducted within the subregion due to the security implications if he is held in Freetown at the Special Court,

Noting that it is not feasible for the trial of former President Taylor to be hosted at the premises of the International Criminal Tribunal for the Prosecution of Persons Responsible for Genocide and Other Serious Violations of International Humanitarian Law Committed in the Territory of Rwanda and Rwandan Citizens Responsible for Genocide and Other Such Violations Committed in the Territory of Neighbouring States between 1 January and 31 December 1994 due to its full engagement on the completion strategy, and that no other international criminal tribunals exist for the trial of former President Taylor in Africa,

Taking note of the exchange of letters dated 29 March 2006 between the President of the Special Court and the Minister for Foreign Affairs of the Netherlands ("the exchange of letters dated 29 March 2006"),

Taking note also of the Memorandum of Understanding dated 13 April 2006 between the Special Court and the International Criminal Court ("the Memorandum dated 13 April 2006"),

Noting that former President Taylor has been brought before the Special Court at its seat in Freetown, and determining that the continued presence of former President Taylor in the subregion is an impediment to stability and a threat to the peace of Liberia and of Sierra Leone and to international peace and security in the region,

Acting under Chapter VII of the Charter,

1. *Takes note* of the intention of the President of the Special Court to authorize a Trial Chamber to exercise its functions away from the seat of the Special Court, and his request to the Government of the Netherlands to host the trial, including any appeal;

2. *Welcomes* the willingness of the Government of the Netherlands, as expressed in the exchange of letters dated 29 March 2006, to host the Special Court for the detention and trial of former President Taylor, including any appeal;

3. *Takes note* of the willingness of the International Criminal Court, as requested by the Special Court and as expressed in the Memorandum dated 13 April 2006, to allow the use of its premises for the detention and trial of former President Taylor by the Special Court, including any appeal;

4. *Requests* all States to cooperate to this end, in particular to ensure the appearance of former President Taylor in the Netherlands for purposes of his trial by the Special Court, and encourages all States to ensure that any evidence or witnesses are, upon the request of the Special Court, promptly made available to the Special Court for this purpose;

5. *Requests* the Secretary-General to assist, as a matter of priority, in the conclusion of all necessary legal and practical arrangements, including for the transfer of former President Taylor to the Special Court in the Netherlands and for the provision of the necessary facilities for the conduct of the trial, in consultation with the Special Court, as well as the Government of the Netherlands;

6. *Requests* the Special Court, with the assistance of the Secretary-General and relevant States, to make the trial proceedings accessible to the people of the subregion, including through video link;

7. *Decides* that the Special Court shall retain exclusive jurisdiction over former President Taylor during his transfer to and presence in the Netherlands in respect of matters within the statute of the Special Court, and that the Netherlands shall not exercise its jurisdiction over former President Taylor except by express agreement with the Special Court;

8. *Decides also* that the Government of the Netherlands shall facilitate the implementation of the decision of the Special Court to conduct the trial of former President Taylor in the Netherlands, in particular by:

(a) Allowing the detention and the trial in the Netherlands of former President Taylor by the Special Court;

(b) Facilitating the transport upon the request of the Special Court of former President Taylor within the Netherlands outside the areas under the authority of the Special Court;

(c) Enabling the appearance of witnesses, experts and other persons required to be at the Special Court under the same conditions and according to the same procedures as applicable to the International Tribunal for the Prosecution of Persons Responsible for Serious Violations of International Humanitarian Law Committed in the Territory of the Former Yugoslavia since 1991;

9. *Decides further* that the measures imposed by paragraph 4 *(a)* of resolution 1521(2003) of 22 December 2003 shall not apply to former President Taylor for the purposes of any travel related to his trial before the Special Court, as well as any travel related to the execution of the judgment, and decides to exempt from the travel ban the travel of any witnesses whose presence at the trial is required;

10. *Recalls* that the costs to be incurred as a result of the trial of former President Taylor in the Netherlands are expenses of the Special Court in the sense of article 6 of the Agreement and that no additional costs can be incurred by any other party without their prior consent;

11. *Recalls also* the Secretary-General's letter dated 5 April 2006 and reiterates its appeal to States to contribute generously to the Special Court, and notes with appreciation the States which have done so in the past;

12. *Decides* to remain seized of the matter.

On the same day, the President of the Court ordered the proceedings to be conducted in The Hague, where the accused was subsequently transferred on 20 June.

The Secretary-General, in a 20 June press statement [SG/SM/10524], encouraged all States to cooperate with the Special Court with respect to Mr. Taylor's trial, by ensuring that evidence and witnesses were made available to the Court upon its request. He also appealed to States to contribute to the Court's budget.

Financing

The General Assembly, in resolution 60/245 [YUN 2005, p. 1483] of 23 December 2005, on a request by the Secretary-General [A/60/572/Add.1] and ACABQ recommendation [A/60/597], approved a subvention in the amount of $11.2 million for the Special Court for Sierra Leone under the 2004-2005 programme budget. The subvention was requested to meet the Court's cash requirements for the period from 1 November to 31 December 2005, and cover the liquidation of outstanding obligations as at 31 December 2005, after the funds appropriated under resolution 59/294 [YUN 2005, p. 1488] for the period from 1 January to 31 December 2005 were fully utilized.

In the first performance report on the utilization of the subvention, submitted in November 2006 under the 2006-2007 programme budget [A/61/593/Add.1], the Secretary-General reported that $4.5 million was remitted to the Court for expenditures from 1 November to 31 December 2005, leaving an unencumbered balance of $6.7 million. Of that amount, $3.4 million was disbursed between January and November 2006; an additional $885,178 was anticipated to be disbursed by the end of 2006 to cover liquidation obligations, and the balance of $1 million in unliquidated obligations would be cancelled. The Assembly was asked to note that the estimated unspent balance of $2.4 million would be surrendered under the programme budget, as at 31 December 2006.

The Assembly, in section VIII of **resolution 61/252** of 22 December (see p. 1616), took note of the performance report on the utilization of the subvention.

Sanctions

The Security Council Committee established pursuant to resolution 1132(1997) [YUN 1997, p. 135] concerning Sierra Leone submitted a 28 December report [S/2006/1043] covering its 2006 activities to monitor and implement the 1998 embargo on the sale or supply of arms to Sierra Leone and the travel ban on leading members of the former military junta in Sierra Leone and of the Revolutionary United Front (RUF), imposed by resolution 1171(1998) [YUN 1998, p. 169].

During 2006, the Committee held one session of informal consultations; it considered the travel ban list on 11 July. The Committee reviewed notifications of 10 August from Denmark of the proposed export of commercial explosives to a private company in Sierra Leone for use in a diamond industry bulk sampling programme, and of 21 April from Switzerland of a proposed donation of certain vehicles, trailers and related spare parts and services to the Consortium for the Rehabilitation and Development of Sierra Leone. In both cases the Committee concluded that the proposed items did not qualify as embargoed items and therefore were not subject to the Committee's further consideration.

The Committee noted that, as of the reporting date, the travel ban list included the names of 30 individuals designated as leading members of the former military junta, the Armed Forces Revolutionary Council and RUF. Since the list was last revised in September 2004 [YUN 2004, p. 223], no further information or recommendation had been received from Sierra Leone. On 14 July, the Committee requested the views of the Government on the future of the travel ban measure, as well as any information or suggestions regarding individuals who remained on the list. A response from the Government was still pending. The Committee approved a 5 December request by Canada, transmitted by the Special Court for Sierra Leone, for a waiver of the travel restriction to enable an accused suspect of the Special Court to receive medical treatment.

During the reporting period, no violations or alleged violations of the sanctions regime were brought to the attention of the Committee. In the light of Sierra Leone's continued progress in its peacebuilding efforts, the Committee Chairperson encouraged members of the Committee and the Security Council to determine the appropriate time to streamline the legal basis for sanctions in Sierra Leone. The Chairperson indicated that the Committee, with a view towards updating the sanctions regime, would ensure that the travel ban list reflected as closely as possible the current situation in Sierra Leone, and in that regard, was awaiting the views of the Government before reviewing the list.

Guinea-Bissau

In 2006, the United Nations Peacebuilding Support Office in Guinea-Bissau (UNOGBIS) continued to assist Guinea-Bissau in its efforts to further consolidate peace, promote national reconciliation and mobilize international financial assistance to enable the Government to meet its financial needs. During the year, political tensions hampered democratic progress in the country and the divisions that surfaced following the 2005 presidential elections polarized the National Popular Assembly, with no side able to assure sustainable support in the Parliament. Some progress was made in launching dialogue initiatives, such as the "Estados Gerais", with the support of the Community of Portuguese-Speaking Countries and the Economic Community of West African States, which established an International Contact Group on Guinea-Bissau. Although the parties made a commitment, in September, to improve the political climate, tensions escalated when former President Koumba Yalá returned to Guinea-Bissau, won the leadership of the Party for Social Renewal at its national congress in November, denounced the Government as illegitimate, and called for the holding of legislative elections before 2008. By year's end, the political situation was severely strained, characterized by bitter disputes among parliamentarians, intra-party divisions and heightened tensions. In the light of the erratic political situation, concerns were raised, as disbursement of the pledged donations made at the donor round table in November hinged upon the precondition of political stability.

The security situation was marked by various incidents throughout the year. In March, the armed forces of Guinea-Bissau launched a month-long military operation against a faction of the Movement of Democratic Forces of Casamance, a separatist group demanding independence from Senegal. The conflict caused the displacement or isolation of some 30,000 people from their homes or communities. Low cash crop yields added more hardship to the country's fragile economic base and compromised the Government's ability to pay salaries and deliver basic services. As dire economic and social conditions persisted, demonstrations and protests, particularly in the public sector, continued to pose a threat to stability in the country. Meanwhile, increasingly large seizures of drugs and weapons elevated concerns that organized crime and drug trafficking were growing in the country.

Throughout the year, UNOGBIS used its good offices to further consolidate peace and build on the progress already achieved. Activities focused on facilitating the national reconciliation and dialogue process, conducting training workshops and galvanizing support for a capacity-building project for Parliament. Moreover, along with key national stakeholders and international partners, UNOGBIS continued to play a critical advisory role in support of national efforts towards security sector reform. As a result, the Government finalized a strategy paper on security sector reform, which was approved by the Council of Ministers, along with a triennial investment plan for $184 million. It also established the National Commission to Combat the Proliferation of Small Arms and Light Weapons.

In view of those developments, the Secretary-General streamlined UNOGBIS mandate to highlight its mediation and good offices functions. Its activities would focus on national reconciliation and dialogue; security sector reform; rule of law and human rights; mainstreaming a gender perspective in peacebuilding; small arms and light weapons proliferation; cooperation with regional organizations, key stakeholders and other international partners; and mobilization of international assistance for reconstruction.

Political and security developments and UNOGBIS activities

Report of Secretary-General (March). In his March report [S/2006/162] on developments in Guinea-Bissau and UNOGBIS activities, the Secretary-General noted that political tensions along personality and party lines continued to hamper further democratic progress. The bitter divisions over the 2005 elections [YUN 2005, p. 293] were mirrored in a National Popular Assembly polarized into two blocs: one, including a dissident faction of the African Party for the Independence of Guinea and Cape Verde (PAIGC), supporting the Government appointed by President João Bernardo Vieira in November 2005; and the other, allied to the former PAIGC Government dismissed by the President in October 2005 [ibid., p. 296]. Hence, the balance of power remained fluid, with neither side able to assure sustainable support in Parliament. PAIGC urged President Vieira to replace the Government led by Prime Minister Aristides Gomes with a broad-based one, drawing from parties not represented in the Assembly. It organized civil actions to protest the Supreme Court's ruling upholding the constitutionality of the President's decision to appoint Mr. Gomes as Prime Minister. Joining forces with 10 smaller parties that had supported its presidential candidate, Malam Bacai Sanhá, PAIGC established the Broad Republican Front, with the aim of preventing a dictatorship. In addition, political controversy surrounded the appointment or replacement of deputies and appointments to parliamentary commissions, with some Government supporters accusing the Assembly Speaker of obstruction and partisanship. UNOGBIS led joint efforts with the Community of Portuguese-Speaking Countries (CPLP) and the Economic Community of West African States (ECOWAS) to get the two sides to resolve their differences constructively. Although the process initiated to bring together senior presidential advisers, government representatives, parliamentary parties and the Assembly's Permanent Commission resulted in the participants affirming their commitment to constructive dialogue and reconciliation, the will to engage in joint-problem solving was still lacking. UNOGBIS convened workshops, including one (2-5 February) that examined the causes of the political crisis and proposed strategies to foster positive developments; and the other, a one-day (7 February) pilot training workshop that focused on leadership and conflict transformation skills for parliamentarians.

In the area of security sector reform, progress was made on 16 January, when the armed forces National Commission on Reconciliation and Reintegration launched the second phase of its sensitization campaign. The Commission's work was expanded to cover the police, security and other paramilitary forces. To consolidate progress already achieved, activities focused on, among other areas, the negative impact of ethnicity in the armed forces; the role the armed forces played in the 2005 presidential elections; and the inclusion in the reconciliation process of Guinea-Bissau citizens who had served in the Portuguese colonial army during the independence struggle. An inter-ministerial committee on security sector reform, established in December 2005 by the Prime Minister [ibid.], was formally launched on 7 February. A steering committee was set up to orient the work of a technical team and approve its proposals prior to submission to the inter-ministerial committee and the Cabinet. The United Kingdom Security Sector Development Advisory Team met in Bissau (20 February–3 March) for its second visit to consult with key stakeholders on the process and content of a security sector review exercise.

An increase in the number and quantity of weapons and drugs seized had not resulted in a reduction in delinquency, implying that the causes were not being addressed. In a mission to Guinea-Bissau (23-27 January) to assess the country's law enforcement capacity, the United Nations Office on Drugs and Crime found that the Government lacked the ability to ensure the execution of sanctions and the capacity to provide border security, which led to international criminal networks using the country as a transit point for drug trafficking. The mission also reported that prison conditions in Bissau, the capital, were appalling and the rehabilitation of detention facilities was a pressing concern.

The Secretary-General observed that the lack of constructive dialogue had undermined the authority of two State institutions: the Supreme Court, which was challenged by opponents of the Government; and the Speaker of Parliament, who was challenged by Government supporters. He stated that it was important for the people of Guinea-Bissau to re-establish the authority of their democratic institutions and urged them to put aside the contradictions of the recent past and join forces to start a process of sustainable reconciliation. He commended the close cooperation among UNOGBIS, ECOWAS and CPLP, as well as their joint initiatives to ensure more constructive partnership in support of Guinea-Bissau. He noted the positive role played by the military leadership in consolidating the recovery process, in particular the directive that the military remain outside the political arena and subordinate itself to the civilian authorities. He encouraged the international community to continue its support to Guinea-Bissau in order to avert worsening social and political tensions.

Launch of military operation against Casamance faction

The Secretary-General reported [S/2006/487] that the armed forces of Guinea-Bissau launched a military operation on 14 March, against a faction of the Movement of Democratic Forces of Casamance (MFDC), led by Salif Sadio, near the border with Senegal. Armed confrontation between the national armed forces and the faction, a separatist group demanding independence or autonomy from Senegal, caused more than 5,500 civilians to flee from the areas in and around the city of São Domingos in northern Guinea-Bissau. Of those, some 3,000 fled to other areas of the country, including to the nearby cities of Ingoré and Cacheu and to a makeshift camp near Bourkadie, and across the border in Senegal.

On 24 March, [AFR/1349], the Under-Secretary-General for Humanitarian Affairs and Emergency Relief Coordinator, Jan Egeland, called upon all parties to cease their hostilities, which had endangered the lives of thousands. He expressed concern over the anti-tank and anti-personnel landmines that had been planted in the conflict area, particularly in the light of the authorities' recent encouragement of the internally displaced and refugees to return to their homes. The World Food Programme and the United Nations Children's Fund provided food, essential drugs and clean drinking water to affected populations.

On 14 April, President Vieira announced that Guinea-Bissau troops would continue their offensive in the north until all Senegalese rebel bases established there had been destroyed. On 22 April, the military authorities declared that the operation had been successfully completed; Salif Sadio's camps within the national territory had been dismantled and his fighters expelled beyond national borders. No official estimate of casualties was made public.

Overall, the military operations resulted in the displacement of about 10,000 persons, mostly women and children, and isolated some 20,000 from farming and fishing communities. Although hostilities had ended, conditions in the affected villages were not conducive to their return, mainly due to mine risks and the destruction of and damage to their property during the clashes. The Secretary-General indicated that mine risk education and sensitization, as well as mine survey and identification had begun in the areas affected by the clashes and field demining operations were under way. Moreover, in Bissau, the removal of unexploded ordnance continued, and it was likely to be declared mine-free soon.

Aftermath of military operations

Report of Secretary-General (July). In his July report [S/2006/487] on developments in Guinea-Bissau and UNOGBIS activities, the Secretary-General said that the fragility of the political situation was demonstrated by the controversy and tensions that arose over military operations launched in March by Guinea-Bissau armed forces against an MFDC faction (see above), prompting heated debates in Parliament. According to official sources, the operations were undertaken to protect national sovereignty and territorial integrity, as well as civilians against the actions of MFDC rebels. However, some members of the National

Popular Assembly, leaders of political parties, civil society organizations and the media questioned the wisdom of military intervention in view of the country's financial and economic difficulties. In late March, President Vieira consulted with key national actors on ways to address the country's political and socio-economic challenges. Expectations arose that the consultative process could lead to sustainable political dialogue that would allow the State to function more effectively and break the political deadlock. Another positive development was the 7 March launch of the "Estados Gerais" initiative by a group of citizens, under the auspices of UNOGBIS, ECOWAS and CPLP, aimed at creating a space for consensus-building on the sources of instability and root causes of conflict in Guinea-Bissau. Following the visit of a high-level delegation to the country (2-5 May) to assess the political, military, humanitarian and socio-economic situation, ECOWAS Ministers for Foreign Affairs (Monrovia, Liberia, 15 May) discussed a proposal to establish a contact group on Guinea-Bissau to harmonize international strategies in support of the country and mobilize resources for peacebuilding and reconstruction.

UNOGBIS continued to play a critical advisory role in supporting national efforts towards security sector reform. However, conflicting schedules and salary arrears hampered progress in the security sector review process and the drafting of a national security sector reform strategy document. Both exercises would follow a template developed with the assistance of the United Kingdom Security Sector Development Advisory Team, which visited the country in late 2005 and early 2006. A third visit of the Advisory Team was planned for later in the year to assist Guinea-Bissau officials in concluding the review process and finalizing the strategy document.

Guinea-Bissau's socio-economic and financial situation remained difficult, with the Government unable to cover costs related to the minimum functioning of the State, and to meet its external debt service payments. The marketing of cashew nuts, the country's top export, was adversely affected by a 30 per cent increase in the Government's reference price. An IMF mission visited Guinea-Bissau (15-16 March) to assess the Government's performance and agree on a new programme for 2006. A follow-up mission in June (19-20) identified areas of concern in the implementation of that agreement. It was hoped that a donor's conference could be convened in 2006, leading to an emergency post-conflict assistance package. Given the disastrous conditions in the country, Nigeria and ECOWAS offered Guinea-Bissau an emergency financial package to help pay salary arrears. UN agencies submitted a $1.5 billion request to the Central Emergency Response Fund to finance a plan for addressing the urgent needs of the affected population, which would, along with the flash appeal of $3.6 million launched in May, allow Guinea-Bissau to cover humanitarian assistance for six months.

The Secretary-General noted that the slow pace of the country's reconciliation process had delayed both political normalization and the restoration of donor confidence, which could impact the flow of critically needed assistance to the country. He welcomed the steps taken by President Vieira to launch constructive dialogue with relevant stakeholders, raising hopes that institutional stability could be achieved. The Secretary-General stressed the need for joint efforts by all States affected by the Casamance question—the Gambia, Guinea-Bissau and Senegal—to find solutions to the causes of the crisis. He called upon States and institutions to support Guinea-Bissau in the organization and conduct of the dialogue and reconciliation process; the coordination and harmonization of socio-economic and financial assistance packages; preparation for the donor round table later in the year; and assistance in the security sector reform process. He also called upon the international community to respond to the flash appeal to assist the displaced population and refugees.

The Secretary-General said that the mission dispatched by the UN Department of Political Affairs to Guinea-Bissau (22 to 27 May) had reported that political and socio-economic challenges continued to hinder the post-conflict recovery process, with many social indicators being lower than before the 1998-1999 conflict. Interlocutors inside and outside Guinea-Bissau cited the lack of financial resources as a critical factor impeding the Government's recovery efforts and underscored the nexus between insufficient resources and instability. The mission's interlocutors also expressed their appreciation for the positive role played by UNOGBIS in the stabilization of Guinea-Bissau. In that regard, the Secretary-General said that he would make recommendations to the Security Council on the role of the Office in the immediate future and beyond.

Press statement. In a 21 July press statement [SC/8783], the Security Council, which had been briefed the previous day on developments in Guinea-Bissau by the Special Representative, reiterated the Secretary-General's request for the international community to positively respond to the flash appeal to address the needs of the population affected by the military operations. The Council also called upon political leaders in Guinea-Bissau to constructively engage in the dialogue process; encouraged the international community to consider ways to help the Government deal with the prevalence of illegal narcotics trafficking in Guinea-Bissau's coastal islands; reaffirmed its intention to closely follow the developments in the country; and expressed its readiness to consider the Secretary-General's forthcoming recommendations on the future role of UNOGBIS.

Further political developments

Report of Secretary-General (September). In his September report [S/2006/783] on Guinea-Bissau and UNOGBIS activities, the Secretary-General said that the political climate was marked by developments within the country's two main political parties: PAIGC and the Party of Social Renewal (PRS). The PAIGC leadership started negotiations to reintegrate the group of dissidents who had supported President Vieira's candidacy against the party's candidate, Malam Bacai Sanhá, in the 2005 presidential elections. Included in that group of dissidents were Prime Minister Aristides Gomes and the Ministers of Defence and of Natural Resources and Energy. PRS, the party of former President Koumba Yalá, reaffirmed its confidence in the party's leadership and expressed its support for the "Forum para a Convergência do Desenvolvimento", the coalition supporting the Government in Parliament. At their sixth summit (17 July, Bissau), Heads of State and Government of CPLP expressed full support for ECOWAS efforts to establish an International Contact Group on Guinea-Bissau. The Group, at its first meeting (New York, 21 September), decided to assist Guinea-Bissau in strengthening its institutions' capacities; mobilize funds to make up the 2006 budget deficit; and assist in the preparation of the donors round table scheduled to take place in Geneva, from 7 to 8 November, and in the implementation of the reforms in the security and judicial sectors and in public administration. Since the launch of the "Estados Gerais" dialogue initiative in March (see p. 247), discussions supporting it had spread beyond the capital Bissau. On 2 September, over 100 participants attending the dialogue initiative's first regional consultation in Biombo expressed their commitment to move away from conflict and work collectively towards a peaceful future. Preparations were under way by UNOGBIS to launch a capacity-building project in conflict transformation skills for parliamentarians and civil society groups to enhance national stakeholders' capacity to mainstream conflict prevention and resolution into their national programmes.

Progress was made on security matters, with the establishment by Government decree of the National Commission to Combat the Proliferation of Small Arms and Light Weapons (CNLCPAL), thus paving the way for the implementation of the pilot small arms collection and destruction programme within the framework of the UN Coordinating Action on Small Arms mechanism. In other developments, the capital Bissau was declared mine-free as of July; the survey of contaminated areas affected by military operations against Casamance rebels along the border with Senegal was completed; and the demining of secondary roads and affected villages was under way. UNOGBIS continued to support security sector reform. The technical team responsible for drafting the National Security Sector Reform strategy document resumed its work after a three-month interruption, and, in September, the United Kingdom Security Sector Development Advisory Team undertook its third mission to the country to assist Guinea-Bissau authorities in finalizing the document. The National Commission on the Reconciliation of the Armed Forces undertook a sensitization campaign throughout the country, from July to mid-August, with a view to extending the reconciliation process to the paramilitary forces and consolidating civil-military relations. Shortly thereafter, on 28 August, two senior reintegrated officers were summoned by the Military Tribunal to assist in the investigation into an alleged plot against the Chief of General Staff. While no charges were brought against the officers, the incident was criticized as going against the grain of the reconciliation process.

Economic conditions in Guinea-Bissau remained difficult and social tensions escalated, as illustrated by a wave of public sector strikes, including a three-day strike in June over civil service wage arrears. Although the Assembly approved the Government's 2006 budget on 20 July, the country still faced severe financial difficulties, particularly the payment of salary arrears and alleviating the hardship faced by the population. Following a visit to Guinea-Bissau from 18 to 21 August by an IMF mission, the Fund indicated its readiness to approve, pending a successful donors round table, an emergency post-conflict package for 2007.

The Secretary-General remarked that, although a strong commitment to improve the political climate continued to emerge, tensions and difficulties highlighted the ever-present risk of a relapse. The significant drop in cashew nut revenues, a poor rice harvest and the ongoing challenge of salary arrears in the public sector aggravated social tensions. He urged the international community to actively participate in the donors round table in November to help the country address its immediate concerns and move towards the achievement of medium- and long-term development goals. The Secretary-General concluded that the United Nations should remain engaged in Guinea-Bissau and announced his intention to revise UNOGBIS mandate and request its extension until 31 December 2007.

Return of former President Yalá and other developments

Report of Secretary General (December). In his December report on Guinea-Bissau and UNOGBIS [S/2006/946], the Secretary-General stated that, on 28 October, former President Koumba Yalá, who had been away from the country for a year, returned to Guinea-Bissau, announcing his intention to contest the elections for the leadership of PRS, which he intended to lead to victory in the 2008 elections. Mr. Yalá, who was overthrown in a military coup in September 2003 [YUN 2003, p. 227], and was defeated in the first round of the 2005 presidential elections by Messrs. Sanhá and Vieira [YUN 2005, p. 294], won the PRS leadership contest by securing nearly 67 per cent of votes cast at the party's national congress (8-12 November). Political tensions heightened when Mr. Yalá, who had initially supported the establishment of the current Government, declared as illegitimate the Forum para a Convergência do Desenvolvimento, the coalition of parties in the Assembly that supported the Government, as well as the Government itself. Meanwhile, PAIGC leadership, along with former Prime Minister Carlos Gomes and the party's 2005 presidential candidate, Malam Bacai Sanhá, deemed the 2008 legislative elections as unnecessary and instead called for the Government to be replaced by one of national unity. Moreover, opposition parties accused the Government of incompetence and corruption. Concerned by the strained political climate, Prime Minister Aristides Gomes warned that the disbursement of pledged donations made at the donors round table (7-8 November, Geneva) hinged upon the precondition of political stability. In view of the criticisms, President Vieira consulted with various political actors to help stabilize the situation. Further controversy arose when Mr. Yalá stated that he had been asked by the AU to support President Vieira in the second round of the 2005 elections, prompting supporters of the losing candidate, Mr. Sanhá, to accuse the AU of interference in the country's internal affairs and to question the legitimacy of President Vieira's 2005 victory.

Meanwhile, efforts continued to reunify and stabilize PAIGC, which had suffered major internal divisions during the 2005 presidential campaign and elections. Seven leading dissidents were reintegrated into the party's decision-making organ, the Political Bureau, in October. The "Estados Gerais" dialogue initiative, despite resource constraints, continued to make headway, holding a consultation on 29 September, with some 60 representatives of the security forces, including the Chief of General Staff, General Tagme Na Waie attending. UNOGBIS facilitated the national reconciliation and dialogue process by holding two workshops on leadership skills for departmental heads and leaders of parliamentary special commissions, and galvanized support for a capacity-building project for Parliament.

On security matters, the Government finalized its strategy paper on security sector reform in October, which was approved by the Council of Ministers, along with a triennial investment plan costing $184 million. The security sector reform plan envisaged the reduction of the armed forces from 9,650 to 3,440, the streamlining of law enforcement bodies and the creation of a national gendarmerie. UNOGBIS would assist the authorities in carrying out a systematic national information campaign on the modalities of the plan, and would support the national commission to combat the proliferation of small arms and light weapons. During the reporting period, UNOGBIS trained 33 police officers on the code of conduct for law enforcement officers and the use of force and firearms. On 24 September, 674 kilogrammes of cocaine and stockpiles of weapons and communications equipment were seized, raising concerns that organized crime in the country was increasing.

The economic situation remained precarious and continued to compromise the Government's ability to pay civil servants' salaries and to deliver basic services. The gravity of the situation was presented at the donors round table (7-8 November, Geneva), under the theme "Security and Development". Pledges of $262.5 million were made, well short of the overall goal of $538 million, making urgent short-term support vital for closing the 2006-2007 budget gap. Moreover, Government revenue fell below target, despite efforts to improve revenue performance and contain expenditure.

The Secretary-General commended the Government's successful organization of the donors round table, particularly its recognition of the linkage between security, stability and development. He urged political actors in Guinea-Bissau to put the national interest above other considerations, as the country could not afford disruptions at a time when its partners were considering budgetary support and the IMF was planning a mission in January 2007 to discuss emergency assistance. In the light of the IMF decision to support Guinea-Bissau's access to post-conflict assistance, the Secretary-General renewed his appeal to the international community to help close the 2006-2007 budget gap and called on the Government to vigorously pursue good governance and the fight against corruption.

Highlighting the critical advisory role played by UNOGBIS and the United Kingdom Security Sector Development Advisory Team supporting the drafting of the national security sector reform strategy, the Secretary-General encouraged the authorities to keep public administration and security sector reform high on the country's agenda.

Press statement. In a 15 December press statement [SC/8910], the Security Council expressed concern over the precarious political, security and economic conditions in Guinea-Bissau. It urged political leaders to exercise restraint, focus on development, reconciliation and good governance, negotiate solutions to their differences and place the national interest above all. It also called upon the international community, international institutions and donors to continue their support to Guinea-Bissau. The Council also called for the early implementation of the Security Sector Reform Plan.

Further developments. In a later report [S/2007/178], the Secretary-General said that, on 14 December, the commander of the border guards was held hostage by subordinates protesting the non-payment of salary arrears and demanding improved conditions of service. A week later, some 300 former soldiers staged a protest at the secretariat for Veterans Affairs over the non-payment of pension arrears, while another group of protesters prevented people from entering and leaving the Prime Minister's office for two hours. In both cases, General Tagme Na Waie, the Chief of General Staff intervened to appease the protesters.

The socio-economic situation remained fragile. Most of the pledges made at the November donors round table remained outstanding. In mid-December, the World Bank suspended support for a multisector infrastructure rehabilitation project after concluding that a joint venture agreement between the Government and a foreign energy company was incompatible with the project as envisaged. That compromised the expected disbursement of $10 million by the Bank in budgetary support, as well as budgetary support of other partners.

In other developments, the "Estados Gerias" dialogue stalled because of resource constraints. The initiative organized a regional meeting in the Oio Region on 28 November, while preparations for another such meeting in the provincial capital of the south were halted, owing to a lack of financial resources. Although President Viera had called for a debate on a proposed general amnesty for all those involved in the 1980 and 2004 military coups, Parliament did not schedule the debate in its November-December session.

On 5 December, President Viera wrote to the Secretary-General requesting that UNOGBIS and the UN country team be transformed into an integrated office.

Ad hoc advisory group. The Ad Hoc Advisory Group on Guinea-Bissau continued to assist the country with its development priorities. The Group's April report [E/2006/8] highlighted its activities and provided an overview of developments in the country, including the overall economic and social situation. The Economic and Social Council, in **resolution 2006/11** of 26 July (see p. 1086), called upon donors to provide budgetary support to Guinea-Bissau, including through the Emergency Economic Management Fund.

UNOGBIS

The United Nations Peace-building Support Office in Guinea-Bissau (UNOGBIS), a political mission established in 1999 by decision of the Secretary-General and supported by Security Council resolution 1233(1999) [YUN 1999, p. 140], was extended until 31 December 2006. Its mandate had been revised by resolution 1580(2004) [YUN 2004, p. 229] in the face of intensified political turmoil and uncertainty in 2004. The Office was headed by the Representative of the Secretary-General for Guinea-Bissau, João Bernardo Honwana (Mozambique). By an exchange of letters between the Secretary-General and the Security Council President on 5 October [S/2006/790, S/2006/791], the Council noted the Secretary-General's intention to designate Mr. Shola Omoregie (Nigeria) as his Special Representative in Guinea-Bissau and Head of UNOGBIS, effective 3 October, to succeed Mr. Honwana.

During 2006, in line with resolution 1580(2004), the Secretary-General submitted reports on developments in Guinea-Bissau and UNOGBIS in March [S/2006/162], July [S/2006/487], September [S/2006/783] and December [S/2006/946]. A UN assessment mission that visited Guinea-Bissau from 22 to 27 May, concluded that a UN political presence remained vital in that country to contribute to stabilization, without which the full resumption of development assistance and economic investments, essential for sustainable peace and progress, could not be guaranteed. In September, the Secretary-General indicated his intention to slightly revise the Mission's mandate and request its extension through 31 December 2007.

Revision of mandate. In a letter dated 8 December [S/2006/974] to the Security Council, the Secretary-General stated that, while progress had been achieved in Guinea-Bissau, much more remained to be done to consolidate and sustain momentum for democratic governance and to prevent a relapse into conflict. The intensified pressure from major opposition parties on President Vieira to dismiss the Government appointed in October 2005, illustrated the continued volatility of the situation. The Secretary-General drew the attention of the Council of an 8 November letter from Prime Minister Aristides Gomes requesting emergency financial assistance from the UN Peacebuilding and Democracy Funds to fill the budget gaps for 2006 and 2007, which further exemplified the need for continued international engagement in Guinea-Bissau.

In the light of the work that remained, and to allow the Office to continue assisting Guinea-Bissau in its peacebuilding efforts, the Secretary-General recommended the extension of UNOGBIS mandate for one year, until 31 December 2007. The proposed extension would allow UNOGBIS to operate under a streamlined mandate, highlighting its mediation and good offices functions aimed at promoting dialogue and reconciliation. In addition to supporting national reconciliation and dialogue, UNOGBIS activities would focus on assisting with security sector reform; promoting respect for the rule of law and human rights; mainstreaming a gender perspective in peacebuilding activities, in line with Security Council resolution 1325(2000) [YUN 2000, p. 1113]; promoting the peaceful settlement of disputes; helping to mobilize international assistance for reconstruction; facilitating efforts to curb the proliferation of small arms and light weapons; and enhancing cooperation with the AU, ECOWAS, CPLP, the EU and other international partners.

On 13 December, the Security Council took note of the Secretary-General's proposal [S/2007/975] and subsequently accepted his proposal to revise, and recommendation to extend the Mission's mandate until 31 December 2007.

Financing

The General Assembly, in section VI of resolution 60/248 [YUN 2005, p. 1495], had approved a prorated amount for UNOGBIS out of the $100 million authorized for the 26 political missions for the period 1 January to 31 December 2006. In a January report [A/60/585/Add.1] on estimates in respect of special political missions, good offices and other political initiatives authorized by the General Assembly and/or the Security Council, the Secretary-General proposed resource requirements of $3,226,200 for UNOGBIS for the period from 1 January to 31 December 2006.

The Assembly, in section I of **resolution 60/255** of 8 May, approved, as recommended by ACABQ [A/60/7/Add.37], a prorated amount for UNOGBIS out of the additional charge of $202,469,500 against the provision for special political missions already approved under Section 3, Political affairs, of the programme budget for 2006-2007 (see p. 1618).

In a November report [A/61/525/Add.3 & Corr.1], which dealt with estimated requirements for special political missions grouped under Thematic Cluster III (UN offices, peacebuilding support offices, integrated offices and commissions), the Secretary-General proposed requirements for UNOGBIS in the amount of $3,467,700 for the period from 1 January to 31 December 2007, which ACABQ recommended for approval [A/61/640 & Corr.1].

On 22 December, in section VII of **resolution 61/252**, the Assembly endorsed ACABQ recommendations within the appropriation of $230,616,400 authorized under section 3, Political affairs, of the programme budget for the 2006-2007 biennium (see p. 1615).

Cameroon-Nigeria

In 2006, Cameroon and Nigeria continued to cooperate peacefully to advance progress in implementing the 2002 ruling of the International Court of Justice on the land and maritime boundary between them through the Cameroon-Nigeria Mixed Commission. The Secretary-General, through his good offices and with UN Secretariat support, continued to facilitate implementation of that ruling. At their fifth meeting with the Secretary-General, the Heads of State of the two countries reaffirmed their willingness to peacefully implement the judgment of the Court and signed an agreement on the withdrawal and transfer of authority in the Bakassi peninsula. Major progress was achieved during the year with the demarcation of more than 460 kilometres of the land boundary from Lake Chad to the south-west and the withdrawal of Nigerian Armed Forces from the Bakassi peninsula. Hence, three of the four issues—Lake Chad area, Land Boundary and Bakassi Peninsula—addressed by the Court's ruling had been resolved to the satisfaction of the two countries.

Cameroon–Nigeria Mixed Commission

The Cameroon-Nigeria Mixed Commission, the mechanism established by the Secretary-General in 2002 [YUN 2002, p. 1265], at the request of the

Presidents of Nigeria and Cameroon, to facilitate the peaceful implementation of the 10 October 2002 ruling of the International Court of Justice (ICJ) on the border dispute between them [ibid.], remained under the chairmanship of the Special Representative of the Secretary-General for West Africa, Ahmedou Ould-Abdallah (Mauritania). The Commission was responsible for the demarcation of the land boundary between the two countries; the withdrawal of civil administration, military and police forces and transfer of authority in relevant areas along the boundary; the eventual demilitarization of the Bakassi peninsula; the protection of the rights of the affected populations; the development of projects to promote joint economic ventures and cross-border cooperation; and the reactivation of the five-member Lake Chad Basin Commission (Cameroon, Central African Republic, Chad, Niger and Nigeria), created in 1964 to regulate and plan the use of the Lake and other natural resources of the conventional basin.

The Mixed Commission established two subcommissions: one responsible for the demarcation of the 1,700-kilometre land boundary between the two countries, with a joint technical team to carry out field assessments of the boundary and to supervise the demarcation work to be undertaken by outside contractors; and the other to assess the situation of the affected populations and to consider ways to ensure the protection of their rights. Two of the four working groups established by the Commission, the group on the withdrawal of civil administration and military and police forces and the transfer of authority in the Lake Chad area and the group on withdrawal and transfer of authority in the land boundary, completed their work in December 2003 and July 2004, respectively. The remaining two groups, one on withdrawal and transfer of authority in the Bakassi peninsula and the other on the maritime boundary, continued their activities. Since December 2003, the Commission's civilian observer personnel carried out nine follow-up missions to the Lake Chad area and the land boundary and noted that peaceful and good relations prevailed among the population and the new authorities. A UN team based in Dakar, Senegal, provided technical and logistical assistance and substantive support to the Commission and its subsidiary bodies. The United Nations Office for West Africa also supported the work of the Mixed Commission.

In 2006, the activities of the Mixed Commission focused on three core tasks: completing and consolidating the transfer of authority carried out in 2004 and 2005 through monitoring, assessment and support activities; finding definitive solutions to the outstanding maritime boundary issues; and concluding the demarcation process.

The withdrawal of Nigerian armed forces from the Bakassi Peninsula took place on 14 August.

Activities

Progress report. On 28 September [S/2006/778], the Secretary-General informed the Security Council of the latest activities and achievements of the Mixed Commission in implementing the 2002 ICJ ruling. He said that, since his previous report [YUN 2005, p. 297], the Mixed Commission had moved the process smoothly and peacefully and maintained an open dialogue and communication between Cameroon and Nigeria. At the fifth summit (12 June, Greentree, New York, United States) of the Presidents of Cameroon and Nigeria and the Secretary-General to review the Commission's work, the Presidents reaffirmed their commitment to the peaceful implementation of the ICJ ruling, and signed the Greentree Agreement between the Republic of Cameroon and the Federal Republic of Nigeria concerning the modalities of withdrawal and transfer of authority in the Bakassi peninsula, the text of which was transmitted to the Security Council by the Secretary-General on 20 June [S/2006/419]. The Agreement established a Follow-up Committee to monitor its implementation, whose membership, as communicated to the Council by the Secretary-General on 28 June [S/2006/454], comprised Cameroon, Nigeria, the four witnesses to the Agreement (France, Germany, United Kingdom, United States) and the United Nations. The Follow-up Committee met on 10 July and 31 August, and was expected to meet subsequently on a monthly basis.

The UN team of civilian observers of the Mixed Commission was also working with the Follow-up Committee. Following the 14 August withdrawal of Nigerian forces and transfer of authority in the Bakassi peninsula, the Commission planned to recruit and deploy observers to consolidate the achievement, as it had done in the case of the Lake Chad area and along the land boundary. The Commission continued to discuss with Cameroon, Nigeria and development partners projects to promote cross-border cooperation for the benefit of the local population on both sides.

The demarcation exercise progressed steadily, with some 462 kilometres having been demarcated. The exercise would be followed by the emplacement of pillars, a final survey and final mapping. The Commission signed an agreement with the European Commission for a contribution of €4 million to help meet the initial estimated $12 million cost of the entire demarcation exercise [YUN 2005, p. 297]. On the maritime boundary, it was estimated that the delineation would be finalized in 2006, which would allow the Commission to address, as necessary, the tri-point between Cameroon, Equatorial Guinea and Nigeria. Taking into account the progress made in the demarcation exercise and the calendar of activities set out in the Greentree Agreement, it was estimated that the Mixed Commission would not be able to complete its mandate by the end of 2007. The Secretary-General therefore indicated his intention to ask for additional funds from the regular budget for the Commission's work in 2007.

On 17 October [S/2006/819], the Security Council took note of the information provided by the Secretary-General and of his intention to continue the activities of the UN support team to the Cameroon-Nigeria Mixed Commission with funding from the UN regular budget. The Council requested further information and clarification on the activities to be performed by the Mixed Commission in 2007 and following years, as well as those to be undertaken by the UN team of observers. It also urged the parties to the Mixed Commission to work with international donors to seek further voluntary contributions.

Future activities. On 1 November [S/2006/859], in response to the Council's request, the Secretary-General provided information on the Commission's 2007 planned activities and beyond, which included completing the demarcation of an estimated 750 kilometres of the 1,700-kilometre land boundary; carrying out civilian observation activities following the transfer of authority in some 40 villages in the Lake Chad area, along the land boundary and in the Bakassi peninsula; addressing issues related to the needs of affected populations, monitoring the application of international human rights instruments and ensuring respect for their rights; supporting meetings of the Lake Chad Basin Commission; sustaining the efforts of the African Development Bank in the cross-border road project; completing outstanding issues further to the delineation of the maritime boundary; contributing to an agreement on the tri-point between Cameroon, Equatorial Guinea and Nigeria; and seeking further voluntary contributions.

Activities beyond 2007 would focus on continuing the land boundary demarcation exercise estimated to be completed in 2008; monitoring the parties' obligations in conformity with the Greentree Agreement, which defined a zone that would remain under Nigerian administration until 2008; following up on the rights of affected populations in the border areas; continuing to monitor progress in joint economic ventures and cross-border activities; and following up on the activities of the Lake Chad Basin Commission and the Gulf of Guinea Cooperation Council.

At its sixteenth meeting (8 November, Abuja), the Mixed Commission discussed the remaining issue of the maritime boundary and decided that a joint field visit by a UN-led team of experts would be undertaken, from 16 to 26 November, to collect data to enable the physical delineation of the maritime boundary between the two countries. The meeting also pledged to double the teams of surveyors to speed up the process of demarcating the 1,700-kilometre land-boundary [UNOWA/CNMC/2006/03].

Financing

In his January report [A/60/585/Add.1] on estimates in respect of special political missions, good offices and other political initiatives authorized by the General Assembly and/or the Security Council, the Secretary-General proposed resource requirements of $7,339,000 for the Cameroon-Nigeria Mixed Commission for the period from 1 January to 31 December 2006.

The Assembly, in section I of **resolution 60/255** of 8 May, approved, as recommended by ACABQ [A/60/7/Add.37], a prorated amount for the Commission out of the additional charge of $202,469,500 against the provision for special political missions already approved under Section 3, Political affairs, of the programme budget for 2006-2007 (see p. 1618).

In a November report [A/61/525/Add.3 & Corr.1], which dealt with estimated requirements for special political missions grouped under Thematic Cluster III (United Nations offices, peacebuilding support offices, integrated offices and commissions), the Secretary-General proposed requirements for the Commission in the amount of $9,303,000 for the period from 1 January to 31 December 2007, which ACABQ recommended for approval [A/61/640 & Corr.1].

On 22 December, in section VII of **resolution 61/252**, the Assembly endorsed the ACABQ recommendations, including that on the Commission's budget under section 3, Political affairs, of the programme budget for the 2006-2007 biennium (see p. 1615).

Guinea

In 2006, the worsening economic and social conditions in Guinea led to unprecedented national strikes and demonstrations over low wages, soaring prices and Government inefficiency, some of which escalated into violence. In March, a strike that had been ongoing for several days, despite Government appeals for people to return to work, brought the capital city Conakry nearly to a halt. It had also allegedly resulted in the death of an innocent bystander. Stone-throwing youths targeting the cavalcade of President Lansana Conté were met with live fire from the President's bodyguards. Three months later, on 8 June, the main labour unions called a nationwide strike for lower prices for fuel and rice. The teachers' union joined the strike against the poor payment of salaries. Four days into the strike, 11 people were killed in violence linked to anti-Government protests and demonstrations.

The following day, in a 13 June press statement [SG/SM/10514], the Secretary-General expressed his concern over the killing of some 10 students during the demonstrations. Underscoring the need for the non-violent resolution of disputes, he called on the authorities to exercise restraint and appealed to various segments of Guinean society to continue to engage in constructive dialogue to address the challenges facing the country.

The EU Presidency, in a 16 June statement on Guinea [S/2006/451], expressed its concern with regard to the violent clashes between Guinean law enforcement authorities and demonstrators. It reiterated the Secretary-General's appeal to all social and political circles in the country to pursue constructive dialogue and expressed its willingness to provide assistance in the preparations for general elections scheduled for 2007.

Horn of Africa

The political landscape in the Horn of Africa continued to be affected by complex, interlocking conflicts. The Sudan, the largest country in the region, took positive steps to implement the Comprehensive Peace Agreement signed in 2005, including the redeployment of troops and the fulfillment of other security commitments. Nevertheless, areas of the country were still plagued by armed militias, disagreements over borders and disputed oil revenues and the escalating crisis in the Darfur states. A milestone was reached in July, when the Sudan People's Liberation Army (SPLA) pulled its remaining 5,672 soldiers out of eastern Sudan and moved them to the south. The United Nations Mission in the Sudan (UNMIS) closed its eastern Sudan office in September, withdrawing 80 civilian and 250 military staff.

The Sudanese armed forces continued to withdraw from the south, with a target date of July 2007 for complete redeployment to the north. People in the south, however, still faced the threat of renegade bands of former combatants who had failed to join either Sudan's armed forces or the SPLA, as stipulated in the peace agreement. In addition, southerners suffered sporadic attacks by the regionally based Lord's Resistance Army (LRA), until talks mediated by the Government of Southern Sudan led the LRA and Uganda to sign a cessation of hostilities agreement in August.

As southern Sudan struggled to rebuild, demarcation of the North-South border faced serious delays. Government parties disagreed on the status of the National Petroleum Commission—whether it should be advisory or decision-making—and the equitable division of oil revenues between North and South Sudan. The Commissions envisioned in the peace accord were either non-functional or yet to be established, including those dealing with human rights, the civil service and land disputes.

Meanwhile, the crisis in western Sudan's Darfur region continued to deteriorate. African Union-mediated talks in Abuja, Nigeria, culminated in the signing of the Darfur Peace Agreement on 5 May, after months of negotiations. However, the Agreement was signed by the Government and only one of the Darfur rebel groups. The African Union, in January, endorsed a transition from its Mission in the Sudan (AMIS) to a UN peacekeeping operation, which the Security Council approved in March. However, the Sudan did not support the transition, citing threats to its sovereignty. A series of high-level meetings and missions sought to convince the Sudanese Government that the operation would only aim at protecting civilians and help bring peace and stability. On 31 August, the Security Council expanded UNMIS mandate by up to 17,300 international military personnel to be deployed to Darfur. However, that was rejected by the Sudan, which instead showed its intention to pursue a military solution to the crisis.

As the conflict between the Sudanese army and militias intensified, the Secretary-General, on 16 November, convened a high-level meeting in Addis Ababa, Ethiopia, which brought together the five permanent members of the Security Council, the Sudanese Government, States and organizations with political influence in the region and AMIS troop-contributing countries. Participants agreed on a three-phased approach for deploying a hybrid AU-UN force. That was endorsed by the AU on 30

November, by the Council of Ministers of the Sudan on 3 December, and by the Security Council on 19 December. However, by the end of the year, the parties had shown no signs of abandoning the pursuit of their objectives through military means, and the conflict had spilled over into Chad and the Central African Republic.

In Somalia, the year opened on a promising note, with the January signing of the Aden Declaration, brokered by Yemen, to end differences between the President and the Speaker of the Transitional Federal Parliament. With the signing of the Declaration, the Transitional Federal Government and Parliament relocated to Baidoa, 140 miles northwest of Mogadishu, and the Parliament held its first session in February.

February also saw a dramatic shift in Somalia's complicated clan-based balance of power, with the emergence of the Alliance for the Restoration of Peace and Counter-Terrorism (ARPCT), whose aim was to combat the Union of Islamic Courts, accused of supporting terrorism and harbouring foreign terrorism suspects. ARPCT and Islamic Courts fighters engaged in fierce battles in Mogadishu, which killed hundreds and displaced thousands. By June, the Courts had routed ARPCT and established their authority in central and southern Somalia. A sense of law and order returned to Mogadishu for the first time in 15 years.

By contrast, the Transitional Federal Government barely held control of Baidoa, a fact starkly illustrated by the assassination of the Minister for Constitutional Affairs in the city, in July, and by an unsuccessful car bombing attempt on the life of the President on 18 September. The previous day, an Italian Catholic nun was assassinated in Mogadishu. In June, a Swedish cameraman and a journalist were killed while filming a rally in Mogadishu. Those incidents and a number of threats forced the United Nations to curtail its operations and withdraw all international staff from Somalia in October.

As tensions increased, the pace of diplomacy quickened. With the support of the United Nations, the League of Arab States launched a round of talks between the Transitional Federal Government and the Union of Islamic Courts in Khartoum on 22 June. After attending the talks, the Secretary-General's Special Representative for Somalia travelled to Baidoa and Mogadishu in July for separate meetings with the President, Prime Minister and Speaker and with the Chairman of the Courts, obtaining commitments from both sides to continue the dialogue. A second round followed on 2 September in Khartoum.

After their surprisingly quick overthrow of the warlords who had ruled Mogadishu by fear for some 15 years, the Islamic Courts continued to expand the territory under their control. In September, they took control of the strategically important port city of Kismayo. By late October, their forces had flanked Baidoa, cut off its fuel supply and seized control of eight of the country's 18 administrative districts. The Courts vowed to fight any foreign troops opposing them on Somali soil, and declared jihad against Ethiopian forces, which they alleged were already inside the country protecting the Transitional Government.

The Security Council, on 6 December, endorsed the request for a joint peace operation to be deployed by the Intergovernmental Authority for Development (IGAD) and the African Union. However, the military build-up by both sides came to a head on 24 December, when skirmishes threatened the Transitional Government in Baidoa and provoked the full force of the Government, backed by Ethiopian troops. The Courts militia retreated to Mogadishu, which fell to the Transitional Government/Ethiopian coalition on 28 December, and then to Kismayo, which fell soon after.

Notwithstanding multiple efforts, including diplomatic initiatives by the United States and the Ethiopia-Eritrea Boundary Commission, 2006 began and ended with Ethiopia and Eritrea still at a stalemate over the demarcation of the border between them.

The Security Council passed three resolutions reiterating its long-standing call for Ethiopia to enable demarcation of the border and for Eritrea to end its restrictions on the United Nations Mission in Ethiopia and Eritrea (UNMEE). Meanwhile, the situation in the buffer zone, the Temporary Security Zone, and adjacent areas turned tense in mid-October, when some 1,500 Eritrean troops backed by tanks, artillery and air defence equipment, entered the Zone in Sector West. Eritrea later stated that the troops had entered the area to assist with crop harvesting and other development projects.

UNMEE forged ahead with its mandate obligations and kept watch over those developments in spite of a significant reduction in troop levels. This situation was exacerbated by Eritrean restrictions, including the flight ban on the Mission's helicopters imposed in 2005, which greatly curtailed UNMEE capacity to monitor the Zone.

During the year, the Eritrea-Ethiopia Boundary Commission failed to advance its demarcation activities, stalled in 2003, following the rejection by Ethiopia of significant parts of the Commission's

2002 final and binding delimitation decision, previously accepted by both parties. On 27 November, the Commission announced that, because of impediments in fulfilling its mandate, it planned to demarcate the border on maps, leaving the two countries to establish the physical boundary themselves. Ethiopia and Eritrea were given one year to reach agreement on border demarcation, failing which, the locations established in the Commission's 2002 delimitation decision would take effect. Both countries rejected the Commission's proposal: Ethiopia stated that the Commission was acting beyond its mandate, and Eritrea maintained that the Algiers Agreement required the Commission, not the parties, to implement the 2002 delimitation decision.

The deadlock in the search for an agreed political solution to the long-standing conflict concerning the governance of the Territory of Western Sahara continued, with no hope of an early breakthrough. The Secretary-General's Special Envoy intensified his efforts in exploring with the parties, Morocco and the Frente Popular para La Liberación de Saguía el-Hamra de Río de Oro (Frente Popular), the best way to achieve a mutually acceptable solution. However, Morocco reiterated that it would not accept a referendum that would include the option of independence, while Frente Popular maintained that the only way forward was to implement the 2003 Peace Plan for the Self-Determination of the People of Western Sahara, or the 1991 Settlement Plan.

The Secretary-General recommended that the Security Council call upon the parties to enter into open-ended negotiations without preconditions and, rather than just extending the Mandate of the United Nations Mission for the Referendum in Western Sahara, to consider passing a more substantial resolution on the situation in Western Sahara.

In other matters, Mauritius, during the General Assembly's general debate, complained that 38 years after its independence, it still was not able to exercise its sovereignty over the Chagos Archipelago, including Diego Garcia. The United Kingdom maintained that the Territory was British. While it did not recognize Mauritius' sovereignty claim, successive British Governments had given the undertaking that the Territory would be ceded, when no longer required for defence purposes, and that it would liaise closely with Mauritius at that time.

Both the Security Council and the General Assembly discussed the issue of cooperation between the United Nations and the African Union in the areas of peace and security, including in Darfur, and implementation of the 2005 World Summit outcome, in which Member States committed themselves to meeting Africa's special needs. Towards that end, the heads of both organizations signed a declaration entitled "Enhancing UN-AU Cooperation: Framework for the ten-year Capacity-Building Programme for the African Union".

Sudan

Implementation of Comprehensive Peace Agreement

In 2006, limited progress was made in the implementation of the 2005 Comprehensive Peace Agreement signed between the Sudan People's Liberation Movement/Army (SPLM/A) and the Government of the Sudan. While the parties respected the letter of the Agreement, there was an increasing climate of distrust between them. The implementation of several major provisions of the Agreement had fallen behind schedule, important contentious issues remained to be resolved, and the parties continued to contest the interpretation of several aspects of the Agreement. People's expectation of the peace dividend remained high, particularly in the south, but they had seen little improvement in their living conditions. The parties continued to face a growing security problem, which was further aggravated by the activities of the Lord's Resistance Army, operating out of neighbouring Uganda. A Security Council mission visited the Sudan, from 6 to 8 June, to hold talks on the north-south peace accord.

The United Nations Mission in the Sudan (UNMIS) continued to play a key supporting role in the implementation of the Agreement. It completed its deployment in southern Sudan, where the Government of Southern Sudan was working hard to transform the region into a functioning administration. Having fulfilled its mandate in eastern Sudan, UNMIS withdrew from the area. With the deteriorating security situation in the Darfur region and the signing of the Darfur Peace Agreement, the Security Council, in response to a AU request, expanded UNMIS mandate and increased its strength to 17,300 troops in the transition to a UN operation in Darfur.

In October, Eritrean-mediated peace talks between the Government of the Sudan and the Eastern Front rebel movement culminated in the signing of the Eastern Sudanese Peace Agreement.

On 22 October, the Sudan informed the Secretary-General that it had decided to terminate the mission of Special Representative Jan Pronk and requested him to leave the Sudan within 72 hours. The Security Council, on 27 October, backed the Secretary-General's decision to retain Mr. Pronk as his Special Representative to the Sudan. He retained his post until the end of the year, when his contract expired.

Security Council consideration (January). Briefing the Council on 13 January [meeting 5344], Jan Pronk, the Secretary-General's Special Representative for the Sudan and Head of UNMIS, said that, although the January 2005 Comprehensive Peace Agreement between the Sudanese Government and the Sudan People's Liberation Movement/Army (SPLM/A) [YUN 2005, p. 301] remained firm, many in the south had become suspicious and were losing their belief in the north's sincerity, especially regarding the Government's lack of transparency in reporting oil revenues that were supposed to be shared. Matching the cynicism in the south, was suspicion in the north that SPLM did not want to promote national unity as it prepared for the referendum on separation scheduled for 2011. Nonetheless, some progress had been made in the past year. Constitutions for the Sudan and southern Sudan had been adopted, two new Governments had been formed, all institutions required under the Agreement had been established, though some had hardly met and others were facing political disputes, and the redeployment of the Sudanese army away from the south had started. Talks between SPLM and the other armed groups in southern Sudan were proceeding well, which could pave the way for the integration of all combatants into one of the armies or into civil society. However, a great deal still needed to be done. The peace process had to be more inclusive, security laws brought into line with the constitution, disarmament, demobilization and reintegration of combatants begun, resources provided to support the return of displaced persons and refugees, and the rehabilitation and development of the economy started. The unity option should be given a real chance in the 2011 referendum, but the Government in the north should do everything to make that attractive, especially by guaranteeing a fair share of power, resources and income to the people of the south.

The Special Representative also raised concerns over the issue of Abyei, one of the transition areas, where uncertainty about its future status posed a threat. He warned that, in the east, close to the Eritrean border, a confrontation was likely to arise as soon as SPLM withdrew to the south, as it was committed to doing under the Peace Agreement. The Government and the eastern rebels had agreed to start peace discussions, with the Libyan Arab Jamahiria as facilitator. Those talks had not yet started, even though the redeployment deadline of 9 January had passed, thereby creating a void, with the potential for new armed conflict.

Communication. On 3 February [S/2006/95], the Sudan submitted information on progress in implementing the Comprehensive Peace Agreement, including ratification of the Interim National Constitution and those of southern Sudan and the other states, appointments made, and constitutional institutions and implementation bodies established. It also identified implementation priorities for the first quarter of 2006.

Report of Secretary-General (March). In his March report on the Sudan [S/2006/160], submitted pursuant to Security Council resolution 1590(2005) [YUN 2005, p. 305] and covering developments since his December 2005 report [ibid., p. 311], the Secretary-General said that progress in implementing the Comprehensive Peace Agreement was accompanied by worrisome delays. While the National Congress Party (NCP) and SPLM had respected the letter of the Agreement, they had not shown the spirit of cooperation, inclusiveness and transparency envisioned therein. Various commissions called for in the Agreement, including those dealing with human rights, the civil service, elections, land and the protection of the rights of non-Muslims, had not been established.

The Ceasefire Political Commission, mandated to supervise implementation of the ceasefire and settle deadlocks reported by the Ceasefire Joint Military Committee, met for the first time on 23 February. The meeting, attended by the Secretary-General's Special Representative and the UNMIS Force Commander, cleared up procedural questions and approved the Commission's terms of reference. The Fiscal and Financial Allocation and Monitoring Commission and the National Petroleum Commission had been established but were not yet performing their critical functions. However, the parties had moved forward on other tasks. President Omar Hassan Al-Bashir established the Joint Defence Board and appointed the president and members of the Constitutional Court. First Vice-President Salva Kiir and the leader of the South Sudan Defence Forces (SSDF) signed, on 8 January, the Juba Declaration on Unity and Integration of the Sudan People's Liberation Army and the South Sudan Defence Forces. However, by late February, most of the commanders had declared their allegiance to SPLA. As the 9 January deadline for the incorporation of other armed forces into the regular forces of either of the parties or their integration into civil society had not been met, the Ceasefire Joint Military Committee extended the date for the final reporting of armed groups to 9 March. The incorporation issue was not addressed, as the Other Armed Groups Collaborative Committee had not been activated.

President Al-Bashir, during his visit to southern Sudan on 14 February, affirmed the right of the people of that region to vote in the referendum in 2011, and declared that he would prefer separation over war. He reiterated that NCP was ready to share wealth with the south.

The Ugandan rebel group, the Lord's Resistance Army (LRA), remained a concern in southern Sudan, threatening civilians, as well as assistance activities. The already strained relations between the Sudan and Chad deteriorated, following a reported attack by Chadian opposition groups on 18 December 2005 on the Chadian border town of Adre.

The Ceasefire Joint Military Committee, chaired by the UNMIS Force Commander, continued to provide a forum for oversight, coordination and liaison between the parties, facilitating their efforts to implement the Peace Agreement. Both parties selected most of the forces required to form the Joint Integrated Units and moved them to assembly areas. However, although the Sudanese armed forces reported that 15,752 troops were available, and SPLA, 14,929, no Joint Integrated Units had yet been formed. That threatened implementation of the Peace Agreement, as the Units were essential for addressing potential conflicts. Frustration among soldiers, many of whom were not being regularly paid, was on the rise.

The Secretary-General observed that implementation of the Peace Agreement was falling short of expectations. The parties had not yet begun to use effectively the Peace Agreement's institutions to resolve differences. Since the National Petroleum Commission was not fully functional, there was a lack of transparency in the sharing of oil revenues with the Government of Southern Sudan. That complicated relations between SPLM and NCP and eroded the confidence of many southern Sudanese. Security arrangements were proceeding slowly, and any further delay in forming the Joint Integrated Units could weaken the parties' capacity to prevent or address conflicts. The Darfur crisis (see p. 268) was having a negative effect on the Peace Agreement's implementation. Efforts to negotiate an end to that conflict were putting pressure on the relationship between the partners in the Government of National Unity.

Making unity attractive for the people of southern Sudan remained one of the greatest challenges of the interim period. To move forward, the partners in the Government of National Unity needed to confront difficulties together through the Peace Agreement institutions and make the necessary compromises. The United Nations remained committed to implementing peace, however, the growing anti-UN campaign in Khartoum and other cities, as well as personal attacks in the media against the UNMIS leadership, were troubling. People's expectations of the peace dividend were high, particularly in the south, yet they had seen little improvement in their living conditions. Many had returned to their home areas in the south, but no basic infrastructure or social services had been established to receive them. Making the dividends of peace visible to the population was an essential part of implementing the Peace Agreement, said the Secretary-General.

Security Council consideration (March). Briefing the Security Council on 21 March [meeting 5392], the Secretary-General's Special Representative said that, although NCP and SPLM had respected the letter of the Comprehensive Peace Agreement, on the ground, there was an increasing climate of mistrust between them. He noted President Al-Bashir's statement on the 2011 referendum (see above) and Vice-President Kiir declaration, during the first meeting of the Sudan Consortium in Paris (9-10 March), that there was no longer any substantial disagreement on the sharing of oil revenues between the north and the south. Another encouraging sign was the fact that, at that meeting, the two parties united to participate as the Government of National Unity, led by Vice-President Kiir. The commitments made by both the north and the south to ensure transparency and accountability, as well as good financial and economic governance, augured well.

However, southern Sudan was suffering from severe poverty. Since the signing of the Comprehensive Peace Agreement, no tangible reconstruction had taken place. Although people were returning, they lacked the means to reintegrate. There were mines everywhere and work on clearing them had not started. The southern capital city of Juba, already short of water and power, was receiving more and more people, and many villages could hardly sustain the increasing number of their inhabitants because of insufficient food production. The reconstruction and development deficit in the south was the greatest challenge to peace.

The security situation in the south was already showing signs of deterioration. The disarmament of ex-combatants had not yet started, and the incorporation of other armed groups was not taking place smoothly. The situation required a substantial and secured increase in financial resources for disarmament, demobilization and reintegration to take place. Following the decision of Paulino Matip, leader of the former South Sudan Defence Forces, the other southern rebel movement, to integrate his forces into SPLA, violent clashes were witnessed between rival factions. The joint integrated units envisioned by the Comprehensive Peace Agreement were still not functional, which was a matter of great concern. Moreover, the Government had severely curtailed UNMIS freedom of movement in the Abyei area, restricting its operation only to the south of a Government-drawn line, thereby hampering the Mission's ability to monitor troop movements in one of the most contentious areas. In addition, since mid-2005, an increasing number of violent incidents had been witnessed in the south, sometimes due to tribal disputes, the activities of other armed groups, clashes between nomads and farmers or between returning internally displaced persons and local populations, attacks by dissatisfied, unpaid soldiers, and local disputes that turned into a tribal or political confrontation. So far, UNMIS had been able to contain such violence, but tension was mounting.

SECURITY COUNCIL ACTION

On 24 March [meeting 5396], the Security Council unanimously adopted **resolution 1663(2006)**. The draft [S/2006/179] was prepared in consultations among Council members.

The Security Council,

Recalling its previous resolutions, in particular resolutions 1627(2005) of 23 September 2005 and 1653(2006) of 27 January 2006, and the statements by its President, in particular that of 3 February 2006, concerning the situation in the Sudan,

Reaffirming its commitment to the sovereignty, unity, independence and territorial integrity of the Sudan,

Welcoming implementation by the parties of the Comprehensive Peace Agreement of 9 January 2005, and urging them to meet their commitments,

Acknowledging the commitments by troop-contributing countries in support of the United Nations Mission in the Sudan, and encouraging deployment in order for the Mission to support timely implementation of the Comprehensive Peace Agreement,

Reiterating in the strongest terms the need for all parties to the conflict in Darfur to put an end to the violence and atrocities,

Stressing the importance of urgently reaching a successful conclusion of the Abuja Peace Talks, and calling upon the parties to conclude a peace agreement as soon as possible,

Welcoming the communiqué of 10 March 2006 issued by the Peace and Security Council of the African Union at its forty-sixth meeting, and the decision of that Council to support in principle the transition of the African Union Mission in the Sudan to a United Nations operation within the framework of partnership between the African Union and the United Nations in the promotion of peace, security and stability in Africa, to pursue the conclusion of a peace agreement on Darfur by the end of April 2006, and to extend the mandate of the African Union Mission in the Sudan until 30 September 2006,

Expressing its deep concern at the movement of arms and armed groups across borders, such as the long-running and brutal insurgency by the Lord's Resistance Army, which has caused the death, abduction and displacement of many innocent civilians in the Sudan,

Determining that the situation in the Sudan continues to constitute a threat to international peace and security,

1. *Decides* to extend the mandate of the United Nations Mission in the Sudan until 24 September 2006, with the intention to renew it for further periods;

2. *Requests* the Secretary-General to report to the Security Council every three months on the implementation of the mandate of the United Nations Mission in the Sudan;

3. *Reiterates its request*, made in paragraph 2 of its resolution 1590(2005) of 24 March 2005, that the United Nations Mission in the Sudan closely and continuously liaise and coordinate at all levels with the African Union Mission in the Sudan, and urges it to intensify its efforts in this regard;

4. *Requests* that the Secretary-General, jointly with the African Union, in close and continuing consultation with the Council, and in cooperation and close consultation with the parties to the Abuja Peace Talks, including the Government of National Unity, expedite the necessary preparatory planning for transition of the African Union Mission in the Sudan to a United Nations operation, including options for how the United Nations Mission in the Sudan can reinforce the effort for peace in Darfur through additional appropriate transitional assistance to the African Union Mission in the Sudan, including assistance in logistics, mobility and communications, and that the Secretary-General present to the Council by 24 April 2006 for its consideration a range of options for a United Nations operation in Darfur;

5. *Encourages* the Secretary-General to continue to provide the maximum possible assistance to the African Union Mission in the Sudan;

6. *Requests* the Secretary-General and the African Union to consult with international and regional organizations and member States to identify resources to support the African Union Mission in the Sudan during transition to a United Nations operation;

7. *Strongly condemns* the activities of militias and armed groups such as the Lord's Resistance Army, which continue to attack civilians and commit human rights abuses in the Sudan, and in this regard urges the United

Nations Mission in the Sudan to make full use of its current mandate and capabilities;

8. *Recalls* resolution 1653(2006) and its request that the Secretary-General make recommendations to the Council, and looks forward to receiving by 24 April 2006 those recommendations which would include proposals on how United Nations agencies and missions, in particular the United Nations Mission in the Sudan, could more effectively address the problem of the Lord's Resistance Army;

9. *Encourages* the Sudanese parties to finalize the establishment of national institutions for disarmament, demobilization and reintegration of ex-combatants, as stipulated in the Comprehensive Peace Agreement, and to expedite the development of a comprehensive disarmament, demobilization and reintegration programme, with the assistance of the United Nations Mission in the Sudan as provided for in resolution 1590(2005);

10. *Decides* to remain actively seized of the matter.

Report of Secretary-General (June). In his June report [S/2006/426], the Secretary-General said that the parties continued to make slow progress in implementing the Comprehensive Peace Agreement. They had not yet activated the Other Armed Groups Collaborative Committee for overseeing the integration of allied militias into their regular forces. The integration was, therefore, well behind schedule and threatened to ignite further violence. On 7 March, two days before the deadline for incorporating the other armed groups, a convoy of unarmed former SSDF soldiers, currently aligned with SPLA, was attacked near Abyei by another group of SSDF elements aligned with SAF. Thirteen people died and 30 were wounded in the attack.

The Ceasefire Joint Military Committee made slow progress on most issues before it. Both parties failed to provide comprehensive data on their forces. UNMIS observers continued to verify the forces that the parties had moved to assembly areas to form Joint Integrated Units. Some 8,410 SAF troops (out of 15,752 ready for the Units) and 14,446 SPLA troops (out of 14,929 troops reported) had been verified. However, the establishment of the Units remained dependent on decisions still to be taken by the Joint Defence Board.

In a significant step in implementing the Peace Agreement, some 3,000 SPLA soldiers and their families had started moving from eastern Sudan to the south on 20 April. On 11 June, SPLA withdrew from the eastern town of Hameshkoreib, handing over control to State authorities. The redeployment of SAF from the south to the north was also proceeding on schedule.

The Assessment and Evaluation Commission, responsible for monitoring implementation of the Peace Agreement, formed four working groups—on power-sharing, wealth-sharing, security arrangements and the three war-affected areas. Law reform envisaged in the Agreement was progressing slowly. The National Assembly, which convened its second session on 3 April, still needed to adopt a number of key acts, including those required to prepare for midterm elections. The Legislative Assembly of southern Sudan, which convened its second regular session on 10 April, in Juba, had yet to table laws to establish key commissions in the south.

Meeting in April, the SPLM Political Bureau expressed concern over the slow implementation of the Comprehensive Peace Agreement, but reaffirmed its desire for a strong partnership with NCP and a more active role in resolving the conflicts in Darfur and eastern Sudan. The SPLM and NCP leadership councils held their first joint meeting in May, co-chaired by President Al-Bashir and First Vice-President Kiir. Participants affirmed their determination to implement the Peace Agreement and to work as partners for peace and development, but failed to reach agreement on the implementation of the Abyei Boundaries Commission report. They referred the report to the Presidency, with four options: a political agreement; a call on the experts of the Abyei Boundaries Commission to defend their recommendations; refer the matter to the constitutional court; or arbitration by a third party. The parties did agree, however, to form a fully representative transitional administration for Abyei.

Relations between the Sudan and Eritrea improved. The two countries exchanged high-level visits and agreed to restore full diplomatic relations. However, Chad severed diplomatic and economic relations with the Sudan, after a 13 April rebel attack on the Chadian capital of N'Djamena.

UN agencies and partners, including the International Organization for Migration, organized several large-scale returns, including that of 4,000 internally displaced persons from Juba to Jonglei State, and 6,000 from Yei to Bor. The Government of Southern Sudan scaled back its plans to return 501,000 people to their homes during the dry season, setting a new target of 151,000.

The Government of National Unity prudent macroeconomic policies and structural reforms, along with rising oil prices, contributed to robust economic growth, single-digit inflation and high levels of foreign investment. Pro-poor spending was significantly raised under the 2006 budget, but the fast pace of non-concessional borrowing was increasing the already large external debt. At the first meeting of the Sudan Consortium (Paris, 9-10 March), organized by the World Bank, the International Monetary Fund (IMF) and the United Nations, the Government of National Unity and the Government of Southern Sudan committed themselves to transparent budgets. The meeting brought together representatives of 22 donor countries and international institutions to increase resources for development, encourage accountability and good economic governance, and increase the transparency of budgets.

The parties took further steps to implement the Comprehensive Peace Agreement, the Secretary-General observed. Overall, the implementation process remained broadly on track and the parties continued to demonstrate commitment to the spirit of the Agreement. However, there were too many delays in implementation and too few indications of real progress in key areas. The parties did not invest enough in the commissions established under the Peace Agreement, and the spirit of cooperation, inclusiveness and transparency envisioned in the Agreement was sometimes lacking. The Secretary-General urged the parties to establish the Joint Integrated Units, act appropriately on the findings of the investigation into the violent incidents that took place in Abyei on 7 March, and ensure that such tragic incidents were not repeated. He also urged the Presidency to resolve the impasse over the implementation of the Abyei Boundaries Commission recommendations and called on the Government to allow freedom of movement of UN personnel in the Abyei area. In addition, he encouraged the Security Council to consider extending UNMIS monitoring and verification presence in the eastern region, in the light of renewed efforts to organize peace talks between the Government and the Eastern Front. Noting the signing of the Darfur Peace Agreement (see p. 274), the Secretary-General said that efforts to address that crisis should not prejudice work for the recovery of southern Sudan, where the greatest challenge was the creation of a true peace dividend for the people.

Security Council mission

On 26 May [S/2006/341], the Security Council informed the Secretary-General that it had decided to send a mission to the Sudan, Chad and the African Union headquarters in Addis Ababa, from 4 to 10 June. The mission, to be led by Emyr Jones Parry (United Kingdom), would deal with Darfur issues, North-South and southern Sudan issues and Sudan-Chad relations.

In its 22 June report [S/2006/433], the mission reported that it visited Khartoum, Juba and El Fasher in the Sudan; the AU headquarters in Addis Ababa; and N'Djamena and Goz Beida in Chad. In the Sudan, the mission met, among others, with President Al-Bashir, First Vice-President Kiir, Foreign Affairs Minister Lam Akol, SPLM Cabinet Affairs Minister Deng Alor and opposition party leaders. In Chad, the mission met, among others, with President Idriss Déby and his cabinet.

The mission was encouraged by the number of key measures taken to implement the Comprehensive Peace Agreement, but noted the challenges that were undermining its implementation, especially the question of the future status of the Abyei region, the slow pace in setting up the commissions under the Peace Agreement and the lack of a peace dividend for the population, owing to the failure of international donors to live up to their pledges. The Legislative Assembly in Juba raised the issue of power-sharing within the Government of National Unity, complaining that SPLM representatives in Khartoum felt ignored within their ministries, their deputy ministers were bypassed and that parallel institutions answering directly to the President had been created in ministries where SPLM held the post of minister. The Government of Southern Sudan and the international humanitarian community expressed concern over the growing insecurity in some areas of southern Sudan, owing to the activities of militias which had not yet been integrated into SAF or SPLA, and their potential to destabilize the region. A number of humanitarian activities were curtailed due to growing militia activity. Fearing a vacuum of authority and of the rule of law, UN country teams and NGOs urged that UNMIS be sufficiently resourced to deal with the fragile situation. The Government of Southern Sudan was also faced with the challenge of the presence of the LRA, which it wanted expelled from the region.

The mission recommended faster implementation of the Comprehensive Peace Agreement, so that the Sudanese public might not lose faith in it. Given the continuing security concerns in the south, UNMIS should not be affected by the deployment of a UN force in Darfur. The problem of LRA required firm attention and steps should be taken to develop a decisive international response to remove that threat, should peace talks fail. The International Criminal Court indictments against LRA members should be acted upon. International aid agencies and donors should live up to their pledges and not allow the problems in Darfur to detract from the problems in southern Sudan.

Security Council consideration. Briefing the Council on 15 June [meeting 5462], Ambassador Jones Parry, the head of the Council's mission, said that during its visit, the mission stressed the Council's wish to work in partnership with the Government and other main actors to help tackle the range of problems facing the country. However, while the international community's attention was focused on the problems in the Darfur region of the country, the mission left with a clear sense that the Council should not lose sight of the wider problems of the Sudan, in particular in the south. Although the Comprehensive Peace Agreement marked the cessation of hostilities and was moving forward, its implementation was slow and international donations were drying up. Yet, Darfur's future was linked to that of the south and the south's to that of Darfur. A holisitc solution was required to address all the country's problems through a coordinated UN response.

The Council considered the mission's written report on 29 June [meeting 5478].

Report of Secretary-General (September). In his September report [S/2006/728], the Secretary-General said that one year after the inauguration of the Government of National Unity, progress in carrying out commitments under the Comprehensive Peace Agreement was limited and the implementation of several of its major provisions had fallen behind schedule. The parties were unable to resolve important contentious issues and made little progress in the crucial areas of power- and wealth-sharing, including the Abyei situation, the sharing of oil revenues, the north-south border and the question of other armed groups. The parties continued to contest the interpretation of several aspects of the Agreement and neglected other commitments.

UNMIS and the wider UN system continued to play a key role in the implementation of the Agreement, providing good offices and political support to the parties, monitoring and verifying their security arrangements and offering assistance in governance, recovery and development. The parties' efforts to implement the Agreement's security provisions had reduced the likelihood of future conflict. The redeployment of SAF from southern Sudan was generally on schedule, although SPLA had accused SAF of concentrating around oilfields in the region bordering the north and the south, rather than redeploying further north. On 4 July, the Ceasefire Joint Military Committee established that SPLA had completed its redeployment from eastern Sudan. UNMIS verified the redeployment of 5,672 troops out of a declared strength of 8,763; the troops unaccounted for were considered to have abandoned SPLA. The completion of the redeployment marked a milestone in implementing the Agreement, as well as the end of the UNMIS monitoring mandate in the east, allowing the Mission to commence its withdrawal. Some of the Peace Agreement's security mechanisms, such as the Ceasefire Joint Military Committee and the Area Joint Military Committees, were largely functioning and had helped in resolving incidents with the potential for triggering wider conflict, such as the August clash between off-duty SPLA and SAF officers in Rubkona market in Unity State, in which eight civilians and three soldiers were killed.

Southern Sudan continued to suffer from insecurity due to the presence of armed groups, communal violence and forced disarmament campaigns. While SPLA had absorbed much of the former SSDF soldiers, other armed groups remained a major threat, as the schedule for incorporating them had fallen well behind. Although the formation of Joint Integrated Units had been slow, the parties had taken the first step to co-locate such units in Juba, Torit and Khartoum. However, the Units needed additional training, as well as budgetary and material support, for which international assistance would be required. International support would also be important in reforming the national security sector, including the police.

The parties were well behind schedule in implementing the power- and wealth-sharing aspects of the Peace Agreement. Disagreement continued over the National Petroleum Commission, its relationship with the Ministry of Energy and Mining and its participation in oil contract negotiations. The Technical Ad Hoc Border Committee had not yet started substantive work on delineating the north-south border, thereby hindering the fulfilment of obligations relating to military redeployment, the distribution of oil revenues, Joint Integrated Unit formation and preparations for the 2011 referendum to confirm the unity of the Sudan, or allow the secession of the south. Abyei remained a serious potential flashpoint. The local Executive Council (Abyei Area Council) had not yet been appointed, leaving the people of that region without formal policing, public sanitation and health services.

Few of the commissions called for in the Peace Agreement functioned as intended. Hardly any action had been taken to start preparing for national elections, scheduled for mid-2009. However, the National Assembly was emerging as a vibrant forum for political dialogue. Meanwhile, SPLM was facing the challenge of transforming itself from a liberation movement into a political party, reflecting the diversity of the peoples of southern Sudan.

The LRA continued to attack civilians and destabilize the area along the borders with Uganda and the Democratic Republic of the Congo (DRC). Uganda and LRA launched talks, in Juba, on 14 July, mediated by the Government of Southern Sudan. On

26 August, Uganda and LRA signed a cessation of hostilities agreement, which required LRA members to assemble at two designated points in southern Sudan.

Talks between the Government and the Eastern Front, mediated by Eritrea and observed by UNMIS, began in Asmara, Eritrea, on 13 June. Eritrea's role in the talks confirmed the warming of relations between Eritrea and the Sudan; on 12 June, the two countries' Presidents met for the first time in more than five years.

The relatively stable humanitarian situation in southern Sudan led to increased activity and optimism among the international aid community. Between January and early June, international assistance contributed to the building or repairing of 370 kilometres of road, which allowed over 10,000 refugees to return, food to be delivered to 3 million people, as well as polio immunization for 4.8 million children. Donor support continued to lag behind needs, and by the end of August, donor pledges met only 56 per cent, or $896.5 million, of the humanitarian workplan requirements. Only some $430 million of the $2.6 billion needed for post-conflict reconstruction had been committed.

The Government continued to breach the status-of-forces agreement. SAF personnel prevented UNMIS movement north of Abyei, restricting UN monitoring to only 20 per cent of the sector. The Government continued to arrest and detain national UNMIS staff.

The Secretary-General observed that the Comprehensive Peace Agreement was entering a new and challenging phase. In the months ahead, the parties had to make substantial progress in security-sector reform, police reform and restructuring, preparing for the return of internally displaced persons, the national census and future elections, while continuing determined disarmament, demobilization and reintegration programmes. He called upon the international community to support the Sudanese people in meeting those challenges and to lend technical and political assistance to the implementation of the Comprehensive Peace Agreement. He recommended that the Security Council renew UNMIS mandate until 24 September 2007.

Security Council consideration. In presenting the Secretary-General's report to the Security Council on 18 September [meeting 5528], the Special Representative said that UNMIS had completed its deployment in southern Sudan, had fulfilled its mandate in eastern Sudan, and had withdrawn from the area. That withdrawal sent a strong signal to the people of the Sudan that the United Nations, which had come to eastern Sudan at the Government's invitation, had accomplished its task and had left. The Organization continued to monitor the Eritrean-mediated talks between the Government and the Eastern Front and an agreement was expected to be signed later in the year. In the south, the Government of Southern Sudan was working hard to transform the region into a functioning administration. President Kiir reshuffled his cabinet and administration to enhance good governance and abate corruption. His 200-day action plan was intended to put the needs of the people in front.

SECURITY COUNCIL ACTION

On 22 September [meeting 5532], the Security Council unanimously adopted **resolution 1709(2006)**. The draft [S/2006/758] was submitted by the United States.

The Security Council,

Recalling its previous resolutions, in particular resolutions 1590(2005) of 24 March 2005, 1627(2005) of 23 September 2005, 1653(2006) of 27 January 2006, 1663(2006) of 24 March 2006, 1679(2006) of 16 May 2006 and 1706(2006) of 31 August 2006, and the statements by its President, in particular that of 3 February 2006, concerning the situation in the Sudan,

Reaffirming its commitment to the sovereignty, unity, independence and territorial integrity of the Sudan and to the cause of peace,

Noting with deep concern the restrictions placed on movements and materiel of the United Nations Mission in the Sudan and the adverse impact that such restrictions have on the ability of the Mission to perform its mandate effectively,

Expressing its grave concern over the continued deterioration of the humanitarian situation in Darfur, and reiterating in the strongest terms the need for all parties to the conflict in Darfur to put an end to the violence and atrocities in that region,

Determining that the situation in the Sudan continues to constitute a threat to international peace and security,

1. *Decides* to extend the mandate of the United Nations Mission in the Sudan until 8 October 2006, with the intention to renew it for further periods;

2. *Decides also* to remain actively seized of the matter.

On 6 October [meeting 5545], the Security Council unanimously adopted **resolution 1714(2006)**. The draft [S/2006/792] was submitted by the United States.

The Security Council,

Recalling its previous resolutions, in particular resolutions 1590(2005) of 24 March 2005, 1627(2005) of 23 September 2005, 1653(2006) of 27 January 2006, 1663(2006) of 24 March 2006, 1679(2006) of 16 May 2006, 1706(2006) of 31 August 2006 and 1709(2006) of 22 September 2006, and the statements by its President, in particular that of 3 February 2006, concerning the situation in the Sudan,

Reaffirming its commitment to the sovereignty, unity, independence and territorial integrity of the Sudan and to the cause of peace,

Welcoming the progress in the implementation of security arrangements by the parties to the Comprehensive Peace Agreement of 9 January 2005, and calling upon the parties to urgently accelerate progress on implementing these and other aspects of the Agreement,

Welcoming also the full deployment of United Nations forces within the United Nations Mission in the Sudan in those areas of operation in support of the Comprehensive Peace Agreement, and acknowledging the commitment by troop-contributing countries in support of this mission,

Welcoming further the improving humanitarian situation in southern Sudan resulting from progress in the implementation of the Comprehensive Peace Agreement,

Noting with concern the restrictions placed on the movements and materiel of the Mission by the Government of the Sudan and the adverse impact that such restrictions have on the ability of the Mission to perform its mandate effectively,

Expressing its grave concern over the recruitment and use of children in conflict in the Sudan, particularly by other armed groups in southern Sudan,

Expressing its grave concern also over the continued deterioration of the humanitarian situation in Darfur, and reiterating in the strongest terms the need for all parties to the conflict in Darfur, including non-parties to the Darfur Peace Agreement, to put an end to the violence and atrocities in that region,

Welcoming the decision of the Peace and Security Council of the African Union, at its sixty-third meeting, held on 20 September 2006, to extend the mandate of the African Union Mission in the Sudan until 31 December 2006,

Encouraging the efforts of the Secretary-General and the African Union to implement those provisions of resolution 1706(2006) on United Nations assistance to the African Union Mission in the Sudan, and calling upon the parties to the Darfur Peace Agreement and all other parties in Darfur to facilitate this process,

Determining that the situation in the Sudan continues to constitute a threat to international peace and security,

1. *Decides* to extend the mandate of the United Nations Mission in the Sudan until 30 April 2007, with the intention to renew it for further periods;

2. *Requests* the Secretary-General to report to the Security Council every three months on the implementation of the mandate of the Mission;

3. *Calls upon* the parties to the Comprehensive Peace Agreement, the Darfur Peace Agreement and the N'Djamena Humanitarian Ceasefire Agreement to respect their commitments and implement fully all aspects of the Agreements without delay, and calls upon those parties that have not signed the Darfur Peace Agreement to do so without delay and not to act in any way that would impede implementation of the Agreement;

4. *Decides* to remain actively seized of the matter.

Further report of Secretary-General. In a later report [S/2007/42], the Secretary-General said that the Eritrean-mediated talks between the Government and the Eastern Front rebel movement culminated in the signing on 14 October of the Eastern Sudan Peace Agreement. The Agreement was approved by the National Assembly on 6 November and its incorporation into the Constitution was pending discussions between NCP and its allies regarding the allocations of parliamentary seats. The state of emergency was lifted in Kassala state and Red Sea state. The Agreement's implementation, however, was progressing slowly.

A most serious violation of the ceasefire occurred in Malakal, Upper Nile, where heavy fighting between SAF and SPLA, from 27 to 30 November, killed at least 150 people, including civilians. A long-running dispute over the "commissionership" of a county in neighbouring Jonglei state triggered the skirmishes between groups aligned with SAF and the SPLA Joint Integrated Unit contingent, which escalated into a full-scale confrontation. The Ceasefire Joint Military Committee played a key role in bringing the fighting to a halt, and the parties subsequently withdrew to their pre-conflict positions. The failure to integrate other armed groups into existing military structures and to create functioning Joint Integrated Units had left the parties facing a growing security problem, where militia violence, as witnessed in Malakal, could easily erupt and spiral out of control. On 18 November, President Al-Bashir called for better cooperation between NCP and SPLM on security matters, particularly the problem of other armed groups, and stressed the need for the Joint Integrated Units to function in order to secure the border areas and oil installations. The clashes in Malakal led the United Nations to relocate temporarily 230 non-essential UN and NGO personnel. Elsewhere in southern Sudan, unidentified armed men, allegedly belonging to SAF-aligned militia groups, were held responsible for attacks on arterial roads outside Juba, in October and December, killing some 75 people.

UNMIS continued to face considerable challenges in carrying out its mandate. On 26 September, two UNMIS staff members monitoring demonstrations at Khartoum University were detained and threatened by unidentified security personnel. They were subsequently declared personae non gratae and requested to leave the Sudan. On 22 October, the Sudan informed the Secretary-General that it had decided to "terminate" the mission of Special Representative Jan Pronk and requested that he leave the Sudan within 72 hours, reportedly due to comments Mr. Pronk had made on his blog. The United Nations strongly protested that decision. Mr. Pronk returned to UN Headquarters for consultations and later to the Sudan for a short farewell visit prior to the expiration of his contract at the end of the year.

UNMIS

The United Nations Mission in the Sudan (UNMIS), established by Security Council resolution 1590(2005) [YUN 2005, p. 304], was headed by Johannes Pronk, Special Representative of the Secretary-General for the Sudan. UNMIS continued to discharge its mandate, in accordance with resolution 1590(2005), to support implementation of the Comprehensive Peace Agreement signed by the Government of the Sudan and SPLM/A; facilitate and coordinate the voluntary return of refugees and internally displaced persons and humanitarian assistance; assist with humanitarian demining; and protect and promote human rights. Its mandate was extended by the Council three times during the year, the first time until 24 September, the second until 8 October and the third until 30 April 2007.

Following the signing of the Darfur Peace Agreement on 5 May (see p. 274), the Security Council, in resolution 1706(2006) of 31 August (see p. 282), decided to expand UNMIS mandate to deploy to Darfur and to strengthen its size up to 17,300 military personnel, 3,300 civilian personnel and 16 formed police units.

As at 31 December, UNMIS comprised 8,734 troops, 592 military observers and 680 international civilian police.

Appointment. By an exchange of letters between the Secretary-General and the Security Council on 4 [S/2006/8] and 6 [S/2006/9] January, Lieutenant General Jasbir Singh Lidder (India) was appointed UNMIS Force Commander, replacing Major General Fazle Elahi Akbar (Bangladesh).

UNMIS activities

UNMIS continued to assist the parties in implementing the Comprehensive Peace Agreement and resolving conflicts in the Sudan through the provision of good offices and political support. In the east, UNMIS supported the Government and the Eastern Front, the coalition of rebel groups operating along the border with Eritrea, in peace talks. With the completion of SPLA redeployment to the south, UNMIS Redeployment Coordination Headquarters, based in the north-eastern town of Kassala, fulfilled its tasks in eastern Sudan, and the Mission started to withdraw on 1 August.

In the south, UNMIS intensified reconciliation efforts and helped to defuse tensions in areas of potential conflict, in close liaison with the SAF, SPLA and other armed groups. The Mission was able to prevent or manage the escalation of local conflicts, many of them associated with the seasonal movement of people and cattle to the dry-season grazing areas. UNMIS used its good offices to help restore calm in a number of volatile situations, including the clashes in May caused by the forced disarmament campaign in Jonglei and the Rubkona market incident in August. Starting on 11 August, UNMIS convened several emergency meetings of the Area Joint Military Committee to secure a halt to the fighting between the SPLA and the SAF-aligned Pangak Peace Force in the town of Malakal (see p. 264). UNMIS good relations with most commanders of SAF, SPLA and other armed groups proved crucial in defusing the tense situation in Upper Nile State. More broadly, it continued to perform an important early warning role throughout southern Sudan, identifying and addressing intercommunal tensions.

UNMIS also assisted in efforts to implement the Darfur Peace Agreement. The Mission continued to persuade the non-signatory groups to support the Agreement, and participated in the work of the AU-led Joint Commission and Ceasefire Commissions.

UNMIS continued to train the local police. Its mine action teams made major progress in clearing 7 million square metres of suspected dangerous areas and destroying some 2,100 anti-personnel mines, over 900 anti-tank mines and some 270,000 pieces of unexploded ordnance and small-arms ammunition. With the United Nations Children's Fund, it provided mine-risk education to more than 834,000 people. The Mission focused on clearing humanitarian routes, verifying or clearing over 1,200 kilometres of road for emergency deployment and aid delivery and making it possible to drive from Khartoum to the Ugandan border.

Financing of UNMIS

In March [A/60/726 & Corr.1], the Secretary-General submitted the UNMIS performance report for the period from 1 July 2004 to 30 June 2005 [YUN 2005, p. 315], and the UNMIS budget for the period from 1 July 2006 to 30 June 2007, amounting to $1,081,659,300.

In May [A/60/868], ACABQ recommended a reduction of $594,300 in the amount requested. The amount to be appropriated totalled $1,081,065,000.

GENERAL ASSEMBLY ACTION

On 30 June [meeting 92], the General Assembly, on the recommendation of the Fifth Committee, adopted **resolution 60/122 B** [A/60/562/Add.1] without vote [agenda item 140].

Financing of the United Nations Mission in the Sudan

The General Assembly,

Having considered the reports of the Secretary-General on the financing of the United Nations Mission in the Sudan and the related report of the Advisory Committee on Administrative and Budgetary Questions,

Recalling Security Council resolution 1590(2005) of 24 March 2005, by which the Council established the United Nations Mission in the Sudan for an initial period of six months as from 24 March 2005, and the subsequent resolutions by which the Council extended the mandate of the Mission, the latest of which was resolution 1663(2006) of 24 March 2006,

Recalling also its resolutions 59/292 of 21 April 2005 and 60/122 A of 8 December 2005 on the financing of the Mission,

Recalling further its resolution 58/315 of 1 July 2004,

Reaffirming the general principles underlying the financing of United Nations peacekeeping operations, as stated in its resolutions 1874(S-IV) of 27 June 1963, 3101(XXVIII) of 11 December 1973 and 55/235 of 23 December 2000,

Mindful of the fact that it is essential to provide the Mission with the necessary financial resources to enable it to fulfil its responsibilities under the relevant resolutions of the Security Council,

1. *Requests* the Secretary-General to entrust the Head of Mission with the task of formulating future budget proposals in full accordance with the provisions of General Assembly resolutions 59/296 of 22 June 2005 and 60/266 of 30 June 2006, as well as other relevant resolutions;

2. *Takes note* of the status of contributions to the United Nations Mission in the Sudan as at 30 April 2006, including the contributions outstanding in the amount of 52.9 million United States dollars, representing some 4 per cent of the total assessed contributions, notes with concern that only sixty Member States have paid their assessed contributions in full, and urges all other Member States, in particular those in arrears, to ensure payment of their outstanding assessed contributions;

3. *Expresses its appreciation* to those Member States which have paid their assessed contributions in full, and urges all other Member States to make every possible effort to ensure payment of their assessed contributions to the Mission in full;

4. *Expresses concern* at the financial situation with regard to peacekeeping activities, in particular as regards the reimbursements to troop contributors that bear additional burdens owing to overdue payments by Member States of their assessments;

5. *Also expresses concern* at the delay experienced by the Secretary-General in deploying and providing adequate resources to some recent peacekeeping missions, in particular those in Africa;

6. *Emphasizes* that all future and existing peacekeeping missions shall be given equal and non-discriminatory treatment in respect of financial and administrative arrangements;

7. *Also emphasizes* that all peacekeeping missions shall be provided with adequate resources for the effective and efficient discharge of their respective mandates;

8. *Reiterates its request* to the Secretary-General to make the fullest possible use of facilities and equipment at the United Nations Logistics Base at Brindisi, Italy, in order to minimize the costs of procurement for the Mission;

9. *Welcomes* the use of the Entebbe installation to enhance the efficiency and responsiveness of its logistical support operations for peacekeeping missions in the region;

10. *Endorses* the conclusions and recommendations contained in the report of the Advisory Committee on Administrative and Budgetary Questions, subject to the provisions of the present resolution, and requests the Secretary-General to ensure their full implementation;

11. *Reaffirms* its resolution 59/296, and requests the Secretary-General to ensure the full implementation of its relevant provisions and the relevant provisions of its resolution 60/266;

12. *Requests* the Secretary-General to take all necessary action to ensure that the Mission is administered with a maximum of efficiency and economy;

13. *Welcomes* the efforts of the Mission in developing the unified mission concept, and requests the Secretary-General to continue to improve this concept;

14. *Notes with appreciation* the strong coordination between the United Nations Mission in the Sudan and the United Nations country team, and requests the Secretary-General to share the Mission's experiences and lessons learned with other complex peacekeeping missions with a view to increasing their coordination and reducing potential duplication of activities with other entities, and to report thereon to it at its sixty-first session in the context of the overview report of the Secretary-General on progress made in this regard;

15. *Requests* the Secretary-General to continue providing the latest available information on specific management efficiencies achieved as well as future plans in this regard in the unified area-based and decentralized organizational structure of the Mission in the context of the next budget submission;

16. *Also requests* the Secretary-General to ensure that the Mission implementation plan and results-based budgeting are integrated and to report on progress made to the General Assembly in the context of the next budget submission for the Mission;

17. *Further requests* the Secretary-General, in order to reduce the cost of employing General Service staff, to continue efforts to recruit local staff for the Mission against General Service posts, commensurate with the requirements of the Mission;

18. *Requests* the Secretary-General to intensify his ongoing efforts, including through innovative approaches, to ensure the expeditious filling of all vacant posts;

19. *Decides* to establish a Planning Officer post at the P-4 level in the Strategic Planning Office;

20. *Stresses* the crucial role of demining for the speedy and successful implementation of the Mission's mandate, and welcomes the intention of the Mission to ensure successful implementation of this activity through collaboration and coordination with the relevant partners in the field;

21. *Requests* the Secretary-General to continue to enhance coordination and provision of technical advice and operational demining in support of the full deployment of the Mission, in accordance with relevant mandates, and to report thereon in context of the proposed budget for the period from 1 July 2008 to 30 June 2009;

22. *Also requests* the Secretary-General to provide clear information on the budget provision for mine detection and mine-clearing services, including staffing and operational costs, in the Mission's next budget submission;

23. *Welcomes* the increasing use of the inland waterway;

24. *Notes* the considerable reliance on air assets for transportation, and, bearing in mind the expected lifetime of the Mission, requests the Secretary-General to ensure that the Mission also effectively utilizes and, where possible, increases the available road, rail and inland waterway transport modes where they are reliable, cost-effective and safer than air transportation, and also requests the Secretary-General to report on the experience of the Mission in this area and to indicate the actual and expected efficiencies resulting from the use of such modes of transportation as well as a long-term strategy in this regard;

25. *Requests* the Secretary-General to increase the Mission's utilization of information and communication technology tools wherever it is possible and creates efficiencies and to report back on their utilization to the General Assembly at its sixty-second session in the context of the budget submission for the Mission;

26. *Looks forward* to the consideration of the comprehensive report requested in section VIII, paragraph 3, of its resolution 60/266;

27. *Requests* the Secretary-General to ensure that quick-impact projects are implemented in compliance with the original intent of such projects and relevant General Assembly resolutions;

28. *Decides* to approve the resources requested for quick-impact projects in section II of the proposed budget for the Mission for the period from 1 July 2006 to 30 June 2007;

29. *Requests* the Secretary-General to ensure the fullest implementation of the quick-impact projects in the period from 1 July 2006 to 30 June 2007 in the light of the Mission's capacity to undertake these activities;

30. *Reaffirms* the provisions of its resolution 59/296 on disarmament, demobilization and reintegration, and requests the Secretary-General to utilize the proposed resources in accordance with the provisions of that resolution;

31. *Requests* the Secretary-General to ensure that future budget submissions include clear information regarding mandated disarmament, demobilization and reintegration activities, including clear justification for post and non-post resource requirements and their projected impact on the effective delivery of Mission objectives in this field as well as information on the collaboration with all relevant United Nations entities present in the field and acting in this area;

Financial performance report for the period from 1 July 2004 to 30 June 2005

32. *Takes note* of the report of the Secretary-General on the financial performance of the Mission for the period from 1 July 2004 to 30 June 2005;

Budget estimates for the period from 1 July 2006 to 30 June 2007

33. *Decides* to appropriate to the Special Account for the United Nations Mission in the Sudan the amount of 1,126,295,900 dollars for the period from 1 July 2006 to 30 June 2007, inclusive of 1,079,534,400 dollars for the maintenance of the Mission, 38,623,300 dollars for the support account for peacekeeping operations and 8,138,200 dollars for the United Nations Logistics Base at Brindisi, Italy;

Financing of the appropriation

34. *Decides also* to apportion among Member States the amount of 262,802,400 dollars for the period from 1 July to 24 September 2006, in accordance with the levels updated in its resolution 58/256 of 23 December 2003, taking into account the scale of assessments for 2006, as set out in its resolution 58/1 B of 23 December 2003;

35. *Decides further* that, in accordance with the provisions of its resolution 973(X) of 15 December 1955, there shall be set off against the apportionment among Member States, as provided for in paragraph 34 above, their respective share in the Tax Equalization Fund of 5,883,800 dollars, comprising the estimated staff assessment income of 4,726,300 dollars approved for the Mission, the prorated share of 1,013,700 dollars of the estimated staff assessment income approved for the support account and the prorated share of 143,800 dollars of the estimated staff assessment income approved for the United Nations Logistics Base;

36. *Decides* to apportion among Member States the amount of 863,493,500 dollars for the period from 25 September 2006 to 30 June 2007, in accordance with the levels updated in its resolution 58/256 and taking into account the scale of assessments for 2006, as set out in its resolution 58/1 B, and the scale of assessments for 2007, subject to a decision of the Security Council to extend the mandate of the Mission;

37. *Decides also* that, in accordance with the provisions of its resolution 973(X), there shall be set off against the apportionment among Member States, as provided for in paragraph 36 above, their respective share in the

Tax Equalization Fund of 19,332,400 dollars, comprising the estimated staff assessment income of 15,529,400 dollars approved for the Mission, the prorated share of 3,330,800 dollars of the estimated staff assessment income approved for the support account and the prorated share of 472,200 dollars of the estimated staff assessment income approved for the United Nations Logistics Base;

38. *Decides further* that, for Member States that have fulfilled their financial obligations to the Mission, there shall be set off against their apportionment, as provided for in paragraph 34 above, their respective share of the unencumbered balance and other income in the total amount of 2,804,000 dollars in respect of the financial period ended 30 June 2005, in accordance with the levels updated in its resolution 58/256, and taking into account the scale of assessments for 2005, as set out in its resolution 58/1 B;

39. *Decides* that, for Member States that have not fulfilled their financial obligations to the Mission, there shall be set off against their outstanding obligations their respective share of the unencumbered balance and other income in the total amount of 2,804,000 dollars in respect of the financial period ended 30 June 2005, in accordance with the scheme set out in paragraph 38 above;

40. *Decides also* that the net increase of 455,200 dollars in the staff assessment income in respect of the financial period ended 30 June 2005, representing the difference between the additional staff assessment income of 678,100 dollars previously approved under the terms of its resolution 60/122 A for the financial period from 1 July 2004 to 30 June 2005 and the decrease in the staff assessment income of 222,900 dollars in respect of the same financial period, shall be added to the credits from the amount of 2,804,000 dollars referred to in paragraphs 38 and 39 above;

41. *Emphasizes* that no peacekeeping mission shall be financed by borrowing funds from other active peacekeeping missions;

42. *Encourages* the Secretary-General to continue to take additional measures to ensure the safety and security of all personnel under the auspices of the United Nations participating in the Mission, bearing in mind paragraphs 5 and 6 of Security Council resolution 1502(2003) of 26 August 2003;

43. *Invites* voluntary contributions to the Mission in cash and in the form of services and supplies acceptable to the Secretary-General, to be administered, as appropriate, in accordance with the procedure and practices established by the General Assembly;

44. *Decides* to include in the provisional agenda of its sixty-first session the item entitled "Financing of the United Nations Mission in the Sudan".

On 15 November [A/61/598], the Secretary-General informed the Assembly President that UNMIS expansion would require extensive augmentation of the support infrastructure and the building of sustained capabilities, and indicated the extraordinary measures he had authorized in that regard. He noted that, under Assembly resolution 60/122 B, an amount of $1,079.5 million had been appropriated for UNMIS. The light support package recommended by the Secretary-General was being implemented under the existing approved budget.

On 22 December, by **decision 61/552**, the Assembly decided that agenda item "Financing of UNMIS" would remain for consideration during its resumed sixty-first (2007) session.

Situation in Darfur

In 2006, the conflict in the Darfur region of western Sudan, which had erupted in 2003, intensified. The Government of the Sudan continued to confront the two main rebel movements—the Sudan Liberation Movement/Army (SLM/A) and the Justice and Equality Movement (JEM). The AU, through the African Union Mission in the Sudan (AMIS), continued to help the parties to observe the 2004 N'Djamena Humanitarian Ceasefire Agreement [YUN 2004, p. 235] and led international efforts to resolve the crisis, through the inter-Sudanese peace talks, also known as the Abuja talks, which began in 2004. Those talks, supported by international partners and the United Nations, culminated in the signing of the Darfur Peace Agreement on 5 May, 2006. While all parties to the conflict attended the talks, only the Government and the SLM/A faction led by Minni Minawi signed the Agreement. In the light of the conclusion of the Darfur Peace Agreement and the intensification of the fighting, the AU Peace and Security Council, on 15 May, requested further UN assistance to help it fulfill its obligations under the Agreement and that steps be taken to transition from AMIS to a UN operation. The Council responded in resolution 1706(2006) of 31 August, by expanding the mandate of the United Nations Mission in the Sudan (UNMIS) and authorizing an increase in its strength to 17,300 military personnel. However, the Government of the Sudan declared its objection to such a mission. At the same, time the non-signatories to the Darfur Peace Agreement maintained their opposition to the Agreement and created alliances to oppose its implementation. Efforts, led by the AU Special Envoy, were made to persuade the non-signatories to support the Agreement. Pending agreement by the Government of the Sudan to allow a UN operation in Darfur, the AU and the United Nations agreed to assist AMIS in the form of a "light support package" and on 16 November, they further agreed to a phase two "heavy package" of assistance, and to establish an AU-UN hybrid operation in Darfur, with a force that would be predominantly African in nature. On 19 December, the Security Council endorsed those decisions and called on all parties to implement them.

The conflict in Darfur also resulted in an escalation of tension between Chad and the Sudan, despite the signing in February of the Tripoli Agreement on the normalization of relations between the two countries.

Political and security developments

The Secretary-General, in his January report on Darfur [S/2006/59], said that African Union Mission in the Sudan (AMIS) continued to liaise closely with UNMIS through periodic meetings between the United Nations Assistance Cell and the AU Commission in Addis Ababa, Ethiopia. The report of the AU Commission's December 2005 in-depth review of AMIS operations [YUN 2005, p. 335] was considered by the AU Peace and Security Council on 12 January, 2006. In a communiqué issued the same day, the Peace and Security Council noted that, despite serious financial, logistical and other constraints facing AMIS, it had contributed significantly to the protection of the civilian population and the improvement of the security and humanitarian situations in Darfur. The Peace and Security Council supported, in principle, the transition from AMIS to a UN operation and decided to convene at the ministerial level in Addis Ababa, in March, to review the situation and make a final decision on the transfer and its modalities. The Secretary-General said that the United Nations would work closely with the AU and other stakeholders to take the matter forward. The transition itself would be difficult and costly, but, in the meantime, everything possible should be done to support and strengthen the existing AMIS operation, including providing it with the necessary funding.

Security Council consideration (January). On 13 January [meeting 5344], the Special Representative of the Secretary-General for the Sudan, Johannes Pronk, in briefing the Security Council, said that the 31 December 2005 deadline for reaching an agreement on Darfur had passed unnoticed and there seemed to be no sense of urgency. Despite his best efforts, the AU Special Envoy for the Inter-Sudanese Peace Talks on the Conflict in Darfur, Salim A. Salim, could not get the parties to reach an agreement. They could learn from the way the north-south Peace Agreement was reached, whereby the parties agreed upon a sustained and lasting ceasefire first, making it possible to continue negotiations for a fair distribution of power and wealth. However, any agreement reached would be sustainable only if the international community assisted in guaranteeing security. AMIS had done an admirable job but had not been provided with adequate resources and means to prevent attacks. International guarantees would have to be provided to allow internally displaced persons and refugees to return, and the military force to provide such guarantees should be bigger than the current AMIS force, stay long enough to provide confidence, and be an integral element of a unified approach to Darfur, with humanitarian, political, police, legal, human rights, reconstruction and economic development instruments, supported by sanctions.

The AU Special Envoy for the Inter-Sudanese Peace Talks told the Council that the AU mediation intended to ensure that the parties were continuously engaged until a comprehensive agreement was reached on all the major issues that separated them. The negotiations had been characterized by inflexibility, suspicion, lack of confidence and deep distrust. The parties, the Government and the armed movements needed to show more willingness to compromise. As a way forward and to give the Abuja talks fresh momentum, he proposed that efforts be made to ensure the effectiveness of the mechanisms established to implement the N'Djamena Humanitarian Ceasefire Agreement [YUN 2004, p. 235], with credible sanctions for those violating it. The parties should know that they would be held responsible for prolonging the suffering of the people, and would be subject to UN sanctions. There needed to be stronger cohesion, transparency and coordination among regional countries facilitating the peace process. Other external conditions needed to be addressed urgently, especially the tension between Chad and the Sudan. Cohesion and greater coordination between the AU mediation and international partners were essential for the negotiations. AMIS should be strengthened as a matter of priority, including the provision of adequate funding. The Special Envoy appealed to the Council to remain engaged and to send strong signals of its support for the Abuja peace process.

SECURITY COUNCIL ACTION

On 3 February [meeting 5364], following consultations among Security Council members, the President made statement **S/PRST/2006/5** on behalf of the Council:

> The Security Council commends the efforts of the African Union for successful deployment of the African Union Mission in the Sudan and for significant contribution to the provision of a secure environment for civilians and the humanitarian situation in Darfur. The Council welcomes the recognition by the Peace and Security Council of the African Union of the partnership between the African Union and the United Nations in the promotion of peace, security and stability in Africa.

The Security Council takes note of the communiqué of 12 January 2006 issued by the Peace and Security Council, in which it expressed its support, in principle, for a transition from the African Union Mission in the Sudan to a United Nations operation and requested the Chairperson of the Commission of the African Union to initiate consultations with the United Nations and other stakeholders on this matter.

The Security Council therefore requests the Secretary-General to initiate contingency planning without delay, jointly with the African Union, in close and continuing consultation with the Council, and in cooperation and close consultation with the parties to the Abuja Peace Talks, including the Government of National Unity, on a range of options for a possible transition from the African Union Mission in the Sudan to a United Nations operation. Such planning should be undertaken on the basis of a unified, integrated approach; of maximum use of existing resources of the African Union Mission in the Sudan and the United Nations Mission in the Sudan, subject to the agreement of troop-contributing countries; of an assessment, to be confirmed by the Council, of the essential tasks to be carried out in southern Sudan and Darfur with a view to reallocating existing troops and assets to the maximum extent practicable; and of a readiness to review and adjust the current structure of the United Nations Mission in the Sudan, including command and control and logistics, at the earliest opportunity, to make the best use of available resources when the African Union deems a transition feasible and agreeable. The Council will be engaged throughout this process.

The Security Council emphasizes the importance of maintaining strong support for the African Union Mission in the Sudan until any eventual transition is completed. The Council looks forward to an early decision from the Peace and Security Council and will keep this issue under consideration with a view to reviewing the options submitted by the Secretary-General.

The Security Council stresses the importance of urgently reaching a successful conclusion of the Abuja Peace Talks and calls upon all parties to negotiate in good faith in order to reach a peace accord as soon as possible. The Council reiterates in the strongest terms the need for all parties in Darfur to end the violence and atrocities. The Council demands that all parties to the Darfur conflict cooperate fully with the African Union Mission in the Sudan and fulfil all the obligations to which they have committed themselves.

Report of Secretary-General (March). In his March report on Darfur [S/2006/148], submitted in response to Security Council resolutions 1556(2004) [YUN 2004, p. 240], 1564(2004) [ibid., p. 245], 1574(2004) [ibid. p. 252] and 1590(2005) [YUN 2005, p. 305], the Secretary-General said that security problems escalated in January, with banditry, armed clashes and tensions along the Chad border contributing to a dangerous and volatile situation.

The situation worsened in Western Darfur, particularly in Jebel Marra, where about 160 fighters from the Sudan Liberation Army (SLA) attacked SAF in Golo, on 23 January, leading to several days of fighting. On 23 January, SLA fighters ambushed a police unit escorting 80 commercial trucks from Al Fasher to Kabkabiya, killing 20 police officers, including the convoy commander. Attacks on humanitarian workers continued. To reduce their exposure, the United Nations restricted their movements to Geneina, the capital of Western Darfur, and reduced staff levels in the region. In Southern Darfur, fighting erupted in Shaeria between SLA and Government forces on 25 January, and humanitarian convoys were attacked by bandits.

Following the 12 January decision (see p. 269) of the AU Peace and Security Council to support, in principle, a transition from AMIS to a UN operation, demonstrations against the United Nations were held in various parts of Darfur, which were, for the most part, peaceful. However, that decision appeared to have given fresh momentum to the Sudanese parties negotiating in the Abuja peace process. The wealth-sharing commission made significant progress, and the commission on power-sharing and security arrangements finally addressed substantive issues. The commission on security arrangements was broken up into smaller working groups and the pace of negotiations increased significantly, with discussions focusing on ways to revitalize the Joint Commission.

In the area of human rights, the police did not provide protection to civilian populations facing continuing attacks by militias. In Western Darfur, the December 2005 militia attack on Abu Sorouj town [YUN 2005, p. 336] created a retaliatory cycle of violence between the police and local residents. Civilians living close to rebel territory and sharing the same ethnicity were particularly vulnerable to human rights violations by the armed forces. An assessment mission by UNMIS and the Office for the Coordination of Humanitarian Affairs (OCHA) (7-10 January) in Golo, Eastern Jebel Marra (Western Darfur), revealed arbitrary arrests and detentions and intimidation of the population by the armed forces. The deteriorating security situation led to new forced displacements. While some of those displacements were due to inter-tribal conflict, including in the Zalinjei area, where thousands were forced out of their homes in late December 2005 and early January 2006, others were due to fighting between SLA and SAF, supported by militias, especially in the Jebel Marra area, where about 20,000 people were displaced.

Humanitarian efforts conducted in that violent and uncertain environment were hindered by armed hijackings of commercial and humanitarian trucks, including clearly marked World Food Programme (WFP) vehicles. Because of the deteriorating security situation, there was no longer humanitarian access to some 30,000 people in areas north of Geneina, where threats from renegade forces had even grounded humanitarian helicopter flights.

In contrast, the situation in Northern Darfur was relatively positive, as aid workers had good access throughout the state. Aid workers in Darfur were constrained also by frequent administrative delays related to visa extensions, identity documents and travel permits. The resulting denial of access and the inability to move humanitarian goods had a detrimental impact on the affected communities.

As at 3 March, AMIS had 6,898 personnel in Darfur, comprising 4,760 troops, 715 military observers, 1,385 civilian police, 27 international civilian staff and 11 Ceasefire Commission personnel. UNMIS continued to liaise closely with AMIS. In accordance with the 3 February statement by the Security Council President (see p. 269), the Secretary-General started planning the transition from AMIS to a UN operation, in consultation with the AU. A UN-led operation would depend greatly on African contributions and remain part of a cooperative international approach. Sudan's cooperation would be a requirement, and planning would have to take into consideration the violence and human rights violations in the region, the displacement of more than 3 million people and increasing instability near the Chad border. The main objectives of international efforts in Darfur would be to protect civilians and create an environment conducive to national reconciliation. Contingency planning for a possible transition to a UN operation would be guided by those objectives and should be achieved through a multidimensional presence. The Secretary-General appealed to the parties to the AU-led inter-Sudanese peace talks in Abuja to show greater commitment and flexibility to achieve a negotiated settlement. At the same time, recent attacks on AMIS and humanitarian agencies, together with the escalation of violence and the deteriorating conditions for civilians, demonstrated the urgent need to strengthen the international presence on the ground.

Security Council consideration (March). In his 21 March [meeting 5392] briefing to the Security Council, the Special Representative said that, since his last briefing (see p. 269), the towns of Sharia, Graida, Aro Sharow, Tama, Abu Sorouj, Tawila, Labado, Hamada and Khor Abeche all stood witness to cruel atrocities, terror, killings and rape. There was no peace agreement and the killings continued. In Jabll Marra, fighting between the Government and SLA intensified. Along the border with Chad, tensions had heightened, and the area was a "no-go" area for humanitarian workers. In Southern Darfur, militias continued to cleanse village after village and AU commanders on the ground openly spoke about continued support for militias from forces allied to the Government. Rebel movements were more and more fragmented, fighting each other, forming new alliances, and alienating themselves from their representatives at the Abuja peace talks. Demands laid down in Council resolutions were brushed aside, the 2004 N'Djamena Humanitarian Ceasefire Agreement was being violated, and the sanctions foreseen with the establishment of the Security Council Panel of Experts (see p. 292) existed only in theory.

The UN strategy should focus on two objectives: bringing about peace between the warring parties and protecting unarmed civilians, in particular against movements that were not party to the peace talks. Three steps were therefore necessary: the swift conclusion of an agreement in Abuja on power and wealth-sharing, followed by an all-inclusive Darfur-Darfur dialogue between all stakeholders; conclusion of a new ceasefire agreement, with firm implementation provisions and procedures, clear sanctions for violations and a strong peacekeeping force to enforce them; and creation of a large, robust peace force, with a mandate broad enough to meet all possible threats.

Steps should be taken to augment the AU, concurrent with planning for the transition to a UN operation. Public reaction to the transition was not very positive, as evidenced by the carefully orchestrated campaign against UN operations in Darfur. However, many Sudanese people were confused about the United Nations, its Charter, principles and objectives. To redress that situation, the United Nations had to consult with the Government to allay fears, correct perceptions and make clear that the extension of the UN presence in the Sudan was not an infringement on the country's sovereignty. The consent of the Government in the transition to a UN operation would greatly advance the cause of peace in the country.

AU support for UN mission (March). The AU Peace and Security Council, meeting at the ministerial level on 10 March on the situation in Darfur [S/2006/156], decided to support in principle the transition from AMIS to a UN operation. It also extended AMIS mandate until 30 September to contribute to the improvement of the security situation, monitor compliance with the 2004 N'Djamena Humanitarian Ceasefire Agreement and subsequent agreements and assist in confidence-building.

The Security Council, in resolution 1663(2006) of 24 March (see p. 259), welcomed the AU support for the transition to a UN operation in Darfur and its intention to conclude a peace agreement on Darfur by the end of April. The Council requested the Secretary-General to expedite planning for the transition and present a range of options for its consideration.

Report of Secretary-General (April). In his April report on Darfur [S/2006/218], the Secretary-General said that a high level of violence persisted during March, with armed clashes between the parties, including between different SLA factions. In Northern and Southern Darfur, all of the parties pursued a deliberate strategy of targeting civilians to stem alleged support for enemy groups, creating further population movements.

Tensions remain high in Southern Darfur, with increasing inter-tribal clashes and militia attacks. On 14 February, armed tribesmen, allegedly supported by Government forces, attacked an SLA camp near the town of Shearia, and SLA shot down a Government helicopter. Two days later, armed tribesmen attacked several villages south-east of Gereida. The situation in Gereida itself remained tense.

In Western Darfur, attacks on villages, violence in camps for internally displaced persons, the presence of Chadian armed groups and harassment of populations by militias led to further displacement of civilians. In the Jebel Marra area, fighting between the SAF and SLA forced virtually the entire population of the town to flee. In Northern Darfur, Government attacks on villages in the area of Haskanita also forced many inhabitants to do likewise.

Local leaders were arrested for raising concerns about internally displaced persons or providing information to "foreigners". That resulted in internally displaced persons being reluctant to share concerns with the international community. Police harassment and arbitrary arrests of community leaders contributed to a climate of intimidation in South and West Darfur. Civilians sharing the same ethnicity as the rebel groups continued to be targeted for arbitrary arrest and detention.

Humanitarian access continued to be limited in Western Darfur. Only about 50 per cent of the affected populations in the area around, and to the north of Geneina, were accessible to UN operations. There was no humanitarian presence in the Kulbus-Silea area and large parts of Jebel Marra, leaving some 300,000 vulnerable people without assistance. Despite those constraints, the humanitarian situation remained under control due to the efforts of the aid community. In January, WFP delivered 36,000 tons of food to 2.1 million beneficiaries. Nearly 14,200 dedicated national and international humanitarian workers continued to assist some 3.6 million vulnerable people in Darfur, about half of whom were displaced.

The Secretary-General said that the recent escalation in the fighting had forced thousands more civilians to flee their homes, exposing them to a wide range of abuses. He was alarmed by reports of widespread human rights violations in Gereida, Mershing and Shearia in Southern Darfur. The most serious problem was the continued attacks by militias on armed civilians. The Government had to take action to rein in those forces over which it had direct or indirect control, and unless the attacks were halted, it would be difficult to reach a sustainable peace and ceasefire agreement. The Secretary-General welcomed the 12 March remarks by senior AU officials, emphasizing that the parties had to sign the draft enhanced ceasefire agreement. The presentation to the parties of that draft agreement was a positive development and a critical step in achieving a settlement. However, the fragile relationships within and between the movements, as well as among the commanders in the field, posed a challenge to the success of the peace process. The fractures within SLM/A, in particular, were worrisome. Moreover, the heightened violence in Western Darfur and the tenuous relationship between Chad and the Sudan continued to impinge negatively on peace negotiations. While the Tripoli agreement signed, on 8 February (see p. 297), between those two States was an encouraging development, much more needed to be done to reinforce the process. The Secretary-General urged both Chad and the Sudan to take concrete steps towards implementing the Tripoli agreement, with a view to normalizing relations and reducing tensions along the border.

Regarding the transition from AMIS to a UN operation in the Sudan, the Secretary-General noted the concerns of the Sudan and other AU member States on that subject and indicated that he was taking steps to address them. Extensive discussions had been held with the AU Commission on planning for the transition and the next critical step was to send a joint AU/ UN technical assessment mission to Darfur, as well as Chad.

SECURITY COUNCIL ACTION

On 11 April [meeting 5409], following consultations among Security Council members, the President made statement **S/PRST/2006/16** on behalf of the Council:

> The Security Council strongly commends the efforts of the African Union to achieve lasting peace in Darfur, which have its full support. It reiterates in the strongest terms the need for all parties to the conflict in Darfur to put an immediate end to the violence and atrocities; reaffirms its concern that the persisting violence in Darfur might further negatively affect the rest of the country as well as the region, including

the security of Chad; and expresses its utmost concern over the dire consequences of the prolonged conflict in Darfur for the civilian population.

The Security Council regrets the decision of the Government of National Unity not to renew the contract of the Norwegian Refugee Council and expresses its grave concern over the humanitarian consequences. It also regrets the decision of the Government of National Unity to deny the entry of the United Nations Emergency Relief Coordinator to Darfur. It looks forward to the forthcoming briefing by the Emergency Relief Coordinator and to his being able to visit Darfur at the earliest possible opportunity. The Council also calls for an explanation from the Government of National Unity on its decision.

The Security Council reiterates its full support for the Inter-Sudanese Peace Talks on the Conflict in Darfur in Abuja, noting that an inclusive political settlement is key to peace in the Sudan, that the Talks provide a mechanism to achieve such a settlement and that the African Union should maintain leadership. It welcomes the timely involvement of the Chair of the African Union and the President of the Federal Republic of Nigeria in the Talks during their visit to Abuja on 8 April 2006; endorses the decision of the Peace and Security Council of the African Union that 30 April 2006 is the final deadline for reaching an agreement; demands that all parties make the necessary efforts to reach an agreement by this date; and reaffirms its determination to hold accountable those impeding the peace process and committing human rights violations, noting the view of the African Union that the Security Council has a critical role in this respect.

The Security Council commends the African Union for what the African Union Mission in the Sudan has successfully achieved in Darfur despite exceptionally difficult circumstances, and the efforts of Member States and organizations that have assisted the Mission. It reiterates its welcome, in resolution 1663(2006) of 24 March 2006, for the decision of the Peace and Security Council of 10 March 2006 to support in principle the transition of the Mission to a United Nations operation and to extend the mandate of the Mission until 30 September 2006; calls, therefore, upon all parties to take all necessary measures to ensure a smooth and successful transfer to a United Nations operation; urges Member States and international and regional organizations to provide additional assistance to the Mission so that it may be strengthened in line with the conclusions of the report of the joint assessment mission of 10 to 20 December 2005; and calls for the convening of a pledging conference.

The Security Council reiterates its commitment to the sovereignty, unity, independence and territorial integrity of the Sudan, which will be unaffected by the transition to a United Nations operation.

The Security Council stresses that the Secretary-General should consult jointly with the African Union, in close and continuing consultation with the Council, and in cooperation and close consultation with the parties to the Abuja Peace Talks, including the Government of National Unity, on decisions concerning the transition; stresses that a United Nations operation will have strong African participation and character; recalls its request, in resolution 1663(2006), that the Secretary-General expedite the necessary preparatory planning for the transition of the African Union Mission in the Sudan to a United Nations operation; in this regard, calls for a United Nations assessment mission to visit Darfur by 30 April 2006; and calls upon international and regional organizations and Member States to provide every possible additional assistance to a United Nations operation.

Security Council consideration (April). Briefing the Council on 18 April [meeting 5413], the AU Special Envoy to the Inter-Sudanese Peace Talks on Darfur and Chief Mediator said that, although the parties at the Abuja talks had not yet compromised on key issues, a peace agreement was within reach by the 30 April deadline set by the AU. Proposals covering power-sharing, wealth-sharing and security arrangements and the Darfur-Darfur dialogue and consultations, as well as implementation mechanisms were to be presented to the parties before that date. The Government had shown some flexibility on power-sharing and there was hope that differences could be mended. Outstanding issues still remained on wealth-sharing, including the formula for transfers from the national Government to the states and compensation for victims of the conflict. However, security was the most contentious issue. Progress, although slow, was being made in some aspects of the security arrangement negotiations. Efforts by the mediation and the international community to provide assurances and guarantees to the Darfur movements had yet to yield the desired results in the form of a speedy progress towards an agreement. As the security arrangement negotiations progressed, attention was being drawn to the challenges of implementing a future agreement, and the responsibilities it would impose on AMIS. The Special Envoy pleaded with the Council to extend maximum support to AMIS to ensure that the enhanced ceasefire agreement, once signed, was followed up by the empowering of AMIS to cope with its responsibilities. The Council should not wait for the transition from AMIS to the UN force before strengthening the implementation mechanisms of any agreement reached in Abuja.

SECURITY COUNCIL ACTION

On 25 April [meeting 5422], following consultations among Security Council members, the President made statement **S/PRST/2006/17** on behalf of the Council:

> The Security Council reaffirms its commitment to the sovereignty, unity, independence and territorial integrity of the Sudan.
>
> The Council strongly commends and supports the efforts of the African Union to achieve lasting peace in Darfur. It reiterates in the strongest terms the need for all parties to the conflict in Darfur to put an immediate end to the violence and atrocities, reaffirms its concern that the persisting violence in Darfur might further negatively affect the rest of the country as well as the region, including the security of Chad, and expresses its utmost concern over the dire consequences of the prolonged conflict in Darfur for the civilian population. It further reaffirms the right of the displaced persons to return to their homes if they wish to do so.

The Council reiterates its full support for the African Union-led Inter-Sudanese Peace Talks on the Conflict in Darfur in Abuja, in particular the tireless efforts of the Chief Mediator, Mr. Salim A. Salim and his team. It welcomes the developments so far in the negotiations and urges the parties to make speedy progress in concluding a Darfur peace accord.

The Council further reiterates its endorsement of the decision of 10 March 2006 of the Peace and Security Council of the African Union that an accord must be reached by 30 April 2006 and strongly urges that all parties make the necessary efforts to reach an accord by this date.

The Council recognizes that an inclusive political settlement is key to peace in the Sudan, and that the Talks provide a mechanism to achieve such a settlement in Darfur. The Council reiterates its call to all parties to the conflict to fulfil their commitments to conclude a peace accord in the interest of the people of Darfur and the Sudan as a whole.

The Council calls upon and expects the parties in Abuja to consider in good faith proposals to be made by the Chief Mediator with a view to reaching peace, security and stability in Darfur and the Sudan as a whole. It emphasizes that working towards a positive outcome is a collective responsibility of all the parties to the conflict.

The Council commends the various partners and stakeholders for their support to the African Union-led Abuja peace process and encourages them, in particular the United Nations, to continue supporting the parties in the implementation of the peace accord.

EU statement. In a 27 April letter to the Security Council President [S/2006/292], the EU Presidency noted with concern that the Sudan had not authorized representatives of the international community, most recently the United Nations Emergency Relief Coordinator, Jan Egeland, to visit Darfur. The EU recalled that the humanitarian situation in Darfur required sustained action by the international community, and it was committed to providing adequate support and funding. Humanitarian actors should be given free access by all those concerned. The Sudanese Government, the EU stated, had a clear obligation to work with the United Nations and NGOs.

The statement followed a 2 April incident in which Sudan had refused permission for Mr. Egeland's plane to land in the country.

Darfur Peace Agreement and follow-up

The Inter-Sudanese Peace Talks, between representatives of the Government of National Unity, SLM/A factions and the Justice and Equality Movement concluded on 5 May with the finalization of the Darfur Peace Agreement. The 85-page document, prepared by the AU mediation team, led by Salim A. Salim, the AU Special Envoy to the talks and Chief Mediator, covered power-sharing, wealth-sharing, security arrangements and a Darfur-Darfur dialogue and consultation. It was signed by the Government and the Minawi faction of SLM/A.

In the area of power-sharing, the parties agreed on a federal system of government, with the establishment of a Transitional Darfur Regional Authority, which would have jurisdiction over the three Darfur States. They also agreed to hold a referendum no later than July 2010, to determine the future status of Darfur, namely whether to establish a region of Darfur or retain the three States. The northern boundaries of Darfur would return to their position as at 1 January 1956, with an ad hoc technical team to carry out the demarcation process. The Agreement also outlined posts at various levels of government to be allocated to nominees of the movements. In that regard, the parties agreed on the creation of the posts of Senior Assistant to the President, the fourth-ranking member in the Presidency, and Chairperson of the Transitional Darfur Regional Authority, to be nominated from the movements. The Agreement allocated to the movements 12 of the 360 seats in the National Assembly, 21 of the 73 seats in the legislatures of the three Darfur states, as well as the post of Governor in one of the Darfur states and two posts of Deputy Governor in the other two Darfur states. The Agreement also called for measures to address the representation of Darfurians in the national civil service, armed forces and the police.

With regard to wealth-sharing, the Fiscal and Financial Allocation and Monitoring Commission established by the Agreement would decide on a formula for transferring funding from Khartoum to the Darfur states. A Darfur Reconstruction and Development Fund would be established, to which the Government would allocate $300 million in 2006, and not less than $200 million for both 2007 and 2008, and provide an initial $30 million to a compensation fund to address claims of people affected by the conflict.

The Agreement also provided for a Joint Assessment Mission to identify the needs of post-conflict economic recovery, development and poverty eradication in preparation for a donors' conference, to be convened within three months of the signing of the Agreement; the establishment of three State Land Commissions to address issues related to land-use management and natural resource development, and a Darfur Rehabilitation and Resettlement Commission to address the needs of displaced and war-affected persons, including the return to their homes and the provision of basic services.

Concerning security arrangements, the parties agreed to strengthen the existing ceasefire monitoring and verification mechanisms. The Agreement detailed measures for increasing security for internally displaced persons and humanitarian supply routes, including the establishment of demilitarized zones around displaced persons camps, and buffer zones to separate forces on the ground. The Government would submit and implement a plan for the neutralization and disarmament of the Janjaweed and armed militias, while the movements would receive non-military support in assembly areas. With regard to demobilization, disarmament and reintegration, some of the movements' military personnel would be integrated into Sudanese security organs, while others would be provided with social and economic support to assist their return to civilian life. The Agreement established the Darfur Security Arrangements Implementation Commission to coordinate implementation of all security provisions.

The parties also agreed to convene a Darfur-Darfur Dialogue and Consultation, under AU leadership, and in cooperation with international partners, to promote reconciliation and broader ownership of the Darfur peace process. A preparatory committee, representing the Government, movements, civil society organizations, tribal leaders, the United Nations, the EU and the League of Arab States, and to be chaired by the AU, would prepare the agenda of the Darfur-Darfur Dialogue and Consultation, identify the some 800 to 1,000 participants, and determine the venue and funding modalities.

Report of Secretary-General (May). In his May report [S/2006/306], the Secretary-General said that the signing of the Darfur Peace Agreement by the Sudan and the Minawi faction of the SLM/A, paved the way for the restoration of peace, the return of displaced persons and economic recovery and reconstruction. Other rebel leaders, however, had not signed the Agreement and the international community had to convince them to choose peace over conflict for the sake of their people. The Secretary-General noted that, even during the final rounds of talks, all parties continued to engage in violence and attacks against civilians.

On 31 March, the Secretary-General met with the AU Commission Chairman, Alpha Oumar Konaré, to discuss the future of the AU peacekeeping operation, as well as options for a UN peace support operation. A UN delegation travelled to Addis Ababa and consulted with the AU Commission from 12 to 14 April on joint planning for the transition to a UN peace operation. The delegation then travelled to Khartoum where, on 15 April, it met with President Al-Bashir to discuss Sudan's concerns about the transition.

The security situation was marked by armed clashes between the warring parties, acts of banditry, continued infighting between SLA factions and further destabilization along the Chad/Sudan border. In Northern Darfur, clashes between SAF and SLA in Haskanita, Al Lait and Al Tawisa resulted in casualties among combatants and civilians. On 8 April, SAF launched attacks against villages in the Jebel Wana area, in which three SLA soldiers were reportedly killed. Late in March, SAF and armed tribesmen attacked the SLA-controlled village of Debbis. On 7 April, SLA ambushed a large SAF convoy in Jebel Wana, killing about 40 Government soldiers. Government forces then attacked several villages in the area. Meanwhile, tensions between the SLA Minni Minawi faction and the Adbul Wahid faction remained high. The factions clashed on 3 April in Khazan Jedid area, and on 19 April, in the Tawilla area. Other intra-SLA clashes in mid-March and early April led to thousands of people becoming displaced. Instability in Chad complicated the security situation in the border region, with armed groups operating on both sides of the border. New armed groups continued to be formed in Darfur as local populations sought ways to defend themselves against attack, often recruiting people younger than 18 years old.

Displaced persons continued to arrive from villages under attack or caught in the crossfire, swelling the populations in the camps, where harassment by armed elements, criminality and shooting incidents were on the rise. Meanwhile, the ability of the UN and other relief organizations to move freely and assist the populations had been reduced by growing insecurity and funding shortages. Administrative measures taken by the Government further limited humanitarian access. High-ranking State officials and leaders of armed groups were not being held accountable for violence and crimes against civilians. UNMIS continued to report cases of young women and girls being raped or brutalized, but the police had rarely taken action to investigate, arrest or prosecute the perpetrators. In addition, local officials continued to limit UNMIS access to detention facilities.

The Secretary-General noted the dramatic and ongoing deterioration in human rights, security and humanitarian conditions, as reported by the United Nations High Commissioner for Human Rights. Both the High Commissioner and the Under-Secretary-General for Humanitarian Affairs had called attention to the urgent need for the Government to ease travel restrictions and create a safer environment for human rights and humanitarian activities. The Under-Secretary-General was successful in negotiating the reinstatement of the Norwegian Refugee Council, after it was expelled without explanation by the Government of Southern Sudan. The Secretary-General said that every effort had to be made to ensure that the people of Darfur were protected and assisted. The immediate priorities for the international community were the strengthening of AMIS and addressing the continuing humanitarian crisis.

Security Council ministerial meeting (May). Meeting at ministerial level on 9 May [meeting 5434], the Security Council was briefed by the Secretary-General, on the latest developments in the Darfur peace process.

The Secretary-General, welcoming the signing of the Darfur Peace Agreement by the Government and the SLM/A Minawi faction, said that everything should be done to convince the other significant rebel leaders to choose peace over conflict, ensure that those that had signed implemented it and that the people of Darfur could survive the next few months. The United Nation's aim was to agree with the AU on the additional resources AMIS would require to implement key provisions of the Darfur Peace Agreement and then hold a pledging conference in early June. In the meantime, he appealed to all to help AMIS. No less urgent was the need to raise money for emergency relief to deal the worst humanitarian crisis facing the world. The challenge of helping to protect the people of Darfur and implementing the Darfur Peace Agreement would be one of the biggest tests the United Nations had ever faced. It was clear that the follow-on UN force would have to be bigger than AMIS but would need major logistical support from Member States. The Secretary-General said that he had written to President Al-Bashir to seek his support for the assessment mission to Darfur to identify what was needed to implement the Agreement. He appealed to all parties to show respect for the ceasefire in Darfur and prove by their actions their determination to honour the Agreement.

Sudan's representative told the Council that settling the Darfur crisis was a strategic objective of the Government. Anyone who had followed the Abuja peace process would have realized the Sudan's eagerness to achieve a political settlement. The Government had tried to facilitate delivery of humanitarian assistance and improve the security situation for the return of refugees and internally displaced persons. The Sudan was committed to implementing the Agreement in every detail and had begun doing so. The country looked to the Security Council to send a strong message to those who had not signed it to demonstrate a sense of responsibility by doing so, bearing in mind the suffering of the civilians. The historic agreement would thrive only through the support of the international community, which could help revive the tradition of co-existence among the people of Darfur. Hopefully, the same resolve and cooperation would be shown during the challenging task of reconstruction.

The representative welcomed the announcement by the Netherlands that it would host a pledging conference in September.

SECURITY COUNCIL ACTION

On 9 May [meeting 5434], following consultations among Security Council members, the President made statement **S/PRST/2006/21** on behalf of the Council:

> The Security Council strongly welcomes the agreement of 5 May 2006 reached at the Inter-Sudanese Peace Talks in Abuja as a basis for lasting peace in Darfur; commends the signatories to the agreement; expresses its appreciation of the efforts of President Denis Sassou Nguesso of the Republic of the Congo, President Olusegun Obasanjo of the Federal Republic of Nigeria, in his capacity as host of the Talks, and the Special Envoy of the African Union and Chief Mediator Mr. Salim A. Salim; calls upon all the parties to respect their commitments and implement the agreement without delay; urges those movements that have not signed the agreement to do so without delay, noting the benefits it will bring them and the people of Darfur, and not to act in any way that would impede implementation of the agreement; and welcomes the forthcoming meeting of the Peace and Security Council of the African Union on 15 May 2006.
>
> The Security Council commends the African Union for what the African Union Mission in the Sudan has achieved in Darfur despite difficult circumstances; stresses the need for the Mission to be urgently further strengthened in line with the conclusions of the report of the joint assessment mission of 10 to 20 December 2005 so that it is able to support implementation of the Darfur Peace Agreement until a United Nations operation is deployed; calls, in this regard, for the Secretary-General and the African Union to convene a pledging conference without delay; and urges Member States and international and regional organizations to provide every possible assistance to the Mission.
>
> The Council stresses that the Secretary-General should consult jointly with the African Union, in close and continuing consultation with the Council, and in cooperation and close consultation with the parties to the Abuja Peace Talks, including the Government of National Unity, on decisions concerning the transition to a United Nations operation; looks forward to receiving from the Secretary-General at the earliest opportunity detailed planning proposals for a United Nations operation in Darfur; calls, in this regard, for the Government of National Unity to facilitate immediately the visit of a joint United Nations and African Union technical assessment mission to Darfur; encourages the Secretary-General to consult urgently with potential troop-contributing countries on the assets required for a United Nations operation; stresses that a United Nations operation should have strong African participation and character; and calls upon international and regional organizations and Member States to provide the United Nations operation with every possible assistance.
>
> The Council expresses its deep concern over the deteriorating humanitarian situation in Darfur; welcomes the visit of the United Nations Emergency Relief Coordinator, Mr. Jan Egeland; expresses its deep concern at the shortfall in

humanitarian funding; urges Member States to make additional funds available; and calls upon all the Sudanese parties to respect the neutrality, impartiality and independence of humanitarian assistance.

EU statement (May). On 5 May [S/2006/293], in a letter to the Council President, the EU Presidency expressed its commitment to supporting the implementation of the Darfur Peace Agreement, and expressed concern at the ongoing fighting in Darfur and the continued failure of the Sudan to allow the visit of the UN planning team dealing with the transition from AMIS to a UN operation.

AU communiqué. The AU Peace and Security Council, at its fifty-first meeting (Addis Ababa, 15 May) [S/2006/307], endorsed the Darfur Peace Agreement, and decided that it would enter into force on 16 May. It regretted the failure of the SLM/A Abdhul Wahid faction and JEM, led by Khalil Ibrahim, to sign the Agreement. It urged them to do so by 31 May, failing which it would consider measures, including sanctions, to be applied against their leadership. The Peace and Security Council demanded that all Darfur groups immediately commit themselves to be bound by the Agreement, in particular those relating to the Comprehensive Ceasefire. It decided that steps should be taken to effect the transition from AMIS to a UN peacekeeping operation, and urged the UN Security Council and the Government of National Unity to consult towards that end, and ensure the commencement of the UN operation in Darfur at the earliest possible time.

SECURITY COUNCIL ACTION

On 16 May [meeting 5439], the Security Council unanimously adopted **resolution 1679(2006)**. The draft [S/2006/296] was submitted by Argentina, the Congo, Denmark, France, Ghana, Greece, Peru, Slovakia, the United Kingdom, the United Republic of Tanzania and the United States.

The Security Council,

Recalling its previous resolutions concerning the situation in the Sudan, in particular resolutions 1556(2004) of 30 July 2004, 1564(2004) of 18 September 2004, 1574(2004) of 19 November 2004, 1590(2005) of 24 March 2005, 1591(2005) of 29 March 2005, 1593(2005) of 31 March 2005, 1663(2006) of 24 March 2006 and 1665(2006) of 29 March 2006, and the statements by its President concerning the Sudan, in particular the statements of 3 February and 9 May 2006,

Recalling also its resolution 1612(2005) of 26 July 2005 on children and armed conflict, resolution 1325(2000) of 31 October 2000 on women and peace and security, resolution 1674(2006) of 28 April 2006 on the protection of civilians in armed conflict and resolution 1502(2003) of 26 August 2003 on the protection of humanitarian and United Nations personnel,

Reaffirming its strong commitment to the sovereignty, unity, independence and territorial integrity of the Sudan, which would be unaffected by transition to a United Nations operation, as well as of all States in the region, and to the cause of peace, security and reconciliation throughout the Sudan,

Expressing its utmost concern over the dire consequences of the prolonged conflict in Darfur for the civilian population, and reiterating in the strongest terms the need for all parties to the conflict in Darfur to put an immediate end to violence and atrocities,

Welcoming the success of the African Union-led Inter-Sudanese Peace Talks on the Conflict in Darfur in Abuja, in particular the framework agreed between the parties for a resolution of the conflict in Darfur (the Darfur Peace Agreement),

Commending the efforts of President Olusegun Obasanjo of the Federal Republic of Nigeria, host of the Talks; President Denis Sassou Nguesso of the Republic of the Congo, Chair of the African Union; Mr. Salim A. Salim, Special Envoy of the African Union for the Talks and Chief Mediator; the respective delegations to the Talks; and the signatories to the Darfur Peace Agreement,

Stressing the importance of full and rapid implementation of the Darfur Peace Agreement to restore a sustainable peace in Darfur, and welcoming the statement, made on 9 May 2006 by the representative of the Sudan at the special meeting of the Security Council on Darfur, of the Government of National Unity's full commitment to implementing the Darfur Peace Agreement,

Reaffirming its concern that the persisting violence in Darfur might further negatively affect the rest of the Sudan, as well as the region, including the security of Chad,

Noting with deep concern the recent deterioration of relations between the Sudan and Chad, and urging the Governments of both countries to abide by their obligations under the Tripoli Agreement of 8 February 2006 and to implement the confidence-building measures which have been voluntarily agreed upon,

Commending the efforts of the African Union for successful deployment of the African Union Mission in the Sudan, despite exceptionally difficult circumstances, and the role of the Mission in reducing large-scale organized violence in Darfur, and commending further the efforts of Member States and regional and international organizations that have assisted the Mission in its deployment,

Taking note of the communiqués of 12 January, 10 March and 15 May 2006 of the Peace and Security Council of the African Union regarding transition of the African Union Mission in the Sudan to a United Nations operation,

Stressing that a United Nations operation would have, to the extent possible, strong African participation and character,

Welcoming the efforts of Member States and regional and international organizations to maintain and strengthen their support to the Mission and potentially to a follow-on United Nations operation in Darfur, looking forward in particular to the convening of a pledging conference in June 2006, and appealing to African Union partners to provide the necessary support to the Mission to allow it to continue to perform its mandate during the transition,

Determining that the situation in the Sudan continues to constitute a threat to international peace and security,

Acting under Chapter VII of the Charter of the United Nations,

1. *Calls upon* the parties to the Darfur Peace Agreement to respect their commitments and implement the Agreement without delay, urges those parties that have not signed the Agreement to do so without delay and not to act in any way that would impede implementation of the Agreement, and expresses its intention to consider taking, including in response to a request by the African Union, strong and effective measures, such as a travel ban and an assets freeze, against any individual or group that violates or attempts to block the implementation of the Agreement;

2. *Calls upon* the African Union to agree with the United Nations, regional and international organizations and Member States on requirements now necessary, in addition to those identified by the joint assessment mission of 10 to 20 December 2005, to strengthen the capacity of the African Union Mission in the Sudan to enforce the security arrangements of the Darfur Peace Agreement, with a view to a follow-on United Nations operation in Darfur;

3. *Endorses* the decision of the Peace and Security Council of the African Union in its communiqué of 15 May 2006 that, in view of the signing of the Darfur Peace Agreement, concrete steps should be taken to effect the transition from the African Union Mission in the Sudan to a United Nations operation, calls upon the parties to the Agreement to facilitate and work with the African Union, the United Nations, regional and international organizations and Member States to accelerate transition to a United Nations operation, and, to this end, reiterating the requests of the Secretary-General and the Security Council, calls for the deployment of a joint African Union and United Nations technical assessment mission within one week of the adoption of the present resolution;

4. *Stresses* that the Secretary-General should consult jointly with the African Union, in close and continuing consultation with the Council, and in cooperation and close consultation with the parties to the Darfur Peace Agreement, including the Government of National Unity, on decisions concerning the transition to a United Nations operation;

5. *Requests* the Secretary-General to submit recommendations to the Council within one week of the return of the joint African Union and United Nations technical assessment mission on all relevant aspects of the mandate of the United Nations operation in Darfur, including force structure, additional force requirements, potential troop-contributing countries and a detailed financial evaluation of future costs;

6. *Decides* to remain actively seized of the matter.

Speaking after the vote, China said that it had reservations concerning the resolution's invocation of Chapter VII of the Charter, which dealt with action with respect to threats to peace, breaches of the peace, and acts of aggression. The resolution's contents were clearly inconsistent with that wording. On the basis of its political support for the AU in establishing conditions for the speedy implementation of the resolution, China had not pressed its objection, which should not be considered as constituting a precedent. Also, if the United Nations were to deploy a peacekeeping operation in Darfur, the agreement and cooperation of the Government should be obtained. That was a basic principle for deploying all peacekeeping operations. Qatar said that the resolution did not imply that the Security Council was prepared to carry out the transfer of responsibilities from AU forces to a UN force prior to the Sudanese Government's approval.

Further developments

On 17 May [S/2006/302], Sudanese Vice-President Ali Osman Mohamed Taha informed the Security Council of measures the Sudan had taken to improve the situation in Darfur. Those measures included the allocation of 20,000 tons of food to WFP; a call to all Governments, state governments and humanitarian partners to implement an emergency limited-term relief plan; the Government's commitment to provide all available facilities for humanitarian organizations working in Darfur; a direction to the Ministry of Humanitarian Affairs to coordinate its efforts with national and international humanitarian partners to execute the humanitarian emergency action plan; a directive to the Finance Ministry and state governments to begin the execution of an emergency relief plan in preparation for the return of refugees; and the Government's commitment to upholding the ceasefire.

Briefing by Emergency Relief Coordinator (May). Briefing the Security Council on 19 May [meeting 5441] on the situation in Chad and the Sudan, the Under-Secretary-General for Humanitarian Affairs and Emergency Relief Coordinator called for immediate steps to strengthen AMIS, speed up the transition to a UN operation and ensure that the humanitarian lifeline to more than 3 million people was secure and funded. The Under-Secretary-General, who visited the Sudan and eastern Chad between 6 and 11 May, said that attacks on civilians and humanitarian workers were continuing despite the Darfur Peace Agreement. Drawing attention to the $389 million shortfall for Darfur and the $983 total shortfall under the 2006 workplan, he appealed to those donors that had contributed much less than they had done the previous year and to donors in the Gulf region for assistance.

Report of Secretary-General (June). In June [S/2006/430], the Secretary-General reported that, following the failure of Abdul Wahid (SLA/M) and Khalil Ibrahim (JEM) to sign the Darfur Peace Agreement by the 31 May deadline fixed by the AU Peace and Security Council, on 8 June, some senior leaders of the two movements presented to the AU a signed declaration of commitment to the Agreement on behalf of their followers. Despite the signing of the Agreement, fighting continued in several areas. Demonstrations were organized against the Agreement, some of which turned violent. There were several attacks on humanitarian aid workers, while militia groups continued to attack civilian targets and AMIS.

Incidents in Southern Darfur included an attack by SLA against a Government police camp at Abgragel, in which a dozen police officers were killed; an attack against the village of Karbaba by SAF, in which at least seven people were killed; a raid by the Janjaweed militia against the villages of Natiga and Baju Baju, in which 35 civilians were killed; and an attack by armed tribesmen against SLA-controlled villages. In Western Darfur, armed militias attacked SLA at Jebel Muktarin on 5 May; five days later, armed tribesmen, allegedly supported by SAF, attacked the Abdul Wahid SLA-controlled village of Shau Fugo. Tension between Chad and the Sudan heightened insecurity in Western Darfur and contributed to the displacement of the population along the border. There was a reported increase in the presence of Chadian rebels on Sudanese territory, and reports of continued recruitment of civilians by Chadian rebels in internally displaced persons camps in Western Darfur. On 21 May, some 150 armed tribesmen attacked and looted a camp near Gereida. Several protests were organized by communities of internally displaced persons affiliated with groups that did not sign the Peace Agreement, some of which turned violent. Sentiments against the Agreement in the camps led to attacks against AMIS personnel and assets.

The Secretary-General observed that, while the signing of the Darfur Peace Agreement was a significant achievement, the parties, with the assistance of the international community, had to act quickly to begin the implementation process. Disarming the Janjaweed, improving civilian protection and strengthening ceasefire monitoring and verification were absolute priorities. He noted that the AU ceasefire Commission was inaugurated on 13 June, and the Joint Commission would be inaugurated on 23 June. He urged that consultations to ensure the transition to a UN operation take place at the earliest opportunity. In that regard, his Special Envoy to Darfur, Lakhdar Brahimi and the Assistant Secretary-General for Peacekeeping Operations, Hédi Annabi, travelled to Khartoum to consult with the Government and secured agreement for the fielding of the technical assessment mission authorized by the Security Council. The mission, led by the Under-Secretary-General for Peacekeeping Operations, held consultations on 8 June with the AU.

Security Council mission to Chad and the Sudan. The Security Council mission to Chad and the Sudan (4-10 June) [S/2006/433] concluded that the Darfur Peace Agreement could provide a basis for sustained security in Darfur, but efforts would have to continue to get further support from the non-signatories, in particular Abdul Wahid. Those who had signed the Agreement should take immediate steps to implement it, particularly the Government of the Sudan, which should disarm the Janjaweed. The mission called for improved public diplomacy by the United Nations, the AU and the Governments of Chad and the Sudan in explaining the Agreement's benefits to the population of Darfur. The United Nations should work, with the Government of the Sudan's agreement, on deploying a UN force in Darfur, which would take over a strengthened AMIS mandate. There would be a seven-stage process towards full UN operational capacity in Darfur by January 2007. In the meantime, AMIS would need immediate strengthening and reinforcing. The mission called upon the international community to provide AMIS with every possible assistance. Urgent action was also needed by the Government of the Sudan and other Sudanese parties to tackle the serious problem of gender violence.

AU communiqué. In a 27 June communiqué [S/2006/461], adopted at its ministerial-level meeting on the situation in Darfur, the AU Peace and Security Council urged the signatories of the Darfur Peace Agreement to honour their commitments; took note of the steps taken by the AU Commission Chairperson towards its implementation, including the establishment of an implementation team within AMIS; and decided to impose targeted measures, including a travel ban and asset freeze, against all persons or groups undermining the Agreement. It reaffirmed its decision to end AMIS mandate on 30 September and to transition to a UN operation. In the meantime, it approved additional tasks and a new mandate for AMIS, including the protection of civilians.

Communication. On 5 July [S/2006/490], the Sudanese Minister for Foreign Affairs, Lam Akol Ajawin, informed the Security Council that the National Redemption Front (NRF), an alliance of groups that had refused to sign the Darfur Peace Agreement, attacked the town of Hamrat al-Sheikh in Sudan's North Kordofan State on 3 July, in an attempt to impede the implementation of the Agreement. Sudan called on the Council to shoulder its responsibilities to protect the Agreement and take decisive and comprehensive measures against that group, as a deterrent to anyone planning to destroy the Agreement.

Authorization of UN operation in Darfur

The Secretary-General, in his July report [S/2006/591], said that the formation of new alliances among various factions was severely complicating an already complex security situation on the ground. The NRF attack on Government positions in Northern Kordofan on 3 July (see above) had widened the conflict beyond Darfur's eastern border. The Minni Minawi SLM/A faction, supported by SAF, carried out major military operations against non-signatories of the Agreement and villages in areas under their control, resulting in further massive displacements and suffering. There was a growing perception among non-signatories that AMIS was not in a position to implement the Agreement. Some members of the G19, a rebel group that did not support the Agreement, believed that AMIS was not resisting the military operations of the SAF and the SLM/A Minni Minawi faction and threatened to attack AMIS.

The UN/AU technical assessment mission visited the Sudan from 9 to 23 June, during which it consulted with President Al-Bashir and Government officials in Khartoum and with a wide range of stakeholders. It also travelled to Chad to meet with President Idriss Déby. The mission found that the Sudanese people held polarized views about AMIS performance and the necessity of a UN operation. Government officials supported the strengthening of AMIS, but questioned the need for a transition from an AU to a UN operation. On the other hand, representatives of internally displaced persons camps, civil society groups and some political parties voiced serious misgivings about the effectiveness of the protection provided by AMIS and demanded the earliest transition to a UN mission. The mission's findings were presented to President Al-Bashir on 22 June, who reiterated that he and his Government did not accept the transition from AMIS to a UN operation.

On the basis of the mission's report, and in response to Council resolution 1679(2006) (see p. 277), the Secretary-General recommended, subject to the Government of the Sudan's consent, an expansion of the unified UN mission in the Sudan into Darfur as from 1 Janaury 2007. The mission would have as its priority the protection of civilians and would work closely with the Government of National Unity and other key actors towards that end. It would promote and support the parties in implementing the Darfur Peace Agreement. Its main tasks would be in the areas of providing support for the peace process and good offices; the rule of law, governance and human rights; humanitarian assistance, recovery and reintegration; and security and physical protection.

Regarding the size of the force, the assessment mission concluded that the magnitude of the protection task and the need to ensure compliance with the Peace Agreement would require a large, agile and robust military force. The Secretary-General therefore recommended three options: a force of some 17,300 troops, consisting of 14 infantry battalions, three fixed-wing reconnaissance aircraft, up to eight reconnaissance and 18 military utility helicopters; a force of 18,000 troops, four reconnaissance and nine utility helicopters, but with two additional battalions to compensate for the lower respond capacity; or a force of 15,000, with 11 battalions, six additional helicopters and three additional rapid reaction companies.

The Secretary-General urged the Security Council to fully support his proposals. However, securing the Sudanese Government's consent for the UN operation would require continuing intensive discussions by Council members, regional organizations and the United Nations with Khartoum. He reiterated that the Organization had no hidden agenda beyond the urgent need to help the population and prevent the crisis for spreading further, and appealed to the Sudanese authorities to ensure that the United Nations was not misrepresented to suit political ends.

An addendum to the report [S/2006/591/Add.1] estimated the financial implications of a four-month support to AMIS at some $21.2 million, or $53.7 million for more resource-intensive support. The financial implications of expanding UNMIS into Darfur for a 12-month period, based on the three options set out in the report, were estimated at some $1.6 billion, $1.7 billion and $1.4 billion, respectively.

Statement of Secretary-General. On 10 August [S/2006/645], the Secretary-General called on the Security Council to give urgent consideration to the situation in Darfur, following the recent upsurge in violence, mostly in Northern Darfur and areas near the Chad border. The violence emanated principally from fighting between Darfur Peace Agreement signatories and non-signatory groups, between Government forces and rebels in the Jebel Moon area in Western Darfur, and in Southern Darfur. As a result of the fighting and direct targeting of humanitarian workers, only 50 per cent of the civilians affected by the conflict could be reached by humanitarian organizations. The rest, some 1.6 million people, were either inaccessible or could be reached only by putting the lives of aid workers directly at risk.

In the meantime, some progress was made in implementation of the Darfur Peace Agreement. The Government submitted its plan for disarming the Janjaweed to AMIS on 23 June. In respect of power-sharing, the Northern and Southern Darfur assemblies convened emergency sessions to amend their interim state constitutions to allow for increased numbers of ministers and assembly members. Minni Minawi, the head of the only movement signatory to the Peace Agreement, was appointed senior assistant to the President in the Government of National Unity, and representatives of his SLM/A faction met with Government officials in Khartoum to establish joint committees to address implementation of the Agreement. With regard to wealth-sharing, the joint assessment mission called for in the Agreement had been initiated.

Nevertheless, implementation of the Darfur Peace Agreement was behind schedule and faced difficulties. Basic aspects of mechanisms for implementing the ceasefire were yet to be clarified. While the plan for disarming the Janjaweed had been submitted, the Government had not restricted their activity to designated areas by 20 July as required by the Peace Agreement. In relation to power-sharing, the 15 June deadline for the finalization of all senior state and national Government and civil service appointments, the establishment of the Transitional Darfur Regional Authority, the Darfur Reconstruction and Development Fund and the Darfur Rehabilitation and Resettlement Commission, had passed, as well as the 15 July deadline for the establishment of a Compensation Commission.

In that difficult environment, AMIS continued to face enormous challenges, including uncertainty with regard to its funding. Despite a relatively positive result from the 18 July Brussels pledging conference, sufficient funding was not in place to support the Mission for the remainder of its mandate, which was to expire on 30 September.

As to the transition to a UN operation on 1 January 2007, and the Government of the Sudan's opposition to that proposal, the United Nations held intensive consultations to address the Government's concerns, but was unable to achieve a mutually agreeable solution. Moreover, the Sudan's plan for restoring stability and protecting civilians in Darfur (see below) did not indicate a willingness on its part to agree to a transition to a UN operation in Darfur. While the Government maintained its firm opposition to a UN operation, the situation on the ground was deteriorating, and the AU mission's ability to function for the remainder of 2006 was jeopardized by a funding crisis.

Sudan national plan for stability and protection. On 8 August [S/2006/665], the Secretary-General received the Sudanese Government's plan for the restoration of stability and protection of civilians in Darfur, which he transmitted to the Security Council on 17 August. The six-month plan, based on the Darfur Peace Agreement, covered control over the security situation, the attainment of stability, the protection of civilians, the strengthening of mechanisms for enforcing the rule of law, as well as a number of quick-impact economic programmes. While appreciating the role played by the African forces in Darfur, President Al-Bashir emphasized that restoring stability and protecting civilians were central to the responsibilities of the Government of the Sudan.

The elements of the plan were: strengthening cooperation between the Government and UNMIS; gaining control over the security situation and achieving stability; improving the humanitarian situation and preparing an environment to permit the voluntary return of internally displaced persons and refugees; carrying out emergency reconstruction programmes; improving the legal and human rights situations; and addressing political concerns, including through a Darfur-Darfur dialogue conference.

Communications. In a 21 August letter to the Security Council President [S/2006/683], President Al-Bashir listed the steps being taken to implement the Darfur Peace Agreement. He indicated that SLM Chairman Minni Minawi, appointed first senior assistant to the President, was overseeing the formation of a transitional authority in Darfur. Other parties that had signed the Addis Ababa Agreement had begun to work on its implementation. Work had also begun on opening up corridors for sending humanitarian assistance to displaced persons and those in need, and a plan initiated for disarming the militias and incorporating the forces of the liberation movements into SAF. A six-month plan (see above) for returning the security and humanitarian situations to normal had been submitted to the Secretary-General and the Security Council.

Transferring AMIS mandate to UN forces did not find acceptance among large sectors of the Sudanese people. All legislative, parliamentary and executive institutions at every level, including the Government of National Unity, had adopted unanimous resolutions rejecting the transfer. The movements that rejected the Peace Agreement would see the entry of UN forces as an infringement or negation of the Agreement, and would be emboldened to frustrate implementation of the pact. The militias would be suspicious of UN forces and oppose the Government's plan to disarm them. The transfer would create a very disorderly situation, leading to acts of violence and unmanageable confrontations. The Council should therefore be patient and not be in a hurry to adopt a new resolution. It should allow the Government sufficient time to resolve the situation in Darfur, concentrate on implementing the Peace Agreement under the six-month plan and provide support to UNMIS.

On 23 August [S/2006/685], responding to the Secretary-General's request that the Sudan send a high-level representative to the forthcoming Security Council meeting on Darfur, President Al-Bashir said that, while the planned meeting coincided with his appeal for dialogue between the Council and the Sudan, it should be postponed in order to provide more time to prepare for it, and allow for the participation of important regional organizations concerned about the situation in Darfur.

SECURITY COUNCIL ACTION

On 31 August [meeting 5519], the Security Council adopted **resolution 1706(2006)** by vote (12-0-3). The draft [S/2006/699] was submitted by Argentina, Denmark, France, Ghana, Greece, Slovakia, the United Kingdom, the United Republic of Tanzania and the United States.

The Security Council,

Recalling its previous resolutions concerning the situation in the Sudan, in particular resolutions 1556(2004) of 30 July 2004, 1564(2004) of 18 September 2004, 1574(2004) of 19 November 2004, 1590(2005) of 24 March 2005, 1591(2005) of 29 March 2005, 1593(2005) of 31 March 2005, 1663(2006) of 24 March 2006, 1665(2006) of 29 March 2006 and 1679(2006) of 16 May 2006, and the statements by its President concerning the Sudan,

Recalling also its resolution 1325(2000) of 31 October 2000 on women and peace and security, resolution 1502(2003) of 26 August 2003 on the protection of humanitarian and United Nations personnel, resolution 1612(2005) of 26 July 2005 on children and armed conflict, and resolution 1674(2006) of 28 April 2006 on the protection of civilians in armed conflict, which reaffirms, inter alia, the provisions of paragraphs 138 and 139 of the 2005 World Summit Outcome, as well as the report of its mission to the Sudan and Chad from 4 to 10 June 2006,

Reaffirming its strong commitment to the sovereignty, unity, independence and territorial integrity of the Sudan, which would be unaffected by transition to a United Nations operation in Darfur, and to the cause of peace, expressing its determination to work with the Government of National Unity, in full respect of its sovereignty, to assist in tackling the various problems confronting the Sudan and that a United Nations operation in Darfur shall have, to the extent possible, a strong African participation and character,

Welcoming the efforts of the African Union to find a solution to the crisis in Darfur, including through the success of the African Union-led Inter-Sudanese Peace Talks on the Conflict in Darfur in Abuja, in particular the framework agreed between the parties for a resolution of the conflict in Darfur (the Darfur Peace Agreement), commending the efforts of the signatories to the Darfur Peace Agreement, expressing its belief that the Agreement provides a basis for sustained security in Darfur, reiterating its welcome of the statement, made on 9 May 2006 by the representative of the Sudan at the special meeting of the Security Council on Darfur, of the Government of National Unity's full commitment to implementing the Agreement, stressing the importance of launching, with the African Union, the Darfur-Darfur dialogue and consultation as soon as possible, and recognizing that international support for the implementation of the Agreement is critically important to its success,

Commending the efforts of the African Union for the successful deployment of the African Union Mission in the Sudan, as well as the efforts of Member States and regional and international organizations that have assisted it in its deployment, and the role of the African Union Mission in reducing large-scale organized violence in Darfur, recalling the decision of the Peace and Security Council of the African Union of 10 March 2006, and its decision of 27 June 2006, as outlined in paragraph 10 of its communiqué, that the African Union is ready to review the mandate of the Mission in the event that the ongoing consultations between the Government of National Unity and the United Nations conclude on an agreement for a transition to a United Nations peacekeeping operation, stressing the need for the Mission to assist implementation of the Darfur Peace Agreement until transition to the United Nations force in Darfur is completed, welcoming the decision of the Peace and Security Council of 27 June 2006 on strengthening the mandate and tasks of the Mission, including on the protection of civilians, and considering that the Mission needs urgent reinforcing,

Reaffirming its concern that the ongoing violence in Darfur might further negatively affect the rest of the Sudan as well as the region, in particular Chad and the Central African Republic, and stressing that regional security aspects must be addressed to achieve long-lasting peace in Darfur,

Remaining deeply concerned over the recent deterioration of relations between the Sudan and Chad, calling upon the Governments of the two countries to abide by their obligations under the Tripoli Agreement of 8 February 2006 and the agreement between the Sudan and Chad signed at N'Djamena on 26 July 2006 and to begin implementing the confidence-building measures which they have voluntarily agreed upon, welcoming the recent re-establishment of diplomatic relations between the Sudan and Chad, and calling upon all States in the region to cooperate in ensuring regional stability,

Reiterating its strong condemnation of all violations of human rights and international humanitarian law in Darfur, and calling upon the Government of National Unity to take urgent action to tackle gender-based violence in Darfur, including action towards implementing its Action Plan to Combat Violence Against Women in Darfur, with particular focus on the rescission of Form 8 and access to legal redress,

Expressing its deep concern for the security of humanitarian aid workers and their access to populations in need, including refugees, internally displaced persons and other war-affected populations, and calling upon all parties, in particular the Government of National Unity, to ensure, in accordance with relevant provisions of international law, the full, safe and unhindered access of relief personnel to all those in need in Darfur as well as the delivery of humanitarian assistance, in particular to internally displaced persons and refugees,

Taking note of the communiqués of 12 January, 10 March, 15 May and 27 June 2006 of the Peace and Security Council regarding transition of the African Union Mission in the Sudan to a United Nations operation,

Taking note also of the report of the Secretary-General of 28 July 2006 on Darfur,

Determining that the situation in the Sudan continues to constitute a threat to international peace and security,

1. *Decides*, without prejudice to its existing mandate and operations as provided for in resolution 1590(2005) and in order to support the early and effective implementation of the Darfur Peace Agreement, that the mandate of the United Nations Mission in the Sudan shall be expanded as specified in paragraphs 8, 9 and 12 below, that it shall deploy to Darfur, and therefore invites the consent of the Government of National Unity for this deployment, and urges Member States to provide the capability for an expeditious deployment;

2. *Requests* the Secretary-General to arrange the rapid deployment of additional capabilities for the United Nations Mission in the Sudan, in order that it may deploy in Darfur, in accordance with the recommendation contained in his report of 28 July 2006;

3. *Decides* that the United Nations Mission in the Sudan shall be strengthened by up to 17,300 military personnel and by an appropriate civilian component including up to 3,300 civilian police personnel and up to 16 formed police units, and expresses its determination to keep the strength and structure of the Mission under regular review, taking into account the evolution of the situation on the ground and without prejudice to its current operations and mandate as provided for in resolution 1590(2005);

4. *Expresses its intention* to consider authorizing possible additional temporary reinforcements of the military component of the United Nations Mission in the Sudan, at the request of the Secretary-General, within the limits of the troop levels recommended in paragraph 87 of his report of 28 July 2006;

5. *Requests* the Secretary-General to consult jointly with the African Union, in close and continuing consultation with the parties to the Darfur Peace Agreement, including the Government of National Unity, on a plan and timetable for transition from the African Union Mission in the Sudan to a United Nations operation in Darfur; decides that those elements outlined in paragraphs 40 to 58 of the report of the Secretary-General of 28 July 2006 shall begin to be deployed no later than 1 October 2006, that thereafter, as part of the process of transition to a United Nations operation, additional capabilities shall be deployed as soon as feasible and that the United Nations Mission in the Sudan shall take over from the African Union Mission the responsibility for supporting the implementation of the Darfur Peace Agreement upon the expiration of the mandate of the African Union Mission but in any event no later than 31 December 2006;

6. *Notes* that the status-of-forces agreement for the United Nations Mission in the Sudan with the Sudan, as outlined in resolution 1590(2005), shall apply to the operations of the Mission throughout the Sudan, including in Darfur;

7. *Requests* the Secretary-General to take the necessary steps to strengthen the African Union Mission in the Sudan through the use of existing and additional United Nations resources with a view to transition to a United Nations operation in Darfur; and authorizes the Secretary-General during this transition to implement the longer-term support to the African Union Mission outlined in the report of the Secretary-General of 28 July 2006, including provision of air assets, ground mobility package, training, engineering and logistics, mobile communications capacity and broad public information assistance;

8. *Decides* that the mandate of the United Nations Mission in the Sudan in Darfur shall be to support implementation of the Darfur Peace Agreement of 5 May 2006 and the N'Djamena Agreement on Humanitarian Ceasefire on the Conflict in Darfur of 8 April 2004 ("the Agreements"), including by performing the following tasks:

(a) To monitor and verify the implementation by the parties of chapter 3 ("Comprehensive Ceasefire and Final Security Arrangements") of the Darfur Peace Agreement and the N'Djamena Agreement on Humanitarian Ceasefire on the Conflict in Darfur;

(b) To observe and monitor movement of armed groups and redeployment of forces in areas of deployment of the Mission by ground and aerial means in accordance with the Agreements;

(c) To investigate violations of the Agreements and to report violations to the Ceasefire Commission; as well as to cooperate and coordinate, together with other international actors, with the Ceasefire Commission, the Joint Commission and the Joint Humanitarian Facilitation and Monitoring Unit established pursuant to the Agreements, including through provision of technical assistance and logistical support;

(d) To maintain, in particular, a presence in key areas, such as buffer zones established pursuant to the Darfur Peace Agreement, areas inside internally displaced persons camps and demilitarized zones around and inside internally displaced persons camps, in order to promote the re-establishment of confidence, to discourage violence, in particular by deterring use of force;

(e) To monitor transborder activities of armed groups along the Sudanese borders with Chad and the Central African Republic, in particular through regular ground and aerial reconnaissance activities;

(f) To assist with development and implementation of a comprehensive and sustainable programme for disarmament, demobilization and reintegration of former combatants and women and children associated with combatants, as called for in the Darfur Peace Agreement and in accordance with resolutions 1556(2004) and 1564(2004);

(g) To assist the parties, in cooperation with other international actors, in the preparations for and conduct of referendums provided for in the Darfur Peace Agreement;

(h) To assist the parties to the Agreements in promoting understanding of the peace accord and of the role of the Mission, including by means of an effective public information campaign, targeted at all sectors of society, in coordination with the African Union;

(i) To cooperate closely with the Chairperson of the Darfur-Darfur Dialogue and Consultation, provide support and technical assistance to him, and coordinate the activities of other United Nations agencies to this effect, as well as to assist the parties to the Darfur-Darfur Dialogue and Consultation in addressing the need for an all-inclusive approach, including the role of women, towards reconciliation and peacebuilding;

(j) To assist the parties to the Darfur Peace Agreement, in coordination with bilateral and multilateral assistance programmes, in restructuring the police service in the Sudan, consistent with democratic policing, to develop a police training and evaluation programme, and to otherwise assist in the training of civilian police;

(k) To assist the parties to the Darfur Peace Agreement in promoting the rule of law, including an independent judiciary, and the protection of the human rights of all people of the Sudan through a comprehensive and coordinated strategy with the aim of combating impunity and contributing to long-term peace and stability and to assist the parties to the Agreement to develop and consolidate the national legal framework;

(l) To ensure an adequate human rights and gender presence, capacity and expertise within the Mission to carry out human rights promotion, civilian protection and monitoring activities that include particular attention to the needs of women and children;

9. *Decides also* that the mandate of the United Nations Mission in the Sudan in Darfur shall also include the following:

(a) To facilitate and coordinate in close cooperation with relevant United Nations agencies, within its capabilities and in its areas of deployment, the voluntary return of refugees and internally displaced persons, and humanitarian assistance, inter alia, by helping to establish the necessary security conditions in Darfur;

(b) To contribute towards international efforts to protect, promote and monitor human rights in Darfur, as well as to coordinate international efforts towards the protection of civilians with particular attention to vulnerable groups, including internally displaced persons, returning refugees, and women and children;

(c) To assist the parties to the Agreements, in cooperation with other international partners in the mine action sector, by providing humanitarian demining assistance, technical advice, and coordination, as well as mine awareness programmes targeted at all sectors of society;

(d) To assist in addressing regional security issues in close liaison with international efforts to improve the security situation in the neighbouring regions along the borders between the Sudan and Chad and between the Sudan and the Central African Republic, including through the establishment of a multidimensional presence consisting of political, humanitarian, military and civilian police liaison officers in key locations in Chad, including in internally displaced persons and refugee camps, and, if necessary, in the Central African Republic, and to contribute to the implementation of the agreement between the Sudan and Chad signed on 26 July 2006;

10. *Calls upon* all Member States to ensure the free, unhindered and expeditious movement to the Sudan of all personnel, as well as equipment, provisions, supplies and other goods, including vehicles and spare parts, which are for the exclusive and official use of the United Nations Mission in the Sudan in Darfur;

11. *Requests* the Secretary-General to keep the Security Council regularly informed of the progress in implementing the Darfur Peace Agreement, respect for the ceasefire, and the implementation of the mandate of the United Nations Mission in the Sudan in Darfur, and to report to the Council, as appropriate, on the steps taken to implement the present resolution and any failure to comply with its demands;

12. Acting under Chapter VII of the Charter of the United Nations:

(a) *Decides* that the United Nations Mission in the Sudan is authorized to use all necessary means, in the areas of deployment of its forces and as it deems within its capabilities:

—To protect United Nations personnel, facilities, installations and equipment, to ensure the security and freedom of movement of United Nations personnel, humanitarian workers, Assessment and Evaluation Commission personnel, to prevent disruption of the implementation of the Darfur Peace Agreement by armed groups, without prejudice to the responsibility of the Government of the Sudan, and to protect civilians under threat of physical violence;

—In order to support early and effective implementation of the Darfur Peace Agreement, to prevent attacks and threats against civilians;

—To seize or collect, as appropriate, arms or related materiel whose presence in Darfur is in violation of the Agreements and the measures imposed by paragraphs 7 and 8 of resolution 1556(2004), and to dispose of such arms and related materiel as appropriate;

(*b*) *Requests* that the Secretary-General and the Governments of Chad and the Central African Republic conclude status-of forces agreements as soon as possible, taking into consideration General Assembly resolution 58/82 of 9 December 2003 on the scope of legal protection under the Convention on the Safety of United Nations and Associated Personnel, and decides that, pending the conclusion of such an agreement with either country, the model status-of-forces agreement dated 9 October 1990 shall apply provisionally with respect to forces of the Mission operating in that country;

13. *Requests* the Secretary-General to report to the Council on the protection of civilians in refugee and internally displaced persons camps in Chad and on how to improve the security situation on the Chadian side of the border with the Sudan;

14. *Calls upon* the parties to the Darfur Peace Agreement to respect their commitments and implement the Agreement without delay, urges those parties that have not signed the Agreement to do so without delay and not to act in any way that would impede implementation of the Agreement, and reiterates its intention to take, including in response to a request by the African Union, strong and effective measures, such as an assets freeze or travel ban, against any individual or group that violates or attempts to block the implementation of the Agreement or commits human rights violations;

15. *Decides* to remain seized of the matter.

RECORDED VOTE ON RESOLUTION 1706(2006):

In favour: Argentina, Congo, Denmark, France, Ghana, Greece, Japan, Peru, Slovakia, United Kingdom, United Republic of Tanzania, United States.

Against: None.

Abstaining: China, Qatar, Russian Federation.

Speaking after the vote, the United Kingdom said that the tragedy in Darfur had gone on far too long and the transition to a UN operation was the only viable solution. The Sudanese Government's plan (see p. 281) would be a military solution imposed by one of the parties to the conflict, in violation of the Peace Agreement. The resolution sent a clear message from the Council regarding the need for a well-equipped third party to ensure the protection of civilians. The Council was appealing to the Sudanese Government in the strongest possible terms to allow the United Nations to provide assistance. The Council wished to help the Sudan, not to threaten, or undermine it.

China said that, while it concurred that a UN operation should take over from AMIS as soon as feasible, the timing of the vote and the fact that the resolution did not specify "with the consent of the Government" meant it had to abstain.

The Russian Federation said that the Council should support a transition to a UN operation, but with the consent of the Government. Pending the receipt of such consent, the Russian Federation had decided to abstain, although it had no objections in principle to the resolution.

Qatar said that the Council should have given due regard to the principles of international practice before taking up a resolution that would have a bearing on the sovereignty of the Sudan, and made more efforts to prepare the ground for Sudan's voluntary consent. Darfur had undergone many positive developments since the signing of the Peace Agreement. The Sudan had submitted a multifaceted plan to address the situation but, regrettably, the Council had not responded to it or submitted any explicit proposals. Nor had enough efforts been made to engage the Sudan, instead of pressuring it into approving the draft resolution. Qatar would have preferred to support AMIS financially and logistically to enable it to complete its mandate. In addition, the League of Arab States and Qatar had requested a postponement of the Council meeting but the resolution's sponsors wanted its speedy adoption. In the circumstances, Qatar had been unable to support the resolution, given its repercussions and the modalities of its implementation.

Implementation of resolution 1706(2006) and further political developments

Security Council consideration (September). Briefing the Council on 11 September [meeting 5520], the Secretary-General called upon Governments and individual leaders in Africa and beyond who were in a position to influence the Sudanese Government, to bring pressure to bear, and convince Khartoum to accept a UN operation. He condemned the recent offensive by Government forces, which included renewed aerial bombing and the deployment of thousands of troops, in violation of the Darfur Peace Agreement. The various factions had engaged in renewed fighting, bringing even greater misery to the population and making it harder for humanitarian workers to reach them. Twelve aid workers had been killed in the past two months alone, more than in the entire previous two years. He urged Khartoum to embrace resolution

1706(2006), give its consent to the transition and pursue the political process with commitment.

Sudan said that it remained open to dialogue and cooperation with the United Nations, but the Council had ignored or downplayed attacks by rebel groups and had not considered the Government's own detailed plan for stabilizing the situation in Darfur on the basis of the Peace Agreement, even though some Council members had requested a meeting on the plan. Some members had spoken of growing violence in Darfur, without mentioning the perpetrators and without condemning the criminal acts of NRF. In adopting resolution 1706(2006), the Council had taken hasty measures without preparing the political context with all the parties involved, foremost among them, the Sudan. The Council had chosen a confrontational approach, but the Sudan was always ready to engage in dialogue on the basis of respect for its sovereignty and independence.

Report of Secretary-General (September). In his September report on Darfur [S/2006/764], the Secretary-General said that situation in Darfur had deteriorated considerably and the Government's decision to deploy a large number of military troops there signalled its determination to pursue a military solution to the crisis. Although the signatories to the Darfur Peace Agreement maintained the ceasefire between themselves, violence flared between the Agreement's signatories and non-signatories. Two AMIS peacekeepers were killed in the 19 August ambush of an AU fuel convoy at Kuma, and attacks against humanitarian workers continued unabated. Militia groups continued to attack civilians and internally displaced persons, while banditry was rampant across most of Darfur. The region was again descending into a vicious cycle of violence, the Secretary-General noted. On 28 July, SAF, reportedly assisted by Janjaweed militia, clashed with Peace Agreement non-signatory forces in the Jebel Moon area of Western Darfur. On 18 August, assailants believed to belong to non-signatory groups attacked an SAF camp at Goz Mino, killing three soldiers. On 24 August, another armed group ambushed a Government convoy near Abu Soroug, killing the Assistant Commissioner of Kulbus and six others. Government-affiliated militia repeatedly attacked villages near Jebel Marra between 17 July and 2 August, killing 12 civilians. Meanwhile, SAF and troops of the SLM-Minawi faction attacked NRF forces north of El Fasher. Clashes between SAF and NRF continued throughout August.

In Northern Darfur, SLA-Minawi elements, currently aligned with the Government forces, attacked villages near Korma town, killing at least 100 civilians. Those and other clashes resulted in almost 20,000 internally displaced persons arriving in Northern Darfur camps in July. Displaced persons reported indiscriminate killing, rape and abduction, as security in the camps remained precarious. The militarization of some of the camps continued unabated. SLA-Minawi soldiers harassed persons in the camps around El Fasher, while SLA-Abdul Wahid troops harassed civilians in Otash camp in Southern Darfur.

Armed robbery against humanitarian workers grew increasingly brazen. On 15 and 16 August, armed men hijacked and stole three vehicles of the International Committee of the Red Cross (ICRC) near El Fasher, killing one driver. Twelve humanitarian workers died in July and August alone. Sexual violence increased dramatically throughout Darfur, and Government authorities appeared unable or reluctant to address it. The UN Special Rapporteur on the Human Rights Situation in the Sudan, Sima Samar, who visited the country from 11 to 17 August, (see p. 942) was disturbed by the critical human rights situation, and raised concerns with senior Government officials about the killings of civilians, rape, torture and displacement. On many occasions, authorities obstructed UN human rights officers performing their duties, while the intelligence and security service continued to restrict UNMIS access to Darfur detention facilities.

In public statements, the Government continued to reject the Security Council's decision on the transition to a UN peace operation. President Bashir and Vice-President Taha threatened armed resistance and other violence against the United Nations if the decision was implemented. However, the proposed transition was welcomed by senior members of the Sudan People's Liberation Movement and the Darfur rebel groups, as well as northern opposition parties. Demonstrations in support of and against the Council's decision were seen throughout Darfur.

In spite of the efforts of the wider international community and major AU and UN initiatives, no additional signatories joined the Darfur Peace Agreement. Its implementation remained well behind schedule, and the inability of its mechanisms and arrangements to halt the continuing violence undermined its credibility. Efforts by the Government of the Sudan and the international community to persuade Abdul Wahid to sign the Agreement were unsuccessful. Abdul Wahid did not entirely reject the Agreement, but wanted amendments or additions to satisfy his four political demands: a role in reviewing the Janjaweed disarmament; a national Vice-Presidency position for Darfur; more compensation; and the merging of the three Darfur states into one region. At the same time, his authority had reportedly been challenged by several influential commanders and his position and strength within SLA remained unclear. In addition to the Abdul Wahid faction of the SLA, the "anti-Darfur Peace Agreement bloc" consisted of the G19, a group of former disaffected SLA-Abdul Wahid commanders and their followers, JEM, and elements of NRF. JEM, which had taken the toughest line against the Darfur Peace Agreement, had also splintered into the JEM-Wing for Peace supporting the Darfur Peace Agreement, and some JEM commanders in Jebel Moon, who eschewed further intra-rebel violence.

Although the groups that had signed the 8 June Declaration of Commitment to the Darfur Peace Agreement (see p. 279) had been recognized by the AU Peace and Security Council as "partners in the peace process", and had been invited by the Joint Commission to participate in its meetings, the Darfur Peace Agreement signatories opposed any significant role or benefits for them, and the AU and the parties had yet to develop a plan for including them in the implementation process. The Ceasefire Commission continued to meet regularly, but had been largely incapacitated by disagreements over the non-signatories' role and the relationship between the N'Djamena and Darfur Peace Agreement ceasefire commissions.

On 7 August, Minni Minawi was sworn in as Senior Assistant to the President, the fourth-highest position in the National Executive, and as Transitional Darfur Regional Authority Chairman. On 9 September, Minni Minawi announced the formation of seven committees for the implementation of the Darfur Peace Agreement, as a first step towards the implementation of the Agreement, and confirmed that the structures of the Transitional Darfur Regional Authority would include the parties that had signed the 8 June Declaration of Commitment.

UN support for AMIS. On 28 September [S/2006/779], the Secretary-General and the AU Chairperson transmitted to the Security Council President the joint UN/AU proposal for UN support to AMIS in the form of an immediate "light support package", which included logistical and material support, 105 military staff officers, 33 police advisers and 48 civilians to assist in the areas of staff support to AMIS senior management, mine action, public information, humanitarian coordination and support for the Darfur Peace Agreement implementation. The proposal was in response to the AU Peace and Security Council request, made at its 20 September meeting at the level of Heads of State and Government, for support to help AMIS to carry out its mandate under the Darfur Peace Agreement. They also transmitted their joint request of 22 September to President Al-Bashir, requesting his Government's full support in implementing the package.

On 3 October [S/2006/789], President Al-Bashir informed the Security Council President of his personal support for the envisaged UN support to AMIS, and suggested that a protocol be drawn up to spell out the details for implementing the package. He looked forward to more mutual understanding between the Sudan, the United Nations and the AU on cooperation in handling the Darfur situation.

Communication. On 16 October [S/2006/823], the Sudan forwarded to the Security Council six presidential decrees issued on 24 September, establishing implementation mechanisms under the Darfur Peace Agreement: the Transitional Darfur Regional Authority, the Darfur Compensation Commission for War-affected Persons, the Darfur Compensation Fund for War-affected Persons, the Darfur Rehabilitation and Resettlement Commission, the Darfur Reconstruction and Development Fund and the Darfur Boundary Demarcation Commission.

Reports of Secretary-General (November-December). In his November report [S/2006/870], the Secretary-General said that violence had increased in Darfur in September, as fighting between the signatories and non-signatories of the Darfur Peace Agreement intensified, with the Government using aerial bombardment in attacks against villages controlled by NRF and the G19 rebel groups. Tensions between signatories also surfaced for the first time. Although, the ceasefire between the SLA-Minni Minawi faction and the Government held generally throughout Darfur, several incidents revealed tensions between the two signatories of the Darfur Peace Agreement. On 30 August, an SLM-Minawi spokesperson accused the Government and the Janjaweed militia of random killing in Southern Darfur, including the torching of around 13 villages south of Nyala. Meanwhile, fighting between Peace Agreement signatories and non-signatories continued. On 28 August, SAF launched an aerial and ground offensive against NRF forces in the Kafod and Abu Sakin area, 60 kilometres north of El Fasher. Heavy fighting was also reported in Southern Darfur between 10 and 13 September, when SAF troops, assisted by militia and aerial support, launched an offensive against non-signatory groups in Eastern Jebel Marra. In Southern Darfur, on 24 August, an armed group attacked the SAF garrison at Songo, 265 kilometres south of Nyala. Reports were received that Government aircraft had bombed areas near Tura, Sayeh and Um Sidir, in Northern

Darfur, several villages south-west of Tawila, and Hashaba North, and NRF-controlled villages of Anka and Amarai about 50 kilometres north-west of Um Sidir.

September also saw increasing tension between and within rebel groups in Southern Darfur. On 1 September, a group of Massalit SLM-Minawi soldiers attacked their Zaghawa comrades in Gereida. Tensions rose between SLM-Minawi (mainly Zaghawa) and SLM-Free Will (mainly Birgid) in Muhajirya, Southern Darfur, and in October, armed clashes were reported there between SLM-Free Will and SLM-Minawi. Armed banditry and looting targeting humanitarian and commercial traffic also continued to be a major source of insecurity and an indicator of the lawlessness prevailing in Darfur. AU peacekeepers were targeted frequently. On 3 September, 12 armed men disarmed an AU team near the camp in Kassab, Northern Darfur. The next day, armed men ambushed an AMIS patrol on its way from Tina to Kutum, in Northern Darfur.

The Government's military campaign in Northern and Southern Darfur was taking its toll on the civilian population, resulting in indiscriminate killings and other grave abuses against civilians, including death, injury, rape and displacement. The presence of armed groups within camps in Northern Darfur made them increasingly militarized and insecure. There were widespread and persistent reports of violence against civilians in those camps, including murder, physical attack, rape and armed robbery. On 12 September, 10 armed men entered the Tawila Camp, in Northern Darfur. Attacks on female internally displaced persons by armed militia outside the camps were recurrent. The increase in insecurity and military conflict exacerbated the already persistent practice of targeting women and girls with sexual violence. The unwillingness of the authorities to recognize the pervasiveness of that problem and to cast doubt on reported incidents only further burdened the victims and prevented an adequate Government response.

In terms of the implementation of the Darfur Peace Agreement, no new parties joined. The already weak pro-Darfur Peace Agreement bloc was further threatened by frictions between and within rebel groups. In September, both the Agreement's signatories and civil society organizations stepped up efforts to bolster the peace process. The Zaghawa Native Administration spearheaded an initiative aimed at reconciling the SLM-Minawi and some G19 commanders in Northern Darfur. Representatives of the Native Administration met G19 commanders in Gira on 15 September. Talks reportedly also commenced between SLM commanders in Eastern Jebel Marra and the Southern Darfur State authorities. However, the fragility of the rebel groups and alliances further complicated efforts to consolidate political support for the Darfur Peace Agreement. On 23 and 24 September, local media reported frictions within the leadership of SLM-Free Will, whose Secretary-General issued a statement on 22 September relieving the group's Chairman, Abdul Rahman Moussa, of his duties. That move was rejected by other elements within the faction. Moreover, recent conflicts within the SLM-Minawi faction in Gereida and between SLM-Minawi and SLM-Free Will in Muhajirya appeared to have divided the pro-Darfur Peace Agreement parties along ethnic lines.

On 26 August, following amendments in the Northern and Southern Darfur state constitutions, the state Legislative Council in Western Darfur amended its constitution to allow for representation of pro-Darfur Peace Agreement groups in the executive and legislative branches of the State. The Wali (Governor) of Western Darfur approved the amendments, which were awaiting endorsement from the Ministry of Justice in Khartoum.

In September, the AU Darfur Peace Agreement Implementation Team in Khartoum commenced work on the Darfur-Darfur Dialogue and Consultation and circulated a strategy paper outlining the main priorities of the Consultation. The AU named Abdul Mohamed (Ethiopia) as the Chairman of the Preparatory Committee, while consultations continued on the appointment of the Chairperson of the Darfur-Darfur Dialogue and Consultation.

The Secretary-General observed that, five months after the signing of the Darfur Peace Agreement, violence has increased again in Darfur, and thousands of SAF troops had been deployed to the area in clear violation of the Agreement and Security Council resolution 1591(2005) [YUN 2005, p. 319]. He called upon all parties to halt the violence, uphold their obligations under the various agreements and work towards a political solution of the conflict. The suffering of the Darfurian population, he said, had lasted far too long. The gains made in 2005 were coming under strain with humanitarian needs expected to increase. At the same time, the efforts of humanitarian aid workers were being undermined by violence targeted at them. Twelve workers had lost their lives since the Darfur Peace Agreement was signed, more than in the previous two years. The Secretary-General appealed to all parties to respect humanitarian principles, and allow humanitarian actors to provide much-needed assistance and monitor protection concerns without being subject to harassment, looting and killing.

In December [S/2006/1041], the Secretary-General reported that military confrontations between the Government and the non-signatories of the Darfur Peace Agreement reached new heights in October and November, spreading to areas outside Northern Darfur. On 3 October, Janjaweed militias supported by SAF helicopters attacked G19/NRF positions in Malagat, Northern Darfur. In retaliation, NRF attacked an SAF post in Karyare, close to the Chadian border. The combined rebel forces reportedly took control of Karyare on 7 October, with SAF suffering a large number of casualties. Government aircraft subsequently bombed the rebel-held town. On 12 and 13 October, SAF attacked rebel positions in Kulbus, Western Darfur. The Secretary-General's Special Representative, visiting Northern Darfur from 16 to 18 October, appealed to G19 and NRF commanders to cease attacks and obtained pledges from them to act only in self-defence. Meanwhile, SAF continued its attacks, with an aerial bombardment of suspected NRF positions north of Kulbus on 17 October.

Fighting among rebel groups and tribal tensions in areas controlled by parties supporting the Darfur Peace Agreement further hampered its implementation. Clashes resumed between SLM-Minawi and the breakaway faction, SLM-Free Will, in Muhajirya, Southern Darfur. Meanwhile, tensions further increased in Gereida, Southern Darfur, between the Zaghawa-dominated SLM-Minawi and the local Massalit population. Following the 28 September attack on the SLM-Minawi headquarters, members of the Massalit tribe in Gereida revolted against the SLM-Minawi forces, protesting the recent increase in attacks on civilians.

In October, armed militias continued to attack civilians with impunity. Armed elements on camels and in vehicles burned down several villages near the Shadad internally displaced persons camp, south of El Fasher. On 29 October, several hundred Arab militia members, wearing military uniforms and armed with machine guns and rocket-propelled grenades, attacked the villages of Gebasesh, Hijlija, Siberia and Goze Mino in Western Darfur, looting livestock and killing at least 52 people. Government forces from a nearby SAF post did not intervene to stop the attack. Clashes between Janjaweed forces and SLA-Minawi forces on 4 December, forced the relocation of some 135 UN staff to Khartoum.

At the regional level, relations between Chad and the Sudan deteriorated, marked by the attack on an SAF post in Karyare and a new offensive against the Government of Chad by Chadian armed opposition groups based in Darfur. On 25 November, the Chadian rebel group, the Union of Forces for Democracy and Development, took control of the town of Abéché, 900 kilometres east of N'Djamena, which served as a base for dozens of relief organizations. Although the Government of Chad retook the town the next day, the incident undermined the delivery of aid to populations in need. On several occasions, Chadian rebel groups were reported to have crossed the border with the Sudan. The Central African Republic also accused the Sudan of supporting rebels in the country after a rebel group took the town of Bifao near the Chad/ Sudan border.

Little progress was made in the implementation of the Darfur Peace Agreement. However, the hosting by SLM-Minawi on 16 October, of a forum in Khartoum, in anticipation of the Darfur-Darfur Dialogue and Consultation, was seen as a positive development. The forum, attended by a cross-section of approximately 500 Darfurians, as well as SLM-Free Will and senior representatives of the ruling National Congress Party (NCP) and the Sudan People's Liberation Movement, represented the first significant effort by the Darfur Peace Agreement signatories to jointly reach out to civil society. During the last week of November, the AU Special Envoy Salim A. Salim met Sudanese officials, as well as non-signatories to the Agreement to broaden support for the peace process in Darfur. Subsequently, a UNMIS representative and Mr. Salim held bilateral consultations on reinvigorating the political process under a joint AU/UN umbrella and agreed to form a working-level team to prepare for the resumption of talks in January 2007. The team was also mandated to consult with the Agreement's signatories, non-signatories and other local actors and to stress the importance of an immediate cessation of hostilities, a commitment to a ceasefire and the related mechanisms created by the Agreement and a credible Darfur-Darfur Dialogue and Consultation.

Concerning UN support to AMIS, UNMIS had started to implement the "light support package" (see p. 287). On 12 November, President Al-Bashir agreed that a tripartite AU-United Nations-Government of the Sudan mechanism be created to facilitate its implementation. The AU and UNMIS held consultations on the longer-term "heavy" UN support package, which would include substantial air assets, significant military and police advisory capacity, civilian support for the implementation of the Darfur Peace Agreement and a range of UN enabling capabilities.

Addis Ababa high-level consultations. On 16 November, the Secretary-General co-chaired a high-level meeting in Addis Ababa with the AU

Chairperson to identify steps for improving the situation, notably to re-energize the peace process, establish a strengthened ceasefire and delineate the way forward for peacekeeping in Darfur. The meeting, attended by the Government of the Sudan, UN Member States, the EU, the League of Arab States and a number of troop-contributing African countries, produced an understanding that only a negotiated settlement could bring the conflict to an end. It agreed that the Darfur Peace Agreement would remain at the heart of any settlement, but would have to be more inclusive; the various efforts to bring non-signatories on board had to be brought under one umbrella, and the AU and the United Nations were best positioned to lead that process; and, as a next step, the AU and the United Nations would convene a meeting of non-signatories, the SLM-Minawi faction and the Government to resolve outstanding issues by the end of the year.

As to peacekeeping in Darfur, the meeting confirmed that a peacekeeping force could be predominantly African in nature, with troops, as far as possible, sourced from the continent. The United Nations would provide backstopping and command and control structures. To strengthen AMIS in Darfur, the meeting concluded that the United Nations would continue to implement the previously agreed "light support package" for AMIS, in collaboration with the AU and the Sudan; the "heavy support package", or phase two, would be initiated and its implementation facilitated by the tripartite (UN-AU-Government of the Sudan) mechanism established for the light package; an AU-UN hybrid operation would be established, led by a Special Representative and commanded by a Force Commander, jointly appointed by the AU and the United Nations; and the United Nations would provide all required funding for peacekeeping in Darfur. The hybrid operation would, in principle, reflect the recommendations made in the Secretary-General's July report to the Security Council (see p. 280).

Communication. On 30 November [S/2006/961], the AU Peace and Security Council, meeting in Abuja at the level of Heads of State and Government, endorsed the conclusions of the 16 November meeting. In a communiqué issued the same day, the Council indicated, with respect to the AU/UN hybrid operation, that: the Special Representative should be jointly appointed by the AU Commission Chairperson and the Secretary-General, and the Force Commander by the AU Commission Chairperson, in consultation with the Secretary-General; the hybrid mission should benefit from UN backstopping and command and control structures and systems; and the size of the force should be determined by the AU and the United Nations, on the basis of factors on the ground and requirements for effectively discharging its mandate.

The Peace and Security Council extended AMIS mandate, which was due to expire on 31 December, for six months and appealed to the United Nations to consider providing logistical and financial support to the Mission, as envisaged in the conclusions of the Addis Ababa consultation.

On 3 December, the Sudan's Council of Ministers endorsed the Peace and Security Council communiqué of 30 November.

Report of Secretary-General. The Secretary-General, in a later report [S/2007/104], said that the Government of the Sudan had accepted, on 23 December, the three-phased approach to peacekeeping in Darfur–the "light support package", the "heavy support package" and the AU/UN hybrid operation. It also confirmed its readiness to start immediately, through the tripartite committee, implementation of the Addis Ababa conclusions and the Abuja communiqué (see above).

Concerning implementation of the Darfur Peace Agreement, preparatory work for the convening of a conference of non-signatories and rationalization of the various initiatives to broaden the base of the Agreement were ongoing. In December, further progress was made to reinforce the ceasefire mechanism, including the creation of a second chamber of the Ceasefire Commission for non-signatories. In a related development, on 27 December, members of the three non-signatory parties, the SLM-Abdul Wahid, SLM-Abdul Sahif and G19, announced their merger into one movement known as the SLM-Non-Signatory Factions, and a cessation of hostilities unless attacked. They reiterated their commitment to the 2004 N'Djamena Humanitarian Ceasefire Agreement.

The security situation in November and December was characterized by increased violence. SAF, supported by armed militia, clashed with non-signatory forces, especially in Northern and Southern Darfur. In their ongoing efforts to flush out non-signatory combatants, the Government intensified aerial bombardment of their positions, including civilian targets. Tension also persisted along the Sudan-Chad border. Humanitarian organizations and AMIS suffered harassment and attacks, while theft and carjackings of their vehicles reached new heights. Clashes occurred between SAF and the NRF coalition in both Northern and Southern Darfur, especially in Birmaza, Sani Hayi, Umm Sidr, Sayah, Gubba, Dobo (Northern Darfur), Abu Jabre and Adilya (Southern Darfur). On 15 November, SAF forces and armed militia, supported by helicopter gunships, attacked several villages in the Birmaza area. The G19 faction of NRF retaliated by attacking SAF and militia forces, as well as Government property, including the oil installations at Abu Jabre on 26 November. On 4 and 5 December, Government helicopter gunships and aircraft bombed the Adilya area (Southern Darfur) in an attack on NRF forces. On 16 December, SAF and G19 members clashed in Sayah (Northern Darfur), during which nine G19 members were killed and seven of their vehicles destroyed. On 20 December, armed militia and Government forces launched a combined ground and air strike against a joint force of the G19 group, SLM-Abdul Shafi and JEM in Gubba (Northern Darfur).

Much of the violence targeted innocent civilians, in contravention of ceasefire arrangements and international law. On 18 November, SAF and armed militia attacked and burned a significant portion of the village of Buli (Western Darfur), where more than 10,000 internally displaced persons had found refuge, and looted several villages between Rowata and Bul Bul (Western Darfur). Dozens of civilians were killed and thousands displaced in the attacks. Armed militia also attacked and torched several villages, causing the death of many civilians. On 5 and 6 December, Government aircraft bombarded Shagbuba, with ground support from armed militia, and on 9 December, armed men on horseback attacked a commercial vehicle convoy carrying people and medical and other supplies near Runju Runju in the Sirba area (Western Darfur), killing 31 civilians.

Tension along the Sudan-Chad border remained high, following the 25 November capture of the eastern Chadian town of Abéché by Chadian armed opposition groups. On 28 November, Chad declared itself in a "state of war" with the Sudan and on 12 December, fighting between Chadian armed opposition groups and Chadian armed forces broke out at Armankul (Western Darfur).

SECURITY COUNCIL ACTION

On 19 December [meeting 5598], following consultations among Security Council members, the President made statement **S/PRST/2006/55** on behalf of the Council:

> The Security Council endorses the conclusions of the Addis Ababa high-level consultation on the situation in Darfur of 16 November 2006 and the communiqué of the 66th meeting of the Peace and Security Council of the African Union, held in Abuja on 30 November 2006. The Security Council welcomes the stated commitment of the Government of National Unity to the conclusions and the communiqué.
>
> The Council calls for the conclusions and the communiqué to be implemented by all parties without delay, and to this end calls upon all parties to facilitate, per the Addis Ababa and Abuja agreements, the immediate deployment of the United Nations light and heavy support packages to the African Union Mission in the Sudan and a hybrid operation in Darfur, for which backstopping and command and control structures and systems will be provided by the United Nations. The Council requests the Secretary-General to keep it updated.
>
> The Council reaffirms its deep concern about the worsening security situation in Darfur and its repercussions in the region. It stresses that a peaceful settlement to the conflict in Darfur lies in a comprehensive approach with the concerted efforts of all relevant parties, in accordance with the Darfur Peace Agreement, and will contribute to restoring security and stability in the region.

Council press statement. In a 27 December press statement [SC/8931], Security Council members welcomed the report of the visit of the Secretary-General's Envoy, Ahmedou Ould-Abdallah, to the Sudan. In discussing the report, Council members also welcomed the 23 December letter from the President of the Sudan, in which he reconfirmed his commitment to implementing the Addis Ababa and Abuja agreements, in particular, to bring about the cessation of hostilities, revitalise the political process and allow the immediate implementation of the UN three-phased support plan to the AU, culminating in the deployment of a hybrid United Nations-AU force in Darfur.

Briefings by ICC Prosecutor

Presenting his third report to the Security Council on 14 June [meeting 5459], the Prosecutor of the International Criminal Court (ICC), Luis Moreno-Ocampo, said that, given the scale of alleged crimes committed in Darfur, and the complexities of identifying those most responsible, he anticipated the prosecution of a sequence of cases, rather than a single case dealing with the situation as a whole. His Office had gathered significant amounts of information to determine whether the Government had dealt with, or was dealing with, the cases that were likely to be selected for prosecution. The Court's concern was to see that effective justice was delivered to the victims. The Government had provided much information on traditional tribal reconciliation mechanisms in Darfur, but it did not appear to have investigated or prosecuted any cases in such a way as to render those cases inadmissible before the Court. The Government, in responding to the request of the Office, had agreed to allow it to conduct interviews in the country so as to establish a complete account of events in Darfur since 2002. There was a reluctance or inability on the part of witnesses and victims to come forward, and there were allegations of intimidation of complainants, especially regarding rape allegations. The Office of the Prosecutor would, in due course, identify those to be prosecuted on the basis of evidence collected, and present its conclusions to the judges. Cooperation was needed to ensure accountability, not only for past, but for current crimes that continued to affect the displaced populations. International justice efforts should contribute to their protection and the prevention of further crimes. However, more information was needed on groups that continued to attack the displaced population.

Sudan said that the ICC Prosecutor had reflected very important aspects of cooperation established with the Sudanese Government; that cooperation had led to several positive results. The Prosecutor had quickly come to an understanding of the situation during his visit and heard briefings by members of the Sudanese judiciary concerning its independence and relationship with other judicial organs in the country. The Prosecutor had also learned about a great number of cases that had been decided and about charges that had been followed up. Special courts had been established, which had issued many criminal sentences, including execution and life in prison. Measures were also taken to compensate the victims.

Briefing the Council on 14 December [meeting 5589], Mr. Moreno-Ocampo said his Office was completing the investigation and collection of evidence to identify those who bore the greatest responsibility for some of the worst crimes in Darfur, adding that there was reasonable ground to believe that those identified had committed crimes against humanity and war crimes, including persecution, torture, murder and rape. The Sudan had formally advised that it had arrested 14 individuals, but those indications did not appear to render the Court's case inadmissible. His Office had taken more than 100 formal witness statements and screened hundreds of potential witnesses since the start of its investigation, travelling to 17 countries to pursue inquiries. The Sudan had participated in the process. Despite the signing of the Darfur Peace Agreement, there were almost daily allegations of crimes that might fall within the Court's jurisdiction. By completing the investigation, the Office was sending a signal to those who were considering committing further crimes that they could not do so with impunity.

Children and armed conflict

An August report [S/2006/662] of the Secretary-General on children and armed conflict in the Sudan, prepared in response to Security Council resolution 1612(2005) [YUN 2005, p. 863], stated that grave child rights abuses in the Sudan continued largely unabated. The report, which covered the period from May to July, said that parties to the conflict committing grave abuses included SAF, SLA, the Popular Defence Forces, the White Army, the Janjaweed militia, the Lord's Resistance Movement operating out of Uganda and Chadian opposition forces. Individual commanders of the various forces bore responsibility for grave violations by their forces, but the Government of National Unity and the Government of Southern Sudan were also directly accountable for violations by individuals within their command structures. The report highlighted action plans and programmes to address violations, and made recommendations for strengthening the protection of war-affected children, including criminalizing the recruitment and use of children, ensuring that children released from the military received adequate support and taking steps to address the special needs of girls. (For further information on children and armed conflict, see Part II, Chapter II.)

Sanctions Committee

The Security Council, by resolution 1556(2004) [YUN 2004, p. 240], imposed an arms embargo on all non-governmental entities and individuals, including the Janjaweed, operating in Darfur. By resolution 1591(2005) [YUN 2005, p. 319], the Council imposed a travel ban and assets freeze and established a Committee to oversee implementation of those sanctions against individuals to be designated by it. The Secretary-General was requested to appoint a Panel of Experts for six months to assist the work of the Council and the Committee.

The Panel of Experts, established in June 2005 [ibid., p. 322], had as its mandate, to assist the Committee in monitoring implementation of the arms embargo and the sanctions; make recommendations to the Committee on possible Council actions; and provide information on individuals who impeded the peace process, committed violations of international law, or were responsible for offensive military overflights.

Appointment of experts. On 13 January [S/2006/23] and 10 February [S/2006/99], the Secretary-General informed the Council President of the appointment of four members to serve on the Panel of Experts established pursuant to resolution 1591(2005). In addition, on 10 February [S/2006/99], he appointed Bernard Saunders (Canada).

Report of Panel of Experts (January). On 30 January [S/2006/65], the Chairman of the Security Council Committee established pursuant to resolution 1591(2005), submitted to the Council the report of the Panel of Experts on the Sudan. The Panel reported that arms, especially small arms and ammunition, continued to enter Darfur from other countries and regions of the Sudan. Although the Council had imposed an arms embargo on all non-governmental groups, SLM/A and JEM continued to receive arms, ammunition and/or equipment through Chad, Eritrea, the Libyan Arab Jamahiriya, and from numerous other sources. According to numerous reports, they also received financial, political and other material support. It also appeared that the Council's intent to deny arms to the Janjaweed militia was circumvented by the fact that many of the militias were already formally part of the Government's security organs or were incorporated into those organs, especially the Popular Defence Force (PDF), the border intelligence guard, the central reserve police, the popular police and the nomadic police. The Panel believed that Eritrea appeared to have provided arms, logistical support, military training and political support to both JEM and SLA, including in training camps in Eritrea. Reports were also received that the Sudan People's Liberation Movement/Army in southern Sudan had provided training and arms to SLM/A. The Panel also identified ways in which the Government violated the arms embargo.

The Panel identified individuals who had impeded the peace process and committed violations of international humanitarian or human rights law, and provided their names in a confidential annex to the report.

The Sudanese Government and SLA, and to a lesser extent JEM, committed consistent, wilful and systematic violations of the N'Djamena Humanitarian Ceasefire Agreement. Sudan failed to fulfil its agreed commitments to identify, neutralize and disarm militias under its control or influence. It continued to support those militias and on occasion engaged in coordinated military operations with them. Several individuals had been identified as having committed acts intended to impede the work of AMIS, including hostile acts against AMIS personnel.

Having found that Sudan continued to violate the provisions of the arms embargo through the movement of arms into Darfur from other parts of the Sudan and the deployment of additional attack helicopters to Darfur, the experts recommended strengthening that embargo by complementing it with the installation of a verification/inventory component, and extending it to the entire territory, while providing appropriate exemptions for the Government of Southern Sudan and the Government of the Sudan.

The Panel found evidence of widespread violations of international humanitarian law in Darfur during the period 29 March–5 December 2005. The parties to the N'Djamena Humanitarian Ceasefire Agreement and other belligerents operating in Darfur, in particular the non-State militias, had undertaken military operations with scant regard for the principles of distinction, proportionality or military imperative. While all parties had violated the rules and norms of armed conflict, SLA, the Government and the militias had shown the least regard for the welfare of civilians.

The experts proposed that the Committee and the Security Council adopt a zero tolerance approach to violations of the N'Djamena Humanitarian Ceasefire Agreement; and any future ceasefire violation reports verified by the Joint Commission should be used as the basis for direct action by the Committee against the leadership of the violating party and against the local commanders that committed the offending act. In view of the failure of the Sudan to identify, neutralize and disarm militias in Darfur, the Council should consider subjecting individuals identified by the report as failing to disarm the militias to sanctions under resolution 1591(2005). Additional measures should be considered against select Government members, as provided for under Article 41 of the Charter.

Communications. In a 17 January letter [S/2006/31] to the Security Council President and the Secretary-General, the Libyan Arab Jamahiriya, responding to the Panel's report, denied providing arms, ammunition and other military equipment to the armed movements or the other parties. On the contrary, it had requested two AU summit meetings to address the Darfur issue, taken part in all meetings to settle the conflict, participated in the Joint Commission's monitoring of implementation of the ceasefire and called for peace-building meetings. An enclosure to the letter summarized Libya's efforts to assist in resolving the Darfur problem.

In a 1 March letter to the Security Council President [S/2006/136], Sudan's Minister for Foreign Affairs, Lam Akol Ajawin, stated that the country had sought to ensure that the Panel of Experts obtained unimpeded access to any information it desired, including highly secret and important information. It was confident that the Panel would handle that information with the requisite confidentiality, secrecy and institutional treatment that took into account the immunity of leaders and officials. However, the Sudan was shocked to see the secret list prepared by the Panel, containing the names of leaders, ministers and officials, carried by western media. The Sudan expected to receive the Council's assurance that such acts would not be repeated, otherwise it would be compelled to suspend its cooperation.

SECURITY COUNCIL ACTION

On 29 March [meeting 5402], the Security Council unanimously adopted **resolution 1665(2006)**. The draft [S/2006/189] was prepared in consultations, among Council members.

The Security Council,

Recalling its previous resolutions concerning the situation in the Sudan, in particular resolutions 1556(2004) of 30 July 2004, 1591(2005) of 29 March 2005 and 1651(2005) of 21 December 2005, and the statements by its President concerning the Sudan,

Stressing again its firm commitment to the cause of peace throughout the Sudan, including through the African Union-led inter-Sudanese peace talks in Abuja ("Abuja Talks"), full implementation of the Comprehensive Peace Agreement of 9 January 2005, and an end to the violence and atrocities in Darfur,

Urging all parties to the Abuja Talks to reach without further delay an agreement that will establish a basis for peace, reconciliation, stability and justice in the Sudan,

Commending the efforts of, and reiterating its full support for, the African Union, the Secretary-General and the leaders of the region to promote peace and stability in Darfur,

Taking note of the observations and recommendations contained in the report of 9 December 2005 of the Panel of Experts appointed by the Secretary-General pursuant to paragraph 3 *(b)* of resolution 1591(2005) and extended by paragraph 1 of resolution 1651(2005), anticipating the receipt of the second report of the Panel currently under consideration by the Security Council Committee established pursuant to paragraph 3 *(a)* of resolution 1591(2005), and expressing its intent to study further the recommendations of the Panel and to consider appropriate next steps,

Emphasizing the need to respect the provisions of the Charter of the United Nations concerning privileges and immunities, and the Convention on the Privileges and Immunities of the United Nations, as applicable to United Nations operations and persons engaged in such operations,

Reaffirming its commitment to the sovereignty, unity, independence and territorial integrity of the Sudan, and recalling the importance of the principles of good-neighbourliness, non-interference and cooperation in the relations among States in the region,

Determining that the situation in the Sudan continues to constitute a threat to international peace and security in the region,

Acting under Chapter VII of the Charter,

1. *Decides* to extend until 29 September 2006 the mandate of the Panel of Experts originally appointed pursuant to resolution 1591(2005) and extended by resolution 1651(2005), and requests the Secretary-General to take the necessary administrative measures;

2. *Requests* the Panel of Experts to provide, no later than ninety days after the adoption of the present resolution, a midterm briefing on its work to the Security Council Committee established pursuant to paragraph 3 *(a)* of resolution 1591(2005), and a final report to the Council no later than thirty days prior to the termination of its mandate, with its findings and recommendations;

3. *Urges* all States, relevant United Nations bodies, the African Union and other interested parties to cooperate fully with the Committee and the Panel of Experts, in particular by supplying any information at their disposal on implementation of the measures imposed by resolutions 1556(2004) and 1591(2005);

4. *Decides* to remain actively seized of the matter.

Communication. The Secretary-General, on 17 May [S/2006/301], informed the Council that he had appointed four experts to serve on the Panel until 29 September.

Report of Panel of Experts (March). In its March report [S/2006/250], the Panel stated that arms, especially small arms and ammunition, continued to flow into Darfur from other countries and other regions of the Sudan during the January-March period, and the Government continued to move in armed troops and supplies without seeking Committee approval, as required by resolution 1591(2005). Pro-Government Arab militias appeared to be maintaining their stock of weapons and ammunition through support from Government entities, banditry and clandestine sources. Adjacent States had ignored their obligations to abide by the embargo and failed to ensure that persons within their jurisdiction complied with it. SLA violated ceasefire accords by expanding territory under its control, while the Government still had not identified, neutralized and disarmed armed groups.

The Panel recommended, among other things, expanding the embargo to all of the Sudan, with certain exemptions for non-lethal supplies; establishing a verification mechanism and an arms inventory; requiring end-use certification for the sale of military goods and services to the Sudan; and imposing additional measures on the Government and SLA as entities, rather than on individuals, for actions that impeded the peace process. Since the Government continued its offensive military overflights, the Council should consider establishing a no-fly zone over the entire Darfur region for all Government aircraft and those utilized by parties to the conflict.

SECURITY COUNCIL ACTION

On 25 April [meeting 5423], the Security Council adopted **resolution 1672(2006)** by vote (12-0-3). The draft [S/2006/255] was submitted by Argentina, Denmark, France, Japan, Peru, Slovakia, the United Kingdom and the United States.

The Security Council,

Recalling its previous resolutions concerning the situation in the Sudan, in particular resolutions 1556(2004) of 30 July 2004, 1591(2005) of 29 March 2005, 1651(2005) of 21 December 2005 and 1665(2006) of 29 March 2006, and the statements by its President concerning the Sudan,

Stressing again its firm commitment to the cause of peace throughout the Sudan, including through the African Union-led inter-Sudanese peace talks in Abuja ("Abuja Talks"), full implementation of the Comprehensive Peace Agreement of 9 January 2005 and an end to the violence and atrocities in Darfur,

Determining that the situation in the Sudan continues to constitute a threat to international peace and security in the region,

Acting under Chapter VII of the Charter of the United Nations,

1. *Decides* that all States shall implement the measures specified in paragraph 3 of resolution 1591(2005) with respect to the following individuals:

–Major General Gaffar Mohamed Elhassan (Commander of the Western Military Region for the Sudanese Armed Forces)

–Sheikh Musa Hilal (Paramount Chief of the Jalul Tribe in North Darfur)

–Adam Yacub Shant (Sudanese Liberation Army Commander)

–Gabril Abdul Kareem Badri (National Movement for Reform and Development Field Commander);

2. *Decides also* to remain actively seized of the matter.

RECORDED VOTE ON RESOLUTION 1672(2006):

In favour: Argentina, Congo, Denmark, France, Ghana, Greece, Japan, Peru, Slovakia, United Kingdom, United Republic of Tanzania, United States.

Against: None.

Abstaining: China, Qatar, Russian Federation.

Speaking after the adoption of the resolution, the Russian Federation said it had abstained because the resolution might have a negative impact on concluding a peace agreement and would not promote international peace efforts. Sanctions should be linked to promoting the resolution of conflicts and ensuring regional stability. Qatar said that there was no evidence to condemn those individuals identified in the resolution and justify sanctions against them. Given the positive developments at the Abuja peace talks, it would have been preferable to postpone the vote until the end of the process. China said that it had always been careful on the adoption of sanctions, as experience showed that they could not achieve the expected results and victimized the civilian population. In the Sanctions Committee, China had joined others in requesting clarifications on the inclusion of individuals on the sanctions list. Regrettably, such information had yet to be provided, and certain members had requested ending discussions and submitting the resolution to the Council. More importantly, the timing of the vote was not right. The peace talks were at a crucial juncture, and the Council should assist the AU in bringing the Abuja talks to a conclusion. China was concerned about the situation in Darfur, supported the role of AMIS and felt that those responsible for serious violations of international humanitarian law should be brought to justice.

Report of Sanctions Committee (July). Reporting in July [S/2006/543] on its activities from 29 March 2005 to 31 March 2006, the Security Council Committee established pursuant to resolution 1591(2005) said that, by the end of the period under review, it had received replies from 13 countries to its request for information on the steps taken to implement the arms embargo, the travel ban and the assets freeze: Brazil [S/AC.47/2005/1], Russian Federation [S/AC.47/2005/2], Portugal [S/AC.47/2005/3], Lithuania [S/AC.47/2005/4], Bulgaria [S/AC.47/2005/5], Greece [S/AC.47/2005/6], Costa Rica [S/AC.47/2005/7], South Africa [S/AC.47/2005/8] United Kingdom [S/AC.47/2005/9], Switzerland [S/AC.47/2005/10] Canada, [S/AC.47/2005/11], Liechtenstein [S/AC.47/2005/12] and Ukraine [S/SC.47/2006/1].

The Committee held four formal and 12 informal meetings and submitted three 90-day reports to the Council. The Panel of Experts, in its two reports (see above), provided information on individuals who could be subject to the travel ban and the assets freeze. By the end of the period under review, the Committee had not concluded its consideration of the Panel's recommendations, nor had it designated any individual as subject to the targeted sanctions.

SECURITY COUNCIL ACTION

On 29 September [meeting 5543], the Security Council unanimously adopted **resolution 1713(2006)**. The draft [S/2006/775] was submitted by Denmark, France, Ghana, Greece, Slovakia, the United Kingdom and the United States.

The Security Council,

Recalling its previous resolutions concerning the situation in Sudan, in particular resolutions 1556(2004) of 30 July 2004, 1591(2005) of 29 March 2005, 1651(2005) of 21 December 2005 and 1665(2006) of 29 March 2006, and the statements by its President concerning the Sudan,

Stressing again its firm commitment to the cause of peace throughout the Sudan, full implementation of the Comprehensive Peace Agreement of 9 January 2005, full implementation of the framework agreed between the parties for a resolution of the conflict in Darfur (the Darfur Peace Agreement), and an end to the violence and atrocities in Darfur,

Urging those parties that have not signed the Darfur Peace Agreement to do so without delay and not act in any way that would impede the implementation of the Agreement, and further urging that those that have signed the Agreement to implement their obligations without delay,

Deploring the ongoing violence, impunity and consequent deterioration of the humanitarian situation, reiterating its deep concern about the security of civilians and humanitarian aid workers and about humanitarian access to populations in need, and calling upon all parties in Darfur to cease offensive actions immediately and to refrain from further violent attacks,

Commending the efforts of, and reiterating its full support for, the African Union, the Secretary-General and the leaders of the region to promote peace and stability in Darfur,

Recalling the midterm briefing of 25 July 2006 by the Panel of Experts appointed by the Secretary-General pursuant to paragraph 3 *(b)* of resolution 1591(2005) and extended by resolutions 1651(2005) and 1665(2006), anticipating the receipt of the final report of the Panel presented on 31 August 2006 to the Security Council Committee established pursuant to resolution 1591(2005) and currently under consideration, and expressing its intent to study the recommendations of the Panel further and to consider appropriate next steps,

Emphasizing the need to respect the provisions of the Charter of the United Nations concerning privileges and immunities, and the Convention on the Privileges and Immunities of the United Nations, as applicable to United Nations operations and persons engaged in such operations,

Reaffirming its commitment to the sovereignty, unity, independence and territorial integrity of the Sudan, and recalling the importance of the principles of good-neighbourliness, non-interference and cooperation in the relations among States in the region,

Determining that the situation in the Sudan continues to constitute a threat to international peace and security in the region,

Acting under Chapter VII of the Charter,

1. *Decides* to extend until 29 September 2007 the mandate of the Panel of Experts originally appointed pursuant to resolution 1591(2005), previously extended by resolutions 1651(2005) and 1665(2006), and requests the Secretary-General to appoint a fifth member to enable the Panel to better carry out its mission, and to take the necessary administrative measures;

2. *Requests* the Panel of Experts to provide, no later than 29 March 2007, a midterm briefing on its work, and no later than ninety days after the adoption of the present resolution an interim report to the Security Council Committee established pursuant to paragraph 3 (*a*) of resolution 1591(2005), and no later than thirty days prior to the termination of its mandate a final report to the Council with its findings and recommendations;

3. *Urges* all States, relevant United Nations bodies, the African Union and other interested parties to cooperate fully with the Committee and the Panel of Experts, in particular by supplying any information at their disposal on implementation of the measures imposed by resolutions 1556(2004) and 1591(2005);

4. *Decides* to remain actively seized of the matter.

Speaking before the vote, Qatar said that it had repeatedly advised the Panel of Experts and the Security Council Committee on the Sudan to be precise, cautious and professional in addressing the issue of Darfur. Qatar expressed concern that the Panel had hastened to hurl allegations and accusations against Sudanese high officials without respect for legal principles and protocol. The Panel had treated as equals the Government and the rebel groups that were hindering the peace process and ignoring calls to join the Peace Agreement. The experts should be accurate, professional, transparent and non-selective so as to maintain the Council's credibility.

Report of Panel of Experts (August). In its August report [S/2006/795], the Panel of Experts said that blatant violations of the arms embargo by Government forces, allied Janjaweed militias, rebel groups and insurgents from Chad continued unabated. Weapons continued to enter Darfur and rebel forces had shown a notable increase in capacity to engage the Sudanese forces.

Chadian insurgents were contributing to the conflict by reportedly joining Sudanese Government forces and the Janjaweed in their operations against rebel groups. According to reliable reports, the Sudan was re-supplying the Chadian insurgents with weapons and vehicles. Weapons and ammunition had been observed being offloaded at local airports and moved to locations within Darfur. Credible information also indicated that the Government continued to support the Janjaweed by providing weapons and vehicles. The Janjaweed/armed militias appeared to have upgraded their modus operandi from horses, camels and AK-47s to land cruisers, pick-up trucks and rocket-propelled grenades.

The Sudan had not implemented the financial sanctions against the four persons designated in resolution 1672(2006) (see p. 295) and had wilfully avoided its commitment under the resolution. Chad had advised the Panel that it was not implementing the resolution, thus posing a major impediment to peace. The Panel was informed that the Darfur rebels were receiving financial and logistical support from the Sudanese diaspora abroad, and it was awaiting information on the matter from Member States.

The Panel recommended, among other things, that Member States providing arms, ammunition, other military equipment and dual-use items to the Sudan should submit a prior notification to the

Committee; an in-depth assessment be undertaken of the customs and border control capacity of the countries bordering Darfur; and airlines and other related agencies informed of the travel ban.

Appointment of experts. On 29 November [S/2006/926] the Secretary-General appointed until 29 September 2007, five persons to the Panel of Experts established pursuant to resolution 1591(2005).

Report of Sanctions Committee (December). On 28 December, the Sanctions Committee Chairman transmitted to the Council a report [S/2006/1045] on the Committee's activities between 1 April and 31 December. The Committee held six informal consultations and submitted to the Council its fourth, fifth and sixth 90-day reports. It had received no additional replies from Member States on steps taken to implement the sanctions.

Financing of Panel of Experts

On 31 January [A/60/585/Add.1], the Secretary-General submitted to the General Assembly estimated requirements relating to the Panel for the period from 1 January to 31 December 2006, amounting to $1,725,700 net ($1,779,200 gross). ACABQ, on 10 March [A/60/7/Add.37], endorsed that amount.

The General Assembly, on 22 December, by section VII of **resolution 61/252** approved the budget in that amount as part of the $326,500,000 budget for special political missions (see p. 1615).

Chad-Sudan

Tripoli Declaration and Agreement. On 14 February [S/2006/103], the Libyan Arab Jamahiriya transmitted to the Security Council President the Tripoli Declaration concerning the situation between Chad and the Sudan and the Tripoli Agreement to Settle the Dispute between the Republic of Chad and the Republic of the Sudan, adopted on 8 February, in Tripoli, at a summit meeting of the Presidents of the two countries, and those of Burkina Faso and the Central African Republic, under the chairmanship of the Leader of the Libyan Arab Jamahiriya. Also participating were the AU Chairperson, the Secretary-General of the Community of the Sahelo-Saharan States and a representative of the UN Secretary-General. By the Agreement, the parties pledged, among other things, to prevent the use of their territories for subversive activities against the sovereignty and territorial integrity of the other country; prohibit the presence of rebel elements from either country in their respective territories; and normalize diplomatic and consular relations. They also agreed to establish a ministerial committee to follow up on the implementation of the Agreement and a peace and security force to secure the common border.

Communications. On 21 March [S/2006/187], the AU Peace and Security Council, in a communiqué on the implementation of the Tripoli Agreement, took note of steps taken to implement it, including the request that AMIS provide security for the observer posts to be established on Sudanese territory, such as air transportation, communication and training assistance. On 13 April [S/2006/256], Chad's Minister for Foreign Affairs and African Integration told the Secretary-General that, despite the Tripoli Agreement, the Khartoum regime persisted in destabilizing Chad. For several days, mercenaries, acting on behalf of the Government of the Sudan, had been waging an offensive against military garrisons in eastern Chad and a Sudanese refugee camp within Chadian territory. On 13 April, the capital city of N'Djamena was attacked. The attackers were repelled and military equipment destroyed or seized. Several mercenaries were captured, including combatants holding Sudanese nationality. Chad urged that measures be taken under the UN Charter to put an end to the aggression against it and to protect Sudanese refugees sheltering in Chadian territory.

Security Council press statement. In a 13 April press statement [SC/8690], the Security Council President said that the situation in Darfur and the mounting tension at the Chad/Sudanese border were considered by Council members, who were concerned about the recent attacks by armed groups in Chad. Council members urged Chad and the Sudan to respect the Tripoli Declaration and Agreement, fully implement the commitments made therein and facilitate the work of the follow-up mechanisms agreed upon.

SECURITY COUNCIL ACTION

On 25 April [meeting 5425], following consultations among Security Council members, the President made **statement S/PRST/2006/19** on behalf of the Council:

> The Security Council welcomes the briefing by the Secretary-General on 18 April 2006 on relations between Chad and the Sudan and endorses his deep concerns over the political and security situation and the instability along Chad's borders with the Sudan, as well as over the possible spillover effects of these crises on neighbouring countries and the entire region. The Council encourages the Secretary-General to continue his consultations with relevant parties, in particular the African Union, on the matter and requests him to closely follow the situation and continue to keep the Council informed.

The Council welcomes the fact-finding mission dispatched by the African Union to Chad and looks forward to its conclusions.

The Council fully endorses the statement of 13 April 2006 made by the Peace and Security Council of the African Union, in which it strongly condemned the rebel attacks against N'Djamena and the eastern town of Adré, and reiterates that any attempt to seize power by force, pursuant to the 1999 Algiers Declaration of the Organization of African Unity, would be regarded as unacceptable.

The Security Council calls for political dialogue and a negotiated solution to the continuing crisis within Chad.

The Council also reaffirms the sovereignty, independence and territorial integrity of Chad and the Sudan, as well as of all States in the region, and calls upon all Members to refrain in their international relations from the threat or use of force against the territorial integrity or political independence of any State, or in any other manner inconsistent with the purposes of the United Nations.

The Council calls upon States in the region to cooperate in ensuring their common stability.

The Council notes with deep concern the deteriorating relations between Chad and the Sudan and urges the Governments of the two countries to abide by their obligations under the Tripoli Agreement of 8 February 2006 and to urgently start implementing the confidence-building measures which have been voluntarily agreed upon. Both the Sudan and Chad must refrain from any actions that violate the border.

The Council is concerned about the situation of the refugees from the Darfur region of the Sudan and from the Central African Republic, as well as the situation of the thousands of internally displaced persons in Chad. It therefore notes the decision by the Government of Chad not to expel the Sudanese refugees and urges the Government of Chad to continue supporting the efforts of humanitarian and relief agencies in the country in accordance with international principles governing the protection of refugees. The Council further reaffirms the right of all displaced persons who wish to do so to return to their homes. It reminds all Governments in the region of their obligation to respect international humanitarian law. In this regard, the Council calls upon donor countries to provide additional resources to respond to the emergency humanitarian situation in both the Sudan and Chad.

Report of Secretary-General. The Secretary-General, in his May report on Darfur [S/2006/306], said that the Security Council had been informed on 26 April that tension along the border between Chad and the Sudan had increased further, after the Government of Chad accused the Sudan of having supported an apparent coup attempt in Chad on 13 April (see above). The Sudan denied any involvement in the incidents in Chad. It was also reported that elements of the Chadian armed opposition had returned to Western Darfur following those events. On 19 April, Beida in Western Darfur was shelled from a position within Chad.

Security Council consideration. During the Security Council's consideration, on 19 May [meeting 5441], of the situation in Chad and the Sudan, the Under-Secretary-General for Humanitarian Affairs and Emergency Relief Coordinator, said that threats against relief workers and the civilian population in eastern Chad were as serious as those in Darfur. A total of 24 vehicles had been hijacked from humanitarian organizations in eastern Chad in the past few months alone. As a result of the insecurity, UN agencies and NGOs had been forced to reduce staff and programmes in many areas, at a time when needs were increasing, particularly those of the 50,000 new internally displaced persons.

Another major concern in eastern Chad was the targeting of refugees and displaced persons, including children, for recruitment by various armed groups. That development was undermining the civilian and humanitarian character of the camps and further increased their vulnerability to attack. The displaced and the civilian population were also being threatened by militia and rebel attacks and by the almost total lack of law and order in the area. One indication of the lawlessness in eastern Chad was the fact that at least 13,000 people had fled from Chad to Darfur in recent weeks to escape the fighting and the attacks.

The situation in eastern Chad was expected to deteriorate further, and President Déby had made it clear that the Government lacked the capacity to ensure the security and protection of the civilian population and the humanitarian organizations that were there to assist them. That meant that the vacuum was being filled by rebels, militias and others, leaving civilians, the camps and relief workers exposed.

Something had to be done urgently to prevent civilians from being attacked and displaced, refugee camps from being increasingly militarized and potentially embroiled in the conflict, and relief workers from being withdrawn. A number of options could be considered, including assistance to the Government of Chad to enable it to meet its security responsibilities.

Security Council mission. The Security Council mission (see p. 279), which visited Chad and the Sudan from 4 to 10 June [S/2006/433], concluded that the future of Darfur was tied to that of the rest of the Sudan and the wider region, and failure to resolve the Darfur crisis would bring serious regional implications. It was important that the Governments of Chad and the Sudan begin dialogue and implement the Tripoli Agreement. The Council announced its intention to review international protection of the camps in Chad and asked the Secretary-General to make recommendations in that regard. It also recommended an increase in humanitarian aid.

Agreement of 26 July. On 10 August [S/2006/637], Chad transmitted to the Security Council President the 26 July Agreement on the normalization of relations between Chad and the Sudan, finalized by the Minister for Foreign Affairs of the Sudan and the Minister for Foreign Affairs and African Integration of Chad; and the official communiqué of the Chadian Government, following the successful conclusion of the mini-summit held in N'Djamena on 8 August concerning the Chad-Sudan dispute. The leaders agreed to put an end to their dispute through the immediate normalization of diplomatic and economic relations.

Security Council action. The Security Council, in resolution 1706(2006) of 31 August (see p. 282), expanded UNMIS mandate with a view to improving security along the borders between the Sudan, Chad and the Central African Republic, including through the establishment of a multinational presence. The Secretary-General was to report on the protection of civilians in refugee and internally displaced persons camps in Chad and on ways to improve the security situation on the Chadian side of the border with the Sudan. The Secretary-General reported to the Council in December (see p. 300).

Reports of Secretary-General. In September [S/2006/764], the Secretary-General reported that relations between Chad and the Sudan had improved considerably. Under the 26 July Agreement on the normalization of relations (above), both countries agreed to create a political commission to follow up on its implementation and a mixed military commission to monitor the situation along their common borders, as well as deploy a mixed military force to their respective border towns. However, Chadian armed opposition groups remained active in Western Darfur. On 23 August, Chadian officials reportedly arrested seven JEM leaders in N'Djamena. On 28 August, in Khartoum, Chad's Minister for Foreign Affairs stated that his Government intended to hand over 17 JEM and 30 SLA-Abdul Wahid leaders to the AU.

In October [S/2006/1041], bilateral relations between Chad and the Sudan deteriorated, as a result of an attack on an SAF post in Karyare and an offensive against the Government of Chad by Chadian armed opposition groups based in Darfur. On 22 and 23 October, a new Chadian rebel group, the Union of Forces for Democracy, presumably based in Darfur, briefly captured the towns of Goz Beida and Am Timam, before retreating. Violent clashes between the rebels and Chadian armed forces ensued on 29 October, close to the Sudanese border. Chad accused the Sudanese air force of bombing several towns along its eastern frontier, which the Government of the Sudan denied. On many occasions, Chadian rebels were reported to have crossed the border with the Sudan.

On 21 November [S/2007/104], Chad and the Sudan met in Tripoli under a peace initiative by the Libyan Arab Jamahiriya. Egypt, Eritrea and the Central African Republic also attended. On 28 November, Chad declared itself in a "state of war" with the Sudan over the latter's alleged support of Chadian rebels. On 12 December, fighting between Chadian armed opposition groups and the Chadian armed forces at Armankul (Western Darfur) resulted in the displacement of the local population.

SECURITY COUNCIL ACTION

On 15 December [meeting 5595], following consultations among Security Council members, the Council President made statement **S/PRST/2006/53** on behalf of the Council:

The Security Council expresses its grave concern regarding the increase in military activities of armed groups in eastern Chad.

The Council strongly condemns all attempts at destabilization by force, including the recent offensive carried out by these groups in Biltine and Ouaddei in eastern Chad, and supports the statement of the Chairperson of the African Union Commission that those attacks against Chad are a blatant violation of the principles stated in the Constitutive Act of the African Union, including respect for the territorial integrity and unity of member States. The Council reaffirms that any attempt to seize power by force is unacceptable. It recalls the importance of an open political dialogue based on constitutional provisions to foster national reconciliation and durable peace in the country.

The Council expresses its concern regarding the threat that the increase in military activities of armed groups in eastern Chad poses for the safety of the civilian population and of humanitarian personnel and the maintenance of their operations in the eastern part of the country. It reiterates that the presence of a large number of refugees places a heavy burden on the host country and the local communities, and emphasizes the need for humanitarian aid to continue reaching the people in need of assistance without any hindrance. It calls upon the Government of Chad to do all it can to protect its civilian population.

The Council reaffirms its deep concern about the worsening security situation in Darfur. It stresses that a peaceful settlement of the conflict in Darfur, in accordance with the Darfur Peace Agreement and relevant Council resolutions, will contribute to restoring security and stability in the region, in particular in Chad and the Central African Republic, and reaffirms its commitment to the sovereignty, unity, independence and territorial integrity of all States in the region.

The Council expresses its concern over the continuing tensions between Chad and the Sudan, urges the two States to abide fully by the obligations they assumed with regard to respect for and securing of their common border in the Tripoli Agreement of 8 February 2006 and in subsequent agreements concluded between them, and once again urges the States of the region to cooperate with a view to ensuring their common stability.

The Council recalls that it looks forward to a prompt report of the Secretary-General with recommendations, as requested in previous relevant Council resolutions, focusing on ways of improving security conditions on the Chadian side of the border with the Sudan and the monitoring of trans-border activities between Chad, the Sudan and the Central African Republic, bearing in mind the need to foster regional peace and stability.

Report of Secretary-General pursuant to resolution 1706(2006)

In response to Security Council resolution 1706(2006) (see p. 282), the Secretary-General submitted a December report [S/2006/1019] on the multidisciplinary technical assistance mission to Chad and the Central African Republic to investigate the feasibility of establishing a UN operation in the region. The mission, which visited Chad and the Central African Republic from 21 November to 3 December, was not able to visit the north-eastern Central African Republic and eastern Chad, the regions bordering Darfur, due to the security situation. The report provided an overview of the political, security, humanitarian and human rights situations in both countries, in particular, the protection of civilians in refugee camps and internally displaced persons locations in Chad. It also outlined preliminary options on the mandate, structure and concept of operations of a miltinational UN presence in both countries.

In Chad, the mission found that the 8 February Tripoli Agreement (see p. 297) and the 26 July N'Djamena Agreement (see p. 299) had not been implemented and relations between Chad and the Sudan had deteriorated considerably, with both countries accusing each other of supporting rebel groups and/or mercenaries seeking to destabilize their respective Governments. Rebel and criminal activities, as well as inter-ethnic clashes had increased in eastern Chad. On 7 November, Chad called for the limited deployment of an international civilian force to ensure security in the refugee camps in the east of the country and guarantee their neutrality, made up of gendarmes from African countries, and paid for by European countries and the United Nations. On 15 November, Chad alleged that genocide was being committed at the Chad-Sudanese border and accused the Sudan of instigating a "scorched-earth" policy in Darfur and eastern Chad. It called on the international community to deploy a UN force along the border with the Sudan and to effectively implement resolution 1706(2006).

As at November, Chad was hosting 232,000 Sudanese refugees in camps, most of which were located about 50 kilometres away from the border region adjacent to Darfur. In November, the Government of Chad decided that the camps should be located some 500 kilometres further inside the country, and appealed for international assistance to do so. The aim was to ensure the safety of refugees and put to rest the accusations by the Sudan that N'Djamena encouraged Sudanese rebels to use the refugee camps as a rear base. The Government and the Office of the United Nations High Commissioner for Refugees established a technical working group to identify alternative sites.

The mission found that the deployment and sustainment of any UN presence in Chad and the Central African Republic would pose enormous logistical challenges, as the terrain was difficult, weather conditions extreme and infrastructure poor. It therefore proposed two options: a monitoring mission to observe the situation in the border area, provide early warning and contribute towards improving security; or a larger monitoring and protection mission, which would, in addition, deter attacks, and provide protection, within its capabilities, to civilians under imminent threat. The latter option would have a division-sized military contingent and a police component.

The Secretary-General observed that, as there were limited prospects for a meaningful dialogue and reconciliation process between the Governments and the rebels in the two countries, and no signs of a credible and inclusive political process in Darfur, the deployment of a UN peacekeeping force in eastern Chad and the north-eastern Central African Republic would face considerable risks. Unless all the parties concerned were to agree to a ceasefire and engage in an intra- and inter-State dialogue aimed at a political solution, a UN force would be operating in the midst of continuing hostilities and would have no clear exit strategy. The conditions for an effective UN peacekeeping operation did not, therefore, seem to be in place.

However, should the Security Council decide to pursue the idea, it should consider authorizing the deployment of a robust monitoring and protection mission as suggested in the second option (see above). The decision to deploy such a robust UN monitoring and protection mission should be contingent upon a cessation of hostilities and an agreement by all parties to allow the induction of the force, facilitate its operations and fully comply with its mandate. The Governments concerned should engage each other and their respective opposition groups, including armed rebel movements, in a process of dialogue and reconciliation aimed at reaching a political solution. In addition, the Council should ascertain that Member States were prepared to make available the necessary troops and police, and to assist in addressing the logistical challenges. In the meantime, the Council could authorize the dispatch of an advance team to the two countries to collect more information on the situation in the border areas, explore the possibilities for a political agreement, and conduct further detailed planning and logistic preparations, so as to enable the Secretary-General to submit more comprehensive recommendations to the Council.

Somalia

At the beginning of 2006, the prospects for returning Somalia to peace and stability improved, as efforts to end the long-standing political impasse within Somalia's transitional federal institutions resulted in the signing, on 5 January, by Somali President Abdullahi Yusuf and the Speaker of the Transitional Federal Parliament, Sheikh Sharif Sheikh Adan, of the Aden Declaration, in which they pledged to end their differences, relocate the transitional federal institutions to Baidoa, 140 miles northwest of Mogadishu, and hold the first-ever session of the Transitional Federal Parliament. The agreement raised hopes for a resolution of the clan and faction-based conflict that had plagued the country for more than 15 years.

However, political progress was accompanied by increasingly fierce fighting in the capital, Mogadishu, between militias of the Islamic Courts and those of the Alliance for the Restoration of Peace and Counter-Terrorism. Fighting erupted in March and escalated in May, leading to the deaths of at least 220 people. The Security Council in May condemned the clashes and called for an immediate ceasefire. In early June, the Union of Islamic Courts took control of Mogadishu. The League of Arab States arranged a meeting in Khartoum on 22 June, where President Yusuf and representatives of the Union of Islamic Courts agreed to pursue dialogue. The Union gained control of eight of Somalia's 18 administrative regions, and on 26 June, its leaders announced the creation of the Supreme Council of the Islamic Courts. On 4 September, at the second round of peace talks in Khartoum, the parties agreed to reconstitute a joint Somali national army and police and discuss political, power-sharing and security issues at a third round of talks to be held in October.

Clashes between Union militia and forces allied to the Transitional Federal Government renewed on 21 October. On 6 December, as requested by the AU and the Intergovernmental Authority for Development (IGAD), the Security Council authorized the establishment of an AU/IGAD protection and training mission in Somalia to help defend the Transitional Federal Institutions in Baidoa. The Union demanded the withdrawal of Ethiopian troops, which were reportedly assisting the Government, and on 12 December, gave Ethiopia seven days to do so. The Security Council, on 22 December, voiced grave concern at the intensified fighting, as the Transitional Federal Government forces, supported by Ethiopian ground and air forces, engaged with Union forces on a 400-kilometre front. Within days, the Transitional Federal Government/Ethiopian coalition had retaken several towns that had fallen to Union forces, and took control of Mogadishu on 28 December.

The United Nations Political Office in Somalia continued to fulfil its expanded role in Somalia in advancing the cause of peace and national reconciliation. The Office, headed by the Special Representative of the Secretary-General, remained in contact with the parties and worked to get them to resume peace talks.

The Monitoring Group on Somalia, charged with investigating violations of the arms embargo imposed on the country, reported on the activities of the Transitional Federal Government, the Mogadishu-based opposition groups and the militias of the Islamic fundamentalists, and all those who violated the embargo. In May, the Security Council expressed its intention to consider specific action to improve implementation and compliance with the sanctions imposed by resolution 733(1992) [YUN 1992, p. 199]. At the request of the Council, the Secretary-General, in May and December, re-established the Group, each time for a period of six months, in order to continue its functions.

National reconciliation process and security situation

Aden Declaration (January). On 9 January, Somalia transmitted to the Security Council President the Aden Declaration [S/2006/14], signed in Aden, Yemen, on 5 January, by Abdullahi Yusuf Ahmed, President of the Federal Republic of Somalia, and Sharif Hassan Sheikh Adan, Speaker of Somalia's Transitional Federal Parliament. With a view to reconciling and solving the differences of opinion among members of the institutions of State [YUN 2005, p. 344], the two leaders agreed to respect the principles and norms of the Transitional Federal Charter and to hold a session of Parliament within 30 days. They called upon members of Parliament and of the Transitional Federal Government to put aside their differences and unite in the interest of the nation, and called upon the international community to support efforts to convene the first session of the Transitional Federal Parliament inside the country, at a venue to be agreed upon.

On 16 January [S/2006/37], the EU welcomed the Aden Declaration and called upon the members of Parliament and the Government to respond positively to the initiative. It reaffirmed its willingness to provide logistical and financial support to facilitate the work of the Parliament.

AU decision. The AU, at its January Summit (Khartoum, the Sudan, 11-24 January), welcomed the signing of the Aden Declaration. Recalling the decision of its Peace and Security Council on the deployment of an IGAD peace support mission, to be followed by an AU peace support mission, the Summit asked the UN Security Council for an exemption of the arms embargo imposed by resolution 733(1992) [YUN 1992, p. 199] to facilitate the envisaged deployment.

Report of Secretary-General (February). In his February report on the situation in Somalia [S/2006/122], submitted pursuant to the Security Council presidential statement S/PRST/2001/30 [YUN 2001, p. 210], the Secretary-General said that the President, the Speaker and the Prime Minister met again in Nairobi, Kenya, on 14 January, and were joined the following day by Prime Minister Gedi for their first meeting since the May 2005 split within the leadership of the transitional federal institutions, and later with Kenyan President Mwai Kibaki. At those meetings, they underscored their commitment to the Aden Declaration and to the early convening of Parliament. At a meeting with François Lonsény Fall, the Secretary-General's Special Representative for Somalia, the Somali President and Prime Minister requested his assistance in securing a waiver of the UN arms embargo for the training of the Somali national police and army.

After consultations among the leaders of the transitional federal institutions, the Speaker announced, on 30 January, that Baidoa had been selected as the venue of the first session of the Transitional Federal Parliament inside Somalia, to be held on 26 February. There were reports that Prime Minister Gedi had concerns regarding the choice of Baidoa, and the President called upon the international community to help bring the Prime Minister on board. The Secretary-General's Special Representative and a group of ambassadors met in Jawhar with Prime Minister Gedi on 1 February. The Prime Minister expressed concern about the security situation in Baidoa, but reaffirmed his commitment to the Aden Declaration and stated his willingness to work towards resolving outstanding issues with the President.

Insecurity remained a significant problem for aid agencies in much of the country. Inter- and intra-clan clashes over land, water and grazing rights resulted in many civilian casualties, especially in central and southern Somalia, making humanitarian access difficult. Reports indicated continuing violations of the arms embargo, while increasing attacks on ships and other acts of piracy hampered UN relief activities. Piracy had become a major problem along the east coast at Somalia, where more than 34 attacks on commercial shipping had been reported between March 2005 and January 2006. On 21 January 2006, a United States Navy warship captured 10 suspected Somali pirates off the coast of Somalia and handed them over to Kenyan authorities, which had started legal proceedings to prosecute them. Extremist activities were reportedly increasing in Mogadishu and in Lower Juba, and fighting increased between Shariah Court militias and those of other factions in north Mogadishu. Some militias were suspected of having links to Al-Qaida operatives

The humanitarian situation deteriorated significantly, due to the worst drought in a decade. The number of people in need of urgent assistance rose to 1.7 million. In addition, some 400,000 internally displaced persons continued to need assistance and protection. In February, UNDP Somali Emergency Budgetary Support Project planned to pay allowances to members of Parliament and to help establish a Parliament secretariat for its first session. UNDP also funded four policy studies on key civil service issues through its Governance and Financial Services Programme.

The Secretary-General observed that the signing of the Aden Declaration created encouraging prospects for reconciliation among the leaders of the transitional federal institutions. Those leaders faced complex political and security challenges, including the development of a national security and stabilization plan, the promotion of reconciliation and the urgent need to improve the humanitarian situation and the quality of life. The international community should continue supporting the political reconciliation efforts, especially the convening of the Transitional Federal Parliament.

EU statement (March). On 3 March [S/2006/166], the EU welcomed the opening session of the Transitional Federal Parliament in Baidoa on 26 February, and reiterated its intention to maintain its political, moral and material support for the transitional federal institutions.

SECURITY COUNCIL ACTION

On 15 March [meeting 5387], following consultations among Security Council members, the President made statement **S/PRST/2006/11** on behalf of the Council:

The Security Council reaffirms all previous statements by its President and its resolutions concerning the situation in Somalia, in particular the statements by its President of 14 July and 9 November 2005.

The Council welcomes the report of the Secretary-General of 21 February 2006 and reaffirms its commitment to a comprehensive and lasting settlement of the situation in Somalia and its respect for the sovereignty, territorial integrity, political independence and unity of Somalia, consistent with the purposes and principles of the Charter of the United Nations.

The Council commends the efforts of the President of the Somali Republic and the Speaker of the Transitional Federal Parliament towards reconciliation and dialogue, particularly the signing, with the facilitation of the Government of Yemen, of the Aden Declaration on 5 January 2006, which culminated in the convening of the first session of the Transitional Federal Parliament inside Somalia, in Baidoa on 26 February 2006. The Council encourages all leaders and members of the transitional federal institutions to continue their efforts towards inclusive dialogue and consensus-building within the framework of the transitional federal institutions and in accordance with the Transitional Federal Charter of the Somali Republic adopted in February 2004.

The Council welcomes and supports the convening of the first session of the Transitional Federal Parliament and looks forward to sustained sessions of the Transitional Federal Parliament as Somali leaders seek peacefully to resolve their differences. The Council calls upon the Transitional Federal Parliament to promote peace and reconciliation in its work towards implementing the Transitional Federal Charter and encourages the members of the Transitional Federal Parliament to use this opportunity to address key issues of national concern. In this regard, the Council urges the members of the transitional federal institutions to continue to organize their work in accordance with the Transitional Federal Charter, such as the formation of independent commissions and parliamentary committees, which will provide a framework for addressing the complex and divisive issues of the transitional period.

The Council reiterates the urgent need for the rapid finalization of an agreed national security and stabilization plan, to include a comprehensive and verifiable ceasefire agreement, as well as plans for the restoration of public safety and security institutions and the implementation of disarmament, demobilization and reintegration.

The Council reiterates its strong support for the Special Representative of the Secretary-General for Somalia and calls upon all Member States to provide their full and active support in this regard.

The Council remains seriously concerned over the continued intermittent fighting and armed violence, kidnapping and other use of force, particularly in recent incidents in the capital Mogadishu and other parts of Somalia, which have caused loss of life among innocent civilians and have the potential to undermine the current progress achieved by the leaders of the transitional federal institutions. The Council calls upon all the parties to cease all hostilities and resolve their differences peacefully in the spirit of the Aden Declaration through the framework of the transitional federal institutions.

The Council expresses its growing concern over the situation of 1.7 million Somalis in a state of humanitarian emergency or suffering from serious malnutrition, severe livelihood distress and the rising civil and food insecurity in parts of southern Somalia. The Council urges all Somali leaders to ensure complete and unhindered humanitarian access, as well as provide guarantees for the safety and security of the humanitarian aid workers in Somalia. The Council emphasizes the importance of the international commitment and coordinated support for improving the humanitarian situation.

The Council commends the neighbouring countries, the Intergovernmental Authority on Development, the African Union, the League of Arab States, the European Union, the Organization of the Islamic Conference and concerned Member States for their keen interest and persistent efforts in support of the peace, reconciliation and recovery process in Somalia. The Council encourages them to continue to use their influence in support of the transitional federal institutions, in particular to help them in their efforts to move ahead on the key issues of security and national reconciliation.

The Council welcomes the African Union summit decision on Somalia of 25 January 2006, including the possible deployment of an Intergovernmental Authority on Development Peace Support Mission to Somalia, to be followed by an African Union Peace Support Mission. In the event that a national security and stabilization plan includes the need for a peace support mission, the Council reiterates that it expects the African Union and the Intergovernmental Authority to work out a detailed mission plan in close coordination with and with the broad consensus of the transitional federal institutions and consistent with the national security and stabilization plan. The Council stands ready to consider an exemption to the arms embargo imposed against Somalia by Council resolution 733(1992) on the basis of such a mission plan.

The Council takes note of resolution A.979(24), adopted on 23 November 2005 at the twenty-fourth session of the biennial Assembly of the International Maritime Organization, concerning the increasing incidents of piracy and armed robbery against ships in waters off the coast of Somalia. The Council encourages Member States whose naval vessels and military aircraft operate in international waters and airspace adjacent to the coast of Somalia to be vigilant to any incident of piracy therein and to take appropriate action to protect merchant shipping, in particular the transportation of humanitarian aid, against any such act, in line with relevant international law. In this regard, the Council welcomes the communiqué of the meeting of the Council of Ministers of the Intergovernmental Authority on Development, held in Jawhar, Somalia, on 29 November 2005, in which the Council of Ministers decided to coordinate its strategies and action plans to face this common challenge in close collaboration with the international community. The Security Council further urges cooperation among all States, particularly regional States, and active prosecution of piracy offences.

The Council takes note of the annual report of the Security Council Committee established pursuant to resolution 751(1992) concerning Somalia and the midterm briefing of the Monitoring Group on Somalia to the Committee. The Council condemns the increased inflow of weapons into Somalia and the continuous violations of the United Nations arms embargo, and further reminds all States of their obligations to comply fully with the measures imposed by resolution 733(1992) and urges them to take all necessary steps to hold violators accountable. Continued violations of these measures prevent the establishment of a stable and secure environment and undermine the efforts of those who seek to establish peace in Somalia.

The Council reaffirms its full support to the peace process in Somalia and welcomes the commitment of the United Nations to assist in this regard. In this connection, the Council encourages the transitional federal institutions and the international partners to reinvigorate the Coordination and Monitoring Committee in the interest of a more effective international engagement in the peace, reconciliation and recovery process in Somalia.

Fighting in Mogadishu

The political progress in Somalia was accompanied by some of the worst fighting for nearly a decade in Mogadishu, pitting militias loyal to the leaders of the Alliance for the Restoration of Peace and Counter-Terrorism (ARPCT) against those of the Shariah Courts. ARPCT, formed on 18 February and comprising Government ministers, powerful businessmen and faction leaders, had the stated aim of uprooting terrorist elements reportedly linked to some of Mogadishu's Shariah Courts, which, in the absence of a functioning central or city government, provided basic security and social services in the city. While not all of the Shariah Courts had extremist leanings, some had been accused of being responsible for assassinations, terrorist attacks, and harbouring foreign terrorism suspects. However, leaders of the Transitional Federal Government distanced themselves from ARPCT, and urged them to go to Baidoa to work with them in the fight against terrorism.

Fighting erupted in Mogadishu on 22 March, when militia loyal to Abukar Umar Adani, believed to be the main financier of the Shariah Courts, attacked militia loyal to Bashir Raghe Shirar, a prominent businessman and ARPCT member. The fighting was seen as a continuation of the clashes that had taken place in January between the same militias for the control of the port of El-Ma'an. The fighting, which lasted four days, resulted in the death of at least 60 people, most of them civilians. Another intermittent round of clashes continued throughout April, with neither side achieving substantial success, and erupted again on 6 May in North Mogadishu, between militia loyal to the Chairman of the Union of Islamic Courts, Sheikh Sharif Sheikh Ahmed, and others loyal to ARPCT member Nur Hassan Ali "Nur Diqle", leading to the displacement of 17,000 people. Both sides used heavy weapons indiscriminately, killing at least 160 people, mostly civilians. At least 60 people were reported killed in renewed fighting between 24 and 27 May. The fighting ended on 2 June, with the Courts' militias having made significant territorial gains, especially in central Mogadishu. Some ARPCT leaders fled to Jowhar, while others were reported to have regrouped in north Mogadishu. On 4 June, Sharia Courts militias were reported to have taken control of Balad, a town on the road to Jowhar.

Meanwhile, at a Summit held in Nairobi on 20 March, IGAD Heads of State and Government reiterated their decision to deploy a peace support mission to Somalia and urged the UN Security Council to approve a partial lifting of the embargo, not only for the proposed mission but also to enable the Transitional Federal Government to raise a national army and police force.

Security Council press statements (May). In a 16 May press statement [SC/8722], Security Council members expressed concern at the reports of violence in Mogadishu, leading to a large number of casualties, particularly among civilians, and the displacement of thousands of people. They called for an unconditional and immediate ceasefire by the warring parties so as to allow the resumption of humanitarian activities, the rescue of survivors and the recovery of the deceased. They urged all parties to return to dialogue and reconciliation and work within the framework of the transitional federal institutions.

In another statement of 31 May [SC/8735] condemning the resumption of fighting in Mogadishu, Security Council members again called for an immediate and unconditional ceasefire and urged both sides to find solutions within the framework of the Transitional Federal Charter. They reiterated the urgent need for a rapid finalization of an agreed national security and stabilization plan, as called for in presidential statement S/PRST/2006/11 (see p. 303), and called upon Member States to strictly comply with the arms embargo.

Further political developments

Report of Secretary-General (June). Reporting in June [S/2006/418], the Secretary-General said that, following the first extraordinary session of the Transitional Federal Parliament in Baidoa on 26 February, the transitional federal institutions addressed some of the key differences that had divided the leadership and paralysed the political process. Differences over the interim location of the institutions were resolved on 22 April, when the Parliament endorsed Baidoa as the interim seat of the Transitional Federal Government and Parliament. The Parliament established 14 parliamentary committees and set up a national constitutional commission. At a meeting in Baidoa on 21 May, the Council of Ministers adopted the draft national security and stabilization plan, which was submitted to Parliament for consideration. The plan provided for the deployment of an IGAD/AU peace support mission, the details of which were to be prepared in consultation with those institutions.

However, concerns remained about insecurity in Baidoa. On 13 April, an agreement was signed in Wajid, formally ending the dispute between factions of the former Rahanweyn Resistance Army, and reconciling Hassan Mohamed Nur "Shattigudud" with a rival group headed by Mohammed Ibrahim "Habsade". Years of fighting in and around Baidoa had generated a large number of freelance militias without allegiance to any faction leader. The continued activity of those militia posed a significant security challenge to Baidoa and the surrounding areas. Efforts by local leaders to dismantle checkpoints and restore order had limited success. There was an urgent need for those leaders to agree on an appropriate administrative structure and to relocate the freelance and other factional militias to camps outside the city. Some international assistance had been provided for that purpose and the United Nations planned to begin a cash-for-work programme to support the demobilization of some of the encamped militiamen.

The central and southern regions of the country also remained insecure due to the absence of formal State structures, clan disputes and political and resource-related disputes. In Kismayo, which had been relatively calm, the security situation became fragile owing to the emergence of localized disputes along the Lower Juba Valley and a spillover of tension from Mogadishu. However, in the north, "Somaliland" remained relatively peaceful and continued to make substantial progress in development and reconstruction, while intensifying efforts to obtain international recognition. Neighbouring "Puntland" was generally stable, although disagreements remained within the administration. The dispute between "Somaliland" and "Puntland" over the Sool and Sanaag areas continued.

The human rights situation continued to be of great concern. Perpetrators of human rights abuses acted with impunity. Violence against women was endemic and the rights of minority groups remained unprotected. There was no functional administration of justice. Elders dispensed justice through the practice of compensation. In Mogadishu, the Shariah Courts had established their own private detention centres, inaccessible to defence lawyers and human rights defenders. Somali human rights organizations continued to operate in a context of insecurity and fear.

The United Nations and donors provided support for the first session of Parliament in Baidoa, including by rehabilitating the Parliament's facilities and paying stipends to its members. UN programmes and agencies carried out training programmes and workshops for prospective Supreme Court judges, civil society leaders, civil servants and youth, as well as vaccination campaigns against polio, measles and tetanus.

Fighting in Mogadishu and the continuing insecurity in Baidoa risked undermining the significant gains in Somalia's political process, the Secretary-General observed. The priorities were to achieve an enduring ceasefire in Mogadishu, strengthen the transitional federal institutions, and build a bridge between Mogadishu and Baidoa. Effective transitional federal institutions would enable Somalia to strengthen its internal security and deal with such threats as terrorism. There was an urgent need to assist in the establishment of a district administration in Baidoa to provide basic services and enforce public security. Greater international commitment and coordinated support were also needed to alleviate the plight of Somalis and improve the humanitarian situation.

Consolidation of Islamic Courts control of Mogadishu

Report of Secretary-General. After defeating the ARPCT forces in June, the Union of Islamic Courts had consolidated their control over Mogadishu and restored a semblance of security, said the Secretary-General in his October report [S/2006/838]. The fall of Mogadishu was followed by the extension of the Union of Islamic Courts' authority into the regions of Middle Shabelle, Hiran, parts of Galgudud and Mudug, the traditional heartland of the Hawiye clan. The Islamic Courts' influence also extended to the Lower Shabelle and the Lower Juba region. On 26 June, the leaders of the Union of the Islamic Courts announced the creation of the Supreme Council of the Islamic Courts, comprising a 90-member legislative committee, and an executive committee. The rapid expansion of the Courts' influence posed a threat to the transitional federal institutions, which already faced difficulties in extending their authority beyond Baidoa. The Islamic Courts reopened Mogadishu International Airport on 15 July and the main seaport on 23 August; both had been out of operation for more than a decade.

To reduce tension between the Transitional Federal Government and the Courts, the League of Arab States organized a meeting in Khartoum on 22 June, attended by the three main leaders of the transitional federal institutions—the President, the Prime Minister and the Speaker—and by a lower-level delegation of the Islamic Courts. By a communiqué [S/2006/442] issued on the same day, following a meeting of the League's Ministerial Committee on Somalia, in Khartoum, the Somali parties, Somali President Yusuf and representatives of the Union of Islamic Courts conveyed their agreement to recognize the legitimacy of the Somali Transitional Government; recognize the Union of Islamic Courts; continue dialogue without preconditions; bring war criminals to justice; remain committed to the cessation of military campaigns; address security and political issues at the next round of talks on 15 July; and form technical committees to make proposals on those issues. The Committee appealed for rapid assistance, including urgent humanitarian assistance.

EU statements. On 29 June, [S/2006/486], the EU welcomed the agreement, as a basis for negotiation between the two sides and reaffirmed its readiness to provide political and material support.

In a 14 July letter to the Secretary-General [S/2006/561], the EU condemned the fighting in Mogadishu and expressed support for the efforts of the League of Arab States to facilitate dialogue between the Transitional Federal Government and the Union of Islamic Courts.

Soon after signing the agreement (see above), however, each side accused the other of violating it, and the Courts accused the Transitional Federal Government of inviting Ethiopian troops into the country. As a result, the second round of talks scheduled for 15 July, was postponed. The Special Representative, meeting on 25 July in Baidoa with the three leaders of the transitional federal institutions, and later that day in Mogadishu with the head of the executive committee of the Supreme Council of the Islamic Courts, encouraged all parties to send a delegation to Khartoum for the second round of talks.

SECURITY COUNCIL ACTION

On 13 July [meeting 5486], following consultations among Security Council members, the President made statement **S/PRST/2006/31** on behalf of the Council:

> The Security Council reaffirms all previous statements by its President and its resolutions concerning the situation in Somalia, in particular the statement by its President of 15 March 2006.
>
> The Council reiterates its commitment to a comprehensive and lasting settlement of the situation in Somalia and its respect for the sovereignty, territorial integrity, political independence and unity of Somalia, consistent with the purposes and principles of the Charter of the United Nations.
>
> The Council reiterates its strong support for the Special Representative of the Secretary-General for Somalia, Mr. François Fall. The Council encourages Mr. Fall and other United Nations agencies and offices to actively engage in the region to promote peace and stability. It calls upon all Member States to provide him their full support in this regard.
>
> The Council supports the Transitional Federal Government and Transitional Federal Parliament as the internationally recognized authorities to restore peace, stability and governance to Somalia. It notes the importance for stability in Somalia of broad-based and representative institutions and of an inclusive political process, as envisaged in the Transitional Federal Charter.
>
> The Council welcomes the agreement reached in Khartoum on 22 June 2006 between the Transitional Federal Government and the Islamic Courts, transmitted to the President of the Council on 29 June 2006. The Council commends the League of Arab States for facilitating the talks. The Council condemns the recent fighting in Mogadishu and requests all parties to adhere to the ceasefire agreed to on 22 June 2006. In this regard, the Council emphasizes the importance of dialogue between the transitional federal institutions and the Islamic Courts.
>
> The Council therefore urges all parties involved in this dialogue to engage constructively at the next round of talks, scheduled for 15 July 2006, when it looks forward to further progress in pursuit of a lasting political process.
>
> The Council requests all parties inside and outside of Somalia to refrain from action that could provoke or perpetuate violence and violations of human rights, endanger the ceasefire and political process, or further damage the humanitarian situation.
>
> The Council expresses its grave concern at the deteriorating humanitarian situation in Somalia, and demands that all Somali leaders ensure complete and unhindered humanitarian access, as well as providing guarantees for the safety and security of the humanitarian aid workers in Somalia.
>
> The Council commends the African Union and the Intergovernmental Authority on Development for their continuing efforts to promote peace and stability in Somalia and the region. The Council notes their meetings held on 19 June and 28 and 29 June 2006, and welcomes the role of the fact-finding mission of the African Union, the Intergovernmental Authority on Development, the League of Arab States and the European Union to Somalia from 5 to 7 July 2006 in promoting peace, stability and a political process.
>
> The Council welcomes the meeting of the Heads of State and Government of the African Union, held in Banjul on 5 July 2006, and notes the request made at that meeting for the Council to consider an exemption to the arms embargo imposed on Somalia by its resolution 733(1992) of 23 January 1992, to pave the way for the possible deployment of a peace support mission and to help to facilitate the re-establishment of the national security forces of Somalia.
>
> The Council states its willingness, if it judges that a peace support mission would contribute to peace and stability in Somalia, to consider the above request for a peace support mission, on the basis of a detailed mission plan from the Intergovernmental Authority on Development or the African Union.
>
> The Council welcomes the fact that the Transitional Federal Government and the Transitional Federal Parliament were able to agree on 14 June 2006 to adopt the National Security and Stabilization Plan for Somalia. The Council believes that the adoption of a security plan is an important step towards providing a framework for effective security sector reform in Somalia, in order to help to deliver peace for all Somalis.
>
> The Council expresses its readiness to consider a limited modification of the arms embargo to enable the transitional federal institutions, on the basis of a sustainable peace

process, to develop Somalia's security sector and national institutions capable of responding to security issues.

The Council emphasizes, however, the continued contribution made to Somalia's peace and security by the arms embargo, and calls upon all to comply with it. The Council reiterates its intention to consider urgently how to strengthen the effectiveness of the arms embargo.

The Council welcomes the outcome of the first meeting of the International Contact Group on Somalia.

Further peace efforts

Internal squabbles prevented the Transitional Federal Government from establishing its own authority, the Secretary-General said in his October report [S/2006/838]. On 26 July, a number of parliamentarians, including ministers, criticized the leadership style of Prime Minister Gedi and some ministers subsequently resigned. On 30 July, the Prime Minister narrowly survived a parliamentary no-confidence vote. The vote, however, did not resolve the crisis and more ministers resigned. On 5 August, an Ethiopian delegation, led by the Minister for Foreign Affairs, Seyoum Mesfin, arrived in Baidoa on a mediation mission, which led to the signing of a 6 August memorandum of understanding aimed at ending the crisis. On 10 August, the President dissolved the Government and asked Prime Minister Gedi to appoint a leaner, better qualified cabinet. On 18 August, in accordance with the memorandum of understanding, the Prime Minister announced a new Council of Ministers comprising 31 ministers, five ministers of state and 31 assistant ministers. On 18 September, the Parliament endorsed the new Government by 174 votes in favour to 25 against.

The second round of peace talks, which opened in Khartoum on 2 September, under the auspices of the League of Arab States, led to the signing of the 4 September agreement, in which the Transitional Federal Government and the Supreme Council of the Islamic Courts pledged to reconstitute the Somali national army and national police force and reintegrate the forces of the Islamic Courts, the Transitional Federal Government and other armed militias once an agreement on a political programme was in place; discuss political, power-sharing and security issues in a third round of talks, to be held on 30 October in Khartoum; establish a joint committee to follow-up on the agreement; and form a technical committee, consisting of the Arab League presidency (the Sudan), its General secretariat, and Committee on Somalia, and representatives from the Transitional Federal Government and the Islamic Courts. Following the second round of talks, the European Commission offered to establish a task force to facilitate inter-Somali dialogue, which would work with the League of Arab States to provide technical and financial support to the transitional federal institutions and the Islamic Courts for the functioning of the follow-up committees envisaged in the 4 September agreement.

The Secretary-General's Special Representative maintained contact with the Transitional Federal Government and the Supreme Council of the Islamic Courts, urging them to refrain from any provocative actions and to find a negotiated solution. As requested by the Security Council on 13 July, in presidential statement S/PRST/2006/31 (see p. 306), he visited Djibouti, Egypt, Eritrea, Ethiopia, the Sudan, Uganda and Yemen for consultations with the leaders of those countries.

Meeting in Brussels on 17 July, and in Stockholm on 29 August, the International Contact Group on Somalia (Italy, Norway, Sweden, the United Republic of Tanzania, the United Kingdom, the United States) together with the AU, EU, IGAD, the League of Arab States and the United Nations, urged the parties to engage in consultations with a view to resolving their differences, build confidence and address issues of common concern.

On 5 September, a summit meeting of IGAD member States endorsed the deployment plan for the IGAD-led support mission for Somalia, which was approved by the AU Peace and Security Council on 13 September. However, the Supreme Council of the Islamic Courts opposed the proposed peace mission, and in a 24 September letter to UN Security Council members, urged the Council to maintain the arms embargo and to give the Khartoum negotiations a chance.

Security in Baidoa remained unstable. On 28 July, the Minister for Constitutional Affairs, Abdallah Deerow Isaq, was murdered while leaving a mosque after Friday prayers. On 4 September, the Transitional Federal Government police clashed with local clan militias over control of the airport, killing at least 10 militiamen. On 8 September, the Transport Minister, Mohamed Ibrahim Habsade, a former Baidoa faction leader, called on the Transitional Federal Government to relocate from Baidoa, saying that it was no longer welcome there. Following the murder of an Italian nun and her bodyguard in Mogadishu on 17 September, the attempt on the life of the President (see below) and threats against UN staff, the United Nations, in September, relocated its international staff from Baidoa to Nairobi and suspended all missions to Mogadishu. President Yusuf narrowly survived an assassination attempt on 18 September, when a car bomb exploded as he was leaving Parliament. The international community, the transitional federal institutions and the Supreme Council of the Islamic Courts condemned the assassination attempt, in which at least 11 people died. The police arrested three suspects on 29 September.

As some 1.8 million people, mostly along the southern Gedo region and Juba Valley, were in need of critical assistance, the Humanitarian Coordinator for Somalia led three missions to Mogadishu, meeting with leaders of the Islamic Courts, business leaders and civil society groups. The outflow of refugees into Kenya continued unabated, exacerbated by insecurity and the effects of the drought. Since January, some 25,000 new Somali refugees had been registered at the Dadaab refugee camp in Kenya, most of them fleeing clashes between the Islamic Courts and warlord militias in Mogadishu and Kismayo, which came under control of the forces of the Islamic Courts on 24 September.

The seasonal smuggling of Ethiopian migrants and Somali nationals to Yemen from ports in "Puntland" also continued. Reports indicated that since the beginning of 2006, close to 12,000 Somalis and Ethiopians had arrived in Yemen from Bossaso.

The United Nations supported a seminar on the re-establishment of the judiciary, the training and equipping of police cadets in Baidoa, a demobilization and reintegration initiative in "Somaliland" and "Puntland" and a civilian weapons registration project in Hargeisa, the de facto capital of "Somaliland". From June to September, UNICEF provided training on education to 1,779 head teachers and training on peacebuilding to 4,000 teachers.

As later reported by the Secretary-General [S/2007/115], the military forces of the Transitional Federal Government and Ethiopia in December, dislodged the Islamic Courts, which had gained control of eight of Somalia's 18 administrative regions. Clashes between Islamic Courts militia and forces allied to the Transitional Federal Government began on 21 October near the town of Buale, Middle Juba region. Other clashes followed around the town of Burhakaba in the Bay region, 60 kilometres south-east of Baidoa. Remnants of the Islamic Courts were pursued in southern Somalia by forces of the Transitional Federal Government and Ethiopia.

The third round of peace talks was postponed due to differences between the parties. The Islamic Courts demanded the withdrawal of Ethiopian troops from Somalia and objected to Kenya serving as co-chair of the talks on behalf of IGAD. Transitional Federal Parliament Speaker and a number of parliamentarians, who had travelled to Mogadishu, reached an agreement with the Islamic Courts on resuming dialogue, but the Government refused to accept it, as the Speaker had not consulted with the Parliament or the Government. The Special Representative sought to mend the growing rift between the Speaker and the Government and encouraged the Government and the Islamic Courts to return to the Khartoum talks.

The Islamic Courts stated that the deployment of foreign forces was tantamount to an invasion of Somalia by Ethiopia. Intermittent clashes followed in the Bay region, and on 7 December the Islamic Courts took the town of Idale, and reached Daynune, a Government military training camp 30 kilometres south of Baidoa. Both sides accused each other of relying on support from foreign elements. The Defence Chief of the Islamic Courts, on 12 December, gave Ethiopia seven days to withdraw its forces. On 20 December, heavy fighting broke out once more in southern Somalia's Bay region and spread to the central Galkayo, Hiran and Middle Shabelle administrative regions, where Islamic Courts forces confronted warlords of the former ARPCT, who were allied with the Transitional Federal Government. On 23 December, Islamic Courts leaders called for jihad against the Ethiopian troops and appealed to foreign fighters for support. Ethiopia's Prime Minister, Meles Zenawi, on 24 December, stated that his Government had taken self-defense measures and started counter-attacking the aggressive extremist forces of the Islamic Courts and foreign terrorist groups. The Transitional Federal Government forces, supported by Ethiopian ground and air forces, engaged with the Islamic Courts forces on a front stretching more than 400 kilometres, from the Lower Juba Valley in the south to the region of Galkayo in central Somalia. Within days, the towns of Bandiradley (Galkayo), Beletweyne (Hiran), Bulo-barde (Middle Shebelle), Burhakaba (Bay) and Dinsor (Bay) fell to the Transitional Federal Government/Ethiopian coalition. Mogadishu fell to the coalition on 28 December. Meanwhile, heavy rains in November displaced an estimated 454,000 people in the south.

Authorization of IGAD mission in Somalia

On 6 December [meeting 5579], the Security Council unanimously adopted **resolution 1725(2006)**. The draft [S/2006/940] was submitted by the United Republic of Tanzania, Ghana, the Congo and the United States.

The Security Council,

Recalling its previous resolutions concerning the situation in Somalia, in particular resolutions 733(1992) of 23 January 1992, 1356(2001) of 19 June 2001 and

1425(2002) of 22 July 2002, and the statements by its President, in particular the statement of 13 July 2006,

Reaffirming its respect for the sovereignty, territorial integrity, political independence and unity of Somalia,

Reiterating its commitment to a comprehensive and lasting settlement of the situation in Somalia through the Transitional Federal Charter, and stressing the importance of broad-based and representative institutions and of an inclusive political process, as envisaged in the Transitional Federal Charter,

Reiterating its insistence that all Member States, in particular those in the region, should refrain from any action in contravention of the arms embargo and related measures, and should take all actions necessary to prevent such contraventions,

Emphasizing its willingness to engage with all parties in Somalia who are committed to achieving a political settlement through peaceful and inclusive dialogue, including the Union of Islamic Courts,

Underlining the importance for stability in Somalia of broad-based and representative institutions and of an inclusive political process, commending the crucial efforts of the League of Arab States and the Intergovernmental Authority on Development to promote and encourage political dialogue between the transitional federal institutions and the Union of Islamic Courts, expressing its full support for these initiatives, and affirming its readiness to assist, as appropriate, an inclusive political process in Somalia,

Urging both the transitional federal institutions and the Union of Islamic Courts to unite behind and continue a process of dialogue, recommit to the principles of the Khartoum Declaration of 22 June 2006 and the agreements made at the meeting held in Khartoum from 2 to 4 September 2006, and establish a stable security situation inside Somalia,

Calling upon the Union of Islamic Courts to cease any further military expansion and reject those with an extremist agenda or links to international terrorism,

Deploring the bombing in Baidoa on 30 November 2006, and expressing its concern regarding the continued violence inside Somalia,

Welcoming the agreement reached between the Union of Islamic Courts and the Secretariat of the Intergovernmental Authority on Development on 2 December 2006, and encouraging the Intergovernmental Authority to continue discussions with the transitional federal institutions,

Calling upon all parties inside Somalia and all other States to refrain from action that could provoke or perpetuate violence and violations of human rights, contribute to unnecessary tension and mistrust, endanger the ceasefire and political process, or further damage the humanitarian situation,

Taking note of the note verbale dated 16 October 2006 from the Permanent Mission of Kenya to the United Nations addressed to the President of the Security Council, transmitting the text of the deployment plan for a peacekeeping mission of the Intergovernmental Authority on Development in Somalia,

Determining that the situation in Somalia continues to constitute a threat to international peace and security in the region,

Acting under Chapter VII of the Charter of the United Nations,

1. *Reiterates* that the Transitional Federal Charter and the transitional federal institutions offer the only route to achieving peace and stability in Somalia, emphasizes the need for continued credible dialogue between the transitional federal institutions and the Union of Islamic Courts, and affirms, therefore, that the following provisions of the present resolution, based on the decisions of the Intergovernmental Authority on Development and the Peace and Security Council of the African Union, aim solely at supporting peace and stability in Somalia through an inclusive political process and creating the conditions for the withdrawal of all foreign forces from Somalia;

2. *Urges* the transitional federal institutions and the Union of Islamic Courts to fulfil commitments they have made, resume without delay peace talks on the basis of the agreements reached in Khartoum, and adhere to agreements reached in their dialogue, and states its intention to consider taking measures against those that seek to prevent or block a peaceful dialogue process, overthrow the transitional federal institutions by force, or take action that further threatens regional stability;

3. *Decides* to authorize the Intergovernmental Authority on Development and member States of the African Union to establish a protection and training mission in Somalia, to be reviewed after an initial period of six months by the Security Council with a briefing by the Intergovernmental Authority, with the following mandate drawing on the relevant elements of the mandate and concept of operations specified in the deployment plan for the Peacekeeping Mission of the Intergovernmental Authority on Development in Somalia:

(a) To monitor progress by the transitional federal institutions and the Union of Islamic Courts in implementing agreements reached in their dialogue;

(b) To ensure free movement and safe passage of all those involved with the dialogue process;

(c) To maintain and monitor security in Baidoa;

(d) To protect members of the transitional federal institutions and the Transitional Federal Government as well as their key infrastructure;

(e) To train the transitional federal institutions' security forces to enable them to provide their own security and to help to facilitate the re-establishment of national security forces of Somalia;

4. *Endorses* the specification in the deployment plan of the Intergovernmental Authority on Development that those States that border Somalia would not deploy troops to Somalia;

5. *Decides* that the measures imposed by paragraph 5 of resolution 733(1992) and further elaborated in paragraphs 1 and 2 of resolution 1425(2002) shall not apply to supplies of weapons and military equipment and technical training and assistance intended solely for the support of or use by the force referred to in paragraph 3 above;

6. *Encourages* Member States to provide financial resources for the Peacekeeping Mission of the Intergovernmental Authority on Development in Somalia;

7. *Requests* the Secretary-General, in consultation with the African Union Commission and the Secretariat of the Intergovernmental Authority on Development, to report to the Security Council on the implementation of the mandate of the Peacekeeping Mission of the Intergovernmental Authority on Development in Somalia within thirty days, and every sixty days thereafter;

8. *Emphasizes* the continued contribution made to Somalia's peace and security by the arms embargo, demands that all Member States, in particular those of the region, fully comply with it, and reiterates its intention to consider urgently ways to strengthen its effectiveness, including through targeted measures in support of the arms embargo;

9. *Decides* to remain actively seized of the matter.

Statement by Eritrea. In a 15 December letter to the Secretary-General [S/2006/1009], Eritrean President, Isaias Afwerki, said that at its June and August meetings at the Foreign Minister level, IGAD had decided to promote sustainable peace in Somalia by supporting the dialogue initiated in Khartoum. While there was consensus among IGAD member States on Somalia's political realities, there was no understanding to deploy a peacekeeping force in support of one faction or to request a partial lifting of the arms embargo. Several IGAD members, including Eritrea, had insisted that any peacekeeping arrangement would follow the achievement of a viable framework for a political solution. Arrangements for a peacekeeping force had been considered merely on a contingency basis, and for eventual reactivation when and if necessary. Thus, Security Council resolution 1725(2006) did not reflect the unified position of IGAD. He urged the United Nations not to become a party to a misguided approach that would sow further conflict and suffering in Somalia and the region as a whole.

SECURITY COUNCIL ACTION

On 22 December [meeting 5611], following consultations among Security Council members, the President made statement **S/PRST/2006/59** on behalf of the Council:

The Security Council expresses its deep concern over the continued violence inside Somalia, in particular the recent intensified fighting between the Union of Islamic Courts and the transitional federal institutions.

The Council calls upon all parties to draw back from conflict, recommit to dialogue, immediately implement resolution 1725(2006) and refrain from any actions that could provoke or perpetuate violence and violations of human rights, contribute to unnecessary tension and mistrust, endanger the ceasefire and political process or further damage the humanitarian situation.

The Council reaffirms its respect for the sovereignty, territorial integrity, political independence and unity of Somalia.

The Council reaffirms its commitment to a comprehensive and lasting settlement of the situation in Somalia through the Transitional Federal Charter, stressing the importance of broad-based and representative institutions and of an inclusive political process, as envisaged in the Transitional Federal Charter.

The Council reiterates that the Transitional Federal Charter and the transitional federal institutions offer the only route to achieving peace and stability in Somalia, and emphasizes the need for continued credible dialogue between the transitional federal institutions and the Union of Islamic Courts. The Council therefore urges the transitional federal institutions and the Union of Islamic Courts to fulfil commitments they have made, resume without delay peace talks on the basis of the agreements reached in Khartoum, and adhere to agreements reached in their dialogue and establish a stable security situation inside Somalia. The Council welcomes all regional and international efforts to promote and encourage political dialogue between the transitional federal institutions and the Union of Islamic Courts and expresses its full support for these initiatives.

Security Council consideration (December). Briefing the Security Council on 26 December [S/PV/5614], the Secretary-General's Special Representative said that the crisis in Somalia had escalated dangerously, involving foreign forces and the use of heavy weapons and aircraft, which had dealt a serious blow to an early resumption of peace talks. The fighting had also compounded an already serious humanitarian crisis, resulting in additional displacement of populations. In a 22 December statement, the Secretary-General deplored the fighting and called on both sides to cease hostilities and resume peace talks without delay or preconditions. He expressed concern at reports of the involvement of foreign forces in the conflict and implored all concerned to respect Somalia's sovereignty and territorial integrity. The Secretary-General spoke with the Prime Minister of Ethiopia and the President of Kenya on 26 December and reiterated the need to encourage the Somali partners to resume peace talks. On 4 December, the Islamic Courts pledged to consider the Special Representative's appeal to return to dialogue, but denied that they were harbouring international terrorist suspects. They reiterated their invitation for an international fact-finding mission to visit Somalia to verify that claim. The International Contact Group on Somalia, meeting on 19 December, in Nairobi, to discuss the worsening situation, also called on the parties to resume direct talks and to guarantee support and unhindered access for humanitarian assistance. On 20 December, the EU Commissioner, on a visit to Somalia, discussed the possibility of establishing the joint verification mechanism proposed at previous rounds of the Khartoum talks and presented both sides with a draft memorandum of understanding on avoiding conflicts and resuming dialogue, which they did not accept.

Report of Secretary-General on IGASOM. On 28 December [S/2006/1042] the Secretary-General, in his first report on the implementation of the mandate of an IGAD Peacekeeping Mission in Somalia (IGASOM), as requested by resolution 1725(2006), said that, while Uganda and the Sudan had initially indicated their willingness to provide the first two battalions for IGASOM, the Sudan recently voiced its opposition to the intervention of foreign troops in Somalia, while Uganda expressed reluctance to deploy its troops in the absence of a secure environment. No other troop-contributing countries seemed to have been identified, and there was no information on whether financial resources and logistical support for deploying IGASOM had been secured.

United Nations Political Office for Somalia

The United Nations Political Office for Somalia (UNPOS), established in 1995 [YUN 1995, p. 402] and headed by the Secretary-General's Special Representative, continued to assist in advancing the cause of peace and reconciliation in Somalia. The Office, through the United Nations Trust Fund for Peacebuilding in Somalia, carried out three projects, focusing on the reconstitution and revival of the judiciary, the establishment of a national reconciliation commission and the organization of a seminar on federalism and constitutional affairs. The judiciary project sought to assist in establishing a judicial commission to rebuild the domestic justice system in accordance with Somali legal traditions and the rule of law through training and capacity-building for judges and other court personnel. The national reconciliation commission project sought to build national capacity to meet the reconciliation objectives defined in the Transitional Federal Charter. A five-day seminar in May, in Baidoa, on federalism and constitutional affairs, organized to help members of Parliament prepare for the drafting of a new federal constitution, saw more than 180 of the 275 members of Parliament attending. The Office also established a security sector technical working group to provide a forum for coordinating security sector reform.

On 20 April [S/2006/261], the Secretary-General informed the Security Council of his intention to extend the mandate of his Special Representative for Somalia and Head of the UNPOS until 8 May 2007. On 25 April [S/2006/262], the Council took note of that intention.

Financing

The Secretary-General, in his March report [A/60/585/Add.1] on estimates in respect of special political missions, good offices and other political initiatives authorized by the General Assembly and/or the Security Council, presented resource requirements for the Office from 31 January to 31 December in the amount of $7,129,200 net ($7,770,400 gross). ACABQ on 10 March [A/60/7/Add.37] endorsed that request.

The General Assembly, on 22 December, in section VII of **resolution 61/252** approved the budget in that amount, as part of the $326,500,000 budget of special political missions (see p. 1615).

Arms embargo

The Security Council, by resolution 751(1992) [YUN 1992, p. 202], established a Committee (Committee on sanctions against Somalia) to oversee the arms embargo imposed on Somalia by resolution 733(1992) [ibid., p. 199]. A Panel of Experts was established by resolution 1425(2002) [YUN 2002, p. 206] to generate information on the arms embargo violations. The Panel of Experts was succeeded by a Monitoring Group established by resolution 1519(2003) [YUN 2003, p. 254] to focus on arms embargo violations.

On 22 May [S/2006/313] and 15 December [S/2006/986], the Secretary-General informed the Security Council of the experts he had appointed to the Monitoring Group.

Report of Monitoring Group (May). As requested by Security Council resolution 1630(2005) [YUN 2005, p. 349], the Nairobi-based Monitoring Group of four experts re-established by the Secretary-General for a period of six months [ibid., p. 350], continued to investigate arms embargo violations, update the draft list of individuals and entities violating the embargo and make recommendations.

In its 5 April report [S/2006/229], which the Committee transmitted to the Council on 4 May, the Group said that arms embargo violations and the militarization of central and southern Somalia continued. Violations were related to arms and ammunition, military advice and training, military materiel and equipment, and financial support. The arms embargo violators were the three principal antagonists—the Transitional Federal Government, the Mogadishu-based opposition groups and militant Islamic fundamentalists—as well as the business elite, pirate groups, and clans involved in feuds over natural resources and other issues.

Like the other main contenders, the Islamic fundamentalists contending for political power in Somalia through violent means obtained arms and equipment in violation of the arms embargo on a sustained basis. All parties obtained their supplies from three basic sources: a widening circle of States that clandestinely provided support to the antagonist of their choice; the arms supermarket in Mogadishu, the Bakaraaha Arms Market; and individuals and businesses. While States were the main suppliers of military support and funding, powerful individuals and businesses also channelled arms, military equipment and financial support to the antagonist of their choice.

The Monitoring Group uncovered the existence of a number of Mogadishu-based business cartels and associated businesses with sprawling business empires inside and outside of Somalia, generating millions of dollars each year, portions of which were spent to maintain well-equipped militias and support warlords. They also had direct relationships with the militant fundamentalists; in some cases, they were themselves militants. Business cartels, associated businesses and local administrations created a powerful cross-clan web of economic vested interests. Their combined economic, military and political strength was powerful enough to maintain a status quo that preserved their interests and bring the process of establishing a new government to a standstill. Supplies violating the embargo were shipped from Djibouti, Eritrea, Ethiopia, Italy, Saudi Arabia and Yemen.

The report recommended an integrated arms embargo on Somalia, complemented by an embargo on the export of charcoal and fish, and a ban on foreign vessels fishing in Somali waters, in order to curtail funds to embargo violators who accrued revenues from exporting charcoal and issuing rights to foreign businesses for fishing in the Somali exclusive economic zone. It also recommended targeted sanctions against individuals and entities violating the embargo.

SECURITY COUNCIL ACTION

On 10 May [meeting 5435], the Security Council unanimously adopted **resolution 1676(2006)**. The draft [S/2006/287] was prepared in consultations among Council members.

The Security Council,

Reaffirming its previous resolutions and the statements by its President concerning the situation in Somalia, in particular resolution 733(1992) of 23 January 1992, which established an embargo on all deliveries of weapons and military equipment to Somalia (hereinafter referred to as "the arms embargo"), and resolutions 1519(2003) of 16 December 2003, 1558(2004) of 17 August 2004, 1587(2005) of 15 March 2005 and 1630(2005) of 14 October 2005,

Reaffirming also the importance of the sovereignty, territorial integrity, political independence and unity of Somalia,

Reiterating the urgent need for all Somali leaders to take tangible steps to continue political dialogue,

Reiterating its strong support for the Special Representative of the Secretary-General for Somalia,

Stressing the need for the transitional federal institutions to continue working towards establishing effective national governance in Somalia,

Commending the efforts of the African Union and the Intergovernmental Authority on Development in support of the transitional federal institutions, and welcoming the continued support of the African Union for national reconciliation in Somalia,

Taking note of the report of the Monitoring Group of 5 April 2006 submitted pursuant to paragraph 3 *(i)* of resolution 1630(2005) and the observations and recommendations contained therein,

Condemning the significant increase in the flow of weapons and ammunition supplies to and through Somalia, which constitutes a violation of the arms embargo and a serious threat to the Somali peace process,

Concerned about the increasing incidents of piracy and armed robbery against ships in waters off the coast of Somalia, and their impact on security in Somalia,

Reiterating its insistence that all Member States, in particular those in the region, should refrain from any action in contravention of the arms embargo and should take all necessary steps to hold violators accountable,

Reiterating and underscoring the importance of enhancing the monitoring of the arms embargo in Somalia through persistent and vigilant investigation into the violations, bearing in mind that strict enforcement of the arms embargo will improve the overall security situation in Somalia,

Determining that the situation in Somalia constitutes a threat to international peace and security in the region,

Acting under Chapter VII of the Charter of the United Nations,

1. *Stresses* the obligation of all Member States to comply fully with the measures imposed by resolution 733(1992);

2. *Expresses its intention*, in the light of the report of the Monitoring Group of 5 April 2006, to consider specific actions to improve implementation of and compliance with the measures imposed by resolution 733(1992);

3. *Requests* the Secretary-General, in consultation with the Security Council Committee established pursuant to resolution 751(1992) (hereinafter referred to as "the Committee"), to re-establish within thirty days of the date of adoption of the present resolution, and for a period of six months, the Monitoring Group referred to in paragraph 3 of resolution 1558(2004), with the following mandate:

(a) To continue the tasks outlined in paragraphs 3 (a) to (c) of resolution 1587(2005);

(b) To continue to investigate, in coordination with relevant international agencies, all activities, including in the financial, maritime and other sectors, which generate revenues used to commit arms embargo violations;

(c) To continue to investigate any means of transport, routes, seaports, airports and other facilities used in connection with arms embargo violations;

(d) To continue refining and updating information on the draft list of those individuals and entities who violate the measures implemented by Member States in accordance with resolution 733(1992), inside and outside Somalia, and their active supporters, for possible future measures by the Council, and to present such information to the Committee as and when the Committee deems appropriate;

(e) To continue making recommendations based on its investigations, on the previous reports of the Panel of Experts appointed pursuant to resolutions 1425(2002) of 22 July 2002 and 1474(2003) of 8 April 2003, and on the previous reports of the Monitoring Group appointed pursuant to resolutions 1519(2003), 1558(2004), 1587(2005) and 1630(2005);

(f) To work closely with the Committee on specific recommendations for additional measures to improve overall compliance with the arms embargo;

(g) To assist in identifying areas where the capacities of States in the region can be strengthened to facilitate the implementation of the arms embargo;

(h) To provide to the Council, through the Committee, a midterm briefing within ninety days of its establishment;

(i) To submit, through the Committee, for consideration by the Council, a final report covering all the tasks set out above, no later than fifteen days prior to the termination of the mandate of the Monitoring Group;

4. *Also requests* the Secretary-General to make the necessary financial arrangements to support the work of the Monitoring Group;

5. *Reaffirms* paragraphs 4, 5, 7, 8 and 10 of resolution 1519(2003);

6. *Requests* the Committee, in accordance with its mandate and in consultation with the Monitoring Group and other relevant United Nations entities, to consider the recommendations contained in the report of the Monitoring Group of 5 April 2006 and recommend to the Council ways to improve implementation of and compliance with the arms embargo, in response to continuing violations;

7. *Also requests* the Committee to consider, when appropriate, a visit to Somalia and/or the region by its Chairman and those he may designate, as approved by the Committee, to demonstrate the determination of the Council to give full effect to the arms embargo;

8. *Decides* to remain actively seized of the matter.

Report of Monitoring Group (October). In accordance with the above Security Council resolution, the Monitoring Group issued its report on 16 October [S/2006/913], which the Committee transmitted to the Council on 21 November. The Group said that the Union of Islamic Courts had become the pre-eminent force in central and southern Somalia and had consolidating its grip in the areas under its control, while the much weaker Transitional Federal Government, was attempting to hold on to its tenuous power base in Baidoa.

Those developments were accompanied by rampant arms flows to the Transitional Government and the Union of Islamic Courts. Behind the scenes, large cargo aircraft and ocean-going dhows clandestinely delivered arms and military support from States, arms-trading networks and others. Both contenders were engaged in an aggressive military build-up, which involved obtaining a wide variety of arms, including surface-to-air missiles, military materiel and trucks and land cruisers used as mobile weapons platforms. Both sides, especially the Islamic Courts, had the financial capacity to maintain their military machinery and were supported by the presence inside Somalia of combat troops, military trainers and advisers from certain States. Eritrea supported the Islamic Courts, and Ethiopia and Uganda, the Transitional Government.

The Monitoring Group requested information on their activities from several States, businesses and other entities. Some of the respondents provided information that was not relevant to the questions asked, others gave conflicting responses, and all denied any involvement in violating the arms embargo.

To offset the momentum towards a military catastrophe, the Group recommended strengthening the arms embargo through an all-border surveillance and interdiction effort to curtail or cut off the flow of arms and materiel by air, sea and land; applying financial sanctions on significant Somali businesses; and pursuing a high-level international diplomatic effort to disengage States from contributing to the military build-up.

SECURITY COUNCIL ACTION

On 29 November [meeting 5575], the Security Council unanimously adopted **resolution 1724(2006)**. The draft [S/2006/921] was submitted by Qatar.

The Security Council,

Reaffirming its previous resolutions and the statements by its President concerning the situation in Somalia, in particular resolution 733(1992) of 23 January 1992, which established an embargo on all deliveries of weapons and military equipment to Somalia (hereinafter referred to as "the arms embargo"), and resolutions 1519(2003) of 16 December 2003, 1558(2004) of 17 August 2004,

1587(2005) of 15 March 2005, 1630(2005) of 14 October 2005 and 1676(2006) of 10 May 2006,

Reaffirming also the importance of the sovereignty, territorial integrity, political independence and unity of Somalia,

Stressing the need for the transitional federal institutions to continue working towards establishing effective national governance in Somalia,

Reiterating the urgent need for all Somali leaders to take tangible steps to continue political dialogue,

Commending the efforts of the African Union, the Intergovernmental Authority on Development and the League of Arab States for their continued support for national reconciliation in Somalia, and urging both the transitional federal institutions and the Union of Islamic Courts to recommit to the principles of the Khartoum Declaration of 22 June 2006 and the agreements made at the meeting held in Khartoum from 2 to 4 September 2006 and to engage in the next round of talks without further delays,

Reiterating its strong support for the Special Representative of the Secretary-General for Somalia,

Taking note of the report of the Monitoring Group of 16 October 2006 submitted pursuant to paragraph 3 *(i)* of resolution 1676(2006) and the observations and recommendations contained therein,

Condemning the significant increase in the flow of weapons and ammunition supplies to and through Somalia, which constitutes a violation of the arms embargo and a serious threat to peace and stability in Somalia,

Reiterating its insistence that all Member States, in particular those in the region, should refrain from any action in contravention of the arms embargo and should take all necessary steps to hold violators accountable,

Reiterating and underscoring the importance of enhancing the monitoring of the arms embargo in Somalia through persistent and vigilant investigation into the violations, bearing in mind that strict enforcement of the arms embargo will improve the overall security situation in Somalia,

Determining that the situation in Somalia constitutes a threat to international peace and security in the region,

Acting under Chapter VII of the Charter of the United Nations,

1. *Stresses* the obligation of all Member States to comply fully with the measures imposed by resolution 733(1992);

2. *Expresses its intention*, in the light of the report of the Monitoring Group of 16 October 2006, to consider specific action to improve implementation of and compliance with measures imposed by resolution 733(1992);

3. *Requests* the Secretary-General, in consultation with the Security Council Committee established pursuant to resolution 751(1992) (hereinafter referred to as "the Committee"), to re-establish within thirty days of the date of adoption of the present resolution, and for a period of six months, the Monitoring Group referred to in paragraph 3 of resolution 1558(2004), with the following mandate:

(a) To continue the tasks outlined in paragraphs 3 (a) to (c) of resolution 1587(2005);

(b) To continue to investigate, in coordination with relevant international agencies, all activities, including in the financial, maritime and other sectors, which generate revenues used to commit arms embargo violations;

(c) To continue to investigate any means of transport, routes, seaports, airports and other facilities used in connection with arms embargo violations;

(d) To continue refining and updating information on the draft list of those individuals and entities who violate the measures implemented by Member States in accordance with resolution 733(1992), inside and outside Somalia, and their active supporters, for possible future measures by the Council, and to present such information to the Committee as and when the Committee deems appropriate;

(e) To continue making recommendations based on its investigations, on the previous reports of the Panel of Experts appointed pursuant to resolutions 1425(2002) of 22 July 2002 and 1474(2003) of 8 April 2003, and on the previous reports of the Monitoring Group appointed pursuant to resolutions 1519(2003), 1558(2004), 1587(2005), 1630(2005) and 1676(2006);

(f) To work closely with the Committee on specific recommendations for additional measures to improve overall compliance with the arms embargo;

(g) To assist in identifying areas where the capacities of States in the region can be strengthened to facilitate the implementation of the arms embargo;

(h) To provide to the Council, through the Committee, a midterm briefing within ninety days of its establishment, and to submit progress reports to the Committee on a monthly basis;

(i) To submit, through the Committee, for consideration by the Council, a final report covering all the tasks set out above, no later than fifteen days prior to the termination of the mandate of the Monitoring Group;

4. *Also requests* the Secretary-General to make the necessary financial arrangements to support the work of the Monitoring Group;

5. *Reaffirms* paragraphs 4, 5, 7, 8 and 10 of resolution 1519(2003);

6. *Requests* the Committee, in accordance with its mandate and in consultation with the Monitoring Group and other relevant United Nations entities, to consider the recommendations contained in the reports of the Monitoring Group of 5 April and 16 October 2006 and recommend to the Council ways to improve implementation of and compliance with the arms embargo, in response to continuing violations;

7. *Decide*s to remain actively seized of the matter.

Communcation. On 29 November [S/2006/943], Uganda, in its response to the Monitoring Group's report, objected to its inclusion in the list of arms embargo violators and questioned the Monitoring Group's methodology and conclusions. Affirming its commitment to the arms embargo, Uganda denied the allegations in the report and challenged the Monitoring Group to provide evidence implicating it.

Financing of Monitoring Group

On 31 January [A/60/585/Add.1], the Secretary-General submitted to the General Assembly estimated financial requirements for the Monitoring Group, from 1 January to 31 December 2006, amounting to $1,626,600 net ($1,646,900 gross).

ACABQ, on 10 March [A/60/7/Add.37], endorsed that amount. The General Assembly on 22 December, in section VII of **resolution 61/252** (see p. 1615) approved the budget in that amount, as part of the $326,500,000 budget for special political missions.

Eritrea-Ethiopia

The United Nations, in 2006, maintained its presence in Eritrea and Ethiopia to assist both countries in implementing the June 2000 Agreement on Cessation of Hostilities and the December 2000 Comprehensive Peace Agreement, both signed in Algiers (the Algiers Agreements), which regulated their border dispute that had led to armed conflict in 1998 and subsequent intermittent fighting. The United Nations Mission in Ethiopia and Eritrea (UNMEE), established in 2000, continued to monitor the border region, also referred to as the Temporary Security Zone, which marked the formal separation of forces, and to support the work of the five-member Eritrea-Ethiopia Boundary Commission, the neutral body mandated under the terms of the Peace Agreement to delimit and demarcate the colonial treaty border. During the year, the Security Council extended the UNMEE mandate five times.

To resolve the impasse between the two countries, the United States, in January, launched a new peace initiative, which was endorsed by the Security Council. The Council, on 24 February, urged both countries to abide by the Boundary Commission's decisions. During the year, Eritrea imposed new restrictions on UNMEE monitoring and verification activities and detained several UNMEE personnel. The situation deteriorated in October, when some 1,500 Eritrean troops and 15 tanks entered the Temporary Security Zone. On 17 October, the Council called on Eritrea to withdraw and urged both sides to exercise restraint. At year's end, some 2,000 Eritrean troops remained inside the Zone, equipped with battle tanks, anti-aircraft guns and rocket launchers.

During the year, the Boundary Commission failed to advance its demarcation activities, stalled since 2003, following the rejection by Ethiopia of significant parts of the Commission's 2002 final and binding delimitation decision, previously accepted by both parties. Ethiopia maintained that specific delimitation problems on the ground should be resolved through negotiations by the parties, while Eritrea pointed out that the Commission's 2002 delimitation decision was final. On 27 November, the Commission announced that, because of impediments in fulfilling its mandate, it planned to demarcate the border on maps, leaving the two countries to establish the physical boundary. The Commission decided to give Ethiopia and Eritrea one year to reach an agreement on border demarcation. If they failed to do so, the locations established in its 2002 delimitation decision would take effect. Ethiopia and Eritrea rejected the proposal. Eritrea maintained that the Algiers Agreements required the Commission, not the parties, to implement the 2002 delimitation decision, while Ethiopia held the view that the Commission was acting beyond its mandate.

Implementation of Algiers Agreements

Report of Secretary-General (January). In his January report on Ethiopia and Eritrea [S/2006/1], submitted pursuant to security Council resolution 1320(2000) [YUN 2000, p. 174], the Secretary-General said that, despite the efforts of the international community, the situation between Ethiopia and Eritrea had deteriorated as a result of the protracted stalemate caused by Ethiopia's non-compliance with the implementation of the Boundary Commission's decisions [YUN 2002, p. 187], lack of dialogue between the two countries, the dangerous escalation of tension, including the forward movement of troops and heightened military activity in and around the Temporary Security Zone, and the exacerbation of the situation caused by the restrictions imposed by Eritrea on UNME, including most recently, the helicopter ban and the arbitrary demand that Mission staff of certain nationalities be removed. Since the situation had become untenable as a result of those restrictions, and in response to Security Council presidential statement S/PRST/2005/62 [YUN 2005, p. 363], the Secretary-General proposed options for the future of the Mission: maintain its current configuration but with a diminished monitoring capacity, with the hope that diplomatic initiatives would unblock the current stalemate; relocate the entire UNMEE headquarters and related units from Asmara to Addis Ababa, leaving only a small liaison office in the Eritrean capital; transform UNMEE into an observer mission, either on both sides of the Temporary Security Zone or exclusively on the Ethiopian side, with limited monitoring and conflict prevention capabilities; deploy a strong preventive force entirely south of the Temporary Security Zone currently held by Ethiopia; downgrade UNMEE to a liaison mission, maintaining a small office in each capital, while pursuing efforts towards a political solution; or withdraw UNMEE entirely. While none of the options was perfect, the Council would have to take into consideration the objective reality on the ground, the attitudes of the parties and the international community's commitment to the implementation of the Algiers Agreements [YUN 2000, p. 173].

Communication (January). On 2 January [S/2006/3], Eritrea stated that for four years, Ethiopia had flouted international law and continued to occupy its sovereign territories and to reject the award of the Eritrea-Ethiopia Boundary Commission. The Council, by failing to exercise its moral and legal responsibilities in regard to Ethiopia's rejection of the Commission's final and binding award, was condoning the violation of the rule of law and potentially sowing the seeds of tension and instability in the region.

Statement by Algiers Agreements Witnesses. The United States, on 22 February [S/2006/126], transmitted to the Security Council President the statement issued the same day by the Witnesses to the Algiers Agreements (the African Union, Algeria, the European Union, the United Nations and the United States) following their meeting in New York, in which they endorsed the United States' diplomatic initiative (see above) to resolve the impasse in the peace process; stressed that the parties had to implement the Algiers Agreements fully and without qualifications uphold their commitment to the binding determinations of the Boundary Commission; urged the Commission to meet with the parties and consider holding technical discussions, supported by a neutral facilitator, to assist with the demarcation process; and urged the parties not to restrict UNMEE operation.

SECURITY COUNCIL ACTION

On 24 February [meeting 5380], following consultations among Security Council members, the President made statement **S/PRST/2006/10** on behalf of the Council:

> The Security Council welcomes the successful convening of the meeting of the Witnesses to the Algiers Agreements in New York on 22 February 2006 and their efforts to resolve the current impasse between Eritrea and Ethiopia, in order to promote stability between the parties and lay the foundation for sustainable peace in the region.
>
> The Council calls upon both parties to show maximum restraint and refrain from any threat or use of force against each other.
>
> The Council emphasizes that both parties bear the primary responsibility for the full, unconditional and expeditious implementation of the Algiers Agreements.
>
> The Council recalls that, under the Algiers Agreements, both Eritrea and Ethiopia have agreed to accept the delimitation and demarcation decisions of the Eritrea-Ethiopia Boundary Commission as final and binding.
>
> In this regard, the Council calls upon both sides to cooperate with the Boundary Commission to implement its decisions without further delay.
>
> The Council urges the Boundary Commission to convene a meeting with the parties to prepare to resume demarcation and strongly urges the two parties to attend the Boundary Commission meeting and to cooperate with and abide by the requirements specified by the Boundary Commission, in order to successfully conclude the demarcation process.
>
> The Council commends the role of the United Nations Mission in Ethiopia and Eritrea and expresses once again its deep appreciation for the contribution and dedication of the troop-contributing countries to the work of the Mission.
>
> The Council demands that the parties permit the Mission to perform its duties without restrictions and provide the Mission with the access, assistance, support and protection required for the performance of these duties, including its mandated task to assist the Boundary Commission in the expeditious and orderly implementation of the delimitation decision, in accordance with Council resolutions 1430(2002) and 1466(2003).
>
> The Council calls upon Member States to provide continued support for the Mission and contributions to the trust fund established pursuant to Council resolution 1177(1998) and referred to in article 4, paragraph 17, of the comprehensive Peace Agreement signed by the Governments of Ethiopia and Eritrea on 12 December 2000, in order to support the demarcation process.

Report of Secretary-General (March). In his March report [S/2006/140], the Secretary-General said that, while there had been no serious incidents, the military situation remained tense. Since their redeployment from forward positions in December 2005, as requested by the Security Council in resolution 1640(2005) [YUN 2005, p. 360], Ethiopia's armed forces remained deployed south of the Temporary Security Zone in a defensive posture. On the Eritrean side, Eritrea's defence forces conducted training exercises in the areas adjacent to the Zone. UNMEE observed the continued presence of groups of armed personnel inside the Zone at more than 15 locations. Since they refused to identify themselves, UNMEE suspected that at least some of them could be regular troops rather than militia.

Eritrea's restrictions on UNMEE continued to inhibit its ability to carry out its task. UNMEE patrols experienced restrictions on their freedom of movement inside the Zone, especially in Sectors West and Centre. As a result of the helicopter ban and restrictions on ground patrols, UNMEE could monitor only about 40 per cent of the territory in its area of responsibility. However, the Mission, to the extent possible, continued to carry out its major monitoring and verification functions, carrying out more than 100 patrols per day and maintaining dozens of checkpoints.

At the thirty-fourth meeting of the Military Coordination Commission (Nairobi, Kenya, 13 January), Eritrea stated that it could not accept Security Council resolution 1640(2005) because it dealt with secondary issues, while overlooking Ethiopia's intransigence with regard to border demarcation. Ethiopia expressed concern over the degradation of the Mission's monitoring capability due to Eritrea's restrictions, as well as its expulsion of UNMEE staff of selected nationalities. Both countries expressed appreciation for UNMEE work and reaffirmed their commitment to peace. As at 28 February, the UNMEE military component stood at 3,355, comprising 3,069 troops, 78 headquarters staff and 208 military observers.

On 1 March, an Indian peacekeeper who had suffered a cardiac arrest in Adigrat (Ethiopia) died after having been evacuated to Addis Ababa, instead of the UNMEE hospital in Asmara because of the helicopter ban, including on aerial medical evacuations. That was the tenth instance since Eritrea imposed the helicopter ban in October 2005, in which UNMEE had to carry out medical evacuation by alternative means. The temporary relocation of staff, in December 2005, following Eritrea's demand that UNMEE personnel of certain nationalities leave the country, limited the Mission's operations, with most civilian components seriously understaffed. On 23 January, Eritrea imposed new immigration regulations on UNMEE personnel, requiring them to apply for entry and exit visas five days prior to arrival or departure. The new procedures presented further unacceptable operational constraints and contravened the model status-of-forces agreement and the UN Charter. Furthermore, between 11 and 14 February, Eritrean security personnel detained 27 locally recruited UNMEE staff.

The United States diplomatic initiative and the 22 February meeting of the Algiers Agreements Witnesses were positive developments aimed at ending the stalemate, the Secretary-General observed. In view of those developments, the Security Council had decided to maintain UNMEE current configuration. In the circumstances, he recommended that the Council extend the Mission's mandate for two to three months to allow the diplomatic process to proceed and the forthcoming meeting of the Boundary Commission to bear fruit.

Report of Boundary Commission (March). The Boundary Commission, in its twentieth report [S/2006/140, annex II], issued in March and covering its activities from 1 December 2005 to 28 February 2006, stated that, although there had been little change in the situation, it was seeking to arrange a meeting with the parties in March as a further attempt to secure the consent of the parties to the resumption of the demarcation process interrupted in 2003.

Security Council press statement. By a 3 March press statement [SC/8656], Security Council members expressed their condolences at the death of a member of UNMEE Indian contingent (see above) and stated their concern that the death occurred in the circumstances of the "unacceptable restrictions" imposed by Eritrea on UNMEE operations, which had grave implications for staff safety and should be lifted without further delay.

Communication. On 6 March [S/2006/143], Eritrea expressed its condolences over the death on 1 March of the Indian peacekeeper, Kamble Ramesh Annappa. While his death was to be mourned, it was sad that the Security Council and the Secretary-General, in recent statements, had chosen to politicize it and blame it on Eritrea, which had no control over what happened in Ethiopia. The circumstances, including the location of the incident and the medical response time, raised more questions. It would have been more appropriate to look into the UNMEE mechanisms for coping with emergencies than to link the incident to Eritrea's restrictions. Eritrea refused to be used as a scapegoat and could not accept statements that failed to honestly assess incidents that occurred outside of its jurisdiction.

SECURITY COUNCIL ACTION

On 14 March [meeting 5384], the Security Council unanimously adopted **resolution 1661(2006)**. The draft [S/2006/155] was prepared in consultations among Council members.

The Security Council,

Reaffirming all its previous resolutions and the statements by its President pertaining to the situation between Ethiopia and Eritrea, and the requirements contained therein, including in particular resolutions 1622(2005) of 13 September 2005 and 1640(2005) of 23 November 2005, as well as the statement by its President of 24 February 2006,

Stressing its unwavering commitment to the peace process and to the full and expeditious implementation of the comprehensive Peace Agreement signed by the Governments of Ethiopia and Eritrea on 12 December 2000 and the preceding Agreement on the Cessation of Hostilities signed on 18 June 2000 ("the Algiers Agreements"),

Stressing further that lasting peace between Ethiopia and Eritrea (hereinafter referred to as the parties) as well as in the region cannot be achieved without the full demarcation of the border between the two parties, and recalling that both parties have agreed to accept the delimitation and demarcation decisions of the Eritrea-Ethiopia Boundary Commission as final and binding,

Reaffirming its strong commitment to ensure that the two parties permit the United Nations Mission in Ethiopia and Eritrea to perform its duties without restrictions and provide the Mission with the access, assistance, support and protection required for the performance of these duties, and, in this regard, stressing that the demarcation of the border cannot proceed effectively unless the Mission is allowed full freedom of movement throughout its area of operations,

Welcoming the successful convening of the meeting of the Witnesses to the Algiers Agreement in New York on 22 February 2006, as well as the convening of the meeting of the Boundary Commission in London on 10 March 2006,

Bearing in mind the reports of the Secretary-General of 3 January and 6 March 2006 and the options on the future of the Mission contained therein,

1. *Decides* to extend the mandate of the United Nations Mission in Ethiopia and Eritrea for a period of one month, until 15 April 2006;

2. *Demands* that the two parties fully comply with resolution 1640(2005), in particular paragraphs 1 and 5 thereof;

3. *Decides* to remain actively seized of the matter.

On 13 April [meeting 5410], the Council unanimously adopted **resolution 1670(2006)**. The draft [S/2006/232] was prepared in consultations among Council members.

The Security Council,

Reaffirming all its previous resolutions and the statements by its President pertaining to the situation between Ethiopia and Eritrea, and the requirements contained therein, including in particular resolutions 1640(2005) of 23 November 2005 and 1661(2006) of 14 March 2006, as well as the statement by its President of 24 February 2006,

Stressing its unwavering commitment to the peace process and to the full and expeditious implementation of the comprehensive Peace Agreement signed by the Governments of Ethiopia and Eritrea on 12 December 2000 and the preceding Agreement on Cessation of Hostilities signed on 18 June 2000 ("the Algiers Agreements"),

Stressing further that lasting peace between Ethiopia and Eritrea (hereinafter referred to as the parties) as well as in the region cannot be achieved without the full demarcation of the border between the two parties, and recalling that both parties have agreed to accept the determinations of the Eritrea-Ethiopia Boundary Commission as final and binding,

Reaffirming its strong commitment to ensure that the two parties permit the United Nations Mission in Ethiopia and Eritrea to perform its duties without restrictions and provide the Mission with the access, assistance, support and protection required for the performance of these duties, and, in this regard, stressing that demarcation of the border cannot proceed unless the Mission is allowed full freedom of movement throughout its area of operations,

Welcoming once again the successful convening of the meeting of the Witnesses to the Algiers Agreement in New York on 22 February 2006, as well as the convening of the meeting of the Boundary Commission in London on 10 March 2006, and looking forward to the next meeting of the Boundary Commission,

Stressing that the unacceptable restrictions on the Mission, which must be lifted, have drastically reduced the operational capacity of the Mission and could lead to serious implications for the future of the Mission,

Commending the role of the Mission, and expressing once again its deep appreciation for the contribution and dedication of the troop-contributing countries to the work of the Mission, despite the immense difficulties which they are facing,

Mindful of the reports of the Secretary-General of 3 January and 6 March 2006 and the options on the future of the Mission contained therein,

1. *Decides* to extend the mandate of the United Nations Mission in Ethiopia and Eritrea for a period of one month, until 15 May 2006;

2. *Demands* that the parties fully comply with resolution 1640(2005), in particular paragraphs 1 and 5 thereof;

3. *Calls upon* Member States to provide continued support for the Mission and contributions to the trust fund established pursuant to resolution 1177(1998) of 26 June 1998 and referred to in article 4, paragraph 17, of the comprehensive Peace Agreement signed by the Governments of Ethiopia and Eritrea on 12 December 2000, in order to support the demarcation process;

4. *Affirms its intention*, in the event that it determines that the parties have not demonstrated full compliance with resolution 1640(2005) by the beginning of May 2006, to review the mandate and troop level of the Mission by 15 May 2006, with a view to a decision on possible adjustments of the Mission, as outlined in the report of the Secretary-General of 3 January 2006, including, inter alia, a transformation into an observer mission;

5. *Decides* to remain actively seized of the matter.

On 15 May [meeting 5437], the Security Council unanimously adopted **resolution 1678(2006)**. The draft [S/2006/289] was prepared in consultations among Council members.

The Security Council,

Reaffirming all its previous resolutions and the statements by its President pertaining to the situation between Ethiopia and Eritrea (hereinafter referred to as the parties), and the requirements contained therein, including in particular resolutions 1640(2005) of 23 November 2005, 1661(2006) of 14 March 2006 and 1670(2006) of 13 April 2006, as well as the statement by its President of 24 February 2006,

Stressing its unwavering commitment to the peace process and to the full and expeditious implementation of the comprehensive Peace Agreement signed by the Governments of Ethiopia and Eritrea on 12 December 2000

and the preceding Agreement on Cessation of Hostilities signed on 18 June 2000 ("the Algiers Agreements"),

Bearing in mind the progress achieved at the meeting of the Eritrea-Ethiopia Boundary Commission held in London on 10 March 2006, and looking forward to a positive outcome at the next meeting of the Boundary Commission on 17 May 2006,

1. *Decides* to extend the current mandate of the United Nations Mission in Ethiopia and Eritrea until 31 May 2006;

2. *Demands* that the parties fully comply with resolution 1640(2005), in particular paragraphs 1 and 5 thereof;

3. *Calls once again upon* Member States to provide continued support for the Mission and contributions to the trust fund established in support of the demarcation process;

4. *Decides*, in the event that it determines that the parties have not demonstrated full compliance with resolution 1640(2005), in the light of the outcome of the meeting of the Eritrea-Ethiopia Boundary Commission on 17 May 2006, that it shall adjust the mandate and troop level of the Mission by the end of May 2006;

5. *Requests* the Secretary-General to report to the Security Council on the parties' compliance with resolution 1640(2005) within seven days of the adoption of the present resolution, and to provide to the Council any further recommendations on adjusting the Mission to focus on support for the demarcation process;

6. *Decides* to remain actively seized of the matter.

Boundary Commission meeting (May). On 21 May [S/2006/362], the Boundary Commission President transmitted to the Secretary-General a report on the Commission's meeting with the parties on 17 May, in London. At that meeting, the Commission announced its intention, as a first step towards the resumption of the demarcation process, to re-open its field offices in Addis Ababa and Asmara. However, progress in that regard was impeded by UN administrative procedures and the need for the re-establishment of arrangements to ensure the security of the Commission's field personnel. Eritrea had submitted a security plan in 2003, but Ethiopia had not yet done so. The Commission reiterated its request that Ethiopia produce by 19 May a security plan based on the assumption that UNMEE would continue to play its part in the demarcation process.

The full resumption of UNMEE role for the continuation of the demarcation process was discussed. The Commission was advised that any significant reduction in the size of UNMEE would seriously impair its ability to protect the surveyors and demining personnel. The parties did not disagree with that assessment and Eritrea expressed the hope that its Government would be able to withdraw the restrictions affecting the Commission's work. Ethiopia, while accepting the Commission's 2002 decision, maintained that, difficulties in demarcating the border could only be resolved by negotiations between the parties, thus implying that the decision of the Commission with which Ethiopia did not agree might not be binding.

The meeting decided that demarcation would resume as soon as the Commission was assured that UNMEE would be retained in the area at a level to enable it to provide adequate support to the field staff; the parties should confirm their proposed security arrangements; contracts could be concluded with the surveyors and the contractors; and both parties should cooperate fully with the Commission in the field. The Commission proposed convening a further meeting on 15 June.

Communications. On 22 May [S/2006/323], Ethiopia submitted to the Security Council and the Secretary-General a report on its compliance with resolution 1640(2005) and its cooperation with the United States-led peace initiative. The report said that Ethiopia had fully complied with the requirements of that resolution and was cooperating with the peace initiative. Ethiopia had accepted resuming border demarcation with the support of a neutral facilitator, and to entering into normalization talks. It was committed to the peaceful settlement of all disputes with Eritrea in accordance with the Algiers Agreements, fully supported the new peace initiative and had demonstrated its willingness to cooperate with the Boundary Commission. Eritrea, on the other hand, had rejected resolution 1640(2005), and continued to deploy its military forces in the Temporary Security Zone, prevent UNMEE from fulfilling its mandate and place obstacles to border demarcation and the peace initiative. Ethiopia called on the Council to ensure that Eritrea restored the integrity of the Zone, removed all restrictions against UNMEE and entered into political dialogue.

Ethiopia, on 25 May [S/2006/328], transmitted to the Council a letter from its Legal Counsel, addressed to the President of the Boundary Commission. The Legal Counsel said that Eritrea, in a 22 May letter, had misrepresented Ethiopia's actions toward the Commission. Eritrea had erected practical barriers to demarcation activities and had refused to honor the Commission's instructions to withdraw from the Zone and remove restrictions against UNMEE. Ethiopia, unlike Eritrea, had sent senior government officials to attend Commission meetings, had appointed field liaision officers and was eager to submit a security plan so that demarcation could resume. Ethiopia rejected Eritrea's assertion that Ethiopia alone was responsible for the current delays. It was Eritrea that had raised physical barriers to demarcation and, in its 22 May letter, had refused to remove them. Ethiopia was committed to settling all disputes peacefully, supported the new peace initiative and had shown willingness to cooperate with the Boundary Commission.

SECURITY COUNCIL ACTION

On 31 May [meeting 5450], the Security Council unanimously adopted **resolution 1681(2006)**. The draft [S/2006/343] was prepared in consultations, among Council members.

The Security Council,

Reaffirming all its previous resolutions and the statements by its President pertaining to the situation between Ethiopia and Eritrea (hereinafter referred to as the parties) and the requirements contained therein, including in particular resolutions 1320(2000) of 15 September 2000, 1430(2002) of 14 August 2002, 1466(2003) of 14 March 2003, 1640(2005) of 23 November 2005 and 1678(2006) of 15 May 2006, as well as the statement by its President of 24 February 2006,

Stressing its unwavering commitment to the peace process and to the full and expeditious implementation of the comprehensive Peace Agreement signed by the Governments of Ethiopia and Eritrea on 12 December 2000 and the preceding Agreement on Cessation of Hostilities signed on 18 June 2000 ("the Algiers Agreements"), and the importance of prompt implementation of the decision of the Eritrea-Ethiopia Boundary Commission as a basis for peaceful and cooperative relations between the parties,

Reaffirming the integrity of the Temporary Security Zone as provided for in the Agreement on Cessation of Hostilities, and recalling the objectives of its establishment and the commitment of the parties to respect the Zone,

Stressing further that the full demarcation of the border between the two parties is vital to lasting peace between Ethiopia and Eritrea as well as in the region, and recalling that both parties have agreed to accept the delimitation and demarcation determinations of the Boundary Commission as final and binding,

Welcoming the convening of the meetings of the Boundary Commission in London on 10 March and 17 May 2006, and supporting the ongoing Boundary Commission process,

Reaffirming its strong commitment to ensure that the two parties, as agreed by them, permit the United Nations Mission in Ethiopia and Eritrea to perform its duties and provide the Mission with the access, assistance, support and protection required for the performance of these duties,

Commending the role of the Mission, and expressing once again its deep appreciation for the contribution and dedication of the troop-contributing countries to the work of the Mission, despite the immense difficulties which they are facing,

Welcoming the intention of the Secretary-General to keep the operations of the Mission under close review while continuing to take into account developments on the ground and the views of the parties, and to revert to the Security Council with recommendations, as appropriate, for further adjustments to the mandate, force levels and concept of operation of the Mission as soon as warranted,

Having considered the reports of the Secretary-General of 3 January and 6 March 2006 and the options on the future of the Mission contained therein,

Noting paragraph 4 of resolution 1678(2006),

1. *Decides* to extend the mandate of the United Nations Mission in Ethiopia and Eritrea for a period of four months, until 30 September 2006;
2. *Authorizes* the reconfiguration of the military component of the Mission, and, in this regard, approves the deployment within the Mission of up to 2,300 troops, including up to 230 military observers, with the existing mandate, as stipulated in resolution 1320(2000) and further adjusted in resolution 1430(2002);
3. *Demands* that the parties fully comply with resolution 1640(2005);
4. *Calls upon* both parties to cooperate fully with the Eritrea-Ethiopia Boundary Commission, in order to resume the demarcation process, stresses that the parties have primary responsibility for the implementation of the Algiers Agreements, and calls again upon the parties to implement completely and without further delay the decision of the Boundary Commission and to create the necessary conditions for demarcation to proceed expeditiously;
5. *Demands* that the parties provide the Mission with the access, assistance, support and protection required for the performance of its duties, including its mandated task to assist the Boundary Commission in the expeditious and orderly implementation of the delimitation decision, in accordance with resolutions 1430(2002) and 1466(2003), and demands that any restrictions be lifted immediately;
6. *Calls upon* Member States to provide continued support for the Mission and contributions to the trust fund established pursuant to resolution 1177(1998) of 26 June 1998 and referred to in article 4, paragraph 17, of the comprehensive Peace Agreement signed by the Governments of Ethiopia and Eritrea on 12 December 2000, in order to support the demarcation process;
7. *Requests* the Secretary-General to keep the Security Council closely and regularly informed of progress towards the implementation of the present resolution;
8. *Decides* to remain actively seized of the matter.

Report of Secretary-General (September). In his September report [S/2006/749], the Secretary-General said that the military situation in the Temporary Security Zone and the adjacent areas remained generally stable but tense. Ethiopian troops continued to train and maintain defence facilities in areas adjacent to the Zone, but without any significant change in their strength close to the Zone's southern boundary. On the Eritrean side, Eritrean forces carried out routine training and maintenance activities outside the Zone but had not significantly increased their deployment inside the Zone and adjacent area. However, some 650 additional militia had entered the Zone in Sector West, reportedly for farming activities. Eritrea's restrictions on UNMEE, including on the freedom of movement in Sectors West and Centre of the Zone, continued to impede the Mission's ability to effectively monitor the Zone and the adjacent area on the Eritrean side.

At the thirty-seventh meeting of the Military Coordination Commission (Nairobi, 30 July), Ethiopia expressed concern over the drastic reduction of UNMEE strength which, coupled with Eritrea's restrictions, further affected the Mission's ability to carry out its tasks. Eritrea, for its part, regretted the lack of progress in demarcating the border and argued that the downsizing of UNMEE would not resolve the stalemate. Both reaffirmed their commitment to the peace process. Following Eritrea's expression of concern about the constraints of holding future commission meetings in Nairobi, the parties agreed to meet in a third country in the region, to be determined, and requested UNMEE to facilitate the meeting.

Since early May, Eritrea had detained some 29 locally recruited UNMEE staff, usually on the grounds that they were required to fulfil national service obligations. Four of them remained in detention, despite strong UNMEE protests. On 28 August, Eritrea arrested and detained a UN Volunteer, alleging that he was involved in smuggling Eritreans out of the country. The Mission neither received a proper explanation nor was allowed access to the detainee, which prevented it from investigating Eritrea's allegations. Moreover, on 5 September, Eritrea announced its decision to declare five UN security officers "persona non grata" for performing activities incompatible with their duty, without substantiating the allegation.

In compliance with resolution 1681(2006) (see p. 320), the UNMEE military component was reduced to 2,300 troops, including 230 military observers. By the end of August, UNMEE completed its reconfiguration plan, while ensuring that it had sufficient capability to fulfil its mandate. It maintained the same number of posts and military observer team sites and conducted on average the same number of patrols. However, its operational capacity was overstretched, adding considerable strain on the military observers, as well as on the contingents.

Landmines and unexploded ordnance continued to pose a threat in the Zone and the adjacent areas. The UNMEE demining units, together with a commercial clearance contractor, cleared an additional area of 593,000 square metres and 540 kilometres of road. In all, an area of 30 square kilometres was surveyed and assessed to be mine-free, enabling UNMEE to return three tracts of land to civilian use. The Mission destroyed more than 200 unexploded ordnance and four anti-personnel mines. UNMEE provided mine risk education to 4,101 inhabitants, focusing on those who had recently returned from internally displaced persons camps.

The June meeting of the Boundary Commission did not take place as Eritrea refused to attend. It also refused to attend the meeting planned for 24 August, while Ethiopia did not respond to the invitation.

Expressing concern about the untenable stalemate in the peace process four years after the 2002 decision of the Boundary Commission, the Secretary-General observed that the parties' political will to finally resolve the issue and implement the Commission's decision remained elusive. The meetings of the Boundary Commission and the ongoing United States diplomatic initiative, supported by the Security Council, gave the parties a unique opportunity to resolve the stalemate. The Secretary-General recommended that the Security Council extend UNMEE mandate for six months, until 31 March 2007.

Report of Boundary Commission (September). The Boundary Commission, in its twenty-first report [S/2006/749, annex II] issued in September, and covering its activities from 21 May to 31 August, stated that Eritrea had declined to attend the 15 June meeting because it felt that Ethiopia had still not accepted the delimitation decision without qualification. The Commission held an internal meeting on 15 June, believing that it might be helpful in reopening its field offices in Asmara and Addis Ababa. In spite of the lack of cooperation from the parties, the Commission, with UNMEE assistance, reopened its field office in Addis Ababa on 7 August, but was unable to reopen one in Asmara. On 21 August, Eritrean President Isaias set out a number of fundamental issues that needed to be settled before other aspects of the process could be addressed, including Ethiopia's acceptance of the Boundary Commission decision before any other matters could be discussed. The Commission met from 22 to 24 August, without the participation of the parties, to review the situation and consider how best to advance its work. Its next meeting was scheduled for November.

SECURITY COUNCIL ACTION

On 29 September [meeting 5540], the Security Council unanimously adopted **resolution**

1710(2006). The draft [S/2006/776] was prepared in consultations among Council members.

The Security Council,

Reaffirming all its previous resolutions and the statements by its President pertaining to the situation between Ethiopia and Eritrea (hereinafter referred to as the "parties") and the requirements contained therein, including in particular resolutions 1320(2000) of 15 September 2000, 1430(2002) of 14 August 2002, 1466(2003) of 14 March 2003, 1640(2005) of 23 November 2005 and 1681(2006) of 31 May 2006,

Stressing its unwavering commitment to the peace process and to the full and expeditious implementation of the comprehensive Peace Agreement signed by the Governments of Ethiopia and Eritrea on 12 December 2000 and the preceding Agreement on Cessation of Hostilities signed on 18 June 2000 (the "Algiers Agreements"), and the importance of prompt implementation of the decision of the Eritrea-Ethiopia Boundary Commission as a basis for peaceful and cooperative relations between the parties,

Reaffirming the integrity of the Temporary Security Zone as provided for in the Agreement on Cessation of Hostilities of 18 June 2000, and recalling the objectives of its establishment and the commitment of the parties to respect the Zone,

Commending the efforts made by the United Nations Mission in Ethiopia and Eritrea and its military and civilian personnel to accomplish its duties, despite the difficult circumstances,

Stressing further that the full demarcation of the border between the two parties is vital to lasting peace between Ethiopia and Eritrea as well as in the region, and recalling that both parties have agreed to accept the delimitation and demarcation determinations of the Boundary Commission as final and binding,

Expressing its full support for the ongoing process, aimed at implementing the final and binding decision of the Boundary Commission,

Taking note of the statement by the Mission of 25 September 2006 on allegations against Mission staff,

Having considered the report of the Secretary-General of 19 September 2006,

1. *Decides* to extend the mandate of the United Nations Mission in Ethiopia and Eritrea for a period of four months, until 31 January 2007;

2. *Reiterates its demand*, expressed in paragraph 1 of resolution 1640(2005), that Eritrea reverse, without further delay or preconditions, all restrictions on the movement and operations of the Mission, and provide the Mission with the access, assistance, support and protection required for the performance of its duties, and in this regard expresses its deep concern at the recent expulsion of Mission personnel by Eritrea;

3. *Reiterates its call*, expressed in paragraph 2 of resolution 1640(2005), for the parties to show maximum restraint and refrain from any threat or use of force against each other;

4. *Reiterates its demand*, expressed in paragraph 5 of resolution 1640(2005), that Ethiopia accept fully and without delay the final and binding decision of the Eritrea-Ethiopia Boundary Commission and take immediately concrete steps to enable, without preconditions, the Commission to demarcate the border completely and promptly;

5. *Regrets* the lack of progress on demarcation, calls upon both parties to cooperate fully with the Boundary Commission, including attending meetings of the Commission, stresses that the parties have primary responsibility for the implementation of the Algiers Agreements, and calls again upon the parties to implement completely and without further delay or preconditions the decision of the Commission and to take concrete steps to resume the demarcation process;

6. *Demands* that the parties provide the Mission with the access, assistance, support and protection required for the performance of its duties, including its mandated task to assist the Boundary Commission in the expeditious and orderly implementation of the delimitation decision, in accordance with resolutions 1430(2002) and 1466(2003), and demands that any restrictions be lifted immediately;

7. *Intends*, in the event that it determines that the parties have not demonstrated progress towards demarcation by 31 January 2007, to transform or reconfigure the Mission as the Security Council may decide;

8. *Also intends* to review the situation before 30 November 2006, in order to prepare for possible changes by 31 January 2007, and to that end requests the Secretary-General to present updated options for possible changes to the mandate of the Mission;

9. *Expresses its willingness* to reconsider any changes to the Mission that it may make in accordance with paragraph 7 above in the light of subsequent progress towards demarcation, and also expresses its readiness to take further decisions to ensure that the Mission will be able to facilitate demarcation as progress becomes possible;

10. *Calls upon* Member States to provide contributions to the trust fund established pursuant to resolution 1177(1998) of 26 June 1998 and referred to in article 4, paragraph 17, of the comprehensive Peace Agreement signed by the Governments of Ethiopia and Eritrea on 12 December 2000, in order to support the demarcation process;

11. *Expresses its deep appreciation* for the contribution and dedication of the troop-contributing countries to the work of the Mission;

12. *Decides* to remain actively seized of the matter.

Violation of the Temporary Security Zone

The Secretary-General reported [S/2006/992] that the security situation in and around the Temporary Security Zone had deteriorated further. On 16 October, in the most serious violation of the Zone's integrity, some 400 Eritrean soldiers, along with military vehicles, six battle tanks and one anti-aircraft gun entered the Zone's Sector West. At the same time, some 1,000 Eritrean troops, with artillery guns, rocket-propelled grenades and 10 battle tanks, forcefully passed the UNMEE checkpoint at Maileba heading towards Om Hajer located in the Zone's Sector West. In the following two weeks, Eritrea sent some 745 additional troops and stopped all movement of UNMEE patrols in the area.

On the same day, the Secretary-General stated that the incursion constituted a major breach of the ceasefire and urged Eritrea to withdraw. While some Eritrean forces withdrew or moved out temporarily, some 2,000 troops remained inside the Zone, equipped with battle tanks, anti-aircraft guns and multi-barrel rocket launchers. Eritrea stated that the troops had been moved to "help harvest crops" from state-owned farms in the area, and that their movements were "a natural decision" due to development projects in the area. Ethiopia condemned the incursion as a provocation and a flagrant violation of the Algiers Agreements.

Security Council press statement. In a 17 October press statement [SC/8854], Security Council members expressed their concern over reports that Eritrean Defence Forces had moved approximately 1,500 troops and 15 tanks into the Temporary Security Zone. Such actions were contrary to the 2000 Agreement on Cessation of Hostilities and violated the integrity of the Zone. Security Council members called upon Eritrea to immediately withdraw its troops and to extend its full cooperation to UNMEE, particularly in maintaining the ceasefire arrangements. They called upon both parties to show maximum restraint and to refrain from any threat or use of force against each other.

Communication. On 23 October [S/2006/840], Eritrea expressed concern about the Security Council's press statement on its troop movements to the southwestern part of its territory to conduct developmental work. Eritrea's troop movements to its own sovereign territory constituted neither an incursion nor a breach of the Algiers Agreements. The Council's concern was misplaced and the blame for not advancing in the peace process ought to be placed where it belonged. The Eritrean Defence Forces had been building and maintaining basic infrastructure in all parts of the country. Eritrea had refrained from deploying its defence forces in the southern part of the country bordering Ethiopia, with the expectation that the border would be demarcated expeditiously, in accordance with the Boundary Commission's decision.

Eritrea had exercised maximum restraint for over four years, refraining from any developmental work in its border territories to allow maximum time and opportunity for the Council to use its leverage over Ethiopia's intransigence. Eritrea would therefore exercise its legitimate right of vigorously pursuing its development policy in its own sovereign territory.

Despite having acted in good faith in all its commitments, Eritrea continued to be targeted unjustly by some Council members. In that connection, the Council should take the necessary steps to implement the Boundary Commission decision without interfering in the Commission's mandate.

Boundary Commission demarcation decision

On 9 November, the Boundary Commission President informed the Secretary-General that he intended to convene a meeting with both Governments on 20 November, in The Hague, to discuss a proposal to demarcate the border between Eritrea and Ethiopia by coordinates, thus avoiding the need to place boundary pillars on the ground. The Commission also invited the Witnesses to the Algiers Agreements to the meeting. The Commission had to take that action because of the persistent lack of cooperation by the parties, neither of which had granted it access to the border area to erect boundary pillars on the ground and complete the demarcation process. Using image-processing and terrain-modelling to demarcate the boundary, by identifying the location of boundary points by both grid and geographical coordinates, allowed a degree of accuracy that did not differ significantly from pillar site assessment and emplacement undertaken in the field.

Communications. On 15 November [S/2006/890], Ethiopia expressed dismay at the Commission's 20 November demarcation decision, which noted that, since the Commission's 2002 delimitation decision [YUN 2002, p. 187], a careful process had been established, involving field work for demarcating the boundary. Ethiopia, although concerned that the process did not conform to international practice, as it did not allow sufficient consideration of anomalies between the 2000 delimitation decision and the realities on the ground, had been encouraged by the Commission's recognition that those difficulties existed and that a cooperative process was needed.

Meanwhile, Eritrea had moved troops in the Temporary Security Zone, placed restrictions on UNMEE, stalled the demarcation process and asserted its right to seize by force territory allocated to it under the delimitation decision. Against that background, it was impossible to understand the Commission's plan to issue a demarcation decision, notwithstanding the parties' and Witnesses' understanding that final demarcation would be impossible without a cooperative process.

Since the Commission's President did not provide a clear indication of the nature of the proposed demarcation decision, Ethiopia would not be able to comment on it at the proposed meeting. The issuance of a demarcation decision was inconsistent with the Commission's responsibilities and mandate. Noting the 9 November letter of the Boundary Commission President to the Security Council, which suggested that action by the Commission, at its proposed 20 November meeting, would complete the demarcation process and fulfill a precondition for "transfer of territorial control", Ethiopia said that any decision purporting to effect a final demarcation under those circumstances would be invalid; therefore, there was no question of a transfer of territorial control.

Ethiopia urged the Commission to withdraw that communication and cancel the meeting. If the Commission wished to proceed along that path, Ethiopia would have to conclude that, by its own action, the Commission had lost its mandate under the Algiers Agreements.

On 20 November [S/2006/905], Eritrea stated that it could not agree with the Boundary Commission's decision to schedule a meeting to reconsider the modalities for demarcating the boundary. Had Ethiopia complied with its obligations to cooperate with the Commission in demarcating the boundary, the process would have been completed years ago. From Ethiopia's response to the Commission, it was clear that Ethiopia's position had not changed and the country would not implement the award.

Eritrea remained committed to the delimitation/demarcation process of the Algiers Agreements and the Commission 2002 Award. The Commission should face the problem of Ethiopia's non-compliance directly rather than search for ways to avoid the issue. To alter or modify the terms of the award would be beyond the Commission's authority. Any attempt to accommodate Ethiopia's demands to change the boundary ruling would therefore be *ultra vires* and without effect.

Boundary Commission statement. The Commission, meeting in The Hague on 20 November, in the presence of the Witnesses, including the United Nations, explained its decision to demarcate the boundary by coordinates and invited the Witnesses to express their views. At the end of the meeting, the Commission informed the participants that it would issue a statement on the issue.

On 27 November, the Commission, in a statement [S/2006/992, enclosure], announced that the most practical way to carry out its mandate was to provide the parties with the list of boundary points that it had identified by the techniques indicated on 9 November. The list provided the locations at which, if allowed, the Commission would construct permanent pillars. The list and explanatory comments annexed to the Commission's statement were accompanied by 45 maps illustrating the boundary points. The boundary so illustrated did not differ significantly from the one identified in the 2000 delimitation decision, although two areas (Tserona and Zalambessa) had been clarified. Since the Commission could not remain in existence indefinitely, it proposed that the Parties, over the next 12 months, consider their positions and seek to reach agreement on the emplacement of pillars. If, by the end of that period, the parties failed to do so or permit the Commission to resume its activity, the boundary would automatically stand as demarcated and the Commission would deem its mandate as fulfilled. In the meantime, the Commission remained in existence and until such time as the boundary was finally demarcated, the 2002 demarcation decision was the only valid legal description of the boundary. The Commission urged the parties to cooperate with it to expeditiously implement the demarcation of the border.

Further developments

Report of Secretary-General (December). In his December special report on Ethiopia and Eritrea [S/2006/992], submitted pursuant to Security Council resolution 1710(2006) (see p. 322), the Secretary-General said that the security situation in and around the Temporary Security Zone had deteriorated further. On 16 December, Eritrean armed militia stopped at gunpoint, threatened and temporarily detained an UNMEE patrol inside the Zone's Sector West. On 22 December, about 350 Eritrean militias entered the Zone in Sector Centre.

Eritrea instituted further measures, which affected UNMEE ability to perform its tasks. It imposed a ceiling on the purchase of diesel fuel and turned down the Mission's request to import diesel fuel directly. That situation severely restricted the Mission's operation, forcing it to introduce austerity measures. Eritrea stated, on 1 November, that it did not recognize the appointment of Azouz Ennifar (Tunisia) as the Secretary-General's Acting Special Representative, even though he had been appointed since 11 August. Mr. Ennifar had to relocate to Addis Ababa. Eritrea then stated that UNMEE officials could have their visas revoked if they attended functions in Addis Ababa convened by Mr. Ennifar. On 29 November, Eritrea stated that Mr. Ennifar should not be maintained as the Head of the Mission and not decide on operational issues related to the border question, regardless of his location. On 6 November, Eritrea notified UNMEE that, owing to the threat of bird flu, it had banned the importation of any supplies of poultry products by UNMEE and had prohibited their consumption.

The thirty-eighth meeting of the Military Coordination Commission could not be held, as Ethiopia requested a postponement because of Eritrea's incursion in the Temporary Security Zone. Eritrea said that it would suspend participation in the Commission until Ethiopia rescinded its request for a postponement, which it said, amounted to a withdrawal from the Agreement on Cessation of Hostilities.

The crippling Eritrean restrictions, the Secretary-General said, presented a challenge to several core principles of UN peacekeeping: the safety of its personnel, the need for freedom of movement, the exclusively international character of the personnel working under the UN flag and the Secretary-General's prerogative to appoint the required staff. UNMEE had to operate under unacceptable conditions for far too long, and he feared that, if allowed to continue, it could have very serious implications for the wider concept of peacekeeping.

Despite its reduced relevance, UNMEE presence still helped to some extent to reduce the risk of the conflict flaring up again, and remained a political, operational and psychological obstacle to any precipitous action that might result from the current situation, where the two armies were already directly facing each other, without a separation zone.

In the light of the developments that had taken place, the Secretary-General proposed that the Security Council, in considering future options for UNMEE, authorize a reduction in the Mission's strength from 2,300 to 1,700 military personnel. That option would allow the current observation capacity to be maintained, while reducing the overall strength. Contingents in all check posts at key and sensitive points of entry and exit from the Zone would also be reduced, while UN Military Observers would carry out patrolling tasks. The Mission would maintain its presence inside the Zone and the adjacent areas. If, however, there was no progress in the coming months towards implementation of the Commission's recommendation, the Council could consider converting UN operations into an observer mission, supported by a smaller protection force of 800 personnel, while removing all permanent observer sites, or converting it into a liaison mission, with 30 to 40 military liaison officers.

Communication (December). On 28 December [S/2006/1036], Eritrea, responding to the Secretary-General's report (see above), said it had been accused of rejecting the appointment of the Acting Special Representative, without mention of its concerns or the patience it had shown in getting clarifications, or the facts surrounding the nomination of another person for the post of Acting Special Representative, Tuliameni Kalomoh (Namibia), prior to that of Mr. Ennifar. The failure to mention Eritrea's acceptance of Mr. Kalomoh's nomination was a serious omission, as was the fact that Mr. Ennifar's nomination was done without an explanation as to why Mr. Kalomoh's had been dropped. The démarche presented by Eritrea on 1 November to the Secretary-General's Office was further evidence of its attempts not to embarrass anyone.

In that 1 November démarche, Eritrea said that it had agreed to Mr. Kalomoh's nomination after it was notified in May. Soon thereafter, the appointment of Mr. Ennifar was forwarded without any explanation as to why the former nominee was dropped. Stressing that the whole exercise lacked standard diplomatic practice, Eritrea asked for justifications and requested remedial action. Its request, however, was completely ignored, and Eritrea learned of Mr. Ennifar's appointment through the grapevine. It reaffirmed that it had neither agreed to the appointment of Mr. Ennifar as the Special Representative, nor recognized him as the Acting Special Representative, and urged the Secretary-General to appoint a Special Representative and communicate the designated representative to Eritrea through diplomatic channels.

UNMEE

The United Nations Mission in Ethiopia and Eritrea (UNMEE), established by Security Council resolution 1312(2000) [YUN 2000, p. 174], continued in 2006 to monitor and verify implementation of the 2000 Algiers Agreement on Cessation of Hostilities between Ethiopia and Eritrea [ibid., p. 173]. Its core operations, as revised by resolution 1320(2000) [ibid., p. 176] and 1430(2002) [YUN 2002, p. 189], were devoted to observation, reporting, analysis, identification of potential flashpoints and preventive action, chairing the Military Coordination Commission and assisting the Boundary Commission (see below). The area under constant monitoring was within and around the Temporary Security Zone, a 25-kilometre-wide buffer zone separating Eritrea and Ethiopia, which for operational purposes was divided into Sector West, Sector Centre and Sub-Sector East (formerly Sector East). UNMEE was headquartered in Addis Ababa and Asmara and maintained an office in Adigrat, Ethiopia.

On the recommendation of the Secretary-General, the Security Council extended UNMEE mandate five times during the year, the last time until 31 January 2007.

The Special Representative of the Secretary-General for Eritrea and Ethiopia, Legwaila Joseph Legwaila (Botswana), who had headed UNMEE since 2000, left in April. His deputy, Azouz Ennifar (Tunisia), who acted in the capacity of Officer-in-Charge, was appointed Acting Special Representative in August. In November, Eritrea refused to accept Mr. Ennifar's appointment, and in December, he was relocated to Addis Ababa.

By an exchange of letters between the Secretary-General and the Security Council [S/2006/235, S/2006/236], Major General Mohammad Taisir Masedeh (Jordan) was appointed UNMEE Force Commander as of 9 April, replacing Major General Rajender Singh (India).

UNMEE Financing

At its resumed sixtieth session, the General Assembly considered the Secretary-General's performance report on UNMEE budget for the period 1 July 2004 to 30 June 2005, and the proposed UNMEE budget for 1 July 2006 to 30 June 2007 [YUN 2005, p. 353], and the related ACABQ report [A/60/790].

GENERAL ASSEMBLY ACTION

On 30 June [meeting 92], the General Assembly, on the recommendation of the Fifth Committee [A/60/920], adopted **resolution 60/272** without vote [agenda item 143].

Financing of the United Nations Mission in Ethiopia and Eritrea

The General Assembly

Having considered the reports of the Secretary-General on the financing of the United Nations Mission in Ethiopia and Eritrea and the related report of the Advisory Committee on Administrative and Budgetary Questions,

Bearing in mind Security Council resolution 1312(2000) of 31 July 2000, by which the Council established the United Nations Mission in Ethiopia and Eritrea, and the subsequent resolutions by which the Council extended the mandate of the Mission, the latest of which was resolution 1681(2006) of 31 May 2006,

Recalling its resolution 55/237 of 23 December 2000 on the financing of the Mission and its subsequent resolutions thereon, the latest of which was resolution 59/303 of 22 June 2005,

Reaffirming the general principles underlying the financing of United Nations peacekeeping operations, as stated in General Assembly resolutions 1874(S-IV) of 27 June 1963, 3101(XXVIII) of 11 December 1973 and 55/235 of 23 December 2000,

Noting with appreciation that voluntary contributions have been made to the Mission,

Mindful of the fact that it is essential to provide the Mission with the necessary financial resources to enable it to fulfil its responsibilities under the relevant resolutions of the Security Council,

1. *Requests* the Secretary-General to entrust the Head of Mission with the task of formulating future budget proposals in full accordance with the provisions of General Assembly resolutions 59/296 of 22 June 2005 and 60/266 of 30 June 2006, as well as other relevant resolutions;

2. *Takes note* of the status of contributions to the United Nations Mission in Ethiopia and Eritrea as at 30 April 2006, including the contributions outstanding in the amount of 29 million United States dollars, representing some 2.6 per cent of the total assessed contributions, notes with concern that only eighteen Member States have paid their assessed contributions in full, and urges all other Member States, in particular those in arrears, to ensure payment of their outstanding assessed contributions;

3. *Expresses its appreciation* to those Member States which have paid their assessed contributions in full, and urges all other Member States to make every possible effort to ensure payment of their assessed contributions to the Mission in full;

4. *Expresses concern* at the financial situation with regard to peacekeeping activities, in particular as regards the reimbursements to troop contributors that bear additional burdens owing to overdue payments by Member States of their assessments;

5. *Also expresses concern* at the delay experienced by the Secretary-General in deploying and providing adequate resources to some recent peacekeeping missions, in particular those in Africa;

6. *Emphasizes* that all future and existing peacekeeping missions shall be given equal and non-discriminatory treatment in respect of financial and administrative arrangements;

7. *Also emphasizes* that all peacekeeping missions shall be provided with adequate resources for the effective and efficient discharge of their respective mandates;

8. *Reiterates its request* to the Secretary-General to make the fullest possible use of facilities and equipment at the United Nations Logistics Base at Brindisi, Italy, in order to minimize the costs of procurement for the Mission;

9. *Endorses* the conclusions and recommendations contained in the report of the Advisory Committee on Administrative and Budgetary Questions subject to the provisions of the present resolution, and requests the Secretary-General to ensure their full implementation;

10. *Recalls* its request as contained in section XIV, paragraph 4, of its resolution 59/296;

11. *Decides* to finance resources for conduct and discipline capacity equivalent to 622,300 dollars under general temporary assistance;

12. *Requests* the Secretary-General to ensure the full implementation of the relevant provisions of its resolutions 59/296 and 60/266;

13. *Also requests* the Secretary-General to take all necessary action to ensure that the Mission is administered with a maximum of efficiency and economy;

14. *Further requests* the Secretary-General, in order to reduce the cost of employing General Service staff, to continue efforts to recruit local staff for the Mission against General Service posts, commensurate with the requirements of the Mission;

Financial performance report for the period from 1 July 2004 to 30 June 2005

15. *Takes note* of the report of the Secretary-General on the financial performance of the Mission for the period from 1 July 2004 to 30 June 2005;

Budget estimates for the period from 1 July 2006 to 30 June 2007

16. *Decides* to appropriate to the Special Account for the United Nations Mission in Ethiopia and Eritrea the amount of 182,237,800 dollars for the period from 1 July 2006 to 30 June 2007, inclusive of 174,679,200 dollars for the maintenance of the Mission, 6,243,100 dollars for the support account for peacekeeping operations and 1,315,500 dollars for the United Nations Logistics Base;

Financing of the appropriation

17. *Decides also* to apportion among Member States the amount of 45,559,450 dollars for the period from 1 July to 30 September 2006, and, subject to a decision of the Security Council to extend the mandate of the Mission, to apportion the amount of 45,559,450 dollars for the period from 1 October to 31 December 2006, in accordance with the levels updated in General Assembly resolution 58/256 of 23 December 2003, and taking into account the scale of assessments for 2006, as set out in its resolution 58/1 B of 23 December 2003;

18. *Decides further* that, in accordance with the provisions of its resolution 973(X) of 15 December 1955, there shall be set off against the apportionment among Member States, as provided for in paragraph 17 above, their respective share in the Tax Equalization Fund of 1,091,375 dollars for the period from 1 July to 30 September 2006, comprising the estimated staff assessment income of 890,925 dollars approved for the Mission, the prorated share of 175,550 dollars approved for the support account, and the prorated share of 24,900 dollars approved for the United Nations Logistics Base and their respective share in the Tax Equalization Fund of 1,091,375 dollars for the period from 1 October to 31 December 2006, comprising the estimated staff assessment income of 890,925 dollars approved for the Mission, the prorated share of 175,550 dollars approved for the support account and the prorated share of 24,900 dollars approved for the United Nations Logistics Base;

19. *Decides* that, for Member States that have fulfilled their financial obligations to the Mission, there shall be set off against their apportionment, as provided for in paragraph 17 above, their respective share of the unencumbered balance and other income in the total amount of 32,154,200 dollars in respect of the financial period ended 30 June 2005, in accordance with the levels updated in General Assembly resolution 58/256, and taking into account the scale of assessments for 2005, as set out in its resolution 58/1 B;

20. *Decides also* that, for Member States that have not fulfilled their financial obligations to the Mission, there shall be set off against their outstanding obligations their respective share of the unencumbered balance and other income in the total amount of 32,154,200 dollars in respect of the financial period ended 30 June 2005, in accordance with the scheme set out in paragraph 19 above;

21. *Decides further* that the decrease of 556,500 dollars in the estimated staff assessment income in respect of the financial period ended 30 June 2005 shall be set off against the credits from the amount of 32,154,200 dollars referred to in paragraphs 19 and 20 above;

22. *Emphasizes* that no peacekeeping mission shall be financed by borrowing funds from other active peacekeeping missions;

23. *Encourages* the Secretary-General to continue to take additional measures to ensure the safety and security of all personnel under the auspices of the United Nations participating in peacekeeping operations, bearing in mind paragraphs 5 and 6 of Security Council resolution 1502(2003) of 26 August 2003;

24. *Invites* voluntary contributions to the Mission in cash and in the form of services and supplies acceptable to the Secretary-General, to be administered, as appropriate, in accordance with the procedure and practices established by the General Assembly;

25. *Decides* to include in the provisional agenda of its sixty-first session the item entitled "Financing of the United Nations Mission in Ethiopia and Eritrea".

On 22 December, the Assembly considered the Secretary-General's report on the revised budget for the UNMEE for the period from 1 July 2006 to 30 June 2007 [A/61/521 & Corr.1], showing revised cost estimates totalling $145,516,400; and the related ACABQ report [A/61/575], which recommended an amount of $137,385,100.

On 22 December [meeting 84], the General Assembly, on the recommendation of the Fifth Committee [A/61/617] adopted **resolution 61/248 A** without vote [agenda item 139].

Financing of the United Nations Mission in Ethiopia and Eritrea

The General Assembly,

Having considered the report of the Secretary-General on the financing of the United Nations Mission in Ethiopia and Eritrea and the related report of the Advisory Committee on Administrative and Budgetary Questions,

Bearing in mind Security Council resolution 1312(2000) of 31 July 2000, by which the Council established the United Nations Mission in Ethiopia and Eritrea, and the subsequent resolutions by which the Council extended the mandate of the Mission, the latest of which was resolution 1710(2006) of 29 September 2006,

Recalling its resolution 55/237 of 23 December 2000 on the financing of the Mission and its subsequent resolutions thereon, the latest of which was resolution 60/272 of 30 June 2006,

Reaffirming the general principles underlying the financing of United Nations peacekeeping operations, as stated in General Assembly resolutions 1874(S-IV) of 27 June 1963, 3101(XXVIII) of 11 December 1973 and 55/235 of 23 December 2000,

Noting with appreciation that voluntary contributions have been made to the Mission,

Mindful of the fact that it is essential to provide the Mission with the necessary financial resources to enable it to fulfil its responsibilities under the relevant resolutions of the Security Council,

1. *Requests* the Secretary-General to entrust the Head of Mission with the task of formulating future budget proposals in full accordance with the provisions of General Assembly resolutions 59/296 of 22 June 2005 and 60/266 of 30 June 2006, as well as other relevant resolutions;

2. *Takes note* of the status of contributions to the United Nations Mission in Ethiopia and Eritrea as at 30 September 2006, including the contributions outstanding in the amount of 49.2 million United States dollars, representing some 4.4 per cent of the total assessed contributions, notes with concern that only thirty-nine Member States have paid their assessed contributions in full, and urges all other Member States, in particular those in arrears, to ensure payment of their outstanding assessed contributions;

3. *Expresses its appreciation* to those Member States which have paid their assessed contributions in full, and urges all other Member States to make every possible effort to ensure payment of their assessed contributions to the Mission in full;

4. *Expresses concern* at the financial situation with regard to peacekeeping activities, in particular as regards the reimbursements to troop contributors that bear additional burdens owing to overdue payments by Member States of their assessments;

5. *Also expresses concern* at the delay experienced by the Secretary-General in deploying and providing adequate resources to some recent peacekeeping missions, in particular those in Africa;

6. *Emphasizes* that all future and existing peacekeeping missions shall be given equal and non-discriminatory treatment in respect of financial and administrative arrangements;

7. *Also emphasizes* that all peacekeeping missions shall be provided with adequate resources for the effective and efficient discharge of their respective mandates;

8. *Reiterates its request* to the Secretary-General to make the fullest possible use of facilities and equipment at the United Nations Logistics Base at Brindisi, Italy, in order to minimize the costs of procurement for the Mission;

9. *Endorses* the conclusions and recommendations contained in the report of the Advisory Committee on Administrative and Budgetary Questions, and requests the Secretary-General to ensure their full implementation;

10. *Reaffirms* its resolution 59/296, and requests the Secretary-General to ensure the full implementation of its relevant provisions and the relevant provisions of its resolution 60/266;

11. *Requests* the Secretary-General to take all necessary action to ensure that the Mission is administered with a maximum of efficiency and economy;

12. *Also requests* the Secretary-General, in order to reduce the cost of employing General Service staff, to continue efforts to recruit local staff for the Mission against General Service posts, commensurate with the requirements of the Mission;

13. *Further requests* the Secretary-General, in view of the recent reconfiguration and reduction in the strength of the Mission, to rejustify all posts and to report thereon to the General Assembly in the context of the budget of the Mission for the period from 1 July 2007 to 30 June 2008;

Revised budget estimates for the period from 1 July 2006 to 30 June 2007

14. *Decides* to reduce the appropriation of 174,679,200 dollars authorized for the maintenance of the Mission for the period from 1 July 2006 to 30 June 2007 under the terms of its resolution 60/272 by the amount of 37,294,100 dollars, to 137,385,100 dollars;

15. *Also decides* to reduce the amount of staff assessment income for the period from 1 July 2006 to 30 June 2007 from 3,563,700 dollars to 2,751,000 dollars;

Financing of the appropriation

16. *Further decides* to apportion among Member States the amount of 53,824,800 dollars, inclusive of the amount of 3,121,550 dollars for the support account for peacekeeping operations and 657,750 dollars for the United Nations Logistics Base, at a monthly rate of 8,970,800 dollars for the period from 1 January to 30 June 2007, in addition to the amount of 91,118,900 dollars already apportioned for the period from 1 July to 31 December 2006, subject to a decision of the Security Council to extend the mandate of the Mission, in accordance with the levels updated in General Assembly resolutions 58/256 of 23 December 2003 and 61/243 of 22 December 2006, and taking into account the scale of assessments for 2007, as set out in Assembly resolution 61/237 of 22 December 2006;

17. *Decides* that, in accordance with the provisions of its resolution 973(X) of 15 December 1955, there shall be set off against the apportionment among Member States, as provided for in paragraph 16 above, their respective share in the Tax Equalization Fund of 1,370,050 dollars for the period from 1 January to 30 June 2007, comprising the estimated staff assessment income of 969,150 dollars approved for the Mission, the prorated share of 351,100 dollars approved for the support account and the prorated share of 49,800 dollars approved for the United Nations Logistics Base;

18. *Emphasizes* that no peacekeeping mission shall be financed by borrowing funds from other active peacekeeping missions;

19. *Encourages* the Secretary-General to continue to take additional measures to ensure the safety and security of all personnel under the auspices of the United Nations participating in peacekeeping operations, bearing in mind paragraphs 5 and 6 of Security Council resolution 1502(2003) of 26 August 2003;

20. *Invites* voluntary contributions to the Mission in cash and in the form of services and supplies acceptable to the Secretary-General, to be administered, as appropriate, in accordance with the procedure and practices established by the General Assembly;

21. *Decides* to continue its consideration of this question at its resumed sixty-first session.

On 22 December, by **decision 61/552**, the Assembly decided that the agenda item on the financing of the United Nations Mission in Ethiopia and Eritrea, would remain for consideration during its resumed sixty-first (2007) session.

North Africa

Western Sahara

The year 2006 proved to be another frustratingly uneventful one for the United Nations in Western Sahara, with continuing deadlock in the search for an agreed political solution to the long-standing conflict. The United Nations Mission for the Referendum in Western Sahara (MINURSO) continued to monitor compliance by Morocco and the Frente Popular para la Liberación de Saguía el-Hamra y de Río de Oro (Frente Polisario) with the 1991 ceasefire that ended their armed hostilities over the disputed governance of the Territory of Western Sahara.

The Secretary-General's Personal Envoy, Peter van Walsum, continued to explore with the parties, as well as with Algeria and other countries, how best to achieve a mutually acceptable solution. Morocco reiterated its non-acceptance of a referendum that would include the option of independence, while Frente Polisario reaffirmed that the only way forward was to implement either the 2003 peace plan proposed by the previous Personal Envoy, James Baker III, or the 1991 settlement plan proposed by the Secretary-General and approved by the Security Council, which provided for self-determination through a referendum, with independence as an option. The Secretary-General urged the parties to enter into negotiations without preconditions, and called on Member States not to acquiesce to the temptation of maintaining the status quo. However, the positions of the parties remained far apart, and efforts by the Secretary-General and his Personal Envoy to initiate direct negotiations were unsuccessful. Given the continuing impasse, the Secretary-General proposed that the Security Council prepare for a more substantial resolution on the situation concerning Western Sahara.

As recommended by the Secretary-General, the Security Council extended the MINURSO mandate twice, the second time until 30 April 2007.

Peacemaking efforts

Security Council consideration (January). Briefing the Security Council on 18 January in closed consultations, the Secretary-General's Personal Envoy for Western Sahara, Peter van Walsum, pointed out that, since Morocco's rejection in 2004 [YUN 2004, p. 275] of the 2003 Peace Plan for self-determination of the People of Western Sahara [YUN 2003, p. 259], the Plan was never mentioned again in a Council resolution, nor had any country with close ties to Morocco tried to persuade it to reconsider its position. Mr. Van Walsum concluded that the Council was firm in its opinion that it could only contemplate a consensual solution. In that context, he did not see how he could draft a new plan to replace the 2003 Peace Plan. A new plan would be doomed to rejection by Morocco, unless it excluded the provision for a referendum with independence as an option. On the other hand, the United Nations could not endorse a plan that excluded a genuine referendum, while claiming to provide for the self-determination of the people of Western Sahara.

However, what was unthinkable in a Council-endorsed plan might not be beyond the reach of direct negotiations, he said. Once the Council recognized the political reality that Morocco would not give up its sovereignty claim, it would realize that there were only two options left: indefinite prolongation of the deadlock in anticipation of a different political reality, or direct negotiations between the parties. He dismissed the first option, calling a continuation of the impasse a recipe for violence. What remained therefore was a recourse to direct negotiations, which should be held without preconditions. The objective should be to accomplish what no plan could—work out a compromise between international legality and political reality that would produce a just, lasting and mutually acceptable political solution providing for self-determination. After years of reliance on UN-sponsored plans, it should be made clear to the parties that the United Nations was taking a step back and that the responsibility rested with them. That did not mean that the parties would henceforth be on their own. There seemed to be a consensus in the Council that any solution had to be found in the framework of the United Nations. Mr. van Walsum urged the Council to invite Algeria to participate in the negotiations, and called on those Council members who had been supporting Morocco's position to do all in their power to make the negotiations succeed.

Communications. Morocco, in a 26 January letter to the Secretary-General [S/2006/52], said that under the 1991 ceasefire [YUN 1991, p. 796], the buffer strip between the defensive wall and the border with Algeria was designed to mitigate tensions between the two countries and prevent any risk of escalation. There was never any question of sanctioning a division of the Territory or legitimizing the idea of "liberated territory", as that was an uninhabited buffer strip. Morocco had, at every opportunity, drawn UN attention to violations of the buffer strip. In 2000, the United Nations, having concluded that the referendum proposed in the 1990 settlement plan could not be carried out, sought an alternative political solution. Increasingly, however, the other parties to the dispute, rather than engaging in genuine negotiations, were attempting to establish a fait accompli in the buffer strip by constructing buildings, carrying on "diplomatic activities" there and even signing contracts of convenience with oil companies for oil prospecting. Such actions, which were illegal, were aimed at giving credence to the existence of a "pseudo-republic of Sahara" on territorial grounds. As long as there was no agreement on a political solution, Morocco, under the 1975 Madrid Accord concluded with Spain, remained the sole competent administrative authority over the entire Territory. That authority was confirmed by the 1990 settlement plan [YUN 1990, p. 919] and reinforced by the 2001 Framework Agreement on the Status of Western Sahara [YUN 2001, p. 216]. The other parties, in disregard of international law, were laying greater obstacles in the path of international efforts to reach a negotiated solution. Those parties should fulfil their obligations, refrain from entering into agreements or contracts involving the Territory and show the necessary political will by participating in the internationally-supported negotiations. Morocco was prepared to initiate negotiations, and would soon submit a proposal on autonomy.

Responding to Morocco, Frente Polisario Secretary-General Mohamed Abdelaziz, in a 7 February letter transmitted to the Council by Namibia [S/2006/84], recalled that, since May 1991, Moroccan "occupying forces" had been stationed inside and to the west of the defensive wall, by which Morocco had divided the Territory into two parts, while Saharawi forces had been positioned outside the defensive wall and eastwards. Contrary to Morocco's claims, there was currently a liberated area of Western Sahara and another under Morocco's illegal occupation. Frente Polisario and the international community did not recognize any valid legal title to Morocco's presence. The 1975 Madrid Accords, whereby the former colonial power renounced its responsibilities as an administering Power, were an illegal transaction that did not alter the colonial nature of the problem. The International Court of Justice, in 1975, denied any validity to Morocco's territorial claims, and the Legal Counsel, in 2002, had stated that the Madrid Accords did not confer on Morocco the status of administering Power. Morocco's presence in the Territory was therefore illegal. The United Nations was dealing with a decolonization question, which should be resolved in conformity with the Charter and the resolutions elaborated by its supreme bodies, which had unequivocally affirmed the right of the people of Western Sahara to decide their future through a self-determination referendum. In several resolutions, the Security Council had advocated a referendum to enable the Saharawi people to choose independence, autonomy or integration into the occupying Power. The Council could not resign itself to a dangerous stalemate. Only the resumption of the Council-approved referendum process offered real possibilities for resolving the conflict. Any other approach would imply the renunciation of the Charter, the legitimization of a "colonial fait accompli" and the establishment of force in international relations.

In a further communication of 24 February [S/2006/129], Morocco said that it had learned that the other parties were organizing, on 28 February, on the eastern side of the berm, a march of some 3,000 to 4,000 people from the Tindouf camps, accompanied by foreign guests, and planned to cross over it. Morocco requested the Secretary-General to draw the attention of the other parties to the illegal nature of the demonstration and the danger it posed to the participants, and to take all necessary steps to prevent it from taking place.

Report of Secretary-General (April). In his April report [S/2006/249], submitted in response to Security Council resolution 1634(2005) [YUN 2005, p. 369] and covering developments since his October 2005 report [ibid., p. 369], the Secretary-General said that his Personal Envoy had undertaken an exploratory mission to the region from 11 to 17 October, during which he met, among others, with King

Mohammed VI of Morocco and Prime Minister Driss Jettou; Frente Polisario Secretary-General Abdelaziz and other senior officials and sheikhs; Algerian President Abdelaziz Bouteflika; and Mauritania's Head of State, Colonel Ely Ould Mohamed Vall. Following the visit, the Personal Envoy informed the Secretary-General that the question was still at an impasse, with no agreement on how to enable the people of Western Sahara to exercise their right to self-determination. Morocco reiterated that it would not accept a referendum that would include the option of independence, while advocating negotiations to achieve a just, lasting and mutually acceptable political solution, and made it clear that those negotiations would have to be only about the Territory's autonomy status. Frente Polisario, with Algeria's support, maintained that the only way forward was to implement either the 2003 Peace Plan for the Self-Determination of the People of Western Sahara or the 1991 Settlement Plan. Any other course would be unacceptable to Frente Polisario. Mauritania reiterated its strict neutrality. During meetings in Rabat, Morocco, Tindouf and Algiers, Algeria, and Nouakchott, Mauritania, all officials confirmed their commitment to cooperating with the United Nations in reaching a solution, as a prerequisite for the region's stability and development.

After two rounds of consultations, in October 2005 and February 2006, involving France, Spain, the United Kingdom, the United States, the AU Commission Chairperson and senior EU authorities, the Personal Envoy perceived the emergence of a consensus on the need to reach a solution as soon as possible to enable the people of Western Sahara to exercise their right to self-determination.

The Secretary-General observed that forces outside the region militated against the negotiations option. Although no country would admit that it favoured a continuation of the impasse, Western Sahara was not high on the political agenda in most capitals, and great store was set by continuing good relations with both Morocco and Algeria. Those two factors constituted a powerful temptation to acquiesce to the continuation of the impasse. The Security Council could not afford to adopt such an attitude, while the situation deteriorated from potential instability to a threat to international peace and security. The Council and individual Member States should rise to the occasion and do all in their power to help negotiations get off the ground. The objective of negotiations should be a just, lasting and mutually acceptable political solution, providing for the self-determination of the people of Western Sahara.

Turning to recent developments, the Secretary-General said that, on 6 November 2005, a ceremony was held in Laayoune to mark the thirtieth anniversary of Morocco's "Green March" into the Territory. From 24 to 28 February 2006, Frente Polisario celebrated the thirtieth anniversary of the "Saharan Arab Democratic Republic" in Tindouf, Algeria, and Tifariti, Western Sahara. On 20 March, King Mohammed VI of Morocco paid a five-day visit to Laayoune and announced the appointment of a new President and other high-level officials to the Royal Advisory Council for Saharan Affairs in an effort to revive that body, which comprised traditional leaders (sheikhs), civil society representatives and elected members.

On 25 March, the King of Morocco granted pardons to 216 prisoners, including 30 Saharan activists. Pro-Saharan demonstrators were organized in Laayoune, Boujdour, Dakhla and Smara to welcome their release and demand the release of 37 more political prisoners. According to media reports, Moroccan security forces intervened to disperse the demonstrators, resulting in a number of arrests. On 28 March, Mr. Abdelaziz wrote again to the Secretary-General expressing concern about the human rights abuses perpetrated by Moroccan security forces, particularly in Smara, where several people were reportedly detained and some, including women, injured on 26 March. Mr. Abdelaziz, who travelled to UN Headquarters and met with the Secretary-General on 3 April, expressed concern about the situation.

As to MINURSO, the Secretary-General said that the Mission's new concept of operations, which took effect in October 2005 [ibid., p. 364], had resulted in a 25 per cent increase in the number of ground patrols compared to the period covered in the previous report. Frente Polisario lifted the restrictions on the movement of MINURSO observers that had been in place for several years, allowing access to its military units for inspection. New violations of the military agreement occurred during the period under review. From 14 October 2005 to 15 March 2006, MINURSO observed eight violations by the Royal Moroccan Army and four by Frente Polisario—a decrease of almost 50 per cent compared to the previous period. They included continued incursions into the buffer strip by armed elements from both sides, construction of new physical structures and movement of weapons and military units without prior notification or MINURSO approval. One such violation was Frente Polisario's concentration of military forces during the 27 February military parade in Tifariti, involving some 2,600 troops, 150 camels and 40 armoured personnel carriers. MINURSO continued to observe long-standing violations by both parties, including the presence of radar equipment and improvement of the defence infrastructure, including expansions of the berm by the Royal Moroccan Army, and the continued deployment of military personnel and infrastructure improvements by Frente Polisario in the "Spanish Fort" area. The parties continued to cooperate with MINURSO in the marking and disposal of mines and unexploded ordnance. On 27 February, Frente Polisario destroyed 3,100 anti-personnel mines and an anti-tank mine near Tifariti.

With regard to assistance to Western Saharan refugees, following the joint Office of the United Nations High Commissioner for Refugees (UNHCR)-World Food Programme (WFP) decision to reduce the number of assisted beneficiaries from 158,000 to 90,000, UNHCR and WFP representatives met with senior officials of Algeria and Frente Polisario to review the issue. Between 50,000 and 60,000 refugees in the Tindouf area were left homeless after their shelters were destroyed by heavy rainfalls and flash floods from 9 to 11 February. UNHCR, WFP and the Algerian Red Crescent immediately put in place an emergency response mechanism, while Algeria dispatched a humanitarian convoy. MINURSO assisted by providing water tanks and by coordinating assistance.

UNHCR and MINURSO resumed, on 25 November 2005, the programme of exchange of family visits between the Territory and the refugee camps in the Tindouf area, after an eleven-month hiatus. As at 15 March 2006, some 610 persons had taken the weekly UN flights to and from the Territory and the Tindouf area refugee camp, and over 17,000 candidates were on the waiting list.

The Secretary-General recommended that MINURSO mandate be extended for a further period of six months, until 31 October.

Communications. Responding to the Secretary-General's report, Algeria, in a 24 April letter [S/2006/258] to the Secretary-General and the Security Council President, recalled that Western Sahara was a decolonization question, under the responsibility of the United Nations, which should see that process to conclusion. The 1988 United Nations Plan, the 1997 Houston Accords and the 2003 Baker Plan, accepted by the parties and endorsed by the Security Council, provided that the question could only be settled through the expression of the will of the people of Western Sahara. On the pretext that one party had rejected those plans, the United Nations intended to withdraw from a settlement process in which it bore political, legal and moral responsibility. Algeria could not support or accept the shift in approach recommended by the Personal Envoy and endorsed by the Secretary-General. It regretted that the United Nations would sacrifice compliance with international law for realpolitik. The only valid negotiations, which should be limited to Morocco and Frente Polisario, were those dealing with the modalities for implementing the Council-approved 2003 Peace Plan. Only that plan, which represented a delicate compromise between the positions of the parties, could ensure a just and lasting settlement in accordance with the Charter and international law.

Namibia, in a 26 April letter [S/2006/266] to the Secretary-General and the Security Council President, expressed concern at the attempts to legalize the occupation of Western Sahara through proposed solutions that were based on the denial of the right of the Western Saharan people to self-determination. Any attempt to depart from the 2003 Peace Plan for the Self-Determination of the People of Western Sahara, the only viable peaceful solution to the conflict which provided for a referendum, was unacceptable. Namibia urged the United Nations, particularly the Security Council to reject any attempt to deny the people of Western Sahara their right to self-determination and independence, reiterated its support for the implementation of all General Assembly and Security Council resolutions aimed at holding a referendum and urged Morocco to accept the right of the people of Western Sahara to self-determination. Namibia also requested that the Security Council mandate MINURSO to monitor and submit reports on human rights violations.

SECURITY COUNCIL ACTION

On 28 April [meeting 5431], the Security Council unanimously adopted **resolution 1675(2006)**. The draft [S/2006/268] was submitted by France, the Russian Federation, Spain, the United Kingdom and the United States.

The Security Council,

Recalling all its previous resolutions on Western Sahara, including resolution 1495(2003) of 31 July 2003, resolution 1541(2004) of 29 April 2004, and resolution 1634(2005) of 28 October 2005,

Reaffirming its commitment to assist the parties to achieve a just, lasting and mutually acceptable political solution which will provide for the self-determination of the people of Western Sahara in the context of arrangements consistent with the principles and purposes of the Charter of the United Nations, and noting the role and responsibilities of the parties in this respect,

Reiterating its call upon the parties and States of the region to continue to cooperate fully with the United Nations to end the current impasse and to achieve progress towards a political solution,

Having considered the report of the Secretary-General of 19 April 2006,

1. *Reaffirms* the need for full respect of the military agreements reached with the United Nations Mission for the Referendum in Western Sahara with regard to the ceasefire;

2. *Calls upon* Member States to consider voluntary contributions to fund confidence-building measures that allow for increased contact between separated family members, especially family unification visits;

3. *Requests* the Secretary-General to provide a report on the situation in Western Sahara before the end of the mandate period;

4. *Requests* the Secretary-General to continue to take the necessary measures to achieve actual compliance in the Mission with the United Nations zero-tolerance policy on sexual exploitation and abuse, including the development of strategies and appropriate mechanisms to prevent, identify and respond to all forms of misconduct, including sexual exploitation and abuse, and the enhancement of training for personnel to prevent misconduct and ensure full compliance with the United Nations code of conduct, requests the Secretary-General to take all necessary action in accordance with the Secretary-General's bulletin on special measures for protection from sexual exploitation and sexual abuse and to keep the Council informed, and urges troop-contributing countries to take appropriate preventive action including conducting pre-deployment awareness training, and to take disciplinary action and other action to ensure full accountability in cases of such conduct involving their personnel;

5. *Decides* to extend the mandate of the Mission until 31 October 2006;

6. *Decides* to remain seized of the matter.

Letter of Secretary-General (June). In a 26 June letter [S/2006/466] to the Security Council President, the Secretary-General said that his April report had referred to certain factors that could constitute a powerful temptation to acquiesce in the continuation of the impasse for several more years. It was feared that many countries might find the status quo more tolerable than any of the possible solutions. Although he had stated that the Council could not afford to adopt such an attitude, resolution 1675(2006) (see above) did not reflect his recommendations. There was a danger in prolonging the impasse, and everyone should do everything possible to move the process forward. His Personal Envoy was preparing to visit the region again, to explore how the parties and the neighbouring States could help the Council to go beyond just extending MINURSO mandate. That opportunity should not be lost and Council members should use the next four months to prepare for a more substantial resolution.

On 30 June [S/2006/467], the Council informed the Secretary-General that it had taken note of his suggestion.

Report of Secretary-General (October). In his October report [S/2006/817], submitted in response to Security Council resolution 1675(2006), the Secretary-General said that the parties should drop any preconditions and begin negotiations to try to find a lasting solution. Such preconditions—Morocco's demand that its sovereignty over Western Sahara be recognized and Frente Polisario's demand that there should be a referendum, with independence as an option—should be raised by the respective parties during the negotiations instead.

However, such negotiations would not get off the ground unless the Security Council made it absolutely clear that the exercise of self-determination was the only agreed aim of the negotiations. The fact that the Council had acquiesced in Morocco's rejection of a referendum with independence as an option did not imply that it had rejected such a referendum itself. If either party could not accept that open-ended approach, there would be no negotiations. That would be a setback for Morocco, which was anxious to obtain international recognition of its sovereignty over Western Sahara, and for Frente Polisario, for, as the impasse continued, the international community would grow more accustomed to Moroccan control over Western Sahara. Frente Polisario would be well advised to enter into negotiations immediately, while there was still consensus in the Council that a negotiated political solution had to provide for self-determination. Any proposal should be judged on its potential for being an exercise of the right to self-determination.

The Secretary-General recommended that the Council call upon the parties to enter into negotiations without preconditions, with a view to achieving a just, lasting and mutually acceptable political solution that would provide for the self-determination of the people of Western Sahara. Algeria and Mauritania should be invited to those negotiations. Once the parties had responded favourably, he would submit further proposals on the format of the negotiations and the UN role.

Nothing that the two military sides did not have direct contact with each other 15 years after the ceasefire went into effect, which had had a negative effect on mutual confidence and prevented the adoption of procedures for stabilizing the situation during critical periods, the Secretary-General invited the parties to establish direct cooperation through a joint military verification commission or other fora.

Turning to other developments, the Secretary-General said that, in a 29 July speech, the King of Morocco had referred to the Moroccan initiative to find a political solution, which included a proposed autonomy plan for Western Sahara, and his decision to strengthen the Royal Advisory Council for Saharan Affairs, whose members had been invited to submit views on the plan. The King stated that the international community's reaction had been positive, thanks to Morocco's wish to cooperate with all parties towards realizing the full potential of a common regional future.

On 22 April, the King ordered the release of 46 prisoners, including 38 Saharan activists who had been jailed in 2005 for participating in demonstrations for self-determination. Their release sparked demonstrations in towns across the Territory, with consequent allegations of further arrests and detention of demonstrators by Moroccan authorities. Violent confrontations were reported between Moroccan security forces and demonstrators, leading to arrests and detentions. Frente Polisario Secretary-General Abdelaziz, in letters to the Secretary-General in May and June, alleged human rights abuses by Moroccan authorities in the Territory, including detention, torture, lack of judicial due process and the disappearance of political prisoners and human rights activists. Morocco, on 2 June, called for UN intervention to stop oppression in the Tindouf camps, following alleged reports of unrest there. On 26 July, Morocco singed a fisheries agreement with the EU, granting EU fishing vessels access to territorial waters off Morocco, not excluding the waters off Western Sahara. On 23 May, Mr. Abdelaziz deplored Morocco's exploitation of Western Sahara's natural resources, stating that certain clauses of the fishing agreement constituted a breach of international law and might complicate the situation.

The Secretary-General's Envoy held consultations with both sides, neighbouring States and other parties. Algeria reiterated that it was not a party to the conflict and that any negotiations should be between Morocco and Frente Polisario. Mauritania once again stressed its strict neutrality, but also its strong support for UN effort to reach a mutually acceptable solution. The Personal Envoy explained to the parties that he had advocated negotiations because, given the Security Council's firm rejection of a non-consensual solution, they were the only alternative to indefinite prolongation of the impasse. Frente Polisario officials replied that it would opt for the continuation of the impasse, while realizing that that would lead to renewed armed struggle and that the pressure of frustrated young Saharans might be impossible to resist.

Besides the position taken by the parties in prolonging the impasse, the positions adopted by third countries could also hinder the search for a negotiated solution, the Secretary-General observed. Most third countries were anxious to be strictly impartial by trying to please both parties. While they showed understanding for Morocco's reluctance to see a territory the size of the United Kingdom, with only a few hundred thousand inhabitants, become a fully independent State, they were opposed to exerting pressure on Frente Polisario to accept Moroccan sovereignty over Western Sahara and be content with a referendum without the option of independence. The Special Envoy underlined that negotiations would have only one Council-endorsed objective: to achieve a just, lasting and mutually acceptable political solution that would provide for the self-determination of the people of Western Sahara. However, the negotiations would not get off the ground unless the Security Council made it absolutely clear that they would have to be open-ended.

During the period under review, MINURSO observed eight new violations of the military agreement by Morocco and five by Frente Polisario—a decrease of almost 50 per cent compared with the same period in 2005. From the start, both parties had imposed restrictions on the freedom of movement of MINURSO military observers. On 1 June, MINURSO started to record such restrictions as violations of the military agreement. During the period 1 June –1 October, MINURSO recorded 539 such violations by Morocco and 86 by Frente Polisario.

MINURSO general food distribution programme continued to support 90,000 beneficiaries deemed most vulnerable in the Tindouf refugee camps, and provided an extra 35,000 food rations for refugees affected by the February torrential rains. A supplementary feeding programme reached some 9,500 pregnant and nursing women, as well as children under 5 years old. In August, MINURSO assisted 15 migrants from sub-Saharan Africa stranded in the "no-man's land" south of the berm, near the Mauritanian border, with basic medical assistance, blankets, food and water. The Secretary-General recommended that the Mission's mandate be extended until 30 April 2007.

The Office of the United Nations High Commissioner for Human Rights (OHCHR) conducted a mission to Rabat, Laayoune and the camps in the Tindouf area from 15 to 23 May and to Algiers on 19 June, to gather information on the human rights situation in Western Sahara and the refugee camps in Algeria. The OHCHR delegation, which enjoyed very good cooperation by all parties, was to report to the High Commissioner and make recommendations on improving protection of the rights of the people of Western Sahara. The report, transmitted on 15 September as a confidential document to Algeria, Morocco and Frente Polisario, was leaked to the press.

In a later report [S/2007/202], the Secretary-General said that the King of Morocco, in a 6 November statement, confirmed that his Government was developing an autonomy proposal, with a view to finding a political solution. The ongoing consultations on that initiative would be completed on a broad basis. Morocco remained committed to cooperating with the United Nations in its efforts to find a consensual political solution to which all parties could adhere.

Demonstrations by Saharans calling for respect for human rights and the right to self-determination were reported to have continued in the Territory. On 11 December, Frente Polisario Secretary-General Abdelaziz wrote to the UN Secretary-General to protest the brutal repression and arrest of demonstrators by Moroccan security forces during protests to mark International Human Rights Day on 10 December.

SECURITY COUNCIL ACTION

On 31 October [meeting 5560], the Security Council unanimously adopted **resolution 1720(2006)**. The draft [S/2006/850] was submitted by France, Russian Federation, Spain, the United Kingdom and the United States.

The Security Council,

Recalling all its previous resolutions on Western Sahara, including resolution 1495(2003) of 31 July 2003, resolution 1541(2004) of 29 April 2004, and resolution 1675(2006) of 28 April 2006,

Reaffirming its strong support for the efforts of the Secretary-General and his Personal Envoy,

Reaffirming its commitment to assist the parties to achieve a just, lasting and mutually acceptable political solution which will provide for the self-determination of the people of Western Sahara in the context of arrangements consistent with the principles and purposes of the Charter of the United Nations, and noting the role and responsibilities of the parties in this respect,

Reiterating its call upon the parties and States of the region to continue to cooperate fully with the United Nations to end the current impasse and to achieve progress towards a political solution,

Having considered the report of the Secretary-General of 16 October 2006,

1. *Reaffirms* the need for full respect of the military agreements reached with the United Nations Mission for the Referendum in Western Sahara with regard to the ceasefire;

2. *Calls upon* Member States to consider voluntary contributions to fund confidence building measures that allow for increased contact between separated family members, especially family unification visits;

3. *Requests* the Secretary-General provide a report on the situation in the Western Sahara before the end of the mandate period;

4. *Requests* the Secretary-General to continue to take the necessary measures to ensure full compliance in Mission with the United Nations zero-tolerance policy on sexual exploitation and abuse and to keep the Council informed, and urges troop-contributing countries to take appropriate preventive action, including pre-deployment awareness training, and other action to ensure full accountability in cases of such conduct involving their personnel;

5. *Decides* to extend the mandate of the Mission until 30 April 2007;

6. *Decides* to remain seized of the matter.

Following the adoption of the resolution, the United States, the United Kingdom and France urged the parties to use the next six months to finally break the impasse. The United States urged Morocco to move quickly to fulfil its promises to table a comprehensive and credible autonomy proposal for Western Sahara and to engage in serious discussions with all Saharawi people, including Polisario, in a way that could form the basis for a new, UN-led negotiating process. The United States asked the Secretary-General to examine the mechanisms and timetable for the Mission's dismantlement, should MINURSO continue to be ineffective in fulfilling its mandate or the concerned parties prove unable to make substantial progress towards a political solution. The United Kingdom restated that the only solution had to be a mutually acceptable one and provide for the self-determination of the people of Western Sahara.

GENERAL ASSEMBLY ACTION

The General Assembly, in December, examined the Secretary-General's July report [A/61/121] summarizing his 1 July 2005–30 June 2006 reports to the Security Council on the question of Western Sahara and the relevant chapter in the report [A/61/23] of the Special Committee on decolonization for 2006 (see p. 719).

On 14 December [meeting 79], the Assembly, on the recommendation of the Fourth (Special Political and Decolonization) Committee [A/61/415], adopted **resolution 61/125** by recorded vote (70-150-91) [agenda item 39].

Question of Western Sahara

The General Assembly,

Having considered in depth the question of Western Sahara,

Reaffirming the inalienable right of all peoples to self-determination and independence, in accordance with the principles set forth in the Charter of the United Nations and General Assembly resolution 1514(XV) of 14 December 1960 containing the Declaration on the Granting of Independence to Colonial Countries and Peoples,

Recalling its resolution 60/114 of 8 December 2005,

Recalling also all resolutions of the General Assembly and the Security Council on the question of Western Sahara,

Recalling further Security Council resolutions 658(1990) of 27 June 1990 and 690(1991) of 29 April 1991, by which the Council approved the settlement plan for Western Sahara,

Recalling Security Council resolutions 1359(2001) of 29 June 2001 and 1429(2002) of 30 July 2002, as well as 1495(2003) of 31 July 2003, in which the Council expressed its support of the peace plan for self-determination of the people of Western Sahara as an optimum political solution on the basis of agreement between the two parties, and resolutions 1541(2004) of 29 April 2004, 1570(2004) of 28 October 2004, 1598(2005) of 28 April 2005, 1634(2005) of 28 October 2005 and 1675(2006) of 28 April 2006,

Taking note of the responses of the parties and neighbouring States to the Personal Envoy of the Secretary-General concerning the peace plan contained in the report of the Secretary-General of 23 May 2003,

Reaffirming the responsibility of the United Nations towards the people of Western Sahara,

Noting with satisfaction the entry into force of the ceasefire in accordance with the proposal made by the Secretary-General, and stressing the importance it attaches to the maintenance of the ceasefire as an integral part of the settlement plan,

Underlining, in this regard, the validity of the settlement plan, while noting the fundamental differences between the parties in its implementation,

Stressing that the lack of progress in the settlement of the dispute on Western Sahara continues to cause suffering to the people of Western Sahara, remains a source of potential instability in the region and obstructs the economic development of the Maghreb region and that, in view of this, the search for a political solution is critically needed,

Welcoming the efforts of the Secretary-General and his Personal Envoy in search of a mutually acceptable political solution, which will provide for self-determination of the people of Western Sahara,

Having examined the relevant chapter of the report of the Special Committee on the Situation with regard to the Implementation of the Declaration on the Granting of Independence to Colonial Countries and Peoples,

Having also examined the report of the Secretary-General,

1. *Takes note* of the report of the Secretary-General;

2. *Underlines* Security Council resolution 1495(2003), in which the Council expressed its support of the peace plan for self-determination of the people of Western Sahara as an optimum political solution on the basis of agreement between the two parties;

3. *Underlines also* that the parties reacted differently to this plan;

4. *Continues to support strongly* the efforts of the Secretary-General and his Personal Envoy to achieve a mutually acceptable political solution to the dispute over Western Sahara;

5. *Commends* the Secretary-General and his Personal Envoy for their outstanding efforts and the two parties for the spirit of cooperation they have shown in the support they provide for those efforts;

6. *Calls upon* all the parties and the States of the region to cooperate fully with the Secretary-General and his Personal Envoy;

7. *Reaffirms* the responsibility of the United Nations towards the people of Western Sahara;

8. *Calls upon* the parties to cooperate with the International Committee of the Red Cross in its efforts to solve the problem of the fate of the people unaccounted for, and calls upon the parties to abide by their obligations under international humanitarian law to release without further delay all those held since the start of the conflict;

9. *Requests* the Special Committee on the Situation with regard to the Implementation of the Declaration on the Granting of Independence to Colonial Countries and Peoples to continue to consider the situation in Western Sahara and to report thereon to the General Assembly at its sixty-second session;

10. *Invites* the Secretary-General to submit to the General Assembly at its sixty-second session a report on the implementation of the present resolution.

RECORDED VOTE ON RESOLUTION 61/125:

In favour: Algeria, Angola, Antigua and Barbuda, Argentina, Armenia, Austria, Bahamas, Barbados, Belize, Bolivia, Botswana, Chad, Chile, Côte d'Ivoire, Croatia, Cuba, Democratic People's Republic of Korea, Dominica, Ecuador, Estonia, Ethiopia, Fiji, Finland, Germany, Greece, Grenada, Guyana, Haiti, Hungary, Iceland, Ireland, Italy, Jamaica, Lao People's Democratic Republic, Lesotho, Liechtenstein, Malawi, Mauritius, Mexico, Mozambique, Myanmar, Namibia, Nauru, Netherlands, New Zealand, Nigeria, Norway, Panama, Papua New Guinea, Russian Federation, Rwanda, Saint Lucia, Saint Vincent and the Grenadines, Slovakia, Slovenia, South Africa, Suriname, Sweden, Switzerland, Timor-Leste, Trinidad and Tobago, Tuvalu, Uganda, United Kingdom, United Republic of Tanzania, Uruguay, Venezuela, Viet Nam, Zambia, Zimbabwe.

Against: None.

Abstaining: Albania, Andorra, Australia, Azerbaijan, Bahrain, Bangladesh, Benin, Bosnia and Herzegovina, Brazil, Bulgaria, Burkina Faso, Burundi, Cambodia, Cameroon, Canada, Central African Republic, Comoros, Congo, Costa Rica, Czech Republic, Democratic Republic of the Congo, Denmark, Djibouti, Dominican Republic, Egypt, El Salvador, Equatorial Guinea, France, Gabon, Georgia, Ghana, Guatemala, Guinea, Guinea-Bissau, Honduras, India, Indonesia, Iraq, Israel, Japan, Jordan, Kazakhstan, Kiribati, Kuwait, Latvia, Lebanon, Lithuania, Luxembourg, Madagascar, Malaysia, Maldives, Malta, Marshall Islands, Micronesia (Federated States of), Moldova, Monaco, Mongolia, Morocco, Nepal, Nicaragua, Niger, Oman, Palau, Paraguay, Peru, Philippines, Portugal, Qatar, Republic of Korea, Samoa, San Marino, Sao Tome and Principe, Saudi Arabia, Senegal, Serbia, Sierra Leone, Singapore, Solomon Islands, Spain, Sri Lanka, Swaziland, Tajikistan, Thailand,

The former Yugoslav Republic of Macedonia, Togo, Tonga, Ukraine, United Arab Emirates, United States, Vanuatu, Yemen.

MINURSO

The United Nations Mission for the Referendum in Western Sahara (MINURSO), established by Security Council resolution 690(1991) [YUN 1991, p. 794], continued in 2006 to monitor compliance with the 1991 formal ceasefire [ibid., p. 796] between Frente Polisario and Morocco. Monitoring was carried out by the Mission's military observers through a combination of ground and air patrols and observation posts, and through inspections of larger-than-company-size military units of Frente Polisario and the Royal Moroccan Army (RMA). The main focus was on military activities close to the berm, the defensive sand wall built by RMA between 1981 and 1987 across Western Sahara, extending from the north-east corner down to the south-west, near the Mauritanian border.

Military Agreement No.1, which MINURSO signed separately with the parties [YUN 1998, p. 194], remained the basic legal instrument governing the ceasefire monitoring of the five parts into which, for operational purposes, the disputed territory of Western Sahara was divided: one five-kilometre-wide buffer strip to the east and south of the berm; two restricted areas—one, 25 kilometres wide east of the berm and the other, 30 kilometres wide west of it; and two areas with limited restrictions that encompassed the remainder of the Territory. Bilateral military agreements Nos. 2 and 3 [YUN 1999, p. 180], committing both parties to cooperating with MINURSO in the exchange of mine-related information, marking of mined areas, and clearance and destruction of mines and unexploded ordnance, remained in force.

MINURSO maintained its headquarters in Laayoune, Western Sahara; a liaison office in Tindouf, Algeria; and nine military-observer team sites located across the Territory, four on the Moroccan-controlled side and five on the Frente Polisario side.

On the recommendation of the Secretary-General, the Council extended MINURSO mandate twice during the year, the first time until 31 October 2006 and the second until 30 April 2007.

MINURSO financing

The General Assembly, at its resumed sixtieth session, considered the Secretary-General's report [A/60/724] on the MINURSO budget for the period from 1 July 2006 to 30 June 2007, showing cost estimates of $42,804,400; of the ACABQ report thereon, and the report on MINURSO financial performance for the period from 1 July 2004 to 30 June 2005 [YUN 2005, p. 366].

GENERAL ASSEMBLY ACTION

On 30 June [meeting 92], the General Assembly, on the recommendation of the Fifth Committee [A/60/927], adopted **resolution 60/280** without vote [agenda item 152].

Financing of the United Nations Mission for the Referendum in Western Sahara

The General Assembly,

Having considered the reports of the Secretary-General on the financing of the United Nations Mission for the Referendum in Western Sahara and the related report of the Advisory Committee on Administrative and Budgetary Questions,

Recalling Security Council resolution 690(1991) of 29 April 1991, by which the Council established the United Nations Mission for the Referendum in Western Sahara, and the subsequent resolutions by which the Council extended the mandate of the Mission, the latest of which was resolution 1675(2006) of 28 April 2006,

Recalling also its resolution 45/266 of 17 May 1991 on the financing of the Mission and its subsequent resolutions and decisions thereon, the latest of which was resolution 59/308 of 22 June 2005,

Reaffirming the general principles underlying the financing of United Nations peacekeeping operations, as stated in General Assembly resolutions 1874 (S-IV) of 27 June 1963, 3101(XXVIII) of 11 December 1973 and 55/235 of 23 December 2000,

Noting with appreciation that voluntary contributions have been made to the Mission,

Mindful of the fact that it is essential to provide the Mission with the necessary financial resources to enable it to fulfil its responsibilities under the relevant resolutions of the Security Council,

1. *Requests* the Secretary-General to entrust the Head of Mission with the task of formulating future budget proposals in full accordance with the provisions of General Assembly resolutions 59/296 of 22 June 2005 and 60/266 of 30 June 2006, as well as other relevant resolutions;

2. *Takes note* of the status of contributions to the United Nations Mission for the Referendum in Western Sahara as at 30 April 2006, including the contributions outstanding in the amount of 45.5 million United States dollars, representing some 8 per cent of the total assessed contributions, notes with concern that only seventy-one Member States have paid their assessed contributions in full, and urges all other Member States, in particular those in arrears, to ensure payment of their outstanding assessed contributions;

3. *Expresses its appreciation* to those Member States which have paid their assessed contributions in full, and urges all other Member States to make every possible

effort to ensure payment of their assessed contributions to the Mission in full;

4. *Expresses concern* at the financial situation with regard to peacekeeping activities, in particular as regards the reimbursements to troop contributors that bear additional burdens owing to overdue payments by Member States of their assessments;

5. *Also expresses concern* at the delay experienced by the Secretary-General in deploying and providing adequate resources to some recent peacekeeping missions, in particular those in Africa;

6. *Emphasizes* that all future and existing peacekeeping missions shall be given equal and non-discriminatory treatment in respect of financial and administrative arrangements;

7. *Also emphasizes* that all peacekeeping missions shall be provided with adequate resources for the effective and efficient discharge of their respective mandates;

8. *Reiterates its request* to the Secretary-General to make the fullest possible use of facilities and equipment at the United Nations Logistics Base at Brindisi, Italy, in order to minimize the costs of procurement for the Mission;

9. *Endorses* the conclusions and recommendations contained in the report of the Advisory Committee on Administrative and Budgetary Questions, and requests the Secretary-General to ensure their full implementation;

10. *Reaffirms* its resolution 59/296, and requests the Secretary-General to ensure the full implementation of its relevant provisions and the relevant provisions of its resolution 60/266;

11. *Requests* the Secretary-General to take all necessary action to ensure that the Mission is administered with a maximum of efficiency and economy;

12. *Also requests* the Secretary-General, in the context of the next performance report, to report any savings or efficiencies resulting from the military operational audit of June 2005;

13. *Further requests* the Secretary-General, in order to reduce the cost of employing General Service staff, to continue efforts to recruit local staff for the Mission against General Service posts, commensurate with the requirements of the Mission;

Financial performance report for the period from 1 July 2004 to 30 June 2005

14. *Takes note* of the report of the Secretary-General on the financial performance of the Mission for the period from 1 July 2004 to 30 June 2005;

Budget estimates for the period from 1 July 2006 to 30 June 2007

15. *Decides* to appropriate to the Special Account for the United Nations Mission for the Referendum in Western Sahara the amount of 44,460,000 dollars for the period from 1 July 2006 to 30 June 2007, inclusive of 42,619,400 dollars for the maintenance of the Mission, 1,520,300 dollars for the support account for peacekeeping operations and 320,300 dollars for the United Nations Logistics Base;

Financing of the appropriation

16. *Decides also* to apportion among Member States the amount of 14,820,000 dollars for the period from 1 July to 31 October 2006, in accordance with the levels updated in General Assembly resolution 58/256 of 23 December 2003, and taking into account the scale of assessments for 2006 as set out in its resolution 58/1 B of 23 December 2003;

17. *Decides further* that, in accordance with the provisions of its resolution 973(X) of 15 December 1955, there shall be set off against the apportionment among Member States, as provided for in paragraph 16 above, their respective share in the Tax Equalization Fund of 800,534 dollars, comprising the estimated staff assessment income of 735,467 dollars approved for the Mission, the prorated share of 57,000 dollars of the estimated staff assessment income approved for the support account and the prorated share of 8,067 dollars of the estimated staff assessment income approved for the United Nations Logistics Base;

18. *Decides* to apportion among Member States the amount of 29,640,000 dollars for the period from 1 November 2006 to 30 June 2007, at a monthly rate of 3,705,000 dollars, in accordance with the levels updated in General Assembly resolution 58/256, and taking into account the scale of assessments for 2006 as set out in its resolution 58/1 B, and the scale of assessments for 2007, subject to a decision of the Security Council to extend the mandate of the Mission;

19. *Decides also* that, in accordance with the provisions of its resolution 973(X), there shall be set off against the apportionment among Member States, as provided for in paragraph 18 above, their respective share in the Tax Equalization Fund of 1,601,066 dollars, comprising the estimated staff assessment income of 1,470,933 dollars approved for the Mission, the prorated share of 114,000 dollars of the estimated staff assessment income approved for the support account and the prorated share of 16,133 dollars of the estimated staff assessment income approved for the United Nations Logistics Base;

20. *Decides further* that, for Member States that have fulfilled their financial obligations to the Mission, there shall be set off against their apportionment, as provided for in paragraph 16 above, their respective share of the unencumbered balance and other income in the total amount of 1,483,200 dollars in respect of the financial period ended 30 June 2005, in accordance with the levels updated in its resolution 58/256, and taking into account the scale of assessments for 2005, as set out in its resolution 58/1 B;

21. *Decides* that, for Member States that have not fulfilled their financial obligations to the Mission, there shall be set off against their outstanding obligations their respective share of the unencumbered balance and other income in the total amount of 1,483,200 dollars in respect of the financial period ended 30 June 2005, in accordance with the scheme set out in paragraph 20 above;

22. *Decides also* that the decrease of 597,000 dollars in the estimated staff assessment income in respect of the financial period ended 30 June 2005 shall be set off

against the credits from the amount of 1,483,200 dollars referred to in paragraphs 20 and 21 above;

23. *Emphasizes* that no peacekeeping mission shall be financed by borrowing funds from other active peacekeeping missions;

24. *Encourages* the Secretary-General to continue to take additional measures to ensure the safety and security of all personnel under the auspices of the United Nations participating in the Mission, bearing in mind paragraphs 5 and 6 of Security Council resolution 1502(2003) of 26 August 2003;

25. *Invites* voluntary contributions to the Mission in cash and in the form of services and supplies acceptable to the Secretary-General, to be administered, as appropriate, in accordance with the procedure and practices established by the General Assembly;

26. *Decides* to include in the provisional agenda of its sixty-first session the item entitled "Financing of the United Nations Mission for the Referendum in Western Sahara".

In December, the Secretary-General submitted the performance report [A/61/683] on the MINURSO budget for the period from 1 July 2005 to 30 June 2006.

On 22 December, by **decision 61/552**, the Assembly decided that agenda item "Financing of MINURSO" would remain for consideration during its resumed sixty-first (2007) session.

Other issues

Libyan Arab Jamahiriya

On 22 December, by **decision 61/552**, the General Assembly decided that the agenda item "Declaration of the Assembly of Heads of State and Government of the Organization of African Unity on the aerial and naval military attack against the Socialist People's Libyan Arab Jamahiriya by the present United States Administration in April 1986" would remain for consideration during its sixty-first (2007) session.

Mauritius–United Kingdom/France

On 22 September [A/61/PV.16], Mauritius' Prime Minister, Navinchandra Rangolaam, speaking during the General Assembly's general debate, drew attention to the fact that, 38 years after its independence, Mauritius had still not been able to exercise its sovereignty over the Chagos Archipelago, including Diego Garcia. The Archipelago was excised from the territory of Mauritius by the former colonial Power to be subsequently used for military purposes behind Mauritius' back, in total disregard of Assembly resolutions 1514(XV) [YUN 1960, p. 49] and 2066(XX) [YUN 1965, p. 587]. That exercise also involved the displacement of the inhabitants of the Chagos from their homeland, thereby denying them their fundamental human rights. Mauritius called once again upon the United Kingdom to pursue constructive dialogue with Mauritius to enable it to exercise its sovereignty over the Chagos Archipelago. Mauritius viewed positively the visit jointly organized by its Government and the United Kingdom in April to enable the former inhabitants of the Chagos to visit the Archipelago for the first time since their displacement to pay respects at their relatives' graves.

Mauritius also hoped to continue meaningful dialogue with France on the sovereignty of Tromelin, and viewed the Agreement reached in Paris, at the expert level, in January, to set up a French-Mauritanian joint commission for the co-management of the Tromelin Zone as a positive first step.

On 29 September [A/61/488], the United Kingdom, in the exercise of its right of reply, maintained that the British Indian Ocean Territory was British and had been since 1814, and did not recognize Mauritius' sovereignty claim. However, the British Government recognized Mauritius as the only State which had a right to assert a claim of sovereignty whenever the United Kingdom relinquished its own sovereignty. Successive British Governments had given undertakings to Mauritius that the Territory would be ceded when no longer required for defence purposes. The British Government remained open to discussions regarding arrangements governing the British Indian Ocean Territory or the future of the Territory; and had stated that when the time came for the Territory to be ceded, it would liaise closely with the Government of Mauritius.

Cooperation between the AU and the UN system

On 31 May [meeting 5448], the Security Council was briefed by the AU Chairman, President Denis Sassou-Nguesso of the Congo, who expressed the AU deep gratitude to the Council for its efforts and determination in supporting peace and security on the continent. The Council's stabilizing action and partnership with the AU should be encouraged. Both institutions were striving to harmonize their undertakings, including through regular consultations. The way the AU and the Council together managed such complex issues, as Côte d'Ivoire and the situation in the Darfur region of the Sudan, were testimony to the relevance of that vision.

The partnership between the two organizations was based on a vision that there could be no peace without development, or development without peace. Issues of economic and social development, poverty elimination, national reconciliation, good governance and social justice were closely linked, and should be dealt with appropriately. The partnership between the United Nations, the AU and Africa's subregional communities should be strengthened. The AU and the United Nations had a common will to put an end to conflicts in Africa by making the best use of all the means that international cooperation provided, particularly in the framework of the partnership between the two organizations.

The Secretary-General, on 11 December [A/61/630], informed the General Assembly President of the Secretariat's efforts to implement the 2005 World Summit Outcome [YUN 2005, p. 48], in which Member States had committed themselves to meeting Africa's special needs and agreed to develop and implement a 10-year plan for capacity building with the AU. To further the World Summit Outcome, the Secretary-General and AU Commission Chairperson Alpha Oumar Konaré, signed in Addis Ababa, on 16 November, a declaration entitled "Enhancing UN-AU Cooperation: Framework for the Ten-Year Capacity-Building Programme for the African Union", which reflected a shared commitment to maintaining peace and security, promoting human rights and post-conflict reconstruction and advancing Africa's development and regional integration. The declaration provided a framework for UN system-wide support to the capacity-building efforts of the AU Commission and the regional economic communities. Both sides agreed on strategic priorities and political aspects of their relationship. Mr. Konaré stated the need for the United Nations and other partners to promote African integration, including by helping the AU Commission to become a real executive body. If the AU had the capacity to undertake certain tasks in Africa, it would unburden the United Nations. The United Nations-AU cooperation within the 10-year programme covered a much wider spectrum than the cooperation between the United Nations and the defunct Organization for African Unity, the Secretary-General said.

The Secretary-General, in his consolidated report [A/61/256] on cooperation between the United Nations and regional organizations, said that the AU 10-year capacity-building plan would be the overall framework under which the UN system could enhance its various activities in Africa and its cooperation with the AU, covering all aspects of UN assistance to the organizations.

On 22 December, by **decision 61/552**, the Assembly decided that agenda item on "Cooperation between the United Nations and the AU" would remain for consideration during its resumed sixty-first (2007) session.

Chapter III

Americas

During 2006, the United Nations continued to advance the cause of lasting peace, human rights, sustainable development and the rule of law in the Americas. In Guatemala, following the 2005 establishment of a joint UN office for monitoring and reporting human rights in the country, the Government and the United Nations signed, in December 2006, an agreement to create an International Commission against Impunity in Guatemala.

Although the political and security situation in Haiti remained challenging, significant progress was made in the democratic process, with the holding of successful national, municipal and local elections. With the support of the United Nations Stabilization Mission in Haiti (MINUSTAH) and the Organization of American States (OAS), presidential and legislative elections were held in February and April, and municipal and local elections in December, in a relatively calm manner. The new Government launched its long-term agenda for the modernization of the State and economic rebirth, as well as plans for improving living conditions in Haiti and reforming the Haitian National Police (HNP). In response to a request by the President for development support, a high-level delegation from the Caribbean Community (CARICOM) visited Haiti and discussed prospects for the full integration of the country into that organization, including the common market. Despite the political progress achieved, the security situation in the country remained precarious. Demonstrations, outbreaks of violence and attacks by armed groups, particularly against MINUSTAH and HNP continued, and in some areas, increased. The Mission's mandate was expanded to accommodate its post-electoral role in Haiti, which related to HNP reform, ensuring a safe and stable environment and strengthening State institutions. In November, the HNP started the vetting process to assess the professional skills and disciplinary background of police officers. MINUSTAH supported the training and institutional development of the police. By year's end, some 10,650 HNP officers and civilian employees had been registered within a UN police database, which would also serve HNP.

In other developments in the region, the General Assembly again called on States to refrain from promulgating laws and measures, such as the ongoing embargo against Cuba by the United States. The Assembly also considered activities undertaken by the United Nations to strengthen cooperation with CARICOM and OAS.

Central America

In 2006, Central America continued to consolidate peace and build democratic and equitable societies upon the foundation developed in years of successful UN peacemaking efforts. In support of those efforts, the United Nations continued to assist the region through development programming, the good offices of the Secretary-General and other means.

In September [meeting 17], the Nicaraguan Minister for Foreign Affairs, in briefing the General Assembly on the situation of the country, indicated that Nicaragua was experiencing a new political, economic and social reality. It envisaged the establishment of a Central American customs union, as well as an association agreement between the European Union and Central America, which would include a free trade agreement. On 5 November, in general elections held in Nicaragua, Daniel Ortega of the Sandinista National Liberation Front (FSLN) was elected President for a five-year term.

Two years after the ending of the mandate of the United Nations Verification Mission in Guatemala (MINUGA) in 2004 [YUN 2004, p. 287], the country continued to build upon the foundation developed in previous years. Following the establishment of a joint UN office for monitoring and reporting human rights in Guatemala, and pursuant to the Secretary-General's 2005 recommendation that the issue of impunity should be addressed as it related to illegal security forces and other clandestine organizations [YUN 2005, p. 375], the Government and the United Nations signed an agreement in December to create an International Commission against Impunity in Guatemala (see p. 870).

The Assembly, by **decision 61/552** of 22 December, decided that the item "The situation in Central America: progress in fashioning a region of peace, freedom, democracy and development" would remain for consideration during its resumed sixty-first (2007) session.

Communications. On 24 April [A/60/820-S/2006/265], Panama transmitted to the Secretary-General, the "Panama Declaration", adopted by Colombia, Costa Rica, the Dominican Republic, El Salvador, Guatemala, Honduras, Nicaragua and Panama at the Ministerial Conference on International Co-operation against Terrorism and Transnational Organized Crime (Panama City, Panama, 4-7 April) (see p. 73).

On 30 August [A/61/343], the Dominican Republic transmitted to the General Assembly a Declaration adopted as the outcome document of the Regional Consultation on Migration, Remittances and Development in Latin America and the Caribbean (Dominican Republic, 27-28 July), which brought together 75 representatives from 13 countries in the region.

Cuba, on behalf of the Non-Aligned Movement, transmitted to the Secretary-General, on 19 September [A/61/472-S/2006/780], documents adopted at the Fourteenth Conference of Heads of State or Government of the Non-Aligned Movement (Havana, Cuba, 11-16 September), which summarized political issues concerning Latin America and the Caribbean, and stressed the need for action by the international community to declare the Caribbean Sea as a "special area" for sustainable development.

Haiti

During 2006, although the political and security situation in Haiti remained challenging, significant progress was made in the democratic process, with the completion of the electoral calendar and installation of a new Government. In January, the Transitional Authorities announced the postponement of the elections due to logistical and technical difficulties. However, with the support of the United Nations Stabilization Mission in Haiti (MINUSTAH) and the Organization of American States (OAS), national elections were held in February, and local and municipal elections in December—the first such elections in ten years. The incoming administration promulgated President René Préval's recovery plan, the *Programme d'apaisement social,* to improve living conditions in Haiti in the short term. In August, a plan for the reform of the Haitian National Police (HNP) was adopted by the Government. In response to the President's request for development support, a high-level delegation from the Caribbean Community and Common Market (CARICOM) visited Haiti and discussed with Haitian authorities prospects for the full integration of the country into the organization, as well as the possibility of opening a CARICOM office in Port-au-Prince. Although the security situation remained stable and calm, demonstrations and sporadic violence by armed groups continued, and in some areas, attacks against MINUSTAH and the HNP increased, resulting in fatalities. MINUSTAH mandate was expanded to accommodate its post-electoral role in Haiti relating to HNP reform, modernization of the State and ensuring a safe and stable environment to facilitate economic reactivation. In November, HNP started a vetting process, utilizing MINUSTAH expertise, to assess the professional skills and disciplinary background of police officers. MINUSTAH also supported the training and institutional development of the police. By year's end, some 10,650 HNP officers and civilian employees had been registered. In addition to providing security support, MINUSTAH monitored the human rights situation, provided humanitarian assistance and coordinated its activities with regional organizations.

Political and security situation

National dialogue and electoral process

Haitian authorities and MINUSTAH continued to focus their efforts on organizing credible and timely elections. On 7 January, a new electoral calendar established by presidential decree scheduled the first round of national elections to be held on 7 February; the second round on 19 March; the swearing in of the new President on 29 March; and the holding of municipal and local elections on 30 April. Prime Minister Gérard Latortue had previously announced that, while his Government would formally resign on 7 February, it would carry out ongoing business until the new Government took office. The Secretary-General said that the postponement underlined the degree to which preparations for the elections continued to be complicated by a politically and technically fragile decision-making process in Haiti.

SECURITY COUNCIL ACTION

On 6 January [meeting 5343], following consultations among Security Council members, the President made statement **S/PRST/2006/1** on behalf of the Council:

> The Security Council reiterates its full support for the work of the United Nations Stabilization Mission in Haiti and the Special Representative of the Secretary-General for Haiti, Mr. Juan Gabriel Valdés.
>
> The Council reiterates that the future holding of elections is a fundamental step towards the restoration of democracy and stability in Haiti. The Council takes

note with concern of the new postponement of the elections in Haiti and, in this regard, trusts that the delay in the electoral calendar will enable the resolution of logistical and technical problems in order to ensure transparent, inclusive, free and fair elections.

The Council urges the Transitional Government of Haiti and the Provisional Electoral Council to expeditiously announce new and definitive dates for the elections, the first round to be held within weeks, but no later than 7 February 2006, and to ensure that the elections take place in accordance with international democratic standards and under conditions conducive to the widest possible participation. The Security Council calls upon all relevant international stakeholders to continue to collaborate closely with the Transitional Government and other national authorities in this endeavour. The revised electoral calendar and corresponding budget should be realistic and comprehensive, and should encompass national, municipal and local elections.

The Council reaffirms that security remains an essential element for the holding of free and equitable elections. The Council expresses its concern over the deterioration of security conditions in Port-au-Prince and urges the Haitian National Police and the Mission to continue their efforts to further intensify their cooperation to improve the security situation in order to restore and maintain the rule of law. In this regard, the Council pays tribute to those Mission peacekeepers that have been killed or injured in the line of duty.

The Council is of the view that, after the elections, a period of fundamental importance for long-term stability will follow. National reconciliation and political dialogue should continue to be promoted as a means to ensure long-term stability and good governance.

The Council reaffirms that open and credible elections, based on ownership by the Haitian people, are paramount to the consolidation of democratic institutions and procedures, but it recognizes at the same time that they do not constitute the sole means to address the longer-term problems that Haiti faces in the security sector and in the restoration of the rule of law, both of which are critical to stability and sustainable development. The Council welcomes, accordingly, the decision taken by the donor community to extend the Interim Cooperation Framework until December 2007 in order to assist the new elected Government to continue reconstruction efforts. The Council reaffirms that short-, medium- and long-term strategies, within a unified framework, are needed to ensure coordination and continuity in the international assistance to Haiti.

Statement by Secretary-General. In a 7 January press statement [SG/SM/10296], the Secretary-General said that he was saddened to learn of the death of Lieutenant General Urano Teixeira da Matta Bacellar (Brazil), MINUSTAH Force Commander, who had been found dead in his accommodations that morning. He indicated that a full investigation was being conducted.

Report of Secretary-General (February). In his February report on MINUSTAH [S/2006/60], the Secretary-General said that technical and logistical arrangements for the elections had progressed with the support of MINUSTAH and the Organization of American States (OAS), which played a lead role in the voter registration process. By the end of January, over 80 per cent of national identity cards had been distributed, nearly all voting centre supervisors recruited and polling workers identified. Remaining tasks included the training of poll workers, relocation of some voting centres; the resolution of technical problems; and preparations for municipal and local elections, which involved some 9,000 positions and a ballot printing process encompassing 700 districts.

Additional funding would be required for holding the elections, as delays, the need for more rapid execution to compensate for them, and technical limitations on the ground had led to an increase in the budget, which totalled $73.2 million, some $12.4 million over the original figure.

The overall security environment in most of the country remained stable. Progress was made in the Capital, Port-au-Prince, including the Bel-Air district, where there had been problems previously. Nevertheless, the security situation had worsened in other parts of the capital, such as Cité Soleil, where gangs remained active and continued to attack peacekeepers. The Secretary-General observed that, while MINUSTAH authorized strength was adequate to maintain basic security, stability during the elections could be enhanced if one or more Member States backed up MINUSTAH capabilities. In the interim, specialized military engineering equipment was being sought for security operations in Cité Soleil.

Emphasis was placed on the reform and restructuring of HNP, which continued to be inhibited by professional, technical and logistical shortcomings. Demonstrations staged against HNP Director General Mario Andrésol and the vandalizing of MINUSTAH vehicles exemplified the potential for resistance to HNP reform efforts. Joint bodies, such as a MINUSTAH/HNP steering committee to oversee progress in reform implementation,and MINUSTAH/HNP planning teams, were established. To provide a basis for a comprehensive reform process, MINUSTAH worked with HNP to register current officers. By the end of January, 4,492 national police officers and staff had been registered. A certification programme was also envisaged to promote HNP reform, whereby MINUSTAH would issue provisional certification for individual HNP officers and units. The certification, which would be valid for one year, would be renewed based on their observance of standards of conduct and satisfactory results from the vetting process. Haitian authorities would implement MINUSTAH recommendations, remain responsible for all personnel decisions and ensure that uncertified individuals did not serve in HNP. The process would terminate upon final certification of all HNP personnel and when the institution no longer required ongoing monitoring.

The Secretary-General stressed that HNP reform should be reinforced by efforts to improve the judicial system. A MINUSTAH review of the justice and corrections systems revealed a number of serious weaknesses, such as non-conformance with international standards; corruption at all levels of the legal system; prolonged and arbitrary detentions; and inadequate infrastructure to accommodate the increasing number of detainees, posing security and human rights concerns. The Secretary-General said that an extended programme of international assistance would be required to enhance the professional capacity of the judicial system. He recommended the incorporation of appropriately qualified experts within MINUSTAH, who would serve as a professional resource for judicial actors in the offices of the prosecutor, investigating magistrates and trial judges.

The Secretary-General concluded that significant progress had been made toward laying the basis for an inclusive democratic transition, but Haitian authorities had to complete the remaining preparations to support free, fair and transparent elections. MINUSTAH would redouble efforts to curb criminality and violence in the country, particularly in the capital, at a time when perceptions of insecurity could have an impact on public confidence.

The Secretary-General emphasized that the success of the new administration would depend on continued long-term international institution- and capacity-building assistance, in addition to enhanced security, to contribute to stability and facilitate economic and social development. As the registration of HNP officers would be completed in the coming months, intensified HNP reform efforts might involve demands beyond minustah's current capacity, particularly in providing technical assistance for strengthening rule-of-law institutions and policy-level advice to related ministries. He recommended that the Mission be extended for a six-month interim period to allow for further consultation and assessment regarding MINUSTAH role in the post-electoral environment, for which recommendations would be presented to the Security Council.

SECURITY COUNCIL ACTION

On 14 February [meeting 5372], the Security Council unanimously adopted **resolution 1658(2006)**. The draft [S/2006/97] was prepared in consultations among Council members.

The Security Council,

Reaffirming its previous resolutions on Haiti, in particular resolutions 1542(2004) of 30 April 2004, 1576(2004) of 29 November 2004 and 1608(2005) of 22 June 2005, as well as the relevant statements by its President,

Reaffirming its strong commitment to the sovereignty, independence, territorial integrity and unity of Haiti,

Congratulating the Haitian people on the successful holding of the first round of Haiti's elections on 7 February 2006, and commending the Haitian authorities, the United Nations Stabilization Mission in Haiti, the Organization of American States and relevant international stakeholders for their efforts in this regard,

Welcoming the progress achieved thus far in Haiti's political process, and urging all Haitians to continue to participate in it, and to accept peacefully its outcome,

Reaffirming the important role that the Mission, with the support of the international community, including regional and subregional organizations, has in supporting Haiti's national elections, as well as municipal and local elections scheduled to take place on 30 April 2006,

Looking forward to the early inauguration of the elected President, and emphasizing that, after that event, national reconciliation, inclusiveness and political dialogue will continue to be of fundamental importance for the long-term political, social and economic stability of Haiti,

Recognizing that the installation of the new Government will represent a major event that will mark a new chapter in the efforts of the international community in Haiti,

Emphasizing that security, the rule of law, political reconciliation and economic and social development remain key to the stability of Haiti,

Underscoring that security remains an essential element for the completion of the electoral process, and calling upon Haitians to renounce all forms of violence,

Expressing its full support for the efforts of the Mission to continue to assist the Haitian authorities to ensure a secure and stable environment after the elections,

Stressing that the consolidation of Haitian democratic institutions will be crucial for achieving stability and development, and that the Mission and the international community should continue to assist in building the capacity of national and local authorities and institutions,

Recognizing that the rule of law and respect for human rights are vital components of democratic societies, reaffirming the mandate of the Mission in this respect, and calling upon the Haitian authorities to undertake a comprehensive reform in all areas of the rule of law and to promote and protect human rights and fundamental freedoms,

Calling upon the Mission and the Haitian National Police to enhance coordination and to cooperate with other international stakeholders to effect the reform of the Haitian National Police and to finalize the overall reform plan requested in its resolution 1608(2005) as soon as possible,

Encouraging the Mission to further explore possibilities for greater support to reform, modernize and strengthen the judiciary and correctional systems, including through the provision of targeted technical assistance to rule-of-law institutions,

Stressing the importance of rapid progress on disarmament, demobilization and reintegration,

Welcoming the extension of the Interim Cooperation Framework until December 2007, urging the Haitian authorities to continue to make progress in its implementation in close cooperation with all relevant international stakeholders, and reiterating the commitment of the international community to provide long-term support for the Haitian people, including to achieve and sustain stability and combat poverty,

Recognizing the progress achieved thus far in the disbursement of pledged assistance, and encouraging the international financial institutions and donors to continue to disburse promptly the funds pledged,

Noting that the Haitian people must take responsibility for achieving stability, social and economic development and law and order,

Recalling paragraph 3 of its resolution 1608(2005),

Determining that the situation in Haiti continues to constitute a threat to international peace and security,

Acting under Chapter VII of the Charter of the United Nations, as described in section I of paragraph 7 of resolution 1542(2004),

1. *Decides* to extend the mandate of the United Nations Stabilization Mission in Haiti, as contained in resolutions 1542(2004) and 1608(2005), until 15 August 2006, with the intention to renew for further periods;

2. *Welcomes* the report of the Secretary-General of 2 February 2006, and supports the recommendations contained therein;

3. *Requests* the Secretary-General to report to the Security Council, as soon as possible after the conclusion of Haiti's electoral process and drawing, as appropriate, on consultations with the elected Government of Haiti, on whether to restructure the mandate of the Mission after the new Government takes office, including recommendations on ways in which the Mission can support reform and strengthening of key institutions;

4. *Decides* to remain seized of the matter.

Elections

Presidential and legislative elections (February)

The first round of presidential and legislative elections, held on 7 February, were regarded as a success. For the first time in recent history, the legitimacy of the elections was not contested. Due to the fragile security situation in Port-au-Prince during the preceding months, MINUSTAH had stepped up its activities to promote a safe environment and the isolated incidents that occurred resulted from long queues at polling stations. The Secretary-General appealed for all to respect the official results, which would be announced by the Provisional Electoral Council.

SECURITY COUNCIL ACTION

On 9 February [meeting 5368], following consultations among Security Council members, the President made statement **S/PRST/2006/7** on behalf of the Council:

The Security Council commends the Haitian people on the holding of the first round of national elections on 7 February 2006 with high voter turnout, and congratulates them on taking this fundamental step towards the restoration of democracy and stability in their country. The Council calls upon all parties to respect the outcome of the elections, remain engaged in the political process and renounce all forms of violence. The Council wishes to thank the United Nations Stabilization Mission in Haiti, the Organization of American States and others in the international community for providing crucial assistance to the Transitional Government and the Provisional Electoral Council during this period.

The Council underlines the fact that the electoral process should lead to the inauguration of a representative government. The Council reiterates the importance of national, municipal and local elections as pillars of democratic governance in Haiti. The Council emphasizes that, once the new government takes office, Haitians should continue to promote national reconciliation and political dialogue in order to strengthen their democracy and to ensure social, economic and political stability.

The Council, while recognizing the importance of the elections for democratic institutions and procedures, stresses that they do not constitute the sole means to address Haiti's longer-term problems and that significant challenges remain, in particular, in the fields of rule of law, security and development. Tackling these challenges will require a long-term engagement of the international community.

On the same date, the Council [meeting 5367], in a closed meeting with the troop-contributing countries, heard a briefing by the Assistant Secretary-General for Peacekeeping Operations.

Polling aftermath. On 12 February, street protests erupted following the release of partial results of the presidential elections by the Provisional Electoral Council, which showed that Presidential candidate René Préval's lead had dropped from over 60 per cent to below the 50 per cent threshold required to win the election in the first round. By the next day, large-scale demonstrations took place country-wide, stretching the ability of MINUSTAH to maintain a secure and stable environment, and forcing the erection of roadblocks along main thoroughfares and the temporary closure of the Port-au-Prince airport. Protesters overran the hotel where the Provisional Electoral Council media centre was located and surrounded the tabulation centre, causing both centres to temporarily suspend their activities. On 14 February, after two days of demonstrations and negotiations between the main political actors, the Provisional Electoral Council decided to allocate an unusually high proportion of blank ballots (4.3 per cent), on a pro rata basis, among all the candidates according to the number of votes they had received, and thereby, declared Mr. Préval the winner of the presidential election, with an absolute majority of 51.2 per cent of the votes. Although the procedure and its subsequent result were politically criticized by some of the candidates, including runner-up Leslie Manigat, who received 12 per cent of the votes, no one legally challenged the outcome.

Statement by Secretary-General. In a 17 February statement [SG/SM/10353], the Secretary-General welcomed the results of the Haitian Presidential election, and congratulated Mr. René Préval on his victory. He commended the Haitian people for their commitment to the democratic process and stressed the importance of national reconciliation and the holding of local and municipal elections as early as possible to complete the electoral cycle.

Security Council consideration. On 22 February [meeting 5377], the Security Council heard a briefing by the Interim Prime Minister, Mr. Gérard Latortue, who said that the Transitional Government had accomplished its mission to organize free, fair, democratic, transparent and inclusive elections, with the participation of all Haitian political actors. He expressed gratitude to the 43 countries that had contributed troops and police to ensure the country's stability and conveyed condolences to the families of the MINUSTAH soldiers who had lost their lives. After highlighting MINUSTAH efforts to improve relations with HNP, collaborate with various segments of Haitian society in the public and private sectors, provide security to facilitate a high participation rate during the elections and assist the Provisional Electoral Council, he encouraged the Council to visit Haiti to demonstrate the international community's support for the democratic process in the country. While the Interim Prime Minister welcomed the Council's decision to extend MINUSTAH's mandate for six months, he pointed out that new changes to support MINUSTAH would have to be considered, in consultation with the new Government. He also underlined the need for assistance in institution-building, improving the judicial system and professionalizing the national police.

Security Council consideration. On 27 March, the Security Council met [meeting 5397] to discuss the question of Haiti and heard statements by the Secretary-General, President-elect René Préval and the Secretary-General's Special Representative Juan Gabriel Valdés.

The Secretary-General said that Haiti was beginning a long journey towards a stable and democratic future and deserved assistance to meet that goal. President-elect Préval's efforts to encourage broad political reconciliation required generous support. While it was crucial that a multidimensional peacekeeping operation continue in Haiti following the February elections, MINUSTAH could only address the most urgent needs, and bilateral assistance would be required to build on those efforts.

President-elect Préval stated that the large turnout by the Haitian people at the elections demonstrated their desire to take part in national reconstruction and improve their living conditions. Citing chronic insecurity, poverty, widespread unemployment and the dilapidated state of basic infrastructure as challenges to be addressed, he called for a renewal of the international community's commitment to a long-term assistance programme for Haiti. He emphasized that the Interim Cooperation Framework [YUN 2004, p. 296], a set of priorities and targets to address Haiti's urgent and medium-term development needs, which had been extended to December 2007, should be taken into account. He also called for support from the international community for the disarmament, demobilization and reintegration programme and from MINUSTAH to help reform of the police and the Haitian judicial system.

The Secretary-General's Special Representative Juan Valdés reiterated the need to strengthen State institutions, security and rule of law, along with the launch of a sustainable socio-economic development process. He welcomed the decision taken by the Caribbean Community and Common Market (CARICOM) to re-establish its relations with the Government and the renewal of commitments by Argentina, Brazil and Chile to contribute troops to MINUSTAH.

At the Council's resumed session [meeting 5397], OAS expressed its commitment to supporting long-term institution-building and reconstruction in Haiti and stressed the importance of maintaining the time frame for completing the second round of legislative elections, scheduled for 21 April, and the holding of municipal and local elections on 18 June. It would also continue to support the Haitian registry and identification system for future electoral processes and help build a solid, professional and permanent electoral institution.

SECURITY COUNCIL ACTION

On 27 March [meeting 5397], following consultations among Security Council members, the President made statement **S/PRST/2006/13** on behalf of the Council:

The Security Council commends the Haitian people on the successful completion of the first round of their electoral process, congratulates Mr. René García Préval on his election as President, and looks forward to working with the new Government to help to build a better future for Haiti. This process will give Haiti a unique opportunity to break with the violence and political instability of the past. The Council expresses its full support for the work of the United Nations Stabilization Mission in Haiti and the Special Representative of the Secretary-General for Haiti, Mr. Juan Gabriel Valdés.

The Council welcomes the announcement by the Haitian authorities that the second round of parliamentary elections will be held on 21 April 2006, which will allow the prompt inauguration of the President-elect. The Council emphasizes that timely municipal and local elections are also fundamentally important to complete Haiti's electoral process and to strengthen its democratic institutions. The Council urges the Transitional Government of Haiti and the Provisional Electoral Council, with the support of the international community, to continue to ensure that the electoral process is conducted in a transparent and credible manner. The Security Council reiterates its call upon all parties to respect the outcome of the elections, remain engaged in the political process, and promote national reconciliation and inclusiveness in order to reach consensus on the basic policies that Haiti should pursue to bolster its democratic transition.

The Council stresses the need to ensure a secure and stable environment in Haiti and expresses its support for the continued efforts of the Mission to assist the Haitian authorities in that respect. The Council, in that regard, encourages all troop- and police-contributing countries to remain engaged in the Mission. The Council reaffirms that the establishment of the rule of law, including the protection of human rights, institutional capacity-building and rapid progress on disarmament, demobilization and reintegration will be crucial to Haiti's future over the next few years. To this end, the sustained political will and the common strategic vision of the Haitian authorities and the international community are essential. In this context, the Council underlines the urgent need to proceed with a thorough and comprehensive reform of the Haitian National Police in line with its resolution 1608(2005) as well as concurrent justice reform.

The Council is aware that sustainable development in Haiti remains essential to the stability of the country. In that regard, the Council reiterates the need for the quick implementation of highly visible and labour-intensive projects that help to create jobs and deliver basic social services. Recognizing progress already made in donor efforts, the Council calls upon donors and relevant stakeholders to work with the new Government through the Interim Cooperation Framework to reassess assistance priorities in a targeted way and to work in close coordination, as appropriate, with the Mission. The Council reiterates its willingness to cooperate with the newly elected authorities in order to address the long-term challenges facing Haiti.

Legislative elections (April)

Although the second round of legislative elections were held in an atmosphere of calm on 21 April, two voting stations were closed in Grande Saline due to violent confrontations between supporters of rival political parties. On 9 May, pending run-off elections in localities where the electoral process had been disrupted or appeals had been upheld, 27 out of 30 senators and 88 out of 99 deputies were sworn into office. Front de l'Espoir (LESPWA), the coalition of President-elect Préval, won 11 seats in the Senate, followed by the Organisation du peuple en lutte with 4 seats. LESPWA also gained the most seats in the House of Deputies, a total of 20, with Fusion winning 15 seats.

On 14 May, Mr. Préval assumed office as President of Haiti, called for dialogue to bring stability to the country and acknowledged the efforts of the international community and MINUSTAH.

SECURITY COUNCIL ACTION

On 15 May [meeting 5438], following consultations among Security Council members, the President made statement **S/PRST/2006/22** on behalf of the Council:

The Security Council congratulates Mr. René García Préval on his inauguration as President of the Republic of Haiti. The Council also congratulates all newly elected parliamentarians and calls upon them to recognize the importance of the mandate given to them by the Haitian people to work constructively to build a better future for their country. To this end, the Council urges the executive and legislative powers to establish a fruitful and collaborative relationship. The Council stresses that the timely holding of municipal, local and remaining parliamentary elections is fundamental to democratic governance.

The Council underlines the fact that many challenges remain to be tackled, including the need to ensure a secure and stable environment in Haiti, strengthen its democratic institutions, foster national reconciliation, inclusiveness and political dialogue, promote and protect human rights and the rule of law, and build governmental capacity, and welcomes the commitment of Mr. Préval in this regard. The Council also emphasizes the need to reform and strengthen Haiti's police, judiciary and correctional systems, and, in this regard, looks forward to the results of the discussions between the United Nations Stabilization Mission in Haiti and the new authorities on how to address these and other security-related issues. Recognizing that development remains essential to Haiti's stability, the Council calls upon donors and relevant stakeholders to continue to assess and coordinate assistance priorities, in close cooperation with the new Government, taking into account existing mechanisms such as the Interim Cooperation Framework. The Council reiterates the need for the quick implementation of highly visible and labour-intensive projects that help to create jobs and deliver basic social services. In this regard, the Council looks forward to the upcoming meeting to be held in Brasilia on 23 May 2006.

The Council welcomes the intention of the Caribbean Community to reintegrate Haiti fully into the activities of the Community. The Council also expresses its appreciation for the contribution of the Organization of American States to the electoral process. In this regard, the Council supports the commitment of the new Haitian authorities to enhance cooperation with regional partners in order to address issues related to regional stability.

The Council expresses its full support for the continued efforts by the Mission and the international community to assist Haiti in its ongoing transition, and requests that the Mission work closely with the new authorities in the implementation of its mandate. The Council looks forward to the report of the Secretary-General requested in resolution 1658(2006) on whether to restructure the mandate of the Mission and reiterates its willingness to cooperate with the newly elected authorities to address the long-term challenges facing Haiti. The Council would like also to thank the Special Representative of the Secretary-General for his tireless efforts and dedication to the success of the United Nations presence in Haiti.

Municipal and local elections (December)

In December [S/2006/1003], the Secretary-General reported the successful completion of the electoral process, after the holding of municipal and local elections. On 3 December, some 29,000 candidates competed for approximately 8,000 municipal and local positions—the first such elections in 10 years—and a second round was held for 3 senatorial and 11 deputy seats, which had been postponed from the previous legislative elections due to voting interruptions. The Provisional Electoral Council assumed increased responsibility for technical and administrative aspects of the process, including full responsibility for the training and payment of 40,000 poll workers. MINUSTAH provided logistic and security assistance, including the recruitment and training of some 4,000 electoral guards. Although some security incidents occurred, voter turnout was higher than expected, approximately 30 per cent, and Haitian electoral authorities were generally satisfied with the process. Nevertheless, a number of appeals were anticipated.

Further political and security developments

MINUSTAH post-election role

Report of Secretary-General. In July [S/2006/592], the Secretary-General reported that President Préval had ratified the appointment of Jacques Edouard Alexis as Prime Minister on 30 May. A process of consultation that preceded President Préval's inauguration led to an agreement on a multi-party Government, reflecting a spirit of political diversity. The 18-member cabinet contained representatives for seven political formations, including Alyans, Fanmi Lavalas, Fusion, LESPWA, Movement pour l'instauration de la democratie en Haiti and l'Organisation du peuple en lutte et Union. The Government's agenda—presented by Prime Minister Alexis in early June—which focused on the modernization of the State and on wealth creation, was approved by the Senate and the House of Deputies. President Préval's recovery plan, the Programme d'apaisement social, which responded to immediate social needs, was also submitted for approval.

Overall, the security situation remained stable. However, in early July, violence and criminal activities by armed groups increased sharply. Killings and kidnappings dominated media reports and public debate, prompting criticism of the Government and MINUSTAH by political and civil society groups. In response, MINUSTAH and the Government designed an integrated security plan, with increased checkpoints and joint patrols, which was launched on 10 July. Other destabilizing factors included elements of the former military who remained scattered throughout the country; the dysfunctional state of the rule-of-law institutions; fragile political alliances; and continued drug and arms trafficking, which gave rise to gang criminality, engendered corruption and undermined efforts to reduce armed violence and strengthen State institutions.

Pursuant to Security Council resolution 1658(2006) (see p. 344), a thorough assessment of MINUSTAH mandate in Haiti was carried out, involving exchanges between MINUSTAH and UN Headquarters, as well as with international partners. In June, a UN team visited Haiti to discuss with Haitian authorities and other actors MINUSTAH role in the post-electoral period. The need to specify a clear division of labour among the relevant actors was stressed.

With regard to the modernization of the State, MINUSTAH would focus on providing support to the rule-of-law sector and State administration, particularly outside Port-au-Prince, where MINUSTAH often represented the largest, and in some areas, the only, international presence and where local authorities were weak or non-existent. In the area of economic reactivation, MINUSTAH would continue to ensure a secure and stable environment, whereby Haitians and international actors could pursue their activities in safety. MINUSTAH components that focused on cross-cutting issues, including human rights, gender, child protection and HIV/AIDS would work to ensure the mainstreaming of such matters. During the post-electoral period, MINUSTAH would continue to ensure a secure and stable environment, work with Haitian authorities on appropriate security measures and pave the way for HNP to assume full responsibility for security in the country. Specifically, MINUSTAH troops and police units would patrol towns and their surroundings; protect key installations and UN personnel and facilities; provide operational support to HNP and MINUSTAH police operations; facilitate access of humanitarian workers to Haitians in need; and protect civilians under imminent threat. As gang violence and kidnappings were the main factors destabilizing security, without significant added special police capacities, MINUSTAH's ability to respond to crime would be limited. There was need for an enhanced security presence at key land border crossing points and selected ports to assist in extending State authority; increased support to the Haitian coast guard to respond to illicit activities in the coastal areas; and increased technical assistance from MINUSTAH military and police components to address specific issues, such as smuggling and the lack of proper customs administration in Haiti. To fulfil those responsibilities, MINUSTAH troops would continue to be deployed in all 10 regions of the country and would require expanded specific capacities, including engineering personnel, dump trucks, military police, and the deployment of sufficient aviation capabilities to maintain its airlifting capacity. The force strength would be maintained at its authorized ceiling of 7,500 troops, and its police strength increased to 1,951. It would also be provided with special weapons and tactics (SWAT) personnel and equipment and 16 corrections officers. Downsizing of international security components would take place progressively as HNP built up its capacity to handle primary security functions. MINUSTAH should also assist the Haitian authorities in the development and implementation of a disarmament and violence reduction programme.

The Secretary-General reported that an HNP reform plan, which had been finalized and was awaiting endorsement by the *Conseil supérieur de la police nationale*, estimated that essential policing functions in Haiti could be discharged by 12,000 well-trained and well-equipped officers, a figure that could be achieved in five years. The plan anticipated between 18,000 to 20,000 officers to implement the full range of Haitian security sector responsibilities, including border and coastal monitoring, fire fighting and responding to serious security threats. The MINUSTAH police component would assist in HNP reform and restructuring through a programme of monitoring, mentoring and field training at HNP stations and commissariats. Particular emphasis would be placed on the vetting process, to be conducted by 50 investigative teams and supported by MINUSTAH human rights experts. Fifty-four officers with specialized skills in investigation, database programming, engineering, finance, communication systems and training would be required, as well as experts in counter-kidnapping and anti-gang operations.

To strengthen the judicial system, MINUSTAH could provide experts to serve as a professional resource to the Ministry of Justice and other key justice institutions. It would continue to assist the Provisional Electoral Council in completing the electoral cycle, and in collaboration with the United Nations Development Programme (UNDP), support democratic governance and the strengthening of State institutions. To that end, the establishment of a MINUSTAH parliamentary liaison office in the capital to provide hands-on assistance to parliamentarians was envisaged.

The Secretary-General recommended that the Security Council approve the proposals regarding MINUSTAH mandate and resources and extend the Mission for a 12-month period, as the minimum time needed to establish a solid basis for rule of law reform, achieve some initial results and make progress towards democratic governance. He called on the international community to complement MINUSTAH activities, in particular regional partners such as OAS and CARICOM. He further appealed to donors to provide their support in the context of the 25 July pledging conference held in Port-au-Prince.

Secretary-General's visit to Haiti. On the occasion of his first official visit to Haiti on 3 and 4 August [SG/T/2506], the Secretary-General met with MINUSTAH staff and contingent commanders and addressed HNP and the MINUSTAH police component at the Haitian Police Academy. He also met with President Préval and other senior Haitian officials. In a joint press conference with the President, he announced that he had asked the Security Council to extend MINUSTAH mandate for 12 months instead of the customary six, due to the difficulties that lay ahead for the country.

Security Council consideration. On 8 August [meeting 5506], the Security Council, in a closed meeting with the troop-contributing countries, heard a briefing by Edmond Mulet, Special Representative of the Secretary-General and Head of MINUSTAH.

SECURITY COUNCIL ACTION

On 15 August [meeting 5513], the Security Council unanimously adopted **resolution 1702(2006)**. The draft [S/2006/648] was prepared in consultations among Council members.

The Security Council,

Reaffirming its previous resolutions on Haiti, in particular resolutions 1542(2004) of 30 April 2004, 1576(2004) of 29 November 2004, 1608(2005) of 22 June 2005 and 1658(2006) of 14 February 2006, as well as the relevant statements by its President,

Reaffirming its strong commitment to the sovereignty, independence, territorial integrity and unity of Haiti,

Welcoming the successful and peaceful political transition to an elected Government, as well as the election of a new President and Parliament, which will give Haiti a unique opportunity to break with the violence and political instability of the past,

Welcoming also the political agenda of the Government of Haiti on the modernization of State institutions and on wealth creation and the adoption, by the Haitian authorities, of the 'Programme d'apaisement social' to respond to Haiti's immediate social needs,

Emphasizing that security, the rule of law and institutional reform, national reconciliation and sustainable economic and social development remain key to the stability of Haiti,

Recognizing that the United Nations Stabilization Mission in Haiti constitutes a key actor in the continuing stabilization of the country, and expressing its appreciation for its efforts to continue to assist the Government of Haiti to ensure a secure and stable environment,

Reaffirming the importance of appropriate expertise on issues relating to gender in peacekeeping operations and post-conflict peacebuilding in accordance with its resolution 1325(2000) of 31 October 2000, recalling the need to address violence against women and children, and encouraging the Mission as well as the Government of Haiti to actively address these issues,

Condemning all violations of human rights in Haiti, calling upon all Haitians to renounce violence, and recognizing, in this context, that the rule of law and respect for human rights are vital components of democratic societies,

Urging the Government of Haiti to undertake, in coordination with the international community, a comprehensive reform of the police, judiciary and correctional systems, to promote and protect human rights and fundamental freedoms and to end impunity,

Welcoming the final approval by the Government of Haiti of its Haitian National Police Reform Plan, and calling upon it to implement the Plan as soon as possible,

Recognizing that conditions for conventional disarmament, demobilization and reintegration do not currently exist in Haiti and that alternative programmes are required to address local conditions and to further the goal of disarmament, demobilization and reintegration,

Underlining the need for the quick implementation of highly effective and visible labour-intensive projects that help to create jobs and deliver basic social services, and emphasizing the importance of quick-impact projects in the post-electoral phase,

Welcoming the outcomes of the ministerial donor meeting on Haiti, held in Brasilia on 23 May 2006, as well as those of the International Conference of Donors for the Social and Economic Development of Haiti, held in Port-au-Prince on 25 July 2006,

Expressing its support for the extension of the Interim Cooperation Framework until September 2007, and urging the Government of Haiti to continue to make progress in its implementation in close cooperation with all relevant international stakeholders,

Welcoming the readmittance of Haiti to the Councils of the Caribbean Community, and calling upon the Mission to continue to work closely with the Organization of American States and the Caribbean Community,

Welcoming also the appointment of a new Special Representative of the Secretary-General for Haiti with overall authority on the ground for the coordination and conduct of all the activities of the United Nations agencies, funds and programmes in Haiti,

Paying tribute to the continued support of the international community, particularly the Core Group, interested stakeholders, donors and regional organizations, for Haiti and the Mission, which remains essential to the achievement of stability and development,

Expressing its gratitude to the troops and police personnel of the Mission and to their countries,

Noting that the Haitian people and their Government hold the ultimate responsibility for achieving political stability, social and economic development and law and order,

Determining that the situation in Haiti continues to constitute a threat to international peace and security,

Acting under Chapter VII of the Charter of the United Nations, as described in section I of paragraph 7 of resolution 1542(2004),

1. *Decides* to extend the mandate of the United Nations Stabilization Mission in Haiti, as contained in its resolutions 1542(2004) and 1608(2005), until 15 Febru-

ary 2007, with the intention to renew for further periods;

2. *Welcomes* the report of the Secretary-General of 28 July 2006, and supports the priorities set out therein;

3. *Decides* that the Mission shall consist of a military component of up to 7,200 troops of all ranks and a police component of up to 1,951 officers;

4. *Authorizes* the Mission to deploy 16 corrections officers seconded from Member States in support of the Government of Haiti to address the shortcomings of the prison system;

5. *Urges* Member States to provide enough well-qualified, particularly francophone, police candidates, to ensure full staffing of the Mission police and, in particular, to provide specific expertise in anti-gang operations, corrections and other specializations identified as necessary in the report of the Secretary-General;

6. *Urges* the Haitian authorities to complete the run-off legislative, local and municipal elections as soon as feasible, and calls upon the Mission to provide all appropriate assistance in this regard, consistent with its mandate, and with the support of regional and subregional organizations;

7. *Reaffirms its call upon* the Mission to support the constitutional and political process in Haiti, including through good offices, and to promote national dialogue and reconciliation;

8. *Welcomes* the important contribution provided by the Mission in capacity- and institution-building at all levels, and calls upon the Mission to expand its assistance to support the Government of Haiti in strengthening State institutions, especially outside Port-au-Prince;

9. *Underlines* the importance of the continuing support of the Mission for the institutional strengthening of the Haitian National Police, and in this regard requests the Haitian authorities, especially the Haitian National Police, and the Mission to achieve optimal coordination in order to counter crime and violence, particularly in urban areas, taking into account the needs expressed by the Secretary-General for specialized capacities to enhance the ability of the Mission in this field;

10. *Strongly supports*, in this regard, the intention of the Secretary-General to maximize the crime prevention role of the Mission, particularly with regard to the threat of gang violence and kidnapping;

11. *Requests* the Mission to reorient its disarmament, demobilization and reintegration efforts, to further that goal, towards a comprehensive community violence reduction programme adapted to local conditions, including assistance for initiatives to strengthen local governance and the rule of law and to provide employment opportunities to former gang members, and at-risk youth, in close coordination with the Government of Haiti and other relevant actors, including the donor community;

12. *Urges* donors engaged in supporting the implementation of the reform of the Haitian National Police by the Haitian authorities to coordinate their activities closely with the Mission;

13. *Reaffirms* the mandate of the Mission to provide operational support to the Haitian Coast Guard, and invites Member States, in coordination with the Mission, to engage with the Government of Haiti in order to address cross-border drug and arms trafficking control;

14. *Decides* that the Mission, consistent with its existing mandate under resolution 1542(2004) to assist with the restructuring and maintenance of the rule of law, public safety and public order, shall provide assistance and advice to the Haitian authorities, in consultation with relevant actors, in monitoring, restructuring, reforming and strengthening the justice sector, including through technical assistance to review all relevant legislation, the provision of experts to serve as professional resources, the rapid identification and implementation of mechanisms to address prison overcrowding and prolonged pretrial detention and the coordination and planning of these activities, and invites the Government of Haiti to take full advantage of that assistance;

15. *Reaffirms* the human rights mandate of the Mission, and calls upon the Haitian authorities to undertake a comprehensive reform in all areas of rule of law and to promote and protect human rights and fundamental freedoms;

16. *Recognizes* the progress achieved thus far in the disbursement of pledged assistance, welcomes the pledges of donors, and notes the need for these funds to be rapidly disbursed, given that further sustained and generous international assistance will be essential for the Haitian people and their Government to succeed in pursuing its programme for social and economic development;

17. *Requests* the Mission to continue to implement quick-impact projects;

18. *Calls upon* the Mission to enhance its coordination with the United Nations country team and with the various development actors in Haiti in order to ensure greater efficiency in development efforts and to address urgent development problems;

19. *Reaffirms* the need to maintain a proactive communications and public outreach strategy to improve public understanding of the mandate and role of the Mission in Haiti and to deliver messages to the Haitian people directly;

20. *Requests* the Secretary-General to report to the Security Council on the implementation of the mandate of the Mission no later than 31 December 2006;

21. *Decides* to remain seized of the matter.

HNP reform plan

On 31 August [S/2006/726], the Secretary-General transmitted to the Security Council the Haitian National Police Reform Plan, submitted to him by Jean Rénalde Clérismé, the Haitian Minister for Foreign Affairs, who confirmed the Government's adoption of the plan on 8 August. The plan, which had been elaborated in coordination with MINUSTAH, was based on findings made by the Interim Cooperation Framework 2004-2006 and included the anticipated size, standards, implementation timetable and resources required. According to the plan, essential policing functions would require 14,000 trained and equipped officers. That target would be achieved over a five-year period, at a rate of 1,500 new officers per year, reaching 9,000 officers by 2008 and 14,000 by 2011. The review of current personnel, leading to final certification, would remain a priority and would target the disciplinary and training record of each officer. The plan reflected a general consensus that 18,000 to 20,000 police and security officers would be required to cover the full range of security needs in Haiti. It also provided for the development of capabilities, such as a Coast Guard, border patrol and surveillance, fire brigades and penal system. According to the estimate for personnel expenditures, the national budget could support the HNP staffing increase. However, as the budget allocation for capital investments was insufficient, HNP development would rely heavily on external funding sources. The overall cost of HNP reform was estimated at $700 million.

Mr. Clérismé stressed that, although the Haitian Government would implement the HNP reform plan in close cooperation with MINUSTAH and the international community, its success depended on the ongoing support of the latter. Detailed implementation plans for each HNP functional area would be developed, focusing on execution modalities, as well as the roles and responsibilities of the international community, in coordination with bilateral and multilateral donors.

End-of-year developments

Report of Secretary-General (December). In his December report on MINUSTAH [S/2006/1003], the Secretary-General said that, while the overall security environment remained stable, with much of the violence taking place in the capital, armed attacks against MINUSTAH and violent demonstrations increased. On 19 July, armed groups, frustrated over the Government's perceived inaction in meeting their amnesty demands in return for participation in a disarmament programme, fired weapons and created panic near Cité Soleil. The following day, they opened fire on MINUSTAH and a nearby HNP station, resulting in the injury of one police officer, the death of five gang members and the injury of another five. Over the two-day period, six civilians were killed, 80 injured and an unknown number abducted. On 25 August, Haitian and MINUSTAH officials agreed to an enhanced security plan, establishing 12 additional HNP/MINUSTAH checkpoints and 23 more HNP checkpoints around Port-au-Prince, in addition to the redeployment of three MINUSTAH platoons from the outlying regions to Cité Soleil. By mid-September, the situation had improved, and after joint MINUSTAH/HNP meetings with local residents and community leaders, HNP subsequently resumed patrols in the area during daylight hours. On 24 October, tensions again escalated as a group of 30 students protested a UN Day ceremony, holding anti-MINUSTAH placards and calling for the withdrawal of peacekeepers. The next day, 600 students held a similar protest near the Presidential Palace and erected roadblocks with burning tires. The Minister for Foreign Affairs, who had urged students not to resort to violence, remarked that the demonstrations illustrated the public's impatience with the lack of social progress. Progress was made with the apprehension of an armed group leader who had been linked to large-scale killings in Martissant in 2005 and 2006.Ongoing violence had taken a toll on MINUSTAH troops and police, with the death of two MINUSTAH and one HNP soldiers, with seven officers having been murdered in the capital since August. In the light of the fragile security situation, the Secretary-General stressed that an international security presence in Haiti should continue and future reductions in MINUSTAH troop and police strength should be linked to proportionate increases in the ability of that country's institutions to assume relevant tasks and to any changes in the security environment.

In the area of disarmament, demobilization and reintegration (DDR), MINUSTAH worked with national authorities to develop a DDR process appropriate to the country's needs. On 29 August, the Government appointed a seven-member National Commission for Disarmament, Dismantlement and Reintegration, which had taken the lead in implementing its DDR programme. However, progress remained limited, with only two groups of 104 individuals having formally entered the programme. Meanwhile, in collaboration with the Government, MINUSTAH and UNDP continued to strengthen the legislative framework for small arms control; build community capacity for violence reduction; and maintain a focus on women affected by violence and children associated with armed groups.

An update on HNP reform provided information on the implementation status of its three main pillars: vetting, training and the strengthening of institutional capacities. On 9 November, HNP announced the beginning of the vetting process, which would assess professional skills and disciplinary background and draw on the efforts of combined MINUSTAH and Haitian police teams. In December, the 25 most senior HNP officers, including the

Director General and Inspector General took part in the process, along with 10 HNP investigators, who would be involved in the vetting process. By December, some 8,070 HNP officers and 1,580 civilian employees had been registered within a UN police database. A further 600 HNP candidates, including 30 women, would begin training in January 2007.

The implementation of the Prime Minister's *Programme d'apaisement social* had not advanced significantly. At the International Conference for Haiti's Economic and Social Development (Port-au-Prince, 25 July), donors pledged $750 million to finance the budget deficit and the Government's public investment programme for the next fiscal year. They reiterated their long-term support for the Government's reform efforts in economic governance, fighting corruption, smuggling and tax evasion, and reaffirmed their willingness to support the reform of HNP and the judicial system, as well as efforts for social development and the DDR process. The follow-up conference (Madrid, Spain, 30 November) further helped to maintain international focus on Haiti and resulted in other sizeable pledges.

In the area of regional cooperation, the report summarized the 18 October visit to Haiti by a high-level CARICOM delegation, which met with Haitian authorities and discussed prospects for the full integration of the country into that organization, including the common market. The visit coincided with a CARICOM assessment mission, which considered the possibilities of opening an office in Port-au-Prince. Those initiatives were conducted within the framework of CARICOM's response to a request from President Préval for support for Haiti's development.

The Secretary-General concluded that the Haitian Government would continue to face significant challenges, including issues such as the distribution of responsibilities between central and local authorities; how best to meet the country's security requirements; an appropriate response to armed groups and the development of relevant DDR programmes; finalization of justice system reform plans and the adoption of key related bills; resolution of the problem of pre-trial detentions; and adoption of a legislative framework for the Office of the Ombudsman. He stressed that, unless swift results were achieved in those areas, the situation in Haiti could deteriorate. He recommended the extension of MINUSTAH's mandate for a further 12-month period, with its authorized capacity ceilings remaining at 7,200 troops and 1,951 police officers.

Programme of support for Haiti

Ad Hoc Advisory Group. The Ad Hoc Advisory Group on Haiti, mandated by resolution 2004/322 [YUN 2004, p. 939] to follow and advise on the long-term development of the country, submitted a May report [E/2006/69 & Corr.1] to the Economic and Social Council, which summarized the political, social and economic situation in Haiti and presented information on international support provided to the country since the 2005 substantive session of the Council. It elaborated on prospects for assistance in the post-electoral context and made recommendations to Haitian authorities and their development partners. Progress highlighted in the report included the preparation by Haitian national authorities of an interim Poverty Reduction Strategy Paper (PRSP); the development and attribution of "scores" for the accomplishment of ICF objectives; the identification by the International Monetary Fund and the World Bank of Haiti as one of 11 countries that could qualify for debt relief under the Heavily Indebted Poor Countries Initiative (HIPC); and the creation by the interim Government of a strategic "think tank" to work at the technical level on a long-term development plan for the country, in partnership with the Advisory Group and other actors.

On 26 July, the Economic and Social Council adopted **resolution 2006/10** on the Ad Hoc Advisory Group on Haiti (see p. 1087).

MINUSTAH

In 2006, the United Nations Stabilization Mission in Haiti (MINUSTAH), established by Security Council resolution 1542(2004) [YUN 2004, p. 294], continued to focus on ensuring a secure and stable environment, supporting the electoral process and reform of rule-of-law structures, strengthening State institutions, providing humanitarian and development assistance and protecting and promoting human rights. In February, its mandate was extended to August 2006. In August, pursuant to Security Council resolution 1658(2006), the structure of the Mission was enhanced and its mandate extended to 15 February 2007 (see p. 344).

Appointments. By an exchange of letters between the Secretary-General and the Security Council President on 18 [S/2006/32] and 20 [S/2006/33] January, Lieutenant General José Elito Carvalho de Siqueira (Brazil) was appointed Force Commander of MINUSTAH to replace General Teixeira da Matta Bacellar.

In May, by an exchange of letters with the Council President [S/2006/303, S/2006/304], the Secretary-General appointed Edmond Mulet (Guatemala) as his Special Representative in Haiti and Head of MINUSTAH to replace Juan Valdés, who would complete his assignment on 31 May.

In July, the Secretary-General informed the Council of his intention to add Bolivia to the list of troop-contributing countries to MINUSTAH, of which it took note [S/2006/586, S/2006/587].

MINUSTAH activities

During 2006, the Secretary-General reported to the Security Council on MINUSTAH activities and developments in Haiti for the periods 7 October 2005 to 2 February 2006 [S/2006/60], 3 February to 28 July [S/2006/592] and 29 July to 19 December [S/2006/1003]. In addition to the political and security aspects, the reports summarized MINUSTAH activities dealing with human rights; child protection; the humanitarian and development situations; gender issues; the prevention of HIV/AIDS; the implementation of the Interim Cooperative Framework; UN country team activities; the conduct and discipline of UN personnel; and Mission support.

Human rights. The human rights situation in Haiti continued to fall short of acceptable standards, with armed gangs being responsible for killings, kidnappings, armed robberies, extortion and harassment. Mob violence, including lynchings and the destruction of property, remained widespread and summary executions perpetrated by HNP officers continued to occur. In February, former Prime Minister Yvon Neptune and former Minister for the Interior Jocelerme Privert remained incarcerated. Mr. Neptune was granted provisional release on 27 July and four high-profile Fanmi Lavalas activists were released on 8 August, after two and half years of pre-trial detention. In October, the United Nations High Commissioner for Human Rights expressed concern over prison overcrowding and pre-trial detentions in Haiti. With the support of the High Commissioner's Office, MINUSTAH augmented its training, civic education and advisory services. MINUSTAH, in collaboration with HNP, developed training materials for mainstreaming human rights standards into all aspects of basic police training.

Child protection. Grave violations against children, especially in areas affected by armed violence, remained a serious concern, as well as widespread rape and other forms of sexual abuse of girls. MINUSTAH and the United Nations Children's Fund (UNICEF) initiated a campaign encouraging political parties and civil society representatives to include child protection in the political agendas of election candidates. To facilitate disarmament and the reintegration of children associated with armed groups, MINUSTAH, UNICEF and local partners advocated the development of transitional justice mechanisms, such as conditional amnesty for such children, as Haitian criminal law did not allow for disarmament of children recruited by armed gangs without punishment. Strengthening of the HNP *Brigade de protection des mineurs* (Brigade for the Protection of Minors) and the institution of a training programme for the police on children's rights were stressed as priorities, as was the resumed functioning of the juvenile court.

Humanitarian situation. MINUSTAH continued to respond to the humanitarian situation in Haiti. In August, Hurricane Ernesto killed four people, left 515 in temporary shelters, and destroyed 83 houses and damaged another 759. It prompted the activation of the UN contingency plan for natural disasters and the establishment by MINUSTAH of a joint operations coordination centre. Heavy rains in September and October caused a succession of floods and landslides, also resulting in fatalities, infrastructure damage to two hospitals and eight water supply systems, and the destruction or damage of 792 houses. MINUSTAH worked with local authorities to clear a major drainage channel in Cap Haïtien following landslides there.

Development. In June, President Préval proposed a recovery plan, the *Programme d'apaisement social*, to improve living conditions in Haiti in the short-term, by ensuring access to basic services such as, electricity, garbage disposal and employment generation (see p. 353). At the High-level International Meeting on Haiti (Brasilia, Brazil, 23 May), participants discussed the Interim Cooperation Framework (ICF), which had been extended from September 2006 to 2007 [YUN 2005, p. 390]. Donors reiterated their support for ICF and aligning it with the *Programme d'apaisement social*. To that end, under the auspices of the UN Resident Coordinator, donors formed a *Comité de partenariat* with the Government. In December, the Secretary-General reported that steps had been taken to ensure enhanced coordination among the UN country team, MINUSTAH and development actors in Haiti, as well as improved monitoring and reporting on the impact of humanitarian and development efforts.

Gender. Following its activities to promote women's participation in the electoral process, MINUSTAH, as a member of the National Coordination Committee on the Prevention of Violence against Women, intensified its work in that area, in order to strengthen prevention and develop activities to fight violence against women. Statistics provided by local authorities revealed that a large number of rapes had been carried out under the intimidation of weapons; there was a high occurrence of gang rapes; and 50 per cent of the rape victims were minors.

However, few cases were reported due to the lack of confidence in the justice system and fears of retribution. MINUSTAH was involved in programmes to establish a database for harmonizing data collection on violence; create reception units for women exposed to violence within HNP stations; and to institute a national non-governmental organization (NGO) created by men for men to combat violence against women. MINUSTAH also continued its policy of training all categories of Mission personnel in sexual exploitation and abuse prevention, conducting outreach activities with the local community and enforcing off-limit locations.

Other activities. The UN country team continued to implement its mandated activities in the areas of food aid to vulnerable populations, rehabilitation of schools, legal aid for children at odds with the law, psychosocial assistance to women and girl victims of sexual violence, HIV/AIDS prevention, distribution of medical equipment and electricity generators, technical assistance to farmers and employment generation. Stabilization of the security situation made it possible for humanitarian and development actors to provide aid to groups most affected by the chronic emergency conditions. A UN country team task force for Cité Soleil, established to coordinate the conduct of assessment missions to, and interventions in the shantytown, comprised representatives of MINUSTAH, donors and NGOs.

Financing of MINUSTAH

In January [A/60/646], the Secretary-General submitted the performance report on the budget of MINUSTAH for the period from 1 July 2004 to 30 June 2005, in which he recommended that the General Assembly decide on the treatment of the unencumbered balance of $1,374,000 for the period ended 30 June 2005 and interest income of $2,000 for the period ended 30 June 2004.

On 28 March [A/60/728], the Secretary-General submitted to the Assembly MINUSTAH budget for the period from 1 July 2006 to 30 June 2007, which amounted to $490,636,200 gross and provided for the deployment of 7,500 military personnel, 1,897 UN police officers, including 1,000 formed units, 510 international staff, 1,072 national staff and 189 United Nations Volunteers.

In its May report [A/60/869], the Advisory Committee on Administrative and Budgetary Questions (ACABQ) identified reductions totalling $385,300. It therefore recommended that the Assembly appropriate $490,250,900 for the period 1 July 2006 to 30 June 2007; and that the unencumbered balance and the amount resulting from other income and adjustments for the period 1 July 2004 to 30 June 2005 be credited to Member States in a manner to be determined by the Assembly.

GENERAL ASSEMBLY ACTION

On 30 June [meeting 92], the General Assembly, on the recommendation of the Fifth (Administrative and Budgetary) Committee [A/60/541/Add.1], adopted **resolution 60/18 B**, without vote [agenda item 145].

Financing of the United Nations Stabilization Mission in Haiti

B

The General Assembly,

Having considered the reports of the Secretary-General on the financing of the United Nations Stabilization Mission in Haiti and the related report of the Advisory Committee on Administrative and Budgetary Questions,

Recalling Security Council resolution 1529(2004) of 29 February 2004, by which the Council declared its readiness to establish a United Nations stabilization force to support continuation of a peaceful and constitutional political process and the maintenance of a secure and stable environment in Haiti,

Recalling also Security Council resolution 1542(2004) of 30 April 2004, by which the Council decided to establish the United Nations Stabilization Mission in Haiti for an initial period of six months, and the subsequent resolutions by which the Council extended the mandate of the Mission, the latest of which was resolution 1658(2006) of 14 February 2006,

Recalling further its resolution 58/315 of 1 July 2004,

Recalling its resolution 58/311 of 18 June 2004 on the financing of the Mission and its subsequent resolutions thereon, the latest of which was resolution 60/18 A of 23 November 2005,

Reaffirming the general principles underlying the financing of United Nations peacekeeping operations, as stated in General Assembly resolutions 1874 (S-IV) of 27 June 1963, 3101 (XXVIII) of 11 December 1973 and 55/235 of 23 December 2000,

Mindful of the fact that it is essential to provide the Mission with the necessary financial resources to enable it to fulfil its responsibilities under the relevant resolutions of the Security Council,

1. *Requests* the Secretary-General to entrust the Head of Mission with the task of formulating future budget proposals in full accordance with the provisions of General Assembly resolutions 59/296 of 22 June 2005 and 60/266 of 30 June 2006, as well as other relevant resolutions;

2. *Takes note* of the status of contributions to the United Nations Stabilization Mission in Haiti as at 30 April 2006, including the contributions outstanding in the amount of 66.8 million United States dollars, representing some 11 per cent of the total assessed contributions, notes with concern that only thirty-five Member States have paid their assessed contributions in full, and

urges all other Member States, in particular those in arrears, to ensure payment of their outstanding assessed contributions;

3. *Expresses its appreciation* to those Member States which have paid their assessed contributions in full, and urges all other Member States to make every possible effort to ensure payment of their assessed contributions to the Mission in full;

4. *Expresses concern* at the financial situation with regard to peacekeeping activities, in particular as regards the reimbursements to troop contributors that bear additional burdens owing to overdue payments by Member States of their assessments;

5. *Also expresses concern* at the delay experienced by the Secretary-General in deploying and providing adequate resources to some recent peacekeeping missions, in particular those in Africa;

6. *Emphasizes* that all future and existing peacekeeping missions shall be given equal and non-discriminatory treatment in respect of financial and administrative arrangements;

7. *Also emphasizes* that all peacekeeping missions shall be provided with adequate resources for the effective and efficient discharge of their respective mandates;

8. *Reiterates its request* to the Secretary-General to make the fullest possible use of facilities and equipment at the United Nations Logistics Base at Brindisi, Italy, in order to minimize the costs of procurement for the Mission;

9. *Endorses* the conclusions and recommendations contained in the report of the Advisory Committee on Administrative and Budgetary Questions, subject to the provisions of the present resolution, and requests the Secretary-General to ensure their full implementation;

10. *Requests* the Secretary-General to ensure that future budget submissions include clear information regarding mandated disarmament, demobilization and reintegration activities, including clear justification for post and non-post resource requirements and their projected impact on the effective delivery of the Mission's objectives in this field, as well as information on collaboration with all relevant United Nations entities present in the field and acting in this area;

11. *Also requests* the Secretary-General to ensure the coordination and collaboration of efforts with the United Nations agencies, funds and programmes, to report on progress made and to provide a clear description of their respective roles and responsibilities in future budget submissions;

12. *Further requests* the Secretary-General to review the use of consultants required for disarmament, demobilization and reintegration in order to ensure the successful implementation of the mandated programmes, and to report thereon in the performance report;

13. *Requests* the Secretary General to ensure that the utilization of these resources takes fully into account the functions performed by existing capacities;

14. *Looks forward* to the consideration of the comprehensive report requested in section VIII, paragraph 3, of its resolution 60/266;

15. *Requests* the Secretary-General to ensure that quick-impact projects are implemented in compliance with the original intent of such projects and relevant General Assembly resolutions;

16. *Decides* to approve the resources requested for quick-impact projects in the proposed budget for the Mission for the period from 1 July 2006 to 30 June 2007, in the interim, bearing in mind Security Council resolution 1608(2005) of 22 June 2005 and relevant presidential statements;

17. *Requests* the Secretary-General to ensure full implementation of the quick-impact projects for the financial period 2006/07;

18. *Notes* that full information on the need for the establishment of an off-site, in-theatre secondary disaster recovery and business continuity centre for the Mission has yet to be provided, and requests the Secretary-General to provide comprehensive and detailed information in this regard in the context of the budget for the Mission for the period from 1 July 2007 to 30 June 2008;

19. *Requests* the Secretary-General, in future budget submissions, to ensure that resource requirements for national interpreters include full justification of the rationale for the number of interpreters, taking fully into account the principles of efficiency, ensuring effective implementation of the Mission mandate and the requirements of the various components of the Mission in the field;

20. *Also requests* the Secretary-General, in this regard, to rejustify the need for five administrative staff in the light of the experience of the Mission in the context of the next budget submission for the Mission;

21. *Further requests* the Secretary-General to continue to report on specific management improvements achieved, taking fully into account relevant recommendations of the Advisory Committee;

22. *Requests* the Secretary-General to ensure the full implementation of relevant provisions of its resolutions 59/296 and 60/266;

23. *Also requests* the Secretary-General to take all necessary action to ensure that the Mission is administered with a maximum of efficiency and economy;

24. *Further requests* the Secretary-General, in order to reduce the cost of employing General Service staff, to continue efforts to recruit local staff for the Mission against General Service posts, commensurate with the requirements of the Mission;

Financial performance report for the period from 1 July 2004 to 30 June 2005

25. *Takes note* of the report of the Secretary-General on the financial performance of the Mission for the period from 1 July 2004 to 30 June 2005;

Budget estimates for the period from 1 July 2006 to 30 June 2007

26. *Decides* to appropriate to the Special Account for the United Nations Stabilization Mission in Haiti the amount of 510,394,700 dollars for the period from 1 July 2006 to 30 June 2007, inclusive of 489,207,100 dollars for the maintenance of the Mission, 17,500,200

dollars for the support account for peacekeeping operations and 3,687,400 dollars for the United Nations Logistics Base;

Financing of the appropriation

27. *Also decides* to apportion among Member States the amount of 63,799,300 dollars for the period from 1 July to 15 August 2006, in accordance with the levels updated in General Assembly resolution 58/256 of 23 December 2003, and taking into account the scale of assessments for 2006 as set out in its resolution 58/1 B of 23 December 2003;

28. *Further decides* that, in accordance with the provisions of its resolution 973(X) of 15 December 1955, there shall be set off against the apportionment among Member States, as provided for in paragraph 27 above, their respective share in the Tax Equalization Fund of 1,455,800 dollars, comprising the estimated staff assessment income of 1,174,800 dollars approved for the Mission, the prorated share of 246,100 dollars of the estimated staff assessment income approved for the support account and the prorated share of 34,900 dollars of the estimated staff assessment income approved for the United Nations Logistics Base;

29. *Decides* to apportion among Member States the amount of 446,595,400 dollars for the period from 16 August 2006 to 30 June 2007 at a monthly rate of 42,532,892 dollars, in accordance with the levels updated in General Assembly resolution 58/256, and taking into account the scale of assessments for 2006, as set out in its resolution 58/1 B, and the scale of assessments for 2007, subject to a decision of the Security Council to extend the mandate of the Mission;

30. *Also decides* that, in accordance with the provisions of its resolution 973(X), there shall be set off against the apportionment among Member States, as provided for in paragraph 29 above, their respective share in the Tax Equalization Fund of 10,190,500 dollars, comprising the estimated staff assessment income of 8,223,900 dollars approved for the Mission, the prorated share of 1,722,400 dollars of the estimated staff assessment income approved for the support account and the prorated share of 244,200 dollars of the estimated staff assessment income approved for the United Nations Logistics Base;

31. *Further decides* that, for Member States that have fulfilled their financial obligations to the Mission, there shall be set off against their apportionment, as provided for in paragraph 27 above, their respective share of the unencumbered balance and other income in the total amount of 6,646,600 dollars in respect of the financial period ended 30 June 2005, in accordance with the levels updated in its resolution 58/256, and taking into account the scale of assessments for 2005 as set out in its resolution 58/1 B;

32. *Decides* that, for Member States that have not fulfilled their financial obligations to the Mission, there shall be set off against their outstanding obligations their respective share of the unencumbered balance and other income in the total amount of 6,646,600 dollars in respect of the financial period ended 30 June 2005, in accordance with the scheme set out in paragraph 31 above;

33. *Also decides* that the decrease of 909,400 dollars in the estimated staff assessment income in respect of the financial period ended 30 June 2005 shall be set off against the credits from the amount of 6,646,600 dollars referred to in paragraphs 31 and 32 above;

34. *Emphasizes* that no peacekeeping mission shall be financed by borrowing funds from other active peacekeeping missions;

35. *Encourages* the Secretary-General to continue to take additional measures to ensure the safety and security of all personnel under the auspices of the United Nations participating in the Mission, bearing in mind paragraphs 5 and 6 of Security Council resolution 1502(2003) of 26 August 2003;

36. *Invites* voluntary contributions to the Mission in cash and in the form of services and supplies acceptable to the Secretary-General, to be administered, as appropriate, in accordance with the procedure and practices established by the General Assembly;

37. *Decides* to include in the provisional agenda of its sixty-first session the item entitled "Financing of the United Nations Stabilization Mission in Haiti".

The Assembly, by **decision 61/552** of 22 December, decided that the item entitled "Financing of the United Nations Stabilization Mission in Haiti" would remain for consideration during its resumed sixty-first (2007) session.

Other questions

Cuba-United States

On 8 February [A/60/676], Cuba transmitted to the Secretary-General a statement concerning the expulsion of a group of Cuban businessmen from the Hotel María Isabel Sheraton in Mexico City on 3 February, in application of the Helms-Burton Act and requesting that the document be circulated under the agenda item on the necessity of ending the United States' economic, commercial and financial embargo against Cuba.

Report of Secretary-General. On 8 August [A/61/132], in response to General Assembly resolution 60/12 [YUN 2005, p. 394], the Secretary-General forwarded information received from 96 States, one non-member State, the European Union and 20 UN bodies and specialized agencies, as at 21 July 2006, on the implementation of that resolution. The text of the resolution had called on States to refrain from the unilateral application of economic and trade measures against other States, and urged them to repeal or invalidate such measures.

GENERAL ASSEMBLY ACTION

On 8 November [meeting 50], the General Assembly adopted **resolution 61/11** [draft: A/61/L.10] by recorded vote (183-4-1) [agenda item 18].

Necessity of ending the economic, commercial and financial embargo imposed by the United States of America against Cuba

The General Assembly,

Determined to encourage strict compliance with the purposes and principles enshrined in the Charter of the United Nations,

Reaffirming, among other principles, the sovereign equality of States, non-intervention and non-interference in their internal affairs and freedom of international trade and navigation, which are also enshrined in many international legal instruments,

Recalling the statements of the Heads of State or Government at the Ibero-American Summits concerning the need to eliminate unilateral application of economic and trade measures by one State against another that affect the free flow of international trade,

Concerned at the continued promulgation and application by Member States of laws and regulations, such as that promulgated on 12 March 1996 known as the "Helms-Burton Act", the extraterritorial effects of which affect the sovereignty of other States, the legitimate interests of entities or persons under their jurisdiction and the freedom of trade and navigation,

Taking note of declarations and resolutions of different intergovernmental forums, bodies and Governments that express the rejection by the international community and public opinion of the promulgation and application of measures of the kind referred to above,

Recalling its resolutions 47/19 of 24 November 1992, 48/16 of 3 November 1993, 49/9 of 26 October 1994, 50/10 of 2 November 1995, 51/17 of 12 November 1996, 52/10 of 5 November 1997, 53/4 of 14 October 1998, 54/21 of 9 November 1999, 55/20 of 9 November 2000, 56/9 of 27 November 2001, 57/11 of 12 November 2002, 58/7 of 4 November 2003, 59/11 of 28 October 2004 and 60/12 of 8 November 2005,

Concerned that, since the adoption of its resolutions 47/19, 48/16, 49/9, 50/10, 51/17, 52/10, 53/4, 54/21, 55/20, 56/9, 57/11, 58/7, 59/11 and 60/12, further measures of that nature aimed at strengthening and extending the economic, commercial and financial embargo against Cuba continue to be promulgated and applied, and concerned also at the adverse effects of such measures on the Cuban people and on Cuban nationals living in other countries,

1. *Takes note* of the report of the Secretary-General on the implementation of resolution 60/12;

2. *Reiterates its call upon* all States to refrain from promulgating and applying laws and measures of the kind referred to in the preamble to the present resolution, in conformity with their obligations under the Charter of the United Nations and international law, which, inter alia, reaffirm the freedom of trade and navigation;

3. *Once again urges* States that have and continue to apply such laws and measures to take the necessary steps to repeal or invalidate them as soon as possible in accordance with their legal regime;

4. *Requests* the Secretary-General, in consultation with the appropriate organs and agencies of the United Nations system, to prepare a report on the implementation of the present resolution in the light of the purposes and principles of the Charter and international law and to submit it to the General Assembly at its sixty-second session;

5. *Decides* to include in the provisional agenda of its sixty-second session the item entitled "Necessity of ending the economic, commercial and financial embargo imposed by the United States of America against Cuba".

RECORDED VOTE ON RESOLUTION 61/11:

In favour: Afghanistan, Albania, Algeria, Andorra, Angola, Antigua and Barbuda, Argentina, Armenia, Australia, Austria, Azerbaijan, Bahamas, Bahrain, Bangladesh, Barbados, Belarus, Belgium, Belize, Benin, Bhutan, Bolivia, Bosnia and Herzegovina, Botswana, Brazil, Brunei Darussalam, Bulgaria, Burkina Faso, Burundi, Cambodia, Cameroon, Canada, Cape Verde, Central African Republic, Chad, Chile, China, Colombia, Comoros, Congo, Costa Rica, Croatia, Cuba, Cyprus, Czech Republic, Democratic People's Republic of Korea, Democratic Republic of the Congo, Denmark, Djibouti, Dominica, Dominican Republic, Ecuador, Egypt, Equatorial Guinea, Eritrea, Estonia, Ethiopia, Fiji, Finland, France, Gabon, Gambia, Georgia, Germany, Ghana, Greece, Grenada, Guatemala, Guinea, Guinea-Bissau, Guyana, Haiti, Honduras, Hungary, Iceland, India, Indonesia, Iran, Ireland, Italy, Jamaica, Japan, Jordan, Kazakhstan, Kenya, Kiribati, Kuwait, Kyrgyzstan, Lao People's Democratic Republic, Latvia, Lebanon, Lesotho, Liberia, Libyan Arab Jamahiriya, Liechtenstein, Lithuania, Luxembourg, Madagascar, Malawi, Malaysia, Maldives, Mali, Malta, Mauritania, Mauritius, Mexico, Moldova, Monaco, Mongolia, Montenegro, Morocco, Mozambique, Myanmar, Namibia, Nauru, Nepal, Netherlands, New Zealand, Niger, Nigeria, Norway, Oman, Pakistan, Panama, Papua New Guinea, Paraguay, Peru, Philippines, Poland, Portugal, Qatar, Republic of Korea, Romania, Russian Federation, Rwanda, Saint Kitts and Nevis, Saint Lucia, Saint Vincent and the Grenadines, Samoa, San Marino, Sao Tome and Principe, Saudi Arabia, Senegal, Serbia, Seychelles, Sierra Leone, Singapore, Slovakia, Slovenia, Solomon Islands, Somalia, South Africa, Spain, Sri Lanka, Sudan, Suriname, Swaziland, Sweden, Switzerland, Syrian Arab Republic, Tajikistan, Thailand, The former Yugoslav Republic of Macedonia, Timor-Leste, Togo, Tonga, Trinidad and Tobago, Tunisia, Turkey, Turkmenistan, Tuvalu, Uganda, Ukraine, United Arab Emirates, United Kingdom, United Republic of Tanzania, Uruguay, Uzbekistan, Vanuatu, Venezuela, Viet Nam, Yemen, Zambia, Zimbabwe.

Against: Israel, Marshall Islands, Palau, United States.

Abstaining: Micronesia.

Communications. Cuba, on 21 March [S/2006/180], requested that the four items it had previously submitted to the Council be retained on the list of matters of which the Council was seized.

Cuba transmitted to the Secretary-General the 15 August [A/61/280] declaration of the Committee on Constitutional and Legal Affairs of its National

Assembly expressing outrage at the ruling of the United States Court of Appeal in Atlanta, Georgia, vacating the verdict of the panel of three judges that had rescinded the judgment handed down in Miami against five Cuban anti-terrorist heroes.

Cooperation between the United Nations and regional organizations

Caribbean Community

The Secretary-General, in response to General Assembly resolution 59/138 [YUN 2004, p. 306], submitted, in his August consolidated report [A/61/256 & Add.1] on cooperation between the United Nations and regional organizations, a summary of UN-Caribbean Community (CARICOM) collaborative activities, which highlighted consultations with the Department of Political Affairs on the holding of the fourth general meeting between CARICOM representatives and the UN system. Participants would review progress in the implementation of UN-CARICOM cooperation and discuss measures to strengthen cooperation between the two organizations. The report also covered CARICOM activities with various UN system bodies to address issues such as the import and export of firearms; terrorism and organized crime; sustainable and social development; statistics; gender; censuses in the Caribbean region; childhood education; and HIV/AIDS.

GENERAL ASSEMBLY ACTION

On 4 December [meeting 65], the General Assembly adopted **resolution 61/50** [draft: A/61/L.29 & Add.1] without vote [agenda item 108(*e*)].

Cooperation between the United Nations and the Caribbean Community

The General Assembly,

Recalling its resolutions 46/8 of 16 October 1991, 49/141 of 20 December 1994, 51/16 of 11 November 1996, 53/17 of 29 October 1998, 55/17 of 7 November 2000, 57/41 of 21 November 2002 and 59/138 of 10 December 2004,

Bearing in mind the provisions of Chapter VIII of the Charter of the United Nations on the existence of regional arrangements or agencies for dealing with such matters relating to the maintenance of international peace and security as are appropriate for regional action and other activities consistent with the purposes and principles of the United Nations,

Bearing in mind also the assistance given by the United Nations towards the maintenance of peace and security in the Caribbean region,

Recalling the signing, on 27 May 1997, by the Secretary-General of the United Nations and the Secretary-General of the Caribbean Community of a cooperation agreement between the secretariats of the two organizations,

Bearing in mind that, in its resolutions 54/225 of 22 December 1999, 55/203 of 20 December 2000, 57/261 of 20 December 2002 and 59/230 of 22 December 2004, it recognized the importance of adopting an integrated management approach to the Caribbean Sea area in the context of sustainable development,

Bearing in mind also that in the United Nations Millennium Declaration, adopted by resolution 55/2 of 8 September 2000, Heads of State and Government resolved to address the special needs of small island developing States by implementing the Barbados Programme of Action and the outcome of the twenty-second special session of the General Assembly rapidly and in full,

Noting that the World Summit on Sustainable Development considered the specific issues and problems facing small island developing States, taking note in this regard of the Monterrey Consensus of the International Conference on Financing for Development, and noting the outcome of the International Meeting to Review the Implementation of the Programme of Action for the Sustainable Development of Small Island Developing States,

Noting also that the Caribbean region is the second most hazard-prone region in the world and is frequently exposed to devastating hazards including earthquakes, floods, hurricanes and volcanic eruptions,

Noting further that the Caribbean region has been hard hit, and in some cases devastated, by hurricanes in the recent past, and concerned that their frequency, intensity and destructive power continue to pose a challenge to the development of the region,

Noting that the Declaration of Commitment on HIV/AIDS adopted by the General Assembly in resolution S-26/2 of 27 June 2001 recognized the Caribbean region as having the second-highest rate of infection after sub-Saharan Africa and that the region therefore needs special attention and assistance from the international community,

Noting also the commitment undertaken by the international community in the Political Declaration on HIV/AIDS, adopted by the High-level Meeting on HIV/AIDS on 2 June 2006, to assist low- and middle-income countries in achieving universal access to comprehensive HIV/AIDS prevention programmes, treatment, care and support by 2010,

Affirming the need to strengthen the cooperation that already exists between entities of the United Nations system and the Caribbean Community in the areas of economic and social development, as well as the areas of political and humanitarian affairs,

Convinced of the need for the coordinated utilization of available resources to promote the common objectives of the two organizations,

Having considered the report of the Secretary-General on cooperation between the United Nations and regional and other organizations,

1. *Takes note* of the report of the Secretary-General, in particular part one, section IV, on the Caribbean Community, as well as efforts to strengthen cooperation;

2. *Calls upon* the Secretary-General of the United Nations, in association with the Secretary-General of the Caribbean Community, as well as the relevant regional organizations, to continue to assist in furthering the development and maintenance of peace and security within the Caribbean region;

3. *Invites* the Secretary-General to continue to promote and expand cooperation and coordination between the United Nations and the Caribbean Community in order to increase the capacity of the two organizations to attain their objectives;

4. *Urges* the specialized agencies and other organizations and programmes of the United Nations system to cooperate with the Secretary-General of the United Nations and the Secretary-General of the Caribbean Community in order to initiate, maintain and increase consultations and programmes with the Caribbean Community and its associated institutions in the attainment of their objectives, with special attention to the areas and issues identified at the third general meeting between representatives of the Caribbean Community and its associated institutions and of the United Nations system, held in New York on 12 and 13 April 2004, as set out in the report of the Secretary-General, as well as in resolutions 54/225, 55/2, 55/203 and S-26/2 and the decisions of the World Summit on Sustainable Development, and the International Meeting to Review the Implementation of the Programme of Action for the Sustainable Development of Small Island Developing States, as well as the Monterrey Consensus of the International Conference on Financing for Development;

5. *Invites* the organizations of the United Nations system as well as Member States to increase financial and other assistance to the countries of the Caribbean Community to help to implement the priorities of the Caribbean Regional Strategic Framework for HIV/AIDS, which sets out realistic targets for reducing the rate of new infections, raising the quality and coverage of care, treatment and support and building institutional capacity, and to cope with the problems and the burden caused by the HIV/AIDS pandemic;

6. *Invites* the Secretary-General to consider utilizing a strategic programming framework modality to strengthen the coordination and cooperation between the two secretariats as well as between the United Nations field offices and the Caribbean Community;

7. *Calls upon* the United Nations, the specialized agencies and other organizations and programmes of the United Nations system to assist the countries of the Caribbean in addressing the social and economic consequences of the vulnerability of Caribbean economies and the challenges that this poses for achieving the Millennium Development Goals and the goal of sustainable development;

8. *Reaffirms* the objective of strengthening the implementation of the Mauritius Strategy for the Further Implementation of the Programme of Action for the Sustainable Development of Small Island Developing States, including through the mobilization of financial and technological resources, as well as capacity-building programmes;

9. *Welcomes* the initiatives of Member States in assisting in the cooperation between the United Nations and the Caribbean Community, and encourages their continuing efforts;

10. *Recommends* that the fourth general meeting between representatives of the Caribbean Community and its associated institutions and of the United Nations system be held in the Caribbean in early 2007 in order to review and appraise progress in the implementation of the agreed areas and issues and to hold consultations on such additional measures and procedures as may be required to facilitate and strengthen cooperation between the two organizations;

11. *Requests* the Secretary-General to submit to the General Assembly at its sixty-third session a report on the implementation of the present resolution;

12. *Decides* to include in the provisional agenda of its sixty-third session the sub-item entitled "Cooperation between the United Nations and the Caribbean Community".

Cooperation with OAS

In response to General Assembly resolution 59/257 [YUN 2004, p. 307] on cooperation between the United Nations and the Organization of American States (OAS), the Secretary-General, in his consolidated report on cooperation between the United Nations and regional organizations [A/61/256 & Add.1], reviewed the close cooperation between OAS and the UN Regional Centre for Peace, Disarmament and Development in Latin America and the Caribbean, which had maintained the joint UN-OAS small arms and light weapons administrations and had developed, with other partners, an integrated weapons management system to register firearms, ammunition and explosives and manage weapons facilities. OAS activities with the International Labour Organization to establish national labour councils, promote social dialogue, organize training and promote human rights and the application of international labour standards were also highlighted.

By **decision 61/552** of 22 December, the Assembly decided that the item entitled "Cooperation between the United Nations and the Organization of American States" would remain for consideration during its resumed sixty-first (2007) session.

Chapter IV

Asia and the Pacific

In 2006, the United Nations continued to face significant political and security challenges in Asia and the Pacific, especially in Afghanistan and Iraq, as it sought to restore peace and stability and promote economic and social development in the region. In Afghanistan, further progress was made to advance that country's development and strengthen the rule of law. In that regard, more than 60 countries attended the London Conference on Afghanistan (31 January–1 February), pledging $10.5 billion in new financial assistance. Participants adopted the Afghanistan Compact, a blueprint for action in the areas of security, governance, human rights, the anti-narcotics struggle and development. However, the year also saw an increase in insurgent activities, especially in the south, which hampered the ability of the United Nations and its partners to provide development assistance. In November, a Security Council mission to Afghanistan assessed the situation there and made recommendations for strengthening the country's governance institutions and addressing the security concerns.

The International Security Assistance Force (ISAF), a multinational force established by Security Council resolution 1386(2001), continued to assist the Government in maintaining security. In October it assumed responsibility for all international military operations in Afghanistan. The North Atlantic Treaty Organization (NATO) continued its role as lead command for ISAF.

The United Nations Assistance Mission in Afghanistan (UNAMA) continued to coordinate international humanitarian and development activities, assist the Government in building institutions and foster political dialogue. In March, the Security Council extended UNAMA mandate for an additional year. In December, the General Assembly, by resolution 61/18, called on the Government to continue to address the security and development challenges, with the support of the international community.

In Iraq, strides were made in returning the country to democratic and constitutional rule. In April, the Parliament elected Jalal Talabani as President, and a new Government was formed in May, headed by Prime Minister Jawad Nouri Al-Maliki. Nevertheless, sectarian and other violence continued, with an escalation of bombings, murders and kidnappings. The bombing of a Shiite Shrine on 22 February ignited ferocious attacks between Shiites and Sunnis, which resulted in the deaths of hundreds of people. On 23 November, more than 200 people were killed in explosions in Baghdad's Shiite-dominated Sadr City district.

The United Nations Assistance Mission in Iraq (UNAMI) continued to promote dialogue, advise the Government on developing civil and social services, foster human rights protection and legal reforms, and contribute to the coordination of development and reconstruction efforts. In August, the Security Council extended UNAMI mandate for another year.

The United Nations continued to follow up on issues relating to Iraq's 1990 invasion of Kuwait, the repatriation of the remains of Kuwaiti and third-country nationals, the return of Kuwaiti property, including the national archives, and compensation for losses and damage.

The United Nations Office in Timor-Leste (UNOTIL) addressed the crisis that erupted in that country, as a result of grievances by members of the security forces. Clashes occurred between protesters and security forces in April and between the police and the armed forces in May. To restore order, the Government sought military assistance from Australia, Malaysia, New Zealand and Portugal. The Prime Minister was forced to resign in June, and the Secretary-General appointed a Special Envoy to promote negotiations. The international security forces, in cooperation with the Government and the United Nations, restored order. In August, the Security Council, which had scaled back its operation in Timor-Leste, was forced to establish a new missions, the United Nations Integrated Mission in Timor-Leste (UNMIT).

Following Iran's decision to resume uranium enrichment-related activities, the Security Council, in July, mandated a suspension of such activities and in December imposed sanctions against the country. Iran maintained that its nuclear programme was entirely peaceful and in line with its engagements under the 1968 Treaty on the Non-Proliferation of Nuclear Weapons.

In response to the Democratic People's Republic of Korea's (DPRK) multiple ballistic missile launches on 5 July, the Security Council, on 15 July, demanded that the country suspend such activities. After the DPRK informed the Council that it had conducted an underground nuclear weapon test on 9 October, the Council, by resolution 1718(2006), imposed sanctions on the country. The DPRK maintained that such activities were merely defensive and were prompted by the hostile policies of the United States.

Mass demonstrations in Nepal in April forced the Nepalese King to restore Parliament and hand over power to an alliance of mainstream political parties. In August, the Secretary-General appointed a Personal Representative for Nepal to act as the senior United Nations political interlocutor. Negotiations between the Maoists and the new Government led to a Comprehensive Peace Agreement signed on 21 November, which ended a decade-long conflict that had killed some 13,000 people. The United Nations was requested to supervise the management of arms and armed personnel of both sides, continue human rights monitoring and assist in elections scheduled for 2007.

The United Nations also continued to assist Cambodia in setting up a tribunal to prosecute senior leaders responsible for crimes committed between 1975 and 1979; provide good offices for democratization and national reconciliation in Myanmar; and support Tajikistan in its peacebuilding efforts. It expressed concern over the 5 December military takeover in Fiji, and was requested to keep on the agenda the issue of the Greater Tunb, Lesser Tunb and Abu Musa islands in the Persian Gulf.

Afghanistan

Situation in Afghanistan

In 2006, the international community continued to assist the Government of Afghanistan to lay the foundation for peace and stability and the restoration of economic and social development, through support provided by the United Nations Assistance Mission in Afghanistan (UNAMA), under the direction of the Special Representative of the Secretary-General and Head of Mission, and the International Security Assistance Force (ISAF), led by the North Atlantic Treaty Organization (NATO).

The Secretary-General submitted two progress reports to the General Assembly and the Security Council on the situation in Afghanistan and on UNAMA activities: one [A/60/712-S/2006/145] covering events from August 2005 to March 2006, and the other [A/61/326-S/2006/727] from April to September. ISAF activities were reported to the Council by the NATO Secretary-General through the UN Secretary-General [S/2006/318, S/2006/765]. The Council extended UNAMA mandate until 23 March 2007 (**resolution 1662(2006)**) (see p. 365), and ISAF authorization until 13 October 2007 (**resolution 1707(2006)**) (see p. 381). The Council endorsed (**resolution 1659(2006)**) (see p. 363) the "Afghanistan Compact", adopted on 31 January at the London Conference on Afghanistan (see p. 363). A Council mission visited Afghanistan from 11 to 16 November. In February, Tom Koenigs (Germany) replaced Jean Arnault (France) as the Secretary-General's Special Representative for Afghanistan and Head of UNAMA.

Security Council consideration (January). On 17 January [meeting 5347], the Security Council heard a briefing by the Secretary-General's Special Representative, Jean Arnault, who said that, almost four years after the signing of the 2001 Agreement on provisional arrangements in Afghanistan pending the re-establishment of permanent government institutions (the Bonn Agreement) [YUN 2001, p. 263], the political transition had been completed, with the inauguration, on 19 December 2005, of the new Afghan National Assembly [YUN 2005, p. 403]. Following the inauguration of the National Assembly, Yunus Qanooni, a leading opposition figure, was elected chair of the Lower House (Wolesi Jirga) and Sibghatullah Mojaddedi chair of the Upper House (Mesharano Jirga). Both houses made progress in discussions on their rules of procedure. However, no agreement was reached on the rule relating to the process by which parliament would exercise its constitutional prerogative of endorsing members of the cabinet. At the request of the President, those appointments would be reviewed after the London Conference on Afghanistan. The Government also decided to establish a Ministry of Parliamentary Affairs to facilitate interaction between the cabinet and the National Assembly.

The cabinet, on 12 December 2005, had approved the National Action Plan on Peace, Reconciliation and Justice, which sought to address the needs of victims of the conflict through reparation, truth-seeking, stronger justice institutions and national reconciliation. While the Plan's implementation faced objections by some groups, a conference on transitional justice in December had revealed broad support for truth-finding, justice and the vetting of Government officials.

National and international partners had agreed on a strategy for disbanding illegal armed groups, which were linked to factions, organized crime and the drug trade. Herat and Kapisa were the first two provinces to implement the strategy.

However, the south had seen an increase in attacks by anti-Government elements, with 13 suicide attacks in the past 10 weeks. On 15 January, in Kandahar, the political director of the Canadian Provincial Reconstruction Team in that region was killed, as well as three soldiers and two civilians in Kandahar city in separate incidents. Attacks against international forces were carried out in parts of the country where such attacks had been rare, and violence and threats against local officials, religious leaders and schools intensified, particularly in the south and south-east. Security remained at the heart of Government and international efforts as it limited the United Nations ability to operate throughout the country. However, the Special Representative observed that the magnitude of the tasks in consolidating peace should not detract from the fact that the Afghans had successfully defied violent extremism and hardship to lay the foundations for a democratic and peaceful State.

Press statement (January). In a 17 January press statement, Security Council members condemned the terrorist attacks in Kandahar province on 14, 15 and 16 January, for which the Taliban had claimed responsibility. They expressed their condolences for the many Afghan victims of those attacks, and for those killed and injured in the attack against the Canadian Provincial Reconstruction Team. The Council stressed that the attacks underlined the necessity to improve safety and security in the country and urged the parties concerned to make every effort to bring the perpetrators to justice.

London Conference on Afghanistan. The International Conference on Afghanistan was held in London from 31 January to 1 February. Co-chaired by Afghan President Hamid Karzai, British Prime Minister Tony Blair and the UN Secretary-General, under the theme "building on success", the Conference signaled the international community's determination to continue to assist the Afghan Government in improving the lives of its people and support a programme of State building under Afghan leadership, in accordance with national priorities. The Conference adopted the Afghanistan Compact [S/2006/90], a five-year peacebuilding agenda in the areas of security, governance, the rule of law and human rights, economic and social development and counter-narcotics. The Compact identified over 40 measurable and time-bound benchmarks and established a results-oriented action plan. To increase transparency and coordination, the Compact provided for the establishment of a Joint Coordination and Monitoring Board, to be co-chaired by the Government and the United Nations. Participating countries and organizations announced $10.5 billion in financial assistance.

Afghanistan, in a 6 February letter of its Minister for Foreign Affairs, expressed the country's appreciation for the international community's continued support. It observed that the benchmarks and timelines for progress set in the Compact were challenging, but achievable and would make a difference in the lives of ordinary Afghans. It welcomed the leading role of the United Nations in the new Coordination and Monitoring Board, and hoped that the Security Council would reflect, in its resolutions, the continuing importance of international support for the country's reconstruction.

Security Council consideration (February). At the Security Council's 10 February session [meeting 5369] on the situation in Afghanistan, Under-Secretary-General for Peacekeeping Operations Jean-Marie Guéhenno said that the Afghanistan Compact, launched at the London Conference on Afghanistan, was an ambitious agenda committing Conference participants to a sustained and prolonged engagement in the country's future. It was a realistic reflection of what was required to consolidate State-building efforts in Afghanistan and to enable nascent democratic institutions created by the Bonn process to meet the country's basic needs. The Compact's timelines and benchmarks were the criteria against which the efforts of the international community in Afghanistan would be judged. The United Nations stood ready to assist the Afghan Government and the international community to meeting those goals. The Afghan Government committed itself to meeting a wide range of goals over the next five years and unveiled strategies for doing so in a number of sectors, including the Afghanistan National Development Strategy: an interim strategy for Security, Governance, Economic Growth and Poverty Reduction [S/2006/105] and the Afghanistan National Drug Control Strategy [S/2006/106]. The pledges made by the international community should be brought to bear on the Compact if the promise of the London Conference was to be fulfilled.

SECURITY COUNCIL ACTION

On 15 February [meeting 5374], the Security Council unanimously adopted **resolution 1659(2006)**. The draft [S/2006/102] was prepared in consultations among Council members.

The Security Council,

Reaffirming its previous resolutions on Afghanistan, in particular resolutions 1378(2001) of 14 November 2001, 1383(2001) of 6 December 2001 and 1589(2005) of 24 March 2005,

Reaffirming its full commitment to the sovereignty, independence, territorial integrity and national unity of Afghanistan,

Pledging its continued support for the Government and people of Afghanistan as they rebuild their country, strengthen the foundations of a constitutional democracy and assume their rightful place in the community of nations,

Stressing the inalienable right of the people of Afghanistan freely to determine their own future,

Determined to assist the Government and people of Afghanistan in building on the successful completion of the Bonn process,

Recognizing the interconnected nature of the challenges ahead, and affirming that sustainable progress on security, governance and development, which necessarily involves capacity-building, is mutually reinforcing,

Recognizing also the continuing importance of fighting terrorist and narcotics threats and addressing threats posed by the Taliban, Al-Qaida and other extremist groups,

Stressing that regional cooperation constitutes an effective means to promote security and development in Afghanistan,

Welcoming the letter dated 6 February 2006 from the Minister for Foreign Affairs of Afghanistan informing the Secretary-General of the launch of the "Afghanistan Compact" in London on 31 January 2006,

1. *Endorses* the Afghanistan Compact and the annexes thereto as providing the framework for the partnership between the Government of Afghanistan and the international community which underlies the mutual commitments set out in the Compact;

2. *Calls upon* the Government of Afghanistan, and all members of the international community and international organizations, to implement in full the Compact and the annexes thereto;

3. *Affirms* the central and impartial role of the United Nations in Afghanistan, including the coordination of efforts in implementing the Compact, and looks forward to the early formation of the Joint Coordination and Monitoring Board, co-chaired by the Government of Afghanistan and the United Nations with a secretariat function to support it;

4. *Welcomes* the interim Afghanistan National Development Strategy presented by the Government of Afghanistan and the political, security and financial pledges made by participants at the London Conference on Afghanistan, held on 31 January and 1 February 2006, notes that financial assistance available for the implementation of the Strategy has now reached 10.5 billion United States dollars, and also notes the intention of the Government of Afghanistan to seek debt relief through the Paris Club;

5. *Recognizes* the risk that opium cultivation, production and trafficking poses to the security, development and governance of Afghanistan as well as to the region and internationally, welcomes the updated National Drug Control Strategy presented by the Government of Afghanistan at the London Conference, and encourages additional international support for the four priorities identified in the Strategy, including through contribution to the Counter-Narcotics Trust Fund;

6. *Acknowledges* the continuing commitment of the North Atlantic Treaty Organization to lead the International Security Assistance Force, and welcomes the adoption by the Organization of a revised Operational Plan allowing the continued expansion of the Force across Afghanistan, closer operational synergy with Operation Enduring Freedom, and support, within means and capabilities, to Afghan security forces in the military aspects of their training and operational deployments;

7. *Declares its willingness* to take further action to support the implementation of the Compact and the annexes thereto, on the basis of timely reports by the Secretary-General which encompass recommendations on the future mandate and structure of the United Nations Assistance Mission in Afghanistan;

8. *Decides* to remain actively seized of this matter.

Report of Secretary-General (March). In his March report on the situation in Afghanistan and its implications for international peace and security [A/60/712-S/2006/145], submitted in response to Security Council resolution 1589(2005) [YUN 2005, p. 399], and General Assembly resolutions 60/32A [ibid., p. 404] and 60/32B [ibid., p. 1000], the Secretary-General summarized key developments since his 12 August 2005 report [ibid., p. 401]. Since its inauguration on 19 December 2005, the National Assembly had focused primarily on administrative matters and issues of public concern, including threats to the country's security, devoting four days of debate to that issue. Security was also the focus of President Karzai's dialogue with Pakistani authorities during his visit to Islamabad from 15 to 17 February. On 27 February, the lower house decided to exercise its constitutional authority to review and approve the Cabinet on an individual rather than a collective basis. Impatient at the lack of meaningful progress on issues of national concern, a number of civil society groups formed the Coordination Office for Civil Organizations to lobby the Assembly on human rights reform.

The Secretary-General noted that, while the completion of the Bonn Agreement marked a significant achievement in Afghanistan's political transition, progress was needed across a number of interrelated areas. Following consultations with the Afghan Government, he proposed a new mandate for UNAMA. Under that mandate, the mission would provide political and strategic advice for the peace process and good offices; assist in the coordination and monitoring of the Afghanistan Compact and co-chair the Compact's Joint Coordination and Monitoring Board; continue to promote human rights; provide technical assistance in sectors where the United Nations had a comparative advantage; and manage all UN humanitarian, relief, recovery, reconstruction and development activities. The mission would retain its current structure, with some modifications in scope and size depending on security conditions. He recommended that UNAMA mandate be extended for a further 12 months until 24 March 2007.

The Secretary-General observed that security remained foremost among the challenges facing Afghanistan. The fertile ground for anti-Government violence and terrorism was not limited to the unmet needs of ordinary Afghan citizens. The sources of support for the insurgency and for anti-Government terrorist operations needed to be tackled. Afghanistan could only become a place of stability if the causes of violence and distrust, including all its domestic and external dimensions, were resolutely addressed, including the disarmament of illegally armed groups and the development of credible and sustainable national security institutions.

The Afghanistan Compact and the Interim Afghanistan National Development Strategy provided an unprecedented opportunity to ensure that the Government and the international community worked together on a common plan towards shared objectives. The Secretary-General called upon the Afghan Government to do its utmost to meet the benchmarks set out in those documents and upon the participants in the London Conference to show continuing generosity and commitment in making available the resources for realizing that vision.

Security Council consideration (March). At the 14 March Security Council meeting on the situation in Afghanistan [meeting 5385], the Special Representative of the Secretary-General and Head of UNAMA, Tom Koenigs, said two priorities were essential to the success of the Afghanistan Compact: Afghanistan's institutions had to be strengthened to the point where they were effective enough to deliver basic services, and the strategy for tackling security challenges had to evolve to meet outstanding threats. The prevalence of attacks in the south of the country pointed to a consolidation of the command and control networks of the Taliban, Al-Qaida and associated groups; redoubled international effort was needed to dismantle structures threatening the security of both Afghanistan and Pakistan.

A key challenge under the Afghanistan Compact was to extend the reach of the Government at the local level. That would require a greater official, civil society and private sector presence in areas not yet touched by recovery efforts and would challenge the Government to make functioning institutions of justice and the rule of law more and more a reality. Those expectations could only be met by reforming and strengthening the Government institutions necessary to develop human capital, harness the potential of agriculture and natural resources and set the conditions for the emergence of a vibrant private sector. Having completed its support for the Bonn process, an expanded UNAMA, as proposed by the Secretary-General, would support the Government in its efforts to extend its reach to underserved areas in Afghanistan.

SECURITY COUNCIL ACTION

On 23 March [meeting 5393], the Security Council unanimously adopted **resolution 1662(2006)**. The draft [S/2006/175] was prepared in consultations among Council members.

The Security Council,

Recalling its previous resolutions on Afghanistan, in particular resolution 1589(2005) of 24 March 2005, in which it extended the mandate of the United Nations Assistance Mission in Afghanistan until 24 March 2006, and resolution 1659(2006) of 15 February 2006, in which it endorsed the Afghanistan Compact,

Reaffirming its strong commitment to the sovereignty, independence, territorial integrity and national unity of Afghanistan,

Reaffirming, in this context, its support for the implementation by the Government of Afghanistan and all members of the international community and international organizations of the Compact under the ownership of the Afghan people, and its support for the interim Afghanistan National Development Strategy,

Pledging its continued support for the Government and people of Afghanistan as they build on the successful completion of the Bonn process in rebuilding their country, strengthening the foundations of a constitutional democracy and assuming their rightful place in the community of nations,

Stressing the inalienable right of the people of Afghanistan freely to determine their own future, and welcoming the successful holding of the parliamentary and provincial elections on 18 September 2005,

Determined to assist the Government and people of Afghanistan in building on the successful London Conference on Afghanistan, held on 31 January and 1 February 2006,

Recognizing the interconnected nature of the challenges in Afghanistan, affirming that sustainable progress on security, governance and development as well as the cross-cutting issue of counter-narcotics, which necessarily involves capacity-building, is mutually reinforcing, and welcoming the continuing efforts of the Government of Afghanistan and the international community to address these challenges,

Recognizing also the continuing importance of combating increased terrorist attacks caused by the Taliban, Al-Qaida and other extremist groups and narcotics threats,

Expressing its concern at the increasing threat to the local population, national security forces, international military and international assistance efforts by extremist activities, and stressing the importance of the security and safety of the United Nations staff,

Recalling the importance of the Kabul Declaration on Good-neighbourly Relations (Kabul Declaration) of 22 December 2002, and stressing that regional cooperation constitutes an effective means to promote security and development in Afghanistan,

Expressing its appreciation and strong support for the ongoing efforts of the Secretary-General and his Special Representative for Afghanistan,

Stressing the central and impartial role that the United Nations continues to play in promoting peace and stability in Afghanistan, including the coordination and monitoring of efforts in implementing the Compact,

1. *Welcomes* the report of the Secretary-General of 7 March 2006;

2. *Also welcomes* the United Nations' long-term commitment to work with the people and Government of Afghanistan;

3. *Decides* to extend the mandate of the United Nations Assistance Mission in Afghanistan, as set out in the report of the Secretary-General, for an additional period of twelve months from the date of adoption of the present resolution;

4. *Reiterates its call upon* the Government of Afghanistan, and all members of the international community and international organizations, to implement in full the Afghanistan Compact and the annexes thereto;

5. *Emphasizes* the importance of meeting the benchmarks and timelines of the Compact for progress on security, governance and development, as well as the cross-cutting issue of counter-narcotics, and of increasing the effectiveness and coordination of the assistance to Afghanistan;

6. *Calls upon* all Afghan parties and groups to engage constructively in the peaceful political development of the country and avoid resorting to violence;

7. *Welcomes* the substantial progress in the disarmament, demobilization and reintegration process in accordance with the Bonn Agreement of 5 December 2001, including the completion of disarmament and demobilization, encourages the Government of Afghanistan to complete the disarmament, demobilization and reintegration process by June 2006, calls for determined efforts by the Government, including its security authorities, to disband illegal armed groups and to dispose of ammunition stockpiles, and requests the international community to extend further assistance for those efforts, taking fully into account the guidance by the Mission;

8. *Also welcomes* the development of the Afghan National Army and the Afghan National Police and the ongoing efforts to increase their capabilities as important steps towards the goal of Afghan security forces providing security and ensuring the rule of law throughout the country, and further welcomes in this regard the outcome of the Doha Conference on Border Management in Afghanistan of 28 February 2006;

9. *Further welcomes* the inauguration of the new Afghan National Assembly, commends Afghan efforts to ensure its efficient functioning, which will be critical to the political future of Afghanistan, welcomes the international efforts to provide technical assistance, and encourages all the institutions to work in a spirit of cooperation;

10. *Calls upon* the Government of Afghanistan to ensure continued public administrative reform and anti-corruption efforts, as described in the Compact;

11. *Welcomes* the finalization of the ten-year strategy for justice reform in Afghanistan, as detailed in the paper entitled "Justice for all" presented by the Ministry of Justice, and invites the Government of Afghanistan, with the assistance of the international community, to continue to work towards the establishment of a fair and transparent justice system, including the reconstruction and reform of the correctional system, as highlighted in the Compact, in order to strengthen the rule of law throughout the country and eliminate impunity;

12. *Calls for* full respect for human rights and international humanitarian law throughout Afghanistan, in this regard, requests the Mission, with the support of the Office of the United Nations High Commissioner for Human Rights, to continue to assist in the full implementation of the human rights provisions of the Afghan Constitution and international treaties to which Afghanistan is a State party, in particular those regarding the full enjoyment by women of their human rights, commends the Afghan Independent Human Rights Commission for its courageous efforts to monitor respect for human rights in Afghanistan as well as to foster and protect those rights, welcomes the adoption of the Action Plan on Peace, Justice and Reconciliation on 12 December 2005, and encourages international support for the Action Plan;

13. *Welcomes* the interim Afghanistan National Development Strategy presented at the London Conference on Afghanistan, calls upon the Government of Afghanistan to further provide strong leadership in its implementation, and encourages the fulfilment of the pledges made by the participants at the Conference, including financial assistance available for the implementation of the Strategy, which has reached 10.5 billion United States dollars;

14. *Recognizes* the risk that opium cultivation, production and trafficking poses to the security, development and governance of Afghanistan as well as to the region and internationally, welcomes the updated National Drug Control Strategy presented by the Government of Afghanistan at the London Conference, calls upon the Government, with support provided by the international community, to pursue early implementation of the Strategy, and encourages additional international support for the four priorities identified in the Strategy, including through contributions to the Counter-Narcotics Trust Fund;

15. *Emphasizes* the important role in monitoring the implementation of the Compact to be played by the Joint Coordination and Monitoring Board, which will be co-

chaired by the Special Representative of the Secretary-General and the Government of Afghanistan and supported by a small secretariat;

16. *Welcomes* the proposal of the Secretary-General to extend the reach of regional offices, security circumstances permitting;

17. *Calls upon* all Afghan and international parties to continue to cooperate with the Mission in the implementation of its mandate and to ensure the security and freedom of movement of its staff throughout the country;

18. *Calls upon* the Government of Afghanistan, with the assistance of the international community, including the Operation Enduring Freedom coalition and the International Security Assistance Force, in accordance with their respective designated responsibilities as they evolve, to continue to address the threat to the security and stability of Afghanistan posed by the Taliban, Al-Qaida, other extremist groups and criminal activities;

19. *Encourages* the promotion of confidence-building measures between Afghanistan and its neighbours in the spirit of the Kabul Declaration in order to foster dialogue and cooperation in the region in full respect for the principles of territorial integrity, mutual respect, friendly relations and non-interference in each other's internal affairs;

20. *Requests* the Secretary-General to report to the Security Council every six months on developments in Afghanistan;

21. *Decides* to remain actively seized of the matter.

Press statements (May and July). In a 15 May press statement [SC/8720], Security Council members condemned the terrorist attack on a United Nations Children's Fund (UNICEF) vehicle in Herat province on 12 May, which had claimed the lives of two UNICEF staff and a non-governmental organization doctor. They stressed the importance of the security and safety of UN staff. In another statement of 26 July [SC/8787], Council members, following a briefing by the Special Representative, expressed their concern over the situation in Afghanistan, against the background of increasing activity by the Taliban and other groups. They expressed their support for the efforts of the Afghan Security Forces to maintain security, with the cooperation of ISAF and Operation Enduring Freedom; reaffirmed that progress on security, governance, development and counter-narcotics were mutually reinforcing; welcomed efforts by the Government and Parliament to ensure a democratic debate; expressed hope that the pace of reform would accelerate; took note of Afghan efforts to implement the Afghan Compact; encouraged the international community to further strengthen its support under the Compact's framework; and reaffirmed the Council's strong support of UNAMA activities.

Second Tokyo Conference on Afghanistan. The Second Tokyo Conference on Consolidation of Peace in Afghanistan (Tokyo, Japan, 5 July), held under the co-chairmanship of Afghanistan, Japan and the United Nations, was attended by some 53 States and 15 international organizations. The Conference recognized that the achievements made in Afghanistan had not yet been consolidated sufficiently for the nation-building process to be considered self-sustaining and that the situation remained fragile, especially in view of the tense security atmosphere in the country. It examined the status of implementation of the programme for the disbandment of illegally armed groups and expressed its dissatisfaction with progress made so far. It requested Afghan and international stakeholders to further enhance efforts so that the programme could be completed by the end of 2007. The Conference appreciated that the Government of Afghanistan, in a statement of its President, had reiterated its strong commitment to stand firm on the disbandment of illegally armed groups and to accomplish it at any cost, despite the difficulties and challenges that lay ahead. The Conference stressed the need for robust engagement in that regard by the Ministry of the Interior, the Ministry of Defence and the National Directorate for Security.

The Conference congratulated all stakeholders on the completion of the disarmament, demobilization and reintegration process in June, under which some 63,380 ex-combatants had been disarmed, 62,044 demobilized and 55,804 reintegrated. It noted that the United Nations Development Programme (UNDP) would continue to provide for the needs of the ex-combatants for another 18 months. The Conference noted that, to achieve security on the basis of the rule of law and good governance in accordance with the Afghanistan Compact, both Afghan and international stakeholders would have to cooperate more fully to advance simultaneously the enhancement of the Afghan National Army and reform of the Afghan National Police and judicial police, the disbandment of illegally armed groups and counter-narcotic activities.

Report of Secretary-General (September). In his September report on the situation in Afghanistan and its implications for peace and security [A/61/326-S/2006/727], submitted in response to Security Council resolution 1662(2006) and General Assembly resolutions 60/32 A [YUN 2005, p. 404] and 60/32 B [ibid., p. 1000], the Secretary-General summarized key developments since his March report (see p. 364), the most significant of which was the upsurge in violence, particularly in the south, southeast and east of Afghanistan. An estimated 2,000 people, at least one third of them civilians, had died in the fighting since the beginning of the year, a three- to four fold increase in the rate of casualties compared to 2005, with close to 500 incidents involving anti-Government elements per month.

The growing number of casualties in the south was due to a rise in anti-Government attacks and a corresponding increase in offensive military operations by the Afghan National Army and its international partners. In the south-east, where major military operations were only just getting under way, insurgent activity went largely unchecked. Suicide attacks at mid-August numbered 65, against 17 during all of 2005. The violence, with a quantitative spike in insurgent activities and a qualitative shift in operations, represented a watershed. At no time since the fall of the Taliban in 2001, had the threat to Afghanistan's transition been so severe.

The insurgency was conducted mostly by Afghans operating inside the country's borders, but its leaders relied on support and sanctuary from outside the country. It was centred in and around the provinces of Farah, Hilmand, Kandahar and Uruzgan, but anti-government operations also continued in parts of the east and south-east, and were the cause for concern in Wardak and Logar provinces, close to the capital. The insurgency covered a broad arc of mostly Pashtun-dominated territory, extending from Kunar province in the east to Farah province in the west and increasingly was affecting the southern fringe of the central highlands, in Ghor and Day Kundi provinces.

The five leadership centres of the insurgency were the wing of the Hezb-i-Islami party led by Gulbuddin Hekmatyar, in Kunar province; the Taliban northern command for Nangarhar and Laghman provinces; networks led by Jalaluddin Haqqani, a former Taliban minister, mainly for Khost and Paktya provinces; the Wana Shura for the Paktika province; and the Taliban southern command for the provinces of Zabul, Kandahar, Hilmand, and Uruzgan. The leaders appeared to act in loose coordination, and some benefited from financial and operational links with drug trafficking networks. The Taliban southern command established parallel civil administrations and courts in its area of operations. The leadership relied heavily on cross-border fighters, many of whom were Afghans drawn from nearby refugee camps and radical seminaries in Pakistan. They were typically indoctrinated, unemployed young men whose sense of identity had been blurred by years in exile, who were trained and paid to serve as medium-level commanders, leading operations inside Afghanistan, and were able to retreat to safe havens outside the country. The insurgency's foot soldiers were locally recruited Afghans, driven by poverty, poor education and disenchantment with their place in society.

Dialogue with elders, clerics and community leaders revealed several grievances which, if addressed, could significantly weaken support for the insurgency. Government corruption at the provincial and district levels, particularly within the police and the judiciary, had alienated local populations, as had unfulfilled expectations of development following the fall of the Taliban. Imbalances in the distribution of power between different Pashtun tribes at the provincial level contributed to a sense of marginalization felt by entire tribes. Conservative elements of the population, mostly in rural areas, viewed the Government's social policies as insufficiently protective of, or even harmful to, religious, tribal and cultural norms. A sense of volatility had also gripped Kabul, triggered by the riots that broke out there on 29 May, following a tragic traffic incident involving United States–led coalition forces. At least 25 people died on that day and several properties were looted or burned.

On the political side, the National Assembly was functioning effectively. It had reviewed internal rules of procedures, defined the membership of standing committees, discussed issues such as national security and the national budget and held hearings for high-level appointments. The Assembly replaced five of the 25 cabinet ministers proposed by President Karzai and endorsed eight of the nine Supreme Court justices, including the Chief Justice, leaving only two positions unconfirmed: the head of the Central Bank and the ninth member of the Supreme Court. However, several Assembly members continued to maintain links with illegally armed groups and criminal networks. Reports of corruption were rife, and traditional power brokers and former commanders repeatedly threatened and intimidated elected representatives.

Provincial councils continued to function in varying degrees in all 34 provinces. Appointments of highly qualified officials in some provinces had led to notable improvements, and UNAMA and international agencies were providing technical assistance to the councils.

As called for in the Afghanistan Compact, a Joint Coordination and Monitoring Board was established to provide high-level coordination and political guidance for implementing the Compact's benchmarks. The 28-member Board comprised seven Afghan and 21 international members, including the six largest contributors of development assistance (Germany, India, Japan, the United Kingdom, the United States and the European Union); three neighbouring countries (China, Iran and Pakistan);

countries in three regions (the Russian Federation, Saudi Arabia and Turkey); the international military supporters (Canada, France, Italy, the Netherlands, NATO and coalition forces); and the World Bank and the Asian Development Bank. The Board met on 30 April and 30 July. It considered an action plan for power sector reform, which aimed to define a midterm energy sector strategy.

Press statement (September). In an 11 September press statement [SC/8825], Security Council members condemned suicide bombings in Kabul and other parts of Afghanistan, including the one on 10 September that killed Governor Abdul Hakim Tanaiwal of Paktya province.

Security Council consideration. On 9 October, the Security Council met in closed session [meeting 5548], during which it was briefed by the Special Representative of the Secretary-General and the Executive Director of the United Nations Office on Drugs and Crime. In a press statement issued on the same date [SC/8850], Council members expressed their concern at the security situation, particularly in the south and south-east, and at the increase in the cultivation and trafficking of opium. They expressed their belief that the building of sound and resilient institutions would provide solutions to Afghanistan's long-term problems. Council members welcomed the fact that the Joint Coordination and Monitoring Board had begun to work on improving coordination of the international community's engagement in the country and the extension of UNAMA presence in new provinces; and efforts by the Government and its neighbouring partners to foster trust and cooperation. The Council affirmed its willingness to send a mission to review the situation and give Afghanistan and its people a message of assurance of the Council's commitment.

Later developments. In a later report [A/61/799-S/2007/152], the Secretary-General reported that insurgency-related violence peaked in September but receded thereafter due to intensive security efforts and the onset of winter. Despite high losses of personnel, indications pointed to an insurgency emboldened by their strategic successes, rather than disheartened by tactical failures. They continued to mount widespread roadblocks on the ring road connecting Kabul to Kandahar and Herat and to target senior public officials and community leaders, including the head of the Kandahar Department of Women's Affairs and the Governor of Paktya province (see above), who were assassinated in September and October, respectively. In the central and south-east regions, military operations conducted by Government and international military forces managed to clear areas only temporarily. The peace agreement concluded on 5 September between Pakistan and the local Taliban of North Waziristan did not prevent the use of the tribal area as a staging ground for attacks on Afghanistan. Security incidents involving insurgents instead rose by 50 per cent in Khost and 70 per cent in Paktika, between September and November, accompanied by intensified propaganda activities. There were reports of cross-border movement in both directions. Local communities had begun entering into accords with the Government and the insurgents in order to limit the damage of warfare. One such agreement reached in September with local elders from Musa Qala district in Helmand province, under which the district would not be used as a staging ground for insurgent attacks in exchange for the withdrawal of international military forces, led to five months of relative stability. However, suicide attacks increased significantly, with a record of 21 suicide bombings in September, dropping to 15 per month by the end of the year.

At the political level, parliamentarians and party leaders announced in November the formation of the National United Council, an alliance of prominent jihadis, leftists and ethno-nationalists, whose platform included support for decentralization and federalism, regularizing the presence of international military forces and resolving border disputes. Relations between Afghanistan and Pakistan remained tense. Commitments to cooperate in resolving cross-border issues had yet to realize their full potential. In summit talks between the Presidents of both countries in September, both the insurgency and the counter-terrorism efforts were prioritized. Also in September, at a meeting in Washington, D.C., the Presidents of Afghanistan, Pakistan and the United States agreed on a proposal to hold peace jirgas (gatherings of tribal and community leaders).

The third meeting of the Joint Coordination and Monitoring Board of the Afghanistan Compact, held in November, identified key priorities to be met, including the reform of the Ministry of the Interior; aid-effectiveness; capacity-building; the strengthening of institutions, particularly the justice sector; anti-corruption efforts; impunity; and counter-narcotics efforts. The meeting stressed the need for an outcome-based assessment of expenditures by the donor community and the Government and a new strategy for private sector development.

GENERAL ASSEMBLY ACTION

On 28 November [meeting 58], the General Assembly adopted **resolution 61/18 A** [draft: A/61/L.25 & Add.1] without vote [agenda item 16].

The situation in Afghanistan

The General Assembly,

Recalling its resolutions 60/32 A and B of 30 November 2005 and all its previous relevant resolutions,

Recalling also all relevant Security Council resolutions and statements by the President of the Council on the situation in Afghanistan, in particular the most recent resolutions 1659(2006) of 15 February 2006, 1662(2006) of 23 March 2006 and 1707(2006) of 12 September 2006, as well as the statement by the President of the Council on 26 July 2006,

Expressing its strong commitment to the implementation of the Afghanistan Compact and the annexes thereto, launched at the London Conference on Afghanistan held on 31 January and 1 February 2006, which provide the framework for the partnership between the Government of Afghanistan and the international community,

Reaffirming its strong commitment to the sovereignty, independence, territorial integrity and national unity of Afghanistan, and respecting its multicultural, multi-ethnic and historical heritage,

Recognizing the urgent need to tackle the challenges in Afghanistan, including terrorist threats, the fight against narcotics, the lack of security, in particular in the south and east, the comprehensive nationwide disbandment of illegal armed groups and the development of Afghan Government institutions, including at the subnational level, the strengthening of the rule of law, the acceleration of justice sector reform, the promotion of national reconciliation, without prejudice to the fulfilment of the measures introduced by the Security Council in its resolution 1267(1999) of 15 October 1999 and other relevant resolutions, and an Afghan-led transitional justice process, the safe and orderly return of Afghan refugees and internally displaced persons, the promotion and protection of human rights and the advancement of economic and social development,

Expressing in this context its deep concern over attacks against both Afghan and foreign nationals committed to supporting the consolidation of peace, stability and development in Afghanistan, in particular United Nations and diplomatic staff, national and international humanitarian and development personnel, Afghan National Security Forces, the International Security Assistance Force, as well as the Operation Enduring Freedom coalition, and noting with concern that the lack of security is causing some organizations to cease or curtail their humanitarian and development work in some parts of Afghanistan,

Recognizing the progress achieved, while nonetheless remaining deeply concerned about the problem of millions of anti-personnel landmines and explosive remnants of war, which constitute a great danger for the population and a major obstacle for the resumption of economic activities and for recovery and reconstruction efforts,

Noting that, despite improvements in building the security sector, increased terrorist attacks caused by the Taliban, Al-Qaida and other extremist groups, in particular in the south and east of Afghanistan over the past months, and the lack of security caused by criminal activity and the illicit production of and trafficking in drugs, remain a serious challenge, threatening the democratic process as well as reconstruction and economic development,

Noting also that the responsibility for providing security and law and order throughout the country resides with the Government of Afghanistan supported by the Assistance Force and the Operation Enduring Freedom coalition, recognizing the institutional progress achieved in this respect, deeply concerned about the recent increase in violence, and stressing the importance of further extending central government authority to all parts of Afghanistan,

Commending the Afghan National Army and the Afghan National Police, the Assistance Force and the Operation Enduring Freedom coalition for their efforts to improve security conditions in Afghanistan,

Acknowledging, in this context, that the Afghan National Army and the Afghan National Police require additional support to enhance their capability, including through the provision of more modern equipment,

Stressing that regional cooperation constitutes an effective means to promote security and development in Afghanistan,

Reaffirming in this context its continued support for the spirit and the provisions of the Bonn Agreement of 5 December 2001, of the Berlin Declaration, including the annexes thereto, of 1 April 2004 and of the Afghanistan Compact of 31 January 2006, and pledging its continued support, after the successful completion of the political transition, to the Government and people of Afghanistan as they rebuild their country, strengthen the foundations of a constitutional democracy and resume their rightful place in the community of nations,

Applauding the inauguration of the Afghan National Assembly on 19 December 2005, which completes the Bonn process, as well as the constitution of the provincial councils,

Welcoming the constitution of the national Government, and noting the importance of it being representative of the ethnic diversity of the country and ensuring also the adequate participation of women,

Welcoming also the finalization of the ten-year strategy for justice reform in Afghanistan, and expressing its appreciation for the appointment and confirmation of a highly qualified Supreme Court,

Welcoming further, in this regard, the guarantee of human rights and fundamental freedoms for all Afghans in the new Constitution as a significant step towards an improved situation of human rights and fundamental freedoms, in particular for women and children,

Recalling Security Council resolution 1325(2000) of 31 October 2000 on women and peace and security, and applauding the progress achieved in the empowerment of women in Afghan politics as historic milestones in the political process, which will help to consolidate durable peace and national stability in Afghanistan, while noting the need to promote the empowerment of women also at the provincial level,

Noting at the same time with concern reports of continued violations of human rights and of international humanitarian law and violent or discriminatory practices, in particular against women and girls, in certain parts of the country, and stressing the need for adherence to international standards of tolerance and religious freedom,

Welcoming the presentation of the interim Afghanistan National Development Strategy and the adoption of the first report on the Millennium Development Goals by the Government of Afghanistan as well as the further efforts of the Government to achieve the Millennium Development Goals,

Welcoming also the continuing and growing ownership of the rehabilitation and reconstruction efforts by the Government of Afghanistan, and emphasizing the crucial need to achieve ownership in all fields of governance and to improve institutional capabilities, including at the provincial level, in order to use aid more effectively,

Expressing its appreciation for the humanitarian assistance work of the international community in the reconstruction and development of Afghanistan, recognizing the necessity of further addressing the slow pace of change in the living conditions of the Afghan people, and noting the need to strengthen the capacity of the Government of Afghanistan to deliver basic services and to promote development,

Welcoming the continuous return of refugees and internally displaced persons, while noting with concern that conditions in parts of Afghanistan are not yet conducive to safe and sustainable returns to some places of origin and that the high concentration of returns to major urban areas has placed an extreme burden on limited urban resources,

Aware of the high vulnerability of Afghanistan to natural disasters and harsh climate conditions, in particular drought or flooding,

Expressing its appreciation for the work of the provincial reconstruction teams and of the executive steering committee,

Recognizing that the social and economic development of Afghanistan, specifically the development of alternative gainful and sustainable livelihoods in the formal productive sector, is an important element of the successful implementation of the comprehensive Afghan national drug control strategy and depends to a large extent on enhanced international cooperation with the Government of Afghanistan,

Welcoming the launching on 31 January 2006 of the updated National Drug Control Strategy at the London Conference on Afghanistan,

Deeply concerned about the increased cultivation, production of and trafficking in narcotic drugs in Afghanistan, which is undermining stability and security as well as the political and economic reconstruction of Afghanistan and has dangerous repercussions in the region and far beyond, and commending in this context the publication of the updated National Drug Control Strategy and the reaffirmed commitment of the Government of Afghanistan to rid the country of this pernicious production and trade, including by decisive law enforcement measures,

Expressing its appreciation and strong support for the central and impartial role that the Secretary-General and his Special Representative continue to play in the consolidation of peace and stability in Afghanistan, and underlining the coordinating role of the United Nations in continuing to ensure a seamless transition, under Afghan leadership, from humanitarian relief to recovery and reconstruction,

Welcoming, in this context, the establishment of the Joint Coordination and Monitoring Board pursuant to the Afghanistan Compact as an instrument to further improve coordination between the Government of Afghanistan and its international partners and to monitor the implementation of all benchmarks,

Recognizing the need for a continued strong international commitment to humanitarian assistance and for programmes, under the ownership of the Government of Afghanistan, of recovery, rehabilitation and reconstruction, and expressing, at the same time, its appreciation to the United Nations system and to all States and international and non-governmental organizations whose international and local staff continue to respond positively to the humanitarian, transition and development needs of Afghanistan despite increasing security concerns and difficulties of access in certain areas,

1. *Welcomes* the report of the Secretary-General and the recommendations contained therein;

2. *Strongly condemns* the upsurge of violence throughout Afghanistan, in particular in the southern and eastern parts, owing to the increased violent and terrorist activity by the Taliban, Al-Qaida, other extremist groups and those involved in the narcotics trade, which has resulted in increased casualties among Afghan civilians, Afghan National Security Forces, the International Security Assistance Force and the Operation Enduring Freedom coalition, as well as among the personnel of Afghan and international aid agencies and all other humanitarian workers;

3. *Stresses* the importance of the provision of sufficient security, welcomes the expansion of the presence of the Assistance Force in southern and eastern Afghanistan, and calls upon Member States to continue contributing personnel, equipment and other resources to the Assistance Force and to further develop the provincial reconstruction teams in close coordination with the Government of Afghanistan and the United Nations Assistance Mission in Afghanistan;

4. *Expresses its appreciation* for the work of the Assistance Mission, and welcomes the extension of its presence in additional provinces, which thus ensures that the United Nations fulfils its essential coordinating role, and encourages the Assistance Mission to continue expansion of its presence throughout the country;

5. *Calls upon* the Government of Afghanistan, with the assistance of the international community, including through the Operation Enduring Freedom coalition and the Assistance Force, in accordance with their respective designated responsibilities, to continue to address the threat to the security and stability of Afghanistan posed by the Taliban, Al-Qaida and other extremist groups as well as by criminal violence, in particular violence involving the drug trade;

6. *Urges* the Government of Afghanistan and local authorities to take all possible steps to ensure the safe and unhindered access of United Nations, development and humanitarian personnel to all affected populations;

7. *Strongly condemns* all acts of violence and intimidation, in particular that directed against development and humanitarian personnel and United Nations and associated personnel as well as against Afghan civilians, including women activists, regrets the loss of life and physical harm, and urges the Government of Afghanistan and local authorities to make every effort, in accordance with General Assembly resolution 60/123 of 15 December 2005, to bring to justice the perpetrators of attacks, to ensure the safety, security and free movement of all United Nations, development and humanitarian personnel and to protect the property of the United Nations and of development or humanitarian organizations;

8. *Welcomes* the successful completion of the disarmament, demobilization and reintegration of former Afghan combatants, which started in October 2003;

9. *Also welcomes* the launching of the programme of disbandment of illegal armed groups, and stresses the importance of advancing its full implementation throughout the country under Afghan ownership, while ensuring further coordination and coherence with other relevant efforts regarding security sector reform and community development;

10. *Further welcomes*, in this context, the commitment of the President of Afghanistan to stand firm on the disbandment of illegal armed groups, at the Second Tokyo Conference on Consolidation of Peace in Afghanistan on 5 July 2006, and encourages the Government of Afghanistan to work actively at national, provincial and local levels to advance this commitment;

11. *Welcomes* the development of the new professional Afghan National Army and the Afghan National Police, calls for accelerated efforts to modernize and strengthen both institutions, welcomes the progress made in the creation of a fair and effective justice system as important steps towards the goal of strengthening the Government of Afghanistan, providing security and ensuring the rule of law throughout the country, and urges the international community to continue to support the efforts of the Government of Afghanistan in these areas in a coordinated manner;

12. *Also welcomes* the completion of the disarmament and demobilization of child soldiers in the Afghan Military Forces, stresses the importance of the reintegration of child soldiers and of care for other children affected by war, commends the Government of Afghanistan for its efforts in this regard, and encourages it to continue efforts in cooperation with the United Nations;

13. *Expresses its concern* about the recruitment and use of child soldiers by illegal armed groups in Afghanistan, reiterates the importance of ending the use of children contrary to international law, and welcomes the accession by Afghanistan to the Convention on the Rights of the Child and the two optional protocols thereto;

14. *Urges* the Government of Afghanistan to meet its responsibilities under the Convention on the Prohibition of the Use, Stockpiling, Production and Transfer of Anti-personnel Mines and on Their Destruction, to cooperate fully with the mine action programme coordinated by the United Nations, and to eliminate all existing stocks of anti-personnel landmines;

15. *Recognizes* the completion of the establishment of democratic institutions according to the Bonn process, notes the challenges lying ahead identified in the Afghanistan Compact, and calls upon the international community to continue to provide sustained support;

16. *Notes with concern* the negative impact of the security situation on the enjoyment of human rights, and calls for all parties to fully respect human rights and international humanitarian law throughout Afghanistan and, with the assistance of the Afghan Independent Human Rights Commission and of the Assistance Mission, to fully implement the human rights provisions of the new Afghan Constitution, and commends the commitment of the Government of Afghanistan in this respect;

17. *Calls for* the full respect of the human rights and fundamental freedoms of all, without discrimination of any kind, including on the basis of gender, ethnicity or religion, in accordance with obligations under the Afghan Constitution and international law;

18. *Stresses* the need to ensure respect for the right to freedom of expression and the right to freedom of thought, conscience or belief;

19. *Continues to emphasize* the necessity of investigating allegations of current and past violations of human rights and of international humanitarian law, including violations committed against persons belonging to ethnic and religious minorities, as well as against women and girls, of facilitating the provision of efficient and effective remedies to the victims and of bringing the perpetrators to justice in accordance with international law;

20. *Reiterates* the important role of the Afghan Independent Human Rights Commission in the promotion and protection of human rights and fundamental freedoms, stresses the need to expand its range of operation in all parts of Afghanistan in accordance with the Afghan Constitution, welcomes the adoption by the Government of Afghanistan of the Action Plan on Peace, Justice and Reconciliation, and stresses the importance of judicial accountability of human rights offenders in accordance with national and international law;

21. *Recalls* Security Council resolution 1325(2000) on women and peace and security, commends the efforts of the Government of Afghanistan to mainstream gender issues and to protect and promote the equal rights of women and men as guaranteed, inter alia, by virtue of its ratification of the Convention on the Elimination of All Forms of Discrimination against Women, and by the Afghan Constitution, welcomes the level of participation of Afghan women in the parliamentary and provincial council elections, including the election of female candidates to these bodies, and reiterates the continued importance of the full and equal participation of women in all spheres of Afghan life;

22. *Welcomes* the presentation of the interim national action plan for women in Afghanistan currently under

consultation and the significant efforts by the Government of Afghanistan to counter discrimination, urges the Government to actively involve all elements of Afghan society, in particular women, in the development and implementation of relief, rehabilitation, recovery and reconstruction programmes, and encourages the collection and use of statistical data on a sex-disaggregated basis to provide information on gender-based violence and accurately track the progress of the full integration of women into the political, economic and social life of Afghanistan;

23. *Recognizes* the significant progress achieved on gender equality in Afghanistan in recent years, and strongly condemns incidents of discrimination and violence against women in Afghanistan, wherever they occur;

24. *Welcomes* the initiative of the Government of Afghanistan to formulate a national plan of action on combating child trafficking, encourages the Government to formulate the plan of action guided by the Protocol to Prevent, Suppress and Punish Trafficking in Persons, Especially Women and Children, supplementing the United Nations Convention against Transnational Organized Crime, and stresses the importance of considering becoming a party to the Protocol;

25. *Urges* the Government of Afghanistan to continue to effectively reform the public administration sector in order to implement the rule of law and to ensure good governance and accountability at both national and local levels, and stresses the importance of meeting the respective benchmarks of the Afghanistan Compact, with the support of the international community;

26. *Encourages* the Government of Afghanistan to vigorously pursue its efforts to establish a more effective, accountable and transparent administration at all levels of Government leading the fight against corruption in accordance with the Afghanistan Compact, and notes with concern the effects of administrative corruption with regard to security, good governance and combating the narcotics industry;

27. *Stresses once again* the need for further progress on a comprehensive judicial reform in Afghanistan, and urges the Government of Afghanistan and the international community to devote resources also to the reconstruction and reform of the prison sector in order to improve respect for the rule of law and human rights therein, while reducing physical and mental health risks to inmates;

28. *Urges* the Government of Afghanistan to address, with the assistance of the international community, the question of claims for land property through a comprehensive land titling programme, including formal registration of all property and improved security of property rights, and welcomes the steps already taken by the Government in this regard;

29. *Welcomes* the presentation of the interim Afghanistan National Development Strategy at the London Conference on Afghanistan, underlines the need to finalize the Strategy as soon as possible, and urges the international community actively to support this process;

30. *Reiterates* the necessity of providing Afghan children with educational and health facilities in all parts of the country, recognizing the special needs of girls, strongly condemns terrorist attacks on education facilities, and encourages the Government of Afghanistan, with the assistance of the international community, to expand these facilities, to train professional staff and to promote full and equal access to them by all members of Afghan society, including in remote areas;

31. *Expresses its appreciation* to those Governments that continue to host Afghan refugees, acknowledging the huge burden they have so far shouldered in this regard, and reminds them of their obligations under international refugee law with respect to the protection of refugees, the principle of voluntary return and the right to seek asylum and to allow international access for their protection and care;

32. *Urges* the Government of Afghanistan, acting with the support of the international community, to continue and strengthen its efforts to create the conditions for the voluntary, safe, dignified and sustainable return and reintegration of the remaining Afghan refugees and internally displaced persons;

33. *Calls for* the provision of continued international assistance to the large numbers of Afghan refugees and internally displaced persons to facilitate their voluntary, safe and orderly return and sustainable reintegration into society so as to contribute to the stability of the entire country;

34. *Welcomes* the efforts to date of the Afghan authorities to carry out the updated National Drug Control Strategy presented at the London Conference on Afghanistan on 31 January 2006, and urges the Government of Afghanistan to take decisive action, in particular to stop the processing of and trade in drugs, by pursuing the concrete steps set out in the Strategy and in the Afghanistan Compact;

35. *Calls upon* the international community to assist the Government of Afghanistan in carrying out its National Drug Control Strategy, aimed at eliminating the cultivation, production, trafficking in and consumption of illicit drugs, including through increased support for Afghan law enforcement and criminal justice agencies, rural development, demand reduction, the elimination of illicit crops, increasing public awareness and building the capacity of drug control institutions;

36. *Expresses concern* about the recent increase in the cultivation of opium, notes that opium cultivation, and the related drug production and trafficking, pose a serious threat to security, the rule of law and development in Afghanistan, urges the Government of Afghanistan, supported by the international community, to work to mainstream counter-narcotics throughout all the national programmes, commends the efforts of the Government in this regard, and urges it to increase its efforts against opium cultivation;

37. *Encourages* the international community to increasingly channel counter-narcotics funding through the Government of Afghanistan's counter-narcotics trust fund;

38. *Urges* the Government of Afghanistan, while carrying out its National Drug Control Strategy, to pro-

mote the development of sustainable livelihoods in the formal production sector as well as other sectors, thus improving substantially the lives, health and security of the people, particularly in rural areas, and calls upon the international community, in cooperation with the Government, to continue to assist it in this regard;

39. *Supports* the fight against the illicit trafficking in drugs and precursors within Afghanistan and in neighbouring States and countries along trafficking routes, including increased cooperation among them to strengthen anti-narcotic controls to curb the drug flow;

40. *Welcomes* the outcome of the Second Ministerial Conference on Drug Trafficking Routes from Afghanistan, organized by the Government of the Russian Federation in cooperation with the United Nations Office on Drugs and Crime, held in Moscow from 26 to 28 June 2006, within the framework of the Paris Pact initiative, and therefore calls upon States to strengthen international and regional cooperation to counter the threat to the international community posed by the illicit production of and trafficking in drugs;

41. *Also welcomes* the establishment of the Joint Coordination and Monitoring Board for the implementation of the political commitments of the Afghanistan Compact, and expresses its appreciation for the support to the Assistance Mission and the Government of Afghanistan by the international members of the Board;

42. *Endorses* the key principles for cooperation between the Government of Afghanistan and the international community as referred to in the Afghanistan Compact: respect for the pluralistic culture, values and history of Afghanistan, based on Islam; partnership between the Government of Afghanistan, with its sovereign responsibilities, and the international community, with a central and impartial coordinating role for the United Nations; further engagement of participation and aspiration to ownership of the Afghan people; pursuit of fiscal, institutional and environmental sustainability; building of lasting Afghan capacity and effective State and civil society institutions; ensuring balanced and fair allocation of domestic and international resources throughout the country; recognition of equal rights and responsibilities of men and women in all policies; promotion of regional cooperation; and fight against corruption, and ensuring public transparency and accountability;

43. *Commends* the continuing efforts of the signatories of the Kabul Declaration on Good-neighbourly Relations of 22 December 2002 to implement their commitments under the Declaration, including, within that framework, those under the Kabul Declaration of 5 December 2005, adopted at the first Regional Economic Cooperation Conference, and furthermore calls upon all other States to respect and support the implementation of those provisions and to promote regional stability;

44. *Welcomes* efforts by the Governments of Afghanistan and its neighbouring partners to foster trust and cooperation with each other, and looks forward, where appropriate, to increasing cooperation between Afghanistan and all its neighbouring and regional partners against the Taliban, Al-Qaida and other extremist groups and in promoting peace and prosperity in Afghanistan, in the region and beyond;

45. *Appreciates* the efforts of the members of the Tripartite Commission, namely, Afghanistan, Pakistan and the United States of America, to continue to address cross-border activities and to broaden its cooperation, welcomes the participation of the Assistance Force, and calls upon the international community to support those efforts;

46. *Invites* all States, intergovernmental and non-governmental organizations providing assistance to Afghanistan to focus on institution-building in a coordinated manner and to ensure that such work complements and contributes to the development of an economy characterized by sound macroeconomic policies, the development of a financial sector that provides services, inter alia, to microenterprises, small and medium-sized enterprises and households, transparent business regulations and accountability;

47. *Encourages* the international community, including all donor nations, to assist the Government of Afghanistan in making capacity-building and human resources development a cross-cutting priority;

48. *Urges* the international community, in accordance with the Afghanistan Compact, to increase the proportion of donor assistance channelled directly to the core budget, as agreed bilaterally between the Government of Afghanistan and each donor, as well as through other more predictable core budget funding modalities in which the Government participates, such as the Afghanistan Reconstruction Trust Fund, the Law and Order Trust Fund and the Counter-Narcotics Trust Fund;

49. *Urgently appeals* to all States, the United Nations system and international and non-governmental organizations to continue to provide, in close coordination with the Government of Afghanistan and in accordance with its national development strategy, all possible and necessary humanitarian, recovery, reconstruction, financial, technical and material assistance for Afghanistan;

50. *Emphasizes* the need to maintain, strengthen and review civil-military relations among international actors, as appropriate, at all levels in order to ensure complementarity of action based on the different mandates and comparative advantages of the humanitarian, development, law enforcement and military actors present in Afghanistan, bearing in mind the central and impartial coordinating role of the United Nations;

51. *Requests* the Secretary-General to report to the General Assembly every six months during its sixty-first session on developments in Afghanistan, as well as on the progress made in the implementation of the present resolution;

52. *Decides* to include in the provisional agenda of its sixty-second session the item entitled "The situation in Afghanistan".

Security Council mission

On 9 November [S/2006/875], the Security Council President informed the Secretary-General of the Council's decision to send a mission to Afghanistan.

The mission, to be led by Kenzo Oshima (Japan), would assure the Afghan society of the international community's continued commitment to the Afghan process based on the Afghanistan Compact and Council resolution 1662(2006) (see p. 365); demonstrate the Council's support of Afghan efforts in the areas of security, governance and development; review progress in those areas, with particular emphasis on counter-narcotics, disarmament, demobilization and reintegration-disbandment of illegally armed groups, human rights protection, public and justice sector reforms and rule of law issues; and review the status of international assistance. The mission, which took place between 11 and 16 November, visited Kabul, Qalat and Mazari Sharif but was unable to visit Kandahar city due to security concerns. It also visited Pakistan. During its stay in Afghanistan, the mission held discussions with President Karzai and members of his Government, the National Security Council, governors, members of the upper and lower houses of the National Assembly, civil society, NGOs, ISAF, UNAMA, and UN agencies. It also received statements from Human Rights Watch and Amnesty International.

In its report to the Council in December [S/2006/935], the mission found that the spread of insurgency and terrorist activity by the Taliban, Al-Qaida and other extremists groups linked to the illegal drug trade, coupled with corruption and failures of governance and the rule of law, collectively posed a grave threat to reconstruction and nation-building in Afghanistan. However, the mission was convinced that the Government and the international community had established a sound strategy for overcoming those challenges. The Council should ensure that the international community's commitment to that shared strategy remained firm and enduring. The Afghanistan Compact, adopted at the London Conference on Afghanistan (see p. 363), should move to serious action and consistent implementation. The mission encouraged the Government to transform its ownership of the Compact into further action, with a view to striving towards the benchmarks contained therein. The mission urged the international community, especially the participants in the London Conference on Afghanistan, to continue their financial and political support towards the achievement of those benchmarks and the Compact's overall goals. NATO and other countries were urged to maintain and increase their commitment to ISAF to meet the challenges of the current security environment. International military forces should enhance their cooperation with the Government, remain committed to respecting international human rights law and international humanitarian law, avoid civilian casualties and respect local culture and traditions. The mission affirmed the importance of establishing a strong and sustainable National Army and urged donors and the Government to redouble their efforts to establish a trusted and effective National Police throughout the country. It concluded that considerable investment would be required before the Compact's security benchmarks could be achieved. The National Auxiliary Police had to be properly funded and monitored and the international community should revitalize its support to Afghanistan's efforts to implement the programme to disband illegally armed groups. The mission urged the Government, as a matter of high priority, to establish the rule of law and good governance throughout the country, including by strengthening justice sector institutions and provincial governments. More effective mechanisms for strategic planning, funding and coordination of rule of law programmes were required. Donors should increase the coherence and scale of assistance in the development of Afghanistan's human capital, especially for the reform of the country's civil service. Technical assistance efforts should be assessed so as to maximize its use. The mission urged the Government to reinforce its commitment to human rights and reconciliation through increased support to the Afghan Independent Human Rights Commission and the implementation of the Action Plan for Peace, Justice and Reconciliation in Afghanistan, as required by the Afghanistan Compact. The Government and donors should also make the empowerment of women a cross-cutting priority and defend the Afghan Constitution's provisions relating to the rights of women.

The international community and the Government were encouraged to implement programmes that generated employment given that the dearth of such programmes contributed significantly to the recruitment of insurgents. In that regard, the coordination mechanism of the Joint Coordination and Monitoring Board should be further improved and focused on delivery. The mission urged the Government and the international community to further strengthen and diversify legal livelihoods so that rural communities could move away from the illegal cultivation of opium poppy and pursue legitimate economic opportunities. They should also step up activity to arrest and prosecute major drug traffickers regardless of their position and status and implement all aspects of the National Drug Control Strategy.

The mission urged the Governments of Afghanistan and Pakistan to increase dialogue and collaboration in the face of the growing threat to their shared security and looked forward to the outcome of plans by both countries to hold jirgas to improve security and stability. The mission also recommended that the list established pursuant to Council resolution 1267(1999) [YUN 1999, p. 265] should continue to be updated on the basis of the most recent information available.

Security Council consideration. The Security Council twice considered the mission's report on its visit to Afghanistan. On 22 November [meeting 5570], it heard an oral report by the head of the mission, Ambassador Kenzo Oshima, who presented the full report to the Council on 7 December [meeting 5581].

At the 22 November meeting, he said that the Afghan partnership that had begun in Bonn in late 2001 was largely on track. Gains in establishing democratic institutions and improving the welfare of the population had consolidated. However, the year had witnessed the rise in the Taliban-led insurgency and social ills, including the upsurge in illegal drug production and trafficking, against the backdrop of weak State and provincial institutions. Problems of security and the rule of law, and the accompanying endemic corruption and impunity, had compromised public confidence, giving rise to a sense of backsliding. In the circumstances, it was important to stress that the international community's commitment of support for Afghanistan remained firm and sustained and that the Afghanistan Compact was the best strategic framework for cooperation.

Overall security was the number-one concern. After an upsurge in security incidents before summer, there were signs that insurgent and terrorist violence had begun to subside. The insurgency had to be dealt with through robust military and law-enforcement actions. Measures should also address the growing frustration among ordinary Afghans. President Karzai told the mission that the Government's failure to show its capability to provide security, as well as economic and social services, in the countryside, had increased disillusionment and partly contributed to the surge in violence. The President also conceded that the continued influence and tolerance of the activities of warlords had contributed to the loss of faith by the people. The narcotics issue, which, according to the President, was a direct result of the desperation of the people, should be addressed as a matter of priority. In the area of reconstruction, the achievements by the Government and the people were to be highly commended. All those issues should be addressed as a matter of the highest priority and the Afghan Government, with the international community's backing, should take immediate and effective steps to re-establish trust among the people.

Speaking during the Council's 7 December consideration of the mission's report, Afghanistan's representative said that, despite achievements made, the prevailing security situation and the slow pace of development remained in the forefront of the country's challenges. He appealed for additional resources for Afghanistan's security institutions as a means of improving the overall security situation. He also highlighted the need for the initiation and implementation of major construction projects and the expeditious provision of basic services so that tangible and visible improvements in the daily lives of the people might be achieved. The representative called for sustained international support for the implementation of the Afghanistan Compact and the interim national development strategy, especially the need to channel donor assistance through the national budget. Noting the significant challenges being faced in the fight against narcotics, he reiterated that particular focus should be accorded to providing alternative crops to farmers as an essential element of a successful counter-narcotics strategy. On the instructions of President Karzai, the Afghan Government had embarked upon a comprehensive initiative to enhance transparency and good governance, including the establishment of an anti-corruption commission, headed by the Chief Justice of the Supreme Court, to propose additional recommendations for further action by the President.

Pakistan's representative said that his country had a vital stake in peace and stability in Afghanistan. There could be no doubt about its commitment to bring security to the border regions of both countries, but the responsibility had to be joint. He noted that the international community had avoided addressing the problem of Afghan refugees, 3 million of whom were still in Pakistan, and that the issue did not figure in the report of the Council's mission. Pakistan would continue to provide cooperation and support to Afghanistan, but that country's problems needed to be addressed in a holistic approach based on political reconciliation, improved security and governance and rapid and large-scale economic and social development and reconstruction.

Sectoral issues

Judicial system and the rule of law

Although some progress in reform was being made, Afghanistan's justice system continued to suffer from severe and systemic problems, including a lack of sufficiently qualified judges, prosecutors and lawyers, and the necessary infrastructure to administer justice effectively. Institutionalized corruption, political interference, lengthy pre-trial detentions, the lack of availability of legal representation and other due process violations remained the norm and contributed to the low level of public trust in the justice system. With the support of the United Nations and donor nations, judges and prosecutors were being trained, more defendants were receiving legal representation, courthouses and prisons were being rebuilt or refurbished and the capacity of the permanent justice institutions had been enhanced. Key legislation had been put in place and a new criminal code, an anti-terrorism law, a new law on the organization of the prosecutor's office and a law establishing an independent bar association were being drafted. In December, the Afghanistan rule of law coordination meeting in Dubai, United Arab Emirates, saw renewed commitments to reform the justice sector. Consensus emerged in favour of a multi-donor funding mechanism or a justice trust fund. The international community was supporting justice institutions to finalize a detailed sectoral reform strategy to achieve the benchmarks of the Afghanistan National Development Strategy.

Widespread corruption in the justice system remained a serious concern. The appointment of a reform-oriented Supreme Court Chief Justice and Attorney General in 2006 was a promising development. The composition of the new Supreme Court reflected a fairly even ethnic balance, but did not include women. Challenges facing the judiciary included low level of education and competency, inadequate salaries, insecure career progression, tenure and personal safety. Only a third of the 1,415 judges had higher education, and there was a lack of fundamental judicial competencies. Some 170 new judges were finishing their training under the auspices of the Supreme Court but another 300 posts, out of a total of 1,884 approved positions, would need to be filled. However, the failure to ensure a secure environment for courts and judicial personnel undermined the reform efforts, as well as the capacity of the legal system to act impartially and independently. The situations regarding prisons remained serious. With international support, significant reforms were being carried out, including major prison projects for two new facilities in Gardez and Mazar-e-Sharif, a women's facility and a juvenile reformatory in Kabul. As part of the Government's anti-narcotics strategy, the construction of a high security unit at Pol-e-Charkhi prison for high-profile drug offenders was nearing completion.

Security sector reform

The National Police continued to make modest strides in developing as a dependable public security provider. According to the Interior Ministry, the force consisted of 65,497 police officers and patrolmen. The restructuring of the leadership continued, and the second-tier restructuring culminated on 4 June, when President Karzai appointed 86 one-star police generals selected from a list of 275 officers. With growing insecurity in the south, 2,100 more officers were deployed there, and highway police officers to the Border Police in unstable areas. The police continued to face daunting challenges: weak command and control arrangements, insufficient administrative and logistical support, widespread lack of discipline, rampant corruption and disregard for human rights and due process. As a result, the level of public trust in the police remained low. The police had limited ability to project itself outside Kabul, and once deployed, officers lacked sufficient leadership, equipment and facilities to perform their role. At all but the most senior levels, illiteracy remained a problem, with an estimated 70 per cent illiteracy rate. The budget of the UNDP-administered Law and Order Trust Fund for Afghanistan, which provided remuneration and other support to the police, was increased to $169 million for the year, but a $27 million shortfall for salaries remained, affecting implementation of the new police salary regime, food allowances and severance packages.

Disarmament, demobilization and reintegration and disbandment of armed groups

On 26 January, the Government and its international partners agreed on a national strategy to disband armed groups, which provided for close coordination, with initiatives aimed at extending the rule of law, good governance, security and development assistance. The programme would offer time-bound opportunities for voluntary and negotiated compliance, failing which the Ministry of the Interior could enforce compliance, using State security forces. The main phase of the programme was launched in five provinces between 1 May and 7 June, but compliance had been disappointing, with few commanders willing to take part in the programme. The largest impediment to implementation was the mounting alarm over the insurgency in the southern provinces. At the conference on disarmament, demobilization and reintegration and disbandment of illegally armed groups, which took place in July, donors pledged $90 million, most of which was allocated to disbandment development projects. In response to the stalled implementation of the programme, a joint review panel was commissioned in September, which identified the need to renew Government commitment to the programme, focus on those groups engaged in criminal activity and ensure flexibility in awarding development projects to districts where groups were positively engaged with the programme. In November, President Karzai convened a meeting to discuss the state of the programme and a way forward.

The final reintegration portion of the process of Afghan New Beginnings Programme for disarmament, demobilization and reintegration, which ended in 2005 [YUN 2005, p. 407] was completed on 30 June. Over 63,000 former combatants were disarmed, some 62,000 were demobilized and almost 56,000 took advantage of one of the reintegration packages.

Counter-narcotics activities

Afghanistan remained the world's largest opium supplier, with an estimated export value of $2.7 billion in 2005. That thriving economy, equivalent to more than 50 per cent of the country's legal gross domestic revenues, provided fertile ground for criminal networks, illegally armed groups and extremist elements, and posed a profound threat to achieving peace and stability. The 2006 eradication campaign, which the United Nations Office on Drugs and Crime (UNDOC) estimated destroyed around 15,000 hectares of opium poppy, was marred by corruption.

On 3 September, UNDOC and the Ministry of Counter-Narcotics presented the findings of the Office's opium survey, which indicated that poppy cultivation increased 59 per cent during the year, from 104,000 to 165,000 hectares. Opium production increased from 4,100 to 6,100 tons. Afghanistan accounted for 92 per cent of the total world supply of opium and its derivative, heroin. The increase occurred mainly in the southern provinces, primarily Helmand, where cultivation soared 162 per cent to 69,324 hectares. Six provinces, mainly in the central region, remained poppy-free, while eight provinces, mainly in the north, experienced a decrease, with the notable exception of Badakshan province. The sizeable 2006 harvest came in spite of increased eradication programmes.

Progress was made in strengthening law enforcement. In the first half of the year, the National Police and its specially trained counter-narcotics unit seized over 66 tons of narcotics (including opium, heroin and cannabis) and 13,000 litres of precursor chemicals used in refining drugs. The Counter Narcotics Tribunal and the Counter Narcotics Criminal Justice Task Force, established in 2005, were fully operational. Several hundred cases had been processed in Kabul, in accordance with the Counter Narcotics law. The Counter Narcotics Trust Fund, a Government-executed fund with resources of over $70 million, became operational early in the year; projects promoting alternative livelihoods and reducing drug demand, with funding of over $10 million, were approved. In November, the Ministry of Counter-Narcotics established a Good Performance Fund to reward six poppy-free provinces. The other eight "good performers" provinces would also receive funding under the programme.

Communication. On 15 February, Afghanistan transmitted to the Security Council President Afghanistan's National Drug Strategy [S/2006/106], which the country had presented at the London Conference.

Recovery, rehabilitation and reconstruction

Following a drought affecting up to 2.5 million people, which caused a severe harvest shortfall, a joint Government–United Nations drought appeal for $76 million was launched on 25 July, covering the July to December period. The Government's Emergency Response Commission led the drought response, with support from designated ministries, the Food and Agriculture Organization of the United Nations, UNAMA, UNICEF and the World Food Programme.

Inflation fell to an estimated 7 per cent, and revenue collection in 2005/06 reached 5.5 per cent of gross domestic product, largely on account of higher customs receipts. The share of operating expenditures financed by domestic revenues rose from 47 per cent in 2003/04 to 59 per cent in 2005/06, and was budgeted at 63 per cent in 2006/07, still not enough to reach fiscal sustainability.

Insecurity seriously limited the capacity of the United Nations and aid organizations to deliver humanitarian programmes in insurgency-affected areas, with most districts in the south chronically or temporarily inaccessible. UNICEF and the World Health Organization faced serious obstacles in conducting polio immunization campaigns there, and 25 of the 26 reported polio cases were in the south. However, UN agencies and UNAMA continued to be present in the south, south-east and east, and under a UNICEF immunization programme there some 2.3 million children under five were vaccinated against polio from 22 to 24 January. Despite the prevailing situation, Afghan refugees continued to return, mostly from Pakistan, and the Office of the United Nations High Commissioner for Refugees (UNHCR) was prepared to assist 220,000 returnees for the year.

New mechanisms to elaborate and implement Afghanistan's long-term development strategy were formulated. The Interim Afghanistan National Development Strategy set out the strategic priorities and plans for achieving the Government's development vision, mirroring the three pillars of the Afghanistan Compact—security; governance, rule of law and human rights; and economic and social development. Eight consultative groups were launched in May to coordinate strategic guidance on development priorities in each sector. The Government's Oversight Committee, the ministerial body responsible for implementing the interim Strategy, had been given responsibility for reporting to the Joint Coordination and Monitoring Board on progress made towards achieving the benchmarks of the Afghanistan Compact. Some 22 technical working groups were set up under the consultative groups to develop detailed strategies, annual action plans and projects for each line ministry, which were to be reviewed in September and October.

Social aspects

The deteriorating security situation seriously affected human rights, with civilians at times becoming indirect victims of attacks by insurgents and military forces. Women continued to face restrictions in exercising their rights, including discrimination, obstacles to access to education, restrictions on movement and pervasive violence. The marked increase in attacks on schools since late 2005 compromised the right to education, especially in the south and south-east. The Education Ministry, UNICEF and other partners set up a national task force to strengthen the protection of students, teachers, school officials and schools, and facilitate a rapid response to incidents. The Afghan Independent Human Rights Commission released in May a report on economic and social rights, which found that half of the 8,000 people interviewed did not have access to safe drinking water. There was a widespread lack of adequate housing, compounded by insecurity of tenure and impunity for violators. Accessibility to and quality of clinics and hospitals remained insufficient for 40 per cent of the respondents. The report concluded that a lack of basic economic and social rights was the primary cause of displacement and the main obstacle to the integration of internally displaced persons and returnees.

On 19 March, four television journalists were detained overnight by the National Directorate for Security for interviewing a Taliban leader in Helmand. Also in March, the case of an Afghan citizen who risked being sentenced to death for having converted from Islam to Christianity attracted world attention. In similar cases, Afghan citizens were accused of apostasy by local religious leaders and were forced to leave the country.

On 10 December, President Karzai launched the action plan for transitional justice and declared 10 December as national remembrance day.

UNAMA

The United Nations Assistance Mission in Afghanistan (UNAMA), established by Security Council resolution 1401(2002) [YUN 2002, p. 264] to promote, among other things, national reconciliation and the responsibilities entrusted to the United Nations under the Bonn Agreement, comprised the Office of the Special Representative, as well as three sub-components: two substantive pillars, one political (Pillar I) and one relief, recovery and development (Pillar II), and an administrative component. UNAMA was headquartered in Kabul, with regional offices in Bamyan, Gardez, Herat, Jalalabad, Kandahar, Kunduz and Mazar-e-Sharif and sub-offices regional offices in Faryab and Badakhstan. Pursuant to Security Council resolution 1662(2006) (see p. 365), two new provincial sub-offices were opened in Kunar and Zabul provinces. UNAMA was headed by the Special Representative of the Secretary-General. In February, Tom Koenigs (Germany) replaced Jean Arnault (France) as Special Representative and Head of UNAMA. By resolution 1662(2006) (see p. 365), the Security Council extended UNAMA mandate until 23 March 2007.

UNAMA financing

In May, the Secretary-General submitted the UNAMA budget for the period 1 April to 31 December 2006, totalling $59,835,200 gross ($54,890,600 net) [A/60/585/Add.3], part of which would be met from the unencumbered balance of $2,780,900 remaining from the appropriation totalling $13,616,900 for the period 1 January to 31 March, approved by the General Assembly in **resolution 60/255** (see p. 1618).

The Advisory Committee on Administrative and Budgetary Questions (ACABQ), in its report [A/60/7/Add.39] on the proposed budget, recommended that the total be reduced to $59,647,600 gross ($54,744,100 net).

On 30 June, by **resolution 60/281** (see p. 1621), the General Assembly approved a budget of $59,647,600 gross ($54,744,100 net).

In December, the Secretary-General submitted the UNAMA budget for the period 1 January to 31 December 2007, totalling $74,169,900 gross ($67,532,900 net) [A/61/525/Add.4]. ACABQ's comments on the proposal were contained in its December report [A/61/640 & Corr.1] on estimates in respect of special political missions, good offices and other political initiatives authorized by the General Assembly and/or the Security Council. On 22 December, the General Assembly, by section VII of **resolution 61/252** (see p. 1614) approved the budget in that amount as part of the $326,500,000 approved for special political missions.

International Security Assistance Force

During the year, the Secretary-General submitted to the Security Council, in accordance with Council resolutions 1386(2001) [YUN 2001, p. 267] and 1510(2003) [YUN 2003, p. 310], reports in May [S/2006/318] and September [S/2006/765] on the activities of International Security Assistance Force (ISAF). Activities from August to the end of the year were covered in later reports [S/2007/48, S/2007/306].

ISAF continued to assist the Government in improving the security situation, as mandated by resolution 1510(2003), executing its mission in the north, west and capital regions through regular operations. Joint security patrols with both the Afghan National Army and, to a lesser extent, the Afghan National Police increased. The development of Afghan national security forces continued to be at the forefront of ISAF mission, with a particular focus on developing the National Army.

On 31 July, ISAF, led by NATO, took over the Regional Command South from the United States–led coalition forces, completing the third stage of its nationwide expansion. That expansion concluded when Regional Command East came under ISAF authority on 5 October, and ISAF assumed responsibility for all international military operations throughout Afghanistan, with the exception of counter-terrorist operations, and provided a single point of interface with the Government and the international community.

As at 19 November, ISAF had increased from 10,177 to 32,886 personnel from the 26 NATO nations and 681 from non-NATO nations.

Beginning on 6 June, ISAF participated as a full member in the Tripartite Commission, which brought together every two months Afghan, Pakistani and international military staff to improve regional security and stability.

On the security front, the trend towards greater use of improvised explosive devices and suicide attacks continued. Suicide attacks in 2006 grew five-fold, compared to 2005, with 130 suicide events in 2006 against 25 in 2005. Insurgent activity increased markedly in April-July, with opposition forces mounting large, coordinated attacks in the south and east. Operational successes by ISAF in the south were complemented by operations led by Afghan security forces in the east, where increased cross-border infiltration was reported.

The number of insurgent attacks in Kabul decreased significantly, mostly due to increased counter-insurgency operations by the Afghan National Security Forces and ISAF, including the disruption of improvised explosive device cells, increased security around Kabul Centre and key Government installations, effective outreach to traditional and tribal leaders and coordinated use of reconstruction and development funds. However, insurgents seemed to have switched their focus towards "softer" targets of the National Security Forces and the Government in Kabul's outlying districts. The situation in the west was relatively stable, and in the north incidents were at a level comparable to that of the previous year. In the south—the focus of the Taliban insurgency—the Taliban threatened to take over Kandahar city, but were repulsed by ISAF and driven out of the city. In the east, the crossing of insurgents from Pakistan's federally administered tribal areas remained a concern. ISAF operations had a significant effect on insurgent activity, pushing them away from the interior and into the border regions and reducing the effectiveness of attacks. Counter-insurgency operations and deteriorating winter weather helped to reduce the ability of the opposing forces to conduct attacks.

Various local security arrangements were implemented. In September, the Government of Pakistan signed an agreement with local leaders to reduce the Government's military presence and give tribal entities more autonomy, in return for an end to support for crossborder fighters. Tribes on both sides of the Afghanistan-Pakistan border in the Kunar and Nuristan regions signed a cross-border security arrangement in December.

Provincial reconstruction teams engaged local populations, in line with the development goals of the Government, to strengthen the perception that ISAF could provide security for reconstruction and development. On 16 August, the President endorsed the ISAF concept of Afghan development zones in the south. The zones corresponded to strategically important locations where improving security and governance would lead to more effective development. A reconciliation programme focused on the south and east, aiming at Taliban and members of the Hezb-e-Islami Gulbuddin faction.

Communication. By an 11 September letter addressed to the Security Council President [S/2006/725], Afghanistan expressed its appreciation for the role played by ISAF in improving the security in Kabul and through its programme of phased expansion in the north, west and south of the country. It welcomed the prospect of ISAF continuing operation in the country until such time as its security forces were fully able to provide security to the nation, and hoped that the Council would reflect in its resolutions the paramount importance of fulfilling the ISAF mandate.

SECURITY COUNCIL ACTION

On 12 September [meeting 5], the Security Council unanimously adopted **resolution 1707(2006)**. The draft [S/2006/723] was prepared in consultation among Council members.

The Security Council,

Reaffirming its previous resolutions on Afghanistan, in particular resolutions 1386(2001) of 20 December 2001, 1413(2002) of 23 May 2002, 1444(2002) of 27 November 2002, 1510(2003) of 13 October 2003, 1563(2004) of 17 September 2004, 1623(2005) of 13 September 2005 and 1659(2006) of 15 February 2006,

Reaffirming its strong commitment to the sovereignty, independence, territorial integrity and national unity of Afghanistan,

Reaffirming its resolutions 1368(2001) of 12 September 2001 and 1373(2001) of 28 September 2001, and reiterating its support for international efforts to root out terrorism in accordance with the Charter of the United Nations,

Recognizing that the responsibility for providing security and law and order throughout the country resides with the Afghans themselves, and welcoming the cooperation of the Government of Afghanistan with the International Security Assistance Force,

Recognizing once again the interconnected nature of the challenges in Afghanistan, reaffirming that sustainable progress on security, governance and development, as well as on the cross-cutting issue of counter-narcotics, is mutually reinforcing, and welcoming the continuing efforts of the Government of Afghanistan and the international community to address these challenges,

Stressing, in this regard, the importance of the Afghanistan Compact and the annexes thereto, launched at the London Conference on Afghanistan on 31 January 2006, which provide the framework for the partnership between the Government of Afghanistan and the international community,

Expressing its concern about the security situation in Afghanistan, in particular the increased violent and terrorist activity by the Taliban, Al-Qaida, illegal armed groups and those involved in the narcotics trade, which has resulted in increased Afghan civilian casualties,

Reiterating its call upon all Afghan parties and groups to engage constructively in the peaceful political development of the country and to avoid resorting to violence, including through the use of illegal armed groups,

Stressing, in this context, the importance of the security sector reform, including further strengthening of the Afghan National Army and Police, disbandment of illegal armed groups, justice sector reform and counter-narcotics,

Expressing in this context its support for the Afghan security forces, with the assistance of the International Security Assistance Force and the Operation Enduring Freedom coalition, in contributing to security in Afghanistan and in building the capacity of the Afghan security forces, and welcoming the extension of the Force into southern Afghanistan, with effect from 31 July 2006, the planned further expansion of the Force into eastern Afghanistan and the increased coordination between the Force and the coalition,

Expressing its appreciation to the United Kingdom of Great Britain and Northern Ireland for taking over the lead from Italy in commanding the Force, and recognizing with gratitude the contributions of the North Atlantic Treaty Organization and many nations to the Force,

Determining that the situation in Afghanistan still constitutes a threat to international peace and security,

Determined to ensure the full implementation of the mandate of the Force, in consultation with the Government of Afghanistan,

Acting, for these reasons, under Chapter VII of the Charter,

1. *Decides* to extend the authorization of the International Security Assistance Force, as defined in resolutions 1386(2001) and 1510(2003), for a period of twelve months beyond 13 October 2006;
2. *Authorizes* the Member States participating in the Force to take all necessary measures to fulfil its mandate;
3. *Recognizes* the need to further strengthen the Force, and in this regard calls upon Member States to contribute personnel, equipment and other resources to the Force, and to make contributions to the trust fund established pursuant to resolution 1386(2001);
4. *Calls upon* the Force to continue to work in close consultation with the Government of Afghanistan and the Special Representative of the Secretary-General for Afghanistan, as well as with the Operation Enduring Freedom coalition in the implementation of the mandate of the Force;
5. *Requests* the leadership of the Force to provide quarterly reports on implementation of its mandate to the Security Council, through the Secretary-General;
6. *Decides* to remain actively seized of the matter.

Sanctions

United Nations sanctions-related activities were guided by the measures adopted by Security Council resolution 1617(2005) [YUN 2005, p. 410] against Osama bin Laden, Al-Qaida, the Taliban, their associates and associated entities, which further refined the financial measures, travel ban and arms embargo imposed on those persons identified in the consolidated list created pursuant to resolution 1267(1999) [YUN 1999, p. 265].

Sanctions Committee activities

The Al-Qaida and Taliban Sanctions Committee, established pursuant to resolution 1267(1999), submitted a report [S/2007/59] on its activities from 1 January to 31 December 2006. During that period, the Committee held three formal meetings and 38 informal meetings at the expert level.

The Committee continued to consider notifications and requests submitted by Member States pursuant to resolution 1452(2002) [YUN 2002, p. 280] seeking exceptions to the sanctions provisions. It received 41 such requests. It updated its Consolidated List of individuals and entities belonging to or associated with Al-Qaida and the Taliban on the basis of information provided by Member States. The List continued to be the key instrument for States in enforcing and implementing the arms embargo, the travel ban and the assets freeze against listed individuals and entities. The Committee added the names of 18 individuals and six entities, de-listed three individuals, and in one case was unable to accede to a request for de-listing a suggested individual.

The Committee received requests from States seeking assistance in confirming the identity of certain individuals for the purpose of implementing the sanctions, in particular with regard to the assets freeze. It assisted those States by providing liaison with designating States. The Committee also increased cooperation with the International Criminal Police Organization (Interpol). It continued the practice, begun in December 2005, of issuing Interpol–Security Council special notices, 275 of which were issued during the year. It also strengthened cooperation with the Organization for Security and Cooperation in Europe, the International Civil Aviation Organization and the International Air Transport Association.

To comply with its obligation under resolution 1617(2005) to submit an analytical assessment of action taken by Member States to implement the sanctions, the Committee requested the Monitoring Team to provide a preliminary assessment of States' compliance, which the Team submitted on 27 October [S/2006/1046]. The Committee's own conclusions were contained in its assessment [S/2006/1046], submitted to the Security Council on 20 December. The assessment aimed to assist the Council in improving the sanctions, encouraging States to implement them, providing feedback for reporting States and encouraging non-reporting States to submit their reports.

The Committee also considered the recommendations contained in the Monitoring Team's fourth and fifth reports (see below), and on 8 August [S/2006/635] and 20 December [S/2006/1047] forwarded to the Security Council reports containing its position on the Team's recommendations.

Monitoring Team

The Analytical Support and Sanctions Monitoring Team (the Monitoring Team), established by Security Council resolution 1526(2004) [YUN 2004, p. 332] and extended by resolution 1617(2005) [YUN 2005, p. 410], had the mandate of collating, assessing, monitoring, reporting on and making recommendations on the implementation of measures imposed by that resolution.

The Monitoring Team visited 25 States, including a further visit to Afghanistan. At the request of Member States, it continued to organize regional meetings with the heads and deputy heads of intelligence and security services to discuss how the sanctions could be adapted to address changes in the threat posed by Al-Qaida-related terrorism.

Report of Monitoring Team (March). Pursuant to Council resolution 1617(2005), the Sanctions Committee Chairman, on 8 March [S/2006/154], transmitted to the Council President the fourth report of the Monitoring Team. The report noted that both the core Al-Qaida leaders in Afghanistan and the more active leadership in Iraq were striving to extend their influence. Though their tactics, methodology and messages differed, Al-Qaida and Taliban leaders and associated groups would continue their assault on international peace and security unless met by a sustained and coordinated response.

Implementation of the sanctions by Member States continued to improve, albeit with disparities between regions and individual States. The Consolidated List of individuals and entities belonging to or associated with the Taliban and Al-Qaida continued to be developed in scope and accuracy, and Member States increasingly regarded it as a critical element in the international response to terrorism. While the List was a preventive measure, most of the listed Al-Qaida-related persons had in fact been charged or convicted.

The amount of money frozen under the Al-Qaida/Taliban sanctions continued to increase, but at a decreasing rate. There had been improvements in the increasingly sophisticated global financial sectors, but there were continuing areas of concern, including those resulting from a lack of resources in less developed States. Despite the travel ban, listed persons continued to cross borders. A joint Interpol/Security Council initiative resulted in an international notice, complete with identity, description, photographs and fingerprints for persons on the List.

The report contained an annex on litigation by or relating to individuals on the Consolidated List.

Report of Monitoring Team (September). The Sanctions Committee Chairman, on 18 September [S/2006/750], transmitted to the Council President the fifth report of the Monitoring Team. According to the report, over the past six months, the Al-Qaida/Taliban sanctions had focused on the need to improve procedures for adding to and removing names from the Consolidated List; make the sanctions more effective and relevant to the threat; and increase the involvement of as wide a range of Member States as possible. As at the end of July, the List had 478 entries: 142 individuals and one entity associated with the Taliban, and 213 individuals and 122 entities associated with Al-Qaida. The List contained the names of 19 de-listed individuals and entities. The Monitoring Team had made several recommendations on listing and de-listing over the past two years, and there had been additional proposals from States, as well as at least three major academic studies on the fairness of the sanctions. The matter was at the top of the Sanctions Committee's agenda.

Resolution 1617(2005) [YUN 2005, p. 410] had called on Member States to use a checklist to report by 1 March, on actions taken to implement the sanctions against individuals and entities added to the Consolidated List between 29 July 2005 and 31 January 2006. By the end of July 2006, 53 States had returned their checklists and six had requested extensions.

As at July, 35 States had frozen $91.4 million under the sanctions, mainly in bank accounts.

The Team continued to gather information from States on their assessment of the sanctions regime and on their difficulties with implementation. While support for the Committee's work remained robust, States were often frustrated that their problems, especially as regards the travel ban and the arms embargo, were still far from solution. However, several States had introduced new counter-terrorism measures and the Team believed that progress in implementation remained steady.

States were increasingly willing to cooperate to prevent the movement of terrorists and their supporters across borders, and those efforts had made a difference; but listed persons continued to travel, and the problems of unpoliced borders and widely available stolen, falsified or forged documents remained persistent and difficult to address.

The Committee believed that the arms embargo should take into account the evolution in terrorists' tactics in order to address the threat posed by listed individuals and entities. States needed a clearer definition of their obligations under the arms embargo in order to better implement it. Another widespread frustration among States was a lack of proper knowledge and understanding of the nature of the threat and the best way to deal with it. The transnational nature of Al-Qaida and the subversive appeal of its message left many States at a loss, seeing ways to suppress but not to defeat the problem. The Team continued to bring together groups of very senior intelligence and security officials to discuss those issues and contacted many others to help to identify new measures and actions that the Committee could consider.

Annexed to the report was information on a cover sheet for Member State submissions to the Committee, litigation by or relating to individuals on the Consolidated List, and the Interpol-UN Security Council poster on persons subject to sanctions.

Assessment of sanctions implementation. In response to Council resolution 1617(2005) [YUN 2005, p. 410], the Sanctions Committee Chairman, on 20 December [S/2006/1046], transmitted to the Council an assessment of action taken by Member States to implement the sanctions, based on the Monitoring Team's report on the subject. During the reporting period (1 August 2005–30 September 2006), six additional States had submitted reports pursuant to resolution 1455(2003) [YUN 2003, p. 311], bringing the total to 147. In addition, 55 States had submitted checklists under resolution 1617(2005).

The threat from Al-Qaida and the Taliban was constantly changing and continued to grow, and it was vital to design and implement the sanctions with a great deal of precision. Some States, in addition to complying with the assets freeze, travel ban and arms embargo, had implemented non-mandatory measures contained in Security Council resolutions that were designed to strengthen the efficiency of the sanctions. The number of States that had circulated the Consolidated List to the relevant authorities and agencies reached 169. In July, measures were introduced to improve the List and, in November, the guidelines regarding the List were revised.

The Suspicious Transaction Reporting system had proven effective in countering the financing of Al-Qaida and Taliban-sponsored terrorism, and at least 110 States established financial intelligence units to provide the capability to analyse the system, while banks and financial institutions had become more aware of the financial sanctions. States were making greater efforts to implement the travel ban, even if some had not reported cases of violation by listed individuals. However, implementation of the arms embargo seemed less effective.

The Committee concluded that States had made conscientious efforts to implement the sanctions measures, but it wished to see them to do so with more vigour. It also wanted the reporting cycle, pursuant to resolution 1455(2003) [YUN 2003, p. 311], to be completed by obtaining and considering the remaining 44 implementation reports, and stressed that those States that had already reported should update the information provided, so that the Committee could be aware of efforts, or challenges and problems encountered.

Noting that the level of sanctions implementation varied, the Committee intended to address the difficulties facing States in their implementation, in particular with regard to the accuracy of the Consolidated List and listing and de-listing procedures. The Committee was aware that actual sanction implementation might be below the capacity of some States, and intended to deal with compliance, especially by States known to be vulnerable to terrorist threats, in a more systematic and focused manner, including through possible action to address incomplete sanction implementation.

SECURITY COUNCIL ACTION

On 22 December [meeting 5609], the Security Council unanimously adopted **resolution 1735(2006)**. The draft [S/2006/1013] was submitted by Argentina, Denmark, France, Greece, Japan, Peru, the Russian Federation, Slovakia, the United Republic of Tanzania, the United Kingdom and the United States.

The Security Council,

Recalling its resolutions 1267 (1999) of 15 October 1999, 1333 (2000) of 19 December 2000, 1363 (2001) of 30 July 2001, 1373 (2001) of 28 September 2001, 1390 (2002) of 16 January 2002, 1452 (2002) of 20 December 2002, 1455 (2003) of 17 January 2003, 1526 (2004) of 30 January 2004, 1566 (2004) of 8 October 2004, 1617 (2005) of 29 July 2005, 1624 (2005) of 14 September 2005 and 1699 (2006) of 8 August 2006, and the relevant statements by its President,

Reaffirming that terrorism in all its forms and manifestations constitutes one of the most serious threats to peace and security and that any acts of terrorism are criminal and unjustifiable regardless of their motivations, whenever and by whomsoever committed, and reiterating its unequivocal condemnation of Al-Qaida, Osama bin Laden, the Taliban, and other individuals, groups, undertakings and entities associated with them, for ongoing and multiple criminal terrorist acts aimed at causing the death of innocent civilians and other victims, destruction of property and greatly undermining stability,

Expressing its deep concern about the increased violent and terrorist activities in Afghanistan of the Taliban and Al-Qaida, and other individuals, groups, undertakings and entities associated with them,

Reaffirming the need to combat by all means, in accordance with the Charter of the United Nations and international law, threats to international peace and security caused by terrorist acts, stressing in this regard the important role that the United Nations plays in leading and coordinating this effort,

Stressing that terrorism can only be defeated by a sustained and comprehensive approach involving the active participation and collaboration of all States and international and regional organizations to impede, impair, isolate and incapacitate the terrorist threat,

Emphasizing that dialogue between the Security Council Committee established pursuant to resolution 1267(1999) ("the Committee") and Member States is vital to the full implementation of measures,

Recognizing that one of the most effective means of dialogue between the Committee and Member States is through direct contact, including country visits,

Welcoming the expanded cooperation with INTERPOL, including the establishment of "INTERPOL-United Nations Security Council Special Notices" and the passage of resolution 1699(2006), and encouraging Member States to work within the framework of INTERPOL and other international and regional organizations in order to reinforce the implementation of the measures against Al-Qaida, Osama bin Laden and the Taliban, and other individuals, groups, undertakings and entities associated with them,

Noting the need for robust implementation of the measures in paragraph 1 below as a significant tool in combating terrorist activity,

Reiterating that the measures referred to in paragraph 1 below are preventative in nature and are not reliant upon criminal standards set out under national law,

Underscoring that, in giving effect to the measures in paragraph 1 of resolution 1617(2005) and other relevant resolutions, full account is to be taken of the provisions regarding exemptions in paragraphs 1 and 2 of resolution 1452(2002),

Taking note of the Committee document on the arms embargo, which is intended to be a useful tool to assist States in the implementation of the measures in paragraph 1 (*c*) below,

Expressing its deep concern about the criminal misuse of the Internet by Al-Qaida, Osama bin Laden and the Taliban, and other individuals, groups, undertakings and entities associated with them, in furtherance of terrorist acts,

Noting with concern the changing nature of the threat presented by Al-Qaida, Osama bin Laden and the Taliban, and other individuals, groups, undertakings and entities associated with them, in particular the ways in which terrorist ideologies are promoted,

Stressing the importance of meeting all aspects of the threat that Al-Qaida, Osama bin Laden and the Taliban, and other individuals, groups, undertakings and entities associated with them represent to international peace and security,

Acting under Chapter VII of the Charter,

Measures

1. *Decides* that all States shall take the following measures as previously imposed by paragraph 4 (*b*) of resolution 1267(1999), paragraph 8 (*c*) of resolution 1333(2000) and paragraphs 1 and 2 of resolution 1390(2002) with respect to Al-Qaida, Osama bin Laden and the Taliban, and other individuals, groups, undertakings and entities associated with them, as referred to in the list created pursuant to resolutions 1267(1999) and 1333(2000) ("the Consolidated List"):

(*a*) Freeze without delay the funds and other financial assets or economic resources of those individuals, groups, undertakings and entities, including funds derived from property owned or controlled, directly or indirectly, by them or by persons acting on their behalf or at their direction, and ensure that neither these nor any other funds, financial assets or economic resources are made available, directly or indirectly, for the benefit of such persons by their nationals or by persons within their territory;

(*b*) Prevent the entry into or the transit through their territories of those individuals, provided that nothing in this paragraph shall oblige any State to deny entry into or require the departure from its territories of its own nationals and that this paragraph shall not apply where entry or transit is necessary for the fulfilment of a judicial process, or the Security Council Committee established pursuant to resolution 1267(1999) ("the Committee") determines on a case-by-case basis only that entry or transit is justified;

(*c*) Prevent the direct or indirect supply, sale or transfer to those individuals, groups, undertakings and entities, from their territories or by their nationals outside their territories, or using their flag vessels or aircraft, of arms and related materiel of all types, including weapons and ammunition, military vehicles and equipment, paramilitary equipment, and spare parts for the aforementioned, and technical advice, assistance or training related to military activities;

2. *Reminds* States of their obligation to freeze without delay the funds and other financial assets or economic resources pursuant to paragraph 1 (*a*) above;

3. *Confirms* that the requirements in paragraph 1 (*a*) above apply to economic resources of every kind;

4. *Calls upon* States to redouble their efforts to implement the measures in paragraphs 1 (*b*) and (*c*) above;

Listing

5. *Decides* that, when proposing names to the Committee for inclusion on the Consolidated List, States shall act in accordance with paragraph 17 of resolution 1526 (2004) and paragraph 4 of resolution 1617 (2005) and provide a statement of case; the statement of case should provide as much detail as possible on the basis(es) for the listing, including: (i) specific information supporting a determination that the individual or entity meets the criteria above; (ii) the nature of the information; and (iii) supporting information or documents that can be provided; States should include details of any connection between the proposed designee and any currently listed individual or entity;

6. *Requests* designating States, at the time of submission, to identify those parts of the statement of case which may be publicly released for the purposes of notifying the listed individual or entity, and those parts which may be released upon request to interested States;

7. *Calls upon* States to use the cover sheet in annex I to the present resolution when proposing names for the Consolidated List, in order to ensure clarity and consistency in requests for listing;

8. *Directs* the Committee to encourage the submission of names from Member States for inclusion on the Consolidated List;

9. *Also directs* the Committee to encourage States to submit additional identifying and other information on listed individuals and entities, including updates on assets frozen and the movement of listed individuals as such information becomes available;

10. *Decides* that the Secretariat shall, after publication but within two weeks after a name has been added to the Consolidated List, notify the permanent mission of the country or countries where the individual or entity is believed to be located and, in the case of individuals, the country of which the person is a national (to the extent this information is known), and include with this notification a copy of the publicly releasable portion of the statement of case, a description of the effects of designation, as set forth in the relevant resolutions, the procedures of the Committee for considering de-listing requests, and the provisions of resolution 1452(2002);

11. *Calls upon* States receiving notification as in paragraph 10 above to take reasonable steps according to their domestic laws and practices to notify or inform the listed individual or entity of the designation and to include with this notification a copy of the publicly releasable portion of the statement of case, a description of the effects of designation, as provided in the relevant resolutions, the procedures of the Committee for considering de-listing requests, and the provisions of resolution 1452(2002);

12. *Encourages* States to submit to the Committee for inclusion on the Consolidated List names of individuals and entities participating in the financing or support of acts or activities of Al-Qaida, Osama bin Laden and the Taliban, and other individuals, groups, undertakings and entities associated with them, as described in paragraph 2 of resolution 1617(2005), by any means, including but not limited to using proceeds derived from illicit cultivation

and production of and trafficking in narcotic drugs originating in Afghanistan and their precursors;

De-listing

13. *Decides* that the Committee shall continue to develop, adopt and apply guidelines regarding the de-listing of individuals and entities on the Consolidated List;

14. *Decides also* that the Committee, in determining whether to remove names from the Consolidated List, may consider, among other things, (i) whether the individual or entity was placed on the Consolidated List due to a mistake of identity, or (ii) whether the individual or entity no longer meets the criteria set out in relevant resolutions, in particular resolution 1617(2005); in making the evaluation in (ii) above, the Committee may consider, among other things, whether the individual is deceased, or whether it has been affirmatively shown that the individual or entity has severed all association, as defined in resolution 1617(2005), with Al-Qaida, Osama bin Laden, the Taliban, and their supporters, including all individuals and entities on the Consolidated List;

Exemptions

15. *Decides further* to extend the period for consideration by the Committee of notifications submitted pursuant to paragraph 1 (*a*) of resolution 1452(2002) from forty-eight hours to three working days;

16. *Reiterates* that the Committee must make a negative decision on notifications submitted pursuant to paragraph 1 (*a*) of resolution 1452(2002) in order to prevent the release of funds and other financial assets or economic resources that have been determined by the notifying State(s) to be necessary for basic expenses;

17. *Directs* the Committee to review its guidelines with respect to the provisions of paragraph 1 (*a*) of resolution 1452(2002) as reiterated in paragraph 15 above;

18. *Encourages* States that submit requests to the Committee, pursuant to paragraph 1 (*b*) of resolution 1452(2002), to report in a timely way on the use of such funds, with a view to preventing such funds from being used to finance terrorism;

Measures—implementation

19. *Encourages* States to identify, and if necessary introduce, adequate procedures to fully implement all aspects of the measures described in paragraph 1 above;

20. *Stresses* that the measures imposed by paragraph 1 (*a*) above apply to all forms of financial resources, including but not limited to those used for the provision of Internet hosting or related services, used for the support of Al-Qaida, Osama bin Laden and the Taliban, and other individuals, groups, undertakings and entities associated with them;

21. *Directs* the Committee to identify possible cases of non-compliance with the measures pursuant to paragraph 1 above, and requests the Chairman, in his periodic reports to the Council pursuant to paragraph 31 below, to provide progress reports on the work of the Committee on this issue;

22. *Requests* States to ensure that the most up-to-date version of the Consolidated List is promptly made available to relevant Government offices and other relevant bodies, in particular, those offices responsible for the assets freeze and border control;

23. *Requests* the Secretary-General to take the necessary steps to increase cooperation between the United Nations and relevant international and regional organizations, including INTERPOL, the International Civil Aviation Organization, the International Air Transport Association, and the World Customs Organization, in order to provide the Committee with better tools to fulfil its mandate more effectively and to give Member States better tools to implement the measures referred to in paragraph 1 above;

The Taliban

24. *Encourages* States to submit names of individuals and entities currently associated with the Taliban to the Committee for inclusion on the Consolidated List;

25. *Directs* the Committee to encourage States to provide additional identifying and other information on listed Taliban individuals and entities;

26. *Also directs* the Committee to work, in accordance with its guidelines, to consider requests for inclusion on the Consolidated List of names of individuals and entities associated with the Taliban, and to consider petitions for the removal of listed members and/or associates of the Taliban who are no longer associated with the Taliban;

Coordination

27. *Reiterates* the need for ongoing close cooperation and exchange of information among the Committee, the Security Council Committee established pursuant to resolution 1373 (2001) concerning counter-terrorism (the Counter-Terrorism Committee) and the Security Council Committee established pursuant to resolution 1540 (2004), as well as their respective groups of experts, including enhanced information-sharing, coordinated visits to countries, technical assistance and other issues of relevance to all three Committees;

Outreach

28. *Further reiterates* the importance of having the Committee follow up via oral and/or written communications with Member States regarding effective implementation of the sanctions measures;

29. *Strongly encourages* Member States to send representatives to meet the Committee for more in-depth discussion of relevant issues;

30. *Requests* the Committee to consider, where and when appropriate, visits to selected countries by the Chairman and/or Committee members to enhance the full and effective implementation of the measures referred to in paragraph 1 above, with a view to encouraging States to comply fully with the present resolution and resolutions 1267(1999), 1333(2000), 1390(2002), 1455(2003), 1526(2004) and 1617(2005);

31. *Also requests* the Committee to report orally, through its Chairman, at least every one hundred and eighty days, to the Council on the overall work of the Committee and the Analytical Support and Sanctions Monitoring Team ("Monitoring Team"), and, as appropriate, in conjunction with the reports of the Chairmen of the Counter-Terrorism Committee and the Committee

established pursuant to resolution 1540(2004), including briefings for all interested Member States;

Monitoring Team and reviews

32. *Decides*, in order to assist the Committee in the fulfilment of its mandate, to extend the mandate of the current New York–based Monitoring Team, appointed by the Secretary-General pursuant to paragraph 20 of resolution 1617(2005), for a further period of eighteen months, under the direction of the Committee with the responsibilities outlined in annex II to the present resolution, and requests the Secretary-General to make the necessary arrangements to this effect;

33. *Decides also* to review the measures described in paragraph 1 above with a view to their possible further strengthening in eighteen months, or sooner if necessary;

34. *Decides further* to remain actively seized of the matter.

ANNEX I

Cover sheet

CONSOLIDATED LIST: COVER SHEET FOR MEMBER STATE SUBMISSIONS TO THE COMMITTEE

Please complete as many of the following fields as possible:

I. IDENTIFIER INFORMATION—for Individuals

Where possible, note the nationality or cultural or ethnic sources of names/aliases. Provide all available spellings.	**Surname/ Family Name/Last Name**	**First Name**	**Additional name (e.g. father's name or middle name), where applicable**	**Additional name (e.g. grand-father's name), where applicable**	**Additional name, where applicable**	**Additional name, where applicable**
Full Name: (in original and Latin script)						
Aliases/ "Also Known As" (A.K.A.s): Note whether it is a strong or weak alias. — Current						
Former						
Other nom de guerre, pseudonym:			**Title:** Honorary, professional, or religious title			
Employment/Occupation: Official title/position			**Nationality/Citizenship:**			
Date of Birth: (DD/MM/YYYY)			**Passport Details:** (Number, issuing date and country, expiry date)			
Alternative Dates of Birth (if any): (DD/MM/YYYY)			**National Identification Number(s), Type(s):** (e.g. Identity card, Social Security)			
Place of Birth: (provide all known details including city, region, province/state, country)			**Address(es):** (provide all known details, including street address, city, province/state, country)			
Alternative Place(s) **of Birth** (if any): (city, region, province/state, country)			**Previous Address(es):** (provide all known details, including street address, city, province/state, country)			
Gender:			**Languages spoken:**			
Father's full name:			**Mother's full name:**			
Current location:			**Previous location(s):**			
Undertakings and entities owned or controlled, directly or indirectly by the individual (see UNSCR 1617 (2005), para. 3):						
Website Addresses:						
Other relevant detail: (such as physical description, distinguishing marks and characteristics)						

IDENTIFIER INFORMATION—For Groups, Undertakings, or Entities	
Name:	
Also Known As (A.K.A.s): Where possible, note whether it is a strong or weak A.K.A.	**Now Known As (N.K.A.s)**
	Formerly Known As (F.K.A.s)
Address(es): Headquarters and/or branches. Provide all known details, including street address, city, province/state, country	
Tax Identification Number: (or local equivalent, type)	
Other Identification Number and type:	
Website Addresses:	
Other Information:	

II. BASIS FOR LISTING

May the Committee publicly release the following information? Yes No

May the Committee release the following information to Member States? Yes No

Complete one or more of the following:

	(*a*) participating in the financing, planning, facilitating, preparing, or perpetrating of acts or activities by, in conjunction with, under the name of, on behalf of, or in support of Al-Qaida (AQ), Usama bin Laden (UBL), or the Taliban, or any cell, affiliate, splinter group or derivative thereof.[1] • Name(s) of cell, affiliate, splinter group or derivate thereof:
	(*b*) supplying, selling or transferring arms and related materiel to AQ, UBL or the Taliban, or any cell, affiliate, splinter group or derivative thereof.[1] • Name(s) of cell, affiliate, splinter group or derivate thereof:
	(*c*) recruiting for AQ, UBL or the Taliban, or any cell, affiliate, splinter group or derivative thereof.[1] • Name(s) of cell, affiliate, splinter group or derivate thereof:
	(*d*) otherwise supporting acts or activities of AQ, UBL or the Taliban, or any cell, affiliate, splinter group or derivative thereof.[1] • Name(s) of cell, affiliate, splinter group or derivate thereof:
	(*e*) Other association with AQ, UBL or the Taliban, or any cell, affiliate, splinter group or derivative thereof. • Briefly explain nature of association and provide name of cell, affiliate, splinter group or derivate thereof:
	(*f*) Entity owned or controlled, directly or indirectly, by, or otherwise supporting, an individual or entity on the Consolidated List.[2] • Name(s) of individual or entity on the Consolidated List:

Please attach a Statement of the Case which should provide as much detail as possible on the basis(es) for listing indicated above, including:

(1) specific information supporting the association or activities alleged;

(2) the nature of the information (e.g., intelligence, law enforcement, judicial, media, admissions by subject, etc.) and

(3) supporting information or documents that can be provided. Include details of any connection with a currently listed individual or entity. Indicate what portion(s) of the Statement of Case the Committee may publicly release or release to Member States.

[1] S/RES/1617 (2005), para. 2.

[2] S/RES/1617 (2005), para. 3.

III. POINT OF CONTACT

The individual(s) below may serve as a point-of-contact for further questions on this case:

(THIS INFORMATION SHALL REMAIN CONFIDENTIAL)

Name:	*Position/Title:*

ANNEX II

In accordance with paragraph 32 of this resolution, the Monitoring Team shall operate under the direction of the Security Council Committee established pursuant to resolution 1267(1999) and shall have the following responsibilities:

(a) To collate, assess, monitor and report on and make recommendations regarding implementation of the measures, including implementation of the measures in paragraph 1 *(a)* of this resolution as it pertains to preventing the criminal misuse of the Internet by Al-Qaida, Osama bin Laden, the Taliban, and other individuals, groups, undertakings and entities associated with them, to pursue case studies, as appropriate; and to explore in depth any other relevant issues as directed by the Committee;

(b) To submit a comprehensive programme of work to the Committee for its review and approval, as necessary, in which the Monitoring Team should detail the activities envisaged in order to fulfil its responsibilities, including proposed travel, based on close coordination with the Counter-Terrorism Committee Executive Directorate ("CTED") and the group of experts of the Security Council Committee established pursuant to resolution 1540(2004) to avoid duplication and reinforce synergies;

(c) To submit, in writing, two comprehensive, independent reports to the Committee, one by 30 September 2007 and the other by 31 March 2008, on implementation by States of the measures referred to in paragraph 1 of this resolution, including specific recommendations for improved implementation of the measures and possible new measures;

(d) To analyse reports submitted pursuant to paragraph 6 of resolution 1455(2003), the checklists submitted pursuant to paragraph 10 of resolution 1617(2005), and other information submitted by Member States to the Committee as instructed by the Committee;

(e) To work closely and share information with CTED and the group of experts of the Committee established pursuant to resolution 1540(2004) to identify areas of convergence and overlap and to help to facilitate concrete coordination, including in the area of reporting, among the three Committees;

(f) To assist the Committee with its analysis of non-compliance with the measures referred to in paragraph 1 of this resolution by collating information collected from Member States and submitting case studies, both on its own initiative and upon the Committee's request, to the Committee for its review;

(g) To present to the Committee recommendations which could be used by Member States to assist them with the implementation of the measures referred to in paragraph 1 of this resolution and in preparing proposed additions to the Consolidated List;

(h) To consult with Member States in advance of travel to selected Member States, based on its programme of work as approved by the Committee;

(i) To encourage Member States to submit names and additional identifying information for inclusion on the Consolidated List, as instructed by the Committee;

(j) To study and report to the Committee on the changing nature of the threat of Al-Qaida and the Taliban and the best measures to confront it, including by developing a dialogue with relevant scholars and academic bodies, in consultation with the Committee;

(k) To consult with Member States and other relevant organizations, including regular dialogue with representatives in New York and in capitals, taking into account their comments, especially regarding any issues that might be contained in the reports of the Monitoring Team referred to in paragraph *(c)* of this annex;

(l) To consult with Member States' intelligence and security services, including through regional forums, in order to facilitate the sharing of information and to strengthen enforcement of the measures;

(m) To consult with relevant representatives of the private sector, including financial institutions, to learn about the practical implementation of the assets freeze and to develop recommendations for the strengthening of that measure;

(n) To work with relevant international and regional organizations in order to promote awareness of, and compliance with, the measures;

(o) To assist other subsidiary bodies of the Security Council, and their expert panels, upon request, with enhancing their cooperation with INTERPOL, referred to in resolution 1699(2006);

(p) To report to the Committee, on a regular basis or when the Committee so requests, through oral and/or written briefings on the work of the Monitoring Team, including its visits to Member States and its activities;

(q) Any other responsibility identified by the Committee.

Iraq

Situation in Iraq

In 2006, the United Nations, through the Secretary-General's Special Representative for Iraq and the United Nations Assistance Mission for Iraq (UNAMI), continued to assist Iraq in its transition to democratic governance and in promoting reconstruction and reconciliation. On 10 August, by resolution 1700(2006) (see p. 398), the Security Council extended UNAMI mandate until 10 August 2007. On 28 November, by resolution 1723(2006) (see p. 403), the Council extended the mandate of the 29-country Multinational Force until 31 December 2007.

Election results

Following the 15 December 2005 elections [YUN 2005, p. 427] for a new 275-seat Council of Representatives and the protests about irregularities after the partial results were announced, the International Mission for Iraq Elections, an international non-governmental body composed mainly of independent electoral management bodies, deployed a monitoring team to Iraq as part of its observation mandates from 1 to 18 January 2006. The International Mission concluded that the election had generally met international standards, paving the way for the announcement of uncertified results on 20 January. The Transitional Electoral Panel decided upon 12 appeals to those uncertified results, thereby allowing the Electoral Commission to announce the certified results on 10 February.

The election resulted in 12 political entities and coalitions, representing a broad political, ethnic and religious spectrum, winning seats in the Council of Representatives. The United Iraqi Alliance remained the largest political bloc, with 128 seats, followed by the Kurdish Gathering, 53; the Tawafoq Iraqi Front, 44; the Iraqi National List, 25; the Sunni-dominated National Iraqi Dialogue Front, 11; the Islamic Union of Kurdistan, 5; the Liberation and Reconciliation Gathering, 3; and the Progressives List, 2. The Al-Rafedeen List, Iraqi Turkoman Front, Mithal al-Aloosi List for the Iraqi Nation and Al Ezediah Movement for Progress and Reform obtained one seat each. With the announcement of the results, the political transition timetable set forth in the Transitional Administrative Law [YUN 2004, p. 346] and endorsed by resolution 1546(2004) [ibid., p. 348] was completed.

SECURITY COUNCIL ACTION

On 14 February [meeting 5371], following consultations among Security Council members, the President made statement **S/PRST/2006/8** on behalf of the Council:

> The Security Council welcomes the announcement by the Independent Electoral Commission of Iraq on 10 February 2006 of the certified election results for the Iraqi Council of Representatives. The Security Council is particularly encouraged that political parties representing all of Iraq's communities participated in the election, as demonstrated by the high voter turnout across Iraq. The Council commends and congratulates the people of Iraq for demonstrating their commitment to a peaceful, democratic political process, and for having braved difficult conditions and the threat of violence to cast their votes.
>
> The Council stresses the importance of inclusiveness, national dialogue and unity as Iraq's political development moves forward. The Council calls upon Iraq's political leaders to work with resolve towards the formation of a fully inclusive Government, which will strive to build a peaceful, prosperous, democratic and united Iraq. The Council urges all Iraqis to participate in the peaceful political process and calls upon those who continue to use violence to lay down their arms. The Council unanimously condemns acts of terrorism in Iraq. Such acts should not be allowed to disrupt Iraq's political and economic progress.
>
> The Council gives special recognition to the Independent Electoral Commission of Iraq for its role in organizing and administering the elections. The Council also commends the Secretary-General and the United Nations for successfully assisting election preparations, and notes in particular the role of the United Nations Assistance Mission for Iraq. The Council also appreciates the assistance given by other international actors, including European Union electoral experts and the International Mission for Iraqi Elections.
>
> The Council underlines the need for continued and enhanced international support from all States and relevant international organizations to assist Iraq's wide-ranging political, economic and social development. The Council calls upon the United Nations to play the fullest possible role in Iraq. It also calls upon all other international actors, particularly Iraq's neighbours, to conform to relevant Council resolutions and consider also how they can reinforce their contribution at this important time. In this context, the Council also looks forward to the continued efforts of the League of Arab States in support of the political process endorsed in Council resolutions 1546(2004) and 1637(2005).
>
> The Council reaffirms its support for a federal, democratic, pluralist and unified Iraq, in which there is full respect for human rights.

Inauguration of newly elected Government

The Council of Representatives held its first session on 16 March. On 23 April, it elected Jalal Talabani as the new President of Iraq, and Adel Abdul Mahdi (United Iraqi Alliance) and Tareq al-Hashemi (Tawafoq) as Vice-Presidents. The Parliament also elected its Speaker, Mahmoud al-Mashhadani (Tawafoq Iraqi Front) and two Deputy Speakers, Arif Tayfour (Kurdish Alliance) and Khaled al-Attiyya (United Iraqi Alliance). Nouri Jawad al-Maliki was appointed Prime Minister-designate, and in accordance with the Constitution, President Talabani charged him with forming the Council of Ministers.

On 20 May, the Council of Representatives approved the appointment of the new Government for a four-year term, with Jawad al-Maliki as Prime Minister and Barham Saleh (Patriotic Union of Kurdistan) and Salam al-Zubaie (General Conference for the People of Iraq) as Deputy Prime Ministers. It also approved the appointment of 37 ministers, including 26 ministers and 11 ministers of State, as well as a 34-point government programme concentrating on measures to improve security, combat corruption, promote national unity and strengthen government institutions. Four women were appointed to the Cabinet. Three ministerial posts remained to be filled—Defence, Interior and National Security Affairs.

Communications. On 12 April [S/2006/247], the Ministerial Committee on Iraq of the League of Arab States, meeting in Cairo, issued a statement reaffirming its commitment to preserving Iraq's identity as a member of the wider Arab world and to working to ensure respect for Iraq's unity and sovereignty, independence, non-intervention in its internal affairs and respect for the will of its people. It welcomed the convening of an Iraqi Islamic Reconciliation Conference in Jordan on 22 April, and supported the proposal to convene a full Iraqi national reconciliation conference in Baghdad in June.

On 3 June [S/2006/449], Honduras welcomed the successful formation of a Government by the people of Iraq and reiterated its support for the country.

SECURITY COUNCIL ACTION

On 24 May [meeting 5444], following consultations among Security Council members, the President made statement **S/PRST/2006/24** on behalf of the Council:

> The Security Council welcomes the inauguration on 20 May 2006 of Iraq's constitutionally elected Government and congratulates the people of Iraq on this milestone in their country's political transition.
>
> The Council is particularly encouraged by the fact that the Government is representative of Iraq's many diverse communities and expresses its hope that the Ministers of Defence, Interior and National Security Affairs will be appointed as soon as possible. The Council encourages the new Government to work tirelessly to promote national reconciliation through dialogue and inclusion and to build an atmosphere in which sectarianism is rejected. The Council, at the same time, urges all Iraqis to participate in the political process peacefully, demanding that those who continue to use violence lay down their arms. The Council wholly condemns acts of terrorism in Iraq, including recent horrific attacks on civilians and religious sites aimed callously at provoking intercommunal tensions.
>
> The Council underlines the high expectations in the new Government to deliver improvements in security and stability, in human rights and the rule of law, in the provision of essential services, and in economic progress and prosperity. The Council urges the Government to work effectively and energetically to this end. The Council also strongly urges all States and relevant international organizations to continue and enhance their help to Iraq's sovereign Government at this crucial time. The Council notes the particular role of Iraq's neighbours and calls upon them to conform to relevant Council resolutions and to examine how they can reinforce their contribution. In this context, the Council also looks forward to the continued efforts of the League of Arab States, including the forthcoming conference in Baghdad, in support of the political process that the Council has endorsed.
>
> The Council reaffirms its support for a federal, democratic, pluralist and unified Iraq, as a responsible member of the international community, in which there is stability, prosperity and full respect for human rights and the rule of law. The Council also reaffirms the independence, sovereignty, unity and territorial integrity of Iraq.

Terrorist violence

Press statement. In a 22 February press statement [SC/8647], Security Council members condemned that morning's attack on the holy Shrine of Imams Ali al-Hadi and al-Hasan al-Askari in Samarra and the ensuing attacks on other religious sites. Council members urged the Iraqi people to defy their perpetrators by showing restraint and unity, and called on political leaders to work with resolve towards the formation of a fully inclusive Government.

In a 5 June press statement [SC/8738], Council members condemned the 3 June attack against employees of the Russian Embassy in Baghdad, which resulted in the killing of one embassy employee and the kidnappings of four others, including a diplomat. The Russian Federation's Foreign Ministry confirmed, on 26 June, that the four had been killed.

In a 29 June presidential statement, S/PRST/2006/29 (see p. 71), Council members condemned that crime and urged all States to cooperate in bringing to justice the perpetrators, organizers and sponsors.

International Compact with Iraq

The Secretary-General reported that, on 16 June, he had accepted the Iraqi Government's request that the United Nations provide support in developing the International Compact with Iraq. The Compact, a Government initiative for a new partnership with the international community, presented a five-year national vision for Iraq aimed at consolidating peace and pursuing political, economic and social development. Its primary focus would be to build a framework for Iraq's economic transformation and its integration into the regional and global economies. The Compact was co-chaired by Deputy Prime Minister Barham Salih and UN Deputy Secretary-General Mark Malloch Brown. The Secretary-General's Special Representative would be the UN Focal Point for the Compact in Iraq.

On 5 and 6 July, the Deputy Secretary-General visited Baghdad to consult with the Government, the United Nations Development Group, UN agencies, the World Bank and the donor community on the process of developing the Compact. The co-chairs appointed an executive committee, comprising representatives of the Government, the United Nations, the World Bank, the International Monetary Fund, the Arab Fund for Economic and Social Development and the Islamic Development Bank, to manage the process towards the adoption of the Compact and beyond. The Compact was formally launched on 27 July. It was envisaged that the finalized Compact, including key priorities, benchmarks and commitments, would be presented by the Government of Iraq by the end of 2006. To engage in a strategy dialogue on the future of Iraq, the Secretary-General proposed convening, on 18 September, a meeting of Foreign Ministers in New York to review progress in the implementation of Security Council resolution 1546(2004) and the UN commitment to provide the necessary assistance to the Government of Iraq. The meeting would provide an opportunity to review the progress being made by the Government in the political, security and economic fields, and to seek broader international support and engagement with the Government and for the Government to present an outline of its programme for the reconstruction of Iraq over the next five years inside the framework of the International Compact.

The European Union (EU), in a 1 August statement [S/2006/678], welcomed the launching of the Compact and underlined its readiness to participate in its preparation and follow-up. It underlined the importance of Iraqi ownership in developing the Compact, the involvement of the international community, the participation of Iraq's neighbours and regional partners, and a longer-term perspective and need for monitoring the Compact's implementation.

Communications. The ninth meeting of Foreign Ministers of Iraq's neighbouring countries (Tehran, Iran, 8-9 July), in a final communiqué [S/2006/505], expressed support for Iraq's Government and National Assembly, the Government priorities and the Prime Minister's reconciliation plan (see below); and called on countries and international institutions to provide assistance to Iraq's development and reconstruction. The Ministers stressed the importance of expanded cooperation between Iraq and its neighbouring countries to combat terrorism, expressed concern over the continued presence of terrorist groups in the country, and expressed their support for the efforts made by the Government and Parliament to combat terrorism and to prevent terrorist groups from using Iraqi territory to carry out operations against neighbouring countries.

National reconciliation

Faced with growing violence and insecurity, particularly in Baghdad and the southern and western regions, the new Government of Iraq, in response to those challenges, focused its political efforts on promoting national reconciliation and dialogue. On 14 June, the Government launched a security plan for Baghdad to address the increased violence and growing criminality, which were undermining those efforts. The second phase of the Baghdad security plan was initiated at the beginning of August with the redeployment of additional troops of the Multinational Force to the capital. On 25 June, the Prime Minister, Nouri al-Maliki, unveiled the 24-point National Reconciliation Plan, which called for a qualified amnesty, the release of detainees, the reform of the legal and judicial systems, the provision of assistance to areas prone to violence, the facilitation of dialogue on constitutional and related matters, and the resolution of the problem of militias. The Plan also acknowledged the idea of an Iraqi-led Baghdad peace initiative, emphasized the need for regional support to achieve peace and stability, and recognized the efforts of the League of Arab States to convene a conference on Iraqi national accord (see below). The Plan also provided for the establishment of the High Committee for National Reconciliation, which held its first session on 22 July. The composition of the Committee was yet to be finalized owing to a difference in views concerning membership criteria.

In his statement marking the launch of the National Reconciliation Plan, the Secretary-General's Special Representative commended the efforts of the Government in promoting dialogue and peace, called upon all concerned, including regional and international actors, to support the initiative, and reiterated the UN's commitment to facilitating and assisting in the implementation of the issues outlined in the reconciliation project.

Communications. The League of Arab States' Preparatory Committee for the Conference on Iraqi National Accord, meeting in Cairo from 25 to 27 July [S/2006/614], agreed that all Iraqi parties should commit to achieving reconciliation and national accord in a single unified process. All proposed initiatives, in particular the efforts of President Talabani and the initiative launched by Prime Minister al-Maliki, should lead to the goal of attaining national reconciliation that would confirm respect for Iraq's sovereignty and the unity of its people and territory. Participants also agreed, among other things, on the need to put an end to the deterioration of the security situation, acts of violence and terrorism and factional and ethnic tensions, as well as forced displacement and abductions; to review the controversial clauses on the Constitution; and to hold accountable and punish those responsible for the commission of crimes against the Iraqi people before and since 9 April 2003. The Committee added to the agenda of the Conference the items on ending the state of sectarian and ethnic tension and forced displacement. Noting that a number of the confidence-building measures agreed upon at its 2005 Cairo meeting [YUN 2005, p. 426] had not been implemented satisfactorily, the Committee requested the Secretary-General to continue to coordinate with all the initiatives proposed, with a view to bringing about national accord. He should liaise with the Government of Jordan to set the date for the conference of Iraqi religious leaders and the Organization of the Islamic Conference to convene the Mecca Conference of Islamic Scholars.

Meanwhile, Prime Minister al-Maliki pushed forward the implementation of his National Reconciliation Plan. Following a conference of tribal leaders in August, he held a meeting with a cross-section of civil society figures and institutions on 16 September. On 2 October, the Prime Minister announced a four-point Ramadan Accord, supported by major political parties, which included the establishment of local security committees composed of political, religious, police and army figures. He also initiated direct contact with Iraqi opposition groups within Iraq and in Egypt, Jordan and other neighbouring counties. Reconciliation initiatives in Iraq were complemented by the efforts of regional actors. On 20 October, Iraqi Shiite and Sunni religious leaders, in a meeting sponsored by the Organization of the Islamic Conference, issued a declaration calling for an end to sectarian bloodshed. The agreement was welcomed by political and religious leaders both inside and outside of Iraq.

In a statement following its meeting in Cairo on 5 December [S/2006/963], the League of Arab States' Ministerial Committee on Iraq affirmed respect for Iraq's unity, sovereignty, independence and identity; rejection of calls for partition or division; and non-intervention in its internal affairs. It affirmed also that national accord was the key to a solution, and that achieving national reconciliation was fundamental for bringing stability. It condemned terrorist and criminal acts, sectarian violence, murder and forced displacement; expressed concern over the chaotic security situation; supported the Government in its effort to cope with such acts; and demanded that it dissolve the militias and put an end to unlawful armed acts. It welcomed the 20 October Mecca Declaration (see above), which rejected accusations of religious infidelity on the part of any component of the Iraqi people. It affirmed the need to foster the spread of humanitarian values; launch efforts aimed at defusing the factional and sectarian situation; and build the armed forces and security forces in accordance with a clearly defined timetable synchronized with the departure of foreign forces and the achievement of full Iraqi sovereignty. It called for the holding of the Conference on Iraqi National Accord and that the preparatory work continue for the holding of that conference withing four months. It requested the Secretary-General to pursue the necessary contacts with the Iraqi parties.

Trial and sentencing of Saddam Hussein

The trial of former President Saddam Hussein and seven co-defendants continued. Following the ejection from the courtroom of Barzan Hassan by the presiding judge on 29 January in the wake of an outburst, which amounted to contempt, Mr. Hussein walked out of the courtroom, followed by his team of privately retained counsel. The defence counsel for Mr. Hussein and his co-defendants failed to appear in court on 1 February and was replaced by an Iraqi Higher Tribunal duty counsel, as provided for under Iraqi law. Those of the accused who appeared in court on 1 February signalled their disquiet with the replacement of their counsel and none of the accused appeared the next day. They were, however, compelled to appear in court on the order of the presiding judge on 13 February. The court heard additional witnesses on 13 and 14 February. The privately retained counsel was not reinstated by the Trial Chamber and the right of the defendants to legal counsel of their choice, together with the conduct of the court to maintain order in the trial, remained key issues of concern. The Trial of Mr. Hussein in the Iraqi Higher Tribunal resumed, entering a new phase with the commencement of testimonies by the defendants. The Higher Tribunal announced the conclusion of the investigation of the Anfal campaign. That case was thus referred to the court, which was to set a date for the commencement of the trial.

On 21 June, following the assassination of Khamis al-Obeidi, a lawyer representing Saddam Hussein, the defence counsel boycotted several court sessions. On 27 July, the court recessed until 16 October, when it was scheduled to announce the verdict of the Dujail case. The current trial, relating to the Anfal campaign in northern Iraq against the

Kurdish population during the late 1980s, began on 21 August. Mr. Hussein and his co-defendants were charged with war crimes and crimes against humanity. Saddam Hussein and Ali-Hassan al-Majid were also charged with genocide.

On 5 November, the Iraqi Higher Criminal Tribunal sentenced Mr. Hussein and two co-defendants to death for their role in the 1984 execution of 148 people convicted of involvement in the attempted assassination of the former President in Dujail. On the same day, UN High Commissioner for Human Rights, Louise Arbour, urged the Iraqi authorities to ensure that the right of appeal would be fully respected.

On 26 December, the Appeals Chamber of the Iraqi High Tribunal unanimously dismissed the appeals of Mr. Hussein and his two co-defendants, Barzan al-Tikriti and Awad al-Bandar, upholding all three death sentences. The Appeals Chamber returned the case of a fourth defendant, Taha Yassin Ramadan, to the Iraqi High Tribunal for re-sentencing, recommending a harsher sentence than the term of life imprisonment that he had received. The Special Rapporteur on the independence of judges and lawyers, in a 27 December statement, expressed concern at the grave shortcomings in the trial and the failure to address them. He urged the Government not to carry out the death sentences following an allegedly procedurally flawed legal process. The UN High Commissioner for Human Rights called for restraint by the Iraqi authorities and reiterated her concerns about the appeal process and fairness of the original trial. Saddam Hussein, however, was executed on 30 December.

UN Assistance Mission for Iraq

The United Nations Assistance Mission for Iraq (UNAMI), established by Security Council resolution 1500(2003) [YUN 2003, p. 346], continued to support the Secretary-General in the fulfilment of his mandate under Council resolution 1483(2003) [ibid., p. 338], and extended by resolution 1546(2004) [YUN 2004, p. 348]. The Secretary-General's Special Representative and his substantive, security and administrative support staff were based in Baghdad, with regional offices in Basra and Erbil. Most humanitarian project planning and management activities were conducted from Amman, Jordan. The primary logistics support base was in Kuwait.

During the year, the Secretary-General submitted four reports on UNAMI activities [S/2006/137, S/2006/360, S/2006/706, S/2006/945].

Report of Secretary-General (March). In his seventh report on UNAMI activities [S/2006/137], submitted in response to resolution 1546(2004), the Secretary-General summarized developments since his December 2005 report [YUN 2005, p. 426]. While Iraq had met all the key benchmarks of its timetable, it continued to face formidable political, security and economic challenges. Sectarian violence, as demonstrated by the 22 February bombing of the Shia shrine of Imams Ali-Hadi and al-Askari in Samarra and its aftermath, had emerged as a main threat to security and stability. Mutual trust and national reconciliation should remain the top priority, and the political and civil society leadership should commit itself to the unconditional respect for human rights and the rule of law. In this endeavour, Iraq would continue to require sustained international support in the years to come.

UNAMI continued to support Government efforts in the areas of reconstruction, development and humanitarian assistance and maintained its leading role in donor coordination. Together with UN agencies, programmes and funds, UNAMI focused on strengthening management capacities in ministries, providing and coordinating basic services and restoring infrastructure. UNAMI Office of Constitutional Support assisted in the constitutional review process envisaged by the Constitution and in the development of legislation, institutions and processes for implementing the Constitution effectively. It developed an action plan on federalism and decentralization, the rule of law and human rights and national reconciliation.

Military operations by the Multinational Force (MNF) and Iraqi security forces, especially in Al Anbar governorate, raised a number of human rights concerns, especially allegations of restrictions on freedom of movement, excessive use of force and evictions and demolitions. Those allegations were raised by the Special Representative during his visit to Ramadi and Fallujah on 20 and 21 February.

The Secretary-General observed that the completion of the transition should encourage Iraq's political and economic integration into the region. There was a need to consider new ways of promoting greater regional engagement between Iraq and its neighbours. It was also time to normalize Iraq's international status, particularly in the Security Council. While political facilitation would remain a priority for UNAMI in 2006, the Mission intended to strengthen activities in the areas of reconstruction and development. It would therefore maintain an important role in donor coordination and increase assistance in strengthening the management capacities of ministries, coordinating the provision of basic services and supporting the restoration of public infrastructure.

The security situation continued to be a source of concern, as demonstrated by the large number of civilian casualties as a result of terrorist, insurgent, paramilitary and military action. Also of concern was the increasingly sectarian nature of the violence, particularly in ethnically mixed areas, with almost daily reports of intercommunal intimidation, murder and attacks against sacred buildings. The role of militias and irregular armed elements remained disturbing. Training Iraqi security forces was indispensable for improving security, but ultimately, the best way to address the security situation was to ensure an inclusive political process and rapid improvement in the basic living conditions of the people.

The human rights situation was also worrisome. UNAMI Human Rights Office continued to receive consistent allegations of human rights violations, and had corroborated claims through contacts with key ministries, local authorities and civil society. The Office developed a robust human rights strategy and coordinated efforts to set up a strong national human rights protection system, while working to strengthen the capacities of key ministries and civil society organizations to promote and protect human rights.

In such a political and security environment, UNAMI continued to face operational constraints and needed a dedicated protection force for all its activities. Steps should be taken to provide UNAMI with the necessary level of support, including by developing a new integrated UN complex.

As at 31 January, contributions to the UN Development Group Iraqi Trust Fund amounted to $903.4 million. A total of 83 projects valued at $759.3 million had been approved, contracts worth $564.2 million had been initiated and $430.1 million disbursed.

Security Council consideration (March). On 15 March [meeting 5386], the Council was briefed by the Secretary-General's Special Representative for Iraq, Ashraf Jehangir Qazi. Despite achieving the political transition benchmarks, Mr. Qazi said, Iraq continued to face enormous security, political and reconstruction challenges. However, those achievements had provided a basis for the next phase of the political process, one characterized by a sovereign and democratically elected Government. The 22 February bombing of the Shia Shrine in Samarra and its violent aftermath had shown that the transition was increasingly threatened by inter-sectarian violence, exacerbated by the continuing insurgency and counter-insurgency, acts of terror and a deteriorating human rights situation. While sectarian fissures had always been an integral part of Iraq's political history, they had come to dominate and almost define the country's politics and its prospects. There was growing mistrust between the communities. Unless political leaders undertook to overcome the sectarian divide, efforts to promote security and strengthen national cohesion would be undermined. The Office of the Special Representative had stepped up its engagement with political, religious and civic leaders to encourage greater intercommunal understanding, including through the Political Consultative Committee formed in response to the Samarra attack and its aftermath. Together with the United Nations Educational, Scientific and Cultural Organization and the United Nations Development Programme, UNAMI had launched an initiative to assist the Government in restoring the Samarra shrine and other religious sites damaged during the recent violence.

The situation remained tense and volatile, and recent developments had made negotiations on government formation more difficult, creating a dangerous political vacuum. The situation also hampered the implementation of infrastructural and income-generating projects. If not addressed, violence would prevent donor programmes from having an impact.

Iraq's stability was intrinsically linked to the stability in the region and vice versa. UNAMI remained engaged with the countries of the region, and in the past 18 months, the Special Representative and his deputies had visited the Islamic Republic of Iran, Jordan, Kuwait, the Syrian Arab Republic and Turkey. To increase regional engagement, he proposed the establishment of a regional contact group that would bring together Iraq's regional neighbours to discuss how to improve stability in Iraq.

In such a political and security environment, UN staff members remained at risk of becoming targets of violence. If a more robust role was expected of the United Nations in the next phase of the political transition, the necessary capacities within UNAMI would have to be enhanced.

The United States, on behalf of the 29 countries comprising the Multinational Force, said that insurgents and terrorists remained capable of carrying out attacks to destabilize the Government and disrupting democracy. More than 80 per cent of attacks were concentrated in four of Iraq's 18 provinces. While the attacks had been targeted against coalition forces, most victims were civilians. Iraqi security forces continued to grow and increasingly conduct independent operations. MNF continued to train, mentor and equip Iraqi security forces and to hand over battle responsibilities. As at 6 March, 101 Iraqi army and special operations battalions were conducting counter-insurgency operations, 59 of which were taking the lead. Sixty-five per cent of Baghdad was under the control of Iraqi forces, which numbered some 240,000 troops. MNF continued to provide security for the United Nations. UNAMI had made essential contributions, particularly to the elections and the formation of the Government. The international community, particularly Iraq's neighbours and especially Syria and Iran, should do more to prevent foreign fighters from entering Iraq.

Iraq said that the country would need the active engagement of the United Nations and to that end had asked for an increase in UNAMI staff operating throughout Iraq and its participation in the constitutional phase and in reconstruction. It welcomed the Secretary-General's statement that it was time to normalize Iraq's relationship with the Security Council by lifting the barriers and sanctions introduced when the country was under a dictatorship. Iraq reiterated its request that the Council review and rescind prior mandates imposed upon Iraq's previous regime, as they were no longer relevant.

Communication. On 23 March [A/60/732-S/2006/182], the Permanent Observer of Palestine drew the Secretary-General's attention to the plight of a group of 89 Palestinians, nearly half of them children, who had fled the violence in Iraq and were stranded in no-man's-land on the Iraqi-Jordanian border. Some 23,000 Palestinians were registered as refugees in Iraq, and the Palestinian community in Iraq was fearful of violence against them, especially after 10 Palestinians had been killed and several kidnapped in Baghdad the previous week. The United States President, acting on recommendations from military commanders, had authorized a decrease in the number of United States combat brigades from 17 to 15, and other coalition partners were planning similar measures. That decision reflected the growing capability of the Iraqi security forces.

Report of Secretary-General (June). In his report on UNAMI operations [S/2006/360], the Secretary-General said that his Special Representative remained in close contact with all key Iraqi political leaders to facilitate negotiations on Government formation and to promote inter- and intra-communal dialogue. He held meetings with a broad spectrum of religious, tribal, political, civil society and community leaders to explore options for developing an Iraqi-led Baghdad peace initiative, with a view to promoting inter-communal dialogue and confidence-building measures so as to curb sectarian violence in Baghdad. The Special Representative also met with leaders from neighbouring countries in Amman, Jordan, from 8 to 10 March, with cabinet members of the United States Government and the President of the World Bank in Washington, D.C., from 17 to 20 March, and with several local Iraqi leaders, including Grand Ayatollah Al-Sistani and Sayyid Moqtada al-Sadr and other senior clerics during his visit to Najaf from 18 to 19 April.

Despite the prevailing security conditions, the United Nations undertook an increasing number of missions to assess the impact of the Organization's ongoing activities in the country. Most of the quick-impact projects, at a cost of $40 million, focusing on the provision of basic services in health, education, water and sanitation, were successfully concluded. UNAMI led the donor community in the preparation of key recommendations on reconstruction and development. The Mission also promoted the use of resources by Iraqi authorities for rebuilding damaged cultural and religious sites.

Sectarian violence and ongoing military activities continued to affect the lives of Iraqi civilians, large numbers of whom were displaced. Since the Samarra attack of 22 February (see p. 391), between 70,000 and 90,000 persons had been displaced. UN agencies continued to provide food, shelter and non-food items as resources permitted. In response to the displacements, UNAMI mobilized UN agencies and donors through the Emergency Working Group to devise a rapid response initiative to address short-term needs, using the accrued interest of the United Nations Development Group Iraq Trust Fund.

The Mission continued to work with Iraqi ministries, judicial institutions and civil society organizations to support the establishment of a strong national human rights protection system. In close cooperation with Iraqi authorities and donors, it was developing a comprehensive strategy on the rule of law to address challenges faced by the judiciary, and with the Office of the UN High Commissioner for Human Rights, was also supporting the establishment of an independent national Human Rights Commission, as foreseen in the constitution.

As to the security situation, the lethal character of the attacks was marked by large numbers of casualties, especially among civilians. Much of the violence stemmed from acts perpetrated by both sides of the Sunni-Shiite sectarian divide. The month of March was the fourth deadliest since May 2003, with twice as many Iraqis killed as in December 2005. The situation in Basra remained tense and MNF had restricted the freedom of movement in the area. In Erbil, the situation remained relatively calm, allowing for a modest expansion of the UN presence into an area office. The Secretary-General observed that the formation on 20 May of the first constitutionally elected Government, represented the culmination of the country's political transition. Iraq's political leaders had demonstrated that they could rise to the challenge and engage in a spirit of compromise to form an inclusive and democratic Government. However, the protracted nature of the negotiations and the deterioration of the security situation following the Samarra bombing indicated that the Iraqi people had arrived at an important turning point. If the Government was able to develop and implement a concrete national agenda to quickly address the basic needs and concerns of all communities, the country could be put on a path towards peace and prosperity. On the other hand, unless a strong dynamic towards national reconciliation was generated, the danger of polarization, sectarian strife and, potentially, civil war would increase. The Government should be empowered and enabled to demonstrate to the Iraqi people that their participation in the elections would lead to improvements in their daily lives. National reconciliation had become an imperative. Iraq's neighbours and other countries had an important support role to play in that regard. To that end, in addition to supporting the League of Arab States Conference on Iraqi National Accord in Baghdad, the United Nations was looking into establishing a contact group, composed of Iraq and its neighbours, as a forum for dialogue on mobilizing greater international support for Iraq and on ways to promote stability in the country. With the election of a new Government, the international community had the opportunity to help accelerate the country's recovery by fulfilling pledges of assistance, increasing levels of debt forgiveness and agreeing on an Iraqi-led framework for mobilizing international assistance.

Security Council consideration (June). Briefing the Security Council on 15 June on the situation concerning Iraq [meeting 5463], Angela Kane, Assistant Secretary-General for Political Affairs, said that of particular concern was the mounting loss of civilian life as a result of insecurity, huge levels of violence and a breakdown of law and order. Intercommunal violence and criminal activities had compounded insurgent violence as threats to national security. Among the most affected provinces were Anbar, Baghdad, Ninewa, Salahuddin and, more recently, Basra and Diyala, where the Government declared a month-long state of emergency on 31 May. In Baghdad, the Medico-Legal Institute confirmed that more than 6,000 bodies were received in the first five months of 2006 alone. As a result, since late February, more than 100,000 people had been internally displaced, adding to a total of some 1.3 million internally displaced persons countrywide. Upon taking office, Prime Minister al-Maliki had singled out improving security and promoting reconciliation as his key priorities. However, achieving results in those areas would require time.

Efforts by MNF to speed up training and equipping the Iraqi security forces remained indispensable. A determined effort was needed to control militias and other unauthorized forces, so as to re-establish a State monopoly on weapons. In tackling violence, both the Iraqi security forces and MNF should act in accordance with international human rights and humanitarian law. The Government should make it a priority to set a robust human rights agenda, establish an independent national human rights commission and a centre for missing and disappeared persons. Human rights protection should include investigating all allegations of violations and bringing perpetrators to justice. The United Nations remained concerned about the large number of detainees held in detention centres countrywide without investigation or criminal charges.

Iraq had a strong foundation for national reconciliation, but to succeed the political process had to be inclusive. There had to be political will by all Iraqi leaders to work towards that end and effective mechanisms to promote dialogue and consensus-building had to be put in place. The review of the country's Constitution agreed by Iraqi leaders could be an effective vehicle for advancing the process of national reconciliation, and the United Nations hoped that the new parliament would address, as a matter of priority, the early establishment of a constitutional review committee as provided for under the Constitution.

At the international level, there was an opportunity to build a deeper consensus in support of Iraq's transition. Priorities included fulfilling existing pledges, debt forgiveness and support for reconstruction and foreign investment. UNAMI and the United Nations country team continued to support the Government in establishing effective, transparent and accountable public institutions, providing access to basic services and restoring public infrastructure.

Reporting to the Council on behalf of the 29 countries of the Multinational Force, the United States said a striking development had occurred on 7 June, with the killing of the Al-Qaida terrorist leader, Abu Musab al-Zarqawi, and one of his key associates, Sheikh Abd al-Rahman. However, he had been replaced, and the terrorist organization still posed a threat, as its members would continue to attempt to intimidate the Iraqi people and threaten the Government.

Iraqi Foreign Minister Hoshyar Zebari said that, while the country's new Constitution and the formation of the first constitutional Government testified to historical progress towards a pluralistic, federal and united democracy, a difficult and destructive security situation persisted. Thus, continued cooperation between Iraqi forces and MNF was vital for security and for attaining the goal of self-sufficiency. At the same time, security operations had to go hand in hand with initiatives to promote national consensus, tolerance, justice and respect for human rights.

Extension of UNAMI mandate

On 1 August [S/2006/601], the Secretary-General recommended that UNAMI mandate be extended for a further period of 12 months. Despite severe operational and security constraints, UNAMI had further grown in size and expanded its activities beyond Baghdad. It had 396 international civilian and military personnel in Iraq, including up to 300 in Baghdad, 74 in Erbil and 22 in Basra. The Mission had advised and supported the Independent Electoral Commission, the Transitional Government and the Transitional National Assembly on the election process; promoted dialogue and consensus-building on the drafting of a Constitution; advised the Government on developing civil and social services; contributed to the coordination and delivery of reconstruction, development and humanitarian assistance; helped to promote human rights protection, national reconciliation and judicial and legal reform; and advised the Government on planning for the eventual conduct of a comprehensive census. The Secretary-General's Special Representative and his team were rendering their good offices and providing political facilitation to the new Government, based on the contacts UNAMI had established with a wide spectrum of interlocutors.

SECURITY COUNCIL ACTION

On 10 August [meeting 5510], the Security Council unanimously adopted **resolution 1700(2006)**. The draft [S/2006/629] was submitted by the United Kingdom and the United States.

The Security Council,

Recalling all its previous relevant resolutions on Iraq, in particular resolutions 1500(2003) of 14 August 2003, 1546(2004) of 8 June 2004, 1557(2004) of 12 August 2004 and 1619(2005) of 11 August 2005,

Reaffirming the independence, sovereignty, unity and territorial integrity of Iraq,

Recalling the establishment on 14 August 2003 of the United Nations Assistance Mission for Iraq, the mandate of which was extended most recently on 11 August 2005, and reaffirming that the United Nations should play a leading role in assisting the efforts of the Iraqi people and Government in strengthening institutions for representative government, and in promoting national dialogue and unity,

Stressing that this Iraqi national dialogue, which the Mission should assist, is crucial for the political stability and unity of Iraq,

Welcoming the request conveyed in the letter dated 3 August 2006 from the Minister for Foreign Affairs of Iraq to the Secretary-General expressing the view of the constitutionally elected Government of Iraq that there continues to be a vital role for the Mission in assisting Iraqi efforts to build a productive and prosperous nation at peace with itself and its neighbours,

Taking note of the letter dated 1 August 2006 from the Secretary-General addressed to the President of the Security Council, and expressing its appreciation for the role that the United Nations is playing in Iraq with the support of the international community,

Welcoming the Secretary-General's agreement, as requested by the Government of Iraq, that the United Nations, as co-chair, will provide strong support for the International Compact with Iraq, launched on 27 July 2006 with a joint statement by the Government of Iraq and the United Nations,

1. *Decides* to extend the mandate of the United Nations Assistance Mission for Iraq for another period of twelve months from the date of the present resolution;

2. *Expresses its intention* to review the mandate of the Mission in twelve months or sooner, if requested by the Government of Iraq;

3. *Requests* the Secretary-General to update the Security Council on a regular basis on the latest developments of the International Compact with Iraq;

4. *Decides* to remain seized of the matter.

Report of Secretary-General (September). In his report on UNAMI activities [S/2006/706], the Secretary-General said that his Special Representative was in close contact with all key political, community and religious leaders to promote the National Reconciliation Plan unveiled on 25 June by Prime Minister al-Maliki (see p. 392).

In response to a 2 July request from the Council of Representatives, UNAMI Electoral Assistance Team provided assistance in drafting the legal framework for establishing a permanent electoral commission. UNAMI also provided guidance to the Government on addressing the needs of internally displaced persons and gave grants to non-governmental organizations for providing services to communities. In the light of the growing violence and insecurity, the Government launched, on 14 June, a security plan for Baghdad to address the increased level of violence and growing criminality. The second phase of that plan was initiated at the beginning of August with the deployment of additional MNF troops.

On 8 June, the Council of Representatives completed the Government formation process by approving the appointment of Mohammed Abdulqadir al-Obaidi as Minister for Defence, Jawad Bolani from the Al-Fadila party of the United Iraqi Alliance as Minister of the Interior, and Sherwan al-Waili from Al-Daawa of the United Iraqi Alliance as Minister of State for National Security. Prior to its August recess, the Parliament established 19 of its 24 parliamentary committees. However, extensive debate on rules of procedure and the powers of the Speaker delayed parliamentary deliberations and the work of the committees. On 16 and 25 July, the Council of Representatives conducted its first and second readings of the draft law on the establishment of the Independent High Electoral Commission. It extended the Commission's caretaker mandate until 10 October and continued consultations on the draft law for the establishment of a national human rights commission.

Iraq continued to experience an acute human rights and humanitarian crisis. There were reports that militia elements had infiltrated governmental and law enforcement institutions, thus undermining the confidence of the Iraqi people in State institutions. The existence of death squads, some of which were linked to armed militias, and even to sectors of Government security forces, was highlighted by the daily appearance, in various parts of the country, of dozens of bodies of murdered persons bearing signs of torture and execution. The violence in Iraq continued to affect civilians disproportionately. According to figures provided by the Ministry of Health, 3,149 civilians were killed in June, while at least 3,438 were reportedly killed in July.

The number of detainees held in the country was also a source of concern. The Ministry of Human Rights reported that approximately 26,398 detainees were being held in detention centres countrywide as at the end of July, including some 13,000 in the custody of the Multinational Force. The Secretary-General said that he was concerned that arbitrary detention and torture of detainees in Iraqi prisons continued to be widespread. On 1 June, a joint inspection of a prison site by representatives of the Iraqi Government and MNF found 1,431 detainees with signs of physical and psychological abuse. A total of 52 arrest warrants had been issued against officials of the Ministry of the Interior, but they had yet to be served.

The security situation in Iraq varied widely. After Baghdad, the western province of Al-Anbar was considered the most dangerous area in the country. As a result, the United Nations was unable to conduct operations there. In Baghdad, many districts had been effectively out of bounds for UN operations for extended periods. Meanwhile, the situation in Basra remained tense and MNF had made arrests of high-profile militia leaders in the province. In response, the levels of violence increased, including indirect attacks in the Basra Palace area, which housed UN offices. As a result, the United Nations temporarily relocated some members of its liaison detachment staff from Basra. The Organization's presence and its ability to operate effectively in Iraq remained severely constrained by the security environment.

The Secretary-General observed that, if current patterns of discord and violence prevailed for much longer, there was a grave danger of a breakdown of the Iraqi State, and potentially of civil war, which would be detrimental not only to the Iraqi people, but also to countries in the region and the international community in general. The Secretary-General hoped that the Iraqi people would resolve to unite with a view to building a better future for all, with support from the region and the international community in general.

Security Council consideration (September). On 14 September [meeting 5523], the Council was briefed by the Secretary-General's Special Representative for Iraq, who said the key challenge for the Government was to develop a truly national agenda that was responsive to the needs and aspirations of all Iraqis. The Prime Minister had laid out a range of initiatives in his National Reconciliation Plan and had taken steps to broaden support for his Government and to increase the effectiveness of the Iraqi security forces. The Plan included the Baghdad Peace Initiative, aimed at establishing a basis for mutual trust and protection among Baghdad's diverse communities. The Government was seeking to establish a dialogue with those who had remained outside the political process.

Insurgent, militia and terrorist attacks, as well as gross violations of human rights, continued to inflict untold suffering. Given Iraq's importance and potential, its neighbours and the international community had a vital stake in helping Iraq become a peaceful, stable and prosperous partner. The International Compact with Iraq (see p. 391) could become an important vehicle towards that end. At the preparatory meeting in Abu Dhabi, on 10 September, the Government outlined the key priorities on which to form the Compact, such as effective public resource management, economic reform in private sector development and social sector reforms. The Government had also pledged its commitment to tackling corruption and creating a transparent and efficient oil sector. The Government's commitment to make urgent progress on national reconciliation, political inclusion and consensus-building deserved the full support of the region and the international community. The time had come to hold focused discussions on how best to assist Iraq. The international community should provide real support for Iraq's efforts to transform itself into a participatory and institutionalized democracy.

The United States representative said that the insurgency remained potent and viable, although its visibility had been overshadowed by the increase in sectarian violence, which defined the emerging nature of the violence. The security plan for Baghdad, "Operation Together Forward", an Iraqi-planned and led operation involving Iraqi police, army and the national police supported by the Multinational Forces, increased patrols and checkpoints in all areas of Baghdad, while concentrating on areas of the city that had witnessed increases in violence and sectarian killings. In July, during his visit to the United States, Prime Minister al-Maliki and President George W. Bush announced an adjustment to the plan, whereby Multinational Forces and Iraqi units would be repositioned from less active areas in the country. The plan appeared to have reduced violence in the north of the city. Attacks on the Iraqi infrastructure continued to adversely affect oil revenues and the availability of electricity. Sectarian violence was gradually spreading north into Diyala province and Kirkuk, as Sunni, Shia and Kurdish groups competed for provincial influence. Meanwhile, Al-Qaida continued its intimidation. On 13 July, Iraq achieved another milestone with the transfer of security responsibility in Al-Muthana province from the Multinational Force. Dhi Qar province appeared ready to assume security independence, and several other provinces would likely meet the transition criteria by the end of the year. In August, the Fourth Iraqi Army Division headquarters officially assumed responsibility from the 101 United States Airborne Division, representing the halfway mark of the goal of putting all Iraqi security forces in the lead of coordinating, planning and conducting security operations in Iraq. The Joint Committee to Achieve Iraqi Security Self-reliance announced by Prime Minister al-Maliki and President George W. Bush on 25 July would develop a conditions-based road map for full transition of security responsibility.

Report of Secretary-General (December). In his report on UNAMI activities [S/2006/945], the Secretary-General said civilian casualties had reached an all-time high as a result of increased sectarian violence, insurgent and terrorist attacks and criminal activities.

The joint effort of the Government and MNF to stem the rising level of violence under the Baghdad security plan appeared to have had very limited success. Control of access to and from Baghdad, curfew extensions and house-to-house cordon and search operations were some of the additional security measures employed to stabilize the capital. Despite those efforts, in large areas of Baghdad and other parts of the country, insurgent and militia activities remained uncontrolled. Among the most serious incidents was the terrorist attacks in Sadr City on 23 November, which left over 200 people dead and scores injured, deepening public concern over the Government's ability to control the security environment. Initiatives to promote national reconciliation did not appear to have had a significant impact on the scale and nature of the violence in the country. The Government had also been unable to supplement its security initiatives with the implementation of projects to improve the delivery of essential services, provide jobs and rebuild socio-economic infrastructure.

At the political level, the Council of Representatives adopted legislation on the import and retailing of oil products, a law on national investments and amendments to the criminal code and the general prosecution law of 1979. It also adopted the law on the formation of regions, following a compromise under which the law would not be implemented for 18 months and the Constitutional Review Committee would be given one year to complete its work. On 25 September, the Council established the 27-member Constitutional Review Committee, which held its first formal session on 15 November. The Council also renewed for another 30 days the state of emergency that had been in place across the country since November 2004, with the exception of the Kurdistan region. On 24 September, a draft constitution for the Kurdistan region was read in the Kurdistan National Assembly and submitted for a period of public comment that would run through April 2007.

The United Nations, as co-chair of the International Compact with Iraq, continued to support the Government in developing the Compact document and assisted in organizing the high-level and technical meetings of the Compact's Preparatory Group. A high-level meeting at UN Headquarters on 18 September, attended by the Security Council permanent members, Iraq's neighbouring countries, key donors and representatives of regional and international organizations, reviewed Government progress in the political, security and economic fields. On 10 September, the UN Deputy Secretary-General and Iraq's Deputy Prime Minister co-chaired the first high-level meeting of the International Compact Preparatory Group in Abu Dhabi, United Arab Emirates. Participants adopted the Abu Dhabi Declaration, which recognized the need to finalize the Compact through national, regional and international consultations. On 31 October, the Preparatory Group's second high-level meeting in Kuwait City focused on substantive issues related to the Compact document and its implementation.

The Secretary-General's Special Representative continued his consultations with a broad spectrum of key political, civil society, tribal and religious leaders to promote dialogue and address the volatile security situation. UNAMI Office of Constitutional Support continued to assist the Parliament in developing legislation for implementing the Constitution, and had engaged key members of Parliament on the establishment of the Constitutional Review Committee and relevant legislative issues. UNAMI and UN agencies, programmes and funds continued to strengthen ministerial capacities, provide access to basic services and restore public infrastructure. UNAMI Human Rights Office continued to work with Iraqi institutions, including the Higher Judicial Council, the Ministry of Human Rights and the Ministry of Justice, to strengthen the rule of law and create a strong national human rights protection system.

As of 31 October, total contributions to the UN Development Group Iraq Trust Fund reached $1.1 billion. Some 104 projects valued at $869 million were approved for funding as at the end of October. Contracts worth $664 million (76 per cent of approved funding) had been initiated and $558 million (64 per cent of approved funding) had been disbursed. Strong progress was made in delivering basic services. Ten quick-impact projects in education, health, water and sanitation had led to the rehabilitation of 262 schools, 192 primary health centres and 160 water and sanitation systems, thus keeping polio and cholera under control.

The Secretary-General observed that, while Iraq had made efforts to improve security and promote national reconciliation, it needed to develop a fully inclusive political process focused on bringing all disenfranchised and marginalized communities into the political mainstream; establish a monopoly over the use of force through the security and law enforcement instruments within the rule of law; and cultivate a regional environment that was supportive of Iraq's transition. The constitutional review process which had just begun offered a real opportunity to reach a broad consensus on the fundamental issues that continued to divide the country. The Secretary-General urged Iraqi leaders and key international actors to demonstrate their commitment and make the review a top priority. He suggested that it might be worthwhile to consider a larger framework for fostering dialogue and understanding at all levels under an arrangement, similar to that in Afghanistan, which would bring together all Iraqi political parties, possibly outside Iraq.

Security Council consideration (December). On 11 December [meeting 5583], the Security Council was briefed by the Secretary-General's Special Representative for Iraq, who said that efforts by the Government and MNF had not prevented a continuous deterioration of the security situation. Initiatives such as the 2 October Ramadan declaration had had no impact on the violence and bloodshed, while the Baghdad Security Plan had not expanded beyond the initially selected areas. The violence seemed to be out of control.

While eight governorates out of 18 accounted for 80 per cent of the attacks against MNF and the Iraq security forces, those governorates accounted for a significant proportion of the population. Restoring peace and stability in Baghdad was critical for the peace and stability of Iraq as a whole. Nor could multilateral partnerships, such as the International Compact for Iraq, be expected to realize their potential, as they were predicated on the Government being able to implement the requisite political, security, economic and social reforms. Given the lack of political unity, the fragmentation of society and the paralysing levels of violence, it was unrealistic to expect the Government and Parliament to bring about progress without regional and international cooperation.

Vigorous efforts were under way to build up the armed forces and put in place effective command and control, disciplinary and organizational structures. Significant progress was being made in some respects. Even under the best circumstances, developing self-sufficient and professional security forces would take years. The key issues confronting Iraq were not amenable to solutions based on force alone. Excessive reliance on the use of force could preclude negotiated compromise, the only sound basis for stability. A collective sense of urgency, resolve and compromise was essential. The international community and regional States had a real stake in assisting the Government to overcome the challenges it faced.

To replace the climate of fear and mistrust, a reconciliation process should address sensitive issues, rather than postpone considering them. A genuine constitutional review process could provide the framework for national reconciliation. Technical revision needed to be backed by political negotiation on key issues, aimed at making the Constitution a workable national framework.

The issues on which consensus was urgent were clear: a political vision for the new Iraq; a fair sharing of oil revenues; a realistic sharing of powers; the development of security forces into genuine national institutions; the disbanding of militias and other illegal armed groups; ensuring effective human rights protection; encouraging civil society to foster the emergence of issue-based, non-sectarian politics; and finding a way to discuss the future of the Multinational Force's role as a key component of national reconciliation.

The United States, reporting on behalf of the Multinational Force, said the Force continued to play a vital role in security and stability and to work with the authorities toward a transition of responsibility to Iraqi forces. As at 13 November, six Iraqi army divisions headquarters, 30 brigade headquarters and 91 battalions, representing some 70 per cent of the Iraqi army, had the security lead in their areas of operation. MNF had transferred 55 of the 110 forward operating bases to Iraqi control. It also transferred Dhi Qar Province to provincial Iraqi control. The Government, with MNF, had identified a force structure that would provide a basis for transitioning Iraq to security self-reliance. The authorized end-strength of the force was 137,500 personnel, including one Iraqi command and 10 divisions. The Ministry of the Interior, with MNF assistance, had begun to assess National Police battalions' capabilities, reinforce police training and establish practices for continuing education. The end-strength of those forces was fixed at 188,200 trained and equipped personnel.

The Parliament, on 10 October, adopted a new foreign investment law and a federal regions law that would allow Iraq's provinces to hold referendums to merge themselves into larger federal regions. The Council of Ministers, on 26 November, endorsed the International Compact.

The rise in sectarian violence had become the greatest threat to security and stability. In response, Iraq's Prime Minister had announced a four-point plan on 2 October to unite Shia and Sunni parties behind the drive to stop sectarian killings. The Government had also sponsored four reconciliation conferences across Iraq to promote national dialogue and solicit recommendations for action.

Report of the Secretary-General. In a later report [S/2007/126], the Secretary-General stated that, on 16 and 17 December, Prime Minister al-Maliki hosted a conference of political parties and entities as part of the Government's national reconciliation plan. The event was largely attended by political parties within the National Unity Government, while those with ties to the Ba'ath Party, the Sadrist bloc, the Iraqiya list of Ayad Allawi, and the Iraqi Front for National Dialogue led by Saleh al-Mutlak did not officially attend. However, numerous members of each group participated in their own personal capacity. The conference concluded with a statement recommending, among other items, the dissolution of militias, the expedited withdrawal of the multinational force, and the re-incorporation of veteran army personnel.

UNAMI financing

The Secretary-General, on 5 December [A/61/525/Add.5], submitted the UNAMI budget for the period 1 January to 31 December 2007, totalling $169,394,700 net ($176,496,000 gross).

The General Assembly, on 22 December, by section VII of **resolution 61/252** (see p. 1614), approved the budget in that amount as part of the $326,500,000 budget of special political missions.

Multinational force

On 9 June [S/2006/377], Iraq, noting that, in accordance with Security Council resolution 1637(2005) [YUN 2005, p. 429], the mandate of the Multinational Force (MNF) was due for review, stated that the continuation of the Force's mandate remained necessary and requested the continued assistance of the international community in providing security and stability.

Press statement (June). In a 15 June press statement [SC/8752], Security Council members agreed to continue the MNF mandate in accordance with resolution 1637(2005). Welcoming the progress made in recruiting, training and equipping Iraqi security forces and their increasing responsibilities on the ground, Council members looked forward to the day when Iraqi forces would assume full responsibility for maintaining security and stability, thus allowing the completion of MNF mandate.

On 14 November [S/2006/888], Iraq requested the extension of MNF mandate for another 12 months, which was subject to periodic reviews before 15 June 2007. The United States, on 17 November [S/2006/899], confirmed the readiness of MNF unified command to continue to fulfil its mandate.

SECURITY COUNCIL ACTION

On 28 November [meeting 5574], the Security Council unanimously adopted **resolution**

1723(2006). The draft [S/2006/919] was submitted by Denmark, Japan, Slovakia, the United Kingdom and the United States.

The Security Council,

Welcoming the formation of a national unity government in Iraq with a detailed political, economic and security programme and a strong national reconciliation agenda, and looking forward to the day that Iraqi forces assume full responsibility for the maintenance of security and stability in their country, thus allowing the completion of the multinational force mandate and the end of its presence in Iraq,

Welcoming also the progress made to date in the training and equipping of Iraqi security forces as well as in the transfer of security responsibilities to those forces in Al Muthanna and Dhi Qar provinces, and looking forward to the continuation of that process during 2007,

Recalling all of its previous relevant resolutions on Iraq,

Reaffirming the independence, sovereignty, unity and territorial integrity of Iraq,

Reaffirming also the right of the Iraqi people freely to determine their own political future and control their own national resources,

Welcoming the continuing work of the Government of Iraq towards a federal, democratic, pluralistic and unified Iraq, in which there is full respect for human rights,

Welcoming also the vital role played by the Government of Iraq in continuing to promote national dialogue and reconciliation in pursuit of an atmosphere in which sectarianism is totally rejected, including the National Reconciliation Plan announced by Iraqi Prime Minister al-Maliki, stressing the importance of the rapid implementation of the Plan, and reaffirming the willingness of the international community to work closely with the Government of Iraq to assist these reconciliation efforts,

Recognizing the International Compact with Iraq, an initiative of the Government of Iraq to create a new partnership with the international community and to build a strong framework for Iraq's continued political, security and economic transformation and integration into the regional and global economy, and welcoming the important role that the United Nations is playing by jointly chairing the Compact with the Government of Iraq,

Calling upon the international community, particularly countries in the region and Iraq's neighbours, to support the Iraqi people in their pursuit of peace, stability, security, democracy and prosperity, and noting that the successful implementation of the present resolution will contribute to regional stability,

Demanding that those who use violence in an attempt to subvert the political process lay down their arms and participate in the political process, and encouraging the Government of Iraq to continue to engage with all those who renounce violence,

Reaffirming that acts of terrorism must not be allowed to disrupt Iraq's political and economic transition, and further reaffirming the obligations of Member States under resolution 1618(2005) of 4 August 2005 and other relevant resolutions and international conventions with respect, inter alia, to terrorist activities in and from Iraq or against its citizens,

Recognizing the request, conveyed in the letter dated 11 November 2006 from the Prime Minister of Iraq to the President of the Security Council, which is annexed to the present resolution, to retain the presence of the multinational force in Iraq, and affirming the common goals therein: Iraqi assumption of recruiting, training, equipping and arming of the Iraqi security forces, Iraqi assumption of command and control over Iraqi forces, and the transfer of responsibility for security to the Government of Iraq,

Recognizing also the importance of the consent of the sovereign government of Iraq for the presence of the multinational force and of close coordination and partnership between the multinational force and that government,

Welcoming the willingness of the multinational force to continue efforts to contribute to the maintenance of security and stability in Iraq, including participating in the provision of humanitarian and reconstruction assistance, as described in the letter dated 17 November 2006 from the Secretary of State of the United States of America to the President of the Security Council, which is annexed to the present resolution,

Recognizing the tasks and arrangements set out in the letters annexed to resolution 1546(2004) of 8 June 2004 and the cooperative implementation by the Government of Iraq and the multinational force of those arrangements,

Affirming the importance that all forces promoting the maintenance of security and stability in Iraq act in accordance with international law, including obligations under international humanitarian law, and cooperate with the relevant international organizations, and welcoming their commitments in this regard,

Recalling the establishment of the United Nations Assistance Mission for Iraq on 14 August 2003, and affirming that the United Nations should continue to play a leading role in assisting the Iraqi people and Government with further political and economic development, including advising and supporting the Government of Iraq, providing strong support in developing the International Compact with Iraq, contributing to the coordination and delivery of reconstruction, development and humanitarian assistance, and promoting the protection of human rights, national reconciliation, as well as judicial and legal reform in order to strengthen the rule of law in Iraq,

Recognizing that international support for security and stability is essential to the well-being of the people of Iraq as well as the ability of all concerned, including the United Nations, to carry out their work on behalf of the people of Iraq, and expressing its appreciation for contributions by Member States in this regard under resolutions 1483(2003) of 22 May 2003, 1511(2003) of 16 October 2003, 1546(2004) and 1637(2005) of 8 November 2005,

Recognizing also that the Government of Iraq will continue to have the primary role in coordinating international assistance to Iraq, and reaffirming the importance of international assistance and development of the Iraqi economy and the importance of coordinated donor assistance,

Recognizing further the significant role of the Development Fund for Iraq and the International Advisory and Monitoring Board in helping the Government of Iraq to ensure that Iraq's resources are being used transparently and equitably for the benefit of the people of Iraq,

Stressing the responsibility of the Iraqi authorities to undertake all appropriate steps to prevent attacks on the diplomatic personnel accredited in Iraq in accordance with the Vienna Convention on Diplomatic Relations of 1961,

Determining that the situation in Iraq continues to constitute a threat to international peace and security,

Acting under Chapter VII of the Charter of the United Nations,

1. *Notes* that the presence of the multinational force in Iraq is at the request of the Government of Iraq and reaffirms the authorization for the multinational force as set forth in resolution 1546(2004), and decides to extend the mandate of the multinational force as set forth in that resolution until 31 December 2007, taking into consideration the letter dated 11 November 2006 from the Prime Minister of Iraq and the letter dated 17 November 2006 from the Secretary of State of the United States of America;

2. *Decides* that the mandate for the multinational force shall be reviewed at the request of the Government of Iraq or no later than 15 June 2007, and declares that it will terminate this mandate earlier if requested by the Government of Iraq;

3. *Decides also* to extend until 31 December 2007 the arrangements established in paragraph 20 of resolution 1483(2003) for the deposit into the Development Fund for Iraq of proceeds from export sales of petroleum, petroleum products and natural gas and the arrangements referred to in paragraph 12 of resolution 1483(2003) and paragraph 24 of resolution 1546(2004) for the monitoring of the Development Fund for Iraq by the International Advisory and Monitoring Board;

4. *Decides further* that the provisions in paragraph 3 above for the deposit of proceeds into the Development Fund for Iraq and for the role of the International Advisory and Monitoring Board shall be reviewed at the request of the Government of Iraq or no later than 15 June 2007;

5. *Requests* that the Secretary-General continue to report to the Security Council on the operations in Iraq of the United Nations Assistance Mission for Iraq on a quarterly basis;

6. *Requests* that the United States of America, on behalf of the multinational force, continue to report to the Council on the efforts and progress of the force on a quarterly basis;

7. *Decides* to remain actively seized of the matter.

ANNEX I

Letter dated 11 November 2006 from Mr. Nuri Kamel al-Maliki, Prime Minister of Iraq, to the President of the Security Council

Iraq has taken in the specified time the steps required for the completion of the political process, in particular the drafting of a permanent Constitution and the laying of foundations for building its political and legal institutions. In May 2006, the constitutionally elected Council of Representatives formed a Government of national unity. The steps for building a democratic, federal and united Iraq were consolidated by the commitment of the Government to adopt a dialogue and national reconciliation scheme, secure broad political participation, monitor human rights, establish the rule of law and economic development and provide services to citizens.

Establishing security and securing permanent stability are among the highest priorities of the Iraqi Government's programme to realize the desired peace and prosperity for the Iraqi people. However, terrorists and forces hostile to democracy continue to target innocent citizens and the various State institutions.

Security and stability in Iraq are the responsibility of the Iraqi Government. The Security Council affirmed in its resolution 1546(2004) that Iraqi security forces would play a progressively greater role in enabling the Iraqi Government to assume that responsibility, diminishing and thereby ending the role of the multinational force, when the responsibility for security of the Iraqi security forces increases and expands. From the experience of the past two and a half years, it was established that the Iraqi security forces, which operated under the command of the Iraqi Government, had acquired new experiences and responsibilities and had grown in size, experience and capacity, demonstrated by their increased ability to assume full responsibility in the fields of security and defence.

We started to reap the fruits of success when our forces assumed responsibility for security in the governorates of Al Muthanna and Dhi Qar. In September 2006, the Ministry of Defence assumed the operational command and control of the ground, naval and air force commands. It also assumed operational command and control over two military divisions, indicating an increase in the ability of the Iraqi Army to assume the leadership in providing security to the Iraqi people. The Iraqi Government is also relentlessly working on building the necessary administrative and logistics system to make our Iraqi forces self-sufficient.

It is the intention of the Iraqi Government to continue increasing the number of governorates that fall fully under the control of the Iraqi authorities during 2006, until all 18 are under their control. When the responsibilities for security are transferred to the Iraqi authorities in a certain governorate, the multinational force will be present in its bases and can provide support to Iraqi security forces at the request of the Iraqi authorities, in accordance with an agreement that allocates the authorities and responsibilities between the two sides.

We have agreed on three common goals: first, assumption by Iraq of recruiting, training, equipping and arming of Iraqi security forces; second, assumption by Iraq of command and control over Iraqi forces; and third, transferring responsibility for security to the Government of Iraq. We have formed a high-level working group that will provide recommendations on how best to achieve these goals. It has also been agreed to work towards the

Iraqi authorities' assuming the apprehension, detention and imprisonment tasks on the basis of an agreement to be reached between the Government of Iraq and the multinational force.

Hence, the Iraqi Government requests the extension of the mandate of the multinational force in accordance with Security Council resolutions 1546(2004) and 1637(2005) and the letters attached thereto for another 12 months starting on 31 December 2006, provided that the extension is subject to a commitment by the Council to end the mandate at an earlier date if the Iraqi Government so requests and that the mandate is subject to periodic review before 15 June 2007. The Iraqi Government requests the termination of the mission of the United Nations Monitoring, Verification and Inspection Commission due to the completion of its tasks. The Iraqi Government believes that the time has come to terminate the war compensations that were imposed on Iraq.

The Iraqi Government realizes that the provisions of resolution 1546(2004) relating to the depositing of revenues in the Development Fund for Iraq and the role of the International Advisory and Monitoring Board help to ensure the use of the natural resources of Iraq for the benefit of the people of Iraq. We recognize that the fund plays an important role in convincing donors and creditors that Iraq is managing its resources and debts in a responsible way for the Iraqi people. This role is vital, especially since Iraq is seeking to form a new partnership with the international community to build a vital network for economic transformation and integration in the economies of the region and the world through the International Compact with Iraq. We ask the Security Council to extend the mandate of the Development Fund for Iraq and the International Advisory and Monitoring Board for another 12 months and to review this mandate based on the request of the Iraqi Government before 15 June 2007.

The people of Iraq are determined to establish a stable and peaceful democracy for themselves and a proper basis for building a vital economy. This vision for the future of Iraq cannot become a reality without the help of the international community.

We realize that the Security Council intends to append the present letter to the special resolution concerning Iraq that is being prepared. Meanwhile, I ask that the present letter be distributed to the members of the Security Council as soon as possible.

ANNEX II

Letter dated 17 November 2006 from Ms. Condoleezza Rice, Secretary of State of the United States of America, to the President of the Security Council

Having reviewed the request of the Government of Iraq to extend the mandate of the Multinational Force (MNF) in Iraq and following consultations with the Government of Iraq, I am writing to confirm, consistent with this request, that MNF under unified command stands ready to continue to fulfil its mandate as set out in Security Council resolution 1546(2004) and extended by Security Council resolution 1637(2005).

The Government of Iraq and MNF in Iraq continue to improve their cooperation through a security partnership to combat the challenges that threaten Iraq's security and stability. This partnership has evolved over time to incorporate the increasing leadership by Iraqi security forces in fighting and deterring terrorism and other violent acts throughout Iraq's 18 provinces. In the context of this partnership, MNF is prepared to continue to undertake a broad range of tasks to contribute to the maintenance of security and stability and to ensure force protection, acting under the authorities set forth in resolution 1546(2004), including the tasks and arrangements set out in the letters annexed thereto, and in close cooperation with the Government of Iraq. The forces that make up MNF will remain committed to acting consistently with their obligations and rights under international law, including the law of armed conflict.

Iraqi security forces have already made substantial progress this year in developing their capabilities and, as a result, they are shouldering a greater portion of the responsibility for Iraq's security. This progress is most notable in their assumption of security responsibility in Dhi Qar and Al Muthanna and the assumption of operational command and control over the Ground, Naval, and Air Force Commands and two Iraqi military divisions by the Ministry of Defense.

The Government of Iraq and MNF have agreed on three common goals: Iraqi assumption of recruiting, training, equipping and arming of the Iraqi security forces; Iraqi assumption of command and control over Iraqi forces; and transferring responsibility for security to the Government of Iraq. We look forward to recommendations from the newly formed high-level working group on how these goals can best be achieved. The strong partnership between the Government of Iraq and MNF is a vital factor in fulfilling these goals. Together we will build towards the day when the Iraqi forces assume full responsibility for the maintenance of security and stability in Iraq.

The co-sponsors intend to annex this letter to the resolution on Iraq that is under consideration. In the meantime, I request that you provide copies of the present letter to members of the Council as quickly as possible.

International Advisory and Monitoring Board

The International Advisory and Monitoring Board for Iraq (IAMB), established by Security Council resolution 1483(2003) [YUN 2003, p. 338] to ensure that the Development Fund for Iraq was used in a transparent manner for the benefit of the Iraqi people and that Iraqi export sales of petroleum products were consistent with international market best practices, continued to oversee the auditing of the Fund.

Communication. On 9 June [S/2006/377], Iraq requested the Council to approve the continuation of the Development Fund for Iraq and IAMB, as those mechanisms had demonstrated that Iraq's oil resources were being used transparently and had confirmed for donors and creditors that Iraq was managing its resources and debts responsibly.

IAMB report (February/June). In a 12 June letter [S/2006/394], submitted by the Secretary-General to the Security Council President, the Secretary-General's representative on IAMB provided an update of the Board's activities. The January report indicated that IAMB had received, in October 2005, the reports by an independent auditor on the Fund's operations for the period 1 January to 30 June 2005. The reports highlighted numerous exceptions to administrative and accounting procedures by Iraq's spending ministries and United States agencies. The auditor continued to face lack of cooperation by some ministries and required the intervention of the Ministry of Finance to conduct or complete its work. IAMB was briefed by representatives of the Iraqi Government on the implementation of the recommendations contained in the audits and on measures taken to address the shortcomings identified by IAMB and in the audit reports. The Government reported a number of steps, including the enactment of a Financial Management Law, which set out a structured process for formulating the budget, as well as reporting requirements to increase accountability and transparency; establishment of a department within the Board of Supreme Audit (BSA) to follow up on all audit and investigation reports, and of a specialized directorate within each ministry to audit and oversee public funds administered by them. With regards to contracts administered by United States agencies, United States representatives informed IAMB that Iraq's Finance Minister had signed, in December 2005, a memorandum extending the authority of the United States Chief of Mission and Commander of the Multinational Force to continue to administer those contracts until year's end in view of the small number of remaining contracts.

Of the 24 sole-sourced contracts, with a value of $2 billion, 23 ($563 million) were audited by an independent auditor and one ($1.4 billion) by the United States Special Inspector General for Iraq Reconstruction. The independent audit revealed exceptions in a number of cases, including insufficient documentation to justify non-competitive contracting, lack of support for the provision of services or receipt of goods, and discrepancies in the amounts billed. The 26 January 2006 report of the United States Special Inspector General on the Development Fund for Iraq noted deficiencies in contract-award documentation. It concluded that the Coalition Provisional Authority South-Central Region had failed to adequately manage its Rapid Regional Response Programme contracts and micro-purchases. IAMB had requested a briefing on the matter.

The June report stated that the briefing took place on 5 April, at which clarification was provided. At a meeting in May, in Washington, D.C., IAMB was briefed by the Fund's independent auditor on the status of the audit of the Fund's resources and disbursements, and of the oil export sales from 1 July to 31 December 2005. The BSA President provided a summary of the main findings of recent audits. Representatives of the United States Department of Defense briefed IAMB on pending audits. On the review of the remaining sole-sourced contracts awarded by the Coalition Provisional Authority and funded from the Fund, the representatives indicated that the follow-up audit of such contracts had only recently been awarded, and was expected to be completed by September. One of IAMB main concerns had been the absence of metering for crude oil production, and it had recommended in 2004 the expeditious installation of metering equipment in accordance with standard oil industry practices. The Iraqi Government informed IAMB, in March, that the Oil Ministry had concluded an agreement with the United States to rebuild the metering system in the Basrah oil port of the Southern Oil State Company, expected to be completed by year's end. Welcoming those developments, IAMB reiterated that key actions, especially the installation of an oil metering system, should be comprehensive and were taking a long time to implement.

Communication. In November [S/2006/888], Iraq requested the Security Council to extend the mandate of the Development Fund for Iraq and IAMB for another 12 months. That was vital since Iraq was seeking to form a new partnership with the international community through the International Compact with Iraq.

The Council, in **resolution 1723(2006)** (see p. 402) of 28 November, approved the request.

UN Monitoring, Verification and Inspection Commission and IAEA activities

UNMOVIC

On 23 May [S/2006/339] and 17 November [S/2006/907], the Secretary-General proposed to the Security Council the appointment of Francis C. Record (United States) to the United Nations

Monitoring, Verification and Inspection Commission (UNMOVIC) College of Commissioners, to replace Stephen G. Rademaker (United States), and of Robert Witajewski (United States) to replace Francis C. Record. The Council agreed to those proposals [S/2006/340, S/2006/908].

Reports of UNMOVIC. As called for in resolution 1284(1999) [YUN 1999, p. 230], UNMOVIC submitted to the Council, through the Secretary-General, quarterly reports on its activities. Throughout the year, the UNMOVIC Acting Executive Chairman continued to provide monthly briefings to the Council President and kept the Secretary-General informed about the Commission's activities.

The February report [S/2006/133] stated that, during the period from 1 December 2005 to 28 February 2006, the Commission's experts had reviewed information on hazardous items and materials at the former Iraqi chemical warfare production at the Muthanna State Establishment, and compiled a detailed inventory of the site on the basis of existing records. Under a handover protocol agreed between Iraq and UNMOVIC in 1994, the Iraqi Government still had obligations concerning the security and safety of the site. The UNMOVIC College of Commissioners shared the Chairman's concern that the handover protocol for the Muthanna plant was not being implemented. They welcomed the fact that the Compendium of Iraq's weapons of mass destruction (WMD) programmes was nearing completion and noted the Chairman's intention to produce a version without any proliferation-sensitive or other confidential information for open access.

The May report [S/2006/342], covering the period 1 March to 31 May, said that on 7 April, Iraq had informed the Chairman that it intended to accede to the Convention on the Prohibition of the Development, Production, Stockpiling and Use of Chemical Weapons and on Their Destruction [YUN 1992, p. 65], and had requested that UNMOVIC provide the full and final disclosure relating to chemical weapons that was provided by Iraq's National Monitoring Directorate to the UN Special Commission in 1996. On 10 April, the Chairman proposed to the Council President that UNMOVIC provide Iraq with the document duly redacted for proliferation-sensitive content. On 24 May, the Council suggested that the Chairman provide Iraq with the relevant sections of the currently accurate, full and complete declaration, transmitted by the National Monitoring Directorate in December 2002, having due regard to disposing of proliferation-sensitive documents and materials. UNMOVIC transmitted the relevant sections to Iraq on 30 May. The College of Commissioners discussed the revised summary of the Compendium on Iraq's WMD and made additional comments.

The August report [S/2006/701], covering the period 1 June to 31 August, said that on 21 June, the United States Director of National Intelligence declassified key parts from a National Ground Intelligence Center report on the recovery of approximately 500 chemical munitions that contained degraded mustard or sarin nerve agent. The munitions, recovered since 2003, were of pre-1991 Gulf war origin, and despite efforts to locate and destroy Iraq's chemical munitions, more were thought to still exist. The declassified points indicated that, while the agents had degraded over time, chemical warfare agents remained hazardous and potentially lethal. An annex to the UNMOVIC report provided information on the possible conditions of remaining Iraqi chemical warfare agents and associated munitions.

The November report [S/2006/912] covering the period from 1 September to 30 November, stated that, in view of its plans to accede to the Chemical Weapons Convention, Iraq, on 18 August, requested copies of "certificates of destruction" of the chemical weapons-related material and equipment that was destroyed under UN supervision, as well as a copy of the 1994 handover protocol between Iraq and the UN Special Commission on the transfer of the Muthanna chemical warfare agent production site to the custody of Iraq. The protocol, providing an account of destruction activities conducted at Muthanna between 1992 and 1994 and setting out safety and security measures to be applied at the site, remained in force. On 6 September, Iraq sought a copy of UNMOVIC working document of 6 March 2003 on unresolved disarmament issues and Iraq's responses thereto. The Commission's experts prepared the relevant documents, eliminated proliferation and other sensitive information and provided Iraq with materials covering both requests. The materials included several destruction certificates, the handover protocol and 54 documents regarding unresolved disarmament issues. The College of Commissioners noted the continuation and possible expansion of agricultural activities outside and within the Muthanna perimeter close to the bunkers in which a variety of chemical munitions filled with nerve agents were known to have been stored, which might pose safety and health hazards.

Communication. On 14 November [S/2006/888], Iraq's Minister for Foreign Affairs requested the termination of UNMOVIC due to the completion of its task.

Escrow account

On 7 February [S/2006/93], the Secretary-General proposed to the Security Council that, following a request from Iraq, $416,871 of the balance of $112.2 million in the UNMOVIC escrow account, established under Council resolution 1284(1999) [YUN 1999, p. 230] and related resolutions, be credited against assessments issued in respect of Iraq's obligations for UN regular budget, peacekeeping, the tribunals and the capital master plan. On 10 February [S/2006/94], the Council approved that proposal.

Also on 4 December [S/2006/987], the Secretary-General informed the Council President that, on 14 November, the Minister had requested him to transfer $40 million of the balance in the UNMOVIC account to the Permanent Mission of Iraq, to be used to purchase facilities near United Nations Headquarters and to renovate the headquarters of the Mission and the residence of the Permanent Representative. The balance in the account stood at about $105.7 million, and making that transfer would leave a balance of $65.7 million. While that balance would be adequate at current expenditure levels, it would be insufficient should expenditures return to the levels of previous years.

On 15 December [S/2006/988], the Council proposed that the $40 million be transferred to the Development Fund for Iraq, taking into consideration that the remaining balance in the UNMOVIC account should be sufficient to finance its current activities.

Reports of Board of Auditors

On 21 August, the Secretary-General transmitted to the Security Council the report [S/2006/672] of the Board of Auditors on the financial statements of the escrow account for the financial period ended 31 December 2004. According to the report, the shortfall of income over expenditure for the period was $245.7 million. Total expenditure decreased from $9.7 billion in 2003 to $368.8 million in 2004 and total assets from $18.8 million in 2003 to $3.6 million in 2004, attributable mainly to the settlement of unliquidated obligations and transfers to the Development Fund for Iraq.

The Board reviewed five major accounts: revenues; expenditures on humanitarian supplies; assets; liabilities, which were essentially unliquidated obligations for approved/amended contracts; and reserves and fund balances as at 31 December 2004. The Board noted that a total of 202 letters of credit amounting to $248.7 million, which expired on 1 October 2004 and earlier, were still included in the Banque Nationale de Paris (BNP) Paribas liability report; the balance of unliquidated obligations, as at 31 December 2004, disclosed a $35 million difference with the BNP Paribas liability report; letters of credit amounting to $31.1 million, which expired in 2004, owing to failure of suppliers to deliver, were cancelled; the currency amounts of obligations raised/closed in the financial period 2004 were translated, using exchange rates other than the 31 December 2004 rates; the shipment and validity dates of certain letters of credit were repeatedly extended since the contracts were amended under Council resolution 1483(2003) [YUN 2003, p. 338]; and the $580,000 payable to the German Government remained outstanding since 1992, owing to differing opinions on whether Germany could be reimbursed under resolution 986(1995) [YUN 1995, p. 475].

The Board recommended that the administration of the account coordinate with BNP Paribas on the cancellation of expired letters of credit, particularly those without valid claims; reconcile the balances of unliquidated obligations against the BNP Paribas liability report on a per obligation basis and reflect the adjustment in the related financial period; ensure that all transactions for a particular period were taken up during the same period; coordinate with the Integrated Management Information System (IMIS) on the currency exchange rates used in the translation of balances of obligations raised or closed as at cut-off date; review the obligations related to amended contracts and effect the adjustments in IMIS; and, with UNMOVIC, determine whether the payable to the German Government represented a valid claim.

Also on 21 August, the Secretary-General transmitted to the Council the report [S/2006/673] of the Board of Auditors on the financial statements of the escrow account for the biennium ended 31 December 2005. According to the report, as at 31 December 2005, cash and term deposits and cash pool amounted to $1.6 billion, which adequately covered the $1.2 billion in unliquidated obligations arising from approved contracts for current and prior periods. The total reserves and fund balances decreased from $3.2 billion in 2003 to $28 million in 2005, due to the transfer of funds to the Development Fund for Iraq. The income shortfall for the biennium was $165.7 million, compared to the $286 million surplus for the 2002-2003 biennium. Total income decreased by 98 per cent between 2003 and 2005. The closure of the programme in November 2003 and the transfer of funds to the Development Fund for Iraq during the 2004-2005 biennium had drastically reduced the programme's funds. The non-cancellation of the expired letters of credit hampered the complete liquidation of the programme and held up cash collaterals associated with each expired letter of credit.

As at 31 December 2005, a reserve of $114 million remained in the escrow account for UNMOVIC activities. During the biennium ended 31 December 2005, administrative expenditure amounted to $32 million.

The Board recommended that the administration of the account make representation to the Security Council and the Iraqi Government to resolve the issue of contracts with expired letters of credit; continue to coordinate with the designated bank for the release of the cash collateral associated with each expired letter of credit in order to adjust the unliquidated obligations at the time the cash collateral was released by the bank; begin evaluation of UNMOVIC mandate in the light of current events and invite the Security Council to decide the final course of action; and facilitate completion of the final inventory necessary to update the UNMOVIC records of non-expendable property lost or stolen.

IAEA

IAEA reports. In accordance with Security Council resolution 1051(1996) [YUN 1996, p. 218], the International Atomic Energy Agency (IAEA) submitted to the Council, through the Secretary-General, two consolidated six-monthly reports, on 10 May [S/2006/291] and 9 October [S/2006/797], on the Agency's verification activities in Iraq.

In May, IAEA said that, since 17 March 2003, it had not been in a position to implement its mandate in Iraq under Council resolution 687(1991) [YUN 1991, p. 172] and related resolutions. The number of IAEA staff assigned to follow the situation in Iraq was kept at a minimum, reflecting the level of headquarters activities being implemented pursuant to the relevant Council resolutions. During the period under review, IAEA had further developed its archive system for storing and retrieving information collected and generated in the course of its activities in Iraq. Satellite imagery of the most significant sites continued to be collected and assessed. Under IAEA monitoring and verification plans, Iraq and States that either exported to or imported from Iraq had to report to IAEA certain items, in accordance with the export-import mechanism approved by the Council in resolution 1051(1996). Iraq also had to declare semi-annually changes that had occurred or were foreseen at sites deemed relevant by IAEA. During the past six months, the Agency had received no reports from Iraq or other States in that regard.

In October, IAEA reported that, during the period under review, it continued to systematically collect and assess satellite imagery of the most significant sites, and provided training on nuclear material accountancy and control for the newly established Iraqi National Monitoring Directorate.

Iraq-Kuwait

Oil-for-food programme: high-level Independent Inquiry Committee

Under the oil-for-food programme, established by Security Council resolution 986(1995) [YUN 1995, p. 475], Iraq had been authorized to sell petroleum and petroleum products to finance humanitarian assistance, thereby alleviating the adverse consequences of the sanctions imposed by the Council. The programme was phased out in November 2003 [YUN 2003, p. 362]. In March 2004 [YUN 2004, p. 364], the Secretary-General informed the Council that he intended to establish an independent, high-level inquiry on matters arising from news reports and commentaries that had questioned the programme's administration and management, including allegations of fraud and corruption. A high-level Independent Inquiry Committee, headed by Paul A. Volcker, was formed in April 2004 [ibid.]. In its final report, submitted on 7 September 2005 [YUN 2005, p. 1475], the Committee found evidence of mismanagement in the programme and of corruption within the United Nations and by contractors. It also found that the responsibility for the failures was broadly shared, starting with Member States and the Council itself.

On 24 March [S/2006/194], the Secretary-General informed the Council President of his decision to extend the Office of the Independent Inquiry Committee until 31 December to allow it to continue to handle enquiries from Member States' law-enforcement authorities in follow-up to the findings contained in the Committee's final report. The Council, on 28 March [S/2006/195], took note of that decision.

United Nations Iraq Account

Following the termination of all activities under the oil-for-food programme in 2003 [YUN 2003, p. 366], the United Nations retained responsibility for the administration and execution of letters of credit issued under the programme by the bank holding the United Nations Iraq Account, Banque Nationale de Paris (BNP) Paribas, for purchasing humanitarian supplies for the south/centre of Iraq, until such letters were executed or expired, in accordance with Security Council resolution 1483(2003) [ibid., p. 338].

The Secretary-General, in a 10 July letter [S/2006/510] to the Council President, said that he had asked the Secretariat to consult with the Iraqi authorities on terminating the operations of the oil-for-food programme. Funding had been retained in the Account for 524 letters of credit that were reported by BNP Paribas as open as at 30 November 2005. Subsequently, 16 letters of credit were paid in full, 32 were reinstated for making payments to suppliers who delivered goods in Iraq, and 209 were partially paid and/or balances of letters of credit cancelled. The Iraqi authorities made 104 requests for amendments and reinstatements to existing letters of credit, as a result of which shipment dates and validity dates were extended for certain letters of credit. After processing all amendment requests received on or before 31 December 2005 from the Iraqi authorities, and making payments to suppliers for goods delivered in Iraq, the Account, as at 31 May, retained funding for 331 letters of credit worth $1.1 billion.

However, the Iraqi authorities continued to send additional requests for further amendments past the deadlines approved by the Council. The UN Controller requested clarifications from the Iraqi authorities on various issues, and received clarifications on the need for further amendments to extend the validity of the letters of credit. The Secretary-General concurred with the 91 requests made by the Iraqi authorities, and asked the Controller to consult with them and make the final amendment to the letters of credit that needed an extension, on condition that those amendments be considered as final. Such consultations should recognize that ongoing projects under the oil-for-food programme should be brought to a conclusion within 10 months, while complying with the provisions of Council resolution 1483(2003).

On the unresolved matter of the satisfaction of claims from suppliers, 203 of the 331 outstanding letters of credit, as at 31 May, fell into that category, with an approximate value of $300 million. The United Nations was not in a position to satisfy such claims without authentication documents from Iraq, and the Secretary-General asked the Council to urge the Iraqi authorities to process such documents promptly.

A balance of funds ($187 million) was due to be transferred to the Development Fund of Iraq, in accordance with Council resolution 1483(2003). However, until the issue of claims from suppliers was resolved, those funds would be held in the Account as a reserve for any unanticipated claims from suppliers.

On 11 August [S/2006/646], the Council President informed the Secretary-General that Council members, noting with concern that the question of processing the authentication documents remained unresolved, urged the Secretariat to consult with the Iraqi Government in order to find a final resolution to the remaining issues and achieve an orderly termination of the programme.

POWs, Kuwaiti property and missing persons

Reports of Secretary-General. In response to Security Council resolution 1284(1999) [YUN 1999, p. 230], the Secretary-General submitted reports in June [S/2006/428] and December [S/2006/948] on Iraq's compliance with its obligations regarding the repatriation or return of all Kuwaiti and third-country nationals or their remains, and on the return of all Kuwaiti property, including archives, seized by Iraq during its occupation of Kuwait, which began in August 1990 [YUN 1990, p. 189]. The High-level Coordinator for compliance by Iraq with its obligations regarding the return of Kuwaiti nationals and property, Yuli M. Vorontsov (Russian Federation), briefed the Council throughout the year.

In June, the Secretary-General reported that, in May, the Iraqi Government had returned Kuwaiti property located in Tunisia to Kuwait, namely an airplane engine, spare parts and accessories belonging to the Kuwait Airways Corporation, which were removed from the wing of an Iraqi Airways Company 747 aircraft stationed in Tozeur, Tunisia. There was no progress on returning the Kuwaiti national archives and related documents, and it might not be possible to ascertain whether they were destroyed or were still hidden at one or several locations. Kuwait considered their return essential.

On 28 June [S/2006/468], the Secretary-General informed the Council President that the activities related to the return of all Kuwaiti and third-country nationals or their remains had slowed down, and requested the Council to reduce the frequency of reports from every four months to every six months. The Council President, on 30 June [S/2006/469], informed the Secretary-General that the Council members had taken note of his intention.

In his December report, the Secretary-General said that Kuwait had advised the High-level Coordinator that the total number of identified persons had reached 230. The names of the 230 Kuwaiti and third-country nationals whose remains had been identified were annexed to the report. Owing to the security situation in Iraq, the Kuwaiti technical teams had not been able, in 2006, to conduct significant assessment work, have access to known mass graves or locate new graves. Cooperation between Iraq, Kuwait and Saudi Arabia on searching burial sites of persons unaccounted for by Iraq after the 1991 Gulf War [YUN 1991, p. 167] had led to the repatriation of nine human remains to Iraq from Kuwait. However, the fate of 370 Kuwaiti and third-country nationals was still unknown.

Press statement. In a 13 December press statement [SC/8899] by its President, Security Council members welcomed progress on identifying and recovering the remains of Kuwaitis and other nationals missing, but expressed concern over the fate of those whose whereabouts remained unknown. Council members noted the resolution of all issues relating to the transfer of Kuwaiti spare parts on board Iraqi Airways planes in Tunisia but regretted that there had been no developments in locating the missing Kuwaiti national archives.

UN Iraq-Kuwait Observation Mission

Financing

The United Nations Iraq-Kuwait Observation Mission (UNIKOM) discharged its functions until 6 October 2003, in accordance with its terms of reference, as expanded by Security Council resolution 806(1993) [YUN 1993, p. 406].

The Secretary-General, on 13 January, submitted to the General Assembly a final performance report on UNIKOM [A/60/651], providing information on assets, outstanding liabilities and fund balances as at 30 June 2005. The fund balance stood at $46,529,000. The Secretary-General proposed that two thirds of the cash balance of $27,844,700 be returned to the Government of Kuwait, and the remaining balance of $13,922,300 be credited to Member States. The Advisory Committee on Administrative and Budgetary Questions (ACABQ) [A/60/788], noting that the arrangement of returning two thirds of the unencumbered balance to Kuwait and one third to Member States had been applied since 1 November 1993, recommended that the Assembly accept the Secretary-General's proposal.

GENERAL ASSEMBLY ACTION

On 30 June [meeting 92], the General Assembly, on the recommendation of the Fifth (Administrative and Budgetary) Committee [A/60/922], adopted **resolution 60/274** without vote [agenda item 146 *(a)*].

Financing of the United Nations Iraq-Kuwait Observation Mission

The General Assembly,

Having considered the report of the Secretary-General on the financing of the United Nations Iraq-Kuwait Observation Mission and the related report of the Advisory Committee on Administrative and Budgetary Questions,

Expressing its appreciation for the substantial voluntary contributions made to the Observation Mission by the Government of Kuwait and the contributions of other Governments,

1. *Takes note* of the proposal of the Secretary-General contained in paragraph 14 of his report;

2. *Also takes note* of the status of contributions to the United Nations Iraq-Kuwait Observation Mission as at 30 April 2006, including the contributions outstanding in the amount of 3.9 million United States dollars, representing some 1 per cent of the total assessed contributions, notes with concern that only one hundred and forty-one Member States have paid their assessed contributions in full, and urges all other Member States, in particular those in arrears, to ensure the payment of their outstanding assessed contributions;

3. *Expresses its continued appreciation* of the decision of the Government of Kuwait to defray two thirds of the cost of the Observation Mission, effective 1 November 1993;

4. *Expresses its appreciation* to those Member States which have paid their assessed contributions in full, and urges all other Member States to make every possible effort to ensure payment of their assessed contributions to the Observation Mission in full;

5. *Endorses* the conclusions and recommendations contained in the report of the Advisory Committee on Administrative and Budgetary Questions;

6. *Decides* that, taking into account the voluntary contributions of the Government of Kuwait, two thirds of the cash balance available as at 30 June 2005 in the amount of 27,844,700 dollars shall be returned to the Government of Kuwait;

7. *Also decides* that Member States that have fulfilled their financial obligations to the Observation Mission shall be credited with their respective share of the remaining balance as at 30 June 2005 in the amount of 13,922,300 dollars, in accordance with the levels set out in General Assembly resolution 55/235 of 23 December 2000, as adjusted by the Assembly in its resolution 55/236 of the same date and its resolution 57/290 A of 20 December 2002, and taking into account the scale of assessments for 2003, as set out in its resolutions 55/5 B of 23 December 2000 and 57/4 B of 20 December 2002;

8. *Further decides* that, for Member States that have not fulfilled their financial obligations to the Observation Mission, their respective share of the remaining balance as at 30 June 2005 in the amount of 13,922,300 dollars shall be set off against their outstanding obligations, in accordance with the scheme set out in paragraph 7 above;

9. *Encourages* Member States that are owed credits for the closed peacekeeping mission accounts to apply those credits to any accounts where the Member State concerned has outstanding assessed contributions;

10. *Decides* that updated information on the financial position of the Observation Mission shall be included in the report on the updated position of closed peacekeeping missions to be considered by the General Assembly at its sixty-first session under the agenda item entitled "Administrative and budgetary aspects of the financing of the United Nations peacekeeping operations";

11. *Also decides* to delete from its agenda the item entitled:

"Financing of the activities arising from Security Council resolution 687(1991):

"*(a)* United Nations Iraq-Kuwait Observation Mission;

"*(b)* Other activities".

UN Compensation Commission and Fund

The United Nations Compensation Commission (UNCC), established in 1991 [YUN 1991, p. 195] for the resolution and payment of claims against Iraq for losses and damages resulting from its 1990 invasion and occupation of Kuwait [YUN 1990, p. 189], continued in 2006 to expedite the settlement of claims through the United Nations Compensation Fund, which was established at the same time as the Commission.

On 19 January the Commission paid out $284.8 million to eight Governments for distribution to 42 claimants; $248.4 million, on 27 April, to six governments for distribution to 25 claimants; $396.5 million, on 27 July, to four Governments for distribution to 31 claimants; and $417.8 million, on 26 October, to seven Governments for distribution to 46 claimants; bringing the overall amount of compensation made available by the Commission to $21.4 billion.

Governing Council. The Commission's Governing Council held three sessions in Geneva during the year—the fifty-ninth (7-9 March) [S/2006/238], the sixtieth (27-29 June) [S/2006/530] and the sixty-first (31 October–3 November) [S/2006/881]—at which it considered the reports and recommendations of the Panels of Commissioners appointed to review specific instalments of various categories of claims. The Governing Council also acted on the Executive Secretary's report submitted at each session, which, in addition to providing a summary of the previous period's activities, covered the processing, withdrawal and payment of claims.

Other matters considered by the Council included the processing and payment of claims, the distribution of payments, the transparency of the distribution process and the return of undistributed funds.

Oversight activities

On 21 August [S/2006/674], the Secretary-General transmitted to the Security Council the report of the Board of Auditors on UNCC financial statements for the biennium ended 31 December 2005. The Board reported that the financial statements presented fairly the financial position as at 31 December 2005, and the results of its operations and cash flows, in accordance with UN system accounting standards. UNCC expenditure for the 2004-2005 biennium was $2.1 billion, comprising awards of $2 billion, administrative expenses of $58.9 million and $6.6 million in other expenses. The Board made recommendations to improve financial management and payments in respect of those findings and of a number of less significant issues. It also recommended that, with the United Nations, the Commission should decide on a completion strategy.

On 22 December, the Assembly decided that the item on the "Consequences of the Iraqi occupation of and aggression against Kuwait", would remain for consideration during its resumed sixty-first (2007) session (**decision 61/552**).

Timor-Leste

The United Nations Office in Timor-Leste (UNOTIL), established by Security Council resolution 1599(2005) [YUN 2005, p. 440], continued to carry out its mandate of supporting the development of critical State institutions, the police and the Border Patrol Unit, and observing democratic governance and human rights. With the improvement of the situation in the country, the United Nations prepared to scale back its operations in Timor-Leste. However, tensions escalated, in April and May, within the Timorese security forces, which led to the establishment of a new UN mission. On 25 August, the Council established the United Nations Integrated Mission in Timor-Leste (UNMIT) for an initial six-month period. In December, the Secretary-General appointed Atul Khare (India) as his Special Representative for Timor-Leste and Head of UNMIT.

United Nations Office in Timor-Leste

Report of Secretary-General (January). In response to Security Council resolution 1599(2005) [YUN 2005, p. 440], the Secretary-General submitted a January report [S/2006/24] covering UNOTIL activities since his August 2005 report [ibid., p. 444]. During that period, the overall situation remained calm, except for a few isolated incidents involving the incursion of formed militias, which led to a number of arrests by the Timorese police. The most serious border incident, which occurred on 6 January, led to the death of three infiltrators.

On 12 January, Timor-Leste and Australia signed an agreement on the sharing of natural resources from the Timor Sea, allocating 50 per cent of the revenues to Timor-Leste. That would provide the country with the much-needed means to promote development and improve living conditions. The agreement did not affect the positions and claims of both countries in respect to maritime boundaries.

UNOTIL continued to coordinate donor assistance for the country's sustainable and long-term development and for ensuring a smooth transition from UNOTIL to a development assistance framework. It continued to support training in democratic governance and human rights for Timorese public officials and civil society, and capacity development of State institutions, civil society and development partners.

To support the development of critical State institutions, 39 UNOTIL advisers conducted training and transferred skills and knowledge to their Timorese counterparts in the justice sector, the Office of the President and the National Parliament, as well as across various Government institutions. In the justice sector, 23 civilian advisers provided training and performed line functions in all four district courts. Under the UNOTIL training programme for judges, prosecutors and defence lawyers, 27 national judicial actors had begun on-the-job training in the courts under the supervision of experienced international judges, prosecutors and public defenders.

Six UNOTIL legal advisers assisted in drafting legislation and streamlining procedures within the Council of Ministers and provided support to the Parliament in the exercise of its legislative powers. One UNOTIL adviser on the Petroleum Fund, assigned to the Prime Minister's Office, advised the Prime Minister during negotiations over the sharing of natural resources in the Timor Sea, which led to the 12 January agreement with Australia.

The UN system, together with donors, continued to provide assistance to help Timor-Leste meet its social, economic and human development needs. The World Bank coordinated the consolidation support programme, which contributed some $10 million per year to Timor-Leste's budget, while monitoring progress in the areas of governance, basic service delivery and job creation. Since August 2005, the World Bank administered the Trust Fund for Timor-Leste, assisted in the establishment of the Petroleum Fund, the rehabilitation of 22 market sites, the training of 4,000 new entrepreneurs at five business development centres and the construction of six schools. The International Monetary Fund (IMF) assisted the Timorese authorities in addressing key policy issues, including how best to employ growing oil and gas revenues so as to improve infrastructure and social services. The United Nations Development Programme (UNDP) supported the development of institutional, organizational and human resource capacities. It provided training to judges, prosecutors and public defenders, supported the development of local government, implemented community activation programmes, and a rural project on sustainable water and energy services. The Food and Agriculture Organization of the United Nations (FAO), the World Health Organization (WHO), the United Nations Children's Fund (UNICEF) and other agencies provided support in their areas of expertise.

The Secretary-General observed that Timor-Leste had made further progress towards establishing effective democratic governance. The successful conclusion of local elections, the adoption of key legislation and the improved observance of human rights by the police were examples of such progress. Relations with neighbouring countries continued to improve. However, the situation remained fragile. Crucial State institutions, in particular the justice sector, were weak, mainly due to a lack of qualified personnel. According to some assessments, it might take years for the Parliament to be able to function without international support. Time would also be required for democratic governance and human rights to take root. The international community should therefore remain engaged in Timor-Leste.

Security Council consideration (January). On 23 January [meeting 5351], Sukehiro Hasegawa (Japan), the Secretary-General's Special Representative and Head of UNOTIL, said that the past five months had been productive for UNOTIL in implementing Security Council mandated programmes and preparing to transfer capacity-building support functions to UN agencies and development partners. Since 2002, international advisers provided by the United Nations and bilateral development partners had made great progress in building Timorese capacity to administer public institutions. As a result, the number of UN international advisers had declined from nearly 300 three years earlier to about 100 by the end of 2005. The UNOTIL civilian advisers had accelerated efforts to transfer skills and knowledge, and their Timorese counterparts demonstrated increased ability to carry out their duties. Yet, national capacities in highly technical areas, such as justice and finance, remained extremely weak. International advisory support, especially in those two areas, would be required for some years to come.

In the areas of democratic governance and human rights, the Office of the Provedor for Human Rights and Justice made great progress in drafting a strategic plan and establishing a complaint-handling system in preparation for the opening of the Office to the public in March. Under the leadership of Minister for Foreign Affairs and Cooperation José Ramos-Horta, Timor-Leste demonstrated a commitment to establishing a normative international human rights framework through the early ratification of core human rights treaties. The Commission for Reception, Truth and Reconciliation completed its report and made specific recommendations.

Timor-Leste had made major progress in peacebuilding, but peace remained fragile. In 2007, for the first time since the restoration of independence, presidential and parliamentary elections would take place. Those elections would be a critical test for the nascent democratic State. An electoral needs assessment mission fielded in November 2005 had concluded that, for the elections to be free and fair, Timor-Leste needed international assistance and a strong political presence.

Timor-Leste's President, Xanana Gusmão, addressed the report of the Commission for Reception, Truth and Reconciliation, current developments and challenges and ongoing needs and expectations vis-à-vis the international community. He noted a number of concerns with the Commission's recommendations, especially regarding justice, the payment of reparations to victims, the establishment of an international tribunal, renewing the contracts of international judges who served on the Special Panels for Serious Crimes, and the enhancement of the allocation of resources to the investigation and trial of all crimes committed between 1975 and 1999. He regretted that the United Nations had not shown any interest or support for the Commission's recommendation for the establishment of a Commission for Truth and Friendship as a counter to punitive justice. There were many valuable recommendations that deserved in-depth study by the Timorese society and particularly by the political forces of the nation.

Noting that UNOTIL mandate was due to end on 20 May, he expressed Timor Leste's gratitude for the role it had played in the country's recent history. He appealed to the international community to continue to assist the country in meeting some of the most critical needs, a request which had been conveyed by the Timorese Prime Minister to the Secretary-General and the Security Council President. He asked the Security Council to consider establishing a special political office in the country after the end of UNOTIL mandate on 20 May. In view of the upcoming national elections in 2007, the proposed UN presence should have an electoral assistance component to provide the Government with technical and logistical support; 15 to 20 military liaison personnel to be deployed along the border with Indonesia in order to prevent tensions and encourage cooperation between the two countries' security forces; police training, for which Timor-Leste continued to need assistance; and civilian advisers for the justice and finance sectors.

Communications. The formal request for the establishment of a post-UNOTIL special political office was conveyed on 20 January [S/2006/39] by Timor-Leste's Prime Minister Mari Alkatiri to the Secretary-General. The request was reiterated on 2 March by Foreign Affairs Minister Ramos-Horta [S/2006/157] and on 2 April [S/2006/230] by President Gusmão, who requested that all UN agencies should be integrated into the special political office as a unified UN presence under the command of a senior UN representative.

On 28 March [S/2006/196], the Council President requested the Secretary-General to present options on how the United Nations could best assist Timor-Leste following the end of UNOTIL mandate, paying attention to the best modality for assisting the country in organizing the 2007 national elections, maximum use of efficient coordination with bilateral and multilateral donors on post-conflict peacebuilding and capacity-building assistance, respect for Timor Leste's sovereignty, bearing in mind that the rules and processes governing the elections should be part of a broad national consensus, and the report of the 2005 United Nations electoral needs assessment mission.

Report of Secretary-General. The Secretary-General, in his April end-of-mandate report [S/2006/251 & Corr.1] reviewing the activities of UNOTIL since January, recommended the establishment of a small integrated United Nations office for 12 months beginning on 21 May. The office, which would comprise civilian, police and military elements, would have as its mandate to support Timor-Leste in organization of the 2007 presidential and parliamentary elections; support and guide the country in consolidating democratic development and political stability and facilitate dialogue among Timorese stakeholders; support the national police, the Government in liaising with the Indonesian military, and the Timorese Border Patrol Unit; and assist in building the capacity of State and Government institutions, including national capacity and mechanisms for the protection of human rights and the promotion of justice and reconciliation. The Office, to be headed by a Special Representative of the Secretary-General, who would also serve as the UN resident coordinator, would have an Electoral Support and Advisory Section, a Political Advisory Section, a Police Training and Advisory Section, a Military Liaison and Advisory Section, a Civilian Advisory Section, a Human Rights Support Section and an administrative support office.

Given the considerable UN investment in the country over more than six years, the Secretary-General said, it was in the international community's interest to assist Timor-Leste in consolidating the achievements made. By providing assistance through the proposed office, the United Nations could better enable the Government to make further advances in fostering peace, stability and democracy.

In other developments, the Secretary-General reported that, on 8 February, around 400 members of the Timorese armed forces demonstrated in front of the office of the President, demanding a response to their 15 January petition concerning alleged discrimination in promotions and ill-treatment against members from non-eastern areas of the country. The following day, the demonstrators, who had not returned to their bases since signing the petition, agreed to return to the military base at Metinaro. The armed forces' Chief of Staff had established a commission of inquiry to investigate the allegations, but little progress was made because the protesting soldiers refused to cooperate with it. Meanwhile, more soldiers joined the protestors, culminating, in mid-March, in the dismissal of 594 soldiers, or almost 40 per cent of the armed forces. In his address to the nation on 23 March, the President stated that, as Commander-in-Chief, he respected the decision of the armed forces Commander to dismiss all 594 protesting troops, but that, as President, he found that it focused more on military discipline and failed to address the root causes of the problems.

Violent incidents took place in the Timor-Leste capital, Dili, in late March, involving stone throwing, fights and vandalism, which created anxiety among the population. After three days, following appeals from the President, the Prime Minister and the Foreign Affairs Minister, the situation returned to normal. The police arrested 48 suspects, eight of whom were among the dismissed soldiers. On 12 April, the President met with the Prime Minister and the Commander-in-Chief of the armed forces, Brigadier-General Taur Matan Ruak, who agreed to take steps to end the impasse, including a legal review of the soldiers' contracts and the continuation of payment of their salaries until the process was completed.

The situation along the Timorese-Indonesian border remained calm, but with a porous and inadequately guarded border separating the two countries, there were occasional reports of illegal entries into Timor-Leste. The two coutries continued to maintain cordial relations. On 17 February, President Gusmão met with Indonesian President Susilo Bambang Yudhoyono, in Bali, Indonesia, to discuss the report of the Commission for Reception, Truth and Reconciliation, the joint investigation into the 6 January border incident and the strengthening of bilateral relations.

UNOTIL continued to work towards a smooth transition to a development assistance framework and encouraged donor assistance for projects aimed at long-term development. It continued to review issues related to the development of institutional capacity, together with representatives of State institutions and civil society, the UN system and development partners. The Secretary-General's Special Representative, who also served as Resident Coordinator and headed the UN country team, spearheaded efforts to enhance coordination and integration of UN system activities.

Security Council consideration (May). On 5 May [meeting 5432], the Secretary-General's Special Representative, in briefing the Security Council on events in Timor-Leste, said that, as the situtation had undergone a rapid change since the Secretary-General's last report, Council members might need to adjust their perceptions and assumptions. The dismissed soldiers staged a demonstration on 24 April, demanding an independent commission to address the issue of discrimination and an investigation into their grievances. While they remained peaceful throughout the four-day demonstration, on 28 April, a mob of young people and some political elements attacked Government buildings. As the police were unable to deal with the situation, the Government deployed the military to restore law and order. Government offices were damaged and cars, shops and houses destroyed during the riots. Although the damages were small, the psychological impact turned out to be immense. As many as 14,000 people in Dili became internally displaced as they sought refuge in churches, public buildings and the UNOTIL headquarters compound. According to UNOTIL estimates, five people were killed and at least 60 injured. Such developments were a reminder that the country's democracy was still fragile. The Special Representative said that he agreed with President Gusmão on the need to strengthen the institutional foundation of the Ministry of Defence and the armed forces, particularly their capacity to manage their human resources development. In that regard, the United Nations would respond to the President's request for the provision of civilian advisers to assist in the drafting and implementation of the organic law and in setting up management mechanisms for both the Ministry and the armed forces.

In preparation for the elections, the Government had moved swiftly towards finalizing the draft electoral laws for submission to the Parliament. The continued presence of the UN police would be essential to ensure that law and order, and respect for human rights, were maintained. The impartiality of the police could not be guaranteed in a tense political electoral environment.

The Timor-Leste Minister for Foreign Affairs and Cooperation, Ramos-Horta, told the Council that the incidents in Dili the previous week were a wake-up call that the apparent tranquillity in the country should not be taken for granted, and that urgent measures should be taken to prevent a relapse into violence and instability. While the Government and people were determined to ensure that the 2007 elections would be held in a free, fair and credible manner, those incidents indicated that threats remained to the country's fragile peace and stability. On 27 April, Prime Minister Alkatiri and President Gusmão announced the establishment of an investigative commission to look into the allegations contained in the 15 January petition. In conversations held prior to 28 April, the leader of the 594 petitioners, Lieutenant Gastão Salsinha, stated that he would accept the commission's conclusions and recommendations. The leadership of the defence forces promised to do likewise. On 4 May, Lieutenant Salsinha reiterated that his group would abide by the commission's findings and recommendations. The Government also established a commission to verify the data on the dead and wounded and another to look into losses incurred by individuals and to propose ways to assist them. The Minister reassured the Council that the Government was in full control of the situation and public administration continued to function. The armed forces had returned to their barracks and the police was in charge of law and order. The proposals contained in the Secretary-General's report for a continued UN presence represented the bare minimum that the country required. In the light of the latest developments, it was desirable to have once again a robust international police force during the period leading to the national elections at company strength.

SECURITY COUNCIL ACTION

On 12 May [meeting 5436], the Security Council unanimously adopted **resolution 1677(2006)**. The draft [S/2006/290] was prepared in consultations among Council members.

The Security Council,

Recalling its relevant resolutions on the situation in Timor-Leste, in particular resolution 1599(2005) of 28 April 2005,

Expressing its deep concern over the incidents of 28 and 29 April 2006 as well as the ensuing situation, and acknowledging the actions of the Government of Timor-Leste to establish an investigation into the incidents, their effects and their causes,

Remaining fully committed to the promotion of long-lasting stability in Timor-Leste,

1. *Decides* to extend the mandate of the United Nations Office in Timor-Leste until 20 June 2006;
2. *Requests* the Secretary-General to provide the Security Council by 6 June 2006 with an update on the situation in Timor-Leste and the role of the United Nations in Timor-Leste following the expiration of the mandate of the Office with a view to taking further action on the subject;
3. *Encourages* the Government and other State institutions of Timor-Leste, with assistance from the Office within its current mandate, to address the causes of the violence in order to prevent a recurrence of such incidents;
4. *Decides* to remain actively seized of the matter.

Escalation of violence

The ramifications of the violence of 28 April (see p. 415) were far-reaching. Most of the "594 Group" of petitioners moved to the western highland towns of Gleno and Aileu. On 3 May, Major Alfredo Reinado, commanding officer of the military police, broke away from the Timorese armed forces, the Falintil-Forças Armadas de Defesa de Timor-Leste (F-FDTL), along with two other senior officers from western districts. On 8 May, about 500 persons, including some petitioners, surrounded the office of the Regional Secretary of State in Gleno, the district capital of Ermera. They attacked two unarmed Timorese national police (PNTL) officers of eastern origin, who had been persuaded to disarm by a commander of western origin, causing the death of one and serious injury to the other. That incident exacerbated tensions within PNTL, setting easterners against westerners and officers loyal to the Minister of the Interior, Rogério Lobato, against those who opposed him. Those cleavages were most pronounced at the PNTL headquarters in Dili, within the Dili district command and in the PNTL specialized units. On 23 May, an armed group led by Major Reinado, who had come down to Dili from his base in Aileu, engaged F-FDTL soldiers and

PNTL officers in a protracted exchange of fire that resulted in deaths on both sides. The following day, the F-FDTL headquarters in Tasi Tolu (to the west of Dili) was attacked by an armed group reportedly consisting of petitioners, PNTL officers and civilians. The residence of the Commander of the armed forces, Brigadier-General Taur Matan Ruak, also came under attack, reportedly by an armed group of PNTL officers and civilians. Following those confrontations, a number of PNTL officers of eastern origin threw in their lot with F-FDTL, taking refuge at the F-FDTL training centre at Metinaro to the east of Dili.

Requests for assistance. Against that background, on 24 May [S/2006/319], President Gusmão, Prime Minister Alkatiri and the President of the National Parliament informed the Secretary-General of their urgent request to the Governments of Australia, Malaysia, New Zealand and Portugal for police and military assistance. On the same day [S/2006/320, S/2006/321], Australia and New Zealand indicated that they were giving serious consideration to the request and urged the Council to give urgent attention to the situation that had developed in Timor-Leste. On 25 May, Australia informed the Council President that it had agreed to immediately commence deployment of security forces to Timor-Leste, New Zealand [S/2006/327] announced the initial deployment of aircraft and military personnel and Portugal [S/2006/326] considered deploying a force of the Portuguese gendarmerie. Portugal said that it was consulting with Australia, Malaysia and New Zealand, which had all agreed to coordinate efforts. It believed that a multinational deployment would profit from a Security Council decision confirming its full international authority.

Further developments. On 25 May, F-FDTL members reportedly accompanied by police and civilian elements sympathetic to them, launched armed attacks against the PNTL national headquarters and the PNTL Dili district headquarters. The UNOTIL Chief Military Training Adviser and Chief Police Training Adviser negotiated an agreement with the F-FDTL Commander, under which PNTL officers were to be allowed to leave the PNTL headquarters under UN auspices, provided that they were first disarmed. As UNOTIL police and military training advisers were escorting the PNTL officers, F-FDTL soldiers reportedly opened fire, killing eight PNTL officers and injuring more than 25 of the group, including two UNOTIL police training advisers. Also on 25 May, the Secretary-General appointed Ian Martin (United Kingdom) as his Special Envoy to assess the situation and facilitate dialogue among the various parties.

SECURITY COUNCIL ACTION

On 25 May [meeting 5445], following consultations among Security Council members, the President made statement **S/PRST/2006/25** on behalf of the Council:

> The Security Council received briefings from the Secretariat on the situation in Timor-Leste on 24 and 25 May 2006.
>
> The Council expresses its deep concern at developments in Timor-Leste, recognizes the urgency of the deteriorating security situation and condemns acts of violence against people as well as destruction of property.
>
> The Council urges the Government of Timor-Leste to take all necessary steps to end the violence with due respect for human rights and to restore a secure and stable environment.
>
> The Council urges all parties in Timor-Leste to refrain from violence and to participate in the democratic process.
>
> The Council acknowledges the request made by the Government of Timor-Leste to the Governments of Portugal, Australia, New Zealand and Malaysia to dispatch defence and security forces under bilateral arrangements.
>
> The Council welcomes the positive responses made by the Governments concerned and fully supports their deployment of defence and security forces to urgently assist Timor-Leste in restoring and maintaining security.
>
> The Council looks forward to close cooperation between the United Nations Office in Timor-Leste and the forces of the Governments concerned.
>
> The Council welcomes the initiatives of the Secretary-General, including his intention to send a special envoy to Timor-Leste in order to facilitate the political dialogue.
>
> The Council requests the Secretary-General to follow closely the situation in Timor-Leste and to report on developments, as necessary.
>
> The Council will continue to monitor closely the situation in Timor-Leste and confirms that it will act, as appropriate.

Communications. On 26 May, Portugal informed the Council President [S/2006/337] that it had begun deploying a gendarmerie force in response to Timor-Leste's request.

Also on 26 May, the Secretary-General informed the Council President [S/2006/338] that the situation had worsened, with the reported deaths, on 25 May, of nine Timorese police officers and injuries to almost 30 others, including two UN police advisers, as a result of gunshot wounds following an attack on the police headquarters (see above). Gunshots had reportedly been heard during the day throughout Dili and in the surrounding hills. The Secretary-General contacted President Gusmão and Prime Minister Alkatiri and signalled the UN's readiness to facilitate negotiations. With the concurrence of the Timorese leaders, the Secretary-General requested his Special Envoy to travel to Timor-Leste to assess the situation. He also spoke with the Prime Ministers of Australia, Malaysia, New Zealand and Portugal, who welcomed that action and pledged to send defence and security forces to Timor-Leste.

In an 8 June letter addressed to the Secretary-General [S/2006/391], Timor-Leste invited the United Nations to establish an independent Special Inquiry Commission to review the incidents of 28 and 29 April, and 23, 24 and 25 May and other related events or issues which contributed to the crisis. In response, the Secretary-General, on 12 June, requested the United Nations High Commissioner for Human Rights to establish such a Commission.

On 13 June, the Secretary-General transmitted to the Council President [S/2006/383], an 11 June request from the Timorese President, the President of the Parliament and the Prime Minister, for the immediate establishment of a UN police force in Timor-Leste, for a minimum of one year, to maintain law and order and re-establish confidence among the people, until the Timorese police was reorganized as an independent and professional law enforcement agency. The Government also said that a robust UN police, military and civilian mission to succeed UNOTIL was indispensable. Timor-Leste reiterated that request on 4 August [S/2006/620], informing the Council President that, along with a strong civilian component, the new mission should have a police force of considerable strength, backed by a small military force.

Security Council consideration (June). The Secretary-General, addressing the Security Council on 13 June [meeting 5457], said he was deeply concerned about the evolution of the situation since the incidents of 28 and 29 April. The violence and unrest were particularly painful in many respects and reflected shortcomings not only on the part of Timor-Leste, but of the international community in sustaining Timor-Leste's nation-building process. The lesson to be learned was that institution-building was not a simple process that could be completed within a few short years. He said that the United Nations was determined not to abandon Timor-Leste at its critical time of need and appealed to the Security Council to stand united in supporting the country's return to normality.

Mr. Martin, the Secretary-General's Special Envoy for Timor-Leste, said that during his visit to the country from 29 May to 7 June, he held discussions across the political spectrum, including with senior officials, key members of the opposition, the Defence Force Commander, the Bishop of Dili, civil society representatives and the diplomatic community.

While he was in Dili, the two senior constitutional bodies that advised the President—the Council of State and the Superior Council for Defence and Security—had agreed upon a framework and a plan of action, within which the political leadership would address the crisis. That involved the President assuming the main responsibility for defence and security, in close collaboration with the Prime Minister and the President of the Parliament. All those responsible for security matters expressed their commitment to work together within that framework.

The Portuguese-led police force began operations in Dili, and police officers from Australia, Malaysia and New Zealand would soon begin patrolling. However, all that in itself would not end the security crisis. The leaders of the demonstrating soldiers had told him that they would take no offensive armed action and would respect the President's authority. However, weapons from the defence force and the police had been distributed to civilians, including former resistance fighters. The President's action plan provided for the return and audit of weapons of the security forces, but, as long as the armed groups remained disaffected, the security situation would remain unresolved.

The elections set for May 2007 would provide the arena where political competition should be democratically resolved. However, sections of the population did not accept that the Government should remain in place until then. Such opposition was reported to be widespread in western districts and within the Church. A sizeable demonstration in Dili had called for the resignation of the Prime Minister. Soldiers, ex-soldiers and their leaders considered that a precondition for dialogue.

However, the most serious underlying cause of the crisis, and the biggest challenge for future stability, lay in the security sector. The crisis revealed political cleavages, not only between the defence force and the police, but also within each institution. Initial recruits to the defence force had been from the former fighters of the Armed Forces of National Liberation of East Timor (FALINTIL) and their selection had been controversial ever since. Later recruits were mostly from western districts, many of whom had since alleged discrimination by eastern officers. Initial recruitment in the police had also been controversial, with criticism of the absorption of officers from the Indonesian police. The national command structure and at least two of the Dili police special units had disintegrated during the violence, although the police in the districts had largely continued their regular duties.

The immediate issues were thus the future of soldiers or ex-soldiers outside the command of the defence force, and the re-establishment of a national police command structure and a Dili police force. The sudden elevation of east-west friction as a central factor in the crises in the army and defence force was potentially the most dangerous cleavage for national unity. Although that division had some historical roots, political and religious leaders maintained that it was not deep-seated.

Politically, the crisis was centred upon the dominance of the ruling party, the Revolutionary Front for the Independence of East Timor (FRETILIN), and the challenges to it. Critics accused its leaders of heading the country towards a one-party system, by using its dominant position in Parliament, its superior political machinery, and its access to power and State resources. The leaders' perspective was that the crisis stemmed from the failure of the opposition parties and domestic critics, including the Church, to challenge the Government democratically and to create an institutional crisis and even bring about a military coup. The crisis was exacerbated by the fact that the opposition saw President Gusmão as a guarantor of pluralism. However, while he remained the country's most important national figure and had the legitimacy of direct election, the presidency was constitutionally almost powerless.

As for the role the Timorese people wanted the United Nations to play, there was a need for an impartial investigation of recent events, particularly the disputed number of killings that occurred in Dili on 28 and 29 April, and the killing by soldiers of unarmed police officers under UN escort on 25 May, as well as several other incidents.

SECURITY COUNCIL ACTION

On 20 June [meeting 5469], the Security Council unanimously adopted **resolution 1690(2006)**. The draft [S/2006/414] was prepared in consultations among Council members.

The Security Council,

Recalling its relevant resolutions on the situation in Timor-Leste, in particular resolutions 1599(2005) of 28 April 2005 and 1677(2006) of 12 May 2006,

Expressing deep concern over the volatile security situation in Timor-Leste and its serious humanitarian repercussions,

Condemning continuing acts of violence against people and destruction of property,

Welcoming the initiatives taken by the Secretary-General, including the work of his Special Envoy for Timor-Leste to assess the situation on the ground,

Taking note of the letter dated 11 June 2006 from the President of the Democratic Republic of Timor-Leste, the President of the National Parliament and the Prime Minister of Timor-Leste addressed to the Secretary-General, as well as the letter dated 8 June 2006 from the Minister for Foreign Affairs and Cooperation and Minister for Defence of Timor-Leste addressed to the Secretary-General,

Reaffirming its full commitment to the sovereignty, independence, territorial integrity and national unity of Timor-Leste,

Remaining fully committed to the promotion of long-lasting stability in Timor-Leste,

1. *Decides* to extend the mandate of the United Nations Office in Timor-Leste until 20 August 2006 with a view to planning for the role of the United Nations following the expiration of the mandate of the Office;

2. *Expresses its appreciation and full support* for the deployment of international security forces by the Governments of Portugal, Australia, New Zealand and Malaysia in response to the request of the Government of Timor-Leste and their activities aimed at restoring and maintaining security in Timor-Leste, notes with appreciation that the work of those international forces is also facilitating the provision of humanitarian assistance and humanitarian access to the people of Timor-Leste in need, and encourages those countries to continue to inform the Security Council of their activities;

3. *Calls upon* the international security forces to continue to work in close coordination with the Government of Timor-Leste as well as the United Nations Office in Timor-Leste;

4. *Urges* all parties in Timor-Leste to refrain from violence and to participate in the democratic process;

5. *Requests* the Secretary-General to provide to the Council by 7 August 2006 a report on the role for the United Nations in Timor-Leste following the expiration of the mandate of the United Nations Office in Timor-Leste, taking into account the current situation and the need for a strengthened presence of the United Nations;

6. *Welcomes* the initiative of the Secretary-General to request the United Nations High Commissioner for Human Rights to take the lead in establishing an independent special inquiry commission in response to the request made by the Government of Timor-Leste in the letter dated 8 June 2006, and requests the Secretary-General to keep the Council informed on this matter;

7. *Calls upon* the donor community to respond urgently and positively to the flash appeal launched by the United Nations on 12 June 2006 for humanitarian assistance to Timor-Leste;

8. *Decides* to remain actively seized of the matter.

Communications (June-July). On 27 June [S/2006/440], Australia informed the Council President that it had deployed some 2,650 Defence Force personnel in Timor-Leste, together with some 200 Federal Police providing security and assessing law-enforcement needs. Working with forces from Malaysia, New Zealand and Portugal, and in cooperation with the Government, they had secured the area around Dili, allowing humanitarian agencies to move freely in the city, and provided increased access to the outside districts. The security situation had improved but remained tense. Dili continued to experience sporadic outbreaks of disorder, arson, looting and violence, mostly due to communal gang conflict. Fighting between the armed forces and the police had ceased, but tensions remained. Progress was made in securing the weapons of rebel military groups.

On 20 July [S/2006/559], New Zealand informed the Council President that a contingent of 25 police personnel had begun community policing work to help restore the rule of law. Their three-month deployment was in addition to the 190 Defence Force personnel who had been in Timor-Leste since late May–early June.

Report of Secretary-General (August). In his 8 August report to the Security Council on Timor-Leste [S/2006/628], submitted in response to resolution 1690(2006) (see p. 419), the Secretary-General said the crisis was far from resolved, and many of the underlying factors could only be addressed in the longer term.

Following a meeting of the Council of State on 29 and 30 May, President Gusmão announced that he was assuming responsibility for defence and national security in his capacity as Commander-in-Chief of the armed forces. On 1 June, following an extraordinary meeting of the Council of Ministers, Prime Minister Alkatiri announced that, in response to a request from President Gusmão, the Defence and Interior Ministers had resigned.

As decided by the Council of State, the Secretary-General's Special Envoy accompanied Foreign Affairs Minister Ramos-Horta, who had also assumed the defence portfolio, to meet with the petitioners, Major Reinado and armed forces leaders. After meeting President Gusmão on 15 June, Major Reinado and members of his group began handing over weapons to the international forces.

On 19 June, President Gusmão requested a group of civilians to hand over their weapons. The group's leaders stated that they had received their weapons in early May on the orders of Prime Minister Alkatiri and former Interior Minister Lobato and had been instructed to use them against political opponents. The next day, the Prime Minister's Office denied the allegations. On the same day, the Office of the Prosecutor-General issued an arrest warrant for Mr. Lobato for alleged involvement in distributing weapons to civilians. That evening, President Gusmão informed the Prime Minister that the evidence implicating him in the distribution of arms required him to resign or be dismissed. A 21 June meeting of the Council of State convened to address the issue ended inconclusively with a request by the Prime Minister for more time to consult with his party. On the same day, the President announced, in a message broadcast to the nation, his intention to resign on 23 June if the Prime Minister did not accept responsibility for the crisis and resign. However, on 22 June, the Fretilin Central Committee reaffirmed its support for Prime Minister Alkatiri. In response, Mr. Ramos-Horta and a number of other ministers and officials announced their resignations on 25 and 26 June. On 26 June, the Prime Minister announced he was ready to resign so as to avoid the resignation of the President. Later that day, the Office of the President stated that the President had received the Prime Minister's letter of resignation.

A stand-off between the President and Fretilin over the appointment of a new Prime Minister and the formation of a new government brought further insecurity. Several thousand demonstrators, mostly from western districts, had come into Dili to call for the Prime Minister's resignation. Meanwhile, several thousand ruling party supporters, mostly from eastern districts, gathered just outside the capital in support of their party. Mr. Alkatiri addressed the party supporters outside Dili, and the television broadcast of part of his address sparked several hours of street protests and house burning in the city. The international forces were able to calm the situation. The anti-Alkatiri demonstrators returned to their districts, and the pro-Alkatiri demonstrators went to Dili, where discipline was maintained and further violence avoided, owing to their leaders' actions and to a major operation by the international forces.

Following discussions with President Gusmão, the ruling party agreed to discuss the objectives of a transitional government, as proposed by the President, together with possible candidates for Prime Minister and two Deputy Prime Ministers, before making any formal proposal. On 8 July, after consultations with all parties, President Gusmão announced that Mr. Ramos-Horta would be the new Prime Minister. On 10 July, he was sworn in by the President, together with two Deputy Prime Ministers. The new Council of Ministers was announced on 14 July. Most of its members were reappointed to their previous portfolios and two ruling party "reformers" entered the cabinet for the first time. In his inaugural address on 10 July and in other public statements, Prime Minister Ramos-Horta sought to embrace constituencies, such as the Church and civil society, which often felt excluded by the previous Government, and pledged to focus on the needs of youth and resistance veterans.

The crisis had led to the displacement of about two thirds of Dili's inhabitants. As of mid-July, 72,000 internally displaced persons were receiving food aid in 62 makeshift camps scattered throughout Dili, and up to 80,000 people had fled to the countryside. An inter-agency flash appeal for $19.6 million was issued on 12 June to ensure that resources were available for essential humanitarian needs until mid-September.

Timor-Leste and Indonesia continued to maintain cordial relations. Indonesia closed the borders in late May at the height of the violence. On 17 June, President Yudhoyono and President Gusmão met in Bali, Indonesia, to discuss the situation in Timor-Leste. Following that meeting, two crossing points on the border were reopened to allow Indonesians and other non-Timorese with Indonesian visas to enter West Timor. On 13 July, Indonesia reopened its borders with Timor-Leste.

Security Council consideration (August). Briefing the Security Council on 15 August [meeting 5512], the Secretary-General's Special Envoy for Timor-Leste said the Council was asked to mandate a large mission after downsizing former missions. That might be seen as a reversal, but Timor-Leste was a sovereign State, which had struggled hard for its independence. Its second constitutional Government represented a political compromise, forged to manage the most serious crisis faced by the State and to steer the country towards its first post-independence elections. International support had achieved much. The Secretary-General's proposals would establish a more coordinated partnership between Timor-Leste and the international community. The mission should play key roles in the governance of the security sector, administration of justice and the functioning of democratic institutions. The central failure revealed by the crisis had been in the security sector and reforming the police sector was a core task. However, the wider issue was a fundamental review of the whole security sector to clarify the roles of the defence force and the police in relation to each other. The challenge to the justice system as it confronted serious crimes was greater than ever, and the protection of human rights needed strengthening. The twin challenges faced by the Government, aided by the Church and civil society, were dialogue across political divisions and community reconciliation, in particular between east and west. The new mission should be ready to support that process.

SECURITY COUNCIL ACTION

On 18 August [meeting 5514], the Security Council unanimously adopted **resolution 1703(2006)**. The draft [S/2006/660] was prepared in consultations among Council members.

The Security Council,

Reaffirming its previous resolutions on the situation in Timor-Leste, in particular resolutions 1599(2005) of 28 April 2005, 1677(2006) of 12 May 2006 and 1690(2006) of 20 June 2006,

Taking note of the report of the Secretary-General of 8 August 2006 and his report of 26 July 2006 on justice and reconciliation for Timor-Leste,

Taking note also of the letters dated 4 August and 9 August 2006 from the Prime Minister of Timor-Leste to the Secretary-General,

1. *Decides* to extend the mandate of the United Nations Office in Timor-Leste until 25 August 2006;
2. *Decides also* to remain actively seized of the matter.

Assessment mission

Further to the 11 June request from Timor-Leste's President, Prime Minister and President of Parliament (see p. 418) for the immediate establishment of a UN police force in Timor-Leste, the Secretary-General asked his Special Envoy to lead a multidisciplinary assessment mission to Timor-Leste, in order to develop recommendations on the future UN presence, as requested by the Council in resolution 1690(2006) (see p. 419).

The assessment mission recommended a number of key principles for a new UN mission. First, the development of institutions in a new State required not only skilled personnel, but also the establishment of institutional systems, standards, norms and values based on democratic principles. The commitment by the international community to assist the country should be a long-term one, and extend beyond the lifetime of a new mission, sustained by UNDP and other UN agencies, funds and programmes and development partners. Second, a new mission should recognize the success so far achieved in developing many aspects of governance in Timor-Leste, making a comprehensive UN involvement in those areas unnecessary. Third, a transfer of responsibility from UNOTIL to UN agencies, funds and programmes and development partners was in progress and should not be reversed. Most importantly, the underlying causes of the crisis necessitated an increased focus on economic and social development, reaching the marginalized and disenfranchised populations in the rural districts.

On that basis, the assessment mission made recommendations on the new UN mission's priorities in the areas of good offices and reconciliation, electoral support, security sector support, promotion of human rights and justice, institutional capacity-building, governance and development, humanitarian support, gender, and public information. The Secretary-General recommended the establishment of such a mission, with the mandate to support the Government in its efforts to consolidate political stability and enhance democratic governance; bring about national reconciliation; support the 2007 electoral process; ensure, through the presence of UN police, the restoration and maintenance of security; assist in liaising with the Indonesian military; and assist in strengthening the national human rights capacity.

Communications. On 14 August [S/2006/651], Prime Minister Ramos-Horta, noting that the recent incidents had left the country with a dysfunctional police force, agreed with the Secretary-General's proposal that the UN police in the new mission would have exclusive police authority. On 16 August [S/2006/668], Prime Minister Ramos-Horta requested the United Nations to observe and verify the election process, including the legislative and presidential elections scheduled for April and May 2007.

Establishment of UN Integrated Mission in Timor-Leste

On 25 August [meeting 5516], the Security Council unanimously adopted **resolution 1704(2006)**. The draft [S/2006/686] was submitted by Japan.

The Security Council,

Reaffirming its previous resolutions on the situation in Timor-Leste, in particular resolutions 1599(2005) of 28 April 2005, 1677(2006) of 12 May 2006, 1690(2006) of 20 June 2006 and 1703(2006) of 18 August 2006,

Welcoming the report of the Secretary-General of 8 August 2006,

Commending the people and the Government of Timor-Leste for their action to resolve their political conflicts and the creation of the new Government, and expressing its concern over the still fragile security, political and humanitarian situation in Timor-Leste, in the light of the threat of weapons unaccounted for and the significant number of internally displaced persons,

Taking note of the letters dated 4 August, 9 August and 11 August 2006 from the Prime Minister of Timor-Leste to the Secretary-General,

Reaffirming its full commitment to the sovereignty, independence, territorial integrity and national unity of Timor-Leste and to the promotion of long-lasting stability in Timor-Leste,

Expressing its appreciation and full support for the deployment of international security forces by the Governments of Portugal, Australia, New Zealand and Malaysia in response to the requests of the Government of Timor-Leste, and their activities aimed at restoring and maintaining security in Timor-Leste,

Welcoming the establishment and initiation of the tasks of the Independent Special Commission of Inquiry for Timor-Leste in response to the request made by the Government of Timor-Leste in the letter dated 8 June 2006, and looking forward to its report by 7 October 2006,

Expressing its view that the presidential and parliamentary elections scheduled for 2007, to be held for the first time since the country's independence, will be a significant step forward in the process of strengthening the fragile democracy of Timor-Leste,

Reaffirming the need for credible accountability for the serious human rights violations committed in East Timor in 1999, and welcoming the report of the Secretary-General of 26 July 2006 on justice and reconciliation for Timor-Leste,

Further commending the United Nations Office in Timor-Leste, under the leadership of the Special Representative of the Secretary-General for Timor-Leste, as well as the good offices and assessment work of the Special Envoy of the Secretary-General for Timor-Leste, and expressing its appreciation to those Member States which have provided support to the Office,

Taking into account that, while the manifestations of the current crisis in Timor-Leste are political and institutional, poverty and its associated deprivations, including high urban unemployment, especially for youth, also contributed to the crisis,

Paying tribute to Timor-Leste's bilateral and multilateral partners for their invaluable assistance, particularly with regard to institutional capacity-building and social and economic development, recognizing that there has been a considerable degree of success in the development of many aspects of governance in Timor-Leste, and expressing its view that a transfer of responsibility for various areas of support from the Office to the United Nations agencies, funds and programmes and other development partners should not be reversed,

Reaffirming its resolution 1325(2000) of 31 October 2000 on women and peace and security and its resolution 1502(2003) of 26 August 2003 on the protection of humanitarian and United Nations personnel,

Welcoming the efforts of the United Nations to sensitize United Nations personnel in the prevention and control of HIV/AIDS and other communicable diseases in all its established operations,

Noting the existence of challenges to the short- and long-term security and stability of an independent Timor-Leste, and determining that preserving the country's stability is necessary for the maintenance of peace and security in the region,

1. *Decides* to establish a follow-on mission in Timor-Leste, the United Nations Integrated Mission in Timor-Leste, for an initial period of six months, with the intention to renew for further periods, and further decides that the Mission shall consist of an appropriate civilian component, including up to 1,608 police personnel, and an initial component of up to 34 military liaison and staff officers;

2. *Requests* the Secretary-General to review the arrangements to be established between the Mission and the international security forces, having consulted all stakeholders, including the Government of Timor-Leste and the contributors to the international security forces, and present his views no later than 25 October 2006, and affirms that the Security Council shall consider possible adjustments in the Mission structure, including the nature and size of the military component, taking into account the above views of the Secretary-General;

3. *Decides* that the Mission shall be headed by a Special Representative of the Secretary-General for Timor-Leste, who shall direct the operations of the Mission and coordinate all United Nations activities in Timor-Leste;

4. *Decides also* that the Mission shall have the following mandate:

(a) To support the Government of Timor-Leste and relevant institutions with a view to consolidating stability, enhancing a culture of democratic governance and facilitating political dialogue among Timorese stakeholders in their efforts to bring about a process of national reconciliation and to foster social cohesion;

(b) To support Timor-Leste in all aspects of the 2007 presidential and parliamentary electoral process, including through technical and logistical support, electoral policy advice and verification or other means;

(c) To ensure, through the presence of United Nations police, the restoration and maintenance of public security in Timor-Leste through the provision of support to the Timorese national police, as outlined in the report of the Secretary-General, which includes interim law enforcement and public security until the national police is reconstituted, and to assist with the further training, institutional development and strengthening of the national police as well as the Ministry of the Interior, and also assist in the planning and preparation of electoral-related security arrangements to adequately prepare the national police for performing its roles and responsibilities during the conduct of the 2007 elections;

(d) To support the Government of Timor-Leste to liaise on security tasks and to establish a continuous presence in the three border districts alongside armed United Nations police officers assigned to district police stations, through the impartial presence of United Nations military liaison officers;

(e) To assist the Government of Timor-Leste in conducting a comprehensive review of the future role and needs of the security sector, including the Falintil-Forças Armadas de Defesa de Timor-Leste, the Ministry of Defence, the Timorese national police and the Ministry of the Interior, with a view to supporting the Government, through the provision of advisers and in cooperation and coordination with other partners, in strengthening institutional capacity-building, as appropriate;

(f) To assist, in cooperation and coordination with other partners, in further building the capacity of State and Government institutions in areas where specialized expertise is required, such as in the justice sector, and to promote a 'compact' between Timor-Leste and the international community for coordinating Government, United Nations and other multilateral and bilateral contributors to priority programmes;

(g) To assist in further strengthening the national institutional and societal capacity and mechanisms for monitoring, promoting and protecting human rights and for promoting justice and reconciliation, including for women and children, and to observe and report on the humanrights situation;

(h) To facilitate the provision of relief and recovery assistance and access to the Timorese people in need, with a particular focus on the segment of society in the most vulnerable situatin, including internally displaced persons and women and children;

(i) To assist in the implementation of the relevant recommendations contained in the report of the Secretary-General on justice and reconciliation for Timor-Leste, including to assist the Office of the Prosecutor-General of Timor-Leste, through the provision of a team of experinced investigative personnel, to resume investigative functions of the former Serious Crimes Unit, with a view to completing investigations into outstanding cases of serious human rights violations committed in the country in 1999;

(j) To cooperate and coordinate with United Nations agencies, funds and programmes as well as all relevant partners, including the international financial institutions and donors, in carrying out tasks mentioned above as relevant, with a view to making maximum use of existing and forthcoming bilateral and multilateral assistance to Timor-Leste in post-conflict peacebuilding and capacity-building, and to support the Government and relevant institutions, in cooperation and coordination with other partners, in designing poverty reduction and economic growth policies and strategies to achieve the development plan of Timor-Leste;

(k) To mainstream gender perspectives and those of children and youth throughout the policies, programmes and activities of the Mission, and, working together with United Nations agencies, funds and programmes, support the development of a national strategy to promote gender equality and the empowerment of women;

(l) To provide objective and accurate information to the Timorese people, particularly regarding the forthcoming 2007 elections, while promoting an understanding of the work of the Mission, and to assist in building local media capacity;

(m) To ensure, within its capability and areas of deployment, and in coordination with the international security forces, the security and freedom of movement of United Nations and associated personnel, and protect United Nations personnel, facilities, installations and equipment and humanitarian assets associated with the operation; and

(n) To monitor and review progress in *(a)* to *(m)* above;

5. *Calls upon* the international security forces to fully cooperate with and provide assistance to the Mission for the implementation of the mandate mentioned above;

6. *Requests* that the Secretary-General and the Government of Timor-Leste conclude a status-of-forces

agreement within thirty days of the adoption of the present resolution, taking into consideration General Assembly resolution 60/123 of 15 December 2005 on the safety and security of humanitarian personnel and protection of United Nations personnel, and decides that, pending the conclusion of such agreement, the agreement between the Government of Timor-Leste and the United Nations concerning the status of the United Nations Mission of Support in East Timor of 20 May 2002 shall apply provisionally, mutatis mutandis, in respect of the United Nations Integrated Mission in Timor-Leste;

7. *Calls upon* all parties in Timor-Leste to cooperate fully in the deployment and operations of the Mission and the international security forces, in particular in ensuring the safety, security and freedom of movement of United Nations personnel as well as associated personnel throughout Timor-Leste;

8. *Encourages* the Government of Timor-Leste and the Office of the President to create a mechanism to ensure high-level coordination on all matters related to the mandate of the Mission;

9. *Further encourages* Timor-Leste to enact a set of electoral legislation which provides for the 2007 elections to be supervised, organized, administered and conducted in a free, fair and transparent manner, with due respect for the need to establish an independent mechanism, and reflects general consensus within Timor-Leste regarding the appropriate modalities for the 2007 electoral process;

10. *Urges* the development partners, including the United Nations agencies and multilateral financial institutions, to continue providing resources and assistance for the preparations for the 2007 elections and other projects towards sustainable and long-term development in Timor-Leste;

11. *Takes note* of the findings contained in the report of the Commission of Experts transmitted on 15 July 2005, welcomes the efforts so far by Indonesia and Timor-Leste in pursuance of truth and friendship, encourages the two Governments and the Commissioners to make every effort to strengthen the efficiency and credibility of the Commission of Truth and Friendship in order to ensure further conformity with human rights principles, with a view to ensuring credible accountability, and welcomes the proposal of the Secretary-General to create a programme of international assistance to Timor-Leste, consisting of a community restoration programme and a justice programme, including the establishment of a solidarity fund by the United Nations to accept voluntary contributions from Member States for the purpose of funding those programmes;

12. *Requests* the Secretary-General to keep the Council closely and regularly informed of developments on the ground, including, in particular, the state of preparations for the 2007 elections and of the implementation of the mandate of the Mission, and to submit a report no later than 1 February 2007, with recommendations for any modifications such progress might allow to the size, composition, mandate and duration of the Mission presence;

13. *Also requests* the Secretary-General to take the necessary measures to achieve actual compliance in the Mission with the United Nations zero-tolerance policy on sexual exploitation and abuse, including the development of strategies and appropriate mechanisms to prevent, identify and respond to all forms of misconduct, including sexual exploitation and abuse, and the enhancement of training for personnel to prevent misconduct and ensure full compliance with the United Nations code of conduct, requests the Secretary-General to take all necessary action in accordance with the Secretary-General's bulletin on special measures for protection from sexual exploitation and sexual abuse and to keep the Council informed, and urges troop-contributing countries to take appropriate preventive action, including conducting pre-deployment awareness training, and to take disciplinary action and other action to ensure full accountability in cases of such conduct involving their personnel;

14. *Decides* to remain actively seized of the matter.

On 30 October [S/2006/923], the Secretary-General informed the Council President of his intention to appoint Mr. Atul Khare (India) as his Special Representative for Timor-Leste and Head of UNMIT. On 29 November [S/2006/924], Council members took note of his intention.

Independent Special Commission

The Secretary-General, on 17 October [S/2006/822], transmitted to the Council President the report of the Independent Special Commission of Inquiry for Timor-Leste, which he had received from the United Nations High Commissioner for Human Rights.

The Commission, headed by Paulo Sérgio Pinheiro (Brazil), was to establish the facts and circumstances relevant to incidents that took place on 28 and 29 April and 23, 24 and 25 May and related events or issues that contributed to the crisis, clarify responsibility and recommend measures of accountability for alleged crimes and serious human rights violations. After interviewing more than 200 witnesses and considering some 2,000 documents, during its visits to Timor-Leste from 4 to 11 August and 4 to 15 September, the Commission established a detailed and accurate narrative of the events, and determined the responsibility of various actors and institutions.

The Commission's mandate included establishing individual criminal responsibility, but the Commission was neither a tribunal nor a prosecuting authority, and made no conclusions about the guilt beyond reasonable doubt of specific persons. Rather, it identified individuals suspected of participation in serious criminal activity and recommended that they be prosecuted, including persons holding public office and senior security officials. The Commission also identified others with respect to whom further investigation might lead to criminal prosecution.

The Commission recommended measures of accountability to be accomplished through the judicial system. That system should be reinforced, as it was vital to Timor-Leste that justice be done and seen to be done. A culture of impunity would threaten the foundations of the State. If peace and democracy were to be advanced, justice should be effective and visible. That would require a substantial and long-term effort by the Government and its international partners.

The Commission concluded that the events were the expression of deep-rooted problems inherent in fragile State institutions and a weak rule of law. The events exposed many deficiencies and failures, particularly in the two institutions at the centre of the crisis, the armed forces and the police, along with the Defence Ministry and the Interior Ministry charged with their oversight. The absence of comprehensive regulatory frameworks and the bypassing of institutional mechanisms greatly contributed to the crisis. The report's conclusions, findings and recommendations should be viewed as the foundation for strengthening State institutions and the rule of law.

Among other things, the Commission found that the Government was insufficiently proactive in addressing the lack of a national security policy and problems evident within and between the armed forces and the police; and had failed to follow the legislative procedures in calling out the armed forces on 28 April, a matter for which those members of the Crisis Cabinet who made the decision, and in particular the former Prime Minister, bore responsibility.

The armed forces were ill prepared to provide military assistance to the civil power, a matter for which responsibility rested with the Defence Minister and the Chief of the Defence Force. The planning and response to the violence by the police were deficient, a matter for which the police General Commander and the Interior Minister bore responsibility. No massacre of 60 people occurred on 28 and 29 April. The abandonment of post on 24 May by the police General Commander was a serious dereliction of duty, and the Interior Minister failed to respond to the breakdown in the police's chain of command. The Chief of the Defence Force could not be held criminally responsible for the 25 May shooting of police officers by armed forces soldiers, but he failed to exhaust all avenues to either prevent or stop the confrontation.

There was an absence of systematic control over weapons and ammunition within the security sector, particularly within the police. The Interior Minister and the General Commander bypassed procedures by irregularly transferring weapons within the institution. Police and armed forces weapons were distributed to civilians. In arming civilians, the Interior Minister, the Defence Minister and the Chief of Defence acted without lawful authority and created a potentially dangerous situation. The former Prime Minister failed to denounce the transfer of weapons in the face of credible information that such transfer was ongoing and involved Government members. The President's 23 March speech was perceived as divisive. Finally, certain individuals were criminally responsible for the incidents of violence.

The Commission issued 21 recommendations, including prosecuting numerous persons suspected of participation in criminal activity; further investigating those persons involved in the events and acts of violence for which the Commission could not identify those responsible; subjecting State officials to disciplinary procedures and administrative sanctions; establishing robust and independent police and military oversight; handling criminal cases related to the events within the district court system; and having at least one international judge participate in the proceedings. A senior international prosecutor should be appointed Deputy Prosecutor General to investigate and prosecute impartially and without political interference. International legal actors should take the lead in investigations and prosecutions, supported by national prosecutors.

The Government should provide reparations for those who suffered as a result of the events, especially those who suffered the death of a family member, significant injury and the destruction of their residences. Those institutions bearing responsibility for the events should acknowledge publicly their responsibility.

Communications. In a 19 October letter [S/2006/831] to the Secretary-General, Prime Minister Ramos-Horta noted that resolution 1704(2006) (see p. 422) requested the Secretary-General to review by 25 October, in consultation with Timor-Leste, the arrangements between UNMIT and the international security forces. Mr. Ramos-Horta said that the multinational security forces (known as Joint Task Force 631) had quickly quelled the violence and stabilized the situation, and continued to do so in an exemplary manner. That had enabled the Timorese leadership to focus on nation-building priorities, such as service provision, especially to the poor; assistance to internally displaced persons; and institution-building. It also enabled the 700-strong UN police to carry out policing functions, while working with Timorese institutions and authorities to reconstitute the national police. The arrangement by which the UN police undertook the State function of law and order and the international forces provided security was working well. Australia, which provided some 1,000 troops, had advised that it was willing to stay at least until the 2007 elections and beyond. Other States had indicated that they would consider deploying troops as part of a regional multinational security force. It was the wish of all State institutions, including the President, for that arrangement to continue, with the approval of the Security Council.

On 26 October [S/2006/849], Australia informed the Council President of the assistance the international security force it was leading provided to UNMIT. On 31 December [S/2006/1022], President Gusmão told the Secretary-General that, with elections planned for early 2007, he was concerned with the unstable security conditions that still affected parts of the country. He therefore wanted to see the UN police reinforced by a further integrated police unit from Portugal.

Later developments

In a later report on UNMIT [S/2007/50], the Secretary-General said that the grievances of the dismissed F-FDTL "Petitioners", which triggered the April-May security and political crisis were yet to be resolved. Most of the 594 dismissed soldiers remained in their home villages, mostly in the western region, while the Government continued to extend the financial subsidy programme for individual soldiers. A "Commission of Notables", established in May to address the petitioners' allegations, continued to examine the issue. In addition, the armed group led by fugitive F-FDTL Military Police Commander, Major Alfredo Reinado, who escaped from Becora Prison with 56 others on 30 August, continued to be a cause of concern. The F-FDTL Command, on behalf of the Government, initiated a dialogue with Major Reinado on 21 December, to bring about the cantonment of his armed group.

UNMIT police continued to restore and maintain public order, particularly in Dili. While the overall security situation remained volatile, the trend was towards increasingly longer periods of calm and fewer outbreaks of violence, due, in part, to the increased presence of UNMIT police officers in communities. Civil disturbance incidents in Dili decreased from an average of 20 to 30 daily in September and October, to between 10 and 15 from November to the end of the year. The signing of the "Arrangement on the Restoration and Maintenance of Public Safety in Timor-Leste and Assistance to the Reform, Restructuring and Rebuilding of the Timorese National Police (PNTL) and the Ministry of Interior" between the Government and UNMIT on 1 December clarified the roles and responsibilities of UNMIT police and its relationship with PNTL and the Ministry of the Interior. Under that agreement, a comprehensive assessment of PNTL commenced as a basis for developing a reform, restructuring and rebuilding plan. Also, in view of the volatile security situation, UNMIT drafted a security plan to ensure the necessary security coverage throughout the country from the election period through the immediate post-election period. The Secretary-General supported the President's 31 December request (see above) for a reinforcement of the UNMIT police deployment by a unit from Portugal to help address the security challenges during that period.

Following the findings of the Independent Special Commission of Inquiry (see p. 424) that an alleged massacre by F-FDTL did not take place during the events of April/May, the Government, on 11 November, informed UNMIT and the international security forces of its intention to normalize F-FDTL operations, and was devising a plan for doing so. The Government, with UNMIT support, initiated a comprehensive review of the entire security sector through a joint working group on security sector reform, the first meeting of which took place on 18 December.

As a result of the political impasse in the aftermath of the crisis in April/May, steps were taken by the national leadership and other actors towards national dialogue and political reconciliation. Following the issuance of the report of the Independent Special Commission of Inquiry, the Parliament established, on 8 November, a seven-member ad hoc parliamentary commission to study it. Their findings were submitted on 12 December. Also in November, under the auspices of President Gusmão's Dialogue Commission, mid-level political dialogue events, primarily involving political parties and civil society, took place, followed by a high-level political dialogue, with the participation of top state officials, political party leaders and the commanders of the Timorese armed forces and the national police. The long-awaited public meeting between President Gusmão and former Prime Minister Alkatiri on 8 December, the first since the latter's resignation, was a promising development towards restitution of a cooperative relationship in promoting national objectives.

On 10 December, a traditional peace ceremony publicly brought together the national leadership, including President Gusmão, Prime Minister Ramos-Horta, President of Parliament Francisco

"Lu-Olo" Guterres and former Prime Minister Alkatiri. It included a public acknowledgement of collective responsibility for the crisis by President Gusmão on behalf of the organs of state sovereignty. Similar statements of apology were made by the Commander of the Timorese armed forces and the former General Commander of the Timorese national police on behalf of their respective national security institutions. Concurrent with those high-level activities, community-level dialogue progressed under the Government-led "Simu-Malu" ("to receive each other") programme and the President's Dialogue Commission. The community-based activities, which were principally held in Dili, were aimed at facilitating the reintegration of internally displaced persons and addressing the societal fragmentation that followed the east-west violence and inter-gang fighting in various neighbourhoods, particularly around the internally displaced persons' camps. Those activities, which were supported by UNMIT and UN agencies, contributed to the reduction in violent incidents between sections of some internally displaced persons' camps and surrounding neighbourhood gangs. On 1 December, the Council of Ministers approved measures for assistance and repatriation to victims of the crisis. Meanwhile, the trial of the former Minister of the Interior, Rogerio Lobato, charged with embezzlement, unlawful use of weapons, and manslaughter, commenced on 30 November, but was adjourned because of the absence of one of the co-defendants. On 29 November, the Prosecutor-General requested UN assistance in recruiting an international prosecutor as Deputy Prosecutor.

Progress continued towards establishing the legal and regulatory framework for the elections. The Laws on the National Commission on Elections , as well as on the Parliamentary and Presidential Elections, were adopted by the Parliament and entered into force on 29 December.

Justice and reconciliation

On 26 July, the Secretary-General submitted to the Security Council a report [S/2006/580] on justice and reconciliation for Timor-Leste. That was in response to a 2005 request of the Council [YUN 2005, p. 444], which, before further considering the report of the Commission of Experts [ibid., p. 443] on the prosecution of human rights violations committed during the events of 1999, had requested of the Secretary-General a report on justice and reconciliation, taking into account the report of the Commission of Experts and the views of Indonesia and Timor-Leste.

The Secretary-General observed that, since the events of 1999 [YUN 1999, p. 288], a great deal of effort had been made by the United Nations to review progress towards justice and reconciliation for Timor-Leste, including the establishment of the Commission of Experts. The Commission of Truth and Friendship, jointly established by Indonesia and Timor-Leste, was a unique vehicle for advancing bilateral relations between them, which he hoped would succeed in revealing the truth about the 1999 events. The looting and vandalism that occurred from 29 to 30 May and 5 June of that year, had caused serious concern that they might have resulted in the loss of vital records relating to justice and reconciliation and carried security implications for victims, witnesses and suspects alike. The closure of the serious crimes process pursuant to Security Council resolution 1543(2004) left a number of issues unresolved, including the question of how to address the more than 300 arrest warrants that were still outstanding; and how to address the hundreds of indicted persons residing in Indonesia, among others.

The Secretary-General concluded that the pursuit of justice and reconciliation was a process that evolved over time, but the challenges were more complex for Timor-Leste, given that the process was both national and bilateral. While he was encouraged by the efforts of Timor-Leste and Indonesia to seek the truth and achieve reconciliation, they also had a responsibility to ensure accountability and end impunity. The international community had a responsibility to uphold the universal principles of human rights on which a credible process of justice and reconciliation had to rest.

Therefore, for a practically feasible approach to justice and reconciliation, he recommended that the Council, pending any further consideration of the report of the Commission of Experts, should endorse the Commission's findings, welcome the efforts of Indonesia and Timor-Leste to make the joint Commission on Truth and Friendship work, and encourage them and the Commissioners to strengthen its efficiency and credibility, including through a review of the amnesty clause, to ensure conformity with international standards and principles. The two Governments should also strengthen the capacity of their judicial systems, in particular as regards the prosecution of serious human rights violations committed in East Timor in 1999.

The Council should endorse the creation by the United Nations of an international assistance programme for Timor-Leste, consisting of: a United Nations solidarity fund for a community restoration programme and a justice programme, funded by voluntary contributions; a community restoration programme to support the Timorese people and to provide collective restorative measures to victims and their immediate relatives, including the provision of qualified teachers, school equipment and health, social and psychological services; individual restorative measures to assist the most vulnerable victims and families of victims of the most serious human rights violations; and reconciliatory measures, including public acknowledgment of the crimes, the location of the remains of victims, the restoration of cemeteries and the construction of memorials to victims and veterans.

The Council should also create a justice programme, which would include the establishment, within the Office of the Prosecutor General, of an experienced investigative team, led by an international serious-crimes investigator, to complete the investigations into serious crimes committed in 1999; and international assistance to Timor-Leste's justice and the rule of law sector in order to strengthen its capacity to prosecute those crimes.

Financing of UN operations

In 2006, the General Assembly considered the financing of four UN missions in Timor-Leste—the United Nations Mission of Support in East Timor (UNMISET), the United Nations Office in Timor-Leste (UNOTIL), the United Nations Integrated Mission in Timor-Leste (UNMIT) and the United Nations Mission in East Timor (UNAMET). UNMISET was established by Council resolution 1410(2002) [YUN 2002, p. 321] to assist the administrative, law enforcement and public security critical to Timor-Leste's viability and political stability. UNOTIL was established by Council resolution 1599(2005) [YUN 2005, p. 440] to support and monitor progress in developing critical State institutions and observance of democratic governance and human rights. UNMIT was established by Council resolution 1704(2006) (see p. 422) to support the Government in consolidating stability, enhancing a culture of democratic governance and facilitating political dialogue; support the country in all aspects of the 2007 presidential and parliamentary elections; ensure the maintenance of public security; assist the Government in reviewing the role and needs of the security sector; strengthen capacity for promoting human rights, justice and reconciliation; and assist in implementing the Secretary-General's recommendations on justice and reconciliation. UNAMET was established by Council resolution 1246(1999) [YUN 1999, p. 283] to conduct the 1999 popular consultations on East Timor's autonomy [ibid., p. 288]; its mandate ended on 30 November, 1999, in accordance with resolution 1262(1999) [ibid., p. 287].

UNMISET

On 30 June [meeting 92], the General Assembly considered the UNMISET performance report for the period 1 July 2004 to 30 June 2005 [A/60/614], the report on the final disposition of UNMISET assets [A/60/703] and the related ACABQ report [A/60/789]. The Assembly, on the recommendation of the Fifth Committee [A/60/919], adopted **resolution 60/271** without vote [agenda item 142].

Financing of the United Nations Mission of Support in East Timor

The General Assembly,

Having considered the reports of the Secretary-General on the financing of the United Nations Mission of Support in East Timor, and the related report of the Advisory Committee on Administrative and Budgetary Questions,

Recalling Security Council resolution 1272(1999) of 25 October 1999 regarding the establishment of the United Nations Transitional Administration in East Timor and the subsequent resolutions by which the Council extended the mandate of the Transitional Administration, the last of which was resolution 1392(2002) of 31 January 2002, by which the mandate was extended until 20 May 2002,

Recalling also Security Council resolution 1410(2002) of 17 May 2002, by which the Council established the United Nations Mission of Support in East Timor as of 20 May 2002 for an initial period of twelve months, and the subsequent resolutions by which the Council extended the mandate of the Mission, the last of which was resolution 1573(2004) of 16 November 2004, by which the Council extended the mandate of the Mission for a final period of six months until 20 May 2005,

Recalling further its resolution 54/246 A of 23 December 1999 on the financing of the United Nations Transitional Administration in East Timor and its subsequent resolutions on the financing of the United Nations Mission of Support in East Timor, the latest of which was resolution 59/13 B of 22 June 2005,

Reaffirming the general principles underlying the financing of United Nations peacekeeping operations, as stated in General Assembly resolutions 1874(S-IV) of 27 June 1963, 3101(XXVIII) of 11 December 1973 and 55/235 of 23 December 2000,

Noting with appreciation that voluntary contributions have been made to the Mission and to the Trust Fund for the United Nations Transitional Administration in East Timor,

1. *Takes note* of the status of contributions to the United Nations Transitional Administration in East Timor and the United Nations Mission of Support in East Timor as at 30 April 2006, including the contribu-

tions outstanding in the amount of 36.1 million United States dollars, representing some 2 per cent of the total assessed contributions, notes with concern that only one hundred and five Member States have paid their assessed contributions in full, and urges all other Member States, in particular those in arrears, to ensure payment of their outstanding assessed contributions;

2. *Expresses its appreciation* to those Member States that have paid their assessed contributions in full, and urges all other Member States to make every possible effort to ensure payment of their assessed contributions to the Transitional Administration and the Mission in full;

3. *Endorses* the conclusions and recommendations contained in the report of the Advisory Committee on Administrative and Budgetary Questions;

Financial performance report for the period from 1 July 2004 to 30 June 2005

4. *Takes note* of the report of the Secretary-General on the financial performance of the Mission for the period from 1 July 2004 to 30 June 2005;

5. *Decides* that Member States that have fulfilled their financial obligations to the Mission shall be credited with their respective share of the unencumbered balance and other income in the total amount of 16,775,900 dollars in respect of the financial period ended 30 June 2005, in accordance with the levels updated in its resolution 58/256 of 23 December 2003, and taking into account the scale of assessments for 2005, as set out in its resolution 58/1 B of 23 December 2003;

6. *Decides also* that, for Member States that have not fulfilled their financial obligations to the Mission, their share of the unencumbered balance and other income in the total amount of 16,775,900 dollars in respect of the financial period ended 30 June 2005 shall be set off against their outstanding obligations in accordance with the scheme set out in paragraph 5 above;

7. *Decides further* that the decrease of 408,700 dollars in the estimated staff assessment income in respect of the financial period ended 30 June 2005 shall be set off against the credits from the amount of 16,775,900 dollars referred to in paragraphs 5 and 6 above;

8. *Encourages* Member States that are owed credits for the closed peacekeeping mission accounts to apply those credits to any accounts where the Member State concerned has outstanding assessed contributions;

Final disposition of the assets of the United Nations Mission of Support in East Timor

9. *Takes note* of the report of the Secretary-General on the final disposition of the assets of the Mission;

10. *Decides* to include in the provisional agenda of its sixty-first session the item entitled "Financing of the United Nations Mission of Support in East Timor".

In December [A/61/670], the Secretary-General submitted to the General Assembly UNMISET performance report for the period from 1 July 2005 to 30 June 2006.

On 22 December, the Assembly decided that the item on the financing of UNMISET would remain for consideration during the sixty-first (2007) session (**decision 61/552**).

UNOTIL

In June [A/60/585/Add.4], the Secretary-General, in his report on estimates in respect of special political missions, good offices and other political initiatives authorized by the General Assembly and/or the Security Council, proposed resource requirements for UNOTIL for the period from 21 June to 31 August 2006, estimated at $5,253,500 ($5,776,200 gross). ACABQ endorsed [A/60/7/Add.41] the amount proposed by the Secretary-General.

On 30 June, by **resolution 60/281** (see p. 1621), the Assembly approved a budget of $5,253,500 ($5,776,200 gross).

UNMIT

In August [A/61/231], the Secretary-General requested that the General Assembly include in the agenda of its sixty-first session an additional item "Financing of the United Nations Integrated Mission in Timor-Leste".

In October [A/61/519], he submitted to the Assembly a report on UNMIT financing from 25 August 2006 to 31 March 2007. Pending the submission of a full budget for UNMIT to the Assembly's resumed sixty-first (2007) session, the Secretary-General requested authority to enter into commitments for the Mission for the period 25 August 2006 to 31 March 2007 in the amount of $172,528,600, inclusive of the amount of $49,961,500 previously authorized by ACABQ.

In November [A/61/567], ACABQ recommended a reduction of commitments for establishing and maintaining the Mission for the period indicated to $170,221,100, inclusive of the amount of $49,961,500 previously authorized by the Committee.

In a 15 November letter to the Assembly President [A/61/598], the Secretary-General reported on the extraordinary measures he had authorized to enable the Secretariat to implement effectively Security Council resolution 1704(2006) (see p. 422). He said that approval of the initial financing request would permit the formulation of more detailed budgetary proposals for consideration at its resumed sixty-first (2007) session.

GENERAL ASSEMBLY ACTION

On 22 December [meeting 84], the General Assembly, on the recommendation of the Fifth Committee [A/61/644], adopted **resolution 61/249** without vote [agenda item 151].

Financing of the United Nations Integrated Mission in Timor-Leste

The General Assembly,

Having considered the report of the Secretary-General on the financing of the United Nations Integrated Mission in Timor-Leste and the related report of the Advisory Committee on Administrative and Budgetary Questions,

Recalling Security Council resolution 1704(2006) of 25 August 2006, by which the Council decided to establish a follow-on mission in Timor-Leste, the United Nations Integrated Mission in Timor-Leste, for an initial period of six months, with the intention to renew it for further periods,

Recognizing that the costs of the Mission are expenses of the Organization to be borne by Member States in accordance with Article 17, paragraph 2, of the Charter of the United Nations,

Reaffirming the general principles underlying the financing of United Nations peacekeeping operations, as stated in General Assembly resolutions 1874(S-IV) of 27 June 1963, 3101(XXVIII) of 11 December 1973 and 55/235 of 23 December 2000,

Mindful of the fact that it is essential to provide the Mission with the financial resources necessary to enable it to fulfil its responsibilities under the relevant resolution of the Security Council,

1. *Requests* the Secretary-General to entrust the Head of Mission with the task of formulating future budget proposals in full accordance with the provisions of General Assembly resolutions 59/296 of 22 June 2005 and 60/266 of 30 June 2006, as well as other relevant resolutions;

2. *Expresses concern* at the financial situation with regard to peacekeeping activities, in particular as regards the reimbursements to troop contributors that bear additional burdens owing to overdue payments by Member States of their assessments;

3. *Also expresses concern* at the delay experienced by the Secretary-General in deploying and providing adequate resources to some recent peacekeeping missions, in particular those in Africa;

4. *Emphasizes* that all future and existing peacekeeping missions shall be given equal and non-discriminatory treatment in respect of financial and administrative arrangements;

5. *Also emphasizes* that all peacekeeping missions shall be provided with adequate resources for the effective and efficient discharge of their respective mandates;

6. *Recalls* its resolution 60/266, section VI, paragraph 1, and emphasizes the importance of ensuring coordination and collaboration of efforts with the United Nations agencies, funds and programmes and the implementation of a unified workplan, and requests the Secretary-General to report to the General Assembly on measures taken and progress made and to provide clear descriptions of respective roles and responsibilities in future budget submissions;

7. *Reiterates its request* to the Secretary-General to make the fullest possible use of facilities and equipment at the United Nations Logistics Base at Brindisi, Italy, in order to minimize the costs of procurement for the Mission;

8. *Endorses* the conclusions and recommendations contained in the report of the Advisory Committee on Administrative and Budgetary Questions, subject to the provisions of the present resolution, and requests the Secretary-General to ensure their full implementation;

9. *Notes* the additional information provided by the Secretary-General on the ability to finance twenty-two general temporary assistance positions for the backstopping of the Mission at United Nations Headquarters in the amount of 2,307,500 United States dollars from the resources approved for the support account for peacekeeping operations for the period from 1 July 2006 to 30 June 2007;

10. *Authorizes* the Secretary-General to finance up to twenty-two general temporary assistance positions at United Nations Headquarters to provide support for the deployment of the Mission from the resources approved for the support account for peacekeeping operations for the period from 1 July 2006 to 30 June 2007, to be reported to the General Assembly in the context of the performance report on the support account for the period;

11. *Reaffirms* its resolution 59/296, and requests the Secretary-General to ensure the full implementation of its relevant provisions and the relevant provisions of its resolution 60/266;

12. *Requests* the Secretary-General to take all necessary action to ensure that the Mission is administered with a maximum of efficiency and economy;

13. *Also requests* the Secretary-General, in order to reduce the cost of employing General Service staff, to continue efforts to recruit local staff for the Mission against General Service posts, commensurate with the requirements of the Mission;

14. *Further requests* the Secretary-General to make greater use of national staff;

Budget estimates for the period from 25 August 2006 to 31 March 2007

15. *Authorizes* the Secretary-General to establish a special account for the United Nations Integrated Mission in Timor-Leste for the purpose of accounting for the income received and expenditure incurred in respect of the Mission;

16. *Also authorizes* the Secretary-General to enter into commitments for the Mission for the period from 25 August 2006 to 31 March 2007 in a total amount not exceeding 170,221,100 dollars, inclusive of the amount of 49,961,500 dollars previously authorized by the Advisory Committee on Administrative and Budgetary Questions under the terms of section IV of General Assembly resolution 49/233 A of 23 December 1994;

Financing of the commitment authority

17. *Decides* to apportion among Member States the amount of 143,140,420 dollars for the period from 25 August 2006 to 25 February 2007, in accordance with the levels updated in General Assembly resolutions 58/256 of 23 December 2003 and 61/243 of 22 December 2006,

and taking into account the scale of assessments for 2006, as set out in its resolution 58/1 B of 23 December 2003, and the scale of assessments for 2007, as set out in its resolution 61/237 of 22 December 2006;

18. *Also decides* that, in accordance with the provisions of its resolution 973(X) of 15 December 1955, there shall be set off against the apportionment among Member States, as provided for in paragraph 17 above, their respective share in the Tax Equalization Fund of the amount of 2,046,840 dollars, representing the estimated staff assessment income approved for the Mission for the period from 25 August 2006 to 25 February 2007;

19. *Further decides* to apportion among Member States the amount of 27,080,680 dollars for the period from 26 February to 31 March 2007 at the monthly rate of 23,556,753 dollars, in accordance with the levels updated in General Assembly resolution 61/243, and taking into account the scale of assessments for 2007, as set out in its resolution 61/237, subject to a decision of the Security Council to extend the mandate of the Mission;

20. *Decides* that, in accordance with the provisions of its resolution 973(X), there shall be set off against the apportionment among Member States, as provided for in paragraph 19 above, their respective share in the Tax Equalization Fund of the amount of 387,360 dollars, representing the estimated staff assessment income approved for the Mission for the period from 26 February to 31 March 2007;

21. *Emphasizes* that no peacekeeping mission shall be financed by borrowing funds from other active peacekeeping missions;

22. *Encourages* the Secretary-General to continue to take additional measures to ensure the safety and security of all personnel under the auspices of the United Nations participating in the Mission, bearing in mind paragraphs 5 and 6 of Security Council resolution 1502(2003) of 26 August 2003;

23. *Invites* voluntary contributions to the Mission in cash and in the form of services and supplies acceptable to the Secretary-General, to be administered, as appropriate, in accordance with the procedure and practices established by the General Assembly;

24. *Decides* to keep under review during its sixty-first session the item entitled "Financing of the United Nations Integrated Mission in Timor-Leste".

Also on 22 December, the General Assembly decided that the item on the financing of the UNMIT remained for consideration during its sixty-first (2007) session (**decision 61/552**).

UNAMET

On 22 December, the General Assembly decided that the item on the financing of the United Nations Mission in East Timor (UNAMET) [YUN 1999, p. 280] would remain for consideration during its sixty-first (2007) session (**decision 61/552**).

Iran

In 2006, the United Nations addressed Iran's nuclear programme. On 6 June, China, France, Germany, the Russian Federation, the United Kingdom and the United States made proposals to Iran for resolving the issues concerning that programme. On 31 July, the Security Council, by resolution 1696(2006), demanded a suspension of the country's nuclear enrichment and reprocessing activities, threatening sanctions for non-compliance. Iran, in its 22 August reply to the six-country proposal, expressed its readiness to negotiate an agreement with those States, but reaffirmed its right to develop its peaceful nuclear programme. On 23 December, by resolution 1737(2006), the Council imposed sanctions on Iran related to its nuclear and ballistic missile programmes, as well as an assets freeze and a travel ban for certain persons and entities. The Council also established a Committee to oversee implementation of the relevant measures and to undertake the tasks set out in paragraph 18 of the resolution.

IAEA action (February). Having determined in 2005 [YUN 2005, p. 607] that Iran's history of concealment of its nuclear activities and the resulting lack of confidence in its nuclear programme being exclusively for peaceful purposes raised questions that were within the competence of the Security Council, on 4 February [GOV/2006/14], the Board of Governors of the International Atomic Energy Agency (IAEA) requested the IAEA Director General to transmit to the Council all IAEA reports and resolutions relating to the implementation of the Safeguards Agreement between Iran and IAEA under the 1968 Treaty on the Non-Proliferation of Nuclear Weapons (NPT), adopted by the General Assembly in resolution 2373(XXII) [YUN 1968, p. 177]. He should also report on the steps required of Iran to re-establish full and sustained suspension of all enrichment-related and reprocessing activities and to consider the construction of a research reactor moderated by heavy water.

In response to that resolution, the Secretary-General transmitted to the Council on 6 February [S/2006/80] the reports requested, as submitted to him by the IAEA Director General. In his report, the Director-General said that the Agency was informed by Iran on 3 January of its decision to resume research and development on the peaceful nuclear programme which it had suspended. Consequently, as requested by Iran, the Agency removed seals applied at Natanz, Farayand Technique and Pars Trash facilities, which had been used for monitoring the suspension of enrichment-related activities.

SECURITY COUNCIL ACTION

On 29 March [meeting 5403], following consultations among Security Council members, the President made statement **S/PRST/2006/15** on behalf of the Council:

The Security Council reaffirms its commitment to the Treaty on the Non-Proliferation of Nuclear Weapons and recalls the right of States parties, in conformity with articles I and II of the Treaty, to develop research, production and use of nuclear energy for peaceful purposes without discrimination.

The Council notes with serious concern the many reports and resolutions of the International Atomic Energy Agency relating to the Islamic Republic of Iran's nuclear programme reported to it by the Director General of the Agency, including resolution GOV/2006/14 adopted on 4 February 2006 by the Board of Governors of the Agency.

The Council also notes with serious concern that the report of the Director General of 27 February 2006 lists a number of outstanding issues and concerns, including topics which could have a military nuclear dimension, and that the Agency is unable to conclude that there are no undeclared nuclear materials or activities in the Islamic Republic of Iran.

The Council further notes with serious concern the Islamic Republic of Iran's decision to resume enrichment-related activities, including research and development, and to suspend cooperation with the Agency under the Additional Protocol.

The Council calls upon the Islamic Republic of Iran to take the steps required by the Board of Governors, notably in paragraph 1 of its resolution GOV/2006/14, which are essential to build confidence in the exclusively peaceful purpose of its nuclear programme and to resolve outstanding questions, and underlines, in this regard, the particular importance of re-establishing full and sustained suspension of all enrichment-related and reprocessing activities, including research and development, to be verified by the Agency.

The Council expresses the conviction that such suspension and full, verified Iranian compliance with the requirements set out by the Board of Governors would contribute to a diplomatic, negotiated solution that guarantees that the Islamic Republic of Iran's nuclear programme is for exclusively peaceful purposes, and underlines the willingness of the international community to work positively for such a solution, which will also benefit nuclear non-proliferation elsewhere.

The Council strongly supports the role of the Board of Governors and commends and encourages the Director General and the secretariat of the Agency for their ongoing professional and impartial efforts to resolve outstanding issues in the Islamic Republic of Iran, and underlines the necessity of the Agency continuing its work to clarify all outstanding issues relating to the Islamic Republic of Iran's nuclear programme.

The Council requests in 30 days a report from the Director General on the process of Iranian compliance with the steps required by the Board of Governors, to the Board and, in parallel, to the Council for its consideration.

IAEA report. In response to the Council's request, the IAEA Director General, on 28 April [S/2006/270], reported to the Council President that all nuclear material declared by Iran to the Agency was accounted for, and apart from small quantities previously reported to the Board, no other undeclared material had been found. However, gaps remained with respect to the scope and content of Iran's centrifuge programme. The Agency was therefore unable to provide assurance about the absence of undeclared nuclear material and activities.

After more than three years of IAEA efforts, the gaps in knowledge continued to be a matter of concern. Progress required transparency and cooperation by Iran, beyond safeguards measures, to understand the 20 years of its undeclared activities. Iran had continued to facilitate the implementation of the Safeguards Agreement and agreed to some transparency measures, including providing access to certain military sites. The Agency needed Iran to take additional measures, including providing access to documentation, dual-use equipment and individuals, to be able to verify the scope and nature of the enrichment programme, the purpose and use of the dual-use equipment and material and studies which could have a military dimension.

With Iran's decision to stop implementing the provisions of the Model Protocol Additional to Safeguards Agreements [YUN 1997, p. 486] and to confine verification to the implementation of the Safeguards Agreement, IAEA ability to clarify those issues and confirm the absence of undeclared nuclear material and activities would be further limited.

Six-nation package. On 13 July [S/2006/521], France transmitted to the Council President the proposals of China, France, Germany, the Russian Federation, the United Kingdom and the United States for a comprehensive long-term arrangement providing for cooperation with Iran based on mutual respect and the establishment of international confidence on the exclusively peaceful nature of Iran's nuclear programme. The package had been offered in Tehran on 6 June by Javier Solana, the European Union (EU) High Representative for Common Foreign and Security Policy.

The agreement, to be deposited with IAEA and endorsed by a Security Council resolution, would reaffirm Iran's right to develop nuclear energy for peaceful purposes in conformity with its NPT obligations; reaffirm support for the development of a civil nuclear energy programme; support the building of new light water reactors through international joint projects, in accordance with the IAEA statute and NPT; and suspend discussion of Iran's nuclear programme in the Council.

In exchange, Iran would commit to addressing all of IAEA outstanding concerns; suspend all enrichment-related and reprocessing activities, to be verified by IAEA; and resume the implementation of the Additional Protocol.

The proposal included a list of areas of future nuclear, political and economic cooperation to be covered during the negotiations. The incentives included promoting Iran's membership in the World Trade Organization, the lifting of United States and European restrictions on the export of civilian aircraft and telecommunications equipment, and help in building light water nuclear power reactors.

In a 12 July press statement [S/2006/573], the Ministers for Foreign Affairs of China, France, Germany, the Russian Federation, the United Kingdom and the United States and the High Representative of the European Union reported that they had agreed, on 1 June at a meeting in Vienna, on a set of far-reaching proposals as a basis for negotiation with Iran, including cooperation in the political, economic and nuclear areas [S/2006/521] (see above). If Iran decided not to engage, further steps would have to be taken in the Security Council. Although the offer was made to Iran on 6 June, there was no indication that Iran was ready to engage seriously on the substance of the proposals, and had not taken any steps to allow negotiations to begin, specifically on the suspension of all enrichment-related and reprocessing activities. They therefore had no choice but to seek a Council resolution making the IAEA-required sanctions mandatory. If Iran did not comply, they would work to adopt measures under Chapter VII, Article 41, of the UN Charter. They asked Iran to respond positively to the substantive proposals.

SECURITY COUNCIL ACTION

On 31 July [meeting 5500], the Security Council adopted **resolution 1696(2006)** by vote (14-1). The draft [S/2006/589] was submitted by France, Germany and the United Kingdom.

The Security Council,

Recalling the statement by its President of 29 March 2006,

Reaffirming its commitment to the Treaty on the Non-Proliferation of Nuclear Weapons, and recalling the right of States parties, in conformity with articles I and II of the Treaty, to develop research, production and use of nuclear energy for peaceful purposes without discrimination,

Noting with serious concern the many reports of the Director General of the International Atomic Energy Agency and resolutions of the Board of Governors of the Agency relating to the Islamic Republic of Iran's nuclear programme reported to it by the Director General, including resolution GOV/2006/14 adopted by the Board of Governors on 4 February 2006,

Noting with serious concern also that the report of the Director General of 27 February 2006 lists a number of outstanding issues and concerns on the Islamic Republic of Iran's nuclear programme, including topics which could have a military nuclear dimension, and that the Agency is unable to conclude that there are no undeclared nuclear materials or activities in the Islamic Republic of Iran,

Noting with serious concern further the report of the Director General of 28 April 2006 and the findings therein, including that, after more than three years of Agency efforts to seek clarity about all aspects of the Islamic Republic of Iran's nuclear programme, the existing gaps in knowledge continue to be a matter of concern, and that the Agency is unable to make progress in its efforts to provide assurances about the absence of undeclared nuclear material and activities in the Islamic Republic of Iran,

Noting with serious concern that, as confirmed by the report of the Director General of 8 June 2006, the Islamic Republic of Iran has not taken the steps required of it by the Board of Governors, reiterated by the Security Council in the statement by its President of 29 March 2006, and which are essential to build confidence, and, in particular, the Islamic Republic of Iran's decision to resume enrichment-related activities, including research and development, its recent expansion of and announcements about such activities, and its continued suspension of cooperation with the Agency under the Additional Protocol,

Emphasizing the importance of political and diplomatic efforts to find a negotiated solution guaranteeing that the Islamic Republic of Iran's nuclear programme is exclusively for peaceful purposes, and noting that such a solution would benefit nuclear non-proliferation elsewhere,

Welcoming the statement made by the Minister for Foreign Affairs of France, Mr. Philippe Douste-Blazy, on behalf of the Ministers for Foreign Affairs of China, France, Germany, the Russian Federation, the United Kingdom of Great Britain and Northern Ireland and the United States of America and the High Representative of the European Union in Paris on 12 July 2006,

Concerned by the proliferation risks presented by the Iranian nuclear programme, mindful of its primary responsibility under the Charter of the United Nations for the maintenance of international peace and security, and being determined to prevent an aggravation of the situation,

Acting under Article 40 of Chapter VII of the Charter in order to make mandatory the suspension required by the Agency,

1. *Calls upon* the Islamic Republic of Iran without further delay to take the steps required by the Board of Governors of the International Atomic Energy Agency in its resolution GOV/2006/14, which are essential to build confidence in the exclusively peaceful purpose of its nuclear programme and to resolve outstanding questions;

2. *Demands*, in this context, that the Islamic Republic of Iran suspend all enrichment-related and reprocessing activities, including research and development, to be verified by the Agency;

3. *Expresses the conviction* that such suspension as well as full, verified Iranian compliance with the requirements set out by the Board of Governors would contribute to a diplomatic, negotiated solution that guarantees that the Islamic Republic of Iran's nuclear programme is for exclusively peaceful purposes, underlines the willingness of the international community to work positively for such a solution, encourages the Islamic Republic of Iran, in conforming to the above provisions, to re-engage with the international community and with the Agency, and stresses that such engagement will be beneficial to the Islamic Republic of Iran;

4. *Endorses*, in this regard, the proposals of China, France, Germany, the Russian Federation, the United Kingdom of Great Britain and Northern Ireland and the United States of America, with the support of the High Representative of the European Union, for a long-term comprehensive arrangement which would allow for the development of relations and cooperation with the Islamic Republic of Iran based on mutual respect and the establishment of international confidence in the exclusively peaceful nature of the Islamic Republic of Iran's nuclear programme;

5. *Calls upon* all States, in accordance with their national legal authorities and legislation and consistent with international law, to exercise vigilance and prevent the transfer of any items, materials, goods and technology that could contribute to the Islamic Republic of Iran's enrichment-related and reprocessing activities and ballistic missile programmes;

6. *Expresses its determination* to reinforce the authority of the Agency process, strongly supports the role of the Board of Governors, commends and encourages the Director General and the secretariat of the Agency for their ongoing professional and impartial efforts to resolve all remaining outstanding issues in the Islamic Republic of Iran within the framework of the Agency, underlines the necessity of the Agency continuing its work to clarify all outstanding issues relating to the Islamic Republic of Iran's nuclear programme, and calls upon the Islamic Republic of Iran to act in accordance with the provisions of the Additional Protocol and to implement without delay all transparency measures as the Agency may request in support of its ongoing investigations;

7. *Requests*, by 31 August 2006, a report from the Director General primarily on whether the Islamic Republic of Iran has established full and sustained suspension of all activities mentioned in the present resolution, as well as on the process of Iranian compliance with all the steps required by the Board of Governors and with the above provisions of the present resolution, to the Board and, in parallel, to the Council for its consideration;

8. *Expresses its intention*, in the event that the Islamic Republic of Iran has not by that date complied with the present resolution, then to adopt appropriate measures under Article 41 of Chapter VII of the Charter of the United Nations to persuade the Islamic Republic of Iran to comply with the present resolution and the requirements of the Agency, and underlines that further decisions will be required should such additional measures be necessary;

9. *Confirms* that such additional measures will not be necessary in the event that the Islamic Republic of Iran complies with the present resolution;

10. *Decides* to remain seized of the matter.

RECORDED VOTE ON RESOLUTION 1696(2006):

In favour: Argentina, China, Congo, Denmark, France, Ghana, Greece, Japan, Peru, Russian Federation, Slovakia, United Kingdom, United Republic of Tanzania, United States.

Against: Qatar.

Speaking after the adoption of the text, Qatar said it disagreed with the decision to submit the resolution when its region was "inflamed". Proceeding to action at such a critical time neither served regional security nor Council unity. There was no harm in exhausting all possible means to identify Iran's real intentions and the degree of its willingness to cooperate, especially since it had not rejected the package offered by China, France, Germany, the Russian Federation, the United Kingdom and the United States; it had simply asked for some time to consider it. The Council had certainly waited longer to act on much more burning issues. Qatar was committed to ensuring that the Middle East became a nuclear-weapons-free zone, but failure to take into account those concerns, as well as the situation in the region, was not helpful.

The United States said that Iran had defied the international community by continuing its pursuit of nuclear weapons, and its continued defiance demanded a strong response from the Council. The pursuit of nuclear weapons was a direct threat to international peace and security and demanded a clear statement by the Council. The resolution sent an unambiguous message to Iran, namely, to take the steps required by the IAEA Board of Governors, including full and sustained suspension of all enrichment-related and reprocessing activities. Iran should understand that the United States and others would ensure that financial transactions associated with proliferation activities would be scrutinized.

The text was the first Council resolution on Iran in response to its nuclear programme, reflecting the gravity of the situation and the Council's determination.

Iran said that its peaceful nuclear programme posed no threat to international peace and security, and therefore dealing with the issue in the Council was unwarranted and void of any legal basis or practical utility. Far from reflecting the international community's concerns, the sponsors' approach flouted the stated position of the overwhelming majority of Member States. The Council's action, which was the culmination of efforts aimed at making the suspension of uranium enrichment mandatory, violated international law, the NPT and IAEA resolutions. It also ran counter to the views of the majority of Member States, which the Council was obliged to represent. The sole reason for pushing the Council to take action was that Iran had decided, after over two years of negotiations, to resume the exercise of its inalienable right to nuclear technology for peaceful purposes, by partially reopening its fully safeguarded facilities and ending a voluntary suspension.

Iran's right to enrich uranium was recognized under the NPT. Upholding the right of State parties to international regimes was as essential as ensuring respect for their obligations. Those regimes, including the NPT, were sustained by a balance between rights and obligations. Iran's statement before the Council was reproduced as a Council document [S/2006/603].

In response to the Council's request, the IAEA Director General, on 31 August [S/2006/702], reported to the Council President that Iran had been providing the Agency with access to nuclear material and facilities and with the required reports. Although Iran had provided the Agency with some information on product assays at the Pilot Fuel Enrichment Plant, it continued to deny access to certain operating records at the Plant. Iran had not addressed the long-outstanding verification issues or removed uncertainties associated with some of its activities. It had not suspended its enrichment-related activities, nor acted in accordance with the provisions of the Additional Protocol. IAEA remained unable to make progress in verifying the correctness and completeness of Iran's declarations so as to confirm the peaceful nature of its nuclear programme.

Iran response to six-nation package. In a 22 August response to the six-country package (see p. 432) [A/61/514-S/2006/806], transmitted to the Secretary-General, Iran said that it considered the 6 June proposals as containing useful foundations for comprehensive long-term cooperation between the two sides. It was prepared for the removal of the concerns of the two sides through negotiations and was ready for long-term cooperation in security, economic and political energy areas.

However, while Iran accepted the core idea of the proposal and the negotiating approach, certain points needed to be expressed. The proposal lacked reference to irreversible guarantees, which were essential in nuclear matters. The proposal was ambiguous as to the purpose and procedures of the proposed negotiations and lacked clarity as to the relationship and link between the processes of Iran's interaction and collaboration with IAEA and the negotiations between Iran and its counterparts. The proposal was also ambivalent on the central point of Iran's nuclear activities and the way to resolve it. Iran's firm position was that it had the right to pursue its intended peaceful nuclear programme; it was obligated to comply with all its commitments under its bilateral agreement with IAEA and allow the Agency to perform its responsibilities in relation to Iran's activities; and as an IAEA member, it had the right to receive technical support. Iran was prepared to negotiate on those principles. It proposed collaboration with IAEA and negotiations with Iran's counterparts without clarifying the link between the two processes. IAEA was the main avenue for resolving the issue. An agreement would be possible if all sides limited their expectations and actions to the framework of internationally accepted norms, particularly the NPT. While the package recognized Iran's right to a peaceful nuclear programme and activity, it was mute on its scope and exercise. There was a need to clarify whether enrichment and nuclear fuel cycle for peaceful use were under consideration, and whether the NPT was the basis for determining it.

As to the issues of the suspension of Iran's dossier in the Security Council, and suspension of Iran's enrichment activities, the correct approach should be for the Council to take the Iran nuclear dossier off its agenda and resolve that the IAEA process, supported by negotiations, was the logical approach to the issue.

Under the negotiations, the parties should be entitled to be informed of non-diversion of Iran's peaceful nuclear activities within the NPT and IAEA frameworks; for its part, Iran would provide the utmost cooperation for IAEA inspections. If all such requirements were met, Iran was ready to implement voluntarily the Additional Protocol. Iran was also ready to guarantee that it would not abandon membership of IAEA and NPT, but that was conditional to the other party's commitment to creating a nuclear-free zone in the Middle East; convincing the countries of the region to join the NPT and implement the Additional Protocol; and preventing hostile acts against Iran.

Communications. On 13 October, France sent to the Security Council President two lists of items, material, equipment, goods and technology, one related to nuclear programmes [S/2006/814] and the other to ballistic missiles programmes [S/2006/815]. On 7 December, the United Kingdom sent to the Council President related guidelines [S/2006/985] for sensitive missile-relevant transfers.

SECURITY COUNCIL ACTION

On 23 December [meeting 5612], the Security Council unanimously adopted **resolution 1737(2006).** The draft [S/2006/1010] was submitted by France, Germany and the United Kingdom.

The Security Council,

Recalling the statement by its President of 29 March 2006, and its resolution 1696(2006) of 31 July 2006,

Reaffirming its commitment to the Treaty on the Non-Proliferation of Nuclear Weapons, and recalling the right of States parties, in conformity with articles I and II of the Treaty, to develop research, production and use of nuclear energy for peaceful purposes without discrimination,

Reiterating its serious concern over the many reports of the Director General of the International Atomic Energy Agency and resolutions of the Board of Governors of the Agency related to the Islamic Republic of Iran's nuclear programme reported to it by the Director General, including resolution GOV/2006/14 adopted by the Board of Governors on 4 February 2006,

Reiterating its serious concern also that the report of the Director General of 27 February 2006 lists a number of outstanding issues and concerns on the Islamic Republic of Iran's nuclear programme, including topics which could have a military nuclear dimension, and that the Agency is unable to conclude that there are no undeclared nuclear materials or activities in the Islamic Republic of Iran,

Reiterating its serious concern further over the report of the Director General of 28 April 2006 and the findings therein, including that, after more than three years of Agency efforts to seek clarity about all aspects of the Islamic Republic of Iran's nuclear programme, the existing gaps in knowledge continue to be a matter of concern, and that the Agency is unable to make progress in its efforts to provide assurances about the absence of undeclared nuclear material and activities in the Islamic Republic of Iran,

Noting with serious concern that, as confirmed by the reports of the Director General of 8 June, 31 August and 14 November 2006, the Islamic Republic of Iran has not established full and sustained suspension of all enrichment-related and reprocessing activities as set out in resolution 1696(2006), nor resumed its cooperation with the Agency under the Additional Protocol, nor taken the other steps required of it by the Board of Governors, nor complied with the provisions of resolution 1696(2006), which are essential to build confidence, and deploring the Islamic Republic of Iran's refusal to take these steps,

Emphasizing the importance of political and diplomatic efforts to find a negotiated solution guaranteeing that the Islamic Republic of Iran's nuclear programme is exclusively for peaceful purposes, noting that such a solution would benefit nuclear non-proliferation elsewhere, and welcoming the continuing commitment of China, France, Germany, the Russian Federation, the United Kingdom of Great Britain and Northern Ireland and the United States of America, with the support of the High Representative of the European Union, to seek a negotiated solution,

Determined to give effect to its decisions by adopting appropriate measures to persuade the Islamic Republic of Iran to comply with resolution 1696(2006) and with the requirements of the Agency, and also to constrain the Islamic Republic of Iran's development of sensitive technologies in support of its nuclear and missile programmes, until such time as the Security Council determines that the objectives of the present resolution have been met,

Concerned by the proliferation risks presented by the Iranian nuclear programme and, in this context, by the Islamic Republic of Iran's continuing failure to meet the requirements of the Board of Governors and to comply with the provisions of resolution 1696(2006), mindful of its primary responsibility under the Charter of the United Nations for the maintenance of international peace and security,

Acting under Article 41 of Chapter VII of the Charter,

1. *Affirms* that the Islamic Republic of Iran shall without further delay take the steps required by the Board of Governors of the International Atomic Energy Agency in its resolution GOV/2006/14, which are essential to build confidence in the exclusively peaceful purpose of its nuclear programme and to resolve outstanding questions;

2. *Decides*, in this context, that the Islamic Republic of Iran shall without further delay suspend the following proliferation-sensitive nuclear activities:

(a) All enrichment-related and reprocessing activities, including research and development, to be verified by the Agency; and

(b) Work on all heavy water-related projects, including the construction of a research reactor moderated by heavy water, also to be verified by the Agency;

3. *Decides also* that all States shall take the necessary measures to prevent the supply, sale or transfer directly or indirectly from their territories, or by their nationals or using their flag vessels or aircraft to, or for the use in or benefit of, the Islamic Republic of Iran, and whether or not originating in their territories, of all items, materials, equipment, goods and technology which could contribute to the Islamic Republic of Iran's enrichment-related, reprocessing or heavy water-related activities, or

to the development of nuclear weapon delivery systems, namely:

(a) Those set out in sections B.2, B.3, B.4, B.5, B.6 and B.7 of INFCIRC/254/Rev.8/Part 1 in document S/2006/814;

(b) Those set out in sections A.1 and B.1 of INFCIRC/254/Rev.8/Part 1 in document S/2006/814, except the supply, sale or transfer of:

(i) Equipment covered by B.1 when such equipment is for light water reactors;

(ii) Low-enriched uranium covered by A.1.2 when it is incorporated in assembled nuclear fuel elements for such reactors;

(c) Those set out in document S/2006/815, except the supply, sale or transfer of items covered by 19.A.3 of Category II;

(d) Any additional items, materials, equipment, goods and technology, determined as necessary by the Security Council or the Committee established pursuant to paragraph 18 below (hereinafter 'the Committee'), which could contribute to enrichment-related, reprocessing or heavy water-related activities, or to the development of nuclear weapon delivery systems;

4. *Decides further* that all States shall take the necessary measures to prevent the supply, sale or transfer directly or indirectly from their territories, or by their nationals or using their flag vessels or aircraft to, or for the use in or benefit of, the Islamic Republic of Iran, and whether or not originating in their territories, of the following items, materials, equipment, goods and technology:

(a) Those set out in INFCIRC/254/Rev.7/Part 2 in document S/2006/814 if the State determines that they would contribute to enrichment-related, reprocessing or heavy water-related activities;

(b) Any other items not listed in document S/2006/814 or document S/2006/815 if the State determines that they would contribute to enrichment-related, reprocessing or heavy water-related activities, or to the development of nuclear weapon delivery systems;

(c) Any further items if the State determines that they would contribute to the pursuit of activities related to other topics about which the Agency has expressed concerns or identified as outstanding;

5. *Decides* that, for the supply, sale or transfer of all items, materials, equipment, goods and technology covered by documents S/2006/814 and S/2006/815 the export of which to the Islamic Republic of Iran is not prohibited by paragraph 3 (*b*), paragraph 3 (*c*) or paragraph 4 (*a*) above, States shall ensure that:

(a) The requirements, as appropriate, of the Guidelines as set out in documents S/2006/814 and S/2006/985 have been met; and

(b) They have obtained and are in a position to exercise effectively a right to verify the end-use and end-use location of any supplied item; and

(c) They notify the Committee within ten days of the supply, sale or transfer; and

(d) In the case of items, materials, equipment, goods and technology contained in document S/2006/814, they also notify the Agency within ten days of the supply, sale or transfer;

6. *Decides also* that all States shall also take the necessary measures to prevent the provision to the Islamic Republic of Iran of any technical assistance or training, financial assistance, investment, brokering or other services, and the transfer of financial resources or services, related to the supply, sale, transfer, manufacture or use of the prohibited items, materials, equipment, goods and technology specified in paragraphs 3 and 4 above;

7. *Decides further* that the Islamic Republic of Iran shall not export any of the items in documents S/2006/814 and S/2006/815 and that all Member States shall prohibit the procurement of such items from the Islamic Republic of Iran by their nationals, or using their flag vessels or aircraft, and whether or not originating in the territory of the Islamic Republic of Iran;

8. *Decides* that the Islamic Republic of Iran shall provide such access and cooperation as the Agency requests to be able to verify the suspension outlined in paragraph 2 above and to resolve all outstanding issues, as identified in Agency reports, and calls upon the Islamic Republic of Iran to ratify promptly the Additional Protocol;

9. *Decides also* that the measures imposed by paragraphs 3, 4 and 6 above shall not apply where the Committee determines in advance and on a case-by-case basis that such supply, sale, transfer or provision of such items or assistance would clearly not contribute to the development of the Islamic Republic of Iran's technologies in support of its proliferation-sensitive nuclear activities and of the development of nuclear weapon delivery systems, including where such items or assistance are for food, agricultural, medical or other humanitarian purposes, provided that:

(a) Contracts for delivery of such items or assistance include appropriate end-user guarantees; and

(b) The Islamic Republic of Iran has committed not to use such items in proliferation-sensitive nuclear activities or for the development of nuclear weapon delivery systems;

10. *Calls upon* all States to exercise vigilance regarding the entry into or transit through their territories of individuals who are engaged in, directly associated with or providing support for the Islamic Republic of Iran's proliferation-sensitive nuclear activities or for the development of nuclear weapon delivery systems, and decides in this regard that all States shall notify the Committee of the entry into or transit through their territories of the persons designated in the annex to the present resolution (hereinafter 'the annex'), as well as of additional persons designated by the Council or the Committee as being engaged in, directly associated with or providing support for the Islamic Republic of Iran's proliferation-sensitive nuclear activities and for the development of nuclear weapon delivery systems, including through the involvement in procurement of the prohibited items, goods, equipment, materials and technology specified by and under the measures in paragraphs 3 and 4 above, except where such travel is for activities directly related to the items in paragraphs 3 (*b*) (i) and (ii) above;

11. *Underlines* that nothing in paragraph 10 above requires a State to refuse its own nationals entry into its territory, and that all States shall, in the implementation of paragraph 10 above, take into account humanitarian considerations as well as the necessity to meet the objectives of the present resolution, including where article XV of the statute of the Agency is engaged;

12. *Decides* that all States shall freeze the funds, other financial assets and economic resources which are on their territories at the date of adoption of the present resolution or at any time thereafter, that are owned or controlled by the persons or entities designated in the annex, as well as those of additional persons or entities designated by the Council or by the Committee as being engaged in, directly associated with or providing support for the Islamic Republic of Iran's proliferation-sensitive nuclear activities or for the development of nuclear weapon delivery systems, or by persons or entities acting on their behalf or at their direction, or by entities owned or controlled by them, including through illicit means, and that the measures in this paragraph shall cease to apply in respect of such persons or entities if, and at such time as, the Council or the Committee removes them from the annex, and decides further that all States shall ensure that any funds, financial assets or economic resources are prevented from being made available by their nationals or by any persons or entities within their territories, to or for the benefit of these persons and entities;

13. *Decides also* that the measures imposed by paragraph 12 above do not apply to funds, other financial assets or economic resources that have been determined by the relevant States:

(a) To be necessary for basic expenses, including payment for foodstuffs, rent or mortgage, medicines and medical treatment, taxes, insurance premiums and public utility charges or exclusively for payment of reasonable professional fees and reimbursement of incurred expenses associated with the provision of legal services, or fees or service charges, in accordance with national laws, for routine holding or maintenance of frozen funds, other financial assets and economic resources, after notification by the relevant States to the Committee of the intention to authorize, where appropriate, access to such funds, other financial assets or economic resources and in the absence of a negative decision by the Committee within five working days of such notification;

(b) To be necessary for extraordinary expenses, provided that such determination has been notified by the relevant States to the Committee and has been approved by the Committee;

(c) To be the subject of a judicial, administrative or arbitral lien or judgement, in which case the funds, other financial assets and economic resources may be used to satisfy that lien or judgement provided that the lien or judgement was entered into prior to the date of the present resolution, is not for the benefit of a person or entity designated pursuant to paragraphs 10 and 12 above, and has been notified by the relevant States to the Committee;

(d) To be necessary for activities directly related to the items specified in paragraphs 3 *(b)* (i) and (ii) above and have been notified by the relevant States to the Committee;

14. *Decides further* that States may permit the addition to the accounts frozen pursuant to the provisions of paragraph 12 above of interest or other earnings due on those accounts or payments due under contracts, agreements or obligations that arose prior to the date on which those accounts became subject to the provisions of the present resolution, provided that any such interest, other earnings and payments continue to be subject to these provisions and are frozen;

15. *Decides* that the measures in paragraph 12 above shall not prevent a designated person or entity from making payment due under a contract entered into prior to the listing of such a person or entity, provided that the relevant States have determined that:

(a) The contract is not related to any of the prohibited items, materials, equipment, goods, technologies, assistance, training, financial assistance, investment, brokering or services referred to in paragraphs 3, 4 and 6 above;

(b) The payment is not directly or indirectly received by a person or entity designated pursuant to paragraph 12 above;

and after notification by the relevant States to the Committee of the intention to make or receive such payments or to authorize, where appropriate, the unfreezing of funds, other financial assets or economic resources for this purpose, ten working days prior to such authorization;

16. *Decides also* that technical cooperation provided to the Islamic Republic of Iran by the Agency or under its auspices shall only be for food, agricultural, medical, safety or other humanitarian purposes, or where it is necessary for projects directly related to the items specified in paragraphs 3 *(b)* (i) and (ii) above, but that no such technical cooperation shall be provided that relates to the proliferation-sensitive nuclear activities set out in paragraph 2 above;

17. *Calls upon* all States to exercise vigilance and prevent specialized teaching or training of Iranian nationals, within their territories or by their nationals, of disciplines which would contribute to the Islamic Republic of Iran's proliferation-sensitive nuclear activities and to the development of nuclear weapon delivery systems;

18. *Decides* to establish, in accordance with rule 28 of its provisional rules of procedure, a Committee of the Security Council consisting of all the members of the Council, to undertake the following tasks:

(a) To seek from all States, in particular those in the region and those producing the items, materials, equipment, goods and technology referred to in paragraphs 3 and 4 above, information regarding the actions taken by them to implement effectively the measures imposed by paragraphs 3, 4, 5, 6, 7, 8, 10 and 12 above and whatever further information it may consider useful in this regard;

(b) To seek from the Secretariat of the Agency information regarding the actions taken by the Agency to

implement effectively the measures imposed by paragraph 16 above and whatever further information it may consider useful in this regard;

(*c*) To examine and take appropriate action on information regarding alleged violations of the measures imposed by paragraphs 3, 4, 5, 6, 7, 8, 10 and 12 above;

(*d*) To consider and decide upon requests for exemptions set out in paragraphs 9, 13 and 15 above;

(*e*) To determine as may be necessary additional items, materials, equipment, goods and technology to be specified for the purpose of paragraph 3 above;

(*f*) To designate as may be necessary additional individuals and entities subject to the measures imposed by paragraphs 10 and 12 above;

(*g*) To promulgate guidelines as may be necessary to facilitate the implementation of the measures imposed by the present resolution and include in such guidelines a requirement for States to provide information, where possible, as to why any individuals and/or entities meet the criteria set out in paragraphs 10 and 12 above and any relevant identifying information;

(*h*) To report at least every ninety days to the Council on its work and on the implementation of the present resolution, with its observations and recommendations, in particular on ways to strengthen the effectiveness of the measures imposed by paragraphs 3, 4, 5, 6, 7, 8, 10 and 12 above;

19. *Decides also* that all States shall report to the Committee within sixty days of the adoption of the present resolution on the steps they have taken with a view to implementing effectively paragraphs 3, 4, 5, 6, 7, 8, 10, 12 and 17 above;

20. *Expresses the conviction* that the suspension set out in paragraph 2 above, as well as full, verified Iranian compliance with the requirements set out by the Board of Governors of the Agency, would contribute to a diplomatic, negotiated solution that guarantees that the Islamic Republic of Iran's nuclear programme is for exclusively peaceful purposes, underlines the willingness of the international community to work positively for such a solution, encourages the Islamic Republic of Iran, in conforming to the above provisions, to re-engage with the international community and with the Agency, and stresses that such engagement will be beneficial to the Islamic Republic of Iran;

21. *Welcomes* the commitment of China, France, Germany, the Russian Federation, the United Kingdom of Great Britain and Northern Ireland and the United States of America, with the support of the High Representative of the European Union, to a negotiated solution to this issue, and encourages the Islamic Republic of Iran to engage with their proposals of June 2006, which were endorsed by the Council in resolution 1696(2006), for a long-term comprehensive agreement which would allow for the development of relations and cooperation with the Islamic Republic of Iran based on mutual respect and the establishment of international confidence in the exclusively peaceful nature of the Islamic Republic of Iran's nuclear programme;

22. *Reiterates its determination* to reinforce the authority of the Agency, strongly supports the role of the Board of Governors of the Agency, commends and encourages the Director General and the Secretariat of the Agency for their ongoing professional and impartial efforts to resolve all remaining outstanding issues in the Islamic Republic of Iran within the framework of the Agency, and underlines the necessity of the Agency continuing its work to clarify all outstanding issues relating to the Islamic Republic of Iran's nuclear programme;

23. *Requests* within sixty days a report from the Director General on whether the Islamic Republic of Iran has established full and sustained suspension of all activities mentioned in the present resolution, as well as on the process of Iranian compliance with all the steps required by the Board of Governors and with the other provisions of the present resolution, to the Board and, in parallel, to the Council for its consideration;

24. *Affirms* that it shall review the actions of the Islamic Republic of Iran in the light of the report referred to in paragraph 23 above, to be submitted within sixty days, and:

(*a*) That it shall suspend the implementation of measures if and for so long as the Islamic Republic of Iran suspends all enrichment-related and reprocessing activities, including research and development, as verified by the Agency, to allow for negotiations;

(*b*) That it shall terminate the measures specified in paragraphs 3, 4, 5, 6, 7, 10 and 12 above as soon as it determines that the Islamic Republic of Iran has fully complied with its obligations under the relevant resolutions of the Council and met the requirements of the Board of Governors, as confirmed by the Board;

(*c*) That it shall, in the event that the report referred to in paragraph 23 above shows that the Islamic Republic of Iran has not complied with the present resolution, adopt further appropriate measures under Article 41 of Chapter VII of the Charter of the United Nations to persuade the Islamic Republic of Iran to comply with the present resolution and the requirements of the Agency, and underlines that further decisions will be required should such additional measures be necessary;

25. *Decides* to remain seized of the matter.

ANNEX

A. Entities involved in the nuclear programme

1. Atomic Energy Organisation of Iran
2. Mesbah Energy Company (provider for A40 research reactor—Arak)
3. Kala-Electric (aka Kalaye Electric) (provider for PFEP—Natanz)
4. Pars Trash Company (involved in centrifuge programme, identified in IAEA reports)
5. Farayand Technique (involved in centrifuge programme, identified in IAEA reports)
6. Defence Industries Organisation (overarching MODAFL-controlled entity, some of whose subordinates have been involved in the centrifuge programme making components, and in the missile programme)

7. 7th of Tir (subordinate of DIO, widely recognized as being directly involved in the nuclear programme)

B. Entities involved in the ballistic missile programme

1. Shahid Hemmat Industrial Group (SHIG) (subordinate entity of AIO)
2. Shahid Bagheri Industrial Group (SBIG) (subordinate entity of AIO)
3. Fajr Industrial Group (formerly Instrumentation Factory Plant, subordinate entity of AIO)

C. Persons involved in the nuclear programme

1. Mohammad Qannadi, AEOI Vice President for Research and Development
2. Behman Asgarpour, Operational Manager (Arak)
3. Dawood Agha-Jani, Head of the PFEP (Natanz)
4. Ehsan Monajemi, Construction Project Manager, Natanz
5. Jafar Mohammadi, Technical Adviser to the AEOI (in charge of managing the production of valves for centrifuges)
6. Ali Hajinia Leilabadi, Director General of Mesbah Energy Company
7. Lt Gen Mohammad Mehdi Nejad Nouri, Rector of Malek Ashtar University of Defence Technology (chemistry dept, affiliated to MODALF, has conducted experiments on beryllium)

D. Persons involved in the ballistic missile programme

1. Gen Hosein Salimi, Commander of the Air Force, IRGC (Pasdaran)
2. Ahmad Vahid Dastjerdi, Head of the AIO
3. Reza-Gholi Esmaeli, Head of Trade and International Affairs Dept, AIO
4. Bahmanyar Morteza Bahmanyar, Head of Finance and Budget Dept, AIO

E. Persons involved in both the nuclear and ballistic missile programmes

Maj Gen Yahya Rahim Safavi, Commander, IRGC (Pasdaran)

Speaking before the vote, the Russian Federation said the main thrust of the resolution was the Council's support for IAEA activities on the issue at hand. The long and complex consultations had focused on confirming the measures that Iran needed to take to ensure confidence in its nuclear programme, as formulated by the IAEA Board. It was crucial that the restrictions on cooperation with Iran applied to the areas that had caused IAEA concern. Cooperation with Iran in areas not restricted by the draft resolution should not be subjected to its terms. A solution to the Iranian nuclear problem could be found exclusively in the political, diplomatic and legal framework. In that context, the measures provided for in the draft resolution should be taken in line with Article 41 of the Charter and not commit to the use of force.

The United States said that the resolution sent Iran an unambiguous message that there were serious repercussions for its continuing disregard of its obligations. The resolution would hopefully convince Iran that the best way to ensure its security and end its isolation was to end its nuclear weapons programme and take steps to restore international confidence. The text provided an important basis for action, compelling all Member States to deny Iran the equipment, technology, technical assistance and financial assistance that could contribute to nuclear-sensitive activities. In the face of non-compliance by Iran, the United States would not hesitate to return to the Council for further action.

Speaking after the vote, the United Kingdom recalled that, following adoption of the first such Council resolution on 31 July mandating IAEA-required suspension by Iran of its enrichment-related and reprocessing activities, that country had "simply thumbed its nose at the Council and defied international law". However, the door was not closed to Iran. The EU remained committed to seeking a diplomatic, negotiated solution. If Iran did not change course, the Council had committed itself, in the resolution, to further measures. Iran, therefore, faced a choice, and the vote indicated the gravity of that choice. Iran would hopefully heed the Council's decision and return to negotiations to resolve the nuclear dossier, thereby opening the way for the EU and Iran to start a new and wider relationship to their mutual benefit, and to the benefit of international peace and security.

China stressed that sanctions were not the end, but a means to urge Iran to return to negotiations. The sanctions were limited and reversible, and targeted at proliferation-sensitive nuclear activities and the development of nuclear-weapon delivery systems. Explicit provisions indicated that, if Iran suspended its enrichment-related and reprocessing activities and complied with the relevant Council texts and IAEA requirements, the Council would suspend and even terminate the sanctions. The text welcomed the commitment of China, France, Germany, the Russian Federation, the United Kingdom and the United States to a negotiated solution, and encouraged Iran to engage with them for a long-term agreement leading to the development of relations and cooperation based on mutual respect and the establishment of international confidence in the peaceful nature of Iran's nuclear programme.

Iran said it was a sad day for the non-proliferation regime. The Council was imposing sanctions on a member of NPT which, unlike Israel, had never attacked or threatened to use force against any Member State; had categorically rejected the development, stockpiling and use of nuclear weapons on ideological and strategic grounds; and was prepared to provide guarantees that it would never withdraw from NPT. Iran had placed all its nuclear facilities under IAEA safeguards, had fully implemented the Additional Protocol for more than two years, and had stated its readiness to resume its implementation. Iran had also allowed more than 2,000 "person days of IAEA scrutiny" of all of its related and unrelated facilities, resulting in repeated statements by the Agency on the absence of any evidence of diversion. It had suspended its lawful enrichment activities for over two years, as verified by IAEA, to build confidence and provide an opportunity for a mutually acceptable solution, presented far-reaching proposals to ensure permanent non-diversion, and called for unconditional negotiations to find a mutually acceptable solution.

Bringing Iran's peaceful nuclear programme to the Council by a few permanent members, particularly the United States, was not aimed at a solution or helping negotiations, but at compelling Iran to abandon its rights under NPT to peaceful nuclear technology. Suspension was not a solution, but a temporary measure to allow time to find a real solution. Moreover, such a suspension had been in place for two years, as verified by IAEA, during which nothing had been done to find an agreement. However, Iran was prepared to go to any length to allay the so-called proliferation concerns. Iran's statement was circulated to Council members as document [S/2006/1024].

Democratic People's Republic of Korea

Communications. On 4 July [S/2006/481], Japan requested an immediate meeting of the Security Council to consider the launch of ballistic missiles by the Democratic People's Republic of Korea (DPRK).

On 6 July [S/2006/493], the DPRK informed the Council President that the missile launches (5 July) were part of routine military exercises to increase the nation's self-defence capacity. The country's exercise of its legitimate right was bound neither to any international law nor to bilateral or multilateral agreements. The DPRK was not a signatory to the missile technology control regime. The moratorium on long-range missile test-firing, to which the DPRK agreed in 1999, was valid only when bilateral dialogue was under way. However, the current United States administration had scrapped all the agreements concluded with the DPRK by its preceding administration and scuttled the bilateral dialogue. The DPRK had already clarified, in March 2005, that its moratorium on missile test-firing had lost its validity.

The same could be said of the moratorium on the test-firing of long-range missiles, which the DPRK had agreed with Japan in the 2002 Pyongyang Declaration. The country had expressed its intention to extend that moratorium beyond 2003, on the premise that Japan would normalize its relations with the DPRK, but Japan did not honour its commitment.

The joint statement of the six-party talks of 19 September 2005 set out the commitments to be fulfilled by the six countries (China, the DPRK, Japan, the Republic of Korea, the Russian Federation and the United States) to the talks on denuclearizing the Korean peninsula. The United States immediately applied financial sanctions against the DPRK, escalated pressure in various fields, and carried out large-scale military exercises targeted against the DPRK. There was therefore no need for the country to unilaterally put on hold the missile launch in such a situation. Nevertheless, the country remained committed to denuclearizing the Korean peninsula in a negotiated manner.

Communications. On 6 July [S/2006/514], the EU condemned the missile test launches and urged the DPRK to return to the six-party talks. Honduras, on 7 July [S/2006/498], condemned the missile programme and called on the DPRK to halt it.

SECURITY COUNCIL ACTION

On 15 July [meeting 5490], the Security Council unanimously adopted **resolution 1695(2006)**. The draft [S/2006/488] was prepared in consultations among Council members.

The Security Council,

Reaffirming its resolutions 825(1993) of 11 May 1993 and 1540(2004) of 28 April 2004,

Bearing in mind the importance of maintaining peace and stability on the Korean peninsula and in north-east Asia at large,

Reaffirming that the proliferation of nuclear, chemical and biological weapons, as well as their means of delivery, constitutes a threat to international peace and security,

Expressing grave concern at the launch of ballistic missiles by the Democratic People's Republic of Korea, given the potential of such systems to be used as a means to deliver nuclear, chemical or biological payloads,

Registering profound concern at the Democratic People's Republic of Korea's breaking of its pledge to maintain its moratorium on missile launching,

Expressing further concern that the Democratic People's Republic of Korea endangered civil aviation and shipping through its failure to provide adequate advance notice,

Expressing grave concern about the Democratic People's Republic of Korea's indication of possible additional launches of ballistic missiles in the near future,

Expressing its desire for a peaceful and diplomatic solution to the situation, and welcoming efforts by members of the Security Council as well as other Member States to facilitate a peaceful and comprehensive solution through dialogue,

Recalling that the Democratic People's Republic of Korea launched an object propelled by a missile without prior notification to the countries in the region which fell into the waters in the vicinity of Japan on 31 August 1998,

Deploring the announcement by the Democratic People's Republic of Korea of its withdrawal from the Treaty on the Non-Proliferation of Nuclear Weapons (the Treaty) and its stated pursuit of nuclear weapons in spite of its Treaty and International Atomic Energy Agency safeguards obligations,

Stressing the importance of the implementation of the joint statement issued on 19 September 2005 by China, the Democratic People's Republic of Korea, Japan, the Republic of Korea, the Russian Federation and the United States of America,

Affirming that such launches jeopardize peace, stability and security in the region and beyond, particularly in the light of the claim by the Democratic People's Republic of Korea that it has developed nuclear weapons,

Acting under its special responsibility for the maintenance of international peace and security,

1. *Condemns* the multiple launches by the Democratic People's Republic of Korea of ballistic missiles on 5 July 2006 local time;

2. *Demands* that the Democratic People's Republic of Korea suspend all activities related to its ballistic missile programme and, in this context, re-establish its pre-existing commitments to a moratorium on missile launching;

3. *Requires* all Member States, in accordance with their national legal authorities and legislation and consistent with international law, to exercise vigilance and prevent missile and missile-related items, materials, goods and technology being transferred to the Democratic People's Republic of Korea's missile or weapons of mass destruction programmes;

4. *Also requires* all Member States, in accordance with their national legal authorities and legislation and consistent with international law, to exercise vigilance and prevent the procurement of missiles or missile-related items, materials, goods and technology from the Democratic People's Republic of Korea, and the transfer of any financial resources in relation to the Democratic People's Republic of Korea's missile or weapons of mass destruction programmes;

5. *Underlines*, in particular to the Democratic People's Republic of Korea, the need to show restraint and refrain from any action that might aggravate tension, and to continue to work on the resolution of non-proliferation concerns through political and diplomatic efforts;

6. *Strongly urges* the Democratic People's Republic of Korea to return immediately to the six-party talks without precondition, to work towards the expeditious implementation of the joint statement of 19 September 2005, in particular to abandon all nuclear weapons and existing nuclear programmes, and to return at an early date to the Treaty on the Non-Proliferation of Nuclear Weapons and International Atomic Energy Agency safeguards;

7. *Supports* the six-party talks, calls for their early resumption, and urges all the participants to intensify their efforts for the full implementation of the joint statement of 19 September 2005 with a view to achieving the verifiable denuclearization of the Korean peninsula in a peaceful manner and to maintaining peace and stability on the Korean peninsula and in north-east Asia;

8. *Decides* to remain seized of the matter.

Following its adoption, Japan said that the resolution marked an important step forward in promoting peace and security on the Korean peninsula and North-East Asia. The Council had acted swiftly and robustly in response to the DPRK launching of the barrage of ballistic missiles on 5 July. Through the resolution, the Council had sent an unmistakable message to the country, and had agreed on binding measures to deal with the situation. Japan had already taken unilateral measures against the DPRK, including the continuation of export-control measures on missiles and weapons of mass destruction-related goods and services against the DPRK.

The United States noted that it was the first Council resolution on the DPRK since 1993, reflecting the gravity of the situation and the unity and determination of the Council. It expressed the hope that the DPRK would make the strategic decision that pursuing weapons of mass destruction programmes and threatening acts made it less, not more, secure.

Urging all parties to practice restraint, China said it was opposed to any acts that would lead to further tension, and hoped that the resolution would help all parties to act calmly and continue diplomatic efforts to denuclearize the Korean peninsula and normalize relations between the countries concerned. Maintaining peace and stability on the Korean peninsula was in the common interests of the international community and the North-East Asian countries, and was the fundamental starting point for China in handling Korean peninsula affairs.

The DPRK said that the Council was not justified in taking up his country's missile launch exercise, both in view of the competence of the Council and international law. The DPRK rejected the resolution.

While the DPRK was committed to denuclearizing the peninsula, the country would continue its launch exercises as part of efforts to bolster its self-defence. It had no option, but to take strong actions, should any country take issue with the exercises and apply pressure on it.

Expressing appreciation for the Council's unanimous adoption of the resolution, the Republic of Korea said it had been following North Korea's activities, warning the DPRK not to conduct any missile launches. The Republic of Korea urged the DPRK to refrain from any further provocative actions, return to the six-party talks and comply with international non-proliferation efforts.

Communication. On 16 July [S/2006/535], the DPRK Minister for Foreign Affairs said that his country rejected totally the resolution adopted by the Security Council, which was a result of the hostile policy of the United States against the DPRK, and did not consider itself bound by it. The DPRK intended to bolster its deterrent to ensure its legitimate defence by all possible means.

SECURITY COUNCIL ACTION

On 6 October [meeting 5546], following consultations among Security Council members, the President made statement **S/PRST/2006/41** on behalf of the Council:

The Security Council expresses its deep concern over the statement of 3 October 2006 by the Ministry of Foreign Affairs of the Democratic People's Republic of Korea, in which it stated that the Democratic People's Republic of Korea would conduct a nuclear test in the future.

The Council reaffirms that the proliferation of weapons of mass destruction and their means of delivery constitutes a threat to international peace and security. The Council deplores the Democratic People's Republic of Korea's announcement of withdrawal from the Treaty on the Non-Proliferation of Nuclear Weapons (the Treaty) and its stated pursuit of nuclear weapons in spite of its Treaty and International Atomic Energy Agency safeguards obligations. The Council deems that, should the Democratic People's Republic of Korea carry out its threat of a nuclear weapon test, it would jeopardize peace, stability and security in the region and beyond.

The Council underlines that such a test would bring universal condemnation by the international community and would not help the Democratic People's Republic of Korea to address the stated concerns, particularly with regard to strengthening its security. The Council urges the Democratic People's Republic of Korea not to undertake such a test and to refrain from any action that might aggravate tension, to work on the resolution of non-proliferation concerns and to facilitate a peaceful and comprehensive solution through political and diplomatic efforts. The Council reiterates the need for the Democratic People's Republic of Korea to comply fully with all the provisions of Council resolution 1695(2006).

The Council supports the six-party talks and calls for their early resumption with a view to achieving the verifiable denuclearization of the Korean peninsula in a peaceful manner and to maintaining peace and stability on the Korean peninsula and in north-east Asia.

The Council urges the Democratic People's Republic of Korea to return immediately to the six-party talks without precondition, and to work towards the expeditious implementation of the joint statement of 19 September 2005, and in particular to abandon all nuclear weapons and existing nuclear programmes.

The Council will be monitoring this situation closely. The Council stresses that a nuclear test, if carried out by the Democratic People's Republic of Korea, would represent a clear threat to international peace and security and that, should the Democratic People's Republic of Korea ignore calls of the international community, the Council will act consistent with its responsibility under the Charter of the United Nations.

Communication (October). On 11 October [S/2006/801], the DPRK informed the Security Council President that, on 9 October, it had successfully conducted an underground nuclear test under secure conditions as a new measure for bolstering its war deterrent for self-defence. The test was entirely attributable to the United States nuclear threat, sanctions and pressure. The DPRK has exerted every possible effort to settle the nuclear issue through dialogue and negotiations, prompted by its desire to realize the denuclearization of the Korean peninsula. However, the current United States administration had responded with the policy of sanctions and blockade, and the DPRK was compelled to prove its possession of nukes to protect its sovereignty and right to existence. The country remained unchanged in its will to denuclearize the peninsula through dialogue and negotiations. The country's nuclear test did not contradict the 19 September 2005 joint statement under which it committed itself to dismantling its nuclear weapons and abandoning the nuclear programme.

The DPRK was ready for both dialogue and confrontation. If the United States increased pressure upon the DPRK, persistently doing harm to it, it would continue to take countermeasures, considering that as a declaration of a war.

On 13 October [A/61/528-S/2006/825], the extraordinary meeting of the Coordinated Bureau of the Non-Aligned Movement expressed its concern, while recognizing the complexities arising from the nuclear test in the Korean peninsula. It called on the parties concerned to exercise restraint, discontinue nuclear tests and not to transfer nuclear-weapons-related materials, equipment and technology.

On the same date [S/2006/814, S/2006/815, S/2006/816], France transmitted to the Council President lists of items, materials, equipment, goods and technology related to ballistic missile programmes, nuclear programmes and other weapons of mass destruction programmes.

SECURITY COUNCIL ACTION

On 14 October [meeting 5551], the Security Council unanimously adopted **resolution 1718(2006).** The draft [S/2006/805] was prepared in consultation among Council members:

The Security Council,

Recalling its previous relevant resolutions, including resolutions 825(1993) of 11 May 1993 1540(2004) of 28 April 2004 and, in particular, resolution 1695(2006) of 15 July 2006, as well as the statement by its President of 6 October 2006,

Reaffirming that the proliferation of nuclear, chemical and biological weapons, as well as their means of delivery, constitutes a threat to international peace and security,

Expressing the gravest concern at the claim by the Democratic People's Republic of Korea that it conducted a test of a nuclear weapon on 9 October 2006, and at the challenge such a test constitutes to the Treaty on the Non-Proliferation of Nuclear Weapons and to international efforts aimed at strengthening the global regime of non-proliferation of nuclear weapons, and the danger it poses to peace and stability in the region and beyond,

Expressing its firm conviction that the international regime on the non-proliferation of nuclear weapons should be maintained, and recalling that the Democratic People's Republic of Korea cannot have the status of a nuclear-weapon State in accordance with the Treaty on the Non-Proliferation of Nuclear Weapons,

Deploring the Democratic People's Republic of Korea's announcement of withdrawal from the Treaty on the Non-Proliferation of Nuclear Weapons and its pursuit of nuclear weapons,

Deploring further that the Democratic People's Republic of Korea has refused to return to the six-party talks without precondition,

Endorsing the joint statement issued on 19 September 2005 by China, the Democratic People's Republic of Korea, Japan, the Republic of Korea, the Russian Federation and the United States of America,

Underlining the importance that the Democratic People's Republic of Korea respond to other security and humanitarian concerns of the international community,

Expressing profound concern that the test claimed by the Democratic People's Republic of Korea has generated increased tension in the region and beyond, and determining, therefore, that there is a clear threat to international peace and security,

Acting under Chapter VII of the Charter of the United Nations, and taking measures under Article 41 thereof,

1. *Condemns* the nuclear test proclaimed by the Democratic People's Republic of Korea on 9 October 2006 in flagrant disregard of its relevant resolutions, in particular resolution 1695(2006), as well as of the statement by its President of 6 October 2006, including that such a test would bring universal condemnation of the international community and would represent a clear threat to international peace and security;

2. *Demands* that the Democratic People's Republic of Korea not conduct any further nuclear test or launch of a ballistic missile;

3. *Demands also* that the Democratic People's Republic of Korea immediately retract its announcement of withdrawal from the Treaty on the Non-Proliferation of Nuclear Weapons;

4. *Demands further* that the Democratic People's Republic of Korea return to the Treaty on the Non-Proliferation of Nuclear Weapons and International Atomic Energy Agency safeguards, and underlines the need for all States parties to the Treaty to continue to comply with their Treaty obligations;

5. *Decides* that the Democratic People's Republic of Korea shall suspend all activities related to its ballistic missile programme and in this context re-establish its pre-existing commitments to a moratorium on missile launching;

6. *Decides also* that the Democratic People's Republic of Korea shall abandon all nuclear weapons and existing nuclear programmes in a complete, verifiable and irreversible manner, shall act strictly in accordance with the obligations applicable to parties under the Treaty on the Non-Proliferation of Nuclear Weapons and the terms and conditions of its International Atomic Energy Agency safeguards agreement and shall provide the Agency transparency measures extending beyond these requirements, including such access to individuals, documentation, equipment and facilities as may be required and deemed necessary by the Agency;

7. *Decides further* that the Democratic People's Republic of Korea shall abandon all other existing weapons of mass destruction and ballistic missile programmes in a complete, verifiable and irreversible manner;

8. *Decides* that:

(a) All Member States shall prevent the direct or indirect supply, sale or transfer to the Democratic People's Republic of Korea, through their territories or by their nationals, or using their flag vessels or aircraft, and whether or not originating in their territories, of:

(i) Any battle tanks, armoured combat vehicles, large-calibre artillery systems, combat aircraft, attack helicopters, warships, missiles or missile systems as defined for the purpose of the United Nations Register of Conventional Arms, or related materiel, including spare parts, or items as determined by the Security Council or the Committee established pursuant to paragraph 12 below (the Committee);

(ii) All items, materials, equipment, goods and technology as set out in the lists in documents S/2006/814 and S/2006/815, unless within fourteen days of the adoption of the present resolution the Committee has amended or completed their provisions, also taking into account the list in document S/2006/816, as well as other items, materials, equipment, goods and technology, determined by the Council or the Committee, which could contribute to the Democratic People's Republic of Korea's nuclear-related, ballistic missile-related or other weapons of mass destruction-related programmes;

(iii) Luxury goods;

(b) The Democratic People's Republic of Korea shall cease the export of all items covered in subparagraphs *(a)* (i) and (ii) above and that all Member States shall prohibit the procurement of such items from the Democratic People's Republic of Korea by their nationals, or using their flag vessels or aircraft, and whether or not originating in the territory of the Democratic People's Republic of Korea;

(c) All Member States shall prevent any transfers to the Democratic People's Republic of Korea by their nationals or from their territories, or from the Democratic People's Republic of Korea by its nationals or from its territory, of technical training, advice, services or assistance related to the provision, manufacture, maintenance or use of the items in subparagraphs *(a)* (i) and (ii) above;

(d) All Member States shall, in accordance with their respective legal processes, freeze immediately the funds, other financial assets and economic resources which are on their territories at the date of the adoption of the present resolution or at any time thereafter, that are owned or controlled, directly or indirectly, by the persons or entities designated by the Committee or by the Council as being engaged in or providing support for, including through other illicit means, the Democratic People's Republic of Korea's nuclear-related, other weapons of mass destruction-related and ballistic missile-related programmes, or by persons or entities acting on their behalf or at their direction, and ensure that any funds, financial assets or economic resources are prevented from being made available by their nationals or by any persons or entities within their territories, to or for the benefit of such persons or entities;

(e) All Member States shall take the necessary steps to prevent the entry into or transit through their territories of the persons designated by the Committee or by the Council as being responsible for, including by supporting or promoting, policies of the Democratic People's Republic of Korea in relation to the Democratic People's Republic of Korea's nuclear-related, ballistic missile-related and other weapons of mass destruction-related programmes, together with their family members, provided that nothing in this paragraph shall oblige a State to refuse its own nationals entry into its territory;

(f) In order to ensure compliance with the requirements of this paragraph, and thereby preventing illicit trafficking in nuclear, chemical or biological weapons, their means of delivery and related materials, all Member States are called upon to take, in accordance with their national authorities and legislation, and consistent with international law, cooperative action, including through inspection of cargo to and from the Democratic People's Republic of Korea, as necessary;

9. *Decides also* that the provisions of paragraph 8 *(d)* above do not apply to financial or other assets or resources that have been determined by relevant States:

(a) To be necessary for basic expenses, including payment for foodstuffs, rent or mortgage, medicines and medical treatment, taxes, insurance premiums and public utility charges, or exclusively for payment of reasonable professional fees and reimbursement of incurred expenses associated with the provision of legal services, or fees or service charges, in accordance with national laws, for routine holding or maintenance of frozen funds, other financial assets and economic resources, after notification by the relevant States to the Committee of the intention to authorize, where appropriate, access to such funds, other financial assets and economic resources and in the absence of a negative decision by the Committee within five working days of such notification;

(b) To be necessary for extraordinary expenses, provided that such determination has been notified by the relevant States to the Committee and has been approved by the Committee; or

(c) To be the subject of a judicial, administrative or arbitral lien or judgement, in which case the funds, other financial assets and economic resources may be used to satisfy that lien or judgement, provided that the lien or judgement was entered prior to the date of the present resolution, is not for the benefit of a person referred to in paragraph 8 *(d)* above or an individual or entity identified by the Council or the Committee, and has been notified by the relevant States to the Committee;

10. *Decides further* that the measures imposed by paragraph 8 *(e)* above shall not apply where the Committee determines on a case-by-case basis that such travel is justified on the grounds of humanitarian need, including religious obligations, or where the Committee concludes that an exemption would otherwise further the objectives of the present resolution;

11. *Calls upon* all Member States to report to the Council within thirty days of the adoption of the present resolution on the steps they have taken with a view to implementing effectively the provisions of paragraph 8 above;

12. *Decides* to establish, in accordance with rule 28 of its provisional rules of procedure, a Committee of the Security Council consisting of all the members of the Council, to undertake the following tasks:

(a) To seek from all States, in particular those producing or possessing the items, materials, equipment, goods and technology referred to in paragraph 8 *(a)* above, information regarding the actions taken by them to implement effectively the measures imposed by paragraph 8 above and whatever further information it may consider useful in this regard;

(b) To examine and take appropriate action on information regarding alleged violations of measures imposed by paragraph 8 above;

(c) To consider and decide upon requests for exemptions set out in paragraphs 9 and 10 above;

(d) To determine additional items, materials, equipment, goods and technology to be specified for the purpose of paragraphs 8 *(a)* (i) and (ii) above;

(*e*) To designate additional individuals and entities subject to the measures imposed by paragraphs 8 (*d*) and (*e*) above;

(*f*) To promulgate guidelines as may be necessary to facilitate the implementation of the measures imposed by the present resolution;

(*g*) To report at least every ninety days to the Council on its work, with its observations and recommendations, in particular on ways to strengthen the effectiveness of the measures imposed by paragraph 8 above;

13. *Welcomes and encourages further* the efforts by all States concerned to intensify their diplomatic efforts, to refrain from any actions that might aggravate tension and to facilitate the early resumption of the six-party talks, with a view to the expeditious implementation of the joint statement issued on 19 September 2005 by China, the Democratic People's Republic of Korea, Japan, the Republic of Korea, the Russian Federation and the United States of America, to achieve the verifiable denuclearization of the Korean peninsula and to maintain peace and stability on the Korean peninsula and in north-east Asia;

14. *Calls upon* the Democratic People's Republic of Korea to return immediately to the six-party talks without precondition and to work towards the expeditious implementation of the joint statement issued on 19 September 2005 by China, the Democratic People's Republic of Korea, Japan, the Republic of Korea, the Russian Federation and the United States of America;

15. *Affirms* that it shall keep the actions of the Democratic People's Republic of Korea under continuous review and that it shall be prepared to review the appropriateness of the measures contained in paragraph 8 above, including the strengthening, modification, suspension or lifting of the measures, as may be needed at that time in the light of the Democratic People's Republic of Korea's compliance with the provisions of the resolution;

16. *Underlines* that further decisions will be required, should additional measures be necessary;

17. *Decides* to remain actively seized of the matter.

Following the adoption of the resolution, the United States said the test posed one of the gravest threats to international peace and security that the Council had ever had to confront. The resolution sent a strong and clear message to the DPRK and other would-be proliferators that they would meet with serious repercussions in continuing to pursue weapons of mass destruction. In response to the DPRK provocation, the United States would increase its defense cooperation with its allies to protect against the DPRK aggression, and to prevent that country from importing or exporting nuclear and other missile technologies.

China agreed that the Council's action should both indicate the international community's firm position and help create conditions for the peaceful solution to the DPRK nuclear issue through dialogue. Sanctions were not the end in themselves. China did not approve of the practice of inspecting cargo to and from the DPRK, and urged the countries concerned to adopt a responsible attitude in that regard, refraining from taking any provocative steps that could intensify the tension. China still believed that the six-party talks were the realistic means of handling the issue. It also firmly opposed the use of force.

The Russian Federation said that the resolution contained a set of carefully targeted measures, aimed at dealing with the main problem: to make the DPRK correct its dangerous course, return to NPT, and resume, without preconditions, its participation in the six-party talks. That could be done only through political and diplomatic means. The Council should exercise strict control over the measures to be taken against the DPRK, and the resolution reflected concern over the humanitarian consequences of sanctions.

The DPRK rejected the resolution, saying that it was "gangster-like" of the Council to adopt such a coercive resolution against it, while neglecting the nuclear threat posed by the United States against the DPRK. The Council had completely lost its impartiality and persisted in applying double standards. The 9 October test, a further measure for bolstering the country's deterrent for self-defence, was a response to the United States threat, sanctions and pressure. The DPRK had made every effort to settle the issue through dialogue and negotiations, but the United States administration had responded with a policy of sanctions and blockade. The DPRK would feel no need for even a single nuclear weapon once it was no longer exposed to the United States threat. Instead, the United States had manipulated the Council into adopting a resolution pressurizing Pyongyang.

Security Council Committee. On 20 October [S/2006/833], Council members elected Peter Burian (Slovakia) as Chairman and Argentina and Qatar as Vice-Chairmen, until 31 December, of the Security Council Committee established pursuant to resolution 1718(2006). On 1 November [S/2006/853 & Corr.1], the Committee chairman transmitted to the Council President a list of items, materials, equipment, goods and technology related to other weapons of mass destruction programmes.

In November-December, 41 States and the EU [S/AC.49/2006/1-S/AC.49/2006/8 & Add.1; S/AC.49/2006/30 & Add.1; S/AC.49/2006/31 & Add.1; S/AC.49/2006/33-34] reported to the Committee Chairman on steps they had taken to implement the Council's resolution.

Other matters

Cambodia

In 2006, the Secretary-General continued to put in place arrangements for the entry into force of the Agreement between the United Nations and the Royal Government of Cambodia concerning the Prosecution under Cambodian Law of Crimes Committed During the Period of Democratic Kampuchea. The Agreement, approved by the General Assembly in resolution 57/228 [YUN 2003, p. 385], regulated cooperation between the United Nations and the Royal Government of Cambodia in bringing to trial senior leaders of Democratic Kampuchea and those who were most responsible for the crimes committed during the period 17 April 1975–6 January 1979. The Agreement provided, among other things, the legal basis and the principles and modalities of such cooperation.

On 6 March, in accordance with the Agreement, the Secretary-General communicated to Cambodia the nominations of international judges and prosecutors of the Extraordinary Chambers for the Prosecution under Cambodian Law of Crimes Committed during the Period of Democratic Kampuchea. On 4 May, the Supreme Council of the Magistracy of Cambodia selected and appointed international judges to the Trial Chamber, the Supreme Court and the Pre-Trial Chamber, as well as the international co-investigating Judge and the international co-prosecutor. The Supreme Council also appointed national judges, co-investigating judges and co-prosecutors from among serving Cambodian judges and prosecutors. On 3 July, the national and international judicial officers were sworn in during a ceremony held at Phnom Penh's Royal Palace.

In July, a Rules and Procedure Committee and a Judicial Administration Committee were appointed. The draft rules of procedure were completed in October and submitted to a plenary session of the Extraordinary Chamber for adoption. At its November session, the plenary failed to adopt the draft rules of procedure, because of disagreement over the role of the defence and the right of foreign lawyers to appear before the Extraordinary Chambers. To move the process forward, the plenary created a Review Committee to resolve those issues. Once consensus was reached a new plenary would be called to adopt them.

The Office of the Co-Prosecutors became operational in July and prepared standard operating procedures pending the adoption of the draft rules of procedure. The co-investigating judges took up their functions in September when their Office became operational. The head of the Defence Support Section took up his office in October.

On 6 February, by **decision 60/553**, the Assembly concurred with the Secretary-General's recommendation in his report on Khmer Rouge trials [YUN 2004, p. 380] that the international judges, the international co-prosecutor and the international co-investigating judge should be deemed UN officials for the purposes of their terms and conditions of service, and approved the granting of that status.

Fiji

In a 29 November press statement [SC/8881], delivered by the Security Council President, Council members expressed concern about the challenges posed by the Fiji Military Commander, Josaia Voreqe Bainimarama, to the Government of Prime Minister Laisenia Qarase. They called upon the Fiji military to avoid taking any action that would undermine the rule of law and run counter to the interests of the people of Fiji. They encouraged the Secretary-General to continue to use his good offices to help resolve the dispute in an orderly and peaceful manner.

In another statement issued on 7 December [SC/8894], Council members expressed concern about the situation in Fiji, where the Military Forces Commander had announced that the military had taken over the executive authority from the democratically elected Government. They expressed their hope that a peaceful solution to the situation would be achieved and that the Government would be reinstated as soon as possible. Council members welcomed and supported efforts by the Pacific Islands Forum, regional and international entities and the Secretary-General to resolve the situation.

India-Pakistan

During the year, steady and meaningful progress was achieved by India and Pakistan in their bilateral dialogue, agreed to in 2004 [YUN 2004, p. 382]. On 13 February [S/2006/104], Pakistan informed the Security Council that the Foreign Secretaries of both countries had met in New Delhi on 17 and 18 January to commence the third round of talks under the India-Pakistan composite dialogue framework. The two Foreign Secretaries held a detailed exchange of views on Jammu and Kashmir and agreed to continue the dialogue in a purposeful and forward-looking manner to find a peaceful and negotiated final settlement. They noted with satisfaction the opening of the five crossing points across the line of control and expressed the hope that the process of promoting greater interaction between divided families would get further impetus.

The United Nations Military Observer Group in India and Pakistan (UNMOGIP) continued in 2006 to monitor the situation in Jammu and Kashmir.

Myanmar

In 2006, the Secretary-General continued to provide his good offices in the pursuit of national reconciliation and democratization in Myanmar. Under-Secretary-General for Political Affairs, Ibrahim Gambari, who visited the country from 18 to 20 May—the first high-level talks between the United Nations and Myanmar in more than two years—discussed with the Myanmar authorities improved safety and access for humanitarian assistance, restraint in military operations that affected civilians and the possibility of internal dialogue that could lead to national reconciliation. Mr. Gambari visited Myanmar again from 9 to 12 November.

Press statement. On 16 May [SG/S/10464], the Spokesman for the Secretary-General announced the visit (18-20 May) to Myanmar by the Under-Secretary-General, Ibrahim Gambari, to assess developments in the country and see what more could be done, including by the United Nations, to move the country in the direction of all-inclusive democracy, sustainable development and national reconciliation. The Under-Secretary-General would convey a clear message that Myanmar's prospects for improved relations with the international community would depend on tangible progress in restoring democratic freedom and full respect for human rights.

Report of Special Rapporteur. According to the Special Rapporteur of the Human Rights Council [A/61/369 and Corr.1], who was not allowed in the country, the number of political prisoners was estimated at 1,185. On 27 May, the house arrest of National League for Democracy (NLD) General Secretary Daw Aung San Suu Kyi was further prolonged by 12 months, in spite of various international appeals, including by the Secretary-General. From April to July, 1,038 NLD members were reportedly forced to resign from the party following intimidation and threats. Grave human rights violations had taken place with impunity, authorized by "security laws". The continued misuse of the legal system led to the criminalization of the exercise of fundamental freedoms by political opponents, human rights defenders and victims of human rights abuses.

Press statement. In another statement issued on 30 May [SG/SM/10485], the Secretary-General expressed disappointment that the Myanmar authorities had extended the detention under house arrest of Daw Aung San Suu Kyi and other political detainees and indicated his intention to make every effort to secure their release. The Secretary-General urged the authorities to take the steps they had discussed with Under-Secretary-General Gambari during his May visit to the country (see above).

On 7 June [SG/SM10505], the Secretary-General welcomed the release from prison of Su Su Nway, who had been imprisoned since October 2005. He urged the Myanmar authorities to follow up that measure with further action that would alleviate the political atmosphere, including lifting the remaining restrictions on Daw Aung San Suu Kyi and other political leaders.

On 1 September [SG/SM/10297], he accepted with regret the resignation of Tan Sri Razali Ismail, his Special Envoy for Myanmar since 2000.

Security Council consideration. The Security Council, on 15 September [meeting 5526], decided, by vote (10-4-1), to include the item "The situation in Myanmar" on its agenda and to consider it after 19 September. The action came after the United States informed the Council President, on 15 September [S/2006/742], that the United States and other Council members were concerned about the deteriorating situation in Myanmar, which was likely to endanger the maintenance of international peace and security.

Addressing the Council, the United States recalled that in his December 2005 and June 2006 briefings to the Council, Mr. Gambari had described the grave human rights and humanitarian conditions in Myanmar, including the detention of more than 1,100 political prisoners, as well as the outflow from the country of refugees, drugs, HIV/AIDS and other diseases. As those conditions threatened to have a destabilizing impact on the region, the United States requested that the situation be placed on the Council's agenda, and that a senior Secretariat official brief Member States on the implications of that situation for international peace and security. Since the adoption of resolution 688(1991) [YUN 1991, p. 204] on the massive flow of Iraqi refugees across the country's borders, such matters had been deemed threats to international peace and security.

China said that only threats to international peace and security warranted inclusion on the Council's agenda. If other issues, such as human rights, refugees, drugs and HIV/AIDS, were also considered for inclusion, any country facing similar issues could be inscribed in the agenda as well. Few countries in the region thought the situation in Myanmar was a threat to peace and security, and the fact that some countries across the ocean thought otherwise was a far cry from reality. Requesting the Council to discuss a country's internal affairs would undermine the Council's authority. Myanmar's efforts to solve its own problems had been recognized, and the situation was gradually improving. Following his visit in May, Mr. Gambari had indicated that Myanmar was ready to collaborate with the United Nations and turn over a new leaf. On 10 July, the Non-Aligned Movement expressed its opposition to the item's inclusion on the Council's agenda and, in August, the Chair of Association of South-East Asian Nations (ASEAN) visited Myanmar. The international community had achieved some hard-won gains, and an intervention by the Council would have a negative impact. So long as the situation in Myanmar did not threaten international peace and security, the question should not be included in the Council's agenda.

Qatar noted that Myanmar's neighbours did not consider the country's human rights situation to constitute a threat to regional peace and security and felt that the door should be left open for the relevant organs to deal with such questions. Including the question on the Council's agenda was inappropriate and would close diplomatic channels to the competent international human rights institutions.

At a resumed, closed Council meeting on 29 September [meeting 5526], Council members, Mr. Gambari and the representative of Myanmar had an exchange of views on the item "The situation in Myanmar".

Communication. On 8 December [S/2006/969], Cuba, on behalf of the Non-Aligned Movement, conveyed to the Council President the concerns of the Movement on the intention expressed by a permanent member of the Council to present a draft resolution on Myanmar. The movement did not consider the situation in Myanmar a threat to international peace and security, and opposed attempts to categorize Myanmar as such. Neighbouring countries that were members of the Movement stated that the situation did not threaten regional peace and stability. The position of the Movement was therefore that the situation in Myanmar should not be on the Council's agenda.

Nepal

The Secretary-General continued to work closely with all sides to encourage a negotiated political solution to a conflict in Nepal that had claimed more than 13,000 lives. In April, mass demonstrations across the country, with strong participation by women and marginalized groups, brought an end to King Gyanendra's direct rule, led to the restoration of Parliament and a mutual ceasefire, and opened the way for further negotiations between the Seven-Party Alliance of mainstream political parties and the Communist Party of Nepal (Maoist).

Communication. In a 30 January statement [S/2006/77] on the political situation in Nepal, Austria, on behalf of the European Union (EU), condemned the use of force to suppress the Nepalese people's exercise of the rights to freedom of assembly and expression; found the Government's restrictions on society, political parties and civil society disproportionate; called upon King Gyanendra, the Government and the security forces to restore political and civil liberties and release all political prisoners and human rights defenders; condemned the resumption of Maoist violence, including the murder of an election candidate; regretted the Government's failure to seize the opportunity to declare a truce provided by the Maoists' unilateral ceasefire; underlined that for elections to be meaningful they should be held in consultation with the political parties; and said that the lack of such consultation meant that the planned municipal elections were likely to polarize positions.

Secretary-General's letter (November). The Secretary-General reported to the Council President [S/2006/920] that, on 9 August, Nepal's Prime Minister Girija Prasad Koirala and Communist Party Chairman Pushpa Kamal Dahal (Prachanda), in identical letters, had informed him that peace talks between the Seven-Party Alliance forming the Government of Nepal and the Communist Party of Nepal (Maoist) led to the conclusion, on 8 November, of an agreement, which outlined the next steps in the political process leading to free and fair elections for a Constituent Assembly in 2007. By that Agreement, the parties agreed on the cantonment of the combatants of the Maoist People's Liberation Army and the storage of arms and ammunition on both sides. That was consolidated by a Comprehensive Peace Agreement signed on 21 November, by which the parties declared their commitment to transforming the ceasefire into permanent peace. The Secretary-General appointed Ian Martin (United Kingdom) as his Personal Representative to undertake consultations with all parties in order to build on the common understanding that had emerged.

Arising out of those agreements, the Government and the Communist Party requested UN assistance in creating a free and fair atmosphere for the election of a constituent Assembly and the peace process; in human rights monitoring through the Office of the UN High Commissioner for Human Rights in Nepal; in monitoring the code of conduct during the ceasefire; deploying civilian personnel to monitor and verify the confinement of Communist Party combatants and their weapons within designated cantonment areas; monitoring the Nepal Army to ensure that it remained in its barracks and its weapons were not used for or against any side; and providing election observation for the election of the Constituent Assembly. Nepal also requested further UN assistance to help verify and monitor the cantonment of the Maoist combatants, monitor and inspect the storing of all arms and ammunition held by the Communist Party and the Army, and monitor the election of the Constituent Assembly, to be held by mid-June 2007.

In response to those requests, the Secretary-General indicated that he intended to deploy a technical assessment mission to determine logistical and security requirements and develop an integrated concept of operations for a UN political mission in Nepal; an advance group of up to 35 monitors to serve as the vanguard for the proposed UN monitoring presence for the management of arms and armed personnel; and an initial team of up to 25 electoral personnel to provide technical advice and support to the Nepalese electoral authorities and the parties. He also informed the Council that once consultations with the parties had progressed sufficiently and the logistical support and security requirements for a fully fledged mission had been assessed, he would propose to the Council a concept of operations for such a mission.

On 28 November, following tripartite negotiations with the Secretary-General's Personal Representative and his advisers, the parties reached agreement on the modalities for the monitoring of arms and armies, which detailed the arrangements for the UN's role. The Personal Representative signed the agreement as a witness on 8 December.

SECURITY COUNCIL ACTION

On 1 December [meeting 5576], following consultations among Security Council members, the President made statement **S/PRST/2006/49** on behalf of the Council:

> The Security Council warmly welcomes the signing on 21 November 2006 by the Government of Nepal and the Communist Party of Nepal (Maoist) of a Comprehensive Peace Agreement, and the stated commitment of both parties to transforming the existing ceasefire into a permanent peace.
>
> The Council notes the request of the parties for United Nations assistance in implementing key aspects of the Agreement, in particular monitoring of arrangements relating to the management of arms and armed personnel of both sides and election monitoring. The Council agrees that the United Nations should respond positively and expeditiously to this request for assistance.
>
> The Council welcomes and expresses support for the intention of the Secretary-General to send a technical assessment mission to Nepal with a view to proposing, following close consultations with the parties, a fully developed concept of United Nations operations, including a United Nations political mission to deliver the assistance requested, and to dispatch an advance deployment of essential personnel of up to 35 monitors and 25 electoral personnel.
>
> The Council stands ready to consider the formal proposals of the Secretary-General as soon as the technical assessment is complete.

Report of Secretary-General (December). In his 20 December report on children and armed conflict in Nepal [S/2006/1007], submitted further to resolution 1612(2005) [YUN 2005, p. 863], the Secretary-General provided information on compliance and progress in ending the recruitment and use of children and other grave violations committed against children in situations of armed conflict. The November Comprehensive Peace Agreement had committed the parties to reintegrating children associated with armed groups into their families. The report made recommendations for stronger action to protect war-affected children.

Tajikistan

In 2006, with the assistance of the United Nations Tajikistan Office of Peacebuilding (UNTOP), the Government of Tajikistan took further steps to consolidate peace in that country. In view of the important role being played by UNTOP and the country's continuing need for assistance in the area of peacebuilding, the Secretary-General announced, on 26 May [S/2006/355], his intention to continue UNTOP activities for a further year, until 1 June 2007. The Security Council on 31 May [S/2006/356] took note of his intention.

UNTOP, established in 2000 [YUN 2000, p. 315], following the withdrawal of the United Nations Mission of Observers in Tajikistan (UNMOT), continued to foster national dialogue and reconciliation, assist in strengthening democratic institutions and conflict-prevention mechanisms, promote the rule of law and build human rights capacity. UNTOP developed a technical assistance project for the November presidential elections, executed in cooperation with national electoral authorities. A national dialogue project in political pluralism and peace consolidation brought together in 2005-2006 more than 500 Government officials, political party activists and civil society representatives in meetings across the country. The project provided a forum for building trust and consensus on issues relating to the sustainability of the peace process. Training seminars on human rights and conflict management involved more than 900 community leaders, educators, lawyers and local officials. Training for Interior Ministry personnel on international legal standards in police operations involved 40 instructors and more than 1,000 Interior Ministry staff.

The 2006 UN Appeal for Tajikistan, issued in January by the Office of the UN Resident Coordinator, requested $51.3 million for the country's development needs.

United Arab Emirates–Iran

Greater Tunb, Lesser Tunb and Abu Musa

On 10 February [S/2006/112], the United Arab Emirates requested that the Security Council retain on its agenda for 2006 the item entitled "Letter dated 3 December 1971 from the Permanent Representatives of Algeria, Iraq, the Libyan Arab Jamahiriya and the People's Democratic Republic of Yemen to the United Nations addressed to the President of the Security Council", concerning Iran's occupation of Greater Tunb, Lesser Tunb and Abu Musa, until a settlement of the dispute was reached through direct negotiations or through recourse to the International Court of Justice.

In communications issued between 15 March and 8 December [A/60/722-S/2006/169, A/61/620-S/2006/949], the United Arab Emirates transmitted to the Secretary-General statements made by the Ministerial Council of the Gulf Cooperation Council reiterating its support of the sovereignty of the United Arab Emirates over the islands.

The League of Arab States, in communications transmitted between 13 March and 14 September [S/2006/168, S/2006/285, S/2006/745], informed the Security Council President of the adoption of a decision and two resolutions denouncing the Iranian occupation of Greater Tunb, Lesser Tunb and Abu Musa, and affirming the sovereignty of the United Arab Emirates over the three islands. The League also called upon the Secretary-General and the Council President to maintain the issue among the matters of which the Security Council was seized until Iran ended its occupation.

In letters transmitted between 24 March and 27 September [S/2006/191, S/2006/200, S/2006/381, S/2006/787], Iran stated that the three islands were an integral and eternal part of the Iranian territory and rejected any claims to the contrary. It continued to emphasize the importance of negotiations between itself and the United Arab Emirates to improve bilateral relations and remove any misunderstandings between the two countries.

Regional meetings

On 27 June [A/60/910-S/2006/444], Kazakhstan transmitted to the Secretary-General the Declaration of the Second Summit of the Conference on Interaction and Confidence Building Measures in Asia (CICA) (Almaty, 17 June), which addressed political, security and development issues affecting the region.

Chapter V

Europe and the Mediterranean

The restoration of peace and stability in the post-conflict countries in the Europe and Mediterranean region advanced in 2006, as efforts to re-establish their institutions and social and economic infrastructure continued. However, a number of issues remained unresolved.

Led by the European Union (EU), the international community continued to assist Bosnia and Herzegovina to move towards full integration into Europe through the EU Stabilization and Association Process. The country adopted an EU integration strategy, its first long-term strategic document leading towards full EU membership, and made progress in meeting the North Atlantic Treaty Organization Partnership for Peace requirements, which culminated in an invitation for Bosnia and Herzegovina to join the Partnership. In October, domestic authorities successfully carried out the country's first self-organized general elections since the war ended in 1995. The Security Council, in a November resolution, authorized Member States, acting through or in cooperation with the EU, to establish, for a further 12 months, a multinational stabilization force (the European Union Force) and welcomed the NATO decision to continue its presence in Bosnia and Herzegovina.

In Kosovo (Serbia and Montenegro), the United Nations Interim Administration Mission in Kosovo (UNMIK) continued to assist in the building of a modern, multi-ethnic society. The overall security situation in the province remained stable, allowing UNMIK to continue to monitor progress towards the fulfillment of the benchmarks set out in the 2004 Kosovo Standards Implementation Plan and the 2001 Constitutional Framework for Provisional Self-Government, including transferring authority to Kosovo's domestic institutions. The year began with several leadership changes following the January death of Kosovo's President, Ibrahim Rugova, and with the opening of negotiations to determine the final status of the province. Increased efforts by the Provisional Institutions to reach out to minority communities, including Kosovo Serb communities with close ties to Belgrade (Serbia and Montenegro), met with challenges throughout the year as relations with Belgrade deteriorated. However, significant progress towards European integration was made by the new leadership of Kosovo in August when its Government adopted a European Partnership Action Plan. In November, the Secretary-General's Special Envoy for the future status of Kosovo announced that the presentation of the Settlement Proposal would be delayed until the end of January 2007 to allow for the holding of parliamentary elections in Serbia.

In a historic referendum in May, Montenegro voted to separate from Serbia. In June, the General Assembly welcomed Montenegro to membership in the United Nations.

Renewed efforts were made to end the stalemate in the Georgian Abkhaz peace process. During the year, the Special Representative of the Secretary-General in Georgia convened the first session of the resumed Coordination Council of the Georgian and Abkhaz sides, which had not met since 2001. Senior officials of the Group of Friends of the Secretary-General (France, Germany, Russian Federation, United Kingdom, United States) continued to encourage dialogue on the basis of the 2001 Basic Principles for the Distribution of Competencies between Tbilisi (the Georgian Government) and Sukhumi (the Abkhaz leadership). A difficult and complex situation prevailed on the ground, however, with Abkhaz authorities claiming that Georgian forces had violated the 1994 Agreement on a Ceasefire and Separation of Forces (Moscow Agreement), and Georgia demanding the withdrawal of Russian peacekeeping forces from the conflict zone. Compliance with the Moscow Agreement and with Security Council resolutions 858(1993) and 937(1994) was monitored by the United Nations Observer Mission in Georgia (UNOMIG) and by a collective peacekeeping force of the Commonwealth of Independent States.

No progress was made towards settling the conflict between Armenia and Azerbaijan over the occupied Nagorny Karabakh region in Azerbaijan. In December, Nagorny Karabakh held an independence referendum, the results of which were rejected by Azerbaijan, several neighbouring States and the Organization of the Islamic Conference, and its status remained uncertain at year's end.

Similarly, a 17 September independence referendum in the Transnistrian region of Moldova was rejected by Moldova and by the newly-formed Organization for Democracy and Economic

Development–GUAM, which consisted of Azerbaijan, Georgia, the Republic of Moldova and Ukraine.

In the Mediterranean, the situation in Cyprus remained unresolved. During an overview mission to the country in July by the UN Under-Secretary-General for Political Affairs, Greek Cypriot and Turkish Cypriot leaders signed a set of principles and a decision on cooperation and began to meet regularly regarding issues affecting the day-to-day life of the Cypriot people. Despite such progress, serious tensions continued to exist between the two Cypriot communities. The United Nations Peacekeeping Force in Cyprus continued to cooperate with its UN partners and the two communities to facilitate projects of benefit to Greek and Turkish Cypriots in the buffer zone and to advance towards the goal of restoring normal conditions and humanitarian functions in Cyprus.

Bosnia and Herzegovina

During 2006, the European Union (EU) continued to lead the international community's efforts to assist the two entities comprising the Republic of Bosnia and Herzegovina—the Federation of Bosnia and Herzegovina (where mainly Bosnian Muslims (Bosniacs) and Bosnian Croats resided) and Republika Srpska (where mostly Bosnian Serbs resided)—in implementing the 1995 General Framework Agreement for Peace in Bosnia and Herzegovina and the annexes thereto (the Peace Agreement) [YUN 1995, p. 544]. The Office of the High Representative for the Implementation of the Peace Agreement, was responsible for the Agreement's civilian aspects [YUN 1996, p. 293], while the European Union Police Mission in Bosnia and Herzegovina (EUPM) helped to develop sustainable policing arrangements. The EU Force (EUFOR) mission was responsible for the Agreement's military aspects, which were transferred to it by the North Atlantic Treaty Organization (NATO) in December 2004 [YUN 2004, p. 401]. The Peace Implementation Council (PIC) and its Steering Board continued to oversee and facilitate the Agreement's implementation.

The High Representative reported on progress made in the Agreement's implementation process and related political developments in the country during the year in the context of his mission implementation plan, which set out a number of core tasks to be accomplished [YUN 2003, p. 401]. Bosnia and Herzegovina undertook several reforms, particularly with regard to the rule of law, refugee return, police restructuring, defence and economic development, in accordance with European standards, and continued to work towards full integration into Europe through the EU Stabilization and Association Process and NATO Partnership for Peace requirements. In March, Bosnia and Herzegovina adopted an EU integration strategy, its first long-term strategic document leading towards full EU membership and, in November, it was invited to join the Partnership for Peace. The country's October general elections were the first since the war to be wholly organized and run by domestic authorities.

Implementation of Peace Agreement

Civilian aspects

The civilian aspects of the 1995 Peace Agreement entailed a wide range of activities, including humanitarian aid, infrastructure rehabilitation, establishment of political and constitutional institutions, promoting respect for human rights and the holding of free and fair elections. The High Representative for the Implementation of the Peace Agreement, who chaired the PIC Steering Board and other key implementation bodies, was the final authority with regard to implementing the civilian aspects of the Peace Agreement [YUN 1995, p. 547]. The reports on EUPM activities were submitted by the High Representative to the Security Council President through the Secretary-General.

Office of High Representative

Reports of High Representative. On 30 January [S/2006/61], the Security Council President informed the Secretary-General that the Council welcomed the 2005 PIC decision [YUN 2005, p. 460] to appoint Christian Schwarz-Schilling (Germany) to succeed Lord Paddy Ashdown as the High Representative for Bosnia and Herzegovina, effective 31 January 2006.

The new High Representative reported to the Security Council, through the Secretary-General, on the peace implementation process for the periods 1 February to 30 June 2006 [S/2006/810] and 1 July to 31 March 2007 [S/2007/253]. (For details on the specific topics of the reports see below.)

The Council considered the High Representative's report covering the latter half of 2005 [ibid.] on 18 April, and his report covering the first half of 2006 on 8 and 21 November.

On 21 November, the Council adopted resolution 1722(2006) (see p. 457).

Mission implementation plan

The High Representative, briefing the Security Council on 18 April [meeting 5412], during consideration of his report covering the latter half of 2005 [YUN 2005, p. 460], said that he saw three priorities for Bosnia and Herzegovina in 2006: constitutional reform; the general elections in October; and the ongoing stability and association agreement negotiations with the EU. In his October report [S/2006/810], he stated that his Office had endeavoured to implement its work plan and the revised Mission Implementation Plan (MIP), which was approved by PIC in March, but its efforts had been hampered by the politicking that led up to the 1 October elections. Three core tasks of the MIP remained incomplete: rule of law; reforming the economy; and institution-building.

In January, the EU adopted a revised European Partnership with Bosnia and Herzegovina and judged that the conclusion of the Stabilization and Association Agreement depended, in particular, on progress achieved by the country in developing its legislative framework and administration capacity, the implementation of police reform, the adoption and implementation of all necessary public broadcasting legislation and full cooperation with the International Tribunal for the Former Yugoslavia (ICTY) (see p. 1484). In March, the country's Council of Ministers adopted an action plan to address the European Partnership priorities; in April, it adopted an EU integration strategy, its first long-term strategic document setting out the steps and benchmarks required in order to fulfil membership criteria.

Police restructuring, which was to take place through a phased implementation plan and which would require that legislative and budgetary competencies for all police matters be vested at the State level, faced significant challenges during the year. Immediately upon taking office at the end of February, Prime Minister Milorad Dodik of Republika Srpska launched an attack on the legitimacy of the Police Restructuring Directorate Steering Board and continued to obstruct reforms throughout the year. Despite Serb determination to maintain the name Republika Srpska for police forces deployed on its territory, the Steering Board finally opted for a model based on State and local police authorities with no place for entity police forces. Republika Srpska responded by unilaterally downgrading its participation in the Steering Board to that of observer. In December, the Directorate completed its final report on a proposed plan for the implementation of the reform of police structures and forwarded it to the Council of Ministers for review in 2007.

No progress was made during the year in apprehending Radovan Karadzić, Ratko Mladić and other main indictees not yet in the custody of ICTY, a situation that had so far disqualified Bosnia and Herzegovina from joining the NATO Partnership for Peace. Nonetheless, in November, NATO invited the country to join the Partnership, together with Serbia and with Montenegro, stressing that the three countries were expected to improve their coordination with ICTY.

In May, EU Foreign Ministers expressed the EU readiness to, in principle, reinforce its engagement in the country in the context of the envisaged closure of the Office of the High Representative. On 23 June, the PIC Steering Board decided that the Office should immediately begin preparations to close as of 30 June 2007, taking into account the situation of Bosnia and Herzegovina and the region. In October, the EU Secretary-General and High Representative for Common Foreign and Security Policy, Javier Solana, and the EU Commissioner for Enlargement, Olli Rehn, submitted their second joint report on a reinforced EU presence in Bosnia and Herzegovina; on 23 November, the High Representative submitted a detailed proposal for the consideration of the EU General Affairs and External Relations Council on the mandate, structure and resources required for such a reinforced engagement. However, due to such factors as the virtual halt in reform and a prolonged void in government following the October elections, the issue of the Office's closure remained uncertain at the end of 2006.

Civil affairs

The High Representative, in his report covering the first half of 2006 [S/2006/810], noted that a recent accentuation of dangers and divisions in Bosnia and Herzegovina had not only made the passage of reform legislation impossible, but had also poisoned political discourse. Politicians in Republika Srpska, referring to the 21 May independence referendum in Montenegro (see p. 472) and the Kosovo (Serbia) final status talks (see p. 466), claimed the right to a referendum on the future of Republika Srpska. On the other hand, some Bosniac politicians suggested that Republika Srpska be abolished. The first six months of the year comprised two distinct periods: one of high expectations and optimism resulting from the unprecedented six-party agreement on constitutional reform that, after several months of intensive talks, was signed on 18 March; and a subsequent period of political antagonism, increasingly underscored by nationalist rhetoric following the narrow defeat of that constitutional reform package in the lower House on 26 April. The second half of the year was dominated by the general election campaign and the subsequent negotiations to form new governments at the state, entity and cantonal levels.

The first general elections since the war to be wholly organized and run by the domestic authorities took place peacefully and successfully on 1 October. The results showed that the traditional nationalist parties that had dominated the political scene in the country since the first free elections in 1990 had weakened. However, the parties that employed the most vociferous rhetoric during the campaign were also the biggest winners. The Alliance of Independent Social Democrats (SNSD) won 41 of the 83 seats in the National Assembly of Republika Srpska, coming close to an absolute majority and more than doubling its previous 19 seats. By contrast, the Serbian Democratic Party (SDS) saw its tally fall from 26 to 17 seats. In the Federation, the Party for Democratic Action (SDA) retained its position as the biggest Bosniac party, with 28 seats in the lower House. However, its rival, the Party for Bosnia and Herzegovina (SBiH), increased its seats from 15 to 24 and its candidate, Haris Silajdžić, defeated SDA leader Sulejman Tihić in the race for the Bosniac place on the country's Presidency. Despite the success of the elections, both the intense pre-election environment and the complicated post-election situation were far from conducive to the implementation of reforms; by the end of 2006, only Republika Srpska had a reconstructed government.

Beginning on 1 January, Bosnia and Herzegovina had a single defence ministry and military force. The Defence Minister, Nikola Radovanović, oversaw what was expected to be a two-year period of implementation and integration, while a team of defence ministry experts began the process of planning, organizing, coordinating, and monitoring the transfer of all defence functions and personnel to state level. NATO continued to assist in the process and the Office of the High Representative provided political support to entity authorities with regard to implementation. The formation of the new Armed Forces of Bosnia and Herzegovina was slated to be completed by the end of 2007.

On 23 January, the EU repealed its long-standing arms embargo on Bosnia and Herzegovina.

The unification of the Mostar city administration slowed considerably during the first half of 2006, with little if any progress made in finalizing the systematization of the administration, forming an urban planning institution, resolving the status of Hercegovacka Radio-Television and various cultural institutions, or forming a single public utility company. The High Representative therefore appointed a special envoy to mediate, arbitrate or recommend other solutions to outstanding disputes. Despite resolution by the envoy of several long-standing issues, the High Representative was obliged, in December, to impose solutions pertaining to urban and spatial planning that he had recommended but had been unable to convince the polarized parties to adopt. Brcko District was also characterized by mounting disputes within the majority coalition and declining effectiveness on the part of the Government, all of which were exacerbated by the State-wide election campaign and other factors. A working group, initiated by the United States Government in November 2005 to find long-term political solutions to problems plaguing Brcko's relationship with the State, began work during the year. The Brcko District Office in the Council of Ministers opened in March.

The State Court, in addition to handling a number of ongoing complex war crimes trials, initiated trials of cases transferred from ICTY (Savo Todović, Mitar Rašević, Paško Ljubičić). A first instance verdict of crimes against humanity was handed down in another case transferred from ICTY (Radovan Stanković). Although there was little or no progress in capturing remaining ICTY fugitives, Republika Srpska, in December, adopted a new action plan directed at locating, apprehending or arranging the voluntary surrender of such fugitives.

Judicial reform

Although the Rule of Law Department of the Office of the High Representative had closed at the end of 2005, the Office, mindful that work remained to be done to ensure that past reforms were fully implemented, established a unit for that task. The Office also identified systemic problems in the work of prosecutors, facilitated improved cooperation between them and the police and produced an analysis of strategies and best practices in the prosecution of organized crime in other European countries and distributed it to local prosecutors. It further contributed to ensuring the successful transition of the Registry of the State Court to full domestic ownership by concluding a new registry agreement. Of particular importance in that agreement were provisions authorizing the High Judicial and Prosecutorial Council to appoint all judges to the State Court and all prosecutors to the State Prosecutor's Office, and the provisions reorganizing the Registry and its financing. The agreement also provided for the integration of national Registry staff into domestic judicial institutions from 2006 to 2009, with the goal of ensuring that Bosnia and Herzegovina assumed full responsibility for the State Court and Prosecutor's Office with regard to finance, administration and personnel matters. A further aim was to guarantee the long-term sustainability and capacity of domestic judicial institutions to process war crimes and organized crime cases.

Economic reform

Although the pace of economic reform slowed during the first half of 2006, economic growth during the year remained relatively robust. It was estimated that real gross domestic product (GDP) would grow by 5.7 per cent in 2006, compared with 5 per cent in 2005.

The value-added tax (VAT) was introduced on 1 January at a single rate of 17 per cent. Actual revenues from the tax far exceeded initial projections, reaching a final total of some 4 billion convertible marka (KM). However, there was intense disagreement over revenue allocation among the entities and Brcko District. The contention also caused delays in reaching an agreement on the National Fiscal Council, which, by the end of 2006, still had no basis in law. The introduction of VAT had an impact on retail prices, producing a one-time rise in the average rate of inflation to 6.8 per cent. Exports rose and the High Representative reported that, with improved statistics, the current account deficit should show a narrowing from 21 per cent of GDP in 2005 to about 13.5 per cent in 2006. The external deficit, however, remained very large.

Economic policy advances were confirmed during the year by the decision of Moody's Investor Service to upgrade the country's key debt rating from B3 to B2. Moody's highlighted, in particular, the resolution of the longstanding issue of compensation for frozen foreign currency deposits, plans to deal with the other internal debts, restitution and the smooth introduction of the VAT.

Progress in improving the business environment, restructuring corporations and making structural reforms slowed in 2006. The absence of political interest or will stymied privatization efforts in the Federation, although there was significant overall progress in the Republika Srpska in privatizing a number of large companies. The country also faced the challenge of increasing power generation capacity and creating an overall national infrastructure policy in the face of a marked increase in demand for most modes of transportation.

In December, Bosnia and Herzegovina joined the Central European Free Trade Agreement, which provided the Western Balkan States with a single set of trade rules harmonized with those of the EU.

Public administration reform

In his October report [S/2006/810], the High Representative stated that the authorities of Bosnia and Herzegovina continued to engage actively in the process of public administration reform during the first half of 2006. The National Public Administration Reform Coordinator finalized the first draft of the national public administration reform strategy and an action plan for adoption by the State, entities and Brcko District. The strategy encompassed human resources; legislative drafting; administrative procedures; information technology; institutional communications; and public finance. On 22 June, the three Prime Ministers and the Brcko mayor publicly endorsed the strategy. Although six intergovernmental working groups were established to implement the action plan, the High Represetative stated, in a later report [S/2007/253], that implementation had not begun in earnest at the end of 2006.

Media development

The final handover of responsibility for public broadcasting by the Office of the High Representative to domestic institutions was delayed in 2006. Republika Srpska adopted its public broadcasting law on 11 May, but the Croats invoked the Vital National Interest Procedure, referring to the constitutional court the 4 April Federation public broadcasting law. On 19 July, the entity court ruled in their favour. In November, the Bosniac club in the Federation House of Peoples appealed to the Constitutional Court of Bosnia and Herzegovina, seeking to reverse the entity court's ruling. While no decision had been made on the matter as at 31 December, the Office of the High Representative continued to meet regularly with the public broadcasting service governors and other stakeholders to discuss the course of reform and encourage measures to modernize and streamline the system.

Relations with other countries

During the first half of 2006, regional issues had a significant impact on Bosnia and Herzegovina. The start of Kosovo status talks in February (see p. 466) and the independence referendum in Montenegro (see p. 472) encouraged politicians and commentators in Serbia and Republika Srpska to draw false parallels between the future of Kosovo and Montenegro and that of the Republika. In his report covering the latter half of 2006 [S/2007/253], the High Representative noted that uncertainty over the future status of Kosovo and related delays had had an especially negative influence during the 2006 election campaign and thereafter. Accordingly, the risk of regional instability was a factor in his decision not to close the Office of the High Representative on the target date of 30 June 2007, as originally set by PIC in June. The High Representative also noted that, while the NATO invitation to Bosnia and Herzegovina to join the Partnership for Peace had a reassuring effect, any perceived lowering of international interest in Bosnia and Herzegovina or any apparent weakening of resolve to uphold its sovereignty and territorial integrity could invite trouble in the country.

Bosnia and Herzegovina continued to have minor border disputes with Serbia and Croatia, though the potential quarrel over Zagreb's plan to build a bridge between the mainland and the Pelješac peninsula that would have restricted Bosnia and Herzegovina's access to the Adriatic had abated. Another long-standing irritant to regional relations—the constitutional bans on extradition of their nationals by Croatia and Serbia—remained unresolved, although cooperation among prosecutors continued to improve.

Communication. In an 8 November letter [S/2006/874] to the Security Council President, Serbia stated that it had consistently supported all efforts towards stability, democracy and social and economic prosperity in Bosnia and Herzegovina. Both countries were committed to the European principles and values that led to EU accession, including strengthening regional cooperation among Western Balkan States.

SECURITY COUNCIL ACTION

On 21 November [meeting 5567], the Security Council, having considered the High Representative's report for the period from 1 February to 30 June 2006 [S/2006/810] and a 12 October letter from the Secretary-General [S/2006/809], which transmitted the seventh report on the activities of the EU military mission in Bosnia and Herzegovina (see p. 462), unanimously adopted **resolution 1722(2006)**. The draft [S/2006/900] was prepared in consultations among Council members.

The Security Council,

Recalling all its previous relevant resolutions concerning the conflicts in the former Yugoslavia and the relevant statements by its President, including resolutions 1031(1995) of 15 December 1995, 1088(1996) of 12 December 1996, 1423(2002) of 12 July 2002, 1491(2003) of 11 July 2003, 1551(2004) of 9 July 2004, 1575(2004) of 22 November 2004 and 1639(2005) of 21 November 2005,

Reaffirming its commitment to the political settlement of the conflicts in the former Yugoslavia, preserving the sovereignty and territorial integrity of all States there within their internationally recognized borders,

Emphasizing its full support for the continued role in Bosnia and Herzegovina of the High Representative for Bosnia and Herzegovina,

Underlining its commitment to support the implementation of the General Framework Agreement for Peace in Bosnia and Herzegovina and the annexes thereto (collectively the "Peace Agreement"), as well as the relevant decisions of the Peace Implementation Council,

Recalling all the agreements concerning the status of forces referred to in appendix B to annex 1-A of the Peace Agreement, and reminding the parties of their obligation to continue to comply therewith,

Recalling also the provisions of its resolution 1551(2004) concerning the provisional application of the status-of-forces agreements contained in appendix B to annex 1-A of the Peace Agreement,

Emphasizing its appreciation to the High Representative, the Commander and personnel of the multinational stabilization force (the European Union Force), the Senior Military Representative and personnel of the North Atlantic Treaty Organization Headquarters Sarajevo, the Organization for Security and Cooperation in Europe, the European Union and the personnel of other international organizations and agencies in Bosnia and Herzegovina for their contributions to the implementation of the Peace Agreement,

Emphasizing that a comprehensive and coordinated return of refugees and displaced persons throughout the region continues to be crucial to lasting peace,

Recalling the declarations of the ministerial meetings of the Peace Implementation Council,

Recognizing that full implementation of the Peace Agreement is not yet complete, while paying tribute to the achievements of the authorities at State and entity level in Bosnia and Herzegovina and of the international community in the eleven years since the signing of the Peace Agreement,

Emphasizing the importance of Bosnia and Herzegovina's progress towards Euro-Atlantic integration on the basis of the Peace Agreement, while recognizing the importance of Bosnia and Herzegovina's transition to a functional, reform-oriented, modern and democratic European country,

Taking note of the reports of the High Representative, including his latest report, of 6 October 2006,

Determined to promote the peaceful resolution of the conflicts in accordance with the purposes and principles of the Charter of the United Nations,

Recalling the relevant principles contained in the Convention on the Safety of United Nations and Associated Personnel of 9 December 1994 and the statement by its President of 9 February 2000,

Welcoming and encouraging efforts by the United Nations to sensitize peacekeeping personnel in the prevention and control of HIV/AIDS and other communicable diseases in all its peacekeeping operations,

Taking note of the conclusions of the Ministers for Foreign Affairs of the European Union at their meeting of 12 June 2006, which refer to the requirement for the European Union Force to remain in Bosnia and Herzegovina beyond 2006, and confirm the intention of the European Union to take the steps necessary to that end,

Recalling the letters between the European Union and the North Atlantic Treaty Organization sent to the Security Council on 19 November 2004 on how those organizations will cooperate together in Bosnia and Herzegovina, in which both organizations recognize that the European Union Force will have the main peace stabilization role under the military aspects of the Peace Agreement,

Recalling also the confirmation by the Presidency of Bosnia and Herzegovina, on behalf of Bosnia and Herzegovina, including its constituent entities, of the arrangements for the European Union Force and the North Atlantic Treaty Organization Headquarters presence,

Welcoming the increased engagement of the European Union in Bosnia and Herzegovina and the continued engagement of the North Atlantic Treaty Organization,

Further welcoming tangible signs of Bosnia and Herzegovina's progress towards the European Union, and, in particular, the progress made in the negotiations of Bosnia and Herzegovina with the European Union on a Stabilization and Association Agreement, and calling upon the authorities in Bosnia and Herzegovina to implement in full their undertakings, including on police reform, as part of that process,

Determining that the situation in the region continues to constitute a threat to international peace and security,

Acting under Chapter VII of the Charter,

1. *Reaffirms once again its support* for the General Framework Agreement for Peace in Bosnia and Herzegovina and the annexes thereto (collectively the "Peace Agreement"), as well as for the Dayton Agreement on Implementing the Federation of Bosnia and Herzegovina of 10 November 1995, and calls upon the parties to comply strictly with their obligations under those Agreements;

2. *Reiterates* that the primary responsibility for the further successful implementation of the Peace Agreement lies with the authorities in Bosnia and Herzegovina themselves and that the continued willingness of the international community and major donors to assume the political, military and economic burden of implementation and reconstruction efforts will be determined by the compliance and active participation by all the authorities in Bosnia and Herzegovina in implementing the Peace Agreement and rebuilding a civil society, in particular in full cooperation with the International Tribunal for the Prosecution of Persons Responsible for Serious Violations of International Humanitarian Law Committed in the Territory of the Former Yugoslavia since 1991, in strengthening joint institutions, which foster the building of a fully functioning self-sustaining State able to integrate itself into the European structures, and in facilitating returns of refugees and displaced persons;

3. *Reminds* the parties once again that, in accordance with the Peace Agreement, they have committed themselves to cooperate fully with all entities involved in the implementation of this peace settlement, as described in the Peace Agreement, or which are otherwise authorized by the Security Council, including the International Tribunal for the Former Yugoslavia, as it carries out its responsibilities for dispensing justice impartially, and underlines that full cooperation by States and entities with the Tribunal includes, inter alia, the surrender for trial or apprehension of all persons indicted by the Tribunal and the provision of information to assist in Tribunal investigations;

4. *Emphasizes its full support* for the continued role of the High Representative for Bosnia and Herzegovina in monitoring the implementation of the Peace Agreement and giving guidance to and coordinating the activities of the civilian organizations and agencies involved in assisting the parties to implement the Peace Agreement, and reaffirms that, under annex 10 of the Peace Agreement, the High Representative is the final authority in theatre regarding the interpretation of civilian implementation of the Peace Agreement and that, in case of dispute, he may give his interpretation and make recommendations, and make binding decisions as he judges necessary on issues as elaborated by the Peace Implementation Council in Bonn, Germany, on 9 and 10 December 1997;

5. *Expresses its support* for the declarations of the ministerial meetings of the Peace Implementation Council;

6. *Reaffirms* its intention to keep implementation of the Peace Agreement and the situation in Bosnia and Herzegovina under close review, taking into account the reports submitted pursuant to paragraphs 18 and 21 below, and any recommendations those reports might include, and its readiness to consider the imposition of measures if any party fails significantly to meet its obligations under the Peace Agreement;

7. *Recalls* the support of the authorities of Bosnia and Herzegovina for the European Union Force and the continued North Atlantic Treaty Organization presence and their confirmation that both are the legal successors to the Stabilization Force for the fulfilment of their missions for the purposes of the Peace Agreement, its annexes and appendices and relevant Security Council resolutions and can take such actions as are required, including the use of force, to ensure compliance with annexes 1-A and 2 of the Peace Agreement and relevant Council resolutions;

8. *Pays tribute* to those Member States which participated in the multinational stabilization force (the European Union Force) and in the continued North Atlantic Treaty Organization presence, established in accordance with its resolution 1575(2004) and extended by its resolution 1639(2005), and welcomes their willingness to assist the parties to the Peace Agreement by continuing to deploy a multinational stabilization force (the

European Union Force) and by maintaining a continued North Atlantic Treaty Organization presence;

9. *Welcomes* the intention of the European Union to maintain a European Union military operation to Bosnia and Herzegovina from November 2006;

10. *Authorizes* the Member States acting through or in cooperation with the European Union to establish for a further period of twelve months, starting from the date of adoption of the present resolution, a multinational stabilization force (the European Union Force) as a legal successor to the Stabilization Force under unified command and control, which will fulfil its missions in relation to the implementation of annexes 1-A and 2 of the Peace Agreement in cooperation with the North Atlantic Treaty Organization Headquarters presence in accordance with the arrangements agreed between the North Atlantic Treaty Organization and the European Union as communicated to the Security Council in their letters of 19 November 2004, which recognize that the European Union Force will have the main peace stabilization role under the military aspects of the Peace Agreement;

11. *Welcomes* the decision of the North Atlantic Treaty Organization to continue to maintain a presence in Bosnia and Herzegovina in the form of a North Atlantic Treaty Organization Headquarters in order to continue to assist in implementing the Peace Agreement in conjunction with the European Union Force, and authorizes the Member States acting through or in cooperation with the North Atlantic Treaty Organization to continue to maintain a North Atlantic Treaty Organization Headquarters as a legal successor to the Stabilization Force under unified command and control, which will fulfil its missions in relation to the implementation of annexes 1-A and 2 of the Peace Agreement in cooperation with the European Union Force in accordance with the arrangements agreed between the North Atlantic Treaty Organization and the European Union as communicated to the Security Council in their letters of 19 November 2004, which recognize that the European Union Force will have the main peace stabilization role under the military aspects of the Peace Agreement;

12. *Reaffirms* that the Peace Agreement and the provisions of its previous relevant resolutions shall apply to and in respect of both the European Union Force and the North Atlantic Treaty Organization presence as they have applied to and in respect of the Stabilization Force and that, therefore, references in the Peace Agreement, in particular in annex 1-A and the appendices thereto, and in relevant resolutions to the Implementation Force and/or the Stabilization Force, the North Atlantic Treaty Organization and the North Atlantic Council shall be read as applying, as appropriate, to the North Atlantic Treaty Organization presence, the European Union Force, the European Union and the Political and Security Committee and Council of the European Union respectively;

13. *Expresses its intention* to consider the terms of further authorization as necessary in the light of developments in the implementation of the Peace Agreement and the situation in Bosnia and Herzegovina;

14. *Authorizes* the Member States acting under paragraphs 10 and 11 above to take all necessary measures to effect the implementation of and to ensure compliance with annexes 1-A and 2 of the Peace Agreement, stresses that the parties shall continue to be held equally responsible for the compliance with those annexes and shall be equally subject to such enforcement action by the European Union Force and the North Atlantic Treaty Organization presence as may be necessary to ensure implementation of those annexes and the protection of the European Union Force and the North Atlantic Treaty Organization presence;

15. *Authorizes* Member States to take all necessary measures, at the request of either the European Union Force or the North Atlantic Treaty Organization Headquarters, in defence of the European Union Force or the North Atlantic Treaty Organization presence respectively, and to assist both organizations in carrying out their missions, and recognizes the right of both the European Union Force and the North Atlantic Treaty Organization presence to take all necessary measures to defend themselves from attack or threat of attack;

16. *Authorizes* the Member States acting under paragraphs 10 and 11 above, in accordance with annex 1-A of the Peace Agreement, to take all necessary measures to ensure compliance with the rules and procedures governing command and control of airspace over Bosnia and Herzegovina with respect to all civilian and military air traffic;

17. *Demands* that the parties respect the security and freedom of movement of the European Union Force, the North Atlantic Treaty Organization presence and other international personnel;

18. *Requests* the Member States acting through or in cooperation with the European Union and the Member States acting through or in cooperation with the North Atlantic Treaty Organization to report to the Security Council on the activity of the European Union Force and the North Atlantic Treaty Organization Headquarters presence respectively, through the appropriate channels and at least at three-monthly intervals;

19. *Invites* all States, in particular those in the region, to continue to provide appropriate support and facilities, including transit facilities, for the Member States acting under paragraphs 10 and 11 above;

20. *Reiterates its appreciation* for the deployment by the European Union of its Police Mission to Bosnia and Herzegovina since 1 January 2003;

21. *Requests* the Secretary-General to continue to submit to the Security Council reports from the High Representative, in accordance with annex 10 of the Peace Agreement and the conclusions of the Peace Implementation Conference held in London on 4 and 5 December 1996, and later Peace Implementation Conferences, on the implementation of the Peace Agreement and in particular on compliance by the parties with their commitments under that Agreement;

22. *Decides* to remain seized of the matter.

European Union missions in Bosnia and Herzegovina

EUPM

Reports of EU Secretary-General. As requested by the Security Council in presidential statement S/PRST/2002/33 [YUN 2002, p. 363], the EU Secretary-General reported to the Council, through the UN Secretary-General, on the activities of the European Union Police Mission (EUPM). On 19 January [S/2006/62], he noted that EUPM had made considerable advances in developing sustainable policing arrangements under the ownership of Bosnia and Herzegovina. They included: the transformation of the State Investigation and Protection Agency into an operational policy agency with enhanced and executive powers to fight major and organized crime; and the solid development of other institutions in cooperation with the European Commission (EC), including the Ministry of Security and the State Border Service. He stated that he would continue to keep the Council updated on the progress of the Mission's follow-on phase, which was launched on 1 January. He submitted two reports on the subject during the year.

In the first report covering the period from 1 January to 30 June [S/2006/644], the EU Secretary-General noted that the first five months of 2006 were a transitional period for EUPM, characterized by the development of a refocused mandate, the reduction of Mission strength and the establishment of new structures. EUPM took the lead role in coordinating the policing aspects of the European Security and Defence Policy efforts against organized crime and assisted local authorities in planning and conducting major organized crime investigations. Among other activities, EUPM assisted the local police in the planning and execution of a number of operations for illegally stored weapons, a continuing problem affecting safety and security in the country, and introduced a case management system to track all investigations of the State Investigation and Protection Agency (SIPA) in order to monitor progress, identify weaknesses and give appropriate advice. Following a review, the system was extended to the entire Mission. EUPM continued to monitor investigations in support of the police's fight against organized crime. In June, the Bosnia and Herzegovina strategy for the fight against organized crime and corruption for the period 2006-2009 (National Action Plan), drafted by a locally owned business group that was chaired by the Minister for Security, and assisted by the EU Crime Strategy Group, was adopted by the Council of Ministers. In view of the importance of monitoring the wider criminal justice bodies to ensure the integrity and effectiveness of the system in dealing with organized crime, a new unit, the Criminal Justice Interface Unit, was created, with the task of identifying and addressing deficiencies in police and prosecutorial cooperation.

While the provision of technical assistance and equipment had already proved beneficial, EUPM continued to liaise with international bodies and diplomatic missions to establish better coordination arrangements for donations, and, in turn, to strengthen local police capacity. Together with the Office of the High Representative and the Directorate for the Implementation of Police Restructuring, the Mission helped to finalize a draft cantonal law on police officials in order to regulate their powers and their employment-related legal status. By the end of 2006, the model law had been adopted by six of the 10 cantons. EUPM also participated in the development of draft legislative amendments and a draft Council of Ministers decision on obligations for telecommunication providers, which were completed in May, and worked towards strengthening internal and external control, inspection and accountability of the police. EUPM continued to monitor and provide advisory support to both SIPA and the State Border Service, including reviewing amendments to SIPA books of rules and planning and conducting operations for the arrest, detention and transfer of suspected war criminals.

In a report covering the period from 1 July to 31 December [S/2007/118], the EU Secretary-General said that the Mission continued to address the fragmentation in the police system by supporting cantons in developing cantonal laws on police officials; facilitating the development of a new model law on police officials; and helping to develop 26 complementary by-laws on police issues.

With regard to the fight against organized crime, the EUFOR mission in Bosnia and Herzegovina turned all organized crime-related planning support over to EUPM at the end of September. As to deficiencies in relations between police and prosecutors, EUPM encouraged and supported the State Prosecutor's initiatives, although limited, to play a coordinating role in dealing with some of the concerns identified by the new Criminal Justice Interface Unit. It also worked with partner agencies to advise on improvements in the legislative and regulatory framework for major and organized criminal investigations. The Mission continued to identify areas for inspections and oversee the work of internal control functions, or prosecutors, as cases were passed to them, to ensure that the cases progressed through to a final, conclusive and appropriate result. It supported SIPA in monitoring the newly established case management system, made progress in the build-up of permanent headquarters and regional offices and advised SIPA in the training of its first class of cadets.

EUPM continued to follow the implementation and finalization of projects launched during 2003-2005 in close cooperation with the Bosnia and Herzegovina police experts co-located within the department. It also provided legal and technical advice in the drawing up of a memorandum of understanding, adopted in November, relating to the establishment of a new telecommunication system for law enforcement agencies and played a coordinating role in facilitating the participation of all law enforcement agencies in securing EU funding.

On 31 December, the Mission numbered 414 personnel (166 international police officers, 29 international civilian experts and 219 national staff). All 25 EU member States and 8 non-EU contributing States participated in the Mission in 2006. In January, Brigadier General Vincenzo Coppola (Italy) succeeded Commissioner Kevin Carty (Ireland) as Head of Mission/Police Commissioner.

Police decertification

The decertification of police officers by the International Police Task Force (IPTF) police reconstruction process, instituted in 2001 [YUN 2001, p. 332], continued to concern the Bosnia and Herzegovina authorities. The European Commission for Democracy through Law had also considered the matter in 2005 and recommended that the United Nations review the decisions that had denied certification [YUN 2005, p. 464]. In a 30 January letter [S/2006/64], Bosnia and Herzegovina drew the Security Council's attention to the challenges by 150 of the country's former police officers to their decertification by IPTF and requested the Council to consider offering the 150 decertified officers the right to appeal and have their cases re-examined.

In August, the High Representative asked the Council President to request the United Nations to determine a review mechanism for the cases, while he explored other options. In December, the Bosnia and Herzegovina Council of Ministers adopted a decision on the establishment of a national commission for the review of individual cases of decertified police officers who had initiated legal proceedings. Given the implications of such a decision, notably with regard to relevant Security Council resolutions and annex 11 of the General Framework Agreement for Peace [YUN 1995, p. 544], the High Representative called upon the Council of Ministers to contact the Security Council and the UN Secretariat as a matter of urgency.

EUFOR

The EU Force (EUFOR) mission in Bosnia and Herzegovina executed the military aspects of the Peace Agreement as specified in annexes 1-A and 2, which were transferred to it by NATO in December 2004 [YUN 2004, p. 401]. Its activities were described in four reports, covering the periods 1 March to 31 May [S/2006/476], 1 June to 31 August [S/2006/809], 1 September to 30 November [S/2006/1035], and 1 December 2006 to 28 February 2007 [S/2007/268], submitted by the EU Secretary-General and High Representative for the Common Foreign and Security Policy, in accordance with Security Council resolution 1575(2004) [YUN 2004, p. 401].

As at 30 November, EUFOR strength stood at around 5,700 troops from 34 countries.

During 2006, EUFOR main task was to conduct and support operations in cooperation with local authorities and law enforcement agencies. Particular focus was given to targeting organized crime, especially illegal logging and fuel smuggling, and weapons collection. In June, it handed over to Bosnia and Herzegovina responsibility for the management of airspace above 10,000 feet, while retaining control of airspace below that level.

Serbia and Montenegro

The authorities and population of the Kosovo province of Serbia and Montenegro continued to receive UN assistance in 2006 in building a multi-ethnic society. The United Nations Interim Administration Mission in Kosovo (UNMIK), together with the Kosovo's leadership, led efforts to strengthen the Provisional Institutions of Self-Government, mainly the Kosovo Assembly and the Kosovo Government, and transferred authority to those institutions, in accordance with the 2001 Constitutional Framework for Provisional Self-Government [YUN 2001, p. 352]. It also monitored progress towards achieving the eight standards set out in the 2003 "standards for Kosovo" document [YUN 2003, p. 420], under which Kosovo was expected to develop stable democratic institutions under UNMIK administration before any decision could be made on its future status.

Throughout the year, the Secretary-General's Special Envoy for the future status process for Kosovo, Martti Ahtisaari, organized direct talks between representatives of Serbia and the Kosovo province on decentralization of Kosovo's governmental and administrative functions and other issues. Underlying the negotiations to determine Kosovo's final status were several political challenges, including the issue of northern Kosovo, where Kosovo Serbs were in the majority. Despite increased efforts by the Provisional Institutions to reach out to minority communities, Kosovo Serb participation in governance remained marginal, especially at the central level. Belgrade continued to discourage Kosovo Serb participation in the province's governing bodies and, in response to some violent incidents that were viewed as possible ethnically motivated, several Kosovo Serb-majority municipalities cut off contacts with the Provisional Institutions.

The death of Kosovo's President Ibrahim Rugova in January led to leadership changes, including the election by the Kosovo Assembly of his successor, Fatmir Sejdiu, and a new Prime Minister, Agim Çeku. Significant progress was made in European integration work with the adoption by the Government of Kosovo in August of a European Partnership Action Plan.

In May, Montenegro voted to separate from Serbia, becoming an independent Republic. On 28 June, the General Assembly admitted Montenegro to membership in the United Nations.

Situation in Kosovo

Guided by Martti Ahtisaari (Finland), the Special Envoy appointed by the Secretary-General in 2005 [YUN 2005, p. 472], negotiations took place throughout 2006 to determine the final status of the Serbia and Montenegro province of Kosovo. Work continued towards the full implementation of Security Council resolution 1244(1999) [YUN 1999, p. 353], which set out the modalities for a political solution to the crisis in the province, and of resolutions 1160(1998) [YUN 1998, p. 369], 1199(1998) [ibid., p. 377], 1203(1998) [ibid., p. 382] and 1239(1999) [YUN 1999, p. 349]. The civilian aspects of resolution 1244(1999) were implemented by UNMIK and the military aspects by the international security presence (KFOR), led by NATO.

Appointment of Special Representative. On 14 August [S/2006/656], the Secretary-General informed the Security Council of his intention to appoint Joachim Rücker (Germany) to replace Søren Jessen-Petersen (Denmark) as his Special Representative for Kosovo and Head of UNMIK. The Council took note of that intention on 16 August [S/2006/657].

Security Council consideration (February). On 14 February [meeting 5373], the Security Council discussed the situation in Kosovo. It had before it the Secretary-General's 25 January report [S/2006/45], which mainly covered developments during the second half of 2005 [YUN 2005, p. 472]. The Special Representative informed the Council that three major issues defined recent politics in Kosovo: the January death of President Rugova and the orderly transition to a new President; the opening of the status process; and the continued and revitalized push for progress on standards implementation, decentralization and the full inclusion of minorities in the creation of Kosovo's future. The latter part of 2005 had seen a noticeable slow-down in the pace of implementation of standards in Kosovo, particularly with regard to minority rights. However, critical observations made to the Kosovo authorities had an effect and a number of fresh initiatives were taken to push standards implementation forward through short-term, results-oriented governmental action plans. The Special Representative stated that decentralization remained a key issue, not least in terms of minority rights. It was vital that Kosovo's institutions and the international community reach out as much as possible to the Kosovo Serb minority, and that Belgrade encourage and support Kosovo Serb participation in the province's institutions.

Report of Secretary-General (June). The Secretary-General reported in June [S/2006/361] that the political process to determine the future status talks of Kosovo was underway. Major changes occurred early in the year in the leadership of the Provisional Institutions of Self-Governance in Kosovo following the death of President Rugova on 21 January; his 26 January funeral was a major public event that took place without incident. On 10 February, a new President, Fatmir Sejdiu, was elected by the Assembly of Kosovo. After the governing coalition parties reached an agreement regarding changes in the leadership of the Provisional Institutions, Prime Minister Bajram Kosumi announced his resignation on 1 March. The head of the Kosovo Protection Corps (KPC), Agim Çeku, was elected as his successor on 10 March. The new Prime Minister accelerated the pace of standards implementation and acknowledged a direct link between the Provisional Institutions' ability to improve performance on standards and the possible outcome of the discussions on Kosovo's future status. The Kosovo negotiating team welcomed the statement by the Contact Group (France, Germany, Italy, the Russian Federation, the United Kingdom and the United States) on the political process to determine Kosovo's future status, following their 30

January meeting in London, and produced detailed proposals for decentralization and a plan for the future governance of Mitrovica district.

Despite increased efforts by the President, the Prime Minister and the Kosovo negotiating team to reach out to minority communities, Kosovo Serb participation in the governance structures of the province remained marginal, particularly at the central level. The efforts of the new leadership to rebuild confidence with the Kosovo Serb community were dealt a severe blow in March, when Serbia's Coordination Centre for Kosovo and Metohija demanded that Kosovo Serb municipal employees choose either to be on the payroll of the Provisional Institutions or on that of the parallel structures sponsored by Belgrade. All Kosovo Serb education workers resigned from their posts in the Provisional Institutions, although they continued to perform their functions, receiving payments from Belgrade. The Secretary-General, his Special Representative and his Special Envoy expressed concerns regarding the pressure from Belgrade on that issue. The Secretary-General called on Belgrade to assist Kosovo Serbs wanting to work within the Institutions and not to hamper them. The Kosovo Ministry of Local Government Administration, with the assistance of UNMIK and other international partners, made progress on decentralization, despite the continued lack of participation of Kosovo Serbs. A draft law on local self-government and a concept paper on local finance were produced.

The security situation in Kosovo remained generally stable, although fragile, and was not affected by the changes in the political leadership or by the start of the future status process. The level of inter-ethnic incidents remained low. UNMIK moved forward with the transfer of further competencies to the Provisional Institutions in the area of the rule of law, while retaining overall authority for peace and justice, without prejudice to Security Council resolution 1244(1999). Senior officers of the newly established Kosovo Ministry of Justice, Ministry of Internal Affairs and Kosovo Judicial Council were appointed in January and the Special Representative promulgated a regulation on the regulatory framework for the justice system in Kosovo. Challenges in promoting returns and integrating returnees remained significant during the reporting period. An eight-month consultation and review of the policy and process regarding communities, returns and sustainable solutions was concluded in April at a two-day joint Provisional Institutions/UNMIK workshop on a new strategy and action plan on communities and returns for Kosovo.

Security Council consideration (June). The Special Representative, briefing the Security Council on 20 June [meeting 5470], reported an across-the-board revitalization of the standards implementation process in Kosovo. The pace of policy implementation had been matched by a far greater willingness on the part of the province's new leadership to take the lead in reaching out to minority communities, in particular to Kosovo Serbs. Despite those efforts, however, the situation of many Kosovo Serbs remained very difficult. The Special Representative called on the Serbian authorities to work with the United Nations and the Kosovo Government to provide factual information about current events, so as not to promote a climate of fear and further isolate the Kosovo Serb minority. A further concern was the Serbian Government's directive obliging Kosovo Serbs to choose between their Belgrade and Pristina salaries (see above), which was a divisive move and did a disservice to Kosovo Serbs. The Special Representative called on Belgrade to withdraw that damaging directive.

While UNMIK was not a player in the status negotiations, its activities in Kosovo had to be consistent with and supportive of them. With the process gaining momentum, the end of UNMIK mandate was drawing near and tensions could rise, increasing the risk of security incidents. The Special Representative was concerned that violent crimes could quickly become politicized and used to provoke tensions and divisions, in particular in the northern part of Kosovo. In that context, it was important that political actors in the region did not foment instability. UNMIK was working closely with KFOR on strategies to respond to any eventuality and to keep down the risk of incidents that could escalate into something worse.

The Special Representative welcomed the signing, on 6 June, of a returns protocol between UNMIK, Belgrade and Pristina (see below), which would enable the return of displaced persons to take place on an agreed basis. He also noted that progress had been made also in the development and performance of the Kosovo Police Service (KPS). However, more needed to be done in several areas, including in the field of justice and the rule of law.

Report of Secretary-General (September). The Secretary-General, in a September report [S/2006/707], said that the political situation in Kosovo, from May to August, was dominated by the future status process and the underlying political challenges. Foremost among those was the issue of governance of the portion of Kosovo territory north of the Ibar River. Relations between Kosovo Albanians and Kosovo Serbs, particularly in the northern region, were still affected by apprehensiveness. In May, several highly publicized security incidents affected Kosovo Serbs but were not necessarily of an inter-ethnic nature. Nonetheless, the incidents were denounced by some Kosovo Serb leaders and Serbian authorities as inter-ethnic attacks. A 5 June protest demonstration was attended by some 800 Kosovo Serbs in Zveçan municipality. Subsequently, the municipality, along with two others, declared the cessation of contacts with the Provisional Institutions of Self-Government. On 17 July, the Municipal Assembly Presidents of the three northern municipalities requested the withdrawal of Kosovo Albanian members of the KPS border police in the northern region. While rejecting contacts with the Provisional Institutions, the municipalities maintained cooperation with UNMIK. Although Kosovo Serbs from northern Kosovo participated in the future status talks as part of the Belgrade delegation, Belgrade continued to discourage Kosovo Serb participation in Kosovo's governing bodies.

In close coordination with KFOR, UNMIK police and KPS took measures to enhance security throughout Kosovo, with particular attention to the north, including programmes to enhance relations between the police and minority communities. Border and boundary controls were strengthened through the deployment of international officers. The Kosovo Ministry of Internal Affairs continued to make generally satisfactory progress towards its full establishment and took an active and positive role in the finalization of terms of reference for the Municipal Community Safety Councils and Local Public Safety Committees. Additional competencies in the justice sector were transferred to the Kosovo Ministry of Justice, while UNMIK retained overall authority in the area of justice. No significant progress was made in investigating and prosecuting cases related to the violence of March 2004 [YUN 2004, p. 405].

With regard to decentralization, UNMIK liaised with local stakeholders and evaluated proposals on the delineation of new municipal boundaries and the transfer of competencies from central institutions to the proposed new municipal units. Despite earlier progress, the establishment of three pilot municipal units—two in Kosovo Albanian areas and one in a Kosovo Turkish-majority area—faced challenges due to a lack of capacity. Following consultations with all key political actors in Kosovo, the Special Representative decided on 16 June to postpone the 2006 Kosovo municipal elections for up to 12 months to maintain focus on the future status process.

In response to a notable increase in reports of vandalism against Serbian Orthodox Church sites, KPS developed operational plans to increase security, especially at churches undergoing restoration. After an intervention by the Secretary-General's Special Envoy, the Kosovo Assembly included two key passages on religious communities in the Law on Cultural Heritage. The reconstruction of Serbian Orthodox Churches damaged or destroyed during the violence of March 2004 [ibid.] moved forward.

On 6 June, the Special Representative and the Belgrade and Pristina representatives on the Working Group on Returns signed the Protocol on Voluntary and Sustainable Returns, which signalled the operational and technical cooperation of Belgrade and Pristina to improve conditions for, and facilitate returns of, internally displaced persons to Kosovo. The Protocol had an immediate effect, with more than 70 families agreeing to return to one Serb-majority village. However, displaced persons continued to cite economic and security factors as the primary reasons for their reluctance to return; the number of minority returns remained unsatisfactory.

On 9 August, the Government of Kosovo adopted a European Partnership Action Plan to replace the 2004 Kosovo Standards Implementation Plan [YUN 2004, p. 408]. The new Plan incorporated the values and principles of the Standards in the process of the European integration work.

Security Council consideration (September). The Special Representative, briefing the Security Council on 13 September [meeting 5522], said that the future status process would continue to dominate the political agenda in Kosovo until its final status was determined. The pace of standards implementation remained at the rate reported in his previous briefing in June (see above). The standards programme received even greater attention since the Contact Group presented the Government, on 9 June, with a list of 13 priorities, drawn largely from the results of an April UNMIK technical assessment on standards implementation. Most of the priorities had been achieved and the remaining areas were on track. The situation in northern Kosovo was of particular concern. Referring to the May security incidents that had induced three northern provinces to sever cooperation with the Pristina authorities (see above), the Special Representative stated that violent crimes were to be deplored wherever they occurred and prosecuted with the full force of the law. However, attempts to portray Kosovo as a place where non-Albanians, in particular Kosovo Serbs, were under constant attack and were victims of daily ethnic crimes, were unjustified. Belgrade retained a powerful influence over the attitudes of the Kosovo Serbs, including through its continued directive that Serbs in the public service should either leave the Provisional Institutions' payroll or lose the extra salaries and other benefits paid by Belgrade (see above). The Special Representative hoped for a clear signal from Belgrade, including the withdrawal of that directive, that the future of Kosovo Serbs was in Kosovo if they so wished.

With regard to the justice system, the Special Representative said that efforts to reappoint all judges and prosecutors on the basis of a reassessment of their credentials should contribute to an improvement and should begin soon. As to the economy, the legal and institutional framework for a functioning market economy was largely in place, but increased private sector development was needed to extricate Kosovo's economy from a cycle of low growth, unemployment and a large trade imbalance. With regard to the possible termination of the UNMIK mandate, he informed the Council that an EU planning team was in Pristina to examine future involvement in the police and justice sectors, and a separate team was advising Brussels on the composition of the future international civilian office.

Report of Secretary-General (November). In a November report covering mid-August to the end of October [S/2006/906], the Secretary-General stated that the issue of decentralization had led to protests in a number of Kosovo Albanian-majority municipalities affected by the proposed decentralization plan. Grenade attacks against Kosovo Serbs in August and September, along with subsequent protests, further raised tensions in the province. Despite those incidents, however, the overall number of potentially ethnically motivated crimes had decreased considerably over the course of the year. An October referendum in Kosovo on the new Serbian Constitution, which described the province as an integral part of Serbia, was conducted without incident. The start of the party election process of the Democratic League for Kosovo (LDK) was a source of pressure on the unity of the Kosovo negotiating team. In September, LDK proposed President Sejdiu as its candidate for the party's chief position, despite the stipulation in the constitutional framework that the President of Kosovo should not hold any other office or employment. Despite being informed by the Special Representative that he should either resign as President or not accept the role of party president, President Sejdiu accepted the nomination.

UNMIK and the Provisional Institutions continued to transfer aspects of security to greater local control. The establishment of the Kosovo Ministry of Justice proceeded well and the consolidation of the Ministry of Internal Affairs progressed, with UNMIK and donor agencies focusing on four priority areas: clarification of the role and authority of the Ministry vis-à-vis KPS; the creation of capacity for managing migration and repatriation; improved capability for emergency preparedness and response; and civil registration and documentation.

The Secretary-General noted that sustained progress on standards was an encouraging feature throughout 2006. The Provisional Institutions were also creating structures and work plans to implement the European Partnership Action Plan, adopted in August (see p. 464). Within the region, two bilateral free trade agreements were signed on 28 September and 19 October, with Croatia and Bosnia Herzegovina, respectively. Negotiations on a single agreement for the region of South-East Europe concluded in Brussels on 20 October. On 24 August, the Special Representative signed a regulation that transformed the Banking and Payments Authority of Kosovo into the Central Banking Authority of Kosovo. The newly established body produced the province's first balance-of-payments report, in accordance with International Monetary Fund guidelines.

The Special Representative noted a decrease in incidents reported against Serbian Orthodox Church sites, and UNMIK intervened through the Provisional Institutions to stop illegal constructions in the vicinity of the cultural heritage sites included by the Special Envoy in the list of sites for proposed protective zones.

Security Council consideration (December). Briefing the Security Council on 13 December [meeting 5588], the Special Representative reported on several areas of progress. He highlighted the effort to create the conditions for the return of internally displaced persons. Large reconstruction projects were nearly completed in several villages, including one near Mitrovica. However, those efforts would have limited impact if more was not done—particularly by Belgrade—to encourage returns when the conditions for them had been created. There had also been a sharp drop in the number of incidents that were possibly ethnically motivated. UNMIK continued to monitor those incidents very carefully, and put a high priority on all those in which police suspected ethnic or political motives. The Mission had also been working intensively to address the supply of electricity in the province, which was another important concern.

With regard to the status process (see below), the Special Representative said that further delay would entail significant political and economic costs for Kosovo, its neighbours, the region as a whole and the international community; it would raise tensions and play into the hands of extremists on all sides. Once a status decision was made, UNMIK would need to provide for an orderly and smooth handover to future local and international institutions established under the status settlement. Kosovo would need a new constitutional arrangement to replace the constitutional framework, which relied on UNMIK, and elections would follow. The Special Representative advocated early and prudent transition planning, and stated that it was important that the future International Civilian Office, which was being prepared by the EU and the United States, be fully operational when Kosovo's status was decided.

Communications. On 20 September [A/61/375], Serbia transmitted a statement in exercise of its right of reply to remarks made by Albania in the General Assembly on 20 September [A/61/PV.13]. Serbia observed that Albania had openly advocated the independence of the Kosovo province of Serbia, thereby supporting the break-up of Serbia's territorial integrity. The position expressed by Albania was contrary to the interest of stability in the Western Balkan region.

In a 6 October letter [A/61/508], Albania stated that it had been playing a helpful and moderating role in the region. It believed that the situation in Kosovo would be better served if all interested parties offered their continuous support for the Special Envoy and his mandate.

Kosovo future status process

In his June report on UNMIK [S/2006/361], the Secretary-General said that, during the first four months of 2006, the efforts of his Special Envoy for the future status process for Kosovo, Martti Ahtisaari, appointed in 2005 [YUN 2005, p. 472], had focused on bringing representatives of Belgrade and Pristina together in direct talks to discuss practical issues. During the four rounds of talks on the decentralization of Kosovo's governmental and administrative functions and others on cultural heritage, religious sites and economic issues, there was some convergence of views on specific points, but in many areas the proposals of the parties remained far apart. The Special Envoy also held parallel consultations on developments in the future status process with a range of interested Member States and regional organizations.

Direct talks continued during the following months, including the first high-level meeting (Vienna, 24 July) between delegations headed by the President and the Prime Minister of Serbia and the President and the Prime Minister of Kosovo [S/2006/707]. The meeting provided the parties with an opportunity to present their proposals on Kosovo's future status at the political level, but they also reiterated their divergent positions on substantial autonomy (Serbia) and independence (Kosovo). Further rounds of direct talks between the parties revealed that they remained far apart on most issues.

On 20 November [S/2006/906], the Secretary-General reported that the future status process continued to advance between mid-August and the end of October. The Special Envoy convened further rounds of direct talks between Belgrade and Pristina on decentralization, and cultural and religious heritage rights in September. However, no major shifts of position resulted. Following those talks, the Special Envoy brought the sides together to discuss the delineation of new municipalities, including Mitrovica, but there was no substantial progress.

In a later report [S/2007/134], the Secretary-General stated that the Special Envoy had announced, on 10 November, that his presentation to the parties of the Settlement Proposal would be delayed until after 21 January 2007 to allow for the holding of parliamentary elections in Serbia.

Later developments

Reporting on developments during the latter part of the year [S/2007/134], the Secretary-General said that the November announcement by his Special Envoy that his presentation of the Kosovo Settlement Proposal to the parties would be delayed until after 21 January was received with deep disappointment by Kosovo Albanians. Kosovo Serbs continued to take very little part in the political institutions. Against a background of active discouragement from Belgrade, Kosovo Serbs in the Assembly and the Government had not taken up their seats and the only Kosovo Serb Minister in the Government, the Minister for Communities and Returns, was forced to resign on 27 November, following allegations of financial irregularities and mismanagement. Three Kosovo Serb municipalities in the north of the province continued to boycott most contacts with Pristina and were nearly fully dependent on Serbian state financial support. In December, President Sejdiu emerged victorious from LDK party elections but suspended his role as party leader in order to retain his post as President, as required by the constitutional framework.

The Government continued to make progress on standards implementation, with the Agency for

European Integration becoming the main coordinating mechanism on standards within the Provisional Institutions, and the European Partnership Action Plan representing the main guiding tool for Kosovo's European integration process. Preparations and planning for the handover of UNMIK responsibilities at the end of its mandate following a political settlement intensified. They were carried out by five technical working groups dealing with rule of law, governance, civil administration, legislation, economy and property. Good progress was made in preparing for the transition at both the political and technical levels. With regard to the economy, the first draft of the Kosovo Development Strategy and Plan was completed at the end of December, though much work remained to be done on prioritizing its proposed policy measures and formulating concrete, cost-specific projects. On 19 December, UNMIK, on behalf of Kosovo, signed the enlarged Central Europe Free Trade Area Agreement, which constituted a single free trade agreement among its parties and was designed to simplify trade relations among them, giving them access to a large market of consumers. Several significant projects also moved forward in the energy and telecommunications sectors.

During the year, the number of returns and repatriations to Kosovo remained low, due primarily to a lack of economic opportunities, uncertainty about the future status of Kosovo and, to a much lesser degree than in the past, security factors. Some 3,600 persons were involuntarily repatriated from host countries during 2006, and another 90,000 Kosovars were subject to deportation and return to Kosovo, adding urgency to the Government/UNMIK plan to address reintegration needs.

Progress on standards implementation

The Secretary-General transmitted to the Security Council the technical assessments of progress in implementing the eight standards for Kosovo (functioning democratic institutions, rule of law, freedom of movement, returns and integration, economy, property rights, dialogue with Belgrade, KPC), which it had to meet to comply with Council resolution 1244(1999) [YUN 1999, p. 353], the Constitutional Framework for Provisional Self-Government [YUN 2001, p. 352], the original standards/benchmarks endorsed by the Council in presidential statement S/PRST/2002/11 [YUN 2002, p. 369] and the 2004 Kosovo Standards Implementation Plan [YUN 2004, p. 408]. The assessments, prepared by the Special Representative, were annexed to the Secretary-General's five reports to the Council on UNMIK covering 2006 [S/2006/45, S/2006/361, S/2006/707, S/2006/906, S/2007/134].

In his November assessment [S/2006/906], the Special Representative outlined progress made in standards implementation and listed 13 implementation priorities, identified by the Contact Group in June (see p. 462), which primarily addressed community-related issues.

Functioning democratic institutions. In 2006, improvements were made in the handling of Government and Assembly business following the change of leadership of those institutions in March. The Assembly adopted a comprehensive reform plan in June, resulting in more regular and frequent plenary sessions, improved forward planning and greater transparency and coordination between the Presidency, committee chairpersons and the leaders of parliamentary groups. The Office of Gender Equality was fully established within the Office of the Prime Minister and, in May, the Government approved a long-term strategy to increase the number and improve the position of women in the Provisional Institutions. The Independent Media Council was established in August, which subsequently created working groups on the future licensing process and related guidelines, cable regulation and advertising policies, and the protection of minors. On 27 July, the Assembly adopted the Law on Languages (a Contact Group priority), which provided for full equality of Albanian and Serbian as official languages of Kosovo.

The withdrawal from the payroll of the Provisional Institutions of large numbers of Kosovo Serb teachers, health-care workers and administrative staff weakened the link between Kosovo Serbs and local institutions, while strengthening parallel structures supported by Belgrade. Boycotts by three northern Kosovo Serb municipalities of most contacts with Pristina had a similar effect. The Government continued to hold in trust the salaries of the Kosovo Serbs who had left the payroll of the Provisional Institutions.

Rule of law. The establishment of the new Ministries of Internal Affairs and Justice was slow but orderly and a more extensive set of competencies was transferred to them in 2006. New ministers for both departments were appointed in March. In February, the Kosovo Assembly adopted the Law on the Kosovo Judicial Institute, which established the Institute as an independent body to coordinate the training of judges and judicial and prosecutorial candidates. It also approved the long-awaited Anti-Corruption Action Plan. In December, a two-week anti-corruption campaign publicized a confidential hotline for citizens to report corruption cases. During the year, 24 people were arrested and 1 person was convicted on corruption charges.

Insufficient progress was made in investigating and prosecuting cases relating to the riots of March 2004 [YUN 2004, p. 405], a Contact Group priority. Local courts were handling cases against 513 persons: 423 were convicted, 8 were acquitted, charges were dropped against 19 and cases were pending against 63 persons.

Freedom of movement. Freedom of movement in Kosovo improved during the year, and the police continued to assess the security situation as stable but fragile. Regular surveys showed that 94 per cent of minorities travelled outside their areas of residence and their perception of freedom of movement remained good. In an effort to ensure access of all communities to the police, police substations were opened in 18 minority communities (a Contact Group priority) and more openings were expected. Local Public Safety Committees were established in 14 areas. Following an August hand grenade attack on a bar in Mitrovica, the main bridge across the Ibar River was closed for several weeks.

Returns and reintegration. In April, a workshop on a Strategic Framework on Communities and Returns was held, with significant participation from representatives of the internally displaced from Serbia and Montenegro, to finalize the policy for achieving sustainable solutions for the displaced population and to stabilize the life of communities in Kosovo. Communities and mediation committees were established in all municipalities and human rights units were formed in all ministries. On 6 June, a returns protocol, signed by UNMIK, Pristina and Belgrade, sought to improve conditions for returns and enhance capacity for implementation of return projects through measures such as providing access to basic services for the returnees and promoting integration of internally displaced persons. An increasing number of municipalities showed considerable progress in taking over the ownership of the returns process. However, lack of funding remained the single most important obstacle to returns. Central-level involvement was also impeded by serious financial and administrative management problems in the Ministry of Returns and Communities.

Major progress was made in completing the reconstruction and compensation programme relating to the unrest of March 2004 [ibid.] (a Contact Group priority). On 16 June, the Special Representative, at the request of Prime Minister Çeku, assigned KPC a major role in completing the reconstruction work in Svinjarë and in utilizing KPC humanitarian and public services to help resolve other pending claims relating to the reconstruction. KPC held meetings in the municipality with all stakeholders, including internally displaced persons, the receiving community and municipal officers, and established a decision-making board which began to hold regular meetings.

Despite progress made throughout the year, only 1,608 minorities (593 Serbs) returned to Kosovo voluntarily in 2006. That was the lowest minority returns figure since 2001 and the lowest Kosovo Serb returns figure since proper monitoring was established in 2000. The low figures were partly due to the improper management of the Ministry of Communities and Returns in the previous years. On 27 November, the Minister of Communities and Returns resigned following many months of criticism from the international community. His replacement quickly established a more productive relationship with the international community and initiated the restructuring of the Ministry.

Economy. Privatization in Kosovo continued to accelerate. The Board of the Kosovo Trust Agency met regularly, approving the launch of new waves of privatization. By the end of the year, 393 new companies derived from the assets of 256 socially owned enterprises had been tendered for sale, 216 contracts were signed and 85 contracts were pending signature. The total privatization proceeds amounted to €267,784,767. The Advisory Board of the Investment Promotion Agency was established and held its first meeting in January. The incorporation of UNMIK Railways, District Heating into the Kosovo electricity company (KEK) completed the incorporation of all major publicly owned enterprises in Kosovo.

Following a mid-year review, the Special Representative promulgated in September the 2006 budget for Kosovo. The Ministry of Finance and Economy continued to enforce the authorized ceiling on the wage bill and, on 7 September, the Government imposed a hiring freeze, with the exception of a few employment categories. At year's end, spending on wages and salaries appeared to be broadly in line with the mid-year review; however, it was 10.1 per cent lower than budgeted, mostly due to underspending in capital projects.

Property rights. Legal reform relating to property rights moved forward slowly. Draft laws on housing and the treatment of illegal construction, plus other bills to ensure compliance with European Standards, were sent to the Kosovo Assembly for approval. The Kosovo Property Agency was established on 4 March as an independent body and successor to the Housing and Property Directorate. The Agency received, registered and assisted the courts in resolving conflict-related private immovable property claims (including those related to agricultural and commercial property), enforced related decisions and administered abandoned properties. By the end of 2006, the Agency had received over 8,500 claims and the first decisions were expected in March 2007. The Agency and the Government agreed to implement a pilot project on the rental scheme (a Contact Group priority) that included properties under Agency administration, the owners of which were identified and would be able to receive the rent collected. A Kosovo-wide information campaign against illegal occupation, which was still a common phenomenon, was also implemented.

Cultural heritage. Early in the year, the Ministry of Culture, Youth and Sport launched a youth information campaign on cultural heritage; ministers and officials gave presentations in the 12 municipalities most affected by the violence of March 2004 [ibid.] on the importance of cultural heritage in Kosovo. Meetings of cultural coordinators from Pristina and Belgrade resulted in the establishment of four working groups on: return of documents; return of artefacts; archaeology; and artist-to-artist exchange. Reconstruction and restoration of cultural heritage sites continued and progress was made on the inventory of cultural heritage, with 2,847 objects entered into a central database by the end of December.

Following a February request by minority representatives, the Ministry of Culture, Youth and Sport stopped the approval process by the Kosovo Assembly of the draft law on cultural heritage. The Council of Europe agreed to assist the Ministry and the Parliamentary Committee to redraft the law. A revised Law was promulgated on 6 November. As required by the Law, the Ministry of Culture, Youth and Sports began working with the Assembly to establish the multi-ethnic Kosovo Council for Cultural Heritage.

Dialogue with Belgrade. Direct dialogue with Belgrade continued during the year. The Working Group on Missing Persons met in March and May, and held numerous meetings with the International Committee of the Red Cross and the UNMIK Office on Missing Persons and Forensics. In April, the Government issued a statement declaring its commitment to the dialogue, and appealed to the public to come forward with information on missing persons. In June, the Working Group on Returns met in Belgrade and agreed to establish at least one sub-working group to deal with various technical issues, including tracking the implementation of the Returns Protocol.

Kosovo Protection Corps. Sylejman Selimi replaced Agim Çeku as Commander of the Kosovo Protection Corps (KPC) following Mr. Çeku's election as Prime Minister in March (see p. 462). KPC performed its functions in accordance with the law and its disciplinary code. Its activities included involvement in remedial action against natural disasters (flooding and a landslide), returns, and other humanitarian projects, such as rubble-clearing, road-building, constructing fire-stations, medical assistance, mine risk education, snow-clearing and monitoring reconstructed properties until returnees were ready to move in.

In August, 20 minority community members joined KPC (from the Bosniac, Croat, Egyptian, Kosovo Serb and Roma communities), 19 of them entering the active contingent. By October, the Corps had 223 non-Albanian members, including 58 Serbs, as compared to 180 non-Albanian members at the start of the year. Women were represented at all levels of KPC and continued to occupy relatively more senior ranks in comparison with men.

UN Interim Administration Mission in Kosovo

The United Nations Interim Administration Mission in Kosovo (UNMIK), established in 1999 [YUN 1999, p. 357] to facilitate a political process to determine Kosovo's political future, comprised five components referred to as pillars: interim administration (led by the United Nations); institution-building (led by the Organization for Security and Cooperation in Europe (OSCE)); economic reconstruction (led by the EU); humanitarian affairs (led by the Office of the United Nations High Commissioner for Refugees (UNHCR)); and police and justice (led by the United Nations). UNMIK was headed by the Special Representative of the Secretary-General, Joachim Rücker.

The Secretary-General reported to the Security Council on UNMIK activities and developments in Kosovo for the periods 1 January to 30 April [S/2006/361], 1 May to 14 August [S/2006/707] and 15 August to 31 October [S/2006/906]. Activities during the remainder of the year were covered in a later report [S/2007/134].

Financing

On 30 June [meeting 92], the General Assembly, having considered the Secretary-General's performance report on the UNMIK budget covering the period from 1 July 2004 to 30 June 2005 [A/60/637 & Corr.1], the Secretary-General's report on the UNMIK budget for 1 July 2006 to 30 June 2007 [A/60/684 & Corr.1] and the report of the Advisory Committee on Administrative and Budgetary Questions (ACABQ) thereon [A/60/809], adopted, on the recommendation of the Fifth (Administrative and Budgetary) Committee [A/60/923], **resolution 60/275** without vote [agenda item 147].

Financing of the United Nations Interim Administration Mission in Kosovo

The General Assembly,

Having considered the reports of the Secretary-General on the financing of the United Nations Interim Administration Mission in Kosovo and the related report of the Advisory Committee on Administrative and Budgetary Questions,

Recalling Security Council resolution 1244(1999) of 10 June 1999 regarding the establishment of the United Nations Interim Administration Mission in Kosovo,

Recalling also its resolution 53/241 of 28 July 1999 on the financing of the Mission and its subsequent resolutions thereon, the latest of which was resolution 59/286 B of 22 June 2005,

Acknowledging the complexity of the Mission,

Reaffirming the general principles underlying the financing of United Nations peacekeeping operations, as stated in General Assembly resolutions 1874(S-IV) of 27 June 1963, 3101(XXVIII) of 11 December 1973 and 55/235 of 23 December 2000,

Mindful of the fact that it is essential to provide the Mission with the necessary financial resources to enable it to fulfil its responsibilities under the relevant resolution of the Security Council,

1. *Requests* the Secretary-General to entrust the Head of Mission with the task of formulating future budget proposals in full accordance with the provisions of General Assembly resolutions 59/296 of 22 June 2005 and 60/266 of 30 June 2006, as well as other relevant resolutions;

2. *Takes note* of the status of contributions to the United Nations Interim Administration Mission in Kosovo as at 30 April 2006, including the contributions outstanding in the amount of 58.7 million United States dollars, representing some 2 per cent of the total assessed contributions, notes with concern that only eighty-three Member States have paid their assessed contributions in full, and urges all other Member States, in particular those in arrears, to ensure payment of their outstanding assessed contributions;

3. *Expresses its appreciation* to those Member States which have paid their assessed contributions in full, and urges all other Member States to make every possible effort to ensure payment of their assessed contributions to the Mission in full;

4. *Expresses concern* at the financial situation with regard to peacekeeping activities, in particular as regards the reimbursements to troop contributors that bear additional burdens owing to overdue payments by Member States of their assessments;

5. *Also expresses concern* at the delay experienced by the Secretary-General in deploying and providing adequate resources to some recent peacekeeping missions, in particular those in Africa;

6. *Emphasizes* that all future and existing peacekeeping missions shall be given equal and non-discriminatory treatment in respect of financial and administrative arrangements;

7. *Also emphasizes* that all peacekeeping missions shall be provided with adequate resources for the effective and efficient discharge of their respective mandates;

8. *Reiterates its request* to the Secretary-General to make the fullest possible use of facilities and equipment at the United Nations Logistics Base at Brindisi, Italy, in order to minimize the costs of procurement for the Mission;

9. *Endorses* the conclusions and recommendations contained in the report of the Advisory Committee on Administrative and Budgetary Questions, subject to the provisions of the present resolution, and requests the Secretary-General to ensure their full implementation;

10. *Recalls* its request as contained in section XIV, paragraph 4, of its resolution 59/296;

11. *Decides* to finance resources for conduct and discipline capacity equivalent to 601,300 dollars under general temporary assistance;

12. *Requests* the Secretary-General to ensure the full implementation of the relevant provisions of its resolutions 59/296 and 60/266;

13. *Also requests* the Secretary-General to take all necessary action to ensure that the Mission is administered with a maximum of efficiency and economy;

14. *Further requests* the Secretary-General, in order to reduce the cost of employing General Service staff, to continue efforts to recruit local staff for the Mission against General Service posts, commensurate with the requirements of the Mission;

Financial performance report for the period from 1 July 2004 to 30 June 2005

15. *Takes note* of the report of the Secretary-General on the financial performance of the Mission for the period from 1 July 2004 to 30 June 2005;

Budget estimates for the period from 1 July 2006 to 30 June 2007

16. *Decides* to appropriate to the Special Account for the United Nations Interim Administration Mission in Kosovo the amount of 227,400,400 dollars for the period from 1 July 2006 to 30 June 2007, inclusive of 217,962,000 dollars for the maintenance of the Mission, 7,795,800 dollars for the support account for peacekeeping operations and 1,642,600 dollars for the United Nations Logistics Base;

Financing of the appropriation

17. *Decides also* to apportion among Member States the amount of 227,400,400 dollars, in accordance with the levels updated in General Assembly resolution 58/256 of 23 December 2003, and taking into account the scale of assessments for 2006, as set out in its resolution 58/1 B

of 23 December 2003, and the scale of assessments for 2007;

18. *Decides further* that, in accordance with the provisions of its resolution 973(X) of 15 December 1955, there shall be set off against the apportionment among Member States, as provided for in paragraph 17 above, their respective share in the Tax Equalization Fund of the amount of 17,537,800 dollars, comprising the estimated staff assessment income of 16,536,600 dollars approved for the Mission, the prorated share of 876,900 dollars of the estimated staff assessment income approved for the support account and the prorated share of 124,300 dollars of the estimated staff assessment income approved for the United Nations Logistics Base;

19. *Decides* that, for Member States that have fulfilled their financial obligations to the Mission, there shall be set off against their apportionment, as provided for in paragraph 17 above, their respective share of the unencumbered balance and other income in the amount of 10,423,600 dollars in respect of the financial period ended 30 June 2005, in accordance with the levels updated in General Assembly resolution 58/256, and taking into account the scale of assessments for 2005, as set out in its resolution 58/1 B;

20. *Decides also* that, for Member States that have not fulfilled their financial obligations to the Mission, there shall be set off against their outstanding obligations their respective share of the unencumbered balance and other income in the amount of 10,423,600 dollars in respect of the financial period ended 30 June 2005, in accordance with the scheme set out in paragraph 19 above;

21. *Decides further* that the increase of 84,100 dollars in the estimated staff assessment income in respect of the financial period ended 30 June 2005 shall be added to the credits from the amount of 10,423,600 dollars referred to in paragraphs 19 and 20 above;

22. *Emphasizes* that no peacekeeping mission shall be financed by borrowing funds from other active peacekeeping missions;

23. *Encourages* the Secretary-General to continue to take additional measures to ensure the safety and security of all personnel under the auspices of the United Nations participating in the Mission, bearing in mind paragraphs 5 and 6 of Security Council resolution 1502(2003) of 26 August 2003;

24. *Invites* voluntary contributions to the Mission in cash and in the form of services and supplies acceptable to the Secretary-General, to be administered, as appropriate, in accordance with the procedure and practices established by the General Assembly;

25. *Decides* to include in the provisional agenda of its sixty-first session the item entitled "Financing of the United Nations Interim Administration Mission in Kosovo".

By **decision 61/552** of 22 December, the Assembly decided that the agenda item on the financing of UNMIK would remain for consideration during its resumed sixty-first (2007) session.

Also on 22 December, the Secretary-General submitted to the Assembly the performance report for UNMIK covering 1 July 2005 to 30 June 2006 [A/61/675].

International security presence (KFOR)

In accordance with resolution 1244(1999) [YUN 1999, p. 353], the Secretary-General transmitted to the Security Council reports on the activities during 2006 of the international security presence in Kosovo (KFOR), also known as Operation Joint Guard, covering the periods 1 to 31 January [S/2006/210], 1 to 28 February [S/2006/228], 1 to 31 March [S/2006/288], 1 to 30 April [S/2006/368], 1 to 31 May [S/2006/574], 1 to 31 June [S/2006/643], 1 to 31 July [S/2006/720], 1 to 31 August [S/2006/830], 1 to 31 October [S/2007/39], 1 to 30 November [S/2007/53] and 1 to 31 December [S/2007/130]. As at 25 December, the force, which operated under NATO leadership, comprised 14,498 troops, including 2,537 from non-NATO countries.

KFOR continued to handle incidents related to unexploded ordnance, illegal weapons possession, drugs, human trafficking and smuggling. It also carried out operations to prevent ethnic violence and protect patrimonial sites and monitored possible threats against international organizations and military bases. It continued to improve its crowd and riot control capabilities so as to be better prepared to counter any resurgence of violence.

Pristina Airport investigation

OIOS report. On 14 March [A/60/720 & Corr.1], the Office of Internal Oversight Services (OIOS) reported to the General Assembly on the investigation conducted by the Investigations Task Force into fraud and corruption allegations at Pristina Airport. The Task Force was jointly established in 2003 by OIOS, the EU European Anti-fraud Office (OLAF), UNMIK and its Financial Investigations Unit to identify fraud and corruption in UNMIK, all publicly owned enterprises in Kosovo and institutions funded from the Kosovo consolidated budget.

Between 2004 and 2005, the Task Force submitted 33 reports to the Special Representative covering institutional and administrative shortcomings and flaws, primarily in the area of procurement. Nine cases were referred, through the Special Representative, to the UNMIK Department of Justice for further criminal investigation. The findings and the resultant actions by UNMIK showed a lack of accountability in the operation, management and supervision of the airport.

In an exchange of correspondence with the Task Force, OIOS and OLAF in 2005, the Special Representative stated that, in most instances, no administrative action against airport managers would be taken. The Special Representative, supported by a legal opinion from the UN Office of Legal Affairs, had asserted that it was outside OIOS jurisdiction to report to the Assembly on the results of the Task Force investigations. However, OIOS, citing Assembly resolution 48/218 B [YUN 1994, p. 1362], stated that it had an obligation to report to the Assembly on matters that provided insight into the effective utilization and management of resources and the protection of assets. It was the view of OIOS, shared by OLAF, that UNMIK had the responsibility to combat corruption vigorously, including by addressing all issues raised by the Task Force, to ensure that the future of Kosovo was based on sound management and international standards in the area of anti-corruption prevention and investigation to reduce long-term problems. OIOS was concerned that the Special Representative's failure to address many of the recommendations of the Task Force and his reluctance to consider any of the OIOS recommendations would allow the ongoing problem of corruption to prevail.

The 11 OIOS recommendations, based on the findings of the Task Force investigations, included: the creation of a viable, long-term anti-corruption entity responsible for administrative investigations in the public sector; the evaluation of the performance of all managers of Pristina Airport; the provision of resources for regular external audits of all publicly owned enterprises; the introduction of procedures for the regular disclosure of assets of staff of publicly owned enterprises; and the introduction of the concept of merit-based employment in all public institutions.

Note by Secretary-General. In May [A/60/720/Add.1], the Secretary-General, commenting on the OIOS report, provided details of the structural and management reforms undertaken and completed by UNMIK since 2003 to address the issues of governance, fraud and corruption in publicly owned enterprises, including Pristina Airport. It also provided information on the status of implementation of the recommendations made in the OIOS report.

By **decision 60/551 C** of 7 July, the Assembly deferred until its sixty-first session consideration of the OIOS report on the investigation by the Investigations Task Force into allegations of fraud and corruption at Pristina Airport and the Secretary-General's comments theron.

Montenegro independence

In a 21 May referendum, the Republic of Montenegro, one of the two constituent Republics of Serbia and Montenegro [YUN2003, p. 412], voted for independence.

On 24 May [S/2006/335], Austria drew attention to a statement by the EU Presidency welcoming the referendum on the independence of Montenegro and calling on all sides to accept the result. On 7 June [S/2006/412], Austria drew attention to an EU Presidency statement, in which the EU reiterated its full respect for the decision of Montenegro and called on Belgrade and Podgorica to pursue a dialogue on their future relations.

Admission to UN membership

On 16 June [A/60/890-S/2006/409], the Secretary-General transmitted to the General Assembly and the Security Council a 5 June letter from the President of the Republic of Montenegro, in which he formally requested admission of the Republic to membership in the United Nations.

On 22 June, the Council President issued statement **S/PRST/2006/27**, in which the Council recommended to the Assembly that Montenegro be admitted as a Member of the United Nations. On the same day, the Council adopted **resolution 1691(2006)** making the same recommendation.

On 28 June, the Assembly adopted **resolution 60/264,** in which it admitted the Republic of Montenegro to membership in the United Nations (see p. 1592).

Georgia

In 2006, efforts continued to advance the Georgian Abkhaz peace process, based on the 2001 Basic Principles for the Distribution of Competences between Tbilisi (Georgia's Government) and Sukhumi (the Abkhaz leadership) [YUN 2001, p. 386]. That document was intended to serve as a framework for substantive negotiations on the status of Abkhazia as a sovereign entity within the State of Georgia.

In May, the Secretary-General's Special Representative for Georgia convened the first session of the resumed Coordinating Council of the Georgian and Abkhaz sides, which had not met since 2001 [YUN 2001, p. 378], followed by a meeting of the Council's working groups on security (June) and on the return of internally displaced persons and refugees (July). The Group of Friends of the

Secretary-General on Georgia (France, Germany, Russian Federation, the United Kingdom and the United States) continued to meet throughout the year, with the participation of the parties, and some of their high-level representatives visited conflict regions in Georgia. Georgian and Abkhaz representatives to the Group of Friends recognized the importance of a package of documents on the non-use of force and welcomed the planned registration of returnees in the Gali district.

Despite some political progress, the situation on the ground remained difficult and complex. In July, a large-scale law enforcement operation was launched by Georgian forces in the upper Kodori Valley, which the Abkhaz side declared a gross violation of the 1994 Agreement on a Ceasefire and Separation of Forces (Moscow Agreement) [YUN 1994, p. 583]. Also in July, Georgia's Parliament, maintaining that Russian Federation peacekeepers had ignored violations of human rights perpetrated by the Sukhumi separatist regime, adopted a resolution to begin the suspension of peacekeeping operations and requested the immediate withdrawal of Russian peacekeeping forces from the country. Abductions and, in some cases, killings continued in the Gali and Zugdidi conflict regions throughout the year, prompting several investigations by the United Nations Observer Mission in Georgia. In October and December, UNOMIG and peacekeeping forces of the Commonwealth of Independent States, with security guarantees from the parties, launched joint patrols in the Kodori Valley region.

UN Observer Mission in Georgia

The United Nations Observer Mission in Georgia (UNOMIG), established by Security Council resolution 858(1993) [YUN 1993, p. 509], continued to monitor compliance with the 1994 Moscow Agreement [YUN 1994, p. 583] and to fulfil other tasks, as mandated by Council resolution 937(1994) [ibid., p. 584]. The Mission operated in close collaboration with the collective peacekeeping forces of the Commonwealth of Independent States (CIS) located in the zone of conflict since 1994 [ibid., p. 583]. The Council extended the Mission's mandate three times during the year, the first time until 31 March, the second until 15 October, and the third until 15 April 2007.

UNOMIG main headquarters was located in Sukhumi (Abkhazia, Georgia), with some administrative headquarters in Pitsunda, a liaison office in the Georgian capital of Tbilisi and team bases and a sector headquarters in the Gali and Zugdidi sectors. A team base in the Kodori Valley was manned by observers operating from Sukhumi. As at December 2006, UNOMIG strength stood at 127 military observers and 14 civilian police officers.

In August [S/2006/539, S/2006/540], Jean Arnault (France) succeeded Heidi Tagliavini (Switzerland) as the Secretary-General's Special Representative for Georgia and head of UNOMIG. He was assisted by the UNOMIG Chief Military Observer, Major General Niaz Muhammed Khan Khattak (Pakistan).

Political aspects of the conflict

Report of Secretary-General (January). In a 13 January report to the Security Council [S/2006/19], the Secretary General described the situation in Abkhazia, Georgia, and UNOMIG operations during the latter part of 2005 [YUN 2005, p. 485].

Security Council consideration. During closed sessions of the Security Council on 26 January [meetings 5357, 5358], the Special Representative of the Secretary-General and Head of UNOMIG, Heidi Tagliavini, briefed Council members on the situation in Abkhazia. Countries contributing troops to UNOMIG attended the earlier session.

SECURITY COUNCIL ACTION

On 31 January [meeting 5363], the Council, having considered the Secretary-General's 13 January report, unanimously adopted **resolution 1656(2006)**. The draft [S/2006/58] was prepared in consultations among Council members.

The Security Council,

Recalling its relevant resolutions on the issue, in particular resolution 1615(2005) of 29 July 2005,

Taking note of the meeting of the Group of Friends of the Secretary-General on Georgia scheduled to take place in Geneva on 2 and 3 February 2006,

1. *Decides* to extend the mandate of the United Nations Observer Mission in Georgia until 31 March 2006;
2. *Decides also* to remain actively seized of the matter.

Meeting of Group of Friends (February). Senior representatives of the Group of Friends of the Secretary-General on Georgia (France, Germany, Russian Federation, the United Kingdom and the United States) met, with the participation of the parties (Geneva, 2-3 February). The Group underlined the need for a peaceful settlement of the conflict within the framework of the relevant Security Council resolutions and reaffirmed its commitment to the sovereignty, independence and territorial integrity of Georgia within internationally recognized borders. They agreed on the need to address the core political issues of the conflict, in addition to continuing work on confidence-building measures. They supported the registration of returnees in the Gali district by the Office of the United Nations High Commissioner for Refugees (UNHCR), which was to commence in April.

In separate consultations with the parties, the Group of Friends stressed the urgent need for tangible results in the peace process and urged them to finalize, without delay, the package of documents on the non-use of force and on the return of internally displaced persons and refugees, and to follow up on a possible meeting of their highest leadership. They stressed the need for the Georgian side to address legitimate Abkhaz security concerns and to avoid actions that might be seen as threatening. They also underlined the need for the Abkhaz side to address the issues of return and the security and human rights concerns of returnees, open a UN human rights sub-office in Gali, and take other measures. Georgian and Abkhaz representatives recognized the importance of finalizing the non-use of force documents and welcomed the planned registration of returnees in the Gali district. They expressed individual concerns, but also acknowledged the need to maintain a constructive and results-oriented dialogue on those issues.

Report of Secretary-General (March). In a March report on the situation in Abkhazia, Georgia [S/2006/173], the Secretary-General stated that, on 24 January, at its Gali sector headquarters, UNOMIG had chaired a ministerial-level meeting between Georgian and Abkhaz representatives on security issues, in particular in the Gali district. The parties signed a protocol in which they agreed to intensify cooperation in order to combat and prevent criminal activities and, for that purpose, to nominate coordinators at the regional level, exchange relevant operational information, elaborate a joint action plan and appoint focal points for the mass media to provide verified information about the situation on the ground. In February, the Parliament of Georgia adopted a resolution requesting the Georgian Government to pursue a revision of the 1992 Sochi agreement relating to South Ossetia and the replacement of the peacekeeping forces there by an international peacekeeping operation. The Secretary-General noted that a meeting had been held between the two sides on avian flu prevention and described the February meeting of the Group of Friends (see above).

The Secretary-General stated that it was essential for the Georgian and Abkhaz sides to follow up actively on the understandings reached at the meeting of the Group of Friends. In particular, early finalization of the documents on the non-use of force and on the return of internally displaced persons and refugees would be a strong indication of their commitment to make tangible progress in the peace process. As UNOMIG continued to play a key role in maintaining stability in the conflict zone and in facilitating progress toward a sustainable political solution of the conflict, the Secretary-General recommended that the Mission's mandate be extended until 30 September. He urged the parties to ensure the security and freedom of movement of all UNOMIG personnel and, as a matter of priority, bring the perpetrators of criminal acts against the Mission to justice.

Communications. On 16 February [A/60/685], Georgia transmitted to the General Assembly the text of a resolution adopted by its Parliament concerning the situation and conduct of peacekeeping operations in the Former Autonomous Region of South Ossetia, which it assessed as extremely negative. Among other things, the Parliament instructed the Georgian Government to replace Russian Federation peacekeeping forces in the district with an effective international peacekeeping operation.

On 28 March [S/2006/188], Georgia drew the Security Council's attention to positive developments in the conflict resolution process in Abkhazia but observed that there was increasing public distrust in Georgia of the Russian peacekeeping forces. It stated that there was an alarming increase in the number of criminal offenses where evidence showed that the culprits were the peacekeepers themselves, and that there were cases where local criminals and peacekeepers had colluded, resulting in raids, trafficking and killing of ethnic Georgian civilians. The Russian Federation, it said, continued to seize property in Abkhazia. Georgia called for the United Nations to consider new options for setting in motion the process of returns for refugees and displaced persons.

SECURITY COUNCIL ACTION

On 28 March, in a closed session [meeting 5398], the Security Council and troop-contributing countries to UNOMIG were briefed by the UN Department of Peacekeeping Operations (DPKO).

On 31 March [meeting 5405], the Council, having considered the Secretary-General's March report (see above), unanimously adopted **resolution 1666(2006)**. The draft [S/2006/201] was submitted by France, Germany, the Russian Federation, Slovakia, the United Kingdom and the United States.

The Security Council,

Recalling all its relevant resolutions, in particular resolution 1615(2005) of 29 July 2005,

Welcoming the report of the Secretary-General of 17 March 2006,

Supporting the sustained efforts of the Secretary-General and of his Special Representative for Georgia, with the assistance of the Russian Federation in its capacity as facilitator, as well as of the Group of Friends of the Secretary-General on Georgia and of the Organization for Security and Cooperation in Europe,

Stressing the importance of close and effective cooperation between the United Nations Observer Mission in Georgia and the peacekeeping force of the Commonwealth of Independent States as they currently play an important stabilizing role in the conflict zone, and recalling that a lasting and comprehensive settlement of the conflict will require appropriate security guarantees,

1. *Reaffirms* the commitment of all Member States to the sovereignty, independence and territorial integrity of Georgia within its internationally recognized borders, and supports all efforts of the United Nations and the Group of Friends of the Secretary-General on Georgia which are guided by their determination to promote a settlement of the Georgian-Abkhaz conflict only by peaceful means and within the framework of the Security Council resolutions;

2. *Recalls*, with a view to achieving a lasting and comprehensive settlement, its support for the principles contained in the paper on "Basic Principles for the Distribution of Competences between Tbilisi and Sukhumi", and welcomes additional ideas that the sides would be willing to offer with a view to conducting creatively and constructively a political dialogue under the aegis of the United Nations;

3. *Calls upon* the two sides to make full use of all existing mechanisms as described in the relevant Council resolutions in order to come to a peaceful settlement, and to comply fully with previous agreements and understandings regarding ceasefire, non-use of violence and confidence-building measures;

4. *Urges* both parties to finalize without delay the package of documents on the non-use of violence and on the return of refugees and internally displaced persons for the Gali district and to undertake the necessary steps to secure the protection and dignity of the civilian population, including the returnees;

5. *Calls upon* both parties to follow up on their expressed readiness for a meeting of their highest authorities without preconditions;

6. *Urges* the Georgian side to address seriously legitimate Abkhaz security concerns, to avoid steps which could be seen as threatening and to refrain from militant rhetoric;

7. *Urges* the Abkhaz leadership to address seriously the need for a dignified return of internally displaced persons and refugees, including their security and human rights concerns, to publicly reassure the local population, particularly in the Gali district, that their residency rights and identity will be respected, and to move without delay on implementing past commitments relating to United Nations police advisers, a United Nations human rights sub-office and the language of instruction;

8. *Underlines* the fact that it is the primary responsibility of both sides to provide appropriate security and to ensure the freedom of movement of the United Nations Observer Mission in Georgia, the peacekeeping force of the Commonwealth of Independent States and other international personnel, and calls upon both sides to fulfil their obligations in this regard;

9. *Supports* all efforts by the Georgian and Abkhaz sides to engage constructively in economic cooperation as envisaged in the Geneva meetings and complemented by the working groups established in Sochi, Russian Federation, in March 2003, including, security conditions permitting, the rehabilitation of infrastructure, and welcomes the intention expressed by Germany to host a meeting on economic cooperation and confidence-building measures, pending progress in the conflict resolution process;

10. *Welcomes* the efforts being undertaken by the Mission to implement the Secretary-General's zero-tolerance policy on sexual exploitation and abuse and to ensure full compliance of its personnel with the United Nations code of conduct, requests the Secretary-General to continue to take all necessary action in this regard and to keep the Council informed, and urges troop-contributing countries to take appropriate preventive action, including conducting predeployment awareness training, and to take disciplinary action and other action to ensure full accountability in cases of such conduct involving their personnel;

11. *Decides* to extend the mandate of the Mission for a new period terminating on 15 October 2006, subject to a review, as appropriate, of its mandate by the Council in the event of changes in security conditions, including changes in the mandate of the peacekeeping force of the Commonwealth of Independent States;

12. *Requests* the Secretary-General to continue to keep the Council regularly informed and to report three months from the date of adoption of the present resolution on the situation in Abkhazia, Georgia, in particular on progress in negotiations on the documents on the non-use of violence and the return of refugees and internally displaced persons;

13. *Strongly supports* the efforts of the Special Representative of the Secretary-General for Georgia, and calls upon the Group of Friends of the Secretary-General to continue giving her their steadfast and unified support;

14. *Decides* to remain actively seized of the matter.

Meeting of Group of Friends (May). High-level representatives of the Group of Friends of the Secretary-General on Georgia and the Special Representative of the Secretary-General for Georgia held meetings with the President and senior members of the Government of Georgia and with the Abkhaz leadership at the highest level (22-25 May). The Group reaffirmed the proposals and concerns expressed by the Security Council in resolution 1666(2006) (see above), in particular the human rights situation in the Gali district, the return of displaced persons and refugees and the non-use of force. The Group welcomed steps taken by both sides to establish a closer dialogue and encouraged them to focus on practical steps to build confidence.

Report of Secretary-General (June). In a 26 June report on the situation in Abkhazia, Georgia [S/2006/435], the Secretary-General stated that recent efforts by his Special Representative to facilitate dialogue between the Georgian and Abkhaz sides included a 29 March visit to Sukhumi by a senior Georgian official and a 2 May meeting between the Special Representative and senior officials of the Russian Federation. On 15 May, the Special Representative convened the first session of the resumed Coordinating Council of the Georgian and Abkhaz sides, which had not met since 2001 [YUN 2001, p. 378]. Among other things, the participants agreed on an agenda and a schedule of meetings for the Council's three working groups (security concerns; the return of internally displaced persons and refugees; socio-economic issues). They also confirmed their intention to continue work on the set of documents on the non-use of force and the safe and dignified return of internally displaced persons and refugees, and on preparations for a meeting of their highest authorities.

The Secretary-General noted, however, that new tensions had emerged between Georgia and the Russian Federation following a Russian ban on some Georgian imports and the establishment of a Georgian governmental commission to assess the implications of a possible withdrawal of Georgia from CIS. Georgia protested the Russian Federation's April decision to lift restrictions on foreign nationals crossing the Abkhaz section of the Russian-Georgian border, and visits that Russian officials had made to Sukhumi without prior agreement with Tbilisi. The Secretary-General urged the Georgian and Abkhaz sides to implement the understandings reached during the February meeting of the Group of Friends (see p. 473), in particular regarding a high-level meeting between the parties and the early finalization of documents on the non-use of force and on returns.

Security Council consideration. On 11 July, during a closed session [meeting 5483], the Security Council heard statements on the situation in Georgia by the Speaker of the Parliament of Georgia and the representative of the Russian Federation.

Report of Secretary-General (September). Reporting in September on the situation in Abkhazia, Georgia [S/2006/771], the Secretary-General indicated that a new and tense situation had emerged between the Georgian and Azkhaz sides, in particular as a result of the Georgian special operation in the upper Kodori Valley (see p. 479). Following the resumption of the Coordinating Council on 15 May (see above), the first session of the resumed working group on security matters was held; the Georgian and Abkhaz sides tasked their regional coordinators with preparing a plan of action for combating crime and building trust in the zones of conflict. On 11 July, the first session of the resumed working group on the return of internally displaced persons and refugees took place; the sides exchanged views on issues relating to dignified returns, in the first instance to the Gali district, and outlined their approaches on how to improve the situation in the district. They agreed to recommend participation of their respective representatives on educational issues at the next session and to continue discussions on the verification of returnees to the Gali district. The two meetings took place against the backdrop of Abkhaz objections to the composition of the Georgian delegation to the Coordinating Council and its working groups, which resulted in several delays before the meetings could be held.

On 18 July, the Parliament of Georgia adopted a resolution calling on the Government to start procedures for the immediate suspension of the peacekeeping operations in the country and to request the immediate withdrawal of Russian Federation peacekeeping forces from Georgian territory. It also requested the Government to start working immediately on a change of the peacekeeping format and the deployment of international police forces in South Ossetia and Abkhazia and inform the international community of its plans for the peaceful resolution of the conflicts. The Abkhaz side stated that a withdrawal of the CIS Collective Peacekeeping Forces would lead to an escalation of tensions and a resumption of hostilities. It reiterated its firm opposition to any change in the negotiation and peacekeeping mechanisms. By early September, the Government of Georgia insisted that new momentum could be given to the settlement process only through amendments to the peace process mechanisms involving, in particular, broader international participation in the peacekeeping force. On 22 September, President Saakashvili presented Georgia's proposals on the resolution of the conflicts, which included the demilitarization of Abkhazia and South Ossetia, direct dialogue between the parties, the establishment of an international police presence followed by the signing of a comprehensive pledge on the non-use of force, and economic rehabilitation.

Relations between the two sides took a turn for the worse on 25 July when Georgia launched a large-scale special operation in the upper Kodori Valley (see p. 479). Throughout that tense period, the Deputy Special Representative was in constant contact with both parties in order to avoid any escalation of the situation. UNOMIG requested security guarantees for joint patrols in the upper Kodori Valley and continued to be guided by agreements between the parties and the relevant Security Council resolutions. It also stressed that independent verification of the situation in the Kodori Valley was overdue and hoped that the parties would reach an agreement on that issue. In August, the UN High Commissioner for Refugees visited Georgia, including Sukhumi, Gali and Zugdidi. In September, a DPKO fact-finding mission visited the country to review the security and crime situation in the conflict zone and identify possible steps to enhance the effectiveness of law enforcement and cooperation between the parties.

The Secretary-General stated that several issues related to the events in the Kodori Valley were of special relevance: the commitment of both sides to providing advance notification and full transparency in the movement of those pieces of military equipment and armed personnel that were permitted under the Moscow Agreement; maintaining open channels of communication and dialogue; and agreement on the modalities for the monitoring of the Kodori Valley. He recommended an extension of UNOMIG mandate until 15 April 2007.

Communication. On 19 July [S/2006/555], the Russian Federation informed the Secretary-General that it considered the Georgian Parliament's decision to end peacekeeping operations in Abkhazia and South Ossetia to be a provocative step designed to aggravate tensions, destroy the existing format of negotiations and shatter the framework of legal agreements for the peaceful settlement of the Georgian-Abkhaz and Georgian-South Ossetia conflicts. The Russian Federation would take such measures as were necessary to ensure compliance with existing international agreements, prevent the destabilization of the situation in the region and protect the rights of Russian citizens living there.

SECURITY COUNCIL ACTION

On 6 October, during a closed session [meeting 5544], the Security Council and troop-contributing countries were briefed by the new Special Representative of the Secretary-General for Georgia and Head of UNOMIG, Jean Arnault.

On 13 October [meeting 5549], the Council, having considered the Secretary-General's September report (see above), unanimously adopted **resolution 1716(2006).** The draft [S/2006/804] was submitted by France, Germany, the Russian Federation, Slovakia and the United Kingdom.

The Security Council,

Recalling all its relevant resolutions, in particular resolution 1666(2006) of 31 March 2006,

Welcoming the report of the Secretary-General of 28 September 2006 on the activities of the United Nations Observer Mission in Georgia,

Supporting the sustained efforts of the Secretary-General and of his Special Representative for Georgia, with the assistance of the Russian Federation in its capacity as facilitator, as well as of the Group of Friends of the Secretary-General on Georgia and of the Organization for Security and Cooperation in Europe,

Regretting the continued lack of progress on key issues of a comprehensive settlement of the Georgian-Abkhaz conflict,

Acknowledging with concern the observation of the Secretary-General that a new and tense situation has emerged between the Georgian and the Abkhaz sides, in particular as a result of the Georgian special operation in the upper Kodori Valley,

1. *Reaffirms* the commitment of all Member States to the sovereignty, independence and territorial integrity of Georgia within its internationally recognized borders, and supports all efforts by the United Nations and the Group of Friends of the Secretary-General on Georgia which are guided by their determination to promote a settlement of the Georgian-Abkhaz conflict only by peaceful means and within the framework of the Security Council resolutions;

2. *Recalls*, with a view to achieving a lasting and comprehensive settlement, its support for the principles contained in the paper on "Basic Principles for the Distribution of Competences between Tbilisi and Sukhumi", and welcomes additional ideas that the sides would be willing to offer with a view to conducting creatively and constructively a political dialogue under the aegis of the United Nations;

3. *Having in mind* the relevant Council resolutions containing an appeal to both sides to refrain from any action that might impede the peace process, expresses its concern with regard to the actions of the Georgian side in the Kodori Valley in July 2006, and to all violations of the Agreement on a Ceasefire and Separation of Forces signed at Moscow on 14 May 1994, and other Georgian-Abkhaz agreements concerning the Kodori Valley;

4. *Urges* the Georgian side to ensure that the situation in the upper Kodori Valley is in line with the Moscow Agreement and that no troops unauthorized by the Agreement are present;

5. *Notes with satisfaction* the resumption of joint patrols in the upper Kodori Valley by the United Nations Observer Mission in Georgia and the peacekeeping force of the Commonwealth of Independent States, and reaffirms that such joint patrols should be conducted on a regular basis;

6. *Urges* both parties to comply fully with previous agreements and understandings regarding ceasefire, non-use of violence and confidence-building measures, and stresses the need to strictly observe the Moscow Agreement in the air, on the sea and on land, including in the Kodori Valley;

7. *Acknowledges* the important role of the peacekeeping force of the Commonwealth of Independent States and of the Mission in the Georgian-Abkhaz conflict zone, stresses the importance of close and effective cooperation between the Mission and the peacekeeping force as they currently play a stabilizing role in the conflict zone, looks to all sides to continue to extend the necessary cooperation to them, and recalls that a lasting and comprehensive settlement of the conflict will require appropriate security guarantees;

8. *Once again urges* the Georgian side to address seriously legitimate Abkhaz security concerns, to avoid steps which could be seen as threatening and to refrain from militant rhetoric and provocative actions, especially in the upper Kodori Valley;

9. *Urges* the Abkhaz leadership to address seriously the need for a dignified return of internally displaced persons and refugees, including their security and human rights concerns, to publicly reassure the local population, particularly in the Gali district, that their residency rights and identity will be respected, and to move without delay on implementing past commitments relating to United Nations police advisers, a United Nations human rights sub-office and the language of instruction;

10. *Urges* both parties to finalize without delay the package of documents on the non-use of violence and on the return of refugees and internally displaced persons for the Gali district and to undertake necessary steps to secure the protection and dignity of the civilian population, including the returnees;

11. *Commends* the presentation by both sides of ideas as a basis for dialogue, and calls upon the two sides to resume this dialogue by using all existing mechanisms as described in the relevant Council resolutions in order to come to a peaceful settlement;

12. *Calls upon* both parties to follow up on their expressed readiness for a meeting of their highest authorities without preconditions and to maintain open channels of communication to build confidence, and encourages further contacts between representatives of civil society;

13. *Calls upon* the Secretary-General to explore with the sides ways and means to build confidence, in particular by improving the welfare and security of the inhabitants of Gali and Zugdidi districts;

14. *Supports* all efforts by the Georgian and Abkhaz sides to engage constructively in economic cooperation as envisaged in the Geneva meetings and complemented by the working groups established in Sochi, Russian Federation, in March 2003, including, security conditions permitting, the rehabilitation of infrastructure, and welcomes the intention expressed by Germany to host a meeting on economic cooperation and confidence-building measures, pending progress in the conflict resolution process;

15. *Underlines* that it is the primary responsibility of both sides to provide appropriate security and to ensure the freedom of movement of the Mission, the peacekeeping force of the Commonwealth of Independent States and other international personnel, and calls upon both sides to fulfil their obligations in this regard;

16. *Welcomes* the efforts being undertaken by the Mission to implement the Secretary-General's zero-tolerance policy on sexual exploitation and abuse and to ensure full compliance of its personnel with the United Nations code of conduct, requests the Secretary-General to continue to take all necessary action in this regard and to keep the Council informed, and urges troop-contributing countries to take appropriate preventive action, including conducting predeployment awareness training, and to take disciplinary action and other action to ensure full accountability in cases of such conduct involving their personnel;

17. *Decides* to extend the mandate of the Mission for a new period terminating on 15 April 2007;

18. *Requests* the Secretary-General to include detailed information on developments in the Kodori Valley and on the progress on efforts for the return of refugees and internally displaced persons, particularly to the Gali district, in his next report on the situation in Abkhazia, Georgia;

19. *Strongly supports* the efforts of the Special Representative of the Secretary-General for Georgia, and calls upon the Group of Friends of the Secretary-General to continue giving him their steadfast and unified support;

20. *Decides* to remain actively seized of the matter.

Communications. On 4 September [S/2006/709], Georgia informed the Security Council President of violations of human rights perpetrated by the Abkhaz armed forces against Georgians in the Gali district, within sight of the CIS peacekeeping forces. Georgia observed that those events supported the correctness of its Parliament's decision on the withdrawal of Russian peacekeepers from the conflict zone and to replace them by an international component. In a 9 October letter to the Secretary-General [A/61/505], Georgia stated that the Russian authorities had begun retaliatory measures against Georgian citizens and ethnic Georgians, including women and children, on the territory of Russia.

On 13 October [S/2006/807], Georgia emphasized that Security Council resolution 1716(2006) (see above) recognized that a new reality had emerged in the upper Kodori Valley as a result of the Georgian operation there (see p. 480). Patrols, which had been impossible since 2003 because of lack of security, had resumed.

On 23 October [A/61/536], Georgia transmitted to the Secretary-General a statement by its Minister of Foreign Affairs, Gela Bezhuashvili, in response to comments made by the Russian Federation

President, Vladimir Putin, at an informal EU summit (Lahti, Finland, 20 October). The Minister said that President Putin had deliberately misrepresented the nature of the tensions between Russia and Georgia. There had never been a genocide against the people of South Ossetia and the ethnic cleansing in Abkhazia was carried out by troops sponsored by the Russian Federation.

In a 25 October letter [S/2006/845], Georgia expressed its deep concern regarding recent Abkhaz military exercises in the Upper Tkvarcheli region at a location where the Georgian Minister of the Interior was present. It strongly protested what it considered to be a deliberate provocation with the aim of escalating tension in the conflict zone and requested the international community to undertake measures to prevent future recurrences.

On 2 November [A/61/569-S/2006/880], Ukraine, on behalf of the Organization for Democracy and Economic Development-GUAM (Azerbaijan, Georgia, the Republic of Moldova and Ukraine), welcomed Georgia's decision to repatriate Russian servicemen detained on its territory. It also welcomed the Russian Federation's undertaking to remove its military bases and facilities from the territory of Georgia in 2008. GUAM called on States to refrain from unilateral acts directed at Georgia with a view to severing economic, humanitarian and other inter-State contacts, and expressed the conviction that problems, including those related to conflict settlement, should be resolved at the negotiating table.

Later report of Secretary-General. In a report on the situation in Abkhazia, Georgia, during late 2006 [S/2007/15], the Secretary-General stated that, since the adoption of resolution 1716(2006) (see p. 477), both sides had agreed to work towards its implementation. However, recent developments in the Georgian-controlled upper Kodori Valley (see below) had caused the Abkhaz side to delay the resumption of formal dialogue. A similar situation had emerged in South Ossetia, where the Georgian Government protested the November independence referendum organized by the South Ossetia leadership. Weekly quadripartite meetings on security issues between the parties, UNOMIG and the CIS peacekeeping force were suspended following the resignation of the Georgian coordinator in November; a new coordinator had not yet been appointed. The Joint Fact Finding Group opened new cases, investigating incidents in the Gali district, including the September unidentified overflight of the security zone and restricted weapons zone, and the 25-26 December killings (see below). UNOMIG also closely observed two Abkhaz military exercises conducted outside the security and restricted weapons zones, on 26 September and from 8 to 10 November.

The Secretary-General condemned the recent acts of violence in the conflict zone and urged both parties to work together to identify and bring to justice those responsible. He appealed to them to engage in dialogue to prevent an escalation of the situation on the ground and reaffirmed UNOMIG readiness to assist in that respect.

Communications. On 26 July [S/2006/597], Finland, on behalf of the EU, expressed deep concern about continuing tensions between Georgia and the Russian Federation and recent incidents in South Ossetia. It was particularly worried by the recent closure of the only recognized border crossing between the two States and emphasized the importance of ensuring freedom of movement of goods and people. It urged the parties to do their utmost to promote stability and peaceful development in the region. It regretted the cancellation of the July meeting of the Joint Control Commission on South Ossetia.

Referring to the 12 November referendum in South Ossetia (see above), Moldova, on 13 November [A/61/573], transmitted to the Secretary-General an 11 November declaration by its Ministry of Foreign Affairs, which stated that it considered the referendum to be a destabilizing step and a display of separatism. In solidarity with the EU and the United States, it would not recognize the referendum or the presidential elections held in South Ossetia on the same day. On 20 November [S/2006/955], Finland, on behalf of the EU, transmitted a statement supporting Georgia's sovereignty and territorial integrity within its internationally recognized borders. It reiterated that it did not recognize the referendum, the presidential elections, or their respective outcomes.

On 7 December [A/61/619], Georgia expressed deep concern regarding statements in support of the independence of Abkhazia and South Ossetia by the Russian Federation State Duma. It appealed to international organizations, parliamentary assemblies and parliaments of friendly States to support Georgia in its difficult but legitimate quest for common democratic and just values.

Situation on the ground

Kodori Valley

On 25 July, Georgia launched a large-scale operation in the upper Kodori Valley, the stated objective of which was to restore law and order in the area. Georgia, which controlled the upper valley, provided, without detail, advance notice of the impending operation to the Abkhaz side, which controlled the lower valley. The Abkhaz side declared the operation a gross violation of the 1994 Moscow Agreement [YUN 1994, p. 583], aimed at taking over a strategically important bridgehead for the further build-up of the Georgian military presence. It put its forces on high alert, deployed military units just outside the lower valley and threatened to retaliate in the event of an incursion by the Georgian side into that part of the valley. The Government of Georgia stressed that the forces involved in the operation belonged to the Ministry of the Interior or were military assets on loan to that Ministry; that it was conducting not a military but a law enforcement operation against a defiant local armed group; and that the operation would not spill over into Abkhaz-controlled territory. On 27 July, President Saakashvili announced the completion of the operation and the relocation of the Tbilisi-based Government of the Autonomous Republic of Abkhazia to the upper Kodori Valley, a decision that he described as a first important step towards extending Georgia's jurisdiction in the region. In response, the Abkhaz side stated that it would oppose, even by force, such a relocation, and announced that it had the support of the North Caucasus republics of the Russian Federation, including in the form of volunteers.

In the absence of UNOMIG monitoring of the upper Kodori Valley, which had been suspended since the hostage-taking incident in June 2003 [YUN 2003, p. 439], the Mission was unable to verify the situation there. On 27 and 28 July, UNOMIG established two temporary observation posts in the vicinity of two checkpoints of the CIS peacekeeping force to monitor movement to and from the upper Kodori Valley on a 24-hour basis. Throughout the tense period, the Secretary-General's Deputy Special Representative was in constant contact with both parties in order to avoid an escalation of the situation. The Mission requested security guarantees for a joint patrol, which were eventually granted. Joint UNOMIG-CIS peacekeeping patrols in the upper Kodori Valley took place on 12 October and in the upper and lower valley from 13 to 16 December, with security guarantees and full cooperation provided by both parties. UNOMIG discussed the findings of the patrols, including the discovery of a large amount of ammunition and some weapons, with both sides and the CIS peacekeeping force, with a view to enhancing mutual confidence and transparency. It encouraged dialogue between the parties to discuss their respective security concerns in the valley, emphasized the benefits of regular patrols for improving confidence, and proposed follow-up on joint patrols to maintain the momentum. A serious incident took place in the upper valley on 25 October when three rockets were fired towards Kvemo Azhara village. While the rockets did not explode, the attack's potential to escalate tensions led UNOMIG to dispatch a fact-finding team to the impact sites and to the district from which the Georgian side assessed that the firing had taken place.

Communications. In identical letters dated 26 July [A/60/959, S/2006/576] addressed, respectively, to the Secretary-General and the Security Council President, Georgia categorically ruled out any kind of military operation in the Kodori Gorge. It urged the population to obey the law; in cases of disobedience, the Georgian authorities would exercise their legitimate right to carry out anti-criminal police operations in the region.

In two identical letters of the same date [A/60/960, S/2006/577] addressed, respectively, to the Secretary-General and the Council President, Georgia reiterated that the police operation in the Kodori Gorge took place in full compliance with Georgian laws and its international commitments. It reaffirmed that the operation did not extend to the territory controlled by the Abkhazian de facto authorities, and that special representatives were keeping in contact with them to bring clarity to the state of affairs in the region. On 28 July [A/60/962], Georgia informed the Secretary-General of its continuing intensive consultations with international organizations and others concerned regarding the ongoing police operation in Kodori Gorge.

On 13 September [S/2006/739], Georgia drew the Council's attention to the successful completion of the police operation in the Kodori Valley region. Immediately after the operation, Georgia launched social-economic rehabilitation projects in the region, including the delivery of food aid, the creation of jobs and the reconstruction of bridges. It noted that the restoration of order and security in the Gorge would create the necessary prerequisites for the United Nations to conduct monitoring in the area, which had been halted three years earlier for security reasons [YUN 2003, p. 439].

Gali and Zugdidi sectors

The situation in the Gali sector fluctuated during the year. Following several killings by unidentified armed men in March and reports of the presence of an armed group in the vicinity, Abkhaz law enforcement agencies and the CIS peacekeeping force increased their activities in the area, including joint patrolling. Two reports of violations of the

Moscow Agreement [YUN 1994, p. 583] in the Gali area were issued, one in July when Abkhaz de facto law enforcement agency personnel denied freedom of movement to a UNOMIG patrol, and the second in August when a similar incident took place at an Abkhaz observation post in the restricted weapons zone. Despite a comparatively low level of criminal activity, some incidents were investigated, including the 8 August killing of three persons during an attempted abduction and the 17 August shooting attack against armoured vehicles of a UNOMIG patrol, in which there were no casualties.

The security situation in the Gali sector remained generally calm. However, in September, an overflight by an unidentified aircraft caused both the Georgian and Abkhaz sides to exchange accusations, and live firing along the ceasefire line on 28 September caused protests by the Georgian side. UNOMIG established two temporary posts along the ceasefire line, and no further incidents were observed. In November, several raids were conducted by the Abkhaz militia in the district, resulting in the temporary detention of some local residents. In December, tensions rapidly increased following the arrest in Zugdidi of Pridon Chakaberia, the de facto administrator of the Kvemo Bargebi village in the lower Gali district, and the killings of three members of the Abkhaz militia. The Abkhaz side claimed that those acts were perpetrated by armed groups backed by the Georgian Government, while the Georgian side attributed the killings to Abkhaz inter-factional rivalry and denied any connection with so-called armed groups. At the end of December, the Abkhaz militia detained 66 residents in the lower Gali district, causing apprehension among the local population. In response, UNOMIG launched special patrols and, with the participation of the Chief Military Officer, initiated investigations into the killings. The Secretary-General's Special Representative publicly condemned the violence and appealed to both sides to cooperate in bringing to justice the perpetrators and to engage in dialogue.

The Zugdidi sector was a main transit zone for Georgian military vehicles and aircraft en route to the upper Kodori Valley. UNOMIG maintained special patrols in the sector and observed the movement of vehicles transporting armed and unarmed personnel, stores and fuel, movement of isolated military vehicles and overflight by military helicopters. UNOMIG presented a number of options to the Georgian Ministry of Internal Affairs regarding movements through the security zone that were in line with the Moscow Agreement, which were considered favourably. The Mission called on the authorities to implement those measures soon; together with regular joint patrolling in the upper Kodori Valley, they could contribute to easing tension in the area.

Humanitarian situation and human rights

The UN Human Rights Office in Abhkazia, Georgia, continued to implement the programme for the protection and promotion of human rights by monitoring the human rights situation and taking measures to prevent and redress violations. The Office provided human rights education and technical assistance to strengthen local non-governmental organizations (NGOs) and grass-roots initiatives and investigated reports of violations of due process; arbitrary detention and ill-treatment of detainees; prolonged pre-trial detention; impunity; involuntary disappearances; and arbitrary evictions and other property rights violations. In cooperation with local NGOs, the Office continued its projects dealing with: support for a confidential phone line for detainees; training of prison inmates to facilitate their reintegration into society upon release; free legal aid for vulnerable groups; internet communication between family members separated by conflict; and awareness initiatives on women's and children's rights.

UNOMIG stressed that the implementation of a 15 May de facto Abkhaz parliamentary decree, which resulted in the de facto courts declining as inadmissible claims by property owners displaced by armed conflict and violence since 1992 to repossess their illegally occupied property, discriminated against non-Abkhaz citizens and that the courts' practice was a deterrent to the return and reintegration of internally displaced persons, especially in the areas beyond the Gali district.

UNOMIG continued the implementation of quick-impact humanitarian projects and the first phase of the rehabilitation programme funded by the European Commission. It also secured additional funding for the continued operation of a shuttle bus across the ceasefire line. UN agencies and international NGOs continued to assist vulnerable groups on the Abkhaz side of the ceasefire line. The Mission began preparations for the rehabilitation of several hospitals affected by conflict, including the tuberculosis hospital in Zugdidi. The United Nations Development Programme (UNDP) pursued its integrated area-based recovery programme; some 40 groups were formed and received inputs as part of the agricultural income-generation component. An agricultural youth programme was set up in eight schools in the Zugdidi district and nine in Abkhazia. The implementation of water rehabilitation projects in three urban areas also continued. During the year, the United Nations Development Fund for Women launched an information network to advocate the inclusion of women's needs into ongoing reconstruction and development processes, and the United Nations Children's Fund (UNICEF) continued its immunization programmes and provided district hospitals and rural medical points with medical equipment and supplies. On 1 November, UNHCR opened an office in Sukhumi, in addition to its field office in Gali.

Financing

On 30 June [meeting 92], the General Assembly, having considered the financial performance report on the UNOMIG budget covering 1 July 2004 to 30 June 2005 [A/60/643 & Corr.2], the budget for UNOMIG covering 1 July 2006 to 30 June 2007 [A/60/652], and ACABQ's comments and recommendations thereon [A/60/810], adopted, on the recommendation of the Fifth Committee [A/60/921], **resolution 60/273** without vote [agenda item 144].

Financing of the United Nations Observer Mission in Georgia

The General Assembly,

Having considered the reports of the Secretary-General on the financing of the United Nations Observer Mission in Georgia and the related report of the Advisory Committee on Administrative and Budgetary Questions,

Recalling Security Council resolution 854(1993) of 6 August 1993, by which the Council approved the deployment of an advance team of up to ten United Nations military observers for a period of three months and the incorporation of the advance team into a United Nations observer mission if such a mission was formally established by the Council,

Recalling also Security Council resolution 858(1993) of 24 August 1993, by which the Council established the United Nations Observer Mission in Georgia, and the subsequent resolutions by which the Council extended the mandate of the Observer Mission, the latest of which was resolution 1666(2006) of 31 March 2006,

Recalling further its decision 48/475 A of 23 December 1993 on the financing of the Observer Mission and its subsequent resolutions and decisions thereon, the latest of which was resolution 59/304 of 22 June 2005,

Reaffirming the general principles underlying the financing of United Nations peacekeeping operations, as stated in General Assembly resolutions 1874(S-IV) of 27 June 1963, 3101(XXVIII) of 11 December 1973 and 55/235 of 23 December 2000,

Mindful of the fact that it is essential to provide the Observer Mission with the necessary financial resources to enable it to fulfil its responsibilities under the relevant resolutions of the Security Council,

1. *Requests* the Secretary-General to entrust the Head of Mission with the task of formulating future budget proposals in full accordance with the provisions of General Assembly resolutions 59/296 of 22 June 2005 and 60/266 of 30 June 2006, as well as other relevant resolutions;

2. *Takes note* of the status of contributions to the United Nations Observer Mission in Georgia as at 30 April 2006, including the contributions outstanding in the amount of 16.8 million United States dollars, representing some 6 per cent of the total assessed contributions, notes with concern that only thirty-three Member States have paid their assessed contributions in full, and urges all other Member States, in particular those in arrears, to ensure payment of their outstanding assessed contributions;

3. *Expresses its appreciation* to those Member States which have paid their assessed contributions in full, and urges all other Member States to make every possible effort to ensure payment of their assessed contributions to the Observer Mission in full;

4. *Expresses concern* at the delay experienced by the Secretary-General in deploying and providing adequate resources to some recent peacekeeping missions, in particular those in Africa;

5. *Emphasizes* that all future and existing peacekeeping missions shall be given equal and non-discriminatory treatment in respect of financial and administrative arrangements;

6. *Also emphasizes* that all peacekeeping missions shall be provided with adequate resources for the effective and efficient discharge of their respective mandates;

7. *Reiterates its request* to the Secretary-General to make the fullest possible use of facilities and equipment at the United Nations Logistics Base at Brindisi, Italy, in order to minimize the costs of procurement for the Observer Mission;

8. *Endorses* the conclusions and recommendations contained in the report of the Advisory Committee on Administrative and Budgetary Questions, subject to the provisions of the present resolution, and requests the Secretary-General to ensure their full implementation;

9. *Recalls* its request as stated in section XIV, paragraph 4, of its resolution 59/296;

10. *Decides* to finance resources for conduct and discipline capacity equivalent to 191,200 dollars under general temporary assistance;

11. *Requests* the Secretary-General to ensure the full implementation of the relevant provisions of its resolutions 59/296 and 60/266;

12. *Also requests* the Secretary-General to take all action necessary to ensure that the Observer Mission is administered with a maximum of efficiency and economy;

13. *Further requests* the Secretary-General, in order to reduce the cost of employing General Service staff, to continue efforts to recruit local staff for the Observer Mission against General Service posts, commensurate with the requirements of the Mission;

Financial performance report for the period from 1 July 2004 to 30 June 2005

14. *Takes note* of the report of the Secretary-General on the financial performance of the Observer Mission for the period from 1 July 2004 to 30 June 2005;

Budget estimates for the period from 1 July 2006 to 30 June 2007

15. *Decides* to appropriate to the Special Account for the United Nations Observer Mission in Georgia the amount of 34,827,000 dollars for the period from 1 July 2006 to 30 June 2007, inclusive of 33,377,900 dollars for the maintenance of the Observer Mission, 1,196,900 dollars for the support account for peacekeeping operations and 252,200 dollars for the United Nations Logistics Base;

Financing of the appropriation

16. *Decides also* to apportion among Member States the amount of 10,157,900 dollars for the period from 1 July to 15 October 2006, in accordance with the levels updated in General Assembly resolution 58/256 of 23 December 2003, and taking into account the scale of assessments for 2006, as set out in its resolution 58/1 B of 23 December 2003;

17. *Decides further* that, in accordance with the provisions of its resolution 973(X) of 15 December 1955, there shall be set off against the apportionment among Member States, as provided for in paragraph 16 above, their respective share in the Tax Equalization Fund of 694,300 dollars, comprising the estimated staff assessment income of 649,400 dollars approved for the Observer Mission, the prorated share of 39,300 dollars of the estimated staff assessment income approved for the support account and the prorated share of 5,600 dollars of the estimated staff assessment income approved for the United Nations Logistics Base;

18. *Decides* to apportion among Member States the amount of 24,669,100 dollars for the period from 16 October 2006 to 30 June 2007 at a monthly rate of 2,902,247 dollars, in accordance with the levels updated in General Assembly resolution 58/256, and taking into account the scale of assessments for 2006, as set out in its resolution 58/1 B, and the scale of assessments for 2007, subject to a decision of the Security Council to extend the mandate of the Observer Mission;

19. *Decides also* that, in accordance with the provisions of its resolution 973(X), there shall be set off against the apportionment among Member States, as provided for in paragraph 18 above, their respective share in the Tax Equalization Fund of 1,686,100 dollars, comprising the estimated staff assessment income of 1,577,200 dollars approved for the Observer Mission, the prorated share of 95,400 dollars of the estimated staff assessment income approved for the support account and the prorated share of 13,500 dollars of the estimated staff assessment income approved for the United Nations Logistics Base;

20. *Decides further* that, for Member States that have fulfilled their financial obligations to the Observer Mission, there shall be set off against their apportionment, as provided for in paragraph 16 above, their respective share of the unencumbered balance and other income in the amount of 1,854,900 dollars in respect of the financial period ended 30 June 2005, in accordance with the levels updated in its resolution 58/256, and taking into account the scale of assessments for 2005, as set out in its resolution 58/1 B;

21. *Decides* that, for Member States that have not fulfilled their financial obligations to the Observer Mission, there shall be set off against their outstanding obligations their respective share of the unencumbered balance and other income in the total amount of 1,854,900 dollars in respect of the financial period ended 30 June 2005, in accordance with the scheme set out in paragraph 20 above;

22. *Decides also* that the increase of 37,400 dollars in the estimated staff assessment income in respect of the financial period ended 30 June 2005 shall be added to the credits from the amount of 1,854,900 dollars referred to in paragraphs 20 and 21 above;

23. *Emphasizes* that no peacekeeping mission shall be financed by borrowing funds from other active peacekeeping missions;

24. *Encourages* the Secretary-General to continue to take additional measures to ensure the safety and security of all personnel under the auspices of the United Nations participating in the Observer Mission, bearing in mind paragraphs 5 and 6 of Security Council resolution 1502(2003) of 26 August 2003;

25. *Invites* voluntary contributions to the Observer Mission in cash and in the form of services and supplies acceptable to the Secretary-General, to be administered, as appropriate, in accordance with the procedure and practices established by the General Assembly;

26. *Decides* to include in the provisional agenda of its sixty-first session the item entitled "Financing of the United Nations Observer Mission in Georgia".

By **decision 61/552** of 22 December, the Assembly decided that the agenda item on the financing of UNOMIG would remain for consideration during its resumed sixty-first (2007) session.

Armenia and Azerbaijan

In 2006, Armenia and Azerbaijan maintained their positions with regard to the Nagorno-Karabakh region of Azerbaijan, which had erupted in conflict in 1992 [YUN 1992, p. 388]. Both sides addressed communications regarding the conflict to the Secretary-General. The Organization for Security and Cooperation in Europe (OSCE) Minsk Group (France, the Russian Federation, the United States) continued to mediate the dispute between Armenia and Azerbaijan.

Communications. On 21 February [A/60/686-S/2006/118], Azerbaijan stated that, on 26 February it would commemorate the fourteenth anniversary of the genocide in the town of Khojaly, which was perpetrated by Armenian armed forces in 1992 [ibid.]. In a 24 February letter [A/60/697-S/2006/128], it transmitted the text of an appeal by displaced persons from Khojaly to the United Nations, OSCE and the Council of Europe, which called for a legal and political assessment of the Khojaly genocide. In response to those letters, Armenia, on 24 February [A/60/701-S/2006/132] and 6 March [A/60/710-S/2006/141], stated that the events that led to the deaths of civilians in Khojaly were the result solely of political intrigues and power struggle in Azerbaijan, and that Armenians suffered massacres of their own between 1988 and 1990 in three of Azerbaijan's largest cities.

On 28 June [A/60/911-S/2006/450], Azerbaijan transmitted to the Secretary-General a statement by its Minister for Foreign Affairs concerning massive fires in the eastern occupied territories of Azerbaijan. Satellite images of the affected areas, which, Azerbaijan said, had been seized and settled by Armenians, were attached to the communication. The Minister stated that the separation of the fires by lanes untouched by them, as well as their massive and targeted character, gave reasonable grounds to suggest that they were man-made and intentional; even if they had occurred naturally, however, Armenia, as the occupying power, bore full responsibility for suppressing the fires. On the same date [A/60/915], Azerbaijan transmitted to the Secretary-General a letter from the Secretary-General of the Organization of the Islamic Conference (OIC) concerning the fires in the occupied territories.

Armenia, on 27 June [A/60/961-S/2006/588], stated that Azerbaijan was attempting to create an emergency situation out of the natural phenomenon of grass fires that occurred yearly in the region. Annexed to the letter was the report of an OSCE monitoring team, which had proven Azerbaijan's assertions to be unfounded. In letters of 28 July [A/60/963] and 10 August [A/60/975-S/2006/642], Azerbaijan stated that satellite images of the area in 2005 and 2006 proved that in 2005 the occupied territories had not been touched by fire. It accused Armenia of applying a scorched earth policy.

On 6 December [A/61/618-S/2006/952], Armenia transmitted a Statement on Nagorno-Karabakh adopted by the Ministerial Council of OSCE the previous day. Among other things, the Council called on both sides, with the assistance of the international community, to cooperate in suppressing the fires in the affected territories and to overcome their detrimental consequences.

On 28 August [A/60/995-S/2006/689], Armenia, referring to the draft resolution [A/60/L.60] on the situation in the occupied territories of Azerbaijan submitted to the General Assembly by Azerbaijan (see below), stated that it was politically motivated and was presented under the pretext of the issues of resettlement and fires.

GENERAL ASSEMBLY ACTION

On 7 September [meeting 98], the General Assembly adopted **resolution 60/285** [draft: A/60/L.60/Rev.2] without vote [agenda item 40].

The situation in the occupied territories of Azerbaijan

The General Assembly,

Seriously concerned by the fires in the affected territories, which have inflicted widespread environmental damage,

1. *Stresses* the necessity to urgently conduct an environmental operation to suppress the fires in the affected territories and to overcome their detrimental consequences;

2. *Welcomes* the readiness of the parties to cooperate to that end, and considers such an operation to be an important confidence-building measure;

3. *Takes note* of the intention of the Organization for Security and Cooperation in Europe to organize a mission to the region to assess the short- and long-term impact of the fires on the environment as a step in preparation for the environmental operation;

4. *Calls upon*, in this regard, the organizations and programmes of the United Nations system, in particular the United Nations Environment Programme, in cooperation with the Organization for Security and Cooperation in Europe, to provide all necessary assistance and expertise, including, inter alia, the assessment of and counteraction to the short- and long-term impact of the environmental degradation of the region, as well as in its rehabilitation;

5. *Requests* the Chairman-in-Office of the Organization for Security and Cooperation in Europe to provide a report on this matter to States members of the General Assembly by 30 April 2007.

By **decision 60/564** of 11 September, the Assembly deferred consideration of the agenda item on the situation in the occupied territories of Azerbaijan and included it in the agenda of its sixty-first (2006) session.

Further communications. On 7 July [A/60/933-S/2006/500], Armenia transmitted to the Secretary-General statements by its Foreign Minister and Foreign Ministry on the two statements by the OSCE Minsk Group Co-Chairs on the question of the Nagorno-Karabakh conflict. The Foreign Ministry said that the OSCE Co-Chairs had, for the first time, affirmed that the people of Nagorno-Karabakh should determine their own future status through a referendum. On 21 July [A/60/952-S/2006/564 &

Corr.1], Azerbaijan forwarded statements by its own Foreign Ministry indicating that no progress had been made at the recent OSCE negotiations (Vienna, 22 June). It was concerned that Armenia would soon begin to refer to its forthcoming elections, especially when neutral parties commented on them as being an obstacle to an active and results-oriented peace process.

On 11 December [A/61/627-S/2006/966], Azerbaijan stated that the holding of a so-called constitutional referendum in the occupied Nagorno-Karabakh region violated both the Constitution of Azerbaijan and relevant norms and principles of international law; it also interfered with the peace process. In another letter [A/61/629-S/2006/968] of the same date, Azerbaijan drew the Secretary-General's attention to the reaction of the international community to the referendum, which had been held on 10 December. It pointed out that OSCE, the Council of Europe and the EU had stated that the referendum would not be recognized and could not have any legal validity. In a further 11 December letter [A/61/628-S/2006/967], Azerbaijan transmitted an address by its Minister for Foreign Affairs to the OSCE Ministerial Council (Brussels, 5 December). The Minister called for the complete withdrawal of Armenian troops from the occupied territories of Azerbaijan and the safe and dignified return of the displaced Azerbaijani population to the Nagorno-Karabakh region. On 13 December [A/61/637-S/2006/983], Azerbaijan transmitted two press releases issued by OIC, which also rejected the outcome of the referendum. In letters dated 12 [A/61/649-S/2006/1005] and 20 December [A/61/660-S/2006/1015], Ukraine, on behalf of GUAM (see p. 486), and Turkey, respectively, followed suit.

Armenia, on 22 December [A/61/678-S/2006/1027], stated that the people of Nagorno-Karabakh had demonstrated their ability to rule themselves, protect their territory and freedom and meet their international commitments, including upholding the ceasefire, and that their constitutional referendum was a necessary and overdue step in establishing a basic legal framework in the region.

On 27 December [A/61/684-S/2006/1032], Azerbaijan transmitted to the Secretary-General an appeal by the Congress of National Minorities of Azerbaijan to the United Nations, OSCE, the Council of Europe and the foreign ministries of the Minsk Group countries regarding the so-called constitutional referendum conducted by the illegal military regime in Nagorno-Karabakh. The Congress called on the international community to condemn the referendum, to refuse to recognize the results and to support efforts to find ways to resolve the conflict in compliance with the principle of the territorial integrity of Azerbaijan.

Also transmitted to the Secretary-General during the year were an 8 June joint declaration [A/61/93] by Azerbaijan and Lithuania on enhancing political, economic and social relations between the two countries and a 6 July letter [A/61/126] from Azerbaijan, Georgia and Turkey announcing the inauguration of a new main pipeline to carry crude oil from Azerbaijan, through Georgia, to the Ceyhan export terminal in Turkey.

The General Assembly, by **decision 61/552** of 22 December, decided that the agenda item on the situation in the occupied territories of Azerbaijan would remain for consideration during its resumed sixty-first (2007) session.

Republic of Moldova

In September 2006, the Republic of Moldova reported that the authorities of its breakaway Transnistrian region had carried out a referendum on self-determination.

Communications. On 18 September [A/61/359], Moldova transmitted to the Secretary-General a statement by its Government rejecting the results of a 17 September referendum conducted by the self-proclaimed separatist regime in its Transnistrian region. On 20 September [A/61/364], it submitted a report by the Committee on European Affairs of the New York City Bar Association, which had conducted a year-long study on the Transnistrian region. The study concluded that the Russian Federation's support of the separatist regime in Transnistria could support a serious claim that Russia was violating international law and illegally interfering in Moldova's internal affairs. Ukraine, on 29 September [A/61/491-S/2006/794], transmitted a statement by the Council of Ministers for Foreign Affairs of the GUAM States (see p. 486), which also rejected the Transnistrian referendum, noting that it was illegal and violated the internationally recognized sovereignty and territorial integrity of Moldova.

On 16 October [A/61/518], Moldova transmitted a Declaration from its Parliament, which expressed concern that the Russian State Duma had adopted a declaration on the so-called referendum in Moldova's Transnistrian region, which recognized the referendum as an act of free expression of citizens' will. The Moldovan Parliament called on the Duma to refrain from supporting separatism that could have unpredictable consequences for the entire European continent.

Establishment of GUAM

Communications. On 24 May [A/60/875-S/2006/364], Azerbaijan, Georgia, the Republic of Moldova and Ukraine transmitted to the Secretary-General the Kyiv Declaration on the establishment of the Organization for Democracy and Economic Development-GUAM, the secretariat of which would be in Kyiv, Ukraine. In the annexed Joint Declaration on the Issue of Conflict Settlement, the Heads of State of the four countries said that the settlement of conflicts in the territories of the GUAM States would be carried out exclusively on the basis of respect for sovereignty, territorial integrity and the inviolability of the internationally recognized borders of those States. They stressed that the territory of a State could not be the subject of acquisition or military occupation and underscored the incompatibility of the use of force, the practice of ethnic cleansing and the seizure of territory with universal and European values, the principles and ideals of peace, democracy, stability and regional cooperation. The GUAM States entrusted the Council of Ministers of Foreign Affairs with the task of implementing the provisions of the Declaration.

On 10 August [A/61/195], the GUAM States requested the inclusion in the agenda of the sixty-first (2006) session of the General Assembly of a supplementary item entitled "Protracted conflicts in the GUAM area and their implications for international peace, security and development".

On 22 September [A/61/379], Moldova, referring to the fact that the issue of protracted conflicts in the GUAM area had been placed on the Assembly's agenda, said that protracted or "frozen" conflicts were turning into forgotten conflicts. That situation had done little to help efforts to find solutions to severe political problems in the region, including the Transnistrian issue.

The General Assembly, by **decision 61/552** of 22 December, decided that the agenda item on protracted conflicts in the GUAM area and their implications for international peace, security and development would remain for consideration during its resumed sixty-fist (2007)session.

Cyprus

During 2006, progress in resolving the Cyprus problem remained elusive, despite renewed calls by both the Greek Cypriot and Turkish Cypriot leaders for a resumption of the Secretary-General's mission of good offices, which had been discontinued following the disappointing results of the April 2004 referenda [YUN 2004, p. 440] on the "Comprehensive Settlement of the Cyprus Problem" [ibid., p. 438]. The Secretary-General and the Security Council were of the view that conditions were not yet ripe for the Secretary-General to resume his mission. The Secretary-General's Special Representative in Cyprus focused his efforts on assisting the two sides in implementing their existing agreements aimed at the resumption of negotiations leading to a comprehensive settlement. During an overview mission to Cyprus in July by the UN Under-Secretary-General for Political Affairs, the leaders of both sides signed a set of principles and a decision, which included a commitment to the unification of Cyprus based on a bizonal, bicommunal federation and political equality, and agreed to meet regularly on issues affecting the day-to-day life of the Cypriot people. Several months into the working process, however, differences arose between the two sides regarding the implementation of the agreement.

The United Nations Peacekeeping Force in Cyprus (UNFICYP) continued to cooperate with its UN partners and local actors to facilitate projects for the benefit of both Greek and Turkish Cypriots in and outside the buffer zone and to promote confidence-building measures between them. The Security Council extended the UNFICYP mandate twice during the year, the second time until June 2007.

Incidents and position statements

Communications. Throughout 2006, the Secretary-General received letters from the Government of Cyprus and from Turkish Cypriot authorities containing charges and counter-charges, protests and accusations, and explanations of positions regarding the question of Cyprus. Letters from the "Turkish Republic of Northern Cyprus" were transmitted by Turkey.

In communications dated between 10 January and 12 December, Cyprus reported violations of its national airspace and unauthorized intrusion into the Nicosia flight information region by Turkish military jets and civilian aircraft. [A/60/648-S/2006/16, A/60/729-S/2006/177, A/60/894-S/2006/416, A/60/991-S/2006/691, A/61/542-S/2006/847, A/61/634-S/2006/979]. The "Turkish Republic of Northern Cyprus" refuted those allegations, claiming the existence of two independent States on the island of Cyprus and stating that the flights mentioned took place within the sovereign airspace of the "Turkish Republic of Northern Cyprus" [A/60/656-S/2006/47, A/60/740-S/2006/198, A/60/908-S/2006/439, A/61/336-S/2006/731, A/61/560-S/2006/864, A/61/676-S/2006/1025].

On 24 January [A/60/657-S/2006/48], Turkey informed the Secretary-General that it had prepared a detailed action plan for a transitional process until a comprehensive settlement to the Cyprus problem could be found. The "Turkish Republic of Northern Cyprus", on 2 February [A/60/663-S/2006/72], expressed its full support for Turkey's action plan. By a 31 January letter [A/60/671-S/2006/82], Cyprus expressed its dissatisfaction with the Turkish proposals, stating that they did not contribute to creating the appropriate conditions for resuming negotiations and that their effect would be to widen the gap between the respective positions of the Cypriot and Turkish Governments. In further communications [A/60/841-S/2006/286, A/60/943-S/2006/533, A/61/559-S/2006/863], the "Turkish Republic of Northern Cyprus" reiterated its support for the 2004 "Comprehensive Settlement of the Cyprus Problem" document [YUN 2004, p. 438] and proposed confidence-building measures.

On 15 May [A/60/850-S/2006/300], Cyprus, referring to a communication from the "Turkish Republic of Northern Cyprus" [A/60/841-S/2006/286], clarified that Cyprus remained committed to a fair and sustainable resolution of the Cyprus problem.

On 10 October [A/61/511-S/2006/800], the "Turkish Republic of Northern Cyprus" took issue with some of the remarks made by the President of Cyprus, Tassos Papadopoulus, during his statement to the General Assembly on 19 September [A/61/PV.11].

On 14 November [A/61/579-S/2006/896], Cyprus cited an article in the Turkish Cypriot newspaper *Kibris,* which reported that Turkey was going to finance a project to restore and reorganize the Apostolos Andreas Monastery, including the transformation of the Monastery's annexes into a 120-room hotel. Cyprus strongly protested the project, which would destroy the character of a highly important religious and cultural landmark of Cyprus and would constitute a violation of international humanitarian law and the law of armed conflict with regard to an occupying power's obligations in the field of property rights. In response [A/61/677-S/2006/1026], the "Turkish Republic of Northern Cyprus" refuted those allegations, stating that it had no intention to convert the annexes into a hotel nor to plan any construction on those premises affecting their historical and religious status.

On 29 November [A/61/602-S/2006/929], the "Turkish Republic of Northern Cyprus" complained of maltreatment of Turkish Cypriots visiting the southern part of the island by Greek Cypriot authorities and civilians.

On 28 December [A/61/686-S/2006/1037], the "Turkish Republic of Northern Cyprus" reported that the Cypriot administration was speeding up rearmament efforts.

Good offices mission

During 2006, both the Greek Cypriot and Turkish Cypriot leaders renewed their calls for a resumption of the Secretary-General's mission of good offices. However, the Secretary-General and the Security Council were of the view that the time was not ripe to renew the mission, which had been discontinued following the April 2004 referenda [YUN 2004, p. 440] on the "Comprehensive Settlement of the Cyprus Problem" [ibid., p. 438]. Nevertheless, the Secretary-General met with both leaders during the year and his Special Representative in Cyprus continued to engage with representatives of both sides.

In July, the UN Under-Secretary-General for Political Affairs, Ibrahim Gambari, undertook an overview mission to the region. During a meeting with him, the Greek Cypriot and Turkish Cypriot leaders signed a Set of Principles and a Decision [S/2006/572], in which they agreed, as a contribution to a comprehensive settlement, to begin immediately a two-track process involving discussions by technical committees of issues affecting the day-to-day life of the Cypriot people and, concurrently, consideration by working groups of substantive issues.

Following the emergence of differences between the two sides regarding implementation of the agreement, the Under-Secretary-General, in November, wrote to the two leaders suggesting a way forward. Both sides formally accepted his suggestions on 18 November.

UNFICYP

In 2006, the United Nations Peacekeeping Force in Cyprus (UNFICYP), established in 1964 [YUN 1964, p. 165], continued to monitor the ceasefire lines between the Turkish and Turkish Cypriot forces on the northern side and the Cypriot National Guard on the southern side of the island; to maintain the military status quo and prevent a recurrence of fighting; and to undertake humanitarian and economic activities.

On 1 January, Michael Møller (Denmark) replaced Zbigniew Wlosowicz (Poland) as the

Secretary-General's Special Representative in Cyprus and Chief of Mission. On 6 February [S/2006/91], the Secretary-General informed the Security Council of his intention to appoint Major General Rafael José Barni (Argentina) as Force Commander of UNFICYP, replacing Major General Herbert Figoli (Uruguay). The Council took note of his intention on 9 February [S/2006/92]. Major General Barni began his tour of duty on 6 March.

As at 15 November, UNFICYP comprised 853 troops and 60 civilian police.

Activities

Report of Secretary-General (May). In a 23 May report on UNFICYP [S/2006/315], covering activities from 25 November 2005 to 17 May 2006, the Secretary-General stated that the military and security situation along the ceasefire lines in Cyprus remained generally stable. Although incidents increased during the reporting period, they were minor in nature and included overmanning, enhancements to military positions, stone-throwing, weapon-pointing, and incursions into the buffer zone. Disputes over the demarcation of ceasefire lines and the authority of UNFICYP in the buffer zone increased and a confrontation over the opening of a new crossing point at Ledra Street in old Nicosia heightened tensions in the early weeks of the reporting period. Two violations of the status quo, related to the improvement of one of the Cypriot National Guard's observation posts and the subsequent erection of a new observation post by the Turkish Forces in the same vicinity, had raised tensions in and along the buffer zone. Turkish Forces also continued to man a checkpoint at the Louroujina pocket, despite repeated protests by UNFICYP.

UNFICYP continued to cooperate with its UN partners and both sides to facilitate projects of common benefit for both Greek and Turkish Cypriots in the buffer zone and promote confidence-building measures between them. A bicommunal road construction project in the buffer zone, funded by the EU and implemented by the United Nations Development Programme (UNDP) and the United Nations Office for Project Services, was completed. The Mission continued to work with both sides on enhancing the effectiveness of law enforcement and maintaining law and order in and around the buffer zone; it conducted 64 humanitarian convoys, money deliveries and humanitarian visits in support of the 385 Greek Cypriots and 132 Maronites living in the north. It continued to assist Turkish Cypriots living in the south to obtain identity documents, housing, welfare services, medical care, employment and education. It coordinated with UNDP on two projects: Action for Cooperation and Trust; and Partnership for the Future. The former project contributed to joint activities between the north and south to promote HIV/AIDS awareness and the latter, which focused on the rehabilitation of old Nicosia, provided support to small businesses on both sides of the island. The UNFICYP Mine Action Centre continued to demine the Nicosia area and consultations began in February on extending its activities to the rest of the buffer zone.

UNFICYP observed an emerging trend of increased unauthorized construction of buildings for personal and commercial use and utilization of land outside the areas designated for civilian use in the buffer zone. It initiated discussions with the relevant authorities to establish practical procedures to ensure that civilian use of the buffer zone did not compromise the security situation or hamper UNFICYP ability to carry out its mandate.

During the reporting period, UNFICYP facilitated 43 bicommunal events with the participation of 1,340 people. Regular monthly meetings between the Greek Cypriot and Turkish Cypriot leaders continued under the auspices of the Embassy of Slovakia.

The Secretary-General recommended that the Council extend the UNFICYP mandate until 15 December 2006.

Communication. On 14 June [A/60/892-S/2006/410], the "Turkish Republic of Northern Cyprus" submitted comments on the Secretary-General's report.

SECURITY COUNCIL ACTION

On 15 June [meeting 5465], the Security Council unanimously adopted **resolution 1687(2006)**. The draft [S/2006/393] was submitted by China, France, the Russian Federation, the United Kingdom and the United States.

The Security Council,

Welcoming the report of the Secretary-General of 23 May 2006 on the United Nations operation in Cyprus,

Reiterating its call to the parties to assess and address the humanitarian issue of missing persons with due urgency and seriousness, and welcoming in this regard the resumption of the activities of the Committee on Missing Persons in Cyprus since August 2004, as well as the appointment by the Secretary-General of a third member, who will assume his duties in July 2006,

Noting that the Government of Cyprus has agreed that, in view of the prevailing conditions on the island, it is necessary to keep the United Nations Peacekeeping Force in Cyprus beyond 15 June 2006,

Taking note of the assessment of the Secretary-General that the security situation on the island continues to be stable and that the situation along the Green Line remains calm, and expressing the hope that there will be a decrease in the overall number of incidents involving the two sides,

Urging both sides to avoid any action which could lead to an increase in tension, and, in this context, noting with concern sequential developments in the vicinity of Dherinia, the increase in unauthorized construction of buildings for personal and commercial use in the buffer zone, and developments at certain checkpoints in sector 4, including new restrictions on the freedom of movement of the Force, and encouraging both sides to engage in consultations with the Force on the demarcation of the buffer zone and to respect the mandate and operations of the Force in the buffer zone,

Regretting that the gap between words and deeds remains too great for the Secretary-General to resume fully his mission of good offices and urging progress towards the resumption of negotiations for a comprehensive settlement, and, in this context, welcoming the efforts of the Secretary-General to encourage renewed bicommunal contacts, and the agreement to a proposal to establish a mechanism for bicommunal discussions at the technical level, as well as the agreement of both leaders to meet on the occasion of the installation of the third member of the Committee on Missing Persons in Cyprus,

Welcoming progress in demining, particularly in the Nicosia area, and expressing strong support for the efforts of the Force to extend demining operations to Turkish Forces minefields in the rest of the buffer zone,

Welcoming also the fact that over 10 million crossings by Greek Cypriots to the north and Turkish Cypriots to the south have taken place peacefully, and encouraging the opening of additional crossing points,

Expressing its concern at continued disagreement over construction activity relating to the proposed additional crossing point at Ledra Street, and urging both sides to cooperate with the Force to resolve this issue,

Welcoming the emphasis of the Special Representative of the Secretary-General for Cyprus on greater cohesiveness in the efforts of the United Nations family in Cyprus, as well as the intention of the Secretary-General to keep the operations of the Force under close review while continuing to take into account developments on the ground and the views of the parties, and to revert to the Security Council with recommendations, as appropriate, for further adjustments to the mandate, force levels and concept of operation of the Force as soon as warranted,

Welcoming also all efforts to promote bicommunal contacts and events, including, inter alia, on the part of the United Nations, and urging the two sides to promote further bicommunal contacts and to remove any obstacles to such contacts,

Echoing the Secretary-General's gratitude to the Government of Cyprus and the Government of Greece for their voluntary contributions to the funding of the Force, and his request for further voluntary contributions from other countries and organizations,

Welcoming and encouraging efforts by the United Nations to sensitize peacekeeping personnel in the prevention and control of HIV/AIDS and other communicable diseases in all its peacekeeping operations,

1. *Reaffirms* all its relevant resolutions on Cyprus, in particular resolution 1251(1999) of 29 June 1999 and subsequent resolutions;

2. *Expresses its full support* for the United Nations Peacekeeping Force in Cyprus, including its mandate in the buffer zone, and decides to extend its mandate for a further period ending 15 December 2006;

3. *Calls upon* the Turkish Cypriot side and Turkish forces to restore in Strovilia the military status quo which existed there prior to 30 June 2000;

4. *Encourages* active participation in bicommunal discussions at the technical level, under the leadership of the Special Representative of the Secretary-General for Cyprus, and expresses its full support for the Special Representative;

5. *Requests* the Secretary-General to submit a report on the implementation of the present resolution by 1 December 2006;

6. *Welcomes* the efforts being undertaken by the Force to implement the Secretary-General's zero-tolerance policy on sexual exploitation and abuse and to ensure full compliance of its personnel with the United Nations code of conduct, requests the Secretary-General to continue to take all necessary action in this regard and to keep the Security Council informed, and urges troop-contributing countries to take appropriate preventive action, including conducting predeployment awareness training, and to take disciplinary action and other action to ensure full accountability in cases of such conduct involving their personnel;

7. *Decides* to remain seized of the matter.

Report of Secretary-General (December). On 1 December [S/2006/931], the Secretary-General reported to the Security Council on UNFICYP activities between 18 May and 27 November. He stated that, despite an overall reduction in the number of incidents along the ceasefire lines, the Mission's mandate continued to be challenged by both opposing forces. Significant violations by the Cypriot National Guard included overmanning of an observation post and conducting a military exercise at platoon strength with mortars behind one of their observation posts. Violations by Turkish Forces/Turkish Cypriot Security Forces included the continued manning of an unauthorized checkpoint, the patrolling of the vicinity of the Laroujina pocket and overmanning of a nearby observation post. Attempts to restore the status quo in the area had not progressed. In response, UNFICYP employed standing patrols and, on occasion, reoccupied some of its static observation towers. In June, UNFICYP invited the Cypriot National Guard and the Turkish Forces/Turkish Cypriot Security Forces to submit proposals for unmanning/deconfrontation measures. The opposing forces expressed support for the

Mission's suggestions and agreed to submit a list of deconfrontation measures, but no proposals had yet been received.

UNFICYP continued to work with its UN partners and local actors to facilitate projects of common benefit for Greek and Turkish Cypriots in and outside the buffer zone and to promote confidence-building measures between them, with the goal of restoring normal conditions and humanitarian functions in Cyprus. The Mission facilitated 10 bicommunal events in the buffer zone with the participation of approximately 500 people from both sides. It conducted 62 humanitarian convoys and humanitarian visits in support of Greek Cypriots and Maronites living in the north and continued to assist Turkish Cypriots living in the south. The UNFICYP Mine Action Centre also continued its demining of the region, clearing 12 of the 13 Turkish Forces minefields during the reporting period. It was expected that the last would be cleared before the end of the year.

During the reporting period, there was an increase in farming activities, mainly in the area around Nicosia, by farmers wishing to cultivate land beyond the farming security line established by UNFICYP to prevent tension arising from such activities in the buffer zone, as had happened on several occasions in the past. UNFICYP tightened its procedures for issuing farming permits in order to safeguard property rights and maintain security in the area.

The Mission continued to facilitate the exchange of information on criminal matters between the two communities; liaise with both sides on the preservation and restoration of cultural and religious sites on the island; and coordinate gender-related activities. Significant progress was achieved during the reporting period on the issue of missing persons. At the onset of the crisis in Lebanon (see p. 574), UNFICYP assisted in moving UN personnel and their dependents from Lebanon and supported UN humanitarian and other activities in the region.

The Secretary-General noted with concern the hampering of UNDP activities intended to reduce the socio-economic disparities between the two Cypriot communities. He recommended that the Council extend the UNFICYP mandate until 15 June 2007.

SECURITY COUNCIL ACTION

On 15 December [meeting 5593], the Security Council unanimously adopted **resolution 1728(2006)**. The draft [S/2006/978] was submitted by China, France, the Russian Federation, the United Kingdom and the United States.

The Security Council,

Welcoming the report of the Secretary-General of 1 December 2006 on the United Nations operation in Cyprus,

Noting that the Government of Cyprus has agreed that, in view of the prevailing conditions on the island, it is necessary to keep the United Nations Peacekeeping Force in Cyprus beyond 15 December 2006,

Taking note of the assessment of the Secretary-General that the security situation on the island continues to be generally stable and that the situation along the Green Line remains calm, and welcoming the decrease in the overall number of incidents involving the two sides,

Urging both sides to avoid any action which could lead to an increase in tension, such as military exercises, and, in this context, noting with concern that disagreements have arisen over civilian activities in the buffer zone, including farming and construction, and encouraging both sides to engage in consultations with the Force on the demarcation of the buffer zone, respecting the mandate of the Force, and to reach an agreed approach to the operations of the Force in the buffer zone on the basis of the United Nations 1989 aide-memoire,

Expressing its strong appreciation for the work of the Under-Secretary-General for Political Affairs, Mr. Ibrahim Gambari, in achieving the agreement of 8 July 2006, and welcoming the principles and decisions enshrined therein, including recognition that the status quo is unacceptable and that a comprehensive settlement based on a bicommunal, bizonal federation and political equality, as set out in the relevant Security Council resolutions, is both desirable and possible and should not be further delayed, but noting, with regret, the assessment by the Secretary-General that continued lack of trust between the parties has so far prevented the implementation of any of those decisions, underlining the need to implement the agreement of 8 July without further delay, and expressing the hope that the recent positive reaction of the leaders of both communities to suggestions by the United Nations will result in the finalization of the preparatory phase as soon as possible in order to prepare the ground for fully-fledged negotiations leading to a comprehensive and durable settlement,

Welcoming continued progress in demining, expressing strong support for the efforts of the Force to extend demining operations to Turkish Forces minefields in the rest of the buffer zone, and welcoming the prospect that it could be declared free of mines within two years,

Reiterating its call to the parties to assess and address the humanitarian issue of missing persons with due urgency and seriousness, and welcoming in this regard the resumption of the activities of the Committee on Missing Persons in Cyprus since August 2004, and the progress which has since been made, as well as the appointment by the Secretary-General of a third member,

Welcoming the continuing crossings by Greek Cypriots to the north and Turkish Cypriots to the south which have taken place peacefully, and encouraging early progress on other confidence-building measures, such as the opening of additional crossing points, including at Ledra Street,

Welcoming also all efforts to promote bicommunal contacts and events, including on the part of the United Nations, and urging the two sides to promote further bicommunal contacts and to remove any obstacles to such contacts,

Expressing concern, in this respect, that opportunities for constructive public debate about the future of the island, within and between the communities, are becoming fewer, and that this atmosphere is hampering, in particular, efforts to foster bicommunal activities intended to benefit Greek Cypriots and Turkish Cypriots, and to promote reconciliation and build trust in order to facilitate a comprehensive settlement,

Noting the primary role of the United Nations in assisting the parties to bring the Cyprus conflict and division of the island to a comprehensive and durable settlement,

Reaffirming the importance of the Secretary-General continuing to keep the operations of the Force under close review while continuing to take into account developments on the ground and the views of the parties, and reverting to the Council with recommendations, as appropriate, for further adjustments to the mandate, force levels and concept of operation of the Force as soon as warranted,

Echoing the Secretary-General's gratitude to the Government of Cyprus and the Government of Greece for their voluntary contributions to the funding of the Force, and his request for further voluntary contributions from other countries and organizations,

Welcoming and encouraging efforts by the United Nations to sensitize peacekeeping personnel in the prevention and control of HIV/AIDS and other communicable diseases in all its peacekeeping operations,

1. *Welcomes* the observations contained in the report of the Secretary-General on progress since June 2006, and in particular on developments since 8 July, and expresses its appreciation for his personal efforts over the last ten years, and those of his staff, aimed at achieving a comprehensive solution;

2. *Reaffirms* all its relevant resolutions on Cyprus, in particular resolution 1251(1999) of 29 June 1999 and subsequent resolutions;

3. *Expresses its full support* for the United Nations Peacekeeping Force in Cyprus, including its mandate in the buffer zone, and decides to extend its mandate for a further period ending 15 June 2007;

4. *Calls upon* the Turkish Cypriot side and Turkish forces to restore in Strovilia the military status quo which existed there prior to 30 June 2000;

5. *Expresses its full support* for the process agreed by the leaders, encourages active participation in bicommunal discussions as described in Under-Secretary-General Gambari's letter of 15 November 2006, under the auspices of the Special Representative of the Secretary-General for Cyprus, and calls for the early completion of the preparatory phase so that a fully-fledged good offices process may resume as soon as possible;

6. *Requests* the Secretary-General to submit a report on the implementation of the present resolution by 1 June 2007;

7. *Welcomes* the efforts being undertaken by the Force to implement the Secretary-General's zero-tolerance policy on sexual exploitation and abuse and to ensure full compliance of its personnel with the United Nations code of conduct, requests the Secretary-General to continue to take all necessary action in this regard and to keep the Security Council informed, and urges troop-contributing countries to take appropriate preventive action, including conducting predeployment awareness training, and to take disciplinary action and other action to ensure full accountability in cases of such conduct involving their personnel;

8. *Decides* to remain seized of the matter.

On 22 December, the Assembly decided that the agenda item on the question of Cyprus would remain for consideration during its resumed sixty-first (2007) session (**decision 61/552**).

Financing

On 30 June [meeting 92], the General Assembly, having considered the financial performance report on the UNFICYP budget for 1 July 2004 to 30 June 2005 [A/60/584], the UNFICYP budget for 1 July 2006 to 30 June 2007 [A/60/592] and ACABQ related comments and recommendations [A/60/785], adopted, on the recommendation of the Fifth Committee [A/60/918], **resolution 60/270** without vote [agenda item 139].

Financing of the United Nations Peacekeeping Force in Cyprus

The General Assembly,

Having considered the reports of the Secretary-General on the financing of the United Nations Peacekeeping Force in Cyprus and the related report of the Advisory Committee on Administrative and Budgetary Questions,

Recalling Security Council resolution 186(1964) of 4 March 1964, regarding the establishment of the United Nations Peacekeeping Force in Cyprus, and the subsequent resolutions by which the Council extended the mandate of the Force, the latest of which was resolution 1642(2005) of 14 December 2005,

Recalling also its resolution 47/236 of 14 September 1993 on the financing of the Force for the period beginning 16 June 1993, and its subsequent resolutions and decisions thereon, the latest of which was resolution 59/284 B of 22 June 2005,

Reaffirming the general principles underlying the financing of United Nations peacekeeping operations, as stated in General Assembly resolutions 1874 (S-IV) of 27 June 1963, 3101(XXVIII) of 11 December 1973 and 55/235 of 23 December 2000,

Noting with appreciation that voluntary contributions have been made to the Force by certain Governments,

Noting that voluntary contributions were insufficient to cover all the costs of the Force, including those incurred by troop-contributing Governments prior to 16 June 1993, and regretting the absence of an adequate response to appeals for voluntary contributions, including that contained in the letter dated 17 May 1994 from the Secretary-General to all Member States,

Mindful of the fact that it is essential to provide the Force with the necessary financial resources to enable it to fulfil its responsibilities under the relevant resolutions of the Security Council,

1. *Requests* the Secretary-General to entrust the Head of Mission with the task of formulating future budget proposals in full accordance with the provisions of General Assembly resolutions 59/296 of 22 June 2005 and 60/266 of 30 June 2006, as well as other relevant resolutions;

2. *Takes note* of the status of contributions to the United Nations Peacekeeping Force in Cyprus as at 30 April 2006, including the contributions outstanding in the amount of 16.9 million United States dollars, representing some 6 per cent of the total assessed contributions, notes with concern that only forty-eight Member States have paid their assessed contributions in full, and urges all other Member States, in particular those in arrears, to ensure payment of their outstanding assessed contributions;

3. *Expresses its appreciation* to those Member States that have paid their assessed contributions in full, and urges all other Member States to make every possible effort to ensure payment of their assessed contributions to the Force in full;

4. *Expresses concern* at the financial situation with regard to peacekeeping activities, in particular as regards the reimbursements to troop contributors that bear additional burdens owing to overdue payments by Member States of their assessments;

5. *Also expresses concern* at the delay experienced by the Secretary-General in deploying and providing adequate resources to some recent peacekeeping missions, in particular those in Africa;

6. *Emphasizes* that all future and existing peacekeeping missions shall be given equal and non-discriminatory treatment in respect of financial and administrative arrangements;

7. *Also emphasizes* that all peacekeeping missions shall be provided with adequate resources for the effective and efficient discharge of their respective mandates;

8. *Reiterates its request* to the Secretary-General to make the fullest possible use of facilities and equipment at the United Nations Logistics Base at Brindisi, Italy, in order to minimize the costs of procurement for the Force;

9. *Endorses* the conclusions and recommendations contained in the report of the Advisory Committee on Administrative and Budgetary Questions, subject to the provisions of the present resolution, and requests the Secretary-General to ensure their full implementation;

10. *Recalls* its request as contained in section XIV, paragraph 4, of resolution 59/296;

11. *Decides* to finance resources for conduct and discipline capacity equivalent to 253,900 dollars under general temporary assistance;

12. *Requests* the Secretary-General to ensure the full implementation of the relevant provisions of its resolutions 59/296 and 60/266;

13. *Also requests* the Secretary-General to take all necessary action to ensure that the Force is administered with a maximum of efficiency and economy;

14. *Further requests* the Secretary-General, in order to reduce the cost of employing General Service staff, to continue efforts to recruit local staff for the Force against General Service posts, commensurate with the requirements of the Force;

15. *Requests* the Secretary-General, in view of the recent amendment of the concept of operations and force level of the Force, to conduct a review of the number and grade levels of support staff, including the possibility of utilizing United Nations Volunteers, and to report thereon to the General Assembly in the context of the next budget submission for the Force;

Financial performance report for the period from 1 July 2004 to 30 June 2005

16. *Takes note* of the report of the Secretary-General on the financial performance of the Force for the period from 1 July 2004 to 30 June 2005;

Budget estimates for the period from 1 July 2006 to 30 June 2007

17. *Decides* to appropriate to the Special Account for the United Nations Peacekeeping Force in Cyprus the amount of 46,770,000 dollars for the period from 1 July 2006 to 30 June 2007, inclusive of 44,831,400 dollars for the maintenance of the Force, 1,601,200 dollars for the support account for peacekeeping operations and 337,400 dollars for the United Nations Logistics Base;

Financing of the appropriation for the period from 1 July 2006 to 30 June 2007

18. *Notes with appreciation* that a one-third share of the net appropriation, equivalent to 14,915,300 dollars, will be funded through voluntary contributions from the Government of Cyprus and the amount of 6.5 million dollars from the Government of Greece;

19. *Decides* to apportion among Member States the amount of 25,354,700 dollars at a monthly rate of 2,112,891 dollars, in accordance with the levels updated in its resolution 58/256 of 23 December 2003, and taking into account the scale of assessments for 2006, as set out in its resolution 58/1 B of 23 December 2003, and the scale of assessments for 2007, subject to a decision of the Security Council to extend the mandate of the Force;

20. *Decides also* that, in accordance with the provisions of its resolution 973(X) of 15 December 1955, there shall be set off against the apportionment among Member States, as provided for in paragraph 19 above, their respective share in the Tax Equalization Fund of 2,024,100 dollars, comprising the estimated staff assess-

ment income of 1,818,500 dollars approved for the Force, the prorated share of 180,100 dollars of the estimated staff assessment income approved for the support account and the prorated share of 25,500 dollars of the estimated staff assessment income approved for the United Nations Logistics Base;

21. *Decides further* that, for Member States that have fulfilled their financial obligations to the Force, there shall be set off against their apportionment, as provided for in paragraph 19 above, their respective share of the unencumbered balance and other income in the total amount of 870,911 dollars for the financial period ended 30 June 2005, in accordance with the levels updated in its resolution 58/256, and taking into account the scale of assessments for 2005, as set out in its resolution 58/1 B;

22. *Decides* that, for Member States that have not fulfilled their financial obligations to the Force, there shall be set off against their outstanding obligations their respective share of the unencumbered balance and other income in the total amount of 870,911 dollars in respect of the financial period ended 30 June 2005, in accordance with the scheme set out in paragraph 21 above;

23. *Decides also* that the decrease in the estimated staff assessment income of 339,100 dollars in respect of the financial period ended 30 June 2005 shall be set off against the credits from the amount of 870,911 dollars referred to in paragraphs 21 and 22 above;

24. *Decides further*, taking into account its voluntary contribution for the financial period ended 30 June 2005, that one third of the net unencumbered balance and other income in the amount of 331,400 dollars in respect of the financial period ended 30 June 2005 shall be returned to the Government of Cyprus;

25. *Decides*, taking into account its voluntary contribution for the financial period ended 30 June 2005, that the prorated share of the net unencumbered balance and other income in the amount of 130,989 dollars in respect of the financial period ended 30 June 2005 shall be returned to the Government of Greece;

26. *Decides also* to continue to maintain as separate the account established for the Force for the period prior to 16 June 1993, invites Member States to make voluntary contributions to that account, and requests the Secretary-General to continue his efforts in appealing for voluntary contributions to the account;

27. *Emphasizes* that no peacekeeping mission shall be financed by borrowing funds from other active peacekeeping missions;

28. *Encourages* the Secretary-General to continue to take additional measures to ensure the safety and security of all personnel under the auspices of the United Nations participating in the Force, bearing in mind paragraphs 5 and 6 of Security Council resolution 1502(2003) of 26 August 2003;

29. *Invites* voluntary contributions to the Force in cash and in the form of services and supplies acceptable to the Secretary-General, to be administered, as appropriate, in accordance with the procedure and practices established by the General Assembly;

30. *Decides* to include in the provisional agenda of its sixty-first session the item entitled "Financing of the United Nations Peacekeeping Force in Cyprus".

On 22 December [meeting 84], the Assembly decided that the agenda item on the financing of UNFICYP would remain for consideration during its resumed sixty-first (2007) session (**decision 61/552**).

Other issues

Strengthening of security and cooperation in the Mediterranean

In response to General Assembly resolution 60/94 [YUN 2005, p. 500], the Secretary-General submitted a July report and a December addendum [A/61/123 & Add.1] containing replies received from Algeria, Bolivia, Morocco, Spain and the United Arab Emirates to his 28 February note verbale requesting the views of all Member States on ways to strengthen security and cooperation in the Mediterranean region.

GENERAL ASSEMBLY ACTION

On 6 December [meeting 67], the General Assembly, on the recommendation of the First (Disarmament and International Security) Committee [A/61/399], adopted **resolution 61/101** without vote [agenda item 95].

Strengthening of security and cooperation in the Mediterranean region

The General Assembly,

Recalling its previous resolutions on the subject, including resolution 60/94 of 8 December 2005,

Reaffirming the primary role of the Mediterranean countries in strengthening and promoting peace, security and cooperation in the Mediterranean region,

Welcoming the efforts deployed by the Euro-Mediterranean countries to strengthen their cooperation in combating terrorism, in particular by the adoption of the Euro-Mediterranean Code of Conduct on Countering Terrorism by the Euro-Mediterranean Summit, held in Barcelona, Spain, on 27 and 28 November 2005,

Bearing in mind all the previous declarations and commitments, as well as all the initiatives taken by the riparian countries at the recent summits, ministerial meetings and various forums concerning the question of the Mediterranean region,

Recognizing the indivisible character of security in the Mediterranean and that the enhancement of cooperation among Mediterranean countries with a view to promoting the economic and social development of all peoples of the region will contribute significantly to stability, peace and security in the region,

Recognizing also the efforts made so far and the determination of the Mediterranean countries to intensify the process of dialogue and consultations with a view to resolving the problems existing in the Mediterranean region and to eliminating the causes of tension and the consequent threat to peace and security, and their growing awareness of the need for further joint efforts to strengthen economic, social, cultural and environmental cooperation in the region,

Recognizing further that prospects for closer Euro-Mediterranean cooperation in all spheres can be enhanced by positive developments worldwide, in particular in Europe, in the Maghreb and in the Middle East,

Reaffirming the responsibility of all States to contribute to the stability and prosperity of the Mediterranean region and their commitment to respecting the purposes and principles of the Charter of the United Nations as well as the provisions of the Declaration on Principles of International Law concerning Friendly Relations and Cooperation among States in accordance with the Charter of the United Nations,

Noting the peace negotiations in the Middle East, which should be of a comprehensive nature and represent an appropriate framework for the peaceful settlement of contentious issues in the region,

Expressing its concern at the persistent tension and continuing military activities in parts of the Mediterranean that hinder efforts to strengthen security and cooperation in the region,

Taking note of the report of the Secretary-General,

1. *Reaffirms* that security in the Mediterranean is closely linked to European security as well as to international peace and security;

2. *Expresses its satisfaction* at the continuing efforts by Mediterranean countries to contribute actively to the elimination of all causes of tension in the region and to the promotion of just and lasting solutions to the persistent problems of the region through peaceful means, thus ensuring the withdrawal of foreign forces of occupation and respecting the sovereignty, independence and territorial integrity of all countries of the Mediterranean and the right of peoples to self-determination, and therefore calls for full adherence to the principles of non-interference, non-intervention, non-use of force or threat of use of force and the inadmissibility of the acquisition of territory by force, in accordance with the Charter and the relevant resolutions of the United Nations;

3. *Commends* the Mediterranean countries for their efforts in meeting common challenges through coordinated overall responses, based on a spirit of multilateral partnership, towards the general objective of turning the Mediterranean basin into an area of dialogue, exchanges and cooperation, guaranteeing peace, stability and prosperity, encourages them to strengthen such efforts through, inter alia, a lasting multilateral and action-oriented cooperative dialogue among States of the region, and recognizes the role of the United Nations in promoting regional and international peace and security;

4. *Recognizes* that the elimination of the economic and social disparities in levels of development and other obstacles as well as respect and greater understanding among cultures in the Mediterranean area will contribute to enhancing peace, security and cooperation among Mediterranean countries through the existing forums;

5. *Calls upon* all States of the Mediterranean region that have not yet done so to adhere to all the multilaterally negotiated legal instruments related to the field of disarmament and non-proliferation, thus creating the necessary conditions for strengthening peace and cooperation in the region;

6. *Encourages* all States of the region to favour the necessary conditions for strengthening the confidence-building measures among them by promoting genuine openness and transparency on all military matters, by participating, inter alia, in the United Nations system for the standardized reporting of military expenditures and by providing accurate data and information to the United Nations Register of Conventional Arms;

7. *Encourages* the Mediterranean countries to strengthen further their cooperation in combating terrorism in all its forms and manifestations, including the possible resort by terrorists to weapons of mass destruction, taking into account the relevant resolutions of the United Nations, and in combating international crime and illicit arms transfers and illicit drug production, consumption and trafficking, which pose a serious threat to peace, security and stability in the region and therefore to the improvement of the current political, economic and social situation and which jeopardize friendly relations among States, hinder the development of international cooperation and result in the destruction of human rights, fundamental freedoms and the democratic basis of pluralistic society;

8. *Requests* the Secretary-General to submit a report on means to strengthen security and cooperation in the Mediterranean region;

9. *Decides* to include in the provisional agenda of its sixty-second session the item entitled "Strengthening of security and cooperation in the Mediterranean region".

Stability and development in South-Eastern Europe

On 24 July [A/61/183], Croatia and Serbia drew the Secretary-General's attention to the joint statement made by their Presidents on the occasion of the official visit of Serbia's President, Boris Tadić, to Croatia. On 26 July [A/61/190], Croatia and Montenegro forwarded to the Secretary-General the joint statement made by their Presidents on the occasion of the official visit of Montenegro's President, Filip Vujanović, to Croatia. In both statements, the Presidents announced their commitment to peace, stability and security in South-Eastern Europe.

GENERAL ASSEMBLY ACTION

On 6 December [meeting 67], the General Assembly, on the recommendation of the First Committee [A/61/387], adopted **resolution 61/53** without vote [agenda item 83].

Maintenance of international security—good-neighbourliness, stability and development in South-Eastern Europe

The General Assembly,

Recalling the purposes and principles of the Charter of the United Nations and the Final Act of the Conference on Security and Cooperation in Europe, signed in Helsinki on 1 August 1975,

Recalling also the United Nations Millennium Declaration and the 2005 World Summit Outcome,

Recalling further its previous resolutions on the subject, including resolution 59/59 of 3 December 2004,

Welcoming with appreciation the continuing cooperation among countries in the region of South-Eastern Europe on issues related to security, economy, trade, transport, energy, cross-border cooperation, human rights and justice and home affairs,

Welcoming the Republic of Montenegro as the one hundred and ninety-second State Member of the United Nations,

Reiterating the importance of the South-East European Cooperation Process for further enhancing regional cooperation and stability, which constitutes one of the main elements of the Stabilization and Association Process, and welcoming the positive results of the South-East European Cooperation Process summit meeting, held in Thessaloniki, Greece, on 4 May 2006,

Recalling the conclusions reached at the Summit of the European Council, held in Thessaloniki, Greece, on 19 and 20 June 2003, the decisions of the European Council on the principles, priorities and conditions contained in the European Partnerships with all countries of the Stabilization and Association Process and the outcome of the meeting held in Salzburg, Austria, of Ministers for Foreign Affairs on the European Union Stabilization and Association Process, confirming that the future of the Western Balkans lies in the European Union,

Noting the progress made by the countries of the region, including those of the Stabilization and Association Process, in fulfilling the criteria for membership in the European Union and, in this context, the start of the accession negotiations of Croatia and Turkey, the former Yugoslav Republic of Macedonia becoming a candidate country for membership in the European Union, the signing of the Stabilization and Association Agreement with Albania and the opening of the negotiations for a stabilization and association agreement with Bosnia and Herzegovina and Montenegro, as well as resuming stabilization and association agreement negotiations with Serbia, pending full cooperation with the International Tribunal for the Prosecution of Persons Responsible for Serious Violations of International Humanitarian Law Committed in the Territory of the Former Yugoslavia since 1991,

Stressing the role and responsibility of the United Nations Interim Administration Mission in Kosovo, supported by the Organization for Security and Cooperation in Europe and the European Union, and of the North Atlantic Treaty Organization and its Kosovo Force for further promotion of stability in the region, and noting the Council of the European Union's joint action establishing a European Union planning team,

Reaffirming the validity of the Agreement for the delineation of the borderline between the former Yugoslav Republic of Macedonia and Serbia and Montenegro, signed in Skopje on 23 February 2001, and encouraging the parties to the Agreement and inviting all the parties involved in the process of settlement of the future status of Kosovo to respect the Agreement, to cooperate fully and to prepare for its timely implementation,

Emphasizing the crucial importance of strengthening regional efforts in South-Eastern Europe on arms control, demining, disarmament and confidence-building measures and non-proliferation of weapons of mass destruction, and noting that, in spite of ongoing efforts, the illicit trade in small arms and light weapons in all its aspects persists in some parts of the region,

Reaffirming its support for all regional initiatives on combating the illicit proliferation of small arms and light weapons, including the activities undertaken at the national level for their collection and destruction,

Mindful of the importance of national, regional and international activities aimed at the creation of peace, security, stability, democracy, cooperation and economic development and the observance of human rights and good-neighbourliness in South-Eastern Europe,

Reaffirming its determination that all nations should live together in peace with one another as good neighbours,

1. *Reaffirms* the need for full observance of the Charter of the United Nations;

2. *Calls upon* all States, the relevant international organizations and the appropriate organs of the United Nations to respect and support all the principles of the Charter and the commitments of the Organization for Security and Cooperation in Europe and through further development of regional arrangements, as appropriate, to eliminate threats to international peace and security and to help to prevent conflicts in South-Eastern Europe, which can lead to the violent disintegration of States;

3. *Acknowledges* the positive results achieved so far by the countries of the region, urges them to invest further efforts in consolidating South-Eastern Europe as a region of peace, security, stability, democracy, the rule of law, cooperation and economic development and for the promotion of good-neighbourliness and the observance of human rights, thus contributing to the maintenance of international peace and security and enhancing the prospects for sustained development and prosperity for all peoples in the region as an integral part of Europe, and recognizes the role of the United Nations, the Organization for Security and Cooperation in Europe

and the European Union in successfully promoting regional disarmament;

4. *Supports* the countries of the region in their determination to gradually take over ownership and responsibility for regional cooperation by a phased evolution of the Stability Pact for South-Eastern Europe into a more regionally owned, streamlined and effective regional cooperation framework as set out at the Stability Pact's Regional Table meeting on 30 May 2006 in Belgrade;

5. *Stresses* that every effort should be made to achieve a negotiated settlement in line with Security Council resolution 1244(1999) of 10 June 1999 and the contact group guiding principles; emphasizes the importance of the implementation of the standards for Kosovo; and fully supports the work of the Special Envoy of the Secretary-General and his team on the Kosovo status talks;

6. *Rejects* the use of violence in pursuit of political aims, and stresses that only peaceful political solutions can assure a stable and democratic future for South-Eastern Europe;

7. *Stresses* the importance of good-neighbourliness and the development of friendly relations among States, and calls upon all States to resolve their disputes with other States by peaceful means, in accordance with the Charter;

8. *Urges* the strengthening of relations among the States of South-Eastern Europe on the basis of respect for international law and agreements, in accordance with the principles of good-neighbourliness and mutual respect;

9. *Recognizes* the efforts of the international community, and in particular those of the European Union, the Stability Pact for South-Eastern Europe and other contributors, as well as of the South-East European Cooperation Process as an authentic voice of the region, in promoting the long-term process of democratic and economic development of the region;

10. *Calls upon* all States to intensify cooperation with and render all necessary assistance to the International Tribunal for the Prosecution of Persons Responsible for Serious Violations of International Humanitarian Law Committed in the Territory of the Former Yugoslavia since 1991 to bring all at-large indictees to surrender to the Tribunal in line with Security Council resolutions 1503(2003) of 28 August 2003 and 1534(2004) of 26 March 2004;

11. *Stresses* the importance of enhanced regional cooperation for the development of the South-Eastern European States in the priority areas of infrastructure, transport, trade, energy and environment, as well as in other areas of common interest, and welcomes the Treaty establishing the Energy Community, the establishment of the Regional Cooperation Council and the negotiations for the simultaneous enlargement and amendment of the Central European Free Trade Agreement;

12. *Also stresses* that the further rapprochement of the South-Eastern European States with the Euro-Atlantic institutions will favourably influence the security, political and economic situation in the region, as well as good-neighbourly relations among the States;

13. *Emphasizes* the importance of continuous regional efforts and intensified dialogue in South-Eastern Europe aimed at arms control, disarmament and confidence-building measures, as well as strengthening cooperation and undertaking appropriate measures at the national, subregional and regional levels against the proliferation of weapons of mass destruction and to prevent all acts of terrorism;

14. *Recognizes* the seriousness of the problem of anti-personnel mines and explosive remnants of war in some parts of South-Eastern Europe, welcomes in this context the efforts of the countries in the region and of the international community in support of mine action, and encourages States to join and support these efforts;

15. *Urges* all States to take effective measures against the illicit trade in small arms and light weapons in all its aspects and to help programmes and projects aimed at the collection and safe destruction of surplus stocks of small arms and light weapons, and stresses the importance of closer cooperation among States, inter alia, in crime prevention and combating terrorism, trafficking in human beings, organized crime and corruption, drug trafficking and money-laundering;

16. *Calls upon* all States and the relevant international organizations to communicate to the Secretary-General their views on the subject of the present resolution;

17. *Decides* to include in the provisional agenda of its sixty-third session the item entitled "Maintenance of international security—good-neighbourliness, sability and development n South-Eastern Europe.

Cooperation with the Council of Europe

In a consolidated report on cooperation between the United Nations and regional and other organizations [A/61/256 & Add.1], submitted in response to General Assembly resolution 57/337 [YUN 2003, p. 50] and Security Council resolution 1631(2005) [YUN 2005, p. 97], the Secretary-General described strengthened cooperation with the Council of Europe.

GENERAL ASSEMBLY ACTION

On 13 November [meeting 52], the General Assembly adopted **resolution 61/13** [draft: A/61/L.14 & Add.1] without vote [agenda item 108 *(g)*].

Cooperation between the United Nations and the Council of Europe

The General Assembly,

Recalling the Agreement between the Council of Europe and the Secretariat of the United Nations signed on 15 December 1951 and the Arrangement on Cooperation and Liaison between the Secretariats of the United Nations and the Council of Europe of 19 November 1971,

Recalling also the 2005 World Summit Outcome, approved at the United Nations summit held in New York from 14 to 16 September 2005, including the section on regional organizations, which provides an incentive to reinforce links between the United Nations and regional organizations such as the Council of Europe,

Welcoming the outcome of the Third Summit of the Council of Europe, held in Warsaw on 16 and 17 May 2005, and the fact that on this occasion the Heads of State and Government encouraged cooperation with the United Nations and the specialized agencies, and committed themselves to achieving the Millennium Developments Goals in Europe, including environmental development,

Welcoming also the increasingly close relations between the United Nations and the Council of Europe,

Welcoming further the report of the Secretary-General on cooperation between the United Nations and the Council of Europe,

1. *Considers* that cooperation with the Council of Europe regarding the protection of human rights, the fight against racism, discrimination, xenophobia and intolerance, the protection of the rights of persons belonging to minorities, the prevention of torture and inhuman or degrading treatment or punishment, the fight against trafficking in human beings and violence against women, as well as the protection and promotion of the rights of the child should be reinforced;

2. *Takes note* of the important role of the European Court of Human Rights, and invites the Human Rights Council and the Office of the United Nations High Commissioner for Human Rights to work closely with the Council of Europe, and in particular its Commissioner for Human Rights, in promoting respect for human rights;

3. *Notes* the contribution of the Council of Europe to the protection and strengthening of democracy, inter alia, through the Forum for the Future of Democracy, and welcomes fruitful cooperation between the United Nations and the Council of Europe in the area of democracy, good governance and education for democratic citizenship and human rights, in particular through the strengthening of links between the United Nations Decade of Education for Sustainable Development and the Council of Europe Project on Education for Democratic Citizenship and Human Rights;

4. *Encourages* the development of cooperation, where appropriate, between the United Nations Peacebuilding Commission and the Council of Europe, with a view to promoting post-conflict re-establishment and consolidation of peace in Europe, with full respect for human rights and the rule of law;

5. *Commends* the ongoing cooperation between the Counter-Terrorism Committee and its Executive Directorate and the Council of Europe, as well as the contribution of the Council of Europe to the implementation of Security Council resolutions 1373(2001) of 28 September 2001 and 1624(2005) of 14 September 2005, and calls for the deepening of cooperation in the fight against terrorism, while protecting human rights;

6. *Encourages* cooperation between the two organizations regarding the fight against transnational organized crime, cybercrime, corruption and money-laundering, as well as concerning the promotion of human rights and the rule of law in the information society;

7. *Reiterates its support* for cooperation between the two organizations in the social field, in particular concerning the protection and promotion of the rights and dignity of persons with disabilities, combating poverty and social exclusion and ensuring equal access to social rights for all;

8. *Welcomes* the joint initiatives of the United Nations Educational, Scientific and Cultural Organization and the Council of Europe for the promotion of intercultural dialogue, especially the creation of the Faro Platform of inter-institutional cooperation in 2005, and encourages the continuation of such cooperation, in particular through the European Centre for Global Interdependence and Solidarity of the Council of Europe, and also as regards the promotion of cultural diversity;

9. *Notes* the constructive interest of the Parliamentary Assembly of the Council of Europe in the reform process of the United Nations, and welcomes its proposals for a closer involvement of parliamentarians in the work of the United Nations;

10. *Requests* the Secretaries-General of the United Nations and the Council of Europe to combine their efforts in seeking answers to global challenges, within their respective mandates, and calls upon all relevant United Nations bodies to support the enhancement of cooperation with the Council of Europe in the areas mentioned above;

11. *Decides* to include in the provisional agenda of its sixty-third session the sub-item entitled "Cooperation between the United Nations and the Council of Europe", and requests the Secretary-General to submit to the General Assembly at its sixty-third session a report on cooperation between the United Nations and the Council of Europe in implementation of the present resolution.

Cooperation with the Organization for Security and Cooperation in Europe

On 22 December, the General Assembly decided that the agenda item on cooperation between the United Nations and OSCE would remain for consideration during its resumed sixty-first (2007) session (**decision 61/552**).

Chapter VI

Middle East

Events in the Middle East in 2006 illustrated the magnitude of the instability in the region, the ever-widening divide between Israel and its neighbours, and the bleak chances for achieving peace and security. The kidnapping of Israeli military personnel by Palestinian groups and Hizbullah in Lebanon in separate incidents, the continued firing of Qassam rockets towards Israel and the strong Israeli military response and ensuing humanitarian crisis were major setbacks to progress made the previous year in rebuilding trust and breaking the cycle of bloodshed.

In Palestine, the hope that the democratic process there would lead to a revitalization of the peace process between Israel and the Palestinian Authority (PA) was dashed, following the victory of the Palestinian resistance group Hamas in the January elections and its adherence to its previously held positions regarding Israel and the peace process. The Middle East Quartet (Russian Federation, United States, European Union, United Nations) set out principles which the new PA Government had to adhere to, including the recognition of Israel and the acceptance of previous agreements and obligations, as well as the road map, against which future assistance to the Government would be reviewed. The PA President, Mahmoud Abbas, asked Hamas to form a government in February. Israel immediately halted tax revenue transfers, causing a severe financial crisis throughout the Palestinian territories. In April, international donor funding to the PA was suspended. The increased firing of Qassam rockets from the Gaza Strip into Israel and the kidnapping of an Israeli soldier led to Israeli military action in the Gaza Strip. The Secretary-General dispatched a UN team, headed by Vijay Nambiar, to explore ways to defuse the crisis in the region. By the time a ceasefire between Israel and the Palestinian factions was announced in late November, scores of Palestinians and Israelis had been killed and hundreds others injured. The Occupied Palestinian Territory also saw bouts of inter-factional fighting between the PA and Hamas supporters.

The General Assembly convened its resumed tenth emergency special session in November to discuss the item "Illegal Israeli actions in occupied East Jerusalem and the rest of the Occupied Palestinian Territory". It adopted a resolution which called, among other things, on the Secretary-General to establish a fact-finding mission concerning the attack against the town of Beit Hanoun in the Gaza Strip on 8 November and to report to the Assembly within 30 days. The Secretary-General reported in December that the mission could not be dispatched because Israel had not indicated whether it would extend the necessary cooperation. The emergency session reconvened in December and adopted a resolution on the establishment of the United Nations register of damage caused by the construction of the separation wall in the Occupied Palestinian Territory.

The Middle East Quartet continued to promote the road map initiative as the best solution to the conflict. The road map, endorsed by the Security Council in 2003, aimed to achieve progress through parallel and reciprocal steps by Israel and the PA in the political, security, economic, humanitarian and institution-building areas, under an international monitoring system.

In Lebanon, hostilities between Hizbullah and Israel broke out on 12 July and continued until a UN-brokered ceasefire went into effect on 14 August, though the Israeli naval blockade of Lebanon was only lifted on 8 September. The conflict began with an unprovoked military attack by Hizbullah and the kidnapping of two Israeli soldiers. Israel responded with air strikes and artillery fire on Lebanese civilian infrastructure, an air and naval blockade and a ground invasion of southern Lebanon. Over a thousand civilians were killed, mostly Lebanese, and approximately 1 million people were displaced. In an effort to end the hostilities, the Security Council, on 11 August, unanimously adopted resolution 1701(2006), which was approved by both the Lebanese and Israeli Governments, calling for, among other things, Israel's withdrawal from Lebanon, and the deployment of Lebanese soldiers in southern Lebanon, with the assistance of an enlarged United Nations Interim Force in Lebanon (UNIFIL). The Lebanese army began deploying on 17 August and by the end of the year, for first time in over three decades, had deployed soldiers throughout southern Lebanon. Israeli troops withdrew from Lebanon on 1 October.

The United Nations International Independent Investigation Commission (UNIIIC) continued to investigate the 14 February 2005 assassination of former Lebanese Prime Minister Rafik Hariri and 22 others. On 10 November, the Secretary-General transmitted to the Lebanese Government a draft agreement between the United Nations and Lebanon on the establishment of a special tribunal to try those responsible for the assassination. The treaty still awaited a formal approval by the Government and ratification by the Parliament. Following the 21 November assassination of Minister of Industry Pierre Gemayel, the Security Council invited UNIIIC to extend its technical assistance to the Lebanese authorities in the investigation of Mr. Gemayel's assassination.

The UNIFIL mandate, which was expanded to include tasks related to resolution 1701(2006), was extended three times during the year: in January for six months, in July for one month during the Hizbullah-Israeli conflict in Lebanon, and until 31 August 2007. The mandate of the United Nations Disengagement Observer Force in the Golan Heights was extended twice. The military observers of the United Nations Truce Supervision Organization (UNTSO) were moved from their patrol bases and relocated within UNIFIL, following the 25 July killing of four UNTSO military observers.

The United Nations Relief and Works Agency for Palestine Refugees in the Near East continued to provide education, health and social services to over 4 million Palestinian refugees living in and outside camps in the West Bank and the Gaza Strip, as well as in Jordan.

During the year, the Special Committee to Investigate Israeli Practices Affecting the Human Rights of the Palestinian People and Other Arabs of the Occupied Territories reported to the General Assembly on the situation in the West Bank, including East Jerusalem, and in the Gaza Strip and the Golan Heights. The Committee on the Exercise of the Inalienable Rights of the Palestinian People continued to mobilize international support for the Palestinians.

Peace process

Overall situation

The Secretary-General, in a September report on the peaceful settlement of the question of Palestine [A/61/355-S/2006/748] (see also p. 547), said that the opportunity for the revitalization of the Middle East peace process had not materialized. Violence was on the rise from September 2005 to September 2006, including suicide bombings in Israel by Palestinian militants and indiscriminate rocket and mortar fire at Israel, as well as Israeli aerial strikes, extrajudicial killings of alleged militants, extensive ground operations and tank shelling. There were also incidents of intra-Palestinian violence, primarily in the Gaza Strip.

Elections for the Palestinian Legislative Council were held on 25 January 2006 throughout Gaza and the West Bank, with limited participation of Palestinian residents of East Jerusalem. Official results showed that the Change and Reform list of Hamas had won a majority of seats. Subsequently, the Quartet indicated that future assistance to any Palestinian Government would be reviewed by donors against the commitment of that government to the principles of non-violence, recognition of the right of Israel to exist and acceptance of previous agreements and obligations, including the road map. President Mahmoud Abbas invited Ismail Haniyeh of Hamas to form a Government and urged him to align his government's programme with that of the presidency. In his inauguration speech, Prime Minister Haniyeh stated his respect for the constitutional relationship with President Abbas and the role of the Palestine Liberation Organization (PLO). However, the Government could not commit to the principles articulated by the Quartet. The result of the legislative elections, however, was not without impact on the security sector. The Government of Israel put a stop to the transfer by the international community of equipment for the Palestinian security forces. In addition, President Abbas and the Government made conflicting security appointments and decisions. The Palestinian Minister of Interior deployed in Gaza a new "special force", drawing its members from security services and various factions, in spite of the declaration of President Abbas that the move was illegal. Clashes ensued between the two security forces, and calm was restored only after the President and the Prime Minister agreed to absorb the "special force" into the PA payroll.

After the Israeli general election of 28 March, a coalition Government was formed, led by Prime Minister Ehud Olmert, which expressed its desire to set Israel's permanent borders, preferably through an agreement with the Palestinians. The Israeli Government acknowledged that it would entail a reduction of Israeli settlements in the Occupied Palestinian Territory, but also envisaged the retention of major settlement blocs on occupied land. According to government guidelines, Israel would stand ready to proceed unilaterally should it deem that negotiations with the Palestinian side were not possible.

On 10 May, Palestinian prisoners in Israeli jails, including senior figures from the Palestinian political party Fatah and the militant organization Hamas, drafted a document outlining common political goals aimed at establishing a Palestinian State within the 1967 borders and describing the PLO as the sole legitimate representative of the Palestinian people. Fatah and Hamas reached an agreement on 27 June on a revised version of the document and pledged to make it the basis for establishing a national unity Government.

On 25 June, Palestinian militants attacked an Israeli military base near the Gaza border, killing three Israeli soldiers and capturing one. Israel subsequently launched a wide-ranging military operation in the Gaza Strip with the stated aims of freeing the soldier and putting a halt to rocket fire. The operation included aerial bombardments, ground activities, the arrest of Palestinian cabinet ministers and lawmakers, and the destruction of civilian infrastructure, including the only electric power plant in Gaza, roads and bridges, as well as many other public and private installations. As at September, over 200 Palestinians had been killed.

The Government of Israel failed to implement its obligations under the road map to freeze its settlement activities and dismantle outposts constructed in the West Bank since March 2001, although it had evacuated the Amona settlement outpost in February. In December 2005, it was reported that 3,696 housing units were under construction in the West Bank settlements and another 1,654 in East Jerusalem. Further expansion of the West Bank settlements to the north and south of Jerusalem and in the Jordan Valley were authorized by the Israeli Ministry of Defence.

The pace of the barrier construction in the West Bank accelerated. Land expropriation orders were issued by Israel to allow the extension of the barrier eastward around Jerusalem so as to envelop the settlement of Ma'ale Adumim. The Israeli High Court of Justice rejected a petition against the construction in northern Jerusalem, but ordered the dismantling of 5 kilometres of the barrier east of the settlement of Tzofim. The Israeli Ministry of Defence reportedly ordered a review of the barrier route in order to reduce its impact on Palestinian daily life. The continuing construction of the barrier encroaching on Palestinian land contradicted the legal obligations of Israel set forth in the 9 July 2004 Advisory Opinion of the International Court of Justice [YUN 2004, p. 465] and General Assembly resolution ES-10/15 of 20 July 2004 [ibid]. The Quartet Special Envoy for Gaza Disengagement, James D. Wolfensohn, continued to emphasize that without the re-establishment of free movement in the West Bank, a viable Palestinian economy was not possible. For several months, he endeavoured to advance an agenda covering issues related to movement and reform in the Occupied Palestinian Territory. Under the 2005 Agreement on Movement and Access [YUN 2005, p. 519], the opening of the Rafah crossing for travel between Gaza and Egypt, under the European Union (EU) supervision, initially operated on a daily basis, but since 25 June 2006 was only open sporadically. Likewise, the Karni, Kerem Shalom and Erez crossings did not operate regularly throughout 2006.

After the Palestinian legislative elections in January, Israel declared that the PA had turned effectively into a terrorist entity and decided to withhold the transfer of customs and value-added tax payments it collected on behalf of the PA, thereby depriving it of approximately $50 million per month in revenue. Key donor Governments also withdrew their direct support to the PA, in the light of the failure of the new Palestinian Government to commit to the principles laid out by the Quartet. The ensuing contraction of economic activity reduced domestic tax revenues, resulting in the PA increasingly being unable to meet its financial obligations. It cut most social benefits in February, stopped paying salaries to civil servants as of March and by April, its monthly revenue was estimated to be a mere sixth of its requirement. Aware of the humanitarian consequences of the situation, the Quartet, on 9 May, expressed its willingness to endorse a temporary international mechanism, limited in scope and duration and operating with full transparency and accountability, to ensure the direct delivery of assistance to the Palestinian people. The provision of fuel support costs and payment of allowances to health workers by the EU under the mechanism began in July. Other aspects, including payments of needs-based allowances and other non-salary costs, such as medicines, were also implemented.

Quartet activities. The Quartet continued to monitor the political and economic situation in the Middle East throughout the year. Its representatives met on 30 January [SG/2104], 9 May [SG/SM/10453] and 20 September [SG/2116]. The Quartet also issued statements on 30 March [SG/2110], 17 June [SG/2114] and 22 December [SG/2121]. The mandate of its Special Envoy, James D. Wolfensohn, ended on 30 April. In a 6 April letter to the Security Council President [S/2006/233], the Secretary-General said that members of the Quartet had decided that its Special Envoy and its team should continue to be provided with the support necessary to operate an office in Jerusalem. On 10 April [S/2006/234], the Council welcomed the Secretary-General's proposed arrangements.

Occupied Palestinian Territory

Change in Israeli leadership and Palestinian elections

Communication. On 19 January [A/ES-10/316-S/2006/30], the Permanent Observer of Palestine to the United Nations complained about the systematic efforts by Israel to thwart the Palestinian Legislative elections scheduled for 25 January, including harassment, arrest and detention of election candidates and their staff. Moreover, campaign offices in occupied East Jerusalem had been repeatedly raided and closed down. The Permanent Observer said that Israel's announcement that it would allow the elections to take place, but with the stipulation it would decide who could run campaigns or participate in the elections, was in contravention to the signed agreement regarding the elections and went against the spirit of democracy.

Security Council consideration. The Assistant Secretary-General for Political Affairs, Angela Kane, briefing the Security Council on 31 January [meeting 5361] during its consideration of the situation in the Middle East, including the Palestinian question, said that there had been dramatic developments in both Israel and the Occupied Palestinian Territory. Prime Minister Ariel Sharon suffered a stroke on 4 January and remained in an extremely serious but stable condition. Vice-Prime Minister Ehud Olmert took over as Acting Prime Minister and was subsequently confirmed by the Knesset (Parliament) on 16 January. He confirmed Israel's commitment to resolving the conflict in accordance with the road map, while leaving open the possibility of further unilateral measures in the West Bank.

On 25 January, Palestinian Legislative Council elections were held throughout Gaza and the West Bank, including in East Jerusalem, after the Israeli Cabinet agreed to allow 6,300 of the approximately 120,000 eligible voters to vote in six post offices, consistent with the precedents set by the Oslo Accords and the 1996 and 2005 elections. Overall, 77 per cent of registered voters cast their votes for a new legislature. The election was observed by approximately 20,000 national and 1,000 international observers, who concluded that, overall the campaign was held in a relatively calm atmosphere, with an absence of provocative rhetoric. Israeli authorities generally eased travel through checkpoints to facilitate freedom of movement on election day, although candidates, as well as campaign and election workers, were at times unable to move satisfactorily during the campaign period. The official results announced by the Central Elections Commission showed that the Change and Reform list of Hamas won 74 seats and the Fatah list 45, with the remaining 13 seats going to smaller parties and independents. Consultations on the formation of a Palestinian government were ongoing.

Quartet meeting (January). On 30 January [SG/2104], the Middle East Quartet met in London to discuss the political situation in the aftermath of the election, address the crisis of Palestinian finances and consider the way forward on security-sector performance and reform. The Quartet was briefed by Special Envoy James Wolfensohn and United States Security Coordinator Keith Dayton. Former United States President Jimmy Carter also shared his impressions after having led the electoral observer mission. The Quartet congratulated the Palestinian people on a free, fair and secure electoral process. It welcomed the affirmation of President Abbas that the PA was committed to the road map, previous agreements and obligations between the parties, and a negotiated two-State solution to the Israeli-Palestinian conflict. It held the view that all members of a future Palestinian government should be committed to non-violence, recognition of Israel and acceptance of previous agreements and obligations. While expressing concern about the PA fiscal situation and the need for measures to facilitate the work of the caretaker government to stabilize public finances, and taking into consideration established fiscal-accountability reform benchmarks, the Quartet concluded that it was inevitable that future assistance to any new government would be reviewed by donors against that commitment, including the road map.

SECURITY COUNCIL ACTION

On 3 February [meeting 5365], following consultations among Security Council members, the President made statement **S/PRST/2006/6** on behalf of the Council:

> The Security Council congratulates the Palestinian people on an electoral process that was free, fair and secure. It commends all the parties for the preparation and conduct of the elections, particularly the Central Elections Commission and the Palestinian Authority security forces, for their professionalism.
>
> The Council expresses its expectation that a new government remain committed to realizing the aspirations of the Palestinian people for peace and statehood. The Council welcomes President Abbas' affirmation that the Palestinian

Authority remains committed to the Road Map, previous agreements and obligations between the parties, and a negotiated two-State solution to the Israeli-Palestinian conflict. The Council expresses its view that all members of a future Palestinian government must be committed to the aforementioned instruments and principles.

Cognizant of the humanitarian needs of the Palestinian people, the Council reaffirms its continuing interest in the fiscal stability of the caretaker government, consistent with clear reform and austerity benchmarks. The Council notes that major donors have indicated they will review future assistance to a new Palestinian Authority government against the commitment of that government to the principles of non-violence, recognition of Israel and acceptance of previous agreements and obligations, including the Road Map.

The Council reminds both parties of their obligation under the Road Map and on existing agreements, including on movement and access. It calls upon both parties to avoid unilateral actions which prejudice final status issues. The Council underlines the need for the Palestinian Authority to prevent terrorist attacks and dismantle the infrastructure of terror. It reiterates its view that settlement expansion must stop and its concern regarding the route of the barrier.

The Council reaffirms its profound attachment to the vision of two democratic States, Israel and Palestine, living side by side in peace and security. The Council reiterates the importance of, and the need to achieve, a just, comprehensive and lasting peace in the Middle East, based on all its relevant resolutions, including resolutions 242(1967), 338(1973), 1397(2002) and 1515(2003), the Madrid terms of reference and the principle of land for peace.

Communications. President Abbas, in a speech delivered before the Palestinian Legislative Council on 18 February [A/ES-10/319-S/2006/115], said that election results had brought a new political reality, in which the Hamas movement held a majority in the Legislative Council and would have the task of forming the new government. However, the change should not be used as an excuse for increased aggression against the Palestinian people, or a pretext for blackmail. Palestinians should not be punished for a democratic choice made through the ballot box. President Abbas also stressed that the reform of the National Authority should not end, promising to oversee all reform initiatives to create an Authority that respected the law and was committed to enforcing it. The new government was expected to face up to its challenges, perform its functions capably, honour all signed commitments and act in the national interest.

On 20 February [A/ES-10/320-S/2006/116], the Permanent Observer of Palestine informed the Secretary-General and the Council President that, on 19 February, the Israeli Cabinet had adopted the unilateral measure of freezing the transfer of some $50 million of customs and tax receipts collected on behalf of the PA under the 1994 economic protocol. He called upon the international community, including the Quartet, and in particular the United Nations, to pressure Israel to rescind its decision to withhold funds and not punish the Palestinian people for exercising their democratic right to elect their representatives.

In an earlier communication of 17 February [A/ES-10/318-S/2006/110], the Permanent Observer said that the PLO Executive Committee had, on 16 February, condemned plans by the Israeli Government to isolate the Al-Aghwar (the Jordan Valley) area from the rest of the West Bank by instituting a regime of permits and severe restrictions on the movement of Palestinians in the Jordan Valley. Israel had also begun the construction of the "eastern wall" in the area.

Security Council consideration (February). The Special Coordinator for the Middle East Peace Process and Personal Representative of the Secretary-General, Alvaro de Soto, reporting to the Security Council on 28 February [meeting 5381], noted that a democratically elected government was in the process of being formed in the Occupied Palestinian Territory. It would be led by the Hamas list of Change and Reform, an organization that was formally committed to the destruction of Israel and had a condemnable record of terrorism against that country. On 21 February, President Abbas asked Ismail Haniyeh of Hamas to form the new government. Mr. de Soto observed that Hamas had evolved with respect to its rejection of Palestinian commitments made 13 years ago, but that it was too early to say whether it would continue in the right direction. The choices to be made by Hamas would be the single most important variable that would shape the future of the conflict. Meantime, Israel had halted the transfer of monthly customs and value-added tax payments to the PA and had tightened the closure regime in the Occupied Palestinian Territory. It had also decided to stop the transfer by the international community of equipment for the PA security forces. On 19 February, the day after the inauguration of the Palestinian Legislative Council, Acting Prime Minister Olmert made clear the Israeli Government's view that the PA was turning effectively into a "terrorist Authority" and that Israel would not hold contacts with an Authority that was led partly or completely by Hamas. The Special Envoy reminded Council members of the need to stabilize the PA finances, in the light of its budget deficit of some $260 million resulting from Israel's withholding of taxes and customs duty. While the formation of the new government was awaited in order to assess its commitment to the principles set out by the Quartet, the Council should be alert to the danger posed by cutting off assistance prior to such formation, which might be interpreted by the Palestinians and the Arab world as punishment for the way the Palestinian people voted on 25 January.

Israel, Mr. de Soto continued, was entering the final month of a Knesset election campaign. Since taking over as leader, Acting Prime Minister Olmert had spoken of entering into final status negotiations with the Palestinians should their government accept the principles laid down by the Quartet, and if that did not happen, of the possibility of setting Israel's permanent borders unilaterally, in ways that would keep all of Jerusalem and the large West Bank settlement blocs in Israel and the Jordan Valley under Israeli control.

In other developments, at least 32 Palestinians and one Israeli were killed, and some 130 Palestinians and 25 Israelis wounded. Violence instigated by Palestinians included the almost daily rocket fire against Israeli targets in the vicinity of the Gaza Strip, an attack on an Israeli military post at Erez and violent protests related to the publication in the West of cartoons depicting the Prophet Mohammed. The Israeli Government reported having foiled several suicide bombings by Palestinians and having conducted a series of targeted killings of alleged militants and other security operations. The most extensive military operation was held in Nablus beginning 19 February, resulting in a number of Palestinian deaths. Israel carried out the evacuation of the Amona settlement outpost, despite violent resistance by Israeli settlers. It announced further barrier construction and the building of a road protection fence in the southern West Bank near the original route of the barrier.

Communication. At its ninety-eighth session (Riyadh, Saudi Arabia, 1 March) [A/60/722-S/2006/169], the Ministerial Council of the Gulf Cooperation Council called on the international community to continue to provide financial assistance to the Palestinians and not punish them for exercising their democratic choice; welcomed the EU decision to resume its assistance of €120 million to help meet the basic needs of the Palestinian people; demanded that the international community not pass hasty judgment on the new Palestinian Government and support it; and reaffirmed its support for efforts to bring together different points of view within the Palestinian political spectrum to prevent political differences from overwhelming the interests of the Palestinian people.

Security Council consideration (March). On 28 March, the Palestinian Legislative Council approved the new Palestinian Government, led by Ismail Haniyeh and comprising Hamas members and independents, Assistant Secretary-General for Political Affairs Tuliameni Kalomoh told the Security Council on 30 March during its discussion on the situation in the Middle East, including the Palestinian question [meeting 5404]. The Permanent Observer of Palestine also attended the meeting at his own request [S/2006/197]. The approval followed two months of fruitless discussions on the possibility of forming a national unity government. PA President Abbas swore in the new Government on 29 March. He wrote to Mr. Haniyeh expressing his concern at the Government's draft programme prepared by Hamas and requesting him to align it with that of the Palestinian presidency. The programme outlined by Mr. Haniyeh in his speech before the Legislative Council expressed its respect for the constitutional relationship with President Abbas and its honouring of the relationship with the PLO. It did not, however, acknowledge the status of the PLO as the sole representative of the Palestinian people or the basic tenets of its 1988 declaration of independence, as requested by Fatah and other parties in discussions on a national unity Government.

The PA continued to be unable to meet its financial obligations. Although salary payments were made in February, the PA was unable to pay $15 million to $20 million in unemployment and other social benefits.

Meanwhile, in Israel, the new Kadima party, led by Acting Prime Minister Olmert, won the 28 March Israeli elections, with 28 seats in the Knesset, followed by Labour with 20, Shas 13, Yisrael Beiteinu 12 and Likud 11, with the rest shared by smaller parties. Mr. Olmert stated during the campaign that only the parties committed to the so-called convergence plan would be invited to join a Kadima-led coalition government. That plan involved withdrawal from parts of the West Bank, combined with the annexing of major settlement blocs, with the stated goal of setting Israel's permanent borders by 2010. According to statements made during the campaign, Israel would stand ready to proceed unilaterally should it judge that negotiations with the Palestinian side were not possible. President Abbas had rejected the concept of unilateral measures and indicated his desire to enter into negotiations with Israel at the earliest opportunity.

The Permanent Observer of Palestine said that the Palestinian people could not be punished by anyone for exercising their democratic right to elect their representatives. As in all democratic elections, the people's choice deserved respect and support. In that context, Israel had to release the monthly tax payments belonging to the Palestinian people. The Israeli Government had intensified and accelerated its attempts to carry through with its unilateral actions to further entrench measures already taken by it in the Occupied Palestinian Territory, including East Jerusalem. The political platform of the newly elected Acting Prime Minister was based on a dangerous campaign that called for a unilateral delimitation of the borders of Israel in the next four years, by keeping control of strategic parts of the occupied West Bank, occupied East Jerusalem, the Jordan Valley and three major illegal settlement blocs. That illegal plan was an attempt to legitimize the Israeli settlements and would effectively mean the end of the two-State solution.

Israeli unilateralism and militarism had to be rejected and should not be allowed to replace constructive political dialogue and pragmatism. The unilateral withdrawal from Gaza, since it was not negotiated with the Palestinian side, had proved to be disastrous. In fact, Israel continued to retain ultimate control of the Gaza Strip by regulating its borders, territorial sea and airspace. It also continued with its de facto annexation of huge parts of the West Bank, including East Jerusalem. Israel's pronouncement that it had no partner with whom to negotiate peace should be viewed from the perspective of unilateralism. The PLO was the sole legitimate representative of the Palestinian people and was therefore the only real negotiating partner.

Israel said that Hamas had yet to recognize Israel and renounce terrorism and violence as a means of achieving its goals. In Israel, the parliamentary elections underscored a long-standing commitment to international agreements, but Hamas had vowed to accept only those agreements that matched its interests. Israel remained committed to the road map, with progression based on the fulfilment of successive benchmarks. Unfortunately, the Palestinians had failed to carry out even the first requirement—to fight terrorism and begin to dismantle the terrorist infrastructure. Israel believed that Hamas' victory in the legislative elections could lead to a deterioration of the situation. Israel faced a constant dilemma: safeguarding the security and well-being of its citizens, while minimizing any humanitarian hardships that could affect the Palestinians as a result of terrorism prevention. On 23 March, the security situation permitted the Karni crossing to be reopened, allowing hundreds of truckloads of food, goods and commercial items to be transported to and from the Gaza Strip. Israel was doing everything in its power to ensure that the Palestinian people received all necessary humanitarian assistance. It would like to find a solution to end their suffering and improve the economy, but it could not compromise its own security.

The United States said that it would continue to judge Hamas by its actions and had seen nothing to make it change its position towards Hamas—a designated foreign terrorist organization under United States law. Its position on the provision of assistance to the new PA Government was consistent with that of the Quartet and it expected that measures would be in place to ensure that any such assistance could not be used by those affiliated with such an organization. In addition, the United States Security Coordinator, General Dayton, would have no contact with Palestinian security forces who reported to members of the Hamas-led Cabinet. His role would be redefined in the light of changing circumstances. The United States was continuing discussions with the Quartet to find a way forward and on the best means of supporting the Palestinian people.

The Russian Federation said that, instead of closing doors on prospects for achieving peace and punishing the Palestinians with sanctions and ultimatums, it would focus on joint efforts to establish a mechanism that would ensure reliable monitoring of the provision of donor assistance. It was resolved to carry out its commitment to provide the PA with $10 million.

On behalf of the EU, Austria said that, on the basis of the Palestinian Legislative Council and the new Government committing themselves to existing agreements, the road map, the rule of law and sound fiscal management, as well as the dismantlement of terrorist capabilities and infrastructure, it would continue to support Palestinian economic development and democratic State-building. The EU had mobilized €120 million to meet basic needs and help stabilize the finances of the caretaker Government, but future assistance would be reviewed against the Palestinian commitment to the principles set out by the Quartet for providing such assistance.

Communication. The Council of the League of Arab States, at its eighteenth summit (Khartoum, Sudan, 28-29 March) [S/2006/285], called upon the Arab States to continue to support the PA budget for a further period commencing on 1 April, and the Arab financial and economic funds and institutions to support and intensify programmes to strengthen the Palestinian economic and institutional capacities. It also called upon the international community to continue to provide grants and financial and economic assistance to the PA and respect the Palestinians' choice. It cautioned against continuing the call for the cessation of support for the PA and rejected the assumptions on which those calls were based. It also called attention to the dangerous negative consequences of the economic and social conditions of the Palestinian people.

Quartet meeting (March). In a statement issued on 30 March [SG/2110], following its meeting on the Middle East, the Quartet welcomed President Abbas' call for the new Palestinian Government to commit to a platform of peace but noted that in its programme approved on 28 March, the new Government had not committed to the principles spelled out on 30 January (see p. 501). The Quartet concurred that there would inevitably be an effect on direct assistance to the Government and its ministries, and encouraged continued assistance to meet the basic needs of the Palestinian people.

Communication. The newly appointed PA Minister for Foreign Affairs, in a 4 April letter [A/ES-10/327-S/2006/217], appealed to the Secretary-General to seek within the Quartet the start of earnest dialogue with the PA and its new Government. The PA looked to the international community to respect the democratic choice of the Palestinian people. It hoped that certain States would re-examine the premature stance of withholding assistance and adopting a language of threats rather than dialogue. He said that the blockade and closure of the Gaza Strip had created a tragic humanitarian situation, which numerous international and humanitarian institutions had warned could deteriorate.

Security situation

The security situation in the Occupied Palestinian Territory deteriorated further during 2006. In communications issued between January and April, both Israel and Palestine brought to the attention of the Secretary-General and the Security Council President information on attacks committed by either side. [A/ES-10/314-S/2006/11, A/ES-10/315-S/2006/20, A/ES-10/316-S/2006/30, A/ES-10/317-S/2006/83, A/ES-10/318-S/2006/110, A/ES-10/320-S/2006/116, A/ES-10/321-S/2006/123, A/ES-10/322-S/2006/127, A/ES-10/323-S/2006/144, A/ES-10/324-S/2006/165, A/ES-10/325-S/2006/181, A/60/732-S/2006/182, A/60/742-S/2006/205, A/ES-10/326-S/2006/213, A/ES-10/328-S/2006/220, A/ES-10/329-S/2006/226].

On 5 January, the Permanent Observer of Palestine said that the situation in the Occupied Palestinian Territory had witnessed an unprecedented increase in military aggression and unilateral measures by Israel. Those included the implementation of an Israeli plan to create a buffer zone in the northern Gaza Strip through the shelling and bombing of that area. In addition, Israel refused to implement the internationally brokered 2005 Agreement on Movement and Access, Agreed Principles for the Rafah Crossing [YUN 2005, p. 519], according to which Israel was to allow bus convoy traffic between Gaza and the West Bank.

On 13 January, the Permanent Observer said that Israeli forces had laid siege to the town of Jenin in the West Bank, while carrying out repeated military invasions against the Palestinian civilian population. They had also entered the Jenin refugee camp, killing two Palestinians, and had further tightened the closures on the northern areas of the West Bank from the rest of the Palestinian Occupied Territory. The siege had gravely intensified the socio-economic hardships being suffered by the entire Palestinian population. On 19 January, the Permanent Observer said that Israel was trying to obstruct the Palestinian elections, scheduled for 25 January, by its detention of election candidates and their staff, frequent incursions inside Palestinian centres and the extrajudicial execution of Palestinian activists. Between 7 and 24 February, he complained of Israel's military incursions into Palestinian towns and refugee camps, its restrictions of the movement of Palestinian residents of the West Bank and its decision on 19 February to freeze the transfer of funds belonging to the Palestinian people. In communications received between 6 and 23 March, the Permanent Observer also complained that Israel continued its campaign of extrajudicial executions. Since 9 March, Israeli forces had conducted military incursions into Palestinian cities, refugee camps and villages, causing death and destruction. On 14 March, they stormed the prison in the city of Jericho, killing two Palestinians, injuring 35 and capturing six others (see below).

On 30 March, Israel said that, according to initial reports, a Palestinian, who apparently had been planning to carry out a suicide attack at a crowded destination, had blown himself up next to a car packed with Israelis in the West Bank, killing at least three. Israel called on the international community to condemn the attack and help to bring about the participation of a genuine partner on the Palestinian side who would reject terrorism.

On 3 April, the Permanent Observer complained that Israeli forces stormed the Israeli prison camp in the Negev and forcefully moved 250 Palestinian prisoners and detainees to the central jails in Israel. On 5 April, he reported that Israeli forces carried out air and artillery raids and attacks against the Gaza Strip, using heavy weaponry, including F-16 warplanes, and terrorized the civilian population, causing more death and destruction. The extrajudicial killings also continued.

Security Council consideration (April). The Security Council, at the requests of Bahrain, on behalf of the Arab Group and the League of Arab States

(LAS) [S/2006/227], Yemen, on behalf of the Organization of the Islamic Conference [S/2006/239], and Malaysia [S/2006/240], on behalf of the Non-Aligned Movement, met on 17 April [meeting 5411] to discuss the situation in the Middle East, including the Palestinian question. The Council invited the Permanent Observer of Palestine, at his own request [S/2006/241], and the Permanent Observer for the LAS, at the request of Qatar [S/2006/244], to attend the meeting without the right to vote.

The Permanent Observer of Palestine said that the latest aggression and escalation of military attacks, mostly extrajudicial assassinations, by Israel against the Palestinian people in the occupied territories, and especially in Gaza, began on 7 April. In three days, at least 21 Palestinians were killed, including two children, and scores of others wounded. Those attacks followed the firing of missiles into the compound of the PA President and the PLO Executive Committee on 5 April. President Abbas continued to condemn all acts of violence against civilians, including suicide bombings, in particular the suicide bombing in Tel Aviv that same day. He reiterated that such acts harmed the Palestinian national interest and called on the international community, through the Council, to stop the latest Israeli aggression against the Palestinian people and ensure that Israel complied with its obligations under international law.

Israel said that the Tel Aviv bombing killed 9 people and wounded more than 60 others in yet another act of terrorism. The Palestinian terrorist organizations, Islamic Jihad and the Fatah-linked Al Aqsa Martyrs Brigades, had claimed responsibility. The Hamas spokesperson did not condemn the attack, claiming that "Palestinians had every right to use all means to defend themselves". That terrorist act and those that preceded it were the direct result of an axis of terror, comprised of Iran and Syria, and those terrorist organizations that they had been harbouring and financing, namely Hamas and Hizbullah. Without the capable efforts of the Israeli security forces and the effectiveness of the security fence, there would have been more terrorist attacks. Since January, 11 suicide terrorist attacks had been prevented and 90 potential suicide bombers arrested. Since September 2000, Palestinian terrorists had perpetrated nearly 26,000 attacks against the people of Israel. One of the most serious threats to security in Israel was the persistent fire of Qassam rockets and mortar shells. Since the Israeli withdrawal from the Gaza Strip in September 2005 [YUN 2005, p. 516], more than 500 Qassam rockets had been fired from Gaza, representing the primary form of terrorism against Israel. Israel would not compromise the safety and security of its citizens. While it regretted any loss of life, equating the loss of life caused erroneously by Israel acting in self-defense with a suicide bomber was morally wrong.

The United States said that the burden of responsibility for preventing terrorist attacks rested with the PA. It noted the reactions by several terrorist groups, including Hamas, which defended the act of terror in Tel Aviv. It also noted President Abbas' denunciation of it. Defence or sponsorship of terrorist acts by the Palestinian Cabinet would have the gravest effect on relations between the PA and all States seeking peace in the Middle East. The PA had to be held responsible for enforcing law and order, and for taking immediate action to dismantle the infrastructure of terrorism. So far, it had not taken any action to prevent terrorist attacks or the launching of Qassam rockets into Israel. The United States regretted the loss of innocent life, including in Gaza. It said that the United Nations had to play an even-handed role in the Israeli-Palestinian conflict, encouraging both parties to take the necessary steps to make progress along the road map. Unbalanced resolutions or statements undermined the credibility of the United Nations and its ability to be an honest broker. In consultations on the adoption of a presidential statement, the United States was willing to support a balanced statement, calling on both sides to refrain from causing the situation to escalate, but unfortunately that was not achieved. Israel had a right to defend itself. To condemn it for doing so, while failing to acknowledge the provocation of persistent Qassam rocket attacks or the PA responsibility for taking action to stop them was unworthy of the Security Council. The United States had been concerned about the humanitarian needs of the Palestinian people and on 7 April announced a 57 per cent increase in humanitarian aid, to a total of $245 million. It would also provide $42 million to strengthen civil society and independent institutions.

France said that it condemned the suicide attack committed in Tel Aviv and was shocked by the Hamas spokesman's comments. France appealed for calm and restraint and called on the parties to respect the arrangements agreed upon at the Sharm el-Sheik summit in 2005 [ibid., p. 506]. It believed that the recent escalation called for a strong political response from the international community and regretted that the Council was unable to agree on a balanced draft presidential statement submitted by Qatar, which it supported. A robust initiative by the Quartet that would bring the parties back to the negotiating table was necessary. France indicated that direct EU budgetary assistance had been temporarily suspended until alternative channels could be defined to ensure that such assistance could be clearly targeted to priority needs, such as education and health care.

Egypt said that the latest developments in the Occupied Palestinian Territory had brought the peace process to the threshold of a crucial decision that could determine its future and that of the region. It was incumbent on the Council to take immediate measures to put an end to the situation. Despite the Council's failure to date to issue a presidential statement, the latest events should provide an incentive for it to discharge its responsibilities and adopt a balanced statement that would break the cycle of violence and counter-violence and lead to a resumption of final-status negotiations.

Syria also expressed concern over the Council's failure to shoulder its responsibilities in the maintenance of international peace and security in the Middle East, which was due mainly to the selectivity and double standards applied by some to the question of the Arab-Israeli conflict. While the Arab side complied with Security Council resolutions, despite their unjust nature, some Council members continued to oppose any resolution condemning Israel's policies in the Arab territories and its lack of compliance with the Council's resolutions. Israel's claims accusing Syria and others of terrorism were made to cover up the war crimes committed by Israel against the Palestinian people.

Post-election situation

On 24 April [meeting 5419], the Security Council heard a briefing by the Special Coordinator for the Middle East Peace Process and Personal Representative of the Secretary-General, Alvaro de Soto. He said that a potentially dangerous deterioration of the situation in the Israeli-Palestinian conflict was being witnessed. In the light of the failure of the new Palestinian Government to commit to the principles articulated by the Quartet related to non-violence, the recognition of Israel's right to exist and acceptance of previous commitments and obligations, several key donors, while expressing a desire to meet the basic needs of the Palestinian people had withdrawn direct support to the PA. Others had indicated a willingness to provide funds, and efforts to obtain support continued within the region. The new Government was experiencing grave difficulties in meeting its running costs, including payment of salaries of civil servants and security forces. Lawlessness, already endemic, was worsening amid uncertainties concerning command and control of the security forces and signs of a struggle, still unresolved, between the PA presidency and the new Government. On the Israeli side, negotiations on the formation of a new Cabinet continued. Coalition talks were based on the programme outlined in interim Prime Minister Ehud Olmert's speech on election night, indicating a determination to set the permanent borders of Israel by removing settlements east of the barrier, consolidating the large existing settlement blocs and linking Jerusalem to Ma'ale Adumim. The Israeli caretaker Cabinet decided on 11 April that the PA had become a "terrorist entity".

The growing financial crisis of the PA was due to the fact that revenues were falling sharply as key donors had discontinued direct support, because of the Government's failure to meet Quartet principles; Israel's continued withholding of tax revenues collected on behalf of the PA, although Israel had announced it would use a portion of it to pay electricity, water and fuel bills owed to Israeli companies by the PA; and contraction of economic activity, which was expected to reduce Palestinian domestic tax revenues. Those problems were compounded by a crisis in the banking system and the high wage bill, which had been expanded to unsustainable levels by the PA prior to the assumption of power by the new Government. The PA had yet to pay the March salaries of more than 150,000 civil servants, 70,000 of whom were members of the security forces, who had already vented their anger by taking over government buildings. Protest demonstrations were also held, including at the office of the Special Coordinator in Gaza, against the withdrawal of funding and Israeli military operations. Without additional revenues, the PA might not be able to deliver the basic services needed to sustain the Palestinians and stave off a humanitarian crisis. The Palestinian economy was already depressed by closures, and it had been hoped that the implementation of the 2005 Agreement on Movement and Access would have paved the way to economic revival. Of the six parts of that Agreement, only the Rafah crossing for persons at the southern border of Gaza was operating satisfactorily, monitored by the EU Border Assistance Mission. The Karni crossing—another aspect of the Agreement—reopened in April, but only for few days. In the West Bank, there were 476 checkpoints. In the aftermath of the Tel Aviv suicide bombing on 17 April, measures to divide the West Bank into distinct areas had been solidified.

The Special Coordinator identified a number of key challenges. The security situation had to be stabilized and the responsible authorities had to take firm measures to prevent suicide attacks such as that in Tel Aviv, as well as rocket attacks. The Government of Israel, according to the Secretary-General, had to ensure that its military actions were proportionate and did not endanger the civilian population. The basic needs of the Palestinian people had to be met, with the United Nations continuing to work with all concerned to ensure that was done. Another challenge was to address the new reality that both parties were on quite different trajectories from those of the road map. The Security Council had to deal with the situation with the right mixture of adherence to basic principles and creativity. In that regard, the Secretary-General had invited the Quartet to meet in New York on 9 May to discuss those issues.

Quartet meeting (May). Representatives of the Quartet—United Nations Secretary-General Kofi Annan, Russian Federation Foreign Minister Sergi Lavrov, Austrian Foreign Minister Ursula Plassnik, United States Secretary of State Condoleezza Rice, High Representative for the European Union Common Foreign and Security Policy Javier Solana, and European Commissioner for External Relations Benita Ferrero-Waldner—met in New York on 9 May to discuss the situation in the Middle East. They were joined by the Foreign Ministers of Egypt, Jordan and Saudi Arabia.

In a statement [SG/SM/10453], the Quartet reiterated its concern at the failure of the PA Government to commit itself to the principles it had set out in January, which had affected direct assistance to the Authority. It condemned the Government's failure to take action against terrorism and its justification of the 17 April suicide bombing in Tel Aviv. The Quartet urged the PA to act decisively against terrorism and bring an end to violence. It expressed concern over Israel's military operations that resulted in the loss of lives and called for Israel to bear in mind the potential consequences of its actions. It also expressed concern about settlement expansion and the route of the barrier, and reiterated the importance of both parties avoiding unilateral measures.

Mindful of the needs of the Palestinian people, the Quartet expressed its willingness to endorse a temporary international mechanism, limited in scope and duration and operating with full transparency and accountability, to ensure direct delivery of assistance to the Palestinian people. If those criteria could be met, the mechanism, to be developed by the EU, could begin as soon as possible and be reviewed after three months. The Quartet also urged Israel to take steps to improve the humanitarian situation.

Security Council consideration (May). The Security Council, on 22 May [meeting 5443], heard a briefing by the Under-Secretary-General for Political Affairs, Ibrahim Gambari, on political and security developments in the Middle East. He said that Hamas' takeover of the PA, the interfactional tensions in Gaza and the new Israeli Government created a new set of challenges and opportunities for the international community, including a serious humanitarian situation in the Occupied Palestinian Territory. Some 155,000 Palestinian public-sector workers had not been paid since the end of February, and those salaries accounted for 25 per cent of the Palestinian economy, supporting about 1 million people. The Secretary-General had expressed the hope that the scope of the proposed mechanism for direct assistance to the Palestinian people (see above) would be as broad and non-discriminatory as possible. The United Nations was lending its full support to the EU efforts to establish the mechanism. The largest portion of the shortfall in the PA monthly budget was the Palestinian value-added tax and customs duties, which Israel had not transferred for the third month in a row. On 21 May, the Israeli cabinet decided to spend approximately $11 million of that money on the health sector, in addition to Prime Minister Olmert's pledge to address humanitarian concerns in the Occupied Palestinian Territory. Responding to the Quartet's call for urgent responses for assistance by international organizations, especially UN agencies, a revised consolidated appeal addressing additional humanitarian needs of the Palestinians under the new circumstances would be issued by the end of May. Donors were also called upon to support the emergency activities of the United Nations Relief and Works Agency for Palestine Refugees in the Near East (UNRWA).

A Palestinian national dialogue was planned for 25 May, in Ramallah and Gaza City. Around 500 representatives of political parties, civil society, the private sector, the PA and the PLO were expected to participate. The agenda included measures to reinforce national unity and address the security situation, and the activation of the PLO. As an important precursor to the dialogue, Palestinian political detainees in Israeli prisons, including senior Fatah and Hamas members, announced on 10 May an agreement on common principles for national action and dialogue. The agreement referred to the establishment of a Palestinian State in accordance with the 1967 borders, described the PLO as the sole legitimate representative of the Palestinian people, stated that political action should be based on Arab legitimacy and UN resolutions, and declared that resistance to Israel should be limited to the 1967 borders. Palestinian President Abbas endorsed the document, but the Government's response was more cautious.

Regarding the security situation, five Israelis were wounded by Palestinian violence since the end of April. Some 45 Palestinians had reportedly been killed and 180 injured; 10 of the dead and at least 33 of the wounded were victims of intra-Palestinian fighting. As internal strife, notably in Gaza, between PA police and the new Hamas-led security force had reached worrying proportions, President Abbas made a number of key security appointments, including within the Ministry of the Interior. Subsequently, the Government announced the formation of a new security force controlled by the Ministry. Although President Abbas had declared that move illegal, the Interior Minister deployed 3,000 armed men in Gaza on 17 May. The President responded by ordering all police forces to reinforce deployments in the Gaza Strip, and clashes between PA police and the new Hamas-led security force ensued. The situation remained volatile, but Egypt had made efforts to calm the tensions.

Regarding the barrier construction, on 26 April, Prime Minister Olmert announced his intention to increase the pace of construction and complete the barrier around Jerusalem by the end of the year. The Israeli Cabinet reiterated its commitment to the construction of the barrier and approved a series of changes in the northern West Bank and Jerusalem areas. Meanwhile, construction of Israeli settlements continued. The Defence Ministry authorized the expansion of four West Bank settlements to the north and south of Jerusalem, as well as in the Jordan Valley.

Quartet statement on funding mechanism. In a statement issued on its behalf on 17 June [SG/2114], the Quartet endorsed an EU proposal for a Temporary International Mechanism to facilitate needs-based assistance directly to the Palestinian people, including essential equipment, supplies and support for health services, the uninterrupted supply of fuel and utilities, and basic needs allowances to the poor. The Quartet hoped that other donors, international organizations and Israel would participate in the mechanism, and encouraged donors to respond to humanitarian and other assistance requests by international organizations, especially UN agencies active in the West Bank and Gaza.

Security Council consideration (21 June). In a further briefing to the Security Council on 21 June [meeting 5472], Mr. Gambari reported that, on 10 June, PLO Chairman and PA President Abbas called for a referendum, to be held on 26 July, on the covenant for national reconciliation agreed upon by Palestinian prisoners, called the "National Conciliation Document of the Prisoners" [A/ES-10/345-S/2006/499], adopted on 28 June. Most Palestinian factions, other than Hamas and the Islamic Jihad, supported the document. The PA Government had concerns about aspects of the document and disputed its legality, as well as the desirability of a referendum, and called for a dialogue without deadlines. The security situation in the streets calmed somewhat following consultations between President Abbas and Prime Minister Haniyeh, which led to the announcement that the special force recently created by the Minister of the Interior would be absorbed into the PA payroll after its members had received proper police training. The PA fiscal crisis had not abated. The continued non-transfer of Palestinian value-added tax (VAT) and customs revenues collected by Israel remained the major impediment to fiscal stability. In June, the PA made salary payments to 10,000 of its lowest-paid workers, and a further 90,000 employees each received about $300 in advances, using cash brought by officials and disbursed through local post offices, but some 40,000 remained unpaid. The delivery of some PA services were interrupted, including medical services, and the $11 million VAT and customs revenues Israel promised to spend on medicines had not been realized. Gaza was hit harder by the crisis than the West Bank. Some 40 per cent of those employed in Gaza worked for the PA, where the employment rate was 34 per cent. The World Bank estimated that the continued economic decline, combined with the degradation of public services, would have significant humanitarian impact and longer-term consequences. The Secretary-General welcomed the Quartet's endorsement of a Temporary International Mechanism (see p. 508) to facilitate needs-based assistance directly to the Palestinian people.

Israeli settlement activities and barrier construction continued. On 23 May, the Israeli High Court of Justice approved the route of the barrier in Jerusalem that passed between Ma'ale Adumim and the village of El-Azariyeh. On 15 June, the High Court ordered the dismantling of 5 kilometres of the barrier east of the settlement of Tzofin. According to the High Court, during earlier hearings the State concealed the fact that the existing route was determined partly by a master plan for expanding the settlement and not solely by security considerations. The Minister of Defence reportedly ordered a review of the barrier route so as to reduce its impact on Palestinian daily life.

The level of violence among Palestinians and between them and Israel increased, taking a severe toll on Palestinian civilians in Gaza. In the reporting period, at least 64 Palestinians were killed and 328 injured; 49 of those killed and 259 of the injured were victims of Israeli-Palestinian violence, while the rest were casualties of intra-Palestinian violence. One Israeli was killed and 18 injured in Israeli-Palestinian violence. Israel stepped up its policy of targeted killings of militants and shelling of areas in Gaza, from which rockets continued to be fired at Israeli territory. On 29 May, for the first time since Israel's withdrawal from Gaza, Israeli ground troops entered the Gaza Strip, killing five Palestinians. The Secretary-General was particularly disturbed that, despite his prior expressions of concern, targeted killings continued to be carried out by the Israel Defence Forces, which claimed civilian lives. During the reporting period, the United Nations recorded 176 rockets fired by Palestinian militants from Gaza towards Israeli territory, hitting towns and cities, injuring civilians and damaging private property and government buildings, including a school. For the first time in over a year, Hamas claimed responsibility for rockets launched at Israel. The Secretary-General repeatedly called on the PA to heed the Quartet's call and meet its road map obligations to act decisively against terrorism, including ending indiscriminate rocket attacks that endangered Israeli civilian lives.

Escalation of violence

The PA and Israel continued to inform the Security Council President and the Secretary-General on actions taken by each other. The Permanent Observer of Palestine, in communications [A/ES-10/330-S/2006/279, A/ES-10/331-S/2006/297, A/ES-10/332-S/2006/314, A/ES-10/333-S/2006/330, A/ES-10/335-S/2006/347, A/ES-10/336-S/2006/374, A/ES-10/337-S/2006/378, A/ES-10/338-S/2006/388, A/ES-10/339-S/2006/427], said that Israel continued to kill and injure civilians, destroy property and impose collective punishment on the Palestinian people on a daily basis. In May, 37 Palestinians were killed and 182 injured. He noted that the situation in the Occupied Palestinian Territory continued to deteriorate as a result of the escalation of military attacks by Israel. On 31 May, Israel Defence Forces (IDF) entered the Balata refugee camp and arrested six Palestinians. A series of arrests were also made in other cities and villages. IDF also carried out extrajudicial killings, resulting in the death of a number of Palestinians, including children.

Israel, in its communications [A/60/885-S/2006/382, A/ES-10/334-S/2006/336], said that the situation on the ground was dire. Since October 2005, approximately 600 Qassam rockets had been launched against Israeli cities, kibbutzim and other civilian localities, including strategic installations in the Negev. Some 19 rockets landed on the city of Sderot on 11 June. Israel said that all too often those referred to as Palestinian martyrs were actually terrorists on their way to perpetrate suicide bombing attacks.

On 22 June [A/ES-10/340-S/2006/432], the Permanent Observer of Palestine reported a further Israeli air strike in the southern Gaza Strip, killing two Palestinian civilians and wounding 14.

On 26 June [A/60/905-S/2006/436], Israel said that the previous day, Hamas members infiltrated Israel near the Kerem Shalom border crossing with Gaza, through a tunnel dug 300 metres into Israeli territory. They killed two Israeli soldiers, wounded three, and kidnapped Corporal Gilad Shalit. In a communiqué issued after the attack, which was annexed to Israel's communication, the Israeli cabinet said that it would take all necessary action to bring about the release of Cpl. Shalit, and that the PA would bear full responsibility for any harm to him. It also approved the security establishment's recommendation for urgent military action. Prime Minister Olmert and Defence Minister Amir Peretz would approve actions against targets among the terrorist organizations and the PA.

On 28 [A/ES-10/341-S/2006/443] and 29 [A/ES-10/342-S/2006/460] June, the Permanent Observer of Palestine said that Israel had launched a major air and ground military assault on Gaza. In addition, IDF raided several cities in the Occupied Palestinian Territory, detaining at least 64 Palestinians, the majority of them high-ranking officials, including at least nine PA ministers, as well as the Deputy Prime Minister, 24 members of the Palestinian Legislative Council and several mayors from the West Bank and Gaza.

On 29 June [A/60/912-S/2006/459], Syria said that Israeli military aircrafts had violated its airspace, which was an unjustified act of provocation. It also drew attention to the vast offensive launched by Israel against the Palestinian Occupied Territory. Those acts of aggression constituted unacceptable provocation and were direct attacks. On the same day [S/2006/475], Iran said that Israel's incursion into northern Gaza targeted civilians and civilian infrastructure, destroying, among other things, three bridges, disabling the only power plant, and firing missiles indiscriminately into residential areas. The illegal detention of Palestinian Cabinet ministers and members of Parliament indicated that Israel was intent on rendering the democratically elected Palestinian Government inoperative. Violating Syria's airspace and threatening to hit targets inside that country were equally perturbing. The crisis, if unchecked, could lead to an escalation, engulfing the whole region.

Also on 29 June [A/60/913-S/2006/463], Israel said that a Palestinian terrorist group on 25 June abducted and killed an Israeli civilian, for which the Palestinian terrorist organization, Popular Resistance Committees, claimed responsibility. Furthermore, between 20 and 28 June, 41 Qassam rockets were launched from Gaza towards Israel.

Security Council consideration (30 June). On 30 June [meeting 5481], the Security Council, at the request of Algeria [S/2006/458], as Chairman of the Group of Arab States and on behalf of the League of Arab States, and Qatar [S/2006/462], discussed the situation in the Middle East, including the Palestinian question. The Council President invited, at their own request, Israel's representative and the Permanent Observer of Palestine [S/2006/465] to attend the meeting without the right to vote.

The Assistant Secretary-General for Political Affairs, Angela Kane, said that three Palestinian militant groups—Nasser Salah el-Din Troops of the Popular Resistance Committees; Izz el-Din al-Qassam Brigades, the Hamas military wing; and the newly formed Islamic Army—issued a statement confirming that they were holding Corporal Shalit, who was abducted on 25 June, and would not be released. No information on his health would be provided until Israel released all female and underage Palestinian detainees. President Abbas had called for the release of the soldier and met with Prime Minister Haniyeh and international counterparts. Efforts to secure his release, especially by Egypt, as well as France and Jordan, continued. The Secretary-General consulted with the parties and the Quartet.

The Israeli military operation in Gaza began on 28 June. In a military briefing on 29 June, an IDF spokesperson stated that the ongoing operation was aimed at halting rocket attacks on Israel from northern Gaza and at securing the release of the missing soldier. Between 25 and 30 June, Palestinian militants reportedly fired 17 rockets from Gaza; there were no reported casualties. The Israeli Attorney General said that those Palestinians arrested by Israel, including the Cabinet ministers, would be charged under anti-terrorism legislation.

Ms. Kane also reported that the Palestinian Ministry of the Interior was targeted by an aerial strike and sustained major damage, as well as the power station, leaving over 40 per cent of Gaza without power. Water pipes were also damaged, leaving some 130,00 people without water. Crossing points between Gaza and Israel were closed since the start of the IDF operation, affecting the supply of food and medicines, and the pipeline for fuel into the Gaza Strip had not functioned for five days. The humanitarian consequences of the failure of sanitation systems and private generators would be severe. International efforts were under way to restore the flow of fuel.

The Assistant Secretary-General observed that the slightest turn of events could easily set off another full-scale conflict between Israelis and Palestinians. Nothing justified the holding of hostages, nor the indiscriminate rocket attacks, which the PA should stop. However, Palestinian civilians should not pay the price of those actions. Israel should cease the destruction of civilian infrastructure and allow the flow of humanitarian assistance. All concerned should give dialogue a chance to avert a full-scale confrontation.

The Permanent Observer of Palestine said that the scope and scale of the military assaults and the destruction carried out by IDF in Gaza indicated that the military aggression against the Palestinian population was premeditated and planned. Indeed, well prior to the capture of the Israeli soldier on 25 June, Israel had threatened to launch a major invasion of Gaza and had begun to mobilize its troops. The soldier's capture became the spark or the pretext for the actual launching of the invasion. Israel's air and ground military assault on Gaza was threatening the lives of the defenceless Palestinian civilian population, causing wanton destruction of civilian property and infrastructure and further destabilizing the situation on the ground. The Palestinian population in Gaza was under complete siege, as Israel had also sealed all border crossings. With the deprivation of electricity and clean water, including for hospitals, and the shortages of food and medical supplies, the humanitarian crisis was exacerbated. Israel had also expanded its aggression into the West Bank, resulting in the detention of democratically elected Palestinian officials there also. The operation was undertaken to sabotage the agreement achieved among Palestinian parties for reconciliation and unity, severely hamper the functioning of the PA and ultimately cause its complete collapse. The Palestinian leadership was sparing no effort to resolve the issue of Cpl. Shalit and ensure that he was treated in accordance with international humanitarian law, as well as his being released unharmed, together with efforts to secure agreement among Palestinian parties on the question of national unity. The Security Council and the international community should exert pressure on all parties to move away from aggression and resume negotiations and the peace process.

Israel said that Palestinian terrorist organizations launched a series of attacks after weeks of Israeli restraint in the face of numerous attempted kidnappings and rocket attacks from Gaza. Israel disengaged from Gaza in 2005 [YUN 2005, p. 515], with the hope of creating a window of opportunity and re-energizing the peace process. Instead, the response was an increase in Palestinian terrorist attacks. Gaza had become a terror base, actively supported by the elected Hamas Government, a terrorist regime with a sworn intent to deny Israelis their most fundamental human right and with a radical and militant ideology. Palestinian terrorists had perpetrated suicide bombings, shootings, stabbing attacks, Katyusha and Qassam rocket fire, explosions and Molotov cocktail attacks and other forms of terror. Hamas earlier in the month had declared a ceasefire, which it had also violated. The dangerous realities in the Middle East were further inflamed by the active and direct collaboration between Syria, Iran, Hizbullah and other Palestinian terror groups.

Israel had spared no effort in exploring and exhausting all diplomatic channels. In particular, it gave President Abbas an opportunity to secure Cpl. Shalit's safe release. However, it could not tolerate a situation in which its citizens were being held hostage by members of a terrorist group, such as Hamas. Israel did not disengage from Gaza in order to return to it. The military operation was specific in nature and limited in scope, aimed at preventing Cpl. Shalit from being smuggled outside of Gaza, and was not punishment or retaliation. Israel's goal was in line with its legitimate right to live in security. In the light of the escalation of Palestinian terrorism, Israel had decided to intensify its efforts to arrest those operatives responsible for terrorist attacks, so they could be tried and brought to justice. It urged the international community to apply all possible political pressure on the PA and Hamas to ensure the immediate and safe return of Cpl. Shalit and end the use of Palestinian territory as a base for terrorist operations.

Communications. In communications received between 3 and 12 July [A/ES-10/343-S/2006/479, A/ES-10/344-S/2006/489, A/ES-10/346-S/2006/501, A/ES-10/347-S/2006/519], the Permanent Observer of Palestine said that Israel continued to attack areas in Gaza, endangering the lives of Palestinians and causing further destruction to property and infrastructure, including the offices of Prime Minister Haniyeh, causing severe damage. In an attack launched on 6 July in Gaza, IDF killed at least 21 Palestinians and wounded more than 60 other civilians. On 8 July, Prime Minister Haniyeh called for a truce and for talks aimed at resolving the issue of the Israeli soldier taken prisoner. However, those calls were rejected by the Israeli Government. On 12 July, nine other Palestinian civilians were killed after a 550-pound bomb was dropped by an Israeli warplane in the heavily populated Sheikh Radwan neighbourhood in Gaza City. Israel had also pushed further into central Gaza, taking control of the main north-south road there, while Israeli snipers took positions on the rooftops of buildings and homes, and tanks and bulldozers continued to destroy crops and agricultural land.

On 5 July [A/60/931-S/2006/485], Israel said that between 28 June and 4 July, Palestinian terrorists launched at least 29 Qassam rockets from Gaza towards Israel. The attack on 4 July represented a serious escalation of violence, as the rocket used was an upgraded version, travelling farther into Israeli territory. Between 5 and 9 July [A/60/935-S/2006/502], 22 additional rockets landed on Israeli soil, damaging a factory and a greenhouse, destroying a private home and injuring several people.

On 6 July [S/2006/491], the Coordinating Bureau of the Movement of Non-Aligned Countries issued a statement demanding that Israel immediately cease its military aggression against the Palestinian civilian population. The Ninth Meeting of Foreign Ministers of Iraq's Neighbouring Countries on the Grave Situation in Palestine (Tehran, Iran, 8–9 July) also issued a statement condemning the Israeli military attacks.

Security Council consideration (13 July). On 13 July [meeting 5488], the Security Council, at the request of Algeria [S/2006/458] and Qatar [S/2006/462], discussed the situation in the Middle East. The Council President invited the representative of Israel, and the Permanent Observer of Palestine, at their request [S/2006/520], to participate in the meeting without the right to vote. Council Members had before them the text of a draft resolution submitted by Qatar [S/2006/508], by which the Council would have, among other things, condemned the Israeli military assault, the detention of democratically elected Palestinian and other officials, and the firing of rockets from Gaza into Israel, as well as the abduction of the Israeli soldier by Palestinian armed groups, including the most recent abduction and killing of an Israeli civilian in the West Bank. It also called for the immediate and unconditional release of the abducted soldier, the detained Palestinian ministers and other officials, and called upon Israel to stop its military operations and the PA to take action to bring an end to violence, including the firing of rockets.

The vote on the draft resolution was 10 in favour, 1 against, and 4 abstentions. The draft was therefore not adopted because of the negative vote of a permanent member of the Council.

The United States, in an explanation of vote, said that in the light of the fluid and volatile nature of events on the ground the draft resolution was not only untimely but already outmoded. The major escalation of violence by Hizbullah and the Secretary-General's decision to send a team to the region to help resolve the situation should be reflected in the text. The draft was also unbalanced as it placed demands on one side but not the other in the Middle East conflict and undermined the vision of two democratic States—Israel and Palestine—living side by side in peace and security. It would have also undermined the credibility of the Council. The best way to resolve the crisis was for Hamas to secure the safe and unconditional release of Cpl. Shalit. Establishing the foundations for a lasting peace, however, would require focusing attention not just on Hamas but also on the State sponsors of terror, particularly Syria and Iran, as without that financial and material support, Hamas would be severely crippled in carrying out its terrorist operations. The United States was concerned about the duration of the current difficulties and the lack of a solution, but the issue was whether action by the Council made such a solution more or less likely, and not simply whether the Council seemed "engaged" or not.

Qatar said that it had submitted a balanced draft resolution that reflected the views of the majority of the Council. The Council's failure to assume its responsibilities to put an end to aggression would only encourage the aggressor and lengthen the duration of violence.

Communications. On 18 July [A/ES-10/348-S/2006/538], the Permanent Observer of Palestine said that the Council's inaction on 13 July to adopt a balanced draft resolution had bolstered Israel's perception that it was immune from the law, leading to the imposition of more destruction and human loss on the besieged and devastated population of the Occupied Palestinian Territory. In fact, since 12 July, 23 more Palestinians were killed by IDF. On 13 July, Israel also bombed the Ministry of Foreign Affairs in Gaza City and on 15 July, the Ministry of the Economy. In a further communication [A/ES-10/349-S/2006/554], the Permanent Observer said that, since 13 July, at least 19 Palestinians were killed and 80 others wounded by IDF in a refugee camp in Gaza. The refugee camp at Al-Maghazi in central Gaza was also attacked, resulting in the deaths of 12 Palestinians. Also attacked were the West Bank town of Nablus, the offices of the Palestine News Agency in Ramallah and the headquarters of that town's Governorate.

G-8 Summit statement. The Summit of the Group of Eight (G-8) most industrialized countries (St. Petersburg, Russian Federation, 15-17 July) [S/2006/556] issued a statement on the Middle East calling for the return of the Israeli soldiers in Gaza and Lebanon unharmed; an end to the shelling of Israeli territory; an end to Israeli military operations; the early withdrawal of Israeli forces from Gaza; and the release of the arrested Palestinian ministers and parliamentarians. The goal of the G-8 leaders was an immediate end to the current violence, a resumption of security cooperation between Palestinians and Israelis, and political engagement both among Palestinians and with Israel. The G-8 leaders also called for the immediate expansion of the Temporary International Mechanism for donors established by the Quartet, and Israeli compliance with the 2005 Agreement on Movement and Access.

Mission of Special Adviser. The Special Adviser to the Secretary-General, Vijay Nambiar, who had been dispatched to the Middle East by the Secretary-General to explore ways of defusing the crisis in the region, briefed the Security Council on 21 July [meeting 5493] on the results of his visit, accompanied by Special Coordinator for the Middle East Alvaro de Soto, and Special Envoy Terje Roed-Larsen. Mr. Nambiar first gave an overview of developments since the last briefing by Under-Secretary-General Gambari. The Council President invited the representative of Israel and the Permanent Observer of Palestine at their own request [S/2006/553]. The Secretary-General also attended the meeting.

Mr. Nambiar said that efforts of mediators to obtain the release of the Israeli soldier were unsuccessful and Israel's military operation to secure his return and prevent rocket attacks from Gaza continued. Since 21 June, Palestinian militants fired over 200 rockets from Gaza into southern Israel, striking a number of population centres. At least 147 Palestinians were killed by Israeli forces in Gaza and the West Bank, and more than 450 injured. Five Israelis were killed and at least 25 injured by Palestinian militants, including in rocket attacks. On the humanitarian front, Israel's destruction of parts of the Gaza power station left 1.4 million Palestinians without electricity for about 12 to 18 hours a day. Water was rationed and public health suffered, with insufficient access to clean drinking water. Access into and out of Gaza continued to be severely restricted. Meanwhile, the second window of the Temporary International Mechanism, which provided fuel support financing for the Gaza power plant and other facilities, started on 11 July, with the first transfer by the EU of 300,000 litres of fuel for hospital generators in Gaza. On 27 June, Fatah and Hamas reached an agreement on a revised version of the so-called Prisoners' Document (see p. 508) on which to base the National Unity Government and the PLO reform.

Reporting on his mission to Palestine and Lebanon (see p. 513), Mr. Nambiar said that, on arrival in the region on 14 July, he met with high-level representatives of Egypt, Jordan, Israel, Lebanon, Qatar, Saudi Arabia, the PA, the EU and the League of Arab States. President Abbas was particularly concerned that the crisis in Lebanon involved, among other things, an attempt by non-Palestinian extremists to hijack leadership on the Palestinian issue, and felt it was important to de-link the two crises and for the Palestinian issue to be addressed on its merits. The international community had work to do in assisting the parties to develop a credible political framework that could lead to a comprehensive Middle East peace.

The Permanent Observer of Palestine said that the recent failure of the Security Council to respond appropriately to the Israeli onslaught against the Palestinian civilian population had allowed the Israeli Government to continue to carry out illegal actions with impunity. The Council could not continue to remain passive in the face of such military aggression. It should condemn the most recent Israeli aggression, call for an immediate cessation of hostilities and the immediate withdrawal of Israeli forces to their original positions before the aggression against Gaza began, and release all democratically elected Palestinians. He hoped that the Council would act to address the growing crisis.

Israel said that the Palestinian Observer's description of Israel's actions was as if they came from nowhere. There was no mention of the kidnapping of the Israeli soldier, the firing of hundreds of Qassam rockets by the Hamas-led Government and the fact that Israel had totally withdrawn from Gaza nearly a year ago. Calls had been made for a cessation of hostilities, but Israel had to insist on the cessation of terror. It welcomed the 16 July statement of the G-8 leaders (see p. 513), which provided a basis for progress towards a sustainable peace. As a step towards that goal, Israel demanded that its kidnapped soldiers, including Gilad Shalit, be released immediately.

Communications. On 25 [A/ES-10/350-S/2006/570] and 26 July [A/ES-10/351-S/2006/579], the Permanent Observer of Palestine said Israel continued to use disproportionate force and launch military attacks in the occupied Palestinian territories. On 26 June, backed by tanks and armoured personnel vehicles, IDF pushed two kilometres into northern Gaza.

In communications received between 3 and 21 August [A/ES-10/352-S/2006/613, A/ES-10/353-S/2006/623, A/ES-10/354-S/2006/641, A/ES-10/355-S/2006/669], the Permanent Observer said that IDF continued to carry out its military attacks, including extrajudicial killings, in the Occupied Palestinian Territory, especially in Gaza, and against Lebanon. Since 26 July, IDF had killed at least 32 Palestinians and injured 40 others. A military incursion east of Rafah in southern Gaza injured more than 20 Palestinians. On 4 August, IDF widened its attack in southern Gaza. On 20 August, Israeli forces kidnapped the Secretary-General of the Palestinian Legislative Council, bringing to 30 the number of elected officials kidnapped.

In related developments, the Security Council on 11 August, in resolution 1701(2006) (see p. 583), called for a full cessation of hostilities between Hizbullah and Israel, and for both countries to support a permanent ceasefire and a long-term solution. The UN Secretary-General reported that the ceasefire went into effect on 14 August.

Humanitarian fact-finding mission

At the request of Security Council members during consultations held on 28 July, the Secretary-General transmitted the briefing delivered on the same day by the Under-Secretary-General for Humanitarian Affairs and Emergency Relief Coordinator, Jan Egeland, on the humanitarian situation in the Middle East [S/2006/593].

The Relief Coordinator said he had just returned from a six-day mission to three war zones: Lebanon, northern Israel and Gaza. There was a need to address the armed conflict and the deepening social and economic crisis in Gaza and the Occupied Palestinian Territory as a whole. The destruction of vital civilian infrastructure, such as bridges, roads and the only electrical power plant in Gaza, the ongoing closure of most border crossings into and out of Gaza, and frequent roadblocks were suffocating any attempt at building a viable economic and social infrastructure in the area. As a result, anger and the readiness to resort to militant violence seemed to be growing. The greenhouses erected, as part of the Quartet Special Envoy's efforts, were all destroyed, as were the bridges built by the United Nations Development Programme, with European aid over the years. However, the violence had to stop immediately, the international community had to support the efforts of President Abbas and international mediators to stop militants from firing Qassam rockets at Israeli settlements, and the Israeli soldier held in captivity had to be released. Israel, in turn, had to end its often excessive and disproportionate use of force. The PA needed help to re-establish a social and economic infrastructure that would provide employment and hope and curb the extreme radicalization of youth in Gaza. The Relief Coordinator also called on Israeli authorities to establish a transparent and reliable regime at key crossing points into and out of Gaza, and in that regard proposed a weekly working meeting between IDF and the United Nations to facilitate the transport of humanitarian and other urgently needed goods into Gaza. He recommended a humanitarian truce of at least 72 hours, to be accompanied by a major operation to relocate children, the wounded, the disabled and the elderly who had been unable to escape the fighting in the worst war zones; resupply hospitals and health centres with emergency medical relief items and fuel for generators to avoid a complete breakdown of public health facilities for the thousands wounded; provide water and sanitation facilities, food and other basic supplies to the tens of thousands of the displaced, who were seeking shelter in public buildings in the conflict zones; and establish an emergency communication system to vulnerable communities, allowing the United Nations to address acute needs where and when they arose.

Further developments

Review of peace process

Security Council consideration (August). On 22 August [meeting 5515], the Security Council heard a briefing by the Under-Secretary-General for Political Affairs on the latest political and security developments in the Middle East, including the Palestinian question. The Council invited the representative of Israel and the Permanent Observer of Palestine, at their own request, to participate in the meeting without the right to vote.

The Under-Secretary-General said that, in the light of the emphasis in paragraph 18 of resolution 1701(2006) (see p. 583) on the need for a comprehensive, just and lasting peace in the Middle East, based on Council resolutions, it was necessary to step back from recent events and consider the state of the peace process in the region, taking into account developments since September 2005, when Israel completed its disengagement from Gaza and four West Bank settlements. Led by the Quartet, the international community had worked to ensure that Israel's disengagement would lead the parties back to the road map and the revival of the economy of the Occupied Palestinian Territory. However, those hopes were not fulfilled due to a number of reasons. The first was the political positions and actions of the parties. While President Abbas remained committed to his platform of peace, the Hamas-led PA did not fully commit itself to the basic principles of the peace process: non-violence, recognition of Israel and acceptance of previous agreements. Although factional tensions persisted, a broad spectrum of political and other Palestinian forces were engaged in a dialogue to put in place a national unity government with a new programme. While efforts to strengthen Palestinian border management and security services that fell under the President's purview continued, the Palestinian reform agenda was largely frozen, and with it, Palestinian compliance with its road map obligations. On the Israeli side, the coalition Government stated its readiness to commence negotiations if the PA accepted the basic principles of the peace process and implemented its road map obligations. However, Israel did not transfer some $500 million it owed to the PA and failed to implement its road map obligations, including the freezing of settlement activity and the removal of outposts. Meanwhile, the Israeli Government had been planning to disengage unilaterally from parts of the West Bank, while consolidating its presence in other parts. The second reason for the stagnation of the peace process was the degradation of the PA, the most tangible symbol of Palestinian hopes for statehood, as well as of Israel's hope for a viable partner. The PA performance in the months following the disengagement was at best mixed. The Palestinian wage bill continued to grow, as the PA recruited more officers into the security forces, security in Gaza deteriorated and rocket attacks on Israel continued. By December 2005, key donors were reconsidering their support to the already depleted PA budget. Its domestic revenues plunged further since the January elections. The cumulative worth of value-added tax transfers collected by Israel but withheld from the PA would be between $480 million and $560 million by September 2006. Restrictions on movement meant that the Palestinian Cabinet never met in one place, and ministers were confined either in Gaza or the West Bank. Moreover, several Cabinet members were in Israeli detention, while others were in hiding or abroad, leaving ministries without policy direction and creating disillusionment among managers and employees who remained at their posts. Although the Temporary International Mechanism and the UN consolidated appeal were to ensure that basic goods and services were delivered and that minimum cash payments were made to the needy, they neither generated economic growth nor provided hope for the Palestinians. The third reason was the suffering, destruction and death resulting from violence. Israeli land, air and sea operations, despite reportedly being aimed at militants or military targets, had killed large numbers of civilians, including children, and caused heavy damage to civilian infrastructure, particularly in Gaza. In the West Bank, Israeli incursions were a regular occurrence, in particular in Nablus and Jenin. There had been also several Palestinian suicide attacks in Israeli cities, and civilians living in towns and kibbutzim near Gaza endured regular Qassam rocket attacks. The cycle of attack and counter-attack only led to increased human suffering. In the past year, 41 Israelis were killed and nearly 480 injured, while over 450 Palestinians were killed and over 2,500 injured; 190 of those deaths occurred since the capture of Corporal Shalit on 25 June.

A fourth reason for the lack of progress towards a negotiated two-State solution was the creation of facts on the ground that would appear to prejudice final status issues. Settlement activities continued, with some 3,000 units reportedly under construction within existing settlements, and despite several statements of intent, unauthorized settlement outposts had not been dismantled. The barrier, large parts of which were on the Occupied Palestinian Territory, was 51 per cent completed. Once finished, approximately 60,500 West Bank Palestinians, in addition to the 180,000 Palestinians in East Jerusalem, would reside in areas between the barrier and the Green Line, with restricted access to health, education and employment services in both the West Bank and East Jerusalem. In East Jerusalem, the combination of settlement activity, barrier construction and other administrative measures pointed to the encirclement of the city that was intended to serve as the capital of two States, while effectively dividing the West Bank into two separate geographical areas. A fifth reason was the economic situation, since development was a building-block of peace. According to the UN Office for the Coordination of Humanitarian Affairs, some 70 per cent of Palestinians were living below the poverty threshold and 85 per cent of the population in Gaza was receiving food aid. According to the World Bank, the single biggest impediment to Palestinian economic growth was the closure regime. The number of IDF manned and unmanned physical obstacles in the West Bank increased by 43 per cent since Israel's disengagement from Gaza. The sixth reason for the state of the peace process was the attitudes of ordinary women and men. Opinion polls suggested a woeful decline in confidence in the peace process and in prospects for a negotiated settlement on both sides. The stalled state of the process should therefore be regarded as unacceptable, both on its own merits and because of its broader regional implications. As the Secretary-General had suggested, a renewed international effort was needed in which the various crises in the region were addressed, not in isolation or bilaterally, but as part of a holistic and comprehensive effort, sanctioned and championed by the Security Council, to bring peace and stability to the whole region.

The United States said that it believed that resolution 1701(2006) was an important step forward and when fully implemented would help lay the foundation for a lasting peace in the region. It remained deeply concerned by the ongoing crisis between Israel and the Palestinians, and was keenly aware of its humanitarian impact. The United States had increased humanitarian assistance to more than $270 million, including $50 million in response to the urgent appeal by the United Nations Relief and Works Agency for Palestine Refugees in the Near East (UNRWA) for the West Bank, and had substantively increased its support for the promotion of democracy and civil society and the development of the private sector.

The Permanent Observer of Palestine, noting the ceasefire in place in Lebanon (see p. 585) and the assembling of a force under the Council's supervision to bring peace and security to that country, expressed the hope that the continuing hopes and appeals of the Palestinian people and their leadership would lead to action by the Council. He drew attention to the decision of the Arab Foreign Ministers [S/2006/700] requesting a high-level meeting of the Council in September to discuss the situation in the Middle East, with a view to moving towards the implementation of relevant Council resolutions. Their decision to return to the Council was taken based on their belief in its responsibilities and its rightful role with regard to peace and security, and the upholding of international law.

Israel informed the Council that it too was conscious of the humanitarian needs in Gaza. It had received information that 3,772 truckloads of food, medical equipment and other supplies had already entered Gaza in the past two months, with 664 trucks intending to return with new supplies. That was done in cooperation with the international community's representatives dealing with those humanitarian issues.

The Middle East was a region caught between rifts of extremism, where radicals engaged in fierce battles that had no rules of play. Israel found itself wedged between those currents, trying to navigate a peaceful solution to the turmoil and allowing civilization to grow and prosper as it should. There was a way to a new Palestinian reality, which should begin with the immediate and unconditional release of Gilad Shalit, a halt to the Qassam rocket and terror attacks, and an end to all forms of terror and the uprooting of terrorists who willfully endangered the region.

Communications. On 28 August [A/ES-10/356-S/2006/696], the Permanent Observer of Palestine said that nearly two months had passed and the Israeli military aggression against the Palestinian civilian population had not ceased. On the contrary, IDF continued to kill, injure and destroy, and commit other violations of international law in the Occupied Palestinian Territory. Moreover, according to the 24 August report of the Office for the Coordination of Humanitarian Affairs, some 120 Palestinian structures had been destroyed and another 160 damaged. The humanitarian aid that had reached Gaza was very limited, owing to the complete closure of the Karni crossing point. The Country Director of the World Food Programme had warned that the Gaza economy had reached rock bottom, and the industries that were the backbone of that economy and food system, such as agriculture and fishing, were suffocated by the current situation and risked losing all viability. In another communication issued on 31 August [A/ES-10/357-S/2006/704], the Permanent Observer complained that, while the international community remained silent, Israel continued to wage its military campaign against the Palestinian people, killing at least 22 since 28 August. He again called on the international community to take action to compel Israel to cease its military attacks and abide by international law and the provisions of the Fourth Geneva Convention.

Quartet meeting (September). The Quartet principals, meeting in New York on 20 September [SG/2116], stressed the urgent need to make progress towards a just, lasting and comprehensive peace in the Middle East. They expressed concern at the crisis in Gaza and the continued stalemate between Israel and the Palestinians. The Quartet welcomed the efforts of President Abbas to form a government of national unity, in the hope that the platform for such a government would reflect Quartet principles and allow for early engagement. It encouraged greater donor support to meet the needs of the Palestinian people, with particular emphasis on security-sector reform, reconstruction of damaged infrastructure and economic development. It commended the World Bank and the EU for facilitating needs-based assistance directly to the Palestinian people through the Temporary International Mechanism and endorsed its continuation and expansion for a further three months. The Quartet encouraged Israel and the PA to consider the resumption of transfers of tax and customs revenues collected by Israel on behalf of the PA in order to improve economic and humanitarian conditions. It welcomed the prospect of a meeting between Prime Minister Olmert and President Abbas in the near future and agreed to meet regularly, including with the parties, to monitor developments and discuss the way ahead.

Security Council consideration (September). At the request of the League of Arab States (LAS) [S/2006/700], the Security Council, on 21 September [meeting 5530], considered the situation in the Middle East, including the Palestinian question. The Secretary-General attended the meeting. The PA President and PLO Executive Chairman Abbas was also invited.

The Secretary-General said that the Arab-Israeli conflict, like no other conflict, carried a powerful symbolic and emotional charge for people throughout the world. The narratives of the two sides—dispossession, prolonged occupation and denial of statehood on one side, terrorism and existential threats on the other—stirred the fears and passions of people of many nations. The continued failure to resolve the conflict called into question the legitimacy and effectiveness of the Council itself. The events of the past two months demonstrated how dangerous it was to leave the broader Arab-Israeli conflict unresolved and how interconnected the region's problems were. At the same time, the role of the Council in bringing about the cessation of hostilities between Israel and Hizbullah and charting the way towards a sustainable ceasefire through resolution 1701(2006) showed that it could play a vital role in the search for peace in the region. The resolution stressed the need to achieve a comprehensive, just and lasting peace in the Middle East, based on all relevant Council resolutions. To achieve that, progress had to be made on the issue at the heart of the conflict, which was the problem of Israel and Palestine. Large majorities of Israelis and Palestinians desired peace, and what they needed was a bridge to enable them to reach peace from their current state of conflict. The bridge to peace had to be wide enough to accommodate all who had a legitimate stake in the process, long enough to span the enormous gulf of mistrust that separated the parties, and strong enough to withstand the efforts that would inevitably be made to sabotage it. The existing bridge was badly in need of repair, since both parties had failed to take the concrete actions needed to meet their obligations.

Palestinians living under occupation in Gaza and in the West Bank had neither a State nor a functioning government and looked to the international community for protection, help and hope. If that was not forthcoming, young Palestinians could be attracted by the false promises of those who advocated violence. For their part, Israelis rightly demanded an end to rocket attacks against the towns and kibbutzim of southern Israel, the return of the soldier captured on 25 June, and a Palestinian Authority that accepted basic principles of peace and took credible action to prevent attacks against Israel. Yet, in the absence of a political process, Israelis naturally looked to their own military to deal with security threats. It would be easy for the international community to declare that the parties were not ready for dialogue. Poll after poll showed that people on both sides understood that there was no military solution to the conflict and that a two-State solution could not be achieved through unilateral actions by either side. The Secretary-General said that he believed both Israeli Prime Minister Olmert and Palestinian President Abbas understood those realities and were searching for a way forward. The Quartet, which met on 20 September (see above), encouraged efforts to form a Palestinian national unity government in the hope that its programme would reflect Quartet principles and facilitate early engagement by the international community. During the meeting, the Secretary-General said that he reminded the other Quartet partners that the Quartet itself had to be more active and effective if confidence in the peace process was to be restored. There was a need for all parties to work together in putting in place a credible political process based on dialogue, parallel implementation of obligations, monitoring of performance and clarity as to the end goal.

Bahrain, on behalf of LAS, said that the persistence of the Arab-Israeli conflict had had dire consequences. It was exhausting the resources of the region, creating instability and allowing extremist forces to flourish. The Arab States were deeply concerned over the continuation of the conflict and firmly believed in the urgent need to bring it to a peaceful resolution. It was therefore important to create an environment conducive to peace. Reviving the peace process could mean reinvigorating the road map, which contained the elements for attaining a lasting peace, as well as implementing relevant Council resolutions, the principle of land for peace, and the Arab initiative, while at the same time devising a new and carefully developed mechanism to implement the road map and put the peace process back on track. The main elements of the Arab initiative were: Arab States were prepared to consider the possibility of bringing an end to the Arab-Israeli conflict; enter into a peace agreement between themselves and Israel; establish normal and full relations with Israel in the context of a comprehensive peace, which required full Israeli withdrawal from the occupied Arab territories; arriving at a just and agreed solution to the Palestinian refugee problem, in accordance with General Assembly resolution 194 (III) [YUN 1948-49, p.174]; and acceptance of the establishment of an independent, sovereign Palestinian State, with Jerusalem as its capital. To revive the peace process, the LAS Ministerial Council proposed that the Security Council should agree to: initiate negotiations between the parties, based on agreed terms of reference with a set time frame, assisted by the international community and under the auspices of the Council; request the Secretary-General, in consultation with all parties concerned, including parties to the conflict, the States in the region and the Quartet, to prepare a report on appropriate mechanisms for resuming direct negotiations, including, among other things, options for the format, guarantees, time limits, parameters and role of the Security Council and other third parties, for submission to the Council; and request that the Council remain actively seized of the matter and reconvene at the ministerial level upon submission of the aforementioned report, in order to consider further measures.

Israel said that its Vice-Prime Minister and Minister of Foreign Affairs, Tzipi Livni, had met with Chairman Abbas and both had agreed to re-energize the dialogue and create a permanent channel to advance the process, based on the road map and the principles of peace that had been agreed upon by the parties. There was a common vision for peace that bound together Israelis, moderate Palestinians, other moderates in the region and the international community. Israel was committed to being a partner for peace and to the process of dialogue with all Palestinians who believed in mutual compromise and reconciliation. The road map and the three international (Quartet) conditions (see p. 501) were designed to confront the enemies of peace and ensure that the future Palestinian State envisaged in the two-State solution was not a terror State that perpetuated the conflict, but a peaceful State that ended it. The goal should be to rekindle the road map process, which required genuine consultation, negotiation and agreement between the parties.

Situation in Gaza

Communications. On 3 October [A/61/507-S/2006/798], Israel said that Qassam rockets continued to be fired into Israel by Palestinian terrorists in Gaza on 29 September until the next day, Yom Kippur, the holiest day in the Jewish calendar, which was an affront to Israel's sovereignty. The continuation of Palestinian terror and violence jeopardized the prospects for peace in the region. If such attacks continued, Israel would be forced to exercise its right of self-defence.

In communications received between 4 and 16 October [A/ES-10/358-S/2006/788, A/ES-10/359-S/2006/808, A/ES-10/360-S/2006/818], the Permanent Observer of Palestine complained that IDF had stepped up its military campaign in the Gaza Strip. Those attacks had been accompanied by the announcement by Israeli Defence Minister Amir Peretz, on 15 October, that he had given orders to IDF to intensify their extrajudicial killings and military assaults on the Gaza Strip. Additionally, the Israeli Cabinet alleged receiving reports that "advanced weapons" had entered Gaza and vowed to take action against such a development, which was just another excuse for Israel to continue its incursions. On 13 October, IDF carried out a number of incursions inside Gaza that left 14 Palestinians dead.

Security Council consideration (October). On 19 October [meeting 5552], the Security Council heard a briefing by Special Representative Alvaro de Soto, who said that a deadly crisis continued in Gaza. For many months, Israel had conducted military operations, featuring tank, commando and infantry incursions, targeted killings from the air and firing from the sea, with the stated purpose of preventing the daily Palestinian militant rocket fire into population centres in southern Israel. Those operations intensified after the capture of an Israeli soldier on 25 June and the killing of two others by Palestinian militants who had crossed from Gaza into Israel. Since that time, Israeli operations had killed 295 Palestinians, including 66 children, and injured 1,113 others. However, neither those intensive operations nor the continuing diplomatic efforts had led to the release of the captured soldier or the cessation of the indiscriminate rocket attacks, which had injured 20 Israelis since 25 June. A number of Israeli sources in the IDF and intelligence services claimed that weapons smuggling into Gaza had increased in recent months, including through tunnels under the Philadelphi corridor (a code name used by IDF for the strip of land along the border between Egypt and Israel). IDF forces had recently launched a ground operation along the corridor, and there were reports that it was preparing for a further intensification of its military operations in Gaza. Egyptian officials who were leading diplomatic efforts to resolve the crisis, reported that proposals had been made to address both parties' concerns.

The other crisis that had to be overcome was the political crisis within the PA, which for several months had been governed by a President and a Prime Minister with divergent programmes and polarized by deadly clashes between rival security forces. On 11 September, President Abbas announced that he had agreed with Prime Minister Haniyeh on the political platform of a national unity government. Regrettably, following statements by the Prime Minister calling basic points into question, those efforts did not succeed. UN workers on the ground also reported an increased reliance on traditional law enforcement, as family groupings resorted to self-protection and took justice into their own hands. Members of the civil police had received less than 40 per cent of their salaries since March and only half of them showed up for work. A rolling strike had, in fact, been widespread throughout the public sector since 13 August. As many as three quarters of the medical workers were not turning up for work. In response, UNRWA had to open its medical facilities to non-refugees. The European Commission, in order to mitigate the worst effects of the crisis, renewed and expanded the Temporary International Mechanism, which could neither substitute for the PA nor be sustained financially over time. The continued withholding by Israel of over half a billion dollars of Palestinian value-added tax and customs receipts was the biggest single direct cause of the Palestinian financial crisis.

Another ingredient for restoring hope to the Palestinians would be the implementation of the 2005 Agreement on Movement and Access. The Quartet believed that the Rafah and other crossings had to remain open in accordance with the Agreement. Despite discussions by Quartet members with Israeli authorities on concrete steps to move forward, Israel's policy of near-complete closure of Gaza continued. Meanwhile, obstacles to movement in the West Bank rose by 40 per cent in a year. Settlement activity and the construction of the barrier continued. Prime Minister Olmert announced, in the aftermath of the war in Lebanon, that the plans on which he had been elected, namely, to withdraw Israeli settlements from parts of the West Bank, were on hold. He, however, stated his willingness to meet President Abbas.

The continuing violence in Gaza and southern Israel continued to kill, injure and endanger civilians. Palestinian militant rocket fire should cease, as should Israeli military operations. Both sides should comply with their obligations to respect civilians under international humanitarian law. The virtual siege of Gaza was having a devastating effect on the lives of ordinary Palestinians, stifling hope and fomenting despair, while the continued dangerous launching of rockets at Israeli population centres, such as Sderot, was a source of deep distress for ordinary Israelis. Palestinian institutions continued to be degraded and the suffering of civilians increased, particularly in Gaza. The combination of near total closure of the Gaza Strip, non-payment of public-sector salaries, absence of basic law and order, declining service delivery, continued military strikes by air and land, and the lack of any apparent political horizon was an explosive one—as potentially dangerous for Israel as it was for Palestinians. The route of Palestinian national unity offered the most credible opportunity to stem the slide into anarchy and for the security forces controlled by the presidency and those under the jurisdiction of the Ministry of the Interior to work together to provide basic law and order and prevent attacks against Israel. The United Nations continued to work closely with the Quartet to identify ways to restart the political process between Israel and the Palestinians.

Communications. On 25 October [A/ES-10/362-S/2006/843], the Permanent Observer of Palestine said that, on 19 October, Israeli forces had reoccupied the international Rafah crossing and the Philadelphi route in Gaza for two days. On 23 October, they made an incursion into Beit Hanoun, killing nine Palestinians. On 1 November [A/ES-10/363-S/2006/858], the Permanent Observer accused Israel of further escalating the situation on the ground by expanding the military assault on the Gaza Strip. In Rafah, a large number of armed vehicles, tanks and bulldozers occupied Gaza International Airport on 31 October. He said that official Israeli declarations had also made it clear that the ongoing military assault was the largest of its kind since June. The previous day, Prime Minister Olmert had declared before the Knesset Foreign Affairs and Defence Committee that Israeli forces would expand operations in Gaza. That declaration was endorsed by the Israeli Cabinet. On 3 November [A/ES-10/364-S/2006/862], the Permanent Observer reported that, on 1 November, Israeli forces killed at least 28 Palestinians in the northern Gaza Strip, and on 8 November [A/ES-10/365-S/2006/872], IDF shelled Beit Hanoun, killing another 19 civilians and wounding at least 54.

Security Council consideration (November). At the request of Qatar, on behalf of the Arab Group and LAS [S/2006/868], Azerbaijan, on behalf of the Organization of the Islamic Conference (OIC) [S/2006/869], and Cuba, on behalf of the Non-aligned Movement [S/2006/871], the Security Council, on 9 and 11 November [meetings 5564 and 5565], considered the situation in the Middle East, including the Palestinian question.

Speaking on 9 November, the Assistant Secretary-General for Political Affairs, Angela Kane, said that on 8 November, Israeli forces fired 12 to 15 shells into northwest Beit Hanoun in the northern Gaza Strip, killing at least 18 Palestinians and injuring 55 others. The incident followed a week-long military operation undertaken by IDF in northern Gaza, which, according to IDF, was intended to prevent and disrupt the launching of rockets at Israel and damage terrorist infrastructure in Beit Hanoun. As reported by the World Health Organization, 82 Palestinians were killed and 260 wounded during the incursion. Israel said that Palestinian militants fired 52 rockets and mortars towards Israel between 31 October and 6 November, injuring four Israeli civilians. The United Nations was in contact with the Israeli Government to express concern about the situation in Gaza and continued to call for restraint and the urgent need to protect civilians. The Secretary-General publicly expressed his shock to learn about the 8 November incident and extended his condolences to the families of the victims. Prime Minister Olmert and Defence Minister Peretz expressed their regret over the deaths of Palestinian civilians and announced the suspension of the IDF artillery fire pending an investigation of the circumstances of that incident. Palestinian President Abbas and Prime Minister Haniyeh postponed their talks on the establishment of a new Palestinian government until further notice. Meantime, in Damascus, exiled Hamas leader Khaled Mashaal called for renewed attacks on Israel and urged other militant groups to join the struggle.

Ms. Kane said that the Secretary-General had repeatedly expressed concern about the rising death toll caused by Israeli military operation in Gaza and had reminded both sides of their obligations under international law regarding the protection of civilians. The Palestinians needed a respite from the siege, so that they could see on the horizon a credible, negotiated way out. It was of critical importance that responsible Palestinian forces joined in action to make sure that militant attacks were stopped. It was hoped that the Israelis and the Palestinians would, in the light of the Beit Hanoun tragedy, reflect on the fact that the conflict would not be solved by force and that ways had to be found to bring about negotiations.

On 11 November, a vote was taken on a draft resolution [S/2006/878] submitted by Qatar, by which the Security Council would have, among other measures, condemned the Israeli military operation in the Gaza Strip, including the attack on Beit Hanoun, and the firing of rockets from Gaza into Israel; demanded the immediate cessation of military operations in the Occupied Palestinian Territory and the withdrawal of the Israeli occupying forces from Gaza to positions prior to 28 June 2006; requested the Secretary-General to establish a fact-finding mission on the attack; and called upon the PA to take immediate and sustained action to end the violence, including the firing of rockets on Israeli territory. By a vote of 10 to 1, with 4 abstentions, the draft was not adopted due to the negative vote of a permanent member of the Council.

Speaking before the vote, the United States said that the draft resolution did not display an even-handed characterization of the events in Gaza nor did it advance the cause of Israeli-Palestinian peace. The draft resolution remained an unbalanced text. Its language was biased against Israel and politically motivated. The preambular text equated Israeli military operations, which were legal, with the firing of rockets aimed at civilians into Israel, which was an act of terrorism. Moreover, its characterization of Israeli military actions as excessive and disproportionate constituted a legal judgment that the Council would be ill-advised to make. In addition, the draft resolution called for the establishment of a fact-finding mission, which was unnecessary and would do nothing to improve the situation on the ground. The United States was concerned that there was no reference to terrorism nor any condemnation of the Hamas leadership's statement that Palestinians should resume terror attacks, or of the Hamas military wing's calls to Muslims worldwide to strike American targets.

Speaking after the vote, Qatar said it had submitted a balanced draft resolution, reflecting the views of the majority of Council members, but the Council was nonetheless unable to adopt that text, for reasons which were familiar to all. The Council's failure to do its duty with respect to the deteriorating situation in the occupied Palestinian territories by putting an end to Israeli aggression would lead to the continuation of that aggression and the cycle of violence.

Communications. On 14 November [A/61/574-S/2006/887], Israel said that between 7 and 13 November, 42 mortars and Qassam rockets were fired at Israel by Palestinian terrorists from Gaza, injuring five Israeli civilians. On 15 November [A/61/578-S/2006/891], Israel said that 14 more Qassam rockets were launched by Palestinian terrorists in Gaza, killing one and wounding two other Israelis.

Emergency special session

In accordance with General Assembly resolution ES-10/15 [YUN 2004, p. 465] and at the requests of Qatar [A/ES-10/366], on behalf of LAS and in its capacity as Chairman of the Arab Group, and Cuba [A/ES-10/367], in its capacity as Chairman of the Coordinating Bureau of the Non-Aligned Movement and on behalf of its States members, the tenth emergency special session of the Assembly resumed on 17 November to discuss the "Illegal Israeli actions in occupied East Jerusalem and the rest of the Occupied Palestinian Territory". The session was first convened in April 1997 [YUN 1997, p. 394] and resumed in July and November of that year, then in March 1998 [YUN 1998, p. 425], February 1999 [YUN 1999, p. 402], October 2000 [YUN 2000, p. 421], December 2001 [YUN 2001, p. 414], May 2002 [YUN 2002, p. 428] and in August [ibid., p. 435], September 2003 [YUN 2003, p. 472] and resumed in October [ibid., p. 476] and December [ibid., p. 479], and July 2004 [YUN 2004, p. 465].

The Assembly had before it the draft resolution [A/ES-10/L.19 & Add.1] on illegal Israeli actions. Opening the debate, the Assembly President said that the meeting was held due to the deteriorating situation in the Middle East and the need to establish a just, comprehensive and lasting peace in the region. The situation in the occupied Palestinian territories was deteriorating daily, creating serious humanitarian problems and further exacerbating the already serious political problems. The Assembly had to condemn without distinction the killing of Palestinians and Israeli civilians because arbitrary killings were contrary to international humanitarian law and established legal norms. The situation called for initiatives and solutions to find a genuine resolution to the crisis, beginning with the end to the cycle of violence and a return to the negotiating table.

The Permanent Observer of Palestine said that, through the excessive and indiscriminate use of force, Israel had perpetrated war crimes against Palestinian civilians, such as the killing of 82 civilians near Beit Hanoun on 8 November, in the course of a six-day campaign of aggression. The Security Council had failed to uphold its responsibility due to the negative vote of one of its permanent members on a balanced draft resolution that condemned that act and demanded an investigation into its circumstances. The Assembly resumed its tenth emergency special session in a last-resort effort to defend the principles on which the United Nations was founded and to allow Member States to do collectively what the Council was incapable of doing. Serious and firm action was required, especially with regard to the massacre in Beit Hanoun, to put an end to the Israeli campaign, which intended to destroy an entire people and any hope of reviving the peace process. The Palestinians could not accept Israel's argument that the killings at Beit Hanoun were unintentional. Furthermore, an apology that held the victim responsible for his own death was unacceptable. The perpetrators of those acts should be brought to justice.

Israel said that the real emergency was not in the General Assembly Hall but in Israeli cities like Sderot and Ashkelon, where residents were pounded daily by Qassam rockets. It was in Gaza, where Palestinian terrorists continued to plan and carry out terror attacks. Ever since Israel left Gaza in 2005, the Palestinians had turned Gaza into a staging ground for a war of terror against Israel. In the past year, over 1,000 rockets were fired from Gaza into Israel. Israel responded in self-defence, but during one of its operations, on 8 November, a tragic incident occurred that it deeply regretted. Israel had launched a full investigation and offered medical and other assistance to the injured, in coordination with Palestinian agencies. However, Israel emphasized that, though Palestinians might have been killed by Israeli shells, they were the victims of the PA, which was directly responsible for their deaths and the tragedy of its own people. Convening the emergency special session was yet another example of Member States' misusing and abusing the Assembly's procedures, placing procedure before substance in a not-so-subtle attempt to circumvent the Security Council, and raising questions about the UN role as an honest broker for peace. Contrary to perception, the Council did not fail to act. If there was any failure, it was of the resolutions, both in the Council and the Assembly, to aptly address the origins of the situation. It was also the failure to recognize that Israel's response was a legitimate one, that the source of the conflict was Palestinian terror and that Israel had a right to self-defence, as well as to recognize that the Palestinians could not demand their national rights without fulfilling their national responsibilities. Direct negotiations, based on mutual recognition of rights and responsibilities of both sides, constituted the only mechanism that would bring benefit and progress to the Israelis and the Palestinians. That mechanism was the road map, accepted by Israel and endorsed by the international community.

The United States said that once again the Assembly, meeting in emergency special session, was presented with a one-sided and unbalanced draft resolution addressing the Israel-Palestinian conflict. That type of text served only to exacerbate tensions by serving the interests of elements hostile to Israel's inalienable and recognized right to exist. The challenge of advancing towards the vision of two States—Israel and Palestine—living side by side in peace and security required determined efforts by the parties and the constructive support of countries in the region and the international community. The United Nations was ill-served when its Member States sought to transform the Organization into a forum that was little more than a self-serving and polemical attack against Israel or the United States.

Egypt said that the Assembly could no longer continue to close its eyes to repeated Israeli attacks on the occupied Palestinian territories. It was unacceptable to interpret the legitimate right to self-defence as the right to kill innocent people and to claim that the Beit Hanoun incident was a tactical error. Egypt regretted the use of the veto against two successive Council draft resolutions aimed at protecting the human rights of Palestinians against Israeli aggression. The Assembly, as the principal organ responsible for the protection of human rights, had to intervene through practical measures to ensure that respect and to guarantee that such acts of aggression would not be repeated in the future.

GENERAL ASSEMBLY ACTION

On 17 November [meeting 29], the General Assembly adopted **resolution ES-10/16** [draft: A/ES-10/L.19 & Add.1, as orally revised] by recorded vote (156-7-6) [agenda item 5].

Illegal Israeli actions in Occupied East Jerusalem and the rest of the Occupied Palestinian Territory

The General Assembly,

Recalling its relevant resolutions, including resolutions of the tenth emergency special session,

Reaffirming Security Council resolutions 242(1967) of 22 November 1967, 338(1973) of 22 October 1973, 446(1979) of 22 March 1979, 1322(2000) of 7 October 2000, 1397(2002) of 12 March 2002, 1402(2002) of 30 March 2002, 1403(2002) of 4 April 2002, 1405(2002) of 19 April 2002, 1435(2002) of 24 September 2002, 1515(2003) of 19 November 2003 and 1544(2004) of 19 May 2004,

Reaffirming also the applicability of the rules and principles of international law, including humanitarian and human rights laws, in particular the Geneva Convention relative to the Protection of Civilian Persons in Time of War, of 12 August 1949, to the Occupied Palestinian Territory, including East Jerusalem,

Expressing grave concern at the continued deterioration of the situation on the ground in the Palestinian Territory occupied by Israel since 1967 during the recent period, particularly as a result of the use of force by Israel, the occupying Power, which has caused extensive loss of civilian Palestinian life and injuries, including among children and women,

Deeply deploring the military actions being carried out by Israel, the occupying Power, in the Gaza Strip, which have caused loss of life and extensive destruction of Palestinian property and vital infrastructure,

Deeply deploring also the killing of many Palestinian civilians, including children and women, by Israel, the occupying Power, that took place in Beit Hanoun on 8 November 2006,

Deeply deploring further the firing of rockets from Gaza into Israel,

Emphasizing the importance of the safety and well-being of all civilians and condemning all attacks against civilians on both sides, and stressing that the parties must respect their obligations, including by putting an end to violence,

1. *Calls upon* Israel, the occupying Power, to immediately cease its military operations that endanger the Palestinian civilian population in the Occupied Palestinian Territory, including East Jerusalem, and to immediately withdraw its forces from within the Gaza Strip to positions held prior to 28 June 2006;

2. *Calls for* the immediate cessation of military operations and all acts of violence, terror, provocation, incitement and destruction between the Israeli and Palestinian sides, including extrajudicial executions, bombardment against civilian areas, air raids and the firing of rockets, as was agreed in the Sharm el Sheikh understandings of 8 February 2005;

3. *Requests* the Secretary-General to establish a fact-finding mission on the attack that took place in Beit Hanoun on 8 November 2006 and to report thereon to the General Assembly within thirty days;

4. *Calls upon* Israel, the occupying Power, to scrupulously abide by its obligations and responsibilities under the Geneva Convention relative to the Protection of Civilian Persons in Time of War, of 12 August 1949, in the Occupied Palestinian Territory, including East Jerusalem;

5. *Calls upon* the Palestinian Authority to take immediate and sustained action to bring an end to violence, including the firing of rockets on Israeli territory;

6. *Emphasizes* the need to preserve Palestinian institutions, infrastructure and properties;

7. *Expresses grave concern* about the dire humanitarian situation of the Palestinian people, and calls for the continued provision of emergency assistance to them;

8. *Emphasizes* the urgency of ensuring that medical and humanitarian organizations are granted unhindered access to the Palestinian civilian population at all times and of allowing the severely injured a speedy exit outside the Occupied Palestinian Territory for needed treatment, and emphasizes also the importance of the implementation of the Agreement of Movement and Access of November 2005;

9. *Calls upon* the Quartet, together with the international community, to take immediate steps to stabilize the situation and restart the peace process, including through the possible establishment of an international mechanism for the protection of civilian populations;

10. *Calls upon* the parties, with the support of the international community, to take immediate steps, including confidence-building measures, aimed at the early resumption of direct peace negotiations towards the conclusion of a final peaceful settlement;

11. *Stresses* the importance of and the need to achieve a just, comprehensive, and lasting peace in the Middle East, based on all relevant Security Council resolutions, including resolutions 242(1967), 338(1973), 1397(2002) and 1515(2003), the Madrid terms of reference, the principle of land for peace, the Arab Peace Initiative adopted by the League of Arab States at its fourteenth session, held in Beirut on 27 and 28 March 2002, and the road map;

12. *Requests* the Secretary-General to report to the General Assembly on the implementation of the present resolution in a timely manner;

13. *Decides* to adjourn the tenth emergency special session temporarily and to authorize the President of the General Assembly at its most recent session to resume its meeting upon request from Member States.

RECORDED VOTE ON RESOLUTION ES-10/16:

In favour: Afghanistan, Albania, Algeria, Andorra, Antigua and Barbuda, Argentina, Armenia, Austria, Azerbaijan, Bahamas, Bahrain, Bangladesh, Barbados, Belarus, Belgium, Belize, Benin, Bhutan, Bolivia, Bosnia and Herzegovina, Botswana, Brazil, Brunei Darussalam, Bulgaria, Burkina Faso, Cambodia, Cape Verde, Central African Republic, Chile, China, Colombia, Comoros, Congo, Costa Rica, Croatia, Cuba, Cyprus, Czech Republic, Democratic People's Republic of Korea, Denmark, Djibouti, Dominica, Ecuador, Egypt, El Salvador, Eritrea, Estonia, Ethiopia, Finland, France, Gabon, Gambia, Georgia, Germany, Ghana, Greece, Guatemala, Guinea, Guinea-Bissau, Guyana, Haiti, Hungary, Iceland, India, Indonesia, Iran, Iraq, Ireland, Italy, Jamaica, Japan, Jordan, Kazakhstan, Kenya, Kuwait, Kyrgyzstan, Lao People's Democratic Republic, Latvia, Lebanon, Lesotho, Libyan Arab Jamahiriya, Liechtenstein, Lithuania, Luxembourg, Malawi, Malaysia, Maldives, Mali, Malta, Mauritania, Mauritius, Mexico, Moldova, Monaco, Mongolia, Montenegro, Morocco, Mozambique, Myanmar, Namibia, Nepal, Netherlands, New Zealand, Niger, Nigeria, Norway, Oman, Pakistan, Panama, Paraguay, Peru, Philippines, Poland, Portugal, Qatar, Republic of Korea, Romania, Russian Federation, Saint Lucia, San Marino, Saudi Arabia, Senegal, Serbia, Sierra Leone, Singapore, Slovakia, Slovenia, Solomon Islands, Somalia, South Africa, Spain, Sudan, Suriname, Swaziland, Sweden, Switzerland, Syrian Arab Republic, Tajikistan, Thailand, The former Yugoslav Republic of Macedonia, Timor-Leste, Togo, Trinidad and Tobago, Tunisia, Turkey, Ukraine, United Arab Emirates, United Kingdom, United Republic of Tanzania, Uruguay, Uzbekistan, Venezuela, Viet Nam, Yemen, Zambia, Zimbabwe.

Against: Australia, Israel, Marshall Islands, Micronesia, Nauru, Palau, United States.

Abstaining: Canada, Côte d'Ivoire, Papua New Guinea, Tonga, Tuvalu, Vanuatu.

On 21 December [A/ES-10/374], pursuant to Assembly resolution ES-10/16 (see above), the Secretary-General reported on his efforts to establish a fact-finding mission on the attack that took place in Beit Hanoun on 8 November. He said that, on 1 December, he designated Staffan de Mistura, Director of the United Nations System Staff College, to lead the mission, which was to be supported by a small team, as well as by security and general support staff. The Secretary-General instructed the team to gather no later than 13 December and carry out its assignment in accordance with the terms of reference that he had approved. The Secretariat accordingly informed the Permanent Missions of Israel and Palestine on 1 and 5 December, respectively, and requested that the Israeli Government and the PA extend their cooperation to the mission. The PA agreed to extend its cooperation, but, as at 22 December, Israel had not indicated whether it would do so. For that reason, the Secretary-General regretted that he was unable to dispatch the fact-finding mission and report to the Assembly about the events that occurred in Beit Hanoun.

Further developments

Security Council consideration (November). On 21 November [meeting 5568], the Security Council heard a briefing by Under-Secretary-General for Political Affairs, Ibrahim Gambari, who said that there had been intense confrontations between IDF and Palestinian militants, as the IDF military operation in Gaza entered its sixth month. The operation was aimed at curbing the launching of rockets by Palestinian militants against Israeli civilian targets. In the West Bank and Gaza, a combined total of at least 128 Palestinians were killed and over 380 injured during the past month. One Israeli soldier and one civilian were killed, and many injuries were reported. Palestinian militants fired over 200 rockets and mortars into the western Negev region, causing one death, multiple injuries and significant damage. The town of Sderot, in particular, had borne the brunt of those indiscriminate attacks. Israel also expressed concern that weapons and explosives continued to be smuggled into Gaza, enabling militants to continue and possibly intensify their attacks against Israeli targets.

Palestinian President Abbas continued negotiations on a national unity government with Hamas and other Palestinian factions, and there appeared to be an understanding in principle on the elements for the composition and programme of a new government. Despite the reported progress, the announcement of a full agreement was not imminent, as negotiations encompassed a number of outstanding issues, including the release of the Israeli soldier who remained captive in Gaza.

On the Israeli side, implementation of the 2005 Agreement on Movement and Access had been limited. Despite the stationing of EU observers, the Rafah crossing between Gaza and Egypt had been open only 58 per cent of the scheduled hours, and the Karni crossing only 44 per cent. Export targets for Gaza, established under the Agreement, were also not met, with an average of only 18 truckloads of produce per day being allowed through, instead of the envisaged 150. No Palestinian worker had been allowed to cross at Erez for jobs in Israel since March, and no progress was reported on plans to rebuild the seaport and airport. The Israeli Government had still not presented its plan to reduce closure measures inside the West Bank. Despite the stated intention of the Government to evacuate outposts in accordance with the road map, no action was taken in that regard, which continued to have a direct and far-reaching impact on movement and access, since many of the impediments to Palestinian movement in the West Bank existed primarily to provide security for illegal settlements, as opposed to monitoring movement into Israel proper. Israel also continued construction of the barrier. The Secretary-General's report on the establishment of a register of damage related to Israel's construction of the wall was submitted to the General Assembly on 17 October (see p. 528). The report presented the institutional framework required for the register, the establishment of which was requested by the Assembly.

In another briefing to the Council [meeting 5624], Mr. Gambari said that the ceasefire agreed upon by Prime Minister Olmert and PA President Abbas on 26 November in Gaza remained in place, although, according to Israeli officials, militants fired more than 104 rockets into southern Israel since that date. In the face of those attacks, the Israeli Government showed considerable restraint, and despite its flaws, the ceasefire did reduce violence. Both leaders agreed on 23 December to revive the joint committees established in the Sharm el-Sheikh understandings and resume the work of the quadripartite security committee between Israel, the PA, Egypt and the United States. Prime Minister Olmert undertook to transfer to the Office of President Abbas $100 million of the more than $500 million of Palestinian revenues being withheld. He also agreed to intensify efforts to upgrade the crossings between the Gaza Strip and Israel, ease procedures at a number of checkpoints in the West Bank and remove a number of roadblocks.

Communications. On 22 November [A/61/594-S/2006/916] and 5 December [A/61/608-S/2006/941], Israel said that from 26 November to 4 December, 15 Qassam rockets were fired by Palestinians from Gaza at Israeli communities. Those attacks came after the 26 November ceasefire agreement.

Report of Secretary-General (December). On 11 December [S/2006/956], the Secretary-General submitted his last report on the Middle East as his term in office was to end. During the past ten years, having focused on developments, the current report would focus on the attempts by the international community and the parties to reach a negotiated political solution to an enduring conflict. He stressed that the Middle East faced grim prospects and was more complex, fragile and dangerous than it had been for many years. The various unresolved but increasingly interconnected conflicts in the region both fed and fed off a growing sense of estrangement between peoples of different faiths, with consequences throughout the world. Overall, the instability that prevailed in the Middle East was the greatest regional challenge to international peace and security and needed to be addressed far more thoroughly than it had been to date.

The failure to achieve a just and comprehensive solution to the Arab-Israeli conflict remained the major underlying source of frustration and instability in the region. Other recent conflicts were shaped by that failure, although they inevitably took on a dynamic of their own. The search for stability in Iraq, Lebanon and elsewhere would be greatly served by a concerted effort to address the legitimate aspirations of Israelis, Palestinians, Syrians and Lebanese to achieve two independent and secure States of Israel and Palestine; an end to the occupation of Arab land both in the Occupied Palestinian Territory and the Golan Heights; and the comprehensive, just and lasting peace in the Middle East referred to in Security Council resolution 1701(2006) (see p. 583) and many other resolutions. A regional approach was needed to resolve the various crises and conflicts in the region, not least because progress in each arena was to a large extent dependent on progress in others.

The Secretary-General analysed the post-Oslo era, as well as the Quartet and road map process. Turning to the current situation, he noted that efforts to form a Palestinian national unity government appeared to have stalled. However, a precarious and imperfect ceasefire agreed upon by both sides on 26 November was in place in Gaza, and tentative feelers were put out regarding the possibility of resuming the Israeli-Palestinian dialogue. Negotiations under Egyptian auspices for the release of the Israeli soldier were continuing. Israel's right to self-defence had to be carried out in accordance with international law. The repeated phenomenon of large numbers of civilian casualties from Israeli military operations was not acceptable. Given the complexity of the situation, the continuing high levels of tension and the steep decline in Palestinian living standards since 2000, the UN presence on the ground continued to be of key importance, especially its assistance to meet the basic needs of Palestinians throughout the region. The Secretary-General had also strengthened the Office of the Special Coordinator to consolidate UN leadership on aid policy and common operational issues.

The Secretary-General observed that an enormous responsibility rested on the United Nations to contribute to the resolution of the Arab-Israeli conflict. However, that resolution was difficult to achieve because one side perceived itself as being singled out for unfair criticism, while the other regarded the Organization as ineffective in ensuring compliance with its resolutions. Accusations of double standards were regularly made in both directions, and each with some justification. The Secretary-General expressed the view that until Member States matched their concerns with a concerted effort to empower the United Nations to make a strategic difference, other forums would be sought to ensure effective multilateral engagement on the conflict. In fact, the formation of the Quartet embodied that conviction. However, the divisions which often paralysed the United Nations itself had started to inhibit the capacity of the Quartet to play a beneficial role, which it could do were it to act with determination and consistency. There was, thus, a sense of increased frustration at the Quartet's limited effectiveness, matched by the apparent lack of any alternative mechanism.

The Quartet retained its relevance because of its combination of legitimacy, political strength and economic influence. As for the road map, it was still the reference point around which any effort to re-energize a political effort on the Israeli-Palestinian track should be centred. It remained the only document of recent years accepted—albeit with substantial reservations by Israel—by Palestinian and Israeli leaderships alike, the Arab States and the Security Council. To restore a sense of faith in the practicability of the road map, it was crucial for Quartet members to act together to create the conditions for re-energizing the Israeli-Palestinian peace process. The Quartet had also to find a way to institutionalize its consultations with relevant regional partners and engage the parties directly in its deliberations. Under the revitalized stewardship of the Quartet, it should be possible to re-examine the road map, with a view to restarting its basic goals, principles and "destination", identifying priority action relating to security, as well as economic, humanitarian and institution-building areas, addressing the political issues and negotiations, and updating its timetable. The Quartet should provide greater clarity regarding the parameters of an end-game deal, tackle openly the road map's premise of parallelism and monitoring, and be more open to new ideas and initiatives, with an even-handed and proactive stance.

Several political issues needed to be addressed, including the dilemma posed by Hamas, in order to stem the growing trend towards the disintegration of Palestinian society, renew support for Palestinian institutions, promote efforts to achieve unity among Palestinian factions on basic principles of the peace process and persuade Israel not to pursue any policy that damaged Palestinian institutions. Forging an internal Palestinian consensus around a two-State solution should be seen as a process rather than an event, one that should be encouraged and nurtured. An immediate priority was to devise new ways of protecting Palestinian and Israeli civilians; the monitoring foreseen in the road map could help to ensure far greater accountability. The international community had to find constructive responses to the challenge posed by democratic choices made by the peoples of the region. Victorious parties, even radical ones, needed to acknowledge that with power came responsibilities, including acceptance that the legitimacy and rights of others should be respected and that decisions and agreements by previous Governments could not be ignored without serious consequences.

The Secretary-General urged the Quartet and the Security Council to explore the feasibility of consolidating the current Gaza ceasefire within an international framework. The parameters of the political framework for a permanent solution were clear, but the political will to advance it was not sufficient. In order to halt the violence and open a space for negotiations, a stronger international role was required. Elements for that role could include: consolidating the Gaza ceasefire by working with the parties to define its parameters and rules; extending the ceasefire to the West Bank; promoting unconditional and open-ended talks between the Israeli Prime Minister and the PA President; securing the parties agreement to the deployment of international observers to monitor the ceasefire; establishing with the parties a mechanism for protecting civilians; monitoring the actions of the parties to implement existing commitments and agreements and ensure that the results of monitoring were systematically acted upon; and ensuring that the political framework for negotiations was updated and credible, including clear parameters for the settlement of final status issues, so that the end goal of the process was visible to all concerned. In that regard, the Secretary-General urged members of the Council and the Quartet to consider viable options that would be acceptable to both parties, as an active and systematic third party role was indispensable. Israel had traditionally been suspicious of such roles. However, the record showed that an international presence on the ground had been a key feature of nearly every modus vivendi reached between Israel and its adversaries. The Israeli-Syrian border would not be stable without the peacekeepers of the United Nations Disengagement Observer Force. The situation in Hebron would be even worse without the temporary international presence there. The full disengagement from Gaza would not have been achieved had the EU not stepped forward to monitor the Rafah crossing. The idea of convening an international conference along the lines of the 1991 Madrid conference [YUN 1991, p. 223] should be explored, so that the full regional dimension of the conflict could be addressed. However, the conditions had to be right and the foundations for trust and successful negotiations laid. The Secretary-General expressed deep personal regret that peace in the Middle East had not been achieved.

Security Council consideration (December). On 12 December [meeting 5584], the Security Council discussed the situation in the Middle East, and in particular the Secretary-General's 11 December report (see above).

The Secretary-General said that the situation in the Middle East was more complex, fragile and dangerous than it had been for a very long time. Mistrust between Israelis and Palestinians had reached new heights. The Gaza Strip had become a cauldron of deepening poverty and frustration, despite the withdrawal of Israeli troops and settlements in 2005. In the West Bank also the situation was dire. Settlement activity and construction of the barrier continued, while Israeli obstacles impeded Palestinian movement throughout the area. The PA, paralysed by a debilitating political and financial crisis, was no longer able to provide security or basic services. Israelis, for their part, continued to live in fear of terrorism. They were dismayed by the inadequacy of Palestinian efforts to halt rocket attacks into southern Israel and were alarmed by a Hamas-led Government, which refused to renounce violence and had rejected the basic tenets of the approach to the conflict consistently favoured by a majority of Palestinians. The various conflicts and crises in the region had become evermore intertwined, affecting and shaping each other, thereby making conflict resolution and crisis management more difficult. The international community had to develop a new understanding of the uncertainty engulfing the Middle East and to shoulder full responsibility for resolving it and stabilizing the region.

The Secretary-General offered some thoughts on what the parties themselves, including the Quartet, the Security Council and other UN bodies, might do differently in search for peace, in particular between Israelis and Palestinians, which while no panacea would go a long way toward defusing tensions throughout the region. One of the most frustrating aspects of the Israeli-Palestinian conflict was the apparent inability of many people on both sides to understand the position of the other and the unwillingness of some even to try. It was understandable that Israel and its supporters should seek to ensure its security by persuading Palestinians, Arabs and Muslims to alter their attitude and behaviour towards Israel. However, they were not likely to succeed unless they themselves grasped and acknowledged the fundamental Palestinian grievance, namely, that the establishment of the State of Israel involved the dispossession of hundreds of thousands of Palestinian families, turning them into refugees, and followed 19 years later by a military occupation that brought hundreds of thousands more Palestinians under Israeli rule. Israel was justifiably proud of its democracy and efforts to build a society based on respect for the rule of law, but that democracy could thrive only if the occupation ended. Yet, thousands of Israelis still lived in territories occupied in 1967, and over a thousand more were added every month. As Palestinians watched that activity, they also saw a barrier being built through their land, in contravention of the advisory opinion of the International Court of Justice [YUN 2004, p. 1272], and more than 500 checkpoints erected to control their movement, as well as the heavy IDF presence. Their despair at the occupation only grew, as did their determination to resist it. As a result, some tended to invest much of their trust in those who pursued the armed struggle rather than a peace process that did not seem to yield the coveted goal of an independent State. The Secretary-General said that he agreed with Israel and its supporters that there was a moral and legal difference between terrorists who deliberately targeted civilians and regular soldiers who, in the course of military operations, unintentionally killed or wounded civilians. Yet, the larger the number of civilian casualties during those operations and the more perfunctory the precautions taken to avoid such losses, the more that difference was diminished. The use of military force in densely populated civilian areas produced more death, destruction, recrimination and vengeance, and did little to achieve the desired goal of stopping terrorist attacks. It was understandable also to support the Palestinian people, who had suffered so much, but they and their supporters would never be truly effective if they focused solely on Israel's transgressions, without conceding any justice or legitimacy to Israel's own concerns, and without being willing to admit that Israel's opponents had themselves committed appalling and inexcusable crimes.

The Secretary-General noted that those who complained that the Security Council was guilty of a double standard—applying sanctions to Arab and Muslim Governments, but not to Israel—should be cautious that they themselves did not apply double standards, by holding Israel to a standard of behaviour that they were unwilling to apply to other States, to Israel's adversaries or to themselves. He also said that some might have felt satisfaction at repeatedly passing General Assembly resolutions or holding conferences that condemned Israel's behaviour, but one should also ask whether such steps brought any tangible relief or benefit to the Palestinians. There had been decades of resolutions and a proliferation of special committees, sessions and Secretariat divisions and units. The Secretary-General asked whether any of that had an effect on Israel's policies, other than to strengthen the belief in Israel and among many of its supporters that the United Nations was too one-sided to be allowed a significant role in the Middle East peace process. Even worse, some of the rhetoric used in connection with the issue implied a refusal to concede the very legitimacy of Israel's existence, let alone the validity of its security concerns. The international community could never forget that Jews had very good historical reasons for taking seriously any threat to Israel's existence. Israelis were often confronted with words and actions that seemed to confirm their fear that the goal of their adversaries was to extinguish their existence as a State and as a people. Therefore, those who wanted to be heard on Palestine should not deny or minimize Israel's history or the connection of Jews with their historic homeland. Rather, they should acknowledge Israel's security concerns and make clear that their criticism was rooted, not in hatred or intolerance, but in a desire for justice, self-determination and peaceful coexistence. Perhaps the greatest irony in that sad story was that there was no serious question about the broad outline of a final settlement.

The parties themselves had come close to bridging almost all of the gaps between them. There was every reason for them to try again, with principled, concerted help from the international community. The road would be long and much trust would have to be rebuilt, but the end results should be: two States, Israel and Palestine, within secure, recognized and negotiated boundaries based on those set on 4 June 1967; a broader peace encompassing Israel's other neighbours, namely Lebanon and Syria; normal diplomatic and economic relations; arrangements that would allow Israel and Palestine to establish their internationally recognized capitals in Jerusalem and ensure access for people of all faiths to their holy places; and a solution that respected the rights of Palestinian refugees and was consistent with the two-State solution and with the character of the States in the region. The road map, endorsed by the Council in resolution 1515(2003) [YUN 2003, p. 483], was still the reference point for re-energizing a political effort. Its sponsor, the Quartet, retained its validity because of its singular combination of legitimacy, political strength, and financial and economic clout. However, it should do more to restore faith in its own seriousness and effectiveness, as well as in the road map's practicability, and create the conditions for resuming a viable peace process. Tensions in the region were near the breaking point, as extremism and populism were leaving less political space for moderates, including those States that had reached peace agreements with Israel. Welcomed moves towards democracy, such as elections, had simultaneously posed a quandary in bringing to parties, individuals and movements that opposed the basis of peacemaking approaches. The opportunity for negotiating a two-State solution would last for only so long.

SECURITY COUNCIL ACTION

On 12 December [meeting 5584], following consultations among Security Council members, the President made statement **S/PRST/2006/51** on behalf of the Council:

> The Security Council expresses its deep concern over the situation in the Middle East, with its serious ramifications for peace and security, and underlines the need to intensify efforts to achieve a just, lasting and comprehensive peace in the region.
>
> The Council stresses that there can be no military solution to the problems of the region and that negotiation is the only viable way to bring peace and prosperity to peoples throughout the Middle East.
>
> The Council stresses that the parties must respect their obligations under previous agreements, including by putting an end to violence and all aspects of terrorism.
>
> The Council expresses grave concern over the deteriorating humanitarian situation and calls for the provision of emergency assistance to the Palestinian people through the Temporary International Mechanism, international organizations and other official channels.
>
> The Council welcomes the agreement between Israeli Prime Minister Ehud Olmert and Palestinian Authority President Mahmoud Abbas to establish a mutual ceasefire in Gaza.
>
> The Council welcomes the steps taken by both sides to maintain the ceasefire and expresses its hope that it will lead to a sustained period of calm. It calls upon both sides, therefore, to avoid any actions which could jeopardize further progress. It reiterates its call for an end to all aspects of terrorism and violence as set out in previous statements and resolutions.
>
> The Council is mindful of the need to encourage steps to increase confidence in the peace process.
>
> The Council reiterates its call for the Palestinian Authority Government to accept the three Quartet principles.
>
> The Council reaffirms its profound attachment to the vision of two democratic States, Israel and Palestine, living side by side in peace and security, as envisaged in the Road Map.
>
> The Council underlines that action by the international community cannot be a substitute for determined measures by the parties themselves.
>
> The Council encourages the parties to engage in direct negotiations.
>
> The Council reaffirms the vital role of the Quartet and looks forward to its continued active engagement.
>
> The Council reiterates the importance of, and the need to achieve a just, comprehensive and lasting peace in the Middle East, based on all its relevant resolutions, including resolutions 242(1967), 338(1973) and 1515(2003), the Madrid terms of reference and the principle of land for peace.

Communication (12 December). On 12 December [A/ES-10/373-S/2006/1016], the Permanent Observer of Palestine said that in November alone, IDF killed more than 100 Palestinians, 35 of them children.

Resumed emergency special session

In accordance with General Assembly resolution ES-10/16 (see p. 522) and at the request of Qatar [A/ES-10/370], in its capacity as Chairman of the Arab Group and on behalf of the States members of LAS, Cuba [A/ES-10/371], in its capacity as Chair of the Coordinating Bureau of the Non-Aligned Movement, and Azerbaijan [A/ES-10/372], in its capacity as Chairman of the Organization of the Islamic Conference (OIC) Group, the tenth emergency special session of the Assembly resumed on 15 December. It discussed the Secretary-General's report, prepared pursuant to Assembly resolution ES-10/15, concerning the register of damage caused by Israel's construction of the wall in the Occupied Palestinian Territory, including East Jerusalem (see below); a draft resolution [A/ES-10/L.20] on the establishment of the United Nations register of damage; and the report of the Fifth (Administrative and Budgetary) Committee [A/61/625].

Eastablishment of UN register of damage

In an October report [A/ES-10/361], submitted pursuant to General Assembly resolution ES-10/15 [YUN 2004, p. 465], the Secretary-General described the institutional framework for the establishment of a register of damage caused to all natural or legal persons concerned, in connection with paragraphs 152 and 153 of the advisory opinion of the International Court of Justice of 9 July 2004 [ibid.] on the Legal Consequences of the Construction of a Wall in the Occupied Palestinian Territory, including in and around East Jerusalem.

The Assembly reconvened the emergency special session on 15 December to consider the issue.

GENERAL ASSEMBLY ACTION

On 15 December [meeting 31], the General Assembly adopted **resolution ES-10/17** [draft: A/ES-10/L.20/Rev.1 as orally revised] by recorded vote (162-7-7) [agenda item 5].

Establishment of the United Nations Register of Damage Caused by the Construction of the Wall in the Occupied Palestinian Territory

The General Assembly,

Guided by the principles enshrined in the Charter of the United Nations and the rules and principles of international law, including international humanitarian law and human rights law,

Reaffirming the permanent responsibility of the United Nations towards the question of Palestine until it is resolved in all its aspects in a satisfactory manner on the basis of international legitimacy,

Recalling the relevant resolutions of the Security Council,

Recalling also its relevant resolutions, including the resolutions of its tenth emergency special session on illegal Israeli actions in Occupied East Jerusalem and the rest of the Occupied Palestinian Territory,

Recalling further the advisory opinion rendered on 9 July 2004 by the International Court of Justice on the *Legal Consequences of the Construction of a Wall in the Occupied Palestinian Territory*, and recalling in particular the Court's reply to the question put forth by the General Assembly in resolution ES-10/14 of 8 December 2003, as set forth in the *dispositif* of the advisory opinion,

Recalling in this regard the Court's conclusion that, inter alia, "Israel is under an obligation to make reparation for all damage caused by the construction of the wall in the Occupied Palestinian Territory, including in and around East Jerusalem",

Reaffirming its resolution ES-10/15 of 20 July 2004 entitled "Advisory opinion of the International Court of Justice on the legal consequences of the construction of a wall in the Occupied Palestinian Territory, including in and around East Jerusalem",

Recalling the request made in resolution ES-10/15 for the Secretary-General to establish a register of damage caused to all natural or legal persons concerned in connection with paragraphs 152 and 153 of the advisory opinion,

Noting in this connection the Court's conclusion whereby, inter alia: Israel is accordingly under an obligation to return the land, orchards, olive groves and other immovable property seized from any natural or legal person for purposes of construction of the wall in the Occupied Palestinian Territory. In the event that such restitution should prove to be materially impossible, Israel has an obligation to compensate the persons in question for the damage suffered. The Court considers that Israel also has an obligation to compensate, in accordance with the applicable rules of international law, all natural or legal persons having suffered any form of material damage as a result of the wall's construction,

Deploring the continuing construction, contrary to international law, by Israel, the occupying Power, of the wall in the Occupied Palestinian Territory, including in and around East Jerusalem, against the conclusions of the International Court of Justice in its advisory opinion of 9 July 2004 and resolution ES-10/15 and in breach of the applicable rules and principles of international law,

Recognizing the necessity of accurately documenting the damage caused by the construction of the wall for the purpose of fulfilling the obligation to make the above-mentioned reparations, including restitution and compensation, in accordance with the rules and principles of international law, and noting that the act of registration of damage, as such, does not entail, at this stage, an evaluation or assessment of the loss or damage caused by the construction of the wall,

Taking note with appreciation of the report of the Secretary-General of 17 October 2006 pursuant to resolution ES-10/15,

1. *Reaffirms* its resolution ES-10/15 entitled "Advisory opinion of the International Court of Justice on the legal consequences of the construction of a wall in the Occupied Palestinian Territory, including in and around East Jerusalem", and reiterates the demands made therein, inter alia, the demand that Israel, the occupying Power, comply with its legal obligations as mentioned in the advisory opinion;

2. *Takes note with appreciation* of the report of the Secretary-General submitted pursuant to resolution ES-10/15;

3. *Establishes* the United Nations Register of Damage Caused by the Construction of the Wall in the Occupied Palestinian Territory:

(a) To serve as a record, in documentary form, of the damage caused to all natural and legal persons concerned as a result of the construction of the wall by Israel, the occupying Power, in the Occupied Palestinian Territory, including in and around East Jerusalem;

(b) To be referred to henceforth in brief as the "Register of Damage";

4. *Decides* to set up an office of the Register of Damage, which will be:

(a) Responsible for the establishment and comprehensive maintenance of the Register of Damage;

(b) Composed of a three-member Board and a small secretariat, headed by an Executive Director and consisting of substantive, administrative and technical support staff;

(c) A subsidiary organ of the General Assembly operating under the administrative authority of the Secretary-General;

(d) Established at the site of the United Nations Office at Vienna;

5. *Requests* the Secretary-General to appoint the three-member Board of the Office of the Register of Damage, according to the selection criteria in the above-mentioned report, at the earliest practicable date;

6. *Decides* that the responsibilities assumed by the Board of the Office of the Register of Damage shall be as follows:

(a) The Board shall have overall responsibility for the establishment and maintenance of the Register of Damage;

(b) The Board shall establish the rules and regulations governing the work of the Office of the Register of Damage;

(c) The Board shall determine the eligibility criteria, bearing in mind varying circumstances with regard to the title and residency status of the claimants, for the inclusion of damages and losses caused in the Register of Damage with an established causal link to the construction of the wall;

(d) The Board shall, guided by the relevant findings of the advisory opinion, general principles of international law and principles of due process of law, also determine the criteria of damage and the procedure for the collection and registration of damage claims;

(e) The Board, on the recommendation of the Executive Director, shall have the ultimate authority in determining the inclusion of damage claims in the Register of Damage;

(f) The Board shall meet at least four times each year at the Office of the Register of Damage to determine which claims should be included in the Register of Damage, based on the established objective criteria defined in the rules and regulations;

(g) The Board shall engage, periodically and as deemed necessary, the expertise of technical specialists in relevant fields, inter alia, agriculture, land law, topography and assessment and compensation, to assist it in establishing and maintaining the Register of Damage;

(h) The Board shall render progress reports periodically to the Secretary-General for transmission to the General Assembly, including, as appropriate, possible further steps in connection with paragraphs 152 and 153 of the advisory opinion;

7. *Requests* the Secretary-General to appoint, at the earliest practicable date, the Executive Director of the Office of the Register of Damage, who shall:

(a) Have responsibility for overseeing and administrating the work of the secretariat of the Office of the Register of Damage;

(b) Be responsible for forwarding all damage claims to the Board for its approval for inclusion in the Register of Damage and serve in an advisory capacity to the Board in this regard;

8. *Decides* that the secretariat of the Office of the Register of Damage shall provide substantive, technical and administrative support for the establishment and maintenance of the Register of Damage by undertaking, inter alia, the following functions:

(a) Designing the format of the damage claims;

(b) Administering a public awareness programme to inform the Palestinian public about the possibility of and the requirements for filing a damage claim for registration, including an extensive community outreach programme to explain the purpose of the Register of Damage and provide guidance on how to fill out and submit the claim forms;

(c) Receiving and processing all damage claims and establishing the credibility of the causal link of those claims to the construction of the wall for registration in the Register of Damage;

(d) Submitting all processed damage claims through the Executive Director to the Board for inclusion in the Register of Damage;

(e) Aggregating and maintaining the records of damage claims approved by the Board, including both hard copies of the claims and their electronic version, which shall be maintained at the Office of the Register of Damage;

(f) Providing legal advice regarding the operations of the Office of the Register of Damage and the submitted claims;

9. *Resolves* that the Register of Damage shall remain open for registration for the duration of existence of the wall in the Occupied Palestinian Territory, including in and around East Jerusalem;

10. *Resolves also* that the Office of the Register of Damage shall remain active for the duration of the process of registration and shall carry out the specific functions and directives ascribed to it by the Secretary-General in his report, as set out in the present resolution, and such additional functions as requested by the General Assembly upon recommendation by the Secretary-General;

11. *Calls for* the establishment and operation of the Office of the Register of Damage and the establishment of the Register of Damage itself within six months of the adoption of the present resolution and the immediate undertaking thereafter of the process of registration of damage claims;

12. *Instructs* the Office of the Register of Damage, immediately upon its establishment, to seek the cooperation of the concerned Governments and authorities so as to facilitate its work in connection with the collection, submission and processing of damage claims in the Occupied Palestinian Territory, including East Jerusalem;

13. *Calls upon* the Government of Israel and the Palestinian Authority and relevant Palestinian institutions to cooperate with the Office of the Register of Damage;

14. *Calls upon* the Secretary-General to instruct the United Nations agencies and offices present on the ground in the Occupied Palestinian Territory to lend their support and expertise to the Office of the Register of Damage, upon its request, so as to facilitate its work;

15. *Requests* the Secretary-General to provide the necessary staff and facilities and to make appropriate

arrangements to provide the necessary funds required to carry out the terms of the present resolution;

16. *Also requests* the Secretary-General to report to the General Assembly within six months on the progress made with regard to the establishment and operation of the Office of the Register of Damage and the establishment of the Register of Damage;

17. *Decides* to adjourn the tenth emergency special session temporarily and to authorize the President of the General Assembly at its most recent session to resume the meeting of the special session upon request from Member States.

RECORDED VOTE ON RESOLUTION ES-10/17:

In favour: Afghanistan, Albania, Algeria, Andorra, Angola, Antigua and Barbuda, Argentina, Armenia, Austria, Azerbaijan, Bahamas, Bahrain, Bangladesh, Barbados, Belarus, Belgium, Belize, Benin, Bhutan, Bolivia, Bosnia and Herzegovina, Botswana, Brazil, Brunei Darussalam, Bulgaria, Burkina Faso, Burundi, Cambodia, Cape Verde, Central African Republic, Chile, China, Colombia, Comoros, Congo, Costa Rica, Croatia, Cuba, Cyprus, Czech Republic, Democratic People's Republic of Korea, Denmark, Djibouti, Dominica, Dominican Republic, Ecuador, Egypt, El Salvador, Eritrea, Estonia, Finland, France, Gabon, Gambia, Georgia, Germany, Ghana, Greece, Grenada, Guatemala, Guinea, Guinea Bissau, Guyana, Haiti, Honduras, Hungary, Iceland, India, Indonesia, Iran, Iraq, Ireland, Italy, Jamaica, Japan, Jordan, Kazakhstan, Kenya, Kuwait, Kyrgyzstan, Lao People's Democratic Republic, Latvia, Lebanon, Lesotho, Liberia, Libyan Arab Jamahiriya, Liechtenstein, Lithuania, Luxembourg, Malaysia, Maldives, Mali, Malta, Mauritania, Mauritius, Mexico, Moldova, Monaco, Mongolia, Montenegro, Morocco, Mozambique, Myanmar, Namibia, Nepal, Netherlands, New Zealand, Nicaragua, Niger, Nigeria, Norway, Oman, Pakistan, Panama, Paraguay, Peru, Philippines, Poland, Portugal, Qatar, Republic of Korea, Romania, Russian Federation, Saint Lucia, Saint Vincent and the Grenadines, San Marino, Saudi Arabia, Senegal, Serbia, Singapore, Slovakia, Slovenia, Solomon Islands, Somalia, South Africa, Spain, Sri Lanka, Sudan, Suriname, Sweden, Switzerland, Syrian Arab Republic, Tajikistan, Thailand, The former Yugoslav Republic of Macedonia, Timor-Leste, Togo, Trinidad and Tobago, Tunisia, Turkey, Turkmenistan, Ukraine, United Arab Emirates, United Kingdom, United Republic of Tanzania, Uruguay, Uzbekistan, Venezuela, Viet Nam, Yemen, Zambia, Zimbabwe.

Against: Australia, Israel, Marshall Islands, Micronesia, Nauru, Palau, United States.

Abstaining: Cameroon, Canada, Côte d'Ivoire, Malawi, Papua New Guinea, Tonga, Uganda.

Communications (18-25 December). On 18 [A/61/647-S/2006/1000] and 25 December [A/61/681-S/2006/1029], Israel restated that, despite the 26 November ceasefire, Palestinians continued to fire Qassam rockets at Israel.

In a later communication [A/ES-10/375-S/2007/1], the Permanent Observer of Palestine said that, on 26 December, the Israeli Government announced its plans to construct a new settlement in the West Bank.

Quartet meeting (December). Meeting on 22 December [SG/2121], the Quartet endorsed the continuation of the Temporary International Mechanism for another three months and agreed to review it again at the end of that period.

Jerusalem

East Jerusalem, where most of the city's Arab population lived, remained one of the most sensitive issues in the Middle East peace process and a focal point of concern for the United Nations in 2006.

Committee on Palestinian Rights. In its annual report [A/61/35], the Committee on the Exercise of the Inalienable Rights of the Palestinian People (Committee on Palestinian Rights) said that, on 30 April, the Israeli Cabinet revised the route of the separation wall, which would further consolidate Israeli control over vital parts of the West Bank, including East Jerusalem. The revised route would incorporate over 370,000 settlers, or nearly 87 per cent of the settler population. The wall in the Jerusalem area annexed 228.2 square kilometres of the West Bank, severing East Jerusalem and isolating over 230,000 Palestinian Jerusalemites from the rest of the West Bank. It would further separate over 2 million Palestinians living on the eastern side of the wall from East Jerusalem. The wall would sever East Jerusalem from Bethlehem and Ramallah, communities that were socially, culturally and economically interdependent. In addition, the territorial contiguity of East Jerusalem settlements was being enhanced.

Transfer of diplomatic missions

In letters dated 16 [S/2006/659] and 25 August [A/61/294-S/2006/694], respectively, Costa Rica and El Salvador informed the Secretary-General that they had decided to transfer their embassies in Israel from Jerusalem to the city of Tel Aviv.

On 27 August [A/61/298], the Secretary-General reported that three Member States, including Israel, had replied to his request for information on steps taken or envisaged to implement General Assembly resolution 60/41 [YUN 2005, p.523], which addressed the transfer by some States of their diplomatic missions to Jerusalem, in violation of Security Council resolution 478(1980) [YUN 1980, p. 426]. Israel viewed those resolutions as unbalanced and said that they threatened to prejudice the outcome of the Middle East peace process.

GENERAL ASSEMBLY ACTION

On 1 December [meeting 63], the General Assembly adopted **resolution 61/26** [draft: A/61/L.35 & Add.1] by recorded vote (157-6-10) [agenda item 13].

Jerusalem

The General Assembly,

Recalling its resolution 181 (II) of 29 November 1947, in particular its provisions regarding the City of Jerusalem,

Recalling also its resolution 36/120 E of 10 December 1981 and all subsequent resolutions, including resolution 56/31 of 3 December 2001, in which it, inter alia, determined that all legislative and administrative measures and actions taken by Israel, the occupying Power, which have altered or purported to alter the character and status of the Holy City of Jerusalem, in particular the so-called "Basic Law" on Jerusalem and the proclamation of Jerusalem as the capital of Israel, were null and void and must be rescinded forthwith,

Recalling further the Security Council resolutions relevant to Jerusalem, including resolution 478(1980) of 20 August 1980, in which the Council, inter alia, decided not to recognize the "Basic Law" on Jerusalem,

Recalling the advisory opinion rendered on 9 July 2004 by the International Court of Justice on the *Legal Consequences of the Construction of a Wall in the Occupied Palestinian Territory,* and recalling resolution ES-10/15 of 20 July 2004,

Expressing its grave concern about any action taken by any body, governmental or non-governmental, in violation of the above-mentioned resolutions,

Expressing its grave concern in particular about the continuation by Israel, the occupying Power, of illegal settlement activities, including the so-called E-1 plan, and its construction of the wall in and around East Jerusalem, and the further isolation of the city from the rest of the Occupied Palestinian Territory, which is having a detrimental effect on the lives of Palestinians and could prejudge a final status agreement on Jerusalem,

Reaffirming that the international community, through the United Nations, has a legitimate interest in the question of the City of Jerusalem and the protection of the unique spiritual, religious and cultural dimensions of the city, as foreseen in relevant United Nations resolutions on this matter,

Having considered the report of the Secretary-General,

1. *Reiterates its determination* that any actions taken by Israel, the occupying Power, to impose its laws, jurisdiction and administration on the Holy City of Jerusalem are illegal and therefore null and void and have no validity whatsoever, and calls upon Israel to cease all such illegal and unilateral measures;

2. *Welcomes* the decision of those States that had established diplomatic missions in Jerusalem to withdraw their missions from the city, in compliance with Security Council resolution 478(1980);

3. *Stresses* that a comprehensive, just and lasting solution to the question of the City of Jerusalem should take into account the legitimate concerns of both the Palestinian and Israeli sides and should include internationally guaranteed provisions to ensure the freedom of religion and of conscience of its inhabitants, as well as permanent, free and unhindered access to the holy places by the people of all religions and nationalities;

4. *Requests* the Secretary-General to report to the General Assembly at its sixty-second session on the implementation of the present resolution.

RECORDED VOTE ON RESOLUTION 61/26:

In favour: Afghanistan, Albania, Algeria, Andorra, Antigua and Barbuda, Argentina, Armenia, Austria, Azerbaijan, Bahamas, Bahrain, Bangladesh, Barbados, Belarus, Belgium, Belize, Benin, Bhutan, Bolivia, Bosnia and Herzegovina, Brazil, Brunei Darussalam, Bulgaria, Burkina Faso, Burundi, Cambodia, Canada, Cape Verde, Central African Republic, Chile, China, Colombia, Comoros, Congo, Costa Rica, Croatia, Cuba, Cyprus, Czech Republic, Democratic People's Republic of Korea, Denmark, Djibouti, Dominica, Dominican Republic, Ecuador, Egypt, El Salvador, Eritrea, Estonia, Ethiopia, Finland, France, Georgia, Germany, Ghana, Greece, Grenada, Guatemala, Guinea, Guyana, Haiti, Honduras, Hungary, Iceland, India, Indonesia, Iran, Iraq, Ireland, Italy, Jamaica, Japan, Jordan, Kazakhstan, Kuwait, Kyrgyzstan, Lao People's Democratic Republic, Latvia, Lebanon, Lesotho, Liberia, Libyan Arab Jamahiriya, Liechtenstein, Lithuania, Luxembourg, Malaysia, Maldives, Mali, Malta, Mauritania, Mauritius, Mexico, Monaco, Mongolia, Montenegro, Morocco, Mozambique, Myanmar, Namibia, Nepal, Netherlands, New Zealand, Nicaragua, Niger, Nigeria, Norway, Oman, Pakistan, Panama, Paraguay, Peru, Philippines, Poland, Portugal, Qatar, Republic of Korea, Romania, Russian Federation, Saint Vincent and the Grenadines, Samoa, San Marino, Saudi Arabia, Senegal, Serbia, Seychelles, Sierra Leone, Singapore, Slovakia, Slovenia, Solomon Islands, Somalia, South Africa, Spain, Sri Lanka, Sudan, Suriname, Sweden, Switzerland, Syrian Arab Republic, Tajikistan, Thailand, The former Yugoslav Republic of Macedonia, Timor-Leste, Togo, Trinidad and Tobago, Tunisia, Turkey, Turkmenistan, Ukraine, United Arab Emirates, United Kingdom, Uruguay, Uzbekistan, Venezuela, Viet Nam, Yemen, Zambia.

Against: Israel, Marshall Islands, Micronesia, Nauru, Palau, United States.

Abstaining: Australia, Cameroon, Côte d'Ivoire, Fiji, Malawi, Moldova, Papua New Guinea, Tonga, Uganda, Vanuatu.

Economic and social situation

A May report on the economic and social repercussions of the Israeli occupation on the living conditions of the Palestinian people in the Occupied Palestinian Territory, including Jerusalem, and of the Arab population in the occupied Syrian Golan [A/61/67-E/2006/13] was prepared by the Economic and Social Commission for Western Asia (ESCWA), in accordance with Economic and Social Council resolution 2005/51 [YUN 2005, p. 524] and General Assembly resolution 60/183 [ibid., p. 525]. It covered developments since the last ESCWA report [ibid., p. 523].

The report noted that the occupation of Palestinian territory by Israel continued to deepen the economic and social hardship of Palestinians. Citing the right to self-defence, the Israeli army continued to mount military operations in the Occupied Palestinian Territory, frequently employing arbitrary detention, the disproportionate use of force, home demolition, severe mobility restrictions and closure policies. The Israeli closure system remained a primary cause of poverty and humanitarian crisis, and restricted Palestinian access to health and education services, employment, markets and social and religious networks. Israeli restrictions also impeded humanitarian services to the occupied territory. The United Nations Relief and Works Agency for Palestine Refugees in the Near East (UNRWA) alone incurred over $10 million in losses in 2005. While the Palestinian gross domestic product grew in 2005 by some 6 per cent, economic indicators continued to show negative trends. Unemployment and poverty rates remained high, estimated at 23 per cent and 62 per cent, respectively. Israel's confiscation of Palestinian land and water resources for settlements, and the construction of the West Bank barrier, accelerated during 2005. Israeli settlements, land confiscation and the construction of a barrier isolated occupied East Jerusalem, bisected the West Bank and curtailed normal economic and social life. Refugees, women and children bore a significant brunt of those measures. Malnutrition and other health problems afflicted a growing number of Palestinians at a time of curtailed access to needed services. Some 350,000 children under the age of five suffered from chronic malnutrition.

ECONOMIC AND SOCIAL COUNCIL ACTION

On 27 July [meeting 42], the Economic and Social Council adopted **resolution 2006/43** [draft: E/2006/L.17/rev.1] by recorded vote (45-3-3) [agenda item 11].

Economic and social repercussions of the Israeli occupation on the living conditions of the Palestinian people in the Occupied Palestinian Territory, including East Jerusalem, and the Arab population in the occupied Syrian Golan

The Economic and Social Council,

Recalling General Assembly resolution 60/183 of 22 December 2005,

Recalling also its resolution 2005/51 of 27 July 2005,

Guided by the principles of the Charter of the United Nations affirming the inadmissibility of the acquisition of territory by force and recalling relevant Security Council resolutions, including resolutions 242(1967) of 22 November 1967, 252(1968) of 21 May 1968, 338(1973) of 22 October 1973 and 497(1981) of 17 December 1981,

Recalling the resolutions of the tenth emergency special session of the General Assembly, including ES-10/13 of 21 October 2003, ES-10/14 of 8 December 2003 and ES-10/15 of 20 July 2004,

Reaffirming the applicability of the Geneva Convention relative to the Protection of Civilian Persons in Time of War, of 12 August 1949, to the Occupied Palestinian Territory, including East Jerusalem, and other Arab territories occupied by Israel since 1967,

Stressing the importance of the revival of the Middle East peace process on the basis of Security Council resolutions 242(1967), 338(1973), 425(1978), 1397(2002), 1515(2003) and 1544(2004) and the principle of land for peace, as well as compliance with the agreements reached between the Government of Israel and the Palestine Liberation Organization, the representative of the Palestinian people,

Reaffirming the principle of the permanent sovereignty of peoples under foreign occupation over their natural resources,

Convinced that the Israeli occupation has gravely impeded the efforts to achieve sustainable development and a sound economic environment in the Occupied Palestinian Territory, including East Jerusalem, and in the occupied Syrian Golan,

Gravely concerned about the deterioration of the economic and living conditions of the Palestinian people in the Occupied Palestinian Territory, including East Jerusalem, and of the Arab population of the occupied Syrian Golan and the exploitation by Israel, the occupying Power, of their natural resources,

Gravely concerned also by the formidable impact on the economic and social conditions of the Palestinian people caused by Israel's construction of the wall and its associated regime inside the Occupied Palestinian Territory, including in and around East Jerusalem, and the resulting violation of their economic and social rights, including the right to work, to health, to education and to an adequate standard of living,

Recalling, in this regard, the International Covenant on Civil and Political Rights, the International Covenant on Economic, Social and Cultural Rights and the Convention on the Rights of the Child, and affirming that these human rights instruments must be respected in the Occupied Palestinian Territory, including East Jerusalem, as well as in the occupied Syrian Golan,

Gravely concerned at the extensive destruction by Israel, the occupying Power, of agricultural land and orchards in the Occupied Palestinian Territory, including East Jerusalem, and, in particular, as a result of its construction of the wall, contrary to international law, in the Occupied Palestinian Territory, including in and around East Jerusalem,

Recalling the advisory opinion rendered on 9 July 2004 by the International Court of Justice on the *Legal Consequences of the Construction of a Wall in the Occupied Palestinian Territory*, recalling also General Assembly resolution ES-10/15, and stressing the need to comply with the obligations mentioned therein,

Extremely concerned at the dire humanitarian crisis in the Occupied Palestinian Territory further exacerbated by the current Israeli military operations, the severe restrictions on the Palestinian people, and Israel's withholding of Palestinian tax revenues,

Expressing grave concern at the increasing number of deaths and injuries among civilians, including children,

Commending the important work being done by the United Nations and the specialized agencies in support of the economic and social development of the Palestinian people, as well as the assistance being provided in the humanitarian field,

Conscious of the urgent need for the reconstruction and development of the economic and social infrastructure of the Occupied Palestinian Territory, including East Jerusalem, as well as the urgent need to address the dire humanitarian crisis facing the Palestinian people,

Affirming that the Israeli occupation is a major obstacle to the economic and social development of the Occupied Palestinian Territory, including East Jerusalem, and of the occupied Syrian Golan,

Calling upon both parties to fulfil their obligations under the road map in cooperation with the Quartet,

1. *Calls for* the lifting of the severe restrictions imposed on the Palestinian people, including those arising from the current Israeli military operations, and for other urgent measures to be taken to alleviate the desperate humanitarian situation in the Occupied Palestinian Territory;

2. *Demands* that Israel comply with the Protocol on Economic Relations between the Government of Israel and the Palestine Liberation Organization signed in Paris on 29 April 1994 and urgently transfer Palestinian tax revenues;

3. *Stresses* the need to preserve the national unity and the territorial integrity of the Occupied Palestinian Territory, including East Jerusalem, and to guarantee the freedom of movement of persons and goods in the Territory, including the removal of restrictions on going into and from East Jerusalem, and the freedom of movement to and from the outside world;

4. *Calls upon* Israel to restore and replace the destroyed civilian infrastructure, including the only power station, where Israeli air strikes on Gaza's power plant have had a far reaching impact on Gaza's hospitals, food production facilities, water and sanitation systems; as well as water networks, schools, bridges, the airport, the seaport and Palestinian ministries and institutions;

5. *Urges* the full implementation of the Agreement on Movement and Access of 15 November 2005, particularly the urgent reopening of Rafah and Karni crossings, which is crucial to ensuring the passage of foodstuffs and essential supplies, as well as the access of the United Nations agencies to and within the Occupied Palestinian Territory;

6. *Urges* all parties to respect the rules of international humanitarian law, and to refrain from violence against the civilian population in accordance with the Geneva Convention relative to the Protection of Civilian Persons in Time of War, of 12 August 1949;

7. *Reaffirms* the inalienable right of the Palestinian people and the Arab population of the occupied Syrian Golan to all their natural and economic resources, and calls upon Israel, the occupying Power, not to exploit, endanger or cause loss or depletion of those resources;

8. *Calls upon* Israel, the occupying Power, to cease the dumping of all kinds of waste materials in the Occupied Palestinian Territory, including East Jerusalem, and in the occupied Syrian Golan, which gravely threaten their natural resources, namely, water and land resources, and pose an environmental hazard and health threat to the civilian populations;

9. *Reaffirms* that Israeli settlements in the Occupied Palestinian Territory, including East Jerusalem, and the occupied Syrian Golan, are illegal and an obstacle to economic and social development, and calls for the full implementation of the relevant Security Council resolutions;

10. *Stresses* that the wall being constructed at an accelerated pace by Israel in the Occupied Palestinian Territory, including in and around East Jerusalem, is contrary to international law and is isolating East Jerusalem and dividing up the West Bank and is seriously debilitating to the economic and social development of the Palestinian people, and calls in this regard for full compliance with the legal obligations mentioned in the 9 July 2004 advisory opinion of the International Court of Justice and in General Assembly resolution ES-10/15;

11. *Emphasizes* the importance of the work of the organizations and agencies of the United Nations and of the United Nations Special Coordinator for the Middle East Peace Process and Personal Representative of the Secretary-General to the Palestine Liberation Organization and the Palestinian Authority;

12. *Requests* the Secretary-General to submit to the General Assembly at its sixty-first session, through the Economic and Social Council, a report on the implementation of the present resolution and to continue to include in the report of the United Nations Special Coordinator an update on the living conditions of the Palestinian people, in collaboration with relevant United Nations agencies;

13. *Decides* to include the item entitled "Economic and social repercussions of the Israeli occupation on the living conditions of the Palestinian people in the Occupied Palestinian Territory, including East Jerusalem, and the Arab population in the occupied Syrian Golan" in the agenda of its substantive session of 2007.

RECORDED VOTE ON RESOLUTION 2006/43:

In favour: Albania, Armenia, Austria, Bangladesh, Belgium, Belize, Benin, Brazil, Chad, China, Colombia, Costa Rica, Cuba, Denmark, France, Germany, Guinea, Guyana, Haiti, Iceland, India, Indonesia, Italy, Japan, Lithuania, Madagascar, Mauritania, Mauritius, Mexico, Namibia, Nigeria, Pakistan, Panama, Paraguay, Republic of Korea, Russian Federation, Saudi Arabia, South Africa, Spain, Sri Lanka, Thailand, Tunisia, Turkey, United Arab Emirates, United Republic of Tanzania.

Against: Australia, Canada, United States.

Abstentions: Czech Republic, Poland, United Kingdom.

On the same date (**decision 2006/249**), the Council took note of the Secretary-General's note transmitting the report prepared by ESCWA (see p. 532).

GENERAL ASSEMBLY ACTION

On 20 December [meeting 83], the General Assembly, on the recommendation of the Second (Economic and Financial) Committee [A/61/418], adopted **resolution 61/184** by recorded vote (164-6-9) [agenda item 40].

Permanent sovereignty of the Palestinian people in the Occupied Palestinian Territory, including East Jerusalem, and of the Arab population in the occupied Syrian Golan over their natural resources

The General Assembly,

Recalling its resolution 60/183 of 22 December 2005, and taking note of Economic and Social Council resolution 2006/43 of 27 July 2006,

Recalling also its resolutions 59/251 of 22 December 2004 and 58/292 of 6 May 2004,

Reaffirming the principle of the permanent sovereignty of peoples under foreign occupation over their natural resources,

Guided by the principles of the Charter of the United Nations, affirming the inadmissibility of the acquisition of territory by force, and recalling relevant Security Council resolutions, including resolutions 242(1967) of 22 November 1967, 465(1980) of 1 March 1980 and 497(1981) of 17 December 1981,

Recalling its resolution 2625 (XXV) of 24 October 1970,

Reaffirming the applicability of the Geneva Convention relative to the Protection of Civilian Persons in Time of War, of 12 August 1949, to the Occupied Palestinian Territory, including East Jerusalem, and other Arab territories occupied by Israel since 1967,

Recalling, in this regard, the International Covenant on Civil and Political Rights and the International Covenant on Economic, Social and Cultural Rights, and affirming that these human rights instruments must be respected in the Occupied Palestinian Territory, including East Jerusalem, as well as in the occupied Syrian Golan,

Recalling also the advisory opinion rendered on 9 July 2004 by the International Court of Justice on the *Legal Consequences of the Construction of a Wall in the Occupied Palestinian Territory*, and recalling further its resolution ES-10/15 of 20 July 2004,

Expressing its concern at the exploitation by Israel, the occupying Power, of the natural resources of the Occupied Palestinian Territory, including East Jerusalem, and other Arab territories occupied by Israel since 1967,

Expressing its grave concern at the extensive destruction by Israel, the occupying Power, of agricultural land and orchards in the Occupied Palestinian Territory, including the uprooting of a vast number of fruit-bearing trees,

Expressing its concern at the widespread destruction caused by Israel, the occupying Power, to vital infrastructure, including water pipelines and sewage networks, in the Occupied Palestinian Territory, which, inter alia, pollutes the environment and negatively affects the natural resources of the Palestinian people,

Aware of the detrimental impact of the Israeli settlements on Palestinian and other Arab natural resources, especially as a result of the confiscation of land and the forced diversion of water resources, and of the dire economic and social consequences in this regard,

Aware also of the detrimental impact on Palestinian natural resources being caused by the unlawful construction of the wall by Israel, the occupying Power, in the Occupied Palestinian Territory, including in and around East Jerusalem, and of its grave effect on the natural resources and economic and social conditions of the Palestinian people,

Reaffirming the need for the immediate resumption of negotiations within the Middle East peace process, on the basis of Security Council resolutions 242(1967), 338(1973) of 22 October 1973, 425(1978) of 19 March 1978 and 1397(2002) of 12 March 2002, the principle of land for peace and the Quartet performance-based road map to a permanent two-State solution to the Israeli-Palestinian conflict, as endorsed by the Security Council in its resolution 1515(2003) of 19 November 2003, and for the achievement of a final settlement on all tracks,

Noting the Israeli withdrawal from within the Gaza Strip and parts of the northern West Bank and the importance of the dismantlement of settlements therein as a step towards the implementation of the road map,

Recalling the need to end all acts of violence, including acts of terror, provocation, incitement and destruction,

Taking note with appreciation of the note by the Secretary-General transmitting the report prepared by the Economic and Social Commission for Western Asia on the economic and social repercussions of the Israeli occupation on the living conditions of the Palestinian people in the Occupied Palestinian Territory, including East Jerusalem, and of the Arab population in the occupied Syrian Golan,

1. *Reaffirms* the inalienable rights of the Palestinian people and the population of the occupied Syrian Golan over their natural resources, including land and water;

2. *Calls upon* Israel, the occupying Power, not to exploit, damage, cause loss or depletion of, or endanger the natural resources in the Occupied Palestinian Territory, including East Jerusalem, and in the occupied Syrian Golan;

3. *Recognizes* the right of the Palestinian people to claim restitution as a result of any exploitation, damage, loss or depletion, or endangerment of their natural resources resulting from illegal measures taken by Israel, the occupying Power, in the Occupied Palestinian Territory, including East Jerusalem, and expresses the hope that this issue will be dealt with in the framework of the final status negotiations between the Palestinian and Israeli sides;

4. *Stresses* that the wall being constructed by Israel in the Occupied Palestinian Territory, including in and

around East Jerusalem, is contrary to international law and is seriously depriving the Palestinian people of their natural resources, and calls in this regard for full compliance with the legal obligations mentioned in the 9 July 2004 advisory opinion of the International Court of Justice and in resolution ES-10/15;

5. *Notes* the Israeli withdrawal from within the Gaza Strip and parts of the northern West Bank and the dismantlement of the settlements therein as a step towards the implementation of the road map;

6. *Calls upon* Israel, the occupying Power, in this regard, to comply strictly with its obligations under international law, including international humanitarian law, with respect to the alteration of the character and status of the Occupied Palestinian Territory, including East Jerusalem;

7. *Also calls upon* Israel, the occupying Power, to cease the dumping of all kinds of waste materials in the Occupied Palestinian Territory, including East Jerusalem, and in the occupied Syrian Golan, which gravely threaten their natural resources, namely the water and land resources, and pose an environmental hazard and health threat to the civilian populations;

8. *Further calls upon* Israel to cease its destruction of vital infrastructure, including water pipelines and sewage networks, which, inter alia, has a negative impact on the natural resources of the Palestinian people;

9. *Requests* the Secretary-General to report to it at its sixty-second session on the implementation of the present resolution, and decides to include in the provisional agenda of its sixty-second session the item entitled "Permanent sovereignty of the Palestinian people in the Occupied Palestinian Territory, including East Jerusalem, and of the Arab population in the occupied Syrian Golan over their natural resources".

RECORDED VOTE ON RESOLUTION 61/184:

In favour: Afghanistan, Albania, Algeria, Andorra, Angola, Antigua and Barbuda, Argentina, Armenia, Austria, Azerbaijan, Bahamas, Bahrain, Bangladesh, Barbados, Belarus, Belgium, Belize, Benin, Bhutan, Bolivia, Botswana, Brazil, Brunei Darussalam, Bulgaria, Burkina Faso, Burundi, Cambodia, Cape Verde, Central African Republic, Chile, China, Colombia, Comoros, Congo, Costa Rica, Croatia, Cuba, Cyprus, Czech Republic, Democratic People's Republic of Korea, Denmark, Djibouti, Dominica, Ecuador, Egypt, El Salvador, Eritrea, Estonia, Ethiopia, Finland, France, Gabon, Gambia, Georgia, Germany, Ghana, Greece, Grenada, Guatemala, Guinea, Guinea-Bissau, Guyana, Haiti, Honduras, Hungary, Iceland, India, Indonesia, Iran, Iraq, Ireland, Italy, Jamaica, Japan, Jordan, Kazakhstan, Kenya, Kuwait, Kyrgyzstan, Lao People's Democratic Republic, Latvia, Lebanon, Lesotho, Liberia, Libyan Arab Jamahiriya, Liechtenstein, Lithuania, Luxembourg, Malawi, Malaysia, Maldives, Mali, Malta, Mauritania, Mauritius, Mexico, Moldova, Monaco, Mongolia, Montenegro, Morocco, Mozambique, Myanmar, Namibia, Nepal, Netherlands, New Zealand, Nicaragua, Niger, Nigeria, Norway, Oman, Pakistan, Panama, Paraguay, Peru, Philippines, Poland, Portugal, Qatar, Republic of Korea, Romania, Russian Federation, Saint Lucia, Saint Vincent and the Grenadines, Samoa, San Marino, Sao Tome and Principe, Saudi Arabia, Senegal, Serbia, Sierra Leone, Singapore, Slovakia, Slovenia, Solomon Islands, Somalia, South Africa, Spain, Sri Lanka, Sudan, Suriname, Sweden, Switzerland, Syrian Arab Republic, Thailand, The former Yugoslav Republic of Macedonia, Timor-Leste, Togo, Trinidad and Tobago, Tunisia, Turkey, Turkmenistan, Ukraine, United Arab Emirates, United Kingdom, United Republic of Tanzania, Uruguay, Uzbekistan, Venezuela, Viet Nam, Yemen, Zambia, Zimbabwe.

Against: Australia, Israel, Marshall Islands, Micronesia, Palau, United States.

Abstaining: Cameroon, Canada, Côte d'Ivoire, Dominican Republic, Fiji, Nauru, Tonga, Uganda, Vanuatu.

Other aspects

Special Committee on Israeli Practices

In response to General Assembly resolution 60/104 [YUN 2005, p. 529], the Special Committee to Investigate Israeli Practices Affecting the Human Rights of the Palestinian People and Other Arabs of the Occupied Territories, in October, reported for the thirty-eighth time to the General Assembly on events and the human rights situation in the territories it considered occupied—the Golan Heights, the West Bank, including East Jerusalem, and the Gaza Strip [A/61/500]. Due to the deteriorating security situation in the region, the Committee postponed its annual field visit to the Middle East but held consultation in Geneva (31 July–2 August) with representatives of the concerned countries, as well as with LAS, OIC, UN agencies and non-governmental organizations (NGOs). The Committee's report was therefore based on documents, surveys and case studies made available by Palestinian and Israeli NGOs. An updated report would be submitted to the Assembly in early 2007, upon completion of the rescheduled field visit planned to take place in mid-November.

The Committee observed that, not since the inception of its mandate in 1968, had it ever confronted such anger and misery among the Palestinian people and other Arabs in the occupied territories and disrespect for their basic human rights and fundamental freedoms. Palestinians saw themselves as constant subjects of collective punishments in every area of their daily lives. Since the establishment of the elected Hamas-led Government in March, the shortage of funds resulting from aid cut-off and the non-transfer of taxes and revenues by Israel, leading to severe economic hardships for people in the Occupied Palestinian Territory, were perceived as economic sanctions against the Palestinian people. Some of them, for the first time, were questioning the role of the United Nations in the crisis. The Committee supported the call by the Human Rights Council for the dispatch of an urgent fact-finding mission, headed by the Special Rapporteur on the situation of human rights in the Palestinian territories occupied since 1967. It was of the view that time had come for Israel to grant compensation for the multifaceted damages inflicted in the Occupied Palestinian Territory, not only as a consequence of military incursions and operations but also due to the construction of the separation wall.

The Committee urged the Assembly to consider innovative ways to fulfil its responsibility with respect to all aspects of the question of Palestine until it was resolved in conformity with relevant UN resolutions and the norms of international law, and the inalienable rights of the Palestinians were fully realized, and to that end, provide the Special Committee with a renewed mandate in line with the new realities. It requested the Security Council to ensure implementation of the International Court of Justice advisory opinion and Assembly resolution ES-10/15 requesting Israel to comply with its legal obligation to cease the construction of the wall in the occupied territories, including in and around East Jerusalem, dismantle the segments of the wall already built, repeal all legislative and regulatory acts adopted in view of the construction of the wall, and make reparation for the damage arising from such construction. The Council should also consider instituting sanctions against Israel if it continued to pay no attention to its international obligations; ensure that other States were not taking actions to assist in any way the construction of the wall; and encourage members of the Quartet to fully implement the road map in such a way as to achieve a comprehensive, just and lasting settlement of the conflict.

The Committee called upon Israel, among other measures, to recognize the applicability of the Fourth Geneva Convention in the occupied territories and distinguish in all circumstances between military objectives and civilian persons and objects; cease its policies of excessive use of force and extrajudicial killings of Palestinians, confiscation of Palestinian land and expansion of Jewish settlements in the Occupied Palestinian Territory; restore freedom of movement for the Palestinian population, by lifting road closures, roadblocks and other impediments, such as checkpoints, and stop building roads accessible only to Israeli settlers and preventing easy access to Palestinians; facilitate and implement the reopening of the Gaza airport and seaport; stop construction of the separation wall between Israel and the occupied territories; and stop mass arrests and arbitrary detentions.

The PA should, among other actions, apply the provisions of the Fourth Geneva Convention as relevant to the Occupied Palestinian Territory; abide by pertinent provisions of human rights law and international humanitarian law; restore law and order in the Occupied Palestinian Territory; ensure payment of salary arrears to all civil servants; comply with the requirements of the road map as laid out by the Quartet; stop the cycle of violence and exert control over Palestinian armed groups; arrest and bring to justice those responsible for planning or participating in attacks against civilians; implement legislative and other reforms for greater democratization in the occupied territories, especially in the areas of justice, education, health and employment; and ensure greater protection of women against various forms of violence, including domestic violence, and women's participation in the life of their communities.

The Committee also urged concerned civil society groups and diplomatic, academic and research associations to use their goodwill and influence to make the human rights and humanitarian crisis of Palestinians widely known by all available means, and encouraged international and national media to give accurate and wide coverage to the matter in order to mobilize national and world opinion for a just and lasting settlement of the 38-year-old conflict.

In an addendum to the report [A/61/500/Add.1], the Special Committee said that, after postponing its field visit, initially scheduled for June, then August, it was finally able to visit Egypt, Jordan and Syria (11-22 November). The report was based on the testimonies gathered from Palestinian, Syrian and Israeli witnesses. Following its visit, the Committee could not but emphasize that the harsh military occupation of the occupied territories, with all its negative effects, continued despite the withdrawal of Israeli forces from the Gaza Strip in August 2005. Gaza was still a vast open-air prison, under the strict control of Israeli authorities, which had yet to release their tight grip on the airport and seaport. The checkpoints of Eretz and Karni remained closed for extended periods, seriously hampering any normal flow of people and goods. Increasing restrictions on movement in the West Bank, owing to the expanding construction of the wall and the unabated increase of road closures and checkpoints, continued to affect the living conditions of Palestinians and hampered the creation of a viable Palestinian State. The daily situation of the Palestinian people had worsened because of military incursions, the excessive use of force by the Israeli military and the great number of casualties. Increased violations of the right to life had gone hand in hand with the expansion of the wall, the increasing expropriation of Palestinian land, the intrusive presence of settlers in the occupied territories with their own roads, and the expansion of road closures and fixed or movable checkpoints. Palestinians were losing opportunities for higher education and the development of their talents and skills.

It was not possible to equate the responsibilities of Palestinians and Israelis. The latter bore an added responsibility because of the neglect of their binding obligations, as well as the excessive use of force and the wide range of collective punishments and humiliations imposed on Palestinians as retaliatory measures. The responsibility of the Palestinians could not be excluded either, as rockets launched against Israeli cities took the lives of innocent civilians and attested to the inability of some Palestinian leaders to control the activity of militant armed groups. In addition, the renewed cycle of inter-Palestinian violence affecting families, especially in Gaza, revealed once more the absence of the rule of law and order and the impunity that reigned in the occupied territories. The Committee agreed with Israel's fundamental desire to ensure the security of its citizens against the human and material damage caused by rockets launched from Gaza. However, that could not justify its mistreatment of the Palestinian people.

The Committee, in addition to the recommendations made in its main report, urged the General Assembly and the Security Council to ensure the protection of civilians through, among other measures, the deployment of an international human rights mechanism in the occupied territories and the conduct of a national independent, transparent and comprehensive investigation into allegations of violations of international human rights and humanitarian law, with a view to establishing individual responsibility and accountability, providing avenues for redress and reparation, and preventing the recurrence of such violations. Measures should also be taken to prevent intrusive actions by Israel and any act of desecration against holy sites, or any broader attempt to "Judaize" holy sites, as well as the use of excessive force by IDF. It urged Israel to stop withholding Palestinian tax revenues and major EU donors not to cut international aid. The Committee also drew the attention to the UN responsibility, including as a member of the Quartet, to assist in developing a new and constructive approach towards the conflict, bearing in mind that a durable solution, guaranteeing peace and security to both parties, could only be achieved if respect for their fundamental human rights was at the heart of the peace process.

Report of Secretary-General. On 12 September [A/61/329], the Secretary-General informed the General Assembly that Israel had not replied to his July request for information on steps taken or envisaged to implement Assembly resolution 60/107 [YUN 2005, p. 527] demanding that Israel, among other things, cease all practices and actions that violated the human rights of the Palestinian people, and condemning all acts of terror, provocation, incitement and destruction, especially the excessive use of force by Israeli forces against Palestinian civilians.

Report of Special Rapporteur. The Special Rapporteur on the situation of human rights in the Palestinian territories occupied by Israel since 1967, John Dugard, submitted to the Human Rights Council at its 2006 session his report on the situation of human rights in the Occupied Palestinian Territory [E/CN.4/2006/29], which the Secretary-General transmitted to the General Assembly through a September note [A/61/470].

GENERAL ASSEMBLY ACTION

On 14 December [meeting 79], the General Assembly, on the recommendation of the Fourth (Special Political and Decolonization) Committee [A/61/408], adopted **resolution 61/119** by recorded vote (157-9-14) [agenda item 32].

Israeli practices affecting the human rights of the Palestinian people in the Occupied Palestinian Territory, including East Jerusalem

The General Assembly,

Recalling its relevant resolutions, including resolution 60/107 of 8 December 2005, as well as those adopted at its tenth emergency special session,

Recalling also the relevant resolutions of the Commission on Human Rights and the Human Rights Council,

Bearing in mind the relevant resolutions of the Security Council,

Having considered the report of the Special Committee to Investigate Israeli Practices Affecting the Human Rights of the Palestinian People and Other Arabs of the Occupied Territories and the report of the Secretary-General,

Taking note of the recent reports of the Special Rapporteur of the Human Rights Council on the situation of human rights in the Palestinian territories occupied since 1967,

Recalling the advisory opinion rendered on 9 July 2004 by the International Court of Justice, and recalling also General Assembly resolution ES-10/15 of 20 July 2004,

Noting in particular the Court's reply, including that the construction of the wall being built by Israel, the occupying Power, in the Occupied Palestinian Territory, including in and around East Jerusalem, and its associated regime are contrary to international law,

Recalling the International Covenant on Civil and Political Rights, the International Covenant on Economic, Social and Cultural Rights and the Convention on the Rights of the Child, and affirming that these human rights instruments must be respected in the Occupied Palestinian Territory, including East Jerusalem,

Aware of the responsibility of the international community to promote human rights and ensure respect for international law, and recalling in this regard its resolution 2625 (XXV) of 24 October 1970,

Reaffirming the principle of the inadmissibility of the acquisition of territory by force,

Reaffirming also the applicability of the Geneva Convention relative to the Protection of Civilian Persons in Time of War, of 12 August 1949, to the Occupied Palestinian Territory, including East Jerusalem, and other Arab territories occupied by Israel since 1967,

Reaffirming further the obligation of the States parties to the Fourth Geneva Convention under articles 146, 147 and 148 with regard to penal sanctions, grave breaches and responsibilities of the High Contracting Parties,

Reaffirming that all States have the right and the duty to take actions in conformity with international law and international humanitarian law to counter deadly acts of violence against their civilian population in order to protect the lives of their citizens,

Stressing the need for full compliance with the Israeli-Palestinian agreements reached within the context of the Middle East peace process, including the Sharm El-Sheikh understandings, and the implementation of the Quartet road map to a permanent two-State solution to the Israeli-Palestinian conflict,

Stressing also the need for the full implementation of the Agreement on Movement and Access and the Agreed Principles for the Rafah Crossing, both of 15 November 2005, to allow for the freedom of movement of the Palestinian civilian population within and into and out of the Gaza Strip,

Noting the Israeli withdrawal from within the Gaza Strip and parts of the northern West Bank and the importance of the dismantlement of settlements therein as a step towards the implementation of the road map,

Expressing grave concern about the continuing systematic violation of the human rights of the Palestinian people by Israel, the occupying Power, including that arising from the excessive use of force, the use of collective punishment, the reoccupation and closure of areas, the confiscation of land, the establishment and expansion of settlements, the construction of the wall inside the Occupied Palestinian Territory in departure from the Armistice Line of 1949, the destruction of property and infrastructure, and all other actions by it designed to change the legal status, geographical nature and demographic composition of the Occupied Palestinian Territory, including East Jerusalem,

Gravely concerned about the military actions that have been carried out since 28 September 2000 and that have led to thousands of deaths among Palestinian civilians, including hundreds of children, and tens of thousands of injuries,

Expressing deep concern about the recent deterioration in the humanitarian and security situation in the Gaza Strip, including that resulting from the bombardment against civilian areas, air raids and sonic booms, and the firing of rockets into Israel, and in particular from the military actions carried out by Israel, the occupying Power, that endanger the Palestinian civilian population, and especially deploring the killing of Palestinian civilians, including women and children, that took place in Beit Hanoun on 8 November 2006,

Expressing deep concern also about the vast destruction caused by the Israeli occupying forces, including of religious, cultural and historical sites, of vital infrastructure and institutions of the Palestinian Authority, and of agricultural land throughout Palestinian cities, towns, villages and refugee camps, and expressing deep concern about the short- and long-term detrimental impact of such destruction on the socio-economic and humanitarian conditions of the Palestinian civilian population,

Expressing deep concern further about the Israeli policy of closure and the severe restrictions, including curfews and the permit regime, that continue to be imposed on the movement of persons and goods, including medical and humanitarian personnel and goods, throughout the Occupied Palestinian Territory, including East Jerusalem, and the consequent negative impact on the socio-economic situation of the Palestinian people, which remains that of a dire humanitarian crisis,

Concerned about the continued establishment of Israeli checkpoints in the Occupied Palestinian Territory, including East Jerusalem, and the transformation of several of these checkpoints into structures akin to permanent border crossings inside the Occupied Palestinian Territory, which are severely impairing the territorial contiguity of the Territory and severely undermining efforts to rehabilitate and develop the Palestinian economy,

Expressing deep concern that thousands of Palestinians, including children and women, continue to be held in Israeli prisons or detention centres under harsh conditions that impair their well-being, and expressing concern about the ill treatment and harassment of any of the Palestinian prisoners and all reports of torture,

Convinced of the need for an international presence to monitor the situation, to contribute to ending the violence and protecting the Palestinian civilian population and to help the parties implement the agreements reached and, in this regard, recalling the positive contribution of the Temporary International Presence in Hebron,

Welcoming the Palestinian truce initiative and its acceptance by Israel that came into effect on 26 November 2006, and urging both parties to maintain this truce, which could pave the way for genuine negotiations towards a just resolution of the conflict,

Stressing the necessity for the full implementation of all relevant Security Council resolutions,

1. *Reiterates* that all measures and actions taken by Israel, the occupying Power, in the Occupied Palestinian Territory, including East Jerusalem, in violation of the relevant provisions of the Geneva Convention relative to the Protection of Civilian Persons in Time of War, of 12 August 1949, and contrary to the relevant resolutions of the Security Council, are illegal and have no validity;

2. *Demands* that Israel, the occupying Power, comply fully with the provisions of the Fourth Geneva Convention of 1949 and cease immediately all measures and actions taken in violation and in breach of the Convention, including all of its settlement activities and the construction of the wall in the Occupied Palestinian Territory, including in and around East Jerusalem, as well as the extrajudicial executions;

3. *Condemns* all acts of violence, including all acts of terror, provocation, incitement and destruction, especially the excessive use of force by the Israeli occupying forces against Palestinian civilians, resulting in extensive loss of life and vast numbers of injuries, including among children, massive destruction of homes, properties, agricultural lands and vital infrastructure, and the internal displacement of civilians;

4. *Expresses grave concern* at the use of suicide bombing attacks against Israeli civilians resulting in extensive loss of life and injury;

5. *Notes* the Israeli withdrawal from within the Gaza Strip and parts of the northern West Bank and the dismantlement of the settlements therein as a step towards the implementation of the road map;

6. *Calls upon* Israel, the occupying Power, in this regard, to comply strictly with its obligations under international law, including international humanitarian law, with respect to the alteration of the character and status of the Occupied Palestinian Territory, including East Jerusalem;

7. *Demands* that Israel, the occupying Power, cease all practices and actions that violate the human rights of the Palestinian people, and that it respect human rights law and comply with its legal obligations in this regard;

8. *Urges* Member States to continue to provide emergency assistance to the Palestinian people to alleviate the financial crisis and the dire socio-economic and humanitarian situation being faced by the Palestinian people;

9. *Calls upon* Israel, the occupying Power, to release the tax revenues due to the Palestinian Authority, in accordance with the Paris Economic Protocol of 1994, and to ease the severe closures and restrictions on movement;

10. *Acknowledges* the role the temporary international mechanism plays in assisting directly the Palestinian people, and encourages interested donors to make use of the mechanism;

11. *Emphasizes* the need to preserve the Palestinian institutions and infrastructure for the provision of vital public services to the Palestinian civilian population and the promotion of Palestinian civil, political, economic, social and cultural rights;

12. *Demands* that Israel, the occupying Power, comply with its legal obligations under international law, as mentioned in the advisory opinion rendered on 9 July 2004 by the International Court of Justice and as demanded in resolutions ES-10/15 of 20 July 2004 and ES-10/13 of 21 October 2003, and that it immediately cease the construction of the wall in the Occupied Palestinian Territory, including in and around East Jerusalem, dismantle forthwith the structure situated therein, repeal or render ineffective all legislative and regulatory acts relating thereto, and make reparation for all damage caused by the construction of the wall, which has gravely impacted the human rights and the socio-economic living conditions of the Palestinian people;

13. *Stresses* the need for respect for the unity and territorial integrity of all of the Occupied Palestinian Territory and for guarantees of the freedom of movement of persons and goods within the Palestinian territory, including the removal of restrictions on movement into and from East Jerusalem, and the freedom of movement to and from the outside world;

14. *Also stresses* the need for the full implementation by both parties of the Sharm El-Sheikh understandings and the Agreement on Movement and Access and the Agreed Principles for the Rafah Crossing;

15. *Requests* the Secretary-General to report to the General Assembly at its sixty-second session on the implementation of the present resolution.

RECORDED VOTE ON RESOLUTION 61/119:

In favour: Afghanistan, Albania, Algeria, Andorra, Antigua and Barbuda, Argentina, Armenia, Austria, Azerbaijan, Bahamas, Bahrain, Bangladesh, Barbados, Belarus, Belgium, Belize, Benin, Bhutan, Bolivia, Bosnia and Herzegovina, Botswana, Brazil, Brunei Darussalam, Bulgaria, Burkina Faso, Cambodia, Cape Verde, Central African Republic, Chad, Chile, China, Colombia, Comoros, Congo, Costa Rica, Croatia, Cuba, Cyprus, Czech Republic, Democratic People's Republic of Korea, Denmark, Djibouti, Dominica, Ecuador, Egypt, Eritrea, Estonia, Ethiopia, Finland, France, Gabon, Georgia, Germany, Ghana, Greece, Grenada, Guatemala, Guinea, Guinea-Bissau, Guyana, Haiti, Hungary, Iceland, Indonesia, Iran, Iraq, Ireland, Italy, Jamaica, Japan, Jordan, Kazakhstan, Kenya, Kuwait, Kyrgyzstan, Lao People's Democratic Republic, Latvia, Lebanon, Lesotho, Libyan Arab Jamahiriya, Liechtenstein, Lithuania, Luxembourg, Malaysia, Maldives, Mali, Malta, Mauritania, Mauritius, Mexico, Moldova, Monaco, Mongolia, Montenegro, Morocco, Mozambique, Myanmar, Namibia, Nepal, Netherlands, New Zealand, Niger, Nigeria, Norway, Oman, Pakistan, Panama, Paraguay, Peru, Philippines, Poland, Portugal, Qatar, Republic of Korea, Romania, Russian Federation, Saint Lucia, Saint Vincent and the Grenadines, Samoa, San Marino, Sao Tome and Principe, Saudi Arabia, Senegal, Serbia, Sierra Leone, Singapore, Slovakia, Slovenia, Solomon Islands, South Africa, Spain, Sri Lanka, Sudan, Suriname, Sweden, Switzerland, Syrian Arab Republic, Tajikistan, Thailand, The former Yugoslav Republic of Macedonia, Timor-Leste, Togo, Trinidad and Tobago, Tunisia, Turkey, Turkmenistan, Ukraine, United Arab Emirates, United Kingdom, United Republic of Tanzania, Uruguay, Uzbekistan, Venezuela, Viet Nam, Yemen, Zambia, Zimbabwe.

Against: Australia, Canada, Israel, Marshall Islands, Micronesia, Nauru, Palau, Tuvalu, United States.

Abstaining: Burundi, Cameroon, Côte d'Ivoire, Dominican Republic, El Salvador, Equatorial Guinea, Fiji, Honduras,

Malawi, Nicaragua, Papua New Guinea, Tonga, Uganda, Vanuatu.

By resolution 61/25 of 1 December, the Assembly reaffirmed the right of the Palestinian people to self-determination, including the right to their State, and urged all States and UN specialized agencies and organizations to support the Palestinian people in their quest for self-determination (see p. 548).

Work of Special Committee

In a September report [A/61/330], the Secretary-General stated that, owing to spending limitations affecting the regular budget, the Committee rescheduled its field trip to Egypt, Jordan and Syria, originally planned for June, to 1 to 15 August. However, the deteriorating security situation in the region since July, resulting in the restriction of movement and travel for both the Committee and witnesses, compelled the Committee to postpone its visit. Instead it held consultations in Geneva from 31 July to 2 August, with a view of reviewing the situation and revising plans for its field visit by mid-November. Pursuant to General Assembly resolution 60/104 [YUN 2005, p. 529], the UN Department of Public Information continued to disseminate information on the Committee's activities.

The Committee was finally able to visit the region from 11 to 22 November (see p. 537).

GENERAL ASSEMBLY ACTION

On 14 December [meeting 79], the General Assembly, on the recommendation of the Fourth Committee [A/61/408], adopted **resolution 61/116** by recorded vote (90-9-81) [agenda item 32].

Work of the Special Committee to Investigate Israeli Practices Affecting the Human Rights of the Palestinian People and Other Arabs of the Occupied Territories

The General Assembly,

Guided by the purposes and principles of the Charter of the United Nations,

Guided also by international humanitarian law, in particular the Geneva Convention relative to the Protection of Civilian Persons in Time of War, of 12 August 1949, as well as international standards of human rights, in particular the Universal Declaration of Human Rights and the International Covenants on Human Rights,

Recalling its relevant resolutions, including resolutions 2443 (XXIII) of 19 December 1968 and 60/104 of 8 December 2005, and the relevant resolutions of the Commission on Human Rights and the Human Rights Council,

Recalling also the relevant resolutions of the Security Council,

Taking into account the advisory opinion rendered on 9 July 2004 by the International Court of Justice on the *Legal Consequences of the Construction of a Wall in the Occupied Palestinian Territory*, and recalling in this regard General Assembly resolution ES-10/15 of 20 July 2004,

Convinced that occupation itself represents a gross and grave violation of human rights,

Gravely concerned about the continuing detrimental impact of the events that have taken place since 28 September 2000, including the excessive use of force by the Israeli occupying forces against Palestinian civilians, resulting in thousands of deaths and injuries, the widespread destruction of property and vital infrastructure and the internal displacement of civilians,

Having considered the report of the Special Committee to Investigate Israeli Practices Affecting the Human Rights of the Palestinian People and Other Arabs of the Occupied Territories and the relevant reports of the Secretary-General,

Recalling the Declaration of Principles on Interim Self-Government Arrangements of 13 September 1993 and the subsequent implementation agreements between the Palestinian and Israeli sides,

Welcoming the free and democratic Palestinian Legislative Council elections that took place on 25 January 2006 and welcoming also the efforts to form a national unity government working towards a peaceful resolution of the Israeli-Palestinian conflict, based on relevant United Nations resolutions and the agreements concluded between the two sides,

Expressing the hope that the Israeli occupation will be brought to an early and complete end and that therefore the violation of the human rights of the Palestinian people will cease, and recalling in this regard its resolution 58/292 of 6 May 2004,

1. *Commends* the Special Committee to Investigate Israeli Practices Affecting the Human Rights of the Palestinian People and Other Arabs of the Occupied Territories for its efforts in performing the tasks assigned to it by the General Assembly and for its impartiality;

2. *Reiterates its demand* that Israel, the occupying Power, cooperate, in line with its obligations as a State Member of the United Nations, with the Special Committee in implementing its mandate;

3. *Deplores* those policies and practices of Israel that violate the human rights of the Palestinian people and other Arabs of the occupied territories, as reflected in the report of the Special Committee covering the reporting period;

4. *Expresses grave concern* about the critical situation in the Occupied Palestinian Territory, including East Jerusalem, since 28 September 2000, as a result of unlawful Israeli practices and measures, and especially condemns all Israeli settlement activities and the construction of the wall, as well as the excessive and indiscriminate use of force against the civilian population, including extra-judicial executions;

5. *Welcomes* the free and democratic Palestinian Legislative Council elections that took place on 25 January 2006 and welcomes also the efforts to form a national

unity government working towards a peaceful resolution of the Israeli-Palestinian conflict, based on relevant United Nations resolutions and the agreements concluded between the two sides;

6. *Requests* the Special Committee, pending complete termination of the Israeli occupation, to continue to investigate Israeli policies and practices in the Occupied Palestinian Territory, including East Jerusalem, and other Arab territories occupied by Israel since 1967, especially Israeli violations of the Geneva Convention relative to the Protection of Civilian Persons in Time of War, of 12 August 1949, and to consult, as appropriate, with the International Committee of the Red Cross according to its regulations in order to ensure that the welfare and human rights of the peoples of the occupied territories are safeguarded and to report to the Secretary-General as soon as possible and whenever the need arises thereafter;

7. *Also requests* the Special Committee to submit regularly to the Secretary-General periodic reports on the current situation in the Occupied Palestinian Territory, including East Jerusalem;

8. *Further requests* the Special Committee to continue to investigate the treatment of the thousands of prisoners and detainees in the Occupied Palestinian Territory, including East Jerusalem, and other Arab territories occupied by Israel since 1967;

9. *Requests* the Secretary-General:

(a) To provide the Special Committee with all necessary facilities, including those required for its visits to the occupied territories, so that it may investigate Israeli policies and practices referred to in the present resolution;

(b) To continue to make available such staff as may be necessary to assist the Special Committee in the performance of its tasks;

(c) To circulate regularly to Member States the periodic reports mentioned in paragraph 7 above;

(d) To ensure the widest circulation of the reports of the Special Committee and of information regarding its activities and findings, by all means available, through the Department of Public Information of the Secretariat and, where necessary, to reprint those reports of the Special Committee that are no longer available;

(e) To report to the General Assembly at its sixty-second session on the tasks entrusted to him in the present resolution;

10. *Decides* to include in the provisional agenda of its sixty-second session the item entitled "Report of the Special Committee to Investigate Israeli Practices Affecting the Human Rights of the Palestinian People and Other Arabs of the Occupied Territories".

RECORDED VOTE ON RESOLUTION 61/116:

In favour: Afghanistan, Algeria, Antigua and Barbuda, Armenia, Azerbaijan, Bahrain, Bangladesh, Barbados, Belarus, Belize, Benin, Bhutan, Bolivia, Botswana, Brazil, Brunei Darussalam, Cambodia, Chad, Chile, China, Comoros, Congo, Cuba, Democratic People's Republic of Korea, Djibouti, Dominica, Ecuador, Egypt, Equatorial Guinea, Eritrea, Gabon, Ghana, Grenada, Guinea, Guinea-Bissau, Guyana, India, Indonesia, Iran, Iraq, Jamaica, Jordan, Kenya, Kuwait, Lao People's Democratic Republic, Lebanon, Lesotho, Libyan Arab Jamahiriya, Malaysia, Maldives, Mali, Mauritania, Mauritius, Morocco, Mozambique, Myanmar, Namibia, Nepal, Niger, Nigeria, Oman, Pakistan, Paraguay, Qatar, Saint Lucia, Saint Vincent and the Grenadines, Sao Tome and Principe, Saudi Arabia, Senegal, Sierra Leone, Singapore, South Africa, Sri Lanka, Sudan, Suriname, Syrian Arab Republic, Tajikistan, Togo, Trinidad and Tobago, Tunisia, Turkey, Turkmenistan, United Arab Emirates, United Republic of Tanzania, Uzbekistan, Venezuela, Viet Nam, Yemen, Zambia, Zimbabwe.

Against: Australia, Canada, Israel, Marshall Islands, Micronesia, Nauru, Palau, Tuvalu, United States.

Abstaining: Albania, Andorra, Argentina, Austria, Bahamas, Belgium, Bosnia and Herzegovina, Bulgaria, Burundi, Cameroon, Cape Verde, Central African Republic, Colombia, Costa Rica, Côte d'Ivoire, Croatia, Cyprus, Czech Republic, Denmark, Dominican Republic, El Salvador, Estonia, Ethiopia, Fiji, Finland, France, Georgia, Germany, Greece, Guatemala, Haiti, Honduras, Hungary, Iceland, Ireland, Italy, Japan, Kazakhstan, Kyrgyzstan, Latvia, Liechtenstein, Lithuania, Luxembourg, Malawi, Malta, Mexico, Moldova, Monaco, Mongolia, Montenegro, Netherlands, New Zealand, Nicaragua, Norway, Panama, Papua New Guinea, Peru, Philippines, Poland, Portugal, Republic of Korea, Romania, Russian Federation, Samoa, San Marino, Serbia, Slovakia, Slovenia, Solomon Islands, Spain, Swaziland, Sweden, Switzerland, Thailand, The former Yugoslav Republic of Macedonia, Tonga, Uganda, Ukraine, United Kingdom, Uruguay, Vanuatu.

By **decision 61/552** of 22 December, the Assembly decided that the agenda item entitled "Report of the Special Committee to Investigate Israeli Practices Affecting the Human Rights of the Palestinian People and Other Arabs of the Occupied Territories" would remain for consideration during its resumed sixty-first (2007) session.

Fourth Geneva Convention

Report of Secretary-General. In a September report [A/61/331], the Secretary-General informed the General Assembly that Israel had not replied to his June request for information on steps taken or envisaged to implement Assembly resolution 60/105 [YUN 2005, p. 531] demanding that Israel accept the de jure applicability of the Fourth Geneva Convention to the Occupied Palestinian Territory, including East Jerusalem, and other occupied Arab territories, and that it comply scrupulously with its provisions. The Secretary-General said that he had drawn the attention of all States parties to the Convention to paragraph 3 of resolution 60/105 calling on them to exert all efforts to ensure respect by Israel for the Convention's provisions, and to paragraph 6 of resolution 60/108 [ibid., p. 574] calling on States not to recognize any legislative or administrative measures and actions taken by Israel in the occupied Syrian Golan.

The High Contracting Parties to the Fourth Geneva Convention had ratified the applicability of the

Convention to the Occupied Palestinian Territory at meetings in 1999 [YUN 1999, p. 415] and in 2001 [YUN 2001, p. 425].

GENERAL ASSEMBLY ACTION

On 14 December [meeting 79], the General Assembly, on the recommendation of the Fourth Committee [A/61/408], adopted **resolution 61/117** by recorded vote (165-7-10) [agenda item 32].

Applicability of the Geneva Convention relative to the Protection of Civilian Persons in Time of War, of 12 August 1949, to the Occupied Palestinian Territory, including East Jerusalem, and the other occupied Arab territories

The General Assembly,

Recalling its relevant resolutions, including its resolution 60/105 of 8 December 2005,

Recalling also its resolution ES-10/15 of 20 July 2004,

Bearing in mind the relevant resolutions of the Security Council,

Recalling the Regulations annexed to the Hague Convention IV of 1907, the Geneva Convention relative to the Protection of Civilian Persons in Time of War, of 12 August 1949, and relevant provisions of customary law, including those codified in Additional Protocol I, to the four Geneva Conventions,

Having considered the report of the Special Committee to Investigate Israeli Practices Affecting the Human Rights of the Palestinian People and Other Arabs of the Occupied Territories and the relevant reports of the Secretary-General,

Considering that the promotion of respect for the obligations arising from the Charter of the United Nations and other instruments and rules of international law is among the basic purposes and principles of the United Nations,

Recalling the advisory opinion rendered on 9 July 2004 by the International Court of Justice, and also recalling General Assembly resolution ES-10/15,

Noting in particular the Court's reply, including that the Fourth Geneva Convention is applicable in the Occupied Palestinian Territory, including East Jerusalem, and that Israel is in breach of several of the provisions of the Convention,

Noting the convening, on 15 July 1999, of a Conference of High Contracting Parties to the Fourth Geneva Convention on measures to enforce the Convention in the Occupied Palestinian Territory, including East Jerusalem, and to ensure respect thereof in accordance with article 1 common to the four Geneva Conventions, and stressing the importance of the Declaration adopted by the reconvened Conference on 5 December 2001 and the need for the parties to follow up the implementation of the Declaration,

Welcoming and encouraging the initiatives by States parties to the Convention, both individually and collectively, according to article 1 common to the four Geneva Conventions, aimed at ensuring respect for the Convention,

Stressing that Israel, the occupying Power, should comply strictly with its obligations under international law, including international humanitarian law,

1. *Reaffirms* that the Geneva Convention relative to the Protection of Civilian Persons in Time of War, of 12 August 1949, is applicable to the Occupied Palestinian Territory, including East Jerusalem, and other Arab territories occupied by Israel since 1967;

2. *Demands* that Israel accept the de jure applicability of the Convention in the Occupied Palestinian Territory, including East Jerusalem, and other Arab territories occupied by Israel since 1967, and that it comply scrupulously with the provisions of the Convention;

3. *Calls upon* all High Contracting Parties to the Convention, in accordance with article 1 common to the four Geneva Conventions and as mentioned in the advisory opinion of the International Court of Justice of 9 July 2004, to continue to exert all efforts to ensure respect for its provisions by Israel, the occupying Power, in the Occupied Palestinian Territory, including East Jerusalem, and other Arab territories occupied by Israel since 1967;

4. *Reiterates* the need for speedy implementation of the relevant recommendations contained in the resolutions adopted by the General Assembly at its tenth emergency special session, including resolution ES-10/15, with regard to ensuring respect by Israel, the occupying Power, for the provisions of the Convention;

5. *Requests* the Secretary-General to report to the General Assembly at its sixty-second session on the implementation of the present resolution.

RECORDED VOTE ON RESOLUTION 61/117:

In favour: Afghanistan, Albania, Algeria, Andorra, Antigua and Barbuda, Argentina, Armenia, Austria, Azerbaijan, Bahamas, Bahrain, Bangladesh, Barbados, Belarus, Belgium, Belize, Benin, Bhutan, Bolivia, Bosnia and Herzegovina, Botswana, Brazil, Brunei Darussalam, Bulgaria, Burkina Faso, Burundi, Cambodia, Canada, Cape Verde, Central African Republic, Chad, Chile, China, Colombia, Comoros, Congo, Costa Rica, Croatia, Cuba, Cyprus, Czech Republic, Democratic People's Republic of Korea, Denmark, Djibouti, Dominica, Ecuador, Egypt, El Salvador, Equatorial Guinea, Eritrea, Estonia, Ethiopia, Finland, France, Gabon, Georgia, Germany, Ghana, Greece, Grenada, Guatemala, Guinea, Guinea-Bissau, Guyana, Haiti, Honduras, Hungary, Iceland, India, Indonesia, Iran, Iraq, Ireland, Italy, Jamaica, Japan, Jordan, Kazakhstan, Kenya, Kuwait, Kyrgyzstan, Lao People's Democratic Republic, Latvia, Lebanon, Lesotho, Libyan Arab Jamahiriya, Liechtenstein, Lithuania, Luxembourg, Malaysia, Maldives, Mali, Malta, Mauritania, Mauritius, Mexico, Moldova, Monaco, Mongolia, Montenegro, Morocco, Mozambique, Myanmar, Namibia, Nepal, Netherlands, New Zealand, Nicaragua, Niger, Nigeria, Norway, Oman, Pakistan, Panama, Paraguay, Peru, Philippines, Poland, Portugal, Qatar, Republic of Korea, Romania, Russian Federation, Saint Lucia, Saint Vincent and the Grenadines, Samoa, San Marino, Sao Tome and Principe, Saudi Arabia, Senegal, Serbia, Sierra Leone, Singapore, Slovakia, Slovenia, Solomon Islands, South Africa, Spain, Sri Lanka, Sudan, Suriname, Sweden, Switzerland, Syrian Arab Republic, Tajikistan, Thailand, The former Yugoslav Republic of Macedonia, Timor-Leste, Togo, Tonga, Trinidad and Tobago, Tunisia, Turkey, Turkmenistan, Ukraine, United Arab

Emirates, United Kingdom, United Republic of Tanzania, Uruguay, Uzbekistan, Venezuela, Viet Nam, Yemen, Zambia, Zimbabwe.

Against: Israel, Marshall Islands, Micronesia, Nauru, Palau, Tuvalu, United States.

Abstaining: Angola, Australia, Cameroon, Côte d'Ivoire, Dominican Republic, Fiji, Malawi, Papua New Guinea, Uganda, Vanuatu.

Israeli settlements

Report of Secretary-General. On 12 September [A/61/328], the Secretary-General informed the General Assembly that Israel had not replied to his June request for information on steps taken or envisaged taking to implement the relevant provisions of resolution 60/106 [YUN 2005, p. 532] demanding that Israel, among other things, cease all construction of the wall and new settlements in the Occupied Palestinian Territory, including East Jerusalem.

GENERAL ASSEMBLY ACTION

On 14 December [meeting 79], the General Assembly, on the recommendation of the Fourth Committee [A/61/408], adopted **resolution 61/118** by recorded vote (162-8-10) [agenda item 32].

Israeli settlements in the Occupied Palestinian Territory, including East Jerusalem, and the occupied Syrian Golan

The General Assembly,

Guided by the principles of the Charter of the United Nations, and affirming the inadmissibility of the acquisition of territory by force,

Recalling its relevant resolutions, including resolution 60/106 of 8 December 2005, as well as those resolutions adopted at its tenth emergency special session,

Recalling also relevant Security Council resolutions, including resolutions 242(1967) of 22 November 1967, 446(1979) of 22 March 1979, 465(1980) of 1 March 1980, 476(1980) of 30 June 1980, 478(1980) of 20 August 1980, 497(1981) of 17 December 1981 and 904(1994) of 18 March 1994,

Reaffirming the applicability of the Geneva Convention relative to the Protection of Civilian Persons in Time of War, of 12 August 1949, to the Occupied Palestinian Territory, including East Jerusalem, and to the occupied Syrian Golan,

Considering that the transfer by the occupying Power of parts of its own civilian population into the territory it occupies constitutes a breach of the Fourth Geneva Convention and relevant provisions of customary law, including those codified in Additional Protocol I to the Geneva Conventions,

Recalling the advisory opinion rendered on 9 July 2004 by the International Court of Justice on the *Legal Consequences of the Construction of a Wall in the Occupied Palestinian Territory*, and recalling also General Assembly resolution ES-10/15 of 20 July 2004,

Noting that the International Court of Justice concluded that "the Israeli settlements in the Occupied Palestinian Territory (including East Jerusalem) have been established in breach of international law",

Taking note of the recent report of the Special Rapporteur of the Human Rights Council on the situation of human rights in the Palestinian territories occupied by Israel since 1967,

Recalling the Declaration of Principles on Interim Self-Government Arrangements of 13 September 1993 and the subsequent implementation agreements between the Palestinian and Israeli sides,

Recalling also the Quartet road map to a permanent two-State solution to the Israeli-Palestinian conflict, and noting specifically its call for a freeze on all settlement activity,

Aware that Israeli settlement activities involve, inter alia, the transfer of nationals of the occupying Power into the occupied territories, the confiscation of land, the exploitation of natural resources and other illegal actions against the Palestinian civilian population,

Bearing in mind the detrimental impact of Israeli settlement policies, decisions and activities on efforts to achieve peace in the Middle East,

Expressing grave concern about the continuation by Israel, the occupying Power, of settlement activities, including in and around East Jerusalem, in violation of international humanitarian law, relevant United Nations resolutions and the agreements reached between the parties, and concerned in particular about the construction and expansion of the settlements in Jabal Abu-Ghneim and Ras Al-Amud in and around Occupied East Jerusalem and Israel's intentions to proceed with the so-called E-1 plan, aimed at connecting its illegal settlements around and further isolating Occupied East Jerusalem,

Expressing grave concern also about the continuing unlawful construction by Israel of the wall inside the Occupied Palestinian Territory, including in and around East Jerusalem, and expressing its concern in particular about the route of the wall in departure from the Armistice Line of 1949, which could prejudge future negotiations and make the two-State solution physically impossible to implement and which is causing serious humanitarian hardship and a serious decline of socio-economic conditions for the Palestinian people,

Deeply concerned that the wall's route has been traced in such a way as to include the great majority of the Israeli settlements in the Occupied Palestinian Territory, including East Jerusalem,

Reiterating its opposition to settlement activities in the Occupied Palestinian Territory, including East Jerusalem, and in the occupied Syrian Golan and to any activities involving the confiscation of land, the disruption of the livelihood of protected persons and the de facto annexation of land,

Recalling the need to end all acts of violence, including acts of terror, provocation, incitement and destruction,

Gravely concerned about the dangerous situation resulting from actions taken by the illegal armed Israeli settlers in the occupied territory,

Noting the Israeli withdrawal from within the Gaza Strip and parts of the northern West Bank and the importance of the dismantlement of the settlements therein as a step towards the implementation of the road map,

Taking note of the relevant reports of the Secretary-General,

1. *Reaffirms* that Israeli settlements in the Palestinian territory, including East Jerusalem, and in the occupied Syrian Golan are illegal and an obstacle to peace and economic and social development;

2. *Calls upon* Israel to accept the de jure applicability of the Geneva Convention relative to the Protection of Civilian Persons in Time of War, of 12 August 1949, to the Occupied Palestinian Territory, including East Jerusalem, and to the occupied Syrian Golan and to abide scrupulously by the provisions of the Convention, in particular article 49;

3. *Notes* the Israeli withdrawal from within the Gaza Strip and parts of the northern West Bank and the importance of the dismantlement of the settlements therein as a step towards the implementation of the road map;

4. *Calls upon* Israel, the occupying Power, in this regard, to comply strictly with its obligations under international law, including international humanitarian law, with respect to the alteration of the character and status of the Occupied Palestinian Territory, including East Jerusalem;

5. *Emphasizes* the need for the parties to speedily resolve all remaining issues in the Gaza Strip, including the removal of rubble;

6. *Reiterates its demand* for the immediate and complete cessation of all Israeli settlement activities in all of the Occupied Palestinian Territory, including East Jerusalem, and in the occupied Syrian Golan, and calls for the full implementation of the relevant resolutions of the Security Council;

7. *Demands* that Israel, the occupying Power, comply with its legal obligations, as mentioned in the advisory opinion rendered on 9 July 2004 by the International Court of Justice;

8. *Stresses* the need for full implementation of the relevant Security Council resolutions regarding the Israeli settlements, including Security Council resolution 904(1994), in which, among other things, the Council called upon Israel, the occupying Power, to continue to take and implement measures, including confiscation of arms, with the aim of preventing illegal acts of violence by Israeli settlers, and called for measures to be taken to guarantee the safety and protection of the Palestinian civilians in the occupied territory;

9. *Reiterates its calls* for the prevention of all acts of violence by Israeli settlers, especially against Palestinian civilians and properties, particularly in the light of recent developments;

10. *Requests* the Secretary-General to report to the General Assembly at its sixty-second session on the implementation of the present resolution.

RECORDED VOTE ON RESOLUTION 61/118:

In favour: Afghanistan, Albania, Algeria, Andorra, Antigua and Barbuda, Argentina, Armenia, Austria, Azerbaijan, Bahamas, Bahrain, Bangladesh, Barbados, Belarus, Belgium, Belize, Benin, Bhutan, Bolivia, Bosnia and Herzegovina, Botswana, Brazil, Brunei Darussalam, Bulgaria, Burkina Faso, Burundi, Cambodia, Canada, Cape Verde, Central African Republic, Chad, Chile, China, Colombia, Comoros, Congo, Costa Rica, Croatia, Cuba, Cyprus, Czech Republic, Democratic People's Republic of Korea, Denmark, Djibouti, Dominica, Ecuador, Egypt, El Salvador, Eritrea, Estonia, Ethiopia, Finland, France, Gabon, Georgia, Germany, Ghana, Greece, Grenada, Guatemala, Guinea, Guinea-Bissau, Guyana, Haiti, Honduras, Hungary, Iceland, India, Indonesia, Iran, Iraq, Ireland, Italy, Jamaica, Japan, Jordan, Kazakhstan, Kenya, Kuwait, Kyrgyzstan, Lao People's Democratic Republic, Latvia, Lebanon, Lesotho, Libyan Arab Jamahiriya, Liechtenstein, Lithuania, Luxembourg, Malaysia, Maldives, Mali, Malta, Mauritania, Mauritius, Mexico, Moldova, Monaco, Mongolia, Montenegro, Morocco, Mozambique, Myanmar, Namibia, Nepal, Netherlands, New Zealand, Nicaragua, Niger, Nigeria, Norway, Oman, Pakistan, Panama, Paraguay, Peru, Philippines, Poland, Portugal, Qatar, Republic of Korea, Romania, Russian Federation, Saint Lucia, Saint Vincent and the Grenadines, Samoa, San Marino, Sao Tome and Principe, Saudi Arabia, Senegal, Serbia, Sierra Leone, Singapore, Slovakia, Slovenia, South Africa, Spain, Sri Lanka, Sudan, Suriname, Sweden, Switzerland, Syrian Arab Republic, Tajikistan, Thailand, The former Yugoslav Republic of Macedonia, Timor-Leste, Togo, Trinidad and Tobago, Tunisia, Turkey, Turkmenistan, Ukraine, United Arab Emirates, United Kingdom, United Republic of Tanzania, Uruguay, Uzbekistan, Venezuela, Viet Nam, Yemen, Zambia, Zimbabwe.

Against: Australia, Israel, Marshall Islands, Micronesia, Nauru, Palau, Tuvalu, United States.

Abstaining: Cameroon, Côte d'Ivoire, Dominican Republic, Equatorial Guinea, Fiji, Malawi, Papua New Guinea, Tonga, Uganda, Vanuatu.

Palestinian women

The Secretary-General, in a report [E/CN.6/2006/4] to the Commission on the Status of Women, as requested by the Economic and Social Council in resolution 2005/43 [YUN 2005, p. 534], reviewed the situation of Palestinian women and the assistance provided by UN organizations, from October 2004 to September 2005. He said that the impact of the conflict continued to adversely affect women in all spheres of life. Women and their families lived in a permanent state of insecurity, tension and fear. They were negatively affected by the restrictions on movement, the deteriorating economic conditions, poverty and lack of access to health care and services. Palestinian women continued to bear the combined burdens of occupation and patriarchy, which had deepened their inequality and denied them the possibility for enjoyment of rights, fundamental freedoms and liberty. The outcome document of the 2005 World Summit [ibid., p. 48] highlighted the importance of eliminating all forms of discrimination and violence against women and girls. The important role of women in the prevention and resolution of conflicts and in peacebuilding was also highlighted.

Member States had reaffirmed their commitment to the full and effective implementation of Security Council resolution 1325(2000) on women, peace and security [YUN 2000, p. 1113]. In that regard, it was important that Palestinian women were fully involved in all conflict-resolution and peacebuilding initiatives, including at decision-making levels. United Nations entities continued to make efforts to improve the situation of Palestinian women. The World Bank reported an improved targeting scheme of the Social Safety Net Reform Project to enable poor adult women living on their own due to separation, divorce or widowhood to receive cash assistance from the special hardship case programme. UNRWA continued its microcredit community support programme to promote the socio-economic status and self-reliance of the most vulnerable refugees, including women. UN-Habitat introduced a housing and income-generating programme for widows and underprivileged women in Hebron, with an initial funding of $6.2 million. The United Nations Development Programme established eight centres for the empowerment of community women, while the United Nations Conference on Trade and Development made empowering Palestinian women and fostering their contribution to economic development one of the main objectives of its integrated capacity-building programme. UNRWA assistance to Palestinian refugee women focused on education and technical training, delivery of women-focused health services, social service support and the provision of microfinance and emergency assistance to respond to the urgent needs generated by the ongoing crisis. The newly established Ministry of Women's Affairs undertook important initiatives to promote gender mainstreaming in all ministries. United Nations entities and other international organizations should continue to coordinate and collaborate to provide financial, advisory and technical assistance to the Ministry and gender units to ensure that gender perspectives were identified and addressed in policies and programmes in all policy areas.

ECONOMIC AND SOCIAL COUNCIL ACTION

On 25 July [meeting 38], the Economic and Social Council, on the recommendation of the Commission on the Status of Women [E/2006/27 & Corr.1], adopted **resolution 2006/8** by recorded vote (38-2-1) [agenda item 14 *(a)*].

Situation of and assistance to Palestinian women

The Economic and Social Council,

Having considered with appreciation the report of the Secretary-General on the situation of and assistance to Palestinian women,

Recalling the Nairobi Forward-looking Strategies for the Advancement of Women, in particular paragraph 260 concerning Palestinian women and children, the Beijing Platform for Action adopted at the Fourth World Conference on Women, and the outcome of the twenty-third special session of the General Assembly entitled "Women 2000: gender equality, development and peace for the twenty-first century",

Recalling also its resolution 2005/43 of 26 July 2005 and other relevant United Nations resolutions,

Recalling further the Declaration on the Elimination of Violence against Women as it concerns the protection of civilian populations,

Recalling the importance of the implementation of General Assembly resolution 57/337 of 3 July 2003, on the prevention of armed conflict, and Security Council resolution 1325(2000) of 31 October 2000, on women and peace and security,

Expressing the urgent need for the full resumption of negotiations within the Middle East peace process on its agreed basis and towards the speedy achievement of a final settlement between the Palestinian and Israeli sides,

Concerned about the grave situation of Palestinian women in the Occupied Palestinian Territory, including East Jerusalem, resulting from the severe impact of ongoing illegal Israeli settlement activities and the unlawful construction of the wall in the Occupied Palestinian Territory, including in and around East Jerusalem, as well as the severe consequences arising from Israeli military operations on and sieges of civilian areas, which have impacted detrimentally their social and economic conditions and deepened the humanitarian crisis faced by Palestinian women and their families,

Welcoming the report of the United Nations High Commissioner for Human Rights on the issue of Palestinian pregnant women giving birth at Israeli checkpoints owing to denial of access by Israel to hospitals, with a view to ending this Israeli practice,

Recalling the advisory opinion rendered on 9 July 2004 by the International Court of Justice on the *Legal Consequences of the Construction of a Wall in the Occupied Palestinian Territory,* and recalling also General Assembly resolution ES-10/15 of 20 July 2004,

Recalling also the International Covenant on Civil and Political Rights, the International Covenant on Economic, Social and Cultural Rights and the Convention on the Rights of the Child, and affirming that these human rights instruments must be respected in the Occupied Palestinian Territory, including East Jerusalem,

Expressing its condemnation of all acts of violence, including all acts of terror, provocation, incitement and destruction, especially the excessive use of force against Palestinian civilians, many of them women and children, resulting in injury and loss of human life,

1. *Calls upon* the concerned parties, as well as the international community, to exert all the efforts necessary to ensure the full resumption of the peace process on its agreed basis, taking into account the common ground already gained, and calls for measures for tangible improvement of the difficult situation on the ground and the living conditions faced by Palestinian women and their families;

2. *Reaffirms* that the Israeli occupation remains a major obstacle for Palestinian women with regard to their advancement, self-reliance and integration in the development planning of their society;

3. *Demands* that Israel, the occupying Power, comply fully with the provisions and principles of the Universal Declaration of Human Rights, the Regulations annexed to the Hague Convention Respecting the Laws and Customs of War on Land (Convention IV) of 18 October 1907 and the Geneva Convention relative to the Protection of Civilian Persons in Time of War, of 12 August 1949, in order to protect the rights of Palestinian women and their families;

4. *Calls upon* Israel to facilitate the return of all refugees and displaced Palestinian women and children to their homes and properties, in compliance with the relevant United Nations resolutions;

5. *Calls upon* the international community to continue to provide urgently needed assistance and services in an effort to alleviate the dire humanitarian crisis being faced by Palestinian women and their families and to help in the reconstruction of relevant Palestinian institutions;

6. *Requests* the Commission on the Status of Women to continue to monitor and take action with regard to the implementation of the Nairobi Forward-looking Strategies for the Advancement of Women, in particular paragraph 260 concerning Palestinian women and children, the Beijing Platform for Action and the outcome of the twenty-third special session of the General Assembly, entitled "Women 2000: gender equality, development and peace for the twenty-first century";

7. *Requests* the Secretary-General to continue to review the situation, to assist Palestinian women by all available means, including those set out in the report of the Secretary-General, and to submit to the Commission on the Status of Women at its fifty-first session a report, including information provided by the Economic and Social Commission for Western Asia, on the progress made in the implementation of the present resolution.

RECORDED VOTE ON RESOLUTION 2006/8:

In favour: Albania, Angola, Austria, Belgium, Belize, Benin, China, Colombia, Costa Rica, Cuba, Czech Republic, France, Germany, Guyana, Iceland, India, Indonesia, Italy, Japan, Lithuania, Madagascar, Mauritania, Mexico, Namibia, Nigeria, Pakistan, Panama, Paraguay, Republic of Korea, Russian Federation, Saudi Arabia, South Africa, Spain, Sri Lanka, Thailand, Tunisia, Turkey, United Kingdom.

Against: Australia, United States.

Abstentions: Haiti.

Issues related to Palestine

General aspects

The General Assembly again considered the question of Palestine in 2006. Having discussed the annual report of the Committee on the Exercise of the Inalienable Rights of the Palestinian People (Committee on Palestinian Rights) [A/61/35], the Assembly adopted a resolution reaffirming, among other things, the necessity of achieving a peaceful solution to the Palestine question—the core of the Arab-Israeli conflict—and stressing the need for the realization of the inalienable rights of the Palestinians, primarily the right to self-determination, for Israeli withdrawal from the Palestinian territory occupied since 1967 and for resolving the problem of the Palestine refugees.

In observance of the International Day of Solidarity with the Palestinian People, celebrated annually on 29 November in accordance with Assembly resolution 32/40 B [YUN 1977, p. 304], the Committee held a solemn meeting.

Report of Secretary-General. In a September report on the peaceful settlement of the question of Palestine [A/61/355-S/2006/748], submitted in response to Assembly resolution 60/39 [YUN 2005, p. 536], the Secretary-General made observations on the status of the Israeli-Palestinian conflict and international efforts to move the Middle East peace process forward. On 30 May, he sought information from Egypt, Israel, Jordan, Lebanon, the Syrian Arab Republic and the PLO regarding steps taken to implement the resolution. As at 1 September, Israel and the Permanent Observer of Palestine had responded.

In a 10 August note verbale, Israel said that one year after its withdrawal from the Gaza Strip, in the hope of restarting the peace process, Palestinian terrorism not only continued but had intensified. Israel viewed the resolution as unbalanced, politically motivated and an interference in matters that the parties had agreed to resolve through direct bilateral negotiations. Such a one-sided approach jeopardized the efficacy of the United Nations.

The Permanent Observer, in a 4 August note verbale, said that Israel had not complied with Assembly resolution 60/39 and continued to violate provisions of international law. The situation in the Occupied Palestinian Territory had deteriorated since December 2005, due primarily to the continuation by Israel of its policies and practices against the Palestinian people.

The Secretary-General said that he remained disturbed by the restrictions imposed by Israeli security forces as a result of the construction of the West Bank barrier, checkpoints and other obstacles that had consistently impeded the ability of UN agencies and programmes to provide assistance to Palestinians. The increasingly tight restrictions had hindered the movement of international staff to and from Gaza, while movement of national staff had been more difficult between Jerusalem, where most UN offices were headquartered, and the West Bank, where aid was needed. Of particular concern were incidents that compromised the security of UN staff. The Secretary-General noted that the road map had set the end of 2005 as the target date for settling the Israeli-Palestinian conflict. While that deadline had passed unobserved, the road map remained the agreed framework for achieving a just and lasting peace in the Middle East and an important reference for the future. He regretted that prospects for achieving a two-State solution had not improved over the reporting period. Though realities had changed, it was essential that all parties be encouraged to adopt policies and practices that were conducive to a peaceful solution. In that regard, he welcomed the continued commitment of President Abbas to a platform of peace, and noted with satisfaction Prime Minister Olmert's stated readiness to engage with Palestinian partners.

GENERAL ASSEMBLY ACTION

On 1 December [meeting 63], the General Assembly adopted **resolution 61/25** [draft: A/61/L.34, as orally revised] by recorded vote (157-7-10) [agenda item 14].

Peaceful settlement of the question of Palestine

The General Assembly,

Recalling its relevant resolutions, including those adopted by its tenth emergency special session,

Recalling also its resolution 58/292 of 6 May 2004,

Recalling further relevant Security Council resolutions, including resolutions 242(1967) of 22 November 1967, 338(1973) of 22 October 1973, 1397(2002) of 12 March 2002, 1515(2003) of 19 November 2003 and 1544(2004) of 19 May 2004,

Welcoming the affirmation by the Security Council of the vision of a region where two States, Israel and Palestine, live side by side within secure and recognized borders,

Noting with concern that it has been fifty-nine years since the adoption of resolution 181 (II) of 29 November 1947 and thirty-nine years since the occupation of Palestinian territory, including East Jerusalem, in 1967,

Having considered the report of the Secretary-General submitted pursuant to the request made in its resolution 60/39 of 1 December 2005,

Reaffirming the permanent responsibility of the United Nations with regard to the question of Palestine until the question is resolved in all its aspects in accordance with international law,

Recalling the advisory opinion rendered on 9 July 2004 by the International Court of Justice on the *Legal Consequences of the Construction of a Wall in the Occupied Palestinian Territory*, and recalling also its resolution ES-10/15 of 20 July 2004,

Convinced that achieving a just, lasting and comprehensive settlement of the question of Palestine, the core of the Arab-Israeli conflict, is imperative for the attainment of comprehensive and lasting peace and stability in the Middle East,

Aware that the principle of equal rights and self-determination of peoples is among the purposes and principles enshrined in the Charter of the United Nations,

Affirming the principle of the inadmissibility of the acquisition of territory by war,

Recalling its resolution 2625 (XXV) of 24 October 1970,

Reaffirming the illegality of the Israeli settlements in the Palestinian territory occupied since 1967,

Reaffirming also the illegality of Israeli actions aimed at changing the status of Jerusalem, including measures such as the so-called E-1 plan and all other unilateral measures aimed at altering the status of the city and the territory as a whole,

Reaffirming further that the construction by Israel, the occupying Power, of a wall in the Occupied Palestinian Territory, including in and around East Jerusalem, and its associated regime, are contrary to international law,

Expressing deep concern about the Israeli policy of closure and the severe restrictions, including curfews and the permit regime, that continue to be imposed on the movement of persons and goods, including medical and humanitarian personnel and goods, throughout the Occupied Palestinian Territory, including East Jerusalem, and the consequent negative impact on the socio-economic situation of the Palestinian people, which remains that of a dire humanitarian crisis,

Concerned about the continued establishment of Israeli checkpoints in the Occupied Palestinian Territory, including East Jerusalem, and the transformation of several of these checkpoints into structures akin to permanent border crossings inside the Occupied Palestinian Territory, which are severely impairing the territorial contiguity of the Territory and severely undermining efforts to rehabilitate and develop the Palestinian economy,

Affirming once again the right of all States in the region to live in peace within secure and internationally recognized borders,

Recalling the mutual recognition between the Government of the State of Israel and the Palestine Liberation Organization, the representative of the Palestinian people, and the agreements concluded between the two sides and the need for full compliance with those agreements,

Recalling also the endorsement by the Security Council, in resolution 1515(2003), of the Quartet road map to a permanent two-State solution to the Israeli-Palestinian conflict, and stressing the urgent need for its implementation and compliance with its provisions,

Welcoming the efforts of the Arab Foreign Ministers, demonstrated in the meeting of the Security Council on 21 September 2006, who called for, among other things, a solution to the conflict on the basis of relevant United Nations resolutions, especially from the Security Council, the Arab Peace Initiative and the road map,

Welcoming also the important contribution to the peace process of the United Nations Special Coordinator for the Middle East Peace Process and Personal Representative of the Secretary-General to the Palestine Liberation Organization and the Palestinian Authority, including in the framework of the activities of the Quartet,

Welcoming further the "Stockholm Donor Conference on the Humanitarian Situation in the Palestinian Territories" of 1 September 2006 and encouraging further donor meetings, as well as the establishment of international mechanisms, and in this regard acknowledging the Temporary International Mechanism, to provide assistance to the Palestinian people to alleviate the financial crisis and the dire socio-economic and humanitarian situation being faced by the Palestinian people,

Recognizing the efforts being undertaken by the Palestinian Authority, with international support, to rebuild, reform and strengthen its damaged institutions, and emphasizing the need to preserve the Palestinian institutions and infrastructure,

Expressing its concern over the tragic events that have occurred in the Occupied Palestinian Territory, including East Jerusalem, since 28 September 2000, including the large number of deaths and injuries, mostly among Palestinian civilians, the widespread destruction of public and private Palestinian property and infrastructure, the internal displacement of civilians, and the serious deterioration of the socio-economic and humanitarian conditions of the Palestinian people,

Expressing its grave concern over the repeated military actions in the Occupied Palestinian Territory and the reoccupation of Palestinian population centres by the Israeli occupying forces, and emphasizing in this regard the need for the implementation by both sides of the Sharm el-Sheikh understandings,

Welcoming the Palestinian truce initiative and its acceptance by Israel that came into effect on 26 November 2006, and urging both sides to maintain this truce, which could pave the way for genuine negotiations towards a just resolution to the conflict, and extend it to the West Bank,

Emphasizing the importance of the safety and well-being of all civilians in the whole Middle East region, and condemning all acts of violence and terror against civilians on both sides, including the suicide bombings, the extrajudicial executions and the excessive use of force,

Noting the Israeli withdrawal from within the Gaza Strip and parts of the northern West Bank and the importance of the dismantlement of the settlements therein as a step towards the implementation of the road map,

Stressing the urgent need for sustained and active international involvement, including by the Quartet, to support both parties in revitalizing the peace process towards the resumption and acceleration of direct negotiations between the parties for the achievement of a just, lasting and comprehensive peace settlement, in accordance with the road map,

Welcoming the initiatives and efforts undertaken by civil society in pursuit of a peaceful settlement of the question of Palestine,

Taking note of the findings by the International Court of Justice, in its advisory opinion, including on the urgent necessity for the United Nations as a whole to redouble its efforts to bring the Israeli-Palestinian conflict, which continues to pose a threat to international peace and security, to a speedy conclusion, thereby establishing a just and lasting peace in the region,

1. *Reaffirms* the necessity of achieving a peaceful settlement of the question of Palestine, the core of the Arab-Israeli conflict, in all its aspects, and of intensifying all efforts towards that end;

2. *Also reaffirms* its full support for the Middle East peace process, which began in Madrid, and the existing agreements between the Israeli and Palestinian sides, stresses the necessity for the establishment of a comprehensive, just and lasting peace in the Middle East, and welcomes in this regard the ongoing efforts of the Quartet;

3. *Welcomes* the Arab Peace Initiative adopted by the Council of the League of Arab States at its fourteenth session, held in Beirut on 27 and 28 March 2002;

4. *Calls upon* the parties themselves, with the support of the Quartet and other interested parties, to exert all efforts necessary to halt the deterioration of the situation, to reverse all measures taken on the ground since 28 September 2000 and to immediately resume direct peace negotiations towards the conclusion of a final peaceful settlement on the basis of relevant United Nations resolutions, especially from the Security Council, the Arab Peace Initiative, the terms of reference of the Madrid Conference and the road map;

5. *Calls upon* the Quartet, together with the international community, to take immediate steps, including confidence-building measures between the parties, aimed at stabilizing the situation and restarting the peace process;

6. *Stresses* the need for a speedy end to the reoccupation of Palestinian population centres and for the complete cessation of all acts of violence, including military attacks, destruction and acts of terror;

7. *Also stresses* the need for the immediate implementation of the Sharm el-Sheikh understandings;

8. *Calls upon* both parties to fulfil their obligations in respect of the implementation of the road map by taking parallel and reciprocal steps in this regard, and stresses the importance and urgency of establishing a credible and effective third-party monitoring mechanism, including all members of the Quartet;

9. *Notes* the Israeli withdrawal from within the Gaza Strip and parts of the northern West Bank and the dismantlement of the settlements therein as a step towards the implementation of the road map;

10. *Emphasizes* the need for the parties, with the help of the international community, speedily and fully to resolve all remaining issues in the Gaza Strip, including a durable arrangement for the border crossings, the airport, the construction of the seaport, the removal of the rubble and the establishment of a permanent physical link between the Gaza Strip and the West Bank, and stresses also the need for the full implementation by both parties of the Agreement on Movement and Access and the Agreed Principles for the Rafah Crossing, of 15 November 2005;

11. *Calls upon* Israel, the occupying Power, to comply strictly with its obligations under international law, including international humanitarian law, and that it cease all of its measures that are contrary to international law and unilateral actions in the Occupied Palestinian Territory, including East Jerusalem, that are aimed at altering the character and status of the Territory, including via the de facto annexation of land, and thus at prejudging the final outcome of peace negotiations;

12. *Demands accordingly* that Israel, the occupying Power, comply with its legal obligations under international law, as mentioned in the advisory opinion and as demanded in resolutions ES-10/13 of 21 October 2003 and ES-10/15 of 20 July 2004 and, inter alia, that it immediately cease its construction of the wall in the Occupied Palestinian Territory, including East Jerusalem, and calls upon all States Members of the United Nations to comply with their legal obligations, as mentioned in the advisory opinion;

13. *Reiterates its demand* for the complete cessation of all Israeli settlement activities in the Occupied Palestinian Territory, including East Jerusalem, and in the occupied Syrian Golan, and calls for the full implementation of the relevant Security Council resolutions;

14. *Reaffirms its commitment*, in accordance with international law, to the two-State solution of Israel and Palestine, living side by side in peace and security within recognized borders, based on the pre-1967 borders;

15. *Stresses* the need for:

(a) The withdrawal of Israel from the Palestinian territory occupied since 1967;

(b) The realization of the inalienable rights of the Palestinian people, primarily the right to self-determination and the right to their independent State;

16. *Also stresses* the need for resolving the problem of Palestine refugees in conformity with its resolution 194 (III) of 11 December 1948;

17. *Urges* Member States to expedite the provision of economic, humanitarian and technical assistance to the Palestinian people and the Palestinian Authority during this critical period to help to alleviate the humanitarian crisis being faced by the Palestinian people, rehabilitate the Palestinian economy and infrastructure and support the rebuilding, restructuring and reform of Palestinian institutions;

18. *Requests* the Secretary-General to continue his efforts with the parties concerned, and in consultation with the Security Council, towards the attainment of a peaceful settlement of the question of Palestine and the promotion of peace in the region and to submit to the General Assembly at its sixty-second session a report on these efforts and on developments on this matter.

RECORDED VOTE ON RESOLUTION 61/25:

In favour: Afghanistan, Albania, Algeria, Andorra, Angola, Antigua and Barbuda, Argentina, Armenia, Austria, Azerbaijan, Bahamas, Bahrain, Bangladesh, Barbados, Belarus, Belgium, Belize, Benin, Bhutan, Bolivia, Bosnia and Herzegovina, Brazil, Brunei Darussalam, Bulgaria, Burkina Faso, Burundi, Cambodia, Cape Verde, Central African Republic, Chile, China, Colombia, Comoros, Congo, Costa Rica, Croatia, Cuba, Cyprus, Czech Republic, Democratic People's Republic of Korea, Denmark, Djibouti, Dominica, Dominican Republic, Ecuador, Egypt, El Salvador, Eritrea, Estonia, Ethiopia, Finland, France, Georgia, Germany, Ghana, Greece, Grenada, Guatemala, Guinea, Guyana, Haiti, Honduras, Hungary, Iceland, India, Indonesia, Iran, Iraq, Ireland, Italy, Jamaica, Japan, Jordan, Kazakhstan, Kuwait, Kyrgyzstan, Lao People's Democratic Republic, Latvia, Lebanon, Lesotho, Liberia, Libyan Arab Jamahiriya, Liechtenstein, Lithuania, Luxembourg, Malaysia, Maldives, Mali, Malta, Mauritania, Mauritius, Mexico, Monaco, Mongolia, Montenegro, Morocco, Mozambique, Myanmar, Namibia, Nepal, Netherlands, New Zealand, Nicaragua, Niger, Nigeria, Norway, Oman, Pakistan, Panama, Paraguay, Peru, Philippines, Poland, Portugal, Qatar, Republic of Korea, Romania, Russian Federation, Saint Vincent and the Grenadines, Samoa, San Marino, Saudi Arabia, Senegal, Serbia, Seychelles, Sierra Leone, Singapore, Slovakia, Slovenia, Solomon Islands, Somalia, South Africa, Spain, Sri Lanka, Sudan, Suriname, Sweden, Switzerland, Syrian Arab Republic, Tajikistan, Thailand, The former Yugoslav Republic of Macedonia, Timor-Leste, Togo, Trinidad and Tobago, Tunisia, Turkey, Turkmenistan, Ukraine, United Arab Emirates, United Kingdom, Uruguay, Uzbekistan, Venezuela, Viet Nam, Yemen, Zambia.

Against: Australia, Israel, Marshall Islands, Micronesia, Nauru, Palau, United States.

Abstaining: Cameroon, Canada, Côte d'Ivoire, Fiji, Malawi, Moldova, Papua New Guinea, Tonga, Uganda, Vanuatu.

By **decision 61/552** of 22 December, the Assembly decided that the agenda items entitled "The situation in the Middle East" and "Question of Palestine" would remain for consideration during its resumed sixty-first (2007) session.

Committee on Palestinian Rights

As mandated by General Assembly resolution 60/36 [YUN 2005, p. 538], the Committee on the Exercise of the Inalienable Rights of the Palestinian People reviewed and reported on the Palestine question, and made suggestions to the Assembly and the Security Council.

The Committee followed up on the Palestine-related activities of intergovernmental bodies, such as the African Union, the Non-Aligned Movement and the Organization of the Islamic Conference, and through its Chairman's participation in meetings of those bodies. In March, the Committee's Bureau held consultations with EU representatives as part of the effort to build a constructive relationship on issues of common concern. Throughout the year, the Committee held a number of international meetings, including the United Nations International Meeting in Support of Israeli-Palestinian Peace (Vienna, 27-28 June) and the United Nations International Conference of Civil Society in Support of the Palestinian People (Geneva, 7-8 September).

The Committee's annual report to the Assembly [A/61/35] covered the period from 6 October 2005 to 4 October 2006. The Committee closely monitored the situation on the ground and was alarmed by the steady deterioration of the security and humanitarian situation in the Occupied Palestinian Territory, including East Jerusalem. It expressed particular concern at Israeli incursions into Gaza, which started in June 2006, and its destructive effects on the Palestinian people and their hopes for peace. The Committee called upon Israel to end its military operations in the occupied territories and stop any other measures that further undermined Palestinian institutions. It also condemned the killing of innocent civilians by either side and denounced the rocket attacks on Israel, calling for a cessation of those activities by Palestinian armed groups. The Committee was strongly opposed to the expansion of settlements in the West Bank and efforts to complete the construction of the wall on Palestinian land. It was particularly alarmed by the intention of the Israeli Government to expand large settlement blocks in the West Bank, which would separate it from East Jerusalem, and the southern West Bank from its northern part.

GENERAL ASSEMBLY ACTION

On 1 December [meeting 63], the General Assembly adopted **resolution 61/22** [draft: A/61/L.31 & Add.1] by recorded vote (101-7-62) [agenda item 14].

Committee on the Exercise of the Inalienable Rights of the Palestinian People

The General Assembly,

Recalling its resolutions 181 (II) of 29 November 1947, 194 (III) of 11 December 1948, 3236 (XXIX) of 22 November 1974, 3375 (XXX) and 3376 (XXX) of 10 November 1975, 31/20 of 24 November 1976 and all subsequent relevant resolutions, including those adopted by the General Assembly at its emergency special sessions and resolution 60/36 of 1 December 2005,

Recalling also its resolution 58/292 of 6 May 2004,

Having considered the report of the Committee on the Exercise of the Inalienable Rights of the Palestinian People,

Recalling the mutual recognition between the Government of the State of Israel and the Palestine Liberation Organization, the representative of the Palestinian people, as well as the existing agreements between the two sides and the need for full compliance with those agreements,

Recalling also the Quartet road map to a permanent two-State solution to the Israeli-Palestinian conflict,

Recalling further the advisory opinion rendered on 9 July 2004 by the International Court of Justice on the *Legal Consequences of the Construction of a Wall in the Occupied Palestinian Territory*, and recalling also its resolution ES-10/15 of 20 July 2004,

Reaffirming that the United Nations has a permanent responsibility towards the question of Palestine until the question is resolved in all its aspects in a satisfactory manner in accordance with international legitimacy,

1. *Expresses its appreciation* to the Committee on the Exercise of the Inalienable Rights of the Palestinian People for its efforts in performing the tasks assigned to it by the General Assembly, and takes note of its annual report, including the conclusions and valuable recommendations contained in chapter VII thereof;

2. *Requests* the Committee to continue to exert all efforts to promote the realization of the inalienable rights of the Palestinian people, to support the Middle East peace process and to mobilize international support for and assistance to the Palestinian people, and authorizes the Committee to make such adjustments in its approved programme of work as it may consider appropriate and necessary in the light of developments and to report thereon to the General Assembly at its sixty-second session and thereafter;

3. *Also requests* the Committee to continue to keep under review the situation relating to the question of Palestine and to report and make suggestions to the General Assembly, the Security Council or the Secretary-General, as appropriate;

4. *Further requests* the Committee to continue to extend its cooperation and support to Palestinian and other civil society organizations in order to mobilize international solidarity and support for the Palestinian people, particularly during this critical period of humanitarian hardship and financial crisis, with the overall aim of promoting the achievement by the Palestinian people of its inalienable rights and for a peaceful settlement of the question of Palestine, and to continue to involve additional civil society organizations in its work;

5. *Requests* the United Nations Conciliation Commission for Palestine, established under General Assembly resolution 194 (III), and other United Nations bodies associated with the question of Palestine to continue to cooperate fully with the Committee and to make available to it, at its request, the relevant information and documentation which they have at their disposal;

6. *Invites* all Governments and organizations to extend their cooperation to the Committee in the performance of its tasks;

7. *Requests* the Secretary-General to circulate the report of the Committee to all the competent bodies of the United Nations, and urges them to take the necessary action, as appropriate;

8. *Also requests* the Secretary-General to continue to provide the Committee with all the necessary facilities for the performance of its tasks.

RECORDED VOTE ON RESOLUTION 61/22:

In favour: Afghanistan, Algeria, Angola, Antigua and Barbuda, Argentina, Armenia, Azerbaijan, Bahamas, Bahrain, Bangladesh, Barbados, Belarus, Belize, Benin, Bhutan, Bolivia, Brazil, Brunei Darussalam, Burkina Faso, Burundi, Cambodia, Cape Verde, Central African Republic, Chile, China, Comoros, Congo, Costa Rica, Côte d'Ivoire, Cuba, Cyprus, Democratic People's Republic of Korea, Djibouti, Ecuador, Egypt, El Salvador, Eritrea, Ethiopia, Ghana, Grenada, Guinea, Guyana, Haiti, Honduras, India, Indonesia, Iran, Iraq, Jamaica, Jordan, Kazakhstan, Kuwait, Kyrgyzstan, Lao People's Democratic Republic, Lebanon, Liberia, Libyan Arab Jamahiriya, Malaysia, Maldives, Mali, Malta, Mauritania, Mauritius, Mexico, Morocco, Mozambique, Myanmar, Namibia, Nepal, Niger, Nigeria, Oman, Pakistan, Panama, Paraguay, Philippines, Qatar, Saint Vincent and the Grenadines, Saudi Arabia, Senegal, Seychelles, Sierra Leone, Singapore, Somalia, South Africa, Sri Lanka, Sudan, Suriname, Syrian Arab Republic, Tajikistan, Togo, Trinidad and Tobago, Tunisia, Turkey, Turkmenistan, United Arab Emirates, Uzbekistan, Venezuela, Viet Nam, Yemen, Zambia.

Against: Australia, Canada, Israel, Marshall Islands, Micronesia, Palau, United States.

Abstaining: Albania, Andorra, Austria, Belgium, Bosnia and Herzegovina, Bulgaria, Cameroon, Colombia, Croatia, Czech Republic, Denmark, Dominican Republic, Estonia, Fiji, Finland, France, Georgia, Germany, Greece, Guatemala, Hungary, Iceland, Ireland, Italy, Japan, Latvia, Liechtenstein, Lithuania, Luxembourg, Malawi, Moldova, Monaco, Montenegro, Nauru, Netherlands, New Zealand, Nicaragua, Norway, Papua New Guinea, Peru, Poland, Portugal, Republic of Korea, Romania, Russian Federation, Samoa, San Marino, Serbia, Slovakia, Slovenia, Solomon Islands, Spain, Sweden, Switzerland, Thailand, The former Yugoslav Republic of Macedonia, Tonga, Uganda, Ukraine, United Kingdom, Uruguay, Vanuatu.

Division for Palestinian Rights

Under the guidance of the Committee on Palestinian Rights, the Division for Palestinian Rights of the UN Secretariat continued to prepare studies and research, monitor, collect and disseminate information on issues related to the Palestine question. The Division responded to requests for information and issued the following publications: a monthly bulletin covering action taken by the United Nations and intergovernmental organizations on the issue of Palestine; monthly chronology of developments relating to the question of Palestine, based on media reports and other sources; reports of international meetings and conferences organized under the Committee's auspices; special bulletins and notes on the observance of the International Day of Solidarity with the Palestinian People (29 November); periodic reviews of developments relating to Middle East peace efforts; and the annual compilation of resolutions and decisions of the General Assembly and the Security Council relating to the question of Palestine.

The Committee, in its annual report [A/61/35], requested the Division to continue its programme of publications and other informational activities, as well as research and monitoring, such as the further expansion and development of the United Nations Information System on the Question of Palestine (UNISPAL), the annual training programme for PA staff, and the annual observance of the International Day of Solidarity with the Palestinian People.

GENERAL ASSEMBLY ACTION

On 1 December [meeting 63], the General Assembly adopted **resolution 61/23** [draft: A/61/L.32] by recorded vote (101-7-62) [agenda item 14].

Division for Palestinian Rights of the Secretariat

The General Assembly,

Having considered the report of the Committee on the Exercise of the Inalienable Rights of the Palestinian People,

Taking note in particular of the relevant information contained in chapter V.B of that report,

Recalling its resolution 32/40 B of 2 December 1977 and all subsequent relevant resolutions, including resolution 60/37 of 1 December 2005,

1. *Notes with appreciation* the action taken by the Secretary-General in compliance with its resolution 60/37;

2. *Considers* that the Division for Palestinian Rights of the Secretariat continues to make a useful and constructive contribution by assisting the Committee on the Exercise of the Inalienable Rights of the Palestinian People in the implementation of its mandate;

3. *Requests* the Secretary-General to continue to provide the Division with the necessary resources and to ensure that it continues to carry out its programme of work as detailed in the relevant earlier resolutions, in consultation with the Committee on the Exercise of the Inalienable Rights of the Palestinian People and under its guidance, including, in particular, the organization of international meetings and conferences in various regions with the participation of all sectors of the international community, liaison and cooperation with civil society, the further development and expansion of the documents collection of the United Nations Information System on the Question of Palestine, the preparation and widest possible dissemination of publications and information materials on various aspects of the question of Palestine and the provision of the annual training programme for staff of the Palestinian Authority;

4. *Also requests* the Secretary-General to ensure the continued cooperation of the Department of Public Information and other units of the Secretariat in enabling the Division to perform its tasks and in covering adequately the various aspects of the question of Palestine;

5. *Invites* all Governments and organizations to extend their cooperation to the Division in the performance of its tasks;

6. *Requests* the Division, as part of the observance of the International Day of Solidarity with the Palestinian People on 29 November, to continue to organize, under the guidance of the Committee on the Exercise of the Inalienable Rights of the Palestinian People, an annual exhibit on Palestinian rights or a cultural event in cooperation with the Permanent Observer Mission of Palestine to the United Nations, and encourages Member States to continue to give the widest support and publicity to the observance of the Day of Solidarity.

RECORDED VOTE ON RESOLUTION 61/23:

In favour: Afghanistan, Algeria, Angola, Antigua and Barbuda, Argentina, Azerbaijan, Bahamas, Bahrain, Bangladesh, Barbados, Belarus, Belize, Benin, Bhutan, Bolivia, Brazil, Brunei Darussalam, Burkina Faso, Cambodia, Cape Verde, Central African Republic, Chile, China, Comoros, Congo, Costa Rica, Côte d'Ivoire, Cuba, Cyprus, Democratic People's Republic of Korea, Djibouti, Dominican Republic, Ecuador, Egypt, El Salvador, Eritrea, Ethiopia, Ghana, Grenada, Guinea, Guyana, Haiti, Honduras, India, Indonesia, Iran, Iraq, Jamaica, Jordan, Kazakhstan, Kuwait, Kyrgyzstan, Lao People's Democratic Republic, Lebanon, Liberia, Libyan Arab Jamahiriya, Malaysia, Maldives, Mali, Malta, Mauritania, Mauritius, Mexico, Morocco, Mozambique, Myanmar, Namibia, Nepal, Niger, Nigeria, Oman, Pakistan, Panama, Paraguay, Philippines, Qatar, Saint Vincent and the Grenadines, Saudi Arabia, Senegal, Seychelles, Sierra Leone, Singapore, Somalia, South Africa, Sri Lanka, Sudan, Suriname, Syrian Arab Republic, Tajikistan, Togo, Trinidad and Tobago, Tunisia, Turkey, Turkmenistan, United Arab Emirates, Uruguay, Uzbekistan, Venezuela, Viet Nam, Yemen, Zambia.

Against: Australia, Canada, Israel, Marshall Islands, Micronesia, Palau, United States.

Abstaining: Albania, Andorra, Armenia, Austria, Belgium, Bosnia and Herzegovina, Bulgaria, Burundi, Cameroon, Colombia, Croatia, Czech Republic, Denmark, Estonia, Fiji, Finland, France, Georgia, Germany, Greece, Guatemala, Hungary, Iceland, Ireland, Italy, Japan, Latvia, Liechtenstein, Lithuania, Luxembourg, Malawi, Moldova, Monaco, Montenegro, Nauru, Netherlands, New Zealand, Nicaragua, Norway, Papua New Guinea, Peru, Poland, Portugal, Republic of Korea, Romania, Russian Federation, Samoa, San Marino, Serbia, Slovakia, Slovenia, Solomon Islands, Spain, Sweden, Switzerland, Thailand, The former Yugoslav Republic of Macedonia, Tonga, Uganda, Ukraine, United Kingdom, Vanuatu.

Special information programme

As requested in General Assembly resolution 60/38 [YUN 2005, p. 540], the UN Department of Public Information (DPI) continued its special information programme on the question of Palestine, which included the maintenance of the web page on the question of Palestine, the issuing of press releases and preparation for the annual training programme for Palestinian broadcasters and journalists. The Radio Section provided coverage of various aspects of the question of Palestine in its broadcasts in all six official languages. The *UN News Centre* portal provided extensive coverage on a wide array of related developments and issues. In cooperation with the Foreign Ministry of the Russian Federation, DPI organized an international media seminar on peace in the Middle East (Moscow, 8-9 June).

As in previous years, the network of the United Nations Information Centres (UNICs) and other UN offices carried out activities in connection with the International Day of Solidarity with the Palestinian People. Throughout the year, many UNICs dealt with the Palestine question and organized related outreach activities.

GENERAL ASSEMBLY ACTION

On 1 December [meeting 63], the General Assembly adopted **resolution 61/24** [draft: A/61/L.33] by recorded vote (157-7-9) [agenda item 14].

Special information programme on the question of Palestine of the Department of Public Information of the Secretariat

The General Assembly,

Having considered the report of the Committee on the Exercise of the Inalienable Rights of the Palestinian People,

Taking note in particular of the information contained in chapter VI of that report,

Recalling its resolution 60/38 of 1 December 2005,

Convinced that the worldwide dissemination of accurate and comprehensive information and the role of civil society organizations and institutions remain of vital importance in heightening awareness of and support for the inalienable rights of the Palestinian people,

Recalling the mutual recognition between the Government of the State of Israel and the Palestine Liberation Organization, the representative of the Palestinian people, as well as the existing agreements between the two sides and the need for full compliance with those agreements,

Recalling also the Quartet road map to a permanent two-State solution to the Israeli-Palestinian conflict,

Recalling further the advisory opinion rendered on 9 July 2004 by the International Court of Justice on the *Legal Consequences of the Construction of a Wall in the Occupied Palestinian Territory*,

Reaffirming that the United Nations has a permanent responsibility towards the question of Palestine until the question is resolved in all its aspects in a satisfactory manner in accordance with international legitimacy,

1. *Notes with appreciation* the action taken by the Department of Public Information of the Secretariat in compliance with resolution 60/38;

2. *Considers* that the special information programme on the question of Palestine of the Department is very useful in raising the awareness of the international community concerning the question of Palestine and the situation in the Middle East and that the programme is contributing effectively to an atmosphere conducive to dialogue and supportive of the peace process;

3. *Requests* the Department, in full cooperation and coordination with the Committee on the Exercise of the Inalienable Rights of the Palestinian People, to continue, with the necessary flexibility as may be required by developments affecting the question of Palestine, its special information programme for the biennium 2006-2007, in particular:

(a) To disseminate information on all the activities of the United Nations system relating to the question of Palestine, including reports on the work carried out by the relevant United Nations organizations;

(b) To continue to issue and update publications on the various aspects of the question of Palestine in all fields, including materials concerning the recent developments in that regard, in particular the efforts for peace;

(c) To expand its collection of audio-visual material on the question of Palestine and to continue the production and preservation of such material and the updating of the exhibit in the Secretariat;

(d) To organize and promote fact-finding news missions for journalists to the Occupied Palestinian Territory, including East Jerusalem;

(e) To organize international, regional and national seminars or encounters for journalists, aiming in particular at sensitizing public opinion to the question of Palestine;

(f) To continue to provide assistance to the Palestinian people in the field of media development, in particular to strengthen the annual training programme for Palestinian broadcasters and journalists.

RECORDED VOTE ON RESOLUTION 61/24:

In favour: Afghanistan, Albania, Algeria, Andorra, Angola, Antigua and Barbuda, Argentina, Armenia, Austria, Azerbaijan, Bahamas, Bahrain, Bangladesh, Barbados, Belarus, Belgium, Belize, Benin, Bhutan, Bolivia, Bosnia and Herzegovina, Brazil, Brunei Darussalam, Bulgaria, Burkina Faso, Burundi, Cambodia, Cape Verde, Central African Republic, Chile, China, Colombia, Comoros, Congo, Costa Rica, Côte d'Ivoire, Croatia, Cuba, Cyprus, Czech Republic, Democratic People's Republic of Korea, Denmark, Djibouti, Dominica, Dominican Republic, Ecuador, Egypt, El Salvador, Eritrea, Estonia, Ethiopia, Finland, France, Georgia, Germany, Ghana, Greece, Grenada, Guatemala, Guinea, Guyana, Haiti, Honduras, Hungary, Iceland, India, Indonesia, Iran, Iraq, Ireland, Italy, Jamaica, Japan, Jordan, Kazakhstan, Kuwait, Kyrgyzstan, Lao People's Democratic Republic, Latvia, Lebanon, Liberia, Libyan Arab Jamahiriya, Liechtenstein, Lithuania, Luxembourg, Malaysia, Maldives, Mali, Malta, Mauritania, Mauritius, Mexico, Monaco, Mongolia, Montenegro, Morocco, Mozambique, Myanmar, Namibia, Nepal, Netherlands, New Zealand, Nicaragua, Niger, Nigeria, Norway, Oman, Pakistan, Panama, Paraguay, Peru, Philippines, Poland, Portugal, Qatar, Republic of Korea, Romania, Russian Federation, Saint Vincent and the Grenadines, Samoa, San Marino, Saudi Arabia, Senegal, Serbia, Seychelles, Sierra Leone, Singapore, Slovakia, Slovenia, Solomon Islands, Somalia, South Africa, Spain, Sri Lanka, Sudan, Suriname, Sweden, Switzerland, Syrian Arab Republic, Tajikistan, Thailand, The former Yugoslav Republic of Macedonia, Timor-Leste, Togo, Trinidad and Tobago, Tunisia, Turkey, Turkmenistan, Ukraine, United Arab Emirates, United Kingdom, Uruguay, Uzbekistan, Venezuela, Viet Nam, Yemen, Zambia.

Against: Australia, Israel, Marshall Islands, Micronesia, Nauru, Palau, United States.

Abstaining: Cameroon, Canada, Fiji, Malawi, Moldova, Papua New Guinea, Tonga, Uganda, Vanuatu.

Assistance to Palestinians

UN activities

In response to General Assembly resolution 60/126 [YUN 2005, p. 542], the Secretary-General submitted a May report [A/61/80-E/2006/72] describing United Nations and other assistance to the Palestinian people covering the period from May 2005 to April 2006.

The overall situation during the reporting period was characterized by uncertainty and failed expectations. Despite an apparent stabilization of the economy and growth in private-sector activities after 2003, Palestinians did not benefit comprehensively or equitably. Looking ahead, the number of chronically poor people would likely increase, and public institutions weaken, if major disruptions of aid flows took place. In response, the United Nations, through UNRWA, provided free education to some 254,175 pupils enrolled in 273 UNRWA elementary and preparatory schools. The United Nations Children's Fund (UNICEF) helped to improve teaching and learning processes, while the United Nations Educational, Scientific and Cultural Organization (UNESCO) began work on a joint programme on girls' education and launched a $15.1 million project to support an equitable and efficient funding mechanism for higher education aimed at providing scholarships to some 20,000 Palestinians students and direct grants to universities. The United Nations Development Programme contributed to the Education for All initiative through the construction and rehabilitation of 26 schools, the provision of computers and educational material and teacher training. The World Health Organization invested $2.5 million in technical assistance to the Ministry of Health in such areas as mental health, nutrition, food safety and communicable diseases, while the United Nations Population Fund invested $1.1 million to help improve accessibility to 41 primary health-care facilities. Targeted social assistance was provided by UNRWA and UNICEF. Direct budget assistance of $293 million had so far been provided to the PA by the World Bank-administered multi-donor financial management reform trust fund. The Bank's own operations included emergency services support projects aimed at mitigating the deterioration in service provision by covering municipal services, water and sewage, environmental management, electricity, education community support, land administration, tertiary education and the Social Safety Net Reform Project. Some $15.8 million was invested by UN agencies in technical assistance and capacity-building activities directly benefiting the PA.

In terms of the challenges ahead, the Secretary-General said that it was not yet clear if the PA would be able to pay the salaries of the approximately 152,000 Palestinian employees, including 73,000 security personnel. The donor community was searching for ways to maintain vital support for the Palestinian people, while pressing the PA to accede to the Quartet's three principles (see p. 501). While donors remained committed to averting a new socio-economic crisis in the Territory, PA institutions were facing a serious fiscal threat and the prospect of a temporary international disengagement. The Secretary-General observed that significant financial support from the international community would be needed to avoid further degradation in the quality of life within the Occupied Palestinian Territory, a contraction in the Palestinian economy and an attendant increase in the socio-economic and humanitarian needs of the Palestinian population, and to maintain a basis for long-term economic recovery. With the election of Hamas in January 2006, prospects for continued international financial support for the PA had lessened, leading to a risk of contraction in the Palestinian economy. An estimated 48 per cent of Palestinians were living below the poverty line at the end of 2005, while unemployment levels reached 23.4 per cent.

UNCTAD assistance to Palestinians

At its fifty-third session (Geneva, 27 September–2 and 10 October), the Trade and Development Board of the United Nations Conference on Trade and Development (UNCTAD) considered its report on assistance to the Palestinian people [TD/B/53/2]. The report stated that the development prospects of the economy of the Occupied Palestinian Territory faced unprecedented challenges. The PA had reached a perilous position with regard to its financial solvency and ability to deliver services for which it was designed. In 2006, the Palestinian economy had to cope with a significant reduction in donor aid, while its institutional infrastructure was at risk of erosion and dysfunction. Meanwhile, renewed confrontations and restrictive measures added to the economic decline. Those new constraints complemented long-standing adverse conditions affecting the economy, engendered by prolonged occupation and conflict. In such circumstances, projections implied an economic decline that would result in the halving of per capita incomes from their pre-2000 levels, unemployment for half of the Palestinian workforce and extension of poverty to two out of three households. There was an urgent need, among other things, to respond to Palestinian national development objectives and priorities, work through the informal sector to address unemployment and poverty, manage limited fiscal policy space and establish a development-driven approach to public sector reform.

GENERAL ASSEMBLY ACTION

On 14 December [meeting 79], the General Assembly adopted **resolution 61/135** [draft: A/61/L.47 & Add.1] by recorded vote (159-0-7) [agenda item 69 *(d)*].

Assistance to the Palestinian people

The General Assembly,

Recalling its resolution 60/126 of 15 December 2005, as well as previous resolutions on the question,

Recalling also the signing of the Declaration of Principles on Interim Self-Government Arrangements in Washington, D.C., on 13 September 1993, by the Government of the State of Israel and the Palestine Liberation Organization, the representative of the Palestinian people, and the subsequent implementation agreements concluded by the two sides,

Recalling further the International Covenant on Civil and Political Rights, the International Covenant on Economic, Social and Cultural Rights and the Convention on the Rights of the Child,

Gravely concerned at the deterioration in the living conditions of the Palestinian people, in particular children, throughout the occupied territory, which constitutes a mounting humanitarian crisis,

Conscious of the urgent need for improvement in the economic and social infrastructure of the occupied territory,

Aware that development is difficult under occupation and is best promoted in circumstances of peace and stability,

Noting the great economic and social challenges facing the Palestinian people and their leadership,

Emphasizing the importance of the safety and well-being of all children in the whole Middle East region,

Deeply concerned about the negative impact, including the health and psychological consequences, of violence on the present and future well-being of children in the region,

Conscious of the urgent necessity for international assistance to the Palestinian people, taking into account the Palestinian priorities,

Welcoming the results of the Conference to Support Middle East Peace, convened in Washington, D.C., on 1 October 1993, the establishment of the Ad Hoc Liaison Committee and the work being done by the World Bank as its secretariat and the establishment of the Consultative Group, as well as all follow-up meetings and international mechanisms established to provide assistance to the Palestinian people,

Welcoming also the results of the "Stockholm International Donor Conference on the Humanitarian Situation in the Occupied Palestinian Territories" of 1 September 2006,

Welcoming further the work of the Joint Liaison Committee, which provides a forum in which economic policy and practical matters related to donor assistance are discussed with the Palestinian Authority,

Stressing the continued importance of the Ad Hoc Liaison Committee in the coordination of assistance to the Palestinian people,

Stressing also the need for the full engagement of the United Nations in the process of building Palestinian institutions and in providing broad assistance to the Palestinian people, and welcoming in this regard the support provided to the Palestinian Authority by the Task Force on Palestinian Reform, established by the Quartet in 2002,

Noting, in this regard, the active participation of the United Nations Special Coordinator for the Middle East Peace Process and Personal Representative of the Secretary-General to the Palestine Liberation Organization and the Palestinian Authority in the activities of the Special Envoys of the Quartet,

Welcoming the endorsement by the Security Council, in its resolution 1515(2003) of 19 November 2003, of the performance-based road map to a permanent two-State solution to the Israeli-Palestinian conflict, and stressing the need for its implementation and compliance with its provisions,

Noting the Israeli withdrawal from the Gaza Strip and parts of the northern West Bank as a step towards implementation of the road map,

Having considered the report of the Secretary-General,

Expressing grave concern at the continuation of the recent tragic and violent events that have led to many deaths and injuries, including among children,

1. *Takes note* of the report of the Secretary-General;

2. *Also takes note* of the report of the Personal Humanitarian Envoy of the Secretary-General on the humanitarian conditions and needs of the Palestinian people;

3. *Expresses its appreciation* to the Secretary-General for his rapid response and efforts regarding assistance to the Palestinian people;

4. *Also expresses its appreciation* to the Member States, United Nations bodies and intergovernmental, regional and non-governmental organizations that have provided and continue to provide assistance to the Palestinian people;

5. *Stresses* the importance of the work of the United Nations Special Coordinator for the Middle East Peace Process and Personal Representative of the Secretary-General to the Palestine Liberation Organization and the Palestinian Authority and of the steps taken under the auspices of the Secretary-General to ensure the achievement of a coordinated mechanism for United Nations activities throughout the occupied territories;

6. *Urges* Member States, international financial institutions of the United Nations system, intergovernmental and non-governmental organizations and regional and interregional organizations to extend, as rapidly and as generously as possible, economic and social assistance to the Palestinian people, in close cooperation with the Palestine Liberation Organization and through official Palestinian institutions;

7. *Calls upon* relevant organizations and agencies of the United Nations system to intensify their assistance in response to the urgent needs of the Palestinian people in accordance with priorities set forth by the Palestinian side;

8. *Calls upon* the international community to provide urgently needed assistance and services in an effort to alleviate the dire humanitarian crisis being faced by Palestinian children and their families and to help in the reconstruction of relevant Palestinian institutions;

9. *Welcomes* the role that the temporary international mechanism plays in assisting directly the Palestinian people under the current circumstances, and encourages interested donors to make use of the mechanism;

10. *Urges* Member States to open their markets to exports of Palestinian products on the most favourable terms, consistent with appropriate trading rules, and to implement fully existing trade and cooperation agreements;

11. *Calls upon* the international donor community to expedite the delivery of pledged assistance to the Palestinian people to meet their urgent needs;

12. *Stresses*, in this context, the importance of ensuring the free passage of aid to the Palestinian people and the free movement of persons and goods;

13. *Also stresses* the need for the full implementation by both parties of the Agreement on Movement and Access and of the Agreed Principles for the Rafah Crossing, of 15 November 2005, to allow for the freedom of movement of the Palestinian civilian population within and into and out of the Gaza Strip;

14. *Urges* the international donor community, United Nations agencies and organizations and non-governmental organizations to extend as rapidly as possible emergency economic and humanitarian assistance to the Palestinian people to counter the impact of the current crisis;

15. *Stresses* the need to implement the Paris Protocol on Economic Relations of 29 April 1994, fifth annex to the Israeli-Palestinian Interim Agreement on the West Bank and the Gaza Strip, signed in Washington, D.C., on 28 September 1995, in particular with regard to the

full and prompt clearance of Palestinian indirect tax revenues;

16. *Requests* the Secretary-General to submit a report to the General Assembly at its sixty-second session, through the Economic and Social Council, on the implementation of the present resolution, containing:

(*a*) An assessment of the assistance actually received by the Palestinian people;

(*b*) An assessment of the needs still unmet and specific proposals for responding effectively to them;

17. *Decides* to include in the provisional agenda of its sixty-second session the sub-item entitled "Assistance to the Palestinian people".

RECORDED VOTE ON RESOLUTION 61/135:

In favour: Afghanistan, Albania, Algeria, Andorra, Angola, Argentina, Armenia, Australia, Austria, Azerbaijan, Bahamas, Bahrain, Bangladesh, Barbados, Belarus, Belgium, Belize, Benin, Bhutan, Bolivia, Bosnia and Herzegovina, Botswana, Brazil, Brunei Darussalam, Bulgaria, Burkina Faso, Burundi, Canada, Cape Verde, Central African Republic, Chad, Chile, China, Colombia, Comoros, Congo, Costa Rica, Côte d'Ivoire, Croatia, Cuba, Cyprus, Czech Republic, Democratic People's Republic of Korea, Denmark, Djibouti, Dominican Republic, Ecuador, Egypt, El Salvador, Equatorial Guinea, Eritrea, Estonia, Ethiopia, Finland, France, Gabon, Georgia, Germany, Ghana, Greece, Grenada, Guatemala, Guinea, Guyana, Haiti, Honduras, Hungary, Iceland, India, Indonesia, Iran, Iraq, Ireland, Italy, Jamaica, Japan, Jordan, Kuwait, Kyrgyzstan, Latvia, Lebanon, Lesotho, Libyan Arab Jamahiriya, Liechtenstein, Lithuania, Luxembourg, Madagascar, Malawi, Malaysia, Mali, Malta, Mauritania, Mauritius, Mexico, Monaco, Mongolia, Montenegro, Morocco, Mozambique, Myanmar, Namibia, Nepal, Netherlands, New Zealand, Nicaragua, Niger, Norway, Oman, Pakistan, Panama, Paraguay, Peru, Philippines, Poland, Portugal, Qatar, Republic of Korea, Romania, Russian Federation, Rwanda, Samoa, San Marino, Saudi Arabia, Senegal, Serbia, Sierra Leone, Singapore, Slovakia, Slovenia, Solomon Islands, South Africa, Spain, Sri Lanka, Sudan, Suriname, Swaziland, Sweden, Switzerland, Syrian Arab Republic, Tajikistan, Thailand, The former Yugoslav Republic of Macedonia, Timor-Leste, Togo, Tonga, Trinidad and Tobago, Tunisia, Turkey, Ukraine, United Arab Emirates, United Kingdom, Uruguay, Uzbekistan, Vanuatu, Venezuela, Viet Nam, Yemen, Zambia, Zimbabwe.

Against: None.

Abstaining: Fiji, Israel, Marshall Islands, Micronesia, Nauru, Palau, United States.

UNRWA

The United Nations Relief and Works Agency for Palestine Refugees in the Near East (UNRWA) continued to provide vital education, health, relief and social services, and micro-finance to an ever-growing refugee population in the Gaza Strip, the West Bank, Jordan, Lebanon and the Syrian Arab Republic.

As at 31 December 2006, some 4.5 million refugees were registered with UNRWA, compared to 4.3 million in 2005. Of that number, 3.2 million registered refugees resided outside the 58 recognized refugee camps. The largest refugee population was registered in Jordan (42 per cent), followed by the Gaza Strip (23 per cent), the West Bank (16 per cent), the Syrian Arab Republic (10 per cent) and Lebanon (9 per cent).

In his report on the work of the Agency from 1 January to 31 December 2006 [A/62/13], the UNRWA Commissioner-General drew attention to the developments in the Occupied Palestinian Territory and Lebanon. He said that the armed conflict, closures and the withholding of tax revenues and international donations to the PA had taken an enormous toll on the Palestinian economic and social conditions. The situation in Gaza was particularly grim. UNRWA responded to the emergency situation by providing shelter and other assistance to over 5,000 displaced people, and by delivering water and food to areas isolated by military incursions. In the Israeli-Lebanese war, although the Palestinian refugee camps were not directly targeted, the Palestinian community was substantially affected by the conflict, as some 47 per cent of Palestine refugees lived in urban and rural areas within the Lebanese community. UNRWA responded immediately to that crisis, maintaining essential services, while also commencing an emergency assistance programme to the Palestine refugee population and about 5,500 displaced Lebanese. In total, some 4,127 displaced persons were accommodated by UNRWA in its schools and a further 14,745 persons by Palestinian families in the camps. UNRWA included its emergency needs in the United Nations consolidated appeal launched in July 2006 and received $5.6 million in funding from donors. It participated in an early recovery appeal for Lebanon in the aftermath of the conflict and received $4.9 million for emergency needs, water and sanitation works, immediate shelter repair, psychosocial support, new school infrastructure and the establishment of a programme to reactivate businesses. In October, UNRWA prepared a camp improvement initiative, comprising $50 million worth of projects designed to address the squalid conditions in refugee camps in Lebanon, and had received $21 million by the end of 2006.

The UNRWA reform process aimed at strengthening its management capacity required an investment of $30 million from 2006 to 2009, of which over $2.1 million had been contributed at the end of the reporting period. The process was based on four main "levers" of change: human resources management; programme management, including the establishment of a programme management cycle; leadership and management; and organizational processes.

Advisory Commission. The UNRWA Advisory Commission, in its comments on the Agency's 2006 annual report, transmitted by its Chairperson [A/62/13], expressed concerned over the deteriorating and fragile situations in the Gaza Strip, the West Bank and Lebanon, including their impact on the humanitarian situation and the delivery of humanitarian aid. The Commission commended UNRWA for its efforts in addressing the urgent needs of Palestine refugees who sought the Agency's assistance during the Israeli military operations in the summer. However, factional clashes in the Palestinian Occupied Territory and attacks on UNRWA installations and personnel had negative consequences for the presence of UN international staff in the Gaza Strip.

The Commission commended the Lebanese Government and UNRWA on the dynamic steps taken to secure additional funds for basic living conditions in the Lebanese camps and to address the developmental needs of Palestine refugees. It also commended the Syrian Government on the assistance provided to over 600 Palestinian refugees who had fled the conflict in Iraq. The Commission encouraged the international community to address the humanitarian needs of Palestine refugees.

Concerned over the restrictions imposed by the Israeli authorities both in the West Bank and Gaza, which obstructed Palestinian access to employment, income, essential goods and services, as well as the ability of UNRWA to move staff and humanitarian assistance to those in immediate need, the Commission reiterated the urgent necessity to have them removed as they impeded the movement of UNRWA staff and goods. The Commission expressed its concerns regarding the detention of some UNRWA staff by Israel, and the fact that UNRWA facilities had regularly been subjected to forced entry and obstructions by the Israeli military. It also noted the Agency's demands for compensation for damaged UNRWA installations from the Israeli authorities ($1,048,000), as well as reimbursement of outstanding port charges ($27,756,193), and that henceforth it be exempted from such charges. The Commission called upon the General Assembly to examine that issue at its sixty-second (2007) session and to take it into account in its resolution dealing with UNRWA operations, including a clause calling for the reimbursement of those charges by the Israeli authorities.

The Commission welcomed the organizational development being implemented in UNRWA and commended the Agency's determination to develop a strategic approach to programming. It noted that the UNRWA regular budget grew by 23 per cent, from $ 396.4 million in 2005 to $ 488.6 million in 2006, while expenditures increased by 10.6 per cent, from $ 377.2 million to $ 417.1 million. UNRWA launched an emergency appeal for the West Bank and the Gaza Strip, of which $145 million or 84 per cent had been pledged as at 31 December 2006.

Report of Conciliation Commission. The United Nations Conciliation Commission for Palestine, in its sixtieth report covering the period from 1 September 2005 to 31 August 2006 [A/61/172], submitted in response to General Assembly resolution 60/100 [YUN 2005, p. 545], noted the submission of its August 2005 report [ibid., p. 544] and observed that it had nothing further to report.

Projects and major service areas

UNRWA continued in 2006 to provide education, health, social services and microcredit assistance to Palestinian refugees in its five fields of operations. Education remained the largest programme, accounting for almost 60 per cent of the total budget, followed by health, 18 per cent, relief and social services, 11 per cent, common services, 7 per cent, and operational and technical services, 5 per cent.

The education programme included elementary, preparatory and secondary (in Lebanon only) education for almost half a million children, technical and vocational education, teacher training, placement and career guidance and a limited number of scholarships. Highlights included the launching of a quality assurance framework for UNRWA schools; a joint (health and education departments) review of the psychosocial support programme to improve its effectiveness; plans to expand technical and vocational training in Gaza; and the creation of 200 new places in vocational training. The conflict in the Occupied Palestinian Territory and in Lebanon in 2006 continued to fragment learning patterns for children and impair their educational achievements. To safeguard the educational, emotional and social well-being of pupils, UNRWA arranged extracurricular activities in drama, music, sports, theatre and creative arts through funding made available by UNESCO. In July, 26 UNRWA schools offered emergency accommodation to approximately 4,500 people during the conflict in Lebanon.

The health programme, supervised by the World Health Organization, was aimed to protect, preserve and promote the health status of Palestine refugees within the Agency's area of operations. In 2006, the number of refugees receiving hospital treatment grew by 11.4 per cent, to 68,986, while dental consultations increased by 4.3 per cent, to 683,898; the number of newly registered pregnant women increased by 4.8 per cent, to

91,889, and those receiving post-natal care rose by 3.4 per cent, to 76,813; the number of patients with non-communicable diseases under supervision at UNRWA health facilities increased by 15.1 per cent, to 146,092. Family planning and maternal health-care services benefited from a new health management information system in all 127 UNRWA health centres, which allowed for the rapid interpretation of health-related data and the evaluation of medical outcomes. The health programme introduced a geographic information system at the headquarters level, providing a framework for managing a broad range of public health challenges, in particular, assessing health service availability and accessibility, mapping health events and identifying disease clusters. A new risk-assessment tool was introduced in the non-communicable diseases clinic to better evaluate patients with diabetes and hypertension.

Through the relief and social programme, UNRWA continued to provide a social safety net for the most impoverished Palestine refugees and promote the self-reliance of less advantaged members of the community, especially women, the elderly, youth and those with disabilities. Services included food support, shelter rehabilitation and cash assistance to families living in conditions of special hardship, community-based social services, access to subsidized credit, and the maintenance, updating and preservation of records and documents of 4.3 million registered refugees. The revised bilingual consolidated eligibility and registration instructions were finalized and issued, which provided for the extension of services to families of registered refugee women married to non-refugees. In the process of developing and implementing a "poverty-based" approach for special hardship food aid distributions, the results of the first in-depth, socio-economic survey of 3,603 families living in conditions of special hardship were analysed for policy implications, and disseminated to donors, host authority representatives and relevant staff. The first social services policy and guidelines, designed to clarify and streamline policy issues with regard to the delivery of social services, were also finalized. Selective cash assistance was severely curtailed by agency-wide austerity measures during the year, falling by almost 90 per cent. The worsening socio-economic conditions in the Gaza Strip and West Bank contributed to increasing demands for emergency cash assistance by refugee families.

The Agency's microfinance and micro-enterprise programme—intended to improve the quality of life of micro-enterprise owners, sustain jobs, reduce unemployment and poverty, build household assets, improve housing stock, empower women and provide economic opportunities for youth—had, in 16 years, financed over 126,000 loans totalling $131 million. It was the leading microfinance provider in the Occupied Palestinian Territory and was in the process of pioneering the development of urban microfinance in the Syrian Arab Republic. In 2006, the programme's base loan capital had gone up by $2 million, thereby increasing its credit outreach to the agriculture and food-processing sectors. The programme extended its branch network to 13 offices in 2006, and planned adding five more offices in Jordan and the Syrian Arab Republic in 2007. It successfully tested its new housing microfinance loans product in Gaza and continued to administer and develop the PalFund trust fund, which was supported by the Organization of the Petroleum Exporting Countries Fund for International Development. By the end of 2006, it had financed 7,282 micro-enterprise loans, valued at $7.2 million, in the Occupied Palestinian Territory from a trust fund capital of $2.3 million. In 2006, the programme financed 14,023 loans worth $15.3 million, significantly below its performance targets. Some 36 per cent of financing was in the West Bank, 31 per cent in Gaza, 19 per cent in Jordan and 13 per cent in Syria.

Emergency appeals

The demands on the UNRWA programme of emergency assistance for refugees affected by armed conflict, closures and the deteriorating economic situation in the Occupied Palestinian Territory increased in 2006, due to the deteriorating living conditions in the occupied territories, prompting the Agency to revise its emergency appeal from $95 million to $171 million. The revised appeal was launched in May, as part of a revised consolidated appeals process for the occupied territory. By the end of the year, the Agency had received $145 million or some 84 per cent of the funding requested to support the provision of emergency food aid to 240,000 refugee families, or around 70 per cent of the registered refugee population, and the creation of over 3 million workdays for 50,000 unemployed refugees. The inability of the PA to pay public-sector salaries compelled UNRWA to extend its emergency relief programmes to refugee families, whose main breadwinners were employed by the PA, thereby adding 100,000 people to the rolls of its food distribution system. Emergency operations also included cash assistance to impoverished families, the reconstruction of destroyed shelters, the provision of health care through mobile clinics for families facing access problems in the West Bank and in-kind support to Gaza's municipalities to ensure the maintenance of vital public facilities, including those for water purification, waste water and sewage. The programme also provided shelter, food and water to refugees affected by the main Israeli incursions into Gaza.

GENERAL ASSEMBLY ACTION

On 14 December [meeting 79], the General Assembly, having considered the UNRWA Commissioner-General's report covering the period 1 January to 31 December 2005 [YUN 2005, p. 544], on the recommendation of the Fourth Committee [A/61/407], adopted **resolution 61/112** by recorded vote (173-1-10) [agenda item 31].

Assistance to Palestine refugees

The General Assembly,

Recalling its resolution 194 (III) of 11 December 1948 and all its subsequent resolutions on the question, including resolution 60/100 of 8 December 2005,

Recalling also its resolution 302 (IV) of 8 December 1949, by which, inter alia, it established the United Nations Relief and Works Agency for Palestine Refugees in the Near East,

Recalling further relevant Security Council resolutions,

Aware of the fact that, for more than five decades, the Palestine refugees have suffered from the loss of their homes, lands and means of livelihood,

Affirming the imperative of resolving the problem of the Palestine refugees for the achievement of justice and for the achievement of lasting peace in the region,

Acknowledging the essential role that the United Nations Relief and Works Agency for Palestine Refugees in the Near East has played for more than fifty-six years since its establishment in ameliorating the plight of the Palestine refugees in the fields of education, health and relief and social services,

Taking note of the report of the Commissioner-General of the United Nations Relief and Works Agency for Palestine Refugees in the Near East covering the period from 1 January to 31 December 2005,

Aware of the continuing needs of the Palestine refugees throughout all the fields of operation, namely, Jordan, Lebanon, the Syrian Arab Republic and the Occupied Palestinian Territory,

Expressing grave concern at the especially difficult situation of the Palestine refugees under occupation, including with regard to their safety, well-being and living conditions,

Noting the signing of the Declaration of Principles on Interim Self-Government Arrangements on 13 September 1993 by the Government of Israel and the Palestine Liberation Organization and the subsequent implementation agreements,

Aware of the important role to be played in the peace process by the Multilateral Working Group on Refugees of the Middle East peace process,

1. *Notes with regret* that repatriation or compensation of the refugees, as provided for in paragraph 11 of General Assembly resolution 194 (III), has not yet been effected, that, therefore, the situation of the Palestine refugees continues to be a matter of grave concern and that the Palestine refugees continue to require assistance to meet basic health, education and living needs;

2. *Also notes with regret* that the United Nations Conciliation Commission for Palestine has been unable to find a means of achieving progress in the implementation of paragraph 11 of General Assembly resolution 194 (III), and reiterates its request to the Conciliation Commission to exert continued efforts towards the implementation of that paragraph and to report to the Assembly as appropriate, but no later than 1 September 2007;

3. *Affirms* the necessity for the continuation of the work of the United Nations Relief and Works Agency for Palestine Refugees in the Near East and the importance of its unimpeded operation and its provision of services for the well-being of the Palestine refugees and for the stability of the region, pending the just resolution of the question of the Palestine refugees;

4. *Calls upon* all donors to continue to make the most generous efforts possible to meet the anticipated needs of the Agency, including with regard to increased expenditures arising from the deteriorating socio-economic and humanitarian situation in the region, particularly in the Occupied Palestinian Territory, and those mentioned in recent emergency appeals.

RECORDED VOTE ON RESOLUTION 61/112:

In favour: Afghanistan, Albania, Algeria, Andorra, Angola, Antigua and Barbuda, Argentina, Armenia, Australia, Austria, Azerbaijan, Bahamas, Bahrain, Bangladesh, Barbados, Belarus, Belgium, Belize, Benin, Bhutan, Bolivia, Bosnia and Herzegovina, Botswana, Brazil, Brunei Darussalam, Bulgaria, Burkina Faso, Burundi, Cambodia, Canada, Cape Verde, Central African Republic, Chad, Chile, China, Colombia, Comoros, Congo, Costa Rica, Côte d'Ivoire, Croatia, Cuba, Cyprus, Czech Republic, Democratic People's Republic of Korea, Democratic Republic of the Congo, Denmark, Djibouti, Dominica, Dominican Republic, Ecuador, Egypt, El Salvador, Equatorial Guinea, Eritrea, Estonia, Ethiopia, Finland, France, Gabon, Georgia, Germany, Ghana, Greece, Grenada, Guatemala, Guinea, Guinea-Bissau, Guyana, Haiti, Honduras, Hungary, Iceland, India, Indonesia, Iran, Iraq, Ireland, Italy, Jamaica, Japan, Jordan, Kazakhstan, Kenya, Kuwait, Kyrgyzstan, Lao People's Democratic Republic, Latvia, Lebanon, Lesotho, Libyan Arab Jamahiriya, Liechtenstein, Lithuania, Luxembourg, Malawi, Malaysia, Maldives, Mali, Malta, Mauritania, Mauritius, Mexico, Moldova, Monaco, Mongolia, Montenegro, Morocco, Mozambique, Myanmar, Namibia, Nepal, Netherlands, New Zealand, Nicaragua, Niger, Nigeria, Norway, Oman, Pakistan, Panama, Paraguay, Peru, Philippines, Poland, Portugal, Qatar, Republic of Korea, Romania, Russian Federation, Rwanda, Saint Lucia, Saint Vincent and the Grenadines, Samoa, San Marino, Sao Tome and Principe, Saudi Arabia, Senegal, Serbia, Sierra Leone, Singapore, Slovakia, Slovenia, Solomon Islands, South Africa, Spain, Sri Lanka, Sudan, Suriname, Sweden, Switzerland, Syrian Arab Republic, Tajikistan, Thailand, The former Yugoslav Republic of Macedonia, Timor-Leste, Togo, Tonga, Trinidad and Tobago, Tunisia, Turkey, Turkmenistan, Uganda, Ukraine, United Arab Emirates, United Kingdom, United Republic of Tanzania, Uruguay, Uzbekistan, Venezuela, Viet Nam, Yemen, Zambia, Zimbabwe.

Against: Israel.

Abstaining: Cameroon, Fiji, Marshall Islands, Micronesia, Nauru, Palau, Papua New Guinea, Tuvalu, United States, Vanuatu.

The Assembly, also on 14 December [meeting 79], and on the Fourth Committee's recommendation [A/61/407], adopted **resolution 61/114** by recorded vote (169-6-8) [agenda item 31].

Operations of the United Nations Relief and Works Agency for Palestine Refugees in the Near East

The General Assembly,

Recalling its resolutions 194 (III) of 11 December 1948, 212 (III) of 19 November 1948, 302 (IV) of 8 December 1949 and all subsequent related resolutions, including its resolution 60/102 of 8 December 2005,

Recalling also the relevant Security Council resolutions,

Having considered the report of the Commissioner-General of the United Nations Relief and Works Agency for Palestine Refugees in the Near East covering the period from 1 January to 31 December 2005,

Taking note of the letter dated 28 September 2006 from the Chairperson of the Advisory Commission of the United Nations Relief and Works Agency for Palestine Refugees in the Near East addressed to the Commissioner-General,

Deeply concerned about the critical financial situation of the Agency, as well as about the rising expenditures of the Agency resulting from the deterioration of the socio-economic and humanitarian conditions in the region and their significant negative impact on the provision of necessary Agency services to the Palestine refugees, including its emergency-related and development programmes,

Recalling Articles 100, 104 and 105 of the Charter of the United Nations and the Convention on the Privileges and Immunities of the United Nations,

Recalling also the Convention on the Safety of United Nations and Associated Personnel,

Affirming the applicability of the Geneva Convention relative to the Protection of Civilian Persons in Time of War, of 12 August 1949, to the Palestinian territory occupied since 1967, including East Jerusalem,

Aware of the continuing needs of the Palestine refugees throughout the Occupied Palestinian Territory and in the other fields of operation, namely Jordan, Lebanon and the Syrian Arab Republic,

Gravely concerned about the extremely difficult living conditions being faced by the Palestine refugees in the Occupied Palestinian Territory, including East Jerusalem, particularly in the refugee camps in the Gaza Strip, resulting, inter alia, from the loss of life and injury, the extensive destruction of their shelters, properties and vital infrastructure and the displacement of the Palestine refugees,

Aware of the extraordinary efforts being undertaken by the Agency for the repair or rebuilding of thousands of damaged or destroyed refugee shelters and for the provision of shelter for those refugee families internally displaced as a result of recent Israeli military actions,

Aware also of the valuable work done by the refugee affairs officers of the Agency in providing protection to the Palestinian people, in particular Palestine refugees,

Gravely concerned about the endangerment of the safety of the Agency's staff and about the damage caused to the facilities of the Agency as a result of Israeli military operations during the reporting period,

Deploring the killing of fourteen Agency staff members by the Israeli occupying forces in the Occupied Palestinian Territory since September 2000 and of one Agency staff member by the Israeli air force in Lebanon in August 2006,

Deploring also the killing and wounding of refugee children, including in the Agency's schools, by the Israeli occupying forces,

Expressing deep concern about the policies of closure and severe restrictions that continue to be imposed on the movement of persons and goods throughout the Occupied Palestinian Territory, including East Jerusalem, as well as the continued construction of the wall, contrary to international law, in the Occupied Palestinian Territory, including in and around East Jerusalem, which have had a grave impact on the socio-economic situation of the Palestine refugees and have greatly contributed to the dire humanitarian crisis facing the Palestinian people,

Deeply concerned about the continuing imposition of restrictions on the freedom of movement of the Agency's staff, vehicles and goods, and the harassment and intimidation of the Agency's staff, which undermine and obstruct the work of the Agency, including its ability to provide its essential basic and emergency services,

Recalling the signing, on 13 September 1993, of the Declaration of Principles on Interim Self-Government Arrangements by the Government of Israel and the Palestine Liberation Organization and the subsequent implementation agreements,

Aware of the agreement between the Agency and the Government of Israel,

Taking note of the agreement reached on 24 June 1994, embodied in an exchange of letters between the Agency and the Palestine Liberation Organization,

Recalling the Geneva Conference convened by the United Nations Relief and Works Agency for Palestine Refugees in the Near East and the Swiss Agency for Development and Cooperation on 7 and 8 June 2004 to increase support for the United Nations Relief and Works Agency,

1. *Expresses its appreciation* to the Commissioner-General of the United Nations Relief and Works Agency for Palestine Refugees in the Near East, as well as to all of the staff of the Agency, for their tireless efforts and valuable work, particularly in the light of the difficult conditions during the past year;

2. *Also expresses its appreciation* to the Advisory Commission of the Agency, and requests it to continue its efforts and to keep the General Assembly informed of its activities;

3. *Takes note with appreciation* of the report of the Working Group on the Financing of the United Nations Relief and Works Agency for Palestine Refugees in the Near East and the efforts of the Working Group to assist in ensuring the financial security of the Agency, and requests the Secretary-General to provide the necessary services and assistance to the Working Group for the conduct of its work;

4. *Commends* the continuing efforts of the Commissioner-General to increase the budgetary transparency and efficiency of the Agency, as reflected in the Agency's programme budget for the biennium 2006-2007;

5. *Also commends* the organizational reform measures taken by the Agency to modernize and strengthen its management aimed at enhancing its ability to address the needs of the Palestine refugees;

6. *Endorses*, meanwhile, the efforts of the Commissioner-General to continue to provide humanitarian assistance, as far as practicable, on an emergency basis, and as a temporary measure, to persons in the area who are internally displaced and in serious need of continued assistance as a result of recent incursions in the Occupied Palestinian Territory and hostilities in Lebanon;

7. *Acknowledges* the important support provided by the host Governments to the Agency in the discharge of its duties;

8. *Encourages* the Agency's further consideration of the needs and rights of children in its operations in accordance with the Convention on the Rights of the Child;

9. *Expresses concern* about the temporary relocation of the international staff of the Agency from its headquarters in Gaza City and the disruption of operations at the headquarters;

10. *Calls upon* Israel, the occupying Power, to comply fully with the provisions of the Geneva Convention relative to the Protection of Civilian Persons in Time of War, of 12 August 1949;

11. *Also calls upon* Israel to abide by Articles 100, 104 and 105 of the Charter of the United Nations and the Convention on the Privileges and Immunities of the United Nations in order to ensure the safety of the personnel of the Agency, the protection of its institutions and the safeguarding of the security of its facilities in the Occupied Palestinian Territory, including East Jerusalem;

12. *Urges* the Government of Israel to speedily compensate the Agency for damage to its property and facilities resulting from actions by the Israeli side and to expeditiously reimburse the Agency for port and related charges, including storage, demurrage and transit charges, incurred by the Agency and other financial losses sustained by the Agency as a result of delays and restrictions on movement and access imposed by Israel;

13. *Calls upon* Israel particularly to cease obstructing the movement of the staff, vehicles and supplies of the Agency and to cease the levying of extra fees and charges, which affect the Agency's operations detrimentally;

14. *Requests* the Commissioner-General to proceed with the issuance of identification cards for Palestine refugees and their descendants in the Occupied Palestinian Territory;

15. *Affirms* that the functioning of the Agency remains essential in all the fields of operation;

16. *Notes* the success of the Agency's microfinance and micro-enterprise programmes, and calls upon the Agency, in close cooperation with the relevant agencies, to continue to contribute to the development of the economic and social stability of the Palestine refugees in all the fields of operation;

17. *Reiterates its request* to the Commissioner-General to proceed with the modernization of the archives of the Agency through the Palestine Refugee Records Project, and to indicate progress in her report to the General Assembly at its sixty-second session;

18. *Reiterates its previous appeals* to all States, specialized agencies and non-governmental organizations to continue and to augment the special allocations for grants and scholarships for higher education to Palestine refugees in addition to their contributions to the regular budget of the Agency and to contribute to the establishment of vocational training centres for Palestine refugees, and requests the Agency to act as the recipient and trustee for the special allocations for grants and scholarships;

19. *Urges* all States, specialized agencies and non-governmental organizations to continue and to increase their contributions to the Agency so as to ease the ongoing financial constraints, exacerbated by the current humanitarian situation on the ground that has resulted in rising expenditures, in particular with regard to emergency services, and to support the Agency's valuable and necessary work in assisting the Palestine refugees in all fields of operation.

RECORDED VOTE ON RESOLUTION 61/114:

In favour: Afghanistan, Albania, Algeria, Andorra, Antigua and Barbuda, Argentina, Armenia, Australia, Austria, Azerbaijan, Bahamas, Bahrain, Bangladesh, Barbados, Belarus, Belgium, Belize, Benin, Bhutan, Bolivia, Bosnia and Herzegovina, Botswana, Brazil, Brunei Darussalam, Bulgaria, Burkina Faso, Burundi, Cambodia, Canada, Cape Verde, Central African Republic, Chad, Chile, China, Colombia, Comoros, Congo, Costa Rica, Croatia, Cuba, Cyprus, Czech Republic, Democratic People's Republic of Korea, Democratic Republic of the Congo, Denmark, Djibouti, Dominica, Dominican Republic, Ecuador, Egypt, El Salvador, Equatorial Guinea, Eritrea, Estonia, Ethiopia, Finland, France, Gabon, Georgia, Germany, Ghana, Greece, Grenada, Guatemala, Guinea, Guinea-Bissau, Guyana, Haiti, Honduras, Hungary, Iceland, India, Indonesia, Iran, Iraq, Ireland, Italy, Jamaica, Japan, Jordan, Kazakhstan, Kenya, Kuwait, Kyrgyzstan, Lao People's Democratic Republic, Latvia, Lebanon, Lesotho, Libyan Arab Jamahiriya, Liechtenstein, Lithuania, Luxembourg, Malawi, Malaysia, Maldives, Mali, Malta, Mauritania, Mauritius, Mexico, Moldova, Monaco, Mongolia, Montenegro, Morocco, Mozambique, Myanmar, Namibia, Nepal, Netherlands, New Zealand, Nicaragua, Niger, Nigeria, Norway, Oman, Pakistan, Panama, Paraguay, Peru, Philippines, Poland, Portugal, Qatar, Republic of Korea, Romania, Russian Federation, Saint Lucia, Saint Vincent and the Grenadines, Samoa, San Marino, Sao Tome and Principe, Saudi Arabia, Senegal, Serbia, Sierra Leone, Singapore, Slovakia, Slovenia, Solomon Islands, South Africa, Spain, Sri Lanka, Sudan, Suriname, Sweden, Switzerland, Syrian Arab Republic, Tajikistan, Thailand, The former Yugoslav Republic of Macedonia, Timor-Leste, Togo, Tonga, Trinidad and Tobago, Tunisia, Turkey, Turkmenistan, Ukraine, United Arab Emirates, United Kingdom, United Republic of Tanzania, Uruguay, Uzbekistan, Venezuela, Viet Nam, Yemen, Zambia, Zimbabwe.

Against: Israel, Marshall Islands, Micronesia, Nauru, Palau, United States.

Abstaining: Cameroon, Côte d'Ivoire, Fiji, Papua New Guinea, Swaziland, Tuvalu, Uganda, Vanuatu.

UNRWA financing

UNRWA expended $598.7 million in 2006, against a total regular budget of $639 million, on projects and emergency appeal activities. The largest component was $417.1 million, accounting for nearly 70 per cent of the total expenditure under the regular budget. Emergency appeal activities and projects accounted for 23 per cent and 7 per cent, respectively. The microfinance and micro-enterprise programme made up less than 1 per cent of total expenditure. The unfunded portion of $71.5 million resulted from the difference between the needs-based budget and the contributions donors were prepared to offer. The shortfall necessitated the adoption of stringent austerity measures throughout UNRWA.

Working Group. The Working Group on the Financing of UNRWA met on 1, 12 and 13 September. In its report to the General Assembly [A/61/347], the Working Group said that the UNRWA regular budget (cash and in-kind) for the 2006-2007 biennium was $994.2 million, of which $488.5 million was for 2006 and $505.6 million for 2007. In 2005, the Agency received $341.5 million in income for its planned expenditure, leaving a funding gap of $44.7 million. The anticipated funding gap for 2006, as at 1 September, was $129.1 million. The Agency's regular budget income was expected to be some $359.4 million ($322.5 million in donor contributions, $16.3 million in in-kind contributions, $18.1 million in income from the United Nations and $2.5 million in interest income and exchange rate gains). The project budget deficit for 2005 was $13.9 million and was expected to rise in 2006 to $132.1 million, following the incorporation of key infrastructure provisions from the Agency's 2005-2009 medium-term plan, for which funding had fallen far short of requirements.

The Working Group, noting that, as at 1 September, only 64 per cent of the 2006 budget had been funded, expressed concern over the large funding gap and reiterated that it was the responsibility of the international community to ensure that UNRWA services were maintained at an acceptable level in quantitative and qualitative terms, and that funding kept pace with the natural growth of the refugee population and its changing needs. It also called for the early and complete fulfilment of pledges and other commitments to UNRWA, in particular the reimbursement of value-added tax by the PA, and port and related charges by the Israeli Government. It welcomed UNRWA strengthened focus on strategic planning, monitoring and evaluation of programmes and its commitment to results-based management, ensuring the most effective use of donor funds and a stronger emphasis on well-defined outcomes.

Displaced persons

In a September report [A/61/358], submitted in compliance with General Assembly resolution 60/101 [YUN 2005, p. 548], which called for the accelerated return of all persons displaced as a result of the June 1967 and subsequent hostilities to their homes in the territories occupied by Israel since then, the Secretary-General said that the Agency's information was based on requests by returning registered refugees for the transfer of their entitlements to their areas of return. UNRWA was not involved in the arrangements for the return of either refugees or displaced persons not registered with it. Displaced refugees known by UNRWA to have returned to the West Bank and Gaza Strip since 1967 totalled 26,534. From 1 July 2005 to 30 June 2006, 1,272 refugees registered with UNRWA had returned to the West Bank and 102 to the Gaza Strip from outside the Occupied Palestinian Territory—some of them might not have been displaced since 1967, but were possibly family members of a displaced registered refugee.

GENERAL ASSEMBLY ACTION

On 14 December [meeting 79], the General Assembly, on the recommendation of the Fourth Committee [A/61/407], adopted **resolution 61/113** by recorded vote (170-6-8) [agenda item 31].

Persons displaced as a result of the June 1967 and subsequent hostilities

The General Assembly,

Recalling its resolutions 2252(ES-V) of 4 July 1967, 2341 B (XXII) of 19 December 1967 and all subsequent related resolutions,

Recalling also Security Council resolutions 237(1967) of 14 June 1967 and 259(1968) of 27 September 1968,

Taking note of the report of the Secretary-General submitted in pursuance of its resolution 60/101 of 8 December 2005,

Taking note also of the report of the Commissioner-General of the United Nations Relief and Works Agency for Palestine Refugees in the Near East covering the period from 1 January to 31 December 2005,

Concerned about the continuing human suffering resulting from the June 1967 and subsequent hostilities,

Taking note of the relevant provisions of the Declaration of Principles on Interim Self-Government Arrangements of 13 September 1993 with regard to the modalities for the admission of persons displaced in 1967, and concerned that the process agreed upon has not yet been effected,

1. *Reaffirms* the right of all persons displaced as a result of the June 1967 and subsequent hostilities to return to their homes or former places of residence in the territories occupied by Israel since 1967;

2. *Expresses deep concern* that the mechanism agreed upon by the parties in article XII of the Declaration of Principles on Interim Self-Government Arrangements of 13 September 1993 on the return of displaced persons has not been complied with, and stresses the necessity for an accelerated return of displaced persons;

3. *Endorses*, in the meantime, the efforts of the Commissioner-General of the United Nations Relief and Works Agency for Palestine Refugees in the Near East to continue to provide humanitarian assistance, as far as practicable, on an emergency basis, and as a temporary measure, to persons in the area who are currently displaced and in serious need of continued assistance as a result of the June 1967 and subsequent hostilities;

4. *Strongly appeals* to all Governments and to organizations and individuals to contribute generously to the Agency and to the other intergovernmental and non-governmental organizations concerned for the above-mentioned purposes;

5. *Requests* the Secretary-General, after consulting with the Commissioner-General, to report to the General Assembly before its sixty-second session on the progress made with regard to the implementation of the present resolution.

RECORDED VOTE ON RESOLUTION 61/113:

In favour: Afghanistan, Albania, Algeria, Andorra, Angola, Antigua and Barbuda, Argentina, Armenia, Australia, Austria, Azerbaijan, Bahamas, Bahrain, Bangladesh, Barbados, Belarus, Belgium, Belize, Benin, Bhutan, Bolivia, Bosnia and Herzegovina, Botswana, Brazil, Brunei Darussalam, Bulgaria, Burkina Faso, Burundi, Cambodia, Cameroon, Canada, Cape Verde, Central African Republic, Chad, Chile, China, Colombia, Comoros, Congo, Costa Rica, Croatia, Cuba, Cyprus, Czech Republic, Democratic People's Republic of Korea, Democratic Republic of the Congo, Denmark, Djibouti, Dominica, Dominican Republic, Ecuador, Egypt, El Salvador, Equatorial Guinea, Eritrea, Estonia, Ethiopia, Finland, France, Gabon, Georgia, Germany, Ghana, Greece, Grenada, Guatemala, Guinea, Guinea-Bissau, Guyana, Haiti, Honduras, Hungary, Iceland, India, Indonesia, Iran, Iraq, Ireland, Italy, Jamaica, Japan, Jordan, Kazakhstan, Kenya, Kuwait, Kyrgyzstan, Lao People's Democratic Republic, Latvia, Lebanon, Lesotho, Libyan Arab Jamahiriya, Liechtenstein, Lithuania, Luxembourg, Malaysia, Maldives, Mali, Malta, Mauritania, Mauritius, Mexico, Moldova, Monaco, Mongolia, Montenegro, Morocco, Mozambique, Myanmar, Namibia, Nepal, Netherlands, New Zealand, Nicaragua, Niger, Nigeria, Norway, Oman, Pakistan, Panama, Paraguay, Peru, Philippines, Poland, Portugal, Qatar, Republic of Korea, Romania, Russian Federation, Saint Lucia, Saint Vincent and the Grenadines, Samoa, San Marino, Sao Tome and Principe, Saudi Arabia, Senegal, Serbia, Sierra Leone, Singapore, Slovakia, Slovenia, Solomon Islands, South Africa, Spain, Sri Lanka, Sudan, Suriname, Sweden, Switzerland, Syrian Arab Republic, Tajikistan, Thailand, The former Yugoslav Republic of Macedonia, Timor-Leste, Togo, Tonga, Trinidad and Tobago, Tunisia, Turkey, Turkmenistan, Ukraine, United Arab Emirates, United Kingdom, United Republic of Tanzania, Uruguay, Uzbekistan, Venezuela, Viet Nam, Yemen, Zambia, Zimbabwe.

Against: Israel, Marshall Islands, Micronesia, Nauru, Palau, United States.

Abstaining: Côte d'Ivoire, Fiji, Malawi, Papua New Guinea, Swaziland, Tuvalu, Uganda, Vanuatu.

Property rights

In response to General Assembly resolution 60/103 [YUN 2005, p. 549], the Secretary-General submitted an August report [A/61/278] on steps taken to protect and administer Arab property, assets and property rights in Israel. He indicated that he had transmitted the resolution to Israel and all other Member States, requesting information on any steps taken or envisaged to implement it. A reply was received from Sweden covering various aspects of Assembly resolutions 60/103 and 60/100 [YUN 2005, p. 545] pertaining to assistance to Palestinian refugees. As at 21 August, no information had been received from other Member States.

GENERAL ASSEMBLY ACTION

On 14 December [meeting 79], the General Assembly, on the recommendation of the Fourth Committee [A/61/407], adopted **resolution 61/115** by recorded vote (170-6-8) [agenda item 31].

Palestine refugees' properties and their revenues

The General Assembly,

Recalling its resolutions 194 (III) of 11 December 1948 and 36/146 C of 16 December 1981 and all its subsequent resolutions on the question,

Taking note of the report of the Secretary-General submitted in pursuance of resolution 60/103 of 8 December 2005,

Taking note also of the report of the United Nations Conciliation Commission for Palestine for the period from 1 September 2005 to 31 August 2006,

Recalling that the Universal Declaration of Human Rights and the principles of international law uphold the principle that no one shall be arbitrarily deprived of his or her property,

Recalling in particular its resolution 394(V) of 14 December 1950, in which it directed the Conciliation Commission, in consultation with the parties concerned, to prescribe measures for the protection of the rights, property and interests of the Palestine refugees,

Noting the completion of the programme of identification and evaluation of Arab property, as announced by the Conciliation Commission in its twenty-second progress report, and the fact that the Land Office had a schedule of Arab owners and a file of documents defining the location, area and other particulars of Arab property,

Expressing its appreciation for the work done to preserve and modernize the existing records, including the land records, of the Conciliation Commission and the importance of such records for a just resolution of the plight of the Palestine refugees in conformity with resolution 194(III),

Recalling that, in the framework of the Middle East peace process, the Palestine Liberation Organization and the Government of Israel agreed, in the Declaration of Principles on Interim Self-Government Arrangements of 13 September 1993, to commence negotiations on permanent status issues, including the important issue of the refugees,

1. *Reaffirms* that the Palestine refugees are entitled to their property and to the income derived therefrom, in conformity with the principles of equity and justice;

2. *Requests* the Secretary-General to take all appropriate steps, in consultation with the United Nations Conciliation Commission for Palestine, for the protection of Arab property, assets and property rights in Israel;

3. *Calls once again upon* Israel to render all facilities and assistance to the Secretary-General in the implementation of the present resolution;

4. *Calls upon* all the parties concerned to provide the Secretary-General with any pertinent information in their possession concerning Arab property, assets and property rights in Israel that would assist him in the implementation of the present resolution;

5. *Urges* the Palestinian and Israeli sides, as agreed between them, to deal with the important issue of Palestine refugees' properties and their revenues within the framework of the final status negotiations of the Middle East peace process;

6. *Requests* the Secretary-General to report to the General Assembly at its sixty-second session on the implementation of the present resolution.

RECORDED VOTE ON RESOLUTION 61/115:

In favour: Afghanistan, Albania, Algeria, Andorra, Angola, Antigua and Barbuda, Argentina, Armenia, Australia, Austria, Azerbaijan, Bahamas, Bahrain, Bangladesh, Barbados, Belarus, Belgium, Belize, Benin, Bhutan, Bolivia, Bosnia and Herzegovina, Botswana, Brazil, Brunei Darussalam, Bulgaria, Burkina Faso, Burundi, Cambodia, Canada, Cape Verde, Central African Republic, Chad, Chile, China, Colombia, Comoros, Congo, Costa Rica, Côte d'Ivoire, Croatia, Cuba, Cyprus, Czech Republic, Democratic People's Republic of Korea, Democratic Republic of the Congo, Denmark, Djibouti, Dominica, Dominican Republic, Ecuador, Egypt, El Salvador, Equatorial Guinea, Eritrea, Estonia, Ethiopia, Finland, France, Gabon, Georgia, Germany, Ghana, Greece, Grenada, Guatemala, Guinea, Guinea-Bissau, Guyana, Haiti, Honduras, Hungary, Iceland, India, Indonesia, Iran, Iraq, Ireland, Italy, Jamaica, Japan, Jordan, Kazakhstan, Kenya, Kuwait, Kyrgyzstan, Lao People's Democratic Republic, Latvia, Lebanon, Lesotho, Libyan Arab Jamahiriya, Liechtenstein, Lithuania, Luxembourg, Malaysia, Maldives, Mali, Malta, Mauritania, Mauritius, Mexico, Moldova, Monaco, Mongolia, Montenegro, Morocco, Mozambique, Myanmar, Namibia, Nepal, Netherlands, New Zealand, Nicaragua, Niger, Nigeria, Norway, Oman, Pakistan, Panama, Paraguay, Peru, Philippines, Poland, Portugal, Qatar, Republic of Korea, Romania, Russian Federation, Saint Lucia, Saint Vincent and the Grenadines, Samoa, San Marino, Sao Tome and Principe, Saudi Arabia, Senegal, Serbia, Sierra Leone, Singapore, Slovakia, Slovenia, Solomon Islands, South Africa, Spain, Sri Lanka, Sudan, Suriname, Sweden, Switzerland, Syrian Arab Republic, Tajikistan, Thailand, The former Yugoslav Republic of Macedonia, Timor-Leste, Togo, Tonga, Trinidad and Tobago, Tunisia, Turkey, Turkmenistan, Ukraine, United Arab Emirates, United Kingdom, United Republic of Tanzania, Uruguay, Uzbekistan, Venezuela, Viet Nam, Yemen, Zambia, Zimbabwe.

Against: Israel, Marshall Islands, Micronesia, Nauru, Palau, United States.

Abstaining: Cameroon, Fiji, Malawi, Papua New Guinea, Swaziland, Tuvalu, Uganda, Vanuatu.

Peacekeeping operations

In 2006, the United Nations Truce Supervision Organization (UNTSO), originally set up to monitor the ceasefire called for by the Security Council in resolution S/801 of 29 May 1948 [YUN 1947-48, p. 427] in the newly partitioned Palestine, continued its work. UNTSO unarmed military observers fulfilled evolving mandates—from supervising the original four armistice agreements between Israel and its neighbours (Egypt, Jordan, Lebanon, the Syrian Arab Republic) to observing and monitoring other ceasefires, as well as performing a number of additional tasks. During the year, UNTSO personnel worked with the two remaining UN peacekeeping forces in the Middle East—the United Nations Disengagement Observer Force (UNDOF) in the Golan Heights and the United Nations Interim Force in Lebanon (UNIFIL).

On 29 July [S/2006/595], the Secretary-General informed the Council President that the killing on 25 July of four UNTSO military observers at patrol base Khiam and the incident on 23 July, when a military observer at patrol base Ras was seriously injured, called into question whether UN peacekeeping personnel could be sufficiently protected in their positions. It was the Secretariat's assessment that the risks of continuing staffing the remaining two patrol bases with unarmed military observers outweighed the merits gained from their presence. Accordingly, UNTSO military observers at patrol bases Hin and Mar were relocated to other positions within UNIFIL. Patrol bases Ras and Khiam had not been occupied by UN personnel since 23 and 25 July, respectively. The Secretary-General had asked the Israeli Prime Minister to carry out a joint investigation with the United Nations into the events that led to the death of the military observers at Khiam, and for information about what actions IDF had taken in response to the repeated communications from UNTSO and UNIFIL on the recurring incidents of close firing in the hours before the position was hit directly. The Secretary-General was disturbed to learn that the patrol base and its surroundings had come under renewed firing by IDF in the days following the 25 July incident.

In an exchange of letters of 10 [S/2006/894] and 15 November [S/2006/895] with the Council President, the Secretary-General appointed Major General Ian Campbell Gordon (Australia) as UNTSO Chief of Staff, to replace Major General Clive Lilley, who relinquished his post on 30 November.

Lebanon

Lebanon continued to be the focus of international attention and concern throughout 2006. One of the most serious crises between Israel and Lebanon broke out on 12 July, after the paramilitary group Hizbullah crossed the border and kidnapped two Israeli soldiers whom they brought back to Lebanon. Israel retaliated with ground, air and sea attacks, crossing into Lebanon. Over one thousand Lebanese civilians were killed, thousands more were wounded, and over one million were displaced. On the Israeli side, over one hundred soldiers were killed, as well as 43 civilians. Much of the Lebanese infrastructure was destroyed and Israel imposed a sea and air blockade. With the adoption of Security Council resolution 1701(2006) on 11 August and through the good offices of the Secretary-General, Israel and Lebanon agreed to a ceasefire effective 14 August. The Council's resolution, among other measures, expanded the numbers, mandate and scope of UNIFIL. By the end of the year, in a historic development, the Lebanese armed forces were deployed in the south of the country for the first time in over three decades, as well as along the border with the Syrian Arab Republic.

The United Nations International Independent Investigation Commission (UNIIIC) continued to investigate the 14 February 2005 assassination of former Lebanese Prime Minister Rafik Hariri and 22 others. Following the 21 November 2006 assassination of Minister of Industry Pierre Gemayel, the Security Council invited UNIIIC to extend its technical assistance to Lebanese authorities in the subsequent investigation. On 10 November, the Secretary-General transmitted to the Lebanese Prime Minister the draft agreement between the United Nations and the Lebanese Government on the establishment of a special tribunal to try those individuals responsible for the assassination of Mr. Hariri. Formal approval by the Lebanese Government and ratification by the Lebanese Parliament were still needed before the signing of a treaty between the United Nations and Lebanon.

Monthly briefings on the Palestine question were given to the Security Council by Alvaro de Soto, Special Coordinator for the Middle East Peace Process and Personal Representative of the Secretary-General, Ibrahim Gambari, Under-Secretary-General for Political Affairs, and Angela Kane, Assistant Secretary-General for Political Affairs. Those briefings also covered developments in southern Lebanon. In July, Vijai Nambiar, Special Adviser to the Secretary-General, led a mission to the Middle East, including Lebanon, to explore ways of defusing the crisis in the region. He was accompanied by Terje Roed-Larsen and Mr. de Soto.

The paramilitary group Hizbullah continued to carry out attacks against positions of the Israeli Defence Force (IDF) inside Israel, while the IDF continued attacks within Lebanon. The Shab'a farmlands had been an area of contention since the withdrawal of Israeli forces from Lebanon in June 2000. According to the Lebanese Government, Israel's withdrawal from southern Lebanon was incomplete, as Israeli forces continued to occupy the Shab'a farms, while Israel viewed the area as occupied Syrian territory and thus within the purview of Council resolution 242(1967) [YUN 1967, p. 257] on the Israeli-Syrian conflict, and not resolution 425(1978) [YUN 1978, p. 312], which dealt with Israel's withdrawal from Lebanon. However, Lebanon and the Syrian Arab Republic maintained that the Shab'a farmlands were inside Lebanese territory.

The Personal Representative of the Secretary-General for Lebanon, Geir O. Pedersen, continued to coordinate UN political activities in Lebanon.

Communications. In communications received throughout the year [A/60/644-S/2006/5, A/60/666-S/2006/74, A/60/670-S/2006/81, A/60/708-S/2006/138, A/60/745-S/2006/214, A/60/837-S/2006/277, A/60/866-S/2006/346, A/60/873-S/2006/363, A/60/938-S/2006/518, A/60/939-S/2006/522, A/60/940-S/2006/528, A/60/941-S/2006/529, A/60/942-S/2006/531, A/60/944-S/2006/536, A/60/945-S/2006/537, A/60/948-S/2006/550, A/60/953-S/2006/565, A/60/955-S/2006/571, A/60/956-S/2006/575, A/60/957-S/2006/578, A/60/964-S/2006/599, A/60/966-S/2006/605, A/ES-10/354-S/2006/641, A/60/985-S/2006/684, A/60/988-S/2006/687, A/60/993-S/2006/697, A/60/994-S/2006/698, A/60/997-S/2006/705, A/60/998-

S/2006/711, A/60/1001-S/2006/713, A/60/1003-S/2006/721, A/61/334-S/2006/729, A/61/339-S/2006/732, A/61/356-S/2006/747, A/61/366-S/2006/753, A/61/435-S/2006/763, A/61/467-S/2006/767, A/61/473-S/2006/772, A/61/481-S/2006/782, A/61/482-S/2006/785, A/61/493-S/2006/786, A/61/516-S/2006/813, A/61/527-S/2006/824, A/61/540-S/2006/844, A/61/543-S/2006/852, A/61/555-S/2006/860, A/61/596-S/2006/917, A/61/607-S/2006/937, A/61/626-S/2006/965, A/61/643-S/2006/995, A/61/685-S/20061033], Lebanon reported on Israeli acts of aggression and violations of the Blue Line, the provisional border drawn by the United Nations following the withdrawal of Israeli troops from southern Lebanon in 2000, and consequently of Lebanese sovereignty and territorial integrity. In particular, Lebanon detailed the Israeli military campaign against Lebanese civilians and territory which commenced on 12 July.

In a series of letters [A/60/667-S/2006/76, A/60/867-S/2006/348, A/60/937-S/2006/515], Israel reported on attacks carried out across the Blue Line, as well as the firing of rockets, by Hizbullah and other militias against Israeli civilians and military targets. Israel claimed that those attacks were enabled by the complicity of the Government of Lebanon and the support of the Iranian and Syrian regimes.

In a separate response [A/60/884-S/2006/380], Iran refuted Israel's allegations, regarding them as an attempt to distract the international community from the numerous crimes committed by Israel in the region.

Situation in Lebanon

Report of Secretary-General (January). In a January report [S/2006/26] on developments in the UNIFIL area of operations since his previous report [YUN 2005, p. 567], the Secretary-General said that a fragile political and security environment continued to prevail in Lebanon. In the south, the general situation remained calm, yet volatile for the most part. The greatest cause for concern was the Hizbullah attack across the Blue Line on 21 November 2005 [YUN 2005, p. 569], which was a deliberate act in direct breach of the decisions of the Security Council leading to a heavy exchange of fire between Hizbullah and IDF inside the village of Ghajar. The incident highlighted the need for stronger security control around Ghajar, where UNIFIL had established a static patrol presence on the northern side and was ready to assist the Lebanese Government with its responsibilities in that respect. Continued Israeli air incursions, occasionally reaching far into Lebanese airspace, remained a matter of deep concern. The serious breaches of the ceasefire underlined yet again the urgent need for the Lebanese Government to extend its full authority throughout the south down to the Blue Line and to deploy sufficient numbers of armed security forces to maintain law and order and ensure a calm environment.

The Secretary-General welcomed the Lebanese Government's decision to co-locate the Army Liaison Office with UNIFIL headquarters in Naqoura, appoint liaison officers to UNIFIL field battalions and work more closely with the Force in the field. So that planning for the deployment of additional forces in the south could start without delay, he encouraged the Lebanese Government to accept the UNIFIL Force Commander's proposal to establish a joint planning cell, composed of members of the Lebanese armed forces and UNIFIL. The activities and presence of the Joint Security Force could also be enhanced on the ground, within the limits of its authorized number of 1,000. Additionally, closer coordination between UNIFIL and the Joint Security Force patrols in the area of operation would help to enhance the role and activities of the Lebanese armed forces. In the light of the prevailing conditions in the area, the Secretary-General, as requested by Lebanon on 9 January [S/2006/15], recommended that the Security Council extend UNIFIL mandate until 31 July 2006.

SECURITY COUNCIL ACTION

On 31 January [meeting 5362], the Security Council unanimously adopted **resolution 1655(2006)**. The draft [S/2006/57] was submitted by Denmark, France, Greece, Slovakia, the United Kingdom and the United States.

The Security Council,

Recalling all its previous resolutions on Lebanon, including resolutions 425(1978) and 426(1978) of 19 March 1978 and 1614(2005) of 29 July 2005, as well as the statements by its President on the situation in Lebanon, in particular the statement of 18 June 2000,

Recalling also the letter dated 18 May 2001 from its President to the Secretary-General,

Recalling further the conclusion of the Secretary-General that, as of 16 June 2000, Israel had withdrawn its forces from Lebanon in accordance with resolution 425(1978) and met the requirements defined in the report of the Secretary-General of 22 May 2000, as well as the conclusion of the Secretary-General that the United Nations Interim Force in Lebanon had essentially completed two of the three parts of its mandate, focusing now on the remaining task of restoring international peace and security,

Reaffirming that the Security Council has recognized the Blue Line as valid for the purpose of confirming the withdrawal of Israel pursuant to resolution 425(1978) and that the Blue Line must be respected in its entirety,

Gravely concerned at the persistence of tension and violence along the Blue Line, including the hostilities initiated by Hizbollah on 21 November 2005 and those triggered by the firing of rockets from Lebanon into Israel on 27 December 2005, which demonstrated once more that the situation remains volatile and fragile and underlined yet again the urgent need for the Government of Lebanon to fully extend its authority and exert control and monopoly over the use of force throughout its territory, as outlined in the report of the Secretary-General of 18 January 2006, and concerned also by the continuing Israeli violations of Lebanese airspace,

Recalling its resolution 1308(2000) of 17 July 2000,

Recalling also its resolution 1325(2000) of 31 October 2000,

Recalling further the relevant principles contained in the Convention on the Safety of United Nations and Associated Personnel of 9 December 1994,

Responding to the request of the Government of Lebanon to extend the mandate of the Force for a new period of six months, presented in the letter dated 9 January 2006 from the Chargé d'affaires a.i. of the Permanent Mission of Lebanon to the United Nations addressed to the Secretary-General,

1. *Endorses* the report of the Secretary-General of 18 January 2006 on the United Nations Interim Force in Lebanon;

2. *Decides* to extend the present mandate until 31 July 2006, while emphasizing the interim nature of the Force and looking forward to the early fulfilment of its mandate;

3. *Reiterates its strong support* for the territorial integrity, sovereignty and political independence of Lebanon within its internationally recognized boundaries and under the sole and exclusive authority of the Government of Lebanon;

4. *Condemns* all acts of violence, including the latest serious incidents across the Blue Line initiated from the Lebanese side that have resulted in deaths and injuries on both sides, expresses great concern about these serious breaches and the sea, land and continuing aforementioned air violations of the withdrawal line, and urges the parties to put an end to these violations, to refrain from any act of provocation that could further escalate the tension and to abide scrupulously by their obligation to respect the safety of the Force and other United Nations personnel, including avoiding any course of action which endangers United Nations personnel;

5. *Reiterates its call upon* the parties to continue to fulfil the commitments they have given to respect fully the entire withdrawal line identified by the United Nations, as set out in the report of Secretary-General of 16 June 2000, and to exercise utmost restraint;

6. *Reiterates its call upon* the Government of Lebanon to fully extend and exercise its sole and effective authority throughout the south;

7. *Welcomes* the steps undertaken recently by the Government of Lebanon to strengthen the liaison between its armed forces and the Force, including the establishment of a Lebanese Armed Forces liaison office at Force headquarters in Naqoura, the appointment of liaison officers to the field battalions of the Force, and the appointment of a new government coordinator with the Force, and acknowledges the firm intention of the Government of Lebanon to preserve the security and, to that end, to reinforce the presence of its armed forces in the southern region and to coordinate their activities with the Force;

8. *Urges*, nevertheless, the Government of Lebanon to do more to assert its authority in the south, to exert control and monopoly over the use of force and to maintain law and order on its entire territory and to prevent attacks from Lebanon across the Blue Line, including by deploying additional numbers of Lebanese Armed Forces and Internal Security Forces and taking up the proposals of the Force to enhance coordination between those forces and the Force on the ground and establishing a joint planning cell, as recommended by the Secretary-General in his report;

9. *Requests* the Secretary-General to continue to work with the Government of Lebanon to reinforce its authority in the south, and in particular to facilitate the early implementation of the measures contained in paragraph 8 above;

10. *Supports* the continued efforts of the Force to maintain the ceasefire along the withdrawal line consistent with its remaining task, while stressing the primary responsibility of the parties in this regard, and encourages the Force to focus also on assisting the Government of Lebanon to assert its authority in the south;

11. *Welcomes* the continued contribution of the Force to operational mine clearance, encourages further assistance in mine action by the United Nations to the Government of Lebanon in support of both the continued development of its national mine action capacity and clearance of the remaining mines/unexploded ordnance in the south, commends donor countries for supporting those efforts through financial and in-kind contributions encouraging further international contributions, and stresses the necessity for the provision to the Government of Lebanon and the Force of any additional existing maps and minefield records;

12. *Calls upon* the parties to ensure that the Force is accorded full freedom of movement throughout its area of operation as outlined in the report of the Secretary-General, requests the Force to report any obstruction it may face in the discharge of its mandate, and reiterates its call upon the parties to cooperate fully with the United Nations and the Force;

13. *Welcomes* the efforts being undertaken by the Force to implement the Secretary-General's zero-tolerance policy on sexual exploitation and abuse and to ensure full compliance of its personnel with the United Nations code of conduct, requests the Secretary-General to continue to take all necessary action in this regard and keep the Security Council informed, and urges troop-contributing countries to take appropriate preventive action, including conducting predeployment awareness training, and to take disciplinary action and other action to ensure full accountability in cases of such conduct involving their personnel;

14. *Requests* the Secretary-General to continue consultations with the Government of Lebanon and other parties directly concerned on the implementation of the present resolution and to report thereon to the Council before the end of the present mandate as well as on the activities of the Force and the tasks presently carried out by the United Nations Truce Supervision Organization, and to include in the report an assessment of the progress made by the Government of Lebanon towards extending its sole and effective authority throughout the south;

15. *Expresses its intention* to keep the mandate and structures of the Force under regular review, taking into account the prevailing situation on the ground, the activities actually performed by the Force in its area of operation, its contribution towards the remaining task of restoring international peace and security, the views of the Government of Lebanon and the measures it has taken to fully extend its authority in the south as well as the implications those measures may have, in order to adjust the Force to its mission;

16. *Stresses* the importance of, and the need to achieve, a comprehensive, just and lasting peace in the Middle East, based on all its relevant resolutions, including resolutions 242(1967) of 22 November 1967 and 338(1973) of 22 October 1973.

Political developments

Implementation of Security Council resolution 1559(2004)

On 23 January [meeting 5352], the Security Council considered the Secretary-General's October 2005 report [YUN 2005, p. 564] on the implementation of resolution 1559(2004) [YUN 2004, p. 506]. Following consultations among its members, the President made statement **S/PRST/2006/3** on behalf of the Council:

The Security Council recalls all its previous resolutions on Lebanon, in particular resolutions 1559(2004), 425(1978), 426(1978), 520(1982) and 1614(2005), as well as the statements by its President on the situation in Lebanon, in particular the statements of 18 June 2000, 19 October 2004 and 4 May 2005.

The Council reaffirms its strong support for the sovereignty, territorial integrity, unity and political independence of Lebanon, as well as for the freedom of its press.

The Council welcomes the second semi-annual report of the Secretary-General to the Council, of 26 October 2005, on the implementation of Council resolution 1559(2004).

The Council notes that significant further progress has been made towards the implementation of resolution 1559(2004), in particular through the withdrawal of Syrian forces from Lebanon and the holding of free and credible parliamentary elections in May and June 2005, but it notes also with regret that other provisions of resolution 1559(2004) have yet to be implemented, particularly the disbanding and disarming of Lebanese and non-Lebanese militias and the extension of government control over all Lebanese territory, and free and fair presidential elections conducted according to the Lebanese constitutional rules, without foreign interference and influence.

In this context, the Council commends the Government of Lebanon for the dialogue it initiated in October 2005 with representatives of Lebanese and non-Lebanese militias, for the steps it has taken towards restoring fully its authority throughout its territory and for its stated willingness to establish full diplomatic relations and representation and to demarcate the border between Lebanon and the Syrian Arab Republic. The Council calls upon the Government of Lebanon to sustain its efforts to achieve progress on all these issues in accordance with resolution 1559(2004) and to pursue a broad national dialogue, and the Council calls upon all other parties concerned, in particular the Government of the Syrian Arab Republic, to cooperate to this end.

The Council notes with concern the suggestion in the report that there have been movements of arms and people into Lebanese territory and, in this context, commends the Government of Lebanon for undertaking measures against such movements and calls upon the Government of the Syrian Arab Republic to undertake similar measures.

The Council condemns the continued terrorist attacks in Lebanon, which have resulted in the death or injury of scores of Lebanese citizens, including several prominent Lebanese figures, as part of a deliberate strategy to destabilize the country and to intimidate the Lebanese people, their Government and their media.

The Council warns that those responsible for such crimes must be held fully accountable and will not be permitted to jeopardize the stability, democracy and national unity of Lebanon.

The Council reiterates its call for the full implementation of all requirements of resolution 1559(2004), and urges all concerned parties to cooperate fully with the Council and the Secretary-General to achieve this goal.

The Council commends the Secretary-General as well as his Special Envoy for their efforts and dedication to facilitate and assist in the implementation of all provisions of resolution 1559(2004).

Report of Secretary-General (April). On 18 April [S/2006/248], the Secretary-General submitted his third semi-annual report on the implementation of Council resolution 1559(2004). He stated that, in the six months since his last report [YUN 2005, p. 564], the situation in Lebanon remained tense. The number of terrorist attacks and acts of intimidation decreased significantly, compared to the previous six-month period. However, a general atmosphere of fear and insecurity continued to prevail. Lebanon's political transition continued, but suffered a few setbacks. On 12 December 2005, members of the Amal party and Hizbullah suspended their participation in the cabinet in protest over the Government's request to the United Nations for the creation of an international tribunal to try suspects in the assassination of former Lebanese Prime Minister Hariri (see p. 602). The political process remained deadlocked until the ministers returned to the cabinet on 2 February 2006. Upon the initiative of Speaker of the Lebanese Parliament, Nabih Berri, 14 leaders from Lebanese factions and parties gathered on 2 March for the first session of a national dialogue to discuss the investigation into the Hariri assassination; the Palestinian issue in Lebanon; Syrian Arab Republic-Lebanon relations; the status of the Shab'a farmlands; the fate of the Presidency; and the arms possessed by Hizbullah. A number of agreements were reached on the first four items before the dialogue was adjourned on 3 April.

The Secretary-General observed that the Lebanese had made significant progress towards implementing in full all provisions of resolution 1559(2004). However, the provisions calling for the disbanding and disarmament of all Lebanese and non-Lebanese militias, the extension of the control of the Government of Lebanon over all Lebanese territory, and strict respect of the sovereignty, territorial integrity, unity and political independence of Lebanon under the sole and exclusive authority of the Government had not yet been fully implemented. In addition, there had not been a presidential election process, as called for in the resolution and the Security Council presidential statement of 23 January (see p. 569). There was urgent need to take tangible measures in order to retain the momentum and maintain Lebanon's progress towards full reaffirmation of its sovereignty, territorial integrity, unity and political independence. The implementation of the agreements reached in the national dialogue depended on the cooperation of parties other than the Lebanese themselves, in particular the Syrian Arab Republic, for the full implementation of resolution 1559(2004). The Secretary-General called on Syria to cooperate with Lebanon in establishing embassies, delineating the border between the two countries and undertaking any other measure towards the full implementation of resolution 1559(2004). The delineation of the border between Syria and Lebanon was of crucial importance to a number of explicit operational requirements of resolution 1559(2004). The timely implementation of tangible measures towards that end, as well as towards the disarming and disbanding of Lebanese and non-Lebanese militias, was an important step towards the extension of the Government's control over all its territory. Noting that repeated statements by representatives of the Syrian Government that the Shab'a farms area was Lebanese and not Israeli-occupied Syrian territory, as determined by the United Nations on the basis of the so-called Blue Line, the Secretary-General reiterated his previous caveat that the United Nations determination of the status of the Shab'a farms was without prejudice to any border delineation agreement between Syria and Lebanon. The Shab'a farms status as Israeli-occupied Syrian territory remained valid unless and until the Lebanese and Syrian Governments took steps under international law to alter that status. The existence of armed groups defying the control of the legitimate Government was incompatible with the restoration and full respect of the sovereignty, territorial integrity, unity and political independence of the country.

The national dialogue in Lebanon was a truly historic and unprecedented event. It maked the first time that the Lebanese had come together in that manner to talk frankly with one another about issues that were once considered taboo. The agreement reached in the national dialogue on the arms of Palestinian militias outside Palestinian refugee camps was an important step towards the implementation of resolution 1559(2004). The dialogue was scheduled to reconvene on 28 April to deal with remaining unresolved issues.

The implementation of resolution 1559(2004) was part of a wider process of historical transformation, including investigations into the terrorist assassination of former Prime Minister Hariri and 22 others, as well as other acts of assassination and terror in Lebanon over the previous period, the ongoing effort to reform the electoral processes and the ongoing preparations and subsequent implementation of economic reforms.

Security Council consideration (April). Lebanese Prime Minister Fouad Siniora told the Security Council, during its 21 April [meeting 5417] discussion on the situation in the Middle East, that the process of national dialogue, which brought together 14 representatives of all parliamentary blocs, had achieved significant progress. The Lebanese people showed remarkable resilience in the face of systematic attempts of terrorism and intimidation and demonstrated that they had moved a long way towards a strong, united and stable country. It was a major challenge to put Lebanese-Syrian relations on the right footing. In the national dialogue, it was agreed that those relations should be strong, positive and based on mutual respect, parity and non-interference. However, it required the re-establishment of confidence and acceptance of a truly independent, free and sovereign Lebanon. As to the delineation of the Lebanese Shaba'a farms area, the Syrian Government had been approached on the matter and a positive response was anticipated. However, Lebanon would request the Secretary-General to confirm the specific steps required by the United Nations to recognize Lebanese sovereignty over the territory. With respect to the Palestinian refugees, the Government had initiated efforts to improve their living conditions, in cooperation with the United Nations Relief and Works Agency for Palestine Refugees in the Near East.

Another challenge was reaching agreement on the two remaining issues of the National Dialogue Conference: that of the presidency of the Republic, and Hizbullah's weapons and their role in the defence of Lebanon. The majority in Parliament considered the extension of President Lahoud's term in September 2004 for three more years to have been the result of Syrian coercion and interference, but because that majority was not sufficient to constitutionally shorten the President's extended term, the issue had been referred to the national dialogue in the hope that a consensus could be reached. On the issue of Hizbullah, while there was consensus of the important role it had played in spearheading the resistance to force Israel's withdrawal from Lebanon in 2000, the future role of its weapons in defending Lebanon was a matter of national debate and a major challenge to be addressed in the period ahead.

Lebanon said that what happened in the country had a significant impact on the entire region and stressed its interest in taking responsibility for working together with others against the forces of extremism and despair by addressing their motives.

The Prime Minister of Syria sent a letter to his Lebanese counterpart stating his willingness to demarcate the border between the two countries. The demarcation of the border in the Shaba'a farms, however, would have to await Israel's withdrawal from that area.

Communication. On 24 April [S/2006/259], Syria said the report of the Special Representative of the Secretary-General on the implementation of resolution 1559(2004) exceeded the mandate provided in that resolution. The report mostly focused on issues relating to diplomatic relations and delineation of the borders as factors contributing to the respect of the sovereignty, independence and unity of Lebanese territory. The issue of establishing embassies between Lebanon and Syria was a matter that fell within the domestic jurisdiction of both countries, and could be agreed on when the environment prevailing in relations between them allowed such steps. The report also stated that the reporting period witnessed tense bilateral relations between Syria and Lebanon. That claim had no valid basis on the ground, owing to the fact that the tension was created by some parties in Lebanon to damage relations between the two countries. The call for Syria to implement measures to control its borders with Lebanon was superseded by those already implemented by Syria to stop illegal entry and trafficking to and from Syria. The report, however, failed to refer in detail to arms trafficking into Lebanon by sea, which was directed to some political parties in Lebanon. Syria affirmed that the support of the international community for the efforts of the Lebanese people to enhance its unity and to maintain its independence and sovereignty was the only avenue to ensuring the future of Lebanon. Pressure by certain parties for the Security Council to adopt new resolutions or statements did not calm the situation in Lebanon or the region, but escalated instability and tension.

SECURITY COUNCIL ACTION

On 17 May [meeting 5440], the Security Council adopted **resolution 1680(2006)** by recorded vote (13-0-2). The draft [S/2006/298] was submitted by Denmark, France, Slovakia, the United Kingdom and the United States.

The Security Council,

Recalling all its previous resolutions on Lebanon, in particular resolutions 425(1978) and 426(1978) of 19 March 1978, 520(1982) of 17 September 1982, 1559(2004) of 2 September 2004 and 1655(2006) of 31 January 2006, as well as the statements by its President on the situation in Lebanon, in particular the statements of 18 June 2000, 19 October 2004, 4 May 2005 and 23 January 2006,

Reiterating its strong support for the territorial integrity, sovereignty and political independence of Lebanon within its internationally recognized borders,

Noting positively that further significant progress has been made towards implementing in full all provisions of resolution 1559(2004), in particular through the Lebanese national dialogue, but noting with regret that other provisions of resolution 1559(2004) have not yet been fully implemented, namely the disbanding and disarming of Lebanese and non-Lebanese militias, the extension of the control of the Government of Lebanon over all its territory, the strict respect of the sovereignty, territorial integrity, unity and political independence of Lebanon, and free and fair presidential elections conducted according to the Lebanese constitutional rules, without foreign interference and influence,

Noting with concern the conclusion contained in the report of the Secretary-General that there had been movements of arms into Lebanese territory for militias over the last six months,

Expressing full support for the Lebanese national dialogue, and commending all Lebanese parties for its conduct and for the consensus reached in this context on important matters,

Having heard the address by the Prime Minister of Lebanon to the Security Council on 21 April 2006,

1. *Welcomes* the third semi-annual report of the Secretary-General to the Security Council of 18 April 2006 on the implementation of resolution 1559(2004);

2. *Reiterates its call for* the full implementation of all requirements of resolution 1559(2004);

3. *Reiterates its call upon* all concerned States and parties, as mentioned in the report, to cooperate fully

with the Government of Lebanon, the Security Council and the Secretary-General to achieve this goal;

4. *Strongly encourages* the Government of the Syrian Arab Republic to respond positively to the request made by the Government of Lebanon, in line with the agreements of the Lebanese national dialogue, to delineate their common border, especially in those areas where the border is uncertain or disputed, and to establish full diplomatic relations and representation, noting that such measures would constitute a significant step towards asserting the sovereignty, territorial integrity and political independence of Lebanon and improving the relations between the two countries, thus contributing positively to stability in the region, and urges both parties to make efforts through further bilateral dialogue to this end, bearing in mind that the establishment of diplomatic relations between States, and of permanent diplomatic missions, takes place by mutual consent;

5. *Commends* the Government of Lebanon for undertaking measures against movements of arms into Lebanese territory, and calls upon the Government of the Syrian Arab Republic to take similar measures;

6. *Welcomes* the decision of the Lebanese national dialogue to disarm Palestinian militias outside refugee camps within six months, supports its implementation, and calls for further efforts to disband and disarm all Lebanese and non-Lebanese militias and to restore fully the Government of Lebanon's control over all Lebanese territory;

7. *Reiterates its support* to the Secretary-General and his Special Envoy in their efforts and dedication to facilitate and assist in the implementation of all provisions of resolution 1559(2004);

8. *Decides* to remain seized of the matter.

RECORDED VOTE ON RESOLUTION 1680(2006):

In favour: Argentina, Congo, Denmark, France, Ghana, Greece, Japan, Peru, Qatar, Slovakia, United Kingdom, United Republic of Tanzania, United States.

Against: None.

Abstaining: China, Russian Federation.

Report of Secretary-General (October). On 19 October [S/2006/832], the Secretary-General, in his fourth semi-annual report on the implementation of Council resolution 1559(2004), stated that, since his last report (see p. 569), Lebanon had witnessed political standstill, followed by severe deterioration and prolonged instability. The national dialogue reconvened on 28 April and 16 May to discuss the two remaining issues on its agenda, the Lebanese presidency and Hizbullah's arms, amidst an increasingly tense political climate both domestically and with regard to Lebanese-Syrian relations. On 1 and 2 June, protests and clashes erupted after a television programme appeared to parody the Hizbullah Secretary-General, Hassan Nasrallah. In that context, the national dialogue met again on 8 June, during which Lebanese political leaders agreed on a written code of conduct stipulating that they would refrain from attacking each other, in order to decrease the rising political and sectarian tension. On 29 June, the national dialogue convened for the last time to date and adjourned, having reached no further agreements. On 12 July, hostilities erupted between Israel and Hizbullah, after the latter launched an unprovoked attack across the Blue Line, abducting two Israeli soldiers and killing several others (see p. 574). Since then, a tense political climate prevailed in Lebanon, with a worrying return to the previous year's climate of frequent assassinations and terrorist acts.

Additional progress had been made in recent months in the implementation of Council resolution 1559(2004) with the deployment of the Lebanese Armed Forces in the south of the country for the first time in three decades. Moreover, Lebanese troops had taken up positions along the eastern part of the Blue Line for the first time ever, and had deployed in significant numbers along Lebanon's border with the Syrian Arab Republic. Those steps represented important progress towards the full extension of the Government of Lebanon's control over all Lebanese territory. However, resolution 1559(2004), and in particular its provisions calling for the disbanding and disarmament of all Lebanese and non-Lebanese militias and the strict respect of the sovereignty, territorial integrity, unity, and political independence of Lebanon under the sole and exclusive authority of the Government, had yet to be implemented in full.

Israeli troops, which had entered Lebanon in the course of the July-August conflict, returned beyond the Blue Line on 1 October, except in the divided village of Ghajar. The Secretary-General expected that presence to end rapidly in the context of a trilateral discussion on security arrangements for the village. The Lebanese Government informed the Secretary-General of its continuing efforts to consolidate its full control over all security services. Allegations had at times been made, including by the Lebanese Government, that there continued to be Syrian intelligence activity in Lebanon.

In a meeting with the Secretary-General on 21 April regarding the delineation of the border in the Shab'a Farms area, Prime Minister Siniora enquired as to possible steps that could be taken, from the UN perspective, for the sovereignty of the Shab'a Farms to be transferred from Syria to Lebanon. In the light of Syrian statements indicating that the Shab'a Farms area was Lebanese, and considering the alternative path suggested by the Government of Lebanon in its seven-point plan (see p. 579), the Secretary-General continued to investigate the complicated cartographic, legal and political implications of such an approach and would revert to the Council in due course. In the meantime, he reiterated his urgent call to Syria and Lebanon to undertake the necessary steps to delineate their common border, in fulfilment of relevant Council resolutions.

During the July-August 2006 hostilities, the Lebanese Government reaffirmed its determination to extend its control over all of Lebanon's territory and to establish its monopoly on the legitimate use of force. Prime Minister Siniora's seven-point plan (see p. 579) envisaged that the Lebanese Government would extend its authority over its territory through its own armed forces, such that there would be no weapons or authority other than that of the Lebanese State. The Lebanese Council of Ministers adopted the seven-point plan as the official position of the Government on 27 July. On 7 August, the cabinet decided to send 15,000 Lebanese soldiers to the south, simultaneous with the withdrawal of the occupying Israeli forces beyond the Blue Line.

The national dialogue's decision to disarm Palestinian militias outside the camps had not been implemented within the six-month deadline, which ended on 26 August. The Secretary-General expected that the Lebanese Government would further define a political process and a clear timeline for the full disarmament of Palestinian militias in Lebanon. The national dialogue also discussed the issue of Hizbullah's arms, but did not reach agreement. Hizbullah continued to limit the authority of the Lebanese Government, especially in areas close to the Blue Line. The eventual disarmament of Hizbullah, within the context of the completion of its transformation into a solely political party, was a key element in ensuring a permanent end to the hostilities and a critical provision to be realized in the implementation of resolution 1701(2006) and in the full restoration of Lebanon's sovereignty, territorial integrity and political independence. (The measures to further that purpose provided for in resolution 1701(2006) were being implemented, in particular, the establishment between the Blue Line and the Litani River of an area free of any armed personnel, assets and weapons other than those of the Lebanese Government and UNIFIL. That action constituted an important step towards the disarming of all militias in Lebanon.)

The Secretary-General observed that, in the previous six months, Lebanon suffered a severe setback. Instead of making further strides towards completing its political transformation and reaping the economic rewards of political progress, it had to confront challenges of a magnitude unseen since the end of the civil war. Moreover, since the end of the hostilities in August, a tense political climate prevailed, with manifold challenges for the Lebanese in their quest to reconstruct their country, their polity and economy. In the months ahead, Lebanon would have to engage again in a truly national and inclusive dialogue. The disarming and disbanding of Lebanese and non-Lebanese militias could only be achieved through an inclusive process that addressed the political and economic interests of all Lebanese. The Secretary-General emphasized once again that Hizbullah's transformation into a solely political party was a key element in ensuring a permanent end to hostilities and in restoring Lebanon's sovereignty, territorial integrity and political independence.

SECURITY COUNCIL ACTION

On 30 October [meeting 5559], following consultations among Security Council members, the President made statement **S/PRST/2006/43** on behalf of the Council:

> The Security Council recalls all its previous resolutions on Lebanon, in particular resolutions 425(1978), 426(1978), 520(1982), 1559(2004), 1680(2006) and 1701(2006), as well as the statements by its President on the situation in Lebanon, in particular the statements of 18 June 2000, 19 October 2004, 4 May 2005 and 23 January 2006.
>
> The Council reaffirms its strong support for the territorial integrity, sovereignty, unity and political independence of Lebanon within its internationally recognized borders.
>
> The Council welcomes the fourth semi-annual report of the Secretary-General of 19 October 2006 on the implementation of resolution 1559(2004).
>
> The Council notes that important progress has been made towards the implementation of resolution 1559(2004), in particular through the deployment of the Lebanese Armed Forces in the south of the country for the first time in three decades, but it also notes with regret that some provisions of resolution 1559(2004) have yet to be implemented, namely the disbanding and disarming of Lebanese and non-Lebanese militias, the strict respect for the sovereignty, territorial integrity, unity and political independence of Lebanon, and free and fair presidential elections conducted according to the Lebanese constitutional rules, without any foreign interference and influence.
>
> The Council commends the Government of Lebanon for extending its authority throughout its territory, particularly in the south, and encourages it to continue its efforts in this regard.
>
> The Council reiterates its call for the full implementation of resolution 1559(2004) and urges all concerned States and parties as mentioned in the report to cooperate fully with the Government of Lebanon, the Council and the Secretary-General to achieve this goal.
>
> The Council reaffirms its support to the Secretary-General and his Special Envoy in their efforts and dedication to facilitate and assist in the implementation of all provisions of resolutions 1559(2004) and 1680(2006).
>
> The Council acknowledges the intention of the Secretary-General to revert to the Council in his next report on the implementation of resolution 1701(2006) and looks forward

to his further recommendations on the relevant outstanding issues.

Communications. In separate letters dated 3 [S/2006/865] and 7 [S/2006/877] November, Syria said that the fourth report on the implementation of Security Council resolution 1559(2006), as on the previous three occasions, was prejudiced against Syria and against its efforts to calm the situation in Lebanon and in the region.

Outbreak of hostilities between Israel and Hizbullah

Security Council consideration (14 July). At the request of Lebanon [S/2006/517], the Security Council, on 14 July [meeting 5489], discussed the situation in the Middle East, and in particular the crisis in Lebanon. The Under-Secretary-General for Peacekeeping Operations, Jean-Marie Guéhenno, said that the most serious crisis between Israel and Lebanon since the withdrawal of Israeli forces from south Lebanon in 2000 had broken out, with rising numbers of casualties on both sides. The crisis started on 12 July, when Hizbullah launched several rocket attacks from Lebanese territory across the Blue Line—the border demarcation between Lebanon and Israel established by the United Nations in June 2000—towards IDF positions near the coast and in the area of the Israeli town of Zarit. Shortly afterwards, Hizbullah fighters crossed the Blue Line into Israel and attacked an IDF patrol, capturing two IDF soldiers, killing three others and wounding two more. The captured soldiers were taken into Lebanon. Subsequent to the attack on the patrol, a heavy exchange of fire ensued across the Blue Line between Hizbullah and IDF, with the former targeting IDF positions and Israeli towns south of that Line. Israel retaliated with ground, air and sea attacks. In addition to air strikes on Hizbullah positions, IDF targeted numerous roads and bridges in southern Lebanon, which was intended to prevent Hizbullah from transferring the abducted soldiers. IDF crossed into Lebanon to the area controlled by Hizbullah militia in an attempt to rescue the captured soldiers. It appeared that the incursion was localized and the United Nations Interim Force in Lebanon (UNIFIL) had no reports of additional IDF incursions into Lebanese territory. The Secretary-General condemned the Hizbullah attack and called for the soldiers' immediate and unconditional release.

In the afternoon of 12 July, the Lebanese Government requested UNIFIL to broker a ceasefire. Israel responded that a ceasefire would be contingent upon the return of the captured soldiers. On 13 July, Hizbullah launched numerous rocket attacks on Nahariya, 10 kilometres south of the Blue Line, reportedly killing one Israeli civilian and wounding scores more. Later in the day, two rockets struck the city of Haifa causing some damage to buildings and injuries to several civilians, to which IDF responded by bombing Hizbullah positions; the Bierut international airport, setting fuel depots on fire, as well as a southern suburb of Beirut; the Hizbullah-affiliated Al-Manar television station; and two air bases. Israeli planes also dropped leaflets across Lebanon warning the population to avoid areas known for Hizbullah's presence. It was also reported that intermittent exchanges of fire from both sides continued along the Blue Line. Based on available information, eight IDF soldiers were killed and several wounded, and two Israeli civilians were killed and dozens more wounded. One Lebanese army soldier was reported killed in the attack on an air base, in addition to more than 50 civilians killed and scores wounded. The Personal Representative of the Secretary-General for Lebanon, Mr. Pedersen, expressed alarm at Israel's heavy attacks and the escalation that took place across the Blue Line. He also voiced concern that the Israeli military was enforcing an air and sea blockade, which would increase the hardship of the civilian population in Lebanon. UNIFIL reported several instances of firing close to its positions by both IDF and Hizbullah. Since 12 July, its personnel had been confined to their positions, unable to carry out regular vehicle and helicopter patrols along the Blue Line.

The Under-Secretary-General for Political Affairs, Ibrahim Gambari, said that the Secretary-General was deeply alarmed at the escalation of violence in Lebanon and Israel. Parts of Lebanon were under blockade and heavy Israeli military action, while Israel was being subjected to indiscriminate attacks by Hizbullah forces. The Secretary-General condemned all actions which targeted civilians or which unduly endangered them. He continued to work on the evolving and dangerous situation, and called upon all parties to adhere to their obligations under international humanitarian law and international agreements. He had been in close consultations also with leaders around the world to find an urgent solution to the crisis, urge restraint and prevent the situation from spiralling even further out of control. In that regard, the Secretary-General decided to send a mission to the Middle East to exercise good offices and help defuse the crisis in the region. The team, led by his Special Adviser, Vijay Nambiar, and comprising two other senior UN political officers, Alvaro de Soto and Terje Roed-Larsen, would help to de-escalate the situation by conveying the Secretary-General's call for the release of the captured soldiers, restraint by all parties and a ceasefire. All parties would also be encouraged to use their influence to defuse the situation. The team would also emphasize the Secretary-General's message that both sides respect international humanitarian law and protect civilians and civilian infrastructure.

Lebanon claimed that Israeli forces had launched widespread military operations, deliberately bombing vital installations. Most major bridges had been destroyed, as well as fuel storage tanks at electrical power plants, three runways at Beirut International Airport and many civilian installations and residential buildings. An air and sea blockade had been imposed to isolate Lebanon, cutting off all means of communication. Lebanon condemned the Israeli counter-attacks, which violated all international resolutions, laws, norms and conventions. Lebanon affirmed its right and duty to exercise its sovereignty over all its territory and had been working tirelessly to regain its independence and rebuild institutions, in cooperation with the international community. Israel's attacks hampered the efforts made towards fostering democracy. The Security Council should call for an immediate ceasefire, the lifting of the air and sea blockade and an end to the attacks. It should also take up the root causes and consequences of the current crisis along the Blue Line.

Israel said that its actions were in direct response to an act of war from Lebanon. Although Israel held the Government of Lebanon responsible, it was concentrating its response mainly on Hizbullah strongholds, positions and infrastructure. The hundreds of Katyusha rockets fired from Lebanon in the previous few days demonstrated the magnitude of the immense arsenal of rockets and other weapons that Hizbullah had amassed. Within 48 hours, more than 500 Katyushas and mortar shells were fired into the northern part of Israel, killing two civilians and wounding hundreds more. It was important for the international community to understand that, while Hizbullah executed that terrorism, it was merely the finger on the long-reaching arms of Syria and Iran. The Security Council and the international community had a duty to help the Lebanese people achieve the goal of a free, prosperous and democratic Lebanon.

Communications. On 14 July [S/2006/526], Syria complained that the Security Council Presidency had denied the right of the Syrian delegation to speak at the Council's 14 July meeting, especially since his country was the subject of false accusations and direct threat in the context of Israeli aggression towards Lebanon. The Council President, in his reply of the same day [S/2006/534], said that the meeting was held in accordance with the modalities that were initially decided on 13 July. The Council President had brought to the attention of the Council the requests made by three delegations, including Syria, to participate in the meeting. Council members did not wish to change those modalities and thus Syria was not invited to participate in the meeting.

On 20 July [S/2006/556], the Russian Federation transmitted the text of the statement on the Middle East adopted during the Group of Eight (G-8) Summit in St. Petersburg, Russia. The G-8, expressing its desire to restore peace and supporting the Secretary-General's mission (see above), said that the root cause of the problem in the region was the absence of a comprehensive Middle East peace. The crisis resulted from efforts by extremist forces to destabilize the region and frustrate the aspirations of the Palestinian, Israeli and Lebanese people for peace. In Gaza, elements of Hamas launched rocket attacks against Israel and abducted a soldier (see p. 510), while in Lebanon, Hizbullah, in violation of the Blue Line, attacked Israel from Lebanese territory and killed and captured Israeli soldiers, reversing the positive trends that began with the Syrian withdrawal in 2005 [YUN 2005, p. 560], and undermining the democratically elected Lebanese Government. Those extremists had to immediately halt their attacks. Israel, on the other hand, while exercising the right to defend itself, had to be mindful of the strategic and humanitarian consequences of its actions. The most urgent priority was to create conditions for a cessation of violence that would be sustainable and lay the foundation for a more permanent solution. That required: the return of the Israeli soldiers in Gaza and Lebanon unharmed; an end to the shelling of Israeli territory; an end to Israeli military operations and the early withdrawal of Israeli forces from Gaza; and the release of the arrested Palestinian ministers and parliamentarians. The framework for resolving those disputes was already established by international consensus. The G-8 urged the Security Council to develop a plan for the full implementation of its resolutions 1559(2004) [YUN 20004, p. 506] and 1680(2006) (see p. 571), both of which addressed the underlying causes that gave rise to the current crisis. The G-8 fully supported the Government of Lebanon in asserting its sovereignty, including the deployment of Lebanese Armed Forces to all parts of the country, in particular the South, and the disarming of militias. They would welcome an examination by the Council of the possibility of an international security and monitoring presence, and supported the initiation of a political dialogue between Lebanese and Israeli officials on all issues of concern to them, as well as the economic and humanitarian needs of the Lebanese people, including the convening of a donors conference.

Report on assessment mission and related developments. On 20 July [meeting 5492], the Secretary-General, in his briefing to the Security Council on the situation in the Middle East, said that the conflict that had engulfed Lebanon and northern Israel continued to rage. Over 300 Lebanese were killed and over 600 wounded. Much of the infrastructure in Beirut and around the country was destroyed and Lebanon remained under an Israeli sea and air blockade. Israeli civilians found themselves under constant Hizbullah rocket attacks, which every day reached further into Israeli territory. As at 20 July, 28 Israeli civilians were killed and over 200 wounded. On the humanitarian front, conditions continued to deteriorate. Israeli operations made it impossible for UN agencies and their humanitarian partners to reach almost any part of southern Lebanon to assess needs, or deliver assistance. Based on preliminary information provided by UNIFIL, the national Lebanese Red Cross, the Lebanese Government, and UN agencies were working on the basis of a combined total of up to 500,000 people affected, comprising both internally displaced persons and those under siege. In addition, Syrian authorities reported that more than 140,000 people had crossed into Syria, the majority being nationals of Lebanon, Syria and other Arab countries.

Since the fighting began, the Secretary-General had constantly been in touch with regional and world leaders. The G-8 issued an important statement (see above), but what was urgently needed was an immediate cessation of hostilities to prevent further loss of innocent life and the infliction of further suffering; allow full humanitarian access to those in need; and give diplomacy a chance to work out a practical package of actions that would provide a lasting solution to the crisis. On 13 July, the Secretary-General said he had dispatched an urgent mission to the region, led by his Special Adviser (see p. 574). Hizbullah's provocative attack on 12 July was the trigger for the crisis. It was clear that the Lebanese Government had no advance knowledge of it. The Secretary-General condemned Hizbullah's attacks on Israel and acknowledged Israel's right to defend itself under Article 51 of the UN Charter. He also condemned Hizbullah's disregard for the wishes of the Lebanese Government and the interests of the Lebanese people and the wider region. Israel confirmed that the goal of its operation in Lebanon was not only the return of its captured soldiers, but also to end the threat posed by Hizbullah. The mission was informed that the operation was not yet approaching the achievement of that objective. Israel stated that it had no quarrel with the Government or the people of Lebanon and that it was taking extreme precautions to avoid harm to them. Yet, certain actions had killed or injured Lebanese civilians and military personnel and caused great damage to infrastructure. Hizbullah's actions were deplorable and Israel's excessive use of force was condemned. The mission reported many of its interlocutors in the region as noting that, whatever damage Israel's operations might be doing to Hizbullah's military capabilities, they were doing little or nothing to decrease popular support for Hizbullah in Lebanon, and were actually weakening the Government of Lebanon. The Government of Lebanon, which Israel hoped would extend its control throughout the territory, had itself become a hostage to the crisis, was struggling to deploy its forces in the areas necessary to control Hizbullah, and was appealing to the international community for an immediate humanitarian ceasefire.

Despite the mission's assessment that a full ceasefire remained difficult to achieve, the Secretary-General was of the view that the international community had to make its position clear on the need for an immediate cessation of hostilities and a far greater and more credible effort by Israel to protect civilians and civilian infrastructure while the conditions for such a cessation were developed. Both the deliberate targeting by Hizbullah of Israeli population centres using hundreds of indiscriminate weapons and Israel's disproportionate use of force on the Lebanese population had to stop. The abducted soldiers had to be released as soon as possible and the International Committee of the Red Cross (ICRC) granted immediate access to them. The Israeli Government had to allow humanitarian agencies access to civilians, while the democratically elected Lebanese Government had to be supported in its hour of crisis. In addition to, and parallel with those urgent steps, there was a need to continue diplomatic efforts to develop a political framework that could be implemented as soon as hostilities ceased. Most people in the region rejected a simple return to the status quo ante, since any truce based on such a limited outcome could not be expected to last.

Based on the mission's suggestions, the Secretary-General said that the political basis of any lasting ceasefire had to rest on a number of key elements, including the transfer of the captured Israeli soldiers to legitimate Lebanese authorities, under the auspices of ICRC, with a view to their repatriation to Israel and a ceasefire. On the Lebanese side of the Blue Line, an expanded peacekeeping force would help stabilize the situation, working with the Lebanese Government to assist in strengthening its army and deploying it fully throughout the area. Meanwhile, the Lebanese Government would fully implement Security Council resolutions 1559(2004) and 1680(2006) (see p. 571), to establish Lebanese sovereignty and control. The Prime Minister of Lebanon would confirm to the Secretary-General and the Security Council that the Lebanese Government would respect the Blue Line in its entirety, until agreement on Lebanon's final international boundaries was reached. A donor framework would be established to secure funding for an urgent package of aid, reconstruction and development for Lebanon. A mechanism would be established, composed of key regional and international actors, to monitor and guarantee the implementation of all aspects of the agreement. An international conference should be organized, with broad Lebanese and international participation, to develop precise timelines for the speedy and full implementation of relevant Security Council resolutions and endorse a delineation of Lebanon's international borders, including a final resolution on all disputed areas, especially the Shaba'a Farms. The planning and implementation of those elements should, as far as possible, be done in parallel. There was also a need to develop a peace track for Gaza, where over 100 Palestinians had been killed since 12 July and where, as a result of the destruction by Israel of the Gaza power plant, more than a million people were without electricity for most of the day and night. Israelis in the south continued to endure Qassam rocket attacks, fortunately without casualties. The Secretary-General called for an immediate cessation of indiscriminate and disproportionate violence in the Israeli-Palestinian conflict and for a reopening of closed crossing points, without which Gaza would continue to be sucked into a downward spiral of suffering and chaos and the region would be further inflamed.

Report of Secretary-General on UNIFIL operations (July). In response to resolution 1655(2006) (see p. 567) the Secretary-General submitted a July report on UNIFIL covering the period from January to July [S/2006/560]. The situation in the UNIFIL area of operation, which remained tense and volatile, completely changed on 12 July, when hostilities broke out and the area was plunged into the most serious conflict in decades. Hostilities within and outside the UNIFIL area of operations had continued without interruption since 12 July. Within that area of operations, IDF bombings damaged or destroyed Hizbullah positions in addition to most roads and bridges, obstructing movement throughout the south of the country. On 15 July, UNIFIL was informed by IDF that Israel would establish a "special security zone" between 21 villages along the Blue Line and the Israeli technical fence. IDF also informed UNIFIL that any vehicles entering the area would be shot at. That security zone would be directly within UNIFIL area of operation, which would make it impossible to support many of the Mission's positions that were located in the zone and prevent it from discharging its mandate. UNIFIL was closely coordinating with the Lebanese authorities to address the humanitarian needs of the population that remained in the area. To that end, UNIFIL and the Lebanese authorities established a joint coordination centre for humanitarian activities in two locations: Tyre in the west and Marjayoun in the east. Most requests received by the centre were for humanitarian escorts to relocate civilians, as well as the wounded and dead. The ongoing hostilities and the destruction of roads seriously restricted the mission's freedom of movement and hampered its ability to respond to such requests. UNIFIL requested IDF to authorize "windows" to patrol the Blue Line and to allow the passage of logistical convoys to supply its positions. While UNIFIL was able to send out two logistical convoys, no authorization was given for the patrolling of the Blue Line.

The Secretary-General observed that the hostilities between Hizbullah and Israel since 12 July had radically changed the context in which UNIFIL was operating, and circumstances conducive to UN peacekeeping did not exist. With constant firing along the Blue Line, where roads and bridges and other critical infrastructure throughout its area of operation were destroyed, and where its freedom of movement was continuously impeded, UNIFIL could not resume its work in a meaningful way. A cessation of hostilities would be essential for that to be possible. Noting that UNIFIL mandate would expire on 31 July, the Secretary-General drew attention to Lebanon's 7 July request [S/2006/496] that the Security Council extend that mandate for a further period of six months. However, in a situation where a return to the status quo ante did not appear feasible, and with a view to providing the Security Council the time required to consider all possible options for future arrangements in south Lebanon, the Secretary-General instead recommended that the Council extend the mandate for a period of one month.

SECURITY COUNCIL ACTION

On 31 July [meeting 5501], the Security Council unanimously adopted **resolution 1697(2006).** The draft [S/2006/583] was submitted by France.

The Security Council,

Recalling all its previous resolutions on Lebanon, including resolutions 425(1978) and 426(1978) of 19 March 1978 and 1655(2006) of 31 January 2006 as well as the statements by its President on the situation in Lebanon, in particular the statement of 18 June 2000,

Expressing deepest concern at the escalation of hostilities in Lebanon and Israel since 12 July 2006,

Taking note of the letter dated 7 July 2006 from the Chargé d'affaires a.i. of the Permanent Mission of Lebanon to the United Nations conveying to the Secretary-General the request that the Security Council extend the mandate of the United Nations Interim Force in Lebanon for a further period of six months,

Having examined the report of the Secretary-General of 21 July 2006 on the Force, including the observations contained therein that, as a result of the continuing hostilities along the Blue Line, the Force has been impeded from carrying out its activities effectively, and noting in this context the recommendation of the Secretary-General that the mandate of the Force be extended for a period of one month pending consideration of other options for future arrangements in south Lebanon,

1. *Urges* all concerned parties to abide scrupulously by their obligation to respect the safety of the United Nations Interim Force in Lebanon and other United Nations personnel, and avoid any course of action which might endanger United Nations personnel, and calls upon them to allow the Force to resupply its positions, conduct search and rescue operations on behalf of its personnel and undertake any other measures that the Force deems necessary to ensure the safety of its personnel;
2. *Decides* to extend the mandate of the Force until 31 August 2006;
3. *Decides also* to remain actively seized of the matter.

Safety and security of UN personnel

On 29 July [S/2006/595], the Secretary-General informed the Council President that the killing on 25 July of four members of the Observer Group of the United Nations Truce Supervision Organization (UNTSO) at patrol base Khiam and the incident on 23 July, when a military observer at patrol base Ras was seriously injured, called into question whether UN peacekeeping personnel could be sufficiently protected in their positions. It was the Secretariat's assessment that the risks of continuing to staff the remaining two patrol bases with unarmed military observers outweighed the merits gained from their presence. Accordingly, UNTSO military observers at patrol bases Hin and Mar were relocated to other positions within UNIFIL. Patrol bases Ras and Khiam had not been occupied by UN personnel since 23 and 25 July, respectively. The Secretary-General had asked Israel's Prime Minister to carry out a joint investigation with the United Nations into the events that led to the death of the military observers at patrol base Khiam, and for information about what actions IDF had taken in response to the repeated communications from UNTSO and UNIFIL on the recurring incidents of close firing in the hours before the position was hit. The Secretary-General was disturbed to learn that the patrol base and its surroundings had come under renewed firing by IDF in the days following the 25 July incident.

SECURITY COUNCIL ACTION

On 27 July [meeting 5497], following consultations among Security Council members, the President made statement **S/PRST/2006/34** on behalf of the Council:

The Security Council is deeply shocked and distressed by the firing on a United Nations observer post in southern Lebanon on 25 July 2006 by the Israel Defense Forces, which caused the death of four United Nations military observers.

The Council extends its deepest condolences to the families of those victims and expresses its sympathies to the Governments of Austria, Canada, China and Finland.

The Council calls upon the Government of Israel to conduct a comprehensive inquiry into this incident, taking into account any relevant material from United Nations authorities, and to make the results public as soon as possible.

The Council is deeply concerned about the safety and security of United Nations personnel and, in this regard, stresses that Israel and all concerned parties must comply fully with their obligations under international humanitarian law related to the protection of United Nations and associated personnel and underlines the importance of ensuring that United Nations personnel are not the object of attack.

The Council expresses its deep concern for Lebanese and Israeli civilian casualties and suffering, the destruction of civil infrastructure and the rising number of internally displaced people.

The Council will remain seized of this matter.

Humanitarian situation

On 28 July [S/2006/593], the Under-Secretary-General for Humanitarian Affairs and Emergency Relief Coordinator briefed the Security Council on the humanitarian situation in the Middle East, with particular reference to the Lebanese crisis. He said that the humanitarian situation in Lebanon was dramatic; tens of thousands were fleeing the fighting, hundreds were wounded and dozens died every day. Lebanese and international humanitarian organizations were trying to come to the relief of as many people as possible. The United Nations established humanitarian corridors by land and by sea to Beirut, as well as a notification channel to the Israeli forces to guarantee safe passage for the increasing number of UN convoys. They provided needed relief items to hundreds of thousands of people in the south of Lebanon and other areas, such as the Bekaa Valley.

However, the limited and controlled assistance provided by the United Nations was not enough to prevent the suffering of the civilian population. There was a need for an immediate cessation of hostilities, followed by a ceasefire agreement, the deployment of a security force, and the political settlement of the conflict, as proposed by the Secretary-General. The level of displacement, primarily from southern Lebanon and the southern suburbs of Beirut, had reached approximately 700,000. Some 210,000 fled Lebanon as refugees to neighbouring Syria and 100,000 people were victims of the siege of their homes. The civilian death toll in Lebanon stood at more than 600, according to the Lebanese Minister of Health. The Under-Secretary-General said that he had urged Israeli authorities to review the conduct of the air strikes and bombardments to avoid excessive use of force that inflicted disproportionate suffering on the civilian population. At the same time, he publicly appealed to Hizbullah to stop its tactic of hiding ammunition, arms, or combatants among civilians.

The devastating impact of the conflict on the civilian population was not confined to Lebanon, for hundreds of thousands of Israeli civilians suffered as well. Daily Hizbullah rocket attacks were spreading constant fear and terror among the civilian population. Altogether, more than 1,000 rockets had been fired indiscriminately on the population in northern Israel, leaving some 20 dead and hundreds wounded.

Lebanon's Seven-Point Plan

In Rome, on 26 July [A/60/974-S/2006/639], Lebanese Prime Minister Siniora proposed the Seven-Point Plan, later adopted by the Lebanese Council of Ministers, which called for an immediate and comprehensive ceasefire and a declaration of agreement on the following points: an undertaking to release Lebanese and Israeli prisoners and detainees through the International Committee of the Red Cross; the withdrawal of IDF behind the Blue Line and the return of the displaced to their villages; a commitment from the Security Council to place the Shab'a Farms area and the Kfarshouba Hills under UN jurisdiction until border delineation and Lebanese sovereignty over them were fully settled; the surrender to the United Nations by Israel of all remaining landmine maps in South Lebanon; extension by the Lebanese Government of its authority over its territory through its own legitimate armed forces, so that there would be no weapons or authority other than that of the Lebanese State; enhancement of the UN force operating in South Lebanon in numbers, equipment, mandate and scope of operation to undertake urgent humanitarian and relief work and guarantee stability and security in the South so that those who fled their homes could return; the undertaking by the United Nations, in cooperation with the relevant parties, to once again put into effect the 1949 Armistice Agreement between Lebanon and Israel and to ensure adherence to its provisions, as well as to explore possible amendments to, or development of those provisions; and commitment by the international community to support and assist Lebanon on all levels in facing the burden of the human, social and economic tragedy that had afflicted the country, especially in the areas of relief, reconstruction and rebuilding of the national economy.

The Qana incident

Security Council consideration (July). On 30 July [meeting 5498], the Secretary-General, in his briefing to the Security Council on the situation in the Middle East, reported that, during the previous night, the Israeli air force bombed the village of Qana, in southern Lebanon, where, according to information provided by the Lebanese authorities, at least 54 people were killed, including 37 children. That tragedy had provoked moral outrage throughout the world. Regrettably, some Lebanese people turned their anger against the United Nations, as a large number of protesters broke into UN headquarters in Beirut and set it afire. In the pevious 18 days, several hundred Lebanese citizens were killed, the vast majority of them civilians. During the same period, hundreds of thousands of Lebanese had to flee their homes. Meanwhile, over 50 Israelis died, including 19 civilians, and the population of northern Israel was subjected to intense and continuous rocket fire. Thousands were in shelters. Both sides in the conflict bore a heavy responsibility, and there was strong prima facie evidence that both had committed grave breaches of international humanitarian law. Hizbullah continued to fire rockets indiscriminately into northern Israel from positions apparently located in the midst of civilian populations. Although no one disputed Israel's right to defend itself, it was unfortunate that in doing so, its action led to death and suffering on an entirely unacceptable scale. The most urgent need was to bring the fighting to a halt without further delay. For that, the Council had a solemn responsibility. The Secretary-General therefore reiterated his call for an immediate cessation of hostilities to allow desperately needed humanitarian relief to reach the victims. At the same time, it was necessary to work on the political framework needed for a lasting ceasefire and a sustainable solution, the strengthening of Lebanon's Government, the disarming of all militia and the implementation of all relevant Security Council resolutions. The Secretary-General would work with the Council on the development and deployment of a stabilization force to support the Government of Lebanon in its decision and responsibility to extend its authority throughout the country. He also noted that the Lebanese Government had decided that it would no longer engage in further diplomatic discussions and efforts to find a solution without a ceasefire. The Secretary-General concluded by saying that the authority and standing of the Council were at stake, for people had noticed its failure to act firmly and quickly during the crisis.

Lebanon said that acts of killing and destruction had continued for a third week, and Qana once again had met its fate with Israel, 10 years later. Israel was committing atrocities against humanity, and the fact that such massacres had yet to be addressed by resolutions of the Security Council did not mean that the truth was to remain hidden. That tragedy came at a time when the Government of Lebanon was seeking a window to resolve the crisis. Lebanon was calling upon the Council to bring an end to the firing immediately and to undertake a serious investigation of the massacre and others that Israel had perpetrated on Lebanon over the previous three weeks.

Israel said that it mourned and grieved with the people of Lebanon at the death of the innocent civilians in Kafr Qana. Those people, including women and children, might have been killed by Israeli fire, but they were victims of Hizbullah, and of terror. Kafr Qana had been a long-time hub for Hizbullah, which had been launching missiles from there at Israel. While Israel mourned the deaths of those people, it stressed that it had never targeted innocent people, and particularly not in the recent case of Kafr Qana.

SECURITY COUNCIL ACTION

On 30 July [meeting 5499], following consultations among Security Council members, the President made statement **S/PRST/2006/35** on behalf of the Council:

> The Security Council expresses its extreme shock and distress at the shelling of a residential building by the Israeli Defense Forces in Qana, southern Lebanon, which has caused the killing of dozens of civilians, mostly children, and injured many others. The Council sends its deepest condolences to the families of the victims and to the Lebanese people.
>
> The Council strongly deplores this loss of innocent lives and the killing of civilians in the present conflict and requests the Secretary-General to report to it within one week on the circumstances of this tragic incident.
>
> The Council expresses its concern at the threat of escalation of violence with further grave consequences for the humanitarian situation, calls for an end to violence, and underscores the urgency of securing a lasting, permanent and sustainable ceasefire.
>
> The Council expresses again its utmost concern at the Lebanese and Israeli civilian casualties and human suffering, the widespread destruction of civilian infrastructure, and the increased number of internally displaced persons.
>
> The Council urges all parties to grant immediate and unlimited access to humanitarian assistance.
>
> The Council deplores any action against United Nations personnel and calls for full respect for the safety and security of all United Nations personnel and premises.
>
> The Council affirms its determination to work without any further delay to adopt a resolution for a lasting settlement of the crisis, drawing on diplomatic efforts under way.
>
> The Council remains seized of the matter.

Security Council consideration. On 31 July [meeting 5503], at the request of Lebanon [S/2006/596], the Council discussed the situation in the Middle East. Lebanon said that it wanted to reiterate its call for an immediate and comprehensive ceasefire, and asked the Council to set in motion a process of international investigation with regard to the events of Qana. The Lebanese people perceived the Israeli action to be unjustified collective punishment. Lebanon called upon the Council to put an end to the human tragedy, which could be achieved through the Seven-Point Plan approved by the Council of Ministers (see p. 579).

Israel replied that it had no quarrel and was not at war with Lebanon. It had never in history had any claim over the country, nor over its right to exist as a free, proud and prosperous State. Israel had been compelled to act repeatedly not against Lebanon, but against the forces which Lebanon had allowed itself to be taken hostage by. It had been taken over time and time again by tyrants in the north, namely Syria, which still regarded Lebanon as southern Syria, as well as by terrorist organizations, such as the PLO in the 1980s and Hizbullah in the 1990s. Lebanon had several chances to exert its sovereignty and to take its fate into its own hands, but tragically had not done so. Israel believed that it was time for Lebanon to act.

Report of Secretary-General on Qana incident. Pursuant to Security Council presidential statement S/PRST/2006/35 (see above), the Secretary-General, on 7 August, submitted a report on the circumstances of the 30 July incident in Qana [S/2006/626]. He noted that a proper gathering of all relevant facts and their presentation in a comprehensive report could not be completed in just seven days, especially when the area in question was difficult to access because of ongoing hostilities. Furthermore, UN personnel were not present at the scene when the attack occurred. Information was thus drawn from the official accounts sought from and provided by the Lebanese and Israeli Governments and UN eyewitnesses who visited Qana in the aftermath of the attack. Copies of the Secretariat's notes verbales to the Permanent Missions of Israel and Lebanon and the responses thereto were attached to the report.

The Israeli Government, in a note verbale, said that Qana was the center of Hizbullah's regional headquarters. It contained extensive weapons stockpiles, served as a terrorist haven and was the source for over 150 missiles that were launched into northern Israel. Hizbullah maintained a regional command centre there, which was the planning site for numerous attacks against Israel. On 30 July, according to Israel, the Israeli Air Force attacked missile launch sites in the village. Prior to the operation, Israel had publicly called on the residents to move away from the terrorists and flee from the areas where missiles were being launched. Leaflets were dropped from the air urging civilians to leave the village on account of their own safety, as Hizbullah routinely launched rockets in close proximity to residential buildings. For several days, radio announcements were also made to the public warning of a strike against Hizbullah. Israeli military activity in that area was carried out on the assumption that residents had heeded the warnings and had cleared out.

The Lebanese Government, in its note verbale, said that on July 30, the Israeli Air Force struck a three-storey building in the village of Qana where two extended families had sought shelter. According to the Mayor of Qana, the civilians had taken refuge there because the building had a reinforced basement. They were not able to flee the area because of destroyed roads and the ongoing Israeli attacks. None of the bodies recovered showed that there were any militants present among the civilians, and the rescuers found no weapons in the building that was struck. In an investigation conducted by Lebanese military authorities, there was no indication that rockets were launched next to the building.

The Secretary-General said that he was gravely distressed by the tragic events in Qana and by the overall effect of the conflict on the civilian populations of Lebanon and Israel. According to official Lebanese and Israeli sources, as of 5 August, after 25 days of conflict, more than 933 Lebanese civilians and 35 Israeli civilians had been killed. Approximately 915,000 Lebanese, amounting to one quarter of the country's total population and including more than 80 per cent of the population living south of the Litani River, had been displaced by the conflict, and the majority of those people were in need of assistance. Tens of thousands of Israelis had to take refuge in air raid shelters and many more had fled northern Israel. The attack on Qana should be seen in the broader context of what could, on the basis of preliminary information available to the United Nations, be a pattern of violations of international law, including international humanitarian and human rights law, committed during the course of the hostilities. The effects of the conflict on civilians in Lebanon and Israel rose to a level of seriousness that required further gathering of information, including information on violations of international humanitarian law and international human rights law. Accordingly, he supported the calls for a more comprehensive investigation.

Communications. On 4 [A/60/968-S/2006/621] and 5 August [A/60/969-S/2006/622], respectively, Lebanon and Syria reported that the Israeli air force had targeted civilian farmers in Al Qa'a village in the Bekaa Valley, killing 33 Syrian and Lebanese civilians and wounding 12 more. On 9 August [A/60/972-S/2006/630], Lebanon said that the Israeli air force had targeted a residential building in Beirut, killing 41 civilians and wounding 60 more. That new massacre came on the heels of the second Qana attack and was part of Israel's violations of international humanitarian and human rights law.

Agreement on the cessation of hostilities

On 7 August [A/60/970-S/2006/625], the Lebanese Government reaffirmed, on the basis of the Seven-Point Plan approved by its cabinet, that it was ready to deploy a 15,000-strong Lebanese armed force in the south of the country as IDF withdrew behind the Blue Line, and requested the assistance of additional forces from UNIFIL to facilitate the entry of the Lebanese armed forces into the region.

Security Council consideration (8 August). On 8 August [meeting 5508], the Security Council discussed the situation in the Middle East, in particular a draft resolution on the situation in Lebanon. The Secretary-General attended the meeting.

Qatar said that it was disheartening that the Council had stood idly by, unable to stop the bloodshed that had become a daily occurrence. The draft resolution before the Council should take into account the Arab position expressed by the Council of Ministers of LAS, at an extraordinary meeting held on 7 August in Beirut, at which it adopted Lebanon's Seven-Point Plan. The Council's consideration of the issue should take into account the sociopolitical structure of Lebanese society, as well as its interests, unity, stability and territorial integrity. Qatar drew the Council's attention to the repercussions of adopting a non-enforceable resolution, as that would only complicate matters on the ground and have grave ramifications for Lebanon, other Arab States and all countries of the region.

Lebanon said that, while it appreciated the concern expressed by the international community for the future of Lebanon, support for its democratic Government and attempts to provide a framework for peace and stability, the draft resolution not only fell short of meeting many of its legitimate requests, but might not bring about the results that the international community hoped to achieve. The Lebanese people needed explicit and firm assurance that the integrity of its borders, ground, sea and air space, would be respected by Israel.

Israel said that the critical test the Council faced was not whether it could adopt a resolution, but whether, with the international community, it could adopt a course of action, a blueprint for change, which would end the threat that Hizbullah and its sponsors posed for the peoples of Israel and Lebanon and the region as a whole. Israel added that, while the past four weeks had taken a painful toll on the Lebanese and Israeli people, it had created a new opportunity. Hizbullah's bases had been dismantled and its missile launchers and weapons stockpiles removed; south Lebanon was substantially cleared of the infrastructure of terrorism. As a result, for the first time in six years, there was a possibility that Lebanon and the international community could begin anew and repair the omissions that had led to the crisis. However, that required a strong and effective international force to ensure the dismantling and disarming of terrorist groups; enforceable and effective measures to prevent the continued supply and rearmament of weapons and ammunition; and the Government of Lebanon's willingness and courage to retake control of its destiny, confront terrorists who had wreaked havoc in their society and meet the basic obligations placed by international law and the Council to end the use of its territory as a base to threaten others. Israel wanted a ceasefire that sowed the seeds of a future peace, not conflict.

Security Council consideration (11 August). On 11 August [meeting 5511], the Security Council continued discussion on the situation in the Middle East, and in particular the text of a draft resolution [S/2006/640] on the escalation of hostilities in Lebanon and Israel.

The Secretary-General said that he welcomed wholeheartedly the draft resolution the Council was about to adopt and was relieved that it provided for a full and immediate cessation of hostilities. He expressed his belief that the draft would make it possible to conclude a sustainable and lasting ceasefire agreement in the days ahead, which he hoped could be the beginning of a process to solve the underlying political problems in the region through peaceful means. Yet, he was disappointed that the Council had not reached that point much earlier, as that inability to act sooner had badly shaken the world's faith in its authority and integrity. Noting that Council members were able to resolve their differences, accommodating many points of view, he hoped they would adopt the text unanimously, and work with equal determination to make what they agreed upon fully effective on the ground. First of all, humanitarian convoys and relief workers had to be guaranteed safe passage and access to those who needed help. Secondly, the draft resolution had at its core Lebanon's sovereignty and territorial integrity, consistent with relevant Council resolutions, and the international community had to give the Lebanese Government all possible support to make that sovereignty effective. The Government, acting through its regular armed forces and police, had to be able to assert its authority throughout the country and on all its borders, particularly to prevent illegal and destabilizing flows of arms. Only when there was one authority would there be a chance of lasting stability. The Lebanese State, like any other sovereign State, had to have a monopoly of the use of force on its own territory. That implied a full and swift Israeli withdrawal from Lebanese territory. The decision of the Lebanese Government to deploy 15,000 of the country's armed forces to the south was a significant development, but it needed help. That made the Council's decision to strengthen the mandate and capacity of UNIFIL a vital ingredient of the package. UNIFIL was thus faced with a new task, perhaps even more difficult and dangerous than its previous one. It had to be robust and effective and ensure that no vacuum was left between the Israeli withdrawal and the deployment of Lebanese forces. To carry out its new mandate, it needed to be augmented with the utmost urgency and provided with sophisticated military capabilities. The Secretary-General therefore urged the Council to consult closely with both existing and potential troop contributors, with a view to generating the additional forces needed as quickly as possible. He also appealed to all potential donors to respond swiftly to requests from the Lebanese

Government for financial help to reconstruct its devastated country.

The Lebanese Government would meet on 12 August, and the Israeli Cabinet on 13 August, to review the resolution. The Secretary-General would work to establish with both parties the exact date and time at which the cessation of hostilities would come into effect. The Lebanese people deserved the full support of the United Nations in their effort to cast off the chains of external interference and domestic strife. Doing so would require both the establishment of national consensus among the Lebanese and constructive cooperation, based on mutual goodwill and sustained dialogue, by all relevant parties and actors at the regional level, including the Governments of Syria and Iran. Indeed, since 12 July, the international community had been reminded yet again what a fragile, tense, crisis-ridden region the Middle East had become. The draft resolution that the Council was about to adopt was only one step towards the comprehensive approach that was needed. To prevent another eruption of violence and bloodshed, the international community had to be prepared to offer sustained support and assistance for Lebanon's political and economic reconstruction and address the broader context of crisis in the region.

SECURITY COUNCIL ACTION

On 11 August [meeting 5511], the Security Council unanimously adopted **resolution 1701(2006).** The draft [S/2006/640] was submitted by Denmark, France, Ghana, Greece, Slovakia, the United Kingdom and the United States.

The Security Council,

Recalling all its previous resolutions on Lebanon, in particular resolutions 425(1978) and 426(1978) of 19 March 1978, 520(1982) of 17 September 1982, 1559(2004) of 2 September 2004, 1655(2006) of 31 January 2006, 1680(2006) of 17 May 2006 and 1697(2006) of 31 July 2006, as well as the statements by its President on the situation in Lebanon, in particular the statements of 18 June 2000, 19 October 2004, 4 May 2005, 23 January 2006 and 30 July 2006,

Expressing its utmost concern at the continuing escalation of hostilities in Lebanon and in Israel since Hizbullah's attack on Israel on 12 July 2006, which has already caused hundreds of deaths and injuries on both sides, extensive damage to civilian infrastructure and hundreds of thousands of internally displaced persons,

Emphasizing the need for an end to violence, but at the same time emphasizing the need to address urgently the causes that have given rise to the current crisis, including by the unconditional release of the abducted Israeli soldiers,

Mindful of the sensitivity of the issue of prisoners, and encouraging the efforts aimed at urgently settling the issue of the Lebanese prisoners detained in Israel,

Welcoming the efforts of the Prime Minister of Lebanon and the commitment of the Government of Lebanon, in its seven-point plan, to extend its authority over its territory, through its own legitimate armed forces, such that there will be no weapons without the consent of the Government of Lebanon and no authority other than that of the Government of Lebanon, welcoming also its commitment to a United Nations force that is supplemented and enhanced in numbers, equipment, mandate and scope of operation, and bearing in mind its request in this plan for an immediate withdrawal of the Israeli forces from southern Lebanon,

Determined to act for this withdrawal to happen at the earliest,

Taking due note of the proposals made in the seven-point plan regarding the Sheba'a Farms area,

Welcoming the unanimous decision taken by the Government of Lebanon on 7 August 2006 to deploy a Lebanese armed force of 15,000 troops in South Lebanon as the Israeli army withdraws behind the Blue Line, to request the assistance of additional forces from the United Nations Interim Force in Lebanon, as needed, to facilitate the entry of the Lebanese Armed Forces into the region, and to restate its intention to strengthen the Lebanese Armed Forces with material as needed to enable it to perform its duties,

Aware of its responsibilities to help secure a permanent ceasefire and a long-term solution to the conflict,

Determining that the situation in Lebanon constitutes a threat to international peace and security,

1. *Calls for* a full cessation of hostilities based upon, in particular, the immediate cessation by Hizbullah of all attacks and the immediate cessation by Israel of all offensive military operations;

2. Upon full cessation of hostilities, *calls upon* the Government of Lebanon and the United Nations Interim Force in Lebanon as authorized by paragraph 11 below to deploy their forces together throughout the south, and calls upon the Government of Israel, as that deployment begins, to withdraw all of its forces from southern Lebanon in parallel;

3. *Emphasizes* the importance of the extension of the control of the Government of Lebanon over all Lebanese territory in accordance with the provisions of resolutions 1559(2004) and 1680(2006), and of the relevant provisions of the Taif Accords, for it to exercise its full sovereignty, so that there will be no weapons without the consent of the Government of Lebanon and no authority other than that of the Government of Lebanon;

4. *Reiterates its strong support* for full respect for the Blue Line;

5. *Also reiterates its strong support*, as recalled in all its previous relevant resolutions, for the territorial integrity, sovereignty and political independence of Lebanon within its internationally recognized borders, as contemplated by the Israeli-Lebanese General Armistice Agreement of 23 March 1949;

6. *Calls upon* the international community to take immediate steps to extend its financial and humanitarian assistance to the Lebanese people, including by facilitating the safe return of displaced persons and, under the authority of the Government of Lebanon, reopening airports and harbours, consistent with paragraphs 14 and 15 below, and calls upon it also to consider further assistance in the future to contribute to the reconstruction and development of Lebanon;

7. *Affirms* that all parties are responsible for ensuring that no action is taken contrary to paragraph 1 above that might adversely affect the search for a long-term solution, humanitarian access to civilian populations, including safe passage for humanitarian convoys, or the voluntary and safe return of displaced persons, and calls upon all parties to comply with this responsibility and to cooperate with the Security Council;

8. *Calls for* Israel and Lebanon to support a permanent ceasefire and a long-term solution based on the following principles and elements:

- Full respect for the Blue Line by both parties;
- Security arrangements to prevent the resumption of hostilities, including the establishment between the Blue Line and the Litani river of an area free of any armed personnel, assets and weapons other than those of the Government of Lebanon and of the United Nations Interim Force in Lebanon as authorized in paragraph 11 below, deployed in this area;
- Full implementation of the relevant provisions of the Taif Accords, and of resolutions 1559(2004) and 1680(2006), that require the disarmament of all armed groups in Lebanon, so that, pursuant to the Lebanese Cabinet decision of 27 July 2006, there will be no weapons or authority in Lebanon other than that of the Lebanese State;
- No foreign forces in Lebanon without the consent of its Government;
- No sales or supply of arms and related materiel to Lebanon except as authorized by its Government;
- Provision to the United Nations of all remaining maps of landmines in Lebanon in Israel's possession;

9. *Invites* the Secretary-General to support efforts to secure as soon as possible agreements in principle from the Government of Lebanon and the Government of Israel to the principles and elements for a long-term solution as set forth in paragraph 8 above, and expresses its intention to be actively involved;

10. *Requests* the Secretary-General to develop, in liaison with relevant international actors and the parties concerned, proposals to implement the relevant provisions of the Taif Accords, and resolutions 1559(2004) and 1680(2006), including disarmament, and for delineation of the international borders of Lebanon, especially in those areas where the border is disputed or uncertain, including by dealing with the Sheba'a Farms area, and to present those proposals to the Council within thirty days;

11. *Decides*, in order to supplement and enhance the United Nations Interim Force in Lebanon in numbers, equipment, mandate and scope of operations, to authorize an increase in its force strength to a maximum of 15,000 troops, and that the Force shall, in addition to carrying out its mandate under resolutions 425(1978) and 426(1978):

(a) Monitor the cessation of hostilities;

(b) Accompany and support the Lebanese Armed Forces as they deploy throughout the south, including along the Blue Line, as Israel withdraws its armed forces from Lebanon as provided in paragraph 2 above;

(c) Coordinate its activities related to subparagraph *(b)* above with the Government of Lebanon and the Government of Israel;

(d) Extend its assistance to help ensure humanitarian access to civilian populations and the voluntary and safe return of displaced persons;

(e) Assist the Lebanese Armed Forces in taking steps towards the establishment of the area as referred to in paragraph 8 above;

(f) Assist the Government of Lebanon, at its request, to implement paragraph 14 below;

12. *Acting in support* of a request from the Government of Lebanon to deploy an international force to assist it to exercise its authority throughout the territory, authorizes the United Nations Interim Force in Lebanon to take all necessary action, in areas of deployment of its forces and as it deems within its capabilities, to ensure that its area of operations is not utilized for hostile activities of any kind, to resist attempts by forceful means to prevent it from discharging its duties under the mandate of the Council, and to protect United Nations personnel, facilities, installations and equipment, ensure the security and freedom of movement of United Nations personnel, humanitarian workers and, without prejudice to the responsibility of the Government of Lebanon, protect civilians under imminent threat of physical violence;

13. *Requests* the Secretary-General urgently to put in place measures to ensure that the Force is able to carry out the functions envisaged in the present resolution, urges Member States to consider making appropriate contributions to the Force and to respond positively to requests for assistance from the Force, and expresses its strong appreciation to those who have contributed to the Force in the past;

14. *Calls upon* the Government of Lebanon to secure its borders and other entry points to prevent the entry in Lebanon without its consent of arms or related materiel, and requests the Force, as authorized in paragraph 11 above, to assist the Government of Lebanon at its request;

15. *Decides* that all States shall take the necessary measures to prevent, by their nationals or from their territories or using their flag vessels or aircraft:

(a) The sale or supply to any entity or individual in Lebanon of arms and related materiel of all types, including weapons and ammunition, military vehicles and equipment, paramilitary equipment, and spare parts for

the aforementioned, whether or not these originated in their territories; and

(b) The provision to any entity or individual in Lebanon of any technical training or assistance related to the provision, manufacture, maintenance or use of the items listed in subparagraph *(a)* above; except that these prohibitions shall not apply to arms, related materiel, training or assistance authorized by the Government of Lebanon or by the Force as authorized in paragraph 11 above;

16. *Decides also* to extend the mandate of the Force until 31 August 2007, and expresses its intention to consider in a later resolution further enhancements to the mandate and other steps to contribute to the implementation of a permanent ceasefire and a long-term solution;

17. *Requests* the Secretary-General to report to the Council within one week on the implementation of the present resolution and subsequently on a regular basis;

18. *Stresses* the importance of, and the need to achieve, a comprehensive, just and lasting peace in the Middle East, based on all its relevant resolutions, including resolutions 242(1967) of 22 November 1967, 338(1973) of 22 October 1973 and 1515(2003) of 19 November 2003;

19. *Decides* to remain actively seized of the matter.

Qatar, in explanation of vote [S/2006/655], said that, while thanking France and the United States for their efforts to improve the language of the resolution, it was of the view that the draft lacked balance, overlooked the complicated historical, social and geopolitical factors that had culminated in the current situation, and failed to adequately take into consideration Lebanon's territorial integrity. It did not explicitly address the horrors of destruction caused by Israeli aggression, nor clearly spell out Israel's legal and humanitarian responsibility for that destruction or address in a balanced manner the question of Lebanese prisoners, detainees and abducted persons in Israeli prisons.

Implementation of Security Council resolution 1701(2006)

Cessation of hostilities. On 12 August [S/2006/647], the Secretary-General informed the Security Council President that, as requested of him in resolution 1701(2006), he had agreed with the Prime Ministers of Israel and Lebanon that the cessation of hostilities would come into effect at 0500 GMT on 14 August. On the same date [S/2006/675], the Secretary-General wrote to both countries setting out, in an annex to his letter, expectations on how all the parties concerned would fulfil their obligations with respect to the cessation of hostilities. To facilitate that, the Israeli and Lebanese Armed Forces should each designate a General Officer who would be accessible to the UNFIL Force Commander and authorized to meet with him within 72 hours of the cessation of hostilities to discuss arrangements and timelines for the implementation of paragraph 2 of resolution 1701(2006).

Communications. In identical letters addressed to the Secretary-General and the Security Council President [A/60/982-S/2006/667], Lebanon reported that, on 16 August, the Lebanese Council of Ministers had decided to deploy the Lebanese army in the two regions south of the Litani River, Al-Arqoub Hasbaiya and Marjaayoun, with the mandate to defend the national territory, maintain security and order, preserve and protect the property and livelihood of citizens and prevent the presence of forces of any kind not under the authority of the Lebanese State. In so doing, it would ensure that the Blue Line was respected and laws in force were applied with regard to any weapons not under the authority of the Lebanese State. The army would cooperate with UNIFIL and coordinate with it, as provided for in Security Council resolution 1701(2006).

In other related communication [A/60/979-S/2006/654], Lebanon reported that, on 13 August, the Israeli air force had targeted a residential complex in a district of southern Beirut, killing 15 people.

Report of Secretary-General. On 18 August [S/2006/670], the Secretary-General submitted a progress report on implementation of Security Council resolution 1701(2006). The report focused on the steps taken and measures required to consolidate the cessation of hostilities, in particular the withdrawal and deployment of forces in southern Lebanon and the rapid reinforcement of UNIFIL, and provided an assessment of the humanitarian situation and the action being taken by the United Nations to address it. The Secretary-General intended to submit to the Council by mid-September (see p. 587) a more comprehensive report on significant political developments, which would be informed by the report of mission to the region of his Special Envoys, Terje Roed-Larsen and Vijay Nambiar, whom he had dispatched there on 18 August.

The Secretary-General said that the parties were generally complying with the cessation of hostilities called for in paragraph 1 of resolution 1701(2006). On 12 August, the Government of Lebanon announced its acceptance of that resolution, while the Government of Israel announced, on 13 August, that it would act according to its obligations as outlined in the resolution. However, some of the heaviest fighting of the conflict occurred during the 48-hour period prior to the cessation of hostilities. IDF intensified shelling and aerial bombardment across Lebanon, while Hizbullah launched a barrage of rockets into northern Israel. UNIFIL personnel endured artillery and air-to-ground rocket fire during that period. Guns on all sides fell silent at 0500 hours GMT on 14 August, as agreed, with UNIFIL reporting only isolated violations of the cessation of hostilities since then.

Both parties made constructive efforts to uphold their obligations with regard to the implementation of paragraph 2 of resolution 1701, which called for the joint deployment of Lebanese and UNIFIL forces throughout the south and the simultaneous withdrawal of Israeli forces from the area. On 14 August, just hours after the cessation of hostilities came into effect, the two sides met at the request of the UNIFIL Force Commander, Major-General Pellegrini, to coordinate their respective deployment and withdrawal plans. At that meeting and a subsequent one on 16 August, the Lebanese side confirmed its desire and intention to deploy its forces to the south as quickly as possible, with UNIFIL assistance, and extend its authority in areas vacated by the withdrawing Israeli forces. UNIFIL supported that deployment, which involved three light infantry brigades, one armoured brigade and one armoured regiment. The Israeli side provided information on the areas occupied by its forces north of the Blue Line and expressed its desire to withdraw its forces from all of the sectors as quickly as possible. IDF also provided maps showing mines and unexploded ordnance in the sectors from which it was withdrawing. In accordance with the mutually-agreed phased approach, IDF vacated three sectors on 16 August, and the Lebanese Armed Forces (LAF) subsequently deployed over 1,500 troops in those sectors.

As a reinforced UNIFIL, called for in paragraph 11 of resolution 1701(2006), was a vital part of the package to enable the deployment of LAF to the south and the withdrawal of Israeli forces; monitor compliance with the cessation of hostilities; help ensure humanitarian access to civilian populations and the voluntary and safe return of displaced persons; and establish conditions conducive to concluding a permanent ceasefire agreement and help to implement it, the Secretary-General appealed to leaders around the world for contributions to UNIFIL. At a formal meeting of current and potential troop-contributing countries, on 17 August, Member States generally reacted positively to that approach for reinforcing UNIFIL, and the Department of Peacekeeping Operations presented the concept of operations, force requirements and revisions to the rules of engagement. The most urgent need was to reinforce UNIFIL, between 17 August and 2 September, with up to 3,500 additional personnel, followed by another 3,500 forces between 3 September and 5 October to assist LAF achieve full operational capacity. A final reinforcement of up to an additional 3,000 troops would be required between 5 October and 4 November. The phases of deployment and disposition of UNIFIL troops might need to be adjusted as circumstances dictated, including the required capabilities being made available by Member States, as requested. UNIFIL had established a rear administrative headquarters in Cyprus with facilities provided by the United Nations Peacekeeping Force in Cyprus.

In other areas, the absence of hostilities had greatly improved the frequency and quality of humanitarian assistance. Within 96 hours of the cessation of hostilities, 20 convoys of some 118 trucks were dispatched to locations in the south and the Bekaa valley. A UN vessel delivered food at the port of Tyre and a more regular naval shuttle between Beirut and Tyre was envisaged. The United Nations set up camps in return locations to provide temporary shelter and distributed medicines and medical equipment to hospitals. Rapid needs assessments were conducted, including assessments of infrastructure damage, housing and unexploded ordnance. A three-stage humanitarian action plan laid out a concept of decentralized humanitarian operations in close proximity to target populations, primarily returnees. Existing humanitarian hubs in Beirut and Tyre were further strengthened and additional hubs established in Saida, Tripoli and Zahle. Despite the progress made in reaching people previously cut off from aid supplies, massive access problems remained, particularly because of the enormous damage to most roads and the bridge infrastructure leading to the south, which merited the lifting of the continuing sea and air blockade as soon as possible.

The conflict resulted in considerable unexploded ordnance contamination south of the Litani River and in areas in the south and east of the country, which had already led to many deaths and injuries to returnees. The contamination also hampered humanitarian efforts. The United Nations Mine Action Team supported the structures within the Government of Lebanon and civil society and coordinated with UNIFIL mine clearance assets to ensure the most effective use of resources.

Further communications. On 21 August [A/60/983-S/2006/679], Lebanon said that, between 14 and 20 August, it registered 82 aerial violations by the Israeli air force, the most serious of which was the landing close to the town of Baalbek in eastern Lebanon on 19 August. In addition, Israel continued to consolidate its position at several border points inside Lebanese territory.

On 23 August [A/60/990-S/2006/692], Israel shared with the Security Council President and the Secretary-General the list of the names of the 157 Israeli civilians and soldiers killed between 12 July and 14 August.

Lifting of naval blockade. On 30 August [S/2006/700], LAS informed the Security Council President that the LAS Council, at an extraordinary ministerial meeting (Cairo, Egypt, 20 August), issued a decision calling on the UN Security Council to pressure Israel to immediately lift the air, land and sea blockade imposed by it on Lebanon. It reaffirmed its support for and adoption of the Seven-Point Plan presented by the Lebanese Government (see p. 579).

On 5 September [A/60/1000-S/2006/712], Lebanon said that Israel continued to disregard Council resolution 1701(2006) by attacking Lebanon and violating its sovereignty by imposing an air and sea blockade.

In his September report on the implementation of resolution 1701(2006) [S/2006/730] (see below), the Secretary-General reported that Israel fully lifted the aerial blockade on 6 September and the maritime blockade on 7 September, after his discussions with all concerned parties led to a consensus on the necessary security arrangements to ensure the maintenance of the arms embargo imposed under resolution 1701(2006).

On 8 September [S/2006/733], the Secretary-General informed the Council President that, in accordance with paragraphs 11(f) and 14 of resolution 1701(2006), the United Nations had received a request from the Lebanese Government for assistance with the monitoring and patrolling of Lebanese territorial waters. France, Greece, Italy and the United Kingdom had agreed to provide that assistance on an interim basis. The deployment of those interim naval forces was a prerequisite for the lifting of the naval blockade imposed on Lebanon. UNIFIL had established a naval operations centre at its headquarters in Naqoura to coordinate operational details. In the meantime, preparations for the deployment of a full naval task force under UNIFIL command were proceeding. On 13 September [S/2006/734], the Council took note of the Secretary-General's letter.

Report of Secretary-General (September). On 12 September [S/2006/730], the Secretary-General submitted his second report on the implementation of resolution 1701(2006). He stated that, as at 31 August, official Lebanese figures showed that 1,187 people had died and 4,092 injured as a result of the conflict, many of whom were children, and one million were displaced between 12 July and 14 August, according to the Office for the Coordination of Humanitarian Affairs estimates. The cessation of hostilities on 14 August triggered a massive and speedy return of internally displaced persons and refugees back to their areas of origin. On the Israeli side, from 12 July until 14 August, 43 Israeli civilians and 117 IDF soldiers were killed. In addition, 33 Israelis were wounded seriously and 68 moderately. During that time, 3,970 rockets landed in Israel, 901 of them in urban areas; 300,000 residents were displaced and more than a million were forced to live for some of the time in shelters, according to official Israeli figures.

Since the cessation of hostilities went into effect, the nature of the humanitarian response in Lebanon had seen a rapid transition to early recovery activities and short-term intervention to provide assistance to the large numbers of returnees. The revised UN flash appeal placed emphasis on the clearance of mines and unexploded ordnance, emergency health and education needs and water and sanitation. The Lebanese Government, with UN system, civil society and international institutions support, developed a strategy to address early recovery needs, which laid the basis for longer-term reconstruction. The strategy was presented at the international donors conference (Stockholm, Sweden, 31 August), along with the UN revised flash appeal. More than $900 million was pledged at the meeting to support the Government's short-term efforts.

Given the importance of implementing resolution 1701(2006), the Secretary-General decided to visit the region. He attended the EU extraordinary ministerial-level meeting in Brussels on 25 August, and travelled to Lebanon, Israel, the Occupied Palestinian Territory, Jordan, the Syrian Arab Republic, Iran, Qatar, Saudi Arabia, Egypt, Turkey and Spain in subsequent days. He discerned broad support for the implementation of resolution 1701(2006) and was encouraged by the general commitment to restoring security and stability across the Middle East.

Since his previous report of 18 August (see p. 585), the parties had largely complied with the cessation of hostilities. UNIFIL had, however, observed numerous minor incidents and violations in its area of operation between the Litani River and the Blue Line. On the whole, the ground violations had not been of an offensive and hostile character and the parties seemed determined to uphold the agreement, except for the 19 August violation, when Israeli forces carried out a raid in eastern Lebanon. On the ground, significant progress continued to be made in the gradual withdrawal of Israeli forces and the deployment of LAF. IDF, which had divided the occupied area into 16 sectors and sub-sectors, vacated 9 of them by 7 September, with withdrawal from the others projected for before the end of September. In total, IDF had vacated approximately 65 per cent of the area it occupied when the cessation of hostilities went into effect. A general understanding had been reached that IDF would completely withdraw from Lebanese territory once UNIFIL strength was increased to 5,000 troops and the Lebanese Army was ready to deploy at the full strength of 15,000 troops.

In terms of the arms embargo imposed by resolution 1701(2006) to prevent the entry into Lebanon of arms or related material without its consent, both the Lebanese and the Israeli Governments were in agreement that the embargo underpinned a permanent ceasefire and a long-term solution. The Secretary-General noted the assurances given to him by the Syrian President that, while Syria objected to the presence of foreign troops along its border with Lebanon, it would implement in full paragraph 15 of resolution 1701(2006), including by establishing joint border patrols and control points with the Lebanese authorities. LAF deployed some 8,000 troops along the land border with Syria, and similar measures were taken along the 200-kilometre coastline in order to secure the maritime border. The Lebanese authorities enforced their monopoly on the control and legitimate use of force throughout the country, and the Council of Ministers decided on 4 September to task LAF with exercising control of the Lebanese territorial waters, with UNIFIL support and technical assistance. On 6 September, Prime Minister Siniora wrote to the Secretary-General requesting UN assistance in securing Lebanon's maritime border and entry points. In response to that request, UNIFIL established a naval component.

Regarding land mines and unexploded ordnance, the Israeli authorities assured UNIFIL that all relevant maps of landmines and unexploded ordnance in their possession would be handed over on completion of the withdrawal. While IDF provided some maps to UNIFIL regarding cluster strikes, they were not specific enough to be of use to operators on the ground. Both Lebanese soldiers and civilians continued to be killed by unexploded ordnance; some 14 persons had been killed and 57 injured.

The Secretary-General said that once again part of the Middle East was emerging from war, destruction and crisis. However, he was pleased that the Lebanese Government had decided in clear terms that there could only be one source of law, order and authority. He was also encouraged by the statements made by relevant parties, including Syria and Iran, during his mission to the region. A sustainable long-term solution could only be implemented on the basis of inclusive political processes in Lebanon, as well as in the wider region. Permanent respect of the Blue Line could be sustainable only if, on the Lebanese side, security arrangements were put in place to prevent the resumption of hostilities, including the establishment between the Blue Line and the Litani River of an area free of any armed personnel, assets and weapons other than those of the Lebanese Government or UNIFIL. In addition, all forces other than LAF had to be disarmed. At the same time, on the Israeli side, overflights had to cease completely.

Communication. On 20 September [A/61/367-S/2006/754], Lebanon reported that its efforts to implement resolution 1701(2006) had not been met with equal Israeli compliance. In fact, Israel was still occupying Lebanese territory and violating the resolution on a daily basis.

Report of Secretary-General (December). On 1 December [S/2006/933], the Secretary-General updated his 12 September report (see above) on the implementation of Security Council resolution 1701(2006), in particular on the operations of UNIFIL and other relevant UN activities.

Since 12 September, the military and security situation in the UNIFIL area of operation had further stabilized. The cessation of hostilities was maintained and there were no serious incidents or confrontations. Nevertheless, UNIFIL observed and reported air violations by Israeli jets and unmanned aerial vehicles on an almost daily basis. The Government of Lebanon had protested the overflights as a serious violation of Lebanese sovereignty, in contravention of resolution 1701(2006). Israel, however, maintained that they were not violations, but a necessary security measure; its Minister of Defence linked them to the return of the two IDF soldiers captured by Hizbullah on 12 July, and full respect for the arms embargo established under resolution 1701(2006). Israel continued to withdraw its forces from southern Lebanon, in coordination with UNIFIL, retaining a presence only in the northern part of the village of Ghajar, where UNIFIL was working with LAF and IDF to finalize the final withdrawal and set up temporary security arrangements for the part of the village inside Lebanese territory. In parallel with the withdrawal of Israeli forces, LAF deployed, in coordination with UNIFIL, four brigades throughout the south in the areas vacated by IDF, including along the Blue Line. That deployment, for the first time in decades, was a most notable achievement and a key stabilizing factor. LAF also took steps to ensure that the area between the Litani River and the Blue Line was free of armed personnel, assets and weapons other than those of the Government of Lebanon and UNIFIL. Specifically, LAF established a considerable number of permanent positions and checkpoints and commenced patrols. The Interim Maritime Task Force, under the lead of the Italian Navy, operated in support of the Lebanese Navy to secure Lebanese territorial waters until 15 October, when the UNIFIL Maritime Task Force became operational. The Lebanese authorities reported that they had undertaken a variety of measures to secure their borders and entry points to prevent the illegal entry into Lebanon of arms and related materiel. However, the United Nations continued to receive reports of illegal arms smuggling across the Lebanese-Syrian border, but had not been able to verify them. The Secretary-General dispatched a team of border police experts, as requested by the Lebanese Government, to review the measures put in place and assess the technical assistance needs. Significant deficiencies were found in equipment and training and in coordination among the different government services responsible for the borders, as well as in compliance with basic border security standards. The team did however confirm that the Lebanese authorities had taken steps to improve border security and control, but bilateral assistance was needed to enhance its capabilities. The Secretary-General requested that further specialized equipment and technical know-how be provided.

Following the decision of the Security Council to supplement and enhance the UNIFIL force, as at 28 November, its troop strength was 10,480 all ranks. The completion of the augmentation was expected in December, when UNIFIL force strength would reach approximately 11,500 ground troops, 1,750 naval personnel and 51 military observers from UNTSO.

As at 20 November, the National Demining Office, LAF and the United Nations Mine Action Coordination Centre South Lebanon recorded 822 cluster bomb strike sites. Civilian casualties as at 24 November, totaled 17 killed and 135 injured. Israel had yet to provide UNIFIL with the detailed firing data on its use of cluster munitions.

Further to the Council's request in resolution 1701(2006) to develop proposals for the delineation of Lebanon's international borders, especially in those areas where the border was disputed or uncertain, including the Shab'a Farms area, the Secretary-General appointed a senior cartographer to assume the lead in reviewing relevant material and developing an accurate territorial definition of the Shab'a Farms area. A permanent solution of that issue remained contingent upon the delineation of the border between Lebanon and the Syrian Arab Republic, in fulfilment of relevant Council resolutions. At the same time, and in view of the repeated Syrian statements indicating that the Shab'a Farms area was Lebanese, the Secretary-General continued to take careful note of the alternative path suggested by the Lebanese Government in its seven-point plan for placing the Shab'a Farms under UN jurisdiction until permanent border delineation and Lebanese sovereignty over them were settled.

SECURITY COUNCIL ACTION

On 12 December [meeting 5586], following consultations among Security Council members, the President made statement **S/PRST/2006/52** on behalf of the Council:

The Security Council recalls all its previous resolutions on Lebanon, in particular resolutions 425(1978), 426(1978), 520(1982), 1559(2004), 1680(2006) and 1701(2006), as well as the statements by its President on the situation in Lebanon, in particular the statements of 30 October and 21 November 2006.

The Council reiterates its full support for the legitimate and democratically elected Government of Lebanon, calls for full respect for the democratic institutions of the country, in conformity with the Constitution, and condemns any effort to destabilize Lebanon. The Council calls upon all Lebanese political parties to show responsibility with a view to preventing, through dialogue, further deterioration of the situation in Lebanon. It reaffirms its strong support for the sovereignty, territorial integrity, unity and political independence of Lebanon within its internationally recognized borders and under the sole and exclusive authority of the Government of Lebanon. The Council reiterates its call upon all parties concerned to cooperate fully and urgently with the Council for the full implementation of all relevant resolutions concerning the restoration of the territorial integrity, full sovereignty and political independence of Lebanon.

The Council welcomes the letter dated 1 December 2006 from the Secretary-General to the President of the Council, as well as the previous reports of the Secretary-General of 18 August and 12 September 2006 on the implementation of resolution 1701(2006).

The Council calls for the full implementation of resolution 1701(2006) and urges all concerned parties to cooperate fully with the Council and the Secretary-General to achieve this goal.

The Council welcomes the indication by the Secretary-General of the continuing commitment of the Government of Lebanon and the Government of Israel to all aspects of the implementation of resolution 1701(2006). It urges both Governments to strictly abide by their commitment and to pursue their efforts to achieve a permanent ceasefire and a long-term solution as envisioned in the resolution.

The Council notes that important progress has been made towards the implementation of resolution 1701(2006), in particular through the cessation of hostilities, the imminent withdrawal of all the Israeli forces from southern Lebanon and the deployment of the Lebanese Armed Forces in the south of the country for the first time in three decades, together with the deployment so far of more than 10,000 troops from the reinforced United Nations Interim Force in Lebanon.

The Council welcomes the maintenance of the cessation of hostilities since 14 August 2006, supports the work done by the Force, together with the parties, to finalize the Israeli withdrawal from the remaining area inside Lebanon and set up temporary security arrangements for the part of the village of Ghajar inside Lebanese territory, positively notes the decision of the Israeli Cabinet in this regard, and looks forward to its early implementation.

The Council commends the Government of Lebanon for extending its authority throughout its territory, particularly in the south, and encourages it to continue its efforts in this regard, including through the reinforcement of its capacities along its borders and the exercise of its monopoly of the use of force all over its territory in accordance with relevant Council resolutions.

The Council reiterates its full support to the Force and looks forward to the completion of its deployment early next year as contemplated by the Secretary-General in his letter. It expresses its strong appreciation to Member States that have contributed to the Force in the past and since the adoption of resolution 1701(2006) and notes the establishment of the Strategic Military Cell dedicated to the Force at United Nations Headquarters.

The Council, while expressing deep concern at the continuing Israeli violations of Lebanese airspace, appeals to all parties concerned to respect the cessation of hostilities and the Blue Line in its entirety, to refrain from any act of provocation and to abide scrupulously by their obligation to respect the safety of the Force and other United Nations personnel, including by avoiding any course of action which endangers United Nations personnel and by ensuring that the Force is accorded full freedom of movement throughout its area of operation.

The Council, in this context, reiterates its deep concern at the latest reports, though unverified, of illegal movements of arms into Lebanon. It welcomes the initial steps taken by the Government of Lebanon, notably the deployment of 8,000 troops along the border, to prevent movements of arms in conformity with relevant resolutions, and reiterates its call upon the Government of the Syrian Arab Republic to take similar measures to reinforce controls at the border.

The Council, mindful of the conclusions of the team of border police experts dispatched by the Secretary-General at the request of the Government of Lebanon, invites the Secretary-General to pursue further technical and independent assessment of the situation along the border and to report back to the Council on further findings and recommendations in this regard.

The Council further invites Member States, as recommended by the Secretary-General, to consider possible bilateral assistance to the Government of Lebanon to enhance its border security capacities.

The Council urges all Member States, in particular in the region, to take all necessary measures to implement in full paragraph 15 of resolution 1701(2006), including the arms embargo, and expresses its intention to consider further steps to achieve the goals set out in that paragraph.

The Council welcomes the concrete steps taken by the Government of Lebanon, with the assistance of the Force, to establish between the Blue Line and the Litani river an area free of any armed personnel, assets and weapons other than those of the Government of Lebanon and of the Force, and calls upon the Government of Lebanon to strengthen its efforts to this end. The Council also reiterates its call for the disbanding and disarmament of all militias and armed groups in Lebanon.

The Council expresses deepest concern at the presence in very high numbers of unexploded ordnance in south Lebanon, including cluster munitions. It deplores the death and injury of dozens of civilians, as well as of several deminers, caused by those munitions since the cessation of hostilities. It welcomes the continued contribution of the Force to operational mine clearance, encourages further assistance in mine action by the United Nations to the Government of Lebanon in support of both the continued development of its national mine action capacity and clearance of the remaining mine/unexploded ordnance threat in the south, commends donor countries for supporting these efforts through financial and in-kind contributions and encourages further international contributions and practical cooperation.

The Council reaffirms the urgent need for the unconditional release of the abducted Israeli soldiers.

The Council further encourages efforts aimed at urgently settling the issue of the Lebanese prisoners detained in Israel.

The Council commends the efforts of the Secretary-General and his facilitator to this end and calls upon all parties concerned to support those efforts.

Bearing in mind the relevant provisions of resolutions 1559(2004), 1680(2006) and 1701(2006), in particular on the delineation of the Syrian-Lebanese border, the Council takes note with interest of the appointment by the Secretary-General of a senior cartographer to review relevant material and develop an accurate territorial definition of the Sheba'a Farms area.

The Council notes with appreciation the process launched by the Secretary-General to investigate the cartographic, legal and political implications of the proposal contained in the seven-point plan of the Government of Lebanon and looks forward to its further recommendations on this issue early next year.

The Council calls upon the international community urgently to provide the Government of Lebanon with financial assistance in support of the national early recovery and reconstruction process. It expresses its appreciation to the Member States, United Nations bodies and intergovernmental, regional and non-governmental organizations that have provided and continue to provide assistance to the Lebanese people and Government, and looks forward to the success of the international conference which will be held in Paris on 25 January 2007 in support of Lebanon.

The Council reaffirms its full support to the Secretary-General in his efforts and dedication to facilitate and assist in the fulfilment of all provisions of resolution 1701(2006), and requests the Secretary-General to report on a quarterly basis on the implementation of that resolution, notably on further progress made towards the achievement of a permanent ceasefire and a long-term solution.

UNIFIL

The United Nations Interim Force in Lebanon (UNIFIL) continued to discharge its mandate by observing, monitoring and reporting on developments in its area of operation. Established by Security Council resolution 425(1978), following Israel's invasion of Lebanon [YUN 1978, p. 312], UNIFIL was originally entrusted with confirming the withdrawal of Israeli forces, restoring international peace and security, and assisting Lebanon in regaining authority in southern Lebanon. Following a second invasion in 1982 [YUN 1982, p. 428], the Council, in resolution 511(1982) [ibid., p. 450], authorized the Force to carry out the additional task of providing protection and humanitarian assistance to the local population. Following the withdrawal of Israeli forces from Lebanon in June 2000 [YUN 2000, p. 465], UNIFIL was reinforced in order to monitor those territories previously occupied by Israeli forces, to prevent the recurrence of fighting and create conditions for the restoration of Lebanese authority in the area. The Council extended the UNIFIL mandate thrice, in January for six months, in July for one month and in August for six months.

As a result of the hostilities between Hizbullah and Israel in July and August, the Council increased UNIFIL force strength to a maximum of 15,000 and expanded its scope of operations. It was mandated to monitor the cessation of hostilities; accompany and support LAF as it deployed throughout south Lebanon, including along the Blue Line; coordinate its activities with the Lebanese and Israeli Governments; help ensure humanitarian access to civilian populations and the voluntary and safe return of displaced persons; assist LAF in the establishment between the Blue Line and the Litani river of an area free of any armed personnel, assets and weapons other than those of the Lebanese Government and UNIFIL; and assist the Lebanese Government to secure its borders.

The Force headquarters, based in Naqoura, provided command and control, and liaison with Lebanon and Israel, UNDOF, UNTSO and a number of NGOs. After the July/August hostilities, two sector headquarters, West and East, in Tibnin and Marjayoun, respectively, and a quick reaction force based in Frun were established. UNIFIL air assets were based at the Force headquarters, while its Maritime Task Force operated in Lebanese territorial waters.

On 13 April [S/2006/245], the Secretary-General informed the Security Council President that Ukraine, whose troops had served in UNIFIL since July 2000, would withdraw its engineering and demining unit, to be replaced by China, which would be added to the list of countries that had agreed to provide military personnel to UNIFIL. On 18 April [S/2006/246], the Council took note of the Secretary-General's intention.

Financing

In June, the General Assembly considered the performance report on UNIFIL budget from 1 July 2004 to 30 June 2005 [A/60/629 & Corr.1]. Total expenditure for the period amounted to $89,244,100, compared with a total apportionment of $92,960,300.

The Assembly also had before it the proposed UNIFIL budget for the period from 1 July 2006 to 30 June 2007 [A/60/642 & Corr.1], in the amount of $94,112,400, and the related ACABQ comments and recommendations [A/60/812 & Corr.1].

GENERAL ASSEMBLY ACTION

On 30 June [meeting 92], the General Assembly, on the recommendation of the Fifth (Administrative and Budgetary) Committee [A/60/928], adopted **resolution 60/278** by recorded vote (150-3-1) [agenda item 149 *(b)*].

Financing of the United Nations Interim Force in Lebanon

The General Assembly,

Having considered the reports of the Secretary-General on the financing of the United Nations Interim Force in Lebanon and the related report of the Advisory Committee on Administrative and Budgetary Questions,

Recalling Security Council resolution 425(1978) of 19 March 1978 regarding the establishment of the United Nations Interim Force in Lebanon and the subsequent resolutions by which the Council extended the mandate of the Force, the latest of which was resolution 1655 (2006) of 31 January 2006,

Recalling also its resolution S-8/2 of 21 April 1978 on the financing of the Force and its subsequent resolutions thereon, the latest of which was resolution 59/307 of 22 June 2005,

Reaffirming its resolutions 51/233 of 13 June 1997, 52/237 of 26 June 1998, 53/227 of 8 June 1999, 54/267 of 15 June 2000, 55/180 A of 19 December 2000, 55/180 B of 14 June 2001, 56/214 A of 21 December 2001, 56/214 B of 27 June 2002, 57/325 of 18 June 2003, 58/307 of 18 June 2004 and 59/307,

Reaffirming also the general principles underlying the financing of United Nations peacekeeping operations, as stated in General Assembly resolutions 1874(S-IV) of 27 June 1963, 3101(XXVIII) of 11 December 1973 and 55/235 of 23 December 2000,

Noting with appreciation that voluntary contributions have been made to the Force,

Mindful of the fact that it is essential to provide the Force with the necessary financial resources to enable it to fulfil its responsibilities under the relevant resolutions of the Security Council,

1. *Requests* the Secretary-General to entrust the Head of the United Nations Interim Force in Lebanon with the task of formulating future budget proposals in full accordance with the provisions of General Assembly resolutions 59/296 of 22 June 2005 and 60/266 of 30 June 2006, as well as other relevant resolutions;

2. *Takes note* of the status of contributions to the Force as at 30 April 2006, including the contributions outstanding in the amount of 71 million United States

dollars, representing some 2 per cent of the total assessed contributions, notes with concern that only thirty Member States have paid their assessed contributions in full, and urges all other Member States, in particular those in arrears, to ensure payment of their outstanding assessed contributions;

3. *Expresses its appreciation* to those Member States that have paid their assessed contributions in full, and urges all other Member States to make every possible effort to ensure payment of their assessed contributions to the Force in full;

4. *Expresses deep concern* that Israel did not comply with General Assembly resolutions 51/233, 52/237, 53/227, 54/267, 55/180 A, 55/180 B, 56/214 A, 56/214 B, 57/325, 58/307 and 59/307;

5. *Stresses once again* that Israel should strictly abide by General Assembly resolutions 51/233, 52/237, 53/227, 54/267, 55/180 A, 55/180 B, 56/214 A, 56/214 B, 57/325, 58/307 and 59/307;

6. *Expresses concern* at the financial situation with regard to peacekeeping activities, in particular as regards the reimbursements to troop contributors that bear additional burdens owing to overdue payments by Member States of their assessments;

7. *Also expresses concern* at the delay experienced by the Secretary-General in deploying and providing adequate resources to some recent peacekeeping missions, in particular those in Africa;

8. *Emphasizes* that all future and existing peacekeeping missions shall be given equal and non-discriminatory treatment in respect of financial and administrative arrangements;

9. *Also emphasizes* that all peacekeeping missions shall be provided with adequate resources for the effective and efficient discharge of their respective mandates;

10. *Reiterates its request* to the Secretary-General to make the fullest possible use of facilities and equipment at the United Nations Logistics Base at Brindisi, Italy, in order to minimize the costs of procurement for the Force;

11. *Endorses* the conclusions and recommendations contained in the report of the Advisory Committee on Administrative and Budgetary Questions, and requests the Secretary-General to ensure their full implementation;

12. *Reaffirms* its resolution 59/296, and requests the Secretary-General to ensure the full implementation of its relevant provisions and the relevant provisions of its resolution 60/266;

13. *Notes with great concern* the reported fuel and rations fraud as reported by the Advisory Committee, which was revealed in an investigation undertaken by the Office of Internal Oversight Services at the request of the Force;

14. *Recognizes* that the investigation is still ongoing, and requests the Secretary-General to report in the next budget submission on the status of recovery of the financial loss, if any, to the Force;

15. *Requests* the Secretary-General to take all necessary action to ensure that the Force is administered with a maximum of efficiency and economy;

16. *Also requests* the Secretary-General, in order to reduce the cost of employing General Service staff, to continue efforts to recruit local staff for the Force against General Service posts, commensurate with the requirements of the Force;

17. *Reiterates its request* to the Secretary-General to take the necessary measures to ensure the full implementation of paragraph 8 of its resolution 51/233, paragraph 5 of its resolution 52/237, paragraph 11 of its resolution 53/227, paragraph 14 of its resolution 54/267, paragraph 14 of its resolution 55/180 A, paragraph 15 of its resolution 55/180 B, paragraph 13 of its resolution 56/214 A, paragraph 13 of its resolution 56/214 B, paragraph 14 of its resolution 57/325, paragraph 13 of its resolution 58/307 and paragraph 13 of its resolution 59/307, stresses once again that Israel shall pay the amount of 1,117,005 dollars resulting from the incident at Qana on 18 April 1996, and requests the Secretary-General to report on this matter to the General Assembly at its sixty-first session;

Financial performance report for the period from 1 July 2004 to 30 June 2005

18. *Takes note* of the report of the Secretary-General on the financial performance of the Force for the period from 1 July 2004 to 30 June 2005;

Budget estimates for the period from 1 July 2006 to 30 June 2007

19. *Decides* to appropriate to the Special Account for the United Nations Interim Force in Lebanon the amount of 97,579,600 dollars for the period from 1 July 2006 to 30 June 2007, inclusive of 93,526,200 dollars for the maintenance of the Force, 3,348,000 dollars for the support account for peacekeeping operations and 705,400 dollars for the United Nations Logistics Base;

Financing of the appropriation

20. *Also decides* to apportion among Member States the amount of 8,131,633 dollars for the period from 1 to 31 July 2006, in accordance with the levels updated in General Assembly resolution 58/256 of 23 December 2003, and taking into account the scale of assessments for 2006, as set out in its resolution 58/1 B of 23 December 2003;

21. *Further decides* that, in accordance with the provisions of its resolution 973(X) of 15 December 1955, there shall be set off against the apportionment among Member States, as provided for in paragraph 20 above, their respective share in the Tax Equalization Fund of 414,025 dollars, comprising the estimated staff assessment income of 378,200 dollars approved for the Force, the prorated share of 31,383 dollars of the estimated staff assessment income approved for the support account and the prorated share of 4,442 dollars of the estimated staff assessment income approved for the United Nations Logistics Base;

22. *Decides* to apportion among Member States the amount of 89,447,967 dollars for the period from 1 Au-

gust 2006 to 30 June 2007 at a monthly rate of 8,131,633 dollars, in accordance with the levels updated in its resolution 58/256, and taking into account the scale of assessments for 2006, as set out in its resolution 58/1 B, and the scale of assessments for 2007, subject to a decision of the Security Council to extend the mandate of the Force;

23. *Also decides* that, in accordance with the provisions of its resolution 973(X), there shall be set off against the apportionment among Member States, as provided for in paragraph 22 above, their respective share in the Tax Equalization Fund of 4,554,275 dollars, comprising the estimated staff assessment income of 4,160,200 dollars approved for the Force, the prorated share of 345,217 dollars of the estimated staff assessment income approved for the support account and the prorated share of 48,858 dollars of the estimated staff assessment income approved for the United Nations Logistics Base;

24. *Further decides* that, for Member States that have fulfilled their financial obligations to the Force, there shall be set off against their apportionment, as provided for in paragraphs 20 and 22 above, their respective share of the unencumbered balance and other income in the amount of 8,814,700 dollars in respect of the financial period ended 30 June 2005, in accordance with the levels updated in its resolution 58/256, and taking into account the scale of assessments for 2005, as set out in its resolution 58/1 B;

25. *Decides* that, for Member States that have not fulfilled their financial obligations to the Force, there shall be set off against their outstanding obligations their respective share of the unencumbered balance and other income in the amount of 8,814,700 dollars in respect of the financial period ended 30 June 2005, in accordance with the scheme set out in paragraph 24 above;

26. *Also decides* that the decrease of 521,300 dollars in the estimated staff assessment income in respect of the financial period ended 30 June 2005 shall be set off against the credits from the amount of 8,814,700 dollars referred to in paragraphs 24 and 25 above;

27. *Emphasizes* that no peacekeeping mission shall be financed by borrowing funds from other active peacekeeping missions;

28. *Encourages* the Secretary-General to continue to take additional measures to ensure the safety and security of all personnel under the auspices of the United Nations participating in the Force;

29. *Invites* voluntary contributions to the Force in cash and in the form of services and supplies acceptable to the Secretary-General, to be administered, as appropriate, in accordance with the procedure and practices established by the General Assembly;

30. *Decides* to include in the provisional agenda of its sixty-first session, under the item entitled "Financing of the United Nations peacekeeping forces in the Middle East", the sub-item entitled "United Nations Interim Force in Lebanon".

RECORDED VOTE ON RESOLUTION 60/278:

In favour: Albania, Algeria, Andorra, Angola, Antigua and Barbuda, Argentina, Armenia, Austria, Azerbaijan, Bahrain, Bangladesh, Barbados, Belarus, Belgium, Belize, Benin, Bosnia and Herzegovina, Brazil, Brunei Darussalam, Bulgaria, Burkina Faso, Burundi, Cambodia, Canada, Cape Verde, Chile, China, Colombia, Comoros, Costa Rica, Côte d'Ivoire, Croatia, Cuba, Cyprus, Czech Republic, Denmark, Djibouti, Dominica, Dominican Republic, Ecuador, Egypt, El Salvador, Eritrea, Estonia, Fiji, Finland, France, Gabon, Gambia, Georgia, Germany, Ghana, Greece, Grenada, Guatemala, Guinea, Guyana, Haiti, Hungary, Iceland, India, Indonesia, Iraq, Ireland, Italy, Jamaica, Japan, Jordan, Kazakhstan, Kenya, Kuwait, Kyrgyzstan, Lao People's Democratic Republic, Latvia, Lebanon, Lesotho, Libyan Arab Jamahiriya, Liechtenstein, Lithuania, Luxembourg, Madagascar, Malawi, Malaysia, Maldives, Mali, Malta, Mauritania, Mauritius, Mexico, Monaco, Mongolia, Morocco, Mozambique, Myanmar, Namibia, Nepal, Netherlands, New Zealand, Niger, Nigeria, Norway, Oman, Pakistan, Panama, Papua New Guinea, Paraguay, Peru, Philippines, Poland, Portugal, Qatar, Republic of Korea, Romania, Russian Federation, Saint Lucia, Saint Vincent and the Grenadines, San Marino, Saudi Arabia, Senegal, Serbia, Sierra Leone, Singapore, Slovakia, Slovenia, Solomon Islands, South Africa, Spain, Sri Lanka, Sudan, Suriname, Sweden, Switzerland, Syrian Arab Republic, Thailand, The former Yugoslav Republic of Macedonia, Timor-Leste, Togo, Trinidad and Tobago, Tunisia, Turkey, Uganda, Ukraine, United Arab Emirates, United Kingdom, Uruguay, Venezuela, Viet Nam, Yemen, Zambia, Zimbabwe.

Against: Israel, Palau, United States.

Abstaining: Australia.

On 17 August [A/60/986], the Secretary-General informed the Assembly President that implementation of Security Council resolution 1701(2006), authorizing an expansion of UNIFIL operations, would require extensive augmentation of its support infrastructure and sustainment capabilities. To facilitate and support the rapid deployment of the additional UNIFIL troops, as well as the deployment of LAF within the envisaged time frame, the Secretary-General had authorized extraordinary measures, including the waiver of the two-month notification process to all Member States for gratis personnel to allow existing and potential UNIFIL troop-contributing countries to assist with the urgent need for military planners; the immediate reassignment of civilian personnel without advertisement of the posts and within existing delegations of authority; relief from the current three-month limit on temporary deployment of civilian staff; an immediate increase in the not-to-exceed level of existing main-commodity contracts, in particular for fuel, rations, water and accommodation, for UNIFIL as well as for the United Nations Peacekeeping Force in Cyprus (UNFICYP), which would provide initial forward logistics support to UNIFIL; and an increase in the procurement delegations of UNIFIL and UNFICYP for six months to facilitate the immediate sustainment and development of the expanded Force.

The Secretary-General sought ACABQ concurrence to enter into commitments not to exceed $50 million to meet the most immediate needs of UNIFIL expansion, and had informed the Committee that the appropriation of $97,579,600 approved by the Assembly for UNIFIL for the period from 1 July 2006 to 30 June 2007 in resolution 60/278 (see above) would be utilized flexibly to meet the requirements of UNIFIL expansion. The immediate requirement of $50 million should be supplemented by a request for commitment authority, with assessment, covering the interim period from 11 August 2006 to 31 March 2007, which would be submitted to the Assembly, through ACABQ, for consideration at the regular part of its sixty-first (2006) session. More concrete and detailed budgetary proposals would be formulated for the Assembly's consideration and approval in the main part of that session. A planning team would be deployed to UNIFIL to assess the support requirements needed to implement resolution 1701(2006).

In December, the Assembly considered the Secretary-General's report on the financing of UNIFIL for the period from 1 July 2006 to 31 March 2007 [A/61/588], which contained a request for commitment authority, with assessment, in the amount of $263,364,200, inclusive of the amount of $50 million previously authorized by ACABQ. Total cost estimates, including the $93,526,200 approved in June, amounted to $356,890,400. The Assembly also considered the related ACABQ comments and recommendations thereon [A/61/616].

GENERAL ASSEMBLY ACTION

On 22 December [meeting 84], the General Assembly, on the recommendation of the Fifth Committee [A/61/657], adopted **resolution 61/250 A** by recorded vote (145-3-1) [agenda item 144 *(b)*].

Financing of the United Nations Interim Force in Lebanon

The General Assembly,

Having considered the report of the Secretary-General on the financing of the United Nations Interim Force in Lebanon, the letter dated 17 August 2006 from the Secretary-General addressed to the President of the General Assembly and the related report of the Advisory Committee on Administrative and Budgetary Questions,

Recalling Security Council resolution 425(1978) of 19 March 1978 regarding the establishment of the United Nations Interim Force in Lebanon and the subsequent resolutions by which the Council extended the mandate of the Force, the latest of which was resolution 1701(2006) of 11 August 2006, by which the Council extended the mandate of the Force until 31 August 2007 and authorized an increase in the strength of the Force to a maximum of 15,000 troops,

Recalling also its resolution S-8/2 of 21 April 1978 on the financing of the Force and its subsequent resolutions thereon, the latest of which was resolution 60/278 of 30 June 2006,

Reaffirming its resolutions 51/233 of 13 June 1997, 52/237 of 26 June 1998, 53/227 of 8 June 1999, 54/267 of 15 June 2000, 55/180 A of 19 December 2000, 55/180 B of 14 June 2001, 56/214 A of 21 December 2001, 56/214 B of 27 June 2002, 57/325 of 18 June 2003, 58/307 of 18 June 2004, 59/307 of 22 June 2005 and 60/278,

Reaffirming also the general principles underlying the financing of United Nations peacekeeping operations, as stated in General Assembly resolutions 1874(S-IV) of 27 June 1963, 3101(XXVIII) of 11 December 1973 and 55/235 of 23 December 2000,

Noting with appreciation that voluntary contributions have been made to the Force,

Mindful of the fact that it is essential to provide the Force with the necessary financial resources to enable it to fulfil its responsibilities under the relevant resolutions of the Security Council,

1. *Requests* the Secretary-General to entrust the Head of the United Nations Interim Force in Lebanon with the task of formulating future budget proposals in full accordance with the provisions of General Assembly resolutions 59/296 of 22 June 2005 and 60/266 of 30 June 2006, as well as other relevant resolutions;

2. *Takes note* of the status of contributions to the Force as at 31 October 2006, including the contributions outstanding in the amount of 67.9 million United States dollars, representing some 2 per cent of the total assessed contributions, notes with concern that only thirty-eight Member States have paid their assessed contributions in full, and urges all other Member States, in particular those in arrears, to ensure payment of their outstanding assessed contributions;

3. *Expresses its appreciation* to those Member States that have paid their assessed contributions in full, and urges all other Member States to make every possible effort to ensure payment of their assessed contributions to the Force in full;

4. *Expresses deep concern* that Israel did not comply with General Assembly resolutions 51/233, 52/237, 53/227, 54/267, 55/180 A, 55/180 B, 56/214 A, 56/214 B, 57/325, 58/307, 59/307 and 60/278;

5. *Stresses once again* that Israel should strictly abide by General Assembly resolutions 51/233, 52/237, 53/227, 54/267, 55/180 A, 55/180 B, 56/214 A, 56/214 B, 57/325, 58/307, 59/307 and 60/278;

6. *Expresses concern* at the financial situation with regard to peacekeeping activities, in particular as regards the reimbursements to troop contributors that bear additional burdens owing to overdue payments by Member States of their assessments;

7. *Also expresses concern* at the delay experienced by the Secretary-General in deploying and providing adequate resources to some recent peacekeeping missions, in particular those in Africa;

8. *Emphasizes* that all future and existing peacekeeping missions shall be given equal and non-discriminatory

treatment in respect of financial and administrative arrangements;

9. *Also emphasizes* that all peacekeeping missions shall be provided with adequate resources for the effective and efficient discharge of their respective mandates;

10. *Reiterates its request* to the Secretary-General to make the fullest possible use of facilities and equipment at the United Nations Logistics Base at Brindisi, Italy, in order to minimize the costs of procurement for the Force;

11. *Endorses* the conclusions and recommendations contained in the report of the Advisory Committee on Administrative and Budgetary Questions, and requests the Secretary-General to ensure their full implementation, subject to the provisions of the present resolution;

12. *Takes note* of the proposal for the establishment of the Office of Political and Civil Affairs, as contained in paragraph 19 of the report of the Secretary-General, and requests the Secretary-General to ensure, in reviewing the organizational structure of the Force, that it is in conformity with the mandate of the Force;

13. *Notes* the measures being undertaken by the Secretary-General, as set out in his letter;

14. *Requests* the Secretary-General to further elaborate the rationale for and status of those measures implemented in the context of his next budget submission, during the first part of the resumed sixty-first session;

15. *Emphasizes* that the approval of commitment authority in no way implies approval of the establishment of posts or the creation of new functions;

16. *Recalls* section VIII of its resolution 60/266, and, mindful of the significantly increased size and the increased area of operation of the Force, decides to authorize the provision of 500,000 dollars for quick-impact projects;

17. *Decides* to authorize, without setting a precedent, the utilization of an amount not exceeding 750,000 dollars for temporary fuel assistance for the Force to assist the deployment of the Lebanese Armed Forces in southern Lebanon;

18. *Reaffirms* its resolution 59/296, and requests the Secretary-General to ensure the full implementation of its relevant provisions and the relevant provisions of its resolution 60/266;

19. *Requests* the Secretary-General to take all necessary action to ensure that the Force is administered with a maximum of efficiency and economy;

20. *Also requests* the Secretary-General, in order to reduce the cost of employing General Service staff, to continue efforts to recruit local staff for the Force against General Service posts, commensurate with the requirements of the Force;

21. *Reiterates its request* to the Secretary-General to take the necessary measures to ensure the full implementation of paragraph 8 of its resolution 51/233, paragraph 5 of its resolution 52/237, paragraph 11 of its resolution 53/227, paragraph 14 of its resolution 54/267, paragraph 14 of its resolution 55/180 A, paragraph 15 of its resolution 55/180 B, paragraph 13 of its resolution 56/214 A, paragraph 13 of its resolution 56/214 B, paragraph 14 of its resolution 57/325, paragraph 13 of its resolution 58/307, paragraph 13 of its resolution 59/307 and paragraph 17 of its resolution 60/278, stresses once again that Israel shall pay the amount of 1,117,005 dollars resulting from the incident at Qana on 18 April 1996, and requests the Secretary-General to report on this matter to the General Assembly at its current session;

Budget estimates for the period from 1 July 2006 to 31 March 2007

22. *Authorizes* the Secretary-General to enter into commitments for the Force for the period from 1 July 2006 to 31 March 2007 in a total amount not exceeding 257,340,400 dollars, inclusive of the amount of 50 million dollars previously authorized by the Advisory Committee on Administrative and Budgetary Questions under the terms of section IV of General Assembly resolution 49/233 A of 23 December 1994 and in addition to the amount of 97,579,600 dollars already appropriated for the period from 1 July 2006 to 30 June 2007 under the terms of its resolution 60/278;

23. *Also authorizes* the Secretary-General to enter into commitments for the period from 1 July 2006 to 31 March 2007 in a total amount not exceeding 2,486,900 dollars for the support account for peacekeeping operations and in respect of the backstopping of the Force at Headquarters;

Financing of the commitment authority

24. *Decides* to apportion among Member States the amount of 257,340,400 dollars for the period from 1 July 2006 to 31 March 2007 for the expansion of the Force, in accordance with the levels updated in General Assembly resolutions 58/256 of 23 December 2003 and 61/243 of 22 December 2006, and taking into account the scale of assessments for 2006, as set out in its resolution 58/1 B of 23 December 2003, and the scale of assessments for 2007, as set out in its resolution 61/237 of 22 December 2006;

25. *Also decides* that, in accordance with the provisions of its resolution 973(X) of 15 December 1955, there shall be set off against the apportionment among Member States, as provided for in paragraph 24 above, their respective share in the Tax Equalization Fund of the amount of 2,305,800 dollars of the estimated staff assessment income approved for the Force;

26. *Emphasizes* that no peacekeeping mission shall be financed by borrowing funds from other active peacekeeping missions;

27. *Encourages* the Secretary-General to continue to take additional measures to ensure the safety and security of all personnel under the auspices of the United Nations participating in the Force;

28. *Invites* voluntary contributions to the Force in cash and in the form of services and supplies acceptable to the Secretary-General, to be administered, as appropriate, in accordance with the procedure and practices established by the General Assembly;

29. *Decides* to keep under review during its sixty-first session, under the item entitled "Financing of the United Nations peacekeeping forces in the Middle East",

the sub-item entitled "United Nations Interim Force in Lebanon".

RECORDED VOTE ON RESOLUTION 61/250:

In favour: Afghanistan, Albania, Algeria, Andorra, Antigua and Barbuda, Argentina, Armenia, Austria, Bahamas, Bahrain, Bangladesh, Barbados, Belarus, Belgium, Belize, Benin, Bhutan, Bolivia, Botswana, Brazil, Brunei Darussalam, Bulgaria, Burkina Faso, Cambodia, Canada, Cape Verde, Chile, China, Colombia, Comoros, Congo, Costa Rica, Croatia, Cuba, Cyprus, Czech Republic, Denmark, Djibouti, Dominica, Dominican Republic, Ecuador, Egypt, El Salvador, Eritrea, Estonia, Fiji, Finland, France, Gabon, Georgia, Germany, Ghana, Greece, Grenada, Guatemala, Guinea, Guinea-Bissau, Guyana, Haiti, Honduras, Hungary, Iceland, India, Indonesia, Iraq, Ireland, Italy, Jamaica, Japan, Jordan, Kazakhstan, Kenya, Kuwait, Kyrgyzstan, Latvia, Lebanon, Libyan Arab Jamahiriya, Liechtenstein, Lithuania, Madagascar, Malawi, Malaysia, Maldives, Mali, Malta, Mauritania, Mauritius, Mexico, Moldova, Monaco, Morocco, Mozambique, Namibia, Nepal, Netherlands, New Zealand, Niger, Nigeria, Norway, Oman, Pakistan, Panama, Paraguay, Peru, Philippines, Poland, Portugal, Qatar, Republic of Korea, Romania, Russian Federation, Saint Lucia, Saudi Arabia, Senegal, Serbia, Sierra Leone, Singapore, Slovakia, Slovenia, Solomon Islands, South Africa, Spain, Sri Lanka, Sudan, Suriname, Swaziland, Sweden, Switzerland, Syrian Arab Republic, Thailand, The former Yugoslav Republic of Macedonia, Timor-Leste, Trinidad and Tobago, Tunisia, Turkey, Ukraine, United Arab Emirates, United Kingdom, United Republic of Tanzania, Uruguay, Venezuela, Viet Nam, Yemen, Zambia, Zimbabwe.

Against: Israel, Palau, United States.

Abstaining: Australia.

By **decision 61/552** of 22 December, the Assembly decided that the item on the financing of UN peacekeeping forces in the Middle East would remain for consideration at its resumed sixty-first (2007) session.

Other security issues

Assassination of Industry Minister Pierre Gemayel

On 21 November [meeting 5569], following consultations among Security Council members, the President made statement **S/PRST/2006/46** on behalf of the Council:

The Security Council unequivocally condemns the assassination in Beirut on 21 November 2006 of Minister for Industry Pierre Gemayel, a patriot who was a symbol of freedom and of the political independence of Lebanon. The Council expresses its deepest sympathy and condolences to the family of the victim and to the people and Government of Lebanon.

The Council condemns any attempt to destabilize Lebanon through political assassination or other terrorist acts. The Council is gravely concerned by this assassination and its possible impact on ongoing efforts by the Government and people of Lebanon to solidify democracy, extend the authority of the Government of Lebanon throughout its territory and complete the reconstruction process.

The Council calls upon all parties in Lebanon and the region to show restraint and a sense of responsibility with a view to preventing any further deterioration of the situation in Lebanon. The Council urges all States, in accordance with its resolutions 1373(2001), 1566(2004) and 1624(2005), to cooperate fully in the fight against terrorism.

The Council welcomes the determination and commitment of the Government of Lebanon to bring to justice the perpetrators, organizers and sponsors of this and other assassinations and underlines its determination to support the Government of Lebanon in its efforts to this end.

The Council reaffirms its previous calls upon all parties concerned to cooperate fully and urgently with the Council for the full implementation of all relevant resolutions concerning the restoration of the territorial integrity, full sovereignty and political independence of Lebanon, in particular resolutions 1559(2004), 1595(2005), 1664(2006), 1680(2006) and 1701(2006).

The Council requests the Secretary-General to continue to follow closely and report regularly to the Council on the situation in Lebanon. The Council underlines its readiness to continue to act in support of the legitimate and democratically elected Government of Lebanon.

Communications. On 21 November [S/2006/914], the Secretary-General said that he had received a request from the Lebanese Prime Minister for technical assistance in support of the Lebanese Government's efforts to investigate the murder of Minister Gemayel. The Prime Minister also requested that the United Nations International Independent Investigation Commission (UNIIIC), established to investigate the 2005 assassination of former Prime Minister Rafik Hariri (see below), consult with relevant Lebanese authorities for that purpose. The following day [S/2006/915], the Council invited UNIIIC to extend its technical assistance as appropriate to the Lebanese authorities in the investigation of the assassination of Mr. Gemayel.

Investigation of assassination of former Prime Minister Rafik Hariri

The United Nations International Independent Investigation Commission (UNIIIC), established by Security Council resolution 1595(2005) [YUN 2005, p. 553], continued to assist Lebanese authorities in their investigation of all aspects pertaining to the assassination of former Lebanese Prime Minister Rafiq Hariri and 22 others on 14 February 2005 [ibid., p. 551].

On 11 January [S/2006/17], the Secretary-General informed the Council of his intention to appoint Serge Brammertz (Belgium) as UNIIIC Commissioner to succeed Detlev Mehlis, which the Council noted on 13 January [S/2006/18]. By another exchange of letters with the Council President of 14 and 19 July, respectively [S/2006/541, S/2006/542], Mr. Brammertz's appointment was extended until 31 December, and subsequently by a further exchange of letters of 14 and 19 December, respectively [S/2006/998, S/2006/999], until 15 June 2007.

Report of UNIIIC (March). On 14 March [S/2006/161], the Secretary-General transmitted to the Security Council President the third UNIIIC report on progress in implementing the Commission's mandate, as well as in consolidating its organizational structure and resources. The consolidation provided continuity to UNIIIC core work, following the appointment, in January, of Commissioner Brammertz, and allowed UNIIIC to provide the necessary technical assistance to the Lebanese authorities with regard to the investigation of the terrorist attacks perpetrated in Lebanon since 1 October 2004, as requested by the Council in resolution 1644(2005) [YUN 2005, p. 558]. In the area of cooperation with the Syrian Arab Republic, a common understanding was reached on the operational modalities with regard to the applicable legal framework, access to individuals, sites and information, and communications with the Government.

With the expansion of its mandate and the prospect of the creation of an international tribunal, UNIIIC work entered a new phase. A significant number of new lines of inquiry enabled faster-than-expected progress. Along with the development and refinement of case knowledge, the Commission was confident that its support to the Lebanese authorities would result in a successful outcome to the investigations within a realistic time frame. UNIIIC provided further technical assistance to the Lebanese authorities for their investigations into 14 other alleged terrorist attacks since 1 October 2004. UNIIIC was of the view that it was necessary to make short, medium and long-term investments into the capacity of the relevant Lebanese judicial and law enforcement agencies in specific areas of expertise. Interaction with the Lebanese authorities was close and frequent and UNIIIC would strive not only to maintain that working relationship, but to find ways to further assist and enhance the interaction and information exchange. However, its capacity and mandate to provide technical assistance to the Lebanese authorities were limited. UNIIIC laid the groundwork with the Syrian authorities for improved cooperation and looked forward to receiving timely and relevant responses to its requests, as agreed by the Syrian Government.

Security Council consideration. On 16 March [meeting 5388], in his briefing to the Security Council, UNIIIC Commissioner Serge Brammertz said that the Commission had made further progress in the investigation into the assassination of former Prime Minister Hariri and 22 others. It had gained a better understanding of the crime, its circumstances and modus operandi, had developed new lines of inquiry and pursued and further evaluated existing leads and discarded others. While he understood the public interest in learning further details on the status of certain lines of inquiry, it had been agreed with Lebanon's Prosecutor General not to discuss any of the details at that stage of the proceedings.

UNIIIC also made progress in implementing the request to provide technical assistance to the Lebanese authorities in their investigations of 14 other cases of a possible terrorist nature. It completed its first round of evaluations of all cases and agreed with the Prosecutor General and the investigation judges on what assistance was needed. However, structural problems within Lebanese law enforcement and judicial systems in coping with the demands of those cases had been apparent. More cooperation and communication among the different Lebanese agencies were necessary, as were more specialized investigative capability and forensic expertise. UNIIIC reached an understanding with the Syrian Foreign Ministry on the legal framework for cooperation and access to information, sites and Syrian citizens.

Communication. On 5 May [S/2006/278], Lebanon requested the extension of UNIIIC mandate for one year, from 15 June, and looked forward to the earliest conclusion of the agreement with the United Nations for the establishment of an international court, as provided for in Council resolution 1664(2006) (see p. 601).

Report of UNIIIC (June). In its 10 June report [S/2006/375], UNIIIC stated that considerable progress had been achieved in the Hariri investigation. The Commission has almost completed the critically important work relating to the crime scene, the Hariri convoy and associated events on the day, and by the latter part of the year, it anticipated that the main projects relating to that aspect of the crime would have been completed. The fundamental building blocks for the investigation into the crime, in particular concerning the explosion, the container/carrier and the means of delivery, were largely understood and provided the basis for investigative progress with regard to the perpetrators. The Commission anticipated that an analysis of the results of its recent forensic activities, in particular the exploitation of the crime scene and the blast properties, would lead to the strengthening or exclusion of some of the existing case hypotheses. The Commission was also accelerating its investigation on a number of other fronts. As far as the 14 other cases were concerned, the Commission believed that a more concerted and robust effort was needed to move those investigations forward, and could also conceive of a more proactive role for itself in that respect, including interviewing witnesses, victims or suspects.

Progress was made in consolidating UNIIIC organizational structure and capacity, but it still faced challenges of securing adequate and timely resources, identifying and employing expert staff and resources on short notice, and reaching full operational capacity. As the investigative process progressed and became more complex, assistance from Member States and international organizations would continue to be necessary to ensure stability and continuity in the work of the Commission.

Security Council consideration. On 14 June [meeting 5458], the Security Council was briefed by UNIIIC Commissioner Brammertz, who said that 24 projects were under way concurrently, including forensic examinations of the crime scene and the convoy vehicles; a review of the telecommunications used by the alleged perpetrators; and the interviewing of key witnesses and sensitive sources. Most notably, UNIIIC invested a major 23-day effort in the systematic forensic examination of the immediate circumstances of the Hariri attack, in order to establish a unifying theory on whether the explosion occurred below ground or above ground, whether it consisted of one or two blasts or a combination thereof, and how it was triggered. That would facilitate an understanding of the planning and execution of the crime, the nature and composition of the perpetrating team and its skills and coordination, the time spent to plan the attack, the period during which the decision to assassinate Mr. Hariri was taken, and the extent of the involvement, potential advance knowledge or complicity of other individuals. UNIIIC reached the following preliminary conclusions. One above-ground explosion took place on 14 February 2005 at precisely 12.55 p.m. A large improvised explosive device (IED), placed in a Mitsubishi truck, was detonated as the Hariri convoy passed by. The IED contained a minimum of 1,200 kilogrammes of TNT equivalent. The detonation of the IED was most likely initiated by an individual within or immediately in front of the Mitsubishi vehicle. UNIIIC did not believe that the claim of responsibility expressed in the video delivered to Reuters and Al Jazeera immediately after the attack established the identity of the individual. In fact, DNA analysis of human remains recovered from the crime scene suggested that there was no evidence that the individual claiming responsibility for the attack, namely Ahmed Abu Adass, was the individual who initiated the detonation of the IED. The crime had to be considered a targeted assassination. The large quantity of explosives used elevated the attack to an almost "guaranteed" level. The magnitude of the explosion was designed to ensure the success of the operation even if the Hariri vehicle was not directly hit. The Commission had developed two basic hypotheses regarding the perpetrators of the attack and was developing working hypotheses regarding those who commissioned it. It was also investigating different motives, including political, personal vendettas, financial circumstances and extremists ideologies.

SECURITY COUNCIL ACTION

On 15 June [meeting 5461], the Security Council unanimously adopted **resolution 1686(2006)**. The draft [S/2006/392] was submitted by France, the United Kingdom and the United States.

The Security Council,

Recalling all its previous relevant resolutions, in particular resolutions 1595(2005) of 7 April 2005, 1636(2005) of 31 October 2005, 1644(2005) of 15 December 2005, 1664(2006) of 29 March 2006, 1373(2001) of 28 September 2001 and 1566(2004) of 8 October 2004,

Reaffirming its strongest condemnation of the terrorist bombing of 14 February 2005, as well as of all other attacks in Lebanon since October 2004, and reaffirming also that those involved in these attacks must be held accountable for their crimes,

Having examined the report of the United Nations International Independent Investigation Commission ("the Commission"), submitted pursuant to resolutions 1595(2005), 1636(2005) and 1644(2005),

Commending the Commission for the outstanding professional work it continues to accomplish under difficult circumstances in assisting the Lebanese authorities in their investigation of all aspects of this terrorist act, and taking note of the conclusion of the Commission that, while significant progress has been made, the investigation is not yet complete,

Taking note of the letter dated 4 May 2006 from the Prime Minister of Lebanon to the Secretary-General requesting that the mandate of the Commission be extended for a further period of up to one year from 15 June 2006, and noting the concurrent recommendation of the Commission in that regard,

Recalling its request to the Secretary-General, in resolution 1644(2005), to submit recommendations with regard to the request of the Government of Lebanon to expand the mandate of the Commission to the other terrorist attacks perpetrated in Lebanon since 1 October 2004,

Willing to continue to assist Lebanon in the search for the truth and in holding all those involved in this terrorist attack accountable,

1. *Welcomes* the report of the Commission;

2. *Decides* to extend the mandate of the Commission until 15 June 2007;

3. *Supports* the intention of the Commission, as it deems appropriate and consistent with its mandate, to extend further its technical assistance to the Lebanese

authorities with regard to their investigations into the other terrorist attacks perpetrated in Lebanon since 1 October 2004, and requests the Secretary-General to provide the Commission with the support and resources needed in this regard;

4. *Requests* the Commission to continue to report to the Security Council on the progress of the investigation on a quarterly basis, or at any other time as it deems appropriate;

5. *Decides* to remain seized of the matter.

Report of UNIIIC (September). In a 25 September report [S/2006/760], UNIIIC outlined the progress made in its investigative activities between 15 June and 15 September. That period was marked by the conflict and unstable security situation in Lebanon (see p. 574), and resulted in the temporary relocation of UNIIIC to a base in Cyprus on 21 July, as required by the United Nations. The gradual process of moving international personnel back to Beirut had started. Although UNIIIC faced delays and logistical difficulties in accessing witnesses and information as a result of the conflict, progress was made in all investigative areas. UNIIIC continued to provide technical assistance to Lebanese authorities in their investigation of other attacks perpetrated in Lebanon since 1 October 2004. The expanded mandate given to UNIIIC by Council resolution 1686(2006) (see p. 598) enabled it to take a more proactive role in those cases, resulting in tangible progress both in individual cases and in their potential linkage to each other. The assistance UNIIIC received from States continued to be critical to the progress of the investigation. Cooperation with Syria remained generally satisfactory, and UNIIIC continued to require its full support in providing information and facilitating interviews with individuals located on Syrian territory.

Security Council consideration. On 29 September [meeting 5539], the Security Council heard a briefing by UNIIIC Commissioner Brammertz, who said that in the Hariri investigation, 20 major investigations and analysis projects were ongoing. The focus was on consolidating the results of forensic examination of the crime scene and the blast that killed Mr. Hariri and 22 others. In addition, UNIIIC conducted a significant number of interviews to identify the perpetrators at all levels. The DNA analysis of the human remains found at the crime scene appeared to correspond to the person that allegedly detonated the improvised explosive device, a man in his early twenties. Further forensic tests were taking place to possibly establish the regional origin of that person. Independent tests carried out in two separate environments earlier in 2006, as well as scaling explosion experiments had corroborated UNIIIC findings with regard to the characteristics and nature of the explosion of 14 February 2005. It was estimated that the quantity of the explosive used was closer to 1,800 kilogrammes. UNIIIC also continued to investigate the modus operandi used by the perpetrators, and information suggesting that Rafik Hariri was the subject of earlier surveillances and possibly of earlier attempts to kill him. It was likely that the alleged bombing team knew that electronic countermeasures were in place to protect the convoy and Rafik Hariri and that they chose a method of attack that would not be impeded by such countermeasures. The reduced security arrangements for Mr. Hariri after his resignation as Prime Minister created a number of vulnerabilities, enabling the attack to be perpetrated more easily. The Commission's analysis and investigation of the communications traffic relevant to the case demonstrated a complex network of telecommunications traffic between a number of individuals relevant to the investigation. UNIIIC strategic objectives for the coming months were to undertake approximately 50 key linkage-related interviews, collect and analyse a large amount of already identified electronic data, technical intelligence and documentation and develop its communication and further sensitive sources.

The Commission increased its technical assistance to the Lebanese authorities in the 14 other cases, concentrating on three main areas: forensic investigation and analysis for each case to establish the nature and location of the explosive devices used; communications analysis, in order to lift from the vast amount of communications traffic in Beirut during the period of the attacks those numbers common to some of the attacks, and to link other relevant numbers; and the conduct of interviews, where the interviewees could provide information on individual cases, as well as on multiple cases' commonalities. As a result of the work done during the reporting period, UNIIIC strengthened its preliminary conclusions that the 14 cases were not commissioned and executed by 14 disparate and unconnected persons or groups with separate motives.

Report of UNIIIC (December). In a 12 December report [S/2006/962], UNIIIC described further progress made in its investigative activities between 25 September and 10 December. During that period, UNIIIC returned to Lebanon from Cyprus, where it had temporarily relocated from 22 July to 13 October. Since its return to Lebanon, UNIIIC operated in a volatile political environment, reflected in the 21 November assassination of Industry Minister Pierre Gemayel (see p. 596), and the national and international attention surrounding the establishment of a special tribunal for Lebanon. UNIIIC investigative direction in the Hariri case remained focused on developing crime scene evidence from investigation and forensic analysis, investigating potential perpetrators and collecting evidence relating to the linkage and contextual aspects of the case. UNIIIC, in close cooperation with the Lebanese judiciary, continued to take a proactive role in the other 14 cases. The assassination of Mr. Gemayel led to a 22 November request by the Security Council for UNIIIC to extend technical assistance in the Gemayel case to the Lebanese authorities. That constituted an expansion of its mandate contained in Council resolution 1644(2005) [YUN 2005, p. 558] in relation to the investigation of other terrorist attacks perpetrated in Lebanon since 1 October 2004. UNIIIC responded by providing technical assistance, including forensic support, witness interviews and evidence collection and analysis. UNIIIC interaction with the Lebanese authorities on all matters relevant to its mandate was ongoing. It continued to receive support from Syria in providing information and facilitating interviews with individuals located on Syrian territory. In addition, UNIIIC noted the assistance received from other Member States in response to its requests and highlighted the need for such assistance to be provided in a timely manner.

Security Council consideration. On 18 December [meeting 5597], the Security Council was briefed by UNIIIC Commissioner Brammertz, who reported that the latest forensic results confirmed that it was likely that a person triggered the explosion from within or immediately in front of the Mitsubishi van that carried the explosive device, rather than through the use of a remote-controlled device. Forensic analysis of the human parts belonging to the suspected bomber that were recovered from the crime scene showed that he did not spend his youth in Lebanon, but was situated there in the last two to three months before his death. UNIIIC continued to analyse information relating to Ahmed Abu Adass, in order to establish how he was identified, where and when that occurred, who might have been involved in organizing his appearance in the video in which he claimed responsibility for the assassination, and what happened to him after the video was made and delivered. Individuals associated with Ahmed Abu Adass in Lebanon and elsewhere were also being investigated. UNIIIC analysed information about the increasing threats against and pressure on Mr. Hariri during the last 15 months of his life, which revealed a number of potential motives for his killing, most of which were linked to his political activities. In its assistance to the Lebanese authorities relating to the other 14 cases, UNIIIC interviewed witnesses associated with the victims of the six targeted attacks. A considerable number of links between the six cases, and between those cases and the Rafik Hariri case, emerged from those interviews. The Commission believed that the motive was related to their common objectives and interests, and thus might have been linked by a common intent. As to the technical assistance provided in the investigation of the assassination of Minister Gemayel, UNIIIC helped to identify the perpetrators and the vehicles that were used in the attack, and was working to reconstruct the modus operandi of the assassins. A total of 250 exhibits were sent for forensic research and analysis. It was the UNIIIC preliminary assessment that Mr. Gemayel was the subject of surveillance as part of a planned assassination operation against him.

Syria's cooperation with UNIIIC remained generally satisfactory. Between 25 September and 10 December, UNIIIC submitted 12 formal requests for assistance to Syria and undertook a number of investigation activities and interviews of individuals in that country. It was satisfied with the timeliness and efficiency of Syria's assistance and with the logistical and security arrangements made for its investigation activities on Syrian territory.

In the light of the proposed creation of a special tribunal for Lebanon, UNIIIC intended to realign its objectives and organize its work in a manner that would facilitate the transition to such a tribunal.

Implementation of Security Council resolution 1644(2005)

Report of Secretary-General. Pursuant to Council resolution 1644(2005) [YUN 2005, p. 558], the Secretary-General submitted a March report [S/2006/176] on the nature and scope of the international assistance needed to try those eventually charged with the assassination of former Lebanese Prime Minister Hariri and 22 others before a tribunal of an international character. The Lebanese Government, in 2005 [YUN 2005, p. 558], had requested the establishment of such a tribunal.

Following consultations between UN officials and Lebanese authorities, it became clear that the establishment of a mixed tribunal would best balance the need for Lebanese and international involvement in the work of the proposed tribunal, which would be determined by characteristics, such as the tribunal's founding instrument, jurisdiction, applicable law, location, composition and financial arrangements. There was a common understanding that the tribunal should be established through an agreement concluded between the United Nations and Lebanon, which would determine whether national legislative action was needed for the establishment of the tribunal. Such an approach would not exclude the need for the Security Council to take complementary measures to ensure the effectiveness of and cooperation with the tribunal.

The jurisdiction of the tribunal would be determined with respect to persons involved and acts committed. Paragraph 6 of resolution 1644(2005) provided guidance regarding subject matter jurisdiction, that was, the 14 February 2005 terrorist bombing that killed Mr. Hariri and 22 others. However, the Council provided broad direction regarding personal jurisdiction in resolution 1595(2005) [ibid. p. 553], calling on the Lebanese Government to bring to justice the perpetrators, organizers and sponsors of the crime. That same wording was echoed by the Lebanese authorities during consultations with UN officials, in which they expressed a preference for the tribunal to have personal jurisdiction over all those responsible for the death of Mr. Hariri and 22 others.

The process of choosing the tribunal's applicable law had to take into account the types of crimes committed and respect Lebanon's legal culture, as well as international criminal justice standards developed over the preceding years in the work of other tribunals. Consultations with the Lebanese authorities made it clear that applying Lebanese substantive criminal law would play an important role in ensuring that the tribunal would have a national dimension. The drafting of the rules of procedure of and evidence applicable in the tribunal could benefit from the experience gained in the existing international tribunals, giving due consideration to the specific circumstances of the matter at hand.

The choice of the location of the tribunal should balance the objective of basing a judicial process within the territory of the affected State against the security of the judges, prosecutor and staff of the tribunal, as well as of the witnesses and the accused, and take into account logistical and financial implications. As to the concerns for security, there was a belief among the Lebanese authorities that the tribunal might not be able to operate effectively in Lebanon.

Concerning the tribunal's composition, the Lebanese authorities emphasized that significant international participation would be essential for the tribunal to fulfil its purpose effectively, but it was of the utmost importance that the judges, the prosecutor and other court personnel be selected in a way that ensured the independence, objectivity and impartiality of the judicial process. In terms of financing the tribunal, Lebanese authorities acknowledged that Lebanon should make a financial contribution in keeping with the country's economic situation. It was necessary that sources of funding be found to ensure that the tribunal had adequate funds to guarantee its continuity and effective functioning. The adoption of the legal basis of and framework for the tribunal would not predetermine when it might commence operations, nor prevent the gradual phasing-in of the different elements of the tribunal. In addition, it would be necessary to ensure, at an appropriate time, a smooth transition between the current investigation and a future judicial mechanism.

If the common understanding achieved between the Secretariat and the Lebanese authorities regarding the key issues was acceptable to the Security Council, the Council could consider adopting a resolution requesting the Secretary-General to initiate negotiations with the Lebanese Government aimed at establishing a tribunal of an international character along the lines set forth in the report.

SECURITY COUNCIL ACTION

On 29 March [meeting 5401], the Security Council unanimously adopted **resolution 1664(2006)**. The draft [S/2006/186] was submitted by France, the United Kingdom and the United States.

The Security Council,

Recalling all its previous relevant resolutions, in particular resolutions 1595(2005) of 7 April 2005, 1636(2005) of 31 October 2005 and 1644(2005) of 15 December 2005,

Reiterating its call for the strict respect of the sovereignty, territorial integrity, unity and political independence of Lebanon under the sole and exclusive authority of the Government of Lebanon,

Mindful of the demand of the Lebanese people that all those responsible for the terrorist bombing that killed former Prime Minister of Lebanon Rafiq Hariri and others be identified and brought to justice,

Recalling the letter dated 13 December 2005 from the Prime Minister of Lebanon to the Secretary-General requesting, inter alia, the establishment of a tribunal of an international character to try all those who are found responsible for this terrorist crime, and recalling its request to the Secretary-General, in resolution 1644(2005), to help the Government of Lebanon to identify the nature and scope of the international assistance needed in this regard,

Having examined the report of 21 March 2006 submitted by the Secretary-General pursuant to paragraph 6 of resolution 1644(2005), and welcoming the common understanding reached between the Secretariat and the Lebanese authorities on the key issues regarding the establishment and the main features of a possible tribunal,

Willing to continue to assist Lebanon in the search for the truth and in holding all those involved in this terrorist attack accountable,

1. *Welcomes* the report of the Secretary-General, and requests him to negotiate an agreement with the Government of Lebanon aimed at establishing a tribunal of an international character based on the highest international standards of criminal justice, taking into account the recommendations contained in his report and the views that have been expressed by members of the Security Council;

2. *Acknowledges* that the adoption of the legal basis of, and framework for, the tribunal would not prejudice the gradual phasing-in of its various components and would not predetermine the timing of the commencement of its operations, which will depend on the progress of the investigation;

3. *Requests* the Secretary-General to update the Council on the progress of the negotiation as he deems appropriate and to submit in a timely manner for the consideration of the Council a report on the implementation of the present resolution, in particular on the draft agreement negotiated with the Government of Lebanon, including options for a funding mechanism appropriate to ensure the continued and effective functioning of the tribunal;

4. *Decides* to remain seized of the matter.

Special tribunal for Lebanon

Report of Secretary-General. As requested in Council resolution 1664(2006) (see above), the Secretary-General submitted a November report [S/2006/893] on the establishment of a special tribunal for Lebanon. The report analysed the main features of the statute of the special tribunal and the agreement between the United Nations and the Lebanese Government, and examined the legal nature of the tribunal; its temporal, personal and subject matter jurisdictions; organizational structure and composition; the conduct of the trial process; the location of the tribunal; the funding mechanism; and cooperation with third States. Annexed to the report were the draft agreement between the United Nations and the Lebanese Republic on the establishment of a special tribunal for Lebanon, including the Statute of the Special Tribunal; and an overview of the 14 cases pertaining to attacks perpetrated in Lebanon since 1 October 2004.

On 10 November, the Secretary-General transmitted to the Lebanese Prime Minister the draft agreement between the United Nations and the Lebanese Government on the establishment of a special tribunal for Lebanon. On 13 November, the Prime Minister informed the Secretary-General that the Lebanese Council of Ministers had agreed to the draft and looked forward to the completion of the remaining steps leading to the establishment of the tribunal. On 14 November, Lebanon forwarded to the Secretary-General a copy of observations made by the Lebanese President, including a challenge to the decision of the Council of Ministers. The negotiated instruments were submitted to the Security Council for its consideration.

A 21 November addendum to the Secretary-General's report [S/2006/893/Add.1] contained the statement made by the Under-Secretary-General for Legal Affairs, Nicolas Michel, during informal consulations of the Security Council held on 20 November. He said that the Lebanese constitutional process for the conclusion of an agreement with the United Nations had not been completed. Major steps remained to be taken, in particular formal approval by the Government, which was the prerequisite for the signature of the treaty and its submission for parliamentary approval and, ultimately, its ratification. Only after that process had been completed would Lebanon enter into an internationally binding commitment. The Under-Secretary-General also focused on the six characteristics of the tribunal: its jurisdiction; applicable criminal law; appointment of judges; funding; entry into force of the agreement and commencement of the functioning of the tribunal; and duration of the agreement. Lebanon needed the help of the international community to lay the foundation for lasting peace. As a precondition for that, steps had to be taken to end the impunity of the perpetrators of crimes, such as the assassination of former Prime Minister Hariri. On behalf of the Secretary-General, he invited the Security Council to take a decisive step towards justice and peace in Lebanon by supporting the draft text on the tribunal's establishment and the rest of the process.

Security Council communication. On 21 November [S/2006/911], the Security Council President informed the Secretary-General that the Council welcomed the conclusion of the negotiation with the Lebanese Government, as requested in resolution 1664(2006). The Council also recommended that 51 per cent of the expenses of the tribunal should be borne by voluntary contributions from States, and 49 per cent by the Lebanese Government. The Secretary-General would commence the process of establishing the tribunal when he had sufficient contributions in hand to do so for twelve months, plus pledges equal to the anticipated expenses of the following twenty-four months of the tribunal's operation. Should voluntary contributions be insufficient for the tribunal to implement its mandate, the Secretary-General and the Security Council should explore alternate means of financing the tribunal. The Council invited the Secretary-General to proceed with the final steps for the conclusion of the Agreement.

Communication. On the same date [S/2006/909], Syria said that the special tribunal should not be established until the completion of UNIIIC work. Moreover, it had not been consulted on the drafting of the two documents. Adoption of the statute of the "special tribunal" in such a manner would establish Syria's belief that it had no connection with that tribunal.

Syrian Arab Republic

In 2006, the General Assembly again called for Israel's withdrawal from the Golan Heights in the Syrian Arab Republic, which it had occupied since 1967. The area was effectively annexed by Israel when it extended its laws, jurisdiction and administration to the territory towards the end of 1981 [YUN 1981, p. 309].

The United Nations Disengagement Force (UNDOF) continued to supervise the ceasefire between Israel and the Syrian Arab Republic in the Golan Heights and ensure the separation of forces. The Mission's mandate was extended twice during the year.

Communications. The Syrian Arab Republic, on 4 January [S/2006/6], said that Israel was planning to divide the Syrian occupied village of al-Ghajar by erecting a boundary fence to bisect it. Israel was to transfer all villagers living north of the Blue Line to the southern part of the village and then build a security wall on the Blue Line, ultimately separating the southern and northern parts of the village. The northern part of the village was to remain with Lebanon, while the southern part was to fall under Israeli occupation. The division of the village and transfer of civilian population would lead to the confiscation of a 900-dunum area, thereby altering the demography of the village. Syria called on the international community to prevent al-Ghajar from being divided in a manner counter to international legitimacy and to end the human, social and economic suffering of its inhabitants.

On 29 June [A/60/912-S/2006/459], Syria said that Israeli military aircrafts flew over the Syrian coast on 28 June in violation of international law. The aggression constituted unacceptable and unjustified provocation and was a direct attack.

In identical letters of 5 December addressed to the Secretary-General and the Security Council President [A/61/609-S/2006/947], Syria expressed concern over the situation of Syrian detainees from the occupied Golan who were in Israeli prisons.

Committee on Israeli Practices. According to its annual report [A/61/500 & Add.1], the Committee on Israeli Practices visited Damascus, Syria, between 18 and 22 November. Syria reported to the Committee that Israeli settlement policy and land confiscation in the occupied Syrian Golan continued unabated. Forty-four Israeli settlements built on the ruins of Arab villages destroyed by the occupation had expanded; the largest one, Katzrin, had more than 18,000 settlers. The Government of Israel announced a massive project to encourage settlements in the occupied Golan, with the construction of new neighbourhoods, a factory, a winery and a luxury resort. The occupation authorities pursued their policy of using the water resources of the occupied Syrian Golan for themselves. Agriculture, which was the principal source of livelihood for Syrian Arab citizens of the occupied Golan, suffered from the Israeli policy of restricting their lands and production, while imposing taxes on agricultural products amounting to as much as 50 per cent of their value, leaving very little to the farmer. According to the Syrian report, Israeli mines were still a persistent threat as they were laid in areas adjacent to towns, villages and pastures, threatening the population and farm animals, as well as preventing inhabitants from freely accessing and exploiting their lands. Workers in the occupied Syrian Golan suffered from discrimination in hiring, wages and taxation. Unemployment was high and most of the workers were confined to insecure jobs. The health condition of the Syrian population in the occupied Golan had not improved since 2005, owing to continued lack of hospitals, medical clinics and basic health centres. Women were still deprived of basic health care and other facilities, leading to hard lives with little means to live on when close relatives were detained. Women and children were also among the some 2,500 Syrians held in Israeli detention facilities for the last 38 years. Many women and men in the occupied Golan had been suffering for years from the trauma of the separation of their families, some of whose members remained in Syria, while others were living in the occupied sector.

Reports of Secretary-General. In an August report [A/61/298], the Secretary-General submitted replies from three Member States, in response to his request for information on steps taken or envisaged to implement Assembly resolution 60/40 [YUN 2005, p. 573], which dealt with Israeli policies in the Syrian territory since 1967.

In September [A/61/327], the Secretary-General reported that no reply had been received from Israel to his June request for information on steps taken or envisaged to implement Assembly resolution 60/108

[YUN 2005, p. 574], which called on Israel to desist from changing the physical character, demographic composition, institutional structure and legal status of the Syrian Golan, and from its repressive measures against the population.

GENERAL ASSEMBLY ACTION

On 1 December [meeting 63], the General Assembly adopted **resolution 61/27** [draft: A/61/L.36] by recorded vote (107-6-60) [agenda item 13].

The Syrian Golan

The General Assembly,

Having considered the item entitled "The situation in the Middle East",

Taking note of the report of the Secretary-General,

Recalling Security Council resolution 497(1981) of 17 December 1981,

Reaffirming the fundamental principle of the inadmissibility of the acquisition of territory by force, in accordance with international law and the Charter of the United Nations,

Reaffirming once more the applicability of the Geneva Convention relative to the Protection of Civilian Persons in Time of War, of 12 August 1949, to the occupied Syrian Golan,

Deeply concerned that Israel has not withdrawn from the Syrian Golan, which has been under occupation since 1967, contrary to the relevant Security Council and General Assembly resolutions,

Stressing the illegality of the Israeli settlement construction and other activities in the occupied Syrian Golan since 1967,

Noting with satisfaction the convening in Madrid on 30 October 1991 of the Peace Conference on the Middle East, on the basis of Security Council resolutions 242(1967) of 22 November 1967, 338(1973) of 22 October 1973 and 425(1978) of 19 March 1978 and the formula of land for peace,

Expressing grave concern over the halt in the peace process on the Syrian track, and expressing the hope that peace talks will soon resume from the point they had reached,

1. *Declares* that Israel has failed so far to comply with Security Council resolution 497(1981);

2. *Also declares* that the Israeli decision of 14 December 1981 to impose its laws, jurisdiction and administration on the occupied Syrian Golan is null and void and has no validity whatsoever, as confirmed by the Security Council in its resolution 497(1981), and calls upon Israel to rescind it;

3. *Reaffirms its determination* that all relevant provisions of the Regulations annexed to the Hague Convention of 1907, and the Geneva Convention relative to the Protection of Civilian Persons in Time of War, continue to apply to the Syrian territory occupied by Israel since 1967, and calls upon the parties thereto to respect and ensure respect for their obligations under those instruments in all circumstances;

4. *Determines once more* that the continued occupation of the Syrian Golan and its de facto annexation constitute a stumbling block in the way of achieving a just, comprehensive and lasting peace in the region;

5. *Calls upon* Israel to resume the talks on the Syrian and Lebanese tracks and to respect the commitments and undertakings reached during the previous talks;

6. *Demands once more* that Israel withdraw from all the occupied Syrian Golan to the line of 4 June 1967 in implementation of the relevant Security Council resolutions;

7. *Calls upon* all the parties concerned, the co-sponsors of the peace process and the entire international community to exert all the necessary efforts to ensure the resumption of the peace process and its success by implementing Security Council resolutions 242(1967) and 338(1973);

8. *Requests* the Secretary-General to report to the General Assembly at its sixty-second session on the implementation of the present resolution.

RECORDED VOTE ON RESOLUTION 61/27:

In favour: Afghanistan, Algeria, Antigua and Barbuda, Argentina, Armenia, Azerbaijan, Bahamas, Bahrain, Bangladesh, Barbados, Belarus, Belize, Benin, Bhutan, Bolivia, Brazil, Brunei Darussalam, Burkina Faso, Cambodia, Cape Verde, Central African Republic, Chile, China, Colombia, Comoros, Congo, Costa Rica, Cuba, Democratic People's Republic of Korea, Djibouti, Dominica, Ecuador, Egypt, El Salvador, Eritrea, Ethiopia, Ghana, Grenada, Guatemala, Guinea, Guyana, Honduras, India, Indonesia, Iran, Iraq, Jamaica, Jordan, Kazakhstan, Kuwait, Kyrgyzstan, Lao People's Democratic Republic, Lebanon, Lesotho, Liberia, Libyan Arab Jamahiriya, Malaysia, Maldives, Mali, Mauritania, Mauritius, Mexico, Mongolia, Morocco, Mozambique, Myanmar, Namibia, Nepal, Nicaragua, Niger, Nigeria, Oman, Pakistan, Panama, Paraguay, Peru, Philippines, Qatar, Russian Federation, Saint Vincent and the Grenadines, Saudi Arabia, Senegal, Seychelles, Sierra Leone, Singapore, Somalia, South Africa, Sri Lanka, Sudan, Suriname, Syrian Arab Republic, Tajikistan, Thailand, Timor-Leste, Togo, Trinidad and Tobago, Tunisia, Turkey, Turkmenistan, Uganda, United Arab Emirates, Uruguay, Uzbekistan, Venezuela, Viet Nam, Yemen, Zambia.

Against: Canada, Israel, Marshall Islands, Micronesia, Palau, United States.

Abstaining: Albania, Andorra, Australia, Austria, Belgium, Bosnia and Herzegovina, Bulgaria, Burundi, Cameroon, Côte d'Ivoire, Croatia, Cyprus, Czech Republic, Denmark, Dominican Republic, Estonia, Fiji, Finland, France, Georgia, Germany, Greece, Haiti, Hungary, Iceland, Ireland, Italy, Japan, Latvia, Liechtenstein, Lithuania, Luxembourg, Malawi, Malta, Moldova, Monaco, Montenegro, Nauru, Netherlands, New Zealand, Norway, Papua New Guinea, Poland, Portugal, Republic of Korea, Romania, Samoa, San Marino, Serbia, Slovakia, Slovenia, Solomon Islands, Spain, Sweden, Switzerland, The former Yugoslav Republic of Macedonia, Tonga, Ukraine, United Kingdom, Vanuatu.

On 14 December [meeting 79], the Assembly, under the agenda item on the report of the Committee on Israeli Practices, and on the Fourth Committee's recommendation [A/61/408], adopted **resolution 61/120** by recorded vote (163-2-16) [agenda item 32].

The occupied Syrian Golan

The General Assembly,

Having considered the report of the Special Committee to Investigate Israeli Practices Affecting the Human Rights of the Palestinian People and Other Arabs of the Occupied Territories,

Deeply concerned that the Syrian Golan, occupied since 1967, has been under continued Israeli military occupation,

Recalling Security Council resolution 497(1981) of 17 December 1981,

Recalling also its previous relevant resolutions, the most recent of which was resolution 60/108 of 8 December 2005,

Having considered the report of the Secretary-General submitted in pursuance of resolution 60/108,

Recalling its previous relevant resolutions in which, inter alia, it called upon Israel to put an end to its occupation of the Arab territories,

Reaffirming once more the illegality of the decision of 14 December 1981 taken by Israel to impose its laws, jurisdiction and administration on the occupied Syrian Golan, which has resulted in the effective annexation of that territory,

Reaffirming that the acquisition of territory by force is inadmissible under international law, including the Charter of the United Nations,

Reaffirming also the applicability of the Geneva Convention relative to the Protection of Civilian Persons in Time of War, of 12 August 1949, to the occupied Syrian Golan,

Bearing in mind Security Council resolution 237(1967) of 14 June 1967,

Welcoming the convening at Madrid of the Peace Conference on the Middle East on the basis of Security Council resolutions 242(1967) of 22 November 1967 and 338(1973) of 22 October 1973 aimed at the realization of a just, comprehensive and lasting peace, and expressing grave concern about the stalling of the peace process on all tracks,

1. *Calls upon* Israel, the occupying Power, to comply with the relevant resolutions on the occupied Syrian Golan, in particular Security Council resolution 497(1981), in which the Council, inter alia, decided that the Israeli decision to impose its laws, jurisdiction and administration on the occupied Syrian Golan was null and void and without international legal effect and demanded that Israel, the occupying Power, rescind forthwith its decision;

2. *Also calls upon* Israel to desist from changing the physical character, demographic composition, institutional structure and legal status of the occupied Syrian Golan and in particular to desist from the establishment of settlements;

3. *Determines* that all legislative and administrative measures and actions taken or to be taken by Israel, the occupying Power, that purport to alter the character and legal status of the occupied Syrian Golan are null and void, constitute a flagrant violation of international law and of the Geneva Convention relative to the Protection of Civilian Persons in Time of War, of 12 August 1949, and have no legal effect;

4. *Calls upon* Israel to desist from imposing Israeli citizenship and Israeli identity cards on the Syrian citizens in the occupied Syrian Golan, and from its repressive measures against the population of the occupied Syrian Golan;

5. *Deplores* the violations by Israel of the Geneva Convention relative to the Protection of Civilian Persons in Time of War, of 12 August 1949;

6. *Calls once again upon* Member States not to recognize any of the legislative or administrative measures and actions referred to above;

7. *Requests* the Secretary-General to report to the General Assembly at its sixty-second session on the implementation of the present resolution.

RECORDED VOTE ON RESOLUTION 61/120:

In favour: Afghanistan, Albania, Algeria, Andorra, Antigua and Barbuda, Argentina, Armenia, Australia, Austria, Azerbaijan, Bahamas, Bahrain, Bangladesh, Barbados, Belarus, Belgium, Belize, Benin, Bhutan, Bolivia, Bosnia and Herzegovina, Botswana, Brazil, Brunei Darussalam, Bulgaria, Burkina Faso, Cambodia, Canada, Cape Verde, Central African Republic, Chad, Chile, China, Colombia, Comoros, Congo, Costa Rica, Croatia, Cuba, Cyprus, Czech Republic, Democratic People's Republic of Korea, Denmark, Djibouti, Dominica, Ecuador, Egypt, El Salvador, Eritrea, Estonia, Ethiopia, Finland, France, Gabon, Georgia, Germany, Ghana, Greece, Grenada, Guatemala, Guinea, Guinea-Bissau, Guyana, Honduras, Hungary, Iceland, India, Indonesia, Iran, Iraq, Ireland, Italy, Jamaica, Japan, Jordan, Kazakhstan, Kenya, Kuwait, Kyrgyzstan, Lao People's Democratic Republic, Latvia, Lebanon, Lesotho, Libyan Arab Jamahiriya, Liechtenstein, Lithuania, Luxembourg, Malaysia, Maldives, Mali, Malta, Mauritania, Mauritius, Mexico, Moldova, Monaco, Mongolia, Montenegro, Morocco, Mozambique, Myanmar, Namibia, Nepal, Netherlands, New Zealand, Nicaragua, Niger, Nigeria, Norway, Oman, Pakistan, Panama, Paraguay, Peru, Philippines, Poland, Portugal, Qatar, Republic of Korea, Romania, Russian Federation, Saint Lucia, Saint Vincent and the Grenadines, Samoa, San Marino, Sao Tome and Principe, Saudi Arabia, Senegal, Serbia, Sierra Leone, Singapore, Slovakia, Slovenia, Solomon Islands, South Africa, Spain, Sri Lanka, Sudan, Suriname, Sweden, Switzerland, Syrian Arab Republic, Tajikistan, Thailand, The former Yugoslav Republic of Macedonia, Timor-Leste, Togo, Trinidad and Tobago, Tunisia, Turkey, Turkmenistan, Uganda, Ukraine, United Arab Emirates, United Kingdom, United Republic of Tanzania, Uruguay, Uzbekistan, Venezuela, Viet Nam, Yemen, Zambia, Zimbabwe.

Against: Israel, Tuvalu.

Abstaining: Burundi, Cameroon, Côte d'Ivoire, Dominican Republic, Equatorial Guinea, Fiji, Haiti, Malawi, Marshall Islands, Micronesia, Nauru, Palau, Papua New Guinea, Tonga, United States, Vanuatu.

UNDOF

The mandate of the United Nations Disengagement Force (UNDOF), established by Security Council resolution 350(1974) [YUN 1974, p. 205] to supervise the observance of the ceasefire between Israel and the Syrian Arab Republic in the Golan

Heights and ensure the separation of their forces, was renewed twice in 2006, in June and December, each time for a six-month period.

UNDOF maintained an area of separation, which was some 75 kilometres long and varied in width between approximately 12.5 kilometres in the centre to less than 200 metres in the extreme south. The area of separation was inhabited and policed by the Syrian authorities, and no military forces other than UNDOF were permitted within it.

On 8 February [S/2006/100], the Secretary-General informed the Security Council President of the withdrawal by Canada of its logistic support element from UNDOF and the retention of only two staff officer positions. Following India's offer to replace the Canadian component, the Secretary-General intended to add India to the list of countries that had agreed to provide military personnel to UNDOF. On 13 February [S/2006/101], the Council took note of the Secretary-General's intention.

As at 15 November, UNDOF comprised 1,025 troops from Austria (372), Canada (2), India (190), Japan (30), Nepal (2), Poland (334) and Slovakia (95). It was assisted by 83 UNTSO military observers. Lieutenant-General Bala Nanda Sharma (Nepal) continued as Force Commander.

Reports of Secretary-General. The Secretary-General reported to the Security Council on UNDOF activities between 10 December 2005 and 1 June 2006 [S/2006/333] and between 10 June and 1 December 2006 [S/2006/938]. Both reports noted that UNDOF area of operation remained calm, except in the Shab'a farms area. Between 12 July and 14 August, rockets originating from UNIFIL area of operation hit close to UNDOF installations, destroying one UN unmanned watchtower.

UNDOF continued to supervise the area of separation between Israeli and Syrian troops in the Golan Heights, ensuring by means of fixed positions and patrols that no military forces of either party were deployed there. The Force, accompanied by liaison officers from the parties concerned, carried out fortnightly inspections of equipment and force levels in the area of limitation. As in the past, both sides denied inspection teams access to some of their positions and imposed restrictions on the Force's freedom of movement. UNDOF continued to assist the International Committee of the Red Cross with the passage of persons through the area of separation, and provided medical treatment to the local population upon request. Mines, especially in the area of separation, continued to pose a threat to UNDOF personnel and local inhabitants, and the Force carried out operational mine clearance, supporting UNICEF in mine-awareness activities.

The Secretary-General observed that the situation in the Middle East was tense and was likely to remain so, unless and until a comprehensive settlement covering all aspects of the problem could be reached. He hoped that determined efforts would be made by all concerned to tackle the problem in all its aspects, with a view to arriving at a just and durable peace settlement, as called for by Council resolution 338(1973) [YUN 1973, p. 213]. Stating that he considered the Force's continued presence in the area to be essential, the Secretary-General, with the agreement of both Israel and Syria, recommended, in June, that UNDOF mandate be extended until 30 June 2007.

SECURITY COUNCIL ACTION

On 13 June [meeting 5456], the Security Council unanimously adopted **resolution 1685(2006).** The draft [S/2006/373] was prepared in consultations among Council members.

The Security Council,

Having considered the report of the Secretary-General of 1 June 2006 on the United Nations Disengagement Observer Force, and reaffirming its resolution 1308(2000) of 17 July 2000,

1. *Calls upon* the parties concerned to implement immediately its resolution 338(1973) of 22 October 1973;
2. *Welcomes* the efforts being undertaken by the United Nations Disengagement Observer Force to implement the Secretary-General's zero-tolerance policy on sexual exploitation and abuse and to ensure full compliance of its personnel with the United Nations code of conduct, requests the Secretary-General to continue to take all necessary action in this regard and to keep the Security Council informed, and urges troop-contributing countries to take preventive and disciplinary action to ensure that such acts are properly investigated and punished in cases involving their personnel;
3. *Decides* to renew the mandate of the Force for a period of six months, that is, until 31 December 2006;
4. *Requests* the Secretary-General to submit, at the end of this period, a report on developments in the situation and the measures taken to implement resolution 338(1973).

On 15 December [meeting 5596], the Council unanimously adopted **resolution 1729(2006).** The draft [S/2006/973] was prepared during consultations among Council members.

The Security Council,

Having considered the report of the Secretary-General of 4 December 2006 on the United Nations Disengagement Observer Force, and reaffirming its resolution 1308(2000) of 17 July 2000,

1. *Calls upon* the parties concerned to implement immediately its resolution 338(1973) of 22 October 1973;
2. *Welcomes* the efforts being undertaken by the United Nations Disengagement Observer Force to im-

plement the Secretary-General's zero-tolerance policy on sexual exploitation and abuse and to ensure full compliance of its personnel with the United Nations code of conduct, requests the Secretary-General to continue to take all necessary action in this regard and to keep the Security Council informed, and urges troop-contributing countries to take preventive and disciplinary action to ensure that such acts are properly investigated and punished in cases involving their personnel;

3. *Decides* to renew the mandate of the Force for a period of six months, that is, until 30 June 2007;

4. *Requests* the Secretary-General to submit, at the end of this period, a report on developments in the situation and the measures taken to implement resolution 338(1973).

After adopting each resolution, the President, following consultations among Council members, made identical statements **S/PRST/2006/26** [meeting 5456] on 13 June and **S/PRST/2006/54** [meeting 5596] on 15 December, on behalf of the Council:

"In connection with the resolution just adopted on the renewal of the mandate of the United Nations Disengagement Observer Force, I have been authorized to make the following complementary statement on behalf of the Security Council:

'As is known, the report of the Secretary-General on the United Nations Disengagement Observer Force states in paragraph 12: "... the situation in the Middle East is very tense and is likely to remain so, unless and until a comprehensive settlement covering all aspects of the Middle East problem can be reached". That statement of the Secretary-General reflects the view of the Security Council.'"

Financing

The General Assembly had before it the performance report on UNDOF budget for 1 July 2004 to 30 June 2005 [A/60/628 & Corr.1], which showed expenditures totalling $40,819,900 against an apportionment of $40,902,100. It also had before it the UNDOF budget for the period from 1 July 2006 to 30 June 2007 [A/60/641 & Corr. 2], totalling $39,975,900, and ACABQ comments and recommendations thereon [A/60/811].

GENERAL ASSEMBLY ACTION

On 30 June [meeting 92], the General Assembly, on the recommendation of the Fifth Committee [A/60/925], adopted **resolution 60/277** without vote [agenda item 149 *(a)*].

Financing of the United Nations Disengagement Observer Force

The General Assembly,

Having considered the reports of the Secretary-General on the financing of the United Nations Disengagement Observer Force and the related report of the Advisory Committee on Administrative and Budgetary Questions,

Recalling Security Council resolution 350 (1974) of 31 May 1974 regarding the establishment of the United Nations Disengagement Observer Force and the subsequent resolutions by which the Council extended the mandate of the Force, the latest of which was resolution 1648 (2005) of 21 December 2005,

Recalling also its resolution 3211 B (XXIX) of 29 November 1974 on the financing of the United Nations Emergency Force and of the United Nations Disengagement Observer Force and its subsequent resolutions thereon, the latest of which was resolution 59/306 of 22 June 2005,

Reaffirming the general principles underlying the financing of United Nations peacekeeping operations, as stated in General Assembly resolutions 1874 (S-IV) of 27 June 1963, 3101 (XXVIII) of 11 December 1973 and 55/235 of 23 December 2000,

Mindful of the fact that it is essential to provide the Force with the necessary financial resources to enable it to fulfil its responsibilities under the relevant resolutions of the Security Council,

1. *Requests* the Secretary-General to entrust the Head of Mission with the task of formulating future budget proposals in full accordance with the provisions of General Assembly resolutions 59/296 of 22 June 2005 and 60/266 of 30 June 2006, as well as other relevant resolutions;

2. *Takes note* of the status of contributions to the United Nations Disengagement Observer Force as at 30 April 2006, including the contributions outstanding in the amount of 20.1 million United States dollars, representing some 1 per cent of the total assessed contributions, notes with concern that only forty-nine Member States have paid their assessed contributions in full, and urges all other Member States, in particular those in arrears, to ensure the payment of their outstanding assessed contributions;

3. *Expresses its appreciation* to those Member States which have paid their assessed contributions in full, and urges all other Member States to make every possible effort to ensure payment of their assessed contributions to the Force in full;

4. *Expresses concern* at the financial situation with regard to peacekeeping activities, in particular as regards the reimbursements to troop contributors that bear additional burdens owing to overdue payments by Member States of their assessments;

5. *Also expresses concern* at the delay experienced by the Secretary-General in deploying and providing adequate resources to some recent peacekeeping missions, in particular those in Africa;

6. *Emphasizes* that all future and existing peacekeeping missions shall be given equal and non-discriminatory treatment in respect of financial and administrative arrangements;

7. *Also emphasizes* that all peacekeeping missions shall be provided with adequate resources for the effective and efficient discharge of their respective mandates;

8. *Reiterates its request* to the Secretary-General to make the fullest possible use of facilities and equipment

at the United Nations Logistics Base at Brindisi, Italy, in order to minimize the costs of procurement for the Force;

9. *Endorses* the conclusions and recommendations contained in the report of the Advisory Committee on Administrative and Budgetary Questions, and requests the Secretary-General to ensure their full implementation;

10. *Requests* the Secretary-General to ensure the full implementation of the relevant provisions of its resolutions 59/296 and 60/266;

11. *Also requests* the Secretary-General to take all necessary action to ensure that the Force is administered with a maximum of efficiency and economy;

12. *Further requests* the Secretary-General, in order to reduce the cost of employing General Service staff, to continue efforts to recruit local staff for the Force against General Service posts, commensurate with the requirements of the Force;

Financial performance report for the period from 1 July 2004 to 30 June 2005

13. *Takes note* of the report of the Secretary-General on the financial performance of the Force for the period from 1 July 2004 to 30 June 2005;

Budget estimates for the period from 1 July 2006 to 30 June 2007

14. *Decides* to appropriate to the Special Account for the United Nations Disengagement Observer Force the amount of 41,588,400 dollars for the period from 1 July 2006 to 30 June 2007, inclusive of 39,865,200 dollars for the maintenance of the Force, 1,423,300 dollars for the support account for peacekeeping operations and 299,900 dollars for the United Nations Logistics Base;

Financing of the appropriation

15. *Decides also* to apportion among Member States the amount of 41,588,400 dollars at a monthly rate of 3,465,700 dollars, in accordance with the levels updated in General Assembly resolution 58/256 of 23 December 2003, and taking into account the scale of assessments for 2006, as set out in its resolution 58/1 B of 23 December 2003, and the scale of assessments for 2007, subject to a decision of the Security Council to extend the mandate of the Force;

16. *Decides further* that, in accordance with the provisions of its resolution 973 (X) of 15 December 1955, there shall be set off against the apportionment among Member States, as provided for in paragraph 15 above, their respective share in the Tax Equalization Fund of 1,249,400 dollars, comprising the estimated staff assessment income of 1,066,600 dollars approved for the Force for the period from 1 July 2006 to 30 June 2007, the prorated share of 160,100 dollars of the estimated staff assessment income approved for the support account and the prorated share of 22,700 dollars of the estimated staff assessment income approved for the United Nations Logistics Base;

17. *Decides* that, for Member States that have fulfilled their financial obligations to the Force, there shall be set off against their apportionment, as provided for in paragraph 15 above, their respective share of the unencumbered balance and other income in the amount of 1,983,300 dollars in respect of the financial period ended 30 June 2005, in accordance with the levels updated in its resolution 58/256 and taking into account the scale of assessments for 2005, as set out in its resolution 58/1 B;

18. *Decides also* that, for Member States that have not fulfilled their financial obligations to the Force, there shall be set off against their outstanding obligations their respective share of the unencumbered balance and other income in the amount of 1,983,300 dollars in respect of the financial period ended 30 June 2005, in accordance with the scheme set out in paragraph 17 above;

19. *Decides further* that the decrease of 101,500 dollars in the estimated staff assessment income in respect of the financial period ended 30 June 2005 shall be set off against the credits from the amount of 1,983,300 dollars referred to in paragraphs 17 and 18 above;

20. *Emphasizes* that no peacekeeping mission shall be financed by borrowing funds from other active peacekeeping missions;

21. *Encourages* the Secretary-General to continue to take additional measures to ensure the safety and security of all personnel under the auspices of the United Nations participating in the Force, bearing in mind paragraphs 5 and 6 of Security Council resolution 1502(2003) of 26 August 2003;

22. *Invites* voluntary contributions to the Force in cash and in the form of services and supplies acceptable to the Secretary-General, to be administered, as appropriate, in accordance with the procedure and practices established by the General Assembly;

23. *Decides* to include in the provisional agenda of its sixty-first session, under the item entitled "Financing of the United Nations peacekeeping forces in the Middle East", the sub-item entitled "United Nations Disengagement Observer Force".

Chapter VII

Disarmament

In 2006, the United Nations reinforced efforts to mobilize the international community for concerted and more intensive action towards overcoming current disarmament and non-proliferation challenges, including persisting differences among Member States, which limited progress in multilateral disarmament fora. To that end, the General Assembly declared the 2010s as the Fourth Disarmament Decade, following three previous decades that had covered the 1970s, 1980s and 1990s, all aimed at advancing disarmament norms and measures. In related action, the Assembly continued to promote the idea of convening a fourth special session devoted to disarmament, the aim of which would be to define the future course of action on disarmament and associated international security questions, and enhance the gains made at the first, second and third special sessions held in 1978, 1982 and 1988, respectively. In April, relative progress was made in settling some of the issues dividing Member States on disarmament questions, following the achievement of consensus within the Disarmament Commission on a work programme, which helped resolve a two-year deadlock and consequent suspension of its work. That breakthrough enabled the Commission to resume substantive meetings to consider recommendations for achieving nuclear disarmament and practical confidence-building measures in the field of conventional weapons. Unfortunately, such progress eluded the Conference on Disarmament, which, despite 49 formal and 22 informal meetings, still could not achieve consensus on its programme of work, nor undertake any substantive work on its agenda items for the eighth consecutive year.

In June, the independent international Weapons of Mass Destruction Commission, chaired by the former head of the UN Monitoring,Verification and Inspection Commission, Hans Blix, transmitted its report to the General Assembly containing proposals on how to rid the world of weapons of mass destruction (WMDs) (nuclear, chemical and biological). Determined to further reinforce existing institutional mechanisms for tackling international terrorism, the Assembly adopted, in September, a United Nations Global Counter-Terrorism Strategy, based on earlier recommendations from the Secretary-General. Annexed to that Strategy was a plan of action, by which Member States resolved to take measures to prevent terrorists from acquiring WMDs. On 8 September, the growing movement to fortify the nuclear non-proliferation regime through the adoption of legally-binding agreements designating whole geographic regions as nuclear-weapon-free zones achieved marked progress, following the adoption of the Treaty on a Nuclear-Weapon-Free Zone in Central Asia. It was the fifth Zone of its kind to be declared worldwide and the first to be located entirely in the northern hemisphere.

However, the optimism generated by those encouraging developments was tempered by widespread anxiety following a 9 October announcement by the Democratic People's Republic of Korea that it had tested a nuclear weapon, only a few months after having launched ballistic missiles capable of delivering WMD payloads. Similar concerns were raised by Iran's decision to resume research and development activities on its nuclear energy programme, as well as uranium conversion and enrichment. Alarmed by the potential threat which the actions of both States posed to the nuclear non-proliferation regime and to regional and international stability, the Security Council, in resolutions 1718(2006) (see p. 444) and 1737(2006) (see p. 436), respectively, firmly condemned those activities and imposed an arms embargo and other sanctions against them.

Notable developments in the field of conventional arms control included the Assembly's resolve to begin exploring the possibility of an arms trade treaty, providing common international standards for the import, export and transfer of conventional arms. The Assembly asked the Secretary-General to seek the views of Member States on the idea and to establish a group of governmental experts to examine the feasibility and scope of the proposed instrument and report thereon in 2008.

Member States also continued to deal with disarmament and international security issues stemming from the proliferation of small arms and light weapons, mostly within the framework of the Programme of Action adopted at the 2001 UN Conference on small arms. However, an opportunity for consolidating the gains made since then was missed when the UN Conference to Review progress in implementing the Programme concluded, in July, without adopting a final document, owing to discord among delegates on several small arms-related issues. Despite that setback, the Assembly continued to seek ways of advancing conventional disarmament. It adopted a resolution requesting the Secretary-General to establish another group of governmental experts to examine how to strengthen collaboration in confronting the problem of surplus conventional ammunition stockpiles. Meanwhile, the Group of Governmental Experts appointed by the Secretary-General to review the status of the UN Register of Conventional Arms proposed measures for strengthening its operation and future development, aimed at enhancing transparency in conventional armaments as a major confidence-building measure.

On 12 November, the international framework for tackling humanitarian problems caused by leftover explosives in a post-conflict environment received a boost from the entry into force of the Protocol on Explosive Remnants of War (Protocol V) to the 1980 Convention on Prohibitions or Restrictions on the Use of Certain Conventional Weapons Which May Be Deemed to Be Excessively Injurious or to Have Indiscriminate Effects. At their Third Review Conference, States Parties to that Convention adopted a Final Declaration reaffirming their commitment to comply with the Convention's objectives, and a plan of action outlining specific measures for promoting its universality. The same month, the Sixth Review Conference of the States Parties to the Convention on the Prohibition of the Development, Production and Stockpiling of Bacteriological (Biological) and Toxin Weapons and on Their Destruction adopted a declaration and a series of decisions and recommendations designed to strengthen its effectiveness.

At the bilateral level, Russian President Vladimir Putin proposed negotiations with the United States on a new treaty to replace their 1991 Treaty on the Reduction and Limitation of Strategic Offensive Arms (START I) agreement, which had committed both sides to limiting to approximately 6,000, the number of nuclear warheads they could each deploy, and which was scheduled to expire in 2009. In a related development, the two countries extended for another seven years their 1992 Cooperative Threat Reduction Agreement, designed to prevent the proliferation of WMDs, and launched the Global Initiative to Combat Nuclear Terrorism. Both sides also continued to implement their 2002 Strategic Offensive Reductions Treaty (Moscow Treaty), for reducing the level of their deployed strategic nuclear warheads to between 3000 and 3500 by 31 December 2012.

UN role in disarmament

UN machinery

In 2006, disarmament issues before the United Nations were considered mainly through the Security Council, the General Assembly and its First (Disarmament and International Security) Committee, the Disarmament Commission (a deliberative body) and the Conference on Disarmament (a multilateral negotiating forum, which met in Geneva). In addition, the Organization maintained efforts to engage civil society organizations concerned with disarmament issues.

The UN Department for Disarmament Affairs (DDA) continued to support the work of Member States and treaty bodies, service the Advisory Board on Disarmament Matters and administer the UN disarmament fellowship programme.

Fourth disarmament decade

Concerned with the current disarmament, non-proliferation and international security climate, the General Assembly determined that a fourth disarmament decade could help mobilize international efforts to meet disarmament and related challenges and directed the Disarmament Commission to prepare, in 2009, elements of a draft declaration on the 2010s as the fourth disarmament decade, for consideration during its sixty-fourth (2009) session.

The First Disarmament Decade, covering the 1970s, was proclaimed in 1969 in Assembly resolution 2602 E (XXIV) [YUN 1969, p. 22], the Second, addressing the 1980s, was declared in Assembly resolution 35/46 [YUN 1980, p. 102], while the Third, spanning the 1990s, was initiated in 1989 by Assembly resolution 43/78 L [YUN 1988, p. 46]. All were designed to promote international disarmament and non-proliferation measures, with the ultimate aim of general and complete disarmament under effective international control, and the economic and social advancement of developing countries.

GENERAL ASSEMBLY ACTION

On 6 December [meeting 67], the General Assembly, on the recommendation of the First Committee [A/61/394], adopted **resolution 61/67** by recorded vote (123-1-52) [agenda item 90].

Declaration of a fourth disarmament decade

The General Assembly,

Recalling its previous resolutions on arms control, disarmament and non-proliferation, in particular those relating to its declaration of the First, Second and Third Disarmament Decades,

Reaffirming the validity of the Final Document of the Tenth Special Session of the General Assembly, the first special session devoted to disarmament,

Recalling the conclusion of the Secretary-General in his latest report to the General Assembly on the work of the Organization, inter alia, that if ever there was a time to break the deadlock in multilateral negotiations and bring disarmament back into the limelight of the international agenda, it is now,

Seriously concerned at the current disarmament, non-proliferation and international security climate,

Recognizing the urgent need to mobilize concerted and more intensive global efforts to reverse the current trend in the field of arms control, disarmament and non-proliferation, including, where appropriate, indicative targets for accelerating attainment of the objectives of general and complete disarmament under effective international control,

Conscious of the role that a fourth disarmament decade could play in the mobilization of such global efforts to meet current and emerging challenges in the area of arms control, disarmament, non-proliferation and international security,

Directs the Disarmament Commission, at its 2009 substantive session, to prepare elements of a draft declaration of the 2010s as the fourth disarmament decade and to submit them for consideration by the General Assembly at its sixty-fourth session.

RECORDED VOTE ON RESOLUTION 61/67:

In favour: Afghanistan, Algeria, Angola, Antigua and Barbuda, Argentina, Bahamas, Bahrain, Bangladesh, Barbados, Belarus, Belize, Bhutan, Bolivia, Brazil, Brunei Darussalam, Burkina Faso, Burundi, Cambodia, Cameroon, Canada, Cape Verde, Central African Republic, Chad, Chile, China, Colombia, Comoros, Congo, Costa Rica, Côte d'Ivoire, Cuba, Democratic People's Republic of Korea, Democratic Republic of the Congo, Djibouti, Dominica, Dominican Republic, Ecuador, Egypt, El Salvador, Eritrea, Ethiopia, Fiji, Gabon, Gambia, Ghana, Grenada, Guatemala, Guinea, Guyana, Haiti, Honduras, India, Indonesia, Iran, Iraq, Jamaica, Jordan, Kazakhstan, Kuwait, Kyrgyzstan, Lao People's Democratic Republic, Lebanon, Lesotho, Liberia, Libyan Arab Jamahiriya, Malawi, Malaysia, Maldives, Mali, Mauritania, Mauritius, Mexico, Mongolia, Morocco, Mozambique, Myanmar, Namibia, Nauru, Nepal, Nicaragua, Niger, Nigeria, Oman, Pakistan, Panama, Papua New Guinea, Paraguay, Peru, Philippines, Qatar, Russian Federation, Rwanda, Saint Kitts and Nevis, Saint Lucia, Saint Vincent and the Grenadines, Sao Tome and Principe, Saudi Arabia, Senegal, Sierra Leone, Singapore, Solomon Islands, South Africa, Sri Lanka, Sudan, Suriname, Swaziland, Syrian Arab Republic, Tajikistan, Thailand, Timor-Leste, Togo, Trinidad and Tobago, Tunisia, Turkmenistan, United Arab Emirates, United Republic of Tanzania, Uruguay, Uzbekistan, Venezuela, Viet Nam, Yemen, Zambia, Zimbabwe.

Against: United States.

Abstaining: Albania, Andorra, Armenia, Australia, Austria, Azerbaijan, Belgium, Bosnia and Herzegovina, Bulgaria, Croatia, Cyprus, Czech Republic, Denmark, Estonia, Finland, France, Georgia, Germany, Greece, Hungary, Iceland, Ireland, Israel, Italy, Japan, Latvia, Liechtenstein, Lithuania, Luxembourg, Malta, Moldova, Monaco, Montenegro, Netherlands, New Zealand, Norway, Palau, Poland, Portugal, Republic of Korea, Romania, San Marino, Serbia, Slovakia, Slovenia, Spain, Sweden, Switzerland, The former Yugoslav Republic of Macedonia, Turkey, Ukraine, United Kingdom.

Fourth special session devoted to disarmament

The General Assembly had decided, by resolution 51/45 C [YUN 1996, p. 447], to convene the fourth special session of the Assembly devoted to disarmament in 1999, subject to the emergence of a consensus on its agenda and objectives. It had not been possible to achieve such consensus over the years, despite efforts to facilitate agreement through an open-ended working group established to consider the issue in Assembly resolutions 57/61 [YUN 2002, p. 487] and 59/71 [YUN 2004, p. 522].

By **decision 60/559** of 6 June, 2006, the Assembly decided to re-establish at a later date, an open-ended working group to further consider the objectives and agenda for the session, including the possible establishment of a preparatory committee. In further action, in December (see below), the Assembly established the group and asked it to hold an organizational session to set the date for its 2007 substantive sessions and to report on its work before the end of the Assembly's sixty-first (2006) session.

GENERAL ASSEMBLY ACTION

On 6 December [meeting 67], the General Assembly, on the recommendation of the First Committee [A/61/394], adopted **resolution 61/60** by recorded vote (175-1-0) [agenda item 90 *(dd)*].

Convening of the fourth special session of the General Assembly devoted to disarmament

The General Assembly,

Recalling its resolutions 49/75 I of 15 December 1994, 50/70 F of 12 December 1995, 51/45 C of 10 December 1996, 52/38 F of 9 December 1997, 53/77 AA of 4 December 1998, 54/54 U of 1 December 1999, 55/33 M of 20 November 2000, 56/24 D of 29 November 2001, 57/61 of 22 November 2002 and 59/71 of 3 December 2004, as well as its decisions 58/521 of 8 December 2003, 60/518 of 8 December 2005 and 60/559 of 6 June 2006,

Recalling also that, there being a consensus to do so in each case, three special sessions of the General Assembly devoted to disarmament were held in 1978, 1982 and 1988 respectively,

Bearing in mind the Final Document of the Tenth Special Session of the General Assembly, adopted by consensus at the first special session devoted to disarmament,

Bearing in mind also the ultimate objective of general and complete disarmament under effective international control,

Taking note of paragraph 80 of the Final Document of the Fourteenth Conference of Heads of State or Government of Non-Aligned Countries, held at Havana on 15 and 16 September 2006, which supported the convening of the fourth special session of the General Assembly devoted to disarmament, which would offer an opportunity to review, from a perspective more in tune with the current international situation, the most critical aspects of the process of disarmament and to mobilize the international community and public opinion in favour of the elimination of nuclear and other weapons of mass destruction and of the control and reduction of conventional weapons,

Recalling the United Nations Millennium Declaration, adopted by the Heads of State and Government during the Millennium Summit of the United Nations, held in New York from 6 to 8 September 2000, in which they resolved "to strive for the elimination of weapons of mass destruction, particularly nuclear weapons, and to keep all options open for achieving this aim, including the possibility of convening an international conference to identify ways of eliminating nuclear dangers",

Reiterating its conviction that a special session of the General Assembly devoted to disarmament can set the future course of action in the fields of disarmament, arms control, non-proliferation and related international security matters,

Emphasizing the importance of multilateralism in the process of disarmament, arms control, non-proliferation and related international security matters,

Taking note of the report of the Open-ended Working Group to consider the objectives and agenda, including the possible establishment of the preparatory committee, for the fourth special session of the General Assembly devoted to disarmament,

1. *Decides* to establish an open-ended working group, working on the basis of consensus, to consider the objectives and agenda, including the possible establishment of the preparatory committee, for the fourth special session of the General Assembly devoted to disarmament, taking note of the paper presented by the Chairman of Working Group II during the 1999 substantive session of the Disarmament Commission and the written proposals and views submitted by Member States as contained in the working papers presented during the three substantive sessions of the Open-ended Working Group in 2003 as well as the reports of the Secretary-General regarding the views of Member States on the objectives, agenda and timing of the fourth special session of the General Assembly devoted to disarmament;

2. *Requests* the Open-ended Working Group to hold an organizational session in order to set the date for its substantive sessions in 2007 and to submit a report on its work, including possible substantive recommendations, before the end of the sixty-first session of the General Assembly;

3. *Requests* the Secretary-General, within existing resources, to provide the Open-ended Working Group with the necessary assistance and services as may be required to discharge its tasks;

4. *Decides* to include in the provisional agenda of its sixty-second session the item entitled "Convening of the fourth special session of the General Assembly devoted to disarmament".

RECORDED VOTE ON RESOLUTION 61/60:

In favour: Afghanistan, Albania, Algeria, Andorra, Angola, Antigua and Barbuda, Argentina, Armenia, Australia, Austria, Azerbaijan, Bahamas, Bahrain, Bangladesh, Barbados, Belarus, Belgium, Belize, Bhutan, Bolivia, Bosnia and Herzegovina, Brazil, Brunei Darussalam, Bulgaria, Burkina Faso, Burundi, Cambodia, Cameroon, Canada, Cape Verde, Central African Republic, Chile, China, Colombia, Comoros, Congo, Costa Rica, Côte d'Ivoire, Croatia, Cuba, Cyprus, Czech Republic, Democratic People's Republic of Korea, Democratic Republic of the Congo, Denmark, Djibouti, Dominica, Dominican Republic, Ecuador, Egypt, El Salvador, Eritrea, Estonia, Ethiopia, Fiji, Finland, France, Gabon, Georgia, Germany, Ghana, Greece, Grenada, Guatemala, Guinea, Guyana, Haiti, Honduras, Hungary, Iceland, India, Indonesia, Iran, Iraq, Ireland, Israel, Italy, Jamaica, Japan, Jordan, Kazakhstan, Kuwait, Kyrgyzstan, Lao People's Democratic Republic, Latvia, Lebanon, Lesotho, Liberia, Libyan Arab Jamahiriya, Liechtenstein, Lithuania, Luxembourg, Malawi, Malaysia, Maldives, Mali, Malta, Mauritania, Mauritius, Mexico, Micronesia, Moldova, Monaco, Mongolia, Montenegro, Morocco, Mozambique, Myanmar, Namibia, Nauru, Nepal, Netherlands, New Zealand, Nicaragua, Niger, Nigeria, Norway, Oman, Pakistan, Palau, Panama, Paraguay, Peru, Poland, Portugal, Qatar, Republic of Korea, Romania, Russian Federation, Rwanda, Saint Kitts and Nevis, Saint Lucia, Saint Vincent and the Grenadines, Samoa, San Marino, Sao Tome and Principe, Saudi Arabia, Senegal, Serbia, Sierra Leone, Singapore, Slovakia, Slovenia, Solomon Islands, Somalia, South Africa, Spain, Sri Lanka, Sudan, Suriname, Swaziland, Sweden, Switzerland, Syrian Arab Republic, Tajikistan, Thailand, The former Yugoslav Republic of Macedonia, Timor-Leste, Togo, Trinidad and Tobago, Tunisia, Turkey, Turkmenistan, Ukraine, United Arab Emirates, United Kingdom, United Republic of Tanzania, Uruguay, Uzbekistan, Vanuatu, Venezuela, Viet Nam, Yemen, Zambia, Zimbabwe.

Against: United States.

Abstaining: None.

On 22 December, the Assembly decided that the item on general and complete disarmament would remain for consideration during its resumed sixty-first (2007) session (**decision 61/552**).

Disarmament Commission

In 2006, the Disarmament Commission, comprising all UN Member States, reached consensus on a programme of work, enabling it to resume substantive work it had suspended in 2004 [YUN 2004, p. 523] and 2005 [YUN 2005, p. 579], owing to a deadlock among delegates on a substantive agenda. Following that breakthrough, the Commission held seven plenary meetings and four informal sessions

(New York, 10-28 April) [A/61/42], in addition to an earlier organizational meeting. It adopted two substantive agenda items: recommendations for achieving the objective of nuclear disarmament and non-proliferation of nuclear weapons; (see p. 619) and practical confidence-building measures in the field of conventional weapons (see p. 666) and established a Committee of the Whole and two working groups to consider them.

In accordance with General Assembly resolution 60/91 [ibid., p. 579], the Commission considered measures for improving the effectiveness of its working methods during informal meetings of the whole. Based on the Chairman's summary of the discussions and draft report, the Commission adopted consensus recommendations for consideration by the Assembly on ways to improve some of the organizational and procedural aspects of its work. Other recommendations highlighted the need for the Commission to strengthen dialogue with other bodies of the UN disarmament machinery, such as the First Committee and the Conference on Disarmament; participation by disarmament experts, including those at the United Nations Institute for Disarmament Research (UNIDIR) (see p. 680), in discussions at the Commission's plenary meetings; and improvement by the UN Secretariat of the Commission's website, in order to provide better communication and updated information about its work.

On 28 April, the Commission adopted its report to the Assembly containing those recommendations.

GENERAL ASSEMBLY ACTION

On 6 December [meeting 67], the General Assembly, on the recommendation of the First Committee [A/61/396], adopted **resolution 61/98** without vote [agenda item 92 *(d)*].

Report of the Disarmament Commission

The General Assembly,

Having considered the report of the Disarmament Commission,

Recalling its resolutions 47/54 A of 9 December 1992, 47/54 G of 8 April 1993, 48/77 A of 16 December 1993, 49/77 A of 15 December 1994, 50/72 D of 12 December 1995, 51/47 B of 10 December 1996, 52/40 B of 9 December 1997, 53/79 A of 4 December 1998, 54/56 A of 1 December 1999, 55/35 C of 20 November 2000, 56/26 A of 29 November 2001, 57/95 of 22 November 2002, 58/67 of 8 December 2003, 59/105 of 3 December 2004 and 60/91 of 8 December 2005,

Considering the role that the Disarmament Commission has been called upon to play and the contribution that it should make in examining and submitting recommendations on various problems in the field of disarmament and in the promotion of the implementation of the relevant decisions adopted by the General Assembly at its tenth special session,

1. *Takes note* of the report of the Disarmament Commission;

2. *Reaffirms* the validity of its decision 52/492 of 8 September 1998, concerning the efficient functioning of the Disarmament Commission;

3. *Decides* to adopt the following additional measures for improving the effectiveness of the Disarmament Commission's methods of work:

(a) The Chairpersons and Vice-Chairpersons of the Commission and its subsidiary bodies should be elected at an organizational session of the Commission, if possible at least three months before the beginning of the substantive session; the regional groups should, accordingly, present their candidates as soon as possible to ensure that such elections take place within that time frame;

(b) Member States are encouraged to adopt the draft agenda of the substantive session of the Commission as early as possible at the organizational meetings of the Commission;

(c) Member States are encouraged to present their national working documents to the Commission as early as possible before the beginning of the substantive session to facilitate deliberation in the meetings ahead;

(d) The Commission should make efforts to strengthen dialogue with other bodies of the disarmament machinery of the United Nations, that is, the First Committee of the General Assembly and the Conference on Disarmament;

(e) The Commission is encouraged to invite, as appropriate, experts on disarmament, including those at the United Nations Institute for Disarmament Research, for discussions at its plenary meetings;

(f) The Secretariat is requested to improve the Commission section of the United Nations website to provide better communication and up-to-date information about the work of the Commission, and in particular to make available in a timely manner the information and documentation relevant to the Commission's deliberations;

4. *Reaffirms* the mandate of the Disarmament Commission as the specialized, deliberative body within the United Nations multilateral disarmament machinery that allows for in-depth deliberations on specific disarmament issues, leading to the submission of concrete recommendations on those issues;

5. *Also reaffirms* the importance of further enhancing the dialogue and cooperation between the First Committee, the Disarmament Commission and the Conference on Disarmament;

6. *Requests* the Disarmament Commission to continue its work in accordance with its mandate, as set forth in paragraph 118 of the Final Document of the Tenth Special Session of the General Assembly, and with paragraph 3 of Assembly resolution 37/78 H of 9 December 1982, and to that end to make every effort to achieve specific recommendations on the items on its agenda, taking

into account the adopted "Ways and means to enhance the functioning of the Disarmament Commission";

7. *Recommends* that the Disarmament Commission continue the consideration of the following items at its 2007 substantive session:

(*a*) Recommendations for achieving the objective of nuclear disarmament and non-proliferation of nuclear weapons;

(*b*) Practical confidence-building measures in the field of conventional weapons;

8. *Requests* the Disarmament Commission to meet for a period not exceeding three weeks during 2007, namely from 9 to 27 April, and to submit a substantive report to the General Assembly at its sixty-second session;

9. *Requests* the Secretary-General to transmit to the Disarmament Commission the annual report of the Conference on Disarmament, together with all the official records of the sixty-first session of the General Assembly relating to disarmament matters, and to render all assistance that the Commission may require for implementing the present resolution;

10. *Also requests* the Secretary-General to ensure full provision to the Disarmament Commission and its subsidiary bodies of interpretation and translation facilities in the official languages and to assign, as a matter of priority, all the necessary resources and services, including verbatim records, to that end;

11. *Decides* to include in the provisional agenda of its sixty-second session the item entitled "Report of the Disarmament Commission".

Conference on Disarmament

The Conference on Disarmament, a multilateral negotiating body, held a three-part session in Geneva in 2006 (23 January–31 March, 15 May–30 June and 31 July–15 September) [A/61/27].

The Conference, in 49 formal and 22 informal plenary meetings, continued to consider the cessation of the nuclear arms race and nuclear disarmament; prevention of nuclear war; prevention of an arms race in outer space; effective international arrangements to assure non-nuclear-weapon States against the use or threat of use of nuclear weapons; new types of WMDs and new systems of such weapons; radiological weapons; a comprehensive programme of disarmament; and transparency in armaments. Prior to the adoption of the agenda, France emphasized the importance of addressing "new issues" not previously considered by the Conference, particularly threats to critical physical infrastructure, while Australia proposed the inclusion of man-portable air defence systems (MANPADs) in the agenda, which was considered under the item on transparency in armaments. Other delegations addressed the issue of an arms trade treaty under the item "comprehensive programme of disarmament".

In the light of the unresolved impasse over a substantive programme of work, the last President of the 2005 session (Peru) [YUN 2005, p. 580] and the first President of the 2006 session (Poland), in cooperation with five incoming Presidents for the current year (the Republic of Korea, Romania, the Russian Federation, Senegal and Slovakia), held informal consultations on the possibility of achieving consensus on a programme of work, with a view to commencing substantive work in 2006. That initiative was reinforced with the appointment of six Friends of the Presidents, charged with assisting in reviewing the Conference agenda and enhancing its effectiveness by facilitating consensus on a work programme and augmenting the involvement of civil society. Owing to the lack of progress in resolving the deadlock during the first two weeks of meetings, the Presidents proposed incorporating into traditional general debates structured discussions, whereby each President would focus on two agenda items. That enabled the Conference to double the number of meetings held and to hear an increased number of statements on each item.

Despite those efforts, the Conference, for the eighth consecutive year, was unable to achieve consensus on a programme of work and did not establish or re-establish any mechanism on any of its agenda items. While some delegates did not want linkages established between elements of the programme, others preferred a balanced and comprehensive approach covering all issues and mandates for subsidiary bodies. Even drafting the Conference's annual report to the General Assembly proved contentious, mainly on how to reflect the views expressed about "new issues".

Against that background, the six 2006 Presidents (P-6) submitted at the end of the session a "vision paper" [CD/1809] highlighting their evaluation of the current situation regarding the work of the Conference, lessons to be learned and the possible steps for advancing substantive work. In that context, they advocated that the right conclusions be drawn from the experience of the current session; separate decisions on establishing subsidiary bodies to negotiate and/or consider issues of interest to all delegations; the adoption of a schedule of activities for substantive discussions on all agenda items; consideration of the possibility of establishing subsidiary bodies other than ad hoc committees; the use of focused, structured debates to advance the substantive work of the Conference, pending agreement on the programme of work and/or the establishment of subsidiary bodies; and that experts be invited from capitals and relevant UN bodies and other international organizations. The Conference decided to hold its 2007 session between January and September and asked its current and incoming Presidents to conduct consultations during the intersessional period and make recommendations, taking into account all relevant proposals.

GENERAL ASSEMBLY ACTION

On 6 December [meeting 67], the General Assembly, on the recommendation of the First Committee [A/61/396], adopted **resolution 61/99** without vote [agenda item 92 *(c)*].

Report of the Conference on Disarmament

The General Assembly,

Having considered the report of the Conference on Disarmament,

Convinced that the Conference on Disarmament, as the sole multilateral disarmament negotiating forum of the international community, has the primary role in substantive negotiations on priority questions of disarmament,

Recognizing the need to conduct multilateral negotiations with the aim of reaching agreement on concrete issues,

Recalling, in this respect, that the Conference has a number of urgent and important issues for negotiation,

Taking note of active discussions held on the programme of work during the 2006 session of the Conference, as duly reflected in the report and the records of the plenary meetings,

Taking note also of increased deliberations of the Conference due to the constructive contribution of its member States, focused structured debates on all agenda items including with the participation of experts from capitals, and cooperation between all six Presidents of the Conference in the 2006 session,

Taking note further of significant contributions made during the 2006 session to promote substantive discussions on issues on the agenda, as well as of discussions held on other issues that could also be relevant to the current international security environment,

Stressing the urgent need for the Conference to commence its substantive work at the beginning of its 2007 session,

Recognizing the address of the Secretary-General of the United Nations, as well as the addresses of Ministers for Foreign Affairs and other high-level officials, as expressions of support for the endeavours of the Conference and its role as the sole multilateral disarmament negotiating forum,

Bearing in mind the importance of efforts towards revitalization of the disarmament machinery, including the Conference,

Recognizing the importance of continuing consultations on the question of the expansion of the Conference membership,

1. *Reaffirms* the role of the Conference on Disarmament as the sole multilateral disarmament negotiating forum of the international community;

2. *Calls upon* the Conference to further intensify consultations and explore possibilities with a view to reaching an agreement on a programme of work;

3. *Takes note* of the strong collective interest of the Conference in commencing substantive work as soon as possible during its 2007 session;

4. *Welcomes* the decision of the Conference to request its current President and the incoming President to conduct consultations during the intersessional period and, if possible, to make recommendations, taking into account all relevant proposals, including those submitted as documents of the Conference, views presented and discussions held, and to endeavour to keep the membership of the Conference informed, as appropriate, of their consultations, as contained in paragraph 28 of its report;

5. *Requests* all States members of the Conference to cooperate with the current President and successive Presidents in their efforts to guide the Conference to the early commencement of substantive work in its 2007 session;

6. *Requests* the Secretary-General to continue to ensure the provision to the Conference of adequate administrative, substantive and conference support services;

7. *Requests* the Conference to submit a report on its work to the General Assembly at its sixty-second session;

8. *Decides* to include in the provisional agenda of its sixty-second session the item entitled "Report of the Conference on Disarmament".

Multilateral disarmament agreements

As at 31 December 2006, the following number of States had become parties to the multilateral agreements listed below (in chronological order, with the years in which they were initially signed or opened for signature).

(Geneva) Protocol for the Prohibition of the Use in War of Asphyxiating, Poisonous or Other Gases, and of Bacteriological Methods of Warfare (1925): 133 parties

The Antarctic Treaty (1959): 46 parties

Treaty Banning Nuclear Weapon Tests in the Atmosphere, in Outer Space and under Water (1963): 125 parties

Treaty on Principles Governing the Activities of States in the Exploration and Use of Outer Space, including the Moon and Other Celestial Bodies (1967) [YUN 1966, p. 41, GA res. 2222(XXI), annex]: 98 parties

Treaty for the Prohibition of Nuclear Weapons in Latin America and the Caribbean (Treaty of Tlatelolco) (1967): 39 parties

Treaty on the Non-Proliferation of Nuclear Weapons (1968) [YUN 1968, p. 17, GA res. 2373(XXII), annex]: 190 parties

Treaty on the Prohibition of the Emplacement of Nuclear Weapons and Other Weapons of Mass Destruction on the Seabed and the Ocean Floor and in the Subsoil Thereof (1971) [YUN 1970, p. 18, GA res. 2660(XXV), annex]: 93 parties

Convention on the Prohibition of the Development, Production and Stockpiling of Bacteriological (Biological) and Toxin Weapons and on Their Destruction (1972) [YUN 1971, p. 19, GA res 2826(XXVI), annex]: 155 parties

Convention on the Prohibition of Military or Any Other Hostile Use of Environmental Modification Techniques (1977) [YUN 1976, p. 45, GA res. 31/72, annex]: 72 parties

Agreement Governing the Activities of States on the Moon and Other Celestial Bodies (1979) [YUN 1979, p. 111, GA res. 34/68, annex]: 13 parties

Convention on Prohibitions or Restrictions on the Use of Certain Conventional Weapons Which May Be Deemed to Be Excessively Injurious or to Have Indiscriminate Effects (1981): 102 parties

South Pacific Nuclear-Free Zone Treaty (Treaty of Rarotonga) (1985): 17 parties

Treaty on Conventional Armed Forces in Europe (CFE Treaty) (1990): 30 parties

Treaty on Open Skies (1992): 33 parties

Convention on the Prohibition of the Development, Production, Stockpiling and Use of Chemical Weapons and on Their Destruction (1993): 181 parties

Treaty on the South-East Asia Nuclear-Weapon-Free Zone (Bangkok Treaty) (1995): 10 parties

African Nuclear-Weapon-Free Zone Treaty (Pelindaba Treaty) (1996): 24 parties

Comprehensive Nuclear-Test-Ban Treaty (1996): 137 parties

Inter-American Convention against the Illicit Manufacturing of and Trafficking in Firearms, Ammunition, Explosives, and Other Related Materials (1997): 26 parties

Convention on the Prohibition of the Use, Stockpiling, Production and Transfer of Anti-personnel Mines and on Their Destruction (Mine-Ban Convention, formerly known as Ottawa Convention) (1997): 152 parties

Inter-American Convention on Transparency in Conventional Weapons Acquisitions (1999): 12 parties

Agreement on Adaptation of the CFE Treaty (1999): 4 parties

Treaty on a Nuclear-Weapon-Free Zone in Central Asia (2006): 5 signatories

[*United Nations Disarmament Yearbook*, vol. 31: *2006*, Sales No. E.07.IX.1]

Nuclear disarmament

Report of Secretary-General. In response to General Assembly resolutions 60/70 [YUN 2005, p. 588] and 60/79 [ibid., p. 590], the Secretary-General submitted a July report [A/61/127 & Add.1] assessing efforts to address nuclear disarmament issues, which remained a priority for international peace and security. Pointing to the several disappointing setbacks since 2005, he observed that nuclear disarmament efforts appeared to have stalled, while the international community continued to confront dangers resulting from the development, acquisition and possible use of WMDs, including nuclear weapons and radiological dispersal devices or "dirty bombs". The world was facing increasing challenges regarding compliance with International Atomic Energy Agency (IAEA) safeguards agreements (see p. 640), adding to concerns about the effectiveness of the non-proliferation regime. To reduce such threats, renewed unilateral, bilateral and multilateral efforts were required, particularly by nuclear-weapons States, to reduce existing nuclear arsenals. Despite some progress in that respect, it was of concern that emphasis seemed to have shifted towards acquiring fewer but more powerful weapons. The international community therefore had to continue strengthening existing arms control and disarmament agreements through universal adherence to, full compliance with, and effective implementation of their provisions.

Although the 1968 Treaty on the Non-proliferation of Nuclear Weapons (NPT) [YUN 1968, p. 17, GA res. 2373(XXII), annex] remained the cornerstone of the global non-proliferation regime and the foundation for pursuing nuclear disarmament, the disappointing outcome of the 2005 NPT Review Conference [YUN 2005, p. 597] and of the 2005 World Summit [ibid., p. 47], where diverging views prevented agreement on key disarmament issues, represented two missed opportunities for Member States to address important threats and challenges to the international nuclear non-proliferation regime. Action was therefore needed on many fronts, including strengthening confidence in the integrity of NPT; achieving further irreversible cuts in nuclear arsenals; ensuring that compliance measures were more effective; reducing the threat of proliferation to States and non-state actors; and finding durable ways to reconcile the right to peaceful uses of nuclear technology with the imperative of non-proliferation. Reducing the value of the perceived security benefits of nuclear weapons possession was also necessary, and in that context, the report of the independent international Weapons of Mass Destruction Commission, chaired by Hans Blix (see p. 636), ought to be considered seriously by the international community. Of further concern were the fact that the Comprehensive Nuclear-Test-Ban Treaty (CTBT) (see p. 628) still had not attracted enough ratifications to enable it to enter into force, and the ongoing impasse in the Conference on Disarmament over a substantive work programme (see p. 614). It was critical for the Conference to move forward, as the validity of the multilateral disarmament machinery was beginning to be questioned. Further efforts were also needed to implement fully the seven recommendations identified by the Secretary-General's Advisory Board on Disarmament Matters [YUN 2001, p. 475] to reduce nuclear dangers. Ten years after the 1996 advisory opinion of the International Court of Justice on the *Legality of the Threat or Use of Nuclear Weapons* [YUN 1996, p. 461], related challenges facing multilateral disarmament efforts had increased, as illustrated by the recent discovery of clandestine markets for nuclear technology and the possibility that such weapons could fall into the hands of terrorists. The Organization remained committed to assisting Member States in meeting those challenges.

Conference on Disarmament

In 2006, as in the previous eight years, the Conference on Disarmament did not establish any subsidiary body to address nuclear disarmament, owing to continuing disagreement among delegates over a substantive programme of work (see p. 614). The item was discussed in formal and informal plenary meetings, during which delegates reaffirmed or further elaborated their positions. The Group of 21 (G-21) continued to accord nuclear disarmament the highest priority and drew attention to proposals for the establishment of an ad hoc committee for the complete elimination of nuclear weapons. As distinct from that position, most members of the Western Group and Eastern European Group saw the negotiation of a fissile material cut-off treaty as a priority, with some of them viewing progress on negotiating such a treaty and on the ratification of CTBT as complementary to the undertakings of nuclear-weapon States under NPT. Norway and Sweden proposed the creation of a global inventory of nuclear arsenals and stockpiles under international safeguards to deter non-state actors from stealing such material for terrorist activities.

Fissile material

In 2006, although the unresolved impasse over a comprehensive programme of work again prevented the Conference on Disarmament from establishing an ad hoc committee on the prohibition of the production of fissile material for nuclear weapons and other nuclear explosive devices, the Conference devoted five days of plenary discussions to that item. To enhance the breadth of those discussions, experts were invited from Member States to participate in an exchange of views on specific sub-items relating to fissile materials, including definitions, scope, stocks, compliance and verification. On 18 May, the United States put forward a draft mandate for the Conference to start negotiating a fissile material cut-off treaty, together with a draft text of such a treaty [CD/1777], which received mixed reaction from other delegates. While many Western countries and a number of Latin American States adopted a reserved but generally favourable position towards the proposed draft, several other delegations did not support it, including some Non-Aligned Movement (NAM) States. Diverging issues included the scope of the envisioned agreement and the questions of compliance and verification. A further complicating factor was the link to other core issues which some delegates maintained. China, and several NAM States in particular, were prepared to deal with fissile material only within the framework of a "balanced and comprehensive" programme of work which would include such other core issues as nuclear disarmament, the prevention of an arms race in outer space and negative security assurances (see below).

Security assurances

During consideration by the Conference on Disarmament of the issue of security assurances for non-nuclear-weapon States against the use or threat of use of nuclear weapons, differences continued on the question of the appropriate forum for dealing with the subject and the adequacy of existing security assurances given, either under the nuclear-weapon-free zones regimes, by unilateral declarations or pursuant to Security Council resolutions. While some delegates preferred the Conference on Disarmament as the forum best suited for addressing the subject, others favoured the NPT platform. Most non-nuclear-weapon States maintained that existing security assurances were inadequate and pressed for a universal and legally-binding agreement on such assurances, while France, the Russian Federation, the United Kingdom and the United States stressed that the assurances already pledged, as well as those given within the NPT framework, were sufficiently strong.

Seminar. In August, at the initiative of Senegal, the United Nations Institute for Disarmament Research (UNIDIR) (see p. 680) organized a seminar on negative security assurances (Geneva, 8 August) [CD/1804]. Discussions focused on such assurances as a step towards nuclear disarmament and the related questions of the forum in which to pursue the idea, possible contributions by the Security Council, and relevant articles in nuclear-weapon-free zone treaties that could play a role in securing those assurances.

Communication. In September, the Fourteenth Conference of Heads of State or Government of Non-Aligned Countries (Havana, Cuba, 11-16 September) [A/61/472-S/2006/780] stated that, pending the total elimination of nuclear weapons, which was the only absolute guarantee against the use or threat of use of nuclear weapons, the conclusion of a universal, unconditional and legally binding instrument on security assurances to non-nuclear-weapon States was a priority.

GENERAL ASSEMBLY ACTION

On 6 December [meeting 67], the General Assembly, on the recommendation of the First Committee [A/61/392], adopted **resolution 61/57** by recorded vote (119-1-59) [agenda item 88].

Conclusion of effective international arrangements to assure non-nuclear-weapon States against the use or threat of use of nuclear weapons

The General Assembly,

Bearing in mind the need to allay the legitimate concern of the States of the world with regard to ensuring lasting security for their peoples,

Convinced that nuclear weapons pose the greatest threat to mankind and to the survival of civilization,

Welcoming the progress achieved in recent years in both nuclear and conventional disarmament,

Noting that, despite recent progress in the field of nuclear disarmament, further efforts are necessary towards the achievement of general and complete disarmament under effective international control,

Convinced that nuclear disarmament and the complete elimination of nuclear weapons are essential to remove the danger of nuclear war,

Determined to abide strictly by the relevant provisions of the Charter of the United Nations on the non-use of force or threat of force,

Recognizing that the independence, territorial integrity and sovereignty of non-nuclear-weapon States need to be safeguarded against the use or threat of use of force, including the use or threat of use of nuclear weapons,

Considering that, until nuclear disarmament is achieved on a universal basis, it is imperative for the international community to develop effective measures and arrangements to ensure the security of non-nuclear-weapon States against the use or threat of use of nuclear weapons from any quarter,

Recognizing that effective measures and arrangements to assure non-nuclear-weapon States against the use or threat of use of nuclear weapons can contribute positively to the prevention of the spread of nuclear weapons,

Bearing in mind paragraph 59 of the Final Document of the Tenth Special Session of the General Assembly, the first special session devoted to disarmament, in which it urged the nuclear-weapon States to pursue efforts to conclude, as appropriate, effective arrangements to assure non-nuclear-weapon States against the use or threat of use of nuclear weapons, and desirous of promoting the implementation of the relevant provisions of the Final Document,

Recalling the relevant parts of the special report of the Committee on Disarmament submitted to the General Assembly at its twelfth special session, the second special session devoted to disarmament, and of the special report of the Conference on Disarmament submitted to the Assembly at its fifteenth special session, the third special session devoted to disarmament, as well as the report of the Conference on its 1992 session,

Recalling also paragraph 12 of the Declaration of the 1980s as the Second Disarmament Decade, contained in the annex to its resolution 35/46 of 3 December 1980, which states, inter alia, that all efforts should be exerted by the Committee on Disarmament urgently to negotiate with a view to reaching agreement on effective international arrangements to assure non-nuclear-weapon States against the use or threat of use of nuclear weapons,

Noting the in-depth negotiations undertaken in the Conference on Disarmament and its Ad Hoc Committee on Effective International Arrangements to Assure Non-Nuclear-Weapon States against the Use or Threat of Use of Nuclear Weapons, with a view to reaching agreement on this question,

Taking note of the proposals submitted under the item in the Conference on Disarmament, including the drafts of an international convention,

Taking note also of the relevant decision of the Thirteenth Conference of Heads of State or Government of Non-Aligned Countries, held at Kuala Lumpur on 24 and 25 February 2003, which was reiterated at the Fourteenth Conference of Heads of State or Government of Non-Aligned Countries, held at Havana on 15 and 16 September 2006, as well as the relevant recommendations of the Organization of the Islamic Conference,

Taking note further of the unilateral declarations made by all the nuclear-weapon States on their policies of non-use or non-threat of use of nuclear weapons against the non-nuclear-weapon States,

Noting the support expressed in the Conference on Disarmament and in the General Assembly for the elaboration of an international convention to assure non-nuclear-weapon States against the use or threat of use of nuclear weapons, as well as the difficulties pointed out in evolving a common approach acceptable to all,

Taking note of Security Council resolution 984(1995) of 11 April 1995 and the views expressed on it,

Recalling its relevant resolutions adopted in previous years, in particular resolutions 45/54 of 4 December 1990, 46/32 of 6 December 1991, 47/50 of 9 December 1992, 48/73 of 16 December 1993, 49/73 of 15 December 1994, 50/68 of 12 December 1995, 51/43 of 10 December 1996, 52/36 of 9 December 1997, 53/75 of 4 December 1998, 54/52 of 1 December 1999, 55/31 of 20 November 2000, 56/22 of 29 November 2001, 57/56 of 22 November 2002, 58/35 of 8 December 2003, 59/64 of 3 December 2004 and 60/53 of 8 December 2005,

1. *Reaffirms* the urgent need to reach an early agreement on effective international arrangements to assure

non-nuclear-weapon States against the use or threat of use of nuclear weapons;

2. *Notes with satisfaction* that in the Conference on Disarmament there is no objection, in principle, to the idea of an international convention to assure non-nuclear-weapon States against the use or threat of use of nuclear weapons, although the difficulties with regard to evolving a common approach acceptable to all have also been pointed out;

3. *Appeals* to all States, especially the nuclear-weapon States, to work actively towards an early agreement on a common approach and, in particular, on a common formula that could be included in an international instrument of a legally binding character;

4. *Recommends* that further intensive efforts be devoted to the search for such a common approach or common formula and that the various alternative approaches, including, in particular, those considered in the Conference on Disarmament, be explored further in order to overcome the difficulties;

5. *Also recommends* that the Conference on Disarmament actively continue intensive negotiations with a view to reaching early agreement and concluding effective international agreements to assure the non-nuclear-weapon States against the use or threat of use of nuclear weapons, taking into account the widespread support for the conclusion of an international convention and giving consideration to any other proposals designed to secure the same objective;

6. *Decides* to include in the provisional agenda of its sixty-second session the item entitled "Conclusion of effective international arrangements to assure non-nuclear-weapon States against the use or threat of use of nuclear weapons".

RECORDED VOTE ON RESOLUTION 61/57:

In favour: Afghanistan, Algeria, Angola, Antigua and Barbuda, Azerbaijan, Bahamas, Bahrain, Bangladesh, Barbados, Belize, Bhutan, Brazil, Brunei Darussalam, Burkina Faso, Burundi, Cambodia, Cameroon, Cape Verde, Central African Republic, Chile, China, Colombia, Comoros, Congo, Costa Rica, Cuba, Democratic People's Republic of Korea, Democratic Republic of the Congo, Djibouti, Dominica, Dominican Republic, Ecuador, Egypt, El Salvador, Eritrea, Ethiopia, Fiji, Gabon, Gambia, Ghana, Grenada, Guatemala, Guinea, Guyana, Haiti, Honduras, India, Indonesia, Iran, Iraq, Jamaica, Japan, Jordan, Kazakhstan, Kuwait, Kyrgyzstan, Lao People's Democratic Republic, Lebanon, Lesotho, Liberia, Libyan Arab Jamahiriya, Malawi, Malaysia, Maldives, Mali, Mauritania, Mauritius, Mexico, Mongolia, Morocco, Mozambique, Myanmar, Namibia, Nepal, Nicaragua, Niger, Nigeria, Oman, Pakistan, Panama, Paraguay, Peru, Philippines, Qatar, Rwanda, Saint Kitts and Nevis, Saint Lucia, Saint Vincent and the Grenadines, Samoa, Sao Tome and Principe, Saudi Arabia, Senegal, Sierra Leone, Singapore, Solomon Islands, Somalia, Sri Lanka, Sudan, Suriname, Swaziland, Syrian Arab Republic, Tajikistan, Thailand, Timor-Leste, Togo, Trinidad and Tobago, Tunisia, Turkmenistan, Uganda, United Arab Emirates, United Republic of Tanzania, Uruguay, Uzbekistan, Vanuatu, Venezuela, Viet Nam, Yemen, Zambia, Zimbabwe.

Against: United States.

Abstaining: Albania, Andorra, Argentina, Armenia, Australia, Austria, Belarus, Belgium, Bolivia, Bosnia and Herzegovina, Bulgaria, Canada, Croatia, Cyprus, Czech Republic, Denmark, Estonia, Finland, France, Georgia, Germany, Greece, Hungary, Iceland, Ireland, Israel, Italy, Latvia, Liechtenstein, Lithuania, Luxembourg, Malta, Marshall Islands, Micronesia, Moldova, Monaco, Montenegro, Nauru, Netherlands, New Zealand, Norway, Palau, Poland, Portugal, Republic of Korea, Romania, Russian Federation, San Marino, Serbia, Slovakia, Slovenia, South Africa, Spain, Sweden, Switzerland, The former Yugoslav Republic of Macedonia, Turkey, Ukraine, United Kingdom.

Disarmament Commission

In April [A/61/42], Working Group 1 of the Disarmament Commission considered the item: recommendations for achieving the objective of nuclear disarmament and non-proliferation of nuclear weapons, during a series of meetings held between 18 and 28 April. Those discussions were facilitated by informal consultations conducted by the Group's Chairman and by working/conference room papers submitted by him, which took into consideration the views of delegations and a number of other working papers introduced by them. On 26 April, the Group considered a revised version of the Chairman's working paper [A/CN.10/2006/WG.I/WP.4/Rev.1], which addressed the general principles for achieving the objective of nuclear disarmament and non-proliferation, and set out recommendations for achieving that objective. The Group also had before it the Chairman's revised conference room paper [A/CN.10/2006/WG.I/CRP.1/Rev.1], which elaborated in greater detail on those recommendations, and his draft outline of issues to be further considered by the Group [A/CN.10/2006/WG.I/CRP.7]. The Chairman's papers, however, were not a negotiated position and did not command consensus, as a number of delegates expressed reservations on some of the views contained therein. On 28 April, the Group adopted its report, which the Commission reproduced in its report to the General Assembly.

START and other bilateral agreements and unilateral measures

On 27 January, Ukraine announced that, in line with its international commitments, it had dismantled its last strategic bomber and expected to scrap completely a category of its air-to-surface missiles by May. Those weapons were part of a significant stockpile of nuclear and strategic weapons which it inherited from the former Soviet Union, as did the other three independent States (Belarus, Kazakhstan, the Russian Federation) that emerged when the Union collapsed in 1992. As legal successors of the Union, those States had joined the 1991 Treaty on the Reduction and Limitation of

Strategic Offensive Arms (START I) [YUN 1991, p. 34] between the United States and the former Soviet Union, under which Ukraine committed to voluntarily destroy all of its share of nuclear weapons stockpiles.

In March, the United States and India concluded the United States-India Civil Nuclear Cooperation Initiative on the transfer of peaceful civil-nuclear technology, under which India pledged, for the first time in 30 years, to place its entire civil nuclear programme under the safeguards regime of the International Atomic Energy Agency (IAEA) (see p. 620), and to continue its unilateral moratorium on testing. It would also place the majority of its existing and planned power reactors under international safeguards by 2014. Once the agreement was implemented, potential American and international suppliers could invest in India's safeguarded civil facilities solely for energy production and other peaceful purposes. Given that India remained outside NPT, the agreement received mixed reviews. Sceptics believed it risked weakening the nuclear non-proliferation regime, as India's military nuclear programmes would not be affected or might be enhanced, while optimists countered that it would benefit non-proliferation efforts, as India's military and civil nuclear facilities and programmes would be separated, with the civilian component placed under IAEA safeguards.

During the year, the United States and the Russian Federation continued to implement their 2005 bilateral agreement for combatting the illicit proliferation of man-portable air defence systems (MANPADS), alternatively known as shoulder-fired anti-aircraft missiles, which could threaten global aviation if obtained by criminals, terrorists or other non-state actors. On 19 June, both sides announced that they had extended for another seven years their Cooperative Threat Reduction Umbrella Agreement, signed in 1992, to prevent the proliferation of WMDs and related materials, which was an effective tool in efforts to deny terrorists and proliferators access to those weapons.

On 27 June, Russian President Vladimir Putin urged the United States to begin negotiations on a new weapons treaty to replace the START I agreement, which was scheduled to expire in 2009, and had committed both sides to limit to approximately 6,000 the number of nuclear warheads they could each deploy. Noting that modernization of the global security architecture had become necessary, President Putin called for the renewal of dialogue on key weapons reduction issues. In a 15 July joint statement, the leaders of the two countries launched the Global Initiative to Combat Nuclear Terrorism, designed to help prevent the acquisition, transport, or use by terrorists of nuclear materials and radioactive substances or improvised explosive devices using such material. On 15 September, they signed the Plutonium Disposition Liability Protocol, providing a framework for resolving liability issues for a non-proliferation project for converting excess weapon-grade plutonium into forms unusable for weapons by terrorists and others.

During the year, the Russian Federation and the United States continued to implement their 2002 Strategic Offensive Reductions Treaty (Moscow Treaty) [YUN 2002, p. 493], under which they agreed to reduce the level of their deployed strategic nuclear warheads to between 1700 and 2200 by 31 December 2012. In accordance with the Treaty's provisions, both sides described their plans for achieving the required reductions by the stipulated deadline.

Communication. In September [A/61/72-S/2006/780], the Fourteenth Conference of Heads of State or Government of Non-Aligned Countries (Havana, Cuba, 11-16 September) reaffirmed that nuclear disarmament and the related issue of non-proliferation remained their highest priority and stressed the importance of initiating parallel efforts to achieve both. Concerned at the threat to humanity posed by the continuing existence of nuclear weapons and at the slow progress towards nuclear disarmament, they underscored the need for nuclear-weapon States to implement the unequivocal undertaking they provided during the 2000 Review Conference of the Parties to NPT [YUN 2000, p. 487] to accomplish the total elimination of nuclear weapons, and the urgency of prompt negotiations towards that end.

GENERAL ASSEMBLY ACTION

On 6 December [meeting 67], the General Assembly, on the recommendation of the First Committee [A/61/394], adopted four resolutions and one decision relating to nuclear disarmament. The Assembly adopted **resolution 61/65** by recorded vote (157-7-13) [agenda item 90 *(g)*].

Towards a nuclear-weapon-free world: accelerating the implementation of nuclear disarmament commitments

The General Assembly,

Recalling its resolution 60/56 of 8 December 2005,

Expressing its grave concern at the danger to humanity posed by the possibility that nuclear weapons could be used,

Reaffirming that nuclear disarmament and nuclear non-proliferation are mutually reinforcing processes requiring urgent irreversible progress on both fronts,

Mindful of the contribution of the final report of the Weapons of Mass Destruction Commission,

Recalling the decisions and the resolution on the Middle East of the 1995 Review and Extension Conference of the Parties to the Treaty on the Non-Proliferation of Nuclear Weapons and the Final Document of the 2000 Review Conference of the Parties to the Treaty on the Non-Proliferation of Nuclear Weapons,

Recalling also the unequivocal undertaking by the nuclear-weapon States to accomplish the total elimination of their nuclear arsenals, leading to nuclear disarmament, in accordance with commitments made under article VI of the Treaty on the Non-Proliferation of Nuclear Weapons,

Urging States parties to exert all possible efforts to ensure a successful and productive preparatory process for the 2010 Review Conference of the Parties to the Treaty on the Non-Proliferation of Nuclear Weapons,

1. *Continues to emphasize* the central role of the Treaty on the Non-Proliferation of Nuclear Weapons and its universality in achieving nuclear disarmament and nuclear non-proliferation, and calls upon all States parties to respect their obligations;

2. *Reaffirms* that the outcome of the 2000 Review Conference of the Parties to the Treaty on the Non-Proliferation of Nuclear Weapons sets out the agreed process for systematic and progressive efforts towards nuclear disarmament;

3. *Reiterates its call upon* the nuclear-weapon States to accelerate the implementation of the practical steps towards nuclear disarmament that were agreed upon at the 2000 Review Conference, thereby contributing to a safer world for all;

4. *Calls upon* all States to comply fully with all commitments made regarding nuclear disarmament and nuclear non-proliferation and not to act in any way that may compromise either cause or that may lead to a new nuclear arms race;

5. *Again calls upon* all States parties to spare no effort to achieve the universality of the Treaty on the Non-Proliferation of Nuclear Weapons, and urges India, Israel and Pakistan, which are not yet parties to the Treaty, to accede to it as non-nuclear-weapon States promptly and without conditions;

6. *Condemns* the announced nuclear-weapon test by the Democratic People's Republic of Korea on 9 October 2006, all nuclear-weapon tests by States that are not yet parties to the Treaty on the Non-Proliferation of Nuclear Weapons and any further nuclear-weapon test by any State whatsoever, and urges the Democratic People's Republic of Korea to rescind its announced withdrawal from the Treaty;

7. *Decides* to include in the provisional agenda of its sixty-second session the item entitled "Towards a nuclear-weapon-free world: accelerating the implementation of nuclear disarmament commitments" and to review the implementation of the present resolution at that session.

RECORDED VOTE ON RESOLUTION 61/65:

In favour: Afghanistan, Algeria, Andorra, Angola, Antigua and Barbuda, Argentina, Armenia, Austria, Azerbaijan, Bahamas, Bahrain, Bangladesh, Barbados, Belgium, Belize, Bolivia, Bosnia and Herzegovina, Brazil, Brunei Darussalam, Bulgaria, Burkina Faso, Burundi, Cambodia, Cameroon, Canada, Cape Verde, Central African Republic, Chad, Chile, China, Colombia, Comoros, Congo, Costa Rica, Côte d'Ivoire, Croatia, Cuba, Cyprus, Czech Republic, Democratic Republic of the Congo, Denmark, Djibouti, Dominica, Dominican Republic, Ecuador, Egypt, El Salvador, Eritrea, Estonia, Ethiopia, Fiji, Finland, Gabon, Gambia, Georgia, Germany, Ghana, Grenada, Guatemala, Guinea, Guyana, Haiti, Honduras, Iceland, Indonesia, Iran, Iraq, Ireland, Italy, Jamaica, Japan, Jordan, Kazakhstan, Kuwait, Kyrgyzstan, Lao People's Democratic Republic, Lebanon, Lesotho, Liberia, Libyan Arab Jamahiriya, Liechtenstein, Lithuania, Luxembourg, Malawi, Malaysia, Maldives, Mali, Malta, Marshall Islands, Mauritania, Mauritius, Mexico, Moldova, Mongolia, Montenegro, Morocco, Mozambique, Myanmar, Namibia, Nauru, Nepal, Netherlands, New Zealand, Nicaragua, Niger, Norway, Oman, Panama, Papua New Guinea, Paraguay, Peru, Philippines, Portugal, Qatar, Republic of Korea, Rwanda, Saint Kitts and Nevis, Saint Lucia, Saint Vincent and the Grenadines, Samoa, San Marino, Sao Tome and Principe, Saudi Arabia, Senegal, Serbia, Sierra Leone, Singapore, Slovakia, Solomon Islands, South Africa, Spain, Sri Lanka, Sudan, Suriname, Swaziland, Sweden, Switzerland, Tajikistan, Thailand, The former Yugoslav Republic of Macedonia, Timor-Leste, Togo, Tonga, Trinidad and Tobago, Tunisia, Turkey, Ukraine, United Arab Emirates, United Republic of Tanzania, Uruguay, Uzbekistan, Vanuatu, Venezuela, Viet Nam, Yemen, Zambia, Zimbabwe.

Against: Democratic People's Republic of Korea, France, India, Israel, Pakistan, United Kingdom, United States.

Abstaining: Albania, Australia, Belarus, Bhutan, Greece, Hungary, Latvia, Micronesia, Palau, Poland, Romania, Russian Federation, Slovenia.

The Assembly adopted **resolution 61/74** by recorded vote (167-4-7) [agenda item 90].

Renewed determination towards the total elimination of nuclear weapons

The General Assembly,

Recalling the need for all States to take further practical steps and effective measures towards the total elimination of nuclear weapons, with a view to achieving a peaceful and safe world free of nuclear weapons, and renewing the determination to do so,

Noting that the ultimate objective of the efforts of States in the disarmament process is general and complete disarmament under strict and effective international control,

Recalling its resolution 60/65 of 8 December 2005,

Convinced that every effort should be made to avoid nuclear war and nuclear terrorism,

Reaffirming the crucial importance of the Treaty on the Non-Proliferation of Nuclear Weapons as the cornerstone of the international nuclear disarmament and non-proliferation regime, and expressing regret over the lack of agreement on substantive issues at the Review Conference of the Parties to the Treaty on the Non-Proliferation of Nuclear Weapons, as well as over the elimination of references to nuclear disarmament and non-proliferation in the World Summit Outcome in 2005, the year of the sixtieth anniversary of the atomic bombings in Hiroshima and Nagasaki, Japan,

Recalling the decisions and the resolution of the 1995 Review and Extension Conference of the Parties to the Treaty on the Non-Proliferation of Nuclear Weapons and the Final Document of the 2000 Review Conference of the Parties to the Treaty,

Recognizing that the enhancement of international peace and security and the promotion of nuclear disarmament are mutually reinforcing,

Reaffirming that further advancement in nuclear disarmament will contribute to consolidating the international regime for nuclear non-proliferation and thereby ensuring international peace and security,

Expressing deep concern regarding the growing dangers posed by the proliferation of weapons of mass destruction, inter alia, nuclear weapons, including that caused by proliferation networks,

Condemning the nuclear test proclaimed by the Democratic People's Republic of Korea on 9 October 2006,

1. *Reaffirms* the importance of all States parties to the Treaty on the Non-Proliferation of Nuclear Weapons complying with their obligations under all the articles of the Treaty;

2. *Stresses* the importance of an effective Treaty review process, and calls upon all States parties to the Treaty to work together to ensure that the first session of the Preparatory Committee in 2007 is held constructively, in order to facilitate the successful outcome of the 2010 Review Conference of the Parties to the Treaty on the Non-Proliferation of Nuclear Weapons;

3. *Reaffirms* the importance of the universality of the Treaty, and calls upon States not parties to the Treaty to accede to it as non-nuclear-weapon States without delay and without conditions, and pending their accession to refrain from acts that would defeat the objective and purpose of the Treaty as well as to take practical steps in support of the Treaty;

4. *Encourages* further steps leading to nuclear disarmament, to which all States parties to the Treaty are committed under article VI of the Treaty, including deeper reductions in all types of nuclear weapons, and emphasizes the importance of applying irreversibility and verifiability, as well as increased transparency in a way that promotes international stability and undiminished security for all, in the process of working towards the elimination of nuclear weapons;

5. *Encourages* the Russian Federation and the United States of America to implement fully the Treaty on Strategic Offensive Reductions, which should serve as a step for further nuclear disarmament, and to undertake nuclear arms reductions beyond those provided for by the Treaty, while welcoming the progress made by nuclear-weapon States, including the Russian Federation and the United States, on nuclear arms reductions;

6. *Encourages* States to continue to pursue efforts, within the framework of international cooperation, contributing to the reduction of nuclear-weapons-related materials;

7. *Calls for* the nuclear-weapon States to further reduce the operational status of nuclear weapons systems in ways that promote international stability and security;

8. *Stresses* the necessity of a diminishing role for nuclear weapons in security policies to minimize the risk that these weapons will ever be used and to facilitate the process of their total elimination, in a way that promotes international stability and based on the principle of undiminished security for all;

9. *Urges* all States that have not yet done so to sign and ratify the Comprehensive Nuclear-Test-Ban Treaty at the earliest opportunity with a view to its early entry into force, stresses the importance of maintaining existing moratoriums on nuclear-weapon test explosions pending the entry into force of the Treaty, and reaffirms the importance of the continued development of the Comprehensive Nuclear-Test-Ban Treaty verification regime, including the international monitoring system, which will be required to provide assurance of compliance with the Treaty;

10. *Calls upon* the Conference on Disarmament to immediately resume its substantive work to its fullest, considering the developments of this year in the Conference;

11. *Emphasizes* the importance of the immediate commencement of negotiations on a fissile material cut-off treaty and its early conclusion, and calls upon all nuclear-weapon States and States not parties to the Treaty on the Non-Proliferation of Nuclear Weapons to declare moratoriums on the production of fissile material for any nuclear weapons or other nuclear explosive devices pending the entry into force of the Treaty;

12. *Calls upon* all States to redouble their efforts to prevent and curb the proliferation of nuclear and other weapons of mass destruction and their means of delivery;

13. *Stresses* the importance of further efforts for non-proliferation, including the universalization of the International Atomic Energy Agency comprehensive safeguards agreements and Model Protocol Additional to the Agreement*(s)* between State*(s)* and the International Atomic Energy Agency for the Application of Safeguards approved by the Board of Governors of the International Atomic Energy Agency on 15 May 1997 and the full implementation of Security Council resolution 1540(2004) of 28 April 2004;

14. *Encourages* all States to undertake concrete activities to implement, as appropriate, the recommendations contained in the report of the Secretary-General on the United Nations study on disarmament and non-proliferation education, submitted to the General Assembly at its fifty-seventh session, and to voluntarily share information on efforts they have been undertaking to that end;

15. *Encourages* the constructive role played by civil society in promoting nuclear non-proliferation and nuclear disarmament.

RECORDED VOTE ON RESOLUTION 61/74:

In favour: Afghanistan, Albania, Algeria, Andorra, Angola, Antigua and Barbuda, Argentina, Armenia, Australia, Austria, Azerbaijan, Bahamas, Bahrain, Bangladesh, Barbados, Belarus, Belgium, Belize, Benin, Bolivia, Bosnia and Herzegovina, Brazil, Brunei Darussalam, Bulgaria, Burkina Faso, Burundi, Cambodia, Cameroon, Canada, Cape Verde, Central African Republic, Chad, Chile, Colombia, Comoros, Congo, Costa Rica, Côte d'Ivoire, Croatia, Cyprus, Czech Republic, Denmark, Djibouti, Dominica, Dominican Republic, Ecuador, El Salvador, Eritrea, Estonia, Ethiopia, Fiji, Finland, France, Gabon, Gambia, Georgia, Germany, Ghana, Greece, Grenada, Guatemala, Guyana, Haiti, Honduras, Hungary, Iceland, Indonesia, Iraq, Ireland, Italy, Jamaica, Japan, Jordan, Kazakhstan, Kuwait, Kyrgyzstan, Lao People's Democratic Republic, Latvia, Lebanon, Lesotho, Liberia, Libyan Arab Jamahiriya, Liechtenstein, Lithuania, Luxembourg, Malawi, Malaysia, Maldives, Mali, Malta, Marshall Islands, Mauritania, Mauritius, Mexico, Micronesia, Moldova, Monaco, Mongolia, Montenegro, Morocco, Namibia, Nauru, Nepal, Netherlands, New Zealand, Nicaragua, Niger, Norway, Oman, Palau, Panama, Papua New Guinea, Paraguay, Peru, Philippines, Poland, Portugal, Qatar, Republic of Korea, Romania, Russian Federation, Rwanda, Saint Kitts and Nevis, Saint Lucia, Saint Vincent and the Grenadines, Samoa, San Marino, Sao Tome and Principe, Saudi Arabia, Senegal, Serbia, Sierra Leone, Singapore, Slovakia, Slovenia, Solomon Islands, South Africa, Spain, Sri Lanka, Sudan, Suriname, Swaziland, Sweden, Switzerland, Tajikistan, Thailand, The former Yugoslav Republic of Macedonia, Timor-Leste, Togo, Tonga, Trinidad and Tobago, Tunisia, Turkey, Turkmenistan, Uganda, Ukraine, United Arab Emirates, United Kingdom, United Republic of Tanzania, Uruguay, Uzbekistan, Vanuatu, Venezuela, Viet Nam, Yemen, Zambia, Zimbabwe.

Against: Democratic People's Republic of Korea, India, Pakistan, United States.

Abstaining: Bhutan, China, Cuba, Egypt, Iran, Israel, Myanmar.

The Assembly adopted **resolution 61/78** by recorded vote (115-48-18) [agenda item 90 *(q)*].

Nuclear disarmament

The General Assembly,

Recalling its resolution 49/75 E of 15 December 1994 on a step-by-step reduction of the nuclear threat, and its resolutions 50/70 P of 12 December 1995, 51/45 O of 10 December 1996, 52/38 L of 9 December 1997, 53/77 X of 4 December 1998, 54/54 P of 1 December 1999, 55/33 T of 20 November 2000, 56/24 R of 29 November 2001, 57/79 of 22 November 2002, 58/56 of 8 December 2003, 59/77 of 3 December 2004 and 60/70 of 8 December 2005 on nuclear disarmament,

Reaffirming the commitment of the international community to the goal of the total elimination of nuclear weapons and the establishment of a nuclear-weapon-free world,

Bearing in mind that the Convention on the Prohibition of the Development, Production and Stockpiling of Bacteriological (Biological) and Toxin Weapons and on Their Destruction of 1972 and the Convention on the Prohibition of the Development, Production, Stockpiling and Use of Chemical Weapons and on Their Destruction of 1993 have already established legal regimes on the complete prohibition of biological and chemical weapons, respectively, and determined to achieve a nuclear weapons convention on the prohibition of the development, testing, production, stockpiling, loan, transfer, use and threat of use of nuclear weapons and on their destruction, and to conclude such an international convention at an early date,

Recognizing that there now exist conditions for the establishment of a world free of nuclear weapons, and stressing the need to take concrete practical steps towards achieving this goal,

Bearing in mind paragraph 50 of the Final Document of the Tenth Special Session of the General Assembly, the first special session devoted to disarmament, calling for the urgent negotiation of agreements for the cessation of the qualitative improvement and development of nuclear-weapon systems, and for a comprehensive and phased programme with agreed time frames, wherever feasible, for the progressive and balanced reduction of nuclear weapons and their means of delivery, leading to their ultimate and complete elimination at the earliest possible time,

Reaffirming the conviction of the States parties to the Treaty on the Non-Proliferation of Nuclear Weapons that the Treaty is a cornerstone of nuclear non-proliferation and nuclear disarmament and the importance of the decision on strengthening the review process for the Treaty, the decision on principles and objectives for nuclear non-proliferation and disarmament, the decision on the extension of the Treaty and the resolution on the Middle East, adopted by the 1995 Review and Extension Conference of the Parties to the Treaty on the Non-Proliferation of Nuclear Weapons,

Stressing the importance of the thirteen steps for the systematic and progressive efforts to achieve the objective of nuclear disarmament leading to the total elimination of nuclear weapons, as agreed to by the States parties in the Final Document of the 2000 Review Conference of the Parties to the Treaty on the Non-Proliferation of Nuclear Weapons,

Reiterating the highest priority accorded to nuclear disarmament in the Final Document of the Tenth Special Session of the General Assembly and by the international community,

Reiterating its call for an early entry into force of the Comprehensive Nuclear-Test-Ban Treaty,

Noting with appreciation the entry into force of the Treaty on the Reduction and Limitation of Strategic Offensive Arms (START I), to which Belarus, Kazakhstan, the Russian Federation, Ukraine and the United States of America are States parties,

Noting with appreciation also the entry into force of the Treaty on Strategic Offensive Reductions ("the Moscow Treaty") between the United States of America and the Russian Federation as a significant step towards reducing their deployed strategic nuclear weapons, while calling for further irreversible deep cuts in their nuclear arsenals,

Noting with appreciation further the unilateral measures taken by the nuclear-weapon States for nuclear arms limitation, and encouraging them to take further such measures,

Recognizing the complementarity of bilateral, plurilateral and multilateral negotiations on nuclear disarmament, and that bilateral negotiations can never replace multilateral negotiations in this respect,

Noting the support expressed in the Conference on Disarmament and in the General Assembly for the elaboration of an international convention to assure non-nuclear-weapon States against the use or threat of use of nuclear weapons, and the multilateral efforts in the Conference on Disarmament to reach agreement on such an international convention at an early date,

Recalling the advisory opinion of the International Court of Justice on the *Legality of the Threat or Use of Nuclear Weapons*, issued on 8 July 1996, and welcoming the unanimous reaffirmation by all Judges of the Court that there exists an obligation for all States to pursue in good faith and bring to a conclusion negotiations leading to nuclear disarmament in all its aspects under strict and effective international control,

Mindful of paragraph 64 of the Final Document of the Ministerial Meeting of the Coordinating Bureau of the Movement of Non-Aligned Countries, held in Putrajaya, Malaysia, on 29 and 30 May 2006,

Recalling paragraph 70 and other relevant recommendations in the Final Document of the Fourteenth Conference of Heads of State or Government of Non-Aligned Countries, held in Havana on 15 and 16 September 2006, calling upon the Conference on Disarmament to establish, as soon as possible and as the highest priority, an ad hoc committee on nuclear disarmament and to commence negotiations on a phased programme for the complete elimination of nuclear weapons with a specified time framework,

Reaffirming the specific mandate conferred upon the Disarmament Commission by the General Assembly, in its decision 52/492 of 8 September 1998, to discuss the subject of nuclear disarmament as one of its main substantive agenda items,

Recalling the United Nations Millennium Declaration, in which Heads of State and Government resolved to strive for the elimination of weapons of mass destruction, in particular nuclear weapons, and to keep all options open for achieving this aim, including the possibility of convening an international conference to identify ways of eliminating nuclear dangers,

Reaffirming that, in accordance with the Charter of the United Nations, States should refrain from the use or threat of use of nuclear weapons in settling their disputes in international relations,

Seized of the danger of the use of weapons of mass destruction, particularly nuclear weapons, in terrorist acts and the urgent need for concerted international efforts to control and overcome it,

1. *Recognizes* that, in view of recent political developments, the time is now opportune for all the nuclear-weapon States to take effective disarmament measures with a view to achieving the elimination of these weapons;

2. *Reaffirms* that nuclear disarmament and nuclear non-proliferation are substantively interrelated and mutually reinforcing, that the two processes must go hand in hand and that there is a genuine need for a systematic and progressive process of nuclear disarmament;

3. *Welcomes and encourages* the efforts to establish new nuclear-weapon-free zones in different parts of the world on the basis of agreements or arrangements freely arrived at among the States of the regions concerned, which is an effective measure for limiting the further spread of nuclear weapons geographically and contributes to the cause of nuclear disarmament;

4. *Recognizes* that there is a genuine need to diminish the role of nuclear weapons in strategic doctrines and security policies to minimize the risk that these weapons will ever be used and to facilitate the process of their total elimination;

5. *Urges* the nuclear-weapon States to stop immediately the qualitative improvement, development, production and stockpiling of nuclear warheads and their delivery systems;

6. *Also urges* the nuclear-weapon States, as an interim measure, to de-alert and deactivate immediately their nuclear weapons and to take other concrete measures to reduce further the operational status of their nuclear-weapon systems;

7. *Reiterates its call upon* the nuclear-weapon States to undertake the step-by-step reduction of the nuclear threat and to carry out effective nuclear disarmament measures with a view to achieving the total elimination of these weapons;

8. *Calls upon* the nuclear-weapon States, pending the achievement of the total elimination of nuclear weapons, to agree on an internationally and legally binding instrument on a joint undertaking not to be the first to use nuclear weapons, and calls upon all States to conclude an internationally and legally binding instrument on security assurances of non-use and non-threat of use of nuclear weapons against non-nuclear-weapon States;

9. *Urges* the nuclear-weapon States to commence plurilateral negotiations among themselves at an appropriate stage on further deep reductions of nuclear weapons as an effective measure of nuclear disarmament;

10. *Underlines* the importance of applying the principle of irreversibility to the process of nuclear disarmament, and nuclear and other related arms control and reduction measures;

11. *Underscores* the importance of the unequivocal undertaking by the nuclear-weapon States, in the Final Document of the 2000 Review Conference of the Parties to the Treaty on the Non-Proliferation of Nuclear Weapons, to accomplish the total elimination of their nuclear arsenals leading to nuclear disarmament, to which all States parties are committed under article VI of the Treaty, and the reaffirmation by the States parties that the total elimination of nuclear weapons is the only absolute guarantee against the use or threat of use of nuclear weapons;

12. *Calls for* the full and effective implementation of the thirteen steps for nuclear disarmament contained in the Final Document of the 2000 Review Conference;

13. *Urges* the nuclear-weapon States to carry out further reductions of non-strategic nuclear weapons, based on unilateral initiatives and as an integral part of the nuclear arms reduction and disarmament process;

14. *Calls for* the immediate commencement of negotiations in the Conference on Disarmament on a non-discriminatory, multilateral and internationally and effectively verifiable treaty banning the production of fissile material for nuclear weapons or other nuclear explosive devices on the basis of the report of the Special Coordinator and the mandate contained therein;

15. *Urges* the Conference on Disarmament to agree on a programme of work that includes the immediate commencement of negotiations on such a treaty with a view to their conclusion within five years;

16. *Calls for* the conclusion of an international legal instrument or instruments on adequate security assurances to non-nuclear-weapon States;

17. *Also calls for* the early entry into force and strict observance of the Comprehensive Nuclear-Test-Ban Treaty;

18. *Expresses its regret* that the 2005 Review Conference of the Parties to the Treaty on the Non-Proliferation of Nuclear Weapons was unable to achieve any substantive result and that the 2005 World Summit Outcome adopted by the General Assembly failed to make any reference to nuclear disarmament and nuclear non-proliferation;

19. *Also expresses its regret* that the Conference on Disarmament was unable to establish an ad hoc committee to deal with nuclear disarmament at its 2006 session, as called for in General Assembly resolution 60/70;

20. *Reiterates its call upon* the Conference on Disarmament to establish, on a priority basis, an ad hoc committee to deal with nuclear disarmament early in 2007 and to commence negotiations on a phased programme of nuclear disarmament leading to the eventual total elimination of nuclear weapons;

21. *Calls for* the convening of an international conference on nuclear disarmament in all its aspects at an early date to identify and deal with concrete measures of nuclear disarmament;

22. *Requests* the Secretary-General to submit to the General Assembly at its sixty-second session a report on the implementation of the present resolution;

23. *Decides* to include in the provisional agenda of its sixty-second session the item entitled "Nuclear disarmament".

RECORDED VOTE ON RESOLUTION 61/78:

In favour: Afghanistan, Algeria, Angola, Antigua and Barbuda, Argentina, Bahamas, Bahrain, Bangladesh, Barbados, Belize, Benin, Bhutan, Bolivia, Brazil, Brunei Darussalam, Burkina Faso, Cambodia, Cameroon, Central African Republic, Chile, China, Colombia, Comoros, Congo, Costa Rica, Côte d'Ivoire, Cuba, Democratic People's Republic of Korea, Djibouti, Dominica, Dominican Republic, Ecuador, Egypt, El Salvador, Eritrea, Ethiopia, Fiji, Gabon, Gambia, Ghana, Grenada, Guatemala, Guinea, Guyana, Haiti, Honduras, Indonesia, Iran, Iraq, Jamaica, Jordan, Kenya, Kuwait, Lao People's Democratic Republic, Lebanon, Lesotho, Liberia, Libyan Arab Jamahiriya, Malawi, Malaysia, Maldives, Mali, Mauritania, Mexico, Mongolia, Morocco, Mozambique, Myanmar, Namibia, Nauru, Nepal, New Zealand, Nicaragua, Niger, Nigeria, Oman, Panama, Papua New Guinea, Paraguay, Peru, Philippines, Qatar, Rwanda, Saint Kitts and Nevis, Saint Lucia, Saint Vincent and the Grenadines, Samoa, Sao Tome and Principe, Saudi Arabia, Senegal, Sierra Leone, Singapore, Solomon Islands, South Africa, Sri Lanka, Sudan, Suriname, Swaziland, Syrian Arab Republic, Thailand, Timor-Leste, Togo, Tonga, Trinidad and Tobago, Tunisia, Uganda, United Arab Emirates, United Republic of Tanzania, Uruguay, Vanuatu, Venezuela, Viet Nam, Yemen, Zambia, Zimbabwe.

Against: Albania, Andorra, Australia, Belgium, Bosnia and Herzegovina, Bulgaria, Canada, Chad, Croatia, Cyprus, Czech Republic, Denmark, Estonia, Finland, France, Georgia, Germany, Greece, Hungary, Iceland, Israel, Italy, Latvia, Liechtenstein, Lithuania, Luxembourg, Marshall Islands, Micronesia, Moldova, Monaco, Montenegro, Netherlands, Norway, Palau, Poland, Portugal, Romania, San Marino, Serbia, Slovakia, Slovenia, Spain, Switzerland, The former Yugoslav Republic of Macedonia, Turkey, Ukraine, United Kingdom, United States.

Abstaining: Armenia, Austria, Azerbaijan, Belarus, Cape Verde, India, Ireland, Japan, Kazakhstan, Kyrgyzstan, Malta, Mauritius, Pakistan, Republic of Korea, Russian Federation, Sweden, Tajikistan, Uzbekistan.

The Assembly adopted **resolution 61/85** by recorded vote (118-52-13) [agenda item 97 *(w)*].

Reducing nuclear danger

The General Assembly,

Bearing in mind that the use of nuclear weapons poses the most serious threat to mankind and to the survival of civilization,

Reaffirming that any use or threat of use of nuclear weapons would constitute a violation of the Charter of the United Nations,

Convinced that the proliferation of nuclear weapons in all its aspects would seriously enhance the danger of nuclear war,

Convinced also that nuclear disarmament and the complete elimination of nuclear weapons are essential to remove the danger of nuclear war,

Considering that, until nuclear weapons cease to exist, it is imperative on the part of the nuclear-weapon States to adopt measures that assure non-nuclear-weapon States against the use or threat of use of nuclear weapons,

Considering also that the hair-trigger alert of nuclear weapons carries unacceptable risks of unintentional or accidental use of nuclear weapons, which would have catastrophic consequences for all mankind,

Emphasizing the imperative need to adopt measures to avoid accidental, unauthorized or unexplained incidents arising from computer anomaly or other technical malfunctions,

Conscious that limited steps relating to de-alerting and de-targeting have been taken by the nuclear-weapon States and that further practical, realistic and mutually reinforcing steps are necessary to contribute to the improvement in the international climate for negotiations leading to the elimination of nuclear weapons,

Mindful that a diminishing role for nuclear weapons in the security policies of nuclear-weapon States would positively impact on international peace and security and improve the conditions for the further reduction and the elimination of nuclear weapons,

Reiterating the highest priority accorded to nuclear disarmament in the Final Document of the Tenth Special Session of the General Assembly and by the international community,

Recalling that in the advisory opinion of the International Court of Justice on the *Legality of the Threat or Use of Nuclear Weapons*, it is stated that there exists an obligation for all States to pursue in good faith and bring to a conclusion negotiations leading to nuclear disarmament in all its aspects under strict and effective international control,

Recalling also the call in the United Nations Millennium Declaration to seek to eliminate the dangers posed by weapons of mass destruction and the resolve to strive for the elimination of weapons of mass destruction, particularly nuclear weapons, including the possibility of convening an international conference to identify ways of eliminating nuclear dangers,

1. *Calls for* a review of nuclear doctrines and, in this context, immediate and urgent steps to reduce the risks of unintentional and accidental use of nuclear weapons, including through de-alerting and de-targeting of nuclear weapons;

2. *Requests* the five nuclear-weapon States to take measures towards the implementation of paragraph 1 above;

3. *Calls upon* Member States to take the necessary measures to prevent the proliferation of nuclear weapons in all its aspects and to promote nuclear disarmament, with the objective of eliminating nuclear weapons;

4. *Takes note* of the report of the Secretary-General submitted pursuant to paragraph 5 of General Assembly resolution 60/79 of 8 December 2005;

5. *Requests* the Secretary-General to intensify efforts and support initiatives that would contribute towards the full implementation of the seven recommendations identified in the report of the Advisory Board on Disarmament Matters that would significantly reduce the risk of nuclear war, and also to continue to encourage Member States to endeavour to create conditions that would allow the emergence of an international consensus to hold an international conference as proposed in the United Nations Millennium Declaration, to identify ways of eliminating nuclear dangers, and to report thereon to the General Assembly at its sixty-second session;

6. *Decides* to include in the provisional agenda of its sixty-second session the item entitled "Reducing nuclear danger".

RECORDED VOTE ON RESOLUTION 61/85:

In favour: Afghanistan, Algeria, Angola, Antigua and Barbuda, Bahamas, Bahrain, Bangladesh, Barbados, Belize, Benin, Bhutan, Bolivia, Brazil, Brunei Darussalam, Burkina Faso, Burundi, Cambodia, Cameroon, Cape Verde, Central African Republic, Chad, Chile, Colombia, Comoros, Congo, Costa Rica, Côte d'Ivoire, Cuba, Democratic People's Republic of Korea, Djibouti, Dominica, Dominican Republic, Ecuador, Egypt, El Salvador, Eritrea, Ethiopia, Fiji, Gabon, Gambia, Ghana, Grenada, Guatemala, Guinea, Guyana, Haiti, Honduras, India, Indonesia, Iran, Iraq, Jamaica, Jordan, Kenya, Kuwait, Lao People's Democratic Republic, Lebanon, Lesotho, Liberia, Libyan Arab Jamahiriya, Malawi, Malaysia, Maldives, Mali, Mauritania, Mauritius, Mexico, Mongolia, Morocco, Mozambique, Myanmar, Namibia, Nauru, Nepal, Nicaragua, Niger, Nigeria, Oman, Pakistan, Panama, Papua New Guinea, Peru, Philippines, Qatar, Rwanda, Saint Kitts and Nevis, Saint Lucia, Saint Vincent and the Grenadines, Samoa, Sao Tome and Principe, Saudi Arabia, Senegal, Sierra Leone, Singapore, Solomon Islands, South Africa, Sri Lanka, Sudan, Suriname, Swaziland, Syrian Arab Republic, Thailand, Timor-Leste, Togo, Tonga, Trinidad and Tobago, Tunisia, Turkmenistan, Uganda, United Arab Emirates, United Republic of Tanzania, Uruguay, Vanuatu, Venezuela, Viet Nam, Yemen, Zambia, Zimbabwe

Against: Albania, Andorra, Australia, Austria, Belgium, Bosnia and Herzegovina, Bulgaria, Canada, Croatia, Cyprus, Czech Republic, Denmark, Estonia, Finland, France, Georgia, Germany, Greece, Hungary, Iceland, Ireland, Israel, Italy, Latvia, Liechtenstein, Lithuania, Luxembourg, Malta, Marshall Islands, Micronesia, Moldova, Monaco, Montenegro, Netherlands, New Zealand, Norway, Palau, Poland, Portugal, Romania, San Marino, Serbia, Slovakia, Slovenia, Spain, Sweden, Switzerland, The former Yugoslav Republic of Macedonia, Turkey, Ukraine, United Kingdom, United States.

Abstaining: Argentina, Armenia, Azerbaijan, Belarus, China, Japan, Kazakhstan, Kyrgyzstan, Paraguay, Republic of Korea, Russian Federation, Tajikistan, Uzbekistan.

The Assembly adopted **decision 61/515** by recorded vote (128-3-44) [agenda item 90 *(cc)*].

United Nations conference to identify ways of eliminating nuclear dangers in the context of nuclear disarmament

At its 67th plenary meeting, on 6 December 2006, the General Assembly, on the recommendation of the First Committee, decided, by a recorded vote of 128 to 3, with 44 abstentions, to include in the provisional agenda of its sixty-second session the item entitled "United Nations conference to identify ways of eliminating nuclear dangers in the context of nuclear disarmament".

RECORDED VOTE ON DECISION 61/515:

In favour: Afghanistan, Algeria, Angola, Antigua and Barbuda, Argentina, Armenia, Bahamas, Bahrain, Bangladesh, Barbados, Belarus, Belize, Benin, Bhutan, Bolivia, Brazil, Brunei Darussalam, Burkina Faso, Burundi, Cambodia, Cameroon, Cape Verde, Central African Republic, Chad, Chile, China, Colombia, Comoros, Congo, Costa Rica, Côte d'Ivoire, Cuba, Cyprus, Djibouti, Dominica, Dominican Republic, Ecuador, Egypt, El Salvador, Ethiopia, Fiji, Gabon, Gambia, Ghana, Grenada, Guatemala, Guinea, Guyana, Haiti, Honduras, India, Indonesia, Iran, Iraq, Ireland, Jamaica, Japan, Jordan, Kazakhstan, Kenya, Kuwait, Kyrgyzstan, Lao People's Democratic Republic, Lebanon, Lesotho, Liberia, Libyan Arab Jamahiriya, Malawi, Malaysia, Maldives, Mali, Malta, Mauritania, Mauritius, Mexico, Mongolia, Morocco, Mozambique, Myanmar, Namibia, Nauru, Nepal, New Zealand, Nicaragua, Niger, Nigeria, Oman, Panama, Papua New Guinea, Paraguay, Peru,

Philippines, Qatar, Rwanda, Saint Kitts and Nevis, Saint Lucia, Saint Vincent and the Grenadines, Samoa, Sao Tome and Principe, Saudi Arabia, Senegal, Sierra Leone, Singapore, Solomon Islands, South Africa, Sri Lanka, Sudan, Suriname, Swaziland, Sweden, Syrian Arab Republic, Tajikistan, Thailand, Timor-Leste, Togo, Trinidad and Tobago, Tunisia, Uganda, United Arab Emirates, United Republic of Tanzania, Uruguay, Uzbekistan, Vanuatu, Venezuela, Viet Nam, Yemen, Zambia, Zimbabwe.

Against: France, United Kingdom, United States.

Abstaining: Albania, Andorra, Australia, Austria, Azerbaijan, Belgium, Bosnia and Herzegovina, Bulgaria, Canada, Croatia, Czech Republic, Denmark, Estonia, Finland, Georgia, Germany, Greece, Hungary, Iceland, Israel, Italy, Latvia, Liechtenstein, Lithuania, Luxembourg, Marshall Islands, Moldova, Montenegro, Norway, Palau, Poland, Portugal, Republic of Korea, Romania, Russian Federation, San Marino, Serbia, Slovakia, Slovenia, Spain, Switzerland, The former Yugoslav Republic of Macedonia, Turkey, Ukraine.

Missile defence issues

The subscribing States to the non-legally binding international code of conduct against ballistic missile proliferation, also known as Hague Code of Conduct [YUN 2002, p. 504], at their fifth regular meeting (Vienna, 22-23 June), considered, among other issues, the strengthening of confidence-building measures, such as pre-launch notification and annual declaration of ballistic missiles and space-vehicle launches and related policies. They also discussed the importance of outreach activities, with a view to increasing the number of subscribing States, especially in the Middle East and Africa. The sixth regular meeting of the subscribing States was scheduled to be held in Vienna, between May and June, 2007, to continue discussions on confidence-building measures and the universalization of the Code. At year's end, subscribing States numbered 125.

Report of Secretary-General. In response to General Assembly resolution 59/67 [YUN 2004, p. 537], the Secretary-General submitted a July report [A/61/168] on the issue of missiles in all its aspects, which described the current situation in the field of missiles and identified areas where consensus had been or could be achieved. Most States had agreed that the existing situation regarding missiles was unsatisfactory and ambitious arms control and disarmament measures on missiles were currently unattainable. Consensus was also possible on one category of missile systems, man-portable air defence systems, particularly the need to further explore measures for enhancing their control. The Secretary-General, therefore, recommended sustained UN efforts to strengthen the control of those systems, with a view to enhancing related elements identified in Assembly resolution 60/77 [YUN 2005, p. 624], and to broaden adherence to the controls stipulated by existing multilateral agreements and initiatives dealing with them. He also recommended that the United Nations address the substantive content and appropriateness of missile specific confidence-building measures at regional or global levels, and further investigate them with respect to ballistic missiles.

In October, the Missile Technology Control Regime (MTCR)—an informal and voluntary association of countries sharing the goals of the non-proliferation of unmanned delivery systems capable of delivering WMDs—held its twenty-first plenary meeting (Copenhagen, Denmark, 2-6 October) to review its activities and further strengthen efforts to prevent missile proliferation. Acknowledging the growing risk of WMD proliferation and their means of delivery, as well as the proliferation of missiles in North-East and South Asia, and the Middle East, the Regime partners noted the relevance of Security Council resolutions 1695(2006) (see p. 441) and 1696(2006) (see p. 433) and expressed their determination to implement calls made therein to exercise vigilance and prevent the transfer of any items, materials, goods and technology that could contribute to ballistic missile programmes, where proliferation was a concern. The partners welcomed Denmark's offer to host a conference on missile proliferation in 2007.

GENERAL ASSEMBLY ACTION

On 6 December [meeting 67], the General Assembly, on the recommendation of the First Committee [A/61/394], adopted **resolution 61/59** by recorded vote (115-7-54) [agenda item 90 *(b)*].

Missiles

The General Assembly,

Recalling its resolutions 54/54 F of 1 December 1999, 55/33 A of 20 November 2000, 56/24 B of 29 November 2001, 57/71 of 22 November 2002, 58/37 of 8 December 2003 and 59/67 of 3 December 2004 and its decision 60/515 of 8 December 2005,

Reaffirming the role of the United Nations in the field of arms regulation and disarmament and the commitment of Member States to take concrete steps to strengthen that role,

Realizing the need to promote regional and international peace and security in a world free from the scourge of war and the burden of armaments,

Convinced of the need for a comprehensive approach towards missiles, in a balanced and non-discriminatory manner, as a contribution to international peace and security,

Bearing in mind that the security concerns of Member States at the international and regional levels should be taken into consideration in addressing the issue of missiles,

Underlining the complexities involved in considering the issue of missiles in the conventional context,

Expressing its support for the international efforts against the development and proliferation of all weapons of mass destruction,

1. *Takes note* of the report of the Secretary-General on the issue of missiles in all its aspects, submitted pursuant to resolution 59/67;

2. *Decides* to include in the provisional agenda of its sixty-second session the item entitled "Missiles".

RECORDED VOTE ON RESOLUTION 61/59:

In favour: Afghanistan, Algeria, Angola, Antigua and Barbuda, Argentina, Bahamas, Bahrain, Bangladesh, Barbados, Belarus, Belize, Bhutan, Bolivia, Brazil, Brunei Darussalam, Burkina Faso, Cambodia, Cameroon, Cape Verde, Central African Republic, Chile, China, Colombia, Comoros, Congo, Costa Rica, Cuba, Democratic People's Republic of Korea, Democratic Republic of the Congo, Djibouti, Dominica, Dominican Republic, Ecuador, Egypt, El Salvador, Eritrea, Ethiopia, Fiji, Gabon, Ghana, Grenada, Guatemala, Guinea, Guyana, Haiti, India, Indonesia, Iran, Iraq, Jamaica, Jordan, Kazakhstan, Kuwait, Kyrgyzstan, Lao People's Democratic Republic, Lebanon, Lesotho, Liberia, Libyan Arab Jamahiriya, Malawi, Malaysia, Maldives, Mali, Mauritania, Mauritius, Mexico, Mongolia, Morocco, Mozambique, Myanmar, Namibia, Nepal, Nicaragua, Niger, Nigeria, Oman, Pakistan, Panama, Paraguay, Peru, Philippines, Qatar, Russian Federation, Rwanda, Saint Kitts and Nevis, Saint Lucia, Saint Vincent and the Grenadines, Sao Tome and Principe, Saudi Arabia, Senegal, Sierra Leone, Solomon Islands, Somalia, Sri Lanka, Sudan, Suriname, Swaziland, Syrian Arab Republic, Tajikistan, Thailand, Timor-Leste, Togo, Tonga, Trinidad and Tobago, Tunisia, Turkmenistan, United Arab Emirates, United Republic of Tanzania, Uruguay, Uzbekistan, Venezuela, Viet Nam, Yemen, Zambia, Zimbabwe.

Against: Albania, France, Israel, Micronesia, Palau, United Kingdom, United States.

Abstaining: Andorra, Armenia, Australia, Austria, Azerbaijan, Belgium, Bosnia and Herzegovina, Bulgaria, Burundi, Canada, Croatia, Cyprus, Czech Republic, Denmark, Estonia, Finland, Georgia, Germany, Greece, Honduras, Hungary, Iceland, Ireland, Italy, Japan, Latvia, Liechtenstein, Lithuania, Luxembourg, Malta, Marshall Islands, Moldova, Monaco, Montenegro, Nauru, Netherlands, New Zealand, Norway, Poland, Portugal, Republic of Korea, Romania, Samoa, San Marino, Serbia, Singapore, Slovakia, Slovenia, Spain, Sweden, Switzerland, The former Yugoslav Republic of Macedonia, Turkey, Ukraine.

DPRK missile launch

On 5 July, the Democratic People's Republic of Korea executed a multiple launch of ballistic missiles, subsequently condemned by the Security Council in resolution 1695(2006) (see p. 441), which asked Member States to prevent the procurement of missiles and missile-related items and technology from that country, as well as the transfer of financial resources in relation to its missile or WMD programme.

Comprehensive Nuclear-Test-Ban Treaty

Status

As at 31 December, 177 States had signed the 1996 Comprehensive Nuclear-Test-Ban Treaty (CTBT), adopted by General Assembly resolution 50/245 [YUN 1996, p. 454], and 137 had ratified it. During the year, instruments of ratification were deposited by Andorra, Antigua and Barbuda, Armenia, Bosnia and Herzegovina, Cameroon, Cape Verde, Ethiopia, Suriname, Viet Nam and Zambia, while Montenegro succeeded to the Treaty. In accordance with article xiv, CTBT would enter into force 180 days after the 44 States possessing nuclear reactors, listed in annex 2 of the Treaty, had deposited their instruments of ratification. By year's end, 34 of those States had ratified the Treaty.

Report of Secretary-General. In response to General Assembly resolution 60/95 [YUN 2005, p. 594], the Secretary-General submitted a 12 July report [A/61/134 & Add.1] containing information prepared by the Preparatory Commission for the Comprehensive Nuclear-Test-Ban Treaty Organization (see p. 630) on the efforts of ratifying States towards the Treaty's universalization, and on possibilities for providing assistance on ratification procedures to States requesting it.

Report of Executive Secretary. By a 26 July note [A/61/184], the Secretary-General informed the Assembly of the availability of the report of the Commission's Executive Secretary covering 2005.

Communication. On 20 September [A/61/638], Australia, Canada, Finland, Japan and the Netherlands issued a joint Ministerial Statement, supported by 72 countries, as at 13 December, reaffirming support for CTBT as an initiative that would rid the world of nuclear weapons test explosions and contribute to the reduction of nuclear weapons and the prevention of nuclear proliferation. Noting that 2006 marked the tenth anniversary of the Treaty's opening for signature, they pointed out that its entry into force, within the broader framework of multilateral disarmament and non-proliferation efforts, had become more urgent than ever before. They dedicated themselves towards achieving that goal and appealed to States to maximize efforts in that regard. Those States that had not done so were asked to ratify CTBT, particularly those whose ratification was needed for its entry into force. States were also urged to maintain a moratorium on nuclear weapon test explosions or any other nuclear explosions.

GENERAL ASSEMBLY ACTION

On 6 December [meeting 67], the General Assembly, on the recommendation of the First Committee [A/61/400], adopted **resolution 61/104** by recorded vote (172-2-4) [agenda item 96].

Comprehensive Nuclear-Test-Ban Treaty

The General Assembly,

Reiterating that the cessation of nuclear-weapon test explosions or any other nuclear explosions constitutes an effective nuclear disarmament and non-proliferation measure, and convinced that this is a meaningful step in the realization of a systematic process to achieve nuclear disarmament,

Recalling that the Comprehensive Nuclear-Test-Ban Treaty, adopted by its resolution 50/245 of 10 September 1996, was opened for signature on 24 September 1996,

Stressing that a universal and effectively verifiable Treaty constitutes a fundamental instrument in the field of nuclear disarmament and non-proliferation and that after ten years, its entry into force is more urgent than ever before,

Encouraged by the signing of the Treaty by one hundred and seventy-six States, including forty-one of the forty-four needed for its entry into force, and welcoming the ratification of one hundred and twenty-five States, including thirty-four of the forty-four needed for its entry into force, among which there are three nuclear-weapon States,

Recalling its resolution 60/95 of 8 December 2005,

Welcoming the Final Declaration of the fourth Conference on Facilitating the Entry into Force of the Comprehensive Nuclear-Test-Ban Treaty, held in New York from 21 to 23 September 2005, pursuant to article XIV of the Treaty, and the Ministerial Meeting of States Parties, held in New York on 20 September 2006,

1. *Stresses* the vital importance and urgency of signature and ratification, without delay and without conditions, to achieve the earliest entry into force of the Comprehensive Nuclear-Test-Ban Treaty;

2. *Welcomes* the contributions by the States signatories to the work of the Preparatory Commission for the Comprehensive Nuclear-Test-Ban Treaty Organization, in particular its efforts to ensure that the Treaty's verification regime will be capable of meeting the verification requirements of the Treaty upon its entry into force, in accordance with article IV of the Treaty;

3. *Underlines* the need to maintain momentum towards completion of the verification regime;

4. *Urges* all States to maintain their moratoriums on nuclear-weapon test explosions or any other nuclear explosions and to refrain from acts that would defeat the object and purpose of the Treaty, while stressing that these measures do not have the same permanent and legally binding effect as the entry into force of the Treaty;

5. *Condemns* the nuclear test proclaimed by the Democratic People's Republic of Korea on 9 October 2006, and demands that the Democratic People's Republic of Korea not conduct any further nuclear tests;

6. *Urges* all States that have not yet signed the Treaty to sign and ratify it as soon as possible;

7. *Urges* all States that have signed but not yet ratified the Treaty, in particular those whose ratification is needed for its entry into force, to accelerate their ratification processes with a view to ensuring their earliest successful conclusion;

8. *Urges* all States to remain seized of the issue at the highest political level and, where in a position to do so, to promote adherence to the Treaty through bilateral and joint outreach, seminars and other means;

9. *Requests* the Secretary-General, in consultation with the Preparatory Commission for the Comprehensive Nuclear-Test-Ban Treaty Organization, to prepare a report on the efforts of States that have ratified the Treaty towards its universalization and possibilities for providing assistance on ratification procedures to States that so request it, and to submit such a report to the General Assembly at its sixty-second session;

10. *Decides* to include in the provisional agenda of its sixty-second session the item entitled "Comprehensive Nuclear-Test-Ban Treaty".

RECORDED VOTE ON RESOLUTION 61/104:

In favour: Afghanistan, Albania, Algeria, Andorra, Angola, Antigua and Barbuda, Argentina, Armenia, Australia, Austria, Azerbaijan, Bahamas, Bahrain, Bangladesh, Barbados, Belarus, Belgium, Belize, Bhutan, Bolivia, Bosnia and Herzegovina, Brazil, Brunei Darussalam, Bulgaria, Burkina Faso, Burundi, Cambodia, Cameroon, Canada, Cape Verde, Central African Republic, Chile, China, Comoros, Congo, Costa Rica, Côte d'Ivoire, Croatia, Cuba, Cyprus, Czech Republic, Denmark, Djibouti, Dominica, Dominican Republic, Ecuador, Egypt, El Salvador, Eritrea, Estonia, Ethiopia, Fiji, Finland, France, Gabon, Gambia, Georgia, Germany, Ghana, Greece, Grenada, Guatemala, Guinea, Guyana, Haiti, Honduras, Hungary, Iceland, Indonesia, Iran, Iraq, Ireland, Israel, Italy, Jamaica, Japan, Jordan, Kazakhstan, Kenya, Kuwait, Kyrgyzstan, Lao People's Democratic Republic, Latvia, Lebanon, Lesotho, Liberia, Libyan Arab Jamahiriya, Liechtenstein, Lithuania, Luxembourg, Malawi, Malaysia, Maldives, Mali, Malta, Marshall Islands, Mauritania, Mexico, Micronesia, Moldova, Monaco, Mongolia, Montenegro, Morocco, Mozambique, Myanmar, Namibia, Nauru, Nepal, Netherlands, New Zealand, Nicaragua, Niger, Norway, Oman, Pakistan, Palau, Panama, Papua New Guinea, Paraguay, Peru, Philippines, Poland, Portugal, Qatar, Republic of Korea, Romania, Russian Federation, Rwanda, Saint Kitts and Nevis, Saint Lucia, Saint Vincent and the Grenadines, Samoa, San Marino, Sao Tome and Principe, Saudi Arabia, Senegal, Serbia, Sierra Leone, Singapore, Slovakia, Slovenia, Solomon Islands, South Africa, Spain, Sri Lanka, Sudan, Suriname, Swaziland, Sweden, Switzerland, Tajikistan, Thailand, The former Yugoslav Republic of Macedonia, Timor-Leste, Togo, Tonga, Trinidad and Tobago, Tunisia, Turkey, Ukraine, United Arab Emirates, United Kingdom, United Republic of Tanzania, Uruguay, Uzbekistan, Vanuatu, Venezuela, Viet Nam, Yemen, Zambia, Zimbabwe.

Against: Democratic People's Republic of Korea, United States.

Abstaining: Colombia, India, Mauritius, Syrian Arab Republic.

Preparatory Commission for the CTBT Organization

The Preparatory Commission for the Comprehensive Nuclear-Test-Ban Treaty Organization (CTBTO), established in 1996 [YUN 1996, p. 452], continued to develop the Treaty's verification regime for monitoring Treaty compliance. Further progress was made in setting up the International Monitoring System (IMS) [YUN 1999, p. 472], the global network of 337 facilities (comprising 321 monitoring stations and 16 related laboratories) to be built in 90 countries and designed to detect nuclear explosions prohibited by CTBT via a global satellite communication system. Relevant information would then be transmitted to the International Data Centre (IDC) in Vienna for processing. During the year, installations were completed at 25 additional IMS stations, bringing the total number of completed stations to 244 (76 per cent). Twenty-eight stations were certified as meeting the technical requirements, raising the total number of certified stations to 184 (57 per cent), and 9 laboratories (56 per cent). Planning for the future maintenance of IMS continued, including initiatives to establish a high degree of preparedness to facilitate the rapid resolution of problems. The development of IDC also continued, with 190 (59 per cent) IMS stations connected to IDC operations, thereby enhancing the geographical coverage of data being received. Significant progress was made in transferring existing IDC applications software for monitoring purposes to open source platform, and the 9 October announcement by the DPRK that it had conducted an underground nuclear test provided an opportunity to test the responsiveness of IDC operations. The Global Communications Infrastructure, which provided communication links to IMS sites and National Data Centres also continued to expand throughout the year.

The Preparatory Commission, during the first part of its twenty-sixth session (Vienna, 1 March) [CTBT/PC-26/1], appointed the Chairperson of its Working Group B and held the main part of that session (Vienna, 20-23 June) [CTBT/PC-26/2] to consider the reports of its working groups and to discuss organizational, budgetary and other matters, including a possible contribution to a tsunami warning system. As part I of its twenty-seventh session, the Commission held a special session (Vienna, 13 October) [CTBT/PC-27/1] to consider possible steps to be taken in connection with the DPRK underground nuclear test. At the main part of that session (Vienna, 13-17 November) [CTBT/PC-27/2 & Corr.1], it concluded its deliberations on the reports of its working groups and outstanding issues it had previously considered in June (see above). The Commission adopted its 2007 programme budget in the amounts of $48,277,100 and €48,564,400, of which approximately $18 million and €14 million were earmarked for the IMS network.

Symposium. During the year, the Preparatory Commission organized a scientific symposium on "CTBT: Synergies with science, 1996-2006 and beyond" (Vienna, 31 August–1 September), designed to provide for increased interaction between the scientific community worldwide, the Commission and signatories to the Treaty, in order to increase the ability to build global capacity in science and technology fields relevant to the Commission's activities.

GENERAL ASSEMBLY ACTION

On 4 December [meeting 65], the General Assembly, having considered the report on cooperation between the United Nations and the Preparatory Commission for the Comprehensive Nuclear-Test-Ban Treaty Organization [A/61/184] and the Secretary-General's consolidated report on cooperation between the United Nations and international organizations containing information on the subject [A/61/256], adopted **resolution 61/47** [draft: A/61/L.18] by recorded vote (133-1-0) [agenda item 108 *(s)*].

Cooperation between the United Nations and the Preparatory Commission for the Comprehensive Nuclear-Test-Ban Treaty Organization

The General Assembly,

Taking note of the report of the Secretary-General on cooperation between the United Nations and the Preparatory Commission for the Comprehensive Nuclear-Test-Ban Treaty Organization,

Taking note also of the report of the Executive Secretary of the Preparatory Commission for the Comprehensive Nuclear-Test-Ban Treaty Organization,

Decides to include in the provisional agenda of its sixty-third session the sub-item entitled "Cooperation between the United Nations and the Preparatory Commission for the Comprehensive Nuclear-Test-Ban Treaty Organization".

RECORDED VOTE ON RESOLUTION 61/47:

In favour: Algeria, Andorra, Angola, Antigua and Barbuda, Argentina, Armenia, Australia, Austria, Bahamas, Bahrain, Barbados, Belarus, Belgium, Belize, Bhutan, Bolivia, Bosnia and Herzegovina, Brazil, Brunei Darussalam, Bulgaria, Canada, Cape Verde, Chile, China, Congo, Costa Rica, Croatia, Cuba, Cyprus, Czech Republic, Denmark, Dominica, Dominican Republic, Ecuador, Egypt, El Salvador, Estonia, Ethiopia, Fiji, Finland, France, Georgia, Germany, Greece, Grenada, Guinea, Guyana, Honduras, Hungary, Iceland, India, Indonesia, Iran, Iraq, Ireland, Israel, Italy, Jamaica, Japan, Kuwait, Latvia, Lebanon, Lesotho, Libyan Arab Jamahiriya, Liechtenstein, Lithuania, Luxembourg, Madagascar, Malaysia, Malta, Mauritania, Mauritius, Micronesia, Moldova, Monaco, Montenegro,

Morocco, Mozambique, Myanmar, Netherlands, New Zealand, Niger, Nigeria, Oman, Pakistan, Panama, Papua New Guinea, Paraguay, Peru, Philippines, Poland, Portugal, Qatar, Republic of Korea, Romania, Russian Federation, Saint Kitts and Nevis, Saint Lucia, Saint Vincent and the Grenadines, Samoa, San Marino, Saudi Arabia, Senegal, Serbia, Singapore, Slovenia, Solomon Islands, South Africa, Spain, Sri Lanka, Suriname, Swaziland, Sweden, Switzerland, Tajikistan, Thailand, The former Yugoslav Republic of Macedonia, Togo, Tonga, Trinidad and Tobago, Tunisia, Turkey, Tuvalu, Ukraine, United Arab Emirates, United Kingdom, Uruguay, Vanuatu, Venezuela, Viet Nam, Yemen, Zambia, Zimbabwe.

Against: United States.

Abstaining: None.

Prohibition of the use of nuclear weapons

Owing to the continuing lack of consensus among delegates over a programme of work, the Conference on Disarmament was not able to take action on any of its substantive agenda items, including the question of starting negotiations on a convention on the prohibition of the use of nuclear weapons, as called for in General Assembly resolution 60/88 [YUN 2005, p. 595].

The Assembly, in resolution 61/97 (see below), reiterated its request to the Conference to commence those negotiations and to report thereon.

GENERAL ASSEMBLY ACTION

On 6 December [meeting 67], the General Assembly, on the recommendation of the First Committee [A/61/395] adopted **resolution 61/97** by recorded vote (119-52-10) [agenda item 91 *(h)*].

Convention on the Prohibition of the Use of Nuclear Weapons

The General Assembly,

Convinced that the use of nuclear weapons poses the most serious threat to the survival of mankind,

Bearing in mind the advisory opinion of the International Court of Justice of 8 July 1996 on the *Legality of the Threat or Use of Nuclear Weapons,*

Convinced that a multilateral, universal and binding agreement prohibiting the use or threat of use of nuclear weapons would contribute to the elimination of the nuclear threat and to the climate for negotiations leading to the ultimate elimination of nuclear weapons, thereby strengthening international peace and security,

Conscious that some steps taken by the Russian Federation and the United States of America towards a reduction of their nuclear weapons and the improvement in the international climate can contribute towards the goal of the complete elimination of nuclear weapons,

Recalling that paragraph 58 of the Final Document of the Tenth Special Session of the General Assembly states that all States should actively participate in efforts to bring about conditions in international relations among States in which a code of peaceful conduct of nations in international affairs could be agreed upon and that would preclude the use or threat of use of nuclear weapons,

Reaffirming that any use of nuclear weapons would be a violation of the Charter of the United Nations and a crime against humanity, as declared in its resolutions 1653(XVI) of 24 November 1961, 33/71 B of 14 December 1978, 34/83 G of 11 December 1979, 35/152 D of 12 December 1980 and 36/92 I of 9 December 1981,

Determined to achieve an international convention prohibiting the development, production, stockpiling and use of nuclear weapons, leading to their ultimate destruction,

Stressing that an international convention on the prohibition of the use of nuclear weapons would be an important step in a phased programme towards the complete elimination of nuclear weapons, with a specified framework of time,

Noting with regret that the Conference on Disarmament, during its 2006 session, was unable to undertake negotiations on this subject as called for in General Assembly resolution 60/88 of 8 December 2005,

1. *Reiterates its request* to the Conference on Disarmament to commence negotiations in order to reach agreement on an international convention prohibiting the use or threat of use of nuclear weapons under any circumstances;

2. *Requests* the Conference on Disarmament to report to the General Assembly on the results of those negotiations.

RECORDED VOTE ON RESOLUTION 61/97:

In favour: Afghanistan, Algeria, Angola, Antigua and Barbuda, Argentina, Bahamas, Bahrain, Bangladesh, Barbados, Belize, Benin, Bhutan, Bolivia, Brazil, Brunei Darussalam, Burkina Faso, Burundi, Cambodia, Cameroon, Cape Verde, Central African Republic, Chad, Chile, China, Colombia, Comoros, Congo, Costa Rica, Côte d'Ivoire, Cuba, Democratic People's Republic of Korea, Djibouti, Dominica, Dominican Republic, Ecuador, Egypt, El Salvador, Eritrea, Ethiopia, Fiji, Gabon, Gambia, Ghana, Grenada, Guatemala, Guinea, Guyana, Haiti, Honduras, India, Indonesia, Iran, Iraq, Jamaica, Jordan, Kenya, Kuwait, Lao People's Democratic Republic, Lebanon, Lesotho, Liberia, Libyan Arab Jamahiriya, Malawi, Malaysia, Maldives, Mali, Mauritania, Mauritius, Mexico, Mongolia, Morocco, Myanmar, Namibia, Nepal, Nicaragua, Niger, Nigeria, Oman, Pakistan, Panama, Papua New Guinea, Paraguay, Peru, Philippines, Qatar, Rwanda, Saint Kitts and Nevis, Saint Lucia, Saint Vincent and the Grenadines, Samoa, Sao Tome and Principe, Saudi Arabia, Senegal, Sierra Leone, Singapore, Solomon Islands, South Africa, Sri Lanka, Sudan, Suriname, Swaziland, Syrian Arab Republic, Thailand, Timor-Leste, Togo, Tonga, Trinidad and Tobago, Tunisia, Turkmenistan, Uganda, United Arab Emirates, United Republic of Tanzania, Uruguay, Vanuatu, Venezuela, Viet Nam, Yemen, Zambia, Zimbabwe.

Against: Albania, Andorra, Australia, Austria, Belgium, Bosnia and Herzegovina, Bulgaria, Canada, Croatia, Cyprus, Czech Republic, Denmark, Estonia, Finland, France, Georgia, Germany, Greece, Hungary, Iceland, Ireland, Israel, Italy, Latvia, Liechtenstein, Lithuania, Luxembourg, Malta, Marshall Islands, Micronesia, Moldova, Monaco, Montenegro, Netherlands, New Zealand, Norway, Palau,

Poland, Portugal, Romania, San Marino, Serbia, Slovakia, Slovenia, Spain, Sweden, Switzerland, The former Yugoslav Republic of Macedonia, Turkey, Ukraine, United Kingdom, United States.

Abstaining: Armenia, Azerbaijan, Belarus, Japan, Kazakhstan, Kyrgyzstan, Republic of Korea, Russian Federation, Tajikistan, Uzbekistan.

Advisory opinion of International Court of Justice

Pursuant to General Assembly resolution 60/76 [YUN 2005, p. 596] on the advisory opinion of the International Court of Justice (ICJ) that the threat or use of nuclear weapons was contrary to the UN Charter [YUN 1996, p. 461], the Secretary-General presented information received from eight States (Bolivia, Chile, Cuba, the Democratic People's Republic of Korea, Georgia, Japan, Qatar, the Syrian Arab Republic) on measures they had taken to implement the resolution and towards nuclear disarmament [A/61/127 & Add.1].

GENERAL ASSEMBLY ACTION

On 6 December [meeting 67], the General Assembly, on the recommendation of the First Committee [A/61/394], adopted **resolution 61/83** by recorded vote (125-27-29) [agenda item 90 *(u)*].

Follow-up to the advisory opinion of the International Court of Justice on the *Legality of the Threat or Use of Nuclear Weapons*

The General Assembly,

Recalling its resolutions 49/75 K of 15 December 1994, 51/45 M of 10 December 1996, 52/38 O of 9 December 1997, 53/77 W of 4 December 1998, 54/54 Q of 1 December 1999, 55/33 X of 20 November 2000, 56/24 S of 29 November 2001, 57/85 of 22 November 2002, 58/46 of 8 December 2003, 59/83 of 3 December 2004 and 60/76 of 8 December 2005,

Convinced that the continuing existence of nuclear weapons poses a threat to all humanity and that their use would have catastrophic consequences for all life on Earth, and recognizing that the only defence against a nuclear catastrophe is the total elimination of nuclear weapons and the certainty that they will never be produced again,

Reaffirming the commitment of the international community to the goal of the total elimination of nuclear weapons and the creation of a nuclear-weapon-free world,

Mindful of the solemn obligations of States parties, undertaken in article VI of the Treaty on the Non-Proliferation of Nuclear Weapons, particularly to pursue negotiations in good faith on effective measures relating to cessation of the nuclear-arms race at an early date and to nuclear disarmament,

Recalling the principles and objectives for nuclear non-proliferation and disarmament adopted at the 1995 Review and Extension Conference of the Parties to the Treaty on the Non-Proliferation of Nuclear Weapons,

Emphasizing the unequivocal undertaking by the nuclear-weapon States to accomplish the total elimination of their nuclear arsenals leading to nuclear disarmament, adopted at the 2000 Review Conference of the Parties to the Treaty on the Non-Proliferation of Nuclear Weapons,

Recalling the adoption of the Comprehensive Nuclear-Test-Ban Treaty in its resolution 50/245 of 10 September 1996, and expressing its satisfaction at the increasing number of States that have signed and ratified the Treaty,

Recognizing with satisfaction that the Antarctic Treaty and the treaties of Tlatelolco, Rarotonga, Bangkok, Pelindaba and Semipalatinsk, as well as Mongolia's nuclear-weapon-free status, are gradually freeing the entire southern hemisphere and adjacent areas covered by those treaties from nuclear weapons,

Stressing the importance of strengthening all existing nuclear-related disarmament and arms control and reduction measures,

Recognizing the need for a multilaterally negotiated and legally binding instrument to assure non-nuclear-weapon States against the threat or use of nuclear weapons,

Reaffirming the central role of the Conference on Disarmament as the sole multilateral disarmament negotiating forum, and regretting the lack of progress in disarmament negotiations, particularly nuclear disarmament, in the Conference during its 2006 session,

Emphasizing the need for the Conference on Disarmament to commence negotiations on a phased programme for the complete elimination of nuclear weapons with a specified framework of time,

Expressing its regret over the failure of the 2005 Review Conference of the Parties to the Treaty on the Non-Proliferation of Nuclear Weapons to reach agreement on any substantive issues,

Expressing its deep concern at the lack of progress in the implementation of the thirteen steps to implement article VI of the Treaty on the Non-Proliferation of Nuclear Weapons agreed to at the 2000 Review Conference of the Parties to the Treaty,

Desiring to achieve the objective of a legally binding prohibition of the development, production, testing, deployment, stockpiling, threat or use of nuclear weapons and their destruction under effective international control,

Recalling the advisory opinion of the International Court of Justice on the *Legality of the Threat or Use of Nuclear Weapons*, issued on 8 July 1996,

Taking note of the relevant portions of the report of the Secretary-General relating to the implementation of resolution 60/76,

1. *Underlines once again* the unanimous conclusion of the International Court of Justice that there exists an obligation to pursue in good faith and bring to a conclusion

negotiations leading to nuclear disarmament in all its aspects under strict and effective international control;

2. *Calls once again upon* all States immediately to fulfil that obligation by commencing multilateral negotiations leading to an early conclusion of a nuclear weapons convention prohibiting the development, production, testing, deployment, stockpiling, transfer, threat or use of nuclear weapons and providing for their elimination;

3. *Requests* all States to inform the Secretary-General of the efforts and measures they have taken on the implementation of the present resolution and nuclear disarmament, and requests the Secretary-General to apprise the General Assembly of that information at its sixty-second session;

4. *Decides* to include in the provisional agenda of its sixty-second session the item entitled "Follow-up to the advisory opinion of the International Court of Justice on the *Legality of the Threat or Use of Nuclear Weapons*".

RECORDED VOTE ON RESOLUTION 61/83:

In favour: Afghanistan, Algeria, Angola, Antigua and Barbuda, Argentina, Austria, Bahamas, Bahrain, Bangladesh, Barbados, Belize, Benin, Bhutan, Bolivia, Brazil, Brunei Darussalam, Burkina Faso, Burundi, Cambodia, Cameroon, Cape Verde, Central African Republic, Chad, Chile, China, Colombia, Comoros, Congo, Costa Rica, Côte d'Ivoire, Cuba, Democratic People's Republic of Korea, Djibouti, Dominica, Dominican Republic, Ecuador, Egypt, El Salvador, Eritrea, Ethiopia, Fiji, Gabon, Ghana, Grenada, Guatemala, Guinea, Guyana, Haiti, Honduras, India, Indonesia, Iran, Iraq, Ireland, Jamaica, Jordan, Kenya, Kuwait, Lao People's Democratic Republic, Lebanon, Lesotho, Liberia, Libyan Arab Jamahiriya, Malawi, Malaysia, Maldives, Mali, Malta, Mauritania, Mauritius, Mexico, Mongolia, Morocco, Mozambique, Myanmar, Namibia, Nepal, New Zealand, Nicaragua, Niger, Nigeria, Oman, Pakistan, Panama, Papua New Guinea, Paraguay, Peru, Philippines, Qatar, Rwanda, Saint Kitts and Nevis, Saint Lucia, Saint Vincent and the Grenadines, Samoa, San Marino, Sao Tome and Principe, Saudi Arabia, Senegal, Sierra Leone, Singapore, Solomon Islands, South Africa, Sri Lanka, Sudan, Suriname, Swaziland, Sweden, Syrian Arab Republic, Thailand, Timor-Leste, Togo, Tonga, Trinidad and Tobago, Tunisia, Turkmenistan, Uganda, United Arab Emirates, United Republic of Tanzania, Uruguay, Vanuatu, Venezuela, Viet Nam, Yemen, Zambia, Zimbabwe.

Against: Albania, Belgium, Bulgaria, Czech Republic, Denmark, France, Germany, Greece, Hungary, Iceland, Israel, Italy, Latvia, Lithuania, Luxembourg, Netherlands, Norway, Palau, Poland, Portugal, Russian Federation, Slovakia, Slovenia, Spain, Turkey, United Kingdom, United States.

Abstaining: Andorra, Armenia, Australia, Azerbaijan, Belarus, Bosnia and Herzegovina, Canada, Croatia, Cyprus, Estonia, Finland, Georgia, Japan, Kazakhstan, Kyrgyzstan, Liechtenstein, Marshall Islands, Micronesia, Moldova, Montenegro, Nauru, Republic of Korea, Romania, Serbia, Switzerland, Tajikistan, The former Yugoslav Republic of Macedonia, Ukraine, Uzbekistan.

Non-proliferation issues

Non-Proliferation Treaty

Status

In 2006, the number of States party to the 1968 Treaty on the Non-Proliferation of Nuclear Weapons (NPT), adopted by the General Assembly in resolution 2373(XXII) [YUN 1968, p.17], increased to 190 following Montenegro's ratification. NPT entered into force on 5 March 1970.

2010 review conference

Following consultations, the parties to NPT decided that the first session of the Preparatory Committee for the 2010 Review Conference of the parties would take place in Vienna from 30 April to 11 May, 2007.

Quinquennial review conferences, as called for under article VIII, paragraph 3, of the Treaty, were held in 1975 [YUN 1975, p. 27], 1980 [YUN 1980, p. 51], 1985 [YUN 1985, p. 56], 1990 [YUN 1990, p. 50], 1995 [YUN 1995, p. 189], 2000 [YUN 2000, p. 487] and 2005 [YUN 2005, p. 597].

Communication. The Group of Eight (G-8) major industrialized countries (St. Petersburg, Russian Federation, 15-17 July), in a statement on non-proliferation, reaffirmed their commitment to NPT and called upon States to comply with their obligations under the Treaty regime, including IAEA safeguards and the development of effective measures to prevent trafficking in nuclear equipment, technology and materials.

The Heads of State or Government of Non-Aligned Countries (Havana, Cuba, 11-16 September) [A/61/472-S/2006/780] underlined the importance of establishing subsidiary bodies to the relevant main committees of the 2010 NPT Review Conference to deliberate on practical steps for systematic and progressive efforts to eliminate nuclear weapons; consider and recommend proposals on the implementation of the resolution on the Middle East adopted by the 1995 Review and Extension Conference of NPT [YUN 1995, p. 189]; and consider security assurances.

GENERAL ASSEMBLY ACTION

On 6 December [meeting 67], the General Assembly, on the recommendation of the First Committee [A/61/394], adopted **resolution 61/70** by recorded vote (175-0-3) [agenda item 90].

2010 Review Conference of the Parties to the Treaty on the Non-Proliferation of Nuclear Weapons and its Preparatory Committee

The General Assembly,

Recalling its resolution 2373 (XXII) of 12 June 1968, the annex to which contains the Treaty on the Non-Proliferation of Nuclear Weapons,

Noting the provisions of article VIII, paragraph 3, of the Treaty regarding the convening of review conferences at five-year intervals,

Recalling the outcomes of the 1995 Review and Extension Conference of the Parties to the Treaty on the Non-Proliferation of Nuclear Weapons and of the 2000 Review Conference of the Parties to the Treaty,

Recalling also the decision of the 2000 Review Conference of the Parties to the Treaty on improving the effectiveness of the strengthened review process for the Treaty, which reaffirmed the provisions in the decision on strengthening the review process for the Treaty, adopted by the 1995 Review and Extension Conference of the Parties to the Treaty,

Recalling further that the 2005 Review Conference of the Parties to the Treaty, held from 2 to 27 May 2005, was unable to produce a consensus substantive outcome on the review of the implementation of the provisions of the Treaty,

Noting the decision on strengthening the review process for the Treaty, in which it was agreed that review conferences should continue to be held every five years, and noting that, accordingly, the next review conference should be held in 2010,

Recalling the decision of the 2000 Review Conference that three sessions of the Preparatory Committee should be held in the years prior to the review conference,

1. *Takes note* of the decision of the parties to the Treaty on the Non-Proliferation of Nuclear Weapons, following appropriate consultations, to hold the first session of the Preparatory Committee in Vienna from 30 April to 11 May 2007;

2. *Requests* the Secretary-General to render the necessary assistance and to provide such services, including summary records, as may be required for the 2010 Review Conference of the Parties to the Treaty on the Non-Proliferation of Nuclear Weapons and its Preparatory Committee.

RECORDED VOTE ON RESOLUTION 61/70:

In favour: Afghanistan, Albania, Algeria, Andorra, Angola, Antigua and Barbuda, Argentina, Armenia, Australia, Austria, Azerbaijan, Bahamas, Bahrain, Bangladesh, Barbados, Belarus, Belgium, Belize, Bhutan, Bolivia, Bosnia and Herzegovina, Brazil, Brunei Darussalam, Bulgaria, Burkina Faso, Burundi, Cambodia, Cameroon, Canada, Cape Verde, Central African Republic, Chad, Chile, China, Colombia, Comoros, Congo, Costa Rica, Côte d'Ivoire, Croatia, Cuba, Cyprus, Czech Republic, Denmark, Djibouti, Dominica, Dominican Republic, Ecuador, Egypt, El Salvador, Eritrea, Estonia, Ethiopia, Fiji, Finland, France, Gabon, Gambia, Georgia, Germany, Ghana, Greece, Grenada, Guatemala, Guinea, Guyana, Haiti, Honduras, Hungary, Iceland, Indonesia, Iran, Iraq, Ireland, Italy, Jamaica, Japan, Jordan, Kazakhstan, Kuwait, Kyrgyzstan, Lao People's Democratic Republic, Latvia, Lebanon, Lesotho, Liberia, Libyan Arab Jamahiriya, Liechtenstein, Lithuania, Luxembourg, Malawi, Malaysia, Maldives, Mali, Malta, Mauritania, Mauritius, Mexico, Micronesia, Moldova, Monaco, Mongolia, Montenegro, Morocco, Mozambique, Myanmar, Namibia, Nauru, Nepal, Netherlands, New Zealand, Nicaragua, Niger, Nigeria, Norway, Oman, Palau, Panama, Papua New Guinea, Paraguay, Peru, Philippines, Poland, Portugal, Qatar, Republic of Korea, Romania, Russian Federation, Rwanda, Saint Kitts and Nevis, Saint Lucia, Saint Vincent and the Grenadines, Samoa, San Marino, Sao Tome and Principe, Saudi Arabia, Senegal, Serbia, Sierra Leone, Singapore, Slovakia, Slovenia, Solomon Islands, South Africa, Spain, Sri Lanka, Sudan, Suriname, Swaziland, Sweden, Switzerland, Syrian Arab Republic, Tajikistan, Thailand, The former Yugoslav Republic of Macedonia, Timor-Leste, Togo, Trinidad and Tobago, Tunisia, Turkey, Turkmenistan, Uganda, Ukraine, United Arab Emirates, United Kingdom, United Republic of Tanzania, United States, Uruguay, Uzbekistan, Vanuatu, Venezuela, Viet Nam, Yemen, Zambia, Zimbabwe.

Against: None.

Abstaining: India, Israel, Pakistan.

Non-proliferation of weapons of mass destruction

Security Council Committee on WMDs. On 25 April [S/2006/257 & Corr.1], the Chairman of the Security Council Committee established pursuant to resolution 1540(2004) [YUN 2004, p. 544] to monitor the implementation of measures against the proliferation of WMDs and their means of delivery reported on the status of its work. The Committee had approved four programmes of work, each covering three to four months, for the period from 1 April 2005 to 28 April 2006. Those programmes set goals and provided guidance on issues regarding the examination of national reports; outreach activities and further reporting; and assistance, transparency, and cooperation with international, regional and subregional organizations and other Security Council subsidiary bodies.

The report noted that, as at 20 April, 129 Member States and one organization had submitted first national reports, with 79 of them submitting additional information, and 62 still to submit their first report, 55 of which were in Africa, the Caribbean and the South Pacific. The Committee observed that, international efforts to prevent WMD proliferation could be effective only if all States implemented fully the requirements laid down by resolution 1540(2004) and cooperated closely towards that end. After two years of work, the Committee had a clearer understanding of the challenges to be addressed to ensure full implementation of the resolution, and in that regard, despite the positive response from the majority of States that had developed legislative and other measures for tackling the problem, much more needed to be done. To address some States' lack of capacity and their requests for assistance in that regard, the Committee had designed an outreach strategy, but a coherent strategy on assistance still needed to be developed.

The Committee addressed a series of recommendations to the Council, including that it extend the Committee's mandate for another two years. The Council should also encourage States to provide additional information on national implementation on an ongoing basis; widen and intensify regional and subregional outreach activities so as to guide States in the implementation of their obligations under the resolution; invite States offering and receiving assistance to be proactive on a bilateral basis, in order to contribute to capacity-building; encourage States to use the background information provided through the legislative database developed by the Committee and related advice by international organizations when enacting national implementation laws and measures; continue identifying national practices that might be used to guide States seeking legislative assistance in implementing the resolution; and inform States that had already reported to the Committee that they might be further contacted to take stock of the extent to which they had implemented resolution 1540(2004).

SECURITY COUNCIL ACTION

On 27 April [meeting 5429], the Security Council unanimously adopted **resolution 1673(2006)**. The draft [S/2006/263] was prepared in consultations among Council members.

The Security Council,

Having considered the report of the Security Council Committee established pursuant to resolution 1540(2004) (hereinafter the 1540 Committee), and reaffirming its resolution 1540(2004) of 28 April 2004,

Reaffirming that the proliferation of nuclear, chemical and biological weapons, as well as their means of delivery, constitutes a threat to international peace and security,

Endorsing the work already carried out by the 1540 Committee, particularly in its consideration of the national reports submitted by States pursuant to resolution 1540(2004),

Recalling that not all States have presented to the 1540 Committee their reports on the steps they have taken or intend to take to implement resolution 1540(2004),

Reaffirming its decision that none of the obligations in resolution 1540(2004) shall be interpreted so as to conflict with or alter the rights and obligations of State parties to the Treaty on the Non-Proliferation of Nuclear Weapons, the Convention on the Prohibition of the Development, Production, Stockpiling and Use of Chemical Weapons and on Their Destruction and the Convention on the Prohibition of the Development, Production and Stockpiling of Bacteriological (Biological) and Toxin Weapons and on Their Destruction or alter the responsibilities of the International Atomic Energy Agency or the Organization for the Prohibition of Chemical Weapons,

Noting that the full implementation of resolution 1540(2004) by all States, including the adoption of national laws and measures to ensure the implementation of those laws, is a long-term task that will require continuous efforts at the national, regional and international levels,

Acting under Chapter VII of the Charter of the United Nations,

1. *Reiterates* its decisions taken in, and the requirements of, resolution 1540(2004), and emphasizes the importance for all States to implement fully that resolution;

2. *Calls upon* all States that have not yet presented a first report on steps they have taken or intend to take to implement resolution 1540(2004) to submit such a report to the 1540 Committee without delay;

3. *Encourages* all States that have submitted such reports to provide, at any time or upon the request of the 1540 Committee, additional information on their implementation of resolution 1540(2004);

4. *Decides* to extend the mandate of the 1540 Committee for a period of two years, with the continued assistance of experts, until 27 April 2008;

5. *Decides also* that the 1540 Committee shall intensify its efforts to promote the full implementation by all States of resolution 1540(2004) through a work programme which shall include the compilation of information on the status of the implementation by States of all aspects of resolution 1540(2004), outreach, dialogue, assistance and cooperation, and which shall address, in particular, all aspects of paragraphs 1 and 2 of that resolution, as well as of paragraph 3 thereof, which encompasses *(a)* accountability, *(b)* physical protection, *(c)* border controls and law enforcement efforts, and *(d)* national export and trans-shipment controls, including controls on providing funds and services, such as financing, to such export and trans-shipment, and in that regard:

(a) Encourages the pursuit of the ongoing dialogue between the 1540 Committee and States on the full implementation of resolution 1540(2004), including on further actions needed from States to that end and on technical assistance needed and offered;

(b) Invites the 1540 Committee to explore with States and international, regional and subregional organizations experience-sharing and lessons learned in the areas covered by resolution 1540(2004), and the availability of programmes which might facilitate the implementation of resolution 1540(2004);

6. *Decides further* that the 1540 Committee shall submit to the Security Council a report no later than 27 April 2008 on compliance with resolution 1540(2004) through the achievement of the implementation of its requirements;

7. *Decides* to remain seized of the matter.

International WMD Commission

On 29 June [A/60/934], Sweden, convener of the independent international Weapons of Mass Destruction Commission, transmitted to the Security Council the Commission's report entitled "Weapons of Terror: freeing the world of nuclear, biological and chemical arms". The Commission, noting that nuclear, biological and chemical weapons were the most inhumane of weapons and were designed to terrify and destroy on a far greater scale than conventional weapons, observed that, for as long as States had them, others would want them, and there was a high risk that they would be used by design or accident. Any such use would be catastrophic. While WMDs could not be uninvented, they could be outlawed and their use made unthinkable. To address the loss of momentum and direction in disarmament and non-proliferation in the past decade, the Commission's proposed action under four broad themes: agreement on general principles of action; reduction of the danger posed by current arsenals by ensuring that States did not use them and terrorists did not acquire them; prevention of proliferation by refraining from the development of new weapons systems and discouraging new possessors; and working towards outlawing all WMDs once and for all. In that context, the report outlined 60 specific recommendations relevant to those themes.

New types of weapons of mass destruction

In 2006, the Conference on Disarmament [A/61/27] did not establish any mechanism to consider any of its substantive agenda items, including the item on "new types of weapons of mass destruction and new systems of such weapons; radiological weapons", owing to the continuing deadlock over the contents of a programme of work. Nonetheless, the item was addressed during plenary meetings held between 19 and 23 June, during which delegations reaffirmed their respective positions on the issue.

Terrorism and WMDs

During the year, the United Nations continued to promote international action against terrorism through collaborative efforts with Member States and regional and international organizations, and through the ongoing work of the Counter-Terrorism Committee, established pursuant to Security Council resolution 1373(2001) [YUN 2001, p. 61] (see p. 73).

Reports of Secretary-General. As requested in the 2004 report of the High-level Panel on Threats, Challenges and Change [YUN 2004, p. 54] and in the 2005 World Summit Outcome, contained in resolution 60/1 [YUN 2005, p. 48], the Secretary-General submitted an April report [A/60/825] containing recommendations for a global counter-terrorism strategy (see p. 65).

Based on the recommendations contained in the Secretary-General's report, the General Assembly, by **resolution 60/288** of 8 September (see p. 66), adopted the United Nations Global Counter-Terrorism Strategy, annexed to which was a plan of action by which Member States resolved to prevent and combat terrorism in all its forms and manifestations, and advocated, among other things, measures to help build the capacity of States to prevent terrorists from accessing WMDs.

Pursuant to General Assembly resolution 60/78 [YUN 2005, p. 602], the Secretary-General, in a July report with a later addendum [A/61/171 & Add.1], presented the views of 13 Member States and 11 international organizations, including UN agencies, on measures they had taken to prevent terrorists from acquiring WMDs.

IAEA action. The International Atomic Energy Agency (IAEA) continued to address the terrorist threat through its action plan to combat nuclear terrorism, designed to build Member States' capacity to respond effectively to incidents of nuclear or radiological terrorist attacks. In September, the IAEA General Conference [GC(50)/RES/11], in a resolution on nuclear security: measures to protect against nuclear terrorism, called upon Member States to provide political, financial and technical support to prevent nuclear and radiological terrorism, deny support to non-state actors that had committed or intended to commit such acts and to take all necessary steps required by the Security Council Committee established pursuant to resolution 1540(2004) [YUN 2004, p. 544] to prevent illicit trafficking of nuclear and other radiological material. The Conference had before it a report of the IAEA Director General on nuclear security: measures to protect against nuclear terrorism [GOV/2006/46-GC (50)/13], which highlighted significant accomplishments of the previous year and established future goals and priorities in efforts to protect against nuclear terrorism.

Communication. The Group of Eight (G-8) major industrialized countries (St. Petersburg, Russian Federation, 15-17 July), in a Declaration on Counter-Terrorism, denounced terrorist attacks worldwide and pledged to make every effort to combat the problem. Advocating coordinated action with international partners to reduce further attacks, they resolved to support and strengthen UN counter-terrorism efforts.

The Fourteenth Conference of Heads of State or Government of Non-Aligned Countries (Havana, Cuba, 11-16 September) [A/61/472-S/2006/780] also resolved to take speedy and effective action against terrorist acts and urged States to fulfil their obligations under international law, including by prosecuting or extraditing perpetrators and refraining from assisting them with weapons supplies.

GENERAL ASSEMBLY ACTION

On 6 December [meeting 67], the General Assembly, on the recommendation of the First Committee [A/61/394], adopted **resolution 61/86** without vote [agenda item 90 *(v)*].

Measures to prevent terrorists from acquiring weapons of mass destruction

The General Assembly,

Recalling its resolution 60/78 of 8 December 2005,

Recognizing the determination of the international community to combat terrorism, as evidenced in relevant General Assembly and Security Council resolutions,

Deeply concerned by the growing risk of linkages between terrorism and weapons of mass destruction, and in particular by the fact that terrorists may seek to acquire weapons of mass destruction,

Cognizant of the steps taken by States to implement Security Council resolution 1540(2004) on the non-proliferation of weapons of mass destruction, adopted on 28 April 2004,

Welcoming the adoption, by consensus, of the International Convention for the Suppression of Acts of Nuclear Terrorism on 13 April 2005,

Welcoming also the adoption, by consensus, of amendments to strengthen the Convention on the Physical Protection of Nuclear Material by the International Atomic Energy Agency on 8 July 2005,

Noting the support expressed in the Final Document of the Fourteenth Conference of Heads of State or Government of Non-Aligned Countries, held in Havana on 15 and 16 September 2006, for measures to prevent terrorists from acquiring weapons of mass destruction,

Noting also that the Group of Eight, the European Union, the Regional Forum of the Association of Southeast Asian Nations and others have taken into account in their deliberations the dangers posed by the acquisition by terrorists of weapons of mass destruction, and the need for international cooperation in combating it,

Acknowledging the consideration of issues relating to terrorism and weapons of mass destruction by the Advisory Board on Disarmament Matters,

Taking note of the relevant resolutions adopted by the General Conference of the International Atomic Energy Agency at its fiftieth regular session,

Taking note also of the 2005 World Summit Outcome adopted on 16 September 2005 at the High-level Plenary Meeting of the sixtieth session of the General Assembly and the adoption of the United Nations Global Counter-Terrorism Strategy on 8 September 2006,

Taking note further of the report of the Secretary-General submitted pursuant to paragraphs 3 and 5 of resolution 60/78,

Mindful of the urgent need for addressing, within the United Nations framework and through international cooperation, this threat to humanity,

Emphasizing that progress is urgently needed in the area of disarmament and non-proliferation in order to help to maintain international peace and security and to contribute to global efforts against terrorism,

1. *Calls upon* all Member States to support international efforts to prevent terrorists from acquiring weapons of mass destruction and their means of delivery;

2. *Appeals* to all Member States to consider signing and ratifying the International Convention for the Suppression of Acts of Nuclear Terrorism in order to bring about its early entry into force;

3. *Urges* all Member States to take and strengthen national measures, as appropriate, to prevent terrorists from acquiring weapons of mass destruction, their means of delivery and materials and technologies related to their manufacture, and invites them to inform the Secretary-General, on a voluntary basis, of the measures taken in this regard;

4. *Encourages* cooperation among and between Member States and relevant regional and international organizations for strengthening national capacities in this regard;

5. *Requests* the Secretary-General to compile a report on measures already taken by international organizations on issues relating to the linkage between the fight against terrorism and the proliferation of weapons of mass destruction, to seek the views of Member States on additional relevant measures for tackling the global threat posed by the acquisition by terrorists of weapons of mass destruction and to report to the General Assembly at its sixty-second session;

6. *Decides* to include in the provisional agenda of its sixty-second session the item entitled "Measures to prevent terrorists from acquiring weapons of mass destruction".

Multilateralism in disarmament and non-proliferation

Report of Secretary-General. In response to General Assembly resolution 60/59 [YUN 2005, p. 605], the Secretary-General, in a June report [A/61/114], presented replies received from seven Governments regarding the promotion of multilateralism in the area of disarmament and non-proliferation.

Other developments. European Union (EU) leaders and the United States, at their 2006 Summit (Vienna, 21 June), adopted a declaration pledging to strengthen their strategic partnership through cooperation in tackling mutual challenges, including those relating to international security, particularly counter-terrorism and non-proliferation issues. They agreed to step up cooperation against terrorism, by denying resources (financing, travel and other material support) and shelter to terrorists by preventing the emergence of a new generation of recruits by countering radicalization and promoting tolerance. They would, in addition, work to further implement their 2005 programme of work on the non-proliferation of WMDs [YUN 2005, p. 604] and the full implementation of Security Council resolution 1540(2004) [YUN 2004, p. 544], which was designed to prevent non-state actors from acquiring WMDs.

The Group of Eight (G-8) major industrialized countries (St. Petersburg, Russian Federation, 15-17 July) adopted a statement on non-proliferation, reaffirming their determination to work with other States and institutions in the fight against WMD proliferation, including by preventing those weapons from falling into the hands of terrorists. To that end, they announced their determination to pursue arms control, disarmament and non-proliferation obligations under relevant international treaties and arrangements to which they were parties, called upon other States to do the same and dedicated themselves to reinvigorating relevant multilateral fora, beginning with the Conference on Disarmament.

In December, Ministers from EU member States adopted a concept paper pertaining to the EU WMD and non-proliferation strategy, with a view to creating a cooperative working method within the Union to improve implementation.

GENERAL ASSEMBLY ACTION

On 6 December [meeting 67], the General Assembly, on the recommendation of the First Committee [A/61/394], adopted **resolution 61/62** by recorded vote (120-7-51) [agenda item 90 *(i)*].

Promotion of multilateralism in the area of disarmament and non-proliferation

The General Assembly,

Determined to foster strict respect for the purposes and principles enshrined in the Charter of the United Nations,

Recalling its resolution 56/24 T of 29 November 2001 on multilateral cooperation in the area of disarmament and non-proliferation and global efforts against terrorism and other relevant resolutions, as well as its resolutions 57/63 of 22 November 2002, 58/44 of 8 December 2003, 59/69 of 3 December 2004 and 60/59 of 8 December 2005 on the promotion of multilateralism in the area of disarmament and non-proliferation,

Recalling also the purpose of the United Nations to maintain international peace and security and, to that end, to take effective collective measures for the prevention and removal of threats to the peace and for the suppression of acts of aggression or other breaches of the peace, and to bring about by peaceful means, and in conformity with the principles of justice and international law, adjustment or settlement of international disputes or situations which might lead to a breach of the peace, as enshrined in the Charter,

Recalling further the United Nations Millennium Declaration, which states, inter alia, that the responsibility for managing worldwide economic and social development, as well as threats to international peace and security, must be shared among the nations of the world and should be exercised multilaterally and that, as the most universal and most representative organization in the world, the United Nations must play the central role,

Convinced that, in the globalization era and with the information revolution, arms regulation, non-proliferation and disarmament problems are more than ever the concern of all countries in the world, which are affected in one way or another by these problems and, therefore, should have the possibility to participate in the negotiations that arise to tackle them,

Bearing in mind the existence of a broad structure of disarmament and arms regulation agreements resulting from non-discriminatory and transparent multilateral negotiations with the participation of a large number of countries, regardless of their size and power,

Aware of the need to advance further in the field of arms regulation, non-proliferation and disarmament on the basis of universal, multilateral, non-discriminatory and transparent negotiations with the goal of reaching general and complete disarmament under strict international control,

Recognizing the complementarity of bilateral, plurilateral and multilateral negotiations on disarmament,

Recognizing also that the proliferation and development of weapons of mass destruction, including nuclear weapons, are among the most immediate threats to international peace and security which need to be dealt with, with the highest priority,

Considering that the multilateral disarmament agreements provide the mechanism for States parties to consult one another and to cooperate in solving any problems which may arise in relation to the objective of, or in the application of, the provisions of the agreements and that such consultations and cooperation may also be undertaken through appropriate international procedures within the framework of the United Nations and in accordance with the Charter,

Stressing that international cooperation, the peaceful settlement of disputes, dialogue and confidence-building measures would contribute essentially to the creation of multilateral and bilateral friendly relations among peoples and nations,

Being concerned at the continuous erosion of multilateralism in the field of arms regulation, non-proliferation and disarmament, and recognizing that a resort to unilateral actions by Member States in resolving their security concerns would jeopardize international peace and security and undermine confidence in the international security system as well as the foundations of the United Nations itself,

Noting that the Fourteenth Conference of Heads of State or Government of Non-Aligned Countries, held at Havana on 15 and 16 September 2006, welcomed the adoption of General Assembly resolution 60/59 on the promotion of multilateralism in the area of disarmament and non-proliferation, and underlined the fact that multilateralism and multilaterally agreed solutions, in accordance with the Charter, provide the only sustainable method of addressing disarmament and international security issues,

Reaffirming the absolute validity of multilateral diplomacy in the field of disarmament and non-proliferation, and determined to promote multilateralism as an essential way to develop arms regulation and disarmament negotiations,

1. *Reaffirms* multilateralism as the core principle in negotiations in the area of disarmament and non-proliferation with a view to maintaining and strengthening universal norms and enlarging their scope;

2. *Also reaffirms* multilateralism as the core principle in resolving disarmament and non-proliferation concerns;

3. *Urges* the participation of all interested States in multilateral negotiations on arms regulation, non-proliferation and disarmament in a non-discriminatory and transparent manner;

4. *Underlines* the importance of preserving the existing agreements on arms regulation and disarmament, which constitute an expression of the results of international cooperation and multilateral negotiations in response to the challenges facing mankind;

5. *Calls once again upon* all Member States to renew and fulfil their individual and collective commitments to multilateral cooperation as an important means of pursuing and achieving their common objectives in the area of disarmament and non-proliferation;

6. *Requests* the States parties to the relevant instruments on weapons of mass destruction to consult and cooperate among themselves in resolving their concerns with regard to cases of non-compliance as well as on implementation, in accordance with the procedures defined in those instruments, and to refrain from resorting or threatening to resort to unilateral actions or directing unverified non-compliance accusations against one another to resolve their concerns;

7. *Takes note* of the report of the Secretary-General containing the replies of Member States on the promotion of multilateralism in the area of disarmament and non-proliferation, submitted pursuant to resolution 60/59;

8. *Requests* the Secretary-General to seek the views of Member States on the issue of the promotion of multilateralism in the area of disarmament and non-proliferation and to submit a report thereon to the General Assembly at its sixty-second session;

9. *Decides* to include in the provisional agenda of its sixty-second session the item entitled "Promotion of multilateralism in the area of disarmament and non-proliferation".

RECORDED VOTE ON RESOLUTION 61/62:

In favour: Afghanistan, Algeria, Angola, Antigua and Barbuda, Argentina, Bahamas, Bahrain, Bangladesh, Barbados, Belarus, Belize, Bhutan, Bolivia, Brazil, Brunei Darussalam, Burkina Faso, Burundi, Cambodia, Cameroon, Cape Verde, Central African Republic, Chile, China, Colombia, Comoros, Congo, Costa Rica, Côte d'Ivoire, Cuba, Democratic People's Republic of Korea, Democratic Republic of the Congo, Djibouti, Dominica, Dominican Republic, Ecuador, Egypt, El Salvador, Eritrea, Ethiopia, Fiji, Gabon, Gambia, Ghana, Grenada, Guatemala, Guinea, Guyana, Haiti, Honduras, India, Indonesia, Iran, Iraq, Jamaica, Jordan, Kazakhstan, Kuwait, Kyrgyzstan, Lao People's Democratic Republic, Lebanon, Lesotho, Liberia, Libyan Arab Jamahiriya, Malawi, Malaysia, Maldives, Mali, Mauritania, Mauritius, Mexico, Mongolia, Morocco, Mozambique, Myanmar, Namibia, Nauru, Nepal, Nicaragua, Niger, Nigeria, Oman, Pakistan, Panama, Paraguay, Peru, Philippines, Qatar, Russian Federation, Rwanda, Saint Kitts and Nevis, Saint Lucia, Saint Vincent and the Grenadines, Sao Tome and Principe, Saudi Arabia, Senegal, Sierra Leone, Singapore, Solomon Islands, South Africa, Sri Lanka, Sudan, Suriname, Swaziland, Syrian Arab Republic, Tajikistan, Thailand, Timor-Leste, Togo, Trinidad and Tobago, Tunisia, Turkmenistan, United Arab Emirates, United Republic of Tanzania, Uruguay, Uzbekistan, Venezuela, Viet Nam, Yemen, Zambia, Zimbabwe.

Against: Andorra, Israel, Marshall Islands, Micronesia, Palau, United Kingdom, United States.

Abstaining: Albania, Armenia, Australia, Austria, Azerbaijan, Belgium, Bosnia and Herzegovina, Bulgaria, Canada, Croatia, Cyprus, Czech Republic, Denmark, Estonia, Finland, France, Georgia, Germany, Greece, Hungary, Iceland, Ireland, Italy, Japan, Latvia, Liechtenstein, Lithuania, Luxembourg, Malta, Moldova, Monaco, Montenegro, Netherlands, New Zealand, Norway, Poland, Portugal, Republic of Korea, Romania, Samoa, San Marino, Serbia, Slovakia, Slovenia, Spain, Sweden, Switzerland, The former Yugoslav Republic of Macedonia, Turkey, Ukraine, Vanuatu.

International Atomic Energy Agency

In 2006, the International Atomic Energy Agency (IAEA) continued its work under the three pillars of its mandate—technology, safety and verification—with a special focus on ensuring that nuclear technology contributed to the promotion of peace, health and prosperity.

The fiftieth session of the IAEA General Conference (Vienna, 18-22 September) adopted resolutions and decisions on measures to strengthen international cooperation in nuclear radiation and transport safety and waste management; nuclear security, including measures to protect against nuclear and radiological terrorism; strengthening the Agency's technical cooperation activities, as well as its activities related to nuclear science, technology and applications; strengthening the effectiveness and improving the efficiency of the safeguards system and application of the Model Additional Protocol to Safeguards Agreements; implementation of the NPT safeguards agreement between the Agency and the Democratic People's Republic of Korea and in the Middle East.

IAEA Activities

In its annual report for 2006 [GC(51)/5], the Agency reported on its activities during the period from 1 January to 31 December. It stated that given the expanding interest in nuclear power by countries in meeting their energy needs, IAEA established an interdepartmental Nuclear Power Support Group to provide coordinated support to interested member States considering the introduction or expansion of nuclear power. The Agency assisted Argentina, Hungary, Mexico and Ukraine in extending the operating life of their nuclear power plants through improvements in maintenance, scheduling, training, scientific visits and workshops. Its International Project on Innovative Nuclear Reactors and Fuel Cycles reached 28 members. In July, the Project completed development of a methodology to assess innovative nuclear energy systems, which would be further improved in its second phase. The increasing global demand for energy led to the 29 new requests for energy assessment services, which were responded to in 21 technical cooperation projects approved by the IAEA Board of Governors. In other areas, IAEA assisted 12 countries in decommissioning nuclear facilities. Legal and technical advice was also provided for the decommissioning and clean up of former nuclear sites in Iraq.

In recognition of the challenge of disposing spent nuclear fuel, the Agency organized, in June, a conference in Vienna, which discussed trends and initiatives on spent fuel management. In terms of new approaches to the nuclear fuel cycle, the Agency facilitated discussions on a number of proposals, including the Russian Federation's Global Nuclear Power Infrastructure; the United States Global Nuclear Energy Partnership; the report *Ensuring Security of Supply in the International Nuclear Fuel Cycle* issued by the four commercial enrichment companies; the Concept for a Multilateral Mechanism for Reliable Access to Nuclear Fuel proposed by the six enriched uranium exporting countries; the IAEA Standby Arrangements System for the Assurance of Nuclear Fuel Supply, under IAEA auspices, suggested by Japan; and the Enrichment Bond, proposed by the United Kingdom. During the Agency's fiftieth regular session, it organized a special event entitled "New Framework for the Utilization of Nuclear Energy: Assurances of Supply and Non-Proliferation".

In the application of nuclear science and technology, IAEA continued to assist member States in building capacity to produce crops with improved characteristics. It assisted Peru to develop mutant varieties of barley. With the World Health Organization, it initiated studies to compare radiotherapy techniques for breast cancer and through its Programme of Action on Cancer Therapy helped to raise awareness of the growing cancer epidemic in the developing world.

Concerning nuclear safety and security, the Agency continued to support member States in attaining a high level of safety and security by promoting adherence to international legal instruments. In September, the IAEA Board of Governors approved the publication of the *Fundamental Safety Principles*, a set of ten new principles, consolidating and replacing earlier publications. The Agency developed a new safety review initiative, the Integrated Regulatory Review Service, designed to facilitate the exchange of experience and learning among regulatory bodies, enhance member States' legislative and regulatory infrastructures and harmonize regulatory approaches. IAEA hosted the second review meeting of the Joint Convention on the Safety of Spent Fuel Management and on the Safety of Radioactive Waste Management. It continued to help countries implement the enhanced regime of international legal instruments relevant to nuclear safety, and implemented an updated version of its Nuclear Security Safety Plan, which came into operation in 2006.

In a statement before the General Conference, the Director General provided additional information on the main developments during 2006. He noted that, in celebrating its fiftieth anniversary, the Agency's goal was to broaden awareness of the scope of its mission and activities, its contribution to development, nuclear safety and security and nuclear proliferation, and provide fora to review the challenges and opportunities that lay ahead.

Note by Secretary-General. In August [A/61/266], the Secretary-General informed the General Assembly of the availability of IAEA fiftieth report [GC(50)/4] covering activities in 2005.

The Assembly, in resolution 61/8 of 30 October (see p. 1203), took note of the statement of the IAEA Director General and his report on the work of the Agency for 2006.

IAEA safeguards

As at 31 December, the Model Protocol Additional to Safeguards Agreements strengthening

IAEA safeguards regime, approved by the Board of Governors in 1997 [YUN 1997, p. 486], had been signed and/or approved by 118 States, including the five nuclear-weapon States, and was in force in 78 States.

The IAEA General Conference [GC(50)/RES/14], as in previous years, requested concerned States and other parties to safeguards agreements, including nuclear-weapon States that had not done so, to sign the additional protocols promptly and bring them into force as soon as possible. Noting that Agency safeguards could provide increased assurances that nuclear material had not been diverted and that all such material and related activity of a State had been declared, IAEA called for cooperation among member States in implementing them and advocated the strengthening of innovative technological means for improving their efficiency. It commended member States, notably Japan, that had implemented elements of a plan of action first outlined in a 2000 resolution of the Conference [YUN 2000, p. 505] and updated in September 2006, and recommended that other States consider doing so to facilitate the entry into force of comprehensive safeguards agreements and additional protocols.

In 2006, international concern persisted over DPRK nuclear status, especially following its 9 October announcement that it had tested a nuclear weapon. It took that action despite having been urged against it three days earlier by the Security Council, in statement **S/PRST/2006/41** (see p. 443). The test took place only three months after DPRK executed a multiple launch of ballistic missiles (see p. 441), and one year after its first official announcement that it had manufactured nuclear weapons [YUN 2005, p. 606]. On 14 October, the Council, in resolution 1718(2006) (see p. 444), condemned the test, demanded that DPRK desist from conducting any further nuclear tests or launch of a ballistic missile and imposed an arms embargo and other sanctions on it. DPRK actions raised particular concern, owing to the country continuing refusal to allow IAEA access to verify that it had declared all nuclear material subject to Agency safeguards, a position the country had maintained since December 2002 when it terminated all IAEA verification activities on its territory. The General Conference [GC(50)/RES/15], stressing its desire for a peaceful resolution to the DPRK nuclear issue through dialogue, called on the country to comply fully with NPT, cooperate promptly with the Agency in the full and effective implementation of its safeguards and resolve any outstanding issues.

Considerable international concern also persisted during the year over Iran's nuclear programme. On 3 January, Iran informed IAEA that it was resuming research and development on its peaceful nuclear energy programme, which had been halted as part of its extended voluntary and non-legally-binding suspension of such activities. Shortly thereafter, it removed IAEA seals on enrichment-related equipment and material at some of its facilities.

On 4 February, the IAEA Board of Governors [GOV/2006/14] regretted that, despite its repeated calls for maintaining the suspension of all enrichment-related and reprocessing activities, which was essential to addressing outstanding issues, Iran had resumed uranium conversion and taken steps to resume also enrichment activities. It underlined the need for Iran to re-establish full and sustained suspension of all those activities, including research and development, to be verified by IAEA. It should, among other things, ratify promptly and implement the Model Protocol Additional to Safeguards Agreements and implement transparency measures.

Two days later, the situation deteriorated when Iran informed IAEA of its decision to suspend its voluntary commitment to implement the Additional Protocol and that henceforth, the implementation of safeguards measures would be based only on its comprehensive safeguards agreements with IAEA. The Security Council, in statement **S/PRST/2006/15** of 29 March (see p. 432) and in resolution 1696(2006) of 31 July (see p. 433), expressed concern about Iran's actions and asked it to take the steps required by the Board of Governors, which were essential to build confidence in the peaceful purpose of its nuclear programme. In several situation reports during the year, the IAEA Director General notified the Board of Iran's failure to comply with its demands and of persisting uncertainties regarding the scope and nature of its nuclear programme. Taking those reports into account, the Security Council, in resolution 1737(2006) of 27 December (see p. 436), imposed a nuclear and ballistic missile programmes-related embargo and other sanctions on Iran.

The IAEA mandate to maintain inspections of Iraq's nuclear programme under various Security Council resolutions remained in force in 2006. Accordingly, the Agency continued to consolidate its information assets; collect and analyse new information, including satellite imagery; and update its knowledge of relevant facilities in Iraq. In September, the IAEA Director General, in a statement marking the Agency's fiftieth anniversary, referred to the Council's plans to review the Agency's Iraq mandate, announced in Council resolution 1546(2004) [YUN 2004, p. 348], and expressed the hope that the review would be undertaken as soon as possible, with the aim of normalizing inspections in the country to confirm the absence of any undeclared nuclear activities.

Communications. The Group of Eight (G-8) major industrialized countries (St. Petersburg, Russian Federation, 15-17 July), in a comprehensive statement on non-proliferation, emphasized the importance of the IAEA safeguards system and expressed support for Security Council actions in dealing with the proliferation implications of the missile and nuclear programmes of the DPRK and Iran.

The Heads of State or Government of Non-Aligned Countries (Havana, Cuba, 11-16 September) [A/61/472-S/2006/780], in a statement on the Iran nuclear issue, reaffirmed the inalienable right of all States to develop the capacity to research, produce and use atomic energy for peaceful purposes and emphasized the distinction between the legal obligations of States to their respective safeguards agreements and any confidence-building measures voluntarily undertaken to resolve difficult questions. They believed that all issues on safeguards and verification, including those of Iran, should be resolved within the IAEA framework, based on technical and legal grounds.

Middle East

In 2006, the General Assembly (see below) and the IAEA General Conference [GC(50)/RES/16] again took action regarding the risk of nuclear proliferation in the Middle East. While the Assembly continued to call on the non-party in the region to place all its nuclear facilities under IAEA safeguards, IAEA again affirmed the need for States in the region to accept the application of full-scope Agency safeguards to all their nuclear activities as an important confidence-building measure.

Responding to Assembly resolution 60/92 [YUN 2005, p. 607], the Secretary-General reported in July [A/61/140 (Part II)] that, apart from the IAEA resolution on the application of the Agency's safeguards in the Middle East, which was annexed to his report, he had not received any additional information since his 2005 report.

GENERAL ASSEMBLY ACTION

On 6 December [meeting 67], the General Assembly, on the recommendation of the First Committee [A/61/397], adopted **resolution 61/103** by recorded vote (166-5-6) [agenda item 93].

The risk of nuclear proliferation in the Middle East

The General Assembly,

Bearing in mind its relevant resolutions,

Taking note of the relevant resolutions adopted by the General Conference of the International Atomic Energy Agency, the latest of which is resolution GC(50)/RES/16, adopted on 22 September 2006,

Cognizant that the proliferation of nuclear weapons in the region of the Middle East would pose a serious threat to international peace and security,

Mindful of the immediate need for placing all nuclear facilities in the region of the Middle East under full-scope safeguards of the Agency,

Recalling the decision on principles and objectives for nuclear non-proliferation and disarmament adopted by the 1995 Review and Extension Conference of the Parties to the Treaty on the Non-Proliferation of Nuclear Weapons on 11 May 1995, in which the Conference urged universal adherence to the Treaty as an urgent priority and called upon all States not yet parties to the Treaty to accede to it at the earliest date, particularly those States that operate unsafeguarded nuclear facilities,

Recognizing with satisfaction that, in the Final Document of the 2000 Review Conference of the Parties to the Treaty on the Non-Proliferation of Nuclear Weapons, the Conference undertook to make determined efforts towards the achievement of the goal of universality of the Treaty, called upon those remaining States not parties to the Treaty to accede to it, thereby accepting an international legally binding commitment not to acquire nuclear weapons or nuclear explosive devices and to accept Agency safeguards on all their nuclear activities, and underlined the necessity of universal adherence to the Treaty and of strict compliance by all parties with their obligations under the Treaty,

Recalling the resolution on the Middle East adopted by the 1995 Review and Extension Conference on 11 May 1995, in which the Conference noted with concern the continued existence in the Middle East of unsafeguarded nuclear facilities, reaffirmed the importance of the early realization of universal adherence to the Treaty and called upon all States in the Middle East that had not yet done so, without exception, to accede to the Treaty as soon as possible and to place all their nuclear facilities under full-scope Agency safeguards,

Noting that Israel remains the only State in the Middle East that has not yet become party to the Treaty,

Concerned about the threats posed by the proliferation of nuclear weapons to the security and stability of the Middle East region,

Stressing the importance of taking confidence-building measures, in particular the establishment of a nuclear-weapon-free zone in the Middle East, in order to enhance peace and security in the region and to consolidate the global non-proliferation regime,

Emphasizing the need for all parties directly concerned to consider seriously taking the practical and urgent steps required for the implementation of the proposal to establish a nuclear-weapon-free zone in the region of the Middle East in accordance with the relevant resolutions of the General Assembly and, as a means of promoting this objective, inviting the countries concerned to adhere to the Treaty and, pending the establishment of the zone, to agree to place all their nuclear activities under Agency safeguards,

Noting that one hundred and seventy-six States have signed the Comprehensive Nuclear-Test-Ban Treaty, including a number of States in the region,

1. *Welcomes* the conclusions on the Middle East of the 2000 Review Conference of the Parties to the Treaty on the Non-Proliferation of Nuclear Weapons;

2. *Reaffirms* the importance of Israel's accession to the Treaty on the Non-Proliferation of Nuclear Weapons and placement of all its nuclear facilities under comprehensive International Atomic Energy Agency safeguards, in realizing the goal of universal adherence to the Treaty in the Middle East;

3. *Calls upon* that State to accede to the Treaty without further delay and not to develop, produce, test or otherwise acquire nuclear weapons, and to renounce possession of nuclear weapons, and to place all its unsafeguarded nuclear facilities under full-scope Agency safeguards as an important confidence-building measure among all States of the region and as a step towards enhancing peace and security;

4. *Requests* the Secretary-General to report to the General Assembly at its sixty-second session on the implementation of the present resolution;

5. *Decides* to include in the provisional agenda of its sixty-second session the item entitled "The risk of nuclear proliferation in the Middle East".

RECORDED VOTE ON RESOLUTION 61/103:

In favour: Afghanistan, Albania, Algeria, Andorra, Angola, Antigua and Barbuda, Argentina, Armenia, Austria, Azerbaijan, Bahamas, Bahrain, Bangladesh, Barbados, Belarus, Belgium, Belize, Bhutan, Bolivia, Bosnia and Herzegovina, Brazil, Brunei Darussalam, Bulgaria, Burkina Faso, Burundi, Cambodia, Cape Verde, Central African Republic, Chile, China, Colombia, Comoros, Congo, Costa Rica, Côte d'Ivoire, Croatia, Cuba, Cyprus, Czech Republic, Democratic People's Republic of Korea, Denmark, Djibouti, Dominica, Dominican Republic, Ecuador, Egypt, El Salvador, Eritrea, Estonia, Fiji, Finland, France, Gabon, Gambia, Georgia, Germany, Ghana, Greece, Grenada, Guatemala, Guinea, Guyana, Haiti, Honduras, Hungary, Iceland, Indonesia, Iran, Iraq, Ireland, Italy, Jamaica, Japan, Jordan, Kazakhstan, Kenya, Kuwait, Kyrgyzstan, Lao People's Democratic Republic, Latvia, Lebanon, Lesotho, Liberia, Libyan Arab Jamahiriya, Liechtenstein, Lithuania, Luxembourg, Malawi, Malaysia, Maldives, Mali, Malta, Mauritania, Mauritius, Mexico, Moldova, Monaco, Mongolia, Montenegro, Morocco, Mozambique, Myanmar, Namibia, Nepal, Netherlands, New Zealand, Nicaragua, Niger, Nigeria, Norway, Oman, Pakistan, Panama, Papua New Guinea, Paraguay, Peru, Philippines, Poland, Portugal, Qatar, Republic of Korea, Romania, Russian Federation, Saint Kitts and Nevis, Saint Lucia, Saint Vincent and the Grenadines, Samoa, San Marino, Sao Tome and Principe, Saudi Arabia, Senegal, Serbia, Sierra Leone, Singapore, Slovakia, Slovenia, Solomon Islands, South Africa, Spain, Sri Lanka, Sudan, Suriname, Swaziland, Sweden, Switzerland, Syrian Arab Republic, Tajikistan, Thailand, The former Yugoslav Republic of Macedonia, Timor-Leste, Togo, Trinidad and Tobago, Tunisia, Turkey, Ukraine, United Arab Emirates, United Kingdom, United Republic of Tanzania, Uruguay, Uzbekistan, Vanuatu, Venezuela, Viet Nam, Yemen, Zambia, Zimbabwe.

Against: Israel, Marshall Islands, Micronesia, Palau, United States.

Abstaining: Australia, Cameroon, Canada, Ethiopia, India, Tonga.

Radioactive waste

In 2006, international concern rose over the threat posed by radioactive waste, following the death of 10 persons and hospitalization of 107,000 others from toxins released by some 500 tons of toxic waste dumped on 19 August in various locations in Abidjan, Côte d'Ivoire, by unidentified foreign agents. In a 17 November statement to the General Assembly's Second (Economic and Financial) Committee, Namibia, on behalf of the African Group, highlighted widespread fears about the medium and long-term effects of the toxins on the population and the environment, noting that the dumping violated international toxic waste management instruments. The African Group was determined to work with the EU and other concerned entities to identify the perpetrators. In that context, Namibia introduced a draft resolution [A/C.2/61/L.43] on the issue, requesting the Assembly to condemn the dumping and the perpetrators and to appeal to Member States and international organizations to assist the country in dealing with the problem. The resolution was withdrawn on 8 December because of a lack of consensus, but Nigeria, on behalf of the Group, stated that it reserved the right to draw the attention of the international community to the criminal practice of dumping toxic wastes in developing countries.

During the year, IAEA promoted the safe transport of radioactive material among Member States. It continued to finalize a draft safety guide on compliance assurance with related safety measures and establish recommendations for security during the transport of such waste. Security levels and physical protection measures were expected to be finalized in early 2007. The Agency also assisted Member States to improve their management of radioactive wastes and launched a web-based database of official national records on radioactive discharges submitted by Member States.

In September [GC(50)/RES/10], the IAEA General Conference, recognizing concerns about the potential for damage in the event of an accident while transporting radioactive materials by sea, including pollution of the marine environment, urged its member States that did not have national regulatory documents governing the transport of those materials to adopt them and ensure that they conformed with the amended edition of the IAEA Transport Regulations, adopted in 2005 [YUN 2005, p. 608]. The Conference looked forward to initiating dialogue with the United Nations on reconciling language differences between the IAEA Transport Regulations and the UN Model Regulations on the transport of dangerous goods (see p. 1141).

Conferences. To reinforce its framework for the safe transport of radioactive materials, IAEA held a seminar (Vienna, Austria, 11-12 January) on complex technical issues relating to such transportation. Experts discussed various aspects of the transport of those materials, including regulatory programmes, transport standards and their implementation at national and international levels, and cooperation between national competent authorities on international transport matters. The seminar also reviewed member States' experiences with maritime shipments, risk analyses, emergency response arrangements, the denial of shipments and the Agency's Transport Safety Appraisal Service.

In May, the Agency held a technical meeting of experts to discuss progress on the issue of denials of shipment of radioactive material. It recommended the establishment of a steering committee on denials of shipments of radioactive material. The committee, at its first meeting in November, developed an action plan for promoting progress on such shipments.

The Second Review Meeting (Vienna, 15-24 May) of the Contracting Parties of the Joint Convention on the Safety of Spent Fuel Management and on the Safety of Radioactive Waste Management [YUN 1997, p. 487], which entered into force in 2001 [YUN 2001, p. 487], committed themselves to improving policies and practices, particularly in the areas of national strategies for spent fuel and radioactive waste management, engagement with stakeholders and the public and control of disused sealed sources. However, challenges on a number of potentially risky issues remained, including those relating to clean-up, such as determining unknown locations where contaminated equipment and material might be buried and recovering lost records about the contents of radioactive material stored in waste containers.

Nuclear-weapon-free zones

Africa

As at 31 December, 24 States had ratified the African Nuclear-Weapon-Free Zone Treaty (Treaty of Pelindaba) [YUN 1995, p. 203], which was opened for signature in 1996 [YUN 1996, p. 486]. China, France and the United Kingdom had ratified Protocols I and II thereto, and France had also ratified Protocol III. The Russian Federation and the United States had signed Protocols I and II. The Treaty had 56 signatories. By the terms of the Treaty, ratification by 28 States was required for its entry into force.

Asia

Central Asia

On 8 September, the Treaty on a Nuclear-Weapon-Free Zone in Central Asia opened for signature in Semipalatinsk, Kazakhstan, following eight years of negotiations by the five regional States (Kazakhstan, Kyrgyzstan, Tajikistan, Turkmenistan, Uzbekistan) and the five nuclear-weapon States. First proposed in 1997 [YUN 1997, p. 494], the Zone was the fifth of its kind to be established and the first to be located entirely in the northern hemisphere.

Under the Treaty, it was forbidden to research, develop, manufacture, stockpile, acquire, possess or control nuclear weapons or other nuclear explosive devices.It was also forbidden to dispose in the territories of States within that Zone of radioactive waste by other States and test nuclear weapons or other nuclear explosive devices, within the framework of the Comprehensive Nuclear-Test-Ban Treaty (CTBT) (see p. 628). In signing the Treaty, the Central Asian States undertook to assist efforts for the environmental security of territories contaminated by activities relating to the development, testing or storage of nuclear weapons; conclude and enforce IAEA safeguards agreement and related Additional Protocol; and ensure the physical protection of nuclear material, facilities and equipment, in accordance with established international standards and IAEA guidelines.

The Treaty also provided for the use of nuclear energy for peaceful purposes, and included a Protocol by which nuclear-weapon States would undertake not to use or threaten to use a nuclear-weapon or other nuclear explosive device against parties to the Treaty, nor contribute to any act that violated it. The Treaty would not affect the rights and obligations of the parties under other international treaties concluded prior to its entry into force, a clause that was a major point of contention between the nuclear-weapon States and the regional States. The Treaty, which was of unlimited duration, would not be subject to reservations, but could be amended by consensus. It would enter into force 30 days after the date of deposit of the fifth instrument of ratification. Kyrgyzstan was designated depositary of the Treaty, which was signed during the year by all five Central Asian States.

Communications. In an 8 September statement [A/61/344-S/2006/741], the Foreign Ministers of the five Central Asian States described the Treaty as an initiative that would promote the security of the States parties, an important confidence-building measure and an instrument of regional cooperation.

On 21 September [A/61/466-S/2006/766], Belarus, in its capacity as the Chair of the Council of Foreign Ministers of States members of the Collective Security Treaty Organization, the membership of which included four Central Asian States, welcomed the Treaty as a significant contribution to ensuring global and regional security, nuclear disarmament and non-proliferation.

GENERAL ASSEMBLY ACTION

On 6 December [meeting 67], the General Assembly, on the recommendation of the First Committee [A/61/394], adopted **resolution 61/88** by recorded vote (141-3-37) [agenda item 90 (*bb*)].

Establishment of a nuclear-weapon-free zone in Central Asia

The General Assembly,

Recalling its resolutions 52/38 S of 9 December 1997, 53/77 A of 4 December 1998, 55/33 W of 20 November 2000 and 57/69 of 22 November 2002, and its decisions 54/417 of 1 December 1999, 56/412 of 29 November 2001, 58/518 of 8 December 2003, 59/513 of 3 December 2004 and 60/516 of 8 December 2005,

Convinced that the establishment of nuclear-weapon-free zones contributes to the achievement of general and complete disarmament, and emphasizing the importance of internationally recognized treaties on the establishment of such zones in different regions of the world in the strengthening of the non-proliferation regime,

Considering that the establishment of a nuclear-weapon-free zone in Central Asia on the basis of arrangements freely arrived at among the States of the region constitutes an important step towards strengthening the nuclear non-proliferation regime, promoting cooperation in the peaceful uses of nuclear energy and in the environmental rehabilitation of territories affected by radioactive contamination, and enhancing regional and international peace and security,

Considering also the establishment of a nuclear-weapon-free zone in Central Asia as an effective contribution to combating international terrorism and preventing nuclear materials and technologies from falling into the hands of non-state actors, primarily terrorists,

Reaffirming the universally recognized role of the United Nations in the establishment of nuclear-weapon-free zones,

1. *Welcomes* the signing of the Treaty on a Nuclear-Weapon-Free Zone in Central Asia in Semipalatinsk, Kazakhstan, on 8 September 2006;

2. *Notes* the readiness of the Central Asian countries to continue consultations with the nuclear-weapon States on a number of provisions of the Treaty;

3. *Decides* to include in the provisional agenda of its sixty-third session the item entitled "Establishment of a nuclear-weapon-free zone in Central Asia".

RECORDED VOTE ON RESOLUTION 61/88:

In favour: Afghanistan, Algeria, Angola, Antigua and Barbuda, Argentina, Armenia, Austria, Azerbaijan, Bahamas, Bahrain, Bangladesh, Barbados, Belarus, Belize, Benin, Bhutan, Bolivia, Brazil, Brunei Darussalam, Burkina Faso, Burundi, Cambodia, Cameroon, Cape Verde, Central African Republic, Chad, Chile, China, Colombia, Comoros, Congo, Costa Rica, Côte d'Ivoire, Cuba, Cyprus, Democratic People's Republic of Korea, Djibouti, Dominica, Dominican Republic, Ecuador, Egypt, El Salvador, Eritrea, Ethiopia, Fiji, Gabon, Gambia, Georgia, Ghana, Grenada, Guatemala, Guinea, Guyana, Haiti, Honduras, India, Indonesia, Iran, Iraq, Ireland, Jamaica, Japan, Jordan, Kazakhstan, Kenya, Kuwait, Kyrgyzstan, Lao People's Democratic Republic, Lebanon, Lesotho, Liberia, Libyan Arab Jamahiriya, Liechtenstein, Malawi, Malaysia, Maldives, Mali, Malta, Mauritania, Mauritius, Mexico, Moldova, Mongolia, Morocco, Mozambique, Myanmar, Namibia, Nauru, Nepal, New Zealand, Nicaragua, Niger, Nigeria, Oman, Pakistan, Panama, Papua New Guinea, Paraguay, Peru, Philippines, Qatar, Republic of Korea, Russian Federation, Rwanda, Saint Kitts and Nevis, Saint Lucia, Saint Vincent and the Grenadines, Samoa, Sao Tome and Principe, Saudi Arabia, Senegal, Sierra Leone, Singapore, Solomon Islands, South Africa, Sri Lanka, Sudan, Suriname, Swaziland, Sweden, Switzerland, Syrian Arab Republic, Tajikistan, Thailand, Timor-Leste, Togo, Trinidad and Tobago, Tunisia, Turkmenistan, Uganda, Ukraine, United Arab Emirates, United Republic of Tanzania, Uruguay, Uzbekistan, Vanuatu, Venezuela, Viet Nam, Yemen, Zambia, Zimbabwe.

Against: France, United Kingdom, United States.

Abstaining: Albania, Andorra, Australia, Belgium, Bosnia and Herzegovina, Bulgaria, Canada, Croatia, Czech Republic, Denmark, Estonia, Finland, Germany, Greece, Hungary, Iceland, Israel, Italy, Latvia, Lithuania, Luxembourg, Marshall Islands, Monaco, Montenegro, Netherlands, Norway, Palau, Poland, Portugal, Romania, San Marino, Serbia, Slovakia, Slovenia, Spain, The former Yugoslav Republic of Macedonia, Turkey.

Mongolia

In response to General Assembly resolution 59/73 [YUN 2004, p. 551], the Secretary-General submitted a September report [A/61/164], which reviewed new developments and UN assistance to Mongolia to consolidate and strengthen its nuclear-weapon-free status. The range of relevant activities described in the report related both to Mongolia's nuclear-weapon-free status and the non-nuclear aspects of its international security. The Secretary-General said there was evidence that international recognition of the country's nuclear-weapon-free status was growing. The United Nations was continuing to help in promoting it and would continue to assist Mongolia in coping with economic and ecological vulnerabilities, particularly regarding efforts to follow-up on related recommendations. The Secretary-General hoped that UN assistance would help achieve sustainable development and balanced growth in Mongolia during the current period of political and economic transition, reinforcing its efforts to achieve the Millennium Development Goals [YUN 2000, p. 51].

Communication. On 16 August [A/61/293], Mongolia transmitted a draft report it had prepared on the implementation of the national law on its nuclear-weapon-free status, highlighting various policy initiatives and other activities undertaken since the enactment of that law [YUN 2000, p. 509].

GENERAL ASSEMBLY ACTION

On 6 December [meeting 67], the General Assembly, on the recommendation of the First Committee [A/61/394], adopted **resolution 61/87** without vote [agenda item 90 (*d*)].

Mongolia's international security and nuclear-weapon-free status

The General Assembly,

Recalling its resolutions 53/77 D of 4 December 1998, 55/33 S of 20 November 2000, 57/67 of 22 November 2002 and 59/73 of 3 December 2004,

Recalling also the purposes and principles of the Charter of the United Nations, as well as the Declaration on Principles of International Law concerning Friendly Relations and Cooperation among States in accordance with the Charter of the United Nations,

Bearing in mind its resolution 49/31 of 9 December 1994 on the protection and security of small States,

Proceeding from the fact that nuclear-weapon-free status is one of the means of ensuring the national security of States,

Convinced that the internationally recognized status of Mongolia will contribute to enhancing stability and confidence-building in the region as well as promote Mongolia's security by strengthening its independence, sovereignty and territorial integrity, the inviolability of its borders and the preservation of its ecological balance,

Taking note of the adoption by the Mongolian parliament of legislation defining and regulating Mongolia's nuclear-weapon-free status as a concrete step towards promoting the aims of nuclear non-proliferation,

Bearing in mind the joint statement of the five nuclear-weapon States on security assurances to Mongolia in connection with its nuclear-weapon-free status as a contribution to implementing resolution 53/77 D as well as their commitment to Mongolia to cooperate in the implementation of the resolution, in accordance with the principles of the Charter,

Noting that the joint statement has been transmitted to the Security Council by the five nuclear-weapon States,

Mindful of the support expressed for Mongolia's nuclear-weapon-free status by the Heads of State and Government of Non-Aligned Countries at the Thirteenth Conference of Heads of State or Government of Non-Aligned Countries, held in Kuala Lumpur on 24 and 25 February 2003 and the Fourteenth Conference, held in Havana on 15 and 16 September 2006,

Noting that the States parties and signatories to the Treaties of Tlatelolco, Rarotonga, Bangkok and Pelindaba and the State of Mongolia expressed their recognition and full support of Mongolia's international nuclear-weapon-free status at the first Conference of States Parties and Signatories to Treaties that Establish Nuclear-Weapon-Free Zones, held in Tlatelolco, Mexico, from 26 to 28 April 2005,

Noting also other measures taken to implement resolution 59/73 at the national and international levels,

Welcoming Mongolia's active and positive role in developing peaceful, friendly and mutually beneficial relations with the States of the region and other States,

Having considered the report of the Secretary-General on Mongolia's international security and nuclear-weapon-free status,

1. *Takes note* of the report of the Secretary-General on the implementation of resolution 59/73;

2. *Expresses its appreciation* to the Secretary-General for the efforts to implement resolution 59/73;

3. *Endorses and supports* Mongolia's good-neighbourly and balanced relationship with its neighbours as an important element of strengthening regional peace, security and stability;

4. *Welcomes* the efforts made by Member States to cooperate with Mongolia in implementing resolution 59/73, as well as the progress made in consolidating Mongolia's international security;

5. *Invites* Member States to continue to cooperate with Mongolia in taking the necessary measures to consolidate and strengthen Mongolia's independence, sovereignty and territorial integrity, the inviolability of its borders, its independent foreign policy, its economic security and its ecological balance, as well as its nuclear-weapon-free status;

6. *Appeals* to the Member States of the Asia and Pacific region to support Mongolia's efforts to join the relevant regional security and economic arrangements;

7. *Requests* the Secretary-General and relevant United Nations bodies to continue to provide assistance to Mongolia in taking the necessary measures mentioned in paragraph 5 above;

8. *Requests* the Secretary-General to report to the General Assembly at its sixty-third session on the implementation of the present resolution;

9. *Decides* to include in the provisional agenda of its sixty-third session the item entitled "Mongolia's international security and nuclear-weapon-free status".

South-East Asia

In 2006, the States parties to the Treaty on the South-East Asia Nuclear-Weapon-Free Zone (Bangkok Treaty), which opened for signature in

1995 [YUN 1995, p. 207] and entered into force in 1997 [YUN 1997, p. 495], continued to establish an institutional framework to implement the Treaty. The thirty-ninth Ministerial Meeting of the Association of South-East Asian Nations (ASEAN) (Kuala Lumpur, Malaysia, 25 July) issued a joint communiqué reaffirming the importance of strengthening cooperation in implementing the Treaty, urged nuclear-weapon States to become parties to the Treaty's Protocol as soon as possible and addressed the need to review the Treaty's operation, as provided for under article 20.

Latin America and the Caribbean

In 2006, States parties to the Treaty for the Prohibition of Nuclear Weapons in Latin America and the Caribbean (Treaty of Tlatelolco) [YUN 1967, p. 13] continued to consolidate the treaty regime. The General Assembly of the Organization of American States (OAS), at its thirty-sixth regular session (Santo Domingo, Dominican Republic, 4-6 June) [AG/RES.2245 (XXXVI-O/06], called on regional States that had not done so to sign or ratify amendments to the Treaty. It reaffirmed the importance of strengthening the Agency for the Prohibition of Nuclear Weapons in Latin America and the Caribbean (OPANAL) as the appropriate legal and political forum for ensuring observance of the Treaty in its zone of application and for promoting cooperation with the agencies of other nuclear-weapon-free zones. During the year, a notable source of concern for OPANAL was the interpretation by some nuclear-weapon States of the use of nuclear weapons as a legitimate means of self-defence, which the Agency considered to be contrary to international law.

Communication. On 5 January [A/60/678], Chile transmitted the text of the Declaration of Santiago de Chile, adopted by the nineteenth regular session of OPANAL [YUN 2005, p. 611], which, among other actions, urged the nuclear powers that had signed or ratified Additional Protocols I and II to the Treaty with reservations or unilateral interpretations affecting the denuclearized status of the zone to modify or withdraw those reservations.

Middle East

In response to General Assembly resolution 60/52 on the establishment of a nuclear-weapon-free zone in the Middle East [YUN 2005, p. 612], the Secretary-General, in a July report with later addendum [A/61/140 (part I) & Add.1], provided information on the resolution's implementation. He continued to explore with concerned parties within and beyond the region further ways of promoting the establishment of the zone, but was concerned that developments in the region since his 2005 report [YUN 2005, p. 611] might affect efforts towards that goal. The Secretary-General emphasized the need to continue efforts to achieve a just, lasting and comprehensive peace, and hoped that new impetus could be given to the road map for peace in the region developed by the Middle East Quartet (European Union, the Russian Federation, the United States and the United Nations). He called upon all parties concerned to resume dialogue, with a view to creating stable security conditions that would lead to an eventual settlement and thus facilitate the process of establishing the zone. The report included the views of Bolivia, Canada, Chile, Egypt, Iran, Israel, Jamaica, Japan, Lebanon, the Libyan Arab Jamahiriya, Mauritius, Mexico, Syria and the United Arab Emirates on the establishment of the Middle East zone.

In September, the IAEA General Conference adopted a resolution on the Middle East [GC(50)/RES/16] calling on all parties directly concerned to take the steps required to implement the proposal for a mutually and effectively verifiable nuclear-weapon-free zone in the region.

Communication. The Fourteenth Conference of Heads of State or Government of Non-Aligned Countries (Havana, Cuba, 11-16 September) [A/61/472-S/2006/780] reaffirmed the need for the speedy establishment of a nuclear-weapon-free zone in the Middle East, and called upon all parties concerned to make efforts towards that goal. It stressed that necessary steps ought to be taken in different international fora to establish the zone, pending which, Israel, the only regional State that remained outside the NPT regime, should renounce the possession of nuclear weapons, accede to NPT and place promptly all its nuclear facilities under IAEA full scope safeguards.

On 19 December [A/61/650-S/2006/1008], Iran alleged unlawful possession of nuclear weapons by Israel, adding that the Israeli regime was the only obstacle to the establishment of a nuclear-weapons-free zone in the Middle East. Peace and stability could not be achieved in the region, as the Israeli nuclear arsenal continued to pose a threat there. As such, the Security Council should fulfil its Charter-based responsibility to address the problem and take appropriate action.

GENERAL ASSEMBLY ACTION

On 6 December [meeting 67], the General Assembly, on the recommendation of the First Committee [A/61/391], adopted **resolution 61/56** without vote [agenda item 87].

Establishment of a nuclear-weapon-free zone in the region of the Middle East

The General Assembly,

Recalling its resolutions 3263 (XXIX) of 9 December 1974, 3474 (XXX) of 11 December 1975, 31/71 of 10 December 1976, 32/82 of 12 December 1977, 33/64 of 14 December 1978, 34/77 of 11 December 1979, 35/147 of 12 December 1980, 36/87 A and B of 9 December 1981, 37/75 of 9 December 1982, 38/64 of 15 December 1983, 39/54 of 12 December 1984, 40/82 of 12 December 1985, 41/48 of 3 December 1986, 42/28 of 30 November 1987, 43/65 of 7 December 1988, 44/108 of 15 December 1989, 45/52 of 4 December 1990, 46/30 of 6 December 1991, 47/48 of 9 December 1992, 48/71 of 16 December 1993, 49/71 of 15 December 1994, 50/66 of 12 December 1995, 51/41 of 10 December 1996, 52/34 of 9 December 1997, 53/74 of 4 December 1998, 54/51 of 1 December 1999, 55/30 of 20 November 2000, 56/21 of 29 November 2001, 57/55 of 22 November 2002, 58/34 of 8 December 2003, 59/63 of 3 December 2004 and 60/52 of 8 December 2005 on the establishment of a nuclear-weapon-free zone in the region of the Middle East,

Recalling also the recommendations for the establishment of such a zone in the Middle East consistent with paragraphs 60 to 63, and in particular paragraph 63 *(d)*, of the Final Document of the Tenth Special Session of the General Assembly,

Emphasizing the basic provisions of the above-mentioned resolutions, which call upon all parties directly concerned to consider taking the practical and urgent steps required for the implementation of the proposal to establish a nuclear-weapon-free zone in the region of the Middle East and, pending and during the establishment of such a zone, to declare solemnly that they will refrain, on a reciprocal basis, from producing, acquiring or in any other way possessing nuclear weapons and nuclear explosive devices and from permitting the stationing of nuclear weapons on their territory by any third party, to agree to place their nuclear facilities under International Atomic Energy Agency safeguards and to declare their support for the establishment of the zone and to deposit such declarations with the Security Council for consideration, as appropriate,

Reaffirming the inalienable right of all States to acquire and develop nuclear energy for peaceful purposes,

Emphasizing the need for appropriate measures on the question of the prohibition of military attacks on nuclear facilities,

Bearing in mind the consensus reached by the General Assembly since its thirty-fifth session that the establishment of a nuclear-weapon-free zone in the Middle East would greatly enhance international peace and security,

Desirous of building on that consensus so that substantial progress can be made towards establishing a nuclear-weapon-free zone in the Middle East,

Welcoming all initiatives leading to general and complete disarmament, including in the region of the Middle East, and in particular on the establishment therein of a zone free of weapons of mass destruction, including nuclear weapons,

Noting the peace negotiations in the Middle East, which should be of a comprehensive nature and represent an appropriate framework for the peaceful settlement of contentious issues in the region,

Recognizing the importance of credible regional security, including the establishment of a mutually verifiable nuclear-weapon-free zone,

Emphasizing the essential role of the United Nations in the establishment of a mutually verifiable nuclear-weapon-free zone,

Having examined the report of the Secretary-General on the implementation of resolution 60/52,

1. *Urges* all parties directly concerned to consider seriously taking the practical and urgent steps required for the implementation of the proposal to establish a nuclear-weapon-free zone in the region of the Middle East in accordance with the relevant resolutions of the General Assembly, and, as a means of promoting this objective, invites the countries concerned to adhere to the Treaty on the Non-Proliferation of Nuclear Weapons;

2. *Calls upon* all countries of the region that have not done so, pending the establishment of the zone, to agree to place all their nuclear activities under International Atomic Energy Agency safeguards;

3. *Takes note* of resolution GC(50)/RES/16, adopted on 22 September 2006 by the General Conference of the International Atomic Energy Agency at its fiftieth regular session, concerning the application of Agency safeguards in the Middle East;

4. *Notes* the importance of the ongoing bilateral Middle East peace negotiations and the activities of the multilateral Working Group on Arms Control and Regional Security in promoting mutual confidence and security in the Middle East, including the establishment of a nuclear-weapon-free zone;

5. *Invites* all countries of the region, pending the establishment of a nuclear-weapon-free zone in the region of the Middle East, to declare their support for establishing such a zone, consistent with paragraph 63 *(d)* of the Final Document of the Tenth Special Session of the General Assembly, and to deposit those declarations with the Security Council;

6. *Also invites* those countries, pending the establishment of the zone, not to develop, produce, test or otherwise acquire nuclear weapons or permit the stationing on their territories, or territories under their control, of nuclear weapons or nuclear explosive devices;

7. *Invites* the nuclear-weapon States and all other States to render their assistance in the establishment of the zone and at the same time to refrain from any action that runs counter to both the letter and the spirit of the present resolution;

8. *Takes note* of the report of the Secretary-General;

9. *Invites* all parties to consider the appropriate means that may contribute towards the goal of general and complete disarmament and the establishment of a zone free of weapons of mass destruction in the region of the Middle East;

10. *Requests* the Secretary-General to continue to pursue consultations with the States of the region and other concerned States, in accordance with paragraph 7 of resolution 46/30 and taking into account the evolving situation in the region, and to seek from those States their views on the measures outlined in chapters III and IV of the study annexed to the report of the Secretary-General of 10 October 1990 or other relevant measures, in order to move towards the establishment of a nuclear-weapon-free zone in the Middle East;

11. *Also requests* the Secretary-General to submit to the General Assembly at its sixty-second session a report on the implementation of the present resolution;

12. *Decides* to include in the provisional agenda of its sixty-second session the item entitled "Establishment of a nuclear-weapon-free zone in the region of the Middle East".

South Pacific

In 2006, the number of States that had ratified the 1985 South Pacific Nuclear-Free Zone Treaty (Treaty of Rarotonga) [YUN 1985, p. 58] remained at 17. China and the Russian Federation had ratified Protocols 2 and 3, and France, the United Kingdom and the United States had ratified all three Protocols.

Under Protocol 1, the States internationally responsible for territories situated within the zone would undertake to apply the relevant prohibitions of the Treaty to those territories; under Protocol 2, the five nuclear-weapon States would provide security assurances to parties or territories within the same zone; and under Protocol 3, the five would not carry out nuclear tests in the zone.

Southern hemisphere and adjacent areas

On 6 December [meeting 67], the General Assembly, on the recommendation of the First Committee [A/61/394], adopted **resolution 61/69** by recorded vote (167-3-9) [agenda item 90 *(h)*].

Nuclear-weapon-free southern hemisphere and adjacent areas

The General Assembly,

Recalling its resolutions 51/45 B of 10 December 1996, 52/38 N of 9 December 1997, 53/77 Q of 4 December 1998, 54/54 L of 1 December 1999, 55/33 I of 20 November 2000, 56/24 G of 29 November 2001, 57/73 of 22 November 2002, 58/49 of 8 December 2003, 59/85 of 3 December 2004 and 60/58 of 8 December 2005,

Recalling also the adoption by the Disarmament Commission at its 1999 substantive session of a text entitled "Establishment of nuclear-weapon-free zones on the basis of arrangements freely arrived at among the States of the region concerned",

Determined to pursue the total elimination of nuclear weapons,

Determined also to continue to contribute to the prevention of the proliferation of nuclear weapons in all its aspects and to the process of general and complete disarmament under strict and effective international control, in particular in the field of nuclear weapons and other weapons of mass destruction, with a view to strengthening international peace and security, in accordance with the purposes and principles of the Charter of the United Nations,

Recalling the provisions on nuclear-weapon-free zones of the Final Document of the Tenth Special Session of the General Assembly, the first special session devoted to disarmament,

Stressing the importance of the treaties of Tlatelolco, Rarotonga, Bangkok and Pelindaba establishing nuclear-weapon-free zones, as well as the Antarctic Treaty, to, inter alia, achieve a world entirely free of nuclear weapons,

Underlining the value of enhancing cooperation among the nuclear-weapon-free-zone treaty members by means of mechanisms such as joint meetings of States parties, signatories and observers to those treaties,

Noting the adoption of the Declaration of Santiago de Chile by the Governments of the States members of the Agency for the Prohibition of Nuclear Weapons in Latin America and the Caribbean and the States parties to the Treaty of Tlatelolco, during the nineteenth regular session of the General Conference of the Agency, held in Santiago on 7 and 8 November 2005,

Recalling the applicable principles and rules of international law relating to the freedom of the high seas and the rights of passage through maritime space, including those of the United Nations Convention on the Law of the Sea,

1. *Welcomes* the continued contribution that the Antarctic Treaty and the treaties of Tlatelolco, Rarotonga, Bangkok and Pelindaba are making towards freeing the southern hemisphere and adjacent areas covered by those treaties from nuclear weapons;

2. *Also welcomes* the ratification by all original parties of the Treaty of Rarotonga, and calls upon eligible States to adhere to the Treaty and the protocols thereto;

3. *Further welcomes* the efforts towards the completion of the ratification process of the Treaty of Pelindaba, and calls upon the States of the region that have not yet done so to sign and ratify the Treaty, with the aim of its early entry into force;

4. *Calls upon* all concerned States to continue to work together in order to facilitate adherence to the protocols to nuclear-weapon-free-zone treaties by all relevant States that have not yet adhered to them;

5. *Welcomes* the steps taken to conclude further nuclear-weapon-free-zone treaties on the basis of arrangements freely arrived at among the States of the region concerned, and calls upon all States to consider all relevant proposals, including those reflected in its resolutions on the establishment of nuclear-weapon-free zones in the Middle East and South Asia;

6. *Also welcomes* the signing of the Treaty on a Nuclear-Weapon-Free Zone in Central Asia, in Semipalatinsk, Kazakhstan, on 8 September 2006;

7. *Affirms its conviction* of the important role of nuclear-weapon-free zones in strengthening the nuclear non-proliferation regime and in extending the areas of the world that are nuclear-weapon-free, and, with particular reference to the responsibilities of the nuclear-weapon States, calls upon all States to support the process of nuclear disarmament and to work for the total elimination of all nuclear weapons;

8. *Welcomes* the progress made on increased collaboration within and between zones at the first Conference of States Parties and Signatories to Treaties that Establish Nuclear-Weapon-Free Zones, held in Tlatelolco, Mexico, from 26 to 28 April 2005, at which States reaffirmed their need to cooperate in order to achieve their common objectives;

9. *Congratulates* the States parties and signatories to the treaties of Tlatelolco, Rarotonga, Bangkok and Pelindaba, as well as Mongolia, for their efforts to pursue the common goals envisaged in those treaties and to promote the nuclear-weapon-free status of the southern hemisphere and adjacent areas, and calls upon them to explore and implement further ways and means of cooperation among themselves and their treaty agencies;

10. *Encourages* the competent authorities of the nuclear-weapon-free-zone treaties to provide assistance to the States parties and signatories to those treaties so as to facilitate the accomplishment of the goals;

11. *Decides* to include in the provisional agenda of its sixty-second session the item entitled "Nuclear-weapon-free southern hemisphere and adjacent areas".

RECORDED VOTE ON RESOLUTION 61/69:

In favour: Afghanistan, Albania, Algeria, Andorra, Angola, Antigua and Barbuda, Argentina, Armenia, Australia, Austria, Azerbaijan, Bahamas, Bahrain, Bangladesh, Barbados, Belarus, Belgium, Belize, Bolivia, Bosnia and Herzegovina, Brazil, Brunei Darussalam, Bulgaria, Burkina Faso, Burundi, Cambodia, Cameroon, Canada, Cape Verde, Central African Republic, Chad, Chile, China, Colombia, Comoros, Congo, Costa Rica, Côte d'Ivoire, Croatia, Cuba, Cyprus, Czech Republic, Democratic People's Republic of Korea, Denmark, Djibouti, Dominica, Dominican Republic, Ecuador, Egypt, El Salvador, Eritrea, Estonia, Ethiopia, Fiji, Finland, Gabon, Georgia, Germany, Ghana, Greece, Grenada, Guatemala, Guinea, Guyana, Haiti, Honduras, Hungary, Iceland, Indonesia, Iran, Iraq, Ireland, Italy, Jamaica, Japan, Jordan, Kazakhstan, Kuwait, Kyrgyzstan, Lao People's Democratic Republic, Latvia, Lebanon, Lesotho, Liberia, Libyan Arab Jamahiriya, Liechtenstein, Lithuania, Luxembourg, Malawi, Malaysia, Maldives, Mali, Malta, Mauritania, Mauritius, Mexico, Moldova, Mongolia, Montenegro, Morocco, Mozambique, Myanmar, Namibia, Nauru, Nepal, Netherlands, New Zealand, Nicaragua, Niger, Nigeria, Norway, Oman, Panama, Papua New Guinea, Paraguay, Peru, Philippines, Poland, Portugal, Qatar, Republic of Korea, Romania, Rwanda, Saint Kitts and Nevis, Saint Lucia, Saint Vincent and the Grenadines, Samoa, San Marino, Sao Tome and Principe, Saudi Arabia, Senegal, Serbia, Sierra Leone, Singapore, Slovakia, Slovenia, Solomon Islands, South Africa, Sri Lanka, Sudan, Suriname, Swaziland, Sweden, Switzerland, Syrian Arab Republic, Tajikistan, Thailand, The former Yugoslav Republic of Macedonia, Timor-Leste, Togo, Tonga, Trinidad and Tobago, Tunisia, Turkey, Turkmenistan, Uganda, Ukraine, United Arab Emirates, United Republic of Tanzania, Uruguay, Uzbekistan, Vanuatu, Venezuela, Viet Nam, Yemen, Zambia, Zimbabwe.

Against: France, United Kingdom, United States.

Abstaining: Bhutan, India, Israel, Marshall Islands, Micronesia, Pakistan, Palau, Russian Federation, Spain.

Bacteriological (biological) and chemical weapons

In 2006, as in previous years, the international community continued to address the threat posed by biological and chemical weapons, compounded by globalization and the inherent ease in the movement across borders of dangerous biological and chemical agents. That threat was illustrated in August when 500 tons of deadly chemical agents were illegally dumped in Cote d'Ivoire by unidentified foreign ships. Member States continued to focus on further strengthening the Convention on the Prohibition of the Development, Production and Stockpiling of Bacteriological (Biological) and Toxin Weapons and on Their Destruction (BWC) (see below) and the Convention on the Prohibition of the Development, Production, Stockpiling and Use of Chemical Weapons and on Their Destruction (CWC) (see p. 653). The Security Council Committee established pursuant to Council resolution 1540(2004) [YUN 2004, p. 544] to monitor Member States' implementation of measures to combat the proliferation of WMDs, including chemical and biological weapons, also addressed relevant proposals to the Council.

Bacteriological (biological) weapons convention

Sixth Review Conference

The Sixth Review Conference of the States Parties to BWC (Geneva, 20 November–8 December) [BWC/CONF.VI/6] was held to review the provisions and operation of the Convention. Previous review conferences were held in 1980 [YUN 1980, p. 70], 1986 [YUN 1986, p. 64], 1991 [YUN 1991, p. 52], 1996 [YUN 1996, p. 477] and 2002 [YUN 2002, p. 516].

On 8 December, the Conference adopted by consensus its Final Document [BWC/CONF.VI/6], containing a Declaration and a series of decisions and recommendations. By the Declaration, the States parties reaffirmed their commitment to the Convention's purposes and provisions and declared their determination to comply with their obligations in that regard, convinced that the full implementation of those provisions should facilitate economic and technological development and international cooperation in peaceful biological activities. They reviewed the Convention's 15 articles, and reaffirmed the comprehensive scope of the Convention, which, as defined under article 1, unequivocally covered all naturally or artificially created or altered microbial and other biological agents and toxins and their components. Noting that Iran had proposed amendments to that article and to the title of the Convention to include explicitly the prohibition of the use of biological weapons, the Conference encouraged States parties to convey their views on the proposal to the Russian Federation, in its capacity as the Convention's depositary.

Regarding the provisions of the Convention's other articles, the Conference advocated, among other things, measures to ensure effective national export controls over biological agents and toxins and to protect and safeguard them; constitutional, legislative, administrative and judicial actions to enhance domestic implementation of the Convention; and the promotion of awareness among professionals of the need to report activities that could violate the Convention or related national criminal law. It emphasized the importance of States parties' legal right under the Convention to participate in the exchange of equipment and scientific and technological information for the use of biological agents for peaceful purposes; the need to implement the Convention's procedure for reporting violations of its prohibitions, for which the Security Council was invited to consider and investigate any complaints in that regard; and the indefinite duration of the Convention. Reaffirming the value of Review Conferences for assessing the Convention's implementation, the Conference recommended that they continue to be held every five years, with the Seventh Review Conference being held in Geneva, not later than 2011.

In other decisions and recommendations, the Conference decided that four annual meetings of the States parties should be held as from 2007 and up to the Seventh Review to discuss and promote common understanding and effective action on: how to enhance national implementation of the Convention; regional and subregional cooperation on implementation matters; national, regional and international measures to improve biosafety and the security of pathogens and toxins; oversight, education, awareness raising and the adoption and/or development of codes of conduct for the prevention of misuse of bio-science and technology potentially useful for purposes banned by the Convention; enhancing international cooperation in biological sciences and technology for peaceful purposes; and the provision of assistance and coordination with relevant organizations in cases of alleged use of biological and toxin weapons. Each meeting of the States parties would be preceded by a preparatory experts' meeting, the outcome of which would be considered by the Seventh Review Conference.

To provide administrative support to those meetings and further aid the comprehensive implementation and universalization of the Convention and the exchange of confidence-building measures, the Conference decided that an Implementation Support Unit should be established within the Geneva Branch of the UN Department for Disarmament Affairs. The Unit's mandate would be limited to tasks relating to administrative support and confidence-building measures and would report annually on its activities to the States parties. The Conference also adopted decisions and recommendations to enhance States parties' participation in the confidence-building process and promote the Convention's universalization.

GENERAL ASSEMBLY ACTION

On 6 December [meeting 67], the General Assembly, on the recommendation of the First Committee [A/61/401], adopted **resolution 61/102** without vote [agenda item 97].

Convention on the Prohibition of the Development Production and Stockpiling of Bacteriological (Biological) and Toxin Weapons and on Their Destruction

The General Assembly,

Recalling its previous resolutions relating to the complete and effective prohibition of bacteriological (biological) and toxin weapons and to their destruction,

Noting with satisfaction that there are one hundred and fifty-five States parties to the Convention on the Prohibition of the Development, Production and Stockpiling of Bacteriological (Biological) and Toxin Weapons and on Their Destruction, including all of the permanent members of the Security Council,

Bearing in mind its call upon all States parties to the Convention to participate in the implementation of the recommendations of the Review Conferences, including the exchange of information and data agreed to in the Final Declaration of the Third Review Conference of the Parties to the Convention, and to provide such information and data in conformity with standardized procedure to the Secretary-General on an annual basis and no later than 15 April,

Welcoming the reaffirmation made in the Final Declaration of the Fourth Review Conference that under all circumstances the use of bacteriological (biological) and toxin weapons and their development, production and stockpiling are effectively prohibited under article I of the Convention,

1. *Reaffirms* the call upon all signatory States that have not yet ratified the Convention on the Prohibition of the Development, Production and Stockpiling of Bacteriological (Biological) and Toxin Weapons and on Their Destruction to do so without delay, and calls upon those States that have not signed the Convention to become parties thereto at an early date, thus contributing to the achievement of universal adherence to the Convention;

2. *Welcomes* the information and data provided to date, and reiterates its call upon all States parties to the Convention to participate in the exchange of information and data agreed to in the Final Declaration of the Third Review Conference of the Parties to the Convention;

3. *Appreciates* the significant participation of the States parties at the meetings of States parties and meetings of experts to date and the constructive and useful exchange of information achieved;

4. *Welcomes* the discussion and the promotion of common understanding and effective action on topics agreed upon at the Fifth Review Conference: the adoption of necessary national measures to implement the prohibitions set forth in the Convention, including the enactment of penal legislation, and national mechanisms to establish and maintain the security and oversight of pathogenic micro-organisms and toxins in 2003; enhancing international capabilities for responding to, investigating and mitigating the effects of cases of alleged use of biological or toxin weapons or suspicious outbreaks of disease and strengthening and broadening national and international institutional efforts and existing mechanisms for the surveillance, detection, diagnosis and combating of infectious diseases affecting humans, animals and plants in 2004; and the content, promulgation and adoption of codes of conduct for scientists in 2005;

5. *Recalls* that the Sixth Review Conference was mandated to consider issues identified in the review of the operation of the Convention as provided for in article XII thereof and any possible consensus follow-up action;

6. *Welcomes* the convening of the Sixth Review Conference in Geneva from 20 November to 8 December 2006, pursuant to the decision reached by the Preparatory Committee of the States Parties to the Convention;

7. *Requests* the Secretary-General to continue to render the necessary assistance to the depositary Governments of the Convention and to provide such services as may be required for the implementation of the decisions and recommendations of the Review Conferences;

8. *Decides* to include in the provisional agenda of its sixty-second session, also in view of the outcome of the Sixth Review Conference, the item entitled "Convention on the Prohibition of the Development, Production and Stockpiling of Bacteriological (Biological) and Toxin Weapons and on Their Destruction".

1925 Geneva Protocol

In response to General Assembly resolution 59/70 [YUN 2004, p. 556], the Secretary-General reported, in June [A/61/116], that France, as the depositary of the Protocol for the Prohibition of the Use in War of Asphyxiating, Poisonous or Other Gases, and of Bacteriological Methods of Warfare (the 1925 Geneva Protocol), had received no notice of withdrawals of reservations since the Assembly's adoption of the resolution.

GENERAL ASSEMBLY ACTION

On 6 December [meeting 67], the General Assembly, on the recommendation of the First Committee [A/61/394], adopted **resolution 61/61** by recorded vote (173-0-4) [agenda item 90 *(c)*].

Measures to uphold the authority of the 1925 Geneva Protocol

The General Assembly,

Recalling its previous resolutions on the subject, in particular resolution 59/70 of 3 December 2004,

Determined to act with a view to achieving effective progress towards general and complete disarmament under strict and effective international control,

Recalling the long-standing determination of the international community to achieve the effective prohibition of the development, production, stockpiling and use of chemical and biological weapons as well as the continuing support for measures to uphold the authority of the Protocol for the Prohibition of the Use in War of Asphyxiating, Poisonous or Other Gases, and of Bacteriological Methods of Warfare, signed at Geneva on 17 June 1925, as expressed by consensus in many previous resolutions,

Emphasizing the necessity of easing international tension and strengthening trust and confidence between States,

1. *Takes note* of the note by the Secretary-General;

2. *Renews its previous call* to all States to observe strictly the principles and objectives of the Protocol for the Prohibition of the Use in War of Asphyxiating, Poisonous or Other Gases, and of Bacteriological Methods of Warfare, and reaffirms the vital necessity of upholding its provisions;

3. *Calls upon* those States that continue to maintain reservations to the 1925 Geneva Protocol to withdraw them;

4. *Requests* the Secretary-General to submit to the General Assembly at its sixty-third session a report on the implementation of the present resolution.

RECORDED VOTE ON RESOLUTION 61/61:

In favour: Afghanistan, Albania, Algeria, Andorra, Angola, Antigua and Barbuda, Argentina, Armenia, Australia, Austria, Azerbaijan, Bahamas, Bahrain, Bangladesh, Barbados, Belarus, Belgium, Belize, Bhutan, Bolivia, Bosnia and Herzegovina, Brazil, Brunei Darussalam, Bulgaria, Burkina Faso, Burundi, Cambodia, Cameroon, Canada, Cape Verde, Central African Republic, Chile, China, Colombia, Comoros, Congo, Costa Rica, Côte d'Ivoire, Croatia, Cuba, Cyprus, Czech Republic, Democratic People's Republic of Korea, Democratic Republic of the Congo, Denmark, Djibouti, Dominica, Dominican Republic, Ecuador, Egypt, El Salvador, Eritrea, Estonia, Ethiopia, Fiji, Finland, France,

Gabon, Gambia, Georgia, Germany, Ghana, Greece, Grenada, Guatemala, Guinea, Guyana, Haiti, Honduras, Hungary, Iceland, India, Indonesia, Iran, Iraq, Ireland, Italy, Jamaica, Japan, Jordan, Kazakhstan, Kuwait, Kyrgyzstan, Lao People's Democratic Republic, Latvia, Lebanon, Lesotho, Liberia, Libyan Arab Jamahiriya, Liechtenstein, Lithuania, Luxembourg, Malawi, Malaysia, Maldives, Mali, Malta, Mauritania, Mauritius, Mexico, Moldova, Monaco, Mongolia, Montenegro, Morocco, Mozambique, Myanmar, Namibia, Nepal, Netherlands, New Zealand, Nicaragua, Niger, Nigeria, Norway, Oman, Pakistan, Panama, Paraguay, Peru, Philippines, Poland, Portugal, Qatar, Republic of Korea, Romania, Russian Federation, Rwanda, Saint Kitts and Nevis, Saint Lucia, Saint Vincent and the Grenadines, Samoa, San Marino, Sao Tome and Principe, Saudi Arabia, Senegal, Serbia, Sierra Leone, Singapore, Slovakia, Slovenia, Solomon Islands, South Africa, Spain, Sri Lanka, Sudan, Suriname, Swaziland, Sweden, Switzerland, Syrian Arab Republic, Tajikistan, Thailand, The former Yugoslav Republic of Macedonia, Timor-Leste, Togo, Tonga, Trinidad and Tobago, Tunisia, Turkey, Turkmenistan, Ukraine, United Arab Emirates, United Kingdom, United Republic of Tanzania, Uruguay, Uzbekistan, Vanuatu, Venezuela, Viet Nam, Yemen, Zambia, Zimbabwe.

Against: None.

Abstaining: Israel, Marshall Islands, Palau, United States.

Chemical weapons

Chemical weapons convention

In 2006, Djibouti, Haiti, Liberia, Comoros, the Central African Republic and Montenegro ratified or acceded to the Convention on the Prohibition of the Development, Production, Stockpiling and Use of Chemical Weapons and on Their Destruction (CWC), bringing the total number of States parties to 181. The number of signatories stood at 165. The Convention was adopted by the Conference on Disarmament in 1992 [YUN 1992, p. 65] and entered into force in 1997 [YUN 1997, p. 499].

The eleventh session of the Conference of the States Parties (The Hague, Netherlands, 5-8 December) [C-11/5] considered, among other issues, the status of the Convention's implementation, fostering international cooperation for peaceful purposes in the field of chemical activities, ensuring the Convention's universality and administrative and budgetary matters. The Conference approved or adopted decisions on the status of implementation of article VII of the Convention addressing national implementation measures; extension of deadlines for the destruction of category 1 chemical weapons stockpiles; implementation of the plan of action for the universality of the Convention; the establishment of an Organization for the Prohibition of Chemical Weapons Office in Africa; the establishment of a Committee on Relations with the Host Country; and the establishment of a mechanism to encourage States parties that were in arrears to regularize payment of their outstanding contributions. The Conference decided to hold its twelfth regular session in November 2007, and the thirteenth in December 2008. It scheduled the second Special Session of the States parties to review the Convention's operation for April 2008.

GENERAL ASSEMBLY ACTION

On 6 December [meeting 67], the General Assembly, on the recommendation of the First Committee [A/61/394], adopted **resolution 61/68** without vote [agenda item 90 *(p)*].

Implementation of the Convention on the Prohibition of the Development, Production, Stockpiling and Use of Chemical Weapons and on Their Destruction

The General Assembly,

Recalling its previous resolutions on the subject of chemical weapons, in particular resolution 60/67 of 8 December 2005, adopted without a vote, in which it noted with appreciation the ongoing work to achieve the objective and purpose of the Convention on the Prohibition of the Development, Production, Stockpiling and Use of Chemical Weapons and on Their Destruction,

Determined to achieve the effective prohibition of the development, production, acquisition, transfer, stockpiling and use of chemical weapons and their destruction,

Noting with satisfaction that, since the adoption of resolution 60/67, six additional States have ratified the Convention or acceded to it, bringing the total number of States parties to the Convention to one hundred and eighty,

Reaffirming the importance of the outcome of the First Special Session of the Conference of the States Parties to Review the Operation of the Chemical Weapons Convention, including the Political Declaration, in which the States parties reaffirmed their commitment to achieving the objective and purpose of the Convention, and the final report, which addressed all aspects of the Convention and made important recommendations on its continued implementation,

1. *Emphasizes* that the universality of the Convention on the Prohibition of the Development, Production, Stockpiling and Use of Chemical Weapons and on Their Destruction is fundamental to the achievement of its objective and purpose and acknowledges progress made in the implementation of the action plan for the universality of the Convention, and calls upon all States that have not yet done so to become parties to the Convention without delay;

2. *Underlines* the fact that the Convention and its implementation contribute to enhancing international peace and security, and emphasizes that its full, universal and effective implementation will contribute further to that purpose by excluding completely, for the sake of all humankind, the possibility of the use of chemical weapons;

3. *Stresses* that the full and effective implementation of all provisions of the Convention, including those on

national implementation (article VII) and assistance and protection against chemical weapons (article X), constitutes an important contribution to the efforts of the United Nations in the global fight against terrorism in all its forms and manifestations;

4. *Also stresses* the importance to the Convention that all possessors of chemical weapons, chemical weapons production facilities or chemical weapons development facilities, including previously declared possessor States, should be among the States parties to the Convention, and welcomes progress to that end;

5. *Reaffirms* the obligation of the States parties to the Convention to destroy chemical weapons and to destroy or convert chemical weapons production facilities within the time limits provided for by the Convention;

6. *Notes* that the effective application of the verification system builds confidence in compliance with the Convention by States parties;

7. *Stresses* the importance of the Organization for the Prohibition of Chemical Weapons in verifying compliance with the provisions of the Convention as well as in promoting the timely and efficient accomplishment of all its objectives;

8. *Urges* all States parties to the Convention to meet in full and on time their obligations under the Convention and to support the Organization for the Prohibition of Chemical Weapons in its implementation activities;

9. *Welcomes* progress made in the national implementation of the plan of action on the implementation of article VII obligations and commends the States parties and the Technical Secretariat for assisting other States parties, on request, with the implementation of the follow-up to the plan of action regarding article VII obligations, and urges States parties that have not fulfilled their obligations under article VII to do so without further delay, in accordance with their constitutional processes;

10. *Reaffirms* the importance of article XI provisions relating to the economic and technological development of States parties and recalls that the full, effective and non-discriminatory implementation of those provisions contributes to universality, and also reaffirms the undertaking of the States parties to foster international cooperation for peaceful purposes in the field of chemical activities of the States parties and the importance of that cooperation and its contribution to the promotion of the Convention as a whole;

11. *Notes with appreciation* the ongoing work of the Organization for the Prohibition of Chemical Weapons to achieve the objective and purpose of the Convention, to ensure the full implementation of its provisions, including those for international verification of compliance with it, and to provide a forum for consultation and cooperation among States parties, and also notes with appreciation the substantial contribution of the Technical Secretariat and the Director-General to the continued development and success of the Organization;

12. *Welcomes* the decision of the Conference of the States Parties at its tenth session approving the appointment of Mr. Rogelio Pfirter as the Director-General of the Technical Secretariat of the Organization for the Prohibition of Chemical Weapons;

13. *Also welcomes* the beginning of preparatory work by the States parties on the substance of the Second Special Session of the Conference of the States Parties to Review the Operation of the Chemical Weapons Convention;

14. *Draws attention* to the tenth anniversary of the entry into force of the Convention, on 29 April 2007, which provides a special occasion to publicly renew commitment to the multilateral treaty system and to the objective and purpose of the Convention, and takes note of the unveiling in The Hague on 9 May 2007 of a permanent memorial to all victims of chemical weapons;

15. *Welcomes* the cooperation between the United Nations and the Organization for the Prohibition of Chemical Weapons within the framework of the Relationship Agreement between the United Nations and the Organization, in accordance with the provisions of the Convention;

16. *Decides* to include in the provisional agenda of its sixty-second session the item entitled "Implementation of the Convention on the Prohibition of the Development, Production, Stockpiling and Use of Chemical Weapons and on Their Destruction".

Organization for the Prohibition of Chemical Weapons

In 2006, the Organization for the Prohibition of Chemical Weapons (OPCW) continued to make progress towards the complete elimination of chemical weapons and the threat of their proliferation or use. As at year's end, the six States parties that had declared possession of chemical weapons had between them declared some 487,644 tonnes of chemical weapons and related items. Overall, OPCW verified the destruction of 3,821 tonnes of chemical warfare agents and conducted 42 inspections at 27 chemical weapons storage facilities in six States. States parties also made considerable progress in eliminating the capacity to produce chemical weapons, with five of the remaining 12 chemical weapons production facilities destroyed or converted to other uses. As provided for under article 10 of the Convention, OPCW continued to coordinate efforts to ensure protection against chemical weapons, including through activities for improving international cooperation in the event of an incident involving the release of chemical agents. Under its mandate relating to economic and technological development, OPCW supported 55 new chemistry research projects in 26 States parties.

The OPCW Executive Council held its forty-fourth (14-17 March), forty-fifth (16-19 May), forty-sixth (4-7 July) and forty-seventh (7-10 November) sessions, at which it considered reports on the status of the Convention's implementation, including issues concerning verification activities and the Convention's articles X and XI on assistance and protection against chemical weapons and on economic and technological development, respectively. It adopted decisions on the destruction of chemical weapons and the destruction or conversion of chemical weapons production facilities, and on questions relating to the chemical industry and financial matters. It adopted recommendations regarding the plan of action for implementing article VII obligations on national implementation measures, monitored the implementation of the action plan for the Convention's universality, approved facility agreements between OPCW and a number of States parties and established an open-ended working group to begin preparations for the Second Review Conference of the States Parties, scheduled for 2008.

Cooperation between the United Nations and OPCW

By a 9 October note [A/61/185], the Secretary-General submitted to the General Assembly the 2004 OPCW report and the draft 2005 report, in accordance with the Agreement concerning the Relationship between the United Nations and OPCW, which was signed in 2000 [YUN 2000, p. 516] and entered into force in 2001 [YUN 2001, p. 495].

The Assembly also had before it the Secretary-General's consolidated report on cooperation between the United Nations and other organizations, highlighting cooperation with OPCW [A/61/256].

GENERAL ASSEMBLY ACTION

On 20 December [meeting 83], the General Assembly adopted **resolution 61/224** [draft: A/61/L.49 & Add.1] without vote [agenda item 108 *(n)*].

Cooperation between the United Nations and the Organization for the Prohibition of Chemical Weapons

The General Assembly,

Recalling its resolution 59/7 of 22 October 2004 on cooperation between the United Nations and the Organization for the Prohibition of Chemical Weapons,

Having received the annual report for 2004 and the draft report for 2005 of the Organization for the Prohibition of Chemical Weapons on the implementation of the Convention on the Prohibition of the Development, Production, Stockpiling and Use of Chemical Weapons and on Their Destruction,

1. *Takes note* of the annual report for 2004 and the draft report for 2005 of the Organization for the Prohibition of Chemical Weapons submitted on its behalf by its Director-General;

2. *Welcomes* the announcement of the tenth anniversary of the entry into force of the Convention on the Prohibition of the Development, Production, Stockpiling and Use of Chemical Weapons and on Their Destruction and of the establishment, on 29 April 1997, of the Organization for the Prohibition of Chemical Weapons, which will be celebrated on 9 May 2007 in The Hague, and calls upon Member States to arrange for representation at the appropriate political level;

3. *Decides* to include in the provisional agenda of its sixty-third session the sub-item entitled "Cooperation between the United Nations and the Organization for the Prohibition of Chemical Weapons".

Conventional weapons

Towards an arms trade treaty

In 2006, the General Assembly began to explore the possibility of establishing a legally-binding instrument providing common international standards for the import, export and transfer of conventional arms. Recognizing that the absence of such standards was contributing to conflict, the displacement of people, crime and terrorism, and acknowledging the growing support for the proposed instrument across all regions, the Assembly asked the Secretary-General to establish a group of governmental experts to examine, beginning in 2008, the feasibility, scope and draft parameters for it, which the Assembly would consider at its sixty-third (2008) session. The need for such an instrument had been promoted by the United Kingdom [YUN 2005, p. 621] and was considered throughout the year by members of Control Arms, the international coalition of non-governmental organizations (NGOs) dedicated to raising awareness about the human costs of the unregulated global arms trade.

GENERAL ASSEMBLY ACTION

On 6 December [meeting 67], the General Assembly, on the recommendation of the First Committee [A/61/394], adopted **resolution 61/89** by recorded vote (153-1-24) [agenda item 90].

Towards an arms trade treaty: establishing common international standards for the import, export and transfer of conventional arms

The General Assembly,

Guided by the purposes and principles enshrined in the Charter of the United Nations, and reaffirming its respect for and commitment to international law,

Recalling its resolutions 46/36 L of 9 December 1991, 51/45 N of 10 December 1996, 51/47 B of 10 December 1996, 56/24 V of 24 December 2001 and 60/69 and 60/82 of 8 December 2005,

Recognizing that arms control, disarmament and non-proliferation are essential for the maintenance of international peace and security,

Reaffirming the inherent right of all States to individual or collective self-defence in accordance with Article 51 of the Charter,

Acknowledging the right of all States to manufacture, import, export, transfer and retain conventional arms for self-defence and security needs, and in order to participate in peace support operations,

Recalling the obligations of all States to fully comply with arms embargoes decided by the Security Council in accordance with the Charter,

Reaffirming its respect for international law, including international human rights law and international humanitarian law, and the Charter,

Taking note of and encouraging relevant initiatives, undertaken at the international, regional and subregional levels between States, including those of the United Nations, and of the role played by non-governmental organizations and civil society, to enhance cooperation, improve information exchange and transparency and implement confidence-building measures in the field of responsible arms trade,

Recognizing that the absence of common international standards on the import, export and transfer of conventional arms is a contributory factor to conflict, the displacement of people, crime and terrorism, thereby undermining peace, reconciliation, safety, security, stability and sustainable development,

Acknowledging the growing support across all regions for concluding a legally binding instrument negotiated on a non-discriminatory, transparent and multilateral basis, to establish common international standards for the import, export and transfer of conventional arms,

1. *Requests* the Secretary-General to seek the views of Member States on the feasibility, scope and draft parameters for a comprehensive, legally binding instrument establishing common international standards for the import, export and transfer of conventional arms, and to submit a report on the subject to the General Assembly at its sixty-second session;

2. *Also requests* the Secretary-General to establish a group of governmental experts, on the basis of equitable geographical distribution, informed by the report of the Secretary-General submitted to the General Assembly at its sixty-second session, to examine, commencing in 2008, the feasibility, scope and draft parameters for a comprehensive, legally binding instrument establishing common international standards for the import, export and transfer of conventional arms, and to transmit the report of the group of experts to the Assembly for consideration at its sixty-third session;

3. *Further requests* the Secretary-General to provide the group of governmental experts with any assistance and services that may be required for the discharge of its tasks;

4. *Decides* to include in the provisional agenda of its sixty-second session an item entitled "Towards an arms trade treaty: establishing common international standards for the import, export and transfer of conventional arms".

RECORDED VOTE ON RESOLUTION 61/89:

In favour: Afghanistan, Albania, Algeria, Andorra, Angola, Antigua and Barbuda, Argentina, Armenia, Australia, Austria, Azerbaijan, Bahamas, Bangladesh, Barbados, Belgium, Belize, Benin, Bhutan, Bolivia, Bosnia and Herzegovina, Brazil, Brunei Darussalam, Bulgaria, Burkina Faso, Burundi, Cambodia, Cameroon, Canada, Cape Verde, Central African Republic, Chad, Chile, Colombia, Comoros, Congo, Costa Rica, Côte d'Ivoire, Croatia, Cuba, Cyprus, Czech Republic, Denmark, Djibouti, Dominica, Dominican Republic, Ecuador, El Salvador, Eritrea, Estonia, Ethiopia, Fiji, Finland, France, Gabon, Gambia, Georgia, Germany, Ghana, Greece, Grenada, Guatemala, Guinea, Guyana, Haiti, Honduras, Hungary, Iceland, Indonesia, Ireland, Italy, Jamaica, Japan, Jordan, Kazakhstan, Kenya, Kyrgyzstan, Latvia, Lebanon, Lesotho, Liberia, Liechtenstein, Lithuania, Luxembourg, Malawi, Malaysia, Maldives, Mali, Malta, Mauritania, Mauritius, Mexico, Micronesia, Moldova, Monaco, Mongolia, Montenegro, Morocco, Mozambique, Namibia, Nauru, Netherlands, New Zealand, Nicaragua, Niger, Nigeria, Norway, Palau, Panama, Papua New Guinea, Paraguay, Peru, Philippines, Poland, Portugal, Republic of Korea, Romania, Rwanda, Saint Kitts and Nevis, Saint Lucia, Saint Vincent and the Grenadines, Samoa, San Marino, Sao Tome and Principe, Senegal, Serbia, Sierra Leone, Singapore, Slovakia, Slovenia, Solomon Islands, South Africa, Spain, Sri Lanka, Suriname, Swaziland, Sweden, Switzerland, Tajikistan, Thailand, The former Yugoslav Republic of Macedonia, Timor-Leste, Togo, Tonga, Trinidad and Tobago, Tunisia, Turkey, Uganda, Ukraine, United Kingdom, United Republic of Tanzania, Uruguay, Vanuatu, Zambia.

Against: United States.

Abstaining: Bahrain, Belarus, China, Egypt, India, Iran, Iraq, Israel, Kuwait, Lao People's Democratic Republic, Libyan Arab Jamahiriya, Marshall Islands, Nepal, Oman, Pakistan, Qatar, Russian Federation, Saudi Arabia, Sudan, Syrian Arab Republic, United Arab Emirates, Venezuela, Yemen, Zimbabwe.

Small arms

Reports of Secretary-General. As requested in Security Council Presidential statement S/PRST/2005/7 [YUN 2005, p. 619], the Secretary-General submitted a February report [S/2006/109 & Corr.1] updating the Council on the initiatives undertaken during 2005 to implement the recommendations contained in his 2002 report [YUN 2002, p. 521] on ways the Council could contribute to dealing with the illicit trade in small arms and light weapons.

The Secretary-General reported that the most significant achievement during that period was the adoption by the General Assembly, in decision 60/519 [YUN 2005, p. 621], of the International Instrument to Enable States to Identify and Trace, in a Timely and Reliable Manner, Illicit Small Arms and Light Weapons, thereby fulfilling recommendation 1 in his 2002 report. The effectiveness and relevance of the Instrument would, however, depend on Member States' commitment to implement it fully. Progress had also been made on recommendation 2 concerning the Interpol Weapons Electronic Tracing System, which the Secretary-General noted had been enhanced. He advocated closer cooperation between the United Nations and Interpol in implementing the Instrument. Encouraging developments regarding recommendations 6 to 12 included the continuing attention by the Council to links between the illicit exploitation of natural and other resources and the illicit trade in small arms and light weapons and developing strategies to address the issue; the emphasis placed by the Council on the importance of inter-mission cooperation in the implementation of disarmament, demobilization and reintegration operations, as well as the Assembly's acknowledgment that reinsertion activities were part of those operations; initiatives to control the export, import and transit of small arms and light weapons; the continuing practice of establishing under relevant Council resolutions, mechanisms to support, monitor and assess the implementation of sanctions and provide technical advice to the related sanctions committees to ensure full compliance with the embargoes; and the growing participation of Member States in the two UN reporting instruments on armaments.

Regarding recommendations 3 to 5, on which less progress was achieved, the Secretary-General suggested that the Council call upon Member States to support the inter-agency Coordinating Action on Small Arms mechanism so as to enhance its effectiveness as a platform for developing a coordinated and coherent UN approach to the small arms problem and its relevance as a provider of services to Member States. On recommendation 4, which addressed the need for greater interaction between the Council and the Assembly in tackling the problem, the Secretary-General noted that such interaction would help develop a clear and comprehensive UN policy on small arms and light weapons, which was important in the light of the scheduled conference to review progress in implementing the Programme of Action adopted by the 2001 UN Conference on small arms (see below). Turning to recommendation 5 on the need for Member States to implement Council resolutions on sanctions, the question of enforcement depended on the political will and relevant capacity of Member States, the Secretary-General noted.

In response to General Assembly resolution 60/74 [YUN 2005, p. 623], the Secretary-General submitted a June report, with later addendum [A/61/118 & Add.1], containing the views of eight Member States (Bolivia, Georgia, Lebanon, Mauritius, Mexico, Norway, Panama, Spain) regarding the risks arising from the accumulation of conventional ammunition stockpiles in surplus and ways of strengthening controls on that ammunition at the national level.

He also submitted, as requested in Assembly resolutions 60/71 [YUN 2005, p. 622] and 60/81 [ibid., p. 625], an August report [A/61/288] covering the period from July 2005 to July 2006, which summarized national, subregional and regional activities undertaken to assist States in curbing the illicit trade in small arms and in collecting and disposing of them. The report also provided an overview of activities undertaken by the UN system and Member States to combat the illicit trade in those weapons and to implement the 2001 Programme of Action.

The Secretary-General observed that Member States, international and regional organizations and civil society remained committed to implementing the Programme of Action, as demonstrated by the high number of activities undertaken by States, intergovernmental organizations and NGOs, and by the many practical projects carried out during the reporting period, often through partnerships. Furthermore, although the Conference to review progress in implementing the Programme (see below) underlined continuing differences among Member States on a number of issues, the intensity of discussions at the Conference and the unanimous reaffirmation of support for the Programme illustrated the high degree of importance which the international community continued to accord efforts to combat the illicit trade in small arms and light weapons. Those efforts were advanced by the establishment of a Group of Governmental Experts to consider further steps to enhance international cooperation in preventing, combating and eradicating illicit brokering in small arms. It was noteworthy that the Group of Interested States in Practical Disarmament Measures (see p. 665) had further expanded its activities to include the provision of assistance to NGOs, and the role of regional, subregional and international organizations in promoting the implementation of the 2001 Programme of Action was growing.

Programme of Action on illicit trade in small arms

Review Conference

As recommended in the Programme of Action adopted by the United Nations Conference on the Illicit Trade in Small Arms and Light Weapons in All Its Aspects [YUN 2001, p. 499], and in accordance with General Assembly resolutions 58/241 [YUN 2003, p. 564] and 59/86 [YUN 2004, p. 561], the

UN Conference to Review progress in implementing that Programme was convened (New York, 26 June–7 July) [A/CONF.192/2006/RC/9], with some 2000 representatives from Governments, international organizations and civil society in attendance. The Conference began with a four-day general exchange of views and thematic debate, during which statements were made by numerous participants and international and regional organizations. Participants considered and negotiated the draft final document of the Conference, adopting as the basis of discussion a working paper presented by the President (Sri Lanka) [A/CONF.192/2006/RG/WP.4], which outlined a preamble; concrete measures to strengthen the Programme's implementation at the national, regional and global levels; international cooperation and assistance; and follow-up to the UN Conference on small arms. Between 29 and 30 June, participants submitted up to 325 proposals regarding the Conference outcome. Owing to disagreements among delegates on aspects of those proposals, the President made efforts in a new working paper to reflect a middle ground and appointed facilitators to help delegates achieve compromise language on contentious issues. As those efforts did not succeed, the Conference was not able to conclude a final document and only adopted a consensus procedural report for submission to the General Assembly. The disagreements focused on a number of issues which also did not command consensus at the 2001 UN Conference on small arms [YUN 2001, p. 499], such as the question of whether or not the outcome document should make references to the civilian possession of small arms and light weapons. While the idea was supported by delegates from Latin America and the Caribbean, Africa and the EU, many others disagreed, arguing that the Programme of Action was about the illicit trade in those weapons rather than their legal possession, which was better left to each State to regulate through national laws. Other contentious issues centred on whether or not the Review Conference final document should address the question of small arms ammunition and their transfer to non-state actors; whether the Conference should address the issue of man-portable air defence systems (MANPADS); and the nature of the follow-up process to consider and/or review progress in the implementation of the Programme.

Despite those setbacks, participants reaffirmed strong commitment to the full implementation of the Programme of Action. They saw the Review Conference as having succeeded in refocusing international community attention on the problem of small arms and light weapons, and the importance of the Programme as the main framework for measures to curtail the illegal trade in those weapons. While acknowledging progress at all levels, Member States conceded that more needed to be done to effectively address the small arms scourge. There was also consensus on the need to strengthen and better coordinate international cooperation and assistance for building the capacity of States to implement the Programme.

The Review Conference was preceded by a meeting of its Preparatory Committee (New York, 9-20 January) [A/CONF.192/2006/RC/1], which was also unable to reach agreement on a draft final outcome document for consideration by the Conference. Consequently it adopted a consensus report containing decisions and recommendations relating only to organizational and procedural issues.

Conference preparations and regional consultations. A regional preparatory meeting of the Latin American and Caribbean States (Antigua, Guatemala, 2-4 May) [A/60/876] and a workshop for Asian States (Bangkok, Thailand, 17-19 May) [A/CONF.192/2006/RC/3] were held to promote and contribute regional perspectives on how to better tackle the challenges posed by small arms and light weapons.

The Department for Disarmament Affairs (DDA), in collaboration with the United Nations Development Programme (UNDP), organized a pilot sponsorship programme (New York, 22 June–7 July), to provide funding for the participation in the Review Conference of representatives from national coordinating bodies in 33 States. Under the auspices of the Coordinating Action on Small Arms (CASA) mechanism, established in 1998 [YUN 1998, p. 525] to coordinate UN system action on small arms, DDA collaborated with UNDP to complete a project on capacity development, which assisted 115 States with the process of reporting, within the framework of the Programme of Action. CASA members, comprising 16 UN entities, also addressed multidisciplinary aspects of the small arms scourge and supported the implementation of the Programme. During the year, CASA launched its internet database, designed to facilitate information exchange among members, disseminate information to the public in general and collect data on UN activities relating to small arms. The database also contained country-specific information via country profiles, which, among other things, provided data to help identify areas where international assistance was needed.

Communications. On 29 June [A/CONF.192/2006/RC/6], the Russian Federation circulated the text of a statement issued by Mikhail Kalashnikov, designer of the AK-47 rifle, reputed to be the most widespread military weapon in the world, in which he emphasized the urgency of addressing the small arms scourge and expressed great sorrow that the assault rifle he designed had produced far too many casualties.

The Fourteenth Conference of Heads of State or Government of Non-Aligned Countries (Havana, Cuba, 11-16 September) [A/61/472-S/2006/780], concerned over the illicit transfer, manufacture and circulation of small arms and light weapons, expressed disappointment at the inability of the Review Conference to agree on a final document and encouraged delegations to coordinate efforts in the United Nations, with a view to reaching agreement on a follow-up to the 2001 Programme of Action, to ensure its full implementation.

International instrument

During the year, the Department for Disarmament Affairs promoted the International Instrument to Enable States to Identify and Trace, in a Timely and Reliable Manner, Illicit Small Arms and Light Weapons, adopted in General Assembly decision 60/519 [YUN 2005, p. 621], including by familiarizing relevant stakeholders with its key provisions and organizing workshops on related issues. In collaboration with Interpol, the Department also defined a strategy for cooperation in providing capacity-building assistance for the Instrument's implementation. Given that the Instrument was not legally-binding, its effectiveness depended on the willingness and capacity of States to implement its provisions. Capacity-building was therefore critical, because many States required assistance in developing the technical means for small arms and light weapons marking and record-keeping, and to train enforcement officials in tracing procedures and techniques. The Instrument provided for biennial follow-up reports from States regarding implementation efforts, to be considered at biennial meeting of Member States, the first of which would be held in 2008.

Illicit small arms brokering

Experts group. In accordance with General Assembly resolution 60/81 [YUN 2005, p. 625], the Secretary-General appointed 25 experts from Member States to the Group of Governmental Experts established to consider further steps to enhance international cooperation in preventing, combating and eradicating illicit brokering in small arms and light weapons. The Group, mandated to hold three sessions of one week's duration each, held its first meeting (Geneva, 27 November–1 December), and was expected to conclude its work in 2007, with a report to the Assembly on the outcome of its study.

GENERAL ASSEMBLY ACTION

On 6 December [meeting 67], the General Assembly, on the recommendation of the First Committee [A/61/394], adopted four resolutions relating to conventional weapons and the illicit traffic in small arms and light weapons. The Assembly adopted **resolution 61/66** by recorded vote (176-1-0) [agenda item 90 *(y)*].

The illicit trade in small arms and light weapons in all its aspects

The General Assembly,

Recalling its resolutions 56/24 V of 24 December 2001, 57/72 of 22 November 2002, 58/241 of 23 December 2003, 59/86 of 3 December 2004 and 60/81 of 8 December 2005,

Emphasizing the importance of the continued and full implementation of the Programme of Action to Prevent, Combat and Eradicate the Illicit Trade in Small Arms and Light Weapons in All Its Aspects, adopted by the United Nations Conference on the Illicit Trade in Small Arms and Light Weapons in All Its Aspects,

Welcoming the efforts by Member States to submit, on a voluntary basis, national reports on their implementation of the Programme of Action,

Noting with satisfaction regional and subregional efforts being undertaken in support of the implementation of the Programme of Action, and commending the progress that has already been made in this regard, including tackling both supply and demand factors that are relevant to addressing the illicit trade in small arms and light weapons,

Recognizing the efforts undertaken by non-governmental organizations in the provision of assistance to States for the implementation of the Programme of Action,

Recalling that, as part of the follow-up to the United Nations Conference on the Illicit Trade in Small Arms and Light Weapons in All Its Aspects, it was agreed that meetings of States should be convened on a biennial basis to consider the national, regional and global implementation of the Programme of Action,

Reiterating the significance of the adoption of the International Instrument to Enable States to Identify and Trace, in a Timely and Reliable Manner, Illicit Small Arms and Light Weapons,

Recognizing that illicit brokering in small arms and light weapons is a serious problem that the international community should address urgently, and in this regard welcoming the decision of the General Assembly to establish a group of governmental experts to consider further steps to enhance international cooperation in preventing, combating and eradicating illicit brokering in small arms and light weapons,

Taking note of the report of the Secretary-General on the implementation of resolution 60/81,

Welcoming the fact that the United Nations Conference to Review Progress Made in the Implementation of the Programme of Action to Prevent, Combat and Eradicate the Illicit Trade in Small Arms and Light Weapons in All Its Aspects, held from 26 June to 7 July 2006, highlighted the importance of implementing the Programme of Action in the activities of the international community to prevent, combat and eradicate the illicit trade in small arms and light weapons in all its aspects, beyond 2006,

1. *Encourages* all initiatives, including those of the United Nations, other international organizations, regional and subregional organizations, non-governmental organizations and civil society, for the successful implementation of the Programme of Action to Prevent, Combat and Eradicate the Illicit Trade in Small Arms and Light Weapons in All Its Aspects, and calls upon all Member States to contribute towards the continued implementation of the Programme of Action;

2. *Regrets* the fact that the United Nations Conference to Review Progress Made in the Implementation of the Programme of Action was not able to conclude an outcome document;

3. *Calls upon* all States to implement the International Instrument to Enable States to Identify and Trace, in a Timely and Reliable Manner, Illicit Small Arms and Light Weapons, among others, through the provision of information to the Secretary-General on the name and contact information of the national points of contact and on national marking practices related to markings used to indicate country of manufacture and/or country of import, as applicable;

4. *Decides* that, as stipulated in the Programme of Action, the next biennial meeting of States to consider the national, regional and global implementation of the Programme of Action shall be held no later than in 2008, in New York;

5. *Also decides* that the meeting of States to consider the implementation of the International Instrument to Enable States to Identify and Trace, in a Timely and Reliable Manner, Illicit Small Arms and Light Weapons, shall be held within the framework of the biennial meeting of States;

6. *Recalls* that the group of governmental experts, established to consider further steps to enhance international cooperation in preventing, combating and eradicating illicit brokering in small arms and light weapons is to submit a report on the outcome of its study to the General Assembly at its sixty-second session;

7. *Emphasizes* the fact that initiatives by the international community with respect to international cooperation and assistance remain essential and complementary to national implementation efforts, as well as to those at the regional and global levels;

8. *Continues to encourage* all such initiatives, including regional and subregional ones, to mobilize resources and expertise to promote the implementation of the Programme of Action and to provide assistance to States in its implementation;

9. *Encourages* States to submit national reports on their implementation of the Programme of Action and to include in such reports information on their implementation of the International Instrument to Enable States to Identify and Trace, in a Timely and Reliable Manner, Illicit Small Arms and Light Weapons in accordance with these instruments, and requests the Secretary-General to collate and circulate such data and information provided by States;

10. *Also encourages* States to share information on national experiences relating to best practices in the implementation of the Programme of Action;

11. *Requests* the Secretary-General to report to the General Assembly at its sixty-second session on the implementation of the present resolution;

12. *Decides* to include in the provisional agenda of its sixty-second session the item entitled "The illicit trade in small arms and light weapons in all its aspects".

RECORDED VOTE ON RESOLUTION 61/66:

In favour: Afghanistan, Albania, Algeria, Andorra, Angola, Antigua and Barbuda, Argentina, Armenia, Australia, Austria, Azerbaijan, Bahamas, Bahrain, Bangladesh, Barbados, Belarus, Belgium, Belize, Bhutan, Bolivia, Bosnia and Herzegovina, Brazil, Brunei Darussalam, Bulgaria, Burkina Faso, Burundi, Cambodia, Cameroon, Canada, Cape Verde, Central African Republic, Chad, Chile, China, Colombia, Comoros, Congo, Costa Rica, Côte d'Ivoire, Croatia, Cuba, Cyprus, Czech Republic, Democratic Republic of the Congo, Denmark, Djibouti, Dominica, Dominican Republic, Ecuador, Egypt, El Salvador, Eritrea, Estonia, Ethiopia, Fiji, Finland, France, Gabon, Gambia, Georgia, Germany, Ghana, Greece, Grenada, Guatemala, Guinea, Guyana, Haiti, Honduras, Hungary, Iceland, India, Indonesia, Iran, Iraq, Ireland, Israel, Italy, Jamaica, Japan, Jordan, Kazakhstan, Kuwait, Kyrgyzstan, Latvia, Lebanon, Lesotho, Liberia, Libyan Arab Jamahiriya, Liechtenstein, Lithuania, Luxembourg, Malawi, Malaysia, Maldives, Mali, Malta, Mauritania, Mauritius, Mexico, Micronesia, Moldova, Monaco, Mongolia, Montenegro, Morocco, Mozambique, Myanmar, Namibia, Nauru, Nepal, Netherlands, New Zealand, Nicaragua, Niger, Nigeria, Norway, Oman, Pakistan, Palau, Panama, Papua New Guinea, Paraguay, Peru, Philippines, Poland, Portugal, Qatar, Republic of Korea, Romania, Russian Federation, Rwanda, Saint Kitts and Nevis, Saint Lucia, Saint Vincent and the Grenadines, Samoa, San Marino, Sao Tome and Principe, Saudi Arabia, Senegal, Serbia, Sierra Leone, Singapore, Slovakia, Slovenia, Solomon Islands, South Africa, Spain, Sri Lanka, Sudan, Suriname, Swaziland, Sweden, Switzerland, Syrian Arab Republic, Tajikistan, Thailand, The former Yugoslav Republic of Macedonia, Timor-Leste, Togo, Trinidad and Tobago, Tunisia, Turkey, Turkmenistan, Ukraine, United Arab Emirates, United Kingdom, United Republic of Tanzania, Uruguay, Uzbekistan, Vanuatu, Venezuela, Viet Nam, Yemen, Zambia, Zimbabwe.

Against: United States.

Abstaining: None.

The Assembly adopted **resolution 61/71** without vote [agenda item 90 *(r)*].

Assistance to States for curbing the illicit traffic in small arms and light weapons and collecting them

The General Assembly,

Recalling its resolution 60/71 of 8 December 2005 on assistance to States for curbing the illicit traffic in small arms and collecting them,

Deeply concerned by the magnitude of human casualty and suffering, especially among children, caused by the illicit proliferation and use of small arms and light weapons,

Concerned by the negative impact that the illicit proliferation and use of those weapons continue to have on the efforts of States in the Sahelo-Saharan subregion in the areas of poverty eradication, sustainable development and the maintenance of peace, security and stability,

Bearing in mind the Bamako Declaration on an African Common Position on the Illicit Proliferation, Circulation and Trafficking of Small Arms and Light Weapons, adopted at Bamako on 1 December 2000,

Recalling the report of the Secretary-General entitled "In larger freedom: towards development, security and human rights for all", in which he emphasized that States must strive just as hard to eliminate the threat of illicit small arms and light weapons as they do to eliminate the threat of weapons of mass destruction,

Taking note of the International Instrument to Enable States to Identify and Trace, in a Timely and Reliable Manner, Illicit Small Arms and Light Weapons, adopted in 2005,

Welcoming the expression of support in the 2005 World Summit Outcome for the implementation of the Programme of Action to Prevent, Combat and Eradicate the Illicit Trade in Small Arms and Light Weapons in All its Aspects,

Welcoming also the adoption, at the thirtieth ordinary summit of the Economic Community of West African States, held in Abuja in June 2006, of the Convention on Small Arms and Light Weapons, Their Ammunition and Other Related Materials, in replacement of the moratorium on the importation, exportation and manufacture of small arms and light weapons in West Africa,

Welcoming further the decision taken by the Economic Community to establish a Small Arms Unit responsible for advocating appropriate policies and developing and implementing programmes, as well as the establishment of the Economic Community's Small Arms Control Programme, launched on 16 June 2006 in Bamako, in replacement of the Programme for Coordination and Assistance for Security and Development,

Taking note of the latest report of the Secretary-General on assistance to States for curbing the illicit traffic in small arms and light weapons and collecting them and the illicit trade in small arms and light weapons in all its aspects,

Welcoming, in that regard, the decision of the European Union to significantly support the Economic Community in its efforts to combat the illicit proliferation of small arms and light weapons,

Recognizing the important role that civil society organizations play, in raising public awareness, in efforts to curb the illicit traffic in small arms and light weapons,

Taking note of the report of the United Nations Conference to Review Progress Made in the Implementation of the Programme of Action to Prevent, Combat and Eradicate the Illicit Trade in Small Arms and Light Weapons in All Its Aspects, held in New York from 26 June to 7 July 2006,

1. *Commends* the United Nations and international, regional and other organizations for their assistance to States for curbing the illicit traffic in small arms and light weapons and collecting them;

2. *Encourages* the Secretary-General to pursue his efforts in the context of the implementation of General Assembly resolution 49/75 G of 15 December 1994 and the recommendations of the United Nations advisory missions, aimed at curbing the illicit circulation of small arms and light weapons and collecting them in the affected States that so request, with the support of the United Nations Regional Centre for Peace and Disarmament in Africa and in close cooperation with the African Union;

3. *Encourages* the international community to support the implementation of the Economic Community of West African States Convention on Small Arms and Light Weapons, Their Ammunition and Other Related Materials;

4. *Encourages* the countries of the Sahelo-Saharan subregion to facilitate the effective functioning of national commissions to combat the illicit proliferation of small arms and light weapons, and, in that regard, invites the international community to lend its support wherever possible;

5. *Encourages* the collaboration of civil society organizations and associations of in the efforts of the national commissions to combat the illicit traffic in small arms and light weapons and in the implementation of the Programme of Action to Prevent, Combat and Eradicate the Illicit Trade in Small Arms and Light Weapons in All Its Aspects;

6. *Also encourages* cooperation among State organs, international organizations and civil society in supporting programmes and projects aimed at combating the illicit traffic in small arms and light weapons and collecting them;

7. *Calls upon* the international community to provide technical and financial support to strengthen the capacity of civil society organizations to take action to help to combat the illicit trade in small arms and light weapons;

8. *Invites* the Secretary-General and those States and organizations that are in a position to do so to continue to provide assistance to States for curbing the illicit traffic in small arms and light weapons and collecting them;

9. *Requests* the Secretary-General to continue to consider the matter and to report to the General Assembly at its sixty-second session on the implementation of the present resolution;

10. *Decides* to include in the provisional agenda of its sixty-second session the item entitled "Assistance to States for curbing the illicit traffic in small arms and light weapons and collecting them".

The Assembly adopted **resolution 61/72** by recorded vote (175-1-1) [agenda item 90 *(s)*].

Problems arising from the accumulation of conventional ammunition stockpiles in surplus

The General Assembly,

Mindful of contributing to the process initiated within the framework of the United Nations reform to make the Organization more effective in maintaining peace and security by giving it the resources and tools it needs for conflict prevention, peaceful resolution of disputes, peacekeeping, post-conflict peacebuilding and reconstruction,

Underlining the importance of a comprehensive and integrated approach to disarmament through the development of practical measures,

Taking note of the report of the Group of Experts on the problem of ammunition and explosives,

Recalling the recommendation contained in paragraph 27 of the report submitted by the Chairman of the Open-ended Working Group to Negotiate an International Instrument to Enable States to Identify and Trace, in a Timely and Reliable Manner, Illicit Small Arms and Light Weapons, namely, to address the issue of small arms and light weapons ammunition in a comprehensive manner as part of a separate process conducted within the framework of the United Nations,

Noting with satisfaction the work and measures pursued at the regional and subregional levels with regard to the issue of conventional ammunition,

Recalling its decision 59/515 of 3 December 2004 and its resolution 60/74 of 8 December 2005, by which it decided to include the issue of conventional ammunition stockpiles in surplus in the agenda of its sixty-first session,

1. *Encourages* all interested States to assess, on a voluntary basis, whether, in conformity with their legitimate security needs, parts of their stockpiles of conventional ammunition should be considered to be in surplus, and recognizes that the security of such stockpiles must be taken into consideration and that appropriate controls with regard to the security and safety of stockpiles of conventional ammunition are indispensable at the national level in order to eliminate the risk of explosion, pollution or diversion;

2. *Appeals* to all interested States to determine the size and nature of their surplus stockpiles of conventional ammunition, whether they represent a security risk, if appropriate, their means of destruction, and whether external assistance is needed to eliminate this risk;

3. *Encourages* States in a position to do so to assist interested States within a bilateral framework or through international or regional organizations, on a voluntary and transparent basis, in elaborating and implementing programmes to eliminate surplus stockpiles or to improve their management;

4. *Encourages* all Member States to examine the possibility of developing and implementing, within a national, regional or subregional framework, measures to address accordingly the illicit trafficking related to the accumulation of such stockpiles;

5. *Requests* the Secretary-General to seek the views of Member States regarding the risks arising from the accumulation of conventional ammunition stockpiles in surplus and regarding national ways of strengthening controls on conventional ammunition, and to submit a report to the General Assembly at its sixty-second session;

6. *Decides* to address the issue of conventional ammunition stockpiles in surplus in a comprehensive manner;

7. *Requests* the Secretary-General to establish a group of governmental experts to consider, commencing no later than 2008, further steps to enhance cooperation with regard to the issue of conventional ammunition stockpiles in surplus, and to transmit the report of the group of experts to the General Assembly for consideration at its sixty-third session;

8. *Decides* to include this issue in the provisional agenda of its sixty-third session.

RECORDED VOTE ON RESOLUTION 61/72:

In favour: Afghanistan, Albania, Algeria, Andorra, Angola, Antigua and Barbuda, Argentina, Armenia, Australia, Austria, Azerbaijan, Bahamas, Bahrain, Bangladesh, Barbados, Belarus, Belgium, Belize, Benin, Bhutan, Bolivia, Bosnia and Herzegovina, Brazil, Brunei Darussalam, Bulgaria, Burkina Faso, Burundi, Cambodia, Cameroon, Canada, Cape Verde, Central African Republic, Chad, Chile, China, Colombia, Comoros, Congo, Costa Rica, Côte d'Ivoire, Croatia, Cuba, Cyprus, Czech Republic, Denmark, Djibouti, Dominica, Dominican Republic, Ecuador, Egypt, El Salvador, Eritrea, Estonia, Ethiopia, Fiji, Finland, France, Gabon, Gambia, Georgia, Germany, Ghana, Greece, Grenada, Guatemala, Guinea, Guyana, Haiti, Honduras, Hungary, Iceland, India, Indonesia, Iran, Iraq, Ireland, Israel, Italy, Jamaica, Jordan, Kazakhstan, Kuwait, Kyrgyzstan, Lao People's Democratic Republic, Latvia, Lebanon, Lesotho, Liberia, Libyan Arab Jamahiriya, Liechtenstein, Lithuania, Luxembourg, Malawi, Malaysia, Maldives, Mali, Malta, Mauritania, Mauritius, Mexico, Micronesia, Moldova, Monaco, Mongolia, Montenegro, Morocco, Mozambique, Myanmar, Namibia, Nepal, Netherlands, New Zealand, Nicaragua, Niger, Nigeria, Norway, Oman, Pakistan, Panama, Papua New Guinea, Paraguay, Peru, Philippines, Poland, Portugal, Qatar, Republic of Korea, Romania, Russian Federation, Rwanda, Saint Kitts and Nevis, Saint Lucia, Saint Vincent and the Grenadines, Samoa, San Marino, Sao Tome and Principe, Saudi Arabia, Senegal, Serbia, Sierra Leone, Singapore, Slovakia, Slovenia, Solomon Islands, South Africa, Spain, Sri Lanka, Sudan, Suriname, Swaziland, Sweden, Switzerland, Syrian Arab Republic, Tajikistan, Thailand, The former Yugoslav Republic of Macedonia, Timor-Leste, Togo, Trinidad and Tobago, Tunisia, Turkey, Turkmenistan, Uganda, Ukraine, United Arab Emirates, United Kingdom, United Republic of Tanzania, Uruguay, Uzbekistan, Vanuatu, Venezuela, Viet Nam, Yemen, Zambia, Zimbabwe.

Against: United States.

Abstaining: Japan.

The Assembly adopted **resolution 61/79** without vote [agenda item 90 *(z)*].

Information on confidence-building measures in the field of conventional arms

The General Assembly,

Guided by the purposes and principles enshrined in the Charter of the United Nations,

Bearing in mind the contribution of confidence-building measures in the field of conventional arms, adopted on the initiative and with the agreement of the States concerned, to the improvement of the overall international peace and security situation,

Convinced that the relationship between the development of confidence-building measures in the field of conventional arms and the international security environment can also be mutually reinforcing,

Considering the important role that confidence-building measures in the field of conventional arms can also play in creating favourable conditions for progress in the field of disarmament,

Recognizing that the exchange of information on confidence-building measures in the field of conventional arms contributes to mutual understanding and confidence among Member States,

1. *Welcomes* all confidence-building measures in the field of conventional arms already undertaken by Member States as well as the information on such measures voluntarily provided;

2. *Encourages* Member States to continue to adopt confidence-building measures in the field of conventional arms and to provide information in that regard;

3. *Also encourages* Member States to continue the dialogue on confidence-building measures in the field of conventional arms;

4. *Welcomes* the establishment of the electronic database containing information provided by Member States, and requests the Secretary-General to keep the database updated and to assist Member States, at their request, in the organization of seminars, courses and workshops aimed at enhancing the knowledge of new developments in this field;

5. *Decides* to include in the provisional agenda of its sixty-third session the item entitled "Information on confidence-building measures in the field of conventional arms".

Convention on excessively injurious conventional weapons and Protocols

Status

As at 31 December, the accession of Cameroon and the succession of Montenegro brought to 102 the number of States parties to the 1980 Convention on Prohibitions or Restrictions on the Use of Certain Conventional Weapons Which May Be Deemed to Be Excessively Injurious or to Have Indiscriminate Effects [YUN 1980, p. 76] and its annexed Protocols on Non-Detectable Fragments (Protocol I); on Prohibitions or Restrictions on the Use of Mines, Booby Traps and Other Devices, as amended on 3 May 1996 (Protocol II) [YUN 1996, p. 484]; and on Prohibitions or Restrictions on the Use of Incendiary Weapons (Protocol III). The 1995 Additional Protocol on Blinding Laser Weapons (Protocol IV) [YUN 1995, p. 221], which took effect on 30 July 1998 [YUN 1998, p. 530] had 85 parties following the succession of Montenegro and consent of Cameroon, Georgia and Tunisia in 2006 to be bound by its terms.

The Protocol on Explosive Remnants of War (Protocol V), adopted in 2003 [YUN 2003, p. 566], had 28 parties. The Protocol entered into force on 12 November.

Group of Governmental Experts

The Group of Governmental Experts established by the Second Review Conference of the States Parties to the Convention [YUN 2001, p. 504] to consider the issues of explosive remnants of war, mines other than anti-personnel mines, small-calibre weapons and ammunition, and promotion of compliance with the Convention and its annexed Protocols, held its thirteenth (6-10 March) [CCW/GGE/XIII/7], fourteenth (19-23 June) [CCW/GGE/XIV/5] and fifteenth (28 August–6 September) [CCW/CONF.III/7-CCW/GGE/XV/6] sessions, all in Geneva. The Group discussed issues relating to the weapons under consideration; preparation for the Third Review Conference of the States Parties (see below); universalization of the Convention and its annexed Protocols; the Status of Protocol V on Explosive Remnants of War; options to promote compliance with the Convention; and the possibility of establishing a sponsorship programme under the Convention. The Group also considered working papers and presentations from delegations, international organizations and other participants, including military experts, as well as the reports of its working groups on explosive remnants of war and on mines other than anti-personnel mines, which were annexed to the report of its fifteenth session. On 6 September, the Group adopted its report and a draft declaration on the entry into force later in the year of the Protocol on Explosive Remnants of War (Protocol V) and on the draft final document of the Review Conference, both of which were attached to its report, for consideration by the Conference. It recommended, among other things, that the Conference adopt a plan of action to promote its universality.

Third Review Conference

As requested in General Assembly resolution 60/93 [YUN 2005, p. 627], and as decided by the Second Review Conference [YUN 2001, p. 504], the Third Review Conference of the States Parties to the Convention met (Geneva, 7-17 November) [CCW/CONF.III/11 (Parts I-III)] to review the scope and operation of the Convention and its annexed Protocols, and consider proposals for amending them, as well as for additional protocols relating to other categories of conventional weapons. Preparatory work for the Conference was undertaken by the 2004 [YUN 2004, pp. 562-63] and 2005 [YUN 2005, p. 626] meetings of the States parties and of the Group of Governmental Experts.

The Conference held a general exchange of views during 10 plenary meetings, including a special plenary meeting on 13 November to mark the entry into force of the Convention's Protocol V on Explosive Remnants of War. In that regard, it adopted a declaration reaffirming the parties' conviction of the aim of the Protocol to protect civilians from the effects of those explosives and expressing their determination to ensure universal adherence to the Protocol. On 17 November, the Conference adopted its Final Declaration, by which the States parties, concerned at the humanitarian and development problems caused by the presence of explosive remnants of war, and noting their foreseeable effects on civilian populations, declared their commitment to respect and comply with the objectives and provisions of the Convention and its annexed Protocols and to cooperate in doing so. They committed also to assisting humanitarian demining missions and urged States that had not done so to determine new weapons or means of warfare that needed to be prohibited under international humanitarian law and in line with a related guide published during the year by the International Committee of the Red Cross. The parties decided to: convene urgently an intersessional meeting of governmental experts to consider further application and implementation of existing international humanitarian law to specific munitions that might become explosive remnants of war, focusing in particular on cluster munitions; dedicate up to two days to the issue of mines other than anti-personnel mines during the next meeting of States parties; establish a compliance mechanism applicable to the Convention, and a sponsorship programme within its framework; recommend that the Secretary-General, as the depositary of the Convention and its annexed Protocols, and the President of the Third Review Conference, on behalf of the parties, exercise their authority to achieve the goal of universality; and organize in 2007, a series of activities, including the first Conference of the Parties to Protocol V on Explosive Remnants of War.

The Conference also adopted a plan of action to promote the Convention's universality, which focused on affected States and outlined seven specific courses of action to be followed by the States parties towards achieving that objective.

Annual Conference of States Parties to Amended Protocol II

The Eighth Annual Conference of the States Parties to Amended Protocol II (Geneva, 6 November) [CCW/AP.II/CONF.8/2] reviewed the operation and status of that Protocol, considered related issues and examined national reports received from 44 States parties and the Holy See. The Conference adopted conclusions and recommendations and issued an appeal to States to accede to Amended Protocol II. It recommended that the Secretary-General, as depositary, and the President of the Conference, exercise their authority to achieve the goal of universality of the Protocol and called upon the States parties to promote its wider adherence.

GENERAL ASSEMBLY ACTION

On 6 December [meeting 67], the General Assembly, on the recommendation of the First Committee [A/61/398], adopted **resolution 61/100** without vote [agenda item 94].

Convention on Prohibitions or Restrictions on the Use of Certain Conventional Weapons Which May Be Deemed to Be Excessively Injurious or to Have Indiscriminate Effects

The General Assembly,

Recalling its resolution 60/93 of 8 December 2005,

Recalling with satisfaction the adoption and the entry into force of the Convention on Prohibitions or Restrictions on the Use of Certain Conventional Weapons Which May Be Deemed to Be Excessively Injurious or to Have Indiscriminate Effects, and its amended article 1, and the Protocol on Non-Detectable Fragments (Protocol I), the Protocol on Prohibitions or Restrictions on the Use of Mines, Booby Traps and Other Devices (Protocol II) and its amended version, the Protocol on Prohibitions or Restrictions on the Use of Incendiary Weapons (Protocol III) and the Protocol on Blinding Laser Weapons (Protocol IV),

Recalling the decision of the Second Review Conference of the States Parties to the Convention on Prohibitions or Restrictions on the Use of Certain Conventional Weapons Which May Be Deemed to Be Excessively Injurious or to Have Indiscriminate Effects to establish an open-ended group of governmental experts with two separate coordinators on explosive remnants of war and on mines other than anti-personnel mines,

Recalling also the role played by the International Committee of the Red Cross in the elaboration of the Convention and the Protocols thereto, and welcoming the particular efforts of various international, non-governmental and other organizations in raising awareness of the humanitarian consequences of explosive remnants of war,

1. *Calls upon* all States that have not yet done so to take all measures to become parties, as soon as possible,

to the Convention on Prohibitions or Restrictions on the Use of Certain Conventional Weapons Which May Be Deemed to Be Excessively Injurious or to Have Indiscriminate Effects and the Protocols thereto, as amended, with a view to achieving the widest possible adherence to these instruments at an early date, and so as to ultimately achieve their universality;

2. *Calls upon* all States parties to the Convention that have not yet done so to express their consent to be bound by the Protocols to the Convention and the amendment extending the scope of the Convention and the Protocols thereto to include armed conflicts of a non-international character;

3. *Welcomes with satisfaction* the adoption of the Protocol on Explosive Remnants of War (Protocol V) at the Meeting of the States Parties to the Convention held in Geneva on 27 and 28 November 2003 and its entry into force on 12 November 2006, and calls upon the States that have not yet done so to become parties to the Protocol as soon as possible;

4. *Notes* the decision of the Meeting of the States Parties that the Working Group on Mines Other Than Anti-Personnel Mines would continue its work in 2006 with the mandate to consider all proposals on mines other than anti-personnel mines put forward since the establishment of the Group of Governmental Experts, and to conduct meetings of military experts to provide advice, with the aim of elaborating appropriate recommendations on this issue for submission to the Third Review Conference in 2006;

5. *Also notes* the decision of the Meeting of the States Parties that the Working Group on Explosive Remnants of War would continue its work in 2006 with the mandate to continue to consider, including through participation of legal experts, the implementation of existing principles of international humanitarian law and to further study, on an open-ended basis, with particular emphasis on meetings of military and technical experts, possible preventive measures aimed at improving the design of certain specific types of munitions, including submunitions, with a view to minimizing the humanitarian risk of these munitions becoming explosive remnants of war, and to report on the work done to the Third Review Conference in 2006;

6. *Further notes* the decision of the Meeting of the States Parties that the President-designate should continue to undertake consultations during the intersessional period on possible options with respect to promoting compliance with the Convention and the Protocols thereto, taking into account proposals put forward, and report on the work done to the Third Review Conference in 2006;

7. *Expresses support* for the work conducted by the Group of Governmental Experts, and encourages the President-designate and the Coordinators of the Group to continue their work in preparation for the Third Review Conference, in accordance with the mandates and decisions for 2006, with the aim of achieving a successful Third Review Conference from 7 to 17 November 2006;

8. *Expresses support* for conducting a thorough review at the Third Review Conference of the scope, operation, status and implementation of the Convention and of the Protocols thereto as amended;

9. *Expresses support* for the decisions of the Group of Governmental Experts to recommend to the Third Review Conference a plan of action to promote universality of the Convention and the Protocols thereto, a declaration on the entry into force of Protocol V on explosive remnants of war, as well as a sponsorship programme;

10. *Notes* that, in conformity with article 8 of the Convention, the Review Conference may consider any proposal for amendments to the Convention or the Protocols thereto as well as any proposal for additional protocols relating to other categories of conventional weapons not covered by existing Protocols to the Convention;

11. *Requests* the Secretary-General to render the necessary assistance and to provide such services, including summary records, as may be required for the Eighth Annual Conference of the High Contracting Parties to Amended Protocol II to the Convention on 6 November 2006 and for the Third Review Conference, and for any possible continuation of work after the Conference, should the States parties deem it appropriate;

12. *Also requests* the Secretary-General, in his capacity as depositary of the Convention and the Protocols thereto, to continue to inform the General Assembly periodically, by electronic means, of ratifications and acceptances of and accessions to the Convention, its amended article 1, and the Protocols thereto;

13. *Decides* to remain seized of the matter.

Practical disarmament

Report of Secretary-General. As requested in General Assembly resolution 59/82 [YUN 2004, p. 564], the Secretary-General submitted an August report [A/61/288] describing the activities undertaken by States, including the Group of Interested States established in 1998 [YUN 1998, p. 531] to facilitate international action to assist States in implementing practical disarmament measures. The report, which covered the period from July 2004 to July 2006, noted that the Group provided financial support to project proposals submitted by the Department for Disarmament Affairs and its Regional Centre in Latin America and the Caribbean (see p. 692), the UNDP Bureau for Crisis Prevention and Recovery, and NGOs. The Group of Interested States expanded its focus beyond the consideration of project proposals by initiating discussions on thematic issues relating to the illicit trade in small arms and light weapons, including their impact on humanitarian assistance, human security and development, and on best practices in dealing with those issues. The Group's activities also increased to include assistance to NGOs, which the Secretary-General described as a step in the right direction, given that in most developing countries, NGOs and civil society were often at the forefront in implementing programmes that Governments were not able to conduct owing to the lack of resources.

Practical disarmament measures relating to the collection and control of small arms and light weapons also progressed within the framework of disarmament, demobilization and reintegration programmes, designed to help prevent a relapse into conflict and to facilitate post-conflict reconstruction and peacebuilding. In addition to collecting, storing and/or destroying weapons held by ex-combatants, those programmes also targeted weapons held by non-combatants or civilians, which helped to preserve the overall security balance in immediate post-conflict situations.

Disarmament Commission action. In 2006 [A/61/42], the Disarmament Commission allocated to Working Group II the item entitled "Practical confidence-building measures in the field of conventional weapons", which the Group discussed between 12 and 28 April. It agreed to accept as a basis for its deliberation the Chairman's working paper on the subject. The Group decided to further consider the paper as a possible basis for work in 2007.

GENERAL ASSEMBLY ACTION

On 6 December [meeting 67], the General Assembly, on the recommendation of the First Committee [A/61/394], adopted **resolution 61/76** by recorded vote (179-1-0) [agenda item 90 *(e)*].

Consolidation of peace through practical disarmament measures

The General Assembly,

Recalling its resolutions 51/45 N of 10 December 1996, 52/38 G of 9 December 1997, 53/77 M of 4 December 1998, 54/54 H of 1 December 1999, 55/33 G of 20 November 2000, 56/24 P of 29 November 2001 and 57/81 of 22 November 2002, its decision 58/519 of 8 December 2003 and its resolution 59/82 of 3 December 2004 entitled "Consolidation of peace through practical disarmament measures",

Convinced that a comprehensive and integrated approach towards certain practical disarmament measures often is a prerequisite to maintaining and consolidating peace and security and thus provides a basis for effective post-conflict peacebuilding; such measures include collection and responsible disposal, preferably through destruction, of weapons obtained through illicit trafficking or illicit manufacture as well as of weapons and ammunition declared by competent national authorities to be surplus to requirements, particularly with regard to small arms and light weapons, unless another form of disposition or use has been officially authorized and provided that such weapons have been duly marked and registered; confidence-building measures; disarmament, demobilization and reintegration of former combatants; demining; and conversion,

Noting with satisfaction that the international community is more than ever aware of the importance of such practical disarmament measures, especially with regard to the growing problems arising from the excessive accumulation and uncontrolled spread of small arms and light weapons, including their ammunition, which pose a threat to peace and security and reduce the prospects for economic development in many regions, particularly in post-conflict situations,

Stressing that further efforts are needed in order to develop and effectively implement programmes of practical disarmament in affected areas as part of disarmament, demobilization and reintegration measures so as to complement, on a case-by-case basis, peacekeeping and peacebuilding efforts,

Taking note with appreciation of the report of the Secretary-General on prevention of armed conflict, which, inter alia, refers to the role which the proliferation and the illicit transfer of small arms and light weapons play in the context of the build-up and sustaining of conflicts,

Taking note of the statement by the President of the Security Council of 31 August 2001 underlining the importance of practical disarmament measures in the context of armed conflicts, and, with regard to disarmament, demobilization and reintegration programmes, emphasizing the importance of measures to contain the security risks stemming from the use of illicit small arms and light weapons,

Taking note also of the report of the Secretary-General prepared with the assistance of the Group of Governmental Experts on Small Arms and, in particular, the recommendations contained therein, as an important contribution to the consolidation of the peace process through practical disarmament measures,

Welcoming the work of the Coordinating Action on Small Arms, which was established by the Secretary-General to bring about a holistic and multidisciplinary approach to this complex and multifaceted global problem and to cooperate with non-governmental organizations in the implementation of practical disarmament measures,

Welcoming also the reports of the First and Second Biennial Meetings of States to Consider the Implementation of the Programme of Action to Prevent, Combat and Eradicate the Illicit Trade in Small Arms and Light Weapons in All Its Aspects, held in New York from 7 to 11 July 2003 and from 11 to 15 July 2005, respectively, as well as the report of the Open-ended Working Group to Negotiate an International Instrument to Enable States to Identify and Trace, in a Timely and Reliable Manner, Illicit Small Arms and Light Weapons,

1. *Stresses* the particular relevance of the "Guidelines on conventional arms control/limitation and disarmament, with particular emphasis on consolidation of peace in the context of General Assembly resolution 51/45 N",

adopted by the Disarmament Commission by consensus at its 1999 substantive session;

2. *Takes note* of the report of the Secretary-General on the consolidation of peace through practical disarmament measures, submitted pursuant to resolution 59/82, and once again encourages Member States as well as regional arrangements and agencies to lend their support to the implementation of recommendations contained therein;

3. *Emphasizes* the importance of including in United Nations-mandated peacekeeping missions, as appropriate and with the consent of the host State, practical disarmament measures aimed at addressing the problem of the illicit trade in small arms and light weapons in conjunction with disarmament, demobilization and reintegration programmes aimed at former combatants, with a view to promoting an integrated comprehensive and effective weapons management strategy that would contribute to a sustainable peacebuilding process;

4. *Welcomes* the activities undertaken by the Group of Interested States, and invites the Group to continue to promote, on the basis of lessons learned from previous disarmament and peacebuilding projects, new practical disarmament measures to consolidate peace, especially as undertaken or designed by affected States themselves, regional and subregional organizations as well as United Nations agencies;

5. *Encourages* Member States, including the Group of Interested States, to continue to lend their support to the Secretary-General, relevant international, regional and subregional organizations, in accordance with Chapter VIII of the Charter of the United Nations, and non-governmental organizations in responding to requests by Member States to collect and destroy small arms and light weapons, including their ammunition, in post-conflict situations;

6. *Welcomes* the synergies within the multi-stakeholder process, including Governments, the United Nations system, regional and subregional organizations and institutions as well as non-governmental organizations in support of practical disarmament measures and the Programme of Action to Prevent, Combat and Eradicate the Illicit Trade in Small Arms and Light Weapons in All Its Aspects, in particular, inter alia, through the Coordinating Action on Small Arms;

7. *Thanks* the Secretary-General for his report on the implementation of resolution 59/82, taking into consideration the activities of the Group of Interested States in this regard;

8. *Welcomes* the report of the Secretary-General on disarmament and non-proliferation education, as well as his report on the United Nations Disarmament Information Programme;

9. *Requests* the Secretary-General to submit to the General Assembly at its sixty-third session a report on the implementation of practical disarmament measures, taking into consideration the activities of the Group of Interested States in this regard;

10. *Decides* to include in the provisional agenda of its sixty-third session the item entitled "Consolidation of peace through practical disarmament measures".

RECORDED VOTE RESOLUTION 61/76:

In favour: Afghanistan, Albania, Algeria, Andorra, Angola, Antigua and Barbuda, Argentina, Armenia, Australia, Austria, Azerbaijan, Bahamas, Bahrain, Bangladesh, Barbados, Belarus, Belgium, Belize, Benin, Bhutan, Bolivia, Bosnia and Herzegovina, Brazil, Brunei Darussalam, Bulgaria, Burkina Faso, Burundi, Cambodia, Cameroon, Canada, Cape Verde, Central African Republic, Chad, Chile, China, Colombia, Comoros, Congo, Costa Rica, Côte d'Ivoire, Croatia, Cuba, Cyprus, Czech Republic, Denmark, Djibouti, Dominica, Dominican Republic, Ecuador, Egypt, El Salvador, Eritrea, Estonia, Ethiopia, Fiji, Finland, France, Gabon, Gambia, Georgia, Germany, Ghana, Greece, Grenada, Guatemala, Guinea, Guyana, Haiti, Honduras, Hungary, Iceland, India, Indonesia, Iran, Iraq, Ireland, Israel, Italy, Jamaica, Japan, Jordan, Kazakhstan, Kenya, Kuwait, Kyrgyzstan, Lao People's Democratic Republic, Latvia, Lebanon, Lesotho, Liberia, Libyan Arab Jamahiriya, Liechtenstein, Lithuania, Luxembourg, Malawi, Malaysia, Maldives, Mali, Malta, Mauritania, Mauritius, Mexico, Micronesia, Moldova, Monaco, Mongolia, Montenegro, Morocco, Mozambique, Myanmar, Namibia, Nauru, Nepal, Netherlands, New Zealand, Nicaragua, Niger, Nigeria, Norway, Oman, Pakistan, Palau, Panama, Papua New Guinea, Paraguay, Peru, Philippines, Poland, Portugal, Qatar, Republic of Korea, Romania, Russian Federation, Rwanda, Saint Kitts and Nevis, Saint Lucia, Saint Vincent and the Grenadines, Samoa, San Marino, Sao Tome and Principe, Saudi Arabia, Senegal, Serbia, Singapore, Slovakia, Slovenia, Solomon Islands, South Africa, Spain, Sri Lanka, Sudan, Suriname, Swaziland, Sweden, Switzerland, Syrian Arab Republic, Tajikistan, Thailand, The former Yugoslav Republic of Macedonia, Timor-Leste, Togo, Tonga, Trinidad and Tobago, Tunisia, Turkey, Turkmenistan, Uganda, Ukraine, United Arab Emirates, United Kingdom, United Republic of Tanzania, Uruguay, Uzbekistan, Vanuatu, Venezuela, Viet Nam, Yemen, Zambia, Zimbabwe.

Against: United States.

Abstaining: None.

Transparency

Conference on Disarmament. In 2006 [A/61/27], the Conference on Disarmament was again prevented from establishing or re-establishing any mechanism to deal with any of its agenda items, including the item on transparency in armaments, owing to the unresolved impasse over a substantive programme of work. However, the item was discussed during the focused and structured debates that took place at formal and informal plenary meetings.

UN Register of Conventional Arms

In response to General Assembly resolution 60/226 [YUN 2005, p. 629], the Secretary-General submitted the fourteenth annual report on the United Nations Register of Conventional Arms [A/61/159 & Corr.1, 2 & Add.1 & Corr.1], established in

1992 [YUN 1992, p. 75] to promote enhanced levels of transparency on arms transfers. The report presented information provided by 117 Governments on imports and exports in 2005 in the seven categories of conventional arms covered (battle tanks, armoured combat vehicles, large-calibre artillery systems, attack helicopters, combat aircraft, warships and missiles and missile launchers). Governments also provided information on military holdings and procurement through national production and on small arms and light weapons and national policies. The report indicated a slight increase in the number of submissions.

The report also highlighted the activities undertaken by the Secretariat during the year, through the Department for Disarmament Affairs and in collaboration with Governments and regional organizations, to enhance awareness of the Register and encourage greater participation in it.

Group of Governmental Experts

As requested in General Assembly resolution 60/226 [YUN 2005, p. 629], the Secretary-General, in August [A/61/261], reported on the continuing operation of the Register and its further development, with data provided by a Group of Governmental Experts he had appointed, which completed its work in three sessions held between February and July (New York). The report summarized periodic reviews of the Register undertaken previously, analysed available data on reporting by States, including reporting patterns among regions; assessed the Register's operation; and examined issues relating to its further development, taking into account developments in armaments and military doctrines and the importance of strengthening its relevance and achieving progress towards universal participation.

The Group concluded that significant progress had been made towards achieving a relatively high level of annual participation in the Register since its inception and the United Nations should maintain a central role in sustaining that progress. To strengthen the Register's operation and further development, it recommended, among other things, that the definition for warships (including submarines) be amended to reflect the lowering of tonnage from 750 to 500 tons. Other recommendations were related to the need for Member States in a position to do so to provide data on small arms and light weapons transfers; the achievement of the shared goals of the mechanism, including universal participation; enhancement of awareness of the importance of the Register; and its promotion by the United Nations. In particular, the Department for Disarmament Affairs should overhaul the Register database on its web site to make it more user-friendly and technologically updated.

GENERAL ASSEMBLY ACTION

On 6 December [meeting 67], the General Assembly, on the recommendation of the First Committee [A/61/394], adopted **resolution 61/77** by recorded vote (158-0-21) [agenda item 90 *(aa)*].

Transparency in armaments

The General Assembly,

Recalling its resolutions 46/36 L of 9 December 1991, 47/52 L of 15 December 1992, 48/75 E of 16 December 1993, 49/75 C of 15 December 1994, 50/70 D of 12 December 1995, 51/45 H of 10 December 1996, 52/38 R of 9 December 1997, 53/77 V of 4 December 1998, 54/54 O of 1 December 1999, 55/33 U of 20 November 2000, 56/24 Q of 29 November 2001, 57/75 of 22 November 2002, 58/54 of 8 December 2003 and 60/226 of 23 December 2005 entitled "Transparency in armaments",

Continuing to take the view that an enhanced level of transparency in armaments contributes greatly to confidence-building and security among States and that the establishment of the United Nations Register of Conventional Arms constitutes an important step forward in the promotion of transparency in military matters,

Welcoming the consolidated report of the Secretary-General on the Register, which includes the returns of Member States for 2005,

Welcoming also the response of Member States to the request contained in paragraphs 9 and 10 of resolution 46/36 L to provide data on their imports and exports of arms, as well as available background information regarding their military holdings, procurement through national production and relevant policies,

Welcoming further the inclusion by some Member States of their transfers of small arms and light weapons in their annual report to the Register as part of their additional background information,

Noting the focused discussion on transparency in armaments that took place in the Conference on Disarmament in 2006,

Stressing that the continuing operation of the Register and its further development should be reviewed in order to secure a Register that is capable of attracting the widest possible participation,

1. *Reaffirms its determination* to ensure the effective operation of the United Nations Register of Conventional Arms, as provided for in paragraphs 7 to 10 of resolution 46/36 L;

2. *Endorses* the report of the Secretary-General on the continuing operation of the Register and its further development, and the recommendations ensuing from the consensus report of the 2006 group of governmental experts contained therein;

3. *Decides* to adapt the scope of the Register in conformity with the recommendations contained in the report of the Secretary-General on the continuing operation of the Register and its further development;

4. *Calls upon* Member States, with a view to achieving universal participation, to provide the Secretary-General, by 31 May annually, with the requested data and information for the Register, including nil reports if appropriate, on the basis of resolutions 46/36 L and 47/52 L, the recommendations contained in paragraph 64 of the 1997 report of the Secretary-General on the continuing operation of the Register and its further development, the recommendations contained in paragraph 94 of the 2000 report of the Secretary-General and the appendices and annexes thereto, the recommendations contained in paragraphs 112 to 114 of the 2003 report of the Secretary-General and the recommendations contained in paragraphs 123 to 127 of the 2006 report of the Secretary-General;

5. *Invites* Member States in a position to do so, pending further development of the Register, to provide additional information on procurement through national production and military holdings and to make use of the "Remarks" column in the standardized reporting form to provide additional information such as types or models;

6. *Also invites* Member States in a position to do so to provide additional background information on transfers of small arms and light weapons on the basis of the optional standardized reporting form, as adopted by the 2006 group of governmental experts, or by any other methods they deem appropriate;

7. *Reaffirms its decision*, with a view to further development of the Register, to keep the scope of and participation in the Register under review and, to that end:

(a) Recalls its request to Member States to provide the Secretary-General with their views on the continuing operation of the Register and its further development and on transparency measures related to weapons of mass destruction;

(b) Requests the Secretary-General, with a view to the three-year cycle regarding review of the Register, to ensure that sufficient resources are made available for a group of governmental experts to be convened in 2009 to review the continuing operation of the Register and its further development, taking into account the work of the Conference on Disarmament, the views expressed by Member States and the reports of the Secretary-General on the continuing operation of the Register and its further development;

8. *Requests* the Secretary-General to implement the recommendations contained in his 2000, 2003 and 2006 reports on the continuing operation of the Register and its further development and to ensure that sufficient resources are made available for the Secretariat to operate and maintain the Register;

9. *Invites* the Conference on Disarmament to consider continuing its work undertaken in the field of transparency in armaments;

10. *Reiterates its call upon* all Member States to cooperate at the regional and subregional levels, taking fully into account the specific conditions prevailing in the region or subregion, with a view to enhancing and coordinating international efforts aimed at increased openness and transparency in armaments;

11. *Requests* the Secretary-General to report to the General Assembly at its sixty-second session on progress made in implementing the present resolution;

12. *Decides* to include in the provisional agenda of its sixty-third session the item entitled "Transparency in armaments".

RECORDED VOTE ON RESOLUTION 61/77:

In favour: Afghanistan, Albania, Andorra, Angola, Antigua and Barbuda, Argentina, Armenia, Australia, Austria, Azerbaijan, Bahamas, Bangladesh, Barbados, Belarus, Belgium, Belize, Benin, Bhutan, Bolivia, Bosnia and Herzegovina, Brazil, Brunei Darussalam, Bulgaria, Burkina Faso, Burundi, Cambodia, Cameroon, Canada, Cape Verde, Central African Republic, Chad, Chile, China, Colombia, Congo, Costa Rica, Côte d'Ivoire, Croatia, Cuba, Cyprus, Czech Republic, Denmark, Dominica, Dominican Republic, Ecuador, El Salvador, Eritrea, Estonia, Ethiopia, Fiji, Finland, France, Gabon, Georgia, Germany, Ghana, Greece, Grenada, Guatemala, Guinea, Guyana, Haiti, Honduras, Hungary, Iceland, India, Indonesia, Ireland, Israel, Italy, Jamaica, Japan, Kazakhstan, Kenya, Kyrgyzstan, Lao People's Democratic Republic, Latvia, Lesotho, Liberia, Liechtenstein, Lithuania, Luxembourg, Malawi, Malaysia, Maldives, Mali, Malta, Marshall Islands, Mauritania, Mauritius, Mexico, Micronesia, Moldova, Monaco, Mongolia, Montenegro, Mozambique, Namibia, Nauru, Nepal, Netherlands, New Zealand, Nicaragua, Niger, Nigeria, Norway, Pakistan, Palau, Panama, Papua New Guinea, Paraguay, Peru, Philippines, Poland, Portugal, Republic of Korea, Romania, Russian Federation, Rwanda, Saint Kitts and Nevis, Saint Lucia, Saint Vincent and the Grenadines, Samoa, San Marino, Sao Tome and Principe, Senegal, Serbia, Sierra Leone, Singapore, Slovakia, Slovenia, Solomon Islands, South Africa, Spain, Sri Lanka, Suriname, Swaziland, Sweden, Switzerland, Tajikistan, Thailand, The former Yugoslav Republic of Macedonia, Timor-Leste, Togo, Trinidad and Tobago, Turkey, Turkmenistan, Uganda, Ukraine, United Kingdom, United Republic of Tanzania, United States, Uruguay, Uzbekistan, Vanuatu, Venezuela, Zambia, Zimbabwe.

Against: None.

Abstaining: Algeria, Bahrain, Comoros, Djibouti, Egypt, Iran, Iraq, Jordan, Kuwait, Lebanon, Libyan Arab Jamahiriya, Morocco, Myanmar, Oman, Qatar, Saudi Arabia, Sudan, Syrian Arab Republic, Tunisia, United Arab Emirates, Yemen.

Transparency of military expenditures

In response to General Assembly resolution 60/44 [YUN 2005, p. 630], the Secretary-General, in a July report with later addendum [A/61/133 & Add.1], presented reports from 80 Member States on military expenditures for the latest fiscal year for which data were available. The instrument for reporting those expenditures was that recommended by the Assembly in resolution 35/142 B [YUN 1980, p. 88].

The report also described activities undertaken by the Secretariat, through the Department for Disarmament Affairs, to enhance familiarity with and encourage greater participation in the standardized instrument. Those included assistance in preparing a report entitled "Methodology for the comparison of military expenditures", issued by the Economic

Commission for Latin America and the Caribbean, as part of a larger project on strengthening democratic governance of the security sector in the region. The Department also assisted Nicaragua in facilitating progress on the transparency of military expenditures and held informal consultations with Member States, with a view to encouraging and facilitating their participation in the standardized instrument.

The Assembly, in **decision 61/513** of 6 December, took note of the First Committee's report on the reduction of military budgets [A/61/386].

Verification

In response to General Assembly resolution 59/60 [YUN 2004, p. 568], the Secretary-General submitted a January report, with later addendum [A/60/96/Add.1,2] containing the views of 10 Member States (Bolivia, Cuba, Finland, Iran, Lebanon, Panama, Portugal, Qatar, Serbia (formerly Serbia and Montenegro), Suriname) on the importance of effective verification measures in disarmament agreements.

Panel of experts. As requested in Assembly resolution 59/60, a 16-member Panel of Governmental Experts on Verification in All Its Aspects established by the Secretary-General during the year to explore the issue of verification, including the role of the United Nations, held three sessions between January and August in New York. The Panel considered the issue as it applied to nuclear, radiological, chemical and biological weapons, along with their means of delivery, as well as conventional weapons. It also examined verification as it applied to the activities of States and non-State actors. Specific themes emerging during the Panel's discussions included the concept of verification and related experiences, techniques and methodologies; the need to build synergies between bodies with monitoring and verification responsibilities; capacity-building; the UN role; and the potential contribution of civil society to the verification process. To enable the experts to address the related concerns of Member States, the Secretary-General invited all States to submit to the Panel their views on the subject. Presentations were also made by experts from relevant intergovernmental organizations and NGOs. On 16 October, the Panel's Chairman briefed the First Committee on the Panel's work, noting that its final report, to be issued at a later date, would contain recommendations aimed at developing a basis for a broader consensus on the role of verification in enhancing security for all.

On 6 December, the Assembly encouraged the Panel to conclude its work as soon as possible, and decided to include in the provisional agenda of its sixty-second (2007) session the item entitled "Verification in all its aspects, including the role of the United Nations in the field of verification (**decision 61/514**).

Anti-personnel mines

1997 Convention

The number of States parties to the Convention on the Prohibition of the Use, Stockpiling, Production and Transfer of Anti-personnel Mines and on Their Destruction (Mine-Ban Convention), which was adopted in 1997 [YUN 1997, p. 503] and entered into force in 1999 [YUN 1999, p. 498], reached 152 as at 31 December 2006. During the year, three States ratified to the Convention and one succeeded to it.

Meeting of States parties

In accordance with General Assembly resolution 60/80 [YUN 2005, p 632], the Seventh Meeting of the States Parties to the Convention (Geneva, 18-22 September) [APLC/MSP.7/2006/5] was convened to consider the Convention's general status and operation, and to review the progress made and the challenges remaining in achieving its aims and in the application of the Nairobi Action Plan 2005-2009, adopted at the 2004 Review Conference [YUN 2004, p. 568]. Discussions centered on a number of the Convention's provisions, including the submission of requests for the destruction of anti-personnel mines in mined areas (article 5), transparency measures (article 7) and the facilitation and clarification of compliance (article 8).

On 22 September, the States parties reaffirmed their obligation to ensure the destruction of anti-personnel mines in mined areas under their jurisdiction or control. They decided to establish a process for the preparation, submission and consideration of requests for extension of the deadline for completing such destruction, which article 5 had established at no later than ten years after the Convention's entry into force. Requesting States parties were encouraged to seek the assistance of the Implementation Support Unit in preparing their requests, while those in a position to do so were asked to assist others to fulfil their obligations in that regard and increase funding support to cover the costs of the extension process. The Meeting also adopted a model declaration establishing the voluntary means of reporting the completion of article 5 obligations and scheduled the eighth meeting of the States parties for November 2007, in Jordan.

GENERAL ASSEMBLY ACTION

On 6 December [meeting 67], the General Assembly, on the recommendation of the First Committee [A/61/394], adopted **resolution 61/84** by recorded vote (161-0-17) [agenda item 90 *(x)*].

Implementation of the Convention on the Prohibition of the Use, Stockpiling, Production and Transfer of Anti-personnel Mines and on Their Destruction

The General Assembly,

Recalling its resolutions 54/54 B of 1 December 1999, 55/33 V of 20 November 2000, 56/24 M of 29 November 2001, 57/74 of 22 November 2002, 58/53 of 8 December 2003, 59/84 of 3 December 2004 and 60/80 of 8 December 2005,

Reaffirming its determination to put an end to the suffering and casualties caused by anti-personnel mines, which kill or maim hundreds of people every week, mostly innocent and defenceless civilians, including children, obstruct economic development and reconstruction, inhibit the repatriation of refugees and internally displaced persons and have other severe consequences for years after emplacement,

Believing it necessary to do the utmost to contribute in an efficient and coordinated manner to facing the challenge of removing anti-personnel mines placed throughout the world and to assure their destruction,

Wishing to do the utmost in ensuring assistance for the care and rehabilitation, including the social and economic reintegration, of mine victims,

Welcoming the entry into force, on 1 March 1999, of the Convention on the Prohibition of the Use, Stockpiling, Production and Transfer of Anti-personnel Mines and on Their Destruction, and noting with satisfaction the work undertaken to implement the Convention and the substantial progress made towards addressing the global landmine problem,

Recalling the first to sixth meetings of the States parties to the Convention held in Maputo (1999), Geneva (2000), Managua (2001), Geneva (2002), Bangkok (2003) and Zagreb (2005), and the First Review Conference of the States Parties to the Convention, held in Nairobi (2004),

Recalling also the seventh meeting of the States parties to the Convention, held in Geneva from 18 to 22 September 2006, at which the international community monitored progress and supported continued application of the Nairobi Action Plan 2005-2009 and established priorities to achieve further progress towards ending, for all people and for all time, the suffering caused by anti-personnel mines,

Noting with satisfaction that additional States have ratified or acceded to the Convention, bringing the total number of States that have formally accepted the obligations of the Convention to one hundred and fifty-one,

Emphasizing the desirability of attracting the adherence of all States to the Convention, and determined to work strenuously towards the promotion of its universalization,

Noting with regret that anti-personnel mines continue to be used in conflicts around the world, causing human suffering and impeding post-conflict development,

1. *Invites* all States that have not signed the Convention on the Prohibition of the Use, Stockpiling, Production and Transfer of Anti-personnel Mines and on Their Destruction to accede to it without delay;

2. *Urges* all States that have signed but have not ratified the Convention to ratify it without delay;

3. *Stresses* the importance of the full and effective implementation of and compliance with the Convention, including through the continued implementation of the Nairobi Action Plan 2005-2009;

4. *Urges* all States parties to provide the Secretary-General with complete and timely information as required under article 7 of the Convention in order to promote transparency and compliance with the Convention;

5. *Invites* all States that have not ratified the Convention or acceded to it to provide, on a voluntary basis, information to make global mine action efforts more effective;

6. *Renews its call upon* all States and other relevant parties to work together to promote, support and advance the care, rehabilitation and social and economic reintegration of mine victims, mine risk education programmes and the removal and destruction of anti-personnel mines placed or stockpiled throughout the world;

7. *Urges* all States to remain seized of the issue at the highest political level and, where in a position to do so, to promote adherence to the Convention through bilateral, subregional, regional and multilateral contacts, outreach, seminars and other means;

8. *Invites and encourages* all interested States, the United Nations, other relevant international organizations or institutions, regional organizations, the International Committee of the Red Cross and relevant non-governmental organizations to participate in the eighth meeting of the States parties to the Convention, to be held in Jordan from 18 to 22 November 2007, and in the intersessional work programme established at the first meeting of the States parties and further developed at subsequent meetings of the States parties;

9. *Requests* the Secretary-General, in accordance with article 11, paragraph 2, of the Convention, to undertake the preparations necessary to convene the next meeting of the States parties and, on behalf of the States parties and in accordance with article 11, paragraph 4, of the Convention, to invite States not parties to the Convention, as well as the United Nations, other relevant international organizations or institutions, regional organizations, the International Committee of the Red Cross and relevant non-governmental organizations to attend the eighth meeting of the States parties as observers;

10. *Decides* to remain seized of the matter.

RECORDED VOTE ON RESOLUTION 61/84:

In favour: Afghanistan, Albania, Algeria, Andorra, Angola, Antigua and Barbuda, Argentina, Armenia, Australia, Austria, Azerbaijan, Bahamas, Bahrain, Bangladesh, Barbados, Belarus, Belgium, Belize, Benin, Bhutan, Bolivia, Bosnia and Herzegovina, Brazil, Brunei Darussalam, Bulgaria, Burkina Faso, Burundi, Cambodia, Cameroon,

Canada, Cape Verde, Central African Republic, Chad, Chile, China, Colombia, Comoros, Congo, Costa Rica, Côte d'Ivoire, Croatia, Cyprus, Czech Republic, Denmark, Djibouti, Dominica, Dominican Republic, Ecuador, El Salvador, Eritrea, Estonia, Ethiopia, Fiji, Finland, France, Gabon, Georgia, Germany, Ghana, Greece, Grenada, Guatemala, Guinea, Guyana, Haiti, Honduras, Hungary, Iceland, Indonesia, Iraq, Ireland, Italy, Jamaica, Japan, Jordan, Kenya, Kuwait, Latvia, Lesotho, Liberia, Liechtenstein, Lithuania, Luxembourg, Malawi, Malaysia, Maldives, Mali, Malta, Marshall Islands, Mauritania, Mauritius, Mexico, Micronesia, Moldova, Monaco, Mongolia, Montenegro, Morocco, Mozambique, Namibia, Nauru, Netherlands, New Zealand, Nicaragua, Niger, Nigeria, Norway, Oman, Palau, Panama, Papua New Guinea, Paraguay, Peru, Philippines, Poland, Portugal, Qatar, Romania, Rwanda, Saint Kitts and Nevis, Saint Lucia, Saint Vincent and the Grenadines, Samoa, San Marino, Sao Tome and Principe, Senegal, Serbia, Sierra Leone, Singapore, Slovakia, Slovenia, Solomon Islands, South Africa, Spain, Sri Lanka, Sudan, Suriname, Swaziland, Sweden, Switzerland, Tajikistan, Thailand, The former Yugoslav Republic of Macedonia, Timor-Leste, Togo, Tonga, Trinidad and Tobago, Tunisia, Turkey, Turkmenistan, Uganda, Ukraine, United Arab Emirates, United Kingdom, United Republic of Tanzania, Uruguay, Vanuatu, Venezuela, Yemen, Zambia, Zimbabwe.

Against: None.

Abstaining: Cuba, Egypt, India, Iran, Israel, Kazakhstan, Kyrgyzstan, Lebanon, Libyan Arab Jamahiriya, Myanmar, Pakistan, Republic of Korea, Russian Federation, Syrian Arab Republic, United States, Uzbekistan, Viet Nam.

Other disarmament issues

Prevention of an arms race in outer space

Conference on Disarmament. In the light of the continuing inability of the Conference on Disarmament [A/61/27] to agree on a substantive programme of work (see p. 614), including the establishment of subsidiary bodies to deal with its substantive agenda items, the question of the preparation of an arms race in outer space was considered in plenary meetings held between 8 and 15 June. While there was general agreement on the need to ensure that outer space military and non-military operations were conducted peacefully, delegates continued to differ on the merit of negotiating a legal instrument to prevent an arms race there. Advocates of such an instrument, notably China and the Russian Federation, maintained that conditions were ripe for it, while those opposed to the idea, the United States and the United Kingdom in particular, countered that the existing legal framework was sufficient and that there was no need to negotiate a new one. Several ideas were put forward on how to advance the work of the Conference on the issue, but to no avail.

The General Assembly, in resolution 61/58 (see below), asked the Conference on Disarmament to complete the examination and updating of the mandate on the issue, and establish an ad hoc committee during its 2007 session.

Report of Secretary-General. In accordance with Assembly resolution 60/66 [YUN 2005, p. 635], the Secretary-General submitted an October report [A/61/532] containing the views of eight States (Canada, China, Cuba, Iraq, Japan, Mexico, Mongolia, Russian Federation) on the admissibility of further developing international outer space transparency and confidence-building measures in the interest of maintaining international peace and security.

GENERAL ASSEMBLY ACTION

On 6 December [meeting 67], the General Assembly, on the recommendation of the First Committee [A/61/393], adopted **resolution 61/58** by recorded vote (178-1-1) [agenda item 89].

Prevention of an arms race in outer space

The General Assembly,

Recognizing the common interest of all mankind in the exploration and use of outer space for peaceful purposes,

Reaffirming the will of all States that the exploration and use of outer space, including the Moon and other celestial bodies, shall be for peaceful purposes and shall be carried out for the benefit and in the interest of all countries, irrespective of their degree of economic or scientific development,

Reaffirming also the provisions of articles III and IV of the Treaty on Principles Governing the Activities of States in the Exploration and Use of Outer Space, including the Moon and Other Celestial Bodies,

Recalling the obligation of all States to observe the provisions of the Charter of the United Nations regarding the use or threat of use of force in their international relations, including in their space activities,

Reaffirming paragraph 80 of the Final Document of the Tenth Special Session of the General Assembly, in which it is stated that in order to prevent an arms race in outer space, further measures should be taken and appropriate international negotiations held in accordance with the spirit of the Treaty,

Recalling its previous resolutions on this issue, and taking note of the proposals submitted to the General Assembly at its tenth special session and at its regular sessions, and of the recommendations made to the competent organs of the United Nations and to the Conference on Disarmament,

Recognizing that prevention of an arms race in outer space would avert a grave danger for international peace and security,

Emphasizing the paramount importance of strict compliance with existing arms limitation and disarmament agreements relevant to outer space, including bilateral agreements, and with the existing legal regime concerning the use of outer space,

Considering that wide participation in the legal regime applicable to outer space could contribute to enhancing its effectiveness,

Noting that the Ad Hoc Committee on the Prevention of an Arms Race in Outer Space, taking into account its previous efforts since its establishment in 1985 and seeking to enhance its functioning in qualitative terms, continued the examination and identification of various issues, existing agreements and existing proposals, as well as future initiatives relevant to the prevention of an arms race in outer space, and that this contributed to a better understanding of a number of problems and to a clearer perception of the various positions,

Noting also that there were no objections in principle in the Conference on Disarmament to the re-establishment of the Ad Hoc Committee, subject to re-examination of the mandate contained in the decision of the Conference on Disarmament of 13 February 1992,

Emphasizing the mutually complementary nature of bilateral and multilateral efforts in the field of preventing an arms race in outer space, and hoping that concrete results will emerge from those efforts as soon as possible,

Convinced that further measures should be examined in the search for effective and verifiable bilateral and multilateral agreements in order to prevent an arms race in outer space, including the weaponization of outer space,

Stressing that the growing use of outer space increases the need for greater transparency and better information on the part of the international community,

Recalling, in this context, its previous resolutions, in particular resolutions 45/55 B of 4 December 1990, 47/51 of 9 December 1992 and 48/74 A of 16 December 1993, in which, inter alia, it reaffirmed the importance of confidence-building measures as a means conducive to ensuring the attainment of the objective of the prevention of an arms race in outer space,

Conscious of the benefits of confidence- and security-building measures in the military field,

Recognizing that negotiations for the conclusion of an international agreement or agreements to prevent an arms race in outer space remain a priority task of the Ad Hoc Committee and that the concrete proposals on confidence-building measures could form an integral part of such agreements,

Noting with satisfaction the constructive, structured and focused debate on the prevention of an arms race in outer space at the Conference on Disarmament in 2006,

1. *Reaffirms* the importance and urgency of preventing an arms race in outer space and the readiness of all States to contribute to that common objective, in conformity with the provisions of the Treaty on Principles Governing the Activities of States in the Exploration and Use of Outer Space, including the Moon and Other Celestial Bodies;

2. *Reaffirms its recognition*, as stated in the report of the Ad Hoc Committee on the Prevention of an Arms Race in Outer Space, that the legal regime applicable to outer space does not in and of itself guarantee the prevention of an arms race in outer space, that the regime plays a significant role in the prevention of an arms race in that environment, that there is a need to consolidate and reinforce that regime and enhance its effectiveness and that it is important to comply strictly with existing agreements, both bilateral and multilateral;

3. *Emphasizes* the necessity of further measures with appropriate and effective provisions for verification to prevent an arms race in outer space;

4. *Calls upon* all States, in particular those with major space capabilities, to contribute actively to the objective of the peaceful use of outer space and of the prevention of an arms race in outer space and to refrain from actions contrary to that objective and to the relevant existing treaties in the interest of maintaining international peace and security and promoting international cooperation;

5. *Reiterates* that the Conference on Disarmament, as the sole multilateral disarmament negotiating forum, has the primary role in the negotiation of a multilateral agreement or agreements, as appropriate, on the prevention of an arms race in outer space in all its aspects;

6. *Invites* the Conference on Disarmament to complete the examination and updating of the mandate contained in its decision of 13 February 1992 and to establish an ad hoc committee as early as possible during its 2007 session;

7. *Recognizes*, in this respect, the growing convergence of views on the elaboration of measures designed to strengthen transparency, confidence and security in the peaceful uses of outer space;

8. *Urges* States conducting activities in outer space, as well as States interested in conducting such activities, to keep the Conference on Disarmament informed of the progress of bilateral and multilateral negotiations on the matter, if any, so as to facilitate its work;

9. *Decides* to include in the provisional agenda of its sixty-second session the item entitled "Prevention of an arms race in outer space".

RECORDED VOTE ON RESOLUTION 61/58:

In favour: Afghanistan, Albania, Algeria, Andorra, Angola, Antigua and Barbuda, Argentina, Armenia, Australia, Austria, Azerbaijan, Bahamas, Bahrain, Bangladesh, Barbados, Belarus, Belgium, Belize, Bhutan, Bolivia, Bosnia and Herzegovina, Brazil, Brunei Darussalam, Bulgaria, Burkina Faso, Burundi, Cambodia, Cameroon, Canada, Cape Verde, Central African Republic, Chile, China, Colombia, Comoros, Congo, Costa Rica, Côte d'Ivoire, Croatia, Cuba, Cyprus, Czech Republic, Democratic People's Republic of Korea, Democratic Republic of the Congo, Denmark, Djibouti, Dominica, Dominican Republic, Ecuador, Egypt, El Salvador, Eritrea, Estonia, Ethiopia, Fiji, Finland, France, Gabon, Georgia, Germany, Ghana, Greece, Grenada, Guatemala, Guinea, Guyana, Haiti, Honduras, Hungary, Iceland, India, Indonesia, Iran, Iraq, Ireland, Italy, Jamaica, Japan, Jordan, Kazakhstan, Kuwait, Kyrgyzstan, Lao People's Democratic Republic, Latvia, Lebanon, Lesotho, Liberia, Libyan Arab Jamahiriya, Liechtenstein, Lithuania, Luxembourg, Malawi, Malaysia, Maldives, Mali, Malta, Marshall Islands, Mauritania, Mauritius, Mexico, Micronesia, Moldova, Monaco, Mongolia, Montenegro, Morocco,

Mozambique, Myanmar, Namibia, Nauru, Nepal, Netherlands, New Zealand, Nicaragua, Niger, Nigeria, Norway, Oman, Pakistan, Palau, Panama, Paraguay, Peru, Philippines, Poland, Portugal, Qatar, Republic of Korea, Romania, Russian Federation, Rwanda, Saint Kitts and Nevis, Saint Lucia, Saint Vincent and the Grenadines, Samoa, San Marino, Sao Tome and Principe, Saudi Arabia, Senegal, Serbia, Sierra Leone, Singapore, Slovakia, Slovenia, Solomon Islands, Somalia, South Africa, Spain, Sri Lanka, Sudan, Suriname, Swaziland, Sweden, Switzerland, Syrian Arab Republic, Tajikistan, Thailand, The former Yugoslav Republic of Macedonia, Timor-Leste, Togo, Tonga, Trinidad and Tobago, Tunisia, Turkey, Turkmenistan, Uganda, Ukraine, United Arab Emirates, United Kingdom, United Republic of Tanzania, Uruguay, Uzbekistan, Vanuatu, Venezuela, Viet Nam, Yemen, Zambia, Zimbabwe.

Against: United States.

Abstaining: Israel.

On the same date [meeting 67], the Assembly, on the recommendation of the First Committee [A/61/394], adopted **resolution 61/75** by recorded vote (178-1-1) [agenda item 90 *(o)*].

Transparency and confidence-building measures in outer space activities

The General Assembly,

Recalling its resolution 60/66 of 8 December 2005,

Reaffirming that the prevention of an arms race in outer space would avert a grave danger to international peace and security,

Conscious that further measures should be examined in the search for agreements to prevent an arms race in outer space, including the weaponization of outer space,

Recalling, in this context, its previous resolutions, including resolutions 45/55 B of 4 December 1990 and 48/74 B of 16 December 1993, which, inter alia, emphasize the need for increased transparency and confirm the importance of confidence-building measures as a means conducive to ensuring the attainment of the objective of the prevention of an arms race in outer space,

Recalling also the report of the Secretary-General of 15 October 1993 to the General Assembly at its forty-eighth session, the annex to which contains the study by governmental experts on the application of confidence-building measures in outer space,

Noting the constructive debate which the Conference on Disarmament held on this subject in 2006,

1. *Invites* all Member States to submit to the Secretary-General before its sixty-second session concrete proposals on international outer space transparency and confidence-building measures in the interest of maintaining international peace and security and promoting international cooperation and the prevention of an arms race in outer space;

2. *Requests* the Secretary-General to submit to the General Assembly at its sixty-second session a report with an annex containing concrete proposals from Member States on international outer space transparency and confidence-building measures;

3. *Decides* to include in the provisional agenda of its sixty-second session the item entitled "Transparency and confidence-building measures in outer space activities".

RECORDED VOTE ON RESOLUTION 61/75:

In favour: Afghanistan, Albania, Algeria, Andorra, Angola, Antigua and Barbuda, Argentina, Armenia, Australia, Austria, Azerbaijan, Bahamas, Bahrain, Bangladesh, Barbados, Belarus, Belgium, Belize, Benin, Bhutan, Bolivia, Bosnia and Herzegovina, Brazil, Brunei Darussalam, Bulgaria, Burkina Faso, Burundi, Cambodia, Cameroon, Canada, Cape Verde, Central African Republic, Chad, Chile, China, Colombia, Comoros, Congo, Costa Rica, Côte d'Ivoire, Croatia, Cuba, Cyprus, Czech Republic, Denmark, Djibouti, Dominica, Dominican Republic, Ecuador, Egypt, El Salvador, Eritrea, Estonia, Ethiopia, Fiji, Finland, France, Gabon, Gambia, Georgia, Germany, Ghana, Greece, Grenada, Guatemala, Guinea, Guyana, Haiti, Honduras, Hungary, Iceland, India, Indonesia, Iran, Iraq, Ireland, Italy, Jamaica, Japan, Jordan, Kazakhstan, Kenya, Kuwait, Kyrgyzstan, Lao People's Democratic Republic, Latvia, Lebanon, Lesotho, Liberia, Libyan Arab Jamahiriya, Liechtenstein, Lithuania, Luxembourg, Malawi, Malaysia, Maldives, Mali, Malta, Marshall Islands, Mauritania, Mauritius, Mexico, Micronesia, Moldova, Monaco, Mongolia, Montenegro, Morocco, Mozambique, Myanmar, Namibia, Nepal, Netherlands, New Zealand, Nicaragua, Niger, Nigeria, Norway, Oman, Pakistan, Palau, Panama, Papua New Guinea, Paraguay, Peru, Philippines, Poland, Portugal, Qatar, Republic of Korea, Romania, Russian Federation, Rwanda, Saint Kitts and Nevis, Saint Lucia, Saint Vincent and the Grenadines, Samoa, San Marino, Sao Tome and Principe, Saudi Arabia, Senegal, Serbia, Sierra Leone, Singapore, Slovakia, Slovenia, Solomon Islands, South Africa, Spain, Sri Lanka, Sudan, Suriname, Swaziland, Sweden, Switzerland, Syrian Arab Republic, Tajikistan, Thailand, The former Yugoslav Republic of Macedonia, Timor-Leste, Togo, Trinidad and Tobago, Tunisia, Turkey, Turkmenistan, Uganda, Ukraine, United Arab Emirates, United Kingdom, United Republic of Tanzania, Uruguay, Uzbekistan, Vanuatu, Venezuela, Viet Nam, Yemen, Zambia, Zimbabwe.

Against: United States.

Abstaining: Israel.

Disarmament and development

In 2006, controversy continued to surround the relationship between disarmament and development, with most members of the Non-Aligned Movement, among other Member States, maintaining their call for the implementation of the action programme adopted by the 1987 International Conference on the Relationship between Disarmament and Development [YUN 1987, p. 82], while other States, particularly EU member States and the United States, emphasized that an automatic link between both concepts did not exist.

Report of Secretary-General. As requested in General Assembly resolution 60/61 [YUN 2005, p. 636], the Secretary-General submitted a June report [A/61/98] summarizing the activities undertaken in the past year by partner departments and agencies of the high-level Steering Group on Disarmament and Development. The report noted that the UN inter-agency working group on disarmament, demobilization and reintegration (DDR), comprising 15 UN departments, agencies, funds and programmes, had developed new policies and concepts for planning and implementing DDR operations in a peacekeeping context. Those policies and concepts constituted integrated DDR standards, which recognized the links between the composite processes in DDR operations and the need to coordinate their implementation with longer-term development strategies, including development programmes. DDR programmes, an integral part of peacebuilding, security sector reform and socio-economic rehabilitation efforts, were a central element in wider peace, recovery and development frameworks and strategies. The greatest level of relevant activities were undertaken by the Department of Economic and Social Affairs, UNDP and DDA, through its regional centres.

GENERAL ASSEMBLY ACTION

On 6 December [meeting 67], the General Assembly, on the recommendation of the First Committee [A/61/394], adopted **resolution 61/64** by recorded vote (178-1-2) [agenda item 90 *(k)*].

Relationship between disarmament and development

The General Assembly,

Recalling that the Charter of the United Nations envisages the establishment and maintenance of international peace and security with the least diversion for armaments of the world's human and economic resources,

Recalling also the provisions of the Final Document of the Tenth Special Session of the General Assembly concerning the relationship between disarmament and development, as well as the adoption on 11 September 1987 of the Final Document of the International Conference on the Relationship between Disarmament and Development,

Recalling further its resolutions 49/75 J of 15 December 1994, 50/70 G of 12 December 1995, 51/45 D of 10 December 1996, 52/38 D of 9 December 1997, 53/77 K of 4 December 1998, 54/54 T of 1 December 1999, 55/33 L of 20 November 2000, 56/24 E of 29 November 2001, 57/65 of 22 November 2002, 59/78 of 3 December 2004 and 60/61 of 8 December 2005, and its decision 58/520 of 8 December 2003,

Bearing in mind the Final Document of the Twelfth Conference of Heads of State or Government of Non-Aligned Countries, held in Durban, South Africa, from 29 August to 3 September 1998, and the Final Document of the Thirteenth Ministerial Conference of the Movement of Non-Aligned Countries, held in Cartagena, Colombia, on 8 and 9 April 2000,

Mindful of the changes in international relations that have taken place since the adoption on 11 September 1987 of the Final Document of the International Conference on the Relationship between Disarmament and Development, including the development agenda that has emerged over the past decade,

Bearing in mind the new challenges for the international community in the field of development, poverty eradication and the elimination of the diseases that afflict humanity,

Stressing the importance of the symbiotic relationship between disarmament and development and the important role of security in this connection, and concerned at increasing global military expenditure, which could otherwise be spent on development needs,

Recalling the report of the Group of Governmental Experts on the relationship between disarmament and development and its reappraisal of this significant issue in the current international context,

1. *Stresses* the central role of the United Nations in the disarmament-development relationship, and requests the Secretary-General to strengthen further the role of the Organization in this field, in particular the high-level Steering Group on Disarmament and Development, in order to assure continued and effective coordination and close cooperation between the relevant United Nations departments, agencies and sub-agencies;

2. *Requests* the Secretary-General to continue to take action, through appropriate organs and within available resources, for the implementation of the action programme adopted at the 1987 International Conference on the Relationship between Disarmament and Development;

3. *Urges* the international community to devote part of the resources made available by the implementation of disarmament and arms limitation agreements to economic and social development, with a view to reducing the ever-widening gap between developed and developing countries;

4. *Encourages* the international community to achieve the Millennium Development Goals and to make reference to the contribution that disarmament could provide in meeting them when it reviews its progress towards this purpose in 2006, as well as to make greater efforts to integrate disarmament, humanitarian and development activities;

5. *Encourages* the relevant regional and subregional organizations and institutions, non-governmental organizations and research institutes to incorporate issues related to the relationship between disarmament and development in their agendas and, in this regard, to take into account the report of the Group of Governmental Experts on the relationship between disarmament and development;

6. *Requests* the Secretary-General to report to the General Assembly at its sixty-second session on the implementation of the present resolution;

7. *Decides* to include in the provisional agenda of its sixty-second session the item entitled "Relationship between disarmament and development".

RECORDED VOTE ON RESOLUTION 61/64:

In favour: Afghanistan, Albania, Algeria, Andorra, Angola, Antigua and Barbuda, Argentina, Armenia, Australia, Austria, Azerbaijan, Bahamas, Bahrain, Bangladesh, Barbados, Belarus, Belgium, Belize, Bhutan, Bolivia, Bosnia and Herzegovina, Brazil, Brunei Darussalam, Bulgaria, Burkina Faso, Burundi, Cambodia, Cameroon, Canada, Cape Verde, Central African Republic, Chad, Chile, China, Colombia, Comoros, Congo, Costa Rica, Côte d'Ivoire, Croatia, Cuba, Cyprus, Czech Republic, Democratic People's Republic of Korea, Democratic Republic of the Congo, Denmark, Djibouti, Dominica, Dominican Republic, Ecuador, Egypt, El Salvador, Eritrea, Estonia, Ethiopia, Fiji, Finland, Gabon, Gambia, Georgia, Germany, Ghana, Greece, Grenada, Guatemala, Guinea, Guyana, Haiti, Honduras, Hungary, Iceland, India, Indonesia, Iran, Iraq, Ireland, Italy, Jamaica, Japan, Jordan, Kazakhstan, Kuwait, Kyrgyzstan, Lao People's Democratic Republic, Latvia, Lebanon, Lesotho, Liberia, Libyan Arab Jamahiriya, Liechtenstein, Lithuania, Luxembourg, Malawi, Malaysia, Maldives, Mali, Malta, Marshall Islands, Mauritania, Mauritius, Mexico, Micronesia, Moldova, Monaco, Mongolia, Montenegro, Morocco, Mozambique, Myanmar, Namibia, Nauru, Nepal, Netherlands, New Zealand, Nicaragua, Niger, Nigeria, Norway, Oman, Pakistan, Palau, Panama, Papua New Guinea, Paraguay, Peru, Philippines, Poland, Portugal, Qatar, Republic of Korea, Romania, Russian Federation, Rwanda, Saint Kitts and Nevis, Saint Lucia, Saint Vincent and the Grenadines, Samoa, San Marino, Sao Tome and Principe, Saudi Arabia, Senegal, Serbia, Sierra Leone, Singapore, Slovakia, Slovenia, Solomon Islands, South Africa, Spain, Sri Lanka, Sudan, Suriname, Swaziland, Sweden, Switzerland, Syrian Arab Republic, Tajikistan, Thailand, The former Yugoslav Republic of Macedonia, Timor-Leste, Togo, Tonga, Trinidad and Tobago, Tunisia, Turkey, Turkmenistan, Ukraine, United Arab Emirates, United Kingdom, United Republic of Tanzania, Uruguay, Uzbekistan, Vanuatu, Venezuela, Viet Nam, Yemen, Zambia, Zimbabwe

Against: United States.

Abstaining: France, Israel.

Human rights, human security and disarmament

In 2006, Member States continued to seek ways of limiting or preventing human rights and humanitarian problems in situations of armed conflict, mainly within the framework of the Subcommisson on the Promotion and Protection of Human Rights. According particular attention to preventing human rights violations with small arms, the Subcommission had appointed a Special Rapporteur, Barbara Frey (United States), to conduct a study on the topic [YUN 2002, p. 720]. At its fifty-eighth session (see p. 884), the Subcommission considered the final report along with annexed draft principles on that study prepared by the Special Rapporteur, detailing measures to be taken by States and private actors towards that end.

The related question of the relationship between disarmament and human security continued to be addressed by the United Nations Institute for Disarmament Research (UNIDIR) (see p. 680), which also focused its activities on the small arms problem, the danger posed by explosive remnants of war and disarmament, demobilization and reintegration efforts. In that context, the Institute sought ways to control the rampant spread of small arms and find adequate solutions for the security concerns of local populations.

Arms limitation and disarmament agreements

Pursuant to General Assembly resolution 60/60 [YUN 2005, p. 637], the Secretary-General submitted a June report with later addenda [A/61/113 & Add.1,2], containing information from 11 Member States on measures they had taken to ensure the application of scientific and technological progress in the context of international security, disarmament and related areas, without detriment to the environment or to its effective contribution to attaining sustainable development.

GENERAL ASSEMBLY ACTION

On 6 December [meeting 67], the General Assembly, on the recommendation of the First Committee [A/61/394], adopted **resolution 61/63** by recorded vote (175-1-4) [agenda item 90 *(j)*].

Observance of environmental norms in the drafting and implementation of agreements on disarmament and arms control

The General Assembly,

Recalling its resolutions 50/70 M of 12 December 1995, 51/45 E of 10 December 1996, 52/38 E of 9 December 1997, 53/77 J of 4 December 1998, 54/54 S of 1 December 1999, 55/33 K of 20 November 2000, 56/24 F of 29 November 2001, 57/64 of 22 November 2002, 58/45 of 8 December 2003, 59/68 of 3 December 2004 and 60/60 of 8 December 2005,

Emphasizing the importance of the observance of environmental norms in the preparation and implementation of disarmament and arms limitation agreements,

Recognizing that it is necessary to take duly into account the agreements adopted at the United Nations Conference on Environment and Development, as well as prior relevant agreements, in the drafting and implementation of agreements on disarmament and arms limitation,

Taking note of the report of the Secretary-General submitted pursuant to resolution 60/60,

Mindful of the detrimental environmental effects of the use of nuclear weapons,

1. *Reaffirms* that international disarmament forums should take fully into account the relevant environmental norms in negotiating treaties and agreements on disarmament and arms limitation and that all States, through their actions, should contribute fully to ensuring com-

pliance with the aforementioned norms in the implementation of treaties and conventions to which they are parties;

2. *Calls upon* States to adopt unilateral, bilateral, regional and multilateral measures so as to contribute to ensuring the application of scientific and technological progress within the framework of international security, disarmament and other related spheres, without detriment to the environment or to its effective contribution to attaining sustainable development;

3. *Welcomes* the information provided by Member States on the implementation of the measures they have adopted to promote the objectives envisaged in the present resolution;

4. *Invites* all Member States to communicate to the Secretary-General information on the measures they have adopted to promote the objectives envisaged in the present resolution, and requests the Secretary-General to submit a report containing this information to the General Assembly at its sixty-second session;

5. *Decides* to include in the provisional agenda of its sixty-second session the item entitled "Observance of environmental norms in the drafting and implementation of agreements on disarmament and arms control".

RECORDED VOTE ON RESOLUTION 61/63:

In favour: Afghanistan, Albania, Algeria, Andorra, Angola, Antigua and Barbuda, Argentina, Armenia, Australia, Austria, Azerbaijan, Bahamas, Bahrain, Bangladesh, Barbados, Belarus, Belgium, Belize, Bhutan, Bolivia, Bosnia and Herzegovina, Brazil, Brunei Darussalam, Bulgaria, Burkina Faso, Burundi, Cambodia, Cameroon, Canada, Cape Verde, Central African Republic, Chile, China, Colombia, Comoros, Congo, Costa Rica, Côte d'Ivoire, Croatia, Cuba, Cyprus, Czech Republic, Democratic People's Republic of Korea, Democratic Republic of the Congo, Denmark, Djibouti, Dominica, Dominican Republic, Ecuador, Egypt, El Salvador, Eritrea, Estonia, Ethiopia, Fiji, Finland, Gabon, Gambia, Georgia, Germany, Ghana, Greece, Grenada, Guatemala, Guinea, Guyana, Haiti, Honduras, Hungary, Iceland, India, Indonesia, Iran, Iraq, Ireland, Italy, Jamaica, Japan, Jordan, Kazakhstan, Kuwait, Kyrgyzstan, Lao People's Democratic Republic, Latvia, Lebanon, Lesotho, Liberia, Libyan Arab Jamahiriya, Liechtenstein, Lithuania, Luxembourg, Malawi, Malaysia, Maldives, Mali, Malta, Marshall Islands, Mauritania, Mauritius, Mexico, Micronesia, Moldova, Monaco, Mongolia, Montenegro, Morocco, Mozambique, Myanmar, Namibia, Nauru, Nepal, Netherlands, New Zealand, Nicaragua, Niger, Nigeria, Norway, Oman, Pakistan, Panama, Papua New Guinea, Paraguay, Peru, Philippines, Poland, Portugal, Qatar, Republic of Korea, Romania, Russian Federation, Rwanda, Saint Kitts and Nevis, Saint Lucia, Saint Vincent and the Grenadines, Samoa, San Marino, Sao Tome and Principe, Saudi Arabia, Senegal, Serbia, Sierra Leone, Singapore, Slovakia, Slovenia, Solomon Islands, South Africa, Spain, Sri Lanka, Sudan, Suriname, Swaziland, Sweden, Switzerland, Syrian Arab Republic, Tajikistan, Thailand, The former Yugoslav Republic of Macedonia, Timor-Leste, Togo, Tonga, Trinidad and Tobago, Tunisia, Turkey, Turkmenistan, Ukraine, United Arab Emirates, United Republic of Tanzania, Uruguay, Uzbekistan, Vanuatu, Venezuela, Viet Nam, Yemen, Zambia, Zimbabwe.

Against: United States.

Abstaining: France, Israel, Palau, United Kingdom.

Studies, information and training

Disarmament studies programme

As requested in General Assembly resolution 59/93 [YUN 2004, p. 582], the Secretary-General, in a July report with later addendum [A/61/169 & Add.1], provided information on the implementation of the recommendations contained in the 2002 report [YUN 2002, p. 544] of the Group of Governmental Experts established pursuant to Assembly resolution 55/33 E [YUN 2000, p. 535] to undertake the UN study on disarmament and non-proliferation education. The 2006 report included information provided by eight Member States, five UN bodies and other international organizations, and six NGOs on their activities to promote disarmament and non-proliferation education in the context of the 34 recommendations contained in the Group's report. The Secretary-General concluded that partnerships on the issue had yielded results. Regarding peace education, he reported that youth in four countries around the globe had learned something about their national legislation and regulations on small arms; decision makers in Latin America and the Caribbean familiarized themselves with the concepts and impact of their region's adoption of a Treaty declaring the region a zone free of nuclear weapons; students of global security at the University of Malaga, Spain, would create a virtual library of information about nuclear issues; and many Indonesian Government officials had become aware of their Government's policies and activities at the international level on a wide range of arms control and disarmament issues. The type, quantity and diversity of reports received from Governments and civil society indicated the strong interest in learning the details about weapons and their relationship with and impact on politics, economics, social trends and the environment. Despite fund-raising challenges for all disarmament efforts, particularly for non-proliferation education, the UN study continued to serve as a useful structure for related work and as a point of reference in the field. Efforts should, therefore, continue to be made to implement the study's recommendations.

The Group of Governmental Experts on the continuing operation and further development of the UN Register of Conventional Arms [YUN 2003, p. 568] completed and submitted its report to the General Assembly (see p. 668), while the Group of Governmental Experts on illicit brokering in small arms and light weapons began its work during the year and was expected to conclude in 2007. Also during the year, the Panel of Governmental Experts established by the Secretary-General to explore the issue of verification in all its aspects, pursuant to Assembly resolution 59/60 [YUN 2004, p. 568], began its work.

In 2006, the Assembly, in resolution 61/72 (see p. 661), requested the Secretary-General to establish, no later than 2008, a group of governmental experts to consider further steps to enhance cooperation in confronting surplus conventional ammunition stockpiles, for the Assembly's consideration at its sixty-third (2008) session. By resolution 61/89 (see p. 655), the Assembly asked the Secretary-General to establish a group of governmental experts to examine, commencing in 2008, the feasibility, scope and draft parameters for a comprehensive, legally-binding instrument establishing common international standards for the import, export and transfer of conventional arms, and to report on its studies in 2008.

GENERAL ASSEMBLY ACTION

On 6 December [meeting 67], the General Assembly, on the recommendation of the First Committee [A/61/394], adopted **resolution 61/73** without vote [agenda item 90 *(f)*].

United Nations study on disarmament and non-proliferation education

The General Assembly,

Recalling its resolutions 55/33 E of 20 November 2000, 57/60 of 22 November 2002 and 59/93 of 3 December 2004,

Welcoming the report of the Secretary-General on disarmament and non-proliferation education, in which the Secretary-General reported on the implementation of the recommendations contained in the United Nations study on disarmament and non-proliferation education,

Emphasizing that the Secretary-General concludes in his report that efforts need to be continued to implement the recommendations of the study and follow the good examples of how they are being implemented to stimulate even further long-term results,

Desirous of stressing the urgency of promoting concerted international efforts at disarmament and non-proliferation, in particular in the field of nuclear disarmament and non-proliferation, with a view to strengthening international security and enhancing sustainable economic and social development,

Conscious of the need to combat the negative effects of cultures of violence and complacency in the face of current dangers in this field through long-term programmes of education and training,

Remaining convinced that the need for disarmament and non-proliferation education has never been greater, especially on the subject of weapons of mass destruction, but also in the field of small arms and light weapons, terrorism and other challenges to international security and the process of disarmament, as well as on the relevance of implementing the recommendations contained in the United Nations study,

Recognizing the importance of the role of civil society, including non-governmental organizations, in the promotion of disarmament and non-proliferation education,

1. *Expresses its appreciation* to the Member States, the United Nations and other international and regional organizations, civil society and non-governmental organizations, which, within their purview, implemented the recommendations made in the United Nations study, as discussed in the report of the Secretary-General reviewing the implementation of the recommendations, and encourages them once again to continue applying those recommendations and reporting to the Secretary-General on steps taken to implement them;

2. *Requests* the Secretary-General to prepare a report reviewing the results of the implementation of the recommendations and possible new opportunities for promoting disarmament and non-proliferation education, and to submit it to the General Assembly at its sixty-third session;

3. *Also requests* the Secretary-General to utilize electronic means to the fullest extent possible in the dissemination, in as many official languages as feasible, of information related to that report and any other information that the Department for Disarmament Affairs of the Secretariat gathers on an ongoing basis in regard to the implementation of the recommendations of the United Nations study;

4. *Decides* to include in the provisional agenda of its sixty-third session the item entitled "Disarmament and non-proliferation education".

Disarmament Information Programme

In response to General Assembly resolution 59/103 [YUN 2004, p. 582], the Secretary-General, in July [A/61/215], reported on the performance of the Disarmament Information Programme for the period from July 2004 to June 2006, and on activities planned for the next two years. The report described relevant activities of the Department for Disarmament Affairs and efforts by the UN Department of Public Information (DPI) to raise awareness and understanding of UN work on disarmament and related issues. Those activities included publications, web site access, exhibits, information activities, cooperation with civil society, and radio and television broadcasts. UN information centres, services and offices also took a variety of initiatives in disarmament and arms control, including press and promotional material, workshops, special events, lectures and other programmes. Responding to higher levels of computer literacy and technological capability among its constituents worldwide, the

Programme reoriented its publications to electronic formats, including *The UN Disarmament Yearbook*, the *Occasional Papers* series and "Disarmament Update: New Links". DPI highlighted disarmament and arms control issues of topical interest, especially nuclear weapons and small arms and light weapons, in print, on the Internet and in film, television and radio, using its large network of Information Centres around the world and its outreach activities. Its use of the celebrity appeal of the Messenger of Peace in respect of arms control issues had been particularly effective.

Annexed to the report was information on the status of the Voluntary Trust Fund for the United Nations Disarmament Information Programme, which supported information and outreach activities of the Department for Disarmament Affairs. At the end of the 2004-2005 biennium, the Fund's available balance totalled $318,165.

GENERAL ASSEMBLY ACTION

On 6 December [meeting 67], the General Assembly, on the recommendation of the First Committee [A/61/395], adopted **resolution 61/95** without vote [agenda item 91 *(b)*].

United Nations Disarmament Information Programme

The General Assembly,

Recalling its decision taken in 1982 at its twelfth special session, the second special session devoted to disarmament, by which the World Disarmament Campaign was launched,

Bearing in mind its resolution 47/53 D of 9 December 1992, in which it decided, inter alia, that the World Disarmament Campaign should be known thereafter as the "United Nations Disarmament Information Programme" and the World Disarmament Campaign Voluntary Trust Fund as the "Voluntary Trust Fund for the United Nations Disarmament Information Programme",

Recalling its resolutions 51/46 A of 10 December 1996, 53/78 E of 4 December 1998, 55/34 A of 20 November 2000, 57/90 of 22 November 2002 and 59/103 of 3 December 2004,

Welcoming the report of the Secretary-General,

1. *Takes note with appreciation* of the report of the Secretary-General, in which he underlines that the website of the United Nations Disarmament Information Programme has grown exponentially in content and specialization and is being used by a greater number of Member States and other users;

2. *Commends* the Secretary-General for his efforts to make effective use of the limited resources available to him in disseminating as widely as possible, including by electronic means, information on arms limitation and disarmament to Governments, the media, non-governmental organizations, educational communities and research institutes, and in carrying out a seminar and conference programme;

3. *Stresses* the importance of the Programme as a significant instrument in enabling all Member States to participate fully in the deliberations and negotiations on disarmament in the various United Nations bodies, in assisting them in complying with treaties, as required, and in contributing to agreed mechanisms for transparency;

4. *Commends with satisfaction* the launch of the first online version of *The United Nations Disarmament Yearbook*, the 2004 edition, by the Department for Disarmament Affairs of the Secretariat, together with the 2002 and 2003 archival editions;

5. *Notes with appreciation* the cooperation of the Department of Public Information of the Secretariat and its information centres in pursuit of the objectives of the Programme;

6. *Recommends* that the Programme continue to inform, educate and generate public understanding of the importance of multilateral action and support for it, including action by the United Nations and the Conference on Disarmament, in the field of arms limitation and disarmament, in a factual, balanced and objective manner, and that it focus its efforts:

(a) To continue to publish in all official languages *The United Nations Disarmament Yearbook*, the flagship publication of the Department for Disarmament Affairs;

(b) To continue to maintain the disarmament website as a part of the United Nations website and to produce versions of the site in as many official languages as feasible;

(c) To continue to intensify United Nations interaction with the public, principally non-governmental organizations and research institutes, to help further an informed debate on topical issues of arms limitation, disarmament and security;

(d) To continue to organize discussions on topics of interest in the field of arms limitation and disarmament with a view to broadening understanding and facilitating an exchange of views and information among Member States and civil society;

7. *Recognizes* the important support received from some Governments for the Voluntary Trust Fund for the United Nations Disarmament Information Programme, and invites once again all Member States to make further contributions to the Fund with a view to sustaining a strong outreach programme;

8. *Takes note* of the recommendations contained in the report of the Secretary-General, which reviews the implementation of the recommendations made in the 2002 study on disarmament and non-proliferation education;

9. *Requests* the Secretary-General to submit to the General Assembly at its sixty-third session a report covering both the implementation of the activities of the Programme by the United Nations system during the previous two years and the activities of the Programme contemplated by the system for the following two years;

10. *Decides* to include in the provisional agenda of its sixty-third session the item entitled "United Nations Disarmament Information Programme".

Advisory Board on Disarmament Matters

The Advisory Board on Disarmament Matters, which advised the Secretary-General on the disarmament studies programme and implementation of the Disarmament Information Programme, and served as the Board of Trustees of the United Nations Institute for Disarmament Research (UNIDIR) (see below), held its forty-sixth and forty-seventh sessions (New York, 8-10 February; Geneva, 21-23 June) [A/61/297]. The Board reviewed the issue of disarmament in the light of the 2005 World Summit Outcome [YUN 2005, p. 48]. It discussed measures to prevent the proliferation of weapons systems to non-State actors, the way ahead in building an international security system, and the further development of international norms on small arms and light weapons.

On its review of the World Summit Outcome, the Board recommended incremental steps to help build momentum on such priority issues as WMD terrorism, promoting the universality of WMD treaty regimes and the resumption of substantive work in the Conference on Disarmament; measures to build and restore trust and confidence among States as a basis for disarmament and non-proliferation progress; new thinking aimed at establishing a new international security paradigm; pursuing disarmament and non-proliferation in a mutually complementary manner and adoption of a balanced approach in considering the security concerns of all States and in addressing disarmament, non-proliferation and the peaceful use of nuclear energy; measures to discourage withdrawal from NPT by empowering IAEA to respond decisively to non-compliance, in order to pre-empt any wrong impression that withdrawal from the Treaty was a viable and consequence-free option; widening the scope of the UN Disarmament Fellowship Programme (see below) to include new topics and challenges, such as export controls, national legislation, law enforcement, border controls and illicit trafficking of nuclear material; and encouraging donors to increase their financial support to NGOs involved in disarmament and arms control. The Board also made recommendations for preventing the proliferation of weapons systems to non-State actors, building an international security system, and further developing international norms on small arms and light weapons.

In its capacity as the UNIDIR Board of Trustees (see below), the Board made recommendations concerning the Institute's 2007 work programme and budget.

UN Institute for Disarmament Research

Report of Secretary-General. By a July note [A/61/180], the Secretary-General transmitted to the General Assembly the report of the UNIDIR Director covering the Institute's activities for the period from August 2005 to July 2006, as well as the report of the UNIDIR Board of Trustees on the proposed 2006-2007 programme of work and budget. The Institute's research activities maintained focus on global, regional and human security, which covered the full range of substantive disarmament issues, from small arms to weapons in space. As in previous years, the report drew attention to UNIDIR scope of research activities worldwide, including through conferences, seminars and discussion meetings, and through other networking initiatives with specialized agencies and UN system organizations and institutions. The report also listed UNIDIR publications issued during the reporting period.

Disarmament fellowship, training and advisory services

In July [A/61/130 & Corr.1], the Secretary-General reported that 30 fellows participated in the UN disarmament fellowship, training and advisory services programme, which began in Geneva on 28 August and terminated in New York on 1 November. The programme continued to be structured in three segments, of which the first, traditionally held in Geneva, was designed to acquaint the fellows with various aspects of multilateral negotiations on disarmament. The second segment involved study visits to intergovernmental organizations working on disarmament issues, as well as to Member States. The 2006 programme included visits to China, Germany and Japan, and to UN system organizations in The Hague and Vienna. The third segment, always held in New York, was intended to familiarize the fellows with the work of the General Assembly's First Committee and that of the Department for Disarmament Affairs.

GENERAL ASSEMBLY ACTION

On 6 December [meeting 67], the General Assembly, on the recommendation of the First Committee [A/61/395], adopted **resolution 61/91** without vote [agenda item 91 *(a)*].

United Nations disarmament fellowship, training and advisory services

The General Assembly,

Having considered the report of the Secretary-General,

Recalling its decision, contained in paragraph 108 of the Final Document of the Tenth Special Session of the General Assembly, the first special session devoted to disarmament, to establish a programme of fellowships on disarmament, as well as its decisions contained in annex IV to the Concluding Document of the Twelfth Special Session of the General Assembly, the second special session devoted to disarmament, in which it decided, inter alia, to continue the programme,

Noting that the programme continues to contribute significantly to developing greater awareness of the importance and benefits of disarmament and a better understanding of the concerns of the international community in the field of disarmament and security, as well as to enhancing the knowledge and skills of fellows, allowing them to participate more effectively in efforts in the field of disarmament at all levels,

Noting with satisfaction that the programme has trained a large number of officials from Member States throughout its twenty-eight years of existence, many of whom hold positions of responsibility in the field of disarmament within their own Governments,

Recognizing the need for Member States to take into account gender equality when nominating candidates to the programme,

Recalling all the annual resolutions on the matter since the thirty-seventh session of the General Assembly, in 1982, including resolution 50/71 A of 12 December 1995,

Believing that the forms of assistance available to Member States, in particular to developing countries, under the programme will enhance the capabilities of their officials to follow ongoing deliberations and negotiations on disarmament, both bilateral and multilateral,

1. *Reaffirms* its decisions contained in annex IV to the Concluding Document of the Twelfth Special Session of the General Assembly and the report of the Secretary-General approved by the Assembly in its resolution 33/71 E of 14 December 1978;

2. *Expresses its appreciation* to all Member States and organizations that have consistently supported the programme throughout the years, thereby contributing to its success, in particular to the Governments of Germany and Japan for the continuation of extensive and highly educative study visits for the participants in the programme, and to the Government of the People's Republic of China for organizing a study visit for the fellows in the area of disarmament;

3. *Expresses its appreciation* to the International Atomic Energy Agency, the Organisation for the Prohibition of Chemical Weapons, the Preparatory Commission for the Comprehensive Nuclear-Test-Ban Treaty Organization and the Monterey Institute of International Studies for having organized specific study programmes in the field of disarmament in their respective areas of competence, thereby contributing to the objectives of the programme;

4. *Commends* the Secretary-General for the diligence with which the programme has continued to be carried out;

5. *Requests* the Secretary-General to continue to implement annually the Geneva-based programme within existing resources and to report thereon to the General Assembly at its sixty-third session;

6. *Decides* to include in the provisional agenda of its sixty-third session the item entitled "United Nations disarmament fellowship, training and advisory services".

Regional disarmament

In 2006, the United Nations addressed disarmament and arms control issues at the regional and subregional levels, particularly the halting of the spread of WMDs, strengthening and consolidating nuclear-weapon-free zones (see p. 644), tackling the illicit trade in small arms and light weapons, undertaking confidence- and security-building measures and destroying surplus stocks of conventional armaments. On 22 September, the Seventh High-level Meeting between the United Nations and regional and other intergovernmental organizations considered measures for furthering the pursuit of relevant regional disarmament activities.

In December, the General Assembly, in resolution 61/82 (see p. 683), decided to give urgent consideration to conventional arms control issues at the regional and subregional levels, and encouraged Member States to conclude agreements at those levels to promote disarmament and confidence-building measures.

Reports of Secretary-General. As requested in General Assembly resolution 60/75 [YUN 2005, p. 643], the Secretary-General, in June [A/61/112], presented the views of seven States (Bangladesh, Bolivia, Lebanon, Mauritius, Mexico, Pakistan, Serbia (formerly Serbia and Montenegro) regarding conventional arms control at the regional and subregional levels.

In July [A/61/124], he submitted another report, in response to Assembly resolution 60/64 [YUN 2005, p. 642], containing the views of five States (Bolivia, Mauritius, Pakistan, Poland, Suriname) on confidence-building measures in the regional and subregional context.

GENERAL ASSEMBLY ACTION

On 6 December [meeting 67], the General Assembly, on the recommendation of the First Committee [A/61/394], adopted four resolutions relating to regional disarmament. The Assembly adopted **resolution 61/80** without vote [agenda item 90 *(m)*].

Regional disarmament

The General Assembly,

Recalling its resolutions 45/58 P of 4 December 1990, 46/36 I of 6 December 1991, 47/52 J of 9 December 1992, 48/75 I of 16 December 1993, 49/75 N of 15 December 1994, 50/70 K of 12 December 1995, 51/45 K of 10 December 1996, 52/38 P of 9 December 1997, 53/77 O of 4 December 1998, 54/54 N of 1 December 1999, 55/33 O of 20 November 2000, 56/24 H of 29 November 2001, 57/76 of 22 November 2002, 58/38 of 8 December 2003, 59/89 of 3 December 2004 and 60/63 of 8 December 2005 on regional disarmament,

Believing that the efforts of the international community to move towards the ideal of general and complete disarmament are guided by the inherent human desire for genuine peace and security, the elimination of the danger of war and the release of economic, intellectual and other resources for peaceful pursuits,

Affirming the abiding commitment of all States to the purposes and principles enshrined in the Charter of the United Nations in the conduct of their international relations,

Noting that essential guidelines for progress towards general and complete disarmament were adopted at the tenth special session of the General Assembly,

Taking note of the guidelines and recommendations for regional approaches to disarmament within the context of global security adopted by the Disarmament Commission at its 1993 substantive session,

Welcoming the prospects of genuine progress in the field of disarmament engendered in recent years as a result of negotiations between the two super-Powers,

Taking note of the recent proposals for disarmament at the regional and subregional levels,

Recognizing the importance of confidence-building measures for regional and international peace and security,

Convinced that endeavours by countries to promote regional disarmament, taking into account the specific characteristics of each region and in accordance with the principle of undiminished security at the lowest level of armaments, would enhance the security of all States and would thus contribute to international peace and security by reducing the risk of regional conflicts,

1. *Stresses* that sustained efforts are needed, within the framework of the Conference on Disarmament and under the umbrella of the United Nations, to make progress on the entire range of disarmament issues;

2. *Affirms* that global and regional approaches to disarmament complement each other and should therefore be pursued simultaneously to promote regional and international peace and security;

3. *Calls upon* States to conclude agreements, wherever possible, for nuclear non-proliferation, disarmament and confidence-building measures at the regional and subregional levels;

4. *Welcomes* the initiatives towards disarmament, nuclear non-proliferation and security undertaken by some countries at the regional and subregional levels;

5. *Supports and encourages* efforts aimed at promoting confidence-building measures at the regional and subregional levels to ease regional tensions and to further disarmament and nuclear non-proliferation measures at the regional and subregional levels;

6. *Decides* to include in the provisional agenda of its sixty-second session the item entitled "Regional disarmament".

The Assembly adopted **resolution 61/81** without vote [agenda item 90 *(n)*].

Confidence-building measures in the regional and subregional context

The General Assembly,

Guided by the purposes and principles enshrined in the Charter of the United Nations,

Recalling its resolutions 58/43 of 8 December 2003, 59/87 of 3 December 2004 and 60/64 of 8 December 2005,

Recalling also its resolution 57/337 of 3 July 2003 entitled "Prevention of armed conflict", in which it calls upon Member States to settle their disputes by peaceful means, as set out in Chapter VI of the Charter, inter alia, by any procedures adopted by the parties,

Recalling further the resolutions and guidelines adopted by consensus by the General Assembly and the Disarmament Commission relating to confidence-building measures and their implantation at the global, regional and subregional levels,

Considering the importance and effectiveness of confidence-building measures taken at the initiative and with the agreement of all States concerned and taking into account the specific characteristics of each region, since such measures can contribute to regional stability,

Convinced that resources released by disarmament, including regional disarmament, can be devoted to economic and social development and to the protection of the environment for the benefit of all peoples, in particular those of the developing countries,

Recognizing the need for meaningful dialogue among States concerned to avert conflict,

Welcoming the peace processes already initiated by States concerned to resolve their disputes through peaceful means bilaterally or through mediation, inter alia, by third parties, regional organizations or the United Nations,

Recognizing that States in some regions have already taken steps towards confidence-building measures at the bilateral, subregional and regional levels in the political and military fields, including arms control and disarmament, and noting that such confidence-building measures have improved peace and security in those regions and contributed to progress in the socio-economic conditions of their people,

Concerned that the continuation of disputes among States, particularly in the absence of an effective mechanism to resolve them through peaceful means, may contribute to the arms race and endanger the maintenance of international peace and security and the efforts of the international community to promote arms control and disarmament,

1. *Calls upon* Member States to refrain from the use or threat of use of force in accordance with the purposes and principles of the Charter of the United Nations;

2. *Reaffirms its commitment* to the peaceful settlement of disputes under Chapter VI of the Charter, in particular Article 33, which provides for a solution by negotiation, enquiry, mediation, conciliation, arbitration, judicial settlement, resort to regional agencies or arrangements or other peaceful means chosen by the parties;

3. *Reaffirms* the ways and means regarding confidence- and security-building measures set out in the report of the Disarmament Commission on its 1993 session;

4. *Calls upon* Member States to pursue these ways and means through sustained consultations and dialogue, while at the same time avoiding actions which may hinder or impair such a dialogue;

5. *Urges* States to comply strictly with all bilateral, regional and international agreements, including arms control and disarmament agreements, to which they are party;

6. *Emphasizes* that the objective of confidence-building measures should be to help strengthen international peace and security and be consistent with the principle of undiminished security at the lowest level of armaments;

7. *Encourages* the promotion of bilateral and regional confidence-building measures, with the consent and participation of the parties concerned, to avoid conflict and prevent the unintended and accidental outbreak of hostilities;

8. *Requests* the Secretary-General to submit a report to the General Assembly at its sixty-second session containing the views of Member States on confidence-building measures in the regional and subregional context;

9. *Decides* to include in the provisional agenda of its sixty-second session the item entitled "Confidence-building measures in the regional and subregional context".

The Assembly adopted **resolution 61/82** by recorded vote (177-1-1) [agenda item 90 *(t)*].

Conventional arms control at the regional and subregional levels

The General Assembly,

Recalling its resolutions 48/75 J of 16 December 1993, 49/75 O of 15 December 1994, 50/70 L of 12 December 1995, 51/45 Q of 10 December 1996, 52/38 Q of 9 December 1997, 53/77 P of 4 December 1998, 54/54 M of 1 December 1999, 55/33 P of 20 November 2000, 56/24 I of 29 November 2001, 57/77 of 22 November 2002, 58/39 of 8 December 2003, 59/88 of 3 December 2004 and 60/75 of 8 December 2005,

Recognizing the crucial role of conventional arms control in promoting regional and international peace and security,

Convinced that conventional arms control needs to be pursued primarily in the regional and subregional contexts since most threats to peace and security in the post-cold-war era arise mainly among States located in the same region or subregion,

Aware that the preservation of a balance in the defence capabilities of States at the lowest level of armaments would contribute to peace and stability and should be a prime objective of conventional arms control,

Desirous of promoting agreements to strengthen regional peace and security at the lowest possible level of armaments and military forces,

Noting with particular interest the initiatives taken in this regard in different regions of the world, in particular the commencement of consultations among a number of Latin American countries and the proposals for conventional arms control made in the context of South Asia, and recognizing, in the context of this subject, the relevance and value of the Treaty on Conventional Armed Forces in Europe, which is a cornerstone of European security,

Believing that militarily significant States and States with larger military capabilities have a special responsibility in promoting such agreements for regional security,

Believing also that an important objective of conventional arms control in regions of tension should be to prevent the possibility of military attack launched by surprise and to avoid aggression,

1. *Decides* to give urgent consideration to the issues involved in conventional arms control at the regional and subregional levels;

2. *Requests* the Conference on Disarmament to consider the formulation of principles that can serve as a framework for regional agreements on conventional arms control, and looks forward to a report of the Conference on this subject;

3. *Requests* the Secretary-General, in the meantime, to seek the views of Member States on the subject and to submit a report to the General Assembly at its sixty-second session;

4. *Decides* to include in the provisional agenda of its sixty-second session the item entitled "Conventional arms control at the regional and subregional levels".

RECORDED VOTE ON RESOLUTION 61/82:

In favour: Afghanistan, Albania, Algeria, Andorra, Angola, Antigua and Barbuda, Argentina, Armenia, Australia, Austria, Azerbaijan, Bahamas, Bahrain, Bangladesh, Barbados, Belarus, Belgium, Belize, Benin, Bolivia, Bosnia and Herzegovina, Brazil, Brunei Darussalam, Bulgaria, Burkina Faso, Burundi, Cambodia, Cameroon, Canada, Cape Verde, Central African Republic, Chad, Chile, China, Colombia, Comoros, Congo, Costa Rica, Côte d'Ivoire, Croatia, Cyprus, Czech Republic, Denmark, Djibouti, Dominica, Dominican Republic, Ecuador, Egypt, El Salvador, Eritrea, Estonia, Ethiopia, Fiji, Finland, France, Gabon, Gambia, Georgia, Germany, Ghana, Greece, Grenada, Guatemala, Guinea, Guyana, Haiti, Honduras, Hungary, Iceland, Indonesia, Iran, Iraq, Ireland, Israel, Italy, Jamaica, Japan, Jordan, Kazakhstan, Kenya, Kuwait, Kyrgyzstan, Latvia, Lebanon, Lesotho, Liberia, Libyan Arab Jamahiriya, Liechtenstein, Lithuania, Luxembourg, Malawi, Malaysia, Maldives, Mali, Malta, Marshall Islands, Mauritania, Mauritius, Mexico, Micronesia, Moldova, Monaco, Mongolia, Montenegro, Morocco, Mozambique, Myanmar, Namibia, Nauru, Nepal, Netherlands, New Zealand, Nicaragua, Niger, Nigeria, Norway, Oman, Pakistan, Palau, Panama, Papua New Guinea, Paraguay, Peru, Philippines, Poland, Portugal, Qatar, Republic of Korea, Romania, Russian Federation, Rwanda, Saint Kitts and Nevis, Saint Lucia, Saint Vincent and the Grenadines, Samoa, San Marino, Sao Tome and Principe, Saudi Arabia, Senegal, Serbia, Sierra Leone, Singapore, Slovakia, Slovenia, Solomon Islands, South Africa, Spain, Sri Lanka, Sudan, Suriname, Swaziland, Sweden, Switzerland, Syrian Arab Republic, Tajikistan, Thailand, The former Yugoslav Republic of Macedonia, Timor-Leste, Togo, Tonga, Trinidad and Tobago, Tunisia, Turkey, Turkmenistan, Uganda, Ukraine, United Arab Emirates, United Kingdom, United Republic of Tanzania, United States, Uruguay, Uzbekistan, Vanuatu, Venezuela, Yemen, Zambia, Zimbabwe.

Against: India.

Abstaining: Bhutan.

The Assembly, on the recommendation of the First Committee [A/61/395], adopted **resolution 61/90** without vote [agenda item 91 *(c)*].

United Nations regional centres for peace and disarmament

The General Assembly,

Recalling its resolution 60/83 of 8 December 2005 regarding the maintenance and revitalization of the three United Nations regional centres for peace and disarmament,

Recalling also the reports of the Secretary-General on the United Nations Regional Centre for Peace and Disarmament in Africa, the United Nations Regional Centre for Peace and Disarmament in Asia and the Pacific and the United Nations Regional Centre for Peace, Disarmament and Development in Latin America and the Caribbean,

Reaffirming its decision, taken in 1982 at its twelfth special session, to establish the United Nations Disarmament Information Programme, the purpose of which is to inform, educate and generate public understanding and support for the objectives of the United Nations in the field of arms control and disarmament,

Bearing in mind its resolutions 40/151 G of 16 December 1985, 41/60 J of 3 December 1986, 42/39 D of 30 November 1987 and 44/117 F of 15 December 1989 on the regional centres for peace and disarmament in Nepal, Peru and Togo,

Recognizing that the changes that have taken place in the world have created new opportunities as well as posed new challenges for the pursuit of disarmament, and, in this regard, bearing in mind that the regional centres for peace and disarmament can contribute substantially to understanding and cooperation among States in each particular region in the areas of peace, disarmament and development,

Noting that in paragraph 146 of the Final Document of the Twelfth Conference of Heads of State or Government of the Non-Aligned Countries, held at Durban, South Africa, from 29 August to 3 September 1998, the Heads of State or Government welcomed the decision adopted by the General Assembly on maintaining and revitalizing the three regional centres for peace and disarmament in Nepal, Peru and Togo,

1. *Reiterates* the importance of the United Nations activities at the regional level to increase the stability and security of its Member States, which could be promoted in a substantive manner by the maintenance and revitalization of the three regional centres for peace and disarmament;

2. *Reaffirms* that, in order to achieve positive results, it is useful for the three regional centres to carry out dissemination and educational programmes that promote regional peace and security and that are aimed at changing basic attitudes with respect to peace and security and disarmament so as to support the achievement of the purposes and principles of the United Nations;

3. *Appeals* to Member States in each region and those that are able to do so, as well as to international governmental and non-governmental organizations and foundations, to make voluntary contributions to the regional centres in their respective regions to strengthen their activities and initiatives;

4. *Emphasizes* the importance of the activities of the regional branch of the Department for Disarmament Affairs of the Secretariat;

5. *Requests* the Secretary-General to provide all necessary support, within existing resources, to the regional centres in carrying out their programmes of activities;

6. *Decides* to include in the provisional agenda of its sixty-second session the item entitled "United Nations regional centres for peace and disarmament".

Africa

In 2006, African States continued to address within a regional framework disarmament and non-proliferation issues, focusing in particular on problems relating to small arms and light weapons. Two major developments in that regard were the entry into force, in May, of the Nairobi Protocol for the Prevention, Control and Reduction of Small Arms and Light Weapons in the Great Lakes Region and the Horn of Africa, adopted in 2004 [YUN 2004, p. 571], and the adoption, in June, of the Economic Community of West African States (ECOWAS) Convention on Small Arms and Light Weapons, their Ammunition and Other Related Materials, at the Thirtieth Ordinary Session of ECOWAS Heads of State and Government (Abuja, Nigeria, 14 June). The former, designed to strengthen the Nairobi Declaration [YUN 2000, p. 518], which first drew attention to the small arms scourge in the Great Lakes region and the Horn of Africa, criminalized the illicit trafficking, manufacturing and possession of small arms and light weapons and obliged member States to establish controls over their possession by civilians and accountability for national inventories. The new Convention, on the other hand, had the status of a legally-binding instrument laying down conditions for the transfer of small arms and light weapons and establishing a framework for manufacturing, controlling and managing them. Once the Convention entered into force, it would replace the voluntary ECOWAS Moratorium on small arms, adopted in 1998 [YUN 1998, p. 537].

Another notable development during the year was the launch of the ECOWAS Small Arms Control Project (ECOSAP) as the successor of the Mali-based Programme for Coordination and Assistance for Security and Development, established in 1998 to serve as an operational framework for the small arms Moratorium [ibid.]. The new five-year project would run as a programme, address small arms trafficking in West Africa, help build the capacity of the region's Small Arms Commission and provide technical support to the small arms unit of the ECOWAS secretariat. Elsewhere, efforts continued to encourage members of the Southern African Development Community (SADC) that had not done so, to ratify the 2001 SADC Protocol on the Control of Firearms, Ammunition and Other Related Materials [YUN 2001, p. 511], which entered into force in 2004 [YUN 2004, p. 571].

Standing Advisory Committee

In response to General Assembly resolution 60/87 [YUN 2005, p. 645], the Secretary-General, in September [A/61/365], described the activities of the Standing Advisory Committee on Security Questions in Central Africa since his 2005 report [YUN 2005, p. 644]. He observed that, despite waning financial support and the Committee's consequent inability to fully implement its programme, it continued to play an important role in promoting peace and security in the Central African region. Sustained support to the Committee's activities, mostly through voluntary contributions, was therefore critical to ensuring that it maintained that role. States members of the Committee needed to assume full ownership of its activities, and in that regard, it was critical for the Council for Peace and Security in Central Africa, established in 2000 [YUN 2000, p. 527], to become operational, particularly its early-warning mechanism. It was also vital to strengthen the capacity of the secretariat of the Economic Community of Central African States to enable it to spearhead the implementation of the various declarations, decisions and recommendations of the Committee.

GENERAL ASSEMBLY ACTION

On 6 December [meeting 67], the General Assembly, on the recommendation of the First Committee [A/61/395], adopted **resolution 61/96** without vote [agenda item 91 *(g)*].

Regional confidence-building measures: activities of the United Nations Standing Advisory Committee on Security Questions in Central Africa

The General Assembly,

Bearing in mind the purposes and principles of the United Nations and its primary responsibility for the maintenance of international peace and security in accordance with the Charter of the United Nations,

Recalling its resolutions 43/78 H and 43/85 of 7 December 1988, 44/21 of 15 November 1989, 45/58 M of 4 December 1990, 46/37 B of 6 December 1991, 47/53 F of 15 December 1992, 48/76 A of 16 December 1993, 49/76 C of 15 December 1994, 50/71 B of 12 December 1995, 51/46 C of 10 December 1996, 52/39 B of 9 December 1997, 53/78 A of 4 December 1998, 54/55 A of 1 December 1999, 55/34 B of 20 November 2000, 56/25 A of 29 November 2001, 57/88 of 22 November 2002, 58/65 of 8 December 2003, 59/96 of 3 December 2004 and 60/87 of 8 December 2005,

Considering the importance and effectiveness of confidence-building measures taken at the initiative and with the participation of all States concerned and taking into account the specific characteristics of each region, since such measures can contribute to regional stability and to international peace and security,

Convinced that the resources released by disarmament, including regional disarmament, can be devoted to economic and social development and to the protection of the environment for the benefit of all peoples, in particular those of the developing countries,

Recalling the guidelines for general and complete disarmament adopted at its tenth special session, the first special session devoted to disarmament,

Convinced that development can be achieved only in a climate of peace, security and mutual confidence both within and among States,

Bearing in mind the establishment by the Secretary-General on 28 May 1992 of the United Nations Standing Advisory Committee on Security Questions in Central Africa, the purpose of which is to encourage arms limitation, disarmament, non-proliferation and development in the subregion,

Recalling the Brazzaville Declaration on Cooperation for Peace and Security in Central Africa, the Bata Declaration for the Promotion of Lasting Democracy, Peace and Development in Central Africa and the Yaoundé Declaration on Peace, Security and Stability in Central Africa,

Bearing in mind resolutions 1196(1998) and 1197(1998), adopted by the Security Council on 16 and 18 September 1998 respectively, following its consideration of the report of the Secretary-General on the causes of conflict and the promotion of durable peace and sustainable development in Africa,

Emphasizing the need to strengthen the capacity for conflict prevention and peacekeeping in Africa,

Recalling the decision of the fourth ministerial meeting of the Standing Advisory Committee in favour of establishing, under the auspices of the Office of the United Nations High Commissioner for Human Rights, a subregional centre for human rights and democracy in Central Africa at Yaoundé,

Noting with satisfaction the efforts being made by the countries members of the Economic Community of Central African States to promote peace and security in their subregion, including the convening in N'Djamena, at the initiative of the current Chairman of the Central African Economic and Monetary Community, of two extraordinary sessions of the Conference of Heads of State of the Central African Economic and Monetary Community, for the purpose of considering the risk of destabilization in Chad,

Recalling the Brazzaville Declaration of 2 September 2005 on the situation between the Democratic Republic of the Congo and the Republic of Rwanda,

Taking note of the successful completion of electoral processes in Chad, the Democratic Republic of the Congo, Gabon and Sao Tome and Principe,

Recognizing the importance of disarmament, demobilization and reintegration programmes in strengthening peace, political stability and reconstruction, especially in post-conflict situations,

1. *Takes note* of the report of the Secretary-General on regional confidence-building measures, which deals with the activities of the United Nations Standing Advisory Committee on Security Questions in Central Africa in the period since the adoption by the General Assembly of its resolution 60/87;

2. *Reaffirms its support* for efforts aimed at promoting confidence-building measures at the regional and subregional levels in order to ease tensions and conflicts in Central Africa and to further sustainable peace, stability and development in the subregion;

3. *Encourages* the States members of the Economic Community of Central African States to pursue their efforts to promote peace and security in their subregion;

4. *Notes with satisfaction* that the Democratic Republic of the Congo and Rwanda are pursuing their efforts to strengthen their bilateral relations;

5. *Strongly appeals* to the international community to provide all necessary support for the smooth functioning of the electoral process in the Democratic Republic of the Congo;

6. *Appeals* to the international community to support the efforts undertaken by the States concerned to implement disarmament, demobilization and reintegration programmes;

7. *Reaffirms its support* for the programme of work of the Standing Advisory Committee adopted at the organizational meeting of the Committee, held at Yaoundé from 27 to 31 July 1992;

8. *Notes with satisfaction* the progress made by the Standing Advisory Committee in implementing its programme of work for the period 2005-2006;

9. *Emphasizes* the importance of providing the States members of the Standing Advisory Committee with the essential support they need to carry out the full programme of activities which they adopted at their ministerial meetings;

10. *Welcomes* the creation of a mechanism for the promotion, maintenance and consolidation of peace and security in Central Africa, known as the Council for Peace and Security in Central Africa, by the Conference of Heads of State and Government of the countries members of the Economic Community of Central African States, held at Yaoundé on 25 February 1999, and requests the Secretary-General to give his full support to the effective realization of that important mechanism;

11. *Emphasizes* the need to make the early warning mechanism in Central Africa operational so that it will serve, on the one hand, as an instrument for analysing and monitoring political situations in the States members of the Standing Advisory Committee with a view to preventing the outbreak of future armed conflicts and, on the other hand, as a technical body through which the member States will carry out the programme of work of the Committee, adopted at its organizational meeting held at Yaoundé in 1992, and requests the Secretary-General to provide it with the assistance necessary for it to function properly;

12. *Requests* the Secretary-General and the United Nations High Commissioner for Human Rights to continue to provide their full assistance for the proper functioning of the Subregional Centre for Human Rights and Democracy in Central Africa;

13. *Requests* the Secretary-General, pursuant to Security Council resolution 1197(1998), to provide the States members of the Standing Advisory Committee with the necessary support for the implementation and smooth functioning of the Council for Peace and Security in Central Africa;

14. *Also requests* the Secretary-General to support the establishment of a network of parliamentarians with a view to the creation of a subregional parliament in Central Africa;

15. *Requests* the Secretary-General and the United Nations High Commissioner for Refugees to continue to provide increased assistance to the countries of Central Africa for coping with the problems of refugees and displaced persons in their territories;

16. *Thanks* the Secretary-General for having established the Trust Fund for the United Nations Standing Advisory Committee on Security Questions in Central Africa;

17. *Appeals* to Member States and to governmental and non-governmental organizations to make additional voluntary contributions to the Trust Fund for the implementation of the programme of work of the Standing Advisory Committee;

18. *Thanks* the Secretary-General for sending a multidisciplinary mission from 8 to 22 June 2003 for the purpose of undertaking an assessment of the priority needs of the region and challenges confronting it in the areas of peace, security, economic development, human rights and HIV/AIDS, and in the humanitarian field;

19. *Requests* the Secretary-General to continue to provide the States members of the Standing Advisory Committee with assistance to ensure that they are able to carry on their efforts;

20. *Calls upon* the Secretary-General to submit to the General Assembly at its sixty-second session a report on the implementation of the present resolution;

21. *Decides* to include in the provisional agenda of its sixty-second session the item entitled "Regional confidence-building measures: activities of the United Nations Standing Advisory Committee on Security Questions in Central Africa".

Regional Centre for Peace and Disarmament in Africa

Pursuant to General Assembly resolution 60/86 [YUN 2005, p. 647], the Secretary-General described the activities of the United Nations Regional Centre for Peace and Disarmament in Africa [A/61/137], covering the period from July 2005 to June 2006. The Centre was established in Lomé, Togo, in 1986 [YUN 1986, p. 85].

During the reporting period, the Centre's main areas of focus were: peace and security; arms control and practical disarmament; research, information and publication; and cooperation with regional, subregional and civil society organizations. To strengthen civil-military relations, the Centre developed an African security sector reform programme targeting 12 African countries that were either experiencing difficulties in that area or recovering from armed conflict. The Centre also provided technical support to the Geneva Centre for the Democratic Control of Armed Forces in formulating and adopting a Code of Conduct for the Armed and Security Forces in West Africa, submitted to the ECOWAS Council of Ministers for consideration. The Centre chaired the meeting of independent experts (Abuja, Nigeria, 9-10 March) to review the draft convention for the control of small arms and light weapons in West Africa (see p. 684). In collaboration with the Sahel and West Africa Club of the Organisation for Economic Cooperation and Development, the Centre organized a workshop on human security in West Africa (Lomé, Togo, 28-30 March), which reviewed the state of human security in that subregion and made recommendations for action. Between 11 and 14 April, the Centre participated in the series of meetings conducted by the Security Council Group of Experts on Côte d'Ivoire as part of its multi-country visits to Africa to gather information relating to States' compliance with the Council's arms embargo on Côte d'Ivoire [YUN 2004, p. 186]. The Centre continued to support African countries, especially Burkina Faso, Djibouti, Gabon, Kenya, Mali, Mozambique, Nigeria, South Africa and Togo, in establishing and/or strengthening national commissions for the control of small arms and light weapons, within the context of implementing the small arms transparency and control regime in Africa project, launched in 2003 [YUN 2003, p. 587]. The Centre completed implementation of activities relating to that project, especially the inventory of small arms and light weapons and ammunition production capacities of participating States, as well as the establishment and maintenance of an arms register and a databse on those weapons on the continent. It provided technical expertise to the Nigerian national commission in organizing a training programme (Kaduna, Nigeria, 4-5 May) on enhanced stockpile management and control. The Centre's other notable activities included information exchange with UN system organizations on arms control and disarmament issues, including the promotion of the entry into force of the African Nuclear-Weapon-Free Zone Treaty (Treaty of Pelindaba) (see p. 644); support for the continuing implementation of the ECOWAS Moratorium on small arms; research on issues relating to peace, security and disarmament in Africa; and cooperation with numerous regional organizations and NGOs, including the African Union (AU), in the field of peace, security and disarmament on the continent. In that context, the Centre initiated a partnership programme with the UN Regional Centre for Peace, Disarmament and Development in Latin America and the Caribbean to facilitate the transfer to Africa of the knowledge, skills and best practices from Latin America's law enforcement training courses on the control of the illegal fire arms trade and trafficking. In accordance with General Assembly resolution 60/86, a consultative mechanism for the Centre's reorganization was established to enable it to better fulfil its mandate in responding to Africa's peace and disarmament needs. Open to all interested States, the mechanism held three meetings (New York, 5 May, 5 and 12 June) to consider relevant proposals and recommendations.

GENERAL ASSEMBLY ACTION

On 6 December [meeting 67], the General Assembly, on the recommendation of the First Committee

[A/61/395], adopted **resolution 61/93** without vote [agenda item 91 *(f)*].

United Nations Regional Centre for Peace and Disarmament in Africa

The General Assembly,

Mindful of the provisions of Article 11, paragraph 1, of the Charter of the United Nations stipulating that a function of the General Assembly is to consider the general principles of cooperation in the maintenance of international peace and security, including the principles governing disarmament and arms limitation,

Recalling its resolutions 40/151 G of 16 December 1985, 41/60 D of 3 December 1986, 42/39 J of 30 November 1987 and 43/76 D of 7 December 1988 on the United Nations Regional Centre for Peace and Disarmament in Africa, and its resolutions 46/36 F of 6 December 1991 and 47/52 G of 9 December 1992 on regional disarmament, including confidence-building measures,

Recalling also its resolutions 48/76 E of 16 December 1993, 49/76 D of 15 December 1994, 50/71 C of 12 December 1995, 51/46 E of 10 December 1996, 52/220 of 22 December 1997, 53/78 C of 4 December 1998, 54/55 B of 1 December 1999, 55/34 D of 20 November 2000, 56/25 D of 29 November 2001, 57/91 of 22 November 2002, 58/61 of 8 December 2003, 59/101 of 3 December 2004 and 60/86 of 8 December 2005,

Aware of the important role that the Regional Centre can play in promoting confidence-building and arms-limitation measures at the regional level, thereby promoting progress in the area of sustainable development,

Taking note of the report of the Secretary-General, in which he stated that the Regional Centre continued to operate under enormous uncertainty owing to a persistent decline in voluntary contributions in support of its activities,

Concerned that the activities and staffing of the Regional Centre have been reduced in view of the limited resources at its disposal,

Deeply concerned that, as noted in the report of the Secretary-General, the future of the Regional Centre looks bleak, as there is no foreseeable reliable source of funding that would ensure its operational sustainability,

Bearing in mind the efforts undertaken to mobilize the necessary resources for the operational costs of the Regional Centre,

Conscious of the need to review the mandate and programmes of the Regional Centre in the light of developments in the field of peace and security in Africa since its establishment,

Taking into account the need to establish close cooperation between the Regional Centre and the Peace and Security Council of the African Union, in particular its institutions in the field of peace, disarmament and security, as well as with relevant United Nations bodies and programmes in Africa for greater effectiveness,

Recalling that the General Assembly, in its resolution 60/86, requested the Secretary-General to establish, within existing resources, a consultative mechanism of interested States, in particular African States, for the reorganization of the United Nations Regional Centre for Peace and Disarmament in Africa, and to report thereon to the Assembly at its sixty-first session,

1. *Notes* that the year 2006 commemorates the twentieth anniversary of the establishment of the United Nations Regional Centre for Peace and Disarmament in Africa in Lomé;

2. *Notes with satisfaction* the establishment by the Secretary-General of the Consultative Mechanism for the Reorganization of the United Nations Regional Centre for Peace and Disarmament in Africa and its work aimed at enabling the Centre to effectively fulfil its mandate in responding to the demands and needs of Africa in the field of peace and disarmament;

3. *Requests* the Consultative Mechanism to continue its work, including reviewing the mandate and programmes of the Regional Centre in the light of developments in the field of peace and security in Africa since its establishment, with a view to identifying concrete measures to revitalize the Centre;

4. *Urges* all States, as well as international governmental and non-governmental organizations and foundations, to make voluntary contributions in order to strengthen the programmes and activities of the Regional Centre and facilitate their implementation;

5. *Requests* the Secretary-General to continue to provide the necessary support to the Regional Centre for better achievements and results;

6. *Also requests* the Secretary-General to facilitate close cooperation between the Regional Centre and the African Union, in particular in the areas of peace, security and development, and to continue to provide assistance towards stabilizing the financial situation of the Centre;

7. *Appeals in particular* to the Regional Centre, in cooperation with the African Union, regional and subregional organizations and the African States, to take steps to promote the consistent implementation of the Programme of Action to Prevent, Combat and Eradicate the Illicit Trade in Small Arms and Light Weapons in All Its Aspects;

8. *Requests* the Secretary-General to report to the General Assembly at its sixty-second session on the implementation of the present resolution;

9. *Decides* to include in the provisional agenda of its sixty-second session the item entitled "United Nations Regional Centre for Peace and Disarmament in Africa".

Asia and the Pacific

In 2006, States in Asia and the Pacific continued to address disarmament and non-proliferation issues within the framework of the Association of South-East Asian Nations (ASEAN), its Regional Forum, and the Shanghai Cooperation Organization (SCO) (China, Kazakhstan, Kyrgystan, Russian Federation, Tajikistan, Uzbekistan), which served as a multilateral platform for strengthening regional peace, security and stability. At its sixth summit meeting (Shanghai, China, 15 June), SCO issued a joint communiqué stating that its main priority was to combat the increasing threats posed by terrorism, separatism, extremism and drug trafficking. To that end, it planned to undertake joint anti-terrorism military exercises within the territories of its member States and tackle common military-political or criminal challenges to information security in the region. The summit also adopted declarations by which SCO members committed themselves to enhancing strategic stability and the international regime on the non-proliferation of WMDs; pledged to contribute to the development of a new global security architecture of mutual understanding based on international law; and resolved to enhance the organization's efforts to bring peace, prosperity and harmony to the region.

At the thirty-ninth ASEAN ministerial meeting (Kuala Lumpur, Malaysia, 24-25 July), the Foreign Ministers of ASEAN member States reaffirmed their commitment to promote political and security cooperation in advancing peace, stability and development in the region; condemned terrorism and pledged to help eliminate it; declared continuing support for the implementation of the Treaty on the South-East Asia Nuclear-Weapon-Free Zone (Bangkok Treaty) (see p. 646); and issued a joint declaration with Canada on enhanced cooperation in strengthening measures against the terrorist threat and in tackling the illegal manufacture, possession or trafficking in weapons, ammunition, explosives and other potentially destructive materials or substances.

The non-proliferation of WMDs was the main topic of discussion at a seminar organized by the Regional Forum (Singapore, 27-29 March), at which experts from 25 regional States reaffirmed the seriousness of the threat which those weapons and their means of delivery posed to international security and considered how regional cooperation could be further strengthened to better address the problem. The thirteenth ministerial meeting of the Regional Forum (Kuala Lumpur, Malaysia, 28 July) emphasized the importance of the denuclearization of the Korean Peninsula in maintaining peace and stability in the Asia and Pacific region and discussed related challenges, especially the DPRK test firing of missiles in July (see p. 441), international terrorism and the need to address its root causes, and the continuing threat to human security posed by the illegal use of small arms and light weapons. They reaffirmed their commitment to the implementation of the 2001 Programme of Action adopted by the UN Conference on small arms [YUN 2001, p. 499], as well as the importance of strengthening controls on the transfer of man-portable air defence systems to prevent their acquisition by terrorists. The Ministers also addressed challenges relating to the potential proliferation of WMDs and reaffirmed the importance of NPT and the work of IAEA in dealing with those challenges.

Regional Centre for Peace and Disarmament in Asia and the Pacific

As requested in General Assembly resolution 60/85 [YUN 2005, p. 649], the Secretary-General reported in July on the activities of the United Nations Regional Centre for Peace and Disarmament in Asia and the Pacific for the period from August 2005 to July 2006 [A/61/163]. The Centre was inaugurated in Kathmandu, Nepal, in 1989 [YUN 1989, p. 88].

The Centre maintained efforts to promote disarmament and security by organizing or participating in meetings and conferences. The Centre cooperated with Canada, Japan and UNDP in organizing a workshop for South Asia and South-East Asia (Bangkok, Thailand, 17-19 May) on the implementation of the Programme of Action adopted at the 2001 UN Conference on small arms, designed to prepare the regional States for participation in the conference to review global progress in implementing the Programme. At the initiative of China and with the support of several other Governments, the Centre organized a UN seminar (Beijing, 12-13 July) on implementing Security Council resolution 1540(2004) [YUN 2004, p. 544] on the non-proliferation of WMDs, where participants considered, among other subjects, measures relating to the protection of nuclear, chemical and biological weapons and their means of delivery.

The Centre also organized the eighteenth United Nations Conference on Disarmament Issues (Yokohama, Japan, 21-23 August), which discussed the challenges and risks facing the international non-proliferation regime, notably the nuclear programmes of DPRK and Iran, and global nuclear black market networks. It also explored practical approaches to cope effectively with those challenges. The Centre also helped organize the fifth UN-Republic of Korea Joint Conference on Disarmament and Non-proliferation (Jeju, Republic of Korea, 13-15 December), where participants considered ways to revitalize efforts to curb the proliferation of WMDs.

The Centre addressed disarmament issues in cooperation with regional and subregional organizations and with relevant disarmament-related intergovernmental entities and assisted the five Central Asian States in finalizing the text of the Treaty on a Nuclear-Weapon-Free Zone in Central Asia (see p. 644), and Mongolia, in consolidating its nuclear-weapon-free status (see p. 645).

Communication. On 31 March [A/60/744], the host country of the Centre, Nepal, reaffirmed its desire to relocate the Centre and make it operational within six months of the signing of the host country agreement with the United Nations. It regretted that, despite its expression of readiness, in 2005, to sign that agreement [YUN 2005, p. 649], it had yet to be provided with a comprehensive draft.

GENERAL ASSEMBLY ACTION

On 6 December [meeting 67], the General Assembly, on the recommendation of the First Committee [A/61/395], adopted **resolution 61/94** without vote [agenda item 91 *(e)*].

United Nations Regional Centre for Peace and Disarmament in Asia and the Pacific

The General Assembly,

Recalling its resolutions 42/39 D of 30 November 1987 and 44/117 F of 15 December 1989, by which it established the United Nations Regional Centre for Peace and Disarmament in Asia and renamed it the United Nations Regional Centre for Peace and Disarmament in Asia and the Pacific, with headquarters in Kathmandu and with the mandate of providing, on request, substantive support for the initiatives and other activities mutually agreed upon by the Member States of the Asia-Pacific region for the implementation of measures for peace and disarmament, through appropriate utilization of available resources,

Taking note of the report of the Secretary-General, in which he expresses his belief that the mandate of the Regional Centre remains valid and that the Centre has been a useful instrument for fostering a climate of cooperation for peace and disarmament in the region,

Noting that trends in the post-cold-war era have emphasized the function of the Regional Centre in assisting Member States as they deal with new security concerns and disarmament issues emerging in the region,

Commending the useful activities carried out by the Regional Centre in encouraging regional and subregional dialogue for the enhancement of openness, transparency and confidence-building, as well as the promotion of disarmament and security through the organization of regional meetings, which has come to be widely known within the Asia-Pacific region as "the Kathmandu process",

Expressing its appreciation to the Regional Centre for its organization of meetings, conferences and workshops in the region, held in Kyoto, Japan, from 17 to 19 August 2005; Busan, Republic of Korea, from 1 to 3 December 2005; Bali, Indonesia, on 21 and 22 December 2005; Bangkok, Thailand, from 17 to 19 May 2006; and Beijing, People's Republic of China, on 12 and 13 July 2006,

Welcoming the activities of the Regional Centre in the promotion of disarmament and non-proliferation education in the Asia-Pacific region, as recommended in the United Nations study on disarmament and non-proliferation education,

Noting the important role of the Regional Centre in assisting region-specific initiatives of Member States,

Appreciating highly the overall support that Nepal has extended as the host nation of the headquarters of the Regional Centre,

1. *Reaffirms its strong support* for the forthcoming operation and further strengthening of the United Nations Regional Centre for Peace and Disarmament in Asia and the Pacific;

2. *Underlines* the importance of the Kathmandu process as a powerful vehicle for the development of the practice of region-wide security and disarmament dialogue;

3. *Expresses its appreciation* for the continuing political support and voluntary financial contributions to the Regional Centre, which are essential for its continued operation;

4. *Appeals* to Member States, in particular those within the Asia-Pacific region, as well as to international governmental and non-governmental organizations and foundations, to make voluntary contributions, the only resources of the Regional Centre, to strengthen the programme of activities of the Centre and the implementation thereof;

5. *Requests* the Secretary-General, taking note of paragraph 6 of General Assembly resolution 49/76 D of 15 December 1994, to provide the Regional Centre with the necessary support, within existing resources, in carrying out its programme of activities;

6. *Urges* the Secretary-General to complete, without any further delay, the internal procedure for finalizing the host country agreement and the related memorandum of understanding and to ensure the physical operation of the Regional Centre from Kathmandu within six months of the date of signature of the host country agreement and to enable the Centre to function effectively;

7. *Requests* the Secretary-General to report to the General Assembly at its sixty-second session on the implementation of the present resolution;

8. *Decides* to include in the provisional agenda of its sixty-second session the item entitled "United Nations Regional Centre for Peace and Disarmament in Asia and the Pacific".

Europe

In 2006, European countries addressed security and disarmament issues within the framework of regional institutions, especially the European Union (EU), which enhanced its non-proliferation activities by promoting the implementation of Security Council resolutions 1540(2004) [YUN 2004, p. 544] and 1673(2006) (see p. 635) on the non-proliferation of WMDs. In that regard, it helped fund regional workshops in Asia and the Pacific (Beijing, 12-13 July), Africa (Accra, Ghana, 9-10 November) and Latin America and the Caribbean (Lima, Peru, 27-28 November), all aimed at raising awareness of States' obligations under those resolutions and addressing related regional assistance needs. The EU also provided financial support to IAEA efforts to prevent nuclear terrorism. Accordingly, it developed assistance projects for South-Eastern Europe, the Caucasus and the Mediterranean, Africa, Central Asia and the Middle East, geared to improve the physical protection of nuclear material and facilities, enhance the control of radioactive sources and guard against illicit trafficking in related products. Other projects supported by the EU were aimed at enhancing the CTBT monitoring and verification system (see p. 630), promoting the universalization and national implementation of the Chemical Weapons Convention (see p. 653) and encouraging accession to the Biological Weapons Convention (see p. 650). It also began to implement best practices for the control of dual use items and technology, in accordance with related obligations under Security Council resolution 1540(2004).

In the field of conventional arms control, the EU continued to harmonize its member States' national arms export control policies, in accordance with the 1998 EU Code of Conduct on Arms Exports [YUN 1998, p. 540]. Future priorities in that regard included coordinating outreach efforts, particularly to Western Balkan countries and their neighbours; promoting the Code's principles and criteria; and providing practical and technical assistance towards those objectives. The EU also contributed to international efforts to combat the illicit accumulation of and trafficking in small arms and light weapons and their ammunition, as well as anti-personnel mines and explosive remnants of war. It provided financial support to projects relevant to those issues, which addressed political and legislative processes and the humanitarian and developmental impact of the illicit proliferation and uncontrolled use and misuse of those weapons.

The North Atlantic Treaty Organization (NATO) also addressed regional disarmament and security concerns. Through its Partnership for Peace Trust Fund, NATO provided practical support to nations seeking to implement the Mine-Ban Convention (see p. 670) and the 2001 Programme of Action on small arms. NATO member States also pressed on with efforts to implement the 1990 Treaty on Conventional Armed Forces in Europe (CFE Treaty) [YUN 1990, p. 79]. At the Third Review Conference of the Treaty (Vienna, 30 May–2 June), they discussed developments that should enable the ratification by all members of the 1999 Agreement on the Adaptation of the Treaty [YUN 1999, p. 503], and which were expected to pave the way for its entry into force. The Organization for Security and Cooperation in Europe (OSCE) focused primarily on the implementation of confidence- and security-building measures. It also addressed new threats and security-related concerns, such as illicit trafficking, the small arms scourge and WMDs. It remained involved in the implementation of the 2001 Programme of Action on small arms, notably by initiating discussions on how to counter the illicit transfer of those weapons by private cargo companies, which accounted for a major part of the illegal transport of small arms. Reports by OSCE participating States regarding the Programme's implementation indicated that, in the period between 2001 and 2005, they collectively destroyed some 5.3 million weapons, of which 4.2 million were deemed surplus, and seized 1 million from illegal trafficking.

To enable its participating States to address better the problems relating to man-portable air defence systems, the OSCE forum for security cooperation adopted a decision on best practices regarding national procedures for stockpile management and security of such systems, which would comprise 'annex C' to its *Handbook of Best Practices on Small Arms and Light Weapons*. It also adopted best practice guides on stockpiles of conventional ammunition. Regarding WMDs, OSCE joined the EU in promoting the implementation of Security Council resolution 1540(2004) among its participating States. In that connection, it organized a workshop (Vienna, November), at which participating States agreed to cooperate in furthering UN efforts by promoting lessons learned, sharing experiences and facilitating the identification of assistance needs. Regional disarmament and security concerns in Europe were also addressed by the Stability Pact for South-Eastern Europe [YUN 1999, p. 397], mainly through the convening, training and capacity-building activities of its two most notable initiatives in that subregion: the Regional Arms Control Verification and Implementation Assistance Centre and the South-Eastern and Eastern Europe Clearinghouse for the Control of Small Arms and Light Weapons.

Communication. On 27 June [A/60/910-S/2006/444], Kazakhstan transmitted the text of a Declaration adopted by the second Summit of the Conference on Interaction and Confidence Building Measures in Asia (Almaty, Kazakhstan, 17 June), by which Heads of State or Government of the member States condemned terrorism and separatism, advocated cooperation in preventing the proliferation of WMDs and other international disarmament and security threats and declared their willingness to implement the 2001 Programme of Action on small arms.

Latin America and the Caribbean

In 2006, the EU and Latin American and Caribbean countries resolved, at the fourth Summit of Heads of State and Government (Vienna, 12 May), to reinforce their bi-regional strategic relationship. Consistent with that objective, the Summit adopted the Vienna Declaration, by which the leaders on both sides reaffirmed their commitment to a multilateral approach to current disarmament, non-proliferation and arms control challenges, particularly regarding WMDs, and undertook to cooperate in combating terrorism. In a related development, the Organization of American States (OAS) introduced a multidimensional approach to regional defence and security issues, in particular through the establishment of its Secretariat for Multidimensional Security, incorporating sub-secretariats on terrorism and drug abuse, and a Public Security Department. Building on that shift in focus, the Seventh Conference of the Defence Ministers of the Americas (Managua, Nicaragua, 1-5 October) adopted the Managua Declaration, which recommended, among other actions, measures against all forms of terrorism, the proliferation of small arms and other transnational crime threats. The eighteenth special session of the General Conference of the Agency for the Prohibition of Nuclear Weapons in Latin America and the Caribbean (OPANAL) (Mexico City, 23 November) addressed the concern of its member States that some nuclear-weapon States tended to see the possible use of nuclear weapons as a legitimate means of self-defence, contrary to international law.

Regional Centre

Responding to General Assembly resolution 60/84 [YUN 2005, p. 651], the Secretary-General submitted a July report [A/61/157] describing the activities of the United Nations Regional Centre for Peace, Disarmament and Development in Latin America and the Caribbean for the period from July 2005 to June 2006. The Centre was inaugurated in Lima, Peru, in 1987 [YUN 1987, p. 88].

The Centre helped to promote regional and subregional security; strengthen global security; and foster peace and disarmament education. Activities undertaken in those areas took into account their cross-cutting nature. In February, the Centre reached an agreement with the Regional Centre in Africa (see p. 687) and the International Criminal Police Organization (Interpol) to develop synergies between both regions in combating illicit firearms trafficking. Under the agreement, law enforcement training courses and databases developed by the Centre in Latin America and the Caribbean, would be made available in Africa. The Centre also organized training courses in six countries in Latin America and the Caribbean to assist them in improving control of the legal firearms trade and to prevent illicit trafficking. Up to 720 regional officials were trained by year's end. On 23 February, the Centre agreed to cooperate with the World Centre for Research and Training in the Resolution of Conflicts in Colombia to evaluate national law enforcement courses and prepare training manuals for decision-makers and youth on security issues. In March, it met with the UNDP Regional Bureau to elaborate a new strategic relationship between them for incorporating disarmament and development activities into the assistance provided to the regional States in implementing the Millennium Declaration [YUN 2000, p. 49]. The Centre and its partners helped Argentina improve its capacity to combat crime associated with illicit arms trafficking and use by initiating a pilot programme, using firearms identification, registration and ballistic forensic system to establish links between crimes committed with the same weapon and to identify illicit arms transaction. The initiative, the first of its kind in the region, marked the beginning of the establishment of a region-wide forensic network to assist States in implementing the 2001 Programme of Action on small arms.

On 1 May, the Centre signed an agreement with the Department for Disarmament Affairs and UNDP-Costa Rica to assist that country's Government in reducing the negative impact of firearms violence and insecurity on human development. Under the auspices of the regional clearing house on firearms, ammunition and explosives, the Centre considered ways to assist regional States in enhancing existing controls on their legal arms trade, while preventing illicit trafficking. To help strengthen arms transfer controls in the region, the Centre and its partners organized a regional conference (Antigua, Guatemala, 2-4 May) [A/CONF.192/2006/RC/7], which adopted the Antigua Declaration on a common regional position on the prevention of illicit firearms trafficking. OAS, at its thirty-sixth regular session (Santo Domingo, Dominican Republic, 4-6 June), asked its General Secretariat to work with the Centre and its partners in offering expert training on special techniques for investigating the illicit manufacturing of and trafficking in firearms and ammunition. During the year, the Centre cooperated with regional NGOs to illustrate the impact of illicit firearms trafficking on peoples' daily lives and promote a culture of peace; assisted regional States in weapons destruction exercises under its Lima Challenge project, which had overseen the destruction of some 40,902 firearms and removal of 27,000 others in the past five years; provided further assistance for improving the security of arms storage in the region; collaborated with intergovernmental treaty organizations to promote the signature, ratification and implementation of disarmament-related treaties; and supported Peru's amnesty campaign (23 July 2005 to 17 September 2006) by providing technical and financial resources to enable it to better regulate the possession of firearms, ammunition and explosives in the country.

GENERAL ASSEMBLY ACTION

On 6 December [meeting 67], the General Assembly, on the recommendation of the First Committee [A/61/395], adopted **resolution 61/92** without vote [agenda item 91 *(d)*].

United Nations Regional Centre for Peace, Disarmament and Development in Latin America and the Caribbean

The General Assembly,

Recalling its resolutions 41/60 J of 3 December 1986, 42/39 K of 30 November 1987 and 43/76 H of 7 December 1988 on the United Nations Regional Centre for Peace, Disarmament and Development in Latin America and the Caribbean, with headquarters in Lima,

Recalling also its resolutions 46/37 F of 9 December 1991, 48/76 E of 16 December 1993, 49/76 D of 15 December 1994, 50/71 C of 12 December 1995, 52/220 of 22 December 1997, 53/78 F of 4 December 1998, 54/55 F of 1 December 1999, 55/34 E of 20 November 2000, 56/25 E of 29 November 2001, 57/89 of 22 November 2002, 58/60 of 8 December 2003, 59/99 of 3 December 2004 and 60/84 of 8 December 2005,

Recognizing that the Regional Centre has continued to provide substantive support for the implementation of regional and subregional initiatives and has intensified its contribution to the coordination of United Nations efforts towards peace, disarmament and the promotion of economic and social development,

Welcoming the report of the Secretary-General, which, inter alia, concludes that the Regional Centre has continued to provide assistance to States in the Latin American and Caribbean region in the implementation of regional initiatives in the areas of peace, disarmament and development and that during the period under review such assistance was provided in the area of practical disarmament, such as weapons destruction and training courses; the preparation of national reports on weapons-related instruments; the creation of mechanisms to facilitate the implementation of disarmament treaties; and the provision of forums for discussion among States to facilitate their reaching common positions on disarmament and non-proliferation issues, and welcoming also the Centre's initiation of the process of transferring to the African region its knowledge and best practices in the area of training courses for the law enforcement community on the prevention of illicit firearms trafficking,

Recalling the report of the Group of Governmental Experts on the relationship between disarmament and development, referred to in General Assembly resolution 59/78 of 3 December 2004, which is of utmost interest with regard to the role that the Regional Centre plays in promoting the issue in the region in pursuit of its mandate to promote economic and social development related to peace and disarmament,

Noting that security and disarmament issues have always been recognized as significant topics in Latin America and the Caribbean, the first inhabited region in the world to be declared a nuclear-weapon-free zone,

Welcoming the support provided by the Regional Centre to strengthening the nuclear-weapon-free zone established by the Treaty for the Prohibition of Nuclear Weapons in Latin America and the Caribbean (Treaty of Tlatelolco), as well as to promoting and assisting the ratification and implementation of existing multilateral agreements related to weapons of mass destruction and to promoting peace and disarmament education projects during the period under review,

Bearing in mind the important role that the Regional Centre can play in promoting confidence-building measures, arms control and limitation, disarmament and development at the regional level,

Bearing in mind also the importance of information, research, education and training for peace, disarmament and development in order to achieve understanding and cooperation among States,

Recognizing the need to provide the three United Nations regional centres for peace and disarmament with sufficient financial resources and cooperation for the planning and implementation of their programmes of activities,

1. *Reiterates its strong support* for the role of the United Nations Regional Centre for Peace, Disarmament and Development in Latin America and the Caribbean in the promotion of United Nations activities at the regional level to strengthen peace, stability, security and development among its member States;

2. *Expresses its satisfaction and congratulates* the Regional Centre for the activities carried out in the last year in the areas of peace, disarmament and development, and requests the Centre to take into account the proposals to be submitted by the countries of the region in promoting confidence-building measures, arms control and limitation, transparency, disarmament and development at the regional level;

3. *Expresses its appreciation* for the political support and financial contributions to the Regional Centre, which are essential for its continued operation;

4. *Appeals* to Member States, in particular those within the Latin American and Caribbean region, and

to international governmental and non-governmental organizations and foundations to make and to increase voluntary contributions to strengthen the Regional Centre, its programme of activities and the implementation thereof;

5. *Invites* all States of the region to continue to take part in the activities of the Regional Centre, proposing items for inclusion in its programme of activities and making greater and better use of the potential of the Centre to meet the current challenges facing the international community with a view to fulfilling the aims of the Charter of the United Nations in the areas of peace, disarmament and development;

6. *Recognizes* that the Regional Centre has an important role in the promotion and development of regional initiatives agreed upon by the countries of Latin America and the Caribbean in the field of weapons of mass destruction, in particular nuclear weapons, and conventional arms, including small arms and light weapons, as well as in the relationship between disarmament and development;

7. *Encourages* the Regional Centre to further develop activities in the important area of disarmament and development;

8. *Highlights* the conclusion contained in the report of the Secretary-General that, through its activities, the Regional Centre has demonstrated its role as a viable regional actor in assisting States in the region to advance the cause of peace, disarmament and development in Latin America and the Caribbean;

9. *Requests* the Secretary-General to provide the Regional Centre with all necessary support, within existing resources, so that it may carry out its programme of activities in accordance with its mandate;

10. *Also requests* the Secretary-General to report to the General Assembly at its sixty-second session on the implementation of the present resolution;

11. *Decides* to include in the provisional agenda of its sixty-second session the item entitled "United Nations Regional Centre for Peace, Disarmament and Development in Latin America and the Caribbean".

Chapter VIII

Other political and security questions

The United Nations continued in 2006 to consider political and security questions relating to its efforts to support democratization worldwide, the promotion of decolonization, the Organization's public information activities and the peaceful uses of outer space.

The Sixth International Conference of New or Restored Democracies (October/November) had as its theme "Building capacity for democracy, peace and social progress". It adopted the Doha Declaration, which, stressing the need for systematic implementation of the recommendations of the Sixth Conference and those that had preceded it, established an advisory board and nucleus secretariat to assist the Sixth Conference's Chair to take measures to guarantee appropriate follow-up. Representatives of Governments, parliaments and civil society committed themselves to strengthening their tripartite partnership within the framework of the International Conferences of New or Restored Democracies process.

The Special Committee on the Situation with regard to the Implementation of the Declaration on the Granting of Independence to Colonial Countries and Peoples continued to review progress in implementing the 1960 Declaration, particularly the exercise of self-determination by the remaining Non-Self-Governing Territories.

During the year, the Special Committee organized a Pacific regional seminar in Yanuca, Fiji, as part of its efforts to implement the plan of action for the Second International Decade for the Eradication of Colonialism (2001-2010). It also sent a Special Mission to the Turks and Caicos Islands, at the invitation of the Territory's Chief Minister, to assess the situation on the ground and provide information on how the UN system could provide development assistance. Following a referendum on 30 November, Gibraltar approved a new constitution. During the year, the New Zealand-administered Territory of Tokelau also held a referendum to determine its future status. While the referendum, observed by a four-member UN mission, failed to result in the two-thirds majority needed for a change in the Territory's status, Tokelau and New Zealand agreed to leave the referendum package on the table; a second referendum would be held in 2007.

The Committee on Information continued to review the management and operation of the UN Department of Public Information. At its April/May/August session it considered reports by the Secretary-General on UN public information products and activities in the four years since the reorientation of the Department in 2002. The Dag Hammarskjöld Library continued to focus on follow-up to the new strategic directions for UN libraries outlined by the Secretary-General in 2005, including an expanded role in improving knowledge sharing and internal communications within the UN Secretariat. Regarding the continued rationalization of the UN information centres network that began with the closure in 2003 of information centres in Western Europe, the Department strengthened the centres in Cairo, Egypt, Mexico City and Pretoria, South Africa, by reallocating three Director-level posts to them.

In a December resolution on developments in the field of information and telecommunications in the context of international security, the Assembly called on Member States to consider existing and potential threats in the field of information security, requesting the Secretary-General, with the assistance of a group of governmental experts to be established in 2009, to study such threats and possible cooperative measures to address them. On the role of science and technology in the context of international security and disarmament, the Assembly, also in December, encouraged UN bodies, within existing mandates, to promote the application of science and technology for peaceful purposes.

The Committee on the Peaceful Uses of Outer Space considered the implementation of the recommendations of the Third (1999) United Nations Conference on the Exploration and Peaceful Uses of Outer Space. Its two subcommittees, one of which dealt with scientific and technical matters and the other with legal issues, continued their work. In December, on the Committee's recommendations, the Assembly established the United Nations Platform for Space-based Information for Disaster Management and Emergency Response to provide universal access to all countries and relevant international and regional organizations to space-based information and services relevant to disaster management.

The United Nations Scientific Committee on the Effects of Atomic Radiation held its fifty-fourth session.

General aspects of international security

Support for democracies

UN system activities

In May 2006, the General Assembly considered the November 2005 report of the Secretary-General on support by the UN system of the efforts of Governments to promote and consolidate new or restored democracies [YUN 2005, p. 655].

GENERAL ASSEMBLY ACTION

On 2 May [meeting 78], the General Assembly adopted **resolution 60/253** [draft: A/60/L.53 & Add.1] without vote [agenda item 10].

Support by the United Nations system of the efforts of Governments to promote and consolidate new or restored democracies

The General Assembly,

Bearing in mind the indissoluble links between the principles enshrined in the Universal Declaration of Human Rights and the foundations of any democratic society,

Recognizing that human rights, the rule of law and democracy are interlinked and mutually reinforcing and that they belong to the universal and indivisible core values and principles of the United Nations,

Recalling the United Nations Millennium Declaration adopted by Heads of State and Government on 8 September 2000, in particular paragraphs 6 and 24 thereof, and the 2005 World Summit Outcome,

Recalling also its resolutions 49/30 of 7 December 1994, 50/133 of 20 December 1995, 51/31 of 6 December 1996, 52/18 of 21 November 1997, 53/31 of 23 November 1998, 54/36 of 29 November 1999, 55/43 of 27 November 2000, 56/96 of 14 December 2001, 56/269 of 27 March 2002, 58/13 of 17 November 2003 and 58/281 of 9 February 2004,

Recalling further the declarations and plans of action of the five international conferences of new or restored democracies adopted in Manila in 1988, Managua in 1994, Bucharest in 1997, Cotonou in 2000 and Ulaanbaatar in 2003,

Recalling that the Fifth International Conference of New or Restored Democracies, which was held in Ulaanbaatar from 10 to 12 September 2003, focused on democracy, good governance and civil society,

Noting the results of the Parliamentarians' Forum convened by the Inter-Parliamentary Union and the Parliament of Mongolia on the occasion of the Fifth International Conference, and noting the follow-up work conducted by the Inter-Parliamentary Union in the field of enhancing parliamentary democracy,

Stressing that democracy, development and respect for all human rights and fundamental freedoms are interdependent and mutually reinforcing,

Reaffirming that democracy is a universal value based on the freely expressed will of people to determine their own political, economic, social and cultural systems and their full participation in all aspects of their lives,

Reaffirming also that while democracies share common features, there is no single model of democracy and that it does not belong to any country or region, and reaffirming further the necessity of due respect for sovereignty and the right to self-determination,

Considering the major changes taking place on the international scene and the aspirations of all peoples for an international order based on the principles enshrined in the Charter of the United Nations, including the promotion and respect for human rights and fundamental freedoms for all and other important principles, such as respect for the equal rights and self-determination of peoples, peace, democracy, justice, equality, the rule of law, pluralism, development, better standards of living and solidarity,

Bearing in mind that the activities of the United Nations carried out in support of Governments to promote and consolidate democracy are undertaken in accordance with the Charter and only at the specific request of the Member States concerned,

Taking note with satisfaction of the seminars, workshops and conferences on democratization and good governance convened in 2004 and 2005, including those held under the auspices of the International Conference of New or Restored Democracies,

Taking note of the views expressed by Member States in the debate on this question from the fifty-eighth to the sixtieth session,

Noting that a considerable number of societies have recently undertaken significant efforts to achieve their social, political and economic goals through democratization, good governance practices and the reform of their economies, pursuits that are deserving of the support and recognition of the international community,

Noting with satisfaction that the Sixth International Conference of New or Restored Democracies will be held in Doha from 30 October to 1 November 2006,

Stressing the importance of support by Member States, the United Nations system, the specialized agencies and other intergovernmental organizations for the holding of the Sixth International Conference,

Having considered the report of the Secretary-General,

1. *Takes note with appreciation* of the report of the Secretary-General, and invites Member States to consider the proposals contained therein;

2. *Invites* Member States, the relevant organizations of the United Nations system, other intergovernmental

organizations, national parliaments, including in collaboration with the Inter-Parliamentary Union and other parliamentary organizations, and non-governmental organizations to contribute actively to the follow-up to the Fifth International Conference of New or Restored Democracies and to make additional efforts to identify possible steps in support of the efforts of Governments to promote and consolidate new or restored democracies, including through those steps set out in the Ulaanbaatar Declaration and Plan of Action: Democracy, Good Governance and Civil Society, and to inform the Secretary-General of the actions taken;

3. *Recognizes* that the United Nations has an important role to play in providing timely, appropriate and coherent support to the efforts of Governments to achieve democratization and good governance within the context of their development efforts;

4. *Encourages* the Secretary-General to continue to improve the capacity of the Organization to respond effectively to the requests of Member States by providing coherent and adequate support for their efforts to achieve the goals of good governance and democratization, including through the activities of the Democracy Fund at the United Nations;

5. *Stresses* that the activities of the Organization must be undertaken in accordance with the Charter of the United Nations;

6. *Commends* the Secretary-General, and through him the United Nations system, for the activities undertaken at the request of Governments to support efforts to consolidate democracy and good governance, and requests him to continue those activities;

7. *Welcomes* the work carried out by the follow-up mechanism of the Fifth International Conference and the efforts of the Chair of the Conference to make the Conference and the follow-up thereto more effective and efficient;

8. *Also welcomes* the comprehensive tripartite character (governments, parliaments, civil society) of the Sixth International Conference of New or Restored Democracies, which will allow for greater interaction and cooperation in the common effort of promoting democracy;

9. *Encourages* the Inter-Parliamentary Union to continue to promote the contribution by parliaments worldwide to democracy, including through the process of the International Conference of New or Restored Democracies and the upcoming Parliamentarians' Forum in Doha;

10. *Requests* the Secretary-General to examine options for strengthening the support provided by the United Nations system for the efforts of Member States to consolidate democracy and good governance, including the provision of support to the President of the Fifth International Conference in his efforts to make the Conference and the follow-up thereto more effective and efficient;

11. *Also requests* the Secretary-General to submit to the General Assembly at its sixty-second session a report on the implementation of the present resolution, including the information requested in paragraph 2 above;

12. *Decides* to include in the provisional agenda of its sixty-second session the item entitled "Support by the United Nations system of the efforts of Governments to promote and consolidate new or restored democracies".

Sixth International Conference

The Sixth International Conference of New or Restored Democracies (Doha, Qatar, 29 October–1 November), organized by Qatar in cooperation with the United Nations, had as its theme "Building capacity for democracy, peace and social progress". Over 100 States participated in the Conference, as did parliamentarians and civil society organizations, representing 69 countries and 100 organizations. The Fifth International Conference was held in 2003 [YUN 2003, p. 593].

The Sixth Conference had two main objectives: to enhance the linkages among democracy, peace and social progress in the global development agenda; and to initiate systematic implementation and follow-up steps to consolidate the achievements and recommendations of the earlier International Conferences of New or Restored Democracies, which began in 1988. Interactive dialogues, round tables and forums constituted a major feature of the Doha Conference, which culminated in the adoption of: the Doha Declaration; the Joint Statement by representatives of Governments, parliaments and civil society; and the draft final report.

In the Doha Declaration, participants reaffirmed that the International Conferences had enhanced the international dialogue on concepts and principles of democracy and strengthened cooperation among new and restored democracies, with a view to consolidating the integration of democracy, peace and development.

Stressing that the need for systematic implementation of their recommendations required the establishment of follow-up steps, the participants requested the Sixth Conference's Chair to take measures to guarantee appropriate implementation and follow-up of the recommendations, with the assistance of an eight-member Advisory Board. They also agreed to establish a nucleus secretariat to assist the Chair and Qatar would be responsible for all financial obligations to that effect for three years. Participants requested the Chair, in consultation with the Advisory Board, to submit a progress report to the Seventh (2009) International Conference on the effectiveness of the new secretariat.

Participants welcomed the Secretary-General's establishment of the United Nations Democracy

Fund [YUN, 2005, p. 655] and the support provided to it by Member States and civil society organizations; relevant actors were invited to make use of that strategic and flexible new instrument to further democracy-building efforts.

On the issue of cooperation with the UN system, participants noted the commendable collaboration between the United Nations and the International Conference with respect to promoting and consolidating new and restored democracies, and urged the UN system to continue to provide the necessary technical assistance to member countries upon request. They also urged Qatar, as host Government, to transmit the instruments adopted by the Conference to the General Assembly and initiate actions for continued support by the United Nations.

In the Joint Statement, representatives of Governments, parliaments and civil society committed themselves to strengthening their tripartite partnership through the establishment and enhancement of cooperation and consultation among Governments, parliaments and civil society and, in close cooperation with the United Nations, to organizing national, regional and global meetings, seminars and conferences on democracy promotion.

Communications. On 14 November [A/61/581], Qatar transmitted to the Secretary-General the texts of the Doha Declaration and the Joint Statement, and requested that they be circulated as a General Assembly document during its sixty-first session. On 15 November [A/61/235], Qatar requested the Assembly President to include the item "Support by the United Nations system of the efforts of Governments to promote and consolidate new or restored democracies" in the agenda of the Assembly's sixty-first session.

Qatar also transmitted to the Secretary-General the outcomes of the Parliamentary Meeting and the International Civil Society Forum for Democracy, which took place during the Sixth Conference [A/61/817].

GENERAL ASSEMBLY ACTION

On 22 December [meeting 84], the General Assembly adopted **resolution 61/226** [draft: A/61/L.51 & Add.1] without vote [agenda item 157].

Support by the United Nations system of the efforts of Governments to promote and consolidate new or restored democracies

The General Assembly,

Recalling its resolutions 49/30 of 7 December 1994, 50/133 of 20 December 1995, 51/31 of 6 December 1996, 52/18 of 21 November 1997, 53/31 of 23 November 1998, 54/36 of 29 November 1999, 55/43 of 27 November 2000, 56/96 of 14 December 2001, 56/269 of 27 March 2002, 58/13 of 17 November 2003, 58/281 of 9 February 2004 and 60/253 of 2 May 2006,

Bearing in mind the indissoluble links between the principles enshrined in the Universal Declaration of Human Rights and the foundations of any democratic society,

Recognizing that human rights, the rule of law and democracy are interlinked and mutually reinforcing and that they belong to the universal and indivisible core values and principles of the United Nations,

Recalling the United Nations Millennium Declaration adopted by Heads of State and Government on 8 September 2000, in particular paragraphs 6 and 24 thereof, and the 2005 World Summit Outcome,

Recalling also the declarations and plans of action of the six international conferences of new or restored democracies adopted in Manila in 1988, Managua in 1994, Bucharest in 1997, Cotonou in 2000, Ulaanbaatar in 2003 and Doha in 2006,

Reaffirming that democracy is a universal value based on the freely expressed will of people to determine their own political, economic, social and cultural systems and their full participation in all aspects of their lives,

Reaffirming also that, while democracies share common features, there is no single model of democracy and that democracy does not belong to any country or region, and reaffirming further the necessity of due respect for sovereignty and the right to self-determination and territorial integrity,

Stressing that democracy, development and respect for all human rights and fundamental freedoms are interdependent and mutually reinforcing,

Recognizing that a large number of States are now participating in the international conferences of new or restored democracies and are working together with a host of parliamentarians and international organizations and a large number of non-governmental organizations active in the field of democracy from around the world,

Recognizing also that the international conferences of new or restored democracies over the past eighteen years, since 1988, have strengthened international cooperation among new and restored democracies with a view to consolidating the integration of democracy, peace and development,

Underlining its commitment to, faith in and support for the purposes and principles of the Charter of the United Nations and international law, which are indispensable foundations of a more peaceful, prosperous and just world, and reiterating its determination to foster strict respect for them, and in this regard commending the Secretary-General and the United Nations system for their continuous efforts to consolidate democracy,

Bearing in mind that the activities of the United Nations carried out in support of Governments to promote and consolidate democracy are undertaken in accordance with the Charter and only at the specific request of the Member States concerned,

Expressing its deep appreciation to the Government of Qatar for the successful organization of the Sixth International Conference of New or Restored Democracies,

Recalling that the Sixth International Conference focused on building capacity, democracy and social progress,

Taking note with satisfaction of the deliberations of the Sixth International Conference, which confirmed the commendable efforts of a considerable number of societies that have undertaken concrete actions to achieve better standards of living and solidarity, good governance practices, economic reforms and sustainable development, the rule of law, justice and equality,

1. *Welcomes* the outcome of the Sixth International Conference of New or Restored Democracies, hosted by Qatar and convened in Doha from 29 October to 1 November 2006;

2. *Also welcomes* the special attention given by the Sixth International Conference to the need for the systematic implementation of the recommendations of the international conferences of new or restored democracies, and urges Qatar, as the Chair of the Sixth International Conference, to proceed with the implementation process and to keep the General Assembly informed, as appropriate, of the progress achieved;

3. *Recognizes* the interactions between Governments, parliaments and civil society organizations at all levels in promoting democracy, freedom, equality, participation, respect for human rights and the rule of law;

4. *Welcomes* the tripartite character (Governments, parliaments, civil society) of the Sixth International Conference, which allowed for greater interaction and cooperation in the common effort of promoting democracy;

5. *Urges* the Secretary-General to continue to improve the capacity of the Organization to respond effectively to the requests of Member States by providing adequate support for their efforts to achieve the goals of good governance and democratization, including through the activities of the Democracy Fund at the United Nations;

6. *Requests* the Secretary-General to continue to play an active role in facilitating international cooperation within the framework of the follow-up to the Sixth International Conference, with the support of other parts of the United Nations system providing democracy assistance or advice, including, as appropriate, the Democracy Fund;

7. *Encourages* Governments to strengthen national programmes devoted to the promotion and consolidation of democracy, including through increased bilateral, regional and international cooperation, taking into account innovative approaches and best practices;

8. *Requests* the Secretary-General to include in his report to the General Assembly at its sixty-second session, under the item entitled "Support by the United Nations system of the efforts of Governments to promote and consolidate new or restored democracies", a summary of the results of the Sixth International Conference.

Regional aspects of international peace and security

South Atlantic

The General Assembly, having in 2005 [YUN 2005, p. 657] deferred consideration of the agenda item on the zone of peace and cooperation of the South Atlantic to its 2006 session, decided, by **decision 61/552** of 22 December, that the item would remain for consideration during its resumed sixty-first (2007) session.

Decolonization

The General Assembly's Special Committee on the Situation with regard to the Implementation of the Declaration on the Granting of Independence to Colonial Countries and Peoples (Special Committee on decolonization) held its annual session in New York in two parts–23 February, 29 March and 27 April (first part); and 5-6, 7, 9, 12-13, 15-16, 22 and 30 June (second part). It considered various aspects of the implementation of the 1960 Declaration, adopted by the Assembly in resolution 1514(XV) [YUN 1960, p. 49], including general decolonization issues and the situation in individual Non-Self Governing Territories (NSGTs). In accordance with Assembly resolution 60/112 [YUN 2005, p. 664], the Special Committee transmitted to the Assembly the report on its 2006 activities [A/61/23].

Decade for the Eradication of Colonialism

Pacific regional seminar

As part of its efforts to implement the plan of action for the Second International Decade for the Eradication of Colonialism (2001-2010) [YUN 2001, p. 530], declared by the General Assembly in resolution 55/146 [YUN 2000, p. 548], the Special Committee on decolonization organized a Pacific regional seminar (Yanuca, Fiji, 28-30 November) [A/61/23/Add.1] to assess the implementation of the plan of action. The case of Tokelau received particular attention.

The seminar recommended that the Special Committee continue to monitor the evolution of NSGTs towards achieving self-determination and include the participation of NSGT representatives, on a case-by-case basis, in consultations between the Special Committee and the administering Powers. It should also develop a mechanism to review annually implementation of the Assembly's specific recommendations on decolonization and the plan of action.

The seminar reaffirmed the need for the Special Committee, in collaboration with the UN Department of Public Information (DPI), to embark on a public awareness campaign aimed at fostering an understanding among the people of the Territories of the options of self-determination included in relevant UN resolutions on decolonization. Participants encouraged DPI to continue to disseminate information, using the communications tools available to it. UN information centres (UNICs) could assist in the process. The cooperation of the Electoral Assistance Division of the UN Department of Political Affairs (DPA) should be requested to provide support and assistance for any consultation or monitoring process to be held in NSGTs regarding any act of self-determination.

The seminar supported closer cooperation between the Special Committee and the Economic and Social Council to promote increased UN assistance in the economic and social sphere to NSGTs. It also urged the Special Committee to solicit the Council's assistance regarding the implementation of its resolution 2006/37 (see p. 702) on support to NSGTs by specialized agencies and international institutions associated with the United Nations. The seminar stressed that the wider UN system should continue to explore ways to strengthen measures of support and formulate programmes of assistance to NSGTs and seek concrete proposals for the full implementation of the relevant resolutions by the specialized agencies, as detailed in Assembly resolution 56/67 [YUN 2001, p. 534]. Participants reiterated their support for the current participation of NSGTs in the UN regional commissions and in the specialized agencies, and called for increased involvement of NSGTs in the programmes and activities of the UN system in furtherance of the decolonization process. They recommended that the Special Committee establish closer ties with relevant regional organizations and encouraged NSGTs to develop closer contacts with them.

Participants welcomed the presence of representatives of France, New Zealand and the United States at the seminar and regretted the lack of representation of the United Kingdom. They reiterated their call to all administering Powers to engage the Special Committee in constructive dialogue.

GENERAL ASSEMBLY ACTION

On 14 December [meeting 79], the General Assembly, on the recommendation of the Fourth (Special Political and Decolonization) Committee [A/61/415], adopted **resolution 61/130** by recorded vote (176-3-2) [agenda item 39].

Implementation of the Declaration on the Granting of Independence to Colonial Countries and Peoples

The General Assembly,

Having examined the report of the Special Committee on the Situation with regard to the Implementation of the Declaration on the Granting of Independence to Colonial Countries and Peoples,

Recalling its resolution 1514(XV) of 14 December 1960, containing the Declaration on the Granting of Independence to Colonial Countries and Peoples, and all its subsequent resolutions concerning the implementation of the Declaration, the most recent of which was resolution 60/119 of 8 December 2005, as well as the relevant resolutions of the Security Council,

Bearing in mind its resolution 55/146 of 8 December 2000, by which it declared the period 2001-2010 the Second International Decade for the Eradication of Colonialism, and the need to examine ways to ascertain the wishes of the peoples of the Non-Self-Governing Territories on the basis of resolution 1514(XV) and other relevant resolutions on decolonization,

Welcoming the Plan of Implementation of the Decolonization Mandate 2006-2007, which organizes the actions of the decolonization mandate to be carried out by the wider United Nations system,

Recognizing that the eradication of colonialism has been one of the priorities of the United Nations and continues to be one of its priorities for the decade that began in 2001,

Reconfirming the need to take measures to eliminate colonialism by 2010, as called for in its resolution 55/146,

Reiterating its conviction of the need for the eradication of colonialism, as well as racial discrimination and violations of basic human rights,

Noting with satisfaction the achievements of the Special Committee in contributing to the effective and complete implementation of the Declaration and other relevant resolutions of the United Nations on decolonization,

Stressing the importance of the formal participation of the administering Powers in the work of the Special Committee,

Noting with interest the cooperation and active participation of some administering Powers in the work of the Special Committee, and encouraging the others also to do so,

Taking note that the Pacific regional seminar, originally scheduled to convene from 23 to 25 May 2006 in Timor-Leste, is to be rescheduled to a later date in 2006,

1. *Reaffirms* its resolution 1514(XV) and all other resolutions and decisions on decolonization, including its resolution 55/146, by which it declared the period 2001-2010 the Second International Decade for the Eradication of Colonialism, and calls upon the administering Powers, in accordance with those resolutions, to take all necessary steps to enable the peoples of the Non-Self-Governing Territories concerned to exercise fully as soon as possible their right to self-determination, including independence;

2. *Reaffirms once again* that the existence of colonialism in any form or manifestation, including economic exploitation, is incompatible with the Charter of the United Nations, the Declaration on the Granting of Independence to Colonial Countries and Peoples and the Universal Declaration of Human Rights;

3. *Reaffirms its determination* to continue to take all steps necessary to bring about the complete and speedy eradication of colonialism and the faithful observance by all States of the relevant provisions of the Charter, the Declaration on the Granting of Independence to Colonial Countries and Peoples and the Universal Declaration of Human Rights;

4. *Affirms once again its support* for the aspirations of the peoples under colonial rule to exercise their right to self-determination, including independence, in accordance with relevant resolutions of the United Nations on decolonization;

5. *Calls upon* the administering Powers to cooperate fully with the Special Committee on the Situation with regard to the Declaration on the Granting of Independence to Colonial Countries and Peoples to finalize before the end of 2007 a constructive programme of work on a case-by-case basis for the Non-Self-Governing Territories to facilitate the implementation of the mandate of the Special Committee and the relevant resolutions on decolonization, including resolutions on specific Territories;

6. *Commends* the professional, open and transparent referendum to determine the future status of Tokelau, held under United Nations supervision from 11 to 15 February 2006;

7. *Notes* that the referendum did not produce the two-thirds majority of the valid votes cast required by the General Fono to change the status of Tokelau as a Non-Self-Governing Territory under the administration of New Zealand;

8. *Welcomes* the agreement of New Zealand and the Tokelau Council of Ongoing Government to maintain the referendum package of a draft constitution and draft treaty of free association as a possible future basis for an act of self-determination by Tokelau;

9. *Also welcomes* the dispatch of the United Nations special mission to the Turks and Caicos Islands, at the request of the territorial Government and with the concurrence of the administering Power, which provided information to the people of the Territory on the role of the United Nations in the process of self-determination, on the legitimate political status options, as clearly defined in General Assembly resolution 1541(XV) of 15 December 1960, and on the experiences of other small States which have achieved a full measure of self-government;

10. *Requests* the Special Committee to continue to seek suitable means for the immediate and full implementation of the Declaration and to carry out the actions approved by the General Assembly regarding the International Decade for the Eradication of Colonialism and the Second International Decade for the Eradication of Colonialism in all Territories that have not yet exercised their right to self-determination, including independence, and in particular:

(a) To formulate specific proposals to bring about an end to colonialism and to report thereon to the General Assembly at its sixty-second session;

(b) To continue to examine the implementation by Member States of resolution 1514(XV) and other relevant resolutions on decolonization;

(c) To continue to examine the political, economic and social situation in the Non-Self-Governing Territories, and to recommend, as appropriate, to the General Assembly the most suitable steps to be taken to enable the populations of those Territories to exercise their right to self-determination, including independence, in accordance with relevant resolutions on decolonization, including resolutions on specific Territories;

(d) To finalize before the end of 2007 a constructive programme of work on a case-by-case basis for the Non-Self-Governing Territories to facilitate the implementation of the mandate of the Special Committee and the relevant resolutions on decolonization, including resolutions on specific Territories;

(e) To continue to dispatch visiting missions to the Non-Self-Governing Territories in accordance with relevant resolutions on decolonization, including resolutions on specific Territories;

(f) To conduct seminars, as appropriate, for the purpose of receiving and disseminating information on the work of the Special Committee, and to facilitate participation by the peoples of the Non-Self-Governing Territories in those seminars;

(g) To take all necessary steps to enlist worldwide support among Governments, as well as national and international organizations, for the achievement of the objectives of the Declaration and the implementation of the relevant resolutions of the United Nations;

(h) To observe annually the Week of Solidarity with the Peoples of Non-Self-Governing Territories;

11. *Recognizes* that the plan of action for the Second International Decade for the Eradication of Colonialism, the case-by-case process of assessment of the attainment of self-government in each Territory, and the Plan of Implementation of the Decolonization Mandate 2006-2007 represent an important legislative authority for the attainment of self-government by the end of 2010;

12. *Calls upon* all States, in particular the administering Powers, as well as the specialized agencies and other organizations of the United Nations system, to give effect within their respective spheres of competence to the recommendations of the Special Committee for the

implementation of the Declaration and other relevant resolutions of the United Nations;

13. *Calls upon* the administering Powers to ensure that the economic activities in the Non-Self-Governing Territories under their administration do not adversely affect the interests of the peoples but instead promote development, and to assist them in the exercise of their right to self-determination;

14. *Urges* the administering Powers concerned to take effective measures to safeguard and guarantee the inalienable rights of the peoples of the Non-Self-Governing Territories to their natural resources, including land, and to establish and maintain control over the future development of those resources, and requests the administering Powers to take all necessary steps to protect the property rights of the peoples of those Territories;

15. *Urges* all States, directly and through their action in the specialized agencies and other organizations of the United Nations system, to provide moral and material assistance to the peoples of the Non-Self-Governing Territories, and requests the administering Powers to take steps to enlist and make effective use of all possible assistance, on both a bilateral and a multilateral basis, in the strengthening of the economies of those Territories;

16. *Reaffirms* that the United Nations visiting missions to the Territories are an effective means of ascertaining the situation in the Territories, as well as the wishes and aspirations of their inhabitants, and calls upon the administering Powers to continue to cooperate with the Special Committee in the discharge of its mandate and to facilitate visiting missions to the Territories;

17. *Calls upon* the administering Powers that have not participated formally in the work of the Special Committee to do so at its session in 2007;

18. *Requests* the Secretary-General, the specialized agencies and other organizations of the United Nations system to provide economic, social and other assistance to the Non-Self-Governing Territories and to continue to do so, as appropriate, after they exercise their right to self-determination, including independence;

19. *Approves* the report of the Special Committee on the Situation with regard to the Implementation of the Declaration on the Granting of Independence to Colonial Countries and Peoples covering its work during 2006, including the programme of work envisaged for 2007;

20. *Requests* the Secretary-General to provide the Special Committee with the facilities and services required for the implementation of the present resolution, as well as the other resolutions and decisions on decolonization adopted by the General Assembly and the Special Committee.

RECORDED VOTE ON RESOLUTION 61/130:

In favour: Afghanistan, Albania, Algeria, Andorra, Angola, Antigua and Barbuda, Argentina, Armenia, Australia, Austria, Azerbaijan, Bahamas, Bahrain, Bangladesh, Barbados, Belarus, Belize, Benin, Bhutan, Bolivia, Bosnia and Herzegovina, Botswana, Brazil, Brunei Darussalam, Bulgaria, Burkina Faso, Burundi, Cambodia, Cameroon, Canada, Cape Verde, Central African Republic, Chad, Chile, China, Colombia, Comoros, Congo, Costa Rica, Côte d'Ivoire, Croatia, Cuba, Cyprus, Czech Republic, Democratic People's Republic of Korea, Democratic Republic of the Congo, Denmark, Djibouti, Dominica, Dominican Republic, Ecuador, Egypt, El Salvador, Equatorial Guinea, Eritrea, Estonia, Ethiopia, Fiji, Finland, Gabon, Georgia, Germany, Ghana, Greece, Grenada, Guatemala, Guinea, Guinea-Bissau, Guyana, Haiti, Honduras, Hungary, Iceland, India, Indonesia, Iran, Iraq, Ireland, Italy, Jamaica, Japan, Jordan, Kazakhstan, Kenya, Kuwait, Kyrgyzstan, Lao People's Democratic Republic, Latvia, Lesotho, Libyan Arab Jamahiriya, Liechtenstein, Lithuania, Luxembourg, Madagascar, Malawi, Malaysia, Maldives, Mali, Malta, Marshall Islands, Mauritania, Mauritius, Moldova, Monaco, Mongolia, Montenegro, Morocco, Mozambique, Myanmar, Namibia, Nauru, Nepal, Netherlands, New Zealand, Nicaragua, Niger, Nigeria, Norway, Oman, Pakistan, Palau, Panama, Papua New Guinea, Paraguay, Peru, Philippines, Poland, Portugal, Qatar, Republic of Korea, Romania, Russian Federation, Rwanda, Saint Lucia, Saint Vincent and the Grenadines, Samoa, San Marino, Sao Tome and Principe, Saudi Arabia, Senegal, Serbia, Sierra Leone, Singapore, Slovakia, Slovenia, Solomon Islands, South Africa, Spain, Sri Lanka, Sudan, Suriname, Swaziland, Sweden, Switzerland, Syrian Arab Republic, Tajikistan, Thailand, The former Yugoslav Republic of Macedonia, Timor-Leste, Togo, Tonga, Trinidad and Tobago, Tunisia, Turkey, Tuvalu, Uganda, Ukraine, United Arab Emirates, United Republic of Tanzania, Uruguay, Vanuatu, Venezuela, Viet Nam, Yemen, Zambia, Zimbabwe.

Against: Israel, United Kingdom, United States.

Abstaining: Belgium, France.

Implementation by international organizations

In a March report [A/61/62], the Secretary-General stated that he had brought General Assembly resolution 60/112 [YUN 2005, p. 664] to the attention of specialized agencies and other international institutions associated with the United Nations and had invited them to submit information regarding their implementation activities in support of NSGTs. Replies received from five agencies or institutions were summarized in a May report of the Economic and Social Council President on consultations with the Special Committee on decolonization [E/2006/47]. According to the information provided, a number of specialized agencies and organizations continued to provide support to NSGTs from their own budgetary resources, in addition to their respective contributions as executing agencies of projects funded by the United Nations Development Programme (UNDP), the primary provider of support. Three specialized agencies indicated that they were not currently carrying out any assistance programmes in NSGTs.

ECONOMIC AND SOCIAL COUNCIL ACTION

On 27 July [meeting 41], the Economic and Social Council adopted **resolution 2006/37** [draft:

E/2006/L.27] by recorded vote (29-0-20) [agenda item 9].

Support to Non-Self-Governing Territories by the specialized agencies and international institutions associated with the United Nations

The Economic and Social Council,

Having examined the report of the Secretary-General and the report of the President of the Economic and Social Council containing the information submitted by the specialized agencies and the international institutions associated with the United Nations on their activities with regard to the implementation of the Declaration on the Granting of Independence to Colonial Countries and Peoples,

Having heard the statement by the representative of the Special Committee on the Situation with regard to the Implementation of the Declaration on the Granting of Independence to Colonial Countries and Peoples,

Recalling General Assembly resolutions 1514(XV) of 14 December 1960 and 1541(XV) of 15 December 1960, the resolutions of the Special Committee and other relevant resolutions and decisions, including, in particular, Economic and Social Council resolution 2005/49 of 27 July 2005,

Bearing in mind the relevant provisions of the final documents of the successive Conferences of Heads of State or Government of Non-Aligned Countries and of the resolutions adopted by the Assembly of Heads of State and Government of the African Union, the Pacific Islands Forum and the Caribbean Community,

Conscious of the need to facilitate the implementation of the Declaration on the Granting of Independence to Colonial Countries and Peoples,

Welcoming the participation, in the capacity of observer, of those Non-Self-Governing Territories that are associate members of the regional commissions in world conferences in the economic and social sphere, subject to the rules of procedure of the General Assembly and in accordance with relevant United Nations resolutions and decisions, including resolutions and decisions of the Assembly and the Special Committee on specific Territories,

Noting that only some specialized agencies and organizations of the United Nations system have been involved in providing assistance to Non-Self-Governing Territories,

Welcoming the assistance extended to Non-Self-Governing Territories by certain specialized agencies and other organizations of the United Nations system, in particular the United Nations Development Programme,

Stressing that, because the development options of the small island Non-Self-Governing Territories are limited, there are special challenges to planning for and implementing sustainable development and that those Territories will be constrained in meeting the challenges without the continued cooperation and assistance of the specialized agencies and other organizations of the United Nations system,

Stressing also the importance of securing the resources necessary to fund expanded programmes of assistance for the peoples concerned and the need to enlist the support of all the major funding institutions within the United Nations system in that regard,

Reaffirming the mandate of the specialized agencies and other organizations of the United Nations system to take all appropriate measures, within their respective spheres of competence, to ensure the full implementation of Assembly resolution 1514(XV) and other relevant resolutions,

Expressing its appreciation to the African Union, the Pacific Islands Forum, the Caribbean Community and other regional organizations for the continued cooperation and assistance they have extended to the specialized agencies and other organizations of the United Nations system in this regard,

Expressing its conviction that closer contacts and consultations between and among the specialized agencies and other organizations of the United Nations system and regional organizations help to facilitate the effective formulation of programmes of assistance for the peoples concerned,

Mindful of the imperative need to keep under continuous review the activities of the specialized agencies and other organizations of the United Nations system in the implementation of the various United Nations decisions related to decolonization,

Bearing in mind the extremely fragile economies of the small island Non-Self-Governing Territories and their vulnerability to natural disasters, such as hurricanes, cyclones and sea-level rise, and recalling the relevant resolutions of the General Assembly,

Recalling General Assembly resolution 60/112 of 8 December 2005, entitled "Implementation of the Declaration on the Granting of Independence to Colonial Countries and Peoples by the specialized agencies and the international institutions associated with the United Nations",

1. *Takes note* of the report of the President of the Economic and Social Council, and endorses the observations and suggestions arising therefrom;

2. *Also takes note* of the report of the Secretary-General;

3. *Recommends* that all States intensify their efforts in the specialized agencies and other organizations of the United Nations system of which they are members to ensure the full and effective implementation of the Declaration on the Granting of Independence to Colonial Countries and Peoples by the specialized agencies and the international institutions associated with the United Nations contained in General Assembly resolution 1514(XV), and other relevant resolutions of the United Nations;

4. *Reaffirms* that the specialized agencies and other organizations and institutions of the United Nations system should continue to be guided by the relevant resolutions of the United Nations in their efforts to contribute to the implementation of the Declaration and all other relevant General Assembly resolutions;

5. *Also reaffirms* that the recognition by the General Assembly, the Security Council and other United Nations organs of the legitimacy of the aspirations of the peoples of the Non-Self-Governing Territories to exercise their right to self-determination entails, as a corollary, the extension of all appropriate assistance to those peoples;

6. *Expresses its appreciation* to those specialized agencies and other organizations of the United Nations system that have continued to cooperate with the United Nations and the regional and subregional organizations in the implementation of Assembly resolution 1514(XV) and other relevant resolutions of the United Nations, and requests all the specialized agencies and other organizations of the United Nations system to implement the relevant provisions of those resolutions;

7. *Requests* the specialized agencies and other organizations of the United Nations system and international and regional organizations to examine and review conditions in each Territory so as to take appropriate measures to accelerate progress in the economic and social sectors of the Territories;

8. *Requests* the specialized agencies and other organizations and bodies of the United Nations system and regional organizations to strengthen existing measures of support and to formulate appropriate programmes of assistance to the remaining Non-Self-Governing Territories, within the framework of their respective mandates, in order to accelerate progress in the economic and social sectors of those Territories;

9. *Recommends* that the executive heads of the specialized agencies and other organizations of the United Nations system formulate, with the active cooperation of the regional organizations concerned, concrete proposals for the full implementation of the relevant resolutions of the United Nations and submit the proposals to their governing and legislative organs;

10. *Also recommends* that the specialized agencies and other organizations of the United Nations system continue to review, at the regular meetings of their governing bodies, the implementation of Assembly resolution 1514(XV) and other relevant resolutions of the United Nations;

11. *Welcomes* the continuing initiative exercised by the United Nations Development Programme in maintaining close liaison among the specialized agencies and other organizations of the United Nations system, including the Economic Commission for Latin America and the Caribbean and the Economic and Social Commission for Asia and the Pacific, and in providing assistance to the peoples of the Non-Self-Governing Territories;

12. *Requests* the Department of Public Information of the Secretariat, in consultation with the United Nations Development Programme, the specialized agencies and the Special Committee on the Situation with regard to the Implementation of the Declaration on the Granting of Independence to Colonial Countries and Peoples, to prepare an information leaflet on assistance programmes available to the Non-Self-Governing Territories and to disseminate it widely among them;

13. *Encourages* Non-Self-Governing Territories to take steps to establish and/or strengthen disaster preparedness and management institutions and policies;

14. *Requests* the administering Powers concerned to facilitate, when appropriate, the participation of appointed and elected representatives of Non-Self-Governing Territories in the meetings and conferences of the specialized agencies and other organizations of the United Nations system, in accordance with relevant United Nations resolutions and decisions, including resolutions and decisions of the General Assembly and the Special Committee relating to specific Territories, so that the Territories may benefit from the related activities of those agencies and organizations;

15. *Recommends* that all Governments intensify their efforts in the specialized agencies and other organizations of the United Nations system of which they are members to accord priority to the question of providing assistance to the peoples of the Non-Self-Governing Territories;

16. *Draws the attention* of the Special Committee to the present resolution and to the discussion held on the subject at the substantive session of 2006 of the Economic and Social Council;

17. *Welcomes* the adoption by the Economic Commission for Latin America and the Caribbean of its resolution 574(XXVII) of 16 May 1998 calling for the mechanisms necessary for its associate members, including small island Non-Self-Governing Territories, to participate in the special sessions of the General Assembly, subject to the rules of procedure of the Assembly, to review and assess the implementation of the plans of action of those United Nations world conferences in which the Territories originally participated in the capacity of observer, and in the work of the Economic and Social Council and its subsidiary bodies;

18. *Requests* the President of the Council to continue to maintain close contact on these matters with the Chairman of the Special Committee and to report thereon to the Council;

19. *Requests* the Secretary-General to follow the implementation of the present resolution, paying particular attention to cooperation and integration arrangements for maximizing the efficiency of the assistance activities undertaken by various organizations of the United Nations system, and to report thereon to the Council at its substantive session of 2007;

20. *Decides* to keep these questions under continuous review.

RECORDED VOTE ON RESOLUTION 2006/37:

In favour: Angola, Armenia, Bangladesh, Belize, Benin, Brazil, China, Colombia, Costa Rica, Cuba, Guinea, Guyana, Haiti, India, Indonesia, Madagascar, Mauritania, Mexico, Namibia, Nigeria, Pakistan, Paraguay, Saudi Arabia, South Africa, Sri Lanka, Thailand, Tunisia, United Arab Emirates, United Republic of Tanzania.

Against: None.

Abtaining: Albania, Australia, Austria, Belgium, Canada, Czech Republic, France, Germany, Iceland, Italy, Japan, Lithuania, Mauritius, Poland, Republic of Korea, Russian Federation, Spain, Turkey, United Kingdom, United States.

GENERAL ASSEMBLY ACTION

On 22 December [meeting 84], the General Assembly, on the recommendation of the Fourth Committee [A/61/413], adopted **resolution 61/231** by recorded vote (100-1-52) [agenda item 37].

Implementation of the Declaration on the Granting of Independence to Colonial Countries and Peoples by the specialized agencies and the international institutions associated with the United Nations

The General Assembly,

Having considered the item entitled "Implementation of the Declaration on the Granting of Independence to Colonial Countries and Peoples by the specialized agencies and the international institutions associated with the United Nations",

Having also considered the report of the Secretary-General and the report of the Economic and Social Council on the item,

Having examined the chapter of the report of the Special Committee on the Situation with regard to the Implementation of the Declaration on the Granting of Independence to Colonial Countries and Peoples relating to the item,

Recalling its resolutions 1514(XV) of 14 December 1960 and 1541(XV) of 15 December 1960 and the resolutions of the Special Committee, as well as other relevant resolutions and decisions, including in particular Economic and Social Council resolution 2005/49 of 27 July 2005,

Bearing in mind the relevant provisions of the final documents of the successive Conferences of Heads of State or Government of Non-Aligned Countries and of the resolutions adopted by the Assembly of Heads of State and Government of the African Union, the Pacific Islands Forum and the Caribbean Community,

Conscious of the need to facilitate the implementation of the Declaration on the Granting of Independence to Colonial Countries and Peoples, contained in resolution 1514(XV),

Noting that the large majority of the remaining Non-Self-Governing Territories are small island Territories,

Welcoming the assistance extended to Non-Self-Governing Territories by certain specialized agencies and other organizations of the United Nations system, in particular the United Nations Development Programme,

Also welcoming the current participation in the capacity of observers of those Non-Self-Governing Territories that are associate members of regional commissions in the world conferences in the economic and social sphere, subject to the rules of procedure of the General Assembly and in accordance with relevant United Nations resolutions and decisions, including resolutions and decisions of the Assembly and the Special Committee on specific Territories,

Noting that only some specialized agencies and other organizations of the United Nations system have been involved in providing assistance to Non-Self-Governing Territories,

Stressing that, because the development options of the small island Non-Self-Governing Territories are limited, there are special challenges to planning for and implementing sustainable development and that those Territories will be constrained in meeting the challenges without the continuing cooperation and assistance of the specialized agencies and other organizations of the United Nations system,

Stressing also the importance of securing the necessary resources for funding expanded programmes of assistance for the peoples concerned and the need to enlist the support of all major funding institutions within the United Nations system in that regard,

Reaffirming the mandates of the specialized agencies and other organizations of the United Nations system to take all appropriate measures, within their respective spheres of competence, to ensure the full implementation of General Assembly resolution 1514(XV) and other relevant resolutions,

Expressing its appreciation to the African Union, the Pacific Islands Forum, the Caribbean Community and other regional organizations for the continued cooperation and assistance they have extended to the specialized agencies and other organizations of the United Nations system in this regard,

Expressing its conviction that closer contacts and consultations between and among the specialized agencies and other organizations of the United Nations system and regional organizations help to facilitate the effective formulation of programmes of assistance to the peoples concerned,

Mindful of the imperative need to keep under continuous review the activities of the specialized agencies and other organizations of the United Nations system in the implementation of the various United Nations resolutions and decisions relating to decolonization,

Bearing in mind the extremely fragile economies of the small island Non-Self-Governing Territories and their vulnerability to natural disasters, such as hurricanes, cyclones and sea-level rise, and recalling the relevant resolutions of the General Assembly,

Recalling its resolution 60/112 of 8 December 2005 on the implementation of the Declaration by the specialized agencies and the international institutions associated with the United Nations,

1. *Takes note* of the report of the Secretary-General;

2. *Recommends* that all States intensify their efforts in the specialized agencies and other organizations of the United Nations system in which they are members to ensure the full and effective implementation of the Declaration on the Granting of Independence to Colonial Countries and Peoples, contained in General Assembly resolution 1514(XV), and other relevant resolutions of the United Nations;

3. *Reaffirms* that the specialized agencies and other organizations and institutions of the United Nations system should continue to be guided by the relevant resolutions of the United Nations in their efforts to contribute to the implementation of the Declaration and all other relevant resolutions of the General Assembly;

4. *Reaffirms also* that the recognition by the General Assembly, the Security Council and other United Nations organs of the legitimacy of the aspirations of the peoples of the Non-Self-Governing Territories to exercise their right to self-determination entails, as a corollary, the extension of all appropriate assistance to those peoples;

5. *Expresses its appreciation* to those specialized agencies and other organizations of the United Nations system that have continued to cooperate with the United Nations and the regional and subregional organizations in the implementation of General Assembly resolution 1514(XV) and other relevant resolutions of the United Nations, and requests all the specialized agencies and other organizations of the United Nations system to implement the relevant provisions of those resolutions;

6. *Requests* the specialized agencies and other organizations of the United Nations system and international and regional organizations to examine and review conditions in each Territory so as to take appropriate measures to accelerate progress in the economic and social sectors of the Territories;

7. *Urges* those specialized agencies and organizations of the United Nations system that have not yet provided assistance to Non-Self-Governing Territories to do so as soon as possible;

8. *Requests* the specialized agencies and other organizations and institutions of the United Nations system and regional organizations to strengthen existing measures of support and formulate appropriate programmes of assistance to the remaining Non-Self-Governing Territories, within the framework of their respective mandates, in order to accelerate progress in the economic and social sectors of those Territories;

9. *Requests* the specialized agencies and other organizations of the United Nations system concerned to provide information on:

(a) Environmental problems facing the Non-Self-Governing Territories;

(b) The impact of natural disasters, such as hurricanes and volcanic eruptions, and other environmental problems, such as beach and coastal erosion and droughts, on those Territories;

(c) Ways and means to assist the Territories to fight drug trafficking, money-laundering and other illegal and criminal activities;

(d) The illegal exploitation of the marine resources of the Territories and the need to utilize those resources for the benefit of the peoples of the Territories;

10. *Recommends* that the executive heads of the specialized agencies and other organizations of the United Nations system formulate, with the active cooperation of the regional organizations concerned, concrete proposals for the full implementation of the relevant resolutions of the United Nations and submit the proposals to their governing and legislative organs;

11. *Also recommends* that the specialized agencies and other organizations of the United Nations system continue to review at the regular meetings of their governing bodies the implementation of General Assembly resolution 1514(XV) and other relevant resolutions of the United Nations;

12. *Welcomes* the adoption by the Economic Commission for Latin America and the Caribbean of its resolution 574(XXVII) of 16 May 1998 calling for the creation of mechanisms for the Non-Self-Governing Territories that are associate members of the Commission to participate in the special sessions of the General Assembly, subject to the rules of procedure of the Assembly, to review and assess the implementation of the plans of action of those United Nations world conferences in which the Territories originally participated in the capacity of observer, and in the work of the Economic and Social Council and its subsidiary bodies, and takes note of Commission resolution 598(XXX) of 2 July 2004 on the issue;

13. *Takes note* of resolution 62(XXI) of the Caribbean Development and Cooperation Committee, adopted on 17 January 2006, in which the Committee expressed support for the implementation of Commission resolution 598(XXX) and requested the Commission to disseminate a background note on the matter;

14. *Requests* the Chairman of the Special Committee on the Situation with regard to the Implementation of the Declaration on the Granting of Independence to Colonial Countries and Peoples to continue to maintain close contact on these matters with the President of the Economic and Social Council;

15. *Requests* the Department of Public Information of the Secretariat, in consultation with the United Nations Development Programme, the specialized agencies and the Special Committee, to prepare an information leaflet on assistance programmes available to the Non-Self-Governing Territories and to disseminate it widely in them;

16. *Welcomes* the continuing initiative exercised by the United Nations Development Programme in maintaining close liaison among the specialized agencies and other organizations of the United Nations system, including the Economic Commission for Latin America and the Caribbean and the Economic and Social Commission for Asia and the Pacific, and in providing assistance to the peoples of the Non-Self-Governing Territories;

17. *Encourages* the Non-Self-Governing Territories to take steps to establish and/or strengthen disaster preparedness and management institutions and policies;

18. *Requests* the administering Powers concerned to facilitate, when appropriate, the participation of appointed and elected representatives of Non-Self-Governing Territories in the relevant meetings and conferences of the specialized agencies and other organizations of the United Nations system, in accordance with relevant United Nations resolutions and decisions, including resolutions and decisions of the General Assembly and the Special Committee on specific Territories, so that the Territories may benefit from the related activities of those agencies and organizations;

19. *Recommends* that all Governments intensify their efforts in the specialized agencies and other organizations of the United Nations system of which they are members

to accord priority to the question of providing assistance to the peoples of the Non-Self-Governing Territories;

20. *Requests* the Secretary-General to continue to assist the specialized agencies and other organizations of the United Nations system in working out appropriate measures for implementing the relevant resolutions of the United Nations and to prepare for submission to the relevant bodies, with the assistance of those agencies and organizations, a report on the action taken in implementation of the relevant resolutions, including the present resolution, since the circulation of his previous report;

21. *Commends* the Economic and Social Council for its debate and resolution on this question, and requests it to continue to consider, in consultation with the Special Committee, appropriate measures for the coordination of the policies and activities of the specialized agencies and other organizations of the United Nations system in implementing the relevant resolutions of the General Assembly;

22. *Requests* the specialized agencies to report periodically to the Secretary-General on the implementation of the present resolution;

23. *Requests* the Secretary-General to transmit the present resolution to the governing bodies of the appropriate specialized agencies and international institutions associated with the United Nations so that those bodies may take the necessary measures to implement the resolution, and also requests the Secretary-General to report to the General Assembly at its sixty-second session on the implementation of the present resolution;

24. *Requests* the Special Committee to continue to examine the question and to report thereon to the General Assembly at its sixty-second session.

RECORDED VOTE ON RESOLUTION 61/231:

In favour: Algeria, Angola, Antigua and Barbuda, Australia, Bahamas, Bahrain, Bangladesh, Barbados, Belarus, Belize, Bhutan, Bolivia, Botswana, Brazil, Brunei Darussalam, Cambodia, Cameroon, Cape Verde, Central African Republic, Chile, Colombia, Comoros, Congo, Costa Rica, Cuba, Democratic People's Republic of Korea, Djibouti, Dominica, Ecuador, Egypt, El Salvador, Eritrea, Ethiopia, Fiji, Ghana, Grenada, Guatemala, Guinea, Guinea-Bissau, Guyana, Honduras, India, Indonesia, Iran, Iraq, Jamaica, Jordan, Kenya, Kuwait, Libyan Arab Jamahiriya, Madagascar, Malaysia, Maldives, Mali, Mauritius, Mexico, Morocco, Mozambique, Myanmar, Namibia, Nauru, Nepal, New Zealand, Nicaragua, Niger, Nigeria, Oman, Palau, Panama, Paraguay, Peru, Qatar, Saint Lucia, Saint Vincent and the Grenadines, Sao Tome and Principe, Saudi Arabia, Senegal, Sierra Leone, Singapore, Solomon Islands, South Africa, Sri Lanka, Sudan, Suriname, Swaziland, Syrian Arab Republic, Thailand, Timor-Leste, Tonga, Trinidad and Tobago, Tunisia, United Arab Emirates, United Republic of Tanzania, Uruguay, Uzbekistan, Venezuela, Viet Nam, Yemen, Zambia, Zimbabwe.

Against: United States.

Abstaining: Albania, Andorra, Argentina, Armenia, Austria, Belgium, Bosnia and Herzegovina, Bulgaria, Canada, Croatia, Cyprus, Czech Republic, Denmark, Estonia, Finland, France, Georgia, Germany, Greece, Hungary, Iceland, Ireland, Israel, Italy, Japan, Latvia, Liberia, Liechtenstein, Lithuania, Luxembourg, Malta, Micronesia, Moldova, Monaco, Netherlands, Norway, Poland, Portugal, Republic of Korea, Romania, Russian Federation, San Marino, Serbia, Slovakia, Slovenia, Spain, Sweden, Switzerland, The former Yugoslav Republic of Macedonia, Turkey, Ukraine, United Kingdom.

Military activities and arrangements in colonial countries

In accordance with General Assembly decision 57/525 [YUN 2002, p. 564], Secretariat working papers submitted to the Special Committee on Decolonization on Bermuda [A/AC.109/2006/6], Guam [A/AC.109/2006/8] and the United States Virgin Islands [A/AC.109/2006/11] contained information on, among other subjects, military activities and arrangements by the administering Powers in those Territories.

Economic and other activities affecting the interests of NSGTS

The Special Committee on decolonization continued consideration of economic and other activities affecting the interests of the peoples of NSGTs. It had before it Secretariat working papers containing information on, among other things, economic conditions in Anguilla [A/AC.109/2006/4], Bermuda [A/AC.109/2006/6], the British Virgin Islands [A/AC.109/2006/12], the Cayman Islands [A/AC.109/2006/16], Montserrat [A/AC.109/2006/13], New Caledonia [A/AC.109/2006/14] and the Turks and Caicos Islands [A/AC.109/2006/15].

GENERAL ASSEMBLY ACTION

On 14 December [meeting 79], the General Assembly, on the recommendation of the Fourth Committee [A/61/412], adopted **resolution 61/123** by recorded vote (179-2-2) [agenda item 36].

Economic and other activities which affect the interests of the peoples of the Non-Self-Governing Territories

The General Assembly,

Having considered the item entitled "Economic and other activities which affect the interests of the peoples of the Non-Self-Governing Territories",

Having examined the chapter of the report of the Special Committee on the Situation with regard to the Implementation of the Declaration on the Granting of Independence to Colonial Countries and Peoples relating to the item,

Recalling General Assembly resolution 1514(XV) of 14 December 1960, as well as all other relevant resolutions of the Assembly, including, in particular, resolutions 46/181 of 19 December 1991 and 55/146 of 8 December 2000,

Reaffirming the solemn obligation of the administering Powers under the Charter of the United Nations to promote the political, economic, social and educational advancement of the inhabitants of the Territories under their administration and to protect the human and natural resources of those Territories against abuses,

Reaffirming also that any economic or other activity that has a negative impact on the interests of the peoples of the Non-Self-Governing Territories and on the exercise of their right to self-determination in conformity with the Charter and General Assembly resolution 1514(XV) is contrary to the purposes and principles of the Charter,

Reaffirming further that the natural resources are the heritage of the peoples of the Non-Self-Governing Territories, including the indigenous populations,

Aware of the special circumstances of the geographical location, size and economic conditions of each Territory, and bearing in mind the need to promote the economic stability, diversification and strengthening of the economy of each Territory,

Conscious of the particular vulnerability of the small Territories to natural disasters and environmental degradation,

Conscious also that foreign economic investment, when undertaken in collaboration with the peoples of the Non-Self-Governing Territories and in accordance with their wishes, could make a valid contribution to the socio-economic development of the Territories and also to the exercise of their right to self-determination,

Concerned about any activities aimed at exploiting the natural and human resources of the Non-Self-Governing Territories to the detriment of the interests of the inhabitants of those Territories,

Bearing in mind the relevant provisions of the final documents of the successive Conferences of Heads of State or Government of Non-Aligned Countries and of the resolutions adopted by the Assembly of Heads of State and Government of the African Union, the Pacific Islands Forum and the Caribbean Community,

1. *Reaffirms* the right of peoples of Non-Self-Governing Territories to self-determination in conformity with the Charter of the United Nations and with General Assembly resolution 1514(XV), containing the Declaration on the Granting of Independence to Colonial Countries and Peoples, as well as their right to the enjoyment of their natural resources and their right to dispose of those resources in their best interest;

2. *Affirms* the value of foreign economic investment undertaken in collaboration with the peoples of the Non-Self-Governing Territories and in accordance with their wishes in order to make a valid contribution to the socio-economic development of the Territories;

3. *Reaffirms* the responsibility of the administering Powers under the Charter to promote the political, economic, social and educational advancement of the Non-Self-Governing Territories, and reaffirms the legitimate rights of their peoples over their natural resources;

4. *Reaffirms its concern* about any activities aimed at the exploitation of the natural resources that are the heritage of the peoples of the Non-Self-Governing Territories, including the indigenous populations, in the Caribbean, the Pacific and other regions, and of their human resources, to the detriment of their interests, and in such a way as to deprive them of their right to dispose of those resources;

5. *Reaffirms* the need to avoid any economic and other activities that adversely affect the interests of the peoples of the Non-Self-Governing Territories;

6. *Calls once again upon* all Governments that have not yet done so to take, in accordance with the relevant provisions of General Assembly resolution 2621(XXV) of 12 October 1970, legislative, administrative or other measures in respect of their nationals and the bodies corporate under their jurisdiction that own and operate enterprises in the Non-Self-Governing Territories that are detrimental to the interests of the inhabitants of those Territories, in order to put an end to such enterprises;

7. *Reiterates* that the damaging exploitation and plundering of the marine and other natural resources of the Non-Self-Governing Territories, in violation of the relevant resolutions of the United Nations, are a threat to the integrity and prosperity of those Territories;

8. *Invites* all Governments and organizations of the United Nations system to take all possible measures to ensure that the permanent sovereignty of the peoples of the Non-Self-Governing Territories over their natural resources is fully respected and safeguarded in accordance with the relevant resolutions of the United Nations on decolonization;

9. *Urges* the administering Powers concerned to take effective measures to safeguard and guarantee the inalienable right of the peoples of the Non-Self-Governing Territories to their natural resources and to establish and maintain control over the future development of those resources, and requests the administering Powers to take all necessary steps to protect the property rights of the peoples of those Territories in accordance with the relevant resolutions of the United Nations on decolonization;

10. *Calls upon* the administering Powers concerned to ensure that no discriminatory working conditions prevail in the Territories under their administration and to promote in each Territory a fair system of wages applicable to all the inhabitants without any discrimination;

11. *Requests* the Secretary-General to continue, through all means at his disposal, to inform world public opinion of any activity that affects the exercise of the right of the peoples of the Non-Self-Governing Territories to self-determination in conformity with the Charter and General Assembly resolution 1514(XV);

12. *Appeals* to trade unions and non-governmental organizations, as well as individuals, to continue their efforts to promote the economic well-being of the peoples of the Non-Self-Governing Territories, and also appeals to the media to disseminate information about the developments in this regard;

13. *Decides* to follow the situation in the Non-Self-Governing Territories so as to ensure that all economic activities in those Territories are aimed at strengthening and diversifying their economies in the interest of their peoples, including the indigenous populations, and at

promoting the economic and financial viability of those Territories;

14. *Requests* the Special Committee on the Situation with regard to the Implementation of the Declaration on the Granting of Independence to Colonial Countries and Peoples to continue to examine this question and to report thereon to the General Assembly at its sixty-second session.

RECORDED VOTE ON RESOLUTION 61/123:

In favour: Afghanistan, Albania, Algeria, Andorra, Angola, Antigua and Barbuda, Argentina, Armenia, Australia, Austria, Azerbaijan, Bahamas, Bahrain, Bangladesh, Barbados, Belarus, Belgium, Belize, Benin, Bhutan, Bolivia, Bosnia and Herzegovina, Botswana, Brazil, Brunei Darussalam, Bulgaria, Burkina Faso, Burundi, Cambodia, Cameroon, Canada, Cape Verde, Central African Republic, Chad, Chile, China, Colombia, Comoros, Congo, Costa Rica, Côte d'Ivoire, Croatia, Cuba, Cyprus, Czech Republic, Democratic People's Republic of Korea, Democratic Republic of the Congo, Denmark, Djibouti, Dominica, Dominican Republic, Ecuador, Egypt, El Salvador, Equatorial Guinea, Eritrea, Estonia, Ethiopia, Fiji, Finland, Gabon, Georgia, Germany, Ghana, Greece, Grenada, Guatemala, Guinea, Guinea-Bissau, Guyana, Haiti, Honduras, Hungary, Iceland, India, Indonesia, Iran, Iraq, Ireland, Italy, Jamaica, Japan, Jordan, Kazakhstan, Kenya, Kuwait, Kyrgyzstan, Lao People's Democratic Republic, Latvia, Lesotho, Libyan Arab Jamahiriya, Liechtenstein, Lithuania, Luxembourg, Madagascar, Malawi, Malaysia, Maldives, Mali, Malta, Marshall Islands, Mauritania, Mauritius, Mexico, Micronesia, Moldova, Mongolia, Montenegro, Morocco, Mozambique, Myanmar, Namibia, Nauru, Nepal, Netherlands, New Zealand, Nicaragua, Niger, Nigeria, Norway, Oman, Pakistan, Palau, Panama, Papua New Guinea, Paraguay, Peru, Philippines, Poland, Portugal, Qatar, Republic of Korea, Romania, Russian Federation, Rwanda, Saint Lucia, Saint Vincent and the Grenadines, Samoa, San Marino, Sao Tome and Principe, Saudi Arabia, Senegal, Serbia, Sierra Leone, Singapore, Slovakia, Slovenia, Solomon Islands, South Africa, Spain, Sri Lanka, Sudan, Suriname, Swaziland, Sweden, Switzerland, Syrian Arab Republic, Tajikistan, Thailand, The former Yugoslav Republic of Macedonia, Timor-Leste, Togo, Tonga, Trinidad and Tobago, Tunisia, Turkey, Turkmenistan, Tuvalu, Uganda, Ukraine, United Arab Emirates, United Republic of Tanzania, Uruguay, Vanuatu, Venezuela, Viet Nam, Yemen, Zambia, Zimbabwe.

Against: Israel, United States.

Abstaining: France, United Kingdom.

Dissemination of information

The Special Committee on decolonization held consultations in June with representatives of DPA and DPI on the dissemination of information on decolonization. It also considered a report of the Secretary-General on DPI activities on the topic from June 2005 to March 2006 [A/AC.109/2006/18].

GENERAL ASSEMBLY ACTION

On 14 December [meeting 79], the General Assembly, on the recommendation of the Fourth Committee [A/61/415], adopted **resolution 61/129** by recorded vote (176-3-1) [agenda item 39].

Dissemination of information on decolonization

The General Assembly,

Having examined the chapter of the report of the Special Committee on the Situation with regard to the Implementation of the Declaration on the Granting of Independence to Colonial Countries and Peoples relating to the dissemination of information on decolonization and publicity for the work of the United Nations in the field of decolonization,

Recalling General Assembly resolution 1514(XV) of 14 December 1960, containing the Declaration on the Granting of Independence to Colonial Countries and Peoples, and other resolutions and decisions of the United Nations concerning the dissemination of information on decolonization, in particular Assembly resolution 60/118 of 8 December 2005,

Recognizing the need for flexible, practical and innovative approaches towards reviewing the options of self-determination for the peoples of Non-Self-Governing Territories with a view to implementing the plan of action for the Second International Decade for the Eradication of Colonialism,

Reiterating the importance of dissemination of information as an instrument for furthering the aims of the Declaration, and mindful of the role of world public opinion in effectively assisting the peoples of Non-Self-Governing Territories to achieve self-determination,

Recognizing the role played by the administering Powers in transmitting information to the Secretary-General in accordance with the terms of Article 73 *e* of the Charter of the United Nations,

Also recognizing the role of the Department of Public Information of the Secretariat, through its United Nations information centres, in the dissemination of information at the regional level on the activities of the United Nations,

Recalling its resolution 60/112 of 8 December 2005, in which it requested the Department, in consultation with the United Nations Development Programme, the specialized agencies and the Special Committee, to prepare an information leaflet on assistance programmes available to the Non-Self-Governing Territories and to disseminate it widely in them,

Aware of the role of non-governmental organizations in the dissemination of information on decolonization,

1. *Approves* the activities in the field of dissemination of information on decolonization undertaken by the Department of Public Information and the Department of Political Affairs of the Secretariat, in accordance with the relevant resolutions of the United Nations on decolonization;

2. *Considers it important* to continue and expand its efforts to ensure the widest possible dissemination of information on decolonization, with particular emphasis on the options of self-determination available for the peoples of the Non-Self-Governing Territories, and to this end, requests the Department of Public Information,

including through the United Nations information centres in the relevant regions, to disseminate material to the Non-Self-Governing Territories;

3. *Requests* the Secretary-General to further enhance the information provided on the United Nations decolonization website by including the statements and scholarly papers presented at the regional seminars, as well as the full series of reports of the Special Committee on the Situation with regard to the Implementation of the Declaration on the Granting of Independence to Colonial Countries and Peoples;

4. *Requests* the Department of Public Information to implement the relevant provisions of General Assembly resolution 60/112 on the preparation of an information leaflet on the assistance programmes available to the Non-Self-Governing Territories;

5. *Requests* the Department of Political Affairs and the Department of Public Information to implement the recommendations of the Special Committee to continue their efforts to take measures through all the media available, including publications, radio and television, as well as the Internet, to give publicity to the work of the United Nations in the field of decolonization and, inter alia:

(a) To develop procedures to collect, prepare and disseminate, particularly to the Territories, basic material on the issue of self-determination of the peoples of the Non-Self-Governing Territories;

(b) To seek the full cooperation of the administering Powers in the discharge of the tasks referred to above;

(c) To develop a programme of collaboration with the appropriate regional and intergovernmental organizations, particularly in the Pacific and Caribbean regions, by holding periodic expert briefings and exchanging information;

(d) To encourage the involvement of non-governmental organizations in the dissemination of information on decolonization;

(e) To encourage the involvement of the Non-Self-Governing Territories in the dissemination of information on decolonization;

(f) To report to the Special Committee on measures taken in the implementation of the present resolution;

6. *Requests* all States, including the administering Powers, to accelerate the dissemination of information referred to in paragraph 2 above;

7. *Requests* the Special Committee to continue to examine this question and to report to the General Assembly at its sixty-second session on the implementation of the present resolution.

RECORDED VOTE ON RESOLUTION 61/129:

In favour: Afghanistan, Albania, Algeria, Andorra, Angola, Antigua and Barbuda, Argentina, Armenia, Australia, Austria, Azerbaijan, Bahamas, Bahrain, Bangladesh, Barbados, Belarus, Belgium, Belize, Benin, Bhutan, Bolivia, Bosnia and Herzegovina, Botswana, Brazil, Brunei Darussalam, Bulgaria, Burkina Faso, Burundi, Cambodia, Cameroon, Canada, Cape Verde, Central African Republic, Chad, Chile, China, Colombia, Comoros, Congo, Costa Rica, Côte d'Ivoire, Croatia, Cuba, Cyprus, Czech Republic, Democratic People's Republic of Korea, Democratic Republic of the Congo, Denmark, Djibouti, Dominica, Dominican Republic, Ecuador, Egypt, El Salvador, Equatorial Guinea, Eritrea, Estonia, Ethiopia, Fiji, Finland, Gabon, Georgia, Germany, Ghana, Greece, Grenada, Guatemala, Guinea, Guinea-Bissau, Guyana, Haiti, Honduras, Hungary, Iceland, India, Indonesia, Iran, Iraq, Ireland, Italy, Jamaica, Japan, Jordan, Kazakhstan, Kenya, Kuwait, Kyrgyzstan, Lao People's Democratic Republic, Latvia, Lesotho, Libyan Arab Jamahiriya, Liechtenstein, Lithuania, Luxembourg, Madagascar, Malawi, Malaysia, Maldives, Mali, Malta, Mauritania, Mauritius, Mexico, Moldova, Monaco, Mongolia, Montenegro, Morocco, Mozambique, Myanmar, Namibia, Nauru, Nepal, Netherlands, New Zealand, Nicaragua, Niger, Nigeria, Norway, Oman, Pakistan, Palau, Panama, Papua New Guinea, Paraguay, Peru, Philippines, Poland, Portugal, Qatar, Republic of Korea, Romania, Russian Federation, Rwanda, Saint Lucia, Saint Vincent and the Grenadines, Samoa, San Marino, Sao Tome and Principe, Saudi Arabia, Senegal, Serbia, Sierra Leone, Singapore, Slovakia, Slovenia, Solomon Islands, South Africa, Spain, Sri Lanka, Sudan, Suriname, Swaziland, Sweden, Switzerland, Syrian Arab Republic, Tajikistan, Thailand, The former Yugoslav Republic of Macedonia, Timor-Leste, Togo, Tonga, Trinidad and Tobago, Tunisia, Tuvalu, Uganda, Ukraine, United Arab Emirates, United Republic of Tanzania, Uruguay, Vanuatu, Venezuela, Viet Nam, Yemen, Zambia, Zimbabwe.

Against: Israel, United Kingdom, United States.

Abstaining: France.

Information on Territories

In response to General Assembly resolution 60/110 [YUN 2005, p. 669], the Secretary-General submitted a March report [A/61/70] indicating the dates of transmittal of information on economic, social and educational conditions in NSGTs for the years 2004-2005, under Article 73 *e* of the Charter of the United Nations.

GENERAL ASSEMBLY ACTION

On 14 December [meeting 79], the General Assembly, on the recommendation of the Fourth Committee [A/61/411], adopted **resolution 61/122** by recorded vote (179-0-4) [agenda item 35].

Information from Non-Self-Governing Territories transmitted under Article 73 e of the Charter of the United Nations

The General Assembly,

Recalling its resolution 1970(XVIII) of 16 December 1963, in which it requested the Special Committee on the Situation with regard to the Implementation of the Declaration on the Granting of Independence to Colonial Countries and Peoples to study the information transmitted to the Secretary-General in accordance with Article 73 *e* of the Charter of the United Nations and to take such information fully into account in examining the situation with regard to the implementation of the Declaration, contained in General Assembly resolution 1514(XV) of 14 December 1960,

Recalling also its resolution 60/110 of 8 December 2005, in which it requested the Special Committee to continue to discharge the functions entrusted to it under resolution 1970(XVIII),

Stressing the importance of timely transmission by the administering Powers of adequate information under Article 73 *e* of the Charter, in particular in relation to the preparation by the Secretariat of the working papers on the Territories concerned,

Having examined the report of the Secretary-General,

1. *Reaffirms* that, in the absence of a decision by the General Assembly itself that a Non-Self-Governing Territory has attained a full measure of self-government in terms of Chapter XI of the Charter of the United Nations, the administering Power concerned should continue to transmit information under Article 73 *e* of the Charter with respect to that Territory;

2. *Requests* the administering Powers concerned in accordance with their Charter obligations to transmit or continue to transmit regularly to the Secretary-General for information purposes, subject to such limitation as security and constitutional considerations may require, statistical and other information of a technical nature relating to economic, social and educational conditions in the Territories for which they are respectively responsible, as well as the fullest possible information on political and constitutional developments in the Territories concerned, including the constitution, legislative act or executive order providing for the government of the Territory and the constitutional relationship of the Territory to the administering Power, within a maximum period of six months following the expiration of the administrative year in those Territories;

3. *Requests* the Secretary-General to continue to ensure that adequate information is drawn from all available published sources in connection with the preparation of the working papers relating to the Territories concerned;

4. *Requests* the Special Committee on the Situation with regard to the Implementation of the Declaration on the Granting of Independence to Colonial Countries and Peoples to continue to discharge the functions entrusted to it under General Assembly resolution 1970(XVIII), in accordance with established procedures.

RECORDED VOTE ON RESOLUTION 61/122

In favour: Afghanistan, Albania, Algeria, Andorra, Angola, Antigua and Barbuda, Argentina, Armenia, Australia, Austria, Azerbaijan, Bahamas, Bahrain, Bangladesh, Barbados, Belarus, Belgium, Belize, Benin, Bhutan, Bolivia, Bosnia and Herzegovina, Botswana, Brazil, Brunei Darussalam, Bulgaria, Burkina Faso, Burundi, Cambodia, Cameroon, Canada, Cape Verde, Central African Republic, Chad, Chile, China, Colombia, Comoros, Congo, Costa Rica, Côte d'Ivoire, Croatia, Cuba, Cyprus, Czech Republic, Democratic People's Republic of Korea, Democratic Republic of the Congo, Denmark, Djibouti, Dominica, Dominican Republic, Ecuador, Egypt, El Salvador, Equatorial Guinea, Eritrea, Estonia, Ethiopia, Fiji, Finland, Gabon, Georgia, Germany, Ghana, Greece, Grenada, Guatemala, Guinea, Guinea-Bissau, Guyana, Haiti, Honduras, Hungary, Iceland, India, Indonesia, Iran, Iraq, Ireland, Italy, Jamaica, Japan, Jordan, Kazakhstan, Kenya, Kuwait, Kyrgyzstan, Lao People's Democratic Republic, Latvia, Lesotho, Libyan Arab Jamahiriya, Liechtenstein, Lithuania, Luxembourg, Madagascar, Malawi, Malaysia, Maldives, Mali, Malta, Marshall Islands, Mauritania, Mauritius, Mexico, Micronesia, Moldova, Mongolia, Montenegro, Morocco, Mozambique, Myanmar, Namibia, Nauru, Nepal, Netherlands, New Zealand, Nicaragua, Niger, Nigeria, Norway, Oman, Pakistan, Palau, Panama, Papua New Guinea, Paraguay, Peru, Philippines, Poland, Portugal, Qatar, Republic of Korea, Romania, Russian Federation, Rwanda, Saint Lucia, Saint Vincent and the Grenadines, Samoa, San Marino, Sao Tome and Principe, Saudi Arabia, Senegal, Serbia, Sierra Leone, Singapore, Slovakia, Slovenia, Solomon Islands, South Africa, Spain, Sri Lanka, Sudan, Suriname, Swaziland, Sweden, Switzerland, Syrian Arab Republic, Tajikistan, Thailand, The former Yugoslav Republic of Macedonia, Timor-Leste, Togo, Tonga, Trinidad and Tobago, Tunisia, Turkey, Turkmenistan, Tuvalu, Uganda, Ukraine, United Arab Emirates, United Republic of Tanzania, Uruguay, Vanuatu, Venezuela, Viet Nam, Yemen, Zambia, Zimbabwe.

Against: None.

Abstaining: France, Israel, United Kingdom, United States.

Study and training

In response to General Assembly resolution 60/113 [YUN 2005, p. 670], the Secretary-General submitted a March report [A/61/66] on offers of study scholarships and training facilities for inhabitants of NSGTs during the period 26 March 2005 to 23 March 2006 by the following Member States: Argentina, Cuba, Japan and the United Kingdom. Fifty-eight Member States and one non-member State had made such offers over the years.

GENERAL ASSEMBLY ACTION

On 14 December [meeting 79], the General Assembly, on the recommendation of the Fourth Committee [A/60/414], adopted **resolution 61/124** without vote [agenda item 38].

Offers by Member States of study and training facilities for inhabitants of Non-Self-Governing Territories

The General Assembly,

Recalling its resolution 60/113 of 8 December 2005,

Having examined the report of the Secretary-General on offers by Member States of study and training facilities for inhabitants of Non-Self-Governing Territories, prepared pursuant to its resolution 845(IX) of 22 November 1954,

Conscious of the importance of promoting the educational advancement of the inhabitants of Non-Self-Governing Territories,

Strongly convinced that the continuation and expansion of offers of scholarships is essential in order to meet the increasing need of students from Non-Self-Governing Territories for educational and training assistance, and considering that students in those Territories should be encouraged to avail themselves of such offers,

1. *Takes note* of the report of the Secretary-General;

2. *Expresses its appreciation* to those Member States that have made scholarships available to the inhabitants of Non-Self-Governing Territories;

3. *Invites* all States to make or continue to make generous offers of study and training facilities to the inhabitants of those Territories that have not yet attained self-government or independence and, wherever possible, to provide travel funds to prospective students;

4. *Urges* the administering Powers to take effective measures to ensure the widespread and continuous dissemination in the Territories under their administration of information relating to offers of study and training facilities made by States and to provide all the necessary facilities to enable students to avail themselves of such offers;

5. *Requests* the Secretary-General to report to the General Assembly at its sixty-second session on the implementation of the present resolution;

6. *Draws the attention* of the Special Committee on the Situation with regard to the Implementation of the Declaration on the Granting of Independence to Colonial Countries and Peoples to the present resolution.

Visiting missions

In June, the Special Committee on decolonization considered the question of sending visiting missions to NSGTs [A/61/23]. It adopted a resolution in which it stressed the need to dispatch periodic visiting missions to facilitate the full implementation of the 1960 Declaration on decolonization, called on the administering Powers to cooperate with the United Nations by facilitating UN visiting missions to the Territories under their administration and requested those Powers to consider resuming formal cooperation with the Special Committee. The Chairman was asked to consult with the administering Powers concerned and to report on the results.

The Committee recommended to the General Assembly for adoption draft resolutions on 11 small NSGTs (see p. 719) and on Tokelau (see p. 717), which endorsed a number of conclusions and recommendations concerning the sending of visiting missions to those Territories.

Turks and Caicos Islands mission

In February, the Special Committee on decolonization accepted a July 2005 invitation from the Chief Minister of the Turks and Caicos Islands, Michael Misick, to send a UN Special Mission to the Territory from 2 to 9 April, with the concurrence of the United Kingdom (the administering Power). The objective of the Mission, the first to the Territory since 1980, was to assess the situation on the ground and inform interested groups and the public on matters of self-determination. It would also examine political, economic and social developments in the Territory and provide information on how the UN system could assist the Territory in its development process. On 29 March, the Special Committee decided to shorten the mission by two days given the Organization's budget constraints.

The Special Mission visited the Turks and Caicos Islands from 2 to 7 April. In its April report [A/AC.109/2006/19], the Mission concluded that, while the Territory's political leadership was sufficiently aware of the political alternatives and strategies necessary for achieving a full measure of self-government, many people expressed a general lack of awareness of the issues and were clearly influenced by the perception that continued economic progress was dependent on the maintenance of the colonial condition. The general lack of awareness of the available political options and the self-determination process was very much a function of insufficient information regarding the achievement of self-government. That information deficit spoke to the fundamental deficiency in implementing long-standing UN resolutions on the dissemination of information on decolonization. The Mission observed that a UN public education programme on self-determination would go a long way towards bridging the information deficit in the self-determination process leading to successful decolonization. The best approach would be for the administering Power to join the United Nations in implementing that long-standing UN mandate. The Mission stated that UNDP, given its involvement in constitutional and political evolution in other small island Territories, should consider developing a regional programme on governance, tailor-made to meet the needs of the small island NSGTs it currently served. The Mission was able to accomplish its fundamental goals and, in the process, to gain a more thorough understanding of the challenges and aspirations faced by the Turks and Caicos Islands, whose self-determination could be realized through further engagement with the United Nations on a broad level.

Puerto Rico

In accordance with the Special Committee on decolonization's 2005 resolution concerning the self-determination and independence of Puerto Rico [YUN 2005, p. 671], the Committee's Rapporteur, in an April report [A/AC.109/2006/L.3], provided information on Puerto Rico, including recent political, military and economic developments and UN action.

Following its usual practice, the Committee acceded to requests for hearings from representatives of a number of organizations, who presented their views on 12 and 13 June [A/61/23]. The Committee adopted a resolution, without vote, by which it reaffirmed the inalienable right of the people of Puerto Rico to self-determination and independence; urged the United States to return the occupied land and installations on Vieques Islands and in Ceiba to the people of Puerto Rico; and requested the Rapporteur to report in 2007 on the resolution's implementation.

Territories under review

Falkland Islands (Malvinas)

The Special Committee on decolonization considered the question of the Falkland Islands (Malvinas) on 15 June [A/61/23]; it had before it a Secretariat working paper on the Territory [A/AC.109/2006/17] that addressed constitutional and political developments, mine clearance, economic and social conditions and participation in international organizations and arrangements. It adopted a resolution requesting Argentina and the United Kingdom to consolidate the current process of dialogue and cooperation by resuming negotiations to find a peaceful solution to the sovereignty dispute relating to the Territory as soon as possible.

Argentina, in a 3 January letter to the Secretary-General [A/60/647], recalled its objective of recovering the full sovereignty over the Malvinas, South Georgia and South Sandwich Islands and surrounding maritime areas through peaceful means. It reiterated the need to carry out the numerous UN resolutions and the declarations of the Organization of American States urging the resumption of bilateral negotiations in order to find a just, peaceful and lasting solution to the sovereignty dispute. Reaffirming its readiness to resume negotiations, it called on the British Government to show the same readiness.

In a 31 March response [A/60/743], the United Kingdom stated that it had no doubts about its sovereignty over the Falkland Islands, South Georgia and the South Sandwich Islands and their surrounding maritime areas, and rejected Argentina's claim to sovereignty.

On 27 April [A/60/830], the United Kingdom, referring to a 30 November 2005 communication from Argentina to the United Nations, said that the United Kingdom was fully entitled to extend the Convention on the Prohibition of the Development, Production, Stockpiling and Use of Chemical Weapons and on Their Destruction (see p. 653) to the Falkland Islands, South Georgia and the South Sandwich Islands, and the British Antarctic Territory. The United Kingdom rejected Argentina's claim to sovereignty over those islands and areas and its assertion that they were under illegal occupation by the United Kingdom.

Addressing the General Assembly on 20 September [A/61/PV.13], Argentina's President, Néstor Kirchner, reaffirmed his readiness to engage in constructive dialogue with the United Kingdom and called on that country to heed the international community's request in that regard. In exercise of its right of reply, the United Kingdom, in a 4 October letter to the Assembly President [A/61/535], said that the elected representatives of the Falkland Islands had again asked the Special Committee on decolonization to recognize that they, like any other people, were entitled to exercise the right of self-determination and reiterated that the people of the Falkland Islands did not wish for any change in the Islands' status. The United Kingdom stated that there could be no negotiations on sovereignty unless and until such time as the islanders so wished.

On 22 December, the Assembly decided that the agenda item on the question of the Falkland Islands (Malvinas) would remain for consideration during its resumed sixty-first (2007) session (**decision 61/552**).

Gibraltar

The Special Committee on decolonization considered the question of Gibraltar on 6 June [A/61/23]. It had before it a Secretariat working paper that described political developments and economic and social conditions in the Territory and presented the positions of the United Kingdom (the administering Power), Gibraltar and Spain concerning Gibraltar's future status [A/AC.109/2006/9 & Corr.1].

Gibraltar's Chief Minister, Peter Caruana, in his New Year message, said that there would have to be concessions by all sides regarding the negotiation process with the United Kingdom and Spain within the Trilateral Forum for Dialogue, established in 2005 [YUN 2005, p. 672]. The territorial Government of Gibraltar was not willing to make concessions to Spain on the issue of sovereignty, jurisdiction or control of Gibraltar's airport. Regarding the negotiations between Gibraltar and the United Kingdom on a reformed constitution [YUN 2004, p. 605], the Chief Minister noted that his Government's aim was to establish a modern, non-colonial constitutional relationship between Gibraltar and the United Kingdom. Under the constitution reform, there would be no change to sovereignty. For international legal and political purposes, Gibraltar would remain a dependency of the United Kingdom.

A later Secretariat working paper [A/AC.109/2007/12] reported that, on 27 March, Jack Straw, then Foreign Secretary of the United Kingdom, announced in a written statement to the House of Commons that the details of a new constitution had been agreed between the United Kingdom and Gibraltar. On 30 November, the Gibraltar constitutional referendum was held and the new Constitution was approved by 60.2 per cent of those who voted (60.4 per cent), while 37.8 per cent voted against and the remainder returned blank votes. The United Kingdom informed the Secretary-General [A/61/710] that the new Constitution was given effect by an Order-in-Council on 14 December. The new Constitution provided for a modern relationship between Gibraltar and the United Kingdom that was not based on colonialism.

The later Secretariat working paper [A/AC.109/2007/12] stated that, since its establishment, the Trilateral Forum for Dialogue had held six rounds of discussions. Meeting in Cordoba, Spain, on 18 September, the Minister for Foreign Affairs and Cooperation of Spain, the Minister for Europe of the United Kingdom and the Chief Minister of Gibraltar issued a communiqué containing a package of agreements aimed at enhancing the economic and social development of both Gibraltar and the surrounding region. The communiqué stated that Gibraltar's Government accepted that references to sovereignty in that document were bilateral to the United Kingdom and Spain.

Addressing the Special Committee on decolonization on 6 June [A/AC.109/2006/SR.5], Spain's representative noted that talks had been held in March between the British Government and a delegation from Gibraltar on ways to reform the constitutional order that had been in force in Gibraltar since 1969. The resulting constitutional text could only be regarded as an internal redistribution of powers between the United Kingdom and Gibraltar, aimed at improving the government's efficiency in the Territory, and not at Gibraltar's decolonization. To assert that Gibraltar was no longer an NSGT because of the constitutional reform would be to deny relevant UN resolutions, as well as Spain's historical rights over the Territory.

At the same meeting, Gibraltar's Chief Minister responded that if the Special Committee wished Gibraltar to accept Spanish sovereignty, it was acting outside its mandate, outside the Declaration on the Granting of Independence to Colonial Countries and Peoples and against the wishes of the people of Gibraltar, who would never subjugate their right to decide their own future to Spain's sovereignty claim. The people of Gibraltar had come to believe that the Committee lacked the will to help them secure decolonization in accordance with their wishes. They had, therefore, decided to exercise their right to self-determination through a referendum on a new constitutional relationship with the United Kingdom that was not colonial in nature. If the people of Gibraltar were to accept the revised constitution (see above), the Committee should cease to consider the question of Gibraltar and recommend to the General Assembly that Gibraltar be de-listed. That was for the Committee to decide, however, in accordance with its de-listing criteria.

Speaking before the Fourth Committee on 4 October [A/C.4/61/SR.4], Gibraltar's Chief Minister said there could be no doubt that Gibraltar was a normal case of decolonization, in accordance with the inalienable right to self-determination of its people. Disagreeing with Spain's position that the principle of territorial integrity had priority over the principle of self-determination, he said that decolonization and sovereignty were different questions. On the same day, Spain said that neither the 18 September agreements of the Trilateral Forum for Dialogue on Gibraltar (see above), nor the forthcoming referendum on constitutional reform, altered Spain's position on the question of its sovereignty over Gibraltar.

Responding to Spain's statement on 5 October [A/C.4/61/SR.5], the United Kingdom said the new draft constitution provided for a modern and mature relationship between the United Kingdom and Gibraltar. The referendum on the draft would be an exercise of the right to self-determination by the people of Gibraltar. It was gratifying that, after nearly two years of intense negotiations, the United Kingdom Minister for Europe, the Spanish Minister for Foreign Affairs and the Chief Minister of Gibraltar had been able to announce a first package of agreements, covering Gibraltar airport, border flows, telecommunication and pension issues. Despite the well-known differences on sovereignty matters, it was possible for the three parties to work together for the benefit of all concerned.

In a 29 November letter to the Secretary-General [A/61/604], Spain noted that the 30 November referendum on the new constitution was a purely local initiative that concerned only the authorities of Gibraltar. Nobody could claim that either the referendum or the draft constitution in any way affected the ongoing decolonization process, since Gibraltar's decolonization had to be achieved by means of negotiations between Spain and the United Kingdom, as the Assembly had asserted year after year.

On 14 December (**decision 61/522**), the Assembly urged Spain and the United Kingdom, while listening to the aspirations of Gibraltar, to reach, in the spirit of the 27 November 1984 statement on Gibraltar [YUN 1984, p. 1075], a definitive solution to the question of Gibraltar, in the light of the relevant Assembly resolutions and applicable principles, and in the spirit of the Charter of the United Nations. It also welcomed the successful outcome of the first package of measures concluded in the tripartite Forum for Dialogue on Gibraltar in September.

New Caledonia

The Special Committee on decolonization considered the question of New Caledonia on 16 and 22 June [A/61/23]. It had before it a Secretariat working paper [A/AC.109/2006/14] describing the political situation and economic data and developments in the Territory.

The working paper noted that, following the 2004 elections [YUN 2004, p. 606], which ended the 25-year domination of the Caledonian Government by the Rassemblement pour la Calédonie dans la République (RPCR), the political party that favoured integration with France (the administering Power), and the success of a new party, Avenir Ensemble (AE), the composition of the New Caledonian Government had grown highly complex. Despite considerable institutional and administrative advances, progress was often hindered by friction between RPCR and the pro-independence Front de libération national kanak socialiste (FLNKS), owing to their differing interpretations of collegiality in Government matters and their opposing views on issues, such as voter eligibility, mining initiatives and the implementation of the 1998 Nouméa Accord on New Caledonia's future status [YUN 1998, p. 574]. In January, the Secretary-General received a letter from the National Council for Indigenous Peoples Rights of New Caledonia (CNDPA), expressing its dissatisfaction with the implementation of the Nouméa Accord and asking the United Nations to look into the matter. According to CNDPA, the indigenous Kanak people had been systematically excluded from the process of power transfer mandated by the Accord and were chronically underrepresented in New Caledonia's governmental and social structures.

A later Secretariat working paper [A/AC.109/2007/9] reported that the leader of AE, Harold Martin, was re-elected as President of the Congress, New Caledonia's legislative body, in July. As AE leader, Mr. Martin held talks with RPCR President, Pierre Frogier, to discuss a possible rapprochement between the parties before France's 2007 presidential election. Both parties claimed allegiance to the French political party Union pour un mouvement populaire (UMP). UMP leader Nicolas Sarkozy encouraged AE and RPCR to unify in support of his presidential candidacy.

The working paper noted that political stability in New Caledonia could be undermined by the existence of the "collegiality clause" of the Nouméa Accord, by which the whole Government had to be re-elected by a vote of Congress if one member of the 11-member Government Cabinet resigned and there was no replacement from his or her party. There was a resurgence of inter-ethnic tension between the Kanaks and the settlers from the French territory of Wallis and Futuna, with a number of violent confrontations and acts of arson in suburbs of Nouméa in August.

Addressing the Fourth Committee on 5 October [A/C.4/61/SR.5], Rafael Mapou of the Comité Rheebu Nuu, the Kanak environmental group, said the Kanak people were seeking to recover their sovereignty over their mineral wealth, mainly nickel, which multinational companies sought to appropriate. The decolonization process had already begun and, according to the 1998 Nouméa Accord, should be completed by 2019 at the latest. It was, however, doubtful whether France, the administering Power, was conducting the process in good faith and whether the process could proceed in accordance with the rules set by the international community.

GENERAL ASSEMBLY ACTION

On 14 December [meeting 79], the General Assembly, on the recommendation of the Fourth Committee [A/61/415], adopted **resolution 61/126** without vote [agenda item 39].

Question of New Caledonia

The General Assembly,

Having considered the question of New Caledonia,

Having examined the chapter of the report of the Special Committee on the Situation with regard to the Implementation of the Declaration on the Granting of Independence to Colonial Countries and Peoples relating to New Caledonia,

Reaffirming the right of peoples to self-determination as enshrined in the Charter of the United Nations,

Recalling General Assembly resolutions 1514(XV) of 14 December 1960 and 1541(XV) of 15 December 1960,

Noting the importance of the positive measures being pursued in New Caledonia by the French authorities, in cooperation with all sectors of the population, to promote political, economic and social development in the Territory, including measures in the area of environmental protection and action with respect to drug abuse and trafficking, in order to provide a framework for its peaceful progress to self-determination,

Noting also, in this context, the importance of equitable economic and social development, as well as continued dialogue among the parties involved in New Caledonia in the preparation of the act of self-determination of New Caledonia,

Noting with satisfaction the intensification of contacts between New Caledonia and neighbouring countries of the South Pacific region,

1. *Welcomes* the significant developments that have taken place in New Caledonia since the signing of the Nouméa Accord of 5 May 1998 by the representatives of New Caledonia and the Government of France;

2. *Urges* all the parties involved, in the interest of all the people of New Caledonia, to maintain, in the framework of the Nouméa Accord, their dialogue in a spirit of harmony;

3. *Notes* the relevant provisions of the Nouméa Accord aimed at taking more broadly into account the Kanak identity in the political and social organization of New Caledonia, and also those provisions of the Accord relating to control of immigration and protection of local employment;

4. *Takes note* of the concerns expressed by a group of indigenous people in New Caledonia regarding their underrepresentation in the Territory's governmental and social structures;

5. *Notes* the relevant provisions of the Nouméa Accord to the effect that New Caledonia may become a member or associate member of certain international organizations, such as international organizations in the Pacific region, the United Nations, the United Nations Educational, Scientific and Cultural Organization and the International Labour Organization, according to their regulations;

6. *Also notes* the agreement between the signatories of the Nouméa Accord that the progress made in the emancipation process shall be brought to the attention of the United Nations;

7. *Welcomes* the fact that the administering Power invited to New Caledonia, at the time the new institutions were established, a mission of information which comprised representatives of countries of the Pacific region;

8. *Calls upon* the administering Power to continue to transmit to the Secretary-General information as required under Article 73 *e* of the Charter of the United Nations;

9. *Invites* all the parties involved to continue promoting a framework for the peaceful progress of the Territory towards an act of self-determination in which all options are open and which would safeguard the rights of all sectors of the population, according to the letter and the spirit of the Nouméa Accord, which is based on the principle that it is for the populations of New Caledonia to choose how to control their destiny;

10. *Welcomes* the intention expressed by the French authorities to resolve in the coming years the question of voter registration;

11. *Also welcomes* the measures that have been taken to strengthen and diversify the New Caledonian economy in all fields, and encourages further such measures in accordance with the spirit of the Matignon and Nouméa Accords;

12. *Further welcomes* the importance attached by the parties to the Matignon and Nouméa Accords to greater progress in housing, employment, training, education and health care in New Caledonia;

13. *Notes* the increase by the Government of France in financial assistance to the Territory, amounting to 910 million euros in 2005 for health, education, payment of public-service salaries and funding development schemes;

14. *Acknowledges* the contribution of the Melanesian Cultural Centre to the protection of the indigenous Kanak culture of New Caledonia;

15. *Notes* the positive initiatives aimed at protecting the natural environment of New Caledonia, notably the "Zonéco" operation designed to map and evaluate marine resources within the economic zone of New Caledonia;

16. *Welcomes* the establishment of a new form of cooperation among Australia, France and New Zealand in terms of surveillance of fishing zones, in accordance with the wishes expressed by France during the France-Oceania Summit in July 2003;

17. *Acknowledges* the close links between New Caledonia and the peoples of the South Pacific and the positive actions being taken by the French and territorial authorities to facilitate the further development of those links, including the development of closer relations with the countries members of the Pacific Islands Forum;

18. *Welcomes*, in this regard, the accession by New Caledonia to the status of observer in the Pacific Islands Forum, continuing high-level visits to New Caledonia by delegations from countries of the Pacific region and high-level visits by delegations from New Caledonia to countries members of the Pacific Islands Forum, and notes with satisfaction the request by New Caledonia, with the approval and support of the French authorities, to obtain associate member status in the Pacific Islands Forum;

19. *Welcomes also* the cooperative attitude of other States and Territories in the region towards New Caledonia, its economic and political aspirations and its increasing participation in regional and international affairs;

20. *Welcomes further* the endorsement of the report of the Forum Ministerial Committee on New Caledonia by leaders of the Pacific Islands Forum at its 36th Summit, in October 2005 in Papua New Guinea, and the continuing role of the Forum Ministerial Committee in monitoring developments in the Territory and encouraging closer regional engagements;

21. *Decides* to keep under continuous review the process unfolding in New Caledonia as a result of the signing of the Nouméa Accord;

22. *Requests* the Special Committee on the Situation with regard to the Implementation of the Declaration on the Granting of Independence to Colonial Countries and Peoples to continue the examination of the question

of the Non-Self-Governing Territory of New Caledonia and to report thereon to the General Assembly at its sixty-second session.

Tokelau

On 22 June, the Special Committee on decolonization considered the question of Tokelau (the three small atolls of Nukunonu, Fakaofo and Atafu in the South Pacific), administered by New Zealand [A/61/23]. Before it was a Secretariat working paper [A/AC.109/2006/10] covering constitutional and political developments, external relations and economic and social conditions in the Territory, and presenting the positions of New Zealand and Tokelau on the Territory's future status.

A later Secretariat working paper [A/AC.109/2007/11] reported that the referendum to determine Tokelau's future status took place as planned, with voting in Apia on 11 February (for eligible Tokelauans based in Samoa), and in Atafu, Nukunonu and Fakaofo on 13, 14 and 15 February, respectively. While 60 per cent of registered Tokelauan voters were in favour of self-government in free association with New Zealand, that percentage failed to meet the two-thirds majority needed for a change in the Territory's status. In numbers, a total of 584 voters, or 95 per cent of registered voters, turned out, with 349 voters voting in favour and 232 against. The voting was conducted in the presence of a United Nations monitoring mission (see below), which deemed the election process credible and reflecting the will of the people. Following the referendum, the Tokelau Council of Ongoing Government and New Zealand agreed to leave the referendum package on the table for future consideration. In August, following consultations between the Council of Ongoing Government, the three villages and the General Fono (Tokelau's national representative body), the General Fono decided to hold a second referendum on Tokelau's self-determination in November 2007, using the same self-determination package consisting of a draft constitution and draft treaty of self-determination, and requiring a two-thirds majority for the package to be accepted.

The May report of the four-member UN mission that observed the referendum [A/AC.109/2006/20] noted that extensive dialogue and consultations had taken place on Tokelau's future status, particularly, at the national and village levels, since 2003 when the General Fono had decided to endorse self-government in free association with New Zealand as the choice to be explored with the New Zealand Government. That decision, coupled with the level of agreement of the parties concerned, especially the unanimous support of Tokelau's political leadership at all levels, resulted in the surprise expressed at the referendum's outcome. The voting pattern turned out to be at odds with the stated views of the political leadership, raising some questions about the strength of the decisions taken by traditional leaders.

At the 15 February handing-over ceremony to the new Ulu (the titular head of the Territory, a position that was rotated annually among the three Faipule, or village/atoll representatives), Kolouei O'Brien, the new Ulu-o-Tokelau, expressed surprise at the result of the referendum; however, he stood by the decision that a two-thirds majority was needed for a change in status. Tokelau would remain on the UN list of NSGTs and New Zealand would continue to work with Tokelau to further improve living standards and support any further decisions relating to the Territory's future political status.

Addressing the Special Committee on decolonization on 22 June [A/AC.109/2006/SR.13], the Ulu-o-Tokelau reported that the General Fono, having discussed the referendum result at two meetings, had decided to continue on the path to full self-government in free association with New Zealand, and to meet in August to agree on a new time frame for holding a second referendum. At the same meeting, the Administrator of Tokelau stated that New Zealand would continue to encourage Tokelau in its efforts towards self-government and respect its right to determine the direction and pace of political change.

Addressing the Fourth Committee on 2 October [A/C.4/61/SR.2], New Zealand noted that Tokelau's political leadership, while disappointed with the referendum's outcome, remained committed to the objective of self-government and had asked New Zealand's Government to keep the current draft constitution and draft treaties on the table. New Zealand had agreed and considered the first referendum as one step towards self-determination.

GENERAL ASSEMBLY ACTION

On 14 December [meeting 79], the General Assembly, on the recommendation of the Fourth Committee [A/61/415], adopted **resolution 61/127** without vote [agenda item 39].

Question of Tokelau

The General Assembly,

Having considered the question of Tokelau,

Having examined the chapter of the report of the Special Committee on the Situation with regard to the Implementation of the Declaration on the Granting of Independence to Colonial Countries and Peoples relating to Tokelau,

Recalling its resolution 1514(XV) of 14 December 1960, containing the Declaration on the Granting of Independence to Colonial Countries and Peoples, and all resolutions and decisions of the United Nations relating to Non-Self-Governing Territories, in particular General Assembly resolution 60/116 of 8 December 2005,

Noting with appreciation the continuing exemplary cooperation of New Zealand as the administering Power with regard to the work of the Special Committee relating to Tokelau and its readiness to permit access by United Nations visiting missions to the Territory,

Also noting with appreciation the collaborative contribution to the development of Tokelau by New Zealand and the specialized agencies and other organizations of the United Nations system, in particular the United Nations Development Programme,

Recalling the inauguration in 1999 of a national legislative body, the General Fono, based on village elections by universal adult suffrage and the assumption by that body in June 2003 of full responsibility for the Tokelau budget,

Recalling also the report of the United Nations mission dispatched in August 2002 to Tokelau at the invitation of the Government of New Zealand and the representatives of Tokelau,

Noting that, as a small island Territory, Tokelau exemplifies the situation of most remaining Non-Self-Governing Territories and that, as a case study pointing to successful cooperation for decolonization, Tokelau has wider significance for the United Nations as it seeks to complete its work in decolonization,

Recalling that New Zealand and Tokelau signed in November 2003 a document entitled "Joint statement of the principles of partnership", which sets out in writing, for the first time, the rights and obligations of the two partner countries,

Bearing in mind the decision of the General Fono at its meeting in November 2003, following extensive consultations undertaken in all three villages, to explore formally with New Zealand the option of self-government in free association and its decision in August 2005 to hold a referendum on self-government on the basis of a draft constitution for Tokelau and a treaty of free association with New Zealand,

1. *Notes* that Tokelau remains firmly committed to the development of its capacity for self-government and to an act of self-determination that would result in Tokelau assuming a status in accordance with the options on future status for Non-Self-Governing Territories contained in principle VI of the annex to General Assembly resolution 1541(XV) of 15 December 1960;

2. *Welcomes* the substantial progress made towards the devolution of power to the three taupulega (village councils), in particular the delegation of the Administrator's powers to the three taupulega with effect from 1 July 2004 and the assumption by each taupulega from that date of full responsibility for the management of all its public services;

3. *Recalls* the decision of the General Fono in November 2003, following extensive consultations in all three villages and a meeting of the Special Committee on the Constitution of Tokelau, to explore formally with New Zealand the option of self-government in free association, and the discussions subsequently held between Tokelau and New Zealand pursuant to the General Fono decision;

4. *Recalls also* the decision of the General Fono in August 2005 to hold a referendum on self-government on the basis of a draft constitution for Tokelau and a treaty of free association with New Zealand, and notes the enactment by the General Fono of rules for the referendum;

5. *Welcomes* the invitation extended to the United Nations by Tokelau and New Zealand to monitor Tokelau's act of self-determination;

6. *Acknowledges* Tokelau's initiative in devising a strategic economic development plan for the period 2002-2005, and notes that a strategic plan for the period 2006-2009 is now being developed in consultation with New Zealand;

7. *Also acknowledges* the continuing assistance that New Zealand has committed to promoting Tokelau's welfare, as well as the cooperation of the United Nations Development Programme, including the relief and recovery assistance provided in the aftermath of Cyclone Percy in 2005;

8. *Further acknowledges* Tokelau's need for continued support, given the adjustments that are taking place with the strengthening of its capacity for self-government, and the ongoing responsibility of Tokelau's external partners to assist Tokelau in balancing its desire to be self-reliant to the greatest extent possible with its need for external assistance;

9. *Welcomes* the establishment of the Tokelau International Trust Fund to support the future development needs of Tokelau and the offer of a donor round table by the United Nations Development Programme, and calls upon Member States and international and regional agencies to announce contributions to the Fund and thereby lend practical support to assist this emerging country in overcoming the problems of smallness, isolation and lack of resources;

10. *Also welcomes* the assurance of the Government of New Zealand that it will meet its obligations to the United Nations with respect to Tokelau and abide by the freely expressed wishes of the people of Tokelau with regard to their future status;

11. *Further welcomes* the cooperative attitude of the other States and territories in the region towards Tokelau, and their support for its economic and political aspirations and increasing participation in regional and international affairs;

12. *Welcomes* the associate membership of Tokelau in the United Nations Educational, Scientific and Cultural Organization, and its recent accession to membership in the Forum Fisheries Agency, observer status at the Pacific Islands Forum and associate membership in the South Pacific Applied Geoscience Commission;

13. *Calls upon* the administering Power and United Nations agencies to continue to provide assistance to

Tokelau as it further develops its economy and governance structures;

14. *Welcomes* the actions taken by the administering Power to transmit information regarding the political, economic and social situation of Tokelau to the Secretary-General;

15. *Notes with satisfaction* the successful visit to Tokelau in October 2004 by the Chairman of the Special Committee on the Situation with regard to the Implementation of the Declaration on the Granting of Independence to Colonial Countries and Peoples;

16. *Notes* the considerable progress made towards the adoption of a Constitution and of national symbols by Tokelau, the steps taken by Tokelau and New Zealand to agree to a draft treaty of free association as a basis for an act of self-determination and the support expressed by Tokelauan communities in New Zealand for the move by Tokelau towards self-determination;

17. *Commends* the professional and transparent conduct of the referendum to determine the future status of Tokelau, which was held from 11 to 15 February 2006 and monitored by the United Nations;

18. *Notes* that the referendum failed by a narrow margin to produce the two-thirds majority of the valid votes cast required by the General Fono to change Tokelau's status as a Non-Self-Governing Territory under the administration of New Zealand;

19. *Welcomes* the agreement of New Zealand to the request by the Tokelau Council of Ongoing Government to maintain the referendum package of a draft Constitution and draft Treaty of Free Association as a possible basis for a future act of self-determination by Tokelau;

20. *Requests* the Special Committee to continue to examine the question of the Non-Self-Governing Territory of Tokelau and to report thereon to the General Assembly at its sixty-second session.

Western Sahara

The Special Committee on decolonization considered the question of Western Sahara on 6 June [A/61/23]. A Secretariat working paper [A/AC.109/2006/2] described the Secretary-General's good offices with the parties concerned and actions taken by the General Assembly and Security Council (see p. 329). The Special Committee transmitted the relevant documentation to the Assembly's sixty-first (2006) session to facilitate the Fourth Committee's consideration of the question. The Secretary-General's report on Western Sahara [A/61/121] was submitted to the Assembly in July.

Island Territories

On 16 June, the Special Committee on decolonization [A/61/23] considered working papers on American Samoa [A/AC.109/2006/7], Anguilla [A/AC.109/2006/4], Bermuda [A/AC.109/2006/6], the British Virgin Islands [A/AC.109/2006/12], the Cayman Islands [A/AC.109/2006/16], Guam [A/AC.109/2006/8], Montserrat [A/AC.109/2006/13 & Corr.1], Pitcairn [A/AC.109/2006/5], Saint Helena [A/AC.109/2006/3], the Turks and Caicos Islands [A/AC.109/2006/15], and the United States Virgin Islands [A/AC.109/2006/11], describing political developments and economic and social conditions in each of those 11 island Territories. The Committee approved a two-part consolidated draft resolution for adoption by the General Assembly (see below).

GENERAL ASSEMBLY ACTION

On 14 December [meeting 79], the General Assembly, on the recommendation of the Fourth Committee [A/61/415], adopted **resolutions 61/128 A and B** by recorded vote (173-0-4) [agenda item 39].

Questions of American Samoa, Anguilla, Bermuda, the British Virgin Islands, the Cayman Islands, Guam, Montserrat, Pitcairn, Saint Helena, the Turks and Caicos Islands and the United States Virgin Islands

A

General

The General Assembly,

Having considered the questions of the Non-Self-Governing Territories of American Samoa, Anguilla, Bermuda, the British Virgin Islands, the Cayman Islands, Guam, Montserrat, Pitcairn, Saint Helena, the Turks and Caicos Islands and the United States Virgin Islands, hereinafter referred to as "the Territories",

Having examined the relevant chapter of the report of the Special Committee on the Situation with regard to the Implementation of the Declaration on the Granting of Independence to Colonial Countries and Peoples,

Recalling all resolutions and decisions of the United Nations relating to those Territories, including, in particular, the resolutions adopted by the General Assembly at its sixtieth session on the individual Territories covered by the present resolution,

Recognizing that all available options for self-determination of the Territories are valid as long as they are in accordance with the freely expressed wishes of the peoples concerned and in conformity with the clearly defined principles contained in General Assembly resolutions 1514(XV) of 14 December 1960, 1541(XV) of 15 December 1960 and other resolutions of the Assembly,

Recalling its resolution 1541(XV), containing the principles that should guide Member States in determining whether or not an obligation exists to transmit the information called for under Article 73 *e* of the Charter of the United Nations,

Expressing concern that more than forty-five years after the adoption of the Declaration on the Granting of Independence to Colonial Countries and Peoples, there still remain a number of Non-Self-Governing Territories,

Conscious of the importance of continuing effective implementation of the Declaration, taking into account the target set by the United Nations to eradicate colonialism by 2010 and the plan of action for the Second International Decade for the Eradication of Colonialism,

Recognizing that the specific characteristics and the sentiments of the peoples of the Territories require flexible, practical and innovative approaches to the options of self-determination, without any prejudice to territorial size, geographical location, size of population or natural resources,

Taking note of the stated positions of the Government of the United Kingdom of Great Britain and Northern Ireland and the stated position of the Government of the United States of America on the Non-Self-Governing Territories under their administration,

Taking note also of the stated positions of the representatives of the Non-Self-Governing Territories before the Special Committee and in its regional seminars,

Noting the constitutional developments in some Non-Self-Governing Territories affecting the internal structure of governance about which the Special Committee has received information,

Aware of the importance both to the Territories and to the Special Committee of the participation of elected and appointed representatives of the Territories in the work of the Special Committee,

Convinced that the wishes and aspirations of the peoples of the Territories should continue to guide the development of their future political status and that referendums, free and fair elections and other forms of popular consultation play an important role in ascertaining the wishes and aspirations of the people,

Convinced also that any negotiations to determine the status of a Territory must take place with the active involvement and participation of the people of that Territory, under the supervision of the United Nations, on a case-by-case basis, and that the views of the peoples of the Non-Self-Governing Territories in respect of their right to self-determination should be ascertained,

Aware of the importance of the international financial services for the economies of some of the Non-Self-Governing Territories,

Noting the continued cooperation of the Non-Self-Governing Territories at the local and regional levels, including participation in the work of regional organizations,

Mindful that United Nations visiting and special missions provide an effective means of ascertaining the situation in the Territories, that some Territories have not received a United Nations visiting mission for a long time and that no visiting missions have been sent to some of the Territories, and considering the possibility of sending further visiting missions to the Territories at an appropriate time and in consultation with the administering Powers,

Mindful also that, in order for the Special Committee to enhance its understanding of the political status of the peoples of the Territories and to fulfil its mandate effectively, it is important for it to be apprised by the administering Powers and to receive information from other appropriate sources, including the representatives of the Territories, concerning the wishes and aspirations of the peoples of the Territories,

Recognizing the need for the Special Committee to ensure that the appropriate bodies of the United Nations embark actively on a public awareness campaign aimed at assisting the peoples of the Territories in gaining an understanding of the options of self-determination,

Mindful, in this connection, that the holding of regional seminars in the Caribbean and Pacific regions and at Headquarters and other venues, with the active participation of representatives of the Non-Self-Governing Territories, provides a helpful means for the Special Committee to fulfil its mandate, and that the regional nature of the seminars, which alternate between the Caribbean and the Pacific, is a crucial element in the context of a United Nations programme for ascertaining the political status of the Territories,

Mindful also that the 2006 Pacific regional seminar, originally scheduled to be held in Timor-Leste from 23 to 25 May 2006, is to be rescheduled to a later date in 2006,

Conscious of the particular vulnerability of the Territories to natural disasters and environmental degradation, and, in this connection, bearing in mind the applicability to the Territories of the programmes of action of all United Nations world conferences and special sessions of the General Assembly in the economic and social sphere,

Noting with appreciation the contribution to the development of some Territories by the specialized agencies and other organizations of the United Nations system, in particular the United Nations Development Programme, the Economic Commission for Latin America and the Caribbean and the Economic and Social Commission for Asia and the Pacific, as well as regional institutions such as the Caribbean Development Bank, the Caribbean Community, the Organization of Eastern Caribbean States, the Pacific Islands Forum and the agencies of the Council of Regional Organizations in the Pacific,

Aware that the Human Rights Committee, as part of its mandate under the International Covenant on Civil and Political Rights, reviews the status of the self-determination process of small island Territories under examination by the Special Committee,

Recalling the ongoing efforts of the Special Committee in carrying out a critical review of its work with the aim of making appropriate and constructive recommendations and decisions to attain its objectives in accordance with its mandate,

Recognizing that the annual background working papers prepared by the Secretariat on developments in each of the small Territories, as well as the substantive documentation and information furnished by independent experts, scholars, non-governmental organizations and other independent sources, have provided important inputs in updating the present resolution,

1. *Reaffirms* the inalienable right of the peoples of the Territories to self-determination, in conformity with the Charter of the United Nations and with General Assembly resolution 1514(XV), containing the Declaration on the Granting of Independence to Colonial Countries and Peoples;

2. *Also reaffirms* that, in the process of decolonization, there is no alternative to the principle of self-determination, which is also a fundamental human right, as recognized under the relevant human rights conventions;

3. *Further reaffirms* that it is ultimately for the peoples of the Territories themselves to determine freely their future political status in accordance with the relevant provisions of the Charter, the Declaration and the relevant resolutions of the General Assembly, and in that connection reiterates its long-standing call for the administering Powers, in cooperation with the territorial Governments and appropriate bodies of the United Nations system, to develop political education programmes for the Territories in order to foster an awareness among the people of their right to self-determination in conformity with the legitimate political status options, based on the principles clearly defined in General Assembly resolution 1541(XV);

4. *Requests* the administering Powers to transmit regularly to the Secretary-General information called for under Article 73 *e* of the Charter;

5. *Stresses* the importance of the Special Committee being apprised of the views and wishes of the peoples of the Territories and enhancing its understanding of their conditions, including the nature and scope of the existing political and constitutional arrangements between the Non-Self-Governing Territories and their respective administering Powers;

6. *Reaffirms* the responsibility of the administering Powers under the Charter to promote the economic and social development and to preserve the cultural identity of the Territories, and recommends that priority continue to be given, in consultation with the territorial Governments concerned, to the strengthening and diversification of their respective economies;

7. *Requests* the Special Committee to continue to follow closely the developments in legislation in the area of international financial services and their impact on the economy in some of the Territories;

8. *Requests* the Territories and the administering Powers to take all necessary measures to protect and conserve the environment of the Territories against any degradation, and once again requests the specialized agencies concerned to continue to monitor environmental conditions in the Territories;

9. *Welcomes* the participation of the Non-Self-Governing Territories in regional activities, including the work of regional organizations;

10. *Stresses* the importance of implementing the plan of action for the Second International Decade for the Eradication of Colonialism, in particular by expediting the application of the work programme for the decolonization of each Non-Self-Governing Territory, on a case-by-case basis, and by completing the periodic analyses of the progress and extent of the implementation of the Declaration in each Territory;

11. *Calls upon* the administering Powers to participate in and cooperate fully with the work of the Special Committee in order to implement the provisions of Article 73 *e* of the Charter and the Declaration, and in order to advise the Special Committee on the implementation of provisions under Article 73 *b* of the Charter on efforts to promote self-government in the Territories;

12. *Urges* Member States to contribute to the efforts of the United Nations to usher in a world free of colonialism within the Second International Decade for the Eradication of Colonialism, and calls upon them to continue to give their full support to the Special Committee in its endeavours towards that noble goal;

13. *Notes* that a number of Non-Self-Governing Territories have expressed concern at the procedure followed by some administering Powers, contrary to the wishes of the Territories themselves, of amending or enacting legislation for application to the Territories, either through Orders in Council, in order to apply to the Territories the international treaty obligations of the administering Power, or through unilateral application of laws and regulations;

14. *Takes note* of the constitutional reviews in the Territories administered by the United Kingdom of Great Britain and Northern Ireland, and led by the territorial Governments, designed to address the internal constitutional structure within the present territorial arrangement;

15. *Also takes note* of the report of the Secretary-General on the midterm review of the Second International Decade for the Eradication of Colonialism, and reiterates its long-standing request that the Secretary-General report to the General Assembly at its next session on the implementation of decolonization resolutions adopted since the declaration of the First and Second International Decades;

16. *Reiterates its request* that the Human Rights Committee collaborate with the Special Committee, within the framework of its mandate on the right to self-determination as contained in the International Covenant on Civil and Political Rights with the aim of exchanging information, given that the Committee reviews political and constitutional developments in many of the Non-Self-Governing Territories that are under review by the Special Committee;

17. *Requests* the Special Committee to collaborate with the Permanent Forum on Indigenous Issues and the Committee on the Elimination of Racial Discrimination, within the framework of their respective mandates, with the aim of exchanging information on developments in those Non-Self-Governing Territories which are reviewed by these bodies;

18. *Also requests* the Special Committee to continue to examine the question of the Non-Self-Governing Territories and to report thereon to the General Assembly at its sixty-second session and on the implementation of the present resolution.

B

Individual Territories

The General Assembly,

Referring to resolution A above,

I

American Samoa

Taking note of the working paper prepared by the Secretariat on American Samoa and other relevant information,

Taking note also of the position of the administering Power and the statements made by representatives of American Samoa in the regional seminars expressing satisfaction with the Territory's present relationship with the United States of America,

Noting that the Territory's non-voting delegate to the Congress of the United States of America has formally requested that the administering Power declare its official position on the status of American Samoa before the Special Committee on the Situation with regard to the Implementation of the Declaration on the Granting of Independence to Colonial Countries and Peoples,

Noting with satisfaction the establishment of the Future Political Status Study Commission, which began its work in June 2006, to study alternative forms of future political status open to American Samoa and to assess the advantages and disadvantages of each,

Recalling the negative economic impacts of Cyclone Heta in 2004 and Cyclone Olaf in 2005 on the agricultural sector, noting the importance to the economy of remittances and tourism, and bearing in mind the request of the territorial Government to the administering Power to continue to extend favourable tax benefits with regard to its exports,

1. *Notes* that the Department of the Interior of the United States of America provides that the Secretary of the Interior has administrative jurisdiction over American Samoa;

2. *Also notes* that American Samoa continues to be the only United States Territory to receive financial assistance from the administering Power for the operations of the territorial Government, and calls upon the administering Power to continue to assist the territorial Government in the diversification of its economy;

3. *Welcomes* the invitation extended to the Special Committee by the Governor of American Samoa and reiterated, most recently at the Caribbean regional seminar held in Canouan, Saint Vincent and the Grenadines, from 17 to 19 May 2005, to send a visiting mission to the Territory, calls upon the administering Power to facilitate such a mission, and requests the Chairman of the Special Committee to take all the necessary steps to that end;

4. *Takes note* of the statement of the representative of the Governor of the Territory at the Caribbean regional seminar in 2005 requesting the Special Committee to provide information on the process of self-governance, which could be provided within the context of a visiting mission, or by other acceptable means;

5. *Requests* the administering Power to assist the Territory in facilitating the work of the newly established Future Political Status Study Commission, consistent with Article 73 *b* of the Charter of the United Nations, and calls upon the relevant United Nations organizations to provide assistance to the Territory, if requested, in the context of its public education programme;

II

Anguilla

Taking note of the working paper prepared by the Secretariat on Anguilla and other relevant information,

Taking note also of the constitutional review process resumed by the territorial Government in 2006,

Recalling the holding of the 2003 Caribbean regional seminar in Anguilla, the first time that the seminar had been held in a Non-Self-Governing Territory, and the desire of the territorial Government and the people of Anguilla for a visiting mission by the Special Committee,

Noting the appointment by the administering Power of a new Governor who maintains reserved powers in the Territory,

Aware that the Government has placed a halt on all new and major foreign investment tourism-related projects in order to carefully manage the development of the island's economy to achieve long-term sustainability,

1. *Welcomes* the establishment of a new Constitutional and Electoral Reform Commission in 2006, with the aim of making recommendations to the administering Power on proposed changes to the Constitution in place in the Territory;

2. *Notes* that changes in the visa requirements for Anguillan passport holders entering nearby French Saint Martin could make it more difficult for them to enter the French overseas department, the closest neighbour to the Territory;

3. *Welcomes* the participation of the Territory as an associate member in the Caribbean Community, the Organization of Eastern Caribbean States and the Economic Commission for Latin America and the Caribbean;

III

Bermuda

Taking note of the working paper prepared by the Secretariat on Bermuda and other relevant information,

Conscious of the different viewpoints of the political parties on the future status of the Territory,

Noting the statement of the Premier of Bermuda in his Founder's Day address that there could never be a true democracy as long as the country remains a colony or an overseas dependent Territory, and that only with independence can national unity be forged and pride in being Bermudian fully developed,

Bearing in mind the conclusions in the report of the United Nations special mission to Bermuda, which visited the Territory in March and May 2005,

1. *Welcomes* the dispatch of the United Nations special mission to Bermuda at the request of the territorial

Government and with the concurrence of the administering Power, which provided information to the people of the Territory on the role of the United Nations in the process of self-determination, on the legitimate political status options as clearly defined in General Assembly resolution 1541(XV) of 15 December 1960 and on the experiences of other small States that have achieved a full measure of self-government;

2. *Also welcomes* the 2005 report of the Bermuda Independence Commission, which provides a thorough and meticulous examination of the facts surrounding independence, and takes note of the plans for public meetings and the presentation of a Green Paper to the House of Assembly followed by a White Paper outlining the policy proposals for an independent Bermuda;

3. *Decides* to follow closely the public consultations on the future political status of Bermuda under way in the Territory, and requests the relevant United Nations organizations to provide assistance to the Territory, if requested, in the context of its public education programme;

IV

British Virgin Islands

Taking note of the working paper prepared by the Secretariat on the British Virgin Islands and other relevant information,

Recalling the 1993 report of the Constitutional Commissioners, appointed by the administering Power to review the existing Constitution, and its recommendation to assess the costs, obligations and liabilities of independence, and the 1996 debate on the report in the Legislative Council,

Welcoming the establishment of the Constitutional Commission in 2004 and the completion of its report in 2005 providing recommendations on constitutional modernization, and noting that the Legislative Council of the Territory debated the report in 2005,

Noting the appointment by the administering Power of a new Governor who maintains reserved powers in the Territory,

Also noting that the Territory continues to emerge as one of the world's leading offshore financial centres,

1. *Takes note* of the statement made by the representative of the Legislative Council of the Territory at the Caribbean regional seminar held in Canouan, Saint Vincent and the Grenadines, from 17 to 19 May 2005, who presented an analysis of the internal constitutional review process;

2. *Welcomes* the 2005 report of the Constitutional Commission, which contains a series of recommendations on constitutional advancement, including the scaling back of the powers of the appointed Governor, and also welcomes the discussions which commenced in 2006 between the elected Government and the administering Power on constitutional advancement and devolution of power;

3. *Further welcomes* the ongoing work of the Inter-Virgin Islands Council between the elected Governments of the British Virgin Islands and the United States Virgin Islands as a mechanism for functional cooperation between the two neighbouring Territories;

V

Cayman Islands

Taking note of the working paper prepared by the Secretariat on the Cayman Islands and other relevant information,

Noting the 2002 report of the Constitutional Modernization Review Commission, which contained a draft constitution for the consideration of the people of the Territory, the 2003 draft constitution offered by the administering Power and the subsequent discussions between the Territory and the administering Power in 2003,

Also noting the 2003 visit to the Territory by the Chairman of the Special Committee at the invitation of the Cayman Islands Chamber of Commerce,

1. *Takes note* of the decision by the new territorial Government to reopen discussions with the administering Power in 2006 on constitutional modernization with the aim of ascertaining the views of the people by way of referendum;

2. *Also takes note* of the statement made by the representative of the Non-Governmental Organizations Constitutional Working Group of the Cayman Islands Chamber of Commerce at the Caribbean regional seminar held in Canouan, Saint Vincent and the Grenadines, from 17 to 19 May 2005, which called for a comprehensive educational programme, to be defined by the Special Committee, on the issue of self-determination, as well as a visiting mission to the Territory;

VI

Guam

Taking note of the working paper prepared by the Secretariat on Guam and other relevant information,

Recalling that, in a referendum held in 1987, the registered and eligible voters of Guam endorsed a draft Guam Commonwealth Act that would establish a new framework for relations between the Territory and the administering Power, providing for a greater measure of internal self-government for Guam and recognition of the right of the Chamorro people of Guam to self-determination for the Territory,

Recalling also the requests by the elected representatives and non-governmental organizations of the Territory that Guam not be removed from the list of the Non-Self-Governing Territories with which the Special Committee is concerned, pending the self-determination of the Chamorro people and taking into account their legitimate rights and interests,

Aware that negotiations between the administering Power and the territorial Government on the draft Guam Commonwealth Act are no longer continuing and that Guam has established the process for a self-determination vote by the eligible Chamorro voters,

Cognizant that the administering Power continues to implement its programme of transferring surplus federal land to the Government of Guam,

Noting that the people of the Territory have called for reform in the programme of the administering Power with respect to the thorough, unconditional and expeditious transfer of land property to the people of Guam,

Aware of concerns expressed by many residents regarding the potential social and other impacts of the impending transfer of additional military personnel of the administering Power to the Territory,

Conscious that immigration into Guam has resulted in the indigenous Chamorros becoming a minority in their homeland,

Recalling the dispatch in 1979 of a United Nations visiting mission to the Territory, and noting the recommendation of the 1996 Pacific regional seminar for sending a visiting mission to Guam,

Also recalling the invitation made in 2000 by the Governor and legislature of the Territory to hold the Pacific regional seminar in the Territory and the opposition to the invitation expressed by the administering Power,

1. *Calls once again upon* the administering Power to take into consideration the expressed will of the Chamorro people as supported by Guam voters in the plebiscite of 1987 and as provided for in Guam law, encourages the administering Power and the territorial Government of Guam to enter into negotiations on the matter, and requests the administering Power to inform the Secretary-General of progress to that end;

2. *Requests* the administering Power to continue to assist the elected territorial Government in achieving its political, economic and social goals;

3. *Also requests* the administering Power, in cooperation with the territorial Government, to continue to transfer land to the original landowners of the Territory, to continue to recognize and respect the political rights and the cultural and ethnic identity of the Chamorro people of Guam and to take all necessary measures to respond to the concerns of the territorial Government with regard to the question of immigration;

4. *Further requests* the administering Power to cooperate in establishing programmes specifically intended to promote the sustainable development of economic activities and enterprises, noting the special role of the Chamorro people in the development of Guam;

5. *Takes note* of the request by the elected Governor to the administering Power to lift restrictions to allow for foreign airlines to transport passengers between Guam and the United States of America to provide for a more competitive market and increased visitor arrivals;

VII

Montserrat

Taking note of the working paper prepared by the Secretariat on Montserrat and other relevant information,

Taking note with interest of the statements made and the information on the political and economic situation in Montserrat provided by the Chief Minister of the Territory to the Caribbean regional seminar, held at The Valley, Anguilla, from 20 to 22 May 2003,

Noting with concern the continued consequences of the volcanic eruption, which led to the evacuation of three quarters of the Territory's population to safe areas of the island and to areas outside the Territory, which continues to have enduring consequences for the economy of the island,

Welcoming the continued assistance provided to the Territory by States members of the Caribbean Community, in particular Antigua and Barbuda, which has offered safe refuge and access to educational and health facilities, as well as employment for thousands who have left the Territory,

Noting the continuing efforts of the administering Power and the territorial Government to deal with the consequences of the volcanic eruption,

1. *Calls upon* the administering Power, the specialized agencies and other organizations of the United Nations system, as well as regional and other organizations, to continue to provide assistance to the Territory in alleviating the consequences of the volcanic eruption;

2. *Recalls* the 2002 report of the Constitutional Review Commission, which contains a series of recommendations on constitutional advancement, including the devolution of power from the appointed Governor to the elected Government, and the call in favour of a free-association arrangement;

3. *Welcomes* the convening of a committee of the House of Assembly in 2005 to review the report, and the subsequent discussions between the elected Government and the administering Power on constitutional advancement and devolution of power;

VIII

Pitcairn

Taking note of the working paper prepared by the Secretariat on Pitcairn and other relevant information,

Taking into account the unique nature of Pitcairn in terms of population and area,

Noting the position of the representative of the elected Government, as expressed at the 2004 Pacific regional seminar, that the people of the Territory did not fully understand all the possibilities or the significance of the various self-determination options that might be available to them, and that the review of the Constitution was deferred to after 2006,

1. *Requests* the administering Power to continue its assistance for the improvement of the economic, social, educational and other conditions of the population of the Territory and to continue its discussions with the representatives of Pitcairn on how best to support their economic security;

2. *Takes note* of the position of the representative of the elected Government of the Territory favouring discussions on self-determination in advance of a constitutional review, and notes that a United Nations visiting mission to the Territory would heighten the awareness of the people of their political future;

IX

Saint Helena

Taking note of the working paper prepared by the Secretariat on Saint Helena and other relevant information,

Taking into account the unique character of Saint Helena, its population and its natural resources,

Taking note of the constitutional review process led by the territorial Government and the consultative poll with regard to a new Constitution held in Saint Helena on 25 May 2005,

Aware of the efforts of the administering Power and the territorial authorities to improve the socio-economic conditions of the population of Saint Helena, in particular in the sphere of food production, continuing high unemployment and limited transport and communications,

Noting the importance of improving the infrastructure and accessibility of Saint Helena,

Noting also the importance of the right to nationality for Saint Helenians and their request that it, in principle, be included in the new Constitution,

Noting with concern the problem of unemployment on the island and the joint action of the administering Power and the territorial Government to deal with it,

1. *Welcomes* the continuing constitutional review process and the recent consultative poll led by the Government of Saint Helena in cooperation with the administering Power;

2. *Also welcomes* the decision by the administering Power to provide funding for the construction of an international airport on Saint Helena to become operational in 2010, including all required infrastructure;

3. *Requests* the administering Power and relevant international organizations to continue to support the efforts of the territorial Government to address the socio-economic development challenges, including the high unemployment and the limited transport and communications problems, as well as to support the additional infrastructure required for the airport project;

4. *Calls upon* the administering Power to take into account the concerns of Saint Helenians with regard to the right to nationality;

X

Turks and Caicos Islands

Taking note of the working paper prepared by the Secretariat on the Turks and Caicos Islands and other relevant information,

Recalling the 2002 report of the Constitutional Modernization Review Body, which examined the existing Constitution and made recommendations on the internal structure of government and devolution of power from the appointed Governor to the elected Government,

Welcoming the dispatch of the United Nations special mission to the Turks and Caicos Islands in 2006, at the request of the territorial Government and with the concurrence of the administering Power, which provided information to the people of the Territory on the role of the United Nations in the process of self-determination, on the legitimate political status options as clearly defined in General Assembly resolution 1541(XV) and on the experiences of other small States that have achieved a full measure of self-government,

Taking note of the conclusions of the report of the United Nations special mission to the Turks and Caicos Islands,

1. *Recalls* the statement made by the Chief Minister of the Territory at the Caribbean regional seminar held in Canouan, Saint Vincent and the Grenadines, from 17 to 19 May 2005, that his Government was in favour of a reasonable period of full internal self-government before moving to independence;

2. *Takes note* of the announcement made by the Chief Minister in 2006 of the conclusion of discussions between the territorial Government and the administering Power resulting in an agreement for an advance constitution, which would be circulated to the Government and the opposition for comment and to the general public for information, with the consultative process concluding with a debate in the Legislative Council;

3. *Also takes note* of the significant and steady period of economic expansion, in particular over the last decade, fuelled by the emergence of high-end tourism, and the need for attention to be paid to the enhancement of social cohesion in the Territory;

XI

United States Virgin Islands

Taking note of the working paper prepared by the Secretariat on the United States Virgin Islands and other relevant information,

Taking note with interest of the statements made and the information provided by the representative of the Governor of the Territory at the Caribbean regional seminar held in Canouan, Saint Vincent and the Grenadines, from 17 to 19 May 2005,

Noting the continuing interest of the territorial Government in seeking associate membership in the Organization of Eastern Caribbean States and observer status in the Caribbean Community and the pending request by the Territory to the administering Power for the delegation of authority to proceed, as well as the 2003 resolution of the territorial legislature in support of that request,

Noting also the expressed interest of the territorial Government in being included in regional programmes of the United Nations Development Programme and in the records and archives management programme of the United Nations Educational, Scientific and Cultural Organization,

Recalling that the Territory has not received a United Nations visiting mission since 1977, and bearing in mind the formal request of the Territory for such a mission in 1993 to assist the Territory in its political education process and to observe the Territory's only referendum on political status options in its history,

Noting the ongoing cooperation between the territorial Government and Denmark on the repatriation of artefacts and archives,

Also noting that the convening of a fifth Constitutional Convention to review the existing Revised Organic Act, which organizes the internal governance arrangement, has been postponed to 2007,

1. *Requests* the administering Power to continue to assist the territorial Government in achieving its political, economic and social goals;

2. *Once again requests* the administering Power to facilitate the participation of the Territory, as appropriate, in various organizations, in particular the Organization of Eastern Caribbean States, the Caribbean Community and the Association of Caribbean States;

3. *Calls for* the inclusion of the Territory in regional programmes of the United Nations Development Programme, consistent with the participation of other Non-Self-Governing Territories;

4. *Welcomes* the establishment of the Inter-Virgin Islands Council between the elected Governments of the United States Virgin Islands and the British Virgin Islands as a mechanism of functional cooperation between the two neighbouring Territories;

5. *Notes* the position of the territorial Government supporting the ownership and control of the natural resources of the Territory, including marine resources, and its calls for the return of those marine resources to its jurisdiction;

6. *Welcomes* the cooperation agreements existing between the Territory and Denmark, the former colonial Power of the Territory, on the exchange of artefacts and the repatriation of archival material.

RECORDED VOTE ON RESOLUTIONS 61/128 A and B:

In favour: Afghanistan, Albania, Algeria, Andorra, Angola, Antigua and Barbuda, Argentina, Armenia, Australia, Austria, Azerbaijan, Bahamas, Bahrain, Bangladesh, Barbados, Belarus, Belgium, Belize, Benin, Bhutan, Bolivia, Bosnia and Herzegovina, Botswana, Brazil, Brunei Darussalam, Bulgaria, Burkina Faso, Burundi, Cambodia, Cameroon, Canada, Cape Verde, Central African Republic, Chad, Chile, China, Colombia, Comoros, Congo, Costa Rica, Côte d'Ivoire, Croatia, Cuba, Cyprus, Czech Republic, Democratic People's Republic of Korea, Democratic Republic of the Congo, Denmark, Djibouti, Dominica, Dominican Republic, Ecuador, Egypt, El Salvador, Eritrea, Estonia, Ethiopia, Fiji, Finland, France, Gabon, Georgia, Germany, Ghana, Greece, Grenada, Guatemala, Guinea, Guinea-Bissau, Guyana, Haiti, Honduras, Hungary, Iceland, India, Indonesia, Iran, Iraq, Ireland, Italy, Jamaica, Japan, Jordan, Kazakhstan, Kenya, Kuwait, Kyrgyzstan, Lao People's Democratic Republic, Latvia, Lesotho, Libyan Arab Jamahiriya, Liechtenstein, Lithuania, Luxembourg, Madagascar, Malawi, Malaysia, Maldives, Mali, Malta, Mauritania, Mauritius, Mexico, Moldova, Monaco, Mongolia, Montenegro, Morocco, Mozambique, Myanmar, Namibia, Nauru, Nepal, Netherlands, New Zealand, Nicaragua, Niger, Nigeria, Norway, Oman, Pakistan, Panama, Papua New Guinea, Paraguay, Peru, Philippines, Poland, Portugal, Qatar, Republic of Korea, Romania, Russian Federation, Rwanda, Saint Vincent and the Grenadines, San Marino, Sao Tome and Principe, Saudi Arabia, Senegal, Serbia, Singapore, Slovakia, Slovenia, Solomon Islands, South Africa, Spain, Sri Lanka, Sudan, Suriname, Swaziland, Sweden, Switzerland, Syrian Arab Republic, Thailand, The former Yugoslav Republic of Macedonia, Timor-Leste, Togo, Tonga, Trinidad and Tobago, Tunisia, Turkey, Tuvalu, Uganda, Ukraine, United Arab Emirates, United Kingdom, United Republic of Tanzania, Uruguay, Vanuatu, Venezuela, Viet Nam, Yemen, Zambia, Zimbabwe.

Against: None.

Abstaining: Equatorial Guinea, Israel, Samoa, United States.

Information

UN public information

The General Assembly's Committee on Information, at its twenty-eighth session (New York, 24 April–5 May and 24 August) [A/61/21 & Add.1], continued to consider UN information policies and activities and to evaluate and follow up efforts made and progress achieved in information and communications. The Committee had before it the Secretary-General's report on the activities of the Department of Public Information (DPI). It also considered reports on the continued rationalization of the network of UN information centres; the modernization and integrated management of UN libraries; the UN website: recent developments and progress towards parity among the six official languages of the United Nations (Arabic, Chinese, English, French, Spanish, Russian); and on assessing the effectiveness of UN public information products and activities: the result of a three-year evaluation project.

Those issues and the Secretary-General's report on questions relating to information [A/61/216 & Corr.1] are discussed in the relevant sections below.

At its resumed twenty-eighth session on 24 August [A/61/21/Add.1], the Committee took note of the proposed strategic framework for the period 2008-2009 for programme 23, Public information [A/61/6 (Prog. 23)], as orally amended, which it then forwarded to the Committee for Programme and Coordination for review.

By **decision 61/521** of 14 December, the Assembly increased the membership of the Committee on Information from 108 to 110. On the same date, by **decision 61/413,** the Assembly appointed the Dominican Republic and Thailand as members of the Committee.

GENERAL ASSEMBLY ACTION

On 14 December [meeting 79], the General Assembly, on the recommendation of the Fourth

Committee [A/61/410], adopted **resolutions 61/121 A** and **B** without vote [agenda item 34].

Questions relating to information

A

Information in the service of humanity

The General Assembly,

Taking note of the comprehensive and important report of the Committee on Information,

Also taking note of the report of the Secretary-General on questions relating to information,

Urges all countries, organizations of the United Nations system as a whole and all others concerned, reaffirming their commitment to the principles of the Charter of the United Nations and to the principles of freedom of the press and freedom of information, as well as to those of the independence, pluralism and diversity of the media, deeply concerned by the disparities existing between developed and developing countries and the consequences of every kind arising from those disparities that affect the capability of the public, private or other media and individuals in developing countries to disseminate information and communicate their views and their cultural and ethical values through endogenous cultural production, as well as to ensure the diversity of sources and their free access to information, and recognizing the call in this context for what in the United Nations and at various international forums has been termed "a new world information and communication order, seen as an evolving and continuous process":

(a) To cooperate and interact with a view to reducing existing disparities in information flows at all levels by increasing assistance for the development of communication infrastructures and capabilities in developing countries, with due regard for their needs and the priorities attached to such areas by those countries, and in order to enable them and the public, private or other media in developing countries to develop their own information and communication policies freely and independently and increase the participation of media and individuals in the communication process, and to ensure a free flow of information at all levels;

(b) To ensure for journalists the free and effective performance of their professional tasks and condemn resolutely all attacks against them;

(c) To provide support for the continuation and strengthening of practical training programmes for broadcasters and journalists from public, private and other media in developing countries;

(d) To enhance regional efforts and cooperation among developing countries, as well as cooperation between developed and developing countries, to strengthen communication capacities and to improve the media infrastructure and communication technology in the developing countries, especially in the areas of training and dissemination of information;

(e) To aim at, in addition to bilateral cooperation, providing all possible support and assistance to the developing countries and their media, public, private or other, with due regard to their interests and needs in the field of information and to action already adopted within the United Nations system, including:

(i) The development of the human and technical resources that are indispensable for the improvement of information and communication systems in developing countries and support for the continuation and strengthening of practical training programmes, such as those already operating under both public and private auspices throughout the developing world;

(ii) The creation of conditions that will enable developing countries and their media, public, private or other, to have, by using their national and regional resources, the communication technology suited to their national needs, as well as the necessary programme material, especially for radio and television broadcasting;

(iii) Assistance in establishing and promoting telecommunication links at the subregional, regional and interregional levels, especially among developing countries;

(iv) The facilitation, as appropriate, of access by the developing countries to advanced communication technology available on the open market;

(f) To provide full support for the International Programme for the Development of Communication of the United Nations Educational, Scientific and Cultural Organization, which should support both public and private media.

B

United Nations public information policies and activities

The General Assembly,

Emphasizing the role of the Committee on Information as its main subsidiary body mandated to make recommendations to it relating to the work of the Department of Public Information of the Secretariat,

Reaffirming its resolution 13(I) of 13 February 1946, establishing the Department, which states in paragraph 2 of annex I that "the activities of the Department should be so organized and directed as to promote to the greatest possible extent an informed understanding of the work and purposes of the United Nations among the peoples of the world",

Emphasizing that the contents of public information and communications should be placed at the heart of the strategic management of the United Nations and that a culture of communications and transparency should permeate all levels of the Organization, as a means of fully informing the peoples of the world of the aims and activities of the United Nations, in accordance with the purposes and principles enshrined in the Charter of the United Nations, in order to create broad-based global support for the United Nations,

Stressing that the primary mission of the Department of Public Information is to provide, through its outreach activities, accurate, impartial, comprehensive, timely and relevant information to the public on the tasks and responsibilities of the United Nations in order to strengthen international support for the activities of the Organization with the greatest transparency,

Recalling the comprehensive review of the work of the Department of Public Information, requested by the General Assembly in its resolution 56/253 of 24 December 2001, as well as the report of the Secretary-General entitled "Strengthening of the United Nations: an agenda for further change", and Assembly resolutions 57/300 of 20 December 2002 and 60/109 B of 8 December 2005, which provided an opportunity to take due steps to enhance the efficiency and effectiveness of the Department and to maximize the use of its resources,

Expressing its concern that the gap in information and communication technologies between the developed and the developing countries has continued to widen and that vast segments of the population in developing countries are not benefiting from the present information and communication technologies and, in this regard, underlining the necessity of rectifying the imbalances in the present development of information and communication technologies in order to make it more just, equitable and effective,

Recognizing that developments in the information and communication technologies open vast new opportunities for economic growth and social development and can play an important role in the eradication of poverty in developing countries, and, at the same time, emphasizing that the development of these technologies poses challenges and risks and could lead to the further widening of disparities between and within countries,

Recalling its resolution 59/309 of 22 June 2005 on multilingualism, and emphasizing the importance of making appropriate use of the official languages of the United Nations in the activities of the Department of Public Information, with the aim of eliminating the disparity between the use of English and the five other official languages,

Welcoming Austria to membership in the Committee on Information,

I

Introduction

1. *Reaffirms* its resolution 13(I), in which it established the Department of Public Information, and all other relevant resolutions of the General Assembly related to the activities of the Department, and requests the Secretary-General, in respect of the public information policies and activities of the United Nations, to continue to implement fully the recommendations contained in paragraph 2 of its resolution 48/44 B of 10 December 1993 and other mandates as established by the General Assembly;

2. *Also reaffirms* that the United Nations remains the indispensable foundation of a peaceful and just world and that its voice must be heard in a clear and effective manner, and emphasizes the essential role of the Department of Public Information in this context, the activities of which should be so organized and directed as to promote to the greatest possible extent an informed understanding of the work and purposes of the United Nations among the peoples of the world;

3. *Stresses* the importance of the clear and timely provision of information by the Secretariat to Member States, upon their request, within the framework of existing mandates and procedures;

4. *Reaffirms* the central role of the Committee on Information in United Nations public information policies and activities, including the prioritization of those activities, and decides that recommendations relating to the programme of the Department of Public Information shall originate, to the extent possible, in the Committee and shall be considered by the Committee;

5. *Requests* the Department of Public Information, following the priorities laid down by the General Assembly in its resolution 59/275 of 23 December 2004, and guided by the United Nations Millennium Declaration to pay particular attention to such major issues as the eradication of poverty, conflict prevention, sustainable development, human rights, the HIV/AIDS epidemic, combating terrorism in all its forms and manifestations and the needs of the African continent;

6. *Also requests* the Department of Public Information to pay particular attention to progress in implementing the internationally agreed development goals, including those contained in the Millennium Declaration, and the outcomes of the major related United Nations summits and conferences in carrying out its activities;

7. *Reaffirms* the need to enhance the technological infrastructure of the Department of Public Information on a continuous basis in order to widen its outreach and improve the United Nations website;

8. *Recognizes* the important work carried out by the United Nations Educational, Scientific and Cultural Organization and its collaboration with news agencies and broadcasting organizations in developing countries in disseminating information on priority issues, and encourages continued collaboration between the Department of Public Information and the United Nations Educational, Scientific and Cultural Organization in the promotion of culture and in the fields of education and communication, bridging the existing gap between the developed and the developing countries;

II

General activities of the Department of Public Information

9. *Notes* the report of the Secretary-General on the activities of the Department of Public Information and requests the Secretary-General to continue reporting to the Committee on Information on the activities of the Department at successive sessions;

10. *Acknowledges* that the Department of Public Information has concluded its collaborative project with the Office of Internal Oversight Services on the systematic evaluation of public information products and activities, and notes with appreciation the report of the Secretary-General on the final outcome of this three-year project;

11. *Requests* the Department of Public Information, while acknowledging its commitment to a culture of evaluation, to continue to evaluate its products and activities with the objective of improving their effectiveness, including through interdepartmental consultations;

12. *Reaffirms* that the Department of Public Information is the focal point for information policies of the United Nations and the primary news centre for information about the United Nations, its activities and those of the Secretary-General;

13. *Also reaffirms* the importance of more effective coordination between the Department of Public Information and the Office of the Spokesman for the Secretary-General, and requests the Secretary-General to ensure consistency in the messages of the Organization;

14. *Further reaffirms* that the Department of Public Information must prioritize its work programme while respecting existing mandates and in line with regulation 5.6 of the Regulations and Rules Governing Programme Planning, the Programme Aspects of the Budget, the Monitoring of Implementation and the Methods of Evaluation, to focus its message and better concentrate its efforts and, as a function of performance management, to match its programmes with the needs of its target audiences, on the basis of improved feedback and evaluation mechanisms;

15. *Notes with appreciation* the efforts of the Department of Public Information to continue to publicize the work and decisions of the General Assembly, requests the Department to continue to enhance its working relationship with the Office of the President of the General Assembly and requests the Secretary-General to report thereon to the Committee on Information at its twenty-ninth session;

16. *Requests* the Secretary-General to continue to exert all efforts to ensure that publications and other information services of the Secretariat, including the United Nations website and the United Nations News Service, contain comprehensive, objective and equitable information about the issues before the Organization and that they maintain editorial independence, impartiality, accuracy and full consistency with resolutions and decisions of the General Assembly;

17. *Requests* the Department of Public Information to ensure that United Nations publications are produced in a cost-effective manner and to continue to coordinate closely with all other entities, including all other departments of the Secretariat and funds and programmes of the United Nations system, in order to avoid duplication, within their respective mandates, in the issuance of United Nations publications;

18. *Emphasizes* that the Department of Public Information should maintain and improve its activities in the areas of special interest to developing countries and, where appropriate, other countries with special needs, and that the activities of the Department should contribute to bridging the existing gap between the developing and the developed countries in the crucial field of public information and communications;

19. *Also emphasizes* that the Secretary-General should continue to strengthen the coordination between the Department of Public Information and all other entities, including all other departments of the Secretariat and funds and programmes of the United Nations system, in the context of the client-oriented approach of the Department, which should identify target audiences and develop information programmes and media strategies for priority issues, and emphasizes that public information capacities and activities in other departments should function under the guidance of the Department;

20. *Notes with appreciation* the continued efforts of the Department of Public Information in issuing daily press releases, and requests the Department to continue providing this service to both Member States and representatives of the media, while considering possible means of improving their production process and streamlining their format, structure and length, keeping in mind the views of Member States;

21. *Also notes with appreciation* the efforts of the Department of Public Information to work at the local level with other organizations and bodies of the United Nations system to enhance the coordination of their communication activities, and requests the Secretary-General to report to the Committee on Information at its twenty-ninth session on progress achieved in this regard and on the activities of the United Nations Communications Group;

22. *Calls upon* the Department of Public Information to continue to examine its policies and activities regarding the durable preservation of its radio, television and photographic archives, to take action, within existing resources, to ensure that such archives are preserved and are accessible and to report to the Committee on Information at its twenty-ninth session;

Multilingualism and public information

23. *Emphasizes* the importance of making appropriate use of all the official languages of the United Nations in all the activities of the Department of Public Information, including in presentations to the Committee on Information, with the aim of eliminating the disparity between the use of English and the five other official languages;

24. *Also emphasizes* the importance of ensuring the full, equitable treatment of all the official languages of the United Nations in all the activities of the Department of Public Information and, in this regard, reaffirms its request to the Secretary-General to ensure that the Department has appropriate staffing capacity in all the official languages of the United Nations to undertake all its activities;

25. *Stresses* the importance of fully implementing its resolution 52/214 of 22 December 1997, in section C of which it requested the Secretary-General to ensure that the texts of all new public documents in all six official languages and information materials of the United Nations are made available daily through the United Nations website and are accessible to Member States without delay;

26. *Welcomes* the ongoing efforts of the Department of Public Information to enhance multilingualism in its activities, and requests the Department to continue its endeavours in this regard;

27. *Reiterates* paragraph 4 of section C of its resolution 52/214, and requests the Secretary-General to continue towards completion of the task of uploading all important older United Nations documents on the United Nations website in all six official languages on a priority basis, so that these archives are also available to Member States through that medium;

28. *Reaffirms* that it is important that the Secretary-General include in future programme budget proposals for the Department of Public Information the importance of using all six official languages in its activities;

29. *Welcomes* the work done by the network of United Nations information centres in favour of the publication of United Nations information materials and the translation of important documents in languages other than the United Nations official languages, with a view to reaching the widest possible spectrum of audiences and extending the United Nations message to all the corners of the world in order to strengthen international support for the activities of the Organization;

Bridging the digital divide

30. *Recalls with satisfaction* General Assembly resolution 60/252 of 27 March 2006, in which it endorsed the Tunis Commitment and the Tunis Agenda for the Information Society and proclaimed 17 May annual World Information Society Day, and also recalls the adoption of the Declaration of Principles and the Plan of Action at the first phase of the World Summit on the Information Society, held in Geneva from 10 to 12 December 2003, and in this regard requests the Department of Public Information to contribute to the celebration of this event and to play a role in raising awareness of the possibilities that the use of the Internet and other information and communication technologies can bring to societies and economies, as well as of ways to bridge the digital divide;

31. *Calls upon* the Department of Public Information to contribute to raising the awareness of the international community of the importance of the implementation of the outcome documents of the World Summit on the Information Society;

Network of United Nations information centres

32. *Emphasizes* the importance of the network of United Nations information centres in enhancing the public image of the United Nations and in disseminating messages on the United Nations to local populations, especially in developing countries;

33. *Takes note* of the report of the Secretary-General on the further rationalization of the network of United Nations information centres, and, in this regard, recognizes the constraints of further regionalization as described in paragraph 25 of the report;

34. *Stresses* the importance of rationalizing the network of United Nations information centres, and, in this regard, requests the Secretary-General to continue to make proposals in this direction, including through the redeployment of resources where necessary, and to report to the Committee on Information at its twenty-ninth session;

35. *Reaffirms* that rationalization of United Nations information centres must be carried out on a case-by-case basis in consultation with all concerned Member States in which existing information centres are located, the countries served by those information centres and other interested countries in the region, taking into consideration the distinctive characteristics of each region;

36. *Recognizes* that the network of United Nations information centres, especially in developing countries, should continue to enhance its impact and activities, including through strategic communications support, and calls upon the Secretary-General to submit a report on the implementation of this approach to the Committee on Information at its twenty-ninth session;

37. *Stresses* the importance of taking into account the special needs and requirements of developing countries in the field of information and communications technology for the effective flow of information in those countries;

38. *Also stresses* that the Department of Public Information, through the network of United Nations information centres, should continue to promote public awareness of and mobilize support for the work of the United Nations at the local level, bearing in mind that information in local languages has the strongest impact on local populations;

39. *Further stresses* the importance of efforts to strengthen the outreach activities of the United Nations to those Member States remaining outside the network of United Nations information centres, and encourages the Secretary-General, within the context of rationalization, to extend the services of the network of United Nations information centres to those Member States;

40. *Stresses* that the Department of Public Information should continue to review the allocation of both staff and financial resources to the United Nations information centres in developing countries, emphasizing the needs of the least developed countries;

41. *Encourages* the network of United Nations information centres to continue to develop web pages in local languages, also encourages the Department of Public Information to provide resources and technical facilities, in particular to those information centres whose web pages are not yet operational, and further encourages host countries to respond to the needs of the information centres;

42. *Takes note* of the proposal by the Secretary-General to work closely with the Governments concerned to explore the possibility of identifying rent-free premises, while taking into account the economic condition of the host countries and bearing in mind that such support should not be a substitute for the full allocation of financial resources for the information centres in the context of the programme budget of the United Nations;

43. *Also takes note* of the report of the Secretary-General containing the discussion regarding the creation

of a United Nations information centre in Luanda to address the special needs of Portuguese-speaking African countries, welcomes the offer made by the Government of Angola to host the centre as part of the network of United Nations information centres by providing rent-free premises, and encourages the Secretary-General, within the context of rationalization, to take all necessary measures to accommodate those needs;

III

Strategic communications services

44. *Takes note* of the report of the Secretary-General on the activities of the Department of Public Information and, in this context, reaffirms that the Department of Public Information is the principal department responsible for the implementation of information strategies, as mandated;

45. *Reaffirms* the role of the strategic communications services in devising and disseminating United Nations messages by developing communications strategies, in close collaboration with the substantive departments, United Nations funds and programmes and the specialized agencies, in full compliance with the legislative mandates;

Promotional campaigns

46. *Recognizes* that promotional campaigns aimed at supporting special sessions and international conferences of the United Nations are part of the core responsibility of the Department of Public Information, welcomes the efforts of the Department to examine creative ways in which it can organize and implement these campaigns in partnership with the substantive departments concerned, using the United Nations Millennium Declaration as its guide, and requests the Department to pay particular attention to progress in implementing the internationally agreed development goals, including those contained in the Millennium Declaration, and the outcomes of the major related United Nations summits and conferences in carrying out its activities;

47. *Appreciates* the work of the Department of Public Information in promoting, through its campaigns, issues of importance to the international community, such as United Nations reform, the eradication of poverty, conflict prevention, sustainable development, disarmament, decolonization, human rights, including the rights of women and children and of persons with disabilities, strategic coordination in humanitarian relief, especially in natural disasters and other crises, HIV/AIDS, malaria, tuberculosis and other diseases, the needs of the African continent, combating terrorism in all its forms and manifestations, as well as dialogue among civilizations, the culture of peace and tolerance and the consequences of the Chernobyl disaster, and requests the Department, in cooperation with the countries concerned and with the relevant organizations and bodies of the United Nations system, to continue to take appropriate measures to enhance world public awareness of these and other important global issues;

48. *Invites* the Department of Public Information to continue to work within the United Nations Communications Group to coordinate the preparation and implementation of communication strategies with the heads of information of the agencies, funds and programmes of the United Nations system, and requests the Secretary-General to report to the Committee on Information at its twenty-ninth session on the activities of the Group;

49. *Stresses* the need to continue the renewed emphasis in support of Africa's development, in particular by the Department of Public Information, in order to promote awareness in the international community of the nature of the critical economic and social situation in Africa and of the priorities of the New Partnership for Africa's Development;

Role of the Department of Public Information in United Nations peacekeeping

50. *Requests* the Secretariat to continue to ensure the involvement of the Department of Public Information from the planning stage of future peacekeeping operations through interdepartmental consultations and coordination with other departments of the Secretariat, in particular with the Department of Peacekeeping Operations;

51. *Stresses* the importance of enhancing the public information capacity of the Department of Public Information in the field of peacekeeping operations and its role, in close cooperation with the Department of Peacekeeping Operations, in the selection process of public information staff for United Nations peacekeeping operations or missions, and, in this regard, invites the Department of Public Information to second public information staff who have the necessary skills to fulfil the tasks of the operations or missions, taking into account the principle of equitable geographical distribution in accordance with Chapter XV, Article 101, paragraph 3, of the Charter of the United Nations, and to consider views expressed, especially by host countries, when appropriate, in this regard;

52. *Emphasizes* the importance of the peacekeeping gateway on the United Nations website, and requests the Department of Public Information to continue its efforts in supporting the peacekeeping missions to further develop their websites;

53. *Requests* the Department of Public Information and the Department of Peacekeeping Operations to continue their cooperation in raising awareness of the new realities, successes and challenges faced by peacekeeping operations, especially multidimensional and complex ones, and of the recent surge in United Nations peacekeeping activities, and welcomes efforts by the two Departments to develop and implement a comprehensive communications strategy on current challenges facing United Nations peacekeeping;

54. *Also requests* the Department of Public Information and the Department of Peacekeeping Operations to continue to cooperate in implementing an effective outreach programme to explain the policy of the Organization against sexual exploitation and abuse;

55. *Requests* the Secretary-General to continue to report to the Committee on Information at its successive sessions on the role of the Department of Public Information in United Nations peacekeeping operations;

Role of the Department of Public Information in strengthening dialogue among civilizations and the culture of peace as means of enhancing understanding among nations

56. *Recalls* its resolutions on dialogue among civilizations and the culture of peace and requests the Department of Public Information, while ensuring the pertinence and relevance of subjects for promotional campaigns under this issue, to continue to provide the necessary support for the dissemination of information pertaining to dialogue among civilizations and the culture of peace, as well as the initiative on the Alliance of Civilizations and to take due steps in fostering the culture of dialogue among civilizations and promoting religious and cultural understanding via all mass media, such as the Internet, print, radio and television, and requests the Secretary-General to submit a report in this regard to the Committee on Information at its successive sessions;

IV

News services

57. *Stresses* that the central objective of the news services implemented by the Department of Public Information is the timely delivery of accurate, objective and balanced news and information emanating from the United Nations system in all four mass media—print, radio, television and Internet—to the media and other audiences worldwide, with the overall emphasis on multilingualism, and reiterates its request to the Department to ensure that all news-breaking stories and news alerts are accurate, impartial and free of bias;

58. *Emphasizes* the importance of the Department of Public Information continuing to draw the attention of world media to stories that do not obtain prominent coverage, through the initiative entitled "Ten Stories the World Should Hear More About";

Traditional means of communication

59. *Stresses* that radio remains one of the most cost-effective and far-reaching traditional media available to the Department of Public Information and an important instrument in United Nations activities, including development and peacekeeping, with a view to achieving a broad client base around the world;

60. *Notes* that the international radio broadcasting capacity for the United Nations is an integral part of the activities of the Department of Public Information, and requests the Secretary-General to make every effort to ensure its success and to report on its activities to the Committee on Information at its twenty-ninth session;

61. *Requests* the Secretary-General to continue to make every effort to achieve parity in the six official languages in United Nations radio production;

62. *Notes* the efforts being made by the Department of Public Information to disseminate programmes directly to broadcasting stations all over the world in the six official languages, with the addition of Portuguese, as well as in other languages where possible;

63. *Welcomes* the efforts being made by the Department of Public Information to produce and disseminate television news video and feature material to broadcasters around the world through satellite distribution and web delivery;

64. *Requests* the Department of Public Information to continue building partnerships with local, national and regional broadcasters to extend the United Nations message to all the corners of the world in an accurate and impartial way, and also requests the Radio and Television Service of the Department to continue to take full advantage of the technological infrastructure made available in recent years;

United Nations website

65. *Reaffirms* that the United Nations website is an essential tool for the media, non-governmental organizations, educational institutions, Member States and the general public, and, in this regard, reiterates the continued need for efforts by the Department of Public Information to maintain and improve it;

66. *Recognizes* the efforts made by the Department of Public Information to implement the basic accessibility requirements for persons with disabilities to the United Nations website, calls upon the Department to continue to work towards compliance with all levels of accessibility requirements on all pages of the website with the aim of ensuring its accessibility by persons with different kinds of disabilities, and requests the Secretary-General to report to the Committee on Information at its twenty-ninth session on progress made in this regard;

67. *Reaffirms* the need to achieve full parity among the six official languages on United Nations websites while noting with satisfaction that progress is being made to narrow the gap among different official languages on United Nations websites;

68. *Takes note* of the fact that the multilingual development and enrichment of the United Nations website has improved, although at a slower rate than expected owing to several constraints that need to be addressed, and, in this regard, requests the Department of Public Information, in coordination with content-providing offices, to improve the actions taken to achieve parity among the six official languages on the United Nations website;

69. *Welcomes* the cooperative arrangements undertaken by the Department of Public Information with academic institutions to increase the number of web pages available in some official languages, and requests the Secretary-General to explore additional cost-neutral ways to further extend these cooperative arrangements to include all the official languages of the United Nations;

70. *Reaffirms* section IX, paragraph 2, of its resolution 59/276 of 23 December 2004 on proposals to strengthen the United Nations website;

71. *Reaffirms its request* to the Secretary-General to ensure, while maintaining an up-to-date and accurate website, the adequate distribution of financial and human resources within the Department of Public Information

allocated to the United Nations website among all official languages, taking into consideration the specificity of each official language on a continuous basis;

72. *Recalls* paragraph 74 of its resolution 60/109 B and, in this regard, reiterates that all content-providing offices in the Secretariat should continue their efforts to translate into all official languages all English language materials and databases posted on the United Nations website in the most practical, efficient and cost-effective manner;

73. *Requests* the Secretary-General to continue to take full advantage of recent developments in information technology in order to improve, in a cost-effective manner, the expeditious dissemination of information on the United Nations, in accordance with the priorities established by the General Assembly in its resolutions and taking into account the linguistic diversity of the Organization;

74. *Recognizes* that some official languages use non-Latin and bidirectional scripts and that technological infrastructures and supportive applications in the United Nations are based on Latin script, which leads to difficulties in processing non-Latin and bidirectional scripts, and requests the Department of Public Information, in cooperation with the Information Technology Services Division of the Department of Management, to continue its efforts to ensure that technological infrastructures and supportive applications in the United Nations fully support Latin, non-Latin and bidirectional scripts in order to enhance the equality of all official languages on the United Nations website;

75. *Notes with satisfaction* that United Nations webcast services provide live video of United Nations meetings and events, which is also available in the original language in which it is delivered;

76. *Welcomes* the electronic mail-based United Nations News Service, distributed worldwide in the English and French languages through e-mail by the Department of Public Information, and requests the Department as a matter of priority to continue to examine ways to provide this service in all official languages;

77. *Requests* the Secretary-General to continue to work within the United Nations System Chief Executives Board for Coordination and other appropriate inter-agency bodies to establish a United Nations gateway, an inter-agency search facility in which all entities of the United Nations system should be encouraged to participate, and requests the Secretary-General to report to the Committee on Information at its successive sessions on the activities of the High-level Committee on Management in this regard;

V

Library services

78. *Welcomes* the report of the Secretary-General entitled "Modernization and integrated management of United Nations libraries: update on new strategic directions";

79. *Calls upon* the Department of Public Information to continue to lead the Steering Committee for the Modernization and Integrated Management of United Nations Libraries, and requests the member libraries of the Steering Committee to continue to coordinate closely in the implementation of its programme of work;

80. *Takes note* of the steps taken by the Dag Hammarskjöld Library and the other member libraries of the Steering Committee to align their activities, services and outputs more closely with the goals, objectives and operational priorities of the Organization;

81. *Reiterates* the need to enable the provision of hard copies of library materials to Member States, and notes the efforts of the Secretary-General to enrich, on a multilingual basis, the stock of books and journals in the Dag Hammarskjöld Library, including publications on peace and security and development-related issues, in order to ensure that the Library is enriched and continues to be a broadly accessible resource for information about the United Nations and its activities;

82. *Recognizes* the importance of the depository libraries in disseminating information and knowledge about United Nations activities, and, in this connection, urges the Dag Hammarskjöld Library, in its capacity as the focal point, to continue to take the initiatives necessary to strengthen such libraries by providing regional training and other assistance and by improving their role with the aim of strengthening their support to users in developing countries;

83. *Requests* the Secretary-General to report to the Committee on Information at its twenty-ninth session on the activities of the Steering Committee and the work of the Dag Hammarskjöld Library, including on the application of measures to enhance the effectiveness of the libraries within existing legislative mandates;

84. *Acknowledges* the role of the Dag Hammarskjöld Library, as part of the Outreach Division of the Department of Public Information, in enhancing knowledge-sharing and networking activities to ensure access to the vast store of United Nations knowledge by delegates, permanent missions of Member States, the Secretariat, researchers and depository libraries worldwide, and takes note of the proposal to rename the library the Dag Hammarskjöld Library and Knowledge-Sharing Centre, reflecting its new direction;

85. *Notes* the new approaches taken by the Dag Hammarskjöld Library, in particular the Personal Knowledge Management initiative, to assist representatives of Member States and Secretariat staff in the use of information products and tools as a complement to the traditional training programmes;

86. *Recalls* paragraph 44 of its resolution 56/64 B of 24 December 2001, in which it welcomed the role of the Department of Public Information in fostering increased collaboration among libraries of the United Nations system;

VI

Outreach services

87. *Acknowledges* that the outreach services provided by the Department of Public Information continue to

work towards promoting awareness of the role and work of the United Nations on priority issues;

88. *Notes* the importance of the continued implementation by the Department of Public Information of the ongoing programme for broadcasters and journalists from developing countries and countries with economies in transition, as mandated by the General Assembly, and requests the Department to consider how best to maximize the benefits derived from the programme by reviewing, inter alia, its duration and the number of its participants;

89. *Welcomes* the movement towards educational outreach and the orientation of the *UN Chronicle*, both print and online editions, and, to this end, encourages the *UN Chronicle* to continue to develop co-publishing partnerships, collaborative educational activities and events, including the "Unlearning Intolerance" seminar series, with civil society organizations and institutions of higher learning;

90. *Reaffirms* the important role that guided tours play as a means of reaching out to the general public, including children and students at all levels;

91. *Welcomes* the efforts undertaken by the Department of Public Information in organizing exhibitions on important United Nations-related issues within existing mandates at United Nations Headquarters and at other United Nations offices as a useful tool for reaching out to the general public;

92. *Requests* the Department of Public Information to strengthen its role as a focal point for two-way interaction with civil society relating to the priorities and concerns of the Organization;

93. *Commends* the United Nations Correspondents Association for its ongoing activities and for its Dag Hammarskjöld Memorial Scholarship Fund, which sponsors journalists from developing countries to come to the United Nations Headquarters and report on the activities during the General Assembly, and urges donors to extend financial support to the Fund so that it may increase the number of such scholarships to journalists in this context;

94. *Expresses its appreciation* for the efforts and contribution of United Nations Messengers of Peace, Goodwill Ambassadors and other advocates to promote the work of the United Nations and to enhance international public awareness of its priorities and concerns, and calls upon the Department of Public Information to continue to involve them in its communications and media strategies and outreach activities;

95. *Requests* the Secretary-General to report to the Committee on Information at its next session on the activities being carried out by the Department of Public Information to enhance the public image of the Organization, especially where there is a component of the network of United Nations information centres;

VII

Final remarks

96. *Requests* the Secretary-General to ensure that all reports requested by the Committee on Information are submitted and issued in accordance with the legislative mandate;

97. *Also requests* the Secretary-General to report to the Committee on Information at its twenty-ninth session and to the General Assembly at its sixty-second session on the activities of the Department of Public Information and on the implementation of the recommendations contained in the present resolution;

98. *Requests* the Committee on Information to report to the General Assembly at its sixty-second session;

99. *Decides* to include in the provisional agenda of its sixty-second session the item entitled "Questions relating to information".

DPI activities

In response to General Assembly resolution 60/109 B [YUN 2005, p. 683], the Secretary-General submitted an August report [A/61/216 & Corr.1] covering DPI activities since his February report to the Committee on Information [A/AC.198/2006/5], for the period from July 2005 to February 2006.

DPI continued to address the Organization's strategic priorities and its reform agenda emanating from the 2005 World Summit [YUN 2005, p. 47]. Using a combination of traditional means of communication, such as print and radio, and new information and communication technologies, such as the Internet and webcasting, the Department worked in close cooperation with over 50 "client departments" within the Secretariat and another 26 field offices to further expand its outreach services to Member States, media and civil society. Three sets of collaborators supported the Department's Headquarters staff in their efforts to gain maximum media exposure: the network of UN information centres; the UN family of organizations, who had been integrated into the United Nations Communications Group (see p. 738); and a global network of over 1,500 civil society organizations affiliated with DPI.

In cooperation with the Offices of the General Assembly President and the UN High Commissioner for Human Rights, DPI designed a communications strategy to draw attention to the establishment of the new Human Rights Council (see p. 756). In preparation for the launch of the Secretary-General's May report on migration and development (see p. 1263), DPI undertook a number of media outreach activities, both at Headquarters and through its network of information centres. Months before the June/July United Nations Conference to Review Progress Made in the Implementation of the Programme of Action to Prevent, Combat and Eradicate the Illicit Trade in Small Arms and Light Weapons in All its Aspects (see p. 657) DPI, with the UN Department for Disarmament Affairs, began drafting a communications strategy to promote the Review Conference and the issue.

DPI continued to work closely with the UN Department of Peacekeeping Operations (DPKO) to further develop and refine its global communications strategy in support of UN peace operations. It provided specific support for peacekeeping missions in the field, including developing and implementing a strategy to assist the United Nations Organization Mission in the Democratic Republic of the Congo (see p. 145) in promoting the first elections in that country in more than 40 years, and assisted DPKO in its media relations relating to the Darfur crisis in the Sudan (see p. 268). In preparation for the first meeting of the Organizational Committee of the Peacebuilding Commission in June (see p. 55), DPI prepared a fact sheet, created a website, carried out other media activities and sent guidance and information material to UN information centres to help publicize the Commission's inaugural meeting.

The UN website completed its eleventh year as one of the premier sites providing a wide range of news and information in multiple forms and in multiple languages to users around the world. Enhancing the quality and range of material available in all six official UN languages continued to be a major priority for the Department (see p. 738).

Efforts to strengthen radio programming and to expand partnerships with international broadcasters continued. All six official language radio websites and those for Portuguese and Kiswahili were given major technical overhauls. DPI also made available on the UN Radio website its programming in four Asian languages, namely Bangla, Hindi, Indonesian and Urdu. Improved delivery systems, along with active promotion of its programmes, further expanded UN Radio's potential audience reach.

As part of the DPI continuing effort to draw upon the academic community's involvement in policy thinking and evolution at the United Nations, a new section was created that combined two publications, the *Yearbook of the United Nations* and the *UN Chronicle*, with the provision of print, electronic and convening forums for shared thinking on issues vital to the Organization and its Member States.

The analysis of DPI work with the media, specifically the impact of public information and communications campaigns, was an area in which the Department had been working to establish more systematic assessment. To that end, DPI provided training to staff members by external media monitoring specialists, who also helped to create a media analysis tool for use by communications campaign managers. Also, a pilot project was launched to involve UN information centres in global systematic media monitoring and analysis.

Evaluation of products and activities

In response to General Assembly resolution 60/109 B [YUN 2005, p. 683], the Secretary-General submitted to the Committee on Information a February assessment of the effectiveness of UN public information products and activities: the results of a three-year evaluation project [A/AC.198/2006/4 & Corr.1]. The evaluation was conducted in collaboration with the Office of Internal Oversight Services (OIOS), in accordance with Assembly resolution 57/300 [YUN 2002, p. 1353].

The report stated that the reorientation of DPI, launched in 2002 [YUN 2002, p. 585], allowed the Department to begin working in four main strategic directions: to create a culture of communication through client orientation; to integrate new technologies into all aspects of its work; to make full use of the resources available throughout the UN system by improving the coordination of public information activities; and to strengthen partnerships to maximize global outreach. Based on the DPI/OIOS evaluation of products and activities, the Department identified a set of key findings that corresponded to the strategic directions; they included reaching target audiences; meeting audience needs; raising awareness of key UN issues; effective communications on priority issues; working with the media; working with educators and youth; and coordination and client orientation.

The report concluded that, while the image of the United Nations had been badly bruised, largely because of scandal-driven media coverage, the Organization was still regarded as an important public institution. Although DPI had no illusions about its capacity to counteract much of the negative coverage of the Organization, it had reinforced its media outreach capacity to better tell the UN story, respond to criticism and promote awareness of the Organization's achievements in other areas. It was clear that DPI had to evaluate its programmes and activities on an ongoing basis in order to cope with, and adapt to, the challenges of a rapidly changing international context.

Library services

In 2006, the Dag Hammarskjöld Library continued to implement the new strategic directions for UN libraries outlined by the Secretary-General in his 2005 report to the Committee on Information [YUN 2005, p. 693], including the expanded role given to the Library in improving knowledge sharing and communications within the Secretariat.

Expanding the outreach of depository libraries remained a major focus. As at July, 406 active depository libraries in 145 countries received UN documents and publications. Although changes in information and communication technology made it possible to disseminate information and knowledge through electronic means, the new networks required more support and training for depository libraries. In May, in partnership with Kyung Hee University in the Republic of Korea, a training programme was offered for representatives from nine depository libraries. The Library was exploring other partnerships to further develop training and support for depository libraries and to promote and extend UN outreach capacity, based on that model.

The Library continued to guide the development and expansion of the Organization's Intranet, iSeek, with a view to enhancing and improving that tool for internal organizational communication. In September 2005, iSeek was re-launched; by the end of the year, it was made accessible to all UN information centres. In May 2006, the Economic and Social Commission for Asia and the Pacific became the first overseas office to fully participate in the programme through the launch of its own iSeek page, followed in July by the UN Office at Geneva, which launched its bilingual English-French iSeek. In June, more than 50 participants from New York and other duty stations met to discuss the role of iSeek and how it could be used to support the Secretariat internal communications strategy.

Management of UN Libraries

In response to General Assembly resolution 60/109 B [YUN 2005, p. 683], the Secretary-General submitted to the Committee on Information a February report [A/AC.198/2006/2] on the modernization and integrated management of UN libraries that gave an update on progress made in implementing the new strategic directions for UN libraries that were members of the Steering Committee for the Modernization and Integrated Management of UN Libraries, established in 2003 [YUN 2003, p. 635].

The report noted that UN libraries were moving from their traditional role as independent repositories to networks of knowledge sharing communities, and from building and maintaining book and periodical collections to facilitating a knowledge-enabled environment and information exchange among stakeholders. To reflect those changes and provide a new image, it was proposed that the official name of the Dag Hammarskjöld Library be expanded to the "Dag Hammarskjöld Library and Knowledge Sharing Centre".

In addition to revamping the Organization's Intranet, the Library developed a Secretariat-wide internal communications strategy, the goal of which was to ensure that all Secretariat staff, regardless of duty station, had access to the same level of information. The Library's personal knowledge management programme aimed to create an information management and consulting service to assist staff and UN delegations in dealing with the increasingly complex information environment through direct support services offered on a case-by-case basis to address specific problems. Library professionals were being transformed into networking facilitators, essential team members in the UN community of knowledge workers, who were helping to change the perception of what the Library did and giving it an expanded presence across the Organization.

Recommendations had been made under the capital master plan (see p. 1665) to renovate and redesign the Library, providing an opportunity for more innovation. Another challenge faced by the Dag Hammarskjöld Library, other UN system libraries and libraries worldwide was the shift from print to electronic publishing. Some 70 per cent of commercial journals were available electronically, a trend that had been accompanied by a dramatic increase in subscription prices. The cost of subscribing to such resources represented over 40 per cent of the non-staff resources of the Library's budget.

The report concluded that UN libraries were becoming key players in the field of knowledge sharing and content management for the Organization and were in a position to play a more significant role in the reform process, assisting with internal communications and providing better access to information and knowledge. UN libraries continued to fulfill their original mandates, while adapting innovative approaches, tools and skills for the twenty-first century. Paper collections would be maintained, while new methods of custodianship and preservation would allow library staff to devote more effort to promoting their relevance and value.

UN information centres

In response to General Assembly resolution 60/109 B [YUN 2005, p. 683], the Secretary-General submitted to the Committee on Information a February report [A/AC.198/2006/1] on the continued rationalization of the UN information centres (UNICs) network. The report examined the impact of the changes to the network, including rationalization around regional hubs, which was first proposed to the Assembly in 2002 [YUN 2002, p. 585], on the operation of the network. Following the closure of nine UN information centres in Western Europe at the end of 2003 [YUN 2003, p. 637] and the establishment of a regional hub in Brussels, Belgium, in 2004 [YUN 2004, p. 627], the Department was able to reallocate three Director-level posts to centres in Cairo, Egypt, Mexico City and Pretoria, South Africa. While strengthening the leadership of those centres, DPI had also assigned them greater regional responsibilities. By leveraging the relative strengths of the centres in terms of outreach and information production and by providing them with additional information technology support, the offices were positioned to play an important role in enhancing the activities of the smaller centres in their regions.

DPI made tangible progress towards securing either rent-free or subsidized premises for a number of information centres, with 44 centres operating from offices provided by the local authorities or host country Governments. The UNIC in Sydney, Australia, was in the process of moving to Canberra, where an extrabudgetary contribution by the host Government would cover the cost of the rental of the premises. Through the savings generated, it would be possible to enhance the centre's public information outreach and activities in the South Pacific. Trinidad and Tobago had also pledged to make an extrabudgetary contribution, starting in 2006, to cover the cost of the rental for the UNIC in Port of Spain. The Department had contacted eight other host Governments in locations where the cost of the rental and/or maintenance of premises consumed a large part of the centres' allocation of operational funds.

Noting that only 20 of the 54 UNICs were headed by internationally recruited staff, the report stated that National Information Officers, with their intimate knowledge of the local environment, communications issues and local languages, were the pillars of DPI communications objectives at the country level. In nine locations, UNIC information officers performed National Officer functions at a lower grade level. To remedy that persistent situation, DPI was seeking to convert nine local-level posts to the National Officer category, an objective that would be pursued during the next budgetary exercise. DPI was also working with the UN Office of Human Resources Management to secure the classification of some National Officer posts at the NO-C level, which would have no additional budgetary implications. Although DPI remained open to the proposal of Angola's Government and the Community of Portuguese-speaking Countries with regard to the possibility of opening a UNIC in Luanda to cover Portuguese-speaking African countries and appreciated Angola's offer to provide rent-free premises for such a centre, it was not in a position to cover the considerable one-time and ongoing operational costs of an additional office or to identify the local-level posts needed for that purpose within existing resources. Such an undertaking would be possible only through the closure of one or more currently operating centres.

In late 2005, the Regional United Nations Information Centre for Western Europe in Brussels was renamed the United Nations Regional Information Centre (UNRIC) to increase its visibility in the electronic media, since many web search engines detected the UN connection only when those words appeared at the start of the name. Following UNRIC first operational year in its permanent premises, DPI undertook an initial evaluation of its experience. The evaluation identified the strengths and weaknesses of the Centre as a regional hub and suggested ways to strengthen it. In 2005, the Centre had not yet fully adjusted to the regional approach to information activities and was still grappling with the challenges of a dramatic change in the established patterns of doing business and of serving the media and civil society in a large and distant geographical area from a centralized location.

In his August report to the General Assembly on questions relating to information [A/61/216 & Corr.1], the Secretary-General said that DPI had developed a database for the input of communications workplans by various sections at Headquarters and by the individual information centres. Posted on the newly created internal website, StratCom, the information on the global activities planned for any given strategic communications priority and the status of their implementation were available to programme managers in the Department's Information Centres Service. Further progress had been made in the coordination of communications at the field level. Several country-level communications groups had been established following approval by the United Nations Communications Group (UNCG) in March. UNCG agreed to further strengthen the country- and regional-level groups by promoting joint work programmes and resource-sharing. In addition to strengthening the local web presence (47 UNICs maintained websites in 5 official and 26 unofficial languages), UNICs made progress in developing better online strategies. The technical team in the Brussels UNRIC had developed a content management system that would enable local staff to update and maintain their own websites through a user-friendly interface. Starting with UNICs in sub-Saharan Africa, the project envisioned that all websites maintained by the information centres would be accessible and uniform while still addressing the information needs of their local audiences.

Development of UN website

In response to General Assembly resolution 60/109 B [YUN 2005, p. 683], the Secretary-General submitted to the Committee on Information a February report [A/AC.198/2006/3] on recent developments and progress towards parity among the official languages on the UN website.

Describing the challenge facing the Secretariat in moving towards the goal of parity in the six official languages on the UN website as having many aspects, the report stated that more material was being placed daily on the site by author departments in the working languages, English and French, but overwhelmingly in the former. That constant building of the website was carried out within a decentralized governance structure. DPI worked through the Working Group on Internet Matters, which the Department chaired, as well as bilaterally with other content-providing offices, to promote multilingualism and site coherence in a practical manner.

Despite those issues, technical changes were producing progress towards the language parity goal in a number of ways. Radio files in all the official languages, as well as Kiswahili, Portuguese, Bangla, Hindi, Indonesian and Urdu, were enhancing the site's multilingualism. Webcasting was available in the floor language of meetings and DPI was planning its gradual expansion to the other official languages. With respect to the mandate to publish in the official languages, Member States had recognized the responsibility of individual author departments for producing their websites in the official languages. However, a governance system that would introduce coherence was essential for the website's further development and progress towards language parity.

Another constraint in moving towards language parity was the level of technical expertise available in author departments. DPI was collaborating with the Information Technology Services Division of the Department of Management and other content-providing offices in the search for an enterprise content management system that could handle the language, presentation, multimedia and accessibility requirements of the website, and for a new and improved enterprise search system.

DPI was striving to accelerate the pace of moving towards parity among the official languages on the website, the report concluded, noting that the establishment of new P-4 posts for the website Languages Unit would permit the volume of new material going onto the site to increase and allow for needed maintenance and updating. However, since parity should not be achieved at the cost of quality, the technological infrastructure was being overhauled, a new content management system was being sought and the site was being revamped to provide better navigation and improved access for persons with disabilities.

UN Communications Group

The UN Communications Group (UNCG), established in 2002 [YUN 2002, p. 589], comprised 41 communications offices of the entire UN system; its purpose was to address the common communications challenges facing the system. At a March meeting, the Group endorsed guidelines for country-level communications groups (see p. 737).

At its fifth annual meeting (Vienna, 28-29 June), UNCG members stressed that the Group was the most effective platform for advancing the UN system's common agenda.

Information and telecommunications in the context of international security

In response to General Assembly resolution 60/45 [YUN 2005, p. 695], the Secretary-General, in a July report and later addendum [A/61/161 & Add.1], transmitted the views of seven Member States on the general appreciation of the issues of information security; efforts made at the national level to strengthen information security and promote international cooperation in that area; the content of relevant international concepts aimed at strengthening the security of global information and telecommunications systems; and possible measures that could be taken by the international community to strengthen information security at the global level.

GENERAL ASSEMBLY ACTION

On 6 December [meeting 67], the General Assembly, on the recommendation of the First (Disarmament and International Security) Committee [A/61/389], adopted resolution **61/54** by recorded vote (176-1-0) [agenda item 85].

Developments in the field of information and telecommunications in the context of international security

The General Assembly,

Recalling its resolutions 53/70 of 4 December 1998, 54/49 of 1 December 1999, 55/28 of 20 November 2000, 56/19 of 29 November 2001, 57/53 of 22 November 2002, 58/32 of 8 December 2003, 59/61 of 3 December 2004 and 60/45 of 8 December 2005,

Recalling also its resolutions on the role of science and technology in the context of international security, in which, inter alia, it recognized that scientific and technological developments could have both civilian and military applications and that progress in science and technology for civilian applications needed to be maintained and encouraged,

Noting that considerable progress has been achieved in developing and applying the latest information technologies and means of telecommunication,

Affirming that it sees in this process the broadest positive opportunities for the further development of civilization, the expansion of opportunities for cooperation for the common good of all States, the enhancement of the creative potential of humankind and additional improvements in the circulation of information in the global community,

Recalling, in this connection, the approaches and principles outlined at the Information Society and Development Conference, held in Midrand, South Africa, from 13 to 15 May 1996,

Bearing in mind the results of the Ministerial Conference on Terrorism, held in Paris on 30 July 1996, and the recommendations that it made,

Bearing in mind also the results of the World Summit on the Information Society, held in Geneva from 10 to 12 December 2003 (first phase) and in Tunis from 16 to 18 November 2005 (second phase),

Noting that the dissemination and use of information technologies and means affect the interests of the entire international community and that optimum effectiveness is enhanced by broad international cooperation,

Expressing its concern that these technologies and means can potentially be used for purposes that are inconsistent with the objectives of maintaining international stability and security and may adversely affect the integrity of the infrastructure of States to the detriment of their security in both civil and military fields,

Considering that it is necessary to prevent the use of information resources or technologies for criminal or terrorist purposes,

Noting the contribution of those Member States that have submitted their assessments on issues of information security to the Secretary-General pursuant to paragraphs 1 to 3 of resolutions 53/70, 54/49, 55/28, 56/19, 57/53, 58/32, 59/61 and 60/45,

Taking note of the reports of the Secretary-General containing those assessments,

Welcoming the initiative taken by the Secretariat and the United Nations Institute for Disarmament Research in convening an international meeting of experts in Geneva in August 1999 on developments in the field of information and telecommunications in the context of international security, as well as its results,

Considering that the assessments of the Member States contained in the reports of the Secretary-General and the international meeting of experts have contributed to a better understanding of the substance of issues of international information security and related notions,

Bearing in mind that the Secretary-General, in fulfilment of resolution 58/32, established in 2004 a group of governmental experts, which, in accordance with its mandate, considered existing and potential threats in the sphere of information security and possible cooperative measures to address them and conducted a study on relevant international concepts aimed at strengthening the security of global information and telecommunications systems,

Taking note of the report of the Secretary-General on the Group of Governmental Experts on Developments in the Field of Information and Telecommunications in the Context of International Security, prepared on the basis of the results of the Group's work,

1. *Calls upon* Member States to promote further at multilateral levels the consideration of existing and potential threats in the field of information security, as well as possible measures to limit the threats emerging in this field, consistent with the need to preserve the free flow of information;

2. *Considers* that the purpose of such measures could be served through the examination of relevant international concepts aimed at strengthening the security of global information and telecommunications systems;

3. *Invites* all Member States to continue to inform the Secretary-General of their views and assessments on the following questions:

(*a*) General appreciation of the issues of information security;

(*b*) Efforts taken at the national level to strengthen information security and promote international cooperation in this field;

(*c*) The content of the concepts mentioned in paragraph 2 above;

(*d*) Possible measures that could be taken by the international community to strengthen information security at the global level;

4. *Requests* the Secretary-General, with the assistance of a group of governmental experts, to be established in 2009 on the basis of equitable geographical distribution, to continue to study existing and potential threats in the sphere of information security and possible cooperative measures to address them, as well as the concepts referred to in paragraph 2 above, and to submit a report on the results of this study to the General Assembly at its sixty-fifth session;

5. *Decides* to include in the provisional agenda of its sixty-second session the item entitled "Developments in the field of information and telecommunications in the context of international security".

RECORDED VOTE ON RESOLUTION 61/54:

In favour: Afghanistan, Albania, Algeria, Andorra, Angola, Antigua and Barbuda, Argentina, Armenia, Australia, Austria, Azerbaijan, Bahamas, Bahrain, Bangladesh, Barbados, Belarus, Belgium, Belize, Bhutan, Bolivia, Bosnia and Herzegovina, Brazil, Brunei Darussalam, Bulgaria, Burkina Faso, Burundi, Cambodia, Cameroon, Canada, Cape Verde, Central African Republic, Chile, China, Colombia, Comoros, Congo, Costa Rica, Croatia, Cuba, Cyprus, Czech Republic, Democratic Republic of the Congo, Denmark, Djibouti, Dominica, Dominican Republic, Ecuador, Egypt,

El Salvador, Eritrea, Estonia, Ethiopia, Fiji, Finland, France, Gabon, Gambia, Georgia, Germany, Ghana, Greece, Grenada, Guatemala, Guinea, Guyana, Haiti, Honduras, Hungary, Iceland, India, Indonesia, Iran, Iraq, Ireland, Israel, Italy, Jamaica, Japan, Jordan, Kazakhstan, Kuwait, Kyrgyzstan, Lao People's Democratic Republic, Latvia, Lebanon, Lesotho, Liberia, Libyan Arab Jamahiriya, Liechtenstein, Lithuania, Luxembourg, Malawi, Malaysia, Maldives, Mali, Malta, Marshall Islands, Mauritania, Mauritius, Mexico, Micronesia, Moldova, Monaco, Mongolia, Montenegro, Morocco, Mozambique, Myanmar, Namibia, Nepal, Netherlands, New Zealand, Nicaragua, Niger, Nigeria, Norway, Oman, Pakistan, Palau, Panama, Paraguay, Peru, Philippines, Poland, Portugal, Qatar, Republic of Korea, Romania, Russian Federation, Rwanda, Saint Kitts and Nevis, Saint Lucia, Saint Vincent and the Grenadines, Samoa, San Marino, Sao Tome and Principe, Saudi Arabia, Senegal, Serbia, Sierra Leone, Singapore, Slovakia, Slovenia, Solomon Islands, Somalia, South Africa, Spain, Sri Lanka, Sudan, Suriname, Swaziland, Sweden, Switzerland, Syrian Arab Republic, Tajikistan, Thailand, The former Yugoslav Republic of Macedonia, Timor-Leste, Togo, Tonga, Trinidad and Tobago, Tunisia, Turkey, Turkmenistan, Ukraine, United Arab Emirates, United Kingdom, United Republic of Tanzania, Uruguay, Uzbekistan, Vanuatu, Venezuela, Viet Nam, Yemen, Zambia, Zimbabwe.

Against: United States.

Abstaining: None.

Science and technology in international security and disarmament

On 6 December [meeting 67], the General Assembly, on the recommendation of the First Committee [A/61/390], adopted **resolution 61/55** by recorded vote (108-54-16) [agenda item 86].

Role of science and technology in the context of international security and disarmament

The General Assembly,

Recognizing that scientific and technological developments can have both civilian and military applications and that progress in science and technology for civilian applications needs to be maintained and encouraged,

Concerned that military applications of scientific and technological developments can contribute significantly to the improvement and upgrading of advanced weapons systems and, in particular, weapons of mass destruction,

Aware of the need to follow closely the scientific and technological developments that may have a negative impact on international security and disarmament, and to channel scientific and technological developments for beneficial purposes,

Cognizant that international transfers of dual-use as well as high-technology products, services and know-how for peaceful purposes are important for the economic and social development of States,

Also cognizant of the need to regulate such transfers of dual-use goods and technologies and high technology with military applications through multilaterally negotiated, universally applicable, non-discriminatory guidelines,

Expressing its concern about the growing proliferation of ad hoc and exclusive export control regimes and arrangements for dual-use goods and technologies, which tend to impede the economic and social development of developing countries,

Recalling that in the final document of the Fourteenth Conference of Heads of State or Government of Non-Aligned Countries, held in Havana on 15 and 16 September 2006, it was again noted with concern that undue restrictions on exports to developing countries of material, equipment and technology for peaceful purposes persisted,

Emphasizing that internationally negotiated guidelines for the transfer of high technology with military applications should take into account the legitimate defence requirements of all States and the requirements for the maintenance of international peace and security, while ensuring that access to high-technology products and services and know-how for peaceful purposes is not denied,

1. *Affirms* that scientific and technological progress should be used for the benefit of all mankind to promote the sustainable economic and social development of all States and to safeguard international security, and that international cooperation in the use of science and technology through the transfer and exchange of technological know-how for peaceful purposes should be promoted;

2. *Invites* Member States to undertake additional efforts to apply science and technology for disarmament-related purposes and to make disarmament-related technologies available to interested States;

3. *Urges* Member States to undertake multilateral negotiations with the participation of all interested States in order to establish universally acceptable, non-discriminatory guidelines for international transfers of dual-use goods and technologies and high technology with military applications;

4. *Encourages* United Nations bodies to contribute, within existing mandates, to promoting the application of science and technology for peaceful purposes;

5. *Decides* to include in the provisional agenda of its sixty-third session the item entitled "Role of science and technology in the context of international security and disarmament".

RECORDED VOTE ON RESOLUTION 61/55:

In favour: Afghanistan, Algeria, Angola, Antigua and Barbuda, Bahamas, Bahrain, Bangladesh, Barbados, Belize, Bhutan, Bolivia, Brunei Darussalam, Burkina Faso, Burundi, Cambodia, Cameroon, Cape Verde, Central African Republic, Chile, China, Colombia, Comoros, Congo, Costa Rica, Cuba, Democratic People's Republic of Korea, Democratic Republic of the Congo, Djibouti, Dominica, Dominican Republic, Ecuador, Egypt, El Salvador, Eritrea, Ethiopia, Fiji, Gabon, Ghana, Grenada, Guatemala, Guinea, Guyana, Haiti, Honduras, India, Indonesia, Iran, Iraq, Jamaica, Jordan, Kuwait, Lao People's Democratic Republic, Lebanon, Lesotho, Liberia, Libyan Arab Jamahiriya, Malawi,

Malaysia, Maldives, Mali, Mauritania, Mauritius, Mexico, Mongolia, Morocco, Mozambique, Myanmar, Namibia, Nepal, Nicaragua, Niger, Nigeria, Oman, Pakistan, Panama, Paraguay, Peru, Philippines, Qatar, Rwanda, Saint Kitts and Nevis, Saint Lucia, Saint Vincent and the Grenadines, Sao Tome and Principe, Saudi Arabia, Senegal, Sierra Leone, Singapore, Somalia, Sri Lanka, Sudan, Suriname, Swaziland, Syrian Arab Republic, Thailand, Timor-Leste, Togo, Trinidad and Tobago, Tunisia, Turkmenistan, Uganda, United Arab Emirates, United Republic of Tanzania, Venezuela, Viet Nam, Yemen, Zambia, Zimbabwe.

Against: Albania, Andorra, Australia, Austria, Belgium, Bosnia and Herzegovina, Bulgaria, Canada, Croatia, Cyprus, Czech Republic, Denmark, Estonia, Finland, France, Georgia, Germany, Greece, Hungary, Iceland, Ireland, Israel, Italy, Japan, Latvia, Liechtenstein, Lithuania, Luxembourg, Malta, Marshall Islands, Micronesia, Moldova, Monaco, Montenegro, Netherlands, New Zealand, Norway, Palau, Poland, Portugal, Republic of Korea, Romania, San Marino, Serbia, Slovakia, Slovenia, Spain, Sweden, Switzerland, The former Yugoslav Republic of Macedonia, Turkey, Ukraine, United Kingdom, United States.

Abstaining: Argentina, Armenia, Azerbaijan, Belarus, Brazil, Kazakhstan, Kyrgyzstan, Russian Federation, Samoa, Solomon Islands, South Africa, Tajikistan, Tonga, Uruguay, Uzbekistan, Vanuatu.

Peaceful uses of outer space

The Committee on the Peaceful Uses of Outer Space (Committee on Outer Space), at its forty-ninth session (Vienna, 7-16 June) [A/61/20], discussed ways and means to maintain outer space for peaceful purposes; the spin-off benefits of space technology; space and society; and space and water. It also considered the implementation of the recommendations of the Third (1999) United Nations Conference on the Exploration and Peaceful Uses of Outer Space (UNISPACE III) [YUN 1999, p. 556] and those of the World Summit on the Information Society, which took place in 2003 [YUN 2003, p. 857] and 2005 [YUN 2005, p. 933]. In addition, it reviewed the work of its two subcommittees, one dealing with scientific and technical issues (see p. 746) and the other with legal questions (see p. 749).

GENERAL ASSEMBLY ACTION

On 14 December [meeting 79], the General Assembly, on the recommendation of the Fourth Committee [A/61/406], adopted **resolution 61/111** without vote [agenda item 30].

International cooperation in the peaceful uses of outer space

The General Assembly,

Recalling its resolutions 51/122 of 13 December 1996, 54/68 of 6 December 1999, 59/2 of 20 October 2004 and 60/99 of 8 December 2005,

Deeply convinced of the common interest of mankind in promoting and expanding the exploration and use of outer space, as the province of all mankind, for peaceful purposes and in continuing efforts to extend to all States the benefits derived therefrom, and also of the importance of international cooperation in this field, for which the United Nations should continue to provide a focal point,

Reaffirming the importance of international cooperation in developing the rule of law, including the relevant norms of space law and their important role in international cooperation for the exploration and use of outer space for peaceful purposes, and of the widest possible adherence to international treaties that promote the peaceful uses of outer space in order to meet emerging new challenges, especially for developing countries,

Seriously concerned about the possibility of an arms race in outer space, and bearing in mind the importance of article IV of the Treaty on Principles Governing the Activities of States in the Exploration and Use of Outer Space, including the Moon and Other Celestial Bodies,

Recognizing that all States, in particular those with major space capabilities, should contribute actively to the goal of preventing an arms race in outer space as an essential condition for the promotion and strengthening of international cooperation in the exploration and use of outer space for peaceful purposes,

Considering that space debris is an issue of concern to all nations,

Noting the progress achieved in the further development of peaceful space exploration and applications as well as in various national and cooperative space projects, which contributes to international cooperation, and the importance of further developing the legal framework to strengthen international cooperation in this field,

Convinced of the importance of the recommendations in the resolution entitled "The Space Millennium: Vienna Declaration on Space and Human Development", adopted by the Third United Nations Conference on the Exploration and Peaceful Uses of Outer Space (UNISPACE III), held at Vienna from 19 to 30 July 1999, and the need to promote the use of space technology towards implementing the United Nations Millennium Declaration,

Taking note of the actions already taken as well as those to be embarked upon to further implement the recommendations of UNISPACE III, as reflected in resolution 59/2 and the Plan of Action of the Committee on the Peaceful Uses of Outer Space,

Convinced that the use of space science and technology and their applications in such areas as telemedicine, tele-education, disaster management and environmental protection as well as other Earth observation applications contribute to achieving the objectives of the global conferences of the United Nations that address various aspects of economic, social and cultural development, inter alia, poverty eradication,

Taking note, in that regard, that the 2005 World Summit recognized the important role that science and technology play in promoting sustainable development,

Having considered the report of the Committee on the Peaceful Uses of Outer Space on the work of its forty-ninth session,

1. *Endorses* the report of the Committee on the Peaceful Uses of Outer Space on the work of its forty-ninth session;

2. *Urges* States that have not yet become parties to the international treaties governing the uses of outer space to give consideration to ratifying or acceding to those treaties as well as incorporating them in their national legislation;

3. *Notes* that, at its forty-fifth session, the Legal Subcommittee of the Committee on the Peaceful Uses of Outer Space continued its work, as mandated by the General Assembly in its resolution 60/99;

4. *Endorses* the recommendation of the Committee that the Legal Subcommittee, at its forty-sixth session, taking into account the concerns of all countries, in particular those of developing countries:

(a) Consider the following as regular agenda items:
- (i) General exchange of views;
- (ii) Status and application of the five United Nations treaties on outer space;
- (iii) Information on the activities of international intergovernmental and non-governmental organizations relating to space law;
- (iv) Matters relating to:
  - *a.* The definition and delimitation of outer space;
  - *b.* The character and utilization of the geostationary orbit, including consideration of ways and means to ensure the rational and equitable use of the geostationary orbit without prejudice to the role of the International Telecommunication Union;

(b) Consider the following single issues/items for discussion:
- (i) Review and possible revision of the Principles Relevant to the Use of Nuclear Power Sources in Outer Space;
- (ii) Examination and review of the developments concerning the draft protocol on matters specific to space assets to the Convention on International Interests in Mobile Equipment;

(c) Consider the practice of States and international organizations in registering space objects in accordance with the workplan adopted by the Committee;

5. *Notes* that the Legal Subcommittee, at its forty-sixth session, will submit its proposals to the Committee for new items to be considered by the Subcommittee at its forty-seventh session, in 2008;

6. *Also notes* that, in the context of paragraph 4 *(a)* (ii) above, the Legal Subcommittee, at its forty-sixth session, will reconvene its Working Group and review the need to extend the mandate of the Working Group beyond that session of the Subcommittee;

7. *Further notes* that, in the context of paragraph 4 *(a)* (iv) *a.* above, the Legal Subcommittee will reconvene its Working Group on the item only to consider matters relating to the definition and delimitation of outer space;

8. *Notes* that, in the context of paragraph 4 *(c)* above, the Legal Subcommittee will reconvene its Working Group;

9. *Also notes* that the Scientific and Technical Subcommittee, at its forty-third session, continued its work as mandated by the General Assembly in its resolution 60/99;

10. *Endorses* the recommendation of the Committee that the Scientific and Technical Subcommittee, at its forty-fourth session, taking into account the concerns of all countries, in particular those of developing countries:

(a) Consider the following items:
- (i) General exchange of views and introduction to reports submitted on national activities;
- (ii) United Nations Programme on Space Applications;
- (iii) Implementation of the recommendations of the Third United Nations Conference on the Exploration and Peaceful Uses of Outer Space (UNISPACE III);
- (iv) Matters relating to remote sensing of the Earth by satellite, including applications for developing countries and monitoring of the Earth's environment;

(b) Consider the following items in accordance with the workplans adopted by the Committee:
- (i) Space debris;
- (ii) Use of nuclear power sources in outer space;
- (iii) Near-Earth objects;
- (iv) Space-system-based disaster management support;
- (v) International Heliophysical Year 2007;

(c) Consider the following single issue/item for discussion: examination of the physical nature and technical attributes of the geostationary orbit and its utilization and applications, including in the field of space communications, as well as other questions relating to developments in space communications, taking particular account of the needs and interests of developing countries;

11. *Notes* that the Scientific and Technical Subcommittee, at its forty-fourth session, will submit its proposal to the Committee for a draft provisional agenda for the forty-fifth session of the Subcommittee, in 2008;

12. *Endorses* the recommendation of the Committee that the Committee on Space Research and the International Astronautical Federation, in liaison with member States, be invited to arrange a symposium to address the theme "The use of the equatorial orbit for space applications: challenges and opportunities", with as wide participation as possible, to be held during the first week of the forty-fourth session of the Scientific and Technical Subcommittee;

13. *Agrees* that, in the context of paragraphs 10 *(a)* (ii) and (iii) and 11 above, the Scientific and Technical Subcommittee, at its forty-fourth session, should reconvene the Working Group of the Whole;

14. *Also agrees* that, in the context of paragraph 10 *(b)* (i) above, the Scientific and Technical

Subcommittee could, at any time during its forty-fourth session, reconvene its Working Group on Space Debris to consider comments resulting from the referral of the guidelines to the national level and any further developments, particularly the relationship between the revised draft of the space debris mitigation guidelines and nuclear power sources in outer space;

15. *Further agrees* that, in the context of paragraph 10 *(b)* (ii) above, the Scientific and Technical Subcommittee, at its forty-fourth session, should reconvene its Working Group on the Use of Nuclear Power Sources in Outer Space and that the Working Group should continue its intersessional work on the topics described in the multi-year workplan as amended by the Subcommittee at its forty-second session and as agreed by the Subcommittee at its forty-third session and the Committee at its forty-ninth session;

16. *Agrees* that, in the context of paragraph 10 *(b)* (iii) above, the Scientific and Technical Subcommittee, at its forty-fourth session, should establish, for one year, a working group on near-Earth objects, in accordance with the workplan under this item;

17. *Endorses* the United Nations Programme on Space Applications for 2007, as proposed to the Committee by the Expert on Space Applications and endorsed by the Committee;

18. *Notes with satisfaction* that, in accordance with paragraph 30 of General Assembly resolution 50/27 of 6 December 1995, the African regional centres for space science and technology education, in the French language and in the English language, located in Morocco and Nigeria, respectively, as well as the Centre for Space Science and Technology Education in Asia and the Pacific and the Regional Centre for Space Science and Technology Education for Latin America and the Caribbean, entered into an affiliation agreement with the Office for Outer Space Affairs and have continued their education programmes in 2006;

19. *Agrees* that the regional centres referred to in paragraph 18 above should continue to report to the Committee on their activities on an annual basis;

20. *Notes with satisfaction* the contribution being made by the Scientific and Technical Subcommittee and the efforts of Member States and the Office for Outer Space Affairs to promote and support the activities being organized within the framework of the International Heliophysical Year 2007;

21. *Also notes with satisfaction* that the African Leadership Conference on Space Science and Technology for Sustainable Development, the first of which was hosted by the Government of Nigeria in collaboration with the Governments of Algeria and South Africa from 23 to 25 November 2005, will be held on a biennial basis;

22. *Notes with appreciation* that the Fifth Space Conference of the Americas was held in Quito from 24 to 28 July 2006 under the auspices of the Office for Outer Space Affairs, the European Space Agency and the United Nations Educational, Scientific and Cultural Organization, and that the Government of Chile held a preparatory meeting for that Conference on 28 and 29 March 2006, with support from the Government of Colombia; notes that the theme of the Fifth Conference was "Regional space cooperation for security and human development" and that its results were set out in the Declaration of San Francisco de Quito and in the Plan of Action of the Conference; notes also that Ecuador will serve as secretariat pro tempore of the Conference for a period of three years, during which it will be responsible for the implementation of the recommended activities and programmes, for which purpose it will work in cooperation with the international group of experts; and notes further that the Sixth Space Conference of the Americas will be held in Guatemala in 2009;

23. *Notes with satisfaction* that the Convention on the Establishment of the Asia-Pacific Space Cooperation Organization was opened for signature in Beijing on 28 October 2005, that as at 1 June 2006 the Convention had been signed by nine States and that once the Convention has been ratified by five States, it will enter into force, thereby establishing the organization, with its headquarters in Beijing;

24. *Considers* that it is essential that Member States pay more attention to the problem of collisions of space objects, including those with nuclear power sources, with space debris, and other aspects of space debris, calls for the continuation of national research on this question, for the development of improved technology for the monitoring of space debris and for the compilation and dissemination of data on space debris, also considers that, to the extent possible, information thereon should be provided to the Scientific and Technical Subcommittee, and agrees that international cooperation is needed to expand appropriate and affordable strategies to minimize the impact of space debris on future space missions;

25. *Urges* all States, in particular those with major space capabilities, to contribute actively to the goal of preventing an arms race in outer space as an essential condition for the promotion of international cooperation in the exploration and use of outer space for peaceful purposes;

26. *Emphasizes* the need to increase the benefits of space technology and its applications and to contribute to an orderly growth of space activities favourable to sustained economic growth and sustainable development in all countries, including mitigation of the consequences of disasters, in particular in the developing countries;

27. *Notes* that space science and technology and their applications could make important contributions to economic, social and cultural development and welfare, as indicated in the resolution entitled "The Space Millennium: Vienna Declaration on Space and Human Development";

28. *Reiterates* that the benefits of space technology and its applications should be prominently brought to the attention, in particular, of the major United Nations conferences and summits for economic, social and cultural development and related fields and that the use of space technology should be promoted towards achieving the objectives of those conferences and summits

and for implementing the United Nations Millennium Declaration;

29. *Takes note* of the report of the Secretary-General on the inclusion of the issue of the use of space technology in the reports submitted by the Secretary-General to major United Nations conferences and summits for economic, social and cultural development, and its inclusion in the outcomes and commitments of those conferences and summits;

30. *Notes with satisfaction* the increased efforts of the Committee and its Scientific and Technical Subcommittee as well as the Office for Outer Space Affairs and the Inter-Agency Meeting on Outer Space Activities to promote the use of space science and technology and their applications in carrying out actions recommended in the Plan of Implementation of the World Summit on Sustainable Development ("Johannesburg Plan of Implementation");

31. *Urges* entities of the United Nations system, particularly those participating in the Inter-Agency Meeting on Outer Space Activities, to examine, in cooperation with the Committee, how space science and technology and their applications could contribute to implementing the United Nations Millennium Declaration, particularly in the areas relating to, inter alia, food security and increasing opportunities for education;

32. *Invites* the Inter-Agency Meeting on Outer Space Activities to continue to contribute to the work of the Committee and to report to the Committee and its Scientific and Technical Subcommittee on the work conducted at its annual sessions;

33. *Notes with satisfaction* that the open informal meetings, held in conjunction with the annual sessions of the Inter-Agency Meeting on Outer Space Activities and in which representatives of member States and observers in the Committee participate, provide a constructive mechanism for an active dialogue between the entities of the United Nations system and member States and observers in the Committee;

34. *Encourages* entities of the United Nations system to participate fully in the work of the Inter-Agency Meeting on Outer Space Activities;

35. *Notes* that space technology could play a central role in disaster reduction;

36. *Requests* the Committee to continue to consider, as a matter of priority, ways and means of maintaining outer space for peaceful purposes and to report thereon to the General Assembly at its sixty-second session, and agrees that during its consideration of the matter, the Committee could continue to consider ways to promote regional and interregional cooperation based on experiences stemming from the Space Conference of the Americas, the African Leadership Conference on Space Science and Technology for Sustainable Development and the role space technology could play in the implementation of recommendations of the World Summit on Sustainable Development;

37. *Notes with satisfaction* that the Committee established a closer link between its work to implement the recommendations of UNISPACE III and the work of the Commission on Sustainable Development by contributing to the thematic areas that are addressed by the Commission;

38. *Agrees* that the Director of the Division for Sustainable Development of the Department of Economic and Social Affairs of the Secretariat should be invited to participate in the sessions of the Committee to inform it how it could best contribute to the work of the Commission on Sustainable Development and that the Director of the Office for Outer Space Affairs should participate in the sessions of the Commission to raise awareness and promote the benefits of space science and technology for sustainable development;

39. *Notes with appreciation* that the International Committee on Global Navigation Satellite Systems was established on a voluntary basis as an informal body to promote cooperation, as appropriate, on matters of mutual interest related to civil satellite-based positioning, navigation, timing and value-added services, as well as the compatibility and interoperability of global navigation satellite systems, while increasing their use to support sustainable development, particularly in developing countries;

40. *Notes* the fact that the Office for Outer Space Affairs could integrate into its programme of work a number of actions identified for implementation by the Office in the Plan of Action of the Committee on the Peaceful Uses of Outer Space for the further implementation of the recommendations of UNISPACE III and that some of those actions could be integrated into its programme of work only if additional staff and financial resources were provided;

41. *Urges* all Member States to contribute to the Trust Fund for the United Nations Programme on Space Applications to enhance the capacity of the Office for Outer Space Affairs to provide technical and legal advisory services and initiate pilot projects in accordance with the Plan of Action of the Committee, while maintaining the priority thematic areas agreed by the Committee;

42. *Agrees* that the Committee should continue to consider a report on the activities of the International Satellite System for Search and Rescue as a part of its consideration of the United Nations Programme on Space Applications under the agenda item entitled "Report of the Scientific and Technical Subcommittee" and invites Member States to report on their activities regarding the System;

43. *Requests* the Committee to continue to consider, at its fiftieth session, its agenda item entitled "Spin-off benefits of space technology: review of current status";

44. *Also requests* the Committee, in view of the importance of space and education, to continue to consider, at its fiftieth session, under its agenda item entitled "Space and society", the special theme for the focus of discussions for the period 2004-2006 "Space and education", in accordance with the workplan adopted by the Committee;

45. *Agrees* that the Committee should continue to consider, at its fiftieth session, its agenda item entitled "Space and water";

46. *Also agrees* that a symposium on space and water should be held during the fiftieth session of the Committee;

47. *Notes with satisfaction* that the Committee agreed to consider, at its fiftieth session, under its agenda item entitled "Other matters", the issue of the future role and activities of the Committee and noted that the Chairman of the Committee could conduct intersessional, open-ended informal consultations with a view to presenting to the Committee a list of elements that could be taken into consideration at its next session;

48. *Agrees* to include in the agenda of the fiftieth session of the Committee a new item, entitled "International cooperation in promoting the use of space-derived geospatial data for sustainable development", under a multi-year workplan;

49. *Also agrees* that a panel on space exploration activities, including the participation of the private sector, should be convened during the fiftieth session of the Committee;

50. *Notes with satisfaction* that in accordance with the agreement reached by the Committee at its forty-sixth session on the measures relating to the future composition of the bureaux of the Committee and its subsidiary bodies, on the basis of the measures relating to the working methods of the Committee and its subsidiary bodies, the Group of African States, the Group of Asian States, the Group of Eastern European States, the Group of Latin American and Caribbean States and the Group of Western European and Other States have nominated their candidates for the offices of Chair of the Scientific and Technical Subcommittee, First Vice-Chair of the Committee, Chair of the Legal Subcommittee, Chair of the Committee and Second Vice-Chairman/Rapporteur of the Committee, respectively, for the period 2008-2009;

51. *Endorses* the composition of the bureaux of the Committee and its subsidiary bodies for the period 2008-2009, as reflected in paragraph 50 above, and agrees that the Committee and its Subcommittees should elect their officers at their respective sessions in 2008 in accordance with that composition;

52. *Notes* that each of the regional groups has the responsibility to actively promote the participation in the work of the Committee and its subsidiary bodies of the member States of the Committee that are also members of the respective regional groups, and agrees that the regional groups should consider this Committee-related matter among their members;

53. *Requests* entities of the United Nations system and other international organizations to continue and, where appropriate, to enhance their cooperation with the Committee and to provide it with reports on the issues dealt with in the work of the Committee and its subsidiary bodies.

Implementation of UNISPACE III recommendations

In response to General Assembly resolution 60/99 [YUN 2005, p. 698], the Committee on Outer Space considered the implementation of the recommendations of UNISPACE III [YUN 1999, p. 556]. It had before it a report on the Committee's contribution to the work of the Commission on Sustainable Development (see p. 1212) for the thematic cluster 2006-2007: space for sustainable development [A/AC.105/872], and a conference room paper on strengthening the link between the Committee and the Commission [A/AC.105/2006/CRP.11].

The Committee agreed that the UNISPACE III recommendations were being effectively implemented through the use of multi-year workplans, the establishment of action teams and reports from ad hoc and other groups on their activities, and noted that Member States were contributing to the implementation through a number of national and regional activities. It further noted that the International Committee on Global Navigation Satellite Systems (GNSS) had been established on a voluntary basis as an informal body to promote cooperation on civil satellite-based positioning, navigation, timing and value-added services and to promote the compatibility and interoperability of GNSS systems, while increasing their use to support sustainable development, particularly in developing countries.

The Committee also noted that progress had been made by the Scientific and Technical Subcommittee (see p. 748) with regard to establishing an international entity to coordinate space-based services for use in disaster management [YUN 2005, p. 702]. The General Assembly, by resolution 61/110 (see p. 748), decided to establish the United Nations Platform for Space-based Information for Disaster Management and Emergency Response (SPIDER).

The Committee welcomed the link established between its work on the implementation of the UNISPACE III recommendations and that being carried out by the Commission on Sustainable Development. It agreed that the Director of the Division for Sustainable Development should be invited to participate in the Committee's sessions to inform it of how it could best contribute to the work of the Commission on Sustainable Development and that the Director of the Office of Outer Space Affairs should attend the Commission's sessions with a view to raising awareness and promoting the benefits of space science and technology. It agreed that Member States should provide inputs for the development of a concise document emphasizing the benefits of the use of, and tools offered by, space science and technology and its applications for meeting the challenges faced by developing countries, in particular regarding the issues to be addressed by the Commission on Sustainable Development in 2008-2009. The Scientific and Technical Subcommittee should carry out the first review of the document during its forty-fourth session in 2007.

In accordance with Assembly resolution 60/99 [YUN 2005, p. 698], the Scientific and Technical Subcommittee convened the Working Group of the Whole to consider the implementation of the UNISPACE III recommendations.

Scientific and Technical Subcommittee

The Scientific and Technical Subcommittee of the Committee on Outer Space, at its forty-third session (Vienna, 20 February–3 March) [A/AC.105/869], considered the United Nations Programme on Space Applications and the implementation of the UNISPACE III recommendations. It also dealt with matters relating to remote sensing of the Earth by satellite, including applications for developing countries and monitoring of the Earth's environment; space debris; the use of nuclear power sources in outer space; space-system-based telemedicine; near-Earth objects; space-system-based disaster management support; the examination of the physical nature and technical attributes of the geostationary orbit and its utilization and applications; and the International Heliophysical Year 2007.

UN Programme on Space Applications

The United Nations Programme on Space Applications, as mandated by General Assembly resolution 37/90 [YUN 1982, p. 163], continued to promote the use of space technologies and data for sustainable economic and social development in developing countries and countries with economies in transition through long-term training fellowships, technical advisory services, regional and international training courses and conferences.

The United Nations Expert on Space Applications [A/AC.105/874] said that the Programme continued to support education and training for capacity-building in developing countries through UN-affiliated regional centres for space science and technology education. In accordance with General Assembly resolution 60/99 [YUN 2005, p. 698], representatives of the regional centres in Brazil/Mexico, India, Morocco and Nigeria submitted reports to the Committee on Outer Space. The United Nations/South Africa Training Course on Satellite-Aided Search and Rescue (Cape Town, South Africa, 20-24 November) provided participants from 12 developing countries with an overview of the International Satellite System for Search and Rescue (COSPAS-SARSAT). Under the priority area of space technology for disaster management, the Programme, in cooperation with the Syrian Arab Republic, the European Space Agency (ESA) and the General Organization of Remote Sensing, organized the United Nations/Syrian/ESA Regional Workshop on the Use of Space Technology for Disaster Management in Western Asia and Northern Africa (Damascus, Syrian Arab Republic 22-26 April). Other meetings organized or co-sponsored by the Programme included: the Expert Meeting on Remote Sensing Projects for the Hindu Kush-Himalayan Region (Kathmandu, Nepal, 6-10 March); the United Nations/Zambia/ESA Regional Workshop on the Applications of Global Navigation Satellite System Technologies for Sub-Saharan Africa (Lusaka, Zambia, 26-30 June); the United Nations/China/ESA Training Course on the Use and Applications of Global Navigation Satellite Systems (Beijing, 4-8 December); the expert meeting for the United Nations/India/United States pilot project "Telemedicine in the Reconstruction of Afghanistan" (Cochin, India, 29-31 August); the United Nations/National Aeronautics and Space Administration of the United States Workshop on the International Heliophysical year 2007 and Basic Space Science, hosted by the Indian Institute of Astrophysics (Bangalore, 27 November–1 December); and the fifth United Nations Workshop on Space Law, entitled "Status, Application and Progressive Development of International and National Space Law" (Kyiv, Ukraine, 6-9 November).

Following consideration of the report of the UN Expert on Space Applications [A/AC.105/861] describing 2005 programme activities, those scheduled for 2006 and activities of UN-affiliated regional centres for space science and technology education for 2005, 2006 and 2007, the Subcommittee stressed the need for the Programme to solicit voluntary contributions to support its activities, in order to supplement the Programme's regular budget.

The General Assembly, in resolution 61/111 (see p. 741), endorsed the Programme on Space Applications for 2007, as proposed by the Expert.

Cooperation

The Inter-Agency Meeting on Outer Space Activities, at its twenty-sixth session (Paris, 18-20 January) [A/AC.105/859], discussed the coordination of plans and programmes in the practical application of space technology and related areas; ways and means of establishing inventories of space-related resources, in particular data sets, space-based devices and educational and training materials; involvement of UN entities in the International Charter on "Space and Major Disasters", to which the UN Office on Outer Space Affairs became a cooperating body in 2003 [YUN 2003, p. 643]; space-related outcomes of the 2002 World Summit on Sustainable Development [YUN 2002, p. 821]; electronic information-networking in the UN system; implementation of the UNISPACE III recommendations; participation of UN system entities in the Group on Earth Observations; lessons learned from applications of space technologies in support of disaster relief efforts; and a brochure on the use of space technology by the UN system for achieving development goals.

The Meeting noted the need to devise methods to increase inter-agency collaboration in the area of space-based applications in support of UN operations, such as peacekeeping, emergency response, food security and early recovery. Participants committed themselves to continuing discussions on how to establish effective ways to increase the sharing of information and satellite data and applications. They agreed to strengthen coordination and cooperation to facilitate space-based Earth observations, space technologies, remote sensing and geographical information systems (GIS) to identify, assess and monitor natural and biological hazards and vulnerabilities and enhance early warning for disaster reduction, as requested at the World Conference on Disaster Reduction [YUN 2005, p. 1015] in its main outcome document, the Hyogo Framework for Action 2005-2015. The Meeting reviewed and amended the Secretary-General's draft report on coordination of space-related activities within the UN system: directions and anticipated results for the period 2006-2007 [A/AC.105/858]. It agreed to develop precise guidelines to assist UN entities in preparing their input for the Secretary-General's report, indicating that the draft guidelines would be developed jointly with all of its focal points during the intersessional period. The Meeting also agreed that the Office for Outer Space Affairs should prepare the preliminary draft of the guidelines and post them for discussion on the Meeting's web board by mid-March 2006, that agreement should be reached on the draft guidelines prior to September 2006 and to review and adopt the guidelines at its 2007 session.

The Meeting noted that the Office for Outer Space Affairs had set up a web page to provide links to resources in several areas, including satellite and other data, and agreed that, in order to populate the web page, UN entities should provide the Office with information on links to relevant web resources that could be included in the online inventory of space-related resources. The status of the online inventory would be reviewed in 2007.

Noting the interest of a number of entities in reviewing the lessons learned from the application of space applications in disaster management and reduction, the Meeting agreed that at its next session, UN humanitarian agencies should be invited to discuss the subject.

Scientific and technical issues

In 2006, the Scientific and Technical Subcommittee [A/AC.105/869] continued to emphasize the importance of Earth observation satellite data to support activities in a number of key development areas. It emphasized the importance of providing non-discriminatory access to remote sensing data and to derive information at reasonable cost and in a timely manner and of building capacity for the adoption and use of remote sensing technology to meet the needs of developing countries. It encouraged further international cooperation in the use of remote sensing satellites, in particular by sharing experiences and technologies through bilateral, regional and international collaborative projects.

The Subcommittee agreed that Member States, in particular space-faring countries, should pay more attention to the problem of collisions of space objects, including those with nuclear power sources on board, with space debris and to other aspects of space debris, as well as its re-entry into the atmosphere. It agreed that research on space debris should continue and Member States should make available to all interested parties the results of that research, including information on practices that had proved effective in minimizing the creation of space debris. In accordance with General Assembly resolution 60/99 [YUN 2005, p. 698], the Subcommittee re-established its Working Group on Space Debris to consider the draft space debris mitigation guidelines; it endorsed the Working Group's report, which was annexed to the Subcommittee's report. It agreed that the guidelines would be circulated at the national level to secure consent for their approval by the Subcommittee in 2007.

The Subcommittee also reconvened its Working Group on the Use of Nuclear Power Sources (NPS) in Outer Space and noted the success of the Joint Technical Workshop on the Objectives, Scope and General Attributes of a Potential Technical Safety Framework for Nuclear Power Sources in Outer Space, organized by the Subcommittee and the International Atomic Energy Agency (IAEA) (Vienna, 20-22 February). It requested the Secretariat to distribute the preliminary draft report of the Workshop to IAEA and member States of the Committee for their comment. The Subcommittee endorsed the Working Group's report, which was annexed to its report, and the recommendation that it continue intersessional work on the topics described in the multi-year workplan on the use of NPS adopted in 2003 [YUN 2003, p. 644].

In response to the Subcommittee's request that Member States and regional space agencies continue to report on national research concerning the safety of space objects with NPS, the Secretariat submitted a note containing replies from five Member States [A/AC.105/888].

The Subcommittee noted that space-system-based telemedicine could bridge disparities in the quality of medical services in different parts of a country by providing access to a database of expert knowledge and connectivity for data transfer in areas with underdeveloped infrastructure. It urged Member States to initiate bilateral and multilateral cooperative projects in space-system-based telemedicine in developing countries to bring better health-care services to the populations of those countries. UN specialized agencies involved in health-related areas were urged to explore possibilities of working with Member States in developing and implementing projects in space-system based telemedicine.

Also submitted to the Subcommittee were Secretariat notes on international cooperation in the peaceful uses of outer space [A/AC.105/776 & Add.1,2], containing replies received from 13 Member States, and on information on research in the field of near-Earth objects carried out by Member States, international organization and other entities, containing replies from eight Member States [A/AC.105/863 & Add.1, 2].

Space-based disaster management support

The Scientific and Technical Subcommittee [A/AC.105/869] reviewed the study of the ad hoc expert group on the possibility of creating an international entity to coordinate and optimize the effectiveness of space-based services for use in disaster management. It agreed that the creation of a disaster management international space coordination entity should not lead to duplication of efforts and required close consultation between the ad hoc expert group and other organizations that had related ongoing initiatives.

The Committee on Outer Space [A/61/20] agreed that the entity should be implemented as a programme of the Office for Outer Space Affairs, as an open network of support providers. It further agreed that the proposed programme, which would be named the United Nations Platform for Space-based Information for Disaster Management and Emergency Response (SPIDER), would have offices in Beijing and Bonn, Germany. An annual operating budget of some $1.3 million would be required to cover personnel, facilities and operational costs; two thirds of that amount would be made available by Member States, with the remainder to be provided by the United Nations. The Committee requested the Office for Outer Space Affairs to develop detailed workplans for 2007 and the 2008-2009 biennium, for consideration by the Scientific and Technical Subcommittee. The Committee agreed that the partners implementing the proposed programme should initiate activities in January 2007, or as soon as it was practicable.

GENERAL ASSEMBLY ACTION

On 14 December [meeting 79], the General Assembly, on the recommendation of the Fourth Committee [A/61/406], adopted **resolution 61/110** without vote [agenda item 30].

United Nations Platform for Space-based Information for Disaster Management and Emergency Response

The General Assembly,

Recalling its resolutions 54/68 of 6 December 1999, 59/2 of 20 October 2004 and 59/116 of 10 December 2004,

Seriously concerned about the devastating impact of disasters, causing the loss of lives and property, displacing people from their homes and destroying their livelihoods, and causing tremendous damage to societies around the world,

Equally concerned that disasters reverse, as well as affect and hinder, current and future development efforts in all parts of the world, in particular in developing countries,

Deeply convinced of the urgent need for enhanced coordination efforts at the global level to reduce the impact of disasters,

Recognizing, in that regard, that unnecessary loss of life and property could be avoided if better information were available regarding the risk and onset of disasters, through improved risk assessment, early warning and monitoring of disasters,

Convinced that the use of existing space technology, such as Earth observation and meteorological satellites, communications satellites and satellite navigation and positioning systems, and their applications, can play a vital role in supporting disaster management by providing accurate and timely information for decision-making and re-establishing communication in case of disasters,

Desirous of enhancing international coordination at the global level in disaster management and emergency response through greater access to and use of space-based services for all countries and facilitating capacity-building and institutional strengthening for disaster management, in particular in developing countries,

Having considered the report of the Committee on the Peaceful Uses of Outer Space on the work of its forty-ninth session,

1. *Recognizes* that disasters affect many areas of the Earth and that coordinated international efforts are re-

quired to reduce their impacts, and that space technology and its application can play a vital role in supporting disaster relief operations by providing accurate and timely information and communication support;

2. *Also recognizes* the important role that coordinated applications of space technology can play in the implementation of the Hyogo Declaration and the Hyogo Framework for Action 2005-2015: Building the Resilience of Nations and Communities to Disasters, adopted by the World Conference on Disaster Reduction, held at Kobe, Hyogo, Japan, from 18 to 22 January 2005;

3. *Further recognizes* that different international initiatives aimed at utilizing space-based disaster information and services exist, such as the Integrated Global Observing Strategy Partnership, the Global Earth Observation System of Systems, the Charter on Cooperation to Achieve the Coordinated Use of Space Facilities in the Event of Natural or Technological Disasters and the International Strategy for Disaster Reduction, and that the availability of such services should be promoted among developing countries;

4. *Notes with concern* that unless a global, integrated and coordinated approach is undertaken, building upon the experiences of existing international initiatives, the utilization of space assets in support of disaster management will continue to lag significantly in most parts of the world and that a considerable gap will exist and is likely to remain in all areas of space technology applications to disaster management;

5. *Takes note with appreciation* of the study of the ad hoc expert group established by the Committee on the Peaceful Uses of Outer Space on the possibility of creating an international entity to provide for coordination and the means of realistically optimizing the effectiveness of space-based services for use in disaster management;

6. *Decides* to establish a programme within the United Nations to provide universal access to all countries and all relevant international and regional organizations to all types of space-based information and services relevant to disaster management to support the full disaster management cycle by being a gateway to space information for disaster management support, serving as a bridge to connect the disaster management and space communities and being a facilitator of capacity-building and institutional strengthening, in particular for developing countries;

7. *Agrees* that the programme would be supported through voluntary contributions and through a rearrangement of priorities within the framework of the United Nations reform process and, if necessary, a rearrangement of priorities of the Office for Outer Space Affairs of the Secretariat and that the additional activities would not, as far as possible, have a negative impact on the current programme activities of the Office and should not result in an increase in the total regular budget of the United Nations;

8. *Endorses* the recommendation of the Committee on the Peaceful Uses of Outer Space that the programme have an office in Beijing and an office in Bonn, Germany, and that the activities of the programme be carried out within the proposed implementation framework presented to the Committee;

9. *Notes* that due consideration would be given to the possibility that the programme could have a liaison office in Geneva that would contribute to disseminating and integrating the work of the programme within the disaster reduction and humanitarian response communities;

10. *Takes note with appreciation* of the commitments of support for the establishment of the programme made by Austria, China, Germany and India and the offers of support once it is established made by Algeria, Argentina, Italy, Morocco, Nigeria, Romania, the Russian Federation, Switzerland and Turkey;

11. *Agrees* that the programme should work closely with regional and national centres of expertise in the use of space technology in disaster management to form a network of regional support offices for implementing the activities of the programme in their respective regions in a coordinated manner and to take advantage of the important experience and capabilities being offered, and to be offered, by Member States, particularly by developing countries;

12. *Requests* that the programme also work closely with the international initiatives noted in paragraph 3 above in order to avoid duplication of efforts;

13. *Requests* the Office for Outer Space Affairs to develop a detailed workplan for the programme for 2007 and for the biennium 2008-2009 to be considered during the forty-fourth session of the Scientific and Technical Subcommittee of the Committee on the Peaceful Uses of Outer Space, taking into consideration the commitments received, and in consultation with the representatives of countries that have provided or would be providing commitments, as well as with the representatives of other countries that have indicated their interest in contributing to the development of the workplan;

14. *Agrees* that the partners implementing the programme should endeavour to initiate activities in January 2007 or as soon as it is practicable, in order to enable the programme to begin providing support for disaster management at the earliest possible time.

15. *Also agrees* that the programme should be named the United Nations Platform for Space-based Information for Disaster Management and Emergency Response (SPIDER), and that it should be implemented as a programme of the Office for Outer Space Affairs under the Director of the Office, as an open network of providers of disaster management support, and that the Director of the Office would be responsible for the overall supervision of the programme;

16. *Further agrees* that the programme should report to and receive guidance from the Committee on the Peaceful Uses of Outer Space through the Office for Outer Space Affairs.

Legal Subcommittee

The Legal Subcommittee, at its forty-fifth session (Vienna, 3-13 April) [A/AC.105/871], noted that the Convention on International Interests in

Mobile Equipment, which was opened for signature in 2001 [YUN 2001, p. 570], and its Protocol, known as the Aircraft Protocol, had entered into force on 2 November 2005. In accordance with the Convention, the International Registry on aircraft equipment had been established and had entered into operation on 1 March 2006 for the registration of international interests in aircraft equipment. The International Civil Aviation Organization (ICAO) had assumed the role of Supervisory Authority under the Aircraft Protocol.

The Subcommittee reconvened its Working Group on the Definition and Delimitation of Outer Space, which considered replies from Member States to a questionnaire on possible legal issues with regard to aerospace objects [A/AC.105/635 & Add.1-13, Add.7/Corr.1 & Add.11/Corr.1] and a Secretariat note on national legislation and practice relating to the definition and delimitation of outer space [A/AC.105/865 & Add.1]. The Working Group agreed to develop criteria for analysing the replies to the questionnaire on aerospace objects and invited its Chairman to present to the Legal Subcommittee in 2007 proposals concerning possible ways forward. It decided, among other things, to continue to invite Member States to submit replies to the questionnaire until the Subcommittee could agree on criteria for analysing the replies.

The Subcommittee decided to invite the International Telecommunication Union (ITU) to participate in its sessions on a regular basis and to submit annually reports on its activities relating to the use of the geostationary orbit.

The Subcommittee reconvened its Working Group on the Status and Application of Five UN Treaties on Outer Space [YUN 2001, p. 570]. The Working Group had before it a document on a questionnaire on the possible options for the future development of international space law [A/AC.105/C.2/L.259]. It agreed to recommend to the Subcommittee that Member States be requested to provide information on any action they might have taken as a result of receiving the Secretary-General's model letter, endorsed by the Subcommittee, encouraging participation in the outer space treaties. It also agreed to transfer to the Working Group on the Practice of States and International Organizations in Registering Space Objects the issue of Member States providing information on their current practices regarding on-orbit transfer of ownership of space objects. The Working Group agreed on the text of a document, appended to the report, on the advantages of adherence to the 1971 Convention on International Liability for Damage Caused by Space Objects, adopted by the General Assembly in resolution 2777(XXVI) [YUN 1971, p. 52], and recommended that Secretariat send it to all States that had not yet become parties to the Convention. The Committee on Outer Space [A/61/20] endorsed that recommendation and approved the extension of the Working Group's mandate for one additional year.

The Subcommittee reconvened its Working Group on the Practice of States and International Organizations in Registering Space Objects, which considered notes by the Secretariat on the registration of space objects: harmonization of practices, non-registration of space objects, transfer of ownership and registration/non-registration of 'foreign' space objects [A/AC.105/867 & Corr.1]; and on the benefits of becoming a party to the 1974 Convention on Registration of Objects Launched into Outer Space (the Registration Convention) [A/AC.105/C.2/L.262], contained in Assembly resolution 3235(XXIX) [YUN 1974, p. 63]. Also before the Working Group was a Secretariat paper [A/AC.105/C.2/2006/CRP.5] on States and intergovernmental (or former intergovernmental) organizations that were operating or had operated space objects in Earth orbit or beyond (1957-present), a background paper on the practice of States and international organizations in registering space objects [A/AC.105/C.2/L.255 & Corr.1,2] and statistical information on the number of space objects launched and registered or unregistered between 1957 and 2004 [A/AC.105/C.2/2005/CRP.10].

The Working Group agreed on a set of elements that could constitute the basis for a consensus on specific recommendations and conclusions to be included in the Subcommittee's 2007 report, including benefits of becoming a party to the Registration Convention; adherence to and implementation of the Registration Convention; and registration practice relating to the uniformity of registration on the basis of the Registration Convention or Assembly resolution 1721 B (XVI) or any other basis.

The Subcommittee agreed that it was important to urge greater adherence to the Registration Convention, which would lead to more States registering space objects, and also encourage international organizations to declare their acceptance of the rights and obligations under the Convention. It also noted with concern that in recent years there had been a marked decrease in the registration of objects launched into outer space and that the failure to register those objects undermined the application of the treaties on outer space.

The Committee on Outer Space [A/61/20] agreed that the Subcommittee should reconvene the Working Group in 2007 in order to assist the Subcommittee in preparing the report to be submitted to the Committee on practices of States and international organizations in registering space objects.

The Subcommittee also considered a Secretariat note [A/AC.105/C.2/L.261 & Corr.1,2] and two conference room papers [A/AC.105/C.2/2006/CRP.4 & CRP.6] containing information on activities relating to space law received from four international organizations. It agreed to retain on its agenda the review and possible revision of the Principles Relevant to the Use of Nuclear Power Sources in Outer Space, contained in Assembly resolution 47/68 [YUN 1992, p. 116].

Effects of atomic radiation

At its fifty-fourth session (Vienna, 29 May–2 June) [A/61/46 & Corr.1], the United Nations Scientific Committee on the Effects of Atomic Radiation reviewed documents on the sources and effects of ionizing radiation that it had last considered in 2005 [YUN 2005, p. 706]. While the Committee had originally envisaged the publication of those documents by 2005, limited availability of resources had delayed their development. However, five scientific texts had been approved for publication in the Committee's 2006 report (see below). The Committee also considered drafts of other outstanding documents on: exposures from radiation accidents; exposures from medical uses of radiation; and effects of ionizing radiation on non-human biota.

The Committee had participated in the work of the Chernobyl Forum, which involved eight UN entities and the Governments of Belarus, the Russian Federation and Ukraine, whose mission covered many aspects of the 1986 Chernobyl accident [YUN 1986, p. 584], including the review of the health effects of radiation. The Committee reiterated that the Forum's findings confirmed its own essential scientific conclusions on the health and environmental consequences of radiation exposure due to the Chernobyl accident. It expressed its intention to clarify further the assessment of potential harm from chronic low-level exposures among large populations and the attributability of health effects. It also recognized that some outstanding details merited further scrutiny and that its work to provide the scientific basis for a better understanding of the radiation-related health and environmental effects of the Chernobyl accident needed to continue. However, owing to its participation in the Chernobyl Forum, the Committee's updating of its own assessments of the Chernobyl accident's health and environmental consequences would be extended in order to scrutinize information that had become available more recently.

The Committee summarized the conclusions of five scientific annexes and included them in its report: epidemiological studies of radiation and cancer; epidemiological evaluation of cardiovascular disease and other non-cancer diseases following radiation exposure; non-targeted and delayed effects of exposure to ionizing radiation; effects of ionizing radiation on the immune system; and source-to-effects assessment for radon in homes and workplaces. Recognizing the importance of information from Member States and relevant international organizations for its work, the Committee called on Member States, UN specialized agencies and other international and national scientific bodies, to continue to make available relevant and authorized information for its reviews.

The Committee decided to hold its fifty-fifth session in Vienna from 21 to 25 May 2007.

GENERAL ASSEMBLY ACTION

On 14 December [meeting 79], the General Assembly, on the recommendation of the Fourth Committee [A/61/405], adopted **resolution 61/109** without vote [agenda item 29].

Effects of atomic radiation

The General Assembly,

Recalling its resolution 913 (X) of 3 December 1955, by which it established the United Nations Scientific Committee on the Effects of Atomic Radiation, and its subsequent resolutions on the subject, including resolution 60/98 of 8 December 2005, in which, inter alia, it requested the Scientific Committee to continue its work,

Taking note with appreciation of the work of the Scientific Committee, and of the release of its report on its fifty-fourth session,

Reaffirming the desirability of the Scientific Committee continuing its work,

Concerned about the potentially harmful effects on present and future generations resulting from the levels of radiation to which mankind and the environment are exposed,

Noting the views expressed by Member States at its sixty-first session with regard to the work of the Scientific Committee,

Noting that some Member States have expressed particular interest in becoming members of the Scientific Committee, and expressing its intention to consider the issue further at its next session,

Conscious of the continuing need to examine and compile information about atomic and ionizing radiation and to analyse its effects on mankind and the environment,

1. *Commends* the United Nations Scientific Committee on the Effects of Atomic Radiation for the valuable contribution it has been making in the course

of the past fifty-one years, since its inception, to wider knowledge and understanding of the levels, effects and risks of ionizing radiation, and for fulfilling its original mandate with scientific authority and independence of judgement;

2. *Reaffirms* the decision to maintain the present functions and independent role of the Scientific Committee;

3. *Takes note with appreciation* of the work of the Scientific Committee and of the release of its extensive report to the General Assembly, with scientific annexes, which provides the scientific and world community with the Committee's latest evaluations of the effects of ionizing radiation on human beings;

4. *Requests* the Scientific Committee to continue its work, including its important activities to increase knowledge of the levels, effects and risks of ionizing radiation from all sources;

5. *Endorses* the intentions and plans of the Scientific Committee for completing its present programme of work of scientific review and assessment on behalf of the General Assembly, and requests the Scientific Committee to submit plans for its future programme of work to the General Assembly at its sixty-second session;

6. *Requests* the Scientific Committee to continue at its next session the review of the important problems in the field of ionizing radiation and to report thereon to the General Assembly at its sixty-second session;

7. *Emphasizes* the need for the Scientific Committee to hold regular sessions on an annual basis so that its report can reflect the latest developments and findings in the field of ionizing radiation and thereby provide updated information for dissemination among all States;

8. *Expresses its appreciation* for the assistance rendered to the Scientific Committee by Member States, the specialized agencies, the International Atomic Energy Agency and non-governmental organizations, and invites them to increase their cooperation in this field;

9. *Invites* the Scientific Committee to continue its consultations with scientists and experts from interested Member States in the process of preparing its future scientific reports, and requests the Secretariat to facilitate such consultations;

10. *Welcomes*, in this context, the readiness of Member States to provide the Scientific Committee with relevant information on the effects of ionizing radiation in affected areas, and invites the Scientific Committee to analyse and give due consideration to such information, particularly in the light of its own findings;

11. *Invites* Member States, the organizations of the United Nations system and non-governmental organizations concerned to provide further relevant data about doses, effects and risks from various sources of radiation, which would greatly help in the preparation of future reports of the Scientific Committee to the General Assembly;

12. *Requests* the United Nations Environment Programme to continue providing support for the effective conduct of the work of the Scientific Committee and for the dissemination of its findings to the General Assembly, the scientific community and the public;

13. *Urges* the United Nations Environment Programme to review and strengthen the present funding of the Scientific Committee, pursuant to paragraph 11 of resolution 60/98, and to continue to seek out and consider alternative funding mechanisms to complement existing ones, so that the Committee can discharge the responsibilities and mandate entrusted to it by the General Assembly;

14. *Invites* those Member States that desire to join the Scientific Committee to inform the President of the General Assembly, before 28 February 2007, of their interest, and decides to further consider the question of membership of the Scientific Committee in all its aspects, including financial implications, at the next session.

PART TWO

Human rights

Chapter I

Promotion of human rights

In 2006, the General Assembly established a new subsidiary body—the Human Rights Council—as the Organization's primary mechanism for promoting human rights and fundamental freedoms, in accordance with Member States' resolve at the 2005 World Summit to reform the UN system's human rights machinery. The Council, based in Geneva and comprising 47 members, replaced the 53-member Commission on Human Rights, which had shouldered that responsibility since 1946. All Commission mandates, mechanisms, functions and responsibilities were to be assumed by the Council, which would report directly to the Assembly and whose status and operation would be subject to review within five years.

The Council held its inaugural session in June, followed by two regular sessions to address substantive human rights questions and organizational and administrative matters. To facilitate the transition, the Council extended for one year the mandates and mandate-holders of all the Commission's special procedures. Among them was the Subcommission on the Promotion and Protection of Human Rights, which held its fifty-eight and final session in August and made recommendations on its successor in offering future expert advice to the Council.

The Council also initiated further institutional reforms to improve the operation of the existing framework for promoting and protecting human rights as a whole. To that end, it established three working groups: one to develop the modalities of a universal periodic review mechanism for monitoring Member States' fulfilment of their human rights obligations; the second, to make recommendations for reviewing, improving and rationalizing existing Commission mandates and mechanisms; and the third, to provide proposals on the Council's agenda, annual programme of work, methods of work and rules of procedure.

In July, August, November and December, the Council held special sessions to address the situations in the Palestinian and other occupied Arab territories, Lebanon and the Darfur region of the Sudan.

The Office of the United Nations High Commissioner for Human Rights continued to support, coordinate and strengthen the Organization's human rights programme and related reforms. The High Commissioner made proposals for reforming and improving the operation of the treaty body system. The Office drew up a Strategic Management Plan 2006-2007, the first of its kind, highlighting its priorities and the means by which it hoped to realize the vision of its future direction.

The year also witnessed the entry into force of the Optional Protocol to the Convention against Torture, marking a significant progress in the United Nations efforts to combat torture and other cruel, inhuman or degrading treatment or punishment. In other measures intended to strengthen the legal framework for promoting action against racial discrimination, the Council established an Ad Hoc Committee to elaborate complementary standards, in the form of either a convention or additional protocol(s) to the International Convention on the Elimination of All Forms of Racial Discrimination, in order to fill any gaps in its provisions and provide new normative standards aimed at combating all forms of contemporary racism.

International human rights law was further advanced in 2006 by the Assembly's adoption in December of the Convention on the Rights of Persons with Disabilities and the Optional Protocol thereto, and the International Convention for the Protection of All Persons from Enforced Disappearance.

UN machinery

Commission on Human Rights

Final session

The Commission convened its sixty-second and final session (Geneva, 13 to 27 March) [E/2006/23-E/CN.4/2006/122], during which it held four meetings. It had before it the Secretary-General's notes transmitting its provisional agenda [E/CN.4/2006/1] and annotations thereto [E/CN.4/2006/1/Add.1, 2], and a note by the Secretariat [E/CN.4/2006/8] containing statistical data on its 2005 session, intended to assist with the organization of its work in 2006. The Economic and Social Council, in **resolution 2006/2** of 22 March, requested the Commission to conclude its work and submit its final report, pursuant to General Assembly resolution 60/251 (see p. 757). As recommended by the Assembly, the Council decided to abolish the Commission, with effect from 16 June, thereby cutting short the Commission's session and resulting in the items on its agenda not being considered. On 27 March, the Commission adopted resolution 2006/1, a procedural action by which it concluded its work. The Commission expressed appreciation to those who had helped promote and protect human rights in its 60 years of existence and referred to the newly created Human Rights Council (see p. 757) the documents it had before it, a list of which was annexed to its final report, together with a compilation of all Commission mechanisms that submitted those documents.

The Economic and Social Council took note of the Commission's report on 27 July (**decision 2006/250**).

Statements. Addressing the session, the High Commissioner noted that, despite the Commission's flaws, it was important to celebrate its accomplishments, which the Human Rights Council would have to build on. Among those accomplishments were the drafting by the Commission of the international bill of rights, comprising the Universal Declaration of Human Rights, adopted by General Assembly resolution 217 A (III) [YUN 1948-49, p. 535], and the International Covenants on Civil and Political Rights, and on Economic, Social and Cultural Rights, adopted by Assembly resolution 2200 (XXI) [YUN 1966, pp. 419-423]. Together, those instruments built the framework for international human rights protection and established standards for a wide range of human rights issues. It was a revolutionary step then to assert that human rights constituted the foundation of freedom, justice and peace throughout the world. By recognizing in that context the inherent dignity of the human person and articulating what was necessary to realize and safeguard that dignity, the Commission had helped to redefine the individual's status vis-à-vis the State. The Commission's other accomplishments included: establishment of the system of special procedures, by which it became a human rights protector, in addition to being a promoter; consideration of the human rights situation in specific countries, which enabled it to marshal a global consensus on action to remedy the plight of victims of violations; creation of the first human rights complaints mechanism in the UN system (the "1503 procedure"); and its status as a global forum for dialogue on human rights issues.

The Commission's current Chairperson noted that those achievements had been overshadowed by shortcomings, weaknesses and problems that undermined the Commission's credibility and legitimacy. The establishment of the Council was undoubtedly a positive step for the human rights community. However, its achievements and effectiveness would be assessed in the light of practical experience, which would, in turn, reflect the resolve of Council members and their interaction with non-governmental organizations (NGOs) and civil society. The outgoing Chairperson, who presided over the Commission's sixty-first (2005) session, also highlighted the body's strengths and achievements, noting in particular its role in the establishment of the Council through constructive contribution to preceding discussions and consultations.

Statements focusing on the role of the Commission were also made by regional groups: Morocco, on behalf of the African States; Saudi Arabia, on behalf of the Asian States; Azerbaijan, on behalf of the East European States; Brazil, on behalf of the Latin American and Caribbean States; the Netherlands, on behalf of the Western European and other States; and a representative of the Geneva-based International Service for Human Rights, on behalf of some 265 NGOs involved in the Commission's work.

Thematic procedures

In February, the Secretary-General provided a list of thematic and country-specific procedures and other Commission mechanisms for 2006 [E/CN.4/2006/1/Add.1]. In response to a 2004 Commission resolution [YUN 2004, p. 648], he also submitted a March report [E/CN.4/2006/99] containing references to the conclusions and recommendations of special procedures.

The thirteenth meeting of special rapporteurs/representatives, independent experts and chairpersons of the working groups of the special procedures of the Commission and of the advisory services programme was held in June (see p. 769).

Human Rights Council

Establishment of Human Rights Council

The General Assembly, in follow-up action to its 2005 resolve to create a Human Rights Council [YUN 2005, p. 713] to replace the Commission on Human Rights as the primary mechanism for promoting universal respect for human rights and fundamental freedoms, by resolution 60/251 (see below) established the Council as one of it subsidiary organs. The Council was mandated to address situations of human rights violations and make recommendations thereon, promote the effective coordination and incorporation of human rights within the UN system and undertake universal periodic reviews of Member States' fulfilment of their human rights obligations and commitments. The Assembly would review within five years the Council's work in the light of its mandate.

The Council, to be based in Geneva as had the Commission, would comprise 47 members, elected by the Assembly on the basis of equitable geographical distribution. It should meet regularly, for no less than three sessions a year, including a main session, and could hold special sessions at the request of a Council member if supported by one third of its membership. The Assembly recommended that the Economic and Social Council request the Commission to conclude its work at its sixty-second (2006) session and to abolish it thereafter; this was acted upon on 22 March (see p. 755).

(The details of the mandate and terms of reference for the newly created Human Rights Council are set out in resolution 60/251 below.)

GENERAL ASSEMBLY ACTION

On 15 March [meeting 72], the General Assembly adopted **resolution 60/251** [draft: A/60/L.48] by recorded vote (170-4-3) [agenda items 46 & 120].

Human Rights Council

The General Assembly,

Reaffirming the purposes and principles contained in the Charter of the United Nations, including developing friendly relations among nations based on respect for the principle of equal rights and self-determination of peoples, and achieving international cooperation in solving international problems of an economic, social, cultural or humanitarian character and in promoting and encouraging respect for human rights and fundamental freedoms for all,

Reaffirming also the Universal Declaration of Human Rights and the Vienna Declaration and Programme of Action, and recalling the International Covenant on Civil and Political Rights, the International Covenant on Economic, Social and Cultural Rights and other human rights instruments,

Reaffirming further that all human rights are universal, indivisible, interrelated, interdependent and mutually reinforcing, and that all human rights must be treated in a fair and equal manner, on the same footing and with the same emphasis,

Reaffirming that, while the significance of national and regional particularities and various historical, cultural and religious backgrounds must be borne in mind, all States, regardless of their political, economic and cultural systems, have the duty to promote and protect all human rights and fundamental freedoms,

Emphasizing the responsibilities of all States, in conformity with the Charter, to respect human rights and fundamental freedoms for all, without distinction of any kind as to race, colour, sex, language or religion, political or other opinion, national or social origin, property, birth or other status,

Acknowledging that peace and security, development and human rights are the pillars of the United Nations system and the foundations for collective security and well-being, and recognizing that development, peace and security and human rights are interlinked and mutually reinforcing,

Affirming the need for all States to continue international efforts to enhance dialogue and broaden understanding among civilizations, cultures and religions, and emphasizing that States, regional organizations, non-governmental organizations, religious bodies and the media have an important role to play in promoting tolerance, respect for and freedom of religion and belief,

Recognizing the work undertaken by the Commission on Human Rights and the need to preserve and build on its achievements and to redress its shortcomings,

Recognizing also the importance of ensuring universality, objectivity and non-selectivity in the consideration of human rights issues, and the elimination of double standards and politicization,

Recognizing further that the promotion and protection of human rights should be based on the principles of cooperation and genuine dialogue and aimed at strengthening the capacity of Member States to comply with their human rights obligations for the benefit of all human beings,

Acknowledging that non-governmental organizations play an important role at the national, regional and international levels, in the promotion and protection of human rights,

Reaffirming the commitment to strengthen the United Nations human rights machinery, with the aim of ensuring effective enjoyment by all of all human rights, civil, political, economic, social and cultural rights, including the right to development, and to that end, the resolve to create a Human Rights Council,

1. *Decides* to establish the Human Rights Council, based in Geneva, in replacement of the Commission on Human Rights, as a subsidiary organ of the General Assembly; the Assembly shall review the status of the Council within five years;

2. *Decides* that the Council shall be responsible for promoting universal respect for the protection of all human rights and fundamental freedoms for all, without distinction of any kind and in a fair and equal manner;

3. *Decides also* that the Council should address situations of violations of human rights, including gross and systematic violations, and make recommendations thereon. It should also promote the effective coordination and the mainstreaming of human rights within the United Nations system;

4. *Decides further* that the work of the Council shall be guided by the principles of universality, impartiality, objectivity and non-selectivity, constructive international dialogue and cooperation, with a view to enhancing the promotion and protection of all human rights, civil,

political, economic, social and cultural rights, including the right to development;

5. *Decides* that the Council shall, inter alia:

(a) Promote human rights education and learning as well as advisory services, technical assistance and capacity-building, to be provided in consultation with and with the consent of Member States concerned;

(b) Serve as a forum for dialogue on thematic issues on all human rights;

(c) Make recommendations to the General Assembly for the further development of international law in the field of human rights;

(d) Promote the full implementation of human rights obligations undertaken by States and follow-up to the goals and commitments related to the promotion and protection of human rights emanating from United Nations conferences and summits;

(e) Undertake a universal periodic review, based on objective and reliable information, of the fulfilment by each State of its human rights obligations and commitments in a manner which ensures universality of coverage and equal treatment with respect to all States; the review shall be a cooperative mechanism, based on an interactive dialogue, with the full involvement of the country concerned and with consideration given to its capacity-building needs; such a mechanism shall complement and not duplicate the work of treaty bodies; the Council shall develop the modalities and necessary time allocation for the universal periodic review mechanism within one year after the holding of its first session;

(f) Contribute, through dialogue and cooperation, towards the prevention of human rights violations and respond promptly to human rights emergencies;

(g) Assume the role and responsibilities of the Commission on Human Rights relating to the work of the Office of the United Nations High Commissioner for Human Rights, as decided by the General Assembly in its resolution 48/141 of 20 December 1993;

(h) Work in close cooperation in the field of human rights with Governments, regional organizations, national human rights institutions and civil society;

(i) Make recommendations with regard to the promotion and protection of human rights;

(j) Submit an annual report to the General Assembly;

6. *Decides also* that the Council shall assume, review and, where necessary, improve and rationalize all mandates, mechanisms, functions and responsibilities of the Commission on Human Rights in order to maintain a system of special procedures, expert advice and a complaint procedure; the Council shall complete this review within one year after the holding of its first session;

7. *Decides further* that the Council shall consist of forty-seven Member States, which shall be elected directly and individually by secret ballot by the majority of the members of the General Assembly; the membership shall be based on equitable geographical distribution, and seats shall be distributed as follows among regional groups: Group of African States, thirteen; Group of Asian States, thirteen; Group of Eastern European States, six; Group of Latin American and Caribbean States, eight; and Group of Western European and other States, seven; the members of the Council shall serve for a period of three years and shall not be eligible for immediate re-election after two consecutive terms;

8. *Decides* that the membership in the Council shall be open to all States Members of the United Nations; when electing members of the Council, Member States shall take into account the contribution of candidates to the promotion and protection of human rights and their voluntary pledges and commitments made thereto; the General Assembly, by a two-thirds majority of the members present and voting, may suspend the rights of membership in the Council of a member of the Council that commits gross and systematic violations of human rights;

9. *Decides also* that members elected to the Council shall uphold the highest standards in the promotion and protection of human rights, shall fully cooperate with the Council and be reviewed under the universal periodic review mechanism during their term of membership;

10. *Decides further* that the Council shall meet regularly throughout the year and schedule no fewer than three sessions per year, including a main session, for a total duration of no less than ten weeks, and shall be able to hold special sessions, when needed, at the request of a member of the Council with the support of one third of the membership of the Council;

11. *Decides* that the Council shall apply the rules of procedure established for committees of the General Assembly, as applicable, unless subsequently otherwise decided by the Assembly or the Council, and also decides that the participation of and consultation with observers, including States that are not members of the Council, the specialized agencies, other intergovernmental organizations and national human rights institutions, as well as non-governmental organizations, shall be based on arrangements, including Economic and Social Council resolution 1996/31 of 25 July 1996 and practices observed by the Commission on Human Rights, while ensuring the most effective contribution of these entities;

12. *Decides also* that the methods of work of the Council shall be transparent, fair and impartial and shall enable genuine dialogue, be results-oriented, allow for subsequent follow-up discussions to recommendations and their implementation and also allow for substantive interaction with special procedures and mechanisms;

13. *Recommends* that the Economic and Social Council request the Commission on Human Rights to conclude its work at its sixty-second session, and that it abolish the Commission on 16 June 2006;

14. *Decides* to elect the new members of the Council; the terms of membership shall be staggered, and such decision shall be taken for the first election by the drawing of lots, taking into consideration equitable geographical distribution;

15. *Decides also* that elections of the first members of the Council shall take place on 9 May 2006, and that the first meeting of the Council shall be convened on 19 June 2006;

16. *Decides further* that the Council shall review its work and functioning five years after its establishment and report to the General Assembly.

RECORDED VOTE ON RESOLUTION 60/251:

In favour: Afghanistan, Albania, Algeria, Andorra, Angola, Antigua and Barbuda, Argentina, Armenia, Australia, Austria, Azerbaijan, Bahamas, Bahrain, Bangladesh, Barbados, Belgium, Belize, Benin, Bhutan, Bolivia, Bosnia and Herzegovina, Botswana, Brazil, Brunei Darussalam, Bulgaria, Burkina Faso, Burundi, Cambodia, Cameroon, Canada, Cape Verde, Chile, China, Colombia, Comoros, Congo, Costa Rica, Croatia, Cuba, Cyprus, Czech Republic, Democratic Republic of the Congo, Denmark, Djibouti, Ecuador, Egypt, El Salvador, Estonia, Ethiopia, Fiji, Finland, France, Gabon, Gambia, Germany, Ghana, Greece, Grenada, Guatemala, Guinea, Guinea-Bissau, Guyana, Haiti, Honduras, Hungary, Iceland, India, Indonesia, Iraq, Ireland, Italy, Jamaica, Japan, Jordan, Kazakhstan, Kenya, Kuwait, Kyrgyzstan, Lao People's Democratic Republic, Latvia, Lebanon, Lesotho, Libya, Liechtenstein, Lithuania, Luxembourg, Madagascar, Malawi, Malaysia, Maldives, Mali, Malta, Mauritania, Mauritius, Mexico, Micronesia, Monaco, Mongolia, Morocco, Mozambique, Myanmar, Namibia, Nepal, Netherlands, New Zealand, Nicaragua, Niger, Nigeria, Norway, Oman, Pakistan, Panama, Paraguay, Peru, Philippines, Poland, Portugal, Qatar, Republic of Korea, Republic of Moldova, Romania, Russian Federation, Rwanda, Saint Kitts and Nevis, Saint Lucia, Saint Vincent and the Grenadines, Samoa, San Marino, Sao Tome and Principe, Saudi Arabia, Senegal, Serbia and Montenegro, Sierra Leone, Singapore, Slovakia, Slovenia, Solomon Islands, Somalia, South Africa, Spain, Sri Lanka, Sudan, Suriname, Swaziland, Sweden, Switzerland, Syria, Tajikistan, Thailand, The former Yugoslav Republic of Macedonia, Timor-Leste, Togo, Tonga, Trinidad and Tobago, Tunisia, Turkey, Turkmenistan, Tuvalu, Uganda, Ukraine, United Arab Emirates, United Kingdom, United Republic of Tanzania, Uruguay, Uzbekistan, Vanuatu, Viet Nam, Yemen, Zambia, Zimbabwe.

Against: Israel, Marshall Islands, Palau, United States.

Abstaining: Belarus, Iran, Venezuela.

Election of Council members

In accordance with General Assembly resolution 60/251 (see above), the Assembly, by **decision 60/416** of 9 May, elected 47 members of the Human Rights Council as follows: African group (13), Asian group (13), Eastern European group (6), Latin American and Caribbean group (8), and Western European group and other States (7).

Under the membership terms set out in resolution 60/251, those elected would serve for a period of three years, with effect from 19 June, and would not be eligible for immediate re-election after two consecutive terms. The terms would also be staggered by drawing lots, taking into account equitable regional distribution, in order to determine those who would serve for one, two or three years. By **decision 60/555,** also of 9 May, the Assembly approved the staggering of terms, by which one year was allocated to 14 members, with the African and Asian groups accounting for four seats each, while the other three regional groups accounted for two seats each. The two-year term was approved for 15 members, comprising four each for the African and Asian groups, three for the Latin American and Caribbean group and two each for the Eastern European and Western European groups. Three-year terms were allocated to 18 members, including five each for the African and Asian groups, three for the Latin American and Caribbean group, as well as for the Western European group, and two for the Eastern European group.

In electing the members, the Assembly took into account the contribution of candidates to the promotion and protection of human rights and their voluntary pledges and commitments thereto. The elected members were expected to uphold the highest human rights standards, cooperate with the Council and be reviewed during their term of office, in accordance with a review mechanism to be established by the Council. Rights of membership were subject to suspension by the Assembly in the event that the Member State concerned committed gross and systematic violations of human rights.

Council sessions

During the year, the Human Rights Council held its first (19-30 June) [A/61/53], second (18 September–6 October; 27-29 November) and third (29 November–3 December) [A/62/53] sessions in Geneva. It adopted 14 resolutions, 22 decisions and 2 presidential statements. It also recommended two draft resolutions for adoption by the General Assembly. In addition, the Council held four special sessions (see below).

At its first session, the Council decided, on 19 June [A/61/53 (dec. 1/101)], that its officers would be known as President and Vice-President. It elected its President (Mexico) and four Vice-Presidents (Czech Republic, Jordan, Morocco, Switzerland), with Jordan also serving as Rapporteur. On the same day [A/61/53 (dec. 1/102) (formerly 2006/102)], the Council, to facilitate succession of the Commission and avoid any protection gap during the transitional period, decided to extend exceptionally for one year the mandates and mandate-holders of all the special procedures of the Commission, the Subcommission on the Promotion and Protection of Human Rights (see. p. 762) and the procedure established in accordance with Economic and Social Council resolution 1503(XLVIII) (1503 procedure). The extension would be subject to the review called for in Assembly resolution 60/251. Annexed to the Council's decision was a list of the 56 special procedures concerned.

The Council scheduled the Subcommission's final session, lasting for up to four weeks (see below) to begin on 31 July, and called for a paper on its vision, recommendations for future expert advice to the Council, a detailed list of its ongoing studies and an overall review of its activities, for submission in 2006. The Council further decided that the working groups and the Social Forum of the Subcommission should hold their annual sessions in accordance with current practices, in order to contribute to the Subcommission paper, and that it would consider at its next session all outstanding reports referred to it.

Accordingly, on 6 October [A/62/53 (dec. 2/102)], during the first part of its second session, the Council addressed the status of those reports and asked the Secretary-General and High Commissioner to continue to fulfil their activities, in accordance with all previous decisions adopted by the Commission, and to update relevant reports and studies. On 8 December [A/62/53 (dec. 3/104)], the Council requested the Secretary-General to report to the sixty-first (2006) Assembly session on ways to guarantee the provision of conference services, regular webcast transmission for all Council sessions, timely translation of documentation in all official languages of the United Nations and adequate funding for timely financing of unforeseen and extraordinary expenses arising from the implementation of Council decisions.

Programme of work

The Council held a high-level segment from 19 to 22 June and a general segment on 21 June, and heard statements relating to its mandate and work from Member States and observers. On 30 June [A/61/53 (dec. 1/105)], the Council adopted the draft framework for a programme of work for its first year, and on 6 October [A/62/53 (dec. 2/103)], decided to add to that draft a segment on "follow-up to decisions of the Human Rights Council". On 8 December [A/62/53 (res. 3/4)], it established an open-ended intergovernmental and intersessional working group to formulate recommendations on its agenda, annual programme of work, methods of work and rules of procedure, in accordance with General Assembly resolution 60/251. The Council further decided that the group should meet for 10 days, half of which should be scheduled before the Council's fourth session, and the other half before its fifth session, which should allow sufficient time and flexibility for the fulfilment of the group's mandate. It requested its President to chair the group, and the Office of the High Commissioner for Human Rights (OHCHR) to provide the group with background information. The group should report on its progress at the Council's fourth session.

Special sessions. The Council held its first (5-6 July), second (11 August) [A/61/53], third (15 November) and fourth (12-13 December) [A/62/53] special sessions to consider, respectively, the escalation in 2006 of the situation in the Palestinian and other occupied Arab territories (see p. 969), gross human rights violations by Israel in Lebanon (see p. 964), further violations emanating from Israeli military incursions in the Occupied Palestinian Territory (see p. 969) and the human rights situation in the Darfur region of the Sudan (see p. 942). At each session,it dispatched a fact-finding mission to examine how best to tackle the human rights challenges being faced by the affected population.

On 22 December, the General Assembly took note of the Council's report on its work during the year (**decision 61/547**) and decided that the item on the report of the Council would remain for consideration at its resumed sixty-first (2007) session (**decision 61/552**).

In his report on budgetary implications, the Secretary-General indicated that the expenditure requirements resulting from the Council's resolutions and decisions adopted at its first session and first and second special sessions were estimated at $6,033,300 [A/61/530]. Of that amount, provision had been made for $4,328,600 in the programme budget for the 2006-2007 biennium, and it was anticipated that the balance of $1,704,700 could be absorbed within the resources provided for the biennium. Requirements for the 2008-2009 biennium were estimated at $2,639,300. In a related report [A/61/530/Add.1], he stated that further resolutions and decisions adopted at the Council's resumed second session, third session and third special session had resulted in additional expenditure requirements of $1,571,600. It was envisaged that, to the extent possible, that amount would be accommodated in the existing appropriation for the 2006-2007 biennium and reported in the context of the second performance report for that programme budget cycle. On 18 December [A/C.5/61/SR.34], the Advisory Committee on Administrative and Budgetary Questions (ACABQ) upheld those estimates.

The General Assembly, in Part V of **resolution 61/252** of 22 December (see p. 1615), took note of the Secretary-General's reports on revised estimates resulting from resolutions and decisions adopted by the Council and endorsed the related oral report of ACABQ.

Universal periodic review mechanism

Human Rights Council action. On 30 June [A/61/53 (dec. 1/103)], the Council established an intersessional open-ended, intergovernmental Working Group to develop the modalities of a universal periodic review (UPR) mechanism to examine the fulfilment by each Member State of its human rights obligations and commitments, as called for in General Assembly resolution 60/251. The Working Group, to be chaired by the Council President, should meet for 10 days and allow sufficient time and flexibility for the development of the mechanism. The Council requested OHCHR to provide the Group with background information on existing mechanisms for periodic review and compile the contributions of all stakeholders. The Group was asked to report regularly to the Council, effective September 2006, on progress made in developing modalities for the review. Following the Group's establishment, the Council held four series of intersessional consultations on the UPR between July and September and appointed Council Vice-President Mohammed Loulichki (Morocco) as the Group's facilitator.

Working Group activities. At its first session (20-23 November) [A/HRC/3/3], the intersessional open-ended Working Group held four meetings and discussed a programme of work based on six elements: terms of reference/basis of review, objectives and guiding principles, periodicity and order, process and modalities, outcome and follow-up. The Group focused its attention on the analysis of issues regarding each element and on its reaction to the different proposals and views expressed. It found that stakeholders were eager to establish a credible, effective and manageable UPR mechanism, aimed at improving the respect and promotion of human rights by all States, and that there was an obvious link between UPR and other review processes. However, many complex conceptual and practical issues remained to be addressed. In his preliminary conclusions, the facilitator outlined areas requiring further reflection and discussion, as well as emerging elements of convergence within the Group on each of the six elements. Delegations were invited to study the points raised by stakeholders and direct to the facilitator their comments and observations.

Review of mandates

Human Rights Council action. On 30 June [A/61/53 (dec. 1/104)], the Council, in response to General Assembly resolution 60/251, established an open-ended intergovernmental Working Group to make recommendations on reviewing, improving and rationalizing all mandates, mechanisms, functions and responsibilities of the Commission, in order to maintain a system of special procedures, expert advice and a complaint procedure. The Council designated its President to chair the Group and requested OHCHR to provide it with background information on the functioning of existing mandates and mechanisms, and to compile the contributions of all stakeholders, including the inputs of the special procedures, the Subcommission and NGOs. The Group was asked to report regularly, starting in September 2006.

Prior to the Group's first meeting, the Council President appointed three facilitators to assist in its work: Tomas Husak (Czech Republic) to facilitate the components on special procedures, Mousa Burayzat (Jordan) on expert advice and Blaise Godet (Switzerland) on complaint procedure.

Working Group activities. At its first session (13-24 November), the Working Group on the review of mandates held nine meetings, during which it elaborated on the principles, objectives and structure of the review and held substantive dialogue with delegations and special procedure mandate-holders. Thereafter, the facilitators provided preliminary conclusions from the views expressed. On 30 November [A/HRC/3/4], the Facilitator for the special procedures component, Mr. Husak, reported that substantive discussions within his cluster had focused on: the selection and appointment of mandate-holders; priority areas of mandates; the general criteria for the review, rationalization and harmonization of mandates; ways to achieve coherence and coordination between mandates; relationship with the Council; cooperation by and with Governments; relation between mandate-holders and with other human rights mechanisms and actors; organizational and logistical support of OHCHR to the special procedures; and other issues relating to working methods. Under each topic, the facilitator delineated issues on which there was general agreement and those requiring further consideration.

Facilitator Blaise Godet of the complaint mechanism component, also in preliminary conclusions of the work of his cluster [A/HRC/3/5], highlighted the relevant topics that had been the basis of discussion. Among them were the objective of the mechanism, its scope, admissibility criteria, number of stages in the complaints process, confidentiality, participation of the author of a communication, composition, size and other key questions concerning the working groups examining communications/situations, the Council's consideration of situations, the duration of the process and possible measures to be taken by the Council. The report also highlighted areas on which consensus emerged and those for further discussion. Most notably, consensus emerged in favour of retaining Economic and Social Council resolution 1503 (XVLIII) (1530 procedure) [YUN 1970, p. 530] as a basis of work and to improve it, where necessary, particularly regarding the language of the resolution. Also in a 1 December report [A/HRC/3/6], Mr. Burayzat, facilitator for the cluster which considered the idea of an expert advisory body to assist the Council in its work, summarized seven areas that had received consensus, including the name of the new entity, its membership term and the range of possible tasks it could be assigned. Issues requiring further consultations related to the character, status and structure of the new entity, as well as its functions and size, and the process of selecting the experts that would serve on it.

Further Human Rights Council action. On 6 October [A/61/53 (dec. 2/102)], the Council decided to transmit to the Group the views of the Subcommission on the future expert advice mechanism. On 27 November [A/62/53 (res. 2/1)], the Council requested the Group to review the revised draft manual of the United Nations human rights special procedures of June 2006 and make recommendations on possible additions or amendments thereto, and to draft a code of conduct regulating the work of the special procedures and report thereon at the Council's fourth session.

Subcommission on the Promotion and Protection of Human Rights

In accordance with Council decision 1/102 (see p. 760), the Subcommission on the Promotion and Protection of Human Rights, at its fifty-eighth and final session (Geneva, 7-25 August) [A/HRC/2/2 & Corr.1], adopted 22 resolutions and 12 decisions and recommended 10 draft decisions for adoption by the Council.

It had before it an August note of the Secretariat [A/HRC/Sub.1/58/2] containing statistics relating to its fifty-seventh session [YUN 2005, p. 713]. On 7 August [dec. 2006/101], the Subcommission decided to utilize all three weeks of meeting time it had available to enable it to carry out its programme of work, including the tasks requested by the Council.

On 9 August [dec. 2006/105], the Subcommission established a drafting group to prepare the paper requested by the Council in decision 1/102. The document, which was annexed to the Subcommission's report [A/HRC/2/2 & Corr.1], contained its recommendations for improving and strengthening the network of expert advice mechanisms established by the Economic and Social Council between 1946 and 2006 as part of a system of UN bodies dedicated to promoting and protecting human rights under the primary authority of the Commission. The document also set out the Subcommission's general vision on any similar mechanism that might result from the review to be undertaken by the Council and established the functions to be carried out by such a body. It outlined the issues on which the Council would need advice, in order to facilitate its task of determining which existing or future mechanism was not suitable for providing the required advice. In addition, it addressed the characteristics of any such future mechanism.

Overall, the Subcommission was of the view that the Council's decisions that might imply the extinction of any of the components of the current system should be adopted only after the completion of the review of the status and usefulness of the mandate or mechanism in question, keeping in mind the need to avoid any gaps in the protection of human rights and prevent disruptions in standard-setting activities. It determined that all the mandates and mechanisms listed in the annex to Council decision 1/102 (see p. 759) should continue to exist with their current functions and responsibilities, pending the completion of the review process.

On 25 August [dec. 2006/112], the Subcommission requested its Chairperson to transmit to the Council President the document on its vision and recommendations, which also incorporated related papers called for in Council decision 1/102, including an overview of past and current contributions of the Subcommission, a list of studies it had undertaken between 1956 and 2006, and a list of ongoing studies and reports it had mandated.

Human Rights Council action. On 6 October [A/62/53 (dec. 2/102)], the Council decided to transmit the views of the Subcommission on the Council's future expert advice mechanism to the Working Group on the review of mandates (see p. 761). It also took note of the Subcommission's draft decisions on previously authorized activities, with a view to allowing their continuation, in accordance with decision 1/102 on the extension of mandates and mechanisms.

Report of Subcommission Chairperson. The Council had before it the 2005 report of the Subcommission's Chairperson, Vladimir Kartashkin (Russian Federation), which summarized the Subcommission's work during that year [E/CN.4/2006/82].

Office of the High Commissioner for Human Rights

Reports of High Commissioner. The UN High Commissioner for Human Rights, Louise Arbour

(Canada), in a 21 June report [E/2006/86] to the Economic and Social Council, focused on the legal protection of economic, social and cultural rights and described their relation to civil and political rights. Noting that, although modern conceptions of human rights perceived them in terms of rights of the individual to be free from State interference and abuse of State powers (freedom from the State), as well as rights to State intervention (freedom through the State), the High Commissioner pointed out that the similarity in their nature did not necessarily require the same strategy for protecting all human rights. Strategies to promote and protect human rights should be multidimensional, covering a range of legal, administrative, financial, budgetary, educational and social measures. In particular, the legal protection of economic, social and cultural rights should be an essential element in that strategy, given the recognition of those rights in legally binding treaties and owing to increasing proof that legal protection was effective.

The first step in legal protection was the recognition of economic, social and cultural rights in domestic law, through the incorporation of international norms into the national legal order, and the recognition of those rights in the constitution and legislation or by the judiciary. The second was the provision of legal remedies in cases of breaches of those rights through the courts, administrative tribunals, national human rights institutions and regional and international treaty bodies. In that context, the High Commissioner noted that the drafting of an optional protocol to the International Covenant on Economic, Social and Cultural Rights, establishing an individual communications procedure, should stimulate stronger legal protection of those rights. The report concluded that the protection of all human rights, including through legal means, should be the ultimate goal of the international human rights community. Poverty and exclusion lay behind many of the security threats people faced and, even in prosperous economies, many individuals lived in conditions that amounted to a denial of rights. As such, to reduce economic, social and cultural rights to mere policy objectives or moral commitments rather than legally binding obligations would deny their status as human rights and lessen the likelihood of their realization. The High Commissioner stated that respect for human rights required national and international legal frameworks within which individuals and groups could claim their rights. Only that possibility would give human rights their full meaning.

On 27 July, the Economic and Social Council took note of the report of the High Commissioner (**decision 2006/250**).

The High Commissioner's annual report to the General Assembly [A/61/36] focused on developments relating to the implementation of the Plan of Action and the strategic management of OHCHR [YUN 2005, p. 715], the establishment of the Human Rights Council and treaty body reform. The report discussed major elements of the Plan, particularly country engagement aimed at assisting States to address protection gaps through a consultative process involving Governments, civil society and other national and international counterparts, including the United Nations. In that regard, the Plan anticipated an expansion of geographic desks, increased deployment of human rights staff to countries and regions, the establishment of standing capacities for rapid deployment, investigations, field support, human rights capacity-building, advice and assistance, and work on transitional justice and rule of law. The strengthening of headquarters capacity to support such engagement was also essential. Related developments included the establishment of a rapid response unit within OHCHR to strengthen and coordinate the Office's response to human rights crises and support national human rights institutions. The report also highlighted the OHCHR vision and initiatives to strengthen its field presence through the establishment or expansion of regional and country offices, and to enhance partnerships within the UN system by increasing its engagement with peace missions and stepping up cooperation with humanitarian actors. A notable issue of concern was the closed-door policy of some States and the consequent denial of access to OHCHR, which impeded the accurate assessment of the human rights situation in such States and any possibility of relevant technical assistance.

Also highlighted were OHCHR activities, geared at strengthening its capacities and expertise in strategic thematic areas, including development, poverty reduction and the Millennium Development Goals; economic, social and cultural rights; women's rights; equality and non-discrimination; migration and trafficking; the rule of law and democracy; and human rights responsibilities of businesses. In addition, the report drew attention to OHCHR efforts to facilitate a smooth transition from the Commission on Human Rights to the Human Rights Council, and its readiness to support the work of the two intergovernmental working groups entrusted with the task of reviewing human rights mandates and developing modalities for the universal periodic review (UPR) mechanism. The international community had high expectations of the UPR mechanism, including redressing the selectivity and over-politicization of the consideration of human rights situations in countries, which had plagued the Commission. The report drew attention to OHCHR capacity to strengthen the system and outlined the High Commissioner's proposals for reforming the treaty body system (see p. 769).

On 19 December, the General Assembly took note of the High Commissioner's report (**decision 61/529**).

Strengthening the function of OHCHR

On 29 November [A/62/53 (dec. 2/116)], the Council deferred to its fourth (2007) session consideration of a draft resolution [A/HRC/2/L.24] submitted by China on strengthening OHCHR, which reiterated the need to ensure that necessary resources were provided from the UN regular budget to the Organization's human rights programme to enable OHCHR to carry out its mandate efficiently and expeditiously. It emphasized the need for increasing such resource allocation for advisory services and technical cooperation in human rights, and called on the High Commissioner to continue to strengthen the management structure of her Office and improve its responsiveness in all priority areas, especially regarding economic, social and cultural rights.

Office space

In a 21 June report [A/60/899], the Secretary-General proposed arrangements and related resource requirements concerning additional office accommodation for OHCHR in Geneva. The Secretary-General said that the expanded office accommodation would give rise to additional requirements of $10,451,400, which would be financed through a combination of regular budget resources ($4,975,900) and extrabudgetary resources ($2,759,800), together with the host country contribution of $1,540,300. In June [A/60/7/Add.42], ACABQ recommended acceptance of the Secretary-General's proposals.

On 30 June, the General Assembly authorized the expenditure of the remaining funds appropriated in resolution 60/247 A [YUN 2005, p. 1491] (**decision 60/561**).

Composition of staff

Report of High Commissioner. In response to a 2005 Commission request [YUN 2005, p. 716], the High Commissioner submitted a report [E/CN.4/2006/103] on the composition of OHCHR staff by nationality, grade and gender as at 31 December 2005. The report described the action plan prepared by the High Commissioner for achieving equitable geographical representation, which highlighted the need for the OHCHR recruitment strategy to overcome the chronic shortage of candidates from unrepresented and underrepresented countries. In doing so, the Office would adopt a more proactive approach to recruitment, given that reliance on spontaneous applications had proven insufficient, and strengthen its internal evaluation and selection mechanisms. The High Commissioner had established a series of task forces entrusted with making proposals for the implementation of the plan, one of which recommended measures for broadening the pool of applicants to OHCHR vacancies.

Human Rights Council action. On 29 November [A/62/53 (dec. 2/116)], the Council deferred to its fourth (2007) session consideration of a draft decision [A/HRC/2/L.16] submitted by Cuba, by which the Council would express regret that efforts to address the geographical imbalance in OHCHR staff had not resulted in a significant improvement, and recommend remedial action.

GENERAL ASSEMBLY ACTION

On 19 December [meeting 81], the General Assembly, on the recommendation of the Third Committee [A/61/443/Add.2 and Corr.1], adopted **resolution 61/159** by recorded vote (118-7-55) [agenda item 67 *(b)*].

Composition of the staff of the Office of the United Nations High Commissioner for Human Rights

The General Assembly,

Recalling paragraph 5 *(g)* of its resolution 60/251 of 15 March 2006, in which it decided that the Human Rights Council should assume the role and responsibilities of the Commission on Human Rights relating to the work of the Office of the United Nations High Commissioner for Human Rights, as decided by the General Assembly in its resolution 48/141 of 20 December 1993,

Taking note of all relevant resolutions on this issue adopted by the General Assembly and the Commission on Human Rights,

Taking note also of the relevant reports of the United Nations High Commissioner for Human Rights and the Joint Inspection Unit,

Bearing in mind that the imbalance in the actual composition of the staff could result in diminishing the effectiveness of the work of the Office of the High Commissioner if it is perceived to be culturally biased and unrepresentative of the United Nations as a whole,

Regretting that efforts to address the imbalance regarding the regional geographical diversity of the staff have not resulted in a significant improvement, and noting the low representation from the United Nations regional groups of African, Asian, Eastern European, and

Latin American and Caribbean States in the staff of the Office of the High Commissioner,

Reaffirming that the Fifth Committee is the appropriate Main Committee of the General Assembly entrusted with responsibilities for administrative and budgetary matters,

1. *Decides*, while considering the report of the Joint Inspection Unit:

(a) To provide concrete support and guidance to the United Nations High Commissioner for Human Rights in her ongoing efforts to overcome the status quo;

(b) To allow, in the effort to redress the specific geographical imbalance of the Office of the United Nations High Commissioner for Human Rights, the establishment of a temporary mechanism whereby recruitment of staff in the Office at the P-2 level would not be restricted to successful candidates from the national competitive examination;

(c) To re-evaluate the financing of human rights activities, as noted in the report of the Joint Inspection Unit, with a view to increasing the support from core resources;

2. *Encourages* participation from a broader range of Member States in the associate experts programme, and, in this respect, urges participants to increase sponsorship of associate experts from developing countries;

3. *Requests* the Joint Inspection Unit to assist the Human Rights Council to monitor systematically the implementation of the present resolution, inter alia, by submitting to the Human Rights Council in May 2009 a follow-up comprehensive report on the implementation of the recommendations contained in the report of the Joint Inspection Unit pending their fulfilment;

4. *Requests* the High Commissioner:

(a) To take further measures for the full and effective implementation of the recommendations contained in the report of the Joint Inspection Unit;

(b) To submit a comprehensive and updated report on the basis of paragraph 26 *(e)* of Commission on Human Rights resolution 2005/72 of 20 April 2005 to the Human Rights Council at its fourth session and to the General Assembly at its sixty-third session;

5. *Requests* the President of the General Assembly at its sixty-first session to bring those recommendations to the attention of the Fifth Committee, as soon as possible, for its consideration.

RECORDED VOTE ON RESOLUTION 61/159:

In favour: Afghanistan, Algeria, Angola, Antigua and Barbuda, Argentina, Armenia, Azerbaijan, Bahamas, Bahrain, Bangladesh, Barbados, Belarus, Belize, Benin, Bhutan, Bolivia, Botswana, Brunei Darussalam, Burkina Faso, Burundi, Cambodia, Cameroon, Chile, China, Colombia, Comoros, Congo, Costa Rica, Côte d'Ivoire, Cuba, Democratic People's Republic of Korea, Democratic Republic of the Congo, Djibouti, Dominica, Dominican Republic, Ecuador, Egypt, El Salvador, Eritrea, Ethiopia, Fiji, Gabon, Gambia, Ghana, Grenada, Guatemala, Guinea, Guinea-Bissau, Guyana, Haiti, Honduras, India, Indonesia, Iran, Iraq, Jordan, Kazakhstan, Kenya, Kuwait, Kyrgyzstan, Lao People's Democratic Republic, Lebanon, Lesotho, Liberia, Libya, Madagascar, Malawi, Malaysia, Maldives, Mali, Mauritania, Mauritius, Mexico, Morocco, Mozambique, Myanmar, Namibia, Nauru, Nepal, Nicaragua, Niger, Nigeria, Oman, Pakistan, Paraguay, Peru, Philippines, Qatar, Russian Federation, Rwanda, Saint Lucia, Saint Vincent and the Grenadines, Sao Tome and Principe, Saudi Arabia, Senegal, Sierra Leone, Solomon Islands, Somalia, South Africa, Sri Lanka, Sudan, Suriname, Swaziland, Syrian Arab Republic, Tajikistan, Thailand, Timor-Leste, Togo, Trinidad and Tobago, Tunisia, United Arab Emirates, Uruguay, Uzbekistan, Venezuela, Viet Nam, Yemen, Zambia, Zimbabwe.

Against: Australia, Canada, Israel, Japan, Marshall Islands, Micronesia, United States.

Abstaining: Albania, Andorra, Austria, Belgium, Bosnia and Herzegovina, Brazil, Bulgaria, Croatia, Cyprus, Czech Republic, Denmark, Estonia, Finland, France, Georgia, Germany, Greece, Hungary, Iceland, Ireland, Italy, Latvia, Liechtenstein, Lithuania, Luxembourg, Malta, Moldova, Monaco, Montenegro, Netherlands, New Zealand, Norway, Panama, Papua New Guinea, Poland, Portugal, Republic of Korea, Romania, Samoa, San Marino, Serbia, Singapore, Slovakia, Slovenia, Spain, Sweden, Switzerland, The former Yugoslav Republic of Macedonia, Turkey, Tuvalu, Uganda, Ukraine, United Kingdom, United Republic of Tanzania, Vanuatu.

Management review

JIU Report. By a 27 June note [A/61/115], the Secretary-General transmitted a report of the Joint Inspection Unit (JIU) [JIU/REP/2006/3] on follow-up to the management review of OHCHR undertaken by the Unit in 2003 [YUN 2003, p. 1388] and 2004 [YUN 2004, p. 650]. JIU reported progress in the implementation of the ten recommendations it made in 2003, clarifying in nine cases that it was satisfied with OHCHR initiatives to achieve the intended goals and acknowledging that implementation efforts were "work in progress". The only exception was Recommendation 6 concerning personnel issues and the need to ensure a more balanced geographical distribution of OHCHR staff selection body. In response to the OHCHR position that the membership of its Advisory Review Panel, which oversaw the process of filling some vacancies in the Office, was balanced in terms of gender, nationality, geographic composition and office representation, JIU maintained that the current six-member composition of the Panel did not reflect the UN membership as a whole. It suggested that the High Commissioner review the situation to allow each of the five major geographic regions (Africa, Asia, Eastern Europe, Latin America and the Caribbean, Western Europe) to have at least one representative on the Panel. Also of concern was the imbalance in the geographic distribution of the OHCHR staff in general, which JIU in its 2003 review had noted could only be rectified through a determined management action, and had proposed that the High Commissioner prepare an action plan indicating specific targets and deadlines to be achieved. Although that recommendation was among those described as "work in progress" in the current report, given that the requisite plan had been put in place (see above), the inspectors found it regrettable that the issue had not been dealt with in a sufficiently vigorous manner. They pointed out that the skewed nature of the staff could ultimately diminish the effectiveness of the work of OHCHR if it was perceived to be culturally biased and unrepresentative of the United Nations, and noted that much more could be done to address the problem. In that regard, OHCHR should adopt a more proactive approach to identify and recruit candidates from among the unrepresented or underrepresented countries within the Office. The General Assembly action on the report was contained in resolution 61/159 (see p. 764).

A 29 August addendum [A/61/115/Add.1] containing the Secretary-General's comments on the JIU recommendations stated that the Office mostly agreed with and welcomed the follow-up report of the inspectors and was implementing a management plan of action to resolve recommendations considered as work in progress.

Strategic management plan

During the year, the High Commissioner presented the OHCHR Strategic Management Plan 2006-2007, which articulated how the Office intended to play its role in ensuring that human rights were protected, and change and organize itself, the projects it would implement and how it would prioritize its activities for the next two years. The Plan represented the means by which OHCHR, with the support of Member States, hoped to realize its vision laid out in its 2005 Plan of Action [YUN 2005, p. 715]. It addressed the plan's five focus areas: developing effective and appropriate strategies for country engagement; exercising leadership in the field of human rights; strengthening partnerships; providing high-calibre and strong support for the UN human rights programme; and strengthening the management of OHCHR. Several task forces were established to examine and recommend strategies to advance efforts in each of those areas, with their work incorporated into the Plan.

Right to promote and protect human rights

Human rights defenders

Reports of Special Representative. In her annual report to the Commission [E/CN.4/2006/95], the Secretary-General's Special Representative on human rights defenders, Hina Jilani (Pakistan), described her activities and reflected on the development and implementation of the mandate since its creation in 2000 [YUN 2000, p. 604]. The report also examined the major constraints in implementing the 1998 Declaration on the Right and Responsibility of Individuals, Groups and Organs of Society to Promote and Protect Universally Recognized Human Rights and Fundamental Freedoms (Declaration on human rights defenders), adopted by the General Assembly in resolution 53/144 [YUN 1998, p. 608]. Between December 2004 and December 2005, the Special Representative had sent 310 communications to 68 countries, of which 46 responded, on more than 351 cases, including jointly with other mandates, concerning some 799 alleged violations against defenders and 316 against human rights organizations. The number of urgent appeals and allegation letters sent to Governments had increased markedly since the first year of her mandate.

The Representative's activities focused largely on communications transmitted to Governments, country visits, cooperation with the UN system, intergovernmental organizations and NGOs, the compilation of developments regarding the situation of defenders and the special needs of female defenders. Highlighting the main trends over the past six years in the implementation of the Declaration, the Special Representative found a number of encouraging developments, including the adoption by many States of measures to ensure the personal safety of defenders at imminent risk, the official recognition by several Governments of the status and role of defenders, and government efforts to ensure that domestic legislation reflected States' obligations contained in the Declaration and other human rights standards. Other developments related to the fostering of protection for defenders through increased awareness of the Declaration, action to end the impunity of human rights violators and efforts by regional intergovernmental organizations to create special mechanisms to deal with issues affecting defenders. The Special Representative also highlighted the various initiatives and activities of UN system entities, including OHCHR and the treaty bodies, and by national human rights institutions and civil society, which had facilitated her work and helped promote defenders' rights.

Nonetheless, the Special Representative regretted not being able to achieve the level of effectiveness she sought in certain areas, as insufficient material and human resources prevented her from ensuring effective follow-up to the cases addressed and to related country visits. She stated that the reticence of Governments in extending invitations for country visits was a major impediment to an effective implementation of her mandate. Another major cause for concern was the persistent violation of defenders' rights in many countries, warranting the Special Representative's intervention on several occasions where human rights activists were not allowed to leave their countries to participate in international human rights events, or were molested or subjected to serious reprisals upon their return from such activities. In other instances, she intervened on behalf of individuals targeted for giving information to or lodging complaints with international human rights mechanisms. She was extremely concerned by the murder of some of those affected.

Despite international commitments in some countries, State officials promoted confusion about the role and status of human rights defenders by delivering defamatory and denigrating statements and smear campaigns about their work. The Special Representative was particularly concerned that there was still impunity in an overwhelming majority of violations against defenders, mostly by non-State actors. While drawing attention to the recommendations in her previous reports, she emphasized a number of measures for securing defenders' rights, including the adoption of laws and security policies that recognized the legitimacy of peaceful action to attain economic, social and cultural rights, and increased involvement of the judiciary in ensuring a safe environment for the work of defenders. She also recommended government action to ensure that laws and policies reflected defenders' rights to access information and sites of alleged violations; the development of legal and normative frameworks for the accountability of non-State entities and others who had committed human rights violations, especially against defenders; recognition of defenders' contribution to the restoration of peace and security by ascribing to them a role in peace negotiations and agreements; and establishment by States of a methodology for the prompt investigation of complaints and allegations. In addition, the evaluation of defenders' situation should be used as an indicator for assessing States' compliance with human rights standards and respect for the rule of law.

Two March addenda to the report summarized communications sent to and received from Governments [E/CN.4/2006/95/Add.1 & Corr.1, 2] and provided information on developments regarding the situation of defenders and the implementation of the Declaration in 118 countries over the past six years [E/CN.4/2006/95/Add.5].

A September note of the Secretary-General [A/61/312] transmitted the Special Representative's sixth annual report, in accordance with General Assembly resolution 60/161 [YUN 2005, p. 720], which focused on the right to freedom of assembly in relation to the activities of human rights defenders—one of the principal rights that needed to be guaranteed to enable them to do their work. Without such a guarantee and protection against its violation by State officials or non-State entities, the ability of defenders to fulfil their role would be restricted. Highlighting a worrisome trend of violation of that right, the Representative noted that she had received responses to less than half of the 1,194 communications she had sent to 62 Governments on alleged violations, of which 253 dealt directly with the right to freedom of assembly. Other violations included arrests, violence during assemblies, threats, travel restrictions, prohibition or interruption of assemblies and restrictions imposed through legislation. Particularly vulnerable to violations of the right to freedom of assembly were women defenders, those working on behalf of minorities, and others operating in conflict situations. The Representative recommended that States should ensure the "contextual space" for the activities of defenders, including the rights to peaceful assembly and freedom of expression and association. States should also ensure that their legislation was in line with international standards relating to those rights, and review restrictions imposed by laws and regulations. The Representative urged States to ensure that there were satisfactory complaints review procedures in the event of restrictions being imposed on assemblies and there was no impunity for harm inflicted on defenders who were carrying out collective public action.

On 19 December, the Assembly took note of the Secretary-General's note (**decision 61/529**).

Other aspects

Good governance

In response to a 2005 Commission request [YUN 2005, p. 722], OHCHR, in collaboration with Poland and Australia, organized a conference on anti-corruption, good governance and human rights (Warsaw, Poland, 8-9 November) [A/HRC/4/71], in follow-up to a joint OHCHR-UNDP seminar on a related topic in 2004 [YUN 2004, p.685]. The conference, designed to deepen the understanding of good governance practices in the fight against corruption, identified, explored and clarified the linkages between corruption, human rights and good governance. Participants shared concerns and experiences, and examined, among other things, the impact of corruption on human rights and ways of combating corruption through human rights principles and approaches. Recognizing that corruption impeded the realization of human rights in many ways, they stressed the importance of combating the problem in its various forms, insisting that anti-corruption measures should be effective without compromising human rights, and identified various ways to improve related efforts.

Human rights instruments

General aspects

In 2006, seven UN human rights instruments were in force, whose implementation was being monitored by expert bodies. The instruments and their treaty bodies were: the 1965 International Convention on the Elimination of All Forms of Racial Discrimination [YUN 1965, p. 440, GA res. 2106 A (XX)] (Committee on the Elimination of Racial Discrimination); the 1966 International Covenant on Civil and Political Rights and the Optional Protocol thereto [YUN 1966, p. 423, GA res. 2200 A (XXI)] and the Second Optional Protocol aiming at the abolition of the death penalty [YUN 1989, p. 484, GA res. 44/128] (Human Rights Committee); the 1966 International Covenant on Economic, Social and Cultural Rights [YUN 1966, p. 419, GA res. 2200 A (XXI)] (Committee on Economic, Social and Cultural Rights); the 1979 Convention on the Elimination of All Forms of Discrimination against Women [YUN 1979, p. 895, GA res. 54/4] (Committee on the Elimination of Discrimination against Women); the 1984 Convention against Torture and Other Cruel, Inhuman or Degrading Punishment [YUN 1984, p. 813, GA res. 39/46] and related 2002 Optional Protocol [YUN 2002, p. 631, GA res. 57/199] (Committee against Torture); the 1989 Convention on the Rights of the Child [YUN 1989, p. 560, GA res. 44/25] and Optional Protocols on the involvement of children in armed conflict and on the sale of children, child prostitution and child pornography [YUN 2000, pp. 616 & 618, GA res. 54/263] (Committee on the Rights of the Child); and the 1990 International Convention on the Protection of the Rights of All Migrant Workers and Members of Their Families [YUN 1990, p. 594, GA res. 45/158] (Committee on the Protection of the Rights of All Migrant Workers and Members of Their Families).

Report of Secretary-General. In response to General Assembly resolutions 52/118 [YUN 1997, p. 594] and 53/138 [YUN 1998, p. 612], the Secretary-General submitted a May report, with a later addendum [HRI/GEN/2/Rev.3 & Add.1], containing a compilation in a single volume of guidelines regarding the form and content of reports to be submitted by States parties to the Human Rights Committee, the Committee on Economic, Social and Cultural Rights, the Committee on the Elimination of Discrimination against Women, the Committee on the Elimination of Racial Discrimination, the Committee on the Rights of the Child and the Committee against Torture. In addition, the report provided the consolidated guidelines relating to the initial part of State party reports containing information of a general character ("core documents").

Final report of Special Rapporteur. In a July final report [A/HRC/Sub.1/58/5], submitted in response to a 2005 Subcommission request [YUN 2005, p. 723], the Special Rapporteur on the study of the universal implementation of international human rights treaties, Emmanuel Decaux (France), updated information contained in his 2005 interim report [ibid]. The final report clarified the various commitments undertaken by States and what remained to be done to fully attain universal ratification set by States in 1993. Drawing from a questionnaire he had prepared for the study, the Special Rapporteur addressed the issue of the applicability of international instruments in domestic law and the effective fulfilment of obligations, as well as the legal challenges regarding the nature and scope of international human rights law. Finding that the area to be explored was vast, he considered it necessary for the Human Rights Council to mandate a working group of the Subcommission, or its successor, to carry out periodic and systematic monitoring of the status of international human rights instruments, within the context of the Universal Periodic Review (UPR) (see p. 761). He recommended other measures to ensure momentum to accord international human rights instruments a universal or quasi-universal character. The recent creation of the Council was an opportunity for States to make pledges, including on ratification, thereby bringing the goal of universal ratification closer.

Subcommission action. On 24 August [res.2006/1], the Subcommission requested OHCHR to disseminate the Special Rapporteur's final report widely (see above), and recommended that the Council consider the recommendations contained therein, particularly regarding the need to ensure that the status of international human rights instruments was periodically and systematically monitored under the Council's UPR procedure. It encouraged States to implement the Vienna Declaration and Programme of Action adopted by the 1993 World Conference [YUN 1993, p. 908], with a view to the universal and effective implementation of human rights instruments, and recommended the expansion of technical assistance to facilitate the process. The Subcommission also recommended the convening of seminars to encourage dialogue with States on ratification and best practices.

Human rights treaty body system

Meeting of chairpersons. A May note by the Secretary-General [HRI/MC/2006/1] contained the provisional agenda and annotations for the eighteenth meeting of chairpersons of human rights treaty bodies (see below). In a September note [A/61/385], he submitted the chairperson's report on the meeting (Geneva, 22-23 June), which considered the follow-up to the recommendations of the seventeenth meeting [YUN 2005, p. 723] and reviewed developments relating to the work of the treaty bodies. The meeting also considered the issues of strengthening support to those bodies, enhancing their effectiveness and streamlining their reporting procedures and requirements.

The meeting had before it Secretariat reports on harmonized guidelines on reporting under the international human rights treaties [HRI/MC/2006/3 & Corr.1]; the working methods of the human rights treaty bodies relating to the State party reporting process [HRI/MC/2006/4 & Corr.1]; the practice of human rights treaty bodies with respect to reservations to international human rights treaties [HRI/MC/2005/5/Add.1]; the meeting of the working group on reservations [HRI/MC/2006/5 & Rev.1]; the implementation of recommendations of the fourth inter-committee meeting and the seventeenth meeting of chairpersons [HRI/MC/2006/6]; indicators for monitoring compliance with international human rights instruments [HRI/MC/2006/7]; and a proposal by the Committee on the Elimination of Racial Discrimination on establishing a single body to deal with individual communications [HRI/MC/2006/8/CRP.1].

Also held was the eighth joint meeting of the treaty body chairpersons, special rapporteurs/representatives, independent experts and chairpersons of the working groups of the Commission's special procedures.

The meeting recommended that all treaty bodies consider developing procedures and guidelines for enhanced interaction with special procedures mandate-holders and that the Secretariat seek ways to facilitate that interaction. It also recommended that the Chairpersons of the eighteenth meeting and of the special procedures mandate-holders meeting send a joint letter to the Council President, proposing that the recommendations of those procedures and the concluding observations of treaty bodies form part of the basis of the Universal Periodic Review (see p. 761). It further recommended that treaty bodies consider institutionalizing their relationship with the Council and proposed modalities for such a relationship. Annexed to the report was the report on the fifth inter-committee meeting of human rights treaty bodies (Geneva, 19-21 June), which adopted recommendations on proposals for the reform of the UN human rights framework, harmonization of working methods, the relationship between the Council and treaty bodies, follow-up to concluding observations, reservations, reporting guidelines, standardization of technical terminology, liaison with UN specialized agencies, funds and programmes, NGO participation, national human rights institutions and human rights statistical information.

On 19 December, the General Assembly took note of the report of the Chairpersons' meeting (**decision 61/529**).

Meeting of special rapporteurs, experts and chairpersons. In October [A/HRC/4/43], the High Commissioner transmitted to the Council the report of the thirteenth meeting of special rapporteurs/representatives, independent experts and chairpersons of working groups of the Commission's special procedures and advisory services programme (Geneva, 19-23 June). Participants discussed, among other subjects, the review of mandates to be undertaken by the Council and the role of the special procedures system vis-à-vis the universal periodic review. There was general agreement that mandate-holders should be involved in related discussions. It was stressed that the special procedures represented one of the Commission's greatest achievements and that the periodic review should strengthen the system and ensure that it was based on recommendations adopted by human rights mechanisms.

During the Council's first session, the Chair of the Coordination Committee read a statement in which mandate-holders called on the Council to recognize the special procedures system as an indispensable mechanism for promoting and protecting human rights; provide them with an opportunity to directly and effectively interact with the Council; make their work central to the system of universal periodic review; encourage States to strengthen cooperation with them and implement their recommendations; and recognize the fundamental role of NGOs and regional and national human rights institutions as key partners. They also requested the Secretary-General and the High Commissioner to provide the special procedures with the requisite resources to enable them to respond to the challenges and expectations relating to the reform process.

Reform proposals

Report of High Commissioner. In her annual report to the General Assembly [A/61/36], the High Commissioner proposed that the treaty body system be reformed by unifying the treaty bodies established under the seven principal human rights instruments in a single standing treaty body. The proposal was based on the premise that, despite its achievements, the system, as currently configured, faced serious challenges stemming mainly from the increase in human rights instruments and the growing number of States assuming new legal obligations. Many States accepted the system on a purely formal level, but either did not engage with it or did so in a superficial way, owing to insufficient resources or lack of political will. Some States parties considered the reporting procedures of the treaty bodies overly cumbersome, resulting in many overdue reports. A unified standing treaty body would address those challenges. While some members welcomed the proposal, others opposed it, mostly from the perspective that a unified standing body could undermine the specificity of the seven instruments concerned. A similar division of opinions existed among States and NGOs. However, it was premature to draw definitive conclusions as it appeared that the proposal for such a treaty body, unifying both the reporting and complaints procedures, might not be achievable in the short term.

OHCHR concept paper. A March report of the Secretariat [HRI/MC/2006/2] contained an OHCHR concept paper, which further elaborated on the High Commissioner's proposal for unifying the treaty bodies under a single standing body (see above), provided a basis on which options for reform could be explored, and presented the objectives and guiding principles of the proposal. The report analysed the current system, its achievements and challenges, and identified how a unified treaty body would meet those challenges to ensure a strengthened and more effective monitoring system. Furthermore, it presented ideas on possible reforms, modalities of operation and functions of a unified body, and raised some issues to be considered in its establishment. Several annexes to the paper provided facts and figures about reporting to the human rights treaty bodies and a variety of related information.

Human Rights Committee consideration. The Human Rights Committee, at its eighty-eighth session (16 October–3 November) [A/62/40, Vol. 1], acknowledged that the OHCHR concept paper (see above) could stimulate a serious and constructive debate on the reform of treaty bodies, but the creation of a standing unified treaty body to replace the seven existing ones raised legal and political problems that could not be solved in the short or medium term. It was better to improve coordination of their working methods without necessarily amending the treaties. Questions pertaining to the harmonization of those methods should be approached in such a manner as to facilitate a practical and effective resolution of the problems raised by the separate functioning of the treaty bodies. Consequently, the Committee proposed that the meeting of chairpersons of those treaty bodies and the inter-committee meeting be replaced by a single coordinating body composed of representatives of the various treaty bodies, which would be responsible for oversight of all questions relating to the harmonization of working methods. Such a coordinating body should also promote the exchange of information between the Council and the treaty bodies. The Committee invited the various treaty bodies to amend their rules of procedure, where necessary, in order to promote the harmonization of their working methods, and called for more support and the widest dissemination of their work.

Experts' meeting. An international meeting of experts (Triesenberg, Liechtenstein, 14-16 July) [A/61/351; A/HRC/2/G/5], organized jointly by OHCHR and the Government of Liechtenstein, discussed the High Commissioner's proposal for a unified standing treaty body and other issues relating to the reform of the UN human rights treaty body system. Participants determined that their discussions were not limited to one particular approach to the reform and that the process needed to address all challenges facing the current system and how they could be met.

Human Rights Council action. On 28 November [A/62/53 (res. 2/5)], the Council, noting with appreciation the continuing efforts of Member States, human rights treaty bodies, the High Commissioner and the Secretary-General to improve the effectiveness of the treaty body system, encouraged such efforts and asked the High Commissioner to study various options for reforming the system, seek the views of States and other stakeholders in that regard and report thereon.

Reservations to human rights treaties

Working group on reservations. The Working Group on reservations, established pursuant to the request of the Fourth Inter-Committee Meeting of human rights treaty bodies and the seventeenth meeting of the chairpersons of those bodies [YUN 2005, p. 723], held its first meeting (Geneva, 22-23 June) [HRI/MC/2006/5/Rev.1] to examine the practice of those treaty bodies with respect to reservations to international human rights treaties. The majority of members considered that, although treaty bodies were competent to assess the validity of reservations, in most cases, particularly during the consideration of periodic reports, it was not necessary for them to take a decision on the issue. While any statement made at the time of ratification might be considered as a reservation, care should be exercised in making such a conclusion. However, when reservations were explicitly or implicitly permitted, they could contribute to the attainment of universal ratification. Welcoming the inclusion of a provision on reservations in the draft harmonized guidelines on reporting under international human rights treaties (see p. 768), the Group emphasized the importance of dialogue between treaty bodies and States to distinguish more precisely the scope and consequences of reservations and encourage the State party concerned to reformulate or withdraw its reservations. It also recommended that another meeting be convened, in the light of discussions in the International Law Commission on reservations to treaties (see p. 1523).

Covenant on Civil and Political Rights and Optional Protocols

Accessions and ratifications

As at 31 December, parties to the International Covenant on Civil and Political Rights and the Optional Protocol thereto, adopted by the General Assembly in resolution 2200 A (XXI) [YUN 1966, p. 423], numbered 160 and 109, respectively. During the year, Andorra, Maldives and Montenegro became parties to both instruments, while Bahrain, Indonesia and Kazakhstan became parties to the Covenant, and Turkey to the Optional Protocol.

The Second Optional Protocol, aimed at the abolition of the death penalty, adopted by the Assembly in resolution 44/128 [YUN 1989, p. 484], was acceded to by Andorra, Moldova, Montenegro and Turkey, bringing the total number of States parties to 60, as at 31 December.

Report of Secretary-General. In response to General Assembly resolution 60/149 [YUN 2005, p. 724], which requested the Secretary-General to report on the status of the International Covenants on Human Rights and the Optional Protocols to the International Covenant on Civil and Political Rights, a September report of the Secretary-General [A/61/354] noted that all relevant information on ratifications, accessions, successions, reservations, declarations and objections to reservations was maintained on the websites of the United Nations Office of Legal Affairs Treaty Section (http://untreaty.un.org), and of OHCHR; (http://www.unhchr.ch). Those websites would henceforth constitute the primary means by which the Secretary-General would keep the Assembly informed of the status of those Covenants.

On 19 December, the Assembly noted the Secretary-General's report (**decision 61/529**).

Implementation

Monitoring body. The Human Rights Committee, established under article 28 of the Covenant, held three sessions in 2006: its eighty-sixth, from 13 to 31 March (New York); eighty-seventh, from 10 to 28 July (Geneva) [A/61/40, vol. I]; and eighty-eighth, from 16 October to 3 November (Geneva) [A/62/40, vol. I]. Under article 40, it considered reports from eight States—Bosnia and Herzegovina, Democratic Republic of the Congo, Central African Republic, Honduras, Norway, Republic of Korea, Ukraine, United States—as well as from Hong Kong Special Administrative Region (China) and Kosovo (Serbia), submitted by the United Nations Interim Administration Mission in Kosovo (UNMIK) (see p. 87). The Committee adopted views on communications from individuals alleging violations of their rights under the Covenant, and decided that other such communications were inadmissible. Those views and decisions were annexed to the Committee's reports [A/61/40, vol. II; A/62/40, vol. II].

On 4 January, France terminated the state of emergency it had declared throughout the metropolitan territory in 2005 [YUN 2005, p. 727]. On 7 March, Georgia notified other States through the intermediary of the Secretary-General that it had declared a state of emergency in one district, which was terminated on 16 March. By a notification of 11 April, Ecuador informed the Secretary-General that it had declared a state of emergency on 21 March in a number of provinces and suspended it on 7 April. By several notifications, issued between 18 January and 2 December, Peru stated that it had extended the state of emergency it initially declared in parts of the country in 2003 [YUN 2003, p. 670]. On 24 February, the Philippines informed the Secretary-General that it had declared a state of emergency, and on 5 September, Guatemala notified other States of its declaration of a state of emergency in certain municipalities of one of its departments.

Covenant on Economic, Social and Cultural Rights

Accessions and ratifications

As at 31 December, there were 155 parties to the International Covenant on Economic, Social and Cultural Rights, adopted by the General Assembly in resolution 2200 A (XXI) [YUN 1966, p. 419]. During the year, Indonesia, Kazakhstan, Maldives and Montenegro became parties to the Covenant.

Draft optional protocol

In response to a 2004 Commission request [YUN 2004, p. 663], the open-ended Working Group to consider options regarding the elaboration of an optional protocol to the Covenant held its third session (Geneva, 6-17 February) [E/CN.4/2006/47]. The optional protocol would establish a complaints procedure for individuals or groups who felt that their rights under the Covenant had been violated. After considering preliminary views on options by States and representatives of intergovernmental organizations and NGOs, the Working Group discussed the scope of rights subject to a procedure, the admissibility criteria, merits, friendly settlement of disputes, interim measures and views, inquiry procedure, international cooperation and assistance to countries in implementing human rights obligations, the implications of an optional protocol for national resource allocation, the relationship with existing procedures, and the costs and potential impact of an optional protocol. The Group also discussed with a representative of the Inter-American Court on Human Rights issues relating to the protection of economic, social and cultural rights under the inter-American human rights system.

Most delegations noted that considerable progress had been made in clarifying questions relating to an optional protocol, and that the Group had fulfilled its mandate. Several States called for an extension of the Group's mandate, with a view to drafting and negotiating an optional protocol. Others proposed that the Group's Chairperson, Catarina de Albuquerque (Portugal), be entrusted with the preparation of a first draft, taking into account the views expressed at Group sessions. Others felt, however, that a number of issues remained unresolved and recommended that the Group continue to consider possible elements of a protocol, so as to build consensus on the remaining issues.

Human Rights Council action. On 25 June [A/61/53 (res. 1/3)], the Council extended the mandate of the Working Group for two years, in order to elaborate an optional protocol to the Covenant. It requested the Group's Chairperson to prepare a first draft, including draft provisions corresponding to the various main approaches, to be used as a basis for negotiations. The Group was asked to meet for 10 working days each year and to report thereon.

Implementation

Monitoring body. The Committee on Economic, Social and Cultural Rights held its thirty-sixth (1-19 May) and thirty-seventh (27 November–1 December) sessions in Geneva [E/2007/22]. Its pre-sessional working group also met in Geneva from 22 to 26 May and from 27 November to 1 December, to identify issues to be discussed with reporting States.

On 27 July, the Economic and Social Council took note of the Committee's reports on its thirty-fourth and thirty-fifth sessions, held in 2005 [YUN 2005, p. 727] (**decision 2006/250**).

In 2006, the Committee examined reports, under articles 16 and 17 of the Covenant, submitted by Albania, Canada, El Salvador, Liechtenstein, Mexico, Monaco, Morocco, the Netherlands, Tajikistan and The former Yugoslav Republic of Macedonia.

On 15 May, the Committee held a general discussion on the right to social security, aimed at reviewing the draft general comment prepared by its Rapporteurs. Following the completion of two draft general comments on articles 2.2 (non-discrimination) and 9 (the right to social security), the Committee decided, on 22 November, to elaborate a new general comment on article 15 (the right to participate in cultural life) and requested Jaime Marchan Romero (Ecuador) and Virginia Bonoan-Dandan (Philippines) to serve as Rapporteurs. In the light of the acceptance of new guidelines for preparing common core documents by the human rights treaty monitoring bodies, the Committee decided to review its reporting guidelines and appointed Maria Virginia Brás Gomes (Portugal) as Rapporteur for that task.

Human Rights Council action. On 29 November [A/62/53 (dec. 2/116)], the Council deferred to its fourth session consideration of a draft decision submitted by Algeria, Cameroon, Cuba, Ghana, Libyan Arab Jamahiriya, Mali and South Africa, as well as some non-Council members (Benin, Lesotho, Sudan, Zimbabwe), which called for the initiation of a process, in accordance with international law, particularly international treaties, to rectify the status of the Committee, aimed at placing it on par with other treaty monitoring bodies.

Convention against racial discrimination

Accessions and ratifications

As at 31 December, the number of parties to the International Convention on the Elimination of All Forms of Racial Discrimination, adopted by the General Assembly in resolution 2106 A (XX) [YUN 1965, p. 440], rose to 173, with Andorra, Saint Kitts and Nevis and Montenegro becoming parties during the year.

The Secretary-General reported on the status of the Convention as at 1 July [A/61/260].

A February note of the Secretariat [E/CN.4/2006/13], submitted in response to a 2005 Commission request [YUN 2005, p. 728], described OHCHR efforts towards universal ratification of the Convention and listed six States that had signed but not ratified the Convention and 18 others that had neither signed nor ratified it. OHCHR had sent notes verbales to those 24 States encouraging them to become parties.

Implementation

Monitoring body. The Committee on the Elimination of Racial Discrimination (CERD), established under article 8 of the Convention, held its sixty-eighth (20 February–10 March) and sixty-ninth (31 July–8 August) sessions [A/61/18] in Geneva. The Commission considered reports submitted by Bosnia and Herzegovina, Botswana, Denmark, El Salvador, Estonia, Guatemala, Guyana, Lithuania, Mexico, Mongolia, Norway, Oman, South Africa, Ukraine, Uzbekistan and Yemen. With regard to the Convention's implementation in States parties whose reports were seriously overdue, the Committee adopted a decision on Mozambique, noting that it would proceed with the adoption of concluding observations if the country's overdue report was not received by 30 June. Mozambique provided its second to twelfth periodic report on that day. CERD also adopted decisions on Saint Lucia reminding it of its reporting obligations and urging a response to the Committee's previous communication, and on Ethiopia, regretting the interruption of dialogue with the Committee and urging its prompt submission of its seventh to fifteenth periodic reports, due between 1989 and 2005. To assist in the resumption of dialogue, CERD sent a list of questions to Ethiopia and requested a response by 31 December, but decided that if it did not hear from Ethiopia, it would proceed with the adoption of concluding observations. In the case of Seychelles, one of those whose lack of response the Committee had found regretful in 2005 [YUN 2005, p. 729], it adopted confidential provisional concluding observations.

Under article 14 of the Convention, CERD considered communications from individuals or groups claiming violation by a State party of their rights as enumerated in the Convention. Forty-seven States parties made such declarations and recognized CERD competence to do so: Algeria, Australia, Austria, Azerbaijan, Belgium, Bolivia, Brazil, Bulgaria, Chile, Costa Rica, Cyprus, Czech Republic, Denmark, Ecuador, Finland, France, Georgia, Germany, Hungary, Iceland, Ireland, Italy, Liechtenstein, Luxembourg, Malta, Mexico, Monaco, Netherlands, Norway, Peru, Poland, Portugal, Republic of Korea, Romania, Russian Federation, Senegal, Serbia and Montenegro, Slovakia, Slovenia, South Africa, Spain, Sweden, Switzerland, The former Yugoslav Republic of Macedonia, Ukraine, Uruguay, and Venezuela.

Pursuant to article 15 of the Convention, the Committee was empowered to consider petitions, reports and other information relating to Trust and Non-Self-Governing Territories. It noted, as it had in the past, the difficulty in fulfilling its functions in that regard, owing to the lack of copies of relevant petitions and the fact that the reports received contained scant information relating directly to the Convention's principles and objectives.

The Committee adopted two decisions under its early warning and urgent procedures. The first addressed the situation of the Western Shoshone indigenous peoples and groups in the United States [dec. 1 (68)]. Concerned at the continuing infringement on the affected population's right to ancestral lands and the lack of action to follow-up on its previous concluding observations on the matter, the Committee urged the United States to initiate dialogue with representatives of that community to find a solution acceptable to them. In its second decision, which addressed persons of concern in Suriname [dec. 1 (69)], the Committee drew the attention of the High Commissioner and the Human Rights Council to the alarming situation regarding the rights of indigenous and tribal peoples in that country, asking them to take appropriate measures. Following a general debate on the situation in Lebanon, the Committee issued a statement on 11 August expressing concern that the continuation of the conflict there might intensify racial discrimination and hatred in the region and the wider world. CERD also considered follow-up action to the 2001 World Conference against Racism, Racial Discrimination, Xenophobia and Related Intolerance [YUN 2001, p. 615].

Financial situation. In July [A/61/186], the Secretary-General reported that outstanding States parties' arrears to the Committee as at 1 June totalled $143,770.52. As at 31 December, 43 States parties had accepted an amendment to article 8 of the Convention regarding the financing of CERD [YUN 1992, p. 714]. The amendment would enter into force when accepted by a two-thirds majority of States parties, comprising approximately 114 of the 173 States parties to the Convention.

Election of new members. On 12 January [CERD/SP/SR.30], a meeting of the States parties elected nine members of the Committee to replace those whose terms of office expired on 19 January.

Human Rights Council action. On 8 December [A/62/53 (dec. 3/103)], by a recorded vote of 33 to 12, with 1 abstention, the Council established an Ad Hoc Committee on the Elaboration of Complementary Standards to elaborate complementary standards in the form of either a convention or additional protocol(s) to the International Convention on the Elimination of All Forms of Racial Discrimination, filling the gaps in the Convention and providing new normative standards for combating all forms of contemporary racism. It recommended that the Committee convene annual sessions of 10 working days and hold its first session before the end of 2007, reporting regularly to the Council on progress in elaborating complementary standards. The Council welcomed the High Commissioner's appointment of five experts in that field, with the mandate to produce a base document outlining the substantive gaps in the Convention and make recommendations for bridging them. It requested the experts to finalize their report before the end of June 2007 for submission to OHCHR.

GENERAL ASSEMBLY ACTION

On 19 December [meeting 81], the General Assembly, on the recommendation of the Third Committee [A/61/441], adopted **resolution 61/148** without vote [agenda item 65 *(a)*].

International Convention on the Elimination of All Forms of Racial Discrimination

The General Assembly,

Recalling its previous resolutions on the International Convention on the Elimination of All Forms of Racial Discrimination, most recently resolution 59/176 of 20 December 2004,

Bearing in mind the Vienna Declaration and Programme of Action adopted by the World Conference on Human Rights on 25 June 1993, in particular section II.B of the Declaration, relating to equality, dignity and tolerance,

Reiterating the need to intensify the struggle to eliminate all forms of racism, racial discrimination, xenophobia and related intolerance throughout the world,

Reiterating also the importance of the Convention, which is one of the most widely accepted human rights instruments adopted under the auspices of the United Nations,

Reaffirming that universal adherence to and full implementation of the Convention are of paramount importance for promoting equality and non-discrimination in the world, as stated in the Durban Declaration and Programme of Action adopted by the World Conference against Racism, Racial Discrimination, Xenophobia and Related Intolerance on 8 September 2001,

Mindful of the importance of the contributions of the Committee on the Elimination of Racial Discrimination to the effective implementation of the Convention and to the efforts of the United Nations to combat racism, racial discrimination, xenophobia and related intolerance,

Emphasizing the obligation of all States parties to the Convention to take legislative, judicial and other measures in order to secure full implementation of the provisions of the Convention,

Recalling its resolution 47/111 of 16 December 1992, in which it welcomed the decision, taken on 15 January 1992 by the Fourteenth Meeting of States Parties to the International Convention on the Elimination of All Forms of Racial Discrimination, to amend paragraph 6 of article 8 of the Convention and to add a new paragraph, as paragraph 7 of article 8, with a view to providing for the financing of the Committee from the regular budget of the United Nations, and reiterating its deep concern that the amendment to the Convention has not yet entered into force,

Stressing the importance of enabling the Committee to function smoothly and to have all necessary facilities for the effective performance of its functions under the Convention,

I

Reports of the Committee on the Elimination of Racial Discrimination

1. *Takes note* of the reports of the Committee on the Elimination of Racial Discrimination on its sixty-sixth and sixty-seventh and its sixty-eighth and sixty-ninth sessions;

2. *Commends* the Committee for its contributions to the effective implementation of the International Convention on the Elimination of All Forms of Racial Discrimination, especially through the examination of reports under article 9 of the Convention, action on communications under article 14 of the Convention and thematic discussions, which contribute to the prevention and elimination of racism, racial discrimination, xenophobia and related intolerance;

3. *Calls upon* States parties to fulfil their obligation, under article 9, paragraph 1, of the Convention, to sub-

mit their periodic reports on measures taken to implement the Convention in due time;

4. *Expresses its concern* at the fact that a great number of reports are overdue and continue to be overdue, in particular initial reports, which constitutes an obstacle to the full implementation of the Convention;

5. *Encourages* States parties to the Convention whose reports are seriously overdue to avail themselves of the advisory services and technical assistance that the Office of the United Nations High Commissioner for Human Rights can provide, upon their request, for the preparation of the reports;

6. *Encourages* the Committee to continue to cooperate and exchange information with United Nations bodies and mechanisms, in particular with the Human Rights Council, the Subcommission on the Promotion and Protection of Human Rights and the Special Rapporteur on contemporary forms of racism, racial discrimination, xenophobia and related intolerance, and with intergovernmental organizations, as well as with non-governmental organizations;

7. *Encourages* States parties to the Convention to continue to include a gender perspective in their reports to the Committee, and invites the Committee to take into account a gender perspective in the implementation of its mandate;

8. *Notes with appreciation* the engagement of the Committee in the follow-up to the Durban Declaration and Programme of Action;

9. *Expresses its appreciation* for the efforts made so far by the Committee to improve the efficiency of its working methods, and encourages the Committee to continue its activities in this regard;

10. *Welcomes*, in this regard, measures taken by the Committee to follow up on its concluding observations and recommendations, such as the decision to appoint a follow-up coordinator and to adopt guidelines on the follow-up;

11. *Encourages* the continued participation of members of the Committee in the annual inter-committee meetings and meetings of chairpersons of the human rights treaty bodies, especially with a view to a more coordinated approach to the activities of the treaty body system and standardized reporting;

II

Financial situation of the Committee on the Elimination of Racial Discrimination

12. *Takes note* of the report of the Secretary-General on the financial situation of the Committee on the Elimination of Racial Discrimination;

13. *Expresses its profound concern* at the fact that a number of States parties to the International Convention on the Elimination of All Forms of Racial Discrimination have still not fulfilled their financial obligations, as shown in the report of the Secretary-General, and strongly appeals to all States parties that are in arrears to fulfil their outstanding financial obligations under article 8, paragraph 6, of the Convention;

14. *Strongly urges* States parties to the Convention to accelerate their domestic ratification procedures with regard to the amendment to the Convention concerning the financing of the Committee and to notify the Secretary-General expeditiously in writing of their agreement to the amendment, as decided upon at the Fourteenth Meeting of States Parties to the International Convention on the Elimination of All Forms of Racial Discrimination on 15 January 1992, endorsed by the General Assembly in its resolution 47/111 and further reiterated at the Sixteenth Meeting of States Parties on 16 January 1996;

15. *Requests* the Secretary-General to continue to ensure adequate financial arrangements and to provide the necessary support, including an adequate level of Secretariat assistance, in order to ensure the functioning of the Committee and to enable it to cope with its increasing amount of work;

16. *Also requests* the Secretary-General to invite those States parties to the Convention that are in arrears to pay the amounts in arrears, and to report thereon to the General Assembly at its sixty-third session;

III

Status of the International Convention on the Elimination of All Forms of Racial Discrimination

17. *Takes note* of the report of the Secretary-General on the status of the International Convention on the Elimination of All Forms of Racial Discrimination;

18. *Expresses its satisfaction* at the number of States that have ratified or acceded to the Convention, which now stands at one hundred and seventy-three;

19. *Urges* States parties to comply fully with their obligations under the Convention and to take into consideration the concluding observations and general recommendations of the Committee on the Elimination of Racial Discrimination;

20. *Reaffirms its conviction* that ratification of or accession to the Convention on a universal basis and the implementation of its provisions are necessary for the effectiveness of the fight against racism, racial discrimination, xenophobia and related intolerance and for the implementation of the commitments undertaken under the Durban Declaration and Programme of Action, and expresses its disappointment that universal ratification of the Convention was not achieved by the targeted date of 2005;

21. *Urges* all States that have not yet become parties to the Convention to ratify or accede to it as a matter of urgency;

22. *Urges* States to limit the extent of any reservation they lodge to the Convention and to formulate any reservation as precisely and as narrowly as possible in order to ensure that no reservation is incompatible with the object and purpose of the Convention, to review their reservations on a regular basis with a view to withdrawing them, and to withdraw reservations that are contrary to the object and purpose of the Convention;

23. *Notes* that the number of States parties to the Convention that have made the declaration provided for in article 14 of the Convention now stands at forty-nine, and requests the States parties that have not yet done so to consider making that declaration;

24. *Invites* the Chairman of the Committee on the Elimination of Racial Discrimination to present an oral report on the work of the Committee to the General Assembly at its sixty-third session under the item entitled "Elimination of racism and racial discrimination";

25. *Decides* to consider, at its sixty-third session, under the item entitled "Elimination of racism and racial discrimination", the reports of the Committee on its seventieth and seventy-first and its seventy-second and seventy-third sessions, the report of the Secretary-General on the financial situation of the Committee and the report of the Secretary-General on the status of the Convention.

Convention against torture

Accessions and ratifications

As at 31 December, 144 States were parties to the 1984 Convention against Torture and Other Cruel, Inhuman or Degrading Treatment or Punishment, adopted by the General Assembly in resolution 39/46 [YUN 1984, p. 813]. Andorra, Montenegro and San Marino became parties to the Convention in 2006.

On 22 June, the Optional Protocol to the Convention, which was adopted in Assembly resolution 57/199 [YUN 2002, p. 631] and opened for signature in 2003 [YUN 2003, p. 675], entered into force following the deposit of the twentieth instrument of ratification or accession. During the year, Armenia, Benin, Bolivia, Estonia, Czech Republic, Honduras, Liechtenstein, Maldives, Moldova, Peru, Senegal, Serbia, Spain and Ukraine became parties to the Protocol, bringing the total number of parties to 30. As at 10 July, 52 parties had made the required declarations under articles 21 and 22 (under which a party recognized the competence of the Committee against Torture to receive and consider communications by which a State party claimed that another party was not fulfilling its obligations under the Convention, and from or on behalf of individuals who claimed to be victims of a violation of the Convention's provisions by a State party). Four parties had made the declaration under article 21, bringing the total number of declarations under that article to 56, while six had done so under article 22, bringing the total under that article to 58. Amendments to articles 17 and 18, adopted in 1992 [YUN 1992, p. 735], had been accepted by 27 States parties as at year's end.

Human Rights Council action. In a 30 June statement [A/61/53 (1/PRST/1)], the Council President welcomed the entry into force of the Optional Protocol and reiterated the Assembly's call on States parties, in resolution 60/148 [YUN 2005, p. 815], to consider signing and ratifying the Protocol. The Secretary-General was asked to ensure the provision of adequate staff and facilities for the bodies and mechanisms involved in combating torture and assisting victims of torture.

Establishment of Subcommittee. In accordance with the terms of the Protocol, which provided for the establishment of a Subcommittee on Prevention of Torture and Other Cruel, Inhuman or Degrading Treatment or Punishment (Subcommittee on Prevention) of the Committee against Torture to carry out the functions laid down in the Protocol, the first meeting of the States parties (Geneva, 18 December) [CAT/OP/SP/SR.1] elected the 10 members of the Subcommittee—five were given two-year terms and the other five, four-year terms. Those elected, who were all scheduled to assume office on 1 January 2007, were drawn by secret ballot from among 14 candidates nominated by States parties and circulated by the Secretary-General [CAT/OP/SP/1 & Add.1, 2].

Report of Secretary-General. The Secretary-General reported on the status of the Convention, its Optional Protocol and the declarations provided for in articles 21 and 22, as at 10 July [A/61/279]. On 19 December, the Assembly took note of the report (**decision 61/529**).

Implementation

Monitoring body. The Committee against Torture, established as a monitoring body under the Convention, held its thirty-sixth and thirty-seventh sessions in Geneva from 1 to 19 May [A/61/44] and 6 to 24 November [A/62/44], respectively. Under article 19, it considered reports submitted by Burundi, Georgia, Guatemala, Guyana, Hungary, Mexico, Peru, Qatar, Republic of Korea, the Russian Federation, South Africa, Tajikistan, Togo and the United States.

The Committee continued its work in accordance with article 20, under which it studied reliable information that appeared to contain well-founded indications that torture was systematically practised in a State party. In the framework of its follow-up activities, the Rapporteur on article 20 continued to encourage those States parties on which enquiries had been conducted to implement related recommendations of the Committee. Under article 22, the Committee considered communications submitted by individuals who claimed that their rights under the Convention had been violated by a State party and who had exhausted all available domestic remedies.

Convention on elimination of discrimination against women and Optional Protocol

(For details on the status of the Convention and on the Optional Protocol, see p. 1354.)

Convention on the Rights of the Child

Accessions and ratifications

As at 31 December, the number of States parties to the 1989 Convention on the Rights of the Child, adopted by the General Assembly in resolution 44/25 [YUN 1989, p. 560], rose to 193, with the succession of Montenegro. States parties to the Optional Protocol to the Convention on the involvement of children in armed conflict, adopted in Assembly resolution 54/263 [YUN 2000, p. 615], rose to 110 following ratification by Australia, Belarus, Lao People's Democratic Republic, Slovakia and Thailand. The Optional Protocol on the sale of children, child prostitution and child pornography, also adopted by resolution 54/263, had 115 States parties, with Algeria, Belgium, Brunei Darussalam, Burkina Faso, Cyprus, Dominican Republic, Jordan, Lao People's Democratic Republic, Latvia, Montenegro, Nepal, Sri Lanka, Switzerland and Thailand becoming parties in 2006.

The Secretary-General reported on the status of the Convention and its Optional Protocols as at 30 June [A/61/207].

On 19 December, the Assembly urged States that had not done so to become parties to the Convention and the Optional Protocols thereto, and to strengthen cooperation with the Committee on the Rights of the Child (**resolution 61/146**) (see below).

Implementation

Monitoring body. The Committee on the Rights of the Child (CRC) held its forty-first (9- 27 January) [CRC/C/41/3], forty-second (15 May–2 June) [CRC/C/42/3] and forty-third (11-29 September) [CRC/C/43/3] sessions in Geneva. Each session was preceded by a working group meeting to review State party reports and identify the main questions to be discussed with representatives of the reporting States.

Under article 44 of the Convention, CRC considered initial or periodic reports submitted by Andorra, Azerbaijan, Bangladesh, Belgium, Benin, Canada, Colombia, Congo, Czech Republic, Denmark, El Salvador, Ethiopia, Ghana, Hungary, Iceland, Ireland, Italy, Jordan, Kazakhstan, Kiribati, Latvia, Lebanon, Liechtenstein, Lithuania, Malta, Mauritius, Mexico, Morocco, Oman, Peru, Qatar, Samoa, Saudi Arabia, Senegal, Syria, Swaziland, Switzerland, Thailand, Trinidad and Tobago, Turkey, Turkmenistan, United Republic of Tanzania, Uzbekistan and Viet Nam.

In June, the Committee adopted general comment No. 8 on the rights of the child to protection from corporal punishment and other cruel or degrading forms of punishment, and in September, it adopted general comment No. 9 on the rights of children with disabilities. It also discussed the drafts of other general comments on juvenile justice and the rights of indigenous children, as well as the right of the child to express views and be heard, to which it devoted an annual day of general discussion on 15 September.

The Committee's reports covering its thirty-sixth to forty-first sessions were issued in a consolidated report [A/61/41 & Corr.1]. On 27 July, the Economic and Social Council deferred consideration of the report (**decision 2006/242**), and in subsequent action, took note of it on 11 December (**decision 2006/258**). The General Assembly took note of the report on 19 December (**decision 61/526**).

GENERAL ASSEMBLY ACTION

On 19 December [meeting 81], the General Assembly, on the recommendation of the Third Committee [A/61/439 & Corr.1], adopted **resolution 61/146** by recorded vote (185-1-0) [agenda item 63].

Rights of the child

The General Assembly,

Recalling its previous resolutions on the rights of the child, the most recent of which is resolution 60/231 of 23 December 2005, and its resolution 60/141 of 16 December 2005, as well as Commission on Human Rights resolution 2005/44 of 19 April 2005,

Emphasizing that the Convention on the Rights of the Child must constitute the standard in the promotion and protection of the rights of the child, and bearing in mind the importance of the Optional Protocols to the Convention, as well as other human rights instruments,

Reaffirming the Vienna Declaration and Programme of Action, the United Nations Millennium Declaration and the outcome document of the twenty-seventh special session of the General Assembly on children, entitled "A world fit for children", and recalling the Copenhagen Declaration on Social Development and the Programme of Action, the Dakar Framework for Action adopted at the World Education Forum, the Declaration on Social Progress and Development, the Universal Declaration on the Eradication of Hunger and Malnutrition and the Declaration on the Right to Development,

Recognizing the importance of the integration of child rights issues into the follow-up of the outcome documents of all major United Nations conferences, special sessions and summits,

Taking note with appreciation of the reports of the Secretary-General on progress made towards achieving the commitments set out in the outcome document of the twenty-seventh special session of the General Assembly and on the status of the Convention on the Rights of the Child and the issues raised in Assembly resolution 60/231, as well as the report of the Chairman of the Committee on the Rights of the Child,

Reaffirming that the best interests of the child shall be a primary consideration in all actions concerning children,

Recognizing the importance of incorporating a child-protection perspective across the human rights agenda, as highlighted in the outcome of the 2005 World Summit,

Taking note with appreciation of the attention paid to children in the Convention on the Rights of Persons with Disabilities and in the International Convention for the Protection of All Persons from Enforced Disappearance,

Profoundly concerned that the situation of children in many parts of the world remains critical, in an increasingly globalized environment, as a result of the persistence of poverty, social inequality, inadequate social and economic conditions, pandemics, in particular HIV/AIDS, malaria and tuberculosis, environmental damage, natural disasters, armed conflict, foreign occupation, displacement, violence, terrorism, abuse, exploitation, trafficking in children and their organs, child prostitution, child pornography and child sex tourism, neglect, illiteracy, hunger, intolerance, discrimination, racism, xenophobia, gender inequality, disability and inadequate legal protection, and convinced that urgent and effective national and international action is called for,

Reaffirming the need for mainstreaming a gender perspective in all policies and programmes relating to children, and recognizing the child as a rights holder in all policies and programmes relating to children,

I

Implementation of the Convention on the Rights of the Child and the Optional Protocols thereto

1. *Reaffirms* that the general principles of, inter alia, the best interests of the child, non-discrimination, participation and survival and development provide the framework for all actions concerning children, including adolescents;

2. *Urges* States that have not yet done so to become parties to the Convention on the Rights of the Child and the Optional Protocols thereto as a matter of priority and to implement them fully by, inter alia, putting in place effective national legislation, policies and action plans, strengthening relevant governmental structures for children and ensuring adequate and systematic training in the rights of the child for professional groups working with and for children;

3. *Urges* States parties to withdraw reservations that are incompatible with the object and purpose of the Convention or the Optional Protocols thereto and to consider reviewing other reservations with a view to withdrawing them;

4. *Welcomes* the work of the Committee on the Rights of the Child, and calls upon all States to strengthen their cooperation with the Committee, to comply in a timely manner with their reporting obligations under the Convention and the Optional Protocols thereto, in accordance with the guidelines elaborated by the Committee, and to take into account its recommendations on implementation of the Convention;

5. *Requests* all relevant organs and mechanisms of the United Nations system regularly and systematically to incorporate a strong child rights perspective throughout all activities in the fulfilment of their mandates, as well as to ensure that their staff are trained in child rights matters, and calls upon States to continue to cooperate closely with all those organs and mechanisms, in particular the special rapporteurs and special representatives of the United Nations system;

6. *Encourages* States to strengthen their national statistical capacities and to use statistics disaggregated, inter alia, by age, gender and other relevant factors that may lead to disparities and other statistical indicators at the national, subregional, regional and international levels to develop and assess social policies and programmes so that economic and social resources are used efficiently and effectively for the full realization of the rights of the child;

II

Promotion and protection of the rights of the child

Registration, family relations and adoption or other forms of alternative care

7. *Once again urges* all States parties to intensify their efforts to comply with their obligations under the Convention on the Rights of the Child to preserve the child's identity, including nationality, name and family relations, as recognized by law, to allow for the registration of the child immediately after birth, to ensure that registration procedures are simple, expeditious and effective and provided at minimal or no cost and to raise awareness of the importance of birth registration at the national, regional and local levels;

8. *Encourages* States to adopt and enforce laws and improve the implementation of policies and programmes to protect children growing up without parents or caregivers, recognizing that, where alternative care is necessary, family and community-based care should be promoted over placement in institutions;

9. *Calls upon* States to guarantee, to the extent consistent with the obligations of each State, the right of a child whose parents reside in different States to maintain, on a regular basis, save in exceptional circumstances, personal relations and direct contact with both parents by providing enforceable means of access and visitation in both States and by respecting the principle that both parents have common responsibilities for the upbringing and development of their children;

10. *Also calls upon* States to address and pay particular attention to cases of international parental or familial child abduction, and encourages States to engage in

multilateral and bilateral cooperation to resolve these cases, preferably by accession to or ratification of the Hague Convention on the Civil Aspects of International Child Abduction, and therefore to be in full compliance with the Convention, and to facilitate, inter alia, the return of the child to the country in which he or she resided immediately before the removal or retention;

11. *Further calls upon* States to take all necessary measures to prevent and combat illegal adoptions and all adoptions that are not in the best interests of the child;

Economic and social well-being of children

12. *Calls upon* States and the international community to create an environment in which the well-being of the child is ensured, inter alia, by:

(a) Cooperating, supporting and participating in the global efforts for poverty eradication at the global, regional and country levels, recognizing that strengthened availability and effective allocation of resources are required at all these levels, in order to ensure that all the internationally agreed development and poverty eradication goals, including those set out in the United Nations Millennium Declaration, are realized within their time framework, and reaffirming that investments in children and the realization of their rights are among the most effective ways to eradicate poverty;

(b) Recognizing the right to education on the basis of equal opportunity and non-discrimination by making primary education compulsory and available free to all children, ensuring that all children have access to education of good quality, as well as making secondary education generally available and accessible to all, in particular through the progressive introduction of free education, bearing in mind that special measures to ensure equal access, including affirmative action, contribute to achieving equal opportunity and combating exclusion, and ensuring school attendance, in particular for girls and children from low-income families;

(c) Taking all necessary measures to ensure the right of the child to the enjoyment of the highest attainable standard of health and developing sustainable health systems and social services, ensuring access to such systems and services without discrimination, paying special attention to adequate food and nutrition, to the special needs of adolescents and to reproductive and sexual health, and securing appropriate prenatal and post-natal care for mothers, including measures to prevent mother-to-child transmission of HIV;

(d) Assigning priority to developing and implementing activities and programmes aimed at treating and preventing addictions, in particular addiction to alcohol and tobacco, and the abuse of narcotic drugs, psychotropic substances and inhalants;

(e) Supporting adolescents to be able to deal positively and responsibly with their sexuality in order to protect themselves from HIV/AIDS infection and implementing measures to increase their capacity to protect themselves from HIV/AIDS through, inter alia, the provision of health care, including for sexual and reproductive health, and through preventive education that promotes gender equality;

(f) Putting in place strategies, policies and programmes that identify and address those factors that make individuals particularly vulnerable to HIV infection in order to complement prevention programmes that address activities that place individuals at risk for HIV infection, such as risky and unsafe behaviour and injecting drug use;

(g) Designing and implementing programmes to provide social services and support to pregnant adolescents and adolescent mothers, in particular by enabling them to continue and complete their education;

Violence against children

13. *Welcomes* the United Nations study on violence against children, led by the independent expert for the study, takes fully into account its recommendations, and encourages Member States and requests United Nations entities, regional organizations and civil society, including non-governmental organizations, to widely disseminate and follow up on the study;

14. *Commends* the independent expert for the participatory process through which the report was prepared in close collaboration with Member States, United Nations bodies and organizations, other relevant intergovernmental organizations and civil society, including non-governmental organizations, and in particular for the unprecedented level and quality of participation by children;

15. *Condemns* all forms of violence against children, and urges States to take effective legislative and other measures to prevent and eliminate all such violence, including physical, mental, psychological and sexual violence, torture, child abuse and exploitation, hostage-taking, domestic violence, trafficking in or sale of children and their organs, paedophilia, child prostitution, child pornography, child sex tourism, gang-related violence and harmful traditional practices in all settings;

16. *Also condemns* the abduction of children, in particular extortive abduction and abduction of children in situations of armed conflict, including for the recruitment and use of children in armed conflicts, and urges States to take all appropriate measures to secure their unconditional release, rehabilitation, reintegration and reunification with their families;

17. *Urges* States:

(a) To strengthen efforts to prevent and protect children from all forms of violence through a comprehensive approach and to develop a multifaceted and systematic framework to respond to violence against children, including by giving priority attention to prevention and addressing its underlying causes, which is integrated into national planning processes;

(b) To strive to change attitudes that condone or normalize any form of violence against children;

(c) To end impunity for perpetrators of crimes against children, investigate and prosecute such acts of violence and impose appropriate penalties;

(d) To protect children from all forms of violence or abuse by government officials, such as the police, law enforcement authorities and employees and officials in detention centres or welfare institutions;

(e) To take measures to protect children from all forms of physical and mental violence and abuse in schools, including by using non-violent teaching and learning strategies and adopting classroom management and disciplinary measures that are not based on any form of cruel or degrading punishment, and to establish complaint mechanisms that are age- and gender-appropriate and accessible to children, taking into account children's evolving capacities and the importance of respecting their views;

(f) To take measures to promote constructive and positive forms of discipline and child development approaches in all settings, including the home, schools and other educational settings and throughout care and justice systems;

(g) To take measures to ensure that all those who work with and for children protect children from bullying and implement preventive and anti-bullying policies;

(h) To address the gender dimension of all forms of violence against children and incorporate a gender perspective in all policies adopted and actions taken to protect children against all forms of violence;

(i) To ensure national research and documentation to identify vulnerable groups of children, inform policy and programmes at all levels and track progress and best practices towards preventing all forms of violence against children;

(j) To strengthen international cooperation and mutual assistance to prevent and protect children from all forms of violence and to end impunity for crimes against children;

18. *Recognizes* the contribution of the International Criminal Court in ending impunity for the most serious crimes against children, including genocide, crimes against humanity and war crimes, and calls upon States not to grant amnesties for such crimes;

19. *Calls upon* the relevant organizations of the United Nations system, in particular the Office of the United Nations High Commissioner for Human Rights, the United Nations Children's Fund, the World Health Organization, the International Labour Organization, the Office of the United Nations High Commissioner for Refugees, the United Nations Educational, Scientific and Cultural Organization, the United Nations Office on Drugs and Crime and the Division for the Advancement of Women of the Secretariat, to explore ways and means, within their respective mandates, by which they can contribute more effectively to addressing the need to prevent and to respond to all forms of violence against children;

Non-discrimination

20. *Calls upon* all States to ensure the enjoyment by children of all their civil, political, economic, social and cultural rights without discrimination of any kind;

21. *Notes with concern* the large number of children who are victims of racism, racial discrimination, xenophobia and related intolerance, stresses the need to incorporate special measures, in accordance with the principle of the best interests of the child and respect for his or her views, in programmes to combat racism, racial discrimination, xenophobia and related intolerance, and calls upon States to provide special support and ensure equal access to services for all children;

22. *Calls upon* States to take all necessary measures, including legal reforms where appropriate, to eliminate all forms of discrimination against girls and all forms of violence, including female infanticide and prenatal sex selection, rape, sexual abuse and harmful traditional or customary practices, including female genital mutilation, marriage without the free and full consent of the intending spouses, early marriage and forced sterilization, by enacting and enforcing legislation and by formulating, where appropriate, comprehensive, multidisciplinary and coordinated national plans, programmes or strategies to protect girls;

23. *Also calls upon* States to take the necessary measures to ensure the full and equal enjoyment of all human rights and fundamental freedoms by children with disabilities in both the public and the private spheres, including access to good quality education and health care and protection from violence, abuse and neglect, and to develop and, where it already exists, to enforce legislation to prohibit discrimination against them in order to ensure their inherent dignity, promote their self-reliance and facilitate their active participation and integration in the community, taking into account the particularly difficult situation of children with disabilities living in poverty;

Promoting and protecting the rights of children, including children in particularly difficult situations

24. *Calls upon* all States to prevent violations of the rights of children working and/or living on the street, including discrimination, arbitrary detention and extrajudicial, arbitrary or summary executions, torture and all kinds of violence and exploitation, and to bring the perpetrators to justice, to adopt and implement policies for the protection, social and psychosocial rehabilitation and reintegration of those children and to adopt economic, social and educational strategies to address the problems of children working and/or living on the street;

25. *Also calls upon* all States to protect refugee, asylum-seeking and internally displaced children, in particular those who are unaccompanied, who are particularly exposed to violence and risks in connection with armed conflict, such as recruitment, sexual violence and exploitation, stressing the need for States as well as the international community to continue to pay more systematic and in-depth attention to the special assistance, protection and development needs of those children through, inter alia, programmes aimed at rehabilitation and physical and psychological recovery, and to programmes for voluntary repatriation and, wherever possible, local integration and resettlement, to give priority to family tracing and family reunification and, where appropriate, to cooperate with international humanitarian and refugee organizations, including by facilitating their work;

26. *Further calls upon* all States to ensure, for children belonging to minorities and vulnerable groups, including migrant children and indigenous children, the enjoyment

of all human rights as well as access to health care, social services and education on an equal basis with others and to ensure that all such children, in particular victims of violence and exploitation, receive special protection and assistance;

27. *Calls upon* all States to address, as a matter of priority, the vulnerabilities faced by children affected by and living with HIV, by providing support and rehabilitation to those children and their families, women and the elderly, particularly in their role as caregivers, promoting child-oriented HIV/AIDS policies and programmes and increased protection for children orphaned and affected by HIV/AIDS, ensuring access to treatment and intensifying efforts to develop new treatments for children, and building, where needed, and supporting the social security systems that protect them;

28. *Also calls upon* all States to protect, in law and in practice, the inheritance and property rights of orphans, with particular attention to underlying gender-based discrimination, which may interfere with the fulfilment of these rights;

29. *Further calls upon* all States to translate into concrete action their commitment to the progressive and effective elimination of child labour that is likely to be hazardous or to interfere with the child's education or to be harmful to the child's health or physical, mental, spiritual, moral or social development, to eliminate immediately the worst forms of child labour, to promote education as a key strategy in this regard, including the creation of vocational training and apprenticeship programmes and the integration of working children into the formal education system, and to examine and devise economic policies, where necessary, in cooperation with the international community, that address factors contributing to these forms of child labour;

30. *Urges* all States that have not yet signed and ratified or acceded to the Convention concerning Minimum Age for Admission to Employment, 1973 (Convention No. 138) and the Convention concerning the Prohibition and Immediate Action for the Elimination of the Worst Forms of Child Labour, 1999 (Convention No. 182) of the International Labour Organization to consider doing so;

31. *Calls upon* all States, in particular those States in which the death penalty has not been abolished:

(a) To abolish by law, as soon as possible, the death penalty and life imprisonment without possibility of release for those under the age of 18 years at the time of the commission of the offence;

(b) To comply with their obligations as assumed under relevant provisions of international human rights instruments, including the Convention on the Rights of the Child and the International Covenant on Civil and Political Rights;

(c) To keep in mind the safeguards guaranteeing protection of the rights of those facing the death penalty and the guarantees set out in United Nations safeguards adopted by the Economic and Social Council;

32. *Also calls upon* all States to ensure that no child in detention is sentenced to forced labour or any form of cruel or degrading punishment, or deprived of access to and provision of health-care services, hygiene and environmental sanitation, education, basic instruction and vocational training;

33. *Encourages* States to promote actions, including through bilateral and multilateral technical cooperation and financial assistance, for the social reintegration of children in difficult situations, considering, inter alia, views, skills and capacities that those children have developed in the conditions in which they lived and, where appropriate, with their meaningful participation;

Prevention and eradication of the sale of children, child prostitution and child pornography

34. *Calls upon* all States:

(a) To criminalize and penalize effectively all forms of sexual exploitation and sexual abuse of children, including all acts of paedophilia, including within the family or for commercial purposes, child pornography and child prostitution, child sex tourism, trafficking in children, the sale of children and the use of the Internet for these purposes, and to take effective measures against the criminalization of children who are victims of exploitation;

(b) To ensure the prosecution of offenders, whether local or foreign, by the competent national authorities, either in the country in which the crime was committed, in the country of which the offender is a national or resident, in the country of which the victim is a national, or on any other basis permitted under domestic law, and for these purposes to afford one another the greatest measure of assistance in connection with investigations or criminal or extradition proceedings;

(c) To criminalize and penalize effectively the sale of children, including for the purposes of transfer of organs of the child for profit, to increase cooperation at all levels to prevent and dismantle networks trafficking or selling children and their organs and, for those States that have not yet done so, to consider signing and ratifying or acceding to the Protocol to Prevent, Suppress and Punish Trafficking in Persons, Especially Women and Children, supplementing the United Nations Convention against Transnational Organized Crime;

(d) In cases of trafficking in children, the sale of children, child prostitution and child pornography, to address effectively the needs of victims, including their safety and protection, physical and psychological recovery and full reintegration into society, including through bilateral and multilateral technical cooperation and financial assistance;

(e) To combat the existence of a market that encourages such criminal practices against children, including through the adoption, effective application and enforcement of preventive, rehabilitative and punitive measures targeting customers or individuals who sexually exploit or sexually abuse children, as well as by ensuring public awareness;

(f) To contribute to the elimination of the sale of children, child prostitution and child pornography by adopting a holistic approach, addressing the contributing factors, including underdevelopment, poverty, eco-

nomic disparities, inequitable socio-economic structures, dysfunctional families, lack of education, urban-rural migration, gender discrimination, criminal or irresponsible adult sexual behaviour, child sex tourism, organized crime, harmful traditional practices, armed conflicts and trafficking in children;

Children affected by armed conflict

35. *Strongly condemns* any recruitment or use of children in armed conflict contrary to international law, as well as other violations and abuses committed against children affected by armed conflict, and urges all States and other parties to armed conflict that are engaged in such practices to end them;

36. *Calls upon* States:

(a) When ratifying the Optional Protocol to the Convention on the Rights of the Child on the involvement of children in armed conflict, to raise the minimum age for voluntary recruitment of persons into the national armed forces from that set out in article 38, paragraph 3, of the Convention, bearing in mind that under the Convention persons under 18 years of age are entitled to special protection, and to adopt safeguards to ensure that such recruitment is not forced or coerced;

(b) To take all feasible measures to ensure the demobilization and effective disarmament of children used in armed conflicts and to implement effective measures for their rehabilitation, physical and psychological recovery and reintegration into society, in particular through educational measures, taking into account the rights and the specific needs and capacities of girls;

(c) To ensure timely and adequate funding for rehabilitation and reintegration efforts for all children associated with armed forces and groups, particularly in support of national initiatives, to secure the long-term sustainability of such efforts;

(d) To encourage the involvement of young people in activities concerning the protection of children affected by armed conflict, including programmes for reconciliation, peace consolidation, peacebuilding and children-to-children networks;

(e) To protect children affected by armed conflict, in particular from violations of international humanitarian law and human rights law and to ensure that they receive timely, effective humanitarian assistance, in accordance with international humanitarian law, including the Geneva Conventions of 12 August 1949, and calls upon the international community to hold those responsible for violations accountable, inter alia, through the International Criminal Court;

(f) To take all necessary measures, in accordance with international humanitarian law and human rights law, as a matter of priority, to prevent the recruitment and use of children by armed groups, as distinct from the armed forces of a State, including the adoption of policies that do not tolerate the recruitment and use of children in armed conflict, and legal measures necessary to prohibit and criminalize such practices;

37. *Welcomes* the valuable work of the United Nations Children's Fund, and looks forward to the results of updating the Cape Town principles on child soldiers;

38. *Reaffirms* the essential roles of the General Assembly, the Economic and Social Council and the Human Rights Council for the promotion and protection of the rights and welfare of children, including children affected by armed conflict, and notes the increasing role played by the Security Council in ensuring protection for children affected by armed conflict;

39. *Notes with appreciation* the steps taken regarding Security Council resolution 1612(2005) of 26 July 2005 and the efforts of the Secretary-General to implement the monitoring and reporting mechanism on children and armed conflict in accordance with that resolution, with the participation of and in cooperation with national Governments and relevant United Nations and civil society actors, including at the country level, as well as the work carried out by United Nations child protection advisers in peacekeeping operations;

40. *Welcomes* the appointment of Ms. Radhika Coomaraswamy as the Special Representative of the Secretary-General for Children and Armed Conflict, pursuant to General Assembly resolutions 51/77 of 12 December 1996 and 60/231, and recognizes the progress achieved since the establishment of the mandate of the Special Representative, as extended by resolution 60/231;

41. *Takes note with appreciation* of the report of the Special Representative;

III
Children and poverty

42. *Reiterates* that eradicating poverty is the greatest global challenge facing the world today and an indispensable requirement for sustainable development, in particular for developing countries, and recognizes that chronic poverty remains the single biggest obstacle to meeting the needs and protecting and promoting the rights of children, and that urgent national and international action is therefore required to eliminate it;

43. *Recognizes* that the number of people living in extreme poverty in many countries continues to increase, with women and children constituting the majority and the most affected groups, in particular in the least developed countries and in sub-Saharan Africa;

44. *Also recognizes* that growing inequality within countries is a major challenge to poverty eradication, particularly affecting those living in middle-income countries, and stresses the need to support the development efforts of those countries;

45. *Reaffirms* that democracy, development, peace and security, and the full and effective enjoyment of human rights and fundamental freedoms are interdependent and mutually reinforcing and contribute to the eradication of extreme poverty;

46. *Recognizes* that children living in poverty are deprived of nutrition, water and sanitation facilities, access to basic health-care services, shelter, education, participation and protection, and that while a severe lack of goods and services hurts every human being, it is most threatening and harmful to children, leaving them unable to enjoy their rights, to reach their full potential and to participate as full members of society;

47. *Emphasizes* the critical role of education, both formal and non-formal, in particular basic education and training, especially for girls, in empowering those living in poverty, and in this regard reaffirms the importance of Education for All programmes and the need to bridge the divide between formal and non-formal education, taking into account the need to ensure the good quality of educational services;

48. *Recognizes* the devastating effect of HIV/AIDS, malaria, tuberculosis and other infectious and contagious diseases on human development, economic growth, food security and poverty eradication efforts in all regions, in particular in the least developed countries and in sub-Saharan Africa, and urges Governments and the international community to give urgent priority to preventing and combating those diseases;

49. *Also recognizes* that countries struggle to develop when their children grow up malnourished, poorly educated or ravaged by disease, as these factors can perpetuate the generational cycle of poverty;

50. *Reaffirms* that the primary responsibility for ensuring an enabling environment for securing the well-being of children, in which the rights of each and every child are promoted and respected, rests with each individual State;

51. *Calls upon* all States and the international community to mobilize all necessary resources, support and efforts to eradicate poverty, according to national plans and strategies and in consultation with national Governments, including through an integrated and multifaceted approach based on the rights and well-being of children;

52. *Also calls upon* all States, and the international community, where appropriate:

(a) To integrate the international obligations related to the rights and well-being of the child and the internationally agreed development goals, including the Millennium Development Goals, in national development strategies and plans, including poverty reduction strategy papers where they exist, and calls upon the international community to continue to support developing countries in the implementation of those development strategies and plans;

(b) To ensure a continuum of care from pregnancy through childhood, recognizing that maternal, newborn and child health are inseparable and interdependent, and that the achievement of the Millennium Development Goals must be based on a strong commitment to the rights of women, children and adolescents;

(c) To work for a solid effort of national and international action to enhance children's health, to promote prenatal care and to lower infant and child mortality in all countries and among all peoples;

(d) To develop a national strategy of prevention and treatment to effectively address the condition of obstetric fistula and to further develop a multisectoral, comprehensive and integrated approach to bring about lasting solutions and a meaningful response to the problem of obstetric fistula and related morbidities;

(e) To promote the provision of clean water in all communities for all their children, as well as universal access to sanitation;

(f) To take all necessary measures to eradicate hunger, malnutrition and famine;

(g) To mobilize the necessary additional resources from all sources of financing for development, including domestic resources, international investment flows, official development assistance and external debt relief, and to commit themselves to a universal, open, equitable, rule-based, predictable and non-discriminatory global trading system in order to stimulate development worldwide to ensure the well-being of the most vulnerable sectors of populations, in particular children;

Follow-up

53. *Decides:*

(a) To request the Secretary-General to submit to the General Assembly at its sixty-second session a report on the rights of the child, containing information on the status of the Convention on the Rights of the Child and the issues contained in the present resolution;

(b) To request the Special Representative of the Secretary-General for Children and Armed Conflict to continue to submit reports to the General Assembly and the Human Rights Council on the progress achieved and the remaining challenges on the children and armed conflict agenda;

(c) To invite the independent expert for the United Nations study on violence against children, in cooperation with Member States, relevant organizations and bodies of the United Nations system, in particular the Office of the United Nations High Commissioner for Human Rights, the United Nations Children's Fund, the World Health Organization, the Committee on the Rights of the Child and the Human Rights Council, and regional organizations, national institutions and civil society, including non-governmental organizations, to promote the wide dissemination of the United Nations study on violence against children, to give support to the first year of effective follow-up to its recommendations with an integrated approach that bridges the dimensions of public health, education, child protection and human rights, to submit to the General Assembly at its sixty-second session a report on progress made in the initial phase of the follow-up and to anticipate the necessary strategy for follow-up to the implementation of the study;

(d) To reiterate its invitation to the Chairman of the Committee on the Rights of the Child to present an oral report on the work of the Committee to the General Assembly at its sixty-second session as a way to enhance communication between the Assembly and the Committee;

(e) To pay particular attention to the protection of and the rights of children living in poverty at the commemorative plenary meeting to be held in 2007 devoted to the follow-up to the outcome of the twenty-seventh special session of the General Assembly;

(f) To continue its consideration of the question at its sixty-second session under the item entitled "Promotion and protection of the rights of children", focusing

section III of the resolution on the rights of the child on "Violence against children".

RECORDED VOTE ON RESOLUTION 61/146:

In favour: Afghanistan, Albania, Algeria, Andorra, Angola, Antigua and Barbuda, Argentina, Armenia, Australia, Austria, Azerbaijan, Bahamas, Bahrain, Bangladesh, Barbados, Belarus, Belgium, Belize, Benin, Bhutan, Bolivia, Bosnia and Herzegovina, Botswana, Brazil, Brunei Darussalam, Bulgaria, Burkina Faso, Burundi, Cambodia, Cameroon, Canada, Cape Verde, Central African Republic, Chile, China, Colombia, Comoros, Congo, Costa Rica, Côte d'Ivoire, Croatia, Cuba, Cyprus, Czech Republic, Democratic People's Republic of Korea, Democratic Republic of the Congo, Denmark, Djibouti, Dominica, Dominican Republic, Ecuador, Egypt, El Salvador, Eritrea, Estonia, Ethiopia, Fiji, Finland, France, Gabon, Gambia, Georgia, Germany, Ghana, Greece, Grenada, Guatemala, Guinea, Guinea-Bissau, Guyana, Haiti, Honduras, Hungary, Iceland, India, Indonesia, Iran, Iraq, Ireland, Israel, Italy, Jamaica, Japan, Jordan, Kazakhstan, Kenya, Kuwait, Kyrgyzstan, Lao People's Democratic Republic, Latvia, Lebanon, Lesotho, Liberia, Libyan Arab Jamahiriya, Liechtenstein, Lithuania, Luxembourg, Madagascar, Malawi, Malaysia, Maldives, Mali, Malta, Marshall Islands, Mauritania, Mauritius, Mexico, Micronesia, Moldova, Monaco, Mongolia, Montenegro, Morocco, Mozambique, Myanmar, Namibia, Nauru, Nepal, Netherlands, New Zealand, Nicaragua, Niger, Nigeria, Norway, Oman, Pakistan, Panama, Papua New Guinea, Paraguay, Peru, Philippines, Poland, Portugal, Qatar, Republic of Korea, Romania, Russian Federation, Rwanda, Saint Lucia, Saint Vincent and the Grenadines, Samoa, San Marino, Sao Tome and Principe, Saudi Arabia, Senegal, Serbia, Sierra Leone, Singapore, Slovakia, Slovenia, Solomon Islands, Somalia, South Africa, Spain, Sri Lanka, Sudan, Suriname, Swaziland, Sweden, Switzerland, Syrian Arab Republic, Tajikistan, Thailand, The former Yugoslav Republic of Macedonia, Timor-Leste, Togo, Tonga, Trinidad and Tobago, Tunisia, Turkey, Turkmenistan, Tuvalu, Uganda, Ukraine, United Arab Emirates, United Kingdom, United Republic of Tanzania, Uruguay, Uzbekistan, Vanuatu, Venezuela, Viet Nam, Yemen, Zambia, Zimbabwe.

Against: United States.

Convention on migrant workers

Accessions and ratifications

As at 31 December, the number of parties to the International Convention on the Protection of the Rights of All Migrant Workers and Members of Their Families, adopted by the General Assembly in resolution 45/158 [YUN 1990, p. 594] and which entered into force in 2003 [YUN 2003, p. 676], remained at 34.

In January [E/CN.4.2006/70], the Secretary-General reported on the status of the Convention and efforts made by the Secretariat to promote it.

Implementation

Monitoring body. The Committee on the Protection of the Rights of All Migrant Workers and Members of Their Families held its fourth (24-28 April) [A/61/48] and fifth (30 October–3 November) [A/62/48] sessions in Geneva. In April, the Committee discussed ways to promote the Convention, and towards that end, adopted a written contribution to the High-Level Dialogue of the General Assembly devoted to international migration and development (see p. 1261), in order to highlight the human-rights based approach to migration and development. It also discussed methods of work in relation to the consideration of States parties' reports and considered the initial reports of Mali and Mexico under articles 73 and 74 of the Convention relating to measures taken to give effect to the Convention's provisions. In November, it discussed, among other subjects, follow-up to the High-Level Dialogue and the treaty body reform.

On 19 December, the General Assembly took note of the Committee's reports (**decision 61/529**).

In response to Assembly resolution 60/227 [YUN 2005, p.1176], a July note of the Secretary-General [A/61/120] summarized the Committee's general discussion in December 2005 [YUN 2005, p. 731] on protecting migrant workers' right as a tool to enhance development.

Convention on genocide

As at 31 December, 140 States were parties to the 1948 Convention on the Prevention and Punishment of the Crime of Genocide, adopted by the General Assembly in resolution 260 A (III) [YUN 1948-49, p. 959]. During the year, Andorra and Montenegro became parties to the Convention.

Report of Secretary-General. In response to a 2005 Commission request [YUN 2005, p. 732], the Secretary-General submitted a March report [E/CN.4/2006/84] providing information on the implementation of a five-point action plan to prevent genocide, which he had outlined to the Commission, and on the activities of his Special Adviser on the prevention of genocide since his appointment in 2004 [YUN 2004, p. 730]. Components of the plan included the prevention of armed conflict, which usually provided the context for genocide; protection of civilians; ending impunity through judicial action in both national and international courts; early and clear warning of situations that could potentially degenerate into genocide; and swift and decisive action, including military action. In that context, the Special Adviser, whose mandate derived from the Organization's need to develop a capacity for early warning of potential genocide, had established a small office and created an information exchange system to provide such warnings of situations that could lead to genocide. The report observed that the prevention of genocide presented the international community with the challenge of identifying the warning signs and mobilizing the necessary support for action. It also involved acting comprehensively in four interrelated areas: protecting populations at risk against serious violations of human rights and humanitarian law; establishing accountability; providing humanitarian relief and access to economic, social and cultural rights; and initiating steps to address underlying causes of conflict. The United Nations was committed to overcoming the deficiencies that previously led to failures to act in the face of signs of impending danger. Member States' recognition, expressed in the World Summit outcome document [YUN 2005, p. 48], of the responsibility to protect populations from genocide, war crimes, ethnic cleansing and crimes against humanity was an important step in advancing a common determination to prevent genocide.

Letter by Special Adviser. In an 8 December letter to the Council President [A/HRC/S-4/3], the Special Adviser expressed grave concern about the situation in the Darfur region of the Sudan shortly before the Council's special session on human rights challenges there (see p. 942). Particular concerns included massive and serious violations of human rights and international humanitarian law based on ethnicity, which continued to pose a risk for genocide. Genocide should not be allowed to occur at the beginning of the twenty-first century and under the watch of the newly established Human Rights Council. It was, therefore, imperative that preventive measures be put in place to avoid such a development. It was important that the United Nations, notably the Council, urge all parties to the conflict to abide by international rules. The international community should assist in every effort conducted in good faith to prevent genocide, crimes against humanity and war crimes, and should stand by the victims in Darfur and ensure they were protected. The Council needed to exercise moral leadership in demanding from all relevant actors the adoption of urgent measures to ensure that protection.

Convention on rights of persons with disabilities

During the year, the Ad Hoc Committee established by General Assembly resolution 56/168 [YUN 2001, p. 1012] to consider proposals for a comprehensive and integral international convention on the protection and promotion of the rights and dignity of persons with disabilities finalized the draft convention and draft optional protocol. Both drafts were annexed to its final report, which the Secretary-General transmitted to the Assembly in a 6 December note [A/61/611 & Corr.1]. On 13 December, by resolution 61/106 (see below), the Assembly adopted the Convention on the Rights of Persons with Disabilities and the Optional Protocol to the Convention on the Rights of Persons with Disabilities.

The Convention defined persons with disabilities as including those who had long-term physical, mental, intellectual or sensory impairments which, in interaction with various barriers, might hinder their full and effective participation in society on an equal basis with others. It also defined a set of rights to which they were legally entitled and the obligations of States parties in that regard, in order to empower them in overcoming such barriers. While many of the rights echoed those already affirmed in existing human rights instruments, the new Convention included specific obligations, ensuring that existing rights could be fully realized by persons with disabilities. Specific rights guaranteed by the Convention included the rights to live independently and be included in the community; to personal mobility, habilitation and rehabilitation; and to participation in political, public and cultural life, as well as in recreation and sport. Core provisions covered the rights of affected persons to equality and non-discrimination, access to justice, liberty and security of the person, education, health and work and employment. The Convention also obliged the parties to raise awareness of those rights and ensure access to roads, buildings and information. It provided for the establishment of a Committee on the Rights of Persons with Disabilities, which, upon the Convention's entry into force, would consist of twelve experts and serve to monitor and implement the Convention's provisions. The Optional Protocol, on the other hand, was an integral instrument by which States parties would agree to recognize the competence of the Committee to consider complaints from individuals.

The Convention, expected to open for signature in 2007, would enter into force on the thirtieth day after the deposit of the twentieth instrument of ratification or accession.

GENERAL ASSEMBLY ACTION

On 13 December [meeting 76], the General Assembly adopted **resolution 61/106** [draft: A/61/611] without vote [agenda item 67 *(b)*].

Convention on the Rights of Persons with Disabilities

The General Assembly,

Recalling its resolution 56/168 of 19 December 2001, by which it decided to establish an Ad Hoc Committee, open to the participation of all Member States and observers to the United Nations, to consider proposals for a comprehensive and integral international convention to promote and protect the rights and dignity of persons with disabilities, based on a holistic approach in the work done in the fields of social development, human rights and non-discrimination and taking into account the recommendations of the Commission on Human Rights and the Commission for Social Development,

Recalling also its previous relevant resolutions, the most recent of which was resolution 60/232 of 23 December 2005, as well as relevant resolutions of the Commission for Social Development and the Commission on Human Rights,

Welcoming the valuable contributions made by intergovernmental and non-governmental organizations and national human rights institutions to the work of the Ad Hoc Committee,

1. *Expresses its appreciation* to the Ad Hoc Committee for having concluded the elaboration of the draft Convention on the Rights of Persons with Disabilities and the draft Optional Protocol to the Convention;

2. *Adopts* the Convention on the Rights of Persons with Disabilities and the Optional Protocol to the Convention annexed to the present resolution, which shall be open for signature at United Nations Headquarters in New York as of 30 March 2007;

3. *Calls upon* States to consider signing and ratifying the Convention and the Optional Protocol as a matter of priority, and expresses the hope that they will enter into force at an early date;

4. *Requests* the Secretary-General to provide the staff and facilities necessary for the effective performance of the functions of the Conference of States Parties and the Committee under the Convention and the Optional Protocol after the entry into force of the Convention, as well as for the dissemination of information on the Convention and the Optional Protocol;

5. *Also requests* the Secretary-General to implement progressively standards and guidelines for the accessibility of facilities and services of the United Nations system, taking into account relevant provisions of the Convention, in particular when undertaking renovations;

6. *Requests* United Nations agencies and organizations, and invites intergovernmental and non-governmental organizations, to undertake efforts to disseminate information on the Convention and the Optional Protocol and to promote their understanding;

7. *Requests* the Secretary-General to submit to the General Assembly at its sixty-second session a report on the status of the Convention and the Optional Protocol and the implementation of the present resolution, under a sub-item entitled "Convention on the Rights of Persons with Disabilities".

Annex I

Convention on the Rights of Persons with Disabilities

Preamble

The States Parties to the present Convention,

(*a*) *Recalling* the principles proclaimed in the Charter of the United Nations which recognize the inherent dignity and worth and the equal and inalienable rights of all members of the human family as the foundation of freedom, justice and peace in the world,

(*b*) *Recognizing* that the United Nations, in the Universal Declaration of Human Rights and in the International Covenants on Human Rights, has proclaimed and agreed that everyone is entitled to all the rights and freedoms set forth therein, without distinction of any kind,

(*c*) *Reaffirming* the universality, indivisibility, interdependence and interrelatedness of all human rights and fundamental freedoms and the need for persons with disabilities to be guaranteed their full enjoyment without discrimination,

(*d*) *Recalling* the International Covenant on Economic, Social and Cultural Rights, the International Covenant on Civil and Political Rights, the International Convention on the Elimination of All Forms of Racial Discrimination, the Convention on the Elimination of All Forms of Discrimination against Women, the Convention against Torture and Other Cruel, Inhuman or Degrading Treatment or Punishment, the Convention on the Rights of the Child, and the International Convention on the Protection of the Rights of All Migrant Workers and Members of Their Families,

(*e*) *Recognizing* that disability is an evolving concept and that disability results from the interaction between persons with impairments and attitudinal and environmental barriers that hinders their full and effective participation in society on an equal basis with others,

(*f*) *Recognizing* the importance of the principles and policy guidelines contained in the World Programme of Action concerning Disabled Persons and in the Standard Rules on the Equalization of Opportunities for Persons with Disabilities in influencing the promotion, formulation and evaluation of the policies, plans, programmes and actions at the national, regional and international levels to further equalize opportunities for persons with disabilities,

(*g*) *Emphasizing* the importance of mainstreaming disability issues as an integral part of relevant strategies of sustainable development,

(*h*) *Recognizing also* that discrimination against any person on the basis of disability is a violation of the inherent dignity and worth of the human person,

(*i*) *Recognizing further* the diversity of persons with disabilities,

(*j*) *Recognizing* the need to promote and protect the human rights of all persons with disabilities, including those who require more intensive support,

(*k*) *Concerned* that, despite these various instruments and undertakings, persons with disabilities continue to face barriers in their participation as equal members of society and violations of their human rights in all parts of the world,

(*l*) *Recognizing* the importance of international cooperation for improving the living conditions of persons with disabilities in every country, particularly in developing countries,

(m) *Recognizing* the valued existing and potential contributions made by persons with disabilities to the overall well-being and diversity of their communities, and that the promotion of the full enjoyment by persons with disabilities of their human rights and fundamental freedoms and of full participation by persons with disabilities will result in their enhanced sense of belonging and in significant advances in the human, social and economic development of society and the eradication of poverty,

(n) *Recognizing* the importance for persons with disabilities of their individual autonomy and independence, including the freedom to make their own choices,

(o) *Considering* that persons with disabilities should have the opportunity to be actively involved in decision-making processes about policies and programmes, including those directly concerning them,

(p) *Concerned* about the difficult conditions faced by persons with disabilities who are subject to multiple or aggravated forms of discrimination on the basis of race, colour, sex, language, religion, political or other opinion, national, ethnic, indigenous or social origin, property, birth, age or other status,

(q) *Recognizing* that women and girls with disabilities are often at greater risk, both within and outside the home, of violence, injury or abuse, neglect or negligent treatment, maltreatment or exploitation,

(r) *Recognizing* that children with disabilities should have full enjoyment of all human rights and fundamental freedoms on an equal basis with other children, and recalling obligations to that end undertaken by States Parties to the Convention on the Rights of the Child,

(s) *Emphasizing* the need to incorporate a gender perspective in all efforts to promote the full enjoyment of human rights and fundamental freedoms by persons with disabilities,

(t) *Highlighting* the fact that the majority of persons with disabilities live in conditions of poverty, and in this regard recognizing the critical need to address the negative impact of poverty on persons with disabilities,

(u) *Bearing in mind* that conditions of peace and security based on full respect for the purposes and principles contained in the Charter of the United Nations and observance of applicable human rights instruments are indispensable for the full protection of persons with disabilities, in particular during armed conflicts and foreign occupation,

(v) *Recognizing* the importance of accessibility to the physical, social, economic and cultural environment, to health and education and to information and communication, in enabling persons with disabilities to fully enjoy all human rights and fundamental freedoms,

(w) *Realizing* that the individual, having duties to other individuals and to the community to which he or she belongs, is under a responsibility to strive for the promotion and observance of the rights recognized in the International Bill of Human Rights,

(x) *Convinced* that the family is the natural and fundamental group unit of society and is entitled to protection by society and the State, and that persons with disabilities and their family members should receive the necessary protection and assistance to enable families to contribute towards the full and equal enjoyment of the rights of persons with disabilities,

(y) *Convinced* that a comprehensive and integral international convention to promote and protect the rights and dignity of persons with disabilities will make a significant contribution to redressing the profound social disadvantage of persons with disabilities and promote their participation in the civil, political, economic, social and cultural spheres with equal opportunities, in both developing and developed countries,

Have agreed as follows:

Article 1
Purpose

The purpose of the present Convention is to promote, protect and ensure the full and equal enjoyment of all human rights and fundamental freedoms by all persons with disabilities, and to promote respect for their inherent dignity.

Persons with disabilities include those who have long-term physical, mental, intellectual or sensory impairments which in interaction with various barriers may hinder their full and effective participation in society on an equal basis with others.

Article 2
Definitions

For the purposes of the present Convention:

"Communication" includes languages, display of text, Braille, tactile communication, large print, accessible multimedia as well as written, audio, plain language, human-reader and augmentative and alternative modes, means and formats of communication, including accessible information and communication technology;

"Language" includes spoken and signed languages and other forms of non-spoken languages;

"Discrimination on the basis of disability" means any distinction, exclusion or restriction on the basis of disability which has the purpose or effect of impairing or nullifying the recognition, enjoyment or exercise, on an equal basis with others, of all human rights and fundamental freedoms in the political, economic, social, cultural, civil or any other field. It includes all forms of discrimination, including denial of reasonable accommodation;

"Reasonable accommodation" means necessary and appropriate modification and adjustments not imposing a disproportionate or undue burden, where needed in a particular case, to ensure to persons with disabilities the enjoyment or exercise on an equal basis with others of all human rights and fundamental freedoms;

"Universal design" means the design of products, environments, programmes and services to be usable by all people, to the greatest extent possible, without the need for adaptation or specialized design. "Universal design" shall not exclude assistive devices for particular groups of persons with disabilities where this is needed.

Article 3
General principles

The principles of the present Convention shall be:

(a) Respect for inherent dignity, individual autonomy including the freedom to make one's own choices, and independence of persons;

(b) Non-discrimination;

(c) Full and effective participation and inclusion in society;

(d) Respect for difference and acceptance of persons with disabilities as part of human diversity and humanity;

(e) Equality of opportunity;

(f) Accessibility;

(g) Equality between men and women;

(h) Respect for the evolving capacities of children with disabilities and respect for the right of children with disabilities to preserve their identities.

Article 4
General obligations

1. States Parties undertake to ensure and promote the full realization of all human rights and fundamental freedoms for all persons with disabilities without discrimination of any kind on the basis of disability. To this end, States Parties undertake:

(a) To adopt all appropriate legislative, administrative and other measures for the implementation of the rights recognized in the present Convention;

(b) To take all appropriate measures, including legislation, to modify or abolish existing laws, regulations, customs and practices that constitute discrimination against persons with disabilities;

(c) To take into account the protection and promotion of the human rights of persons with disabilities in all policies and programmes;

(d) To refrain from engaging in any act or practice that is inconsistent with the present Convention and to ensure that public authorities and institutions act in conformity with the present Convention;

(e) To take all appropriate measures to eliminate discrimination on the basis of disability by any person, organization or private enterprise;

(f) To undertake or promote research and development of universally designed goods, services, equipment and facilities, as defined in article 2 of the present Convention, which should require the minimum possible adaptation and the least cost to meet the specific needs of a person with disabilities, to promote their availability and use, and to promote universal design in the development of standards and guidelines;

(g) To undertake or promote research and development of, and to promote the availability and use of new technologies, including information and communications technologies, mobility aids, devices and assistive technologies, suitable for persons with disabilities, giving priority to technologies at an affordable cost;

(h) To provide accessible information to persons with disabilities about mobility aids, devices and assistive technologies, including new technologies, as well as other forms of assistance, support services and facilities;

(i) To promote the training of professionals and staff working with persons with disabilities in the rights recognized in the present Convention so as to better provide the assistance and services guaranteed by those rights.

2. With regard to economic, social and cultural rights, each State Party undertakes to take measures to the maximum of its available resources and, where needed, within the framework of international cooperation, with a view to achieving progressively the full realization of these rights, without prejudice to those obligations contained in the present Convention that are immediately applicable according to international law.

3. In the development and implementation of legislation and policies to implement the present Convention, and in other decision-making processes concerning issues relating to persons with disabilities, States Parties shall closely consult with and actively involve persons with disabilities, including children with disabilities, through their representative organizations.

4. Nothing in the present Convention shall affect any provisions which are more conducive to the realization of the rights of persons with disabilities and which may be contained in the law of a State Party or international law in force for that State. There shall be no restriction upon or derogation from any of the human rights and fundamental freedoms recognized or existing in any State Party to the present Convention pursuant to law, conventions, regulation or custom on the pretext that the present Convention does not recognize such rights or freedoms or that it recognizes them to a lesser extent.

5. The provisions of the present Convention shall extend to all parts of federal States without any limitations or exceptions.

Article 5
Equality and non-discrimination

1. States Parties recognize that all persons are equal before and under the law and are entitled without any discrimination to the equal protection and equal benefit of the law.

2. States Parties shall prohibit all discrimination on the basis of disability and guarantee to persons with disabilities equal and effective legal protection against discrimination on all grounds.

3. In order to promote equality and eliminate discrimination, States Parties shall take all appropriate steps to ensure that reasonable accommodation is provided.

4. Specific measures which are necessary to accelerate or achieve de facto equality of persons with disabilities shall not be considered discrimination under the terms of the present Convention.

Article 6
Women with disabilities

1. States Parties recognize that women and girls with disabilities are subject to multiple discrimination, and in this regard shall take measures to ensure the full and

equal enjoyment by them of all human rights and fundamental freedoms.

2. States Parties shall take all appropriate measures to ensure the full development, advancement and empowerment of women, for the purpose of guaranteeing them the exercise and enjoyment of the human rights and fundamental freedoms set out in the present Convention.

Article 7
Children with disabilities

1. States Parties shall take all necessary measures to ensure the full enjoyment by children with disabilities of all human rights and fundamental freedoms on an equal basis with other children.

2. In all actions concerning children with disabilities, the best interests of the child shall be a primary consideration.

3. States Parties shall ensure that children with disabilities have the right to express their views freely on all matters affecting them, their views being given due weight in accordance with their age and maturity, on an equal basis with other children, and to be provided with disability and age-appropriate assistance to realize that right.

Article 8
Awareness-raising

1. States Parties undertake to adopt immediate, effective and appropriate measures:

(a) To raise awareness throughout society, including at the family level, regarding persons with disabilities, and to foster respect for the rights and dignity of persons with disabilities;

(b) To combat stereotypes, prejudices and harmful practices relating to persons with disabilities, including those based on sex and age, in all areas of life;

(c) To promote awareness of the capabilities and contributions of persons with disabilities.

2. Measures to this end include:

(a) Initiating and maintaining effective public awareness campaigns designed:

(i) To nurture receptiveness to the rights of persons with disabilities;

(ii) To promote positive perceptions and greater social awareness towards persons with disabilities;

(iii) To promote recognition of the skills, merits and abilities of persons with disabilities, and of their contributions to the workplace and the labour market;

(b) Fostering at all levels of the education system, including in all children from an early age, an attitude of respect for the rights of persons with disabilities;

(c) Encouraging all organs of the media to portray persons with disabilities in a manner consistent with the purpose of the present Convention;

(d) Promoting awareness-training programmes regarding persons with disabilities and the rights of persons with disabilities.

Article 9
Accessibility

1. To enable persons with disabilities to live independently and participate fully in all aspects of life, States Parties shall take appropriate measures to ensure to persons with disabilities access, on an equal basis with others, to the physical environment, to transportation, to information and communications, including information and communications technologies and systems, and to other facilities and services open or provided to the public, both in urban and in rural areas. These measures, which shall include the identification and elimination of obstacles and barriers to accessibility, shall apply to, inter alia:

(a) Buildings, roads, transportation and other indoor and outdoor facilities, including schools, housing, medical facilities and workplaces;

(b) Information, communications and other services, including electronic services and emergency services.

2. States Parties shall also take appropriate measures:

(a) To develop, promulgate and monitor the implementation of minimum standards and guidelines for the accessibility of facilities and services open or provided to the public;

(b) To ensure that private entities that offer facilities and services which are open or provided to the public take into account all aspects of accessibility for persons with disabilities;

(c) To provide training for stakeholders on accessibility issues facing persons with disabilities;

(d) To provide in buildings and other facilities open to the public signage in Braille and in easy to read and understand forms;

(e) To provide forms of live assistance and intermediaries, including guides, readers and professional sign language interpreters, to facilitate accessibility to buildings and other facilities open to the public;

(f) To promote other appropriate forms of assistance and support to persons with disabilities to ensure their access to information;

(g) To promote access for persons with disabilities to new information and communications technologies and systems, including the Internet;

(h) To promote the design, development, production and distribution of accessible information and communications technologies and systems at an early stage, so that these technologies and systems become accessible at minimum cost.

Article 10
Right to life

States Parties reaffirm that every human being has the inherent right to life and shall take all necessary measures to ensure its effective enjoyment by persons with disabilities on an equal basis with others.

Article 11
Situations of risk and humanitarian emergencies

States Parties shall take, in accordance with their obligations under international law, including international humanitarian law and international human rights law, all necessary measures to ensure the protection and safety of persons with disabilities in situations of risk, including situations of armed conflict, humanitarian emergencies and the occurrence of natural disasters.

Article 12

Equal recognition before the law

1. States Parties reaffirm that persons with disabilities have the right to recognition everywhere as persons before the law.

2. States Parties shall recognize that persons with disabilities enjoy legal capacity on an equal basis with others in all aspects of life.

3. States Parties shall take appropriate measures to provide access by persons with disabilities to the support they may require in exercising their legal capacity.

4. States Parties shall ensure that all measures that relate to the exercise of legal capacity provide for appropriate and effective safeguards to prevent abuse in accordance with international human rights law. Such safeguards shall ensure that measures relating to the exercise of legal capacity respect the rights, will and preferences of the person, are free of conflict of interest and undue influence, are proportional and tailored to the person's circumstances, apply for the shortest time possible and are subject to regular review by a competent, independent and impartial authority or judicial body. The safeguards shall be proportional to the degree to which such measures affect the person's rights and interests.

5. Subject to the provisions of this article, States Parties shall take all appropriate and effective measures to ensure the equal right of persons with disabilities to own or inherit property, to control their own financial affairs and to have equal access to bank loans, mortgages and other forms of financial credit, and shall ensure that persons with disabilities are not arbitrarily deprived of their property.

Article 13

Access to justice

1. States Parties shall ensure effective access to justice for persons with disabilities on an equal basis with others, including through the provision of procedural and age-appropriate accommodations, in order to facilitate their effective role as direct and indirect participants, including as witnesses, in all legal proceedings, including at investigative and other preliminary stages.

2. In order to help to ensure effective access to justice for persons with disabilities, States Parties shall promote appropriate training for those working in the field of administration of justice, including police and prison staff.

Article 14

Liberty and security of person

1. States Parties shall ensure that persons with disabilities, on an equal basis with others:

(a) Enjoy the right to liberty and security of person;

(b) Are not deprived of their liberty unlawfully or arbitrarily, and that any deprivation of liberty is in conformity with the law, and that the existence of a disability shall in no case justify a deprivation of liberty.

2. States Parties shall ensure that if persons with disabilities are deprived of their liberty through any process, they are, on an equal basis with others, entitled to guarantees in accordance with international human rights law and shall be treated in compliance with the objectives and principles of the present Convention, including by provision of reasonable accommodation.

Article 15

Freedom from torture or cruel, inhuman or degrading treatment or punishment

1. No one shall be subjected to torture or to cruel, inhuman or degrading treatment or punishment. In particular, no one shall be subjected without his or her free consent to medical or scientific experimentation.

2. States Parties shall take all effective legislative, administrative, judicial or other measures to prevent persons with disabilities, on an equal basis with others, from being subjected to torture or cruel, inhuman or degrading treatment or punishment.

Article 16

Freedom from exploitation, violence and abuse

1. States Parties shall take all appropriate legislative, administrative, social, educational and other measures to protect persons with disabilities, both within and outside the home, from all forms of exploitation, violence and abuse, including their gender-based aspects.

2. States Parties shall also take all appropriate measures to prevent all forms of exploitation, violence and abuse by ensuring, inter alia, appropriate forms of gender- and age-sensitive assistance and support for persons with disabilities and their families and caregivers, including through the provision of information and education on how to avoid, recognize and report instances of exploitation, violence and abuse. States Parties shall ensure that protection services are age-, gender- and disability-sensitive.

3. In order to prevent the occurrence of all forms of exploitation, violence and abuse, States Parties shall ensure that all facilities and programmes designed to serve persons with disabilities are effectively monitored by independent authorities.

4. States Parties shall take all appropriate measures to promote the physical, cognitive and psychological recovery, rehabilitation and social reintegration of persons with disabilities who become victims of any form of exploitation, violence or abuse, including through the provision of protection services. Such recovery and reintegration shall take place in an environment that fosters the health, welfare, self-respect, dignity and autonomy of the person and takes into account gender- and age-specific needs.

5. States Parties shall put in place effective legislation and policies, including women- and child-focused legislation and policies, to ensure that instances of exploitation, violence and abuse against persons with disabilities are identified, investigated and, where appropriate, prosecuted.

Article 17

Protecting the integrity of the person

Every person with disabilities has a right to respect for his or her physical and mental integrity on an equal basis with others.

Article 18

Liberty of movement and nationality

1. States Parties shall recognize the rights of persons with disabilities to liberty of movement, to freedom to choose their residence and to a nationality, on an equal basis with others, including by ensuring that persons with disabilities:

(a) Have the right to acquire and change a nationality and are not deprived of their nationality arbitrarily or on the basis of disability;

(b) Are not deprived, on the basis of disability, of their ability to obtain, possess and utilize documentation of their nationality or other documentation of identification, or to utilize relevant processes such as immigration proceedings, that may be needed to facilitate exercise of the right to liberty of movement;

(c) Are free to leave any country, including their own;

(d) Are not deprived, arbitrarily or on the basis of disability, of the right to enter their own country.

2. Children with disabilities shall be registered immediately after birth and shall have the right from birth to a name, the right to acquire a nationality and, as far as possible, the right to know and be cared for by their parents.

Article 19

Living independently and being included in the community

States Parties to the present Convention recognize the equal right of all persons with disabilities to live in the community, with choices equal to others, and shall take effective and appropriate measures to facilitate full enjoyment by persons with disabilities of this right and their full inclusion and participation in the community, including by ensuring that:

(a) Persons with disabilities have the opportunity to choose their place of residence and where and with whom they live on an equal basis with others and are not obliged to live in a particular living arrangement;

(b) Persons with disabilities have access to a range of in-home, residential and other community support services, including personal assistance necessary to support living and inclusion in the community, and to prevent isolation or segregation from the community;

(c) Community services and facilities for the general population are available on an equal basis to persons with disabilities and are responsive to their needs.

Article 20

Personal mobility

States Parties shall take effective measures to ensure personal mobility with the greatest possible independence for persons with disabilities, including by:

(a) Facilitating the personal mobility of persons with disabilities in the manner and at the time of their choice, and at affordable cost;

(b) Facilitating access by persons with disabilities to quality mobility aids, devices, assistive technologies and forms of live assistance and intermediaries, including by making them available at affordable cost;

(c) Providing training in mobility skills to persons with disabilities and to specialist staff working with persons with disabilities;

(d) Encouraging entities that produce mobility aids, devices and assistive technologies to take into account all aspects of mobility for persons with disabilities.

Article 21

Freedom of expression and opinion, and access to information

States Parties shall take all appropriate measures to ensure that persons with disabilities can exercise the right to freedom of expression and opinion, including the freedom to seek, receive and impart information and ideas on an equal basis with others and through all forms of communication of their choice, as defined in article 2 of the present Convention, including by:

(a) Providing information intended for the general public to persons with disabilities in accessible formats and technologies appropriate to different kinds of disabilities in a timely manner and without additional cost;

(b) Accepting and facilitating the use of sign languages, Braille, augmentative and alternative communication, and all other accessible means, modes and formats of communication of their choice by persons with disabilities in official interactions;

(c) Urging private entities that provide services to the general public, including through the Internet, to provide information and services in accessible and usable formats for persons with disabilities;

(d) Encouraging the mass media, including providers of information through the Internet, to make their services accessible to persons with disabilities;

(e) Recognizing and promoting the use of sign languages.

Article 22

Respect for privacy

1. No person with disabilities, regardless of place of residence or living arrangements, shall be subjected to arbitrary or unlawful interference with his or her privacy, family, home or correspondence or other types of communication or to unlawful attacks on his or her honour and reputation. Persons with disabilities have the right to the protection of the law against such interference or attacks.

2. States Parties shall protect the privacy of personal, health and rehabilitation information of persons with disabilities on an equal basis with others.

Article 23

Respect for home and the family

1. States Parties shall take effective and appropriate measures to eliminate discrimination against persons with disabilities in all matters relating to marriage, family, parenthood and relationships, on an equal basis with others, so as to ensure that:

(a) The right of all persons with disabilities who are of marriageable age to marry and to found a family on

the basis of free and full consent of the intending spouses is recognized;

(b) The rights of persons with disabilities to decide freely and responsibly on the number and spacing of their children and to have access to age-appropriate information, reproductive and family planning education are recognized, and the means necessary to enable them to exercise these rights are provided;

(c) Persons with disabilities, including children, retain their fertility on an equal basis with others.

2. States Parties shall ensure the rights and responsibilities of persons with disabilities, with regard to guardianship, wardship, trusteeship, adoption of children or similar institutions, where these concepts exist in national legislation; in all cases the best interests of the child shall be paramount. States Parties shall render appropriate assistance to persons with disabilities in the performance of their child-rearing responsibilities.

3. States Parties shall ensure that children with disabilities have equal rights with respect to family life. With a view to realizing these rights, and to prevent concealment, abandonment, neglect and segregation of children with disabilities, States Parties shall undertake to provide early and comprehensive information, services and support to children with disabilities and their families.

4. States Parties shall ensure that a child shall not be separated from his or her parents against their will, except when competent authorities subject to judicial review determine, in accordance with applicable law and procedures, that such separation is necessary for the best interests of the child. In no case shall a child be separated from parents on the basis of a disability of either the child or one or both of the parents.

5. States Parties shall, where the immediate family is unable to care for a child with disabilities, undertake every effort to provide alternative care within the wider family, and failing that, within the community in a family setting.

Article 24
Education

1. States Parties recognize the right of persons with disabilities to education. With a view to realizing this right without discrimination and on the basis of equal opportunity, States Parties shall ensure an inclusive education system at all levels and lifelong learning directed to:

(a) The full development of human potential and sense of dignity and self-worth, and the strengthening of respect for human rights, fundamental freedoms and human diversity;

(b) The development by persons with disabilities of their personality, talents and creativity, as well as their mental and physical abilities, to their fullest potential;

(c) Enabling persons with disabilities to participate effectively in a free society.

2. In realizing this right, States Parties shall ensure that:

(a) Persons with disabilities are not excluded from the general education system on the basis of disability, and that children with disabilities are not excluded from free and compulsory primary education, or from secondary education, on the basis of disability;

(b) Persons with disabilities can access an inclusive, quality and free primary education and secondary education on an equal basis with others in the communities in which they live;

(c) Reasonable accommodation of the individual's requirements is provided;

(d) Persons with disabilities receive the support required, within the general education system, to facilitate their effective education;

(e) Effective individualized support measures are provided in environments that maximize academic and social development, consistent with the goal of full inclusion.

3. States Parties shall enable persons with disabilities to learn life and social development skills to facilitate their full and equal participation in education and as members of the community. To this end, States Parties shall take appropriate measures, including:

(a) Facilitating the learning of Braille, alternative script, augmentative and alternative modes, means and formats of communication and orientation and mobility skills, and facilitating peer support and mentoring;

(b) Facilitating the learning of sign language and the promotion of the linguistic identity of the deaf community;

(c) Ensuring that the education of persons, and in particular children, who are blind, deaf or deaf blind, is delivered in the most appropriate languages and modes and means of communication for the individual, and in environments which maximize academic and social development.

4. In order to help ensure the realization of this right, States Parties shall take appropriate measures to employ teachers, including teachers with disabilities, who are qualified in sign language and/or Braille, and to train professionals and staff who work at all levels of education. Such training shall incorporate disability awareness and the use of appropriate augmentative and alternative modes, means and formats of communication, educational techniques and materials to support persons with disabilities.

5. States Parties shall ensure that persons with disabilities are able to access general tertiary education, vocational training, adult education and lifelong learning without discrimination and on an equal basis with others. To this end, States Parties shall ensure that reasonable accommodation is provided to persons with disabilities.

Article 25
Health

States Parties recognize that persons with disabilities have the right to the enjoyment of the highest attainable standard of health without discrimination on the basis of disability. States Parties shall take all appropriate measures to ensure access for persons with disabilities to health services that are gender-sensitive, including health-related rehabilitation. In particular, States Parties shall:

(a) Provide persons with disabilities with the same range, quality and standard of free or affordable health care and programmes as provided to other persons, including in the area of sexual and reproductive health and population-based public health programmes;

(b) Provide those health services needed by persons with disabilities specifically because of their disabilities, including early identification and intervention as appropriate, and services designed to minimize and prevent further disabilities, including among children and older persons;

(c) Provide these health services as close as possible to people's own communities, including in rural areas;

(d) Require health professionals to provide care of the same quality to persons with disabilities as to others, including on the basis of free and informed consent by, inter alia, raising awareness of the human rights, dignity, autonomy and needs of persons with disabilities through training and the promulgation of ethical standards for public and private health care;

(e) Prohibit discrimination against persons with disabilities in the provision of health insurance, and life insurance where such insurance is permitted by national law, which shall be provided in a fair and reasonable manner;

(f) Prevent discriminatory denial of health care or health services or food and fluids on the basis of disability.

Article 26

Habilitation and rehabilitation

1. States Parties shall take effective and appropriate measures, including through peer support, to enable persons with disabilities to attain and maintain maximum independence, full physical, mental, social and vocational ability, and full inclusion and participation in all aspects of life. To that end, States Parties shall organize, strengthen and extend comprehensive habilitation and rehabilitation services and programmes, particularly in the areas of health, employment, education and social services, in such a way that these services and programmes:

(a) Begin at the earliest possible stage, and are based on the multidisciplinary assessment of individual needs and strengths;

(b) Support participation and inclusion in the community and all aspects of society, are voluntary, and are available to persons with disabilities as close as possible to their own communities, including in rural areas.

2. States Parties shall promote the development of initial and continuing training for professionals and staff working in habilitation and rehabilitation services.

3. States Parties shall promote the availability, knowledge and use of assistive devices and technologies, designed for persons with disabilities, as they relate to habilitation and rehabilitation.

Article 27

Work and employment

1. States Parties recognize the right of persons with disabilities to work, on an equal basis with others; this includes the right to the opportunity to gain a living by work freely chosen or accepted in a labour market and work environment that is open, inclusive and accessible to persons with disabilities. States Parties shall safeguard and promote the realization of the right to work, including for those who acquire a disability during the course of employment, by taking appropriate steps, including through legislation, to, inter alia:

(a) Prohibit discrimination on the basis of disability with regard to all matters concerning all forms of employment, including conditions of recruitment, hiring and employment, continuance of employment, career advancement and safe and healthy working conditions;

(b) Protect the rights of persons with disabilities, on an equal basis with others, to just and favourable conditions of work, including equal opportunities and equal remuneration for work of equal value, safe and healthy working conditions, including protection from harassment, and the redress of grievances;

(c) Ensure that persons with disabilities are able to exercise their labour and trade union rights on an equal basis with others;

(d) Enable persons with disabilities to have effective access to general technical and vocational guidance programmes, placement services and vocational and continuing training;

(e) Promote employment opportunities and career advancement for persons with disabilities in the labour market, as well as assistance in finding, obtaining, maintaining and returning to employment;

(f) Promote opportunities for self-employment, entrepreneurship, the development of cooperatives and starting one's own business;

(g) Employ persons with disabilities in the public sector;

(h) Promote the employment of persons with disabilities in the private sector through appropriate policies and measures, which may include affirmative action programmes, incentives and other measures;

(i) Ensure that reasonable accommodation is provided to persons with disabilities in the workplace;

(j) Promote the acquisition by persons with disabilities of work experience in the open labour market;

(k) Promote vocational and professional rehabilitation, job retention and return-to-work programmes for persons with disabilities.

2. States Parties shall ensure that persons with disabilities are not held in slavery or in servitude, and are protected, on an equal basis with others, from forced or compulsory labour.

Article 28

Adequate standard of living and social protection

1. States Parties recognize the right of persons with disabilities to an adequate standard of living for themselves and their families, including adequate food, clothing and housing, and to the continuous improvement of living conditions, and shall take appropriate steps to safeguard and promote the realization of this right without discrimination on the basis of disability.

2. States Parties recognize the right of persons with disabilities to social protection and to the enjoyment of that right without discrimination on the basis of disability, and shall take appropriate steps to safeguard and promote the realization of this right, including measures:

(a) To ensure equal access by persons with disabilities to clean water services, and to ensure access to appropriate and affordable services, devices and other assistance for disability-related needs;

(b) To ensure access by persons with disabilities, in particular women and girls with disabilities and older persons with disabilities, to social protection programmes and poverty reduction programmes;

(c) To ensure access by persons with disabilities and their families living in situations of poverty to assistance from the State with disability-related expenses, including adequate training, counselling, financial assistance and respite care;

(d) To ensure access by persons with disabilities to public housing programmes;

(e) To ensure equal access by persons with disabilities to retirement benefits and programmes.

Article 29
Participation in political and public life

States Parties shall guarantee to persons with disabilities political rights and the opportunity to enjoy them on an equal basis with others, and shall undertake:

(a) To ensure that persons with disabilities can effectively and fully participate in political and public life on an equal basis with others, directly or through freely chosen representatives, including the right and opportunity for persons with disabilities to vote and be elected, inter alia, by:

(i) Ensuring that voting procedures, facilities and materials are appropriate, accessible and easy to understand and use;

(ii) Protecting the right of persons with disabilities to vote by secret ballot in elections and public referendums without intimidation, and to stand for elections, to effectively hold office and perform all public functions at all levels of government, facilitating the use of assistive and new technologies where appropriate;

(iii) Guaranteeing the free expression of the will of persons with disabilities as electors and to this end, where necessary, at their request, allowing assistance in voting by a person of their own choice;

(b) To promote actively an environment in which persons with disabilities can effectively and fully participate in the conduct of public affairs, without discrimination and on an equal basis with others, and encourage their participation in public affairs, including:

(i) Participation in non-governmental organizations and associations concerned with the public and political life of the country, and in the activities and administration of political parties;

(ii) Forming and joining organizations of persons with disabilities to represent persons with disabilities at international, national, regional and local levels.

Article 30
Participation in cultural life, recreation, leisure and sport

1. States Parties recognize the right of persons with disabilities to take part on an equal basis with others in cultural life, and shall take all appropriate measures to ensure that persons with disabilities:

(a) Enjoy access to cultural materials in accessible formats;

(b) Enjoy access to television programmes, films, theatre and other cultural activities, in accessible formats;

(c) Enjoy access to places for cultural performances or services, such as theatres, museums, cinemas, libraries and tourism services, and, as far as possible, enjoy access to monuments and sites of national cultural importance.

2. States Parties shall take appropriate measures to enable persons with disabilities to have the opportunity to develop and utilize their creative, artistic and intellectual potential, not only for their own benefit, but also for the enrichment of society.

3. States Parties shall take all appropriate steps, in accordance with international law, to ensure that laws protecting intellectual property rights do not constitute an unreasonable or discriminatory barrier to access by persons with disabilities to cultural materials.

4. Persons with disabilities shall be entitled, on an equal basis with others, to recognition and support of their specific cultural and linguistic identity, including sign languages and deaf culture.

5. With a view to enabling persons with disabilities to participate on an equal basis with others in recreational, leisure and sporting activities, States Parties shall take appropriate measures:

(a) To encourage and promote the participation, to the fullest extent possible, of persons with disabilities in mainstream sporting activities at all levels;

(b) To ensure that persons with disabilities have an opportunity to organize, develop and participate in disability-specific sporting and recreational activities and, to this end, encourage the provision, on an equal basis with others, of appropriate instruction, training and resources;

(c) To ensure that persons with disabilities have access to sporting, recreational and tourism venues;

(d) To ensure that children with disabilities have equal access with other children to participation in play, recreation and leisure and sporting activities, including those activities in the school system;

(e) To ensure that persons with disabilities have access to services from those involved in the organization of recreational, tourism, leisure and sporting activities.

Article 31
Statistics and data collection

1. States Parties undertake to collect appropriate information, including statistical and research data, to enable them to formulate and implement policies to give effect to the present Convention. The process of collecting and maintaining this information shall:

(a) Comply with legally established safeguards, including legislation on data protection, to ensure confidentiality and respect for the privacy of persons with disabilities;

(b) Comply with internationally accepted norms to protect human rights and fundamental freedoms and ethical principles in the collection and use of statistics.

2. The information collected in accordance with this article shall be disaggregated, as appropriate, and used to help assess the implementation of States Parties' obligations under the present Convention and to identify and address the barriers faced by persons with disabilities in exercising their rights.

3. States Parties shall assume responsibility for the dissemination of these statistics and ensure their accessibility to persons with disabilities and others.

Article 32
International cooperation

1. States Parties recognize the importance of international cooperation and its promotion, in support of national efforts for the realization of the purpose and objectives of the present Convention, and will undertake appropriate and effective measures in this regard, between and among States and, as appropriate, in partnership with relevant international and regional organizations and civil society, in particular organizations of persons with disabilities. Such measures could include, inter alia:

(a) Ensuring that international cooperation, including international development programmes, is inclusive of and accessible to persons with disabilities;

(b) Facilitating and supporting capacity-building, including through the exchange and sharing of information, experiences, training programmes and best practices;

(c) Facilitating cooperation in research and access to scientific and technical knowledge;

(d) Providing, as appropriate, technical and economic assistance, including by facilitating access to and sharing of accessible and assistive technologies, and through the transfer of technologies.

2. The provisions of this article are without prejudice to the obligations of each State Party to fulfil its obligations under the present Convention.

Article 33
National implementation and monitoring

1. States Parties, in accordance with their system of organization, shall designate one or more focal points within government for matters relating to the implementation of the present Convention, and shall give due consideration to the establishment or designation of a coordination mechanism within government to facilitate related action in different sectors and at different levels.

2. States Parties shall, in accordance with their legal and administrative systems, maintain, strengthen, designate or establish within the State Party, a framework, including one or more independent mechanisms, as appropriate, to promote, protect and monitor implementation of the present Convention. When designating or establishing such a mechanism, States Parties shall take into account the principles relating to the status and functioning of national institutions for protection and promotion of human rights.

3. Civil society, in particular persons with disabilities and their representative organizations, shall be involved and participate fully in the monitoring process.

Article 34
Committee on the Rights of Persons with Disabilities

1. There shall be established a Committee on the Rights of Persons with Disabilities (hereafter referred to as "the Committee"), which shall carry out the functions hereinafter provided.

2. The Committee shall consist, at the time of entry into force of the present Convention, of twelve experts. After an additional sixty ratifications or accessions to the Convention, the membership of the Committee shall increase by six members, attaining a maximum number of eighteen members.

3. The members of the Committee shall serve in their personal capacity and shall be of high moral standing and recognized competence and experience in the field covered by the present Convention. When nominating their candidates, States Parties are invited to give due consideration to the provision set out in article 4, paragraph 3, of the present Convention.

4. The members of the Committee shall be elected by States Parties, consideration being given to equitable geographical distribution, representation of the different forms of civilization and of the principal legal systems, balanced gender representation and participation of experts with disabilities.

5. The members of the Committee shall be elected by secret ballot from a list of persons nominated by the States Parties from among their nationals at meetings of the Conference of States Parties. At those meetings, for which two thirds of States Parties shall constitute a quorum, the persons elected to the Committee shall be those who obtain the largest number of votes and an absolute majority of the votes of the representatives of States Parties present and voting.

6. The initial election shall be held no later than six months after the date of entry into force of the present Convention. At least four months before the date of each election, the Secretary-General of the United Nations shall address a letter to the States Parties inviting them to submit the nominations within two months. The Secretary-General shall subsequently prepare a list in alphabetical order of all persons thus nominated, indicating the State Parties which have nominated them, and shall submit it to the States Parties to the present Convention.

7. The members of the Committee shall be elected for a term of four years. They shall be eligible for re-election once. However, the term of six of the members elected at the first election shall expire at the end of two years; immediately after the first election, the names of these six members shall be chosen by lot by the chairperson of the meeting referred to in paragraph 5 of this article.

8. The election of the six additional members of the Committee shall be held on the occasion of regular elections, in accordance with the relevant provisions of this article.

9. If a member of the Committee dies or resigns or declares that for any other cause she or he can no longer perform her or his duties, the State Party which nominated the member shall appoint another expert possessing the qualifications and meeting the requirements set out in the relevant provisions of this article, to serve for the remainder of the term.

10. The Committee shall establish its own rules of procedure.

11. The Secretary-General of the United Nations shall provide the necessary staff and facilities for the effective performance of the functions of the Committee under the present Convention, and shall convene its initial meeting.

12. With the approval of the General Assembly of the United Nations, the members of the Committee established under the present Convention shall receive emoluments from United Nations resources on such terms and conditions as the Assembly may decide, having regard to the importance of the Committee's responsibilities.

13. The members of the Committee shall be entitled to the facilities, privileges and immunities of experts on mission for the United Nations as laid down in the relevant sections of the Convention on the Privileges and Immunities of the United Nations.

Article 35
Reports by States Parties

1. Each State Party shall submit to the Committee, through the Secretary-General of the United Nations, a comprehensive report on measures taken to give effect to its obligations under the present Convention and on the progress made in that regard, within two years after the entry into force of the present Convention for the State Party concerned.

2. Thereafter, States Parties shall submit subsequent reports at least every four years and further whenever the Committee so requests.

3. The Committee shall decide any guidelines applicable to the content of the reports.

4. A State Party which has submitted a comprehensive initial report to the Committee need not, in its subsequent reports, repeat information previously provided. When preparing reports to the Committee, States Parties are invited to consider doing so in an open and transparent process and to give due consideration to the provision set out in article 4, paragraph 3, of the present Convention.

5. Reports may indicate factors and difficulties affecting the degree of fulfillment of obligations under the present Convention.

Article 36
Consideration of reports

1. Each report shall be considered by the Committee, which shall make such suggestions and general recommendations on the report as it may consider appropriate and shall forward these to the State Party concerned. The State Party may respond with any information it chooses to the Committee. The Committee may request further information from States Parties relevant to the implementation of the present Convention.

2. If a State Party is significantly overdue in the submission of a report, the Committee may notify the State Party concerned of the need to examine the implementation of the present Convention in that State Party, on the basis of reliable information available to the Committee, if the relevant report is not submitted within three months following the notification. The Committee shall invite the State Party concerned to participate in such examination. Should the State Party respond by submitting the relevant report, the provisions of paragraph 1 of this article will apply.

3. The Secretary-General of the United Nations shall make available the reports to all States Parties.

4. States Parties shall make their reports widely available to the public in their own countries and facilitate access to the suggestions and general recommendations relating to these reports.

5. The Committee shall transmit, as it may consider appropriate, to the specialized agencies, funds and programmes of the United Nations, and other competent bodies, reports from States Parties in order to address a request or indication of a need for technical advice or assistance contained therein, along with the Committee's observations and recommendations, if any, on these requests or indications.

Article 37
Cooperation between States Parties and the Committee

1. Each State Party shall cooperate with the Committee and assist its members in the fulfilment of their mandate.

2. In its relationship with States Parties, the Committee shall give due consideration to ways and means of enhancing national capacities for the implementation of the present Convention, including through international cooperation.

Article 38
Relationship of the Committee with other bodies

In order to foster the effective implementation of the present Convention and to encourage international cooperation in the field covered by the present Convention:

(a) The specialized agencies and other United Nations organs shall be entitled to be represented at the consideration of the implementation of such provisions of the present Convention as falling within the scope of their mandate. The Committee may invite the specialized agencies and other competent bodies as it may consider appropriate to provide expert advice on the implementation of the Convention in areas falling within the scope of their respective mandates. The Committee may invite specialized agencies and other United Nations organs to submit reports on the implementation of the Convention in areas falling within the scope of their activities;

(*b*) The Committee, as it discharges its mandate, shall consult, as appropriate, other relevant bodies instituted by international human rights treaties, with a view to ensuring the consistency of their respective reporting guidelines, suggestions and general recommendations, and avoiding duplication and overlap in the performance of their functions.

Article 39

Report of the Committee

The Committee shall report every two years to the General Assembly and to the Economic and Social Council on its activities, and may make suggestions and general recommendations based on the examination of reports and information received from the States Parties. Such suggestions and general recommendations shall be included in the report of the Committee together with comments, if any, from States Parties.

Article 40

Conference of States Parties

1. The States Parties shall meet regularly in a Conference of States Parties in order to consider any matter with regard to the implementation of the present Convention.

2. No later than six months after the entry into force of the present Convention, the Conference of States Parties shall be convened by the Secretary-General of the United Nations. The subsequent meetings shall be convened by the Secretary-General biennially or upon the decision of the Conference of States Parties.

Article 41

Depositary

The Secretary-General of the United Nations shall be the depositary of the present Convention.

Article 42

Signature

The present Convention shall be open for signature by all States and by regional integration organizations at United Nations Headquarters in New York as of 30 March 2007.

Article 43

Consent to be bound

The present Convention shall be subject to ratification by signatory States and to formal confirmation by signatory regional integration organizations. It shall be open for accession by any State or regional integration organization which has not signed the Convention.

Article 44

Regional integration organizations

1. "Regional integration organization" shall mean an organization constituted by sovereign States of a given region, to which its member States have transferred competence in respect of matters governed by the present Convention. Such organizations shall declare, in their instruments of formal confirmation or accession, the extent of their competence with respect to matters governed by the present Convention. Subsequently, they shall inform the depositary of any substantial modification in the extent of their competence.

2. References to "States Parties" in the present Convention shall apply to such organizations within the limits of their competence.

3. For the purposes of article 45, paragraph 1, and article 47, paragraphs 2 and 3, of the present Convention, any instrument deposited by a regional integration organization shall not be counted.

4. Regional integration organizations, in matters within their competence, may exercise their right to vote in the Conference of States Parties, with a number of votes equal to the number of their member States that are Parties to the present Convention. Such an organization shall not exercise its right to vote if any of its member States exercises its right, and vice versa.

Article 45

Entry into force

1. The present Convention shall enter into force on the thirtieth day after the deposit of the twentieth instrument of ratification or accession.

2. For each State or regional integration organization ratifying, formally confirming or acceding to the present Convention after the deposit of the twentieth such instrument, the Convention shall enter into force on the thirtieth day after the deposit of its own such instrument.

Article 46

Reservations

1. Reservations incompatible with the object and purpose of the present Convention shall not be permitted.

2. Reservations may be withdrawn at any time.

Article 47

Amendments

1. Any State Party may propose an amendment to the present Convention and submit it to the Secretary-General of the United Nations. The Secretary-General shall communicate any proposed amendments to States Parties, with a request to be notified whether they favour a conference of States Parties for the purpose of considering and deciding upon the proposals. In the event that, within four months from the date of such communication, at least one third of the States Parties favour such a conference, the Secretary-General shall convene the conference under the auspices of the United Nations. Any amendment adopted by a majority of two thirds of the States Parties present and voting shall be submitted by the Secretary-General to the General Assembly of the United Nations for approval and thereafter to all States Parties for acceptance.

2. An amendment adopted and approved in accordance with paragraph 1 of this article shall enter into force on the thirtieth day after the number of instruments of acceptance deposited reaches two thirds of the number of States Parties at the date of adoption of the amendment. Thereafter, the amendment shall enter into force for any State Party on the thirtieth day following the deposit of its own instrument of acceptance. An amendment shall

be binding only on those States Parties which have accepted it.

3. If so decided by the Conference of States Parties by consensus, an amendment adopted and approved in accordance with paragraph 1 of this article which relates exclusively to articles 34, 38, 39 and 40 shall enter into force for all States Parties on the thirtieth day after the number of instruments of acceptance deposited reaches two thirds of the number of States Parties at the date of adoption of the amendment.

Article 48
Denunciation

A State Party may denounce the present Convention by written notification to the Secretary-General of the United Nations. The denunciation shall become effective one year after the date of receipt of the notification by the Secretary-General.

Article 49
Accessible format

The text of the present Convention shall be made available in accessible formats.

Article 50
Authentic texts

The Arabic, Chinese, English, French, Russian and Spanish texts of the present Convention shall be equally authentic.

IN WITNESS THEREOF the undersigned plenipotentiaries, being duly authorized thereto by their respective Governments, have signed the present Convention.

Annex II
Optional Protocol to the Convention on the Rights of Persons with Disabilities

The States Parties to the present Protocol have agreed as follows:

Article 1

1. A State Party to the present Protocol ("State Party") recognizes the competence of the Committee on the Rights of Persons with Disabilities ("the Committee") to receive and consider communications from or on behalf of individuals or groups of individuals subject to its jurisdiction who claim to be victims of a violation by that State Party of the provisions of the Convention.

2. No communication shall be received by the Committee if it concerns a State Party to the Convention that is not a party to the present Protocol.

Article 2

The Committee shall consider a communication inadmissible when:

(a) The communication is anonymous;

(b) The communication constitutes an abuse of the right of submission of such communications or is incompatible with the provisions of the Convention;

(c) The same matter has already been examined by the Committee or has been or is being examined under another procedure of international investigation or settlement;

(d) All available domestic remedies have not been exhausted. This shall not be the rule where the application of the remedies is unreasonably prolonged or unlikely to bring effective relief;

(e) It is manifestly ill-founded or not sufficiently substantiated; or when

(f) The facts that are the subject of the communication occurred prior to the entry into force of the present Protocol for the State Party concerned unless those facts continued after that date.

Article 3

Subject to the provisions of article 2 of the present Protocol, the Committee shall bring any communications submitted to it confidentially to the attention of the State Party. Within six months, the receiving State shall submit to the Committee written explanations or statements clarifying the matter and the remedy, if any, that may have been taken by that State.

Article 4

1. At any time after the receipt of a communication and before a determination on the merits has been reached, the Committee may transmit to the State Party concerned for its urgent consideration a request that the State Party take such interim measures as may be necessary to avoid possible irreparable damage to the victim or victims of the alleged violation.

2. Where the Committee exercises its discretion under paragraph 1 of this article, this does not imply a determination on admissibility or on the merits of the communication.

Article 5

The Committee shall hold closed meetings when examining communications under the present Protocol. After examining a communication, the Committee shall forward its suggestions and recommendations, if any, to the State Party concerned and to the petitioner.

Article 6

1. If the Committee receives reliable information indicating grave or systematic violations by a State Party of rights set forth in the Convention, the Committee shall invite that State Party to cooperate in the examination of the information and to this end submit observations with regard to the information concerned.

2. Taking into account any observations that may have been submitted by the State Party concerned as well as any other reliable information available to it, the Committee may designate one or more of its members to conduct an inquiry and to report urgently to the Committee. Where warranted and with the consent of the State Party, the inquiry may include a visit to its territory.

3. After examining the findings of such an inquiry, the Committee shall transmit these findings to the State Party concerned together with any comments and recommendations.

4. The State Party concerned shall, within six months of receiving the findings, comments and recommendations transmitted by the Committee, submit its observations to the Committee.

5. Such an inquiry shall be conducted confidentially and the cooperation of the State Party shall be sought at all stages of the proceedings.

Article 7

1. The Committee may invite the State Party concerned to include in its report under article 35 of the Convention details of any measures taken in response to an inquiry conducted under article 6 of the present Protocol.

2. The Committee may, if necessary, after the end of the period of six months referred to in article 6, paragraph 4, invite the State Party concerned to inform it of the measures taken in response to such an inquiry.

Article 8

Each State Party may, at the time of signature or ratification of the present Protocol or accession thereto, declare that it does not recognize the competence of the Committee provided for in articles 6 and 7.

Article 9

The Secretary-General of the United Nations shall be the depositary of the present Protocol.

Article 10

The present Protocol shall be open for signature by signatory States and regional integration organizations of the Convention at United Nations Headquarters in New York as of 30 March 2007.

Article 11

The present Protocol shall be subject to ratification by signatory States of the present Protocol which have ratified or acceded to the Convention. It shall be subject to formal confirmation by signatory regional integration organizations of the present Protocol which have formally confirmed or acceded to the Convention. It shall be open for accession by any State or regional integration organization which has ratified, formally confirmed or acceded to the Convention and which has not signed the Protocol.

Article 12

1. "Regional integration organization" shall mean an organization constituted by sovereign States of a given region, to which its member States have transferred competence in respect of matters governed by the Convention and the present Protocol. Such organizations shall declare, in their instruments of formal confirmation or accession, the extent of their competence with respect to matters governed by the Convention and the present Protocol. Subsequently, they shall inform the depositary of any substantial modification in the extent of their competence.

2. References to "States Parties" in the present Protocol shall apply to such organizations within the limits of their competence.

3. For the purposes of article 13, paragraph 1, and article 15, paragraph 2, of the present Protocol, any instrument deposited by a regional integration organization shall not be counted.

4. Regional integration organizations, in matters within their competence, may exercise their right to vote in the meeting of States Parties, with a number of votes equal to the number of their member States that are Parties to the present Protocol. Such an organization shall not exercise its right to vote if any of its member States exercises its right, and vice versa.

Article 13

1. Subject to the entry into force of the Convention, the present Protocol shall enter into force on the thirtieth day after the deposit of the tenth instrument of ratification or accession.

2. For each State or regional integration organization ratifying, formally confirming or acceding to the present Protocol after the deposit of the tenth such instrument, the Protocol shall enter into force on the thirtieth day after the deposit of its own such instrument.

Article 14

1. Reservations incompatible with the object and purpose of the present Protocol shall not be permitted.

2. Reservations may be withdrawn at any time.

Article 15

1. Any State Party may propose an amendment to the present Protocol and submit it to the Secretary-General of the United Nations. The Secretary-General shall communicate any proposed amendments to States Parties, with a request to be notified whether they favour a meeting of States Parties for the purpose of considering and deciding upon the proposals. In the event that, within four months from the date of such communication, at least one third of the States Parties favour such a meeting, the Secretary-General shall convene the meeting under the auspices of the United Nations. Any amendment adopted by a majority of two thirds of the States Parties present and voting shall be submitted by the Secretary-General to the General Assembly of the United Nations for approval and thereafter to all States Parties for acceptance.

2. An amendment adopted and approved in accordance with paragraph 1 of this article shall enter into force on the thirtieth day after the number of instruments of acceptance deposited reaches two thirds of the number of States Parties at the date of adoption of the amendment. Thereafter, the amendment shall enter into force for any State Party on the thirtieth day following the deposit of its own instrument of acceptance. An amendment shall be binding only on those States Parties which have accepted it.

Article 16

A State Party may denounce the present Protocol by written notification to the Secretary-General of the United Nations. The denunciation shall become effective one year after the date of receipt of the notification by the Secretary-General.

Article 17

The text of the present Protocol shall be made available in accessible formats.

Article 18

The Arabic, Chinese, English, French, Russian and Spanish texts of the present Protocol shall be equally authentic.

IN WITNESS THEREOF the undersigned plenipotentiaries, being duly authorized thereto by their respective Governments, have signed the present Protocol.

International Convention for protection from enforced disappearance

Human Rights Council action. On 29 June [A/61/53 (res. 1/1)], the Council, recalling the Commission's establishment of an intersessional open-ended working group in 2001 [YUN 2001, p. 643] to elaborate a legally binding instrument for combating enforced disappearance and taking note of the group's conclusion of its work and transmission of the draft instrument to the Commission [YUN 2005, p. 810], adopted the International Convention for the Protection of All Persons from Enforced Disappearance. It also recommended that the General Assembly adopt it, which, thereafter, should be opened for signature in Paris.

On 20 December, the Assembly, in resolution 61/177, adopted the Convention (see below), which defined enforced disappearance as the arrest, detention, abduction or any other form of deprivation of liberty by agents of the State or by persons or groups acting with State authorization, support or acquiescence, followed by a refusal to acknowledge the deprivation of liberty or concealment of the fate of those affected, which placed them outside the protection of the law. Parties to the Convention undertook to: investigate acts of enforced disappearance and to bring those responsible to justice; ensure that it constituted an offence under their criminal law; and establish jurisdiction over the offence when the alleged offenders were within their territory, even if they were not citizens or residents. They also agreed to cooperate in ensuring that offenders were prosecuted or extradited; respect minimum legal standards around the deprivation of liberty, including the right to challenge imprisonment before the courts; establish a register of those currently imprisoned and have it available for inspection by their relatives and counsel; and ensure that victims of or those directly affected by enforced disappearance obtained reparation or compensation. The Convention provided for the establishment of a ten-member Committee on Enforced Disappearances to monitor the compliance of States parties through the review of reports they undertook to submit and of individual complaints.

The Convention would enter into force on the thirtieth day after the deposit of the twentieth instrument of ratification or accession.

GENERAL ASSEMBLY ACTION

On 20 December [meeting 82], the General Assembly, on the recommendation of the Third Committee [A/61/448 & Corr.2, 3], adopted **resolution 61/177** without vote [agenda item 68].

International Convention for the Protection of All Persons from Enforced Disappearance

The General Assembly,

Taking note of Human Rights Council resolution 1/1 of 29 June 2006, by which the Council adopted the International Convention for the Protection of All Persons from Enforced Disappearance,

1. *Acknowledges* the adoption by the Human Rights Council of the International Convention for the Protection of All Persons from Enforced Disappearance;

2. *Adopts* and opens for signature, ratification and accession the International Convention for the Protection of All Persons from Enforced Disappearance, the text of which is annexed to the present resolution;

3. *Recommends* that the Convention be opened for signature at a signing ceremony in Paris.

Annex
International Convention for the Protection of All Persons from Enforced Disappearance

Preamble

The States Parties to this Convention,

Considering the obligation of States under the Charter of the United Nations to promote universal respect for, and observance of, human rights and fundamental freedoms,

Having regard to the Universal Declaration of Human Rights,

Recalling the International Covenant on Economic, Social and Cultural Rights, the International Covenant on Civil and Political Rights and the other relevant international instruments in the fields of human rights, humanitarian law and international criminal law,

Also recalling the Declaration on the Protection of All Persons from Enforced Disappearance adopted by the General Assembly of the United Nations in its resolution 47/133 of 18 December 1992,

Aware of the extreme seriousness of enforced disappearance, which constitutes a crime and, in certain circumstances defined in international law, a crime against humanity,

Determined to prevent enforced disappearances and to combat impunity for the crime of enforced disappearance,

Considering the right of any person not to be subjected to enforced disappearance, the right of victims to justice and to reparation,

Affirming the right of any victim to know the truth about the circumstances of an enforced disappearance and the fate of the disappeared person, and the right to freedom to seek, receive and impart information to this end,

Have agreed on the following articles:

Part I

Article 1

1. No one shall be subjected to enforced disappearance.

2. No exceptional circumstances whatsoever, whether a state of war or a threat of war, internal political instability or any other public emergency, may be invoked as a justification for enforced disappearance.

Article 2

For the purposes of this Convention, "enforced disappearance" is considered to be the arrest, detention, abduction or any other form of deprivation of liberty by agents of the State or by persons or groups of persons acting with the authorization, support or acquiescence of the State, followed by a refusal to acknowledge the deprivation of liberty or by concealment of the fate or whereabouts of the disappeared person, which place such a person outside the protection of the law.

Article 3

Each State Party shall take appropriate measures to investigate acts defined in article 2 committed by persons or groups of persons acting without the authorization, support or acquiescence of the State and to bring those responsible to justice.

Article 4

Each State Party shall take the necessary measures to ensure that enforced disappearance constitutes an offence under its criminal law.

Article 5

The widespread or systematic practice of enforced disappearance constitutes a crime against humanity as defined in applicable international law and shall attract the consequences provided for under such applicable international law.

Article 6

1. Each State Party shall take the necessary measures to hold criminally responsible at least:

(a) Any person who commits, orders, solicits or induces the commission of, attempts to commit, is an accomplice to or participates in an enforced disappearance;

(b) A superior who:

(i) Knew, or consciously disregarded information which clearly indicated, that subordinates under his or her effective authority and control were committing or about to commit a crime of enforced disappearance;

(ii) Exercised effective responsibility for and control over activities which were concerned with the crime of enforced disappearance; and

(iii) Failed to take all necessary and reasonable measures within his or her power to prevent or repress the commission of an enforced disappearance or to submit the matter to the competent authorities for investigation and prosecution;

(c) Subparagraph *(b)* above is without prejudice to the higher standards of responsibility applicable under relevant international law to a military commander or to a person effectively acting as a military commander.

2. No order or instruction from any public authority, civilian, military or other, may be invoked to justify an offence of enforced disappearance.

Article 7

1. Each State Party shall make the offence of enforced disappearance punishable by appropriate penalties which take into account its extreme seriousness.

2. Each State Party may establish:

(a) Mitigating circumstances, in particular for persons who, having been implicated in the commission of an enforced disappearance, effectively contribute to bringing the disappeared person forward alive or make it possible to clarify cases of enforced disappearance or to identify the perpetrators of an enforced disappearance;

(b) Without prejudice to other criminal procedures, aggravating circumstances, in particular in the event of the death of the disappeared person or the commission of an enforced disappearance in respect of pregnant women, minors, persons with disabilities or other particularly vulnerable persons.

Article 8

Without prejudice to article 5,

1. A State Party which applies a statute of limitations in respect of enforced disappearance shall take the necessary measures to ensure that the term of limitation for criminal proceedings:

(a) Is of long duration and is proportionate to the extreme seriousness of this offence;

(b) Commences from the moment when the offence of enforced disappearance ceases, taking into account its continuous nature.

2. Each State Party shall guarantee the right of victims of enforced disappearance to an effective remedy during the term of limitation.

Article 9

1. Each State Party shall take the necessary measures to establish its competence to exercise jurisdiction over the offence of enforced disappearance:

(a) When the offence is committed in any territory under its jurisdiction or on board a ship or aircraft registered in that State;

(b) When the alleged offender is one of its nationals;

(c) When the disappeared person is one of its nationals and the State Party considers it appropriate.

2. Each State Party shall likewise take such measures as may be necessary to establish its competence to exercise jurisdiction over the offence of enforced disappearance when the alleged offender is present in any territory under its jurisdiction, unless it extradites or surrenders him or her to another State in accordance with its international obligations or surrenders him or her to an international criminal tribunal whose jurisdiction it has recognized.

3. This Convention does not exclude any additional criminal jurisdiction exercised in accordance with national law.

Article 10

1. Upon being satisfied, after an examination of the information available to it, that the circumstances so warrant, any State Party in whose territory a person suspected of having committed an offence of enforced disappearance is present shall take him or her into custody or take such other legal measures as are necessary to ensure his or her presence. The custody and other legal measures shall be as provided for in the law of that State Party but may be maintained only for such time as is necessary to ensure the person's presence at criminal, surrender or extradition proceedings.

2. A State Party which has taken the measures referred to in paragraph 1 of this article shall immediately carry out a preliminary inquiry or investigations to establish the facts. It shall notify the States Parties referred to in article 9, paragraph 1, of the measures it has taken in pursuance of paragraph 1 of this article, including detention and the circumstances warranting detention, and of the findings of its preliminary inquiry or its investigations, indicating whether it intends to exercise its jurisdiction.

3. Any person in custody pursuant to paragraph 1 of this article may communicate immediately with the nearest appropriate representative of the State of which he or she is a national, or, if he or she is a stateless person, with the representative of the State where he or she usually resides.

Article 11

1. The State Party in the territory under whose jurisdiction a person alleged to have committed an offence of enforced disappearance is found shall, if it does not extradite that person or surrender him or her to another State in accordance with its international obligations or surrender him or her to an international criminal tribunal whose jurisdiction it has recognized, submit the case to its competent authorities for the purpose of prosecution.

2. These authorities shall take their decision in the same manner as in the case of any ordinary offence of a serious nature under the law of that State Party. In the cases referred to in article 9, paragraph 2, the standards of evidence required for prosecution and conviction shall in no way be less stringent than those which apply in the cases referred to in article 9, paragraph 1.

3. Any person against whom proceedings are brought in connection with an offence of enforced disappearance shall be guaranteed fair treatment at all stages of the proceedings. Any person tried for an offence of enforced disappearance shall benefit from a fair trial before a competent, independent and impartial court or tribunal established by law.

Article 12

1. Each State Party shall ensure that any individual who alleges that a person has been subjected to enforced disappearance has the right to report the facts to the competent authorities, which shall examine the allegation promptly and impartially and, where necessary, undertake without delay a thorough and impartial investigation. Appropriate steps shall be taken, where necessary, to ensure that the complainant, witnesses, relatives of the disappeared person and their defence counsel, as well as persons participating in the investigation, are protected against all ill-treatment or intimidation as a consequence of the complaint or any evidence given.

2. Where there are reasonable grounds for believing that a person has been subjected to enforced disappearance, the authorities referred to in paragraph 1 of this article shall undertake an investigation, even if there has been no formal complaint.

3. Each State Party shall ensure that the authorities referred to in paragraph 1 of this article:

(a) Have the necessary powers and resources to conduct the investigation effectively, including access to the documentation and other information relevant to their investigation;

(b) Have access, if necessary with the prior authorization of a judicial authority, which shall rule promptly on the matter, to any place of detention or any other place where there are reasonable grounds to believe that the disappeared person may be present.

4. Each State Party shall take the necessary measures to prevent and sanction acts that hinder the conduct of an investigation. It shall ensure in particular that persons suspected of having committed an offence of enforced disappearance are not in a position to influence the progress of an investigation by means of pressure or acts of intimidation or reprisal aimed at the complainant, witnesses, relatives of the disappeared person or their defence counsel, or at persons participating in the investigation.

Article 13

1. For the purposes of extradition between States Parties, the offence of enforced disappearance shall not be regarded as a political offence or as an offence connected with a political offence or as an offence inspired by political motives. Accordingly, a request for extradition based on such an offence may not be refused on these grounds alone.

2. The offence of enforced disappearance shall be deemed to be included as an extraditable offence in any extradition treaty existing between States Parties before the entry into force of this Convention.

3. States Parties undertake to include the offence of enforced disappearance as an extraditable offence in any extradition treaty subsequently to be concluded between them.

4. If a State Party which makes extradition conditional on the existence of a treaty receives a request for extradition from another State Party with which it has no extradition treaty, it may consider this Convention as the necessary legal basis for extradition in respect of the offence of enforced disappearance.

5. States Parties which do not make extradition conditional on the existence of a treaty shall recognize the offence of enforced disappearance as an extraditable offence between themselves.

6. Extradition shall, in all cases, be subject to the conditions provided for by the law of the requested State Party or by applicable extradition treaties, including, in particular, conditions relating to the minimum penalty requirement for extradition and the grounds upon which

the requested State Party may refuse extradition or make it subject to certain conditions.

7. Nothing in this Convention shall be interpreted as imposing an obligation to extradite if the requested State Party has substantial grounds for believing that the request has been made for the purpose of prosecuting or punishing a person on account of that person's sex, race, religion, nationality, ethnic origin, political opinions or membership of a particular social group, or that compliance with the request would cause harm to that person for any one of these reasons.

Article 14

1. States Parties shall afford one another the greatest measure of mutual legal assistance in connection with criminal proceedings brought in respect of an offence of enforced disappearance, including the supply of all evidence at their disposal that is necessary for the proceedings.

2. Such mutual legal assistance shall be subject to the conditions provided for by the domestic law of the requested State Party or by applicable treaties on mutual legal assistance, including, in particular, the conditions in relation to the grounds upon which the requested State Party may refuse to grant mutual legal assistance or may make it subject to conditions.

Article 15

States Parties shall cooperate with each other and shall afford one another the greatest measure of mutual assistance with a view to assisting victims of enforced disappearance, and in searching for, locating and releasing disappeared persons and, in the event of death, in exhuming and identifying them and returning their remains.

Article 16

1. No State Party shall expel, return ("refouler"), surrender or extradite a person to another State where there are substantial grounds for believing that he or she would be in danger of being subjected to enforced disappearance.

2. For the purpose of determining whether there are such grounds, the competent authorities shall take into account all relevant considerations, including, where applicable, the existence in the State concerned of a consistent pattern of gross, flagrant or mass violations of human rights or of serious violations of international humanitarian law.

Article 17

1. No one shall be held in secret detention.

2. Without prejudice to other international obligations of the State Party with regard to the deprivation of liberty, each State Party shall, in its legislation:

(a) Establish the conditions under which orders of deprivation of liberty may be given;

(b) Indicate those authorities authorized to order the deprivation of liberty;

(c) Guarantee that any person deprived of liberty shall be held solely in officially recognized and supervised places of deprivation of liberty;

(d) Guarantee that any person deprived of liberty shall be authorized to communicate with and be visited by his or her family, counsel or any other person of his or her choice, subject only to the conditions established by law, or, if he or she is a foreigner, to communicate with his or her consular authorities, in accordance with applicable international law;

(e) Guarantee access by the competent and legally authorized authorities and institutions to the places where persons are deprived of liberty, if necessary with prior authorization from a judicial authority;

(f) Guarantee that any person deprived of liberty or, in the case of a suspected enforced disappearance, since the person deprived of liberty is not able to exercise this right, any persons with a legitimate interest, such as relatives of the person deprived of liberty, their representatives or their counsel, shall, in all circumstances, be entitled to take proceedings before a court, in order that the court may decide without delay on the lawfulness of the deprivation of liberty and order the person's release if such deprivation of liberty is not lawful.

3. Each State Party shall assure the compilation and maintenance of one or more up-to-date official registers and/or records of persons deprived of liberty, which shall be made promptly available, upon request, to any judicial or other competent authority or institution authorized for that purpose by the law of the State Party concerned or any relevant international legal instrument to which the State concerned is a party. The information contained therein shall include, as a minimum:

(a) The identity of the person deprived of liberty;

(b) The date, time and place where the person was deprived of liberty and the identity of the authority that deprived the person of liberty;

(c) The authority that ordered the deprivation of liberty and the grounds for the deprivation of liberty;

(d) The authority responsible for supervising the deprivation of liberty;

(e) The place of deprivation of liberty, the date and time of admission to the place of deprivation of liberty and the authority responsible for the place of deprivation of liberty;

(f) Elements relating to the state of health of the person deprived of liberty;

(g) In the event of death during the deprivation of liberty, the circumstances and cause of death and the destination of the remains;

(h) The date and time of release or transfer to another place of detention, the destination and the authority responsible for the transfer.

Article 18

1. Subject to articles 19 and 20, each State Party shall guarantee to any person with a legitimate interest in this information, such as relatives of the person deprived of liberty, their representatives or their counsel, access to at least the following information:

(a) The authority that ordered the deprivation of liberty;

(b) The date, time and place where the person was deprived of liberty and admitted to the place of deprivation of liberty;

(c) The authority responsible for supervising the deprivation of liberty;

(d) The whereabouts of the person deprived of liberty, including, in the event of a transfer to another place of deprivation of liberty, the destination and the authority responsible for the transfer;

(e) The date, time and place of release;

(f) Elements relating to the state of health of the person deprived of liberty;

(g) In the event of death during the deprivation of liberty, the circumstances

and cause of death and the destination of the remains.

2. Appropriate measures shall be taken, where necessary, to protect the persons referred to in paragraph 1 of this article, as well as persons participating in the investigation, from any ill-treatment, intimidation or sanction as a result of the search for information concerning a person deprived of liberty.

Article 19

1. Personal information, including medical and genetic data, which is collected and/or transmitted within the framework of the search for a disappeared person shall not be used or made available for purposes other than the search for the disappeared person. This is without prejudice to the use of such information in criminal proceedings relating to an offence of enforced disappearance or the exercise of the right to obtain reparation.

2. The collection, processing, use and storage of personal information, including medical and genetic data, shall not infringe or have the effect of infringing the human rights, fundamental freedoms or human dignity of an individual.

Article 20

1. Only where a person is under the protection of the law and the deprivation of liberty is subject to judicial control may the right to information referred to in article 18 be restricted, on an exceptional basis, where strictly necessary and where provided for by law, and if the transmission of the information would adversely affect the privacy or safety of the person, hinder a criminal investigation, or for other equivalent reasons in accordance with the law, and in conformity with applicable international law and with the objectives of this Convention. In no case shall there be restrictions on the right to information referred to in article 18 that could constitute conduct defined in article 2 or be in violation of article 17, paragraph 1.

2. Without prejudice to consideration of the lawfulness of the deprivation of a person's liberty, States Parties shall guarantee to the persons referred to in article 18, paragraph 1, the right to a prompt and effective judicial remedy as a means of obtaining without delay the information referred to in article 18, paragraph 1. This right to a remedy may not be suspended or restricted in any circumstances.

Article 21

Each State Party shall take the necessary measures to ensure that persons deprived of liberty are released in a manner permitting reliable verification that they have actually been released. Each State Party shall also take the necessary measures to assure the physical integrity of such persons and their ability to exercise fully their rights at the time of release, without prejudice to any obligations to which such persons may be subject under national law.

Article 22

Without prejudice to article 6, each State Party shall take the necessary measures to prevent and impose sanctions for the following conduct:

(a) Delaying or obstructing the remedies referred to in article 17, paragraph 2 *(f)*, and article 20, paragraph 2;

(b) Failure to record the deprivation of liberty of any person, or the recording of any information which the official responsible for the official register knew or should have known to be inaccurate;

(c) Refusal to provide information on the deprivation of liberty of a person, or the provision of inaccurate information, even though the legal requirements for providing such information have been met.

Article 23

1. Each State Party shall ensure that the training of law enforcement personnel, civil or military, medical personnel, public officials and other persons who may be involved in the custody or treatment of any person deprived of liberty includes the necessary education and information regarding the relevant provisions of this Convention, in order to:

(a) Prevent the involvement of such officials in enforced disappearances;

(b) Emphasize the importance of prevention and investigations in relation to enforced disappearances;

(c) Ensure that the urgent need to resolve cases of enforced disappearance is recognized.

2. Each State Party shall ensure that orders or instructions prescribing, authorizing or encouraging enforced disappearance are prohibited. Each State Party shall guarantee that a person who refuses to obey such an order will not be punished.

3. Each State Party shall take the necessary measures to ensure that the persons referred to in paragraph 1 of this article who have reason to believe that an enforced disappearance has occurred or is planned report the matter to their superiors and, where necessary, to the appropriate authorities or bodies vested with powers of review or remedy.

Article 24

1. For the purposes of this Convention, "victim" means the disappeared person and any individual who has suffered harm as the direct result of an enforced disappearance.

2. Each victim has the right to know the truth regarding the circumstances of the enforced disappearance, the progress and results of the investigation and the fate

of the disappeared person. Each State Party shall take appropriate measures in this regard.

3. Each State Party shall take all appropriate measures to search for, locate and release disappeared persons and, in the event of death, to locate, respect and return their remains.

4. Each State Party shall ensure in its legal system that the victims of enforced disappearance have the right to obtain reparation and prompt, fair and adequate compensation.

5. The right to obtain reparation referred to in paragraph 4 of this article covers material and moral damages and, where appropriate, other forms of reparation such as:

(a) Restitution;

(b) Rehabilitation;

(c) Satisfaction, including restoration of dignity and reputation;

(d) Guarantees of non-repetition.

6. Without prejudice to the obligation to continue the investigation until the fate of the disappeared person has been clarified, each State Party shall take the appropriate steps with regard to the legal situation of disappeared persons whose fate has not been clarified and that of their relatives, in fields such as social welfare, financial matters, family law and property rights.

7. Each State Party shall guarantee the right to form and participate freely in organizations and associations concerned with attempting to establish the circumstances of enforced disappearances and the fate of disappeared persons, and to assist victims of enforced disappearance.

Article 25

1. Each State Party shall take the necessary measures to prevent and punish under its criminal law:

(a) The wrongful removal of children who are subjected to enforced disappearance, children whose father, mother or legal guardian is subjected to enforced disappearance or children born during the captivity of a mother subjected to enforced disappearance;

(b) The falsification, concealment or destruction of documents attesting to the true identity of the children referred to in subparagraph *(a)* above.

2. Each State Party shall take the necessary measures to search for and identify the children referred to in paragraph 1 *(a)* of this article and to return them to their families of origin, in accordance with legal procedures and applicable international agreements.

3. States Parties shall assist one another in searching for, identifying and locating the children referred to in paragraph 1 *(a)* of this article.

4. Given the need to protect the best interests of the children referred to in paragraph 1 *(a)* of this article and their right to preserve, or to have re-established, their identity, including their nationality, name and family relations as recognized by law, States Parties which recognize a system of adoption or other form of placement of children shall have legal procedures in place to review the adoption or placement procedure, and, where appropriate, to annul any adoption or placement of children that originated in an enforced disappearance.

5. In all cases, and in particular in all matters relating to this article, the best interests of the child shall be a primary consideration, and a child who is capable of forming his or her own views shall have the right to express those views freely, the views of the child being given due weight in accordance with the age and maturity of the child.

Part II

Article 26

1. A Committee on Enforced Disappearances (hereinafter referred to as "the Committee") shall be established to carry out the functions provided for under this Convention. The Committee shall consist of ten experts of high moral character and recognized competence in the field of human rights, who shall serve in their personal capacity and be independent and impartial. The members of the Committee shall be elected by the States Parties according to equitable geographical distribution. Due account shall be taken of the usefulness of the participation in the work of the Committee of persons having relevant legal experience and of balanced gender representation.

2. The members of the Committee shall be elected by secret ballot from a list of persons nominated by States Parties from among their nationals, at biennial meetings of the States Parties convened by the Secretary-General of the United Nations for this purpose. At those meetings, for which two thirds of the States Parties shall constitute a quorum, the persons elected to the Committee shall be those who obtain the largest number of votes and an absolute majority of the votes of the representatives of States Parties present and voting.

3. The initial election shall be held no later than six months after the date of entry into force of this Convention. Four months before the date of each election, the Secretary-General of the United Nations shall address a letter to the States Parties inviting them to submit nominations within three months. The Secretary-General shall prepare a list in alphabetical order of all persons thus nominated, indicating the State Party which nominated each candidate, and shall submit this list to all States Parties.

4. The members of the Committee shall be elected for a term of four years. They shall be eligible for re-election once. However, the term of five of the members elected at the first election shall expire at the end of two years; immediately after the first election, the names of these five members shall be chosen by lot by the chairman of the meeting referred to in paragraph 2 of this article.

5. If a member of the Committee dies or resigns or for any other reason can no longer perform his or her Committee duties, the State Party which nominated him or her shall, in accordance with the criteria set out in paragraph 1 of this article, appoint another candidate from among its nationals to serve out his or her term, subject to the approval of the majority of the States Parties. Such approval shall be considered to have been obtained unless half or more of the States Parties respond negatively within six weeks of having been informed by

the Secretary-General of the United Nations of the proposed appointment.

6. The Committee shall establish its own rules of procedure.

7. The Secretary-General of the United Nations shall provide the Committee with the necessary means, staff and facilities for the effective performance of its functions. The Secretary-General of the United Nations shall convene the initial meeting of the Committee.

8. The members of the Committee shall be entitled to the facilities, privileges and immunities of experts on mission for the United Nations, as laid down in the relevant sections of the Convention on the Privileges and Immunities of the United Nations.

9. Each State Party shall cooperate with the Committee and assist its members in the fulfilment of their mandate, to the extent of the Committee's functions that the State Party has accepted.

Article 27

A Conference of the States Parties will take place at the earliest four years and at the latest six years following the entry into force of this Convention to evaluate the functioning of the Committee and to decide, in accordance with the procedure described in article 44, paragraph 2, whether it is appropriate to transfer to another body—without excluding any possibility—the monitoring of this Convention, in accordance with the functions defined in articles 28 to 36.

Article 28

1. In the framework of the competencies granted by this Convention, the Committee shall cooperate with all relevant organs, offices and specialized agencies and funds of the United Nations, with the treaty bodies instituted by international instruments, with the special procedures of the United Nations and with the relevant regional intergovernmental organizations or bodies, as well as with all relevant State institutions, agencies or offices working towards the protection of all persons against enforced disappearances.

2. As it discharges its mandate, the Committee shall consult other treaty bodies instituted by relevant international human rights instruments, in particular the Human Rights Committee instituted by the International Covenant on Civil and Political Rights, with a view to ensuring the consistency of their respective observations and recommendations.

Article 29

1. Each State Party shall submit to the Committee, through the Secretary-General of the United Nations, a report on the measures taken to give effect to its obligations under this Convention, within two years after the entry into force of this Convention for the State Party concerned.

2. The Secretary-General of the United Nations shall make this report available to all States Parties.

3. Each report shall be considered by the Committee, which shall issue such comments, observations or recommendations as it may deem appropriate. The comments, observations or recommendations shall be communicated to the State Party concerned, which may respond to them, on its own initiative or at the request of the Committee.

4. The Committee may also request States Parties to provide additional information on the implementation of this Convention.

Article 30

1. A request that a disappeared person should be sought and found may be submitted to the Committee, as a matter of urgency, by relatives of the disappeared person or their legal representatives, their counsel or any person authorized by them, as well as by any other person having a legitimate interest.

2. If the Committee considers that a request for urgent action submitted in pursuance of paragraph 1 of this article:

(a) Is not manifestly unfounded;

(b) Does not constitute an abuse of the right of submission of such requests;

(c) Has already been duly presented to the competent bodies of the State Party concerned, such as those authorized to undertake investigations, where such a possibility exists;

(d) Is not incompatible with the provisions of this Convention; and

(e) The same matter is not being examined under another procedure of international investigation or settlement of the same nature;

it shall request the State Party concerned to provide it with information on the situation of the persons sought, within a time limit set by the Committee.

3. In the light of the information provided by the State Party concerned in accordance with paragraph 2 of this article, the Committee may transmit recommendations to the State Party, including a request that the State Party should take all the necessary measures, including interim measures, to locate and protect the person concerned in accordance with this Convention and to inform the Committee, within a specified period of time, of measures taken, taking into account the urgency of the situation. The Committee shall inform the person submitting the urgent action request of its recommendations and of the information provided to it by the State as it becomes available.

4. The Committee shall continue its efforts to work with the State Party concerned for as long as the fate of the person sought remains unresolved. The person presenting the request shall be kept informed.

Article 31

1. A State Party may at the time of ratification of this Convention or at any time afterwards declare that it recognizes the competence of the Committee to receive and consider communications from or on behalf of individuals subject to its jurisdiction claiming to be victims of a violation by this State Party of provisions of this Convention. The Committee shall not admit any communication concerning a State Party which has not made such a declaration.

2. The Committee shall consider a communication inadmissible where:

(a) The communication is anonymous;

(b) The communication constitutes an abuse of the right of submission of such communications or is incompatible with the provisions of this Convention;

(c) The same matter is being examined under another procedure of international investigation or settlement of the same nature; or where

(d) All effective available domestic remedies have not been exhausted. This rule shall not apply where the application of the remedies is unreasonably prolonged.

3. If the Committee considers that the communication meets the requirements set out in paragraph 2 of this article, it shall transmit the communication to the State Party concerned, requesting it to provide observations and comments within a time limit set by the Committee.

4. At any time after the receipt of a communication and before a determination on the merits has been reached, the Committee may transmit to the State Party concerned for its urgent consideration a request that the State Party will take such interim measures as may be necessary to avoid possible irreparable damage to the victims of the alleged violation. Where the Committee exercises its discretion, this does not imply a determination on admissibility or on the merits of the communication.

5. The Committee shall hold closed meetings when examining communications under the present article. It shall inform the author of a communication of the responses provided by the State Party concerned. When the Committee decides to finalize the procedure, it shall communicate its views to the State Party and to the author of the communication.

Article 32

A State Party to this Convention may at any time declare that it recognizes the competence of the Committee to receive and consider communications in which a State Party claims that another State Party is not fulfilling its obligations under this Convention. The Committee shall not receive communications concerning a State Party which has not made such a declaration, nor communications from a State Party which has not made such a declaration.

Article 33

1. If the Committee receives reliable information indicating that a State Party is seriously violating the provisions of this Convention, it may, after consultation with the State Party concerned, request one or more of its members to undertake a visit and report back to it without delay.

2. The Committee shall notify the State Party concerned, in writing, of its intention to organize a visit, indicating the composition of the delegation and the purpose of the visit. The State Party shall answer the Committee within a reasonable time.

3. Upon a substantiated request by the State Party, the Committee may decide to postpone or cancel its visit.

4. If the State Party agrees to the visit, the Committee and the State Party concerned shall work together to define the modalities of the visit and the State Party shall provide the Committee with all the facilities needed for the successful completion of the visit.

5. Following its visit, the Committee shall communicate to the State Party concerned its observations and recommendations.

Article 34

If the Committee receives information which appears to it to contain well-founded indications that enforced disappearance is being practised on a widespread or systematic basis in the territory under the jurisdiction of a State Party, it may, after seeking from the State Party concerned all relevant information on the situation, urgently bring the matter to the attention of the General Assembly of the United Nations, through the Secretary-General of the United Nations.

Article 35

1. The Committee shall have competence solely in respect of enforced disappearances which commenced after the entry into force of this Convention.

2. If a State becomes a party to this Convention after its entry into force, the obligations of that State vis-à-vis the Committee shall relate only to enforced disappearances which commenced after the entry into force of this Convention for the State concerned.

Article 36

1. The Committee shall submit an annual report on its activities under this Convention to the States Parties and to the General Assembly of the United Nations.

2. Before an observation on a State Party is published in the annual report, the State Party concerned shall be informed in advance and shall be given reasonable time to answer. This State Party may request the publication of its comments or observations in the report.

Part III

Article 37

Nothing in this Convention shall affect any provisions which are more conducive to the protection of all persons from enforced disappearance and which may be contained in:

(a) The law of a State Party;

(b) International law in force for that State.

Article 38

1. This Convention is open for signature by all Member States of the United Nations.

2. This Convention is subject to ratification by all Member States of the United Nations. Instruments of ratification shall be deposited with the Secretary-General of the United Nations.

3. This Convention is open to accession by all Member States of the United Nations. Accession shall be effected by the deposit of an instrument of accession with the Secretary-General.

Article 39

1. This Convention shall enter into force on the thirtieth day after the date of deposit with the Secretary-General of the United Nations of the twentieth instrument of ratification or accession.

2. For each State ratifying or acceding to this Convention after the deposit of the twentieth instrument of ratification or accession, this Convention shall enter into force on the thirtieth day after the date of the deposit of that State's instrument of ratification or accession.

Article 40

The Secretary-General of the United Nations shall notify all States Members of the United Nations and all States which have signed or acceded to this Convention of the following:

(a) Signatures, ratifications and accessions under article 38;

(b) The date of entry into force of this Convention under article 39.

Article 41

The provisions of this Convention shall apply to all parts of federal States without any limitations or exceptions.

Article 42

1. Any dispute between two or more States Parties concerning the interpretation or application of this Convention which cannot be settled through negotiation or by the procedures expressly provided for in this Convention shall, at the request of one of them, be submitted to arbitration. If within six months from the date of the request for arbitration the Parties are unable to agree on the organization of the arbitration, any one of those Parties may refer the dispute to the International Court of Justice by request in conformity with the Statute of the Court.

2. A State may, at the time of signature or ratification of this Convention or accession thereto, declare that it does not consider itself bound by paragraph 1 of this article. The other States Parties shall not be bound by paragraph 1 of this article with respect to any State Party having made such a declaration.

3. Any State Party having made a declaration in accordance with the provisions of paragraph 2 of this article may at any time withdraw this declaration by notification to the Secretary-General of the United Nations.

Article 43

This Convention is without prejudice to the provisions of international humanitarian law, including the obligations of the High Contracting Parties to the four Geneva Conventions of 12 August 1949 and the two Additional Protocols thereto of 8 June 1977, or to the opportunity available to any State Party to authorize the International Committee of the Red Cross to visit places of detention in situations not covered by international humanitarian law.

Article 44

1. Any State Party to this Convention may propose an amendment and file it with the Secretary-General of the United Nations. The Secretary-General shall thereupon communicate the proposed amendment to the States Parties to this Convention with a request that they indicate whether they favour a conference of States Parties for the purpose of considering and voting upon the proposal. In the event that within four months from the date of such communication at least one third of the States Parties favour such a conference, the Secretary-General shall convene the conference under the auspices of the United Nations.

2. Any amendment adopted by a majority of two thirds of the States Parties present and voting at the conference shall be submitted by the Secretary-General of the United Nations to all the States Parties for acceptance.

3. An amendment adopted in accordance with paragraph 1 of this article shall enter into force when two thirds of the States Parties to this Convention have accepted it in accordance with their respective constitutional processes.

4. When amendments enter into force, they shall be binding on those States Parties which have accepted them, other States Parties still being bound by the provisions of this Convention and any earlier amendment which they have accepted.

Article 45

1. This Convention, of which the Arabic, Chinese, English, French, Russian and Spanish texts are equally authentic, shall be deposited with the Secretary-General of the United Nations.

2. The Secretary-General of the United Nations shall transmit certified copies of this Convention to all States referred to in article 38.

Other activities

Follow-up to 1993 World Conference

Report of High Commissioner. In a February report [E.CN/4/2006/10] on follow-up to the World Conference on Human Rights [YUN 1993, p. 908], the High Commissioner described OHCHR activities undertaken in the past year, aimed at strengthening country engagement and the Office's thematic expertise at forging linkages between human rights and development, fostering partnerships with civil society and within the UN system and empowering rights-holders. The report presented the High Commissioner's Strategic Management Plan 2006-2007 (see p. 766) and addressed the leadership role of the High Commissioner, against the background of the reform of the UN human rights machinery and the establishment of the Council. The High Commissioner observed that the special procedures, a system developed by the Commission over the years, had played a crucial role and should be transferred to the Council. For its part, the Council should preserve a close relationship with civil society through national institutions and NGOs, and maintain the ability to address human rights violations wherever they occurred. In that regard, the establishment of a universal periodic review system (see p. 761) could prove valuable in reducing the potential for polarization and politicization. It would also be helpful if the Council could meet more frequently and there were increased capabilities in technical cooperation and advisory services.

On 20 December, the Assembly took note of the Third Committee's report [A/61/443/Add.4] on the implementation of and follow-up to the Vienna Declaration and programme of Action, adopted at the 1993 World Conference (**decision 61/530**).

Human rights education

World Programme for Human Rights Education

Report of High Commissioner. In response to a 2005 Commission request [YUN 2005, p. 745], the High Commissioner submitted a February report [E/CN/4/2006/90] on events relating to the World Programme for Human Rights Education, proclaimed by the General Assembly in 2004 [YUN 2004, p. 678], and on associated activities carried out by OHCHR. The Assembly, by resolution 59/113 B [YUN 2005, p. 745], had adopted the Plan of Action for the World Programme's first phase (2005-2007), which focused on primary and secondary school systems. Since the Plan's adoption, OHCHR and the United Nations Educational, Scientific and Cultural Organization (UNESCO) had carried out joint activities to disseminate it, including through a joint message to the Human Rights Education listserv, an international human rights education electronic network that reached out to more than 3,500 human rights educators in some 160 countries. Earlier in the year, the High Commissioner, the UNESCO Director-General and the Council of Europe's Secretary-General had addressed personal letters to education ministers to encourage the Plan's implementation and offer assistance. In further joint action, OHCHR and UNESCO teamed up to publish a booklet on the Plan [ED-2006/WS/53], which provided ideas for developing new initiatives, explaining existing ones and enhancing cooperation and partnership. OHCHR also contributed to the implementation of the World Programme and its Plan of Action by facilitating information-sharing and networking through its online database on human rights education and other training resources, fostering national capacities for human rights education and training through its technical cooperation programme, supporting grass-roots human rights education initiatives through the Assisting Communities Together Project, a joint OHCHR-UNDP initiative providing small grants to NGOs for community-based human rights education and training, and by developing human rights training and education materials and disseminating globally the Universal Declaration of Human Rights.

Subcommission action. On 24 August [res. 2006/19], the Subcommission recommended that human rights treaty bodies, when examining reports of States parties, devote attention to human rights education, particularly in the framework of the World Programme, and that the item be included in the agenda of the annual meeting of the treaty bodies to enable them to make recommendations on how human rights education could contribute to national human rights capacity-building.

Human Rights Council action. On 20 November [A/62/53 (2/116)], the Council deferred to its fourth session consideration of a draft decision submitted by Argentina, Guatemala and Uruguay, together with two non-members of the Council (Costa Rica, Croatia), by which the Council would encourage all States to develop initiatives within the World Programme for Human Rights Education and, in particular, to implement the related Plan of Action. It also requested the High Commissioner and UNESCO to promote and technically assist national implementation of the Plan.

National institutions and regional arrangements

Reports of Secretary-General. In response to a 2005 Commission request [YUN 2005, p. 748], the Secretary-General, in a January report [E/CN.4/2006/102] on national institutions and regional arrangements, provided information on the process utilized by the International Coordinating Committee (ICC) of national human rights institutions to accredit such institutions, in compliance with the principles relating to their status and functioning (Paris Principles), adopted by the General Assembly in 1993 [YUN 1993, p. 898], and on ways of enhancing participation of those institutions in the Commission's work.

To further strengthen the accreditation process, the report noted that ICC, at the request of its members, had instituted a more rigorous review process, which clarified that applications not completed by the two-month deadline prior to the holding of the ICC meeting could not be considered. Consistent with that criteria, national institutions had welcomed a strengthened process and recommendations of a regular reassessment. ICC was expected to make a decision as to the frequency of such reassessment at its next annual meeting. It was therefore recommended that accreditation of national institutions in international forums be commensurate with the institution's accreditation to ICC.

A later report of the Secretary-General [A/HRC/4/91], covering the period from January to December, provided information on OHCHR activities in 2006 to establish and strengthen national human rights institutions, measures taken by Governments and national institutions in that regard, cooperation between international mechanisms and institutions to promote and protect human rights, and the work of institutions on specific issues.

During the year, OHCHR provided advice and information on activities and issues, including on constitutional provisions, enabling legislation, advisory missions and rules and regulations relating to institutions in Angola, Burundi, Cambodia, Chile, Comoros, Côte d'Ivoire, France, Italy, Iraq, Maldives, Lesotho, Nepal, Nigeria, Pakistan, Serbia, Sierra Leone, Sri Lanka, the Sudan, Tajikistan, Timor-Leste, the United Kingdom (regarding Scotland), Uruguay and Zimbabwe. Such support was often provided in collaboration with UNDP and UN missions.

The OHCHR National Institutions Unit, in its capacity as the ICC secretariat, and its Subcommittee on Accreditation, provided substantive support to the seventeenth (Geneva, 12-13 April) and eighteenth (Santa Cruz, Bolivia, 26-27 October) sessions of ICC. In April, ICC considered the existing accreditation process, in light of guidelines for institutions wishing to access the Human Rights Council, and adopted a mechanism for periodic review of accreditation through a five-yearly re-accreditation process. In October, it addressed its accreditation process and the role of national institutions in the Council and the treaty body system. Discussions were also held on national institutions and early warning mechanisms.

OHCHR, in collaboration with Bolivia's national human rights institution and ICC, organized the Eighth International Conference of National Human Rights Institutions (Santa Cruz, Bolivia, 23-27 October), which had as its theme the role of national institutions in migration. The Conference was intended to strengthen cooperation between national institutions on migration as a human rights issue, promote the adoption of related strategies, establish guidelines for national institutions in addressing migrant issues and adopt a declaration on the role of national institutions in dealing with migration and human rights. Participants from 68 countries discussed how best to ensure and implement mechanisms for protecting migrants' rights and committed themselves to increase the positive aspects of migration and better address its negative consequences by adopting the Santa Cruz Declaration and Guidelines [A/HRC/4/91, annex], in which they embraced a human rights-based approach to migration.

Support was given to regional initiatives relating in particular to networks of national human rights institutions. In Africa, OHCHR aided the establishment of such a network, comprising 17 African States and designed to strengthen their effectiveness and encourage cooperation in serving the cause of human rights on the continent. At the subregional level, the Office was involved in consultations resulting in the establishment of a similar network for West African States. National human rights institutions were also assisted and support provided in various regions. In that regard, OHCHR helped organize or took part in numerous meetings, including a seminar aimed at promoting and protecting the right to education in the Americas and the Caribbean (Ecuador, 24-26 May); the eleventh Annual Meeting of the Asia Pacific Forum (Fiji, 31 July–3 August), which discussed the establishment of domestic and regional human rights mechanisms in the Pacific and the rights of human rights defenders; a meeting, under the auspices of the Organization for Security and Cooperation in Europe (OSCE) (Warsaw, Poland, 5 September), which discussed the establishment of a focal point within that Organization to liaise with national human rights institutions; the fourth Round Table of European National Institutions for the Promotion and Protection of Human Rights (27-28 September); the sixth meeting of the European Group of National Human Rights Institutions (Athens, Greece, 28-29 September); and the Fifth General Assembly of the Network of National Human Rights Institutions of the Americas (Buenos Aires, Argentina, 28 November).

OHCHR was also involved in supporting and conducting workshops, training courses and advisory missions to promote the activities of national human rights institutions in the Americas and the Caribbean, Africa, Asia and the Pacific, and Europe. Notable among those were: assessment of draft legislation for establishing a human rights commission in Scotland (January); advisory missions to Tajikistan (21-23 February), Timor Leste (24 March–1 April) and Kosovo, Serbia (16-19 May) to provide advice and support for the establishment of national human rights institutions and for the role of the Ombudsman; a consultation workshop, in collaboration with the UN Mission in the Sudan (UNMIS) (8 May), designed to promote consensus on the draft bill of the National Human Rights Commission Act; an international human rights training programme, under the auspices of the NGO Equitas (Montreal, Canada, 11-30 June); an induction programme for members of the Southern Sudan Human Rights Commission (Juba, the Sudan, 8-11 August); a stakeholder consultation workshop to facilitate the establishment of independent national human rights institutions in Lesotho (20-21 July) and Zimbabwe (21-24 September); a workshop on the mandate and functions of the Ombudsman (Luanda, Angola, 11-13 October), intended to support the work of that office; a mission to the Comoros (31 October–3 November) to assist the Parliament in the final review of enabling legislation for human rights institutions in the country; and a workshop (Rome, 5 December), which discussed the prospects of establishing similar institutions, their core functions, best practices and related draft bills. In the course of those activities, OHCHR assisted UN operations in the Sudan, Sierra Leone, Burundi, Iraq, and Tajikistan.

The report concluded that assistance to national human rights institutions was a key part of OHCHR efforts to engage countries in closing protection gaps. That involvement stemmed from the recognition of those institutions as central to national protection systems and of their role in ensuring that international norms were implemented. With OHCHR support, they had become more engaged in the Council and with treaty bodies and special procedures mandate-holders. OHCHR was responding to the increasing demand from Member States and other stakeholders for expertise, such as on models for establishing a constitutional or legislative framework and the nature, functions, powers and responsibilities of national institutions. The integration of activities relating to national human rights institutions throughout OHCHR had become a reality, and the United Nations could rely on them as implementing partners and not just as beneficiaries.

Regional arrangements

Report of Secretary-General. In response to General Assembly resolution 59/196 [YUN 2004, p. 682], the Secretary-General submitted an October report [A/61/513] on regional arrangements for the promotion and protection of human rights, focusing on OHCHR regional strategies and significant developments since 2005.

The report noted that OHCHR had been pursuing a regional and subregional approach towards more effective human rights promotion and protection, resorting to a broad range of strategies and tools to maximize the incorporation of human rights into the work of the United Nations and regional institutions. The regional approach had proved particularly valuable in engaging countries where OHCHR did not have an office. In Africa, OHCHR continued to provide assistance for incorporating human rights in the policies and programmes of the African Union (AU) through the establishment of new mechanisms, organization of conferences, training and support for peace processes. Within the framework of a global project entitled "Comprehensive support for the African Union in strengthening the promotion and protection of human rights in Africa", OHCHR provided financial and technical support to strengthen the human rights foundation of the AU, in order to maintain its focus on human rights issues and ensure the institutionalization of human rights in its agenda and work programme. With such assistance, AU strategic priorities for the next five years were developed to include a strong human rights agenda, with emphasis on building protection mechanisms at the country, subregional and regional levels through increased support for institutions and civil society organizations.

Through its regional office in Johannesburg, South Africa, OHCHR was responsible for the Centre for Human Rights and Democracy in Central Africa (Yaoundé), which continued to provide technical advice and assistance to the secretariat of the Economic Community of Central African States (ECCAS). The cooperation included the design of a legal framework for information management concerning freedom of movement in the subregion. Through its civil society capacity-building project, the Centre also contributed to the emerging partnership of ECCAS with civil society organizations. OHCHR initiated or participated in numerous activities with other subregional organizations on the continent, such as the Southern African Development Community (SADC) and the Economic Community of West African States (ECOWAS). Those activities included a May meeting between the UN Regional Directors Team for Southern Africa and SADC to discuss collaboration on issues relating to peace and security, political stability, good governance, the rule of law and enhancement of democracy, the fight against poverty, food security, HIV/AIDS, tuberculosis and malaria.

In the Arab region, OHCHR and the League of Arab States cooperated in the revision of the Arab Human Rights Charter, capacity-building for the League staff and the organization of regional conferences on national human rights institutions. Within the framework of memoranda of understanding on human rights cooperation, which it signed previously with the Organization of the Islamic Conference (OIC) and the Islamic Educational, Scientific and Cultural Organization (ISESCO), OHCHR organized activities, including a January training seminar on international and regional systems for the staff of both organizations.

In Asia and the Pacific, the OHCHR regional office for South-East Asia assisted member States of the Association of South-East Asian Nations (ASEAN) in ratifying and implementing international human rights instruments, establishing a regional human rights mechanism, developing legislation in conformity with international human rights standards and building capacity in the administration of justice. The regional office also advised the Economic and Social Commission for Asia and the Pacific on the human rights aspects of its activities and provided support to the resident coordinators and UN country teams in the region.

In Europe, OHCHR maintained close cooperation with the Council of Europe, particularly through its field offices, which facilitated the visit of the High Commissioner in 2006 to the northern Caucasus and South-East Europe. In Bosnia and Herzegovina, OHCHR and the Council of Europe continued cooperation on legal technical expertise, while in Kosovo (Serbia), OHCHR focused on capacity-building and policy advice with the authorities, the ombudsperson and the UN Interim Administration Mission in Kosovo. In the former Yugoslav Republic of Macedonia, cooperation was directed at efforts to promote and follow up the plan of action for the first phase of the World Programme of Human Rights Education.

In Latin America and the Caribbean, the OHCHR regional office continued to organize and participate in various seminars and workshops, and to support the incorporation of human rights in the activities of the Economic Commission for Latin America and the Caribbean and the UN country teams in the region. In collaboration with UNDP, OHCHR supported the UN monitoring process in Ecuador, which led to the appointment and establishment of the Supreme Court of Justice in that country. It provided grants to the Inter-American Institute of Human Rights to support an OHCHR human rights chair at its annual training course, with a view to increasing awareness of UN human rights mechanisms and the work of the Office.

GENERAL ASSEMBLY ACTION

On 19 December [meeting 81], the General Assembly, on the recommendation of the Third Committee [A/61/443/Add.2 & Corr.1], adopted **resolution 61/167** without vote [agenda item 67 *(b)*].

Regional arrangements for the promotion and protection of human rights

The General Assembly,

Recalling its resolution 32/127 of 16 December 1977 and its subsequent resolutions concerning regional arrangements for the promotion and protection of human rights,

Recalling also Commission on Human Rights resolution 1993/51 of 9 March 1993 and its subsequent resolutions in this regard,

Bearing in mind the relevant resolutions of the Commission concerning advisory services and technical cooperation in the field of human rights, including its most recent on that subject, resolution 2004/81 of 21 April 2004,

Bearing in mind also the Vienna Declaration and Programme of Action adopted by the World Conference on Human Rights on 25 June 1993, which reiterates, inter alia, the need to consider the possibility of establishing regional and subregional arrangements for the promotion and protection of human rights where they do not already exist,

Recalling that the World Conference recommended that more resources should be made available for the strengthening of regional arrangements for the promotion and protection of human rights under the programme of technical cooperation in the field of human rights of the Office of the United Nations High Commissioner for Human Rights,

Reaffirming that regional arrangements play an important role in promoting and protecting human rights and should reinforce universal human rights standards, as contained in international human rights instruments,

Welcoming the fact that the Office of the High Commissioner has been systematically pursuing a regional and subregional approach through a variety of complementary means and methods, in order to maximize the impact of the activities of the United Nations at the national level, and that the Office intends to establish new regional offices,

1. *Takes note with satisfaction* of the report of the Secretary-General;

2. *Welcomes* the continuing cooperation and assistance of the Office of the United Nations High Commissioner for Human Rights in the further strengthening of the existing regional arrangements and regional machinery for the promotion and protection of human rights, in particular through technical cooperation aimed at national capacity-building, public information and education, with a view to exchanging information and experience in the field of human rights;

3. *Also welcomes*, in that respect, the close cooperation of the Office of the High Commissioner in the organization of regional and subregional training courses and workshops in the field of human rights, high-level governmental expert meetings and regional conferences of national human rights institutions, aimed at creating greater understanding in the regions of issues concerning the promotion and protection of human rights, improving procedures and examining the various systems for the

promotion and protection of universally accepted human rights standards and identifying obstacles to ratification of the principal international human rights treaties and strategies to overcome them;

4. *Recognizes*, therefore, that progress in promoting and protecting all human rights depends primarily on efforts made at the national and local levels, and that the regional approach should imply intensive cooperation and coordination with all partners involved, while bearing in mind the importance of international cooperation;

5. *Stresses* the importance of the programme of technical cooperation in the field of human rights, renews its appeal to all Governments to consider making use of the possibilities offered by the United Nations under the programme of organizing information or training courses at the national level for government personnel on the application of international human rights standards and the experience of relevant international bodies, and notes with satisfaction, in that respect, the establishment of technical cooperation projects with Governments of all regions;

6. *Welcomes* the growing exchanges between the United Nations and the United Nations human rights treaty bodies, on the one hand, and regional organizations and institutions, such as the African Commission on Human and Peoples' Rights, the Community of Portuguese-speaking Countries, the Council of Europe, the Inter-American Commission on Human Rights, the International Organization of la Francophonie, the League of Arab States, the Organization for Security and Cooperation in Europe and other regional institutions, on the other;

7. *Also welcomes* the placement by the Office of the High Commissioner of regional representatives in subregions and in regional commissions, in particular the deployment to Bishkek of a regional representative for Central Asia;

8. *Further welcomes* the progress achieved in the establishment of regional and subregional arrangements for the promotion and protection of human rights, and, in this regard, notes with interest:

(a) The increasing cooperation between the Office of the High Commissioner and African organizations and suborganizations, in particular the African Union, the Economic Community of Central African States, the Economic Community of West African States and the Southern African Development Community;

(b) The support provided by the Office of the High Commissioner to the African Union for the strengthening of the promotion and protection of human rights in Africa, and welcomes in this regard the establishment of the African Court on Human and Peoples' Rights;

(c) The increased, valuable sharing of concrete national experiences at the thirteenth Workshop on Regional Cooperation for the Promotion and Protection of Human Rights in the Asia-Pacific Region, held in Beijing from 30 August to 2 September 2005, regarding the implementation of the Regional Framework for the Promotion and Protection of Human Rights in the Asia-Pacific Region, which contributes to the enhancement of the promotion and protection of human rights in the region, and welcomes in this regard the establishment in Suva of an office of the High Commissioner for the Pacific region and the steps undertaken by the Office of the High Commissioner to set up a United Nations human rights training and documentation centre for South-West Asia and the Arab region, pursuant to General Assembly resolution 60/153 of 16 December 2005;

(d) The ongoing consultations among Governments aimed at the possible establishment of regional human rights arrangements held in the context of the Regional Framework, with the support and advice of national human rights institutions and civil society organizations of the Asia-Pacific region;

(e) Activities undertaken within the framework of the regional project of the Office of the High Commissioner for the promotion and protection of human rights in the Latin American and Caribbean region and the strengthening of the cooperation between the Office of the High Commissioner, the Inter-American Commission on Human Rights and the Organization of American States;

(f) Activities undertaken within the framework of cooperation between the Office of the High Commissioner and the League of Arab States;

(g) The continued cooperation towards the realization of universal standards between the Office of the High Commissioner and regional organizations in Europe and Central Asia, namely, the Council of Europe, the European Union and the Organization for Security and Cooperation in Europe, in particular for activities at the country level;

9. *Invites* States in areas in which regional arrangements in the field of human rights do not yet exist to consider, with the support and advice of national human rights institutions and civil society organizations, concluding agreements with a view to establishing, within their respective regions, suitable regional machinery for the promotion and protection of human rights;

10. *Requests* the Secretary-General to continue to strengthen exchanges between the United Nations and regional intergovernmental organizations dealing with human rights and to make available adequate resources from within the regular budget of technical cooperation to the activities of the Office of the High Commissioner to promote regional arrangements;

11. *Requests* the Office of the High Commissioner to continue to pay special attention to the most appropriate ways of assisting countries of the various regions, at their request, under the programme of technical cooperation and to make, where necessary, relevant recommendations, and in this regard welcomes the decision of the Office to strengthen national protection systems in accordance with action 2 of the reform programme of the Secretary-General;

12. *Invites* the Secretary-General to provide, in the report that he will submit to the Human Rights Council at its fourth session, information on progress made since the adoption of the Vienna Declaration and Programme of Action on reinforcing the exchange of information

and extending collaboration between the organs of the United Nations dealing with human rights and regional organizations in the field of the promotion and protection of human rights;

13. *Requests* the Secretary-General to submit to the General Assembly at its sixty-third session a report on the state of regional arrangements for the promotion and protection of human rights, formulating concrete proposals and recommendations on ways and means to strengthen cooperation between the United Nations and regional arrangements in the field of human rights, and to include therein the results of action taken in pursuance of the present resolution;

14. *Decides* to consider the question further at its sixty-third session.

Africa

In response to General Assembly resolution 60/151 [YUN 2005, p. 753], the Secretary-General submitted a September report [A/61/352] providing an overview of the activities of the Subregional Centre for Human Rights and Democracy in Central Africa, from November 2005 to September 2006.

Those activities included support to the capacity-building of national human rights institutions through training and technical cooperation activities, human rights education and dissemination of information and documentation; support to peace processes in the subregion; and development of partnerships with UN agencies, research and academic institutions, regional human rights mechanisms and civil society organizations. Within that context, OHCHR supported the International Conference on the Great Lakes region (see p. 124), mostly through participation in related subregional meetings in January and February. The Conference resulted in the incorporation of human rights in all draft protocols, programmes of action and projects, and in the establishment of a regional legal framework on the prevention and elimination of genocide, protection of internally displaced persons, the rights to property of returnees and the media. The Centre also provided support to Governments, national human rights institutions and civil society organizations, such as Cameroon's National Commission on Human Rights and Freedoms, which was assisted in elaborating the human rights curricula for educational institutions, culminating in the adoption in February of the related *Cahiers pédagogiques* that was considered an important contribution to the implementation of the World Programme for Human Rights Education. The Centre and UNDP also developed a project to support Cameroon to consolidate the rule of law and promote human rights, under which they assisted the country's Justice Ministry in publishing the first governmental report on the situation of human rights in Cameroon. In addition, the Centre helped organize a joint subregional workshop on the role of civil society organizations in conflict prevention and peacebuilding in Central Africa (Douala, Cameroon, 10-12 April), aimed at strengthening their role in conflict prevention and peacebuilding. At the request of the Congo, the Centre, with OHCHR and the International Labour Organization (ILO), provided technical assistance in the elaboration of a draft law on pigmies and helped organize two workshops in May and July (Brazzaville, Congo) to ensure the participation of indigenous representatives and civil society in the process.

The Centre maintained its three-month internship programme for four fellows at a time, drawn from among the subregional States, under which the seventeenth, eighteenth and nineteenth batches of interns from seven Central African States completed their training. On the development of partnerships, the Centre continued to advance its collaboration with ECCAS, UN agencies and the UN Department of Political Affairs. It also organized a subregional workshop on human rights-based approaches to development for States members of the Economic and Monetary Community of Central Africa (Yaoundé, 26-28 June), which adopted the Yaoundé Consensus, recommending that participating Governments assess the implementation of human rights treaties at the national level, particularly the submission of reports to the treaty bodies, and to request support from country teams and the Yaoundé Centre in that regard. The Centre's plan of action for 2006–2007 reflected the priority thematic issues relevant to the Central African region, as defined by the High Commissioner's Plan of Action [YUN 2005, p. 715], which included the rule of law and the administration of justice, human rights, human security and development, discrimination and institutional capacity-building.

GENERAL ASSEMBLY ACTION

On 19 December [meeting 81], the General Assembly, on the recommendation of the Third Committee [A/61/443/Add.2 & Corr.1], adopted **resolution 61/158** without vote [agenda item 67 *(b)*].

Subregional Centre for Human Rights and Democracy in Central Africa

The General Assembly,

Recalling its resolution 55/105 of 4 December 2000 concerning regional arrangements for the promotion and protection of human rights,

Recalling also its resolutions 55/34 B of 20 November 2000 and 55/233 of 23 December 2000, section III of its resolution 55/234 of 23 December 2000, and its resolutions 58/176 of 22 December 2003, 59/183 of 20 December 2004 and 60/151 of 16 December 2005 on the Subregional Centre for Human Rights and Democracy in Central Africa,

Recalling further that the World Conference on Human Rights recommended that more resources be made available for the strengthening of regional arrangements for the promotion and protection of human rights under the programme of technical cooperation in the field of human rights of the Office of the United Nations High Commissioner for Human Rights,

Recalling the report of the High Commissioner,

Taking note of the holding of the twenty-third and twenty-fourth ministerial meetings of the United Nations Standing Advisory Committee on Security Questions in Central Africa in Brazzaville from 29 August to 2 September 2006 and in Kigali from 25 to 29 September 2006,

Taking note also of the report of the Secretary-General,

Welcoming the 2005 World Summit Outcome, in particular the decision confirmed therein to double the regular budget of the Office of the High Commissioner over the next five years,

1. *Welcomes* the activities of the Subregional Centre for Human Rights and Democracy in Central Africa at Yaoundé;
2. *Notes with satisfaction* the support provided for the establishment of the Centre by the host country;
3. *Requests* the Secretary-General and the United Nations High Commissioner for Human Rights to provide additional funds and human resources within the existing Office of the United Nations High Commissioner for Human Rights to enable the Centre to respond positively and effectively to the growing needs in the promotion and protection of human rights and in developing a culture of democracy and the rule of law in the Central African subregion;
4. *Requests* the Secretary-General to submit to the General Assembly at its sixty-second session a report on the implementation of the present resolution.

Asia and the Pacific

Human Rights Council action. On 8 December [A/62/53 (dec. 3/102)], the Council decided to convene the next session of the Workshop on Regional Cooperation for the Promotion and Protection of Human Rights in the Asian and Pacific Region in 2007, preferably in the first half of that year.

South West Asia and the Arab region

In response to General Assembly resolution 60/153 [YUN 2005, p. 754], the Secretary-General submitted a 15 September report [A/61/348] providing an overview of OHCHR activities towards the establishment of the United Nations Human Rights and Documentation Centre for South-West Asia and the Arab region, in cooperation with the host country, Qatar. The report noted that OHCHR had allocated human and financial resources for the 2006-2007 biennium to the Centre, which would comprise one international staff at the P-4 level to head the Centre and two locally recruited staff, to be funded by extrabudgetary resources. That staffing level was based on an assessment of the Centre's workload during the inception period. With an overall objective of strengthening a human rights culture and increasing related expertise at the regional and national levels, the Centre would help address two of the four implementation gaps identified in the High Commissioner's plan of action [YUN 2005, p. 715], namely, the knowledge gap and capacity gaps of rights-holders and duty-bearers. The Centre would provide training and expertise on reporting procedures to treaty bodies and assist in preparing user-friendly tools and in training trainers for Government officials, lawmakers and other professional groups and stakeholders. In addition, it would develop information and documentation systems on human rights, especially in Arabic, work with and strengthen national human rights institutions and civil society organizations and contribute to the implementation of the World Programme on Human Rights Education. Extrabudgetary resources amounting to $255,320 were allocated to the Centre for the 2006-2007 biennium.

In June, OHCHR submitted a draft agreement with Qatar and undertook a mission there in connection with plans to inaugurate the Centre during the year. After the mission, OHCHR welcomed the country's offer to provide the premises free of charge and felt it could start operations by year's end. The Office looked forward to finalizing the host country agreement, preferably after Qatar had ratified the Conventions on the Privileges and Immunities of the United Nations and of Specialized Agencies, as well as the medium-term funding agreement. OHCHR and the host country encouraged other countries to contribute to the funding of the Centre to facilitate its rapid development as a reference institution, to the benefit of the people of South-West Asia and the Arab region.

On 19 December, the General Assembly took note of the Secretary-General's report (**decision 61/529**).

Strengthening action to protect human rights

International cooperation in the field of human rights

Human Rights Council action. On 29 November [A/62/53 (dec. 2/116)], the Council deferred consideration of a draft decision [A/HRC/2/L.18] submitted by Cuba, on behalf of the Non-Aligned Movement, which requested the High Commissioner to consult States, intergovernmental organizations and NGOs on ways to enhance international cooperation and dialogue in the UN human rights machinery, aimed at ensuring respect for the principles of universality and non-selectivity in considering human rights issues and eliminating double standards and politicization, in accordance with General Assembly resolution 60/251 (see p. 757).

On 19 December, the Assembly reaffirmed the importance of such cooperation for promoting and protecting human rights (see below).

GENERAL ASSEMBLY ACTION

On 19 December [meeting 81], the General Assembly, on the recommendation of the Third Committee [A/61/443/Add.2 & Corr.1], adopted **resolution 61/168** without vote [agenda item 67 *(b)*].

Enhancement of international cooperation in the field of human rights

The General Assembly,

Reaffirming its commitment to promoting international cooperation, as set forth in the Charter of the United Nations, in particular Article 1, paragraph 3, as well as relevant provisions of the Vienna Declaration and Programme of Action adopted by the World Conference on Human Rights on 25 June 1993, for enhancing genuine cooperation among Member States in the field of human rights,

Recalling its adoption of the United Nations Millennium Declaration on 8 September 2000 and its resolution 60/156 of 16 December 2005, and taking note of Commission on Human Rights resolution 2005/54 of 20 April 2005 on the enhancement of international cooperation in the field of human rights,

Recalling also the World Conference against Racism, Racial Discrimination, Xenophobia and Related Intolerance, held at Durban, South Africa, from 31 August to 8 September 2001, and its role in the enhancement of international cooperation in the field of human rights,

Recognizing that the enhancement of international cooperation in the field of human rights is essential for the full achievement of the purposes of the United Nations, including the effective promotion and protection of all human rights,

Recognizing also that the promotion and protection of human rights should be based on the principle of cooperation and genuine dialogue and aimed at strengthening the capacity of Member States to comply with their human rights obligations for the benefit of all human beings,

Reaffirming that dialogue among religions, cultures and civilizations in the field of human rights could contribute greatly to the enhancement of international cooperation in this field,

Emphasizing the need for further progress in the promotion and encouragement of respect for human rights and fundamental freedoms through, inter alia, international cooperation,

Underlining the fact that mutual understanding, dialogue, cooperation, transparency and confidence-building are important elements in all the activities for the promotion and protection of human rights,

Recalling the adoption of resolution 2000/22 of 18 August 2000, on the promotion of dialogue on human rights issues, by the Subcommission on the Promotion and Protection of Human Rights at its fifty-second session,

1. *Reaffirms* that it is one of the purposes of the United Nations and the responsibility of all Member States to promote, protect and encourage respect for human rights and fundamental freedoms through, inter alia, international cooperation;

2. *Recognizes* that, in addition to their separate responsibilities to their individual societies, States have a collective responsibility to uphold the principles of human dignity, equality and equity at the global level;

3. *Reaffirms* that dialogue among cultures and civilizations facilitates the promotion of a culture of tolerance and respect for diversity, and welcomes in this regard the holding of conferences and meetings at the national, regional and international levels on dialogue among civilizations;

4. *Urges* all actors on the international scene to build an international order based on inclusion, justice, equality and equity, human dignity, mutual understanding and promotion of and respect for cultural diversity and universal human rights, and to reject all doctrines of exclusion based on racism, racial discrimination, xenophobia and related intolerance;

5. *Reaffirms* the importance of the enhancement of international cooperation for the promotion and protection of human rights and for the achievement of the objectives of the fight against racism, racial discrimination, xenophobia and related intolerance;

6. *Considers* that international cooperation in the field of human rights, in conformity with the purposes and principles set out in the Charter of the United Nations and international law, should make an effective and practical contribution to the urgent task of preventing violations of human rights and fundamental freedoms;

7. *Reaffirms* that the promotion, protection and full realization of all human rights and fundamental freedoms should be guided by the principles of universality, non-selectivity, objectivity and transparency, in a manner consistent with the purposes and principles set out in the Charter;

8. *Calls upon* Member States, specialized agencies and intergovernmental organizations to continue to carry out a constructive dialogue and consultations for the enhancement of understanding and the promotion and protection of all human rights and fundamental freedoms, and encourages non-governmental organizations to contribute actively to this endeavour;

9. *Invites* States and relevant United Nations human rights mechanisms and procedures to continue to

pay attention to the importance of mutual cooperation, understanding and dialogue in ensuring the promotion and protection of all human rights;

10. *Requests* the Secretary-General, in collaboration with the United Nations High Commissioner for Human Rights, to consult States and intergovernmental and non-governmental organizations on ways and means to enhance international cooperation and dialogue in the United Nations human rights machinery;

11. *Decides* to continue its consideration of the question at its sixty-second session.

At the same meeting, the Assembly, also on the recommendation of the Third Committee [A/61/443/Add.2 & Corr.1], adopted **resolution 61/166** by recorded vote (86-64-26) [agenda item 67 *(b)*].

Promotion of equitable and mutually respectful dialogue on human rights

The General Assembly,

Guided by the purposes and principles of the Charter of the United Nations, the Universal Declaration of Human Rights, the Vienna Declaration and Programme of Action, the International Covenants on Human Rights and other relevant human rights instruments,

Reaffirming that all human rights are universal, indivisible, interdependent and interrelated and that the international community must treat human rights globally in a fair and equal manner, on the same footing and with the same emphasis, and that the significance of national and regional particularities and various historical, cultural and religious backgrounds must be borne in mind,

Stressing the importance of developing friendly relations among nations based on respect for the principle of equal rights and self-determination of peoples and achieving international cooperation in promoting and encouraging respect for human rights and fundamental freedoms for all,

Emphasizing the responsibilities of all States, in conformity with the Charter, to respect human rights and fundamental freedoms for all, without distinction of any kind as to race, colour, sex, language or religion, political or other opinion, national or social origin, property, birth or other status,

Bearing in mind General Assembly resolution 60/251 of 15 March 2006 entitled "Human Rights Council", in particular the decision of the Assembly that the Council should undertake a universal periodic review, in a manner that ensures universality of coverage and equal treatment with respect to all States, and the decision of the Council on the establishment of an intersessional open-ended intergovernmental working group to develop the modalities of the universal periodic review mechanism, based on an interactive dialogue as well as on objective and reliable information,

Recalling that the General Assembly shall make recommendations for the purpose of promoting international cooperation in the economic, social, cultural, education and health fields, and of assisting in the realization of human rights and fundamental freedoms for all without distinction as to race, sex, language or religion,

Recognizing that politically motivated and biased country-specific resolutions on the situation of human rights severely undermine the principles of objectivity and non-selectivity in the consideration of human rights issues and are counterproductive to the cause of promoting human rights,

1. *Urges* Member States to further strengthen international cooperation in promoting and encouraging respect for human rights in order to enhance dialogue and broaden understanding among civilizations, cultures and religions;

2. *Calls upon* Member States to base their approaches towards development of international dialogue on human rights on the Charter of the United Nations, the Universal Declaration of Human Rights, the Vienna Declaration and Programme of Action and other relevant international human rights instruments and to refrain from approaches that are inconsistent with that international framework;

3. *Reaffirms* that the promotion and protection of human rights and fundamental freedoms, as a legitimate concern of the world community, and the development of international dialogue on human rights should be guided by the principles of universality, non-selectivity, impartiality and objectivity and should not be used for political purposes;

4. *Stresses* the need to avoid politically motivated and biased country-specific resolutions on the situation of human rights, confrontational approaches, exploitation of human rights for political purposes, selective targeting of individual countries for extraneous considerations and double standards in the work of the United Nations on human rights issues;

5. *Affirms* that respect for political, economic and cultural diversity for all contributes to the development of stable and friendly relations among countries and equitable and mutually respectful international dialogue on human rights;

6. *Stresses* the continuing need for unbiased and objective information on the situation of human rights in all countries and the need to present this information in an impartial manner, including through the reports of the special rapporteurs and representatives, independent experts and working groups;

7. *Decides* to consider the matter at its sixty-second session under the item entitled "Promotion and protection of human rights".

RECORDED VOTE ON RESOLUTION 61/166:

In favour: Algeria, Angola, Azerbaijan, Bahrain, Bangladesh, Belarus, Belize, Benin, Bhutan, Bolivia, Botswana, Brunei Darussalam, Cambodia, Central African Republic, China, Colombia, Comoros, Congo, Côte d'Ivoire, Cuba, Democratic People's Republic of Korea, Democratic Republic of the Congo, Ecuador, Egypt, El Salvador, Eritrea, Gabon, Gambia, Guinea, Guinea-Bissau, Haiti, India, Indonesia, Iran, Kazakhstan, Kenya, Kuwait, Kyrgyzstan, Lao People's Democratic Republic, Lebanon, Lesotho, Liberia, Libya, Malaysia, Maldives, Mali, Mauritania, Morocco, Mozambique, Myanmar, Namibia, Nauru, Nepal, Nicaragua, Niger,

Oman, Pakistan, Philippines, Qatar, Russian Federation, Rwanda, Saint Lucia, Sao Tome and Principe, Saudi Arabia, Senegal, Sierra Leone, Singapore, South Africa, Sri Lanka, Sudan, Suriname, Swaziland, Syria, Tajikistan, Thailand, Togo, Trinidad and Tobago, Tunisia, Tuvalu, United Arab Emirates, Uzbekistan, Venezuela, Viet Nam, Yemen, Zambia, Zimbabwe.

Against: Albania, Andorra, Argentina, Australia, Austria, Belgium, Bosnia and Herzegovina, Bulgaria, Canada, Chile, Croatia, Cyprus, Czech Republic, Denmark, Dominican Republic, Estonia, Finland, France, Georgia, Germany, Greece, Guatemala, Honduras, Hungary, Iceland, Ireland, Israel, Italy, Japan, Latvia, Liechtenstein, Lithuania, Luxembourg, Malta, Marshall Islands, Mexico, Micronesia, Moldova, Monaco, Montenegro, Netherlands, New Zealand, Norway, Palau, Panama, Peru, Poland, Portugal, Republic of Korea, Romania, Samoa, San Marino, Serbia, Slovakia, Slovenia, Spain, Sweden, Switzerland, The former Yugoslav Republic of Macedonia, Turkey, Ukraine, United Kingdom, United States, Uruguay.

Abstaining: Antigua and Barbuda, Armenia, Bahamas, Barbados, Brazil, Burundi, Costa Rica, Djibouti, Dominica, Ethiopia, Fiji, Ghana, Guyana, Jamaica, Jordan, Madagascar, Malawi, Mauritius, Nigeria, Papua New Guinea, Paraguay, Solomon Islands, Somalia, Uganda, United Republic of Tanzania, Vanuatu.

Advisory services and technical cooperation

Report of Secretary-General. In accordance with Council decision 2/102 (see p. 762), the Secretary-General submitted a report [A/HCR/4/94 & Corr.1] on advisory services and technical cooperation in the field of human rights, focusing on the work of the Board of Trustees of the Voluntary Fund for Technical Cooperation in the Field of Human Rights, which held its twenty-fourth (30 January–1 February) and twenty-fifth (7-10 November) sessions in Geneva.

At its twenty-fourth session, the Board devoted attention to the implications of the reform of the human rights machinery for the technical cooperation programme, in order to establish clearly defined policy guidelines for staff and ensure understanding and expectations from partners. It recommended that OHCHR seize the moment to reaffirm its position on human rights, in order to prevent the legitimization of misconceptions. Noting that the 2005 World Summit [YUN 2005, p. 47] and the subsequent increase in OHCHR regular budget would raise high expectations, the Board found that the Office needed to be well prepared to acquire the capacity to provide prompt and appropriate responses. It acknowledged the importance of prioritization and recommended that OHCHR develop a long-term vision and strike the difficult balance of respecting set priorities, while maintaining a certain level of flexibility and planning capacity to address emerging situations. Warning, however, of the possible risk of the Office becoming introverted with the envisaged growth and self-strengthening, the Board stressed that securing partnerships was vital and recommended a meeting between the High Commissioner and the UNDP Administrator in that regard.

At its twenty-fifth meeting, the Board held consultations with OHCHR field personnel on progress made, problems encountered and the next steps in implementing the High Commissioner's Strategic Management Plan 2006-2007 (see p. 766) and the 2005 Plan of Action [ibid., p. 715], on which the former was based. It discussed progress made in country engagement in the past year, considered the OHCHR strategy on poverty reduction and engagement with the World Bank and reviewed recent developments in the United Nations, relating especially to the Council, the High-Level Panel on System-wide Coherence, the Peacebuilding Commission and the United Nations Democracy Fund [YUN 2005, p. 655].

The Board held a joint seminar (9-10 November) with members of treaty bodies, representatives of UN agencies and programmes and OHCHR heads of field presences, which discussed, among other things, the implementation of the recommendations of treaty bodies at the national level.

Cooperation with human rights bodies

Report of Secretary-General. A February report of the Secretary-General [E/CN.4/2006/30] described situations in which individuals or NGO members had allegedly suffered intimidation or reprisal for having cooperated with UN human rights bodies regarding human rights violations. The report summarized cases in Brazil, China, Nepal, Thailand, Tunisia and Uzbekistan and expressed concern at the seriousness of the alleged reprisals, with victims suffering egregious violations of rights to liberty and security of person and to life. The gravity of reported acts reinforced the need for all representatives of UN human rights bodies, in cooperation with States, to maintain efforts to help prevent such crimes.

Chapter II

Protection of human rights

In 2006, the United Nations remained actively engaged in protecting human rights, mostly through the activities of its main organs—the General Assembly, the Security Council and the Economic and Social Council—and the newly established Human Rights Council, which assumed the functions of the Commission on Human Rights in the Organization's efforts to overhaul and reform its 60-year old human rights machinery.

The rights of vulnerable groups were especially advanced during the year by the General Assembly's adoption of the Convention on the Rights of Persons with Disabilities and Optional Protocol, intended to empower persons with disabilities to overcome societal barriers and to promote respect for their dignity. In further action, the Assembly adopted the International Convention for the Protection of All Persons from Enforced Disappearance and Optional Protocol, which deemed the phenomenon of systematic and enforced disappearance a crime against humanity and outlined legal obligations to enable States to combat it and protect potential victims. The legal framework for safeguarding indigenous peoples' rights was further fortified by the Human Rights Council's adoption of the United Nations Declaration on the Rights of Indigenous Peoples, which outlined provisions for protecting indigenous rights relative to such crucial issues as self-determination, land use, territories and resources.

In continuing efforts to protect the rights of civilians in conflict situations, the Security Council, in an April resolution, condemned all acts of violence and abuses against civilians in such circumstances and demanded that all parties concerned comply strictly with their obligations under international law. On behalf of children trapped in similar situations of armed conflict and exposed to the risks of extreme human rights violations and abuse, the Council adopted two presidential statements reaffirming its commitment to the protection of their rights. In May, the Council's Working Group on children and armed conflict, established in 2005 to examine compliance with measures for ending the recruitment of child soldiers and other violations against children, began its work. In July, the pressing need to protect human rights in the face of potentially undermining factors in conflict situations was further addressed by the Special Rapporteur on the prevention of human rights violations committed with small arms and light weapons, Barbara Frey (United States), who outlined draft principles for addressing related challenges effectively. Similar principles and/or guidelines were issued or adopted to help advance the rights to adequate housing, water and sanitation, and to address, from a human rights perspective, the problem of extreme poverty, which remained a major theme within the context of economic, social and cultural rights.

Notable developments during the year focusing attention on the protection of key components of civil and political rights included the assessment of the United States detention facility in Guantánamo Bay, Cuba, by four human rights special procedures mandate-holders, who recommended its closure based on findings suggesting the arbitrary detention of some of the inmates, which was promptly rebutted by the United States. On the positive side, international concerns about the continuing practice of torture by some Member States were relatively tempered by the entry into force within the year of the Optional Protocol to the Convention Against Torture and Other Cruel, Inhuman or Degrading Treatment or Punishment.

Progress was maintained regarding follow-up activities to implement the Durban Declaration and Programme of Action, adopted at the 2001 World Conference against Racism, Racial Discrimination, Xenophobia and Related Intolerance. The United Nations High Commissioner for Human Rights, at the request of the Human Rights Council, appointed five experts to study gaps in international instruments to combat racism, while the Assembly decided to convene in 2009 a conference to review the Programme's status of implementation. Underscoring the need to remain proactive in protecting human rights, the Assembly, in a November resolution commemorating the two hundredth anniversary of the abolition of the transatlantic slave trade, denounced it as among the worst human rights violations in the history of humanity, honoured the memory of the victims and acknowledged that its legacy had contributed to racism and prejudice. In related developments, the Assembly condemned all acts of hostage-taking as unjustifiable, described it as a crime and demanded the prompt and unconditional release of all hostages. The Secretary-General announced the establishment of the Organization's outreach programme on the Holocaust, under the auspices of the UN Department of Public Information.

In 2006, the Human Rights Council and the subsidiary body it had inherited from the Commissison on Human Rights, the Subcommission on the Promotion and Protection of Human Rights, established new mandates for special rapporteurs to conduct studies on discrimination against leprosy-affected persons and their families; the implementation in practice of the right to an effective remedy for human rights violations; the accountability of international personnel taking part in peace support operations; and the legal implications of the disappearance of States and other territories for environmental reasons, including global warming. Special rapporteurs, special representatives and independent experts examined, among other issues, contemporary forms of racism; the rights of migrants; freedom of religion or belief; mercenary activity; the independence of the judiciary; extralegal executions; allegations of torture; freedom of expression; human rights and terrorism; the prevention of human rights violations committed with small arms and light weapons; the right to development; economic reform policies; corruption and its impact on the enjoyment of human rights; human rights and extreme poverty; the right to food; the right to adequate housing; the right to education; illicit practices related to toxic and dangerous products and wastes; the right to physical and mental health; violence against women; violence against children; the sale of children, child prostitution and child pornography; children affected by armed conflict; internally displaced persons; and the human rights and fundamental freedoms of indigenous peoples.

Working groups considered the problems of racial discrimination affecting people of African descent, discrimination against minorities, arbitrary detention, enforced or involuntary disappearances, the right to development, working methods and activities of transnational corporations, contemporary forms of slavery and the rights of indigenous peoples.

Civil and political rights

Racism and racial discrimination

Follow-up to 2001 World Conference

Intergovernmental Working Group. At its fourth session (Geneva, 16-27 January) [E/CN.4/2006/18], the Intergovernmental Working Group on the effective implementation of the Durban Declaration and Programme of Action (DDPA), adopted by the 2001 World Conference against Racism, Racial Discrimination, Xenophobia and Related Intolerance [YUN 2001, p. 615], addressed the theme of racism and globalization. The Group had before it a concept paper on that topic [E/CN.4/2006/WG.21/3 & Corr.1], intended to guide panelists in addressing specific challenges noted in DDPA relating to the need to: identify those aspects of globalization that might lead to racism and ensure that globalization became a positive force for everyone; promote respect and preserve cultural diversity within and between communities and nations; consider long-term approaches to all phases of migration, with special attention to its root causes concerning human rights; and analyse how States and international financial institutions' policies and practices might affect national populations in general and indigenous peoples in particular.

Participants emphasized the link between globalization and racial discrimination and discussed the migration dimension of globalization. The Group concluded that, although globalization could contribute to the fight against racism, there was a negative connection between them, similar to the linkages previously established on such issues as poverty, health and education. Pointing out that the process of globalization constituted a powerful and dynamic force that should be harnessed for the benefit, development and prosperity of all countries, the Group recognized, nonetheless, that the opportunities and advantages associated with it were unevenly shared, and its costs unevenly distributed. Finding that developing countries in particular faced special difficulties in responding to the challenges involved, the Group stressed that more equitable international trade that took into consideration the special needs of those countries and the strengthening and enhancement of international cooperation were needed in order to maximize the benefits of globalization for them. It was imperative that a broad strategy be developed to allow the Group to engage in meaningful partnership with such key players as the World Trade Organization (WTO), the International Labour Organization (ILO) and the International Organization for Migration (IOM), with a view to preventing, mitigating and reversing the negative effects of globalization which could aggravate poverty, social exclusion, cultural homogenization and economic disparities along racial lines. The Group urged States to promote a human rights approach to globalization, which would assist in combating racism and ensuring that the benefits of globalization were distributed equitably. In further conclusions and recommendations, the Group recognized that human rights education and cultural diversity could aid efforts to combat racism in a globalized world. It was vital also to ensure the promotion and protection of the human rights of migrants.

Addressing the issue of development, the Group encouraged States to recognize that the lack of progress in the realization of civil and political, as well as economic, social and cultural rights, coupled with the costs of globalization, could promote racial discrimination, and asked them to tackle the problem and ensure universal enjoyment of globalization. The Group advocated a broad, global exchange of "good practices" in combating racism and targeted technical cooperation by the UN system, Governments and other actors to enhance the implementation of DDPA. The Group also considered follow-up to the recommendations of its third session [YUN 2004, p. 686] and recommendations for its future work, highlighting ongoing efforts and activities of the Office of the United Nations High Commissioner for Human Rights (OHCHR) to advance the fight against racial discrimination, in cooperation with other UN entities and non-governmental organizations (NGOs), and through its publications, awareness-raising and outreach activities. The Group determined that a successful strategy to combat racism and racial discrimination on a global scale should focus on reinforcing the implementation of international instruments and elaborating complementary international standards to address substantive and procedural gaps in those instruments. It proposed that a voluntary fund be established to benefit the participation of NGOs in its sessions.

High-Level seminar. During the first week of the session, the Group held a high-level seminar on racism and the Internet and complementary international standards for combating racism, in response to a 2005 Commission request [YUN 2005, p. 758]. Discussions centred on the use of the Internet to disseminate racist material and promote racial hatred and violence. The Group acknowledged that, while the problem had generated responses from a variety of actors, including Governments, the fight against hate speech and racist materials on the Internet faced legal, regulatory, technical, financial and practical challenges, and no single approach could be effective in tackling the problem. The Group concluded that self-regulatory initiatives, combined with education about racist Internet content and the fostering of tolerance could be the most effective way to alleviate the problem. It reminded States that had not done so to adopt legislative and other administrative measures to establish as criminal offences the public distribution through computers of racist or xenophobic material inciting hatred or violence, in compliance with article 4 of the International Convention on the Elimination of All Forms of Racial Discrimination [YUN 1965, p. 440]. The Group suggested that OHCHR should offer technical cooperation to States in dealing with the problem, and identify strategies to support international cooperation and partnership among all stakeholders to enable a globally coordinated development of voluntary codes of conduct, complaint mechanisms and other means to ensure that hate speech was effectively countered.

Regarding complementary international standards, the seminar devoted attention to the implementation of international instruments and the enhancement of their effectiveness in the fight against racism; the identification of gaps in international human rights law, with a view to preparing complementary standards; and outlining the format of those standards to strengthen and update existing instruments. The Group stressed the importance for States to strengthen the implementation of instruments dealing with racism and related phenomena and identified several strategies for doing so. The Group determined that a successful strategy for combating racial discrimination on a global scale should include the need to reinforce implementation of international instruments and the elaboration of complementary standards to address substantive and procedural gaps in those instruments. It considered some of those gaps in the International Convention on the Elimination of All Forms of Racial Discrimination and recommended that OHCHR select five experts to study their content and scope and produce, in consultation with treaty bodies and special procedures, a base document containing recommendations on how to bridge them, including the drafting of a new protocol to the Convention. The Group also proposed that the Committee on the Elimination of Racial Discrimination (CERD) (see p. 773) should study possible measures to strengthen the Convention's implementation through additional recommendations or the update of its monitoring procedures. The Group also made recommendations regarding international complementary standards, some of which were addressed to the General Assembly.

In response to the Council's request (see below), OHCHR elected the following five experts to study the gaps in international instruments to combat racism: Jenny Goldschmidt (Group of Western European and other States); Dimitrina Petrova (Group of Eastern European States); Syafi'i Anwar (Group of Asian States); Tiyajana Maluwa (Group of African States); and Waldo Luis Villalpando (Group of Caribbean and Latin American States).

Human Rights Council action. On 30 June [A/61/53 (res. 1/5)], the Human Rights Council endorsed the Working Group's recommendations and requested OHCHR to select, in consultations with regional groups, five highly qualified experts to study the content and scope of the substantive gaps in international instruments to combat racism, racial discrimination, xenophobia and related intolerance, including the areas identified in the conclusions of the high-level seminar (see above). The experts, in consultation with human rights treaty bodies, the Special Rapporteur on contemporary forms of racism and other mandate-holders, should produce a base document containing recommendations on ways to bridge those gaps, including the drafting of a new optional protocol to the International Convention on the Elimination of All Forms of Racial Discrimination or the adoption of new instruments, such as conventions or declarations. The Council requested CERD to study possible measures for strengthening the implementation of the Convention through additional recommendations or the update of its monitoring procedures and decided that both documents should be presented to the Intergovernmental Working Group at its fifth session. It also extended the Group's mandate for three years.

On 29 November [A/62/53 (dec. 2/116)], the Council deferred to its third session consideration of a draft decision [A/HRC/2/L.27/Rev.2] on global efforts for the total elimination of racism, racial discrimination, xenophobia and related intolerance and the comprehensive implementation of and follow-up to DDPA, submitted by Algeria on behalf of the African Group.

By a recorded vote of 33 to 12, with 1 abstention, the Council, on 8 December [A/62/53 (dec. 3/103)], welcomed the OHCHR appointment of the five experts recommended by the Intergovernmental Working Group (see above) and requested the Group to invite them to the first part of its fifth session to exchange views on complementary standards as a provisional measure pending the completion of their report. The experts would finalize that report before the end of June 2007, for submission to OHCHR, which would ensure its circulation to Governments and other stakeholders, to allow them the opportunity to study the recommendations contained therein. The Group would convene the second part of its fifth session in September 2007 to conclude its deliberations on the question of complementary standards, while continuing its work of ensuring the effective implementation of DDPA. In accordance with the outcome of the 2001 World Conference against racism [YUN 2001, p. 615], the Council also established an Ad Hoc Committee to elaborate complementary standards in the form of either a convention or additional protocol(s) to the International Convention on the Elimination of All Forms of Racial Discrimination, filling existing gaps in the Convention and providing new normative standards aimed at combating all forms of contemporary racism. It recommended that the Ad Hoc Committee report regularly to the Council on the progress of its work. The Council invited the Chairperson of the Intergovernmental Working Group to transmit the report of the five experts to the Ad Hoc Committee, which should convene its first session before the end of 2007. The High Commissioner was asked to strengthen the profile of the OHCHR Anti-Discrimination Unit and provide it with the requisite resources to ensure its effectiveness, especially given current challenges relating to racial and religious discrimination.

Reports of High Commissioner. In accordance with a 2005 Commission request [YUN 2005, p. 758], the High Commissioner submitted a 31 January report [E/CN.4/2006/14] containing the draft basic document on the development of a racial equality index for measuring existing racial inequalities, as proposed by the independent eminent experts appointed to follow-up the implementation of DDPA provisions [YUN 2003, p. 698]. The report discussed the process of constructing the index, highlighted its advantages and disadvantages, the difficulties and challenges involved and how to overcome some of them. Building on earlier research on the issue covered in the High Commissioner's 2005 report [YUN 2005, p. 757], the current report addressed subsequent developments, including efforts already under way to develop such an index, which helped identify core conceptual and methodological issues to be examined. Those issues related to the question of defining race, identifying racialized groups, measuring inequalities and discrimination, national differences in the manifestation of the global phenomenon of racial discrimination, and methodological and data-related questions.

The experts concluded that a racial equality index was technically feasible and had a substantial potential for measuring racial inequalities. It would provide a scientific and comprehensive framework for combating racial discrimination through a system of indicators and could be an important country-specific tool for Member States and other stakeholders to monitor progress in implementing their anti-discrimination policies. However, the non-availability of disaggregated data by ethnicity in many countries was a potential obstacle to the development of the index, although that problem could be resolved over time, since the construction of the index might encourage Member States to make the requisite data available. The report also cautioned against using the index to rank Member States because the situation differed among countries, or to stigmatize or single out minorities. While drawing attention to the financial implication of the index to OHCHR and at the national level, the High Commissioner outlined steps that ought to be taken in the event that the index was authorized. Those included the initiation of another consultation process to provide a detailed description of the index and the indicators to be used in constructing it; ensuring that the process of identifying the population segments and relevant indicators would be participatory at the national level; the development by OHCHR of guidelines for racial and ethnic data collection for the attention of Member States and other stakeholders; the elaboration of a sound, independent and transparent methodology; and a pilot study on a limited set of countries where disaggregated data were available to fine-tune the methodology and make it more efficient and effective.

A 16 February report of the High Commissioner [E/CN.4/2006/15], submitted in response to a 2005 Commission request [YUN 2005, p. 758], described OHCHR efforts to implement the recommendations adopted by the Intergovernmental Working Group on the effective implementation of DDPA at its third session [YUN 2004, p. 687], which focused on racism and health and racism and the Internet and adopted 36 recommendations. In that context, the report summarized information received from 20 States on measures they had taken to combat racism on the Internet. The report concluded that such information illustrated the concern generated by the use of the Internet to incite hatred, but expressed confidence that the completion of efforts to redesign and expand the OHCHR website as a vehicle for combating racism and related phenomena would result in a major improvement in accessing and sharing information on developments relating to anti-discrimination.

In a 28 February report [E/CN.4/2006/10] highlighting steps taken by OHCHR to address its 2005 Plan of Action on the strategic vision for its future direction [YUN 2005, p. 715], the High Commissioner indicated that the Office maintained support for the implementation of DDPA. Through its Anti-Discrimination Unit, OHCHR provided substantive organizational support to the institutional bodies established following the 2001 World Conference against Racism [YUN 2001, p. 615], particularly the Intergovernmental Working Group on the Effective Implementation of DDPA (see p. 820), the Working Group of Experts on People of African Descent (see p. 824) and the group of independent eminent persons (see below). It also undertook cooperative activities with intergovernmental organizations and NGOs.

Report of independent experts. A February Secretariat note [E/CN.4/2006/20] informed the Commission that a third meeting of the independent eminent experts on the implementation of DDPA, appointed in 2003 [YUN 2003, p. 698], did not take place, and as a result, no report on their work would be transmitted to the Commission's sixty-second session.

Report of Secretary-General. In accordance with General Assembly resolution 60/144 [YUN 2005, p. 759], the Secretary-General submitted a September report [A/61/337] summarizing the activities undertaken between August 2005 and June 2006 by States, UN bodies, OHCHR, specialized agencies, international and regional organizations, national human rights institutions, NGOs and youth groups and organizations to implement DDPA. He observed that the adoption by Governments of action plans, in consultation with national human rights institutions, civil society and other institutions created to combat racism, was an important step, even if implementation challenges remained. Steps to combat racism and related phenomena at international and national levels had resulted in the improvement of victims' lives. Unfortunately, much more remained to be done, and the recommendations contained in DDPA provided an agenda for States and other stakeholders to bolster protection against discrimination of all kinds, which would, in turn, foster social harmony.

CERD action. In 2006 [A/61/18], the Committee on the Elimination of Racial Discrimination (CERD) (see p. 773) considered the follow-up to the World Conference against Racism, focusing on the work of the Intergovernmental Working Group (see above), particularly its mandate relating to the preparation of complementary international standards to strengthen and update international instruments against racial discrimination. CERD took note of the Working Group's recommendations that the Committee should continue to develop early warning indicators, including on hate speech; detect outbreaks of racial violence in order to recommend urgent action; and further update its guidelines for State reporting, so as to include the issue of racism on the Internet. The Committee also took note of the Group's request to conduct a further study on possible measures to strengthen the implementation of the International Convention on the Elimination of All Forms of Racial Discrimination.

Working Group on people of African descent. The Working Group of Experts on People of African Descent, established in accordance with DDPA in 2002 [YUN 2002, p. 661] to consider problems of racial discrimination affecting people of African descent, did not meet in 2006. However, on 18 September, the Group's Chairperson-Rapporteur presented to the Human Rights Council the report of the Group's fifth session [YUN 2005, p. 758].

On the same day, Belgium's observer in the Council made a statement in response to the report on the Group's visit to the country in June 2005 [ibid., p. 758].

Review conference. In December (see p. 827), the General Assembly decided to convene in 2009, a review conference on the implementation of DDPA and asked the Council to undertake preparations for the event, and in that regard, to formulate a plan and provide updates and reports on the issue annually, starting in 2007.

Accordingly, the Human Rights Council [A/62/53 (res. 3/2)], by a recorded vote of 34 to 12, with 1 abstention on 8 December, decided that it would act as the Preparatory Committee for the review conference. In that capacity, it would hold a one-week organizational session in May 2007 and two substantive sessions of 10 working days each in 2007 and 2008 in Geneva. At its organizational session, it would decide on the modalities and objectives of the review, which would concentrate on key implementation issues, including further actions, initiatives and practical solutions for combating all the contemporary scourges of racism.

GENERAL ASSEMBLY ACTION

On 19 December [meeting 81], the General Assembly, on the recommendation of the Third (Social, Humanitarian and Cultural) Committee [A/61/441], adopted **resolution 61/149** by recorded vote (179-2-4) [agenda item 65].

Global efforts for the total elimination of racism, racial discrimination, xenophobia and related intolerance and the comprehensive implementation of and follow-up to the Durban Declaration and Programme of Action

The General Assembly,

Recalling its resolution 60/144 of 16 December 2005, in which it reiterated its firm commitment to continue its global efforts towards the total elimination of the scourges of racism, racial discrimination, xenophobia and related intolerance, and towards the effective and comprehensive implementation of and follow-up to the Durban Declaration and Programme of Action adopted by the World Conference against Racism, Racial Discrimination, Xenophobia and Related Intolerance, held in Durban, South Africa, from 31 August to 8 September 2001,

Recalling also its resolution 59/177 of 20 December 2004, in which it firmly consolidated the global drive for the total elimination of racism, racial discrimination, xenophobia and related intolerance and recognized the absolute necessity and the imperative nature of the political will for the achievement of the commitments undertaken in the Durban Declaration and Programme of Action,

Recalling further its resolution 58/160 of 22 December 2003, in which it decided to place emphasis on the concrete implementation of the Durban Declaration and Programme of Action as a solid foundation for a broad-based consensus for further action and initiatives towards the total elimination of the scourge of racism,

Recalling its resolution 57/195 of 18 December 2002, in which it outlined the important roles and responsibilities of the various organs of the United Nations and other stakeholders at the international, regional and national levels, including, in particular, the Commission on Human Rights, and its resolution 56/266 of 27 March 2002, in which it endorsed the Durban Declaration and Programme of Action as constituting a solid foundation for further action and initiatives towards the total elimination of the scourge of racism,

Reiterating that all human beings are born free and equal in dignity and rights and have the potential to contribute constructively to the development and well-being of their societies, and that any doctrine of racial superiority is scientifically false, morally condemnable, socially unjust and dangerous and must be rejected, together with theories that attempt to determine the existence of separate human races,

Convinced that racism, racial discrimination, xenophobia and related intolerance manifest themselves in a differentiated manner for women and girls and may be among the factors leading to a deterioration in their living conditions, poverty, violence, multiple forms of discrimination and the limitation or denial of their human rights, and recognizing the need to integrate a gender perspective into relevant policies, strategies and programmes of action against racism, racial discrimination, xenophobia and related intolerance in order to address multiple forms of discrimination,

Taking note of Human Rights Council resolution 1/5 of 30 June 2006,

Taking note also of Commission on Human Rights resolutions 2002/68 of 25 April 2002, 2003/30 of 23 April 2003, 2004/88 of 22 April 2004 and 2005/64 of 20 April 2005, by which the international community put into effect mechanisms for the effective implementation of the Durban Declaration and Programme of Action,

Underlining the primacy of political will, international cooperation and adequate funding at the national, regional and international levels for the successful implementation of the Durban Programme of Action,

Alarmed at the increase in racist violence and xenophobic ideas in many parts of the world, in political circles, in the sphere of public opinion and in society at large, inter alia, as a result of the resurgent activities of associations established on the basis of racist and xenophobic platforms and charters, and the persistent use of those platforms and charters to promote or incite racist ideologies,

Underlining the importance of urgently eliminating continuing and violent trends involving racism and racial discrimination, and conscious that any form of impunity for crimes motivated by racist and xenophobic attitudes plays a role in weakening the rule of law and democracy, tends to encourage the recurrence of such crimes and requires resolute action and cooperation for its eradication,

Welcoming the determination of the United Nations High Commissioner for Human Rights to profile and increase the visibility of the struggle against racism, racial discrimination, xenophobia and related intolerance and her intention to make this a cross-cutting issue in the activities and programmes of her Office,

Taking note of the report of the Secretary-General, the interim report of the Special Rapporteur on contemporary forms of racism, racial discrimination, xenophobia and related intolerance and Human Rights Council decision 1/102 of 30 June 2006,

I

Basic general principles

1. *Acknowledges* that no derogation from the prohibition of racial discrimination, genocide, the crime of apartheid or slavery is permitted, as defined in the obligations under the relevant human rights instruments;

2. *Expresses its profound concern about and its unequivocal condemnation* of all forms of racism and racial discrimination, including related acts of racially motivated violence, xenophobia and intolerance, as well as propaganda activities and organizations that attempt to justify or promote racism, racial discrimination, xenophobia and related intolerance in any form;

3. *Expresses deep concern* at recent attempts to establish hierarchies among emerging and resurgent forms of racism, racial discrimination, xenophobia and related intolerance, and urges States to adopt measures to address these scourges with the same emphasis and vigour with a view to preventing this practice and protecting victims;

4. *Stresses* that States and international organizations have a responsibility to ensure that measures taken in the struggle against terrorism do not discriminate in purpose or effect on grounds of race, colour, descent or national or ethnic origin, and urges all States to rescind or refrain from all forms of racial profiling;

5. *Recognizes* that States should implement and enforce appropriate and effective legislative, judicial, regulatory and administrative measures to prevent and protect against acts of racism, racial discrimination, xenophobia and related intolerance, thereby contributing to the prevention of human rights violations;

6. *Also recognizes* that racism, racial discrimination, xenophobia and related intolerance occur on the grounds of race, colour, descent or national or ethnic origin and that victims can suffer multiple or aggravated forms of discrimination based on other related grounds, such as sex, language, religion, political or other opinion, social origin, property, birth or other status;

7. *Reaffirms* that any advocacy of national, racial or religious hatred that constitutes incitement to discrimination, hostility or violence shall be prohibited by law;

8. *Emphasizes* that it is the responsibility of States to adopt effective measures to combat criminal acts motivated by racism, racial discrimination, xenophobia and related intolerance, including measures to ensure that such motivations are considered an aggravating factor for the purposes of sentencing, to prevent those crimes from going unpunished and to ensure the rule of law;

9. *Urges* all States to review and, where necessary, revise their immigration laws, policies and practices so that they are free of racial discrimination and compatible with their obligations under international human rights instruments;

10. *Condemns* the misuse of print, audio-visual and electronic media and new communication technologies, including the Internet, to incite violence motivated by racial hatred, and calls upon States to take all necessary measures to combat this form of racism in accordance with the commitments that they have undertaken under the Durban Declaration and Programme of Action, in particular paragraph 147 of the Programme of Action, in accordance with existing international and regional standards of freedom of expression and taking all necessary measures to guarantee the right to freedom of opinion and expression;

11. *Encourages* all States to include in their educational curricula and social programmes at all levels, as appropriate, knowledge of and tolerance and respect for all cultures, civilizations, religions, peoples and countries;

12. *Stresses* the responsibility of States to mainstream a gender perspective in the design and development of prevention, education and protection measures aimed at the eradication of racism, racial discrimination, xenophobia and related intolerance at all levels, to ensure that they effectively target the distinct situations of women and men;

II

International Convention on the Elimination of All Forms of Racial Discrimination

13. *Reaffirms* that universal adherence to and full implementation of the International Convention on the

Elimination of All Forms of Racial Discrimination are of paramount importance for the fight against racism, racial discrimination, xenophobia and related intolerance, including contemporary forms of racism and racial discrimination, and for the promotion of equality and non-discrimination in the world;

14. *Reiterates* the call made by the World Conference against Racism, Racial Discrimination, Xenophobia and Related Intolerance, in paragraph 75 of the Durban Programme of Action, to achieve universal ratification of the Convention by 2005 and for all States to consider making the declaration envisaged under article 14 of the Convention, and endorses the grave concern expressed by the Commission on Human Rights in its resolution 2005/64 to the effect that, with one hundred and seventy-three ratifications and only forty-nine declarations, the deadline for universal ratification decided by the World Conference has, regrettably, not been realized;

15. *Urges*, in the above context, the Office of the United Nations High Commissioner for Human Rights to maintain and issue regular updates on its website of a list of countries that have not yet ratified the Convention and to encourage such countries to ratify it at the earliest;

16. *Expresses its concern* at the serious delays in the submission of overdue reports to the Committee on the Elimination of Racial Discrimination, which impedes the effectiveness of the Committee, makes a strong appeal to all States parties to the Convention to comply with their treaty obligations, and reaffirms the importance of the provision of technical assistance to the requesting countries in the preparation of their reports to the Committee;

17. *Invites* States parties to the Convention to ratify the amendment to article 8 of the Convention on the financing of the Committee, and calls for adequate additional resources from the regular budget of the United Nations to enable the Committee to discharge its mandate fully;

18. *Urges* all States parties to the Convention to intensify their efforts to implement the obligations that they have accepted under article 4 of the Convention, with due regard to the principles of the Universal Declaration of Human Rights and article 5 of the Convention;

19. *Welcomes* the work of the Committee in applying the Convention to the new and contemporary forms of racism and racial discrimination;

20. *Recalls* that the Committee holds that the prohibition of the dissemination of ideas based on racial superiority or racial hatred is compatible with the right to freedom of opinion and expression as outlined in article 19 of the Universal Declaration of Human Rights and in article 5 of the Convention;

21. *Welcomes* the emphasis placed by the Committee on the importance of follow-up to the World Conference and the measures recommended to strengthen the implementation of the Convention as well as the functioning of the Committee;

III

Comprehensive implementation of and follow-up to the Durban Declaration and Programme of Action

22. *Acknowledges* that the outcome of the World Conference against Racism, Racial Discrimination, Xenophobia and Related Intolerance is on an equal footing with the outcomes of all the major United Nations conferences, summits and special sessions in the human rights and social fields;

23. *Also acknowledges* that the World Conference, which was the third world conference against racism, was significantly different from the previous two conferences, as evidenced by the inclusion in its title of two important components relating to contemporary forms of racism, namely, xenophobia and related intolerance;

24. *Emphasizes* that the basic responsibility for effectively combating racism, racial discrimination, xenophobia and related intolerance lies with States, and to this end stresses that States have the primary responsibility to ensure full and effective implementation of all commitments and recommendations contained in the Durban Declaration and Programme of Action;

25. *Also emphasizes* the fundamental and complementary role of national human rights institutions, regional bodies or centres and civil society, working jointly with States towards the achievement of the objectives of the Durban Declaration and Programme of Action;

26. *Welcomes* the steps taken by numerous Governments, in particular the elaboration and implementation of national action plans to combat racism, racial discrimination, xenophobia and related intolerance, and steps taken by national human rights institutions and non-governmental organizations, towards the full implementation of the Durban Declaration and Programme of Action, and affirms this trend as a demonstration of commitment for the elimination of all scourges of racism at the national level;

27. *Calls upon* all States that have not yet elaborated their national action plans on combating racism, racial discrimination, xenophobia and related intolerance to comply with their commitments undertaken at the World Conference;

28. *Calls upon* all States to formulate and implement without delay, at the national, regional and international levels, policies and plans of action to combat racism, racial discrimination, xenophobia and related intolerance, including their gender-based manifestations;

29. *Urges* States to support the activities of existing regional bodies or centres that combat racism, racial discrimination, xenophobia and related intolerance in their respective regions, and recommends the establishment of such bodies in all regions where they do not exist;

30. *Recognizes* the fundamental role of civil society in the fight against racism, racial discrimination, xenophobia and related intolerance, in particular in assisting States to develop regulations and strategies, in taking measures and action against such forms of discrimination and through follow-up implementation;

31. *Decides* that the General Assembly, through its role in policy formulation, the Economic and Social

Council, through its role in overall guidance and coordination, in accordance with their respective roles under the Charter of the United Nations and Assembly resolution 50/227 of 24 May 1996, and the Human Rights Council shall constitute a three-tiered intergovernmental process for the comprehensive implementation of and follow-up to the Durban Declaration and Programme of Action;

32. *Stresses and reaffirms* its role as the highest intergovernmental mechanism for the formulation and appraisal of policy on matters related to the economic, social and related fields, in accordance with Chapter IX of the Charter, including in the comprehensive implementation of and follow-up to the goals and targets set at all the major United Nations conferences, summits and special sessions;

33. *Decides* to convene in 2009 a review conference on the implementation of the Durban Declaration and Programme of Action to be conducted within the framework of the General Assembly, and, to this end, requests the Human Rights Council to undertake preparations for this event, making use of the three existing and ongoing follow-up mechanisms, and to formulate a concrete plan and provide updates and reports on this issue on an annual basis starting in 2007;

34. *Reaffirms* that the Human Rights Council shall have a central role in the monitoring of the implementation of the Durban Declaration and Programme of Action within the United Nations system and in advising the General Assembly thereon;

35. *Expresses its appreciation* for the continuing work in follow-up to the World Conference undertaken by the Intergovernmental Working Group on the Effective Implementation of the Durban Declaration and Programme of Action, the group of independent eminent experts on the implementation of the Durban Declaration and Programme of Action and the Working Group of Experts on People of African Descent;

36. *Welcomes* the conclusions and recommendations agreed upon by the Intergovernmental Working Group on the Effective Implementation of the Durban Declaration and Programme of Action at its fourth session, and welcomes in particular the identification and/or consideration of substantive and procedural gaps, as well as the request for the nomination of five highly qualified experts to further study the content and scope of those gaps, including but not limited to the areas identified in the conclusions of the Chair of the high-level seminar, and, in consultation with human rights treaty bodies, the Special Rapporteur on contemporary forms of racism, racial discrimination, xenophobia and related intolerance and other relevant mandate-holders, to produce a base document that contains concrete recommendations on the means or avenues to bridge those gaps, including but not limited to the drafting of a new protocol to the International Convention on the Elimination of All Forms of Racial Discrimination or the adoption of new instruments, and for the Committee on the Elimination of Racial Discrimination to conduct further study on possible measures to strengthen the implementation of the Convention and its proposals regarding the assessment and evaluation of the implementation of existing international human rights instruments by States parties, and to this end encourages the Intergovernmental Working Group to continue its work related to the preparation of complementary international standards in accordance with the Durban Declaration and Programme of Action;

37. *Acknowledges* the centrality of resource mobilization, effective global partnership and international cooperation in the context of paragraphs 157 and 158 of the Durban Programme of Action for the successful realization of commitments undertaken at the World Conference, and to this end emphasizes the importance of the mandate of the group of independent eminent experts on the implementation of the Durban Declaration and Programme of Action, especially in mobilizing the necessary political will required for the successful implementation of the Declaration and Programme of Action;

38. *Requests* the Secretary-General to provide the necessary resources for the effective fulfilment of the mandates of the Intergovernmental Working Group on the Effective Implementation of the Durban Declaration and Programme of Action, the Working Group of Experts on People of African Descent and the group of independent eminent experts on the implementation of the Durban Declaration and Programme of Action;

39. *Expresses its concern* at the increasing incidence of racism in various sporting events, while noting with appreciation the efforts made by some governing bodies of the various sporting codes to combat racism, and in this regard invites all international sporting bodies to promote, through their national, regional and international federations, a world of sport free from racism and racial discrimination;

40. *Invites*, in this context, the Fédération internationale de football association, in connection with the 2010 soccer World Cup tournament to be held in South Africa, to consider introducing a visible theme on non-racism in football, requests the Secretary-General to bring this invitation to the attention of the Fédération and to bring the issue of racism in sport to the attention of other relevant international sporting bodies, and, in this regard, appreciates the joint efforts of the Government of Germany, the Secretary-General and the Special Rapporteur on contemporary forms of racism, racial discrimination, xenophobia and related intolerance during the 2006 World Cup;

IV

Special Rapporteur on contemporary forms of racism, racial discrimination, xenophobia and related intolerance and follow-up to his visits

41. *Expresses its full support and appreciation* for the work of the Special Rapporteur on contemporary forms of racism, racial discrimination, xenophobia and related intolerance, and encourages its continuation;

42. *Reiterates its call* to all Member States, intergovernmental organizations, relevant organizations of the United Nations system and non-governmental organizations to cooperate fully with the Special Rapporteur,

and calls upon States to consider responding favourably to his requests for visits so as to enable him to fulfil his mandate fully and effectively;

43. *Recognizes with deep concern* the increase in anti-Semitism, Christianophobia and Islamophobia in various parts of the world, as well as the emergence of racial and violent movements based on racism and discriminatory ideas directed against Arab, Christian, Jewish and Muslim communities, as well as all religious communities, communities of people of African descent, communities of people of Asian descent, communities of indigenous people and other communities;

44. *Encourages* closer collaboration between the Special Rapporteur and the Office of the United Nations High Commissioner for Human Rights, in particular the Anti-Discrimination Unit;

45. *Urges* the United Nations High Commissioner for Human Rights to provide States, at their request, with advisory services and technical assistance to enable them to implement fully the recommendations of the Special Rapporteur;

46. *Requests* the Secretary-General to provide the Special Rapporteur with all the necessary human and financial assistance to carry out his mandate efficiently, effectively and expeditiously and to enable him to submit an interim report to the General Assembly at its sixty-second session;

47. *Takes note* of the recommendations contained in the interim report of the Special Rapporteur, and urges Member States and other relevant stakeholders to consider implementing those recommendations;

48. *Requests* the Special Rapporteur to continue giving particular attention to the negative impact of racism, racial discrimination, xenophobia and related intolerance on the full enjoyment of civil, cultural, economic, political and social rights by national or ethnic, religious and linguistic minorities, immigrant populations, asylum-seekers and refugees;

49. *Invites* Member States to demonstrate greater commitment to fighting racism in sport by conducting educational and awareness-raising activities and by strongly condemning the perpetrators of racist incidents, in cooperation with national and international sports organizations;

V

General

50. *Requests* the Secretary-General to submit a report on the implementation of the present resolution to the General Assembly at its sixty-second session;

51. *Decides* to remain seized of this important matter at its sixty-second session under the item entitled "Elimination of racism and racial discrimination".

RECORDED VOTE ON RESOLUTION 61/149:

In favour: Afghanistan, Albania, Algeria, Andorra, Angola, Antigua and Barbuda, Argentina, Armenia, Austria, Azerbaijan, Bahamas, Bahrain, Bangladesh, Barbados, Belarus, Belgium, Belize, Benin, Bhutan, Bolivia, Bosnia and Herzegovina, Botswana, Brazil, Brunei Darussalam, Bulgaria, Burkina Faso, Burundi, Cambodia, Cameroon, Cape Verde, Central African Republic, Chile, China, Colombia, Comoros, Congo, Costa Rica, Côte d'Ivoire, Croatia, Cuba, Cyprus, Czech Republic, Democratic People's Republic of Korea, Democratic Republic of the Congo, Denmark, Djibouti, Dominica, Dominican Republic, Ecuador, Egypt, El Salvador, Eritrea, Estonia, Ethiopia, Fiji, Finland, France, Gabon, Gambia, Georgia, Germany, Ghana, Greece, Grenada, Guatemala, Guinea, Guinea-Bissau, Guyana, Haiti, Honduras, Hungary, Iceland, India, Indonesia, Iran, Iraq, Ireland, Italy, Jamaica, Japan, Jordan, Kazakhstan, Kenya, Kuwait, Kyrgyzstan, Lao People's Democratic Republic, Latvia, Lebanon, Lesotho, Liberia, Libyan Arab Jamahiriya, Liechtenstein, Lithuania, Luxembourg, Madagascar, Malawi, Malaysia, Maldives, Mali, Malta, Mauritania, Mauritius, Mexico, Micronesia, Moldova, Monaco, Mongolia, Montenegro, Morocco, Mozambique, Myanmar, Namibia, Nepal, Netherlands, New Zealand, Nicaragua, Niger, Nigeria, Norway, Oman, Pakistan, Panama, Papua New Guinea, Paraguay, Peru, Philippines, Poland, Portugal, Qatar, Republic of Korea, Romania, Russian Federation, Rwanda, Saint Lucia, Saint Vincent and the Grenadines, Samoa, San Marino, Sao Tome and Principe, Saudi Arabia, Senegal, Serbia, Sierra Leone, Singapore, Slovakia, Slovenia, Solomon Islands, Somalia, South Africa, Spain, Sri Lanka, Sudan, Suriname, Swaziland, Sweden, Switzerland, Syrian Arab Republic, Tajikistan, Thailand, The former Yugoslav Republic of Macedonia, Timor-Leste, Togo, Tonga, Trinidad and Tobago, Tunisia, Turkey, Turkmenistan, Tuvalu, Ukraine, United Arab Emirates, United Kingdom, United Republic of Tanzania, Uruguay, Uzbekistan, Vanuatu, Venezuela, Viet Nam, Yemen, Zambia, Zimbabwe.

Against: Israel, United States.

Abstaining: Australia, Canada, Marshall Islands, Palau.

Commemoration of the abolition of the transatlantic slave trade

On 29 September [A/61/233], Saint Lucia, on behalf of States members of the Caribbean Community, requested the inclusion in the General Assembly's agenda of an item entitled "Commemoration of the two-hundredth anniversary of the abolition of the trans-Atlantic slave trade". Noting that the anniversary would fall in 2007, it suggested that the occasion be marked by a special event that year to honour the memory of the millions who died as a result of slavery, including during their transportation through the Middle Passage, in revolt and resistance to their enslavement. It would also serve as an opportunity to acknowledge the legacy of slavery as being at the heart of situations of profound social and economic inequality, hatred, bigotry, racism and prejudice, which continued to affect people of African descent. The trans-Atlantic slave trade, which lasted for almost 500 years, was responsible for the forced removal of millions of persons, mostly from West Africa, to the "new world" of the Americas, an estimated 13 per cent of whom died as a result of the rigours of the journey, and many others on account of resistance to slavery and of rebellion. Slavery and the slave trade were among the most serious violations of human rights in history, yet it took nearly 200 years for the international community to acknowledge it as a crime against humanity, and the issue of reparations and compensation for that crime remained outstanding.

The General Assembly, in resolution 61/19 of 28 November (see below), honoured the memory of those who died as a result of slavery, recognized that slave trade and slavery were among the worst violations of human rights in the history of humanity and acknowledged that the legacy of that crime was at the heart of situations of profound social and economic inequality, hatred, bigotry, racism and prejudice, which continued to affect people of African descent. It declared 25 March 2007 as the International Day for the Commemoration of the Two-hundreth Anniversary of the Abolition of the Transatlantic Slave Trade.

GENERAL ASSEMBLY ACTION

On 28 November [meeting 59], the General Assembly adopted **resolution 61/19** [draft: A/61/L.28 & Add.1] without vote [agenda item 155].

Commemoration of the two-hundredth anniversary of the abolition of the transatlantic slave trade

The General Assembly,

Reaffirming the Universal Declaration of Human Rights which proclaimed that no one shall be held in slavery or servitude and that slavery and the slave trade shall be prohibited in all their forms,

Recalling that the transatlantic slave trade, which operated between the fifteenth and late nineteenth centuries, involved the forced transportation of millions of Africans as slaves, mostly from West Africa to the Americas, thereby enriching the imperial powers of the time,

Honouring the memory of those who died as a result of slavery, including through exposure to the horrors of the middle passage and in revolt against and resistance to enslavement,

Recognizing that the slave trade and slavery are among the worst violations of human rights in the history of humanity, bearing in mind particularly their scale and duration,

Deeply concerned that it has taken the international community almost two hundred years to acknowledge that slavery and the slave trade are a crime against humanity and should always have been so,

Recalling that slavery and the slave trade were declared a crime against humanity by the World Conference against Racism, Racial Discrimination, Xenophobia and Related Intolerance, held in Durban, South Africa, from 31 August to 8 September 2001,

Acknowledging that the slave trade and the legacy of slavery are at the heart of situations of profound social and economic inequality, hatred, bigotry, racism and prejudice, which continue to affect people of African descent today,

Recalling paragraphs 98 to 106 of the Durban Declaration, and emphasizing, in particular, the importance of the "provision of effective remedies, recourse, redress, and compensatory and other measures at the national, regional and international levels", aimed at countering the continued impact of slavery and the slave trade,

Recognizing the knowledge gap that exists with regard to the consequences created by the slave trade and slavery, and on the interactions, past and present, generated among the peoples of Europe, Africa, Asia and the Americas, including the Caribbean,

Welcoming the work of the International Scientific Committee for the Slave Route Project of the United Nations Educational, Scientific and Cultural Organization, which aims to correct this knowledge gap, and looks forward to its report in due course,

Recalling resolution 28 adopted by the General Conference of the United Nations Educational, Scientific and Cultural Organization at its thirty-first session, proclaiming 2004 the International Year to Commemorate the Struggle against Slavery and its Abolition, and recalling also that 23 August is that Organization's International Day for the Remembrance of the Slave Trade and its Abolition,

Noting that 2007 will mark the two-hundredth anniversary of the abolition of the transatlantic slave trade, which contributed significantly to the abolition of slavery,

1. *Decides* to designate 25 March 2007 as the International Day for the Commemoration of the Two-hundredth Anniversary of the Abolition of the Transatlantic Slave Trade;

2. *Urges* Member States that have not already done so to develop educational programmes, including through school curricula, designed to educate and inculcate in future generations an understanding of the lessons, history and consequences of slavery and the slave trade;

3. *Decides* to convene, on 26 March 2007, a special commemorative meeting of the General Assembly on the two-hundredth anniversary of the abolition of the transatlantic slave trade;

4. *Requests* the Secretary-General to establish a programme of outreach, with the involvement of Member States and civil society, including non-governmental organizations, to appropriately commemorate the two-hundredth anniversary of the abolition of the transatlantic slave trade;

5. *Also requests* the Secretary-General to submit to the General Assembly at its sixty-second session a special report on initiatives taken by States to implement paragraphs 101 and 102 of the Durban Declaration aimed at countering the legacy of slavery and contributing to the restoration of the dignity of the victims of slavery and the slave trade.

On 22 December, the Assembly decided that the item "Commemoration of the two-hundredth anniversary of the abolition of the trans-Atlantic slave trade" would remain for consideration during its resumed sixty-first (2007) session (**decision 61/552**).

Contemporary forms of racism

Reports of Special Rapporteur. In his annual report to the Commission [E/CN.4/2006/16], the Special Rapporteur on contemporary forms of racism, racial discrimination, xenophobia and related intolerance, Doudou Diène (Senegal), described his activities over the past year and highlighted some of the root causes and manifestations of contemporary forms of racism, noting that its resurgence was mainly driven by intolerance and hostility towards immigration; increasing acts of religious defamation, particularly anti-Semitism, Christianophobia and Islamophobia; the increasing rejection of multiculturalism in identity constructs; a tendency to establish a hierarchy in racial discrimination; the increasingly overt intellectual legitimization of racism; the acceptance of racism as normal through the pervasiveness of racist and xenophobic political platforms by extreme right-wing parties; and the increase in racism in sport, in particular football. The worrisome resurgence of anti-Semitism, for example, was illustrated by attacks against young orthodox Jews in parts of the United Kingdom, revisionist literature issued in France and cultural acceptance of related behaviour in the Russian Federation. Regarding the Middle East and the reported denial by the Iranian President that the Holocaust occurred, while advocating the removal of the State of Israel to Europe, the Special Rapporteur observed that such a perspective was a manifestation of anti-Semitism and undermined the position of the international community on the existence of two States, Israel and Palestine. Also of concern were examples of Christianophobia in the form of attacks against places of worship in Nigeria and Pakistan and against the proselytizing of various evangelical movements in parts of Africa, South America and the Caribbean, and Asia. To address the problem, the Special Rapporteur recommended that Member States promote the link between efforts to combat racism and the construction of democratic, interactive and egalitarian multiculturalism, ensuring that cultural diversity became a weapon against racism. The fight against racism needed to involve economic, social and political measures and relate to the question of identity, taking into account the dialectic between respect for the culture and religion of minorities and the promotion of cross-fertilization and interactions among national communities. Efforts on the intellectual front should involve combating, through education and information, ideas and concepts likely to incite or legitimize racism and related phenomena, in particular on the Internet. There was also a need to stress the seriousness of racist and xenophobic practices at entry points to countries, such as airports, train stations and ports. In that regard, it was essential for such areas not to become no-rights zones for immigrants and asylum-seekers. Instead, Member States should recognize the importance of scrupulous respect for fundamental rights, the presence of human rights organizations, proper levels of sanitation and available recourse procedures and defence mechanisms in those places. To eradicate the increase in racism in sport, programmes and initiatives by international sports bodies should be encouraged, and education, awareness-raising and prevention initiatives by Member States promoted. The Special Rapporteur also advocated the promotion by international and national sports bodies of codes of ethics against racism in sport.

In a March addendum to the report [E/CN.4/2006/16/Add.1], the Special Rapporteur summarized communications transmitted to 23 Governments and the European Union regarding cases of racism, racial discrimination, xenophobia and related intolerance, and replies received.

Communication. On 10 March [E/CN.4/2006/G/10], Iran, referring to statements regarding Israel and the Holocaust attributed to its President in the Special Rapporteur's report (see above), noted that its clarification on the issue, provided upon the Special Rapporteur's request, was not reflected in the report. Attached to the communication was a copy of that clarification.

Further reports of Special Rapporteur. In response to a 2005 Commission request [YUN 2005, p. 766], the Special Rapporteur submitted a January report [E/CN.4/2006/54] updating and expanding his 2004 study on political platforms promoting or inciting racial discrimination. Such platforms included all political ideologies, statements, programmes or strategies that advocated racial discrimination or hatred and xenophobia, intended to enable certain groups to gain political power and marginalize others in any given country. The current rise of racism and xenophobia was confirmed by two related factors: their political normalization and exploitation, and their intellectual legitimization. Regarding the former, the Special Rapporteur noted the alarming tendency of parties and groups with racist and xenophobic platforms to penetrate the political agendas of democratic parties under the pretext of combating terrorism, defending the "national identity", promoting "national preference" and combating illegal immigration. That penetration had led to a generalized acceptance of racist and xenophobic statements, writings and deeds, with the political rhetoric of democratic parties gradually borrowing the language, concepts and values of those platforms. That rhetoric became the new political expression of discrimination and xenophobia, and resulted in the rejection or non-recognition of multiculturalism and cultural diversity, as well as the identification of groups that a country needed to protect itself against, namely, non-nationals, immigrants and asylum-seekers. On the question of intellectual legitimization, the Special Rapporteur said that the problem was illustrated by a debate that ensued after the outbreak of unrest in the suburbs of major French cities, in which two eminent French intellectuals, in their interpretation of the problem, seemed to blame the violence on people of African origin or Muslim Arabs.

Overall, the Special Rapporteur concluded that the resurgence of racism and related phenomena reflected a major regression affecting democratic progress. New life had been breathed into ancient and modern forms of racism and racial discrimination. He recommended that the fight against racism, discrimination and xenophobia should be built around a political and legal strategy based on the expression, at the highest level of Government, of a political determination to combat those practices in all their forms, and an ethical, intellectual and cultural strategy for eradicating the deep roots of racist and xenophobic culture and mentality through education, the media and the condemnation of related literature. The impact of racist and xenophobic political platforms on the programmes of democratic parties should be warded off by linking the fight against all forms of racism with the fight against terrorism and illegal immigration. The temptation to criminalize immigrants and asylum-seekers and reduce the problem to a question of security should be rejected. The fight against racism also demanded the construction of democratic, egalitarian and interactive multiculturalism, the promotion of cultural pluralism and the fostering of interactions among different communities.

The Special Rapporteur visited Switzerland (9-13 January) [E/CN.4/2006/16/Add.4; A/HRC/19/Add.2], where he raised key questions concerning the existence of racism in the country, its principal manifestations and how the authorities were addressing the problem, in cooperation with civil society and the communities affected. Within that framework, the Special Rapporteur examined, among other things, the country's linguistic and religious composition, the distinctive features of its federal system, its legislative background in addressing issues relating to racial discrimination and a national referendum on immigration and asylum. He concluded that Switzerland faced a dynamic of racism and xenophobia and that one of the underlying causes was the politicization of identity-related tensions in the country, mostly by political parties with racist and xenophobic platforms, and their ability to implement their programmes through alliances. Like all modern societies, Swiss society was characterized by profound multiculturalism, owing to waves of immigration from European countries and other parts of the world. Refugees and asylum-seekers were being singled out as responsible for rising unemployment or the State debt and there had been a regretful and increasing tendency to criminalize foreigners and immigrants through the enactment of laws that made them legally vulnerable, resulting in their social marginalization and cultural stigmatization.

Pointing to the authorities' lack of clarity or political determination to tackle the problem effectively, the Special Rapporteur observed that, while they recognized the existence of racism and xenophobia in the country, the problem was not deemed to be serious enough, and although the country had adopted several laws concerning respect for and promotion of human rights, the lack of comprehensive national legislation against racism posed a major obstacle to the country's efforts to combat the problem. He made a series of recommendations placing emphasis on the recognition of the dynamic of racism and xenophobia and the expression of the political will to combat those phenomena; the need for a national programme of action against racism and xenophobia comprising national legislation and a cultural and ethical strategy for the long-term construction of a multicultural society based on the recognition and promotion of the cultural, ethnic and religious diversity of Swiss society; and the promotion of interaction and reciprocal knowledge among the various communities making up that society.

In a February report [E/CN.4/2006/17], submitted in response to a 2005 Commission request [YUN 2005, p. 764], the Special Rapporteur examined the situation of Muslim and Arab peoples in various parts of the world, based on information provided by two States, the outcome of a previous expert seminar on the topic and meetings he had held with other sources. The Special Rapporteur found that, since the September 2001 terrorist attacks in the United States [YUN 2001, p. 60], there had been a serious upsurge in discrimination against Muslim and Arab people and acts of violence against their places of worship and culture, mostly manifested through hostility towards the religion of Islam and its believers. In that regard, the politicization of Islam was accompanied by the open validation of Islamophobia in intellectual discourse. Islam was identified with terrorism, and excessive emphasis was placed on containment, mainly from a security perspective and through the control of Muslim education and monitoring of places of worship and congregation. That upsurge in Islamophobia was accompanied by a general increase in the defamation of religions, especially Judaism, Christianity and other spiritual traditions such as Hinduism, Buddhism and traditional religions. Countries witnessing serious outbreaks of Islamophobia shared certain characteristics, including a deep-rooted historical antagonism towards Islam; the popularity of far-right-wing parties and their participation in government; the significance of racist and xenophobic platforms in the programmes of democratic parties; and a lack of will by political leaders to combat racism and Islamophobia. The Special Rapporteur recommended that Member States demonstrate their political commitment to combating all forms of religious defamation, advocate dialogue, and condemn all forms of violence and confrontation in resolving religious tensions between communities. He addressed other recommendations to the Commission on measures for addressing the defamation of religions, the conflation of Islam with violence and terrorism, the relationship between Islamophobia and multiculturalism, and legal standards regarding the matter of religion.

The Special Rapporteur visited the Russian Federation (12-17 June) [A/HRC/4/19/Add.3], following information from NGOs and the media alleging an alarming trend in racism and xenophobia. He found that, while there was no State policy of racism, the society faced an alarming trend of racism and xenophobia, manifested by the increasing racially motivated crimes and attacks, including by neo-Nazi groups, particularly against people of non-Slav appearance from the Caucasus, Africa, Asia or the Arab world; the growing level of violence of those attacks; the extension of violence to human rights defenders, intellectuals and students fighting racism; the relative impunity enjoyed by the perpetrators; the rise of anti-Semitism and other forms of religious intolerance, particularly against Muslims; the increasing importance of political parties with racist and xenophobic platforms; and the virtual correspondence of social, economic and political marginalization with the mapping of ethnic minorities and other groups affected by discrimination. The Special Rapporteur recommended the official recognition of the existence of racism, racial discrimination and xenophobia and the expression of the political will to combat it; the adoption of a federal plan of action to combat the problem, designed in consultation with democratic political parties, independent human rights organizations and the communities concerned; the establishment of an independent institution for human rights promotion and protection and to combat discrimination; and the adoption of legal, cultural and ethical strategies aimed at uprooting the culture and mentality of racism and xenophobia and promoting the construction of a democratic, egalitarian and interactive multiculturalism.

Pursuant to General Assembly resolution 60/144 [YUN 2005, p. 759], the Secretary-General, in September [A/61/335], transmitted the Special Rapporteur's interim report, which summarized his activities during the year, including coordination efforts with other human rights mechanisms, and participation in meetings, conferences, and field missions. The Special Rapporteur's activities focused on monitoring and analysing old and new forms of racism, racial discrimination and xenophobia and promoting a political and legal, and a cultural and ethnic strategy to combat them. He asked the Assembly to draw Member States' attention to the alarming signs of a retreat in the struggle against racism, owing to the growing acceptance of racist content in the programmes of democratic parties, and to the rise in racist political violence. Emphasizing the importance of political will in efforts to combat the problem, the Special Rapporteur noted that the struggle against racism and xenophobia was linked to the recognition and promotion of multiculturalism. He highlighted the need for the Assembly to underline the compatibility and complementarity of the freedoms of expression and of religion in the struggle against all forms of racism. In the spirit of the International Covenant on Civil and Political Rights, adopted by the Assembly in resolution 2200 A (XXI) [YUN 1966, p. 423], he recommended that relevant bodies and mechanisms consider the additional provisions needed to strengthen that complementarity. The Special Rapporteur also advocated action by the International Federation of Football Association (FIFA) to combat racism in sport and by the United Nations to strengthen its role in interreligious and intercultural dialogue, so as to counter religious defamation, including anti-Semitism, Christianophobia, and more particularly, Islamophobia.

In Italy (9-13 October) [A/HRC/4/19/Add.4], the Special Rapporteur found a disturbing trend of xenophobia and manifestations of racism, mainly affecting the Sinti and Roma communities, immigrants and asylum seekers, especially those of African or Eastern European origin, and the Muslim community. The problem was encouraged by the legacy and impact of national policies, the public perceptions of extreme right-wing parties' racist political platforms, and media incitement to racial and religious hatred under the guises of freedom of expression and the need to combat terrorism. That xenophobic trend was also a manifestation of the fear resulting from an identity crisis in Italian society and the challenge of multiculturalism, particularly regarding non-European migrants.

While drawing attention to some positive developments in the Government's efforts to combat those problems, the Special Rapporteur recommended that the Government accord priority to its efforts in that regard and express publicly its disapproval of racist and xenophobic political platforms, and that the country's National Plan of Action for combating racial discrimination be redefined to include a comprehensive strategy for addressing all aspects of the problem and all affected groups, in compliance with DDPA. Other recommendations advocated the improvement of legislation on the issue and the necessary training for judicial and law enforcement agencies; the establishment of an independent national institution for promoting and protecting human rights; severe punishment for the incitement of racial and religious hatred and related crimes; Government action to secure the rights of asylum-seekers, migrants and other national minorities; and the adoption of an ethical and cultural strategy for promoting mutual knowledge and interaction between different communities, and for promoting multiculturalism and the related process of constructing a new multicultural identity.

Incompatibility between democracy and racism

On 27 November [A/62/53 (dec. 2/106)], the Human Rights Council invited OHCHR, in collaboration with the Special Rapporteur, to continue to analyse the issue of incitement and promotion of racism, racial discrimination, xenophobia and related intolerance in political debate. It requested the Special Rapporteur to include in his reports the issue of political participation and representation of groups vulnerable to racism in the decision-making process in governments, parties, parliaments and civil society, taking into consideration their possible contribution to reinforcing the anti-discrimination perspective in political and social life, with a view to strengthening democracy.

GENERAL ASSEMBLY ACTION

On 19 December [meeting 81], the General Assembly, on the recommendation of the Third Committee [A/61/441], adopted **resolution 61/147** by recorded vote (121-4-60) [agenda item 65 *(a)*].

Inadmissibility of certain practices that contribute to fuelling contemporary forms of racism, racial discrimination, xenophobia and related intolerance

The General Assembly,

Guided by the Charter of the United Nations, the Universal Declaration of Human Rights, the International Covenant on Civil and Political Rights, the International Convention on the Elimination of All Forms of Racial Discrimination and other relevant human rights instruments,

Recalling the provisions of Commission on Human Rights resolutions 2004/16 of 16 April 2004 and 2005/5 of 14 April 2005, as well as General Assembly resolution 60/143 of 16 December 2005 on this issue and Assembly resolution 60/144 of 16 December 2005 entitled "Global efforts for the total elimination of racism, racial discrimination, xenophobia and related intolerance and the comprehensive implementation of and follow-up to the Durban Declaration and Programme of Action",

Recalling also the Charter of the Nuremberg Tribunal and the Judgement of the Tribunal, which recognized the Waffen SS organization and all its integral parts as criminal and declared it responsible for many war crimes and crimes against humanity,

Recalling further the relevant provisions of the Durban Declaration and Programme of Action adopted by the World Conference against Racism, Racial Discrimination, Xenophobia and Related Intolerance on 8 September 2001, in particular paragraph 2 of the Declaration and paragraph 86 of the Programme of Action,

Recalling equally the study undertaken by the Special Rapporteur on contemporary forms of racism, racial discrimination, xenophobia and related intolerance, and taking note of his report,

Alarmed, in this regard, at the spread in many parts of the world of various extremist political parties, movements and groups, including neo-Nazis and skinhead groups,

1. *Reaffirms* the provision of the Durban Declaration in which States condemned the persistence and resurgence of neo-Nazism, neo-Fascism and violent nationalist ideologies based on racial and national prejudice and stated that those phenomena could never be justified in any instance or in any circumstances;

2. *Expresses deep concern* over the glorification of the Nazi movement and former members of the Waffen SS organization, including by erecting monuments and memorials as well as holding public demonstrations in the name of the glorification of the Nazi past, the Nazi movement and neo-Nazism;

3. *Notes with concern* the increase in the number of racist incidents in several countries and the rise of skinhead groups, which have been responsible for many of these incidents, as observed by the Special Rapporteur on contemporary forms of racism, racial discrimination, xenophobia and related intolerance;

4. *Reaffirms* that such acts may be qualified to fall within the scope of activities described in article 4 of the International Convention on the Elimination of All

Forms of Racial Discrimination, and that they represent a clear and manifest abuse of the rights to freedom of peaceful assembly and of association as well as the rights to freedom of opinion and expression within the meaning of those rights as guaranteed by the Universal Declaration of Human Rights, the International Covenant on Civil and Political Rights and the International Convention on the Elimination of All Forms of Racial Discrimination;

5. *Stresses* that the practices described above do injustice to the memory of the countless victims of crimes against humanity committed in the Second World War, in particular those committed by the SS organization, and poison the minds of young people, and that those practices are incompatible with the obligations of States Members of the United Nations under its Charter and are incompatible with the goals and principles of the Organization;

6. *Also stresses* that such practices fuel contemporary forms of racism, racial discrimination, xenophobia and related intolerance and contribute to the spread and multiplication of various extremist political parties, movements and groups, including neo-Nazis and skinhead groups;

7. *Emphasizes* the need to take the necessary measures to put an end to the practices described above, and calls upon States to take more effective measures to combat those phenomena and the extremist movements, which pose a real threat to democratic values;

8. *Reaffirms* that, according to article 4 of the International Convention on the Elimination of All Forms of Racial Discrimination, States parties to that instrument are, inter alia, under the obligation:

(*a*) To condemn all propaganda and all organizations that are based on ideas of racial superiority or that attempt to justify or promote racial hatred and discrimination in any form;

(*b*) To undertake to adopt immediate and positive measures designed to eradicate all incitement to, or acts of, such discrimination with due regard to the principles embodied in the Universal Declaration of Human Rights and the rights expressly set forth in article 5 of the Convention;

(*c*) To declare as an offence punishable by law all dissemination of ideas based on racial superiority or hatred, incitement to racial discrimination, as well as all acts of violence or incitement to such acts against any race or group of persons of another colour or ethnic origin, and also the provision of any assistance to racist activities, including the financing thereof;

(*d*) To declare illegal and prohibit organizations and organized and all other propaganda activities that promote and incite racial discrimination and to recognize participation in such organizations or activities as an offence punishable by law;

(*e*) To prohibit public authorities or public institutions, national or local, from promoting or inciting racial discrimination;

9. *Calls upon* those States that have made reservations to article 4 of the International Convention on the Elimination of All Forms of Racial Discrimination to give serious consideration to withdrawing such reservations as a matter of priority;

10. *Recalls* the request of the Commission on Human Rights in its resolution 2005/55 that the Special Rapporteur continue to reflect on this issue, make relevant recommendations in his future reports and seek and take into account in this regard the views of Governments and non-governmental organizations;

11. *Invites* Governments and non-governmental organizations to cooperate fully with the Special Rapporteur in the exercise of the aforementioned task;

12. *Decides* to remain seized of the issue.

RECORDED VOTE ON RESOLUTION 61/147:

In favour: Algeria, Angola, Antigua and Barbuda, Argentina, Armenia, Azerbaijan, Bahamas, Bahrain, Bangladesh, Barbados, Belarus, Belize, Benin, Bhutan, Bolivia, Botswana, Brazil, Brunei Darussalam, Burkina Faso, Burundi, Cambodia, Cameroon, Central African Republic, Chile, China, Colombia, Comoros, Congo, Costa Rica, Côte d'Ivoire, Cuba, Democratic People's Republic of Korea, Democratic Republic of the Congo, Djibouti, Dominica, Dominican Republic, Ecuador, Egypt, El Salvador, Eritrea, Ethiopia, Fiji, Gabon, Gambia, Ghana, Grenada, Guatemala, Guinea, Guyana, Haiti, Honduras, India, Indonesia, Iran, Iraq, Jamaica, Jordan, Kazakhstan, Kenya, Kuwait, Kyrgyzstan, Lao People's Democratic Republic, Lebanon, Lesotho, Liberia, Libyan Arab Jamahiriya, Madagascar, Malawi, Malaysia, Maldives, Mali, Mauritania, Mauritius, Mexico, Mongolia, Morocco, Mozambique, Myanmar, Namibia, Nicaragua, Niger, Nigeria, Oman, Pakistan, Paraguay, Peru, Philippines, Qatar, Russian Federation, Rwanda, Saint Lucia, Saint Vincent and the Grenadines, Sao Tome and Principe, Saudi Arabia, Senegal, Sierra Leone, Singapore, Solomon Islands, Somalia, South Africa, Sri Lanka, Sudan, Suriname, Swaziland, Syrian Arab Republic, Tajikistan, Thailand, Timor-Leste, Togo, Trinidad and Tobago, Tunisia, Turkmenistan, Uganda, United Arab Emirates, Uruguay, Uzbekistan, Venezuela, Viet Nam, Yemen, Zambia, Zimbabwe.

Against: Japan, Marshall Islands, Micronesia, United States.

Abstaining: Albania, Andorra, Australia, Austria, Belgium, Bosnia and Herzegovina, Bulgaria, Canada, Cape Verde, Croatia, Cyprus, Czech Republic, Denmark, Estonia, Finland, France, Georgia, Germany, Greece, Guinea-Bissau, Hungary, Iceland, Ireland, Israel, Italy, Latvia, Liechtenstein, Lithuania, Luxembourg, Malta, Moldova, Monaco, Montenegro, Nauru, Nepal, Netherlands, New Zealand, Norway, Palau, Panama, Papua New Guinea, Poland, Portugal, Republic of Korea, Romania, Samoa, San Marino, Serbia, Slovakia, Slovenia, Spain, Sweden, Switzerland, The former Yugoslav Republic of Macedonia, Turkey, Tuvalu, Ukraine, United Kingdom, United Republic of Tanzania, Vanuatu.

Right to nationality

Report of Secretary-General. Pursuant to a 2005 Commission request [YUN 2005, p. 766], the Secretary-General submitted a report [E/CN.4/2006/88] summarizing information received from six Governments and five intergovernmental organizations and NGOs on human rights and arbitrary deprivation of nationality.

Human Rights Council action. On 27 November [A/62/53 (dec. 2/111)], the Human Rights Council called on its relevant mechanisms and appropriate UN treaty bodies to continue to collect information on the question of human rights and arbitrary deprivation of nationality and to take account of such information, together with any recommendations thereon, in their reports and activities. OHCHR was encouraged to do the same, while the Secretary-General was requested to collect information on the issue for the Council's consideration at its fifth session.

Protection of migrants

Report of Special Rapporteur. In his first report [E/CN.4/2006/73] to the Commission, the Special Rapporteur on the human rights of migrants, Jorge Bustamante (Mexico), described his activities and mandate and highlighted his programme of work and the main situations requiring his attention. He intended to work within the framework of international human rights instruments, including the 1990 International Convention on the Protection of the Rights of All Migrant Workers and Members of Their Families [YUN 1990, p. 594], and to develop the activities undertaken by his predecessor and other special procedures mandate-holders. He would also establish and consolidate follow-up to his own activities, and engage in dialogue, consultations and networking with all interested parties. The Special Rapporteur drew attention to issues in which his predecessors had intervened over the years that deserved further consideration, the first of which was recognition of the demand for the labour of migrant workers in many host countries and the reluctance to meet that demand because of anti-immigrant ideologies that were often tinged with xenophobia and racism. Denial of that demand was also one of the main factors leading to illegal migration. As such, the Special Rapporteur considered the situation of migrants with irregular administrative status to be a priority issue. In that context, he intended to consider information regarding real demand for migrant workers in Member States; data on the numbers involved, with a view to ascertaining the level of acceptance of the demand for immigrant labour; data on indicators of changes in anti-immigrant ideologies, such as statistics on police profiling or hate crimes against aliens; and statistics on crimes and abuses committed against migrants and sanctions imposed.

Another issue of concern to the Special Rapporteur were reports of serious human rights violations committed in the context of legal migration, including complaints of abusive conditions of work, the deduction of wages to pay mediation fees to private recruiting agencies, changes to contracts previously agreed upon, long working hours without overtime pay, payment of wages below what was agreed upon, mistreatment and restrictions to freedom of movement, and complaints of sexual abuse in the case of female migrant workers. The practice of subcontracting work as a means of avoiding labour responsibilities by the main employer made it particularly difficult for migrant workers to claim their rights in the face of abuse. Against that background, the Special Rapporteur determined that all migrants, whether regular or irregular, temporary of permanent, were affected by discrimination and anti-migration ideology. In that context, the issue of protection, especially consular protection, deserved further consideration and examination, as such practices could provide important examples and guidance to Governments seeking to protect migrants from violations and abuse. The Special Rapporteur also considered different aspects of violations against migrant workers and the underlying factors leading to such violations. He intended to continue examining patterns of discrimination suffered by migrants, according priority to the gender dimension of migration, violations by both State and non-State actors and practices that could render migrants vulnerable. He would also focus on the situation of migrant children and continue to address the developmental, economic and social factors at the core of many existing problems.

An addendum to the report [E/CN.4/2006/73/Add.1] summarized the 34 communications the Special Rapporteur and his predecessor had sent to 25 Governments between 1 January and 31 December 2005 and responses thereto regarding individual cases of alleged violations of migrants' rights and general situations concerning their rights in specific countries. Of the 34 communications, three were urgent appeals, while 31 were letters of allegation. Sixteen communications had been transmitted jointly with other special procedures.

In September [A/61/324], the Secretary-General transmitted the Special Rapporteur's interim report to the General Assembly covering his activities between 1 August 2005 and 30 August 2006. The report also focused on the issues which the Special Rapporteur raised at the Assembly's High-level Dialogue on International Migration and Development (see p. 1261). Particularly worrisome was the question of migrants' vulnerability, illustrated by the extent to which their rights and those of other non-nationals in administrative or immigration detention had been limited in many countries.

The Special Rapporteur also addressed the negative consequences of the failure to acknowledge the demand for migrant labour, especially the resulting illegal migration, with the attendant human rights violations and the fuelling of anti-immigration feeling. He concluded that insufficient information and lack of awareness by many sectors of society of the realities of migration contributed to migrants' vulnerability to abuse, particularly the issue of the demand of migrant labour in receiving countries. Governments therefore needed to acknowledge the existence of that demand by collecting and publishing data on the presence of migrant labour by sector of the economy, and adopt immigration policies consistent with receiving countries' demand for migrant labour, which, together with the facilitation of regular migration, should decrease irregular migration. Governments should also undertake public awareness campaigns on the need for migrant labour and on migrants' contributions to their economies. The Special Rapporteur also recommended that the General Assembly should adopt measures to ensure transparency on the demand for migrant labour in receiving countries, with particular attention to irregular migration. Such measures should lead to a new standard for gathering and disclosing information, and would be instrumental in reducing violations of migrants' rights and inducing compliance with international human rights standards.

Further reports of Special Rapporteur. The Special Rapporteur visited the Republic of Korea (5-11 December) [A/HRC/4/24/Add.2] to assess the situation of migrants living in the country, with special attention to female migrants and the impact of new labour systems implemented to regulate unskilled migrant workers living there. He found that, while the country historically saw itself as a mono-ethnic society, with a small Chinese minority, economic growth and globalization had transformed it in the 1980s into an attractive country for migrants. Consequently, the authorities initiated programmes to organize the migration flow but without commensurate attention to the protection of migrants' rights. However, the Government had recognized the vulnerability of unskilled migrant workers and addressed the situation by enacting the Industrial Trainee System and the Act Concerning the Employment Permit for Migrant Workers. Unfortunately, both initiatives had serious pitfalls, since the residence status of migrant workers was tied to their positions with their initial employers, thereby exposing them to greater vulnerability. Migrant women were particularly vulnerable to multiple violations and often fell victim to violence at home, within their families, in their hosting communities and at work. The situation of undocumented children of migrants was also a matter of concern, as their rights to education were not appropriately addressed in line with relevant human rights standards. The Special Rapporteur called on the Government to ratify as a matter of priority the 1990 International Convention on the Protection of the Rights of All Migrant Workers and Members of Their Families [YUN 1990, p. 594]. The Government was also encouraged to revise the Employment Permit System Act to enable unskilled migrant workers to lodge complaints when their rights were violated; consider providing migrant workers with the possibility of family unification; mitigate the requirements so as to allow migrant victims of domestic violence to apply for naturalization; take measures to protect migrants' spouses and facilitate their cultural integration; and regulate the work of international marriage agencies and brokers. The Special Rapporteur also recommended providing incentives for the voluntary return of migrants rather than their expulsion and bringing to justice employers who violated migrants' rights. With regard to migrant children, he proposed that the best interests of the child should govern all regulations or decisions relating to their status, as foreseen in the Convention on the Rights of the Child. In particular, all efforts should be made to ensure that they enjoyed their rights to education and health services.

The Special Rapporteur visited Indonesia (12-21 December) [A/HRC/4/24/Add.3], one of the world's major sources of unskilled international migrant labour, where he examined all aspects of the migration process, particularly the situation of female domestic workers, concern for whose plight was expressed to him by all parties. The Special Rapporteur visited, among other facilities, a detention centre for undocumented migrants entering Indonesia illegally and interviewed some of the detainees. Some of the most poignant testimonies were offered by female migrant domestic workers who had returned to Indonesia by escaping through the jungle or had been deported from the country in which they were employed. Many of them had suffered egregious physical and psychological abuses during their employment abroad, including confiscation of their passports and personal belongings, physical abuse and corporal punishment. Against that background, the Special Rapporteur encouraged Indonesia to uphold its international and national commitments to protect migrants. He also recommended that the Government amend the Memorandum of Understanding signed with Malaysia in May 2006, with a view to improving the regulation and monitoring of the recruitment process, and ratify the 1990 Convention for the protection of migrants and members of their families. The Convention and other international human rights and labour standards should also be incorporated into national legislation.

GENERAL ASSEMBLY ACTION

On 19 December [meeting 81], the General Assembly, on the recommendation of the Third Committee [A/61/443/Add.2 & Corr.1], adopted **resolution 61/165** without vote [agenda item 67 *(b)*].

Protection of migrants

The General Assembly,

Recalling all its previous resolutions on the protection of migrants, the most recent of which is resolution 60/169 of 16 December 2005, and recalling also Commission on Human Rights resolution 2005/47 of 19 April 2005,

Reaffirming the Universal Declaration of Human Rights, which proclaims that all human beings are born free and equal in dignity and rights and that everyone is entitled to all the rights and freedoms set out therein, without distinction of any kind, in particular as to race, colour or national origin,

Reaffirming also that everyone has the right to freedom of movement and residence within the borders of each State, and to leave any country, including his own, and return to his country,

Recalling the International Covenant on Civil and Political Rights and the International Covenant on Economic, Social and Cultural Rights, the Convention against Torture and Other Cruel, Inhuman or Degrading Treatment or Punishment, the Convention on the Elimination of All Forms of Discrimination against Women, the Convention on the Rights of the Child, the International Convention on the Elimination of All Forms of Racial Discrimination and the International Convention on the Protection of the Rights of All Migrant Workers and Members of Their Families,

Recalling also the provisions concerning migrants contained in the outcomes of all major United Nations conferences and summits,

Welcoming the establishment of the Human Rights Council, which is responsible for promoting universal respect for the protection of all human rights and fundamental freedoms for all, without distinction of any kind and in a fair and equal manner,

Welcoming also the convening of the High-level Dialogue on International migration and Development, held in New York on 14 and 15 September 2006 for the purpose of discussing the multidimensional aspects of international migration and development, which recognized the relationship between international migration, development and human rights,

Bearing in mind that policies and initiatives on the issue of migration, including those that refer to the orderly management of migration, should promote holistic approaches that take into account the causes and consequences of the phenomenon, as well as the full respect for the human rights and fundamental freedoms of migrants,

Noting that many migrant women are employed in the informal economy and in less skilled work compared with that of men, which puts those women at greater risk of abuse and exploitation,

Concerned about the large and growing number of migrants, especially women and children, who place themselves in a vulnerable situation by attempting to cross international borders without the required travel documents, and underlining the obligation of States to respect the human rights of those migrants,

Underlining the importance for States, in cooperation with non-governmental organizations, to undertake information campaigns aimed at clarifying opportunities, limitations and rights in the event of migration, so as to enable everyone to make informed decisions and to prevent them from utilizing dangerous means to cross international borders,

Emphasizing the global character of the migratory phenomenon, the importance of international, regional and bilateral cooperation and dialogue in this regard, as appropriate, and the need to protect the human rights of migrants, particularly at a time in which migration flows have increased in the globalized economy and take place in a context of new security concerns,

1. *Requests* States effectively to promote and protect the human rights and fundamental freedoms of all migrants, regardless of their immigration status, especially those of women and children;

2. *Takes note with interest* of the interim report of the Special Rapporteur of the Human Rights Council on the human rights of migrants;

3. *Calls upon* States that have not done so to consider signing and ratifying or acceding to the International Convention on the Protection of the Rights of All Migrant Workers and Members of Their Families as a matter of priority, and requests the Secretary-General to continue his efforts to raise awareness and promote the Convention;

4. *Urges* States parties to the United Nations Convention against Transnational Organized Crime and supplementing protocols thereto, namely, the Protocol against the Smuggling of Migrants by Land, Sea and Air and the Protocol to Prevent, Suppress and Punish Trafficking in Persons, Especially Women and Children, to implement them fully, and calls upon States that have not done so to consider ratifying them as a matter of priority;

5. *Takes note* of the report of the Committee on the Protection of the Rights of All Migrant Workers and Members of Their Families on its third and fourth sessions;

6. *Requests* all States, international organizations and relevant stakeholders to take into account in their policies and initiatives on migration issues the global character of the migratory phenomenon and to give due consideration to international, regional and bilateral cooperation in this field, including by undertaking dialogues on migration that include countries of origin, destination and transit, as well as civil society, including migrants, with a view to addressing, in a comprehensive manner, inter alia, its causes and consequences and the challenge of undocumented or irregular migration, granting priority to the protection of the human rights of migrants;

7. *Expresses concern* about legislation and measures adopted by some States that may restrict the human rights and fundamental freedoms of migrants, and reaffirms that, when exercising their sovereign right to enact and implement migratory and border security measures, States have the duty to comply with their obligations under international law, including international human rights law, in order to ensure full respect for the human rights of migrants;

8. *Requests* States to adopt concrete measures to prevent the violation of the human rights of migrants while in transit, including in ports and airports and at borders and migration checkpoints, to train public officials who work in those facilities and in border areas to treat migrants respectfully and in accordance with the law, and to prosecute, in conformity with applicable law, any act of violation of the human rights of migrants, inter alia, arbitrary detention, torture and violations of the right to life, including extrajudicial executions, during their transit from their country of origin to the country of destination and vice versa, including their transit through national borders;

9. *Calls upon* States to address international migration through international, regional or bilateral cooperation and dialogue and through a comprehensive and balanced approach, recognizing the roles and responsibilities of countries of origin, transit and destination in promoting and protecting the human rights of migrants and avoiding approaches that may aggravate their vulnerability;

10. *Strongly condemns* the manifestations and acts of racism, racial discrimination, xenophobia and related intolerance against migrants and the stereotypes often applied to them, including on the basis of religion or belief, and urges States to apply the existing laws when xenophobic or intolerant acts, manifestations or expressions against migrants occur, in order to eradicate impunity for those who commit xenophobic and racist acts;

11. *Requests* all States, in conformity with national legislation and applicable international legal instruments to which they are party, to enforce labour law effectively, including by addressing violations of such law, with regard to migrant workers' labour relations and working conditions, inter alia, those related to their remuneration and conditions of health, safety at work and the right to freedom of association;

12. *Encourages* all States to remove obstacles that may prevent the safe, unrestricted and expeditious transfer of remittances of migrants to their country of origin or to any other countries, in conformity with applicable legislation, and to consider, as appropriate, measures to solve other problems that may impede such transfers;

13. *Welcomes* immigration programmes, adopted by some countries, that allow migrants to integrate fully into the host countries, facilitate family reunification and promote a harmonious, tolerant and respectful environment, and encourages States to consider the possibility of adopting these types of programmes;

14. *Requests* Member States, the United Nations system, international organizations, civil society and all relevant stakeholders, especially the United Nations High Commissioner for Human Rights and the Special Rapporteur on the human rights of migrants, to ensure that the perspective of the human rights of migrants is included among the priority issues in the ongoing discussions on international migration and development within the United Nations system, bearing in mind the discussions of the High-level Dialogue on International Migration and Development held pursuant to General Assembly resolution 58/208 of 23 December 2003;

15. *Requests* the Secretary-General to report on the implementation of the present resolution at its sixty-second session and decides to examine the question further under the item entitled "Promotion and protection of human rights".

Also on 19 December [meeting 81], the Assembly, on the recommendation of the Third Committee [A/61/443/Add.2 & Corr.1], adopted **resolution 61/162** by recorded vote (122-4-58) [agenda item 67 *(b)*].

Respect for the right to universal freedom of travel and the vital importance of family reunification

The General Assembly,

Recalling its resolution 59/203 of 20 December 2004,

Reaffirming that all human rights and fundamental freedoms are universal, indivisible, interdependent and interrelated,

Recalling the provisions of the Universal Declaration of Human Rights, as well as article 12 of the International Covenant on Civil and Political Rights,

Stressing that, as stated in the Programme of Action of the International Conference on Population and Development, family reunification of documented migrants is an important factor in international migration and that remittances by documented migrants to their countries of origin often constitute a very important source of foreign exchange and are instrumental in improving the well-being of relatives left behind,

Noting with great concern that, while some positive developments have occurred during the past few years in the accomplishment of the objectives highlighted in resolutions 57/227 of 18 December 2002 and 59/203, in particular relating to facilitating the flow of remittances across international borders to help families, in certain cases it has been reported that measures have been adopted that increased the restrictions imposed on documented migrants in relation to family reunification and the possibility of sending remittances to their relatives in the country of origin,

Recalling that the family is the basic unit of society and, as such, should be strengthened, and that it is entitled to receive comprehensive protection and support,

1. *Once again calls upon* all States to guarantee the universally recognized freedom of travel to all foreign nationals legally residing in their territory;

2. *Reaffirms* that all Governments, in particular those of receiving countries, must recognize the vital importance of family reunification and promote its incorporation into national legislation in order to ensure protection of the unity of families of documented migrants;

3. *Calls upon* all States to allow, in conformity with international legislation, the free flow of financial remittances by foreign nationals residing in their territory to relatives in the country of origin;

4. *Also calls upon* all States to refrain from enacting, and to repeal if it already exists, legislation intended as a coercive measure that discriminates against individuals or groups of legal migrants by adversely affecting family reunification and the right to send financial remittances to relatives in the country of origin;

5. *Decides* to continue its consideration of the question at its sixty-third session under the item entitled "Promotion and protection of human rights".

RECORDED VOTE ON RESOLUTION 61/162:

In favour: Afghanistan, Algeria, Angola, Antigua and Barbuda, Argentina, Azerbaijan, Bahamas, Bahrain, Bangladesh, Barbados, Belarus, Belize, Benin, Bhutan, Bolivia, Brazil, Brunei Darussalam, Burkina Faso, Burundi, Cambodia, Cameroon, Cape Verde, Central African Republic, Chile, China, Colombia, Comoros, Congo, Costa Rica, Côte d'Ivoire, Cuba, Democratic People's Republic of Korea, Democratic Republic of the Congo, Djibouti, Dominica, Dominican Republic, Ecuador, Egypt, El Salvador, Eritrea, Ethiopia, Fiji, Gabon, Gambia, Ghana, Grenada, Guatemala, Guinea, Guinea-Bissau, Guyana, Haiti, Honduras, India, Indonesia, Iran, Iraq, Jamaica, Jordan, Kazakhstan, Kenya, Kuwait, Kyrgyzstan, Lao People's Democratic Republic, Lebanon, Lesotho, Liberia, Libyan Arab Jamahiriya, Madagascar, Malawi, Mali, Mauritania, Mauritius, Mexico, Mongolia, Morocco, Mozambique, Myanmar, Namibia, Nepal, Nicaragua, Niger, Nigeria, Oman, Pakistan, Panama, Paraguay, Peru, Philippines, Qatar, Russian Federation, Rwanda, Saint Lucia, Saint Vincent and the Grenadines, Sao Tome and Principe, Saudi Arabia, Senegal, Sierra Leone, Solomon Islands, Somalia, South Africa, Sri Lanka, Sudan, Suriname, Swaziland, Syrian Arab Republic, Tajikistan, Timor-Leste, Togo, Trinidad and Tobago, Tunisia, Tuvalu, Uganda, United Arab Emirates, United Republic of Tanzania, Uruguay, Uzbekistan, Vanuatu, Venezuela, Viet Nam, Yemen, Zambia, Zimbabwe.

Against: Israel, Marshall Islands, Palau, United States.

Abstaining: Albania, Andorra, Armenia, Australia, Austria, Belgium, Bosnia and Herzegovina, Botswana, Bulgaria, Canada, Croatia, Cyprus, Czech Republic, Denmark, Estonia, Finland, France, Georgia, Germany, Greece, Hungary, Iceland, Ireland, Italy, Japan, Latvia, Liechtenstein, Lithuania, Luxembourg, Malaysia, Maldives, Malta, Micronesia, Moldova, Monaco, Montenegro, Netherlands, New Zealand, Norway, Papua New Guinea, Poland, Portugal, Republic of Korea, Romania, Samoa, San Marino, Serbia, Singapore, Slovakia, Slovenia, Spain, Sweden, Switzerland, Thailand, The former Yugoslav Republic of Macedonia, Turkey, Ukraine, United Kingdom.

Other forms of intolerance

Cultural prejudice

Report of High Commissioner. In response to a 2005 Commission request [YUN 2005, p. 772], the High Commissioner submitted a report [E/CN.4/2006/40] summarizing information received from two Governments and the outcome of informal consultations on the possibility of appointing a Special Rapporteur on cultural rights and on steps for promoting and protecting the full enjoyment of such right. The report indicated that views were strongly divided between those who supported the establishment of a new mandate if its scope was clearly defined and coordination with existing procedures was ensured, and others who raised doubts, given that existing mandates could accommodate the proposed functions. It was suggested that the Commission on Human Rights should request special procedures to take into account the cultural dimensions in the exercise of their mandates and include a relevant analysis in their reports to the Council. Treaty bodies, especially the Committee on Economic, Social and Cultural Rights, could be invited to pay greater attention to cultural rights in their analyses and questions to States.

Discrimination against minorities

Report of Independent Expert. In her first report [E/CN.4/2006/74], the Independent Expert on minority issues, Gay McDougall (United States), highlighted UN system developments regarding minority issues and described her mandate, methods of work and some of the activities she had undertaken since her appointment in 2005 [YUN 2005, p. 774]. She noted that the scope of her mandate was determined by the terms of the 1992 Declaration on the Rights of Persons Belonging to National or Ethnic, Religious and Linguistic Minorities, adopted by the General Assembly in resolution 47/135 [YUN 1992, p. 722], and by the provisions of other human rights instruments and international and regional standards. Based on that Declaration, the Independent Expert identified areas of concern relating to minorities around the world, observing that the normative frameworks relating to minority issues were poorly implemented and that the effects of minority rights in the fields of poverty reduction and the promotion of political and social stability required greater understanding and acknowledgement. Minorities all over the world faced serious threats, discrimination and racism, and were frequently excluded from participating fully in the economic, political and social life of their countries. Of particular concern was the proliferation of anti-terrorism measures that violated the rights of minority communities and created a climate that emboldened abusive individuals. The Independent Expert's work would concentrate on three broad strategic objectives: increasing the focus on minority communities in the context of poverty alleviation and development; enhancing the understanding of related issues, in terms of ensuring stable societies; and mainstreaming issues in the work of the United Nations and other multilateral fora.

She intended to collaborate with the Working Group on Minorities (see p. 841), and would highlight the significant benefits to States in recognizing and promoting minority group contributions. In that way, her mandate would address the minority rights component of human rights violations, which was not adequately covered by other mechanisms. She emphasized that respect for minority rights favoured societies in terms of securing the richness of cultural diversity, reflecting their full heritage, contributing to social cohesion and advancing the conditions for political and social stability and peace. To fully exploit those prospects, advances had to be made in promoting minority rights and in highlighting best practices for the effective implementation of those rights in contemporary situations. An anti-discrimination position, while a key element, was not sufficient in itself to fully guarantee minority rights. All States should go beyond that by seeking the goal of equality in diversity, in law and in fact.

The Independent Expert visited Hungary (26 June–3 July)[A/HRC/4/9/Add.2], where there were 13 national and ethnic minority communities who spoke 14 different languages. She found that the Government had demonstrated a high degree of political will in addressing the unique needs and problems of minorities, noting, in that regard, that 12 of those minority communities had effectively been integrated into Hungarian society in socio-economic terms, given that they enjoyed social indicators similar to those of the majority population. That positive outlook was facilitated by the country's system of minority self-government, under which minorities were provided with the financial resources to enable them to preserve and promote their cultural and linguistic autonomy and identity, through the development of related institutions and services. Grants were also provided to assist in establishing such facilities as libraries, museums and heritage centres, theatres, research and educational institutions, and media and publishing outlets, and to organize cultural activities. The only minority community in the country whose situation remained of serious concern was the Roma, who continued to suffer discrimination, exclusion and prejudice, remained the most deprived group with respect to education, employment, health and housing, and suffered disproportionately high levels of extreme poverty. The multiple discrimination faced by Roma women in particular was especially challenging and required targeted attention and dedicated resources from local and regional authorities.

The Independent Expert made recommendations for improving the situation of the Roma in education, employment and housing, and for addressing the extreme poverty affecting them. She cautioned against Government reforms that would diminish attention on Roma issues and advocated the continuation and strengthening of policies favourable to them, including the recruitment of Roma professionals in key Government posts relating to Roma affairs. Regarding other problems affecting Hungarian minorities as a whole, the Independent Expert made recommendations relating to the effective participation of underrepresented minorities in Parliament, including in planning, designing, implementing and evaluating policies and programmes affecting them; steps for meeting their social welfare needs, especially health care, education, housing and social benefits; the implementation by government agencies of legal provisions on anti-discrimination and equal treatment; child protection and other social services; and the collection and use of disaggregated data.

In Ethiopia (28 November–12 December) [A/HRC/4/9/Add.3], which recognized over 80 ethnic groups and as many languages, the Independent Expert found that the Constitution provided a comprehensive foundation for rights, freedoms and equality, departing from the vision of previous Governments, in which a single ethnic group dominated all others. The Constitution brought to the fore the rights of the country's diverse peoples and ethnic communities to political representation in federal structures. However, in some respects, the promise of the Constitution regarding equal participation of minority ethnic groups in democratic decision-making remained unfulfilled. Ethnically-based federalism politicized ethnicity as the most salient individual and group marker, resulting in new dynamics of ethnic division, discrimination and exclusion.

Continuing ethnic conflicts, often caused by land, water and resource issues or due to political factors, undermined the prospects of regional stability and a unified, democratic and prosperous Ethiopia. Minority communities that were discriminated against were frequently victims of such conflict, forcibly displaced from their territories and bereft of the capacity to protect their rights. Some of them, including pastoralist groups, faced severe survival challenges, extreme poverty and food and water insecurity, and a number of them might disappear as distinct groups due to environmental, social and political pressures and assimilation processes. The Independent Expert also expressed concern that a democratic deficit existed in Ethiopia, which might have exacerbated tensions and instability. She advocated checks and balances to ensure the democratic functioning of the federal system and to guarantee the rights of highly disadvantaged communities experiencing political, social and economic inequality. The Government and the regional states should build confidence in democratic processes and ensure good governance, human rights and fundamental freedoms.

As a matter of priority, the Government should depoliticize ethnicity and promote policies of inclusion, shared power and cooperation; release or ensure a fair and speedy trial for detained opposition leaders, journalists, students, and human rights defenders; guarantee freedom of opinion and speech, and the right of peaceful assembly at all times; take urgent and culturally appropriate security measures to ensure the protection of all communities and promote the safe return of those who fled their homes due to violence and conflict; address the needs of historically marginalized ethnic groups in the least developed regions; and convene a national conference on the functioning of the system of ethnic federalism, with the participation of all Ethiopian peoples, political parties, regional authorities and civil society. Other recommendations related to the need to ensure the survival of Ethiopia's small minority groups, the protection and promotion of minority languages and culture, non-discrimination and equality, political participation, poverty reduction, the status of civil society and national human rights institutions, and international assistance.

Working Group activities. The Working Group on Minorities, at its twelfth session (Geneva, 8-11 August) [A/HRC/Sub.1/58/19], reviewed the promotion and practical realization of the 1992 Declaration, examined possible solutions to problems involving minorities, including the promotion of mutual understanding between and among minorities and Governments and effective mechanisms for conflict prevention and resolution. It also recommended further measures to promote and protect minority rights and discussed its future role.

The Group had before it a working paper on integration with diversity in security, policing and criminal justice, submitted by Tom Hadden, Queen's University, Belfast [E/CN.4/Sub.2/AC.5/2006/WP.1] and a conference room paper on a regional perspective on Afro-descendant quality of life prepared by All For Reparations and Emancipation (AFRE), an international NGO [A/HRC/Sub.1/58/AC.5/CRP.1]. It also considered a note verbale from Ethiopia on the human rights situation of minorities in the country [A/HRC/Sub.1/58/AC.5/CRP.2]; a report on the 2005 workshop on conflict prevention and resolution organized by OHCHR [YUN 2005, p. 776]; and a note by the Secretariat reviewing the promotion and practical realization of the 1992 Declaration, which contained a minority profile and matrix completed within the context of the 2006 Minority Fellowship Programme [E/CN.4/Sub.2/AC.5/2006/3]. Other Secretariat notes addressed possible solutions to problems involving minorities, including the promotion of mutual understanding between and among minorities and Governments [E/CN.4/Sub.2/AC.5/2006/4] and the Group's future activities and cooperation with the Independent Expert on Minority Issues (see p. 839) and UN organizations [E/CN.4/Sub.2/AC.5/2006/6].

In recommendations on its future activities, the Group called for its continuation or creation of a smaller expert body to ensure that the Human Rights Council was provided with specialized advice on minority issues. In that context, it proposed intersessional sessions of five working days for the Group or a similar future mechanism, ensuring access to and participation by minority representatives from all regions and serving as a forum for dialogue and mutual understanding on minority rights issues. In other recommendations, the Group and the Independent Expert highlighted the prospects for cooperation and proposed a two-year programme of work, which would include the organization of regional seminars and thematic studies. The Group also recommended that OHCHR continue operating the Minorities Fellowship Programme and identify ways to further engage with minority fellows in that regard. Welcoming the preparation under that programme of a minority profile and matrix, the Group recommended that OHCHR transmit it to minority organizations and Governments as a useful information-gathering tool. The Group advocated inter-agency coordination on minority issues, proposing, in that regard, that OHCHR and the Independent Expert, together with the Group, should call on UN system bodies and other relevant entities to implement the goals of the 1992 Declaration and promote the mainstreaming of a minority perspective in the design, implementation, monitoring and evaluation of relevant policies and programmes.

Subcommission action. In accordance with the recommendations of the Working Group on Minorities (see above), the Subcommission on the Promotion and Protection of Human Rights [A/HRC/2/2], on 24 August [res. 2006/11], called for the continuation of specialized advice to the Council, particularly through its specialized bodies. It recommended that such a future mechanism be convened intersessionally and for at least five working days, and that it ensure access to and participation by minority representatives from all regions and serve as a forum for dialogue and mutual understanding of minority issues. The Subcommission endorsed the request of the Group and the Independent Expert for a two-year programme of work, which would include regional seminars on the situation of Afro-descendants in the Americas and on integration of minority considerations resulting in diversity in security, policing and criminal justice, as well as the preparation of three thematic studies, to be followed by thematic seminars, on positive country experiences on self-government for minorities; ways and means of strengthening the application of the 1992 Declaration; and discrimination against women belonging to minorities. It also recommended that OHCHR continue operating the fellowship programme for minorities as a tool for building capacity among minority representatives and organizations, and called on OHCHR, the Independent Expert and the Working Group to engage the UN system, international financial institutions, regional banks and regional and national development agencies in the implementation of the Declaration, so as to recognize the importance of minority issues as a tool for achieving equal rights.

Leprosy victims

Preliminary report. In response to a 2005 Subcommission request [YUN 2005, p. 778], the Special Rapporteur to prepare a study on discrimination against leprosy victims and their families, Yozo Yokota (Japan), submitted his preliminary report, which focused on his visits to Brazil, Ethiopia and India, and discussed the scope of the issue and new developments [A/HRC/Sub.1/58/CRP.7]. The report also contained a suggested framework for principles and guidelines for eliminating such discrimination. The Special Rapporteur was encouraged by the fact that, despite the previous negative image of the disease, it had become curable, with treatment accessible to everyone. As such, the number of cured victims had grown, while prevalence rates had dropped dramatically in many endemic countries and localities. However, problems remained, given that there were still over half a million leprosy patients worldwide. More efforts would be needed to eradicate the disease completely. The Special Rapporteur recommended that the Subcommission request the Human Rights Council to include the topic of discrimination against leprosy-affected persons and their families among the studies to be conducted by the Subcommission, and that it endorse his proposal to hold two regional workshops in Africa and Asia, respectively, to encourage the participation of representatives of leprosy-affected persons and their organizations in discussions on discrimination against those affected and their families, and that a general consultation be held in Geneva to hear the views of Governments, UN bodies, NGOs and representatives of leprosy-affected persons in drafting the text of principles and guidelines for eliminating such discrimination.

Subcommission action. On 24 August [res. 2006/15], the Subcommission requested Governments that had not yet done so to abolish legislation requiring forced institutionalization of leprosy patients and to provide them with effective, prompt and free treatment; and provide appropriate remedies to former patients forcibly hospitalized and take measures to eradicate discrimination against leprosy-affected persons and their families. Governments were also encouraged to include leprosy education in school curricula, so as to disseminate accurate information about leprosy and leprosy-affected persons and their families and prevent discrimination against them. The Subcommission endorsed Mr. Yokota's proposals to organize two regional workshops in Africa and Asia, respectively, as well as consultations in Geneva to hear the views of Governments. It requested the Council to include the topic of discrimination against leprosy-affected persons and their families among the studies to be conducted by the Subcommission or a new body of experts and appointed Mr. Yokota Special Rapporteur, with the task of conducting a full study on the topic. He was asked to submit a preliminary report in 2007, produce a draft set of principles and guidelines to end discrimination and enter into a dialogue with relevant entities.

Discrimination based on work and descent

Report of Special Rapporteurs. In response to a 2005 Subcommission request [YUN 2005, p. 778], the Special Rapporteurs on discrimination based on work and descent, Yozo Yokota (Japan) and Chin-Sung Chung (Republic of Korea), presented a progress report on that aspect of discrimination [A/HRC/Sub.1/58/CRP.2], which analysed the results of a questionnaire they had sent to Governments, national human rights institutions, UN bodies and NGOs on best practices and measures taken to address discrimination based on work and descent. The report also outlined a revised draft set of principles and guidelines for eliminating such discrimination. The Rapporteurs recommended that the Subcommission endorse their proposal to hold, in 2007, a general consultation meeting in Geneva to hear the views of Governments, UN bodies, NGOs and affected communities in drafting the final text of principles and guidelines, and two regional workshops, one in Asia and one in Africa, to involve the representatives of the affected communities in discussions.

Subcommission action. On 24 August [res. 2006/14], the Subcommission requested the Special Rapporteurs to complete their study on discrimination based on work and descent, finalize the draft principles and guidelines and submit their final report in 2007. It also endorsed their proposals to organize two regional workshops in Africa and Asia, respectively, and a consultation in Geneva during the second quarter of 2007 to receive the views of Governments and other relevant entities. The High Commissioner was asked to assist them.

Non-discrimination

In June, the Special Rapporteur to undertake a study on non-discrimination, Marc Bossuyt (Belgium), informed the Secretariat that he would not be able to submit the interim report on that study, as requested by the Subcommission in 2005 [YUN 2005, p. 779].

Religious intolerance

Reports of Special Rapporteur. In her annual report [E/CN.4/2006/5], the Special Rapporteur on freedom of religion or belief, Asma Jahangir (Pakistan), reviewed her activities, which had focused mainly on the protection of individuals, particularly the monitoring of cases and situations of alleged violations of the right to freedom of religion or belief, based on information provided by individuals and NGOs, and through country visits and communications to Governments to seek clarification on credible allegations received. In that regard, she had sent 84 communications to 36 countries, of which 28 were urgent appeals, and 56, letters of allegation. Some 34 of those communications, which addressed allegations of multiple human rights violations, were transmitted jointly with other special procedures. To increase the effectiveness of communications, the Special Rapporteur developed a framework on communications, annexed to the report, which enabled her to send more precise communications, drawing the attention of Governments to international standards. The Special Rapporteur felt that country visits were the best way to comprehensively assess the status of freedom of religion or belief in a particular country, and welcomed invitations from Azerbaijan and Israel. She reiterated her support for a mechanism to address the situation of countries that consistently failed to cooperate with the special procedures mechanisms regarding country visits, the number of which, she noted, was increasing. The Special Rapporteur also examined, from an international human rights perspective, the positive and negative aspects of freedom of religion or belief of individuals with regard to the wearing of religious symbols. To provide guidance on the applicable human rights standards and their scope, the Special Rapporteur formulated a set of general criteria on religious symbols, including "neutral indicators" and "aggravating indicators", emphasizing that restrictions should not be imposed for discriminatory purposes or applied in a discriminatory manner. Limitations should be directly related to the need on which they were predicated.

The Special Rapporteur noted with concern that, 25 years after the 1981 Declaration on the Elimination of All Forms of Intolerance and of Discrimination Based on Religion or Belief, adopted in General Assembly resolution 36/55 [YUN 1981, p. 881], freedom of religion or belief was not a reality for many individuals throughout the world. Noting that the anniversary was an occasion to reiterate the importance of promoting that freedom, she encouraged Governments and NGOs to challenge the rising trend of religious intolerance, and called for more intergovernmental dialogue to increase the involvement of policymakers in combating it. The Special Rapporteur also observed reports of situations where people deliberately offended the religions of others through expressions made in exercise of the right to freedom of expression. The Special Rapporteur intended to further develop that aspect of her mandate in future activities. An addendum to the report [E/CN.4/2006/5/Add.1] summarized communications which the Special Rapporteur had sent to 36 Governments from 12 November 2004 to 30 November 2005, and the replies thereon, as at 30 January 2006.

The Special Rapporteur visited Azerbaijan (26 February–5 March) [A/HRC/4/21/Add.2] to assess the situation in the light of reports of limitations on the right to freedom of religion or belief and persecution of certain religious groups. She found a generally high level of religious tolerance and harmony, as the country respected the right to freedom of religion or belief. However, that respect was not uniformly observed in all regions, and in some cases, the line between facilitation of religious freedom and control by the authorities might have blurred. Some situations resulted in actual limitations of the right to freedom of religion, such as difficulties in registration and restriction on religious literature, while in others, the control exercised by the authorities extended to forms of persecution, resulting in some religious communities being reluctant to communicate with the Special Rapporteur. It was also disappointing that, in some parts of the country, the level of tolerance between religious communities was sometimes challenged, owing to the actions of the authorities and the negative role played by some media organizations in stigmatizing certain religious communities.

To address those concerns, the Special Rapporteur emphasized that the existence of effective, independent and impartial administrative and judicial mechanisms was crucial. She encouraged the Government and other relevant actors to work towards strengthening democratic institutions. In particular, the Government should ensure that victims of violations of the right to freedom of religion or belief received appropriate redress and that the perpetrators were prosecuted; accord special attention to religious intolerance towards religious minorities; take action to achieve balance between the level of necessary regulation of religious activities and the exercise of the right to freedom of religion; and honour its commitment to the principle of conscientious objection to military service. The Special Rapporteur also encouraged, among other measures, interfaith engagement of religious leaders in the country, dialogue between representatives of religious minorities and the media so as to clarify misunderstandings, and efforts to further strengthen religious tolerance through the production of a school curriculum on the teaching of religion.

In Maldives (6-10 August) [A/HRC/4/21/Add.3], the Special Rapporteur assessed the extent to which the country guaranteed, in law and practice, the freedom to adopt and manifest a religion or belief without coercion, and the extent of discrimination based on such belief, focusing in particular on vulnerable groups, including persons deprived of their liberty, migrant workers, other foreigners and women. She observed that, in Maldives, a traditionally moderate Islamic country, the Government had placed great importance on preserving and promoting national unity. Nonetheless, that concept appeared inextricably linked to that of religious unity, which some interlocutors seemed to equate with religious homogeneity. As such, some of the laws and policies implemented to preserve religious unity might have violated the freedom of religion or belief, particularly in the case of some vulnerable groups, such as migrant workers and other foreigners and persons in detention.

The Special Rapporteur welcomed the Government's position towards the Universal Declaration of Human Rights and its recent accession to the International Covenant on Civil and Political Rights adopted by the General Assembly in resolution 2200 A (XXI) [YUN 1966, p. 423], but expressed regret that it had entered a reservation to article 18 of that Covenant concerning freedom of religion or belief. The Special Rapporteur recommended that the right to that freedom be included in the country's new draft constitution and extended to all persons in the country. She underlined that the designation of Islam as the State religion did not require all citizens to adhere to that religion. She encouraged the Government to take the lead in raising awareness about the freedom of religion or belief, and ensure that no one was detained for the purpose of coercing them to reaffirm their belief in Islam. Her other recommendations related to the freedom to manifest one's religion or belief; the need to combat discrimination based on freedom of religion or belief; and safeguarding the right to that freedom of vulnerable groups who were mostly affected by related violations.

Report of High Commissioner. In response to a 2005 Commission request [YUN 2005, p. 780], the High Commissioner submitted a February report [E/CN.4/2006/12] providing information on follow-up actions taken by Member States, the UN system, human rights mechanisms and OHCHR to promote dialogue among civilizations and religious tolerance. The report noted that, although steps had been taken to counter religious intolerance, serious instances of the problem, as well as discrimination based on religion or belief, were increasing. The defamation of religions was one of its most aggressive manifestations. Member States and other interested parties should strive to counter the phenomenon not only incidentally, but also by strategizing and harmonizing action through legislative, educational and policy measures.

Human Rights Council action. On 30 June [A/61/53 (dec. 1/107)], the Council, taking into account statements at its first session expressing concern over the increasing trend of defamation of religions and incitement to racial and religious hatred, decided by a recorded vote (33-12-1) to request the Special Rapporteur on freedom of religion or belief and the Special Rapporteur on contemporary forms of racism, racial discrimination, xenophobia and related intolerance, as well as the High Commissioner, to report on the phenomenon at its next session.

Further reports of Special Rapporteur. By a September note [A/61/340], the Secretary-General transmitted to the General Assembly the Special Rapporteur's interim report, submitted in accordance with Assembly resolution 60/166 [YUN 2005, p. 783], on her activities, including country visits and communications, and her analysis of recent patterns and trends. The Special Rapporteur discussed the situation of religious minorities, registration and restrictions on freedom of information on religion or belief, conversion and propagation of religion, religious symbols, counter-terrorism and freedom of religion or belief, the right to freedom of religion or belief of persons deprived of their liberty, and religion and the right to freedom of expression. She observed that the right to freedom of religion or belief continued to be challenged in many contexts and in different parts of the world, partly due to a lack of awareness about the right, among both governmental officials and ordinary citizens. That was compounded in some countries by a lack of transparency on the legal and policy frameworks governing the various elements of the right.

Observing a marked increase in the level of religious intolerance in many regions, the Special Rapporteur called for a global strategy to deal with the problem, under UN auspices, which would include regional and subregional approaches to respond to aspects that applied to particular regions. In that regard, she encouraged the United Nations to undertake regional consultations to identify the trends and patterns of religious intolerance in each region and develop policy frameworks for responding to them. Governments were encouraged to cooperate with international and regional organizations to carry out training and awareness raising activities about the right. Even in countries where there was a high level of religious tolerance, there was a need to remain vigilant, and steps should be taken to maintain high levels of tolerance. As to the interrelated nature of freedom of religion or belief and other human rights, the Special Rapporteur noted that the issue arising under her mandate had particularly close links to freedom of association, independence of the judiciary and freedom of expression. With regard to freedom of expression, she called on the media to accommodate the views of religious minorities and allow them to respond to allegations made against them in the press. Noting that the right to disseminate or propagate one's religion peacefully was an important element of freedom of religion or belief, and of freedom of expression, the Special Rapporteur recommended that interreligious communities should consider developing an agreed code of ethics in the pursuit of their missionary work.

On 19 December, the Assembly took note of the Secretary-General's note (**decision 61/529**).

A December report of the Special Rapporteur [A/HRC/4/21], which further highlighted her activities, focused on several issues of concern relating to the vulnerable situation of women, violations linked to counter-terrorism measures and the situation of religious minorities and new religious movements. It also reviewed the framework for communications (see p. 843), including a related online digest which was to be developed as a means of drawing the attention of Governments to relevant international standards on specific issues. In the period from 1 December 2005 to 30 November 2006, the Special Rapporteur sent 64 communications to 34 countries, 27 of which were urgent appeals and 37 letters of allegation, while 39 addressed allegations of multiple human rights violations transmitted jointly with other special procedures. In addition to visits to Azerbaijan and the Maldives (see above), the Special Rapporteur consulted with representatives of the Holy See. Based on the allegations she had received, the Special Rapporteur concluded that the protection of freedom of religion or belief and the implementation of the 1981 Declaration were far from being realized. She emphasized the need to eliminate the root causes of intolerance and discrimination and to remain vigilant with regard to freedom of religion or belief worldwide. It was also crucial to depoliticize issues relating to religion or belief and to bring related discussion fully within the framework of human rights.

Report of Secretary-General. As requested in General Assembly resolution 60/150 [YUN 2005, p. 782], the Secretary-General submitted a September report [A/61/325], which provided an overview of reports relevant to the issues of defamation of religions and the promotion of tolerance for all religions and their value systems by the Special Rapporteur on contemporary forms of racism (see p. 830), the Special Rapporteur on freedom of religion or belief (see p. 843) and the High Commissioner. The report concluded that steps taken by Member States, the UN system and the wider international community indicated their will to counter religious intolerance. However, continuous reporting on allegations of intolerance and discrimination on the grounds of religion or belief signified that much more needed to be done.

On 19 December, the Assembly took note of the Secretary-General's report (**decision 61/529**).

Incitement of racial and religious hatred

In response to a Human Rights Council decision [A/61/53 (dec. 1/107)] (see p. 844), the Special Rapportuer on contemporary forms of racism, racial discrimination, xenophobia and related intolerance (see p. 830) and the Special Rapporteur on freedom of religion or belief (see p. 843) submitted a 20 September report [A/HRC/2/3] on incitement of racial and religious hatred and the promotion of tolerance. The report analysed the political and ideological context of the phenomenon, the trends of racial and religious intolerance, specific and common factors underpinning the defamation of religions, the scope of the right to freedom of religion or belief, and religion and freedom of opinion and expression. The Rapporteurs found that the current trend regarding the incitement of racial and religious hatred was rooted in the fight against terrorism and the emergence of new forms of discrimination. The September 2001 terrorist attacks in the United States [YUN 2001, p. 60] had transformed the fabric of international relations, a major negative impact of which was the ideological inclination of many Governments to consider the security of their country and people as the sum and substance of all human rights. Thus, the rights guaranteed by international human rights instruments were interpreted and implemented in the light of their relevance and contribution to the fight against terrorism, and the respect and exercise of those rights were generally accompanied by restrictions and limitations. In such an ideological context, racial and religious intolerance were legitimized by democratic parties' political use of racism and xenophobia. The trend was accorded further legitimacy by long-term intellectual constructs, which postulated cultural inferiority, religious demonization and the dehumanization of entire races, ethnic groups, communities and peoples. Noting that the phenomenon of globalization had brought new challenges in terms of society's efforts to deal with the use of religious belief for political purposes and the related negative stereotyping of some religions and beliefs, the Rapporteurs observed that religious groups and communities were, in many cases, both the sources and targets of critical expressions, including extreme forms of incitement to violence and hatred against members of a religious group. Against that background, the Special Rapporteurs reviewed the scope of legal provisions in major human rights instruments.

The Rapporteurs recommended that the Council call on Governments to promote the implementation of the Durban Declaration and Programme of Action, which remained the cornerstone in efforts to combat racism and related phenomena, and demonstrate a firm political will and commitment to combating the rise of racial and religious intolerance, particularly the presence of racist and xenophobic platforms in the programmes of democratic parties. That should be accorded priority over convenient governmental political alliances. In addition, Governments should take into account the consequences of their policies on relations with other Member States and avoid policies, postures and statements inspired by the divisive concept of the clash of civilizations. Concerning religious controversies and finding creative ways of dealing with them, the Rapporteurs recommended continuing dialogue and that debate on the issue should be widened and inspired by the spirit of dialogue among religions and cultures. To maintain a pluralist, diverse and tolerant society, Member States should neither stubbornly cling to free speech nor suffocate criticism of a religion by making it punishable by law. Rather, the focus should be on creating a tolerant and inclusive environment in which all religions and beliefs could be exercised free of discrimination or stigmatization. The situation would not be remedied by preventing ideas about religions from being expressed.

Human Rights Council action. On 29 November [A/62/53 (dec. 2/116)], the Council deferred to its third session consideration of a draft decision [A/HRC/2/L.25] on incitement to racial and religious hatred and the promotion of tolerance, by which the Council would take note of related reports of Special Rapporteurs and of the High Commissioner, as well as the implications of pertinent provisions of the International Covenant on Civil and Political Rights, adopted by the General Assembly in resolution 2200 A (XXI) [YUN 1966, p. 423].

GENERAL ASSEMBLY ACTION

On 19 December [meeting 81], the General Assembly, on the recommendation of the Third Committee [A/61/443/Add.2 & Corr.1], adopted **resolution 61/164** by recorded vote (111-54-18) [agenda item 67 *(b)*].

Combating defamation of religions

The General Assembly,

Recalling that all States have pledged themselves, under the Charter of the United Nations, to promote and encourage universal respect for and observance of all human rights and fundamental freedoms without distinction as to race, sex, language or religion,

Recalling also the relevant resolutions of the Commission on Human Rights in this regard,

Recalling further the United Nations Millennium Declaration adopted by the General Assembly on 8 September 2000, welcoming the resolve expressed in the Millennium Declaration to take measures to eliminate the increasing acts of racism and xenophobia in many societies and to promote greater harmony and tolerance in all societies, and looking forward to its effective implementation at all levels, including in the context of the Durban Declaration and Programme of Action adopted by the World Conference against Racism, Racial Discrimination, Xenophobia and Related Intolerance, held in Durban, South Africa, from 31 August to 8 September 2001,

Recalling the proclamation of the Global Agenda for Dialogue among Civilizations, and inviting States, the organizations and bodies of the United Nations system, within existing resources, other international and regional organizations and civil societies to contribute to the implementation of the Programme of Action contained in the Global Agenda,

Welcoming the launch of the Alliance of Civilizations initiative, intended to respond to the need for a committed effort by the international community, in order to promote mutual respect and understanding among different cultures and societies,

Welcoming also the progress achieved in the follow-up to the Durban Declaration and Programme of Action,

Underlining the importance of increasing contacts at all levels in order to deepen dialogue and reinforce understanding among different cultures, religions and civilizations, and noting with regret, in this regard, the cancellation of the meeting on "Civilization and harmony: values and mechanisms of the global order", which was to be held in Turkey in 2004 as a follow-up to the Organization of the Islamic Conference-European Union Joint Forum on the theme "Civilization and harmony: the political dimension", held in Turkey in 2002,

Reaffirming that discrimination against human beings on the grounds of religion or belief constitutes an affront to human dignity and a disavowal of the principles of the Charter,

Convinced that respect for cultural, ethnic, religious and linguistic diversity, as well as dialogue among and within civilizations, is essential for peace, understanding and friendship among individuals and people of the different cultures and nations of the world, while manifestations of cultural prejudice, intolerance and xenophobia towards different cultures and religions generate hatred and violence among peoples and nations throughout the world,

Recognizing the valuable contributions of all religions to modern civilization and the contribution that dialogue among civilizations can make to an improved awareness and understanding of the common values shared by all humankind,

Reaffirming the need for all States to continue international efforts to enhance dialogue and broaden understanding among civilizations, cultures and religions, and emphasizing that States, regional organizations, non-governmental organizations, religious bodies and the media have an important role to play in promoting tolerance, respect for and freedom of religion and belief,

Underlining the important role of education in the promotion of cultural and religious tolerance and the elimination of discrimination based on religion or belief,

Alarmed at the continuing negative impact of the events of 11 September 2001 on Muslim minorities and communities in some non-Muslim countries, the negative projection of Islam in the media and the introduction and enforcement of laws that specifically discriminate against and target Muslims,

Alarmed also at the serious instances of intolerance, discrimination and acts of violence based on religion or belief, intimidation and coercion motivated by extremism, religious or otherwise, occurring in many parts of the world and threatening the enjoyment of human rights and fundamental freedoms,

Noting with concern that defamation of religions is among the causes of social disharmony and leads to violations of human rights,

Deeply alarmed at the rising trends towards discrimination based on religion and faith, including in some national policies and laws that stigmatize groups of people belonging to certain religions and faiths under a variety of pretexts relating to security and illegal immigration, and noting that the increased intellectual and media discourse is among the factors exacerbating such discrimination,

Noting with deep concern the increasing trend in recent years of statements attacking religions, Islam and Muslims in particular, especially in human rights forums,

1. *Expresses its deep concern* about the negative stereotyping of religions and manifestations of intolerance and discrimination in matters of religion or belief still in evidence in some regions of the world;

2. *Strongly deplores* physical attacks and assaults on businesses, cultural centres and places of worship of all religions as well as targeting of religious symbols;

3. *Notes with deep concern* the intensification of the campaign of defamation of religions and the ethnic and religious profiling of Muslim minorities in the aftermath of the tragic events of 11 September 2001;

4. *Expresses its deep concern* that Islam is frequently and wrongly associated with human rights violations and terrorism;

5. *Also expresses its deep concern* about programmes and agendas pursued by extremist organizations and groups aimed at the defamation of religions, in particular when supported by Governments;

6. *Deplores* the use of the print, audio-visual and electronic media, including the Internet, and any other means to incite acts of violence, xenophobia or related intolerance and discrimination against Islam or any other religion;

7. *Recognizes* that, in the context of the fight against terrorism and the reaction to counter-terrorism measures, defamation of religions becomes an aggravating factor that contributes to the denial of fundamental rights and freedoms of target groups, as well as their economic and social exclusion;

8. *Stresses* the need to effectively combat defamation of all religions, Islam and Muslims in particular, especially in human rights forums;

9. *Emphasizes* that everyone has the right to freedom of expression, which should be exercised with responsibility and may therefore be subject to limitations as provided by law and necessary for respect of the rights or reputations of others, protection of national security or of public order, public health or morals and respect for religions and beliefs;

10. *Urges* States to take resolute action to prohibit the dissemination of racist and xenophobic ideas and material aimed at any religion or its followers that constitute incitement to discrimination, hostility or violence;

11. *Also urges* States to provide, within their respective legal and constitutional systems, adequate protection against acts of hatred, discrimination, intimidation and coercion resulting from defamation of religions, to take all possible measures to promote tolerance and respect for all religions and their value systems and to complement legal systems with intellectual and moral strategies to combat religious hatred and intolerance;

12. *Urges* all States to ensure that all public officials, including members of law enforcement bodies, the military, civil servants and educators, in the course of their official duties, respect different religions and beliefs and do not discriminate against persons on the grounds of their religion or belief, and that any necessary and appropriate education or training is provided;

13. *Underscores* the need to combat defamation of religions by strategizing and harmonizing actions at the local, national, regional and international levels through education and awareness-raising;

14. *Urges* States to ensure equal access to education for all, in law and in practice, including access to free primary education for all children, both girls and boys, and access for adults to lifelong learning and education based on respect for human rights, diversity and tolerance, without discrimination of any kind, and to refrain from any legal or other measures leading to racial segregation in access to schooling;

15. *Calls upon* the international community to initiate a global dialogue to promote a culture of tolerance and peace based on respect for human rights and religious diversity, and urges States, non-governmental organizations, religious bodies and the print and electronic media to support and promote such a dialogue;

16. *Affirms* that the Human Rights Council shall promote universal respect for all religious and cultural values and address instances of intolerance, discrimination and incitement of hatred against any community or adherents of any religion;

17. *Calls upon* the United Nations High Commissioner for Human Rights to promote and include human rights aspects in the dialogue among civilizations, inter alia, through:

(*a*) Integrating them into topical seminars and special debates on the positive contributions of cultures, as well as religious and cultural diversity, including through educational programmes, particularly the World Programme for Human Rights Education proclaimed on 10 December 2004;

(*b*) Collaboration by the Office of the United Nations High Commissioner for Human Rights with other relevant international organizations in holding joint conferences designed to encourage this dialogue and promote understanding of the universality of human rights and their implementation at various levels;

18. *Requests* the Secretary-General to submit a report on the implementation of the present resolution, including on the possible correlation between defamation of religions and the upsurge in incitement, intolerance and hatred in many parts of the world, to the General Assembly at its sixty-second session.

RECORDED VOTE ON RESOLUTION 61/164:

In favour: Afghanistan, Algeria, Angola, Antigua and Barbuda, Argentina, Azerbaijan, Bahamas, Bahrain, Bangladesh, Barbados, Belarus, Belize, Benin, Bhutan, Brazil, Brunei Darussalam, Burkina Faso, Burundi, Cambodia, Cameroon, Central African Republic, Chile, China, Comoros, Congo, Costa Rica, Côte d'Ivoire, Cuba, Democratic People's Republic of Korea, Democratic Republic of the Congo, Djibouti, Dominica, Dominican Republic, Ecuador, Egypt, El Salvador, Eritrea, Ethiopia, Gabon, Gambia, Ghana, Grenada, Guatemala, Guinea, Guinea-Bissau, Guyana, Honduras, Indonesia, Iran, Iraq, Jamaica, Jordan, Kazakhstan, Kuwait, Kyrgyzstan, Lao People's Democratic Republic, Lebanon, Lesotho, Liberia, Libyan Arab Jamahiriya, Malaysia, Maldives, Mali, Mauritania, Mauritius, Mexico, Morocco, Mozambique, Myanmar, Namibia, Nicaragua, Niger, Oman, Pakistan, Panama, Paraguay, Peru, Philippines, Qatar, Russian Federation, Rwanda, Saint Lucia, Saint Vincent and the Grenadines, Sao Tome and Principe, Saudi Arabia, Senegal, Sierra Leone, Singapore, Somalia, South Africa, Sri Lanka, Sudan, Suriname, Swaziland, Syrian Arab Republic, Tajikistan, Thailand, Timor-Leste, Togo, Trinidad and Tobago, Tunisia, Turkey, Turkmenistan, United Arab Emirates, Uruguay, Uzbekistan, Venezuela, Viet Nam, Yemen, Zambia, Zimbabwe.

Against: Albania, Andorra, Australia, Austria, Belgium, Bosnia and Herzegovina, Bulgaria, Canada, Croatia, Cyprus, Czech Republic, Denmark, Estonia, Finland, France, Georgia, Germany, Greece, Hungary, Iceland, Ireland, Israel, Italy, Japan, Latvia, Liechtenstein, Lithuania, Luxembourg, Malta, Marshall Islands, Micronesia, Moldova, Monaco, Montenegro, Netherlands, New Zealand, Norway, Palau, Poland, Portugal, Republic of Korea, Romania, Samoa, San Marino, Serbia, Slovakia, Slovenia, Spain, Sweden, Switzerland, The former Yugoslav Republic of Macedonia, Ukraine, United Kingdom, United States.

Abstaining: Armenia, Bolivia, Botswana, Cape Verde, Colombia, Fiji, Haiti, India, Kenya, Madagascar, Malawi, Nepal, Nigeria, Papua New Guinea, Solomon Islands, Tuvalu, United Republic of Tanzania, Vanuatu.

Also on 19 December [meeting 81], the General Assembly, on the recommendation of the Third

Committee [A/61/443/Add.2 & Corr.1], adopted **resolution 61/161** without vote [agenda item 67 *(b)*].

Elimination of all forms of intolerance and of discrimination based on religion or belief

The General Assembly,

Recalling its resolution 36/55 of 25 November 1981, by which it proclaimed the Declaration on the Elimination of All Forms of Intolerance and of Discrimination Based on Religion or Belief,

Recalling also article 18 of the International Covenant on Civil and Political Rights, article 18 of the Universal Declaration of Human Rights and other relevant human rights provisions,

Reaffirming the call of the World Conference on Human Rights upon all Governments to take all appropriate measures in compliance with their international obligations and with due regard to their respective legal systems to counter intolerance and related violence based on religion or belief, including practices of discrimination against women and the desecration of religious sites, recognizing that every individual has the right to freedom of thought, conscience, expression and religion,

Reaffirming also the recognition by the World Conference on Human Rights that all human rights are universal, indivisible, interdependent and interrelated,

Recalling General Assembly resolution 56/6 of 9 November 2001 on the Global Agenda for Dialogue among Civilizations, in which the Assembly recognized the valuable contribution that dialogue among civilizations could make to an improved awareness and understanding of the common values shared by all humankind,

Acknowledging that in order to be effective, such a dialogue should be based on respect for the dignity of adherents of religions and beliefs, as well as respect for diversity and the universal promotion and protection of human rights,

Considering that religion or belief, for those who profess either, is one of the fundamental elements in their conception of life and that freedom of religion or belief should be fully respected and guaranteed,

Considering also that the disregard for and infringement of human rights and fundamental freedoms, in particular the right to freedom of thought, conscience, religion or belief, have brought, directly or indirectly, wars and great suffering to humankind,

Recognizing the importance of promoting dialogue among civilizations in order to enhance mutual understanding and knowledge among different social groups, cultures and civilizations in various areas, including culture, religion, education, information, science and technology, and in order to contribute to the promotion and protection of human rights and fundamental freedoms,

Recalling Commission on Human Rights resolution 2005/40 of 19 April 2005 on the elimination of all forms of intolerance and of discrimination based on religion or belief,

Seriously concerned at all attacks upon religious places, sites and shrines, including any deliberate destruction of relics and monuments,

Seriously concerned also at the misuse of registration procedures as a means to limit the right to freedom of religion or belief of members of certain religious communities and at the limitations placed on religious publications,

Recognizing the important work carried out by the Human Rights Committee in providing guidance with respect to the scope of the freedom of religion or belief,

Convinced of the need to address, for instance, in the context of the Global Agenda for Dialogue among Civilizations and the Alliance of Civilizations the rise in all parts of the world of religious extremism affecting the rights of individuals and groups based on religion or belief, the situations of violence and discrimination that affect many women as a result of religion or belief and the abuse of religion or belief for ends inconsistent with the Charter of the United Nations and other relevant instruments of the United Nations,

Resolved to adopt all necessary and appropriate measures for the speedy elimination of such intolerance based on religion or belief in all its forms and manifestations and prevent and combat discrimination based on religion or belief,

Noting that a formal or legal distinction at the national level between different kinds of religions or faith-based communities may, in some cases, constitute discrimination and may impinge on the enjoyment of the freedom of religion or belief,

Underlining the importance of education in the promotion of tolerance, which involves the acceptance by the public of, and its respect for, diversity, including with regard to religious expressions, and underlining also the fact that education, in particular at school, should contribute in a meaningful way to promoting tolerance and the elimination of discrimination based on religion or belief,

Recalling the importance of the International Consultative Conference on School Education in relation to Freedom of Religion or Belief, Tolerance and Non-Discrimination, held in Madrid from 23 to 25 November 2001, and continuing to invite Governments to give consideration to the Final Document adopted at the Conference,

Emphasizing that States, regional organizations, non-governmental organizations, and religious bodies and the media have an important role to play in promoting tolerance, respect and freedom of religion or belief,

Recognizing the importance of interreligious and intrareligious dialogue and the role of religious and other non-governmental organizations in promoting tolerance in matters relating to religion or belief,

Believing that further intensified efforts are therefore required to promote and protect the right to freedom of thought, conscience, religion or belief and to eliminate all forms of hatred, intolerance and discrimination based on religion or belief, as also noted at the World Conference against Racism, Racial Discrimination, Xenophobia and Related Intolerance,

1. *Welcomes* the work and the report of the Special Rapporteur of the Human Rights Council on freedom of religion or belief;

2. *Condemns* all forms of intolerance and of discrimination based on religion or belief;

3. *Encourages* the efforts made by the United Nations High Commissioner for Human Rights to coordinate in the field of human rights the activities of relevant United Nations organs, bodies and mechanisms dealing with all forms of intolerance and of discrimination based on religion or belief;

4. *Urges* States:

(*a*) To ensure that their constitutional and legislative systems provide adequate and effective guarantees of freedom of thought, conscience, religion and belief to all without distinction, inter alia, by the provision of effective remedies in cases where the right to freedom of thought, conscience, religion or belief, or the right to practise freely one's religion, including the right to change one's religion or belief, is violated;

(*b*) To exert the utmost efforts, in accordance with their national legislation and in conformity with international human rights law, to ensure that religious places, sites, shrines and symbols are fully respected and protected and to take additional measures in cases where they are vulnerable to desecration or destruction;

(*c*) To review, whenever relevant, existing registration practices in order to ensure the right of all persons to manifest their religion or belief, alone or in community with others and in public or in private;

(*d*) To ensure, in particular, the right of all persons to worship or assemble in connection with a religion or belief and to establish and maintain places for these purposes and the right of all persons to write, issue and disseminate relevant publications in these areas;

(*e*) To ensure that, in accordance with appropriate national legislation and in conformity with international human rights law, the freedom of all persons and members of groups to establish and maintain religious, charitable or humanitarian institutions is fully respected and protected;

(*f*) To ensure that no one within their jurisdiction is deprived of the right to life, liberty or security of person because of religion or belief and that no one is subjected to torture or arbitrary arrest or detention on that account and to bring to justice all perpetrators of violations of these rights;

(*g*) To ensure that all public officials and civil servants, including members of law enforcement bodies, the military and educators, in the course of their official duties, respect different religions and beliefs and do not discriminate on the grounds of religion or belief, and that all necessary and appropriate education or training is provided;

5. *Recognizes with deep concern* the overall rise in instances of intolerance and violence directed against members of many religious and other communities in various parts of the world, including cases motivated by Islamophobia, anti-Semitism and Christianophobia;

6. *Expresses concern* over the persistence of institutionalized social intolerance and discrimination practised against many in the name of religion or belief;

7. *Condemns* any advocacy of religious hatred that constitutes incitement to discrimination, hostility or violence, whether it involves the use of print, audio-visual and electronic media or any other means;

8. *Stresses* the need to strengthen dialogue, inter alia, through the Global Agenda for Dialogue among Civilizations and the Alliance of Civilizations;

9. *Invites* States, the Special Rapporteur, the Office of the United Nations High Commissioner for Human Rights and other relevant entities of the United Nations system, such as the United Nations Educational, Scientific and Cultural Organization, and other international and regional organizations and civil society to consider promoting dialogue among civilizations in order to contribute to the elimination of intolerance and discrimination based on religion or belief, inter alia, by addressing the following issues within the framework of international standards of human rights:

(*a*) The rise of religious extremism affecting religions in all parts of the world;

(*b*) The situations of violence and discrimination that affect many women as a result of religion or belief;

(*c*) The use of religion or belief for ends inconsistent with the Charter of the United Nations and other relevant instruments of the United Nations;

10. *Urges* States to step up their efforts to eliminate intolerance and discrimination based on religion or belief, notably by:

(*a*) Taking all necessary and appropriate action, in conformity with international standards of human rights, to combat hatred, intolerance and acts of violence, intimidation and coercion motivated by intolerance based on religion or belief, as well as incitement to hostility and violence, with particular regard to religious minorities, and devoting particular attention to practices that violate the human rights of women and discriminate against women, including in the exercise of their right to freedom of thought, conscience, religion or belief;

(*b*) Promoting and encouraging, through education and other means, understanding, tolerance and respect in all matters relating to freedom of religion or belief;

(*c*) Undertaking all appropriate efforts to encourage those engaged in teaching to cultivate respect for all religions or beliefs, thereby promoting mutual understanding and tolerance;

11. *Invites* Governments, religious bodies and civil society to continue to undertake dialogue at all levels to promote greater tolerance, respect and understanding;

12. *Emphasizes* the importance of a continued and strengthened dialogue among and within religions or beliefs, including as encompassed in the dialogue among civilizations, to promote greater tolerance, respect and mutual understanding;

13. *Also emphasizes* that equating any religion with terrorism should be avoided, as this may have adverse consequences on the enjoyment of the right to freedom

of religion or belief of all members of the religious communities concerned;

14. *Further emphasizes* that, as underlined by the Human Rights Committee, restrictions on the freedom to manifest religion or belief are permitted only if limitations are prescribed by law, are necessary to protect public safety, order, health or morals, or the fundamental rights and freedoms of others, and are applied in a manner that does not vitiate the right to freedom of thought, conscience and religion;

15. *Encourages* the continuing efforts in all parts of the world of the Special Rapporteur to examine incidents and governmental actions that are incompatible with the provisions of the Declaration on the Elimination of All Forms of Intolerance and of Discrimination Based on Religion or Belief and to recommend remedial measures, as appropriate;

16. *Stresses* the need for the Special Rapporteur to continue to apply a gender perspective, inter alia, through the identification of gender-specific abuses, in the reporting process, including in information collection and in recommendations;

17. *Welcomes and encourages* the continuing efforts of all actors in society, including non-governmental organizations and bodies and groups based on religion or belief, to promote the implementation of the Declaration, and further encourages their work in promoting freedom of religion or belief and in highlighting cases of religious intolerance, discrimination and persecution;

18. *Recommends* that the United Nations and other actors, in their efforts to promote freedom of religion or belief, ensure the widest possible dissemination of the text of the Declaration in as many different languages as possible by United Nations information centres and by other interested bodies;

19. *Decides* to continue its consideration of measures to implement the Declaration;

20. *Welcomes* the work of the Special Rapporteur, and urges all Governments to cooperate fully with the Special Rapporteur and to respond favourably to her requests to visit their countries and to provide her with all necessary information so as to enable her to fulfil her mandate even more effectively;

21. *Requests* the Secretary-General to ensure that the Special Rapporteur receives the necessary resources to enable her to discharge her mandate fully;

22. *Requests* the Special Rapporteur to submit an interim report to the General Assembly at its sixty-second session;

23. *Decides* to consider the question of the elimination of all forms of religious intolerance at its sixty-second session under the item entitled "Promotion and protection of human rights".

Right to self-determination

Report of Secretary-General. In response to General Assembly resolution 60/145 [YUN 2005, p. 786], the Secretary-General submitted a September report [A/61/333] summarizing the Commission's consideration of the implementation of the right to self determination. It also outlined the jurisprudence of the Human Rights Committee and the Committee on Economic, Social and Cultural Rights on the treaty-based human rights norms relating to the realization of that right.

On 19 December, the Assembly took note of the Secretary-General's report (**decision 61/528**).

GENERAL ASSEMBLY ACTION

On 19 December [meeting 81], the General Assembly, on the recommendation of the Third Committee [A/61/442], adopted **resolution 61/150** without vote [agenda item 66].

Universal realization of the right of peoples to self-determination

The General Assembly,

Reaffirming the importance, for the effective guarantee and observance of human rights, of the universal realization of the right of peoples to self-determination enshrined in the Charter of the United Nations and embodied in the International Covenants on Human Rights, as well as in the Declaration on the Granting of Independence to Colonial Countries and Peoples contained in General Assembly resolution 1514 (XV) of 14 December 1960,

Welcoming the progressive exercise of the right to self-determination by peoples under colonial, foreign or alien occupation and their emergence into sovereign statehood and independence,

Deeply concerned at the continuation of acts or threats of foreign military intervention and occupation that are threatening to suppress, or have already suppressed, the right to self-determination of peoples and nations,

Expressing grave concern that, as a consequence of the persistence of such actions, millions of people have been and are being uprooted from their homes as refugees and displaced persons, and emphasizing the urgent need for concerted international action to alleviate their condition,

Recalling the relevant resolutions regarding the violation of the right of peoples to self-determination and other human rights as a result of foreign military intervention, aggression and occupation, adopted by the Commission on Human Rights at its sixty-first and previous sessions,

Reaffirming its previous resolutions on the universal realization of the right of peoples to self-determination, including resolution 60/145 of 16 December 2005,

Reaffirming also its resolution 55/2 of 8 September 2000, containing the United Nations Millennium Declaration, and recalling its resolution 60/1 of 16 September 2005, containing the 2005 World Summit Outcome, which, inter alia, upheld the right to self-determination of peoples under colonial domination and foreign occupation,

Taking note of the report of the Secretary-General,

1. *Reaffirms* that the universal realization of the right of all peoples, including those under colonial, foreign and alien domination, to self-determination is a fundamental condition for the effective guarantee and observance of human rights and for the preservation and promotion of such rights;

2. *Declares its firm opposition* to acts of foreign military intervention, aggression and occupation, since these have resulted in the suppression of the right of peoples to self-determination and other human rights in certain parts of the world;

3. *Calls upon* those States responsible to cease immediately their military intervention in and occupation of foreign countries and territories and all acts of repression, discrimination, exploitation and maltreatment, in particular the brutal and inhumane methods reportedly employed for the execution of those acts against the peoples concerned;

4. *Deplores* the plight of millions of refugees and displaced persons who have been uprooted as a result of the aforementioned acts, and reaffirms their right to return to their homes voluntarily in safety and honour;

5. *Requests* the Human Rights Council to continue to give special attention to the violation of human rights, especially the right to self-determination, resulting from foreign military intervention, aggression or occupation;

6. *Requests* the Secretary-General to report on the question to the General Assembly at its sixty-second session under the item entitled "Right of peoples to self-determination".

Right of Palestinians to self-determination

During the year, the General Assembly reaffirmed the right of the Palestinian people to self-determination, including the right to their independent state of Palestine, as well as the right of all States in the region to live in peace within secure and internationally recognized borders. States and UN system specialized agencies were urged to assist Palestinians in the early realization of the right.

GENERAL ASSEMBLY ACTION

On 19 December [meeting 81], the General Assembly, on the recommendation of the Third Committee [A/61/442], adopted **resolution 61/152** by recorded vote (176-5-5) [agenda item 66].

The right of the Palestinian people to self-determination

The General Assembly,

Aware that the development of friendly relations among nations, based on respect for the principle of equal rights and self-determination of peoples, is among the purposes and principles of the United Nations, as defined in the Charter,

Recalling, in this regard, its resolution 2625 (XXV) of 24 October 1970 entitled "Declaration on Principles of International Law concerning Friendly Relations and Cooperation among States in accordance with the Charter of the United Nations",

Bearing in mind the International Covenants on Human Rights, the Universal Declaration of Human Rights, the Declaration on the Granting of Independence to Colonial Countries and Peoples and the Vienna Declaration and Programme of Action adopted at the World Conference on Human Rights on 25 June 1993,

Recalling the Declaration on the Occasion of the Fiftieth Anniversary of the United Nations,

Recalling also the United Nations Millennium Declaration,

Recalling further the advisory opinion rendered on 9 July 2004 by the International Court of Justice on the *Legal Consequences of the Construction of a Wall in the Occupied Palestinian Territory*, and noting in particular the reply of the Court, including on the right of peoples to self-determination, which is a right *erga omnes*,

Recalling the conclusion of the Court, in its advisory opinion of 9 July 2004, that the construction of the wall by Israel, the occupying Power, in the Occupied Palestinian Territory, including East Jerusalem, along with measures previously taken, severely impedes the right of the Palestinian people to self-determination,

Expressing the urgent need for the resumption of negotiations within the Middle East peace process on its agreed basis and for the speedy achievement of a just, lasting and comprehensive peace settlement between the Palestinian and Israeli sides,

Recalling its resolution 60/146 of 16 December 2005,

Affirming the right of all States in the region to live in peace within secure and internationally recognized borders,

1. *Reaffirms* the right of the Palestinian people to self-determination, including the right to their independent State of Palestine;

2. *Urges* all States and the specialized agencies and organizations of the United Nations system to continue to support and assist the Palestinian people in the early realization of their right to self-determination.

RECORDED VOTE ON RESOLUTION 61/152:

In favour: Afghanistan, Albania, Algeria, Andorra, Angola, Antigua and Barbuda, Argentina, Armenia, Austria, Azerbaijan, Bahamas, Bahrain, Bangladesh, Barbados, Belarus, Belgium, Belize, Benin, Bhutan, Bolivia, Bosnia and Herzegovina, Botswana, Brazil, Brunei Darussalam, Bulgaria, Burkina Faso, Burundi, Cambodia, Cameroon, Cape Verde, Chile, China, Colombia, Comoros, Congo, Costa Rica, Côte d'Ivoire, Croatia, Cuba, Cyprus, Czech Republic, Democratic People's Republic of Korea, Democratic Republic of the Congo, Denmark, Djibouti, Dominica, Dominican Republic, Ecuador, Egypt, El Salvador, Eritrea, Estonia, Ethiopia, Fiji, Finland, France, Gabon, Gambia, Georgia, Germany, Ghana, Greece, Grenada, Guatemala, Guinea, Guinea-Bissau, Guyana, Haiti, Honduras, Hungary, Iceland, India, Indonesia, Iran, Iraq, Ireland, Italy, Jamaica, Japan, Jordan, Kazakhstan, Kenya, Kuwait, Kyrgyzstan, Lao People's Democratic Republic, Latvia, Lebanon, Lesotho, Liberia, Libyan Arab Jamahiriya, Liechtenstein, Lithuania, Luxembourg, Madagascar, Malawi, Malaysia, Maldives, Mali, Malta, Mauritania, Mauritius, Mexico, Moldova, Monaco, Mongolia, Montenegro, Morocco, Mozambique, Myanmar,

Namibia, Nepal, Netherlands, New Zealand, Nicaragua, Niger, Nigeria, Norway, Oman, Pakistan, Panama, Papua New Guinea, Paraguay, Peru, Philippines, Poland, Portugal, Qatar, Republic of Korea, Romania, Russian Federation, Rwanda, Saint Lucia, Saint Vincent and the Grenadines, Samoa, San Marino, Sao Tome and Principe, Saudi Arabia, Senegal, Serbia, Sierra Leone, Singapore, Slovakia, Slovenia, Solomon Islands, Somalia, South Africa, Spain, Sri Lanka, Sudan, Suriname, Swaziland, Sweden, Switzerland, Syrian Arab Republic, Tajikistan, Thailand, The former Yugoslav Republic of Macedonia, Timor-Leste, Togo, Trinidad and Tobago, Tunisia, Turkey, Turkmenistan, Tuvalu, Uganda, Ukraine, United Arab Emirates, United Kingdom, United Republic of Tanzania, Uruguay, Uzbekistan, Venezuela, Viet Nam, Yemen, Zambia, Zimbabwe.

Against: Israel, Marshall Islands, Micronesia, Palau, United States.

Abstaining: Australia, Canada, Central African Republic, Nauru, Vanuatu.

Mercenaries

Reports of Working Group. The Working Group on the use of mercenaries, established in a 2005 Commission decision [YUN 2005, p. 788] to continue the work begun by previous mechanisms on mercenaries, held its first session (10-14 October 2005) [E/CN.4/2006/11], at which it addressed its methods of work, including the possible establishment of a complaints mechanism and ways of consulting with private sector actors and field missions. The Group agreed to concentrate initially on two issues: the role of the State as the primary holder of the monopoly of the use of force, and related issues such as sovereignty and State responsibility to protect and ensure respect for human rights by all; and governmental agreements that provided private military and security companies and their employees with immunity for human rights violations.

At a resumed session (13-17 February) [E/CN.4/2006/11/Add.1], the Group adopted its methods of work, including the establishment of a monitoring and complaint mechanism to address complaints regarding mercenaries' activities. It also reviewed several country situations and agreed to establish a network of academics working on the study of mercenarism and related activities; undertake a comparative analysis of national and regional legislation; and recommend the convening of a high-level round table, under UN auspices, to discuss the role of the State as primary holder of the monopoly on the use of force.

In response to Economic and Social Council decision 2005/255 [YUN 2005, p. 788], the Secretary-General, by a September note [A/61/341], transmitted the Working Group's annual report to the General Assembly, which further discussed its methods of work, reviewed its activities since its creation, and analysed responses to a questionnaire on its mandate and work sent to Member States, international organizations and NGOs. Other parts of the report related to the Group's study of the effects of the activities of private companies offering military assistance, consultancy and security services on the international market; mercenaries and mercenary-related activities in different parts of the world; and international and national legislation on the issue of mercenarism. Noting that only 28 States had ratified the International Convention against the Recruitment, Use, Financing and Training of Mercenaries (see below), the Group recommended that Member States that had not yet done so should ratify or accede to the Convention, and incorporate relevant legal norms into their national legislation. To ensure that the military assistance, consultancy and security services offered by private companies did not violate human rights, Governments should set up regulatory mechanisms to control and monitor their activities, including a system of registering and licensing, which would authorize those companies to operate and allow them to be sanctioned when the norms were not respected. Governments that imported such military assistance and services should also establish regulatory mechanisms for registering and licensing the companies providing them.

Human Rights Council action. On 29 November [A/62/53 (dec. 2/116)], the Council deferred to its fourth (2007) session, consideration of a draft decision submitted by Cuba [A/HRC/2/L.19] on the use of mercenaries as a means of violating human rights and impeding the exercise of the right of peoples to self-determination, which called for a high-level round table to discuss the fundamental question of the role of the State as the primary holder of the monopoly of the use of force.

GENERAL ASSEMBLY ACTION

On 19 December [meeting 81], the General Assembly, on the recommendation of the Third Committee [A/61/442], adopted **resolution 61/151** by recorded vote (127-51-7) [agenda item 66].

Use of mercenaries as a means of violating human rights and impeding the exercise of the right of peoples to self-determination

The General Assembly,

Recalling all of its previous resolutions on the subject, including resolution 59/178 of 20 December 2004, and taking note of Commission on Human Rights resolution 2005/2 of 7 April 2005,

Recalling also all of its relevant resolutions, in which, inter alia, it condemned any State that permitted or tolerated the recruitment, financing, training, assembly, transit and use of mercenaries with the objective of overthrowing the Governments of States Members of the United Nations, especially those of developing countries, or of fighting against national liberation movements, and recalling further the relevant resolutions and international instruments adopted by the General Assembly, the Security Council, the Economic and Social Council and the Organization of African Unity, inter alia, the Organization of African Unity Convention for the elimination of mercenarism in Africa, as well as the African Union,

Reaffirming the purposes and principles enshrined in the Charter of the United Nations concerning the strict observance of the principles of sovereign equality, political independence, the territorial integrity of States, the self-determination of peoples, the non-use of force or of the threat of use of force in international relations and non-interference in affairs within the domestic jurisdiction of States,

Reaffirming also that, by virtue of the principle of self-determination, all peoples have the right freely to determine their political status and to pursue their economic, social and cultural development, and that every State has the duty to respect this right in accordance with the provisions of the Charter,

Reaffirming further the Declaration on Principles of International Law concerning Friendly Relations and Cooperation among States in accordance with the Charter of the United Nations,

Alarmed and concerned at the danger that the activities of mercenaries constitute to peace and security in developing countries, in particular in Africa and in small States,

Deeply concerned at the loss of life, the substantial damage to property and the negative effects on the policy and economies of affected countries resulting from criminal mercenary activities,

Extremely alarmed and concerned about recent mercenary activities in Africa and the threat they pose to the integrity of and respect for the constitutional order of those countries,

Convinced that, notwithstanding the way in which they are used or the form that they take to acquire some semblance of legitimacy, mercenaries or mercenary-related activities are a threat to peace, security and the self-determination of peoples and an obstacle to the enjoyment of all human rights by peoples,

1. *Takes note* of the report of the Working Group on the use of mercenaries as a means of violating human rights and impeding the exercise of the right of peoples to self-determination;

2. *Reaffirms* that the use of mercenaries and their recruitment, financing and training are causes for grave concern to all States and violate the purposes and principles enshrined in the Charter of the United Nations;

3. *Recognizes* that armed conflict, terrorism, arms trafficking and covert operations by third Powers, inter alia, encourage the demand for mercenaries on the global market;

4. *Urges once again* all States to take the necessary steps and to exercise the utmost vigilance against the menace posed by the activities of mercenaries and to take legislative measures to ensure that their territories and other territories under their control, as well as their nationals, are not used for the recruitment, assembly, financing, training and transit of mercenaries for the planning of activities designed to impede the right of peoples to self-determination, to destabilize or overthrow the Government of any State or to dismember or impair, totally or in part, the territorial integrity or political unity of sovereign and independent States conducting themselves in compliance with the right of peoples to self-determination;

5. *Requests* all States to exercise the utmost vigilance against any kind of recruitment, training, hiring or financing of mercenaries by private companies offering international military consultancy and security services, as well as to impose a specific ban on such companies intervening in armed conflicts or actions to destabilize constitutional regimes;

6. *Calls upon* all States that have not yet done so to consider taking the necessary action to accede to or ratify the International Convention against the Recruitment, Use, Financing and Training of Mercenaries;

7. *Welcomes* the adoption by some States of national legislation that restricts the recruitment, assembly, financing, training and transit of mercenaries;

8. *Condemns* recent mercenary activities in Africa, and commends the African Governments on their collaboration in thwarting those illegal actions, which posed a threat to the integrity of and respect for the constitutional order of those countries and the exercise of the right of their peoples to self-determination;

9. *Calls upon* States to investigate the possibility of mercenary involvement whenever and wherever criminal acts of a terrorist nature occur and to bring to trial those found responsible or to consider their extradition, if so requested, in accordance with domestic law and applicable bilateral or international treaties;

10. *Condemns* any form of impunity granted to perpetrators of mercenary activities and to those responsible for the use, recruitment, financing and training of mercenaries, and urges all States, in accordance with their obligations under international law, to bring them, without distinction, to justice;

11. *Calls upon* Member States, in accordance with their obligations under international law, to cooperate with and assist the judicial prosecution of those accused of mercenary activities in transparent, open and fair trials;

12. *Requests* the Working Group to continue the work already done by the previous Special Rapporteurs on the strengthening of the international legal framework for the prevention and sanction of the recruitment, use, financing and training of mercenaries, taking into account the proposal for a new legal definition of a mercenary drafted by the Special Rapporteur in his report to the Commission on Human Rights at its sixtieth session;

13. *Requests* the Office of the United Nations High Commissioner for Human Rights, as a matter of priority, to publicize the adverse effects of the activities of mercenaries on the right of peoples to self-determination and, when requested and where necessary, to render advisory services to States that are affected by those activities;

14. *Expresses its appreciation* to the Office of the High Commissioner for convening the third meeting of experts on traditional and new forms of mercenary activities as a means of violating human rights and impeding the exercise of the right of peoples to self-determination, and takes note of the report of the meeting;

15. *Requests* the Working Group to continue to take into account, in the discharge of its mandate, the fact that mercenary activities continue to occur in many parts of the world and are taking on new forms, manifestations and modalities, and, in this regard, requests its members to continue to pay particular attention to the impact of the activities of private companies offering military assistance, consultancy and security services on the international market on the exercise of the right of peoples to self-determination;

16. *Urges* all States to cooperate fully with the Working Group in the fulfilment of its mandate;

17. *Requests* the Secretary-General and the United Nations High Commissioner for Human Rights to provide the Working Group with all the necessary assistance and support for the fulfilment of its mandate, both professional and financial, including through the promotion of cooperation between the Working Group and other components of the United Nations system that deal with countering mercenary-related activities, in order to meet the demands of its current and future activities;

18. *Requests* the Working Group to consult States and intergovernmental and non-governmental organizations in the implementation of the present resolution and to report, with specific recommendations, to the General Assembly at its sixty-second session its findings on the use of mercenaries to undermine the enjoyment of all human rights and to impede the exercise of the right of peoples to self-determination;

19. *Decides* to consider at its sixty-second session the question of the use of mercenaries as a means of violating human rights and impeding the exercise of the right of peoples to self-determination under the item entitled "Right of peoples to self-determination".

RECORDED VOTE ON RESOLUTION 61/151:

In favour: Afghanistan, Algeria, Angola, Antigua and Barbuda, Argentina, Armenia, Azerbaijan, Bahamas, Bahrain, Bangladesh, Barbados, Belarus, Belize, Benin, Bhutan, Bolivia, Botswana, Brazil, Brunei Darussalam, Burkina Faso, Burundi, Cambodia, Cameroon, Cape Verde, Central African Republic, Chile, China, Colombia, Comoros, Congo, Costa Rica, Côte d'Ivoire, Cuba, Democratic People's Republic of Korea, Democratic Republic of the Congo, Djibouti, Dominica, Dominican Republic, Ecuador, Egypt, El Salvador, Eritrea, Ethiopia, Gabon, Gambia, Ghana, Grenada, Guatemala, Guinea, Guinea-Bissau, Guyana, Haiti, Honduras, India, Indonesia, Iran, Iraq, Jamaica, Jordan, Kazakhstan, Kenya, Kuwait, Kyrgyzstan, Lao People's Democratic Republic, Lebanon, Lesotho, Liberia, Libyan Arab Jamahiriya, Madagascar, Malawi, Malaysia, Maldives, Mali, Mauritania, Mauritius, Mexico, Mongolia, Morocco, Mozambique, Myanmar, Namibia, Nepal, Nicaragua, Niger, Nigeria, Oman, Pakistan, Panama, Paraguay, Peru, Philippines, Qatar, Russian Federation, Rwanda, Saint Lucia, Saint Vincent and the Grenadines, Samoa, Sao Tome and Principe, Saudi Arabia, Senegal, Sierra Leone, Singapore, Solomon Islands, Somalia, South Africa, Sri Lanka, Sudan, Suriname, Swaziland, Syrian Arab Republic, Tajikistan, Thailand, Timor-Leste, Togo, Trinidad and Tobago, Tunisia, Tuvalu, Uganda, United Arab Emirates, United Republic of Tanzania, Uruguay, Uzbekistan, Venezuela, Viet Nam, Yemen, Zambia, Zimbabwe.

Against: Albania, Andorra, Australia, Austria, Belgium, Bosnia and Herzegovina, Bulgaria, Canada, Croatia, Cyprus, Czech Republic, Denmark, Estonia, Finland, France, Georgia, Germany, Greece, Hungary, Iceland, Ireland, Israel, Italy, Japan, Latvia, Lithuania, Luxembourg, Malta, Marshall Islands, Micronesia, Moldova, Monaco, Montenegro, Netherlands, Norway, Palau, Poland, Portugal, Republic of Korea, Romania, San Marino, Serbia, Slovakia, Slovenia, Spain, Sweden, The former Yugoslav Republic of Macedonia, Turkey, Ukraine, United Kingdom, United States.

Abstaining: Fiji, Liechtenstein, New Zealand, Papua New Guinea, Switzerland, Tonga, Vanuatu.

1989 International Convention

As at 31 December, 28 States had become parties to the 1989 International Convention against the Recruitment, Use, Financing and Training of Mercenaries, adopted by the General Assembly in resolution 44/34 [YUN 1989, p. 825], following the accession of Moldova in 2006. The Convention entered into force in 2001 [YUN 2001, p. 632].

Administration of justice

Report of High Commissioner. In a February report [E/CN.4/2006/10] highlighting OHCHR efforts to address its 2005 Plan of Action for the future work of the Office [YUN 2005, p. 715], the High Commissioner noted that work continued in the area of administration of justice, including through military tribunals, and on the related issues of the accountability of international personnel taking part in peace support operations, women and children in prison, and the right to a remedy for violations of human rights. OHCHR technical cooperation activities included the training of judges, lawyers and prosecutors and the preparation of human rights education material. It also continued its development of rule of law tools for post-conflict situations to provide practical guidance to field missions and transitional administrations.

Working group activities. Established by the Subcommission on 7 August [dec. 2006/103], the five-member sessional working group on the administration of justice met on 8 and 11 August [A/HRC/Sub.1/58/8]. The group discussed accountability of international personnel taking part in peace support operations; the right to an effective remedy for human rights violations; amnesties, impunity and accountability for violations of international humanitarian law and human rights law; the circumstances in which a party could open fire in international humanitarian law and human rights law; and transitional justice.

The group had before it a January report on the administration of justice through military tribunals [E/CN.4/2006/58], prepared by the Subcommission's Special Rapporteur on the subject, Emmanuel Decaux (France), which presented 20 revised draft principles governing the administration of justice through military tribunals; a working paper by Françoise Hampson (United Kingdom) on the accountability of international personnel taking part in peace support operations [A/HRC/Sub.1/58/CRP.3], which addressed issues relating to criminal and civil liability of UN personnel for their individual actions and the integral question of the UN civil liability for the wrongful actions of its personnel; a working paper by Ms. Hampson and Mohamed Habib Cherif (Tunisia) on the implementation in practice of the right to an effective remedy for human rights violations [A/HRC/Sub.1/58/CRP.4], which considered the mechanisms needed to evaluate whether the right to a remedy was implemented in practice; a working paper by Ms. Hampson on the circumstances in which a party could open fire in the context of the law of armed conflict/international humanitarian law and human rights law [A/HRC/Sub.1/58/CRP.5], which examined the relationship between the applicability of international humanitarian and human rights laws, the related implications for a human rights body and the extraterritorial reach of human rights law; and a preliminary report by Lalaina Rakotoarisoa (Madagascar) on the difficulty of establishing guilt or responsibility in matters of sexual violence [A/HRC/Sub.1/58/CRP.9], which explored how cases of sexual violence could be better examined in law.

In addition, the group considered an informal working paper by Yozo Yokota (Japan) on amnesties, impunity and accountability for violation of international humanitarian law and international human rights law, prepared in response to a 2005 Subcommission request [YUN 2005, p. 790], and which drew a distinction between responsibility and accountability for human rights violations.

At the group's request, an OHCHR representative made a presentation on the work of the United Nations in the field of transitional justice, and highlighted the UN Peacebuilding Commission's intended actions to facilitate transitional justice, including strategies for post-conflict peacebuilding and recovery, and the development of best practices on issues warranting collaboration among political, military and humanitarian actors. A related OHCHR study [E/CN.4/2006/93], which focused on the transitional justice activities of the Office in the field and the human rights components of UN peacekeeping operations, called for the clarification of roles and responsibilities among UN departments, agencies and programmes involved, in order to ensure a greater coherence of approach regarding UN engagement in such activities

Subcommission action. On 24 August [res. 2006/5], the Subcommission, welcoming the report of the working group (see above), reaffirmed the importance of implementing all UN standards on human rights in the administration of justice and called on Member States to ensure the implementation of those standards. It reaffirmed the importance of combating impunity; expressed concern about the use of amnesty as a means of settling conflicts, since it might enable perpetrators of serious human rights violations to escape accountability for their actions; emphasized the importance of accountability of UN staff in peace support operations and of further studies in that area, and welcomed OHCHR release of five publications in the series *Rule-of-law tools for post-conflict States*, focusing on prosecution initiatives, truth and reconciliation commissions, mapping the justice sector, an operational framework for vetting and legal systems monitoring. Noting that the right to an effective remedy remained a significant goal that had yet to be obtained in many States, the Subcommission emphasized the need for further conceptual analysis and study of that subject, recommended to the Human Rights Council that the activity of the working group be continued in the framework of any future expert advice mechanism and invited States, UN bodies, intergovernmental organizations and NGOs to provide information to the group or its successor entity.

On the same day [res. 2006/2], the Subcommission appointed Mr. Cherif as Special Rapporteur to prepare a study on the implementation in practice of the right to an effective remedy for human rights violations based on the working papers submitted by him, Ms. Hampson and jointly by both of them (see above). He was requested to submit a preliminary report, or an expanded working paper should the Council not endorse his appointment, for consideration at the Subcommission's 2007 session or the first session of a future expert advice mechanism, and a progress report and final report in the following years.

Also on 24 August [res. 2006/3], the Subcommission appointed Ms. Hampson as Special Rapporteur with the task of preparing a comprehensive study on the accountability of international personnel taking part in peace support operations, based on her working paper (see p. 856), and requested her to submit a preliminary report to the Subcommission's 2007 session or to the first session of a future expert advice mechanism, and a progress report and final report in the following years. Should she not be appointed Special Rapporteur, she would prepare an updated working paper on the topic.

In further action on 24 August [res. 2006/4], the Subcommission welcomed the preliminary report submitted by Ms. Rakotoarisoa on the difficulty of establishing guilt or responsibility with regard to sexual violence (see p. 856) and asked her to submit an interim report and a final report on the topic in the following year, and failing that, to submit them to the Council or at the first session of a future expert advice mechanism. The Secretary-General was asked to assist her and to invite Governments, UN bodies and specialized agencies and NGOs to provide her with information necessary for preparing her report.

On the same day [dec. 2006/106], the Subcommission requested Vladimir Kartashkin (Russian Federation) to prepare, without financial implications, an expanded working paper on human rights and State sovereignty and to submit it in 2007 to the Subcommission or to any future expert advice mechanism. It also requested Janio Iván Tuñón-Veilles (Panama) [dec. 2006/107] to prepare, without financial implications, a working paper on transitional justice and investigation mechanisms for truth and reconciliation, with an emphasis on experiences in Latin America, and to submit it to the working group at its next session.

Human Rights Council action. On 29 November [A/62/53 (dec. 2/116)], the Council deferred to its fourth (2007) session a draft decision on transitional justice [A/HRC/2/L.36] submitted by Switzerland.

Rule of law

Non-State actors

The expanded working paper on human rights and non-State actors, which the Subcommission requested in 2005 from Gáspár Bíró (Hungary), Antoanella-Iulia Motoc (Romania), David Rivkin (United States) and Ibrahim Salama (Egypt) [YUN 2005, p. 797] was not submitted due to the uncertainty of the transitional period from the Commission on Human Rights to the Human Rights Council.

Humanitarian standards

Report of Secretary-General. In response to a 2004 Commission request [YUN 2004, p. 717], the Secretary-General, in consultation with the International Committee of the Red Cross (ICRC), submitted a March report [E/CN.4/2006/87] highlighting developments between 2004 and 2005 that had contributed to clarifying problems relating to the interpretation and application of relevant standards of humanity. The Secretary-General noted that the need to identify such standards had arisen from situations of internal violence that threatened human dignity and freedom, but they were also aimed at strengthening the protection of individuals by clarifying uncertainties in the application of international law. As such, the process of fundamental standards of humanity should focus on clarifying uncertainties in the application of standards in situations that presented a challenge to their effective implementation. An ICRC study on the rules of customary international humanitarian law had made a significant contribution by clarifying, in particular, rules of international humanitarian law applicable in non-international armed conflict. The Human Rights Committee's adoption of general comment 31 on article 2 of the International Covenant on Civil and Political Rights [YUN 2004, p. 662], as well as the International Court of Justice Advisory Opinion on the *Legal Consequences of the Construction of a Wall in the Occupied Palestinian Territory* [YUN 2004, p. 1272] and its judgment in the *Case Concerning Armed Activities on the Territory of the Congo* [YUN 2005, p. 1380] had reaffirmed the applicability of international human rights law during armed conflict and addressed the relationship between international humanitarian law and international human rights law. To build on that progress, the Commission should keep itself informed of relevant developments, including international and regional case law contributing to the clarification of uncertainties in the application of existing standards. The question of how to secure better compliance with fundamental standards of humanity by non-State actors also merited further consideration.

Civilians in armed conflict

Subcommission action. On 24 August [res. 2006/21], the Subcommission asked the Human Rights Council to call on Member States to consider holding a meeting of the High Contracting Parties to the Geneva Conventions of 1949 to examine possible options for enhanced monitoring of compliance with their obligations under international humanitarian law. It recommended that regional preparatory expert meetings be held, with a view to providing the conference of the High Contracting Parties with lessons learned from recent national conflicts and those of an international character in different parts of the world, and suggestions to remedy protection and monitor gaps. It also recommended that the Subcommission or a future expert advice mechanism should consider as a matter of priority ways of enhancing compliance by States with their obligations under international human rights law applicable in situations of armed conflict, in particular the rights of children.

SECURITY COUNCIL ACTION

On 28 April [meeting 5430], the Security Council unanimously adopted **resolution 1674(2006)**. The draft [S/2006/267] was prepared in consultations among Council members.

The Security Council,

Reaffirming its resolutions 1265(1999) of 17 September 1999 and 1296(2000) of 19 April 2000 on the protection of civilians in armed conflict, its various resolutions on children and armed conflict and on women, peace and security, as well as its resolution 1631(2005) of 17 October 2005 on cooperation between the United Nations and regional organizations in maintaining international peace and security, and further reaffirming its determination to ensure respect for, and follow-up to, those resolutions,

Reaffirming its commitment to the purposes of the Charter of the United Nations as set out in Article 1, paragraphs 1 to 4, and to the Principles of the Charter as set out in Article 2, paragraphs 1 to 7, including its commitment to the principles of the political independence, sovereign equality and territorial integrity of all States, and respect for the sovereignty of all States,

Acknowledging that peace and security, development and human rights are the pillars of the United Nations system and the foundations for collective security and well-being, and recognizing in this regard that development, peace and security and human rights are interlinked and mutually reinforcing,

Expressing its deep regret that civilians account for the vast majority of casualties in situations of armed conflict,

Gravely concerned about the effects of the illicit exploitation of and trafficking in natural resources, as well as the illicit trafficking in small arms and light weapons, and the use of such weapons on civilians affected by armed conflict,

Recognizing the important contribution by regional organizations to the protection of civilians in armed conflict, and acknowledging in this regard, the steps taken by the African Union,

Recognizing also the important role that education can play in supporting efforts to halt and prevent abuses committed against civilians affected by armed conflict, in particular efforts to prevent sexual exploitation, trafficking in humans and violations of applicable international law regarding the recruitment and re-recruitment of child soldiers,

Recalling the particular impact which armed conflict has on women and children, including as refugees and internally displaced persons, as well as on other civilians who may have specific vulnerabilities, and stressing the protection and assistance needs of all affected civilian populations,

Reaffirming that parties to armed conflict bear the primary responsibility to take all feasible steps to ensure the protection of affected civilians,

Bearing in mind its primary responsibility under the Charter for the maintenance of international peace and security, and underlining the importance of taking measures aimed at conflict prevention and resolution,

1. *Notes with appreciation* the contribution of the report of the Secretary-General of 28 November 2005 to its understanding of the issues surrounding the protection of civilians in armed conflict, and takes note of the conclusions contained therein;

2. *Emphasizes* the importance of preventing armed conflict and its recurrence, stresses in this context the need for a comprehensive approach through the promotion of economic growth, poverty eradication, sustainable development, national reconciliation, good governance, democracy, the rule of law, and respect for and protection of human rights, and, in this regard, urges the cooperation of Member States and underlines the importance of a coherent, comprehensive and coordinated approach by the principal organs of the United Nations, cooperating with one another and within their respective mandates;

3. *Recalls* that deliberately targeting civilians and other protected persons as such in situations of armed conflict is a flagrant violation of international humanitarian law, reiterates its condemnation in the strongest terms of such practices, and demands that all parties immediately put an end to such practices;

4. *Reaffirms* the provisions of paragraphs 138 and 139 of the 2005 World Summit Outcome regarding the responsibility to protect populations from genocide, war crimes, ethnic cleansing and crimes against humanity;

5. *Reaffirms also* its condemnation in the strongest terms of all acts of violence or abuses committed against civilians in situations of armed conflict in violation of applicable international obligations with respect in particular to (i) torture and other prohibited treatment, (ii) gender-based and sexual violence, (iii) violence against children, (iv) the recruitment and use of child soldiers, (v) trafficking in humans, (vi) forced displacement, and (vii) the intentional denial of humanitarian assistance, and demands that all parties put an end to such practices;

6. *Demands* that all parties concerned comply strictly with the obligations applicable to them under international law, in particular those contained in the Hague Conventions of 1899 and 1907 and in the Geneva Conventions of 1949 and the Additional Protocols thereto of 1977, as well as with the decisions of the Security Council;

7. *Reaffirms* that ending impunity is essential if a society in conflict or recovering from conflict is to come to terms with past abuses committed against civilians affected by armed conflict and to prevent future such abuses, draws attention to the full range of justice and reconciliation mechanisms to be considered, including national, international and "mixed" criminal courts and tribunals and truth and reconciliation commissions, and notes that such mechanisms can promote not only individual responsibility for serious crimes, but also peace, truth, reconciliation and the rights of the victims;

8. *Emphasizes* in this context the responsibility of States to comply with their relevant obligations to end impunity and to prosecute those responsible for war crimes, genocide, crimes against humanity and serious violations of international humanitarian law, while recognizing, for States in or recovering from armed conflict, the need to restore or build independent national judicial systems and institutions;

9. *Calls upon* States that have not already done so to consider ratifying the instruments of international humanitarian, human rights and refugee law, and to take appropriate legislative, judicial and administrative measures to implement their obligations under those instruments;

10. *Demands* that all States fully implement all relevant decisions of the Council, and, in this regard cooperate fully with United Nations peacekeeping missions and country teams in the follow-up and implementation of these resolutions;

11. *Calls upon* all parties concerned to ensure that all peace processes, peace agreements and post-conflict recovery and reconstruction planning have regard for the special needs of women and children and include specific measures for the protection of civilians including (i) the cessation of attacks on civilians, (ii) the facilitation of the provision of humanitarian assistance, (iii) the creation of conditions conducive to the voluntary, safe, dignified and sustainable return of refugees and internally displaced persons, (iv) the facilitation of early access to education and training, (v) the re-establishment of the rule of law, and (vi) the ending of impunity;

12. *Recalls* the prohibition of the forcible displacement of civilians in situations of armed conflict under circumstances that are in violation of parties' obligations under international humanitarian law;

13. *Urges* the international community to provide support and assistance to enable States to fulfil their responsibilities regarding the protection of refugees and other persons protected under international humanitarian law;

14. *Reaffirms* the need to maintain the security and civilian character of refugee and internally displaced person camps, stresses the primary responsibility of States in this regard, and encourages the Secretary-General, where necessary and in the context of existing peacekeeping operations and their respective mandates, to take all feasible measures to ensure security in and around such camps and of their inhabitants;

15. *Expresses its intention* of continuing its collaboration with the Emergency Relief Coordinator, and invites the Secretary-General to fully associate him from the earliest stages of the planning of United Nations peacekeeping and other relevant missions;

16. *Reaffirms* its practice of ensuring that the mandates of United Nations peacekeeping, political and peacebuilding missions include, where appropriate and on a case-by-case basis, provisions regarding (i) the protection of civilians, particularly those under imminent threat of physical danger within their zones of operation, (ii) the facilitation of the provision of humanitarian assistance, and (iii) the creation of conditions conducive to the voluntary, safe, dignified and sustainable return of refugees and internally displaced persons, and expresses its intention of ensuring that (i) such mandates include clear guidelines as to what missions can and should do to achieve those goals, (ii) the protection of civilians is given priority in decisions about the use of available capacity and resources, including information and intelligence resources, in the implementation of the mandates, and (iii) that protection mandates are implemented;

17. *Reaffirms also* that, where appropriate, United Nations peacekeeping and other relevant missions should provide for the dissemination of information about international humanitarian, human rights and refugee law and the application of relevant Council resolutions;

18. *Underscores* the importance of disarmament, demobilization and reintegration of ex-combatants in the protection of civilians affected by armed conflict, and, in this regard, emphasizes (i) its support for the inclusion in mandates of United Nations peacekeeping and other relevant missions, where appropriate and on a case-by-case basis, of specific and effective measures for disarmament, demobilization and reintegration, (ii) the importance of incorporating such activities into specific peace agreements, where appropriate and in consultation with the parties, and (iii) the importance of adequate resources being made available for the full completion of disarmament, demobilization and reintegration programmes and activities;

19. *Condemns in the strongest terms* all sexual and other forms of violence committed against civilians in armed conflict, in particular women and children, and undertakes to ensure that all peace support operations employ all feasible measures to prevent such violence and to address its impact where it takes place;

20. *Condemns in equally strong terms* all acts of sexual exploitation and abuse of and trafficking in women and children by military, police and civilian personnel involved in United Nations operations, welcomes the efforts undertaken by United Nations agencies and peacekeeping operations to implement a zero-tolerance policy in this regard, and requests the Secretary-General and personnel-contributing countries to continue to take all appropriate action necessary to combat these abuses by such personnel, including through the full implementation, without delay of those measures adopted in the relevant General Assembly resolutions based upon the

recommendations contained in the report of the Special Committee on Peacekeeping Operations;

21. *Stresses* the importance for all, within the framework of humanitarian assistance, of upholding and respecting the humanitarian principles of humanity, neutrality, impartiality and independence;

22. *Urges* all those concerned as set forth in international humanitarian law, including the Geneva Conventions and the Hague Regulations, to allow full unimpeded access by humanitarian personnel to civilians in need of assistance in situations of armed conflict, and to make available, as far as possible, all necessary facilities for their operations, and to promote the safety, security and freedom of movement of humanitarian personnel and United Nations and associated personnel and their assets;

23. *Condemns* all attacks deliberately targeting United Nations and associated personnel involved in humanitarian missions, as well as other humanitarian personnel, urges States on whose territory such attacks occur to prosecute or extradite those responsible, and welcomes in this regard the adoption on 8 December 2005 by the General Assembly of the Optional Protocol to the Convention on the Safety of United Nations and Associated Personnel;

24. *Recognizes* the increasingly valuable role that regional organizations and other intergovernmental institutions play in the protection of civilians, and encourages the Secretary-General and the heads of regional and other intergovernmental organizations to continue their efforts to strengthen their partnership in this regard;

25. *Reiterates* its invitation to the Secretary-General to continue to refer to the Council relevant information and analysis regarding the protection of civilians where he believes that such information or analysis could contribute to the resolution of issues before it, requests him to continue to include in his written reports to the Council on matters of which it is seized, as appropriate, observations relating to the protection of civilians in armed conflict, and encourages him to continue consultations and take concrete steps to enhance the capacity of the United Nations in this regard;

26. *Notes* that the deliberate targeting of civilians and other protected persons, and the commission of systematic, flagrant and widespread violations of international humanitarian and human rights law in situations of armed conflict, may constitute a threat to international peace and security, and, reaffirms in this regard its readiness to consider such situations and, where necessary, to adopt appropriate steps;

27. *Requests* the Secretary-General to submit his next report on the protection of civilians in armed conflict within eighteen months of the date of the present resolution;

28. *Decides* to remain seized of the matter.

On 23 December [meeting 5613], the Security Council unanimously adopted **resolution 1738(2006).** The draft [S/2006/1023] was prepared in consultations among Council members.

The Security Council,

Bearing in mind its primary responsibility under the Charter of the United Nations for the maintenance of international peace and security, and underlining the importance of taking measures aimed at conflict prevention and resolution,

Reaffirming its resolutions 1265(1999) of 17 September 1999, 1296(2000) of 19 April 2000 and 1674(2006) of 28 April 2006 on the protection of civilians in armed conflict and its resolution 1502(2003) of 26 August 2003 on protection of United Nations personnel, associated personnel and humanitarian personnel in conflict zones, as well as other relevant resolutions and statements by its President,

Reaffirming its commitment to the Purposes of the Charter as set out in Article 1, paragraphs 1 to 4, thereof, and to the principles of the Charter as set out in Article 2, paragraphs 1 to 7, thereof, including its commitment to the principles of the political independence, sovereign equality and territorial integrity of all States, and respect for the sovereignty of all States,

Reaffirming that parties to an armed conflict bear the primary responsibility to take all feasible steps to ensure the protection of affected civilians,

Recalling the Geneva Conventions of 12 August 1949, in particular the Third Geneva Convention, on the treatment of prisoners of war, and the Additional Protocols to the Conventions of 8 June 1977, in particular article 79 of the Additional Protocol I regarding the protection of journalists engaged in dangerous professional missions in areas of armed conflict,

Emphasizing that there are existing prohibitions under international humanitarian law against attacks intentionally directed against civilians, as such, which in situations of armed conflict constitute war crimes, and recalling the need for States to end impunity for such criminal acts,

Recalling that the States parties to the Geneva Conventions have an obligation to search for persons alleged to have committed, or to have ordered to be committed a grave breach of these Conventions, and an obligation to try them before their own courts, regardless of their nationality, or may hand them over for trial to another concerned State provided this State has made out a prima facie case against the said persons,

Drawing the attention of all States to the full range of justice and reconciliation mechanisms, including national, international and "mixed" criminal courts and tribunals and truth and reconciliation commissions, and noting that such mechanisms can promote not only individual responsibility for serious crimes, but also peace, truth, reconciliation and the rights of the victims,

Recognizing the importance of a comprehensive, coherent and action-oriented approach, including in early planning, of protection of civilians in situations of armed conflict, stressing, in this regard, the need to adopt a broad strategy of conflict prevention, which addresses the root causes of armed conflict in a comprehensive manner in order to enhance the protection of civilians on a long-term basis, including by promoting sustainable development, poverty eradication, national reconciliation, good governance, democracy, the rule of law and respect for and protection of human rights,

Deeply concerned at the frequency of acts of violence in many parts of the world against journalists, media professionals and associated personnel in armed conflict, in particular, deliberate attacks in violation of international humanitarian law,

Recognizing that the consideration of the issue of protection of journalists in armed conflict by the Security Council is based on the urgency and importance of this issue, and recognizing the valuable role that the Secretary-General can play in providing more information on this issue,

1. *Condemns* intentional attacks against journalists, media professionals and associated personnel, as such, in situations of armed conflict, and calls upon all parties to put an end to such practices;

2. *Recalls*, in this regard, that journalists, media professionals and associated personnel engaged in dangerous professional missions in areas of armed conflict shall be considered as civilians and shall be respected and protected as such, provided that they take no action adversely affecting their status as civilians. This is without prejudice to the right of war correspondents accredited to the armed forces to the status of prisoners of war provided for in article 4.A, paragraph 4 of the Third Geneva Convention of 12 August 1949;

3. *Recalls also* that media equipment and installations constitute civilian objects, and in this respect shall not be the object of attack or of reprisals, unless they are military objectives;

4. *Reaffirms its condemnation* of all incitements to violence against civilians in situations of armed conflict, further reaffirms the need to bring to justice, in accordance with applicable international law, individuals who incite such violence, and indicates its willingness, when authorizing missions, to consider, where appropriate, steps in response to media broadcast inciting genocide, crimes against humanity and serious violations of international humanitarian law;

5. *Recalls its demand* that all parties to an armed conflict comply fully with the obligations applicable to them under international law related to the protection of civilians in armed conflict, including journalists, media professionals and associated personnel;

6. *Urges* States and all other parties to an armed conflict to do their utmost to prevent violations of international humanitarian law against civilians, including journalists, media professionals and associated personnel;

7. *Emphasizes* the responsibility of States to comply with the relevant obligations under international law to end impunity and to prosecute those responsible for serious violations of international humanitarian law;

8. *Urges* all parties involved in situations of armed conflict to respect the professional independence and rights of journalists, media professionals and associated personnel as civilians;

9. *Recalls* that the deliberate targeting of civilians and other protected persons, and the commission of systematic, flagrant and widespread violations of international humanitarian and human rights law in situations of armed conflict may constitute a threat to international peace and security, and reaffirms in this regard its readiness to consider such situations and, where necessary, to adopt appropriate steps;

10. *Invites* States which have not yet done so to consider becoming parties to the Additional Protocols I and II to the Geneva Conventions, of 8 June 1977 at the earliest possible date;

11. *Affirms* that it will address the issue of protection of journalists in armed conflict strictly under the agenda item entitled "Protection of civilians in armed conflict";

12. *Requests* the Secretary-General to include as a sub-item in his next reports on the protection of civilians in armed conflict the issue of the safety and security of journalists, media professionals and associated personnel.

Missing persons

Report of Secretary-General. In response to General Assembly resolution 59/189 [YUN 2004, p. 719], the Secretary-General, in September [A/61/476], summarized replies received from 10 Governments and one international humanitarian organization on the issue of missing persons.

On 19 December, the Assembly took note of the Secretary-General's report (**decision 61/529**). Also, in resolution 61/155 of the same date (see below), the Assembly called on States that were parties to armed conflict to take appropriate measures to prevent persons from going missing in connection with armed conflict and to account for those reported missing as a result of such a situation.

GENERAL ASSEMBLY ACTION

On 19 December [meeting 81], the General Assembly, on the recommendation of the Third Committee [A/61/443/Add.2 & Corr.1], adopted **resolution 61/155** without vote [agenda item 67 *(b)*].

Missing persons

The General Assembly,

Guided by the purposes, principles and provisions of the Charter of the United Nations,

Guided also by the principles and norms of international humanitarian law, in particular the Geneva Conventions of 12 August 1949 and the Additional Protocols thereto of 1977, as well as international standards of human rights, in particular the Universal Declaration of Human Rights, the International Covenant on Economic, Social and Cultural Rights, the International Covenant on Civil and Political Rights, the Convention on the Elimination of All Forms of Discrimination against Women, the Convention on the Rights of the Child and the Vienna Declaration and Programme of Action adopted by the World Conference on Human Rights on 25 June 1993,

Recalling all previous relevant resolutions on missing persons adopted by the General Assembly, as well as the resolutions adopted by the Commission on Human Rights,

Noting with deep concern that armed conflicts are continuing in various parts of the world, often resulting in serious violations of international humanitarian law and human rights law,

Bearing in mind the effective search for and identification of missing persons through traditional forensic methods, and recognizing that great technological progress has been achieved in the field of DNA forensic sciences, which could significantly assist efforts to identify missing persons,

Noting that the issue of persons reported missing in connection with international armed conflicts, in particular those who are victims of serious violations of international humanitarian law and human rights law, continues to have a negative impact on efforts to put an end to those conflicts and causes suffering to the families of missing persons, and stressing in this regard the need to address the issue from a humanitarian perspective, among others,

Recalling the observations and recommendations to address the problems of missing persons and of their families that were adopted at the International Conference of Governmental and Non-Governmental Experts on "The missing: action to resolve the problem of people unaccounted for as a result of armed conflict or internal violence and to assist their families", held in Geneva from 19 to 21 February 2003,

Recalling also the Agenda for Humanitarian Action, in particular its general objective 1, to "respect and restore the dignity of persons missing as a result of armed conflicts or other situations of armed violence and of their families", adopted at the Twenty-eighth International Conference of the Red Cross and Red Crescent, held in Geneva from 2 to 6 December 2003,

Taking note with appreciation of the ongoing regional efforts to address the question of missing persons,

1. *Urges* States strictly to observe and respect and ensure respect for the rules of international humanitarian law, as set out in the Geneva Conventions of 12 August 1949 and, where applicable, in the Additional Protocols thereto of 1977;

2. *Calls upon* States that are parties to an armed conflict to take all appropriate measures to prevent persons from going missing in connection with armed conflict and account for persons reported missing as a result of such a situation;

3. *Reaffirms* the right of families to know the fate of their relatives reported missing in connection with armed conflicts;

4. *Also reaffirms* that each party to an armed conflict, as soon as circumstances permit and, at the latest, from the end of active hostilities, shall search for the persons who have been reported missing by an adverse party;

5. *Calls upon* States that are parties to an armed conflict to take all necessary measures, in a timely manner, to determine the identity and fate of persons reported missing in connection with the armed conflict and, to the greatest possible extent, to provide their family members, through appropriate channels, with all relevant information they have on their fate;

6. *Recognizes*, in this regard, the need for the collection, protection and management of data on missing persons according to international and national legal norms and standards, and urges States to cooperate with each other and with other concerned actors working in this area, inter alia, by providing all relevant and appropriate information related to missing persons;

7. *Requests* States to pay the utmost attention to cases of children reported missing in connection with armed conflicts and to take appropriate measures to search for and identify those children;

8. *Invites* States that are parties to an armed conflict to cooperate fully with the International Committee of the Red Cross in establishing the fate of missing persons and to adopt a comprehensive approach to this issue, including all practical and coordination mechanisms as may be necessary, based on humanitarian considerations only;

9. *Urges* States and encourages intergovernmental and non-governmental organizations to take all necessary measures at the national, regional and international levels to address the problem of persons reported missing in connection with armed conflicts and to provide appropriate assistance as requested by the concerned States, and welcomes, in this regard, the establishment and efforts of commissions and working groups on missing persons;

10. *Calls upon* States, without prejudice to their efforts to determine the fate of persons missing in connection with armed conflicts, to take appropriate steps with regard to the legal situation of the missing persons and that of their family members, in fields such as social welfare, financial matters, family law and property rights;

11. *Invites* relevant human rights mechanisms and procedures, as appropriate, to address the problem of persons reported missing in connection with armed conflicts in their forthcoming reports to the General Assembly;

12. *Requests* the Secretary-General to bring the present resolution to the attention of all Governments, the competent United Nations bodies, the specialized agencies, regional intergovernmental organizations and international humanitarian organizations;

13. *Also requests* the Secretary-General to submit a comprehensive report on the implementation of the present resolution, including relevant recommendations, to the Human Rights Council at its relevant session and to the General Assembly at its sixty-third session;

14. *Decides* to consider the question at its sixty-third session.

Arbitrary detention

Working Group activities. The five-member Working Group on Arbitrary Detention held its forty-fifth (8-12 May), forty-sixth (28 August–1 September) and forty-seventh (15-24 November) sessions, all in Geneva [A/HRC/4/40]. During the year, the Group adopted 47 opinions concerning 104 cases in 23 countries; the texts of those opinions were contained in a separate report [A/HRC/4/40/Add.1]. The Group also transmitted 156 urgent appeals to 58 Governments concerning 1,615 individuals. Responses to 54 of those were received.

The Group discussed the problem of arbitrary detention in the context of the international transfer of detainees, particularly in efforts to counter terrorism. The issue was one of growing concern, as reflected in the rising number of related cases which the Group addressed during the year. The Group argued that both human rights law and the anti-terrorism conventions adopted under UN auspices enshrined a clear preference for extradition as the legal framework for such transfers. As such, the practice of so-called "renditions" was incompatible with international law because it was aimed at avoiding all procedural safeguards.

In applying the principle of non-refoulement, Governments should not only examine whether the person to be removed would be at risk of extrajudicial killing or torture, but also whether there was a substantial risk of arbitrary detention. In that respect, diplomatic assurances could be a legitimate means to protect against arbitrary detention and unfair trial, provided stringent conditions were satisfied. However, the current tendency in the context of countering terrorism was to seek "reverse diplomatic assurances", entailing assurances that a detainee to be transferred would continue to be detained in the country of destination even in the absence of a legal basis. Governments should refuse to give such assurances unless it was in accordance with domestic legislation and the concerned Government's international human rights obligations. Calling on States to join political and technical efforts to address and guarantee the basic needs and rights of people in detention, the Group considered that the minimum conditions for achieving that included the protection of the security, health and nutritional needs of detainees and of their rights to an adequate legal defence and a fair trial.

The Group also discussed concerns arising from country visits, including insufficient resource allocation to the penitentiary system and the resulting failure to protect prisoners' rights; excessive recourse to and duration of pretrial detention; infringements of the right to an effective defence owing to the conditions of detention; and insufficient funding of legal aid programmes. The Group made recommendations for preventing arbitrary detention in the context of the international transfer of detainees and reducing the duration of remand detention. Recommendations were also made regarding the growth in prison populations, particularly in developed countries, detention on remand, alternatives to deprivation of liberty and the international transfer of detainees.

At the invitation of the Government, the Working Group visited Ecuador (12-22 February) [A/HRC/4/40/Add.2], where it toured 13 detention centres and held private meetings with some 200 detainees. Among the issues of concern identified was the divergence between the principles and standards enshrined in the Constitution, the laws in force and observed practices. While under the Constitution pretrial detention should not exceed one year, a 2003 law stipulated that detention under another status (*detención en firme)* should continue even after the pretrial detention period had lapsed. That change in the law had resulted in prison overcrowding, with over 6,000 incarcerated persons awaiting judgement, often for years.

Another cause for concern was the inappropriate implementation of the adversarial system that was introduced by a 2001 Code of Criminal Procedure, which impaired the right to a defence and to fair trial with due process, particularly for the most vulnerable. There was also no genuine system of legal assistance for defendants. The Public Prosecutor's Office had delegated its functions to the Judicial Police, thereby leaving the pretrial inquiry and preliminary investigation phase entirely in the hands of the police. Judges rarely called into question the prosecutors' reports, which undermined the principle of equality of arms between the prosecution and the defence. The Group also found that constitutional remedies, particularly habeas corpus and *amparo*, had little practical effect against arbitrary decisions; a parallel code for the military and police existed; magistrates and judges had a poor public image; and the judicial branch and the penitentiary system were inadequately funded. The material conditions of detention were deplorable and detained immigrants awaiting deportation had neither the resources nor the opportunity to appeal against deportation orders. The Group recommended that the Government provide the judicial branch and prison system with adequate funding and repeal the *detención en firme,* under which more severe sentences were adopted for minor offences, in order to restore the limitations on pretrial detention established by the Constitution. In addition, a genuine public defender system should be established and placed on an equal footing with the Public Prosecutor's Office; people who were arrested should be brought before a judge within 24 hours; minors should not be detained at police stations and pretrial detention centres; the practice of delegating the functions of the Public Prosecutor's Office to the Judicial Police should be stopped; all violations of detainees' rights should be investigated; and persons in pretrial detention should not be held in overcrowded prison and police cells.

In Nicaragua (15-23 May) [A/HRC/4/40/Add.3], the Group visited eight custodial facilities and held private meetings with some 150 detainees selected at random. It identified various positive elements, including the Government's efforts to comply with international standards and to ensure protection for human rights in the criminal justice system, and ongoing work relating to the detention of minors, such as the juvenile delinquency prevention programmes being implemented by a number of institutions and the re-education and rehabilitation of juvenile offenders. Since the promulgation of the Constitution in 1987, Nicaragua had implemented wide-ranging changes to its legal system, which had a positive impact on the democratic functioning of the State and on the protection of human rights.

The Group also identified areas of concern, among which were the lack of compliance with the conditions and time limits stipulated in a new criminal procedural law; the special category of detainees forgotten by both the justice and corrections systems, who referred to themselves as "los Donados" (those who had been effectively dumped as "gifts" on the prison system); and those who had no contact with the outer world and no possibility of availing themselves of the remedies to which they were entitled. The Group also drew attention to the disproportionate severity of criminal penalties handed down for narcotics-related offences. Also of concern was the institution of enforcement by committal, under which a civil court judge could order the detention of a person for up to one year for failing to comply with the conditions of a loan agreement. The Group recommended strict monitoring of compliance by the police of the obligation to bring detainees before a judge within 48 hours of their arrest; substantial improvements to the system for booking detainees in police stations; the revision of drug laws, given the problems experienced in rehabilitating and socially reintegrating prisoners under sentence; and the review of detainees' condition. In general, crime and violence prevention and control methods should be consistent with respect for human rights.

In Honduras (23-31 May) [A/HRC/4/40/Add.4], the Group observed that the legal and institutional framework governing the deprivation of liberty had changed profoundly since the 1990s. The entry into force of a new Criminal Procedure Code in 2002 had expedited criminal proceedings and significantly reduced the number of detainees held on remand, as well as the duration of detention without conviction. Those and other reforms had put Honduras in a much better position to ensure the rights of persons arbitrarily deprived of their liberty. In several areas, widespread arbitrary detentions persisted. The Group expressed concern at the ineffectiveness of the institutions mandated to monitor the legality of detention, the serious shortcomings within the legal aid system, insufficient monitoring of the police during the criminal justice process, and a lack of checks and balances between the police and the judiciary. The powers of the police in the criminal justice process were insufficiently controlled and balanced. The Group also expressed concern about some 1,800 detainees in detention for four and a half years either awaiting trial or release after acquittal because the prosecutor had filed an appeal, and the treatment of members of violent youth gangs (*maras*). The Group recommended that the Government strengthen control over the legality of detention at all stages of the criminal justice process; address the situation of detainees held under the old Criminal Procedure Code; and establish a professionally staffed penitentiary system separate from the police. The Group also stressed the importance of strengthening prevention, law enforcement and criminal justice in dealing with the *maras* in particular, and with crime in general, instead of relaxing the rule of law and protection against arbitrary detention.

In Turkey (9-20 October) [A/HRC/4/40/Add.5], the Group found that the criminal justice and penitentiary systems were well organized, administered and funded. Since the beginning of the 1990s, the law governing detention in the criminal procedure had been reformed, culminating in the entry into force of new criminal laws and related procedure in 2005. In particular, progress was made in the fight against coerced confessions, the shortening of the duration of police custody, the introduction of pretrial detention limits, and the guarantee of an immediate right of access to a lawyer of all persons detained in the criminal process. Nonetheless, the Group expressed concern about the prosecution, trial and detention of terrorism suspects. As the definition of terrorism was overly broad and did not require an offender to commit a serious violent crime, terrorism charges could be used to restrict the non-violent exercise of the rights to freedom of expression, association and assembly. The law also restricted the right of access to counsel for terrorism suspects, and numerous persons accused of terrorism had been held in remand detention for unacceptably long periods without having been judged, in some cases for over more than 10 years. A detainee convicted on terrorism charges faced disproportionately harsh rules governing execution of sentences and access to benefits, particularly conditional release. In terrorism and common criminality cases, the Group criticized the failure to extend the ban on statements made in police custody in the absence of a lawyer to those statements made before the entry into force of the new criminal procedure code. It also expressed concern at the vulnerability of non-Turkish detainees and at persisting problems in the juvenile justice system. The Group recommended that the Government amend the definition of terrorism, release detainees held on remand for more than 10 years without judgement, and make the ban on statements obtained by the police from accused persons in the absence of a lawyer applicable to all pending proceedings. The Government should also ensure that detention was grounded in an appropriate legal framework and was subject to periodic judicial review.

Communication. On 13 February [E/CN.4/2006/G/7], Mexico, in response to a suggestion by the Chairperson-Rapporteur of the Working Group, clarified the circumstances under which one of its nationals was deprived of his liberty and detained. It pointed out that the person in question had been found guilty of the murder of his sister and her spouse, as corroborated by his own confession and by eyewitness accounts. Therefore, the detention of the offender could not be considered arbitrary because it accorded with the country's constitution and legislation, and with international human rights instruments to which Mexico was a party.

Situation of detainees in Guantánamo Bay

In a February report [E/CN.4/2006/120], the Chairperson-Rapporteur of the Working Group on Arbitrary Detention, Leila Zerrougui; the Special Rapporteur on the independence of judges and lawyers, Leandro Despouy; the Special Rapporteur on torture and other cruel, inhuman or degrading treatment or punishment, Manfred Nowak; the Special Rapporteur on freedom of religion or belief, Asma Jahangir; and the Special Rapporteur on the right of everyone to the enjoyment of the highest attainable standard of physical and mental health, Paul Hunt, submitted a joint study on the situation of detainees held since June 2004 at the United States Naval Base at Guantánamo Bay, Cuba. The study by the five mandate-holders, who had monitored the detainees' situation since January 2002 when the detention centre was established, focused on the law and allegations relevant to each of their respective mandates. A visit of the detention facilities, which was to have been a key aspect of the study, was cancelled because the United States Government would not permit private interviews or visits with the detainees, which, according to the mandate-holders, contravened the terms of reference for fact-finding missions by special rapporteurs and undermined an objective and fair assessment of the situation. As such, the study relied on the Government's replies to a joint questionnaire issued by the five mandate-holders concerning detention at Guantánamo Bay, and on interviews with former detainees currently residing or detained in France, Spain and the United Kingdom. Additional information came from responses from lawyers acting on behalf of some of the detainees, public sources, including NGOs, classified official United States documents and media reports.

The five mandate-holders examined, among other things, the legal framework regarding human rights and counter-terrorism measures; the obligations of the United States under international human rights law; the question of limitations and derogations, by which States might limit, restrict or derogate certain rights contained in the 1966 International Covenant on Civil and Political Rights [YUN 1966, p. 423]; and the complementarity of international humanitarian law and human rights law. They observed that international human rights law was applicable to the situation of those detainees and that the United States had not announced any official derogation from the 1966 Covenant or any other international human rights treaty to which it was a party. Under the Covenant, the detainees were entitled to challenge the legality of their detention before a judicial body and to obtain release if the detention was found to lack a proper legal basis. That right was violated. The continuing detention of those being held amounted to arbitrary detention, which also violated the Covenant. The United States operated as judge, prosecutor and defence counsel, in violation of the right to a fair trial before an independent tribunal. Another cause for concern were attempts by the United States Administration to redefine "torture" in the framework of the struggle against terrorism. The interrogation techniques, the excessive violence used in many cases during transportation, the force-feeding of detainees on hunger strike and the lack of an impartial investigation into allegations of torture violated the Convention against Torture. There were also indications that some of the detainees had been victims of violations of the rights to freedom of religion or belief, and to health.

The study recommended that the United States Government expeditiously bring all detainees to trial, in compliance with the International Covenant on Civil and Political Rights, or release them without further delay. Consideration should also be given to having them tried before a competent international tribunal. The Guantánamo Bay detention facilities should be closed promptly, with a possible transfer of detainees to pretrial detention facilities in the United States. In the interim, the Government should refrain from any practice amounting to torture or cruel, inhuman or degrading treatment or punishment, and from violations of the rights to freedom of religion, and to health. It should also refrain from sending the detainees to countries where they might be tortured and ensure that related allegations were investigated by an independent authority, and that persons found responsible for such practices were brought to justice. All five mandate-holders should be granted full and unrestricted access to Guantánamo Bay, including private interviews with detainees.

Annexed to the report was a 31 January response from the United States, in which it objected to most of the report's content and conclusion, noting that the views expressed were largely without merit and not based on the facts. The United States said that it had offered unprecedented access to Guantánamo, similar to that provided to United States congressional delegations, and it was unfortunate that the Special Rapporteurs had rejected the invitation. The report selectively included only those factual assertions needed to support its conclusions, and ignored other facts that would undermine such conclusions. Nowhere did the report set out clearly the legal regime that applied according to United States law. The United States had made clear its position that it was engaged in a continuing armed conflict against Al Qaida, that the law of war applied to the conduct of that war and related detention operations, and that the International Covenant on Civil and Political Rights, by its express terms, applied only to individuals within its territory and subject to its jurisdiction. The report should have presented objective and comprehensive material on all sides of the issue before stating its conclusions.

Impunity

Report of Secretary-General. In response to a 2005 Commission request [YUN 2005, p. 800], the Secretary-General submitted a February report [E/CN.4/2006/89] examining developments in international law and practice relevant to combating impunity, including international jurisprudence and State practice, and the work of OHCHR and other parts of the UN system. The report took into account the updated Set of Principles for the protection and promotion of human rights through action to combat impunity [YUN 2005, p. 800], the 2004 independent study on the subject [YUN 2004, p. 722] and related information received from 11 States and two UN bodies. The report surveyed several OHCHR-supported international commissions of inquiry and fact-finding missions in countries that continued to suffer from conflicts and massive human rights violations, including those established in Timor Leste (then East Timor) in 1999 [YUN 1999, p. 284], Togo in 1990 [YUN 1990, p. 748], the Occupied Palestinian Territory in 2001 [YUN 2001, 735], Côte d'Ivoire in 2004 [YUN 2004, p. 177] and the Darfur region of the Sudan, also in 2004 [ibid, p. 250]. The report also covered the OHCHR fact-finding missions to Uzbekistan [YUN 2005 p. 899] and Togo [ibid., p. 300].

The Secretary-General observed that it was widely recognized that the commissions of inquiry and fact-finding missions could play an important role in combating impunity, and assist UN bodies, including the Commission on Human Rights and the Security Council, in making decisions in the face of serious violations of international human rights and humanitarian law. Those initiatives had increasingly required support, including legal, investigative and forensic expertise, much of which was provided by OHCHR, which, within the framework of the High Commissioner's Plan of Action [YUN 2005, p. 715], was committed to further enhancing its capacity to do so. Increased support for such activities exemplified the nature of OHCHR future work in its quest for a much stronger protection role, especially at the country level.

Human Rights Council action. On 29 November [A/62/53 (dec. 2/116)], the Council deferred to its fourth (2007) session consideration of a draft decision on impunity introduced by Canada [A/HRC/2/L.38/Rev.1], by which the Council would request the High Commissioner to continue to support judicial mechanisms and commissions of inquiry and provide technical and legal assistance in developing national legislation and institutions to combat impunity.

Right to the truth

OHCHR report. As requested by the Commission in 2005 [YUN 2005, p. 801], OHCHR submitted a February study [E/CN.4/2006/91] on the right to truth, based on information received from 11 States and one international organization. The study examined, among other issues, the legal and historical basis for the right, its material scope, entitlement and content. It concluded that the right to the truth about gross violations of human rights and related laws was an inalienable and autonomous right, linked to the duty and obligation of States to protect and guarantee human rights, conduct investigations and guarantee remedy and reparations. That right was also closely linked with other rights, had both an individual and a societal dimension and should be considered as non-derogable and not subject to limitations. While international criminal tribunals, truth commissions, commissions of inquiry, national human rights institutions and other administrative bodies and proceedings constituted important tools for ensuring the right, judicial remedies, such as habeas corpus, were important mechanisms for protecting it. OHCHR recommended further study of the content and scope of the right, including in-depth consideration of its societal and individual dimensions.

Human Rights Council action. On 27 November [A/62/53 (dec. 2/105)], the Council requested OHCHR to prepare a follow-up report on the study, to be examined at its fifth (2007) session.

Independence of the judicial system

Report of Special Rapporteur. The Special Rapporteur on the independence of judges and lawyers, Leandro Despouy (Argentina), submitted a February report [E/CN.4/2006/52], which provided an overview of his 2005 activities. He had transmitted 69 urgent appeals, 16 letters of allegation and 13 press releases to 51 Governments, to which he had received 40 replies. An addendum to the report [E/CN.4/2006/52/Add.1] summarized the allegations and the replies thereto. The report considered issues relating to the administration of justice and the right to the truth, judicial authorities and justice in transitional situations, the Iraqi Special Tribunal and the fight against terrorism and its impact on human rights, especially the situation of persons detained at Guantánamo Bay (see p. 865). The right to the truth was seen as an independent right and as a means of achieving the rights to information, to identity, and especially the right to justice. The report also discussed the issue of legitimacy for the enforcement of the right and the interaction between the courts and the truth commissions. It also reviewed the experiences of individual countries, highlighting what they had in common and the lessons learned. The report highlighted the central role of justice in periods of transition as the keystone of the construction and reconstruction of a country's institutions and emphasized the need to ensure that the measures applied in judicial review procedures were implemented in accordance with the basic principles on the independence of the judiciary. The Special Rapporteur also stressed his reservations regarding the legitimacy of the Iraqi Special Tribunal, the restriction placed on its jurisdiction in terms of people and time, and the breach of international human rights principles and standards resulting from its operation.

In his conclusions and recommendations, the Special Rapporteur highlighted the growing importance of the right to truth and transitional justice. He recommended that the Human Rights Council deal with that right separately, in a more detailed study and develop its potential as a tool for combating impunity. The right should be taken into account also in UN peacekeeping operations and the Organization's other activities. He recommended cooperation between truth commissions and tribunals, the involvement of the international associations of judges and magistrates in addressing specific judicial problems, and timely coordination of the activities of special rapporteurs, OHCHR and other international actors in promoting and consolidating institutions and governance.

The Secretary-General, by a September note [A/61/384], transmitted the Special Rapporteur's report to the General Assembly highlighting his past and planned activities and identifying issues of concern relating to military justice in the context of the trial of civilians, including related national standards in various regions. Recalling the numerous violations of the right to a defence and fair trial owing to the application of military jurisdiction, the Special Rapporteur observed that the wide powers given to military courts in some countries had resulted in repeated violations of the right to a fair trial by a legally established, independent and impartial tribunal. Especially important in that regard were the draft principles governing the administration of justice through military tribunals, drawn up by Subcommission expert Emmanuel Decaux [YUN 2004, p. 789], which were before the Council for consideration prior to submission to the Assembly. Those principles were essential for guaranteeing that the application of military justice was compatible with respect for human rights. Other worrisome issues examined included the situation of detainees at Guantánamo Bay (see p. 865) and the status and operation of the Supreme Iraqi Criminal Tribunal.

The Special Rapporteur urged States to bring their domestic legislation into line with international standards on military jurisdiction, and restrict such jurisdiction exclusively to crimes of a strictly military nature committed by military personnel in active service. Further urging States to respect the integrity of the judicial system and not to set up military or special commissions to try civilians suspected of terrorist or other criminal activities, the Special Rapporteur pointed out that counter-terrorism could not justify the violation of international standards under which all persons had the right to be tried by a competent, independent and impartial tribunal. He urged the United States to comply with the recommendations of the five UN independent experts, the Inter-American Commission on Human Rights and the United States Supreme Court to close the detention centre at Guantánamo Bay and take the measures requested in respect of the situation of the detainees. Regarding the trial of ex-Iraqi President Saddam Hussein and his senior aides, he reiterated that the trial should be conducted in accordance with international standards or an international criminal tribunal should be constituted with UN cooperation. Welcoming the fact that the Extraordinary Chambers in Cambodia had initiated the prosecution of the Khmer Rouge senior leaders for the heinous crimes committed between April 1975 and January 1979, the Special Rapporteur urged the judges to conduct the trials in compliance with international standards on the right to a fair, impartial and independent trial.

Communication. Kyrgyzstan, in a March note [E/CN.4/2006/G/9], provided comments on the Special Rapporteur's report on his 2005 mission to the country [YUN 2005, p. 802].

On 19 December, the General Assembly took note of the Secretary-General's September note (**decision 61/529**).

Human Rights Council action. On 27 November [A/62/53 (dec. 2/110)], the Council requested the Special Rapporteur, in discharging his mandate, and in his 2007 report to the Council, to take into account a 2005 Commission resolution on the independence of the judicial system [YUN 2005, p. 801] and the Subcommission's resolutions and decisions on the issue of the administration of justice through military tribunals.

Capital punishment

Report of Secretary General. In response to a 2005 Commission request [YUN 2005, p. 804], the Secretary-General submitted a February report [E/CN.4/2006/83] supplementing information in his seventh quinquennial report [YUN 2005, p. 803] on capital punishment and implementation of the safeguards guaranteeing protection of the rights of those facing the death penalty, covering the period from January 2004 to December 2005. The report summarized information received from 15 countries and four intergovernmental organizations and NGOs relating to changes in law and practice concerning the death penalty and implementation of the safeguards. During the reporting period, seven countries abolished, the death penalty for all crimes; two limited its use; 21 ratified or signed international instruments abolishing it, two of which did so for peacetime only; seven established a moratorium on executions; and four, along with the Palestinian Authority, reintroduced the death penalty. Overall, at least 7,395 persons were sentenced to death in 64 countries, and some 3,797 executed in 25 countries during 2004. Nonetheless, the Secretary-General concluded that the trend towards the abolition of the death penalty had continued, with the number of countries that were completely abolitionist rising from 77 to 85 and the total number of retentionist countries decreasing from 66 to 65. The number of abolitionists for ordinary crimes stood at 12, while 34 could be considered de facto abolitionists. The report also highlighted initiatives by the Commission and its mechanisms, regional organizations and NGOs regarding relevant international developments and the implementation of safeguards.

Communication. On 12 May [A/60/849], Uzbekistan circulated information regarding the measures it had taken towards abolishing the death penalty by January 2008.

Other issues

Extralegal executions

Reports of Special Rapporteur. The Special Rapporteur on extrajudicial, summary or arbitrary executions, Philip Alston (Australia), in a March report [E/CN.4/2006/53] submitted pursuant to a 2005 Commission request [YUN 2005, p. 809], outlined key measures taken in 2005 towards the goal of eliminating extrajudicial executions; identified ways in which relevant procedures might be developed more effectively to achieve set goals; and highlighted major issues arising at the national level in dealing with extrajudicial executions. In particular, the report focused on the notion of transparency as a key component of the concept of accountability underpinning the international human rights system. In that context, it reviewed issues of concern relating to transparency in investigating violations within the framework of commissions of inquiry and in relation to the death penalty, in armed conflict in respect of accountability for violations of the right to life, and in relation to the shoot-to-kill policies of some Governments in response to particular challenges to law and order, which posed a major threat to human rights-based law enforced approaches. The report also highlighted communications to and from Governments, which were contained in an addendum [E/CN.4/2006/53/Add.1]. Between 1 December 2004 and 30 September 2005, the Special Rapporteur had sent 117 communications to 55 countries and 3 other actors, including 57 urgent appeals and 60 letters of allegation, concerning some 800 individuals. Those appeals involved 373 males, 76 females, 56 minors, 76 members of religious or ethnic minority groups, 29 human rights defenders, 6 journalists and over 200 persons exercising the right to freedom of opinion or expression. Some 18 persons were killed in the name of passion or honour, two for various discriminatory reasons, and nine who were migrants. The proportion of replies to communications remained low at 46 per cent, which meant that approximately half of all communications sent drew no response from the Governments concerned within a reasonable period of time.

The Special Rapporteur recommended that the Human Rights Council should establish a procedure, whereby cases of persistent or problematic non-cooperation with mandate-holders were taken up by the Council. Emphasizing the value of transparency where the death penalty was applied, the report proposed that persons sentenced to death, their families and lawyers should be provided with timely and reliable information about the timing of appeals, clemency petitions and executions. The use of lethal force by law enforcement officers needed to be regulated within the framework of human rights law, and in that regard, the shoot-to-kill rhetoric should never be used, as it risked conveying the message that clear legal standards had been replaced with a vaguely defined licence to kill. Other recommendations advocated the provision of alternative safeguards to ensure the right to life when confronting the threat of suicide bombers; the prompt and thorough investigation during armed conflict of alleged violations of the right; the punishment of those responsible for violations in a manner commensurate with the gravity of their crimes; national investigation of major violations of international human rights or humanitarian law by armed or security forces and a detailed study to identify past problems in that regard; and the need for appropriate mechanisms to ensure police accountability.

In a March report [E/CN.4/2006/53/Add.2], the Special Rapporteur followed up on his country visits to Honduras [YUN 2002, p. 705], Jamaica [YUN 2003, p. 739], Brazil [ibid.] and the Sudan [YUN 2004, p. 727], focusing on measures adopted by those Governments in response to the recommendations contained in his respective reports on those missions. He observed that the overall picture was not encouraging. While some minimal follow-up had occurred in some respects, the recommendations as a whole seemed to have made little impact. Against that background, the Special Rapporteur highlighted the potential usefulness of country visits and noted that a consistent pattern of neglect of related recommendations should ring alarm bells in terms of ensuring that the international human rights regime made a positive difference. To address the situation and enhance the effectiveness and credibility of the Human Rights Council, mandate-holders should be encouraged to rank their recommendations to ensure that they were not all ignored and that priority was not given to the least significant ones. The Council should also call for Governments' response within 12 months of the submission of a country visit report indicating why recommended steps had or had not been taken, and in addition, undertake regular reviews of the situation in the country concerned by inviting mandate-holders to make specific follow-up recommendations to the Council.

In a March report [E/CN.4/2006/53/Add.3], the Special Rapporteur focused on the principle of transparency in relation to the death penalty, a critical area of non-compliance with legal safeguards designed to protect the right to life. Those safeguards reinforced the assumption that, although countries maintaining the death penalty were not prohibited by law from making that choice, they had a clear obligation to disclose the details of their application of the penalty. The report analysed the legal basis of that obligation and examined case studies illustrating the major problems encountered. From that perspective, the report described transparency as one of the fundamental due process safeguards that prevented the arbitrary deprivation of life. Under international human rights law, everyone had the right for criminal charges against them to be adjudicated in public, and secrecy after a conviction was limited by State obligations to ensure due process and the right to freedom from cruel, inhuman or degrading treatment or punishment. The public could not make an informed evaluation of the death penalty in the absence of key pieces of information. In particular, public debate should take place in the light of disclosure by the State of information relating to the number of persons sentenced to death, and of executions actually carried out, of death sentences reversed or commuted on appeal, of instances in which clemency had been granted, of persons remaining under a death sentence and the kinds of offences that had led to the convictions. Despite the critical role of such information in decision-making processes, many States chose secrecy over transparency, claiming that capital punishment attracted widespread public support. In the light of the case studies examined, the report noted that, although the death penalty was not prohibited by international law, its use was potentially inconsistent with respect for the right to life when its administration was cloaked in secrecy.

The Special Rapporteur visited Guatemala (21-25 August) [A/HRC/4/20/Add.2], where he observed continuing violence fed by practices developed during past counter-insurgency efforts. Following the 1996 Peace Accords [YUN 1996, p. 169], which ended decades of civil war between the Government and insurgents, Guatemala had failed to complete the transition to a society in which the right to life was secure. Consequently, it continued to suffer from serious violence, including social cleansing, lynching, increasing incidents of the killing of women, human rights defenders and persons for their sexual identity, as well as prison violence. In some cases, the State bore direct responsibility, as there was evidence of executions of gang members, criminal suspects and other "undesirables" by police personnel, and killings of prison inmates facilitated by the guards. In other cases, State responsibility was indirect. The State was also responsible under human rights law for the many who had been murdered by private individuals.

The Special Rapporteur concluded that the widespread extrajudicial executions in the country were due to a distinct lack of political will. Important legislation was not enacted, nor necessary budget allocations made. In that regard, Guatemala faced a choice: realize the vision of the 1996 Peace Accords or fall back on the brutal tactics of the past. It could choose to implement a working system of criminal justice based on human rights or resort to militarized justice, the execution of suspects by the police and impunity for vigilante justice. Any strategy to confront extrajudicial killings should include measures to root out the practice of social cleansing by Government bodies and reform the criminal justice system to effectively investigate and prosecute murders. In a series of other recommendations, the Special Rapporteur highlighted the need for the country to develop the requisite political will and allocate commensurate resources to enable it to bring crime under control. The Congress needed to enact the legislation relating to the International Commission against Impunity in Guatemala, which it had agreed to establish under a December agreement with the United Nations.

By a 5 September note [A/61/311], the Secretary-General transmitted the interim report of the Special Rapporteur, pursuant to General Assembly resolution 59/197 [YUN 2004, p. 728]. The report, which addressed substantive issues of relevance to his mandate, elaborated on principles of international law applicable to numerous cases which the Special Rapporteur had raised with Governments. In that context, the report explored the standards applicable to the use of lethal force by law-enforcement officials, explained the central concept of due diligence obligations with respect to enforced disappearance and to deaths in custody, and discussed problems raised by legal doctrines that enhanced the role of victims in death penalty cases, both in the decision on whether capital punishment should be carried out and in the actual execution. The Special Rapporteur also addressed the situation of country visits requested and replies received, observing that the prolonged lack of a positive reply by numerous countries, including Council members, was problematic. He recommended that the Assembly appeal to States that had failed to respond to such requests to take appropriate action. In particular, the eight Council members that had not done so should be called upon to honour their obligations to cooperate fully with the Council and its procedures. Reviewing developments following his 2005 visits to Nigeria [YUN 2005, p. 808] and Sri Lanka [ibid., p. 809], the Special Rapporteur noted that there was an urgent need for a robust international human rights monitoring mission in the latter. He also recommended a thorough investigation of all killings that occurred in Lebanon and northern Israel, as well as in Gaza, during the year.

GENERAL ASSEMBLY ACTION

On 19 December [meeting 81], the General Assembly, on the recommendation of the Third Committee [A/61/443/Add.2 & Corr.1], adopted **resolution 61/173** by recorded vote (137-0-43) [agenda item 67 *(b)*].

Extrajudicial, summary or arbitrary executions

The General Assembly,

Recalling the Universal Declaration of Human Rights, which guarantees the right to life, liberty and security of person, the relevant provisions of the International Covenant on Civil and Political Rights and other relevant human rights conventions,

Having regard to the legal framework of the mandate of the Special Rapporteur of the Human Rights Council on extrajudicial, summary or arbitrary executions,

Welcoming the universal ratification of the Geneva Conventions of 12 August 1949, which alongside human rights law provide an important framework of accountability in relation to extrajudicial, summary or arbitrary executions during armed conflict,

Mindful of all its resolutions on the subject of extrajudicial, summary or arbitrary executions and the resolutions of the Commission on Human Rights on the subject,

Noting with deep concern that impunity continues to be a major cause of the perpetuation of violations of human rights, including extrajudicial, summary or arbitrary executions,

Acknowledging that international human rights law and international humanitarian law are complementary and not mutually exclusive,

Noting with deep concern the growing number of civilians and persons *hors de combat* killed in situations of armed conflict and internal strife,

Acknowledging that extrajudicial, summary or arbitrary executions may under certain circumstances amount to genocide, crimes against humanity or war crimes, as defined in international law, including in the Rome Statute of the International Criminal Court,

Affirming the obligation of States to prevent the abuse of persons deprived of their liberty and to investigate and respond to deaths in custody,

Convinced of the need for effective action to prevent, combat and eliminate the abhorrent practice of extrajudicial, summary or arbitrary executions, which represent a flagrant violation of the right to life,

1. *Strongly condemns once again* all the extrajudicial, summary or arbitrary executions that continue to occur throughout the world;

2. *Demands* that all States ensure that the practice of extrajudicial, summary or arbitrary executions is brought to an end and that they take effective action to prevent, combat and eliminate the phenomenon in all its forms;

3. *Reiterates* the obligation of all States to conduct exhaustive and impartial investigations into all suspected cases of extrajudicial, summary or arbitrary executions, to identify and bring to justice those responsible, while ensuring the right of every person to a fair and public hearing by a competent, independent and impartial tribunal established by law, to grant adequate compensation within a reasonable time to the victims or their families, and to adopt all necessary measures, including legal and judicial measures, to put an end to impunity and to prevent the further occurrence of such executions, as recommended in the Principles on the Effective Prevention and Investigation of Extralegal, Arbitrary and Summary Executions;

4. *Calls upon* all States in which the death penalty has not been abolished to comply with their obligations under relevant provisions of international human rights instruments, including in particular articles 6, 7 and 14 of the International Covenant on Civil and Political Rights and articles 37 and 40 of the Convention on the Rights of the Child, bearing in mind the safeguards and guarantees set out in Economic and Social Council resolutions 1984/50 of 25 May 1984 and 1989/64 of 24 May 1989;

5. *Urges* all States:

(*a*) To take all necessary and possible measures, in conformity with international human rights law and international humanitarian law, to prevent loss of life, in particular that of children, during public demonstrations, internal and communal violence, civil unrest, public emergencies or armed conflicts, and to ensure that the police, law enforcement agents, armed forces and other agents acting on behalf of or with the consent or acquiescence of the State act with restraint and in conformity with international humanitarian law and international human rights law, including the principles of proportionality and necessity, and in this regard to ensure that police and law enforcement officials are guided by the Code of Conduct for Law Enforcement Officials and the Basic Principles on the Use of Force and Firearms by Law Enforcement Officials;

(*b*) To ensure the effective protection of the right to life of all persons under their jurisdiction and to investigate promptly and thoroughly all killings, including those targeted at specific groups of persons, such as racially motivated violence leading to the death of the victim, killings of members of national, ethnic, religious or linguistic minorities, of refugees, internally displaced persons, migrants, street children or members of indigenous communities, killings of persons for reasons related to their activities as human rights defenders, lawyers, journalists or demonstrators, killings committed in the name of passion or in the name of honour, all killings committed for any discriminatory reason, including sexual orientation, as well as all other cases where a person's right to life has been violated, and to bring those responsible to justice before a competent, independent and impartial judiciary at the national or, where appropriate, international level, and to ensure that such killings, including those committed by security forces, police and law enforcement agents, paramilitary groups or private forces, are neither condoned nor sanctioned by State officials or personnel;

6. *Also urges* all States to ensure that persons deprived of their liberty are treated humanely and with full respect for their human rights and to ensure that their treatment, including judicial guarantees, and conditions conform to the Standard Minimum Rules for the Treatment of Prisoners and, where applicable, to the Geneva Conventions of 12 August 1949 and the Additional Protocols thereto of 8 June 1977 in relation to all persons detained in armed conflict, as well as to other pertinent international instruments;

7. *Welcomes* the International Criminal Court as an important contribution to ending impunity concerning extrajudicial, summary or arbitrary executions and the fact that one hundred and four States have already ratified or acceded to and a further forty-one States have signed the Rome Statute of the Court, and calls upon all those States that have not ratified or acceded to the Rome Statute to consider doing so;

8. *Encourages* Governments and intergovernmental and non-governmental organizations to organize training programmes and to support projects with a view to training or educating military forces, law enforcement officers and government officials in human rights and

humanitarian law issues connected with their work and to include a gender and child rights perspective in such training, and appeals to the international community and requests the Office of the United Nations High Commissioner for Human Rights to support endeavours to that end;

9. *Takes note* of the interim report of the Special Rapporteur of the Human Rights Council on extrajudicial, summary or arbitrary executions to the General Assembly;

10. *Commends* the important role that the Special Rapporteur plays towards the elimination of extrajudicial, summary or arbitrary executions, and encourages the Special Rapporteur to continue, within his mandate, to collect information from all concerned, to respond effectively to reliable information that comes before him, to follow up on communications and country visits and to seek the views and comments of Governments and to reflect them, as appropriate, in his reports;

11. *Acknowledges* the important role of the Special Rapporteur in identifying cases where extrajudicial, summary and arbitrary executions could amount to genocide and crimes against humanity or war crimes, and urges him to collaborate with the United Nations High Commissioner for Human Rights and, as appropriate, the Special Adviser to the Secretary-General on the Prevention of Genocide, in addressing situations of extrajudicial, summary or arbitrary executions that are of particularly serious concern or in which early action might prevent further deterioration;

12. *Welcomes* the cooperation established between the Special Rapporteur and other United Nations mechanisms and procedures in the field of human rights, and encourages the Special Rapporteur to continue efforts in that regard;

13. *Urges* all States, in particular those that have not done so, to cooperate with the Special Rapporteur so that his mandate can be carried out effectively, including by favourably and rapidly responding to requests for visits, mindful that country visits are one of the tools for the fulfilment of the mandate of the Special Rapporteur, and by responding in a timely manner to communications and other requests transmitted to them by the Special Rapporteur;

14. *Expresses its appreciation* to those States that have received the Special Rapporteur and asks them to examine his recommendations carefully, invites them to inform him of the actions taken on those recommendations, and requests other States to cooperate in a similar way;

15. *Again requests* the Secretary-General to continue to use his best endeavours in cases where the minimum standards of legal safeguards provided for in articles 6, 9, 14 and 15 of the International Covenant on Civil and Political Rights appear not to have been respected;

16. *Requests* the Secretary-General to provide the Special Rapporteur with adequate human, financial and material resources to enable him to carry out his mandate effectively, including through country visits;

17. *Also requests* the Secretary-General to continue, in close collaboration with the High Commissioner, in conformity with the mandate of the High Commissioner established by the General Assembly in its resolution 48/141 of 20 December 1993, to ensure that personnel specialized in human rights and humanitarian law issues form part of United Nations missions, where appropriate, in order to deal with serious violations of human rights, such as extrajudicial, summary or arbitrary executions;

18. *Requests* the Special Rapporteur to submit to the General Assembly at its sixty-second session a report on the situation worldwide in regard to extrajudicial, summary or arbitrary executions and his recommendations for more effective action to combat this phenomenon.

RECORDED VOTE ON RESOLUTION 61/173:

In favour: Afghanistan, Albania, Algeria, Andorra, Angola, Antigua and Barbuda, Argentina, Armenia, Australia, Austria, Barbados, Belarus, Belgium, Belize, Benin, Bhutan, Bolivia, Bosnia and Herzegovina, Botswana, Brazil, Bulgaria, Burkina Faso, Burundi, Cambodia, Cameroon, Canada, Cape Verde, Central African Republic, Chile, Colombia, Congo, Costa Rica, Côte d'Ivoire, Croatia, Cuba, Cyprus, Czech Republic, Denmark, Dominica, Dominican Republic, Ecuador, El Salvador, Eritrea, Estonia, Ethiopia, Fiji, Finland, France, Gabon, Gambia, Georgia, Germany, Ghana, Greece, Grenada, Guatemala, Guinea, Guinea-Bissau, Guyana, Haiti, Honduras, Hungary, Iceland, India, Ireland, Italy, Jamaica, Japan, Jordan, Kazakhstan, Kyrgyzstan, Latvia, Lesotho, Liechtenstein, Lithuania, Luxembourg, Mali, Malta, Mauritania, Mauritius, Mexico, Micronesia, Moldova, Monaco, Mongolia, Montenegro, Morocco, Mozambique, Namibia, Nepal, Netherlands, New Zealand, Nicaragua, Nigeria, Norway, Panama, Paraguay, Peru, Philippines, Poland, Portugal, Republic of Korea, Romania, Russian Federation, Saint Lucia, Saint Vincent and the Grenadines, Samoa, San Marino, Sao Tome and Principe, Serbia, Sierra Leone, Slovakia, Slovenia, Solomon Islands, South Africa, Spain, Suriname, Swaziland, Sweden, Switzerland, Tajikistan, Thailand, The former Yugoslav Republic of Macedonia, Timor-Leste, Togo, Trinidad and Tobago, Tunisia, Turkey, Tuvalu, Ukraine, United Kingdom, Uruguay, Uzbekistan, Vanuatu, Venezuela, Zambia, Zimbabwe.

Against: None.

Abstaining: Bahamas, Bahrain, Bangladesh, Brunei Darussalam, China, Democratic People's Republic of Korea, Democratic Republic of the Congo, Djibouti, Egypt, Indonesia, Iran, Iraq, Israel, Kenya, Kuwait, Lebanon, Liberia, Libyan Arab Jamahiriya, Madagascar, Malawi, Malaysia, Maldives, Marshall Islands, Myanmar, Niger, Oman, Pakistan, Palau, Papua New Guinea, Qatar, Saudi Arabia, Senegal, Singapore, Somalia, Sri Lanka, Sudan, Syrian Arab Republic, Uganda, United Arab Emirates, United Republic of Tanzania, United States, Viet Nam, Yemen.

Disappearance of persons

Working Group activities. The five-member Working Group on Enforced or Involuntary Disappearances held three sessions in 2006, all in Geneva: its seventy-eighth (24-28 April), seventy-ninth (24-28 July) and eightieth (20-29 November) [A/HRC/4/41]. In addition to its core mandate to act as a channel of communication between families of disappeared persons and the Governments concerned, with a view to ensuring that sufficiently documented individual cases were investigated, the Working Group monitored compliance with the 1992 Declaration on the Protection of All Persons from Enforced Disappearance, adopted by the General Assembly in resolution 47/133 [YUN 1992, p. 744]. Cases under active consideration by the Group totalled 41,232, concerning 79 countries. Between November 2005 and November 2006, the Working Group had transmitted 335 new cases of enforced disappearance to 16 Governments, 79 of which allegedly occurred in 2006. Of those cases, 87 were sent as urgent action appeals to 14 countries. The Group also filed 12 other cases jointly with other Commission special procedures and clarified 152 cases in 13 countries. The Group's report summarized information concerning disappearances received from 80 countries.

The Group observed that disappearances tended to occur in States suffering from internal conflict, and that in some cases, radical political changes created conditions that led to hundreds of cases of disappearance, many of which remained unresolved. Noting that the cooperation of Governments was indispensable to discovering the fate or whereabouts of disappeared persons worldwide, the Group urged Governments that had never replied to its requests for information or provided relevant information to fulfil their obligations under the Declaration, and resolutions of the General Assembly and human rights machinery. It was also a matter of concern that disappearances in certain regions and countries were underreported owing to government restrictions on the work of civil society organizations dealing with the issue, including NGOs. The Group reminded Governments that, in combating disappearances, effective preventive measures were crucial, including the harmonization of domestic law with States' obligations under the Declaration, accessible and updated registries of detainees and access to places of detention for relatives and lawyers of detainees, ensuring that detained people were brought before a judicial authority promptly, and bringing to justice persons accused of committing acts of enforced disappearance. Those preventive measures were aimed at democratizing governance structures and making human rights the cornerstone of public policy. The establishment of investigating bodies, truth commissions and war crimes tribunals could lead to the clarification of cases and implementation of compensation policies for victims. However, a further goal of public policy should be the eradication of the culture of impunity in many States for the perpetrators of disappearances.

The Working Group visited Guatemala (19-21 September) [A/HRC/4/41/Add.1] at the invitation of the Government to discuss efforts to address past disappearances in the country. The Group examined the country's constitutional and institutional framework for addressing disappearances and the steps taken and related measures adopted to do so and guarantee victims' rights. The Group found that, although enforced disappearances were no longer a systematic Government policy practice, thousands of unresolved cases remained. While acknowledging the State's goodwill in implementing international human rights standards and its relative progress in that regard, the Group expressed concern about the many obstacles hindering real results. Specific concerns included the lack of coordination of programmes and activities between NGOs and State actors; the lack of economic and material resources and well trained judicial officials to investigate and prosecute perpetrators; inadequate guarantees for the independence of the institution in charge of investigating implicated State officials; impunity for perpetrators; the fact that no one had as yet been convicted for the crime of enforced disappearance; the reported declaration of thousands of habeas corpus applications regarding that crime as null and void; uncertainty regarding the safety of archived information that might be essential in clarifying cases of enforced disappearance; and recurring attacks and intimidation against members of civil society organizations, the judiciary, human rights activists, lawyers and victims' families. Of particular concern was the fact that the Guatemala Criminal Code's definition of enforced disappearance was inconsistent with the definition contained in the Declaration.

The Group recommended the harmonization of domestic laws with international human rights instruments, particularly the Declaration; the creation of an independent National Commission to search for victims of enforced or involuntary disappearance; enactment of legislation on access to public information as legal protection for archived data; upholding the prosecution and punishment of those responsible for enforced disappearance; measures to satisfy the rights of victims; training for justice officials on the crime of enforced disappearance and in the techniques for effective investigation and prosecution of related cases; the application of international standards by the courts regarding their decisions on such cases; and good cooperation and coordination between all State institutions and non-governmental actors in addressing the problem. It further recommended, among other measures, the reopening of suspended habeas corpus procedures and the continuing investigation of cases of disappearance; measures to prevent intimidation and other forms of attacks on witnesses and human rights defenders investigating cases of disappearance; and the provision of information by the Government and other actors for clarifying the nearly 2,000 pending cases of disappearance there.

Report of Secretary-General. Pursuant to General Assembly resolution 59/200 [YUN 2004, p. 731], the Secretary-General submitted an August report [A/61/289] summarizing replies from 16 Governments on measures they had taken to implement the Declaration on the Protection of All Persons from Enforced Disappearances [YUN 1992, p. 744], as well as the obstacles encountered. The report also highlighted the activities of the Working Group on Involuntary Disappearances (see above) and provided information on the Human Rights Council's adoption of the International Convention for the Protection of All Persons from Enforced Disappearance (see p. 800), UN activities undertaken in the past year to promote the Declaration and the obstacles to the realization of its provisions and ways of overcoming them.

On 19 December (**decision 61/529**), the General Assembly took note of the Secretary-General's report.

Holocaust remembrance

Report of Secretary-General. In accordance with General Assembly resolution 60/7 [YUN 2005, p. 811], the Secretary-General reported, in June [A/60/882], on the establishment of an outreach programme on the Holocaust and the United Nations, under the auspices of the UN Department of Public Information. The report highlighted the goals of the programme, its core elements and activities undertaken and planned. The Secretary-General noted that the Department would continue to work with Member States and expand its partnerships with civil society organizations to commemorate the uniqueness of the Holocaust in human history and to draw from it lessons that might help prevent future acts of genocide.

Communications. On 20 January [A/60/655], Iran transmitted a text explaining the position it had intended to present relating to Assembly resolution 60/7 [YUN 2005, p. 811].

On 27 January [A/60/660], the Russian Federation transmitted a communication from Russian President Vladimir Putin to Israeli President Moshe Katsav concerning the International Day of Commemoration in Memory of the Victims of the Holocaust.

Torture and cruel treatment

Reports of Special Rapporteur. In a report to the Commission [E/CN.4/2006/6], the Special Rapporteur on the question of torture, Manfred Nowak (Austria), summarized his activities, discussed his country visit methodology and examined the implications of conditions in countries visited, specifically regarding detention facilities. The report also highlighted developments relating to diplomatic assurances, otherwise referred to as promises or agreements to return alleged terrorist suspects to countries where they might be at risk of torture. The Special Rapporteur noted that such practices circumvented the absolute prohibition of torture and refoulement, particularly in the context of counter-terrorism measures. He reiterated that those assurances were not legally binding, undermined States' obligations to prohibit torture, were ineffective and unreliable in ensuring the protection of returned persons, and should therefore not be resorted to by States. Addressing the distinction between torture and cruel, inhuman or degrading treatment or punishment, the Special Rapporteur observed that, in the aftermath of the September 2001 terrorist attacks in the United States [YUN 2001, p. 60] and other such attacks, an increasing number of Governments had adopted a legal position which, while acknowledging the absolute nature of the prohibition of torture, questioned the absolute nature of the prohibition of cruel, inhuman or degrading treatment or punishment. In particular, it was argued that certain harsh interrogation methods falling short of torture might be justified for the purpose of extracting information in order to prevent future terrorist acts.

The Special Rapporteur concluded that the distinction between those concepts related primarily to the question of personal liberty, adding that the prohibition of cruel, inhuman and degrading treatment was subject to the proportionality principle, which was a precondition for assessing its scope of application. However, where a person was detained or otherwise under the de facto control of another and was rendered powerless, the proportionality test was no longer applicable and the prohibition of torture and cruel, inhuman and degrading treatment or punishment was absolute. That absolute prohibition of the use of any form of physical force or mental coercion applied, first of all, to situations of interrogation by public officials working for the police, the military or the intelligence services.

An addendum to the report [E/CN.4/2006/6/Add.1] summarized requests for information transmitted to Governments and replies received thereto between 1 December 2004 and 15 December 2005. The

Special Rapporteur had sent, occasionally in joint action with other special procedures, 291 letters to 70 Governments and 202 urgent appeals to 56 Governments on behalf of individuals feared to be at risk of torture and other forms of ill-treatment. A further addendum [E/CN.4/2006/6/Add.2] contained information provided by Governments and NGOs in follow-up action to the Special Rapporteur's recommendations following country visits.

The Special Rapporteur visited China at the invitation of the Government (20 November–2 December 2005) [E/CN.4/2006/6/Add.6], where he assessed the situation of torture and other cruel, inhuman or degrading treatment or punishment; promoted preventive mechanisms to eradicate the phenomenon; and initiated cooperation with the Government. He believed that, despite a declining trend, particularly in urban areas, torture remained widespread. The decline was attributable to many measures, including the Government's acknowledgement of the problem in the criminal justice system and the efforts undertaken at the central and provincial levels to combat it. However, other factors accounting for a continuation of torture included rules of evidence that created incentives for interrogators to obtain confessions through torture, the excessive length of time that criminal suspects were held in police custody without judicial control, the absence of a legal culture based on the presumption of innocence and restricted rights and access of defence counsel. The situation was aggravated by the lack of vital social and political institutions, such as a free and investigation-oriented press, citizen-based and independent human rights monitoring organizations, independent commissions visiting places of detention and fair and accessible courts and prosecutors. While the basic conditions in detention facilities seemed generally satisfactory, the Special Rapporteur was struck by the strictness of prison discipline and palpable fear and self-censorship among detainees. The combination of the deprivation of liberty as a sanction for the peaceful exercise of freedom of expression, assembly and religion, with measures of re-education through coercion, humiliation and punishment aimed at admission of guilt and alteration of the personality of detainees, amounted to inhuman or degrading treatment or punishment that was incompatible with the core values of any society based upon a culture of human rights.

The Special Rapporteur recommended measures for adoption by the Government to eradicate torture and ill-treatment. Those recommendations particularly addressed issues relating to the investigation and prosecution of torture; prevention of torture and ill-treatment through safeguards in the criminal justice system; other prevention measures; capital punishment; deprivation of liberty for political crimes; forced re-education; and follow-up action.

In Jordan (25-29 June) [A/HRC/4/33/Add.3], the Special Rapporteur found that torture was alleged to be routinely practiced by the General Intelligence Directorate and Criminal Investigations Department to extract confessions during criminal investigations and obtain intelligence in pursuit of counter-terrorism and national security objectives. Of particular concern were the conditions of detention in prisons and pretrial detention centres, where detainees were subjected to corporal punishment that amounted to torture. The Special Rapporteur attributed the situation to a lack of awareness of the problem and institutionalized impunity, noting that the heads of the security forces and detention facilities he visited had denied any knowledge of torture, despite having been presented with substantiated allegations. Moreover, the provisions and safeguards in Jordanian law to combat torture and ill-treatment were meaningless because the security services were shielded from independent criminal prosecution and judicial scrutiny, as abuses by officials of those services were dealt with by special police, intelligence and military courts. The fact that no official had ever been prosecuted for torture underlined that perspective.

The Special Rapporteur recommended to the Government a number of measures to enable it to comply with its commitment to prevent torture and other forms of ill-treatment. Particular problems addressed in that context included impunity, regarding which he advocated, among other things, action by the highest authorities to clearly indicate that torture and related practices by public officials would not be tolerated and would be prosecuted; the definition of the crime of torture with commensurate penalties, in accordance with the Convention against Torture; the abolition of the special court system within the security forces and the transfer of their jurisdiction to independent public prosecutors and criminal courts; and the establishment of an effective complaints system for torture and abuse leading to criminal investigations. Other recommendations related to safeguards measures against torture, the conditions of detention, preventive action, and international cooperation.

By a 14 August note [A/61/259], the Secretary-General transmitted the Special Rapporteur's interim report, submitted in accordance with General Assembly resolution 60/148 [YUN 2005, p. 815]. The report addressed issues of concern to the Special Rapporteur, particularly regarding overall trends and developments relevant to his mandate. Maintaining focus on the absolute prohibition of torture in the context of counter-terrorism measures, the Special Rapporteur drew attention to the principle of non-admissibility of evidence extracted by torture, consistent with article 15 of the Convention against Torture. Recent key court decisions in that regard revealed an increasing trend towards the use of secret evidence put forward by prosecutors and other authorities in judicial proceedings, with a heavy burden of proof placed on an individual to establish that such evidence was obtained under torture. Such practices potentially undermined the principle of absolute prohibition laid out in article 15. The Special Rapporteur noted that, in the light of well-founded allegations of torture, the burden of proof shifted to the State to establish that evidence invoked against an individual had not been obtained under torture (see p. 776). The Special Rapporteur also discussed the rationale for independent preventive visits to places of detention and the significance of the entry into force of the Optional Protocol to the Convention against Torture. As the most effective instrument established to prevent the practice of torture, he called on States to ratify the Protocol and establish independent and effective national mechanisms empowered to visit places of detention unannounced at any time, conduct private interviews with detainees and have them undergo independent medical examinations.

On 19 December (**decision 61/529**), the General Assembly took note of the Secretary-General's note.

Communication. On 20 September [A/HRC/2/G/4], Uzbekistan transmitted updated information on the recommendations of the former Special Rapporteur following a 2002 visit to the country [YUN 2002, p. 712].

Voluntary fund for victims of torture

Note of Secretary-General. In accordance with a 2005 Commission resolution [YUN 2005, p. 814], a January note of the Secretary-General [E/CN.4/2006/50] updated information contained in his 2005 report on the activities of the United Nations Voluntary Fund for Victims of Torture [YUN 2005, p. 814] and described the Fund's financial needs for 2006 and 2007.

Report of Secretary-General. In his annual report to the General Assembly on the status of the Fund, submitted in July [A/61/226], the Secretary-General described the recommendations of the Fund's Board of Trustees at its twenty-fifth session (Geneva, 5-11 April). Contributions received between April 2005 and July 2006 totalled $17,852, 440, from 36 countries. Against requests amounting to $11,363,743, the Board recommended grants in the amount of $8,797,000 for the period between July 2006 and December 2007 to fund 165 projects in 71 countries. On 10 June, the High Commissioner approved the Board's recommendations on behalf of the Secretary-General. During the year, the Board maintained its practice of financing requests for training and seminars and recommended, in that regard, that $25,000 be allocated to three organizations for training courses. It also allocated $250,000 to the emergency fund. The Board estimated that $12 million would be needed to enable it to assist torture victims in 2008. The report also provided information on policy decisions adopted by the Board to implement the recommendations made by the Office of Internal Oversight Services (OIOS) regarding the Fund's operation in 2004 [YUN 2004, p. 734].

On 19 December, the General Assembly took note of the Secretary-General's report (**decision 61/529**).

GENERAL ASSEMBLY ACTION

On 19 December [meeting 81], the General Assembly, on the recommendation of the Third Committee [A/61/443/Add.1 & Corr.1], adopted **resolution 61/153** without vote [agenda item 67 *(a)*].

Torture and other cruel, inhuman or degrading treatment or punishment

The General Assembly,

Reaffirming that no one shall be subjected to torture or to other cruel, inhuman or degrading treatment or punishment,

Recalling that freedom from torture and other cruel, inhuman or degrading treatment or punishment is a non-derogable right that must be protected under all circumstances, including in times of international or internal armed conflict or disturbance, and that the absolute prohibition of torture and other cruel, inhuman or degrading treatment or punishment is affirmed in relevant international instruments,

Recalling also that a number of international, regional and domestic courts, including the International Tribunal for the Prosecution of Persons Responsible for Serious Violations of International Humanitarian Law Committed in the Territory of the Former Yugoslavia since 1991, have recognized that the prohibition of torture is a peremptory norm of international law and have held that the prohibition of cruel, inhuman or degrading treatment or punishment is customary international law,

Recalling further the definition of torture contained in article 1 of the Convention against Torture and Other Cruel, Inhuman or Degrading Treatment or Punishment,

Noting that under the Geneva Conventions of 1949 torture and inhuman treatment are a grave breach and that under the statutes of the International Tribunal for the Former Yugoslavia and the International Criminal Tribunal for the Prosecution of Persons Responsible for Genocide and Other Serious Violations of International Humanitarian Law Committed in the Territory of Rwanda and Rwandan Citizens Responsible for Genocide and Other Such Violations Committed in the Territory of Neighbouring States between 1 January and 31 December 1994 and the Rome Statute of the International Criminal Court acts of torture constitute war crimes and can constitute crimes against humanity,

Commending the persistent efforts by non-governmental organizations, including the considerable network of centres for the rehabilitation of victims of torture, to combat torture and to alleviate the suffering of victims of torture,

1. *Condemns* all forms of torture and other cruel, inhuman or degrading treatment or punishment, including through intimidation, which are and shall remain prohibited at any time and in any place whatsoever and can thus never be justified, and calls upon all States to implement fully the absolute prohibition of torture and other cruel, inhuman or degrading treatment or punishment;

2. *Emphasizes* that States must take persistent, determined and effective measures to prevent and combat torture and other cruel, inhuman or degrading treatment or punishment, including their gender-based manifestations, and stresses that all acts of torture must be made offences under domestic criminal law;

3. *Also emphasizes* the importance of States ensuring proper follow-up to the recommendations and conclusions of the relevant treaty bodies and mechanisms, including the Committee against Torture and the Special Rapporteur of the Human Rights Council on torture and other cruel, inhuman or degrading treatment or punishment;

4. *Condemns* any action or attempt by States or public officials to legalize, authorize or acquiesce in torture and other cruel, inhuman or degrading treatment or punishment under any circumstances, including on grounds of national security or through judicial decisions;

5. *Stresses* that all allegations of torture or other cruel, inhuman or degrading treatment or punishment must be promptly and impartially examined by the competent national authority, that those who encourage, order, tolerate or perpetrate acts of torture must be held responsible and severely punished, including the officials in charge of the place of detention where the prohibited act is found to have been committed, and takes note in this respect of the Principles on the Effective Investigation and Documentation of Torture and Other Cruel, Inhuman or Degrading Treatment or Punishment (the Istanbul Principles) as a useful tool in efforts to combat torture and of the updated set of principles for the protection of human rights through action to combat impunity;

6. *Emphasizes* that acts of torture are serious violations of international humanitarian law and in this regard constitute war crimes and can constitute crimes against humanity, and that the perpetrators of all acts of torture must be prosecuted and punished;

7. *Urges* States to ensure that any statement that is established to have been made as a result of torture shall not be invoked as evidence in any proceedings, except against a person accused of torture as evidence that the statement was made;

8. *Stresses* that States must not punish personnel who are involved in the custody, interrogation or treatment of any individual subjected to any form of arrest, detention or imprisonment or any other form of deprivation of liberty for not obeying orders to commit or conceal acts amounting to torture or other cruel, inhuman or degrading treatment or punishment;

9. *Urges* States not to expel, return ("refouler"), extradite or in any other way transfer a person to another State where there are substantial grounds for believing that the person would be in danger of being subjected to torture, and recognizes that diplomatic assurances, where used, do not release States from their obligations under international human rights, humanitarian and refugee law, in particular the principle of non-refoulement;

10. *Stresses* that national legal systems must ensure that victims of torture and other cruel, inhuman or degrading treatment or punishment obtain redress, are awarded fair and adequate compensation and receive appropriate social and medical rehabilitation, urges States to take effective measures to this end, and in this regard encourages the development of rehabilitation centres;

11. *Recalls* its resolution 43/173 of 9 December 1988 on the Body of Principles for the Protection of All Persons under Any Form of Detention or Imprisonment, and in this context stresses that ensuring that any individual arrested or detained is promptly brought before a judge or other independent judicial officer in person and permitting prompt and regular medical care and legal counsel as well as visits by family members and independent monitoring mechanisms are effective measures for the prevention of torture and other cruel, inhuman or degrading treatment and punishment;

12. *Reminds* all States that prolonged incommunicado detention or detention in secret places may facilitate the perpetration of torture and other cruel, inhuman or degrading treatment or punishment and can in itself constitute a form of such treatment, and urges all States to respect the safeguards concerning the liberty, security and dignity of the person;

13. *Calls upon* all States to take appropriate effective legislative, administrative, judicial and other measures to prevent and prohibit the production, trade, export and use of equipment that is specifically designed to inflict torture or other cruel, inhuman or degrading treatment;

14. *Urges* all States that have not yet done so to become parties to the Convention against Torture and Other Cruel, Inhuman or Degrading Treatment or Punishment as a matter of priority;

15. *Invites* all States parties to the Convention that have not yet done so to make the declarations provided for in articles 21 and 22 of the Convention concerning inter-State and individual communications, to consider

the possibility of withdrawing their reservations to article 20 of the Convention and to notify the Secretary-General of their acceptance of the amendments to articles 17 and 18 of the Convention as soon as possible;

16. *Urges* States parties to comply strictly with their obligations under the Convention, including, in view of the high number of reports not submitted in time, their obligation to submit reports in accordance with article 19 of the Convention, and invites States parties to incorporate a gender perspective and information concerning children and juveniles and persons with disabilities when submitting reports to the Committee against Torture;

17 *Acknowledges with appreciation* the entry into force of the Optional Protocol to the Convention against Torture and Other Cruel, Inhuman or Degrading Treatment or Punishment, and calls upon States parties to give early consideration to signing and ratifying the Optional Protocol, which provides further measures for use in the fight against and prevention of torture and other cruel, inhuman or degrading treatment or punishment;

18. *Welcomes* the work of the Committee against Torture and its report submitted in accordance with article 24 of the Convention, and recommends that the Committee continue to include information on the follow-up by States to its recommendations;

19. *Calls upon* the United Nations High Commissioner for Human Rights, in conformity with her mandate established by the General Assembly in its resolution 48/141 of 20 December 1993, to continue to provide, at the request of States, advisory services for the prevention of torture and other cruel, inhuman or degrading treatment or punishment, including for the preparation of national reports to the Committee against Torture and for the establishment and operation of national preventive mechanisms, as well as technical assistance for the development, production and distribution of teaching material for this purpose;

20. *Notes with appreciation* the interim report of the Special Rapporteur on torture and other cruel, inhuman or degrading treatment or punishment, and encourages the Special Rapporteur to continue to include in his recommendations proposals on the prevention and investigation of torture and other cruel, inhuman or degrading treatment or punishment, including its gender-based manifestations;

21. *Requests* the Special Rapporteur to continue to consider including in his report information on the follow-up by States to his recommendations, visits and communications, including progress made and problems encountered, and on other official contacts;

22. *Calls upon* all States to cooperate with and assist the Special Rapporteur in the performance of his task, to supply all necessary information requested by the Special Rapporteur, to fully and expeditiously respond to and follow up his urgent appeals, to give serious consideration to responding favourably to requests by the Special Rapporteur to visit their countries and to enter into a constructive dialogue with the Special Rapporteur on requested visits to their countries as well as with respect to the follow-up to his recommendations;

23. *Stresses* the need for the continued regular exchange of views among the Committee against Torture, the Subcommittee on Prevention of Torture and Other Cruel, Inhuman or Degrading Treatment or Punishment, the Special Rapporteur and other relevant United Nations mechanisms and bodies, as well as for the pursuance of cooperation with relevant United Nations programmes, notably the United Nations Crime Prevention and Criminal Justice Programme, with a view to enhancing further their effectiveness and cooperation on issues relating to torture, inter alia, by improving their coordination;

24. *Recognizes* the global need for international assistance to victims of torture, stresses the importance of the work of the Board of Trustees of the United Nations Voluntary Fund for Victims of Torture, and appeals to all States and organizations to contribute annually to the Fund, preferably with a substantial increase in the level of contributions;

25. *Requests* the Secretary-General to continue to transmit to all States the appeals of the General Assembly for contributions to the Fund and to include the Fund on an annual basis among the programmes for which funds are pledged at the United Nations Pledging Conference for Development Activities;

26. *Also requests* the Secretary-General to ensure, within the overall budgetary framework of the United Nations, the provision of adequate staff and facilities for the bodies and mechanisms involved in preventing and combating torture and assisting victims of torture commensurate with the strong support expressed by Member States for preventing and combating torture and assisting victims of torture;

27. *Further requests* the Secretary-General to submit to the Human Rights Council and to the General Assembly at its sixty-second session a report on the status of the Convention and a report on the operations of the Fund;

28. *Calls upon* all States, the Office of the United Nations High Commissioner for Human Rights and other United Nations bodies and agencies, as well as relevant intergovernmental and non-governmental organizations, to commemorate, on 26 June, the United Nations International Day in Support of Victims of Torture;

29. *Decides* to consider at its sixty-second session the reports of the Secretary-General, including the report on the United Nations Voluntary Fund for Victims of Torture, the report of the Committee against Torture and the interim report of the Special Rapporteur on torture and other cruel, inhuman or degrading treatment or punishment.

Freedom of expression

Report of Special Rapporteur. In accordance with a 2005 Commission request [YUN 2005, p. 817], the Special Rapporteur on the promotion and protection of the right to freedom of opinion and expression, Ambeyi Ligabo (Kenya), described his 2005 activities [E/CN.4/2006/55]. He had sent 490 communications to 96 Governments on behalf of 1,328 individuals whose right to freedom of opinion and expression were reportedly threatened or violated, to which he received 206 replies. Of those communications, 304 were urgent appeals, of which 245 were sent jointly with other special procedures, while 181 were allegation letters, 73 of them sent jointly. An addendum to the report [E/CN.4/2006/55/Add.1] summarized the texts of the communications and the replies thereto. The Special Rapporteur also reviewed the final phase of the World Summit on the Information Society [YUN 2005, p. 933] and the human rights situation in Tunisia, which had served as the host country. He examined the shortcomings of the Summit, where human rights issues had been marginalized by a commercial business approach to Internet governance and the attitude of the host country, which demonstrated a tendency to silence human rights activists.

The Special Rapporteur recommended that Governments consider the protection of freedom of opinion and expression as one of the best ways to fight violence and guarantee stability. They should establish an independent authority on communications, entrusted with implementing relevant laws and regulations, and a media ombudsperson to mediate media offences without resorting to criminal law. Such an authority could work to prevent media concentration, in particular the creation of a monopoly that could endanger the pluralism of information and affect media independence. Governments should also increase protection for journalists and other media practitioners from attacks; guarantee freedom of opinion and expression on the Internet, extending to website contributors and bloggers the same protection as other media; and decriminalize defamation and similar offences to alleviate the workload of the judiciary, as related cases could be resolved through the good offices of an independent authority. The Special Rapporteur further recommended that the Commission should request a study on the security of journalists, particularly in situations of armed conflict, which could provide a basis for discussing draft guidelines for protecting journalists and media professionals.

An annex to the report outlined follow-up to the Special Rapporteur's recommendations following his 2004 visit to Serbia and Montenegro [YUN 2004, p. 737] and Italy [ibid., p. 738].

Human Rights Council action. On 29 November [A/62/53 (dec. 2/116)], the Council deferred to its fourth session consideration of a draft decision on freedom of opinion and expression [A/HRC/2/L.42/Rev.1] introduced by Canada, which would have requested the Special Rapporteur to focus in his next report to the Council on the security of journalists, in particular in situations of armed conflict.

Terrorism

Report of Special Rapporteur. Pursuant to a 2005 Commission resolution [YUN 2005, p. 818], the Special Rapporteur on the protection and promotion of human rights while countering terrorism, Martin Scheinin (Finland), submitted a report [E/CN.4/2006/98] summarizing his activities and reviewing communications with Governments between 15 August and 15 December 2005. He had corresponded with 11 States on a variety of relevant issues, including counter-terrorism legislation, states of emergency, suicide bombings and alleged human rights violations, particularly regarding the treatment of terrorism suspects during detention and questioning. The summaries of those communications were contained in an addendum to the report [E/CN.4/2006/98/Add.1]. The Special Rapporteur also discussed the work of the Security Council's Counter-Terrorism Committee (see p. 73) and key issues relevant to his mandate, including the question of defining terrorism, the victims and root causes of terrorism and the activities of non-State actors.

The Special Rapporteur observed that the lack of a universal, comprehensive and precise definition of terrorism posed problems for the effective protection of human rights while countering terrorism. While ongoing work in that regard was encouraging, it was essential to ensure that the term "terrorism" was confined to conduct that was genuinely of a terrorist nature. In that context, and in accordance with Security Council resolution 1566(2004) [YUN 2004, p. 74], terrorism would include acts committed with the intention of causing death or serious bodily injury or the taking of hostages; activities intended to provoke a state of terror, intimidating a population or compelling a Government or international organization to take certain action or abstain from doing so; and conduct that constituted an offence within the scope of international conventions and protocols relating to terrorism. Similarly, the criminalization of conduct in support of terrorist offences should be restricted to offences having all those characteristics, and States should ensure that prescriptions prohibiting terrorist conduct were accessible, precise, applicable to counter-terrorism alone, non-discriminatory and non-retroactive. The Special Rapporteur was concerned that States were not receiving a clear enough message from the Security Council's Counter-Terrorism Committee concerning their duty to respect human rights while countering terrorism. He intended to maintain dialogue with the Committee and the Counter-

Terrorism Executive Directorate, particularly regarding the joint identification and compilation of best practices in the field of effective and human rights-compatible responses to terrorism, and to further consider the position and rights of victims of terrorism, the conditions conducive to terrorism and the question of non-State actors and fundamental standards of humanity.

The Special Rapporteur visited Turkey (16-23 February) [E/CN.4/2006/98/Add.2; A/HRC/4/26/Add.2] to gather information about counter-terrorism initiatives and how they affected human rights. The issues addressed included the definition of terrorism in the country and related matters; freedom of expression, association and assembly; measures to support terrorism victims and the right of the estimated 360,000 persons displaced by associated violence to return to their homes; and ways to further economic, social and cultural rights as a means of preventing terrorism. The Special Rapporteur acknowledged that the country had made significant progress in terms of respect for human rights. Positive practices in that regard included the scheme for compensating victims of terrorism and counter-terrorism operations and the safeguards introduced for terrorism suspects.

He recommended that steps be taken to ensure full compliance of legal and practical counter-terrorism measures with international human rights law, and to bring the definition of terrorist crimes in line with international norms and standards, notably the principle of legality under article 15 of the International Covenant on Civil and Political Rights [YUN 1966, p. 426]. International conventions for the elimination of terrorism [YUN 2001, p. 69] should be taken into account when drafting new legislation against terrorism, and the procedure for designating organizations linked to terrorist crimes as terrorist organizations should be transparent and objective, with the right of appeal to an independent judicial body. The Special Rapporteur pointed out that only full clarity with regard to the definition of acts constituting terrorist crimes could ensure that the crimes of membership, aiding and abetting and what certain authorities referred to as crimes of opinion were not abused for purposes other than fighting terrorism. Other recommendations addressed issues concerning extrajudicial killings and the fight against impunity; and victims of terrorism and the prevention of terrorism.

On 26 May [A/HRC/2/G/3], Turkey transmitted its observations to the Special Rapporteur's report on his visit to the country (see above).

By an August note [A/61/267], the Secretary-General transmitted to the General Assembly a further report of the Special Rapporteur, which summarized his activities since 15 December 2005 and his reflections on the impact of the war on terror on the freedom of association and peaceful assembly and relevant international standards. While acknowledging that the right to such freedom was protected by the International Covenant on Civil and Political Rights, the Special Rapporteur highlighted the need for a successful counter-terrorism strategy that would include a preventive dimension, whereby terrorist groups and organizations involved in planning terrorist acts would be prevented from carrying them out, and sanctioned even if those acts were not committed or attempted. That implied that it was permissible to criminalize preparatory acts of terror, and to take measures against acts that interfered with the freedom of peaceful assembly and of association. States should not, however, abuse the necessity of combating terrorism by resorting to measures that were unnecessarily restrictive of human rights. Highlighting the need for clear legal safeguards to prevent such abuse and provide for remedies where it occurred, the Special Rapporteur said he would continue to work with the High Commissioner and other independent experts to engage with States in upholding human rights and fundamental freedoms in the course of enacting and implementing counter-terrorism legislation or practices. The report also reflected on a number of other relevant issues, including the Secretary-General's report entitled "Uniting against Terrorism: recommendations for a global counter-terrorism strategy" (see p. 65), the definition of terrorism at the domestic level, and the Human Rights Council's ongoing review of mechanisms.

On 19 December, the Assembly took note of the Secretary-General's note (**decision 61/529**).

The Special Rapporteur undertook a study on human rights compliance while countering terrorism in Australia [A/HRC/4/26/Add.3], which was facilitated by responses to a list of related questions he had provided to the Government, the academic community and NGOs in the country. The study reviewed Australia's counter-terrorism framework, legislation and human rights protection, and examined the characterization of terrorism under the country's law and the issues of incitement and sedition. In addition, it analysed the investigative, detention and control measures and considered issues relating to immigration, border control and refugee status. The study identified good practices but noted that there was room for improvement. On the positive side, the Special Rapporteur commended, among other developments, Australia's accession to all universal terrorism-related conventions, leadership in strengthening counter-terrorism in the Asia-Pacific region and adoption of measures capable of protecting the public while avoiding detention. Nonetheless, the study highlighted numerous issues of concern and shortcomings, including a number of actual and potential human rights violations within Australia's counter-terrorism regime. Against that background, the Special Rapporteur urged that the country enact federal legislation to ensure the implementation of the International Covenant on Civil and Political Rights and provide remedial mechanisms for the protection of human rights and freedoms. It should also introduce measures to compensate victims of terrorist acts.

Report of Secretary-General. Pursuant to General Assembly resolution 60/158 [YUN 2005, p. 820], the Secretary-General submitted a September report [A/61/353] covering developments within the UN system relating to human rights and counter-terrorism. The report noted widespread concerns over the alleged use by some Member States of secret detention centres, the practice of irregular transfers of terrorist suspects and the use of diplomatic assurances to justify the return and transfer of suspects to countries where they might be tortured. The Secretary-General called on Member States to reaffirm their commitment to the total prohibition of torture by taking commensurate action in national law, prosecuting those responsible for torture and prohibiting the use of statements extracted under torture. They should ensure access to all prisoners in detention and abolish places of secret detention. Member States should also abide by the principle of non-refoulement. In that regard, the entry into force on 22 June of the Optional Protocol to the Convention against Torture (see p. 776) was a significant development towards ensuring the protection of detainees worldwide, as the Protocol included provisions for visiting detention centers in States parties, which were required to set up national preventive mechanisms against torture. Member States were encouraged to ratify the instrument.

Subcommission action. On 7 August [dec. 2006/102], the Subcommission established a five-member sessional working group to elaborate detailed principles and guidelines concerning the promotion and protection of human rights when combating terrorism (see below).

Working group activities. The working group established to elaborate principles and guidelines when combating terrorism (see above) held two meetings (Geneva, 9-10 August) [A/HRC/Sub.1/58/26], at which it discussed issues relating to its mandate, including, among other things, international judicial cooperation and the rights of victims of terrorist acts. It had before it numerous relevant documents, most notably the report of the sessional working group, which addressed the issue in 2005 [YUN 2005, p. 819]; an updated framework draft of those principles and guidelines contained in an expanded working paper [A/HRC/Sub.1/58/30] submitted by the former Special Rapporteur on Terrorism and Human Rights, Kalliopi K. Koufa (Greece); a working paper on the promotion and protection of human rights when combating terrorism [A/HRC/Sub.1/58/CRP.1 & Corr.1] prepared by Françoise Hampson (United Kingdom); and a working paper on the human rights of victims of terrorist activities [A/HRC/Sub.1/58/CRP.11] from Emmanuel Decaux (France). The group also had before it pertinent reports of the Secretary-General, the Special Rapporteur and the Council of Europe, as well as the OHCHR *Digest of Jurisprudence of the United Nations and Regional Organizations on the Protection of Human Rights while Countering Terrorism*, first compiled in 2003 [YUN 2003, p. 746] and reviewed in 2004 [YUN 2004, p. 739] and 2005 [YUN 2005, p. 818]. The group felt that the draft principles and guidelines was a work in progress which might require several more years to complete, and it was important for such work to continue in a form to be determined by the Human Rights Council. It asked its Chairperson-Rapporteur to prepare, taking into account the comments and observations made during the session, a revised and updated framework draft of principles and guidelines concerning human rights and terrorism, for the Council's consideration. The group also recommended that OHCHR hold a seminar on issues relating to international judicial cooperation.

Subcommission action. On 24 August [res. 2006/20], the Subcommission endorsed the recommendations of the working group (see above); requested Ms. Koufa to update the preliminary framework draft of principles and guidelines based on the group's discussions and the related comments to be submitted to her subsequently; transmitted to the Human Rights Council the updated framework draft for its consideration, recognizing that it would necessitate further elaboration and work; and decided to reconvene the group in 2007 or during the first session of any future expert advice mechanism. It recommended that the Council, in its review of the system of expert advice, consider maintaining the group, in order to carry on the elaboration of the principles and guidelines.

Human Rights Council action. On 27 November [A/62/53 (dec. 2/112)], the Council urged States to ensure that persons deprived of their liberty in the context of counter-terrorism measures, regardless of the place of arrest or of detention, benefited from the guarantees to which they were entitled under international law, including protection against torture, cruel, inhuman or degrading treatment or punishment, protection against refoulement, the review of their detention and, if brought to trial, fundamental judicial guarantees.

GENERAL ASSEMBLY ACTION

On 19 December [meeting 81], the General Assembly, on the recommendation of the Third Committee [A/61/443/Add.2 & Corr.1], adopted **resolution 61/171** without vote [agenda item 67 *(b)*].

Protection of human rights and fundamental freedoms while countering terrorism

The General Assembly,

Reaffirming the purposes and principles of the Charter of the United Nations,

Reaffirming also the fundamental importance, including in response to terrorism and the fear of terrorism, of respecting all human rights and fundamental freedoms and the rule of law,

Recalling its resolutions 57/219 of 18 December 2002, 58/187 of 22 December 2003, 59/191 of 20 December 2004 and 60/158 of 16 December 2005, Commission on Human Rights resolutions 2003/68 of 25 April 2003, 2004/87 of 21 April 2004 and 2005/80 of 21 April 2005 and other relevant resolutions of the General Assembly and the Commission on Human Rights,

Reaffirming that States are under the obligation to protect all human rights and fundamental freedoms of all persons,

Reiterating the important contribution of measures taken at all levels against terrorism, consistent with international law, in particular international human rights law and refugee and humanitarian law, to the functioning of democratic institutions and the maintenance of peace and security and thereby to the full enjoyment of human rights, as well as the need to continue this fight, including through international cooperation and the strengthening of the role of the United Nations in this respect,

Deeply deploring the occurrence of violations of human rights and fundamental freedoms in the context of the fight against terrorism, as well as violations of international refugee law and international humanitarian law,

Recalling the establishment by the Commission on Human Rights, in its resolution 2005/80, of the mandate of the Special Rapporteur on the promotion and protection of human rights and fundamental freedoms while countering terrorism,

Recalling also its resolution 48/141 of 20 December 1993 and, inter alia, the responsibility of the United Nations High Commissioner for Human Rights to promote and protect the effective enjoyment of all human rights,

Welcoming the establishment of the Human Rights Council, which is responsible for promoting universal respect for the protection of all human rights and fundamental freedoms for all, without distinction of any kind and in a fair and equal manner,

Recognizing the importance of the United Nations Global Counter-Terrorism Strategy adopted by the General Assembly on 8 September 2006, and reaffirming its relevant clauses on the measures to ensure respect for human rights for all, international humanitarian law and the rule of law as the fundamental basis for the fight against terrorism,

Reaffirming that acts, methods and practices of terrorism in all its forms and manifestations are activities aimed at the destruction of human rights, fundamental freedoms and democracy, threatening the territorial integrity and security of States and destabilizing legitimately constituted Governments, and that the international community should take the necessary steps to enhance cooperation to prevent and combat terrorism,

Reaffirming its unequivocal condemnation of all acts, methods and practices of terrorism in all its forms and manifestations, wherever and by whomsoever committed, regardless of their motivation, as criminal and unjustifiable, and renewing its commitment to strengthen international cooperation to prevent and combat terrorism,

Reaffirming that terrorism cannot and should not be associated with any religion, nationality, civilization or ethnic group,

Recognizing that the respect for all human rights, the respect for democracy and the respect for the rule of law are interrelated and mutually reinforcing,

Noting the declarations, statements and recommendations of a number of human rights treaty monitoring bodies and special procedures on the question of the compatibility of counter-terrorism measures with human rights obligations,

Recalling Human Rights Council decision 1/102 of 30 June 2006,

1. *Reaffirms* that States must ensure that any measure taken to combat terrorism complies with their obligations under international law, in particular international human rights, refugee and humanitarian law;

2. *Deplores* the suffering caused by terrorism to the victims and their families, and expresses its profound solidarity with them;

3. *Reaffirms* the obligation of States, in accordance with article 4 of the International Covenant on Civil and Political Rights, to respect certain rights as non-derogable in any circumstances, recalls, in regard to all other Covenant rights, that any measures derogating from the provisions of the Covenant must be in accordance with that article in all cases, and underlines the exceptional and temporary nature of any such derogations;

4. *Calls upon* States to raise awareness about the importance of these obligations among national authorities involved in combating terrorism;

5. *Reaffirms* that counter-terrorism measures should be implemented in full consideration of minority rights and must not be discriminatory on the grounds of race, colour, sex, language, religion or social origin;

6. *Urges* States to fully respect non-refoulement obligations under international refugee and human rights law and, at the same time, to review, with full respect for these obligations and other legal safeguards, the validity of a refugee status decision in an individual case if credible and relevant evidence comes to light that indicates that the person in question has committed any criminal acts, including terrorist acts, falling under the exclusion clauses under international refugee law;

7. *Also urges* States, while countering terrorism, to ensure due process guarantees, consistent with all relevant provisions of the Universal Declaration of Human Rights, the International Covenant on Civil and Political Rights and the Geneva Conventions of 1949, in their respective fields of applicability;

8. *Opposes* any form of deprivation of liberty that amounts to placing a detained person outside the protection of the law, and urges States to respect the safeguards concerning the liberty, security and dignity of the person and to treat all prisoners in all places of detention in accordance with international law, including human rights law and international humanitarian law;

9. *Reaffirms* that it is imperative that all States work to uphold and protect the dignity of individuals and their fundamental freedoms, as well as democratic practices and the rule of law, while countering terrorism;

10. *Encourages* States, while countering terrorism, to take into account relevant United Nations resolutions and decisions on human rights, and encourages them to give due consideration to the recommendations of the special procedures and mechanisms and the relevant comments and views of United Nations human rights treaty bodies;

11. *Takes note with interest* of the report of the Secretary-General submitted pursuant to resolution 60/158;

12. *Welcomes* the ongoing dialogue established in the context of the fight against terrorism between the Security Council and its Counter-Terrorism Committee and the relevant bodies for the promotion and protection of human rights, and encourages the Security Council and its Counter-Terrorism Committee to strengthen the links and to continue to develop cooperation with relevant human rights bodies, in particular with the Office of the United Nations High Commissioner for Human Rights, the Special Rapporteur on the promotion and protection of human rights and fundamental freedoms while countering terrorism and other relevant special procedures and mechanisms of the Human Rights Council, giving due regard to the promotion and protection of human rights in the ongoing work pursuant to relevant Security Council resolutions relating to terrorism;

13. *Takes note with appreciation* of the report of the Special Rapporteur submitted pursuant to Commission on Human Rights resolution 2005/80;

14. *Acknowledges with appreciation* the cooperation between the Special Rapporteur and all relevant procedures and mechanisms of the Human Rights Council as well as the United Nations human rights treaty bodies, and urges them to continue their cooperation, in accordance with their mandates, and to coordinate their efforts, where appropriate, in order to promote a consistent approach on this subject;

15. *Requests* all Governments to cooperate fully with the Special Rapporteur in the performance of the tasks and duties mandated, including by reacting promptly to the urgent appeals of the Special Rapporteur and providing the information requested;

16. *Welcomes* the work done by the United Nations High Commissioner for Human Rights to implement the mandate given to her in resolution 60/158, and requests the High Commissioner to continue her efforts in this regard;

17. *Requests* the Secretary-General to submit a report on the implementation of the present resolution to the Human Rights Council and to the General Assembly at its sixty-second session;

18. *Decides* to consider at its sixty-second session the report of the Special Rapporteur on the promotion and protection of human rights and fundamental freedoms while countering terrorism.

Hostage-taking

Human Rights Council action. In a 30 June statement [1/PRST/2], the Council President reaffirmed that acts of hostage-taking, irrespective of who committed them or where they took place, were a crime aimed at the destruction of human rights and were unjustifiable under any circumstances. Condemning such acts, including the related murder of four diplomats at the Russian Federation Embassy in Baghdad, Iraq (see p. 391) and other cases of hostage-taking involving civilians in Iraq, he reaffirmed the need for concerted efforts by all States and the international community to bring the abhorrent practice to an end.

GENERAL ASSEMBLY ACTION

On 19 December [meeting 81], the General Assembly, on the recommendation of the Third Committee [A/61/443/Add. 2 & Corr.1], adopted **resolution 61/172** without vote [agenda item 67 *(b)*].

Hostage-taking

The General Assembly,

Reaffirming the purposes and principles of the Charter of the United Nations,

Recalling the Universal Declaration of Human Rights, which guarantees, inter alia, the right to life, liberty and security of person, freedom from torture and other cruel, inhuman or degrading treatment, freedom of movement and protection from arbitrary detention,

Recalling also the Vienna Declaration and Programme of Action, adopted on 25 June 1993 by the World Conference on Human Rights,

Taking into account the International Convention against the Taking of Hostages, adopted by the General Assembly in its resolution 34/146 of 17 December 1979, which recognizes that everyone has the right to life, liberty and security of person and considers the taking of hostages to be an offence of grave concern to the international community, as well as the Convention on the Prevention and Punishment of Crimes against Internationally Protected Persons, including Diplomatic Agents, adopted by the Assembly in its resolution 3166 (XXVIII) of 14 December 1973,

Bearing in mind the relevant Security Council resolutions condemning all cases of terrorism, including those of hostage-taking, in particular resolution 1440(2002) of 24 October 2002,

Mindful of the fact that hostage-taking constitutes a war crime under the Rome Statute of the International Criminal Court and is also a grave breach of the Geneva Conventions of 12 August 1949 for the protection of victims of war,

Reaffirming its relevant resolutions, including the most recent, resolution 57/220 of 18 December 2002,

Recalling all relevant resolutions of the Commission on Human Rights on the subject, including its most recent, resolution 2005/31 of 19 April 2005 in which it condemned the taking of any person as a hostage, as well as the statement by the President of the Human Rights Council of 30 June 2006 on the same subject,

Concerned that, despite the efforts of the international community, acts of hostage-taking in different forms and manifestations, including, inter alia, those committed by terrorists and armed groups, continue to take place and have even increased in many regions of the world,

Appealing for the humanitarian action of humanitarian organizations, in particular the International Committee of the Red Cross and its delegates, to be respected, in accordance with the Geneva Conventions of 12 August 1949 and the Additional Protocols thereto of 1977,

Recognizing that hostage-taking calls for resolute, firm and concerted efforts on the part of the international community in order, in strict conformity with international human rights standards, to bring such abhorrent practices to an end,

1. *Reaffirms* that hostage-taking, wherever and by whomever committed, is a serious crime aimed at the destruction of human rights and is, under any circumstances, unjustifiable;

2. *Condemns* all acts of hostage-taking, anywhere in the world;

3. *Demands* that all hostages be released immediately and without any preconditions, and expresses its solidarity with the victims of hostage-taking;

4. *Calls upon* States to take all necessary measures, in accordance with relevant provisions of international humanitarian law and international human rights standards, to prevent, combat and punish acts of hostage-taking, including by strengthening international cooperation in this field;

5. *Decides* to remain seized of the matter.

Peace and security

Small arms

Report of Special Rapporteur. In response to a 2005 Subcommission request [YUN 2005, p. 824], the Special Rapporteur on the prevention of human rights violations committed with small arms and light weapons, Barbara Frey (United States), submitted her final report [A/HRC/Sub.1/58/27] containing a comprehensive study on the subject. The study addressed two international legal principles critical for understanding States' obligation to prevent human rights violations committed with small arms, namely, the due diligence responsibilities of States to prevent small arms abuses by private actors, and the significance of the principle of self-defence with regard to States' human rights obligations to prevent small arms-related violence. The due diligence obligation was part of international human rights law, under which States had a primary obligation to maximize human rights protection, especially of the right to life. Minimum effective measures that States should adopt to comply with that obligation should include not only the criminalization of acts of armed violence but the enforcement of a minimum licensing requirement. Although the principle of self-defence also had an important place in international human rights law, it did not provide an independent right to own small arms or reduce the duty of States to use due diligence in regulating civilian arms possession. International law did not support any obligation requiring States to permit access to a gun for self-defence, and the principle of self-defence did not negate the due diligence responsibility of States to keep weapons out of the hands of those most likely to misuse them. The State had particularly acute obligations to protect vulnerable groups, including victims of domestic violence, from abuses with small arms.

To meet their obligations under international human rights law, the Special Rapporteur recommended that States enact and enforce laws and policies to maximize the protection of human rights and minimize violence, including by armed private actors, and ensure public safety in order to reduce the need for people to arm themselves. Other recommended measures included the prohibition of civilian possession of weapons designed for military use and policy measures to decrease the number of weapons in active use and protect those most vulnerable to small arms misuse, including in the context of domestic violence. States should exercise their due diligence responsibilities in the context of self-defence law, particularly the provision that those possessing firearms would act only out of necessity and with proportionality. Above all, the Subcommission needed to clarify the positive responsibilities of States to prevent human rights violations committed with small arms.

In an addendum to the report [A/HRC/Sub.1/58/27/Add.1], the Special Rapporteur outlined draft principles for the prevention of human rights violations committed with small arms.

Subcommission action. On 24 August [res. 2006/22], the Subcommission urged States to adopt laws and policies regarding the manufacture, possession, transfer and use of small arms and light weapons, in line with international human rights and humanitarian law; provide training on the use of firearms by armed forces and law-enforcement personnel; and minimize violence carried out by armed private actors and individuals, including by using due diligence to prevent small arms and light weapons from getting into the hands of those likely to misuse them. To prevent violations with those weapons, the Subcommission requested special procedures, UN human rights monitors in field operations and NGOs to report on human rights violations committed with small arms. It also endorsed the draft principles submitted by the Special Rapporteur (see above), which were annexed to the resolution; encouraged their application by States, intergovernmental organizations and other actors; and transmitted them to the Human Rights Council for consideration and adoption. The Secretariat was requested to transmit the draft principles to UN and regional human rights bodies to assure their dissemination. The Special Rapporteur was asked to update the study on the prevention of human rights violations committed with small arms and light weapons, to be published in all official UN languages as part of the human rights study series.

Economic, social and cultural rights

Right to development

Report of High Commissioner. In response to a 1998 Commission request [YUN 1998, p. 683], the High Commissioner submitted a report [E/CN.4/2006/24 & Corr.1], which summarized OHCHR activities undertaken to implement the right to development, as well as related General Assembly and Commission resolutions. It also provided information on UN system interagency cooperation to implement Commission resolutions.

Pursuant to a 1999 Subcommission request [YUN 1999, p. 652] for the annual transmission of information relating to the realization of the right, the Secretariat, in a June note [E/CN.4/Sub.2/2006/12], drew the Subcommission's attention to the High Commissioner's report.

A further note of the Secretariat [E/CN.4/2006/25], submitted in response to a 2005 Commission request [YUN 2005, p. 825], summarized the views and ideas on the right to development discussed at the Subcommission's 2005 session [ibid., p. 826].

Report of Secretary-General. In accordance with resolution 60/157 [ibid., p. 826], the Secretary-General submitted an August report [A/61/211] supplementing information contained in the High Commissioner's report (see above).

On 19 December, the Assembly took note of the Secretary-General's report (**decision 61/529**).

Working Group activities. The open-ended Working Group on the Right to Development, at its seventh session (Geneva, 9-13 January) [E/CN.4/2006/26], considered options for its future work, the High Commissioner's report (see above) and the 2005 report of its high-level task force [YUN 2005, p. 825]. In its conclusions, the Group recognized the importance of genuine partnerships in realizing the right to development, in line with the Declaration on the Right to Development adopted by the General Assembly in resolution 41/128 [YUN 1986, p. 717]. It noted in that context that the MDG on international cooperation [YUN 2000, p. 51] was a compatible framework. However, the commitments made with respect to the right to development at the highest State level, including the commitment in the Millennium Declaration [ibid., p. 49] to make the right a reality for all, were not always acted upon by policy-makers in relation to development partnerships. It was, therefore, not surprising that the process of monitoring progress had been silent or not sufficiently explicit on human rights and the right to development. The Group also recognized gaps and incoherence between the implementation of the right to development and the practices of development partnerships. The Group agreed that, while adopting agreements and making commitments at such international fora as the World Trade Organization (WTO), States remained accountable for their human rights obligations. Ensuring policy coherence between those obligations and their trade and development engagements was, therefore, a central prerequisite of the right to development. Other conclusions addressed issues relating to development aid, trade, the debt burden of developing countries, technological transfer, the role of the private sector, global governance, migration and regional initiatives.

The Group made recommendations for advancing and realizing the right to development, which included actions to be taken by development practitioners and other entities engaged in monitoring progress towards the MDGs. Notably, it outlined 15 criteria for assessing global partnership from the perspective of the right, to be applied primarily by the parties to a partnership to achieve coherence and accountability. Other recommendations highlighted the role of parliamentary mechanisms, national institutions and civil society; capacity-building in States; entities monitoring the activities of transnational corporations (see p. 896); and the role of UN agencies, funds and programmes, and international financial institutions. In addition, the Group adopted recommendations on its future work.

Human Rights Council action. On 30 June [A/61/53 (res. 1/4)], the Council endorsed the conclusions and recommendations of the Working Group; renewed its mandate for one year; requested the high-level task force on the right to development established by the Group to meet for five working days in 2006, with a view to implementing the Group's recommendations; requested the Working Group to meet in 2007; and asked the Subcommission or its successor mechanism to continue its work on the right, in accordance with relevant resolutions of the General Assembly and the Commission and in compliance with decisions to be taken by the Council.

On 29 November [A/62/53 (dec. 2/116)], the Council deferred to its fourth (2007) session consideration of a draft decision [A/HRC/2/L.15] on the right to development, submitted by Cuba on behalf of the Non-Aligned Movement.

Subcommission action. On 24 August [dec. 2006/108], the Subcommission, reflecting on the 2005 working paper prepared by Florizelle O'Connor (Jamaica) [YUN 2005, p. 826], and taking note of her request for additional time to prepare a further concept paper establishing options for the implementation of the right to development and their feasibility, asked her to submit the paper for consideration at the Subcommission's 2007 session or at the first session of any future expert advice mechanism.

GENERAL ASSEMBLY ACTION

On 19 December [meeting 81], the General Assembly, on the recommendation of the Third Committee [A/61/443/Add.2 & Corr.1], adopted **resolution 61/169** by recorded vote (134-53-0) [agenda item 67 *(b)*].

The right to development

The General Assembly,

Guided by the Charter of the United Nations, which expresses, in particular, the determination to promote social progress and better standards of life in larger freedom, as well as to employ international mechanisms for the promotion of the economic and social advancement of all peoples,

Recalling the Universal Declaration of Human Rights, as well as the International Covenant on Civil and Political Rights and the International Covenant on Economic, Social and Cultural Rights,

Recalling also the outcomes of all the major United Nations conferences and summits in the economic and social fields,

Recalling further that the Declaration on the Right to Development, adopted by the General Assembly in its resolution 41/128 of 4 December 1986, confirmed that the right to development is an inalienable human right and that equality of opportunity for development is a prerogative both of nations and of individuals who make up nations, and that the individual is the central subject and beneficiary of development,

Stressing that the Vienna Declaration and Programme of Action reaffirmed the right to development as a universal and inalienable right and an integral part of fundamental human rights, and the individual as the central subject and beneficiary of development,

Reaffirming the objective of making the right to development a reality for everyone, as set out in the United Nations Millennium Declaration, adopted by the General Assembly on 8 September 2000,

Reaffirming also the universality, indivisibility, interrelatedness, interdependence and mutually reinforcing nature of all civil, cultural, economic, political and social rights, including the right to development,

Expressing concern over the suspension of the trade negotiations of the World Trade Organization, and stressing the need for a successful outcome of the Doha Development Round in key areas such as agriculture, market access for nonagricultural products, trade facilitation, development and services,

Recalling the outcome of the eleventh session of the United Nations Conference on Trade and Development, held in São Paulo, Brazil, from 13 to 18 June 2004, on the theme "Enhancing the coherence between national development strategies and global economic processes towards economic growth and development, particularly of developing countries",

Recalling also all its previous resolutions, Human Rights Council resolution 1/4 of 30 June 2006 and those of the Commission on Human Rights on the right to development, in particular Commission resolution 1998/72 of 22 April 1998, on the urgent need to make further progress towards the realization of the right to development as set out in the Declaration on the Right to Development,

Welcoming the outcome of the seventh session of the Working Group on the Right to Development of the Commission on Human Rights, held in Geneva from 9 to 13 January 2006, as contained in the report of the Working Group,

Recalling the Fourteenth Conference of Heads of State or Government of Non-Aligned Countries, held in Havana on 15 and 16 September 2006, the Ministerial Meeting of the Coordinating Bureau of the Movement of Non-Aligned Countries, held in Putrajaya, Malaysia, on 29 and 30 May 2006, and the Fourteenth Ministerial Conference of the Movement of Non-Aligned Countries, held in Durban, South Africa, from 17 to 19 August 2004,

Reiterating its continuing support for the New Partnership for Africa's Development as a development framework for Africa,

Recognizing that poverty is an affront to human dignity,

Recognizing also that extreme poverty and hunger are a global threat that requires the collective commitment of the international community for its eradication, pursuant to millennium development goal 1, and therefore calling upon the international community, including the Human Rights Council, to contribute towards achieving that goal,

Recognizing further that historical injustices have undeniably contributed to the poverty, underdevelopment, marginalization, social exclusion, economic disparity, instability and insecurity that affect many people in different parts of the world, in particular in developing countries,

Stressing that poverty eradication is one of the critical elements in the promotion and realization of the right to development and that poverty is a multifaceted problem that requires a multifaceted and integrated approach in addressing economic, political, social, environmental and institutional dimensions at all levels, especially in the context of the millennium development goal of halving, by 2015, the proportion of the world's people whose income is less than one dollar a day and the proportion of people who suffer from hunger,

1. *Endorses* the conclusions and recommendations adopted by consensus by the Working Group on the Right to Development of the Commission on Human Rights at its seventh session, and calls for their immediate, full and effective implementation by the Office of the United Nations High Commissioner for Human Rights and other relevant actors;

2. *Recognizes* the relevance of the decisions contained in Human Rights Council resolution 1/4 to renew the mandate of the Working Group and to request the Working Group to meet in the first three months of 2007;

3. *Also recognizes* the relevance of the request of the Human Rights Council to the high-level task force on the right to development to meet before the end of 2006 with a view to implementing the relevant recommendations contained in the report on the seventh session of the Working Group;

4. *Emphasizes* the relevant provisions of General Assembly resolution 60/251 of 15 March 2006 establishing the Human Rights Council, and, in this regard, calls upon the Council:

(*a*) To promote and advance sustainable development and the achievement of the Millennium Development Goals;

(*b*) To agree on a programme that will lead to the elevation of the right to development to the same level, in order that it may be on a par with them, as all other human rights and fundamental freedoms elaborated in the human rights instruments;

5. *Notes with appreciation* that the high-level task force, at its second meeting, examined millennium development goal 8, on developing a global partnership for development, and suggested criteria for its periodic evaluation with the aim of improving the effectiveness of global partnership with regard to the realization of the right to development;

6. *Stresses* the importance of the core principles contained in the conclusions of the Working Group at its third session, congruent with the purpose of international human rights instruments, such as equality, non-discrimination, accountability, participation and international cooperation, as critical to mainstreaming the right to development at the national and international levels, and underlines the importance of the principles of equity and transparency;

7. *Also stresses* that it is important that the high-level task force and the Working Group, in the discharge of their mandates, take into account the need:

(*a*) To promote the democratization of the system of international governance in order to increase the effective participation of developing countries in international decision-making;

(*b*) To also promote effective partnerships such as the New Partnership for Africa's Development and other similar initiatives with the developing countries, particularly the least developed countries, for the purpose of the realization of their right to development, including the achievement of the Millennium Development Goals;

(*c*) To strive for greater acceptance, operationalization and realization of the right to development at the international level, while urging all States to undertake at the national level the necessary policy formulation and to institute the measures required for the implementation of the right to development as a fundamental human right, and also urging all States to expand and deepen mutually beneficial cooperation in ensuring development and eliminating obstacles to development in the context of promoting effective international cooperation for the realization of the right to development, bearing in mind that lasting progress towards the implementation of the right to development requires effective development policies at the national level as well as equitable economic relations and a favourable economic environment at the international level;

(d) To consider ways and means to ensure the operationalization of the right to development as a priority, including through further consideration of the elaboration of a convention on the right to development;

(e) To mainstream the right to development in the policies and operational activities of the United Nations and the specialized agencies, programmes and funds, as well as in policies and strategies of the international financial and multilateral trading system, taking into account in this regard that the core principles of the international economic, commercial and financial spheres, such as equity, non-discrimination, transparency, accountability, participation and international cooperation, including effective partnerships for development, are indispensable in achieving the right to development and preventing discriminatory treatment arising out of political or other non-economic considerations, in addressing the issues of concern to the developing countries;

8. *Recognizes* the relevance of the request to the Subcommission on the Promotion and Protection of Human Rights or its successor expert advice mechanism to pursue its ongoing work on the right to development, in accordance with the relevant provisions of General Assembly and Commission on Human Rights resolutions, and in compliance with decisions to be taken by the Human Rights Council, and requests the Secretary-General to report on progress in this regard to the Assembly at its sixty-second session;

9. *Invites* Member States and all other stakeholders to participate actively in future sessions of the Social Forum, while recognizing the strong support extended to the Forum at its previous three sessions by the Subcommission on the Promotion and Protection of Human Rights;

10. *Reaffirms* the commitment to implement the goals and targets set out in all the outcome documents of the major United Nations conferences and summits and their review processes, in particular those relating to the realization of the right to development, recognizing that the realization of the right to development is critical to achieving the objectives, goals and targets set in those outcome documents;

11. *Also reaffirms* that the realization of the right to development is essential to the implementation of the Vienna Declaration and Programme of Action, which regards all human rights as universal, indivisible, interdependent and interrelated, places the human person at the centre of development and recognizes that, while development facilitates the enjoyment of all human rights, the lack of development may not be invoked to justify the abridgement of internationally recognized human rights;

12. *Stresses* that the primary responsibility for the promotion and protection of all human rights lies with the State, and reaffirms that States have the primary responsibility for their own economic and social development and that the role of national policies and development strategies cannot be overemphasized;

13. *Reaffirms* the primary responsibility of States to create national and international conditions favourable to the realization of the right to development, as well as their commitment to cooperate with each other to that end;

14. *Also reaffirms* the need for an international environment that is conducive to the realization of the right to development;

15. *Stresses* the need to strive for greater acceptance, operationalization and realization of the right to development at the international and national levels, and calls upon States to institute the measures required for the implementation of the right to development as a fundamental human right;

16. *Emphasizes* the critical importance of identifying and analysing obstacles impeding the full realization of the right to development at both the national and the international levels;

17. *Affirms* that, while globalization offers both opportunities and challenges, the process of globalization remains deficient in achieving the objectives of integrating all countries into a globalized world, and stresses the need for policies and measures at the national and global levels to respond to the challenges and opportunities of globalization if this process is to be made fully inclusive and equitable;

18. *Recognizes* that, despite continuous efforts on the part of the international community, the gap between developed and developing countries remains unacceptably wide, that developing countries continue to face difficulties in participating in the globalization process and that many risk being marginalized and effectively excluded from its benefits;

19. *Underlines* the fact that the international community is far from meeting the target set in the United Nations Millennium Declaration of halving the number of people living in poverty by 2015, reaffirms the commitment made to meet that target, and emphasizes the principle of international cooperation, including partnership and commitment, between developed and developing countries towards achieving the goal;

20. *Urges* developed countries that have not yet done so to make concrete efforts towards meeting the targets of 0.7 per cent of their gross national product for official development assistance to developing countries and 0.15 to 0.2 per cent of their gross national product to least developed countries, and encourages developing countries to build on the progress achieved in ensuring that official development assistance is used effectively to help to meet development goals and targets;

21. *Recognizes* the need to address market access for developing countries, including in agriculture, services and non-agricultural products, in particular those of interest to developing countries;

22. *Calls for* the implementation of a desirable pace of meaningful trade liberalization, including in areas under negotiation; implementation of commitments on implementation-related issues and concerns; review

of special and differential-treatment provisions, with a view to strengthening them and making them more precise, effective and operational; avoidance of new forms of protectionism; and capacity-building and technical assistance for developing countries as important issues in making progress towards the effective implementation of the right to development;

23. *Recognizes* the important link between the international economic, commercial and financial spheres and the realization of the right to development, stresses, in this regard, the need for good governance and broadening the base of decision-making at the international level on issues of development concern and the need to fill organizational gaps, as well as strengthen the United Nations system and other multilateral institutions, and also stresses the need to broaden and strengthen the participation of developing countries and countries with economies in transition in international economic decision-making and norm-setting;

24. *Also recognizes* that good governance and the rule of law at the national level assist all States in the promotion and protection of human rights, including the right to development, and agrees on the value of the ongoing efforts being made by States to identify and strengthen good governance practices, including transparent, responsible, accountable and participatory government, that are responsive and appropriate to their needs and aspirations, including in the context of agreed partnership approaches to development, capacity-building and technical assistance;

25. *Further recognizes* the important role and the rights of women and the application of a gender perspective as a cross-cutting issue in the process of realizing the right to development, and notes in particular the positive relationship between women's education and their equal participation in the civil, cultural, economic, political and social activities of the community and the promotion of the right to development;

26. *Stresses* the need for the integration of the rights of children, girls and boys alike, in all policies and programmes, and for ensuring the promotion and protection of those rights, especially in areas relating to health, education and the full development of their capacities;

27. *Welcomes* the Political Declaration on HIV/AIDS adopted at the High-level Meeting of the General Assembly on 2 June 2006, stresses that further and additional measures must be taken at the national and international levels to fight HIV/AIDS and other communicable diseases, taking into account ongoing efforts and programmes, and reiterates the need for international assistance in this regard;

28. *Recognizes* the need for strong partnerships with civil society organizations and the private sector in pursuit of poverty eradication and development, as well as for corporate social responsibility;

29. *Emphasizes* the urgent need for taking concrete and effective measures to prevent, combat and criminalize all forms of corruption at all levels, to prevent, detect and deter in a more effective manner international transfers of illicitly acquired assets and to strengthen international cooperation in asset recovery consistent with the principles of the United Nations Convention against Corruption, particularly chapter V thereof, stresses the importance of a genuine political commitment on the part of all Governments through a firm legal framework, and in this context urges States to sign and ratify as soon as possible, and States parties to implement effectively, the Convention;

30. *Also emphasizes* the need to strengthen further the activities of the Office of the United Nations High Commissioner for Human Rights in the promotion and realization of the right to development, including ensuring effective use of the financial and human resources necessary to fulfil its mandate, and calls upon the Secretary-General to provide the Office of the High Commissioner with the necessary resources;

31. *Reaffirms* the request to the High Commissioner, in mainstreaming the right to development, to undertake effectively activities aimed at strengthening the global partnership for development between Member States, development agencies and the international development, financial and trade institutions, and to reflect those activities in detail in her next report to the Human Rights Council;

32. *Calls upon* the United Nations agencies, funds and programmes, as well as the specialized agencies, to mainstream the right to development in their operational programmes and objectives, and stresses the need for the international financial and multilateral trading systems to mainstream the right to development in their policies and objectives;

33. *Requests* the Secretary-General to bring the present resolution to the attention of Member States, United Nations organs and bodies, specialized agencies, funds and programmes, international development and financial institutions, in particular the Bretton Woods institutions, and non-governmental organizations;

34. *Also requests* the Secretary-General to submit a report to the General Assembly at its sixty-second session and an interim report to the Human Rights Council on the implementation of the present resolution, including efforts undertaken at the national, regional and international levels in the promotion and realization of the right to development, and invites the Chairperson of the Working Group on the Right to Development to present a verbal update to the Assembly at its sixty-second session.

RECORDED VOTE ON RESOLUTION 61/169:

In favour: Afghanistan, Algeria, Angola, Antigua and Barbuda, Argentina, Armenia, Azerbaijan, Bahamas, Bahrain, Bangladesh, Barbados, Belarus, Belize, Benin, Bhutan, Bolivia, Botswana, Brazil, Brunei Darussalam, Burkina Faso, Burundi, Cambodia, Cameroon, Cape Verde, Central African Republic, Chile, China, Colombia, Comoros, Congo, Costa Rica, Côte d'Ivoire, Cuba, Democratic People's Republic of Korea, Democratic Republic of the Congo, Djibouti, Dominica, Dominican Republic, Ecuador, Egypt, El Salvador, Eritrea, Ethiopia, Fiji, Gabon, Gambia, Ghana, Grenada, Guatemala, Guinea, Guinea-Bissau, Guyana, Haiti, Honduras, India, Indonesia, Iran, Iraq, Jamaica, Jordan, Kazakhstan, Kenya, Kuwait, Kyrgyzstan, Lao People's Democratic Republic, Lebanon, Lesotho, Liberia, Libyan

Arab Jamahiriya, Madagascar, Malawi, Malaysia, Maldives, Mali, Mauritania, Mauritius, Mexico, Micronesia, Mongolia, Morocco, Mozambique, Myanmar, Namibia, Nauru, Nepal, Nicaragua, Niger, Nigeria, Oman, Pakistan, Panama, Papua New Guinea, Paraguay, Peru, Philippines, Qatar, Russian Federation, Rwanda, Saint Lucia, Saint Vincent and the Grenadines, Samoa, Sao Tome and Principe, Saudi Arabia, Senegal, Sierra Leone, Singapore, Solomon Islands, Somalia, South Africa, Sri Lanka, Sudan, Suriname, Swaziland, Syrian Arab Republic, Tajikistan, Thailand, Timor-Leste, Togo, Tonga, Trinidad and Tobago, Tunisia, Turkmenistan, Tuvalu, Uganda, United Arab Emirates, United Republic of Tanzania, Uruguay, Uzbekistan, Vanuatu, Venezuela, Viet Nam, Yemen, Zambia, Zimbabwe.

Against: Albania, Andorra, Australia, Austria, Belgium, Bosnia and Herzegovina, Bulgaria, Canada, Croatia, Cyprus, Czech Republic, Denmark, Estonia, Finland, France, Georgia, Germany, Greece, Hungary, Iceland, Ireland, Israel, Italy, Japan, Latvia, Liechtenstein, Lithuania, Luxembourg, Malta, Marshall Islands, Moldova, Monaco, Montenegro, Netherlands, New Zealand, Norway, Palau, Poland, Portugal, Republic of Korea, Romania, San Marino, Serbia, Slovakia, Slovenia, Spain, Sweden, Switzerland, The former Yugoslav Republic of Macedonia, Turkey, Ukraine, United Kingdom, United States.

Human rights and international solidarity

Report of independent expert. By a 1 February note [E/CN.4/2006/96], the High Commissioner transmitted the report of the independent expert on human rights and international solidarity, Rudi Muhammad Rizki (Indonesia), pursuant to a 2005 Commission request [YUN 2005, p. 829]. The report reviewed the expert's approach to his mandate, including the objectives and methodology, and preliminary considerations for refining and developing subsequent reports. The expert would focus on three main areas: international cooperation, global responses to natural disaster and third-generation or collective rights. The expert acknowledged differences of opinion between some Member States with respect to his mandate and the need to avoid duplication of work within the UN system. He highlighted the need to ensure consistency in approaching issues concerning international relations and cooperation, provide a constructive and unifying contribution to the debate on the subject of his mandate and focus on related topics deserving more attention. He stressed that an effective discharge of his mandate would only be possible with the full cooperation of Member States, international organizations and NGOs.

Democratic and equitable international order

Human Rights Council action. On 29 November [A/62/53 (dec. 2/116)], the Council deferred to its fourth (2007) session consideration of a draft decision [A/HRC/2/L.18] on the enhancement of international cooperation in the field of human rights, submitted by Cuba on behalf of the Non-Aligned Movement.

GENERAL ASSEMBLY ACTION

On 19 December [meeting 81], the General Assembly, on the recommendation of the Third Committee [A/61/443/Add.2 & Corr.1], adopted **resolution 61/160** by recorded vote (124-56-4) [agenda item 67 *(b)*].

Promotion of a democratic and equitable international order

The General Assembly,

Recalling its previous resolutions on the promotion of a democratic and equitable international order, including resolution 59/193 of 20 December 2004, and taking note of Commission on Human Rights resolution 2005/57 of 20 April 2005,

Reaffirming the commitment of all States to fulfil their obligations to promote universal respect for, and observance and protection of, all human rights and fundamental freedoms for all, in accordance with the Charter of the United Nations, other instruments relating to human rights and international law,

Affirming that the enhancement of international cooperation for the promotion and protection of all human rights should continue to be carried out in full conformity with the purposes and principles of the Charter and international law as set forth in Articles 1 and 2 of the Charter and, inter alia, with full respect for sovereignty, territorial integrity, political independence, the non-use of force or the threat of force in international relations and non-intervention in matters that are essentially within the domestic jurisdiction of any State,

Recalling the Preamble to the Charter, in particular the determination to reaffirm faith in fundamental human rights, in the dignity and worth of the human person and in the equal rights of men and women and of nations large and small,

Reaffirming that everyone is entitled to a social and international order in which the rights and freedoms set forth in the Universal Declaration of Human Rights can be fully realized,

Reaffirming also the determination expressed in the Preamble to the Charter to save succeeding generations from the scourge of war, to establish conditions under which justice and respect for the obligations arising from treaties and other sources of international law can be maintained, to promote social progress and better standards of life in larger freedom, to practice tolerance and good-neighbourliness, and to employ international machinery for the promotion of the economic and social advancement of all peoples,

Considering the major changes taking place on the international scene and the aspirations of all peoples for an international order based on the principles enshrined in the Charter, including promoting and encouraging respect for human rights and fundamental freedoms for all and respect for the principle of equal rights and self-determination of peoples, peace, democracy, justice, equality, the rule of law, pluralism, development, better standards of living and solidarity,

Considering also that the Universal Declaration of Human Rights proclaims that all human beings are born free and equal in dignity and rights and that everyone is entitled to all the rights and freedoms set out therein, without distinction of any kind, such as race, colour, sex, language, religion, political or other opinion, national or social origin, property, birth or other status,

Reaffirming that democracy, development and respect for human rights and fundamental freedoms are interdependent and mutually reinforcing, and that democracy is based on the freely expressed will of the people to determine their own political, economic, social and cultural systems and their full participation in all aspects of their lives,

Emphasizing that democracy is not only a political concept but that it also has economic and social dimensions,

Recognizing that democracy, respect for all human rights, including the right to development, transparent and accountable governance and administration in all sectors of society, and effective participation by civil society are an essential part of the necessary foundations for the realization of social and people-centred sustainable development,

Noting with concern that racism, racial discrimination, xenophobia and related intolerance may be aggravated by, inter alia, inequitable distribution of wealth, marginalization and social exclusion,

Underlining the fact that it is imperative for the international community to ensure that globalization becomes a positive force for all the world's people, and that only through broad and sustained efforts, based on common humanity in all its diversity, can globalization be made fully inclusive and equitable,

Stressing that efforts to make globalization fully inclusive and equitable must include policies and measures, at the global level, that correspond to the needs of developing countries and countries with economies in transition and are formulated and implemented with their effective participation,

Having listened to the peoples of the world, and recognizing their aspirations to justice, to equality of opportunity for all, to the enjoyment of their human rights, including the right to development, to live in peace and freedom and to equal participation without discrimination in economic, social, cultural, civil and political life,

Resolved to take all measures within its power to secure a democratic and equitable international order,

1. *Affirms* that everyone is entitled to a democratic and equitable international order;

2. *Also affirms* that a democratic and equitable international order fosters the full realization of all human rights for all;

3. *Calls upon* all Member States to fulfil their commitment expressed in Durban, South Africa, during the World Conference against Racism, Racial Discrimination, Xenophobia and Related Intolerance to maximize the benefits of globalization through, inter alia, the strengthening and enhancement of international cooperation to increase equality of opportunities for trade, economic growth and sustainable development, global communications through the use of new technologies, and increased intercultural exchange through the preservation and promotion of cultural diversity, and reiterates that only through broad and sustained efforts to create a shared future based upon our common humanity and all its diversity can globalization be made fully inclusive and equitable;

4. *Affirms* that a democratic and equitable international order requires, inter alia, the realization of the following:

(a) The right of all peoples to self-determination, by virtue of which they can freely determine their political status and freely pursue their economic, social and cultural development;

(b) The right of peoples and nations to permanent sovereignty over their natural wealth and resources;

(c) The right of every human person and all peoples to development;

(d) The right of all peoples to peace;

(e) The right to an international economic order based on equal participation in the decision-making process, interdependence, mutual interest, solidarity and cooperation among all States;

(f) Solidarity, as a fundamental value, by virtue of which global challenges must be managed in a way that distributes costs and burdens fairly, in accordance with basic principles of equity and social justice, and ensures that those who suffer or benefit the least receive help from those who benefit the most;

(g) The promotion and consolidation of transparent, democratic, just and accountable international institutions in all areas of cooperation, in particular through the implementation of the principles of full and equal participation in their respective decision-making mechanisms;

(h) The right to equitable participation of all, without any discrimination, in domestic and global decision-making;

(i) The principle of equitable regional and gender-balanced representation in the composition of the staff of the United Nations system;

(j) The promotion of a free, just, effective and balanced international information and communications order, based on international cooperation for the establishment of a new equilibrium and greater reciprocity in the international flow of information, in particular correcting the inequalities in the flow of information to and from developing countries;

(k) Respect for cultural diversity and the cultural rights of all, since this enhances cultural pluralism, contributes to a wider exchange of knowledge and understanding of cultural backgrounds, advances the application and enjoyment of universally accepted human rights across the world and fosters stable, friendly relations among peoples and nations worldwide;

(l) The right of every person and all peoples to a healthy environment;

(m) The promotion of equitable access to benefits from the international distribution of wealth through enhanced international cooperation, in particular in economic, commercial and financial international relations;

(n) The enjoyment by everyone of ownership of the common heritage of mankind;

(o) The shared responsibility of the nations of the world for managing worldwide economic and social development as well as threats to international peace and security that should be exercised multilaterally;

5. *Stresses* the importance of preserving the rich and diverse nature of the international community of nations and peoples, as well as respect for national and regional particularities and various historical, cultural and religious backgrounds in the enhancement of international cooperation in the field of human rights;

6. *Also stresses* that all human rights are universal, indivisible, interdependent and interrelated and that the international community must treat human rights globally in a fair and equal manner, on the same footing and with the same emphasis, and reaffirms that, while the significance of national and regional particularities and various historical, cultural and religious backgrounds must be borne in mind, it is the duty of States, regardless of their political, economic and cultural systems, to promote and protect all human rights and fundamental freedoms;

7. *Urges* all actors on the international scene to build an international order based on inclusion, justice, equality and equity, human dignity, mutual understanding and promotion of and respect for cultural diversity and universal human rights, and to reject all doctrines of exclusion based on racism, racial discrimination, xenophobia and related intolerance;

8. *Reaffirms* that all States should promote the establishment, maintenance and strengthening of international peace and security and, to that end, should do their utmost to achieve general and complete disarmament under effective international control, as well as to ensure that the resources released by effective disarmament measures are used for comprehensive development, in particular that of the developing countries;

9. *Recalls* the proclamation by the General Assembly of its determination to work urgently for the establishment of an international economic order based on equity, sovereign equality, interdependence, common interest and cooperation among all States, irrespective of their economic and social systems, which shall correct inequalities and redress existing injustices, make it possible to eliminate the widening gap between the developed and the developing countries, and ensure steadily accelerating economic and social development and peace and justice for present and future generations;

10. *Reaffirms* that the international community should devise ways and means to remove the current obstacles and meet the challenges to the full realization of all human rights and to prevent the continuation of human rights violations resulting therefrom throughout the world;

11. *Urges* States to continue their efforts, through enhanced international cooperation, towards the promotion of a democratic and equitable international order;

12. *Requests* the Human Rights Council, the human rights treaty bodies, the Office of the United Nations High Commissioner for Human Rights and the special mechanisms extended by the Human Rights Council and the Subcommission on the Promotion and Protection of Human Rights or its successor expert advice mechanism to pay due attention, within their respective mandates, to the present resolution and to make contributions towards its implementation;

13. *Calls upon* the Office of the High Commissioner to build upon the issue of the promotion of a democratic and equitable international order;

14. *Requests* the Secretary-General to bring the present resolution to the attention of Member States, United Nations organs, bodies and components, intergovernmental organizations, in particular the Bretton Woods institutions, and non-governmental organizations, and to disseminate it on the widest possible basis;

15. *Decides* to continue consideration of the matter at its sixty-third session under the item entitled "Promotion and protection of human rights".

RECORDED VOTE ON RESOLUTION 61/160:

In favour: Algeria, Angola, Antigua and Barbuda, Azerbaijan, Bahamas, Bahrain, Bangladesh, Barbados, Belarus, Belize, Benin, Bhutan, Bolivia, Botswana, Brazil, Brunei Darussalam, Burkina Faso, Burundi, Cambodia, Cameroon, Cape Verde, Central African Republic, China, Colombia, Comoros, Congo, Costa Rica, Côte d'Ivoire, Cuba, Democratic People's Republic of Korea, Democratic Republic of the Congo, Djibouti, Dominica, Dominican Republic, Ecuador, Egypt, El Salvador, Eritrea, Ethiopia, Fiji, Gabon, Gambia, Ghana, Grenada, Guatemala, Guinea, Guinea-Bissau, Guyana, Haiti, Honduras, India, Indonesia, Iran, Iraq, Jamaica, Jordan, Kazakhstan, Kenya, Kuwait, Kyrgyzstan, Lao People's Democratic Republic, Lebanon, Lesotho, Liberia, Libyan Arab Jamahiriya, Madagascar, Malawi, Malaysia, Maldives, Mali, Mauritania, Mauritius, Mongolia, Morocco, Mozambique, Myanmar, Namibia, Nepal, Nicaragua, Niger, Nigeria, Oman, Pakistan, Panama, Papua New Guinea, Paraguay, Philippines, Qatar, Russian Federation, Rwanda, Saint Lucia, Saint Vincent and the Grenadines, Sao Tome and Principe, Saudi Arabia, Senegal, Sierra Leone, Singapore, Solomon Islands, Somalia, South Africa, Sri Lanka, Sudan, Suriname, Swaziland, Syrian Arab Republic, Tajikistan, Thailand, Timor-Leste, Togo, Trinidad and Tobago, Tunisia, Turkmenistan, Tuvalu, Uganda, United Arab Emirates, United Republic of Tanzania, Uruguay, Uzbekistan, Vanuatu, Venezuela, Viet Nam, Yemen, Zambia, Zimbabwe.

Against: Albania, Andorra, Australia, Austria, Belgium, Bosnia and Herzegovina, Bulgaria, Canada, Chile, Croatia, Cyprus, Czech Republic, Denmark, Estonia, Finland, France, Georgia, Germany, Greece, Hungary, Iceland, Ireland, Israel, Italy, Japan, Latvia, Liechtenstein, Lithuania, Luxembourg, Malta, Marshall Islands, Micronesia, Moldova, Monaco, Montenegro, Netherlands, New Zealand, Norway, Palau, Poland, Portugal, Republic of Korea, Romania, Samoa, San Marino, Serbia, Slovakia, Slovenia, Spain, Sweden, Switzerland, The former Yugoslav Republic of Macedonia, Turkey, Ukraine, United Kingdom, United States.

Abstaining: Argentina, Armenia, Mexico, Peru.

Globalization

Report of Secretary-General. In response to General Assembly resolution 60/152 [YUN 2005, p. 830], the Secretary-General submitted an August report [A/61/281] on the views of Member States and UN agencies on the issue of globalization and its impact on the full enjoyment of all human rights, which summarized replies received from two Governments and one UN body.

Human Rights Council action. On 29 November [A/62/53 (dec. 2/116)], the Council deferred to its fourth (2007) session consideration of a draft decision [A/HRC/2/L.23] on globalization and its impact on the full enjoyment of all human rights submitted by China.

GENERAL ASSEMBLY ACTION

On 19 December [meeting 81], the General Assembly, on the recommendation of the Third Committee [A/61/443/Add.2 & Corr.1], adopted **resolution 61/156** by recorded vote (130-54-3) [agenda item 67 *(b)*].

Globalization and its impact on the full enjoyment of all human rights

The General Assembly,

Guided by the purposes and principles of the Charter of the United Nations, and expressing, in particular, the need to achieve international cooperation in promoting and encouraging respect for human rights and fundamental freedoms for all without distinction,

Recalling the Universal Declaration of Human Rights, as well as the Vienna Declaration and Programme of Action adopted by the World Conference on Human Rights on 25 June 1993,

Recalling also the International Covenant on Civil and Political Rights and the International Covenant on Economic, Social and Cultural Rights,

Recalling further the Declaration on the Right to Development adopted by the General Assembly in its resolution 41/128 of 4 December 1986,

Recalling the United Nations Millennium Declaration and the outcome documents of the twenty-third and twenty-fourth special sessions of the General Assembly, held in New York from 5 to 10 June 2000 and in Geneva from 26 June to 1 July 2000, respectively,

Recalling also its resolution 60/152 of 16 December 2005,

Recalling further Commission on Human Rights resolution 2005/17 of 14 April 2005 on globalization and its impact on the full enjoyment of all human rights,

Recognizing that all human rights are universal, indivisible, interdependent and interrelated and that the international community must treat human rights globally in a fair and equal manner, on the same footing and with the same emphasis,

Realizing that globalization affects all countries differently and makes them more exposed to external developments, positive as well as negative, inter alia, in the field of human rights,

Realizing also that globalization is not merely an economic process, but that it also has social, political, environmental, cultural and legal dimensions, which have an impact on the full enjoyment of all human rights,

Reaffirming the commitment contained in paragraphs 19 and 47 of the 2005 World Summit Outcome to promote fair globalization and the development of the productive sectors in developing countries to enable them to participate more effectively in and benefit from the process of globalization,

Realizing the need to undertake a thorough, independent and comprehensive assessment of the social, environmental and cultural impact of globalization on societies,

Recognizing in each culture a dignity and value that deserve recognition, respect and preservation, convinced that, in their rich variety and diversity and in the reciprocal influences that they exert on one another, all cultures form part of the common heritage belonging to all humankind, and aware that the risk of a global monoculture poses more of a threat if the developing world remains poor and marginalized,

Recognizing also that multilateral mechanisms have a unique role to play in meeting the challenges and opportunities presented by globalization,

Emphasizing the global character of the migratory phenomenon, the importance of international, regional and bilateral cooperation and the need to protect the human rights of migrants, particularly at a time in which migration flows have increased in the globalized economy,

Expressing concern at the negative impact of international financial turbulence on social and economic development and on the full enjoyment of all human rights,

Recognizing that globalization should be guided by the fundamental principles that underpin the corpus of human rights, such as equity, participation, accountability, non-discrimination at both the national and the international levels, respect for diversity, tolerance and international cooperation and solidarity,

Emphasizing that the existence of widespread extreme poverty inhibits the full and effective enjoyment of human rights; its immediate alleviation and eventual elimination must remain a high priority for the international community,

Strongly reiterating the determination to ensure the timely and full realization of the development goals and objectives agreed at the major United Nations conferences and summits, including those agreed at the Millennium Summit that are described as the Millennium Development Goals, which have helped to galvanize efforts towards poverty eradication,

Deeply concerned at the inadequacy of measures to narrow the widening gap between the developed and the developing countries, and within countries, which has contributed, inter alia, to deepening poverty and has adversely affected the full enjoyment of all human rights, in particular in developing countries,

Noting that human beings strive for a world that is respectful of human rights and cultural diversity and that, in this regard, they work to ensure that all activities, including those affected by globalization, are consistent with those aims,

1. *Recognizes* that, while globalization, by its impact on, inter alia, the role of the State, may affect human rights, the promotion and protection of all human rights is first and foremost the responsibility of the State;

2. *Emphasizes* that development should be at the centre of the international economic agenda and that coherence between national development strategies and international obligations and commitments is imperative for an enabling environment for development and an inclusive and equitable globalization;

3. *Reaffirms* that narrowing the gap between rich and poor, both within and between countries, is an explicit goal at the national and international levels, as part of the effort to create an enabling environment for the full enjoyment of all human rights;

4. *Reaffirms also* the commitment to create an environment at both the national and the global levels that is conducive to development and to the elimination of poverty through, inter alia, good governance within each country and at the international level, transparency in the financial, monetary and trading systems and commitment to an open, equitable, rule-based, predictable and non-discriminatory multilateral trading and financial system;

5. *Recognizes* that, while globalization offers great opportunities, the fact that its benefits are very unevenly shared and its costs unevenly distributed represents an aspect of the process that affects the full enjoyment of all human rights, in particular in developing countries;

6. *Welcomes* the report of the United Nations High Commissioner for Human Rights on globalization and its impact on the full enjoyment of human rights, which focuses on the liberalization of agricultural trade and its impact on the realization of the right to development, including the right to food, and takes note of the conclusions and recommendations contained therein;

7. *Calls upon* Member States, relevant agencies of the United Nations system, intergovernmental organizations and civil society to promote equitable and environmentally sustainable economic growth for managing globalization so that poverty is systematically reduced and the international development targets are achieved;

8. *Recognizes* that only through broad and sustained efforts, including policies and measures at the global level to create a shared future based upon our common humanity in all its diversity, can globalization be made fully inclusive and equitable and have a human face, thus contributing to the full enjoyment of all human rights;

9. *Underlines* the urgent need to establish an equitable, transparent and democratic international system to strengthen and broaden the participation of developing countries in international economic decision-making and norm-setting;

10. *Affirms* that globalization is a complex process of structural transformation, with numerous interdisciplinary aspects, which has an impact on the enjoyment of civil, political, economic, social and cultural rights, including the right to development;

11. *Affirms also* that the international community should strive to respond to the challenges and opportunities posed by globalization in a manner that ensures respect for the cultural diversity of all;

12. *Underlines*, therefore, the need to continue to analyse the consequences of globalization for the full enjoyment of all human rights;

13. *Takes note* of the report of the Secretary-General, and requests him to seek further the views of Member States and relevant agencies of the United Nations system and to submit a substantive report on the subject to the General Assembly at its sixty-second session.

RECORDED VOTE ON RESOLUTION 61/156:

In favour: Afghanistan, Algeria, Angola, Antigua and Barbuda, Argentina, Armenia, Azerbaijan, Bahamas, Bahrain, Bangladesh, Barbados, Belarus, Belize, Benin, Bhutan, Bolivia, Botswana, Brunei Darussalam, Burkina Faso, Burundi, Cambodia, Cameroon, Cape Verde, Central African Republic, China, Colombia, Comoros, Congo, Costa Rica, Côte d'Ivoire, Cuba, Democratic People's Republic of Korea, Democratic Republic of the Congo, Djibouti, Dominica, Dominican Republic, Ecuador, Egypt, El Salvador, Eritrea, Ethiopia, Fiji, Gabon, Gambia, Ghana, Grenada, Guatemala, Guinea, Guinea-Bissau, Guyana, Haiti, Honduras, India, Indonesia, Iran, Iraq, Jamaica, Jordan, Kazakhstan, Kenya, Kuwait, Kyrgyzstan, Lao People's Democratic Republic, Lebanon, Lesotho, Liberia, Libyan Arab Jamahiriya, Madagascar, Malawi, Malaysia, Maldives, Mali, Mauritania, Mauritius, Mexico, Mongolia, Morocco, Mozambique, Myanmar, Namibia, Nauru, Nepal, Nicaragua, Niger, Nigeria, Oman, Pakistan, Panama, Papua New Guinea, Paraguay, Peru, Philippines, Qatar, Russian Federation, Rwanda, Saint Lucia, Saint Vincent and the Grenadines, Samoa, Sao Tome and Principe, Saudi Arabia, Senegal, Sierra Leone, Solomon Islands, Somalia, South Africa, Sri Lanka, Sudan, Suriname, Swaziland, Syrian Arab Republic, Tajikistan, Thailand, Timor-Leste, Togo, Tonga, Trinidad and Tobago, Tunisia, Turkmenistan, Tuvalu, Uganda, United Arab Emirates, United Republic of Tanzania, Uruguay, Uzbekistan, Vanuatu, Venezuela, Viet Nam, Yemen, Zambia, Zimbabwe.

Against: Albania, Andorra, Australia, Austria, Belgium, Bosnia and Herzegovina, Bulgaria, Canada, Croatia, Cyprus, Czech Republic, Denmark, Estonia, Finland, France, Georgia, Germany, Greece, Hungary, Iceland, Ireland, Israel, Italy, Japan, Latvia, Liechtenstein, Lithuania, Luxembourg, Malta, Marshall Islands, Micronesia, Moldova, Monaco, Montenegro, Netherlands, New Zealand, Norway, Palau, Poland, Portugal, Republic of Korea, Romania, San Marino, Serbia, Slovakia, Slovenia, Spain, Sweden, Switzerland, The former Yugoslav Republic of Macedonia, Turkey, Ukraine, United Kingdom, United States.

Abstaining: Brazil, Chile, Singapore.

Economic reform policies

Reports of independent expert. In a March report [E/CN.4/2006/46], the independent expert on the effects of economic reform policies and foreign debt,

Bernards Mudho (Kenya), reviewed developments regarding the Group of Eight (G-8) major industrialized countries' relief initiative and its implications for the International Monetary Fund (IMF) and the World Bank debt sustainability framework. While welcoming the G-8 political commitment towards a 100 per cent debt cancellation of multilateral debts owed to those two financial institutions by some heavily indebted poor countries (HIPCs) as a step towards broader and deeper debt relief, the expert noted that the international community needed to ensure that such debt relief initiatives represented additional resources. More measures should be considered to secure long-term sustainability through grant-based financing, full cancellation of other official debts of HIPCs and significantly more debt relief for low- and middle-income non-HIPC developing countries. In addition, the expert highlighted the need for new mechanisms to comprehensively address the debt problems of those countries, and to integrate human rights considerations into the macroeconomic approach to debt sustainability analysis. Towards that end, the expert suggested that an independent peer review mechanism be instituted to determine a country's debt sustainability situation and also serve as an accountability mechanism, with the participation of independent national human rights institutions. Pursuant to a 2005 Commission request [YUN 2005, p. 832], the expert also reflected on the proposed draft general guidelines to be followed by States and financial institutions in decision-making on, and execution of, debt repayments and structural reform programmes. He determined that more time was needed to elaborate the guidelines and recommended that the Commission extend by one year the time-frame for doing so, convene expert consultations and urge States, international organizations, civil society and other interested parties to submit their views on elements to be considered in drafting the guidelines.

The expert also submitted the report on his visit to Mozambique [E/CN.4/2006/46/Add.1], where he examined, among other things, the effects of the foreign debt burden on the capacity of the Government to adopt policies and programmes for the enjoyment of economic, social and cultural rights.

By a September note [A/61/464], the Secretary-General transmitted to the General Assembly a report of the independent expert, which reviewed, among other issues, developments relating to the Multilateral Debt Relief Initiative (MDRI) proposed by the G-8 in 2005 [YUN 2005, p. 1057] and which foresaw a 100 per cent debt relief by IMF, the World Bank and the African Development Fund (ADF) for the world's most indebted poor countries, in order to help them achieve the MDGs. Although the Initiative had an overall volume of $50 billion and envisioned providing eligible countries with annual average savings on debt service of about $1.25 billion over a 40-year period, it was unlikely to resolve all the foreign debt problems of poor countries. Furthermore, its impact on the achievement of the MDGs and associated human rights would be long-term and difficult to measure. The expert recommended that follow-up initiatives to MDRI be developed, including further debt relief programmes by other multilateral institutions and initiatives towards a permanent solution to the problems of bilateral and commercial debts. In addition, further steps should be taken towards a more favourable trade system, since the MDG regarding the development of a global partnership for development called for an open trading and financial system that was rule-based and for a comprehensive solution to developing countries' debt problems. The expert invited participating multilateral institutions in MDRI to consider improvements in the eligibility and implementation criteria, particularly a more accurate weighing of MDG criteria for the allocation of related additional funds; the inclusion of non-HIPC countries into the International Development Association's (IDA) and the African Development Fund's parts of the debt relief, as well as a revision of IDA cut-off date for eligible debt.

On 19 December, the Assembly took note of the Secretary-General's note (**decision 61/529**).

Subcommission action. On 24 August [dec. 2006/111], the Subcommission requested the Human Rights Council to authorize it to appoint El-Hadji Guissé (Senegal) as Special Rapporteur on the impact of debt on the enjoyment and exercise of human rights, and requested him to submit his preliminary report to the Subcommission's next session or to the first session of a future expert advice mechanism.

Human Rights Council action. On 27 November [A/62/53 (dec. 2/109)], the Council decided, by a recorded vote of 33 to 13, with 1 abstention, to request the High Commissioner to convene an expert consultation on the drafting of general guidelines to be followed by States and financial institutions in decision-making on, and execution of, debt repayments and structural reform programmes, including those arising from foreign debt relief.

Social Forum

Note by OHCHR. In July [A/HRC/Sub.1/58/SF/2], OHCHR presented the organizational details of the 2006 Social Forum, held in August (see below), in accordance with Economic and Social Council decision 2003/264 [YUN 2003, p. 760] and Human Rights Council decision 1/102 (see p. 759).

Social Forum session. At its fourth session (Geneva, 3-4 August) [A/HRC/Sub.1/58/15], the Social Forum held panel discussions on the feminization of poverty: causes, effects and solutions; women, employment and empowerment through participation; the draft guiding principles on extreme poverty and human rights: the right of the poor; vision and recommendations for expert advice to the Human Rights Council: and the future of the Social Forum. It had before it a working paper on the fight against poverty and the right to participation: the role of women [A/HRC/Sub.1/58/SF/3], submitted by Chin-sung Chung (Republic of Korea), pursuant to a 2005 Subcommission request [YUN 2005, p. 833], and the final report of the ad hoc expert group on the need to develop guiding principles on the implementation of existing human rights norms and standards in the context of the fight against extreme poverty [A/HRC/Sub.1/58/16].

In its conclusions, the Forum acknowledged the increasing feminization of poverty and that women, who were the main actors in combating the problem, were far more vulnerable to poverty than men, owing to the lack of access to assets and opportunities, especially in rural and mountain areas. The Forum determined that gender equality in the social, political and international spheres was necessary to eradicate the feminization of poverty, and addressing the root causes of the problem and the growing gap between the rich and the poor were prerequisites. Similarly, women's empowerment was crucial for eradicating poverty, and could be promoted through employment. As such, education and training were essential for expanding women's opportunities to participate in economic activities and in promoting their social inclusion. Their access to information was a precondition in that regard.

The Forum recommended that States increase women's access to information, establish mechanisms to ensure that gender equality was respected, including in employment, and remove structural barriers and prevent human rights violations impeding women's empowerment and participation. On the question of the Forum's contribution to the Subcommission's report and recommendations on a future expert advice mechanism to the Council, pursuant to Council decision 1/102 (see p. 759), participants agreed that the Forum was a unique and open body bringing fresh perspectives and ideas to the UN human rights system, and should therefore be preserved under the auspices of the Council.

Subcommission action. On 24 August [res. 2006/8], the Subcommission called on the General Assembly to take into account the Forum's conclusions and recommendations within the framework of the review of the first United Nations Decade for the Eradication of Poverty (see p. 993) and recommended that the Human Rights Council preserve the Forum as a unique space for interactive dialogue between the UN human rights system and stakeholders, especially the poor and most vulnerable people. Reaffirming its decision that the Forum meet every year, the Subcommission requested that its next meeting, to be held in 2007 in Geneva, should focus on questions relating to the eradication of poverty in the context of human rights, capturing best practices in the fight against poverty, and discussing the relevant guidelines and reports prepared by the Subcommission, its successor, or other human rights bodies, with civil society. It further recommended that the Council extend the Forum's meeting to five days, to enable it to devote two days of thematic discussions on poverty and human rights and on the work of international human rights mechanisms in the field of economic, social and cultural rights and the right to development in relation to poverty, and one day to an interactive debate with mandate-holders on related issues to formulate conclusions and recommendations. OHCHR was asked to ensure consultation and the broadest possible participation in the Forum, including by establishing partnerships with NGOs, the private sector and international organizations. The Forum was invited to submit to the Council's future expert advice mechanism a separate report containing a comprehensive and detailed summary of its discussions, including recommendations and draft resolutions. The Subcommission also requested the Secretary-General to disseminate information about the Forum.

Transnational corporations

Report of Special Representative. In response to a 2005 Commission request [YUN 2005, p. 834], the Special Representative of the Secretary-General on the issue of human rights and transnational corporations (TNCs) and other business enterprises, John Ruggie (United States), submitted an interim report [E/CN.4/2006/97] that framed the context of his mandate, outlined his strategic approach and summarized his programme of activities. In terms of context, his analysis would be framed by the institutional features of globalization; the overall patterns of alleged corporate abuses and their correlates; and the characteristic strengths and weaknesses of existing responses to deal with human rights challenges. On the question of approach, the Representative would examine the norms on the responsibilities of TNCs and other business enterprises with regard to human rights through principled pragmatism, in terms of an unflinching commitment to the principle of strengthening the promotion and protection of human rights as it related to business, coupled with a pragmatic attachment to what worked best in creating change where it mattered most—in the daily lives of people.

Subcommission action. On 7 August [dec. 2006/104], the Subcommission established a five-member sessional working group on the effects of the working methods and activities of TNCs on the enjoyment of human rights.

Working group activities. The working group on the working methods and activities of TNCs, at its eighth session (Geneva, 8 and 10 August) [A/HRC/Sub.1/58/11], continued its work on the draft norms on the responsibilities of TNCs and other business enterprises, towards the elaboration of a binding instrument. The group's discussion focused on ensuring the implementation of those norms. The group had before it working papers on bilateral and multilateral economic agreements and their impact on the human rights of the beneficiaries [A/HRC/Sub.1/58/CRP.8], prepared by Chin-sung Chung (Republic of Korea) and Florizelle O'Connor (Jamaica), and on the role of States in the guarantee of human rights with reference to the activities of TNCs and other business entities [A/HRC/Sub.1/58/CRP.12], submitted by Gáspár Bíró (Hungary), both pursuant to a 2005 Subcommission request [YUN 2005, p. 835]. The group reviewed activities relating to the responsibilities of businesses with regard to human rights and considered possible situations where those businesses might facilitate or generate violations in different societies and identified appropriate responses. It also considered how to protect individuals or groups from harm caused by business activities and the implementation of Council decision 1/102.

Subcommission action. On 24 August [res. 2006/7], the Subcommission recommended that the Council adopt the draft norms and consider establishing a monitoring body, and that the issue of the working methods and activities of TNCs remain on its agenda and on that of a future expert advice mechanism. The Subcommission further recommended that UN system activities relating to multinational enterprises be coordinated by that mechanism to ensure greater consistency.

Coercive economic measures

Report of Secretary-General. In accordance with General Assembly resolution 60/155 [YUN 2005, p. 835], the Secretary-General submitted an August report [A/61/287], which summarized information received from three States (Cuba, Libyan Arab Jamahiriya, Trinidad and Tobago) on the implications and negative effects of unilateral coercive measures on their populations.

On 19 December, the Assembly took note of the Secretary-General's report (**decision 61/529**).

Human Rights Council action. On 29 November [A/62/53 (dec. 2/116)], the Council deferred to its fourth (2007) session, consideration of a draft decision [A/HRC/2/L.14] on human rights and unilateral coercive measures submitted by Cuba on behalf of members of the Non-Aligned Movement.

GENERAL ASSEMBLY ACTION

On 19 December [meeting 81], the General Assembly, on the recommendation of the Third Committee [A/61/443/Add. 2 & Corr.1], adopted **resolution 61/170** by recorded vote (131-54-0) [agenda item 67 *(b)*].

Human rights and unilateral coercive measures

The General Assembly,

Recalling all its previous resolutions on this subject, the most recent of which was resolution 60/155 of 16 December 2005, and Commission on Human Rights resolution 2005/14 of 14 April 2005,

Reaffirming the pertinent principles and provisions contained in the Charter of Economic Rights and Duties of States proclaimed by the General Assembly in its resolution 3281 (XXIX) of 12 December 1974, in particular article 32 thereof, in which it declared that no State may use or encourage the use of economic, political or any other type of measures to coerce another State in order to obtain from it the subordination of the exercise of its sovereign rights,

Taking note of the report of the Secretary-General, submitted pursuant to Commission on Human Rights resolution 1999/21 of 23 April 1999, and the reports of the Secretary-General on the implementation of resolutions 52/120 of 12 December 1997 and 55/110 of 4 December 2000,

Recognizing the universal, indivisible, interdependent and interrelated character of all human rights, and, in this regard, reaffirming the right to development as an integral part of all human rights,

Recalling that the World Conference on Human Rights, held at Vienna from 14 to 25 June 1993, called upon States to refrain from any unilateral coercive measure not in accordance with international law and the Charter of the United Nations that creates obstacles to trade relations among States and impedes the full realization of all human rights,

Bearing in mind all the references to this question in the Copenhagen Declaration on Social Development adopted by the World Summit for Social Development on 12 March 1995, the Beijing Declaration and Platform for Action adopted by the Fourth World Conference on

Women on 15 September 1995, the Istanbul Declaration on Human Settlements and the Habitat Agenda adopted by the second United Nations Conference on Human Settlements (Habitat II) on 14 June 1996, and their five-year reviews,

Expressing its concern about the negative impact of unilateral coercive measures on international relations, trade, investment and cooperation,

Expressing its grave concern that, in some countries, the situation of children is adversely affected by unilateral coercive measures not in accordance with international law and the Charter that create obstacles to trade relations among States, impede the full realization of social and economic development and hinder the well-being of the population in the affected countries, with particular consequences for women and children, including adolescents,

Deeply concerned that, despite the recommendations adopted on this question by the General Assembly and recent major United Nations conferences, and contrary to general international law and the Charter, unilateral coercive measures continue to be promulgated and implemented with all their negative implications for the social-humanitarian activities and economic and social development of developing countries, including their extraterritorial effects, thereby creating additional obstacles to the full enjoyment of all human rights by peoples and individuals under the jurisdiction of other States,

Bearing in mind all the extraterritorial effects of any unilateral legislative, administrative and economic measures, policies and practices of a coercive nature against the development process and the enhancement of human rights in developing countries, which create obstacles to the full realization of all human rights,

Noting the continuing efforts of the open-ended Working Group on the Right to Development of the Commission on Human Rights, and reaffirming in particular its criteria, according to which unilateral coercive measures are one of the obstacles to the implementation of the Declaration on the Right to Development,

1. *Urges* all States to refrain from adopting or implementing any unilateral measures not in accordance with international law and the Charter of the United Nations, in particular those of a coercive nature with all their extraterritorial effects, which create obstacles to trade relations among States, thus impeding the full realization of the rights set forth in the Universal Declaration of Human Rights and other international human rights instruments, in particular the right of individuals and peoples to development;

2. *Also urges* all States to take steps to avoid and to refrain from adopting any unilateral measures not in accordance with international law and the Charter that impede the full achievement of economic and social development by the population of the affected countries, in particular children and women, that hinder their well-being and that create obstacles to the full enjoyment of their human rights, including the right of everyone to a standard of living adequate for their health and well-being and their right to food, medical care and the necessary social services, as well as to ensure that food and medicine are not used as tools for political pressure;

3. *Invites* all States to consider adopting administrative or legislative measures, as appropriate, to counteract the extraterritorial applications or effects of unilateral coercive measures;

4. *Rejects* unilateral coercive measures with all their extraterritorial effects as tools for political or economic pressure against any country, in particular against developing countries, because of their negative effects on the realization of all the human rights of vast sectors of their populations, in particular children, women and the elderly;

5. *Calls upon* Member States that have initiated such measures to commit themselves to their obligations and responsibilities arising from the international human rights instruments to which they are party by revoking such measures at the earliest possible time;

6. *Reaffirms*, in this context, the right of all peoples to self-determination, by virtue of which they freely determine their political status and freely pursue their economic, social and cultural development;

7. *Urges* the Human Rights Council to take fully into account the negative impact of unilateral coercive measures, including the enactment of national laws and their extraterritorial application, in its task concerning the implementation of the right to development;

8. *Requests* the United Nations High Commissioner for Human Rights, in discharging her functions relating to the promotion, realization and protection of the right to development and bearing in mind the continuing impact of unilateral coercive measures on the population of developing countries, to give priority to the present resolution in her annual report to the General Assembly;

9. *Requests* the Secretary-General to bring the present resolution to the attention of all Member States, to continue to collect their views and information on the implications and negative effects of unilateral coercive measures on their populations and to submit an analytical report thereon to the General Assembly at its sixty-second session, while reiterating once again the need to highlight the practical and preventive measures in this respect;

10. *Decides* to examine the question on a priority basis at its sixty-second session under the sub-item entitled "Human rights questions, including alternative approaches for improving the effective enjoyment of human rights and fundamental freedoms".

RECORDED VOTE ON RESOLUTION 61/170:

In favour: Algeria, Angola, Antigua and Barbuda, Argentina, Armenia, Azerbaijan, Bahamas, Bahrain, Bangladesh, Barbados, Belarus, Belize, Benin, Bhutan, Bolivia, Botswana, Brazil, Brunei Darussalam, Burkina Faso, Burundi, Cambodia, Cameroon, Cape Verde, Central African Republic, Chile, China, Colombia, Comoros, Congo, Costa Rica, Côte d'Ivoire, Cuba, Democratic People's Republic of Korea, Democratic Republic of the Congo, Djibouti, Dominica, Dominican Republic, Ecuador, Egypt, El Salvador, Eritrea, Ethiopia, Fiji, Gabon, Gambia, Ghana, Grenada, Guatemala, Guinea, Guinea-Bissau, Guyana, Haiti, Honduras, India, Indonesia, Iran, Iraq, Jamaica, Jordan, Kazakhstan,

Kenya, Kuwait, Kyrgyzstan, Lao People's Democratic Republic, Lebanon, Lesotho, Liberia, Libyan Arab Jamahiriya, Madagascar, Malawi, Malaysia, Maldives, Mali, Mauritania, Mauritius, Mexico, Mongolia, Morocco, Mozambique, Myanmar, Namibia, Nauru, Nepal, Nicaragua, Niger, Nigeria, Oman, Pakistan, Panama, Papua New Guinea, Paraguay, Peru, Philippines, Qatar, Russian Federation, Rwanda, Saint Lucia, Saint Vincent and the Grenadines, Samoa, Sao Tome and Principe, Saudi Arabia, Senegal, Sierra Leone, Singapore, Solomon Islands, Somalia, South Africa, Sri Lanka, Sudan, Suriname, Swaziland, Syrian Arab Republic, Tajikistan, Thailand, Timor-Leste, Togo, Tonga, Trinidad and Tobago, Tunisia, Turkmenistan, Tuvalu, United Arab Emirates, United Republic of Tanzania, Uruguay, Uzbekistan, Vanuatu, Venezuela, Viet Nam, Yemen, Zambia, Zimbabwe.

Against: Albania, Andorra, Australia, Austria, Belgium, Bosnia and Herzegovina, Bulgaria, Canada, Croatia, Cyprus, Czech Republic, Denmark, Estonia, Finland, France, Georgia, Germany, Greece, Hungary, Iceland, Ireland, Israel, Italy, Japan, Latvia, Liechtenstein, Lithuania, Luxembourg, Malta, Marshall Islands, Micronesia, Moldova, Monaco, Montenegro, Netherlands, New Zealand, Norway, Palau, Poland, Portugal, Republic of Korea, Romania, San Marino, Serbia, Slovakia, Slovenia, Spain, Sweden, Switzerland, The former Yugoslav Republic of Macedonia, Turkey, Ukraine, United Kingdom, United States.

Corruption

Report of Special Rapporteur. In accordance with a 2003 Subcommission request [YUN 2003, p. 764], the Special Rapporteur on corruption and its impact on the enjoyment of human rights, Christy Mbonu (Nigeria), submitted her second progress report [A/HRC/Sub.1/58/CRP.10], which described her recent activities, including a questionnaire she had drafted on the fight against corruption, for transmittal to Member States, specialized agencies, NGOs, members of civil society and banks.

Subcommission action. On 24 August [res. 2006/6], the Subcommission urged States that had not done so to introduce independent mechanisms to prevent and combat corruption through the adoption and implementation of specific anti-corruption legislation, while safeguarding human rights, including due process. It encouraged political leaders to be national examples of probity, integrity and self-esteem; called on civil society, particularly the media and NGOs, to be more involved in preventing and punishing corruption; and endorsed the questionnaire on the fight against corruption contained in the Special Rapporteur's report (see above). The Secretary-General was asked to assist the Special Rapporteur and transmit the questionnaire to Member States, specialized agencies, NGOs, members of civil society and international financial institutions to enable the Special Rapporteur to complete her mandate.

Extreme poverty

Report of independent expert. In accordance with a 2005 Commission request [YUN 2005, p. 838], the independent expert on the question of human rights and extreme poverty, Arjun Sengupta (India), submitted a March report [E/CN.4/2006/43] exploring the link between human rights and extreme poverty. He determined that considering extreme poverty as a violation or denial of human rights would add further value to efforts to combat the problem, and make poverty eradication a social objective trumping other policy objectives. In that regard, it was possible to appeal both to moral entitlements to a life in dignity, and legal obligations, as poverty could be identified with the deprivation of human rights. The expert proposed that the eradication of extreme poverty should be treated as a core right to be realized immediately and given the same priority as other human rights objectives, and accepted by the international community as a human rights obligation. Since poverty was defined as the sum total of income poverty, human development poverty and social exclusion, extreme poverty would be regarded as an extreme form of that situation. However, the definition of poverty would be driven by consensus in various countries, with the predominant consideration being the most vulnerable section of the population suffering from all forms of deprivation. Once such a group was identified, the removal of its conditions of extreme poverty should be taken as a human rights obligation. Even if the countries concerned could not ensure the realization of all human rights, those rights, the denial of which had directly caused extreme poverty, should be subject to immediate fulfilment. The international community and Member States should thus take that up as a core element of their human rights obligations.

In an addendum [E/CN.4/2006/43/Add.1], the expert reported on his visit to the United States, where he found that, despite the country's wealth, the poverty rate remained high relative to other rich nations. Available data indicated that, as at 2004, some 37 million Americans (12.7 percent of the population) lived below the federal poverty line, compared to 34.9 million the previous year. Of the 2004 figure, 15.6 million, accounting for over 5 per cent of the population, lived below 50 per cent of the poverty line, which was equivalent to a situation of extreme poverty. Government programmes had not effectively remedied the vulnerable situation of groups most at risk, notably African Americans, Hispanics, immigrants and single women heading households. Extreme poverty was manifested through food insecurity, the lack of vital health insurance coverage, homelessness and social exclusion, which the expert witnessed in many parts of the country. Extreme poverty in the United States could be eradicated if the country adopted a comprehensive national strategy and programmes based on human rights principles. Social safety nets for poor families should be provided through entitlement programmes, and the full participation of people living in poverty should be ensured in the design, implementation, monitoring and assessment of anti-poverty programmes. The authorities were encouraged to identify, in cooperation with civil society and expert organizations, the fraction of its population suffering from conditions of extreme poverty and adopt legislation to accord them the legal entitlement to anti-poverty programmes, and to seek redress in the courts if they were denied their entitlements. To fund such programmes, the Government could create a fund for the sole purpose of abolishing extreme poverty.

Note by Secretary-General. By a 26 September note [A/61/465], the Secretary-General, referring to General Assembly resolution 59/186 [YUN 2004, p. 760], in which the independent expert was requested to report on his activities at the Assembly's sixty-first (2006) session, drew attention to the reports which the expert had submitted to the Commission in 2005 [YUN 2005, p. 837] and 2006 (see above).

On 19 December, the Assembly took note of the Secretary-General's note (**decision 61/529**).

International declaration

Ad hoc group of experts. In response to a 2004 Subcommission request [YUN 2004, p. 760], José Bengoa (Chile), coordinator of the ad hoc group of experts to prepare a study on a draft international declaration on extreme poverty and human rights, presented its final report [A/HRC/Sub.1/58/16]. The group addressed the importance of the issue of extreme poverty, the concept of extreme poverty, the indivisibility of human rights and their progressive realization, the effective exercise of human rights, and the importance of mechanisms to ensure the participation of persons living in extreme poverty in the decision-making process in society. The group advocated a human-rights based approach in combating extreme poverty, which it believed should cover the duties and responsibilities of national, private and public stakeholders, particularly of States, which bore responsibility for the full realization of human rights. The responsibilities and duties of international stakeholders should also be established, since they often had an impact on initiating or eliminating situations of extreme poverty in a globalized world.

Annexed to the report was a document containing draft guiding principles on the implementation of human rights norms and standards in the context of the fight against extreme poverty, as requested by the Subcommission in 2004 [YUN 2004, p. 760].

Subcommission action. On 24 August [res. 2006/9], the Subcommission welcomed the draft guiding principles (see above), particularly given the extent to which they contributed significantly to the realization of the right to development in all countries and to the implementation of the MDGs; and upheld an approach linking respect for human rights and the adoption of practical measures offering the poor new opportunities. The Subcommission approved the final report of the ad hoc group of experts (see above), as well as the draft guiding principles, and requested the Council to study them, with a view to adopting them and forwarding them to the General Assembly.

Human Rights Council action. On 27 November [A/62/53 (res. 2/2)], the Council affirmed that the fight against extreme poverty had to remain a high priority for the international community. It took note of the draft guiding principles and requested the High Commissioner to circulate them in order to obtain the views of States, intergovernmental organizations, UN agencies, treaty bodies, special procedures, national human rights institutions, NGOs and other parties, and to report to the Council's seventh (2008) session.

GENERAL ASSEMBLY ACTION

On 19 December [meeting 81], the General Assembly, on the recommendation of the Third Committee [A/61/443/Add.2 & Corr.1], adopted **resolution 61/157** without vote [agenda item 67 *(b)*].

Human rights and extreme poverty

The General Assembly,

Reaffirming the Universal Declaration of Human Rights, the International Covenant on Civil and Political Rights, the International Covenant on Economic, Social and Cultural Rights, the Convention on the Elimination of All Forms of Discrimination against Women, the Convention on the Rights of the Child, the International Convention on the Elimination of All Forms of Racial Discrimination and other human rights instruments adopted by the United Nations,

Recalling its resolution 47/196 of 22 December 1992, by which it declared 17 October the International Day for the Eradication of Poverty, and its resolution 50/107 of 20 December 1995, by which it proclaimed the first United Nations Decade for the Eradication of Poverty (1997-2006), as well as its resolution 59/186 of 20 December 2004 and its previous resolutions on human rights and extreme poverty, in which it reaffirmed that extreme poverty and exclusion from society constitute a violation of human dignity and that urgent national and international action is therefore required to eliminate them,

Recalling also its resolution 52/134 of 12 December 1997, in which it recognized that the enhancement of international cooperation in the field of human rights was essential for the understanding, promotion and protection of all human rights,

Reaffirming the internationally agreed development goals, including the Millennium Development Goals,

Deeply concerned that extreme poverty persists in all countries of the world, regardless of their economic, social and cultural situation, and that its extent and manifestations, such as hunger, trafficking in human beings, disease, lack of adequate shelter, illiteracy and hopelessness, are particularly severe in developing countries, while acknowledging the significant progress made in several parts of the world in combating extreme poverty,

Deeply concerned also that gender inequality, violence and discrimination exacerbate extreme poverty, disproportionally impacting women and girls,

Recalling Commission on Human Rights resolution 2005/16 of 14 April 2005, as well as resolution 2005/9 of 8 August 2005 of the Subcommission on the Promotion and Protection of Human Rights,

Welcoming the Summit of World Leaders for Action against Hunger and Poverty of 20 September 2004, convened in New York by the Presidents of Brazil, Chile and France and the Prime Minister of Spain with the support of the Secretary-General,

Recognizing that the eradication of extreme poverty is a major challenge within the process of globalization and requires coordinated and continued policies through decisive national action and international cooperation,

Stressing the necessity of better understanding the causes and consequences of extreme poverty,

Reaffirming that, since the existence of widespread extreme poverty inhibits the full and effective enjoyment of human rights and might, in some situations, constitute a threat to the right to life, its immediate alleviation and eventual eradication must remain a high priority for the international community,

Reaffirming also that democracy, development and the full and effective enjoyment of human rights and fundamental freedoms are interdependent and mutually reinforcing and contribute to the eradication of extreme poverty,

Recalling Human Rights Council decision 1/102 of 30 June 2006,

1. *Reaffirms* that extreme poverty and exclusion from society constitute a violation of human dignity and that urgent national and international action is therefore required to eliminate them;

2. *Reaffirms also* that it is essential for States to foster participation by the poorest people in the decision-making process in the societies in which they live, in the promotion of human rights and in efforts to combat extreme poverty, and that it is essential for people living in poverty and vulnerable groups to be empowered to organize themselves and to participate in all aspects of political, economic and social life, in particular the planning and implementation of policies that affect them, thus enabling them to become genuine partners in development;

3. *Emphasizes* that extreme poverty is a major issue to be addressed by Governments, civil society and the United Nations system, including international financial institutions, and in this context reaffirms that political commitment is a prerequisite for the eradication of poverty;

4. *Reaffirms* that the existence of widespread absolute poverty inhibits the full and effective enjoyment of human rights and renders democracy and popular participation fragile;

5. *Recognizes* the need to promote respect for human rights and fundamental freedoms in order to address the most pressing social needs of people living in poverty, including through the design and development of appropriate mechanisms to strengthen and consolidate democratic institutions and governance;

6. *Reaffirms* the commitments contained in the United Nations Millennium Declaration, in particular the commitments to spare no effort to fight against extreme poverty and to achieve development and poverty eradication, including the commitment to halve, by 2015, the proportion of the world's people whose income is less than one United States dollar a day and the proportion of people who suffer from hunger;

7. *Reaffirms also* the commitment made at the 2005 World Summit to eradicate poverty and promote sustained economic growth, sustainable development and global prosperity for all, including women and girls;

8. *Reaffirms further* the critical role of both formal and informal education in the achievement of poverty eradication and other development goals as envisaged in the Millennium Declaration, in particular basic education and training for eradicating illiteracy, and efforts towards expanded secondary and higher education as well as vocational education and technical training, especially for girls and women, the creation of human resources and infrastructure capabilities and the empowerment of those living in poverty, and in this context reaffirms the Dakar Framework for Action adopted at the World Education Forum in 2000 and recognizes the importance of the United Nations Educational, Scientific and Cultural Organization strategy for the eradication of poverty, especially extreme poverty, in supporting the Education for All programmes as a tool to achieve the millennium development goal of universal primary education by 2015;

9. *Invites* the United Nations High Commissioner for Human Rights to continue to give high priority to the question of the relationship between extreme poverty and human rights, and also invites her to further pursue the work in this area;

10. *Calls upon* States, United Nations bodies, in particular the Office of the United Nations High Commissioner for Human Rights and the United Nations Development Programme, intergovernmental organizations

and non-governmental organizations to continue to give appropriate attention to the links between human rights and extreme poverty, and encourages the private sector and the international financial institutions to proceed likewise;

11. *Welcomes* the efforts of entities throughout the United Nations system to incorporate the Millennium Declaration and the internationally agreed development goals set out therein into their work;

12. *Takes note* of the reports of the independent expert on the question of human rights and extreme poverty submitted to the Commission on Human Rights at its sixty-first and sixty-second sessions and presented to the Human Rights Council at its second session;

13. *Decides* to consider the question further at its sixty-third session under the sub-item entitled "Human rights questions, including alternative approaches for improving the effective enjoyment of human rights and fundamental freedoms".

Right to food

Reports of Special Rapporteur. In response to a 2005 Commission request [YUN 2005, p. 840], the Special Rapporteur on the right to food, Jean Zigler (Switzerland), in a March report [E/CN.4/2006/44], reviewed the definition of the right in an era of globalization. From that perspective, he analysed the primary responsibility of Governments to ensure freedom from hunger for all people at all times. That involved three levels of obligation, to respect, protect and fulfil the right to food, as defined in general comment No. 12 on that right adopted in 1999 by the Committee on Economic, Social and Cultural Rights [YUN 1999, p. 575]. Also discussed were the extraterritorial obligations of States in terms of protecting their citizens from the impact of decisions taken in other countries, as well as the responsibilities of international organizations and private actors regarding the right.

The Special Rapporteur was concerned that global hunger was increasing, with some 852 million people gravely undernourished and millions dying yearly, especially children, owing to the lack of food. Particularly worrisome was the current food crisis affecting many African States. He observed, in that regard, that all human beings had a right to live in dignity, free from hunger. Famine and hunger usually resulted from the action or inaction of Governments. In a world richer than ever, it was unacceptable that people could be left to die of starvation, or to the misery of stunted mental and physical development resulting from chronic malnutrition. The Special Rapporteur recommended action by all Governments to halt the increase in global undernourishment and to combat hunger in Latin American and African countries in particular. He also advocated, among other measures, emergency assistance to refugees, the prevention by Governments of arbitrary and discriminatory actions denying poor people access to food and policies negatively affecting the right to food of people in other countries, and the support and involvement of big TNCs and such international organizations as the World Bank, IMF and the World Trade Organization (WTO) in promoting the realization of the right.

By a September note [A/61/306], the Secretary-General transmitted to the General Assembly the interim report of the Special Rapporteur, in accordance with Assembly resolution 60/165 [YUN 2005, p. 840]. The report reviewed positive developments in Brazil, Guatemala and India, and situations of concern elsewhere, including in Afghanistan, the Democratic People's Republic of Korea, the Darfur region of the Sudan, the Horn of Africa, the Sahel region and Zimbabwe, where the realization of the right to food faced major challenges. The Special Rapporteur had sent 28 communications to 17 Governments and the European Union, mostly together with other special procedures, requesting information on alleged violations of the right to food, particularly regarding the non-fulfillment of State obligations to respect, protect or fulfil the right. The Special Rapporteur noted that many of the ongoing food crises resulted also from debilitating natural disasters, including drought, desertification and land degradation, and increasing conflict over deteriorating resources. He examined the role of the Council in protecting all human rights, including the right to food, highlighting the Council's related action towards the legal protection of indigenous people and the advancement of economic, social and cultural rights, and the right to development.

The Special Rapporteur observed that, despite the increasing recognition of the right to food worldwide, little progress had been made in reducing the global number of people suffering from hunger, which was estimated at 852 million. It was a shame on humanity that every five seconds a child died from hunger and malnutrition. Concluding that hunger was still primarily a rural problem, the Special Rapporteur encouraged investment in rural development and small-scale agriculture and pastoralism. He also advocated that combating hunger should include fighting desertification and land degradation through investments and public policies addressing the specific risks of dry lands. To that end, States parties should implement the United Nations Convention to Combat Desertification [YUN 1994, p. 944]. In other recommendations, the

Special Rapporteur urged Governments to respond to urgent appeals addressing the food crisis.

The Special Rapporteur visited Lebanon (11-16 September) [A/HRC/2/8 & Corr. 1] in the aftermath of the armed hostilities in July and August between Hizbullah and Israel (see p. 574) and following international concerns regarding the impact of the war on the right to food. He found that the destruction of road and transport infrastructure, coupled with the repeated denial of safe transit by Israeli armed forces made it very difficult for humanitarian agencies to transport food and other relief to those in need, especially some 22,000 people trapped in the area south of the Litani River. The destruction of vital infrastructure, particularly agricultural, irrigation and water infrastructure, would also have long-term impacts on livelihoods and access to food and water in the country. Overall, the war severely disrupted the livelihoods of a large part of the population, and the process of reconstruction had been slow. In the light of those findings, the Special Rapporteur made recommendations aimed at improving the right to food of the entire Lebanese population. He recommended, in particular, that violations of the right under international human rights and humanitarian rights be further investigated to determine whether they constituted grave breaches of the Geneva Conventions and Additional Protocol thereto, and war crimes under the Rome Statute of the International Criminal Court.

GENERAL ASSEMBLY ACTION

On 19 December [meeting 81], the General Assembly, on the recommendation of the Third Committee [A/61/443/Add.2 & Corr.1], adopted **resolution 61/163** by recorded vote (185-1-0) [agenda item 67 *(b)*].

The right to food

The General Assembly,

Recalling all its previous resolutions on the issue of the right to food, in particular resolution 60/165 of 16 December 2005, as well as all resolutions of the Commission on Human Rights in this regard,

Recalling also the Universal Declaration of Human Rights, which provides that everyone has the right to a standard of living adequate for her or his health and well-being, including food, the Universal Declaration on the Eradication of Hunger and Malnutrition and the United Nations Millennium Declaration,

Recalling further the provisions of the International Covenant on Economic, Social and Cultural Rights, in which the fundamental right of every person to be free from hunger is recognized,

Bearing in mind the Rome Declaration on World Food Security and the World Food Summit Plan of Action and the Declaration of the World Food Summit: five years later, adopted in Rome on 13 June 2002,

Reaffirming the concrete recommendations contained in the Voluntary Guidelines to Support the Progressive Realization of the Right to Adequate Food in the Context of National Food Security, adopted by the Council of the Food and Agriculture Organization of the United Nations in November 2004,

Reaffirming also that all human rights are universal, indivisible, interdependent and interrelated,

Reaffirming further that a peaceful, stable and enabling political, social and economic environment, at both the national and the international levels, is the essential foundation that will enable States to give adequate priority to food security and poverty eradication,

Reiterating, as in the Rome Declaration on World Food Security and the Declaration of the World Food Summit: five years later, that food should not be used as an instrument of political or economic pressure, and reaffirming in this regard the importance of international cooperation and solidarity, as well as the necessity of refraining from unilateral measures that are not in accordance with international law and the Charter of the United Nations and that endanger food security,

Convinced that each State must adopt a strategy consistent with its resources and capacities to achieve its individual goals in implementing the recommendations contained in the Rome Declaration on World Food Security and the World Food Summit Plan of Action and, at the same time, cooperate regionally and internationally in order to organize collective solutions to global issues of food security in a world of increasingly interlinked institutions, societies and economies where coordinated efforts and shared responsibilities are essential,

Recognizing that the problems of hunger and food insecurity have global dimensions and that they are likely to persist and even to increase dramatically in some regions unless urgent, determined and concerted action is taken, given the anticipated increase in the world's population and the stress on natural resources,

Noting that the global environment continues to suffer degradation, causing a negative impact on the realization of the right to food, in particular in developing countries,

Expressing its deep concern at the number and scale of natural disasters, diseases and pests and their increasing impact in recent years, which have resulted in massive loss of life and livelihood and threatened agricultural production and food security, in particular in developing countries,

Stressing the importance of reversing the continuing decline of official development assistance devoted to agriculture, both in real terms and as a share of total official development assistance,

1. *Reaffirms* that hunger constitutes an outrage and a violation of human dignity and therefore requires the adoption of urgent measures at the national, regional and international levels for its elimination;

2. *Also reaffirms* the right of everyone to have access to safe and nutritious food, consistent with the right to

adequate food and the fundamental right of everyone to be free from hunger, so as to be able to fully develop and maintain their physical and mental capacities;

3. *Considers it intolerable* that every five seconds a child under the age of 5 dies from hunger or hunger-related diseases somewhere in the world, that there are about 854 million undernourished people in the world and that, while the prevalence of hunger has diminished, the absolute number of undernourished people has been increasing in recent years when, according to the Food and Agriculture Organization of the United Nations, the planet could produce enough food to feed 12 billion people, twice the world's present population;

4. *Expresses its concern* that women and girls are disproportionately affected by hunger, food insecurity and poverty, in part as a result of gender inequality and discrimination, that in many countries, girls are twice as likely as boys to die from malnutrition and preventable childhood diseases, and that it is estimated that almost twice as many women as men suffer from malnutrition;

5. *Encourages* all States to take action to address gender inequality and discrimination against women, in particular where it contributes to the malnutrition of women and girls, including measures to ensure the full and equal realization of the right to food and ensuring that women have equal access to resources, including income, land and water, to enable them to feed themselves and their families;

6. *Encourages* the Special Rapporteur of the Human Rights Council on the right to food to continue mainstreaming a gender perspective in the fulfilment of his mandate, and encourages the Food and Agriculture Organization of the United Nations and all other United Nations bodies and mechanisms addressing the right to food and food insecurity to integrate a gender perspective into their relevant policies, programmes and activities;

7. *Encourages* all States to take steps with a view to achieving progressively the full realization of the right to food, including steps to promote the conditions for everyone to be free from hunger and, as soon as possible, to enjoy fully the right to food, and to create and adopt national plans to combat hunger;

8. *Stresses* that improving access to productive resources and public investment in rural development is essential for eradicating hunger and poverty, in particular in developing countries, including through the promotion of investments in appropriate, small-scale irrigation and water management technologies in order to reduce vulnerability to droughts;

9. *Stresses also* the importance of fighting hunger in rural areas, including through national efforts supported by international partnerships to stop desertification and land degradation and through investments and public policies that are specifically appropriate to the risk of drylands, and, in this regard, calls for the full implementation of the United Nations Convention to Combat Desertification in Those Countries Experiencing Serious Drought and/or Desertification, Particularly in Africa;

10. *Acknowledges* that many indigenous organizations and representatives of indigenous communities have expressed in different forums their deep concerns over the obstacles and challenges they face for the full enjoyment of the right to food, and calls upon States to take special actions to combat the root causes of the disproportionately high level of hunger and malnutrition among indigenous peoples and the continuous discrimination against them;

11. *Requests* all States and private actors, as well as international organizations within their respective mandates, to take fully into account the need to promote the effective realization of the right to food for all, including in the ongoing negotiations in different fields;

12. *Stresses* the need to make efforts to mobilize and optimize the allocation and utilization of technical and financial resources from all sources, including external debt relief for developing countries, and to reinforce national actions to implement sustainable food security policies;

13. *Recognizes* the need for a successful conclusion of the Doha Development Round negotiations of the World Trade Organization as a contribution for creating international conditions that permit the realization of the right to food;

14. *Recalls* the importance of the New York Declaration on Action against Hunger and Poverty, and recommends the continuation of efforts aimed at identifying additional sources of financing for the fight against hunger and poverty;

15. *Recognizes* that the promises made at the World Food Summit in 1996 to halve the number of persons who are undernourished are not being fulfilled, and invites once again all international financial and development institutions, as well as the relevant United Nations agencies and funds, to give priority to and provide the necessary funding to realize the aim of halving by 2015 the proportion of people who suffer from hunger, as well as the right to food as set out in the Rome Declaration on World Food Security and the United Nations Millennium Declaration;

16. *Reaffirms* that integrating food and nutritional support, with the goal that all people at all times will have access to sufficient, safe and nutritious food to meet their dietary needs and food preferences for an active and healthy life, is part of a comprehensive response to the spread of HIV/AIDS, tuberculosis, malaria and other communicable diseases;

17. *Urges* States to give adequate priority in their development strategies and expenditures to the realization of the right to food;

18. *Stresses* the importance of international development cooperation and assistance, in particular in activities related to disaster risk reduction and in emergency situations such as natural and man-made disasters, diseases and pests, for the realization of the right to food and the achievement of sustainable food security, while recognizing that each country has the primary responsibility for ensuring the implementation of national programmes and strategies in this regard;

19. *Calls upon* Member States, the United Nations system and other relevant stakeholders to support na-

tional efforts aimed at responding rapidly to the food crises currently occurring across Africa;

20. *Invites* all relevant international organizations, including the World Bank and the International Monetary Fund, to promote policies and projects that have a positive impact on the right to food, to ensure that partners respect the right to food in the implementation of common projects, to support strategies of Member States aimed at the fulfilment of the right to food and to avoid any actions that could have a negative impact on the realization of the right to food;

21. *Takes note* of the interim report of the Special Rapporteur on the right to food, and also takes note of his valuable work in the promotion of the right to food;

22. *Supports* the realization of the mandate of the Special Rapporteur as extended by the Human Rights Council in its decision 1/102 of 30 June 2006;

23. *Requests* the Secretary-General and the United Nations High Commissioner for Human Rights to provide all the necessary human and financial resources for the effective fulfilment of the mandate of the Special Rapporteur;

24. *Welcomes* the work already done by the Committee on Economic, Social and Cultural Rights in promoting the right to adequate food, in particular its General Comment No. 12 (1999) on the right to adequate food (article 11 of the International Covenant on Economic, Social and Cultural Rights), in which the Committee affirmed, inter alia, that the right to adequate food is indivisibly linked to the inherent dignity of the human person and is indispensable for the fulfilment of other human rights enshrined in the International Bill of Human Rights, and is also inseparable from social justice, requiring the adoption of appropriate economic, environmental and social policies, at both the national and the international levels, oriented to the eradication of poverty and the fulfilment of all human rights for all;

25. *Recalls* General Comment No. 15 (2002) of the Committee on the right to water (articles 11 and 12 of the Covenant), in which the Committee noted, inter alia, the importance of ensuring sustainable water resources for human consumption and agriculture in realization of the right to adequate food;

26. *Reaffirms* that the Voluntary Guidelines to Support the Progressive Realization of the Right to Adequate Food in the Context of National Food Security, adopted by the Council of the Food and Agriculture Organization of the United Nations in November 2004, represent a practical tool to promote the realization of the right to food for all, contribute to the achievement of food security and thus provide an additional instrument in the attainment of internationally agreed development goals, including those contained in the Millennium Declaration;

27. *Welcomes* the continued cooperation of the High Commissioner, the Committee and the Special Rapporteur, and encourages them to continue their cooperation in this regard;

28. *Calls upon* all Governments to cooperate with and assist the Special Rapporteur in his task, to supply all necessary information requested by him and to give serious consideration to responding favourably to the requests of the Special Rapporteur to visit their countries to enable him to fulfil his mandate more effectively;

29. *Requests* the Special Rapporteur to submit an interim report to the General Assembly at its sixty-second session on the implementation of the present resolution;

30. *Invites* Governments, relevant United Nations agencies, funds and programmes, treaty bodies and civil society actors, including non-governmental organizations, as well as the private sector, to cooperate fully with the Special Rapporteur in the fulfilment of his mandate, inter alia, through the submission of comments and suggestions on ways and means of realizing the right to food;

31. *Decides* to continue the consideration of the question at its sixty-second session under the item entitled "Promotion and protection of human rights".

RECORDED VOTE ON RESOLUTION 61/163:

In favour: Afghanistan, Albania, Algeria, Andorra, Angola, Antigua and Barbuda, Argentina, Armenia, Australia, Austria, Azerbaijan, Bahamas, Bahrain, Bangladesh, Barbados, Belarus, Belgium, Belize, Benin, Bhutan, Bolivia, Bosnia and Herzegovina, Botswana, Brazil, Brunei Darussalam, Bulgaria, Burkina Faso, Burundi, Cambodia, Cameroon, Canada, Cape Verde, Central African Republic, Chile, China, Colombia, Comoros, Congo, Costa Rica, Côte d'Ivoire, Croatia, Cuba, Cyprus, Czech Republic, Democratic People's Republic of Korea, Democratic Republic of the Congo, Denmark, Djibouti, Dominica, Dominican Republic, Ecuador, Egypt, El Salvador, Eritrea, Estonia, Ethiopia, Fiji, Finland, France, Gabon, Gambia, Georgia, Germany, Ghana, Greece, Grenada, Guatemala, Guinea, Guinea-Bissau, Guyana, Haiti, Honduras, Hungary, Iceland, India, Indonesia, Iran, Iraq, Ireland, Israel, Italy, Jamaica, Japan, Jordan, Kazakhstan, Kenya, Kuwait, Kyrgyzstan, Lao People's Democratic Republic, Latvia, Lebanon, Lesotho, Liberia, Libyan Arab Jamahiriya, Liechtenstein, Lithuania, Luxembourg, Madagascar, Malawi, Malaysia, Maldives, Mali, Malta, Marshall Islands, Mauritania, Mauritius, Mexico, Micronesia, Moldova, Monaco, Mongolia, Montenegro, Morocco, Mozambique, Myanmar, Namibia, Nauru, Nepal, Netherlands, New Zealand, Nicaragua, Niger, Nigeria, Norway, Oman, Pakistan, Palau, Panama, Papua New Guinea, Paraguay, Peru, Philippines, Poland, Portugal, Qatar, Republic of Korea, Romania, Russian Federation, Saint Lucia, Saint Vincent and the Grenadines, Samoa, San Marino, Sao Tome and Principe, Saudi Arabia, Senegal, Serbia, Sierra Leone, Singapore, Slovakia, Slovenia, Solomon Islands, Somalia, South Africa, Spain, Sri Lanka, Sudan, Suriname, Swaziland, Sweden, Switzerland, Syrian Arab Republic, Tajikistan, Thailand, The former Yugoslav Republic of Macedonia, Timor-Leste, Togo, Tonga, Trinidad and Tobago, Tunisia, Turkey, Turkmenistan, Tuvalu, Uganda, Ukraine, United Arab Emirates, United Kingdom, United Republic of Tanzania, Uruguay, Uzbekistan, Vanuatu, Venezuela, Viet Nam, Yemen, Zambia, Zimbabwe.

Against: United States.

Right to adequate housing

Reports of Special Rapporteur. The Special Rapporteur on the right to adequate housing, Miloon Kothari (India), in a March report [E/CN.4/

2006/41], reviewed his activities since his appointment and highlighted progress made in securing the right, as well as issues of concern deserving particular attention. He focused on the far-reaching interface between adequate housing as an economic, social and cultural right, and relevant civil and political rights, such as the right to information and to security of the home. The Special Rapporteur highlighted the main obstacles to the realization of adequate housing as a component of the right to an adequate standard of living, which related mainly to land and property concerns, the impact of natural disasters and humanitarian emergencies, the right to adequate housing in urban and rural areas, housing finance for the poor, and the housing situation of vulnerable or minority groups, including women, homeless persons, children, the elderly, persons with disabilities, indigenous people, refugees and other minorities. The Special Rapporteur also submitted basic principles and guidelines for States on development-based evictions and displacements, which he designed as a practical tool for implementing the right to adequate housing and a further development of the 1997 United Nations Comprehensive Human Rights Guidelines on Development-based Displacement [YUN 1997, p. 676]. The Guidelines, which were annexed to the report, offered several new prescriptions based on experiences gathered since 1997 and clarified States' obligations in addressing evictions.

The Special Rapporteur observed that, within the context of the continuing global housing crisis, concerted international action was required to promote the right to adequate housing. He recommended that his mandate be extended and his proposed guidelines adopted and distributed widely. Land should be recognized as a human right under international human rights law and States should accord priority to agrarian reform and to land and wealth redistribution. In addition, legislation should be enacted and implemented to combat forced evictions, urban apartheid and segregation, unbridled property speculation and indiscriminate escalation of housing and property prices.

Between 16 December 2004 and 1 December 2005, the Special Rapporteur sent 15 communications to 12 Member States and one to the United Nations Interim Administration in Kosovo (UNMIK) (see p. 469) regarding alleged violations of the right to adequate housing and related rights worldwide. Those communications and the replies thereto were summarized in an addendum to his March report [E/CN.4/2006/41/Add.1].

The Special Rapporteur visited Australia (31 July–15 August) [A/HRC/4/18/Add.2] to examine the status of the realization of adequate housing, particularly for specific groups, such as indigenous peoples and women. While acknowledging the Government's good practices in addressing some of the problems relating to the implementation of the right, he was troubled by the situation in parts of the country and determined that Australia, one of the wealthiest developed countries with a relatively small population, had a serious national housing crisis. Mostly affected were vulnerable groups and low- to middle-income households. The country lacked a clear, consistent and holistic housing strategy, and there was no national nor legislative framework to evaluate the outcomes of Government programmes to assess the extent to which the right to adequate housing was being realized. Having also observed major practical problems, including reductions in the public housing stock, soaring private rental rates, a housing affordability crisis and no reduction in the number of homeless persons, the Special Rapporteur concluded that Australia had failed to implement its international legal obligation to progressively realize the human right to adequate housing. He encouraged the Government to make housing a national priority and adopt a comprehensive and coordinated housing policy that addressed structural problems and was based on a human rights approach, with the primary task of meeting the needs of the most vulnerable groups. He also recommended, among other measures, the establishment of a Ministry devoted to housing, a national body representing indigenous people, and vigorous measures to tackle problems of housing affordability and housing and land speculation.

In Spain (20 November–1 December) [A/HRC/4/18/Add.3; A/HRC/7/16/Add.2], where the Special Rapporteur also found a housing crisis, notable concerns related to economic and financial factors, including widespread speculation, affordability problems and the lack of public housing stock, particularly rental housing, all of which negatively impacted the right of large sectors of the population to adequate housing. Acknowledging some positive steps taken by the authorities to address the problem, the Special Rapporteur observed that one of the most significant elements of Spanish housing policy, compared to other European countries, was the priority given to home ownership through such instruments as tax policy and public housing. He determined in that regard that the functioning of the housing market, the current home ownership model and its possible negative impact on low-income housing options should be examined and might necessitate State intervention. The Special Rapporteur made a number of other recommendations, including the adoption of a comprehensive national housing policy based on human rights and the protection of the most vulnerable sections of its population, particularly women, the youth and elderly, people with disabilities and minorities. In addition, there should be heavy penalties for corruption and discrimination in the real estate sector.

The Special Rapporteur visited Lebanon and Israel (7-14 September) [A/HRC/2/7], together with the Special Rapporteur on extrajudicial, summary or arbitrary executions, the Special Rapporteur on the right to the highest attainable standard of physical and mental health, and the Secretary-General's Representative on the human rights of internally displaced persons. The mission, which took place shortly after the 34-day armed hostilities between Israel and Hizbullah in Lebanon from 12 July to 14 August (see p. 574), was intended to study how their conduct of the conflict affected the rights to life, health and housing of the civilian population in both countries. The mission found that, by commission or omission, both sides had violated the principles of international human rights and humanitarian law to varying degrees. In Lebanon, where the Israeli Defence Forces (IDF) had mounted intense air and ground attacks against Hizbullah targets and on Lebanese infrastructure and private homes, the mission found that Israel had failed to distinguish Hizbullah fighters from civilians, and had used cluster munitions, which were notorious for their indiscriminate and often disproportionate impact on civilians. Those attacks had resulted in numerous deaths and injuries to the Lebanese people and the displacement of some 974,184 others, whose homes were destroyed in several villages in southern Lebanon. Many of the affected families were forced to live in insecure housing and poor conditions, without access to water, sanitation, electricity or health care, all of which affected their well-being and contributed to mental health problems, especially among women and children.

In Israel, the mission determined that Hizbullah had also followed a lawless approach in its conduct of the war, having fired thousands of rockets into northern Israel, disregarding the principle of distinction between combatants and civilians and of the prohibition of indiscriminate attacks. Those rocket attacks affected the livelihoods of large parts of the population of northern Israel, killing civilians, damaging up to 12,000 buildings and forcing the evacuation of some 300,000 individuals. Others were forced into shelters in appalling living conditions, where many suffered from anxiety attacks. In the aftermath of the conflict, the civilian population of southern Lebanon continued to suffer as a result of the large-scale destruction and acute danger still posed by unexploded ordnance. To aid the reconstruction efforts in both countries and strengthen the right to adequate housing and other related rights, the mission addressed a series of recommendations to the Governments of Israel and Lebanon, and to Hizbullah, the Human Rights Council, the Commission of Inquiry established pursuant to Council resolution S-2/1 (see p. 965) and the international community.

Communication. On 30 September [A/HRC/2/G/9], Lebanon circulated its observations on the joint report, noting that it did not include sufficient information regarding the scale of the damage and tragedies caused by Israeli attacks on the country.

Women and adequate housing

Report of Special Rapporteur. In response to a 2005 Commission request [YUN 2005, p. 844], the Special Rapporteur on the right to adequate housing (see above) submitted a final report [E/CN.4/2006/118] on women and adequate housing, which analysed obstacles to the effective realization of women's housing rights, such as violence against them, discriminatory cultural and social norms and family or personal laws, privatization and unaffordability of housing, the impact of natural disasters, forced evictions and HIV/AIDS. The Special Rapporteur concluded that States needed to strengthen national legal and policy frameworks for protecting women's rights to adequate housing, land and inheritance, and provide avenues for redress where violations occurred. Pointing to the culture of silence about the global prevalence of violations of women's right to adequate housing and land, he highlighted the need to bridge the gap between legal and policy recognition of that right and for implementation by States of related national programmes. In addition to his previous recommendations, the Special Rapporteur suggested ways to ensure the elaboration of gender-sensitive housing policies and legislation, taking into account the situations of specific groups of women at risk of becoming victims of housing rights violations, such as female-headed households, women from ethnic and national minorities and women in conflict or post-conflict situations. He also recommended the adoption by the Committee on the Elimination of Discrimination against Women (CEDAW) (see p. 1354) of a general recommendation on women's right to adequate housing and land; the harmonization of international human rights instruments and Islamic law on inheritance and property; and the development of gender-sensitive housing policies and legislation. States should diligently investigate and punish acts of violence against women, ensure their access to legal redress and introduce laws on domestic violence that included provisions to protect their right to adequate housing. In post-disaster situations, States, donors and NGOs should ensure that women were able to participate and benefit equally from reconstruction efforts.

Right to education

Reports of Special Rapporteur. The Special Rapporteur on the right to education, Vernor Muñoz Villalobos (Costa Rica), in a February report [E/CN.4/2006/45], focused on the right of girls to education within the context of the MDGs. The report addressed the socio-cultural context of gender discrimination by defining the concept of patriarchalism, which underpinned discriminatory behaviours, and denounced the negative impact on education, especially regarding girls, of the persistent view of education as a service rather than a human right. Pointing to the importance of ensuring girls' access to school and their completion of the education cycle, the Special Rapporteur identified obstacles in that regard, among them, early marriages and pregnancies, child labour (especially domestic work) and armed conflicts. He concluded that the exclusion of girls, which had obstructed efforts at gender parity and equality in education, reflected poverty and other structural factors, as well as a lack of political will by States that did not consider education essential. Many of the serious problems besetting education were rooted in a discriminatory environment, which was why certain educational reforms expected to settle social and economic problems had not been very successful. As a lack of political will, prejudice, social inequality and marginal regard for girls were the basis for those problems, international financial institutions and States should pursue more decisive strategies, integrating human rights completely into public policies to enable the construction of a fairer and more egalitarian world. The reasons for the high dropout and low school enrolment rates among young girls and teenagers should become a major concern of States, relevant not only in educational policy but in all social, cultural and family pursuits, considering that girls' education was inseparably linked to the promotion of social justice and democracy. In additional recommendations highlighting the four components of the right to education—availability, accessibility, acceptability and adaptability—the Special Rapporteur advocated measures for promoting and protecting the right, particularly for girls.

The Special Rapporteur visited Botswana (26 September–4 October 2005) [E/CN.4/2006/45/Add.1], where he found that, although the country had virtually achieved universal primary education and gender equality, it faced challenges in addressing: the multilingual and intercultural nature of its society and the need to ensure that all groups benefited from the education provided; the spread of HIV/AIDS and the resources needed in combating it; the lack of school facilities in many parts of the country; and traditional discrimination, which increased girls' dropout rate at the secondary level, especially due to early pregnancies. The Special Rapporteur noted that the lack of a rights-based approach to education had led to a disparity in educational achievement and seemed to have encouraged the reintroduction of school fees, which was a major step backwards regarding the country's achievement on education. He recommended, among other measures, that the country adopt a rights-based approach by providing a constitutional guarantee for education; withdraw the reintroduction of school fees at junior secondary level and consider alternative ways of sustaining education; implement policies for the recruitment and training of teachers, according priority to those from remote areas; review all curricular materials to eliminate any discriminatory content; and cater to the educational needs of foreign and refugee children, orphaned and pregnant adolescents, nomadic populations and the visually impaired.

In Germany (13-21 February) [A/HRC/4/29/Add.3], the Special Rapporteur analysed the enjoyment of the right to education in the light of four cross-cutting themes: the impact of the German federal system; the reform of the education system; the structure of the education system; and the paradigm shift on migration. He found that, despite the country's extensive public education coverage and high level of school attendance, the educational system's complex structure had resulted in a number of shortcomings, related mostly to the difficulties encountered by children in marginalized groups, particularly people from lower social classes, immigrants or persons with disabilities. That made the educational system somewhat exclusive in nature. The Special Rapporteur recommended that Germany reform its educational system, preserving its current merits, while overcoming its inequalities and the lack of opportunity for certain population sectors.

The Special Rapporteur addressed a series of other recommendations to the Government, including the adoption of uniform safeguards for the right to education; the launching of a national debate on the relationship between the educational system and the phenomenon of exclusion and marginalization of school children; and studies on ways of strengthening the quality of education in the country, and standardizing the salaries and other entitlements of teachers in different school systems and levels. Further studies should be undertaken to clarify the school attendance situation of the children of asylum-seekers, refugee children and those without proper papers, with a view to establishing urgently a legal framework for protecting and promoting their human rights to education.

In Morocco (27 November–5 December) [A/HRC/4/29/Add.2; A/HRC/8/10/Add.2], the Special Rapporteur assessed the realization of the right to education in rural areas and the enjoyment of the right by girls, children with disabilities and other vulnerable groups of children. He acknowledged that the Government had made significant progress in education, owing to various reforms and institutional, legislative and budgetary efforts, which led to a 93 per cent enrolment rate in primary schools in 2006, compared to 40 per cent in the 1960s. There had also been a marked expansion in primary education coverage and a decrease in illiteracy, which, together with the construction of new infrastructure, had facilitated access to education and improved the functioning of schools. Those developments attested to Morocco's growing commitment to human rights and the political will of the State and society. However, not all sectors of the population had benefited, despite the strengthening of the legislative framework for protection and an increase in the education budget. The Special Rapporteur concluded that Morocco had a considerable way to go before it could guarantee all its inhabitants the effective enjoyment of the right to education. The situation illustrated how important it was to ground public policies firmly in human rights, so as to redress social imbalances and disparities in exercising the right. Providing the population with basic services such as drinking water, electricity and sanitation was a major challenge, considering that those services impacted greatly on the realization of the right to education, as did illiteracy and the exclusion of children with disabilities, street children and child workers from the education system. The Special Rapporteur made a series of recommendations for improving the situation, including that the Government redouble efforts to promote universal free education to ensure that children from economically vulnerable families had no difficulty in accessing quality and culturally appropriate education.

Communication. On 17 February [E/CN.4/2006/G/8], Indonesia transmitted the Jakarta Declaration, adopted at the International Conference on the Right to Basic Educations as a Fundamental Human Right and the Legal Framework for its Financing (Jakarta, Indonesia, 2-4 December 2005), organized jointly by Indonesia and UNESCO and designed to promote and safeguard the right to education.

Environmental and scientific concerns

Toxic wastes

Report of Special Rapporteur. In response to a 2005 Commission request [YUN 2005, p. 845], the Special Rapporteur on the adverse effects of the illicit movement and dumping of toxic and dangerous products and wastes on the enjoyment of human rights, Okechukwu Ibeanu (Nigeria), submitted a report [E/CN.4/2006/42] focusing on the human rights impact of the widespread exposure of individuals and communities to toxic chemicals in basic household goods and food. He cited recent studies indicating that man-made toxic chemicals were found in the blood of populations around the world at levels that far exceeded the recommended limits in some cases. Of particular concern was the risk to unborn and younger children of contamination via the mother. Noting that the danger of long-term exposure to a combination of chemicals at low doses had not been thoroughly investigated, the report analysed the human rights dimension of chronic, low-level exposure to toxic chemicals with regard to the rights to life, health, access to information and participation in decision-making processes. It also outlined the obligations of governmental and non-governmental duty bearers in respect of those rights, discussed the value of adopting a human rights approach to chemicals regulation and provided an overview of current regulation efforts at international and regional levels.

The Special Rapporteur observed that poor, vulnerable and marginalized people, particularly in developing countries, suffered disproportionately from exposure to toxic chemicals banned in other parts of the world. They often lacked access to medical attention for related health problems and the capacity and resources to seek redress for the violation of their human rights. From that perspective, the continuing export of electronic wastes from developed to developing countries for recycling or disposal, in conditions which often exposed workers and communities to dangerous toxins, was a burden to developing countries requiring urgent attention from the international community, especially exporting and importing governments. Accordingly, the Special Rapporteur recommended, among other things, that international, regional and national regulatory bodies adopt a human rights approach to chemicals management and that victims of human rights violations arising from the actions of transnational corporations involved be allowed to seek redress in the home country jurisdiction. Governments should also ensure that those corporations operating in their countries were held to account for violating human rights standards. States parties to environmental agreements in developing countries were urged to strengthen their implementation mechanisms to ensure the protection of individuals and communities threatened by the illicit movement and dumping of toxic products and wastes.

An addendum to the report [E/CN.4/2006/42/Add.1] summarized communications which the Special Rapporteur had sent to Governments and other actors in 2005, the responses received, and updates on previously reported cases. Some of those communications were sent jointly with other Commission special procedures.

Disappearance of States for environmental reasons

Working paper. In response to a 2005 Subcommission request [YUN 2005, p. 846], Françoise Hampson (United Kingdom) submitted a working paper [E/CN.4/Sub.2/AC.4/2006/CRP.2] on the human rights situation of indigenous peoples in States and territories threatened with extinction for environmental reasons. Annexed to the paper were a questionnaire on the topic addressed to relevant State ministries or departments for the purpose of gathering legal, statistical and factual data regarding the underlying reasons for the displacement of a population due to environmental threats, and a summary of activities relating to the issue undertaken by civil society groups in the Pacific region in 2005-2006.

Subcommission action. On 24 August [res. 2006/16], the Subcommission endorsed the conclusions and recommendations contained in Ms. Hampson's paper and appointed her Special Rapporteur with the task of preparing a comprehensive study on the legal implications of the disappearance of States and other territories for environmental reasons, with particular reference to the rights of indigenous peoples. She was asked to submit a preliminary report to the Subcommission's next session or to the first session of any future expert advice mechanism, and a progress report and final report in subsequent years. In the event that her appointment was not endorsed by the Human Rights Council, she would prepare an expanded working paper, to be submitted in accordance with the same procedure and schedule. The Secretary-General was asked to assist her, including for attendance at a workshop on the topic scheduled for the first half of 2007 in the South Pacific. States were requested to provide full and timely replies to her questionnaire, authorized by the Commission.

Right to physical and mental health

Report of Special Rapporteur. The Special Rapporteur on the right to the highest attainable standard of physical and mental health, Paul Hunt (New Zealand), in a March report [E/CN.4/2006/48], submitted in accordance with a 2005 Commission request [YUN 2005. p. 847], determined that the right to health could be understood as a right to an effective and integrated health system, encompassing health care and the underlying determinants of health that were responsive to national and local priorities, and accessible to all. Reflecting on the health-related aspects of the MDGs and the 2005 World Summit Outcome [ibid., p. 48], he urged health ministers in low- and middle-income countries to prepare health programmes bold enough to achieve the health-related Goals. Underpinned by the right to health, an effective health system was a core social institution, no less important than a court system or political system. The report also set out a human rights-based approach to health indicators as a way of measuring and monitoring the progressive realization of the right to health. Annexed to the report was an illustration of the application of such an approach to the reproductive health strategy endorsed by the World Health Assembly in 2004.

An addendum to the report [E/CN.4/2006/48/Add.1] summarized communications which the Special Rapporteur had sent to 26 Governments and other actors between December 2004 and December 2005 and the replies received thereto.

The Special Rapporteur visited Sweden (10-18 January) [A/HRC/4/28/Add.2] to examine the Government's efforts to implement the right to health. He found that the country's standard of living, health status and quality of health care were among the best in the world, and that, in addition to its commitment to guaranteeing good health at the national level, the Government had made important contributions through its foreign policies to realizing the right to health and the health-related MDG in developing countries. Nonetheless, despite its ratification of related international treaties, the right was less firmly entrenched in its domestic laws and policies, a major challenge being the integration of the right into domestic policymaking processes. Issues of particular concern related to the accessibility of appropriate health care; the situation of mental health; the status of minorities, including indigenous people, asylum-seekers and foreign nationals; needle exchange by intravenous drug users; and human rights education for health practitioners. The Special Rapporteur advocated the adoption of a human rights-based approach to health indicators, particularly with regard to the collection of disaggregated data on various grounds. He observed in that context that racial and ethnic minorities in Sweden had comparatively poor health status and that shortcomings in disaggregated data collection based on race made it exceedingly difficult to identify the scale and nature of the problem and how to tackle it. While acknowledging sensitivities associated with such data collection, he emphasized the need for appropriate ways of doing so. The Special Rapporteur also highlighted the crucial role of impact assessments of the right to health in integrating the right in Sweden's national and international policymaking processes in a coherent and consistent manner, which was vital for strengthening the realization of the right at the national level.

By a September note [A/61/338], the Secretary-General transmitted to the General Assembly the report of the Special Rapporteur, which examined the relationship between the right to health and two issues at the heart of the MDGs: access to medicines and the reduction of maternal mortality. The report examined the causes of maternal mortality and their relationship to the failure to realize the right, noting that, if properly integrated, the right could help ensure that relevant policies were more equitable, sustainable and robust. The right also provided a powerful campaigning tool in the struggle to reduce maternal mortality. Regarding access to medicines, the report focused on the responsibilities of States and pharmaceutical companies, and the preparation by the Special Rapporteur of guidelines for them on such access. It emphasized the importance for States to maintain updated national medicines policy, a related implementation plan and an essential medicines list, in order to conform with their right-to-health obligations. The report also noted the emerging consensus on the legal and ethical human rights responsibilities of business enterprises, the recognition by some national courts of the impact of pharmaceutical company pricing policies on the human rights of patients, and the steps taken by some companies to affirm those responsibilities.

On 19 December, the Assembly took note of the Secretary-General's note (**decision 61/529**).

Human Rights Council action. On 27 November [A/62/53 (dec. 2/108)], the Council requested the Special Rapporteur, when presenting his report to the Council in the future, to include the possibility of identifying and exploring the key features of an effective, integrated and accessible health system.

Access to medication

Report of Secretary-General. In a January report [E/CN.4/2006/39 & Add.1] submitted in accordance with a 2005 Commission request [YUN 2005, p. 848], the Secretary-General summarized information received from 18 States, four UN bodies and six NGOs on the steps they had taken to improve access to medication in the context of pandemics such as HIV/AIDS, tuberculosis and malaria.

Human Rights Council action. On 27 November [A/62/53 (dec. 2/107)], the Council requested the Secretary-General to continue to solicit comments from Governments, UN bodies, international organizations and NGOs on the steps they had taken to improve access to medication in the context of pandemics such as HIV/AIDS, tuberculosis and malaria and to report to the Council after its fourth session. The Secretary-General was asked to include in his report a study on the exploration of new and innovative financing mechanisms to help improve such access, and an assessment of the impact of intellectual property rights in the context of those pandemics and from a human rights perspective.

Water and sanitation services

Subcommission action. On 24 August [res. 2006/10], the Subcommission adopted the draft guidelines for the realization of the right to drinking water and sanitation, contained in the 2005 report of the Special Rapporteur on the realization of the right, El-Hadji Guissé (Senegal), [YUN 2005, p. 848]. It decided to submit the report and draft guidelines to the Council for adoption and invited Mr. Guissé to continue his work and submit a follow-up report to the next session of the Subcommission or to the first session of a future expert advice mechanism of the Council. The Secretary-General was requested to bring the guidelines to the attention of States, international organizations and NGOs, while the latter were asked to give priority to the implementation of their international obligations in the area of drinking water and sanitation. States were further asked to cooperate in realizing the right.

Human Rights Council action. On 27 November [A/62/53 (dec. 2/104)], the Council, taking note of the draft guidelines (see above), requested OHCHR to conduct a detailed study on the scope and content of the relevant human rights obligations relating to equitable access to safe drinking water and sanitation under international human rights instruments, including conclusions and recommendations thereon, to be submitted prior to the Council's sixth session.

Bioethics

Report of Special Rapporteur. The Special Rapporteur on human rights and the human genome, Antoanella-Iulia Motoc (Romania), was not able to submit the final report on human rights and the human genome requested by the Subcommission in 2005 [YUN 2005, p. 849], owing to the uncertainty of the transitional period from the Commission to the Human Rights Council.

Subcommission action. On 24 August [dec. 2006/110], the Subcommission requested the Special Rapporteur to submit for its consideration or to a future expert advice mechanism or the Council, a final report on human rights and the human genome. The Secretary-General was asked to assist her, including by facilitating contacts with States, intergovernmental organizations and NGOs.

Slavery and related issues

Working group activities. The five-member Working Group on Contemporary Forms of Slavery, at its thirty-first session (Geneva, 8-11 August) [A/HRC/Sub.1/58/25] focused priority attention on the human rights dimensions of prostitution, particularly regarding the impact on human rights of various national responses to that phenomenon, with special attention to initiatives to criminalize or legalize it in order to regulate it. In addition, the Group reviewed the implementation of human rights standards on contemporary forms of slavery and Human Rights Council decision 2006/102 (re-designated 1/102) concerning the extension and review of mandates (see p. 759). In connection with the latter, it considered various alternatives for ensuring that the Council's envisioned expert advice mechanism effectively addressed contemporary forms of slavery.

In its recommendations, the Group reaffirmed that prostitution was incompatible with the dignity and worth of the human person and recommended that the Subcommission or a future expert advice mechanism request a group of experts to undertake, in cooperation with NGOs and States, an in-depth study on the human rights dimension of prostitution, taking into account its transnational dimensions, such as trafficking, irregular migration and financial aspects, including money laundering. The Group recommended that the Subcommission acknowledge in the paper requested by Council decision 1/102, calling for its vision and recommendations on a future expert advice to the Council, the value of the Group's contributions to international awareness and debate concerning all forms of slavery. In other recommendations, the Group outlined a number of possibilities for future reform, including maintaining the Group in its current form, reinforcing its monitoring mandate, and appointing a special rapporteur on contemporary forms of slavery.

Report of Secretary-General. A July report of the Secretary-General [A/HRC/Sub.1/58/AC.2/4], submitted in accordance with a 2005 Subcommission resolution [YUN 2005, p. 849], summarized information provided by 13 Governments, three UN agencies, one international organization and one NGO regarding legal, administrative and other measures taken to deal with slavery-like practices, such as trafficking in human beings, sexual exploitation of children and forced labour.

Subcommission action. On 24 August [res. 2006/17], the Subcommission drew the Human Rights Council's attention to the contribution of the Working Group on Contemporary Forms of Slavery (see above) to the identification of new forms and manifestations of slavery and slavery-like practices and to their eradication. It recommended that the Group be maintained and that the Council recommend to the General Assembly that it intensify efforts to persuade States to ratify international slavery-related treaties, and consider entrusting to the Group a mandate for monitoring the implementation of those treaties. The Council should also consider establishing a special rapporteur on contemporary forms of slavery or merging such a mandate with that of another special rapporteur.

Fund on slavery

Report of Secretary-General. In March [E/CN.4/2006/76], the Secretary-General reported on the financial status of the United Nations Voluntary Trust Fund on Contemporary Forms of Slavery. At its eleventh session (Geneva, 30 January–3 February), the Fund's Board of Trustees had recommended 47 new project grants amounting to $590,300 to assist NGO projects in 22 countries in Africa, the Americas, Asia and Europe, and 12 travel grants amounting to $20,740 to enable NGO representatives to participate in the deliberations of the Working Group on Contemporary Forms of Slavery (see above). The Board estimated that, in order to fulfil its mandate satisfactorily, the Fund would need an additional $1,239,000 before its twelfth session, scheduled for February 2007. On 13 February, the High Commissioner, on behalf of the Secretary-General, approved the Board's recommendations.

Subcommission action. On 24 August [res. 2006/17], the Subcommission recommended that States contribute more generously to the Fund.

Sexual exploitation during armed conflict

Report of High Commissioner. In accordance with a 2005 Subcommission request [YUN 2005, p. 850], the High Commissioner, in a July report [A/HRC/Sub.1/58/23], reviewed the activities of the Commission, the treaty monitoring bodies and other human rights mechanisms, as well as developments regarding systematic rape, sexual slavery and slavery-like practices during armed conflicts. She observed that, despite growing international recognition of the seriousness of sexual violence and slavery-like practices in conflict situations, and the growing commitment to ensuring accountability and redress for those violations, civilian populations, particularly women and children, continued to fall victim to such practices. The fight against impunity should be at the centre of efforts to end those practices, and States had the legal obligation to prosecute those responsible and to respect the right to justice of the victims. At the international level, referring such situations to the International Criminal Court would help to deal with past abuses and prevent future violations.

Subcommission action. On 24 August [res. 2006/18], the Subcommission, deeply concerned that systematic rape, sexual slavery and slavery-like practices were still being used to humiliate civilians and military personnel, destroy society and diminish prospects for a peaceful resolution of conflicts, emphasized that States should provide effective criminal penalties and compensation for unremedied violations in order to end the cycle of impunity with regard to sexual violence committed during armed conflicts. It encouraged States to promote human rights education on the issue, in an effort to prevent the recurrence of such violations, and called on the High Commissioner to submit an updated report to the Subcommission's 2007 session or to its successor body, or, in the absence of either, to the Human Rights Council.

Vulnerable groups

Women

Violence against women

Note by Secretary-General. In accordance with General Assembly resolution 50/166 [YUN 1995, p. 1188], the Secretary-General submitted to the Human Rights Council and the Commission on the Status of Women the report of the United Nations Development Fund for Women (UNIFEM) regarding the Fund's activities to eliminate violence against women [A/HRC/4/69-E/CN.6/2007/6] (see p. 1333).

Reports of Special Rapporteur. In her annual report [E/CN.4/2006/61], the Special Rapporteur on violence against women, its causes and consequences, Yakin Ertürk (Turkey), examined the due diligence standard as a tool for the effective implementation of women's human rights, including the right to live a life free from violence. As defined in the 1993 Declaration on the Elimination of Violence against Women adopted in General Assembly resolution 48/104 [YUN 1993, p. 1046], the concept of due diligence provided a yardstick for determining whether a State had met its obligations in combating violence against women. The concept held that States had a duty to take action to protect women from violence, punish perpetrators and compensate the victims. However, the application of that standard had tended to be limited to responding to violence against women when it occurred, largely neglecting the obligation to prevent and compensate, as well as the responsibility of non-State actors. The current challenge in combating violence against women was the implementation of human rights standards to ensure that the root causes and consequences of the problem were tackled at all levels, from the home to the transnational arena.

Against that background, the potential of the due diligence standard was explored from various perspectives, at the levels of interventions including individual women, the community, the State and transnational fora. For each level, the report outlined recommendations to relevant actors. The report concluded that the universal phenomenon of violence against women was the result of historically unequal power relations between men and women, the response to which had been fragmented and treated in isolation from the wider concern for women's rights and equality owing to a narrow interpretation and application of human rights law. Therefore, the international community should not confine itself to the current conception of due diligence as an element of State responsibility but demand the full compliance of States with international law, including the legal obligation to address the root causes of violence against women and to hold non-State actors accountable for their actions. Only then could progress be made towards a conception of human rights compatible with global aspirations for a just world free of violence. Nonetheless, what was required to meet the standard of due diligence would vary according to the domestic context, internal dynamics, the nature of the actors concerned and the state of international affairs.

An addendum to the report [E/CN.4/2006/61/Add.1] summarized 89 communications and urgent appeals on alleged cases of violence against women, which the Special Rapporteur had transmitted to 34 Governments on behalf of 130 people, and the replies received thereto.

The Special Rapporteur visited Turkey (22-31 May) [A/HRC/4/34/Add.2] to address the occurrence of suicides by women in the eastern and south-eastern parts of the country and reports that their deaths might be instances of murder or forced suicides. In that context, she examined the country's modernization process, including regional specifics and gaps in women's emancipation, as well as the patriarchal factors behind the phenomenon of violence against women in the country, its diverse manifestations and the particular aspect of honour killings. Also examined were responses to the problem by the State and civil society.

The Special Rapporteur observed that, although Turkey's overall national suicide rate was relatively low, the victims comprised far more women than men, which was at odds with global and national trends in general terms. It was notably disturbing that the victims were mostly young women from poor families. Despite the recognition of gender equality in the country and the adoption of legal and institutional measures towards that end, the basic development indicators for women were bleak, and violence against them, pervasive. The situation of women in the eastern regions was particularly worrisome, as their limited access to education, employment, information, health services and justice constrained their rights and ability to negotiate the terms of their existence and to obtain redress for their problems. Honour was of critical importance in the region, as the norm was codified into customary law, and families made efforts to ensure that the honour code was observed by their members, with transgressions seen as stains on the entire family that should be cleansed at all cost, if necessary through murder. Thus, some of the recorded suicide cases appeared to be disguised murders. Despite the Government's statement that all cases of suicide were investigated, and notwithstanding profound legal reforms that entered into force in 2005, many problems persisted, including the lack of sufficient protective mechanisms for women, such as shelters. In her recommendations, the Special Rapporteur called on the Government to ensure women's advancement; strengthen the legal and institutional framework for combating violence against them and implement a zero-tolerance policy in that regard; identify and adjudicate cases of forced suicide and disguised murders; and take additional suicide-prevention measures.

In Sweden (11-21 June) [A/HRC/4/34/Add.3], the Special Rapporteur addressed the discrepancy between the apparent progress in achieving gender equality and continuing reports of violence against women. She examined policy and practice relating to gender equality and the changing demographics of the country. She also considered the manifestations of violence against women, which included intimate-partner violence; rape and sexual coercion; violence against female migrants, asylum-seekers, refugees and ethnic minorities; and violence in the context of prostitution. The Special Rapporteur found that, although gender equality was highly valued in Swedish society and impressive progress had been made towards the achievement of such equality in the public sphere, serious challenges remained. Women remained underrepresented in senior management positions in private business and in such important public institutions as the police and armed forces, and still earned less than their male counterparts in comparable positions. While an equal opportunity agenda had paved the way for significant advances in the public representation of women, it was not effective in addressing the deep-rooted unequal power relations between women and men, which underpinned the continuation of diverse forms of violence against women. Overall, the Government and society appeared determined to combat and eradicate violence against women and the penal law framework addressing the problem was excellent. However, low prosecution and conviction rates indicated the need for improvements in the implementation of that framework. The Special Rapporteur addressed recommendations to the Government for enhancing and reinforcing the institutional framework on gender equality; addressing the root causes of violence against women; prosecuting and punishing perpetrators; protecting women at risk; and expanding the knowledge base on violence against women and related factors. Other recommendations were directed at Swedish municipalities and non-State actors.

The Special Rapporteur visited the Netherlands, (2-12 July) [A/HRC/4/34/Add.4], where she focused on domestic/intimate partner violence, violence in the context of prostitution and the situation of immigrant, asylum-seeking and refugee women, which had gained particular visibility in the context of a wider debate on immigration in the country. She examined changes in the social landscape towards increased diversity, particularly with regard to immigration and shifts in policy considerations; specific policy and practice to promote change for women's emancipation and the manifestations of violence against women and State response thereto. The Special Rapporteur observed that the Netherlands had become a multi-ethnic society with a considerable portion of non-Western immigrants, whose overall socio-economic position was substantially below than that of the average native population, with immigrant women suffering greater marginalization. Although gender equality within native Dutch society had advanced considerably, native Dutch women remained under-represented both in decision-making positions and in the labour market. The Government's gender-mainstreaming strategy did not effectively address persisting inequalities and coordination, monitoring and accountability mechanisms were lacking, as were gender-budgeting practices. Besides equality issues, women faced various types of gender-based violence, and while the Government was committed to combating the problem, it treated it mainly as an integration issue to be addressed within a law-and-order framework. Domestic violence was the most prevalent in that regard, with immigrant women being particularly affected owing to their socio-economic vulnerabilities, coupled with unfavourable cultural perceptions and the tightening of immigration laws. Women in prostitution also faced violence despite the Government's efforts to enforce a zero-tolerance policy towards trafficking and sexual exploitation. The Special Rapporteur recommended that the Government take measures to improve its gender-equality policy and institutional framework; eliminate all forms of discrimination against women; investigate and punish perpetrators of violence against women; address the vulnerabilities of women who were not Dutch citizens; and expand the knowledge base on violence against women, its causes and consequences.

Communication. By a 23 January note [E/CN.4/2006/G/5], Mexico circulated its comments on the Special Rapporteur's report on her 2005 visit to the country [YUN 2005, p. 851].

General Assembly action. The General Assembly, in **resolution 61/143** of 19 December, invited the Human Rights Council and other UN bodies, to discuss, by 2008, the question of violence against women in all its manifestations, bearing in mind the recommendation of the in-depth study on the subject (see p. 1334).

Mainstreaming women's rights

A December report of the Secretary-General [A/HRC/4/68-E/CN.6/2007/5] reviewed the implementation of the 2006 joint work plan of the UN Division for the Advancement of Women and OHCHR, and their proposed joint work plan for 2007. Under both plans, the main joint activities concerned support to human rights treaty bodies, interaction with special procedures mandate holders, support for intergovernmental bodies, technical cooperation, advisory services and meetings, awareness-raising and outreach, and inter-agency cooperation.

Trafficking in women and girls

Report of Special Rapporteur. In response to a 2004 Commission request [YUN 2004, p. 779], the Special Rapporteur on trafficking in persons, especially women and children, Sigma Huda (Bangladesh), submitted a February report [E/CN.4/2006/62] devoted to a study on the relationship between trafficking and commercial sexual exploitation. In that context, the Special Rapporteur provided a legal interpretation of trafficking based on its accepted international definition, as outlined in the Optional Protocol to Prevent, Suppress and Punish Trafficking in Persons, especially Women and Children, which supplemented the United Nations Convention against Transnational Organized Crime, adopted in General Assembly resolution 55/25 [YUN 2000, p. 1048]. She also addressed the issue of commercial sexual exploitation, and highlighted a variety of methods employed to tackle it. Information and data for the study was derived from a questionnaire, which was distributed to Member States, international organizations and NGOs.

The Special Rapporteur concluded that, while the demand created by prostitute users was not the only factor that drove the sex-trafficking market, it was the element that had received the least attention in anti-trafficking initiatives. Related policy had been directed mostly towards detecting, preventing and punishing the conduct of traffickers or stemming the supply of victims through educational campaigns. Such activities, while important and necessary, needed to be complemented by targeted projects that discouraged demand. Reflecting on the complexities of a human rights approach to trafficking, the Special Rapporteur noted that it had been wrongly assumed that such an approach was inconsistent with the punishment of prostitute users under criminal law. That notion could only have derived from the premise that men had a legal right to engage in the use of prostitutes, as had been granted by some domestic legal system. Encouraging the rejection of that premise, since any such right would conflict with the human rights of victims, the Special Rapporteur emphasized that in the face of such conflict of rights, the rights of the trafficking victims should prevail. In other conclusions and recommendations, the Special Rapporteur reviewed the perspectives of questionnaire respondents on how to tackle the demand aspect of trafficking; most of the views expressed related to the need to criminalize the use of prostituted persons and for extraterritorial jurisdiction. The Special Rapporteur examined the key reasons against the idea of legalizing prostitution; non-criminal sanctions against the use of prostituted persons; and the value of information, education and advisory campaigns by community-based organizations aimed at discouraging demand. Consistent with the views of the respondents, the Special Rapporteur supported the idea of criminalizing the use of prostituted persons. She was of the view, however, that the victims should not be punished under the requisite criminal sanction, as domestic laws and policies penalizing them only contributed to their vulnerability to other human rights violations and re-trafficking. Against arguments that criminalization and the exclusive targeting of prostitute-users might unwittingly push prostitution out of sight and make the victims more vulnerable to abuses, the Special Rapporteur countered that legalizing prostitution often made abuses appear legitimate, and had only served to embolden and expand the commercial sex industry in some countries.

An addendum to the report [E/CN.4/2006/62/Add.1] summarized 29 communications concerning a variety of trafficking-related issues, which the Special Rapporteur had sent, jointly with other special procedures, to 22 countries and the Occupied Palestinian Territory between 1 November 2004 and 31 December 2005, and the responses thereto.

The Special Rapporteur visited Bahrain (29 October–1 November), Oman (2-7 November) and Qatar (8-12 November) [A/HRC/4/23/Add.2 & Corr.1], all of which were described as major receiving countries for migrant workers and destinations or transit countries for human trafficking for forced labour, including sexual exploitation. The Special Rapporteur was motivated to undertake the mission by the acknowledgement by the Governments of those three countries that the problem of human trafficking existed within their territories and their willingness to combat it. The Special Rapporteur examined the situation in the three countries, in the context of the obligation of all States to prevent, investigate and punish human trafficking and provide a human rights framework for protecting trafficked persons. Also examined was the process through which migrants in each of the three countries were recruited and employed and the elements giving rise to human trafficking in that context.

The Special Rapporteur found that the main victims were women and girls recruited as domestic workers and entertainers, as well as men in the construction industry and farm work. She highlighted concerns related to the sponsorship system, which rendered foreign migrant workers dependent on their sponsors, thereby increasing their vulnerability and the demand for trafficking, and the situation of domestic workers, given that the labour code in the three countries excluded domestic workers from protection. The Special Rapporteur observed that, despite measures being established or elaborated for tackling the problem, and the existence of a generally strong legal framework for protecting all workers, more was needed to empower and protect foreign migrant workers, monitor the implementation of laws, ensure that the investigation and prosecution of suspected traffickers were carried out and court decisions enforced, and raise the awareness of public officials and the public at large to the problem and the rights of migrant workers. The Special Rapporteur recommended measures to prevent the exploitation of migrant workers and the related problem of human trafficking, protect victims of trafficking in detention centres and punish the perpetrators.

Communication. On 18 January [E/CN.4/2006/G/6], Lebanon transmitted its observations on the Special Rapporteur's report following her 2005 visit to the country [YUN 2005, p. 854].

General Assembly action. On 19 December, the General Assembly adopted **resolution 61/144** on trafficking in women and girls (see p. 1342).

Children

Report of independent expert. Pursuant to General Assembly resolution 60/231 [YUN 2005, p. 855], the Secretary-General, by an August note [A/61/299], transmitted the report of the independent expert for the UN study on violence against children, Paulo Sérgio Pinheiro (Brazil). The in-depth study, conducted in consultation with Governments, regional and subregional organizations and with the participation of children, built on Graça Machel's 1996 study on the impact of armed conflict on children [YUN 1996, p. 800] and addressed the problem in various settings, including within families, schools, alternative care institutions, detention facilities, places where children worked and communities. Affirming that no violence against children was justifiable and that all such violence was preventable, the expert confirmed that the problem existed in every country, cutting across culture, class, education, income and ethnic origin. Although cruel and humiliating punishment, genital mutilation of girls, neglect, sexual abuse, homicide and other forms of violence against children had long been recorded, the grave and urgent nature of the global problem had only recently been revealed. While some violence was unexpected and isolated, the majority of violent acts experienced by children were perpetrated by those close to them, including parents, school mates, teachers, employers, boyfriends or girlfriends. To illustrate the magnitude of the problem, the expert drew attention to World Health Organization (WHO) data estimating that some 53,000 children died worldwide in 2002 as a result of homicide, and 150 million girls and 73 million boys under 18 years experienced sexual violence. Similarly, the International Labour Organization (ILO) estimated that, in 2004, 218 million children were involved in child labour, of whom 126 million worked in hazardous conditions. Many other cases remained hidden, unreported and under-reported owing to fear on the part of the children involved and a lack of safe or trusted ways for reporting abuse.

After analysing numerous initiatives developed by Governments and others in efforts to tackle the problem, the expert acknowledged that some progress had been made towards protecting children from violence, including measures implemented within the framework of various relevant legal instruments, notably the 1989 Convention on the Rights of the Child, adopted in General Assembly resolution 44/25 [YUN 1989, p. 560]. Nonetheless, much remained to be done. He made a series of overarching recommendations that applied to all efforts to prevent violence against children and to respond to it, as well as specific recommendations for tackling the problem in the home and family, schools and other educational settings, institutions for care and detention, the workplace and the community. Both sets of recommendations were addressed primarily to States and invoked their legislative, administrative, judicial, policymaking, service delivery and institutional functions. Others were directed at parents and children and to other important sectors of society, including professional bodies, trade unions, research institutions, employers and non-governmental and community-based organizations. The report also outlined a framework for the implementation of those recommendations and follow-up action at the national, regional and international levels.

The study was accompanied by a book authored by the expert and entitled the *World Report on Violence against Children*, which provided a more detailed account of the issue.

Sale of children, child prostitution and child pornography

Reports of Special Rapporteur. In response to a 2005 Commission request [YUN 2005, p. 862], the Special Rapporteur on the sale of children, child prostitution and child pornography, Juan Miguel Petit (Uruguay), submitted a January report [E/CN.4/2006/67] devoted to the examination of the demand factor in the commercial sexual exploitation of children, with a view to developing appropriate and efficient legal and political policies for dealing with the problem. The report was based on information provided by 28 Governments and several intergovernmental organizations, NGOs and individuals, in response to a questionnaire sent jointly by the Special Rapporteur and his counterpart on trafficking in persons (see p. 915). In addressing the demand factor, the report considered the nature of services deriving from sexual exploitation and the clients of such services and their attitudes. It found that demand was a complex and multifaceted phenomenon, and in any given situation of sexual exploitation, there might be several different kinds of demand generated by different actors at different times. However, some of the factors driving demand included men's demand for prostitution and beliefs about sexual dominance; the impunity of sexual exploiters; the pernicious effects of a globalized free market economy; discriminatory attitudes based on race, colour and ethnicity; armed conflict and political instability; and greed. The demand factor went hand-in-hand with the supply factor, and the reasons that pushed children into sexual exploitation varied from poverty to family disintegration and numerous other elements. The Special Rapporteur recommended that women and children forced into prostitution should not be penalized to ensure they had access to the authorities without fear of sanctions; child sexual exploitation should be criminalized and the consent of the child being trafficked should always be considered irrelevant. In particular, States should ensure that the whole chain of those involved, including pimps, procurers, intermediaries, organizers of child sex tours and parents, were punished. In addition, they should adopt laws providing for the confiscation of assets from traffickers to compensate the victims, ensure that all children under 18 years were protected by law from commercial sexual exploitation and close all loopholes. Other recommendations advocated educational programmes and awareness-raising activities to reduce demand and addressed sexual exploitation by military personnel, including those serving in UN peacekeeping missions.

Between 1 January and 31 December, the Special Rapporteur sent 30 communications to 26 countries regarding alleged cases involving the sale of children, child prostitution and child pornography. Of those, replies were received from 19 countries, with seven other responses addressing communications he had transmitted in previous years. The communications sent and replies thereto were summarized in a separate report [A/HRC/4/31/Add.1].

The Special Rapporteur visited Ukraine (22-27 October) [A/HRC/4/31/Add. & Corr.1], which faced critical political challenges, including the need for a new model of protection for children's rights. After reviewing the country's legal human rights framework, he acknowledged some positive elements, notably that the protection of the rights of children and youth was enshrined in the constitution and protected through national laws, which guaranteed their right to freedom, the inviolability of their person and the protection of their dignity. Several Government programmes and policies were dedicated to addressing trafficking in persons, child prostitution and child pornography, the plight of abandoned or street children, and of victims of trafficking as a whole. Despite those positive elements, major concerns remained, including the slow progress in reforming the social protection system, which left many children and adolescents vulnerable to trafficking and prostitution, and the increasing number of people leaving the country to pursue better prospects abroad, which placed them at risk of internal and international trafficking. Other notable problems included widespread corruption in public administration, particularly in the judiciary, which undermined law enforcement, the delivery of social services and the State's capacity to prevent and redress human rights violations; the lack of a separate juvenile justice system; the desire among many people for full State control and implementation of all social policies; and the multiplicity of public actors providing assistance and care to children.

The Special Rapporteur encouraged the Government to address the problem of corruption firmly, and to better protect children's rights. He recommended the establishment of a separate justice system for them, in conformity with international standards, including separate detention facilities and a high-level independent institution, such as a national commission on children, youth and family dedicated to enforcing children's rights. To be effective, policies and programmes for combating trafficking and sexual exploitation of children needed to address the root causes of the phenomenon, including social exclusion and discrimination, and those mostly affected should be targeted, among them, street children, victims of sexual abuse and domestic violence, children at boarding facilities and from dysfunctional and poor families. The role of local services should be strengthened to proactively serve the interests of children in need, monitor standards of care, develop community child and family protection plans and ensure there was a focal point to coordinate response to problems. Further recommendations addressed, among other things, legislation-related measures, the enhancement of law enforcement and the situation of children in shelters and orphanages.

Children and armed conflict

Reports of Special Representative. In a February report [E/CN.4/2006/66], the Special Representative of the Secretary-General for children and armed conflict, Karin Sham-Poo (Norway) discussed key issues and proposals for more systematic mainstreaming of the matter of children affected by armed conflict into the work of the UN human rights system. The report also updated information on violations against children in conflict situations, so as to bring pressure to bear on parties to conflict responsible for those violations. In that context, the report considered the monitoring and reporting on compliance within the framework of the application campaign launched by the Secretary-General's 2005 report to the Security Council [YUN 2005, p. 862], which aimed to promote the enforcement of international child protection norms and standards. In addition, the report reviewed the role of the UN human rights system in protecting the rights of children affected by armed conflict, highlighting, in particular, the activities of OHCHR, the former Commission on Human Rights and the Committee on the Rights of the Child, the treaty body monitoring the implementation of the Convention on the Rights of the Child (see p. 777). The Representative observed that, although Member States had the primary obligation for enforcing international standards to protect children's rights, the collaboration of relevant UN entities was essential in that regard. The ongoing reform of the human rights system provided a strong momentum for incorporating the issue into the policies, strategic plans and programmes of key UN human rights entities. The Representative called on those entities to ensure that the era of application of international norms and standards for protecting the rights of war-affected children became a reality and addressed related recommendations to OHCHR and the Commission.

In an August report [A/61/275 & Corr.1], the new Special Representative, Radhika Coomaraswamy (Sri Lanka), appointed in April, outlined the key priorities of her Office, including strategies for ensuring the institution of an era of application of international child protection standards and norms, and significant areas of progress by the international community in delivering tangible protection for children affected by armed conflict. The Representative noted that children were being brutalized and callously used to advance the agenda of adults in over 30 situations of concern worldwide. It was estimated that over 2 million of them had been killed in armed conflict situations, with another 6 million permanently disabled, and 250,000 currently engaged as child soldiers. Fortunately, significant advances and momentum had been achieved on the issue, enabling the international community to begin to redress the imbalance between strong protection standards and the grim reality for children on the ground. Practical means and tools had become available to end the impunity of those who systematically committed the most grave violations against children and to usher in an era of application of international child protection standards. It was imperative that the momentum be maintained and the gains already made consolidated and strengthened. However, what was mostly required was the political will and spirit of common purpose and collaboration to ensure that the international community lived up to the promises made to children. Also needed were broader and stronger consensus and action for enforcing international protection standards; equal emphasis on children in all situations of concern and on all grave violations committed against them; deeper collaboration, collective action and pressure by all stakeholders; and the provision by donors of adequate support to ensure the effectiveness and long-term sustainability of intervention programmes for war-affected children.

Report of Secretary-General. Pursuant to Security Council resolution 1612(2005) [YUN 2005, p. 863], the Secretary-General submitted an October report [A/61/529-S/2006/826 & Corr.1] providing information on compliance with Council resolutions on ending the recruitment and use of children and other violations against them in situations of armed conflict. The report also provided information on compliance and progress regarding situations of concern in 19 countries and the Occupied Palestinian Territory, 12 of which were on the Council's agenda; progress made in the implementation of the monitoring and reporting mechanism outlined in the Secretary-General's 2005 report to the Council [YUN 2005, p. 862]; progress in developing and implementing the action plans called for in Council resolution 1539(2004) [YUN 2004, p. 787]; and an assessment of the role and activities of child protection advisers. The Secretary-General observed that, although some progress had been made in the protection of children in a number of situations of armed conflict covered in his 2005 report, new situations of concern had arisen, including the escalation of violence in the Middle East (Lebanon, Israel and the Occupied Palestinian Territory), resulting in thousands of child victims. Evidence suggested that the recruitment and use of child soldiers and other violations were beginning to spread within regions, as rebel groups moved across borders to prey upon vulnerable children, particularly in the Mano River and Great Lakes regions of Africa. Another growing problem was the use of children by mercenaries and mercenary groups. Other challenges included the existence of youth wings of paramilitary organizations, such as in Northern Ireland; the abduction of children as hostages in the Chechen Republic of the Russian Federation; the proliferation of illicit small arms and light weapons in the hands of children; and ways to accommodate the special needs of female combatants and girls associated with armed groups during demobilization, rehabilitation and reintegration exercises.

The Secretary-General recommended that the Council accord equal care and attention to children affected by armed conflict in all situations of concern and equal weight to all categories of grave violations beyond the recruitment and use of child soldiers, including killing, maiming, rape and other sexual violence and abductions of children, as well as attacks against their schools or hospitals and the denial of humanitarian access to them. He encouraged the Council to continue to call on parties to prepare time-bound action plans for halting the recruitment and use of children, and on donors, to ensure that adequate resources and funding were available to Governments and to the United Nations and its partners, for the rehabilitation and reintegration of all children associated with armed forces. Annexed to the report was a list of parties to conflicts in Burundi, Chad, Colombia, Côte d'Ivoire, the Democratic Republic of the Congo (DRC), Myanmar, Nepal, the Philippines, Somalia, Sri Lanka, the Sudan and Uganda, which recruited and used children as soldiers.

In the course of the year, the Secretary-General submitted to the Council and its working group on children and armed conflict (see below) country specific reports regarding the situation of children affected by armed conflict in Burundi [S/2006/851 & Corr.1], the DRC [S/2006/389], Côte d'Ivoire [S/2006/835], Nepal [S/2006/1007], Sri Lanka [S/2006/1006], and the Sudan [S/2006/662], all of which provided information on compliance and progress in ending the recruitment and use of children and other grave violations against them.

Working group activities. In May [S/2006/275], the Working Group of the Security Council on Children and Armed Conflict, established pursuant to Council resolution 1612(2005) [YUN 2005, p. 863], adopted the terms of reference for its work, which would include reviewing the reports of the related monitoring and reporting mechanism, and progress in the implementation of the action plans mentioned in the Council resolution; consideration of other relevant information presented to it; supporting the implementation of resolution 1612(2005); examining information on compliance and progress in ending the recruitment of child soldiers and other violations against children; and making recommendations to the Council on possible measures to promote the protection of children affected by armed conflict.

During the year, the Group held its second (21 February), third (2 May) and fourth (26 June) meetings [S/2006/497], at which it was briefed by senior officials of UN offices and agencies and exchanged views on, among other things, the several situations of concern. The Group's Chairperson noted that it had made a positive start in adopting decisions for its effective functioning, having helped to accelerate the appointment of a new Special Representative of the Secretary-General and following up on and overseeing the establishment of the monitoring and reporting mechanism called for in Council resolution 1612(2005).

The Group embarked on a new phase of its work in June, with the consideration of specific situations of armed conflict involving child victims. In that regard, it had before it country-specific reports of the Secretary-General on Burundi, the DRC, Côte d'Ivoire, Nepal, Sri Lanka, and the Sudan (see above). At its fifth (6 September) [S/2006/724] and sixth (8 November) [S/2006/971] meetings, the Group adopted conclusions on the reports on DRC [S/2006/389] and the Sudan [S/2006/662], respectively. In both cases, it recommended that the Secretary-General and the Security Council strengthen measures for protecting children from abuse and violence, including the protection of girls from rape and other gender-based violence.

Security Council consideration. On 24 July [meeting 5494], the Security Council held a ministerial debate on children and armed conflict based on a concept paper prepared by France [S/2006/494]. Participants focused on an assessment of the ground covered since the adoption of Council resolution 1612(2005) and the prospects for the future. In addition, they considered how to support the monitoring and reporting mechanism provided for in the Council's resolution, particularly regarding political support and necessary resources; how States and other parties concerned could assist the Special Representative in discharging her duties; evaluation of the work of the Council's Working Group on Children and Armed Conflict (see above); how to ensure that the issue of development, particularly in the health and education sectors, was articulated in Council action to ensure that demobilized children were offered the prospect of lasting reintegration; and how to obtain the optimal involvement of regional organizations and civil actors in the Council's strategy for addressing the plight of children affected by armed conflict.

SECURITY COUNCIL ACTION

On 24 July [meeting 5494], following consultations among Security Council members, the President made statement **S/PRST/2006/33** on behalf of the Council:

> The Security Council reiterates its commitment to address the widespread impact of armed conflict on children and its determination to ensure respect for and implementation of its resolution 1612(2005) and all its previous resolutions on children and armed conflict, which provide a comprehensive framework for addressing the protection of children affected by armed conflict.
>
> As part of this comprehensive framework, the Security Council welcomes the progress made since the adoption of resolution 1612(2005), in particular in the following three areas:
>
> — The Council welcomes the appointment of a new Special Representative of the Secretary-General for Children and Armed Conflict, Ms. Radhika Coomaraswamy. The Council also welcomes her field activities in situations of armed conflict and her intention to carry out new visits in such situations. The Council urges parties to armed conflict to cooperate with the Special Representative, as well as with the United Nations Children's Fund and other

relevant United Nations entities, with a view to ending the recruitment and use of child soldiers in violation of applicable international law and all other violations and abuses committed against children by parties to armed conflict.

— The Council welcomes the ongoing implementation of the monitoring and reporting mechanism on children and armed conflict, invites the Secretary-General to accelerate it in accordance with resolution 1612(2005) and looks forward to receiving the forthcoming independent review on the implementation of this mechanism. The Council acknowledges that the application of the mechanism has already produced results in the field and welcomes the efforts by national Governments, relevant United Nations actors and civil society partners to make the mechanism operational. The Council therefore invites relevant States affected by armed conflict that are not yet involved in the implementation of the monitoring and reporting mechanism to join it on a voluntary basis, in cooperation with the Special Representative and the United Nations Children's Fund.

— The Council welcomes the activities of its Working Group on Children and Armed Conflict, as outlined in the report by its Chairman. The Council welcomes the fact that the Working Group has achieved commendable progress in its implementation phase and is now discussing specific reports of the Secretary General on parties in situations of armed conflict. The Council invites the Working Group to propose effective recommendations for consideration by the Council.

The Council underlines the importance of sustained investment in development, especially in health, education and skills training, to secure the successful reintegration of children in their communities and prevent re-recruitment. The specific situation of girls exploited by armed forces and groups must be recognised and adequately addressed.

The Council calls for a reinvigorated effort by the international community to enhance the protection of children affected by armed conflict. In this regard, it invites all parties concerned, including Member States, regional organisations, relevant United Nations entities acting within their mandates, including the United Nations Children's Fund, the United Nations Development Programme, the Office of the United Nations High Commissioner for Refugees, the Office of the United Nations High Commissioner for Human Rights, the International Labour Organization and the United Nations Educational, Scientific and Cultural Organization, international financial institutions including the World Bank, as well as civil society, to build partnerships to that effect. In particular, the Council invites donors to provide additional resources to fund the development of the monitoring and reporting mechanism and the reintegration of children. The Council also looks forward to the contribution of the newly established Peace-building Commission and Human Rights Council to this effort.

The Council looks forward to the next report of the Secretary General on the implementation of resolution 1612(2005) and its previous resolutions on children affected by armed conflict, to be submitted by November 2006, and expresses its determination to address this important issue.

In further action, on 28 November [meeting 5573], following consultations among Council members, the President made statement **S/PRST/2006/48** on behalf of the Council:

The Security Council takes note with appreciation of the sixth report of the Secretary-General on children and armed conflict and the positive developments in the implementation of its resolution 1612(2005), in particular in the five following areas:

The Security Council takes note with appreciation of the first reports of the monitoring and reporting mechanism on children and armed conflict and welcomes the increasing awareness by some parties to armed conflicts of its relevant decisions as well as the development by those parties of action plans to end the recruitment and use of child soldiers in violation of applicable international law.

The Council commends the work carried out to that effect by the Special Representative of the Secretary-General for Children and Armed Conflict, Ms. Radhika Coomaraswamy, including her field activities in the situations of armed conflict.

The Council also commends the work carried out by the United Nations Children's Fund and the child protection advisers of peacekeeping operations in cooperation with other relevant United Nations entities.

The Council welcomes the cooperation extended to the Special Representative, the United Nations Children's Fund and child protection advisers by some parties to armed conflicts in the preparation and implementation of action plans to halt recruitment and use of children in violation of applicable international law.

The Council welcomes the sustained activity of its Working Group on Children and Armed Conflict and its recommendations, and invites it to continue proposing effective recommendations based on timely, objective, accurate and reliable information for consideration and, where appropriate, implementation by the Council.

The Council welcomes the steps taken by national, international and 'mixed' criminal courts and tribunals against those who are alleged to have committed grave violations against children in situations of armed conflict in violation of applicable international law.

However, the Council strongly condemns the continuing recruitment and use of children in armed conflict in violation of applicable international law, the killing and maiming of children, rape and other sexual violence, abductions, denial of humanitarian access to children and attacks against schools and hospitals by parties to armed conflict.

On those bases, the Council reiterates its primary responsibility for the maintenance of international peace and security and, in this connection, its commitment to address the widespread impact of armed conflict on children and its determination to ensure respect for and continued implementation of resolution 1612(2005) and all its previous resolutions on children and armed conflict, including its intention to act, if needed, in accordance with paragraph 9 of resolution 1612(2005).

The Council takes note of the report of the independent review of the monitoring and reporting mechanism for children and armed conflict as called for in resolution 1612(2005).

The Council reiterates its invitation to relevant States affected by armed conflict that are not yet involved in the implementation of the monitoring and reporting mechanism to join it on a voluntary basis, in cooperation with the Special Representative and the United Nations Children's Fund.

The Council also reiterates its call on relevant parties to armed conflict that have not already done so to prepare and implement, as a matter of priority, concrete time-bound action plans to halt the recruitment and use of children in violation of applicable international law, as called for in resolution 1539(2004).

The Council requests the Secretary-General to submit by February 2008 a report on further progress in the implementation of resolution 1612(2005) and its previous resolutions on children and armed conflict which would include:

"Information on compliance by parties to armed conflicts in ending the recruitment or use of children in armed conflict in violation of applicable international law and other violations being committed against children affected by armed conflict;

"Information on progress made in the implementation of the monitoring and reporting mechanism;

"Information on progress made in the development and implementation of the action plans referred to in paragraph 7 of resolution 1612(2005);

"Information on the mainstreaming of child protection in United Nations peacekeeping operations."

Abduction of children in Africa

Report of High Commissioner. In accordance with a 2005 Commission request [YUN 2005, p. 866], the High Commissioner, in a February report [E/CN.4/2006/65] on the abduction of children in Africa, highlighted OHCHR consultations with relevant UN agencies and actions taken to address the phenomenon. It also contained information from Member States, the Special Representative of the Secretary-General for Children and Armed Conflict, and the Office of the United Nations High Commissioner for Refugees (UNHCR), as well as a related desk review. The High Commissioner observed that, although the right of children to be protected from abduction was unquestionable, the phenomenon in Africa remained largely unstudied. Therefore, consultations on the African experience should provide a solid foundation of knowledge to enable the international community to take appropriate action. The comprehensive assessment of the problem would cover two years, with a complete report to the Human Rights Council projected for 2007. To avoid the duplication of work, the mandate of the monitoring and reporting mechanism called for in Security Council resolution 1612(2005) [YUN 2005, p. 863] should be consolidated with the work currently being done, under the Council's direction, to assess the phenomenon of children's abduction in Africa. That would minimize the possibility of redundancy of the efforts of the monitoring and reporting mechanism and the work of several special representatives and rapporteurs.

The elderly

Subcommission action. On 24 August [dec. 2006/109], the Subcommission requested Chin-Sung Chung (Republic of Korea) to prepare a working paper on the human rights of elderly people and to submit it to the next session of the Subcommission or the first session of a successor body.

Mass exoduses

Report of High Commissioner. In response to a 2005 Commission request [YUN 2003, p. 867], the High Commissioner submitted a March report [A/HRC/4/105] reviewing the status of ratification of international instruments relating to mass exoduses, OHCHR activities addressing the issue and information from eight Governments and UNHCR concerning recent developments in that field. The report noted that mass exodus, whether internal or involving the crossing of borders, was a source of great suffering and violations of the human rights and dignity of those affected. Although States had the primary responsibility for protecting displaced populations on their territories, the international community had an obligation to cooperate with affected countries, particularly developing countries. Despite the growing recognition of the magnitude of the problem and its link to human rights, major challenges remained in preventing it and responding appropriately. Therefore, increased cooperation among all actors involved was required to address those challenges and respond to the protection needs of the victims.

Internally displaced persons

Reports of Secretary-General's Representative. In his annual report [E/CN.4/2006/71], the Secretary-General's Representative on the human rights of internally displaced persons (IDPs), Walter Kälin (Switzerland), outlined a conceptual framework for the protection of IDPs, examined his dialogue with Governments and reviewed his efforts to integrate the human rights of IDPs into all parts of the UN system and to promote the 1998 Guiding Principles on Internal Displacement [YUN 1998, p. 675]. The Representative noted that the past year had been marked by significant developments, which provided the basis for future momentum in addressing the protection needs of IDPs, the most notable being the recognition of internal displacement by the 2005 World Summit [YUN 2005, p. 45] as an issue requiring priority action by the international community. The ongoing humanitarian reform at the international level also had the potential to substantially improve the protection of IDPs, by delivering better responses that were marked by predictability, accountability and responsibility. The Representative was heartened by the response to his mainstreaming work and the readiness of the international community to implement the 1998 Guiding Principles at the regional and national levels. Nonetheless, the past year also highlighted new challenges, particularly displacements resulting from natural disasters and alongside conflict-generated displacement.

In his recommendations, the Representative encouraged States confronting internal displacement to prevent and minimize the problem and to seek technical assistance on relevant human rights issues. All States were asked to provide a basis in national law and policy for the 1998 Guiding Principles and to support efforts to build the response capacity of countries affected by internal displacement. The Representative invited the Inter-Agency Standing Committee (IASC) Country Teams to structure their response to internal displacement on the basis of a comprehensive human rights protection framework and to seek a unified and comprehensive institutional response to the phenomenon in all situations. Civil society was asked to continue to gather information on the human rights aspects of the problem and engage in related dialogue with their Government, the Representative, OHCHR and other UN system actors involved in humanitarian responses in their country. OHCHR was encouraged to systematize an Office-wide response to situations of internal displacement, in order to advance at an early stage human rights protection issues to government interlocutors.

An addendum to the report [E/CN.4/2006/71/Add.1] provided a framework for national responsibility based on the 1998 Guiding Principles, produced by the Brookings Institution-University of Bern Project on Internal Displacement, co-directed by the Representative. The framework comprised 12 steps or benchmarks that Governments should consider taking to fulfil their obligations towards their IDP populations: prevent or mitigate displacement; raise national awareness of the problem; collect data on the numbers and conditions of IDPs; promote training on the problem and on the related 1998 Guiding Principles; create a national legal framework for upholding the rights of IDPs; develop a national policy on the problem; designate an institutional focal point to deal with it; encourage national human rights institutions to integrate internal displacement into their work; ensure the participation of IDPs in decision-making; support lasting solutions for the displaced; allocate adequate resources to the problem; and cooperate with international and regional organizations in tackling the problem. The Representative noted that, individually, each of those measures stood to enhance national efforts to better respond to the problem of internal displacement, and collectively, comprised the core components of a comprehensive response to the plight of the millions of persons affected around the world, who relied on their Governments to protect and assist them. As such, the framework, which had become the basis for advocacy efforts on behalf of IDPs, should make it possible to evaluate the extent to which national responsibility was being exercised to respond to the problem. The Representative invited donors to review the benchmarks in reaching funding decisions in support of assistance to Governments dealing with the problem of displacement.

The Representative visited Côte d'Ivoire (17-24 April) [A/HRC/4/38/Add.2] to gain a better understanding of the situation of IDPs there, whose plight had mostly originated from the conflict that erupted in that country in September 2002 [YUN 2002, p. 180]. It was estimated that the country had up to 1 million IDPs. Additional causes of displacement in the country included insecurity regarding political developments, fear of reprisals from one of the two parties to the conflict, the collapse of public administration, the destruction of infrastructure and economic hardship as a consequence of the conflict. The Representative observed that only a small number of displaced persons were housed in camps or shelters, with the great majority taken in by other families in a show of generosity and solidarity by the Ivorian people. It was also gratifying that the authorities were taking the plight of IDPs seriously. However, the protection of IDPs remained in crisis as they continued to live in dire poverty without the capacity to fully enjoy their rights to food, health care, education and freedom of movement. The Representative observed that the dire situation of Côte d'Ivoire's IDP population could further deteriorate unless a proper Government policy was put in place, especially as the host families were beginning to show signs of fatigue. He recommended that the Government, in cooperation with the international community, draw up a political strategy and national plan of action on internal displacement covering all categories of those affected; establish a mechanism to coordinate the work of the various institutions dealing with the problem; ensure the safety of IDPs, particularly in the western part of the country and guarantee their access to humanitarian assistance, especially health care and educational services; ensure their full participation in electoral processes; and raise awareness of their human rights. There was also a need for urgent Government attention to the land issue, which had contributed to the conflict in the country, especially in the west and south.

In Colombia (15-27 June) [A/HRC/4/38/Add.3], the Representative engaged the Government in a dialogue to improve the protection of the country's estimated 3 million IDPs, whose plight had resulted from the country's four-decade conflict between

Government forces and guerilla groups and drug traffickers. The situation of IDPs was one of the most serious in the world, affecting most parts of the country and up to 427,200 households. While commending the Government for having developed far-reaching legislation and policy on IDPs, and for its efforts in responding to their needs, the Representative observed that more needed to be done, as the dynamics of the conflict and the scale of displacement indicated that the response mechanisms were insufficient to address the problem. The Government faced a dual challenge of addressing continuing needs and a growing amount of people in need of sustainable solutions. Especially worrisome was the gap between the policies decided by the central Government and actual implementation in departments and municipalities, which affected the capacities of IDPs to effectively exercise their rights. The Representative addressed a series of recommendations to the Government concerning policy implementation on IDPs; the prevention of displacement; the persistent and multiple causes of the problem; access and registration; the delivery of humanitarian assistance; measures to consolidate and stabilize the socio-economic conditions of IDPs; land issues; prosecution of the crime of forced displacement under Colombian law; the particular situation of women, elderly people and other vulnerable minorities; existing checks and balances in the country; and the role of the international community.

By an August note [A/61/276], the Secretary-General transmitted to the General Assembly the report of the Representative, submitted in accordance with a 2005 Commission request [YUN 2005, p. 870]. The report discussed the Representative's work in terms of dialogue with Governments, mainstreaming the human rights of IDPs into all parts of the UN system, and promoting the use of the 1998 Guiding Principles on Internal Displacement. It also presented the result of the Representative's cooperation with regional organizations and UN partners, as well as a number of capacity-building projects undertaken by the Representative, including an annual course and a manual for legislators on national implementation of the Guiding Principles and several studies relating to IDPs and peace processes. Welcoming the strengthening of his working relationship with Governments, UN agencies and regional organizations over the previous year, the Representative felt that his mandate provided a unique opportunity for advocacy and solutions-oriented discussions on tackling internal displacement. He was encouraged by the innovative efforts of regional organizations to address the challenges of internal displacement in a regional and context-specific environment. To further facilitate the process, the Representative recommended that Governments develop national laws and policies focused on preventing displacement, providing protection during displacement, and finding durable solutions to the problem; recognize that addressing land and property issues was crucial to fostering the long-term sustainability of solutions to displacement; and pay special attention to potentially vulnerable groups of IDPs, whose needs might differ from the general population, including children, women, the elderly, traumatized persons and persons with disabilities. In addition, Governments and regions in political transition, as well as countries engaged in peace processes, should ensure that the rights and needs of IDPs were considered in all negotiations and agreements. Other recommendations were addressed to regional organizations, UN agencies and country teams, donors and the international community.

Regional conference. The first regional conference on internal displacement in West Africa (Abuja, Nigeria, 26-28 April) [A/HRC/4/38/Add.4], organized by Nigeria and co-sponsored by the Representative and a number of other organizations, explored the extent and nature of internal displacement in West Africa, the needs of the displaced and national, regional and international responses. Attended by over 70 participants, the conference recognized that, while Governments bore the primary responsibility for IDPs, civil society groups, donors and subregional, regional and international organizations also had important roles to play in addressing internal displacement in West Africa. Accordingly, it addressed recommendations to Governments, the Economic Community of West African States and the international community.

Persons with disabilities

Report of High Commissioner. In response to a 2005 Commission request [YUN 2005, p. 873], the High Commissioner submitted a January report [E/CN.4/2006/72] on the progress made in implementing the recommendations contained in the 2002 study on the human rights of persons with disabilities [YUN 2002, p. 771] and on the achievements of the relevant parts of the OHCHR work programme. The report also summarized information provided by three States pursuant to the Commission's request, highlighted work undertaken by OHCHR in the field of human rights and disability and made recommendations for enhancing the effectiveness of the human rights machinery in that regard. The High Commissioner noted that OHCHR supported the elaboration of the new international Convention to promote and protect the rights and dignity of persons with disabilities (see p. 785) and considered that such an instrument could strengthen the protection already afforded by existing human rights treaties by tailoring human rights and standards to the situation and needs of persons with disabilities.

Report of Ad Hoc Committee. The Ad Hoc Committee established in General Assembly resolution 56/168 [YUN 2001, p. 1021] to consider proposals for a Comprehensive and Integral International Convention on the Protection and Promotion of the Rights and Dignity of Persons with Disabilities held its seventh session (New York, 16 January–13 February) [A/AC.265/2006/2], at which it considered articles 1 to 34, the preamble and title of the draft convention.

On 26 July, the Economic and Social Council adopted **resolution 2006/16** (see p. 1278) welcoming the Committee's progress in negotiating the draft and inviting Member States and observers to continue to participate actively and constructively in the Committee, with the aim of concluding the draft, to be submitted to the Assembly as a matter of priority, for adoption at its sixty-first (2006) session.

Further reports of Ad Hoc Committee. At its eighth session (New York, 14-25 August) [A/AC.265/2006/4 & Add.1], the Committee completed and adopted the draft text of a 50-article convention and an 18-article optional protocol. It established an open-ended drafting group tasked with ensuring uniformity of terminology in the drafts and harmonizing them in the six official languages of the Organization.

Pursuant to General Assembly resolution 60/232 [YUN 2005, p. 974], the Secretary-General, by a December note [A/61/611], transmitted to the Assembly the final report of the Committee, to which was annexed the draft convention and draft integral optional protocol.

On 13 December, the Assembly, **by resolution 61/106**, adopted those drafts as the *Convention on the Rights of Persons with Disabilities* and *Optional Protocol to the Convention on the Rights of Persons with Disabilities*, respectively (see p. 785).

Indigenous people

Draft declaration of the rights of indigenous peoples

Working group activities. The working group established in 1995 to elaborate a draft declaration on the rights of indigenous peoples [YUN 1995, p. 777], at its resumed eleventh session (Geneva, 30 January–3 February) [E/CN.4/2006/79], continued to discuss articles relating to self-determination; lands, territories and resources; and other articles where potential agreement might be reached. In his opening comments, the Chairperson-Rapporteur noted that the first decade (1994-2004) for indigenous people (see p. 931), which was the initial time frame for the adoption of the declaration, had already ended. He therefore recommended that all delegations be flexible and conciliatory. It was expected that the group was meeting for the last time, making it imperative for efforts to be made to reach consensus. In 10 meetings, attended by a total of 488 participants, the group held consultations on the outstanding articles on which agreement had yet to be reached. Subsequently, the Chairperson-Rapporteur concluded that the Chairman's revised proposals, which had been used a basis for discussion, would serve as a final compromise text. On 27 June, he presented the group's report to the Council.

Human Rights Council action. On 29 June [A/61/53 (res. 1/2)], the Council, by a recorded vote of 30 to 2, with 12 abstentions, adopted the United Nations Declaration on the Rights of Indigenous Peoples, the text of which was annexed to its resolution. It recommended that the General Assembly adopt the 46-article Declaration.

On 8 December [A/62/53 (dec. 3/101)], the Council decided to defer to its next session consideration of a draft decision [A/HRC/2/L.43] on the rights of indigenous peoples.

GENERAL ASSEMBLY ACTION

On 20 December [meeting 82], the General Assembly, on the recommendation of the Third Committee [A/61/448 & Corr.2, 3], adopted **resolution 61/178** by recorded vote (85-0-89) [agenda item 68].

Working group of the Commission on Human Rights to elaborate a draft declaration in accordance with paragraph 5 of General Assembly resolution 49/214 of 23 December 1994

The General Assembly,

Guided by the purposes and principles of the Charter of the United Nations, in particular the principles of self-determination of peoples, respect for the territorial integrity of States and good faith regarding the fulfilment of the obligations assumed by States in accordance with the Charter,

Taking note of the recommendation of the Human Rights Council contained in its resolution 1/2 of 29 June 2006, by which the Council adopted the text of the United Nations Declaration on the Rights of Indigenous Peoples,

Recognizing that the situation of indigenous peoples varies from country to country and from region to region,

1. *Expresses its appreciation* to the Working Group of the Commission on Human Rights for the work done in the elaboration of a draft declaration on the rights of indigenous peoples;

2. *Decides* to defer consideration of and action on the United Nations Declaration on the Rights of Indigenous Peoples to allow time for further consultations thereon;

3. *Also decides* to conclude its consideration of the Declaration, as contained in the annex to the present resolution, before the end of its sixty-first session.

Annex

United Nations Declaration on the Rights of Indigenous Peoples

The Human Rights Council,

Affirming that indigenous peoples are equal to all other peoples, while recognizing the right of all peoples to be different, to consider themselves different, and to be respected as such,

Affirming also that all peoples contribute to the diversity and richness of civilizations and cultures, which constitute the common heritage of humankind,

Affirming further that all doctrines, policies and practices based on or advocating superiority of peoples or individuals on the basis of national origin or racial, religious, ethnic or cultural differences are racist, scientifically false, legally invalid, morally condemnable and socially unjust,

Reaffirming that indigenous peoples, in the exercise of their rights, should be free from discrimination of any kind,

Concerned that indigenous peoples have suffered from historic injustices as a result of, inter alia, their colonization and dispossession of their lands, territories and resources, thus preventing them from exercising, in particular, their right to development in accordance with their own needs and interests,

Recognizing the urgent need to respect and promote the inherent rights of indigenous peoples which derive from their political, economic and social structures and from their cultures, spiritual traditions, histories and philosophies, especially their rights to their lands, territories and resources,

Recognizing also the urgent need to respect and promote the rights of indigenous peoples affirmed in treaties, agreements and other constructive arrangements with States,

Welcoming the fact that indigenous peoples are organizing themselves for political, economic, social and cultural enhancement and in order to bring to an end all forms of discrimination and oppression wherever they occur,

Convinced that control by indigenous peoples over developments affecting them and their lands, territories and resources will enable them to maintain and strengthen their institutions, cultures and traditions, and to promote their development in accordance with their aspirations and needs,

Recognizing that respect for indigenous knowledge, cultures and traditional practices contributes to sustainable and equitable development and proper management of the environment,

Emphasizing the contribution of the demilitarization of the lands and territories of indigenous peoples to peace, economic and social progress and development, understanding and friendly relations among nations and peoples of the world,

Recognizing in particular the right of indigenous families and communities to retain shared responsibility for the upbringing, training, education and well-being of their children, consistent with the rights of the child,

Recognizing that indigenous peoples have the right freely to determine their relationships with States in a spirit of coexistence, mutual benefit and full respect,

Considering that the rights affirmed in treaties, agreements and other constructive arrangements between States and indigenous peoples are, in some situations, matters of international concern, interest, responsibility and character,

Considering also that treaties, agreements and other constructive arrangements, and the relationship they represent, are the basis for a strengthened partnership between indigenous peoples and States,

Acknowledging that the Charter of the United Nations, the International Covenant on Economic, Social and Cultural Rights and the International Covenant on Civil and Political Rights affirm the fundamental importance of the right to self-determination of all peoples, by virtue of which they freely determine their political status and freely pursue their economic, social and cultural development,

Bearing in mind that nothing in this Declaration may be used to deny any peoples their right to self-determination, exercised in conformity with international law,

Convinced that the recognition of the rights of indigenous peoples in this Declaration will enhance harmonious and cooperative relations between the State and indigenous peoples, based on principles of justice, democracy, respect for human rights, non-discrimination and good faith,

Encouraging States to comply with and effectively implement all their obligations as they apply to indigenous peoples under international instruments, in particular those related to human rights, in consultation and cooperation with the peoples concerned,

Emphasizing that the United Nations has an important and continuing role to play in promoting and protecting the rights of indigenous peoples,

Believing that this Declaration is a further important step forward for the recognition, promotion and protection of the rights and freedoms of indigenous peoples and in the development of relevant activities of the United Nations system in this field,

Recognizing and reaffirming that indigenous individuals are entitled without discrimination to all human rights recognized in international law, and that indigenous peoples possess collective rights which are indispensable for their existence, well-being and integral development as peoples,

Solemnly proclaims the following United Nations Declaration on the Rights of Indigenous Peoples as a standard of achievement to be pursued in a spirit of partnership and mutual respect:

Article 1

Indigenous peoples have the right to the full enjoyment, as a collective or as individuals, of all human rights and fundamental freedoms as recognized in the Charter of the United Nations, the Universal Declaration of Human Rights and international human rights law.

Article 2

Indigenous peoples and individuals are free and equal to all other peoples and individuals and have the right to be free from any kind of discrimination, in the exercise of their rights, in particular that based on their indigenous origin or identity.

Article 3

Indigenous peoples have the right to self-determination. By virtue of that right they freely determine their political status and freely pursue their economic, social and cultural development.

Article 4

Indigenous peoples, in exercising their right to self-determination, have the right to autonomy or self-government in matters relating to their internal and local affairs, as well as ways and means for financing their autonomous functions.

Article 5

Indigenous peoples have the right to maintain and strengthen their distinct political, legal, economic, social and cultural institutions, while retaining their right to participate fully, if they so choose, in the political, economic, social and cultural life of the State.

Article 6

Every indigenous individual has the right to a nationality.

Article 7

1. Indigenous individuals have the rights to life, physical and mental integrity, liberty and security of person.

2. Indigenous peoples have the collective right to live in freedom, peace and security as distinct peoples and shall not be subjected to any act of genocide or any other act of violence, including forcibly removing children of the group to another group.

Article 8

1. Indigenous peoples and individuals have the right not to be subjected to forced assimilation or destruction of their culture.

2. States shall provide effective mechanisms for prevention of, and redress for:

(*a*) Any action which has the aim or effect of depriving them of their integrity as distinct peoples, or of their cultural values or ethnic identities;

(*b*) Any action which has the aim or effect of dispossessing them of their lands, territories or resources;

(*c*) Any form of forced population transfer which has the aim or effect of violating or undermining any of their rights;

(*d*) Any form of forced assimilation or integration by other cultures or ways of life imposed on them by legislative, administrative or other measures;

(*e*) Any form of propaganda designed to promote or incite racial or ethnic discrimination directed against them.

Article 9

Indigenous peoples and individuals have the right to belong to an indigenous community or nation, in accordance with the traditions and customs of the community or nation concerned. No discrimination of any kind may arise from the exercise of such a right.

Article 10

Indigenous peoples shall not be forcibly removed from their lands or territories. No relocation shall take place without the free, prior and informed consent of the indigenous peoples concerned and after agreement on just and fair compensation and, where possible, with the option of return.

Article 11

1. Indigenous peoples have the right to practise and revitalize their cultural traditions and customs. This includes the right to maintain, protect and develop the past, present and future manifestations of their cultures, such as archaeological and historical sites, artefacts, designs, ceremonies, technologies and visual and performing arts and literature.

2. States shall provide redress through effective mechanisms, which may include restitution, developed in conjunction with indigenous peoples, with respect to their cultural, intellectual, religious and spiritual property taken without their free, prior and informed consent or in violation of their laws, traditions and customs.

Article 12

1. Indigenous peoples have the right to manifest, practise, develop and teach their spiritual and religious traditions, customs and ceremonies; the right to maintain, protect and have access in privacy to their religious and cultural sites; the right to the use and control of their ceremonial objects; and the right to the repatriation of their human remains.

2. States shall seek to enable the access and/or repatriation of ceremonial objects and human remains in their possession through fair, transparent and effective mechanisms developed in conjunction with indigenous peoples concerned.

Article 13

1. Indigenous peoples have the right to revitalize, use, develop and transmit to future generations their histories, languages, oral traditions, philosophies, writing systems and literatures, and to designate and retain their own names for communities, places and persons.

2. States shall take effective measures to ensure that this right is protected and also to ensure that indigenous peoples can understand and be understood in political, legal and administrative proceedings, where necessary through the provision of interpretation or by other appropriate means.

Article 14

1. Indigenous peoples have the right to establish and control their educational systems and institutions providing education in their own languages, in a manner appropriate to their cultural methods of teaching and learning.

2. Indigenous individuals, particularly children, have the right to all levels and forms of education of the State without discrimination.

3. States shall, in conjunction with indigenous peoples, take effective measures, in order for indigenous individuals, particularly children, including those living outside their communities, to have access, when possible, to an education in their own culture and provided in their own language.

Article 15

1. Indigenous peoples have the right to the dignity and diversity of their cultures, traditions, histories and aspirations which shall be appropriately reflected in education and public information.

2. States shall take effective measures, in consultation and cooperation with the indigenous peoples concerned, to combat prejudice and eliminate discrimination and to promote tolerance, understanding and good relations among indigenous peoples and all other segments of society.

Article 16

1. Indigenous peoples have the right to establish their own media in their own languages and to have access to all forms of non-indigenous media without discrimination.

2. States shall take effective measures to ensure that State-owned media duly reflect indigenous cultural diversity. States, without prejudice to ensuring full freedom of expression, should encourage privately owned media to adequately reflect indigenous cultural diversity.

Article 17

1. Indigenous individuals and peoples have the right to enjoy fully all rights established under applicable international and domestic labour law.

2. States shall, in consultation and cooperation with indigenous peoples, take specific measures to protect indigenous children from economic exploitation and from performing any work that is likely to be hazardous or to interfere with the child's education, or to be harmful to the child's health or physical, mental, spiritual, moral or social development, taking into account their special vulnerability and the importance of education for their empowerment.

3. Indigenous individuals have the right not to be subjected to any discriminatory conditions of labour and, inter alia, employment or salary.

Article 18

Indigenous peoples have the right to participate in decision-making in matters which would affect their rights, through representatives chosen by themselves in accordance with their own procedures, as well as to maintain and develop their own indigenous decision-making institutions.

Article 19

States shall consult and cooperate in good faith with the indigenous peoples concerned through their own representative institutions in order to obtain their free, prior and informed consent before adopting and implementing legislative or administrative measures that may affect them.

Article 20

1. Indigenous peoples have the right to maintain and develop their political, economic and social systems or institutions, to be secure in the enjoyment of their own means of subsistence and development, and to engage freely in all their traditional and other economic activities.

2. Indigenous peoples deprived of their means of subsistence and development are entitled to just and fair redress.

Article 21

1. Indigenous peoples have the right, without discrimination, to the improvement of their economic and social conditions, including, inter alia, in the areas of education, employment, vocational training and retraining, housing, sanitation, health and social security.

2. States shall take effective measures and, where appropriate, special measures to ensure continuing improvement of their economic and social conditions. Particular attention shall be paid to the rights and special needs of indigenous elders, women, youth, children and persons with disabilities.

Article 22

1. Particular attention shall be paid to the rights and special needs of indigenous elders, women, youth, children and persons with disabilities in the implementation of this Declaration.

2. States shall take measures, in conjunction with indigenous peoples, to ensure that indigenous women and children enjoy the full protection and guarantees against all forms of violence and discrimination.

Article 23

Indigenous peoples have the right to determine and develop priorities and strategies for exercising their right to development. In particular, indigenous peoples have the right to be actively involved in developing and determining health, housing and other economic and social programmes affecting them and, as far as possible, to administer such programmes through their own institutions.

Article 24

1. Indigenous peoples have the right to their traditional medicines and to maintain their health practices, including the conservation of their vital medicinal plants,

animals and minerals. Indigenous individuals also have the right to access, without any discrimination, to all social and health services.

2. Indigenous individuals have an equal right to the enjoyment of the highest attainable standard of physical and mental health. States shall take the necessary steps with a view to achieving progressively the full realization of this right.

Article 25

Indigenous peoples have the right to maintain and strengthen their distinctive spiritual relationship with their traditionally owned or otherwise occupied and used lands, territories, waters and coastal seas and other resources and to uphold their responsibilities to future generations in this regard.

Article 26

1. Indigenous peoples have the right to the lands, territories and resources which they have traditionally owned, occupied or otherwise used or acquired.

2. Indigenous peoples have the right to own, use, develop and control the lands, territories and resources that they possess by reason of traditional ownership or other traditional occupation or use, as well as those which they have otherwise acquired.

3. States shall give legal recognition and protection to these lands, territories and resources. Such recognition shall be conducted with due respect to the customs, traditions and land tenure systems of the indigenous peoples concerned.

Article 27

States shall establish and implement, in conjunction with indigenous peoples concerned, a fair, independent, impartial, open and transparent process, giving due recognition to indigenous peoples' laws, traditions, customs and land tenure systems, to recognize and adjudicate the rights of indigenous peoples pertaining to their lands, territories and resources, including those which were traditionally owned or otherwise occupied or used. Indigenous peoples shall have the right to participate in this process.

Article 28

1. Indigenous peoples have the right to redress, by means that can include restitution or, when this is not possible, just, fair and equitable compensation, for the lands, territories and resources which they have traditionally owned or otherwise occupied or used, and which have been confiscated, taken, occupied, used or damaged without their free, prior and informed consent.

2. Unless otherwise freely agreed upon by the peoples concerned, compensation shall take the form of lands, territories and resources equal in quality, size and legal status or of monetary compensation or other appropriate redress.

Article 29

1. Indigenous peoples have the right to the conservation and protection of the environment and the productive capacity of their lands or territories and resources. States shall establish and implement assistance programmes for indigenous peoples for such conservation and protection, without discrimination.

2. States shall take effective measures to ensure that no storage or disposal of hazardous materials shall take place in the lands or territories of indigenous peoples without their free, prior and informed consent.

3. States shall also take effective measures to ensure, as needed, that programmes for monitoring, maintaining and restoring the health of indigenous peoples, as developed and implemented by the peoples affected by such materials, are duly implemented.

Article 30

1. Military activities shall not take place in the lands or territories of indigenous peoples, unless justified by a significant threat to relevant public interest or otherwise freely agreed with or requested by the indigenous peoples concerned.

2. States shall undertake effective consultations with the indigenous peoples concerned, through appropriate procedures and in particular through their representative institutions, prior to using their lands or territories for military activities.

Article 31

1. Indigenous peoples have the right to maintain, control, protect and develop their cultural heritage, traditional knowledge and traditional cultural expressions, as well as the manifestations of their sciences, technologies and cultures, including human and genetic resources, seeds, medicines, knowledge of the properties of fauna and flora, oral traditions, literatures, designs, sports and traditional games and visual and performing arts. They also have the right to maintain, control, protect and develop their intellectual property over such cultural heritage, traditional knowledge, and traditional cultural expressions.

2. In conjunction with indigenous peoples, States shall take effective measures to recognize and protect the exercise of these rights.

Article 32

1. Indigenous peoples have the right to determine and develop priorities and strategies for the development or use of their lands or territories and other resources.

2. States shall consult and cooperate in good faith with the indigenous peoples concerned through their own representative institutions in order to obtain their free and informed consent prior to the approval of any project affecting their lands or territories and other resources, particularly in connection with the development, utilization or exploitation of their mineral, water or other resources.

3. States shall provide effective mechanisms for just and fair redress for any such activities, and appropriate measures shall be taken to mitigate adverse environmental, economic, social, cultural or spiritual impact.

Article 33

1. Indigenous peoples have the right to determine their own identity or membership in accordance with their customs and traditions. This does not impair the

right of indigenous individuals to obtain citizenship of the States in which they live.

2. Indigenous peoples have the right to determine the structures and to select the membership of their institutions in accordance with their own procedures.

Article 34

Indigenous peoples have the right to promote, develop and maintain their institutional structures and their distinctive customs, spirituality, traditions, procedures, practices and, in the cases where they exist, juridical systems or customs, in accordance with international human rights standards.

Article 35

Indigenous peoples have the right to determine the responsibilities of individuals to their communities.

Article 36

1. Indigenous peoples, in particular those divided by international borders, have the right to maintain and develop contacts, relations and cooperation, including activities for spiritual, cultural, political, economic and social purposes, with their own members as well as other peoples across borders.

2. States, in consultation and cooperation with indigenous peoples, shall take effective measures to facilitate the exercise and ensure the implementation of this right.

Article 37

1. Indigenous peoples have the right to the recognition, observance and enforcement of treaties, agreements and other constructive arrangements concluded with States or their successors and to have States honour and respect such treaties, agreements and other constructive arrangements.

2. Nothing in this Declaration may be interpreted as diminishing or eliminating the rights of indigenous peoples contained in treaties, agreements and other constructive arrangements.

Article 38

States, in consultation and cooperation with indigenous peoples, shall take the appropriate measures, including legislative measures, to achieve the ends of this Declaration.

Article 39

Indigenous peoples have the right to have access to financial and technical assistance from States and through international cooperation, for the enjoyment of the rights contained in this Declaration.

Article 40

Indigenous peoples have the right to access to and prompt decision through just and fair procedures for the resolution of conflicts and disputes with States or other parties, as well as to effective remedies for all infringements of their individual and collective rights. Such a decision shall give due consideration to the customs, traditions, rules and legal systems of the indigenous peoples concerned and international human rights.

Article 41

The organs and specialized agencies of the United Nations system and other intergovernmental organizations shall contribute to the full realization of the provisions of this Declaration through the mobilization, inter alia, of financial cooperation and technical assistance. Ways and means of ensuring participation of indigenous peoples on issues affecting them shall be established.

Article 42

The United Nations, its bodies, including the Permanent Forum on Indigenous Issues, and specialized agencies, including at the country level, and States shall promote respect for and full application of the provisions of this Declaration and follow up the effectiveness of this Declaration.

Article 43

The rights recognized herein constitute the minimum standards for the survival, dignity and well-being of the indigenous peoples of the world.

Article 44

All the rights and freedoms recognized herein are equally guaranteed to male and female indigenous individuals.

Article 45

Nothing in this Declaration may be construed as diminishing or extinguishing the rights indigenous peoples have now or may acquire in the future.

Article 46

1. Nothing in this Declaration may be interpreted as implying for any State, people, group or person any right to engage in any activity or to perform any act contrary to the Charter of the United Nations.

2. In the exercise of the rights enunciated in the present Declaration, human rights and fundamental freedoms of all shall be respected. The exercise of the rights set forth in this Declaration shall be subject only to such limitations as are determined by law, in accordance with international human rights obligations. Any such limitations shall be non-discriminatory and strictly necessary solely for the purpose of securing due recognition and respect for the rights and freedoms of others and for meeting the just and most compelling requirements of a democratic society.

3. The provisions set forth in this Declaration shall be interpreted in accordance with the principles of justice, democracy, respect for human rights, equality, non-discrimination, good governance and good faith.

RECORDED VOTE ON RESOLUTION 61/178:

In favour: Afghanistan, Algeria, Angola, Antigua and Barbuda, Australia, Bahamas, Bahrain, Barbados, Belarus, Benin, Bhutan, Botswana, Brunei Darussalam, Burkina Faso, Cameroon, Canada, Cape Verde, Central African Republic, Colombia, Comoros, Congo, Côte d'Ivoire, Democratic Republic of the Congo, Djibouti, Dominica, Egypt, Eritrea, Ethiopia, Gabon, Gambia, Ghana, Grenada, Guinea, Guinea-Bissau, Guyana, Indonesia, Iraq, Jamaica, Kazakhstan, Kenya, Kiribati, Kuwait, Lebanon, Lesotho, Liberia, Libyan Arab Jamahiriya, Madagascar, Malawi, Mali, Mauritania, Mauritius, Micronesia, Mongolia, Morocco, Mozambique, Myanmar, Namibia, New Zealand, Niger, Nigeria, Russian Federation, Rwanda, Saint Lucia, Saint Vincent and the Grenadines, Saudi Arabia, Sierra Leone, Singapore, South Africa, Sudan, Suriname, Swaziland, Syrian Arab Republic, Thailand, Togo, Tunisia, Turkey, Uganda, United Arab Emirates, United Republic of Tanzania, Uzbekistan, Venezuela, Viet Nam, Yemen, Zambia, Zimbabwe.

Against: None.

Abstaining: Albania, Andorra, Argentina, Armenia, Austria, Azerbaijan, Bangladesh, Belgium, Bolivia, Bosnia and Herzegovina, Brazil, Bulgaria, Burundi, Chile, China, Costa Rica, Croatia, Cuba, Cyprus, Czech Republic, Denmark, Dominican Republic, Ecuador, El Salvador, Estonia, Fiji, Finland, France, Georgia, Germany, Greece, Guatemala, Haiti, Honduras, Hungary, Iceland, India, Ireland, Israel, Italy, Japan, Jordan, Latvia, Liechtenstein, Lithuania, Luxembourg, Malaysia, Malta, Marshall Islands, Mexico, Moldova, Monaco, Montenegro, Nauru, Nepal, Netherlands, Nicaragua, Norway, Oman, Pakistan, Palau, Panama, Papua New Guinea, Paraguay, Peru, Philippines, Poland, Portugal, Qatar, Republic of Korea, Romania, Samoa, San Marino, Senegal, Serbia, Slovakia, Slovenia, Solomon Islands, Spain, Sri Lanka, Sweden, Switzerland, The former Yugoslav Republic of Macedonia, Tonga, Trinidad and Tobago, Ukraine, United Kingdom, United States, Uruguay.

Special Rapporteur

Reports of Special Rapporteur. In his fifth annual report [E/CN.4/2006/78], the Special Rapporteur on the situation of human rights and fundamental freedoms of indigenous people, Mr. Rodolfo Stavenhagen (Mexico), addressed the topics of constitutional reform, legislation and implementation of laws regarding the promotion and protection of the rights of indigenous peoples and their application, as well as the implementation of international standards and treaty body decisions. The Special Rapporteur observed that, during the first International Decade of the World's Indigenous People (1994-2004), proclaimed by the General Assembly in resolution 48/163 [YUN 1993, p. 865], many countries had introduced legislative processes and constitutional reforms in recognition of indigenous peoples and their rights. Included in that context was the recognition of languages, cultures and traditions, the need for prior and informed consultation, the regulation of access to natural resources and land, and in some cases, the recognition of autonomy and self-government. Despite those advances, problems remained, the main one being the existence of an implementation gap, resulting from a vacuum between legislation and administrative, legal and political practice. That divide between form and substance violated the human rights of indigenous people. Part of the problem was evident in the scant representation of indigenous people in legislative work, the lack of consultation with them, and biases and prejudices against their rights among legislators and political parties. As such, the problem was not only about legislating on indigenous issues but doing so with the involvement of indigenous people themselves. To narrow the divide was a challenge that needed to be addressed through a programme of action for the human rights of indigenous people in future.

In the meantime, the Special Rapporteur recommended that Governments assign a high priority to the quest for concrete measures and actions to help close the gap; develop a coordinated and systematic policy, with the participation of indigenous peoples, that cut across the various ministries concerned with indigenous issues; establish, in consultation with indigenous peoples' representatives, bodies for consultation and participation on all measures affecting them; establish monitoring and evaluation mechanisms for the implementation of the standards established; and adopt measures to ensure that judicial authorities and public officials had knowledge of the laws, decisions and international commitments concerning indigenous rights. In addition, an international code of conduct for the protection of indigenous peoples' rights should be elaborated for transnational corporations. The rights of indigenous peoples should be kept on the Council's agenda, with a guaranteed role for them in future discussions.

An addendum to the report [A/HRC/4/32/Add.1] summarized 75 communications, including allegation letters and urgent appeals, which the Special Rapporteur had sent to 24 countries, the World Bank, the Asian Development Bank and *l'Agence Française de Développement* regarding alleged violations of indigenous peoples' rights between 1 January and 31 December 2006, and the responses received. Most were sent jointly with other mandate-holders.

In response to a 2005 Commission request [YUN 2005, p. 875], the Special Rapporteur submitted a progress report [E/CN.4/2006/78/Add.4] on preparatory work for his study regarding best practices carried out to implement the recommendations contained in his reports. He intended to submit the study in 2007 and sought inputs from Governments, indigenous organizations, NGOs, UN agencies and programmes, and academic institutions working in that field.

Report of High Commissioner. A February report of the High Commissioner [E/CN.4/2006/77], submitted in accordance with a 2005 Commission request [YUN 2005, p. 876], reviewed OHCHR activities undertaken in 2005 to promote and protect the rights of indigenous people, including through standard-setting, treaty bodies and special procedures; participation in and organization of inter-agency meetings, workshops and seminars; capacity-building of indigenous organizations through human rights training; and country-level activities to assist States in addressing indigenous rights issues. The High Commissioner noted the continuing disadvantaged situation of indigenous peoples in most countries where they faced numerous difficulties, particularly high levels of extreme poverty. That underscored the urgency of adopting the draft declaration on the rights of indigenous peoples (see p. 925). The High Commissioner also underlined the need to improve the human rights of indigenous people at the community level through national programmes and inter-agency cooperation.

Further reports of Special Rapporteur. The Special Rapporteur visited Ecuador (24 April–4 May) [A/HRC/4/32/Add.2], a multi-ethnic country with 14 officially recognized indigenous nationalities accounting for up to 30 per cent of the population. In his examination of the situation of their human rights, the Special Rapporteur focused on a number of priority areas, including the impact of oil exploration on their communities; their situation on the northern border; uncontacted peoples living among them and threats to their existence; the Páramos (heathlands) in the Andean region; population movements and social and economic conditions; social welfare indicators; indigenous political participation and social movements; the administration of justice, especially indigenous justice; the educational system; and matters relating to international cooperation. He acknowledged some encouraging developments, including the fact that the country's constitution embodied specific collective indigenous rights and the establishment of State institutions to address the situation of indigenous peoples, which created opportunities for them to participate in policy implementation; the national recognition of indigenous territories, particularly the Amazon region, which enabled indigenous communities to negotiate agreements governing the use of land and resources; and the capacity of indigenous organizations to serve as a political force in negotiating social and political participation. Nonetheless, problems remained, as indigenous rights recognized in the constitution were yet to be incorporated into corresponding secondary legislation, making the full implementation of those rights difficult. As such, despite the country's economic growth, indigenous economic, social and human development indicators remained below the national average, as indigenous people continued to face rural poverty; low income, unemployment and consequent emigration; limited access to such basic social services as education; the lack of compatible legislation in the area of indigenous justice; and the gradual destruction of their lands.

The Special Rapporteur recommended that Ecuador enact legislation covering the collective rights of the country's indigenous population, in accordance with its constitution and relating to, among other things, the administration of justice; formulate economic development plans and projects and rules governing economic activities on indigenous territories; ensure the right to prior, free and informed consultation and consent, in accordance with international law; strengthen biodiversity and environmental conservation and management; ensure the prevention and punishment of crimes against indigenous people, including, in particular, women; and strengthen local, communal and regional forms of indigenous government. Other recommendations addressed the situation of indigenous people at the country's northern border, and issues relating to consultation, participation and recognition; specific security and justice-related issues; peoples in voluntary isolation; and the need for international cooperation and the involvement of academic institutions.

In Kenya (4-14 December) [A/HRC/4/32/Add.3], the Special Rapporteur identified the challenges facing the country's indigenous minority communities of hunter-gatherers and pastoralists in the arid and semi-arid lands there. They were discriminated against because of livelihoods and cultures, and their lack of legal recognition and empowerment reflected their social, political and economic marginalization. The most notable human rights problem facing them was the loss and environmental degradation of their land, traditional forests and natural resources owing to dispossession, and more recently, inappropriate development and conservation policies, which had aggravated the violation of their economic, social and cultural rights. They were also affected by the lack of social and health services, especially children and women, who also suffered gender inequalities and discrimination with respect to property rights and harmful traditional practices that contributed to the spread of HIV/AIDS. The violence associated with social and ethnic conflicts and the lack of transitional justice and redress had also affected indigenous rights. The Government had embarked on alternative policies for community-driven development of arid and semi-arid lands, affirmative action policies for poverty reduction and a free universal primary education programme, all of which could help to redress historical injustices and improve the overall situation of indigenous communities.

To facilitate the process, the Special Rapporteur addressed recommendations to the Government, including the constitutional recognition of the rights of indigenous communities to their lands and resources and their effective political participation and distinct cultural identity; conduct of a census to provide disaggregated data to better understand their specific needs and facilitate the elaboration of appropriate public policies; and the redefinition of districts and constituencies to provide for a more effective representation of smaller indigenous communities. Numerous other recommendations to the Government addressed challenges relating to land, resource and environmental rights; forest areas; access to justice; social services; and women's rights. Additional measures were directed at the Kenyan National Commission on Human Rights, indigenous communities and organizations, civil society and political parties, the international community, academic institutions and the media.

Pursuant to a 2005 Commission request [YUN 2005, p. 875], the Secretary-General, by an October note [A/61/490], transmitted the third report of Special Rapporteur Rodolfo Stavenhagen to the General Assembly, which focused on the relevance for indigenous people of the draft United Nations Declaration on the Rights of Indigenous Peoples, which the Human Rights Council had adopted at its first session (see p. 925), and which the Special Rapporteur appealed to the Assembly to adopt. The report also outlined the Special Rapporteur's activities in the past 12 months, which included the investigation of situations affecting the human rights and fundamental freedoms of indigenous people, country visits and communications to Governments with respect to alleged violations of those rights worldwide.

On 19 December, the Assembly took note of the Secretary-General's note (**decision 61/527**).

Working Group on Indigenous Populations

Working Group activities. The five-member Working Group on Indigenous Populations held its twenty-fourth session (Geneva, 31 July–4 August) [A/HRC/Sub.1/58/22] to review developments in the promotion and protection of human rights and fundamental freedoms of indigenous populations, with special attention to the evolution of relevant standards. The principal theme of the session was: "Utilization of indigenous peoples' lands by non-indigenous authorities, groups or individuals for military purposes". Other agenda items considered dealt with indigenous peoples and conflict prevention and resolution; standard-setting activities; the Second International Decade of the World's Indigenous Peoples (see below); cooperation with other UN bodies on indigenous issues; follow-up to the 2001 UN conference on racism [YUN 2001, p. 615]; the draft declaration on the rights of indigenous peoples; and the human rights situation of indigenous peoples in States and territories threatened with extinction for environmental reasons.

The Group had before it a note by the Secretariat on the major theme [E/CN.4/Sub.2/AC.4/2006/2]; a report on an expert seminar on indigenous peoples' permanent sovereignty over natural resources and their relationship to land (see p. 936); a working paper by Yozo Yokota and the Saami Council (an NGO) on the review of the draft principles and guidelines on the protection of the heritage of indigenous peoples [E/CN.4/Sub.2/AC.4/2006/5]; a note by the Secretariat containing information on the Group's achievements [E/CN.4/Sub.2/AC.4/2006/CRP.1]; and a working paper by Françoise Hampson on the human rights situation of indigenous peoples in States and other territories threatened with extinction for environmental reasons [E/CN.4/Sub.2/AC.4/2006/CRP.2].

Miguel Alfonso Martínez (Cuba) informed the Secretariat that the additional working paper on indigenous peoples and conflict prevention and resolution, called for in a 2004 Subcommission resolution [YUN 2004, p. 795], could not be submitted due to the uncertainty of the transitional period from the Commission to the Council. In its recommendations, the Group asked Mr. Martínez to submit the requested paper, focusing on conflicts between indigenous traditional sources of authority and State-designated institutions and representatives. It also recommended that the Secretariat assist Ms. Hampson in contacting Governments, including by means of a questionnaire, in order to obtain further information about the scale, nature and urgency of the problem regarding States and territories threatened by extinction for environmental reasons.

The Group, welcoming the General Assembly's proclamation of the Second International Decade of the World's Indigenous People (2004-2013) [YUN 2004, p. 799], proposed including an item on that development on its agenda or that of a new expert body that might be established, in order to consider how it could contribute to the implementation of the programme of action relating to human rights. The Group asked OHCHR to: organize a workshop on indigenous peoples and conflict resolution, if possible in 2007; consult with States, indigenous organizations, the UN system and NGOs on the final draft guidelines relating to indigenous peoples' heritage, for submission to the Group or an alternative body, and on guidelines relating to the principle of free, prior and informed consent based on the Group's work and to publish and disseminated them widely; organize a workshop on indigenous peoples, mining companies and human rights, with a view to preparing guidelines in relation to the private sector, and a seminar on the contemporary sequels of colonialism for indigenous peoples. The Group further asked OHCHR to provide technical cooperation to States wishing to elaborate national legislation on indigenous issues based on existing human rights law; and explore ways of providing guidance to indigenous peoples who were new participants in the Group on how to increase the effectiveness of their contributions. The Group recommended that the Chairperson-Rapporteur submit the Group's report to the sixth session of the Permanent Forum on Indigenous Issues (see p. 935). It proposed that the principal theme for its twenty-fifth session would be: "The impact of private sector activities on indigenous peoples' rights", and adopted its provisional agenda for that session.

Annexed to the Group's report were its recommendations on indigenous populations regarding the two documents which the Council requested from the Subcommission on the question of the Council's future expert advice mechanism (see p. 762) and a related communication of the indigenous peoples' caucus to the President of the Council.

Subcommision action. On 24 August [res. 2006/13], the Subcommission asked the Secretary-General to transmit the Working Group's report on its 2006 session to the High Commissioner, indigenous organizations, Governments, intergovernmental organizations, NGOs, the Human Rights Council, all thematic rapporteurs, special representatives, independent experts, working groups, and treaty bodies. The Council was requested to endorse the participation, for one week, of the Group's Chairperson-Rapporteur at the sixth session of the Permanent Forum on Indigenous Issues in 2007 to enable him to present the Group's report there, and the Chairperson-Rapporteur, to make an oral presentation to the fourteenth annual meeting of special rapporteurs/representatives, independent experts and chairpersons of working groups of the Council's special procedures to substantiate the need for further cooperation with those special procedures.

The Subcommission decided that the Group should adopt the principal theme proposed for its 2007 session (above). It also decided on the Group's agenda for that session, and asked the Secretary-General to prepare an annotated agenda. It requested the Council to authorize 10 meetings for the Group prior to the fifty-ninth session of the Subcommission or the first session of any future expert advice mechanism in 2007. The Group was asked to continue at that session to review the final drafts of the guidelines on the heritage of indigenous people and on free, prior and informed consent, and to explore ways to further strengthen its cooperation with the Permanent Forum and the Special Rappoteur. States were requested to submit to the Group's next session information on conflict resolution and prevention mechanisms available to indigenous people living under their jurisdiction; to promote and protect traditional knowledge of indigenous peoples; and apply the principle of free, prior and informed consent while protecting such knowledge in relations with non-indigenous sections of the population. Mr. Martinez was asked to submit in 2007 the additional working paper on the issue of indigenous peoples and conflict prevention and resolution called for in a 2004 Subcommission resolution [YUN 2004, p. 795], and to prepare a further working paper on the current effects of the colonial era that continued to adversely impact the living conditions of indigenous peoples in various parts of the world. OHCHR was asked to organize, possibly before the end of 2008, a seminar on the contemporary effects of colonialism on indigenous peoples; technical workshops, not later than the end of 2007, to produce a final draft of the guidelines relating to indigenous peoples' heritage, and guidelines on the principle of free, prior and informed consent, which the Office should publish and disseminate widely; and a workshop on indigenous peoples, mining and other private sector companies and human rights, with a view to preparing guidelines based on respect for the cultures, traditions and heritage of indigenous peoples. Welcoming the Council's adoption of the draft declaration on the rights of indigenous peoples (see p. 925), the Subcommission recommended that the General Assembly adopt the draft at its sixty-first (2006) session, and that the item "indigenous issues" be included automatically on the Council's agenda. It stressed the need in that regard for an expert body to advise the Council on the promotion, protection and realization of indigenous peoples' rights, produce in-depth and action-oriented reports and studies, and elaborate norms and other international standards on promoting and protecting indigenous rights.

Seminars. During the year, two expert seminars were held to advance various aspects of indigenous peoples' rights. The first, organized by OHCHR and the Four Nations of Hobbema (Mascwachis Cree Nations), focused on treaties, agreements and other constructive arrangements between States and indigenous peoples (Alberta, Canada, 14-17 November). It explored in particular best practices for implementing treaties and agreements with indigenous peoples at the national and international levels. The second seminar considered the situation of indigenous peoples in initial contact and voluntary isolation in South America's Amazonian basin and El Chaco regions (Santa Cruz de la Sierra, Bolivia, 20-22 November). Both seminars adopted recommendations on how to overcome difficulties and challenges undermining efforts to better address indigenous peoples' needs and rights.

Voluntary Fund for Indigenous Populations

The Board of Trustees of the United Nations Voluntary Fund for Indigenous Populations, at its nineteenth session (Geneva, 13-17 February) [E/CN.4/Sub.2/AC.4/2006/4], recommended 46 travel grants ($244,320) to enable indigenous representatives to attend the Permanent Forum on Indigenous Issues, 45 ($148,115) to enable representatives to attend the Working Group on Indigenous Populations and 10 ($46,900) for representatives to attend the working group on the draft UN declaration on the rights of indigenous peoples. The High Commissioner approved the Board's recommendations on the Secretary-General's behalf on 1 March. Annexed to the report were lists of beneficiaries.

A September report [A/61/376] of the High Commissioner presented an overview of the Fund's activities in 2005 and 2006. The Board had approved its revised cost plan for 2007, which envisaged expenditures of $733,600. However, in view of the substantial increase in the number of applications for grants to attend meetings concerning indigenous rights, the Board estimated that an additional $733,600 would be needed prior to the start of its twentieth session in 2007. As to the future direction of the Fund, the Board recommended expanding the Fund's mandate to include financial support for human rights projects and to allow for grants to support indigenous peoples' participation in meetings of human rights treaty bodies. The Board scheduled its twentieth session from 26 February to 2 March 2007.

On 19 December, the General Assembly took note of the High Commissioner's report (**decision 61/527**).

Subcommission action. On 24 August [res. 2006/13], the Subcommission appealed to Governments, indigenous peoples, governmental organizations, NGOs and other potential donors in a position to do so to contribute to the Fund. It recommended that States consider asking the General Assembly to agree to the Board's recommendation concerning its mandate (above).

Second International Decade of the World's Indigenous People

On 24 August [res. 2006/12], the Subcommission emphasized the need to maintain efforts towards the effective participation of indigenous peoples in the planning, organization and implementation of activities for the Second International Decade of the World's Indigenous People (2004-2013), proclaimed in General Assembly resolution 59/174 [YUN 2004, p. 799]. The High Commissioner was asked to continue to ensure the participation of her Office in the activities of the human rights component of the Decade's programme of action, and the Working Group on Indigenous Populations, to follow closely the activities carried out as part of that component, to contribute to the mid-term and end-term reviews of the Decade in 2010 and 2015, respectively. The Subcommission was of the view that the Group's annual conclusions and recommendations and the experience it had accumulated in its 24-year work could be particularly valuable for planning and implementing the activities of the Decade.

Voluntary Fund for International Decade.

Efforts continued during the year to secure support for the Voluntary Fund for the Second International Decade for the World's Indigenous People, which the General Assembly had requested the Secretary-General to establish within the context of its declaration of the Second Decade in resolution 59/174 [YUN 2004, p. 799]. The new Fund would succeed the pre-existing Fund established for the first Decade pursuant to Assembly resolution 48/163 [YUN 1993, p. 865]. In 2006, the Subcommission, in its resolution 2006/12 (see above), requested the Decade's Coordinator to appeal to Governments and other possible donors to contribute to the Fund.

Permanent Forum on Indigenous Issues

Report of Permanent Forum. The 16-member Permanent Forum on Indigenous Issues, established by Economic and Social Council resolution 2000/22 [YUN 2000, p. 731] to address indigenous issues relating to economic and social development, the environment, health, education and culture, and human rights, at its fifth session (New York, 15-26 May) [E/2006/43], considered as its theme "The Millennium Development Goals and indigenous peoples: redefining the Goals". It recommended four draft decisions for adoption by the Economic and Social Council on the need for an international expert group meeting on the Convention on Biological Diversity and indigenous peoples' human rights; the subject of the coordination segment of the Council's substantive session of 2007; the venue and dates for the Forum's sixth session; and the provisional agenda and documentation for that session. Matters brought to the Council's attention related to that theme, indigenous women, indigenous children and youth, human rights, data collection and disaggregation, the status of Africa's indigenous peoples, the Second International Decade of the world's indigenous people and the Forum's future work.

Note by Secretariat. An April note of the Secretariat [E/C.19/2006/10], submitted in accordance with a 2005 Forum decision [YUN 2005, p. 881], provided information on the Forum's practices and methods of work and on new challenges and recommendations for improvement.

ECONOMIC AND SOCIAL COUNCIL ACTION

On 27 July, the Economic and Social Council deferred consideration of the report of the Permanent Forum on Indigenous Issues, namely, decisions I to IV and the programme budget implications relating to draft decisions I and III (**decision 2006/243**).

On 15 December, the Council authorized a three-day international expert group meeting on the Convention on Biological Diversity international regime on access and benefit-sharing and indigenous people's human rights, with the participation of representatives from the UN system, five Forum members, intergovernmental organizations, experts from indigenous organizations and Member States. It requested that the results of the meeting be reported to the Forum at its 2007 session (**decision 2006/269**).

Also on 15 December, the Council took note of the Forum's report on its fifth session (**decision 2006/273**), decided that its sixth session would be held in New York from 14 to 25 May 2007 (**decision 2006/271**) and approved the provisional agenda and documentation for that session (**decision 2006/272**). It also decided not to take action on the Forum's draft decision II regarding the subject of the Council's coordination segment for its substantive session in 2007 (**decision 2006/270**).

Indigenous peoples' permanent sovereignty over natural resources

In response to a 2005 Commission request [YUN 2005, p. 882], endorsed in Economic and Social Council decision 2005/289 [ibid], OHCHR organized an experts seminar on indigenous peoples' permanent sovereignty over natural resources and their relationship to land (Geneva, 25-27 January) [E/CN.4/Sub.2/AC.4/2006/3], based on previous reports on that theme prepared by Erica-Irene A. Daes (Greece) in 2001 [YUN 2001, p. 693] and 2004 [YUN 2004, p. 800]. The seminar adopted conclusions and recommendations on measures that States could adopt to better protect indigenous peoples' rights to their lands, territories and natural resources. It invited OHCHR to undertake a study and hold a follow-up seminar to assess the role of transnational corporations and international financial institutions in relation to indigenous peoples' rights to lands, territories and resources. The Human Rights Council was asked to establish an effective and inclusive mechanism to ensure access for indigenous peoples to continue to address their concerns and rights.

Chapter III

Human rights country situations

In 2006, human rights situations of concern, particularly regarding alleged violations and how best to assist and guide Governments and national institutions in combating them, were addressed by the General Assembly and the newly established Human Rights Council, as well as by special rapporteurs, the Secretary-General's special representatives and independent experts appointed to examine those situations. A marked escalation of armed conflict in the Darfur region of the Sudan, relations between Israel and Lebanon, and the situation in the occupied Palestinian Territories prompted the Council to convene four special sessions to consider each case. The first and third sessions, held in July and November, respectively, focused on the occupied Palestinian Territories, the second, in August, addressed the situation in Lebanon, and the fourth, in December, considered developments in Darfur. On each occasion, the Council established a high-level mission to assess or investigate the situation and report thereon. As a result of the situation in Lebanon following Israeli military action, the Assembly adopted resolution 61/154 condemning the violence and calling for international assistance to help rebuild the country and rehabilitate the victims.

In Myanmar, the Secretary-General's good offices in facilitating national reconciliation and democratization made relative progress, which encouraged the dispatch of a UN mission to the country to assess the situation and determine how to further help achieve an all-inclusive democracy founded on human rights and humanitarian norms. Building on that development, the Assembly, in resolution 61/232, called on the Government to end the systematic violations of human rights and fundamental freedoms and to release all political prisoners promptly and unconditionally, including the National League for Democracy leader, Aung San Suu Kyi, and others, who had been held for many years. In similar action, the Assembly called for an end to violations and other situations of serious concern in Belarus, the Democratic People's Republic of Korea and Iran.

Also in 2006, the Council, its special procedures and the Office of the High Commissioner for Human Rights strengthened advisory services and technical cooperation for advancing international human rights principles and preventing violations in Afghanistan, Burundi, Cambodia, the Democratic Republic of the Congo, Haiti, Liberia, Sierra Leone, Somalia and Timor-Leste.

General aspects

In accordance with the procedure established by Economic and Social Council resolutions 1503(XLVIII) (1503 procedure) [YUN 1970, p. 530] and 2000/3 [YUN 2000, p. 596] to deal with communications alleging denial or violation of human rights, the Human Rights Council held closed meetings, on 25 September and 2 October, to examine the situation of human rights in Iran, Kyrgyzstan and Uzbekistan.

Human Rights Council action. On 2 October [A/62/53 (dec. 2/101)], the Human Rights Council acknowledged, in the case of Kyrgyzstan that, while the allegations it considered revealed gross human rights violations that were cause for serious concern, the country's new Government had taken positive steps to investigate the matter. Encouraging the Government to continue those efforts, the Council decided to discontinue consideration of the issue and asked the Secretary-General to communicate its decision to the Government.

In earlier action [A/61/53 (dec. 1/102)], the Council had decided to extend exceptionally for one year, subject to the review called for in General Assembly resolution 60/251 (see p. 757), the mandate of the 1530 procedure, along with the other special procedures of the Commission on Human Rights and the Subcommission on the Promotion and Protection of Human Rights. Accordingly, it requested them to continue to implement their mandates, with OHCHR support.

Strengthening country engagements

In a February report [E/CN.4/2006/10], the High Commissioner provided information on OHCHR efforts to strengthen country engagement and increase field operations in support of both rights-holders and duty-bearers in a timely and context-specific manner, in line with the strategic vision for improving OHCHR future operations, contained in its 2005 Plan of Action [YUN 2005, p. 715]. A reform exercise was currently under way within OHCHR to better equip it to implement that new vision, including through the strengthening of geographic desks at headquarters, the establishment of standing capacities for rapid deployment of human rights fact-finding missions and greater collaboration with operational partners, such as UN agencies, country teams and peace missions. It also involved better coordination of various country engagement efforts and assessments among different stakeholders, with a view to defining the most appropriate type of field engagement for enhancing national human rights protection systems. OHCHR currently maintained an operational presence in some 40 countries, and where it did not have a direct presence, it had enhanced support at the regional level, such as in East and Southern Africa, the Middle East and the Gulf, the Pacific, South-East Asia and Latin America.

The High Commissioner, in her visits to a number of countries, including Uganda, as part of a wider UN engagement to assess the human rights situation, found that the main issues of concern in those countries related to impunity, the protection of civilians and gender-based violence. OHCHR made efforts to combat impunity and respond to the causes of violence and related human rights violations. Focusing on three African countries with active peacekeeping operations—Côte d'Ivoire, Liberia, Sierra Leone—had made it possible for OHCHR to develop a coherent strategy, aimed at providing substantial support to human rights units in integrated missions, as part of its 2006-2007 strategic management plan (see p. 766).

Africa

Burundi

Report of independent expert. On 19 September [A/61/360], the Secretary-General transmitted to the General Assembly the interim report of the independent expert on the situation of human rights in Burundi, Akich Okola (Kenya), covering his fifth mission to the country (29 May–10 June). The report focused on governance issues, the transitional justice system and the circumstances of political prisoners. It found that, although the situation was stabilizing following the 2005 elections, the Government's increasing intolerance towards the opposition had eroded progress made in normalizing the political climate. That trend was illustrated by constant harassment by security forces of political opponents and government critics. While the Government seemed occasionally sensitive to its human rights image, it faced tremendous challenges relating to persisting violations, a culture of impunity and the implementation of its programme of reconstruction and development in a context of widespread poverty and slow disbursement of funds pledged by the international community.

Human rights violations were reported on a daily basis, most of them being violations of the rights to life, physical integrity, freedom, safety and inviolability of the person, to freedom of opinion and expression, and to property. The rights of children and women also needed attention, as well as the plight of the Batwa minority. Some 53 persons were reportedly killed, some of whom were summarily executed. Reports of torture were widespread, allegedly inflicted by government forces, police officers, national intelligence agents and members of local administrations. Although efforts were being made to decrease those violations, tremendous challenges for the realization of a culture of human rights remained. The expert urged the Government to speed up the establishment of the transitional justice mechanisms, conclude its investigation of the Gatumba massacre [YUN 2004, p. 149] and ensure that the perpetrators were brought to justice, deal with increasing incidents of sexual violence, and consolidate democracy by demonstrating tolerance towards its critics. He also called on the international community to increase support to the country's justice system and expand humanitarian and development assistance.

The General Assembly took note of the expert's report on 19 December (**decision 61/529**).

In a report on his sixth mission (7–14 October) [A/HRC/4/5], the independent expert made further recommendations.

Democratic Republic of the Congo

Reports of independent expert. In a February report [E/CN.4/2006/113], the independent expert on the situation of human rights in the Democratic Republic of the Congo (DRC), Titinga Frédéric Pacéré (Burkina Faso), analysed information he had received in previous years and up to 10 January 2006. As part of the technical and legal assistance component of his mandate, the expert submitted to the Government an 11 January memorandum containing an analysis of the human rights situation in the country and related recommendations. The issues of concern included, among others, the 2005 massacres and human rights violations perpetrated in South Kivu [YUN 2005, p. 178], cases of murder and assassination, the illegal exploitation of resources, the dire situation of children, insecurity, elections-related problems, population displacement, the management of public demonstrations and the administration of justice. He observed that the human rights situation remained a matter of concern throughout DRC, especially in the eastern region (Ituri, North Kivu and South Kivu) and in northern Katanga, where militias and other local and foreign armed groups, including the Congolese armed forces and the Mai-Mai (a community-based militia group), were committing atrocities and massive violations with impunity. Massacres of civilians, pillaging, mass rape of women and summary executions had undermined the Transitional Government's efforts to improve the situation. The precarious circumstances of unpaid or underpaid civil servants and public officials, the climate of impunity and the threats, harassments and killings to which journalists and human rights defenders were exposed fomented unrest and jeopardized peace prospects. To remedy the situation, the expert recommended speeding up the disarmament of Rwandan militias and their departure from Congolese territory; involving all shades of political opinion in the democratic process; ending the practice by law enforcement agencies of suppressing rallies and demonstrations; establishing mechanisms to combat the culture of impunity, eradicate corruption and end the embezzlement of salaries of public officials, soldiers and police officers; ensuring the independence of the judicial system by revising existing laws and allocating to the system a budget that would guarantee financial independence; and speeding up the return of internally displaced persons and refugees. Given the destitute state of the country's judicial system and the scale of the crimes perpetrated there for over a decade, it was important to establish, by decision of the Security Council, an international criminal tribunal for the DRC or mixed criminal chambers within existing Congolese courts to hear cases involving crimes committed before 1 July 2002.

By a September note, the Secretary-General [A/61/475] transmitted to the General Assembly the expert's progress report, pursuant to Assembly resolution 60/170 [YUN 2005, p. 737]. The report further elaborated on the ongoing and massive violations in virtually all spheres of human rights, as highlighted in the expert's February report (see above), and reiterated his earlier recommendations.

The Assembly took note of the expert's report on 19 December (**decision 61/529**).

Liberia

Report of independent expert. The independent expert on technical cooperation and advisory services in Liberia, Charlotte Abaka (Ghana), visited the country (20-26 February; 13-23 November) [A/HRC/4/6] to review developments there since 2005, including the security situation and the status of the Truth and Reconciliation Commission, the Independent National Human Rights Commission and the Legislature. The expert also examined issues relating to legal reform and the rule of law, the promotion and protection of human rights, and economic, social and cultural rights. She found that, despite a number of positive developments during the year, challenges remained, owing to the failure to effectively tackle some critical human rights issues, especially those affecting the most marginalized and vulnerable in society.

The year began on a promising note, with the enactment in January of amended legislation on rape, designed to give greater legal protection to victims. The act provided for a broader definition of rape, described the offence of gang rape and provided for a presumption against bail for those accused of first-degree rape. While the legislation still needed to be revised, it was encouraging that the proper legislative framework was being put in place. Another promising development was the inauguration, in February, of the Truth and Reconciliation Commission, one of the major mechanisms for national healing and reconciliation. The Commission began its work in October, with the statement-making process. Despite those encouraging initiatives, concerns included the failure of the police and the courts to properly implement the legislation on sexual crimes, which left victims without any effective protection or remedy and resulted in the widespread practice of out-of-court settlements beween the victims and the alleged perpetrators. Such phenomenon, essentially a form of impunity, was a result of the impotence of the justice system, coupled with the country's dire social and economic conditions. In addition, the Truth and Reconciliation Commission had not been able to proceed with public hearings, because the basic administrative and technical procedures were not in place; therefore its functioning and competence had to be reviewed urgently. To function properly, the Commission needed to establish an effective secretariat and submit a strategy document to donors, as opposed to seeking funding for ad hoc activities. The failure to respect, protect and fulfil economic and social rights throughout the country, particularly for workers on the rubber plantations, made daily life for Liberians a constant struggle. As such, it was encouraging that the principle that there could not be sustainable development without good governance had been placed at the centre of the Government's anti-corruption strategies.

The expert concluded that the Liberian society faced enormous human rights challenges on all fronts—civil, political, economic, social and cultural. While the authorities had demonstrated goodwill on several issues, their efforts had been undercut by slow progress and the lack of effective implementation, owing to the lack of capacity, competence and funds. It was incumbent on the Government to lead the way by putting in place concrete and targeted measures, but the international community had a duty to assist it. Foreign judges and prosecutors should be engaged to work as mentors, as a necessary step towards addressing deficiencies in the administration of justice. The expert also proposed the strengthening of the Law Faculty at the University of Liberia and the implementation of special measures to attract more female students; as well as a constitutional amendment to ensure that all international treaties became part of domestic law and the prompt abrogation of discriminatory legislation.

Workshop. A workshop (21 November) organized by the United Nations Mission in Liberia (UNMIL) discussed the follow-up to the expert's 2005 report [YUN 2005, p. 740] and gender-based violence, particularly the status of implementation of Liberia's amended Rape Act (see p. 934). Participants acknowledged that, while the revised legislation provided greater protection, its weak implementation pointed to a clear need for more effective training of investigators, prosecutors and judges. A revision of the legislation to address such vital issues as rape by juveniles and to render out-of-court settlements illegal was urgent. Civil society and government officials expressed serious concerns about UNMIL accountability in cases of alleged rape and sexual assault by members of the Mission. It was argued that those matters be clarified, as justice was needed to be seen to be done and people wanted to know that there was accountability by all.

Sierra Leone

Report of High Commissioner. In response to a 2005 Commission request [YUN 2005, p. 743], the High Commissioner submitted a February report [E/CN.4/2006/106] on assistance to Sierra Leone in the field of human rights, covering developments in 2005. The report examined human rights issues and challenges in the country relating to the right to life and security of the person; the status of amputees; children's rights; gender-based violence and women's rights; the situation of refugees and internally displaced persons; and economic, social and cultural rights. It also discussed the human rights activities of UN bodies in the country, including those of the United Nations Mission in Sierra Leone (UNAMSIL), particularly regarding the monitoring of courts, police stations and prisons; training and capacity-building services; technical cooperation and advocacy; and assistance in efforts to establish a national human rights commission. In addition, it addressed the question of transitional justice and the related work of the Truth and Reconciliation Commission and the Special Court for Sierra Leone, established in 2002 to try those accused of crimes against humanity, war crimes and other serious violations of international humanitarian law [YUN 2002, p. 164].

The High Commissioner observed that Sierra Leone continued to enjoy relative peace and political stability. The Government authorized the Ministry of Justice to establish a human rights commission and had requested technical assistance in that regard. OHCHR responded favourably, and the process of selecting commissioners was under way. On the key issue of reconciliation, the High Commissioner noted the programmes implemented to sensitize the Government and the people to the findings and recommendations of the Truth and Reconciliation Commission. What was required was the actual implementation of those recommendations, without which healing and reconciliation would be compromised and peace undermined. The Government should implement all the recommendations characterized as "imperative", such as abolishing the death penalty, commuting all pending death sentences, repealing criminal sanctions related to freedom of expression and implementing the reparations programme for war-affected victims.

Overall, there was an increasing trend towards respect for human rights, especially civil and political rights. The decentralization of Government and the creation of new local government structures continued to enhance popular participation in governance and the exercise of political rights. However, the enjoyment of social and economic rights was still lagging, owing partly to the poor state of the economy, widespread poverty and high illiteracy levels. Also of major concern was the high level of unemployment, especially among the youth, with the majority of those affected being former combatants. Addressing those problems was one of the most daunting challenges confronting Sierra Leone and its people. The High Commissioner recommended that the human rights situation in the country should continue to be monitored, investigated and documented. The capacity of government institutions, whose mandates impacted on human rights, including the police, prisons, judiciary, army and the ministries of justice, social welfare and gender and children affairs, should be strengthened to promote and protect those rights. In that context, the Government should speed up the establishment of the national human rights commission. The High Commissioner also advocated capacity-building programmes for stakeholders and key institutions, together with the incorporation of human rights education at all levels of the educational system. Those masures should aid the development of a nationwide culture of respect for human rights, create a robust and vibrant civil society and empower the people of Sierra Leone to identify, demand and assert the protection of their rights. As the task of combating impunity and promoting the rule of law primarily fell on national leaders, OHCHR encouraged all interested parties to call upon African leaders to jointly take a position on the surrender to the Special Court for Sierra Leone of former Liberian President Charles Taylor.

Somalia

Report of independent expert. In response to a 2005 Commission request [YUN 2005, p. 743], the independent expert on the situation of human rights in Somalia, Ghanim Alnajjar (Kuwait), submitted a report to the Human Rights Council [A/HRC/2/CRP.2] noting that, between March 2005 and February 2006, Somalia appeared to have moved forward on the difficult road to peace and security. Following the political progress made in 2005, with the establishment of the Transitional Federal Government and the Transitional Federal Parliament, and after several months of political wrangling over the safe relocation of the Government, the year 2006 began with the signing of the Aden Declaration on 5 January, followed by the convening of the Parliament's first session on 26 February. Nevertheless, the country remained characterized by widespread insecurity, extrajudicial killings, arbitrary arrests and detention, threats to press freedoms, violations of women's and children's rights, and infringements of economic, social and cultural rights. The humanitarian situation was also a cause for concern, with over 2 million people, mostly in south and central Somalia, in need of urgent humanitarian assistance due to the severe drought. Children in Somalia, except in Somaliland, had only 13 per cent access rate to education. Women continued to suffer discrimination, and the situation for internally displaced persons was critical and could become worse. In February, over 4,200 people fled to Ethiopia. Human trafficking was also a significant problem. The expert said that the international community should support the Somali leaders and civil society in the crucial human rights work needed if peace and security were to prevail, including by ensuring technical and financial support to strengthen civil society, establishing independent national institutions, protecting internally displaced persons, establishing and upholding the rule of law, and protecting economic, social and cultural rights.

Sudan

Periodic reports of High Commissioner. During the year, the High Commissioner issued five periodic reports on the human rights situation in the Sudan, collectively covering the period from mid-2005 to October 2006. In the January report, which addressed the 2005 developments, the High Commissioner highlighted the Government's efforts to capitalize on the signing of the Comprehensive Peace Agreement [YUN 2005, p. 301], to lay the foundation for a strong institutional human rights framework, including the adoption of an Interim National Constitution, which made international human rights treaties an integral part of its Bill of Rights, and called for an independent advisory human rights commission. Also highlighted were some of the difficulties that prevented those efforts from improving the practical human rights situation on the ground. The report on developments between December 2005 and April 2006 drew attention to specific human rights issues, including persisting sexual and gender-based violence in the Darfur region, the harassment of people expressing human rights concerns, torture and other inhumane treatment of detainees and impunity. The other report, covering the period from May to June 2006, assessed the deepening crisis in Darfur, following the conclusion and signing of the Darfur Peace Agreement (see p. 274), and the ongoing human rights and humanitarian law violations by the parties. The last two reports focused, respectively, on the brutal campaign conducted between August and September 2006 by militia groups against civilians in the Buram locality of South Darfur and the 29 October attack by armed men (Janjaweed) on several villages around the Jebel Moon Area in West Darfur (see p. 289), where hundreds of civilians were feared dead. Collectively, the High Commissioner's periodic reports indicated that Government efforts to improve the human rights situation in the country fell far short of what was envisaged under the peace agreements and the Constitution, and the situation had further deteriorated, as violations persisted. In each report, the High Commissioner outlined the recommendations designed to assist the country in meeting its international and domestic human rights obligations, particularly with regard to the protection of civilians and the need to ensure their full enjoyment of all human rights.

Report of Special Rapporteur. By a 20 September note [A/61/469], the Secretary-General transmitted to the General Assembly the report of the Special Rapporteur on the situation of human rights in the Sudan, Sima Samar (Afghanistan), in accordance with Human Rights Council decision 1/102 (see p. 759), by which the Council extended for one year the mandates of the special procedures established by the former Commission on Human Rights. The report contained the Special Rapporteur's account of her March and August visits to the Sudan. She observed that Sudan's commitment to ending a history of human rights violations had been undermined by the lack of transparency in the reform process and the delays in implementing the 2005 Peace Agreement. Thus, despite other encouraging initiatives by the authorities to strengthen the national framework for promoting human rights, including by facilitating discussions between different stakeholders, bringing perpetrators of abuses to justice, adopting a plan for the protection of civilians in Darfur, improving the prison system, combating violence against women and improving relevant legislation, serious violations continued and threatened the consolidation of peace in the country. Freedoms of expression, association and assembly were being breached, as the security apparatus continued to arrest and detain people arbitrarily, with detainees often subjected to torture and ill-treatment and denied pre- and fair-trial guarantees. Especially targeted were human rights defenders, journalists, students, political opposition parties, internally displaced persons and tribal leaders. The Government also failed to protect economic, social and cultural rights, with widespread poverty and maginalization continuing to cause political unrest throughout the country.

The situation in the Darfur region deteriorated dramatically, despite the signing in May of the Darfur Peace Agreement. Violence escalated between the signatories and non-signatories of the Agreement, all of whom continued to commit serious breaches of human rights and humanitarian law. Darfur-based militias were also reportedly attacking civilians in neighbouring Chad and the Central African Republic. Against that background, impunity and the lack of disarmament were the greatest obstacles to the prevention of future crimes. Efforts to establish accountability and ensure justice and reparation for victims and survivors of the conflict had so far proven inadequate.

The Special Rapporteur recommended that the warring parties respect their international human rights and humanitarian obligations, particularly regarding the protection of civilians. The Government should further protect all human rights and fundamental freedoms by creating conditions in the social, economic, political and other fields and providing legal guarantees to ensure that everyone could enjoy those rights. It should also investigate all reported violations and bring the perpetrators to justice, in order to end the culture of impunity; ensure that amnesty was not granted to perpetrators of large-scale attacks and that those responsible for the most serious violations were not absorbed into the regular armed forces or given government positions; and protect the physical security and freedom of movement of the people of Darfur. Other recommendations were also addressed to the Government of Southern Sudan and the international community.

On 19 December, the General Assembly took note of the report of the Special Rapporteur (**decision 61/529**).

Huan Rights Council action. On 28 November [A/62/53 (dec. 2/115)], the Council, by a recorded vote (25-11-10), called on all parties to end the violations of human rights and international humanitarian law, focusing especially on women, children and other vulnerable groups; enhance accountability and prevent impunity, as stipulated in the Darfur Peace Agreement; and ensure full and unfettered access by OHCHR monitors, in order to facilitate their duties to provide safe and unhindered delivery of humanitarian assistance to those in need in Darfur.

Communications. In a series of communications during the year [A/HRC/2/G/6; A/HRC/2/G/7; A/HRC/2/G/8; A/HRC/3/G/1], the Sudan reflected on the situation in the country, within the context of the deployment of international forces in Darfur, Security Council resolution 1706(2006) (see p. 282) and the country's efforts to implement the 2005 Comprehensive Peace Agreement and the 2006 Darfur Peace Agreement.

Special Human Rights Council session

On 30 November [A/HRC/S-4/1], Finland, on behalf of 35 Council members, requested that a special session be convened on the human rights situation in Darfur. The Council's fourth special session convened in December, in accordance with the terms of General Assembly resolution 61/251 (see p. 757). The first three special sessions took place in July (see p. 969), August (see p. 964) and November (see p. 969).

The fourth special session (Geneva, 12–13 December) held four meetings, at which it heard statements from numerous Council members, including the Sudan, and from intergovernmental and non-governmental organizations (NGOs) [A/HRC/S-4/5]. It also had before it communications from: the Chairperson of the International Commission of Inquiry on Darfur, established pursuant to Security Council resolution 1564(2004) [YUN 2004, p. 245], underlining the importance of the Commission's recommendations [A/HRC/S-4/2]; the Special Adviser to the Secretary-General on the prevention of genocide, emphasizing the need for urgent international action to prevent genocide and other crimes against humanity in Darfur [A/HRC/S-4/3]; and the Special Rapporteur on the situation of human rights in the Sudan (see above) [A/HRC/S-4/4]. The session also considered two notes from the Sudan, one dated 6 December [A/HRC/S-4/G/1], addressing the High Commissioner's observations regarding the country's human rights situation, and the other, dated 11 December [A/HRC/S-4/G/1], providing information on the observations on Darfur by regional and international officials, the number of deceased and displaced persons, government efforts to disarm the Janjaweed and other militias and combat violence against women, the impact and implementation of the Darfur Peace Agreement, the humanitarian situation in Darfur and child recruitment.

On 13 December, the Council adopted decision [A/62/53 (S-4/101)], by which it expressed concern regarding the seriousness of the human rights and humanitarian situation in Darfur and authorized the dispatch of a high-level mission to assess the situation and the country's needs, and report at the Council's fourth (2007) session. The Government was called upon to intensify its cooperation with the Council and its mechanisms, as well as with OHCHR.

Uganda

Following the establishment of an OHCHR office in Uganda and the signing of a memorandum of understanding between the Government and OHCHR, the High Commissioner submitted a March report [E/CN.4/2006/10/Add. 2] providing an overview of the situation of human rights in areas where the Office had established a field presence and which the High Commissioner had visited (7-14 January). The report focused mainly on the situation in northern (Acholiland) and north-eastern (Karamoja subregion) Uganda, and on economic, social and cultural rights, as well as gender issues and women's rights.

Northern Uganda was the main theatre of the Government's 20-year conflict with the Lord's Resistance Army (LRA) (see p. 168), which had displaced an estimated 2 million people, some 1.5 million of whom lived in overcrowded camps, thereby presenting unique challenges to the enjoyment of human rights. The civilian population was also subjected to gross human rights abuses and violations committed by both sides, including abductions, extrajudicial executions, sexual violence and torture, all of which infringed upon the right to life, liberty and security of the person. Other infringements undermined the exercise of the freedom of movement and associated rights, the administration of justice, land rights, and the realization of the rights of women, who were subjected to gender-based violence, including rape, forced marriage, enslavement, killings, mutilation and starvation, as well as the rights of children, who were compelled to walk long distances daily to avoid abduction by the rebels.

In north-eastern Uganda, particularly in Karamoja, insecurity was rooted partly in the traditional culture of cattle rustling and its increasingly violent modern expressions, and partly in the persistent Government neglect, coupled by an unsuccessful disarmament programme, which resulted in serious security concerns, human rights violations, violence and a complete failure to protect civilians. Administration of justice structures and other central government services were virtually non-existent, resulting in the creation of a parallel system of traditional justice based on reprisals and revenge. Regarding economic, social and cultural rights, the High Commissioner drew attention to an overall poor standard of health, which reflected the country's high poverty level and the lack of adequate infrastructure, equipment and trained staff, and highlighted the challenges Uganda faced in addressing the HIV/AIDS epidemic. Considering gender issues, discrimination against women existed widely in all sectors, with traditional practices and persistent gender-based violence further affecting their rights. The High Commissioner's other key observations were the need to overcome the militarization of the civilian administration of justice and law enforcement by strengthening the police force; the importance of ensuring freedom of information and movement, as well as the voluntary and safe return of internally displaced persons in northern Uganda; and the need to reduce the marginalization of Karamoja by strengthening central government services to eradicate poverty, overcome insecurity and foster development.

The OHCHR strategy in Uganda was shaped by the need to respond to two distinct yet historically and economically interlinked situations. While the conflict-affected northern districts required human rights monitoring, reporting and analysis, as well as technical cooperation and strengthening of national capacities, the north-eastern region needed OHCHR to enhance civilian protection, assist in challenging impunity, help restore security through community-based mechanisms and facilitate inter-ethnic dialogue on peace and human rights education. The High Commissioner made recommendations to the Government, the Uganda Human Rights Commission, civil society and the international community regarding the urgent need for a comprehensive strategy for peace, justice and reconciliation for northern Uganda; security issues and the reinstallation of civilian administration of justice; the safe return of displaced persons; land rights issues; and the need to end the marginalization of Karamoja.

In a later report [A/HRC/4/49/Add.2], the High Commissioner further elaborated on the human rights situation in the conflict-affected areas of northern and north-eastern Uganda. It noted that multiparty elections on 23 February, which resulted in the re-election of President Yoweri Museveni, involved incidents of harassment and the arbitrary detention of opposition leaders, killings and apparent politically motivated judicial processes during the immediate pre-election period. Within the context of the peace talks between the Government and LRA, which began in mid-July, OHCHR advocated respect for human rights as an indispensable element for peace and justice, pointing out that granting amnesty for gross human rights violations would not favour the foundation for sustainable peace. In the first half of 2006, although the human rights situation in northern Uganda continued to be characterized by killings, restrictions on movement and the militarization of the civilian administration of justice, the process of establishing accountability for allegations of violations by members of the national and local defence forces improved relatively. There were also some progress in better protecting children's rights, as the Government pledged to cooperate with the Uganda Human Rights Commission, OHCHR and UNICEF towards eliminating the use and recruitment of children in armed forces. The improved security situation in northern Uganda enabled an estimated 300,000 internally displaced persons to leave the overcrowded camps and return to their parishes of origin, but a million others were expected to remain in camps during 2007. In Karamoja, the situation was less encouraging as pastoralist nomadic tribes continued to be affected by high insecurity, owing to the proliferation of firearms, intertribal clashes and traditional cattle rustling, often resulting in criminal acts. The situation was further compounded by the virtual absence of central government services. Significant levels of human rights violations by the defence force also persisted against the civilian population, mostly in connection with the disarmament exercise.

For most of the year, the police in both regions remained underemployed and lacked the capacity and resources to maintain law and order in rural areas. As such, the defence force continued to carry out police functions, for which it was neither trained nor equipped. The combination of inadequate police presence, the lack of professional training and skills and allegations of corruption resulted in low confidence in the policing in conflict-affected areas, and human rights violations not being reported in most cases, particularly gender-based violence. Other problems related to the administration of justice structures and institutions, which were weak in the rural areas in both northern and north-eastern Uganda, and to land rights questions, fuelled by the consequences of displacement, the challenges of post-conflict housing construction and the weakening of traditional cultures. Also of concern were the reported plans by the authorities to promote development and poverty reduction through mechanized farming and the creation of a land market that might lead to further land rights-related disputes.

The High Commissioner recommended, among other things, integrating human rights and justice as key elements for sustainable peace; strengthening the political commitment and judicial processes to investigate, prosecute and punish any human rights violation by government agents; providing adequate security in the return areas for displaced persons; deploying additional personnel and resources to the civilian administration of justice in northern and north-eastern Uganda; establishing land dispute mechanisms capable of dealing with potential disputes arising from the return of displaced persons; and promoting a national dialogue on options for transitional justice.

Americas

Colombia

Reports of High Commissioner. The High Commissioner, in a 16 May report [E/CN.4/2006/9], described the human rights situation in Colombia during 2005 [YUN 2005, p. 885]. In a later report to the Human Rights Council [A/HRC/4/48], she addressed the main human rights developments in that country in 2006, outlining major advances and challenges, the status of the implementation of the recommendations contained in her previous report and additional recommendations for improving the human rights situation there.

The High Commissioner found that the armed conflict between government forces and illegally armed groups, as well as related drug trafficking and other organized crimes, continued to affect Colombians, disrupting democratic institutions and hindering socio-economic development. The conflict was one of the major causes of human rights violations and breaches of international humanitarian law, as it obstructed the authorities' protection efforts and encouraged impunity. As such, the human rights situation in several Colombian regions remained critical, characterized by numerous violations of civil and political rights, including the rights to life and personal integrity, freedom and security, and due process and judicial guarantees. Many of the alleged perpetrators were members of the State security forces, particularly the army and police. Victims included those of indigenous and Afro-Colombian origins, social leaders, human rights defenders, peasants, women, children, union members, journalists and displaced persons. There were also profound violations of economic, social and cultural rights, as illustrated by the fact that 49.2 per cent of the population lived below the poverty line, of which 14.7 per cent lived in extreme poverty. Acute inequality, also a major problem facing the country, was reflected by a wide gap between social strata, income disparities and uneven access to economic, social and cultural rights.

The High Commissioner acknowledged the efforts by the authorities to implement the recommendations contained in her previous reports. They had adopted policies to improve the human rights situation, including by developing a related national plan of action, promulgating various bills designed to protect human rights, adopting measures for eradicating poverty and inequality, initiating reforms for parts of the justice system and developing a strategy to investigate alleged violations and address victims' needs. Noting the need to redouble efforts to create a more adequate basis for formulating public policies to strengthen human rights, the High Commissioner addressed 18 recommendations to the Government and other national institutions, civil society, the international community and illegally armed groups. She suggested, among other things, the continuing implementation of her previous recommendations, collaboration between the Government and OHCHR in addressing challenges to human rights and international humanitarian law, dialogue between the Government and illegally armed groups as a way to achieve a lasting peace, according priority to human rights issues and victims' rights, and observance by members of the armed groups of international humanitarian legal norms prohibiting the murder of protected persons, attacks against civilians, sexual violence, recruitment of children, acts of terrorism, the use of landmines and forced displacement.

Annexed to the report were accounts of cases of human rights violations and breaches of international humanitarian law, and of the situation of groups in conditions of particular vulnerability and discrimination, as well as the activities of OHCHR in Colombia.

Communication. On 15 March [A/HRC/4/G/11], Colombia transmitted its comments on the High Commissioner's report (see above), highlighting the main advances and challenges in public policy and follow-up to the recommendations contained in that report, the process of demobilization and reinsertion of individuals and members of illegally armed groups, and the country's overall human rights situation.

(For information on the visit to Colombia by the Representative of the Secretary-General on internally displaced persons, see p. 923.)

Cuba

Report of Personal Representative. In a report to the Human Rights Council [A/HRC/4/12], the High Commissioner's Personal Representative on the situation of human rights in Cuba, Christine Chanet (France), reviewed factors hindering the realization of human rights in that country, particularly from the perspective of the economic, trade and financial embargo it had faced for over 40 years. As attempts to initiate dialogue with the Cuban authorities remained unsuccessful, the Representative relied on information from the thematic special rapporteurs of the former Commission on Human Rights, who had investigated the human rights issues in Cuba, and from NGOs. Additional insight on the situation came from the report of the Inter-American Commission on Human Rights.

The Representative stated that the restrictions imposed by the embargo were depriving Cuba of vital access to medicines and new medical technology, food, chemicals for water treatment and adequate electricity. The consequential difficulties for Cubans were compounded by even tighter economic and financial restrictions imposed by the United States in

2004 [YUN 2004, p. 806], supplemented by significant limitations on the movement of persons and goods, including a drastic reduction in the frequency of family visits by Cuban-Americans and their capacity to send things to their families. Those restrictions constituted arbitrary interference in the private and family lives of individuals and a disproportionate hindrance to their freedom of movement, thereby infringing on the exercise of their fundamental rights. The embargo further affected the civil and political rights of citizens by provoking the authorities to adopt repressive laws, under which Cubans who allegedly communicated with foreign agents promoting pluralist political principles were liable to punishment. Of particular concern were the arbitrary detention of persons who supported changes in the electoral system and related legislative reforms, mostly writers, human rights defenders and members of opposition trade unions and political parties. Accused persons were often denied access to adequate defence. Particularly alarming were allegations of ill-treatment while in detention. While acknowledging some positive developments in the health and educational systems, efforts to combat discrimination against women in the workplace, ratification of human rights instruments and the release of 18 prisoners on health grounds, the Representative encouraged the authorities to eliminate restrictions on fundamental rights and freedoms of individuals. Accordingly, she recommended 10 measures, among them, halting the prosecution of those exercising the rights enshrined in the Universal Declaration of Human Rights, adopted by General Assembly resolution 217 A(III) [YUN 1948-49, p. 535]. Other recommendations were the release of detained persons who had not committed acts of violence against individuals or property; the reform of laws applied in the criminal prosecution of persons exercising their freedom of expression, demonstration, assembly and association, in order to bring those laws in line with the Universal Declaration of Human Rights; reform of the rules of criminal procedure and regulations relating to travel into and out of Cuba; upholding the moratorium on the death penalty, with a view to its abolition; and establishing a standing independent body empowered to hear complaints from those alleging that their rights were violated.

Guatemala

Reports of High Commissioner. In a February report [E/CN.4/2006/10/Add.1 & Corr. 2], the High Commissioner provided preliminary observations of the human rights situation in Guatemala, within the framework of the 2005 joint agreement between the Government and OHCHR [YUN 2005, p. 374] establishing an OHCHR office in the country to monitor and report on human rights developments. Issues addressed in the report related to violence, the rule of law and impunity, poverty, economic, social and cultural rights, and equality and non-discrimination.

Although the cessation of the conflict and the signing of the peace accords [YUN 1996, p. 168] had ended decades of systematic human rights violations by the State, there was a shift in recent years from political violence to social violence, the High Commissioner noted. It was disquieting to observe the State's ineffectiveness in preventing and investigating acts of violence, as well as punishing those involved, and in embarking on public policies to reduce poverty, discrimination and the lack of opportunity. Combating violence resulting from organized crime and other criminal activities, including by youth gangs and illegal clandestine security bodies, had become a national priority owing to its impact on public security. The ongoing violence had also resulted in an increase in the number of homicides, with 5,338 cases being recorded in 2005. Of notable concern were acts of violence perpetrated by juveniles and by persons in the prison system, as well as against women. Attacks on human rights defenders had increased, the main victims being members of agricultural organizations, trade unions and development and environmental organizations. The State, by not providing the necessary security to prevent violence, had failed to discharge its human rights obligations. Its limited capacity to provide legal and institutional protection for women, in particular the impunity enjoyed by the aggressors and fear among the victims, demonstrated a lack of confidence in the State protection machinery.

The High Commissioner was also concerned at the high levels of poverty and inequality preventing broad segments of the population from enjoying their economic, social and cultural rights, and at the racial discrimination against indigenous communities, including the Maya, Xinca and Garífuna populations, which impeded the enjoyment of their identity and collective rights. On the positive side, however, the new Land Register Act recognized collective registration of ownership of communal lands by indigenous peoples.

The High Commissioner recommended 24 measures to the Government and civil society to help improve the country's human rights situation. Those measures related to prevention and protection issues, the rule of law and impunity, transitional justice, economic and social policy, equality and non-discrimination, the promotion of a culture of human rights, and OHCHR technical cooperation and advisory services.

In a later report [A/HR4/49/Add.1], the High Commissioner described the activities of the OHCHR office in Guatemala in 2006, undertaken in an atmosphere marked by social tension, continuing violence and general insecurity. The office closely monitored the volatile situation hindering the full enjoyment of the right to life and made it imperative for the State to step up preventive measures, and investigate and punish threats to and violations of that right. In particular, it monitored the public security situation and its impact on human rights, the continuing challenges in combating impunity and strengthening the rule of law, the progress and difficulties in implementing the National Compensation Programme for victims of the conflict, the situation of indigenous peoples, the increasing political violence, and the situation of economic, social and cultural rights, and that of human rights defenders. The report noted that homicides had reached their highest level in 10 years, and OHCHR had received information on the alleged involvement of State security officers in extrajudicial executions, facilitated by a climate of impunity. Given the high level of violence, the State had not been able to draw up a public security policy consistent with human rights, while the justice system, despite its continuing modernization and reform programme, was still too weak to confront organized crime.

During the year, the OHCHR office was strengthened through the recruitment of new staff, making it possible to gather more information on the human rights situation in the country and to provide advisory services and technical cooperation to State institutions and civil society organizations. The High Commissioner recommended 18 measures relating to the legislative framework for human rights protection, public security, the rule of law and the need to combat impunity, the situation of indigenous peoples, political rights, violence against women, economic, social and cultural rights, the welfare of human rights defenders, public policy in human rights and OHCHR technical cooperation and advisory services.

(See pp. 870 and 873 respectively, for information on visits to Guatemala in 2006 by the Special Rapporteur on extrajudicial, summary or arbitrary executions and by the Working Group on involuntary disappearances.)

Haiti

Report of independent expert. In a report [A/HCR/4/3] summarizing the human rights situation in Haiti, independent expert Louis Joinet (France) examined the problems stemming from the growing insecurity in the country, including the deteriorating relations between the police and the judicial system, particularly the shortcomings in the police force, the judiciary and the prison system and the rising trend in violent organized crime. Also addressed were a suitable strategy for combating the impunity of what the expert described as "neo-criminals", the need to reform the justice system and the office of the ombudsman and the importance of consolidating the progress made in addressing the status of and violence against women. While acknowledging Haiti's return to constitutional legality, the expert observed that it was still a long way from being a consolidated State based on the rule of law. The goal was to reduce, as a matter of priority, the chronic malfunctions of the State and their impact on human rights in the areas of the police, the judicial system, prisons and more generally in efforts to combat the impunity of perpetrators of particularly serious crimes, such as drug trafficking, murders and kidnappings for ransom. To achieve that, it was necessary to strengthen, through vetting, the police and justice services and launch an ambitious plan of action to reform the judicial system.

The expert noted that, besides ill-treatment in cases of arrest, the police had frequently not observed the time limit for remand in custody, and certain police practices could give rise to dubious financial transactions and abuse of authority. The expert also drew attention to endemic corruption, and the lack of respect for legal principles, with district judges disregarding the legal time limits for the transmission of cases or those without legal competence releasing detainees. The non-observance of the procedure for renewing judges' mandates, chronic absenteeism of certain magistrates, and negligence or professional laxity resulted in the slow process of justice, including extended detention. He deplored the overpopulation in the prison system, aggravated by the dilapidated state of buildings and the lack of safe drinking water and appropriate medical care. Major difficulties were also faced in combating organized crime, especially drug trafficking and an unprecedented wave of murders and kidnappings for ransom.

The expert recommended reinforcing the capacity of the inspection bodies of the police and judiciary to do their job effectively and reduce the malfunctions stemming from individual actions; reforming the judiciary and according high priority to finalizing the three bills relating to the reform of judiciary regulations, the Supreme Council of Justice and the

Judicial Training College; combating extended detention by providing, among other things, the possibility of imposing suspended sentences; providing better legal assistance; and reforming civil status, under the auspices of the National Identification Office, and the land register. He also proposed ways to improve the status of women, including by adopting decrees that categorized rape as a major crime, decriminalized adultery and rejected it as an extenuating circumstance in the murder of a wife or partner, decriminalized abortion, upheld the admissibility of paternity hearings, addressed the status of concubines and regulated domestic work.

By **decision 61/552** of 22 December, the General Assembly decided that the item on the situation of democracy and human rights in Haiti would remain for consideration during its resumed sixty-first (2007) session.

Asia

Afghanistan

Report of High Commissioner. In response to a 2005 Commission request [YUN 2005, 734], the High Commissioner submitted a March report [E/CN.4/2006/108] on the situation of human rights in Afghanistan and the achievements of related technical assistance. Based on the 2005 OHCHR Plan of Action [YUN 2005, p. 715], the report highlighted six main areas where human rights faced particular challenges: poverty, discrimination, armed conflict and violence, impunity, democracy deficits and weak institutions. It acknowledged incremental improvements on some critical issues, including the completion of the disarmament, demobilization and reintegration process, the successful conduct of parliamentary elections, particularly in the empowerment of women, and the application, for the first time, of vetting and complaints procedures to major government programmes. Further indications of progress were the adoption of a constitution, a democratically elected President, improvement in reconstruction efforts, the continuing return of refugees, vibrant media, operational schools in most areas and some functioning institutions, including the Afghanistan Independent Human Rights Commission. However, the overall human rights situation was of great concern, owing mainly to security conditions and weaknesses in governance. Impunity of factional commanders and former warlords, some of whom occasionally received support from the Government and Afghan leaders, undermined justice reform, the freedom of expression, the electoral process, economic development and women's participation in public affairs.

The report determined that a litmus test for improvement would be the will and effort of the Government to implement the Action Plan on Peace, Reconciliation and Justice [ibid., p. 408]. Building on the gains of the past four years, Afghanistan should focus on developing an effective national human rights protection system and, in that context, OHCHR would intensify its technical cooperation programme. The High Commissioner advocated continuing support for the Afghanistan Independent Human Rights Commission; further recommended international political and economic support for the whole spectrum of human rights as reflected in the Afghanistan Compact and the outcome of the London Conference on the country (see p. 363); poverty reduction among the most marginalized and vulnerable sectors; adoption by the Government of a rights-based approach to customary law, in order to protect women and children from detrimental traditional practices; continuing international support to train judicial, police and other government officials in implementing human rights standards relating to women's rights; establishment of a functional, accessible and equitable justice system; appointment of qualified judges; and the introduction of a transparent and merit-based appointment and promotion, transfer and disciplinary mechanism in the judiciary.

Human Rights Council action. On 27 November [A/62/53 (dec. 2/113)], the Human Rights Council requested the High Commissioner to continue, in cooperation with the United Nations Assistance Mission in Afghanistan, to monitor the human rights situation in the country, expand advisory services and technical cooperation in human rights and the rule of law, and report thereon, paying special attention to the rights of women, and on technical assistance provided.

Cambodia

Reports of Special Representative. In an addendum [E/CN.4/2006/110/Add.1] to his previous report [YUN 2005, p. 736], the Secretary-General's Special Representative for human rights in Cambodia, Yash Ghai (Kenya), stated that there had been some encouraging developments, particularly in relation to creating an environment conducive to legitimate political activity in the country. Notable among them were the release from pre-trial detention of persons active in public life, the pardon and restoration of parliamentary immunity granted to members of the Sam Rainsy Party and a statement from the Prime Minister in favour of decriminalizing defamation.

However, the Representative found a number of persisting challenges to the full enjoyment of human rights during his second mission to Cambodia (19-28 March) [A/HRC/4/36], which enabled him to examine the country's adherence to international human rights instruments, effective remedy for human rights violations, and the right to defend human rights and fundamental freedoms of expression, association and assembly. He also considered issues relating to impunity and accountability, rehabilitation and reconstruction of Cambodia from a human rights perspective, problems concerning access to land and livelihoods, and the moral and legal responsibility of the international community to support the country's efforts to strengthen human rights.

The Representative observed that, although overall security had improved following the end of civil conflict, the absence of effective government institutions, basic laws and an impartial judiciary, compounded by continuing impunity, threats against critics of the status quo, increasing landlessness and a growing number of displaced persons, left Cambodians insecure and vulnerable to systemic violations of their rights. Judges were subjected to political interference, murders of journalists and trade union leaders remained unresolved, government critics were being arrested and illegal land grabbing threatened the livelihood of the poor. Some of Cambodia's problems were all familiar, such as entrenched corruption at the highest level, a system based on patronage, the pillaging of natural resources, divide-and-rule tactics, the misuse of State structure to undermine political opposition and enrichment of the few to the neglect of the many. It was regrettable that the Government had not responded to the concerns raised by the special representatives and other UN entities. The international community should therefore press Cambodia to respect its human rights commitments and clearly declare its obligation to stop the abuse of rights and respect the independence of the judiciary.

The Representative also made recommendations relating to the rule of law and the protection of human rights and fundamental freedoms, access to land and livelihoods and adherence to international instruments, all of which, he noted, constituted the minimal elements of a plan of action for human rights in the country.

Democratic People's Republic of Korea

Meetings with Special Representative. In response to a 2005 Commission request [YUN 2005, p. 888], two notes by the Secretariat [E/CN.4/2006/32; A/HRC/4/60] described efforts to provide human rights advisory services to the Democratic People's Republic of Korea (DPRK). The High Commissioner had met with the country's representatives in Geneva on 28 November 2005 and 6 December 2006, during which the prospects for technical cooperation between OHCHR and DPRK were explored in such areas as treaty implementation. Stating that his country did not recognize the Commission resolution giving rise to the meeting, the DPRK representative took note of the High Commissioner's offer of technical assistance but was unable to accept it.

Reports of Special Rapporteur. In a January report [E/CN.4/2006/35], the Special Rapporteur on the situation of human rights in the Democratic People's Republic of Korea, Vitit Muntarbhorn (Thailand), described current concerns. While it was encouraging that the country was a party to key human rights treaties, major challenges remained, particularly regarding the rights to food and life. The food shortage affecting the country since the mid-1990s was not abating, and new policy measures to bring relief to the people had the unforeseen effect of a substantial rise in prices, mostly affecting the urban population who could not fend for themselves. Food shortages affected some 2 million people. Another major concern was the transgressions by the authorities of the right to security of the person, humane treatment, non-discrimination and access to justice. Reforms of the criminal code and criminal procedure code in previous years did not eliminate disturbing reports of appalling prison conditions, torture and inhuman and degrading treatment of prisoners. A related problem was the issue of abductions of foreigners by DPRK agents, including the unresolved cases of Japanese nationals. The ongoing breaches of freedom of movement, asylum and refugee protection were also of concern, as it remained impossible to move in or out of the country without official permission or the threat of penal sanctions. Those affected included DPRK nationals who had sought asylum in neighbouring countries and were forced to return without adequate guarantees of their safety. With regard to the right to self-determination, political participation, access to information, freedoms of expression, belief or opinion, and of association, conscience and religion, there was no ostensible improvement as the opaque and non-democratic nature of the State continued to militate against many of those rights. Of particular concern were the rights of women who were victims of violence, and of children, ageing persons, persons with disabilities and minorities.

The report also summarized the outcome of the Special Rapporteur's visit to the Republic of Korea to assess the impact on that country of the human rights situation in DPRK. Based on lessons learned from the visit, the Special Rapporteur addressed recommendations to both countries for improving the human rights climate in the Korean peninsula as a whole. In particular, he encouraged them to maximize family reunification opportunities and urged DPRK to clarify and resolve the long-standing problem of missing persons, and facilitate access to humanitarian and food aid provided by the Republic of Korea. He also urged the Republic of Korea to continue to accept refugees from DPRK and aid their social recovery and reintegration, and called on DPRK to end transgressions against civil, political, economic, social and cultural rights and to implement effectively the human rights treaties to which it was a party, as well as the recommendations addressed to it by UN human rights mechanisms. The Special Rapporteur outlined additional measures and actions to be taken by DPRK and the international community to better guarantee and safeguard human rights in the country.

In September [A/61/349], the Secretary-General transmitted to the General Assembly the Special Rapporteur's report, which further elaborated on the main human rights challenges in DPRK, as highlighted in the Special Rapporteur's January report (see above). He observed that the situation had deteriorated by mid-year, owing to the missile tests conducted by DPRK in the face of global opposition, which compelled the Security Council to impose an arms embargo and other sanctions on the country (see p. 444). That affected much of the humanitarian aid destined for DPRK and had a serious impact on the population, who also suffeed from the effects of major flooding during the year and the unwillingness of those countries that had previously provided refuge to give access to DPRK citizens. The Special Rapporteur concluded that the human rights situation in DPRK raised continuing cause for concern. To help close the gap between the formal recognition of human rights and the substantive implementation of applicable provisions, the Special Rapporteur addressed additional recommendations to the Government and the international community, most of which echoed the proposals contained in his January report.

Communications. In April [A/60/749] and June [A/61/97], DPRK alleged provocative actions by Japan regarding the issue of Japanese nationals abducted by DPRK agents, which DPRK maintained had already been resolved between both countries. Recent and undisguised anti-DPRK manoeuvres by Japan constituted a flagrant violation of international human rights instruments, especially General Assembly resolution 60/251, which created the Human Rights Council.

In August [A/61/220], Japan stated that the DPRK allegations were groundless and the abduction issue was still unresolved.

GENERAL ASSEMBLY ACTION

On 19 December [meeting 81], the General Assembly, on the recommendation of the Third (Social, Humanitarian and Cultural) Committee [A/61/443/Add.3], adopted **resolution 61/174** by recorded vote (99-21-56) [agenda item 67 *(c)*].

Situation of human rights in the Democratic People's Republic of Korea

The General Assembly,

Reaffirming that States Members of the United Nations have an obligation to promote and protect human rights and fundamental freedoms and to fulfil the obligations that they have undertaken under the various international instruments,

Mindful that the Democratic People's Republic of Korea is a party to the International Covenant on Civil and Political Rights, the International Covenant on Economic, Social and Cultural Rights, the Convention on the Rights of the Child and the Convention on the Elimination of All Forms of Discrimination against Women,

Noting the submission by the Democratic People's Republic of Korea of its second periodic report concerning the implementation of the International Covenant on Economic, Social and Cultural Rights, its second periodic report on the implementation of the Convention on the Rights of the Child and its initial report on the implementation of the Convention on the Elimination of All Forms of Discrimination against Women, as a sign of engagement in international cooperative efforts in the field of human rights,

Taking note of the concluding observations of the treaty monitoring bodies under the four treaties, the most recent of which were given by the Committee on the Elimination of Discrimination against Women in July 2005,

Recalling its resolution 60/173 of 16 December 2005 and Commission on Human Rights resolutions 2003/10 of 16 April 2003, 2004/13 of 15 April 2004 and 2005/11 of 14 April 2005, and mindful of the need for the international community to strengthen its coordinated efforts aimed at urging the implementation of those resolutions,

Taking note of the report of the Special Rapporteur on the situation of human rights in the Democratic People's Republic of Korea, including the specific concerns relating to women's rights, the rights of the child, the rights of the elderly, the rights of persons with disabilities and refugee rights addressed therein,

1. *Expresses its very serious concern* at:

(a) The continued refusal of the Government of the Democratic People's Republic of Korea to recognize the mandate of the Special Rapporteur on the situation of human rights in the Democratic People's Republic of Korea or to extend cooperation to him;

(b) Continuing reports of systemic, widespread and grave violations of human rights in the Democratic People's Republic of Korea, including:

(i) Torture and other cruel, inhuman or degrading treatment or punishment, public executions, extrajudicial and arbitrary detention, the absence of due process and the rule of law, the imposition of the death penalty for political reasons, the existence of a large number of prison camps and the extensive use of forced labour;

(ii) The situation of refugees expelled or returned to the Democratic People's Republic of Korea and sanctions imposed on citizens of the Democratic People's Republic of Korea who have been repatriated from abroad, such as treating their departure as treason, leading to punishments of internment, torture, cruel, inhuman or degrading treatment or the death penalty, and urges all States to ensure respect for the fundamental principle of non-refoulement;

(iii) All-pervasive and severe restrictions on the freedoms of thought, conscience, religion, opinion and expression, peaceful assembly and association, and on equal access to information and limitations imposed on every person who wishes to move freely within the country and travel abroad;

(iv) Continuing violation of the human rights and fundamental freedoms of women, in particular the trafficking of women for the purpose of prostitution or forced marriage, forced abortions, and infanticide of children of repatriated mothers, including in police detention centres and camps;

(v) Unresolved questions of international concern relating to the abduction of foreigners in the form of enforced disappearance, which violates the human rights of the nationals of other sovereign countries;

(vi) The violations of economic, social and cultural rights, which have led to severe malnutrition and hardship for the population in the Democratic People's Republic of Korea;

(vii) Continuing reports of violations of the human rights and fundamental freedoms of persons with disabilities, especially on the use of collective camps and of coercive measures that target the rights of persons with disabilities to decide freely and responsibly on the number and spacing of their children;

2. *Expresses its strong concern* that the Government of the Democratic People's Republic of Korea has not engaged in technical cooperation activities with the United Nations High Commissioner for Human Rights and her Office, despite efforts by the High Commissioner to engage in a dialogue with the authorities of the Democratic People's Republic of Korea in this regard;

3. *Expresses its very deep concern* at the precarious humanitarian situation in the country, compounded by the mismanagement on the part of the authorities, in particular the prevalence of infant malnutrition, which, despite recent progress, continues to affect the physical and mental development of a significant proportion of children, and urges the Government of the Democratic People's Republic of Korea, in this regard, to facilitate the continued presence of humanitarian organizations to ensure that humanitarian assistance is delivered impartially to all parts of the country on the basis of need in accordance with humanitarian principles;

4. *Strongly urges* the Government of the Democratic People's Republic of Korea to respect fully all human rights and fundamental freedoms and, in this regard, to implement fully the measures set out in the above-mentioned resolutions of the General Assembly and the Commission on Human Rights, and the recommendations addressed to the Democratic People's Republic of Korea by the United Nations special procedures and treaty bodies, and to extend its full cooperation to the Special Rapporteur, including by granting him full, free and unimpeded access to the Democratic People's Republic of Korea, and to other United Nations human rights mechanisms;

5. *Decides* to continue its examination of the situation of human rights in the Democratic People's Republic of Korea at its sixty-second session, and to this end requests the Secretary-General to submit a comprehensive report on the situation in the Democratic People's Republic of Korea and the Special Rapporteur to report his findings and recommendations.

RECORDED VOTE ON RESOLUTION 61/174:

In favour: Afghanistan, Albania, Andorra, Argentina, Australia, Austria, Bahamas, Belgium, Belize, Bhutan, Bosnia and Herzegovina, Brazil, Bulgaria, Burundi, Canada, Chile, Comoros, Croatia, Cyprus, Czech Republic, Denmark, Dominican Republic, Ecuador, El Salvador, Eritrea, Estonia, Fiji, Finland, France, Georgia, Germany, Ghana, Greece, Guatemala, Guinea-Bissau, Haiti, Honduras, Hungary, Iceland, Iraq, Ireland, Israel, Italy, Japan, Jordan, Kazakhstan, Latvia, Lebanon, Lesotho, Liberia, Liechtenstein, Lithuania, Luxembourg, Malawi, Maldives, Malta, Marshall Islands, Mexico, Micronesia, Moldova, Monaco, Montenegro, Morocco, Nauru, Netherlands, New Zealand, Nicaragua, Norway, Palau, Panama, Papua New Guinea, Paraguay, Peru, Philippines, Poland, Portugal, Republic of Korea, Romania, Samoa, San Marino, Saudi Arabia, Serbia, Slovakia, Slovenia, Solomon Islands, Spain, Sweden, Switzerland, The former Yugoslav Republic of Macedonia, Timor-Leste, Tonga, Turkey, Tuvalu, Ukraine, United Kingdom, United Republic of Tanzania, United States, Uruguay, Vanuatu.

Against: Algeria, Belarus, China, Congo, Cuba, Democratic People's Republic of Korea, Democratic Republic of the Congo, Egypt, Guinea, Indonesia, Iran, Lao People's Democratic Republic, Libyan Arab Jamahiriya, Pakistan, Russian Federation, Sudan, Syrian Arab Republic, Uzbekistan, Venezuela, Viet Nam, Zimbabwe.

Abstaining: Angola, Antigua and Barbuda, Azerbaijan, Bahrain, Bangladesh, Barbados, Benin, Bolivia, Botswana, Brunei Darussalam, Burkina Faso, Cambodia, Cameroon, Cape Verde, Central African Republic, Colombia, Costa Rica, Côte d'Ivoire, Djibouti, Ethiopia, Guyana, India, Jamaica, Kenya, Kuwait, Kyrgyzstan, Madagascar, Malaysia, Mali, Mauritania, Mauritius, Mozambique, Myanmar, Namibia, Nepal, Niger, Nigeria, Qatar, Rwanda, Sao Tome and Principe, Senegal, Sierra Leone, Singapore, Somalia, South Africa, Sri Lanka, Suriname, Swaziland, Thailand, Togo, Trinidad and Tobago, Turkmenistan, Uganda, United Arab Emirates, Yemen, Zambia.

Iran

The General Assembly, while welcoming encouraging developments in Iran, such as the country's voluntary pledges and commitments on human rights and an October statement by the head of its judiciary regarding the protection of the rights of minors, expressed serious concern about ongoing violations in the country, among them, harassment, intimidation and persecution of human rights defenders and many others. Also of concern was the Government's failure to comply with international standards in the administration of justice. The Assembly called on Iran to take a number of remedial measures to improve the situation.

GENERAL ASSEMBLY ACTION

On 19 December [meeting 81], the General Assembly, on the recommendation of the Third Committee [A/61/443/Add.3], adopted **resolution 61/176** by recorded vote (72-50-55) [agenda item 67 *(c)*].

Situation of human rights in the Islamic Republic of Iran

The General Assembly,

Guided by the Charter of the United Nations, the Universal Declaration of Human Rights, the International Covenants on Human Rights and other international human rights instruments,

Reaffirming that all Member States have an obligation to promote and protect human rights and fundamental freedoms and to fulfil the obligations they have undertaken under the various international instruments in this field,

Mindful that the Islamic Republic of Iran is a party to the International Covenant on Civil and Political Rights, the International Covenant on Economic, Social and Cultural Rights, the International Convention on the Elimination of All Forms of Racial Discrimination and the Convention on the Rights of the Child,

Recalling its previous resolutions on the subject, the most recent of which is resolution 60/171 of 16 December 2005, and recalling also Commission on Human Rights resolution 2001/17 of 20 April 2001,

Noting the submission by the Islamic Republic of Iran of voluntary pledges and commitments on human rights in accordance with General Assembly resolution 60/251 of 15 March 2006,

Noting also the statements made by the Government of the Islamic Republic of Iran on strengthening respect for human rights in the country and promoting the rule of law, and noting further the relevant provisions of its Constitution,

1. *Welcomes:*

(a) The standing invitation extended by the Government of the Islamic Republic of Iran to all human rights thematic monitoring mechanisms in April 2002 and the cooperation extended to the special procedures during their visits, while regretting that no special procedure has been able to visit the Islamic Republic of Iran since July 2005 and expressing its hope that special procedures of the Human Rights Council will be able to visit in the near future;

(b) The report of the Special Rapporteur on violence against women, its causes and consequences on her visit to the Islamic Republic of Iran from 29 January to 6 February 2005;

(c) The report of the Special Rapporteur on adequate housing as a component of the right to an adequate standard of living on his visit to the Islamic Republic of Iran from 19 to 31 July 2005;

(d) The statement by the head of the judiciary of the Islamic Republic of Iran in October 2006 in which he expressed his hope that judges will choose alternative punishments for minors instead of long jail terms for some offences;

(e) The announcement by the head of the judiciary in April 2004 of the ban on torture and the subsequent passage of related legislation by the parliament, which was approved by the Guardian Council in May 2004;

(f) The human rights dialogues between the Islamic Republic of Iran and a number of countries, while urging the Islamic Republic of Iran to intensify those dialogues and ensure that they are held regularly;

(g) The release of some prisoners held without due process of law;

(h) The cooperation with United Nations agencies in developing programmes in the fields of human rights, good governance and the rule of law;

2. *Expresses its serious concern* at:

(a) The continuing harassment, intimidation and persecution of human rights defenders, non-governmental organizations, political opponents, religious dissenters, political reformists, journalists, parliamentarians, students, clerics, academics, webloggers, union members and labour organizers, including through undue restrictions on the freedoms of assembly, conscience, opinion and expression, the threat and use of arbitrary arrest and prolonged detention, targeted at both individuals and their family members, the ongoing unjustified closure of newspapers and blocking of Internet sites and restrictions on the activities of unions and other non-governmental organizations, as well as the absence of many conditions necessary for free and fair elections;

(b) The persistent failure to comply fully with international standards in the administration of justice and, in

particular, the absence of due process of law, the refusal to provide fair and public hearings, the denial of the right to counsel and access to counsel by those detained, the use of national security laws to deny human rights, the prevalent atmosphere of impunity for officials who commit human rights abuses, the harassment, intimidation and persecution of defence lawyers and legal defenders, the adulteration of judicial files, the lack of respect for internationally recognized safeguards, inter alia, with respect to persons belonging to religious, ethnic or national minorities, officially recognized or otherwise, the application of arbitrary prison sentences and the violation of the rights of detainees, including the systematic and arbitrary use of prolonged solitary confinement, the failure to provide proper medical care to those imprisoned, the arbitrary denial of contact between detainees and their family members, and the death of detainees in unclear circumstances or resulting from general mistreatment while in custody;

(c) The continuing use of torture and cruel, inhuman or degrading treatment or punishment such as flogging and amputations;

(d) The continuing of public executions, including multiple public executions, and, on a large scale, of other executions, in the absence of respect for internationally recognized safeguards, and the issuing of sentences of stoning; and, in particular, deplores the execution of persons who were under the age of 18 at the time their offence was committed, contrary to the obligations of the Islamic Republic of Iran under article 37 of the Convention on the Rights of the Child and article 6 of the International Covenant on Civil and Political Rights and in spite of the announcement of a moratorium on juvenile executions;

(e) The continuing violence and discrimination against women and girls in law and in practice, the refusal of the Guardian Council to take steps to address this systemic discrimination and recent arrests of and violent crackdowns on women exercising their right of assembly;

(f) The increasing discrimination and other human rights violations against persons belonging to ethnic and religious minorities, recognized or otherwise, including Arabs, Azeris, Baluchis, Kurds, Christians, Jews, Sufis and Sunni Muslims; the escalation and increased frequency of discrimination and other human rights violations against members of the Baha'i faith, including reports of plans by the State to identify and monitor Baha'is, as noted by the Special Rapporteur on freedom of religion or belief; an increase in cases of arbitrary arrest and detention; the denial of freedom of religion or of publicly carrying out communal affairs; the disregard for property rights, including through de facto expropriation, as noted in the report of the Special Rapporteur on adequate housing as a component of the right to an adequate standard of living; the destruction of sites of religious importance; the suspension of social, educational and community-related activities and the denial of access to higher education, employment, pensions, adequate housing and other benefits; and recent violent crackdowns on Arabs, Azeris, Baha'is, Kurds and Sufis;

3. *Calls upon* the Government of the Islamic Republic of Iran:

(a) To ensure full respect for the rights to freedom of assembly, opinion and expression and for the right to take part in the conduct of public affairs, in accordance with its obligations under the International Covenant on Civil and Political Rights, and, in particular, to end the harassment, intimidation and persecution of political opponents and human rights defenders, including by releasing persons imprisoned arbitrarily or on the basis of their political views; and to increase actions to promote and facilitate human rights education at all levels and to ensure that all those responsible for training lawyers, law enforcement officers, the personnel of the armed forces and public officials include appropriate elements of human rights teaching in their training programme;

(b) To ensure full respect for the right to due process of law, including the right to counsel and access to counsel by those detained, in criminal justice proceedings and, in particular, to ensure a fair and public hearing by a competent, independent and impartial tribunal established by law, to end harassment, intimidation and persecution of defence lawyers and legal defenders and to ensure equality before the law and the equal protection of the law without any discrimination in all instances, including for members of religious, ethnic, linguistic or other minority groups, officially recognized or otherwise;

(c) To eliminate, in law and in practice, the use of torture and other cruel, inhuman or degrading treatment or punishment, such as amputations and flogging and, as previously proposed by the elected Iranian parliament, to accede to the Convention against Torture and Other Cruel, Inhuman or Degrading Treatment or Punishment; and to end impunity for violations of human rights that constitute crimes by bringing the perpetrators to justice in accordance with international standards, noting in this regard, inter alia, the updated set of principles for the protection and promotion of human rights through action to combat impunity;

(d) To abolish, in law and in practice, public executions and other executions carried out in the absence of respect for internationally recognized safeguards, in particular, as called for by the Committee on the Rights of the Child in its report of January 2005, executions of persons who at the time of their offence were under the age of 18, and to uphold the moratoriums on juvenile executions and executions by stoning and to introduce these moratoriums as law in order to completely abolish this punishment;

(e) To eliminate, in law and in practice, all forms of discrimination and violence against women and girls and, as previously proposed by the elected Iranian parliament, to accede to the Convention on the Elimination of All Forms of Discrimination against Women;

(f) To eliminate, in law and in practice, all forms of discrimination based on religious, ethnic or linguistic grounds and other human rights violations against persons belonging to minorities, including Arabs, Azeris,

Baha'is, Baluchis, Kurds, Christians, Jews, Sufis and Sunni Muslims, to refrain from monitoring individuals on the basis of their religious beliefs, to ensure that minorities' access to education is on a par with that of all Iranians and to address these matters in an open manner, with the full participation of the minorities themselves, to otherwise ensure full respect for the right to freedom of thought, conscience, religion or belief of all persons, and to implement the 1996 report of the Special Rapporteur on religious intolerance, which recommended ways in which the Islamic Republic of Iran could emancipate the Baha'i community;

4. *Encourages* the thematic procedures of the Human Rights Council, inter alia, the Special Rapporteur on extrajudicial, summary or arbitrary executions, the Special Rapporteur on torture and other cruel, inhuman or degrading treatment or punishment, the Special Rapporteur on the independence of judges and lawyers, the Special Rapporteur on freedom of religion or belief, the Special Rapporteur on the promotion and protection of the right to freedom of opinion and expression, the Special Representative of the Secretary-General on the situation of human rights defenders, the Working Group on Arbitrary Detention and the Working Group on Enforced or Involuntary Disappearances, to visit or otherwise continue their work to improve the situation of human rights in the Islamic Republic of Iran, and urges the Government of the Islamic Republic of Iran to live up to the commitment it made when it issued a standing invitation to special procedures by cooperating with them, and to illustrate how their subsequent recommendations have been addressed, including the recommendations of special procedures that have previously visited the country;

5. *Decides* to continue its examination of the situation of human rights in the Islamic Republic of Iran at its sixty-second session under the item entitled "Promotion and protection of human rights".

RECORDED VOTE ON RESOLUTION 61/176:

In favour: Albania, Andorra, Argentina, Australia, Austria, Bahamas, Belgium, Belize, Bosnia and Herzegovina, Bulgaria, Burundi, Canada, Chile, Croatia, Cyprus, Czech Republic, Denmark, Dominican Republic, Ecuador, El Salvador, Estonia, Fiji, Finland, France, Germany, Greece, Guatemala, Haiti, Honduras, Hungary, Iceland, Ireland, Israel, Italy, Japan, Kiribati, Latvia, Liechtenstein, Lithuania, Luxembourg, Malta, Marshall Islands, Micronesia, Moldova, Monaco, Montenegro, Nauru, Netherlands, New Zealand, Nicaragua, Norway, Palau, Paraguay, Peru, Poland, Portugal, Romania, Samoa, San Marino, Serbia, Slovakia, Slovenia, Spain, Sweden, Switzerland, The former Yugoslav Republic of Macedonia, Tonga, Tuvalu, Ukraine, United Kingdom, United States, Vanuatu.

Against: Afghanistan, Algeria, Armenia, Azerbaijan, Bahrain, Bangladesh, Belarus, Brunei Darussalam, China, Comoros, Cuba, Democratic People's Republic of Korea, Democratic Republic of the Congo, Djibouti, Egypt, Guinea, India, Indonesia, Iran, Kazakhstan, Kuwait, Kyrgyzstan, Lebanon, Libyan Arab Jamahiriya, Malaysia, Maldives, Mauritania, Morocco, Myanmar, Niger, Oman, Pakistan, Qatar, Russian Federation, Saudi Arabia, Senegal, Somalia, South Africa, Sri Lanka, Sudan, Syrian Arab Republic, Tajikistan, Togo, Tunisia, Turkmenistan, Uzbekistan, Venezuela, Viet Nam, Yemen, Zimbabwe.

Abstaining: Angola, Antigua and Barbuda, Barbados, Benin, Bhutan, Bolivia, Botswana, Brazil, Burkina Faso, Cameroon, Cape Verde, Central African Republic, Colombia, Congo, Costa Rica, Côte d'Ivoire, Eritrea, Ethiopia, Georgia, Ghana, Guinea-Bissau, Guyana, Jamaica, Kenya, Lao People's Democratic Republic, Lesotho, Liberia, Madagascar, Malawi, Mali, Mauritius, Mexico, Mongolia, Mozambique, Namibia, Nepal, Nigeria, Panama, Papua New Guinea, Philippines, Republic of Korea, Rwanda, Sao Tome and Principe, Sierra Leone, Singapore, Solomon Islands, Suriname, Swaziland, Thailand, Trinidad and Tobago, Uganda, United Arab Emirates, United Republic of Tanzania, Uruguay, Zambia.

Myanmar

Reports of Special Rapporteur. In response to a 2005 Commission request [YUN 2005, p. 892], Special Rapporteur Paulo Sérgio Pinheiro (Brazil) submitted a February report on the human rights situation in Myanmar [E/CN.4/2006/34], based on information he had received as at 22 December 2005. He regretted that grave violations of civil and political rights persisted, including intimidation, harassment, arbitrary arrest and imprisonment of persons attempting to exercise those rights. The main targets were members of registered political parties, human rights defenders and democracy advocates. Since July 2005, some 44 people were believed to have been arrested and imprisoned for their political beliefs and activities, and trial procedures and detention conditions were serious cause for concern. There was also evidence of violations of the freedoms of religion and expression, as well as a wide range of economic and social rights. Calling attention to the marked decline in socio-economic conditions and the consequent increase in poverty countrywide, the Special Rapporteur noted that up to a quarter of the population currently lived below the poverty line. State-sponsored practices, such as the imposition of arbitrary taxes, extortion, land and crop confiscation, forced relocations, travel restrictions, financial penalties and the looting of possessions of civilians by military authorities, continued to have a devastating impact on livelihoods. Of particular concern was the deteriorating humanitarian situation, owing partly to the Government's restrictions on the access and activities of international humanitarian agencies in areas of conflict or places populated by ethnic groups, which affected the work of many on the ground, including the International Committee of the Red Cross and the World Food Programme. The Special Rapporteur was also concerned by ongoing internal displacement and the mass exodus of civilian communities, primarily due to the systematic human rights abuses and the conflict between the military authorities and non-State armed groups. As at late 2005, it was understood that some 540,000 people had been displaced in the eastern part of the country, the area most affected by the conflict and government violations.

The Special Rapporteur observed that meaningful political, economic, legislative and judicial reforms were essential for Myanmar to move out of its current quagmire. Economic reform, in particular, was necessary to redress the violation of economic rights in the country, and political reform geared towards resolving the armed conflict was equally necessary, given that the conflict had been the root cause of human rights abuses in Myanmar. While expressing support for the Secretary-General's call for the Government to initiate dialogue with all political parties and ethnic groups [YUN 2005, p. 892], the Special Rapporteur stressed the need to establish confidence in the transition process through the release of all political prisoners and other necessary action to ensure the free participation by all political representatives in that process.

By a 21 September note [A/61/369 & Corr.1], the Secretary-General transmitted to the General Assembly the Special Rapporteur's report covering the period from February to September. As he had not been permitted by Myanmar authorities to undertake a fact-finding visit to the country, the Special Rapportuer relied on information and insight from neighbouring countries. Accordingly, between 11 and 26 February, he visited India, Indonesia, Malaysia and Thailand. He was dismayed that no progress had been made towards genuine democratic reform within the framework of the National Convention, which adjourned in January after meeting for approximately two months. Recommendations put forward by UN bodies had been disregarded by the authorities, as the persecution of political opponents and many others continued, particularly the detention of Daw Aung San Suu Kyi and other members of her party. The culture of impunity remained the main obstacle to efforts to safeguard respect for human rights in the country and create a favourable environment for its realization. That had resulted in widespread and systematic violations, including summary executions, torture, forced labour, sexual violence and the recruitment of child soldiers. Other disturbing violations included restrictions on fundamental freedoms, including of movement, expression, association and assembly; military operations in ethnic areas; access to and control over land and natural resources; deteriorating economic and social conditions and consequent humanitarian challenges; and the Government's failure to finalize its official recognition of and accession to relevant human rights instruments.

The Special Rapporteur, while reaffirming the validity of the recommendations contained in his February report (see above), urged the Government to free all political prisoners and end the harassment and persecution of political opponents and ethnic groups; resume dialogue with all political actors; bring to justice officials alleged to have committed human rights abuses; end the criminalization of the peaceful exercise of fundamental freedoms; establish, with international assistance, an independent and impartial judiciary; facilitate the activities of humanitarian agencies; and respect its obligations to protect civilians from armed conflict.

On 19 December, the General Assembly took note of the report of the Special Rapporteur (**decision 61/529**).

Reports of Secretary-General. In response to General Assembly resolution 60/233 [YUN 2005, p. 894], the Secretary-General submitted a February report [E/CN.4/2006/117] on his good offices' efforts in facilitating national reconciliation and democratization in Myanmar. He announced that, since efforts to engage with the authorities to address international concerns remained stalled, and after having been denied access to the country for approximately two years, his special envoy, Razali Ismail, had stepped down in January upon the expiration of his contract. As the Special Rapporteur (see above) had also not been allowed to visit the country since November 2003, political discussions with the Government took place only on limited occasions outside the country. The Secretary-General noted that representatives of the National League for Democracy (NLD) and other political parties had again not participated in the National Convention, which reconvened between December 2005 and January 2006, and that NLD leader, Daw Aung San Suu Kyi, who had spent approximately 10 years in detention, remained under house arrest. Overall, an estimated 1,147 political prisoners were being held either in prisons or interrogation centres throughout the country. Significant segments of the population faced extremely difficult socio-economic conditions and humanitarian challenges relating to the rapid rise of HIV/AIDS among vulnerable groups, food insecurity, limited health care, inadequate opportunities, forced labour practices and massive displacement owing to unrelenting conflicts in certain parts of the country. Despite the lack of progress in the national reconciliation process, the Secretary-General expressed continuing commitment to making his good offices available and pledged, in the event of progress, to mobilize international assistance to support the authorities in national reconciliation and in the economic, social and political development of the country. He therefore appealed to them to resume promptly substantive political dialogue with representatives of all ethnic groups and political leaders. Following the initiation of dialogue, the remaining constraints on all political leaders should be lifted, NLD offices reopened and political prisoners released.

Also in accordance with resolution 60/233, the Secretary-General in October [A/61/504] further reported on his good offices, which aimed at facilitating national reconciliation and democratization in Myanmar. He noted the relative success in discussions with the Government, resulting in a mission to the country in May, led by the Under-Secretary-General for Political Affairs. The main objective was to meet the top leadership and relevant stakeholders to assess the situation first-hand and determine what more could be done to help move the country towards an all-inclusive democracy, sustainable development and national reconciliation. The mission also sought to address the issue of unhindered access for the delivery of humanitarian assistance to the people of Myanmar. The Secretary-General observed that, despite some follow-up developments that had taken place since the mission, more tangible progress was needed, as a genuine process of democratization and national reconciliation was yet to be launched. Although the Government had announced the resumption in October of the National Convention, which was encouraging, there was no indication that the process would be broadened to include representatives from NLD and certain ethnic political parties. The Secretary-General again called on the authorities to make reform efforts more inclusive and credible when the National Convention reconvened and during the subsequent phases of the road map process, including the drafting of a constitution and the holding of a national referendum. Those steps should start as soon as possible, beginning with confidence-building measures, such as the release of political prisoners and the removal of remaining constraints on political activities.

GENERAL ASSEMBLY ACTION

On 22 December [meeting 84], the General Assembly, on the recommendation of the Third Committee [A/61/443/Add.3], adopted **resolution 61/232** by recorded vote (82-25-45) [agenda item 67 *(c)*].

Situation of human rights in Myanmar

The General Assembly,

Guided by the Charter of the United Nations and the Universal Declaration of Human Rights, and recalling the International Covenants on Human Rights and other relevant human rights instruments,

Reaffirming that all Member States have an obligation to promote and protect human rights and fundamental freedoms and the duty to fulfil the obligations they have undertaken under the various international instruments in this field,

Reaffirming also its previous resolutions on the situation of human rights in Myanmar, the most recent of which is resolution 60/233 of 23 December 2005, those of the Commission on Human Rights, and the conclusions of the International Labour Conference of June 2006,

Bearing in mind Security Council resolution 1325(2000) of 31 October 2000 on women and peace and security, resolutions 1265(1999) of 17 September 1999 and 1296(2000) of 19 April 2000 on the protection of civilians in armed conflict and resolution 1612(2005) of 26 July 2005 on children and armed conflict, the report of the Secretary-General on children and armed conflict and the Security Council discussion on the situation in Myanmar held on 29 September 2006,

Recognizing that respect for human rights, the rule of law, democracy and good governance are essential to achieving sustainable development and economic growth, and affirming that the establishment of a genuine democratic government in Myanmar is essential for the realization of all human rights and fundamental freedoms,

Affirming that the will of the people is the basis of the authority of government and that the will of the people of Myanmar was clearly expressed in the elections held in 1990,

1. *Welcomes:*

(a) The reports of the Special Rapporteur on the situation of human rights in Myanmar and his oral presentations, and the reports of the Secretary-General;

(b) The personal engagement and statements of the Secretary-General with regard to the situation in Myanmar;

(c) The visits of the Under-Secretary-General for Political Affairs to Myanmar in May and November 2006 at the invitation of the Government of Myanmar, and his meetings with senior government officials as well as leaders of the National League for Democracy, including Aung San Suu Kyi;

(d) The efforts of the United Nations and other international humanitarian organizations to deliver urgently needed humanitarian assistance to the most vulnerable people in Myanmar;

(e) The establishment by the Government of Myanmar of a committee for the prevention of military recruitment of underage soldiers and the adoption in November 2004 of an outline plan of action to address the issues of underage recruitment and child soldiers, and the declared willingness of the Government to cooperate with the United Nations and other international organizations to address these issues;

(f) The recent submission by the Government of Myanmar of replies to a number of official communications by the United Nations special procedures on human rights;

(g) The initial measures to combat impunity concerning forced labour, including the six-month moratorium on arrests of individuals who report forced labour and the release of two prominent detainees;

(h) The launching of the Three-Disease Fund with the aim of tackling the severe problems of HIV/AIDS, tuberculosis and malaria in Myanmar;

2. *Expresses grave concern* at:

(a) The ongoing systematic violations of human rights and fundamental freedoms of the people of Myanmar, as described in resolution 60/233 and previous resolutions of the General Assembly and of the Commission on Human Rights, as well as the reports of the Special Rapporteur on the situation of human rights in Myanmar and of the International Labour Organization, including discrimination and violations suffered by persons belonging to ethnic nationalities of Myanmar, including extrajudicial killings, rape and other forms of sexual violence persistently carried out by members of the armed forces; the continuing use of torture, deaths in custody, political arrests and continuing imprisonment and other detention; the continuing recruitment and use of child soldiers and the use of landmines; forced labour, including child labour; trafficking in persons; the denial of freedom of assembly, association, expression and movement; wide disrespect for the rule of law; the confiscation of arable land, crops, livestock and other possessions; and the prevailing culture of impunity;

(b) The attacks by military forces on villages in Karen State and other ethnic States in Myanmar, leading to extensive forced displacements and serious violations of the human rights of the affected populations;

(c) The continuing restrictions on activities of the National League for Democracy and other political parties, and the consistent harassment of their members, as well as of persons belonging to ethnic nationalities and of student leaders, including the extension of the house arrest of the General Secretary of the National League for Democracy, Aung San Suu Kyi, and her deputy, Tin Oo;

(d) The absence of progress towards genuine democratic reform, including the measures hindering representatives of the National League for Democracy and other political parties from participating in an effective and meaningful manner in the National Convention;

(e) The fact that the Special Rapporteur on the situation of human rights in Myanmar and the former Special Envoy of the Secretary-General for Myanmar have been unable to visit the country for almost three years, despite repeated requests;

(f) The continuing denial of the freedom of human rights defenders to pursue their activities;

3. *Strongly calls upon* the Government of Myanmar:

(a) To end the systematic violations of human rights and fundamental freedoms in Myanmar, to fully implement the recommendations of the Special Rapporteur, the General Assembly, the Commission on Human Rights, the International Labour Organization and other United Nations bodies aimed at ensuring full respect for all human rights and fundamental freedoms in Myanmar, and to allow human rights defenders to pursue their activities unhindered and to ensure their safety, security and freedom of movement in that pursuit;

(b) To take urgent measures to put an end to the military operations targeting civilians in the ethnic areas, and the associated violations of human rights and humanitarian law against persons belonging to ethnic nationalities, including widespread rape and other forms of sexual violence persistently carried out by members of the armed forces, and to facilitate a fact-finding mission comprising representatives of relevant United Nations agencies to help to identify measures to alleviate the humanitarian and human rights consequences of the conflict in Karen State and other ethnic States in Myanmar;

(c) To put an immediate end to the continuing recruitment and use of child soldiers, to intensify measures to ensure the protection of children affected by armed conflict, to fully implement the 2004 plan of action, including by intensifying cooperation with the United Nations agencies, in particular the United Nations Children's Fund, and to consider as a matter of high priority signing and ratifying the Optional Protocols to the Convention on the Rights of the Child;

(d) To end the systematic forced displacement of large numbers of persons and other causes of refugee flows to neighbouring countries, to provide the necessary protection and assistance to internally displaced persons, in cooperation with the international community, and to respect the right of refugees to voluntary, safe and dignified return monitored by appropriate international agencies in accordance with international law, including international humanitarian law;

(e) To end impunity, and to this end:

(i) To investigate and bring to justice any perpetrators of human rights violations, including members of the military and other government agents in all circumstances;

(ii) To facilitate a genuinely independent investigation of continuing reports of sexual violence, in particular against women belonging to ethnic nationalities, and other abuse of civilians carried out by members of the armed forces in Shan, Karen, Mon and other States;

(iii) To facilitate a genuinely independent investigation into the attack perpetrated near Depayin on 30 May 2003;

(f) To release all political prisoners immediately and unconditionally, including National League for Democracy leaders Aung San Suu Kyi and Tin Oo, and Shan Nationalities League for Democracy leader Khun Htun Oo and other Shan leaders, as well as former student leaders Min Ko Naing, Ko Ko Gyi, Htay Kywe, Min Zeya and Pyone Cho; to desist from arresting and punishing persons for their peaceful political activities, and to ensure that discipline in prisons does not amount to torture or cruel, inhuman or degrading treatment or punishment, and that conditions of detention otherwise meet international standards, and include the possibility of visiting any detainee, including Aung San Suu Kyi, and to investigate cases of death in custody;

(g) To lift all restraints on peaceful political activity of all persons, including former political prisoners, by, inter alia, guaranteeing freedom of association and freedom of expression, including for free and independent media, and to ensure unhindered access to information for the people of Myanmar;

(h) To urgently resolve the serious issues identified by the International Labour Organization concerning compliance with international labour standards, including to give clear assurances that no action will be taken against persons lodging complaints of forced labour, to resolve outstanding allegations of forced labour, to establish a credible mechanism for dealing with individual complaints of forced labour, to respect the International Labour Organization presence in Myanmar and strengthen it when necessary and ensure the safety, security and freedom of movement of the International Labour Organization liaison officer;

(i) To cooperate fully with the Special Rapporteur, including by granting him full, free and unimpeded access to Myanmar, and with other United Nations human rights mechanisms, and to ensure that no person cooperating with the Special Rapporteur or any international organization is subjected to any form of intimidation, harassment or punishment;

(j) To ensure immediately safe and unhindered access to all parts of Myanmar for the United Nations and international humanitarian organizations and to cooperate fully with those organizations so as to ensure that humanitarian assistance is delivered in accordance with humanitarian principles and reaches the most vulnerable groups of the population in accordance with international law, including applicable international humanitarian law;

(k) To continue to take action to fight the HIV/AIDS epidemic, tuberculosis and malaria;

4. *Calls upon* the Government of Myanmar:

(a) To permit all political representatives and representatives of ethnic nationalities to participate fully in the political transition process without restrictions, and, to this end, to resume, without further delay, dialogue with all political actors, including the National League for Democracy and representatives of ethnic nationalities, to complete the drafting of the Constitution and to ensure that the drafting process responds to the concerns of the ethnic nationalities and to set a clear timetable for the transition to democracy;

(b) To pursue through dialogue and peaceful means the immediate suspension and permanent end of conflict with all ethnic nationalities in Myanmar, and to allow the full participation of representatives of all political parties and representatives of ethnic nationalities in an inclusive and credible process of national reconciliation;

(c) To fulfil its obligations to restore the independence of the judiciary and due process of law, and to take further steps to reform the system of administration of justice;

5. *Requests* the Secretary-General:

(a) To continue to provide his good offices and to pursue his discussions on the situation of human rights and the restoration of democracy with the Government and the people of Myanmar, including all relevant parties to the national reconciliation process in Myanmar, and to offer technical assistance to the Government in this regard;

(b) To give all necessary assistance to enable his Special Envoy, once appointed, and the Special Rapporteur to discharge their mandates fully and effectively;

(c) To report to the General Assembly at its sixty-second session on the progress made in the implementation of the present resolution;

6. *Decides* to continue the consideration of the question at its sixty-second session, on the basis of the report of the Secretary-General and the interim report of the Special Rapporteur.

RECORDED VOTE ON RESOLUTION 61/232:

In favour: Afghanistan, Albania, Andorra, Angola, Argentina, Armenia, Australia, Austria, Bahamas, Belgium, Bolivia, Bosnia and Herzegovina, Brazil, Bulgaria, Burundi, Canada, Chile, Congo, Croatia, Cyprus, Czech Republic, Denmark, Dominican Republic, Ecuador, El Salvador, Estonia, Finland, France, Georgia, Germany, Greece, Guatemala, Honduras, Hungary, Iceland, Ireland, Israel, Italy, Japan, Kazakhstan, Kuwait, Latvia, Lebanon, Liechtenstein, Lithuania, Luxembourg, Malta, Mauritius, Mexico, Micronesia, Moldova, Monaco, Morocco, Nauru, Netherlands, New Zealand, Nicaragua, Nigeria, Norway, Palau, Panama, Paraguay, Peru, Poland, Portugal, Republic of Korea, Romania, Saudi Arabia, Serbia, Slovakia, Slovenia, Spain, Sweden, Switzerland, The former Yugoslav Republic of Macedonia, Timor-Leste, Turkey, Ukraine, United Kingdom, United Republic of Tanzania, United States, Uruguay.

Against: Algeria, Azerbaijan, Bangladesh, Belarus, Brunei Darussalam, Cambodia, China, Cuba, Egypt, Guinea, India, Indonesia, Iran, Lao People's Democratic Republic, Libyan Arab Jamahiriya, Malaysia, Myanmar, Pakistan, Russian Federation, Sudan, Syrian Arab Republic, Uzbekistan, Venezuela, Viet Nam, Zimbabwe.

Abstaining: Antigua and Barbuda, Bahrain, Barbados, Belize, Benin, Bhutan, Botswana, Burkina Faso, Cape Verde, Colombia, Comoros, Costa Rica, Democratic People's Republic of Korea, Djibouti, Ethiopia, Fiji, Ghana, Guinea-Bissau, Guyana, Jamaica, Jordan, Kenya, Kyrgyzstan, Malawi, Mali, Mauritania, Mozambique, Namibia, Nepal, Niger, Philippines, Qatar, Rwanda, Sierra Leone, Singapore, Solomon Islands, South Africa, Sri Lanka, Suriname, Swaziland, Thailand, Trinidad and Tobago, United Arab Emirates, Yemen, Zambia.

Nepal

Reports of High Commissioner. Pursuant to a 2005 Commission request [YUN 2005, p. 741], the High Commissioner submitted a February report [E/CN.4/2006/107] on the situation of human rights and the activities of her Office in Nepal during the period from 1 September 2005 to January 2006. She observed that, despite a marked reduction in killings during a four-month unilateral ceasefire by the Communist Party Nepal-Maoist (CPN), which lasted until early January 2006, OHCHR-Nepal continued to receive information about the killing of civilians and members of security forces, as well as abductions, other violence and threats against government officials, teachers, journalists and human rights defenders perpetrated by both sides. Arbitrary arrest and detention of suspected CPN members or sympathizers also persisted, reinforced by the absence of guarantees in the country's anti-terrorist legislation. Allegations received by OHCHR-Nepal indicated that torture was routine, despite the Government's denials of its systematic nature and statements that it was taking appropriate action.

It was regrettable that the efforts of the security forces were not adequate to investigate violations and hold accountable those responsible, and that relatively light sentences were imposed in the few cases in which action was taken. Also of major concern were the activities of armed groups, such as extortion, assaults and killings of suspected Maoists. In some cases, the State had tolerated or colluded with those groups. Children's rights to life, physical integrity, health and education were repeatedly violated by both sides. Women did not fare any better, as they suffered several conflict-related and other human rights abuses, including torture in the course of search operations by both sides, and were affected by discriminatory legislation and practices, despite recent action by the Supreme Court. Public protests intensified in January, when the authorities introduced an extensive ban on demonstrations to prevent one in the capital, Kathmandu, and arrested more than 100 political and civil society leaders at their homes. Blanket bans on demonstrations were imposed also in many municipalities to prevent the exercise of the right to freedom of peaceful assembly. Restrictions on the freedom of expression included a media ordinance, which entrenched Government efforts to ban the broadcasting of news on FM radio stations, and a consistent pattern of threats and harassment of journalists by the authorities in rural districts. In a related development, a government-imposed code of conduct for NGOs instituted constraints on the membership, objectives and functioning of related organizations, including those of human rights defenders. The conflict aggravated poverty, social inequalities and discrimination, with the rights to health, food and other economic, social and cultural rights all at risk. In addition to monitoring and investigating human rights violations, OHCHR-Nepal provided advisory services and support to a variety of partners in the country, particularly the authorities. It continued to work with the National Human Rights Commission and convened and chaired the United Nations Inter-Agency Human Rights Protection Working Group.

By a September note [A/61/374], the Secretary-General transmitted the High Commissioner's report on the human rights situation and OHCHR activities in Nepal, which examined the protest movement launched on 5 April by the Seven-Party Alliance (SPA) (see p. 449) and associated political developments and their impact on human rights. The protests led to the reinstatement of the House of Representatives, facilitated the formation of a coalition Government and a cessation of military operations in the conflict, the restoration of democratic rights and the relaunching of peace talks between the Government and CPN. Both parties requested UN assistance in a number of areas, including the monitoring of the ceasefire and human rights. A major improvement in the human rights situation was the restoration, for the most part, of the rights to freedom of association, expression and assembly, and the related lifting of bans on demonstrations, except in one area of Kathmandu, and the release of all political detainees. The cessation of hostilities resulted in an end to conflict-related violations, including extrajudicial executions, detention, torture and ill-treatment in army barracks of those suspected of links to CPN. The parties also reached a series of agreements, which included broad references underlining the importance of human rights, and respect for international human rights and humanitarian law in the conduct of security forces and CPN activists. Nonetheless, problems persisted with regard to the activities of other armed groups that were involved in killings and abductions, accountability for past violations, which became a key issue of debate in the peace process, the problem of internal displacement resulting from violations of human rights and international humanitarian law and the social exclusion and marginalization of such vulnerable groups as women, children and ethnic minorities.

The High Commissioner concluded that the improvements made in human rights remained fragile and any setback to the peace process risked a negative and potentially devastating impact on that situation. Major challenges revolved around law enforcement and the justice system and the weakness or absence of enforcement agencies in terms of their limited capacity or will to maintain law and order and protect civilians. Strengthening them would be essential for ensuring that the electoral process for a Constituent Assembly could be organized without fear, intimidation or more serious abuses. However, holding to account those responsible for violence and human rights violations, thereby ending the climate of impunity on both sides, had to be a priority.

On 19 December, the General Assembly took note of the report of the High Commissioner (**decision 61/529**).

Human Rights Council action. On 27 November [A/62/53 (dec. 2/114)], the Human Rights Council welcomed the significant improvement of human rights in Nepal, in the light of the success of the democratic movement and the conclusion of a comprehensive peace agreement stressing commitment to human rights and including the establishment of a truth and reconciliation commission. Underlining the need to address the challenges ahead, such as the consolidation of the rule of law and the strengthening of protection for victims of human rights violations, the Council called on all stakeholders to ensure full respect for human rights, welcomed the Government's cooperation with OHCHR and the Council's special procedures, and asked the High Commissioner to report in 2007.

Sri Lanka

On 29 November [A/62/53 (dec. 2/116)], the Human Rights Council deferred to its fourth (2007) session consideration of a draft decision on Sri Lanka [A/HRC/2/L.37] put forward by Finland on behalf of the European Union (EU), by which the Council would express concern at the recent escalation of violence in Sri Lanka and the increasing violations of human rights and humanitarian law, and call upon the parties to put an immediate end to those violations and guarantee access and protection of humanitarian workers.

Timor-Leste

Commission of Inquiry. In October [S/2006/822], the High Commissioner submitted to the Secretary-General, for transmission to the Security Council, the report of the Independent Special Commission of Inquiry for Timor-Leste established under the auspices of the High Commissioner to investigate the April/May events (see p. 415), which escalated into a serious crisis that claimed many lives and wounded numerous others, and during which egregious human rights violations were allegedly committed.

Turkmenistan

Report of Secretary-General. In response to General Assembly resolution 60/172 [YUN 2005, p. 897], the Secretary-General submitted an October report on the situation of human rights in Turkmenistan [A/61/489]. The report described efforts to implement resolution 60/172 highlighting cooperation with numerous UN treaty bodies and entities, as well as other organizations and institutions, among them, OHCHR, the special procedures established by the Commission on Human Rights and assumed by the Human Rights Council, the Organization for Security and Cooperation in Europe (OSCE), the International Committee of the Red Cross and the International Labour Organization (ILO). It also highlighted specific human rights issues, including restrictive laws that affected the work of human rights defenders and reports of intimidation, harassment, constant surveillance, arbitrary arrests, imprisonment and ill-treatment and reprisals against relatives. Also of concern were restrictions on the freedoms of movement and association, of expression and the media, and of thought, conscience, religion or belief, as well as the substandard prison conditions and reports of torture, the lack of confidence in the judicial system and violations of women's rights.

The Secretary-General concluded that gross and systematic violations of human rights were continuing, despite the Government's gestures and demonstrated readiness to engage with the international community and the human rights mechanisms. He called upon the Government to report to UN treaty bodies on the implementation of human rights instruments in the country; cooperate with the thematic mechanisms of the Council by extending invitations to visit the country; improve the environment for human rights defenders and ensure that those currently held in custody were afforded the full protection of international human rights instruments to which Turkmenistan was a party; stop the use of torture; and ensure that all prisoners had access to lawyers of their choice and independent observers.

On 19 December, the General Assembly took note of the Secretary-General's report (**decision 61/529**).

Uzbekistan

Communications. On 24 March [E/CN.4/2006/G/12], Uzbekistan circulated its comments on the High Commissioner's report on the OHCHR investigative mission to neighbouring Kyrgyzstan, where survivors of the violent events in May 2005 in the Uzbek city of Andijan had fled [YUN 2005, p. 899]. Uzbekistan complained that the mission report distorted the true situation and was based on statements by individuals who had participated in terrorist activities and escaped from detention. In a 30 June aide-memoire [A/60/914], it outlined its observations on the issues raised in General Assembly resolution 60/174 [YUN 2005, p. 900] on the human rights situation in the country.

Report of Secretary-General. In response to Assembly resolution 60/174, and as a follow-up to the findings of the 2005 OHCHR mission, the Secretary-General submitted an October report on the situation of human rights in Uzbekistan [A/61/526]. The report described developments in the aftermath of the Andijan incidents, in particular the implementation of the recommendations of the OHCHR mission, the trial of those involved, the situation of eyewitnesses and others who reported on the incidents and the Government's cooperation with UN human rights bodies and mechanisms and with other organizations and institutions. Encouraging developments included the Government's accession to important human rights instruments and the submission of integral periodic reports to the treaty bodies, and presidential decrees introducing habeas corpus and abolishing the death penalty with effect from 1 January 2008. However, no response had been received from the Government regarding permission to conduct an international investigation into the Andijan incidents, as recommended by the OHCHR mission. It was particularly disturbing that OHCHR and other international organizations had not been given access to the country to conduct investigations. Meanwhile, worrisome violations of human rights persisted in relation to fair and accessible trials, the question of torture, freedom of religion or belief, the conduct of the electoral process, the treatment of NGOs, the protection of journalists and human rights defenders and the functioning of an independent media.

While welcoming the encouraging initiatives taken by the Government, the Secretary-General concluded that its lack of response to the call for the establishment of an international commission of inquiry and the ongoing allegations of human rights violations demonstrated that the country's human rights situation had not improved. He called upon the Government to implement fully and promptly the recommendations of the OHCHR mission, particularly the granting of permission to establish a commission of inquiry into the Andijan events. The Government should also implement fully the recommendations contained in the April report on related trials issued by the OSCE and its Office for Democratic Institutions and Human Rights, protect and safeguard the rights of eyewitnesses and their families, as well as of journalists, human rights defenders and other members of civil society, facilitate access to returning asylum-seekers and refugees, and cooperate with the High Commissioner's Regional Representative and the Human Rights Council's special procedures.

By **decision 61/529** of 19 December, the General Assembly took note of the Secretary-General's report.

Europe and the Mediterranean

Belarus

Report of Special Rapporteur. The Special Rapporteur on the situation of human rights in Belarus, Adrian Severin (Romania), reported [A/HRC/4/16] to the Human Rights Council that the Government of Belarus, as in previous years, had not responded positively to his requests to visit the country. To fulfil his mandate, he had to rely on information gathered during his mission in early 2006 to the Russian Federation and on consultations and discussions in Geneva, Strasbourg and Brussels with delegates, NGOs, UN specialized agencies, OSCE and the Council of Europe. The report described the status of civil, political, economic, social and cultural rights, all of which, it noted, had deteriorated steadily. There were systematic violations of citizens' rights to participate effectively in the conduct of public affairs. Human rights protection mechanisms remained extremely weak, as there was neither a national human rights institution nor a genuine, independent legislative branch, and the judicial system was subservient to the executive branch. Illustrating the problem was the fact that the March presidential elections, in which the incumbent President claimed victory with over 80 per cent of the vote, reportedly did not comply with standards for democratic elections (see below). Other major problems concerned the justice system, particularly the application of the death penalty, with Belarus being the only country in Europe that still applied it, the harsh conditions of pre-trial detention, the practice of torture and other inhuman treatment, as well as the excessive use of force by the police. There were also reports of numerous violations of the freedoms of opinion and expression, the media, assembly and association, and religion, as well as breaches of economic and social rights and of the rights of women and other minorities.

The Special Rapporteur reaffirmed the validity of the conclusions and recommendations contained in his 2005 report [YUN 2005, p. 902], which had been reinforced by identical assessments from other special procedures and Euro-Atlantic organizations. As opposed to the Government's failure to implement those recommendations, the Special Rapporteur acknowledged the cooperation of the Belarusian political opposition and civil society and proposed that they be encouraged and supported. He asked the Council to request OHCHR to establish a group of legal experts to investigate the disappearance and murders of several politicians and journalists and collaborate with other international organizations to convene an international conference on the situation of human rights in Belarus. He further recommended, among other measures, the establishment of an international fund for promoting human rights in the country, an extension of his mandate in terms of time, scope and means, and enhanced cooperation between regional organizations and the United Nations and between the Council and OHCHR.

Communication. On 7 June, the OSCE Office for Democratic Institutions and Human Rights published the findings of its election observation mission, which monitored the 19 March presidential elections in Belarus. The mission identified shortcomings in the exercise and made recommendations for improvement.

The General Assembly, in resolution 61/175 (see below), urged the Belarusian Government to rectify those shortcomings and bring the country's electoral processes in line with international standards, particularly those of OSCE.

GENERAL ASSEMBLY ACTION

On 19 December [meeting 81], the General Assembly, on the recommendation of the Third Committee [A/61/443/Add.3], adopted **resolution 61/175** by recorded vote (72-32-69) [agenda item 67 *(c)*].

Situation of human rights in Belarus

The General Assembly,

Guided by the purposes and principles of the Charter of the United Nations, the provisions of the Universal Declaration of Human Rights, the International Covenants on Human Rights and other applicable human rights instruments,

Reaffirming that all States have an obligation to promote and protect human rights and fundamental freedoms and to fulfil their international obligations,

Mindful that Belarus is a party to the International Covenant on Civil and Political Rights and the Optional Protocols thereto, the International Covenant on Economic, Social and Cultural Rights, the International Convention on the Elimination of All Forms of Racial Discrimination, the Convention against Torture and Other Cruel, Inhuman or Degrading Treatment or Punishment, the Convention on the Elimination of All Forms of Discrimination against Women and the Optional Protocol thereto, and the Convention on the Rights of the Child and the Optional Protocol thereto on the sale of children, child prostitution and child pornography,

Recalling Commission on Human Rights resolutions 2003/14 of 17 April 2003, 2004/14 of 15 April 2004 and 2005/13 of 14 April 2005, and Human Rights Council decision 1/102 of 30 June 2006,

Concerned that the presidential election of 19 March 2006 was severely flawed and fell significantly short of the commitments of Belarus to the Organization for Security and Cooperation in Europe to hold a free and fair election, and that the situation of human rights in Belarus in 2005 was steadily deteriorating, as documented in the final report of the Office for Democratic Institutions and Human Rights of the Organization for Security and Cooperation in Europe and in the report of the Special Rapporteur on the situation of human rights in Belarus,

Noting that the Belarusian authorities have decided to hold local elections on 14 January 2007, and expressing its hope that those will be free and fair, in full respect of international electoral standards,

1. *Expresses deep concern:*

(a) About the failure of the Government of Belarus to cooperate fully with all the mechanisms of the Human Rights Council, in particular with the special rapporteurs on the situation of human rights in Belarus, while noting the serious concern relating to the deterioration of the human rights situation in Belarus expressed by seven independent human rights experts of the United Nations in a statement issued on 29 March 2006;

(b) That in spite of detailed recommendations by the Organization for Security and Cooperation in Europe and dialogue between the Government and the Organization for Security and Cooperation in Europe following previous elections, Belarus again failed to meet its commitments to hold free and fair elections, including through the arbitrary use of State power against opposition candidates, routine harassment, the detention and arrest of political and civil society activists, the obstruction of the access of opposition candidates to State media, the negative portrayal in the State media of opposition candidates and activists, including human rights defenders, and the serious shortcomings of the vote count, which lacked minimum transparency;

(c) About continuing reports of harassment, arbitrary arrest and detention of up to one thousand persons, including opposition candidates, before and after the election of 19 March 2006;

(d) About the continuing and expanding criminal prosecutions, lack of due process and closed political trials of leading opposition figures and human rights defenders;

(e) About the continuing harassment and detention of Belarusian journalists covering local opposition demonstrations, and that senior officials of the Government of Belarus were implicated in the enforced disappearance and/or summary execution of three political opponents of the incumbent authorities in 1999 and of a journalist in 2000 and in the continuing investigatory cover-up, as documented in the report adopted in resolution

1371(2004) of 28 April 2004 by the Parliamentary Assembly of the Council of Europe;

(f) About the decision of the Belarusian authorities to revoke the teaching licence of the European Humanities University in Minsk and to terminate the lease of its buildings, forcing the University in Belarus to close down;

(g) About persistent reports of harassment and closure of non-governmental organizations, national minority organizations, independent media outlets, religious groups, opposition political parties, independent trade unions and independent youth and student organizations, and the harassment and prosecution of individuals, including students engaged in the promotion and protection of human rights, the rule of law and democracy;

2. *Urges* the Government of Belarus:

(a) To bring the electoral process and legislative framework into line with international standards, especially those of the Organization for Security and Cooperation in Europe, demonstrate such commitment through the upcoming local elections in January 2007 and rectify the shortcomings of the electoral process, identified by the Office for Democratic Institutions and Human Rights in its report of 7 June 2006, including, inter alia, election laws and practices that restrict campaigning opportunities for de facto opposition candidates, arbitrary application of electoral laws, including on registration of candidates, obstruction of the right of access to the media, biased presentation of the issues by the State media and falsification of vote counts;

(b) To cease politically motivated prosecution, harassment and intimidation of political opponents, pro-democracy activists and human rights defenders, students, independent media, religious organizations, educational institutions and civil society actors; and to cease the harassment of students and to create the conditions whereby they can continue their studies in Belarus;

(c) To respect the rights to freedom of speech, assembly and association and to release immediately all political prisoners and other individuals detained for exercising those rights;

(d) To suspend from their duties officials implicated in any case of enforced disappearance, summary execution and torture and other cruel, inhuman or degrading treatment or punishment, pending investigation of those cases, and to ensure that all necessary measures are taken to investigate fully and impartially such cases and to bring the alleged perpetrators to justice before an independent tribunal, and, if found guilty, to ensure that they are punished in accordance with the international human rights obligations of Belarus;

(e) To investigate and hold accountable those responsible for the mistreatment and detention of domestic and foreign journalists in connection with the election of 19 March 2006 and post-election demonstrations;

(f) To uphold the right to freedom of religion or belief, including the ability to maintain communications with individuals and communities in matters of religion and belief at the national and international levels;

(g) To investigate and hold accountable those responsible for the mistreatment, arbitrary arrest and incarceration of civic and political activists leading up to and following the presidential election of March 2006 and to release immediately and unconditionally all political prisoners;

(h) To carry out all other steps called for by the Commission on Human Rights in its resolution 2005/13;

3. *Insists* that the Government of Belarus cooperate fully with all the mechanisms of the Human Rights Council, in particular with the Special Rapporteur appointed pursuant to Commission on Human Rights resolution 2004/14 and whose mandate was extended in Commission resolution 2005/13, as well as with the Representative of the Organization for Security and Cooperation in Europe on freedom of the media.

RECORDED VOTE ON RESOLUTION 61/175:

In favour: Afghanistan, Albania, Andorra, Argentina, Australia, Austria, Bahamas, Belgium, Bosnia and Herzegovina, Bulgaria, Canada, Chile, Croatia, Cyprus, Czech Republic, Denmark, Dominican Republic, El Salvador, Estonia, Fiji, Finland, France, Georgia, Germany, Greece, Guatemala, Haiti, Honduras, Hungary, Iceland, Ireland, Israel, Italy, Japan, Latvia, Liechtenstein, Lithuania, Luxembourg, Malta, Marshall Islands, Micronesia, Moldova, Monaco, Montenegro, Netherlands, New Zealand, Nicaragua, Norway, Palau, Paraguay, Peru, Poland, Portugal, Republic of Korea, Romania, San Marino, Serbia, Slovakia, Slovenia, Spain, Sweden, Switzerland, The former Yugoslav Republic of Macedonia, Timor-Leste, Tonga, Turkey, Tuvalu, Ukraine, United Kingdom, United States, Uruguay, Vanuatu.

Against: Algeria, Armenia, Bangladesh, Belarus, China, Cuba, Democratic People's Republic of Korea, Democratic Republic of the Congo, Egypt, Ethiopia, India, Indonesia, Iran, Kazakhstan, Kyrgyzstan, Lebanon, Libyan Arab Jamahiriya, Malaysia, Mauritania, Morocco, Myanmar, Pakistan, Qatar, Russian Federation, South Africa, Sudan, Syrian Arab Republic, Tajikistan, Uzbekistan, Venezuela, Viet Nam, Zimbabwe.

Abstaining: Angola, Antigua and Barbuda, Bahrain, Barbados, Belize, Benin, Bhutan, Botswana, Brazil, Brunei Darussalam, Burkina Faso, Burundi, Cameroon, Cape Verde, Central African Republic, Colombia, Comoros, Congo, Costa Rica, Côte d'Ivoire, Djibouti, Ecuador, Eritrea, Ghana, Guinea, Guinea-Bissau, Guyana, Jamaica, Jordan, Kenya, Kuwait, Lao People's Democratic Republic, Lesotho, Liberia, Madagascar, Malawi, Mali, Mauritius, Mexico, Mongolia, Mozambique, Namibia, Nepal, Niger, Nigeria, Panama, Papua New Guinea, Philippines, Rwanda, Samoa, Sao Tome and Principe, Saudi Arabia, Senegal, Sierra Leone, Singapore, Solomon Islands, Somalia, Sri Lanka, Suriname, Swaziland, Thailand, Togo, Trinidad and Tobago, Turkmenistan, Uganda, United Arab Emirates, United Republic of Tanzania, Yemen, Zambia.

Cyprus

Report of Secretary-General. In response to a 2005 Commission request [YUN 2005, p. 902] and in accordance with Human Rights Council decision 2/102 (see p. 760), the Secretary-General transmitted an OHCHR report [A/HRC/4/59], which provided an overview of human rights issues in Cyprus, covering the period up to 28 December 2006. The report noted that human rights concerns there stemmed from the division of the island and related mainly to the freedom of movement, human trafficking, discrimination, property rights, the question of missing persons, the right to education and freedom of religion. Restrictions on the freedom of movement applied particularly in military zones in the northern part of the country, where some areas were completely inaccessible, even to relatives of the inhabitants. There was also the disturbing trend of implementing policies that impinged on the ability of organizations and individuals to carry out activities and projects designed to contribute to bi-communal contacts and cooperation throughout the island. As a result, UN entities, particularly UNDP, were hampered in implementing projects that benefited both Greek and Turkish Cypriots in areas of common concern. Also disturbing was the fact that a number of serious human rights violations remained unpunished, especially regarding law enforcement agencies, due mostly to the lack of cooperation between both sides. Other issues of concern pertained to the problem of discrimination, the loss of property rights and the right to an effective remedy. While acknowledging the measures being taken to address the issues of missing persons, the right to education, freedom of movement and the preservation and restoration of cultural and religious rights, the report underlined specific challenges to the status of economic rights. Despite the relative narrowing of the gap in standards of living between the Greek Cypriots and the Turkish Cypriots, overall economic opportunities in the northern part of the island remained limited. It was hoped, however, that the situation might yet improve with the implementation within the year of the European Council regulation establishing an instrument of support for encouraging the economic development of the Turkish Cypriot community, and with the pending adoption of a regulation on direct trade. The overall human rights situation would greatly benefit from a comprehensive settlement of the Cyprus problem, given the obstacle which the persisting de facto partition posed to the enjoyment of human rights.

Communication. On 12 May [A/HRC/2/G/2], Turkey transmitted the Turkish Cypriot views on the Secretary-General's report covering the 2005 developments on human rights issues in Cyprus [YUN 2005, p. 902].

Middle East

Lebanon

Special Human Rights Council session

The second special session of the Human Rights Council was held on 11 August in Geneva, at the request of Tunisia [A/HRC/S-2/1], on behalf of the Group of Arab States and the Organization of the Islamic Conference, and backed by 23 States members of the Council. Convened in accordance with General Assembly resolution 60/251 (see p. 757), the session considered and took action on gross human rights violations by Israel in Lebanon, including the Qana massacre (see p. 579), the countrywide targeting of innocent civilians and the destruction of vital civilian infrastructure, which occurred during the Israel-Lebanon conflict (see p. 574).

The second special session held three meetings, at which it heard statements from numerous Council members, including from the parties concerned, intergovernmental organizations and NGOs [A/HRC/S-2/2]. Addressing the session, the High Commissioner noted that the increasing toll of civilian deaths and injuries in Lebanon and Israel, the massive displacement of populations and the destruction of civilian infrastructure in Lebanon required the Council's intervention to impress upon the parties the urgent need to comply with their obligations under international human rights and humanitarian law. Highlighting the sanctity of the right to life, which was the most basic human right, the High Commissioner drew attention to the actions by both parties in violating that right, particularly Israel's 30 July attack on a residential building in Qana and Hizbullah's unrelenting shelling of densely populated centres in Northern Israel. The High Commissioner suggested that the requested inquiry into those incidents should be concerned primarily with the plight of victims and lay the foundation for possible measures of reparation and accountability.

The Council, by a recorded vote of 27 to 11, with 8 abstentions, adopted resolution [A/61/53 (S-2/1)], by which it condemned Israeli violations of human rights and breaches of international humanitarian law in Lebanon, including the bombardment of Lebanese civilian populations, and the massacres in Qana and other Lebanese towns, which resulted in thousands of deaths and injuries, mostly of children and women, and the displacement of 1 million civilians. It called upon Israel to abide by its obligations under international human rights law and humanitarian law, especially the Convention on the Rights of the Child, and asked all concerned parties to respect those same laws, refrain from violence against the civilian population and treat all detainees in accordance with the 1949 Geneva Conventions. The Council established a high-level commission of inquiry, comprising eminent experts on both human rights and humanitarian law, to investigate the systematic targeting and killing of civilians by Israel in Lebanon, examine the types of weapons used by Israel and their conformity with international law, assess the extent and impact of Israeli attacks on human life, property and the environment and report thereon in September. The international community was asked to provide Lebanon with humanitarian and financial assistance to help deal with the humanitarian challenges, including the rehabilitation of victims, the return of displaced persons and the restoration of essential infrastructure.

Commission of Inquiry on Lebanon

The three members of the Commission of Inquiry on Lebanon (João Clemente Baena Soares, Mohamed Chande Othman, Stelios Perrakis) were appointed on 1 September by the Human Rights Council President, pursuant to Council resolution S- 2/1 (see above), based on their expertise in human rights and international humanitarian law, and their integrity, impartiality and independence. The Commission, which visited Lebanon from 23 September to 7 October, 17 to 21 October, and 23 November, submitted its report and findings to the Council [A/HRC/3/2].

The report provided an overview of the 33-day conflict and its historical background, addressed applicable legal principles and analysed the impact of the conflict on life in Lebanon. The Commission observed that the principle of humanity and humanitarian considerations (Martens clause) was not respected during the conflict. Consequently, the conflict had a devastating effect, especially in southern Lebanon, resulting in the death of some 1,191 persons, 4,409 others injured and more than 900,000 displaced from their homes. It further observed a significant pattern of excessive, indiscriminate and disproportionate use of force against Lebanese civilians and other targets by the Israeli Defence Forces (IDF), which failed to distinguish civilians from combatants, and civilian objects from military targets, in violation of international humanitarian law. The IDF did not give effective warning, as legally required, and where warnings were given, they often did not allow sufficient time for the population to leave. In any event, civilians remained at risk of being attacked if they left and lacked access to safe humanitarian exit corridors. There were also various cases of direct attacks on medical and relief personnel, who faced many obstacles and IDF-imposed constraints in reaching civilians in need of medical care and humanitarian assistance. One of the most striking aspects of the conflict was the massive displacement of civilians, owing mainly to a climate of fear and panic from IDF warnings, threats and attacks. The Commission highlighted a number of concerns about the protection of those affected, which the Government estimated at nearly a quarter of the population, of whom approximately 735,000 sought shelter within Lebanon, while another 230,000 fled abroad.

Also of concern were the cases of persons who were detained, mistreated and/or abducted and transferred to Israel before their release; the impact of the conflict on vulnerable groups, including women, children, the elderly and migrant workers; and the extensive damage to civilian infrastructure in Lebanon, which hampered the free movement of the displaced, the transportation of humanitarian assistance and the delivery of many vital social services and devastated the environment. The damage to buildings and other facilities was so severe that the Commission considered it would take Lebanon years to rebuild, with the help of the international community. The Commission was not persuaded by Israel's reasons for attacking civilian infrastructure and found no justification for the 30 direct attacks by the IDF on the United Nations Interim Force in Lebanon (UNIFIL) (see p. 578), which resulted in deaths and injuries to UN personnel. While none of the weapons used by the IDF was deemed illegal under international humanitarian law, the Commission determined that the way in which some weapons were used in some instances, particularly cluster munitions, was excessive and not justified by any reason of military necessity and violated international humanitarian law. It also found evidence of Hizbullah using towns and villages, as well as UNIFIL posts, as deliberate "shields" for the firing of its rockets, but found no evidence that it had used human shields.

The Commission concluded that the conflict gave rise to two pertinent issues: Israel's international responsibility under international law, international humanitarian law and human rights; and the accountability of individuals for serious humanitarian and human rights violations. It addressed to the Council recommendations on five broad areas, including the need for humanitarian assistance and reconstruction efforts in Lebanon. Considering the consequences of the conflict and its effects on the Lebanese population, notably in the south, the Commission proposed that the Council promote initiatives and call for the mobilization of the international community to assist Lebanon and its people. The Council should encourage UN organs, agencies and institutions to work together in a comprehensive and coordinated programme with the Government to improve living conditions and enable the population to fully enjoy their human rights. It should further encourage the UN system and the Bretton Woods Institutions (the World Bank Group and the International Monetary Fund) to facilitate reconstruction efforts in the country; call on the Secretary-General to evaluate the humanitarian assistance provided to civilians by the UN system and other relief organizations; call for the mobilization of professional and technical expertise in coping with the ecological disaster on the marine environment on the Lebanese coast and beyond; and establish a follow-up procedure on the measures to be taken for the rebuilding of Lebanon and for reparations to victims. Other recommendations addressed action to meet the needs of vulnerable groups, ways to promote respect for international humanitarian law, the urgent need to include cluster munitions in the list of weapons banned under international humanitarian law, and the importance of promoting the legal means for individuals to redress violations of international humanitarian law and human rights.

Human Rights Council action. On 8 December [A/62/53 (res. 3/3)], the Human Rights Council took note of the report of the Commission of Inquiry (see above) and asked the High Commissioner to consult with the Government of Lebanon on its findings and on the relevant recommendations contained therein, and to report to the Council in 2007.

(See pp. 903 and 907, respectively, for information on the September visits to Lebanon by the Special Rapporteur on the right to food, and to Israel and Lebanon jointly by the Special Rapporteurs on extrajudicial, summary or arbitrary executions, on the right of everyone to the enjoyment of the highest attainable standard of physical and mental health, on adequate housing as a component of the right to an adequate standard of living, and the Representative of the Secretary-General on the human rights of internally displaced persons.)

GENERAL ASSEMBLY ACTION

On 19 December [meeting 81], the General Assembly, on the recommendation of the Third Committee [A/61/443/Add.2], adopted **resolution 61/154** by recorded vote (112-7-64) [agenda item 67 *(b)*].

The human rights situation arising from the recent Israeli military operations in Lebanon

The General Assembly,

Reaffirming the Universal Declaration of Human Rights and the Vienna Declaration and Programme of Action of 1993, and recalling the International Covenant on Civil and Political Rights, the International Covenant on Economic, Social and Cultural Rights, the Convention on the Rights of the Child and other human rights instruments,

Guided by relevant human rights instruments and international humanitarian law, in particular the Hague Conventions of 1899 and 1907 respecting the Laws and Customs of War on Land, which prohibit attacks on and bombardment of civilian populations and objects and lay down obligations for general protection against dangers arising from military operations against civilian objects, hospitals, relief materials and means of transportation,

Recalling the commitments of the High Contracting Parties to the Geneva Conventions of 12 August 1949 and the Additional Protocols thereto of 1977,

Recalling also the World Declaration on the Survival, Protection and Development of Children and the Plan of Action for Implementing the World Declaration on the Survival, Protection and Development of Children in the 1990s adopted by the World Summit for Children, held in New York on 29 and 30 September 1990,

Stressing that the right to life constitutes the most fundamental of all human rights,

Emphasizing that human rights law and international humanitarian law are complementary and mutually reinforcing,

Bearing in mind Security Council resolution 1701(2006) of 11 August 2006 and the statement by the President of the Council of 30 July 2006,

Bearing in mind also Human Rights Council resolution S-2/1 entitled "The grave situation of human rights in Lebanon caused by Israeli military operations", adopted by the Council at its second special session on 11 August 2006,

1. *Condemns* all acts of violence against civilians, including the bombardment by Israeli military forces of Lebanese civilians causing extensive loss of life and injuries, including among children, immense destruction of homes, properties, agricultural lands and vital civilian infrastructure, and the displacement of up to one million Lebanese civilians and outflows of refugees fleeing heavy shelling and bombardment directed against the civilian population, thus exacerbating the magnitude of human suffering in Lebanon;

2. *Emphasizes* the importance of the safety and well-being of all children;

3. *Expresses deep concern* about the negative consequences, including the mental and psychological impact, of the Israeli military operations for the well-being of Lebanese children;

4. *Emphasizes* that attacks against civilians, wherever they may occur, are contrary to international humanitarian law and constitute flagrant violations of human

rights, condemns the killing of children, women, the elderly and other civilians in Lebanon, underlines that there should be no impunity for such acts, and calls particularly upon Israel to abide scrupulously by its obligations under human rights law, in particular the Convention on the Rights of the Child, and international humanitarian law;

5. *Deplores* the death of more than 1,100 civilians, one third being children, as a result of the Israeli military operations in Lebanon;

6. *Strongly condemns* the deliberate use by Israel of cluster munitions in Lebanon, most of which had been used in the seventy-two hours directly preceding the cessation of hostilities and after the adoption of Security Council resolution 1701(2006), which left over one million unexploded cluster bomblets, threatening the lives of children and civilians and adversely affecting recovery and rebuilding efforts;

7. *Deplores* the environmental degradation caused by Israeli air strikes against power plants in Lebanon and their adverse impact on the health and well-being of children and other civilians;

8. *Calls upon* the international community to urgently provide the Government of Lebanon with financial assistance in support of the national early recovery, reconstruction and enhancing the national economy, including the rehabilitation of victims, return of displaced persons and restoration of the essential infrastructure, and expresses its appreciation to the Member States, United Nations bodies and intergovernmental, regional and non-governmental organizations that have provided and continue to provide assistance to the people and Government of Lebanon.

RECORDED VOTE ON RESOLUTION 61/154:

In favour: Afghanistan, Algeria, Antigua and Barbuda, Argentina, Armenia, Azerbaijan, Bahamas, Bahrain, Bangladesh, Barbados, Belarus, Belize, Benin, Bhutan, Bolivia, Botswana, Brazil, Brunei Darussalam, Burkina Faso, Cambodia, Cape Verde, Chile, China, Colombia, Comoros, Congo, Côte d'Ivoire, Cuba, Democratic People's Republic of Korea, Democratic Republic of the Congo, Djibouti, Dominica, Ecuador, Egypt, El Salvador, Eritrea, Gabon, Gambia, Ghana, Grenada, Guatemala, Guinea, Guinea-Bissau, Guyana, India, Indonesia, Iran, Iraq, Jamaica, Jordan, Kazakhstan, Kuwait, Kyrgyzstan, Lao People's Democratic Republic, Lebanon, Lesotho, Liberia, Libyan Arab Jamahiriya, Madagascar, Malawi, Malaysia, Maldives, Mali, Mauritania, Mauritius, Mongolia, Morocco, Mozambique, Myanmar, Namibia, Nepal, Niger, Nigeria, Oman, Pakistan, Panama, Paraguay, Peru, Philippines, Qatar, Russian Federation, Saint Lucia, Saint Vincent and the Grenadines, Sao Tome and Principe, Saudi Arabia, Senegal, Sierra Leone, Singapore, Somalia, South Africa, Sri Lanka, Sudan, Suriname, Swaziland, Syrian Arab Republic, Tajikistan, Thailand, Timor-Leste, Togo, Trinidad and Tobago, Tunisia, Turkey, Turkmenistan, United Arab Emirates, United Republic of Tanzania, Uruguay, Uzbekistan, Venezuela, Viet Nam, Yemen, Zambia, Zimbabwe.

Against: Australia, Canada, Israel, Marshall Islands, Micronesia, Palau, United States.

Abstaining: Albania, Andorra, Angola, Austria, Belgium, Bosnia and Herzegovina, Bulgaria, Burundi, Cameroon, Central African Republic, Costa Rica, Croatia, Cyprus, Czech Republic, Denmark, Dominican Republic, Estonia, Ethiopia, Fiji, Finland, France, Georgia, Germany, Greece, Honduras, Hungary, Iceland, Ireland, Italy, Japan, Kenya, Latvia, Liechtenstein, Lithuania, Luxembourg, Malta, Mexico, Moldova, Monaco, Montenegro, Netherlands, New Zealand, Nicaragua, Norway, Papua New Guinea, Poland, Portugal, Republic of Korea, Romania, Samoa, San Marino, Serbia, Slovakia, Slovenia, Solomon Islands, Spain, Sweden, Switzerland, The former Yugoslav Republic of Macedonia, Tonga, Tuvalu, Ukraine, United Kingdom, Vanuatu.

Territories occupied by Israel

In 2006, human rights questions, including cases of violations in the territories occupied by Israel following the 1967 hostilities in the Middle East were addressed by the Human Rights Council. Political and other aspects were considered by the General Assembly, its Special Committee to Investigate Israeli Practices Affecting the Human Rights of the Palestinian People and Other Arabs of the Occupied Territories (Committee on Israeli Practices), and other bodies (see PART ONE, Chapter VI).

Report of Secretary-General. In response to a 2005 request of the Commission on Human Rights [YUN 2005, p. 904], the Secretary-General reported that he had brought the Commission's resolution on the occupied Syrian Golan to the attention of all Governments, specialized agencies, regional intergovernmental organizations and international humanitarian organizations [E/CN.4/2006/27]. It was also communicated to the Committee on Israeli Practices, the Committee on the Exercise of the Inalienable Rights of the Palestinian People (Committee on Palestinian Rights) and the United Nations Relief and Works Agency for Palestine Refugees in the Near East (UNRWA). Related activities undertaken by the UN Department of Public Information and its Information Centres and Services were contained in the report on the work of the Committee on Israeli Practices (see p. 536).

Note by Secretariat. By a 9 January note [E/CN.4/2006/28], submitted in response to a 2005 Commission request to the High Commissioner on the issue of Palestinian pregnant women giving birth at Israeli checkpoints [YUN 2005, p. 904], the Secretariat stated that, since the High Commissioner's 2005 report on the issue [ibid., p. 905], no further replies had been received from the Permanent Mission of Israel and the Permanent Observer Mission of Palestine to the United Nations regarding the implementation of the Commission's resolution.

Reports of Special Rapporteur (Janaury). In a January report [E/CN.4/2006/29], Special Rapporteur John Dugard (South Africa) described the human rights situation in the Occupied Palestinian Territory, against the backdrop of Israel's successful evacuation of settlers and the withdrawal of its defence forces from the Gaza Strip and parts of the West Bank [YUN 2005, p. 515]. While acknowledging that as an important step towards resolving the conflict in the region, the Special Rapporteur noted that the withdrawal did not by itself end the occupation of the territory. Israel still retained effective control over the territory through its restrictions of the airspace, territorial sea and external land boundaries, and continued to assert military power by means of sonic booms and repeated air strikes which, although targeting militants, had killed and injured innocent bystanders. Israel also continued its construction of a wall within the Palestinian territory, in defiance of the 2004 Advisory Opinion of the International Court of Justice [YUN 2004, p. 465], causing great hardship to Palestinian communities within the vicinity of the wall, many of which were denied access to family, hospitals and schools in the West Bank and their lands beyond the wall. Consequently, many were leaving their homes, compelled to be internally displaced. The construction of the wall, which was also affecting the character of East Jerusalem, was intended to reduce the number of Palestinians in the city by transferring them to the West Bank. Little progress was made in operationalizing the register or mechanism for compiling and compensating those suffering as a result of the wall. Elsewhere, Israeli policies were designed to drive Palestinians from the Jordan Valley area, as Palestinian land was confiscated, homes destroyed, access denied to non-Jordan Valley residents and water and electricity services curtailed. Other human rights violations continued, notably the situation of some 9,000 prisoners in Israeli jails, further restrictions to the freedom of movement, high unemployment, extreme poverty and difficulties concerning health and education facilities, as well as the effect of the occupation on women. Noting that the primary responsibility for resolving the Israeli/Palestinian conflict rested with the Middle East Quartet (Russian Federation, United States, European Union, United Nations), the Special Rapporteur observed that the Quartet's road map, which formed the basis for negotiations, was outdated. A new road map was needed that would take account of current political realities and be anchored in respect for human rights and the rule of law in the conflict resolution process.

Human Rights Council action. On 30 June [A/61/53 (dec. 1/106)], the Human Rights Council, by a recorded vote of 29 to 12, with 5 abstentions, requested the relevant special rapporteurs to report on the issue during its next session, at which it would undertake substantive consideration of the human rights violations and implications of the Israeli occupation of Palestine and other Arab territories.

Special Rapporteur's visit (June). In a later visit to the Occupied Palestinian Territory (9-17 June) [A/HRC/2/5], the Special Rapporteur found that the human rights situation there had deteriorated substantially, following the abduction of an Israeli soldier by Palestinian militants, the firing of Qassam rockets into Israel and Israel's military response, causing numerous deaths and injuries. Israel's siege of Gaza took the form of the bombardment and destruction of public utilities, including all six transformers of the only power plant there, the main water pipelines and sewage networks, and frequent closure of the only fuel pipeline into the Gaza Strip. The substantial reduction in electricity, fuel and water supply impacted severely on the daily life of Palestinians. Israel also bombarded several public buildings and facilities. Many Palestinians were forced to flee their homes and were sheltered by UNRWA. The Israeli military incursions were accompanied by heavy shelling and the bombardment of houses, resulting in the deaths of many civilians. The attacks on the el-Maghazi refugee camp from 19 to 31 July were typical of those incursions.

In other developments, the 500,000 Palestinians living near the wall required permits to cross it, with about 40 per cent of permit applications refused. Israel also continued to use the wall to implement its policy of "de-Palestinization" of Jerusalem, while Israeli settlements in the West Bank and East Jerusalem continued to expand, in violation of the Fourth Geneva Convention. The difficulties facing Palestinians in terms of restricted access to their lands and social services were exacerbated by the proliferation of checkpoints, which rose from 376 in 2005 to 500 as at June 2006. The demolition of houses remained a regular feature of the occupation, with the family life of Palestinians further undermined by a number of Israeli laws and practices. At least 4 out of 10 Palestinians lived below the official poverty line. Rising unemployment, which stood at 40 per cent, was aggravated by the fact that the public sector, accounting for 23 per cent of total employment in the Palestinian territory, was unpaid because of the withholding of funds owed to the Palestinian Authority by the Israeli Government. In addition, the United States and the European Union cut off funds to the Palestinian Authority, on the grounds that Hamas, elected to office in January 2006, was listed under their laws as a terrorist organization.

In his conclusions, the Special Rapporteur observed that Israel had violated the prohibition of the indiscriminate use of military power against civilians and civilian objects, and its use of force was disproportionate and excessive. It was therefore in violation of important norms of human rights and international humanitarian law. While it was readily conceded that Israel faced a security threat and was entitled to defend itself, it should not be forgotten that the root cause of that threat was the continuing occupation of land belonging to a people who wished to exercise its right to self-determination in an independent State. It was unfortunate that the Middle East Quartet had resorted to punitive measures to compel Hamas to change its ideological stance or bring about a regime change. Questioning whether the UN position in that regard was consistent with the UN Charter, the Special Rapporteur stressed that the Organization needed to show more concern for the human rights of Palestinians and appealed to the wider international community to address their plight.

The report of the Special Rapporteur on his June visit to the Occupied Palestinian Territory was transmitted to the General Assembly by the Secretary-General in a September note [A/61/470].

On 19 December, the Assembly took note of the report of the Special Rapporteur (**decision 61/529**).

Human Rights Council special sessions

At the request of Tunisia [A/HRC/S-1/1], backed by 21 Member States, the Human Rights Council held its first special session to consider the escalation of the situation in the Palestinian and other occupied Arab territories. The session, convened in accordance with General Assembly resolution 60/251 (see p. 757), was held on 5 and 6 July, during which statements were heard from Council members, representatives of the concerned parties, observer States and intergovernmental organizations.

On 6 July, the Council, by a recorded vote of 29 to 11, with 5 abstentions, adopted resolution [A/61/53 (S-1/1)], as orally amended, by which it expressed concern at violations of the Palestinian people's rights caused by the Israeli occupation, including the extensive Israeli military operations against Palestinians there. It demanded that Israel end its military occupation, abide by international humanitarian and human rights laws, refrain from imposing collective punishment on Palestinian civilians, release arrested Palestinians and treat detained persons in accordance with the Geneva Conventions. Calling for a negotiated solution to the crisis, the Council decided to dispatch an urgent fact-finding mission to the Occupied Palestinian Territory, headed by the Special Rapporteur, and recommended that the Assembly endorse its decision.

In his report on his December visit to the Occupied Palestinian Territory [A/HRC/4/17], the Special Rapporteur stated that Beit Hanoun in northern Gaza, with a population of 40,000, was subjected to a six-day Israeli military action in November, during which 82 Palestinians, half of them civilians, were killed by the IDF and more than 260 injured and hundreds of males between the ages of 16 and 40 arrested. Residents were confined to their homes as a result of a curfew, while tanks and bulldozers destroyed 279 homes, as well as public buildings, electricity networks, schools and hospitals. The 8 November assault culminated with the shelling of a home, killing 19 persons and wounding 55 others. Israel justified the attack on Beit Hanoun as a defensive operation aimed at preventing the launching of Qassam rockets into Israel, thousands of which had been fired into civilian areas, killing two Israelis and wounding 30 others. The Special Rapporteur said that such actions could not be condoned and constituted a war crime; however, Israel's response had been disproportionate.

On 10 November [A/HRC/S-3/1], Bahrain and Pakistan, with the support of 24 Council members, requested the convening of a further Council special session to consider and take action on the gross human rights violations resulting from Israeli military incursions in the Occupied Palestinian Territory, including the recent one in northern Gaza and the assault on Beit Hanoun.

The Council convened its third special session on 15 November [A/HRC/S-3/2], and by a recorded vote of 32 to 8, with 6 abstentions, adopted resolution [A/62/53 (res. S-3/1)], in which it condemned the Israeli killing of Palestinian civilians, including women, children and medics in Beit Hanoun and other Palestinian towns and villages, and called for the perpetrators to be brought to justice. Denouncing the massive destruction of Palestinian homes, property and infrastructure, the Council expressed alarm at the gross and systematic violations of human rights of the Palestinian people by Israel and called for urgent international action to put an end to those violations and protect the Palestinian civilians, in compliance with international human rights and humanitarian laws. It also decided to dispatch urgently a high-level fact-finding mission, to be appointed by the Council President, to Beit Hanoun to assess the situation of victims, address survivors' needs and make recommendations on ways to protect Palestinian civilians against any further Israeli assaults. The mission was asked to report no later than the middle of December on progress in fulfilling its mandate, with the assistance of the Secretary-General and the High Commissioner.

Further developments

Communication. In a January letter to the High Commissioner [E/CN.4/2006/G.4], Syria drew attention to Israeli practices aimed allegedly towards the partitioning of the occupied Syrian village of Al-Ghajar, through the displacement of its inhabitants and the construction of a separation wall between the inhabitants and their own lands, in violation of international law.

Human Rights Council action. By a recorded vote of 32 to 1, with 14 abstentions, the Human Rights Council, on 27 November [A/62/53 (res. 2/3)], expressed concern at the suffering of citizens in the Occupied Syrian Golan due to the violation of their fundamental human rights since the Israeli military occupation of 1967. It called on Israel to comply with relevant General Assembly and Security Council resolutions, desist from changing the physical character, demographic composition, institutional structure and legal status of the occupied Syrian Golan, stop imposing Israeli citizenship and identity cards on Syrian citizens, and refrain from repressive measures and other practices mentioned in the report of the Committee on Israeli Practices (see p. 536). Emphasizing that displaced persons in those territories should be allowed to return to their homes and recover their property, the Council determined that all legislative and administrative measures and actions taken or to be taken by Israel, which purportedly altered the character and legal status of the Occupied Syrian Golan, were null and void and violated international law. It called on Member States not to recognize any such measures and asked the Secretary-General to bring the resolution to the attention of Governments, competent UN organs, specialized agencies, as well as international and regional intergovernmental and humanitarian organizations, and to report on it in 2007.

On 27 November [res. 2/4], the Council, by a recorded vote of 45 to 1, with 1 abstention, expressed grave concern at the continuing Israeli settlement and related activities, which changed the physical character and demographic composition of the occupied territories, including East Jerusalem and the Syrian Golan, and at the continuing construction of the wall inside the Occupied Palestinian Territory. It urged Israel to reverse the settlement policy, prevent any new installation of settlers, and demanded that it implement the recommendations regarding the settlements outlined in a 2001 report of the High Commissioner [YUN 2001, p. 776], and comply with its legal obligations, as mentioned in the 2004 Advisory Opinion of ICJ [YUN 2004, p.465]. Welcoming the Palestinian truce initiative and its acceptance by Israel, which came into effect on 26 November (see p. 524), the Council urged the parties to maintain the truce, as it could pave the way for genuine negotiations towards a just resolution of the conflict. It also called on Israel to implement serious measures, including the confiscation of arms and enforcement of criminal sanctions, aimed at preventing acts of violence by Israeli settlers, and to guarantee the safety and protection of Palestinian civilians and property in the Occupied Palestinian Territory, including East Jerusalem.

On 8 December [res. 3/1], the Council, by a recorded vote of 34 to 1, with 12 abstentions, regretted that its resolution of 6 July on the human rights situation in the Occupied Palestinian Territory, adopted at its first special session (see p. 969), had not been implemented and called for its speedy implementation, including the dispatch of an urgent fact-finding mission. It also asked the Special Rapporteur to report in 2007 on the implementation of the resolution.

Further reports of Special Rapporteur. On 20 December [A/HRC/4/116], the Special Rapporteur reported that he had not been able to undertake the fact-finding mission requested in Council resolutions S-1/1 (see p. 969) and S-3/1 (see above) because of the failure of the Government of Israel to consent to such a mission, despite efforts between July and September to obtain its cooperation. However, he was able to obtain the required consent in his capacity as Special Rapporteur, which enabled him to undertake another visit to the Occupied Palestinian Territory in December. He found that violations of human rights law and international humanitarian law persisted in Gaza, the West Bank and other areas. Continuing military incursions and attacks had destroyed or damaged homes, schools, hospitals, mosques, public buildings, bridges, water pipelines, electricity networks and agricultural lands. In Gaza, where Beit Hanoun was particularly affected by heavy attacks that either killed or wounded many civilians, economic sanctions continued to have a major impact on the people. In the West Bank, Israel's construction of the wall and the unrelenting proliferation of checkpoints remained serious obstructions to the freedom of movement and to other social values.

Numerous other human rights challenges highlighted in the Special Rapporteur's earlier reports also persisted. Those responsible for committing war crimes by firing shells and rockets into civilian areas without any apparent military advantage should be apprehended and prosecuted. That applied to Palestinians who fired Qassam rockets into Israel, as well as to members of the IDF who had committed such crimes on a much greater scale. While individual accountability was important, the responsibility of the State of Israel for the violation of peremptory norms of international law in its actions against the Palestinian people should not be overlooked. Elements of Israel's military occupation of the Occupied Palestinian Territory constituted forms of colonialism, and were contrary to international law. Thus, a further advisory opinion should be sought from ICJ on the legal consequences of such prolonged occupation. The Occupied Palestinian Territory was the only instance of a developing country that was denied the right to self-determination, and the failure of developed States to put an end to that situation jeopardized the future of international protection of human rights.

PART THREE

Economic and social questions

Chapter I

Development policy and international economic cooperation

The global economy started 2006 on a strong note, with a number of major developed economies rebounding from the notable slowdown in 2005 and many developing countries maintaining the momentum of broad and solid growth. A measurable moderation in global economic growth was expected for the second half of 2006, however, with the annual growth of world gross domestic product at about 3.6 per cent, the same pace as in 2005, and marginally higher than projected at the beginning of the year. A number of downside risks were expected to weigh on the economy, namely large global imbalances, persistently higher oil prices, the cooling off in the housing sector in a number of countries and rising interest rates worldwide.

With uneven progress in achieving the Millennium Development Goals (MDGs), adopted by the General Assembly in 2000, and staggering levels of human deprivation, the Organization continued, in 2006, to focus on the global development agenda. Highlighting the nexus between achieving the MDGs and global economic stability and prosperity, the Secretary-General's High-level Panel on UN system-wide coherence in the areas of development, humanitarian assistance and the environment proposed a series of reforms to enable the UN system to deliver better on the promises made in the 2000 Millennium Declaration, and reaffirmed in the 2005 World Summit Outcome.

During the year, the General Assembly convened a high-level meeting on the midterm comprehensive global review of the implementation of the Programme of Action for the Least Developed Countries (LDCs) for the Decade 2001-2010. In the Declaration adopted by the meeting, the Assembly reaffirmed that the Programme of Action, adopted at the Third United Nations Conference on LDCs in 2001, constituted a fundamental framework for a strong global partnership whose goal was to accelerate sustained economic growth, sustainable development and poverty eradication in the LDCs. For its part, the Economic and Social Council, during its high-level segment, considered the theme "creating an environment at the national and international levels conducive to generating full and productive employment and decent work for all, and its impact on sustainable development". The Council's coordination segment was devoted to the issue of sustained economic growth for social development, including the eradication of poverty and hunger. In other development-related activities, the international community observed the International Day for the Eradication of Poverty and welcomed the observance of the International Year of Microcredit, 2005. Requesting the submission of a comprehensive evaluation of the implementation of the first UN Decade for the Eradication of Poverty (1997-2006) at its 2007 session, the Assembly recognized the contribution of the first UN Decade and noted interest in the proclamation of a second UN decade for the eradication of poverty.

Arising from the need to link the outcomes of the 2005 World Summit on the Information Society with the broader UN development agenda, the Secretary-General, in March, launched the Global Alliance for Information and Communication Technologies (ICT) and Development to build on the work of the ICT Task Force, whose four-year mandate expired at the end of 2005. In other follow-up action to the World Summit, the United Nations Chief Executives Board endorsed the establishment of the United Nations Group on the Information Society. The Economic and Social Council decided to enlarge the membership of the Commission on Science and Technology for Development by including ten new members

The Commission on Sustainable Development, in overseeing the follow-up to the 2002 World Summit on Sustainable Development, which reviewed progress in implementing Agenda 21, the action plan on sustainable development adopted by the 1992 United Nations Conference on Environment and Development, focused on the thematic cluster of energy for sustainable development, industrial development, air pollution/atmosphere and climate change. It also reviewed progress in the implementation of the Programme of Action for the Sustainable Development of Small Island Developing States and the Mauritius Strategy for the Further Implementation of the Programme of Action.

Regarding other countries in special situations, the Assembly decided to conduct a midterm review, in 2008, of the Almaty Programme of Action, adopted in 2003 by the International Ministerial Conference of Landlocked and Transit Developing Countries and Donor Countries and International Finance and Development Institutions on Transit Transport Cooperation.

International economic relations

Development and international economic cooperation

A number of UN bodies addressed development and international economic cooperation issues during 2006, including the General Assembly and the Economic and Social Council.

On 20 December, the Assembly took note of the report of the Second (Economic and Financial) Committee [A/61/420] on its discussion of macroeconomic policy questions (**decision 61/535**).

Economic and Social Council consideration. On 24 April, the Economic and Social Council held its ninth special high-level meeting with the Bretton Woods institutions (the World Bank Group and the International Monetary Fund), the World Trade Organization (WTO) and the United Nations Conference on Trade and Development [A/61/3]. It had before it a March note [E/2006/48 & Corr.1] by the Secretary-General on coherence, coordination and cooperation in the context of the implementation of the Monterrey Consensus [YUN 2002, p. 953] and the 2005 World Summit Outcome [YUN 2005, p. 48]. A summary of the meeting [A/61/81-E/2006/73] by the Council President outlined the four sub-themes discussed during the special meeting: implementation of and support for national development strategies towards the achievement of the internationally agreed development goals, including the Millennium Development Goals (MDGS) [YUN 2000, p. 51]; fulfilling the development dimension of the Doha work programme: next steps, including in the area of "Aid for Trade"; external debt: implementing and building on current initiatives to enhance debt sustainability; and supporting the development efforts of middle-income developing countries.

At its high-level segment (3-5 July), the Council considered the theme of creating an environment at the national and international levels conducive to generating full and productive employment and decent work for all, and its impact on sustainable development (see p. 1594). Activities included a high-level policy dialogue on important developments in the world economy and international economic cooperation with the executive heads of UN system financial and trade institutions.

During its coordination segment (6, 7, 10 and 17 July), the Council discussed sustained economic growth for social development, including the eradication of poverty and hunger (see p. 1594).

Globalization and interdependence

In response to General Assembly resolution 60/204 [YUN 2005, p. 911], the Secretary-General submitted an August report on the role of innovation, science and technology in pursuing development in the context of globalization [A/61/286], which addressed some of the most pressing concerns of developing countries, including building national scientific societies in the areas of education, capacity-building in agriculture, promoting private technology transfer and research, improving infrastructure for promoting technology and innovation, making effective use of information and communication technologies (ITC), and nurturing appropriate institutions. The report also discussed the role of international strategies in fostering knowledge innovation, such as promoting research and development networks through open access regimes, pursuing the development dimensions of intellectual property rights, and nurturing alliances, such as South-South cooperation. It also examined the role of the United Nations.

The report stated that the growing gap in technological and scientific capabilities between developed and developing countries impeded the capacity of many developing countries to participate fully in the global economy. While several emerging economies had made significant breakthroughs in their scientific and technological capacities, including forward-looking economic policies that engaged the private sector, academia and industry in using scientific and technological knowledge in accomplishing their developmental goals, more needed to be done at both the national and international levels. Poorer countries needed to develop a sound scientific base in terms of human talent and to encourage the application of scientific solutions to their domestic developmental concerns. Global rules governing scientific knowledge needed to be more flexible so as to foster scientific learning. Multilateral institutions and regional development organizations had a critical role to play in that regard.

At the national level, the Secretary-General recommended that policies supporting scientific education be developed, as well as for retaining scientific talent in order to stem the brain drain. Linkages between technology-based industry, academia and government should be created and Governments needed to engage the private sector and promote business activities in science through fiscal incentives, direct public credit and subsidies that lowered the cost of innovative investment. They should take the initiative in acquiring the technical knowledge available through international and indigenous construction and engineering firms. National innovation systems in developing countries should focus on overcoming the "domestic technology gap" by guaranteeing the access to technology of farmers and small urban producers.

At the international level, an international database on knowledge and research information should be created. Other recommendations included: establishing a technology development consortium among companies by mobilizing and pooling research and development resources; creating a network of major development institutions and industrial enterprises able to meet human resource training needs; developing a network of knowledge-sharing among innovation actors; and ensuring that South-South cooperation was designed to leverage all technical knowledge available and applied wherever needed. In pursuing the mandates of the World Summit on the Information Society [YUN 2005, p. 933] and the 2005 World Summit, the United Nations should play an increasingly active role in ensuring that developing countries were able to achieve their goals in the area of innovation, science and technology.

Communication. On 3 October [A/61/486], South Africa transmitted to the Secretary-General the ministerial statement adopted at the thirtieth annual meeting of Foreign Ministers of the Group of 77 and China (New York, 22 September), which welcomed the holding of the Meeting of Ministers of Science and Technology of the Group of 77 (Rio de Janeiro, Brazil, 3 September), and the decision to launch the Consortium on Science, Technology and Innovation for the South, in accordance with the mandate of the Second South Summit [YUN 2005, p. 983].

GENERAL ASSEMBLY ACTION

On 20 December [meeting 83], the General Assembly, on the recommendation of the Second Committee [A/61/424/Add.1], adopted **resolution 61/207** without vote [agenda item 55 *(a)*].

Role of the United Nations in promoting development in the context of globalization and interdependence

The General Assembly,

Recalling its resolutions 53/169 of 15 December 1998, 54/231 of 22 December 1999, 55/212 of 20 December 2000, 56/209 of 21 December 2001, 57/274 of 20 December 2002, 58/225 of 23 December 2003, 59/240 of 22 December 2004 and 60/204 of 22 December 2005 on the role of the United Nations in promoting development in the context of globalization and interdependence,

Recalling also the 2005 World Summit Outcome and all relevant General Assembly resolutions, in particular those that have built upon the 2005 World Summit Outcome, in the economic, social and related fields, including General Assembly resolution 60/265 of 30 June 2006 on follow-up to the development outcome of the 2005 World Summit, including the Millennium Development Goals and the other internationally agreed development goals,

Recalling further its resolution 57/270 B of 23 June 2003 on the integrated and coordinated implementation of and follow-up to the outcomes of the major United Nations conferences and summits in the economic and social fields,

Emphasizing the need to fully implement the global partnership for development and enhance the momentum generated by the 2005 World Summit in order to operationalize and implement the commitments made in the outcomes of the major United Nations conferences and summits, including the 2005 World Summit, in the economic, social and related fields,

Reaffirming the resolve expressed in the United Nations Millennium Declaration to ensure that globalization becomes a positive force for all the world's people,

Recognizing that all human rights are universal, indivisible, interdependent and interrelated,

Noting that particular attention must be given, in the context of globalization, to the objective of protecting, promoting and enhancing the rights and welfare of women and girls, as stated in the Beijing Declaration and Platform for Action,

Reaffirming the commitment to eradicate poverty and hunger and promote sustained economic growth, sustainable development and global prosperity for all and to promote the development of the productive sectors in developing countries to enable them to participate more effectively in and benefit from the process of globalization,

Reaffirming also its strong support for fair globalization and its resolve to achieve the goals of full and productive employment and decent work for all, and in this regard recalling the ministerial declaration adopted on 5 July 2006 by the high-level segment of the substantive session of the Economic and Social Council on the theme "Creating an environment at the national and international levels conducive to generating full and productive employment and decent work for all, and its impact on sustainable development",

Reaffirming further the commitment to broaden and strengthen the participation of developing countries and countries with economies in transition in international economic decision-making and norm-setting, and to that end stressing the importance of continuing efforts to reform the international financial architecture, and acknowledging the need for continued discussion on the issue of the voting power of developing countries in the Bretton Woods institutions, which remains a concern,

Reaffirming its commitment to governance, equity and transparency in the financial, monetary and trading systems and its commitment to open, equitable, rule-based, predictable and non-discriminatory multilateral trading and financial systems,

Recognizing that countries diverge greatly in terms of their abilities to access, diffuse and use scientific and technological knowledge, most of which is generated in developed countries,

Recognizing also that developing countries have varying capacities to translate scientific and technological knowledge into goods and services and to invest in human resources and entrepreneurial capacity-building

1. *Takes note* of the report of the Secretary-General;

2. *Recognizes* that some countries have successfully adapted to the changes and benefited from globalization but many others, especially the least developed countries, have remained marginalized in the globalizing world economy, and recognizes also that, as stated in the Millennium Declaration, the benefits are very unevenly shared, while the costs are unevenly distributed;

3. *Reaffirms* the need for the United Nations to play a fundamental role in the promotion of international cooperation for development and the coherence, coordination and implementation of development goals and actions agreed upon by the international community, and resolves to strengthen coordination within the United Nations system in close cooperation with all other multilateral financial, trade and development institutions in order to support sustained economic growth, poverty eradication and sustainable development;

4. *Underlines* that in addressing the linkages between globalization and sustainable development, particular focus should be placed on identifying and implementing mutually reinforcing policies and practices that promote sustained economic growth, social development and environmental protection and that this requires efforts at both the national and international levels;

5. *Reaffirms* that good governance is essential for sustainable development; that sound economic policies, solid democratic institutions responsive to the needs of the people and improved infrastructure are the basis for sustained economic growth, poverty eradication and employment creation; and that freedom, peace and security, domestic stability, respect for human rights, including the right to development, and the rule of law, gender equality, market-oriented policies and an overall commitment to just and democratic societies are also essential and mutually reinforcing;

6. *Reaffirms also* that good governance at the international level is fundamental for achieving sustainable development, that, in order to ensure a dynamic and enabling international economic environment, it is important to promote global economic governance through addressing the international finance, trade, technology and investment patterns that have an impact on the development prospects of developing countries and that to this end the international community should take all necessary and appropriate measures, including ensuring support for structural and macroeconomic reform, a comprehensive solution to the external debt problem and increasing the market access of developing countries;

7. *Underlines* the fact that the increasing interdependence of national economies in a globalizing world and the emergence of rule-based regimes for international economic relations have meant that the space for national economic policy, i.e., the scope for domestic policies, especially in the areas of trade, investment and industrial development, is now often framed by international disciplines and commitments and global market considerations, that it is for each Government to evaluate the trade-off between the benefits of accepting international rules and commitments and the constraints posed by the loss of policy space and that it is particularly important for developing countries, bearing in mind development goals and objectives, that all countries take into account the need for appropriate balance between national policy space and international disciplines and commitments;

8. *Reaffirms* that each country has primary responsibility for its own development, that the role of national policies and development strategies cannot be overemphasized in the achievement of sustainable development and that national efforts should be complemented by supportive global programmes, measures and policies aimed at expanding the development opportunities of developing countries, while taking into account national conditions and ensuring respect for national ownership, strategies and sovereignty;

9. *Stresses* the special importance of creating an enabling international economic environment through strong cooperative efforts by all countries and institutions to promote equitable economic development in a world economy that benefits all people;

10. *Invites* developed countries, in particular major industrialized economies, to take into account the effect of their macroeconomic policies on international growth and development;

11. *Recognizes*, at the same time, that domestic economies are now interwoven with the global economic system and that, inter alia, the effective use of trade and investment opportunities can help countries to fight poverty;

12. *Stresses* that, in the increasingly globalizing interdependent world economy, a holistic approach to the interconnected national, international and systemic challenges of financing for development, namely, sustainable, gender-sensitive and people-centred development, is essential and that such an approach must open up opportunities for all and help to ensure that resources are created and used effectively and that solid and accountable institutions are established at all levels;

13. *Recognizes* that the gap in technology and scientific capabilities between developed and developing countries, especially the least developed countries, is a continuing concern, as it impedes the capacity of many developing countries to participate fully in the global economy;

14. *Recognizes also* that science and technology are vital for sharing the benefits of globalization, and stresses that the technology gap between developed and developing countries constitutes a major challenge for developing countries in their efforts to achieve development goals, including the Millennium Development Goals;

15. *Recognizes further* that making globalization a positive force for all can be accomplished through the involvement, cooperation and partnership of Governments and other stakeholders and that promoting international cooperation for development and promoting policy coherence on global development issues are indispensable to that end;

16. *Urges* the international community to continue to work towards facilitating an adequate diffusion of scientific and technical knowledge and transfer of, access to and acquisition of technology for developing countries;

17. *Stresses* the need to promote and facilitate access to the development, transfer and diffusion of technologies for the developing countries through the articulation of policies and measures to foster an enabling environment to facilitate the acquisition and development of technology and to enhance innovation capacity, on the basis of the mandates contained in the Doha Ministerial Declaration;

18. *Calls for* technical and financial assistance to developing countries in their efforts to build the human and institutional capacity needed to pursue policies that strengthen their national innovation systems and that encourage investments in science and technology education not only for the generation of new technologies but also for the acquisition of the capacities to adapt science and technology developed elsewhere to local conditions;

19. *Recognizes* that science and technology, including information and communication technologies, are vital for the achievement of development goals and that international support can help developing countries to benefit from technological advancements and enhance their productive capacity, and in this regard reaffirms the commitment to promoting and facilitating, as appropriate, access to and the development, transfer and diffusion of technologies, including environmentally sound technologies and corresponding know-how, for developing countries;

20. *Welcomes* existing mechanisms and initiatives which assist developing countries in accessing technologies, encourages the strengthening and enhancement of existing mechanisms and the consideration of initiatives, including the creation of international databases on knowledge and research information, so as to assist developing countries in accessing technologies and know-how for creating technology-based enterprises and upgrading existing industries, and also encourages the strengthening of assistance to developing countries to enhance digital opportunities for all people, putting the potential of information and communication technologies to work in accessing technologies and know-how;

21. *Encourages* existing arrangements and the further promotion of regional, subregional and interregional joint research and development projects by, where feasible, mobilizing existing scientific and research and development resources and by networking sophisticated scientific facilities and research equipment;

22. *Requests* the Secretary-General to submit to the General Assembly at its sixty-second session a report on globalization and interdependence on the theme "Impact that, inter alia, international commitments, policies and processes can have on the scope and the implementation of national development strategies" under the item entitled "Globalization and interdependence".

On 20 December, the Assembly, by **decision 61/537**, took note of the report of the Second Committee [A/61/424] on its consideration of the agenda item on globalization and interdependence.

Also on the same day, the Assembly, by **decision 61/538**, took note of the report of the Second Committee [A/61/424/Add.3] on its consideration of culture and development.

Industrial development

In response to General Assembly resolution 59/249 [YUN 2004, p. 825], the Secretary-General transmitted, in September [A/61/305], the report of the Director-General of the United Nations Industrial Development Organization (UNIDO) on industrial development cooperation, which highlighted the implementation of programmes in the priority areas outlined in UNIDO medium-term programme framework, its cooperation with other UN system organizations, and contributions to the New Partnership for Africa's Development (NEPAD) [YUN 2001, p. 899]. UNIDO continued to adapt its responses to the changing industrial development environment and Member States' requirements, focusing on its three thematic priority areas of poverty reduction through productive activities, trade capacity-building, and energy and environment. South-South cooperation was given particular attention as a means of promoting industrial development and stimulating the growth of trade and technology diffusion to achieve the MDGs, especially in Africa and the least developed countries (LDCs). The report also highlighted UNIDO support for NEPAD and its efforts to strengthen partnerships with other UN bodies and contribute to greater programmatic coherence in UN system development activities, including at the field level.

The report concluded that, despite the rapid economic development of some newly industrialized countries, especially China, the global industrial landscape continued to show the division between North and South, and a growing gap within the South itself, with LDCs facing an ever-increasing challenge to integrate into the world economy. Extreme poverty and environmental degradation posed great challenges in finding a path towards sustained economic growth and sustainable development. Rapid but sustainable industrial development was crucial for disadvantaged regions, the creation of youth employment, the diffusion of cleaner production and renewable energy technologies, as well as the integration of developing countries into global value chains. The new industrial realities, market failures and inadequate capabilities created an urgent need for accelerated South-South cooperation, as a supplement to North-South cooperation, for poverty reduction. Increased productive capacities in the South were needed to enhance trade, technology and investment flows among developing countries. Given the crucial contribution of sustainable industrial development for achieving the MDGS, UNIDO would continue to play a role in private sector development, productivity growth, trade capacity-building, corporate social responsibility, environmental protection, energy efficiency and the promotion of renewable energies. In Africa, UNIDO would continue to focus on NEPAD objectives under its African Productive Capacity Initiative and on regional integration and cooperation. Its interventions in sub-Saharan Africa and the LDCs would be expanded through a stronger field presence and increased private sector partnerships. Through its collaboration with various multilateral institutions, the organization would further strengthen its efforts in system-wide coherence and collaboration, and continue to seek synergies through inter-agency approaches.

GENERAL ASSEMBLY ACTION

On 20 December [meeting 83], the General Assembly, on the recommendation of the Second Committee [A/61/426/Add.2], adopted **resolution 61/215** without vote [agenda item 57 *(b)*].

Industrial development cooperation

The General Assembly,

Recalling its resolutions 46/151 of 18 December 1991, 49/108 of 19 December 1994, 51/170 of 16 December 1996, 53/177 of 15 December 1998, 55/187 of 20 December 2000, 57/243 of 20 December 2002 and 59/249 of 22 December 2004 on industrial development cooperation,

Recalling also the United Nations Millennium Declaration, the Monterrey Consensus of the International Conference on Financing for Development and the Plan of Implementation of the World Summit on Sustainable Development ("Johannesburg Plan of Implementation"),

Recalling further the 2005 World Summit Outcome,

Recalling its resolution 60/265 of 30 June 2006 on the follow-up to the development outcome of the 2005 World Summit, including the Millennium Development Goals and the other internationally agreed development goals,

Noting that the reform of the United Nations Industrial Development Organization has enabled it to become more focused, effective and efficient and more capable of delivering concrete outcomes and providing valuable contributions to the achievement of the internationally agreed development goals, including the Millennium Development Goals,

Noting also the attention given by the United Nations Industrial Development Organization to poverty eradication through its priorities,

Noting further the prevailing industrial gap and disparities between developed and developing countries,

Recognizing the role of the business community, including the private sector, in enhancing the dynamic process of the development of the industrial sector, and underlining the importance of the benefits of foreign direct investment in that process,

Recognizing also the importance of the transfer of technology on mutually agreed terms to the developing countries as well as countries with economies in transition as an effective means of international cooperation in the pursuit of poverty eradication and sustainable development,

Noting that the Commission on Sustainable Development at its fourteenth session discussed, inter alia, industrial development,

1. *Takes note* of the report of the Director-General of the United Nations Industrial Development Organization;

2. *Reaffirms* that industrialization is an essential factor in the sustained economic growth, sustainable development and eradication of poverty of developing countries as well as countries with economies in transition, and in the creation of productive employment, income generation and the facilitation of social integration, including the integration of women into the development process;

3. *Stresses* the critical role of productive capacity-building and industrial development for the achievement of the internationally agreed development goals, including the Millennium Development Goals;

4. *Takes note* of the comprehensive review of the activities of the United Nations Industrial Development Organization conducted in line with its corporate strategy, which has enabled it to become a more focused, effective and efficient organization, especially for developing countries as well as countries with economies in transition, capable of delivering concrete outcomes and providing valuable contributions to the achievement of the internationally agreed development goals, including the Millennium Development Goals;

5. *Emphasizes* the necessity of favourable national and international measures for the industrialization of developing countries, and urges all Governments to adopt and to implement development policies and strategies to unleash the productivity growth potential through private-sector development, the diffusion of environmentally sound and emerging technologies, investment pro-

motion, enhanced access to markets and the effective use of official development assistance to enable developing countries to achieve the internationally agreed development goals, including the Millennium Development Goals, and to make this process sustainable;

6. *Stresses* the importance of strengthening North-South industrial development cooperation and trade, underlines the importance of a positive investment and business climate, and emphasizes furthermore the importance of North-South trade-related technology diffusion, which has a positive impact on productivity in high-technology industries and on technology-intensive manufacturing activities in developing countries, in promoting the expansion, diversification and modernization of productive capacities;

7. *Recognizes* the importance of South-South cooperation in the area of industrial development, and in this regard encourages the international community, including the international financial institutions, to support the efforts of developing countries, inter alia, through triangular cooperation;

8. *Confirms* the contribution of industry to social development, especially in the context of the linkages between industry and agriculture, and notes that, within the totality of these interlinkages, industry serves as a powerful source of the employment generation, income creation and social integration required for the eradication of poverty;

9. *Calls for* the continuing use of official development assistance for industrial development in the developing countries as well as countries with economies in transition, calls upon donor countries and recipient countries to continue to cooperate in their efforts to achieve greater efficiency and effectiveness of the official development assistance resources devoted to industrial development cooperation and to support the efforts of developing countries as well as countries with economies in transition to promote industrial development cooperation among themselves, and underlines the importance of mobilizing funds for industrial development at the country level, including private funding and funds from relevant development finance institutions;

10. *Also calls for* the continuing use of all other resources, including private and public, foreign and domestic resources, for industrial development in the developing countries as well as countries with economies in transition;

11. *Reiterates* the importance of cooperation and coordination within the United Nations system in providing effective support for the sustainable industrial development of developing countries as well as countries with economies in transition, and calls upon the United Nations Industrial Development Organization to continue to carry out its central role in the field of industrial development according to its mandate;

12. *Encourages* the United Nations Industrial Development Organization to continue to enhance its effectiveness, relevance and development impact by, inter alia, strengthening its cooperation with other institutions of the United Nations system at all levels;

13. *Calls upon* the United Nations Industrial Development Organization to participate actively in coordination at the field level through the common country assessment and the United Nations Development Assistance Framework processes and sector-wide approaches;

14. *Emphasizes* the need to promote the development of microenterprises and small and medium-sized enterprises, including by means of training, education and skills enhancement, with a special focus on agro-industry as a provider of livelihoods for rural communities;

15. *Stresses* the need for the United Nations Industrial Development Organization to promote, within its mandate, the development of competitive industries in developing countries as well as countries with economies in transition, especially in least developed countries and landlocked developing countries;

16. *Encourages* the United Nations Industrial Development Organization to increase its contributions to achieve the objectives of the New Partnership for Africa's Development with a view to further strengthening the industrialization process in Africa;

17. *Invites* the United Nations Industrial Development Organization to continue to build and strengthen its partnership with other United Nations organizations with complementary mandates and activities with a view to achieving greater effectiveness and development impact and promoting increased coherence within the United Nations system;

18. *Recognizes* the importance of information in the replication of best practices in processing, design and marketing, and also recognizes the importance of and encourages South-South cooperation in this respect;

19. *Takes note* of the important role played by the United Nations Industrial Development Organization in the fields of private- and public-sector industrial development, productivity growth, trade capacity-building, corporate social responsibility, environmental protection, energy efficiency and the promotion of renewable energies;

20. *Encourages* the United Nations Industrial Development Organization to develop further its global forum capacity according to its mandate, with the aim of enhancing, in the context of the globalization process, a common understanding of global and regional industrial sector issues and their impact on poverty eradication and sustainable development, and calls for further strengthening of the demand-driven integrated programme approach at the field level;

21. *Requests* the Secretary-General to submit to the General Assembly at its sixty-third session a report on the implementation of the present resolution.

Sustainable development

Implementation of Agenda 21, the Programme for the Further Implementation of Agenda 21 and the Johannesburg Plan of Implementation

In 2006, several UN bodies, including the General Assembly, the Economic and Social Council and the Commission on Sustainable Development, considered the implementation of outcomes of the 2002 World Summit on Sustainable Development [YUN 2002, p. 821], particularly the Johannesburg Declaration and Plan of Implementation, which outlined actions and targets for stepping up implementation of Agenda 21—a programme of action for sustainable development worldwide, adopted at the 1992 United Nations Conference on Environment and Development [YUN 1992, p. 672]—and of the Programme for the Further Implementation of Agenda 21, adopted by the Assembly at its nineteenth special session in 1997 [YUN 1997, p. 792].

Commission on Sustainable Development consideration. The Commission on Sustainable Development, at its fourteenth session (New York, 22 April 2005 and 1-12 May 2006) [E/2006/29], discussed, in line with the multi-year programme adopted by the Economic and Social Council in resolution 2003/61 [YUN 2003, p. 842], the thematic cluster for the 2006-2007 implementation cycle—energy for sustainable development, industrial development, air pollution/atmosphere and climate change.

Intersessional events. The following intersessional events took place in 2006 in preparation for its fourteenth session: International Symposium on Natural Gas and Sustainable Development (Doha, Qatar, 7-8 February); Ninth Special Session of the Governing Council/Global Ministerial Environment Forum (Dubai, United Arab Emirates, 7-9 February); World Bank Energy Week (Washington, D.C., 6-10 March); African Ministerial Conference on Hydropower and Sustainable Development (South Africa, 8-10 March; Symposium on Energy and Sustainable Development (Baku, Azerbaijan, 28-30 March); and Climate Change and Sustainable Development: an international workshop to strengthen research and understanding (New Delhi, India, 7-8 April).

Thematic issues. For its consideration of the thematic issues for 2006-2007, energy for sustainable development, industrial development, air pollution/atmosphere and climate change, the Commission had before it reports of the Secretary-General on overview of progress towards sustainable development: a review of the implementation of Agenda 21, the Programme for the Further Implementation of Agenda 21 and the Johannesburg Plan of Implementation [E/CN.17/2006/2] (see p. 1204); energy for sustainable development, industrial development, air pollution/atmosphere and climate change: integrated review of progress in meeting the goals, targets and commitments of Agenda 21, the Programme for the Further Implementation of Agenda 21 and the Plan of Implementation of the World Summit on Sustainable Development [E/CN.17/2006/3]; partnerships for sustainable development [E/CN.17/2006/6]; and integrated review of the thematic cluster of energy for sustainable development, industrial development, air pollution/atmosphere and climate change in small island developing States [E/CN.17/2006/7] (see p. 1212). It also considered a note by the Secretariat [E/CN.17/2006/4 & Add.1-5, & Add.4/Corr.1] on the outcomes of the regional implementation meetings, as well as notes by the Secretariat on discussion papers submitted by major group [E/CN.17/2006/5 & Add.1-9] and on the outcome of the International Symposium on Integrated Implementation of Sustainable Development Goals [E/CN.17/2006/8].

Implementation activities

In response to General Assembly resolution 60/193 [YUN 2005, p. 918], the Secretary-General, in August [A/61/258], reported on the implementation of Agenda 21, the Programme for the Further Implementation of Agenda 21 and the outcomes of the World Summit on Sustainable Development. The report provided an update on actions taken by Governments, UN system organizations and major groups in advancing implementation of sustainable development goals and targets, including through partnerships for sustainable development. It contained an overview of salient trends in implementation, a summary of the outcome of the work of the Commission on Sustainable Development at its fourteenth session and the 2006 substantive session of the Economic and Social Council, as well as a summary of regional activities. It also provided highlights of ongoing inter-agency activities in the thematic areas of energy for sustainable development, industrial development, air pollution/atmosphere and climate change.

The report showed that there was a broad range of implementation activities at all levels. Significant progress was made in education for sustainable development and the commitment of business to sustainable development. A salient emerging trend since the World Summit on Sustainable Development was a deepening commitment to sustainable development, as characterized by further implementation action and the increasingly diverse group of actors. The Council, at its high-level segment, focused on full and productive employment and decent work for all as a foundation for sustainable development. As a review session, the fourteenth session of the Commission on Sustainable Development focused on identifying barriers and constraints, as well as lessons learned and best practice in the implementation in the thematic cluster of energy for sustainable development, industrial development, air pollution/atmosphere, and climate change. At the inter-agency level, the UN system Chief Executives Board for Coordination (CEB), through its High-level Committee on Programmes (HLCP), continued to provide overall guidance to the work of UN-Energy and other inter-agency cooperation initiatives in sustainable development.

At the regional level, UN regional commissions, regional development banks and other regional organizations continued to expedite implementation of sustainable development goals and targets. Major groups continued to contribute to sustainable development by utilizing their expertise and knowledge to promote education in sustainable development, raise awareness of social, economic and environmental issues and monitor progress towards the implementation of sustainable development.

The Secretary-General recommended that the General Assembly call on Governments, UN system organizations and major groups to redouble their efforts to implement Agenda 21, the Programme for the Further Implementation of Agenda 21 and the Johannesburg Plan of Implementation. He urged Governments to continue their support to the Commission on Sustainable Development by organizing intersessional activities, making available to the Secretariat for broader dissemination, success stories, best practices and case studies, and by contributing to the Commission's trust fund in support of its work. He invited CEB to continue monitoring, through HLCP, the operational efficiency and effectiveness of inter-agency collaborative mechanisms, including UN-Energy. The Secretary-General also called on donors to target funding support to developing countries in support of their efforts to overcome barriers and constraints identified during the Commission's fourteenth (review) session (see above).

GENERAL ASSEMBLY ACTION

On 20 December [meeting 83], the General Assembly, on the recommendation of the Second Committee [A/61/422/Add.1 & Corr.1], adopted **resolution 61/195** without vote [agenda item 53 *(a)*].

Implementation of Agenda 21, the Programme for the Further Implementation of Agenda 21 and the outcomes of the World Summit on Sustainable Development

The General Assembly,

Recalling its resolutions 55/199 of 20 December 2000, 56/226 of 24 December 2001, 57/253 of 20 December 2002 and 57/270 A and B of 20 December 2002 and 23 June 2003, respectively, and its resolutions 58/218 of 23 December 2003, 59/227 of 22 December 2004 and 60/193 of 22 December 2005,

Recalling also the Rio Declaration on Environment and Development, Agenda 21, the Programme for the Further Implementation of Agenda 21, the Johannesburg Declaration on Sustainable Development and the Plan of Implementation of the World Summit on Sustainable Development ("Johannesburg Plan of Implementation"), as well as the Monterrey Consensus of the International Conference on Financing for Development,

Reaffirming the commitment to implement Agenda 21, the Programme for the Further Implementation of Agenda 21, the Johannesburg Plan of Implementation, including the time-bound goals and targets, and the other internationally agreed development goals, including the Millennium Development Goals,

Recalling the 2005 World Summit Outcome,

Reaffirming the decisions taken at the eleventh session of the Commission on Sustainable Development,

Reiterating that sustainable development in its economic, social and environmental aspects is a key element of the overarching framework for United Nations activities, and reaffirming the continuing need to ensure a balance among economic development, social development and environmental protection as interdependent and mutually reinforcing pillars of sustainable development,

Reaffirming that eradicating poverty, changing unsustainable patterns of production and consumption and protecting and managing the natural resource base of economic and social development are overarching objectives of and essential requirements for sustainable development,

Recognizing that eradicating poverty is the greatest global challenge facing the world today and an indispensable requirement for sustainable development, in particular for developing countries, and that although each country has the primary responsibility for its own sustainable development and poverty eradication and the role of national policies and development strategies cannot be overemphasized, concerted and concrete measures are required at all levels to enable developing countries to achieve their sustainable development goals as related to the internationally agreed poverty-related targets and goals, including those contained in Agenda 21, the relevant outcomes of other United Nations conferences and the United Nations Millennium Declaration,

Recognizing also that good governance within each country and at the international level is essential for sustainable development,

Recalling that the Johannesburg Plan of Implementation designated the Commission to serve as the focal point for discussion on partnerships that promote sustainable development and contribute to the implementation of intergovernmental commitments in Agenda 21, the Programme for the Further Implementation of Agenda 21 and the Johannesburg Plan of Implementation,

Recalling also the decision of the Commission at its eleventh session that the Commission, during review years, should discuss the contribution of partnerships towards supporting the implementation of Agenda 21, the Programme for the Further Implementation of Agenda 21 and the Johannesburg Plan of Implementation with a view to sharing lessons learned and best practices, identifying and addressing problems, gaps and constraints, and providing further guidance, including on reporting, during policy years, as necessary,

Looking forward to the upcoming cycles of the work programme of the Commission as adopted at its eleventh session and their contributions to the further implementation of Agenda 21, the Programme for the Further Implementation of Agenda 21 and the outcomes of the World Summit on Sustainable Development,

Recalling the decision of the Commission at its eleventh session, endorsed by the Economic and Social Council in its resolution 2003/61 of 25 July 2003, that the Commission, at its policy sessions, to be held in April/May of the second year of the cycle, would take policy decisions on practical measures and options to expedite implementation in the selected thematic cluster of issues, taking account of the discussions of the Intergovernmental Preparatory Meeting, the reports of the Secretary-General and other relevant inputs,

Recalling also the decision of the Commission at its eleventh session that the discussions of the Intergovernmental Preparatory Meeting would be based on the outcome of the review session and reports of the Secretary-General, as well as other relevant inputs, and that, on the basis of those discussions, the Chair would prepare a draft negotiating document for consideration at the policy session,

Recognizing the importance of the Intergovernmental Preparatory Meeting to discuss policy options and possible actions to address the constraints and obstacles in the process of implementation identified during the review year,

Noting with satisfaction that the Commission at its fourteenth session undertook an in-depth evaluation of progress in implementing Agenda 21, the Programme for the Further Implementation of Agenda 21 and the Johannesburg Plan of Implementation, focusing on the thematic cluster of issues on energy for sustainable development, industrial development, air pollution/atmosphere and climate change, and identified best practices, constraints and obstacles in the process of implementation,

1. *Takes note* of the report of the Secretary-General on the activities undertaken in the implementation of Agenda 21, the Programme for the Further Implementation of Agenda 21 and the outcomes of the World Summit on Sustainable Development;

2. *Reiterates* that sustainable development is a key element of the overarching framework for United Nations activities, in particular for achieving the internationally agreed development goals, including the Millennium Development Goals, and those contained in the Johannesburg Plan of Implementation;

3. *Calls upon* Governments, all relevant international and regional organizations, the Economic and Social Council, the United Nations funds and programmes, the regional commissions and the specialized agencies, the international financial institutions, the Global Environment Facility and other intergovernmental organizations, in accordance with their respective mandates, as well as major groups, to take action to ensure the effective implementation of and follow-up to the commitments, programmes and time-bound targets adopted at the World Summit on Sustainable Development, and encourages them to report on concrete progress in that regard;

4. *Calls for* the effective implementation of the commitments, programmes and time-bound targets adopted at the World Summit on Sustainable Development and for the fulfilment of the provisions relating to the means of implementation, as contained in the Johannesburg Plan of Implementation;

5. *Reiterates* that the Commission on Sustainable Development is the high-level body responsible for sustainable development within the United Nations system and serves as a forum for the consideration of issues related to the integration of the three dimensions of sustainable development, and calls upon Governments to support the work of the Commission;

6. *Encourages* Governments to participate at the appropriate level with representatives, including ministers, from the relevant departments and organizations working in the areas of energy for sustainable development, industrial development, air pollution/atmosphere and climate change, as well as finance, in the fifteenth session of the Commission and its Intergovernmental Preparatory Meeting;

7. *Recalls* the decision of the Commission at its eleventh session that activities during Commission meetings should provide for the balanced involvement of participants from all regions, as well as for gender balance;

8. *Invites* donor countries to consider supporting the participation of representatives from the developing countries in the areas of energy for sustainable development, industrial development, air pollution/atmosphere and climate change in the fifteenth session of the Commission and its Intergovernmental Preparatory Meeting;

9. *Reaffirms* the objective of strengthening the implementation of Agenda 21, including through the mobilization of financial and technological resources, as well as capacity-building programmes, in particular for developing countries;

10. *Also reaffirms* the objective of enhancing the participation and effective involvement of civil society and other relevant stakeholders in the implementation of Agenda 21, as well as promoting transparency and broad public participation;

11. *Further reaffirms* the need to promote corporate responsibility and accountability as envisaged by the Johannesburg Plan of Implementation;

12. *Reaffirms* the need to promote the development of microenterprises and small and medium-sized enterprises, including by means of training, education and skill enhancement, with a special focus on agro-industry as a provider of livelihoods for rural communities;

13. *Requests* the secretariat of the Commission to make arrangements to facilitate the balanced representation of major groups from developed and developing countries in the sessions of the Commission;

14. *Also requests* the secretariat of the Commission to coordinate the participation of the relevant major groups in the discussions at the fifteenth session of the Commission, including the Intergovernmental Preparatory Meeting;

15. *Reiterates* its invitation to the relevant United Nations agencies, programmes and funds, the Global Environment Facility and international and regional financial and trade institutions, within their mandates, to participate actively in the work of the Commission;

16. *Requests* the Secretary-General, in reporting to the Commission at its fifteenth session, on the basis of appropriate inputs from all levels, to submit thematic reports on each of the four issues contained in the thematic cluster of issues on energy for sustainable development, industrial development, air pollution/atmosphere and climate change, taking into account their interlinkages, while addressing the cross-cutting issues, including means of implementation identified by the Commission at its eleventh session, and taking into account also the relevant provisions of paragraphs 10, 14 and 15 of draft resolution I adopted by the Commission at its eleventh session;

17. *Encourages* Governments and organizations at all levels, as well as major groups, including the scientific community and educators, to undertake results-oriented initiatives and activities to support the work of the Commission and to promote and facilitate the implementation of Agenda 21, the Programme for the Further Implementation of Agenda 21 and the Johannesburg Plan of Implementation, including through voluntary multi-stakeholder partnership initiatives;

18. *Underlines* the importance of setting aside adequate time for all envisaged activities in the policy session, including for negotiations on policy options and possible actions, at the fifteenth session of the Commission, and in this regard notes the importance of having all required documents, including the Chair's draft negotiating document, made available for consideration prior to the beginning of the session;

19. *Decides* to include in the provisional agenda of its sixty-second session the sub-item entitled "Implementation of Agenda 21, the Programme for the Further Implementation of Agenda 21 and the outcomes of the World Summit on Sustainable Development", and requests the Secretary-General, at that session, to submit a report on the implementation of the present resolution.

On 20 December, the General Assembly also took note of the report of the Second Committee [A/61/422] on sustainable development (**decision 61/536**).

Commission on Sustainable Development

The Commission on Sustainable Development held its fourteenth session in New York on 22 April 2005 and from 1 to 12 May 2006 [E/2006/29]. On 12 May, the Commission held the first meeting of the fifteenth session, at which it elected the members of its Bureau [E/2007/29]. The Commission's high-level segment focused on the role of the private sector in implementing sustainable development in relation to the thematic cluster of issues for the Commission's 2006-2007 implementation cycle, namely energy for sustainable development, industrial development, air pollution/atmosphere and climate change. On 3 May, the Commission held a multi-stakeholder dialogue with representatives of major groups on their role in promoting implementation activities in relation to the thematic cluster, including in the areas of education, raising public awareness, disseminating information and knowledge and fostering partnership initiatives. It devoted its session on 9 May to monitoring progress on the implementation of the Programme of Action for the Sustainable Development of Small Island Developing States and the Mauritius Strategy for the Further Implementation of the Programme of Action for the Sustainable Development of Small Island Developing States (see p. 1016). A partnerships fair provided an opportunity for registered partnerships to showcase progress in their activities, network with other partnerships and identify new partners. A learning centre offered 17 courses on the themes of the fourteenth session, as well as on cross-cutting issues related to gender, financing and development strategies.

The Commission recommended to the Economic and Social Council for adoption a draft decision on the Commission's report on its fourteenth session and the provisional agenda for the fifteenth session.

The Commission had before it letters dated 31 January from China transmitting the Beijing Declaration on Renewable Energy for Sustainable Development [E/CN.17/2006/9], and the Beijing Declaration on Hydropower and Sustainable Development [E/CN.17/2006/10]; a 22 February letter from Qatar transmitting the conclusions and recommendations of the International Symposium on Natural Gas and Sustainable Development [E/CN.17/2006/11]; a 16 January letter from Austria transmitting the executive summary of the fifth meeting of the Global Forum on Sustainable Energy [E/CN.17/2006/13]; and a 10 April letter from Azerbaijan transmitting the Baku Declaration on Energy Efficiency and Sustainable Development in the Caspian Sea region and Other Oil Producing and Exporting Countries [E/CN.17/2006/14]. It also considered a report prepared by the Mountain Partnership secretariat entitled "The Mountain

Partnership: activities and achievements" [E/CN.17/2006/12] (see p. 1022).

The Council, on 24 July, took note of the report of the Commission on its fourteenth session [E/2006/29] and approved the provisional agenda for the fifteenth (2007) session (**decision 2006/228**).

Follow-up to 2005 World Summit, MDGs, internationally agreed development goals

The Secretary-General, in his annual report on the work of the Organization [A/61/1], noted that since 2000, the United Nations, together with Government, civil society, business and science leaders, had given spirit to the commitment to "spare no effort" to free fellow men, women and children from the abject and dehumanizing conditions of extreme poverty. The result had been dramatically increased global attention on the full one sixth of humanity still living in the most extreme form of poverty, measured as income of less than one dollar per day. That political momentum offered the opportunity to build on recent development successes. The Multilateral Debt Relief Initiative had followed a prompt timetable towards completion; international malaria control efforts were gathering speed, backed by increased donor assistance; momentum was under way to launch the African Green Revolution agreed upon at the 2005 World Summit; and recent global commitments had also prompted new notions for increasing investment to tackle broader development priorities. The UN country teams were helping many countries to prepare and implement Millennium Development-based national development strategies, and the Organization collaborated with Governments and other stakeholders to support "millennium villages" throughout Africa, which were transforming themselves from areas of chronic hunger by tripling their crop production. Thanks to efforts by the World Health Organization and the United Nations Children's Fund (UNICEF) and others, progress was being made to slow the spread of infectious diseases.

Despite those advances, progress remained incomplete. International financial instruments were still inadequate for achieving the MDGs. Many of the new promises would take years to materialize, making it difficult for low-income countries to begin real investment scale-up. Another cause for concern was the suspension of negotiations of the WTO Doha Development Round.

Noting that world leaders at the 2005 Millennium Summit had agreed to several important targets, the Secretary-General recommended that those commitments be incorporated into the targets used to follow up on the MDGs. That included: a new target under Goal 1: to make the goals of full and productive employment and decent work for all, including for women and young people, a central objective of national and international policies and national development strategies; a new target under Goal 5: to achieve universal access to reproductive health by 2015; a new target under Goal 6: to come as close as possible to universal access to treatment for HIV/AIDS by 2010; and a new target under Goal 7: to significantly reduce the rate of loss of biodiversity by 2010. Technical work to select the appropriate indicators would be undertaken by the Inter-agency and Expert Group on the Millennium Development Goal Indicators, so as to build on the Ministerial Declaration on Employment Generation and Decent Work, adopted by the Economic and Social Council, which called for the development of a 10-year action plan (see p. 977).

The *Millennium Development Goals Report 2006*, published by the Department of Economic and Social Affairs [Sales No. E.06.I.18], provided the latest and most comprehensive figures available on the achievement of the eight MDGs. Similar data would be collected and presented each year until 2015, the target date for achieving the MDGs, in order to give further direction and focus to international cooperation and national action. The report stated that, while the challenges presented by the MDGs were staggering, there were clear signs of hope. Developed countries had confirmed their commitment to the Goals through increased aid and enhanced debt relief. Much more needed to be done, both by developed countries in increasing their support and by developing countries in using foreign assistance and their own resources more effectively.

GENERAL ASSEMBLY ACTION

On 30 June [meeting 92], the General Assembly adopted **resolution 60/265** [draft: A/60/L.59] without vote [agenda items 46 & 120].

Follow-up to the development outcome of the 2005 World Summit, including the Millennium Development Goals and the other internationally agreed development goals

The General Assembly,

Recalling the 2005 World Summit Outcome,

Recalling also the outcomes of the major United Nations conferences and summits in the economic, social and related fields, including the development goals and objectives contained therein, and recognizing the vital role played by these conferences and summits in shaping a broad development vision and in identifying commonly agreed objectives, which have contributed to improving human life in different parts of the world,

Recalling further its resolutions 50/227 of 24 May 1996 and 57/270 B of 23 June 2003,

Recalling all relevant General Assembly resolutions, in particular those that have built upon the 2005 World Summit Outcome, in the economic, social and related fields, adopted during the sixtieth session of the General Assembly,

Recognizing that the internationally agreed development goals, including the Millennium Development Goals, offer a framework for planning, reviewing and assessing the activities of the United Nations for development,

Reaffirming that development is a central goal by itself and that sustainable development in its economic, social and environmental aspects constitutes a key element of the overarching framework of United Nations activities,

Emphasizing the need to fully implement the global partnership for development and enhance the momentum generated by the 2005 World Summit in order to operationalize and implement, at all levels, the commitments in the outcomes of the major United Nations conferences and summits, including the 2005 World Summit, in the economic, social and related fields,

Recognizing the action already under way by all Member States, the United Nations system and other international, regional and national forums and organizations and the progress made to implement the internationally agreed development goals, including the Millennium Development Goals,

Recognizing also that the achievement of many of the internationally agreed development goals, including the Millennium Development Goals, in many countries is currently off track, and emphasizing that vigorous implementation of all development commitments will be needed without delay if the Goals are to be achieved,

Remaining concerned that Africa is the only continent currently not on track to achieve any of the goals of the United Nations Millennium Declaration by 2015, and in this regard emphasizing that concerted efforts and continued support are required to fulfil the commitments to address the special needs of Africa,

Also remaining concerned by the lack of and/or uneven progress made by least developed countries, landlocked developing countries and small island developing States in achieving the internationally agreed development goals including the Millennium Development Goals, and in this regard reiterating the importance of strengthening global partnership in the follow-up to and implementation of the Brussels Programme of Action for the Least Developed Countries for the Decade 2001-2010, the Almaty Programme of Action: Addressing the Special Needs of Landlocked Developing Countries within a New Global Framework for Transit Transport Cooperation for Landlocked and Transit Developing Countries and the Mauritius Strategy for the Further Implementation of the Programme of Action for the Sustainable Development of Small Island Developing States,

Reaffirming the commitment to sound policies, good governance at all levels and the rule of law, to mobilizing domestic resources, attracting international flows, promoting international trade as an engine for development and increasing international financial and technical cooperation for development, sustainable debt financing and external debt relief and to enhancing the coherence and consistency of the international monetary, financial and trading systems,

Reaffirming also that each country must take primary responsibility for its own development and that the role of national policies and development strategies cannot be overemphasized in the achievement of sustainable development, and recognizing that national efforts should be complemented by supportive global programmes, measures and policies aimed at expanding the development opportunities of developing countries, while taking into account national conditions and ensuring respect for national ownership, strategies and sovereignty,

Reaffirming further the commitments to the global partnership for development set out in the Millennium Declaration, the Monterrey Consensus and the Johannesburg Plan of Implementation,

1. *Calls for* concerted efforts by all to ensure the timely and full realization of the development goals and objectives agreed at the major United Nations conferences and summits, including the Millennium Development Goals, which have helped to galvanize efforts towards poverty eradication;

2. *Calls upon* all Member States and the United Nations system, and invites international organizations and institutions, including the Bretton Woods institutions and the World Trade Organization, to translate all commitments made at the major United Nations conferences and summits, including the 2005 World Summit, in the economic, social and related fields into concrete and specific actions in order to, inter alia, achieve the internationally agreed development goals, including the Millennium Development Goals, and calls for the efficient use of monitoring and follow-up mechanisms to ensure that these commitments and actions are effectively implemented;

3. *Stresses* the need for the United Nations to play a fundamental role in the promotion of international cooperation for development and the coherence, coordination and implementation of the internationally agreed development goals, including the Millennium Development Goals, and actions agreed upon by the international community, and resolves to strengthen coordination within the United Nations system in close cooperation with all other multilateral financial, trade and development institutions in order to support sustained economic growth, poverty and hunger eradication and sustainable development;

4. *Emphasizes* that the United Nations system has an important responsibility to assist Governments to stay fully engaged in the follow-up to and implementation of agreements and commitments reached at the major United Nations conferences and summits, including the 2005 World Summit, and invites its intergovernmental

bodies to further promote the implementation of the outcomes of the major United Nations conferences and summits;

5. *Also emphasizes* the need to fully implement the global partnership for development and enhance the momentum generated by the 2005 World Summit in order to operationalize and implement, at all levels, the commitments in the outcomes of the major United Nations conferences and summits, including the 2005 World Summit, in the economic, social and related fields, decides to strengthen the existing mechanisms and, as appropriate and where needed, to consider establishing effective mechanisms to monitor, review and follow up the implementation of the outcomes of all the major United Nations conferences and summits in the social, economic and related fields, and stresses that all countries should promote policies coherent and consistent with the commitments of the major United Nations conferences and summits, including those systemic in nature;

6. *Welcomes* the efforts by developing countries to adopt and implement national development strategies to achieve their national development priorities as well as the internationally agreed development goals and objectives, including the Millennium Development Goals, calls upon those countries that have not yet done so to adopt such strategies by 2006, and in this regard calls upon developed countries and the international community to support these efforts as set out in the 2005 World Summit Outcome, including through increased resources;

7. *Calls upon* all countries to promote good governance, which is essential for sustainable development, and reaffirms that sound economic policies, solid democratic institutions responsive to the needs of the people and improved infrastructure are the basis for sustained economic growth, poverty eradication and employment creation and that freedom, peace and security, domestic stability, respect for human rights, including the right to development, the rule of law, gender equality and market-oriented policies and an overall commitment to just and democratic societies, are also essential and mutually reinforcing;

8. *Resolves* to pursue good governance and sound macroeconomic policies at all levels and to support developing countries in their efforts to put in place the policies and investments to drive sustained economic growth, promote small and medium-sized enterprises and employment generation and stimulate the private sector;

9. *Reaffirms* that good governance at the international level is fundamental for achieving sustainable development, that, in order to ensure a dynamic and enabling international economic environment, it is important to promote global economic governance through addressing the international finance, trade, technology and investment patterns that have an impact on the development prospects of developing countries, and that, to that end, the international community should take all necessary and appropriate measures, including ensuring support for structural and macroeconomic reform, a comprehensive solution to the external debt problem and increasing the market access of developing countries;

10. *Urges* countries that have not done so to consider signing, ratifying and implementing the United Nations Convention against Corruption, and calls for the implementation of actions to make the fight against corruption a priority at all levels;

11. *Calls for* the effective management of public finances in all countries to achieve and maintain macroeconomic stability and long-term growth, as well as the effective and transparent use of public funds;

12. *Reiterates* that the increasing interdependence of national economies in a globalizing world and the emergence of rule-based regimes for international economic relations have meant that the space for national economic policy, that is, the scope for domestic policies, especially in the areas of trade, investment and industrial development, is now often framed by international disciplines, commitments and global market considerations, that it is for each Government to evaluate the trade-off between the benefits of accepting international rules and commitments and the constraints posed by the loss of policy space and that it is particularly important for developing countries, bearing in mind development goals and objectives, that all countries take into account the need for appropriate balance between national policy space and international disciplines and commitments;

13. *Resolves* to encourage greater direct investment, including foreign investment, in developing countries and countries with economies in transition to support their development activities and to enhance the benefits they can derive from such investments, including, in this regard:

(a) Continuing to support efforts by developing countries and countries with economies in transition to create a domestic environment conducive to attracting investments through, inter alia, achieving a transparent, stable and predictable investment climate with proper contract enforcement and respect for property rights and the rule of law and pursuing appropriate policy and regulatory frameworks that encourage business formation;

(b) Putting into place policies to ensure adequate investment in a sustainable manner in health, clean water and sanitation, housing and education and in the provision of public goods and social safety nets to protect vulnerable and disadvantaged sectors of society;

(c) Inviting national Governments seeking to develop infrastructure projects and generate foreign direct investment to pursue strategies with the involvement of both the public and private sectors and, where appropriate, international donors;

(d) Calling upon international financial and banking institutions to consider enhancing the transparency of risk rating mechanisms; sovereign risk assessments, made by the private sector, should maximize the use of strict, objective and transparent parameters, which can be facilitated by high-quality data and analysis;

(e) Underscoring the need to sustain sufficient and stable private financial flows to developing countries and countries with economies in transition, that it is im-

portant to promote measures in source and destination countries to improve transparency and the information about financial flows to developing countries, particularly countries in Africa, the least developed countries, small island developing States and landlocked developing countries, and that measures that mitigate the impact of excessive volatility of short-term capital flows are important and must be considered;

14. *Acknowledges* recent increases and commitments to substantial increases in official development assistance, while recognizing that a substantial increase in such assistance is required to achieve the internationally agreed goals, including the Millennium Development Goals, within the respective time frames, and in this regard stresses the importance of the fulfilment of those commitments;

15. *Welcomes* the increased resources that are becoming available as a result of the establishment of timetables by many developed countries to achieve the target of 0.7 per cent of gross national product for official development assistance, as well as the target of 0.15 per cent to 0.20 per cent for least developed countries, and urges those developed countries that have not yet done so to make concrete efforts in this regard in accordance with their commitments;

16. *Also welcomes* recent efforts and initiatives to enhance the quality of aid and to increase its impact, including the Paris Declaration on Aid Effectiveness, and calls for concrete, effective and timely action in implementing all agreed commitments on aid effectiveness, with clear monitoring and deadlines, including through further aligning assistance with countries' strategies, building institutional capacities, reducing transaction costs and eliminating bureaucratic procedures, making progress on untying aid, enhancing the absorptive capacity and financial management of recipient countries and strengthening the focus on development results;

17. *Calls upon* developed countries to ensure that information on their efforts to increase the volume of official development assistance is made available to the relevant United Nations intergovernmental bodies, including through making best use of sources such as the Development Assistance Committee of the Organization for Economic Cooperation and Development;

18. *Welcomes* the progress in the Multilateral Debt Relief Initiative, and calls for its full and timely implementation and the provision of additional resources to ensure that the financial capacity of the international financial institutions is not reduced;

19. *Calls for* the consideration of additional measures and initiatives aimed at ensuring long-term debt sustainability through increased grant-based financing, cancellation of 100 per cent of the official multilateral and bilateral debt of heavily indebted poor countries and, where appropriate, and on a case-by-case basis, significant debt relief or restructuring for low- and middle-income developing countries with an unsustainable debt burden that are not part of the Heavily Indebted Poor Countries Initiative, as well as the exploration of mechanisms to comprehensively address the debt problems of those countries;

20. *Calls upon* Member States to address the development needs of low-income developing countries by working in competent multilateral, regional and international forums to help them to meet, inter alia, their financial, technical and technological requirements, in support of national development strategies;

21. *Calls for* continued support for the development efforts of middle-income developing countries, including through targeted and substantial technical assistance, and the promotion of new partnerships and cooperation arrangements, including bilateral arrangements, as well as by working in competent multilateral, regional and international forums, in support of national development strategies;

22. *Acknowledges* the vital role the private sector can play in generating new investments, employment and financing for development;

23. *Emphasizes* the importance of recognizing and addressing the specific concerns of countries with economies in transition, including through policy advice and substantial and targeted technical assistance, so as to help them to benefit more from globalization, with a view to their full integration into the world economy;

24. *Reaffirms* the commitment to broaden and strengthen the participation of developing countries and countries with economies in transition in international economic decision-making and norm-setting, to that end stresses the importance of continuing efforts to reform the international financial architecture, noting that enhancing the voice and participation of developing countries and countries with economies in transition in the Bretton Woods institutions remains a continuous concern, and in this regard calls for further and effective progress;

25. *Requests* the specialized agencies and invites the Bretton Woods institutions and the World Trade Organization to keep the General Assembly informed about their contribution to the implementation of the outcomes of all major United Nations conferences and summits in the economic, social and related fields, including the 2005 World Summit Outcome;

26. *Stresses* the need to identify, develop and promote innovative and additional sources of financing for development to increase and supplement traditional sources of financing;

27. *Reaffirms* the commitments made in the Doha Ministerial Declaration and the decision of the General Council of the World Trade Organization of 1 August 2004 to fulfil the development dimension of the Doha Development Agenda, which places the needs and interests of developing and least developed countries at the heart of the Doha work programme, and calls for the successful and timely completion of the Doha round of trade negotiations with the fullest realization of the development dimensions of the Doha work programme;

28. *Calls for* the implementation of commitments made in the Brussels Programme of Action on the objective of duty-free and quota-free market access for all

products of the least developed countries to the markets of developed countries, as well as to the markets of developing countries in a position to do so, and support for efforts to overcome their supply-side constraints;

29. *Encourages* the continued promotion of South-South cooperation, which complements North-South cooperation as an effective contribution to development and as a means to share best practices and provide enhanced technical cooperation, and encourages continued international support for South-South cooperation, including regional and interregional cooperation, through, inter alia, triangular cooperation;

30. *Calls upon* Member States to achieve the goal of universal access to reproductive health by 2015, as set out at the International Conference on Population and Development, integrating this goal in strategies to attain the internationally agreed development goals, including the Millennium Development Goals, aimed at reducing maternal mortality, improving maternal health, reducing child mortality, promoting gender equality, combating HIV/AIDS eradicating poverty;

31. *Remains convinced* that progress for women is progress for all, and reaffirms that full and effective implementation of the goals and objectives of the Beijing Declaration and Platform for Action and the outcome of the twenty-third special session of the General Assembly entitled "Women 2000: gender equality, development and peace for the twenty-first century", is an essential contribution to achieving the internationally agreed development goals, including the Millennium Development Goals, and resolves to promote gender equality and eliminate pervasive gender discrimination;

32. *Calls for* the full implementation of Agenda 21 and the Johannesburg Plan of Implementation, taking into account the Rio principles, calls for the promotion of the integration of the three components of sustainable development, economic development, social development and environmental protection, as mutually reinforcing pillars, and to that end calls for concrete action;

33. *Reaffirms* that the eradication of hunger and poverty, changing unsustainable patterns of production and consumption and protecting and managing the natural resource base of economic and social development are overarching objectives of and essential requirements for sustainable development, and invites all countries to promote sustainable consumption and production patterns, with the developed countries taking the lead and all countries benefiting from the process, taking into account the Rio principles, including the principle of common but differentiated responsibilities as set out in principle 7 of the Rio Declaration on Environment and Development, as called for in the Johannesburg Plan of Implementation;

34. *Emphasizes* the need to meet all the commitments and obligations undertaken in the United Nations Framework Convention on Climate Change and other relevant international agreements, including, for many countries, the Kyoto Protocol to the Convention;

35. *Reaffirms* the commitment to moving forward the global discussion on long-term cooperative action to address climate change, in accordance with the principles enshrined in the United Nations Framework Convention on Climate Change, and to that end encourages the parties to the Convention to continue the dialogue as decided at the eleventh session of the Conference of the Parties to the Convention;

36. *Calls upon* the United Nations system to continue to mainstream the special needs of Africa in all its normative and operational activities;

37. *Calls for* the full, timely and effective achievement of the goals and targets of the Brussels Programme of Action, the Almaty Programme of Action, the Barbados Programme of Action and the Mauritius Strategy to address the special needs of least developed countries, landlocked developing countries and small island developing States;

38. *Also calls for* the promotion and facilitation of, as appropriate, access to and the development, transfer and diffusion of technologies, including new and advanced environmentally sound technologies and corresponding know-how, to developing countries;

39. *Invites* national Governments seeking to develop infrastructure projects and to generate foreign direct investment to pursue strategies with the involvement of both the public and private sectors and, where appropriate, international donors, and in this regard calls for support to complement and enhance investments in infrastructure in developing countries and countries with economies in transition consistent with national priorities and strategies;

40. *Urges* countries to continue to take actions to implement quick-impact initiatives;

41. *Calls for* action to address and promote conditions for cheaper, faster and safer transfers of remittances in both source and recipient countries and, as appropriate, to encourage opportunities for development-oriented investment in recipient countries by beneficiaries that are willing and able to do so;

42. *Stresses* the important nexus between international migrations and development, and looks forward to the General Assembly High-level Dialogue on International Migration and Development to be held at Headquarters on 14 and 15 September 2006 as an opportunity to discuss the multidimensional aspects of international migration and development in order to identify appropriate ways and means to maximize their development benefits and minimize their negative impacts;

43. *Reiterates its strong support* for fair globalization and its resolve to make the goals of full and productive employment and decent work for all, including for women and young people, a central objective of relevant national and international policies as well as national development strategies, including poverty reduction strategies, as part of efforts to achieve the Millennium Development Goals;

44. *Calls upon* all Member States to support the implementation of Education for All programmes and to achieve universal primary education by 2015;

45. *Reiterates* that the eradication of poverty, hunger and malnutrition, particularly as they affect children, is

crucial for the achievement of the Millennium Development Goals and that rural and agricultural development should be an integral part of national and international development policies, calls for increased productive investment in rural and agricultural development to achieve food security, in this regard calls for enhanced support for agricultural development and trade capacity-building in the agricultural sector in developing countries, including by the international community and the United Nations system, and encourages support for commodity development projects, especially market-based projects, and for their preparation under the Second Account of the Common Fund for Commodities;

46. *Calls upon* all countries to pursue all necessary efforts to scale up nationally driven, sustainable and comprehensive responses to achieve broad multisectoral coverage for prevention, treatment, care and support, with full and active participation of people living with HIV, vulnerable groups, most affected communities, civil society and the private sector, towards the goal of universal access to comprehensive prevention programmes, treatment, care and support by 2010;

47. *Calls for* active international cooperation in the control of infectious diseases, based on the principles of mutual respect and equality, with a view to strengthening capacity-building in public health, especially in developing countries, including through the exchange of information and the sharing of experience, as well as research and training programmes focusing on surveillance, prevention, control, response and care and treatment in respect of infectious diseases, and vaccines against them;

48. *Emphasizes* the need to strengthen the role of the General Assembly as the highest intergovernmental mechanism for the formulation and appraisal of policy on matters relating to coordinated and integrated follow-up to the major United Nations conferences and summits in the economic, social and related fields;

49. *Reiterates* that the Economic and Social Council should continue to strengthen its role as the central mechanism for system-wide coordination and thus promote the integrated and coordinated implementation of and follow-up to the outcomes of the major United Nations conferences and summits in the economic, social and related fields, in accordance with the Charter of the United Nations and General Assembly resolution 50/227;

50. *Underscores* the fact that the functional commissions, when mandated, should continue to have the primary responsibility for the review and assessment of progress made in implementing the outcomes of the United Nations conferences and summits in the economic, social and related fields;

51. *Stresses* that all relevant organs, organizations and bodies of the United Nations should, in accordance with their respective mandates, strengthen their focus on the implementation of and follow-up to the outcome of the 2005 World Summit on development and the other major United Nations conferences and summits;

52. *Recalls* the role of the United Nations Conference on Trade and Development as the focal point within the United Nations for the integrated treatment of trade and development and interrelated issues in the areas of finance, technology, investment and sustainable development, and invites the Trade and Development Board to contribute, within its mandate, to the implementation and to the review of progress made in the implementation of the outcomes of the major United Nations conferences and summits, under its relevant agenda items;

53. *Resolves* to accelerate the implementation of the measures and mechanisms defined in its resolution 57/270 B on integrated and coordinated implementation of and follow-up to the outcomes of the major United Nations conferences and summits in the economic and social fields;

54. *Reiterates its request* to the Statistical Commission to refine and finalize indicators to assess the implementation of commitments and the achievement of development goals at the national, regional and international levels;

55. *Emphasizes* the need for a substantial increase in resources for operational activities for development on a predictable, continuous and assured basis to enable the United Nations funds and programmes and the specialized agencies to contribute effectively to the implementation of the outcomes of the major United Nations conferences and summits in the economic, social and related fields, and reiterates the need for continuous overall improvement in the effectiveness, efficiency, management and impact of the United Nations system in delivering its development assistance;

56. *Decides* to dedicate a specific meeting focused on development, including an assessment of progress over the previous year, at each session of the General Assembly during the debate on the follow-up to the Millennium Declaration and the 2005 World Summit Outcome;

57. *Invites* the regional commissions, in cooperation with regional organizations and other regional processes, as appropriate, to further contribute within their respective mandates to implementation and reviews of outcomes of the major United Nations conferences and summits in the economic, social and related fields;

58. *Requests* the Secretary-General, in his capacity as the Chairman of the United Nations System Chief Executives Board for Coordination, to continue to include in the annual overview report of the Chief Executives Board information on the mainstreaming, integration and coordination of development activities at the Secretariat level;

59. *Encourages and supports* development frameworks initiated at the regional level, such as the New Partnership for Africa's Development and similar efforts in other regions;

60. *Reiterates its resolve* to enhance the contribution of non-governmental organizations, civil society, the private sector and other stakeholders in national development efforts, as well as to promote the global partnership for development;

61. *Stresses* the importance of promoting corporate responsibility and accountability;

62. *Emphasizes* the need for adequate and substantive preparation for the review conference on the implementation of the Monterrey Consensus, as set out in General Assembly resolution 60/188 of 22 December 2005;

63. *Requests* the Secretary-General to report on progress made in the implementation of the development outcome of the 2005 World Summit in the framework of the comprehensive report on the follow-up to the Millennium Declaration and the 2005 World Summit Outcome.

Recommendations of High-level Panel on UN system-wide coherence

In a November note [A/61/583], the Secretary-General transmitted the report of the High-level Panel on UN system-wide coherence in the areas of development, humanitarian assistance and the environment, entitled "Delivering as one" (see p. 1584). The report put forward a series of recommendations to overcome the fragmentation of the United Nations so that the system could deliver as one, in true partnership with and serving the needs of all countries in their efforts to achieve the MDGs and other internationally agreed development goals. Achieving the MDGs and wider internationally agreed development goals was central to global economic stability and prosperity. While the United Nations had played a crucial role in articulating the MDGs, without ambitious and far-reaching reforms, it would be unable to deliver on its promises and maintain its legitimate position at the heart of the multilateral system. The High-level Panel's recommendations were based on five strategic directions, including ensuring coherence and consolidation of UN activities, in line with the principle of country ownership, establishing appropriate governance, managerial and funding mechanisms to empower and support consolidation and overhauling the UN system's business practices.

In terms of development, the Panel stated that, to bring real progress towards the MDGs and other internationally agreed development goals, the UN system needed to deliver as one at the country level. To do so, it should have an integrated capacity to provide a coherent approach to cross-cutting issues, including sustainable development, gender equality and human rights. The Panel therefore recommended the establishment of One United Nations at the country level, with one leader, one programme, one budget, and, where appropriate, one office. One third of UN country programmes included more than 10 agencies, with almost one third of them spending less than $2 million each. One United Nations would consolidate all programme activities at the country level. The Panel also recommended that five One United Nations country pilots be established by 2007, and, subject to review, 20 more One UN country programmes by 2009, 40 by 2010 and all other appropriate programmes by 2012. At the Headquarters level, the Panel recommended the establishment of a Sustainable Development Board to oversee the One United Nations country programmes by merging the existing joint meetings of the boards of United Nations Development Programme (UNDP), United Nations Population Fund, UNICEF and the World Food Programme, which would report to the Economic and Social Council. The Board would endorse the One United Nations country programme, allocate funding and evaluate its performance. It would maintain a strategic overview of the system to drive coordination and joint planning and to monitor overlaps and gaps. The Secretary-General should appoint a Development Coordinator, with responsibility for the performance and accountability of UN development activities. The Coordinator would be supported by a high-level coordination group comprising heads of principal development agencies. The UNDP Administrator would serve as the Coordinator. The Secretary-General should also establish an independent task force to further eliminate duplication within the UN system and consolidate UN entities, where necessary. The task force should report by the end of 2007, with clear recommendations for early implementation. Regarding results-based funding, performance and accountability, the Panel recommended the establishment of an MDG funding mechanism to provide multi-year funding for the One United Nations country programmes, as well as for agencies that were performing well. The Sustainable Development Board would govern the mechanism, with donor contributions being voluntary.

Eradication of Poverty

International Day for the Eradication of Poverty

In response to General Assembly resolution 60/209 [YUN 2005, p. 922] on implementation of the first United Nations Decade for the Eradication of Poverty (1997-2006), the Secretary-General submitted a September report [A/61/308] on the observance of the International Day for the Eradication of Poverty, held each year on 17 October, as declared by the Assembly in resolution 47/196 [YUN 1992, p. 538]. The Secretary-General was requested to review the observance of the International Day, and identify lessons learned and ways to promote the mobilization of all stakeholders in the fight against poverty.

The report provided a brief overview of the link between the observance of the International Day and human rights, followed by a discussion of key elements of the relationship between poverty and human rights. The report also provided a review of the observance of the International Day by Member States, the UN system, non-governmental organizations (NGOs) and civil society. In addition to responses to a questionnaire sent to Member States and UN entities, the review took into account the report on the outcome of an international seminar organized by an NGO as a civil society initiative. The international seminar (Montreal, Canada, 22-26 May) reviewed the International Day on the basis of 175 responses to a questionnaire sent to NGOs and civil society organizations.

The report concluded that poverty was both a cause and a consequence of the denial of human rights. The defence of economic, social and cultural rights, as well as political and civil rights, was therefore an essential tool in the fight against poverty. The International Day represented an opportunity to acknowledge the efforts and struggles of people living in poverty, a chance for them to make their concerns heard and a moment to recognize that poor people were in the forefront in the fight against poverty. The International Day could be an important tool to support national efforts to eradicate poverty, by promoting dialogue and collaboration among stakeholders. Beyond raising awareness of the need to eradicate poverty or its human rights dimensions, the lessons learned from the International Day's observance pointed to its potential to serve as a rallying point for the global and national campaigns to realize the MDGs, particularly the goal to eradicate poverty and hunger. To promote the observance of the International Day, the Assembly could encourage Member States, the UN system and all stakeholders to ensure that human rights were incorporated into development discussions as a key tool in poverty eradication, enhance community participation, and strengthen civil society as key instruments in promoting respect for human rights and poverty eradication.

Review of UN Decade for Eradication of Poverty

Commission for Social Development. The Commission for Social Development, at its forty-fourth session (New York, 18 February 2005 and 8-17 February and 22 March 2006) [E/2006/26], considered as its priority theme "Review of the first Decade on the Eradication of Poverty (1997-2006)", proclaimed by the General Assembly in resolution 52/193 [YUN 1997, p. 822]. The Commission had before it a report of the Secretary-General [E/CN.5/2006/3] on the subject. The review focused on key developments during the first Decade, including the strengthened commitment to poverty eradication at the national and international levels, the evolution of strategies for poverty eradication, the enhanced coordination within the UN system to support efforts of Member States and the obstacles and challenges facing development partners. The report noted that progress in poverty eradication over the Decade was mixed. The proportion of people living on less than a dollar a day had declined from 27.9 to 21.3 per cent between 1990 and 2001, a transition of some 18 million persons out of extreme poverty. However, there were glaring disparities at the regional level. While global poverty reduction had been driven by the success of East Asia and the Pacific and South Asia, which were on track to achieving the MDG target of halving extreme poverty by 2015, all other regions had experienced setbacks, and some countries were at severe risk of falling short of that goal. Sub-Saharan Africa was the least likely to achieve the income poverty target, and only eight African countries were on track to halving poverty by 2015. The incidence of poverty was much lower in Latin America and the Caribbean, but progress in further reducing it was slow. In Europe and Central Asia, poverty rates had risen since 1990.

The mixed results showed that many countries continued to face deep-rooted obstacles and challenges in trying to hasten poverty reduction. While average per capita income growth had increased from 1.5 per cent per annum in 1990s to 3.4 per cent in 2000, Sub-Saharan Africa had only posted an average rate of 1.2 per cent a year since 2000. Another challenge was rising inequality within countries, with gender inequality being a major barrier to progress in reducing income poverty. In addition, there was a deep division between rural and urban communities, and strong evidence of a link between poverty reduction and agricultural growth. Other major factors affecting poverty reduction were HIV/AIDS, particularly in Sub-Saharan Africa, and armed conflicts. Among the lessons learned over the Decade were the need for a participatory process that was country-driven and promoted ownership as a necessary precondition for the successful implementation of policies and programmes; poverty reduction strategies reflecting the specific context of a country's level of development and priorities; and programmes that promoted the empowerment, representation and participation of marginalized groups.

The report concluded that the Decade provided the first long-term vision for poverty reduction and eradication in an integrated and coordinated way and the summits and conferences convened during the Decade reinforced their urgency and primacy within the UN development agenda, including the MDGs. The urgency of achieving the MDGs, especially the eradication of poverty, could not be overstated. The 2005 World Summit [YUN 2005, p. 47] had called on each developing country in extreme poverty to adopt by 2006 and begin to implement a national development strategy to meet the MDG targets by 2015. That would require a scaling up of public investments, capacity-building and domestic resource mobilization, together with predictable and effective support of official development assistance.

The Secretary-General urged countries with extreme poverty to make every effort to adopt by 2006 and begin to implement a national development strategy in order to halve poverty by 2015; ensure that poverty eradication policies and programmes included measures to foster social integration, including by providing marginalized socio-economic sectors and groups with equal access to opportunities; adopt full, productive and decent employment as a central objective of national and international macroeconomic policies, and fully integrate that objective in poverty reduction strategies; and set time-bound goals and targets for expanding employment and reducing unemployment.

The Commission held a panel discussion on the subject on 8 February, 2006. The panel discussed progress made over the Decade, key challenges in Africa, access to financial resources and international cooperation. The Panel stressed that unless there was a radical change in how poverty was addressed the MDGs would not be achieved. Growth alone was insufficient to reduce poverty. There was therefore a need to link growth centres with the rest of the population so that the benefits of growth were broad-based and widespread. The private sector also had an important role to play in poverty reduction.

The Commission, by decision [E/2006/26 (dec.44/102)], decided to transmit the Chairperson's summary of the panel discussion to the coordination segment of the Economic and Social Council, whose priority theme was "Sustained economic growth for social development, including the eradication of poverty and hunger" (see p. 1594).

Reports of Secretary-General. In April, the Secretary-General submitted a report [E/2006/56] on sustained economic growth for social development, including poverty eradication and hunger, which the Economic and Social Council, by decision 2005/221 [YUN 2005, p. 1540], had adopted as its theme for its 2006 coordination segment.

Responding to resolution 60/130 [ibid., p. 1189], the Secretary-General submitted a June report [A/61/99] on the follow-up to the outcome of the 1995 World Summit for Social Development [YUN 1995, p. 1113] and of the twenty-fourth special session of the General Assembly. The report provided an overview of the substantive discussions on the review of the United Nations Decade for the Eradication of Poverty (1997-2006) during the forty-fourth (2006) session of the Commission for Social Development (see p. 1272), and analysed the message of the 1995 World Summit on Social Development on poverty eradication in the current global context.

The Economic and Social Council, by **decision 2006/220** of 17 July, took note of the Secretary-General's report on sustained economic growth for social development, including poverty eradication and hunger. It deferred until a resumed session the finalization of the multi-year work programme for its coordination segment.

GENERAL ASSEMBLY ACTION

On 20 December [meeting 83], the General Assembly, on the recommendation of the Second Committee [A/61/426/Add.1], adopted **resolution 61/213** without vote [agenda item 57 *(a)*].

Implementation of the first United Nations Decade for the Eradication of Poverty (1997-2006)

The General Assembly,

Recalling its resolutions 47/196 of 22 December 1992, 48/183 of 21 December 1993, 50/107 of 20 December 1995, 56/207 of 21 December 2001, 57/265 and 57/266 of 20 December 2002, 58/222 of 23 December 2003, 59/247 of 22 December 2004 and 60/209 of 22 December 2005,

Recalling also the United Nations Millennium Declaration, adopted by Heads of State and Government on the occasion of the Millennium Summit, and their commitment to eradicate extreme poverty and to halve, by 2015, the proportion of the world's people whose income is less than one dollar a day and the proportion of people who suffer from hunger,

Recalling further the 2005 World Summit Outcome,

Recalling its resolution 60/265 of 30 June 2006 on the follow-up to the development outcome of the 2005 World Summit, including the Millennium Development Goals and the other internationally agreed development goals,

Recalling also its resolution 61/16 of 20 November 2006 on the strengthening of the Economic and Social Council,

Recalling further the outcomes of the World Summit for Social Development and the twenty-fourth special session of the General Assembly,

Expressing its deep concern that, even after the first United Nations Decade for the Eradication of Poverty, the number of people living in extreme poverty in many countries continues to increase, with women and children constituting the majority and the most affected groups, in particular in the least developed countries and in sub-Saharan Africa,

Encouraged by reductions in poverty in some countries in the recent past, and determined to reinforce and extend this trend to benefit people worldwide,

Recognizing that mobilizing financial resources for development at the national and international levels and the effective use of those resources are central to a global partnership for development in support of the achievement of the internationally agreed development goals, including the Millennium Development Goals,

Acknowledging that sustained economic growth, supported by rising productivity and a favourable environment, including private investment and entrepreneurship, is necessary to eradicate poverty, achieve the internationally agreed development goals, including the Millennium Development Goals, and realize a rise in living standards,

Underlining the priority and urgency given by the Heads of State and Government to the eradication of poverty, as expressed in the outcomes of the major United Nations conferences and summits in the economic and social fields,

1. *Recognizes* the contribution that the first United Nations Decade for the Eradication of Poverty (1997–2006) has made to poverty eradication, and notes the interest expressed for the proclamation of a second United Nations decade for the eradication of poverty;

2. *Also recognizes* that during the implementation of the Decade the international community adopted, inter alia, the United Nations Millennium Declaration, the Monterrey Consensus of the International Conference on Financing for Development, the internationally agreed development goals, including the Millennium Development Goals, and the 2005 World Summit Outcome, all of which are mechanisms to focus national, regional and international efforts towards achieving poverty eradication;

3. *Reiterates* that eradicating poverty is the greatest global challenge facing the world today and an indispensable requirement for sustainable development, in particular for developing countries;

4. *Urges* all Governments, the international community, including the United Nations system, and all other actors to continue to pursue seriously the objective of the eradication of poverty;

5. *Reiterates* the need to strengthen the leadership role of the United Nations in promoting international cooperation for development, critical for the eradication of poverty;

6. *Welcomes* the observance of the International Day for the Eradication of Poverty and the International Human Solidarity Day in order to raise public awareness to promote the eradication of poverty and extreme poverty in all countries, in this regard recognizes the useful role the observance of the days continues to play in raising public awareness and mobilizing all stakeholders in the fight against poverty, and encourages a participatory approach to the International Day for the Eradication of Poverty;

7. *Stresses* the importance of ensuring, at the intergovernmental and inter-agency levels, coherent, comprehensive and integrated activities for the eradication of poverty in accordance with the outcomes of the major United Nations conferences and summits in the economic, social and related fields;

8. *Calls upon* donor countries to continue to give priority to the eradication of poverty in their assistance programmes and budgets, on either a bilateral or a multilateral basis;

9. *Requests* the Secretary-General to submit to the General Assembly at its sixty-second session a comprehensive report evaluating the implementation of the first United Nations Decade for the Eradication of Poverty, including recommendations on maintaining the momentum generated by the implementation of the Decade;

10. *Recognizes* the useful role the observance of the International Day for the Eradication of Poverty continues to play in raising public awareness and mobilizing all stakeholders in the fight against poverty, and requests the Secretary-General to take into account his report on the observance of the Day, as well as all other relevant reports concerning poverty eradication, in preparing his comprehensive report on the implementation of the Decade;

11. *Decides* to include in the provisional agenda of its sixty-second session the item entitled "Implementation of the first United Nations Decade for the Eradication of Poverty (1997-2006)".

On 20 December, the Assembly, by **decision 61/540**, took note of the report of the Second Committee [A/61/426] on the eradication of poverty and other development issues.

Evaluation

Responding to a request of the Committee for Programme and Coordination (CPC) at its forty-third session [YUN 2003, p. 1430], the Office of Internal Oversight Services (OIOS) submitted a report [E/AC.51/2006/3] on the usefulness of its pilot thematic evaluation of linkages between headquarters and field activities: a review of best practices for poverty eradication in the framework of the Millennium Declaration [YUN 2000, p. 49], which was presented to the Committee at its 2005 session [YUN 2005, p. 928]. OIOS concluded that the evaluation had provided a sound and useful system-wide assessment of an issue of relevance and significance to the United Nations. Feedback on the evaluation was positive, with both UN stakeholders and Member States rating its overall quality as excellent or good. High ratings were also given to the clarity and relevance of the report's findings, the adequacy of the evaluation methodology and the report's overall structure. Suggestions for improving the pilot thematic evaluation included stronger follow-up and accountability mechanisms, more targeted analyses and greater reference to the wider UN environment, including a discussion of the significance of coordination between Member States and UN entities. While OIOS acknowledged the limitations to the report, it noted that no other evaluation office in the Secretariat was positioned to undertake an evaluation of such a cross-cutting nature. OIOS concluded that the experience of the pilot thematic evaluation was sufficiently positive to warrant the regular conduct of thematic evaluations in the future.

CPC, at its forty-sixth (2006) session (14 August–8 September) [A/61/16], considered the OIOS report on the usefulness of the pilot thematic evaluation and agreed that OIOS should continue to undertake a thematic evaluation for submission to the Committee.

International Year of Microcredit, 2005

Report of Secretary-General. Responding to General Assembly resolution 59/246 [YUN 2004, p. 838], the Secretary-General submitted a September report [A/61/307] on the observance of the International Year of Microcredit, 2005. The report provided information on the commemorative activities and initiatives undertaken at all levels to achieve the objectives of the Year, as well as an overview of national efforts.

The Secretary-General noted that the Year had contributed substantially to increasing global awareness about microcredit and microfinance as important tools in the fight against poverty and towards achieving the MDGs. It served as a platform for building partnerships between Governments, UN system organizations, microfinance institutions, the private sector and other actors, and provided an effective forum for sharing experiences and good practices in building more inclusive financial sectors for improving the access by poor people to financial services. The momentum created by the Year underscored the potential role of microcredit and microfinance as tools for poverty eradication, and provided new impetus for putting best practices into action and enhancing efforts to build inclusive financial sectors to meet the needs and demands of poor people everywhere. Major activities carried out during the Year, in particular the "Blue Book" project, an invaluable tool and guide for policymakers in developing countries seeking to build inclusive financial services, and the Data project, had an important impact on further promoting the commitment to develop inclusive financial sectors. In addition, the Global Microentrepreneurship Awards served to celebrate and reward microentrepreneurs around the world. An important outcome of the Year was the establishment of the United Nations Advisers Group on Inclusive Financial Sectors, which would provide, over a two-year period, guidance to the United Nations and seek ways to make a broad variety of financial services accessible to the poor and to small enterprises across the globe.

In the light of the Year's success, the Secretary-General recommended that the Assembly urge Member States, the UN system and all stakeholders to fully exploit the role of microcredit and microfinance as tools for poverty eradication, building on the partnerships developed during the International Year, and ensure that best practices were widely disseminated and implemented. The Assembly should also recognize that the majority of the world's poor still did not have access to financial services, and welcome, in that regard, the convening of the UN Advisers Group on Inclusive Financial Sectors to promote the building of inclusive financial sectors to meet the needs and demands of poor people everywhere, building on the success of the "Blue Book".

Microcredit summit. The Gobal Microcredit Summit 2006 was held in Halifax, Nova Scotia, Canada, from 12 to 15 November. Attended by over 2,000 delegates from some 110 countries, the Summit assessed progress made towards the Microcredit Summit Campaign goal of reaching 100 million of the world's poorest people by the end of 2005 and the launching of the second phase of the Campaign, with a view to ensuring that 175 million of the world's poorest families received credit for self-employment and other business services by the end of 2015; and that 100 million families were lifted above the dollar a day threshold for purchasing power parity between 1990 and 2015.

Nobel Peace Prize. The 2006 Nobel Peace Prize was awarded to Muhammad Yunus (Bangladesh) for his pioneering use of microfinance, including microcredit in reducing poverty.

GENERAL ASSEMBLY ACTION

On 20 December [meeting 83], the General Assembly, on the recommendation of the Second Committee [A/61/246/Add.1], adopted **resolution 61/214** without vote [agenda item 57 *(a)*].

Role of microcredit and microfinance in the eradication of poverty

The General Assembly,

Recalling its resolutions 52/193 and 52/194 of 18 December 1997, 53/197 of 15 December 1998, 58/221 of 23 December 2003 and 59/246 of 22 December 2004,

Recognizing the need for access to financial services, in particular for the poor, including access to microcredit and microfinance,

Recognizing also that microfinance, including microcredit programmes, has succeeded in generating productive self-employment and proved to be an effective tool in assisting people in overcoming poverty and reducing their vulnerability to crisis, and has led to their growing participation, in particular the participation of women, in the mainstream economic and political processes of society,

Recognizing further that the majority of the world's poor still do not have access to financial services and that microcredit and microfinance are the subject of significant demand worldwide,

Bearing in mind the importance of microfinance instruments, such as credit, savings and other financial products and services, in providing access to capital for people living in poverty,

Bearing in mind also that microcredit programmes have especially benefited women and have resulted in the achievement of their empowerment,

Noting with appreciation the establishment of the United Nations Advisers Group on Inclusive Financial Sectors to promote the building of inclusive financial sectors to meet the needs and demands of poor people everywhere, building on the creation of the "Blue Book" as a tool for policymakers seeking to build more inclusive financial sectors,

Noting events organized for the promotion of inclusive financial sectors, including the convening of the Global Microcredit Summit in Halifax, Canada, from 12 to 15 November 2006,

Welcoming the efforts made in the field of property rights, and noting that an enabling environment at all levels, including transparent regulatory systems and competitive markets, fosters the mobilization of resources and access to finance for people living in poverty,

Noting with appreciation the contribution of awards and prizes to increasing the visibility and awareness of the role of microfinance, including microcredit, in the eradication of poverty, most notably the awarding of the 2006 Nobel Peace Prize,

1. *Takes note* of the report of the Secretary-General on the observance of the International Year of Microcredit, 2005, and on the role of microcredit and microfinance in the eradication of poverty;

2. *Welcomes* the successful observance of the International Year of Microcredit, 2005, which constituted a special occasion to raise awareness and share best practices and lessons learned on microcredit and microfinance;

3. *Recognizes* that access to microcredit and microfinance can contribute to the achievement of the goals and targets of major United Nations conferences and summits in the economic and social fields, including those contained in the United Nations Millennium Declaration, in particular the goals relating to poverty eradication, gender equality and the empowerment of women;

4. *Notes* the lack of relevant statistical data on inclusive financial sectors, in particular microcredit and microfinance programmes, in particular at the national and regional levels, and in this regard invites the international community, in particular the donor community, to support developing countries in collecting and preserving necessary statistical data and information on this issue, specifically on defining and measuring access to financial services and products at the country level and measuring the type, quality and usage of such services and products over time;

5. *Calls upon* Member States, the United Nations system and other relevant stakeholders to fully maximize the role of microfinance tools, including microcredit for poverty eradication and especially for the empowerment of women, and to ensure that best practices in the microfinance sector are widely disseminated;

6. *Calls upon* Member States, the United Nations system, the Bretton Woods institutions and other relevant stakeholders to support, in a coordinated manner, the efforts of developing countries in capacity-building for microcredit and microfinance institutions, including by improving their policy and regulatory framework;

7. *Invites* Member States to consider adopting policies to facilitate the expansion of microcredit and microfinance institutions in order to service the large unmet demand among poor people for financial services, including the identification and development of mechanisms to promote access to sustainable financial services, the removal of institutional and regulatory obstacles and the provision of incentives to microfinance institutions that meet national standards for delivering such financial services to the poor;

8. *Requests* the Secretary-General to submit to the General Assembly at its sixty-third session a report on the implementation of the present resolution, under the item entitled "Eradication of poverty and other development issues".

Rural development

On 10 February, the Economic and Social Council, by **decision 2006/212**, decided to consider, at its regular organizational session in February 2007, the proposal to include a discussion on promoting an integrated approach to rural development in developing countries for poverty eradication and sustainable development at a future substantial session of the Council.

Science and technology for development

Commission on Science and Technology for Development

The Commission on Science and Technology for Development held its ninth session in Geneva from 15 to 19 May [E/2006/31]. It considered as its main substantive theme "Bridging the technology gap between and within nations". The Commission had before it the Secretary-General's report on the subject [E/CN.16/2006/2]; a March Secretariat note on the implementation of and progress made on decisions taken at the Commission's eighth (2005) session [E/CN.16/2006/3]; a summary report on the Commission's Panel on bridging the technology gap between and within nations [E/CN.16/2006/CRP.1], prepared by the United Nations Conference on Trade and Development (UNCTAD) secretariat; and an informal paper containing a compilation of reports from countries on national experiences [E/CN.16/2006/CRP.2].

The Commission recommended a draft resolution and a draft decision for adoption by the Economic and Social Council. It brought to the Council's attention a decision by which it took note of the Secretary-General's report on the theme of the ninth session and a Secretariat note on the implementation of and progress made on decisions taken during the 2005 session [E/2006/31 (dec.9/101)]. The Commission chose as the substantive theme for its tenth (2007) session "Promoting the building of a people-centred, development-oriented and inclusive information society, with a view to enhancing digital opportunities for all people".

By **decision 2006/254** of 28 July, the Council deferred consideration of the Commission's report until its resumed substantive session.

In resolution 2006/46 of the same date (see p. 1001), the Council defined the role of the Commission in follow-up to the World Summit on the Information Society and in that regard, reviewed the Commission's mandate, composition, working methods, multi-stakeholder approach, Secretariat support and reporting arrangements. The Council also enlarged the Commission by ten new members.

In accordance with that decision, the Council, by **decision 2006/267** of 15 December, decided that the distribution of the ten new seats would be as follows: three seats for the Group of African States; two seats for the Group of Asian States; one seat for the Group of Eastern European States; two seats for the Group of Latin American and Caribbean States; and two seats for the Group of Western European and other States. It also decided that, initially, the terms of office of the new members should coincide with the existing terms of membership, the dates to be determined by lot for each region and that the elections of the ten new members would be held at the Council's organizational session in 2007.

On 15 December, by **decision 2006/268**, the Council deferred further consideration of the Commission's report on its ninth session until its 2007 organizational session.

Bridging the technology gap

The Commission had before it a March report [E/CN.16/2006/2] by the Secretary-General on bridging the technology gap between and within nations, which examined the extent of the gap; drew on policy lessons from countries that had successfully moved up the technology ladder; and elaborated policy frameworks for developing countries to build up their technological capabilities. According to the report, the technology gap between and within nations was wide and substantial, severely limiting developing countries' efforts in meeting the MDGs. The North-South gap in the generation and application of new and emerging technologies and their contribution to economic and social development constituted a "technological divide" that had to be bridged if developing countries were to participate in a globally inclusive information society. Most developing countries were unlikely to narrow the technology gap without making science and technology top priorities in their development agenda. To do so, they needed access to new and emerging technologies, including technology transfer, technical cooperation and building a scientific and technological capacity to participate in the development and adaptation of those technologies to local conditions. Also required were a solid scientific base, domestic capacity-building and raising human capital.

The Secretary-General recommended that the Commission consider promoting networking and facilitating information flows and sharing of national experiences in building technological capabilities and narrowing the technology gap. Other recommendations included: promoting the establishment of national science and technology parks as a means of fostering technological innovation and development; providing a forum for developing countries within UNCTAD Science and Technology for Development Network to share success stories and lessons learned in national efforts to apply science and technology for development; encouraging UNCTAD to continue providing its expertise and analytical skills for science, technology and innovation policy reviews; and encouraging UN system bodies to work cooperatively in the context of the UN-Biotech, and within an integrated framework on biotechnology, to help developing countries build national productive capacity in biotechnology.

The Secretary-General also recommended that Governments undertake needs assessment to determine whether or not existing science, technology and innovation policies effectively served their national development goals, especially in the context of meeting the MDGs. They should also strengthen the linkages between public research and private industry; improve national mechanisms for the promotion of knowledge-based and innovative enterprises through various interventions and incentives; adopt special measures to retain and attract young and talented scientists and technologies; and encourage venture capital from both public and private sources to assist product development and commercialization of new and emerging technologies.

Information and communication technologies

During 2006, the United Nations continued to consider how the benefits of new technologies, especially information and communication technologies (ICT), could be made available to all, in keeping with recommendations contained in the ministerial declaration adopted by the Economic and Social Council at its 2000 high-level segment [YUN 2000, p. 799], the Millennium Declaration [ibid., p. 49] and the Geneva Declaration of Principles and Plan of Action [YUN 2003, p. 857], adopted at the first phase of the World Summit on the Information Society [ibid.], and the Tunis Commitment and the Tunis Agenda, adopted at the second phase of the World Summit [YUN 2005, p. 933]. The UN ICT Task Force continued its substantive work as a global forum on integrating information on ICT into development programmes.

World Summit on the Information Society

Report of World Summit. In accordance with General Assembly resolution 59/220 [YUN 2004, p. 845], the Secretary-General of the International Telecommunication Union (ITU), by a March note [A/60/687], transmitted the report of the 2005 World Summit on the Information Society [YUN 2005, p. 933]. The ITU Secretary-General noted that the Assembly had assigned a major role in the implementation and follow-up of the Tunis Agenda [ibid.] to many parts of the UN system, in addition to Governments and other stakeholders. Pursuant to the Tunis Agenda, ITU, the United Nations Educational, Scientific and Cultural Organization (UNESCO) and UNDP had been asked to organize meetings on the modalities of facilitation/moderation of the 11 Action Lines established by the Geneva Plan of Action, adopted at the first part of the Summit [YUN 2003, p. 857]. The Tunis documents emphasized the need to adopt a multistakeholder approach to implementation activities, with the full engagement of the private sector and civil society, in keeping with the Summit's preparatory process. System-wide follow-up of the Summit outcomes had been requested of the Economic and Social Council, including reform of the Commission on Science and Technology for Development. The report also noted that, in 2006, the UN Secretary-General would convene a Forum on Internet Governance in Greece (see p. 1003).

GENERAL ASSEMBLY ACTION

On 27 March [meeting 74], the General Assembly adopted **resolution 60/252** [draft: A/60/L.50] without vote [agenda item 49].

World Summit on the Information Society

The General Assembly,

Recalling its resolutions 56/183 of 21 December 2001, 57/238 of 20 December 2002, 57/270 B of 23 June 2003 and 59/220 of 22 December 2004,

Recalling also the Declaration of Principles and the Plan of Action adopted by the World Summit on the Information Society at its first phase, held in Geneva from 10 to 12 December 2003, as endorsed by the General Assembly,

Recalling further the 2005 World Summit Outcome,

Recognizing that the implementation and follow-up of the World Summit should be an integral part of the integrated follow-up of the major United Nations conferences and summits in the economic, social and related fields and should contribute to the achievement of the internationally agreed development goals, including the Millennium Development Goals, and should not require the creation of any new operational bodies,

Acknowledging the urgent need to bridge the digital divide and to assist developing countries, including least developed countries, landlocked developing countries and small island developing States, and countries with economies in transition to benefit fully from the potential of information and communication technologies,

Reaffirming the potential of information and communication technologies as powerful tools to foster socio-economic development and contribute to the realization of the internationally agreed development goals, including the Millennium Development Goals,

Stressing the importance of the contribution of the Summit to the building of a people-centred, inclusive and development-oriented information society so as to enhance digital opportunities for all people in order to help to bridge the digital divide,

Acknowledging with appreciation the role played by the International Telecommunication Union in the organization of the two phases of the Summit,

1. *Expresses its gratitude* to the Government of Tunisia for having hosted the second phase of the World Summit on the Information Society in Tunis from 16 to 18 November 2005;

2. *Takes note* of the note by the Secretary-General transmitting the report of the Secretary-General of the International Telecommunication Union on the second phase of the Summit;

3. *Endorses* the Tunis Commitment and the Tunis Agenda for the Information Society adopted by the Summit at its second phase;

4. *Welcomes* the contribution of Member States, relevant United Nations bodies and other intergovernmental organizations, non-governmental organizations, civil society and the private sector to the success of the Tunis phase of the Summit;

5. *Also welcomes* the strong development orientation of the outcomes of both the Geneva and the Tunis phases of the Summit, and urges their full implementation;

6. *Further welcomes* progress achieved by the Summit towards a multi-stakeholder approach in building a people-centred, inclusive and development-oriented information society, and acknowledges that Governments could play an important role in that process;

7. *Welcomes* the Digital Solidarity Fund, established in Geneva as an innovative financial mechanism of a voluntary nature, open to interested stakeholders, with the objective of transforming the digital divide into digital opportunities for the developing world by focusing mainly on specific and urgent needs at the local level and seeking new voluntary sources of "solidarity" financing;

8. *Reiterates* that the process towards enhanced cooperation to be started by the Secretary-General will involve all relevant organizations and all stakeholders in their respective roles, as mentioned in paragraph 71 of the Tunis Agenda;

9. *Invites* the Secretary-General, in an open and inclusive process, to convene a new forum for multi-stakeholder policy dialogue called the Internet Governance Forum, in accordance with the decisions made at the Tunis phase of the Summit;

10. *Welcomes* the importance attached by the Summit, as reflected in the Tunis Agenda, to multi-stakeholder implementation at the international level, which should be organized taking into account the themes and action lines in the Geneva Plan of Action and moderated or facilitated by United Nations agencies, where appropriate;

11. *Urges* Member States, relevant United Nations bodies and other intergovernmental organizations, as well as non-governmental organizations, civil society and the private sector, to contribute actively, inter alia by initiating actions, where appropriate, to the implementation and follow-up of the outcomes of the Geneva and Tunis phases of the Summit;

12. *Requests* the Economic and Social Council to oversee the system-wide follow-up of the Geneva and Tunis outcomes of the Summit, and to that end requests the Council, at its substantive session of 2006, to review the mandate, agenda and composition of the Commission on Science and Technology for Development, including considering strengthening the Commission, taking into account the multi-stakeholder approach;

13. *Decides* to proclaim 17 May annual World Information Society Day to help to raise awareness of the possibilities that the use of the Internet and other information and communication technologies can bring to societies and economies, as well as of ways to bridge the digital divide;

14. *Also decides* to conduct an overall review of the implementation of the Summit outcomes in 2015;

15. *Requests* the Secretary-General to submit to the General Assembly through the Economic and Social Council, by June 2006, a report on the modalities of the inter-agency coordination of the implementation of the Summit outcomes, including recommendations on the follow-up process, for consideration at the substantive session of the Council.

Follow-up to World Summit

Report of Secretary-General. Responding to Assembly resolution 60/252 (see above), the Secretary-General submitted a June report [A/60/1005-E/2006/85 & Corr.1] on modalities of inter-agency coordination of the implementation of the outcomes of the World Summit on the Information Society, including recommendations on the follow-up process.

The Secretary-General noted that the implementation of the Summit outcomes was challenging for many reasons, including the complex and interconnected nature of the issues involved, the rapidity of change in ICT and the cross-cutting nature of the issue. In implementation of the Tunis Agenda, a multistakeholder meeting was convened in February, in Geneva, at which provisional focal points were identified for each of the Agenda's 11 action lines. In May, in conjunction with the celebration of World Information Society Day, action line meetings were held to develop work programmes.

In keeping with the Tunis Agenda request that the Secretary-General, in consultation with the Chief Executives Board for Coordination (CEB), establish a UN group on the information society to facilitate the implementation of the Summit outcomes, CEB, in April, approved the establishment of such a group. The Group would act as an information and coordination nexus between multiple stakeholders for the inter-agency activities associated with the implementation of the Summit outcomes; promote a coordinated approach to substantive policy issues related to implementation of the Plan of Action and the Tunis Agenda, thereby contributing to improving UN system policy coherence; interface with country-level coordination arrangements spearheaded by the resident coordinator and the United Nations Development Group to mainstream the Summit outcomes in the United Nations Development Assistance Framework/common country assessment and poverty reduction strategy papers; and support Governments in incorporating Summit outcomes and ICT into their national development strategies and e-strategies. The report outlined a number of activities the group would undertake towards the achievement of that goal.

The Secretary-General recommended that the Economic and Social Council note the actions taken by CEB to establish the UN group on the information society and request to be kept informed of progress in its work. Noting that the Assembly would carry out an overall review of the Summit in 2015, the Secretary-General recommended also that the Assembly use the opportunity to place such a review in the context of the broader review of the internationally agreed development goals, including the MDGs. The review could be conducted at the Council's coordination segment, drawing on the work of the Commission on Science and Technology for Development. In its review of the Commission, the Council should organize in alternate years, review and policy sessions. To assist the Council in carrying out its functions, the Commission could undertake a thematic review of follow-up of outcomes of the World Summit. To that end, the Council might wish to strengthen the Commission by reviewing its mandate, composition and agenda and the modalities of its new functions related to such follow-up. In assisting the Council in the oversight of the system-wide follow-up to the Summit outcomes, the Commission could draw upon the work of the UN group on the information society (see p. 1004).

Regarding follow-up activities, the report described the launch by the Secretary-General of the Global Alliance for ICT and Development (see p. 1004); the establishment of a small secretariat in Geneva to assist in the convening of the multi-stakeholder policy dialogue called the Internet Governance Forum; and the creation, on 17 May, of a multi-stakeholder advisory group to assist him in that task. On 19 May, the substantive priorities for the Forum's first meeting were further clarified. Greece offered to host the meeting (Athens, 30 October–2 November).

ECONOMIC AND SOCIAL COUNCIL ACTION

On 28 July [meeting 43], the Economic and Social Council adopted **resolution 2006/46** [draft: E/2006/L.34] without vote [agenda item 6 and 13 *(b)*].

Follow-up to the World Summit on the Information Society and review of the Commission on Science and Technology for Development

The Economic and Social Council,

Welcoming the outcomes of the World Summit on the Information Society,

Recalling the Declaration of Principles and the Plan of Action, adopted by the World Summit on the Information Society at its first phase, held in Geneva from 10 to 12 December 2003, and endorsed by the General Assembly, and the Tunis Commitment and the Tunis Agenda for the Information Society, adopted by the World Summit on the Information Society at its second phase, held in Tunis from 16 to 18 November 2005, and endorsed by the General Assembly,

Recalling also the 2005 World Summit Outcome,

Taking note of the report of the Secretary-General on modalities of the inter-agency coordination of the implementation of the outcomes of the World Summit on the Information Society, including recommendations on the follow-up process, which reviews the actions taken since the convening of the Summit and emphasizes the need for full implementation of its decisions,

Taking note also of the ongoing United Nations reform process,

Recalling General Assembly resolution 60/252 of 27 March 2006, in which the Assembly requested the Council to oversee the system-wide follow-up to the Geneva and Tunis outcomes of the Summit, and to that end requested the Council, at its substantive session of 2006, to review the mandate, agenda and composition of the Commission on Science and Technology for Development, including considering strengthening the Commission, taking into account the multi-stakeholder approach,

Bearing in mind its decision 1992/218 of 30 April 1992 and resolution 1992/62 of 31 July 1992, by which the Council established the Commission on Science and Technology for Development and defined its terms of reference, as well as its decision 2005/308 of 27 July 2005 on the methods of work of the Commission,

Recognizing the need to strengthen the Commission in order to enable it to undertake activities defined by the Summit, taking into account the multi-stakeholder approach,

Recalling General Assembly resolution 57/270 B of 23 June 2003 on integrated and coordinated implementation of and follow-up to the major United Nations conferences and summits in the economic and social fields,

Recognizing that the implementation of and follow-up to the outcomes of the World Summit on the Information Society should be an integral part of the integrated follow-up to major United Nations conferences and summits in the economic, social and related fields and should contribute to the achievement of the internationally agreed development goals, including the Millennium Development Goals, and should not require the creation of any new operational bodies,

Acknowledging the urgent need to bridge the digital divide and to assist developing countries, including those countries with special needs as stated in the Summit outcome documents, to benefit fully from the potential of information and communication technologies,

Stressing the importance of the Summit outcomes to the building of a people-centred, inclusive and development-oriented information society so as to enhance digital opportunities for all people in order to help to bridge the digital divide,

Welcoming the multi-stakeholder participation in the Summit and in its follow-up as a constructive way of dealing with present and future challenges in building the information society,

Reaffirming the need for ensuring an effective partnership and cooperation between Governments and the relevant actors of civil society, including non-governmental organizations, the academic and scientific communities and the private sector, in the implementation of and follow-up to the outcomes of the Summit,

Taking note of the action taken by the Secretary-General to convene the Internet Governance Forum,

Taking note also of the request to the Secretary-General to start a process towards enhanced cooperation, as referred to in paragraphs 69 to 71 of the Tunis Agenda,

Taking note further of the establishment, within the United Nations System Chief Executives Board for Coordination, of the United Nations Group on the Information Society, consisting of the relevant United Nations bodies and organizations, with the mandate to facilitate the implementation of the Summit outcomes, and noting the importance of having the Council kept informed of the progress in its work as a part of the annual reporting on the work of inter-agency bodies to the Council,

Acknowledging with appreciation the role played by the United Nations Conference on Trade and Development in providing secretariat support to the Commission on Science and Technology for Development,

Follow-up to the World Summit on the Information Society

1. *Welcomes* the strong development orientation of the outcomes of both the Geneva and the Tunis phases of the Summit, and urges their full implementation;

2. *Decides* to carry out its responsibilities for overseeing the system-wide follow-up to the Summit outcomes in the context of its annual consideration of the integrated and coordinated implementation of and follow-up to major United Nations conferences and summits in its coordination segment on the basis of a thematic approach and a multi-year programme, in accordance with General Assembly resolution 57/270 B, on the basis of the work of the Commission on Science and Technology for Development and drawing upon other relevant inputs;

3. *Takes note* of the important role of United Nations regional commissions, and encourages them to undertake specific activities in accordance with the Summit outcomes;

Role of the Commission on Science and Technology for Development

Mandate

4. *Decides* that, in accordance with General Assembly resolutions 57/270 B and 60/252, the Commission shall effectively assist the Economic and Social Council as the focal point in the system-wide follow-up, in particular the review and assessment of progress made in implementing the outcomes of the Summit, while at the same time maintaining its original mandate on science and technology for development, also taking into account the provisions of paragraph 60 of the 2005 World Summit Outcome;

5. *Agrees* that the system-wide follow-up shall have a strong development orientation;

6. *Decides* that, in the exercise of its responsibility as defined in paragraph 4 above, the Commission shall review and assess progress made in implementing the outcomes of the Summit and advise the Council thereon, including through the elaboration of recommendations to the Council aimed at furthering the implementation of the Summit outcomes, and that to that end, the Commission shall:

(a) Review and assess progress at the international and regional levels in the implementation of action lines, recommendations and commitments contained in the outcome documents of the Summit;

(b) Share best and effective practices and lessons learned and identify obstacles and constraints encountered, actions and initiatives to overcome them and important measures for further implementation of the Summit outcomes;

(c) Promote dialogue and foster partnerships, in coordination with other appropriate United Nations funds, programmes and specialized agencies, to contribute to the attainment of the Summit objectives and the implementation of its outcomes and to use information and communication technologies for development and the achievement of internationally agreed development goals, with the participation of Governments, the private sector, civil society, the United Nations and other international organizations in accordance with their different roles and responsibilities;

Composition

7. *Decides also* that the Commission shall be strengthened in its substantive capacity and enhanced through effective and meaningful participation of Member States in its work, and that the Commission shall be enlarged by the inclusion of ten new members, which shall be elected bearing in mind the principle of balanced and equitable geographical distribution and in accordance with procedures and timetables to be established by the Council, from among the States Members of the United Nations or States members of specialized agencies;

Working methods

8. *Decides further* that the Commission shall meet annually for a period of five working days in Geneva on a trial basis, with the Commission reviewing this arrangement after two years and making recommendations to the Council thereon;

9. *Decides* that, in line with Economic and Social Council decision 2005/308 and in the exercise of its responsibilities as defined in paragraph 4 above, the Commission shall continue working on the basis of biennial action cycles;

10. *Decides also*, taking into account the Commission's mandates as set out in paragraph 4 above, that at its next session the Commission shall develop its agenda and a multi-year work programme;

11. *Recommends* that the Commission provide for Governments, the private sector, civil society, the United

Nations and other international organizations to participate effectively in its work and contribute, within their areas of competence, to its deliberations;

12. *Decides* that future sessions of the Commission will increasingly be conducted in the form of interactive dialogue;

13. *Decides also* that, in addition to its traditional working practices, the Commission will continue to explore development-friendly and innovative uses of electronic media, drawing upon existing online databases on best practices, partnership projects and initiatives, as well as other collaborative electronic platforms, which would allow all stakeholders to contribute to follow-up efforts, share information, learn from the experience of others and explore opportunities for partnerships;

Multi-stakeholder approach

14. *Decides further* that, while using the multi-stakeholder approach effectively, the intergovernmental nature of the Commission should be preserved;

15. *Decides* that:

(a) Pursuant to Economic and Social Council resolution 1996/31 of 25 July 1996, non-governmental organizations and civil society entities not in consultative status with the Council, but which received accreditation to the World Summit on the Information Society, may participate, upon approval by the Council in a timely manner, on an exceptional basis and without prejudice to the established rules of the United Nations, in the next two meetings of the Commission, this provision being based on the understanding that, in the meantime, said organizations and entities will apply for consultative status with the Council in accordance with existing rules and procedures, and that in accordance with Council resolution 1996/31, the Committee on Non-Governmental Organizations is invited to consider such applications, in accordance with the rules and procedures of the United Nations, and to do so as expeditiously as possible;

(b) On an exceptional basis, without prejudice to existing rules of procedure, business sector entities including the private sector, in particular those that received accreditation to the Summit, may participate, upon approval by the Council in a timely manner, in the work of the Commission in accordance with the rules of procedure of the Council;

16. *Decides also* that every effort should be made by the Commission, in collaboration with relevant United Nations bodies and other interested parties, to mobilize and ensure the meaningful and effective participation, including by providing assistance on a voluntary basis, of all stakeholders from developing countries, including non-governmental organizations, small- and medium-sized enterprises, industry associations and development actors;

Secretariat support

17. *Requests* the Secretary-General to ensure effective and adequate secretariat support by the United Nations Conference on Trade and Development for the Commission, to enable it to fulfil its mandate as outlined in paragraph 4 above, while ensuring in this regard close collaboration with other relevant United Nations organizations and specialized agencies;

Reporting

18. *Also requests* the Secretary-General to inform the Commission on the progress made in the implementation of the Summit outcomes as a part of his annual reporting to the Commission;

19. *Requests* the Commission to submit to the Council, within its annual report, information on the progress made in the implementation of and follow-up to the Summit outcomes at the regional and international levels;

20. *Decides* to keep the General Assembly apprised, through its annual report on progress made in the implementation of and follow-up to the World Summit outcomes, taking into account the work of the Commission on Science and Technology for Development.

The inaugural meeting of the Internet Governance Forum (Athens, Greece, 30 October–2 November) addressed issues of Internet openness, security, diversity and access. It was attended by more than 1,300 participants from Governments, the private sector, civil society, academia and the Internet community. Participants recognized that the Internet was the backbone infrastructure of the global information and exchange society and argued that the structure and modality of its management should be such as to allow innovation without excessive central control. Specific issues discussed included the Domain Name System and the Root Zone File, and universal control by the United States Government. Several partnerships called "dynamic coalitions" were formed on issues such as multilingualism, digital identities and the Internet Bill of Rights.

UN role in ICT development

ICT Task Force. In May, the Secretary-General submitted to the Economic and Social Council the fourth annual report [E/2006/63] of the Information and Communication Technologies Task Force, which was established in 2001 [YUN 2001, p. 763] to provide a global forum on integrating ICT into development programmes and a platform for promoting public and private partnerships to help bridge the digital divide and foster digital opportunity. The report noted that the Task Force had achieved its key objectives, meeting a recognized need for a truly global policy forum and platform for multi-stakeholder interaction and consensus-building on ways to harness the potential of ICT for servicing and advancing development. It was able to influence policy dialogue and to foster progress in the use of ICT for development by creating a non-confrontational, non-negotiating and open platform for promoting cross-sectoral dialogue on key policy issues and concerns. The Task Force was also successful in functioning in a cost-effective manner by joining with a large number of partners. However, the impact and sustainability of the Task Force's initiatives and activities were at times constrained by its make-up, procedures and practices, including limited membership, inadequate representation and contribution by various stakeholder groups, lack of clarity in the division of responsibilities among its different components, absence of uniform policies on the formation of partnerships, limited resources and a narrow funding base and a lack of measurable objectives and regular evaluation. The mission of the recently launched Global Alliance for ICT and Development (see below) would contribute to linking the outcomes of the World Summit on the Information Society with the broader UN development agenda.

The Council (**decision 2006/251**) took note of the report, and the launching of the Global Alliance. It asked the Secretary-General to include information on the Alliance activities in his annual report to the Council.

Global Alliance for ICT and Development. The Secretary-General reported [E/2006/63] that, with the mandate of the ICT Task Force having expired at the end of 2005, the Global Alliance for ICT and Development, launched by the Secretary-General in March 2006, would build on and advance the work of the Task Force, as well as the experience of the World Summit on the Information Society process in addressing core issues related to the role of ICT in economic development, the eradication of poverty and the realization of the MDGs. In his report on modalities of inter-agency coordination of the implementation of the World Summit outcomes [A/60/1005-E/2006/85], the Secretary-General described the Global Alliance as an initiative for promoting multi-stakeholder dialogue and providing an innovative, inclusive and interactive channel for multi-stakeholder input to the Council's policy debate. The Global Alliance's inaugural meeting (Kuala Lumpur, Malaysia, 19-20 June) attracted extensive participation by Governments, business, media and civil society leaders, academia and the technical community. Funded by voluntary contributions, the Alliance would provide an inclusive multi-stakeholder global platform and forum for policy dialogue on the use of ICT for advancing the achievement of internationally agreed development goals. It would function primarily as a decentralized network, building on the experience of the ICT Task Force and other initiatives, and help to link other initiatives to provide a global platform, making extensive use of online networking and collaborative tools. The Alliance would report periodically to the Secretary-General.

CEB consideration. At its eleventh session (Villiers-le-Mahieu, France, 27-28 February) [CEB/2006/3], the CEB High-level Committee on Management endorsed the guidelines prepared by the ad hoc working group of the ICT Network. The guidelines, which were agreed upon by the ICT Network and the International Computer Centre, were intended to enhance coordination of the work of the two bodies.

The annual CEB overview report for coordination for 2005-2006 [E/2006/66], indicated that, in response to a request addressed by the Tunis Agenda, the Secretary-General endorsed the establishment of a UN group on the information society to coordinate UN system activities within the implementation and follow-up framework of the World Summit on the Information Society. Led by ITU, UNESCO and UNDP, the group would incorporate the information society agenda into the activities and programmes of CEB members, avoid duplication, facilitate synergies between organizations to maximize joint efforts and promote public awareness. The group would act as an information and coordination nexus for inter-agency activities associated with both the implementation of the Action Lines and follow-up processes in the Economic and Social Council and other bodies.

Report of Secretary-General. In response to General Assembly resolution 57/295 [YUN 2002, p. 836], the Secretary-General submitted an August report [A/61/254] on progress in developing a comprehensive UN system ICT strategy. The report noted that CEB, supported by its High-level Committees on Programme and Management and its ICT Network, had made significant progress in translating the UN system ICT strategic framework into specific initiatives and projects, including the elaboration of a knowledge-sharing and knowledge management strategy and the launch of activities to pursue the priority initiatives identified in the strategic framework.

By **decision 61/534** of 20 December, the Assembly took note of the Secretary-General's report on ICT for development: progress in the implementation of resolution 57/295.

Economic and social trends

According to the *Trade and Development Report, 2006* [Sales No. E.06.II.D.6], published by UNCTAD, the expansion of world output continued unabated in 2005, and was expected to maintain its pace, with a projected gross domestic product (GDP) growth of 3.6 per cent in 2006. Output growth in developed countries was likely to continue at 2.5 to 3 per cent, despite high prices for oil and industrial raw materials and a tendency towards more restrictive monetary policies. While turbulence in the financial markets had not yet adversely affected global growth to any appreciable extent, the risks of a slowdown were increasing. Economic growth in East and South Asia, which had exceeded 7 per cent in 2005, was expected to continue at similar rates in 2006. Other parts of the developing world would also continue to grow relatively quickly. For 2006, a growth rate of 4.6 per cent in Latin America, 6 per cent in Africa and in the Commonwealth of Independent States (CIS) should be possible; in West Africa, growth would probably remain at around 5 per cent.

To some extent, developing countries had themselves contributed to setting the pace for global growth, with strong investment dynamics and an overall growth rate of about 6 per cent for the group as a whole. Rapid growth in China and India had contributed to that outcome, not only because of their weight as large economies, but also because they served as an engine for trade. Moreover, their rapid growth, combined with their increasingly intense use of energy and metals, had sustained international demand for a wide range of primary commodities.

Another remarkable feature in the evolution of the world economy had been the ability of many African countries to maintain high growth rates since 2003. Regional growth had accelerated every year since then, and the 6.6 per cent growth expected for sub-Saharan Africa in 2006 was the highest rate of a sub-region after East Asia. In the United States, a more neutral monetary policy, a likely slowdown of housing prices and the impact of high energy prices were expected to decelerate private consumption and investment in the second half of 2006. While United States exports had recovered somewhat since 2003, imports would continue outpacing exports. The opposite was true for Western Europe, where, despite a modest recovery of domestic demand, exports remained the driving force for output growth in the major economies. In Japan, the long deflationary phase appeared to have come to an end. GDP growth would remain stable at 2.8 per cent, but the foreseeable end of an expansionary monetary policy associated with fiscal consolidation measures might temper that growth.

However, there were serious imbalances in the world economy, which suggested the need for caution in assessing prospects for the coming years, as their correction could have strong repercussions on developing countries.

The report on the *World Economic Situation and Prospects 2006* [Sales No.E.06.II.C.2], prepared jointly by the UN Department of Economic and Social Affairs and UNCTAD, stated that world economic growth, which had slowed in the course of 2005, was expected to continue at a moderate pace in the near term. Part of the global slowdown was a result of the maturing of the cyclical recovery in a number of economies and the associated unwinding of earlier policy stimuli. However, economic growth would remain notably stronger in developing rather than in developed economies, but both groups of countries would experience a slowdown from 2004. The still rather robust performance in the developing world relied in part on very strong and sustained growth in China and India. High commodity prices had been an important factor in spurring growth in many of the net exporters of oil and other primary commodities. The group of least developed countries (LDCs) had benefited from those favourable circumstances and its overall growth performance had been better than average.

In developed countries, the deceleration of growth in the United States economy during 2005 was expected to continue into 2006, as it was increasingly challenged by a number of structural macroeconomic weaknesses, including low (and even negative) household savings rate and the large and growing external deficit and associated indebtedness. The probability of a cooling down of buoyant house prices, sustained high energy prices and rising interest rates constituted important downside risks. The Canadian economy was expected to grow at a pace near its potential, aided by high commodity export prices and relatively flexible monetary policies. The growth outlook for Western Europe remained lacklustre, particularly for Germany, Italy and the Netherlands. In contrast, growth of the economies of the new European Union members was expected to strengthen as a result of stronger exports and increased long-term investment.

Among the economies in transition, growth in the CIS, which was expected to remain robust, benefited from higher commodity prices and domestic demand expansion owing to rising real wages and expansionary policies. Growth in South-Eastern Europe was expected to remain strong, but with some deceleration. Africa's growth outlook remained optimistic, although subject to both economic and political risks. The Japanese economic expansion was expected to continue, while Australia and New Zealand continued to witness moderate growth. While the outlook for economic growth in East Asia remained strong, the downside risks had increased, particularly in view of higher oil prices. Only marginal growth was expected in South Asia for 2006, while growth in Western Asia was expected to maintain a robust pace. A modest slowdown was expected in Latin America and the Caribbean. Mexico and Central America faced increasing pressure in their manufacturing sectors from international competitors.

The *World Economic and Social Survey 2006* [Sales No.E.06.II.C.1], entitled "Diverging Growth and Development", focused on the causes and implications of the income divergence between countries. By many measures, world inequality was high and rising. In the industrialized world, the income level over the past five decades had grown steadily, while it failed to do so in many developing countries. Only a few developing countries had been growing at sustained rates in recent decades, including China and India.

Rising inequality between countries was the result of differences in economic performance over several decades, the report noted. Even the growth experiences among the developing countries differed greatly. Widening income disparities among developing countries had become prominent after 1980 as a result, in part, of a limited number of success stories of sustained economic growth, most of them in East Asia. In other parts of the world, a much larger number of countries had suffered growth collapses with long-lasting impacts on living conditions. Economists had no conclusive answers regarding the precise causes of growth successes and failures. A newly emerging consensus was that the search for answers should not merely focus on economic factors, but take into account the historical and institutional setting of each country. While productivity growth in developed countries relied mainly on technological innovation, in developing countries, growth and development were much less about pushing the technology frontier and more about changing the structure of production and to direct it towards activities with higher levels of productivity. Increased integration into the world economy had exacerbated the divergence in growth performance among countries. While trade could help stimulate growth, it was not a matter of how much countries exported, but rather what they exported. Faster overall economic growth driven by trade was associated with more dynamic export structures. Another force for growth divergence was foreign direct investment (FDI). While it brought finance and technology, FDI was mostly attracted to countries with higher incomes and better-developed markets, infrastructure and human capital. Moreover, countries with substantial increases in FDI had not all witnessed a strengthening of their economic growth. There was also no evidence that private non-FDI financial flows had consistently led to increased investment and growth in developing countries. Part of the growth divergence was also attributable to gaps in public investment in, and spending on, infrastructure and human development.

The report concluded that success in development depended both on country efforts and on an appropriate international environment. Greater income divergence was partly explained by a rising number of growth collapses. Countries with weak economic structures and institutions and low infrastructural and human development had less capacity to gain from integrating global markets. Such conditions made it more difficult for developing countries to grow out of poverty and reduce their vulnerability to global shocks. The problem of rising global inequality therefore had an important bearing on the implementation of the UN development agenda, making the achievement of the MDGs and other internationally agreed development goals more difficult and affecting global security. Failure to redress growing global inequality could thus have wide-ranging consequences for human development.

In April, an overview [E/2006/50] of the *World Economic and Social Survey 2006* was submitted to the Economic and Social Council

In July, the Council, by **decision 2006/219**, took note of the *World Economic and Social Survey 2006: Diverging Growth and Development*.

Human Development

The *Human Development Report 2006* [Sales No. 06.III.B.1], prepared by UNDP, discussed the issue of power, poverty and the global water crisis and how it influenced human potential and progress towards achieving the MDGs. The report focused on ending the crisis in water and sanitation; water for human consumption; the vast deficit in sanitation; water scarcity, risk and vulnerability; water competition in agriculture; and managing transboundary waters. The report noted that water, a basic human right, was at the heart of a crisis that threatened life and destroyed livelihoods on a devastating scale. Overcoming the crisis in water and sanitation was one of the great human development challenges of the early twenty-first century. Water security was an integral part of the broader concept of human security, and apart from the highly visible destructive impacts on people, water insecurity violated some of the most basic principles of social justice, including equal citizenship, equality of opportunity and fair distribution. The MDGs provided a benchmark for measuring progress towards the human right to water. Even if the targets for water and sanitation were achieved, there would still be more than 800 million people without water and 1.8 billion without sanitation in 2015.

The report ranked 177 countries in its human development index by combining indicators of life expectancy, educational attainment and adjusted per capital income, among other factors. Of the countries listed, 63 were in the high human development category, 83 in the medium category and 31 in the low category.

UNDP consideration. In response to General Assembly resolution 57/264 [YUN 2002, p. 841], UNDP submitted to its Executive Board an update [DP/2006/19] on consultations that took place in the preparation of the *Human Development Report*.

In June [E/2006/35 (dec 2006/27)], the Board took note of the update.

New global human order

The General Assembly, by **decision 61/552** of 22 December, decided that the item "The role of the United Nations in promoting a new global human order" would remain for consideration during its sixty-first resumed (2007) session.

Development policy and public administration

Committee for Development Policy

Seventh session

The Economic and Social Council, having considered the report of the Committee for Development Policy (CDP)on its seventh session [YUN 2005, p. 937], adopted **resolution 2006/1** [draft: E/2005/L.52] without vote [agenda item 2].

Report of the Committee for Development Policy on its seventh session

The Economic and Social Council,

Recalling General Assembly resolution 59/209 of 20 December 2004 on a smooth transition strategy for countries graduating from the list of least developed countries,

Recalling also its resolution 2004/66 of 5 November 2004,

1. *Takes note* of the report of the Committee for Development Policy;
2. *Endorses* the request of the Committee to be informed by the Secretary-General during the transition period of the implementation of the transition strategy for graduating countries and of their development progress, as laid out in General Assembly resolution 59/209, in order to enable the Committee to carry out the function assigned to it in paragraph 12 of that resolution;
3. *Notes* the work done by the Committee, as described in chapter IV of its report, regarding general principles and the refinement of criteria with a view to achieving the objective of equal treatment of countries in similar situations;
4. *Requests* the Committee to continue developing a consistent set of criteria that can be applied to all recommendations regarding the inclusion in and graduation from the list of least developed countries.

Eighth session

CDP, at its eighth session (New York, 20-24 March) [E/2006/33], addressed three major themes: creating an environment at the national and international levels conducive to generating full and productive employment and decent work for all, and its impact on sustainable development; coping with economic vulnerability and instability; and the triennial review of the identification of LDCs.

CDP believed that creating an environment for full and productive employment and decent work for all should be a key objective of domestic economic and social policy, as productive employment was central to fighting poverty and providing adequate social security. The international community should make the objective of reaching full productive employment and decent work for all an integral part of trade, financial arrangements and development assistance to developing countries, particularly the LDCs. National development strategies should enhance coherence between financial and economic policies, on the one hand, and employment, labour market policies and social development on the other. In addition, a viable strategy for implementing productive employment and decent work in the poorest countries should encompass support for traditional sectors.

The Committee was also of the view that countries that had been successful in preventing or managing shocks had done so by adopting a long-term strategy shaped by the constructive use of local knowledge. It called on the international community to assist developing countries, particularly the LDCs, in strengthening capacity in several key areas, and provide technical assistance to the LDCs in responding to the vulnerability caused by environmental stress or ecological damage.

In its triennial review of the list of LDCs, CDP considered three dimensions of a country's state of development, including income level (gross national income per capita), stock of human assets (human assets index) and economic vulnerability (economic vulnerability index). To be added to the list, a country had to satisfy the threshold for inclusion based on all three criteria. To be eligible for graduation, a country had to reach the thresholds for graduation for at least two of the three criteria, or its gross national income per capita had to exceed twice the threshold level. To be recommended for graduation, a country had to be found eligible for graduation in two consecutive triennial reviews. The report emphasized the need for further methodological refinements in the design and application of the criteria.

By **decision 2006/253** of 28 July, the Economic and Social Council deferred consideration of the CDP report on its eighth session until its resumed substantive session.

By **decisions 2006/265** and **2006/266** of 15 December, the Council deferred consideration of CDP recommendations at its eighth session on the LDCs to its 2007 substantive and organizational sessions, respectively.

Public administration

Committee of Experts on Public Administration. In accordance with Economic and Social Council **decision 2006/203**, the Committee of Experts on Public Administration held its fifth session in New York, from 27 to 31 March [E/2006/44]. The Committee had before it Secretariat reports on: innovations in governance and public administration for the achievement of the internationally agreed development goals, including the MDGs [E/C.16/2006/2]; bottom-up approach and methodologies for developing foundations and principles of sound public administration: questionnaires [E/C.16/2006/3]; definition of basic concepts and terminologies in governance and public administration [E/C.16/2006/4]; and review of UN activities in the area of public administration [E/C.16/2006/5].

Regarding innovations in governance and public administration, the Committee advised the Secretariat to facilitate innovations in Member States by, among other things, maximizing the use of the UN Online Network in Public Administration and Finance as a repository of innovations in governance. It also recommended that the Secretariat focus on good policies and legislation for innovation and on mainstreaming successful knowledge systems as a national policy tool. The Secretariat was advised to examine several key questions to better assist Member States in introducing change in the public sector, including how to build political coalitions to support and validate the innovation process. The Secretariat should also devise tools and methods for risk assessment and change management in the public sector, and focus on uncovering, from a practical point of view, the complex "black box" of the process through which innovations in government came about.

Concerning the bottom-up approach in developing sound public administration principles, the Committee stressed that the United Nations played a major role in sensitizing Member States and local stakeholders about the need to institute policies that enhanced opportunities for citizen participation. In that regard, the Secretariat should place its technical advisory facilities at Member States' disposal, especially those that sought assistance on the design of instruments for monitoring and evaluating participatory processes and their impact on citizens. The Committee decided that the topic of participatory governance should remain on its agenda.

On the issue of a compendium of basic terminology in governance and public administration, the Committee agreed on the need for a common language to facilitate communication on public administration issues brought before the Council and other UN entities. Regarding the terminologies and concepts presented by the Secretariat in its note [E/C.16/2006/4], the Committee noted that there were analytical and normative uses of the terms included in the report. In the light of the value of the exercise, the Committee recommended to the Council that it be further developed and included in the agenda for the Committee's 2007 session. It also set up a working group composed of public administration scholars and practitioners to discuss issues ranging from the scope of the exercise, to the title of the volume, and the development of the glossary.

The Committee emphasized the importance of UN Public Service Day (23 June) and the presentation of the UN Public Service Awards, and called on Member States to participate in the Awards programme. To enhance the programme's impact, the Committee recommended that the Secretariat explore the possibility of linking up with national and regional public administration awards programmes with a view to sharing information. The Committee also reviewed preparations for the seventh Global Forum on Reinventing Government, scheduled to take place in June 2007 in Vienna. It encouraged the Secretariat to continue tracking the impact of the Forums on the dissemination of best practices in the field of governance and public administration.

ECONOMIC AND SOCIAL COUNCIL ACTION

On 28 July [meeting 43], the Economic and Social Council, on the recommendation of the Committee of Experts on Public Administration [E/2006/44], adopted **resolution 2006/47** without vote [agenda item 13 *(g)*].

Report of the Committee of Experts on Public Administration on its fifth session and dates, venue and provisional agenda for the sixth session of the Committee

The Economic and Social Council,

Recalling its resolutions 2003/60 of 25 July 2003, 2005/3 of 31 March 2005 and 2005/55 of 21 October 2005,

Emphasizing that good governance and transparent and accountable public administration at the national and international levels will contribute to the achievement of the internationally agreed development goals, including the Millennium Development Goals,

Recognizing that Member States stand to gain from the sharing of experiences in public administration innovation,

Taking note of the Brisbane Declaration on Community Engagement, adopted at the first International Conference on Engaging Communities, held in Brisbane, Australia, from 14 to 17 August 2005,

Taking note also of the Seoul Declaration on Participatory and Transparent Governance, adopted at the sixth Global Forum on Reinventing Government, held in Seoul from 24 to 27 May 2005,

Noting the recommendations of the *World Public Sector Report, 2005: Unlocking the Human Potential for Public Sector Performance*, highlighting the strategic importance of improving the quality of human resources in the public sector as a means of developing strong institutions for public administration,

Emphasizing the important role of the United Nations in documenting and disseminating global best practices in governance and public administration for the purpose of contributing to the achievement of the internationally agreed development goals, including the Millennium Development Goals,

1. *Takes note* of the report of the Committee of Experts on Public Administration on its fifth session;

2. *Encourages* Governments to create an environment that is supportive of further improving an effective public administration, including through change management, risk assessment and innovation, as appropriate, in order to provide better services to their citizens;

3. *Encourages* Member States to strengthen citizen trust in government by fostering public citizen participation in key processes of public policy development, public service delivery and public accountability;

4. *Requests* all Member States to abide by the principles of proper management of public affairs and public property, and fairness, responsibility and equality before the law, including the need to safeguard integrity and foster a culture of transparency, accountability and rejection of corruption at all levels and in all its forms, and in that regard urges Member States that have not yet done so to consider enacting laws to accomplish those ends;

5. *Recognizes* the role that the United Nations Public Service Awards could play in promoting and disseminating best practices in the field of public administration, and in this regard requests the Secretariat to enhance the information to be provided to Member States on the Awards, with a view to encouraging greater participation;

6. *Requests* the Secretariat to continue to assist Member States, upon their request, in developing e-government tools to improve participation, transparency, accountability and service delivery, and to increase the sharing of information, products and resources throughout the United Nations public administration network;

7. *Welcomes* the convening of the seventh Global Forum on Reinventing Government, to be held in Vienna in 2007, and in this connection encourages the active participation of Governments, as well as civil society organizations and the private sector, in the exchange of innovations and best practices that promote trust in government;

8. *Approves* the decision of the Committee to work according to a multi-year programme and to link it more closely to the theme of the high-level segment of the substantive session of the Economic and Social Council and the United Nations Public Service Awards, based on the following priority areas:

2007

- Participatory governance and citizens' engagement in policy development, service delivery and budgeting

2008

- Capacity-building for development, including post-conflict reconstruction of public administration and crisis/disaster management

2009

- Building transparency, accountability and trust, including leadership development, through the tools of information and communication technologies

9. *Also approves* the convening of the sixth session of the Committee in the second quarter of 2007;

10. *Further approves* the following agenda for the sixth session of the Committee:

    1. Participatory governance and citizens' engagement in policy development, service delivery and budgeting.
    2. Compendium of basic United Nations terminology in governance and public administration.
    3. Review of the United Nations programme in public administration and finance.
    4. A public administration perspective on the theme of the high-level segment of the Economic and Social Council

Groups of countries in special situations

On 13 September, the General Assembly, on the recommendation of the General Committee, included in the agenda of the sixty-first session the item entitled "Groups of countries in special situations", covering LDCs and landlocked and transit developing countries, and allocated it to the Second Committee.

By **decision 61/539** of 20 December, the General Assembly took note of the report of the Second Committee on groups of countries in special situations [A/61/425].

Least developed countries

The special problems of the officially designated least developed countries (LDCs) were considered in several UN forums in 2006, particularly in connection with the implementation of the Brussels Declaration and Programme of Action for LDCs for the Decade 2001-2010, adopted at the Third United Nations Conference on LDCs in 2001 [YUN 2001, p. 770], and endorsed by the General Assembly in resolution 55/279 in July of that year [ibid., p. 771]. World leaders, in the 2005 World Summit Outcome document [YUN 2005, p. 48], reaffirmed their commitment to addressing the special needs of LDCs, and urged all countries and the UN system to speedily meet the goals and targets of the Brussels Programme, particularly the official development assistance target. CDP and UNCTAD also considered LDC-related issues. In September, the Assembly held a high-level meeting on the midterm comprehensive global review of the implementation of the Programme of Action for the LDCs for the Decade 2001-2010.

LDC list

The number of countries officially designated as LDCs remained at 50. Although Cape Verde and Maldives were recommended for graduation from the list, the process would take place over a three-year period, as decided by General Assembly resolution 59/209 [YUN 2004, p. 854]. Regarding Maldives, the Assembly, in resolution 60/33 [YUN 2005, p. 942], deferred, until January 2008, the start of the three-year transition period for its graduation, following the destruction and damage caused by the 26 December 2004 Indian Ocean tsunami to the country's social and economic infrastructure and disruption of its development plans.

The full list of LDCs comprised: Afghanistan, Angola, Bangladesh, Benin, Bhutan, Burkina Faso, Burundi, Cambodia, Cape Verde, Central African Republic, Chad, Comoros, Democratic Republic of the Congo, Djibouti, Equatorial Guinea, Eritrea, Ethiopia, Gambia, Guinea, Guinea-Bissau, Haiti, Kiribati, Lao People's Democratic Republic, Lesotho, Liberia, Madagascar, Malawi, Maldives, Mali, Mauritania, Mozambique, Myanmar, Nepal, Niger, Rwanda, Samoa, Sao Tome and Principe, Senegal, Sierra Leone, Solomon Islands, Somalia, Sudan, Timor-Leste, Togo, Tuvalu, Uganda, United Republic of Tanzania, Vanuatu, Yemen and Zambia.

Smooth transition strategy

CDP consideration. At its eighth session (New York, 20-24 March) [E/2006/33], the Committee for Development Policy (CDP), which was responsible for adding countries to or graduating them from the LDC list, conducted a triennial review of the status of LDCs, taking into consideration the three dimensions of a country's state of development, namely, gross national income (GNI), per capita; the human assets index (HAI) and the economic vulnerability index (EVI). It also took into consideration the principles identified by the Committee at its 2005 session [YUN 2005, p. 942], including: identification of low-income countries suffering from severe structural handicaps; equitable treatment of the countries over time; stability of the criteria; and the need for flexibility in applying the three criteria.

In its review, the Committee noted that of a total of 50 LDCs, 36 countries had failed to meet any of the graduation criteria, while seven other countries had met no more than one of the three graduation criteria. Of the remaining seven countries, two were to be graduated in accordance with Assembly resolutions 59/209 [YUN 2004, p. 854], 59/210 [ibid., p. 855] and 60/33 [YUN 2005, p. 942] (Cape Verde at the end of 2007 and Maldives in January 2011), one was recommended for graduation (Samoa) and four were found eligible for graduation for the first time (Equatorial Guinea, Kiribati, Tuvalu and Vanuatu).

The Committee recommended to the Economic and Social Council that Papua New Guinea be included in the list of LDCs (subject to the Government's acceptance) and that Samoa be graduated from the list. It expected UNCTAD to prepare vulnerability profiles for Equatorial Guinea, Kiribati, Tuvalu and Vanuatu. In 2008, the Committee should identify the countries which were likely to be recommended for inclusion or graduation in order to facilitate timely and in-depth collection of data on those countries.

The Committee agreed that there was scope and need for further methodological refinements in the design and application of the criteria. In particular, given the incidence of HIV, the life expectancy at birth should be used as a component of HAI, as soon as reliable data became available. Regarding the large number of LDCs which did not meet any of the criteria for graduation and were not likely to meet the MDGs, the Committee recommended that priority attention be given to those countries in order to design appropriate policy interventions. It suggested that graduating countries be assisted in obtaining information about the range of development assistance to implement a smooth transition.

Communications. On 19 July [E/2006/91], Papua New Guinea requested that the Council defer consideration of the subject of the country's inclusion in the list of LDCs to its 2007 substantive session. On 20 July [E/2006/90], Samoa, recalling its earlier request to CDP that its graduation from the list be deferred, requested the Council's sympathetic consideration with respect to reforming the graduation rule by making the EVI one of the two criteria to be met before graduation from the LDCs list.

By **decision 2006/265** of 15 December, the Economic and Social Council took note of the CDP recommendation that Papua New Guinea be included in the list of LDCs, as well as that country's 21 July letter to the UN Secretariat, and deferred consideration of the Committee's recommendation until its 2007 substantive session.

By **decision 2006/266** of the same date, the Council deferred until its 2007 organizational session consideration of the CDP recommendation that Samoa be graduated from the list of LDCs.

Programme of Action (2001-2010)

In accordance with General Assembly resolution 59/244 [YUN 2004, p. 857] and Economic and Social Council resolution 2005/44 [YUN 2005, p. 943], the Secretary-General submitted, in May, the fourth annual progress report [A/61/82-E/2006/74 & Corr.1] on the implementation of the Programme of Action for the LDCs for the Decade 2001-2010.

The report noted that, despite improved economic performance, extreme poverty, while decreasing in a few LDCs, was increasing in many others. In an unprecedented reversal of historical trends, life expectancy was declining in several LDCs in Africa most affected by HIV/AIDS and civil strife, while other social indicators, including gender equality, were improving, due to donor support to the social sectors. If current trends persisted, however, very few LDCs would meet the objectives, goals and targets of the Brussels Programme of Action. Fast population growth, rapid urbanization, environmental degradation and HIV/AIDS aggravated extreme poverty in the LDCs, and climate change was a new challenge for sustainable development in those countries, particularly in Africa and the small islands.

The Secretary-General recommended that LDCs integrate the objectives, goals and targets of the Programme of Action into their MDG-based national development strategies, with the support of their development partners through the common country assessment/United Nations Development Assistance Frameworks and poverty reduction strategy papers processes. The integrated investment and operational frameworks should be underpinned by a bottom-up and needs-based assessment and supported by a number of "quick-win" interventions. Keeping the promises on aid, debt relief, market access and technical assistance was crucial for breaking the poverty trap of LDCs and maintaining the credibility of the Programme of Action.

ECONOMIC AND SOCIAL COUNCIL ACTION

On 27 July [meeting 42], the Economic and Social Council adopted **resolution 2006/41** [draft: E/2006/L.29, as orally corrected], without vote [agenda item 6 *(b)*].

Implementation of the Programme of Action for the Least Developed Countries for the Decade 2001-2010

The Economic and Social Council,

Recalling the Brussels Declaration and the Programme of Action for the Least Developed Countries for the Decade 2001-2010,

Recalling also its decision 2001/320 of 24 October 2001, in which it decided to establish, under the regular agenda item entitled "Integrated and coordinated implementation of and follow-up to the major United Nations conferences and summits", a regular sub-item entitled "Review and coordination of the implementation of the Programme of Action for the Least Developed Countries for the Decade 2001-2010",

Recalling further the Ministerial Declaration of the high-level segment of its substantive session of 2004 on the theme "Resources mobilization and enabling environment for poverty eradication in the context of the implementation of the Programme of Action for the Least Developed Countries for the Decade 2001-2010",

Recalling its resolution 2005/44 of 27 July 2005,

Recalling also General Assembly resolution 60/228 of 23 December 2005 and Assembly decision 60/556 of 16 May 2006,

1. *Takes note* of the annual progress report of the Secretary-General on the implementation of the Programme of Action for the Least Developed Countries for the Decade 2001-2010;

2. *Reiterates its deep concern* over the insufficient progress achieved in the implementation of the Programme of Action, and stresses the need to address areas of weakness in its implementation;

3. *Urges* the least developed countries and their bilateral and multilateral development partners to undertake increased efforts and to adopt speedy measures urgently with a view to meeting the goals and targets of the Programme of Action in a timely manner;

4. *Invites* the high-level meeting on the midterm comprehensive global review of the implementation of the Programme of Action, to be held in New York on 18 and 19 September 2006, to identify results-based measures so as to speed up progress in the implementation of the Programme of Action;

5. *Stresses*, within the context of the annual global reviews, as envisaged in the Programme of Action, the need to assess the implementation of the Programme of Action sector by sector, and in this regard invites all relevant organizations, consistent with their respective mandates, to report on the progress made in its implementation using quantifiable criteria and indicators to be measured against the goals and targets of the Programme of Action;

6. *Requests* the Secretary-General to submit an annual progress report on the implementation of the Programme of Action in a more analytical and results-oriented way, by placing greater emphasis on the progress achieved by the least developed countries and their development partners in its implementation.

UNDP action. The Executive Board of the United Nations Development Programme/United Nations Population Fund, at its annual session (New York, 20-27 January) [E/2006/35], reiterated its call upon donor countries and other countries in a position to do so to provide and sustain additional funding support for United Nations Capital Development Fund programmes and activities in the LDCs (dec.2006/4).

Trade and Development Board Action. The UNCTAD Trade and Development Board, at its fifty-third session (Geneva, 27 September–2 October, 10 October), [A/61/15 (Part IV)] adopted agreed conclusions [486(LIII)] on the review of progress in the implementation of the Programme of Action for the LDCs. The Board underlined the urgent need for continued national efforts accompanied by increased and sustained international support in order for the LDCs to achieve the poverty reduction goals of the Brussels Programme of Action and the Millennium Declaration [YUN 2000, p. 49]. It acknowledged that policies complemented by good governance at all levels should better address the challenge of developing and utilizing productive capacities in most LDCs, including strengthening the design of national development plans and poverty reduction strategies and international support measures in favour of LDCs. The Board stressed the need to maintain the momentum of increasing official development assistance flows, and increase the share of development aid for national programmes and projects. It reiterated that the Integrated Framework for Trade-related Technical Assistance to LDCs remained a key instrument in strengthening LDCs institutional capacities, with a view to enhancing their capacity to benefit from participation in the multilateral trading system. The Board recommended that UNCTAD should continue to support the LDCs in formulating and implementing policies and strategies, including through participation in the poverty reduction strategy paper process. In that context, LDCs were encouraged to integrate relevant policy conclusions and recommendations of the *LDC Report 2006* into the design and implementation of national policies, including in the poverty reduction strategy papers, the enhanced Integrated Framework and the Aid for Trade initiative.

GENERAL ASSEMBLY ACTION

On 20 December [meeting 83], the General Assembly, on the recommendation of the Second Committee [A/61/425/Add.1], adopted **resolution 61/211** without vote [agenda item 56 *(a)*].

Third United Nations Conference on the Least Developed Countries

The General Assembly,

Recalling the Brussels Declaration and the Programme of Action for the Least Developed Countries for the Decade 2001-2010,

Recalling also the United Nations Millennium Declaration, in particular paragraph 15 thereof, in which the Heads of State and Government undertook to address the special needs of the least developed countries,

Recalling further its resolution 57/270 B of 23 June 2003 on the integrated and coordinated implementation of and follow-up to the outcomes of the major United Nations conferences and summits in the economic and social fields,

Recalling the 2005 World Summit Outcome,

Recalling also its resolution 60/228 of 23 December 2005,

Recalling further its resolution 61/1 of 19 September 2006,

Reaffirming its resolution 60/265 of 30 June 2006 on the follow-up to the development outcome of the 2005 World Summit, including the Millennium Development Goals and the other internationally agreed development goals,

Taking note of the Ministerial Declaration of the high-level segment of the 2004 substantive session of the

Economic and Social Council on the theme "Resources mobilization and enabling environment for poverty eradication in the context of the implementation of the Programme of Action for the Least Developed Countries for the Decade 2001-2010",

1. *Takes note* of the report of the Secretary-General;

2. *Welcomes* the contributions made in the lead-up to the midterm comprehensive global review of the implementation of the Programme of Action for the Least Developed Countries for the Decade 2001-2010, including the elaboration of the Cotonou Strategy for the Further Implementation of the Programme of Action for the Least Developed Countries for the Decade 2001-2010 as an initiative owned and led by the least developed countries;

3. *Reaffirms its commitment* to the Declaration adopted by Heads of State and Government and heads of delegations participating in the high-level meeting of the General Assembly on the midterm comprehensive global review of the implementation of the Programme of Action, in which they recommitted themselves to addressing the special needs of the least developed countries by making progress towards the goals of poverty eradication, peace and development;

4. *Acknowledges* the findings of the midterm comprehensive global review, which stressed that despite some progress in the implementation of the Programme of Action, the overall socio-economic situation in the least developed countries continues to be precarious and requires attention and that, given current trends, many least developed countries are unlikely to achieve the goals and objectives set out in the Programme of Action;

5. *Stresses* that the internationally agreed development goals, including the Millennium Development Goals, can be effectively achieved in the least developed countries through, in particular, the timely fulfilment of the seven commitments of the Programme of Action;

6. *Reaffirms* that the Programme of Action constitutes a fundamental framework for a strong global partnership, whose goal is to accelerate sustained economic growth, sustainable development and poverty eradication in the least developed countries;

7. *Also reaffirms* that progress in the implementation of the Programme of Action will require effective implementation of national policies and priorities for the sustained economic growth and sustainable development of the least developed countries, as well as strong and committed partnership between those countries and their development partners;

8. *Underscores* the fact that for the further implementation of the Programme of Action, the least developed countries and their development partners must be guided by an integrated approach, a broader genuine partnership, country ownership, market considerations and results-oriented actions;

9. *Urges* the least developed countries to strengthen the implementation of the Programme of Action through their respective national development framework, including, where they exist, Poverty Reduction Strategy Papers, the common country assessment and the United Nations Development Assistance Framework;

10. *Urges* development partners to exercise individual best efforts to continue to increase their financial and technical support for the implementation of the Programme of Action;

11. *Encourages* the United Nations Resident Coordinator system to assist the least developed countries in translating goals and targets of the Programme of Action into concrete actions in the light of their national development priorities;

12. *Encourages* the Resident Coordinator system and country teams, as well as country-level representatives of the Bretton Woods institutions, bilateral and multilateral donors and other development partners, to collaborate with and provide support to, as appropriate, the relevant development forums and follow-up mechanisms;

13. *Invites* the organizations of the United Nations system and other multilateral organizations that have not yet done so to mainstream the implementation of the Brussels Declaration and the Programme of Action within their programmes of work as well as in their intergovernmental processes and to undertake within their respective mandates multi-year programming of actions in favour of the least developed countries;

14. *Stresses*, within the context of the annual global reviews, as envisaged in the Programme of Action, the need to assess the implementation of the Programme of Action sector by sector, and in this regard invites the United Nations system and all relevant international organizations, consistent with their respective mandates, to report on the progress made in its implementation using quantifiable criteria and indicators to be measured against the goals and targets of the Programme of Action and to participate fully in reviews of the Programme of Action at the national, subregional, regional and global levels;

15. *Also stresses* the crucial importance of integrated and coordinated follow-up, monitoring and reporting for the effective implementation of the Programme of Action at the national, subregional, regional and global levels;

16. *Requests* the Secretary-General to ensure, at the Secretariat level, the full mobilization and coordination of all parts of the United Nations system to facilitate coordinated implementation as well as coherence in the follow-up to and monitoring and review of the Programme of Action at the national, subregional, regional and global levels, including through such coordination mechanisms as the United Nations System Chief Executives Board for Coordination, the United Nations Development Group, the Executive Committee on Economic and Social Affairs and the Inter-agency Expert Group on the Millennium Development Goals Indicators;

17. *Reiterates its invitation* to the organs, organizations and bodies of the United Nations system, and other relevant multilateral organizations, to provide full support to and cooperation with the Office of the High Representative for the Least Developed Countries, Landlocked Developing Countries and Small Island Developing States;

18. *Requests* the Secretary-General to elaborate and submit to the General Assembly at its sixty-second session a detailed and clearly defined advocacy strategy

aimed at raising awareness about the objectives, goals and commitments of the Programme of Action with a view to facilitating its effective and timely implementation;

19. *Also requests* the Secretary-General to submit an annual analytical and results-oriented progress report on the further implementation of the Programme of Action and to make available adequate resources, within existing resources, for the preparation of such a report.

Midterm Comprehensive Global Review of the Programme of Action

In accordance with General Assembly **decision 60/556** of 16 May, the General Assembly convened the high-level meeting on the midterm comprehensive global review of the implementation of the Programme of Action for LDCs on 18 and 19 September. The organizational arrangements for the meeting were contained in a March note of the Secretary-General [A/60/738].

The high-level meeting, was preceded by the Ministerial Meeting of Least Developed Countries for the Midterm Comprehensive Global Review of the Brussels Programme of Action (Cotonu, Benin, 5-8 June), which adopted the Cotonu Ministerial Declaration and Strategy for the Further Implementation of the Programme of Action for the Least Developed Countries for the Decade 2001-2010 [A/61/117]; informal interactive hearings with representatives of non-governmental and civil society organizations and the private sector (New York, 22 June) on the theme "Forging partnership with civil society and the private sector for poverty reduction in LDCs" [A/61/162]; and a preparatory meeting of experts (New York, 5-7 September) [A/61/323], which proposed a draft resolution for adoption by the Assembly.

The overall theme of the high-level meeting was "Programme of Action for the Least Developed Countries for the Decade 2001-2010: Redeeming the commitments".

The meeting had before it a July report of the Secretary-General on the midterm comprehensive global review of the implementation of the Programme of Action [A/61/173 & Corr.1]. The report noted that over the past five years, both the LDCs and their development partners had progressed in implementing the actions assigned to them in the Brussels Programme of Action. The LDCs had strengthened their policy and governance and reform efforts, while development partners provided increased development assistance, enhanced debt relief and some additional trade opportunities, yielding tangible results in the LDCs. Economic growth had risen towards the target of 7 per cent, and there had been progress towards several quantitative goals for human development. Most LDCs had adjusted their development strategies and actions to give greater attention to poverty reduction. In addition, there had also been a resurgence in international cooperation for development and the emergence of a wide degree of consensus on the actions required to achieve development, as well as a continuing expansion of programmes to confront specific development challenges facing the world's poorest, such as the Heavily Indebted Poor Countries and the Enhanced Heavily Indebted Poor Countries Initiatives, the Education for All Fast Track Initiative, the Global Fund to Fight AIDS, Tuberculosis and Malaria and others. Official development assistance to LDCs rose by 75 per cent between 2001 and 2004 and increased further in 2005. Other developing countries were also increasing resource flows to the LDCs, including through South-South arrangements.

The improvement, however, had been modest and, for the LDCs, the absolute levels of deprivation remained higher than in other developing countries, with income poverty largely unchanged. More substantial success depended on full delivery by all stakeholders on their commitments in the Brussels Programme.

According to the report, LDCs should continue to improve governance, including by building human and institutional capacities, and give greater attention to gender equality, agriculture, infrastructure and HIV/AIDS. Development partners, including other developing countries, should increase their support to the LDCs. All developed countries should strive to reach the agreed quantitative and qualitative goals for their official development assistance to the LDCs. Efforts to reduce external debt in the LDCs should be sustained. Commitments to reduce the obstacles to exports from LDCs should be translated into action without delay. The UN system should enhance support to the LDCs and improve its effectiveness. The private sector should seize the investment opportunities in the LDCs, and civil society should sustain its actions in support of those countries.

The report concluded that the Brussels Programme of Action should remain the framework for national and international efforts to advance development in the LDCs. In particular, the partnership that the Programme embodied had to be sustained, with mutual recognition of the efforts, successes and challenges of all involved. The focus of attention of that partnership should be on the full implementation of the agreed commitments and actions contained in the Programme and related undertakings, attuned to country circumstances.

UNCTAD report. As part of its contribution to the September high-level meeting, UNCTAD submitted a report [UNCTAD/LDC/2006/3] containing the results of a project designed to provide a qualitative assessment of progress in the implementation of the Programme of Action in selected countries. The report provided an overview and synthesis of the country case studies and national reports, including policy lessons from the experiences of countries covered by the project. It also put forward policy conclusions and recommendations aimed at assisting the further implementation of actions and commitments of the Programme of Action at the national and international levels.

According to the report, the most striking feature of the progress made since 2001 was the strong engagement of development partners in meeting commitments with respect to aid, debt relief and market access. In contrast to the 1990s, there was a significant increase in aid and important progress on debt relief. Efforts to increase development finance for the LDCs had been complemented with new initiatives to improve market access. While growth rates and investment ratios in LDCs had not achieved the ambitious targets of the Programme of Action, the growth and investment performance in the LDC group as a whole was better during the period 2001-2004 than during the 1990s. There were, however, certain disturbing features in meeting targets, including: growing divergences amongst LDCs in terms of growth performance; mixed progress towards human development goals, their economic vulnerability and the unclear nature of the sustainability of recent improvements. Ultimately, the increased external resources being provided by development partners would not translate into sustained economic and social progress unless development finance for LDCs continued to be scaled up, was complemented with more effective trade development measures and linked to efforts to develop domestic productive capacities.

GENERAL ASSEMBLY ACTION

On 19 September [meeting 9], the General Assembly adopted **resolution 61/1** [draft: A/61/L.2], without vote [agenda item 56 *(a)*].

Declaration of the high-level meeting of the sixty-first session of the General Assembly on the midterm comprehensive review of the implementation of the Programme of Action for the Least Developed Countries for the Decade 2001-2010

The General Assembly,

Having considered the report of the preparatory meeting of experts on the midterm comprehensive global review of the implementation of the Programme of Action for the Least Developed Countries for the Decade 2001-2010, held in New York from 5 to 7 September 2006,

Noting with appreciation the contribution made by the least developed countries and their development partners, the organizations of the United Nations system and other intergovernmental organizations, as well as non-governmental organizations, to the process of the midterm review of the Programme of Action,

Adopts the following Declaration:

Declaration of the high-level meeting of the sixty-first session of the General Assembly on the midterm comprehensive global review of the implementation of the Programme of Action for the Least Developed Countries for the Decade 2001-2010

We, Heads of State and Government and heads of delegations participating in the high-level meeting of the General Assembly on the midterm comprehensive global review of the implementation of the Programme of Action for the Least Developed Countries for the Decade 2001-2010, held on 18 and 19 September 2006:

1. Recommit ourselves to meeting the special needs of the least developed countries by making progress towards the goals of poverty eradication, peace and development through the improvement of the quality of lives of people in the least developed countries and the strengthening of their abilities to build a better future for themselves and develop their countries, as committed to in the Programme of Action for the Least Developed Countries for the Decade 2001-2010;

2. Reaffirm that the Programme of Action constitutes a fundamental framework for a strong global partnership whose goal is to accelerate sustained economic growth, sustainable development and poverty eradication in the least developed countries;

3. Also reaffirm that the primary responsibility for development in the least developed countries rests with those countries themselves, but that their efforts need to be given concrete and substantial international support from Governments and international organizations in a spirit of shared responsibility through genuine partnerships, including with civil society and the private sector;

4. Support the smooth transition strategy developed for the graduation of countries from the list of least developed countries and, in this regard, affirm the need for the international community to render necessary support to the graduation of the least developed countries with a view to averting the disruption of their development projects and programmes and allowing them to continue developing;

5. Stress that the internationally agreed development goals, including the Millennium Development Goals, can be effectively achieved in the least developed countries through, in particular, the timely fulfilment of the seven commitments of the Programme of Action;

6. Note that, while the Programme of Action has, since its adoption, registered some progress in its implementation, at the same time the overall socio-economic situation in the least developed countries continues to be precarious;

7. Stress that, given current trends, many least developed countries are unlikely to achieve the goals and objectives set out in the Programme of Action;

8. Emphasize, however, that many least developed countries, with the support of their development partners, have, despite many difficulties, produced notable achievements through wide-ranging and far-reaching reforms;

9. Acknowledge the significant efforts by development partners in the implementation of the Programme of Action, also acknowledge that there is more to be done to implement the Programme of Action, in particular in the area of poverty eradication, and recognize that the situation in the least developed countries requires continued attention;

10. Recognize that it is important to achieve the goals and targets of the Programme of Action in a timely manner and, in this regard, welcome the elaboration of the Cotonou Strategy for the Further Implementation of the Programme of Action for the Least Developed Countries for the Decade 2001-2010 as an initiative owned and led by least developed countries;

11. Welcome the measures taken by developed and developing countries, as well as by multilateral organizations, to promote South-South cooperation and call upon them to continue to enhance their resources and efforts for capacity-building and development in the least developed countries, including the sharing of best practices in the sustainable development of the least developed countries;

12. Call upon the international community and the United Nations system and its agencies to continue to assist in the implementation of the Programme of Action, taking into account the conclusions of the midterm comprehensive global review;

13. Invite the Economic and Social Council to continue to ensure the annual review of the implementation of the Programme of Action, taking into account the concrete and quantifiable achievements produced in the realization of the agreed objectives.

Island developing States

During 2006, UN bodies continued to review progress in the implementation of the Programme of Action for the Sustainable Development of Small Island Developing States (Barbados Programme of Action), adopted at the 1994 Global Conference on the subject [YUN 1994, p. 783]. Member States also reviewed the Mauritius Strategy for Further Implementation of the Programme of Action for the Sustainable Development of Small Island Developing States, adopted by the 2005 International Meeting to Review the Implementation of the 1994 Programme of Action [YUN 2005, p. 946].

Commission on Sustainable Development consideration. In accordance with the decision of its thirteenth (2005) session, the Commission on Sustainable Development devoted one day (9 May) of its fourteenth session (New York, 22 April 2005, 1-12 May) [E/2006/29] to monitoring progress on the implementation of the Programme of Action for the Sustainable Development of Small Island Developing States and the Mauritius Strategy. the review was conducted through three panel-led discussions addressing the Commission's thematic cluster of issues. Panel one reviewed energy efficiency, energy access and the development and expanded use of renewable technologies in small island developing States; Panel two reviewed innovative strategies to enhance industrial development in those States; and Panel three addressed efforts to mitigate air pollution and promote adaptation to climate change in small island developing States.

To assist in the review, the Secretary-General submitted a February report [E/CN.17/2006/7] on the integrated review of the thematic cluster of energy for sustainable development, industrial development, air pollution/atmosphere and climate change in small island developing States. The report stated that small island developing States would continue to tackle the fundamental challenge of managing competing priorities for development with limited resources. The pursuit of innovative financing and new partnerships to meet the challenge would therefore remain a priority. With deep political commitment, small island developing States had expressed the need to strengthen integrated decision-making and implementation to ensure a well-coordinated, multisectoral approach to resilience-building through enhanced energy efficiency, alternative energy and management of pollution, promotion of industrial development and climate-change adaptation. The development and implementation of national sustainable development strategies in small island developing States was an important step in that regard.

Small island developing States continued to focus attention on the strengthening of institutional and human capacities to facilitate vulnerability assessment, energy management, disaster preparedness and mitigation at the national level, supported by action at the regional level. Long-term attention would need to be paid to the development of specialized skills sets in relevant fields, such as climate modeling for small island developing States, disaster management and scientific and technological research for the development of renewable energy sources. The expansion of trade would continue to be the main source of income for small island developing States, and support would be required for diversification strategies, the development of niche markets and the exploration of innovations in industry.

Report of Secretary-General. In an August report [A/61/277], submitted in accordance with General Assembly resolution 60/194 [YUN 2005, p. 949], the Secretary-General described progress made towards the implementation of the Mauritius Strategy for the Further Implementation of the Programme of Action for the Sustainable Development of Small Island Developing States. He reported on the follow-up consultations to strengthen implementation of the Strategy, efforts to strengthen regional infrastructure for doing so, the review conducted by the Commission on Sustainable Development (see above) and the incorporation of small island developing States issues in the UN system.

The Secretary-General concluded that much of the follow-up to the International Meeting had focused on establishing frameworks, setting the foundation and shaping the programmes for effective implementation of the Mauritius Strategy. Small island developing States were poised to pursue implementation of the Mauritius Strategy in a more coordinated fashion, with international community's support. To that end, the UN Department of Economic and Social Affairs (DESA) would work to promote coherent support from the UN system for small island developing States through a strengthened inter-agency consultative process. Attention would also be given to a resource mobilization strategy and the promotion of partnership initiatives. The role played by civil society in the implementation of the Mauritius Strategy needed to be strengthened, and a greater role for the academic communities and the private sector encouraged. Emphasis would be placed on strengthening both technical and institutional capacities in small island developing States. DESA would continue to emphasize the importance of support for the preparation of national sustainable development strategies in all small island developing States as an integral first step towards promoting a well-coordinated, interdisciplinary approach to their sustainable development. Work on the Pacific national sustainable development strategies would continue, and the initiation of a similar project in the Caribbean would be pursued.

Regional meetings. In 2006, three regional meetings to follow up implementation of the Mauritius Strategy were held for the Caribbean (Saint Kitts and Nevis, 5-7 October) [A/61/76-E/2006/51], the Atlantic, Indian Ocean, Mediterranean and South China Seas (Baie Lazare, Seychelles, 26-28 October) [A/61/75-E/2006/49]; and the Pacific (Apia, Samoa, 17-19 October) [A/61/72-E/2006/54].

GENERAL ASSEMBLY ACTION

On 20 December [meeting 83], the General Assembly, on the recommendation of the Second Committee [A/61/422/Add.2], adopted **resolution 61/196** without vote [agenda item 53 *(b)*].

Follow-up to and implementation of the Mauritius Strategy for the Further Implementation of the Programme of Action for the Sustainable Development of Small Island Developing States

The General Assembly,

Reaffirming the Declaration of Barbados and the Programme of Action for the Sustainable Development of Small Island Developing States, adopted by the Global Conference on the Sustainable Development of Small Island Developing States, and recalling its resolution 49/122 of 19 December 1994 on the Global Conference,

Reaffirming also the Mauritius Declaration and the Mauritius Strategy for the Further Implementation of the Programme of Action for the Sustainable Development of Small Island Developing States ("Mauritius Strategy for Implementation"), adopted by the International Meeting to Review the Implementation of the Programme of Action for the Sustainable Development of Small Island Developing States on 14 January 2005, and recalling its resolutions 59/311 of 14 July 2005 and 60/194 of 22 December 2005,

Recalling the 2005 World Summit Outcome,

Welcoming the decision taken by the Commission on Sustainable Development at its thirteenth session to devote one day of its review sessions to the review of the implementation of the Mauritius Strategy for Implementation, focusing on that year's thematic cluster, as well as on any new developments in the sustainable development efforts of small island developing States using existing modalities, and to request the Secretary-General to submit a report to the Commission at its review session on progress in and obstacles to sustainable development in small island developing States, including recommendations to enhance the implementation of the Mauritius Strategy for Implementation,

Recognizing the urgent need to mobilize resources from all sources for the effective implementation of the Mauritius Strategy for Implementation,

1. *Takes note* of the report of the Secretary-General;

2. *Welcomes* the renewed commitment of the international community to the implementation of the Programme of Action for the Sustainable Development of Small Island Developing States;

3. *Urges* Governments and all relevant international and regional organizations, United Nations funds, programmes, specialized agencies and regional commissions, international financial institutions and the Global Environment Facility, as well as other intergovernmental organizations and major groups, to take timely action for the effective implementation of and follow-up to the Mauritius Declaration and the Mauritius Strategy for Implementation, including the further development

and operationalization of concrete projects and programmes;

4. *Calls for* the full and effective implementation of the commitments, programmes and targets adopted at the International Meeting to Review the Implementation of the Programme of Action for the Sustainable Development of Small Island Developing States and, to this end, for the fulfilment of the provisions for the means of implementation, as contained in the Mauritius Strategy for Implementation, and encourages small island developing States and their development partners to continue to consult widely in order to develop further concrete projects and programmes for the implementation of the Mauritius Strategy for Implementation;

5. *Invites* the Commission on Sustainable Development to devote one half day of its Intergovernmental Preparatory Meeting to discussing policy options for addressing the barriers and constraints facing small island developing States in the four thematic areas of the session, taking into account the review of the implementation of the Mauritius Strategy for Implementation conducted during the fourteenth session of the Commission;

6. *Encourages* the implementation of partnership initiatives, within the framework of the Mauritius Strategy for Implementation, in support of the sustainable development of small island developing States;

7. *Reiterates its request* to the Secretary-General to strengthen the Small Island Developing States Unit of the Department of Economic and Social Affairs of the Secretariat, as called for in its resolutions 57/262 of 20 December 2002, 58/213 A of 23 December 2003, 59/229 of 22 December 2004, 59/311 and 60/194, and urges the Secretary-General to ensure that the Unit is sufficiently and sustainably staffed without delay to undertake its broad range of mandated functions with a view to facilitating the full and effective implementation of the Mauritius Strategy for Implementation, within existing resources, including by redeploying resources;

8. *Calls for* the provision of new and additional voluntary resources for the revitalization of the Small Island Developing States Information Network;

9. *Requests* the relevant agencies of the United Nations system, within their respective mandates, to mainstream the Mauritius Strategy for Implementation in their work programmes and to establish a focal point for matters related to small island developing States within their respective secretariats;

10. *Requests* the Secretary-General to submit a report to the General Assembly at its sixty-second session on the follow-up to and implementation of the Mauritius Strategy for Implementation;

11. *Decides* to include in the provisional agenda of its sixty-second session, under the item entitled "Sustainable development", the sub-item entitled "Follow-up to and implementation of the Mauritius Strategy for the Further Implementation of the Programme of Action for the Sustainable Development of Small Island Developing States".

Landlocked developing countries

Report of Secretary-General. In response to General Assembly resolution 60/208 [YUN 2005, p. 951], the Secretary-General submitted a September report [A/61/302] on the progress made in the implementation of the Almaty Programme of Action: Addressing the Special Needs of Landlocked Developing Countries within a New Global Framework for Transit Transport Cooperation for Landlocked and Transit Developing Countries. The Programme of Action was adopted by the International Ministerial Conference of Landlocked and Transit Developing Countries and Donor Countries and International Financial and Development Institutions on Transit Transport Cooperation in 2003 [YUN 2003, p. 875].

The report analysed the overall socio-economic situation in landlocked developing countries and action taken to implement the Almaty Programme of Action in the priority areas of fundamental transit policy issues, infrastructure development and maintenance, international trade and trade facilitation, international support measures and implementation and review of the United Nations.

The report concluded that the high cost of international trade was a serious constraint to trade and economic development of landlocked developing countries. Because they depended on their transit neighbours for access to and from the sea, efficient transit systems required closer and effective cooperation and collaboration between those countries and their transit neighbours. In that context, regional economic integration efforts and subregional and bilateral transit cooperation agreements played a critical role in establishing efficient transit transport systems, and the role of regional and subregional organizations should be further strengthened to monitor and review implementation of the Almaty Programme of Action. The UN Office of the High Representative for the Least Developed Countries, Landlocked Developing Countries and Small Island Developing States should strengthen its cooperation with those organizations. The international community should provide greater market access for goods originating in landlocked developing countries in order to mitigate high trade transaction costs stemming from their geographical disadvantages. Donor countries and international financial and development institutions were invited to make voluntary contributions to the trust fund established to facilitate the follow-up to the implementation of the outcome of the Almaty International Ministerial Conference.

Communications. On 6 July [A/61/126], Azerbaijan, Georgia and Turkey informed the Secretary-General of the inauguration of the Baku-

Tbilisi-Ceyhan (BTC) main pipeline for the export of crude oil, which was scheduled to take place on 13 July in Ceyhan, Turkey. The recent joining of Kazakhstan to the BTC project fostered cooperation between the landlocked States of Azerbaijan and Kazakhstan, on the one hand, and the transit States of Georgia and Turkey, on the other. On 25 July [A/61/181], Azerbaijan transmitted to the Secretary-General a communiqué from its Ministry of Foreign Affairs on the global energy issues adopted at the Group of Eight Summit (St. Petersburg, Russian Federation,15-17 July).

On 10 August [A/60/977], Armenia complained against efforts by Turkey and Azerbaijan to connect the two countries via Georgia in circumvention of the extensive network of railroads in the region.

On 28 September [A/61/486], South Africa transmitted to the Secretary-General the ministerial statement adopted at the thirtieth annual meeting of ministers of foreign affairs of the Group of 77 developing nations and China (New York, 22 September), in which the ministers stressed the importance of the full implementation of the Almaty Programme of Action and noted the convening of the first summit meeting of landlocked developing countries (Havana, Cuba, 14 September).

On 4 October [A/C.2/61/3], the Lao People's Democratic Republic transmitted to the Secretary-General the Declaration adopted at the Meeting of Heads of State or Government of the Group of Landlocked Developing Countries (Havana, Cuba, 14 September), which called on the UN system and other international organizations to redouble efforts to assist landlocked and transit developing countries in implementing the Almaty Programme of Action. It also called for a mid-term review of the Programme of Action in 2008, to be preceded by thematic and regional or subregional reviews.

GENERAL ASSEMBLY ACTION

On 20 December [meeting 83], the General Assembly, on the recommendation of the Second Committee [A/61/425/Add.2], adopted **resolution 61/212** without vote [agenda item 56 *(b)*].

Groups of countries in special situations: specific actions related to the particular needs and problems of landlocked developing countries: outcome of the International Ministerial Conference of Landlocked and Transit Developing Countries and Donor Countries and International Financial and Development Institutions on Transit Transport Cooperation

The General Assembly,

Recalling its resolutions 58/201 of 23 December 2003 and 60/208 of 22 December 2005,

Recalling also the United Nations Millennium Declaration and the 2005 World Summit Outcome,

Taking note of the Declaration of the Heads of State or Government of Landlocked Developing Countries,

Recalling the Asunción Platform for the Doha Development Round,

Recognizing that the lack of territorial access to the sea, aggravated by remoteness from world markets, and prohibitive transit costs and risks continue to impose serious constraints on export earnings, private capital inflow and domestic resource mobilization of landlocked developing countries and therefore adversely affect their overall growth and socio-economic development,

Expressing support to those landlocked developing countries that are emerging from conflict, with a view to enabling them to rehabilitate and reconstruct, as appropriate, political, social and economic infrastructure and to assisting them in achieving their development priorities in accordance with the goals and targets of the Almaty Programme of Action: Addressing the Special Needs of Landlocked Developing Countries within a New Global Framework for Transit Transport Cooperation for Landlocked and Transit Developing Countries,

Recalling the New Partnership for Africa's Development, an initiative for accelerating regional economic cooperation and development, as many landlocked and transit developing countries are located in Africa,

Welcoming the convening of the Economic and Social Commission for Asia and the Pacific Ministerial Conference on Transport, held in Busan, Republic of Korea, on 10 and 11 November 2006, which adopted the Busan Declaration on Transport Development in Asia and the Pacific,

1. *Takes note* of the report of the Secretary-General on the implementation of the Almaty Programme of Action: Addressing the Special Needs of Landlocked Developing Countries within a New Global Framework for Transit Transport Cooperation for Landlocked and Transit Developing Countries;

2. *Reaffirms* the right of access of landlocked countries to and from the sea and freedom of transit through the territory of transit countries by all means of transport, in accordance with the applicable rules of international law;

3. *Also reaffirms* that transit countries, in the exercise of their full sovereignty over their territory, have the right to take all measures necessary to ensure that the rights and facilities provided for landlocked countries in no way infringe their legitimate interests;

4. *Encourages* donor countries and multilateral and regional financial and development institutions, in particular the World Bank, the Asian Development Bank, the African Development Bank and the Inter-American Development Bank, to provide landlocked and transit developing countries with appropriate technical and financial assistance in the form of grants or concessionary loans for the implementation of the five priorities outlined in the Almaty Programme of Action, in particular for the construction, maintenance and improvement of their transport, storage and other transit-related facili-

ties, including alternative routes and improved communications, to promote subregional, regional and interregional projects and programmes;

5. *Reaffirms* the importance of trade and trade facilitation as one of the priorities of the Almaty Programme of Action, and calls for the early resumption and successful development-oriented outcome of the Doha Round of trade negotiations, adhering fully to the agreed mandate in the Doha Ministerial Declaration, the framework adopted by the General Council of the World Trade Organization in its decision of 1 August 2004 and the Hong Kong Ministerial Declaration;

6. *Emphasizes* that assistance for the improvement of transit transport facilities and services should be integrated into the overall economic development strategies of the landlocked and transit developing countries and that donor countries should consequently take into account the requirements for the long-term restructuring of the economies of the landlocked developing countries;

7. *Recalls* that landlocked and transit developing countries have the primary responsibility for implementing the Almaty Programme of Action, as envisaged in its paragraphs 38 and 38 bis;

8. *Emphasizes* that South-South cooperation and triangular cooperation with the involvement of donors should be further promoted, as well as cooperation among subregional and regional organizations;

9. *Calls upon* the relevant organizations of the United Nations system and other international organizations, including the regional commissions, the United Nations Development Programme, the United Nations Conference on Trade and Development, the World Bank, the World Customs Organization, the World Trade Organization and the International Maritime Organization, to integrate the Almaty Programme of Action into their relevant programmes of work, and encourages them to continue their support to the landlocked and transit developing countries, inter alia, through well-coordinated and coherent technical assistance programmes in transit transport;

10. *Requests* the Office of the High Representative for the Least Developed Countries, Landlocked Developing Countries and Small Island Developing States, in accordance with the mandate given by the General Assembly in its resolution 56/227 of 24 December 2001 and in the Almaty Programme of Action and the Almaty Declaration, to continue its cooperation and coordination with organizations within the United Nations system, particularly those engaged in operational activities on the ground in landlocked and transit developing countries, to ensure effective implementation of the Almaty Programme of Action in line with Assembly resolution 57/270 B of 23 June 2003, and also requests the Office to intensify the efforts to establish effective indicators to measure the progress in the implementation of the Almaty Programme of Action, in close cooperation with relevant organizations;

11. *Decides* to hold a midterm review meeting of the Almaty Programme of Action in 2008, in accordance with paragraph 49 of the Almaty Programme of Action; the review should be preceded, where necessary, by national, subregional, regional and substantive preparations in a most effective, well-structured and broad participatory manner and should be organized within existing resources; intergovernmental mechanisms at the global and regional levels, including those of United Nations regional commissions, as well as relevant substantive material and statistical data, should be effectively utilized in the review process; also in accordance with paragraph 49, the Office of the High Representative should coordinate the preparatory process and United Nations system organizations, including the United Nations Conference on Trade and Development, the United Nations Development Programme, the regional commissions and relevant international and regional organizations, within their respective mandates, should provide necessary support to the review process;

12. *Encourages* donor countries and the international financial and development institutions as well as private entities to make voluntary contributions to the trust fund established by the Secretary-General to support the activities related to the follow-up to the implementation of the outcome of the Almaty International Ministerial Conference;

13. *Decides* to include in the provisional agenda of its sixty-second session the item entitled "Specific actions related to the particular needs and problems of landlocked developing countries: outcome of the International Ministerial Conference of Landlocked and Transit Developing Countries and Donor Countries and International Financial and Development Institutions on Transit Transport Cooperation";

14. *Requests* the Secretary-General to submit to the General Assembly at its sixty-second session a report on progress made in the preparation for the midterm review meeting.

Economies in transition

In response to General Assembly resolution 59/243 [YUN 2004, p. 863], the Secretary-General submitted an August report [A/61/269] on progress made in integrating the economies in transition into the world economic system during 2004-2005. The report examined the advances made in integration through trade in goods and services, capital flows and labour migration, focusing in particular on the role that the enlargement of the European Union (EU) had played in the progress of some countries. The report discussed advances in restructuring the markets of economies in transition and in building market-support institutions. It described the major economic trends and indicators of trade and financial integration, and progress in policy and institutional reforms undertaken by the economies in transition in support of their integration into the world economy.

The report concluded that the progress economies in transition had made in integrating their markets into the global economy had been greatly helped by favourable conditions, such as growing world trade, high commodity prices and the low cost of international finance. At the same time, that progress was achieved in a more stable and predictable political and economic environment, underpinned by prudent fiscal policy and a stable monetary stance in several countries of the region. Against that background, some economies had moved ahead with reforms, creating the institutions needed for an effectively functioning market economy. The pace and pattern of that integration varied widely across countries. While the resource-rich countries, particularly in the Commonwealth of Independent States benefited from high commodity prices, their growth performance remained vulnerable to the volatility in world commodity prices.

The report noted that most Central and Eastern European countries were integrated in producer-driven trade networks in high value added sectors, such as the automotive industry, electronics and information technology. South-Eastern Europe was, however, integrated in buyer-driven trade networks in low value added sectors such as textiles, clothing and agriculture. Further integration of the capital markets of transition economies led to strong credit growth, both in the new EU members and in South-Eastern Europe. The macroeconomic policies of the new EU members were anchored to the adoption of the single currency as a further step in economic integration, together with fostering growth in order to sustain real convergences and creating employment. In the short run, however, fast adoption of the euro might lead to a slowdown of GDP growth and loss of income, both before and after adoption. Rapid fiscal consolidation of those countries would require austerity measures, including cuts in social spending and forfeited public investment.

GENERAL ASSEMBLY ACTION

On 20 December [meeting 83], the General Assembly, on the recommendation of the Second Committee [A/61/425/Add.5], adopted **resolution 61/210** without vote [agenda item 55 *(e)*].

Integration of the economies in transition into the world economy

The General Assembly,

Recalling its resolutions 47/187 of 22 December 1992, 48/181 of 21 December 1993, 49/106 of 19 December 1994, 51/175 of 6 December 1996, 53/179 of 15 December 1998, 55/191 of 20 December 2000, 57/247 of 20 December 2002 and 59/243 of 22 December 2004,

Recalling also the 2005 World Summit Outcome and relevant General Assembly resolutions adopted at the sixtieth session which contain provisions on addressing the special needs of the countries with economies in transition,

Reaffirming the need for the full integration of the countries with economies in transition into the world economy, and in this regard stressing the importance of ensuring a conducive national and international environment,

Noting that some of those countries have evolved from the status of economies in transition into functioning market economies,

Noting also that in some economies in transition this progress has been slower, resulting in lower aggregate development levels and lower per capita income,

Taking into account the fact that, despite some progress in the fight against poverty, its level is still high in many countries with economies in transition, particularly in the rural areas,

Stressing the importance of continued international assistance to countries with economies in transition to support their efforts towards market-oriented reforms, institution-building, infrastructure development and achieving macroeconomic and financial stability and economic growth, and to ensure that they are fully integrated into the world economy,

Recognizing, in particular, the need to enhance the capacity of those countries to utilize effectively the benefits of globalization, including those in the field of information and communication technologies, and to respond more adequately to its challenges,

Recognizing also the role that the private sector plays in the socio-economic development of those countries and their integration into the world economy, and stressing the importance of continuing efforts to create a favourable environment for private investment and entrepreneurship,

Recognizing further the continuing need for favourable conditions for market access of exports from countries with economies in transition, in accordance with multilateral trade agreements,

Recognizing the important role that foreign direct investment can play in those countries, and stressing the need to create an enabling environment, both domestically and internationally, to attract more foreign direct investment to those countries,

Taking note of the report of the Secretary-General,

1. *Welcomes* the measures taken by the organizations of the United Nations system to implement General Assembly resolutions on the integration of the economies in transition into the world economy;

2. *Calls upon* the organizations of the United Nations system, including the regional commissions, and invites the Bretton Woods institutions, in collaboration with relevant non-United Nations multilateral and regional institutions, to continue to conduct analytical activities and provide policy advice and targeted and substantial technical assistance to the Governments of the countries with economies in transition aimed at strengthening

the social, legal and political framework for completing market-oriented reforms, supporting national development priorities with a view to sustaining the positive trends and reversing any declines in the economic and social development of those countries;

3. *Emphasizes* in this regard the importance of the further integration of the countries with economies in transition into the world economy, taking into account, inter alia, the relevant provisions of the Monterrey Consensus of the International Conference on Financing for Development, the Johannesburg Declaration on Sustainable Development and the Plan of Implementation of the World Summit on Sustainable Development ("Johannesburg Plan of Implementation");

4. *Stresses* the need to focus international assistance, while supporting and complementing domestic efforts and resources, on those countries with economies in transition facing particular difficulties in socio-economic development, implementing market-oriented reforms and meeting internationally agreed development goals, including the Millennium Development Goals;

5. *Welcomes* the efforts and progress made by countries with economies in transition in implementing policies that promote sustained economic growth and sustainable development, including, inter alia, by promoting competition, regulatory reform, good governance and the rule of law, the fight against corruption, respect for property rights and expeditious contract enforcement, and calls upon the United Nations system, and invites the Bretton Woods institutions, to highlight the successful models as good practices;

6. *Also welcomes*, in this regard, efforts made by countries with economies in transition to improve governance and institutional capabilities, which contribute to using aid more effectively;

7. *Encourages* the countries with economies in transition to continue implementing and, where appropriate, to improve measures to sustain and advance the positive trends mentioned above;

8. *Welcomes* the aspiration of the countries with economies in transition to the further development of regional, subregional and interregional cooperation, and invites the United Nations system to enhance dialogue with and increase support to the regional and subregional cooperation organizations whose membership includes countries with economies in transition and whose efforts include assisting their members to fully integrate into the world economy;

9. *Reaffirms* the commitment to broaden and strengthen the participation of developing countries and countries with economies in transition in international economic decision-making and norm-setting, and to that end stresses the importance of continuing efforts to reform the international financial architecture;

10. *Recognizes* the importance of infrastructure development for diversifying the economies of the countries with economies in transition, and for enhancing their competitiveness and increasing their gains from trade, and encourages Member States, the United Nations and other relevant stakeholders to support such infrastructure development efforts in this regard;

11. *Reaffirms* the commitment to work to accelerate and facilitate the accession of developing countries and countries with economies in transition to the World Trade Organization, consistent with its criteria, recognizing the importance of universal integration in the rules-based global trading system;

12. *Requests* the Secretary-General to prepare, in close consultation with the countries with economies in transition, a report on the implementation of the present resolution containing, inter alia, substantial recommendations, including on the strengthening of cooperation between the United Nations system and those countries, and to submit the report to the General Assembly at its sixty-third session.

Poor mountain countries

The Commission on Sustainable Development, at its fourteenth session (New York, 22 April 2005, 1-12 May) [E/2006/29], considered an April report [E/CN.17/2006/12] on the Mountain Partnership: activities and achievements. The Mountain Partnership, originally known as the International Partnership for Sustainable Development in Mountain Regions, was a multistakeholder, voluntary alliance dedicated to improving the well-being, livelihoods and opportunities of mountain people and the protection and stewardship of mountain environments around the world. Launched in 2002 at the World Summit on Sustainable Development [YUN 2002, p. 821], its membership comprised over 130 member organizations and Governments.

Chapter II

Operational activities for development

In 2006, the UN system provided development assistance to developing countries and those with economies in transition, mainly through the United Nations Development Programme (UNDP), the central UN funding body for technical assistance. UNDP income remained unchanged from 2005, at $5.1 billion. Total expenditure for all programme activities and support costs in 2006 was $4.8 billion, compared to $4.4 billion the previous year. Technical cooperation funded through other sources included $48.7 million provided through the programme executed by the UN Department of Economic and Social Affairs, $191.2 million through the United Nations Fund for International Partnerships (UNFIP), and $25.6 million through the United Nations Capital Development Fund (UNCDF).

In 2006, UNFIP and the United Nations Democracy Fund were consolidated with Partnership Advisory Services and Outreach to form the United Nations Office for Partnerships. The Office served as a gateway for new alliances and partnerships for the UN system to work more effectively with the private sector and civil society.

The Secretary-General, in April, reported on progress in the implementation of General Assembly resolution 59/250 on the 2004 triennial comprehensive policy review of operational activities for development of the UN system. The report contained a matrix of steps taken and the results of specific actions against benchmarks and targets for the UN system as a whole. The Secretary-General recommended that the Economic and Social Council use the assessment of progress to lay out guidelines for the 2007 triennial comprehensive policy review. In July, the Council asked him to focus the analysis for the 2007 policy review within the context of the implementation of the Millennium Development Goals.

Project delivery by the United Nations Office for Project Services (UNOPS) dropped to $706 million, 9.7 per cent less than the projected figure for the year. In May, the Secretary-General appointed Jan Mattson (Sweden) as UNOPS Executive Director. In line with reform measures proposed in the 2005 action plan to restore UNOPS financial viability, the Office relocated its headquarters to Copenhagen, Denmark, which became operational on 1 July.

In 2006, 7,623 volunteers working for the UNDP-administered United Nations Volunteers programme carried out 7,856 assignments in 144 countries.

In March, the UNDP Administrator reported on the implementation of the third cooperation framework for South-South cooperation (2005-2007), which was endorsed by the UNDP/United Nations Population Fund (UNFPA) Executive Board in 2005. In June, the Board requested UNDP to further emphasize the Programme's multi-year funding framework driver of development effectiveness dealing with South-South solutions and to promote its further impact.

UNCDF completed a strategic review of its 2005-2007 business plan and used its conclusions to prepare a detailed investment plan for the 2006-2007 period. Consistent with UN reform initiatives, UNCDF continued to decentralize its operations and improve its efficiency and effectiveness. By April, the streamlining of UNCDF headquarters to focus on strategic functions and management was largely completed. In June, the UNDP/UNFPA Executive Board asked the UNDP Administrator and the UNCDF Executive Secretary to finalize the strategic agreement between the two bodies, setting forth the key elements of their strategic, operational and financial partnership.

System-wide activities

Operational activities segment of Economic and Social Council

The Economic and Social Council, during its 2006 substantive session [A/61/3/Rev.1], and as decided on 10 February (**decision 2006/210**), considered the question of operational activities of the United Nations for international development cooperation at meetings from 11 to 13 and 26 July. On 22 March (**decision 2006/215**), the Council decided to devote the work of the operational activities segment to examining those activities in order to evaluate the implementation of General Assembly resolution 59/250 [YUN 2004, p. 868] on the 2004 triennial comprehensive policy review of operational activities for development of the UN system, with a view to ensuring its full implementation, including through a comprehensive review of trends and perspectives in funding for development cooperation. In that context, the Council applied Assembly decision 60/547 [YUN 2005, p. 958]. It also held discussions on the follow-up to policy recommendations of the Assembly and the Council, and the reports of the Executive Boards of the United Nations Development Programme (UNDP)/United Nations Population Fund (UNFPA), the United Nations Children's Fund (UNICEF) and the World Food Programme (WFP).

Among the documents before the Council were reports of the Secretary-General on the comprehensive statistical data on operational activities for development for 2004 [A/61/77-E/2006/59], funding options and modalities for financing operational activities for development of the UN system [YUN 2005, p. 956] and progress in the implementation of resolution 59/250 [E/2006/58], as well as a note by the Secretary-General on the review of trends and perspectives in funding for development, 2006 [E/2006/60] (see sections below).

On 11 and 12 July respectively, the Council held panel discussions on the comprehensive review of trends and perspectives in funding for development cooperation and, with the UN country team from Indonesia, on the role of UN development cooperation in pursuit of employment creation and decent work: results, coherence and system-wide support through the United Nations Development Assistance Framework (UNDAF). It also held a dialogue with heads of UN funds and programmes on the reports of all the Executive Boards.

Implementation of resolution 59/250

In April [E/2006/58], the Secretary-General reported on progress in the implementation of General Assembly resolution 59/250 [YUN 2004, p. 868]. The report highlighted the UN development system's actions to integrate activities with national plans and priorities to ensure greater national ownership over assistance provided by the UN system, strengthen support to national capacity-building, increase the UN system capacity to contribute to development results and pursue UN development system reform. The report also contained a matrix, outlining the steps taken and results of specific actions against benchmarks and targets set for the UN system as a whole. The elements of the matrix followed the structure and sequence of the 12 sections of resolution 59/250. A comprehensive analysis of the implementation of the resolution would be submitted to the Assembly in 2007 in the context of the triennial comprehensive policy review.

The Secretary-General reported that UNDAFS with harmonized programme cycles had been completed in 83 countries at the end of 2005. System-wide coherence was being strengthened, particularly by strengthening country-level coordination systems, and the linkages between the normative work and UN system operational activities, and by tightly managing entities dealing with development, humanitarian assistance and the environment. Some UN country teams supported government coordination for planning and tracking progress on overall support for transition from recovery to development. The UN Office for the Coordination of Humanitarian Affairs and the United Nations Development Group (UNDG) member organizations developed a joint programme for coordination during the transition phase from relief to development. The UNDG working group on capacity development formulated operational guidance for UN country teams on increasing the effectiveness of their support to national capacity development. While efforts to foster teamwork among UN system organizations were recognized, their participation in country-level activities and coordination mechanisms still differed in level and quality, and in some cases was inadequate. For non-resident agencies, a wide range of tools and mechanisms were employed to promote their participation in country development work, but there were constraints due to insufficient capacity to respond to requests for participation and insufficient staffing of resident coordinators' offices. In keeping with efforts to build a more unified United Nations, members of the Executive Committee for Economic and Social Affairs organized their policy development and analytical work around strategic objectives and strengthened linkages with the operational work of the UN system through close collaboration with UNDG and the Executive Committee.

Regarding the reform of the UN development system, the Secretary-General said that harmonization measures should be associated with tangible achievements in terms of actual simplification of processes and a significant reduction in the administrative and procedural burdens on organizations and their national partners. UN funds and programmes were discussing with their Executive Boards the simplification of their country programming arrangements. The harmonization and simplification of rules and procedures throughout the UN system were critical to rationalizing the country presence of UN organizations. The model joint office presented the most integrated and efficient use of resources; the first pilot joint office in Cape Verde was established in January and additional pilots were being developed for different country situations.

Joint programmes were encouraged, and in early 2006 more than 160 such programmes were reported. However, the differing cost recovery rates and methods used in the UN system were causing unnecessary confusion among stakeholders and delays in the development of joint programmes, as well as problems in the participation of UN organizations in multi-donor trust funds.

Continuous review of the progress of reform was crucial to improving the efficiency and effectiveness of the UN development system. Country teams were conducting common annual reviews of progress towards the expected results defined in the UNDAF results matrix, and joint evaluations of total UN system contributions to development at the country level were planned by members of the United Nations Evaluation Group.

The Secretary-General recommended, among other things, that the Economic and Social Council use the assessment of progress achieved in the implementation of resolution 59/250 in 2006 to lay out broad guidelines for the 2007 triennial comprehensive policy review, emphasizing areas on which the report on the review should focus. The Council should request the Secretary-General, in assessing the implementation of resolution 59/250 in preparation for the review, to take into account the relevant intergovernmental decisions made in the context of the follow-up to the 2005 World Summit Outcome, adopted by the Assembly in resolution 60/1 [YUN 2005, p. 48]. The Council should stress that UN system support to national capacity development be designed to strengthen national ownership and leadership over external assistance and aid coordination, particularly in the context of new aid modalities, including sector-wide approaches and general budget support, and should call for more systematic UN capacity development efforts to support national development strategies and for strengthening arrangements to facilitate country participation in development work.

The Secretary-General, in a May note [E/2006/60], reviewed trends and perspectives in funding for development cooperation, as well as those of bilateral official development assistance (ODA). The report discussed funding of UN development cooperation, the role of multilateral and regional development banks and global funds, innovative sources of financing for development, South-South cooperation and financing from private grants.

According to the report, ODA for development programmes and projects, excluding debt relief and emergency aid, recorded the largest increase in many years, marking the reversal of a declining trend that began in 1985. However, ODA forecast still fell short of the $150 billion needed to meet the Millennium Development Goals (MDGS) [YUN 2000, p. 51]. Overall, the share of ODA contributions to the UN development system was between 13 and 14 per cent over the past five years, as against 9 per cent in the early 1990s. That positive trend should, however, be interpreted with caution as the increase was mostly due to supplementary funding. Meanwhile, core resources did not grow significantly over the period 1993-2003, and in 2004 were only 70 per cent of other resources; even the dollar amount of core resources fell. Such a trend would have significant implications for the funding of the UN system if it were to continue. In addition to multilateral development banks, which focused on middle-income countries, whose combined net flows surpassed those of the World Bank, global funds constituted a growing source of financing for development cooperation. Pledges by the International Development Association increased from $23 billion in 2002-2005 to $33 billion in 2005-2008. Global funds were particularly successful in mobilizing significant additional resources to address worldwide socio-economic challenges. Innovative financing mechanisms were another potential source of financing for development cooperation. At the international conference on "solidarity and globalization" (Paris, 28 February–1 March), 13 countries agreed to initiate procedures to levy a tax on airline tickets to fund the fight against HIV/AIDS, tuberculosis and malaria. Another 25 countries pledged to contribute funds in lieu of the tax to a central account created for the proceeds from that tax. A proposal to establish a new global fund, the international drug purchase facility, was also reviewed at the conference. Another proposal was the International Finance Facility, launched in the context of a pilot project on immunization, to raise $4 billion over ten years.

Private grants, which included private foundation expenditures and corporate donations, were also a source of financing for development.

ECONOMIC AND SOCIAL COUNCIL ACTION

On 26 July [meeting 40], the Economic and Social Council adopted **resolution 2006/14** [draft: E/2006/L.28, orally corrected] without vote [agenda item 3 *(a)*].

Progress in the implementation of General Assembly resolution 59/250 on the triennial comprehensive policy review of operational activities for development of the United Nations system

The Economic and Social Council,

Recalling General Assembly resolution 59/250 of 22 December 2004 on the triennial comprehensive policy review of operational activities for development of the United Nations system,

Recalling also its resolution 2005/7 of 20 July 2005,

Emphasizing the importance of the triennial comprehensive policy review of operational activities for development, through which the General Assembly establishes key system-wide policy orientations for the development cooperation and country-level modalities of the United Nations system,

Reaffirming its role in providing coordination and guidance to the United Nations development system to ensure that those policy orientations are implemented on a system-wide basis, in accordance with General Assembly resolutions 48/162 of 20 December 1993, 50/227 of 24 May 1996 and 57/270 B of 23 June 2003,

Reaffirming also that the fundamental characteristics of operational activities for development of the United Nations system should be, inter alia, their universal, voluntary and grant-based nature, their neutrality and their multilateralism, as well as their ability to respond to the development needs of recipient countries in a flexible manner, and that operational activities are carried out for the benefit of recipient countries, at the request of those countries and in accordance with their own policies and priorities for development,

Stressing that the purpose of reform is to make the United Nations development system more efficient and effective in supporting developing countries in their efforts to achieve the internationally agreed development goals, on the basis of their national development strategies, and stressing also that reform should enhance organizational efficiency and achieve concrete development results,

Emphasizing that operational activities for development of the United Nations system should be valued and assessed on the basis of their impact on recipient countries as contributions to enhance their capacity to pursue poverty eradication, sustained economic growth and sustainable development,

1. *Takes note* of the report of the Secretary-General;

Funding of operational activities for development of the United Nations system

2. *Also takes note* of the report of the Secretary-General on the funding options and modalities for financing operational activities for development of the United Nations system;

3. *Recognizes* the importance of further considering funding options and modalities for financing the operational activities for development of the United Nations system, with the aim of generating, on a voluntary basis, adequate resources including core resources, and increasing the reliability and predictability thereof to achieve the internationally agreed development goals, including the Millennium Development Goals;

4. *Stresses* that increased funding to achieve the internationally agreed development goals, including the Millennium Development Goals, should be combined with higher quality and better delivery of aid, simplified and harmonized operational processes, reduced transactions costs, more effective use of resources and enhanced national ownership;

5. *Emphasizes* that increasing financial contributions to the United Nations development system is key to achieving the Millennium Development Goals, and in that regard recognizes the mutually reinforcing links between increased effectiveness, efficiency and coherence of the United Nations development system, achieving concrete results in assisting developing countries in eradicating poverty and achieving sustained economic growth and sustainable development through operational activities for development and the overall resourcing of the United Nations development system;

6. *Stresses* that core resources, because of their untied nature, continue to be the bedrock of the operational activities for development of the United Nations system, and in that regard notes that the overall increase in core resources has not been sustained and that the overall volume of core resources fell in 2004 in some parts of the system, and also notes that some targets of the multi-year funding frameworks and strategies of the United Nations funds and programmes and the specialized agencies have not been met;

7. *Notes* that the increased use of restrictively earmarked non-core resources reduces the influence of the governing bodies and can lead to the fragmentation of operational activities for development of the United Nations system and can thus constrain their effectiveness;

8. *Also notes* the establishment of the thematic trust funds linked to agency-specific funding frameworks and strategies established by the respective governing bodies as a funding modality complementary to core resources, while recognizing that non-core resources are not a substitute for core resources and that unearmarked contributions are vital for the coherence and harmonization of the operational activities for development;

9. *Requests* the Secretary-General, in consultation with the United Nations Development Group, to provide, in view of the preparations for the 2007 triennial comprehensive policy review, a consolidated overview of the biennial costs of the resident coordinator function and its current funding mechanisms;

10. *Takes note* of the report of the Secretary-General on the comprehensive statistical data on operational activities for development for 2004, as well as the note by the Secretary-General on the review of trends and perspectives in funding for development cooperation;

11. *Requests* the Secretary-General, in order to enhance understanding of funding trends in the United Nations development system and humanitarian field, to further refine data contained in that report, with a view to promoting a concerted effort by entities of the United Nations system to standardize data and statistical practices that reflect funding for operational activities for development, including a better distinction between funding for humanitarian assistance and for long-term development cooperation channelled through the funds, programmes and specialized agencies of the United Nations system and the Secretariat, in collaboration with organizations repository of relevant information and statistics, as appropriate;

12. *Notes* the importance of enhancing the predictability, sustainability and increase of funding, in this context notes the introduction by most United Nations funds, programmes and organizations of multi-year funding frameworks and strategies, and requests the Secretary-General, in view of the 2007 triennial comprehensive policy review, to provide information on the status of the use, efficiency and harmonization of those instruments;

National capacity-building

13. *Stresses* that developing countries, in their efforts to meet the internationally agreed development goals, including the Millennium Development Goals, should be supported by the United Nations system in the development and enhancement of their national capacities consistent with their needs, with the aim of strengthening national ownership and leadership over external assistance and aid coordination in support of their national development strategies, including further strengthening of their capacity to utilize effectively the various aid modalities, including system-wide approaches and budget support;

14. *Also stresses* the need for a systematic and comprehensive United Nations capacity-building effort that would support the preparation and implementation of national development strategies, which should benefit from strengthened linkages between the normative work of the United Nations system and its operational activities;

15. *Notes* the establishment of a United Nations Development Group working group on capacity development, and in this regard looks forward to the improvements in the effectiveness of United Nations country teams in enhancing capacity-building and national ownership of the development process by developing countries, while expressing concern about the poor quality of reporting by the United Nations system on measures and results of the efforts to address the sustainability of capacity-building, relating in particular to the use of national execution, national expertise and technologies, and in that regard requests the Secretary-General to report on progress made using existing reporting mechanisms;

16. *Reiterates* that the United Nations development system should use, to the fullest extent possible, national execution and available national expertise and technologies as the norm in the implementation of operational activities, and in this context notes the decisions by some governing bodies of the United Nations funds and programmes to strengthen the implementation modalities of national execution;

17. *Notes* the various activities undertaken by the United Nations development system to strengthen capacity-building of developing countries, but recognizes that developing countries, in order to meet the internationally agreed development goals, including the Millennium Development Goals, should have access to new and emerging technologies, including information and communication technologies, which requires technology transfer, technical cooperation and the building and nurturing of scientific and technological capacity to participate in the development and adaptation of these technologies to local conditions, and in that regard urges Member States and the United Nations system to ensure the promotion and transfer of new and emerging technologies to developing countries;

Transaction costs and efficiency

18. *Also notes* the efforts of the funds, programmes and specialized agencies of the United Nations system to examine ways to further simplify their rules and procedures and, in that context, to accord the issue of simplification and harmonization high priority, and further notes the steps taken, including: the promotion of common shared support services including the development of banking, administrative and financial procedures; the agreement by the United Nations System Chief Executives Board for Coordination on harmonized definitions and principles for cost recovery; and the establishment of the first joint office pilots and various hosting arrangements for non-resident agencies and agencies that have smaller programmes by resident agencies, consistent with their respective mandates;

19. *Encourages* the funds, programmes and specialized agencies of the United Nations system to step up their efforts, in consultation with national Governments and in accordance with their developments needs and priorities, to, inter alia, rationalize their country presence through common premises and co-location, further implement the joint office model, where appropriate, expand common shared support services, including security, information technology, telecommunications, travel, banking and administrative and financial procedures including for procurement, harmonization of the principles of cost-recovery policies, including that of full cost recovery, and alignment of the regional technical support structures and regional bureaux at headquarters level, including their regional coverage, as well as further simplification and harmonization measures, and to continue to monitor and assess experiences undergone and lessons learned;

Common country assessment/ United Nations Development Assistance Framework

20. *Welcomes* the efforts made so far by the United Nations system in the use of the common country assessment and the United Nations Development Assistance Framework in order to achieve greater country-level programmatic coherence within the system in alignment with national priorities and to foster teamwork among the organizations of the system;

21. *Encourages* the United Nations development system to foster a more inclusive approach to assisting developing countries in obtaining information about and better access to the expertise and services available within the system, in particular in non-resident agencies, and in that regard calls for the strengthening and effective use of arrangements such as system-wide knowledge management;

22. *Recognizes* that resident coordinators, in meeting their obligation to ensure effective and efficient coordination of operational activities, have the responsibility to

inform, in regular consultation with national Governments, the relevant United Nations organizations, funds and programmes of existing opportunities consistent with their respective mandates for their possible participation in country-level development processes;

23. *Notes* the progress made in developing simplified programming processes and tools and the efforts to enhance the capacity of United Nations country teams to develop strategically focused, demand-driven and results-based joint programmes, aligned with national priorities, and, in that regard, encourages assessment of experiences and lessons learned;

24. *Invites* the United Nations system and the Bretton Woods institutions to continue to explore ways to enhance their dialogue and, in full accordance with the priorities of recipient country Governments, to ensure greater consistency between their strategic frameworks used at the country level;

Resident coordinator system

25. *Reaffirms* that the resident coordinator system, within the framework of national ownership, has a key role to play in the effective and efficient functioning of the United Nations system at the country level, including in the formulation of the common country assessment and the United Nations Development Assistance Framework, and is a key instrument for the efficient and effective coordination of the operational activities for development of the United Nations system, and requests the United Nations system, including the funds and programmes, the specialized agencies and the Secretariat, to enhance support to the resident coordinator system;

26. *Takes note*, in that regard, of reports on the improved training provided to the resident coordinators, and urges continued consideration of these and other proposals on support to the resident coordinator system;

27. *Calls for* an acceleration of the development and implementation of a comprehensive accountability framework for resident coordinators, as well as performance appraisal tools and procedures for them;

28. *Reiterates* the need to ensure the functioning of the resident coordinator system in a participatory, collegial and accountable manner;

Country-level capacity of the United Nations system

29. *Also reiterates* the need for the range and level of skills and expertise assembled by the United Nations system at the country level to be commensurate with that needed to deliver on the priorities specified in each country's United Nations Development Assistance Framework, in line with the national development strategies and plans, including poverty reduction strategy papers where they exist, and to correspond to the technical backstopping and capacity-building needs and requirements of developing countries;

30. *Underscores* the importance of reducing the administrative and procedural burden at the country level in the design and delivery of development assistance, on the entities of the United Nations system and recipient countries in order to optimize the impact of such assistance on the development process of countries;

Evaluation of operational activities for development

31. *Emphasizes* the importance of national ownership and leadership of the evaluation process of operational activities for development and of building national evaluation capacities, including through the intergovernmental process aimed at providing coherent guidance to the United Nations funds and programmes as well as the specialized agencies, and also emphasizes the importance of the independence and impartiality of the evaluation function within the United Nations system;

32. *Takes notes* of the endorsement in 2005 of the norms and standards for evaluation by the United Nations system, through the United Nations Evaluation Group, as constituting a contribution to strengthening evaluation as a United Nations system function;

33. *Notes* the adoption by some United Nations organizations of evaluation policies that have been developed based on the norms and standards for evaluation endorsed by the United Nations Evaluation Group, and looks forward to further progress in that regard;

34. *Recalls* the need for country-level evaluations of the United Nations Development Assistance Framework at the end of the programming cycle, based on the results matrix of the framework, with full participation and leadership of the recipient Government;

Regional dimension

35. *Notes* the initiatives and efforts of a number of funds, programmes and agencies to decentralize and regionalize their activities in order to improve their efficiency and their response to national needs;

36. *Requests* the Secretary-General, in consultation with the United Nations System Chief Executives Board for Coordination and the United Nations Development Group, to encourage the funds, programmes and agencies to seek, within their decentralization and regionalization efforts, synergies and complementarities with each other and the regional commissions;

37. *Also requests* the Secretary-General to provide, in view of the preparations for the 2007 triennial comprehensive policy review, information on progress made in the alignment of the regional coverage of regional bureaux and regional technical support structures of the funds, programmes and agencies;

Gender

38. *Notes* the efforts made within entities of the United Nations system to mainstream a gender perspective and to pursue gender equality in their country programmes, planning instruments and sector-wide programmes;

39. *Notes* that recent reviews of accountability mechanisms have found some persistent weaknesses in tracking allocations and expenditures for gender equality in the United Nations system;

40. *Recognizes* that gender-related targets have not yet been met for the recruitment of resident coordinators and that further measures would need to be taken in that regard, and urges the United Nations system within this context to do more, with due regard to representation of

women from developing countries and keeping in mind the principle of equitable geographical representation;

South-South cooperation and development of national capacities

41. *Calls upon* all the entities of the United Nations system to further enhance their support to South-South cooperation;

42. *Reiterates* the need to mobilize additional resources for enhancing South-South cooperation, including from both the United Nations system and donors and through triangular cooperation;

43. *Recognizes* that, while most United Nations entities have focal points to promote South-South cooperation, there is a need for uniform information-sharing standards among United Nations entities to enable system-wide overview of progress made in that regard;

Transition from relief to development

44. *Notes* the ongoing work within the United Nations system to address the complex issue of transition from relief to development to enable the United Nations system, the wider donor community and the affected State to approach transition with a coherent response and strategy;

45. *Encourages* further efforts to build levels of national capacities during the transition from relief to development by, inter alia, adopting policies to systematically implement capacity-building;

46. *Notes* the efforts by the United Nations Development Programme, the Office for the Coordination of Humanitarian Affairs of the Secretariat and the United Nations Development Group office to develop a joint programme to provide joint coordination support during the transition on an institutionalized basis, and requests further information on the progress made in that regard;

47. *Encourages* the Emergency Relief Coordinator to coordinate closely with national authorities so as to make optimal use of available national capacity in relief efforts;

48. *Calls upon* the relevant United Nations entities to further increase efforts, where appropriate, with due consideration given to national data, to harmonize data collection and information management during the transition phase of relief to development and to make that information available to the Member State concerned;

49. *Also calls upon* the relevant United Nations entities to support national efforts directed towards data collection and information evaluation through capacity-building and technical cooperation;

50. *Stresses* the need for adequate, sustained and timely resources to be devoted to the recovery phase in situations of transition from relief to development;

Guidelines for the next triennial comprehensive policy review

51. *Requests* the Secretary-General to focus the analysis for the triennial comprehensive policy review in 2007, within the context of the implementation of the internationally agreed development goals, including the Millennium Development Goals, on:

(a) Status of the implementation of the required actions set out by the General Assembly in its resolution 59/250;

(b) Assessment of the efficiency and effectiveness of the assistance that the United Nations development system provides to developing countries in order to support their efforts to eradicate poverty and achieve sustained economic growth and sustainable development;

(c) Review of the concrete steps taken and progress made by the United Nations development system to ensure country ownership and leadership of United Nations operational activities, including through alignment with national efforts and priorities and identification of further steps needed in that regard, for the consideration of Member States;

(d) Identification of measures and actions required for further improvement in coherence, efficiency and effectiveness of the operational activities for development of the United Nations system at the country and regional levels including, as appropriate, quantifiable time-bound targets, wherever possible;

(e) Identification of further ways to strengthen the efforts of the United Nations system in building capacities in order to assist developing countries to eradicate poverty and to achieve sustained economic growth and sustainable development;

(f) Continued assessment of the extent to which organizations of the United Nations system, within their organizational mandates, have mainstreamed a gender perspective in their country programmes, planning instruments and sector-wide programmes and articulated specific country-level goals and targets in this field in accordance with national development strategies;

(g) Lessons drawn from experiences with the common country assessment/United Nations Development Assistance Framework process as well as options and recommendations for further improvements;

(h) Ways to improve the support to South-South cooperation and enhance its development effectiveness;

(i) Adequacy, predictability and long-term stability of the United Nations development funding, in the light of the challenges that the achievement of the internationally agreed development goals present to the developing countries and the international community, and to suggest further steps accordingly, and the identification of ways to ensure adequate, predictable and stable funding, including through an assessment of the extent to which the increased use of results-based management and programming tools and multi-year funding frameworks and strategies has contributed to this;

(j) Assessment of the adequacy of human resources available within the United Nations system, in particular at the country level, to support national efforts and priorities, including national capacity-building;

(k) Assessment of steps taken and identification of further measures to support the resident coordinator system and to improve its adequacy, accountability and efficiency in order to implement an effective United Nations strategy at the country level, in alignment with national priorities;

(*l*) Identification of options for encouraging the most qualified persons to apply to become resident coordinators;

(*m*) Identification of results, outcomes and lessons learned at the country level from evaluation activities and their use, as appropriate, in improving development results and outcomes and increasing the coherence, effectiveness and quality of programming at the country level;

(*n*) Further identification of the steps needed to streamline and strengthen the United Nations development system to ensure a smooth transition from relief to development.

Financing of operational activities in 2005

The UN system expenditures on operational activities, excluding loans through the World Bank Group, totalled $13,702 million in 2005 [A/62/74-E/2007/54], the most recent year for which figures were available (compared to $11,377 million in 2004). Of that amount, $3,653 million was distributed in development grants by UNDP and UNDP-administered funds, $2,892 million by WFP, $3,32 million by specialized agencies ($2,726 million from extrabudgetary sources and $597 million from regular budgets), $1,960 million by UNICEF, $1,142 million by the Office of the United Nations High Commissioner for Refugees (UNHCR), and $388 million by UNFPA; $344 million was distributed in loan disbursements by the International Fund for Agricultural Development (IFAD).

The UNDP Administrator, in a July report on the UN system's technical cooperation expenditures in 2005 [DP/2006/38 & Add.1], said that the $12.2 billion in technical cooperation (not including the UNHCR and IFAD figures) was the highest level of expenditure for the previous decade and reflected an overall increase of 22.2 per cent over 2004. Increased expenditures of 45.9 per cent ($2 billion) were posted by UNICEF; 29.7 per cent ($3.6 billion) by UNDP; 26.7 per cent ($3.3 billion) by specialized agencies, funds and programmes; and 22.1 per cent ($388 million) by UNFPA. WFP, a key partner in the development process, reported a small decline from 2004 of 0.2 per cent in total delivery.

By region, Africa received the largest amount of development assistance (28.9 per cent or $3.5 billion), followed by Asia and the Pacific (22.3 per cent or $2.7 billion), the Arab States (19.1 per cent or $2.3 billion), Latin America and the Caribbean (14.9 per cent or $1.8 billion), and Europe and the Commonwealth of Independent States (CIS) (4.5 per cent or $549 million). Other global and interregional activities received 10.3 per cent or $1.3 billion. Five countries received 23 per cent of total UN system expenditures in 2005: the Sudan ($954 million), Afghanistan ($542 million), Ethiopia ($477 million), Iraq ($418 million) and Indonesia ($383 million). The health and humanitarian assistance sectors together accounted for 41.8 per cent of the total expenditure, or $5.2 billion.

At the 2006 United Nations Pledging Conference for Development Activities (New York, 15 November) [A/CONF.208/2006/3], Governments pledged contributions to UN programmes and funds dealing with development. The Conference noted that several Governments would communicate their pledges to the Secretary-General as soon as they were able to do so.

In August [A/CONF.208/2006/2], the Secretary-General provided a statement of contributions pledged or made at the 2005 Pledging Conference, as at 30 June 2006, to 25 funds and programmes, amounting to a total of some $605.3 million.

Technical cooperation through UNDP

In November [E/2007/5], the UNDP Administrator and the UNFPA Executive Director issued a joint report on progress towards implementing resolution 59/250 on the triennial comprehensive policy review of operational activities for development of the UN system [YUN 2004, p. 868], including UNDP activities in 2006. Through its Bureau for Crisis Prevention and Recovery, UNDP supported Member States in reducing risks posed by, and in recovering quickly from, the impact of natural disasters, as well as in achieving a peaceful and lasting management of conflicts and disputes prior to the emergence of violence, and a lasting recovery from conflict. Towards those ends, the Bureau designed a five-year strategy for the period 2007-2011, a key element of which was the active promotion of women as central partners in crisis prevention and recovery efforts. UNDP helped Member States to develop conflict management capacity by providing assistance in mainstreaming conflict analysis into development plans and programmes, and in building indigenous mediation capacity through governmental and civil society institutions and processes, consensus on social and economic issues, and an infrastructure for peace.

Regarding post-conflict recovery, UNDP supported Member States in transitional recovery, security reform and transitional justice, small arms reduction, disarmament and demobilization, and mine action. It implemented systematic large-scale measures to generate economic livelihoods and opportunities for communities, especially for internally displaced persons and refugees in Afghanistan, the Democratic Republic of the Congo, Haiti, Indonesia, Iraq, Sri Lanka, the Sudan and Uganda. UNDP also supported access to justice, especially for rural communities, in Haiti, Sierra Leone and the Sudan; the reform and strengthening of the penal system in Haiti and Sierra Leone; multi-stakeholder dialogues on security-sector reform in Haiti and the Sudan, and on transitional justice in Bosnia and Herzegovina, Serbia and Montenegro; and the strengthening of police capabilities for conflict management and community policing in Albania and Sierra Leone. It launched a global initiative to mainstream disaster-risk reduction into development programming, focussing on programme capacities that included disaster concerns in United Nations and UNDP development planning. UNDP continued to support countries affected by the 2004 Indian Ocean tsunami [YUN 2004, p. 952], especially Indonesia, the Maldives, Sri Lanka and Thailand, and with the World Bank, set up a joint task force on scaling up support for the MDGs, as a basis for future collaborative work.

The Economic and Social Council, by **decision 2006/236** of 26 July, took note of the joint report of the UNDP Administrator and the UNFPA Executive Director on the 2005 activities [YUN 2005, p. 962].

UNDP/UNFPA Executive Board

In 2006, the UNDP/UNFPA Executive Board held its first (20-27 January) and second (11-13 September) regular sessions in New York and an annual session (12-23 June) in Geneva [E/2006/35].

At the first regular session, the Board adopted 10 decisions, including one giving an overview of the Board's actions taken at that session [E/2006/35 (dec. 2006/10)]. Others dealt with the UNDP multi-year funding framework (MYFF), 2008-2011 (see p. 1040); the UNDP report on the assessment mission to Myanmar (see p. 1032); the evaluation of gender mainstreaming and the gender action plan (see p. 1035); budgeting and programme decision-making processes of the United Nations Capital Development Fund (UNCDF); the organizational assessment of the United Nations Development Fund for Women (UNIFEM) (see p. 1359); activities of the United Nations Office for Project Services (UNOPS) (see p. 1046); the Executive Board's working methods (see p. 1031); implementation by UNDP, UNFPA and UNOPS of the recommendations of the Board of Auditors (see p. 1042); and cost-efficient approaches to providing programme-level data (see p. 1037).

At its annual session, the Executive Board adopted 17 decisions. In addition to an overview that summarized the actions taken at that session [dec. 2006/27], other decisions dealt with the periodic report of the UNFPA Executive Director on evaluation, and his report for 2005 and funding commitments to UNFPA (see PART THREE, Chapter VIII); internal audit and oversight for UNDP, UNFPA and UNOPS (see p. 1043); improving the working methods of the Executive Board and the election of its Bureau (see p. 1031); UNCDF (see p. 1050); the Evaluation Office report on the role and contributions of UNDP in the HIV and AIDS response in Southern Africa and Ethiopia (see p. 1034); UNOPS (see p. 1046); the United Nations Volunteers programme (see p. 1049); the annual report of the UNDP Administrator on evaluation (see p. 1039); evaluation policy (see p. 1039); UNIFEM (see PART THREE, Chapter X); the report on UNDP performance and results for 2005 in the implementation of the MYFF, 2004-2007 (see p. 1040); preparation of the MYFF, 2008-2011 (see p. 1040); funding commitments to UNDP (see p. 1041); and South-South cooperation (see p. 1050).

At its second regular session, the Board adopted 10 decisions, including an overview [dec. 2006/37] and one welcoming Montenegro as a new UNDP programme country. Other decisions dealt with the annual review of the UNDP financial situation for 2005 (see p. 1040); the report of the Inter-Agency Procurement Services Office for the 2004-2005 biennium (see p. 1044); the determination of UNDP cost recovery rates (see p. 1041); the report of the independent assessment mission to Myanmar (see p. 1032); the progress report on UNOPS activities (see p. 1046); the UNFPA 2005 financial review and the Fund's role in emergency preparedness, humanitarian response, transition and recovery (see PART THREE, Chapter III); and the review of the UNDP/UNFPA country programme approval process (see p. 1038).

The Economic and Social Council, by **decision 2006/236** of 26 July, took note of the report of the UNDP/UNFPA Executive Board on its 2006 first regular session [DP/2006/15] and the decisions adopted by the Board [DP/2006/16].

Working methods

On 27 January [dec. 2006/7], the UNDP/UNFPA Executive Board decided to continue discussions and consultations on its working methods as part of the ongoing process of improving and streamlining its work, and in consultation with Member States, requested that suggestions for further enhancing those methods be presented at the Board's 2006 annual session, including on the early election of the Bureau at the last meeting of the second regular session in September.

On 22 June [dec. 2006/14], the Executive Board decided to convene in early January of each year, starting in 2007, the first meeting of its subsequent first regular session to elect a new President and other members of its Bureau, and requested UNDP and UNFPA to submit a draft work plan for each subsequent year at the second regular meeting of the Board.

In a 23 June decision [dec. 2006/25], the Board took note of the guidelines on its working methods, which were annexed to the decision, emphasizing their non-binding nature. Among the issues covered by the guidelines were the Board's sessions, its agenda and documentation, the decision-making process and the conduct of business. The Board decided to review periodically its working methods, aimed at further improving and streamlining its work.

UNDP/UNFPA reports

Human Development Report

The Executive Board, at its annual session in June, considered an April update [DP/2006/19] on the *Human Development Report* consultations, submitted in response to General Assembly resolution 57/264 [YUN 2002, p. 841]. The Human Development Report Office, charged with preparing the report (see p. 1006), held five informal consultations with Board members on a concept note for the report, including its outline, statistics, structure and message.

The Board took note of the updated report in June [dec. 2006/27].

UNDP operational activities

Country and regional programmes

The UNDP/UNFPA Executive Board, at its January session [dec. 2006/10], approved regional programme documents for Europe and CIS, 2006-2010, the Arab States, 2006-2009; including country programme documents for Albania, Afghanistan, Bangladesh, Belarus, Bulgaria, Burkina Faso, Cambodia, Cape Verde, Chad, China, Georgia, Ghana, Guyana, Indonesia, the Libyan Arab Jamahiriya, Namibia, Peru, Swaziland, Turkey, the Turks and Caicos Islands, Uganda, Ukraine and Viet Nam.

Also in January [dec. 2006/2], the Board took note of the UNDP Administrator's note on assistance to Myanmar [DP/2006/4], requested the Administrator to take account and implement the findings of the independent assessment mission to that country and recommended that UNDP continue to administer the UN HIV/AIDS Fund and engage the international community in supporting the fight against HIV/AIDS in Myanmar.

At its annual session in June [dec. 2006/27], the Board took note of draft country programme documents and the comments made thereon for Egypt, Ethiopia, Gabon, Guinea, Moldova, Morocco, Mozambique, Sao Tome and Principe, Syria, Thailand, Tunisia and Yemen. It also took note of the one-year extensions of the country programmes for Bhutan, Costa Rica, Haiti, Kuwait, Lebanon, Malawi, Nepal, Nicaragua, Rwanda, Sri Lanka, Togo, and Trinidad and Tobago. The Board approved the second one-year extension of the country programmes for the Democratic Republic of the Congo (DRC) and Liberia.

At its second regular session in September [dec. 2006/37], the Board took note of the draft country programme documents and the comments made thereon for Algeria, Belize, Brazil, Chile, the Central African Republic, Croatia, the Democratic People's Republic of Korea, the Dominican Republic, El Salvador, Eritrea, the Gambia, Honduras, Jamaica, the Lao People's Democratic Republic, Mongolia, Montenegro, Panama, Paraguay, Saudi Arabia, Senegal, the Seychelles, Somalia, South Africa, the United Republic of Tanzania, Uruguay, Zambia and Zimbabwe. It approved the two-year extension of the country programme for the Sudan for 2007-2008, and took note of the first one-year extensions of the first country programmes for Colombia, Equatorial Guinea and Suriname, and the regional programmes for Africa and Asia and the Pacific.

Also in September [dec. 2006/31], the Board took note of the Administrator's July note [DP/2006/43] on assistance to Myanmar, and requested the Administrator to take account of and implement the findings of the assessment mission to that country, as appropriate, under the Human Development Initiative. It approved the extension of the current phase of the Initiative for the 2008-2010 period, to be prepared in 2007, with the understanding that formal presentation would be made to the Board in September 2007.

In a decision welcoming Montenegro as a new UNDP programme country [dec. 2006/32], the Board authorized the Administrator to proceed with programme development in the country, at the request of and in close cooperation with the Government and other stakeholders, taking into account other development activities being undertaken.

UNDP programme results

UNDP activities for the 2004-2006 period of the 2004-2007 MYFF were organized under five practice areas: poverty reduction, fostering democratic governance, crisis prevention and recovery, energy and environment, and responding to HIV/AIDS.

Poverty reduction

In 2006, local resources committed to poverty reduction and achievement of the MDGs doubled, comprising 66 per cent ($2.1 billion) of the total expenditure for the practice area. The largest area of work in support of poverty reduction was local policy initiatives, including microfinance, though demand dropped to 38 per cent of the total practice expenditure, from slightly less than half in 2004 and 2005; the drop was attributed to increased support to meet the MDG targets. UNDP supported 105 countries with MDG country reporting and poverty monitoring during the year.

Democratic governance

Under the practice area of fostering democratic governance, UNDP work in justice and human rights grew rapidly, nearly doubling in expenditure, from $65 million in 2004 to $103 million in 2006. Although that increase constituted only 8 per cent of the total democratic governance portfolio, justice and human rights work represented the highest demand of any service in the practice area, with 75 per cent of all programme countries reporting outcomes against that service line. UNDP helped build the capacity of national human rights commissions in Azerbaijan, Ethiopia, Maldives, Nepal and Rwanda, and supported national human rights action plans for Cape Verde and Moldova. The smallest component of the portfolio—e-governance and access to information—represented less than 2 per cent of total expenditure, but grew quickly from $13 million in 2004 to $22 million in 2006, with one fifth of programme countries reporting.

Crisis prevention and recovery

Under the crisis prevention and recovery practice, UNDP played a central role in the development of a joint United Nations-World Bank post-conflict needs assessment for multi-stakeholder assessment and planning exercises. The international community applied that approach in Haiti, Iraq, Liberia, the Sudan and Somalia. Following a joint review in 2006, the exercises were expected to become standard practice, to inform national transition and development plans, prepare donor conferences and form the foundation for coherent implementation plans, aid coordination and priority-setting among national and international partners.

Environment and energy

UNDP continued to promote the vital role of the environment and energy in achieving the long-term goal of sustainable development. The practice area comprised 19 per cent of all reported outcomes in 2006, but UNDP work in the area was generally under-represented. About 34 per cent of all environmental outcomes reported by country offices were associated with support for frameworks and strategies for sustainable development, which facilitated country-driven integration of environmental sustainability into national development frameworks, including poverty reduction strategies; 84 countries were engaged in the service line in 2006. UNDP ensured that environmental concerns were adequately reflected in the economic development and poverty reduction strategy and district development plans in Rwanda. Ghana used strategic environmental assessment (SEA) processes to mainstream dry land development issues in district-level planning, and Iran developed a national SEA framework for its energy sector. Twenty-one countries reported outcomes under the control of the ozone-depleting substances and persistent organic pollutants service line.

Response to HIV/AIDS

In 2006, UNDP realigned its service lines for a more strategic and complementary AIDS response to focus on AIDS and human development, governance of the AIDS response, and the issue of AIDS, human rights and gender. It also helped strengthen gender analysis of AIDS policies and plans, and addressed gender-related vulnerability of women and girls in planning processes. Strategies were in place for the economic empowerment of women living with HIV in Asia, and the promotion of women's rights to inheritance and property in Ethiopia. In South Asia, a regional initiative addressed the nexus of the vulnerability of women and girls to trafficking and AIDS, including through a partnership with 13 civil society organizations and technical support to the regional task force on mobility; the initiative was estimated to have reached 600,000 women. UNDP worked with the National People's Congress in China to support the drafting of national laws protecting the rights of people living with HIV; in March, the national legislative body passed the national HIV regulation. In the Arab States, initiatives with religious leaders promoted human rights and gender equality, resulting in the formation of the first Arab Religious Leaders Network responding to AIDS.

The Political Declaration on HIV/AIDS, adopted by the General Assembly in **resolution 60/262** in June (see p. 1411), highlighted the need for greater flexibility in trade-related aspects of intellectual property rights for access to affordable AIDS treatment. In that regard, UNDP provided guidance and technical support to 28 countries in Africa, Asia, Latin America and the Caribbean to develop enabling trade policies.

Evaluation of AIDS response. At its annual session in June, the UNDP/UNFPA Executive Board considered an April report [DP/2006/29] summarizing the key findings of the evaluation of UNDP role in and contribution to the HIV/AIDS response in Southern Africa and Ethiopia, undertaken by the UNDP Evaluation Office. Country assessments were conducted in Angola, Botswana, Lesotho, Malawi, Mozambique, Namibia, South Africa, Swaziland, Zambia and Zimbabwe. Ethiopia was also included, since it suffered from chronic food shortage and famine, and was estimated to have the second highest number of AIDS-infected people in Africa. The objective of the evaluation was to assess whether UNDP was targeting the right areas and taking the correct approach, as well as the outcomes of its strategy, programmes and projects in addressing HIV/AIDS at the country level. The evaluation was expected to assist the UNDP country offices concerned in positioning themselves for an increasingly effective role in combating HIV/AIDS. Its findings were expected to contribute to future UNDP strategies and programmes on HIV/AIDS.

The evaluation determined that UNDP played multiple roles in the HIV/AIDS response at the country level, but risked losing relevance in some cases, as the environment for its engagement changed. Limited attention to monitoring, evaluation and exit strategies impeded UNDP effectiveness and the sustainability of its interventions. Overall, the evaluation found UNDP supporting programmes and activities, including development programmes for HIV/AIDS-related leadership training, capacity development and policy support to national HIV/AIDS commissions and councils, and decentralized HIV/AIDS responses at the provincial, district and local government levels.

UNDP signature accomplishment lay in moving HIV/AIDS paradigms from biomedical to development perspectives in almost all the case-study countries. However, together with its partners, it had achieved only limited change in translating awareness and policy acceptance into actions, especially beyond the HIV/AIDS sector. In addition, the recent growth in external financial resources and the consequential prominence of treatment created the danger that developmental approaches to combating the epidemic might lose attention. The report described specific findings with regard to the relevance and effectiveness of UNDP role and contributions, the strategy and management of the UNDP HIV/AIDS response, and the monitoring, evaluation and sustainability of that response.

The evaluation's overall recommendation was that in Southern Africa—the subregion with the most severe HIV/AIDS problem in the world—country offices in the case-study countries had to demonstrate a much higher level of urgency in their HIV/AIDS work. Since total UNDP spending on HIV/AIDS was not large enough to have a significant impact on the epidemic at the country level, it was particularly important that its HIV/AIDS resources were strategically used, and coherent approaches developed for leveraging partner resources to achieve the scale of outcomes required in countries with very severe epidemics.

The evaluation recommended that country offices clarify strategic direction, formulate or update UNDP HIV/AIDS country strategies and integrate them into national HIV/AIDS strategies and programmes, shift programme focus, strengthen HIV/AIDS capacity and foster a culture of monitoring and evaluation. It also recommended that the UNDP Regional Bureau for Africa assume new leadership roles, the Bureau for Development Policy review the corporate HIV/AIDS strategy; the Bureau of Management accelerate implementation of the financial management improvement programme; the Office of the Associate Administrator clarify working relationships; and the UNDP/UNFPA Executive Board monitor the implementation of the recommendations and request a report for the 2007 annual session. With the support of a team drawn from all concerned headquarters units and the Regional Centre, each UNDP country office and other units concerned should develop, by September 2006, an action plan for the implementation of the recommendations.

UNDP management, responding to the report, in June [DP/2006/30], noted the concern raised regarding the limited change in translating awareness and policy acceptance into actions and the limited attention paid to monitoring, evaluation and exit strategies, which had impeded UNDP effectiveness and the sustainability of its interventions. The Regional Bureau for Africa, the Bureau for Development Policy and the Evaluation Office would work to strengthen the monitoring and evaluation dimensions of programmes and adjust strategies to focus on implementation issues. Management underlined that the focus on treatment provided an opportunity to discuss the human development impact of the epidemic with ministries and patent offices. Management also noted and/or endorsed the evaluation's specific findings relating to the relevance and effectiveness of UNDP role and contributions in the HIV/AIDS response in Southern Africa and Ethiopia and the strategy and management of the UNDP response.

Management endorsed fully the evaluation's overarching recommendation that country offices in the case-study countries in Southern Africa had to demonstrate a much higher level of urgency in the HIV/AIDS work. Many of the recommendations detailed in the evaluation report had been implemented, including the review of the UNDP corporate strategy on HIV/AIDS, the prioritization of integrating HIV/AIDS into poverty reduction strategies; the development of a corporate strategy on HIV/AIDS and gender, and the strengthening of the capacity of the resident coordinator system to respond to HIV/AIDS. The Regional Bureau for Africa and the Bureau for Development Policy were committed to developing, by September, an action plan to implement the remaining recommendations.

On 23 June [dec. 2006/16], the UNDP/UNFPA Executive Board welcomed the evaluation report and encouraged UNDP to address the recommendations made therein, particularly those dealing with the need for capacity-building, national ownership and working close with stakeholders.

Programme planning and management

Gender issues

The UNDP/UNFPA Executive Board, at its January session, considered a report [DP/2006/5] summarizing the findings of a global evaluation of gender mainstreaming in UNDP. Its objectives were to take stock of what UNDP had done to institute gender mainstreaming policies and ensure their implementation, and assess UNDP overall performance in gender mainstreaming and the promotion of gender equality. The evaluation assessed the attention accorded to gender relations in country-level policies, programmes and institutional measures.

The evaluation concluded that UNDP lacked the capacity and institutional framework for a systematic, effective gender mainstreaming approach. Among key shortcomings, it found that gender mainstreaming was not visible or explicit; there was no corporate strategic plan for putting the gender mainstreaming policy into effect; steps had been simplistic; and UNDP had not acted on previous assessments identifying similar shortcomings and had sent mixed signals about its commitment and expectations. The initiatives that had shown results were probably not sustainable, as they depended on individual interest and effort rather than a systematic corporate approach. The results that were achieved were based on a convergence of several elements, including a strong commitment from management, a clear and proactive strategy and policy, qualified senior expertise, awareness of gender mainstreaming as an organizational responsibility, systematic training, and dedicated financial resources.

The report stated that gender mainstreaming required long-term commitment, consistent effort, and resources. UNDP needed proactive leadership and clear commitment, with accountability and incentives, a clear articulation of its gender mainstreaming mandate, enhanced capacities, stable core financial commitments, strengthened partnership and clarification of the relationship between UNDP and UNIFEM; and an institutional structure to ensure that gender mainstreaming needs were met. Recommendations arising from the evaluation included measures to: provide the needed leadership; establish accountability; retain programmatic gender mainstreaming strategy and gender-focused programmes; strengthen the institutional framework for gender mainstreaming, place gender expertise in country offices, strengthen gender mainstreaming capacities of UNDP staff, and advocacy and partnerships; make adequate financial resources available; and clarify the relationship between UNDP and UNIFEM, and strengthen coordination and cooperation. The UNDP/UNFPA Executive Board should promote accountability for gender mainstreaming within UNDP, monitor the follow-up to the evaluation, and review its progress by 2008 and report to the Board.

UNDP management, in its response to the evaluation [DP/2006/7], acknowledged that, despite the adoption of a gender policy in 2002, proper accountability for the policy and performance measures were inadequate. UNDP needed to make serious efforts to implement its policy, increase its capacities and resources for gender mainstreaming, track progress in gender equality, and invest in women's empowerment.

UNDP management also recognized that it had not sufficiently showcased results at the country level, or the significant progress made at the corporate level. UNDP was taking concerted action to establish a stronger institutional base, capacities and accountability mechanisms to enhance and track gender mainstreaming performance and results. It was confident that its achievements, together with the new commitments to staffing, funding and leadership included in its response, would position UNDP strongly for success in delivering further results in gender mainstreaming.

The Executive Board also considered a progress report [DP/2006/8] on the implementation of the 2005 UNDP gender action plan. The report detailed progress towards the specific goals of building internal capacities for gender mainstreaming, ensuring systematic gender mainstreaming in all programmes, supporting the United Nations Resident Coordinator system, developing mainstreaming tools, knowledge products and best practices, and aligning human resources policies and practices with commitment to gender balance.

There had been major progress in mainstreaming gender into all UNDP interventions, but that progress had not been adequately reflected in the MYFF reports. UNDP needed to invest further in internal capacities and partnerships with UNIFEM and other UN organizations, and to allocate core programme resources to empower women in all the core practice areas. The report highlighted measures taken at the country offices to mainstream gender in each of the UNDP practice areas (see above).

Gender action plan (2006-2007). At its January session, the Executive Board considered the UNDP gender action plan for 2006-2007 [DP/2006/9], which was requested by the Board in 2005 [YUN 2005, p. 969]. The UNDP gender policy was based on a two-pronged approach to achieving gender equality: integrating a gender perspective into all policies and programmes across each UNDP core priority, and investing dedicated resources in specific interventions that empowered women, reduced their vulnerability, built their leadership, provided them with access to resources and protected their human rights. The 2006-2007 gender action plan was designed to strengthen UNDP capacities at all levels and enhance its delivery of gender-responsive policies and programmes in a systematic, visible and measurable way. In response to the main areas of concern identified in the evaluation report (see above), the two-year action plan was built around four goals aimed at: establishing commitment and accountability at all levels; building capacities for gender training, knowledge-sharing and networking; increasing communication and visibility for good practices; and aligning core and non-core resources with commitments. The plan included outcomes, outputs and results indicators for each year, and identified responsible parties for each of the goals. UNDP would scale up UNIFEM innovations and strengthen its capacity to address the feminization of poverty and HIV/AIDS, the vulnerability of women and girls to crises and violations of their rights, the exclusion of women and girls from decision-making and their lack of access to resources and energy services. Results-based management and performance management systems would reflect the priority accorded to those issues, and institutional scorecards would help measure progress and results through the MYFF and track investments through the Atlas enterprise resource planning system.

Executive Board action. In January [dec. 2006/3], the Executive Board endorsed the 2006-2007 gender action plan, and requested the Administrator to ensure that it was translated by the regional and thematic bureaux into multi-year gender action plans for their respective regions or thematic areas. It asked that the annual reports of the Administrator and on the MYFF include reporting on progress in achieving gender equality results. The Board commended the UNDP policy on gender balance and diversity, and requested the Administrator to set benchmarks for reaching a fifty-fifty gender balance in senior management by 2010. It asked UNDP to take the issue of empowerment of women for gender equality into account when devising and implementing gender equality strategies; track allocations and expenditures for gender equality results and develop clear reporting guidelines on the gender driver in the MYFF by December 2006; speed up the implementation of General Assembly resolution 59/250 on the triennial comprehensive policy review [YUN 2004, p. 868], focusing on gender equality and gender mainstreaming; and make use of gender disaggregated data and quantitative and qualitative information. It also requested UNDP to increase the number of senior gender equality experts and develop competency profiles for all staff. It welcomed the Administrator's decision to establish and chair a gender steering and an implementation committee to review results in gender mainstreaming and the achievement of gender equality. It asked him to create incentive and accountability systems for staff at all operational levels, and maintain senior management commitment to ensuring that UNDP maximized its achievement of gender equality results. The Administrator should identify further measures, including evaluating the position and mandate of the gender unit in the Bureau for Development Policy, to increase the profile of the UNDP gender policy and the attention given to its implementation. The Administrator, in his capacity as Chair of the United Nations Development Group (UNDG), should advocate for and support the strengthening of UN country team capacity to achieve gender equality results within UNDAFs, and ensure that the greatest possible attention was given to the achievement of gender equality results in the UN reform process. He should report on progress in implementing the decision, the management response and the gender action plan at the first regular session in January 2007, particularly on progress in implementing the commitments in the response concerning the clarification of the respective roles and responsibilities of UNDP and UNIFEM.

Programming arrangements

Joint programming

In response to the 2005 decisions of the Executive Boards of UNDP/UNFPA [YUN 2005, p. 970] and UNICEF [ibid., p. 1293], those agencies issued in April [DP/2006/33-DP/FPA/2006/11] a comprehensive report on joint programming, as outlined in the 2004 UNDG guidance note on the subject [YUN 2004, p. 884]. The report described the efforts made by them to support joint programmes, assessed the lessons learned from and benefits of such programming, as well as the limits of its application, and provided an overview of the current status of implementation of joint programmes. (For more information on UNICEF role in joint programming, see p. 1378.)

The joint programmes implemented in 2005 were the first to be developed within the context of a full inter-organization programme cycle at the country level. UNDG promoted joint programmes where they added value, while UNDP, UNFPA and UNICEF each established support mechanisms at their headquarters to advise UN country teams on organization-specific issues. At the country level, coordination of and information on joint programmes were increasingly centred in the Resident Coordinator's office. A key development was the creation, in 2005, of the joint programmes database on the UNDG website. The database drew initially on information provided by resident coordinators' offices, and when fully developed should provide a comprehensive view of collective joint programming activity.

The report identified a number of positive experiences and benefits of joint programming, such as increased commitment by UNDG organizations to work together, reduced transaction costs and duplication of activities, improved information and knowledge base in countries, increased coherence of activities, maintained focus on organizational mandates, and ensured transparency and accountability, the ability to reach particularly marginalized populations, facilitation of swift responses to crises, and leveraging of additional resources.

The report identified a number of challenges. Despite positive impacts, joint programmes were not always used effectively. Those formulated before 2005 did not always address UNDAF outputs. A reduction in collaboration following the completion of UNDAF also reduced the emergence of joint programmes from the common country assessment (CCA)/UNDAF process. Joint programmes did not always merit the transaction costs incurred in developing them and there was limited use of joint programmes in the broader national context. The focus of the guidance note led to the perception that joint programming promoted UN-centred programmes rather than partnerships. Bilateral donors had limited knowledge of joint programme fund management options, while monitoring and evaluation of programme impact needed to be improved.

The schedule envisaged completion of the roll-out of joint programming in all countries by 2008, with the largest block of countries (37) presenting draft country programme documents in 2008 and 33 in 2007.

A full evaluation of joint programming and programmes should be undertaken once there was sufficient experience from which to draw meaningful results. The evidence indicated that the guidance note and the CCA/UNDAF process together had effectively addressed some of the challenges faced in the early years of promoting joint programmes, but more sustained efforts were necessary to enable them to meet their full potential to provide a coherent, effective and efficient UN response to support countries in addressing national priorities and attaining the MDGs. Joint programmes would be an integral part of the proposed improvements in the UN country programming process. A continuous flow from planning to programming in the common country programming process should promote the participation of the full capacity of the UN system, including non-resident and specialized UN organizations, in joint programmes.

Provision of programme-level data

In response to a 2005 Executive Board decision [YUN 2005, p. 971], UNDP and UNFPA submitted a joint conference room paper [DP/2006/CRP.2-DP/FPA/2006/CRP.1] on cost-efficient approaches to providing programme data as part of their programming and reporting cycles. The paper discussed the respective reporting systems of UNDP and UNFPA, the issues and challenges of presenting programme-level data, and the United Nations harmonization and simplification process. It also contained recommendations for UNDP/UNFPA-specific approaches to sharing programme-level data, as well as approaches for both bodies.

For UNDP, the scope for provision of data in terms of the 2005 MYFF was limited, but initial assessments for programme-level data could be considered for specific categories of countries in accordance with criteria agreed to by the Executive Board. Alternatively, the groundwork could be laid for the development of some programme reporting system for the 2004-2007 cumulative report for countries that could be of special interest to the Board, including the least developed and landlocked countries. The report recommended that the two bodies maintain periodic consultations with the Board to review information requirements and address any additional information needs. The preparation by UNDP and UNFPA of new MYFFs, to be submitted to the Board in September 2007, provided an opportunity to review the focus and structure of the frameworks to ensure that they fully conformed to the emerging role of UN development organizations in the context of UN reform and the new development architecture. (For information on UNFPA-specific recommendations, see p. 1264.)

In January [dec. 2006/9], the Executive Board encouraged the UNDP Administrator and the UNFPA Executive Director to improve the results-based management systems of their respective organizations and interact proactively with the Executive Board in that regard. They should ensure that country and regional programme results and performance data consolidated over the programme duration were made available at the end of the country and regional programme cycles.

Country programme approval process

In response to the 2005 decisions of the UNDP/UNFPA Executive Board [YUN 2005, p. 970] and the UNICEF Executive Board [ibid., p. 1293], UNDP, UNFPA and UNICEF issued in April [DP/2006/34-DP/FPA/2006/12] a joint report presenting options for modifying the harmonized country programme approval process by their governing bodies and WFP. Annexed to the report were the UNDG process for simplifying and harmonizing the UN programming and documentation process, an outline of the contents of a consolidated UNDAF, and the format for a simplified presentation of organization-specific contributions to the consolidated UNDAF.

The report described a set of principles for the simplification and harmonization process which clarified results and defined accountabilities. The overarching principle affirmed national ownership and leadership of the approval process, its products and results. The primary principle was that the United Nations should make a collective, strategic contribution in response to national priorities and internationally agreed development goals, including the MDGS [YUN 2000. p. 51]. The purpose of simplification was to enable the United Nations to unleash its potential to support national priorities and demonstrate its continuing relevance and effectiveness. Simplification and harmonization should lead to reduced transaction costs.

Under the proposal to improve the appraisal process, the standard format used for governing body review and approval of programme contributions from agencies to the consolidated UNDAF would be aligned with UNDAF. The simplified formats would form part of an overall consolidated UNDAF document, developed under national leadership. Governing body members would continue to review, comment on and approve the organization-specific planned results and resources for the programme of cooperation in a particular country. The consolidated document would be signed by the Government, the resident coordinator and members of the UN country team, following approval of the organization-specific contributions by the Executive Boards. If the organization-specific section was not approved after the first review, the remainder of the consolidated UNDAF would proceed while further consultations took place. The improvements responded to General Assembly resolution 59/250 [YUN 2004, p. 868], and further promoted UN reform and harmonization. The report proposed that the modified approach for country programming should be adopted by all countries presenting new programmes for approval in 2007 and be assessed after one year. Those countries, together with the respective UN country teams, could decide whether they wished to opt for the modified approach or continue using the current multiple-document system. However, that alternative would incur significant costs, as it would entail the operation of parallel country programme preparation and approval processes, and would not fully realize the benefits of the modified approach. The report also presented three options in respect of the harmonized mechanism to be used for Executive Board approval of the revised organization-specific contributions to the consolidated UNDAF: electronic posting; electronic posting with a hard copy; or approval on a no-objection basis at the next Executive Board session.

In September [dec. 2006/36], the UNDP/UNFPA Executive Board decided that, in order to reduce the time frame for the country programme approval process and create more scope for synchronizing it with the length of national programme cycles, draft country programme documents would continue to be presented for discussion at its annual session. The revised programme documents would then be posted on the website of the organization no later than six weeks after the discussion, and a hard copy provided, upon request, to Board members by the secretariat. The country programmes would then be approved by the Board at its second regular session on a no-objection basis without presentation or discussion, unless at least five members informed the secretariat in writing before the session of their wish to bring a particular country programme before the Board. Approval of country programmes for which revised programme documents were not posted within six weeks would be postponed until the Board's first regular session in 2007. The submission and approval of country programmes would continue to follow the guidelines for length and content adopted by the Board in 2001 [YUN 2001, p. 799]. Continued efforts should be made to improve results-based planning and management and strengthen the alignment of country programmes with national strategies and the approved medium-term strategic plan. The UNDP and UNFPA country programme documents should contribute to be derived from national plans and strategies, as well as from the outcomes established in UNDAF.

Monitoring and evaluation

In May [DP/2006/27 & Corr.1], the UNDP Administrator, in his annual report on evaluation covering the period from March 2005 to February 2006, described the scope of coverage of evaluations of UNDP and its associated funds and programmes. The report presented the major findings, analysed the UNDP contribution to selected development results and highlighted factors that affected success. It also outlined significant organizational issues and lessons learned, and described the effect of resource mobilization strategies on the strength of UNDP role as a neutral broker and the challenges faced in complementing advocacy and policy dialogue work with greater downstream relevance and effectiveness. A proposed 2006-2007 programme of work for the Evaluation Office was also outlined in the report.

A total of 300 evaluations were conducted during the year. The conduct of outcome evaluations increased dramatically, with 69 conducted in 2005, representing an 86 per cent increase over the 2004 figure. Lessons learned from evaluations conducted in several countries indicated that, in order for UNDP to be influential in sensitive areas, it had to earn trust and respect across the spectrum of national stakeholders. Where relationships between the State and society were highly polarized, as in post-conflict environments, UNDP effectiveness in empowering civil society through technical and financial support might challenge its position as a trustworthy government partner. Conflict of interest and confusion of roles might arise where UNDP sought to combine the roles of policy coordinator, donor, rights advocate, neutral broker and project implementer. In particular, areas where UNDP had a comparative advantage, but was unlikely to mobilize external resources, could be crowded out by activities for which cost-sharing assistance was more readily available and government consent easier to secure.

While there had been significant achievements in fostering debate on key developmental issues, UNDP performance in implementing programmes and piloting practical experiences was mixed. It appeared more effective when its comparative advantages in resource and knowledge mobilization and policy dialogue were complemented by better programme coordination and monitoring. The findings confirmed that UNDP needed to move from a mainly project-based approach towards one that addressed broad development issues at the local, national or regional levels. The potential for enhancing strategic management and focus through the UNDP results-based management system was still not being fully exploited. Discrepancies were evident between what was formally stated in programme documents and what was actually being done; the way in which strategic results were formulated in those documents did not always constitute useful planning tools for setting priorities, defining programmes strategically or cultivating partnerships. The evaluations also revealed that responsiveness to Governments and adaptability to change were critical for achieving results. The findings suggested that staff capacity for clear and focused programming needed to be developed further, and monitoring systems that had the country programme as their unit of analysis needed to be established. Flexible management procedures allowing for strategic changes during implementation were also key factors for greater impact.

At its June session, the UNDP/UNFPA Executive Board considered a May note [DP/2006/28] on the UNDP evaluation policy. The note established the guiding principles and norms, explained key evaluation concepts, outlined the main organizational roles and responsibilities, and defined the types of evaluation covered. It also identified the key elements of a system for learning and knowledge management and outlined the capacity and resource requirements to enhance excellence in the development of an evaluation culture and a learning organization. The policy sought to increase transparency, coherence and efficiency in generating and using evaluative knowledge for organizational learning and effective management, and to support accountability. It applied to UNDP and its associated funds and programmes, including UNIFEM and the United Nations Volunteers (UNV) programme, the United Nations Capital Development Fund (UNCDF), and all UNDP-managed programmes, irrespective of funding source.

In June [dec. 2006/19], the Executive Board took note of the Administrator's annual report on evaluation and the identification of key organizational lessons. It encouraged the Administrator to make better use of evaluations and further strengthen the quality, efficiency and utility of decentralized evaluations and to provide a separate management response to key and recurring issues identified in the annual reports on evaluations. The Board approved the evaluation agenda for 2006-2007.

Also in June [dec. 2006/20], the Board approved the UNDP evaluation policy and noted that the mandate of the Evaluation Office was to evaluate the effectiveness and efficiency of UNDP programmes and results. It requested UNDP to conduct evaluations of its operations at the country level, in consultation with Governments; provide, for information, an evaluation plan developed in consultation with respective Governments as an annex to programme documents submitted to the Board, and submit a triennial review of the evaluation policy, as of the 2009 annual session. The Board requested the Administrator to further strengthen the evaluation function based on the policy and stressed the need for UNDP to assist Governments in developing national evaluation capacities.

Funding strategy

Multi-year funding framework, 2004-2007

At its June meeting, the Executive Board had before it the multi-year funding framework (MYFF) report [DP/2006/17 & Corr.1] on UNDP performance and results for 2005 [YUN 2005, p. 961] and a statistical analysis [DP/2006/17/Add.2], as well as a UNDP and UNFPA joint report [DP/2006/17/Add.1-DP/FPA/2006/2 (Part II)], which provided a synopsis of management responses to key recommendations of the Joint Inspection Unit (JIU) in 2005 that were of specific relevance to those organizations.

At the same meeting [dec. 2006/22], the Executive Board took note of the UNDP report on its performance and results for 2005 and reaffirmed its commitment to results-based management. It requested the Administrator to continue to include in future reports analytical information about strategic outcomes based on MYFF indicators and explanations of significant deviations from expected results. The Board also asked UNDP to continue to strengthen the MYFF drivers of development effectiveness, namely, advocating for and fostering an enabling policy environment, forging partnerships for results and developing national capacities. Concerned at the low emphasis placed on the drivers of development effectiveness—(enhancing national ownership, seeking South-South solutions and promoting gender equality)—the Board requested UNDP to increase emphasis on those drivers.

MYFF, 2008-2011

In January [dec. 2006/1], the Executive Board took note of the report on the timeline for the preparation of the UNDP end-of-cycle assessment of performance, 2004-2007 [DP/2006/3], which included a road map for the preparation of the MYFF, 2008-2011. It invited the UNDP Administrator to submit a paper on the emerging strategic vision, programme directions and organizational strategy for discussion during its annual session in June, as well as an annotated outline of the MYFF, 2008-2011, to the Board at its first regular session in January 2007 and a draft version at its annual session in June 2007.

In June [dec. 2006/23], the Board encouraged UNDP to hold informal meetings with member States on the preparation of the MYFF, 2008-2011, including on the existing practice areas, service lines and drivers of development effectiveness, in order to better understand how they shaped programming.

Financing

The UNDP Administrator, in his annual review of the financial situation for 2006 [DP/2007/41 & Add.1 & Add.1/Corr.1], reported that total contributions decreased in nominal terms by 1 per cent, from $4.8 billion in 2005 to $4.7 billion in 2006. Net contributions to regular resources increased slightly from $915 million in 2005 to $916 million in 2006. Regular resource contributions amounted to $0.9 billion and for other resources $3.8 billion. Expenditures under regular resources increased by 6 per cent to $903 million, from $849 million in 2005. Contributions from the top 15 bilateral donor members of the Development Assistance Committee of the Organisation for Economic Co-operation and Development (OECD/DAC)—Belgium, Canada, Denmark, Finland, France, Germany, Ireland, Japan, the Netherlands, Norway, Spain, Sweden, Switzerland, United Kingdom, United States)—increased in nominal terms by 3 per cent to $886 million, while the value in real terms remained at $821 million.

Programme expenditure, including programme support to the resident coordinator system, development support services and the UNDP economist programme, increased by 7 per cent to $557 million. By appropriation group, 55 per cent of the expenditure went to programme support activities, 24 per cent to the UN system operational activities, 20 per cent to management and administration, and 1 per cent to support UNCDF. By region, Africa recorded the highest expenditure of regular resources, with $237 million, followed by Asia and the Pacific with $145 million, Europe and CIS with $45 million, the Arab States with $35 million and Latin America with $31 million; the expenditure for global and other programmes was $53 million.

At the end of 2006, the balance of unexpended regular resources stood at $244 million, an increase of 3 per cent over the 2005 figure of $238 million. UNDP held investments for regular resources totalling $317 million, excluding the operational reserve.

For other resources activities—local resources (government, cost-sharing and cash-counterpart contributions), donor cost-sharing, trust funds, UNV programme (see p. 1049), management services agreements, the Junior Professional Officer programme and the reserve for field accommodation—overall income decreased by $15 million, from $4.1 billion in 2005 to $4.08 billion in 2006. Net contributions, interest and other income received totalled $3.8 billion, of which 36 per cent ($1.4 billion) came from local resources; 32 per cent ($1.2 billion) was contributed by non-bilateral/multilateral sources; 27 per cent ($1 billion) from bilateral OECD/DAC donors; and 5 per cent ($200 million) came from other sources.

In September [dec. 2006/28], the Executive Board took note of the Administrtor's annual review of the financial situation for 2005 [YUN 2005, p. 92].

Regular funding commitments to UNDP

In June [DP/2006/18], UNDP submitted a report on the status of regular funding commitments to the Programme and its associated funds and programmes for 2006 and onward. Provisional data showed that contributions to regular resources for 2005 reached $921 million, a 9.4 per cent increase ($79 million) over the $842 million achieved in 2004. For the first time since 1995, UNDP received contributions to regular resources exceeding the $900 million level, and thus surpassed the interim 2005 target of the MYFF, 2004-2007. However, current projections suggested that, based on the official UN exchange rates as of 1 May 2006, contributions would reach approximately $955 million, $45 million short of the MYFF target for 2006. Thirteen OECD/DAC members increased their contributions to regular resources in 2005; three by 20 per cent or more, another four by 10 per cent or more, and all but two paid their contributions in full in 2005. Estimates suggested that almost all OECD/DAC donors would maintain or increase their contributions, and one had committed to increasing its contributions regularly over the full period of the MYFF. Six of the programme countries made contributions to UNDP regular resources in excess of $1 million. As in 2003 and 2004, 11 OECD/DAC donor countries provided fixed payment schedules in 2005, but many of them did not adhere to those schedules. Although a number of donors did not pay significant proportions of their pledges until the last quarter of 2005, it did not become necessary to use the operational reserve.

In June [dec. 2006/24] the Executive Board took note of the report on the status of regular funding commitments to UNDP and its associated funds and programmes for 2006 and onwards. It welcomed the fact that UNDP had achieved the 2005 annual funding target of the MYFF, 2004-2007, but noted with concern that current projections suggested that contributions would fall short of the MYFF 2006 funding target. Countries that had not yet done so were requested to provide contributions to regular resources for 2006, and those that had already contributed were asked to consider supplementing their contributions, so as to maintain the momentum in rebuilding the UNDP regular resource base. The Board requested member States to give priority to regular (core) resources over other (non-core) resources. It asked UNDP to continue to reduce its dependency on a few large donors and broaden its donor base. Member States in a position to do so were encouraged to announce multi-year pledges and payment schedules over the period of the MYFF, 2004-2007, and adhere to such schedules thereafter.

In September [dec. 2006/28], the Board again encouraged member States in a position to do so to increase regular resources funding, bearing in mind the 2007 MYFF target of $1.1 billion, and announce multi-year funding pledges.

Cost recovery

In response to a 2005 Executive Board decision [YUN 2005, p. 975], UNDP submitted an August report [DP/2006/41] detailing the current practice in determining specific cost-recovery rates and cost-recovery criteria in different countries. Since the policy was introduced in 2004 [YUN 2004, p. 889], UNDP had been aligning all existing and new donor agreements to the new rates, in order to achieve proportional funding of support costs from all resources. The gradual adjustment of general management support (GMS) rates, from 3 to 5 per cent to 5 to 7 per cent for third party contributions and trust funds, had not yet been fully met. Approximately 50 per cent of offices had reached the effective minimum policy target average of 5 per cent GMS. In the case of programme country cost-sharing contributions, the policy target of 3 per cent had been met fully.

UNDP, UNFPA, UNICEF and WFP agreed, through the UNDG Management Group, to charge 7 per cent to all multi-donor trust funds, joint programmes and joint offices. For some organizations, the rate harmonization exercise resulted in a somewhat higher applicable rate than what would have been negotiated on a bilateral basis, while for others the rate was lower. For UNDP, the harmonized rate for specific joint funds and programmes reduced flexibility during negotiations with donors.

The UNDP cost-recovery policy was informed by several cost attribution and classification principles: each source of funding should be attributed to all costs for the necessary management provided by the organization; all costs could be classified as "direct costs", "fixed indirect costs" and "variable indirect costs"; and cost recovery would generally apply to variable indirect costs, or indirect costs above the base structure of the organization. Country offices identified the generic criteria that guided their determination of a specific GMS rate, taking into consideration the nature and complexity of project management requirements, the size of contribution, the centrally established rate, the continuation of legacy rates established at lower levels than the approved rates, and the exigencies of partnership building and donor negotiations. It was not viable to single out a specific formula that would inform a country office's determination of specific rates within the 5 to 7 per cent bracket to fit diverse project types and execution modalities. Ultimately, the criteria for determining the GMS rate had to be based on the project's actual operational environment, taking into account managerial assessment of the nature and complexity of projects and differences in costs among offices.

The report concluded that legislation of strict GMS cost-recovery rates for specific execution modalities would not be in the interest of broad partnership-building or in line with the basic objectives of simplification and harmonization. The determination of a specific rate based on project parameters would be administratively burdensome and run the risk of either grossly oversimplifying or inadequately capturing the cost of management arrangements for a specific project. It was imperative to keep the policy guidance simple, preserve a degree of flexibility and continue to build on existing opportunities for inter-agency harmonization. By the end of 2007, UNDP would be in a position to report fully on the effectiveness of its cost-recovery policy and propose adjustments, pending the outcome of the review of the corporate financial model.

In September [dec. 2006/30], the Executive Board took note of the report on the current practice in determining specific cost-recovery rates and criteria, and reiterated that UNDP had to ensure full recovery, at an aggregate level, of all actual costs incurred in implementing activities financed from UNDP third-party cost-sharing, trust fund contributions and programme country cost-sharing. It noted with concern that the relative share of regular resources available to UNDP had decreased and encouraged donors to increase contributions to regular resources. The Board stressed that other resources should support MYFF priorities, and that regular resources should not subsidize the support costs for programmes funded by other resources. UNDP was encouraged to apply procedures that reduced transaction costs for programmes funded by other resources. The Board asserted that the basic objectives of simplification, harmonization and fiscal prudence should guide the cost-recovery policy. It again requested UNDP to review its policy in time for the MYFF, 2008-2011, and report to the Board at its annual session in 2007. The policy review should include lessons learned and provide sufficient detailed analysis for the Board to make a decision on a new, comprehensive cost-recovery policy. In that regard, the Board requested a detailed financial and substantive analysis of current cost-recovery practices and estimated GMS costs by funding modality, execution modality and nature of project. It also requested a proposal for cost-recovery policy options. It asked the Administrator, in cooperation with the UNDG members, to report in 2007 on the progress towards harmonization on cost recovery, including information on cost-recovery methodologies.

Audit reports

The UNDP/UNFPA Executive Board, at its January session, considered the Administrator's follow-up report [DP/2006/13] on the implementation of recommendations of the Board of Auditors for the 2002-2003 biennium [YUN 2004, p. 1396]. The report updated information provided in the Administrator's 2005 implementation report

[YUN 2005, p. 975], and the 2005 report of the Board of Auditors on the implementation of its recommendations relating to the 2002-2003 biennium [ibid., p. 1503]. The report indicated the priority accorded to each recommendation and the time frame for its implementation. Details and the current implementation status of each recommendation were provided in an annex.

Of the 80 recommendations made by the Board of Auditors, 65 per cent had been implemented and 35 per cent were in the process of being implemented, as at 15 October 2005. UNDP put into effect tools and processes to promote transparency in reporting and re-emphasize accountability and responsiveness to audit recommendations, including implementation of a web-based dashboard to track audit recommendations and a quality assurance function within the UNDP Bureau of Management to analyse systematic issues arising from audit observations.

In January [dec. 2006/8], the Executive Board noted the progress made by UNDP and the United Nations Office for Project Services (UNOPS) in implementing the recommendations of the Board of Auditors for the 2002-2003 biennium and the specific efforts made by management to improve transparency and promote managerial accountability and ownership in dealing with audit recommendations. It asked the management of UNDP, UNFPA and UNOPS to build on progress achieved, continue to implement the recommendations and strengthen management and control systems, including risk-management systems that conformed to best practices in monitoring compliance with the respective codes of ethics and professional conduct of the three bodies. The Board also asked the management to intensify fraud prevention and anti-corruption measures, communicate to all staff members and partner organizations a zero-tolerance attitude with regard to the mismanagement of funds, and further strengthen systems for reporting and investigating possible fraud or misuse of funds.

In June [DP/2006/31], the Administrator submitted the 2005 annual report on the internal audit and oversight services provided by the UNDP Office of Audit and Performance Review (OAPR). The report contained: selection criteria of the country offices audited; audit recommendations presented by frequency of occurrence and priority, and further analysis of the causes of audit issues; a report on the status of the most frequent and highest priority recommendations, according to the framework approved in a 2004 Board decision [YUN 2004, p. 891]; the results of the review of internal audit resources; and management responses and actions taken on significant issues raised in internal audit reports. It also discussed the development of risk management, strengthening the analysis of outcomes of audits of non-governmental organizations (NGO)/nationally-executed (NEX) projects and training provided to field-based staff to follow up on NGO/NEX audit findings and recommendations.

OAPR developed a risk-assessment model for country offices, to identify offices to be audited in 2006. A new model, to be introduced during the year, was being developed for headquarters, to ensure that audit resources were applied in high-risk areas of operation. OAPR introduced enterprise risk management towards the end of 2005. With the UNDP Bureau of Management, regional bureaus and PricewaterhouseCoopers, it conducted a survey of the current risk culture at UNDP and held two workshops, at which participants drew an initial risk map for UNDP. The results of the workshops were presented at the UNDP Global Management Team meeting in January 2006, and a road map for implementing enterprise risk-management was developed.

In 2005, 41 audits were conducted; 37 audit reports were issued, 17 of which were for 2004 and 20 for 2005 containing 1,144 recommendations, while the remaining 21 reports for 2005 would be out by June 2006. The management of the country offices responded well to the audit findings, providing full explanations and clarifications, agreeing with the recommendations and indicating a time frame, and the staff and office responsible for implementation. At the end of 2005, the overall implementation rate by country offices was 81 per cent.

Audit activities undertaken at UNDP headquarters in New York in 2005 consisted of a review of the overall project management for the introduction of the first phase of the Atlas enterprise resource planning system, launched in 2004 [YUN 2004, p. 889], resulting in 48 recommendations. A post implementation review of Atlas in UNDP, UNFPA and UNOPS resulted in 80 agency-wide recommendations, while a review of the risks associated with information security at headquarters led to 54 recommendations. At the end of 2005, the implementation rate for headquarters audits was 48 per cent.

In June [dec. 2006/13], the Executive Board welcomed the reports of the Administrator, OAPR [DP/2006/32] (see p. 1049) and the UNFPA Executive Director (see p. 1268) on internal audit and oversight, the creation of an independent audit and oversight committees in UNDP and UNFPA, and the progress made in executing its 2005 decision on internal audit and oversight, and requested UNDP, UNOPS and UNFPA to take further steps to comply with that decision. The Board expressed support for continued strengthening of the internal audit and oversight services of the three UN bodies, and requested an assessment of the resources required. It supported the initiatives of the audit offices in promoting a risk-management culture and requested them to accelerate the development of appropriate, compatible enterprise risk-management systems. The Board also requested UNDP, UNOPS and UNFPA to include clearer, more analytical content in their reports, which should identify risk areas and show their evolution, analyse the causes of the risk, and recommend systems for improvement. It asked that the findings and the risk-based analyses be included in the reports presented to the Board.

The UNDP Administrator and the Executive Directors of UNOPS and UNFPA should include in their respective annual audit and oversight reports: a summary containing key and recurrent findings; a table identifying unresolved audit findings by year and prioritization category; and an explanation of findings that were unresolved for 18 months or more. They should harmonize their audit and management response systems and provide an interim report at the Board's 2007 annual session and separate management responses to key and recurring issues identified in their annual internal audit reports. They were also asked, taking into account the necessity to mitigate the high-risk areas identified in their respective reports, to inform the Board, at its 2007 annual session, on measures to promote the use of national execution.

Procurement

According to the 2005 annual statistical report on procurement [DP/2006/40 & Corr.1], total procurement by the UN system under all sources of funding in 2005 was $8.3 billion, representing an increase of $1.8 billion over the previous year. The share of procurement from developing countries was 43.1 per cent, an increase of 2 per cent from 2004. Under UNDP funding, total procurement was $1.2 billion, of which the share from developing countries was 55.9 per cent, a decrease of 3.2 per cent from 2004.

The UNDP Administrator, in his update of the activities of the Inter-Agency Procurement Services Office (IAPSO) for the 2004-2005 biennium [DP/2006/39], reported that procurement volume handled by IAPSO nearly doubled between 2002 and 2005, due mainly to its deepening relationships with key clients, especially UNDP country offices. Total turnover in 2004 was $141.6 million, with an average fee of 3.3 per cent; corresponding figures for 2005 were $193.2 million and 2.8 per cent. The net operating surplus was about 0.4 per cent of the turnover for the biennium, while the cash reserve increased by about $1.4 million. IAPSO continued to develop its e-procurement system launched in 2002 [YUN 2002, p. 873], further customizing it to support complex procurement and supply chain management for drugs and associated products to address tuberculosis as part of IAPSO services to the Global Drug Facility, and interfacing it with the UNDP Atlas enterprise resource planning system.

In September [dec. 2006/29], the UNDP/UNFPA Executive Board took note of the report on the activities of IAPSO and its continuing self-financing status. It encouraged IAPSO to continue to develop its procurement capabilities, and recommended that it continue to improve the quality and cost-effectiveness of its procurement outcomes in the global supply markets.

Other technical cooperation

Development Account

In response to General Assembly resolution 60/246 [YUN 2005, p. 1489], which requesting him to provide to the Assembly, at its sixty-first session, recommendations on how additional resources in the region of $5 million could be added to the Development Account, the Secretary-General submitted an August report [A/61/282] on the identification of additional resources for the Account. The report discussed the established procedure for, and the possibility of, identifying and transferring savings within the UN programme budget to the Account and the experience in the identification of savings.

The report concluded that, in accordance with resolutions 52/12 B [YUN 1997, p. 1392] and 54/15 [YUN 1999, p. 1307], surpluses from efficiency gains should be identified in the context of budget performance reports and credited to the Development Account. However, in the absence of a reliable method to determine the cost of outputs and services, efficiency savings could not be identified with sufficient precision. Therefore, the Secretary-General could not currently make recommendations on how resources in the region of $5 million could be added to the Account. The results of the re-costing exercise for the 2006-2007 biennium led to an initial appropriation of $13,954,100, as compared with $13,065,000 in previous bienniums, an increase of $889,100. Under financial regulations 5.3 and 5.4, surpluses arising from the regular budget operations at the end of the financial period were to be returned to Member States. While those regulations had been suspended in the past to deal with the Organization's financial problems or to finance specific reform or restructuring activities, any decisions in that regard would relate exclusively to the Assembly's role in conducting a thorough analysis and approval of human and financial resources. Therefore, any future increase in funding levels for the Development Account was subject to the Assembly's consideration of competing priorities for the use of the overall UN programme budget.

The Secretary-General recommended that the Assembly should decide whether the re-costing of the Development Account should be continued beyond the 2006-2007 biennium. In the light of competing priorities, it might also wish, at its sixty-second (2007) session, to consider the use of budget surpluses at the end of the current financial period as a means of increasing the funding level of the Account.

In September [A/61/479], the Advisory Committee on Administrative and Budgetary Questions (ACABQ) said that it would be for the Assembly to decide, as a matter of policy, whether to deviate from the full application of the financial regulations for the purposes of retaining funds to augment the Account. ACABQ pointed out that the re-costing of the Account was a one-time exercise approved by the Assembly, and any decision to continue beyond the 2006-2007 biennium would require further Assembly decision.

The Assembly, in section IV of **resolution 61/252** of 22 December (see p. 1614), took note of the Secretary-General's report on the subject and the related ACABQ report. It regretted that the Secretary-General was not able to provide recommendations on how additional resources in the region of $5 million could be added to the Account and requested him to submit to the Assembly a comprehensive report setting out recommendations on how to do so without using surpluses. The Assembly decided to appropriate, under section 34, Development Account, of the 2006-2007 programme budget $2.5 million as an immediate exceptional measure to address the lack of transfer of resources to the Account. It requested the Secretary-General to provide recommendations to the Assembly on the identification of a further $2 million in the context of his comprehensive report; assess the impact of the Development Account in terms of its aims and purposes, and report thereon to the Assembly at its sixty-second session.

UN activities

Department of Economic and Social Affairs

During 2006, the UN Department of Economic and Social Affairs (DESA) had approximately 470 technical cooperation projects under execution in a dozen substantive sectors, with a total expenditure of $48.7 million. Projects financed by UNDP represented $6.2 million, and those by trust funds, $42.5 million. On a geographical basis, the Department's technical cooperation programme included expenditures of $31 million for interregional and global programmes, $8.5 million in Asia and the Pacific, $5.7 million in Africa, $2.7 million in the Middle East and $0.8 million in the Americas.

Distribution of expenditures by substantive sectors was as follows: associate expert programme, $24 million; programme support, $7.1 million; socio-economic governance management, $6.3 million; governance and public administration, $5.7 million; water, $2.1 million; knowledge management, $1 million; energy, $0.9 million; statistics $0.9 million; population, $0.2 million; infrastructure, $0.2 million; social development, $0.1 million; advancement of women, $0.1 million; and the United Nations Forum on Forests, $0.1 million. Of the total delivery of $48.7 million, the associate expert programme comprised 49 per cent, programme support, 15 per cent; and socio-economic governance management, 13 per cent.

On a component basis, the DESA delivery in 2006 included $41 million for project personnel, $3.1 million for training, $2.1 million for sub-contracts, $2 million for equipment and $0.5 million for miscellaneous expenses.

The total expenditure for DESA against the UN regular programme for technical cooperation was $5.1 million. Distribution of expenditures by division was as follows: public administration and Development management, $2 million; sustainable development, $1.2 million; statistics, $0.8 million; social policy and development, $0.7 million; advancement of women, $0.2 million; population, $0.1 million; and administrative support, $0.1 million. On a component basis, expenditure for 2006 included $3.3 million for advisory services, $0.9 million for meetings, $0.5 million for travel and $0.4 million for consultants' fees and travel.

The total expenditure against the United Nations Development Account (see above) was $1.5 million in 2006. Distribution of expenditures by division was as follows: Advancement of Women, $0.4 million; Office of Economic and Social Council Support and Coordination, $0.4 million;

Statistics, $0.4 million; Development Policy and Planning, $0.1 million; Public Administration and Development Management, $0.1 million; and Social Policy and Development, $0.1 million. On a component basis, expenditure included $0.7 million for meetings, $0.3 million for consultant fees and travel, $0.2 million for travel, $0.2 million for equipment and $0.1 million for contractual services.

UN Office for Partnerships

In 2006, the United Nations Fund for International Partnerships (UNFIP)—which managed the United Nations Foundation, a public charity established by Robert E. Turner in 1998 [YUN 1998, p. 1297], and the United Nations Democracy Fund (UNDEF), set up in 2005 [YUN 2005, p. 655] to provide assistance for projects to strengthen democratic institutions—were consolidated with Partnership Advisory Services and Outreach to form the United Nations Office for Partnerships. The Secretary-General's report [A/62/220] provided information on the 2006 activities of UNFIP and UNDEF (see relevant sections below) and in the area of partnership advisory services and outreach.

The Office for Partnerships served as a gateway for new alliances and partnerships for the UN system to work more effectively with the private sector and civil society. In 2006, it handled nearly 500 inquiries from the private sector, NGOs and foundations wishing to collaborate with the UN systems.

UN Fund for International Partnerships

The United Nations Fund for International Partnerships (UNFIP) was established in 1998 [YUN 1998, p. 1297] to manage the process of grant allocations through the United Nations Foundation, to channel Robert E. Turner's gift of stock valued at some $1 billion to the United Nations. A total of $191.2 million was programmed for 2006, of which $180.5 million was geared for eight projects related to children's health, $3.2 million for three population and women projects; $1 million for six environment projects; $0.1 million for two projects for peace, security and human rights, and $6.4 million for five projects outside the four focus areas. The Foundation's allocations to UNFIP projects and activities since 1998 had reached $994.4 million for 400 projects, implemented by 39 UN agencies covering activities in 123 countries. Its work enabled the United Nations to benefit from the support of other donors and partners in the amount of $561 million. The partnership with the Foundation generated an additional $355 million in parallel contributions. The Foundation was working on a second phase, which was expected to yield an additional $1 billion from other partners, to be managed through UNFIP.

On 22 December (**decision 61/549**), the General Assembly took note of the Secretary-General's report on UNFIP activities in 2005 [YUN 2005, p. 977].

United Nations Democracy Fund

The United Nations Democracy Fund (UNDEF) was established in 2005 [YUN 2005, p. 655], under UNFIP management and administration, to provide assistance to projects that consolidated and strengthened democratic institutions. The Fund's Advisory Board held its first meeting on 6 March and subsequent meetings on 18 July and 12 December, while its Programme Consultative Group met on 24 March, 21 June and 14 August. A total of $36 million was programmed for 125 UNDEF projects in 2006, of which $10 million was for 35 projects related to civic education, electoral support and political parties; $9.8 million for 32 projects for democratic dialogue and constitutional processes; $5.2 million for 20 projects for civil society empowerment; $5.8 million for 20 projects for accountability, transparency and integrity; $3.1 million for 11 projects for human rights and fundamental freedoms; and $2 million for 7 projects for access to information. The UN Office for Partnerships was developing a monitoring and evaluation strategy to measure impact and had reserved 10 per cent of each grant for evaluation. It convened UNDEF donor meetings on 1 May and 11 October to inform donors of its activities and seek guidance on strategic matters. During the year, nine States made first-time contributions to the Fund.

UN Office for Project Services

The United Nations Office for Project Services (UNOPS) was established in 1995 [YUN 1995, p. 900], in accordance with General Assembly decision 48/510 [YUN 1994, p. 806], as a separate, self-financing entity of the UN system to act as a service provider to UN organizations. It offered a broad range of services, from overall project management to the provision of single inputs.

2006 activities

The UNDP/UNFPA Executive Director, in his annual report on UNOPS activities for 2006 [DP/2007/31], said that steady progress had placed UNOPS on firmer footing as a reliable, viable service provider for the UN system and other clients. As part of an ongoing financial clean-up exercise (see p. 1048), financial procedures were reinforced and strengthened to improve data integrity, and business processes were reviewed to enhance the timeliness and accuracy of financial data. As a result, UNOPS submitted its 2006 financial statements and project financial statements to UNDP and other major clients in a timely manner.

UNOPS business acquisition decreased to $884 million, from $1 billion in 2005, but surpassed the target of $713 million for the implementation portfolio by 24 per cent. Half of its business acquisition derived from emergency and post-conflict operations and the other half related to UN development work. Two thirds of new business required project management services.

The 2006 unaudited financial statements showed that project delivery dropped to $706 million, $75.4 million (9.7 per cent) less than the projected figure of $781.4 million submitted by the Executive Director in January, and $197.4 million (21.9 per cent) less than the 2005 delivery of $903.4 million. The decrease in delivery was attributed principally to reduced activities associated with the elections in Afghanistan.

The total UNOPS income in 2006 was $62.9 million, exceeding the 2006 forecast of $59.4 million. Project services continued to provide the largest percentage of total UNOPS income ($53.4 million, or 84.9 per cent); service revenue totalled $9.5 million, or 15.1 per cent of the total.

Administrative expenditures reached $54.6 million, including a net $7.7 million by Denmark for expenses related to the relocation of UNOPS headquarters to Copenhagen (see below). The 2006 surplus of $8. million increased the operational reserve to $13.3 million.

Budget estimates

Projected financial results for 2005 and projections for 2006

In response to a 2005 UNDP/UNFPA Executive Board decision on measures aimed at restoring the financial viability of UNOPS [YUN 2005, p. 980], the acting UNOPS Executive Director submitted a progress report in January [DP/2006/11], which provided an update on the implementation of the decision, and a revised budget projection for 2005 and financial projections for 2006 and 2007.

Projected revenue for 2005 totalled $67.3 million, including $55.7 million from project implementation services, $9.4 million in services-only revenue, and $2.2 million in interest and rental revenue. Year-end delivery projection for 2005 was expected to reach $835 million. Total projected expenditures for 2005 reached $64 million, including $2.1 million in payments to UNDP related to the Atlas system and PeopleSoft human resources management system, and $2.9 million in other reimbursement costs. The ending fund balance as at 31 December 2005 was projected at $3.4 million.

As at 29 December 2005, business acquisition stood at a record $1.01 billion.

Total revenue for 2006 was projected at $59.4 million, including $51.5 million in total implementation of project portfolio revenue, $4.5 million in "service only" revenue and $3.4 million in interest, rental and other revenue. Total administrative expenditures were expected to reach $52.8 million. The project delivery forecast for 2006 was $781.3 million. The ending fund balance was projected at $10 million.

UNOPS action plan

In a January report [DP/2006/11], the acting UNOPS Executive Director provided an update on the status of implementation of a 2005 Executive Board decision [YUN 2005, p. 980] on the reform measures proposed in the 2005 UNOPS action plan [ibid., p. 979] aimed at restoring financial viability.

The reform measures included the relocation of UNOPS headquarters from New York and rationalization of its support services structure into a global service centre. A recommendation was made that UNOPS relocate its headquarters functions and Europe-based operations to Copenhagen, Denmark, in the first half of 2006. A grant provided by Denmark would cover all expenditures associated with the relocation and transition programme. The Office would pursue a three-pronged strategic direction, consisting of fixed-cost reduction, enhanced operating efficiency and restoration of its overall business prowess. The strategic direction would provide savings of $10 million in 2006 and a similar amount in 2007. The relocation costs were estimated at $6.3 million in 2006 and $1 million in 2007, all of which would be absorbed by the grant provided by Denmark.

During the first quarter of 2006, UNOPS would conduct a comprehensive review of its business portfolio aimed at streamlining the delivery of services. Overall financial performance was expected to improve, with a projected income of $6.5 million. Activity-based costing pilots would be introduced to price service delivery more accurately, and a new UNOPS pricing policy would be instituted by midyear. UNOPS would also revise and adjust its most basic business processes to enhance efficiency and reduce costs. The report described contingency measures that would be put in place to monitor and meet business and financial projections.

At its January session [dec. 2006/6], the UNDP/UNFPA Executive Board took note of the report of the acting UNOPS Executive Director, and welcomed the progress made and action taken to implement the Board's 2005 decision on restoring the Office's financial viability, its transparent approach to making management decisions and determination to improve accuracy in costing and enhance business efficiency.

On 15 May, the Secretary-General appointed Jan Mattsson (Sweden) as Executive Director of UNOPS, effective 12 June.

In his annual report, submitted in June [DP/2006/22], the Executive Director said that the new UNOPS headquarters in Copenhagen had been integrated with existing UN offices, complying fully with UN security requirements, and would begin operations on 1 July. UNOPS would maintain a presence in New York to ensure an effective liaison with governing bodies and support service to New York-based client organizations. It transferred its lease obligation at the Chrysler Building in New York, scheduled to expire on 31 December 2014, to an outside tenant, effective 1 September 2006, resulting in a projected $21.8 million fixed-cost reduction over the remaining lease period.

Progress was recorded in the realignment of UNOPS client divisions. As at 1 July, UNOPS regional presence in Africa was consolidated into one office in Nairobi, Kenya, and the European presence would be based in Copenhagen by 31 December, with a liaison presence remaining in Geneva to interact with client organizations there. The service capacity in Dubai, United Arab Emirates, was reconfigured to function as a regional presence supporting service provision in the Middle East and provide emergency and rapid-response capacity on a needs-based, full cost-recovery basis. The Asia-Pacific Regional Office in Bangkok, Thailand, would continue its current operations.

In a June conference room paper [DP/2006/CRP.3], UNOPS, following discussions with the Board of Auditors and the ACABQ secretariat, submitted to the Executive Board for approval a proposed course of action to ensure the successful resubmission of its financial statements by 30 November. The paper outlined specific tasks called for by the Board of Auditors with regard to deferred expenditure, suspense accounts, accounts payable, aging of accounts receivable and inter-fund balances. UNOPS would put in place a dedicated financial clean-up project team to prepare the adjusted financial statements to audit, identify the procedural and systems weaknesses that led to persistent deficiencies in UNOPS accounting practices and establish a system of controls to prevent recurrence of the problems. The Executive Board took note of the paper.

Also in June [dec. 2006/17], the Executive Board welcomed the appointment of the new UNOPS Executive Director, took note of his annual report, and welcomed the further progress made in the implementation of its 2005 decision on restoring the Office's financial viability, and encouraged UNOPS to continue to focus on the work areas contained in that decision. The Board requested UNOPS to improve its accuracy in costing and enhance business efficiency, and inform the Board, at its September session, of progress achieved in implementing the action plan, so as to ensure the availability of certified statements by 30 November.

In response to the Board's request, the Executive Director, in August [DP/2006/45], submitted a progress report on UNOPS activities, which, among other subjects, discussed the UNOPS business strategy for 2006 and beyond and the preparation of the 2004-2005 financial statements. He said that the UNOPS business strategy would target a broad client base with project management and procurement needs. Emphasis would be placed on operations in selected countries that would benefit from a strong UNOPS field presence, thereby allowing for greater specialization, a reduction of overhead costs and improvement in the competitive pricing of UNOPS services.

The goal of becoming a world-class provider of management services would require effective implementation of several important initiatives, including: radically improved financial management practices; a human-resource strategy that encompassed all staff and project personnel, aimed at recruiting, developing and retaining the best possible talent; internationally recognized certification in project management, procurement, and finance at the organizational level and individually for managers and staff; knowledge-sharing in functional management areas and programmatic practices; and rapid development and implementation of solid performance management at all organizational levels, including pricing policy, activity-based costing, reengineered business processes and relevant information technology support. In the short term, UNOPS would focus on building a solid reputation for excellence among its clients, rather than on growth, and establish a "balanced scorecard" system as a central tool for managing performance and holding managers accountable for their contributions to the corporate strategy. An outline of the performance areas to be monitored against targets was annexed to the report.

UNOPS established the project team to clean up data and prepare financial statements for submission by 30 November, as requested by the Executive Board in June. Although solid advances were being made, the Board was asked to take note of several risks to meeting the November deadline, including the need to review many more years of accounts than previously anticipated.

In September [dec. 2006/33], the Executive Board took note of the Executive Director's progress report on UNOPS activities and requested UNOPS to report on its financial, administrative and operational situation at the Board's first regular session in 2007.

Audit reports

The Executive Board, at its January session, considered a report [DP/2006/14] on the implementation of the recommendations of the Board of Auditors for the 2002-2003 biennium [YUN 2004, p. 1397], which updated information provided in a 2005 implementation report [YUN 2005, p. 980]. At the same session [dec. 2006/8], the Executive Board took note of progress made by UNOPS in implementing the recommendations of the Board of Auditors.

In May [DP/2006/32], the UNDP Office of Audit and Performance Review (OAPR) submitted to the UNOPS Executive Director its annual report on internal audit and investigation services for 2005. The report set out initiatives undertaken to strengthen oversight in UNOPS, including helping management in strengthening the governance of oversight, improving the planning and execution of internal audit, and enhancing coordination with management, the external auditor and other oversight bodies. In response to requests made by the Executive Board in 2005 [YUN 2005, p. 975], the report prioritized recommendations based on risks and analysed issues based on frequency of occurrence, as well as the underlying causes of the issues. The status of the most frequent and highest priority recommendations was updated, based on the framework approved by the Board in 2004 [YUN 2004, p. 891]. The report presented management responses to audit recommendations.

The Executive Director established the Risk Management and Oversight Committee in 2005 to assist in fulfilling the Executive Director's responsibilities regarding management and reporting, internal controls, risk management and matters relating to external and internal audits. The Committee also made several recommendations, which the Executive Director agreed to implement, including the establishment of an internal control framework and a policy to prevent and detect fraud both aimed at strengthening internal control and accountability.

OAPR said that 26 audit reports were issued in 2005, of which 22 were initiated and completed during the year. Four pertained to audits carried forward from 2004. The reports contained 157 recommendations for improving internal controls and organizational efficiency. The organizational units concerned provided written responses to the draft audit reports, indicating the actions taken or were being taken to address the audit issues and recommendations.

In June [dec. 2006/13], the Executive Board welcomed the UNOPS report on internal audit and oversight.

UN Volunteers

In 2006, the number of volunteers working for the UNDP-administered United Nations Volunteers (UNV) programme dropped to 7,623, from 8,122 in 2005. The volunteers, representing 163 nationalities, carried out 7,856 assignments in 144 countries; volunteers from developing countries represented 76 per cent of the total number. Women accounted for 36.2 per cent of the total in 2006, compared to 36.5 per cent in 2005. By region, 51 per cent of assignments were carried out in Africa, 18 per cent in Asia and the Pacific, 14 per cent in Latin America and the Caribbean, 10 per cent in the Arab States and 7 per cent in Europe and CIS.

The UNDP Administrator, in his annual report on the UNDP financial situation [DP/2007/41 & Add.1 & Add.1/Corr.1], said that the 2006 income relating to the Special Voluntary Fund, cost-sharing, trust funds and full funding arrangements was $20.2 million, a reduction of $6 million compared to the $26.2 million received in 2005. Programme expenditure was $19 million, marginally higher than the 2005 expenditure of $18.4 million.

In June [dec. 2006/18], the Executive Board took note of the report [DP/2006/24] on UNV activities for 2004-2005. It welcomed UNV efforts to develop and apply a business model and results framework that highlighted UNV areas of distinct contribution to development and peace, and allowed for enhanced analysis and understanding of UNV activities and impact on the achievement of the MDGs. The Board invited the Administrator to pay particular attention to the achievement of results and sustainability in the further implementation of the MDGs and in his reporting. It welcomed the increased involvement of nationally recruited volunteers in UNV activities and encouraged continued efforts in that regard. It also encouraged UNV to continue to increase its focus on assisting programme countries in developing sustainable national capacities. The Board took special note of the UNV commitment to strengthening gender equality in all its work, including by increasing the percentage of women volunteers. It reaffirmed the importance of the Special Voluntary Fund and urged donors and other countries in a position to do so to continue to support the Fund. The Board also reaffirmed its support for the UNV role as focal point for the follow-up to the International Year of Volunteers (2001) [YUN 2001, p. 814]. It invited the Administrator to report on the implementation of the decision in his biennial report, to be submitted in 2008.

Economic and technical cooperation among developing countries

South-South cooperation

In response to a 2005 UNDP/UNFPA Executive Board decision endorsing the third cooperation framework for South-South cooperation (2005-2007) [YUN 2005, p. 982], the Administrator submitted a March report [DP/2006/21] on the implementation of the framework. The report described achievements under the framework's three policy and operational support platforms: to support policy dialogue and follow-up to major intergovernmental conferences; help create an enabling environment and partnership mechanisms for expanded South-South business cooperation and technology exchanges for poverty reduction; and support a more robust information system for managing and sharing Southern development knowledge and solutions. It also discussed efforts to promote South-South initiatives for disaster-risk management and recovery.

The total regular (core) resources allocated yearly to the Special Unit for South-South Cooperation amounted to $3.5 million. The total available resources from 2005 to 2007 amounted to $14.6 million. Some $4.7 million was disbursed in 2005. Resources managed by the Special Unit, as at 31 December 2005, amounted to $24,702.

The Administrator concluded that, in the first phase of the implementation of the framework, the Special Unit's efforts had concentrated on building and strengthening broad-based partnerships. Its efforts to involve the private sector and civil society throughout the South, had invited innovative ideas on how to broaden and strengthen South-South involvement in development. While preparing for long-term results through such programmes as the Global Asset and Technology Exchange and the Global Science Corps, the Special Unit had also responded to the short-term needs of countries, including those affected by the 2004 tsunami, with grants and strategies designed to bring communities back quickly into the global economy.

In June [dec. 2006/26], the Executive Board took note of the report on the implementation of the third cooperation framework for South-South cooperation. It requested UNDP to emphasize further its 2004-2007 multi-year funding framework (MYFF) driver of development effectiveness that sought South-South solutions (see p. 1040) and promote its impact, and to report to the Board, at its 2007 annual session, on further efforts to mainstream that driver. The Administrator was also requested to report to the Board on efforts to mobilize additional resources from donors and other voluntary sources, as well as through triangular cooperation, for enhancing South-South cooperation. In addition, he was asked to support the Special Unit for South-South Cooperation in fostering cooperation among developing countries and in seeking support for such efforts through partnerships within the UN system and through triangular cooperation. The Board encouraged all countries in a position to do so to contribute to the United Nations Fund for South-South Cooperation (formerly the Voluntary Trust Fund for the Promotion of South-South Cooperation), which was included in the United Nations Pledging Conference for Development Activities.

UN Capital Development Fund

The United Nations Capital Development Fund (UNCDF) fully achieved its targeted programme results and outcomes in 2006, a transitional year for the Fund. Contributions to UNCDF regular resources increased from $9.5 million in 2005 to $13.9 million in 2006 [DP/2007/41 & Add.1 & Add.1/Corr.1]. Other resources contributions decreased from $10.3 million to $8.1 million. Overall expenditures totalled 25.6 million, with programme expenditure from regular resources increasing from $11.6 million in 2005 to $17.2 million in 2006, and other resources expenditures increasing from $7.6 million to $8.4 million. UNCDF maintained its operational reserve level at $22.6 million; total unexpended resources increased to $38 million.

At its January session, the UNDP/UNFPA Executive Board considered the UNCDF report on its budgeting and decision-making processes [DP/2006/10], submitted in response to a 2005 Board decision

[YUN 2005, p. 987]. Following the appointment of its new Executive Secretary on 1 August 2005, UNCDF began a strategic review of its 2005-2007 business plan [ibid., p. 986]. Initial results suggested that the niches in which the Fund operated were viable and that it had significant comparative advantages in each of them. It was clear that UNCDF products and services were in great demand and benefited the least developed countries (LDCs) considerably.

Concerning business development and resource mobilization, UNCDF was in the early stages of articulating and implementing its business development strategy. Much work remained to be done to mobilize sufficient financial resources to allow UNCDF to meet the goals in the business plan. The budget forecast suggested that a minimum of $37 million in 2006 and $49 million in 2007, consisting of both core and non-core resources, had to be mobilized for programming, over and above the $5 million provided by UNDP for administrative costs in 2006-2007 biennium budget. Of those amounts, roughly $18 million had been committed for 2006 and $7 million for 2007. Key elements of the UNCDF business development and resource mobilization plan would be to broaden and diversify the donor base; attract additional development partner funding; seek long-term, predictable funding from donors and partners; assure local government and microfinance institution funding participation in all programmes; develop one or two large thematic or regional programmes for funding; and work closely with UNDP to strengthen partnerships and mobilize resources.

UNCDF began a restructuring process in August 2005 to decentralize its operations to the regional and country levels, and significantly reduce its headquarters staff. The alignment of UNCDF regional and country presence with the business plan began in October 2005 and was expected to be completed by 30 June 2006.

In January [dec. 2006/4], the Executive Board took note of the report on UNCDF budgeting and decision-making processes and welcomed the appointment of the new UNCDF Executive Secretary. It encouraged the Fund to continue its strategic review of the business plan and complete its detailed investment plan for 2006-2007. The Executive Secretary was requested to report in June on the status of the strategic review and implementation of the business plan, including, in particular, the business development strategy, the managing-for-results strategy, the organizational structure, and staffing, and budgetary arrangements. The UNDP Administrator and the Executive Secretary were asked to finalize a memorandum of understanding between UNDP and UNCDF, setting out the key elements of their strategic, operational and financial partnership, and report on the arrangements to the Board in June. The Board again asked UNDP to assist UNCDF in mobilizing resources for sustaining its local development and microfinance activities, and donor and other countries in a position to do so to provide and sustain additional funding support for UNCDF programmes and activities in the LDCs.

In April [DP/2006/23], UNCDF submitted to the Executive Board its results-oriented annual report, which provided an overview of UNCDF performance for each of the sub-goals of local development, microfinance and organizational performance and, in response to the Board's January decision (see above), updated information on the status of the strategic review and implementation of the business plan.

In the first quarter of 2006, UNCDF completed the strategic review of the business plan and prepared a detailed investment plan for 2006-2007; the investment plan was annexed to the report. The number of LDCs in which UNCDF planned to invest by 2007 increased to 45, of which 28 were to be covered specifically in the microfinance practice area.

UNCDF sought to expand its donor base and improve burden-sharing for non-earmarked resources. UNDP and UNCDF collaborated with member States during the resources mobilization process and agreed to adjust the mobilization incentive structure at the country level to ensure that mobilized resources for UNCDF were included in the balanced scorecard of the country office concerned. UNCDF was also pursuing financial support on a programme basis at the country level.

UNCDF was at the final stage of refining the coherent managing-for-results framework. Its strategic results framework was close to finalization and would be used for reporting on results in 2006 and 2007. The strategic results framework linked UNCDF results in the local development and microfinance practice areas to MDG objectives and the UNDP results framework, and identified core indicators that could be measured through monitoring and evaluation and used for management and reporting purposes.

Consistent with UN reform initiatives, UNCDF continued restructuring to achieve greater decentralization and improve its operating efficiency and effectiveness. By April 2006, the streamlining of the UNCDF headquarters to focus on strategic functions and management had been largely completed.

A closer working relationship was established between UNCDF and UNDP in monitoring and evaluation, resulting in, among other things, a common evaluation policy for UNDP and its associated funds and programmes, which was submitted to the Executive Board for approval in June. UNCDF also adopted the UNDP balanced scorecard tool for assessing organizational performance. The number of joint UNCDF/UNDP programmes grew in 2005 and included a joint regional programme for building inclusive financial sectors in Africa. The Fund also sought to formulate joint programmes with the UNDP Bureau for Crisis Prevention and Recovery, and work with the regional bureaux in providing technical support to their microfinance activities. UNCDF expanded its presence in the UNDP regional service centres in Dakar (Senegal), Johannesburg (South Africa), and Bangkok (Thailand). The two bodies were preparing a draft strategic partnership agreement to address strategic and operational issues.

Total core and non-core income only reached $21 million in 2005. Core income was $10.7 million, down substantially from $17.6 million in 2004. If UNCDF was able to mobilize resources as set forth in its business plan, core income and core programme expenditure would be in balance at around $18 million in 2006 and 2007. Overall delivery against core resources stood at 74 per cent. Programme delivery and the ratio of administrative to programmatic expenses were affected negatively by the impact of the change management process and the fact that most UNCDF-supported projects were either at the end or in the early stage of their implementation cycle in 2005.

There was an upward trend in both core and non-core programme expenditures compared to 2004, with non-core expenditures making up 39 per cent of total programme expenditures.

In June [dec. 2006/15], the Executive Board welcomed the 2005 UNCDF results-oriented annual report, but noted that the Fund's resource mobilization had fallen short of the requirements set forth in its investment and business plans. It stressed the need to strengthen UNCDF financial situation and reiterated its call to donor countries and those in a position to do so to provide and sustain additional funding support for UNCDF programmes and activities in the LDCs. The Board reiterated its call to UNDP to assist UNCDF in mobilizing the resources necessary to sustain the Fund's activities and the implementation of its investment plan. The UNDP Administrator and the UNCDF Executive Secretary were requested to finalize the strategic agreement between their organizations and report to the Board at its first regular session in 2007. They were also asked to explore ways to cooperate on strategic planning, funding, programming arrangements and the results framework in the context of the preparation of the UNDP 2008-2011 MYFF.

Chapter III

Humanitarian and special economic assistance

In 2006, the United Nations, through the Office for the Coordination of Humanitarian Affairs (OCHA), continued to mobilize and coordinate humanitarian assistance to respond to international emergencies. During the year, consolidated inter-agency appeals were launched for Burundi, the Central African Republic, Chad, the Congo, Côte d'Ivoire, the Democratic Republic of the Congo (DRC), the Great Lakes region, Guinea, Guinea-Bissau, the Horn of Africa, Kenya, Lebanon, Liberia, Nepal, the Occupied Palestinian Territory, Somalia, the Sudan, Timor-Leste, Uganda, West Africa and Zimbabwe. OCHA received contributions for natural disaster assistance totaling $257.3 million.

The Ad Hoc Advisory Groups on Burundi, Guinea-Bissau and Haiti continued to develop long-term programmes of support for those countries. Due to progress made in Burundi and the Ad Hoc Group's conclusion that the situation in the country would be better addressed by the newly established Peacebuilding Commission, the Economic and Social Council terminated the mandate of the Ad Hoc Advisory Group in Burundi.

Efforts continued to implement the Hyogo Declaration and the Hyogo Framework for Action 2005-2015, the 10-year plan for reducing disaster risks, adopted at the World Conference on Disaster Reduction in 2005. In line with the Framework, activities were also undertaken to strengthen the International Strategy for Disaster Reduction. Further progress was made in the development and implementation of the Indian Ocean Tsunami Warning and Mitigation System.

During the year, the Economic and Social Council considered ways to strengthen UN humanitarian assistance coordination by implementing improved humanitarian response at all levels, including strengthening capacity, with particular attention to recent humanitarian emergencies. Implementation of the humanitarian reform agenda, which was initiated in late 2005, advanced following the Humanitarian Response Review. OCHA established the Humanitarian Reform Support Unit to support Humanitarian Coordinators, field teams and agencies in driving forward the reform agenda. The year witnessed the launch of the "cluster leadership approach", an initiative whereby humanitarian clusters or groups of humanitarian organizations and stakeholders worked together to enhance the effectiveness of response, as well as the Central Emergency Response Fund, an upgraded cash-flow mechanism for the initial phase of humanitarian emergencies. The High-level Panel on UN System-wide Coherence in the areas of development, humanitarian assistance and the environment, established in response to the 2005 World Summit Outcome, presented a report entitled, "Delivering as one", which included recommendations relevant to the humanitarian reform agenda.

Humanitarian assistance

Coordination

Humanitarian affairs segment of the Economic and Social Council

The humanitarian affairs segment of the Economic and Social Council (14 and 17-18 July) [A/61/3/Rev.1] considered, in accordance with Council **decision 2006/214**, the strengthening of UN humanitarian assistance coordination: implementing improved humanitarian response at all levels, including strengthening capacity, with particular attention to recent humanitarian emergencies including severe natural disasters. It also convened panels on the sub-themes of gender-based violence in humanitarian emergencies and chronically underfunded emergencies. A panel discussion on risk reduction in the recovery process was also held. On 12 May, the Council decided to hold an informal event on 14 July to discuss relief to development (**decision 2006/217**).

The Council considered the Secretary-General's June report [A/61/85-E/2006/81] on strengthening the coordination of UN emergency humanitarian assistance, submitted in response to General Assembly resolution 60/124 [YUN 2005, p. 991] and Council resolution 2005/4 [ibid., p. 990]. The report summarized humanitarian developments over the proceeding year, particularly with regard to disasters, complex emergencies and population movements, and addressed the themes of the Council's humanitarian affairs segment (see above), as well as issues related to restrictions on humanitarian access, civil-military coordination and integrated missions. It also examined some of the key improvements to humanitarian activities and focused on technical proposals for strengthening response capacities at all levels.

According to the report, during the preceding year, developments in the humanitarian environment were characterized by more natural disasters of exceptional magnitude and worrying trends in complex emergencies. Twenty-seven tropical storms, including 13 hurricanes, ravaged communities in 12 countries, and humanitarian emergencies arising from conflicts continued to challenge the humanitarian community. The impact of those crises on vulnerable countries and communities would require continued attention in order to avert increased displacement, development setbacks and enduring poverty. Although disaster mortality rates had declined in the last two decades, the number of people affected by them was three times higher, and economic losses increased fivefold. The 18 per cent rise in the number of reported large-scale disasters in the past year, the growing frequency and severity of hydro-meteorological hazards (floods, droughts, windstorms), the threat of geological hazards, such as earthquakes, volcanoes and tsunamis, which were the deadliest natural hazards in 2005, and the effects of shorter drought cycles on populations in the Horn of Africa, underpinned the overall trend that disasters were becoming more frequent, severe and destructive.

The humanitarian system itself, with its many actors with varying skills and priorities, had yet to employ those resources to optimum effect. The system was not mobilizing as quickly as possible the people with the right skills and, in the case of the Sudan, continued to import staff, technology and supplies, when local sources might be more effective. International responders were sometimes too slow to coordinate with government and local actors in large-scale disasters. Moreover, respect and application of the principles guiding humanitarian activities continued to be uneven in many areas. Therefore, strengthening the coordination of UN emergency humanitarian assistance would require the reorientation of humanitarian systems.

With regard to disaster management, an approach was needed that would address the interconnected nature of threats and vulnerabilities on a global scale, including strategic disaster planning and preparedness at regional, national and local levels, sustaining high levels of assistance for post-disaster recovery and reconstruction, and prioritizing risk reduction. Targeting disaster "hot spots" was identified as an important starting point. A regional and long-term approach to humanitarian crises was also emphasized. In that connection, the launch, in April, by the Secretary-General of a $426 million regional consolidated appeal to address life-saving needs and the underlying causes of vulnerability to drought in the Horn of Africa (see p. 1105), and the establishment of a temporary position of relief coordinator for tsunami-affected countries were positive developments.

The Emergency Relief Coordinator, together with his humanitarian partners, embarked on several initiatives, based on the guidance provided by the Council in resolution 2005/4, to improve the predictability, accountability and effectiveness of humanitarian response, including the development of the "cluster leadership approach", which entailed humanitarian clusters or groups of humanitarian organizations and other stakeholders working together to collectively identify gaps in and enhance the effectiveness of responses. At the global level, the approach would strengthen system-wide preparedness and technical capacity by designing global "cluster leads" accountable for ensuring predictable and effective inter-agency responses. Cluster leads were established in nine areas, including traditional relief and assistance (water and sanitation, nutrition, health and emergency shelter); service provision (emergency telecommunications and logistics) and cross-cutting issues (camp coordination/management, early recovery and protection). At the country level, the approach would seek to improve the delivery of assistance by identifying and ensuring predictable leadership in key areas/sectors; creating stronger partnerships among actors in critical gap areas; strengthening the cluster responsibility of the Humanitarian Coordinator; and improving strategic, field-level coordination and prioritization. The cluster approach was implemented in the Pakistan earthquake response, as well as in the DRC, Liberia, Somalia and Uganda. In March, the Secretary-General issued a global cluster appeal for $39.7 million to fund the initial implementation of nine clusters at the global level (see p. 1057). Other developments included the creation of a pool of pre-certified candidates that could be deployed for short-term and/or immediate assignment as humanitarian coordinators; the 9 March launch of the new Central Emergency Response Fund (CERF) (see p. 1061); and the establishment of an Advisory Group on the use and impact of the Fund. Future initiatives for improving the humanitarian response system would involve developing more formal structures for interaction with non-UN actors, such as host and neighbouring Governments, regional organizations, non-governmental organizations (NGOs), the International Red Cross and Red Crescent Movement, in order to build on their capacities and expertise.

Efforts to strengthen local, national and regional capacities to prepare and respond to crises included mapping national and local response capacities, overcoming coordination challenges, and advocating for funds from donors. The report provided information on restrictions on humanitarian access; gender-based violence in emergencies; trends and patterns relating to chronically underfunded crises; the need for improved standby arrangements to enhance civil-military coordination and the availability of military assets during crises; and improvements to the integrated mission process, including the February issuance of the Note of Guidance on Integrated Missions (see p. 82), which specified the working relationships of humanitarian, development, military and political actors.

The Secretary-General recommended that Member States, donors and humanitarian organizations invest in preparedness, early recovery and risk reduction activities as part of humanitarian response, particularly in high-risk areas, and support regional appeals and coordination mechanisms to promote coherence of response and recovery activities and the most effective use of resources. Governments with internally displaced persons (IDPs) or populations at risk of displacement should review and amend their legislation, with a view to building their capacity to assist and protect IDPs, and request international assistance to support them in that task.

The Secretary-General proposed a series of actions for Member States, donors, humanitarian organizations, UN system organs, Governments and NGOs regarding implementing improved humanitarian response; strengthening local, national and regional capacities to prepare for and respond to crises; and the application of humanitarian principles, and other issues of concern, including on humanitarian access and the development by UN system organizations of parameters for international emergency response.

Reports of Secretary-General. The Council also had before it the reports of the Secretary-General on humanitarian assistance and rehabilitation for El Salvador and Guatemala (see p. 1104); on strengthening emergency relief, rehabilitation, reconstruction and prevention in the aftermath of the South Asian earthquake disaster in Pakistan (see p. 1106); and on strengthening emergency relief, rehabilitation, reconstruction, recovery and prevention in the aftermath of the Indian Ocean tsunami disaster (see p. 1100).

ECONOMIC AND SOCIAL COUNCIL ACTION

On 18 July [meeting 30], the Economic and Social Council adopted **resolution 2006/5** [draft: E/2006/L.13, orally revised] without vote [agenda item 5].

Strengthening of the coordination of emergency humanitarian assistance of the United Nations

The Economic and Social Council,

Reaffirming General Assembly resolution 46/182 of 19 December 1991 and the guiding principles contained in the annex thereto, and recalling other relevant Assembly and Economic and Social Council resolutions and agreed conclusions of the Council,

Welcoming the fact that at the humanitarian affairs segment of its substantive session of 2006, the Council considered the theme "Strengthening of the coordination of United Nations humanitarian assistance: implementing improved humanitarian response at all levels, including strengthening capacity, with particular attention to recent humanitarian emergencies including severe natural disasters",

Welcoming also the fact that the Council held panels on gender-based violence in humanitarian emergencies and chronically underfunded emergencies,

Recognizing the clear relationship between emergency, rehabilitation, and development and that, in order to ensure a smooth transition from relief to rehabilitation and development, emergency assistance must be provided in ways that will be supportive of recovery and long-term development, and that emergency measures should be seen as a step towards long-term development,

Recalling the Hyogo Declaration and the Hyogo Framework for Action 2005-2015: Building the Resilience of Nations and Communities to Disasters, as adopted at the World Conference on Disaster Reduction, held in Kobe, Hyogo, Japan, from 18 to 22 January 2005,

1. *Takes note* of the report of the Secretary-General;

2. *Also takes note* of the reports of the Secretary-General on humanitarian assistance and rehabilitation for El Salvador and Guatemala, on strengthening emergency relief, rehabilitation, reconstruction and prevention in the aftermath of the South Asian earthquake disaster in Pakistan, and on strengthening emergency relief, rehabilitation, reconstruction, recovery and prevention in the aftermath of the Indian Ocean tsunami disaster;

3. *Requests* the Secretary-General to encourage the relevant organizations of the United Nations system to continue to identify and use, as appropriate and available, local resources and expertise from within the affected country and/or its neighbours in response to humanitarian needs;

4. *Encourages* Member States to continue their efforts in preparedness and disaster risk reduction, and encourages the international community and relevant United

Nations entities, within their respective mandates, to support national efforts in this regard;

5. *Requests* the relevant organizations of the United Nations system to continue to engage systematically with relevant authorities and organizations at the regional and national levels to support efforts to strengthen humanitarian response capacities at all levels, in particular through preparedness programmes, with a view to improving the overall adequacy of the deployment of resources;

6. *Stresses* that the United Nations system should make efforts to enhance existing humanitarian capacities, knowledge and institutions, including, as appropriate, through the transfer of technology and expertise to developing countries;

7. *Emphasizes*, in this regard, the importance of strengthening health sector humanitarian response capacity, and calls upon the relevant entities of the United Nations and all States to cooperate in this regard;

8. *Encourages* all States to strengthen their capacity to respond to natural and man-made disasters, including by establishing or strengthening national contingency plans and developing or strengthening, as appropriate, disaster management institutions, also encourages the sharing of knowledge and experience among States, and further encourages the international community to support, upon request, national efforts in this regard;

9. *Also encourages* national Governments to create an enabling environment for capacity-building of local authorities and local and national non-governmental and community-based organizations, and encourages the relevant entities of the United Nations system and other relevant institutions and organizations to support national authorities in their capacity-building programmes designed to enhance the participation and contribution of local authorities and local and national non-governmental and community-based organizations, including through technical cooperation, and long-term partnerships based on the recognition of their important role in providing humanitarian assistance;

10. *Recognizes* the importance of involving, as appropriate, relevant entities, including non-governmental organizations, that provide humanitarian assistance in national and local coordination efforts, and invites those entities to participate in the improvement of humanitarian assistance, as appropriate;

11. *Invites* the relevant United Nations humanitarian entities to continue their efforts to coordinate, as appropriate, with the International Red Cross and Red Crescent Movement in the provision of humanitarian assistance;

12. *Requests* the Secretary-General to continue to develop more systematic links with Member States offering military assets for natural disaster response in order to identify the availability of such assets, and to report to the General Assembly through the Economic and Social Council in this regard;

13. *Recalls* the 2003 "Guidelines on the Use of Military and Civil Defence Assets to Support United Nations Humanitarian Activities in Complex Emergencies" as well as the 1994 "Guidelines on the Use of Military and Civil Defence Assets in Disaster Relief", and stresses the value of their use and of the development by the United Nations, in consultation with States and other relevant actors, of further guidance on civil-military relations in the context of humanitarian activities and transition situations;

14. *Reiterates* its request to the Secretary-General to report to the General Assembly through the Economic and Social Council on progress achieved in developing and improving mechanisms for the use of emergency standby capacities;

15. *Requests* the Office for the Coordination of Humanitarian Affairs of the Secretariat to continue to improve the analysis and reporting of comprehensive financial information through its Financial Tracking Service, and encourages Member States, multilateral and private donors, relevant United Nations humanitarian agencies and non-governmental organizations to provide timely and accurate information on contributions;

16. *Encourages* the relevant United Nations entities to continue to provide timely information, through existing channels, on the results achieved in the use of funds made available for humanitarian assistance;

17. *Takes note* of the efforts by the United Nations system to further enhance the coordination of its emergency humanitarian assistance;

18. *Welcomes* efforts to strengthen the humanitarian response capacity of and the support to the United Nations resident/humanitarian coordinators and to United Nations country teams, including through the provision of necessary training, the identification of resources and improving the identification and selection of United Nations resident/humanitarian coordinators, to help to provide a timely, predictable and appropriate response to humanitarian needs and to further improve United Nations coordination activities at the field level, and requests the Secretary-General to continue efforts in this regard;

19. *Stresses* the importance of a coordinated process of assessing lessons learned in the international response to a given humanitarian emergency;

20. *Welcomes* the establishment of the Central Emergency Response Fund, as set out in General Assembly resolution 60/124 of 15 December 2005, and looks forward to receiving the report to be submitted to the Assembly on the use of the Fund with a view to maximizing its impact and improving its functioning;

21. *Encourages* the international community to provide humanitarian assistance in proportion to needs and on the basis of needs assessments, with a view to ensuring a more equitable distribution of humanitarian assistance across humanitarian emergencies, including those of a protracted nature, as well as fuller coverage of the needs of all sectors, and to this end requests United Nations organizations, including the United Nations country teams, to continue developing, and improving where appropriate, transparent needs-assessment mechanisms;

22. *Re-emphasizes* that the discussions of humanitarian policies and activities by the General Assembly and the Economic and Social Council should be continuously

revitalized by Member States with a view to enhancing their relevance, efficiency and impact;

23. *Recommends* that the General Assembly, in order to have a more focused discussion on humanitarian issues, explore the possibility at its sixty-first session of reallocating to the plenary of the Assembly the sub-items of its agenda related to the strengthening of the coordination of humanitarian and disaster relief assistance of the United Nations currently considered by the Second Committee;

24. *Encourages* Member States to continue to strengthen cooperation and coordination between the General Assembly and the Economic and Social Council on humanitarian issues, based on their respective mandates and taking into account comparative advantages and existing complementarities of the two bodies;

25. *Decides* to continue to use informal settings, as they exist within its humanitarian segment, as an opportunity for Member States to be informed about and exchange views on humanitarian issues;

26. *Requests* the Secretary-General to include in his report lessons learned and best practices in the implementation of the pilot projects using the cluster approach, in consultation with affected countries and with the active involvement of relevant United Nations humanitarian entities;

27. *Also requests* the Secretary-General to reflect the progress made in the implementation of and follow-up to the present resolution in his next report to the Economic and Social Council and the General Assembly on the strengthening of the coordination of emergency humanitarian assistance of the United Nations.

Humanitarian reform agenda

During 2006, significant progress was made in implementing the humanitarian reform agenda, initiated in 2005 by the Inter-Agency Standing Committee (IASC), following the review of the humanitarian response system commissioned by the United Nations Emergency Relief Coordinator [YUN 2005, p. 991]. The Humanitarian Response Review had identified the low level of preparedness of humanitarian organizations in terms of human resources and sectoral capacities, and made recommendations on strengthening humanitarian response. The reform agenda aimed at introducing new measures for enhancing response capacity, accountability, predictability and partnership, in order to reach more beneficiaries in a more effective and timely manner. More effective partnerships between UN and non-UN humanitarian actors would provide the foundation for successful humanitarian reform and focus on three IASC-endorsed pillars: more adequate, timely and flexible humanitarian financing, including through the Central Emergency Response Fund (see p. 1061); a strengthened Humanitarian Coordinator system, providing more strategic leadership and coordination at the intersectoral and sectoral levels; and implementation of the "cluster approach" to build up capacities in gap areas (see below).

During the year, OCHA established the Humanitarian Reform Support Unit to provide support to humanitarian coordinators, field teams and agencies in driving forward the agenda. The Unit's priorities were to ensure clarity on the agreed IASC and UN policies related to the reform and effectively communicate them to stakeholders, ensure the consistency of approach for successful implementation, and support implementation, monitoring and evaluation of the reform, at headquarters and field levels.

Global Cluster Capacity-Building. In its report on the implementation of global cluster capacity-building [OCHA/CAP/2007/5], under the cluster leadership approach (see p. 1054), OCHA emphasized that the "cluster approach" was one element of the reform package. The revised *Cluster Appeal for Improving Humanitarian Response Capacity*, consolidating the budgets for each of the nine gap areas of the clusters' global-level capacity building requirements, totaled $38.6 million. Progress was made in implementing the approach, with cluster working groups reporting achievements such as enhanced coherence and synergies between different operational agencies; clearer understanding of global capacity and ongoing gaps; improved predictability and accountability for the sector/area of response concerned; and improved partnerships at the field level as a direct result of efforts at the global level. Factors hampering the process included late pledges and contributions, translating the partnership ethos fostered at headquarters to the field, clarifying services that could and could not be provided to field teams in new emergencies and the complexity in establishing clear relationships with field-level sectoral/cluster groups. To ensure that implementation of the humanitarian reform agenda was fully field-driven and responsive to field-level requirements, clusters concluded that guidelines, tools and procedures that had been agreed to should be systematically field-tested and applied, and effective mechanisms for monitoring and evaluating the impact of the global cluster capacity-building on the field response should be established.

In resolution 61/134, the Assembly requested the Secretary-General to report on lessons learned and best practices in the implementation of pilot projects using the cluster approach at its sixty-second (2007) session (see p. 1058).

GENERAL ASSEMBLY ACTION

On 14 December [meeting 79], the General Assembly adopted **resolution 61/134** [draft: A/61/L.46 & Add.1] without vote [agenda item 69 *(a)*].

Strengthening of the coordination of emergency humanitarian assistance of the United Nations

The General Assembly,

Reaffirming its resolution 46/182 of 19 December 1991 and the guiding principles contained in the annex thereto, other relevant General Assembly and Economic and Social Council resolutions and agreed conclusions of the Council,

Taking note of the report of the Secretary-General on the strengthening of the coordination of emergency humanitarian assistance of the United Nations,

Taking note also of the report of the Secretary-General on the Central Emergency Response Fund,

Reaffirming the principles of neutrality, humanity, impartiality and independence for the provision of humanitarian assistance,

Noting with grave concern the number and scale of natural disasters and their increasing impact within recent years, and reaffirming the need for sustainable measures at all levels to reduce the vulnerability of societies to natural hazards using an integrated, multi-hazard approach, and the importance of including disaster risk reduction as part of long-term and sustainable development strategies, taking into account the Hyogo Declaration and the Hyogo Framework for Action 2005-2015: Building the Resilience of Nations and Communities to Disasters,

Noting also with grave concern that violence, including gender-based violence and violence against children, continues to be deliberately directed against civilian populations in many emergency situations,

Emphasizing the need to mobilize adequate resources for humanitarian assistance and with a view to ensuring more equitable distribution across humanitarian emergencies as well as fuller coverage of the needs in all sectors,

Noting with appreciation the efforts made by the United Nations to improve humanitarian response, including by strengthening humanitarian response capacities, by improving humanitarian coordination, and by enhancing predictable and adequate funding,

1. *Takes note with appreciation* of the outcome of the ninth humanitarian affairs segment of the Economic and Social Council, held during its substantive session of 2006;

2. *Requests* the Emergency Relief Coordinator to continue his efforts to strengthen the coordination of humanitarian assistance, and calls upon relevant United Nations and other relevant intergovernmental organizations, as well as other humanitarian and relevant development actors, to continue to work with the Office for the Coordination of Humanitarian Affairs of the Secretariat to enhance the coordination, effectiveness and efficiency of humanitarian assistance;

3. *Calls upon* the relevant organizations of the United Nations system and, as appropriate, other relevant humanitarian actors, to pursue efforts to improve the humanitarian response to natural and man-made disasters and complex emergencies by further strengthening the humanitarian response capacities at all levels, by continuing to strengthen the coordination of humanitarian assistance at the field level, including with national authorities of the affected State, as appropriate, and by further enhancing transparency, performance and accountability;

4. *Encourages* States to create an enabling environment for the capacity-building of local authorities and local and national non-governmental and community-based organizations in providing humanitarian assistance;

5. *Emphasizes* the fundamentally civilian character of humanitarian assistance, reaffirms the leading role of civilian organizations in implementing humanitarian assistance, particularly in areas affected by conflicts, and affirms the need, in situations where military capacity and assets are used to support the implementation of humanitarian assistance, for their use to be in conformity with international humanitarian law and humanitarian principles;

6. *Requests* the Secretary-General to continue to develop more systematic links with Member States offering military assets for natural disaster response in order to identify the availability of such assets;

7. *Requests* the Secretary-General, in consultation with States and relevant organizations, to further develop and improve, as required, mechanisms for the use of emergency standby capacities, including, where appropriate, regional humanitarian capacities, under the auspices of the United Nations, inter alia, through formal agreements with appropriate regional organizations;

8. *Recognizes* the benefits of engagement of and coordination with relevant humanitarian actors to the effectiveness of humanitarian response, and encourages the United Nations to pursue recent efforts to strengthen partnerships at the global level with the International Red Cross and Red Crescent Movement, relevant humanitarian non-governmental organizations and other participants of the Inter-Agency Standing Committee;

9. *Reiterates* the need for a more effective, efficient, coherent, coordinated and better-performing United Nations country presence, with a strengthened role for the senior United Nations resident official responsible for the coordination of United Nations humanitarian assistance, including appropriate authority, resources and accountability;

10. *Requests* the Secretary-General to strengthen the support provided to United Nations resident/humanitarian coordinators and to United Nations country teams, including through the provision of necessary training, the identification of resources, and improving the identification and selection of United Nations resident/humanitarian coordinators;

11. *Calls upon* relevant United Nations organizations to support the improvements of the consolidated appeals process, inter alia, by engaging in the preparation of needs analysis and common action plans, in order to

further development of the process as an instrument for United Nations strategic planning and prioritization, and by involving other relevant humanitarian organizations in the process, while reiterating that consolidated appeals are prepared in consultation with affected States;

12. *Calls upon* United Nations humanitarian organizations to further develop common mechanisms to improve their transparency and the reliability of their humanitarian needs assessments, to assess their performance in assistance, and to ensure the most effective use of humanitarian resources by these organizations;

13. *Calls upon* donors to provide adequate, predictable and flexible resources based on and in proportion to assessed needs, and to encourage efforts to implement the principles of Good Humanitarian Donorship;

14. *Welcomes* the establishment of the Central Emergency Response Fund as set out in resolution 60/124 of 15 December 2005 and the fact that fifty-four donors have pledged 297.9 million United States dollars in the first year of operations, notes the assessment of the Secretary-General on its initial functioning, as reflected in his report on the Fund, and looks forward to the independent review in 2008;

15. *Also welcomes* the Secretary-General's efforts to set up appropriate reporting and accountability mechanisms for the Fund, and stresses the importance of ensuring that the resources are allocated and used in the most efficient, effective and transparent manner possible;

16. *Urges* all Member States and invites the private sector and all concerned individuals and institutions to consider making voluntary contributions to the Fund, reaffirms the target of 500 million dollars by 2008, and emphasizes that contributions should be additional to current commitments to humanitarian programming and not to the detriment of resources made available for international cooperation for development;

17. *Reiterates* that the Office for the Coordination of Humanitarian Affairs should benefit from adequate and more predictable funding;

18. *Urges* all Member States to take effective measures to address gender-based violence in humanitarian emergencies, and to make all possible efforts to ensure that their laws and institutions are adequate to prevent, promptly investigate and prosecute acts of gender-based violence;

19. *Calls upon* all Member States and encourages the relevant organizations of the United Nations to strengthen support services, including psychosocial support, to victims of gender-based violence in humanitarian emergencies;

20. *Calls upon* all States and parties in complex humanitarian emergencies, in particular in armed conflicts and in post-conflict situations, in countries in which humanitarian personnel are operating, in conformity with the relevant provisions of international law and national laws, to cooperate fully with the United Nations and other humanitarian agencies and organizations and to ensure the safe and unhindered access of humanitarian personnel as well as delivery of supplies and equipment in order to allow them to perform efficiently their task of assisting the affected civilian population, including refugees and internally displaced persons;

21. *Reaffirms* the obligation of all States and parties to an armed conflict to protect civilians in armed conflicts in accordance with international humanitarian law, and invites States to promote a culture of protection, taking into account the particular needs of women, children, older persons and persons with disabilities;

22. *Calls upon* States to adopt preventive measures and effective responses to acts of violence committed against civilian populations in armed conflicts as well as to ensure that those responsible are promptly brought to justice, as provided for by national law and obligations under international law;

23. *Recognizes* the Guiding Principles on Internal Displacement as an important international framework for the protection of internally displaced persons, and encourages Member States and humanitarian agencies to continue to work together in endeavours to provide a more predictable response to the needs of internally displaced persons, and in this regard calls for international support, upon request, to capacity-building efforts of States;

24. *Re-emphasizes* the importance of the discussion of humanitarian policies and activities in the General Assembly and the Economic and Social Council and that these discussions should be continuously revitalized by Member States with a view to enhancing their relevance, efficiency and impact;

25. *Encourages* Member States to continue to strengthen cooperation and coordination between the General Assembly and the Economic and Social Council on humanitarian issues, based on their respective mandates and taking into account comparative advantages and existing complementarities of the two bodies;

26. *Decides*, in order to have a more focused and consolidated discussion on humanitarian issues, that the sub-items of its agenda related to the strengthening of the coordination of humanitarian and disaster relief assistance of the United Nations currently considered by the Second Committee shall be reallocated to its plenary as of its sixty-second session;

27. *Recalls* the request to the Secretary-General, in the ninth humanitarian affairs segment of the Economic and Social Council, to include in his report lessons learned and best practices in the implementation of the pilot projects using the cluster approach, in consultation with affected countries and with the active involvement of relevant United Nations humanitarian entities;

28. *Requests* the Secretary-General to report to the General Assembly at its sixty-second session, through the Economic and Social Council at its substantive session of 2007, on progress made in strengthening the coordination of emergency humanitarian assistance of the United Nations and to submit a report to the Assembly through the Council on the detailed use of the Central Emergency Response Fund.

On 20 December, by **decision 61/543**, the General Assembly took note of the Second (Economic and Financial) Committee's report [A/61/429] on strengthening of the coordination of UN humanitarian and disaster relief assistance, including special economic assistance.

High-level Panel on UN System-wide Coherence

In a November note [A/61/583], the Secretary-General transmitted to the General Assembly the report of the High-Level Panel on UN System-wide Coherence in the areas of development, humanitarian assistance and the environment, entitled "Delivering as one" (see p. 1584). The Panel, established by the Secretary-General, in follow-up to the 2005 World Summit and its Outcome document [YUN 2005, p. 48], to advise on further strengthening of the management and coordination of UN operational activities to more effectively achieve internationally agreed development goals, in particular, the Millennium Development Goals (MDGs) [YUN 2000, p. 51], undertook a thorough assessment of the strengths and weaknesses of the UN system and made recommendations for it to overcome its fragmentation and deliver as one.

With regard to humanitarian assistance, the report recommended that, based on the coordination and leadership roles of the Emergency Relief Coordinator at the global level and the humanitarian coordinator at the country level, partnership arrangements should be strengthened, ensuring the participation of the cluster lead agency approach. The Central Emergency Response Fund (see p. 1061) should be fully funded to its three-year target of $500 million from additional resources and consideration should be given to substantially increasing it over the next five years, following a performance review. Humanitarian agencies should clarify their mandates and enhance their cooperation on IDPs.

On transition from relief to development, the repositioned United Nations Development Programme (UNDP) should become the UN leader and coordinator for early recovery, and adequate funding for the UN role in early recovery should be ensured, even before a donor conference was held or a UN/World Bank Multi-Donor Trust Fund was operational. If the Peacebuilding Fund or the UNDP Thematic Trust Fund for Crisis Prevention and Recovery were not able to provide immediate resources, a related country-specific fund for early recovery could be set up. In order to build long-term food security and break the cycle of recurring famines, especially in sub-Saharan Africa, the World Food Programme (WFP), the Food and Agriculture Organization of the United Nations (FAO) and the International Fund for Agricultural Development should review their respective approaches and enhance inter-agency coordination.

As to risk reduction, UN efforts should be enhanced through the full implementation and funding of international agreements and other recent initiatives and the involvement of communities. The United Nations should also continue to build innovative disaster assistance mechanisms, such as private risk insurance markets, as means to provide contingency funding for natural disasters and other emergencies. Consideration should also be given to efforts, such as the WFP pilot humanitarian insurance policy in Ethiopia, for providing coverage in the case of an extreme drought.

The Secretary-General endorsed the Panel's recommendations and called on the General Assembly to support and implement them.

UNFPA emergency preparedness, crisis response and recovery strategy. In an August report [DP/FPA/2006/14], the United Nations Population Fund (UNFPA) presented to the UNDP/UNFPA Executive Board a three-year strategy (2007-2009) to ensure that key issues in the Programme of Action of the 1994 International Conference on Population and Development [YUN 1994, p. 955] were integrated into the emergency preparedness, crisis response and recovery programmes of national entities and civil society, regional institutions and the international humanitarian system, through improved awareness and commitment, enhanced capacity and strengthened partnerships. The strategy sought to enhance the capacity of UNFPA and its partners to respond more effectively to issues of gender, reproductive health and data in crisis and recovery settings.

Executive Board action. The UNDP/UNFPA Executive Board, at its annual session (Geneva, 12-23 June) [E/2006/35 (dec. 2006/35)], endorsed the strategy and encouraged UNFPA to align it with its medium-term strategic plan, and agreed to maintain the emergency fund at $3 million.

UN and other humanitarian personnel

In response to General Assembly resolution 60/123 [YUN 2005, p. 1523], the Secretary-General, in a September report [A/61/463], outlined the threats against the safety and security of humanitarian and UN personnel over the preceding year. He indicated that humanitarian personnel continued to face situations of extreme risk in order to achieve their mandates and according to a comparison study, international aid workers would rank as one of the most hazardous civilian occupations.

The Assembly, in **resolution 61/133** of 14 December, called on Governments and parties in complex humanitarian emergencies to ensure the safe and unhindered access of humanitarian personnel (see p. 1684).

Resource mobilization

Central Emergency Response Fund

On 9 March, the Central Emergency Response Fund (CERF), formerly known as the Central Emergency Revolving Fund, a cash-flow mechanism for the initial phase of humanitarian emergencies established in 1992 [YUN 1992, p. 584], was launched. The Fund was upgraded by General Assembly resolution 60/124 [YUN 2005, p. 991] to include a grant element, targeted at $450 million, to ensure the availability of immediate resources to support humanitarian crises and address underfunded emergencies. The loan element of the Fund continued to operate as a distinct and separately managed revolving fund with a target of $50 million. In April, the twelve-member CERF Advisory Group was established to provide policy guidance and expert advice to the Secretary-General on the use and impact of the Fund; it held meetings in May and October. In October, the Secretary-General issued a bulletin [SGB/2006/10] setting out the modalities for the operation of the Fund. As at 31 December, a total of $259.3 million in CERF funds had been allocated to 34 countries and the Occupied Palestinian Territory.

Report of Secretary-General. In his September report on CERF [A/61/85/Add.1-E/2006/81/Add.1], the Secretary-General indicated that, with the implementation of the upgraded Fund, great progress had been made in promoting early action and response to reduce loss of life; enhancing response to time-critical requirements; and strengthening core elements of humanitarian response in underfunded crises. While the timely disbursement of funds was an issue, adjustments were under way to accelerate those processes. Pledges to the CERF grant element totaled $273.7 million, of which $261.9 million had been transferred to the Fund, leaving $11.8 million still outstanding. The Emergency Relief Coordinator committed $157.5 million to 25 countries from the CERF grant element, comprising $80.6 million to support rapid response and $76.8 million for underfunded emergencies. With regard to the Fund's loan element, as at 31 August, eight loans had been disbursed from the Fund amounting to $43.2 million. The Secretary-General said that the future success of the Fund depended on replenishing it and increasing overall levels, based on the demonstrated effectiveness of the Fund, in order to reach the three-year target of $500 million endorsed by the General Assembly.

Advisory Group meeting. At its 12 October meeting [A/61/550], the CERF Advisory Group reviewed progress and made recommendations on the use and management of the Fund, as well as on the contribution goal for 2007. It advocated the early attainment of the $500 million target and urged Member States to consider making multi-year pledges and to participate in the high-level donor's conference (New York, 7 December).

Consolidated appeals

The consolidated appeals process (CAP), an inclusive and coordinated programme cycle for analysing context, assessing needs and planning prioritized humanitarian response, was the humanitarian sector's main strategic planning and programming tool. In 2006, the United Nations and its humanitarian partners issued consolidated appeals seeking $5.1 billion in assistance for the Central African Republic, Chad, the Congo, the Great Lakes region (Burundi, the DRC, Rwanda, Uganda, the United Republic of Tanzania), the Horn of Africa (Djibouti, Eritrea, Kenya, Somalia), Lebanon, Nepal, the Occupied Palestinian Territory, the Sudan, Timor-Leste, the West Africa subregion (Benin, Burkina Faso, Cape Verde, Côte d'Ivoire, the Gambia, Ghana, Guinea, Guinea-Bissau, Liberia, Mali, Mauritania, the Niger, Nigeria, Senegal, Sierra Leone and Togo) and Zimbabwe. Separate appeals were launched for Burundi, Côte d'Ivoire, the DRC, Guinea, Guinea-Bissau, Kenya, Liberia, Somalia and Uganda.

The latest available data indicated that 66 per cent ($3.36 billion) of requirements had been met.

White Helmets

In response to General Assembly resolution 58/118 [YUN 2003, p. 922], the Secretary-General, in a September report [A/61/313], provided an overview of progress made since the inception of the "White Helmets" initiative, which was established by Argentina in 1993 to promote the concept of pre-identified standby and trained teams of volunteers from various national volunteer corps to support immediate relief, rehabilitation, construction and development activities. The initiative was administered by UNDP. The report, which covered the period from July 2003 to July 2006, highlighted programme activities and their results, existing mechanisms and partnerships, financing and resources mobilization, and concluded with recommendations on the future of the initiative.

GENERAL ASSEMBLY ACTION

On 20 December [meeting 83], the General Assembly, on the recommendation of the Second Committee [A/61/429/Add.2], adopted **resolution 61/220** without vote [agenda item 69 *(c)*].

Participation of volunteers, "White Helmets", in the activities of the United Nations in the field of humanitarian relief, rehabilitation and technical cooperation for development

The General Assembly,

Reaffirming its resolutions 50/19 of 28 November 1995, 52/171 of 16 December 1997, 54/98 of 8 December 1999, 56/102 of 14 December 2001 and 58/118 of 17 December 2003,

Reaffirming also its resolutions 46/182 of 19 December 1991, 47/168 of 22 December 1992, 48/57 of 14 December 1993, 49/139 A and B of 20 December 1994, 50/57 of 12 December 1995 and 51/194 of 17 December 1996 and Economic and Social Council resolutions 1995/56 of 28 July 1995 and 1996/33 of 25 July 1996,

Emphasizing the need for coordination between relief and development activities in the context of humanitarian emergencies, taking into account the internationally agreed development goals, including those contained in the United Nations Millennium Declaration,

Recognizing that the international community, in addressing the growing magnitude and complexity of man-made and natural disasters and chronic situations characterized by hunger, malnutrition and poverty, must rely not only on the formulation of a well-coordinated global response within the framework of the United Nations but also on the promotion of a smooth transition from relief to rehabilitation, reconstruction and development,

Recalling once again that prevention, preparedness and contingency planning for emergencies on a global level depend, for the most part, on the strengthening of local and national response capacities, on the availability of financial resources, both domestic and international, and on the effective use of those resources,

Recognizing the need to integrate a gender perspective in the design and implementation of all phases of disaster management,

1. *Takes note* of the report of the Secretary-General, prepared in pursuance of its resolution 58/118 on the participation of volunteers, "White Helmets", in the activities of the United Nations in the field of humanitarian relief, rehabilitation and technical cooperation for development, especially in the three main areas on which action has been focused, namely dissemination of the concept of volunteerism, support to Latin American and Caribbean countries and response to requests for emergency assistance;

2. *Recognizes* the effort being made by the White Helmets initiative to strengthen national and regional agreements aimed at facilitating coordination between the United Nations system and trained standby national volunteer corps, in accordance with accepted United Nations procedures, through the United Nations Volunteers and other agencies of the system;

3. *Notes* the emphasis placed on the development of mechanisms to facilitate the local management of humanitarian emergencies, through the organization and participatory involvement and empowerment of affected communities and the training of the members of local volunteer corps;

4. *Recognizes* the effort of the White Helmets model in helping to involve stricken populations or those at risk in the tasks of planning, training, mobilizing and providing immediate response in disaster situations;

5. *Notes* the importance of international efforts being made by the White Helmets initiative to strengthen the comprehensive regional mechanisms for managing prevention and response activities in emergency and disaster situations, in particular its model for setting up regional networks of focal points, with a view to linkage with other international structures;

6. *Encourages* Member States to identify their respective national focal points for the White Helmets in order to continue to provide the United Nations system with an accessible global network of rapid response facilities in the event of humanitarian emergencies;

7. *Takes note* of the efforts made by the World Food Programme and the White Helmets to coordinate integration mechanisms that allow for joint action in the framework of food security, on the basis of their general agreements of 1998;

8. *Encourages* operational partners of the United Nations system, in particular the United Nations Volunteers and the World Health Organization, in providing psychosocial support to the disaster-affected population in emergency and disaster situations, to draw, as appropriate, upon the voluntary expertise of the White Helmets, which has been successfully tested, as indicated by the Secretary-General in his report;

9. *Recognizes* that the White Helmets initiative can play an important role in the promotion, diffusion and implementation of the decisions adopted in the United Nations Millennium Declaration, and invites Member States in a position to do so to consider means to ensure the integration of the White Helmets initiative into their programme activities and to make financial resources available to the Special Voluntary Fund of the United Nations Volunteers;

10. *Invites* the Secretary-General, on the basis of the extensive international work experience acquired by the White Helmets, as recognized by the General Assembly since the adoption of its resolution 49/139 B, the first resolution on the White Helmets initiative, and in view of the success of coordinated actions carried out with, inter alia, the United Nations Children's Fund, the World Food Programme, the Office for the Coordination of Humanitarian Affairs of the Secretariat, the United Nations Development Programme and the United Nations Volunteers, to suggest measures to enhance the integration of the White Helmets initiative with the work of the United Nations system, and to report thereon to the Assembly at its sixty-fourth session in a separate section of the annual

report on strengthening of the coordination of emergency humanitarian assistance of the United Nations.

New international humanitarian order

Report of Secretary-General. In response to General Assembly resolution 59/171 [YUN 2004, p. 910], the Secretary-General, in an August report [A/61/224], provided information on the further development of the agenda for the new international humanitarian order. The report examined the five key issues that were the cornerstones for contemporary humanitarian action around the world: prevention; access to people in need; the right to humanitarian assistance; local capacity-building; and burden-sharing. Humanitarian issues requiring greater attention at the international level were also identified. The Secretary-General recommended, among others, that research be undertaken on the role of armed forces in socio-economic development, given the useful role they played in assisting disaster victims; and that the transition from relief to development be further analysed and the nexus between human rights and humanitarian issues investigated by the Human Rights Council. He also emphasized the need to identify and analyse emerging humanitarian problems, such as the increasing number of internally displaced persons compared to that of refugees and the failure to meet their needs satisfactorily, the role of terrorism and internal conflicts in creating victims and the growing number of beggars and street children, especially in developing countries. International efforts should also be made to reduce poverty and help solve the problems facing Third World countries.

Communication. Bosnia and Herzegovina transmitted to the General Assembly a 14 December 2005 document [A/60/627] entitled "Declaration relating to basic tenets of humanitarian action in emergency situations", which was prepared in close collaboration with the Independent Bureau for Humanitarian Issues and in consultation with a number of independent experts, in the context of the Secretary-General's reports related to the promotion of a new international humanitarian order. Bosnia and Herzegovina requested the views of Member States so that the document could be finalized for adoption by the Assembly and implemented in order to improve humanitarian assistance in emergency situations.

GENERAL ASSEMBLY ACTION

On 19 December [meeting 81], the General Assembly, on the recommendation of the Third (Social, Humanitarian and Cultural) Committee [A/61/436], adopted **resolution 61/138** without vote [agenda item 41].

New international humanitarian order

The General Assembly,

Recalling its resolution 59/171 of 20 December 2004, all previous resolutions concerning the promotion of a new international humanitarian order and all relevant resolutions, in particular resolution 46/182 of 19 December 1991, on the strengthening of the coordination of humanitarian emergency assistance of the United Nations, and the annex thereto,

Noting with appreciation the continuing efforts of the United Nations system to increase its capacity and that of its Member States to provide assistance to victims of humanitarian emergencies,

Taking note of the report of the Secretary-General,

1. *Recognizes* the need for the further strengthening of national, regional and international efforts to address humanitarian emergencies;

2. *Invites* Member States, the Office for the Coordination of Humanitarian Affairs of the Secretariat, relevant entities of the United Nations system, and intergovernmental and non-governmental organizations, including the Independent Bureau for Humanitarian Issues, to reinforce activities and cooperation so as to continue to develop an agenda for humanitarian action;

3. *Requests* the Secretary-General to continue to strengthen efforts in the humanitarian field and to report thereon to the General Assembly at its sixty-third session.

Humanitarian activities

Africa

Central African Republic

The UN Consolidated Inter-Agency Appeal for the Central African Republic, launched for $38 million in 2006, received 63 per cent of its target ($24 million).

Although international attention to the humanitarian crisis in the Central African Republic increased in 2006, the situation deteriorated severely in the north as the country was drawn into the crisis in Chad and the Darfur region of the Sudan, resulting in an armed rebellion against the Government (see p. 162). One million persons were directly impacted by hostilities in the north, with at least 100 villages having been burnt within the past year. Forced to flee their homes, some 150,000 were internally displaced, while an additional 70,000 left the country. Other humanitarian concerns included malnutrition, maternal and infant mortality, decreased life expectancy and the prevalence of HIV/AIDS. Humanitarian activity was hampered by the limited capacity of local and national actors, a shortage of NGOs, low funding levels, the lack of infrastructure and the worsening security situation. Despite those obstacles, it was estimated that humanitarian organizations had saved some 250,000 lives through the provision of food, medical services and supplies, drinking water and sanitation products, and 120,000 lives were protected by measles vaccinations. In addition, some 90,000 people in extreme need of protection enjoyed adequate protection.

Chad

The UN Consolidated Inter-Agency Appeal for Chad sought $193.4 million in 2006, of which 80 per cent ($155.6 million) was received.

During 2006, the humanitarian situation in Chad worsened due to the escalation of political tensions, the deterioration of the security environment within the country, and developments in the neighbouring countries of the Sudan (Darfur) and the Central African Republic. Increased rebel and bandit attacks on humanitarian aid workers and reports of human rights abuses further exacerbated the situation. As at January, Chad was host to some 234,000 Sudanese and 45,000 Central African Republic refugees. Violence in eastern Chad resulted in the displacement of 53,000 Chadians, and the influx of an additional 60,000 refugees was expected owing to the crisis situation in northern Central African Republic. Aid agencies were able to stabilize the humanitarian conditions and provide essential services for the Sudanese refugees spread over a 600 kilometre border in eastern Chad. However, in southern Chad, where sporadic influxes of Central African Republic refugees continued, food assistance providers faced severe challenges. Gross imbalances in funding hampered the humanitarian community in implementing its response strategy, which was further complicated by the political and security developments in the country. Funding shortfalls forced UN agencies to further prioritize their activities in order to continue to provide the most urgent, life-saving assistance to the beneficiaries.

The Congo

The 2006 UN Consolidated Inter-Agency Appeal for the Congo, amounting to $27.1 million, received 48 per cent ($13 million) of its request.

Successive conflicts in the Congo over the preceding decade had destroyed basic social infrastructure, including roadways, schools and health centres, creating a humanitarian crisis. Half of the Congolese population lived on less than one dollar a day; malaria claimed four out of ten deaths; and over 10 per cent of children died before five years of age. During 2006, in the Pool region, some 7,800 persons were temporarily displaced to other localities within the Pool and security remained unstable, with recurrent acts of violence hampering humanitarian activity. The humanitarian situation in the Congo was further exacerbated by Ebola epidemics, natural disasters and subregional instability, which led to the influx of additional refugees. As the country was already host to 47,000 refugees, mostly from the DRC, further deterioration of the situation in that country remained a constant threat to peace in the Congo. Moreover, some 11,000 Congolese had taken refuge in neighbouring countries and were awaiting return to their country.

In 2006, strategic priorities for the humanitarian community focused on saving lives and reducing vulnerabilities for affected populations, estimated at 1.2 million persons. Major constraints to humanitarian efforts included insufficient funding; withdrawal of major humanitarian actors from the Pool region; poor infrastructure and inability to transport supplies; lack of reliable data on the needs, priorities and locations of vulnerable persons; and the difficulty in developing a common view on the level of urgency for humanitarian activities in the Pool region.

Great Lakes region

The UN Consolidated Inter-Agency Appeal for the Great Lakes region, launched for a total of $149.4 million to cover 2006, received 72 per cent ($108.1 million) of that amount. In addition to the regional appeal, individual country appeals were made for Burundi, the DRC and Uganda.

In 2006, prospects for peace in the Great Lakes region continued to improve, providing new hopes for the establishment of security. However, due to high structural poverty, lack of infrastructure, and the ongoing vulnerability of populations, humanitarian needs remained immense. During the year, four strategic objectives were pursued by the humanitarian community in the region: strengthening a coordinated and collaborative approach; enhancing preparedness, response capacity and timeliness of action; improving the protection of the environment; and providing life-saving and life-enhancing assistance in conjunction with country-level structures.

Burundi

The UN Consolidated Inter-Agency Appeal for Burundi, launched for $118.6 million in 2006, obtained 45 per cent ($53.8 million) of its goal.

In 2006, the last remaining rebel group, the National Liberation Forces, signed a ceasefire agreement, which lead to improved protection for populations in the Bujumbura Mairie and Bubanza provinces. The United Nations Integrated Office in Burundi was established and the Peacebuilding Commission selected Burundi as one of its first two focus countries (see p. 154). Nevertheless, the year was characterized by a low level of return of displaced populations and unforeseen movements, such as the arrival of some 20,000 Rwandan asylum seekers, the return of 13,000 Burundian asylum seekers from the United Republic of Tanzania, and the expulsion of 3,000 Burundians living without refugee status in the United Republic of Tanzania. Overall, there were some 100,000 IDPs in Burundi and 395,000 Burundian refugees in countries of asylum. Extreme poverty, malnourishment, food security and the strained health care infrastructure remained issues of concern. The humanitarian community conducted early warning and rapid response activities in the areas of food security, agriculture and nutrition. It also responded to localized natural disasters, such as rain, hailstorms and floods. Multisector activities undertaken by the Office of the United Nations High Commissioner for Refugees (UNHCR) and partner NGOs resulted in the construction of over 16,300 houses, which benefited returning families.

Democratic Republic of the Congo

The UN Consolidated Inter-Agency Appeal for the DRC sought $696 million in 2006, of which 51 per cent ($354.1 million) was received.

In 2006, localized armed conflicts created numerous population displacements in the eastern zones of the country. On the average, some 88,000 persons per month, mostly women and children, were newly displaced during the first half of the year. However, the total number of displaced persons in the DRC, approximately 1.1 million, had fallen by 33 per cent since 2005. The successful holding of presidential elections (see p. 134) and unification of the army facilitated an improvement in the security situation, prompting the return of refugees and displaced populations and access by the humanitarian community to previously isolated populations. Since the beginning of the year, 35,000 Congolese refugees had returned, 25,000 of whom had been repatriated by UNHCR, and between April and September, 490,000 displaced persons had returned to their villages of origin. However, the presence of militias and lack of adequate infrastructure hampered the return to normal life. Other areas of concern included preventable and treatable illnesses, HIV/AIDS, sexual violence, access to drinking water, malnutrition and children associated with armed groups, estimated at 33,000.

Uganda

The UN Consolidated Inter-Agency Appeal for Uganda requested $263.4 million to cover 2006 requirements, of which 86 per cent ($225.8 million) was received.

In 2006, partly due to implementation of the cluster approach (see p. 1054), progress was made in addressing the vulnerabilities of some 1.5 million IDPs and improving response, which limited the potentially high fatality rates following outbreaks of cholera and measles. The Agreement on the Cessation of Hostilities signed in August between the Government and the Lord's Resistance Army (LRA) (see p. 120) and improved security during the latter half of the year renewed hopes for a negotiated solution to the conflict and the return of IDPs to their homes of origin. The humanitarian community provided protection for IDPs and other vulnerable populations, including 216,000 registered refugees, and delivered food to 1.5 million IDPs, 183,300 refugees, 414,500 school children and 372,550 other vulnerable individuals. Improved security conditions allowed the phasing out of emergency assistance for approximately 170,000 IDPs. Other assistance focused on agriculture; health, nutrition and HIV/AIDS; water and sanitation; education; early recovery support; and mine action. However, inadequate funding made sectoral coverage uneven and not always timely, undermining efforts to promote an integrated approach to addressing the causes of vulnerability. Moreover, some of the hardest-hit, such as the Teso and Karamoja subregions, received only a fraction of the level of resources channeled to other areas.

Communication. In January [S/2006/13], Canada indicated that some 1.7 million displaced persons, almost 90 per cent of the population of northern Uganda, were confined to 200 squalid and unsafe camps as a result of the conflict that had plagued that region for the past twenty years. Each week, 1,000 civilians died from war-related causes and 300,000 displaced children under 5 years of age suffered from preventable diseases. Insecurity made it difficult for aid agencies to gain access to the areas in need. Canada requested that the Security Council place the issue on its agenda, and proposed a number of steps the Council might take, including calling on all States to respond to the severe humanitarian emergency through the allocation of funds for humanitarian services in the affected areas.

Emergency Relief Coordinator mission. On 22 November [meeting 5571], the Under-Secretary-General for Humanitarian Affairs and Emergency Relief Coordinator, in briefing the Security Council on his mission to the Sudan and his meetings with LRA leaders, reported that the cessation of hostilities had been largely respected, allowing hundreds of thousands of IDPs to start to return to northern Uganda. In his meetings with LRA leaders, he reiterated his demand that they release abducted women and children and allow the sick to go to hospital. He called for continued funding for the mediation effort and for ceasefire monitoring through the OCHA-led Juba Initiative Project.

Kenya

The UN Consolidated Inter-Agency Appeal for Kenya requested $35.3 million to cover 2006 requirements, of which 105 per cent ($36.9 million) was received.

The unpredictability of the political situation in Somalia and the potential of a wider civil war resulted in influx of refugees into north-eastern Kenya. Intra- and inter-clan fighting and the impact of drought and destitution were other factors influencing refugee migration. From January through August, some 24,000 refugees from Baidoa, Kismayo and Mogadishu entered the Dadaab refugee complex in north-eastern Kenya. From September to October, refugee migration accelerated drastically, with arrivals increasing from an average of 300 to 800 per day. On 10 October, over 1,400 refugees arrived. As at mid-October, the Somali population in the three Dadaab refugee camps totaled 160,000. Health and water services were severely stretched and there was a high incidence of child malnutrition and substantial risk of disease outbreaks.

Somalia

In response to General Assembly resolution 60/219 [YUN 2005, p. 997], the Secretary-General, in his July consolidated report [A/61/209], provided information on humanitarian assistance and relief provided by the United Nations and its partners in Somalia in 2006.

With the already dire humanitarian situation having been further aggravated, in 2005, by the failed *deyr* rainy season and the onset of the worse drought in more than a decade, some 1.7 million people were in urgent need of assistance by early January 2006. Southern Somalia was worst hit, including the Gedo, Middle and Lower Juba, Bakool and Bay regions, where 1.4 million people were in need of critical assistance. Northern Gedo and the riverine areas of the Juba Valley were at moderate risk of famine. In March, the 2006 Consolidated Appeal for Somalia was revised to $331 million, up from $174 million, to benefit 2.1 million people, including 400,000 IDPs. Although initial good *gu* rains in southern and north-west Somalia in April and May had replenished water catchments and improved water access for drought-affected pastoral and agro-pastoral communities, an FAO analysis indicated that southern Somalia would remain in a state of humanitarian emergency until December, and areas of central and northern Somalia would be in an acute food and livelihood crisis. Other humanitarian concerns included the emergence of new cases of polio; the presence of armed militias and inter and intra-clan conflicts; the targeting of young women and other vulnerable groups by organized smuggling rings in Puntland; and the situation of IDPs and their protection. The latest round of fighting in Mogadishu in May resulted in 320 deaths and the displacement of some 17,800 persons.

In addition to the security issues, particularly in Southern and Central Somalia, which had restricted access to communities affected by drought, harassment and exploitation, the humanitarian community was further constrained by flooding, the continuing lack of infrastructure and sustainable access and humanitarian space, poor operational capacity and delayed funding. The Secretary-General observed that the onset of rains had not ended the emergency and it would take at least five years for Somalia to fully recover from the crisis, especially pastoralists who had lost their livestock. He called on the donor community to provide more flexible emergency funding, invest in the operational capacity of NGOs and increase their commitments to the non-food sectors.

The revised 2006 UN Consolidated Inter-Agency Appeal for Somalia, launched for $323.8 million, as a complement to the Horn of Africa regional appeal (see p. 1105), met 58 per cent ($186.7 million) of requirements.

(See also p. 1106 under "Disaster assistance".)

Sudan

The UN Consolidated Inter-Agency Appeal for the Sudan Work Plan 2006 (Humanitarian Action component), which sought $1.6 billion to provide 5.5 million people with relief assistance during the year, received 66 per cent ($1.1 billion) of that amount.

In 2006, the Sudan's humanitarian needs remained immense, despite progress in the implementation of the Comprehensive Peace Agreement [YUN 2005, p. 302], and the signing of the Darfur

Peace Agreement, in May, by the Government of the Sudan and the Minni Minawi faction of the Sudan Liberation Movement/Army (see p. 274). In southern Sudan, the continued return of the largest displaced population in the world continued to pose significant challenges. In Darfur, with the continuing violence and insecurity, the humanitarian situation was a cause of great concern. Four million people, including 2 million IDPs in Darfur, continued to rely on humanitarian assistance, while several thousand additional people were displaced. During the year, approximately 350,000 IDPs and refugees returned to southern Sudan, with some 26,000 of that number receiving support from the United Nations and its partners. Challenges affecting the implementation of humanitarian activities included the deteriorating security situation and human rights violations; tensions in parts of the country, including the Eastern region and Abyei; repeated outbreaks of diseases, such as acute diarrhoea/cholera and meningitis; the fragile food security situation in locations, such as Northern Bahr el-Ghazal and Eastern Equatoria; and minimal communications facilities and infrastructure.

Emergency Relief Coordinator mission. On 22 November [meeting 5571], the Emergency Relief Coordinator, in his briefing to the Security Council on his mission to Darfur, indicated that attacks on villages and the displacement of tens of thousands of civilians had reached horrific levels. Due to militia attacks and banditry, more than 95 per cent of all roads in West Darfur were no-go areas for the United Nations and NGOs, and an increasing number of camps had been cut off from adequate and reliable assistance. In some instances, all basic humanitarian services had been shut down. Approximately 4 million people, two-thirds of the population, were in need of emergency assistance and the number of IDPs had risen to an unprecedented 2 million. He called for an immediate cessation of hostilities and implementation of all freedom of movement guarantees.

West Africa

The UN Consolidated Inter-Agency Appeal for the West Africa subregion, which sought $245.8 million in 2006 to assist beneficiaries in Benin, Burkina Faso, Cape Verde, Côte d'Ivoire, the Gambia, Ghana, Guinea, Guinea-Bissau, Liberia, Mali, Mauritania, the Niger, Nigeria, Senegal, Sierra Leone and Togo, received 94 per cent ($231.8 million) of the requirement.

While the overall humanitarian situation had improved over the past year in the subregion, particularly in Liberia, Togo and the Niger, there were still unacceptable levels of human distress and suffering due to malfunctioning political systems, under-nutrition, forced displacement, floods and health epidemics. An estimated 300,000 children were dying annually as a result of under-nutrition, and endemic and epidemic communicable diseases, such as cholera, meningitis and yellow fever, caused extensive human suffering and distress. Interdependent conflicts and humanitarian crises, which erupted simultaneously or fuelled each other, caused movements of populations in need of assistance and protection. The volatile situation in Côte d'Ivoire continued to threaten regional stability, while in Liberia, despite significant improvements in the political climate and humanitarian situation, the majority of that country's population remained without access to adequate basic services, and high levels of insecurity and vulnerability persisted. A fundamental challenge facing partners in the region was finding ways to adequately advocate for and respond to humanitarian situations beyond agreed emergency thresholds. Promoting system-wide and coordinated responses within a region-based perspective had become the focus of the humanitarian community in West Africa. Humanitarian stakeholders had agreed on three priority trans-national humanitarian issues that had to be addressed in the subregion: food security and nutrition in the Sahel; rapid response to health crises; and protection and population movements.

Côte d'Ivoire

The UN Consolidated Inter-Agency Appeal for Côte d'Ivoire sought $43.5 million to meet 2006 requirements, and received 52 per cent ($22.7 million) of that amount.

In 2006, political advances made in Côte d'Ivoire during the first half of the year had translated into slight improvements in the security situation and the humanitarian situation. However, poverty continued to affect many households and vulnerable groups witnessed a persistent degradation of their conditions. The social fabric, weakened by the increased number of IDPs, which stood at approximately 700,000, deteriorated further due to conflicts surrounding the issue of mobile identification courts. Visits to health structures remained low despite the revival of primary health systems in the underserved zones in 2005. Access to water was a crucial problem, particularly in the rebel-controlled Centre, North and West regions, where, due to lack of maintenance, water treatment stations had deteriorated and high rates of breakdowns of water supply systems continued. Low redeployment of the administration in the rebel-controlled areas impeded access to basic social services for women and children, while the influx of displaced persons weakened the capacities of the available social services in the Government-controlled South.

Guinea

The UN Consolidated Inter-Agency Appeal for Guinea, launched for $25.2 million in 2006, met 63 per cent ($15.8 million) of that target.

In 2006, Guinea continued to cope with IDPs and refugees from Côte d'Ivoire, Liberia and Sierra Leone. Added to the tremendous burden of hosting them was the lack of international assistance, resulting in increased poverty, high inflation and the breakdown of social services and infrastructure. Over 50 per cent of the population were living on 20 dollars or less per month, and with little or no access to food security, health, water and sanitation and education facilities. No significant reform action had been taken to address the declining socio-economic situation, including the decreasing gross national product, rising inflation, devaluation of the national currency, stagnation of salaries and deterioration of basic social infrastructure and services that had not been maintained or supported. The humanitarian situation was also characterized by high mortality, morbidity and malnutrition rates, particularly among children under 5 years of age and pregnant women, as well as by outbreaks and recurrence of epidemics, such as cholera, yellow fever, meningitis and polio. Priorities for the humanitarian community focused on reducing malnutrition, morbidity and mortality rates and improving access to basic social services, effective health care and adequate levels of medical services, including malaria treatment.

Guinea-Bissau

The UN Consolidated Inter-Agency Appeal for Guinea-Bissau sought $3.6 million to meet 2006 requirements, and received 56 per cent ($2 million) of that amount.

From mid-March to the end of April, armed confrontation between a faction of the Movement of Democratic Forces of Casamance, a Senegalese separatist group, and the Guinea-Bissau army near São Domingos on the western part of Guinea-Bissau's border with Senegal resulted in the destruction, burning or looting of 14 villages, causing some 10,000 people to flee, including 2,500 who had crossed the border into Senegal. The main concern for the affected population was the lack of safety and protection from anti-tank and anti-personnel landmines and explosive remnants of war, which threatened safe access to their homes and livelihoods. Major routes and villages, as well as homes and farming fields, were suspected of being contaminated with explosive devices, and reports indicated 13 landmine-related deaths and several people being wounded. For five weeks, an estimated 20,000 people had been isolated within the landmine-contaminated area in Varela and Susana, unable to use their main sources of supply or access services through normal routes. Other critical needs included food, safe water and non-food items, such as mosquito nets, cooking utensils, blankets, clothing and latrines. The humanitarian community responded by transporting food aid and medicines across the river by canoe.

(See also p. 1085 under "Special economic assistance".)

Liberia

The UN Consolidated Inter-Agency Appeal for Liberia, launched for $145.2 million in 2006, met 51 per cent ($74.8 million) of requirements.

While the Government of Liberia had made significant achievements during the previous year and had advanced along the path of recovery and rehabilitation, the extent of destruction from 14 years of civil strife remained a factor hindering progress. Health care, safe water and appropriate sanitation, shelter and education eluded the majority of Liberians. Nevertheless, the Government continued to lead efforts to make improvements in social services. Shortly after taking office, the President developed and successfully implemented a 150-day plan to address some of the immediate needs of the population and to demonstrate its commitment to deliver on election pledges. The Liberian Government launched the interim poverty reduction strategy paper to address the country's endemic poverty issues and build the foundation for development through 2008, which would be followed by an MDG-based poverty reduction strategy covering 2008-2011.

(See also p. 1081 under "Special economic assistance".)

Zimbabwe

The UN Consolidated Inter-Agency Appeal for Zimbabwe requested $425.8 million to cover 2006 requirements, of which 64 per cent ($273.3 million) was received.

In 2006, the humanitarian situation in Zimbabwe was characterized by acute humanitarian needs, such as food security, protection from cholera, and assistance for mobile and vulnerable people affected by the land reform programme, Murambatsvina/Operation Restore Order launched in May 2005 [YUN 2005, p. 371], and more recent evictions. More protracted, chronic vulnerabilities, such as inadequate access to basic social services, insufficient agricultural inputs and disrupted livelihoods, as well as the continuing economic decline, the large number of migrants and the HIV/AIDS pandemic, with an average of 3,000 deaths per week, further impacted the overall humanitarian situation in the country. Zimbabwe's population of 11.8 million comprised a number of vulnerable groups, including, among others, 1.8 million living with HIV/AIDS; 1.4 million children who had lost one or both parents; 1.4 million living in rural food-insecure communities; and some 700,000 people affected by Operation Restore Order. During the year, humanitarian efforts focused on reducing morbidity and mortality rates, increasing access to basic social services, preventing further deterioration of livelihoods, providing protection to the most vulnerable groups and reducing the impact of HIV/AIDS.

Asia

Afghanistan

The Secretary-General, in response to General Assembly resolution 60/32 B [YUN 2005, p. 1000], submitted a March report [A/60/712-S/2006/145] on emergency international assistance in Afghanistan, which provided an update on reconstruction efforts, including political, economic and social, and humanitarian activities in the country during the period from 13 August 2005 to 7 March 2006. Further humanitarian developments were included in his September report (see below) on the situation in Afghanistan, covering the period from 8 March to 11 September 2006. (For political aspects, see p. 362.)

Despite the significant transformation in Afghanistan's political landscape over the previous four years, particularly the completion of the Bonn process, and the December 2005 inauguration of a representative and fully elected National Assembly [YUN 2005, p. 403], the foundations of the State remained weak, in 2006, with limited capacity to deliver basic services to the majority of Afghans. In addition, Afghanistan continued to face challenges in the areas of security, governance, rule of law and human rights; sustainable economic and social development; and combating the illegal narcotics industry. The London Conference on Afghanistan, the Afghan Government and the international community reaffirmed their commitment to the long-term future of the country with the launch of the Afghanistan Compact, which earmarked critical areas for activity during the next five years (see p. 363). The Interim Afghanistan National Development Strategy, which was also presented at the Conference, identified four priority sources of growth in Afghanistan, including agriculture, the productive use of State assets, mining and other extractive industries, and regional transit and trade. The security situation, however, was of foremost concern, characterized by extremist activity and the continuing development of the tempo and sophistication of insurgent and other anti-Government elements.

Although the capacity of Afghanistan institutions to manage humanitarian crises had improved, it remained highly dependent on external actors. To address that vulnerability, in December 2005, with UN assistance, the Government established a National Emergency Operation Centre. In 2006, humanitarian efforts focused on the delivery of some 21,000 metric tons of food and more than 10,000 family packs of non-food items to vulnerable populations throughout the country. Emergency relief was provided to several hundred families in the north and northeast affected by avalanches and landslides in January and February. Afghan and UN agencies also provided assistance to the earthquake-affected regions in Kashmir-Pakistan. From 22 to 24 January, the United Nations Children's Fund vaccinated 2.3 million children against the poliomyelitis virus in the south, south-east and east of the country and from August 2005 to February 2006, UNHCR assisted 34,280 refugees returning from Iran and 235,600 from Pakistan.

In September [A/61/326-S/2006/727], the Secretary-General reported that the upsurge in violence during the reporting period, particularly in the south, south-east and east of the country, and the resulting insecurity had taken a toll on the capacity of the United Nations and aid organizations to deliver their humanitarian programmes in insurgency-affected areas. The majority of the districts in the south were chronically or temporarily inaccessible to UN movements. UN agencies and the United Nations Assistance Mission in Afghanistan explored new ways of delivering their services to populations in those areas. Despite the prevailing situation, Afghan refugees continued to return, with over 122,000 having returned, mostly from Pakistan.

The severe drought in Afghanistan affected 2.5 million people and the total shortfall for the current harvest, which had been estimated at 1.2 million tons of cereal, further exacerbated the situation. Initial projections by the International Monetary Fund of a 12 per cent growth rate in Afghanistan in 2006 had been scaled back to 10 per cent in the light of the drought and its impact on the country's agriculture. To address the crisis, a joint Government-United Nations drought appeal for $76 million was launched on 25 July to cover the period from July to December 2006. In October, an extension of that appeal, until the start of the main harvest in April 2007, was launched, calling for an additional $43.3 million.

In **resolution 61/18** of 28 November (see p. 369), the Assembly called on the international community to support Afghanistan's national development strategy, by providing all possible and necessary humanitarian, recovery, reconstruction, financial, technical and material assistance.

Lebanon

The UN Consolidated Inter-Agency Appeal for the crisis in Lebanon, launched for $96.5 million in 2006, received 123 per cent of its target ($119 million).

In July, violence erupted in Lebanon between the paramilitary group Hizbullah and Israel (see p. 574), with the civilian population caught in the middle. Hundreds of people were killed and more than 1,500 wounded within the first two weeks of the conflict. As the humanitarian situation worsened, an estimated 700,000 people fled their homes, including some 150,000 who crossed the border into Syria. The conflict also affected some 100,000 people from 20 different countries, who were living in Lebanon and required assistance to evacuate. Moreover, Israeli military operations caused substantial damage to infrastructure, such as power plants, seaports, and fuel depots. Bridges and road networks were systematically destroyed, leaving entire communities in the South inaccessible, posing a challenge to humanitarian efforts to deliver assistance. The initial consolidated flash appeal launched on 24 July sought $155 million, and was later revised to $96.5 million to reflect the rapidly changing humanitarian situation following the cessation of hostilities on 14 August and the return of more than 90 per cent of Lebanon's displaced population.

Nepal

The UN Consolidated Inter-Agency Appeal for Nepal, which sought $67.5 million in 2006, received 85 per cent (57.1 million) of the requirements.

In 2006, after ten years of insurgency and counter-insurgency that had cost an estimated 13,000 lives, as well as considerable economic and social damage, progress was made in Nepal towards achieving lasting peace and addressing the causes of the conflict. A year-long process of negotiation between the Government and the Communist Party of Nepal-Maoist and a successful people's movement led to the end to the 14-month direct rule of King Gyanendra and the signing of the Comprehensive Peace Agreement in November. However, Nepal's economic performance continued to be low and many key humanitarian indicators, which had verged on emergency thresholds for years, were further aggravated by the conflict, including acute malnutrition in children under five and maternal mortality. Ongoing strikes and ethnic and regional tensions hindered the population's access to basic services, particularly emergency medical care, and food insecurity remained a concern, with some 39 out of 75 districts suffering from food deficit. Three consecutive harvests had failed due to drought, floods and landslides. In addition, some 107,000 Bhutanese refugees living in camps in Eastern Nepal for the last 16 years remained completely reliant on international aid. Many IDPs who had started returning to their places of origin since the April ceasefire faced protection issues, particularly their ability to return and reoccupy land and property safely. Assistance efforts centred on improving access to vulnerable groups; monitoring the human rights situation; providing basic humanitarian services; and developing systems for needs assessment and the coordination of emergency preparedness.

Palestine

The UN Consolidated Inter-Agency Appeal for the Occupied Palestinian Territory, which sought $394.9 million in 2006, received 69 per cent ($273.6 million) of the requirements.

In 2006, political, economic and social conditions sharply deteriorated in Palestine. The political impasse was characterized by Israeli economic and military pressure, including the withholding of Palestinian tax revenues, increasing divisions within the Palestinian Authority, and the diversion of direct international assistance away from key Palestinian institutions. Intensified restrictions on the movement of Palestinian goods, workers, businessmen, officials and public service providers further crippled the economy. Normal market mechanisms had faltered and dependency on aid had risen. Poverty rates stood at 65.8 per cent and continued to increase, while food insecurity rose to 13 per cent during the year. A wave of public sector strikes debilitated the delivery of public services and led to the closure of public schools and hospital wards in the West Bank. Moreover, failing public security structures had given way to the fragmentation of armed factions and private militias. Although the international community tried to spare ordinary Palestinians the worst effects of the crisis by supporting the Temporary International Mechanism (see p. 508) and pledging increased humanitarian assistance, the situation at the end of the year was worse that in 2005. Following the May revision of the appeal, humanitarian assistance focused on supporting the continuation of essential social services and cushioning the deepening humanitarian crisis.

Sri Lanka

In 2006, renewed and escalating levels of open warfare in North and East Sri Lanka shattered the fragile ceasefire, causing grave humanitarian consequences, including the displacement of over 200,000 civilian casualties. Protection issues and human rights violations were of great concern, particularly in the light of the unprecedented killing of 17 Action contre la faim workers in August, which dealt a severe blow to the humanitarian community and its efforts. A humanitarian action plan for Sri Lanka was launched in October, as a programming and coordinating platform, which outlined immediate and prioritized interventions for the affected populations. Total requirements of the action plan amounted to $30 million.

Timor-Leste

The UN Consolidated Inter-Agency Appeal for Timor-Leste, launched for $24.2 million in 2006, received 103 per cent of its target ($25.1 million).

In April and May, hostilities erupted in the capital, Dili, resulting in the displacement of 150,000 people. As the outbreak of fighting was followed by an absence of law and order in the capital, communal fighting between westerners and easteners, as well as looting and burning of houses and Government buildings at the hands of youth gangs continued. An estimated 4,000 houses and many businesses, public buildings, shops, and essential utilities were affected. International forces deployed at the Government's request reduced the violence and looting. However, the precarious security situation led to a humanitarian situation characterized by an increased number of IDPs in already-established camps and an increase in the overall number of camps in the capital. Assistance focused on addressing the immediate needs of IDPs, including food, protection and emergency shelter, health, and water and sanitation.

Europe

North Caucasus (Russian Federation)

In 2006, the joint recovery-oriented, humanitarian and development assistance operation, conducted by nine UN agencies and thirteen NGOs in Chechnya and its neighbouring republics under the Inter-Agency Transitional Workplan for North Caucasus, had developed largely as anticipated. Although serious concerns about violence and insecurity remained, the security situation allowed for more access and project activity than in previous years, particularly in Chechnya where the United Nations, ICRC, and NGOs had a much greater presence. In some areas, where NGOs and UN agencies provided humanitarian assistance in the past few years, the Government was gradually gaining its capacity and taking over. In addition, emergency humanitarian relief was being reduced, which was evident by the shift in the priorities of assistance providers in the food security and agriculture sectors toward livelihood support. Requirements sought for the Transitional Workplan for 2006 were revised in July to $81.9 million, of which $34.9 million (43 per cent) was received.

Special economic assistance

African economic recovery and development

New Partnership for Africa's Development

The General Assembly, by resolution 57/7 [YUN 2002, p. 910], endorsed the Secretary-General's recommendation [ibid., p. 909] that the New Partnership for Africa's Development (NEPAD), adopted in 2001 by the Assembly of Heads of State and Government of the Organization of African Unity [YUN 2001, p. 900], should be the framework within which the international community should concentrate its efforts for Africa's development.

Report of Secretary-General (March). In response to a request of the Committee for Programme and Coordination (CPC) [YUN 2005, p. 1004], the Secretary-General submitted a March report [E/AC.51/2006/6] on UN system support for NEPAD, which detailed work undertaken since mid-2005 around the seven thematic clusters corresponding to the Partnership's priorities and strategies: infrastructure development; governance, peace and security; agriculture, trade and market access; environment, population and urbanization; human resources development, employment and HIV/AIDS; science and technology; and communication, advocacy and outreach. In addition, three selected policy issues in the implementation of NEPAD were examined: innovative approaches developed for funding NEPAD programmes; efforts towards NEPAD advocacy and awareness-raising; and challenges and constraints faced by the UN system in supporting NEPAD. The report also examined issues of coordination, collaboration and funding. In terms of innovative approaches for funding NEPAD priorities, the International Monetary Fund (IMF) provided direct financial support and debt relief. In January, it gave 100 per cent relief on debt owed to it by 13 low-income sub-Saharan African countries that had reached the completion point under the Heavily Indebted Poor Countries (HIPC) Debt Initiative launched in 1996 [YUN 1996, p. 867]. In February, the World Bank created its Catalytic Growth Fund, which was an innovative step for increasing NEPAD project funding. One of the Fund's goals was to scale up regional investments that represented a clear opportunity to supply regional public goods. UNDP mobilized $7.1 million in funding for an African Union (AU) capacity-building project, for which its contribution was $2.5 million. The report concluded with recommendations for improving coordination and strengthening collaboration.

CEB report. The United Nations System Chief Executives Board for Coordination (CEB), in its annual report for 2005-2006 [E/2006/66], identified the system's support to NEPAD as one of the priority issues for inter-agency attention, particularly in addressing poverty and hunger, in addition to migration and the increasing international movement of peoples. Efforts to combine immediate assistance for the poor and hungry with long-term development programmes included the establishment or strengthening of collaborative programmes under the aegis of NEPAD. The report also underscored that NEPAD support should be sustained and proactive, while remaining sensitive to Africa's ownership of the programme. Further programme development by the system in support of Africa would be guided by, and drawn on, the resolve expressed in the World Summit Outcome [YUN 2005, p. 48] to strengthen cooperation with NEPAD.

Advisory Panel report. On 13 July [A/61/138], the Secretary-General transmitted to the General Assembly the second report of the Advisory Panel on International Support for NEPAD, established in 2004 [YUN 2004, p. 924], entitled "From commitments to results: moving forward NEPAD implementation", which reflected progress achieved since the previous report [YUN 2005, p. 1004], and underscored the importance of undertaking policy measures to accelerate the implementation of NEPAD.

During the past year, a growing level of support had coalesced into new momentum for international action in Africa. In order to build on the momentum of those commitments, the Panel recommended the renewal of efforts to complete the stalemated Doha round of trade negotiations (see p. 1111), as well as more efficient and comprehensive monitoring of NEPAD aid by the inclusion of potential partners, such as Brazil, China, India and the Republic of Korea. With regard to debt relief, the Multilateral Debt Relief Initiative (MDRI), agreed on by the 2005 G-8 Summit [YUN 2005, p. 1057] and which took effect on 1 July, should include both HIPC-eligible African countries that had not met performance criteria, and non-HIPC African countries; the Bretton Woods institutions (the World Bank Group and the IMF) and the African Development Bank (ADB) should fully implement commitments made by the three financial institutions with respect to MDRI; and the Office of the Special Adviser on Africa should be updated on the implementation of those new steps. The Panel made several recommendations on measures for reinforcing international support, such as developing a framework to resolve the institutional relationship between the AU Commission and the NEPAD secretariat; enhancing linkages and coordination between African countries, regional economic communities, AU, ADB, and ECA; reflecting NEPAD priorities in national development strategies and engaging African finance ministers fully in the NEPAD implementation process; strengthening partnerships between the Government, the private sector and civil society via multi-stakeholder consultations; and embarking on an effective communication and outreach strategy to build public awareness of NEPAD, mobilize stakeholder groups for action and report on progress made in NEPAD implementation.

The Panel further recommended that the UN system should review and reinforce its modalities of work in Africa, including the framework for coordination and collaboration, and the consultative mechanism between the two organizations should reflect the wide-ranging nature of such cooperation. The UN system should also develop an integrated framework for supporting the AU Commission. With regard to monitoring the implementation of NEPAD, the importance of deepening international support to improve the availability of current and reliable data and indicators was stressed, as was the need to consolidate the results of different monitoring mechanisms in one report. The Panel also proposed strengthening the Office of the Special Adviser on Africa to provide that service and to support the UN overall responsibility for monitoring the performance of donors and partners.

CPC action. CPC, at its forty-sixth session (14 August–8 September) [A/61/16 & Corr.1], endorsed the recommendations in the Secretary-General's report on NEPAD (see p. 1071) and reiterated the critical roles of CEB and the Office of the Special Adviser for the advocacy and fostering of international support for NEPAD at the global level. The Committee recommended that the Assembly ask the Secretary-General to continue to strengthen the Office of the Special Adviser and request the Office to provide leadership and coordinated support to African countries, ECA and the AU. Concerned by coordination, collaboration and funding issues hindering the full and effective implementation of NEPAD, it urged components of the UN system to ensure the proper utilization of talents and resources. The Committee also stressed the need for inter-agency coordination; regular and periodic dialogue with ECA, the AU and the NEPAD secretariat; inter-agency joint planning; and monitoring of international commitments in support of NEPAD to avoid duplication.

CPC called on CEB to ensure that support for NEPAD remained a UN system priority and encouraged CEB member organizations to further align their priorities with those of NEPAD and scale up their efforts in support of it. The Committee also recommended that the Assembly consider the recommendations contained in the Joint Inspection Unit (JIU) report on measures to strengthen UN system support to NEPAD (see p. 1075).

Report of Secretary-General (September). In response to General Assembly resolution 60/222 [YUN 2005, p. 1005], the Secretary-General submitted, in September, the fourth consolidated report [A/61/212] on progress achieved to implement and support NEPAD, which highlighted significant developments in the past year, including actions undertaken by African countries and organizations, the response of the international community and support by the UN system. The report's release also marked the fifth anniversary of NEPAD.

The Secretary-General observed that progress made in the previous 12 months, in both regional efforts to implement NEPAD and in the commitments made by the international community, provided the basis for proclaiming a new momentum in Africa's development. ADB had funded 25 projects and programmes worth $630 million in the period 2002-2005, mobilized $1.6 billion in co-financing, and had funding in the pipeline for 2006 worth $472 million. Other advancements included the establishment of the Infrastructure Consortium for Africa, and the NEPAD Spatial Development Programme aimed at the sustainable provision of integrated transport, in addition to the ongoing development of transboundary water resources management and of the Inga power resources in the DRC to increase electricity generation.

During the year, the e-Africa Commission focused on three major components of the NEPAD e-Schools Initiative (Demonstration Project, Business Plan and the Satellite Network), and on the broadband information and communication technologies network. In total, 13 African countries were involved in the NEPAD e-schools programme and efforts would be made to encompass all 20 countries into the first phase of the programme. A meeting of information and communication ministers responsible for technologies in Eastern and Southern Africa (Johannesburg, South Africa, 8 June) supported the development of a policy framework under which the broadband information and communication technologies infrastructure network could be brought into fruition.

Activities undertaken to advance various education projects included mobilizing financing for conferences related to "Basic education and Education for All"; developing a research and development database for secondary schools in Africa in support of the "Building capacity in education, research and development in Africa" project; and finalizing a scheme to mainstream gender-responsive pedagogy in sub-Saharan school systems for the "Gender equality in primary and secondary schools in Africa" project. Initiatives promoting science and technology resulted in the launch of the Centre for Mathematics, Science and Technology Education in Africa, a flagship project of NEPAD. Teachers from more than 20 countries had undergone training at the Centre.

On strengthening African health systems, the partnership between NEPAD and the World Health Organization (WHO) culminated in the launch of the Global Health Workforce Alliance and in the development of the "Treat, train and retain" initiative, which consolidated efforts to address both HIV/AIDS and health system challenges. NEPAD collaboration with the Joint United Nations Programme on HIV/AIDS continued, particularly in its office for Southern and East Africa, and in the field of mainstreaming, political support and engagement, and monitoring and evaluation.

Significant steps were taken towards implementing the NEPAD Environment Initiative. The revised draft of the NEPAD subregional environment plans was pending ministerial adoption in the respective subregions. Three priority projects per subregion had been identified at the eleventh session of the African Ministerial Conference on the Environment (Brazzaville, Congo, 22-26 May). In addition, an agreement between NEPAD and the Development Bank of South Africa on a joint capacity-building programme for accelerating implementation of the NEPAD Environment Action Plan in five subregional African economic communities was in the final stages. Implementation of the Africa Stockpiles Programme, one of the priority projects of the Plan, took centre stage, with two countries having begun implementation and five others scheduled to start during the second half of 2006.

NEPAD prepared a comprehensive data set of indicators in the field of science, technology and innovation, which were designed to guide countries in the preparation of national science and technology strategies and plans. Efforts continued to implement the NEPAD/African Biosciences Initiative, a cluster of three science and technology flagship programmes (biodiversity, biotechnology and indigenous knowledge systems) launched in 2005. In that connection, regional networks had been established covering the African continent. In addition, the panel of eminent African scientists and policy analysts summoned in 2005 by AU/NEPAD to prepare a policy position on the development and use of genetically modified crops and other biotechnology products [YUN 2005, p. 1005], identified specific issues that required a common African approach, particularly in the transboundary movement of genetically modified products and their impact on African economies.

Progress continued in the implementation of the three-year comprehensive strategic plan for strengthening gender mainstreaming and deepening civil society involvement, through the main institutional mechanisms, namely, the Gender and Civil Society Organizations Unit at the NEPAD secretariat, the NEPAD Gender Task Force and the NEPAD-civil society think tank. With regard to the African Peer Review Mechanism (APRM), an African self-monitoring mechanism established by the AU in 2003 [YUN 2003, p. 938], 25 countries had acceded to it since its inception. Support missions aimed at evaluating the preparedness and national capacity for self-assessment and for preparing national action plans had taken place in five countries since January, and the African Peer Review panel had undertaken one review mission in July. The commitment of African countries to APRM was amplified by recent trends and developments in the region, such as the adoption by several countries of new policy measures to strengthen accountability and transparency, developing equal opportunity acts and drafting legislation on freedom of information acts, as well as by the convening of the sixth African Governance Forum (Kigali, Rwanda, May) on the theme "Implementing the APRM: opportunities and challenges".

Accomplishments attributed to the international community in support of NEPAD encompassed the establishment by the United Kingdom of an independent, high-level Africa Progress Panel to track aid promises made at the 2005 G-8 Summit [YUN 2005, p. 1057]; the April announcement by the Republic of Korea of the Initiative for Africa's Development; the establishment by the European Union of a fund for infrastructure projects in Africa; and the operation in ten African countries of the Millennium Villages Project, which contributed to implementation of quick impact initiatives. Other developments highlighted the significant increases in official development assistance (ODA) to Africa; the substantial progress made in extending and deepening debt relief provision to African countries; the cancellation of partial debt, entire debt or bilateral debt by donor countries or institutions; the delivery of HIPC Initiative debt relief, which benefited 15 African countries, as at June; and the establishment of the Multilateral Debt Relief Initiative (MDRI) (see p. 1130). In the trade sector, developed countries had pledged to grant duty- and quota-free market access to at least 97 per cent of products originating from least developed countries by 2008, with the exception of some 300 sensitive products, such as sugar and rice. The previous year had also witnessed several aid-for-trade commitments from developed countries, which aimed to help developing countries expand their capacity to export.

The Secretary-General concluded that, while the past year had witnessed considerable support for Africa from the international community, as well as the determination of Africa and its development partners to make progress on agreed programmes and commitments, the momentum was not yet strong enough to be irreversible. A number of policy measures and practical actions needed to be taken to strengthen the impetus to implement NEPAD. He urged African Governments to address issues, such as integrating NEPAD into AU structures and processes, providing greater support for the private sector and promoting more outreach to civil society. The delivery of pledges and commitments made to Africa should be in a timely manner and at a much faster pace, particularly by the G-8 countries. Progress on debt write-off should be matched by corresponding efforts to meet the desired annual level of ODA, with a view to achieving the long-term targets for Africa. The increased flow of ODA to Africa should be met with corresponding efforts to simplify the complex administrative and reporting procedures in order to minimize delays in the release of resources for approved programmes.

The diversification of Africa's economic and export structures was essential to the sustained growth and development of the region.

Strengthening UN system support to NEPAD

JIU report. In a March note [A/61/69], the Secretary-General transmitted the report of the Joint Inspection Unit (JIU) on further measures to strengthen UN support to NEPAD, which examined regional collaboration of UN agencies in Africa and its effectiveness, particularly through the meetings convened by the Economic Commission for Africa (ECA). The report considered strategic policy issues; representation of UN system organizations at the regional and subregional levels in Africa; the clusters approach as a mechanism for regional consultations; the role of ECA; and the role of CEB. It identified factors inhibiting effective regional collaboration, and proposed measures to enhance coordination and collaboration in support of NEPAD. The report concluded that there was a need to establish a strategic dialogue, and determine and follow up on a framework for institutionalized cooperation between the UN system, including ECA on the one hand, and the AU Commission, including the NEPAD secretariat, on the other.

Among other measures proposed, JIU recommended that the General Assembly request the Secretary-General to invite the AU to the annual consultative meetings, with a view to ensuring effective collaboration and consultations; conduct an independent study of the potential benefits of establishing regional and subregional hubs for UN representation in Africa; review the institutional architecture of the UN system in Africa to avoid duplication and overlapping, cut costs and improve policy and operational coherence; direct ECA to review the efficiency of the clustering arrangement and report before the next annual consultation meetings; request the Executive Heads of UN organizations concerned to ensure that each cluster gave due focus on a few joint UN regional and subregional projects; request the Secretary-General to enhance the capacity of the ECA Office of Policy and Programme Coordination by redeploying staff from other UN entities; and report to the Assembly's sixty-first session on efforts and measures taken to strengthen ECA capacity in coordinating the work of those agencies. The General Assembly and legislative bodies should increase their support for the clusters' joint programmes/projects and CEB should provide a clear-cut policy directive to ensure consistency and effective implementation towards that end.

In a July note [A/61/69/Add.1], the Secretary-General transmitted to the General Assembly his comments and those of the CEB on the JIU report on strengthening NEPAD (see above). CEB member organizations concurred in general with the report's recommendations.

GENERAL ASSEMBLY ACTION

On 22 December [meeting 84], the General Assembly adopted **resolution 61/229** [draft: A/61/L.23/Rev.1 & Add.1] without vote [agenda item 62 *(a)*].

New Partnership for Africa's Development: progress in implementation and international support

The General Assembly,

Recalling its resolution 57/2 of 16 September 2002 on the United Nations Declaration on the New Partnership for Africa's Development,

Recalling also its resolution 57/7 of 4 November 2002 on the final review and appraisal of the United Nations New Agenda for the Development of Africa in the 1990s and support for the New Partnership for Africa's Development and resolutions 58/233 of 23 December 2003, 59/254 of 23 December 2004 and 60/222 of 23 December 2005 entitled "New Partnership for Africa's Development: progress in implementation and international support",

Recalling further the 2005 World Summit Outcome, including the recognition of the need to meet the special needs of Africa,

Bearing in mind that African countries have primary responsibility for their own economic and social development and that the role of national policies and development strategies cannot be overemphasized, and also the need for their development efforts to be supported by an enabling international economic environment, and in this regard recalling the support given by the International Conference on Financing for Development to the New Partnership,

Stressing the need to implement various commitments by the international community regarding the economic and social development of Africa,

1. *Welcomes* the fourth consolidated report of the Secretary-General;

2. *Reaffirms its full support* for the implementation of the New Partnership for Africa's Development;

3. *Recognizes* the progress made in the implementation of the New Partnership as well as regional and international support for the New Partnership, while acknowledging that much needs to be done in its implementation;

4. *Reaffirms* the resolve to provide assistance for prevention and care, with the aim of ensuring an AIDS, malaria- and tuberculosis-free generation in Africa, and of achieving as closely as possible the goal of universal access by 2010 to HIV/AIDS treatment in African countries, to encourage pharmaceutical companies to make drugs, including antiretroviral drugs, that are affordable and accessible in Africa and to ensure increased bilateral

and multilateral assistance, where possible on a grant basis, to combat malaria, tuberculosis and other infectious diseases in Africa through the strengthening of health systems;

5. *Reaffirms its full support* for the implementation of the Declaration of Commitment on HIV/AIDS, adopted at the twenty-sixth special session of the General Assembly on 27 June 2001, and the Political Declaration on HIV/AIDS, adopted by the Assembly on 2 June 2006;

I

Actions by African countries and organizations

6. *Welcomes* the progress made by the African countries in fulfilling their commitments in the implementation of the New Partnership to deepen democracy, human rights, good governance and sound economic management, and encourages African countries, with the participation of stakeholders, including civil society and the private sector, to intensify their efforts in this regard by developing and strengthening institutions for governance, creating an environment conducive to involving the private sector, including small and medium-size firms, in the New Partnership implementation process and to attracting foreign direct investment for the development of the region;

7. *Also welcomes* the good progress that has been achieved in implementing the African Peer Review Mechanism, in particular the completion of the peer review process in some countries, further welcomes the progress in implementing the recommendations of those reviews, and in this regard urges African States to consider joining the Mechanism process as soon as possible and to strengthen the Mechanism process for its efficient performance;

8. *Further welcomes and appreciates* the continuing and increasing efforts of African countries to mainstream a gender perspective and the empowerment of women in the implementation of the New Partnership;

9. *Stresses* that conflict prevention, management and resolution and post-conflict consolidation are essential for the achievement of the objectives of the New Partnership, and welcomes in this regard the cooperation and support granted by the United Nations and development partners to the African regional and subregional organizations in the implementation of the New Partnership;

10. *Welcomes* the efforts by African countries to achieve food and nutrition security by adopting appropriate strategies inspired by the Comprehensive Africa Agricultural Development Programme and by debates at various summits, such as at the New Partnership's Fish for All Summit, held in Abuja from 22 to 25 August 2005, and the Africa Fertilizer Summit, endorsed by the African Union on 29 August 2005 and held from 9 to 13 June 2006, and the New Partnership's Food Security Summit, held in Abuja from 4 to 7 December 2006;

11. *Emphasizes* the importance for African countries to continue to coordinate, on the basis of national strategies and priorities, all types of external assistance in order to integrate effectively such assistance into their development processes;

12. *Recognizes* the important role that African regional economic communities can play in the implementation of the New Partnership, and in this regard encourages African countries and the international community to give regional economic communities the necessary support to strengthen their capacity;

13. *Supports* the ongoing efforts by the African Union to improve the coordination between the New Partnership secretariat, the African Union Commission, the regional economic communities and African States;

14. *Encourages* the establishment of national institutional mechanisms for further domestication and integration of the priorities and objectives of the New Partnership in national policies and programmes;

II

Response of the international community

15. *Welcomes* the efforts by development partners to strengthen cooperation with the New Partnership;

16. *Also welcomes* the various important initiatives of Africa's development partners in recent years, and emphasizes in this regard the importance of coordination in such initiatives on Africa;

17. *Recognizes* the important role that South-South cooperation can play in supporting Africa's development efforts, including implementation of the New Partnership, and in this regard welcomes the convening of the Beijing Summit of the Forum on China-Africa Cooperation on 4 and 5 November 2006 and the Africa-Latin America Summit, held in Abuja on 30 November and 1 December 2006;

18. *Welcomes* the ongoing initiatives on the follow-up to the second Asia-Africa summit, held in Jakarta on 22 and 23 April 2005, aimed at promoting greater partnership and cooperation between Africa and other regions;

19. *Urges* continued support of measures to address the challenges of poverty eradication and sustainable development in Africa including, as appropriate, debt relief, improved market access, support for the private sector and entrepreneurship, enhanced official development assistance and increased flows of foreign direct investment, and transfer of technology;

20. *Reiterates* the need for all countries and relevant multilateral institutions to continue efforts to enhance coherence in their trade policies towards African countries, and acknowledges the importance of efforts to fully integrate African countries into the international trading system through initiatives such as building Africa's capacity to compete and the provision of assistance to address the adjustment challenges of trade liberalization;

21. *Calls for* a comprehensive and sustainable solution to the external debt problems of African countries, including cancellation or restructuring for heavily indebted African countries not part of the Heavily Indebted Poor Countries Initiative that have unsustainable debt burdens, and emphasizes the importance of debt sustainability;

22. *Welcomes* the recent pledges by the Group of Eight countries to double by 2010 official development assistance to Africa, looks forward to the realization of

those pledges, and urges donors to continue to improve the quality of aid in accordance with the Paris Declaration on Aid Effectiveness: Ownership, Harmonization, Alignment, Results and Mutual Accountability, adopted at the High-level Forum on the question of "Joint Progress towards Enhanced Aid Effectiveness: Harmonization, Alignment, Results", held in Paris from 28 February to 2 March 2005, and to ensure that the increase in official development assistance translates into the actual flow of financial resources to developing countries;

23. *Recognizes* the need for national Governments and the international community to make continued efforts to increase the flow of new and additional resources for financing for development from all sources, public and private, domestic and foreign, to support the development of African countries;

24. *Welcomes* the efforts by development partners to align their financial and technical support to Africa more closely to the priorities of the New Partnership, as reflected in national poverty reduction strategies or in similar strategies, and encourages development partners to increase their efforts in this regard;

25. *Invites* developed countries to promote investment by their private sectors in Africa, to help African countries attract investments and promote policies conducive to attracting domestic and foreign investment, such as encouraging private financial flows and promoting and maintaining macroeconomic stability, to encourage and facilitate the transfer of the technology needed to African countries on favourable terms, including on concessional and preferential terms, as mutually agreed, and to assist in strengthening human and institutional capacities for the implementation of the New Partnership, consistent with its priorities and objectives and with a view to furthering Africa's development at all levels;

26. *Requests* the United Nations system to continue to provide assistance to the African Union and the New Partnership secretariat and to African countries in developing projects and programmes within the scope of the priorities of the New Partnership;

27. *Invites* the Secretary-General, as a follow-up to the 2005 World Summit, to urge the United Nations development system to assist African countries in implementing quick-impact initiatives through, inter alia, the Millennium Villages Project;

28. *Decides* to hold within existing resources a high-level meeting on Africa's development needs: state of implementation of various commitments, challenges and the way forward during its sixty-third session, the focus and modalities of which will be decided upon at its sixty-second session;

29. *Requests* the Secretary-General to promote greater coherence in the work of the United Nations system in support of the New Partnership, on the basis of the agreed clusters;

30. *Also requests* the Secretary-General to continue to take measures to strengthen the Office of the Special Adviser on Africa in order to enable it to effectively fulfil its mandate, including monitoring and reporting on progress related to meeting the special needs of Africa;

31. *Further requests* the Secretary-General to submit a comprehensive report on the implementation of the present resolution to the General Assembly at its sixty-second session on the basis of inputs from Governments, organizations of the United Nations system and other stakeholders in the New Partnership, such as the private sector and civil society.

Social dimensions of NEPAD

ECONOMIC AND SOCIAL COUNCIL ACTION

On 26 July [meeting 40], the Economic and Social Council, on the recommendation of the Commission for Social Development [E/2006/26], adopted **resolution 2006/17** without vote [agenda item 14 *(b)*].

Social dimensions of the New Partnership for Africa's Development

The Economic and Social Council,

Recalling the World Summit for Social Development, held in Copenhagen from 6 to 12 March 1995, and the twenty-fourth special session of the General Assembly, entitled "World Summit for Social Development and beyond: achieving social development for all in a globalizing world", held in Geneva from 26 June to 1 July 2000,

Reaffirming the United Nations Millennium Declaration of 8 September 2000, the United Nations Declaration on the New Partnership for Africa's Development of 16 September 2002, and General Assembly resolution 57/7 of 4 November 2002 on the final review and appraisal of the United Nations New Agenda for the Development of Africa in the 1990s and its support for the New Partnership for Africa's Development,

Welcoming the conclusions of the African Union Extraordinary Summit on Employment and Poverty Alleviation, held in Ouagadougou on 8 and 9 September 2004,

Recognizing the commitments made in meeting the special needs of Africa at the 2005 World Summit,

Cognizant of the link between priorities of the New Partnership for Africa's Development and the United Nations Millennium Declaration, in which the international community committed itself to addressing the special needs of Africa, and the need to achieve the internationally agreed development goals, including those set out in the Millennium Declaration,

Bearing in mind that African countries have primary responsibility for their own economic and social development, that the role of national policies and development strategies cannot be overemphasized and that their development efforts need to be supported by an enabling international economic environment, and in this regard recalling the support given by the International Conference on Financing for Development to the New Partnership,

1. *Welcomes* the adoption of the chapter entitled "Sustainable development for Africa" in the Plan of Implementation of the World Summit on Sustainable Development ("Johannesburg Plan of Implementation");

2. *Emphasizes* that economic development, social development and environmental protection are interdependent and mutually reinforcing components of sustainable development;

3. *Welcomes* the progress made by the African countries in fulfilling their commitments in the implementation of the New Partnership for Africa's Development to deepen democracy, human rights, good governance and sound economic management, and encourages African countries, with the participation of stakeholders, including civil society and the private sector, to intensify their efforts in this regard by developing and strengthening institutions for governance and creating an environment conducive to attracting foreign direct investment for the development of the region;

4. *Emphasizes* that democracy, respect for all human rights and fundamental freedoms, including the right to development, transparent and accountable governance and administration in all sectors of society, and effective participation by civil society, non-governmental organizations and the private sector are among the indispensable foundations for the realization of social and people-centred sustainable development;

5. *Welcomes* the good progress that has been achieved in implementing the African Peer Review Mechanism, in particular the completion of the self-assessment process in some countries, the hosting of country support missions and the launching of the national preparatory process for the Peer Review in others, and urges African States to join the Peer Review, as a matter of priority, as soon as possible, and to strengthen the Peer Review process to ensure its efficient performance;

6. *Welcomes* the efforts made by African countries and regional and subregional organizations, including the African Union, in developing sectoral policy frameworks and implementing specific programmes of the New Partnership as well as mainstreaming a gender perspective and the empowerment of women;

7. *Emphasizes* the importance of African countries continuing to coordinate, on the basis of national strategies and priorities, all types of external assistance, including that provided by multilateral organizations, in order to effectively integrate such assistance into their development processes;

8. *Encourages* further integration of the priorities and objectives of the New Partnership into the programmes of the regional structures and organizations by African countries;

9. *Recalls* that the African Union and the regional economic communities have a critical role to play in the implementation of the New Partnership, and in that regard encourages African countries, with the assistance of their development partners, to increase their support to enhance the capacities of those institutions;

10. *Emphasizes* that progress in the implementation of the New Partnership depends also on a favourable national and international environment for Africa's growth and development, including measures to promote a policy environment conducive to private sector development and entrepreneurship;

11. *Recognizes* that, while social development is primarily the responsibility of Governments, international cooperation and assistance are essential for the full achievement of that goal;

12. *Welcomes* the efforts by development partners to strengthen cooperation with the secretariat of the New Partnership;

13. *Welcomes also* the contribution made by Member States to the implementation of the New Partnership in the context of South-South cooperation, and in that regard encourages the international community, including the international financial institutions, to support the efforts of African countries, including through triangular cooperation;

14. *Acknowledges* the various important initiatives of Africa's development partners in recent years, including those of the Organization for Economic Cooperation and Development, the Africa Action Plan of the Group of Eight, the European Union, the Tokyo International Conference on African Development, including the Africa-Asia Business Forum, the report of the United Kingdom Commission for Africa entitled *Our Common Interest,* and the Africa Partnership Forum, and in that regard emphasizes the importance of coordination in such initiatives on Africa;

15. *Acknowledges also* the important role of the Africa Partnership Forum, as set out in the revised terms of reference dated 5 October 2005, which include catalysing action on the measures taken to meet the commitments that Africa and its development partners have made and coordinating support for African priorities and the New Partnership, and encourages the Africa Partnership Forum to strengthen its efforts in that regard;

16. *Urges* continuing support of measures to address the challenges of poverty eradication and sustainable development in Africa, including, as appropriate, debt relief, improved market access, support for the private sector and entrepreneurship, enhanced official development assistance, increased foreign direct investment and the transfer of technology;

17. *Welcomes* the recent increase in official development assistance pledged by many of the development partners, including the commitments of the Group of Eight and the European Union, which will lead to an increase in official development assistance to Africa of 25 billion United States dollars per year by 2010, and encourages all development partners to ensure aid effectiveness through the implementation of the Paris Declaration on Aid Effectiveness: Ownership, Harmonization, Alignment, Results and Mutual Accountability, of 2005;

18. *Recognizes* the need for national Governments and the international community to make continued efforts to increase the flow of new and additional resources for financing for development from all sources, public and private, domestic and foreign, to support the development of African countries;

19. *Welcomes* the efforts by development partners to align their financial and technical support to Africa more closely with the priorities of the New Partnership, as reflected in national poverty reduction strategies or in

similar strategies, and encourages development partners to increase their efforts in that regard;

20. *Acknowledges* the activities of the Bretton Woods institutions and the African Development Bank in African countries, and invites those institutions to continue their support for the implementation of the priorities and objectives of the New Partnership;

21. *Invites* the Secretary-General, as a follow-up to the 2005 World Summit, to urge the organizations of the United Nations system to assist African countries to implement quick-impact initiatives, based on their national development priorities and strategies, to enable them to achieve the Millennium Development Goals, and in that respect acknowledges recent commitments by some donor countries;

22. *Notes* that the entities of the United Nations system have been actively using the regional consultation mechanism as a vehicle for fostering collaboration and coordination at the regional level, and encourages them to intensify their efforts in developing and implementing joint programmes in support of the New Partnership at the regional level;

23. *Encourages* the United Nations funds and programmes and the specialized agencies to continue to strengthen further their existing coordination and programming mechanisms and the simplification and harmonization of planning, disbursement and reporting procedures as a means of enhancing support for African countries in the implementation of the New Partnership;

24. *Notes* the growing collaboration among the entities of the United Nations system in support of the New Partnership, and requests the Secretary-General to promote greater coherence in the work of the United Nations system in support of the New Partnership, on the basis of the agreed clusters;

25. *Welcomes* the report of the Secretary-General's Advisory Panel on International Support for the New Partnership for Africa's Development, and looks forward to its supplementary report, including recommendations on the actions to enhance support for the implementation of the New Partnership;

26. *Requests* the Commission for Social Development to continue to raise awareness of the social dimensions of the New Partnership and its implementation and to provide recommendations on the measures to achieve this during the policy session in 2008;

27. *Requests* the Secretary-General to continue to take measures to strengthen the Office of the Special Adviser on Africa, and requests the Office to collaborate with the Department for Economic and Social Affairs of the Secretariat and to include the social dimensions of the New Partnership in its comprehensive reports to the General Assembly at its sixty-first session;

28. *Encourages* continued focus on the situation of social groups and persons infected with and affected by HIV and AIDS, malaria and other infectious diseases;

29. *Decides* that the Commission for Social Development should continue to give prominence to the social dimensions of the New Partnership for Africa's Development during its forty-fifth session.

Angola

In response to General Assembly resolution 59/216 [YUN 2004, p. 927], the Secretary-General, in his July consolidated report [A/61/209] on humanitarian assistance and rehabilitation for selected countries and regions, described the political and socio-economic situation in Angola and provided information on humanitarian assistance and relief provided by the United Nations and its partners in 2006.

Four years after the cessation of hostilities in Angola [YUN 2002, p. 221], consolidation of the peace process had become a reality and the country had moved from an emergency and humanitarian assistance phase to one of recovery, reconstruction and development. Therefore, special economic assistance focused on new challenges linked to national recovery and reconstruction efforts. Despite limited international community support, Angola had been innovative in finding ways to rebuild the country, such as maximizing South-South cooperation with Brazil, China and India to obtain loans in support of national reconstruction, and utilizing its immense oil reserves as collateral, with the aim of realizing impressive economic growth through oil revenues and stabilized inflation rates. However, one of the country's greatest challenges was addressing the need for growth with equity, sustainability and human development. Angola's population remained one of the poorest in the world, and the Government faced the difficult task of finding ways to improve their living conditions and achieve the MDGs. However, with political will, decisive action and firm support of the international community, the Government could enhance its ability to undertake the extensive reforms, capacity development and employment creation necessary for development. Improvements in some of the social indicators, such as increased enrolment in primary schools, rehabilitation and construction of social infrastructures, and increased delivery of social services, including health, education, electricity, and water and sanitation were positive developments. Major demining efforts were under way throughout the country and were central to immediate plans to sustain peace and improve human security. Since late 2005, the majority of IDPs, refugees and demobilized soldiers had been or were in the process of being reintegrated into communities. Institutional reform activities, supported by UN programmes, were also ongoing and encompassed areas, such as decentralization and local governance; modernization of public financial management systems; judicial training and reform; environmental sustainability; civil protection systems; micro-entrepreneurship development; the informal sector; and the employment generation strategy. On the political front, preparatory activities for the 2007 presidential elections and the adoption of the UN Convention against Corruption by the National Assembly in May [YUN 2003, p. 1126], signaled the Government's commitment to democratic processes, improved governance and transparency and accountability.

The Secretary-General observed that, despite its wealth in diamonds, oil and water resources, and its agricultural potential, Angola was plagued by high levels of corruption and huge deficits in capacity-building and retention, democratic processes, human rights and the rule of law. Hence, fostering good governance and management in Angola represented a major challenge for the UN system and the international community. On the other hand, there were opportunities for continuing economic growth, and for efforts to engage national and foreign investors by promoting economic diversification, the decentralization programme and improvements in areas, such as general public expenditure management and business legal framework. The Secretary-General called upon the international community to support the Government and its development partners, especially civil society organizations and the private sector, to build the path for long-term development.

GENERAL ASSEMBLY ACTION

On 20 December [meeting 83], the General Assembly, on the recommendation of the Second Committee [A/61/429/Add.1 & Corr.1], adopted **resolution 61/219** without vote [agenda item 69 *(b)*].

International assistance for the economic rehabilitation of Angola

The General Assembly,

Recalling all previous resolutions in which it called upon the international community to continue to render material, technical and financial assistance for the economic rehabilitation of Angola, including resolution 59/216, adopted by consensus on 22 December 2004,

Recalling also that the Security Council, in its resolution 922(1994) of 31 May 1994 and subsequent resolutions adopted as from 2001, the President of the Security Council, in statements on Angola, and the General Assembly, in all of its resolutions on international assistance for the economic rehabilitation of Angola, have, inter alia, called upon the international community to provide economic assistance to Angola,

Bearing in mind that the main responsibility for improving the humanitarian situation and creating the conditions for long-term development and poverty reduction in Angola lies with the Government of Angola, together with, where appropriate, the participation of the international community,

Noting the importance of international engagement for the consolidation of peace in Angola,

Noting with satisfaction the successful implementation of and effective compliance with the provisions of the Lusaka Protocol,

Noting that an economically revived and democratic Angola will contribute to regional stability,

Noting with satisfaction the recent election of Angola as Chair of the Peacebuilding Commission,

Recalling the first Round-Table Conference of Donors, held in Brussels from 25 to 27 September 1995,

Welcoming the efforts made by donors and United Nations agencies, funds and programmes to provide humanitarian, economic and financial assistance to Angola,

1. *Takes note* of the report of the Secretary-General on humanitarian assistance and rehabilitation for selected countries and regions;

2. *Recognizes* the primary responsibility of the Government of Angola for the welfare of its citizens, including returning refugees and internally displaced persons, together with the support of the international community;

3. *Recognizes also* the efforts undertaken by the Government of Angola towards ensuring the maintenance of the peace and national security so necessary for the reconstruction, rehabilitation and economic stabilization of the country, and in this context encourages the Government, with the support of the international community, to continue its efforts for poverty reduction and the achievement of sustained economic growth and sustainable development, including, inter alia, social reintegration, mine action, rural development and food security, gender mainstreaming, education and the rehabilitation of social and economic infrastructures;

4. *Welcomes* the continued commitment of the Government of Angola to improve governance, transparency and accountability in the management of public resources, including natural resources, encourages the Government of Angola to continue its efforts to that end, and calls upon international organizations and others in a position to do so to assist the Government of Angola in this endeavour, including through the promotion of responsible business practices;

5. *Recognizes* the role that South-South cooperation is playing in the reconstruction and rehabilitation of the economy of Angola;

6. *Welcomes* the commitment of the Government of Angola to the development and strengthening of its democratic institutions, encourages the Government of Angola, with the necessary support of the international community, to continue its efforts with a view to holding legislative and presidential elections, as both would accelerate and consolidate the democratic development of the country, and in this regard welcomes the beginning of the voter registration process on 15 November 2006

as part of the road map for the holding of legislative and presidential elections;

7. *Commends* the Government of Angola for its leadership, coordination and successful implementation of the programme for disarmament, demobilization and reintegration and for ensuring the delivery of humanitarian assistance to those in need, all of which contribute to placing the country on the path to sustained economic growth and sustainable development;

8. *Expresses its appreciation* to the international community, the United Nations agencies, funds and programmes, and the governmental and non-governmental organizations that are participating in humanitarian assistance programmes in Angola, including mine-action activities, and appeals for their continued contribution to humanitarian mine-action activities in a manner complementary to that of the Government;

9. *Expresses its gratitude* to donors and United Nations agencies, funds and programmes for the assistance provided to Angola in support of initiatives and programmes for the alleviation of the humanitarian crisis and poverty eradication.

Liberia

In response to General Assembly resolution 59/219 [YUN 2004, p. 929], the Secretary-General, in his July consolidated report [A/61/209], provided information on humanitarian assistance and relief provided by the United Nations and its partners in Liberia in 2006.

Despite the dedication of the newly elected Government and the progress achieved in Liberia, severe institutional, material and national capacity restraints affected efforts to achieve the MDGs, particularly in the area of human resources. Several constraints had been identified, including the lack of resources and the transition from the humanitarian to the development context. Many NGOs were phasing out their activities, particularly in the health sector, and donor funding was increasingly difficult to attract. Delay in the disbursement of pledged funds resulted in considerable delays in the delivery of assistance. Other constraints included the lack of reliable data and information management systems at the national and country levels; inadequate basic social services and infrastructure; and the high level of formal unemployment, estimated at 85 per cent, with youth being one of the worst-affected segments of the population. Regional security issues also remained a concern.

The Secretary-General said that, for substantial progress to be made, massive pro-poor economic recovery efforts were essential. Donor support was urgently needed to help the new Government to commence large-scale service provision and meet the expectations of the Liberian people. He added that the scale and timeliness of resource availability were of the essence. With regard to the forthcoming launch of the interim poverty reduction strategy, he urged development partners to focus on attracting investment into the country and stabilizing the economic environment in order to foster economic growth. He also called on the UN system and other development partners to increase support in the areas of education and health care, particularly child mortality and maternal health.

GENERAL ASSEMBLY ACTION

On 20 December [meeting 83], the General Assembly, on the recommendation of the Second Committee [A/61/429/Add.1 & Corr.1], adopted **resolution 61/218** without vote [agenda item 69 *(b)*].

Humanitarian assistance and reconstruction of Liberia

The General Assembly,

Recalling its resolutions 45/232 of 21 December 1990, 46/147 of 17 December 1991, 47/154 of 18 December 1992, 48/197 of 21 December 1993, 49/21 E of 20 December 1994, 50/58 A of 12 December 1995, 51/30 B of 5 December 1996, 52/169 E of 16 December 1997, 53/1 I of 16 November 1998, 55/176 of 19 December 2000, 57/151 of 16 December 2002 and 59/219 of 22 December 2004,

Having considered the report of the Secretary-General on humanitarian assistance and rehabilitation for selected countries and regions,

Commending the Economic Community of West African States, the African Union, the International Contact Group on the Mano River Basin, the United Nations system and its specialized agencies, donor countries and institutions, and governmental and non-governmental organizations for their continued support for the peacebuilding process and the development of Liberia,

Commending also the United Nations Mission in Liberia for its important role in the maintenance of peace and stability in the country,

Noting with appreciation the holding of democratic elections in October and November 2005, which culminated in the inauguration in January 2006 of the first democratically elected woman president in Africa,

Noting the progress made in a number of areas, including the consolidation of governmental authority throughout the country, evidenced by the national development agenda, which encompasses four benchmarks: security, good governance and the rule of law, economic revitalization and infrastructure, and basic services, which are also important elements for sustainable economic growth and development,

Realizing that, in spite of the positive gains of the recent past, the situation in Liberia remains fragile and still constitutes a threat to international peace and security in the subregion,

1. *Expresses its gratitude* to the Economic Community of West African States, the African Union, donor countries and institutions, the United Nations system

and its specialized agencies and non-governmental organizations for their valuable support in their adoption of a comprehensive approach to peacebuilding in Liberia and the subregion;

2. *Commends* the Secretary-General for his continued efforts in mobilizing the international community, the United Nations system and other organizations to provide assistance to Liberia;

3. *Invites* all States and intergovernmental and non-governmental organizations to provide assistance to Liberia to facilitate the continued creation of an enabling environment for the promotion of peace, socio-economic development and regional security, including by emphasizing capacity-building, institution-building and employment generation in their work and ensuring that such work complements and contributes to the development of an economy characterized by a predictable investment climate conducive to entrepreneurship, good governance and the rule of law;

4. *Invites* the international community to provide financial and technical assistance to support the Government's national reconstruction and development agenda, including the poverty reduction strategy process and the Millennium Development Goals;

5. *Notes with appreciation* the round-table conference of donors for the rehabilitation and reconstruction of Liberia planned for early 2007, and invites the participation of the United Nations system and its specialized agencies in close collaboration with the Government of Liberia and its development partners;

6. *Urges* the Government to continue to create an environment conducive to the promotion of socio-economic development, peace and security in the country, to the reintegration of internally displaced persons and to its commitment to ensure the upholding of human rights, the rule of law and national reconciliation;

7. *Appeals* to the international community and intergovernmental and non-governmental organizations to provide adequate assistance to programmes and projects identified in the present report of the Secretary-General;

8. *Requests* the Secretary-General:

(a) To continue his efforts in coordinating the work of the United Nations system and to mobilize financial, technical and other assistance for the rehabilitation and reconstruction of Liberia;

(b) To report to the General Assembly at its sixty-third session on the implementation of the present resolution;

9. *Decides* to consider at its sixty-third session the status of international assistance for the rehabilitation and reconstruction of Liberia.

Mozambique

In response to General Assembly resolution 59/214 [YUN 2004, p. 930], in his July consolidated report [A/61/209], the Secretary-General provided information on humanitarian assistance and relief provided by the United Nations and its partners in Mozambique in 2006.

In 2006, Mozambique, like other countries in the Southern Africa region, faced the triple threat of a fatal combination of HIV/AIDS, food insecurity and weakened capacity of Government bodies to deliver critical services. Although the UN Integrated Framework on HIV/AIDS was developed to ensure that no less than 25 per cent of each UN agency's budget was spent on HIV/AIDS mitigation, in Mozambique, that budget allocation was 33 per cent.

In addition, with some two-thirds of its population living in rural areas, Mozambique's economy was predominantly based on agriculture. However, the country was also vulnerable to recurring natural disasters such as floods and cyclones, droughts and pests. A four-year drought had caused the food security situation to deteriorate gradually and in mid-2005, the Government appealed for food aid for an estimated 800,000 people. WFP delivered aid to a peak of more than 568,000 drought-affected people in March, and conducted school feedings and implemented community safety net activities for people affected by HIV/AIDS in those same areas. Circumstances improved as the 2005-2006 rainy season was good in most areas. As of May, the food security situation was better and conditions appeared favourable for the second season. The Food and Agriculture Organization of the United Nations (FAO) ensured that more than 30,000 vulnerable households had seeds and other agricultural input for the 2005-2006 planting season and plans were under way to assist an additional 45,000 families across the country. In March, the Council of Ministers approved a new National Disaster Management Institute strategy for 2006-2013, which had a strong focus on prevention and mitigation activities in arid and semi-arid areas.

African countries emerging from conflict

In response to Economic and Social Council resolution 2004/59 [YUN 2004, p. 932], the Secretary-General submitted a May report [E/2006/64], which assessed the work of the two ad hoc advisory groups on African countries emerging from conflict, Burundi (see p. 1084) and Guinea-Bissau (see p. 1085), since the last assessment in 2004 [YUN 2004, p. 931]. The report highlighted the added value of the groups, particularly their work in promoting coordinated support to those countries through a comprehensive approach to relief, peace and development. It also analysed the limits encountered in the work of the groups and assessed implementation of their recommendations, focusing on lessons learned that could be used in the context of future UN efforts in post-conflict recovery and peacebuilding.

The continued mobilization of international support to the countries was a key contribution of the groups, as they helped to sensitize the international community to the assistance needs of Burundi and Guinea-Bissau. The open, transparent and participatory approach utilized by the groups made it possible to reach out to other important entities, such as the Bretton Wood institutions, the European Commission, the AU and donors, thereby constituting a platform for cooperation with a wide range of development partners, without applying criteria of hard conditionality. Another tangible outcome of the groups' recommendations was the creation of the Emergency Economic Management Fund for providing direct assistance. However, for several reasons, progress in their work had been unequal, highlighting the limits of the groups as a mechanism for mobilizing support to post-conflict countries. First, the work of the ad hoc advisory groups was contingent on the political situation in the countries concerned. During the period under review, both Burundi and Guinea-Bissau had organized presidential and parliamentary elections, which had resulted in a "wait and see" approach from donors. Other hindering factors included the groups' limited expertise and willingness to get involved in the modalities of the delivery of development assistance; limited interaction with regional and other organizations; lack of interaction between the Security Council and Economic and Social Council on the situation in Burundi and Guinea-Bissau; difficulty in sustaining the time and attention of ad hoc advisory group members; and the limited UN capacity to provide services to the groups.

The Secretary-General observed that the theme of post-conflict recovery and peacebuilding had gained importance within the international community, particularly at the United Nations. However, since nearly half of countries emerging from conflict relapsed into violence within five years, research had indicated that those countries needed strong international assistance for at least 10 years. The ad hoc advisory groups were the first institutionalized mechanism to address the issue in a comprehensive way and constituted an "avant-garde" that could inspire future similar work. In that connection, the establishment of the Peacebuilding Commission, as a permanent organ to address such complex issues (see p. 55), aimed to strengthen the approach. He recommended that, once operational, the Commission should consider the work of the ad hoc advisory groups and use the lessons learned from the experience, such as the need to implement appropriate mechanisms to mobilize donors and promote the translation of pledges into disbursements; define a vision of long-term rehabilitation and support; remain engaged in favour of the countries concerned by means of concrete development support, even when the political situation could lead to a "wait and see" approach; maximize the work of UN entities to complement the policy approach of intergovernmental bodies with support at the technical and operational level; and ensure good articulation with regional partners and countries concerned, including regional and subregional organizations, regional development banks and the regional commissions.

ECONOMIC AND SOCIAL COUNCIL ACTION

On 26 July [meeting 39], the Economic and Social Council adopted **resolution 2006/13** [draft: E/2006/L.20] without vote [agenda item 7 *(g)*].

Assessment of the ad hoc advisory groups of the Economic and Social Council on African countries emerging from conflict

The Economic and Social Council,

Recalling its resolutions 2003/50 of 24 July 2003 and 2004/59 of 23 July 2004,

1. *Takes note with appreciation* of the report of the Secretary-General;

2. *Commends* the ad hoc advisory groups for their innovative and constructive work in promoting international provision of support to Guinea-Bissau and Burundi and sensitizing a wide range of development partners to their specific needs through the partnership approach that has been adopted by the advisory groups;

3. *Also commends* the ad hoc advisory groups for promoting a comprehensive approach to political stability and economic and social development, based on an integrated approach to relief, rehabilitation, reconstruction and development, and for fostering interaction and coordination among United Nations system and other actors working in the countries concerned;

4. *Welcomes* the increased collaboration fostered by the ad hoc advisory groups with the United Nations system organizations and the Bretton Woods institutions, and encourages further coordination with those bodies;

5. *Calls upon* the national authorities of Guinea-Bissau and Burundi and their development partners to give due consideration to the recommendations formulated by the ad hoc advisory groups on the elaboration of a long-term vision for the development of those countries;

6. *Invites* the donor community to translate pledges made for support to the countries concerned, inter alia, through the United Nations consolidated appeals for humanitarian assistance, into disbursements, including, where appropriate, its consideration of providing direct budgetary support in order to ensure the delivery of concrete benefits to the populations concerned and to sustain peacebuilding efforts;

7. *Acknowledges* the value of the lessons learned from the ad hoc advisory groups, and decides to bring this experience to the attention of relevant United Nations bodies.

Burundi

Pursuant to resolution 2005/33 [YUN 2005, p. 1009], the Ad Hoc Advisory Group on Burundi, established by the Economic and Social Council in resolution 2003/16 [YUN 2003, p. 947], transmitted an April report [E/2006/53] on the situation in Burundi since the substantive session of the Council in 2005 [YUN 2005, p. 1009]. The report highlighted the humanitarian situation in Burundi, assessed international donor support and made a number of recommendations.

The report showed that, while progress had been made with regard to political and security aspects, the humanitarian situation and development perspectives remained a concern mainly due to the persistent acute food crisis, caused by heavy dependence on subsistence agriculture, land fragmentation and deterioration of the soils, as well as droughts, crop diseases and political insecurity. In 2006, an estimated 2.2 million Burundians were expected to be in need of food aid, of a total population of 8 million. The situation also impacted on the flow of refugees.

Although economic growth had increased with the end of the conflict and was expected to reach 6 per cent between 2006 and 2008, and public finances had improved owing to the interim debt relief granted to the country, Burundi's economy remained dependent on the fluctuation of commodity prices. The agricultural sector, particularly coffee, accounted for 50 per cent of gross domestic product and 85 per cent of export earnings. It was therefore essential to create opportunities for public and private investment, develop infrastructure and encourage the diversification of activitiess.

International assistance to Burundi increased over the past year. However, humanitarian requirements had risen by 62 per cent, compared to previous years, due to the increasing need to support returnees and engage in community recovery. Implementation of recovery programmes were poorly funded compared to the agriculture and health sectors. Hence, the Group emphasized that international support to Burundi should increasingly be provided under the prism of the transition from relief to development. Financial backing was also needed for the UNHCR contingency plan for refugee returnees. Two donor conferences had been planned during the period. The first conference (Bujumbura, Burundi, 28 February) discussed a one-year support programme aimed at addressing the most pressing needs of the people. The Government presented an emergency programme for 2006 based on its long-term vision entitled "Integral human development of Burundi", costing $178 million, which was covered by the pledges made. The second conference, scheduled for September, would mobilize donors around the poverty reduction strategy paper and its three-year implementation plan. A national committee for aid coordination established by the Government to increase dialogue with donors was expected to play an important role in preparing for the conference.

The Group called on the donor community to respond generously in support of Burundi, particularly longer-term support. It observed that most of the Group's recommendations [E/2004/11] to the Council had been or were being implemented and encouraged Burundi to continue on the course of agreed reforms. As the United Nations Operation in Burundi was phasing out, it stressed the importance of Burundi's relations with bilateral and multilateral parties. The Group concluded that, in the post-transition phase, consideration of international assistance to Burundi would be better dealt with by the newly established Peacebuilding Commission.

On 26 July, by resolution 2006/12, the Economic and Social Council terminated the mandate of the Ad Hoc Advisory Group on Burundi (see below).

(For more information on the situation in Burundi, see p. 148.)

ECONOMIC AND SOCIAL COUNCIL ACTION

On 26 July [meeting 39], the Economic and Social Council adopted **resolution 2006/12** [draft: E/2006/L.19] without vote [agenda item 7 *(g)*].

Ad Hoc Advisory Group on Burundi

The Economic and Social Council,

Recalling its resolutions 2002/1 of 15 July 2002, 2003/16 of 21 July 2003, 2003/50 of 24 July 2003, 2004/2 of 3 May 2004, 2004/59 and 2004/60 of 23 July 2004, 2005/1 of 1 March 2005 and 2005/33 of 26 July 2005 and its decision 2003/311 of 22 August 2003,

1. *Takes note with appreciation* of the report of the Ad Hoc Advisory Group on Burundi;

2. *Expresses its appreciation* to the Government and people of Burundi for the successful conclusion of the political transition;

3. *Commends* the Government of Burundi for its efforts to consolidate the authority of the institutions concerned and to engage in economic and social recovery;

4. *Expresses concern* as to the high level of vulnerability of the population in Burundi, including refugees returning to Burundi, commends donors for their continued humanitarian assistance, and encourages them to provide funds for the United Nations consolidated ap-

peals for 2006, including the contingency plan elaborated by the United Nations High Commissioner for Refugees for refugee return;

5. *Commends* the authorities of Burundi for preparing an emergency programme and finalizing the poverty reduction strategy paper and its three-year implementation plan;

6. *Encourages* the Government of Burundi to continue to pursue peace talks to achieve permanent peace and stability in Burundi;

7. *Commends* the Government of Burundi on its efforts to improve governance, and in this regard encourages it to continue its fight against corruption;

8. *Commends* those donors that have increased their support to Burundi, and calls for rapid disbursement of funds committed at the conference of development partners, held on 28 February 2006 in Bujumbura;

9. *Invites* donor countries and the institutions concerned to take part in the donor conference organized by the Government of Burundi to be held in Bujumbura in the third quarter of 2006, to work with the National Committee for Aid Coordination established by the Government to increase dialogue with donors, and to support the Government with commensurate means and resources, including, where appropriate, to consider providing direct budgetary support;

10. *Commends* the Advisory Group for its innovative and constructive work in support of Burundi, and welcomes the decision of the Peacebuilding Commission to address the needs of Burundi;

11. *Decides* to terminate the mandate of the Advisory Group.

Guinea-Bissau

In response to resolution 2005/32 [YUN 2005, p. 1011], the Ad Hoc Advisory Group on Guinea-Bissau reported, in April [E/2006/8], on developments in the country, which included the overall economic and social situation, on the Group's activities since its last report [YUN 2005, p. 1010], the current status of international donor support, and the medium to long-term perspective on the situation in the country.

The economic and social situation in Guinea-Bissau remained difficult, with an annual growth rate of 3.5 per cent in 2005—barely sufficient to slow the worsening living conditions—and the worrisome state of public revenues. A cholera epidemic, which began in June 2005 and involved over 25,000 cases, the highest in the West Africa region, finally ended in February 2006. The Group highlighted the work of the UN country team, particularly in the areas of health and education. However, it remained concerned by the lack of progress in the overall socio-economic situation in the country, where 65 per cent of the population lived below the poverty line; 44 per cent had no access to safe drinking water; 36 per cent were food insecure; 30 per cent of children under five were malnourished; and 60 per cent of the working force was unemployed. Those difficult conditions continued to push the population to take desperate measures to reach Europe to find employment.

On 22 March, the Group met to discuss the situation in the country and expressed concern that the military action by the Government of Guinea-Bissau along the border with Senegal and its implications on the socio-economic situation could have far-reaching consequences, including the potential to destabilize the already tense situation in the subregion. Delays in the political process generated a "wait and see attitude" by bilateral donors. The Government had also built up additional debt by turning to short-term commercial loans to pay civil service arrears. A joint high-level delegation, including the West African Economic and Monetary Union, the Central Bank of West African States, the West African Development Bank and the Economic Community of West African States visited Guinea-Bissau in February to explore possible financial and technical assistance to the country, including the payment of civil service salaries for February and March, salary arrears from 2000 to 2005 and the debt in the first trimester of 2006 to the IMF and the World Bank. The Group welcomed the decision by UNDP to extend the Emergency Economic Management Fund through the end of 2006, which would allow the monitoring of new emergency budget support. The Group encouraged donors to contribute to the Fund as a way to assist the Government in meeting its emergency needs, noted that Guinea-Bissau was among the 40 countries that had created the "Leading Group on Solidarity Levies" to fund development projects and encouraged the countries involved to consider Guinea-Bissau as a potential recipient of such innovative mechanisms. In addition, preparations for the donor round-table conference resumed following the approval of the Government's programme by Parliament in March. The Group emphasized that the conference was crucial, as Guinea-Bissau was dependent on the international community for 80 per cent of its resources and noted the EU decision to increase assistance to Guinea-Bissau for the 2002-2007 national indicative programme by €10.7 million, including €5 million for budget support. To put Guinea-Bissau on the path to sustainable development, the Group urged the Government to help the international community to put in place a comprehensive economic diversification strategy.

Despite political and institutional instability, the frequent changes in leadership after short periods of relative stability and the military action by the Armed Forces of Guinea-Bissau, which had led to a period of stagnation in resource mobilization, the Group observed that there had been clear overall progress in improving public administration, transparency and accountability in the public sector. Moreover, following the successful completion of article IV consultations in March, the IMF had indicated that the performance of the previous 12 months was encouraging and the outlook was favourable. Hence, the Group concluded that there was room for flexibility in the provision of budgetary support to the Government in the short-term and in assisting the country in the longer-term with its poverty reduction plan. In the light of the above, the Group indicated that Guinea-Bissau should continue to receive sustained support from the international community and invited the Economic and Social Council to consider recommending Guinea-Bissau as one of the first cases to be considered by the Peacebuilding Commission.

(For more information on the situation in Guinea-Bissau, see p. 244.)

ECONOMIC AND SOCIAL COUNCIL ACTION

On 26 July [meeting 39], the Economic and Social Council adopted **resolution 2006/11** [draft: E/2006/L.21] without vote [agenda item 7 *(g)*].

Ad Hoc Advisory Group on Guinea-Bissau

The Economic and Social Council,

Recalling its resolutions 2002/1 of 15 July 2002, 2003/1 of 31 January 2003, 2003/53 of 24 July 2003, 2004/1 of 3 May 2004, 2004/59 and 2004/61 of 23 July 2004, 2005/2 of 1 March 2005 and 2005/32 of 26 July 2005 and its decision 2002/304 of 25 October 2002,

Welcoming the successful conclusion of the second round of presidential elections on 24 July 2005 and the formal completion of the transitional period, and encouraging the Government of Guinea-Bissau to continue its efforts to further deepen transparency and good governance,

Recognizing the continuing efforts of the Government of Guinea-Bissau to improve its management of public administration and to strengthen economic reforms,

Expressing concern at the emerging food crisis in the southern part of the country, and in this regard expressing appreciation for the continuing efforts of the World Food Programme to assist vulnerable populations in Guinea-Bissau,

Welcoming the positive and constructive role of the Ad Hoc Advisory Group on Guinea-Bissau in supporting the country in its pursuit of its pressing short- and long-term development objectives,

1. *Takes note with appreciation* of the report of the Ad Hoc Advisory Group on Guinea-Bissau;

2. *Invites* the donor community to provide support, including its consideration of providing, where appropriate, the budgetary support needed to enable the minimum functioning of the State, in particular by providing additional contributions through the Emergency Economic Management Fund managed by the United Nations Development Programme;

3. *Notes* the importance of funding the country's poverty reduction strategy plan, and expresses concern that the two previous donor round-table conferences did not take place as scheduled, and in that regard encourages all partners of Guinea-Bissau to participate in the donor round-table conference scheduled to be held in the last quarter of 2006;

4. *Reaffirms* the need to create an enabling environment in Guinea-Bissau for the promotion of sustainable development in the country, expresses support for the efforts of Guinea-Bissau to carry out economic reforms, and in that regard renews its invitation to the authorities and all relevant actors of Guinea-Bissau to consolidate political and institutional stability;

5. *Urges* the international community to remain engaged with Guinea-Bissau, and in that regard decides to extend the mandate of the Advisory Group until the substantive session of 2007 of the Economic and Social Council.

Other economic assistance

Haiti

In response to Economic and Social Council resolution 2005/46 [YUN 2005, p. 1012], the Ad Hoc Advisory Group on Haiti reported in May [E/2006/69 & Corr.1] on the political, economic and social situation in the country, international support since the 2005 substantive session of the Council and prospects for assistance in the post-electoral context. Although the two-year transition period was drawing to a close with the holding of presidential and legislative elections on 7 February and 21 April 2006, respectively, and local and municipal elections scheduled for June, the political situation remained unstable. In the light of the escalating killings and kidnappings in the capital, the Advisory Group stated that the fight against armed gangs, illegal trafficking and violent crime had to remain a priority of the Haitian authorities and international actors. On the socio-economic situation, 75 per cent of the population lived in poverty, with over 50 per cent in extreme poverty and 80 per cent of the active population without regular, remunerative employment. Economic stagnation was linked to political instability, as it had a negative impact on the efficiency of Haitian institutions and on the macroeconomic framework, which had been characterized by persistent inflation and fiscal deficits. In the first quarter of 2006, the Group interacted with Haitian development actors and their international counterparts and held meetings to discuss the challenges of international support to Haiti and prospects for future assistance. Fulfilment of the commitments of international donors under the Interim Cooperation Framework (ICF) improved during the reporting period. In terms of current support to Haiti, $750 million had been disbursed by the end of December 2005, representing some 69.1 per cent of pledges from the 2004 donor conference. Other developments highlighted by the Group, included the establishment of a strategic think tank to draft a long-term development plan for the country; the preparation of the Interim Poverty Reduction Strategy Paper (PRSP) by Haitian authorities, built on the ICF; and an April report, in which IMF and the World Bank identified Haiti as one of 11 countries that could qualify for debt relief under a new round of the HIPC Initiative. As the World Bank and UNDP interlocutors of the Group underscored the fact that the new Government would need additional funding, a high-level ministerial meeting was scheduled for 23 May in Brasilia and a donor conference and pledging session for July in Port-au-Prince.

The Group called on national stakeholders to continue efforts to successfully conclude the electoral process and on international stakeholders to provide support in that regard. Appropriate assistance should be given through the ICF, which had been extended by the Brussels international conference until the end of 2007. Sustained support would be needed to enhance the new Government's capacity to define the national poverty reduction strategy and implement appropriate policies accordingly. The Group recommended that the Council extend its mandate until 2007, in order to help the new Government in the promotion of a long-term development strategy for ensuring socio-economic recovery and political stability and to provide recommendations thereon.

Communication. On 29 June [E/2006/88], Haiti transmitted to the Economic and Social Council a letter from Prime Minister Edouard Alexis, in which he expressed his intention to move forward with the long-term programme and requested that the mandate of the Ad Hoc Advisory Group on Haiti be extended to help the country pursue the national struggle against poverty. The Group's interlocutor in the Government would be primarily the strategic think tank, whose mandate would be to develop a long-term vision for sustainable development and a programme for its implementation covering the next 15 years.

ECONOMIC AND SOCIAL COUNCIL ACTION

On 26 July [meeting 39], the Economic and Social Council adopted **resolution 2006/10** [draft: E/2006/L.11] without vote [agenda item 7 *(d)*].

Ad Hoc Advisory Group on Haiti

The Economic and Social Council,

Recalling its resolutions 2004/52 of 23 July 2004 and 2005/46 of 27 July 2005 and its decision 2004/322 of 11 November 2004,

1. *Takes note with appreciation* of the report of the Ad Hoc Advisory Group on Haiti;

2. *Commends* the Government and people of Haiti for the successful legislative and presidential elections, and welcomes the support provided by the international community to this process;

3. *Welcomes* the extension of the time frame for the Interim Cooperation Framework to allow for the preparation of a national poverty reduction strategy and the continued support provided by donors, the United Nations system and the Bretton Woods institutions under the Framework;

4. *Decides* to extend the mandate of the Advisory Group until the substantive session of the Economic and Social Council in July 2007, with the purpose of following closely and providing advice on Haiti's long-term development strategy to promote socio-economic recovery and stability, with particular attention to the need to ensure coherence and sustainability in international support for Haiti, based on the long-term national development priorities, building upon the Interim Cooperation Framework and the forthcoming poverty reduction strategy, and stressing the need to avoid overlap and duplication with respect to existing mechanisms;

5. *Expresses its satisfaction* to the Secretary-General for the support provided to the Advisory Group, and requests him to continue to support the Group's activities adequately;

6. *Requests* the Advisory Group, in accomplishing its mandate, to continue to cooperate with the Secretary-General, the United Nations Development Group, relevant United Nations funds and programmes and specialized agencies, the Bretton Woods institutions, regional organizations and institutions, including the Organization of American States and the Caribbean Community, the Inter-American Development Bank and other major stakeholders;

7. *Also requests* the Advisory Group to submit a report on its work, with recommendations, as appropriate, to the Economic and Social Council at its substantive session of 2007;

8. *Decides* that the work of the Advisory Group will be reviewed at the substantive session of 2007, with a view to considering whether to continue its mandate, based on the Council's consideration of the report of the Group and the situation then prevailing in Haiti, with

due account being taken of the creation of the Peacebuilding Commission.

Montenegro

The Secretary-General, in his July consolidated report on humanitarian assistance and rehabilitation [A/61/209], provided information on major developments in Montenegro and challenges to the delivery of development assistance.

In the Republic of Montenegro, admitted as a UN member on 28 June, following the 21 May independence referendum (see p. 472) dissolving the State Union of Serbia and Montenegro, 12 per cent of the population continued to live below the poverty line, while some 30 per cent was economically vulnerable. Along with internally displaced persons and refugees, the Roma minority was the most vulnerable and socially excluded group, with a 53 per cent poverty rate. Concerns were expressed that the high poverty rate in the north (19.3 per cent, representing 45 per cent of the total poor) and political polarization could potentially grow into social tensions and instability, especially in the post-referendum period. While the country had recorded improvements in development, economic growth and the human development index, labour retrenchment during the lengthy economic transition had resulted in growing numbers of poor people and a widening gap between the rich and the poor.

The Secretary-General recommended the inclusion of vulnerable social groups, such as refugees, IDPs, Roma and other marginalized groups within the poverty reduction strategy and development opportunities, through economic development, long-term investments and employment generation programmes for hard-to-employ groups. Recommendations were also made to address the need for public administration reform, capacity development and environmental governance, particularly with regard to achieving sustainable development that relied on tourism, renewable energy sources, forestry and organic production in an environmentally responsible manner.

The Philippines

On 11 August, the oil tanker, Solar, sunk off the coast of Guimaras Island in the Philippines, spilling some 50,000 gallons of oil into the sea, polluting more than 300 kilometres of coastline and threatening fishing, as well as other islands of the Philippines. A state of emergency was declared in the country on 25 August.

GENERAL ASSEMBLY ACTION

On 20 December [meeting 83], the General Assembly, on the recommendation of the Second Committee [A/61/429/Add.1 & Corr.1], adopted **resolution 61/217** without vote [agenda item 69 *(b)*].

Special economic assistance for the Philippines

The General Assembly,

Concerned about the oil spill from the oil tanker that sank thirteen nautical miles off the south-western coast of the Province of Guimaras in the central Philippines on 11 August 2006, resulting in that country's unprecedented maritime ecological disaster,

Aware that the geographical features and location of the Philippines make it prone to natural and man-made disasters,

Acknowledging with appreciation the timely assistance extended by the international donor community, in particular the Governments of Australia, France, Germany, Indonesia, Japan and the United States of America, as well as the United Nations Development Programme, the United Nations Environment Programme, the United Nations Children's Fund, the Food and Agriculture Organization of the United Nations and the International Maritime Organization,

Noting the immediate response by the Government of the Philippines to this ecological disaster, which is straining its limited resources in the needed massive clean-up operations, and its request for international support,

1. *Expresses its solidarity and support* to the Government and people of the Philippines;
2. *Invites* Member States and concerned United Nations bodies, as well as international financial institutions and development agencies, to provide additional economic and technical assistance in the post-disaster recovery and rehabilitation processes;
3. *Invites* the international community and the United Nations system and other international organizations to increase their support for the strengthening of the disaster risk management and disaster preparedness capacity of the Philippines;
4. *Requests* the Secretary-General to report to the General Assembly at its sixty-second session, as part of his consolidated report submitted under the sub-item entitled "Special economic assistance to individual countries or regions", on the collaborative effort extended to the Philippines and the progress made in the relief, rehabilitation and clean-up efforts in the affected communities.

(See also p. 1106 under "Disaster assistance".)

Serbia

In response to General Assembly resolution 59/215 [YUN 2004, p. 939], the Secretary-General, in his July consolidated report on humanitarian assistance and rehabilitation [A/61/209], provided information on major developments in Serbia and challenges to the delivery of development assistance, which were impacted by the political situation. In Serbia, which became a separate State following Montenegro's 21 May referendum and declaration of independence, living standards were rising, but some groups continued to suffer and pockets of deep poverty remained. The poverty rate was estimated at 10.5 per cent and unemployment at 27 per cent. Serbia also hosted the highest number of vulnerable groups in the region, including 107,000 registered refugees; 160,000 formerly registered refugees; 208,000 IDPs from the Serbian province of Kosovo; and between 100,000 to 500,000 Roma. The UN country team and the Council of Ministers signed the United Nations Development Assistance Framework (UNDAF) 2005-2009 [YUN 2005, p. 958], a framework to guide resource mobilization for the improvement of governance and institutional capabilities to use aid more effectively. The Government sought to maintain a high level of development assistance until 2010-2011, as a decrease in external funding could adversely impact the smooth implementation of democratic reforms. Meanwhile, Serbia's EU integration process was put on hold as a result of poor cooperation with the International Tribunal for the Former Yugoslavia in the Hague.

The Secretary-General recommended the use of area-based development in addressing the vulnerability of groups at the local level in the development context. The priority for the humanitarian community was redressing the obstacles facing marginalized and vulnerable groups, such as Roma, refugees and IDPs. Statistical data on the situation of those groups were also needed, particularly the Roma, whose numbers appeared to be significantly underestimated by official statistics. As the Government of Serbia had underscored the need for continued donor humanitarian support to UN agencies to meet the immediate basic needs of vulnerable populations, and taking into account resolution of the status of the province of Kosovo, the United Nations would continue to seek international community support in the next two to three years, specifically for the return and local integration of IDPs.

Third States affected by sanctions

In response to General Assembly resolution 60/23 [YUN 2005, p. 1447], the Secretary-General submitted an August report [A/61/304], which highlighted measures taken to further improve the procedures and working methods of the Security Council and its sanctions committees related to assistance to third States affected by the application of sanctions, recent developments concerning the activities and the role of the Assembly and the Economic and Social Council and arrangements in the Secretariat in the area of assistance to those States.

The Assembly took action with regard to the Secretary-General's report in **resolution 61/38** (see p. 1532).

Disaster response

In 2006, the incidence and severity of disasters associated with natural hazards, such as earthquakes, floods and droughts, continued to rise at a steady rate, with 426 disasters affecting 143 million people. Disasters involving geological hazards remained the deadliest, such as the May earthquake that struck the Indonesian island of Java, killing over 5,700 people and leaving 1.5 million homeless (see p. 1106). Hydro-meteorological hazards inflicted more than $2.1 billion in economic losses. The total cost of natural disasters was estimated at $34.6 billion in economic damages. Moreover, the loss of family members, assets and livelihoods, disruption of markets and price increases, and damage to local environments and natural resources, created challenges for the affected communities which could last for years.

While excessive rains and severe flooding in the Horn of Africa displaced more than 650,000 people, erratic and insufficient rainfall led to reduced water, drought and food insecurities in Djibouti, Eritrea, Ethiopia, Kenya and Somalia. Heavy rains coupled with an unprecedented number of cyclones and tropical storms caused extensive flooding across southern Africa, affecting more than 1 million people. Some 12,000 families in the Tindouf region of Algeria hosting refugee camps were affected by rains and flooding. In Angola, a cholera epidemic claimed 1,650 lives and a March outbreak of acute diarrhoea in Botswana resulted in 22,062 cases and 446 deaths.

Typhoons and floods in South-East Asia affected close to 8 million people in the Philippines, where massive landslides in the Southern Leyte province killed 154 and led to the evacuation of 18,862 people. Inadequate and uneven rainfall in Afghanistan prolonged the drought there, resulting in a lost harvest and food supplies being per cent below annual needs. In March and April, a series of earthquakes in the Lorestan Province of western Iran impacted over 160,000 people, and partially or completely destroyed over 35,000 homes.

Central and Latin America were severely affected by floods. Heavy rains in January and February triggered major floods across Bolivia, killing 23 people, affecting 27,500 families and leading to the evacuation of 9,374 families. Floods affected around 3,500 families in Guyana, and in five coastal provinces of Ecuador, flooding and mudslides provoked by heavy rains caused 16 deaths and affected 28,000 families. Torrential rains flooded the entire south and parts of the central Amazonian lowlands in Suriname, damaging 30,000 square kilometers of land.

The avian influenza virus H5N1 continued to spread and in some countries had become endemic. There was growing international recognition of the potential for avian and human influenza to undermine development. In July, the UN Consolidated Action Plan for Avian and Human Influenza was issued to ensure that all countries were adequately protected. In November, the Plan was revised and an appeal for $327 million was launched.

International cooperation

Report of Secretary-General. In response to General Assembly resolution 60/125 [YUN 2005, p. 1022], the Secretary-General, in a September report [A/61/314], highlighted the key challenges faced by the international community in improving international response to natural disasters and strengthening the capacity of disaster-prone countries in disaster management. The report stated that the role of the international community was to support local, national and regional capacities to prepare for, respond to and recover from disasters, and to strengthen capacities when they were deficient. However, efforts to strengthen indigenous response capabilities frequently remained peripheral to the concerns and focus of international responders, and international relief assistance often bypassed indigenous response mechanisms, thereby undermining them.

The report emphasized the need for capacity development and for equipping local, national and regional stakeholders with skills, knowledge and resources to face the challenges posed by disaster risks. Capacity-strengthening efforts needed to reach out to local actors. Among international actors, UN country teams were well placed to identify gaps in disaster-prone countries, define interventions and build the necessary partnerships for long-term engagement. However, their disaster management capacity was often weak, particularly in early warning, preparedness and contingency planning, and risk reduction mainstreaming. Efforts to strengthen those areas were under way in Latin America and the Caribbean, Central Asia and other regions. To strengthen the rapid response capacity of the international community, the report identified several key avenues, such as promoting the use of a common methodology in the response to sudden-onset emergencies and expanding the number of countries and organizations participating in international response networks. It also called for the strengthening of other tools, including the WFP Humanitarian Early Warning Service, the Central Register of Disaster Management Capacities, information and communication technologies, satellite-derived mapping, preliminary damage assessment using remote sensing and image analysis, and military assets.

The report also considered human rights and disasters, humanitarian accountability in disasters, addressing acute environmental issues in disasters, better engagement of external actors and post-disaster recovery. Since it entered into force on 8 January 2005, the Tampere Convention on the Provision of Telecommunication Resources for Disaster Mitigation and Relief Operations [YUN 1998, p. 840] had been ratified by 35 States.

The Secretary-General recommended that international humanitarian agencies and organizations should reorient their disaster response policies and practices from the delivery of goods and services to supporting and strengthening local, national and regional capacities for disaster management. OCHA should review the usefulness of the Central Register of Disaster Management Capacities and propose options for making it more relevant; it should review the use of military assets in disasters to ascertain their cost-effectiveness, and incorporate guidance and mechanisms for their use into the 1994 Oslo Guidelines [YUN 1994, p. 823]. UN agencies and organizations working with OCHA and the Global Compact [YUN 2000, p. 989] should establish standby partnerships with the private sector to augment its capacity to respond to disasters and to bring it more effectively into coordination mechanisms. Member States were encouraged to support the ICRC international disaster response law programme, participate in regional disaster response networks, ratify the Tampere Convention, develop emergency response telecommunication capacities, establish rosters of telecommunication resources to be made available during emergencies, and incorporate disaster risk reduction measures into their relief, reconstruction and development activities. In addition, international humanitarian agencies and organizations should strengthen accountability to both beneficiaries and donors, regularly report on measures taken in that connection, and ensure greater coherence among such initiatives.

SPIDER programme. On 4 August [A/AC.105/873], the Committee on the Peaceful Uses of Outer Space (see p. 748) provided information on the study conducted by its ad hoc expert group on the possibility of creating an international coordination entity for optimizing the effectiveness of space-based services in disaster management, which included the proposed implementation framework for the entity.

On 14 December, the General Assembly observed that the use of space technology, such as Earth observation and satellites and satellite navigation and positioning systems, could play a vital role in supporting disaster management. In the light of the study, the Assembly decided to establish the United Nations Platform for Space-based Information for Disaster Management and Emergency Response (SPIDER), as an open network of providers of disaster management support (**resolution 61/110**).

GENERAL ASSEMBLY ACTION

On 14 December [meeting 79], the General Assembly adopted **resolution 61/131** [draft: A/61/L.42 & Add.1] without vote [agenda item 69 *(a)*].

International cooperation on humanitarian assistance in the field of natural disasters, from relief to development

The General Assembly,

Reaffirming its resolution 46/182 of 19 December 1991, the annex to which contains the guiding principles for the strengthening of the coordination of emergency humanitarian assistance of the United Nations system, as well as all its resolutions on international cooperation on humanitarian assistance in the field of natural disasters, from relief to development, and recalling the resolutions of the humanitarian segments of the substantive sessions of the Economic and Social Council,

Recognizing the importance of the principles of neutrality, humanity, impartiality and independence for the provision of humanitarian assistance,

Reiterating that independence means the autonomy of humanitarian objectives as distinct from the political, economic, military or other objectives that may be pursued by any actor with regard to areas where humanitarian action is being implemented,

Welcoming the Hyogo Declaration, the Hyogo Framework for Action 2005-2015: Building the Resilience of Nations and Communities to Disasters and the common statement of the special session on the Indian Ocean disaster: risk reduction for a safer future, as adopted by the World Conference on Disaster Reduction, held in Kobe, Hyogo, Japan, from 18 to 22 January 2005,

Emphasizing that the affected State has the primary responsibility in the initiation, organization, coordination and implementation of humanitarian assistance within its territory and in the facilitation of the work of humanitarian organizations in mitigating the consequences of natural disasters,

Emphasizing also the responsibility of all States to undertake disaster preparedness, response and mitigation efforts in order to minimize the impact of natural disasters, while recognizing the importance of international cooperation in support of the efforts of affected countries which may have limited capacities in this regard,

Noting the critical role played by local resources, and by existing in-country capacities, in natural disaster management and risk reduction, disaster response, rehabilitation and development,

Recognizing the importance of international cooperation in support of the efforts of the affected States in dealing with natural disasters in all their phases, and of strengthening the response capacity of countries affected by disaster,

Noting with appreciation the important role played by Member States, including developing countries, that have granted necessary and continued generous assistance to countries and peoples stricken by natural disasters,

Recognizing the significant role played by national Red Cross and Red Crescent societies, as part of the International Red Cross and Red Crescent Movement, in disaster preparedness and risk reduction, disaster response, rehabilitation and development,

Emphasizing the importance of addressing vulnerability and integrating risk reduction into all phases of natural disaster management, post-natural disaster recovery and development planning,

Welcoming the work carried out by the Intergovernmental Oceanographic Commission of the United Nations Educational, Scientific and Cultural Organization in the setting up of regional tsunami early warning systems, in the Indian Ocean, the Mediterranean and the north-east Atlantic, and noting with appreciation the convening of the Third International Conference on Early Warning, held in Bonn, Germany, from 27 to 29 March 2006,

Recognizing that efforts to achieve economic growth, sustainable development and internationally agreed development goals, including the Millennium Development Goals, can be adversely affected by natural disasters, and noting the positive contribution that those efforts can make in strengthening the resilience of populations to such disasters,

Emphasizing, in this context, the important role of development organizations in supporting national efforts to mitigate the consequences of natural disasters,

1. *Takes note* of the reports of the Secretary-General entitled "International cooperation on humanitarian assistance in the field of natural disasters, from relief to development"; "Strengthening of the coordination of emergency humanitarian assistance of the United Nations"; "Strengthening emergency relief, rehabilitation, reconstruction, recovery and prevention in the aftermath of the Indian Ocean tsunami disaster"; and "Central Emergency Response Fund";

2. *Expresses its deep concern* at the number and scale of natural disasters and their increasing impact, resulting in massive losses of life and property worldwide, in particular in vulnerable societies lacking adequate capac-

ity to mitigate effectively the long-term negative social, economic and environmental consequences of natural disasters;

3. *Calls upon* States to fully implement the Hyogo Declaration and the Hyogo Framework for Action 2005-2015: Building the Resilience of Nations and Communities to Disasters, in particular those commitments related to assistance for developing countries that are prone to natural disasters and for disaster-stricken States in the transition phase towards sustainable physical, social and economic recovery, for risk-reduction activities in post-disaster recovery and for rehabilitation processes;

4. *Calls upon* all States to adopt, where required, and to continue to implement effectively, necessary legislative and other appropriate measures to mitigate the effects of natural disasters and integrate disaster risk-reduction strategies into development planning, and in this regard requests the international community to continue to assist developing countries as well as countries with economies in transition;

5. *Welcomes* the effective cooperation among the affected States, relevant bodies of the United Nations system, donor countries, regional and international financial institutions and other relevant organizations, such as the International Red Cross and Red Crescent Movement, and civil society, in the coordination and delivery of emergency relief, and stresses the need to continue such cooperation and delivery throughout relief operations and medium- and long-term rehabilitation and reconstruction efforts, in a manner that reduces vulnerability to future natural hazards;

6. *Reiterates* the commitment to support the efforts of countries, in particular developing countries, to strengthen their capacities at all levels in order to prepare for and respond rapidly to natural disasters and mitigate their impact;

7. *Stresses* that, to increase further the effectiveness of humanitarian assistance, particular international cooperation efforts should be undertaken to enhance and broaden further the utilization of national and local capacities and, where appropriate, of regional and subregional capacities of developing countries for disaster preparedness and response, which may be made available in closer proximity to the site of a disaster, and more efficiently and at lower cost;

8. *Also stresses*, in this context, the importance of strengthening international cooperation, particularly through the effective use of multilateral mechanisms, in the timely provision of humanitarian assistance through all phases of a disaster, from relief and mitigation to development, including the provision of adequate resources;

9. *Welcomes* the role of the Office for the Coordination of Humanitarian Affairs of the Secretariat as the focal point within the overall United Nations system for the promotion and coordination of disaster response among United Nations humanitarian organizations and other humanitarian partners;

10. *Also welcomes*, so as to increase further the effectiveness of humanitarian assistance, the incorporation of experts from developing countries that are prone to natural disasters into the United Nations Disaster Assessment and Coordination system, and the work of the International Search and Rescue Advisory Group in assisting such countries in strengthening urban search and rescue capacities and establishing mechanisms for improving their coordination of national and international response in the field, and recalls in this regard its resolution 57/150 of 16 December 2002 entitled "Strengthening the effectiveness and coordination of international urban search and rescue assistance";

11. *Requests* the Secretary-General, in consultation with States and relevant organizations, to continue to explore ways to strengthen the rapid response capacities of the international community to provide immediate humanitarian relief, building on existing arrangements and ongoing initiatives;

12. *Requests* the Secretary-General to develop more systematic links with Member States offering military assets for natural disaster response in order to identify the availability of such assets;

13. *Notes* that the Central Register of Disaster Management Capacities, including the Directory of Advanced Technologies for Disaster Response, has the potential to support planning preparedness and response activities, and requests the Secretary-General to propose options to enhance its relevance;

14. *Encourages* donors to consider the importance of ensuring that assistance in the case of higher-profile natural disasters does not come at the expense of those natural disasters that may be relatively lower-profile, bearing in mind that the allocation of resources should be driven by needs;

15. *Recognizes* that information and telecommunication technology can play an important role in disaster response, encourages Member States to develop emergency response telecommunication capacities, and encourages the international community to assist the efforts of developing countries in this area, where needed;

16. *Encourages* States that have not acceded to or ratified the Tampere Convention on the Provision of Telecommunication Resources for Disaster Mitigation and Relief Operations, which entered into force on 8 January 2005, to consider doing so;

17. *Encourages* the further use of space-based and ground-based remote-sensing technologies, as well as the sharing of geographical data, for the prevention, mitigation and management of natural disasters, where appropriate;

18. *Encourages* Member States, relevant United Nations organizations and international financial institutions to enhance the global capacity for sustainable post-disaster recovery in areas such as coordination with traditional and non-traditional partners, identification and dissemination of lessons learned, development of common tools and mechanisms for recovery needs assessment, strategy development and programming, and incorporation of risk reduction into all recovery processes, and welcomes the ongoing efforts to this end;

19. *Requests* the United Nations system to improve its coordination of disaster recovery efforts, from relief to development, inter alia, by strengthening institutional, coordination and strategic planning efforts in disaster recovery, in support of national authorities;

20. *Stresses* the importance of rapid access to funds to ensure a more predictable and timely United Nations response to humanitarian emergencies, and welcomes in this regard the establishment of the Central Emergency Response Fund in its resolution 60/124 of 15 December 2005;

21. *Requests* the Secretary-General to continue to improve the international response to natural disasters, and to report thereon to the General Assembly at its sixty-second session.

Disaster reduction

International Strategy for Disaster Reduction

In response to General Assembly resolution 60/195 [YUN 2005, p. 1018], the Secretary-General, in an August report [A/61/229 & Corr.1], provided an overview on implementation of the International Strategy for Disaster Reduction (ISDR), adopted by the programme forum of the International Decade for Natural Disaster Reduction (1990-2000) in 1999 [YUN 1999, p. 859] and endorsed by the Assembly in resolution 54/219 [ibid., p. 861]. It also detailed efforts to implement the Hyogo Framework for Action, the 10-year plan for reducing disaster risks, adopted at the 2005 World Conference on Disaster Reduction [YUN 2005, p. 1015] and endorsed by the Assembly in resolution 60/195 [ibid., p. 1018].

Significant steps were taken to implement the Hyogo Framework for Action at the national, regional and international levels, with a focus on its five priority areas: disaster risk reduction as a priority, with a strong institutional basis; risk assessment and early warning; building a culture of safety and resilience; reduction of underlying risk factors; and strengthened disaster preparedness and response. The Strategy secretariat supported those efforts. At the national level, 40 countries reported concrete activities promoting disaster reduction in one or more of the Framework priority areas and 60 Governments had officially designated focal points for implementing the Framework. Lack of resources, however, remained an obstacle to the implementation of disaster risk reduction. Regional strategies and networks were being developed to provide mutual support and coherent action. In June, the World Bank approved a new Global Facility for Disaster Reduction and Recovery, which would support national capacity-building in 86 high-risk countries.Some 32 multiple disaster-prone countries had been identified in the initial phase under the Facility. UNDP and the Strategy secretariat developed guidelines to assist UN country teams in integrating disaster reduction into common country assessments and UNDAFs. A February meeting on capacity-development, organized by the UN inter-agency Disaster Management Training Programme, produced core principles to guide capacity development for Hyogo Framework implementation plans.

A survey of existing capacities and gaps in early warning systems conducted by the Strategy secretariat, in collaboration with the World Meteorological Organization (WMO) and OCHA, found that considerable progress had been made in developing the knowledge and technical tools required to assess risks and to generate and communicate forecasts and warnings. However, in many developing countries, warning systems lacked basic equipment, skills and financial resources. Moreover, systems were non-existent for some hazards, such as tsunamis and landslides. The weakest elements in the early warning chain were the dissemination of warnings and the preparedness to respond. The survey recommended that Governments build national people-centred early warning systems and that a comprehensive global early warning system be built based on existing capacities. The outcome of the Third International Conference on Early Warning (Bonn, Germany, 27-29 March) included a checklist of good practices in early warning, a compendium of more than 100 early warning projects, and the launch of a consolidated advisory package for national action plans aimed at interested Governments of tsunami-affected countries. The Strategy cluster/platform on knowledge of and education for disaster risk reduction education, convened by UNESCO, launched its 2006-2007 campaign "Disaster risk reduction begins at school", which aimed at mobilizing Governments, communities and individuals to integrate disaster risk reduction into school curricula in high-risk countries.

Activities to reduce risk factors focused on the environment, food security, health, and community-based risk and management. Substantial efforts were also needed to address the vulnerability of buildings, critical facilities, urban risks, environmental management practices and social protection. To strengthen preparedness and response, the Inter-Agency Standing Committee identified generic indicators, benchmarks and related guidance material to facilitate, monitor and measure the impact of interventions to strengthen at-risk communities' resilience and capacities to deal with disaster events. The Committee adopted the In-Country Self Assessment Tool for Natural Disaster Response Preparedness, which provided a focus for promoting concrete actions in disaster response preparedness. In addition, organizations, such as OCHA, FAO, WHO, the UN Volunteers and WFP were restructuring their preparedness programmes in line with the Hyogo Framework.

Activities of the Strategy secretariat in support of the Framework centred on developing support capacities; draft guidelines for national actors on implementing the Hyogo Framework; guidance on reporting and developing indicators of progress in disaster risk reduction; the prototype of a Web-based clearing house called "Prevention Web"; and regional outreach to national actors. Efforts continued to reform ISDR and strengthen the institutional framework of the Strategy. A core element in the strengthened Strategy system was the establishment of a successor to the Inter-Agency Task Force on Disaster Reduction, to be named the "Global Platform for Disaster Risk Reduction". The Global Platform would be open to Member States, UN agencies, funds and programmes, the Red Cross and Red Crescent Movement, international and regional organizations, NGOs, academia and the private sector. It would serve as the Global policy forum for disaster reduction, provide strategic guidance and coherence for the implementation of the Hyogo Framework, share experience among stakeholders and prepare recommendations for UN governing bodies. The Strategy secretariat also revised and adapted its structure and work programme to support the implementation of the Framework.

The Secretary-General observed that the shared will to tackle the challenges of disaster reduction required more sustained investment in risk reduction by Member States and donors. The Strategy's 2007 joint work programme and budget represented an important step forward in achieving complementary action among international organizations in that direction. Realignment of the policies of international financial institutions was also necessary to support the mainstreaming of disaster reduction into development investment. While acknowledging the contributions received from several Governments, the European Commission and various private donors to the UN Trust Fund for Disaster Reduction, the Secretary-General indicated that funding for the secretariat was unpredictable and insufficient in the face of the growing demands from Governments and agencies for services and assistance. He recommended that the Assembly endorse the processes for strengthening the Strategy system, reconsider its current funding exclusively from extrabudgetary resources and allocate resources from the UN regular budget to the Strategy secretariat. He encouraged donors and funding institutions to invest in disaster risk reduction as an integral and targeted component of humanitarian assistance and development, and Governments to set public spending targets on multi-year disaster risk reduction programmes at national and regional levels. Member States were invited to engage in the Global Platform, develop national and local capacities to implement the Hyogo Framework and establish programmes and reporting systems in support of their disaster reduction initiatives. The Secretary-General called on Member States and Strategy stakeholders to augment their financial contributions to the UN Trust Fund for Disaster Reduction to ensure adequate support for implementing the Framework and recommended that States invest more in climate monitoring and hazard risk management and risk reduction, and develop a global early warning system for all hazards and communities as recommended in the Global Survey of Early Warning Systems.

2006 International Conference on Disaster Reduction. The International Conference on Disaster Reduction, organized by the United Nations Educational, Scientific and Cultural Organization, the Global Alliance for Disaster Reduction, and the United Nations International Strategy for Disaster Reduction, was held from 27 August to 1 September, in Davos, Switzerland. The purpose of the Conference was to advance the vision of the 2005 World Conference for Disaster Reduction [YUN 2005, p. 1015] and expand understanding of what was needed to mainstream and integrate risk management across various fields. It discussed risks related natural hazards and technology failures, as well as human-induced risk factors. The Conference adopted the Davos 2006 Declaration, participants self-commitment for action.

GENERAL ASSEMBLY ACTION

On 20 December [meeting 83], the General Assembly, on the recommendation of the Second Committee [A/61/422/Add.3], adopted **resolution 61/198** without vote [agenda item 53 *(c)*].

International Strategy for Disaster Reduction

The General Assembly,

Recalling its resolutions 44/236 of 22 December 1989, 49/22 A of 2 December 1994, 49/22 B of 20 December 1994, 53/185 of 15 December 1998, 54/219 of 22 December 1999, 56/195 of 21 December 2001, 57/256 of 20 December 2002, 58/214 of 23 December 2003, 59/231 of 22 December 2004 and 60/195 of 22 December 2005 and Economic and Social Council resolutions 1999/63 of 30 July 1999 and 2001/35 of 26 July 2001, and taking into due consideration its resolution 57/270 B of 23 June 2003 on integrated and coordinated implementation of and follow-up to the outcomes of the major United Nations conferences and summits in the economic and social fields,

Recalling also the 2005 World Summit Outcome,

Reaffirming the Hyogo Declaration, the Hyogo Framework for Action 2005-2015: Building the Resilience of Nations and Communities to Disasters and the common statement of the special session on the Indian Ocean disaster: risk reduction for a safer future, as adopted by the World Conference on Disaster Reduction,

Recognizing that the Hyogo Framework for Action complements the Yokohama Strategy for a Safer World: Guidelines for Natural Disaster Prevention, Preparedness and Mitigation and its Plan of Action,

Reaffirming its role of providing policy guidance on the implementation of the outcomes of the major United Nations conferences and summits,

Recalling that the Inter-Agency Task Force for Disaster Reduction has been serving as the main forum within the United Nations system for devising strategies and policies for disaster reduction and ensuring complementarity of action by agencies involved in disaster reduction, mitigation and preparedness,

Expressing its appreciation for the work the Inter-Agency Task Force for Disaster Reduction has been carrying out in its mandated functions,

Expressing its deep concern at the number and scale of natural disasters and their increasing impact within recent years, which have resulted in massive loss of life and long-term negative social, economic and environmental consequences for vulnerable societies throughout the world, in particular in developing countries,

Reiterating that, although natural disasters damage the social and economic infrastructure of all countries, the long-term consequences of natural disasters are especially severe for developing countries and hamper the achievement of their sustainable development,

Recognizing that disaster risk reduction is a cross-cutting issue in the context of sustainable development,

Recognizing also the clear relationship between development, disaster risk reduction, disaster response and disaster recovery and the need to continue to deploy efforts in all these areas,

Recognizing further the urgent need to further develop and make use of the existing scientific and technical knowledge to build resilience to natural disasters, and emphasizing the need for developing countries to have access to appropriate, advanced, environmentally sound, cost-effective and easy-to-use technologies so as to seek more comprehensive solutions to disaster risk reduction and to effectively and efficiently strengthen their capabilities to cope with disaster risks,

Emphasizing that disaster risk reduction, including reducing vulnerability to natural disasters, is an important element that contributes to the achievement of sustainable development,

Stressing the importance of advancing the implementation of the Plan of Implementation of the World Summit on Sustainable Development and its relevant provisions on vulnerability, risk assessment and disaster management,

Recognizing the need to continue to develop an understanding of, and to address, socio-economic activities that exacerbate the vulnerability of societies to natural disasters and to build and further strengthen community capability to cope with disaster risks,

Noting with appreciation the convening of the Third International Conference on Early Warning, held in Bonn, Germany, from 27 to 29 March 2006,

1. *Takes note* of the report of the Secretary-General on the implementation of the International Strategy for Disaster Reduction;

2. *Recalls* that the commitments of the Hyogo Declaration and the Hyogo Framework for Action 2005-2015: Building Resilience of Nations and Communities to Disasters include the provision of assistance for developing countries that are prone to natural disasters and disaster-stricken States in the transition phase towards sustainable physical, social and economic recovery, for risk-reduction activities in post-disaster recovery and for rehabilitation processes;

3. *Welcomes* the progress made in the implementation of the Hyogo Framework for Action, and stresses the need for a more effective integration of disaster risk reduction into sustainable development policies, planning and programming; for the development and strengthening of institutions, mechanisms and capacities to build resilience to hazards; and for a systematic incorporation of risk-reduction approaches into the implementation of emergency preparedness, response and recovery programmes;

4. *Calls upon* the international community to fully implement the commitments of the Hyogo Declaration and the Hyogo Framework for Action;

5. *Invites* Member States, the United Nations system, international financial institutions, regional bodies and other international organizations, including the International Federation of Red Cross and Red Crescent Societies, as well as relevant civil society organizations, to support, implement and follow up the Hyogo Framework for Action;

6. *Calls upon* the United Nations system, international financial institutions and international organizations to integrate the goals of and take into full account the Hyogo Framework for Action in their strategies and programmes, making use of existing coordination mechanisms, and to assist developing countries with those mechanisms to design and implement, as appropriate, disaster risk-reduction measures with a sense of urgency;

7. *Also calls upon* the United Nations system, the international financial institutions and regional banks and other regional and international organizations to support, in a timely and sustained manner, the efforts led by disaster-stricken countries for disaster risk reduction, in post-disaster recovery and rehabilitation processes;

8. *Recognizes* that each State has the primary responsibility for its own sustainable development and for taking effective measures to reduce disaster risk, includ-

ing for the protection of people on its territory, infrastructure and other national assets from the impact of disasters, including the implementation of and follow-up to the Hyogo Framework for Action, and stresses the importance of international cooperation and partnerships to support those national efforts;

9. *Also recognizes* the efforts made by Member States to develop national and local capacities to implement the Hyogo Framework for Action, including through the establishment of national platforms for disaster reduction, and encourages Member States that have not done so to develop such capacities;

10. *Invites* Governments and relevant international organizations to consider disaster risk assessment as an integral component of development plans and poverty eradication programmes;

11. *Stresses* that continued cooperation and coordination among Governments, the United Nations system, other organizations, regional organizations, non-governmental organizations and other partners, as appropriate, are considered essential to address effectively the impact of natural disasters;

12. *Notes* all the regional and subregional initiatives developed in order to achieve disaster risk reduction, and reiterates the need to further develop regional initiatives and risk-reduction capacities of regional mechanisms where they exist and to strengthen them and encourage the use and sharing of all existing tools;

13. *Recognizes* the importance of linking disaster risk management to regional frameworks, as appropriate, such as the African Regional Strategy for Disaster Reduction developed within the New Partnership for Africa's Development, to address issues of poverty eradication and sustainable development;

14. *Calls upon* the international community to support the development and strengthening of institutions, mechanisms and capacities at all levels, in particular at the community level, that can systematically contribute to building resilience to hazards;

15. *Notes* the proposed establishment of a Global Platform for Disaster Risk Reduction as the successor mechanism of the Inter-Agency Task Force for Disaster Reduction, and, taking into account the implementation of the Hyogo Framework for Action, decides that the Global Platform shall have the same mandate as the Inter-Agency Task Force for Disaster Reduction, and requests the Secretary-General to include information on the Global Platform, for consideration by the General Assembly, in his next report;

16. *Decides* that the proposed establishment of the Global Platform should continue to be carried out in an inclusive and transparent manner and be open to all Member States;

17. *Recognizes* the importance of integrating a gender perspective as well as engaging women in the design and implementation of all phases of disaster management, particularly at the disaster risk-reduction stage;

18. *Expresses its appreciation* to those countries that have provided financial support for the activities of the Strategy by making voluntary contributions to the United Nations Trust Fund for Disaster Reduction;

19. *Encourages* the international community to provide adequate voluntary financial contributions to the Trust Fund, in the effort to ensure adequate support for the follow-up activities to the Hyogo Framework for Action, and to review the current usage and feasibility for the expansion of the Fund, inter alia, to assist disaster-prone developing countries to set up national strategies for disaster risk reduction;

20. *Encourages* Governments, multilateral organizations, international and regional organizations, international and regional financial institutions, the private sector and civil society to systematically invest in disaster risk reduction with a view to implementing the objectives of the Strategy;

21. *Recognizes* the need for adequate financial and administrative resources for the International Strategy for Disaster Reduction secretariat, requests the Secretary-General to allocate such resources, within existing resources, for the activities and effective functioning of the inter-agency secretariat for the International Strategy for Disaster Reduction, and also requests the Secretary-General to report on this as appropriate;

22. *Requests* the Secretary-General to submit a report on the result of the Global Survey of Early Warning Systems, including his recommendations on how to address associated technical, financial and organizational gaps and needs;

23. *Stresses* the need to foster better understanding and knowledge of the causes of disasters, as well as to build and strengthen coping capacities through, inter alia, the transfer and exchange of experiences and technical knowledge, educational and training programmes for natural disaster risk reduction, access to relevant data and information and the strengthening of institutional arrangements, including community-based organizations;

24. *Emphasizes* the need for the international community to maintain its focus beyond emergency relief and to support medium- and long-term rehabilitation, reconstruction and risk reduction, and stresses the importance of implementing programmes related to the eradication of poverty, sustainable development and disaster risk-reduction management in the most vulnerable regions, particularly in developing countries prone to natural disasters;

25. *Stresses* the need to address risk reduction of and vulnerabilities to all natural hazards, including geological and hydrometeorological hazards, in a comprehensive manner;

26. *Requests* the Secretary-General to submit to the General Assembly at its sixty-second session a report on the implementation of the present resolution, under the item entitled "Sustainable development".

Natural disasters and vulnerability

In response to General Assembly resolution 60/196 [YUN 2005, p. 1020], in which the Inter-Agency Task Force was encouraged to make available to relevant UN entities, information on options for disaster reduction, including severe natural hazards and extreme weather-related disasters and vulnerabilities, in August [A/61/229 & Corr.1], the Secretary-General provided an update on activities undertaken to reduce vulnerability to severe climate-related hazards. He stated that severe weather and climate events were the dominant hazards behind disaster statistics and the past two years had witnessed the occurrence of unusual extreme events, such as the intensity and location of tropical cyclones. The Intergovernmental Panel on Climate Change (see p. 1228) would provide an updated assessment of those changes and their consequences in 2007. Many States were developing strategies and measures to reduce their vulnerability to climate variability and change through national adaptation programmes of action, under the auspices of the UN Framework Convention on Climate Change (see p. 1219). Efforts by the International Strategy for Disaster Reduction secretariat and its partners were also ongoing to promote the converging goals of disaster reduction and climate change adaptation at the international level.

GENERAL ASSEMBLY ACTION

On 20 December [meeting 83], the General Assembly, on the recommendation of the Second Committee [A/61/422/Add.3], adopted **resolution 61/200** without vote [agenda item 53 *(c)*].

Natural disasters and vulnerability

The General Assembly,

Recalling its decision 57/547 of 20 December 2002 and its resolutions 58/215 of 23 December 2003, 59/233 of 22 December 2004 and 60/196 of 22 December 2005,

Reaffirming the Johannesburg Declaration on Sustainable Development and the Plan of Implementation of the World Summit on Sustainable Development ("Johannesburg Plan of Implementation"),

Reaffirming also the Hyogo Declaration and the Hyogo Framework for Action 2005-2015: Building the Resilience of Nations and Communities to Disasters, adopted by the World Conference on Disaster Reduction,

Recalling the 2005 World Summit Outcome,

Recognizing the need to continue to develop an understanding of, and to address, the underlying risk factors, as identified in the Hyogo Framework for Action, including socio-economic factors, that exacerbate the vulnerability of societies to natural hazards, to build and further strengthen the capacity at all levels to cope with disaster risks and to enhance resilience against hazards associated with disasters, while also recognizing the negative impact of disasters on economic growth and sustainable development, in particular in developing countries and disaster-prone countries,

Recognizing also the need to integrate a gender perspective in the design and implementation of all phases of disaster risk reduction management, with a view to reducing vulnerability,

Noting that the global environment continues to suffer degradation, adding to economic and social vulnerabilities, in particular in developing countries,

Taking into account the various ways and forms in which all countries, in particular the more vulnerable countries, are affected by severe natural hazards such as earthquakes, tsunamis, landslides and volcanic eruptions and extreme weather events such as heat waves, severe droughts, floods and storms, and the El Niño/La Niña events which have global reach,

Expressing deep concern at the recent increase in the frequency and intensity of extreme weather events and associated natural disasters in some regions of the world and their substantial economic, social and environmental impacts, in particular upon developing countries in those regions,

Taking into account that geological and hydrometeorological hazards and their associated natural disasters and their reduction must be addressed in a coherent and effective manner,

Noting the need for international and regional cooperation to increase the capacity of countries to respond to the negative impacts of all natural hazards, including earthquakes, tsunamis, landslides and volcanic eruptions and extreme weather events such as heat waves, severe droughts and floods, and associated natural disasters, in particular in developing countries and disaster-prone countries,

Bearing in mind the importance of addressing disaster risks related to changing social, economic, environmental conditions and land use, and the impact of hazards associated with geological events, weather, water, climate variability and climate change, in sector development planning and programmes as well as in post-disaster situations,

1. *Takes note* of the report of the Secretary-General on the implementation of its resolution 60/196 of 22 December 2005;

2. *Urges* the international community to continue to address ways and means, including through cooperation and technical assistance, to reduce the adverse effects of natural disasters, including those caused by extreme weather events, in particular in vulnerable developing countries, including least developed countries and in Africa, through the implementation of the International Strategy for Disaster Reduction, including the Hyogo Framework for Action 2005-2015: Building the Resilience of Nations and Communities to Disasters, and encourages the institutional arrangement for the International Strategy to continue its work in this regard;

3. *Recognizes* that each State has the primary responsibility for its own sustainable development and for taking effective measures to reduce disaster risk, including for the protection of people on its territory, infrastructure and other national assets from the impact of disaster, including the implementation and follow-up of the Hyogo

Framework for Action, and stresses the importance of international cooperation and partnerships to support those national efforts;

4. *Stresses* the importance of the Hyogo Declaration and the Hyogo Framework for Action and the priorities for action that States, regional and international organizations and international financial institutions as well as other concerned actors should take into consideration in their approach to disaster risk reduction and implement, as appropriate, according to their own circumstances and capacities, bearing in mind the vital importance of promoting a culture of prevention in the area of natural disasters, including through the mobilization of adequate resources for disaster risk reduction, and of addressing disaster risk reduction, including disaster preparedness at the community level, and the adverse effects of natural disasters on efforts to implement national development plans and poverty reduction strategies with a view to achieving the internationally agreed development goals, including the Millennium Development Goals;

5. *Encourages* Governments, through their respective International Strategy for Disaster Reduction national platforms and national focal points for disaster risk reduction, in cooperation with the United Nations system, the International Federation of Red Cross and Red Crescent Societies and other stakeholders, to strengthen capacity-building in the most vulnerable regions, to enable them to address the social, economic and environmental factors that increase vulnerability, and to develop measures that will enable them to prepare for and cope with natural disasters, including those associated with earthquakes and extreme weather events, and encourages the international community to provide effective assistance to developing countries in this regard;

6. *Emphasizes*, in order to build resilience, particularly in developing countries, especially those vulnerable among them, the importance of addressing the underlying risk factors identified in the Hyogo Framework for Action and the importance of promoting the integration of risk reduction associated with geological and hydrometeorological hazards in disaster risk reduction programmes;

7. *Stresses* that, in order to reduce vulnerability to natural hazards, risk assessments should be integrated into disaster risk reduction programmes at national and local levels;

8. *Encourages* the institutional arrangement for the International Strategy for Disaster Reduction to continue, within its mandate, particularly the Hyogo Framework for Action, to enhance the coordination of activities to promote natural disaster risk reduction and to make available to the relevant United Nations entities information on options for natural disaster risk reduction, including severe natural hazards and extreme weather-related disasters and vulnerabilities;

9. *Stresses* the importance of close cooperation and coordination among Governments, the United Nations system, and other international and regional organizations, as well as non-governmental organizations and other partners such as the International Federation of Red Cross and Red Crescent Societies, as appropriate, taking into account the need for the development of disaster management strategies, including the effective establishment of early warning systems that are, inter alia, people-centred, while taking advantage of all available resources and expertise for that purpose;

10. *Also stresses* that, to reduce vulnerability to all natural hazards, including geological and hydrometeorological events and associated natural disasters, closer and more systematic cooperation, and information-sharing on disaster preparedness between the scientific community and disaster managers at all levels should be strengthened;

11. *Encourages* the Conference of the Parties to the United Nations Framework Convention on Climate Change and the parties to the Kyoto Protocol to the United Nations Framework Convention on Climate Change to continue to address the adverse effects of climate change, especially in developing countries that are particularly vulnerable, in accordance with the provisions of the Convention, and also encourages the Intergovernmental Panel on Climate Change to continue to assess the adverse effects of climate change on the socio-economic and natural disaster reduction systems of developing countries;

12. *Stresses* the need to address risk reduction of and vulnerabilities to all natural hazards including geological and hydrometeorological hazards;

13. *Requests* the Secretary-General to report to the General Assembly at its sixty-third session on the implementation of the present resolution, and decides to consider the issue of natural disasters and vulnerability at that session, under the sub-item entitled "International Strategy for Disaster Reduction" of the item entitled "Sustainable development".

El Niño

In response to General Assembly resolution 59/232 [YUN 2004, p. 949], the Secretary-General, in August [A/61/229 & Corr.1], provided an update on the El Niño phenomenon and on international activities to reduce its impact. Scientific institutions continued to monitor the Pacific Ocean for signs of changes that could lead to either an El Niño or, its opposite, La Niña event. Consultations with the global forecast centres and other experts from around the world were coordinated by WMO. Over the previous two years, the El Niño phenomenon had not exhibited major fluctuations of the type that had devastated countries in 1997 and 1998. However, as historical patterns indicated that it was likely to reoccur, effective preparations needed to be maintained and developed during the quiet years.

To strengthen its operation, the International Research Centre on the El Niño Phenomenon, established in 2003 [YUN 2003, p. 961], undertook three types of activities: monitoring and analysing the El Niño phenomenon through collaboration with international monitoring centres, enhancing regional and international recognition and support for the Centre, and developing tools for decision makers and Government authorities to reduce the impact of the El Niño phenomenon. The Centre produced regionally coordinated monthly seasonal forecasts, and under WMO guidance, cooperated in the exchange of information with the Intergovernmental Authority on Development Climate Prediction and Applications Centre in Nairobi, Kenya, and the Beijing Climate Centre of the Chinese Meteorological Agency. It had also formalized partnerships with several national oceanographic institutions of south-eastern Pacific countries. In collaboration with the Andean national meteorological and hydrological services, the Centre developed several regional project proposals to improve climate information and forecast services and enhance climate risk management in the region.

GENERAL ASSEMBLY ACTION

On 20 December [meeting 83], the General Assembly, on the recommendation of the Second Committee [A/61/422/Add.3], adopted **resolution 61/199** without vote [agenda item 53 *(c)*].

International cooperation to reduce the impact of the El Niño phenomenon

The General Assembly,

Recalling its resolutions 52/200 of 18 December 1997, 53/185 of 15 December 1998, 54/220 of 22 December 1999, 55/197 of 20 December 2000, 56/194 of 21 December 2001, 57/255 of 20 December 2002 and 59/232 of 22 December 2004 and Economic and Social Council resolutions 1999/46 of 28 July 1999, 1999/63 of 30 July 1999 and 2000/33 of 28 July 2000,

Noting that the El Niño phenomenon has a recurring character and that it can lead to extensive natural hazards with the potential to seriously affect humankind,

Reaffirming the importance of developing strategies at the national, subregional, regional and international levels that aim to prevent, mitigate and repair the damage caused by natural disasters that result from the El Niño phenomenon,

Noting that technological developments and international cooperation have enhanced the capabilities for the prediction of the El Niño phenomenon and thereby the potential for the preventive actions that may be taken to reduce its negative impacts,

Taking into account the Johannesburg Declaration on Sustainable Development and the Plan of Implementation of the World Summit on Sustainable Development ("Johannesburg Plan of Implementation"), in particular paragraph 37 *(i)* thereof,

Reaffirming the Hyogo Declaration and the Hyogo Framework for Action 2005-2015: Building the Resilience of Nations and Communities to Disasters,

1. *Recognizes* the ongoing efforts made by the Government of Ecuador, the World Meteorological Organization and the inter-agency secretariat for the International Strategy for Disaster Reduction which have led to the establishment of the International Centre for the Study of the El Niño Phenomenon at Guayaquil, Ecuador, and encourages them to continue their support for the advancement of the Centre;

2. *Also recognizes* the technical and scientific support of the World Meteorological Organization to produce regionally coordinated monthly seasonal forecasts;

3. *Encourages*, in this regard, the World Meteorological Organization to strengthen the exchange of information with the relevant institutions;

4. *Welcomes* the activities undertaken so far to strengthen the International Centre for the Study of the El Niño Phenomenon, through collaboration with international monitoring centres, including the national oceanographic institutions, and efforts to enhance regional and international recognition and support for the Centre and to develop tools for decision-makers and Government authorities to reduce the impact of the El Niño phenomenon;

5. *Calls upon* the Secretary-General and the relevant United Nations organs, funds and programmes, in particular those taking part in the International Strategy for Disaster Reduction, and the international community to adopt, as appropriate, the necessary measures to strengthen the International Centre for the Study of the El Niño Phenomenon, and invites the international community to provide scientific, technical and financial assistance and cooperation for this purpose, as well as to strengthen, as appropriate, other centres devoted to the study of the El Niño phenomenon;

6. *Welcomes* the decision made by the Government of Spain and the Permanent Commission for the South Pacific to become new permanent members of the International Board of the Centre, as well as their commitment to provide economic and technical support;

7. *Underscores* the importance of maintaining the El Niño/Southern Oscillation observation system, continuing research into extreme weather events, improving forecasting skills and developing appropriate policies for reducing the impact of the El Niño phenomenon and other extreme weather events, and emphasizes the need to further develop and strengthen these institutional capacities in all countries, in particular in developing countries;

8. *Requests* the Secretary-General to include a section on the implementation of the present resolution in his report to the General Assembly at its sixty-third session on the implementation of the International Strategy for Disaster Reduction.

Disaster assistance

Indian Ocean tsunami aftermath

Eighteen months after the 2004 Indian Ocean earthquake and resulting tsunami [YUN 2004, p. 952], 42,883 people were still listed as missing. Work on long-term reconstruction was ongoing, with permanent schools, highways, harbours and homes under construction, and livelihood restoration programmes and support to communities in social services were underway. Construction of permanent housing was the priority but most of the affected countries had encountered common challenges, including insecure land tenure, increasing costs of building materials, the need for community consultation in housing construction, and lack of infrastructure at new housing sites.

Multi-agency assessment teams had revised the estimated amount needed for long-term recovery, from $10 billion to approximately $11 billion. Official and private pledges for recovery reached just over $12 billion. The Tsunami Trust Fund established to manage contributions for recovery and reconstruction operations, and managed by OCHA on behalf of more than 60 public and private donors and 14 recipient organizations, received nearly $75 million during the 2005-2006 financial year. As at 18 December, more than $72 million of those funds had been allocated to 67 projects in seven countries. The Multi-Donor Voluntary Trust Fund on Tsunami Early Warning Arrangements in the Indian Ocean and Southeast Asia, established by the United Nations Economic and Social Commission for Asia and the Pacific (ESCAP) in late 2005, opened for its first round of funding in 2006 and welcomed proposals from eligible regional, subregional and national organizations.

Report of Secretary-General. In response to General Assembly resolution 60/15 [YUN 2005, p. 1028], the Secretary-General submitted a May report [A/61/87-E/2006/77] on strengthening emergency relief, rehabilitation, reconstruction, recovery and prevention in the aftermath of the Indian Ocean tsunami. The report provided an overview of the tsunami and its impact on affected countries, as well as an update on the recovery process at the 18-month mark. It identified the key challenges and lessons learned in efforts to build back better and examined successes and hindrances in tsunami response, with a focus on long-term recovery. Themes discussed included coordination, models of Government recovery institutions, assessments of damages and needs, transparency and accountability, community participation in recovery, economic diversification, risk reduction, human rights and environmental issues.

The Secretary-General provided recommendations to both the Economic and Social Council and the General Assembly on each theme. On coordination, he proposed that the UN develop a flexible model for support to recovery coordination that could be quickly deployed in a post-disaster setting. Adequate resources should be allocated to support coordination both in the recovery and relief phases, and the efforts of international NGOs should be supported and more effectively utilized. Continued reform of recovery institutions and harmonization of laws and policies to facilitate effective international response were needed to address the varying levels of disaster preparedness. A consistent methodology for accurate needs and damage assessment for the early phase of recovery should be developed and aid agencies should increase support for national capacity to develop baseline data and guarantee ongoing data collection and analysis during recovery. The Secretary-General stressed the need for financial transparency and accountability to donors and recommended support for the Development Assistance Databases and for the Tsunami Recovery Impact Assessment and Monitoring System. Other recommendations addressed issues such as community-driven development; early emphasis on protection and restoration of livelihoods; enhanced coordination; economic diversification and long-term economic planning; risk reduction and humanitarian and development planning; tsunami warning; human rights and equity in assistance; gender considerations; integration of environmental aspects of recovery, planning and implementation; waste management programmes; and environmental governance.

With regard to risk reduction, the Secretary-General reported that a mechanism had been established under the Intergovernmental Oceanographic Commission (IOC) to develop the regional tsunami early warning system. Observation and warning systems were being upgraded and an initial system was expected to be completed by July. Since 20 of the 29 countries participating in the Indian Ocean warning system lacked national plans for a tsunami early warning and response system, in March, a consortium of international partners offered to support Governments that had fallen behind in developing national capacity. The Secretary-General recommended that the Intergovernmental Coordination Group for the Indian Ocean Tsunami Warning and Mitigation System (ICG-IOTWS) (see p. 1101) be utilized as the primary mechanism for regional coordination and encouraged to factor in broader disaster management and development perspectives wherever possible. He also called for the incorporation of disaster risk reduction into relief and development planning and for tsunami warning systems to be linked to other hazard warning systems.

Regional workshops. The regional workshop on "Mitigation, Preparedness and Development for Tsunami Early Warning Systems in the Indian Ocean (Bangkok, 14-16 June), jointly organized by the UN-ISDR secretariat, ESCAP, IOC-UNESCO and ISDR Asia Partnership, addressed the societal aspects of tsunami early warning systems and initiated a three-way dialogue among partners from technical, disaster risk reduction and development communities. The principal outcome of the workshop was the endorsement of the proposal to establish a working group under ICG-IOTWS on mitigation, preparedness and development to complement the existing ICG-IOTWS technical working groups, and develop terms of reference for the new working group. The meeting agreed on the terms of reference, which included priority actions for its consideration. The workshop agreed that societal issues affected all aspects of the early warning system design and operation and were critical to its effectiveness, but had not been given sufficient attention. In that connection, emphasis was placed on the benefits of linkages between the working groups of ICG-IOTWS to harmonize their work and to accommodate those connections. Participants also called for more regional and international efforts to support the development and implementation of national-level standard operating procedures for tsunami early warning systems.

ICG-IOTWS working groups. Within ICG-IOTWS, five Intersessional Working Groups conducted significant work on data collection and exchange, hazard identification and modeling, as well as the establishment of warning systems. A proposed draft terms of reference for a sixth Working Group on Mitigation, Preparedness and Response was considered at the third session of the IOC ICG-IOTWS (Bali, 31 July–2 August) and the sixth group was formed.

World Tourism Organization. In October, the World Tourism Organization (UNWTO), in collaboration with Germany, established the Consulting Unit on Biodiversity and Tourism for Tsunami Affected Countries. The Unit, located in Bonn, provided consultancy and advisory support services to national and local governments in the 2004 tsunami-affected countries to help them redevelop their tourism infrastructure. As reconstruction and rehabilitation of tourism infrastructures in tsunami-hit areas offered a unique opportunity to link tourism and nature conservation through integrated tourism and biodiversity management, the UNWTO Consulting Unit focused on implementing sustainable tourism strategies in line with the Guidelines on Biodiversity and Tourism Development of the Convention on Biological Diversity (CBD).

Tsunami Consortium. On 15 November, at the fifth session of the Global Consortium for Tsunami Recovery held at UNICEF headquarters in New York, the Secretary-General's Special Envoy for Tsunami Recovery, former United States President, William J. Clinton, lauded the successes achieved in areas devastated by 2004 Indian Ocean disaster. However, he asserted that Governments should start preparing for future disasters immediately and that greater support and funding for local disaster-management authorities were needed. The fourth meeting of the Consortium, also in New York, was held on 28 April.

On 21 December, the Special Envoy issued a report on the first two years of the recovery process entitled "Key Propositions for Building Back Better", which described major achievements realized among the devastated communities across the Indian Ocean region and presented ten propositions that captured key lessons learned from the tsunami recovery effort. The report stressed that it was vital for recovery plans to identify mechanisms to reduce the risk of future disasters and that resources for implementing such plans had to be included from the outset. In addition, ambitious legislation needed to be followed by ambitious long-term financial investment and training, as well as broader incorporation of risk reduction in recovery and development strategies.

GENERAL ASSEMBLY ACTION

On 14 December [meeting 79], the General Assembly adopted **resolution 61/132** [draft: A/61/L.44 & Add.1] without vote [agenda item 69 *(a)*].

Strengthening emergency relief, rehabilitation, reconstruction and prevention in the aftermath of the Indian Ocean tsunami disaster

The General Assembly,

Recalling its resolutions 46/182 of 19 December 1991, 57/152 of 16 December 2002, 57/256 of 20 December 2002, 58/25 of 5 December 2003, 58/214 and 58/215 of 23 December 2003, 59/212 of 20 December 2004, 59/231 and 59/233 of 22 December 2004, 59/279 of 19 January 2005 and 60/15 of 14 November 2005,

Noting the Declaration on Action to Strengthen Emergency Relief, Rehabilitation, Reconstruction and Prevention in the Aftermath of the Earthquake and Tsunami Disaster of 26 December 2004, adopted at the special meeting of leaders of the Association of Southeast Asian Nations, held in Jakarta on 6 January 2005,

Recalling the Hyogo Declaration and the Hyogo Framework for Action 2005-2015, as well as the common statement of the special session on the Indian Ocean disaster, adopted at the World Conference on Disaster Reduction, held in Kobe, Hyogo, Japan, from 18 to 22 January 2005,

Taking note of the report of the Secretary-General,

Taking note with appreciation of the convening of the Global Consortium for Tsunami-Affected Countries by the Office of the United Nations Special Envoy for Tsunami Recovery in April 2006, which brought together national Governments, United Nations agencies, other intergovernmental organizations, the international financial institutions, consortia of non-governmental organizations and donor Governments with the aim of identifying common priorities and implementing actions towards achieving community-driven development, meeting funding gaps, fostering accountability and transparency, integrating disaster risk reduction, disaster resilience and an effective early warning system that is, inter alia, people-centred into national development plans, building social and physical infrastructure and supporting microfinance activities,

Welcoming the convening of the final meeting of the Global Consortium for Tsunami-Affected Countries in New York on 15 November 2006, chaired by Mr. William Jefferson Clinton, former President of the United States of America, in his capacity as Special Envoy for Tsunami Recovery, which aimed to review the progress made and to identify key recovery and reconstruction goals,

Noting with appreciation the convening of the Third International Conference on Early Warning, in Bonn, Germany, from 27 to 29 March 2006,

Stressing the need to develop and implement risk reduction strategies and to integrate them, where appropriate, into national development plans, in particular through the implementation of the International Strategy for Disaster Reduction, so as to enhance the resilience of populations in disasters and reduce the risks to them, their livelihoods, the social and economic infrastructure and environmental resources, and stressing also the need for Governments to develop and implement effective national plans for hazard warning systems with a disaster risk reduction approach,

Emphasizing that disaster reduction, including reducing vulnerability to natural disasters, is an important element that contributes to the achievement of sustainable development,

Welcoming the role of the Intergovernmental Oceanographic Commission of the United Nations Educational, Scientific and Cultural Organization in the establishment and implementation of the Indian Ocean Tsunami Warning and Mitigation System, given the importance of strengthening regional and subregional cooperation and coordination, which is essential for effective early warning system arrangements for tsunamis,

Noting the communiqué relating to support for tsunami and multi-hazard warning systems within the context of the Global Earth Observation System of Systems, which supports the interoperability of systems and free and open real-time data exchange, adopted at the third Earth Observation Summit, in Brussels, on 16 February 2005,

Welcoming the establishment of the Multi-Donor Voluntary Trust Fund on Tsunami Early Warning Arrangements in the Indian Ocean and Southeast Asia, and inviting Governments, donor countries, relevant international organizations, international and regional financial institutions, the private sector and civil society to consider contributing to the Trust Fund through financial contributions and technical cooperation to support the establishment of the tsunami early warning system in accordance with the needs of the countries of the Indian Ocean and Southeast Asia so that the Trust Fund contributes to the development of an integrated early warning system based on adequate resources and comprising a network of collaborative centres connected to the global system,

Stressing the need for continued commitment to assist the affected countries and their peoples, particularly the most vulnerable groups, to fully recover from the catastrophic and traumatic effects of the disaster, including in their medium- and long-term rehabilitation and reconstruction efforts, and welcoming Government and international assistance measures in this regard,

1. *Notes with appreciation* the efforts by the Governments of affected countries to undertake the rehabilitation and reconstruction phase, as well as in enhancing financial transparency and accountability, with respect to the channelling and utilization of resources, including, as appropriate, through the involvement of international public auditors;

2. *Commends* the prompt response, continued support, generous assistance and contributions of the international community, donor Governments, civil society, the private sector and individuals, in the relief, rehabilitation and reconstruction efforts, which reflect the spirit of international solidarity and cooperation to address the disaster;

3. *Takes note with appreciation* of the continued work of Mr. William Jefferson Clinton, former President of the United States of America, the United Nations Special Envoy for Tsunami Recovery, and his various initiatives, and encourages his efforts to continue sustaining the political will and to promote the identification of priorities and integration of efforts of the international community, particularly regional and international financial institutions, civil society and the private sector, to support medium- and long-term rehabilitation, reconstruction and risk reduction efforts led by the Governments of affected countries;

4. *Encourages* donor communities and international and regional financial institutions, as well as the private sector and civil society, to strengthen partnerships and to continue to support the medium- and long-term re-

habilitation and reconstruction needs of the affected countries;

5. *Encourages* the continued effective coordination among the Governments of affected countries, relevant bodies of the United Nations system, international organizations, donor countries, regional and international financial institutions, civil society, the International Red Cross and Red Crescent Movement and private sectors involved in rehabilitation and reconstruction efforts, in order to ensure the effective implementation of existing joint programmes and to prevent unnecessary duplication and reduce vulnerability to future natural hazards, as well as to adequately respond to the remaining humanitarian needs, where needed;

6. *Stresses* the need for the development of stronger institutions, mechanisms and capacities at the regional, national and local levels, as affirmed in the Hyogo Declaration and the Hyogo Framework for Action 2005-2015, and the promotion of public education, awareness and community participation, in order to systematically build resilience to hazards and disasters, as well as reduce the risks and the vulnerability of populations to disasters, including an effective and sustained tsunami warning system, particularly in tsunami-prone countries;

7. *Calls upon* States to fully implement the Hyogo Declaration and the Hyogo Framework for Action 2005-2015, in particular those commitments related to assistance for developing countries that are prone to natural disasters and for disaster-stricken States in the transition phase towards sustainable, physical, social and economic recovery, for risk-reduction activities in post-disaster recovery and for rehabilitation processes;

8. *Stresses* the importance of and the need for regular updating of recovery assessment by the Governments of affected countries, the United Nations system and international and regional financial institutions, based on the affected countries' national data and utilizing a consistent methodology, in order to reassess progress and identify gaps and priorities, with the participation of the local community during the recovery and reconstruction phase in order to build back better;

9. *Emphasizes* the need to promote transparency and accountability among donors and recipient countries by means of, inter alia, a unified financial and sectoral information online tracking system, and highlights the importance of timely and accurate information on assessed needs and the sources and uses of funds, and the continued support of donors, where needed, for further development of online tracking systems in the affected countries;

10. *Stresses* the need for relevant bodies of the United Nations system, international organizations, regional and international financial institutions, civil society and the private sector to implement programmes according to assessed needs and agreed priorities of the Governments of tsunami-affected countries and to ensure full transparency and accountability for their programme activities;

11. *Notes with appreciation* the efforts of international agencies, donor countries and relevant civil society organizations in supporting the Governments of affected countries to develop national capacity for tsunami warning and response so as to increase public awareness and provide community-based support for disaster risk reduction;

12. *Encourages* international agencies and Governments to enhance and accelerate their support for the development, implementation and maintenance of the Indian Ocean Tsunami Warning and Mitigation System, under the Intergovernmental Oceanographic Commission, as the appropriate vehicle for the rapid and timely exchange of alerts and related information required to deliver effective tsunami warnings at the national level;

13. *Requests* the Secretary-General to continue to explore ways to strengthen the rapid response capacities of the international community to provide immediate humanitarian relief, building on existing arrangements and ongoing initiatives;

14. *Encourages* the Emergency Relief Coordinator to continue his efforts to strengthen the coordination of humanitarian assistance, and calls upon relevant United Nations organizations and other humanitarian and relevant development actors to work with the Office for the Coordination of Humanitarian Affairs of the Secretariat to enhance the coordination, effectiveness and efficiency of humanitarian assistance;

15. *Urges* Governments and the United Nations system, in planning for disaster preparedness and responding to natural disasters, and in implementing recovery, rehabilitation and reconstruction efforts, to integrate a gender perspective and to ensure that women take an active and equal role in all phases of disaster management;

16. *Stresses* the importance of a coordinated process of assessing lessons learned in the international response to a given humanitarian emergency, and notes the efforts of Governments of the affected countries, donor Governments and international organizations in providing reports on evaluations of and lessons learned from the Indian Ocean tsunami disaster;

17. *Requests* the Secretary-General to report to the General Assembly at its sixty-second session on the implementation of the present resolution under the item entitled "Strengthening of the coordination of humanitarian and disaster relief assistance of the United Nations, including special economic assistance", through the Economic and Social Council at its substantive session of 2007.

Oversight activities

OIOS audit and investigative reviews

The General Assembly, in **resolution 60/259** of 8 May (see p. 1649), welcomed the comprehensive tsunami risk assessments undertaken jointly by the Office of Internal Oversight Services (OIOS) with UN funds and programmes and specialized agencies, and requested that the Secretary-General ensure that they cooperated with OIOS in the preparation of a consolidated report on audits and investigative reviews of tsunami relief operations and that OIOS report to the Assembly at its sixty-first (2006) session.

In response to that request, OIOS submitted a December report [A/61/669] on the subject, which explained its inability to finalize an agreement on the preparation of the consolidated report because UN funds and programmes and specialized agencies were not able to share their internal audit reports, as they were restricted to their respective management and governing bodies in accordance with their mandates. Furthermore, there was no established protocol or coordinating mechanism for sharing oversight information that could be used by UN system entities. The report submitted summarized the results of OIOS activities to oversee the tsunami relief operations, discussed its assessment of internal control and risk management frameworks and highlighted areas of concern regarding the oversight of complex inter-agency programmes being implemented by a number of UN system agencies.

OIOS found that the design of mechanisms to manage tsunami relief activities needed to be refined. Expenditure tracking was not planned to present a comprehensive picture of resource utilization and the pro bono services provided by PricewaterhouseCoopers could have been better utilized. Several agencies had implemented their own mechanisms to reduce the level of vulnerability to fraud and corruption, and while several conferences had highlighted concern with issues of transparency, strengthening safeguards against corruption and ensuring effective project implementation, no common risk management policy was formulated. Therefore, efforts to identify and manage risks were piecemeal rather than integrated. OIOS oversight of tsunami relief activities also included an audit of OCHA and UNHCR in Indonesia and a risk assessment of UNHCR in Sri Lanka. It had also submitted in 2005 a report concerning an investigation of risks of fraud in tsunami disaster relief in Jakarta and the Ache province of Indonesia. OIOS issued three recommendations to strengthen management, oversight, internal control and risk management of tsunami programmes: the Secretary-General should create an institutionalized framework for management and oversight for future complex inter-agency programmes which involved the participation of more than one UN system entity; formulate an internal control policy document for inter-agency activities, including the requirements for joint oversight for endorsement by the General Assembly and the Economic and Social Council; and establish an integrated risk management framework for complex inter-agency programmes, such as tsunami relief operations, involving participating UN system entities.

Other disaster assistance

Central America

In response to General Assembly resolution 60/220 [YUN 2005, p. 1030], the Secretary-General submitted a May report [A/61/78-E/2006/61] on humanitarian assistance and rehabilitation for El Salvador and Guatemala. The report identified lessons learned with regard to coordination of response and recovery, resource mobilization, use of military assets, information management and incorporation of risk-reduction measures in response, recovery and development processes, and highlighted key issues from the ongoing recovery effort in the two countries, particularly the successes and challenges to the response and recovery effort linked to tropical storm Stan in October 2005.

According to the report, despite the sustained efforts shown by all actors involved, the magnitude of the disasters in both countries exceeded the financial and organizational capacity of their Governments and highlighted the weaknesses in their emergency and response plans, as well as those of UN system agencies, and in the early warning and community preparedness of populations at risk. Tropical storm Stan left compelling evidence that community-based early warning and preparedness had to be stepped up and made an integral part of recovery, reconstruction and development plans. The impact of the 2005 hurricane season revealed the need to harmonize and coordinate better preparedness and response protocols among government agencies, UN agencies, NGOs and civil society organizations.

The Secretary-General recommended that UN humanitarian agencies should reaffirm their commitment to supporting Central American Governments in the formulation and implementation of policies and institutional arrangements for risk identification, early warning, risk preparedness and vulnerabilities. The United Nations should continue to assist countries in formulating disaster preparedness and response plans, with clear definitions of roles, responsibilities and communication lines, and support them in establishing information management systems to ensure timely and adequate decision-making in emergency situations. The Organization should also develop stand-by arrangements and operating procedures to improve civil-military coordination in disaster-prone countries. Greater efforts should be made to ensure the mobilization of resources and Member States should allocate additional resources to the United Nations to enhance its cooperation with Central American Governments and their national and local structures.

In resolution 2006/5 of 18 July, the Economic and Social Council took note of the Secretary-General's report (see p. 1055).

Ethiopia

In 2006, successive years of drought, failed agricultural seasons, livestock loss, asset depletion and chronic structural weaknesses in Ethiopia had culminated in the need to assist approximately 9.8 million people, comprising 2.6 million emergency food recipients, and another 7.2 million through the Productive Safety Net Programme. The Government of Ethiopia and its humanitarian partners began preparations for a crisis in the southern and southeastern pastoral and agro-pastoral areas of Somali and Oromiya regions, which had not received rain for some time. The threat of the avian influenza was a concern, as were unpredictable needs, such as those resulting from floods and other fast-onset disasters. In January, a humanitarian appeal for $166 million was launched to provide food aid to 2.6 million beneficiaries, of which 69 per cent were in the critically affected pastoralist areas.

From January to April, persistent dry conditions increased the vulnerability of populations in drought areas. However, heavy rains in April and May caused sporadic flooding, impeded humanitarian access and raised concerns regarding the spread of water-borne diseases. The situation was aggravated by the country's deteriorating economic conditions and security concerns. During the last week of October, the Wabi-Sheblle River burst its banks and flooded the Lower Sheblle areas of the Gode and Afder zones. Overflow of the Weyib and Fafen rivers also inundated parts of the Liben and Korahe zones, respectively. The flooding reportedly killed 80 people and affected an estimated 362,000, of which 122,500 were displaced. The floods washed away livestock and damaged the already scarce infrastructure, including bridges and roads, which hindered emergency relief efforts. Meanwhile, epidemics of water-borne diseases increased in the flooded areas, particularly diarrhoea.

In November, a joint Government-UN emergency flood appeal for Somali Regional State 2006 sought $7 million to meet non-food requirements, as well as immediate rehabilitation needs for the flood-affected areas.

Horn of Africa

The UN Consolidated Inter-Agency Appeal for the Horn of Africa sought $120 million to assist beneficiaries in Djibouti, Eritrea and Kenya, and received 36 per cent ($43.7 million) of that amount. In addition to the regional appeal, individual country appeals were made for Kenya and Somalia.

In 2006, the situation in the drought-affected areas in the Horn of Africa (Djibouti, Eritrea, Ethiopia, Kenya and Somalia) remained critical. In November 2005, early warning systems had indicated that erratic and insufficient rainfall trends would result in reduced water, pasture, and food availability in the region. By early 2006, the situation had worsened and assessments revealed that the scale and severity of the crisis had escalated dramatically. The number of people estimated at risk was over 15 million, of which more than 8 million were identified as being in need of urgent emergency assistance, including 1.6 million children below the age of five years. Malnutrition was the main threat, compounded by preventable diseases, which were the main causes of illness and death during drought. The border areas of southern Ethiopia, northern and northeastern Kenya, and southern Somalia—areas linked by ethnic affiliations, livelihood structures and fluid population and livestock movements—were the worst hit, and were at moderate to high-risk of famine within six months. In Djibouti and some coastal areas in Eritrea, insufficient rainfall also had a significant impact.

A revised UN Consolidated Appeal for the drought in Somalia was launched as a complement to the emergency appeal for the Horn of Africa (see p. 1066).

Kenya

In early October, incessant short rains in Kenya and heavy flooding led to the loss of 19 lives, affecting 30,000, and displacing some 8,000 people in Isiolo, Garissa, Kisumu, Lodwar, Mandera, Moyale, Turkana and Wajir in the Coastal, Western and Northern Eastern Provinces of Kenya. By November, the rains had intensified and the resulting flooding impacted an estimated 300,000 people. A preliminary emergency appeal in the amount of $7.9 million for six months was launched. However, in December, the heavy rainfall spread to the western region of Kenya, particularly affecting Busia (Budalangi). Dykes along the Nyando River were completely destroyed, causing large-scale destruction of property and flooding of farming land along the flood plain. Some 12,000 households had been displaced and were in urgent need of relief assistance and other services. A revised emergency humanitarian appeal was launched on 7 December, which sought $21.8 million to assist 563,000 people for four months. The appeal was later revised to $50.6 million.

Somalia

In 2006, Somalia was hit by the worst flooding in recent history, which was the latest in a long series of disasters in the country, including a devastating three-year drought that had officially ended the previous year [YUN 2005, p. 997]. The humanitarian crisis had deepened, particularly in the southern and central areas of the country, along the Shabelle and Juba valley river basins. Some 350,000 people along the riverine areas were reported displaced, inundated or otherwise seriously affected by the floods. Floods displaced entire communities, submerged villages, destroyed granaries, cut off feeder roads, blocked or damaged irrigation and flood relief infrastructures and inundated thousands of hectares of farmland in the South/Central area covering Gedo, Juba Valley, Hiran and Shabelle Valley Regions. Access to the affected areas remained a challenge for the humanitarian community. The fragile political and security environment remained a concern to the humanitarian community and prompted it to engage in high-level advocacy efforts to ensure the preservation of humanitarian space for aid delivery.

The UN Consolidated Inter-Agency Appeal for the Somalia Flood Response Plan sought $28.6 million, of which 48 per cent ($13.7 million) was received.

Indonesia

On 27 May, an earthquake registering 5.9 on the Richter scale struck Indonesia's central island of Java, which impacted five districts within Yogyakarta province and six within neighbouring Central Java province. The earthquake severely damaged infrastructure, in particular housing. The two worst-affected districts were Bantul in Yogyakarta and Klaten in Central Java. Some 5,744 people were killed and more than 45,000 injured. Over 350,000 houses were destroyed and 278,000 suffered lesser damage, affecting 2.7 million people altogether, and rendering some 1.5 million homeless. Total damages and losses were estimated at $3.1 billion. National response to the earthquake was decisive and swift, especially in the light of attention and resources already focused on Mt. Merapi Volcano, which had started erupting the previous month and was still a threat to the population living on its slopes.

The emergency earthquake response plan for Indonesia for 2006 sought $80.1 million.

Philippines

In 2006, between 25 September and 1 December, the Philippines was struck by three extreme typhoons, followed by a lower order typhoon on 9 December, triggering landslides, flash floods, mudslides and widespread flooding, and causing destruction and damage to homes, community buildings, communications, infrastructure, roads, bridges, agricultural crops and fishing farms. Typhoon Reming, also called Durian, which hit on 30 November was the most destructive, affecting the provinces of Albay, Catanduanes and Camarines Sur in southeastern Luzon Island. Significant damage was recorded also in Mindoro Oriental, Marinduque, Batangas, Laguna, Mindoro Occidental and Romblon provinces. Over a thousand people were killed, 180,000 houses totally destroyed, and as at 12 December, close to 8 million people were affected to varying degrees by the events. Cumulative economic losses were estimated at $300 million, while estimated damages arising from disasters prior to the four deadly typhoons amounted to $439 million. Overall estimated losses for the country for 2006 totalled $1.6 billion.

The humanitarian appeal for the Philippines typhoon, launched in December, sought $46 million to meet the urgent relief and recovery needs of the most vulnerable persons affected by the four typhoons for a twelve-month period through December 2007.

South Asia earthquake

In response to General Assembly resolution 60/13 [YUN 2005, p. 1034], the Secretary-General, in a May report [A/61/79-E/2006/67] on strengthening emergency relief, rehabilitation, reconstruction and prevention in the aftermath of the South Asian earthquake disaster in Pakistan, identified key lessons learned from the humanitarian response and provided an update on the ongoing relief and recovery efforts.

The Secretary-General recommended that UN humanitarian agencies and relevant international organizations and civil society groups should strengthen national and local capacities in support of the Government of Pakistan, including stand-by arrangements and in-country training programmes. Disaster relief and recovery assistance providers should make better use of local skills, expertise and materials when responding to disasters and take concrete steps to maximize the participation of beneficiaries in the planning and implementation of recovery programmes. The Government of Pakistan, other Governments in disaster-prone countries, major providers of military assets and UN humanitarian agencies should strengthen the understanding and implementation of principles and procedures for the use of military assets in disaster response. Relevant UN organizations, in support of Pakistan, should strengthen in-country disaster risk management capacity at all levels, including the community level. UN organizations and Member States should consider a designated resource mobilization tool for recovery, including transitional recovery strategies complete with costed transitional results matricies.

By resolution 2006/5 of 18 July, the Economic and Social Council took note of the Secretary-General's report (see p. 1055).

Tajikistan

On 29 July, two earthquakes registering 4.5 and 5.0 on the Richter scale struck Tajikistan, affecting at least five settlements in the Qumsangir District, as well as areas south of the capital Dushanbe and east of Shartuuz. Some 16,512 people were affected, with 19 injuries. The relatively low number of casualties was due to the stronger earthquake taking place during the daytime. However, the region's infrastructure was seriously damaged, including nine schools, four health centres and a central hospital, four transformers, 2 kilometres of electrical lines, a pumping station and 20 administrative buildings. Homeless families sought temporary shelter with family members or in makeshift shelters in the back yards of their homes. A total of 1,083 houses were fully damaged and more than 1,500 partially damaged. Total damages were estimated at $22 million.

The humanitarian appeal launched in September sought $1 million for a six-month period to provide 500 winter tents, material support for the reconstruction of 200 houses and the rehabilitation of schools.

Chernobyl aftermath

On 28 April, the General Assembly convened a special commemorative meeting to observe the twentieth anniversary of the Chernobyl nuclear power plant accident on 26 April 1986 [YUN 1986, p. 584], and to honour the memory of the victims. It was also an occasion to remember the heroism of the emergency workers who had responded in the days following the disaster; the deprivation of more than 330,000 residents of the area who had been evacuated from contaminated regions; and the suffering of millions of people living in affected areas, who, over the past two decades, had had to cope with the physical and psychological effects of the accident. The Assembly heard statements from several speakers on the suffering caused by the disaster and lessons learned, such as the importance of the safe use of nuclear power, providing the public with credible and transparent information in the event of any crisis, and ensuring broad public participation in decisions involving any potentially hazardous technology. Many of those addressing the meeting believed the best way for the international community to pay homage to those who had suffered from Chernobyl was to provide generous support to programmes designed to help traumatized communities regain self-sufficiency and affected families to resume normal, healthy lives.

On the same date, the General Assembly invited the UNDP Administrator, the UN Coordinator of International Cooperation on Chernobyl and the UNICEF Executive Director to make statements at the commemorative meeting (**decision 60/502 B**).

Communications. In a 23 March letter [A/60/734], the Russian Federation transmitted the text of the statement by Heads of State of the Commonwealth of Independent States (CIS), which was adopted on 26 August 2005 in Kazan, Russian Federation, and addressed to CIS member States and the world community in connection with the 20-year anniversary of the Chernobyl accident.

On 27 April [A/61/74], Belarus transmitted the summary of the international conference on the theme "Chernobyl 20 years after: strategy for recovery and sustainable development of the affected regions" (Minsk, 19-21 April).

Chapter IV

International trade, finance and transport

In 2006, world merchandise trade expanded at a rapid pace, with the volume of world exports growing an estimated 10 per cent, from 7.3 per cent in 2005. The strong growth of world trade, which was bolstered by broad-based import demand across a majority of economies, was, however, expected to moderate to about 7 per cent. The United States remained the major locomotive for world trade, with its demand accounting for some 13 per cent of the world total. Import demand in the European Union (EU) accelerated, reflecting a better-than-expected growth recovery in Western Europe, as well as in most developing countries and the economies in transition. Demand in the oil-exporting and mineral- and metal-exporting economies in Africa, Latin America and Western Asia grew at double digits, driven by strong consumption demand and demand for new production capacity and infrastructure. Demand for primary commodities also remained strong, owing in particular to the continued rapid pace of industrialization of China and India and other emerging developing countries.

The net transfers of financial resources from developing to developed countries increased from $533 billion in 2005 to $662 billion in 2006. The net transfers of financial resources from transition economies also increased in 2006, from $112 billion to $133 billion. The level of net private capital flows to developing countries and transition economies in 2006 were high in historical terms, although lower than that recorded during the previous year, with the financial-market turbulence in the second quarter of the year contributing to the moderation. Recognizing the urgent need to enhance the coherence, governance and consistency of the international monetary, financial and trading systems, the General Assembly noted that developing countries as a whole continued to experience a net outflow of financial resources and, in that regard, requested the Secretary-General to analyse the reasons and consequences and to report thereon. The Assembly underlined the importance of promoting international financial stability and sustainable growth, as well as national efforts to increase resilience to financial risk and measures to mitigate the impact of excessive volatility of short-term capital flows.

In April, the ninth high-level meeting between the Economic and Social Council and the Bretton Woods institutions (the World Bank Group and the International Monetary Fund), the World Trade Organization (WTO) and the United Nations Conference on Trade and Development (UNCTAD) discussed coherence, coordination and cooperation in the context of the implementation of the Monterrey Consensus, adopted at the 2002 International Conference on financing for Development, and of the 2005 World Summit Outcome. The Assembly decided to hold the Follow-up International Conference on Financing for Development to Review the Implementation of the Monterrey Consensus in the second half of 2008, and intergovernmental consultations in 2007.

In July, the multilateral trading system suffered a serious setback when a meeting of trade ministers from the G-6 countries (Australia, Brazil, India, Japan, the United States and the EU) failed to break the impasse in the five-year long Doha Round of international trade negotiations. The indefinite suspension of the Doha Round cast serious uncertainty on the status of the negotiations, which were expected to conclude in December, with a single undertaking among the 149 WTO members that would build on and deepen liberalization in WTO agreements and usher in a stronger focus on the development dimension. Expressing serious concern at the suspension of the negotiations and calling for their early resumption, the Assembly appealed to developed countries to demonstrate the flexibility and political will necessary to break the impasse and stressed that in order for the Doha Round to be concluded satisfactorily, the negotiations should result in the establishment of rules and disciplines in the area of agriculture.

At its twenty-third special session, the Trade and Development Board (TDB), the governing body of UNCTAD, conducted a mid-term review of the implementation of the São Paulo Consensus, adopted in 2004 by the eleventh session of the Conference (UNCTAD XI). TDB adopted an agreed outcome on the mid-term review, which, among other things, reaffirmed the work of UNCTAD three pillars of research and analysis, consensus building and technical cooperation. It also adopted agreed conclusions on the review of progress in the implementation of the Programme of Action for the Least Developed Countries 2001-2010; economic development in

Africa: doubling aid—making the "big push" work; and decisions on the review of UNCTAD technical cooperation activities and the timing of its 2007 session.

The International Trade Centre, operated jointly by UNCTAD and WTO, increased its delivery of technical assistance by 15 per cent to $25.3 million.

UNCTAD XI follow-up

Mid-term review

As decided in 2004 [YUN 2004, p. 956], the Trade and Development Board (TDB) of the United Nations Conference on Trade and Development (UNCTAD) conducted a mid-term review of UNCTAD XI at the first (Geneva, 8-12 May) and third (3-10 October) parts of its twenty-third special session. At the first part of the special session, it had before it a report by the UNCTAD secretariat [TD/B (S-XXIII)/2] on the implementation of the São Paulo Consensus, adopted in 2004 by the eleventh session of UNCTAD [YUN 2004, p. 954]. The report was structured along the lines of the main chapters of the Consensus, namely: development strategies in a globalizing world economy; building productive capacities and international competitiveness; assuring development gains from the international trading system and trade negotiations; and partnership for development. Two addenda to the report [TD/B(S-XXIII)/2/Add. 1, 2] contained a matrix detailing the mandates of the Consensus, the activities carried out by UNCTAD in implementing them, and a brief review of lessons learned.

The report concluded that implementation of the Consensus spanned an extensive programme of activities under the three pillars of research and analysis, intergovernmental processes and technical cooperation. UNCTAD reports, parliamentary documentation and studies covered strategic issues in the world economy, including the macroeconomic situation, trade, debt, poverty, investment, finance and interdependence. Its databases and analytical tools were used in the analyses and provided direct assistance to member States in relation to debt management, trade negotiations and trade procedures. While considerable interest had been generated in UNCTAD intergovernmental bodies, clear conclusions were necessary to serve as the basis for further secretariat work, including technical cooperation. Although technical cooperation funding had increased, some heavy demands were still being met through co-funding by beneficiaries. In the medium and longer terms, there was a need to nurture self-sustaining capacity, including human, regulatory and institutional frameworks. In that respect, various partnerships and other cooperative arrangements had proven to be valuable mechanisms, making the best use of resources and maximizing the impact of UNCTAD work.

TDB, at its May session, was unable to reach an agreed conclusion. Its report [TD/B(S-XXIII)/4] therefore included only the Chairperson's summary and summaries of formal statements.

At the third part of its special session in October, TDB adopted an agreed outcome of the mid-term review [TD/B(S-XXIII)/7 (Vol.1)], in which it requested UNCTAD to further cooperate and strengthen synergies and complementarities with other international organizations, and continue to analyse the impact of international policies and processes on the scope for implementing national development strategies, taking into account the need of all countries for appropriate balance between national policy space and international disciplines and commitments. UNCTAD should identify policy options and development opportunities and challenges in regional integration and South-South cooperation, debt and debt sustainability, and the financial services sector in developing countries. It should strengthen and disseminate its analytical and research work, in particular the *Trade and Development Report*, the *Least Developed Countries Report* and the annual report on *Economic Development in Africa*, and improve its outreach activities, including technical assistance. UNCTAD was encouraged to enhance its work on the Integrated Framework, strengthen national ownership of the process of incorporating trade into national development strategies, and examine the mutual benefits of transit transport agreements. TDB also requested UNCTAD to analyse the impact of foreign direct investment on the development of host countries, continue its work on corporate responsibility and positive corporate contributions, further its analysis of the transfer and diffusion of technology, strengthen the implementation of activities relating to its insurance programme, particularly for African countries and least developed countires (LDCs), as well as its work on science and technology for development, and integrate that work into its contribution to the follow-up and implementation of the relevant action lines relating to the 2005 World Summit [YUN 2005, p. 47] and the World Summit on the Information Society [ibid., p. 933]. As the UN system focal point for the integrated treatment of trade and development, TDB requested UNCTAD to continue its work on trade in goods, services and commodities.

In terms of its partnership for development, TDB asked the UNCTAD secretariat to ensure that all partnerships were operational, and invited donors to provide sustained resources to strengthen such partnerships. TDB reaffirmed that the work of UNCTAD three pillars (see p. 1142) should contribute directly to implementation of the Consensus and integrated follow-up to the outcomes of the major UN conferences and summits, as well as the accomplishment of the internationally agreed development goals, including the Millennium Development Goals (MDGs) [YUN 2000, p. 51]. UNCTAD should respond to the needs, concerns and priorities of its membership. Measures to strengthen the organization should take into account the need for it to remain responsive and accountable to member States, while maintaining its intellectual independence and rigour of research and analysis.

Regarding the way forward, TDB agreed that UNCTAD played an important role in forging consensus on development-related issues and in supporting the development of policy options that harnessed emerging opportunities, while assisting developing countries and countries with economies in transition in addressing the challenges of globalization. It should increase its support for South-South cooperation and regional and interregional initiatives. The Board also agreed that, to maximize the benefits of globalization for developing countries, UNCTAD should, among other actions, revitalize the global partnership for development by contributing to global consensus building on trade-and-development related issues, promote efforts to deliver on development-related commitments, and strengthen global structures to ensure stable, complementary and mutually reinforcing multilateral trading, monetary and financial systems that would advance the development of all countries. It should contribute to increasing coherence between national and development strategies and international monetary, financing and trading systems; contribute to the implementation of the outcome of the High-level Comprehensive Mid-term Review of the Programme of Action for the LDCs, 2001-2010 [YUN 2001, p. 770]; strengthen its work on good governance at the national and international levels; provide a forum for intergovernmental development-oriented dialogue on the range of policy options available; assist in ensuring that trade-related policies and processes, as well as efforts to resolve trade and development problems associated with commodity dependence, helped to maximize development gains and contribute to poverty eradication; strengthen South-South cooperation; and ensure that its technical cooperation was demand-driven, needs-based and tailored to countries and/or regions. In terms of UN reform, TDB agreed that UNCTAD intergovernmental machinery should contribute to the outcome of the UN reform process and address its implications for UNCTAD.

International trade

The *World Economic Situation and Prospects 2007* [Sales No.E.2007.II.C.2], jointly issued by UNCTAD and the UN Department of Economic and Social Affairs (DESA), stated that in 2006, world merchandise trade expanded at a rapid pace, characterized by a sizeable increase in the value of trade flows of both oil and non-oil commodities, mainly due to higher prices and a notable increase in the volume of trade flows of capital goods, driven by the recovery in global investment. The volume growth of world exports was estimated to be above 10 per cent in 2006, up from 7.3 per cent in 2005, while its value increased by some 16 per cent. The strong growth of world trade was bolstered by broad-based import demand across a majority of economies. Import demand for capital goods increased with the recovery of business investment in several economies. Demand for primary commodities remained strong, owing, in particular, to the pace of industrialization in China, India and other emerging developing countries.

The United States remained the major locomotive for world trade, with its import demand accounting for 13 per cent of the world total. In 2006, the total value of the United States imports increased by about 12 per cent, to an estimated $2.2 trillion. Import demand increased in all categories, but the demand for oil and raw materials surged the most, with oil alone increasing by $70 billion. In the aggregate, the import volume grew by an estimated 6 per cent in 2006, decelerating somewhat from the previous year, and below the average import growth of the last decade.

Import demand in the European Union (EU) accelerated, reflecting a better-than-expected growth recovery in Western Europe. By volume, import growth accelerated to nearly 10 per cent, following a continued boom in the new EU member States. In most developing economies and economies in transition, import demand also accelerated during 2006, owing to sustained economic growth in those economies, as well as continued improvement in the terms of trade for a large number of economies. Real import demand in the oil-exporting and mineral- and metal-exporting economies in Africa, Latin America and Western Asia grew by double digits, driven by strong consumption demand. Import demand in Asian economies was also strong, although most of them were facing some deterioration in their terms of trade.

Regarding exports, the report stated that the strength of world trade had also been broadly shared across countries, with developing countries as a group gaining market shares. Developed countries maintained, at 60 per cent, the largest share of the world export trade. United States exports increased by an estimated 12 per cent in value terms and by more than 10 per cent in volume terms. Exports of capital goods led the expansion, fuelled by the investment recovery in much of the world, especially in Europe and Japan. In Western Europe, export growth accelerated to almost 10 per cent in volume terms, with the United Kingdom and Germany posting the strongest gains, while Italy and Spain were sluggish, curbed by declining competitiveness as a consequence of rising production costs. Japan's export volume increased at about 9 per cent. Asia led developing-country export growth, with most economies in East Asia maintaining export growth revenue of between 10 to 20 per cent, and China exceeding 20 per cent. In Western Asia, export revenue increased substantially, driven mainly by the higher price of oil exports. The volume of African exports expanded, albeit at a lower pace than in 2005. In Latin America and the Caribbean, export revenues increased by some 20 per cent, boosted largely by the continued improvement in commodity prices, while the volume of exports increased by about 8 per cent. Among the economies in transition, export revenues in the resource-rich countries of the Commonwealth of Independent States (CIS) expanded further. The imbalances in trade accounts across regions, which had widened during 2006, accounted for a large proportion of global imbalances in current accounts.

The *Trade and Development Report, 2006* [Sales No. E.06.II.D.6] discussed, among other issues, commodity prices and terms of trade; export opportunities for developing countries, including market access conditions, non-tariff measures and import demand growth in developing countries' trading partners; and restrictions imposed by international agreements on policy autonomy, such as the Agreement on Trade-related Investment Measures, the Agreement on Subsidies and Countervailing Measures, and the Agreement on the Trade-related Aspects of Intellectual Property Rights, as well as industrial tariffs.

Multilateral trading system

Report of Secretary-General. In response to General Assembly resolution 60/184 [YUN 2005, p. 1042], the Secretary-General submitted an August report [A/61/272] on international trade and development, prepared in collaboration with UNCTAD. The report reviewed recent developments in international trade and the trading system, in particular the multilateral trade negotiations under the Doha programme since the Sixth Ministerial Conference of the World Trade Organization in December 2005 [YUN 2005, p. 1041], and their implications for developing countries.

The report recognized international trade as a powerful engine of growth, development and poverty eradication, particularly in developing countries, as seem from the increase in the share of exports of goods and services in gross domestic product (GDP). The rising proportion of trade in the GDP of developing countries was primarily due to their greater integration into the world economy and strong trade performance of dynamic developing countries, in South and East Asia and Latin America. In 2005, world merchandise exports recorded a robust growth of 13.8 per cent, or $10.3 trillion in value. Developing countries expanded their exports at a faster pace (21.3 per cent) than developed countries (9.2 per cent), to reach $3.7 trillion. As a result, their share in world trade exceeded 35 per cent for the first time since 1948. Over two-thirds of developing-country exports were composed of manufactured goods. Primary commodity exports remained important for Africa and the LDCs. Trade in services had become the new growth area for a number of countries, with a significant contribution to GDP and employment in both developed and developing countries. Notwithstanding that overall positive performance, many developing countries, especially in Africa, LDCs and small and vulnerable economies, remained marginalized from the expanding international trade. Their participation in international trade remained vulnerable to factors, such as structural problems related to the building of competitive supply capacities and diversification of production towards new and dynamic sectors of trade. Against that backdrop, all countries needed to participate actively in the multilateral trading system, shaping development-friendly rules and disciplines to take advantage of the opportunities emerging from the international trading system.

Negotiating frameworks

Suspension of Doha Round negotiations

As noted in the Secretary-General's August report on international trade and development [A/61/272], 2006 was a landmark year for the multilateral trading system and the World Trade

Organization (WTO). Following the Sixth WTO Ministerial Conference in 2005 [YUN 2005, p. 1041], the post-session negotiations focused on establishing modalities in agriculture and non-agriculture market access by 30 April 2006, so as to conclude the negotiations by the end of the year. Attention was given to issues considered essential for an across-the-board bargain, including domestic support and market access. Greater effort was called for from the United States to remove agricultural domestic support, including cotton, and from the EU to cut agricultural tariffs more substantially, as well as from large developing countries to make greater reductions in industrial tariffs and provide substantial offers in services. Trade ministers from Australia, Brazil, India, Japan, the United States and the EU met in July to break the impasse but were unsuccessful. The negotiations broke down on the issue of agriculture, as the gap between the levels of ambition of market access and domestic support remained too wide. The WTO Director-General proposed a suspension of the negotiations across all areas to review the situation, examine available options and review positions, which members generally supported. The Doha Round was thus effectively suspended without an indicative date for its resumption or a road map for the way forward. The suspension of the Round cast uncertainty over the prospects of the negotiations, with the timing and conditions for resumption unclear as that depended also on the renewal of the trade promotion authority of the United States President, which was due to expire in June 2007. The suspension of the Round called for careful reflection on the modus operandi of the trade negotiations and the definition and scope of the trade agenda.

The Secretary-General concluded that the suspension indicated that the Doha Round and the multilateral trading system had reached a critical phase, and confidence-building, political decisions and compromises, especially by major players, were needed to unlock the stalemate, particularly on agriculture, and move the process forward towards a timely conclusion. It was imperative that efforts be devoted to resuming negotiations at the earliest possible date, so that the development promises of Doha could be fully delivered, placing the needs and interests of developing countries at the heart of the negotiations and incorporating them in a balanced and development-oriented outcome, including in terms of enhanced and predictable market access and entry opportunities for developing country exports; improved support aimed at building trade-related infrastructure and competitive supply capacity; effective and operational special and differential treatment; and full provision of duty-free and quota-free market access for the LDCs.

UNCTAD consideration. On 27 September, during its fifty-third session (Geneva, 27 September–2 and 10 October), TDB conducted an in-depth review of development issues in the post-Doha work programme. It had before it an August UNCTAD secretariat note [TD/B/53/5], which reviewed developments in negotiations under the WTO Doha Work Programme since 2005, particularly the outcomes of the Sixth WTO Ministerial Conference and the impact of the suspension of negotiations in July, with particular focus on assuring development gains from the international trading system and trade negotiations.

In October [TD/B/53/L.6], the TDB President, in a summary of the discussions, reported on the implications of the suspension of the Doha negotiations and possible ways forward aimed at an early resumption of negotiations. There was agreement that the suspension did not call into question the relevance and importance of WTO as the central pillar of the international trading system, but created uncertainty regarding the timing of resumption, and the quality, ambition and balance of a possible final package. There remained a window of opportunity for concluding the round in 2007 if an early resumption took place between November 2006 and March 2007. Participants called for the earliest realistically possible resumption of the negotiations. While all countries had the responsibility to demonstrate renewed political will and additional flexibilities commensurate with their capacity to restart the round, the key players needed to play the leadership role.

It was stressed that the suspension should not lead to a lowering of ambitions in the development dimension of the round, especially increased market access and entry opportunities for developing countries, matched by "good policy space" and enhanced supply and production capacity, competitiveness and trade-related infrastructure. The view was expressed that flexibilities should not lead to protectionism and the special problems faced by net food-importing developing countries and preference-dependent countries needed to be addressed. The importance of achieving a comparable degree of ambition and balance in agriculture and non-agricultural market access was also stressed. Progress in other areas was also important, including special and differential treatment, implementation issues, trade facilitation, and rules, such as those relating to fishery subsidies and anti-dumping.

GENERAL ASSEMBLY ACTION

On 20 December [meeting 83], the General Assembly, on the recommendation of the Second (Economic and Financial) Committee [A/61/432], adopted **resolution 61/186** by recorded vote (129-2-52) [agenda item 51 *(a)*].

International trade and development

The General Assembly,

Recalling its resolutions 56/178 of 21 December 2001, 57/235 of 20 December 2002, 58/197 of 23 December 2003, 59/221 of 22 December 2004 and 60/184 of 22 December 2005 on international trade and development,

Recalling also the provisions of the United Nations Millennium Declaration pertaining to trade and related development issues, as well as the outcomes of the International Conference on Financing for Development, the World Summit on Sustainable Development and the 2005 World Summit Outcome,

Recalling further its resolution 60/265 of 30 June 2006 on follow-up to the development outcome of the 2005 World Summit, including the Millennium Development Goals and other internationally agreed development goals,

Reaffirming the value of multilateralism to the global trading system and the commitment to achieving a universal, rule-based, open, non-discriminatory and equitable multilateral trading system that contributes to growth, sustainable development and employment generation in all sectors, and emphasizing that bilateral and regional trading arrangements should contribute to the goals of the multilateral trading system,

Stressing the importance of open, transparent, inclusive, democratic and more orderly processes and procedures for the effective functioning of the multilateral trading system, including in the decision-making process, so as to enable developing countries to have their vital interests duly reflected in the outcome of trade negotiations,

Reiterating that development concerns form an integral part of the Doha Development Agenda, which places the needs and interests of developing and least developed countries at the heart of the Doha Work Programme,

Noting that agriculture lags behind the manufacturing sector in the process of establishment of multilateral disciplines and in the reduction of tariff and non-tariff barriers, and that, since most of the world's poor make their living from agriculture, the livelihood and standards of living of many of them are seriously jeopardized by the serious distortions in production and trade in agricultural products caused by the high levels of export subsidies, trade-distorting domestic support and protectionism by many developed countries,

Taking note of the report of the Trade and Development Board as well as the report of the Secretary-General,

1. *Expresses serious concern* at the indefinite suspension of the trade negotiations of the World Trade Organization and considers it a serious setback for the Doha Round, which places development at the heart of the multilateral trading system, and calls upon the developed countries to demonstrate the flexibility and political will necessary to break the current impasse in the negotiations, and also calls for an early resumption of negotiations adhering to the development imperatives and commitments of the Doha Ministerial Declaration, the decision of the General Council of the World Trade Organization of 1 August 2004 and the Hong Kong Ministerial Declaration;

2. *Stresses* that in order for the Doha Round to be concluded satisfactorily, the negotiations should result in the establishment of rules and disciplines in the area of agriculture, adhering to the development imperatives and commitments of the Doha Ministerial Declaration, the decision of the General Council of the World Trade Organization of 1 August 2004 and the Hong Kong Ministerial Declaration;

3. *Also stresses* the need for negotiations of the World Trade Organization in non-agricultural market access to live up to the development imperatives and commitments of the Doha Ministerial Declaration, the decision of the General Council of the World Trade Organization of 1 August 2004 and the Hong Kong Ministerial Declaration;

4. *Underlines* the fact that the increasing interdependence of national economies in a globalizing world and the emergence of rule-based regimes for international economic relations have meant that the space for national economic policy, that is, the scope for domestic policies, especially in the areas of trade, investment and industrial development, is now often framed by international disciplines, commitments and global market considerations, that it is for each Government to evaluate the trade-off between the benefits of accepting international rules and commitments and the constraints posed by the loss of policy space, and that it is particularly important for developing countries that all countries take into account the need for appropriate balance between national policy space and international disciplines and commitments;

5. *Expresses its deep concern* at the imposition of laws and other forms of coercive economic measures, including unilateral sanctions against developing countries, which undermine international law and the rules of the World Trade Organization and also severely threaten the freedom of trade and investment;

6. *Reaffirms* the commitments made at the Fourth Ministerial Conference of the World Trade Organization and at the Third United Nations Conference on the Least Developed Countries, in this regard calls upon developed countries that have not already done so to provide immediate, predictable, duty-free and quota-free market access on a lasting basis to all products originating from all least developed countries, also calls upon developing countries that are in a position to do so to extend duty-free and quota-free market access to exports of these countries, and in this context reaffirms the need to consider additional measures for progressive improvement in market access for least developed countries;

7. *Also reaffirms* the commitment to actively pursue the work programme of the World Trade Organization with respect to addressing the trade-related issues and concerns affecting the fuller integration of countries with small, vulnerable economies into the multilateral trading system in a manner commensurate with their special circumstances and in support of their efforts towards sustainable development, in accordance with paragraph 35 of the Doha Ministerial Declaration;

8. *Recognizes* the special problems and needs of the landlocked developing countries within a new global framework for transit transport cooperation for landlocked and transit developing countries, calls in this regard for the full and effective implementation of the Almaty Programme of Action, and stresses the need for the implementation of the São Paulo Consensus, in particular paragraphs 66 and 84 thereof, by the relevant international organizations and donors in a multistakeholder approach;

9. *Also recognizes* the need to ensure that the comparative advantage of developing countries is not undermined by any form of protectionism, including the arbitrary and abusive use of non-tariff measures, non-trade barriers and other standards to unfairly restrict the access of developing countries' products to developed countries' markets, reaffirms in this regard that developing countries should play an increasing role in the formulation of, inter alia, safety, environment and health standards, and recognizes the need to facilitate the increased and meaningful participation of the developing countries in the work of relevant international standard-setting organizations;

10. *Further recognizes* that South-South trade should be enhanced and that further market access should continue to stimulate South-South trade;

11. *Recognizes* the role that a successful conclusion of the ongoing third round of negotiations on the Global System of Trade Preferences among Developing Countries can play in South-South trade;

12. *Calls for* accelerating the work on the development-related mandate concerning the Agreement on Trade-related Aspects of Intellectual Property Rights in the Doha Ministerial Declaration, especially on issues of making intellectual property rules fully support the objectives of the Convention on Biological Diversity;

13. *Also calls for* facilitating the accession of all developing countries, in particular the least developed countries, and countries emerging from conflict that apply for membership in the World Trade Organization, bearing in mind paragraph 21 of resolution 55/182 of 20 December 2000 and subsequent developments, and calls for the effective and faithful application of the World Trade Organization guidelines on accession by the least developed countries;

14. *Emphasizes* the need for further work to foster greater coherence between the multilateral trading system and the international financial system, and invites the United Nations Conference on Trade and Development, in fulfilment of its mandate, to undertake the relevant policy analysis in those areas and to operationalize such work, including through its technical assistance activities;

15. *Invites* donors and beneficiary countries to implement the recommendations of the Task Force on Aid for Trade established by the Director-General of the World Trade Organization, which aims to support developing and least developed countries to build their supply and export capacities, including infrastructure and institutions development, and the need to increase their exports, and stresses in this regard the urgent need for its effective operationalization with sufficient additional, non-conditional and predictable funding;

16. *Welcomes* the effort being made for operationalization of the Enhanced Integrated Framework for Trade-related Technical Assistance to Least Developed Countries with increased additional, non-conditional and predictable financial resources to enhance the export and supply capacities of the least developed countries, and urges the development partners to increase their contributions to the Integrated Framework Trust Fund on a multi-year basis;

17. *Reiterates* the important role of the United Nations Conference on Trade and Development as the focal point within the United Nations system for the integrated treatment of trade and development and interrelated issues in the areas of finance, technology, investment and sustainable development, and calls upon the international community to work towards the strengthening of the Conference, to enable it to enhance its contribution in its three major pillars, namely, consensus-building, research and policy analysis, and technical assistance, especially through increased core resources of the Conference;

18. *Invites* the United Nations Conference on Trade and Development, in accordance with its mandate, to monitor and assess the evolution of the international trading system and of trends in international trade from a development perspective, and, in particular, to analyse issues of concern to developing countries, supporting them in building capacities to establish their own negotiating priorities and negotiate trade agreements, including under the Doha Work Programme;

19. *Reaffirms* the fundamental role that competition law and policy can play for sound economic development and the validity of the Set of Multilaterally Agreed Equitable Principles and Rules for the Control of Restrictive Business Practices, as well as the important and useful role that the United Nations Conference on Trade and Development plays in this field, and decides to convene in 2010, under the auspices of the United Nations Conference on Trade and Development, a sixth United Nations conference to review all aspects of the Set;

20. *Urges* donors to provide the United Nations Conference on Trade and Development with the increased resources necessary to deliver effective and demand-driven assistance to developing countries, as well as to enhance their contributions to the trust funds of the Integrated Framework for Trade-related Technical Assistance to Least Developed Countries and the Joint Integrated Technical Assistance Programme;

21. *Requests* the Secretary-General, in collaboration with the secretariat of the United Nations Conference on Trade and Development, to submit to the General Assembly at its sixty-second session a report on the implementation of the present resolution and on developments in the multilateral trading system, under the sub-item entitled "International trade and development" of the item entitled "Macroeconomic policy questions".

RECORDED VOTE ON RESOLUTION 61/186:

In favour: Afghanistan, Algeria, Angola, Antigua and Barbuda, Argentina, Armenia, Azerbaijan, Bahamas, Bahrain, Bangladesh, Barbados, Belarus, Belize, Benin, Bhutan, Bolivia, Botswana, Brazil, Brunei Darussalam, Burkina Faso, Burundi, Cambodia, Cameroon, Cape Verde, Central African Republic, Chile, China, Colombia, Comoros, Congo, Costa Rica, Côte d'Ivoire, Cuba, Democratic People's Republic of Korea, Democratic Republic of the Congo, Djibouti, Dominica, Dominican Republic, Ecuador, Egypt, El Salvador, Eritrea, Ethiopia, Fiji, Gabon, Gambia, Ghana, Grenada, Guatemala, Guinea, Guinea-Bissau, Guyana, Haiti, Honduras, India, Indonesia, Iran, Iraq, Jamaica, Jordan, Kazakhstan, Kenya, Kuwait, Kyrgyzstan, Lao People's Democratic Republic, Lebanon, Lesotho, Liberia, Libyan Arab Jamahiriya, Madagascar, Malawi, Malaysia, Maldives, Mali, Mauritania, Mauritius, Micronesia, Mongolia, Morocco, Mozambique, Myanmar, Namibia, Nepal, Nicaragua, Niger, Nigeria, Oman, Pakistan, Panama, Papua New Guinea, Paraguay, Peru, Philippines, Qatar, Saint Kitts and Nevis, Saint Lucia, Saint Vincent and the Grenadines, Samoa, Sao Tome and Principe, Saudi Arabia, Senegal, Sierra Leone, Singapore, Solomon Islands, Somalia, South Africa, Sri Lanka, Sudan, Suriname, Swaziland, Syrian Arab Republic, Thailand, Timor-Leste, Togo, Tonga, Trinidad and Tobago, Tunisia, Turkmenistan, Uganda, United Arab Emirates, United Republic of Tanzania, Uruguay, Uzbekistan, Vanuatu, Venezuela, Viet Nam, Yemen, Zambia, Zimbabwe.

Against: Moldova, United States of America.

Abstaining: Albania, Andorra, Australia, Austria, Belgium, Bulgaria, Canada, Croatia, Cyprus, Czech Republic, Denmark, Estonia, Finland, France, Georgia, Germany, Greece, Hungary, Iceland, Ireland, Israel, Italy, Japan, Latvia, Liechtenstein, Lithuania, Luxembourg, Malta, Marshall Islands, Mexico, Monaco, Montenegro, Netherlands, New Zealand, Norway, Palau, Poland, Portugal, Republic of Korea, Romania, Russian Federation, San Marino, Serbia, Slovakia, Slovenia, Spain, Sweden, Switzerland, The former Yugoslav Republic of Macedonia, Turkey, Ukraine, United Kingdom.

Trade policy

Trade in goods and services, and commodities

The Commission on Trade in Goods and Services, and Commodities, at its tenth session (Geneva, 6-10 February) [TD/B/COM.1/80], had before it the following documentation: an UNCTAD secretariat note on commodity policies for development: a new framework for the fight against poverty [TD/B/COM.1/75]; a report of the expert meeting on dynamic and new sectors of world trade [TD/B/COM.1/EM.28/5]; a report of the expert meeting on methodologies, classifications, quantifications and development impacts on non-tariff barriers [TD/B/COM.1/EM.27/3]; an UNCTAD secretariat note on market access, market entry and competitiveness [TD/B/COM.1/76]; and a report of the expert meeting on distribution services [TD/B/COM.1/EM.29/3]. Also before the Commission were UNCTAD secretariat notes on trade in services and development implications [TD/B/COM.1/77], trade, environment and development [TD/B/COM.1/70] and a progress report on the implementation of the Commission's agreed conclusions and recommendations, including post-Doha follow-up [TD/B/COM.1/78].

The Commission's report contained the Chairman's summary of the high-level event on climbing the trade and development ladder: trade and development index (TDI). Participants welcomed UNCTAD efforts in elaborating the TDI and emphasized its utility as a monitoring and policy tool. They requested UNCTAD to use the TDI framework to undertake country-level and thematic work, and prepare a study on progress in the implementation of the Brussels Programme of Action for LDCs for the Decade 2001-2010 [YUN 2001, p. 770], which should be made available to the Mid-Term Review of that Programme in September (see p. 1109). Participants also welcomed the UNCTAD Secretary-General's intention to constitute an Advisory Board to guide future work on TDI, and took note of the key theme of the 2006 issue of the UNCTAD report *Developing Countries in International Trade*, namely institutions for trade and development.

On commodities and development, participants recognized that the development of the commodity sector was a prerequisite for progress in poverty reduction and realizing the benefits of globalization in developing countries, particularly LDCs and small island developing States. They urged developing country Governments to facilitate regional commodity trade and remove barriers to trade resulting from deficiencies in physical, administrative and commercial infrastructure. Strategic commodity-related information and market intelligence were seen as key factors to improving competitiveness and enhancing the functioning of commodity sectors.

Regarding non-tariff barriers (NTBs), UNCTAD was requested to improve its classification of those barriers by identifying and adding new ones. As a longer-term agenda, it should focus on better defining, classifying and quantifying NTBs, in cooperation with all stakeholders. In the short-term, it should help developing countries to build their capacities to deal with NTB-related negotiating issues. In terms of trade in services and development implications, the report stressed the need for an assessment of the impact of liberalization to assist developing countries in formulating their policy decisions in areas that required further reform, identify actions needed to support the development of sectors; and devise an appropriate negotiating strategy. In the broader development discourse, it was important to analyse how the multilateral trading system addressed issues like striking the balance between efficiency and equity; minimizing the social negative impact of globalization; recognizing policy space; deepening coherence; and enhancing synergies between different policies, countries and institutions. Participants regarded the trade negotiations of the BioFuels Initiative as particularly timely and appropriate, as developing countries wishing to produce and export biofuels required access to information, know-how and technical assistance. The appropriateness of developing partnerships and synergy with other institutions and initiatives was stressed in order to maximize the Initiative's results.

On 10 February, the Commission took note of the reports of the expert meetings and the secretariat's progress report on the implementation of the agreed conclusions and recommendations of the Commission on its ninth (2005) session [YUN 2005, p. 1045], including post-Doha follow-up.

At its thirty-eighth executive session (Geneva, 20 April) [A/61/15], TDB took note of the Commission's report and approved the provisional agenda for its eleventh (2007) session, as well as the topic of expert meetings for 2006.

Subsidiary bodies. In 2006, a number of expert meetings took place, all in Geneva, on issues to be considered by the Commission.

The Ad Hoc Expert Meeting on Logistics Services (13 July) [TD/B/COM.1/AHM.1/3] had before it a note on the subject [TD/B/COM.1/AHM.1/2], which discussed the main features of the logistics services market; international trade in logistics services; and benefits, preconditions to successful liberalization and concerns to be addressed. In its policy conclusions, the Meeting highlighted government policies that acted as barriers to efficient logistics services, primarily customs inefficiencies, including excessive paperwork, extensive formalities, limits on the size and value of shipments, and limited hours of services. While it was important for countries to have access to high-quality and efficient logistics services, it was also important to determine how developing countries could maximize their participation in and partake of the benefits of liberalization of those services. The importance of building regulatory frameworks, including competition rules and proper sequencing for developing countries to benefit fully from the liberalization of logistics services, was reiterated. The Meeting put forward a number of issues for UNCTAD future work, including: analysing how developing countries could maximize their participation in and partake of the benefits of liberalization of logistics services, in terms of both users and suppliers of those services; identifying policy options and the regulatory framework for ensuring the quality and availability of logistics services and the proper sequencing of reforms for developing countries to benefit fully from their liberalization; further exploring the linkages between trade facilitation and liberalization of logistics services; analysing the operation of oligopolies in the logistics services sector and related development impacts; examining the effects of anti-competitive practices in the logistics-related services on developing countries' integration into world trade and their development opportunities; and providing technical assistance and capacity building to developing countries, particularly landlocked and least developed countries.

The Expert Meeting on Universal Access to Services (14-16 November) [TD/B/COM.1/EM.30/3] had before it an UNCTAD secretariat note on the subject [TD/B/COM.1/EM.30/2]. While addressing universal access on a cross-cutting basis, the Meeting focused on water and sanitation, health, education and telecommunications.

The Meeting stressed the need to recognize the primacy of the State's role in ensuring universal access to essential services, either directly or through targeted policies at the national and subnational levels. Universal access objectives needed to reflect national development objectives and be forward looking, with poverty being a policy priority. However, merely establishing national universal access policies was not sufficient. Appropriate regulations and institutions were also required, and universal access needed to be designed and applied using nationally agreed public services principles to ensure that broad-based economic and social development goals were advanced at the national level, including by local actors and small providers/operators. The Meeting recommended that UNCTAD should strengthen its work on universal access to services. With a view to achieving the MDGs, it should support developing countries in their assessment of the role of the State, privatization and trade liberalization in essential services; work to achieve a better understanding of the definition, scope, classification and coverage of essential services; analyse best practices and appropriate policies to promote access to universal services; work on developing countries' policies and regulations; identify ways of overcoming challenges facing those countries in their access to essential services; identify ways to improve infrastructure and policy frameworks for essential services providers in developing countries; analyse regulatory and competition-related issues; contribute to international, regional and national efforts to improve statistical data collection and availability; and assist developing countries in improving their understanding of the linkages between the General Agreement on Trade in Services negotiations and universal access to services, including through studies and expert meetings analysing issues related to domestic regulation and subsidies.

The Expert Meeting on the Participation of Developing Countries in New and Dynamic Sectors of World Trade: Review of the Energy Sector (29 November–1 December) [TD/B/COM.1/EM.31/3] had before it an UNCTAD secretariat note on the subject [TD/B/COM.1/EM.31/2], which focused on the adjustment to higher and more volatile oil prices and opportunities offered by biofuels production and exports. The Meeting noted that dramatic changes had taken place in world energy markets, the implications of which were potentially serious for economic growth and development, particularly for the LDCs and Africa. However, the new situation also offered opportunities for developing countries in terms of accessing new markets and reducing poverty. The Meeting recommended a broad set of actions, including a world energy policy that fostered cooperation and dialogue between producers and consumers and the creation of an oil stabilization fund to operate during times of crisis and an African oil fund to help mitigate the effects of high oil prices on poor oil-importing African countries. Regarding biofuels, the Meeting recommended that, before putting in place national biofuel strategies, countries should decide whether biofuel production was intended for transportation fuel security or for broader energy replacement and the economic and environmental impacts. A major preoccupation addressed during the Meeting was that rapid growth in demand for energy feedstocks, such as corn, sugar cane and oil beans, could divert too much cropland to fuel crops and imperil food security. A related issue was the impact of rising prices of agricultural commodities, due to their use as energy feedstocks, on different segments of the population in developing countries. Increased international trade in biofuels and related feedstocks provided win-win opportunities to all countries, and a more liberal trade regime would greatly contribute to the achievement of the economic, energy efficiency, environmental and social goals through enhanced biofuels production and use. Concerning oil and gas in Africa and the LDCs, a key issue was how to invest the windfall gains from high oil prices to secure future development requirements. The Meeting identified five critical areas where there was need for building rigorous plans for developing the energy sector, namely: analysing trends in the changing oil sector to catalyse development and reduce poverty; developing policies to assist importers in the context of high and volatile prices; encouraging the development-oriented use of windfall gains; avoiding "resource curse" impacts by increasing local content and developing linkages with other sectors; and building a level playing field in the production and trade of biofuels by removing trade obstacles, barriers and subsidies. Participants urged UNCTAD to strengthen its work in energy, trade and sustainable development, with emphasis on monitoring and analysing the trade and development implications of the changing energy economy and national and international energy policies; fostering policy dialogue on energy security, sustainable development and poverty reduction in developing countries; and assisting energy-exporting developing countries in formulating policies and strategies for the development-oriented use of windfall gains. The Meeting recommended that energy, trade and sustainable development issues be kept high on the agenda of UNCTAD XII, to be held in Ghana in 2008. It also called for the further enhancement of institutional arrangements within UNCTAD in dealing with energy issues, including biofuels.

The Expert Meeting on Enabling Small Commodity Producers and Processors in Developing Countries to Reach Global Market (11-13 December) [TD/B/COM.1/EM.32/3] had before it an UNCTAD secretariat note on the subject [TD/B/COM.1/EM.32/2]. The Meeting considered solutions and challenges to the integration into the supply chains of those commodity sectors in poor developing countries. The Meeting recommended that the Commission consider at its 2007 session proposals with regard to UNCTAD future work on enabling small commodity producers and processors in developing countries to reach global markets. UNCTAD was urged to remain one of the international organizations that reminded the world about the increasing difficulties that small commodity producers faced in reaching global markets, especially since the liberalization of most commodity sectors. It should analyse cost compliance and assess certification issues so that additional barriers to trade could be avoided. UNCTAD was encouraged to develop its programme further to meet country-specific needs in capacity-building and technical cooperation in finance and risk management. Given the close relationship between the MDGs relating to poverty reduction and the development of rural productivity and trade, the

Meeting stressed the importance of establishing an international task force on commodities. It also emphasized the role of the international community in addressing trade policies to create a fair and level playing field and in enhancing development cooperation.

Interdependence and global economic issues

TDB, in October [TD/B/3/8], considered interdependence and global economic issues from a trade and development perspective: global partnership and national policies for development. For its consideration of the topic, the Board had before it the *Trade and Development Report, 2006* [Sales No. E.06.II.D.6]. In presenting the *Report*, the UNCTAD Secretary-General said that he agreed with the assertion of the WTO Director-General that, while trade could lead to development and poverty alleviation, it was only one ingredient in a policy mix that should include effective institutions and quality of governance. Acknowledging that trade liberalization would not be sufficient to achieve the economic growth and development needed to reduce poverty, and that the MDG targets for 2015 could only be met if many developing countries grew at a faster rate, the Secretary-General said that economic policies should be devised to enable the developing countries acquire the productive and trade capacities for coping with global economic interdependence. The last 15 years of traditional trade reforms had resulted in both positive and negative outcomes in terms of GDP and employment. Countries that had undertaken cautious reforms and applied proactive industrial policies had enjoyed remarkable success. Developing countries that had diversified their industrial base and trade pattern had performed better than those that relied mainly on commodities. Recent windfall gains from increased commodity prices were not a basis for sustained development. Sound economic management and institutions remained crucial for economic growth, together with proactive policies. While policies that had succeeded in some countries might not be easily adopted in others, there were common principles applicable to all.

Trade promotion and facilitation

In 2006, UN bodies maintained assistance to developing countries and transition economies in promoting their exports and facilitating their integration into the multilateral trading system. The main originator of technical cooperation projects in that area was the International Trade Centre, under the joint sponsorship of UNCTAD and WTO.

International Trade Centre

In 2006, the UNCTAD/WTO International Trade Centre (ITC) increased its delivery of technical assistance by 15 per cent to $25.3 million (excluding support costs), from $22.1 million in 2005 [ITC/AG/(XL)/210]. Assistance was provided to 153 countries under ITC global, regional and country track. Africa remained the main recipient of ITC assistance, with the share of total resources increasing from 33 to 37 per cent, followed by Asia and the Pacific, 30 per cent, Eastern Europe and the Commonwealth of Independent States, 9 per cent, Latin America and the Caribbean, 7 per cent and the Arab States, 5 per cent. The rest, 12 per cent, went to global programmes. The share of assistance going to LDCs also increased, from 37 to 40 per cent of total ITC delivery.

ITC provided targeted assistance to exporting enterprises under country programmes or at the requests of its clients. Enterprises received support in developing export plans, improving product quality and packaging, obtaining greater access to trade finance, acquiring market analysis skills, making more efficient use of information and communication technology, and establishing direct contact with buyers. To develop the capacity of trade service providers to support businesses, ITC helped to build trade capacity in several trade support institutions, including the development of market analysis and trade information management skills, export strategy and implementation skills, and skills for bringing the enterprise to the market. ITC also supported policy-makers in facilitating the export business environment and assisted a growing number of countries in developing national export strategies that were compatible with national planning frameworks.

A new ITC senior management team was constituted. One of its first challenges was to initiate a change management process, with a view to steering the organization to greater heights and making it a centre of technical excellence. A number of thematic working groups were set up to review the main findings and recommendations of the ITC external evaluation, which was sponsored by a group of donors, and to make suggestions for implementing its recommendations. The groups reviewed the ITC mission and vision, results-based management and the relationship with its parent bodies, ITC tools and services, responses to the MDGs and its country focus and performance standards. The results formed the basis for the establishment of a new business model.

JAG action. The ITC Joint Advisory Group (JAG), at its thirty-ninth session (Geneva, 24-28

April) [ITC/AG(XXXIX)/208], considered the reports on ITC 2005 activities [YUN 2005, p. 1049] and on its technical cooperation projects in 2005 [ITC/AG(XXXIX)/206/Add.1], and the report of the Consultative Committee of the ITC Global Trust Fund [ITC/AG(XXXIX)/207].

The Group also considered the 2008-2009 Strategic Framework and the external evaluation of ITC. Statements were made by the WTO Director-General, the UNCTAD Secretary-General and the ITC Executive Director. The Group took note of the report of the Consultative Committee.

Pledges of trust fund contributions to ITC were announced by Canada, China, Denmark, France, Germany, India, Ireland, Italy, Japan, the Netherlands, Norway, Sweden, Switzerland, the United Kingdom and the European Commission.

In terms of the external evaluation of ITC, the Group noted that the evaluation had been positive, with beneficiaries and development partners perceiving ITC as possessing the capacity, neutrality and impartiality to support their integration into the trading system and their trade development goals. ITC comparative advantage rested on its technical expertise in trade development, its convening power, experience in networking and entrepreneurial and responsive approach. The evaluation contained 34 strategic and operational recommendations, the majority of which were addressed to ITC and seven key ones to its stakeholders. Recommendations to ITC called for it to increase the scale of its operations with a greater contribution to the MDGs, and creation of a reporting and monitoring system. ITC should assess needs more systematically, better measure the costs of producing its tools, and monitor their use to ensure relevance and cost-effectiveness. It should also carry forward its results-based management efforts as a priority. The recommendations to donor Governments called for increased harmonization of financial support to reduce transaction costs and improve overall coherence and effectiveness, and for increasing multi-year commitments to reduce the adverse effects of late arrival of funds.

The Group supported the recommendations on increased harmonization of financial support, including multi-year commitments, but stressed that those commitments should not restrict the flexibility of donors to respond to evolving needs. The Group also noted that the Evaluation Report was an important tool for the ITC new senior management to reflect how the Centre could evolve and that the management response already provided a clear direction on the way forward.

ITC administrative arrangements

The General Assembly, in **resolution 61/253 A** of 22 December (see p. 1612), approved revised appropriations for the 2006-2007 biennium for ITC in the amount of $26,901,500.

Enterprise, business facilitation and development

The Commission on Enterprise, Business Facilitation and Development, at its tenth session (Geneva, 21-24 February) [TD/B/COM.3/76], considered UNCTAD secretariat notes on efficient transport and trade facilitation to improve participation by developing countries in international trade [TD/B/COM.3/72]; progress reports on the implementation of the Commission's agreed recommendations at its ninth session [YUN 2005, p. 1050]; promoting transnational corporations small and medium-sized enterprises (TNC-SME) linkages to enhance the productive capacity of developing countries' firms: a policy perspective [TD/B/COM.3/75]; trade in services and development implications [TD/B/COM.1/77]; efficient transport and trade facilitation to improve participation by developing countries in international trade [TD/B/COM.3/80]; information and communication technology (ICT) and e-business for development [TD/B/COM.3/81]; and using ICTs to achieve growth and development [TD/B/COM.3/EM.29/2].

In its agreed recommendations on improving the competitiveness of SMEs through enhancing productive capacity, the Commission requested the UNCTAD secretariat to continue exploring successful policies to promote enterprise development in developing countries, including export orientation and supply side policies, so as to build and maintain their ability to compete successfully in international markets and create new and dynamic capabilities to facilitate internal linkages between export-led growth and the domestic economy. UNCTAD should undertake research and policy analysis and provide technical assistance and policy advice reflecting development needs and priorities of recipient countries.

In its recommendation on efficient transport and trade facilitation, the Commission asked UNCTAD to monitor and analyse issues and developments relating to international transport and trade facilitation and their implications for developing countries; compare developing countries' practices with international transport and trade facilitation standards; undertake research and assist developing countries to participate in trade facilitation and transport and logistics services negotiating processes; provide technical assistance and capacity-building activities in transport and trade facilitation; and cooperate with other international, intergovernmental and non-governmental organizations and other cooperative mechanisms in carrying out the secretariat's work programme in international transport and trade facilitation.

On ICT and e-business strategies for development, the Commission asked UNCTAD to undertake research and policy-oriented analytical work on the implications for economic development of the different aspects of ICT and e-business; continue work on ICT measurement; provide a forum for international discussion and exchange of experiences on ICTs, e-business, their applications to promote trade and development and policies aimed at creating an enabling environment for the information economy; contribute to capacity-building in technology and ICTs for development; further explore the potential benefit of free and open source software for developing countries; support the implementation and follow-up to the World Summit on the Information Society [YUN 2005, p. 933]; and ensure the development perspective of the Information Economy Report and include it in the Commission's agenda.

In April [A/61/15], TDB took note of the Commission's report, approved the provisional agenda for its eleventh (2007) session, as well as the topics of expert meetings for 2006.

Subsidiary bodies. A number of expert meetings were held in Geneva during the year. The Expert Meeting on ICT Solutions to Facilitate Trade at Border Crossings and Ports (16-18 October) [TD/B/COM.3/EM.27/3] had before it an UNCTAD secretariat note on the subject [TD/B/COM.3/EM.27/2]. The meeting discussed ICTs in global trade and transport, rules and standards and their implementation, ICTs in ports and international transport and at customs and border crossings and proposed strategies for a way forward.

The report noted that a key challenge in introducing ICT in transport and trade was promoting trade, while at the same time protecting a country's revenue and security interests. The right sequencing during the introduction of trade facilitation measures was fundamental, given the functional linkages among them. One particular obstacle was the legal recognition of electronic documents. The harmonization and alignment of national legislation and regulations with international rules and standards were essential for any national trade facilitation strategy. Global operability was another key issue for further advances in the introduction and use of ICTs. Another obstacle was the legal recognition of electronic alternatives to traditional paper documents.

The Expert Meeting on Best Practices and Policy Options in the Promotion of SME-TNC Business Linkages (6-8 November) [TD/B/COM.3/EM.28/3] had before it an UNCTAD secretariat note on developing business linkages [TD/B/COM.3/EM.28/2]. The Meeting focused on the development and effective implementation of those linkages and identified key success factors to address the constraints faced by developing countries, particularly the LDCs. It also considered the role of UNCTAD and donors in technical assistance programmes based on partnerships between TNCs and SMEs. Experts agreed that there was a need for greater cooperation at policy and implementation levels to provide an environment conducive for the development of domestic enterprises, and that a systematic policy approach to linkage building in developing countries was necessary, including improving the general investment environment and specific development policies. Among the main lessons learned from successful business linkages were the need to make them an important component of building productive capacities, and part of the Aid for Trade Initiative so as to create a coherent policy framework. Linkage programmes should be designed to strengthen the absorptive capacities of domestic enterprises and address financing requirements for SME upgrading. Experts requested UNCTAD to continue its policy, research and technical assistance activities and participate in the Aid for Trade Initiative. It should also generate a coordinating mechanism and initiate a business linkages networking mechanism.

The Expert Meeting in Support of the Implementation and Follow-up of the World Summit on the Information Society: using ICTs to Achieve Growth and Development (4-5 December) [TD/B/COM.3/EM.29/3] had before it an UNCTAD secretariat note on the subject [TD/B/COM.3/EM.29/2]. The Meeting discussed the impact of ICTs on productivity and growth and on business sectors, ICTs and international trade in goods and services, and ICTs, labour markets and employment, and society. Experts stressed that ICTs were part of a bigger picture for economic and social development, and the conditions under which they could have a positive impact on the economy were becoming clear. ICT application and use, facilitated by the right enabling conditions, were key in that regard. ICT-enabled offshoring of services was a potential source of growth and jobs in the providing countries and productivity and competitiveness in client countries. ICT policies were dynamic tools that needed to be continuously updated to keep up with national, international and technological developments. It was important for UNCTAD to continue its work and define a concrete, strategic road map for its contribution to the implementation and follow-up of the World Summit on the Information Society outcomes.

Commodities

The UNCTAD/DESA report *World Economic Situation and Prospects 2007* [Sales No.E.07.II.C.2] stated that non-oil primary commodity prices generally followed an upward trend from January to May 2006, with prices increasing on average by 22 per cent in United States dollar terms and 19 per cent in Special Drawing Rights (SDRs). From May onwards, however, the situation changed as the composite price fell by 4 per cent in dollar terms and by 3 per cent in SDR terms. The bulk of the reversal took place in May and June, when the turmoil in international financial and commodity markets resulted in a decrease in composite non-oil commodity prices by 5 per cent in dollar terms (4 per cent in SDR terms). The rise in prices over the first ten months of 2006 was mainly driven by the boom in metal and mineral prices (more than 40 per cent), as well as increases in the prices of some vegetable oilseeds. The gradual rise of international crude oil prices and the slight strengthening of world economic growth during the year were the most important factors behind the non-oil commodity price increases, with prices of substitutes for oil-based products taking off as a result. Rapidly expanding Chinese demand was a particularly important factor for many commodities. Food prices rose by 12 per cent from January to May, then fell by 7 per cent from May to October. Prices of agricultural raw materials rose by 16.5 per cent in the first six months of the year, but registered a 15 per cent decline between June and October. The prices for metals and minerals soared by about 45 per cent.

The price of oil price was marked by both strong gains and considerable volatility, reaching a record high of nearly $80 per barrel (pb) in August, following the shutdown of the Prudhoe Bay field in Alaska for pipeline repairs and the heightened uncertainty about the Iranian nuclear issue. By late October, as growth in oil demand showed signs of moderating and supply-side fears calmed, the price dropped by about 25 per cent to below $60 pb. In general, tight worldwide oil production and refinery capacity, coupled with a solid global oil demand, were the fundamental factors behind the uptrend in oil prices, while geopolitical tensions were among the major factors driving volatility.

Report of Secretary-General. As requested by the General Assembly in resolution 59/224 [YUN 2004, p. 969], the Secretary-General submitted a July report on world commodity trends and prospects [A/61/202]. The report provided an overview of developments in commodity markets over the past few years, with an emphasis on the factors underlying the recent commodity price boom and its effects on commodity exporting developing countries, as well as the main factors behind the price increases, including the growing importance of South-South trade.

According to the report, since 2003, international commodity prices had recovered considerably. As most developing countries depended on commodity exports, the price rise had been, on average, a positive factor for economic growth in those countries. The impact, however, measured by the change in the countries' terms of trade and the portion of the increased revenues retained in the economy, varied widely. While it was unlikely that the price increases constituted a break with the declining long-term trend in real prices, they provided an opportunity for developing countries to address urgent development and other challenges, such as distributing the benefits to disadvantaged segments of society, reducing poverty and settling on a sustainable growth path.

The suspension of the Doha round of trade negotiations (see p. 1111) meant that expected improvements in the functioning of world markets for agricultural products and supportive measures for developing countries, including through the Aid for Trade mechanism, were unlikely to materialize in the short term. Accordingly, the development of the commodity sector would rely fundamentally on commodity-specific policies at the international, regional and national levels. Such policies should target LDC country producers and those in other developing countries that had been left out of the development process. In the past few years, trade among developing countries had provided almost all the dynamic stimulus to commodity markets. Growing Asian demand for commodities was partly behind the expansion of South-South trade, as well as the sustained rise in commodity prices. The Aid for Trade mechanism should be pursued independently of developments in the Doha round and not be considered solely as a means to help countries adjust to trade liberalization.

Regarding the implementation of resolution 59/224, the intergovernmental organizations identified in the resolution continued to give priority to commodity issues in their work programmes. The International Task Force on Commodities launched at UNCTAD XI [YUN 2004, p. 954] had, regrettably, not entered into force, owing to the absence of financial support from Member States.

GENERAL ASSEMBLY ACTION

On 20 December [meeting 83], the General Assembly, on the recommendation of the Second Committee [A/61/420/Add.4], adopted resolution **61/190** without vote [agenda item 51 *(d)*].

Commodities

The General Assembly,

Recalling its resolution 59/224 of 22 December 2004, and stressing the urgent need to ensure its full implementation,

Recalling also the United Nations Millennium Declaration adopted by Heads of State and Government on 8 September 2000, the 2005 World Summit Outcome adopted on 16 September 2005 and its resolution 60/265 of 30 June 2006 on the follow-up to the development outcome of the 2005 World Summit, including the Millennium Development Goals, and the other internationally agreed development goals,

Recalling further the International Conference on Financing for Development and its outcome,

Recalling the Plan of Implementation of the World Summit on Sustainable Development,

Recalling also the Programme of Action for the Least Developed Countries for the Decade 2001-2010 and the outcome of the high-level meeting of the sixty-first session of the General Assembly on the midterm comprehensive global review of the implementation of the Programme of Action for the Least Developed Countries for the Decade 2001-2010, held in New York on 18 and 19 September 2006, and taking note of the Least Developed Countries Report, 2004,

Taking note of the Arusha Declaration and Plan of Action on African Commodities adopted at the African Union Conference of Ministers of Trade on Commodities, held in Arusha, United Republic of Tanzania, from 21 to 23 November 2005, and endorsed by the Executive Council of the African Union at its eighth ordinary session, held in Khartoum from 16 to 21 January 2006,

Taking note also of the reports of the Trade and Development Board on its fifty-third session, held in Geneva from 27 September to 2 October and on 10 October 2006, and its twenty-third special session, held in Geneva from 8 to 11 May, from 12 to 15 June and from 3 to 10 October 2006,

Recognizing that many developing countries are highly dependent on primary commodities as their principal source of export revenues, employment, income-generation and domestic savings, and as the driving force of investment, economic growth and social development,

Deeply concerned that, despite the recent increase in some commodity prices, the causes underlying the declining price trend in other commodities have not been addressed, including supply capacity problems, difficulties with effective participation in value chains and lack of diversification of their production and export base, all of which prevent many developing countries from obtaining full benefits from the current positive conditions,

Recognizing that trade in commodities is a fundamental component of international trade,

Taking note of the targets set out in the Rome Declaration on World Food Security and the Plan of Action of the World Food Summit and the outcome document of the World Food Summit: five years later, which reaffirms the pledge to end hunger and poverty,

1. *Reiterates* the importance of maximizing the contribution of the commodity sector to sustained economic growth and sustainable development, while continuing with diversification efforts in commodity-dependent developing countries;

2. *Recalls* the potential of regional integration and cooperation to improve the effectiveness of traditional commodity sectors and support diversification efforts;

3. *Recognizes* that developed countries account for two thirds of non-fuel commodity imports, and expresses the urgent need for supportive international policies and measures to improve the functioning of the commodity markets through efficient and transparent mechanisms, including commodity exchanges;

4. *Reiterates* the importance of expanded South-South trade and investment in commodities;

5. *Emphasizes* the need for efforts by the developing countries that are heavily dependent on primary commodities to continue to promote a domestic policy and an institutional environment that encourage diversification and liberalization of the trade and export sectors and enhance competitiveness;

6. *Reaffirms* that each country has primary responsibility for its own economic and social development, and recognizes that an effective enabling environment at the national and international levels entails, inter alia, a sound macroeconomic framework, competitive markets, clearly defined property rights, an attractive investment climate, good governance, the absence of corruption and well-designed regulatory policies that protect the public interest and generate public confidence in market operations;

7. *Also reaffirms* the commitments made in the Doha Ministerial Declaration, the Hong Kong Ministerial Declaration and the decision of the General Council of the World Trade Organization of 1 August 2004 to meaningfully integrate the developing and the least developed countries into the multilateral trading system, and calls for the successful and timely completion of the Doha round of trade negotiations with the full realization of the development dimensions of the Doha Work Programme;

8. *Expresses concern* over the suspension of the Doha Round of trade negotiations, and calls for their early resumption and successful development-oriented outcome adhering fully to the agreed mandate in the Doha Ministerial Declaration, the Framework adopted by the General Council of the World Trade Organization in its decision of 1 August 2004 and the Hong Kong Ministerial Declaration;

9. *Calls upon* developed countries and developing countries declaring themselves in a position to do so to provide duty-free and quota-free market access on a lasting basis for all products originating from all least developed countries, consistent with the Hong Kong Ministerial Declaration;

10. *Encourages* developing countries, with the necessary support of donor countries and the international community, to formulate specific commodity policies so as to contribute to the facilitation of trade expansion, the reduction of vulnerability and the improvement of livelihood and food security, by:

(a) Creating an enabling environment that encourages the participation of rural producers and small farmers;

(b) Continuing the diversification of the commodity sector and enhancing its competitiveness in developing countries that are heavily dependent on commodities;

(c) Increasing technology development and improving information systems, institutions and human resources;

11. *Stresses* that the adoption or enforcement of any measures necessary to protect human, animal and plant life or health should not be applied in a manner that would constitute arbitrary or unjustifiable use of non-tariff measures, non-trade barriers or other standards to unfairly restrict access of developing countries' products, reaffirms in this regard that developing countries should play an increasing role in the formulation of, inter alia, safety, environmental and health standards, and recognizes the need to facilitate the increased and meaningful participation of developing countries in the work of relevant international standard-setting organizations;

12. *Calls for* capacity-building support by the relevant international organizations and by developed countries, encourages the private sector, in the context of corporate responsibility and accountability as well as responsible business practices, to enable developing countries to put in place measures that are appropriate and necessary for meeting market requirements and standards, inter alia, quality control standards, and invites the relevant intergovernmental organizations to establish procedures for elaborating product and process standards that take into account the interests and capabilities of developing countries without jeopardizing the legitimate objective for developed as well as developing countries of protecting human, animal and plant life or health consistent with the General Agreement on Tariffs and Trade and the relevant agreements of the World Trade Organization;

13. *Invites* international financial organizations, other donors and the United Nations Conference on Trade and Development to revisit the operational modalities of international commodity, as well as to consider finance and risk management facilities and programmes;

14. *Stresses* that technical assistance and capacity-building aimed at improving the competitiveness of commodity producers is particularly important, and urges the donor community to increase resources for commodity-specific, financial and technical assistance, in particular for human and institutional capacity-building, as well as infrastructure development of developing countries, with a view to reducing their institutional bottlenecks and transaction costs and enhancing their commodity trade and development in accordance with national development plans;

15. *Emphasizes* the importance of official development assistance for agriculture and rural development, and in this regard calls upon the donor community to reinforce its assistance in those sectors, and to increase its financial and technical support for activities aimed at addressing commodity issues, in particular the needs and problems of commodity-dependent developing countries;

16. *Invites* developing countries, in cooperation with developed countries and relevant international organizations, to establish medium- and long-term commodity development programmes geared towards enhancing research for product diversification and improving the production, productivity, value addition and competitiveness of developing countries' commodities;

17. *Underlines* the need to strengthen the Common Fund for Commodities, and encourages it, in cooperation with the International Trade Centre UNCTAD/WTO, the United Nations Conference on Trade and Development and other relevant bodies, to continue to strengthen the activities covered by its Second Account in developing countries with its supply chain concept of improving access to markets and reliability of supply, enhancing diversification and addition of value, improving the competitiveness of commodities, strengthening the market chain, improving market structures, broadening the export base and ensuring the effective participation of all stakeholders;

18. *Calls upon* developed countries, the United Nations Conference on Trade and Development and other relevant international organizations to support training and awareness-building programmes on the functioning of commodity exchanges and their use, in a development-oriented manner, in supporting and enabling small farmers and in supporting capacity-building programmes in developing countries in accordance with national development plans;

19. *Reiterates* the role of the United Nations Conference on Trade and Development in addressing commodities issues in a comprehensive way in accordance with relevant General Assembly resolutions and the provisions of the São Paulo Consensus, adopted by the Conference at its eleventh session, and in this regard calls upon the donor community to provide the resources required to enable the Conference to undertake these activities;

20. *Expresses concern* that the International Task Force on Commodities launched at the eleventh session of the United Nations Conference on Trade and Development has not yet entered into force, and calls upon interested stakeholders to provide voluntary financial support for the timely establishment of the Task Force;

21. *Requests* the Secretary-General, in collaboration with the Secretariat of the United Nations Conference on Trade and Development, to submit a report with recommendations on the implementation of the present resolu-

tion and to report on world commodity trends and prospects to the General Assembly at its sixty-third session;

22. *Decides* to include in the provisional agenda of its sixty-third session, under the item entitled "Macroeconomic policy questions", the sub-item entitled "Commodities".

Individual commodities

Timber. The United Nations Conference for the Negotiation of a Successor Agreement to the International Tropical Timber Agreement, 1994 [YUN 1994, p. 887] reconvened in 2006 (Geneva, 16-27 January) [TD/TIMBER.3/12]. On 27 January, the Conference adopted the text of the International Tropical Timber Agreement, 2006. The Agreement's objectives were to promote the expansion and diversification of international trade in tropical timber from sustainably managed and legally harvested forests, and the sustainable management of tropical producing forests by, among other measures, providing a framework for international cooperation and policy development and a forum for consultation to promote non-discriminatory timber trade practices; enhancing members' capacity to implement strategies for achieving exports of tropical timber; promoting understanding of the structural conditions in international markets and research and development; developing mechanisms to secure new and additional financial resources; improving market intelligence and encouraging information sharing; promoting increased processing of tropical timber; supporting tropical timber reforestation; improving marketing and distribution; strengthening members' capacity for the dissemination of statistics on their trade in timber and information on sustainable forestry management, and encouraging them to develop national utilization and conservation policies; improving forest law enforcement; and promoting access to and transfer of technologies and technical cooperation to implement the Agreement's objectives.

The International Tropical Timber Organization, established by the International Tropical Timber Agreement, 1983 [YUN 1983, p. 557] would continue to administer the Agreement's provisions and operation. The Agreement established the International Tropical Timber Council, which would serve as the Organization's highest authority. The Agreement also established the Special Account and the Bali Partnership Fund to receive voluntary contributions. The Organization's headquarters would be in Yokohama, Japan.

The Agreement would be opened for signature at UN Headquarters in New York from 3 April 2006 until one month after the date of its entry into force. It would enter into force definitively on 1 February 2008 or on any date thereafter, if 12 Governments of producers holding at least 60 per cent of the total votes as set out in annex A of the Agreement and 10 Governments of consumers as listed in annex B and accounting for 60 per cent of the global import volume of tropical timber in the reference year 2005 had signed the Agreement or had ratified, accepted or approved it. If the Agreement did not enter into force definitely on that date, it would enter into force provisionally or within six months thereafter if 10 Governments of producers holding at least 50 per cent of the total votes as set out in annex A and seven Governments of consumers as listed in annex B and accounting for 50 per cent of the global import volume of tropical timber in the reference year 2005 had signed the Agreement or had ratified, accepted or approved it. If the requirements for entry into force were not met on 1 September 2008, the UN Secretary-General would invite those Governments which had signed, ratified, accepted or approved the Agreement to meet and decide whether to put the Agreement into force provisionally or definitely among themselves in whole or in part. Governments which decided to do so would meet from time to time to review the situation.

As at 31 December, seven States had signed the Agreement.

Olive oil and table olives. As at 31 December, the International Agreement on Olive Oil and Table Olives, 1986, as amended and extended, 1993 [YUN 1993, p. 760], until December 2005, had 15 parties.

Sugar. As at 31 December, the International Sugar Agreement, 1992 [YUN 1992, p. 625] had 22 signatories and 48 parties. During the year, Cameroon and Guatemala became parties.

Coffee. As at 31 December, the International Coffee Agreement 2001 [YUN 2001, p. 880] had 35 signatories and 65 parties. During the year, Ghana, Latvia, Panama, Poland and Slovakia became members.

Cocoa. As at 31 December, the International Cocoa Agreement, 2001 [YUN 2001, p. 880] had 15 parties.

Common Fund for Commodities

The 1980 Agreement establishing the Common Fund for Commodities [YUN 1990, p. 621], a mechanism intended to stabilize the commodities market by helping to finance buffer stocks of specific commodities and such commodity development activities as research and marketing, entered into force in 1989, and the Fund became operational later that year. As at 31 December 2006, there were 111 parties to the Agreement. In 2006, the Fund proposed that a Global Initiative on Commodities be undertaken.

Finance

Financial Policy

The *World Economic and Social Survey 2006* [Sales No. E.06.II.C.1], which focused on the causes and implications of the income divergence between countries, stated that world inequality was high and rising. The income gap between the industrialized economies and developing countries continued to widen. At the same time, however, the growth experiences among the developing countries differed greatly. Developing countries had done very well recently. Indeed, current trends indicated that the period 2004-2006 would show fairly widespread growth in those countries. As those favourable conditions would not be permanent, the continuation of strong growth would depend on the ability of developing countries to use the dividends of the current positive conjuncture for investments in the interest of long-term economic development. Strong and sustainable growth made it easier to achieve greater macroeconomic stability. However, macroeconomic stability entailed more than just preserving price stability and sustainable fiscal balances. It was also about avoiding large swings in economic activity and employment, maintaining sustainable external accounts and avoiding exchange-rate overvaluation. The frequency of financial crises in developing countries indicated that macroeconomic stability was about maintaining well-regulated domestic financial sectors, sound balance sheets within the banking system and sound external debt structures. A majority of developing countries had enjoyed robust growth and a relatively stable macroeconomic environment in the 1960s. In the decades thereafter, the fast-growing East Asian economies had managed to achieve much greater macroeconomic stability than the much slower growing countries in Latin America and Africa. Macroeconomic stability and growth mutually reinforced each other. While moderating inflation and exercising fiscal prudence as sensible macroeconomic policy objectives were not subject to dispute, there were concerns that, in practice, countries might have emphasized those objectives at the cost of considering other dimensions of macroeconomic stability. The fiscal policy stance in African and Latin American countries had been highly pro-cyclical and was often induced by the pro-cyclical effects of volatile capital flows. In East Asia, fiscal policies were either neutral, with respect to the business cycle, or counter-cyclical. Macroeconomic volatility tended to be much higher at lower levels of development, particularly because of the greater vulnerability of developing countries to external shocks. For many developing-countries, the space for conducting counter-cyclical macroeconomic policies was limited, as the available fiscal and foreign exchange resources tended to be small relative to the size of the external shocks they faced. Governments could take measures to enhance the scope for counter-cyclical policies by improving the institutional framework for macroeconomic policymaking. A major challenge for multilateral financial institutions was to help developing countries mitigate the damaging effects of volatile capital flows and provide counter-cyclical financing mechanisms to compensate for the inherent pro-cyclical movement of private capital flows. A number of options were available to dampen the pro-cyclicality of capital flows, including the adoption of financial instruments that reduced currency mismatches and linked debt-service obligations to developing countries' capacity to pay. Multilateral surveillance, primarily by the International Monetary Fund (IMF), should remain at the centre of crisis prevention efforts.

The UNCTAD/DESA report *World Economic Situation and Prospects 2007* [Sales No.E.06.II.C.2] stated that on the macroeconomic front, 2006 was characterized by a general trend of monetary tightening, as the central banks of many economies continued to raise interest rates. The monetary policy stance, however, remained accommodative in most economies, and benchmark interest rates in world capital markets were still relatively low, compared to historical levels, either in nominal or in real terms. Another feature of macroeconomic policy was a notable improvement in the fiscal position of a large number of countries, mainly due to stronger-than-anticipated government revenues resulting from robust economic growth. In the future, macroeconomic policies were expected to face more challenges. As the cyclical expansion of the world economies tapered off, central banks were likely to face competing demands. In addition, as growth was expected to moderate, further cyclical increases in fiscal revenues would weaken, and in some countries structural problems in government finance would have to be addressed.

Financial Flows

According to the UNCTAD/DESA report on the world economic situation and prospects, in 2006, developing economies further increased their net outward transfers of financial resources to developed countries to an estimated $657.7 billion. Net transfers from economies in transition rose to $125.1 billion. At the same time, however, both developing countries and economies in transition did enjoy substantial private inflows, and for the Highly Indebted Poor Countries (HIPCs), important increases in aid flows and debt write-offs. The level of private capital flows, although lower than that recorded the previous year, remained high in historical terms. The financial-market turbulence in the second quarter of the year, the slowdown in net borrowing from commercial banks and bond creditors because of pre-financing of obligations due in 2006, and bond buy-back contributed to the moderation. Bond lending and commercial bank lending to developing countries also slowed down. Worldwide, foreign direct investment (FDI) flows increased for the third consecutive year to $1.2 trillion in 2006; $800 billion to developed countries, $368 billion to developing countries, and $62 billion to the economies in transition. Among developing regions, Asia and Oceania received the largest share, $230 billion, followed by South, East and South-East Asia, $186.7 billion. Africa's share increased from $30.7 billion in 2005 to $38.8 billion in 2006.

Aid to Africa

The UNCTAD Trade and Development Board (TDB), at its fifty-third session [A/61/15], considered an UNCTAD secretariat overview of economic development in Africa on doubling aid: making the "big push" work" [TD/B/53/4]. The overview stated that the commitments to doubling the amount of aid to Africa by 2015 and the continent's recent economic performance had raised hopes that Africa could sustain its current growth performance as a basis for meeting the MDGs. After two decades of adjustment without growth, there were some real signs of improving economic performance in Africa. Real progress had been recorded on some issues, such as debt relief and public health and education, which would have a direct bearing on poverty reduction prospects, and the international community, after retreating in the late 1990s, had recovered its faith in official development assistance (ODA), with a promise to double aid to Africa by 2015. Concerns remained, however, with respect to the effectiveness of aid, the absorptive capacities of recipients and whether aid could raise growth and help reduce poverty. The continent was already behind in meeting the MDGs and getting back on track implied, in some estimates, sustained growth of 8 per cent annually for the next decade, well above the expected 5.5 per cent GDP growth for the continent as a whole. Although high energy and mineral prices had brought large gains to some African countries, there was little impact in terms of reducing poverty and inequality and raising employment. While a "big push" designed to instigate a virtual circle of higher rates of savings, investment and economic growth was necessary for a permanent reduction in poverty, the quality of both the aid supplied by donors and the policies pursued by recipients were critical factors for success and for eventually ending the need for aid. Aid had not always succeeded in accelerating growth and development. The sheer multiplicity of donors, with different outlooks, accounting systems and priorities had created a chaotic landscape of aid. A greater multilateralization of aid could help to reduce unnecessary and costly competition among donors and reduce administrative costs. Reform of the multilateral aid institutions was also necessary. The time was right to revisit the idea of a UN funding window for African development. A new international architecture for aid would have to encourage and supplement national resource mobilization and fill the gap between national rates of saving and the investment required to meet national development goals, including the MDGs. The United Kingdom had called for a Marshall Plan for Africa, in recognition of the fact that piecemeal approaches to aid had not stimulated recovery and a more coordinated approach was required.

TDB [A/61/15], in agreed conclusions adopted on 7 November [agreed conclusions 487 (LIII)], noted the international community's commitment to doubling aid to Africa. It welcomed the efforts made in raising fundamental questions with regard to: emphasizing the context of increased ownership for African countries with regard to designing and implementing policies consonant with their specific development challenges and priorities; good governance at all levels; the share and volume of multilateral aid; the multilateral structures and modalities for effective aid delivery; and positive aid experiences gained in different countries. It invited Governments to consider those issues, with a view to further enhancing the impact and effectiveness of aid, and agreed that UNCTAD should continue to undertake critical and in-depth analysis and provide policy advice on African development.

International financial system

Report of Secretary-General. In response to General Assembly resolution 60/186 [YUN 2005, p. 1055], the Secretary-General submitted a July report [A/61/136] on the international financial system and development, which complemented his report [A/61/253] (see p. 1135) on follow-up and implementation of the outcome of the International Conference on Financing for Development [YUN 2002, p. 953]. The report surveyed the recent evolution of international official and private capital flows to developing countries, the growth of foreign exchange reserves and efforts to reinforce the role of the international financial system in supporting financial stability. It noted that developing countries and economies in transition continued to make increasing net outward transfers of financial resources to developed countries. Those transfers had been accompanied by increasing net private capital inflows, partially offset by the accumulation of official foreign reserves invested in government securities of major developed countries.

The report noted that the IMF had conducted a medium-term strategic policy review of its role in the international financial system, the major conclusion of which was that, since international policy coordination was most effective when undertaken within a multilateral institution, IMF role in multilateral surveillance should be strengthened. Steps should also be taken to restore IMF to its primary role as the central institution for fostering global financial stability and growth and the forum for cooperation and decision-making on the global international monetary and financial system. At its 2006 spring meeting, the International Monetary and Financial Committee supported proposals to strengthen the IMF role in addressing systematic issues, including correcting global imbalances through enhanced multilateral dialogue. However, the Fund's effectiveness and credibility depended on the adequate voice and participation of all its members. The need for changes in representation and the distribution of quotas to reflect the increased economic importance of emerging market economies and ensure that low-income countries were adequately represented had been recognized. A two-stage approach to reform, in which ad hoc quota increases for the most under-represented countries would be agreed in the near term, seemed to have major support and was to be considered at the Fund's September annual meeting.

In his conclusions, the Secretary-General stated that multilateral surveillance and associated policy coordination and cooperation remained at the centre of crisis prevention efforts. The recent agreement to strengthen IMF surveillance was a welcome development. The effectiveness of multilateral dialogue would depend, however, on adequate voice and participation of all countries. Therefore, it was critically important that the ongoing consideration of the governance structure of international financial institutions should result in prompt decisions on comprehensive reform and a timetable for action. In a number of emerging market countries, despite strong policies and massive reserve holdings, underlying structural vulnerabilities still existed. That called for a further exploration of appropriate international and regional financial instruments to help prevent and manage crises. The international community should continue to assist low-income countries in addressing the macroeconomic aspects of the development challenge, including maintaining macroeconomic stability and debt sustainability.

Meeting of IMF Board of Governors. The IMF Board of Governors (Singapore, 18 September) approved a governance reform resolution, which included voting right increases for China, Mexico, the Republic of Korea and Turkey, and a commitment to increase basic votes and adjust the quota formula within two years. The resolution called for a doubling of basic votes that would respect the existing voting share of low-income countries as a group, as well as for subsequently safeguarding the proportion of basic votes in total voting power.

IMF/World Bank Development Committee. The joint IMF/World Bank Development Committee, in a communiqué issued following its 18 September meeting (Singapore), stated that pledges made to substantially increase ODA, including a doubling of aid to Africa, had to be delivered in a predictable manner, and urged those donors that had not done so to make concrete efforts to meet the target of 0.7 per cent of gross national income as ODA. It asked the World Bank to develop a framework for its role in the provision of global and regional public goods, including criteria for its involvement and financing modalities, and to deliver on its commitments to aid effectiveness, including the implementation of best practice principles identified in the Bank's conditionality review. International commitments to improve aid effectiveness embodied in the Paris Declaration on Aid Effectiveness [YUN 2005, p. 957] should be translated into action at the country level. The Committee urged developing countries to prepare well-defined and costed programmes for using scaled-up aid to step up the poverty reduction effort.

In an earlier communiqué, following its 23 April meeting (Washington, D.C.), the Committee called for rapid progress in implementing the framework agreed in the Paris Declaration on Aid Effectiveness through improved modalities and a stronger focus on results. It noted the importance of continued development progress in middle income countries and emerging market countries, and asked the Bank to refine its engagement strategy with those countries by its next meeting, taking into account their contributions to poverty reduction and global public goods, access to market financing and remaining development challenges. The Committee agreed on the need to improve governance in all countries, and to explore ways to help developing countries enhance their access to affordable, sustainable and reliable modern energy services over the long term, while paying attention to local and global environmental considerations.

GENERAL ASSEMBLY ACTION

On 20 December [meeting 83], the General Assembly, on the recommendation of the Second Committee [A/61/420/Add.2], adopted **resolution 61/187** without vote [agenda item 51 *(b)*].

International financial system and development

The General Assembly,

Recalling its resolutions 55/186 of 20 December 2000 and 56/181 of 21 December 2001, both entitled "Towards a strengthened and stable international financial architecture responsive to the priorities of growth and development, especially in developing countries, and to the promotion of economic and social equity", as well as its resolutions 57/241 of 20 December 2002, 58/202 of 23 December 2003, 59/222 of 22 December 2004 and 60/186 of 22 December 2005,

Recalling also the United Nations Millennium Declaration and its resolution 56/210 B of 9 July 2002, in which it endorsed the Monterrey Consensus of the International Conference on Financing for Development, and the Plan of Implementation of the World Summit on Sustainable Development ("Johannesburg Plan of Implementation"),

Recalling further the 2005 World Summit Outcome,

Recalling its resolution 60/265 of 30 June 2006 on the follow-up to the development outcome of the 2005 World Summit, including the Millennium Development Goals and the other internationally agreed development goals,

Emphasizing that the international financial system should further sustain economic growth and support sustainable development and hunger and poverty eradication, while allowing for the coherent mobilization of all sources of financing for development, including the mobilization of domestic resources, international investment flows, official development assistance, external debt relief and an open, equitable, rule-based, predictable and non-discriminatory global trading system,

Stressing the importance of commitment to sound domestic financial sectors, which make a vital contribution to national development efforts, as an important component of an international financial architecture that is supportive of development,

Stressing also that good governance at the international level is fundamental for achieving sustainable development, in this regard reiterating the importance of promoting global economic governance by addressing the international finance, trade, technology and investment patterns that have an impact on the development prospects of developing countries in order to ensure a dynamic and enabling international economic environment, and reiterating also that, to this effect, the international community should take all necessary and appropriate measures, including ensuring support for structural and macroeconomic reform, finding a comprehensive solution to the external debt problem and increasing the market access of developing countries,

Reaffirming the commitment to broaden and strengthen the participation of developing countries and countries with economies in transition in international economic decision-making and norm-setting, stressing to that end the importance of continuing efforts to reform the international financial architecture, and acknowledging the need for continued discussion on the issue of voting power of developing countries in the Bretton Woods institutions, which remains a concern,

Recognizing the urgent need to enhance the coherence, governance and consistency of the international monetary, financial and trading systems and the importance of ensuring their openness, fairness and inclusiveness in order to complement national development efforts to ensure sustained economic growth and the achievement of the internationally agreed development goals, including the Millennium Development Goals,

Emphasizing the need for additional stable and predictable financing to help developing countries undertake investment plans to achieve internationally agreed development goals,

Recognizing, in this regard, the value of developing innovative sources of financing from various sources on a public, private, domestic and external basis to increase and supplement traditional sources of financing,

Welcoming the contribution to the mobilization of resources for development through innovative financing initiatives taken by groups of Member States,

Reiterating the need to strengthen the leadership role of the United Nations in promoting development,

1. *Takes note* of the report of the Secretary-General;

2. *Notes* that global economic growth and a stable international financial system, inter alia, can support the ability of developing countries to achieve internationally agreed development goals, including the Millennium Development Goals, and stresses the importance of cooperative efforts by all countries and institutions to cope with the risks of financial instability;

3. *Emphasizes* that economic growth should be further strengthened and sustained, noting that global economic growth depends on national economic growth and that implementation of sound macroeconomic policies at

all levels could significantly contribute to a revitalization of economic growth;

4. *Invites* the World Bank, the International Monetary Fund, the regional development banks and other relevant institutions to further integrate development dimensions into their strategies and policies, consistent with their respective mandates, and to fully implement the principles stated in those strategies and policies, in particular the objectives of pro-poor growth and poverty reduction;

5. *Notes* that developing countries as a whole continue to experience a net outflow of financial resources, and requests the Secretary-General, in continuing collaboration with international financial institutions and other relevant bodies, to analyse the range of reasons and consequences for this in his report under this item;

6. *Also notes* that some developing countries have net inflows of financial resources, and requests the Secretary-General, in continuing collaboration with international financial institutions and other relevant bodies, to analyse the range of reasons and consequences for this in his report under this item;

7. *Underlines* the importance of promoting international financial stability and sustainable growth, and welcomes the efforts undertaken to this end by the International Monetary Fund and the Financial Stability Forum, as well as the consideration by the International Monetary and Financial Committee of ways to sharpen tools designed to promote international financial stability and enhance crisis prevention, inter alia, through an even-handed implementation of surveillance, including at the regional level, and a sharpening of surveillance of capital markets and systemically and regionally important countries, with a view, inter alia, to the early identification of problems and risks, integrating debt sustainability analysis, the fostering of appropriate policy responses, the possible provision of financing and other instruments designed to prevent the emergence or spread of financial crises and further improvements in the transparency of macroeconomic data and statistical information on international capital flows;

8. *Also underlines* the importance of efforts at the national level to increase resilience to financial risk, and in this regard welcomes progress that has been made in recent years, stresses the importance of better assessment of a country's debt burden and its ability to service that debt in both crisis prevention and resolution, and welcomes the ongoing work of the International Monetary Fund on assessing debt sustainability;

9. *Recognizes* the need for multilateral surveillance to remain at the centre of crisis prevention efforts and that surveillance should focus not only on crisis-prone countries but also on the stability of the system as a whole;

10. *Reiterates* that measures to mitigate the impact of excessive volatility of short-term capital flows and to improve transparency of and information about financial flows are important and must be considered;

11. *Notes* the impact of financial crises or risk contagion in developing countries and countries with economies in transition, regardless of their size, and in this regard welcomes the efforts of the international financial institutions, in their support to countries, to continuously adapt their array of financial facilities and resources, drawing on a full range of policies, taking into account the effects of economic cycles, as and where appropriate, having due regard to sound fiscal management and the specific circumstances of each case, so as to prevent and respond to such crises in a timely and appropriate way;

12. *Underscores* the importance of competitive and inclusive private and public financial markets in mobilizing and allocating savings towards productive investment and thus making a vital contribution to national development efforts and to an international financial architecture that is supportive of development;

13. *Invites* the international financial and banking institutions to consider enhancing the transparency of risk-rating mechanisms, noting that sovereign risk assessments made by the private sector should maximize the use of strict, objective and transparent parameters, which can be facilitated by high-quality data and analysis, and encourages relevant development institutions, including the United Nations Conference on Trade and Development, to continue their work on this issue, including its potential impact on the development prospects of developing countries;

14. *Stresses* the importance of strong domestic institutions in promoting business activities and financial stability for the achievement of growth and development, inter alia, through sound macroeconomic policies and policies aimed at strengthening the regulatory systems of the corporate, financial and banking sectors, and also stresses that international cooperation initiatives in those areas should encourage flows of capital to developing countries;

15. *Notes* the holding of the annual meeting of the International Monetary Fund, in September 2006, stresses the importance of early agreement on a credible and time-bound package of quota and voice reforms in the Fund, reiterates the need to effectively address the issue of enhancing the voice and participation of developing countries in the Bretton Woods institutions, encourages the Bretton Woods institutions to take further and effective measures, and invites the World Bank and the Fund to continue to provide information on this issue, using existing cooperation forums, including those involving Member States;

16. *Emphasizes* that it is essential to ensure the effective and equitable participation of developing countries in the formulation of financial standards and codes, underscores the need to ensure their implementation, on a voluntary and progressive basis, as a contribution to reducing vulnerability to financial crisis and contagion, and notes that more than one hundred countries have participated in or agreed to participate in the joint World Bank-International Monetary Fund financial sector assessment programme;

17. *Notes* the proposal to use special drawing rights allocations for development purposes, and considers that any assessment of special drawing rights allocations must respect the Articles of Agreement of the International

Monetary Fund and the established rules of procedure of the Fund, which requires taking into account the global need for liquidity at the international level;

18. *Also notes* the initial discussion in the International Monetary Fund on a new liquidity instrument that would enable high-access financial support to developing countries that have market access and strong economic policies but nonetheless remain vulnerable to shocks;

19. *Invites* the multilateral and regional development banks and development funds to continue to play a vital role in serving the development needs of developing countries and countries with economies in transition, including through coordinated action, as appropriate, and stresses that strengthened regional development banks and subregional financial institutions add flexible financial support to national and regional development efforts, thus enhancing their ownership and overall efficiency, and are an essential source of knowledge and expertise for their developing country members;

20. *Calls for* the continued effort of the multilateral financial institutions, in providing policy advice, technical assistance and financial support to member countries, to work on the basis of nationally owned reform and development strategies, to pay due regard to the special needs and implementing capacities of developing countries and countries with economies in transition and to minimize the negative impacts of the adjustment programmes on the vulnerable segments of society, while taking into account the importance of gender-sensitive employment and hunger and poverty eradication policies and strategies;

21. *Stresses* the need to continuously improve standards of corporate and public sector governance, including accounting, auditing and measures to ensure transparency, noting the disruptive effects of inadequate policies;

22. *Requests* the Secretary-General to submit a report to the General Assembly at its sixty-second session on the implementation of the present resolution;

23. *Decides* to include in the provisional agenda of its sixty-second session, under the item entitled "Macroeconomic policy questions", the sub-item entitled "International financial system and development".

Debt problems of developing countries

Report of Secretary-General. In response to General Assembly resolution 60/187 [YUN 2005, p. 1058], the Secretary-General submitted a July report [A/61/152] on recent developments in the external debt of developing countries, which reviewed the implementation of the Heavily Indebted Poor Countries (HIPC) Initiative, launched in 1996 [YUN 1996, p. 867], and the financing challenges for low-income countries. It also addressed the challenges related to private debt flows and financing of development in low-income countries.

The report concluded that, against a backdrop of favourable market conditions, the external debt situation of developing countries further improved in 2005. Global growth boosted their exports, allowing foreign exchange reserve build-ups. Low interest rates and ample liquidity in international capital markets provided opportunities to raise low-cost capital and implement active debt management by repaying high-cost debt and pre-financing future capital needs. Developing countries also attracted foreign investors' interest in local currency debt issued on domestic and international capital markets. That rosy picture, however, should not lead to complacency, as the future was fraught with uncertainty and risks. Global current account imbalances among major trading countries had reached dangerously high levels. The immediate concern was the risk of reverse capital flows and abrupt withdrawal of those flows from emerging markets. The evolution of the international financial system towards a more private-based system of capital flows raised many challenges.

Despite a general improvement in the external debt situation, a large number of countries could be characterized as severely indebted. Innovative approaches could be introduced to allow a larger amount of debt swaps to finance MDG projects in debtor countries. The Paris Club (group of creditor countries) Evian approach could also provide bolder debt reductions for heavily-indebted middle-income countries. The full implementation of the HIPC Initiative and the Multilateral Debt Relief Initiative (MDRI), announced by the G-8 (Group of most industrialized countries) in 2005 [YUN 2005, p. 1057], might be made more expeditious, in order to allow the remaining eligible countries to benefit from needed debt reductions. Beyond those debt relief initiatives, the question of adequate financing of the development of low-income countries needed to be addressed in a flexible way.

Other actions. The joint IMF/World Bank Development Committee, in a communiqué issued following its 23 April meeting (Washington, D.C.), welcomed recent progress in implementing the MDRI, and, in particular, the cancellation by IMF of the MDRI debt of the first 19 countries. It urged donors to secure their financing commitments to achieve full compensation of the International Development Association's (IDA) reflows and ensure that the initiative was truly additional to existing commitments. The Committee called on the World Bank and the IMF to make proposals to further refine the debt sustainability framework for low-income countries.

In a communiqué issued following its 18 September meeting (Singapore), the Committee, noting that 2006 marked the tenth anniversary the

HIPC Initiative, welcomed the substantial reduction of debt stocks. It noted the increase of poverty-reducing expenditures of the 29 HIPCs that had reached the decision point. The Committee welcomed the decision to allow the sunset clause to take effect at end-2006 and grandfather the countries that were assessed to have met the HIPC criteria based on end-2004 data, as well as the implementation of the MDRI by the IMF, IDA and the African Development Fund. It, however, cautioned against excessive borrowing after the relief, which could lead to the re-emergence of debt distress. The Committee underscored the importance of the Joint Debt Sustainability Framework of the Fund and the Bank for low-income countries in helping to ensure that new borrowing in post-MDRI countries did not undermine their long-term debt sustainability. It stressed the importance of implementing the Bank's approach to dealing with the issue of free riding, as well as the need to address the issue of official creditors' coordination.

The UNCTAD/DESA report *World Economic Situation and Prospects 2007* stated that, by September 2006, 29 countries had reached the decision point under the HIPC Initiative—the point at which the international community committed to providing a country with additional assistance beyond traditional debt relief. Of those countries, 20 had reached the completion point, while the remaining nine were in the interim stage between the decision and completion points. Three countries were expected to complete the Initiative by the end of 2006. The sunset clause had been extended at the end of 2006 for countries that had yet to participate in the enhanced Initiative. The IMF and World Bank had identified 11 countries that were potentially eligible for assistance under the extended clause, including four additional countries identified as being eligible in 2006. Five of those eligible countries had yet to start an IMF- or IDA-supported programme, and were required to do so before the sunset clauses' expiration in order to meet the necessary eligibility requirements.

One issue of concern was the return of countries to rising debt ratios after having reached the completion point. According the World Bank, 11 of 13 countries experienced deteriorated debt positions since reaching that point, eight of which had debt ratios that exceeded HIPC thresholds of sustainability.

GENERAL ASSEMBLY ACTION

On 20 December [meeting 83], the General Assembly, on the recommendation of the Second Committee [A/61/420/Add.3], adopted **resolution 61/188** without vote [agenda item 51 *(c)*].

External debt crisis and development

The General Assembly,

Recalling its resolutions 58/203 of 23 December 2003, 59/223 of 22 December 2004 and 60/187 of 22 December 2005 on external debt crisis and development,

Recalling also the International Conference on Financing for Development and its outcome, which recognizes sustainable debt financing as an important element for mobilizing resources for public and private investment,

Recalling further the United Nations Millennium Declaration adopted on 8 September 2000,

Recalling the 2005 World Summit Outcome,

Recalling also its resolution 60/265 of 30 June 2006 on follow-up to the development outcome of the 2005 World Summit, including the Millennium Development Goals and other internationally agreed development goals,

Recalling further its resolution 57/270 B of 23 June 2003,

Noting with satisfaction the improvement in the external debt situation of developing countries as a group in the course of the past year, but concerned that there remains a number of low- and middle-income developing countries that are still facing difficulties in finding a durable solution to their external debt problems, which could adversely affect their sustainable development,

Welcoming the fact that the Heavily Indebted Poor Countries Initiative has enabled heavily indebted poor countries to markedly increase their expenditures on health, education and other social services consistent with national priorities, development plans, and internationally agreed development goals, including the Millennium Development Goals,

Welcoming also the Multilateral Debt Relief Initiative, which will enable a marked increase in expenditures on health, education and other social services consistent with national priorities and development plans by heavily indebted poor countries,

Stressing the importance of addressing the challenges of those heavily indebted poor countries that are facing difficulties in reaching the completion point under the Heavily Indebted Poor Countries Initiative, and expressing concern that some heavily indebted poor countries continue to face substantial debt burdens and need to avoid rebuilding unsustainable debt burdens after reaching the completion point under the Initiative,

Emphasizing that debt sustainability is essential for underpinning growth, and underlining the importance of debt sustainability to the efforts to achieve national development goals, including the Millennium Development Goals, and that countries should direct those financial resources freed through debt relief, in particular through debt reduction and cancellation, towards activities consistent with poverty eradication, sustained economic growth and sustainable development and the achievement of the internationally agreed development goals, including the Millennium Development Goals,

Convinced that enhanced market access for goods and services of export interest to developing countries contributes significantly to debt sustainability in those countries,

1. *Takes note* of the report of the Secretary-General;

2. *Emphasizes* the special importance of a timely, effective, comprehensive and durable solution to the debt problems of developing countries, since debt financing and relief can be an important source of capital for economic growth and development;

3. *Also emphasizes* that creditors and debtors must share responsibility for preventing unsustainable debt situations;

4. *Reiterates* that debt sustainability depends on a confluence of many factors at the international and national levels, emphasizes that country-specific circumstances and the impact of external shocks should be taken into account in debt sustainability analyses, underscores the fact that no single indicator should be used to make definitive judgements about debt sustainability, and, in this regard, while acknowledging the need to use transparent and comparable indicators, invites the International Monetary Fund and the World Bank, in their assessment of debt sustainability, to take into account fundamental changes caused by, inter alia, natural disasters, conflicts and changes in global growth prospects or in the terms of trade, especially for commodity-dependent developing countries, and to continue to provide information on this issue using existing cooperation forums, including those involving Member States;

5. *Underlines* the fact that the long-term sustainability of debt depends, inter alia, on the economic growth, mobilization of domestic resources and export prospects of debtor countries and, hence, on the creation of an enabling international environment conducive to development, progress in following sound macroeconomic policies, transparent and effective regulatory frameworks and success in overcoming structural development problems;

6. *Welcomes* the introduction of the Multilateral Debt Relief Initiative, and calls for its full and timely implementation and the provision of additional resources to ensure that the financial capacity of the international financial institutions is not reduced;

7. *Emphasizes* in this regard that debt relief does not replace other sources of financing;

8. *Urges* donors to ensure that their commitments to the Multilateral Debt Relief Initiative and the Heavily Indebted Poor Countries Initiative be additional to existing aid flows, and underlines that full compensation by donors on the basis of fair burden-sharing for the Multilateral Debt Relief Initiative costs of relevant financial institutions is essential;

9. *Notes with concern* that, in spite of the progress achieved, some countries that have reached the completion point of the Heavily Indebted Poor Countries Initiative have not been able to achieve lasting debt sustainability, stresses the importance of promoting responsible borrowing and lending and the need to help those countries to manage their borrowing and to avoid a build-up of unsustainable debt, including through the use of grants and concessional loans, underscores the importance of the joint Debt Sustainability Framework of the International Monetary Fund and the World Bank for low-income countries in helping to ensure that new borrowing in post-Multilateral Debt Relief Initiative countries does not undermine their long-term debt sustainability, looks forward to the review of the Framework, and encourages the application of the improved Framework in lending and borrowing decisions;

10. *Welcomes and encourages* the efforts of the heavily indebted poor countries, calls upon them to continue to improve their domestic policies and economic management, inter alia, through poverty reduction strategies, and to create a domestic environment conducive to private-sector development, economic growth and poverty reduction, including a stable macroeconomic framework, transparent and accountable systems of public finance, a sound business climate and a predictable investment climate, and in this regard invites creditors, both private and public, who are not yet fully participating in the Heavily Indebted Poor Countries Initiative to substantially increase their participation in the delivery of debt relief, and invites the international financing institutions and the donor community to continue to provide adequate and sufficiently concessional financing;

11. *Stresses* that debt relief can play a key role in liberating resources that should be directed towards activities consistent with poverty eradication, sustained economic growth and sustainable development and the achievement of the internationally agreed development goals, including the Millennium Development Goals, and in this regard urges countries to direct those resources freed through debt relief, in particular through debt cancellation and reduction, towards those objectives;

12. *Calls for* the consideration of additional measures and initiatives aimed at ensuring long-term debt sustainability through increased grant-based financing, cancellation of 100 per cent of the official multilateral and bilateral debt of heavily indebted poor countries and, where appropriate, and on a case-by-case basis, significant debt relief or restructuring for low- and middle-income developing countries with an unsustainable debt burden that are not part of the Heavily Indebted Poor Countries Initiative, as well as the exploration of mechanisms to comprehensively address the debt problems of those countries;

13. *Encourages* the Paris Club, in dealing with the debt of low- and middle-income debtor countries that are not part of the Heavily Indebted Poor Countries Initiative, to take into account their medium-term debt sustainability in addition to their financing gaps, and takes note with appreciation of the Evian approach of the Paris Club in providing terms of debt relief tailored to the specific needs of debtor countries while preserving debt cancellation for heavily indebted poor countries;

14. *Stresses* the need to significantly address debt problems of middle-income developing countries, and in this regard stresses the importance of the Evian ap-

proach of the Paris Club as a practical means to address this issue;

15. *Invites* creditors and debtors to continue to use, where appropriate and on a case-by-case basis, mechanisms such as debt swaps for alleviating the debt burden of low- and middle-income developing countries with an unsustainable debt burden that are not eligible for the Heavily Indebted Poor Countries Initiative, and takes note of the discussions and assessment by the Paris Club of the proposal for "Debt for Equity in Millennium Development Goal Projects";

16. *Stresses* the need to continue to take effective measures, preferably within the existing frameworks, to address the debt problems of the least developed countries, including through cancellation of the multilateral and bilateral debt owed by least developed countries to creditors, both public and private;

17. *Reiterates* its invitation to the World Bank and the International Monetary Fund to keep the overall implications of the debt sustainability framework for low-income countries under review, calls for transparency in the computation of the country policy and institutional assessments, and takes note of the disclosure of the country performance ratings of the International Development Association that form part of the framework;

18. *Notes* that credit rating agencies play an important role in determining countries' access to international capital markets and the cost of such borrowing, and, in this regard, calls upon the international financial and banking institutions to consider enhancing the transparency of risk rating mechanisms, and notes that sovereign risk assessments made by the private sector should maximize the use of strict, objective and transparent parameters, which can be facilitated by high-quality data and analysis;

19. *Invites* donor countries, taking into account country-specific debt sustainability analyses, to continue their efforts to increase bilateral grants to developing countries, which could contribute to debt sustainability in the medium to long term, and recognizes the need for countries to be able to invest, inter alia, in health and education while maintaining debt sustainability;

20. *Welcomes* the efforts of, and calls upon, the international community to provide flexibility, and stresses the need to continue those efforts in helping post-conflict developing countries, especially those that are heavily indebted and poor, to achieve initial reconstruction for economic and social development;

21. *Welcomes also* the efforts of, and invites, creditors to provide flexibility to developing countries affected by natural disasters on a case-by-case basis so as to allow them to address their debt concerns;

22. *Welcomes further* the efforts of, and calls upon, the international community to support institutional capacity-building in developing countries for the management of financial assets and liabilities and to enhance sustainable debt management as an integral part of national development strategies;

23. *Invites* the United Nations Conference on Trade and Development, the International Monetary Fund and the World Bank, in cooperation with the regional commissions, development banks and other relevant multilateral financial institutions and stakeholders, to continue cooperation in respect of capacity-building activities in developing countries in the area of debt management;

24. *Calls upon* all Member States and the United Nations system, and invites the Bretton Woods institutions and the private sector, to take appropriate measures and actions for the implementation of the commitments, agreements and decisions of the major United Nations conferences and summits, in particular those related to the question of the external debt problems of developing countries;

25. *Requests* the Secretary-General to submit to the General Assembly at its sixty-second session a report on the implementation of the present resolution and to include in that report a comprehensive and substantive analysis of the external debt situation and debt-servicing problems of developing countries;

26. *Decides* to include in the provisional agenda of its sixty-second session, under the item entitled "Macroeconomic policy questions", the sub-item entitled "External debt crisis and development".

Financing for development

Follow-up to International Conference on Financing for Development

High-level meeting of the Economic and Social Council, Bretton Woods institutions, WTO and UNCTAD. In accordance with Economic and Social Council **decision 2006/202** of 7 February, the ninth special high-level meeting of the Council, the Bretton Woods institutions (the World Bank Group and IMF), WTO and UNCTAD was held in New York on 24 April. The meeting addressed the theme of coherence, coordination and cooperation in the context of the implementation of the Monterrey Consensus and the 2005 World Summit Outcome. Before it was a note by the Secretary-General on the subject [E/2006/48], providing information and raising a number of questions on four subthemes: implementation of and support for national development strategies towards the achievement of internationally agreed development goals, including the MDGs; fulfilling the development dimension of the Doha work programme; external debt: implementing and building on current initiatives to enhance debt sustainability; and supporting the development efforts of middle-income countries.

The Council President, in his summary of the proceedings [A/61/81-E/2006/73], noted the view of participants that 2005-2006 was a positive period for development, with a growing world economy, increased aid and reductions in debt due to official debt relief, progress in new and innovative sources of financing and expanding private capital flows to developing countries. Yet the risks posed by the large and still growing imbalances and the likelihood that many countries would not reach the MDGs persisted. The year 2005 was also a milestone for the global partnership for development, as a result of which the international development agenda had taken a significant step forward. Noting the convergence of development cooperation institutions in the pursuit of internationally agreed development goals, participants stressed the importance of continuing to build on that approach and enhance coherence among organizations that played a key role in assisting countries to achieve the MDGs. Participants stated that national development strategies were the launching pad for development efforts, adding that such strategies should reflect the conditions in the respective country. It was agreed that an increase in the volume, quality and effectiveness of aid was necessary, especially ODA. It was noted that the stability of aid flows was important and multi-year funding could enhance aid predictability, thus facilitating a smoother implementation of national development strategies. Support was expressed for continuing work on innovative sources of finance, including the expansion of pilot projects, such as the air-ticket solidarity contribution and the International Financial Facility for Immunization. On debt sustainability, speakers stressed that developing countries needed sustainable debt levels in order to make progress on the internationally agreed development goals. In terms of supporting the development efforts of middle-income developing countries, speakers stressed the need for special international financial support to target the poor within those countries.

ECONOMIC AND SOCIAL COUNCIL ACTION

On 28 July [meeting 43], the Economic and Social Council adopted **resolution 2006/45** [draft: E/2006/L.34] without vote [agenda item 6 *(a)*].

Follow-up to the International Conference on Financing for Development

The Economic and Social Council,

Recalling the International Conference on Financing for Development, held in Monterrey, Mexico, from 18 to 22 March 2002, and General Assembly resolutions 56/210 B of 9 July 2002, 57/250, 57/272 and 57/273 of 20 December 2002, 57/270 B of 23 June 2003, 58/230 of 23 December 2003, 59/225 of 22 December 2004 and 60/188 of 22 December 2005,

Recalling also its resolutions 2002/34 of 26 July 2002, 2003/47 of 24 July 2003 and 2004/64 of 16 September 2004,

Recalling further the 2005 World Summit Outcome,

Recalling General Assembly resolution 60/265 of 30 June 2006,

1. *Takes note* of the summary by the President of the Economic and Social Council of the special high-level meeting of the Council with the Bretton Woods institutions, the World Trade Organization and the United Nations Conference on Trade and Development, held in New York on 24 April 2006, and of the note by the Secretary-General on coherence, coordination and cooperation in the context of the implementation of the Monterrey Consensus and the 2005 World Summit Outcome, prepared in collaboration with the major institutional stakeholders and other relevant organizations of the United Nations system;

2. *Recalls* paragraph 9 of the Monterrey Consensus of the International Conference on Financing for Development and, building on the experience of the special high-level meeting of the Economic and Social Council with the Bretton Woods institutions, the World Trade Organization and the United Nations Conference on Trade and Development, requests the President of the Economic and Social Council, with the support of the Financing for Development Office of the Secretariat, to initiate consultations, including with all major institutional stakeholders, on how to enhance the impact of the special high-level meeting of the Council, in order:

(a) To focus the special high-level spring meeting on specific issues, in the context of the implementation of the Monterrey Consensus, within the holistic integrated approach of the Consensus, in consultation with all major institutional stakeholders, and to report thereon to the Council well in advance of the meeting, and, in this regard, underlines the importance of transparency and openness with respect to Member States;

(b) To finalize the preparations well in advance of the meeting, in order to facilitate the participation of all participants and ensure high-level participation;

(c) To discuss innovative ways and mechanisms to enhance interactions between the Council and the major institutional stakeholders in preparation for the special high-level meeting of the Economic and Social Council with the Bretton Woods institutions, the World Trade Organization and the United Nations Conference on Trade and Development;

(d) To request the regional commissions, with the support of regional development banks, as appropriate, and in cooperation with the relevant United Nations entities, to continue to strengthen their efforts in addressing regional and interregional aspects of the follow-up to the International Conference on Financing for Development, in the context of General Assembly resolution 58/230, to undertake specific activities, and to provide inputs to the follow-up to the Conference, including the spring meeting of the Economic and Social Council;

(e) To continue to involve all relevant stakeholders, including civil society organizations and the private sector, in accordance with the rules of procedure of the Economic and Social Council and the accreditation procedures and modalities of participation utilized at the Conference and its preparatory process.

Report of Secretary-General. In response to General Assembly resolution 60/188 [YUN 2005, p. 1061], the Secretary-General submitted an August report [A/61/253] on follow-up to and implementation of the outcome of the International Conference on Financing for Development [YUN 2002, p. 953], including recommendations for action. Prepared in consultation with major institutional stakeholders in the financing for development process, the report was meant to be read in conjunction with the reports of the Secretary-General on: the international financial system and development [A/61/136] (see p. 1127); external debt crisis and development [A/61/152] (see p. 1130); and international trade and development [A/61/272] (see p. 1111), as well as his note on coherence, coordination and cooperation in the context of the implementation of the Monterrey Consensus [E/2006/48] (see p. 1133) and the summary of the President of the Economic and Social Council on the special high-level meeting of the Council with the Bretton Woods institutions, WTO and UNCTAD [A/61/81-E/2006/73] (see p. 1133). The report also incorporated the implications of the Outcome of the 2005 World Summit [YUN 2005, p. 47] for the financing for development process.

The report reflected progress in the areas of mobilizing domestic resource, in increasing both official assistance and private financial flows and in providing more extensive debt relief. However, progress in trade, which had a larger and more permanent potential benefit for developing countries, had stalled and prospects for completion of the Doha round of multilateral trade negtiations (see p. 1111) by the end of 2006 were negligible. It also outlined the activities undertaken to ensure the participation of all stakeholders through continued discussions of issues relevant to the follow-up process.

Communications. South Africa, in a 28 September letter to the Secretary-General [A/61/486], transmitted the ministerial statement adopted at the thirtieth annual meeting of Ministers of Foreign Affairs of the Group of 77, in which they reiterated the significance of increased financing for development, including the need to meet the long-standing target of 0.7 per cent of gross national product for ODA to developing countries, wider and deeper debt relief, as well as ongoing efforts for identifying additional, innovative sources of financing.

China, Ethiopia, and the Congo, in a 15 November letter to the Secretary-General [A/61/580-S/2006/897], transmitted the Declaration of the Beijing Summit of the Forum on China-Africa Cooperation, which, among other things, urged the developed countries to increase ODA and honour their commitments to opening their market and to debt relief.

GENERAL ASSEMBLY ACTION

On 20 December [meeting 83], the General Assembly, on the recommendation of the Second Committee [A/61/421], adopted **resolution 61/191** without vote [agenda item 52].

Follow-up to and implementation of the outcome of the International conference on Financing for Development

The General Assembly,

Recalling the International Conference on Financing for Development, held in Monterrey, Mexico, from 18 to 22 March 2002, and its resolutions 56/210 B of 9 July 2002, 57/250 of 20 December 2002, 57/270 B of 23 June 2003, 57/272 and 57/273 of 20 December 2002, 58/230 of 23 December 2003, 59/225 of 22 December 2004 and 60/188 of 22 December 2005, as well as Economic and Social Council resolutions 2002/34 of 26 July 2002, 2003/47 of 24 July 2003, 2004/64 of 16 September 2004 and 2006/45 of 28 July 2006,

Recalling also the 2005 World Summit Outcome,

Recalling further its resolution 60/265 of 30 June 2006 on the follow-up to the development outcome of the 2005 World Summit, including the Millennium Development Goals and the other internationally agreed development goals,

Taking note of the report of the Secretary-General,

Having considered the summary by the President of the Economic and Social Council of the special high-level meeting of the Council with the Bretton Woods institutions, the World Trade Organization and the United Nations Conference on Trade and Development, held in New York on 24 April 2006,

Welcoming with appreciation the offer of the Government of Qatar to host the follow-up international conference to review the implementation of the outcome of the International Conference on Financing for Development, in accordance with paragraph 73 of the Monterrey Consensus and resolution 60/188,

1. *Decides* that the Follow-up International Conference on Financing for Development to Review the Implementation of the Monterrey Consensus will be held in Doha in the second half of 2008, at a date to be determined by the General Assembly in consultation with the host country, taking into due consideration the regular schedule of meetings of the United Nations;

2. *Decides also*, in accordance with resolution 60/188, to commence the preparatory process for the review conference during the present session of the Assembly, and to this end requests the President of the Assembly to hold, starting in 2007, direct intergovernmental consultations of the whole with the participation of all Member States and the major institutional stakeholders involved in the financing for development process, on all issues related to the review conference, and in this regard decides that these consultations must be open, inclusive and transparent;

3. *Reiterates* that the review conference should assess progress made, reaffirm goals and commitments, share

best practices and lessons learned, and identify obstacles and constraints encountered, actions and initiatives to overcome them and important measures for further implementation, as well as new challenges and emerging issues;

4. *Reaffirms* its resolve to continue to make full use of the existing institutional arrangements for reviewing the implementation of the Monterrey Consensus, out in paragraph 69 of the Consensus and in line with resolution 57/270 B, including the high-level dialogues convened by the Assembly and the spring meetings of the Economic and Social Council with the Bretton Woods institutions, the World Trade Organization and the United Nations Conference on Trade and Development, bearing in mind the need to enhance the effectiveness of the follow-up process of the Monterrey Consensus;

5. *Stresses* the importance of the full involvement of all relevant stakeholders in the implementation of the Monterrey Consensus at all levels, and also stresses the importance of their full participation in the Monterrey follow-up process, in accordance with the rules of procedure of the General Assembly, in particular the accreditation procedures and modalities of participation utilized at the Conference and in its preparatory process;

6. *Decides* to hold the 2007 High-level Dialogue on Financing for Development in the fourth quarter of 2007, at a specific date to be determined by the President of the General Assembly in consultation with Member States;

7. Decides also that the modalities for holding the 2007 High-level Dialogue will be the same as those used in the 2005 High-level Dialogue, as described in General Assembly resolution 59/293 of 27 May 2005;

8. *Requests* the Secretary-General to prepare a note on the organization of work of the High-level Dialogue;

9. *Decides* to include in the provisional agenda of its sixty-second session the item entitled "Follow-up to and implementation of the outcome of the International Conference on Financing for Development";

10. *Requests* the Secretary-General to submit a report on the implementation of commitments agreed at the International Conference on Financing for Development under that item, to be prepared in full collaboration with the major institutional stakeholders, as an input to the High-level Dialogue.

By **decision 61/552** of 22 December, the Assembly decided that the agenda item on follow-up to and implementation of the outcome of the International Conference on Financing for Development would remain for consideration at its resumed sixty-first (2007) session.

Investment, technology and related financial issues

The UNCTAD Commission on Investment, Technology and Related Financial Issues held its tenth session in Geneva from 6 to 10 March [TD/B/COM.2/71].

For its consideration of policy issues related to investment and development, the Commission had before it the *World Investment Report 2005: Transnational Corporations and the Internationalization of R&D* [UNCTAD/WIR/2005)]; the report of the Expert Meeting on Positive Corporate Contributions to the Economic and Social Development of Host Developing Countries [YUN 2005, p. 1067]; and the report of the Expert Meeting on Capacity Building in the Area of foreign direct investment (FDI): Data Compilation and Policy Formulation in Developing Countries [ibid.]. For issues related to investment arrangements, the Commission considered an UNCTAD secretariat note on international investment rule-setting: trends, emerging issues and implications [TD/B/COM.2/68], and a final, in-depth evaluation report of the UNCTAD work programme on capacity building in developing countries on issues in international investment agreements [UNCTAD/ITE/IIT/2005/6]. For its consideration of investment policy reviews (IPRs): exchange of national experiences, the Commission had before it the *Investment Policy Review of Colombia* [UNCTAD/ITE/IPC/MISC/2005/11] and a summary of deliberations on science and technology and innovation policy review of Iran [TD/B/COM.2/69]. For its consideration of the reports of the Commission's subsidiary bodies, it considered the Intergovernmental Working Group of Experts report on International Standards of Accounting and Reporting on its twenty-second session [TD/B/COM.2/ISAR/31].

The Commission, in agreed recommendations, urged UNCTAD to further understanding on FDI and development. It requested the secretariat to intensify technical cooperation in capacity-building in FDI statistics in developing countries, including by assisting them in strengthening regional cooperation, organizing meetings on FDI statistics and policy formulation, and assessing FDI impact on development. UNCTAD should serve as the UN system focal point for matters related to international investment agreement, and advance understanding of related issues and their development dimension, including with reference to investor-State dispute resolution. Welcoming the in-depth impact evaluation of the work programme on international investment agreements, the Commission called for increased support to technical assistance and capacity-building. It commended the programme of IPRs and asked the secretariat to ensure that the development needs and priorities of countries under review formed an integral part of IPR and its follow-up mechanism. The Commission noted the guidance on corporate governance disclosure prepared by the Intergovernmental Working Group of Experts on International Standards of Accounting and Reporting, and recommended wide dissemination of the guidance to improve corporate governance disclosures in order to facilitate investment and enhance the transparency and stability of the investment environment.

The Commission took note of the reports of the two Expert Meetings and the UNCTAD secretariat's progress report on the implementation of the Commission's agreed conclusions and recommendations [TD/B/COM.2/70]. It took note of the report of the Intergovernmental Working Group on International Standards of Accounting and Reporting, endorsed the agreed conclusions contained therein and approved the provisional agenda for that body's twenty-third session. The Commission also approved the provisional agenda for its eleventh (2007) session and the topics for the two Expert Meetings and Ad Hoc Expert Meeting for 2006 (see below).

In April [A/61/15], TDB took note of the Commission's report, approved the provisional agenda for its eleventh (2007) session, as well as the topics of expert meetings for 2006.

Subsidiary bodies. In 2006, three expert meetings took place, all in Geneva. The Expert Meeting on Building Productive Capacities (4-6 September) [TD/B/COM.2/EM.19/3] considered an UNCTAD secretariat note on the issue [TD/B/COM.2/EM.19/2]. The Meeting focused on the development and effective utilization of productive capacities, and the role of the UNCTAD technical assistance programmes on insurance. Experts recognized that liberalization reforms in developing countries had not always yielded the expected benefits of successful integration into the global economy, and overcoming constraints required broad-based capacity building at the national level, supported by development partners. They identified the principal supply constraints affecting capacity building, including an inadequate regulatory environment, weak public institutional and administrative capacity, poor and inefficient infrastructure and a limited resource base. Experts also identified the need for effective investment policy measures in labour, taxation, competition policy, exchange control and intellectual property protection. They noted the role of the UNCTAD IPRs and called for effective implementation of the recommendations. While the Experts welcomed the scaling up of ODA flows, they pointed to the need to channel increasing resources to specific infrastructure development and productive capacity building programmes, and for policy makers in developing countries to pay more attention to the SME sector and strengthen entrepreneurship. The Experts called for a more detailed examination of the problems related to privatization and the lessons to be learned for the efficient administration of that process, as well as the need for accompanying policy and regulatory institutions. In addition, they stressed the importance of synergies between ODA and FDI, particularly for the development of infrastructure. The Experts also noted the challenges that developing countries, particularly in Africa, faced in the area of insurance.

The Expert Meeting on FDI in Natural Resources (20-22 November) [TD/B/COM.2/EM.20/3] had before it an UNCTAD secretariat note on transnational corporations, extractive industries and development: implications for policies [TD/B/COM.2/EM.20/2]. The Experts stressed the strategic importance of natural resources and highlighted the need for adequate policy space for countries to ensure that FDI contributed to their priorities and national development objectives. They agreed that recent commodity price increases had had a notable influence on investment decisions, and had affected policies concerning the entry and operations of transnational corporations (TNCs) in extractive industries. The Experts also discussed the usefulness of international investment agreements, and the potential impacts of TNC involvement in resource extraction and related policy implications. In the light of the cyclical nature of commodity markets, it was argued that countries should design policies to ensure long-term sustainable investment, including flexible contracts that were cost and price indexed, which would better align the interests of both countries and companies. The Experts stressed the need for improving governance in resource-rich countries to ensure a fair distribution of revenues between Governments and firms, as well as sustainable development and poverty reduction. Regarding future operations, a number of recommendations were made, including increased technical assistance for developing countries to improve regulatory frameworks and institutional capacities, as well as further policy analysis on ways to encourage industrialization and diversification based on resource extraction, and on ways to improve mining taxation schemes. Developing countries also needed to develop their geological survey so as to strengthen their bargaining positions. The scope for South-South collaboration in developing development-friendly policies and institutions regulating the involvement of TNCs in extractive industries should be further explored.

The Ad Hoc Expert Meeting on Advocacy for Investment Policies with Particular Reference to the

Development Dimension (23-24 November) [TD/B/COM.2/AHM.1/3] had before it a note prepared by the UNCTAD secretariat on policy advocacy in investment promotion [TD/B/COM.2/AHM.1/2]. The Meeting discussed policy advocacy in investment and the efforts of countries, mostly through investment promotion agencies (IPAs), to influence policy change so as to improve their investment environments in order to attract increased levels of FDI. Experts stressed that policy advocacy work should be based on comprehensive long-term strategies that contained measures for improving the investment climate and the involvement of stakeholders from the private and public sectors. A number of recommendations were made for follow-up work between IPAs and international partners, including the holding of capacity-building workshops to train IPAs in establishing, implementing and evaluating a full range of tools for policy advocacy. IPAs should tap partners like UNCTAD for assistance in developing specific tools for policy advocacy, including business forums and public/private partnerships. Investment policy reviews should be conducted, followed by advocacy plans of action and implementation reviews.

Competition law and policy

The Meeting of the Ad Hoc Expert Group on Competition Law and Policy (Geneva, 30 October), held within the context of the seventh meeting of the intergovernmental Group of Experts on Competition Law and Policy (Geneva, 31 October-2 November) (see below), focused on two issues: the relationship between competition law and policy and subsidies; and the analysis of cooperation and dispute settlement mechanisms relating to competition policy in regional free trade agreements, taking into account issues of particular concern to small and developing countries.

The Intergovernmental Group of Experts on Competition Law and Policy, at its seventh session (Geneva, 31 October–2 November) [TD/B/COM.2/CLP/57], held consultations and discussions regarding peer reviews on competition law and policy; review of the Model Law on Competition and studies related to the provisions of the 1980 Set of Rules for the Control of Restrictive Business Practices (known as the Set) [YUN 1980, p. 626]; the UNCTAD work programme, including capacity-building and technical assistance on competition law and policy; and the provisional agenda of the Group's next session.

The Group had before it an UNCTAD secretariat note on recent improvement cases involving more than one country [TD/RBP/CONF16/5/Rev.1-TD/B/COM.2/CLP/53]; voluntary peer review of competition policy: Tunisia [UNCTAD/DITC/CLP/2006/2]; experiences gained so far on international cooperation on competition policy issues and the mechanisms used [TD/RBP/CONF.6/12/Rev.1–TD/B/COM2./CLP/21/Rev.4]; roles of possible dispute mediation mechanisms and alternative arrangements, including voluntary peer reviews, in competition law and policy [TD/RBP/CONF.6/11/Rev.1–TD/B/COM.2/CLP/37/Rev.3]; ways in which possible international agreements on competition might apply to developing countries, including through preferential or differential treatment, with a view to enabling those countries to introduce and enforce competition law and policy consistent with their level of economic development [TD/RBP/CONF.6/9/Rev.1–TD/B/COM.2/CLP/46/Rev.2]; best practices for defining respective competences and settling of cases, which involved joint action by competition authorities and regulatory bodies [TD/RBP/CONF.6/13/Rev.1-TD/B/COM.2/CLP/44/Rev.2]; review of capacity-building and technical assistance on competition law and policy [TD/B/COM.2/CLP/54]; Voluntary Peer Review of Competition Policy: Tunisia [UNCTAD/DITC/CLP/2006]; handbook on competition legislation [TD/B/COM.2/CLP/50]; and a directory of competition authorities [TD/B/COM.2/CLP/51].

In its agreed conclusions, the Group called on States to increase cooperation between competition authorities and Governments in order to strengthen international action against anti-competitive practices as covered by the Set, especially at the international level; such competition should take particular note of the needs of developing countries and economies in transition. It expressed appreciation to Tunisia for volunteering for a peer review during the seventh session and decided that UNCTAD should undertake further voluntary peer reviews on the competition law and policy of member States or regional groupings of States, back-to-back with the Group's eighth session. The Group took note of the continued implementation of national economic reforms aimed at establishing competition rules and strengthening of bilateral and multilateral cooperation in the area of competition. The UNCTAD secretariat should prepare for consideration at the Group's eighth session a study on competition issues at national and international levels in the energy sector. It should continue publishing as non-sessional documents and include in its website a series of documents, including a further revised and updated version of the Model Law on Competition on the basis of submissions to be received from member States no later than 31 January 2007. The Group recommended that its eighth session consider several issues for better implementation of the Set, namely: competition at national and international levels: energy; competition policy and the exercise of intellectual property rights; and criteria for evaluating the effectiveness of competition authorities.

International standards of accounting and reporting

The Intergovernmental Working Group of Experts on International Standards of Accounting and Reporting (ISAR), at its twenty-third session (Geneva, 10-12 October) [TD/B/COM.2/ISAR/35], had before it an UNCTAD secretariat note on the review of practical implementation issues of international financial reporting standards (IFRS) [TD/B/COM.2/ISAR/33], and case studies on Brazil, Germany, India, Jamaica and Kenya [TD/B/COM.2/ISAR/33/ Add.1-5]. The Experts also considered a report on guidance on corporate responsibility indicators in annual reports [TD/B/COM.2/ISAR/34], a study on the "2006 Review of the implementation status of corporate responsibility indicators" [TD/B/COM.2/ISAR/CRP.2], as well as the annual review of corporate governance disclosure contained in the document entitled "2006 Review of the implementation status of corporate governance disclosures" [TD/B/COM.2/ISAR/CRP.3].

In its agreed conclusions, the Working Group reiterated the importance of principles-based, high-quality financial reporting standards for the coherence and efficient functioning of financial infrastructure, and the mobilization of financial resources for developing countries and transition economies. The Working Group, recognizing that, following the widespread adoption of IFRS in 2005, various stakeholders, including regulators, preparers, users and auditors, continued to encounter various practical implementation challenges, stressed that an effective regulatory regime, an adequate audit system and professional education requirements, should be in place to facilitate the implementation of IFRS. Also observing that IFRS were initially formulated for large listed companies of developed financial markets, the Working Group emphasized that the issue of accounting by small and medium-sized enterprises (SMEs) had to be addressed separately to enable the vast majority of those enterprises around the world to meet their user reporting needs in a cost-effective and useful manner. The Working Group discussed the initiatives by the International Accounting Standards Board (IASB) and other standards setters to develop standards to meet the financial reporting requirements for SMEs and resolved to support such endeavours and provide inputs to the processes. The Group identified the need to update guidance to level 3 SMEs that addressed the accounting and reporting needs of micro-enterprises, and requested UNCTAD to reconvene a Consultative Group to assess the feedback on the practical use of the level 2 and 3 SME guidance; to facilitate ISAR input into the deliberations on accounting by SMEs currently taking place within the IASB and the International Federation of Accountants; and to update its level 3 SME guidance.

Regarding the comparability of indicators on corporate responsibility, the Working Group recognized the increased interest among corporate responsibility reporters in creating more concise, useful and performance-oriented reports. The Group agreed that UNCTAD should further refine and finalize the guidance on selected corporate responsibility indicators and their measurement methodology, with a view to providing a voluntary technical tool for enterprises. It should coordinate that work with other international organizations along with private and public sector stakeholders. The Group considered the results of the annual review of corporate governance disclosure contained in the "2006 Review of the implementation status of corporate governance disclosures" and commended the survey for its quality. The Group further recommended the voluntary use of an ISAR index on corporate governance disclosure as an innovative practical tool for improving corporate transparency.

The Commission on Investment, Technology and Related Financial Issues, in March [TD/B/COM.2/71], took note of the Intergovernmental Working Group's report on its twenty-second session [YUN 2005, p. 1068] and endorsed its agreed conclusions.

Taxation

The Economic and Social Council, by decision **2006/213** of 10 February, deferred consideration of the report of the first session of the Committee of Experts on International Cooperation in Tax Matters [YUN 2005, p. 1069] until its 2006 substantive session in Geneva.

On 28 July [meeting 43], the Council adopted **resolution 2006/48** [draft: E/2006/L.12 & 36] without vote [agenda item 13 *(h)*].

Committee of Experts on International Cooperation in Tax Matters

The Economic and Social Council,

Recalling its resolution 2004/69 of 11 November 2004, in which the Council decided that the Ad Hoc Group of Experts on International Cooperation in Tax Matters should be renamed the Committee of Experts on International Cooperation in Tax Matters,

Recognizing the call made in the Monterrey Consensus of the International Conference on Financing for Development for the strengthening of international tax cooperation through enhanced dialogue among national tax authorities and greater coordination of the work of the concerned multilateral bodies and relevant regional organizations, giving special attention to the needs of developing countries and countries with economies in transition,

Taking note of the report of the Secretary-General on the implementation of and follow-up to commitments and agreements made at the International Conference on Financing for Development and the recommendations contained therein,

Recognizing the need for an inclusive, participatory and broad-based dialogue on international cooperation in tax matters,

Noting the activities developing within the concerned multilateral bodies and relevant regional organizations,

1. *Takes note with appreciation* of the report of the Committee of Experts on International Cooperation in Tax Matters on its first session;

2. *Recognizes* that the Committee agreed to create, as necessary, ad hoc subcommittees composed of experts and observers who would work throughout the year according to the Committee's rules of procedure to prepare and determine the supporting documentation for the agenda items, including requests for papers by independent experts, for consideration at its regular session;

3. *Notes* that four subcommittees on substantial matters, namely, treaty abuses, mutual assistance in collecting tax debts, definition of permanent establishment, and exchange of information, and two working groups, on international tax arbitration and the Manual for the Negotiation of Bilateral Tax Treaties between Developed and Developing Countries, were created at the first session;

4. *Recognizes* that in order to deal with issues relating to the agenda on a continuous basis, subcommittees should use electronic communications where possible, but that the efficient operation of these subcommittees may in future require some face-to-face meetings;

5. *Invites* the Committee to continue to organize training workshops for developing countries and countries with economies in transition as part of the work required to carry out its mandate, which includes making recommendations on capacity-building and providing technical assistance;

6. *Requests* the Secretary-General to establish a trust fund to supplement regular budget resources, which would receive voluntary contributions from Member States and other institutions interested in providing financing for the Committee's activities in supporting international cooperation in tax matters, including support for the participation of experts from developing countries;

7. *Decides* that the second session of the Committee shall be convened in Geneva from 30 October to 3 November 2006;

8. *Approves* the provisional agenda for the second session of the Committee, as contained in paragraph 122 of its report on its first session.

Second meeting of Committee of Experts. Pursuant to Council resolution 2006/48 (above), the second session of the Committee of Experts on International Cooperation in Tax Matter was held in Geneva from 30 October to 3 November [E/2006/45]. The session discussed improper use of treaties; mutual assistance in collection of taxes; definition of permanent establishment; taxation of development projects; exchange of information; revision of the United Nations Manual for the Negotiation of Bilateral Tax Treaties between Developed and Developing Countries; treatment of Islamic financial institutions; and dispute resolution.

The Committee decided that the subcommittee on treaty abuses should continue its work in drafting a new Commentary on article 1 of the United Nations Model Convention, which would include both practical examples and possible wording of anti-abuse clauses, focusing on improper use by taxpayers. To better reflect its work, the subcommittee would be renamed the subcommittee on improper uses of treaties. In terms of definition of permanent establishment, the Committee agreed that attention should be paid to taxation of services related to articles 14 and 5 of the Model Convention and to taxation of technical fees. The subcommittee was mandated to propose a draft article and Commentary, reflecting both its further work and what had been agreed during the current session. Regarding taxation of development projects, the Committee invited the International Tax Dialogue to do further work on the subject, with donor agency participation. The Committee invited the subcommittee on exchange of information to finalize the proposed article and Commentary on exchange of information so that it could agree to the suggested changes at the next session. The Committee also acknowledged the need for updating the United Nations Manual for the Negotiation of Bilateral Tax Treaties between Developed and Developing Countries, taking into account changes to the Model Convention and its Commentary. The Committee decided that further work was needed to obtain a better understanding of the issues involved in the treatment of Islamic financial institutions, and set up a new subcommittee on dispute resolution to address that issue in place of the current working group. With regard to the update of the Commentaries, it agreed that all experts would read the Commentaries by the end of the year and identify changes to be made. It also decided to hold the Committee's third session from 29 October to 2 November.

Transport

Maritime transport

The Review of Maritime Transport, 2006 [Sales No. E.06.II.D.7] reported that world seaborne trade recorded another consecutive annual increase in 2005, reaching a record high of 7.1 billion tons. The annual growth rate was 3.8 per cent, compared to 5.3 per cent for 2004. The world merchant fleet expanded to 960 deadweight tons (dwt) at the beginning of 2006, a 7.2 per cent increase and the highest since 1989. New building deliveries increased to 70.5 dwt, and tonnage broken up and lost was a modest 6.3 million dwt, leaving a net gain of 64.2 million dwt. The fleet of oil tankers and dry bulk carriers, which together made up 72.9 per cent of the total world fleet, increased by 5.4 per cent and 7.9 per cent, respectively. The container ship fleet increased by 13.3 per cent to 111.1 million dwt, and the liquefied gas carriers fleet by 7.5 per cent 24.2 million dwt. Registration of ships by developed market economy countries and major open-registry countries accounted for 26.9 and 45 per cent of the world fleet, respectively. Open registries increased their tonnage by 6.9 per cent; two thirds of that beneficially owned fleet was owned by market-economy and developing countries. Developing countries' share reached 22.7 per cent, or 218.3 million dwt, of which 171.6 million dwt was registered in Asia.

Transport of dangerous goods

The Committee of Experts on the Transport of Dangerous Goods and on the Globally Harmonized System of Classification and Labelling of Chemicals (GHS), at its third session (Geneva, 14 December) [ST/SG/AC.10/34, Add. 1 & Corr.1, Add. 2 & Corr.1 & 3 & Corr.1], considered the reports of the Subcommittee of Experts on the Transport of Dangerous Goods on its twenty-ninth (3-11 July) [ST/SG/AC.10/C.3/58 & Add.1-2] and thirtieth (4-12 December) [ST/SG/AC.10/C.3/60] sessions; and of the Subcommittee of Experts on the Globally Harmonized System of Classification and Labelling of Chemicals (GHS) on its eleventh (12-14 July) [ST/SG/AC.10/C.4/22] and twelfth (12-14 December) [ST/SG/AC.10/C.4/24] sessions, all held in Geneva.

The Committee took note of Economic and Social Council resolution 2005/53 [YUN 2005, p. 1070] and decision 2005/201 C [ibid., p. 1624]. The Committee also noted that the secretariat had published the fourteenth revised edition of the recommendations on the Transport of Dangerous Goods, *Model Regulations* [ST/SG/AC.10/1/Rev.14], Amendment 1 to the fourth revised edition of the Recommendations on the Transport of Dangerous Goods, *Manual of Test and Criteria* [ST/SG/AC.10/11/Rev.4/Amdt.1], and the first revised edition of the *Globally Harmonized System of Classification and Labelling of Chemicals* [ST/SG/AC.10/30/Rev.1], adopted by the Committee in 2003 [YUN 2003, p. 993] in all UN official languages.

The Committee endorsed the reports of the Subcommittee of Experts on the Transport of Dangerous Goods, including the amendments to the existing recommendations on the transport of dangerous goods and the new recommendations. It also endorsed the reports of the Subcommittee of Experts on the GHS, including amendments to the existing text and the new provisions adopted; approved the work programme of the two subcommittees, as well as the list of tasks assigned to the Organisation for Economic Cooperation and Development in relation to health hazards and hazards to the environment; agreed on the schedule of meetings for 2007-2008; and adopted a draft resolution for consideration by the Economic and Social Council in 2007.

UNCTAD institutional and organizational questions

In 2006, the Trade and Development Board (TDB), the governing body of UNCTAD, held the following sessions, all in Geneva: thirty-eighth executive session (20 April); first part of its twenty-third special session (8-11 May); second part of its twenty-third special session (12-16 June); thirty-ninth executive session (30 June); fifty-third session (27 September–2 October and 10 October); resumed fifty-third session (10 October); and third part of its twenty-third special session (3-10 October) [A/61/15].

In April, TDB took note of the reports of its subsidiary bodies and approved the modalities, roadmap and provisional agenda for its Mid-term Review (see p. 1109). It also welcomed the report and resolution of the Fifth United Nations Conference to Review All Aspects of the Set of Multilaterally Agreed

Equitable Principles and Rules for the Control of Restrictive Business Practices [YUN 2005, p. 1068], and approved a revised UNCTAD calendar of meetings for 2006.

On 15 June, TDB adopted an agreed outcome, ad referendum [TD/B (S-XXIII)/5], on strengthening UNCTAD three pillars of research and analysis, consensus building and technical cooperation. TDB stressed that UNCTAD research and analysis should help advance consensus on important trade and development-related issues, including implementation of the outcomes of the major UN conferences and summits. It should be development-oriented, independent and grounded in solid evidence, and provide ahead-of-the-curve and innovative work on trade and development and related issues, challenging conventional wisdom when necessary, and examining all related issues of the international economic system in the context of their relationship with trade and development, including the areas of debt, finance, intellectual property, technology, globalization and sustainable development. It further agreed that UNCTAD should enhance its research and analytical work for all developing countries and countries with economies in transition. TDB recommended also that UNCTAD research and analysis should be strengthened in the context of trade and development, including, among other things: recognizing the need for diversity in national policies; examining systemic issues of the international economy of particular importance to developing countries; and developing an effective dissemination and communication strategy, targeted at a wider audience, including policy makers and other stakeholders. On the issue of consensus building, TDB recommended that the UNCTAD consensus building pillar be strengthened, including by providing a more focused input from the Board to the General Assembly's consideration of the agenda item on international trade and development; considering the creation of a Commission on Globalization and Systemic Issues; and ensuring predictable financing of experts from developing countries and countries with economies in transition in UNCTAD expert meetings. TDB agreed that there was a need to ensure transparency, efficiency, effectiveness and accountability in all UNCTAD technical cooperation activities. It urged donors to work towards predictable funding, based on needs, concerns and developing countries' priorities in order to allow increased sustainability of technical assistance activities. The Board recommended that the UNCTAD technical assistance pillar be strengthened by ensuring more cross-divisional cooperation in order to reflect the systemic perspective of the key interrelated issues of the international economic agenda in the design and implementation of technical cooperation activities; improving management, evaluation and reporting of all technical cooperation activities according to UN Rules and Regulations; and introducing an information sharing system to enhance the flow of information on technical cooperation.

On 30 June, TDB took note of the Secretary-General's report on activities undertaken by UNCTAD in favour of Africa [TD/B/EX(39)/2].

In September, TDB adopted a decision on the review of UNCTAD technical cooperation activities [decision 488 (LIII)]. It took note of: the report of the Working Party on its forty-seventh session (see below) and the report on UNCTAD assistance to the Palestinian people.

In October, TDB adopted an agreed outcome of the mid-term review of UNCTAD XI, as well as agreed conclusions on the review of progress in the implementation of the Programme of Action for the LDCs for the decade 2001-2010 [agreed conclusions 486 (LIII)], and on economic development in Africa: doubling aid–making the "big push" work [agreed conclusions 487 (LIII)]. It also decided to hold its fifty-fourth regular (2007) session during the first two weeks of October [decision 489 (LIII)]. TDB took note of the report on UNCTAD contribution to the review of progress made in the implementation of the outcomes of major UN conferences and summits; of the oral report on UNCTAD XI multi-stakeholder partnerships; of the report on the hearing with civil society; and of the report of the Working Party on its forty-sixth session. It endorsed the agreed conclusions of the Working Party on the review of the UNCTAD section of the proposed UN 2008-2009 Strategic Framework. It took note of the report of UNCITRAL on its thirty-ninth session (New York, 19 June–7 July); the report of the ITC UNCTAD/WTO Joint Advisory Group on its thirty-ninth session; and the report by the President of the Advisory Body set up in accordance with the Bangkok Plan of Action on the implementation of courses by the secretariat in 2005-2006. It decided to submit text to the General Assembly for adoption within the framework of the resolution on international trade and development and agreed that the general system of preferences Certificate of Origin Form A would be accepted until stock ran out.

Working Party. The UNCTAD Working Party on the Medium-term Plan and Programme Budget held two sessions in 2006, all in Geneva: the forty-sixth session (28-29 June) [TD/B/WP/186] and the forty-seventh session (11-14 September) [TD/B/WP/191].

Technical cooperation

In a July report [TD/B/WP/188 & Corr.1 & Add.1,2], the UNCTAD Secretary-General provided a review of technical cooperation activities in 2005. The size of contributions to UNCTAD voluntary trust funds reached its highest level, $34.8 million, or a 30 per cent increase over the previous year. Most of the increase was attributable to contributions from developing countries in support of self-financed activities in their own countries. Developed countries contributions accounted for 45.6 per cent ($15.8 million) of overall contributions, a contraction of 8 per cent compared to 2004. Contributions from developing countries almost doubled to reach some $10.4 million, or some 30 per cent of the total contribution to the trust funds. Contributions from multilateral organizations also increased. Total expenditures on UNCTAD technical cooperation remained at $30.5 million.

By region, $5.9 million went to Asia and the Pacific, $5.1 million to Africa, $2.3 million to Latin America and the Caribbean and $1.1 million to Europe. Some $15.9 million went to interregional projects. The LDCs accounted for 37 per cent of the total delivery. By programme, services infrastructure for development and trade efficiency accounted for 36.7 per cent of the total expenditure; international trade in goods and services and commodities, 29.1 per cent; globalization and development strategies, 13.8 per cent; and investment, technology and enterprise development, 13 per cent. The balance of 7.3 per cent went to programmes for least developed, landlocked and island developing countries (3.7 per cent); UN regular programme of technical cooperation (2.7 per cent); executive direction and management and support services, (0.7 per cent) and resources management service (0.2 per cent). Major technical assistance programmes in order of expenditure included: Automated System for Customs Data ($8.7 million); trade negotiations and commercial diplomacy ($4.1 million); trade, environment and development ($3.2 million); and policy and capacity building ($2.9 million).

Technical cooperation strategy

The Working Party on the Medium-term Plan and the Programme Budget, at its forty-seventh session in September [TD/B/WP/191], considered a July report on UNCTAD technical cooperation activities in 2005 (see above). It adopted a draft decision for adoption by TDB on the review of UNCTAD technical cooperation activities and their financing.

On 10 October [A/61/15 (dec. 488 (LIII))], TDB took note of the report on UNCTAD technical cooperation activities in 2005 and requested the secretariat to introduce further improvements in the reports, including in the statistical annex. It reiterated the importance of ensuring an equitable distribution of resources among the developing country regions and countries with economies in transition in the overall delivery of technical cooperation. Welcoming the fact that a significant part of UNCTAD technical assistance was provided through interregional activities, it urged donors and the secretariat to further enhance their assistance to those countries. The secretariat was requested to ensure that the technical assistance provided was demand-driven and met the beneficiaries' development goals and objectives. It called for implementation of the recommendations on technical cooperation emanating from the Mid-term Review process, and requested the secretariat to report on progress made in that regard to the next session of the Working Party dealing with technical cooperation. TDB looked forward to commencing intergovernmental consultations, which might include the report of the Panel of Eminent Persons, established by the UNCTAD Secretary-General, on possible ways of enhancing the development impact of UNCTAD technical assistance. In that regard, it took note of the efforts envisaged by the secretariat to enhance the coherence and interdivisional nature of technical cooperation programmes and activities, including streamlining projects into thematic clusters and programmes and closing inactive operations.

Evaluation

In July, an independent team submitted an evaluation of UNCTAD trade-related technical assistance and capacity building on accession to WTO [TD/B/WP/190], in response to a request by the Working Party on the Medium-term Plan and Programme Budget, at its forty-third session [YUN 2004, p. 988]. The evaluation focused on technical cooperation projects for WTO accession implemented by UNCTAD.

The report stated that UNCTAD technical assistance and capacity building activities were relevant, focused, pro-development and responsive to the changing needs of the beneficiary countries. Accession to WTO was a very complex and complicated process, and recipient countries relied heavily on UNCTAD to provide objective, evidence-based and development-focused support. Its continued engagement in broad-based technical assistance and capacity building activities were fully supported by beneficiary countries. It was suggested that international agencies/donor countries should work more closely in partnership with UNCTAD to ensure that technical assistance and capacity building programmes on accession were strategically and systematically integrated. The impact and effectiveness of the programme could be further improved by establishing efficient inter-agency coordination structures in the beneficiary countries. Predictable financing and availability of more staff were necessary ingredients to ensure the programme's future.

At its forty-seventh session in September [TD/B/WP/191], the Working Party, in its agreed conclusions, welcomed the report's recommendations and requested the UNCTAD Secretary-General to implement them and to report on progress made in that regard at the Working Party's next session on technical cooperation. He should also ensure that integral support, including post-accession assistance, was provided, the internal resource base of the programme strengthened, and close collaboration with WTO and other relevant organizations enhanced. The Working Party encouraged donors to increase financial support for the technical cooperation programme and called on the international community to enhance donor coherence and coordination in assistance for the accession process.

TDB, in October [A/61/15], endorsed the agreed conclusions of the Working Party.

Medium-term plan and programme budget

At its forty-sixth session (Geneva, 28-29 June) [TD/B/WP/186], the Working Party reviewed the UNCTAD section of the proposed 2008-2009 Strategic Framework. In agreed conclusions, the Working Party concurred with the draft Strategic Plan as amended [TD/B/WP/L.119/Rev.1], while noting that new developments could affect the document's content. It reiterated the importance of consultative processes between the secretariat and member States in making decisions with programmatic implications and requested the secretariat to hold regular briefings on the progress of programme implementation. It requested the UNCTAD Secretary-General to ensure the integrity of the mandates of all subprogrammes and ensure that the transfer of the Africa subprogramme to the new Division for Africa, Least Developed Countries and Special Programmes would strengthen the subprogramme, while maintaining its integrity. The Working Party stressed the need to strengthen the development dimension in the implementation of the programmes and ensure a development focus in new initiatives. It encouraged the secretariat to make further efforts in improving the indicators of achievement, including by measuring achievements through a comprehensive set of multi-dimensional indicators and by better reflecting the qualitative aspects of programme outputs and contributions.

In October [A/61/15], TDB took note of the Working Party's report on its forty-sixth session and endorsed the agreed conclusions.

Chapter V

Regional economic and social activities

In 2006, the five regional commissions of the United Nations continued to provide technical cooperation, including advisory services, to their member States. They also promoted programmes and projects and provided training to enhance national capacity-building in various sectors. All of them—the Economic Commission for Africa (ECA), the Economic Commission for Europe (ECE), the Economic Commission for Latin America and the Caribbean (ECLAC), the Economic and Social Commission for Asia and the Pacific (ESCAP) and the Economic and Social Commission for Western Asia (ESCWA)—held regular sessions during the year.

The executive secretaries of the commissions continued to meet periodically to exchange views and coordinate activities and positions on major development issues. In July, the Economic and Social Council held an interactive dialogue with the executive secretaries on the theme "The regional dimension of creating an environment conducive to generating full and productive employment, and decent work for all, and its impact on sustainable development".

During the year, the Council endorsed the ECE workplan on reform and its revised terms of reference. The General Assembly welcomed ECA efforts to conduct a comprehensive review in order to reposition the Commission to respond better to the challenges facing Africa. ESCWA approved in principle the establishment of an ESCWA Technology Centre and adopted the Intergovernmental Agreement on the Trans-Asian Railway Network. Its Ministers of Transport adopted draft declarations on road safety and transport, aimed at developing integrated intermodal transport and logistics systems. ECLAC asked its Executive Secretary to coordinate annual regional reports with other UN agencies, funds and programmes on progress made toward achieving the Millennium Development Goal (MDG) on hunger and poverty reduction, and to coordinate, in 2010, a regional inter-agency report summing up progress during the 2006-2010 period on all MDG targets. It asked its Executive Secretary to support the Montevideo resolution on shaping the future of social protection: access, financing and solidarity. The Council approved the admission of Japan as a member of ECLAC. In addition, ECLAC admitted the Turks and Caicos Islands as an associate member.

Regional cooperation

In 2006, the United Nations continued to strengthen cooperation among its five regional commissions, between them and other UN entities, and with regional and international organizations.

On 10 February (**decision 2006/211**), the Economic and Social Council decided that the theme for the regional cooperation item at its 2006 substantive session would be "The regional dimension of creating an environment conducive to generating full and productive employment, and decent work for all, and its impact on sustainable development". Accordingly, the Council held an interactive dialogue with the executive secretaries of the regional commissions on that subject on 6 July.

Meetings of executive secretaries. The executive secretaries of the regional commissions met from 3 to 7 July (Geneva), and from 17 to 19 October (New York) [E/2006/15, E/2007/15].

At their meetings, the executive secretaries focused mainly on the 2005 World Summit and its outcome contained in resolution 60/1 [YUN 2005, p. 48], progress made toward achieving internationally agreed development goals, including the Millennium Development Goals (MDGs) [YUN 2000, p. 51], the World Summit on the Information Society [YUN 2005, p. 933] and the efforts of the regional commissions to mainstream a regional dimension into the Organization's overall work in the economic and social sectors. They exchanged views also on the UN reform process, among other subjects, and on the problem of unemployment in their regions.

In their view, the World Summit Outcome underlined the need to bring the commissions' analytical and normative work and the regional dimension of development to bear on development work at the country level through strengthened coordination among the Organization's country teams and the regional commissions. The commissions also kept under review the follow-up actions needed to implement the World Summit Outcome and the subsequent initiatives taken by the General Assembly on the review of mandates, reform of the Economic and Social Council and the creation of the Peacebuilding Commission.

In compliance with the 2005 World Summit Outcome, the executive secretaries coordinated the efforts of the regional commissions in reviewing all mandates older than five years, resulting in a call for strengthening the global and regional linkages of mandates in tourism, trade and investment, information and communication technology, and population and migration. They welcomed the Secretary-General's initiative to strengthen system-wide coherence in order to provide more streamlined and cost-effective services for developing countries, including the least developed countries (LDCs), landlocked developing countries and small island developing States, and countries with economies in transition. In follow-up to the World Summit on the Information Society, they agreed to promote interregional cooperation and exchange of experiences among the commissions, by, among other things, undertaking projects under the United Nations Development Account and cooperating with the Digital Solidarity Fund. They also exchanged views on unemployment in their regions and held two interregional seminars (Bangkok, 20-21 April) on their respective region's macroeconomic situation, development challenges and infrastructure development, as well as on public-private partnerships and other multiple sources of financing. Given the growing need for a coordinated approach on a variety of issues and for programme effectiveness and cooperation among the regional commissions, the executive secretaries decided to organize meetings of the chiefs of programme planning, as a subsidiary structure to their meeting, which would report to them through the Regional Commissions New York Office. The meetings would support the strengthening of interregional cooperation and cooperation among the commissions and ensure more coherence in programme planning and results-based budgeting.

Review and reform of regional commissions

In a May report [E/2006/15], the Secretary-General updated the Economic and Social Council on actions taken by the regional commissions to implement the guidance given in Council resolution 1998/46 [YUN 1998, p. 1262] on mainstreaming the regional dimension into the work of the United Nations and enhancing the coherence of UN activities at the regional level. The report highlighted the reforms and programmatic adjustments undertaken in ECE, ECA, ESCAP and ESCWA. The commissions, while preparing the 2006-2007 programme budget, had significantly streamlined their programme structures and undertaken a detailed review of outputs associated with low priority and obsolete mandates.

An addendum to the report [E/2006/15/Add.1] contained the texts of resolutions and decisions adopted at recent meetings of the regional commissions and drawn to the Council's attention for consideration or action.

By **decision 2006/246** of 27 July, the Council took note of the Secretary-General's report and addendum. By the same decision, it took note of the summaries of: *Economic trends, as well as risks and opportunities, for the economies in the Economic Commission for Europe region* [E/2006/16]; the *Overview of the Economic Report on Africa 2006: "Recent economic trends in Africa and prospects for 2006"* [E/2006/17]; the *Economic and Social Survey of Asia and the Pacific, 2006* [E/2006/18]; *Latin America and the Caribbean: economic situation and outlook, 2005-2006* [E/2006/19]; and the *Survey of Economic and Social Developments in the* ESCWA *region 2005-2006* [E/2006/20].

The Council adopted resolutions on the workplan on reform of ECE and revised terms of reference of the Commission (resolution 2006/38); the admission of Japan as a member of ECLAC (resolution 2006/39); the date and venue of the thirty-second session of ECLAC (resolution 2006/40); and a decision changing the dates of the twenty-ninth session of ECA (decision 2006/205).

(For the summaries of economic surveys covering the regions and the texts of the resolutions, see the relevant sections of this chapter.)

Africa

In accordance with Economic and Social Council **decision 2006/205** of 7 February, the thirty-ninth session of the Economic Commission for Africa (ECA)/Conference of African Ministers of Finance, Planning and Economic Development, was held in Ouagadougou, Burkina Faso, from 10 to 14 May, under the theme "Meeting the challenge of employment in Africa".

The session considered the report and major recommendations of the twenty-fifth meeting of the Committee of Experts of the Conference of African Ministers of Finance, Planning and Economic Development [E/ECA/CM.39/8], which preceded the session (Ouagadougou, 10-13 May), and discussed the session's agenda and statutory issues. It also had before it the ECA 2006 annual report [E/ECA/CM.39/2]; the 2005 Survey of Economic and Social Conditions in Africa [E/ECA/CM.39/3/Rev.1]; an issues paper on meeting the challenge of employment in Africa [E/ECA/CM.39/4]; a report on progress and challenges in aligning poverty reduction strategies with the MDGS [E/ECA/CM.39/5]; a note by the secretariat entitled "Follow-up to the 2005 World Summit Outcome: ECA Response" [E/ECA/CM.39/6]; a note by the Executive Secretary on repositioning ECA to better respond to Africa's priorities [E/ECA/CM.39/7]; an African LDCs strategy paper for the further implementation of the Programme of Action for the Least Developed Countries for the Decade 2001-2010 [E/ECA/CM.39/12]; a joint report of the ECA, African Union Commission and the United Nations Development Programme (UNDP) on the: proceedings of the African plenary on national poverty reduction strategies and the implementation of the MDGS [E/ECA/CM.39/10]; and an outcome statement entitled "African plenary on national poverty reduction strategies and the implementation of the MDGS" that was adopted by the ECA, the African Union Commission and UNDP during their 26-28 March, 2006 meeting in Cairo [E/ECA/CM.39/11].

The Ministers adopted a ministerial statement [E/ECA/CM.39/9/Rev.1], in which they committed to incorporating employment objectives into national development strategies and policies in order to create decent jobs in Africa, and increasing domestic resource mobilization efforts, while urging development partners to honour their aid commitments to Africa and to fully implement and expand the Multilateral Debt Relief Initiative [YUN 2005, p. 1057]. They also undertook to include employment criteria in investment promotion policies and improve the quality of public finance management, alongside the development of accurate statistical and information systems to monitor the impact of policies. The Ministers expressed concern over the lack of comprehensive implementation of the 2004 Ouagadougou Plan of Action, the failure to integrate employment into national development strategies, and weak subregional and national coordination. They acknowledged the particularly fragile situation of African countries emerging from conflict and asked ECA to set up a Technical Capacity Building Forum and a funding initiative to support job creation and re-establish economic development management systems. To stimulate transformation and diversification, they undertook to adopt growth oriented macro- and micro-economic policies; identify and promote labour-absorbing sectors; enhance labour mobility and pursue an integrated rural development approach. Recognizing that stronger regional integration could stimulate job creation, the Ministers committed to ratifying bilateral and regional protocols on the free cross-border movement of goods and people and urged development partners to level the trade playing field for African countries, including by removing constraints imposed by the World Trade Organization (WTO) Agreements on Trade-Related Aspects of Intellectual Property Rights (TRIPS) and Trade-Related Investment Measures. The Ministers took note of the African Union (AU) Migration Policy Framework and Common African Position on International Migration and pledged to actively help shape the UN Secretary-General's initiative on international migration (see p. 1259).

The Ministers welcomed the Executive Secretary's initiative for repositioning ECA to improve the delivery of services. They encouraged him to pursue the proposal to refocus ECA work around two pillars: promoting regional integration; and meeting Africa's special needs and the global challenges facing the continent, as well as strengthening statistics and ECA subregional offices. The Ministers encouraged ECA to pay attention to the special needs of conflict and post-conflict countries and make peace, security and post-conflict recovery, reconstruction and rehabilitation one of its major areas of work.

Economic trends

In 2006, Africa's gross domestic product (GDP) grew by 5.7 per cent, up from 5.3 per cent in 2005, according to the Overview of the economic and social conditions in Africa 2007 [E/2007/17]. The growth was attributed to good macroeconomic management, strong demand for and higher prices of primary commodities, such as crude oil, metals and minerals, as well as debt relief, increased external capital flows and an improved political climate. North Africa led the continent with a GDP growth rate of 6.6 per cent, followed by Southern Africa at 5.9 per cent. However, West Africa's growth dropped to 4.2 per cent in 2006, from 5.4 per cent in 2005, East Africa from 6.1 per cent in 2005 to 5.8 per cent in 2006 and Central Africa, from 3.6 to 3.3 per cent. Higher oil prices resulted in stronger growth in North Africa, which grew from 5.2 to 6.6 per cent, due to steady growth in the secondary and tertiary sectors. By country, eight of the top 10 growth performers achieved the 7 per cent growth rate threshold estimated as needed to reach the MDGS (Angola, the Congo, Ethiopia, Liberia, the Libyan Arab Jamahiriya, Mauritania, Mozambique, the

Sudan), while five others (Comoros, Côte d'Ivoire, Seychelles, Swaziland, Zimbabwe) exhibited the weakest performance.

The average fiscal position on the continent continued to be positive, with an average budget balance of 0.1 per cent of GDP in 2006, compared to 0.4 per cent in 2005. That was largely driven by the sizeable fiscal surpluses recorded by many oil-exporting countries. However, 30 countries had budget deficits, up from 27 in 2005, owing to oil price increases that resulted in higher government expenditures. The inflation outlook remained satisfactory, with a majority of countries recording single-digit inflation rates. Only Zimbabwe, with an inflation rate of 1,216 per cent, and Guinea, with a rate of 27 per cent, were the main exceptions. However, the average consumer price inflation rate increased to 9.9 per cent in 2006, from 8.5 per cent in 2005, fuelled largely by higher oil prices and the subsequent increase in production costs and lower output. The continent's oil-exporting countries recorded increasing trade surpluses, while oil importing countries, particularly the landlocked developing countries, saw their trade deficit deteriorate from 4 per cent of GDP to 11 per cent. The continent's total external debt stock stood at $244 billion and debt-service obligations remained almost unchanged at 4.1 per cent in 2006.

Africa/China Forum. On 15 November [A/61/580-S/2006/897], China, the Congo and Ethiopia transmitted to the Secretary-General the text of the speeches made at the Beijing Summit of the Forum on China-Africa Cooperation (4 November) and the Declaration of the Beijing Summit of the Forum on China-Africa Cooperation. The Forum adopted the Beijing Action Plan of the Forum on China-Africa Cooperation (2007-2009).

Activities in 2006

The ECA programme of work in 2006 was organized under eight subprogrammes: facilitating economic and social policy analysis; fostering sustainable development; strengthening development management; harnessing information for development; promoting trade and regional integration; promoting the advancement of women; supporting subregional activities for development; and development planning and administration [E/ECA/CM.39/2].

Facilitating economic and social policy analysis

In 2006, ECA continued to help member States strengthen their capacity to design and implement appropriate policies to achieve sustained economic growth for poverty reduction, in line with the priorities of the Millennium Declaration [YUN 2000, p. 49] and the New Partnership for Africa's Development (NEPAD) [YUN 2001, p. 900]. Particular emphasis was placed on monitoring and tracking Africa's economic performance; conducting research and policy analysis on macroeconomic, financial and social issues; and strengthening the statistical capacities of African countries for monitoring progress toward the MDGs. ECA organized, with the AU and the African Development Bank, the African Plenary on Poverty Reduction Strategies and the Implementation of the MDGs (Cairo, Egypt, March). Its new subprogramme on social development was responsible for issues relating to the MDGs and poverty analysis and monitoring.

ECA convened an African regional meeting in February, in preparation for the global mid-term review of the Brussels Programme of Action for the Least Developed Countries for the Decade 2001-2010 [YUN 2001, p. 770] (see p. 1014), during which it agreed on a set of actions to expedite progress toward meeting the Programme of Action's targets. An African plenary meeting in March, in Cairo, Egypt, on poverty-reduction strategies and implementation of the MDGs resulted in the launch of an Internet-based Poverty Reduction Strategy Knowledge Network linking scholars and practitioners worldwide. In addition, ECA collaborated in the holding of the second Forum on African Statistical Development (Addis Ababa, 9-10 February) to review and endorse the Regional Reference Strategic Framework for African Statistical Development, which provided an action framework for African statistical development over the next 10 years. In collaboration with the UN Statistics Division and other partners, it organized a meeting in February (Cape Town, South Africa) on the 2010 round of population and housing censuses.

The secretariat submitted to the Commission's May session an issues paper on employment in Africa [E/ECA/CM.39/4], which identified the continent's main employment challenges and provided recommendations on how to integrate employment into national development policies.

New Partnership for Africa's Development

ECA continued to contribute to the implementation of NEPAD, a programme for the continent's development that was initiated by African leaders in 2001 [YUN 2001, p. 900]. Most NEPAD priorities were at the core of the ECA mandate and were supported through its analytical work and technical assistance in infrastructure development, governance, peace and security, agriculture, trade and market access, environment, population and urbanization, human resources development, employment, HIV/AIDS, science and technology and communication and outreach.

ECA provided substantive technical support to two major AU/NEPAD Summits related to the implementation of the NEPAD Comprehensive African Agricultural Development Programme. The African Fertilizer Summit (Abuja, Nigeria, June) called on ECA to collaborate with regional partners in following up on the implementation of its resolutions on the establishment of regional fertilizer procurement and distribution facilities, and of an African Fertilizer Development Financing Facility.

Under the ECA repositioning exercise, the NEPAD Unit was merged into the subprogramme on regional integration to enhance synergies and strengthen ECA role in coordinating regional support to NEPAD. The new Division, NEPAD and Regional Integration, reviewed the regional consultations among UN system agencies in support of NEPAD in order to improve its effectiveness and impact. The Division collaborated with the NEPAD secretariat in organizing capacity-building workshops that led to the further elaboration of implementation strategies for NEPAD priorities. In November, ECA convened the seventh regional consultations meeting of UN agencies with the AU Commission, the regional economic communities and the African Development Bank, which adopted recommendations for strengthening coordination and revitalizing the Cluster System (see p. 1071); fostering subregional coordination; improving coordination between the AU and African regional institutions; monitoring and evaluating actions and outcomes; and mobilizing resources and enhancing capacity.

Information for development

ECA activities on harnessing information for development had the objective of further strengthening the growth of a sustainable information society in Africa that better addressed the continent's development challenges. Its work focused on: harnessing information technology for development through implementation of the African Information Society Initiative [YUN 1996, p. 880]; strengthening geo-information systems for sustainable development; and improving access to information through enhanced library services.

To bridge the digital divide and strengthen information and communication technology (ICT) application in the economic sectors, ECA launched an ICT trade and economic growth initiative in partnership with Canada, to support the use of ICTs in economic performance and growth, build competitiveness, and increase growth in traditional and emerging sectors of African economies and the continent's export base in IT-enabled services (ITES). Since September 2005, ECA and the Economic Community of West African States had been working to create a subregional ICT policy framework that would address the challenges of building the information society, including harmonizing national ICT policies and plans. It also supported the Economic Community of Central African States and the Central African Economic and Monetary Community (CEMAC) in implementing the e-CEMAC 2010 initiative. ECA also assisted the East African Community in developing its Regional e-Government Framework, which was aimed at information sharing and promoting collaboration on cross-border data flow issues.

ECA continued to implement its initiative, SCAN-ICT, with the objective of building and strengthening the capacity of member States to develop indicators and benchmarks for monitoring and assessing information society trends. In late 2006, Cameroon, the Gambia, Ghana, Mauritius and Rwanda began developing web-based resources and databases to collect core ICT for development indicators. The regional information society indicators database for Africa would eventually be integrated into a global database to allow for comparison.

Information for development-related knowledge resources were produced and widely disseminated during 2006, including two video programmes entitled "Ensuring ICT for All" and "Community-based access: ensuring multi-stakeholder dialogue".

Sustainable development

ECA activities in fostering sustainable development aimed to promote awareness of the environmental foundations of sustainable development, with particular emphasis on integrating environmental sustainability into national development processes and poverty reduction strategies so that environmental degradation would not undermine socio-economic development. They focused on: reinforcing the links among food security, population, environment and human settlements; improving stewardship of natural resources by strengthening sustainable exploration capacity; and building capacity to use science and technology for sustainable development.

ECA work on trade and development sought to promote sustainable development by enhancing the capacity of Governments, businesses and civil society to integrate environmental considerations into trade and financial policies and practices, as well as plans for achieving the MDGs and poverty reduction. The impact in member States was reflected in the increase in the number of countries that were redefining their national strategies to include an environmental component. At a regional ECA workshop (Addis Ababa, February), participants expressed concern that environmental issues had not been taken as seriously in trade negotiations within the WTO framework due to the weak negotiating capacities of African countries. They called for awareness raising and advocacy among African leaders on the importance of environmental issues and allocating more resource for the sector.

ECA continued to play a critical role in the AU-ECA-African Development Bank Joint Initiative on Land Policy, which supported NEPAD efforts and programmes related to agricultural development, environmental management, peace-building and post-conflict reconstruction. ECA hosted a multi-stakeholder consultative workshop in March, which provided a platform for gaining consensus on the main land issues and pillars and the critical steps that would guide the formulation and implementation of the continental framework for land policy in Africa, modalities for building institutional capacity and partnerships for resource mobilization, development and implementation of the framework.

Development management

Addressing the challenge of establishing and sustaining good governance practices for broad stakeholder participation in the development process and strengthening the foundations for sustainable development in Africa remained the central objective of ECA work under its subprogramme on strengthening development management.

In March, ECA launched the first African Governance Report. The report, intended to promote consensus-building on key issues and develop, sustain and internalize the norms of good governance in Africa, provided significant input to the African Peer Review Mechanism (APRM) process in several countries. Indicators covered 27 countries and focused on issues of political representation, institutional effectiveness, and economic management and corporate governance. Several ad hoc expert group meetings and workshops were organized to review the results of research, analytical studies and publications prepared by the secretariat. They focused on best practices in participatory development; public financial management and accountability in the context of budget transparency in Africa; and the role of Africa's civil society in implementing the APRM. ECA also organized the sixth African Governance Forum on "Implementing the African Peer Review Mechanism: challenges and opportunities" (Kigali, Rwanda, 9-11 May), in collaboration with UNDP and the African Development Bank. The Forum, which brought together participants from 32 African countries, took stock of experiences countries had gained thus far and explored how the APRM could be incorporated into the region's development efforts. Several countries presented reports resulting from national preparatory consultations. The Forum, in its key recommendations, called for further strengthening and adjustment of APRM processes to facilitate speedy implementation; mainstreaming the APRM into African countries' development plans and strategies in order to avoid duplication and secure greater coherence; creating partnerships and resource sharing arrangements among member States; and mutual learning through advocacy and awareness-building.

Promoting trade and regional integration

In 2006, ECA continued to help accelerate the integration of Africa into the global economy and strengthen regional integration through the promotion of intraregional and international trade and physical integration.

The African Trade Policy Centre, established in 2004 [YUN 2004, p. 998] to strengthen ECA capacity on trade-related issues, conducted in February a training session on international trade negotiations for African embassies based in Addis Ababa, with the aim of helping member States integrate trade into development plans. The Centre also conducted a far-reaching study on mainstreaming trade.

ECA and the AU launched their second report on regional integration in Africa entitled *Assessing Regional Integration in Africa II: Rationalizing Regional Economic Communities* during the AU Summit of Heads of State (Banjul, Gambia, 1-2 July). The report examined the challenges that the proliferation of those communities and their overlapping mandates posed for Africa's integration, as well as their effectiveness in achieving the objectives of the Abuja Treaty, which aimed to establish the African Economic Community. The report recommended that regional economic communities rationalize their institutional settings and strengthen them with technical, legal and financial resources.

Transport and communications

An important objective of ECA work in infrastructure development was to help set up an efficient, integrated and affordable transport and communications system, as a basis for Africa's physical integration and to facilitate national and international traffic. ECA conducted a study on the current status of transport development in Africa, the findings of which were fed into a symposium (Ouagadougou, Burkina Faso, May) on "Financing Transport Infrastructure Development in Africa", organized in cooperation with the African Development Bank. ECA also undertook preparatory activities for the fourth African Road Safety Congress, as well as for the first United Nations Global Road Safety Week, both scheduled for 2007.

Integration of women in development

The overall objective of the ECA subprogramme on promoting the advancement of women was to mainstream gender into development policies, programmes and structures of member States in order to ensure parity in resource distribution and enable women to participate in strategic decisions in economic and social development.

ECA provided national-level support to effectively implement the methods set forth in the Easy Reference Guidebook on Mainstreaming Unpaid Work and Household Production in National Statistics, Policies and Programmes [YUN 2005, p. 1083]. It also continued to develop and refine the gender-aware model to evaluate the impact of policies on poverty reduction and implemention of the MDGs in African countries. To address the lack of progress towards gender equality and women's advancement, ECA developed the African Gender and Development Index (AGDI), which contained a quantitative assessment of gender inequality in the social, economic and political sectors and a qualitative measurement of the extent to which member States had effectively implemented the conventions on gender equality and women's rights. AGDI country studies conducted in 12 countries were synthesized for publication in the Africa Women's report. In July, a subregional workshop was organized in Tunisia to assist Northern African members States in drawing up national action plans to accelerate efforts to address the commitments outlined in the Outcome and Way Forward document of Beijing + 10 [ibid., p. 1247]. ECA, in collaboration with the UNDP Regional Gender Programme of Africa Bureau set up an African Women's Human Rights Observatory, as a complementary source of data for awareness-raising and analysis to inform policy debates and sound policy-making.

Subregional offices

ECA five subregional offices (SROs), located in East Africa (Kigali, Rwanda), Southern Africa (Lusaka, Zambia), West Africa (Niamey, Niger), North Africa (Rabat, Morocco) and Central Africa (Yaounde, Cameroon), continued to promote the harmonization of national policies to support integration efforts and help countries consolidate regional economic communities in the overall AU framework and attain the goals set by NEPAD. A major priority was to support member States and the regional economic communities in translating NEPAD priorities into concrete projects and programmes at the country and subregional levels, particularly in trade, infrastructure, human capacity development, gender mainstreaming, agriculture, food security and the environment.

The SROs served as the ECA operational arm, facilitating subregional economic cooperation and integration, as well as centres for policy dialogue, through workshops, training, data collection and knowledge sharing. In addition, they collaborated with other UN agencies in their respective subregions within the context of the UN Resident Coordinator system and the Common Country Assessment/United Nations Development Assistance Framework to implement operational activities at the national level.

Strengthening of subregional offices

Review by Executive Secretary. The Executive Secretary, in his comprehensive review of ECA, presented at the thirty-ninth session of the Commission, confirmed that, in the light of the AU Commission agenda, as well as from the perspective of NEPAD, the SROs were among the most important instruments in enabling ECA to make meaningful contributions to meeting Africa's challenges. For them to play their role effectively, within the overall exercise for repositioning the Commission, action had to be taken in a number of key areas. Their mandate and mission had to be refocused; their products and services better designed; their delivery model revamped; their modalities improved through enhanced partnerships; and their resource base and use of ICTS significantly strengthened.

ECA, in the Ministerial Statement [E/ECA/CM.39/9/Rev.1] of its thirty-ninth session, supported the proposal to strengthen the SROs. In resolution 844(XXXIX), the Ministers invited the Secretary-General to support the ECA renewal and reform process by providing it, including the SROs, with adequate resources.

OIOS report. As requested in resolution 60/235 [YUN 2005, p. 1085], the Secretary-General, in September, submitted to the General Assembly a report of the Office of Internal Oversight Services (OIOS) on enhancing the role of the SROs [A/61/471].

The report examined the new strategic direction for the SROs, including a refocused mandate and mission, improved products and services and expected results; a new institutional governance framework; an SRO-driven planning and programming framework for ECA; improved modalities through enhanced partnerships; a strengthened resource base; and operational elements.

The report outlined the plan of action for strengthening ECA based on the OIOS recommendations. The report found that the SROs were a vital part of ECA. However, their mandate as the ECA operational arm, facilitators of subregional economic cooperation and integration and centres for policy dialogue was only partially fulfilled. Their core functions were inadequately funded, their role unclear, their visibility and outreach limited, and their support to regional economic communities varied in scope and effectiveness. Initiative, flexibility and multidisciplinary teamwork needed to be promoted. The impact of SROs could be enhanced through: more focused programming of activities; creative dissemination of information emphasizing electronic space and scaling-up of ICT capabilities; aligning staff expertise and skills with subregional priorities; and reliable mechanisms for cooperation between SROs and ECA headquarters. OIOS made 14 recommendations on a wide range of issues aimed at strengthening the SROs capacity to deliver programmes, improve coordination and energize their value for the UN system. The implementation of the action plan would be supported by a number of operational processes. Annexed to the report were the current and proposed ECA organizational structure and proposed staffing and a summary of specific actions to be taken in respect to the OIOS recommendations.

ACABQ report. The Advisory Committee on Administrative and Budgetary Questions (ACABQ), in its October report on enhancing the role of the SROs [A/61/544], noted the 14 recommendations by OIOS to strengthen the capacity of SROs, and that implementation of the action plan was under way, with activities planned for the 2006-2007 and 2008-2009 bienniums, and funding of the additional resources required during the current biennium would be provided through redeployment of staff and non-post resources to the SROs. ACABQ requested that progress toward achieving the ECA target of deploying up to 30 per cent of its staff to SROs by the 2008-2009 biennium be monitored and included in future reports. It also welcomed the results achieved in reducing the vacancy rate. However, the Advisory Committee felt that ECA current repositioning policy aimed at shifting towards operational rather than analytical work raised fundamental questions about the respective roles of the ECA headquarters and the SROs, as well as their integration with other UN entities in the region. It urged ECA to continue to review and define the role of the SROs, with a view to achieving synergies and optimal use of resources. ACABQ also requested that the budget proposals for the 2008-2009 biennium identify a clear link between requested financial and human resources and mandated activities, with the number and level of posts fully justified.

GENERAL ASSEMBLY ACTION

On 22 December [meeting 84], the General Assembly, on the recommendation of the Fifth (Administrative and Budgetary) Committee [A/61/652], adopted **resolution 61/234** without vote [agenda items 116 & 117].

Enhancing the role of the subregional offices of the Economic Commission for Africa

The General Assembly,

Recalling its resolution 60/235 of 23 December 2005,

Having considered the report of the Secretary-General on enhancing the role of the subregional offices of the Economic Commission for Africa and the related report of the Advisory Committee on Administrative and Budgetary Questions,

1. *Takes note* of the report of the Secretary-General and the report of the Advisory Committee on Administrative and Budgetary Questions;

2. *Recalls* its resolution 59/275 of 23 December 2004, in which it decided that the development of Africa should be among the priorities of the Organization for the period 2006-2007;

3. *Recalls also* its resolutions 57/2 of 16 September 2002 and 57/7 of 4 November 2002, and stresses the important role played by the Economic Commission for Africa in coordinating the activities of the United Nations system at the regional level in support of the New Partnership for Africa's Development;

4. *Recalls further* its resolution 60/1 of 16 September 2005 and its commitment to address the special needs of Africa;

5. *Welcomes* the efforts by the Economic Commission for Africa to conduct a comprehensive review aimed at repositioning it to better respond to the challenges facing Africa and to implement the recommendations of the Office of Internal Oversight Services of the Secretariat;

6. *Recalls its request* to the Secretary-General in paragraph 12 of its resolution 60/235 to submit a comprehensive plan of action to strengthen the subregional offices, and notes with appreciation the steps taken to define the role and mission of the subregional offices so as to address the recommendations made by the Office of Internal Oversight Services;

7. *Recalls* paragraphs 9 and 12 of its resolution 60/235 and its request to the Secretary-General, in the context of the plan of action, to ensure that adequate resources are provided to the Economic Commission for Africa and its subregional offices to continue their support for the New Partnership for Africa's Development and the regional economic communities of Africa, as well as to ensure the full implementation of the recommendations of the Office of Internal Oversight Services;

8. *Recalls also* its concern expressed in paragraph 8 of its resolution 60/235, and notes that the repositioning exercise and implementation of the recommendations of the Office of Internal Oversight Services will be addressed through a redeployment of post and non-post resource requirements in the biennium 2006-2007 and that the Secretary-General will address remaining proposals for resources and reorganization in the context of the proposed programme budget for the biennium 2008-2009;

9. *Requests* the Secretary-General, in the context of his report on the comprehensive information and communication technology strategy of the Organization, to be submitted to the General Assembly at the first part of its resumed sixty-first session, to include detailed information on the implementation of paragraph 6 of its resolution 60/235.

Development, planning and administration

The objective of the subprogramme on development planning and administration, implemented by the African Institute for Economic Development and Planning (IDEP), was to enhance national capacity for formulating and implementing development policies and economic management through training. During 2006, IDEP trained 95 mid-career and senior officials from member States and the regional economic communities. IDEP main challenge was mobilizing extrabudgetary resources to meet the need for accelerated expansion in human capacity within African economic policy institutions.

ECA, at its thirty-ninth session, decided that to enable IDEP to play a more effective role, its structure and capacity should be reviewed and strengthened sequentially. The review was undertaken and its report would be presented to ECA at its fortieth (2007) session.

Construction of office facilities at ECA

In response to General Assembly resolution 56/270 [YUN 2002, p. 1458], the Secretary-General submitted a July report [A/61/158] on progress in the construction of additional office facilities at ECA headquarters in Addis Ababa. The report contained an update of actions taken to implement the project since the issuance of his previous report [YUN 2005, p. 1086]. It presented a breakdown of the cost plan ($11,383,300), as approved by Assembly resolution 60/248 [ibid., p. 1494]. The report noted that additional land had been allocated by the host country to accommodate the expansion and action remained to be taken to finalize the host country agreement. The project time schedule was revised to include the construction of two additional floors simultaneously with the original approved project. Final construction documents were being completed and the selection of a general contractor was expected to be finalized in early 2007, with construction work to begin immediately thereafter.

ACABQ, in its September report on the project [A/61/362], noted that the cost increase resulting from the expansion of the scope of the project was in accordance with resolution 60/248 and that it had received assurance that no further increases were anticipated. It recommended that the Assembly take note of the Secretary-General's July report on construction progress.

The Assembly, in section II of **resolution 61/252** of 22 December (see p. 1614), took note of Ethiopia's efforts in facilitating the construction of additional office facilities for ECA in Addis Ababa, the Secretary-General's report thereon, and ACABQ observations.

Regional cooperation

Cooperation between UN and SADC

The Secretary-General, in his consolidated report on cooperation between the United Nations and regional organizations [A/61/256 & Add.1], described cooperation between the Organization and its agencies funds and programmes with the Southern African Development Community (SADC), especially in the area of technical cooperation. ECA collaborated with SADC through its subregional office for Southern Africa in the development of policy frameworks for transport, ICT, mining, energy, gender, agriculture and HIV/AIDS. The two bodies were expected to sign a cooperation agreement covering regional integration, capacity-building and human resources development and resource mobilization for regional multisectoral projects and programmes.

GENERAL ASSEMBLY ACTION

On 4 December [meeting 65], the General Assembly adopted **resolution 61/51** [draft: A/61/L.37 & Add.1] without vote [agenda item 108 *(t)*].

Cooperation between the United Nations and the Southern African Development Community

The General Assembly,

Recalling its resolution 37/248 of 21 December 1982 and all other relevant General Assembly resolutions and decisions on the promotion of cooperation between the United Nations and the Southern African Development Community, including resolutions 57/44 of 21 November 2002 and 59/140 of 15 December 2004 and decision 56/443 of 21 December 2001,

Recalling also its resolution 59/49 of 2 December 2004, in which it decided to invite the Community to participate in its sessions and its work in the capacity of observer,

Recognizing that cooperation between the Community and the United Nations system has continued to deepen,

Commending States members of the Community for demonstrating continued commitment to deeper and more formal arrangements for cooperation among themselves towards regional integration,

Welcoming the continued commitment made by the States members of the Community to deepen democracy, human rights, good governance and sound economic management,

Expressing satisfaction over continued efforts to bring peace to the Democratic Republic of the Congo, launched by the Community in collaboration with the African Union, the United Nations and other entities, and recognizing that the recent elections undertaken in the Democratic Republic of the Congo to end the current transition period by the establishment of elected institutions at all levels are an essential element of the peace process,

Noting with concern that the HIV/AIDS pandemic has reached crisis proportions in the region, and that other communicable diseases, such as malaria and tuberculosis, are having far-reaching social and economic consequences,

Expressing concern over the persistent natural disasters in countries of the region,

Welcoming the efforts of the Community to make southern Africa a landmine-free zone,

Recognizing the important role that women play in the development of the region,

Recognizing also the important role of civil society and the private sector in the development of the region,

1. *Takes note* of the report of the Secretary-General on cooperation between the United Nations and regional and other organizations;

2. *Expresses its appreciation* to the United Nations funds and programmes as well as the international community for the assistance given to the Southern African Development Community;

3. *Welcomes* the decision of the Heads of State and Government of the Southern African Development Community at the summit held in Maseru on 17 and 18 August 2006 to convene a conference on poverty and development, to which the international community will be invited;

4. *Also welcomes* the progress made by the Community on gender and development towards achieving the target of 30 per cent representation of women in decision-making, and its commitment to the new target of 50 per cent;

5. *Notes with satisfaction* the commitment of States members of the Community to scale up the implementation of regional economic integration through, inter alia, the launching of a free trade area by 2008 and the preparations for a custom union by 2010;

6. *Expresses its support* for the economic reforms being implemented by States members of the Community, in pursuance of their shared vision of creating a strengthened regional economic community through deeper economic integration;

7. *Calls upon* the international community to strengthen support for the measures taken by the Community in fighting HIV and AIDS, as well as other communicable diseases such as malaria and tuberculosis, including commitments on the follow-up to the outcome of the twenty-sixth special session of the General Assembly, and the implementation of the Declaration of Commitment on HIV/AIDS;

8. *Recognizes* the vulnerability of the Community subregion to natural disasters, and in this regard calls upon the international community to provide the required assistance to strengthen the Community's disaster preparedness and early-warning capacity;

9. *Urges* the United Nations, its related bodies and the international community to continue to support the Community in building its capacity in negotiations on trade;

10. *Appeals* to the international community and to relevant organizations and bodies of the United Nations system to continue providing financial, technical and material assistance to the Community to support its efforts to fully implement the Regional Indicative Strategic Development Plan and the New Partnership for Africa's Development as well as towards the achievement of other internationally agreed development goals, including the Millennium Development Goals;

11. *Appeals* to the United Nations, its related bodies and the international community to continue to assist and support the Community in its demining activities, and welcomes the progress made so far by its member States;

12. *Calls upon* the international community, in particular the United Nations system, to continue to contribute to the promotion of peace and stability in the Democratic Republic of the Congo and to assist in the rehabilitation and economic reconstruction of that country;

13. *Also calls upon* the international community to continue to assist the Democratic Republic of the Congo through the provision of humanitarian, financial and material assistance to alleviate the suffering of the Congolese people, in particular the children, women and the elderly, and calls upon the Government of the Democratic Republic of the Congo to implement economic and social policies and programmes that will improve the lives of the people of the Democratic Republic of the Congo;

14. *Urges* the United Nations funds and programmes and the international community to continue to provide technical assistance to national vulnerability assessment committees that have been established in the States members of the Community;

15. *Calls upon* the international community to support the efforts of the Community in capacity-building and in addressing the new challenges, opportunities and consequences presented to the economies in the region arising from the process of globalization and liberalization;

16. *Requests* the Secretary-General, in consultation with the Executive Secretary of the Community, to enhance contacts aimed at promoting and harmonizing further cooperation between the United Nations and the Community;

17. *Also requests* the Secretary-General to submit to the General Assembly at its sixty-third session a report on cooperation between the United Nations and the Southern African Development Community.

Cooperation between UN and ECCAS

The Secretary-General, in his consolidated report on cooperation between the United Nations and regional organizations [A/61/256 & Add.1], described cooperation between the Organization and its agencies funds and programmes with the Economic Community of Central African States (ECCAS). The United Nations considered the reinforcement of cooperation with ECCAS as an important step in strengthening the capacity of that subregional body to effectively promote peace as a prerequisite for development in Central Africa. It therefore gave priority to strengthening ECCAS capacity for conflict prevention, early warning, electoral assistance and peacekeeping. Through its subregional office for Central Africa, ECA supported ECCAS in strengthening its capacity to harmonize programmes and activities in selected sectors; implementing the Central Africa Transport Master Plan to support trade development and foster economic integration; assisting ECCAS member States on trade-related issues; and developing a Central Africa e-strategy for promoting ICT in socio-economic activities and the development of the information society.

The General Assembly, by **decision 61/552** of 22 December, decided that the agenda item on cooperation between the United Nations and ECCAS would remain for consideration during its resumed sixty-first (2007) session.

Asia and the Pacific

The Economic and Social Commission for Asia and the Pacific (ESCAP) held its sixty-second session in Jakarta, Indonesia, in two parts: the senior officials segment from 6 to 8 April and the ministerial segment from 10 to 12 April [E/2006/39]. The session's theme topic was "Enhancing regional cooperation in infrastructure development, including that related to disaster management". The Commission discussed policy issues in the ESCAP region; implementation of the Jakarta Declaration on Millennium Development Goals in Asia and the Pacific: the Way Forward 2015; key developments and activities at the regional level; least developed countries, landlocked developing countries and small island developing States; management issues; ESCAP technical cooperation activities; reports of regional intergovernmental bodies; and the activities of the Advisory Committee of Permanent Representatives and Other Representatives Designated by Members of the Commission [E/ESCAP/1384].

The Ministerial Round Table on Enhancing Regional Cooperation in Infrastructure Development, including that Related to Disaster Management was divided into two sessions. The first session consisted of a presentation by the Executive Secretary on the theme topic (see above) and had before it a note by the secretariat [E/ESCAP/1362] on the subject, while the second session heard presentations from delegations.

A special session on the Intergovernmental Agreement on the Trans-Asian Railway Network was also held, as well as a briefing on the avian influenza.

On 12 April [E/2006/39 (dec. 62/2)], the Commission adopted the draft report on its sixty-second session, noting that, except for references to "the Commission elected" or "the Commission endorsed", all statements therein referred to views expressed by one or more delegates, and not to official views or decisions of the Commission.

Economic trends

According to the summary of the *Economic and Social Survey of Asia and the Pacific, 2007* [E/2007/18], the developing Asia-Pacific economies grew at a rate of 7.9 per cent, up from 7.6 per cent the previous year, and were for the eighth consecutive year the fastest-growing economies in the world, accounting for more than one-third of global growth in 2006, while the developed countries grew by 2.2 per cent. The region as a whole, which accounted for more than one third of global growth, was becoming the locomotive of that growth. The expansion was concentrated in the industrial and services sectors, with agriculture growing at a lesser pace.

Economic growth was broad-based, with all subregions performing robustly. North and Central Asia was one of the world's fastest-growing regions, led by Azerbaijan, with a blistering growth rate of 34.5 per cent, followed by Turkmenistan, 14 per cent, Kazakhstan, 10.5 per cent, and the Russian Federation, 6.7 per cent. The demand for services grew as the hydrocarbon sector expanded.

East and North-East Asia achieved an impressive average economic growth of 8.5 per cent in 2006, led once again by China, which achieved a rate of 10.7 per cent. China served as an export platform for the region, while its enormous demand for raw materials and fuels continued to keep global oil and commodity prices high, aiding oil and commodity exporters throughout the region.

South and South-West Asia continued to experience strong economic expansion in 2006, with India, the largest economy in the subregion, leading the growth momentum by expanding 9.2 per cent, and Afghanistan, Bangladesh, Pakistan and Sri Lanka posting growth rates of more than 6.5 per cent, driven largely by gains in industry and services. Exports to all the subregion's countries increased, but imports rose even faster. The increase, due partly to higher oil prices, widened the current account surplus of Iran, the subregion's only net oil exporter, but increased the current accounts deficits in Pakistan, Sri Lanka and Turkey.

Economic growth in the South-East Asian subregion was a robust 5.9 per cent in 2006, up from 5.6 per cent in 2005. Strong external demand, especially for electronics and, to a lesser extent, commodities, was the primary source of growth. As a result, the subregion's major economies posted current account surpluses, ranging from 25.9 per cent in Singapore to 0.9 per cent in Viet Nam. However, as in other subregions, higher oil prices created inflationary pressure.

With few exceptions, the Pacific island countries showed positive economic growth, ranging from slightly less than 2 per cent in Tonga to more than 6 per cent in Vanuatu. Growth was led by the primary sector in Papua New Guinea and the service sector in the smaller countries. Most of the subregion's countries maintained trade deficits, as imports, pushed higher by rising oil prices, continued to outpace exports.

All three developed countries of the region—Australia, Japan and New Zealand—enjoyed modest growth in 2006, expanding 2.2 per cent on average. Higher labour incomes supported household consumption in Australia and New Zealand, while sluggish labour incomes eroded it in Japan. The fiscal positions of Australia and New Zealand remained strong, but Japan's large debt accumulated during the decade-long recession of the 1990s still haunted its fiscal outlook.

Policy issues

The macroeconomic policy challenges facing Asia and the Pacific included high and volatile oil prices, which created inflationary pressures, depleted current account balances and reduced foreign reserves in some countries. Regional growth had so far been resilient to rising oil prices, aided by strong exports, high capital flows and a benign global economic environment, but further world oil hikes would adversely affect that growth, as well as inflation and current account balances.

The low level of domestic demand in East Asian economies had given rise to two interrelated concerns: the increased reliance on exports to drive economic growth, thus exposing those countries to the risk of a significant decline in external demand conditions; and the vulnerability of the region. Further financial reforms were needed to promote private investment in East Asia, including implementation of an improved risk-management system and prudential minimum payment and income requirements for credit cards to curb the excessive growth of consumer credit.

In mid-2006, the region's equity markets experienced their greatest drop since 2004. All countries in the region were affected, suffering record falls for the year and a reversal of the sustained period of increases in financial asset values. The uncertainty in financial markets warranted careful monitoring of the economic vulnerability of the region's countries in order to recognize danger signs as soon as possible.

Moreover, structural problems could hinder sustained growth and development in the future. ESCAP was bearing an increasing share of the regional and global environmental production-related burden. The failure of national policies to address growing environmental pressures would thwart growth; urgent strategies for "green" growth were needed.

There was evidence that urban poverty was growing rapidly, as urban slum-dwellers experienced the cumulative impact of an oversupply of labour, tenure insecurity, poor infrastructure, pollution and congestion. If that challenge went unmet, economic growth would be offset by increasingly high costs to keep urban centres functioning, making it more difficult to achieve the MDGS.

With regard to WTO, ESCAP developing economies were likely to be challenged to make concessions of a commercial value so that developed countries would remain committed to the Doha Development Agenda, adopted by WTO in 2001 [YUN 2001, p. 1432]. Revival of the Doha Development Round should be a priority for the region. Failure to conclude the

Doha Round was partly responsible for the proliferation of the bilateral and regional trading agreements.

At its 2006 session, ESCAP considered a report on the current economic situation in the region and related policy issues [E/ESCAP/1360] and the *Economic and Social Survey of Asia and the Pacific, 2006* [ST/ESCAP/2396].

The Commission noted that the region continued to enjoy robust economic growth, although high and unsustainable oil prices, increasing current account balances, the slow growth of global trade and the threat of the avian influenza pandemic had adversely affected business activity. Poverty, inequality and environmental decay were major challenges for the region, as well as raising the investment rate, which was necessary for achieving higher economic growth. Achieving the MDGs required an effective long-term strategy that included pro-poor economic growth and faster human development. Noting the problems faced by the region concerning unemployment and underemployment, the Commission stated that measures were needed to improve the functioning of labour markets and productivity and ensure that the workforce was provided with the relevant skills to succeed in the rapidly changing global economy. It urged the secretariat to continue to build capacity in the region to address unemployment and other emerging social issues. It emphasized that trade and investment and open economies were essential for ensuring economic growth and sustainable development. The Commission called for a strong commitment by member countries to strengthen social infrastructure and enhance efforts to empower vulnerable groups.

The Commission expressed support for the Asia-Pacific Business Forum 2006, organized by ESCAP, Indonesia and others, at the Commission's sixty-second session. The Forum was important in building and strengthening public-private partnerships.

Activities in 2006

Poverty reduction

The Commission had before it the report of the third session (Bangkok, 29 November–1 December) of the Committee on Poverty Reduction [E/ESCAP/CRP(3)/Rep], which analysed poverty in the informal sector, statistical challenges to assessing the achievement of the MDGs and other internationally agreed development goals, strengthening national statistical capacity by promoting the 2010 round of population and housing censuses and programme planning and evaluation.

The Committee recognized that the commitment contained in the Jakarta Declaration on Millennium Development Goals in Asia and the Pacific: The Way Forward 2015 [A/60/313, annex] and Commission resolution 62/1 of 12 April 2006 (see p. 1158) on achieving the MDGs in the ESCAP region should form the basis for enhanced, sustained and concurrent actions at the regional level to reduce poverty and accelerate achievement of the MDG targets. Noting that several countries were finding it difficult to cost the MDGs, which was essential for mobilizing the necessary resources, the Committee asked the secretariat to help link countries that needed such assistance with relevant agencies, such as the UNDP Regional Centre in Colombo, Sri Lanka.

The Committee recommended that the ESCAP secretariat should take more initiatives to assist member States to develop their respective informal sectors, particularly to build capacities for data collection and analysis, and develop and promote small and medium-sized enterprises and microfinance. It expressed the need for guidelines and a common definition of the informal sector to facilitate international comparison of that sector in Asia and the Pacific, and for the dissemination of international standards and methodologies employed in informal sector measurement. The secretariat should compile information on survey design and methodologies implemented in the region to disseminate best practices and inform future activities and collaborate with other regional and subregional bodies in informal sector measurement initiatives.

The Committee supported the secretariat's initiatives to improve the availability of data for assessing the progress made in achieving the MDGs, and endorsed the specific approaches proposed for strengthening national statistical capacity for data analysis and production through the use of administrative records and registers, and the 2010 round of population and housing censuses. The secretariat should also promote stronger coordination within national statistical systems and between them and international custodian agencies for MDG-related indicators. The Committee underscored the importance of the proposed ESCAP regional census programme.

The Commission also had before it notes by the secretariat on confronting poverty reduction in Asia and the Pacific [E/ESCAP/1365], a summary of progress in the implementation of resolutions relating to poverty reduction [E/ESCAP/1364 & Add.1], and a report on the implementation of the Jakarta Declaration [E/ESCAP/1363].

On 12 April [E/2006/39 (res. 62/1)], the Commission welcomed the efforts of countries that had national development strategies to meet the poverty reduction MDG, and invited countries that had not done so to make concrete efforts in that regard. It took note of the regional partnership on the MDGS among ESCAP, UNDP and the Asian Development Bank, which provided a consolidated regional platform to support the achievement of the goals. The Commission asked the Executive Secretary to strengthen political dialogue for development, including on technical assistance and capacity-building, in cooperation with other UN bodies and relevant organizations, with a view to developing appropriate ways to expedite achievement of the MDGS in ESCAP. The Executive Secretary should continue to assist ESCAP members and associate members to achieve the MDGS through capacity-building and technical cooperation; increase the effectiveness of ESCAP regional advisory services and its subsidiary bodies; continue to assess progress toward achieving the goals in Asia and the Pacific in cooperation with relevant international organizations and transmit a progress assessment to the Economic and Social Council; and develop recommendations for achieving the MDGS by 2015 in the form of a regional road map.

Statistics

During its sixty-second session (Jakarta, 6-12 April), the Commission had before it the annual report of the Statistical Institute for Asia and the Pacific [E/ESCAP/1381], whose statute was revised in 2005 by Economic and Social Council resolution 2005/36 [YUN 2005, p. 1091]. The report highlighted major developments of the Institute in 2005, the decisions and recommendations of the first session of its Governing Council under the revised statute; administrative matters and the programme of work and pledges and contributions.

On 12 April [E/2006/39 (res. 62/10)], the Commission invited members and associate members to give priority to strengthening their official statistical systems, and encouraged them, along with relevant international organizations and institutions with advanced statistical systems, to share expertise and information on their methodological, technological and managerial practices in statistical offices for the benefit of other countries in the region. It requested the Executive Secretary to assist them in developing their statistical systems; strengthening their capacity to monitor progress toward achieving the internationally agreed development goals; implementing international statistical standards in the region; facilitating regional discussion and the sharing of information and good practices on official statistics, international capacity-building activities and the dissemination and use of data; and coordinating with regional and international agencies to collect official statistical data from members and associate members to avoid duplicating efforts and minimize the response burden on national statistical systems.

Managing globalization

The Commission had before it reports [E/ESCAP/1366, E/ESCAP/1368-1371] on key developments and activities at the regional level with regard to managing globalization, as well as a summary [E/ESCAP/1367 & Corr.1] of progress in implementing resolutions related to that theme.

On 12 April, the Commission [E/2006/39 (res. 62/6)], requested that the Executive Secretary continue, in collaboration with regional and global partners, to undertake policy-oriented analytical work and provide technical assistance to ESCAP members and associate members in order to increase their human and institutional capacity to negotiate, conclude and implement multilateral and regional trade agreements, with a specific focus on strengthening the WTO/ESCAP Programme of Technical Assistance for Asia and the Pacific; formulate and implement trade facilitation and e-commerce practices for enhancing international competitiveness; create a domestic policy environment conducive to the development of small and medium-sized enterprises and the mobilization of stable financial and investment flows; and promote a competitive knowledge-based economy through the development of science-based knowledge and technology transfer. The resolution also called on the Executive Secretary to evaluate and analyse regional and bilateral trade agreements involving ESCAP members; strengthen the Asia-Pacific Trade Agreement to promote regional cooperation in trade and related issues; organize policy dialogues in the context of managing globalization; and undertake trade capacity-building assistance to accord priority to the special needs of least developed countries, landlocked developing countries, countries with economies in transition and small island developing States.

The report of the Committee on Managing Globalization on its Third Session (Bangkok, 12-14 September, 10-12 October) [E/ESCAP/CMG(3/I) Rep, E/ESCAP/CMG/(3/II)Rep] requested that the secretariat continue its trade facilitation work to fight poverty and achieve the internationally agreed development goals, and called for the expansion of the Asia-Pacific trade and investment agreements database by including analytical indicators and trade statistics for benchmarking and measuring the trade and development performance of regional and bilateral trade agreements. The secretariat was also asked to develop modalities for regional cooperation mechanisms for supply-side capacity-building, with a focus on small and medium-sized enterprises, as well as promote the exchange of ideas and cooperation in trade facilitation among member countries, in close cooperation with other international organizations. The Committee underscored the importance of the Ministerial Conference on Transport (Busan, Republic of Korea, 6-11 November), which focused its high-level discussion on major issues related to regional transport infrastructure development and facilitation.

The secretariat was asked to coordinate the regional follow-up to the World Summit on the Information Society [YUN 2005, p. 933] and implement its outcome, as well as assist countries in the use of information communication and space technology. The Committee recommended that the Third Ministerial Conference on Space Applications for Sustainable Development in Asia and the Pacific, to be held in 2007, should focus on policy issues to assist Commission members and associate members in the use of space technology and other ICTs for achieving internationally agreed development goals.

In terms of environmental concerns, the Committee, welcoming the publication of the report *State of the Environment in Asia and the Pacific 2005*, recommended stronger regional cooperation to address that report's findings. It requested the secretariat to continue supporting member countries in improving their capacity to develop and implement the Clean Development Mechanism and other projects aimed at reducing greenhouse gas emissions. In terms of natural disaster reduction, the secretariat should conduct a study reviewing all regional efforts to develop early-warning systems and promote regional cooperation in natural disaster risk management. The Committee supported the proposal for the trans-Asian energy system and asked the secretariat to organize workshops, seminars and consultations with member States to consider the initiative.

Least developed, landlocked and island developing countries

Least developed countries

The Commission, on 12 April [E/2006/39 (res. 62/11)], reaffirmed its commitment to the implementation of the Programme of Action for the Least Developed Countries for the Decade 2001-2010 [YUN 2001, p. 770], so that the Asia and Pacific LDCs could attain the internationally agreed development goals. It took note of the regional review of the Programme of Action (Bangkok, 14-15 March) and requested members and associate members to fulfil their commitments contained therein. The Commission recognized the need for coherent results-based national development strategies aimed at poverty reduction, as envisaged in the Programme of Action; and emphasized the need for appropriate strategies and greater political will by the LDCs, as well as continued commitment by their development partners to addressing emerging challenges. It also requested the Executive Secretary to ensure that ESCAP activities took into account the special needs of the LDCs; analyse and disseminate information on their economic and social development for submission to ESCAP thematic committees and intergovernmental committees to promote greater awareness of their concerns; explore with donors the possibility of establishing a fund to support the participation of the LDCs in key ESCAP meetings; and assist them in formulating appropriate development strategies and policies in line with the Programme of Action.

Special Body on Least Developed and Landlocked Developing Countries

The Special Body on Least Developed and Landlocked Developing Countries, at its eighth session (Almaty, Kazakhstan, 15-16 May) [E/ESCAP/63/18], considered issues relating to inter-country energy cooperation to enhance energy security for sustainable development and widen access to energy services in least developed and landlocked developing countries and international migration and development in those countries. The Special Body noted that the Commission's activities in 2006 for the LDCs were in line with the Programme of Action for the Least Developed Countries for the Decade 2001-2010, while for the landlocked developing countries they were in line with the Almaty Programme of Action.

To ensure that those countries were able to attain their internationally agreed development goals, the Commission noted the need for a regional road map to ensure the implementation of the Jakarta Declaration on Millennium Development Goals in Asia and the Pacific: the way forward 2015, adopted in 2005 at the Regional Ministerial Meeting on the Millennium Development Goals in Asia and the Pacific [E/ESCAP/1363]; the commitment of adequate resources; and the participation of all stakeholders.

The Commission noted that, in addition to the evaluation of transit trade and transport, the establishment of economic infrastructure and trade facilitation measures and enhanced regional cooperation between landlocked and transit developing countries were essential for addressing the high transport and logistical costs in landlocked developing countries. It requested the secretariat to facilitate the dissemination of good practices in the diverse areas of development cooperation among least developed, landlocked and small island developing States.

Island developing countries

Special Body on Pacific Island Developing Countries

The Special Body on Pacific Island Developing Countries, on its ninth session (Jakarta, Indonesia, 4-5 April) [E/ESCAP/1373], considered issues relating to the creation of employment and income-earning opportunities for vulnerable groups in Pacific island developing countries and the follow-up to the Mauritius Strategy for the Further Implementation of the Programme of Action for the Sustainable Development of Small Island Developing States [YUN 2005, p. 946] at regional and subregional levels. The Special Body asked Governments in the subregion to address inequities in employment and wealth, noting that experience in many countries had shown that rapid economic growth was not sufficient to generate employment and income-generating opportunities for all, including vulnerable groups, such as women, youth and people with disabilities. Low economic growth, especially when populations were growing at higher rates, meant that employment in the formal sector was unlikely to expand sufficiently to absorb the increase in the labour force in most Pacific countries. Promoting the rights of vulnerable groups and implementing active labour-market programmes were important.

The Commission endorsed the recommendations contained in the report, especially those on the creation of employment and income-earning opportunities for vulnerable groups, follow-up to the Mauritius Strategy and the Commission activities in the Pacific. Specifically, the Commission recommended that the programme of work of the secretariat should mainstream the priorities and commitments of the Mauritius Strategy. It also proposed the establishment of dedicated satellite communications infrastructure in the light of the difficulties of small island developing States, and that a regional review of the implementation of the Mauritius Strategy be conducted in 2008.

Also before the Commission was a secretariat note [E/ESCAP/1361] entitled "Policy issues for the ESCAP region: strengthening Pacific island developing countries and territories through regional cooperation", which highlighted the constraints those countries faced in their quest for economic growth and sustainable development. Supporting the 2005 Pacific Plan for strengthening regional cooperation and integration, the report suggested that Pacific island developing States create greater links to the economic dynamism of Asian countries, especially in trade and investment, infrastructure and ICT.

On 12 April [E/2006/39 (res. 62/9)], the Commission reaffirmed its support for the issues identified by the Mauritius Strategy and stressed that the Strategy's successful implementation depended on shared responsibility and strengthened partnerships, including with civil society and the private sector. The Commission requested the Executive Secretary to ensure that ESCAP activities took into account the special needs of the small island developing States, as contained in the Mauritius Strategy; review, analyse and disseminate information on economic and social development in those States; provide regional inputs into the final review of the Strategy's implementation; and report to the Commission at its sixty-fourth (2008) session.

Also on 12 April [E/2006/39 (res. 62/12)], the Commission requested that the Executive Secretary take into account the development approach to regionalism and the priorities set out in the Pacific Plan for Strengthening Regional Cooperation and Integration in technical cooperation activities for Pacific Island developing countries; undertake research and analysis and provide advice and technical assistance aimed at building the capacity of Pacific island developing countries to benefit from their relations with Asian countries in trade and investment, as well as investigate options for convening a forum in 2007 to share Asian and Pacific experiences in tourism development; and promote the South-South cooperation to help Pacific island countries implement the Mauritius Strategy.

Economic and technical cooperation

In 2006, ESCAP received $14.5 million for technical cooperation activities [E/ESCAP/63/28], down from $25.4 million in 2005. Of that amount, $6.1 million was received from the UN system, and $6.9 million from donor and participating countries, more than half of which came from developing member countries. Japan, the Republic of Korea and China were the top contributors. In addition to cash contributions, countries provided, on a non-reimbursable basis, a total of 148 work-months of the services of experts in various disciplines.

Transport, communications, tourism and infrastructure development

The Ministerial Conference on Transport (Busan, Republic of Korea, 6-11 November) [E/ESCAP/63/13] adopted the Busan Declaration on Transport Development in Asia and the Pacific, including the Regional Action Programme for Phase I (2007-2011). The Conference also adopted the Ministerial Declaration on improving Road Safety in Asia and the Pacific, and supported the establishment of a forum of Asian ministers of transport as a formal regional mechanism to facilitate close collaboration and interaction on emerging issues.

On 12 April [E/2006/39 (res. 62/4)], the Commission adopted the Intergovernmental Agreement on the Trans-Asian Railway network, finalized in 2005 at the intergovernmental meeting convened for that purpose [YUN 2005, p. 1094]. It invited all relevant ESCAP members to become parties to ensure its rapid entry into force, and international and regional financial institutions and multilateral and bilateral donors to consider providing further financial and technical support to develop and operationalize the network. The Commission encouraged landlocked developing countries and their transit neighbours to work together so that the Trans-Asian Railway and Asian Highway networks could provide further tangible transit transport opportunities within the scope of the Almaty Programme of Action [YUN 2003, p. 875]. It also requested the Executive Secretary to assist member countries in becoming parties to the Agreement, accord priority to developing the Railway network within the ESCAP programme of work, collaborate with international and regional financial institutions, multilateral and bilateral donors and international organizations to develop it, and continue to develop an integrated, international, intermodal transport network in Asia and an integrated Euro-Asian transport system.

The Commission, on 12 April [E/2006/39 (res. 62/3)], welcomed the adoption of the Bali Declaration on Sustainable Tourism Development and the Plan of Action for Sustainable Tourism Development in Asia and the Pacific, phase II (2006-2012), including its Regional Action Programme for Sustainable Tourism Development (2006-2012), adopted by the 2005 High-level Intergovernmental Meeting on Sustainable Tourism Development [YUN 2005, p. 1094]. It invited members and associate members to participate actively in the implementation of the Bali Declaration and Plan of Action, including its Regional Action Programme; identify areas for action to further enhance tourism's contribution to socio-economic development and poverty reduction, using the Bali Declaration and the Plan of Action as guidelines; appoint a focal point for coordinating implementation of the Plan of Action at the national level; minimize the adverse socio-cultural and environmental impacts of tourism; promote the Global Code of Ethics on Tourism of the World Tourism Organization (UNWTO); support tourism-related local economic activities; and promote women's empowerment and participation in tourism. The Commission also requested the Executive Secretary to accord priority to the secretariat's activities in tourism; encourage implementation of the Regional Action Programme; conduct a regional study on the role of tourism in socio-economic development; enhance the role of tourism in socio-economic development and poverty reduction, the facilitation of travel and the development of transport and other tourism-related infrastructure. He should also promote regional and subregional cooperation and cooperate with UNWTO and other relevant institutions.

The Commission considered a note by the secretariat entitled "Policy issues for the ESCAP region: enhancing regional cooperation in infrastructure development, including that related to disaster management" [E/ESCAP/1362], which contained the results of a study on the theme of the Commission's sixty-second session (see p. 1155). The study analysed the role of investment and regional cooperation in infrastructure development in the areas of transport, energy, ICT, water and disaster management, noting that adequate investment was necessary to maintain ESCAP strong performance in growth and development. It proposed several options for mobilizing financial resources towards that end: expanding the involvement of the Asian Development Bank in infrastructure financing by refocusing its mandate from development in general to infrastructure development; creating a subsidiary of the Bank exclusively for infrastructure funding; expanding the mandate and scope of the Asian Bond Fund; and setting up a new institution, such as an Asia-Pacific investment bank, for cross-border financial intermediation and lending to public and private infrastructure projects.

During the session, the Commission held a Ministerial Round Table on its theme topic, which summarized the contents of the theme study, and highlighted the importance of infrastructure development in enhancing economic growth and social development and the crucial role of regional cooperation. It also examined regional financial cooperation and featured a presentation by the Executive Secretary on the financial needs of infrastructure development, the resource gap and the options available to bridge that gap.

On 12 April [E/2006/39 (res. 62/2)], the Commission invited members and associate members to implement policies for infrastructure development, taking into account the need to provide high economic and social benefits to poor, rural people; enhance the efficiency and quality of infrastructure facilities and services; implement good public and corporate governance principles throughout the infrastructure development process through transparent legal frameworks for private sector involvement and public procurement systems; create an enabling environment for promoting public-private partnerships; and strengthen national and regional preparedness in disaster risk management and response capability. The Commission also requested the Executive Secretary to enhance regional cooperation in infrastructure development through capacity-building and technical cooperation; forge closer cooperation with UN bodies, development agencies and multilateral financing institutions, as well as donors, to strengthen global partnerships for infrastructure development; and assist members and associate members to develop policy responses for promoting renewable environmentally friendly energy sources, energy efficiency and related infrastructure.

Also before the Commission was the report of the Mekong River Commission [E/ESCAP/63/31]. The Mekong Commission Council approved the 2006-2010 Strategic Plan on water resources development. The plan included an integrated water resources management approach, with emphasis on basin-wide development plans, fuller integration and cooperation with the work of regional development partners and dialogue partners (China and Myanmar). In June, the Council signed the Procedures for the Maintenance of Flows on the Mainstream.

Science and technology

The Commission had before it the report of the Asian and Pacific Centre for Transfer of Technology [E/ESCAP/1378 & Corr.1] on its 2005 activities and on the first session of its Governing Council (February 2006) devoted to technology capacity-building, the promotion and management of innovation and subregional and regional networking. To promote and manage innovation, the Centre implemented a project, funded by India, for providing advisory services and organizing expert group meetings for senior policymakers and national workshops for key actors in the innovation system.

The Commission also had before it the report of the Coordinating Committee for Geoscience Programmes in East and Southeast Asia [E/ESCAP/1385] on its work for 2005, which focused on enhanced coordination of the geoscience programmes of geoscience institutions in member countries, continued human resources development, institutional capacity-building and greater flow of technical information between members and cooperating countries and organizations. The Commission took note of the work of the Committee.

Information and communication technologies

The Commission emphasized the importance of information, communication and space technology (ICST) for sustainable economic and social development, and expressed support for the outcomes of the World Summit on the Information Society [YUN 2005, p. 1096].

On 12 April [E/2006/39 (res. 62/5)], the Commission invited members and associate members to participate actively in implementing the Summit outcomes, including through the Regional Action Plan. It invited international and regional organizations to cooperate with ESCAP and donor countries and agencies, and NGOs to contribute technical and financial resources for the regional implementation of the Summit outcomes. The Commission welcomed the offer of Malaysia to host the Third Ministerial Conference on Space Applications for Sustainable Development in Asia and the Pacific in 2007. The Executive Secretary was requested to promote information exchange and best practices at the regional level and facilitate policy debate on the use of ICT for development; organize expert group meetings, in coordination with the International Telecommunication Union and other relevant organizations, to promote capacity-building in developing countries for monitoring the information society; assist member States with technical and relevant information for developing regional strategies and implementing regional conference outcomes focusing on communication technology applications; and build capacity consistent with the Summit outcomes and encourage all stakeholders to transform the digital divide into digital opportunities and bring the benefits of ICT to everyone.

In preparation for the Third Ministerial Conference, the secretariat organized regional consultative meetings to discuss issues of common concern and identify a framework of cooperation in space-based ICT. It also carried out preparatory missions in July and October. National consultations were also held with space agencies and relevant user organizations in Australia, China, Fiji, India, Japan, Kazakhstan, Malaysia, the Republic of Korea and Samoa. The Meeting of Eminent Persons on Information, Communication and Space Technology in Preparation for the Ministerial

Conference (Bangkok, 3-4 August) recommended priority areas, while the third session (part II) of the Committee on Managing Globalization (Bangkok, 10-12 October) recommended focusing on policy issues in the use of space technology and ICTs for achieving internationally agreed development goals.

The twelfth-session of the Intergovernmental Consultative Committee on the Regional Space Applications Programme for Sustainable Development (Daejeon, Republic of Korea, 17-19 October), held in conjunction with the High-level Expert Group Meeting in Preparation for the Third Ministerial Conference, reviewed the background documents for the Third Ministerial Conference, including the draft ministerial declaration.

Environment and sustainable development

The Commission noted the secretariat's activities relating to environment and sustainable development, especially those relating to implementation of the Johannesburg Plan of Implementation of the World Summit on Sustainable Development [YUN 2002, p. 822] and for achieving the MDGs. The Commission recommended the continuation of activities to promote "green growth", especially technical assistance for capacity-building, and enhanced regional and subregional cooperation. It underscored the need for sustainable and eco-efficient natural resources management and recommended the promotion of initiatives such as the "3 Rs" (reduce, reuse and recycle).

The Commission noted the activities undertaken in the framework of the International Decade for Action "Water for Life", 2005-2015 [YUN 2003, p. 1034], and in preparation for the Fourth World Water Forum, held in Mexico City in 2006.

The Commission emphasized the importance of the secretariat's work in promoting regional and subregional cooperation for the diversification of energy resources, the development of environmentally sound energy technologies and alternative and renewable energy sources, such as microhydro, biogas, biofuel and geothermal, including small-scale projects aimed at poverty reduction. The secretariat was asked to promote the replication of successfully implemented projects in sustainable energy development, such as the initiatives under the ESCAP project on pro-poor public-private partnerships. The Commission highlighted the importance of energy security in achieving sustainable economic growth in the region, and asked the secretariat to facilitate, formulate and implement an integrated trans-Asia energy system aimed at safeguarding the supply of energy resources to final consumption destinations within the region.

The Commission noted that air pollution in mega-cities was a serious problem, and underlined the importance of continued support to implement the Kitakyushu Initiative for a Clean Environment [YUN 2000, p. 936], which had successfully addressed urban pollution, and of maintaining the sustainable development of biological resources to further economically develop the region. In that regard, the secretariat was requested to help member countries create a national biological resource centre and act as a focal point for a regional biological resource network to facilitate the transfer of biological resource management technologies.

Agriculture and development

The annual report of the Asian and Pacific Centre for Agricultural Engineering and Machinery (APCAEM) [E/ESCAP/1379] reviewed the administrative and financial status of the APCAEM work programme in 2005. Financial contributions by China and Finland enabled APCAEM to recruit a new Director, an assistant in information technology and a programme assistant. An expert on non-reimbursable loans, provided by the Republic of Korea, also reported for duty. The realignment of the thematic focus on three core areas, the study on agricultural engineering in support of the Kyoto Protocol to the United Nations Framework Convention on Climate Change [YUN 1997, p. 1048] and nine related project proposals emphasized the Centre's role in achieving its environmental objectives. The report contained the recommendations of the APCAEM Governing Board (November 2005) on the Centre's operations, the medium-term strategy and the 2006-2007 operational workplan. The Board recommended that the current name of the Centre be retained for the next few years, in view of the revised Statute of the Centre adopted in 2005 [YUN 2005, p. 1100].

Social development

The Commission considered a note by the secretariat on progress in addressing persistent and emerging social issues [E/ESCAP/1372], which contained the report of the second session of the Committee on Emerging Social Issues [YUN 2005, p. 1106] and information on progress attained in implementing the Commission's recent resolutions relating to that theme, including resolution 60/1 [YUN 2004, p. 1001] on the Shanghai Declaration.

The Commission noted the conclusions and recommendations of the Committee and affirmed the importance of the goals in poverty eradication, employment expansion and social integration adopted by the 1995 World Summit for Social Development [YUN 1995, p. 1113]. The Commission emphasized the importance of addressing the issue of youth unemployment, including among rural youth, young people with disabilities and minority youth, and called on the secretariat to provide technical support to help develop and strengthen skills training, social protection and education for youth, as well as national laws and policies on youth.

The Commission called on the secretariat to give greater focus to analysing the family as a changing institution and examining the links between family well-being, effective public policies, social services and intergenerational relationships. The Commission acknowledged the link between migration and economic and social development, and called for strengthened cooperation on migration and on protecting the rights of migrant workers.

Addressing women's issues, the Commission noted the high level of commitment shown by many countries towards ensuring gender equality and recognizing the role of women in development and poverty reduction.

The Commission agreed on the importance of transparency and the exchange of information and technical cooperation at the bilateral, regional and global levels in order to tackle effectively the spread of avian influenza across the region. It requested the secretariat to collaborate with other UN agencies to help member countries create multisectoral capacity for surveillance and a global early warning system against communicable diseases, as well as build stockpiles of vaccines and pharmaceuticals. The secretariat should work with the World Health Organization and other agencies to create capacity in strengthening primary health care and health systems as a means of achieving the MDGS. The Commission stressed the need to tackle communicable diseases in an effective manner, while avoiding duplication of work.

On 12 April [E/2006/39 (res. 62/8)], the Commission noted that a number of ESCAP members had already achieved the goal of universal primary education and many others were on track to doing so within the framework of the International Plan of Action for the United Nations Literacy Decade [YUN 2002, p. 1134]. It encouraged those members that had not yet achieved the education goal to devise strategies for reaching the poorest and most marginalized groups and seek alternative formal and non-formal approaches to learning, with a view to achieving the Decade's goals. It invited ESCAP members and associate members, as well as relevant intergovernmental and non-governmental organizations, to intensify efforts to implement the International Plan of Action as a central focus of Education for All; invited the international community and relevant intergovernmental and non-governmental organizations to lend financial and material support to ESCAP members in achieving the Decade's goals; and encouraged them to strengthen their national and professional educational institutions with a view to expanding capacity, developing valid and reliable literacy data and promoting good quality education. The Executive Secretary was asked to assess the implementation of the International Plan of Action for the Decade.

The third session of the Committee on Emerging Social Issues (Bangkok, 12-14 December) [E/ESCAP/CESI(3)/Rep] examined key issues of international migration in the ESCAP region and reviewed ESCAP activities in advance of the High-level Dialogue on International Migration and Development (New York, 14-15 September) (see p. 1261), as well as its outcome. During the session, Mongolia sponsored a draft resolution on sustainable health financing toward achieving universal coverage of health care in Asia and the Pacific, which would be submitted at the Commission's sixty-third (2007) session. In that regard, the Committee requested that the secretariat create a forum for sharing experiences and knowledge on the options for strengthening health systems and providing sustainable financing of health care and universal health care coverage. The secretariat was asked to provide technical assistance to integrate health concerns into economic and trade policies and technical expertise to utilize the flexibilities available under current trade regimes, including the TRIPS agreement, in order to protect public health.

The Committee welcomed the proposal to convene in 2008 the mid-point review meeting on implementation of the Plan of Action on Population and Poverty, which was adopted at the Fifth Asian and Pacific Conference on Population and Poverty. The Committee also expressed support for the high-level meeting on the review and appraisal of implementation of the 2002 Madrid International Plan of Action on Ageing [YUN 2002, p. 1194] and the Macao Plan of Action on Ageing for Asia and the Pacific [YUN 1998, p. 942], scheduled for October 2007 in Macao, China, and urged members and associate members to review and appraise national policies and strategies on ageing. The Committee expressed its support for a regional consultation on implementation of the World Programme of Action for Youth to the Year 2000 and Beyond [YUN 1995, p. 1211], as called for by the General Assembly resolution 60/2 on policies and programmes involving youth [YUN 2005, p. 1296]. The Committee encouraged ESCAP to continue to provide policy assistance to its members and associate members in accordance with the global and regional mandate on disability.

Regarding gender concerns, the Committee welcomed the proposal to convene the next Regional Review of the Implementation of the Beijing Platform for Action [YUN 2005, p. 1104], and asked the secretariat to formulate a long-term and comprehensive framework for the region in the form of a declaration on gender and development, including emerging challenges and opportunities, and to serve as the regional machinery for gender mainstreaming and a forum for the exchange of good practices and experiences on gender and development.

Natural disasters

The Commission had before it the reports of the Typhoon Committee [E/ESCAP/1387] and the Panel of Tropical Cyclones [E/ESCAP/1388]. The Commission recognized the work of the Typhoon Committee and noted the commitment and support of the Committee's members and donors. It asked the Committee to pursue closer collaboration with intergovernmental bodies. The Commission also noted the work of the Panel on Tropical Cyclones in 2005 under the meteorological, hydrological, natural disaster prevention and preparedness, training and research components of its work programme. The Commission was also informed of the Panel's request to the World Meteorological Organization (WMO) to upgrade the Global Telecommunication System (GTS) in some Panel member countries in order to address the requirements for tsunami-related information exchange in the Indian Ocean Rim. It noted that financial support for GTS upgrade had been obtained for Bangladesh, Myanmar and Pakistan. Recognizing the importance of tsunami early warning, the Commission requested WMO and ESCAP and international organizations to increase their assistance to the Panel and its members.

The Commission underscored the adverse impact of natural disasters on the economic development and growth of countries in the region. It expressed appreciation for the secretariat's work in enhancing the capacity of member States in disaster management and noted the need to continue activities in disaster management and preparedness. It invited member States to make use of the Multi-Donor Voluntary Trust Fund on Tsunami Early Warning Arrangements in the Indian Ocean and Southeast Asia [YUN 2005, p. 1107] for capacity-building in the development of tsunami early warning systems, as well as to consider contributing to the Fund.

On 12 April [E/2006/39 (res. 62/7)], the Commission emphasized the importance of international cooperation, including South-South cooperation, in planning, implementation, information collection and knowledge sharing in regional tsunami early warning systems. It recognized the important role of the Trust Fund as a means of contributing to the International Oceanographic Commission of the United Nations Educational, Scientific and Cultural Organization for building and enhancing tsunami early warning capacities at various levels, and for strengthening regional and subregional cooperation and coordination for effective early warning systems for tsunamis. It invited Governments, donor countries, relevant international organizations, international and regional financial institutions, as well as the private sector and civil society, to consider contributing to the Trust Fund, and requested the Executive Secretary to ensure that the Trust Fund was administered efficiently, effectively and transparently.

Also on 12 April, by decision [E/2006/39 (dec. 62/1)], the Commission deferred consideration of the draft resolution submitted by Iran entitled "Establishment of the Asian and Pacific Centre for ICST-enabled Disaster Management" until its sixty-third (2007) session.

Programme and organizational questions

The Commission welcomed the programme performance report for 2004-2005 [E/ESCAP/1374 & Corr.1]. It endorsed the proposed programme changes for the 2006-2007 biennium [E/ESCAP/1375] and noted the adjustments to the programme of work to cope with changing mandates and circumstances. The Commission endorsed the programme overview for the draft strategic framework for the 2008-2009 biennium [E/ESCAP/1376 & Corr.1] for eventual incorporation into the proposed biennial programme. It also provided comments on ESCAP efforts on regional and subregional partnerships to expedite achievement of the MDGs in the region.

Monitoring and evaluation

The Commission considered an overview of ESCAP guidelines for programme monitoring, review and evaluation [E/ESCAP/1377]. The Commission stressed the importance of results-based management and expressed support for related secretariat initiatives, which could help it to focus on organizational learning and the incorporation of lessons learned into future programme and project planning.

ESCAP sixty-third session

In view of the significance of 2007 as the sixtieth anniversary of the founding of ESCAP, the Commission decided to keep open the date and venue of the session for further consideration by ESCAP members that might have an interest in hosting it. In that regard, the secretariat would consult with the Advisory Committee of Permanent Representatives and Other Representatives Designated by Members of the Commission.

The Commission agreed on "Development of health systems in the context of enhancing economic growth towards achieving the Millennium Development Goals in Asia and the Pacific" as the theme topic for its sixty-third session.

UN-Economic Cooperation Organization relations

The Secretary-General, in his consolidated report on cooperation between the United Nations and regional and other intergovernmental organizations [A/61/256 & Add.1], outlined the UN cooperation with the Economic Cooperation Organization.

GENERAL ASSEMBLY ACTION

On 13 November [meeting 52] the General Assembly adopted **resolution 61/12** [draft: A/61/L.8 & Add.1] without vote [agenda item 108 *(i)*].

Cooperation between the United Nations and the Economic Cooperation Organization

The General Assembly,

Recalling its resolution 48/2 of 13 October 1993, by which it granted observer status to the Economic Cooperation Organization,

Recalling also its previous resolutions on cooperation between the United Nations and the Economic Cooperation Organization, in which it invited various specialized agencies as well as other organizations and programmes of the United Nations system and relevant international financial institutions to join in the efforts to implement the economic programmes and projects of the Economic Cooperation Organization,

Appreciating the technical and financial assistance extended by the United Nations system and the relevant international and regional organizations to the Economic Cooperation Organization for its economic programmes and projects, and encouraging them to continue their support,

Welcoming the endeavours of the Economic Cooperation Organization to consolidate its ties with the United Nations system and the relevant international and regional organizations for the development and promotion of projects in all priority areas,

Expressing its support for the relevant plans and programmes as well as the institutional changes in the Economic Cooperation Organization made with a view to achieving internationally agreed development goals, including those contained in the United Nations Millennium Declaration,

Expressing its grave concern and sympathy over the human casualties caused by the worst natural disasters and their devastating impact on the socio-economic situation in the Economic Cooperation Organization region, which is prone to disasters such as earthquakes, floods and drought,

1. *Takes note with appreciation* of the report of the Secretary-General on the implementation of resolution 59/4 of 22 October 2004, and expresses satisfaction at the mutually beneficial interaction between the United Nations and the Economic Cooperation Organization;

2. *Takes note* of the Baku Declaration, adopted at the ninth Economic Cooperation Organization summit, held in Baku on 5 May 2006, which provides guidelines to the Organization in areas such as trade, transportation, energy, agriculture, industry, health and the environment;

3. *Welcomes* the adoption by the Council of Ministers of the Economic Cooperation Organization at its fifteenth meeting of "ECO Vision 2015" as the basic reference document of the Economic Cooperation Organization, in line with the Millennium Development Goals, inter alia, in which the establishment of a free trade area in the region, facilitation of trade and investment information networking, transportation, the promotion of small- and medium-sized enterprises and utilization of new and renewable technologies are highlighted;

4. *Calls for* the strengthening of technical assistance of the World Trade Organization, the United Nations Conference on Trade and Development and other trade-related United Nations bodies, such as the International Trade Centre UNCTAD/WTO, to States members of the Economic Cooperation Organization, taking into account the fact that the member States are developing countries and countries with economies in transition, some of which are in the process of becoming members of the World Trade Organization and that their access to world markets and increasing intraregional and interregional trade through the implementation of regional trade agreements will boost their efforts to achieve their development goals;

5. *Notes with satisfaction* the implementation of the Programme of Action of the Economic Cooperation Organization Decade of Transport and Communications (1998-2007), which is supported by technical assistance from the Economic and Social Commission for Asia and the Pacific and the United Nations Conference on Trade and Development, especially for the elimination of non-physical barriers on main transit-transport routes of the region;

6. *Welcomes* the signing by most States members of the Economic Cooperation Organization of the Intergovernmental Agreement on the Asian Highway Network, which has been launched under the auspices of the Economic and Social Commission for Asia and the Pacific, and calls upon the member States concerned to

contribute to the operationalization of the project by identifying their priority investment projects;

7. *Expresses its appreciation* for the efforts of the Economic Cooperation Organization in developing a regional energy trade with the cooperation and active participation of subregional and international organizations such as the Economic and Social Commission for Asia and the Pacific, the World Bank, the Asian Development Bank and the Islamic Development Bank;

8. *Appreciates* that the Regional Programme for Food Security of the Economic Cooperation Organization has been formulated with the technical and financial assistance of the Food and Agriculture Organization of the United Nations and contributions of the Islamic Development Bank, invites the relevant United Nations bodies, other international organizations and donor agencies to assist the Secretariat of the Economic Cooperation Organization in the efficient implementation of the Regional Programme, which contains eleven regional projects and several national projects, and, in this framework, expresses its appreciation for the signing and launching in early 2006 of the Technical Cooperation Programme for Strengthening Seed Supply in the Economic Cooperation Organization Region of the Food and Agriculture Organization of the United Nations and the Economic Cooperation Organization;

9. *Notes with satisfaction* the enhancement of cooperation between the United Nations Industrial Development Organization and the Economic Cooperation Organization, especially in such areas as industrial cooperation strategy, the transfer of technology, plans of action for small- and medium-sized enterprises and standardization, and invites the United Nations Industrial Development Organization to continue contributing to relevant activities and projects of the Economic Cooperation Organization;

10. *Expresses its satisfaction* at the identification of new fields of cooperation within the framework of the Economic Cooperation Organization and at establishing a new directorate of human resource and sustainable development to enhance cooperation on such important issues as health, the alleviation of poverty and human and sustainable development, and recommends that all relevant United Nations bodies, including the Division for Sustainable Development of the Department of Economic and Social Affairs of the Secretariat, the World Health Organization, the United Nations Population Fund, the United Nations Development Programme and the Office for the Coordination of Humanitarian Affairs of the Secretariat, extend technical and financial support to the Economic Cooperation Organization in its endeavour to enhance cooperation in the above-mentioned areas;

11. *Welcomes* the signing of memorandums of understanding between the Economic Cooperation Organization and the World Meteorological Organization and the United Nations Environment Programme, and calls for the effective implementation of the memorandums;

12. *Takes note* of the contribution made by the Drug Coordination Control Unit of the Economic Cooperation Organization in compiling and disseminating drug-related data and in organizing training programmes/courses in the field of drug control for the experts of the member States, with the technical and financial assistance of the United Nations Office on Drugs and Crime and the European Union, and invites the donor agencies to assist the Economic Cooperation Organization in funding the projects jointly prepared by the United Nations Office on Drugs and Crime and the Secretariat of the Economic Cooperation Organization;

13. *Welcomes* efforts of the Economic Cooperation Organization towards enabling conditions for Afghanistan to assume a more active role in the region in order to benefit from increased trade and export opportunities, and, while taking note of the valuable contribution of the Economic Cooperation Organization in improving the extent and scope of the reintegration of Afghanistan into regional cooperation schemes, appreciates the operationalization of the Special Fund of the Economic Cooperation Organization to finance some priority projects in Afghanistan, and invites the relevant United Nations agencies, such as the United Nations Development Programme and the United Nations Assistance Mission in Afghanistan, to cooperate with the Secretariat of the Economic Cooperation Organization for the successful implementation of its current programmes and projects and the Plan of Action for the Rehabilitation and Reconstruction of Afghanistan, and of a new plan after its expiry in 2007;

14. *Invites* the United Nations system, its relevant bodies and the international community to continue to provide technical assistance, as appropriate, to the States members of the Economic Cooperation Organization in developing and enhancing their early warning systems, preparedness, capacity for timely response and rehabilitation, with a view to reducing human casualties and mitigating the socio-economic impact of natural disasters and infectious diseases;

15. *Takes note with appreciation* of the strides made by the Economic Cooperation Organization in the sphere of external relations, and expresses its desire for the strengthening of the Organization's relations with other international/regional organizations through the establishment of a mechanism to accord it the status of observer/dialogue partner and through the activation of contact groups in the relevant international forums;

16. *Requests* the Secretary-General to submit to the General Assembly at its sixty-third session a report on the implementation of the present resolution;

17. *Decides* to include in the provisional agenda of its sixty-third session the sub-item entitled "Cooperation between the United Nations and the Economic Cooperation Organization".

UN-Pacific Islands Forum cooperation

The Secretary-General, in his consolidated report on cooperation between the United Nations and regional and other intergovernmental organizations [A/61/256 & Add.1], outlined UN cooperation with the Pacific Islands Forum. On 10 April, ESCAP and the Pacific Islands Forum secretariat held the first Pacific Leaders' UN-ESCAP Special Session, which allowed Pacific leaders to highlight their development needs. ESCAP, in collaboration with the Forum and UNDP, initiated a project on the theme "Enhancing Pacific connectivity", which would study ICT applications, including satellite infrastructure in the Pacific. ESCAP worked with the Forum secretariat to assess the adjustment costs that Pacific countries would have to bear as a result of providing greater market access to EU members as part of the Economic Partnership Agreement.

GENERAL ASSEMBLY ACTION

On 4 December [meeting 65], the General Assembly adopted **resolution 61/48** [draft: A/61/L.20/Rev.1 & Add.1] without vote [agenda item 108 *(r)*].

Cooperation between the United Nations and the Pacific Islands Forum

The General Assembly,

Recalling its resolutions 49/1 of 17 October 1994 and 59/20 of 8 November 2004,

Welcoming the ongoing efforts towards closer cooperation between the United Nations and the Pacific Islands Forum and its associated institutions,

Bearing in mind that the Pacific Islands Forum, established in 1971, promotes regional cooperation and integration among its members through trade, investment, economic development and political and international affairs, to achieve their shared goals of economic growth, sustainable development, good governance and security,

Recalling the importance of the internationally agreed development goals set out in the United Nations Millennium Declaration, the Monterrey Consensus of the International Conference on Financing for Development, the Plan of Implementation of the World Summit on Sustainable Development ("Johannesburg Plan of Implementation") and the Mauritius Strategy for the Further Implementation of the Programme of Action for the Sustainable Development of Small Island Developing States ("Mauritius Strategy for Implementation"),

Taking note of the special circumstances pertaining to the continued presence of radioactive contaminants in certain Pacific Islands Forum nations,

Recalling that one of the purposes of the United Nations is to achieve international cooperation in addressing international problems of an economic, social, cultural or humanitarian character,

Reaffirming the commitment of leaders at the 2005 World Summit, and bearing in mind the call thereat for a stronger relationship between the United Nations and regional and subregional organizations,

Affirming the need to strengthen the cooperation that already exists between entities of the United Nations system and the Pacific Islands Forum in the areas of peace and security, sustainable development, environmental protection and good governance,

Noting that many Pacific Islands Forum nations depend upon the continued existence of sustainable marine ecosystems,

Welcoming the support and assistance given by the United Nations towards the maintenance of peace and security in the Pacific Islands Forum region,

Taking note of the Communiqué of the Thirty-seventh Pacific Islands Forum, held at Nadi, Fiji, on 24 and 25 October 2006,

Mindful of the need for coordinated and effective utilization of available resources in pursuing the common objectives of the two organizations,

Having considered the report of the Secretary-General on cooperation between the United Nations and regional and other organizations,

1. *Takes note* of the report of the Secretary-General, in particular part one, section XII, on cooperation between the United Nations and the Pacific Islands Forum, and encourages further such cooperation;

2. *Notes with satisfaction* that regular consultations continue at all levels between the United Nations and the Secretariat of the Pacific Islands Forum, including participation at the annual consultations between the Secretary-General and heads of regional organizations;

3. *Invites* the Secretary-General of the United Nations to take the necessary measures, in consultation with the Secretary-General of the Pacific Islands Forum, to promote and expand cooperation and coordination between the two secretariats in order to increase the capacity of the organizations to attain their common objectives;

4. *Welcomes* the ongoing work of various international organizations and United Nations agencies, funds and programmes in advancing knowledge in the key strategic areas related to governance, security, economic growth, trade and sustainable development, as well as in the implementation of the internationally agreed development goals, including those contained in the United Nations Millennium Declaration, in the Pacific island countries;

5. *Recognizes* the challenges that Pacific island countries are facing in combating the HIV/AIDS pandemic, and in this regard urges the international community, including the United Nations system, to support Pacific island countries in their efforts to implement the Political Declaration on HIV/AIDS, adopted by the General Assembly at its sixtieth session on 2 June 2006, including the commitment to set, in 2006, ambitious national targets that reflected the urgent need to scale up significantly towards the goal of universal access to comprehensive prevention programmes, treatment, care and support by 2010;

6. *Urges* Governments and all relevant international and regional organizations, the Economic and Social Council, United Nations funds, programmes and regional economic commissions, specialized agencies, international financial institutions and the Global Environment Facility, as well as other intergovernmental organizations and major groups, to take timely actions

to support Pacific island countries in their efforts to ensure the effective implementation of and follow-up to the Johannesburg Declaration on Sustainable Development, the Johannesburg Plan of Implementation and the Mauritius Strategy for Implementation;

7. *Notes* the importance of the United Nations Global Counter-Terrorism Strategy adopted on 8 September 2006, and in this regard calls for the support of the United Nations system and other international partners in assisting Pacific island countries in their efforts to implement it;

8. *Welcomes* the ongoing efforts of the Pacific Islands Forum to promote, primarily through the Regional Security Committee, law enforcement cooperation, the rule of law and regional peace and security, including combating all types of terrorism, in implementing the core United Nations treaties on anti-terrorism, anti-money-laundering, transnational crime and the financing of terrorism;

9. *Requests*, in this regard, that the United Nations continue to assist the Pacific Islands Forum in facilitating among its members the timely implementation of relevant United Nations mandates, and invites States to contribute to the Biketawa Trust Fund, which is administered by the Pacific Islands Forum for confidence-building measures and conflict prevention;

10. *Welcomes* the significant efforts of the Pacific Islands Forum in enhancing peace and security in the region, including through the Regional Assistance Mission to Solomon Islands;

11. *Notes with appreciation* the role of the United Nations in the Bougainville peace process in Papua New Guinea and the steady progress being made by the parties;

12. *Welcomes* the establishment of the Peacebuilding Commission and the Peacebuilding Fund, and calls upon the Secretary-General and other relevant actors to give consideration to using these and other mechanisms to support post-conflict peacebuilding activities, reconstruction and institution-building efforts in Pacific island countries, particularly on the island of Bougainville and in Solomon Islands;

13. *Requests* that the Department of Political Affairs of the Secretariat and the United Nations Development Programme, in cooperation with the Pacific Islands Forum, promote joint cooperative needs assessment missions in the region to determine additional support to enhance peacebuilding and reconciliation processes and to complement the activities of regional missions and mechanisms;

14. *Calls upon* the international community to provide, where appropriate, technical and financial support to Pacific island countries in combating the illicit traffic in small arms and light weapons through, inter alia, the implementation of the Programme of Action to Prevent, Combat and Eradicate the Illicit Trade in Small Arms and Light Weapons in All Its Aspects;

15. *Notes* the importance of the United Nations field presence in Pacific island countries for enhancing the cooperation with the United Nations system and its development agencies needed to implement the internationally agreed development goals, including the Millennium Development Goals and the Mauritius Strategy for Implementation;

16. *Welcomes*, in this regard, the endorsement by the Secretary-General of the establishment of an expanded and joint in-country presence of the United Nations in Kiribati, the Marshall Islands, Micronesia (Federated States of), Nauru, Palau, Solomon Islands, Tuvalu and Vanuatu;

17. *Expresses*, in this regard, its appreciation for the support and cooperation of the Pacific Islands Forum members in fulfilling host-country obligations and other operational modalities;

18. *Notes* the efforts of the United Nations, in cooperation with the Pacific Islands Forum, in respect of considering ways to assist Nauru, and in this regard calls upon the United Nations system to support implementation of the Republic of Nauru preparatory assistance project of the United Nations Development Programme as well as that country's national sustainable development strategy;

19. *Also notes* the participation of Pacific leaders at the special session of the Economic and Social Commission for Asia and the Pacific held in Jakarta on 10 April 2006, and takes note of the project "Enhancing Pacific connectivity";

20. *Welcomes* the adoption of the Pacific Plan by Pacific Islands Forum leaders at the Thirty-sixth Pacific Islands Forum, in Madang, Papua New Guinea, during the leaders' Forum Retreat on 26 October 2005, which is aimed at enhancing regional integration and cooperation among its members and cooperation with the international community, including the United Nations system;

21. *Also welcomes* the leadership role of the Pacific Islands Forum in furthering the implementation of the 1995 Agreement for the Implementation of the Provisions of the United Nations Convention on the Law of the Sea of 10 December 1982 relating to the Conservation and Management of Straddling Fish Stocks and Highly Migratory Fish Stocks, particularly in the convening of the negotiations for, and the adoption of, the Convention on the Conservation and Management of Highly Migratory Fish Stocks in the Western and Central Pacific Ocean;

22. *Further welcomes* the decision to convene the Pacific regional seminar on decolonization in Nadi, Fiji, from 28 to 30 November 2006;

23. *Urges* the United Nations to support Pacific island countries in pursuing initiatives for enhancing South-South cooperation among themselves and also with other developing countries;

24. *Takes note* of the steps taken by the Pacific Islands Forum to solidify its partnership with non-State actors in the region in promoting governance and sustainable development issues;

25. *Recognizes* the burden placed on small States by growing international reporting requirements, and encourages the investigation of innovative reporting

modalities, including regional reporting, where appropriate;

26. *Calls upon* the Office of the United Nations High Commissioner for Human Rights to provide technical support to Pacific Islands Forum members to contribute to the regional efforts in promoting awareness and knowledge of all international human rights treaties and instruments;

27. *Requests* the Secretary-General to submit to the General Assembly at its sixty-third session a report on the implementation of the present resolution;

28. *Decides* to include in the provisional agenda of its sixty-third session the sub-item entitled "Cooperation between the United Nations and the Pacific Islands Forum".

The General Assembly also had before it the communiqué of the thirty-seventh Pacific Islands Forum (Fiji, 24-25 October) [A/61/558], which included the Nadi decisions on the Pacific Plan on economic growth, sustainable development and good governance, as well as the Declaration on Deep-Sea Bottom Trawling to Protect Biodiversity in the High Seas.

UN-ASEAN cooperation

On 4 December [meeting 65], the General Assembly, having considered UN cooperation with the Association of South-East Asian Nations (ASEAN), as outlined in the Secretary-General's consolidated report on cooperation between the United Nations and regional and other intergovernmental organizations [A/61/256 & Add.1], adopted **resolution 61/46** [draft: A/61/L.13 & Add.1] without vote [agenda item 108 *(c)*].

Cooperation between the United Nations and the Association of Southeast Asian Nations

The General Assembly,

Bearing in mind the aims and purposes of the Association of Southeast Asian Nations, as enshrined in the Bangkok Declaration of 8 August 1967, in particular the maintenance of close and beneficial cooperation with existing international and regional organizations with similar aims and purposes,

Recalling its resolution 59/5 of 22 October 2004 on cooperation between the United Nations and the Association,

Noting with appreciation the report of the Secretary-General on cooperation between the United Nations and the Association,

Noting with satisfaction that the activities of the Association are consistent with the purposes and principles of the United Nations,

Welcoming the ongoing efforts that strengthen the cooperation between the United Nations system and the Association,

Welcoming also the participation of the Association in the high-level meetings between the United Nations and regional organizations, as well as the collaboration between the Association and the Economic and Social Commission for Asia and the Pacific to promote dialogue and cooperation among regional organizations in Asia and the Pacific,

1. *Welcomes* the holding of the Second Association of Southeast Asian Nations-United Nations Summit at United Nations Headquarters on 13 September 2005, chaired jointly by Prime Minister Dato' Seri Abdullah Ahmad Badawi of Malaysia, the rotating Chair of the Association of Southeast Asian Nations Standing Committee and the Secretary-General of the United Nations, and attended by the leaders of the Association, as well as the heads of various United Nations agencies, funds and programmes;

2. *Acknowledges* the commitment of the leaders of the Association and the Secretary-General of the United Nations to further broaden cooperation between the Association and the United Nations, in the areas mentioned in the joint communiqué of the Second Association of Southeast Asian Nations-United Nations Summit;

3. *Continues to encourage* both the United Nations and the Association to further strengthen and expand their areas of cooperation;

4. *Welcomes* the Association as an observer in the General Assembly;

5. *Encourages* the United Nations and the Association to convene Association of Southeast Asian Nations-United Nations summits regularly;

6. *Commends* the President of the General Assembly, the Secretary-General of the United Nations and the Ministers for Foreign Affairs of the States members of the Association for their efforts to hold regular meetings, on an annual basis, with the presence of the Secretary-General of the Association, during the regular session of the Assembly, with a view to further strengthening the cooperation between the United Nations and the Association;

7. *Takes note* of the efforts of the Association to hold meetings with other regional organizations at the fringes of the sessions of the General Assembly to promote cooperation in support of multilateralism;

8. *Requests* the Secretary-General to submit to the General Assembly at its sixty-third session a report on the implementation of the present resolution;

9. *Decides* to include in the provisional agenda of its sixty-third session the sub-item entitled "Cooperation between the United Nations and the Association of Southeast Asian Nations".

The General Assembly also had before it the joint communiqué of the Second ASEAN-United Nations Summit (New York, 13 September 2005) [A/61/517], which addressed areas of common interest to the two organizations.

Europe

The Economic Commission for Europe (ECE), at its sixty-first session (Geneva, 21-23 February) [E/2006/37], considered the economic situation in Europe on the basis of the *Economic Survey of Europe, 2005, No. 2* [Sales No. E.05.II.E.17].

The Commission noted the success of the Second Regional Implementation Forum on Sustainable Development [YUN 2005, p. 1113]. It stated that the assessment of the region's progress in implementing sustainable development commitments in the areas of energy for sustainable development, atmosphere/air pollution, climate change, industrial development and cross-cutting issues had clearly shown the different challenges and experiences of countries in the region. The Commission Chairperson's summary of the Forum [E/ECE/1442] was submitted to the fourteenth session of the Commission on Sustainable Development (New York, 1-12 May) (see p. 982) (conclusion 9). The Commission expressed appreciation for the secretariat note on the promotion of information and communication technology (ICT) application in its work programme and in the ECE secretariat, including e-applications [E/ECE/1443], which provided updated information on the development and use of ICT applications. It emphasized the need to keep ICT issues under review (conclusion 10).

The Commission also discussed ECE technical cooperation activities in 2005 [E/ECE/1441 & Add.1]. It expressed its appreciation for the work of the regional advisers and stressed the need for interlinkages between the Technical Cooperation Unit and the new subprogramme and to discuss further the issue of the ECE technical cooperation strategy at the Executive Committee. The Commission took note of the technical cooperation carried out with subregional groupings and urged the secretariat to reinforce such cooperation. Further, it welcomed the approval of concrete projects and project proposals by the special session of the regional advisory committee of the Special Programme for the Economies of Central Asia, and urged members who were also members of the Development Assistance Committee of the Organisation for Economic Cooperation and Development to support the inclusion of the ECE on their list of main international organizations (conclusion 8).

After reviewing Conference Paper 2 on the ECE Strategic Framework for 2008-2009, the report of the Group of Experts on the Programme of Work [E/ECE/1440 & Add.1] and an oral report by the Chair, the Commission supported the Group of Experts' comments and asked the Executive Secretary to take them into account when finalizing his submission to UN headquarters (conclusion 7).

In the economic context of ECE reform: challenges, policy responses and the ECE role, the Commission took note of the wide range of views raised during the debate on the economic context in which the ECE was operating and urged sectoral committees and the Executive Committee to take them into account.

The Executive Secretary submitted a note on achieving the internationally agreed development goals, including the MDGs [E/ECE/1438], which reviewed ECE contribution and progress thus far to achieving the goals in the region.

Economic trends

According to the *World Economic Situation and Prospects 2007*, economic growth in Western Europe grew an estimated 2.5 per cent, the fastest growth rate since 2000, and well above potential growth estimates. Growth reached a cyclical peak in the second quarter of 2006, with the euro area recording the strongest performance of all the major developed economies. Growth decelerated in the second half of the year, but remained relatively strong. The brunt of the slowdown was expected to occur in 2007. Growth picked up in Germany, Italy and the United Kingdom. Spain, where growth decelerated to just above 3 per cent, continued to have the strongest growth performance.

Growth in the region was anchored by domestic demand, particularly investment expenditure, as well as strong export performance, but net trade made a minimal impact as imports, boosted by the strong domestic demand and appreciated currencies. Exports were expected to decelerate with the slowing of external demand, and the further appreciation of the euro meant that exporters would face difficulties maintaining market share.

In contrast, economic activity in most of the eight new European Union (EU) member States in Central Europe and the Baltic region continued to be dynamic in 2006. Aggregate GDP in the region grew by 5.7 per cent. That reflected a rebound in Poland, record high growth in the Czech Republic and Slovakia, and an exceptionally strong performance in the Baltic States.

Vibrant growth prevailed in South-East Europe, with aggregate GDP increasing by some 6 per cent, boosted by the strong upturn in Romania, where GDP growth accelerated by more than 2 percentage points, and buoyant domestic demand. Bulgaria,

Croatia and Romania, the EU accession candidates in the subregion, continued to benefit from rising investor and consumer confidence. Strong GDP growth in Bosnia and Herzegovina suggested that the prolonged period of sluggish recovery might be over. The formal dissolution of the federal State of Serbia and Montenegro (see p. 472) did not have major economic implications, as the two entities had already been performing as separate economies. South-East Europe's short-term outlook was positive, with domestic demand driving growth.

The pace of economic expansion in the Commonwealth of Independent States continued in 2006, reaching 7.5 per cent, up from 6.8 per cent in 2005. That outcome was largely due to higher international prices for oil, gas, metals and cotton, relatively low interest rates in international capital markets and increasing domestic demand throughout the subregion.

Activities in 2006

Trade

The Committee on Trade, at its first session (Geneva, 21-23 June) [ECE/TRADE/C/2006/18], approved: the renewal of the mandate of the Ad Hoc Group on Market Surveillance for a further two years; its revised terms of reference; the proposals contained in the document of the Working Party of Regulatory Cooperation and Standardization Policies (WP.6) entitled "WP.6 Vision, Mission, Strategic Directions for 2006-2009 and Work Plan for 2006-2007"; and changes in the UN Centre for Trade Facilitation and Electronic Business (UN/CEFACT) 2004-2005 and 2007-2008 programmes of work. The Committee proposed transition procedures in the document entitled "Strengthening agricultural quality standards work in the UNECE: draft transition plan" and requested the secretariat to revise it for submission to the next intersessional meeting. It approved the addition of the outputs from the extrabudgetary project "On-line Russian language resources for WTO negotiations and agreements" to its 2006-2007 programme of work, provided that adequate funding was obtained for its implementation; and decided to use the "Accomplishments Accounts" for evaluating the Committee's work. It also approved the change to the 2006-2007 programme of work [ECE/TRADE/C/2006/14] as modified during the sessions; and its 2008-2009 programme of work [ECE/TRADE/C/2006/12].

The Committee asked its secretariat to publish the proceedings of the Committee's annual International Forum entitled "A Common Regulatory Language for Global Trade" (Geneva, 20-21 June), with a view to disseminating information to interested parties. Having endorsed the document on strengthening itself [ECE/TRADE/C/2006/3], the Committee asked the secretariat, the bureau and its subsidiary bodies to define priorities and corresponding methods to improve communications, as well as implement the evaluation plan for the next three to four years, as reflected in the expected accomplishments and indicators from the strategic frameworks for 2006-2007 and 2008-2009; develop and support capacity-building activities and clearly define a role for itself that was distinct from that of its subsidiary bodies. The Committee adopted its revised terms of reference with agreed changes [ECE/TRADE/C/2006/10].

The Director of the ECE Trade and Timber Division introduced the draft transition plan drawn up by the secretariat, following the request in the ECE Reform Plan [YUN 2005, p. 1114] to strengthen ECE work in agricultural quality standards. The Committee supported it and urged the Organisation for Economic Co-operation and Development (OECD) secretariat to comment on the draft text so that a final version could be considered in 2006 by the OECD Scheme for the Application of International Standards for Fruit and Vegetables and by the Commission. The Committee, having endorsed the report of the 2005 session of the Working Party on Agricultural Quality Standards (WP.7), asked the secretariat to prepare for the autumn 2006 Bureau meeting a briefing on the relationship between the Codex Alimentarius and the WP.7. An addendum to the Committee's report [ECE/TRADE/C/2006/18/Add.1] contained the draft transition plan for agricultural quality standards work.

The Committee also decided to hold its second session from 22 to 26 October 2007, and asked the Bureau to develop an improved structure for Committee sessions.

Timber

The Timber Committee, at its sixty-fourth session (Geneva, 3-6 October) [ECE/TIM/2006/8], held a policy forum on "Public procurement policies for wood and paper products and their impact on sustainable forest management and timber markets", in collaboration with the Food and Agriculture Organization of the United Nations (FAO). The forum noted that such policies were developing rapidly and should be monitored regularly, and that countries should be requested to include the latest developments in that regard in their national markets in 2007 and subsequent years. Having reviewed the market for forest products and considered forecasts for 2006 and 2007, with a focus on how China's forest products trade was reshaping the market, the Committee approved a market statement. It also noted the inadequacy of information on markets for certified forest products and asked the ECE/FAO Working Party on Forest Economics and Statistics to continue to examine ways to improve the situation. It proposed that the theme for the 2007 policy forum should be "Mobilizing wood resources for raw material, energy or climate change: finding solutions at the policy level".

The Committee also reported on the implementation of ECE reform [ECE/TIM/2006/2], including revised terms of reference, the framework of cooperation with the Ministerial Conference on the Protection of Forests in Europe (MCPFE) and strengthening the monitoring of policies and institutions.

Taking note of the close cooperation on European forestry issues between ECE, FAO and MCPFE, the Committee welcomed the proposal to organize a European Forest Week in 2008. The Committee agreed to present proposals for cooperation with the Committee on Sustainable Energy. It asked its secretariat to look into the issue related to the Almaty Guidelines on Promoting the Application of the Principles of the Aarhus Convention in International Forums.

The Committee reviewed its 2008 activities and programme of work and evaluations of the 2004-2005 biennium. It agreed to post the discussion paper on "International Forest Sector Institutions and Policy Instruments in Europe: A Source Book" on its website and to update it regularly.

Transport

The sixty-eighth session of the Inland Transport Committee (Geneva, 7-9 February) [ECE/TRANS/166 & Add.1] reviewed, among other topics, intersectoral activities; the transport situation in ECE member countries and emerging development trends; transport and security; assistance to countries with economies in transition; the application status of international ECE transport agreements and conventions; transport trends and economics; road transport; road traffic safety; harmonization of vehicle registration; rail, inland water and intermodal transport and logistics; border crossing facilitation; transport of dangerous goods and perishable foodstuffs; transport statistics; and the Committee's strategic objectives and programme of work.

The Committee adopted a resolution on the implementation of the amendments to the European Agreement on the Work of Crews of Vehicles engaged in International Road Transport, particularly the introduction of the digital tachograph, and a resolution on the first United Nations Global Road Safety Week, to be held in April 2007.

The Committee adopted the text of the Convention on International Customs Transit Procedures for the Carriage of Goods by Rail under Cover of Senior Management Groups (SMGS) Consignment Notes, as approved by the Working Party in February, and which included amendments required by the UN Office of Legal Affairs for the Secretary-General to become depositary to the Convention. It decided that the Convention would be open for signature in Geneva from 1 June 2006 for a period of one year. The secretariat was entrusted with the verification and preparation of the final text. It also approved the ECE Transport Division's Strategic Framework for 2008-2009.

Energy

The Committee on Sustainable Energy, at its fifteenth session (Geneva, 28-30 November) [ECE/ENERGY/68 & Add.1], discussed implementation of ECE reform; emerging energy security risks; energy for sustainable development; global harmonization of energy reserves and resources technology; regulation and investment in the electric industry; mitigating environmental and social consequences of coal production; natural gas; energy efficiency, import dependence and climate change; and the work of the Regional Adviser on Energy.

On emerging energy security risks and risk mitigation, including the work of the Energy Security Forum, the Committee recommended that it undertake a broadly shared intergovernmental expert dialogue on energy security in data and information sharing and increased transparency; infrastructure investment and financing; legal, regulatory and policy framework; harmonization of standards; research, development and deployment of new technologies; and investment/transit safeguards and burden sharing. It also agreed to seek strategic guidance from ECE on those areas.

The Committee also took note of the report of the December 2005 meeting of its Extended Bureau [ENERGY/2005/6] and reviewed the activities of its subsidiary bodies. It adopted its revised terms of reference and agreed upon its structure, which included the establishment of the Ad Hoc Group of Experts on Cleaner Electricity Production from Coal and Other Fossil Fuels and the discontinuation of the Ad Hoc Group of Experts on Coal in

Sustainable Development, the Ad Hoc Group of Experts on Electric Power and the Joint Energy and Environment Task Force on Reforming Energy Prices for Sustainable Energy Development.

Environment

The Committee on Environmental Policy, at its thirteenth session (Geneva, 9-11 October) [ECE/CEP/138], held in-depth discussion on major policy issues including environmental policy and international competitiveness, as well as ECE reform and its implications for the Committee's activities, financial assistance to countries with economies in transition and countries contribution to ECE trust funds and reviewed its 2007-2008 programme of work. The Committee, having considered a paper [ECE/CEP/2006/4 & Add.1] on environmental policy and international competitiveness, invited the secretariat to prepare a revised draft and to produce a second paper on low-income economies in the ECE region. It reviewed the environmental performance of Ukraine and adopted the related recommendations, and approved the outline of a discussion paper to be submitted to the Belgrade Ministerial Conference "Environment for Europe". The Committee welcomed the achievements of the working group on environmental monitoring and assessment and favoured strengthening further the monitoring and assessment activities, in particular capacity-building in ECE. It acknowledged progress achieved under ECE multilateral agreements and their protocols and emphasized the importance of strengthening activities related to their implementation.

The Committee adopted its programme of work for 2007-2008, taking into account the evaluation for the 2004-2005 biennium. It approved the updated criteria for financial support, which was annexed to its report.

The fourth session of the Steering Committee for Transport, Health and Environment Pan-European Programme (Geneva, 10-11 April) [ECE/AC.21/2006/10], assessed progress made in implementing its work programme and provided guidance for its further implementation. It also discussed preparations for the third High-level Meeting on Transport, Environment and Health, to be held in 2008.

The second meeting of the ECE Steering Committee on Education for Sustainable Development (Geneva, 4-5 December) [ECE/CEP/AC.13/2006/3 & Corr.1] heard reports from countries on the implementation of the ECE strategy for education for sustainable development. It endorsed the "input" and "output" and "outcome" indicators prepared by the Expert Group, which was tasked with revising them. The Committee stressed the importance of stable and predictable funding for the effective implementation of the strategy and decided to bring the issue of funding to the attention of Ministers at the Belgrade meeting (see below).

The second (Geneva, 29-30 June) [ECE/CEP/AC.11/2006/2] and third (Geneva, 12-13 October) [ECE/CEP/AC.11/2006/9] meetings of the Ad Hoc Preparatory Working Group of Senior Officials for the preparation of the Sixth Ministerial Conference "Environment for Europe" to be held in Belgrade, Serbia, in October 2007, discussed the provisional agenda for the Conference and the preparation of the ministerial declaration and other administrative and procedural matters. Proposals were made regarding the possible elements of the declaration. It was of the view that the declaration should focus on a limited number of issues and address the priority needs of countries beyond the Belgrade Conference and identify appropriate mechanisms for addressing those needs.

Housing and land management

The Committee on Housing and Land Management, at its sixty-seventh session (Geneva, 18-20 September) [ECE/HBP/142 & Add.1], discussed implementation of its work plan on ECE reform; decided that experts on real estate should be integrated into the existing Working Party on Land Administration as observers; and adopted its new terms of reference, as well as those of the Working Party on Land Administration and the Advisory Network. It adopted its programme of work for 2007-2008 and made decisions on its various programme elements, including the outcome of the World Urban Forum (Vancouver, Canada, 19-23 June), country profiles on the housing sector, improvement of urban environmental performance, land registration and land markets and housing modernization and management. Further, it invited its Bureau to help the secretariat formulate expected accomplishments and indicators of achievement when preparing the biennial budget plan.

During the session, Ministers responsible for housing, special planning and land administration discussed social and economic integration through human settlements development, and the multi-family housing sector: ownership, maintenance, renewal and management. They adopted a Ministerial Declaration on Social and Economic Challenges in Distressed Urban Areas in the ECE Region, which reaffirmed the goals and challenges of the ECE Strategy for a Sustainable Quality of Life in Human Settlements in the Twenty-first Century and committed themselves to contributing to social inclusion through the development of affordable housing, and by further addressing effective management of multi-family housing estates and supporting activities in land administration and spatial planning. It decided to convene the next high-level meeting in 2011 to assess progress in the implementation of those commitments.

The Committee discussed the impact of the provisions of the Declaration on its programme of work and agreed to contribute to its implementation in the next five years, with an emphasis on priority areas such as policy tools for affordable and adequate housing, improving management and maintenance of the multi-family housing stock, functioning spatial planning systems and effective integrated housing and land management policies.

Statistics

The Conference of European Statisticians, at its fifty-fourth session (Paris, 13-15 June) [ECE/CES/70], considered the implications of the meetings of its parent bodies—the February session of ECE and the March session of the UN Statistical Commission (see p. 1465). The Conference decided that its Bureau would review health statistics coordination activities and discuss the need to set up a body to coordinate work on globalization statistics; approved the procedure for preparing and adopting standards, recommendations, handbooks and best practices; approved the strategy for coordinating technical cooperation in the ECE region [ECE/CES/2006/3]; and considered ways to improve international work on crime statistics.

It adopted the Guidelines and Core Principles on Managing Statistical Confidentiality and Microdata Access [ECE/CES/2006/6] and recommendations for the 2010 Censuses of Population and Housing.

During the Conference, seminars were held on population and housing censuses and on human resources and training.

Economic cooperation and integration

The Committee on Economic Cooperation and Integration, at its first session (Geneva, 27-28 September) [ECE/CECI/2006/6], adopted its terms of reference [ECE/CECI/2006/2]. It also adopted its 2006-2008 programme of work, and invited international organizations to become active partners in its implementation and the secretariat to establish expert networks in all its thematic areas. The Committee established the Team of Specialists on Innovation and Competitiveness Policies and the Team of Specialists on Intellectual Property. It decided to convene its second meeting in December 2007.

The Team of Specialists on Intellectual Property, at its first meeting (Geneva, 23-24 November) [ECE/CECI/IP/2006/1], discussed the challenges countries in the region faced in terms of the commercialization of intellectual property assets, including the importance of public-private partnerships, transfer of technology offices, training centres for intellectual property specialists and greater funding for research and development. It also discussed the challenges faced in protecting and enforcing intellectual property rights (IPR), including its links to public health and safety standards, and the need to make them more consistent across borders. The Team adopted its 2007 programme of work and agreed to hold its next meeting in July 2007, back-to-back with the meeting on IPR protection and transforming research and design into intangible assets in transition economies.

Operational activities

Operational activities, as described in a note by the Executive Secretary [E/ECE/1441], were mostly carried out through capacity-building workshops, seminars, study tours, policy advisory services and field projects. Activities were funded from the UN regular budget and the UN Development Account, together with extrabudgetary resources and ad hoc and in-kind contributions. Of the $1,376,529 provided by the regular budget, 26 per cent went to industrial restructuring and enterprise development, 15 per cent to sustainable energy, 14 per cent each to statistics and the environment, 13 per cent to transport, 10 per cent to trade development and 7 per cent to management of technical cooperation activities. Extrabudgetary expenditure from ECE general trust funds, local trust funds and other sources totalled $7,640,165.

Proposals, together with the ECE/ESCAP workplan for 2005-2007 in support of the UN Special Programme for the Economies of Central Asia (SPECA), were approved at the Special Session of the SPECA Regional Advisory Committee [YUN 2005, p. 1114]. New areas of technical cooperation under SPECA included trade, statistics and ICT.

Programme and organizational questions

ECE reform

The Commission recommended that the Economic and Social Council endorse the ECE reform [YUN 2005, p. 1114]. It adopted the revised Rules of Procedure for the Commission [E/ECE/1437], and the revised Terms of Reference provisionally, pending their endorsement by the Economic and Social Council. The Commission also adopted the Terms of Reference and Rules of Procedure of the Executive Committee. The Commission asked the Sectoral Committees to strengthen intersectoral activities and approaches among themselves, in order to promote a more coherent ECE and implement the provisions of ECE reform related to cooperation with other organizations. The Commission also had before it a report of the Ad-Hoc Informal Meeting held on 2 December [E/ECE/1439], which included the Chairperson's concluding remarks on ECE reform at the November 2005 meeting of the Intergovernmental Open-ended Negotiations Committee.

The Commission noted that resolutions on Economic and Social Council Reform and Follow-up to the development outcome of the 2005 World Summit, including the Millennium Development Goals and other internationally agreed development goals, which were being negotiated in New York, would impact ECE work.

Concerning organizational changes in the secretariat, the Commission took note of the new organizational structure presented by the Executive Secretary, slated for implementation before April 2006, and asked the Executive Committee to inform member States of any further measures, particularly regarding staff deployment and mobility.

ECONOMIC AND SOCIAL COUNCIL ACTION

On 27 July [meeting 41], the Economic and Social Council adopted **resolution 2006/38** [draft: E/2006/15/Add.1] without vote [agenda item 10].

Workplan on reform of the Economic Commission for Europe and revised terms of reference of the Commission

The Economic and Social Council,

Noting the adoption by the Economic Commission for Europe, in formal segment, at its meeting of 2 December 2005, of the workplan on reform of the Commission, and noting also the adoption by the Commission, at its sixty-first session, held in Geneva from 21 to 23 February 2006, of its revised rules of procedure,

Noting also the provisional adoption by the Economic Commission for Europe at its sixty-first session of the revised terms of reference of the Commission, pending their endorsement by the Economic and Social Council,

Noting further that the General Assembly, in its resolution 60/248 of 23 December 2005, welcomed the workplan on reform of the Economic Commission for Europe, decided that the Commission should implement the adopted measures and, to that end, requested the Secretary-General to allocate the requisite resources within section 19, Economic development in Europe, of the proposed programme budget for the biennium 2006-2007,

1. *Endorses* the workplan on reform of the Economic Commission for Europe, as set out in annex I of the present resolution;

2. *Also endorses* the revised terms of reference of the Economic Commission for Europe, as set out in annex II of the present resolution.

Annex I

Workplan on reform of the Economic Commission for Europe

1. Based on the recommendations on the role, mandate and functions of the Economic Commission for Europe as reflected in the report on the state of the Commission, the Commission adopts the following decision:

I. Mission statement

2. The Economic Commission for Europe as a multilateral platform facilitates greater economic integration and cooperation among its fifty-five member States and promotes sustainable development and economic prosperity through:

(a) Policy dialogue;

(b) Negotiation of international legal instruments;

(c) Development of regulations and norms;

(d) Exchange and application of best practices as well as economic and technical expertise;

(e) Technical cooperation for countries with economies in transition.

3. The Economic Commission for Europe contributes to enhancing the effectiveness of the United Nations through the regional implementation of outcomes of global United Nations conferences and summits.

II. Governance structure

4. The governance structure shall be reformed in order to enhance accountability, transparency and the horizontal coherence of the activities of the organization with a view to enabling the organization to better respond to the needs of its member States.

5. The existing terms of reference and rules of procedure of the Economic Commission for Europe will be amended accordingly.

A. The Commission

6. The Commission is the highest decision-making body of the organization.

7. It is responsible for taking strategic decisions on the programme of work of the Commission and the allocation of resources without prejudice to the competence of the Fifth Committee.

8. It also provides a forum for a policy dialogue at a high level on economic development for the region.

9. The Commission meets once every two years in Geneva as of 2007, taking into account the provisions of rules 1 and 2 of the rules of procedure. At its 2009 session, the Commission will review the reform of the

Commission including the question of frequency of its sessions.

10. The Commission is chaired by the representative of the country elected by the Commission for the period of the biennium. The Chair is assisted by two Vice-Chairs who will be the representatives of two countries elected at the same session.

B. The Executive Committee

11. The implementation of the overall guidance set by the Commission is entrusted to the Executive Committee.

12. Representatives of all States members of the Commission participate in the Executive Committee.

13. The Chairs of the Sectoral Committees—or the Vice-Chairs—are regularly invited to the meetings of the Executive Committee.

14. The Executive Secretary or his representative takes part in the meetings of the Executive Committee.

15. The Executive Committee is presided by a representative of the country that chairs the Commission. The Chairman of the Executive Committee is assisted by two Vice-Chairs elected by the Executive Committee, for a period of one year, the term being renewable.

16. In the period between the biennial sessions of the Commission, the Executive Committee acts on behalf of the Commission and can seize itself of all matters related to Commission activities in conformity with the terms of reference.

17. In particular, the Executive Committee:

(a) Prepares the sessions of the Commission;

(b) Reviews, evaluates and approves in due time the programmes of work of the sectoral committees, including intersectoral activities and relations with other international organizations, based on the criteria that shall be defined by the Executive Committee and that shall include coherence with the overall objective of the Commission, coordination with other subprogrammes and resource implications;

(c) Approves the set-up, renewal, discontinuance, terms of reference and workplans of groups under the Sectoral Committees, based on the criteria of their relevance to the subprogramme, resource implications, and avoidance of duplication and overlap in respect of the activities of the Commission;

(d) Examines with the Chairs and Vice-Chairs of the Sectoral Committees, their report on the implementation of their programme of work and other relevant issues;

(e) Ensures coherence between subprogrammes, inter alia, by encouraging horizontal communication within the organization;

(f) Deals with all matters related to programme planning, administrative and budget issues, including extrabudgetary funding;

(g) Discusses with the Executive Secretary, initiatives taken by the Secretariat and the work undertaken by the Office of the Executive Secretary.

18. The ad hoc informal sessions of the Commission, the Bureau of the Commission, the Group of Experts on the Programme of Work, and the Steering Committee are hereby discontinued. The governance role formerly filled by these bodies shall be performed by the Executive Committee. The existing monthly briefings by the Secretariat will be replaced by a regular briefing which shall take place as a rule during the meetings of the Executive Committee.

19. The Executive Committee meets when necessary.

20. All decisions are adopted in formal sessions. For formal sessions, interpretation shall be provided and documentation for decision shall be available in all official languages of the Commission. The Executive Committee may also meet in informal mode.

21. The terms of reference and the rules of procedure of the Executive Committee shall be adopted by the Commission.

C. The Sectoral Committees

22. The reference to "Principal subsidiary bodies" is discontinued and replaced by reference to "Sectoral Committees".

23. Each subprogramme of the programme of work is attributed to a Sectoral Committee.

24. Each Sectoral Committee is responsible for the preparation and implementation of its programme of work under the conditions defined by the Commission and the Executive Committee. The terms of reference of the Sectoral Committees shall be approved by the Commission.

25. The Sectoral Committees are the following:

(a) Committee on Environmental Policy;

(b) Committee on Inland Transport;

(c) Committee on Statistics, further referred to as the Conference of European Statisticians;

(d) Committee on Sustainable Energy;

(e) Committee on Trade;

(f) Committee on Timber;

(g) Committee on Housing and Land Management;

(h) Committee on Economic Cooperation and Integration.

26. All Committees shall have reviewed by the end of February 2007:

(a) Their subsidiary intergovernmental bodies in accordance with the guidelines for the establishment and functioning of teams of specialists within the Commission, which shall have been previously reviewed by member States;

(b) Conference servicing needs, with a view to rationalizing them, and shall submit proposals on possible streamlining to the Executive Committee.

27. The Sectoral Committees report once a year and upon request to the Executive Committee, through a meeting with their Chairs and Vice-Chairs.

28. Sectoral Committees will jointly prepare and submit proposals to the Executive Committee on issues and activities of common interest.

D. The Secretariat

29. The Secretariat services the intergovernmental structure entrusted with the implementation of the programme of work.

III. Priorities of the programme of work

30. In order to respond to the actual needs expressed by member States, the programme of work will be restructured. Elements of the subprogrammes of work that are not mentioned below will be maintained. This reform will be implemented within existing budgetary resources.

A. Environment subprogramme

31. The subprogramme shall increase its focus on:

(a) Member States' implementation of their decisions and commonly agreed goals, including those adopted in the Environment for Europe process, the Eastern Europe, Caucasus and Central Asia Environment Strategy, and the Commission's environmental conventions;

(b) Strengthening work on environmental performance reviews and environmental monitoring and assessment, which lays the necessary foundation for evaluating environmental protection and the implementation of these decisions.

32. Greater efforts shall be directed towards the implementation of the Commission's environmental programme, notably through further capacity-building and workshops at subregional levels.

33. The Committee on Environmental Policy shall study ways and means to strengthen cooperation with the United Nations Environment Programme and all other relevant United Nations institutions and international organizations in order to optimize the implementation of the programme of work in the region and shall submit proposals to the Executive Committee.

34. The Committee on Environmental Policy shall, in cooperation with the Committee on Inland Transport and in consultation with the World Health Organization, strengthen activities relating to: *(a)* the Transport, Health and Environment Pan European Programme, including sustainable financing and staffing for the clearing house; and *(b)* environmental aspects of transportation, and submit proposals thereon to the Executive Committee.

B. Transport subprogramme

35. The Committee on Inland Transport shall strengthen activities in the fields of border-crossing and trade facilitation in cooperation with the Committee on Trade and submit proposals thereon to the Executive Committee.

36. The Committee on Inland Transport shall, in cooperation with the Committee on Environmental Policy and in consultation with the World Health Organization, strengthen activities relating to: *(a)* the Transport, Health and Environment Pan European Programme, including sustainable financing and staffing for the clearing house; and *(b)* environmental aspects of transportation, and submit proposals thereon to the Executive Committee.

37. The Committee on Inland Transport shall submit proposals to the Executive Committee on ways and means of monitoring and strengthening the implementation of the Commission's key legal instruments on transport, including on road safety.

38. The Committee on Inland Transport shall submit proposals to the Executive Committee on ways and means to strengthen Euro-Asia transport links.

39. The Committee on Inland Transport shall submit proposals to the Executive Committee on ways and means:

(a) To strengthen the Customs Convention on the International Transport of Goods under Cover of TIR Carnets (TIR Convention);

(b) To improve transparency in managing the TIR Convention.

C. Subprogramme on statistics

40. The coordination of international statistical work, methodological work and technical cooperation activities shall be strengthened.

41. In order to provide member States with user-oriented statistics, the Conference of European Statisticians shall submit proposals to the Executive Committee on the actual production of statistics of member States. The contents of the online database shall be reviewed and improved accordingly.

42. The functioning and accessibility of the online database shall be improved in order to facilitate the dissemination of statistics.

43. The publication of "Trends" is discontinued. The production of other publications shall be reviewed by the Conference of European Statisticians which will submit proposals to the Executive Committee.

44. The resources allocated to the processing of data by this subprogramme shall be reduced owing to the overall reduction of activities in the field of economic analysis.

D. Subprogramme on economic cooperation and integration

45. This subprogramme will address key aspects of economic development and integration and focus mainly on countries with economies in transition in order to:

(a) Deliver policy advice;

(b) Facilitate policy dialogue, and exchange of experience and best practices;

(c) Develop guidelines.

46. To this extent, the subprogramme will deal with:

(a) Application of experience gained, lessons learned and best practices conducive to economic growth and innovative development. This work shall be demand-driven and focused on specific topics and may be entrusted by the Committee to external experts and relevant organizations and institutions, in particular those from countries with economies in transition. The initial list to be considered by the Committee may include such issues as:

(i) Promoting effective public investment and regulatory policies;

(ii) Strengthening the competitiveness of the economy through innovative development;

(iii) Development of financial systems and services;

(iv) Application and adaptation of economic analysis;

(b) Elaboration of recommendations aimed at creating a policy, financial and regulatory environment conducive to economic development, investment and innovation through:

(i) Creation and development of enterprises and entrepreneurship;

(ii) Promotion of knowledge-based economies and innovation;

(iii) Promotion of an effective system of protection of intellectual property rights;

(iv) Promotion of corporate governance, rule of law and public-private partnerships through the improvement of transparency and investor confidence, including the establishment of guidelines thereto;

(c) Definition by the Sectoral Committee of the modalities of the integration of existing activities in the new subprogramme, with a view to continuing valuable work in the areas mentioned above, with the Sectoral Committee reporting to the Executive Committee.

47. Networks of experts, advisers and decision-makers shall be set up in order to provide a platform for exchange of national policy experiences and development of standards and best models on these matters.

48. The activities of this subprogramme shall build, inter alia, on the results of the work carried out by other relevant organizations and institutions operating in this field, including United Nations organizations, with which synergies should be improved.

49. Based on the overall framework above, member States shall approve the strategic framework no later than end of March 2006, and the Committee on Economic Cooperation and Integration shall submit proposals on its terms of reference and programme of work to the Executive Committee for approval as soon as possible and, at the latest, within one year from the date of the adoption of the present decision.

50. The Executive Committee will review the subprogramme on economic cooperation and integration no later than three years from the date of the adoption of the present decision with a view to assessing whether the level of resources is appropriate and optimizing the programme if necessary.

51. A regional adviser shall be allocated to this subprogramme.

E. Subprogramme on sustainable energy

52. The Committee on Sustainable Energy shall streamline its activities and improve cooperation with other relevant institutions, in particular the International Energy Agency and the Energy Charter process. This cooperation could take the form of joint activities, memorandums of understanding, and participation of members of other relevant organizations in the activities of the subprogramme and vice versa.

53. The Committee on Sustainable Energy shall strengthen activities in the fields of energy efficiency, cleaner energy production, energy security and diversification of energy sources, taking into account environmental concerns. Special attention should be given to cooperation with the Committee on Environmental Policy, the Committee on Inland Transport and the Committee on Timber.

F. Trade development subprogramme

54. Activities in the field of trade facilitation shall continue and focus on supporting the development of standards carried out by the United Nations Centre for Trade Facilitation and Electronic Business.

55. The Committee on Trade shall review the programme on regulatory cooperation and standardization policies.

56. The activities in the field of agricultural quality standards shall be strengthened. Consultations shall be initiated with the Organization for Economic Cooperation and Development in order to concentrate the activities of the two organizations within the Economic Commission for Europe.

57. The Sectoral Committee is renamed the "Committee on Trade".

58. The subprogramme is renamed the "Trade subprogramme".

G. Timber subprogramme

59. The Committee on Timber shall submit proposals to the Executive Committee on the development of increased cooperation between the Ministerial Conference for the Protection of Forests in Europe and the Commission, and shall explore the possibility of a formal framework for this cooperation.

60. The Committee on Timber shall submit proposals to the Executive Committee on ways and means to strengthen its monitoring and analysis activities relating to forest policy and institutions.

61. The subprogramme is renamed the "Subprogramme on timber and forestry".

H. Human settlements subprogramme

62. The following programme elements are discontinued:

(a) Development of human settlements statistics;

(b) Major trends characterizing human settlements development.

63. The activities and related resources in the field of real estate (currently carried out under the Industrial restructuring and enterprise development subprogramme) shall be integrated in the subprogramme. The Sectoral Committee shall submit proposals to the Executive Committee on the modalities of this integration.

64. The activities and related resources in the field of population (currently carried out under the Economic analysis subprogramme) shall be integrated in the subprogramme.

65. The subprogramme is renamed the "Subprogramme on housing, land management and population".

66. The Sectoral Committee is renamed the "Committee on Housing and Land Management".

67. The intergovernmental governance of population activities shall be assured by the Executive Committee.

I. Economic analysis and industrial restructuring and enterprise development subprogrammes

68. These subprogrammes as well as the related intergovernmental structures will be discontinued.

IV. Technical cooperation

69. Technical cooperation, which forms an integral part of the Commission's activities, has to focus on the countries with economies in transition and has to be demand-driven.
70. The Commission's technical cooperation shall concentrate on the sectors where the Commission has in-house expertise and comparative advantage over other organizations. It should be coherent with and support the implementation of the agreed work programmes.
71. The coordination of the Commission's technical cooperation shall be ensured by the Technical Cooperation Unit reporting directly to the Executive Secretary with appropriate resources for carrying out its functions.
72. The intergovernmental governance of technical cooperation shall be assured by the Executive Committee.
73. The impact of the Technical Cooperation Strategy, endorsed by the Commission at its annual session of 2004, shall be assessed by the Executive Committee and the Strategy will be reviewed if necessary.
74. Member States shall review, no later than two months after the adoption of this decision, the resource allocation among subprogrammes concerning the regular programme of technical cooperation (section 23 of the regular budget) as foreseen in the decision related to this subject.
75. The use of the Commission's regional advisers shall be strengthened by enabling their participation in capacity-building activities.
76. Evaluations of separate subprogrammes' technical cooperation activities shall be conducted on a regular basis. A common policy and practice for these evaluations shall be implemented.

V. Cross-sectoral issues

A. Millennium Development Goals

77. In order to contribute to the implementation of the Millennium Development Goals, the Commission shall:

(a) Offer a platform to all stakeholders for sharing their information, views and experience, and for improving the coordination of these activities;

(b) Set up and maintain a database on Millennium Development Goal indicators using the database and dissemination infrastructure of the statistical subprogramme.

78. The Commission shall cooperate with the United Nations Development Programme to this extent and within existing resources.

B. Gender issues

79. The Commission shall pay particular attention to the gender dimension of development, as a priority cross-cutting theme, by identifying good practices in further mainstreaming gender issues in its various subprogrammes and activities, taking into account the economic areas addressed by the regional review of the implementation of the Beijing Declaration and Platform for Action. This should apply across both regular and operational activities.

C. The private sector and non-governmental organizations

80. The Sectoral Committees shall review and report to the Executive Committee on the involvement of the private sector and non-governmental organizations, in order to strengthen and further improve their relationship and to increase resources and contributions of expertise with a view to optimizing the implementation of the programme of work.

VI. Relations with other organizations

81. In order to increase the impact of its work, the Commission shall reinforce its cooperation with key international organizations and institutions in all relevant areas of its work.
82. In particular, regular consultation shall be fostered with other pan-European organizations.
83. In addition to the specific cooperations identified under the different subprogrammes, the cooperation with the United Nations Development Programme should be strengthened. The Secretariat shall explore ways and means to improve the synergy between the organization and the Programme.
84. The Economic Commission for Europe shall seek to reinforce partnerships with other United Nations regional commissions, in particular the Economic and Social Commission for Asia and the Pacific, the Economic Commission for Africa and the Economic and Social Commission for Western Asia. The Secretariat shall assess the possibilities for strengthening the United Nations Special Programme for the Economies of Central Asia.
85. The Secretariat shall keep member States informed of these proceedings through the Executive Committee.
86. The implementation of the memorandum of understanding with the Organization for Security and Cooperation in Europe is entrusted to the Office of the Executive Secretary and the Executive Committee shall monitor this implementation.
87. After consultations with other organizations and upon the recommendation of the Secretariat, the Executive Committee shall decide on the opportunity for the Commission's engagement in the development of an early warning mechanism.

VII. Management

A. Coordination tasks

88. The Office of the Executive Secretary is entrusted with:

(a) The follow-up of the implementation of horizontal and sectoral issues arising from the relevant multilateral commitments such as those made at the General

Assembly, the Economic and Social Council and United Nations global conferences and summits, as well as the provision of inputs required by these global bodies and by the Secretary-General;

(b) The coordination of intersectoral and cross-sectoral activities;

(c) The coordination of Commission inputs into the monitoring of implementation of the commitments of the Organization for Security and Cooperation in Europe in the fields of economics and the environment;

(d) Reporting to the Executive Committee on the progress in the implementation of any follow-up of agreed measures.

B. Programme planning and budget

89. The Commission shall strengthen its programme planning, monitoring and evaluation resources and improve the training of its managers in the application of pertinent skills.

90. A dedicated unit for planning, monitoring and evaluation shall be established and attached to the Office of the Executive Secretary in order to secure the continuous involvement of senior management.

91. To facilitate the assessment of programme performance:

(a) The strategic framework (biennial programme plan) will be consolidated with the programme budget narratives in order to emphasize the linkage between expected accomplishments and outputs financed by the regular budget and extrabudgetary funds;

(b) In its reporting to the Executive Committee, the Secretariat shall provide, in a user-friendly format, complete information about the allocation of resources from the regular budget and of extrabudgetary resources to the subprogrammes and programme items within their respective programmes of work.

92. The Sectoral Committees together with the Secretariat will take into account the results of the assessment and evaluations when preparing the strategic frameworks for their respective subprogrammes and, subsequently, the programme narratives.

93. The Secretariat shall provide information to the Executive Committee on cost implications for any programmatic changes proposed for the next biennium during the preparatory process of the programme budget.

94. Any change in resources (both regular and extrabudgetary) materializing after the adoption of the programme budget by the General Assembly shall be presented to the Executive Committee for approval.

C. Monitoring and evaluation, including reporting on performance

95. The Sectoral Committees shall provide complete information concerning the allocation of resources according to programme items within the programme of work of their respective subprogrammes.

96. The Executive Committee shall examine the advisability of developing "downstream" indicators with the Secretariat so as to better reflect actual accomplishments of the Commission, in particular relating to the use and relevance of the Commission's soft legislation tools, norms and standards.

97. The Commission shall develop and streamline its evaluation functions and practices in conformity with the relevant decision of the Commission and in compliance with the instructions of the Office of Internal Oversight Services. This also applies to technical cooperation activities.

D. Human resources

98. The Executive Secretary shall:

(a) Improve communication, coordination and cooperation across the divisions and subprogrammes;

(b) Promote, through human resources management, staff mobility and skill enhancement in order to ensure that staff members periodically change divisions and subprogrammes, and encourage staff members to gain experience in other United Nations and international organizations, as well as in the field.

99. The Secretariat shall provide systematic programme planning, monitoring and evaluation training to its programme managers, in particular in cooperation with the Management Consulting Section of the Office of Internal Oversight Services. Priority will be given to such training in the training budget allocated to the Commission.

100. The Secretariat shall analyse the merits of using the United Nations Office for Project Services for the implementation of its extrabudgetary projects and will present suggestions to the Executive Committee.

E. Public relations, communication and corporate image

101. To improve its own corporate image and to attract more attention to its achievements, the Secretariat shall enhance its communications, public relations and contacts with the media by making more and better-targeted materials and publications available on the Internet in all official languages of the Commission and producing appropriate printed materials in quantities that correspond to actual demand.

102. To improve its communication with member States the Secretariat shall update, in consultation with member States, the lists of its contacts in government agencies and among governmental experts and address its communications at the appropriate level and through transparent channels.

VIII. Resources

103. The redeployment shall be implemented within existing resources.

104. The abolition of the subprogrammes on Economic analysis (excluding the Population Activities Unit) and industrial restructuring and enterprise development will free:

(a) One D and 12 P posts from Economic analysis;

(b) Four P posts from industrial restructuring and enterprise development;

(c) Two P posts from statistics (owing to the reduction of activities related to Economic analysis);

for a total of one D and 18 P posts.

105. These posts are redeployed to strengthen other subprogrammes/entities. The redeployments, with their justification given through reference to the relevant paragraph(s) of the present annex, are as follows:

(a) Environment: two P posts (paragraphs 31, 32, 34 and 53);

(b) Transport: two P posts (paragraphs 35-39 and 53);

(c) Statistics: one P post (paragraphs 40-42 and 77);

(d) Economic cooperation and integration: one D and eight P posts (paragraphs 45-51);

(e) Sustainable energy: one P post (paragraph 53);

(f) Trade development: one P post (paragraphs 35 and 56);

(g) Timber: one P post (paragraphs 53, 59 and 60);

(h) Office of the Executive Secretary and information activities: two P posts (paragraphs 86, 89-94, 97 and 101);

for a total of one D and 18 P posts.

Annex II

Draft revised terms of reference and rules of procedure of the Economic Commission for Europe

Terms of reference

1. The Economic Commission for Europe, acting within the framework of the policies of the United Nations and subject to the general supervision of the Economic and Social Council shall, provided that the Commission takes no action in respect of any country without the agreement of the Government of that country:

(a) Initiate and participate in measures for facilitating concerted action for the economic development and integration of Europe, for raising the level of European economic activity, and for maintaining and strengthening the economic relations of the European countries both among themselves and with other countries of the world;

(b) Make or sponsor such investigations and studies of economic and technological problems of and developments within member countries of the Commission and within Europe generally as the Commission deems appropriate;

(c) Undertake or sponsor the collection, evaluation and dissemination of such economic, technological and statistical information as the Commission deems appropriate.

2. Cancelled.

3. Cancelled.

4. The Commission is empowered to make recommendations on any matter within its competence directly to its member Governments, Governments admitted in a consultative capacity under paragraph 8 below, and the specialized agencies concerned. The Commission shall submit for the prior consideration of the Economic and Social Council any of its proposals for activities that would have important effects on the economy of the world as a whole.

5. The Commission may, after discussion with any specialized agency functioning in the same general field and with the approval of the Economic and Social Council, establish such subsidiary bodies as it deems appropriate for facilitating the carrying out of its responsibilities.

6. The Commission shall submit to the Economic and Social Council a full report on its activities and plans, including those of any subsidiary bodies, once a year, and shall make interim reports at each regular session of the Council.

7. A complete list of countries members of the Economic Commission for Europe is contained in the appendix to the present annex.

8. The Commission may admit, in a consultative capacity, European nations that are not States Members of the United Nations, and shall determine the conditions under which they may participate in its work, including the question of voting rights in the subsidiary bodies of the Commission.

9. Cancelled.

10. Cancelled.

11. The Commission shall invite any State Member of the United Nations not a member of the Commission to participate in a consultative capacity in its consideration of any matter of particular concern to that non-member.

12. The Commission shall invite representatives of specialized agencies and may invite representatives of any intergovernmental organizations to participate in a consultative capacity in its consideration of any matter of particular concern to that agency or organization, following the practices of the Economic and Social Council.

13. The Commission shall make arrangements for consultation with non-governmental organizations that have been granted consultative status by the Economic and Social Council, in accordance with the principles approved by the Council for this purpose and contained in Council resolution 1296(XLIV) of 23 May 1968, parts I and II.14.

14. The Commission shall take measures to ensure that the necessary liaison is maintained with other organs of the United Nations and with the specialized agencies.

15. The Commission shall adopt its own rules of procedure, including the method of selecting its Chairman.

16. The administrative budget of the Commission shall be financed from the funds of the United Nations.

17. The Secretary-General of the United Nations shall appoint the staff of the Commission, which shall form part of the United Nations Secretariat.

18. The headquarters of the Commission shall be located at the seat of the European Office of the United Nations.
19. Cancelled.
20. The Economic and Social Council shall, from time to time, undertake special reviews of the work of the Commission.

Rules of procedure

Chapter I
Sessions

Rule 1

Sessions of the Commission shall be held:

(a) On dates fixed by the Commission, after consultation with the Executive Secretary, at previous meetings;

(b) Within thirty days of the communication of a request to that effect by the Economic and Social Council;

(c) At the request of the majority of the members of the Commission, after consultation with the Executive Secretary;

(d) On such other occasions as the Chairperson, in consultation with the Vice-Chairpersons and the Executive Secretary, deems necessary.

Rule 2

Sessions shall ordinarily be held at the United Nations Office at Geneva. The Commission may, with the concurrence of the Secretary-General, decide to hold a particular session elsewhere.

Rule 3

The Executive Secretary shall, at least forty-two days before the commencement of a session of the Commission, distribute a notice of the opening date of the session, together with a copy of the provisional agenda. The basic documents relating to each item appearing in the provisional agenda of a session shall be transmitted not less than forty-two days before the opening of the session, with the provision that, in exceptional cases, the Executive Secretary may, for reasons to be stated in writing, transmit such documents not less than twenty-one days before the opening of the session.

Rule 4

The Commission shall invite any State Member of the United Nations not a member of the Commission to participate in a consultative capacity in its consideration of any matter of particular concern to that State.

Chapter II
Agenda

Rule 5

The provisional agenda for each session shall be drawn up by the Executive Secretary in consultation with the Chairperson, the two Vice-Chairpersons and the Executive Committee.

Rule 6

The provisional agenda for any session shall include:

(a) Items arising from previous sessions of the Commission;

(b) Items proposed by the Economic and Social Council;

(c) Items proposed by any member of the Commission;

(d) Items proposed by a specialized agency in accordance with the agreements of relationship concluded between the United Nations and such agencies;

(e) Any other items that the Chairperson or the Executive Secretary sees fit to include.

Rule 7

The first item in the provisional agenda for each session shall be the adoption of the agenda.

Rule 8

The Commission may amend the agenda at any time.

Chapter III
Representation and credentials

Rule 9

Each member shall be represented on the Commission by an accredited representative.

Rule 10

A representative may be accompanied to the sessions of the Commission by alternate representatives and advisers and, when absent, he may be replaced by an alternate representative.

Rule 11

The credentials of each representative appointed to the Commission, together with a designation of alternate representatives, shall be submitted to the Executive Secretary without delay.

Chapter IV
Officers

Rule 12

The Commission shall, at each biennial session, elect a country from among its members to hold the chair for the period of the biennium. The representative of the elected country will be the Chairperson. The Commission will also, at the same meeting, elect two countries whose representatives will become the Vice-Chairpersons for the period of the biennium.

Rule 13

If the Chairperson is absent from a meeting, or any part thereof, one of the Vice-Chairpersons, designated by the Chairperson, shall preside.

Rule 14

If the representative of the country holding the position of Chairperson or Vice-Chairperson of the Commission ceases to represent his or her country, the new representative of that country shall become the new Chairperson or Vice-Chairperson for the unexpired portion of the term. If the representative of the country holding the position of Chairperson or Vice-Chairperson is so incapacitated that he or she can no longer hold office, the alternate representative shall become the new Chairperson or Vice-Chairperson for the unexpired portion of the term.

Rule 15

The Vice-Chairperson acting as Chairperson shall have the same powers and duties as the Chairperson.

Rule 16

The Chairperson or the Vice-Chairperson acting as Chairperson shall participate in the meetings of the Commission as such and not as the representative of the member by whom he or she was accredited. The Commission shall admit an alternate representative to represent that member in the meetings of the Commission and to exercise its right to vote.

Chapter V
Intersessional committee (Executive Committee)

Rule 17

The Commission shall adopt the terms of reference and the rules of procedure of its intersessional governing committee (Executive Committee) and may amend these when necessary. The Commission provides general guidance to the Executive Committee.

Chapter VI
Subsidiary bodies other than the intersessional committee

Rule 18

After discussion with any specialized agency functioning in the same general field, and with the approval of the Economic and Social Council, the Commission may establish such continuously acting subcommissions or other subsidiary bodies as it deems necessary for the performance of its functions and shall define the powers and composition of each of them. Such autonomy as may be necessary for the effective discharge of the technical responsibilities laid upon them may be delegated to them.

Rule 19

The Commission may establish or discontinue such committees and subcommittees as it deems necessary to assist it in carrying out its tasks.

Rule 20

Subsidiary bodies shall adopt their own rules of procedure unless otherwise decided by the Commission.

Rule 21

Subsidiary bodies should, as in rules 52 and 53, consult those non-governmental organizations in general consultative status with the Economic and Social Council that, because of their importance as regards their activity and the number of their members in Europe, play a part in the economic life of Europe, on questions within the competence of the Commission and deemed of interest to such organizations. These organizations could in appropriate cases be invited to be represented at meetings of subsidiary bodies.

Chapter VII
Secretariat

Rule 22

The Executive Secretary shall act in that capacity at all meetings of the Commission and of its subsidiary bodies. He or she may appoint another member of the staff to take his or her place at any meeting.

Rule 23

The Executive Secretary or his or her representative may at any meeting make either oral or written statements concerning any question under consideration.

Rule 24

The Executive Secretary shall direct the staff provided by the Secretary-General and required by the Commission, and its subsidiary bodies.

Rule 25

The Executive Secretary shall be responsible for the necessary arrangements being made for meetings.

Rule 26

The Executive Secretary, in carrying out his or her functions, shall act on behalf of the Secretary-General.

Chapter VIII
Conduct of business

Rule 27

A majority of the members of the Commission shall constitute a quorum.

Rule 28

In addition to exercising the powers conferred upon him or her elsewhere by these rules, the Chairperson shall declare the opening and closing of each meeting of the Commission, shall direct the discussion, shall ensure the observance of these rules, and shall accord the right to speak, put questions to the vote, and announce decisions. The Chairperson may also call a speaker to order if his or her remarks are not relevant to the subject under discussion.

Rule 29

During the discussion of any matter, a representative may raise a point of order. In this case the Chairperson shall immediately state his or her ruling. If it is challenged, the Chairperson shall forthwith submit his or her ruling to the Commission for decision and it shall stand, unless overruled.

Rule 30

During the discussion of any matter, a representative may move the adjournment of the debate. Any such motion shall have priority. In addition to the proposer of the motion, one representative shall be allowed to speak in favour of, and one representative against, the motion.

Rule 31

A representative may at any time move the closure of the debate whether or not any other representative has signified his or her wish to speak. Not more than two representatives may be granted permission to speak against the closure.

Rule 32

The Chairperson shall take the sense of the Commission on a motion for closure. If the Commission is in favour of the closure, the Chairperson shall declare the debate closed.

Rule 33

The Commission may limit the time allowed to each speaker.

Rule 34

Principal motions and resolutions shall be put to the vote in the order of their submission, unless the Commission decides otherwise.

Rule 35

When an amendment revises, adds to or deletes from a proposal, the amendment shall be put to the vote first, and if it is adopted, the amended proposal shall then be put to the vote.

Rule 36

If two or more amendments are moved to a proposal, the Commission shall vote first on the amendment furthest removed in substance from the original proposal, then, if necessary, on the amendment next furthest removed, and so on, until all the amendments have been put to the vote.

Rule 37

The Commission may, at the request of a representative, decide to put a motion or proposal to the vote in parts. If this is done, the text resulting from the series of votes shall be put to the vote as a whole.

Chapter IX
Voting

Rule 38

Each member of the Commission shall have one vote.

Rule 39

Decisions of the Commission shall be made by a majority of the members present and voting.

Rule 40

The Commission shall take no action in respect of any country without the agreement of the Government of that country.

Rule 41

The Commission shall normally vote by show of hands. If any representative requests a roll-call, a roll-call shall be taken in the English alphabetical order of the names of the members.

Rule 42

All elections shall be decided by secret ballot, unless, in the absence of any objection, the Commission decides to proceed without taking a ballot on an agreed candidate or slate.

Rule 43

If a vote is equally divided upon matters other than elections, a second vote shall be taken. If this vote also results in equality, the proposal shall be regarded as rejected.

Chapter X
Languages

Rule 44

English, French and Russian shall be the working languages of the Commission.

Rule 45

Interventions made in any of the working languages shall be interpreted into the other working languages.

Chapter XI
Records

Rule 46

Suspended.

Rule 47

Suspended.

Rule 48

Suspended.

Rule 49

As soon as possible, the text of all reports, resolutions, recommendations and other formal decisions taken by the Commission and its subsidiary bodies shall be communicated to the members of the Commission, to the consultative members concerned, to all other States Members of the United Nations and to the specialized agencies.

Chapter XII
Publicity of meetings

Rule 50

The meetings of the Commission shall ordinarily be held in public. The Commission may decide that a particular meeting or particular meetings shall be held in private.

Chapter XIII
Consultation with specialized agencies and the International Atomic Energy Agency

Rule 51

(a) Where an item proposed for the provisional agenda for a session contains a proposal for new activities to be undertaken by the United Nations relating to matters that are of direct concern to one or more specialized agencies or the International Atomic Energy Agency, the Executive Secretary shall enter into consultation with the agency or agencies concerned and report to the Commission on the means of achieving coordinated use of the resources of the respective agencies.

(b) Where a proposal put forward in the course of a meeting for new activities to be undertaken by the United Nations relates to matters that are of direct concern to one or more specialized agencies or the International Atomic Energy Agency, the Executive Secretary shall, after such consultation as may be possible with the representatives

at the meeting of the other agency or agencies concerned, draw the attention of the meeting to these implications of the proposal.

(*c*) Before deciding on proposals referred to above, the Commission shall satisfy itself that adequate consultations have taken place with the agencies concerned.

Chapter XIV
Relations with non-governmental organizations

Rule 52

Non-governmental organizations in general or in special consultative status with the Economic and Social Council may designate authorized representatives to sit as observers at public meetings of the Commission. Organizations on the Roster may have representatives present at such meetings as are concerned with matters within their field of competence. Non-governmental organizations in general consultative status with the Council may circulate to the members of the Commission written statements and suggestions on matters within their competence. Non-governmental organizations in special consultative status with the Council or on the Roster may submit such statements and suggestions to the Executive Secretary. The Executive Secretary shall prepare and distribute at each session of the Commission a list of such communications received, briefly indicating the substance of each of them. Upon the request of any member of the Commission, the Executive Secretary shall reproduce in full and distribute any such communication.

Rule 53

The Commission at its discretion may consult with non-governmental organizations in general or in special consultative status with the Economic and Social Council or on the Roster on matters concerning which the Commission regards these organizations as having special competence or knowledge. Such consultations may be arranged at the invitation of the Commission or at the request of the organization. In the case of non-governmental organizations in general consultative status, consultations should normally be held with the Commission itself. In the case of non-governmental organizations in special consultative status or on the Roster, consultations might be effected either directly or through ad hoc committees.

Chapter XV
Reports

Rule 54

The Commission shall submit to the Economic and Social Council a full report on its activities and plans, including those of any subsidiary bodies, once a year, and shall make interim reports at each regular session of the Council.

Chapter XVI
Amendments and suspensions

Rule 55

Any of these rules of procedure may be amended or suspended by the Commission provided that the proposed amendments or suspensions do not attempt to set aside the terms of reference laid down by the Economic and Social Council.

Appendix

List of countries members of the
Economic Commission for Europe
(as at 9 January 2006)

Albania
Andorra
Armenia
Austria
Azerbaijan
Belarus
Belgium
Bosnia and Herzegovina
Bulgaria
Canada
Croatia
Czech Republic
Denmark
Estonia
Finland
France
Georgia
Germany
Greece
Hungary
Iceland
Ireland
Israel
Italy
Kazakhstan
Kyrgyzstan
Latvia
Liechtenstein
Lithuania
Luxembourg
Malta
Monaco
Netherlands
Norway
Poland
Portugal
Republic of Moldova
Romania
Russian Federation
San Marino
Serbia
Slovakia
Slovenia
Spain
Sweden
Switzerland
Tajikistan
The former Yugoslav Republic of Macedonia
Turkey
Turkmenistan
Ukraine
United Kingdom of Great Britain and Northern Ireland
United States of America
Uzbekistan

Regional cooperation

The Secretary-General's consolidated report on cooperation between the United Nations and regional and other intergovernmental organizations [A/61/256] outlined UN cooperation with the Black Sea Economic Cooperation Organization.

GENERAL ASSEMBLY ACTION

On 20 October [meeting 39], the General Assembly adopted **resolution 61/4** [draft: A/61/L.4 & Add.1] without vote [agenda item 108 *(d)*].

Cooperation between the United Nations and the Black Sea Economic Cooperation Organization

The General Assembly,

Recalling its resolution 54/5 of 8 October 1999, by which it granted observer status to the Black Sea Economic Cooperation Organization, as well as its resolutions 55/211 of 20 December 2000, 57/34 of 21 November 2002 and 59/259 of 23 December 2004, on cooperation between the United Nations and the Black Sea Economic Cooperation Organization,

Recalling also that one of the purposes of the United Nations is to achieve international cooperation in solving international problems of an economic, social or humanitarian nature,

Recalling further the Articles of the Charter of the United Nations that encourage activities through regional cooperation for the promotion of the purposes and principles of the United Nations,

Recalling its Declaration on the Enhancement of Cooperation between the United Nations and Regional Arrangements or Agencies in the Maintenance of International Peace and Security of 9 December 1994,

Recognizing that any dispute or conflict in the region impedes cooperation, and stressing the need to solve such a dispute or conflict on the basis of the norms and principles of international law,

Convinced that the strengthening of cooperation between the United Nations and other organizations contributes to the promotion of the purposes and principles of the United Nations,

Recalling the report of the Secretary-General submitted pursuant to resolution 59/259,

1. *Encourages* efforts within the Black Sea Economic Cooperation Organization to consider ways and means of enhancing the contribution of the Organization to security and stability in the region;

2. *Welcomes* the signing in Athens on 3 December 2004 of the Additional Protocol on Combating Terrorism to the Agreement among the Governments of the Black Sea Economic Cooperation Organization Participating States on Cooperation in Combating Crime, in Particular in its Organized Forms;

3. *Also welcomes* the activities of the Black Sea Economic Cooperation Organization aimed at strengthening regional cooperation in various fields, such as energy, transport, institutional reform and good governance, trade and economic development, banking and finance, communications, agriculture and agro-industry, health care and pharmaceuticals, environmental protection, tourism, science and technology, exchange of statistical data and economic information, collaboration among Customs services, and combating organized crime and illicit trafficking in drugs, weapons and radioactive material, acts of terrorism and illegal migration, or in any other related area;

4. *Encourages* the activities of the Black Sea Economic Cooperation Organization aimed at the elaboration and realization of specific joint regional projects, particularly in the field of transport and energy infrastructure, focused on security of supply of respective services to the economies of the region;

5. *Welcomes* the operationalization and financing of projects by the Project Development Fund of the Black Sea Economic Cooperation Organization to the benefit of the sustainable development of the Black Sea region;

6. *Takes note* of the positive contributions of the Parliamentary Assembly of the Black Sea Economic Cooperation Organization, the Business Council, the Black Sea Trade and Development Bank and the International Centre for Black Sea Studies to the strengthening of multifaceted regional cooperation in the Black Sea area;

7. *Appeals* for greater cooperation between the Black Sea Economic Cooperation Organization and international financial institutions in co-financing feasibility and pre-feasibility studies of the projects in the Black Sea area;

8. *Takes note* of the cooperation between the Black Sea Economic Cooperation Organization and the World Bank and the World Trade Organization and the working contacts with the World Tourism Organization, aimed at promoting the sustainable development of the Black Sea region;

9. *Also takes note* of the importance attached by the Black Sea Economic Cooperation Organization to the strengthening of relations with the European Union, and supports the efforts of the Organization to take concrete steps to advance this cooperation in line with the provisions of the Komotini statement of 23 April 2005, as reinforced by the Chisinau Declaration of 28 October 2005 and the Bucharest statement of 26 April 2006, issued by the Council of Ministers for Foreign Affairs of the States members of the Black Sea Economic Cooperation Organization;

10. *Further takes note* of the cooperation established between the Black Sea Economic Cooperation Organization and other regional organizations and initiatives;

11. *Invites* the Secretary-General to strengthen dialogue with the Black Sea Economic Cooperation Organization with a view to promoting cooperation and coordination between the two secretariats;

12. *Invites* the specialized agencies and other organizations and programmes of the United Nations system to cooperate with the Black Sea Economic Cooperation Organization in order to continue programmes with the Organization and its associated institutions for the achievement of their objectives;

13. *Requests* the Secretary-General to submit to the General Assembly at its sixty-third session a report on the implementation of the present resolution;

14. *Decides* to include in the provisional agenda of its sixty-third session the sub-item entitled "Cooperation between the United Nations and the Black Sea Economic Cooperation Organization".

Latin America and the Caribbean

At its thirty-first session (Montevideo, Uruguay, 20-24 March) [LC/G.2318], the Economic Commission for Latin America and the Caribbean (ECLAC) considered a document [LC/G.2295(SES.31/4)] entitled "Shaping the Future of Social Protection: Access, Financing and Solidarity," which proposed the creation of a new social protection covenant designed to build bridges between economic, social and cultural rights, as well as create institutions and policies to enforce them; analysed the region's situation in three areas related to social protection: health systems, pension systems and social programmes to combat poverty; and formulated proposals for reform. It held a high-level seminar on that subject, which included panel discussions on social protection coverage and rights; health service financing and delivery; pension system reform; and social programmes, human capital and inclusion. Chilean President Michelle Bachelet addressed the Commission, describing the main points of her Government's social policies, including reform of the pension system and health care reform; changes in pre-school education and the first four years of primary education, and job creation in the framework of decent employment; plans for overcoming extreme poverty; and an equal opportunity plan. The Commission also had before it reports of the Committee on South-South Cooperation and the ECLAC sessional Ad Hoc Committee on Population and Development.

ECLAC adopted a number of resolutions, among them, the Montevideo resolution on Shaping the Future of Social Protection: Access, Financing and Solidarity [res. 626(XXXI)]; and two resolutions, one on the admission of Japan as a member State of ECLAC [res. 627(XXXI)] and the other on the venue of the Commission's thirty-second session [res. 631(XXXI)], which it recommended to the Economic and Social Council for adoption. It also adopted resolutions on international migration [res. 615(XXXI)]; population and development: priority activities for the period 2006-2008 [res. 616(XXXI)]; the Statistical Conference of the Americas [res. 617(XXXI)]; the Regional Conference on Women in Latin America and the Caribbean [res. 618(XXXI)]; ECLAC calendar of conferences for 2006-2008 [res. 619(XXXI)]; South-South Cooperation [res. 620(XXXI)]; the Caribbean Development and Cooperation Committee [res. 621(XXXI)]; the Central American Economic Cooperation Committee [res. 622(XXXI)]; ECLAC priorities and programme of work for the 2008-2009 biennium [res. 623(XXXI)]; support for the United Nations Stabilization Mission in Haiti [res. 624(XXXI)]; ECLAC activities in relation to follow-up to the MDGS [res. 625(XXXI)]; the admission of the Turks and Caicos Islands as an associate member of ECLAC [res. 628(XXXI)]; follow-up to the Plan of Action for the Information Society in Latin America and the Caribbean [res. 629(XXXI)]; and support for the work of the Latin American and Caribbean Institute for Economic and Social Planning [res. 630(XXXI)].

Economic trends

According to the Latin America and the Caribbean: economic situation and outlook, 2006-2007 [E/2007/19], 2006 was the fourth consecutive year of positive growth and the third year of more than 4 per cent growth. Its GDP expanded by 5.6 per cent, equal to a 4.1 per cent rise in per capita GDP. The international environment remained favorable, and the volume of goods and services exports was up by 8.4 per cent for the region as a whole. Higher prices for the region's main export products translated into an improvement in its terms-of-trade, equivalent to over 7 per cent. As a result of those gains in earnings, together with increased remittances from abroad, the rise in national income, 7.3 per cent, again exceeded GDP growth.

Boosted by strong labour demand, the employment rate rose by 0.5 per cent, to 54 per cent of the working-age population, the highest rate in 15 years. The unemployment rate in the region dropped 0.4 per cent. Only Brazil saw a rise in unemployment. Regional inflation continued its downward trend, with a rate of 4.8 per cent, compared to 6.1 per cent in 2005. The region recorded a surplus on its balance-of-payments current account for the fourth consecutive year, which was estimated at $51 billion or 1.8 per cent of GDP.

Activities in 2006

Development policy and regional economic performance

The ECLAC Economic Development Division continued to report on the macroeconomic performance of both individual countries and the region as a whole in its publications *Economic Survey of Latin America and the Caribbean* and *Preliminary Overview of the Economies of Latin America and the Caribbean.* It also continued to publish working documents in the Macroeconomics of Development Series.

In the framework of the Macroeconomic Dialogue Network (REDIMA) [YUN 2005, p. 1115], ECLAC contributed to regional integration and macroeconomic policy coordination by fostering network activities and sharing best practices. As for productive development, it provided technical cooperation to 28 stakeholders, including five countries, to formulate innovative development plans and national systems of innovation, and to four countries to develop a methodology for creating clusters and local networks of small and medium-sized enterprises and to support institutions.

ECLAC, in resolution [res. 629(XXXI)], requested that the secretariat support countries of the region in formulating national strategies to reach the goals of the Plan of Action for the Information Society in Latin America and the Caribbean (ELAC 2007) [YUN 2005, p. 935], through technical cooperation and studies; promote measures to launch and support the working groups for implementing the Plan of Action; maintain and develop indicators for the on-going assessment and dissemination of progress achieved in the region, especially with respect to the goals of ELAC 2007, provide technical support for organizing the high-level follow-up meeting on the Plan of Action, to be held in San Salvador, El Salvador, in 2007; support countries participating in ELAC 2007 in organizing a regional follow-up meeting to assess the application of the Regional Plan of Action and renew it within the framework of the process intended to achieve the MDGs and the targets set forth in the Plan of Action; and collaborate with the Caribbean Development and Cooperation Committee to finalize, with the European Commission and other donors, the agreement to fund the Caribbean activities related to follow-up to ELAC 2007 and the World Summit on the Information Society [ibid., p. 933].

The Commission, in resolution [res. 630(XXXI)], noted that the resolutions adopted at the twenty-third meeting of the Presiding Officers of the Regional Council for Planning of the Latin American and Caribbean Institute for Economic and Social Planning (ILPES) [ibid., p. 1115] provided for approval of the report of the Institute in the 2004-2005 biennium, the programme of work for the 2006-2007 biennium and the report on ILPES financial situation. The Commission requested that ILPES work in relation to planning be strengthened, while attributing importance to the exchange of experiences, the visions of the countries, and short- and long-term economic, social and territorial dimensions.

In resolution [res. 620(XXXI)], the Commission took note of the document on the activities of the ECLAC system to promote and support South-South cooperation during the 2004-2005 biennium, and underscored the need to expand support for the activities of Governments in the region to improve and expand the use of South-South cooperation mechanisms and modalities in public economic and social development policy and in building national capacities to deal with natural disasters; and for studies to assess the various cooperation options for middle-income countries. It requested the Executive Secretary to strengthen activities aimed at incorporating South-South cooperation modalities into the secretariat's programme of work for the 2008-2009 biennium, particularly technical cooperation financed with extrabudgetary resources; as well as strategic partnerships with countries, cooperation institutions and international cooperation agencies to increase North-South and South-South cooperation and triangular cooperation; and intensify contacts and collaboration with development agencies and UN system organizations to foster interregional cooperation in the context of globalization.

International trade and integration

The 2006 activities of the ECLAC Division of International Trade and Integration concentrated on increasing regional awareness of the implications and impact of the adoption of new trade rules and disciplines and on strengthening understanding and analytical knowledge of ways of improving linkages with the global economy. ECLAC provided technical support for hemispheric integration and, with financial support from the Canadian International Development Agency, implemented national trade capacity-building strategies for member countries of the Free Trade Agreement of the Americas. Some 17 missions were organized to provide technical assistance on various aspects of trade agreements, including rules of origin and the projected impact of trade agreement negotiations, using General Computing Equilibrium Models; and 12 technical cooperation missions concentrated specifically on the World Trade Organization (WTO) Doha Round on multilateral trade negotiations (see p. 1111) process. Support for the region's Governments in the light of the uncertainty generated by the breakdown of the WTO negotiations was also discussed at a meeting of experts on foreign trade held in May in Santiago, Chile. In that context, ECLAC continued providing technical cooperation in negotiating and administering trade agreements by launching a joint initiative on South America cooperation and integration with the Andean Community. ECLAC started a project to strengthen competition in the Central American Isthmus, in response to Governments' requests to develop a legal and institutional framework. In 2006, five countries enacted laws and an Intergovernmental Working Group on Competition was set up, involving the competition authorities of Central America.

The Division also organized eight missions to provide policy recommendations on trade relations between China and Latin America, reflecting the growing importance of China as a trade partner for the region. The Division published *Latin America and the Caribbean in the World Economy, 2005: Trends 2006* [LC/G.2341-P].

ECLAC, in collaboration with the United Nations Conference on Trade and Development, organized a joint Conference on Globalization of Research and Development by Transnational Corporations: Policy Challenges and Opportunities for Latin America and the Caribbean (Santiago, 17 January).

Social development and equity

The main activities of ECLAC Social Development Division in 2006 focused on applied research and the strengthening of the institutional capacity of Governments and other stakeholders in the social policy field to design, implement and assess policies, programmes and projects to enhance social equity and integration and to use and exchange information in designing and implementing social policies and programmes.

It continued the ECLAC/World Food Programme agreement [YUN 2005, p. 1116], with the development of subregional and national diagnostic studies on the cost of hunger and malnutrition, and the creation of a methodology adaptable to different areas of development, which led to concrete proposals for achieving the MDGS.

The Division updated poverty, social expenditure, labour market and income distribution databases for at least 18 countries and planned to expand that database. The 2006 edition of the *Social Panorama of Latin America* included new data from 45 countries and territories on 38 indicators for the follow-up to the MDGS.

In that regard, Commission resolution [res. 625(XXXI)] requested the Executive Secretary to coordinate annual regional reports on advances made toward achieving the development goal of reducing hunger and poverty, as well as a regional inter-agency report summing up progress during 2006-2010 regarding all MDG targets.

In the Montevideo resolution [res. 626(XXXI)] on shaping the future of social protection: access, financing and solidarity, the Commission requested the Executive Secretary to widely disseminate the document "Shaping the Future of Social Protection: Access, Financing and Solidarity", and promote its review by political, social, academic and business spheres and civil society organizations. It urged the Executive Secretary to undertake a more in-depth analysis of efforts to develop countercyclical public finances to give continuity to social policies; reform of social policy financing; the creation of solidarity mechanisms to permit equitable access to health services for the entire population; mechanisms for progressing in terms of pension coverage, solidarity and viability; the impacts of reforms on gender equity; ways of complementing short-term programmes for alleviating poverty; best practices applied in social programmes; and methods for ensuring that public policies contributed to social cohesion.

Sustainable development and human settlements

During 2006, the ECLAC Sustainable Development and Human Settlements Division focused on analysing public policies and articulating policy recommendations, with special emphasis on the Plan of Implementation for the World Summit on Sustainable Development [YUN 2002, p. 821], and a focus on urban poverty, urban public services, public spaces and urban sustainability analysis.

It provided technical cooperation services related to public efficiency in the management of human settlements, urban environmental management and ways to reduce air pollution in cities. ECLAC supported countries of the region in international fora on the reduction in emissions from deforestation and forest degradation, and strengthened sustainable policies by developing new instruments for policy makers. The Division organized 12 technical assistance missions in 10 countries and disseminated its methodology through 15 workshops.

At the third session of the World Urban Forum (Vancouver, Canada, 19-23 June), the Regional Meeting of Ministers and High-level Authorities of the Housing and Urban Development Sector (MINURVI) presented a report on progress in the region related to the Habitat Agenda, Agenda 21 and the Human Settlements Regional Action Plan for Latin and the Caribbean in five key thematic issues: production and improvement of urban land; provision and access to basic services and infrastructure and housing; provision and improvement of public areas and social services; the development of productive activities; and the generation of employment and income. ECLAC also provided support to the fifteenth MINURVI meeting in October in Montevideo, Uruguay.

The first regional forum for implementing the decisions adopted at the World Summit on Sustainable Development was held in January. It studied the current situation and prospects for cooperation in the region in terms of three key issues to be discussed by ECLAC: energy for sustainable development, industrial development and air pollution/atmosphere and climate change.

Population and development

In 2006, the ECLAC Latin American and Caribbean Demographic Centre (CELADE)-

Population Division focused on technical cooperation and support for policymaking, including developing mechanisms for the application of the 2002 Madrid International Plan of Action on Ageing [YUN 2002, p. 1194] and its regional implementation strategy [YUN 2004, p. 1023]. It produced technical assistance documents for use by countries; a methodological guide for the development of advocacy strategies and a guide to participatory evaluations of programmes directed by older persons. In December, it conducted a training workshop on indicators of quality of life in old age for professionals from 13 countries. The Centre provided support to the meeting of the Ad Hoc Committee on Population and Development, held during ECLAC thirty-first session, in follow-up to the Programme of Action of the International Conference on Population and Development (ICPD). The regional perspective on international migration, human rights and development, presented at ECLAC thirty-first session, gave rise to a series of presentations, short-term advisory services and meetings. The sixteenth Ibero-American Summit of Heads of State (Montevideo, Uruguay, 3-5 November) adopted the Montevideo Commitment on Migration and Development, which called upon ECLAC to coordinate a study on the social and economic impact of the insertion of migrants in receiving countries.

In resolution [res. 616(XXXI)], the Commission called upon the countries in the region to provide the resources to implement key measures of the ICPD Programme of Ation, with special reference to the agreements contained in resolution 604(XXX), adopted at its thirtieth session [YUN 2004, p. 1023], and the Madrid International Plan of Action and its Regional Strategy, particularly within the framework of policies aimed at reducing social and ethnic inequalities, overcoming gender inequality and eradicating poverty. It urged the international community to increase technical and financial cooperation to fulfil those objectives. The Commission also asked the secretariat, in coordination with organizations of the Inter-Agency Group on Ageing and the competent institutions of the host country, to organize a regional intergovernmental conference in 2007 to review and assess the advances of countries in the region in applying the Regional Strategy and to prepare the relevant substantive documentation. The secretariat should also organize a special event to mark the fiftieth anniversary of CELADE in 2007. The Commission recommended that, at its 2008 session, the Ad Hoc Committee should analyse the issue of demographic changes from a gender perspective, their influence on development and impact on poverty and inequality.

The Commission, in its resolution on international migration [res. 615(XXXI)], urged Governments that had not yet done so to consider signing and ratifying the UN legal instruments that aimed to promote and protect migrants' human rights as mechanism for full integration, and to define the trafficking in persons in any form as an offence. It welcomed the commitments regarding international migration contained in the Declaration of Salamanca, adopted at the fifteenth Ibero-American Summit of Heads of State and Government, and the organization of an Ibero-American meeting on migration in July 2006 in Madrid. It asked the Executive Secretary to inform the Ibero-American secretariat of the special interest of all member countries in participating in that meeting and of the choice of migration for shared development as the theme of the sixteenth Ibero-American Summit.

The Executive Secretary should form an inter-agency group to follow up on issues relating to international migration and development in the region and foster coordination and coherence among the activities of UN system bodies.

Integration of women in development

The work of ECLAC Women and Development Unit focused on promoting the adoption of policies to mainstream the gender perspective into priority areas of government agendas in economic policy, employment, poverty, social protection, institutional development and security, as well as the increased use of monitoring tools, such as gender indicators and planning. ECLAC continued to design, assess and execute national, subregional and regional projects with the United Nations Development Fund for Women on the status of women in the region and on mainstreaming the gender perspective in the main spheres of the regional development process in the ECLAC region.

The Unit promoted gender-disaggregated data as a basis of social analysis and policymaking with respect to gender issues. In the Caribbean subregion, an agreement was concluded between national statistical offices and national mechanisms for the advancement of women in nine countries and territories. The Unit also provided support to CELADE in processing household survey data for Latin American countries, in developing gender indicators for the Caribbean, as part of a wider inter-agency project, as well as training materials on gender-related issues.

The thirty-ninth Meeting of Presiding Officers of the Regional Conference on Women in Latin America and the Caribbean (Mexico City, 11-12 May) [LC/L.2599] analysed the mainstreaming of gender perspectives in public policies and the sustainability of gender machinery. At its fortieth meeting (Santiago, 3-4 October) [LC/L.2598 (MDM. 40/2)], the Presiding Officers requested the organization of an International Seminar on Gender Parity and Political Participation in Latin America and the Caribbean.

The Commission, in resolution [res. 618(XXXI)], noted the reports and agreements of the thirty-seventh [YUN 2004, p. 1024] and thirty-eighth [YUN 2005, p. 1117] meetings of the Presiding Officers of the Regional Conference on Women in Latin America and the Caribbean and invited member countries to consider implementing them. It also welcomed the announcement by the Executive Secretary concerning gender mainstreaming throughout ECLAC programme of work, and requested that the secretariat incorporate the analysis of unremunerated work performed by women and their contribution to social protection and caregiving and report to the Commission in 2008.

Economic statistics and technical cooperation

During 2006, the work of the ECLAC Statistics and Economic Projections Division centred on: institutional strengthening, human resources, statistical capacity-building and strengthening of international cooperation. The Division continued efforts to create technical capacities in national accounts and external-sector statistics among the countries of the region; organized workshops and seminars on national accounts, external trade and international classifications; provided technical assistance in the systematization, production and analysis of information; produced and disseminated comparable social, environmental and economic indicators; and developed quantitative methodologies to produce new indicators and utilize existing ones to analyse and formulate public policies in the region. The Division continued to publish the *Statistical Yearbook for Latin America and the Caribbean*.

In 2006, ECLAC convened the sixth meeting of the Executive Committee of the Statistical Conference of the Americas of the Economic Commission for Latin America and the Caribbean (Madrid, Spain, 25-26 September) [LC/L.2651]. Participants adopted the final draft strategic plan 2005-2015, incorporating the provisions of Economic and Social Council resolution 2006/6 on strengthening statistical capacity (see p. 1472); approved the draft provisional agenda for the fourth meeting of the Statistical Conference, to be held in July 2007 in Santiago; and entrusted the secretariat with preparing a comprehensive report on all activities carried out under the Programme of Regional Statistical Work for Latin America and the Caribbean, July 2005–June 2007.

The Commission, in resolution [res. 617(XXXI)], welcomed the decision to establish a strategic plan for the statistical conference for 2005-2015 and entrusted the Statistical Conference of the Americas with the task of promoting the importance of scaling up to best international practices in terms of the standards of quality, comparability and transparency of national statistics in the region.

Natural resources and infrastructure

The ECLAC Natural Resources and Infrastructure Division conducted work on strengthening institutional capacity in the countries of the region to formulate policies and regulatory mechanisms for sustainable natural-resource management and infrastructures. It provided technical assistance regarding issues related to energy, including renewable energy, access to affordable energy and energy intensity of growth; water, including water-resources legislation and management and drinking water supply and sanitation services; and mining, including environmental impacts, social problems, distribution of rents and fiscal policies. In terms of infrastructure and public utilities, it helped beneficiary countries to define the optimal combination of regulation and market competition in each sector. The Division disseminated research findings and policy recommendations, participated in the fourth World Water Forum (Mexico City, 16-22 March) and presented proposals on the Framework Agreement on Energy Complementarities. It carried out a study on a methodological proposal for evaluating multinational infrastructure projects; provided support to the Initiative for the Integration of Regional Infrastructure in South America [YUN 2005, p. 1117] on the integrated development of the Amazon Axis; and coordinated the binational project on the Asuncion-Montevideo corridor.

Production and management

The ECLAC Division of Production, Productivity and Management addressed issues in the agricultural, manufacturing and services sectors, including production structure and dynamics, productivity and competitiveness, patterns of investment and international integration, the information society, and knowledge, innovation, technological capacities and vocational training. It provided technical assistance to 28 member States and other stakeholders to formulate innovation development plans and develop national systems of innovation. It helped four countries develop a methodology to establish working groups at the local level for the creation of clusters and local networks of SMEs.

The Division collaborated with the Statistics and Economic Projections Division in elaborating a core list of information and communication technology (ICT) indicators for the region. It produced several publications, including *Foreign Investment in Latin America and the Caribbean* and others on various issues related to productive development. New topics, such as the information society, the service sector and biofuels, were integrated into the Division's programme of work.

In terms of the Regional Plan of Action for the Information Society in Latin America and the Caribbean [YUN 2005, p. 1118], the Division was active in follow-up. It also prepared an extensive number of ICT-related publications and training manuals, as well as facilitated discussions to define priorities for the ELAC 2010 draft plan.

Subregional activities

Caribbean

The ECLAC subregional headquarters for the Caribbean in Port of Spain, Trinidad and Tobago, which was also the secretariat of the Caribbean Development and Cooperation Committee (CDCC), continued to provide technical cooperation and applied research for the subregion. Its priorities in economic development were influenced by the proposal to fully establish in 2008 a Caribbean Community single market economy. It also focused on strengthening competitiveness, especially the export performance of private businesses, and increasing the level and quality of foreign investment flows. In terms of social development, its priorities were on demographic issues, poverty and social vulnerability, analysis of women's political participation and unpaid work and the impact of migration on the region.

Activities in the environment and information technology areas continued to be linked to implementation of the Mauritius Strategy for the Further Implementation of the Programme of Action for the Sustainable Development of Small Island Developing States. [YUN 2005, p. 946]. CDCC set up a regional coordinating mechanism (RCM) to implement the Mauritius strategy in the Caribbean. The subregional headquarters in Port of Spain would serve as the RCM secretariat for the next two years. The Division also supported the development of alternative sources of energy in the Caribbean, mainly biofuels in Guyana and Jamaica and geothermal energy in Montserrat.

In the areas of statistics and social development, the subregional headquarters continued to provide information on the benefits of data sharing and addressed issues related to data ownership. In terms of implementing the MDGs, the secretariat prepared a social development framework to promote sustained social development in the Caribbean and the achievement of the Goals in the subregion.

At its twenty-first session (Port of Spain, 16-17 January) [LC/CAR/L.86], CDCC adopted resolutions on assistance to its associate member countries; creation of a temporary mechanism for regional follow-up of the Tunis phase of the World Summit on the Information Society and the ELAC 2007 Action Plan; policy research in the area of social vulnerability and alienation; establishment of a regional coordination mechanism for the implementation of the Mauritius Strategy; and support for efforts in natural disasters.

The Commission, in resolution [res. 621(XXXI)], endorsed the CDCC resolutions adopted at the Committee's twenty-first session pertaining to the work of the ECLAC subregional headquarters in the Caribbean and called upon the secretariat to support the mobilization of additional resources for the full implementation of the programme of work for the Caribbean.

In a resolution on support for the United Nations Stabilization Mission in Haiti [res. 624(XXXI)], the Commission trusted that ECLAC participation in favour of Haiti would be reinforced to encompass all the spheres envisaged in the Mission's mandate and attributed special importance to that country's economic and social development. It recommended that cooperation activities in Haiti be continued and broadened, in close coordination with the Haitian Government.

Mexico and Central America

The ECLAC subregional headquarters in Mexico provided analyses, training and technical assistance to countries in the subregion. It worked with member States on trade-related capacity-building through a technical cooperation project funded by the Canadian International Development Agency to respond to applied research, training and information dissemination needs identified by countries of the subregion. In terms of competition policy, it launched a project to strengthen competition in Central America in response to the urgent need of Governments to develop a legal and institutional framework in an area where little analysis was available. An Intergovernmental Competition Working Group for the competition authorities of Central America was set up. In order to build up the capacity of member States in fiscal and monetary policy issues, ECLAC prepared a study on the advances, limitations and challenges of launching a new fiscal pact for the region, which was presented at the REDIMA seminar in Managua, Nicaragua, in May, and organized training courses in macroeconomic modelling. ECLAC was actively involved, with the Inter-American Development Bank, as the technical secretariat for the Central American Energy Emergency Plan developed during the 2004-2005 biennium, and created an action matrix for the development and integration of the subregion's energy sectors.

Concerning the impact of the Central America-United States Free Trade Agreement on the agricultural and rural sectors, ECLAC worked in collaboration with other organizations and national research institutes in Central America to analyse the impact of the Agreement on economic growth, employment, salaries, income distribution and poverty in rural zones, using general economic equilibrium modes.

The Commission, in its resolution on the Central American Economic Cooperation Committee [res. 622(XXXI)], affirmed that the Committee was a forum for reflection and analysis of the subregion's economic and social problems and could provide important inputs in reinforcing Governments' capacity in designing, implementing, following up and assessing public policy in general, especially trade, macroeconomic and microeconomic, social and environmental policies.

Programme and organizational questions

By resolution [res. 623(XXXI)], the Commission approved the draft 2008-2009 programme of work of the ECLAC system [LC/G.2297(SES.31/6)], which encompassed the progressive consolidation of macroeconomic stability, improved integration in the world economy, an increase in social cohesion and in the region's production potential, enhancement of sustainable development policies, gender mainstreaming in public policies and the strengthening of global institutions.

In other action, it approved its proposed calendar of conferences [LC/G.2298(SES.31/7)] for 2006-2008 [res. 619(XXXI)], and decided to maintain the current intergovernmental structure and pattern of meetings.

Venue and participation in ECLAC thirty-second session

By resolution [res. 631(XXXI)], the Commission recommended that the Economic and Social Council approve the decision to hold ECLAC thirty-second session in Santo Domingo de Guzman, Dominican Republic, in 2008.

ECONOMIC AND SOCIAL COUNCIL ACTION

On 27 July [meeting 41], the Economic and Social Council, on the recommendation of ECLAC [E/2006/15/Add.1], adopted resolution **2006/40** without vote [agenda item 10].

Venue of the thirty-second session of the Economic Commission for Latin America and the Caribbean

The Economic and Social Council,

Bearing in mind paragraph 15 of the terms of reference and rules 1 and 2 of the rules of procedure of the Economic Commission for Latin America and the Caribbean,

Considering the invitation of the Government of the Dominican Republic to host the thirty-second session of the Commission,

1. *Expresses its gratitude* to the Government of the Dominican Republic for its generous invitation;
2. *Notes* the acceptance by the Economic Commission for Latin America and the Caribbean of this invitation with pleasure;
3. *Endorses* the decision of the Commission to hold its thirty-second session in Santo Domingo in 2008.

Membership

By resolution [res. 627(XXXI)], the Commission recommended that the Economic and Social Council approve the admission of Japan as a member of ECLAC and authorize the amendment of paragraph 3*(a)* of the Commission's terms of reference to include Japan's name after that of Italy.

By resolution [res. 628(XXXI)], the Commission decided to grant the Turks and Caicos Islands associate membership in ECLAC.

ECONOMIC AND SOCIAL COUNCIL ACTION

On 27 July [meeting 41], the Economic and Social Council, on the recommendation of ECLAC [E/2006/15/Add.1], adopted resolution **2006/39** without vote [agenda item 10].

Admission of Japan as a member of the Economic Commission for Latin America and the Caribbean

The Economic and Social Council,

Bearing in mind that the Economic Commission for Latin America and the Caribbean was established by the Economic and Social Council by its resolution 106(VI) of 25 February 1948, in which the Council stated that membership in the Commission should be open to States Members of the United Nations in North, Central and South America and in the Caribbean area, and to France, the Netherlands and the United Kingdom of Great Britain and Northern Ireland,

Bearing in mind also that the Commission was established on the basis of the participation by all the countries of Latin America and the Caribbean and those that have had special relations with the region of a historical, cultural, geographical or economic nature,

Recalling that, in this spirit, the Commission subsequently admitted, as members, Spain in 1979, Portugal in 1984, Italy in 1990, and Germany in 2005,

Considering that the Government of Japan has communicated to the Commission, through the Executive Secretary, its desire to be admitted as a member of the Commission,

1. *Welcomes with satisfaction* the request of the Government of Japan that it be admitted to membership of the Economic Commission for Latin America and the Caribbean;

2. *Approves* the admission of Japan as a member of the Commission, and authorizes the amendment of paragraph 3 *(a)* of the terms of reference of the Commission to include the name of Japan after that of Italy.

Cooperation between UN and SELA

On 22 December the General Assembly, having considered the Secreary-General's report on cooperation between the United Nations and the Latin American Economic System (SELA) [A/61/256/Add.1], (**decision 61/552**), decided that the agenda item on the subject would remain for consideration during its resumed sixty-first (2007) session.

Western Asia

The Economic and Social Commission for Western Asia (ESCWA) held its twenty-fourth session (Beirut, Lebanon, 8-11 May) [E/2006/41], the first biennial session in an even year, in accordance with its 2005 decision to hold sessions in even years only [YUN 2005, p. 1120].

The ministerial segment, which took the form of a round table on general policy issues in the ESCWA region, addressed new challenges in the region and their impact on ESCWA work, particularly youth unemployment problems, and the achievement of the MDGs. The other items on the Commission's agenda, including the report of the Executive Secretary on the activities of the Commission, management issues and progress by Yemen in the implementation of the Programme of Action for the Least Developed Countries for the Decade 2001-2010, were addressed by the Senior Officials segment.

The Commission adopted several resolutions, including those to be brought to the attention of the Economic and Social Council (see below).

Economic trends

In 2006, the ESCWA region marked its fourth consecutive year of robust economic expansion, according to the summary of the survey of economic and social developments in the ESCWA region, 2006-2007 [E/2007/20]. Recent favourable external economic conditions, represented by high oil prices, continued to buoy the region, and together with various efforts of intraregional cooperation, helped to minimize the adverse effects of conflict that would otherwise have been more devastating to and increased the vulnerability of the region. Although the rate of GDP expansion slowed in 2006, as compared with the previous year, it was still high in most countries. Excluding Iraq, Lebanon and the Palestinian territory, where regional conflicts and political instabilities reduced economic potential significantly and security pressures pushed down business and consumer confidence, GDP growth in the region stood at an estimated 5.6 per cent in 2006, down from 6.9 per cent in 2005. Growth was stable in the countries of the Gulf Cooperation Council (GCC), at 5.9 per cent on average, after registering 7.3 per cent in 2005, fuelled by crude oil production and exports, as well as the development of non-oil sectors, such as financial services and construction. The more diversified economies experienced growth of 5.1 per cent, down from 6 per cent the previous year, and were sheltered from the potential foreign exchange constraints that could otherwise hamper growth of domestic demands. In Egypt and Jordan, the industrial sector developed rapidly and strong confidence in business and consumption led to faster recoveries in stock market performance. The conflict-affected economies of Iraq, Lebanon and the Palestinian territory posted negative GDP growth for the most part, with Palestinian economy shrinking 6.9 per cent and Lebanon's by 5 per cent. Iraq's economy grew 8 per cent, versus 10 per cent the previous year. The construction sector was strong in the subregion, reflecting high inflows in foreign capital, as well as fiscal capital expenditure, which sustained domestic demand and offset factors that dented business and consumer confidence.

The average inflation rate stood at 6.7 per cent in 2006, up from 4.4 per cent in 2005, fuelled by high international commodity prices.

Oil

In 2006, despite the weaker than expected demand growth, crude oil prices continued to be historically high. The crude oil price of the Organization of Petroleum Exporting Countries (OPEC) reference basket averaged $61.8 per barrel in 2006, compared to $50.6 in 2005. The tight supply-demand condition in fuel products continued to be the bottleneck in refinery capability, while the speculative factor, owing to ample global monetary liquidity, caused a rapid price hike until the summer, followed by a rapid plunge toward year's end. The total crude oil production of ESCWA OPEC members (Kuwait, Qatar, Saudi Arabia, United Arab Emirates) declined slightly in 2006, from the 2005 level of 19.4 million barrels per day. However, the high oil prices resulted in a 25.7 per cent increase in gross oil export revenues to $401 billion for the region.

Trade

In 2006, the United States-Middle East Free Trade Area was still under negotiation. A free trade agreement was signed between Oman and the United States in January; a free trade pact between Bahrain and the United States in August; and the United Arab Emirates was negotiating an accord with the United States. Parallel to those developments and within the framework of the Euro-Mediterranean Partnership, the Agadir Agreement between Egypt, Jordan, Morocco and Tunisia came into effect, aimed at establishing a free trade agreement between the four Arab Mediterranean countries with benefits of preferential access to European Union (EU) markets. The GCC was engaged in trade negotiations with the EU to set up a free trade agreement, and was considering free trade pacts with China, India and Singapore.

Activities in 2006

In 2006, ESCWA activities under its 2006-2007 draft work programme [E/ESCWA/23/7] continued to focus on the four pivotal priorities: globalization and regional integration, social policies, water and energy, and information and communication technologies; and the advancement and empowerment of women, national statistical capacity-building, especially in monitoring the attainment of the MDGs, and the special needs of countries emerging from conflict. ESCWA later proposed changes to realign the work programme with the 2005 World Summit Outcome and the outcome of the second phase of the World Summit of the Information Society, among other things [E/ESCWA/24/6(Part II)Rev.1].

Attainment of the MDGs

During the Commission's twenty-fourth session, a round-table discussion took place on the achievement of the MDGs [YUN 2000, p. 51] in ESCWA member countries. The round-table had before it a report [E/ESCWA/24/4(Part III)], which summarized progress in the implementation of the Damascus Declaration, adopted by the Commission and endorsed by the Economic and Social Council in resolution 2005/50 [YUN 2005, p. 1121], and in the achievement of the MDGs, particularly in Iraq and the Palestinian territory. The report also reviewed development-related events in the Arab region and the challenges faced in achieving the MDGs, in the light of the outcome of the 2005 World Summit.

World Summit follow-up

On 11 May [E/2006/41 (res. 269(XXIV))], the Commission adopted the draft strategic framework for 2008-2009, which addressed the main critical areas of importance to Western Asia and the priorities identified in the 2005 World Summit Outcome; approved the changes proposed to the ESCWA programme of work for 2006-2007; and called upon member countries to work toward achieving the Summit objectives. It requested the Executive Secretary to increase coherence and synergy with other regional UN organizations, and foster partnerships and cooperation with them.

Economic development and cooperation

In 2006, ESCWA published the *Annual Review of Developments in Globalization and Regional Integration in the Arab Countries, 2006* [E/ESCWA/GRID/2006/3], which focused on assessing the involvement of Arab economies in selected global economic sectors: tourism, trade, investment, oil and gas. It also examined the progress made by Arab countries in integrating into the global economy and expediting Arab economic integration.

A pre-feasibility study on the establishment of the ESCWA Technology Centre for Development [E/ESCWA/ICTD/2006/WP.1] was reviewed by the third meeting of the ESCWA Consultative Committee on Scientific and Technological Development and Technological Innovation (Beirut, 6-7 March).

On 11 May [E/2006/41 (res. 274(XXIV))], the Commission, recognizing the role of science and technology in accelerating development and as one of the priorities of the United Nations, and bearing in mind the pre-feasibility study on the establishment of the ESCWA Technology Centre, approved in principle the establishment of such a centre. It requested the secretariat to follow up with member countries with respect to hosting the centre and securing its financial sources, and to take the necessary actions aimed at establishing it.

On the same day [E/2006/41 (res. 270(XXIV))], the Commission, noting with concern the problems associated with financial sector development in facing the recent volatility in market behaviour that could have serious repercussions for socio-economic development and the attainment of the MDGs in the region, urged member countries to take appropriate macroeconomic policy measures and develop regulatory frameworks that would help stabilize and promote orderly and transparent performance in financial markets. The secretariat should monitor and analyse, in cooperation with relevant regional and international institutions, the possible consequences of financial market instability, with a view to assessing the impact of such events on regional socio-economic development and to undertake regular and timely forecasts and policy analyses of current and emergent macroeconomic trends.

Development and regional cooperation

On 11 May [E/2006/41 (res. 271(XXIV))], the Commission, recalling its 2005 resolution on development and regional cooperation under unstable conditions [YUN 2005, p. 1122], requested member states to intensify efforts to attain peace, security and stability at the regional and international levels. It asked the ESCWA secretariat to enhance the capacity of countries to assess, predict and respond to socio-economic challenges posed by conflict and instability through monitoring, analysing and reporting on their repercussions on socio-economic development; formulate and implement operational activities for rehabilitation and development in conflict-stricken areas; assist conflict countries with improvements in good governance, public administration, rule of law and socio-economic decision-making; and support the activities of the Peacebuilding Commission in the ESCWA region. Further, it requested that the international community lift the economic, political and financial embargoes imposed on the Palestinian people and assist in liberating them from Israeli occupation, meet Palestinian basic humanitarian needs, and rehabilitate its economic and social sectors.

Technical cooperation

ESCWA first *Technical Cooperation Report 2006* [E/ESCWA/PPTCD/2007/Technical Material.1] documented the Commission's technical cooperation activities in managing water and energy resources; promoting social policies; stimulating economic development and integration; harnessing ICT for development; developing statistical capacities; empowering women; and assisting conflict-stricken countries. It also discussed ESCWA Technical Cooperation Strategy adopted in 2005 [YUN 2005, p. 1122] to help clarify the Commission's position concerning the provision of technical cooperation, improve its delivery, effectiveness and efficiency and lay the groundwork for its development.

The Commission, on 11 May [E/2006/41 (res. 275(XXIV))], recalling its 2005 resolution on strengthening technical cooperation in ESCWA, requested the secretariat to continue to implement the Strategy and take appropriate measures to launch the technical cooperation information and knowledge-sharing network. It approved the multi-year funding plan and requested that member countries and donors make voluntary annual contributions through the ESCWA Trust Fund for Regional Activities, project/activity agreements between ESCWA and donors, or agreements for in-kind cooperation and support. The secretariat should prepare a specific plan of action for partnership development and resource mobilization.

The Commission also considered the report by the Executive Secretary on ESCWA technical cooperation programme and regional advisory services [E/ESCWA/24/5(Part III)] undertaken in 2005.

Transport

The Committee on Transport, at its seventh session (Beirut, 17-19 April) [E/ESCWA/GRID/2006/IG.1/4], recommended that ESCWA adopt the plan of action for implementation of the Agreement on International Railways in the Arab Mashreq [YUN 2002, p. 1019] and a draft resolution concerning follow-up to implementation of components of the Integrated Transport System in the Arab Mashreq for submission to ESCWA twenty-fourth session.

In other action, the Committee urged countries that had not yet signed or ratified the Agreement on International Roads in the Arab Mashreq [YUN 2001, p. 928] to do so and urged all countries to review the report of the ESCWA consultant on follow-up to the plan of action for implementing the Agreement. It also urged countries that had not yet signed or ratified the Memorandum of Understanding (MOU) concerning cooperation in maritime transport in the Arab Mashreq [YUN 2005, p. 1123] to do so, and asked ESCWA to prepare a draft plan of action for implementing the MOU for circulation at an expert group meeting in September and to submit it to the eighth session of the Committee. The Committee also made recommendations with regard to: the regional road transport information system; road safety; the programme or work for the 2006-2007 biennium; the holding of annual sessions; and the annual follow-up reports on the implementation of the Committee's recommendations.

On 11 May [E/2006/41 (res. 279(XXIV))], the Commission, in follow-up to implementation of components on the Integrated Transport System in the Arab Mashreq, urged member countries to complete implementation of the plan of action for the Agreement on International Roads in the Arab Mashreq by the time specified and begin implementation of the plan of action for the Agreement on Railways in Arab Mashreq. It also urged member countries that had not yet signed or ratified the MOU on Cooperation in the Field of Maritime Transport in the Arab Mashreq to do so and requested that the secretariat follow up and submit an annual report to the Committee on Transport on progress made on the two Agreements, the MOU, priority routes M40 and M45, the national committees for the facilitation of transport and trade and road safety.

Information

A workshop on ICT policymaking in ESCWA member countries (Beirut, 2-4 May) resulted in the formation of an initial network of ICT policymakers aimed at sharing experiences and knowledge in the field of ICT strategies and their implementation. Topics and issues of concern for the region were also discussed through an online forum managed by ESCWA.

On 11 May [E/2006/41 (res. 273(XXIV))], the Commission, guided by the 2005 Tunis Agenda for the Information Society adopted at the second phase of the World Summit on the Information Society [YUN 2005, p. 933], and considering the 2004 Damascus Call for Partnership and the work carried out by ESCWA in developing the Regional Plan of Action for Building the Information Society, called on the secretariat to provide member countries with technical assistance to implement national plans of action through workshops, advisory services and other means of technical cooperation in areas related to formulation and implementation of national ICT strategies, capacity-building, multistakeholder partnerships and ICT applications for socio-economic development. It also called on the secretariat, in coordination with member countries, to participate actively in implementing the Regional Plan of Action and continually update that Plan as progress was made in achieving its objectives. The Executive Secretary was asked to submit a report at ESCWA twenty-fifth session on follow-up to the Tunis Agenda, implementation of the plans of action regarding progress achieved in member countries, and ESCWA efforts in that regard.

Statistics

The Commission had before it reports by the Executive Secretary on the development of statistical work in the ESCWA region, including a report on streamlining the work of the Commission [E/ESCWA/24/6(Part I)/Add.1], which provided an overview of changes in the statistical programme in the light of the restructuring of ESCWA in 2003, the audits and reviews by the Office of Internal Oversight Services (OIOS) and ESCWA internal evaluation.

On 11 May [E/2006/41 (res. 276(XXIV))], ESCWA called on member countries to improve their national institutional statistical frameworks, including national statistical development strategies, in accordance with the Fundamental Principles of Official Statistics of the UN Statistical Commission. It urged them to step up efforts to produce and disseminate reliable and timely indicators of progress in achieving national and international development goals, including the MDGs. The Commission requested the secretariat to continue supporting member countries through expert group meetings, training workshops and advisory services to improve the coverage, quality and comparability of qualitative statistics and data, particularly in such emerging fields as the 2010 Round of Population and Housing Censuses and MDG-related issues, and to implement the draft strategic framework for the 2008-2009 biennium with respect to the statistics subprogramme. Further, it urged donors, regional and international financial institutions and the private sector to support ESCWA efforts to assist member countries in building their national statistical capacities.

Social development

On 11 May [E/2006/41 (res. 277(XXIV))], the Commission, taking into consideration its 2005 resolution on social policies [YUN 2005, p. 1124], the progress made in ESCWA in concluding a MOU with the Government of Bahrain on that issue, and the successful National Conference for Social Policies (Bahrain, 24-25 April), which recommended the holding of an Arab forum on social policies in the Arab region, requested the secretariat to organize the forum, with the aim of increasing interest in integrated and effective social policies, promoting dialogue and the exchange of views, and strengthening coordination mechanisms. It urged member countries to adopt an integrated social policy approach and called upon them to make use of ESCWA analytical activities and technical and advisory services.

The Commission had before it a review of progress made by Yemen in 2001-2005 in implementing the Programme of Action for the Least Developed Countries for the Decade 2001-2010 [E/ESCWA/24/7], which noted that Yemen had made strenuous efforts to achieve economic and social development, which had produced good results, given the limited financial and human resources available.

Youth

During its annual session, the Commission held a round-table discussion on facing youth unemployment problems in the ESCWA region. It had before it a report on the subject [E/ESCWA/24/4(Part II)/Rev.1], which examined the scope of the problem, the characteristics of unemployed youth, youth and emigration, the impact of youth unemployment on Arab economies and the gap between education outputs and labour market needs, as well as initiatives to address the problem. It proposed two major initiatives in that regard. The first called for the establishment of a regional observatory to monitor international experiences by focusing on policies that had successfully eradicated the problem and setting up a database on the issue in general and on the impact on youth in each Arab country in particular, with the aim of designing and disseminating indicators to track changes in employment. The second entailed the creation of a regional fund to finance prototype initiatives for youth employment, beginning with an in-depth feasibility study of the design for such a fund and ways to finance and manage it.

On 11 May [E/2006/41 (res. 272 (XXIV))], the Commission called upon member countries to include youth policies in their national development strategies by mainstreaming the youth perspective into all planning processes; preparing national youth policies; and devising political action plans for youth employment in order to limit the migration of a skilled and creative workforce. Member countries were asked to make available up-to-date and accurate national statistics on youth unemployment, collect periodic data on all youth-related issues, including employment, education and health; and carry out studies on factors leading to unemployment and their impact, with a view to devising appropriate policies to resolve the problem. The secretariat should help develop statistical indicators on youth employment, and incorporate them into development indicators, including those for the MDGs, as well as devise, in cooperation with relevant Arab and international organizations, a mechanism for establishing a system to provide information on Arab labour markets. Member countries should encourage the exchange of labour, in particular well-qualified youth labour, among the countries of the region, thereby helping to circulate financial resources within the region and contribute to regional development as a whole.

Women

On 11 May [E/2006/41 (res. 278(XXIV))], the Commission, considering that several regional countries had suffered from instability because of war and conflicts, the negative impacts of which affected women more, affirmed the need for member countries and the secretariat to accord the exceptional needs of women living in unstable conditions the requisite importance in their plans and programmes. The secretariat should also examine the situation of women in those ESCWA member countries suffering from occupation, war and conflict, and help build their capacities in conflict resolution and peacebuilding. The Commission urged member countries to increase their representation, participation and empowerment of women at all levels of decision-making and in conflict resolution and peace-building processes.

Programme and organizational questions

The Commission had before it reports by the Executive Secretary on progress made during the 2004-2005 biennium in implementing the programme of work [E/ESCWA/24/5(Part I)], on a proposed multi-year funding plan [E/ESCWA/24/5(Part IV)], the 2006-2007 draft work programme [E/ESCWA/23/7], proposed programme changes for the 2006-2007 biennium [E/ESCWA/24/6(Part II)/Rev.1] and the draft strategic framework for the 2008-2009 biennium [E/ESCWA/24/6(Part III)].

The Commission decided to form a technical committee to follow up on implementation of programme activities and support ESCWA in achieving its aims. The Commission adopted the proposed programme budget changes for the 2006-2007 biennium and the draft strategic framework for the 2008-2009 biennium.

OIOS report. An OIOS report on the inspection of ESCWA programme and administrative management [A/61/61] observed that ESCWA consistently strove to attain its vision of becoming an action-oriented regional centre of excellence, in particular by applying an integrated and disciplinary approach to addressing the regional challenges of globalization and development in the context of the MDGs. OIOS observed that UN tools for results-based management were consistently promoted and that ESCWA was one of the most advanced entities in that regard. However, its organizational structure had to be normalized; the Statistical Division needed to be re-established; ESCWA comparative advantages had to be reassessed and its collaborative networking with regional partners strengthened; information and knowledge management advanced; and the executive management culture made more consistent, objective and transparent. A note by the Secretary-General [A/61/61/Add.1] transmitting his comments on that report provided clarification on issues raised by OIOS, particularly those regarding the organizational structure, information and knowledge management, programme support and executive management.

On 22 December, the General Assembly, by **decision 61/551 A**, decided that the agenda item on the report of OIOS on the inspection of the programme and administrative management of ESCWA and the note by the Secretary-General transmitting his comments on that report would remain for consideration during its resumed sixty-first (2007) session.

Cooperation with LAS

In follow-up to the Commission's 2005 resolution on strengthening the cooperation between the Commission and the League of Arab States (LAS) [YUN 2005 p. 1125], the seventy-seventh regular session of LAS Social and Economic Council (Abu Dhabi, United Arab Emirates, 13-16 February) adopted a resolution calling for an MOU between the two bodies on the mechanisms for economic and social cooperation. The ESCWA secretariat was following up on the matter and would submit a report on it during the Commission's twenty-fifth session.

The Secretary-General, in his consolidated report on cooperation between the United Nations and regional organizations [A/61/256], described cooperation between LAS and the United Nations, including with ESCWA.

The General Assembly, in **resolution 61/14** of 13 November (see p. 1599), noted the report.

ESCWA twenty-fifth session

During its twenty-fourth session, the Commission decided to hold its twenty-fifth session in Beirut, Lebanon, in April 2008.

Chapter VI

Energy, natural resources and cartography

The conservation and use of energy and natural resources continued to be the focus of several UN bodies in 2006, including the Commission on Sustainable Development, which commenced its second two-year implementation cycle on the theme: energy for sustainable development, industrial development, air pollution/atmosphere and climate change. The Commission considered energy for poverty eradication, energy security and efficiency and cleaner energy technologies, and reviewed progress in meeting the goals, targets and commitments of Agenda 21, the 2002 World Summit on Sustainable Development and the 2005 Mauritius Strategy for the Further Implementation of the Programme of Action for the Sustainable Development of Small Island Developing States.

The Director General of the International Atomic Energy Agency (IAEA), Mohamed ElBaradei, in presenting the Agency's 2005 report, cited its emphasis on the role of energy for development, describing the energy shortage in developing countries as a staggering impediment to development.

The Fourth World Water Forum, under the theme "Local actions for a global challenge", adopted a Ministerial Declaration reaffirming the critical importance of water for sustainable development. The role of water in development was also highlighted in the second edition of the *World Water Development Report: Water, a shared responsibility*, and was the major theme of the *Human Development Report 2006*, "Beyond scarcity: power, poverty and the global water crisis".

The Seventeenth United Nations Regional Cartographic Conference for Asia and the Pacific adopted resolutions on mitigating large-scale disaster, marine administration and spatial data infrastructure support. The twenty-third session of the United Nations Group of Experts on Geographical Names continued to support United Nations Conferences on the Standardization of Geographical Names.

Energy and natural resources

The Commission on Sustainable Development, at its fourteenth session (New York, 1-12 May) [E/2006/29] (see p. 1212), focused on the thematic cluster of energy for sustainable development, industrial development, air pollution/atmosphere and climate change in the first year of its two-year (2006-2007) work cycle.

Throughout the session, the Commission held thematic discussions on various aspects of the issue of energy. Those issues included: improving access to reliable, affordable, economically viable, socially acceptable and environmentally sound energy services; enhancing energy efficiency to address air pollution and atmospheric problems, combat climate change and promote industrial development, including improved transmission of electricity and end-use efficiency in commercial and residential sectors; meeting growing needs for energy services through increased use of renewable energy and greater reliance on advanced technologies, including advanced and fossil fuel technologies; investing in energy and industrial development: challenges and opportunities; and addressing energy, industrial development, air pollution/atmosphere and climate change in an integrated manner, focusing on interlinkages and cross-cutting issues.

During its high-level segment (10-12 May), the Commission identified a number of challenges to be addressed in the course of the policy year, with a view to strengthening implementation of Agenda 21 (the 1992 action plan for sustainable development) [YUN 1992, p. 672], the Johannesburg Plan of Implementation of the 2002 World Summit on Sustainable Development [YUN 2002, p. 821] and the Mauritius Strategy for the Further Implementation of the Programme of Action for the Sustainable Development of Small Island Developing States [YUN 2005, p. 946], and facilitating the achievement of the Millennium Development Goals (MDGs) [YUN 2000, p. 51]. The challenges included integrating energy for sustainable development, industrial development, air pollution/atmosphere and climate change in national sustainable development strategies, poverty reduction strategies and national development plans and ensuring a long-term integrated approach to implementation; providing energy for all—access to reliable and affordable energy services for sustainable development; promoting energy efficiency; and strengthening the development, use and transfer of clean energy technologies.

Documents before the Commission included the Secretary-General's report [E/CN.17/2006/3] on energy for sustainable development, industrial development, air pollution/atmosphere and climate change: integrated review of progress in meeting the goals, targets and commitments of Agenda 21, the Programme for the Further Implementation of Agenda 21 [YUN 1997, p. 792] and the Plan of Implementation of the World Summit on Sustainable Development. In the report, the Secretary-General explained that, while energy was essential to poverty reduction and economic development, including industrial development, fossil fuel combustion for energy, industry and transport was a major source of air pollution and greenhouse gas emissions. While some progress had been achieved since the 2002 World Summit on Sustainable Development, some 2.4 billion people had no access to modern energy services, and about one quarter of the world population lived without electricity. Concerns over energy security had been heightened with recent significant increases in energy prices. Addressing the world's growing demand for energy resources and ensuring the reliability of global energy supplies on a fair and stabilized energy market called for comprehensive and integrated policies that considered both demand and supply.

The Commission also had before it a series of discussion papers submitted by major groups on the session's overarching theme of energy for sustainable development, industrial development, air pollution/atmosphere and climate change [E/CN.17/2006/5 & Add.1-9]. The discussion papers reflected the views of the major groups on the status of implementation of commitments related to the thematic cluster and proposed solutions to meet challenges and overcome problems.

In another report before the Commission [E/CN.17/2006/7], the Secretary-General reviewed progress in small island developing States in carrying out the Mauritius Strategy for the Further Implementation of the Programme of Action for the Sustainable Development of Small Island Developing States [YUN 2005, p. 946]. The report noted that the development of renewable energy technologies and the promotion of their use, including through public education, remained a priority for many small island developing States, particularly through public education and awareness. Small island developing States continued to focus on strengthening institutional and human capacities to facilitate vulnerability assessment, energy management, and disaster preparedness and mitigation.

A number of intersessional meetings were held in 2006, including the Baku Symposium on Energy Efficiency and Sustainable Development (Baku, Azerbaijan, 28-30 March) [E/CN.17/2006/14] and the International Symposium on Natural Gas and Sustainable Development (Doha, Qatar, 6-8 February) [E/CN.17/2006/11].

Energy

Nuclear energy

By an August note [A/61/266], the Secretary-General transmitted to the General Assembly the 2005 report of the International Atomic Energy Agency (IAEA). Presenting the report on 30 October [A/61/PV.42], the IAEA Director General said that, for the past five decades, the role of nuclear power had been shaped by many factors, such as growing energy needs, economic performance, the availability of other energy sources, the quest for energy independence, environmental factors, nuclear safety and proliferation of concerns and advances in nuclear technology. IAEA had recently begun emphasizing the role of energy for development as the energy shortage in developing countries was a staggering impediment to their development. The IAEA offered energy assessment services for building a State's capability for energy analysis and energy planning, taking into account the country's economic, environmental and social development needs. Noting that, as a sophisticated technology, nuclear power required a correspondingly sophisticated infrastructure, the Director General said that the Agency had recently published guidance on the infrastructure needed for countries to introduce nuclear power, and for those countries which had chosen nuclear power as part of their energy mix, there was much that IAEA could do to make that option accessible, affordable, safer and secure. Its technical cooperation programme was focused on the sharing of knowledge and expertise to promote sustainable growth and human security as a contribution to the Millennium Development Goals, with much of its scientific work devoted to the transfer of peaceful nuclear technology in health, agriculture, industry, water management and environmental preservation. The safety and security of nuclear activities around the globe remained key elements of the IAEA mandate, and it was clear that the sustained effort to build a global nuclear safety regime was paying off.

The Director General reported on the challenges facing the nuclear non-proliferation and arms control regime (see p. 633), and the Agency's nuclear verification efforts in connection with the Democratic People's Republic of Korea (see p. 441) and Iran. (see p. 431). He reiterated his call for the development of a new, multilateral approach to the nuclear fuel cycle as a key measure to strengthen non-proliferation and cope with the expected expansion of nuclear power use.

GENERAL ASSEMBLY ACTION

On 30 October [meeting 43], the General Assembly adopted **resolution 61/8** [draft: A/61/L.9 & Add.1] by recorded vote (114-1-1) [agenda item 81].

Report of the International Atomic Energy Agency

The General Assembly,

Having received the report of the International Atomic Energy Agency for 2005,

Taking note of the statement by the Director General of the International Atomic Energy Agency, in which he provided additional information on the main developments in the activities of the Agency during 2006,

Recognizing the importance of the work of the Agency,

Recognizing also the cooperation between the United Nations and the Agency and the Agreement governing the relationship between the United Nations and the Agency as approved by the General Conference of the Agency on 23 October 1957 and by the General Assembly in the annex to its resolution 1145(XII) of 14 November 1957,

1. *Takes note with appreciation* of the report of the International Atomic Energy Agency;

2. *Takes note* of resolutions GC(50)/RES/10A on measures to strengthen international cooperation in nuclear, radiation and transport safety and waste management; GC(50)/RES/10B on transport safety; GC(50)/RES/11 on progress on measures to protect against nuclear and radiological terrorism; GC(50)/RES/12 on strengthening of the Agency's technical cooperation activities; GC(50)/RES/13 on strengthening the Agency's activities related to nuclear science, technology and applications, comprising GC(50)/RES/13 A on non-power nuclear applications, GC(50)/RES/13 B on nuclear power applications and GC(50)/RES/13 C on nuclear knowledge; GC(50)/RES/14 on strengthening the effectiveness and improving the efficiency of the safeguards system and application of the Model Additional Protocol; GC(50)/RES/15 on the implementation of the Agreement between the Agency and the Democratic People's Republic of Korea for the application of safeguards in connection with the Treaty on the Non-Proliferation of Nuclear Weapons; GC(50)/RES/16 on the application of Agency safeguards in the Middle East; and decisions GC(50)/DEC/11 on the amendment to article XIV. A of the Statute and GC(50)/DEC/12 on the amendment to article VI of the Statute, adopted on 22 September 2006 by the General Conference of the Agency at its fiftieth regular session;

3. *Reaffirms its strong support* for the indispensable role of the Agency in encouraging and assisting the development and practical application of atomic energy for peaceful uses, in technology transfer to developing countries and in nuclear safety, verification and security;

4. *Appeals* to Member States to continue to support the activities of the Agency;

5. *Requests* the Secretary-General to transmit to the Director General of the Agency the records of the sixty-first session of the General Assembly relating to the activities of the Agency.

RECORDED VOTE ON RESOLUTION 61/8:

In favour: Albania, Algeria, Andorra, Angola, Antigua and Barbuda, Argentina, Armenia, Australia, Austria, Bahrain, Belarus, Belgium, Belize, Brazil, Brunei Darussalam, Bulgaria, Burkina Faso, Canada, Cape Verde, Chad, Chile, China, Colombia, Comoros, Costa Rica, Croatia, Cuba, Czech Republic, Denmark, Djibouti, Ecuador, Egypt, Eritrea, Estonia, Finland, France, Georgia, Germany, Greece, Guatemala, Guinea, Guinea-Bissau, Guyana, Haiti, Honduras, Hungary, Iceland, India, Indonesia, Iran, Iraq, Ireland, Israel, Italy, Japan, Kenya, Kuwait, Lao People's Democratic Republic, Latvia, Lebanon, Libyan Arab Jamahiriya, Liechtenstein, Lithuania, Luxembourg, Madagascar, Malaysia, Maldives, Malta, Mauritius, Mexico, Moldova, Monaco, Mongolia, Montenegro, Morocco, Myanmar, Netherlands, New Zealand, Nigeria, Norway, Oman, Pakistan, Paraguay, Peru, Philippines, Poland, Portugal, Qatar, Republic of Korea, Romania, Russian Federation, San Marino, Saudi Arabia, Serbia, Singapore, Slovenia, Somalia, South Africa, Spain, Sri Lanka, Sweden, Switzerland, Syrian Arab Republic, Thailand, Togo, Tunisia, Turkey, Ukraine, United Arab Emirates, United Kingdom, United States, Venezuela, Viet Nam, Yemen.

Against: Democratic People's Republic of Korea.

Abstaining: Zambia.

Natural resources

Water resources

The Fourth World Water Forum (Mexico City, 16-22 March), which coincided with the observance of World Water Day on 22 March, was held under the theme "Local actions for a global challenge". Discussions were held on five framework themes: water for growth and development; implementing integrated water resources management; water supply and sanitation for all; water management for food and the environment; and risk management. Six ministerial roundtables focused on water efficiency and transfer of water-related technologies; capacity-building for effective water management and basic sanitation at the local level; water for the environment; the decentralization process, governance, institutions and the enhancement of stakeholder participation; financing local water and sanitation initiatives; and development and strengthening of national water monitoring mechanisms and targeting. The Forum adopted a Ministerial Declaration reaffirming the critical importance of water for sustainable development and underlined the need to include water and sanitation priorities in national processes, particularly national sustainable development and poverty reduction strategies. The Declaration recognized the importance of domestic and international capacity-building policies and cooperation to mitigate water-related disasters and welcomed the launch by the Commission on Sustainable Development of the Water Action and Networking Database.

During the Forum, the Secretary-General's Advisory Board on Water and Sanitation, established in 2004 to give advice and galvanize action in those areas, published a document entitled "The Compendium of Actions", also known as the Hashimoto Action Plan, which outlined a global workplan to ensure the attainment of the MDGs for water and sanitation.

The second edition of the *World Water Development Report: Water, a shared responsibility*, was published by the United Nations Educational, Scientific and Cultural Organization on behalf of the UN system's World Water Assessment Programme.

The *Human Development Report 2006*, entitled "Beyond scarcity: power, poverty and the global water crisis", discussed ways to end the crisis in water and sanitation; water for human consumption; the deficit in sanitation; water scarcity, risk and vulnerability; water competition in agriculture; managing transboundary waters; and human development indicators. The report acknowledged the growing recognition that the world faced a crisis that, left unchecked, would derail progress towards the MDGs and hold back human development. Setting out the challenges to access to clean water and sanitation, the report argued that the roots of the crisis in water could be traced to poverty, inequality and unequal power relationships, as well as flawed water management policies that exacerbated scarcity.

On 9 August, the Secretary-General launched the UN-MTV global campaign on the world water crisis, the objective of which was to educate young people about its devastating impact.

The Commission on Sustainable Development also continued its consideration of water resources. In a report [E/CN.17/2006/2] before the Commission, the Secretary-General discussed access to safe drinking water and adequate sanitation, noting that investments in access to water supply and sanitation yielded very high rates of return, making them extremely attractive from a social investment standpoint. Improved water supplies and sanitation created savings in terms of time, which could, in turn, translate into higher economic output and productivity, as well as greater school attendance. Reduced incidence of waterborne diseases was another significant source of benefits. South Asia had made the greatest progress in providing access to safe drinking water, with coverage having increased from 71 to 84 per cent between 1990 and 2002. Northern Africa, Latin America and the Caribbean, and Western Asia had achieved coverage levels of about 90 per cent. Progress in sub-Saharan Africa was also impressive, with coverage having increased from 49 to 58 per cent between 1990 and 2002. The situation in Oceania, however, had not improved much between 1990 and 2002, with almost half of the population still not served by improved water supply.

In terms of protecting and managing the natural resource base for development, the report noted that the need to balance water use and development with securing the vital services provided by water-based ecosystems would continue to increase with human population growth and associated changes in land use. While preparation of water management and efficiency plans, as agreed during the World Summit on Sustainable Development, was viewed as an important step towards achieving that balance, evidence suggested that progress on that goal had been uneven.

Cartography

UN Regional Cartographic Conference for Asia and the Pacific

The Seventeenth United Nations Regional Cartographic Conference for Asia and the Pacific (Bangkok, Thailand, 18-22 September) [E/CONF.97/7] was held in accordance with Economic and Social Council decision 2004/304 [YUN 2004, p. 1035]. The work of the Conference centred around three technical committees on: Geographical Information System, remote sensing and geodesy for disaster management; spatial data infrastructure capacity-building and its development in Asia and the Pacific; and geospatial fundamental data, including collection, management and dissemination thereof.

The Conference adopted resolutions on mitigating large-scale disaster, regional geodesy, marine administration, spatial data infrastructure support, fundamental data, and Timor-Leste spatial data infrastructure. In another resolution, the Conference recommended to the Economic and Social Council that the Eighteenth United Nations Regional Cartographic Conference for Asia and the Pacific be convened in 2009.

Standardization of geographical names

In accordance with Economic and Social Council decision 2004/303 [YUN 2004, p. 1035], the twenty-third session of the UN Group of Experts on Geographical Names (Vienna, 28 March–4 April) [E/2006/57] presented its major findings, focusing primarily on its work in supporting the United Nations Conferences on the Standardization of Geographical Names and the contribution it provided to Member States in the geographical information field, particularly in the context of natural-disaster preparedness and responding to humanitarian needs. The Group of Experts considered the reports of ten working groups and 18 linguistic/geographical divisions on their regions. The Experts accepted the provisional agenda for the twenty-fourth session, to be held in 2007 in conjunction with the Ninth UN Conference on the Standardization of Geographical Names.

The Council, by **decision 2006/229** of 24 July, took note of the report of the session.

Chapter VII

Environment and human settlements

In 2006, the United Nations and the international community continued to work towards protecting the environment through the application of legally binding instruments and the activities of the United Nations Environment Programme (UNEP).

The ninth special session of the UNEP Governing Council/seventh Global Ministerial Environmental Forum considered, in the form of ministerial consultations, the policy issues of energy and the environment and tourism and the environment and a summary of the consultations submitted by the Governing Council President, entitled "United Arab Emirates Initiative". The UNEP Executive Director elaborated a ten-point strategy to facilitate more effective and coordinated delivery of UNEP services and support within the context of the Bali Strategic Plan for Technology Support and Capacity-building.

The first session of the International Conference on Chemicals Management adopted the Strategic Approach to International Chemicals Management (SAICM) in February. The Governing Council subsequently endorsed SAICM and requested the Executive Director to establish and assume overall administrative responsibility for its secretariat.

UNEP issued the final report of the Global International Waters Assessment, which confirmed that pressures from human activities had weakened the ability of aquatic ecosystems to perform essential functions, thus compromising human well-being and development. The Economic and Social Council, on the recommendation of the United Nations Forum on Forests, set four Global Objectives on Forests and agreed to work to achieve them by 2015. The Council adopted a number of measures to strengthen the international arrangement on forests. The Assembly declared 2011 the International Year of Forests and 2010 the International Year of Biodiversity.

Donor countries pledged $3.1 billion to the fourth replenishment of the Global Environment Facility (GEF) to fund operations between 2006 and 2010. The GEF Council, the Facility's governing body, endorsed the replenishment in August.

In March, the General Assembly elected Mr. Achim Stiener (Germany) as Executive Director of UNEP for a four year term of office.

The United Nations Human Settlements Programme (UN-Habitat) continued to support the implementation of the 1996 Habitat Agenda and the Millennium Development Goals. It adopted a comprehensive and results-based approach to mobilize, guide and coordinate more effective and cohesive responses to the urbanization of poverty and social exclusion at the national and international levels.

In June, the Assembly re-elected Ms. Anna Kajumulo Tibaijuka (United Republic of Tanzania) as UN-Habitat Executive Director for a further four-year term of office.

Environment

UN Environment Programme

Governing Council/Ministerial Forum

The ninth special session of the Governing Council (GC) of the United Nations Environment Programme (UNEP), also serving as the seventh Global Ministerial Environmental Forum (GMEF), was held in Dubai, United Arab Emirates, from 7 to 9 February [A/61/25].

Ministerial-level consultations (7-9 February) discussed the policy themes of energy and the environment (see p. 1213), chemicals management (see p. 1247), and tourism and the environment (see p. 1213). GC/GMEF had before it a January discussion paper [UNEP/GCSS.IX/9] containing a synopsis of background papers on the three themes. Ministerial consultations also discussed international environmental governance, with a particular focus on the issue of universal membership of the Governing Council (see p. 1208).

The Committee of the Whole [UNEP/GCSS.IX/11] considered assessment, monitoring and early warning: state of the environment (see p. 1211); follow-up to the 2002 World Summit on Sustainable Development [YUN 2002, p. 821]: contribution of UNEP to the fourteenth (2006) session of the Commission on Sustainable Development (see p. 985); international environmental governance; and implementation of the UNEP programme of work and the decisions of the Governing Council [UNEP/GCSS.IX/INF/5].

The General Assembly, in resolution 61/205 of 20 December (see below), took note of the Governing Council's report on its ninth special session.

Subsidiary body

In 2006, the Committee of Permanent Representatives, which was open to representatives of all UN Member States and members of specialized agencies, held an extraordinary meeting on 19 January [UNEP/CPR/94/3] and regular meetings on 14 March [UNEP/CPR/95/2], 29 June [UNEP/CPR/96/2], 27 September [UNEP/CPR/97/2] and 13 December [UNEP/CPR/98/2]. The Committee discussed, among other matters, preparations for the Governing Council's twenty-fourth session; implementation of UNEP programme of work and relevant GC/GMEF decisions; and the status of the Environment Fund.

GENERAL ASSEMBLY ACTION

On 20 December [meeting 83], the General Assembly, on the recommendation of the Second (Economic and Financial) Committee [A/61/422/Add.7], adopted **resolution 61/205** without vote [agenda item 53 *(g)*].

Report of the Governing Council of the United Nations Environment Programme on its ninth special session

The General Assembly,

Recalling its resolutions 2997(XXVII) of 15 December 1972, 53/242 of 28 July 1999, 56/193 of 21 December 2001, 57/251 of 20 December 2002, 58/209 of 23 December 2003, 59/226 of 22 December 2004 and 60/189 of 22 December 2005,

Recalling also the 2005 World Summit Outcome,

Recognizing the need for more efficient environmental activities in the United Nations system, and noting the need to consider possible options to address this need,

Taking into account Agenda 21 and the Plan of Implementation of the World Summit on Sustainable Development ("Johannesburg Plan of Implementation"),

Reaffirming the role of the United Nations Environment Programme as the principal body within the United Nations system in the field of environment, which should take into account, within its mandate, the sustainable development needs of developing countries, as well as countries with economies in transition,

Emphasizing that capacity-building and technology support for developing countries, as well as countries with economies in transition, in environment-related fields are important components of the work of the United Nations Environment Programme,

Recognizing the need to accelerate implementation of the Bali Strategic Plan for Technology Support and Capacity-building of the United Nations Environment Programme,

1. *Takes note* of the report of the Governing Council of the United Nations Environment Programme at its ninth special session and the decision contained therein;

2. *Takes note also* of the report of the Secretary-General on universal membership of the Governing Council/Global Ministerial Environment Forum of the United Nations Environment Programme;

3. *Notes* that the Governing Council of the United Nations Environment Programme at its ninth special session discussed all components of the recommendations on international environmental governance as contained in its decision SS.VII/1, and also notes the continued discussions scheduled for the twenty-fourth session of the Governing Council;

4. *Emphasizes* the need to further advance and fully implement the Bali Strategic Plan for Technology Support and Capacity-building, and, in this regard, calls upon Governments as well as other stakeholders that are in a position to do so to provide the necessary funding and technical assistance for its full implementation, and also calls upon the United Nations Environment Programme to continue its efforts to fully implement the Bali Strategic Plan through strengthened cooperation with other stakeholders, based on their comparative advantages;

5. *Welcomes* the endorsement of the Strategic Approach to International Chemicals Management by the Governing Council/Global Ministerial Environment Forum of the United Nations Environment Programme at its ninth special session, and invites Governments, regional economic integration organizations, intergovernmental organizations and non-governmental organizations to engage actively and cooperate closely to support the Strategic Approach implementation activities of the United Nations Environment Programme, including the Strategic Approach Quick Start Programme, including through providing adequate resources, as appropriate;

6. *Emphasizes* the need to further enhance coordination and cooperation among the relevant United Nations organizations in the promotion of the environmental dimension of sustainable development, and welcomes the continued active participation of the United Nations Environment Programme in the United Nations Development Group and the Environment Management Group;

7. *Also emphasizes* the need for the United Nations Environment Programme, within its mandate, to further contribute to sustainable development programmes, the implementation of Agenda 21 and the Johannesburg Plan of Implementation, at all levels, and to the work of the Commission on Sustainable Development, bearing in mind the mandate of the Commission;

8. *Recognizes* the need to strengthen the scientific base of the United Nations Environment Programme, as recommended by the intergovernmental consultation on strengthening the scientific base of the Programme, including the reinforcement of the scientific capacity of

developing countries, as well as countries with economies in transition, including through the provision of adequate financial resources;

9. *Reiterates* the need for stable, adequate and predictable financial resources for the United Nations Environment Programme, and, in accordance with General Assembly resolution 2997(XXVII), underlines the need to consider the adequate reflection of all administrative and management costs of the Programme in the context of the United Nations regular budget;

10. *Invites* Governments that are in a position to do so to increase their contributions to the Environment Fund;

11. *Emphasizes* the importance of the Nairobi headquarters location of the United Nations Environment Programme, and requests the Secretary-General to keep the resource needs of the Programme and the United Nations Office at Nairobi under review so as to permit the delivery, in an effective manner, of necessary services to the Programme and to the other United Nations organs and organizations in Nairobi;

12. *Decides* to consider, if necessary, the issue of universal membership of the Governing Council/Global Ministerial Environment Forum of the United Nations Environment Programme at its sixty-fourth session, while noting the differences in views expressed so far on this important but complex issue;

13. *Decides* also to include in the provisional agenda of its sixty-second session, under the item entitled "Sustainable development", a sub-item entitled "Report of the Governing Council of the United Nations Environment Programme on its twenty-fourth session".

International environmental governance

The Governing Council considered a report of the Executive Director on international environmental governance [UNEP/GCSS.IX/3], which discussed the implementation of the Bali Strategic Plan for Technology Support and Capacity-building (see below), adopted by the Council in 2005 [YUN 2005, p. 1135]; developments with respect to universal membership of GC/GMEF; strengthening of UNEP scientific base, including examination of the Environment Watch proposal (see p. 1211); and of UNEP financing (see p. 1219); multilateral environmental agreements (see p. 1210); and enhanced UN system coordination, including the Environmental Management Group.

Also before the Council was a report of the Executive Director on the outcome of intergovernmental meetings of relevance to GC/GMEF [UNEP/GCSS.IX/8].

Report of Secretary-General. In response to General Assembly resolution 59/226 [YUN 2004, p. 1037], the Secretary-General submitted an August report [A/61/322] on establishing universal membership for GC/GMEF, which outlined consideration of the issue under the auspices of GC/GMEF and summarized the views of Member States. The Secretary-General recommended that the Assembly decide on a further process to consider the question of universal membership of GC/GMEF in the light of its consideration of the institutional framework for UN environmental activities in follow-up to the 2005 World Summit Outcome, adopted by the Assembly in resolution 60/1 [YUN 2005, p. 48]. The Assembly took action on the report in resolution 61/205 (see p. 1207).

Environmental Management Group

The Chairman of the United Nations Environmental Management Group (EMG), an inter-agency advisory group set up in 1999 to coordinate UN system activities in addressing the major challenges in UNEP work programme [YUN 1999, p. 974], convened a High-level Forum of the Group's members (Geneva, 24 January) [UNEMG/HLF/12] to ascertain their views and recommendations on reviving and strengthening EMG and more effectively addressing existing and emergent environmental challenges in a coherent and coordinated manner. The Forum considered the Group's terms of reference, working methods, including the need to improve operational links with other UN inter-agency and coordination mechanisms, membership, support structure and other issues. It concluded that, in a changing international context, it was necessary to clarify EMG terms of reference. UN agencies, Governments and the international community had the means to transform the Group into an effective, authoritative, service- and results-oriented mechanism to further UN system-wide coherence and coordination in the areas of the environment and human settlements. The UN system needed an effective mechanism to discuss and agree on a more coordinated, productive and cost-effective way of tackling environmental and human settlements challenges. The Forum also discussed the elements of a short-term workplan.

EMG also held a partnership forum (Curitiba, Brazil, 26 March) and a forum on UN reform initiatives (Geneva, 3-4 July) [UNEMG/FUNRI/3].

Bali Strategic Plan for Technology Support and Capacity-building

In response to a 2005 Governing Council decision, the Executive Director submitted a report [UNEP/GCSS.IX/3/Add.1] on the implementation of the Bali Strategic Plan for Technology Support and Capacity-building, adopted by the High-level Open-ended Intergovernmental Working Group on an Intergovernmental Strategic Plan for Technology Support and Capacity-building in 2004 [YUN 2004, p. 1040], and by the Council in 2005 [YUN 2005, p. 1135]. Since the adoption of the Plan, the Executive Director had strengthened and enhanced the delivery of capacity-building and technology transfer; conducted a preliminary inventory and analysis of regional and national needs and priorities for environmental capacity-building and technology support; strengthened cooperation between regional and subregional intergovernmental bodies to ensure better implementation of the Plan; conducted an in-depth analysis of existing and planned capacity-building and technology support activities within the framework of the UNEP 2006-2007 programme of work; and strengthened UNEP collaboration with the United Nations Development Programme (UNDP). He also reviewed UNEP operational modalities to facilitate the implementation of the Plan, and UNEP and UNDP project development, approval and implementation procedures to identify possible areas for increased efficiency. Within the overall framework of the approved 2006-2007 programme of work, UNEP support to the implementation of the Bali Strategic Plan met the requirements for: assistance to country-driven needs assessments and priority setting; focused implementation of the capacity-building and technology support aspects of the work programme; strengthening activities for enhanced delivery of UNEP implementation of the Plan; and improved cooperation with Plan partners. The report also described the 2006-2007 resource mobilization strategy for implementing the Plan.

The Executive Director concluded that the 2006-2007 biennium was a transition period with regard to the implementation of the Bali Strategic Plan, during which UNEP would test and develop operational methods and concepts to enable all partners to work together effectively to tackle priority country needs. UNEP financial management and oversight capacity would be enhanced on the basis of the expected recommendations of the UNEP management review, and results-based monitoring and reporting strengthened. A reorientation of the way UNEP conducted business would be initiated during the biennium. Once country needs and priorities were identified and adopted by the relevant national forums, the challenge would be to gradually address them in a coordinated and phased manner, and thereafter amend the needs assessment. Deeper and more comprehensive cooperation with UNDP, including in support to countries towards achieving the Millennium Development Goals (MDGs) [YUN 2000, p. 51], would be a key priority beyond the 2006-2007 biennium. Knowledge management would continue to be one of UNEP major contributions to the implementation of the Plan. Implementation would be an interactive process with the participation of all major stakeholders. The Executive Director would keep Governments regularly informed on steps taken to strengthen implementation.

In a further report on implementation of the Bali Strategic Plan [UNEP/GCSS.IX/INF/13], the Executive Director set out the components for capacity-building and technology support activities in the UNEP programme of work for the 2006-2007 biennium.

A January note by the Executive Director [UNEP/GCSS.IX/INF/15] contained information on the status of pilot projects for the implementation of the Bali Strategic Plan in Burkina Faso, the Gambia, Kenya, Lesotho, Rwanda and Tunisia. A workshop for technical experts, including Government and UNDP country office focal points from the pilot countries, organized by UNEP (Nairobi, 16-20 January) to determine progress made and chart the way forward, noted that the implementation process in the six countries began with the signing of memorandums of understanding between the UNEP/UNDP country offices and the Governments of those countries. Following a consultative review meeting (27-28 October), the countries embarked on a process of sensitization and national consultations, involving public institutions, the private sector, civil society, research institutions and the donor community. Preliminary results from the exercise indicated that, in general, individual countries had the requisite technical capacity to undertake the pilot project, but required further technical support in communication and information sharing, resource mobilization, and South-South cooperation. The pilot countries were urged to strengthen the focal points for the Bali Plan by defining clearly their roles and responsibilities. UNEP and UNDP should set up a network to help countries and other stakeholders share experiences and information. Regional offices of multilateral organizations involved in the implementation of the Bali Plan should establish a framework for effective coordination of Plan activities. The report concluded that, although individual countries were at different stages of implementation of the pilot project, they needed to finalize the needs assessment reports, complete the development of technology support and capacity-building plans, and obtain donor commitment. The six countries were committed to completing the pilot activities by the end of April. The note also contained a declaration adopted by the Heads of State and Government of the pilot countries (Khartoum, Sudan, 22 January) welcoming the implementation of the Bali Strategic Plan in Africa.

In a December report [UNEP/GC/24/3/Add.1], the Executive Director outlined progress achieved in the implementation of the Bali Strategic Plan during 2006 and planned activities for 2007, and set out the strategy for implementing the Plan in the 2008-2009 biennium and beyond. In order to implement the Plan fully, UNEP had to accept the findings of the UN reform processes. In response to the 2005 World Summit Outcome, adopted by the General Assembly in resolution 60/1 [YUN 2005, p. 48], the Assembly President established an informal consultative process on the institutional framework of environmental activities within the United Nations. The process concluded its first round of consultations in June and was scheduled to resume consultations in January 2007, at which time it would consider the recommendations of the High-level Panel on United Nations System-wide Coherence in the Areas of Development, Humanitarian Assistance and the Environment, formed by the Secretary-General in February. In its final report, transmitted by the Secretary-General in November [A/61/583], the Panel recommended that the Bali Strategic Plan be implemented strategically at the country level; where necessary, UNEP should participate in UN country teams through the resident coordinator system. The Assembly's informal consultative process requested closer cooperation between UNEP regional offices and UNDP country offices, and the Plan provided the framework for responding to that request.

An overarching objective of UNEP implementation efforts in 2006 was to bring its normative, scientific and technical work closer to the operational activities conducted by stakeholders in sustainable development, in accordance with national priorities. UNEP implementation activities, described in an annex to the report, focused on the development of environmental law; compliance with and enforcement of multilateral environmental agreements; environmental aspects of national sustainable development plans; integrated environmental assessment and networking; environmentally sound technologies; sustainable consumption and production; biosafety; freshwater resources; oceans, seas and coastal areas; chemicals and waste management; environmental emergency preparedness and response; and post-conflict assessment.

UNEP assisted countries in identifying their needs, including capacity-building and technology support priorities for each subregion and for individual countries. UNEP also undertook a comprehensive review of needs assessment methodologies. Advances were made also in setting up processes to deliver the Plan support activities more effectively, including the establishment of the South-South coordination unit, increased dialogue and partnership with UNDP, and involvement in the United Nations Development Group (UNDG).

From October 2005 to March 2006, a review of UNEP was conducted by Dahlberg Global Development Advisors, in response to the implications of implementing the Bali Strategic Plan. The review, which considered UNEP programme implementation mechanisms and administrative structures, as well as ways to operationalize the Plan, generated several recommendations for improving management efficiency. It recognized that the Plan required UNEP to shift focus from its traditional core competencies in the analytical and normative areas, as well as advocacy, towards also meeting more country-driven needs. UNEP established task forces on: the Bali Strategic Plan, management and administration, and information and communication technology. The task forces reviewed UNEP operations and made a series of short, medium and long-term recommendations to help UNEP better implement the Plan. A number of further priority actions to ensure that the support activities for the Plan continued to drive programme implementation in 2007 and beyond were identified. The priority actions dealt with the key issues of focusing UNEP future; needs assessment; partnerships; strategic presence; developing and utilizing UNEP staff capacities; ensuring that the UNEP structure delivered Plan objectives; building quality and coherence in the design and execution of UNEP work; accountability in the delivery of UNEP work; financing; and communication and outreach.

The Executive Director, drawing on the work of the task forces and the Dahlberg review, elaborated a ten-point strategy that would be implemented beginning in 2007 to facilitate the more effective and coordinated delivery of UNEP services and support within the context of the Bali Strategic Plan. Under the strategy, UNEP would: integrate capacity-building and support into its 2008-2009 programme of work; ensure the UNEP structure supported better delivery of the Plan; focus UNEP activities; establish a strategic presence and strategic partnerships in the context of the Global Environment Facility (GEF); engage UN country teams, UNDG and EMG; streamline and strengthen partnerships, including the strategic partnership with UNDP; and increase South-South programmes. New and additional finance mechanisms and fund-raising strategies would need to be developed by UNEP in order to fully implement the Plan. To that end, the report described practical suggestions to reorient internal resource allocation, such as refocusing partnership and framework agreements with donor countries to promote projects to implement capacity-building and technology support activities; expanding private sector collaboration; using the Plan as a tool to assist countries in fund-raising; and mobilizing other donors, including through joint proposals with UNDP or GEF.

The Executive Director concluded that the full and coordinated implementation of the Bali Strategic Plan implied significant changes for UNEP and the way it conducted its work. It would have to transform the systems and processes for project implementation, increase dramatically the amount of work undertaken with and through UN and non-UN partners, strengthen UNEP regional offices and other mechanisms for establishing a strategic presence in countries and regions, and integrate fully into UN country teams and programmes. Changes were also required in the activities and outputs contained in the UNEP programme of work so as to ensure a greater integration of technology support and capacity-building components. It was evident that UNEP had responded to the Plan and brought about many of those changes, but more was needed before it could implement technology support and capacity-building activities effectively and efficiently, and respond to country needs in a more timely fashion.

The Assembly, in resolution 61/205 of 20 December (see p. 1207), called on Governments and other stakeholders in a position to do so to provide the necessary funding and technical assistance for the full implementation of the Bali Strategic Plan, and on UNEP to continue to implement the Plan through strengthened cooperation with other stakeholders, based on their comparative advantages.

UNEP activities

Monitoring and assessment

In response to a 2005 Governing Council decision [YUN 2005, p. 1136], the Executive Director circulated an updated proposal for the Environment Watch assessment framework [ibid., p. 1135]. In addition, a needs assessment exercise was undertaken to determine which elements of the Environment Watch system were already in place, and identify where capacities needed to be strengthened. Comments on the proposal received from Governments and other institutions, summarized in the Executive Director's report on international environmental governance [UNEP/GCSS.IX/3], formed the basis for a further updated proposal, which was submitted by the Executive Director in January [UNEP/GCSS.IX/3/Add.2] and considered by the Council in February. Council representatives generally felt that the proposal required further improvement before being considered for approval, but that its capacity-building and technology support elements were too important to be held up by continued consideration.

The Executive Director undertook further consultations and deliberations to clarify points raised by Governments regarding the proposal. The consultations included an informal global expert meeting on environmental information networking, hosted by the European Environment Agency (Copenhagen, Denmark, 22-23 May); informal regional expert group meetings on environmental information networking; an expert meeting on tools for capacity-building in the context of the Bali Strategic Plan; and informal bilateral consultations with interested partners and agencies. Based on the consultations, the Executive Director proposed shifting the focus of the Environment Watch proposal to a multi-year strategy, known as Environment Watch Strategy: Vision 2020. The proposed strategy, which was outlined in a December report of the Executive Director [UNEP/GC/24/3/Add.2], set out a bottom-up, incremental approach to achieving, by 2020, enhanced institutional, scientific and technological infrastructures and capacities for cooperation on keeping the state of the environment under review and providing timely, accurate, credible, relevant and consistent environmental data and information for environmental governance. The strategy had three objectives: to build national institutional and technological capacity in developing countries and countries with economies in transition for collecting, managing, analysing and disseminating environmental data and information for decision-making; to connect national, international, scientific and technical capacities and efforts to keep the state of the environment under review and to promote the exchange of priority environmental data and information; and to enhance interaction between scientists and decision-makers through timely, credible, legitimate and relevant assessments of the state of and outlook for the environment. During implementation of the UNEP programme of work, the Strategy would be further improved by the Executive Director, in close cooperation with Governments and a consortium of international organizations and financial institutions. Capacity-building and technology support to developing countries and countries with economies in transition would be provided by UNEP or a consortium partner.

In February, the Governing Council considered a report by the Executive Director [UNEP/GCSS.

IX/10] summarizing issues emanating from UNEP activities in the area of assessment, monitoring and early-warning.

Support to Africa

In 2006, UNEP continued to work closely with African subregional organizations to finalize subregional action plans for the Environment Initiative of the New Partnership for Africa's Development (NEPAD). With assistance from Norway, UNEP supported Cameroon, Ethiopia, Ghana, the Libyan Arab Jamahiriya and Mozambique in the development of their NEPAD National Action Plans on a pilot basis. UNEP also served as the secretariat for the African Ministerial Conference on the Environment, and provided substantive support for the eleventh regular session of the Conference (Brazzaville, Congo, 25-26 May), which reviewed the Action Plan for the NEPAD Environment Initiative.

Water policy and strategy

In response to a 2005 Governing Council decision [YUN 2005, p. 1137], the Executive Director submitted to the Council's ninth special session the first draft of the UNEP updated water policy and strategy, focusing on freshwater resources [UNEP/GCSS.IX/4]; the updated policy and strategy was first submitted in 2004 [YUN 2004, p. 1042], and was revised in 2005 [YUN 2005, p. 1136]. The latest update built on UNEP mandates on water rather than defining any new policy, and focused on strategic principles and key components for implementing those mandates. Once adopted, the update would provide strategic direction for UNEP activities related to water for six years, and a basis for the development of the UNEP biennial programmes of work. It was proposed that the implementation of the mandated UNEP functions in the area of water, particularly at the national and regional level, should be an integral component of the delivery of the Bali Strategic Plan for Technology Support and Capacity-building.

In a November report [UNEP/GC/24/4], the Executive Director discussed the status of implementation of the Governing Council's 2005 decision on the updated UNEP water policy and strategy [YUN 2005, p. 1137], and the implementation of the policy and strategy itself. He reported that, within the framework of the Bali Strategic Plan, UNEP and the national water agency of Brazil signed a memorandum of understanding on the establishment of a GEMS/Water focal point in Latin America. As a result, 1,000 new monitoring stations were established in Brazil by the end of October, and similar increases were expected in all Latin American countries. The GEMS/Water global monitoring network grew to over 2,700 stations, with over two million data points.

The atmosphere

The Atmospheric Brown Cloud project continued to study the three kilometre-deep pollution blanket that formed over parts of Asia during the monsoon season. By 2006, Atmospheric Brown Cloud obsevatories were operational in India, Japan, the Republic of Korea, Maldives, Nepal and Thailand. A team for assessing impacts on agriculture, water supply and public health was also established.

Environment and sustainable development

In response to a 2005 Governing Council decision [YUN 2005, p. 1138], the Executive Director submitted an October progress report [UNEP/GC/24/5] on UNEP activities in small island developing States (SIDS). The report, which followed the structure of the Mauritius Strategy for the Further Implementation of the Programme of Action for the Sustainable Development of Small Island Developing States [YUN 2005, p. 946], described activities related to climate change; natural and environmental disasters; waste management; coastal, marine, freshwater, land, energy, tourism and biodiversity resources; capacity development and education; capacity-building in environmental law, including multilateral environmental agreements; governance; and trade and finance. The report also discussed additional UNEP activities in the Caribbean. A Pacific subregional strategy for 2006-2010 was being implemented by the UNEP Regional Office for Asia and the Pacific, focusing on promoting regional cooperation, strengthening the environment community, identifying and addressing emerging environment issues, and demonstration projects.

Commission on Sustainable Development consideration. The Commission on Sustainable Development, at its fourteenth session (New York, 1-12 May) [E/2006/29], considered, for its 2006-2007 implementation cycle, the thematic cluster issues of energy for sustainable development, industrial development, air pollution and the atmosphere, and climate change (see p. 982). The Commission had before it a February report of the Secretary-General [E/CN.17/2006/7] reviewing the status of progress in SIDS in the implementation of the Mauritius Strategy, with specific focus on the thematic cluster issues, and a report on the activities and achievements of the Mountain Partnership [E/CN.17/2006/12] (see p. 1241).

Energy and the environment

On 8 February, GC/GMEF held ministerial consultations on policy issues relating to energy and the environment. The Council/Forum had before it a note by the Executive Director [UNEP/GCSS.IX/INF/11] summarizing UNEP energy programme, and the current status of major trends in and future prospects for renewable energy. The ultimate objective of the energy programme was to help bring about a global shift to energy systems that were less disruptive to the environment, did not harm human health, and supported sustainable development. UNEP helped Governments and the private sector to improve overall planning and management of energy systems, deploy and use renewable and low- and non-carbon energy technologies, direct financing to energy efficiency and renewable energy investments, increase the efficiency with which energy was transformed and used, and develop alternatives to, and shift consumer preferences away from, energy intensive products and services. UNEP focused on promoting robust analysis of different technology options to help stakeholders make better policy and investment decisions. The nucleus of UNEP energy work was the Energy Branch in the Division of Technology, Industry and Economics (DTIE), comprising of the Energy and Transport Policy Unit, which promoted policies that placed energy and transport within the broader sustainable development context, and the Renewable Energy and Finance Unit, which steered project developers and the investment community toward greater support of renewable energy and energy efficiency projects. UNEP, through the Energy and Transport Policy Unit and a link to the International Partnership on a Hydrogen Economy, helped developing countries better understand the technical and economic issues involved and the associated policy implications. It intended to place more emphasis on promoting the use of clean fossil fuel technologies, particularly the transfer of improved technologies to developing countries. Through its Renewable Energy and Finance Unit, UNEP anticipated expanding joint efforts with financial institutions and others to build longer-term partnerships with a more strategic orientation.

GC/GMEF also had before it a background paper on energy and the environment [UNEP/GCSS.IX/9/Add.1]. Its President submitted a summary of the ministerial consultations to the Council/Forum. The summary, entitled the "United Arab Emirates Initiative", was annexed to the Council's report on its ninth special session [A/61/25]. While there was no consensus on a number of the issues contained in the Initiative, ministers and heads of delegations agreed that it should be transmitted to the fourteenth (2006) session of the Commission on Sustainable Development for its consideration.

Tourism and the environment

On 8 February, GC/GMEF held ministerial consultations on the policy issues of energy and the environment (see above) and tourism and the environment. The Council/Forum had before it a note by the Executive Director on UNEP activities in tourism and the UNEP tourism strategy [UNEP/GCSS.IX/INF/12]. UNEP strategic goals and objectives in tourism were to support the integration of sustainability in tourism policies in developing, emerging and post-conflict countries. Its work addressed key barriers to the integration of sustainability in the decision-making processes of the private sector, public policy makers and consumers. UNEP tourism strategy would be based on two interconnected work programmes: a sustainable policy support programme aimed at providing information and technical expertise to national authorities on the integration of sustainability in national and local tourism policies; and a programme to support the integration of sustainable production and consumption in the tourism industry. UNEP cooperation with the World Tourism Organization (UNWTO) would focus on linking the joint UNEP/UNWTO/United Nations Educational, Scientific and Cultural Organization (UNESCO) Tour Operators' Initiative for Sustainable Tourism Development to local authorities and destination management organizations; developing a sustainability programme for the UNWTO Business Council; and supporting the integration of sustainability in national and local policies. UNEP tourism programme was implemented through activities targeting the tourism industry, the public sector and consumers.

GC/GMEF also had before it a background paper on tourism and the environment [UNEP/GCSS.IX/9/Add.3]. Its President, in his summary of the ministerial consultations entitled the "United Arab Emirates Initiative", which was annexed to the Council's report [A/61/25], said that Ministers and heads of delegation concurred that the tourism sector could contribute significantly to environmental protection, the conservation and restoration of biological diversity, and the sustainable use of natural resources. Governments should involve and support indigenous peoples and local communities in the development of criteria, indicators, early warning systems and guidelines that embraced both the cultural and ecological aspects of biodiversity. While there was no consensus on a number of the issues contained in the Initiative, ministers and heads of delegations agreed that it should be transmitted to the fourteenth (2006) session of the Commission on Sustainable Development for consideration.

Policy and advisory services

Trade and the environment

In 2006, UNEP initiated a two-year project, implemented jointly by the UNEP-United Nations Conference on Trade and Development (UNCTAD) Capacity Building Task Force (CBTF) on Trade, Environment and Development, the secretariat of the Convention on International Trade in Endangered Species of Wild Fauna and Flora, and the Graduate Institute of Development Studies, to enhance the capacity of developing countries and countries with economies in transition to assess, design and implement effective national wildlife trade policies. CBTF, together with the International Federation of Organic Agricultural Movements, facilitated the assessment of the organic sector and the harmonization of organic agriculture standards in Kenya, the United Republic of Tanzania and Uganda, under the East Africa Organic Agriculture initiative. UNEP Economics and Trade Branch, in collaboration with the International Institute for Sustainable Development, updated the Environment and Trade Handbook to enable Governments to develop practical approaches to integrating policies in those two sectors.

Coordination and cooperation

Business and industry

UNEP and the International Chamber of Commerce hosted the twenty-third Annual Consultative Meeting on Business and Industry (Paris, 26-27 October), which discussed energy and climate challenges and corporate responsibility in industrial development. Six Principles for Responsible Investment, drafted by institutional investors at the request of the Secretary-General, were launched in April. The Principles were supported by more than 90 institutions, representing over $5 trillion in assets. The globally applicable, sustainable reporting guidelines developed by the Global Reporting Initiative, a multi-stakeholder process and independent institution established in 2002 [YUN 2002, p. 1038], were launched in October, with UNEP involvement. UNEP also conducted a workshop on business and climate change at the annual meeting of the Global Compact National Networks (Barcelona, Spain, 26-27 September).

Labour and the environment

UNEP hosted the first meeting of the Trade Union Assembly on Labour and the Environment (Nairobi, 15-17 January) [UNEP/DPDL/TUALE/1], which brought together over 150 representatives of labour organizations, trade unions, Governments, the private sector and UN bodies to discuss synergies between labour and the environment and ways to establish partnerships and framework agreements for joint environmental policy design and implementation. The Assembly adopted the Workers Initiative for a Lasting Legacy, which confirmed the commitment of unions to advance sustainable development and the MDGs. The Initiative endorsed efforts to strengthen cooperation between trade unions and UNEP, the International Labour Organization (ILO), the World Health Organization (WHO), and other organizations, and mapped out steps for joint follow-up action.

The Trade Union Regional Conference on Labour and the Environment in Latin America (São Paulo, Brazil, 17-19 April) aimed to establish a framework for discussion, adoption and extension of common strategies in the work of trade unions on sustainable development and the environment in that region. At the African Trade Union Conference on Labour and Environment (Johannesburg, South Africa, 28-29 July), UNEP presented the key environmental challenges and messages outlined in the second Africa Environment Outlook report [YUN 2005, p. 1136].

Environmental emergencies

In 2006, UNEP worked with partners to establish, inform and implement an environmental agenda for recovery. In the aftermath of the 2004 Indian Ocean tsunami [YUN 2004, p. 952], UNEP cleared 89 islands of hazardous waste; the three remaining affected islands were cleared in 2006. UNEP also worked to restore coastal habitats. Guided by the 2005 Hyogo Framework for Action 2005-2015 [YUN 2005, p. 1016], UNEP strengthened its engagement in the UN International Strategy for Disaster Reduction (ISDR) by increasing its institutional capacity for assessing risk and vulnerabilities; generating and applying risk information; improving preparedness for effective response; and introducing programmes that addressed underlying risk factors. In Africa, UNEP, ISDR and UNDP launched an initiative to incorporate disaster risk reduction into development practice, including environmental management. In Indonesia, UNEP conducted two missions to identify disaster-related capacity and developed the Strategic Framework for Disaster Risk Reduction and Recovery to help the country in its national disaster risk reduction efforts. UNEP and the ISDR Environment and Disaster Working Group convened the plenary session on Environment and Vulnerability at the International Conference on Disaster Reduction, (Davos, Switzerland, 27 August–1 September) (see p. 1094). In Sri Lanka and Morocco, national and local authorities were trained in disaster preparedness. In July, the European Commission concluded a partnership with UNEP to implement a new project on disaster reduction through awareness, preparedness and prevention mechanisms in coastal settlements in Asia. The project aimed to minimize casualties, as well as property and environmental damage from natural and man-made disasters in tsunami-affected tourism destinations in India and Thailand.

During the year, the Joint UNEP/Office for the Coordination of Humanitarian Affairs Environment Unit coordinated responses to a number of environmental emergencies, including an oil spill in the Philippines, floods in Suriname; an earthquake and a hot mud flow on the island of Java, Indonesia; an oil spill affecting the Syrian Arab Republic, an oil slick affecting Lebanon (see below) and other consequences of the conflict between Israel and the paramilitary group Hizbullah in Lebanon (see p. 574); forest fires in the Nagorny-Karabakh region of Azerbaijan; and toxic waste dumping in Côte d'Ivoire.

Oil slick in Lebanon

On 15 July, following the outbreak of hostilities in Lebanon between Israel and the paramilitary group Hizbullah (see p. 574), Israel was reported to have destroyed oil storage tanks near the El-Jiyeh electric power plant in Lebanon, causing an oil slick that covered the entirety of the Lebanese coastline and other coastal areas.

GENERAL ASSEMBLY ACTION

On 20 December [meeting 83], the General Assembly, on the recommendation of the Second Committee [A/61/422/Add.1 & Corr.1], adopted **resolution 61/194** by recorded vote (170-6-0) [agenda item 53 *(a)*].

Oil slick on Lebanese shores

The General Assembly,

Reaffirming the outcome of the United Nations Conference on the Human Environment, especially principle 7 of the Declaration of the Conference, which requested States to take all possible steps to prevent pollution of the seas,

Emphasizing the need to protect and preserve the marine environment in accordance with international law,

Taking into account the 1992 Rio Declaration on Environment and Development, especially principle 16, which stipulates that the polluter should, in principle, bear the cost of pollution, and taking into account also chapter 17 of Agenda 21,

Noting with great concern the environmental disaster caused by the destruction by the Israeli Air Force on 15 July 2006 of the oil storage tanks in the direct vicinity of the El-Jiyeh electric power plant in Lebanon, causing an oil slick that covered the entirety of the Lebanese coastline and extended beyond,

Noting with appreciation the assistance offered by donor countries and international organizations for the early recovery and reconstruction of Lebanon through bilateral and multilateral channels, including the Stockholm Conference for Lebanon's Early Recovery, held on 31 August 2006,

1. *Expresses its deep concern* over the adverse implications of the destruction by the Israeli Air Force of the oil storage tanks in the direct vicinity of the Lebanese El-Jiyeh electric power plant for the achievement of sustainable development in Lebanon;

2. *Considers* that the oil slick has heavily polluted the shores of Lebanon and consequently has serious implications for human health, biodiversity, fisheries and tourism, all four of which in turn have serious implications for livelihoods and the economy of Lebanon;

3. *Calls upon* the Government of Israel to assume responsibility for prompt and adequate compensation to the Government of Lebanon for the costs of repairing the environmental damage caused by the destruction, including the restoration of the marine environment;

4. *Encourages* Member States, regional and international organizations, regional and international financial institutions, and non-governmental organizations and the private sector to provide financial and technical assistance to the Government of Lebanon in support of its efforts to clean up the polluted shores and sea of Lebanon with a view to preserving its ecosystem;

5. *Requests* the Secretary-General to submit to the General Assembly at its sixty-second session a report on the implementation of the present resolution under the item entitled "Sustainable development".

RECORDED VOTE ON RESOLUTION 61/194:

In favour: Afghanistan, Albania, Algeria, Andorra, Angola, Antigua and Barbuda, Argentina, Armenia, Austria, Azerbaijan, Bahamas, Bahrain, Bangladesh, Barbados, Belarus, Belgium, Belize, Benin, Bhutan, Bolivia, Botswana, Brazil, Brunei Darussalam, Bulgaria, Burkina Faso, Burundi, Cambodia, Cape Verde, Central African Republic, Chile, China, Colombia, Comoros, Congo, Costa Rica, Côte d'Ivoire, Croatia, Cuba, Cyprus, Czech Republic, Democratic People's Republic of Korea, Denmark, Djibouti, Dominica, Dominican Republic, Ecuador, Egypt, Eritrea, Estonia, Ethiopia, Fiji, Finland, France, Gabon, Gambia, Georgia, Germany, Ghana, Greece, Grenada, Guatemala, Guinea, Guinea-Bissau, Guyana, Haiti, Honduras, Hungary,

Iceland, India, Indonesia, Iran, Iraq, Ireland, Italy, Jamaica, Japan, Jordan, Kazakhstan, Kuwait, Kyrgyzstan, Lao People's Democratic Republic, Latvia, Lebanon, Lesotho, Liberia, Libyan Arab Jamahiriya, Liechtenstein, Lithuania, Luxembourg, Madagascar, Malawi, Malaysia, Maldives, Mali, Malta, Mauritania, Mauritius, Mexico, Moldova, Monaco, Mongolia, Montenegro, Morocco, Mozambique, Myanmar, Namibia, Nepal, Netherlands, New Zealand, Nicaragua, Niger, Nigeria, Norway, Oman, Pakistan, Panama, Papua New Guinea, Paraguay, Peru, Philippines, Poland, Portugal, Qatar, Republic of Korea, Romania, Russian Federation, Saint Kitts and Nevis, Saint Lucia, Saint Vincent and the Grenadines, Samoa, San Marino, Sao Tome and Principe, Saudi Arabia, Senegal, Serbia, Sierra Leone, Singapore, Slovakia, Slovenia, Solomon Islands, Somalia, South Africa, Spain, Sri Lanka, Sudan, Suriname, Swaziland, Sweden, Switzerland, Syrian Arab Republic, Thailand, The former Yugoslav Republic of Macedonia, Timor-Leste, Togo, Trinidad and Tobago, Tunisia, Turkey, Uganda, Ukraine, United Arab Emirates, United Kingdom, United Republic of Tanzania, Uruguay, Uzbekistan, Vanuatu, Venezuela, Viet Nam, Yemen, Zambia, Zimbabwe.

Against: Australia, Canada, Israel, Marshall Islands, Palau, United States.

Abstaining: None.

Global Environment Facility

The Global Environment Facility (GEF), a joint programme of UNDP, UNEP and the World Bank, established in 1991 [YUN 1991, p. 505] to help solve global environmental problems, was the designated financial mechanism for the 1992 Convention on Biological Diversity [YUN 1992, p. 683] (see p. 1223), the 1992 United Nations Framework Convention on Climate Change [ibid., p. 681] (see p. 1219), and the 1994 United Nations Convention to Combat Desertification [YUN 1994, p. 944] (see p. 1225), and served as the interim financial mechanism for the 2001 Stockholm Convention on Persistent Organic Pollutants (POPs) [YUN 2001, p. 971] (see p. 1247).

As at June, the cumulative UNEP/GEF work programme was financed to $1.1 billion, including $535 million in GEF grant funding, involving activities in 153 countries. UNEP helped countries meet their obligations to the global environmental conventions through GEF enabling activities addressing biodiversity, biosafety, climate change, POPs and capacity-building needs assessment for global environmental management.

In August, donors pledged $3.1 billion to the fourth GEF replenishment to fund operations between 2006 and 2010. The GEF Council, the Facility's governing body, endorsed the fourth replenishment at a special meeting held in Cape Town, South Africa, on 28 August.

On 13 September [UNEP/GC/24/INF/13], the GEF Chief Executive Officer and Chairperson informed the UNEP Executive Director that the third GEF Assembly (Cape Town, 29-30 August) had approved an amendment to the Instrument for the Establishment of the Restructured Global Environment Facility, providing the GEF Council with authority to decide the location of its meetings. The Executive Director, in his capacity as head of a GEF Implementing Agency, was requested to facilitate its adoption by the UNEP Governing Council.

Memorandum of understanding

In a 22 November note [UNEP/GC/24/INF/9], the Executive Director informed GC/GMEF that no memorandum of understanding had been concluded between UNEP and other UN system organizations since the Executive Director's 2005 report on the subject [YUN 2005, p.114].

Participation of civil society

In response to a 2003 Governing Council decision [YUN 2003, p. 1046], the Executive Director submitted a midterm progress report [UNEP/GCSS.IX/7] on the implementation of the UNEP Tunza strategy (2003-2008) for the engagement and involvement of young people in environmental issues [YUN 2002, p. 1040]. The report described UNEP activities in the four Tunza focus areas of information exchange, awareness-building, youth in decision-making processes, and capacity-building. Since its adoption, the strategy had generated extensive interest from children and youth organizations, UN and international partners, and the private sector. As a result, UNEP expanded its network for children and youth organizations, increased the substantive base of its processes for young people, signed several partnership agreements with youth-related organizations, and increased the frequency and regularity of its conferences and publications for children and youth. Despite substantial funding from Bayer AG, the German-based chemical and health care company, in the amount of €1 million annually, full implementation of the strategy was hampered by inadequate human and financial resources.

UNEP held the 2006 Tunza International Children's Conference on the Environment (Putrajaya, Malaysia, 26-30 August), which was attended by 250 children between the ages of 10 and 14 from more than 67 countries. The Conference, which had as its theme "Save a Tree, Save our Lungs", adopted the Tunza Environmental Contract, in which participants pledged to protect and raise awareness about the environment and the Tunza programme. Each child would plant a minimum of 20 trees each year, help organize a tree planting week in schools or communities and promote recycling. UNEP would establish an online network and bulletin board for the participants, and provide a certification scheme for those who fulfilled the Contract.

UNEP also organized the first Africa Youth Conference on the Environment in the margins of the eleventh regular session of the African Ministerial Conference on the Environment (Brazzaville, Congo, 22-26 May). The Conference was aimed at promoting networking among young people and youth organizations in Africa, in order to maximize youth participation in environmental issues. The "Africa Environmental Outlook for Youth" report was launched during the Conference.

UNEP and the Japan-based Global Sports Alliance organized the fourth Global Forum for Sport and the Environment (Lausanne, Switzerland, 30 November–1 December), which brought together international sports organizations, sporting goods manufacturers, civil society organizations, the media and sports personalities to review sport's impact on and contribution to the environment. Participants also discussed the integration of environmental issues in the development of sports facilities and equipment and the running of sports events.

The seventh Global Civil Society Forum (Dubai, United Arab Emirates, 5-6 February) [UNEP/GCS/7/1] adopted a resolution on chemicals management and submitted it to the first session of the International Conference on Chemicals Management (see p. 1246). It also discussed the outcomes of the Conference; international environmental governance; recommendations to GC/GMEF on tourism and on energy; reports of the Forum's working groups on sustainable tourism, energy for sustainable development and international environmental governance; outcomes of the first Trade Union Assembly on Labour and the Environment (see p. 1214); the perspectives of business and industry and youth on the policy issues considered by the Forum; the Global Environment Outlook (see p. 1218); and civil society engagement with GC/GMEF.

The global civil society statement to the ninth (2006) session of GC/GMEF was contained in a note by the Executive Director [UNEP/GCSS.IX/INF/7]. Regional civil society statements from the African, Asia and the Pacific, European, Latin America and the Caribbean, North American, and West Asian regions were also submitted [UNEP/GCSS.IX/INF/7/Add.1-6].

Cooperation with UN-Habitat

A November progress report [UNEP/GC/24/INF/14], prepared jointly by the Executive Directors of UNEP and UN-Habitat, summarized the objectives and institutional aspects of cooperation between the two organizations; reviewed joint activities; described regional cooperation; presented the results of cooperation; and outlined opportunities for future cooperation. The two programmes were developing a strategic framework for long-term cooperation.

Gender and the environment

In response to a 2005 Governing Council decision on gender equality in the field of the environment [YUN 2005, p. 1142], the Executive Director, in an October report [UNEP/GC/24/8], summarized progress made by UNEP in implementing that decision, and addressed the issues of equal participation in decision-making, gender mainstreaming in environmental policies and programmes, and the assessment of the effects on women of environmental policies.

UNEP, in partnership with the Women's Environment and Development Organization, developed and circulated a questionnaire to the UNEP Committee of Permanent Representatives, permanent missions to the United Nations in Geneva and ministries responsible for the environment, with the aim of sharing examples of gender-sensitive environmental initiatives. UNEP would use the responses to develop a plan for technical assistance to countries, build capacities and develop gender policies and plans of action. The two bodies also developed a mentorship project proposal entitled "Wings on Waves: A Mentorship Programme to Build Young Women's Environmental Leadership", which aimed at creating a cadre of young environmentalists who would take future leadership roles in policy and programme development.

UNEP addressed the issue of gender balance in its activities and formulated plans for the collection of gender-disaggregated data. All UNEP divisions and offices worked to strengthen the involvement of women in their activities and ensure gender balance in participation in capacity-building and training courses. The UNEP Programme Coordination and Management Unit led efforts to improve gender sensitivity in project cycle management.

In June, UNEP held a Senior Management Group Workshop on gender mainstreaming, which considered and adopted a Gender Plan of Action which stipulated that all relevant UNEP environmental policies, programmes and initiatives should be gender-sensitive and employ a conceptual framework that incorporated gender equality and equity. The Plan called for high-level and sustained commitment to internal capacity-building on gender mainstreaming, changes in policy and practice and accountability for implementation, as well as resource mobilization and human resources management. The Plan contained objectives, action steps, a timeline and success indicators. UNEP would implement the Plan of Action in 2006, 2007 and 2008 in collaboration with the internal network of gender focal points, as well as women's groups, gender-environment organizations, scientific institutions, the Network of Women Ministers of Environment, ministries of environment, secretariats of multilateral environmental agreements and other UN organizations. An important outcome of the Plan would be the appointment of a new Senior Gender Advisor in 2007, in the office of the Executive Director, to increase the internal capacity of UNEP and foster external partnerships

The UNEP Environmental Education and Training Unit streamlined gender issues in its activities, including the development of gender-sensitive publications and toolkits, and the release of materials to promote equality between men and women in their behavioural patterns in relation to the environment. A project proposal was developed to improve environmental management and expand gender equity and women's rights through collaboration with the United Nations Committee on the Elimination of Discrimination against Women and other relevant human rights bodies.

Recognizing that women's empowerment was an effective tool to combat poverty, hunger and environmental degradation, UNEP intensified efforts to ensure the full implementation of the Governing Council's 2005 decision on gender and the environment.

General Assembly issues

The Executive Director provided information on issues arising from resolutions adopted by the General Assembly in 2005 that called for action by, or were of relevance to, UNEP [UNEP/GCSS.IX/INF/3].

Global Environment Outlook Year Book

UNEP published the Global Environment Outlook (GEO) *Year Book 2006*, which presented a global and regional overview of the state of the environment; highlighted the linkages between environmental well-being, vulnerability and poverty; provided recent findings on the value of ecosystem services; and described new findings on polar and ocean changes. The *Year Book 2006* focused on the environmental, socio-economic and public health impacts of energy-related air pollution.

Administrative and budgetary matters

Budget execution

A January note by the Executive Director [UNEP/GCSS.IX/INF/4] contained information on the execution of the UNEP 2004-2005 biennial budget, showing total provisional income for the biennium, including from the UN regular budget, the Environment Fund, trust funds, trust fund support and earmarked contributions, amounting to $383.6 million, and expenditures totalling $290.1 million. The balance in the funds, as at 31 December 2005, was projected at $93.6 million.

Board of Auditors report

A November note by the Executive Director [UNEP/GC/24/INF/7] contained the report of the Board of Auditors, which included the financial report and audited financial statements for the biennium ended 31 December 2005 [A/61/5/Add.6]. UNEP financial statements covered the major funds, including the Environment Fund, general trust funds, the Multilateral Fund for the Implementation of the Montreal Protocol on Substances that Deplete the Ozone Layer, Technical Cooperation Trust Funds and other trust funds. The Environment Fund reported a total income of $121.2 million, against expenditures of $126.3 million, resulting in a net shortfall of $5 million (4 per cent), as compared with $11.2 million in 2002-2003. The general trust funds showed a shortfall of income relative to expenditure of $2.1 million, compared to $8.6 million for 2002-2003. The increase in income was sufficient to cope with increased expenditures, which were attributable to a rise in the costs of contractual services of $66 million (71 per cent), from $93 million in 2002-2003 to $159 million in 2004-2005, as well as an increase in staff and other personnel costs of $38 million (22 per cent), from $178 million in 2002-2003 to over $217 million in 2004-2005. The Multilateral Fund reported a net shortfall of income over expenditures of $44.6 million, compared with a net excess of income over expenditures of $16.2 million for 2002-2003.

The Board made recommendations relating to unliquidated obligations; the submission of travel claims; financial management and control; cash management; non-expendable property; consultancy services; gender distribution; inactive trust funds; programme management; voluntary contributions receivable; and the presentation and disclosure of financial statements of the Multilateral Fund.

Strengthening of UNEP financing

In response to a 2005 Governing Council decision [YUN 2005, p. 1145], the Executive Director submitted a note [UNEP/GCSS.IX/INF/6] providing information on all aspects of the financial strengthening of UNEP. He reported that UNEP had been successful in implementing the resources mobilization strategy approved by GC/GMEF in 2001 [YUN 2001, p. 953], achieving a 44 per cent increase in contributions over the 2001-2005 period, well within the strategic target of 5-10 per cent annual increase in financial resources envisaged in the strategy. In 2005, 121 donor countries made pledges and contributions to the Environment Fund of approximately $59.2 million.

The introduction of the pilot phase of the voluntary indicative scale of contributions, which began in 2003 [YUN 2003, p. 1048] and was extended to 2004-2005 [YUN 2004, p. 1049], proved to be an efficient approach in stimulating additional contributions to the Environment Fund. By November 2005, more than 75 per cent of contributions paid were above or close to the levels proposed in the voluntary indicative scale, compared to 80 per cent in 2004. The introduction of the pilot phase resulted in a significant broadening of the donor base, higher voluntary payments to the Environment Fund, improved financial stability, and higher predictability of voluntary contributions. In accordance with the Governing Council's 2005 decision, UNEP prepared a new voluntary indicative scale for the 2006-2007 biennium, which took into consideration an increased level of annual contributions, from $65 million to $72 million. Donors were notified of the proposed scale and invited to inform the Executive Director of whether they intended to use it. By November 2005, more than 75 per cent of donor countries supported the proposed scale and agreed to make their contributions accordingly; about 15 percent agreed with the need to strengthen UNEP financing and declared increased contributions in the next biennium, though still below the proposed levels; and 7 per cent confirmed the same level of payments in 2006-2007, which were below the invited level of voluntary contributions.

In the 2004-2005 period, direct support to the UNEP work programme from trust funds was expected to reach approximately $79 million, which was about 30 per cent higher than the figure of $60 million for the 2002-2003 biennium. The amount of trust fund support fees charged to UNEP trust funds was expected to increase from $17.4 million in 2002-2003 to $20.9 in 2004-2005.

In the 2004-2005 biennium, UNEP received $10.5 million from the UN regular budget, 17 per cent more than the figure of $9 million for the 2002-2003 biennium. It was expected that UNEP would receive an additional $1.5 million from the UN regular budget in the 2006-2007 biennium.

In 2005, the Executive Director initiated a comprehensive review of UNEP, including its management and organization. The main goals of the review were to analyse the mechanisms for project planning, development and implementation and allocation of resources; make recommendations for improving and streamlining the planning, programming and budgetary process, as well as the implementation of the Bali Strategic Plan on Technology Support and Capacity-building, adopted by the Council in 2005 [YUN 2005, p. 1135]; and develop appropriate programmatic and management performance indicators. During the second phase of the review, UNEP would receive and select recommendations for implementation. The long-term aim of the review project was to improve UNEP organizational effectiveness, including the management of financial resources.

Election of Executive Director

By **decision 60/409 B** of 16 March, the General Assembly, on the proposal of the Secretary-General [A/60/718], elected Mr. Achim Steiner (Germany) as Executive Director of UNEP for a four-year term of office beginning on 15 June 2006 and ending on 14 June 2010.

International conventions and mechanisms

In response to General Assembly resolutions 60/197 [YUN 2005, p. 1146], 60/201 [ibid., p. 1151] and 60/202 [ibid., p. 1149], the Secretary-General, by an August note [A/61/225], transmitted reports submitted by the secretariats of the United Nations Framework Convention on Climate Change (see below), the United Nations Convention to Combat Desertification in Those Countries Experiencing Serious Drought and/or Desertification, Particularly in Africa (see p. 1225), and the Convention on Biological Diversity) (see p. 1223), respectively.

Climate change convention

As at 31 December, 190 States and the European Commission (EC) were parties to the United Nations Framework Convention on Climate Change (UNFCCC), which was opened for signature in 1992

[YUN 1992, p. 681] and entered into force in 1994 [YUN 1994, p. 938].

As at 31 December, 168 States and the EC were parties to the Kyoto Protocol to the Convention [YUN 1997, p. 1048], which entered into force in 2005 [YUN 2005, p. 1146].

The twelfth session of the Conference of the Parties to UNFCCC (Nairobi, 6-17 November) [FCCC/CP/2006/5 & Add.1] decided to allow Croatia to add to its 1990 level of greenhouse gas emissions not controlled by the Montreal Protocol on Substances that Deplete the Ozone Layer [YUN 1985, p. 804], in order to establish the level of emissions for the base year for implementation of its commitments under article 4, paragraph 2, of the Convention. It also decided to continue the pilot phase for activities implemented jointly by developed country parties and other parties included in annex I to reduce greenhouse gases or enhance their removal. Other decisions related to capacity building; the development and transfer of technologies; the operation of the Special Climate Change Fund; the review of the Convention's financial mechanism; additional guidance to the Global Environment Facility (GEF) as an operating entity of the financial mechanism; and other administrative and financial matters.

The second Conference of the Parties serving as the meeting of the Parties to the Kyoto Protocol, held concurrently with the twelfth Conference of the Parties [FCCC/KP/CMP/2006/10 & Add.1], adopted an amendment, proposed by Belarus, to annex B to the Protocol, which listed the quantified emission limitation or reduction commitment as a percentage of base year or period for each party to the Protocol. Other decisions related to the Protocol's clean development mechanism; implementation of article 6 of the Protocol dealing with the transfer or acquisition of emission reduction units; the Protocol's Compliance Committee; the Adaptation Fund; capacity building under the Protocol; the review of the Protocol pursuant to article 9; submissions by Italy regarding forest management under article 3 of the Protocol; privileges and immunities for individuals serving on constituted bodies under the Protocol; and administrative, financial and institutional matters.

In August, the Executive Board of the Protocol's clean development mechanism issued its annual report to the Conference of the Parties serving as the Meeting of the Parties to the Protocol [FCCC/KP/CMP/2006/4 & Corr.1] covering the period from 28 November 2005 to 21 July 2006; a November addendum to the report [FCCC/KP/CMP/2006/4/Add.1 (Parts I & II)] covering the period 22 July–1 November contained the clean development mechanism management plan 2007-2008.

The Subsidiary Body for Scientific and Technological Advice (SBSTA) [FCCC/SBSTA/2006/5 & Add.1] and the Subsidiary Body for Implementation (SBI) [FCCC/SBI/2006/11] held their twenty-fourth sessions in Bonn, Germany, on 18-26 May and 18-25 May, respectively. SBSTA [FCCC/SBSTA/2006/11] and SBI [FCCC/SBI/2006/28] also held their twenty-fifth sessions (Nairobi, 6-14 November) in 2006.

GENERAL ASSEMBLY ACTION

On 20 December [meeting 83], the General Assembly, on the recommendation of the Second Committee [A/61/422/Add.4], adopted **resolution 61/201** by recorded vote (137-0-47) [agenda item 53 *(d)*].

Protection of global climate for present and future generations of mankind

The General Assembly,

Recalling its resolution 54/222 of 22 December 1999, its decision 55/443 of 20 December 2000 and its resolutions 56/199 of 21 December 2001, 57/257 of 20 December 2002, 58/243 of 23 December 2003, 59/234 of 22 December 2004 and 60/197 of 22 December 2005 and other resolutions relating to the protection of the global climate for present and future generations of mankind,

Recalling also the provisions of the United Nations Framework Convention on Climate Change, including the acknowledgement that the global nature of climate change calls for the widest possible cooperation by all countries and their participation in an effective and appropriate international response, in accordance with their common but differentiated responsibilities and respective capabilities and their social and economic conditions,

Recalling further the United Nations Millennium Declaration, in which Heads of State and Government resolved to make every effort to ensure the entry into force of the Kyoto Protocol and to embark on the required reduction in emissions of greenhouse gases,

Recalling the Johannesburg Declaration on Sustainable Development, the Plan of Implementation of the World Summit on Sustainable Development ("Johannesburg Plan of Implementation"), the Delhi Ministerial Declaration on Climate Change and Sustainable Development, adopted by the Conference of the Parties to the United Nations Framework Convention on Climate Change at its eighth session, held in New Delhi from 23 October to 1 November 2002, the outcome of the ninth session of the Conference of the Parties, held in Milan, Italy, from 1 to 12 December 2003, the outcome of the tenth session of the Conference of the Parties, held in Buenos Aires from 6 to 18 December 2004, and the outcome of the eleventh session of the Conference of the Parties and the first session of the Conference of the Parties serving as the Meeting of the Parties to the Kyoto

Protocol, held in Montreal, Canada, from 28 November to 10 December 2005,

Reaffirming the Mauritius Declaration and the Mauritius Strategy for the Further Implementation of the Programme of Action for the Sustainable Development of Small Island Developing States,

Recalling the 2005 World Summit Outcome,

Remaining deeply concerned that all countries, in particular developing countries, including the least developed countries and small island developing States, face increased risks from the negative effects of climate change, and stressing the need to address adaptation needs relating to such effects,

Noting that one hundred and eighty-nine States and one regional economic integration organization have ratified the Convention,

Noting also that, to date, the Kyoto Protocol to the United Nations Framework Convention on Climate Change has attracted one hundred and sixty-six ratifications, including from parties mentioned in annex I to the Convention, which account for 61.6 per cent of emissions,

Noting further the work of the Intergovernmental Panel on Climate Change and the need to build and enhance scientific and technological capabilities, inter alia, through continuing support to the Panel for the exchange of scientific data and information, especially in developing countries, and noting the pending release of the fourth assessment report,

Reaffirming its commitment to the ultimate objective of the Convention, namely, to stabilize greenhouse gas concentrations in the atmosphere at a level that prevents dangerous anthropogenic interference with the climate system,

Taking note of the report of the Executive Secretary of the United Nations Framework Convention on Climate Change on the work of the Conference of the Parties to the Convention,

1. *Calls upon* States to work cooperatively towards achieving the ultimate objective of the United Nations Framework Convention on Climate Change;

2. *Notes* the commitments, initiatives and processes undertaken within the framework of the United Nations Framework Convention on Climate Change, as well as the Kyoto Protocol thereto for those which are parties to it, to meet the ultimate objective of the Convention;

3. *Also notes* that States that have ratified the Kyoto Protocol welcome the entry into force of the Protocol on 16 February 2005 and strongly urge States that have not yet done so to ratify it in a timely manner;

4. *Stresses* that the seriousness of climate change argues for the implementation of the provisions of the Framework Convention;

5. *Notes with interest* the activities undertaken under the flexible mechanisms established by the Kyoto Protocol;

6. *Takes note* of the outcome of the eleventh and twelfth sessions of the Conference of the Parties to the Framework Convention and the first and second sessions of the Conference of the Parties serving as the Meeting of the Parties to the Kyoto Protocol;

7. *Takes note with appreciation* of the outcome of the fourth replenishment of the Global Environment Facility Trust Fund, including the pledges made by the international community to the Trust Fund at the third Global Environment Facility Assembly, held in Cape Town, South Africa, on 29 and 30 August 2006, and stresses the importance of the fulfilment of the commitments;

8. *Also takes note with appreciation* of the hosting by the Government of Kenya of the twelfth session of the Conference of the Parties to the Framework Convention and the second session of the Conference of the Parties serving as the Meeting of the Parties to the Kyoto Protocol, held in Nairobi from 6 to 17 November 2006, and further takes note with appreciation of the offer of the Government of Indonesia to host the thirteenth session of the Conference of the Parties and the third session of the Meeting of the Parties to the Kyoto Protocol, to be held in Bali from 3 to 14 December 2007;

9. *Notes* the ongoing work of the liaison group of the secretariats and offices of the relevant subsidiary bodies of the Framework Convention, the United Nations Convention to Combat Desertification in Those Countries Experiencing Serious Drought and/or Desertification, Particularly in Africa, and the Convention on Biological Diversity, and encourages cooperation to promote complementarities among the three secretariats while respecting their independent legal status;

10. *Endorses* the continuation of the institutional linkage of the secretariat of the Framework Convention to the United Nations until such time as a review is deemed necessary by the Conference of the Parties or the General Assembly;

11. *Invites* the secretariat of the Framework Convention to report to the General Assembly at its sixty-second session on the work of the Conference of the Parties;

12. *Invites* the conferences of the parties to the multilateral environmental conventions, when setting the dates of their meetings, to take into consideration the schedule of meetings of the General Assembly and the Commission on Sustainable Development so as to ensure the adequate representation of developing countries at those meetings;

13. *Decides* to include in the provisional agenda of its sixty-second session the sub-item entitled "Protection of global climate for present and future generations of mankind".

RECORDED VOTE ON RESOLUTION 61/201:

In favour: Afghanistan, Algeria, Angola, Antigua and Barbuda, Argentina, Armenia, Azerbaijan, Bahamas, Bahrain, Bangladesh, Barbados, Belarus, Belize, Benin, Bhutan, Bolivia, Botswana, Brazil, Brunei Darussalam, Burkina Faso, Burundi, Cambodia, Cameroon, Cape Verde, Central African Republic, Chile, China, Colombia, Comoros, Congo, Costa Rica, Côte d'Ivoire, Cuba, Democratic People's Republic of Korea, Democratic Republic of the Congo, Djibouti, Dominica, Dominican Republic, Ecuador, Egypt, El Salvador, Eritrea, Ethiopia, Fiji, Gabon, Gambia, Ghana, Grenada, Guatemala, Guinea, Guinea-Bissau, Guyana, Haiti, Honduras, India, Indonesia, Iran, Iraq, Jamaica,

Japan, Jordan, Kazakhstan, Kenya, Kuwait, Kyrgyzstan, Lao People's Democratic Republic, Lebanon, Lesotho, Liberia, Libyan Arab Jamahiriya, Madagascar, Malawi, Malaysia, Maldives, Mali, Marshall Islands, Mauritania, Mauritius, Mexico, Micronesia, Mongolia, Morocco, Mozambique, Myanmar, Namibia, Nauru, Nepal, Nicaragua, Niger, Nigeria, Oman, Pakistan, Palau, Panama, Papua New Guinea, Paraguay, Peru, Philippines, Qatar, Republic of Korea, Russian Federation, Saint Kitts and Nevis, Saint Lucia, Saint Vincent and the Grenadines, Samoa, Sao Tome and Principe, Saudi Arabia, Senegal, Sierra Leone, Singapore, Solomon Islands, Somalia, South Africa, Sri Lanka, Sudan, Suriname, Swaziland, Syrian Arab Republic, Thailand, Timor-Leste, Togo, Tonga, Trinidad and Tobago, Tunisia, Turkmenistan, Uganda, United Arab Emirates, United Republic of Tanzania, United States, Uruguay, Uzbekistan, Vanuatu, Venezuela, Viet Nam, Yemen, Zambia, Zimbabwe.

Against: None.

Abstaining: Albania, Andorra, Australia, Austria, Belgium, Bulgaria, Canada, Croatia, Cyprus, Czech Republic, Denmark, Estonia, Finland, France, Georgia, Germany, Greece, Hungary, Iceland, Ireland, Israel, Italy, Latvia, Liechtenstein, Lithuania, Luxembourg, Malta, Moldova, Monaco, Montenegro, Netherlands, New Zealand, Norway, Poland, Portugal, Romania, San Marino, Serbia, Slovakia, Slovenia, Spain, Sweden, Switzerland, The former Yugoslav Republic of Macedonia, Turkey, Ukraine, United Kingdom.

Vienna Convention and Montreal Protocol

As at 31 December, 190 States and the EC were parties to the 1985 Vienna Convention for the Protection of the Ozone Layer [YUN 1985, p. 804], which entered into force in 1998 [YUN 1998, p. 810].

Parties to the Montreal Protocol, which was adopted in 1987 [YUN 1987, p. 868], numbered 190 States and the EC; the 1990 Amendment to the Protocol, 183 and the EC; the 1992 Amendment, 174 and the EC; the 1997 Amendment, 148 and the EC; and the 1999 Amendment, 120 and the EC.

The eighteenth Meeting of the Parties to the Montreal Protocol on Substances that Deplete the Ozone Layer (New Delhi, India, 30 October–3 November) [UNEP/OzL.Pro.18/10] updated the code of conduct for the members of the Ozone secretariat's Technology and Economic Assistance Panel (TEAP), technical options committees and temporary subsidiary bodies and decided to convene, in 2007, a two-day open-ended dialogue on key challenges to be faced by the Protocol. Other decisions related to ratification of the Convention, the Protocol and the amendments thereto; essential-use exemptions for the production of chloroflourocarbons used in metered-dose inhalers for 2007-2008, and the difficulties faced by manufacturers in some States parties; an essential-use exemption for chloroflourocarbon-113 for aerospace applications in the Russian Federation for 2007; terms of reference for case studies on the environmentally sound destruction of ozone-depleting substances; sources of carbon tetrachloride emissions and opportunities for reductions; sources of n-propyl bromide emissions, available alternatives and opportunities for reductions; and future work following the Ozone secretariat workshop (Montreal, Canada, 7 July) [UNEP/OzL.Pro/Workshop.2/2] on the 2005 special report of the Intergovernmental Panel on Climate Change and TEAP on protecting the ozone layer and global climate system [YUN 2005, p. 1148]. Decisions were also made on critical use exemptions for methyl bromide for 2007 and 2008; cooperation between the Protocol and the International Plant Protection Convention on the use of alternatives to methyl bromide for quarantine and pre-shipment; laboratory and analytical critical uses of methyl bromide; the treatment of stockpiled ozone-depleting substances; preventing illegal trade in ozone-depleting substances; Mexico's request for a change in baseline data for 1998 for its consumption of carbon tetrachloride; the establishment of licensing systems under the Protocol; data and information provided by the parties to the Protocol; compliance issues; and administrative and budgetary matters.

The Implementing Committee under the Non-compliance Procedure held its thirty-sixth (Montreal, Canada, 30 June–1 July) [UNEP/OzL.Pro/ImpCom/36/7] and thirty-seventh (New Delhi, India, 25-27 October) [UNEP/OzL.Pro/ImpCom/37/7] meetings.

Convention on air pollution

As at 31 December, 50 States and the EC were parties to the 1979 Convention on Long-Range Transboundary Air Pollution [YUN 1979, p. 710], which entered into force in 1983 [YUN 1983, p. 645]. Eight protocols to the Convention dealt with the programme for monitoring and evaluation of the pollutants in Europe (1984), the reduction of sulphur emissions or their transboundary fluxes by at least 30 percent (1985), the control of emissions of nitrogen oxides or their transboundary fluxes (1988), the control of volatile organic compounds or their transboundary fluxes (1991), further reduction of sulphur emissions (1984), heavy metals (1998), persistent organic pollutants (POPs) (1998) and the abatement of acidification, eutrophication and ground-level ozone (1999).

The twenty-third session of the Executive Body for the Convention (Geneva, 11-14 December) [ECE/EB.AIR/89 & Corr.1, 2 & Add.1] adopted decisions on data availability under the Convention; the structure and functions of the Implementation Committee and its procedures for the review of compliance by the parties to the protocols to the Convention; accreditation of non-governmental organizations

(NGOs) to attend meetings under the Convention; funding for travel by Convention secretariat staff; the participation of countries with economies in transition in the activities of the Executive Body; and compliance with reporting obligations.

Convention on Biological Diversity

As at 31 December, 189 States and the EC were parties to the 1992 Convention on Biological Diversity [YUN 1992, p. 638], which entered into force in 1993 [YUN 1993, p. 210].

At year's end, the number of parties to the Cartagena Protocol on Biosafety, which was adopted in 2000 [YUN 2000, p. 973] and entered into force in 2003 [YUN 2003, p. 1051], stood at 136 States and the EC. During the year, 7 countries became parties to the Protocol.

The eighth meeting of the Conference of the Parties to the Convention (Curitiba, Brazil, 20-31 March) [UNEP/CBD/COP/8/31] adopted the programme of work on island biodiversity and the framework for a cross-cutting initiative on biodiversity for food and nutrition. In a decision on the Global Initiative on Communication, Education and Public Awareness, the Conference adopted the implementation plan for the Initiative and invited the General Assembly to consider for adoption a draft resolution proclaiming 2010 as the International Year of Biodiversity (see p. 1225). Other decisions adopted by the Conference related to the biological diversity of dry and sub-humid lands, inland water ecosystems, marine and coastal ecosystems and forests; the Global Taxonomy Initiative; access and benefit sharing; article 8(j) of the Convention on traditional knowledge; the *Global Biodiversity Outlook 2* report, launched on 20 March, and national reporting and the third *Outlook* report; implementation of the Convention and its Strategic Plan (2002-2010), adopted in 2002 [YUN 2002, p. 1045]; implementation of the findings of the Millennium Ecosystem Assessment (see p. 1228); scientific and technical cooperation and the clearing house mechanism; technology transfer and cooperation; and the framework for monitoring and implementing the 2010 target for a significant reduction in the rate of loss of biological diversity, adopted in 2002 [YUN 2002, p. 1045]. Further decisions dealt with private sector engagement; cooperation with other conventions and international organizations and initiatives; protected areas; incentive measures; alien species that threatened ecosystems, habitats or species; impact assessment; liability and redress for damage to biological diversity; biological diversity and climate change; the potential impact of the avian influenza on biodiversity; and administrative and budgetary matters.

Economic and Social Council action. On 15 December (**decision 2006/269**), the Economic and Social Council authorized a three-day international expert group meeting on the Convention in Biological Diversity international regime on access and benefit-sharing and indigenous people's human rights, with the participation of representatives from the UN system and five members of the Permanent Forum on Indigenous Issues (see p. 936). It also invited other interested intergovernmental organizations, experts from indigenous organizations and interested Member States to participate, and requested that the meeting's results be reported to the Permanent Forum at its sixth (2007) session.

Cartagena Protocol on Biosafety

The third meeting of the Conference of the Parties to the Convention serving as the Meeting of the Parties to the Cartagena Protocol on Biosafety (Curitiba, Brazil, 13-17 March) [UNEP/CBD/BS/COP-MOP/3/15] adopted an updated action plan for building capacities for the effective implementation of the Protocol and a format for national reporting. Other decisions dealt with compliance; the operation and activities of the Biosafety Clearing-House; strengthening the roster of experts on biosafety; cooperation with other organizations, conventions and initiatives; the handling, transport, packaging and identification of living modified organisms; risk assessment and management; liability and redress under the Protocol; the need for a permanent technical advisory subsidiary body; assessment and review of the implementation of the Protocol; and administrative, budgetary and other issues.

GENERAL ASSEMBLY ACTION

On 20 December [meeting 83], the General Assembly, on the recommendation of the Second Committee [A/61/422/Add.6], adopted **resolution 61/204** without vote [agenda item 53 *(f)*].

Convention on Biological Diversity

The General Assembly,

Recalling its resolutions 55/201 of 20 December 2000, 56/197 of 21 December 2001, 57/253 and 57/260 of 20 December 2002, 58/212 of 23 December 2003, 59/236 of 22 December 2004 and 60/202 of 22 December 2005,

Recalling also the 2005 World Summit Outcome,

Reiterating that the Convention on Biological Diversity is the key international instrument for the conservation and sustainable use of biological resources and the fair and equitable sharing of benefits arising from the use of genetic resources,

Noting that one hundred eighty-eight States and one regional economic integration organization have ratified the Convention,

Recalling the commitments of the World Summit on Sustainable Development to pursue a more efficient and coherent implementation of the three objectives of the Convention and the achievement by 2010 of a significant reduction in the current rate of loss of biological diversity, which will require action at all levels, including the implementation of national biodiversity strategies and action plans and the provision of new and additional financial and technical resources to developing countries,

Concerned by the continued loss of biological diversity, and acknowledging that an unprecedented effort would be needed to achieve by 2010 a significant reduction in the rate of loss of biological diversity,

Acknowledging the contribution that the ongoing work of the Intergovernmental Committee on Intellectual Property and Genetic Resources, Traditional Knowledge and Folklore, of the World Intellectual Property Organization, can make in enhancing the effective implementation of the provisions of the Convention on Biological Diversity,

Noting the contribution that South-South cooperation can make in the area of biological diversity,

Taking note of the reports of the Millennium Ecosystem Assessment,

Expressing its deep appreciation to the Government of Brazil for hosting the eighth meeting of the Conference of the Parties to the Convention on Biological Diversity and the third meeting of the Conference of the Parties to the Convention serving as the Meeting of the Parties to the Cartagena Protocol on Biosafety, held in Curitiba from 20 to 31 March, and from 13 to 17 March 2006, respectively,

Expressing its deep appreciation also to the Government of Germany for its offer to host the ninth meeting of the Conference of the Parties to the Convention on Biological Diversity and the fourth meeting of the Conference of the Parties to the Convention serving as the Meeting of the Parties to the Cartagena Protocol on Biosafety in 2008,

1. *Takes note* of the report of the Executive Secretary of the Convention on Biological Diversity, transmitted by the Secretary-General to the General Assembly at its sixty-first session;

2. *Notes* the outcome of the eighth meeting of the Conference of the Parties to the Convention on Biological Diversity;

3. *Notes also* the outcome of the third meeting of the Conference of the Parties to the Convention serving as the Meeting of the Parties to the Cartagena Protocol on Biosafety;

4. *Notes further* the progress made with respect to the achievement of the three objectives set out in the Convention on Biological Diversity;

5. *Urges* all Member States to fulfil their commitments to significantly reduce the rate of loss of biodiversity by 2010, and emphasizes that this will require an appropriate focus on the loss of biodiversity in their relevant policies and programmes and the continued provision of new and additional financial and technical resources to developing countries, including through the Global Environment Facility;

6. *Reiterates* the commitment of States parties to the Convention on Biological Diversity and the Cartagena Protocol on Biosafety to support the implementation of the Convention and the Protocol, as well as other biodiversity-related agreements and the Johannesburg commitment to a significant reduction in the rate of loss of biodiversity by 2010, and to continue to negotiate within the framework of the Convention, bearing in mind the Bonn Guidelines, an international regime to promote and safeguard the fair and equitable sharing of benefits arising out of the utilization of genetic resources, and urges all States to commit to significantly reducing the rate of loss of biodiversity by 2010 and to continue ongoing efforts to elaborate and negotiate an international regime on access to genetic resources and benefit-sharing;

7. *Notes* the progress made in the Ad Hoc Open-ended Working Group on Access and Benefit-sharing towards elaborating and negotiating the international regime, as well as the decision of the eighth meeting of the Conference of the Parties to complete the work of the Ad Hoc Open-ended Working Group at the earliest possible time, before the tenth meeting of the Conference of the Parties to be held in 2010, and urges parties to make every effort to complete the work within the established time frame;

8. *Reaffirms* the commitment, subject to national legislation, to respect, preserve and maintain the knowledge, innovations and practices of indigenous and local communities embodying traditional lifestyles relevant to the conservation and sustainable use of biological diversity, promote their wider application with the approval and involvement of the holders of such knowledge, innovations and practices and encourage the equitable sharing of the benefits arising from their utilization;

9. *Notes* the progress made in the thematic programmes of work of the Convention on Biological Diversity;

10. *Notes also* the progress made at the third meeting of the Conference of the Parties to the Convention serving as the Meeting of the Parties to the Cartagena Protocol on Biosafety and the continuing efforts made towards the implementation of the Protocol, and stresses that this will require the full support of parties and of relevant international organizations, in particular with regard to the provision of assistance to developing countries, as well as countries with economies in transition, in capacity-building for biosafety;

11. *Takes note with appreciation* of the outcome of the fourth replenishment of the Global Environment Facility, including the pledges made by the international community to the Global Environment Facility Trust Fund, at the third Global Environment Facility Assembly, held in Cape Town, South Africa, on 29 and 30 August 2006, and stresses the importance of fulfilment of the commitments;

12. *Invites* the countries that have not yet done so to ratify or to accede to the Convention;

13. *Invites* the parties to the Convention that have not yet ratified or acceded to the Cartagena Protocol on Biosafety to consider doing so;

14. *Invites* countries to consider ratifying or acceding to the International Treaty on Plant Genetic Resources for Food and Agriculture;

15. *Encourages* developed countries parties to the Convention to contribute to the relevant trust funds of the Convention, in particular so as to enhance the full participation of the developing countries parties in all of its activities;

16. *Urges* parties to the Convention on Biological Diversity to facilitate the transfer of technology for the effective implementation of the Convention in accordance with its provisions;

17. *Takes note* of the ongoing work of the liaison group of the secretariats and offices of the relevant subsidiary bodies of the United Nations Framework Convention on Climate Change, the United Nations Convention to Combat Desertification in Those Countries Experiencing Serious Drought and/or Desertification, Particularly in Africa, and the Convention on Biological Diversity, and further encourages continuing cooperation in order to promote complementarities among the secretariats, while respecting their independent legal status;

18. *Stresses* the importance of reducing duplicative reporting requirements of the biodiversity-related conventions, while respecting their independent legal status and their independent mandates;

19. *Invites* the Executive Secretary of the Convention on Biological Diversity to continue reporting to the General Assembly on the ongoing work regarding the Convention, including its Cartagena Protocol;

20. *Decides* to include in the provisional agenda of its sixty-second session, under the item entitled "Sustainable development", the sub-item entitled "Convention on Biological Diversity".

International Year of Biodiversity (2010)

On 20 December [meeting 83], the General Assembly, on the recommendation of the Second Committee [A/61/422/Add.6], adopted **resolution 61/203** without vote [agenda item 53 *(f)*].

International Year of Biodiversity, 2010

The General Assembly,

Recalling chapter 15 of Agenda 21 on the conservation of biological diversity adopted by the United Nations Conference on Environment and Development,

Recalling also the Convention on Biological Diversity, which was ratified by one hundred and eighty-eight States and one regional economic integration organization, and the Cartagena Protocol on Biosafety to the Convention on Biological Diversity,

Recalling the commitment of the World Summit on Sustainable Development to a more effective and coherent implementation of the three objectives of the Convention, and the target to achieve by 2010 a significant reduction in the current rate of loss of biodiversity,

Recalling also the Plan of Implementation of the World Summit on Sustainable Development ("Johannesburg Plan of Implementation"),

Recalling further the 2005 World Summit Outcome,

Recalling the need to expedite the implementation of the Global Initiative on Communication, Education and Public Awareness of the Convention on Biological Diversity,

Concerned by the continued loss of biological diversity, and acknowledging that an unprecedented effort would be needed to achieve by 2010 a significant reduction in the rate of loss of biological diversity,

Deeply concerned by the social, economic, environmental and cultural implications of the loss of biodiversity, including negative impacts on the achievement of the Millennium Development Goals, and stressing the necessity to adopt concrete measures in order to reverse it,

Taking note of the reports of the Millennium Ecosystem Assessment,

Conscious of the need for effective education to raise public awareness for achieving the threefold objective of the Convention and the 2010 biodiversity target,

1. *Declares* 2010 the International Year of Biodiversity;

2. *Designates* the secretariat of the Convention on Biological Diversity as the focal point for the International Year of Biodiversity, and invites the secretariat to cooperate with other relevant United Nations bodies, multilateral environmental agreements, international organizations and other stakeholders, with a view to bringing greater international attention to bear on the issue of the continued loss of biodiversity;

3. *Invites* Member States to consider establishing national committees for the International Year of Biodiversity;

4. *Encourages* Member States and other stakeholders to take advantage of the International Year of Biodiversity to increase awareness of the importance of biodiversity by promoting actions at the local, regional and international levels;

5. *Invites* Member States and relevant international organizations to support the activities to be organized by developing countries, especially least developed countries, landlocked developing countries and small island developing States, and countries with economies in transition;

6. *Invites* relevant international organizations as well as relevant global and regional environmental conventions to communicate to the focal point for the International Year of Biodiversity efforts made towards the successful implementation of the objective of the Year;

7. *Requests* the Secretary-General to submit to the General Assembly at its sixty-sixth session a report on the implementation of the present resolution.

Convention to combat desertification

As at 31 December, the total number of parties to the 1994 United Nations Convention to Combat Desertification in Those Countries Experiencing

Serious Drought and/or Desertification, Particularly in Africa (UNCCD) [YUN 1994, p. 944], which entered into force in 1996 [YUN 1996, p. 958], remained at 190 States and the EC.

The Secretary-General, in his August report on the implementation of UN environmental conventions [A/61/225], provided information on the implementation of UNCCD.

GENERAL ASSEMBLY ACTION

On 20 December [meeting 83], the General Assembly, on the recommendation of the Second Committee [A/61/422/Add.5], adopted **resolution 61/202** without vote [agenda item 53 *(e)*].

Implementation of the United Nations Convention to Combat Desertification in Those Countries Experiencing Serious Drought and/or Desertification, Particularly in Africa

The General Assembly,

Recalling its resolution 60/201 of 22 December 2005 and other resolutions relating to the United Nations Convention to Combat Desertification in Those Countries Experiencing Serious Drought and/or Desertification, Particularly in Africa,

Reaffirming the Plan of Implementation of the World Summit on Sustainable Development ("Johannesburg Plan of Implementation"), which recognizes the Convention as one of the tools for poverty eradication,

Recalling the 2005 World Summit Outcome,

Reaffirming the universal membership of the Convention, and acknowledging that desertification and drought are problems of a global dimension in that they affect all regions in the world,

Noting that the timely and effective implementation of the Convention would help to achieve the internationally agreed development goals, including the Millennium Development Goals, and encouraging affected country parties to include, as appropriate, in their national development strategies measures to combat desertification,

Recognizing the need for the provision of adequate resources for Global Environment Facility focal areas, including a focus on land degradation, primarily desertification and deforestation,

Stressing the need for further diversification of funding sources to address land degradation, in accordance with articles 20 and 21 of the Convention,

Noting the decision of the Conference of the Parties to the Convention at its seventh session to establish an ad hoc intergovernmental intersessional working group with the mandate to review the report of the Joint Inspection Unit in full and, building on the results of that review and other inputs, to develop a draft ten-year strategic plan and framework to enhance the implementation of the Convention,

Recognizing the need to provide the secretariat of the Convention with stable, adequate and predictable resources in order to enable it to continue to discharge its responsibilities in an efficient and timely manner, and further recognizing the provision in section A on budget reform in the decision of the Conference of the Parties at its seventh session on the programme and budget for the biennium 2006-2007, including the request that the Executive Secretary take additional measures necessary to address the recommendations of the Joint Inspection Unit, ensure that the financial rules are fully respected in the future and report on this matter to the meeting of the Bureau and in the performance report for the biennium 2006-2007,

Noting the decision of the Conference of the Parties at its seventh session to introduce the euro as the budget and accounting currency from 2008-2009,

Recalling its resolution 58/211 of 23 December 2003, in which it declared 2006 the International Year of Deserts and Desertification,

Noting the activities undertaken within the framework of the celebration of the Year,

Underlining the importance of the issue of desertification in the process of the Commission on Sustainable Development, in particular in the context of its sixteenth and seventeenth sessions dealing with thematic clusters on agriculture, rural development, land, drought and desertification,

1. *Takes note* of the report of the Secretary-General;

2. *Reaffirms* its resolve to support and strengthen the implementation of the United Nations Convention to Combat Desertification in Those Countries Experiencing Serious Drought and/or Desertification, Particularly in Africa to address causes of desertification and land degradation, as well as poverty resulting from land degradation, through, inter alia, the mobilization of adequate and predictable financial resources, the transfer of technology and capacity-building at all levels;

3. *Reiterates its call* upon Governments, where appropriate, in collaboration with relevant multilateral organizations, including the Global Environment Facility implementation agencies, to integrate desertification into their plans and strategies for sustainable development;

4. *Takes note with appreciation* of the outcome of the fourth replenishment of the Global Environment Facility Trust Fund, including the pledges made by the international community to the Trust Fund at the third Global Environment Facility Assembly, held in Cape Town, South Africa, on 29 and 30 August 2006, and stresses the importance of the fulfilment of the commitments;

5. *Invites* the Global Environment Facility to continue to make resources available for capacity-building activities in affected country parties implementing the Convention;

6. *Welcomes* the establishment of the ad hoc intergovernmental intersessional working group with the mandate to review the report of the Joint Inspection Unit in full and, building on the results of that review and other inputs, to develop a draft ten-year strategic plan and framework to enhance the implementation of the Convention, for submission to the Conference of the Parties to the Convention at its eighth session, and invites parties to the Convention, as well as other stakeholders, to sub-

mit views and comments to the working group in order to assist it in its work;

7. *Invites* parties to contribute on a voluntary basis either to the Supplementary Fund or in kind to cover the cost of the activities of the intergovernmental intersessional working group in order to allow it to fulfil its mandate;

8. *Requests* the Secretary-General, taking into account the institutional linkage and related administrative arrangements between the Convention secretariat and the United Nations Secretariat, to facilitate the implementation of decision 23 of the Conference of the Parties at its seventh session pertaining to the introduction of the euro as the budget and accounting currency of the Convention;

9. *Invites* Member States to be represented at the highest appropriate level at the sessions of the Conference of the Parties to the Convention;

10. *Expresses its appreciation* for the financial contributions made by countries and other relevant stakeholders to carry out activities in the context of the celebration of the International Year of Deserts and Desertification;

11. *Requests* the secretariat of the Commission on Sustainable Development to work closely with the secretariat of the Convention in the preparations for the sixteenth and seventeenth sessions of the Commission in the areas relevant to the Convention;

12. *Takes note* of the ongoing work of the liaison group of the secretariats and offices of the relevant subsidiary bodies of the United Nations Framework Convention on Climate Change, the United Nations Convention to Combat Desertification in Those Countries Experiencing Serious Drought and/or Desertification, Particularly in Africa, and the Convention on Biological Diversity, and further encourages continuing cooperation in order to promote complementarities among the secretariats, while respecting their independent legal status;

13. *Decides* to include in the provisional agenda of its sixty-second session the sub-item entitled "Implementation of the United Nations Convention to Combat Desertification in Those Countries Experiencing Serious Drought and/or Desertification, Particularly in Africa";

14. *Requests* the Secretary-General to report to the General Assembly at its sixty-second session on the implementation of the present resolution.

International Year of Deserts and Desertification

As part of its contributions to the International Year of Deserts and Desertification (2006), declared by the General Assembly in resolution 58/211 [YUN 2003, p. 1055], UNEP launched the *Global Deserts Outlook*, the first thematic report in UNEP Global Environment Outlook (GEO) series of assessments. The report, prepared by international experts, traced the history and biodiversity of deserts; assessed likely changes due to human activity and climate change; and presented policy options that could help Governments provide a more sustainable future for deserts and exploit their potential for generating solar power and supporting industries. UNEP also contributed to the organization of the International Scientific Conference on the Future of Drylands (Tunis, Tunisia, 19-21 June) and the Joint International Conference: Desertification and the International Policy Imperative (Algiers, Algeria, 17-19 December). The UNCCD secretariat, together with Algeria, China and Italy, organized the Beijing Conference on Women and Desertification (Beijing, 29 May–1 June), which highlighted the fundamental role played by women as the main stakeholders in managing natural resources, food production and meeting household needs, including energy and water, in rural areas affected by desertification and drought. In July [ICCD/CRIC(5)/10], the secretariat issued an interim report on the status of the observance of the International Year under the theme "Protection of the biological diversity of the drylands".

Environmental activities

Follow-up to the 2000 Millennium Summit and 2005 World Summit

In response to the Outcome of the 2005 World Summit [YUN 2005, p. 48], the Secretary-General, in November [A/61/583], transmitted to the General Assembly the report of the High-level Panel on United Nations System-wide Coherence in the areas of development, humanitarian assistance and the environment. The report, entitled "Delivering as One", put forward a series of recommendations to overcome the fragmentation of the UN system, so that it could deliver as one, in partnership with and serving the needs of all countries in their efforts to achieve the Millennium Development Goals (MDGs) [YUN 2000, p. 51], and other internationally agreed development goals.

The report stated that environmental priorities had too often been isolated from economic development priorities. However, global environmental degradation, including climate change, would have far-reaching economic and social implications for the world's ability to meet the MDGs. Because the impacts were global and felt disproportionately by the poor, coordinated multilateral action to promote environmental sustainability was urgently required. The Panel recommend that international environmental governance be strengthened and made more coherent in order to improve the effectiveness and targeted actions of UN system environmental activities. To improve system-wide coherence, the Secretary-General should commission an independent assessment of international environmental governance within the UN system. UNEP should be upgraded and given real authority as the UN system environmental policy pillar. UN entities should cooperate more effectively on a thematic basis and through partnerships, with a dedicated agency at the centre. As the major financial mechanism for the global environment, the Global Environment Facility should be strengthened to help developing countries build their capacity, and its resources significantly increased to address the challenge posed by climate change and other environmental issues. The Panel also made a number of recommendations to: ensure that the United Nations helped countries to incorporate environmental issues in their strategies and actions; elevate the status of sustainable development in the UN institutional architecture and in country activities; and achieve the balance among the three pillars—economic, social and environmental—of sustainable development.

Millennium Ecosystem Assessment

The UNEP Governing Council considered a note by the Executive Director [UNEP/GCSS.IX/INF/8] on the findings of the Millennium Ecosystem Assessment (MA), a four-year international assessment, launched in 2001, to evaluate the state of major ecosystems and their links with human well-being. Annexed to the note were extracts from two key MA reports released when the Assessment was completed in 2005: *Living Beyond Our Means: Natural Assets and Human Well-being*, and *Ecosystems and Human Well-being* [YUN 2005, p. 1154].

The atmosphere

Intergovernmental Panel on Climate Change

The twenty-fifth session of the Intergovernmental Panel on Climate Change (IPCC) (Port Louis, Mauritius, 26-28 April) adopted the 2006 IPCC guidelines for national greenhouse gas inventories, rules of procedure for the election of the IPCC bureau and task force bureaus, and the policy and process for admitting observer organizations. It adopted decisions on its programme and budget for 2006-2009, the revised budget for 2006 and the budget for 2007, and further work on emissions scenarios. The Panel also discussed a proposal for a special report on renewable energy; matters related to the United Nations Framework Convention on Climate Change; progress reports of the IPCC working groups; and administrative issues.

Terrestrial ecosystems

Deforestation and forest degradation

United Nations Forum on Forests

The United Nations Forum on Forests (UNFF), at its sixth session (New York, 13-24 February) [E/2006/42 & Corr.2], in its decision (6/1) brought to the attention of the Economic and Social Council, accredited three intergovernmental organizations: the Commission des Forêts d'Afrique Centrale, the Secretariat of the Pacific Community, and the Asia Forest Partnership. UNFF recommended a draft resolution for adoption by the Council on the outcome of the sixth session, containing four global objectives on forests, which focused on urgent priorities for the implementation of sustainable forest management. In resolution 2006/49 (see below), the Council agreed to work to achieve progress towards the achievement of those goals by 2015. The Forum also recommended draft decisions on the proclamation of an International Year of Forests (2011), the report on its sixth session, and the dates, venue and provisional agenda for its seventh (2007) session.

The Forum had before it a note by its secretariat [E/CN.18/2006/2 & Corr.1] on the implementation of a 2005 UNFF decision dealing with the completion of its review process [YUN 2005, p. 1154]; a 29 November 2005 note from Germany [E/CN.18/2006/3] containing the final report of the International Expert Meeting on scoping for a future agreement on forests (Berlin, 16-18 November 2005); a Secretariat note on the accreditation of intergovernmental organizations to UNFF [E/CN.18/2006/4]; and a 21 February letter from Austria [E/CN.18/2006/5] containing an EU proposal on a possible structure and elements of an outcome document of the sixth (2006) UNFF session.

On 24 July, the Council decided that the seventh session of UNFF would be held in New York from 16 to 27 April 2007 (**decision 2006/231**). On 28 July, the Council took note of the report of UNFF on its sixth (2006) session and approved the provisional agenda for its seventh (2007) session (**decision 2006/255**).

ECONOMIC AND SOCIAL COUNCIL ACTION

On 28 July [meeting 43], the Economic and Social Council, on the recommendation of the United Nations Forum on Forests [E/2006/42 & Corr. 2], adopted **resolution 2006/49** without vote [agenda item 13 *(i)*].

Outcome of the sixth session of the United Nations Forum on Forests

The Economic and Social Council,

Recalling and reaffirming its resolution 2000/35 of 18 October 2000,

Also recalling General Assembly resolution 57/270 B of 23 June 2003,

Further recalling the 2005 World Summit Outcome,

Reaffirming its commitment to the Rio Declaration on Environment and Development, including that States have, in accordance with the Charter of the United Nations and the principle of international law, the sovereign right to exploit their own resources pursuant to their own environmental and developmental policies and the responsibility to ensure that activities within their jurisdiction or control do not cause damage to the environment of other States or of areas beyond the limits of national jurisdiction and to the common but differentiated responsibilities of countries, as set out in principle 7 of the Rio Declaration; the Non-Legally Binding Authoritative Statement of Principles for a Global Consensus on the Management, Conservation and Sustainable Development of All Types of Forests (Forest Principles); chapter 11 of Agenda 21; the proposal for action of the Intergovernmental Panel on Forests/Intergovernmental Forum on Forests; resolutions and decisions of the United Nations Forum on Forests; the Johannesburg Declaration on Sustainable Development and the Plan of Implementation of the World Summit on Sustainable Development; the Monterrey Consensus of the International Conference on Financing for Development; and the internationally agreed development goals, including the Millennium Development Goals,

Recalling the existing international legally binding instruments relevant to forests,

Recognizing the importance of the multiple economic, social and environmental benefits derived from goods and services provided by forests and trees outside forests,

Emphasizing that sustainable forest management can contribute significantly to sustainable development, poverty eradication and the achievement of internationally agreed development goals, including the Millennium Development Goals,

Expressing its concern about continued deforestation and forest degradation, as well as the slow rate of afforestation and forest cover recovery and reforestation, and the resulting adverse impact on economies, the environment, including biological diversity, and the livelihoods of at least a billion people and their cultural heritage, and emphasizing the need for more effective implementation of sustainable forest management at all levels to address these critical challenges,

Recognizing the special needs and requirements of countries with fragile forest ecosystems, including those of low forest cover countries,

Emphasizing that effective implementation of sustainable forest management is critically dependent upon adequate resources, including financing, capacity development and the transfer of environmentally sound technologies, and recognizing in particular the need to mobilize increased financial resources, including from innovative sources, for developing countries, including least developed countries, landlocked developing countries and small island developing States, as well as countries with economies in transition,

Recognizing the important contribution of voluntary public-private partnerships and private sector initiatives at all levels to achieving effective implementation of sustainable forest management and supporting national strategies, plans and priorities related to forests,

Also recognizing the need to strengthen political commitment and collective efforts at all levels, to include forests on national and international development agendas, to enhance national policy coordination and international cooperation and to promote intersectoral coordination at all levels for the effective implementation of sustainable management of all types of forests,

Welcoming the accomplishments of the international arrangement on forests since its inception, including the joint initiatives of the Collaborative Partnership on Forests,

Re-emphasizing the importance of the United Nations Forum on Forests as an intergovernmental body on forests within the United Nations and the continued supporting role of the Collaborative Partnership on Forests, and the need for the Forum to continue to provide the Partnership with clear guidance,

Recognizing the need to strengthen interaction between the global forest policy dialogue and regional and subregional level processes,

1. *Decides* to strengthen the international arrangement on forests through the following measures;

2. *Agrees* that to achieve its main objective, as set out in Economic and Social Council resolution 2000/35, the international arrangement on forests will perform the following additional principal functions:

(a) Enhance the contribution of forests to the achievement of the internationally agreed development goals, including the Millennium Development Goals, and to the implementation of the Johannesburg Declaration on Sustainable Development and the Plan of Implementation of the World Summit on Sustainable Development, bearing in mind the Monterrey Consensus of the International Conference on Financing for Development;

(b) Encourage and assist countries, including those with low forest cover, to develop and implement forest conservation and rehabilitation strategies, increase the area of forests under sustainable management and reduce forest degradation and the loss of forest cover in order to maintain and improve their forest resources with a view to enhancing the benefits of forests to meet present and future needs, in particular the needs of indigenous peoples and local communities whose livelihoods depend on forests;

(c) Strengthen interaction between the United Nations Forum on Forests and relevant regional and subregional forest-related mechanisms, institutions and instruments, organizations and processes, with participation of major groups, as identified in Agenda 21 and relevant stakeholders to facilitate enhanced coopera-

tion and effective implementation of sustainable forest management, as well as to contribute to the work of the Forum;

Global objectives on forests

3. *Decides*, with a view to achieving the main objective of the international arrangement on forests and enhancing the contribution of forests to the achievement of the internationally agreed development goals, including the Millennium Development Goals, in particular with respect to poverty eradication and environmental sustainability, and emphasizing in this regard the importance of political commitment and action at all levels for effective implementation of the sustainable management of all types of forests, to set the following shared global objectives on forests and to agree to work globally and nationally to achieve progress towards their achievement by 2015:

Global objective 1

Reverse the loss of forest cover worldwide through sustainable forest management, including protection, restoration, afforestation and reforestation, and increase efforts to prevent forest degradation;

Global objective 2

Enhance forest-based economic, social and environmental benefits, including by improving the livelihoods of forest dependent people;

Global objective 3

Increase significantly the area of protected forests worldwide and other areas of sustainably managed forests, as well as the proportion of forest products from sustainably managed forests;

Global objective 4

Reverse the decline in official development assistance for sustainable forest management and mobilize significantly increased new and additional financial resources from all sources for the implementation of sustainable forest management;

4. *Agrees* that countries, while taking national sovereignty, practices and conditions into account, should make all efforts to contribute to the above-mentioned global objectives through the development or indication of voluntary national measures, policies, actions or specific goals;

Means of implementation

5. *Urges* countries to make concerted efforts to secure sustained high-level political commitment to strengthen the means of implementation, including financial resources, to provide support, in particular for developing countries, including least developed countries, landlocked developing countries and small island developing States, as well as countries with economies in transition, in order to achieve the global objectives and to promote sustainable forest management by:

(a) Reversing the decline in official development assistance for sustainable forest management;

(b) Mobilizing and providing significant new and additional resources for sustainable forest management from private, public, domestic and international sources to and within developing countries, especially the least developed countries, landlocked developing countries and small island developing States, as well as countries with economies in transition;

(c) Strengthening, through new and additional financial resources, provided on a voluntary basis, existing forest-related funds hosted by members of the Collaborative Partnership on Forests, including the National Forest Programme Facility, the Programme on Forests and the Bali Partnership Fund, to support national forest programmes and national actions aimed at implementing sustainable forest management as well as integrating forest issues in national development programmes and, where appropriate, poverty reduction strategies;

(d) Inviting the governing bodies of the National Forest Programme Facility, the Programme on Forests and the Bali Partnership Fund to enhance their contribution to sustainable forest management and the achievement of the global objectives by effectively managing and coordinating among themselves to facilitate access to the funds by developing countries, as well as countries with economies in transition, as appropriate;

(e) Assessing and reviewing the current funding mechanisms, including, if appropriate, the possibility of setting up a voluntary global funding mechanism as a contribution towards achieving the global objectives and implementing sustainable forest management;

(f) Inviting members of the Collaborative Partnership on Forests, in particular the World Bank, as host of the Programme on Forests, to maintain and enhance support to analytical work and knowledge generation and to develop new tools and approaches to key issues within the forest sector, in particular those relevant to the global objectives, in order to support developing countries, as well as countries with economies in transition, in accessing additional national and international funding;

(g) Welcoming the ongoing work of the Global Environment Facility to clarify its focal area strategies and operational programmes, and in this context inviting the Global Environment Facility Council to fully consider the potential for strengthened support of the Facility for sustainable forest management, including the option to establish a separate operational programme on forests, without prejudicing other operational programmes;

(h) Inviting the governing bodies of international financial institutions, development agencies and regional banks to consider ways to generate and facilitate access to resources and to respond to requests from developing countries to finance forest-related activities;

(i) Creating an effective enabling environment for investment in sustainable forest management, including to avoid the loss of forest cover and forest degradation and to support reforestation, afforestation and forest restoration;

(j) Creating an enabling environment for the involvement of and investment by local communities and other forest users in sustainable forest management;

(*k*) Further developing innovative financial mechanisms for generating revenue to support sustainable forest management;

(*l*) Encouraging the development of mechanisms, including systems for attributing proper value, as appropriate, to the benefits derived from goods and services provided by forests and trees outside forests, consistent with relevant national legislation and policies;

(*m*) Fostering access, where appropriate, by households and communities to forest resources and markets;

(*n*) Supporting livelihoods and income diversification from forest products and services for small-scale forest owners, indigenous peoples, including forest-dependent local communities and poor people living in and around forest areas, consistent with sustainable forest management objectives;

6. *Also urges* countries to make concerted efforts to develop and implement national forest programmes, policies and strategies, as appropriate, in order to achieve the global objectives set out in the present resolution and to promote sustainable forest management, through capacity-building and transfer of environmentally sound technologies, including traditional technologies, and taking into account economic, social and environmental priorities specific to countries by:

(*a*) Providing greater support to scientific and technological innovations for sustainable forest management, including innovations that help local communities undertake sustainable forest management;

(*b*) Enhancing the capacity of countries, in particular developing countries, to significantly increase the production of forest products from sustainably managed forests;

(*c*) Integrating national forest programmes or other forest strategies into national strategies for sustainable development, relevant national action plans and, where appropriate, poverty reduction strategies;

(*d*) Promoting international cooperation, including South-South cooperation and triangular cooperation;

(*e*) Promoting the active participation and empowerment of all forest-related stakeholders, especially local and forest-dependent communities, indigenous peoples, women and small-scale private forest owners and forest workers, in the development and implementation of sustainable forest management policies and programmes;

(*f*) Strengthening of mechanisms that enhance sharing and use of best practices in sustainable forest management;

(*g*) Strengthening the capacity of countries to address illegal practices according to national legislation and illegal international trade in forest products in the forest sector, through the promotion of forest law enforcement and governance at the national and subnational and regional and subregional levels, as appropriate;

(*h*) Encouraging the private sector, including timber processors, exporters, and importers, as well as civil society organizations, to develop, promote and implement voluntary instruments with a view to adopting good business practices and improving market transparency;

Enhanced cooperation and cross-sectoral policy and programme coordination

7. *Encourages* countries to enhance cooperation and cross-sectoral policy and programme coordination in order to achieve the global objectives set out in the present resolution and to promote sustainable forest management by:

(*a*) Facilitating implementation of the proposals for action of the Intergovernmental Panel on Forests/Intergovernmental Forum on Forests through clustering and further simplification of the language, as needed, taking into account existing work, and through promoting greater stakeholder understanding of the intent of these proposals;

(*b*) Strengthening forest education and research and development through global, regional and subregional networks, as well as relevant organizations, institutions and centres of excellence in all regions of the world, particularly in developing countries, as well as countries with economies in transition;

(*c*) Strengthening cooperation and partnerships at the regional level, as needed:

(*i*) To increase political, financial and technical support and capacity;

(ii) To develop regional strategies and plans for implementation;

(iii) To collaborate on implementation activities;

(iv) To exchange experiences and lessons learned;

(*d*) Establishing or strengthening multi-stakeholder partnerships and programmes;

8. *Invites* the Collaborative Partnership on Forests to enhance cooperation and cross-sectoral policy and programme coordination by promoting the exchange of forest management-related experiences and good practices and considering the feasibility of serving as a clearing house to facilitate access by developing countries, as well as countries with economies in transition, to better technology for sustainable forest management;

9. *Invites* the relevant multilateral environmental agreements, instruments, processes and United Nations bodies to improve collaboration and cooperation with the international arrangement on forests;

Working modalities

10. *Decides* that, following its seventh session in 2007, the Forum shall meet biennially for a period of up to two weeks on the basis of a focused multi-year programme of work to be adopted by the Forum at its seventh session;

11. *Invites* forest-related regional and subregional bodies, mechanisms and processes, in coordination with the Forum secretariat, as appropriate, to strengthen collaboration and to provide input to the work of the Forum by:

(*a*) Raising awareness of the work of the Forum at the regional and subregional levels;

(*b*) Addressing topics identified in the multi-year programme of work, with a view to sharing with the Forum regional and subregional perspectives on these topics;

(*c*) Encouraging participation of interested members of the Forum, especially from within the region, as well as members of the Collaborative Partnership on Forests, relevant regional organizations and major groups;

12. *Decides* that the Forum will seek to strengthen interaction with major groups and other forest stakeholders in meetings of the Forum;

13. *Recommends* that country-led initiatives address issues identified in the multi-year programme of work for a given cycle;

14. *Emphasizes* that ad hoc expert groups referred to in paragraph 4 (*k*) of Economic and Social Council resolution 2000/35 could be convened to address issues identified in the multi-year programme of work;

15. *Stresses* that the Forum should consider inputs from regional and subregional forest-related bodies, mechanisms and processes and from country-led initiatives, as well as from major groups;

16. *Reaffirms* that the Forum should continue to support participants from developing countries, with priority given to the least developed countries, as well as from countries with economies in transition, in accordance with General Assembly decision 58/554 of 23 December 2003;

17. *Decides* to consider ways of strengthening the secretariat of the Forum, within existing resources, as well as through increased voluntary extrabudgetary resources in order to enable it to fulfil its function more effectively, bearing in mind paragraph 163 *(b)* of the 2005 World Summit Outcome;

18. *Calls upon* interested donor Governments, financial institutions and other organizations to make voluntary financial contributions to the United Nations Forum on Forests Trust Fund, and urges other countries in a position to do so and other interested parties to contribute to the Trust Fund;

Monitoring, assessment and reporting

19. *Agrees* that countries should, on a voluntary basis, submit national reports to the Forum, in accordance with a timetable established by the Forum, on progress made in implementing national measures, policies, actions or specific objectives towards achieving the global objectives set out in the present resolution, taking into consideration, as appropriate, the seven thematic elements of sustainable forest management;

20. *Invites* the member organizations of the Collaborative Partnership on Forests, in collaboration with the Forum, to further harmonize processes for voluntary monitoring, assessment and reporting, taking into account the seven thematic elements for sustainable forest management, with a view to reducing the reporting burden on countries;

21. *Also invites* the Collaborative Partnership on Forests to continue to report in a consolidated manner to the Forum on its initiatives and activities, including progress on the means of implementation, in support of the work of the Forum;

Collaborative Partnership on Forests

22. *Reaffirms* that the Forum will provide guidance to the Collaborative Partnership on Forests, and invites members of the Collaborative Partnership on Forests:

(*a*) To strengthen their collaboration and coordination on forest issues in order to foster progress towards sustainable forest management at the global, regional and national levels;

(*b*) To continue and further develop its ongoing initiatives on monitoring, assessment and reporting on forest resources, on streamlining national forest reporting, on the sourcebook on funding for sustainable forest management, on harmonizing forest-related definitions and on the Global Forest Information Service;

(*c*) To translate relevant policy recommendations of the Forum into their programmes of work;

(*d*) To explore ways to involve major groups in the activities of the Collaborative Partnership on Forests and to strengthen the Partnership's contribution to activities at the regional level;

(*e*) To provide, if requested by the Forum, an assessment of scientific knowledge-based actions needed to achieve sustainable forest management and the global objectives at all levels;

(*f*) To continue to strengthen the Tehran Process, consistent with their mandates and programmes of work, through developing and implementing strategies on conservation and rehabilitation of forests in low forest cover countries;

23. *Welcomes* the joint initiative by the International Union of Forest Research Organizations, the Center for International Forestry Research and the International Centre for Research in Agroforestry, in collaboration with other members of the Collaborative Partnership on Forests, on science and technology in support of the Forum by assessing available information and producing reports on forests-related issues of concern to the Forum;

24. *Urges* States members of the governing bodies of the member organizations of the Collaborative Partnership on Forests to help ensure that their forest-related priorities and programmes are integrated and mutually supportive, consistent with their mandates;

25. *Urges* countries and parties interested in the work of the Collaborative Partnership on Forests to support its joint initiatives by making voluntary financial contributions to the respective lead organizations of the Partnership, as appropriate;

Non-legally binding instrument

26. *Emphasizes* the importance of strengthening political commitment and action at all levels to implement effectively the sustainable management of all types of forests and to achieve the global objectives set out in the present resolution by requesting the Forum to conclude and adopt at its seventh session a non-legally binding instrument on all types of forests, in order to facilitate the work of the Forum in this regard;

27. *Requests* the secretariat of the Forum to circulate to the member States, by 31 July 2006, a compilation of the draft indicative elements and other proposals submitted by members during the sixth session, which

are contained in the annex to the present resolution, as well as any further proposals submitted by members by 30 June 2006;

28. *Invites* the member States to provide comments on the compilation circulated by the Forum secretariat by 31 August 2006, and requests the secretariat to circulate these comments to the member States;

29. *Decides* that the Forum should, within its existing resources, convene an open-ended ad hoc expert group for up to five days to consider the content of the non-legally binding instrument to assist the Forum in its deliberations, drawing on the compilation and comments referred to in paragraphs 27 and 28 above; the group should be convened in time to allow its outputs to be made available in all languages before the seventh session of the Forum and should be open to all member States, members of the organizations of the Collaborative Partnership on Forests and representatives of major groups;

30. *Invites* the member States to consider sponsoring country-led initiatives to contribute to the work of the Forum, emphasizing that such initiatives should be open to and facilitate participation by all members of the Forum, as well as members of the Collaborative Partnership on Forests and representatives of major groups;

31. *Also invites* member States to contribute to the United Nations Forum on Forests Trust Fund in support of the actions outlined in paragraphs 29 and 30 above;

32. *Decides* that the effectiveness of the international arrangement on forests will be reviewed in 2015 and that on this basis a full range of options will be considered, including a legally binding instrument on all types of forests, strengthening the current arrangement, continuation of the current arrangement and other options;

Input to the Commission on Sustainable Development

33. *Decides also* that the Forum should contribute relevant input, as appropriate, to the 2012-2013 cycle of the Commission on Sustainable Development.

Annex

Elements or proposals for a non-legally binding instrument on forests

I. Proposal of the African Group

Elements of a voluntary code/guidelines/international understanding

1. Enhanced capacity-building mechanisms.
2. Recognition of the global importance of forests.
3. Must facilitate or attract strong political support.
4. Must build on strengthening subregional initiatives.
5. Must provide for technological transfer as a means for achievement of sustainable forest management.
6. Must address the three elements (social, environmental and economic) of sustainable forest management.
7. Should include reference to the role of major groups.
8. Should accommodate regional nuances and variations.
9. Should have appropriate institutional arrangements for implementation, including strengthening the role of the Collaborative Partnership on Forests.
10. Clear funding mechanisms to ensure that implementation is facilitated in developing countries.
11. Effective institutional arrangements and working modalities.
12. Enhanced international cooperation and assistance.

II. Proposal of Australia

Potential elements of a voluntary international instrument to support sustainable forest management

Summary

1. **Purpose and preamble**

   Including an explanation of context and relationship to other instruments.

2. **Adoption/endorsement**

3. **Principles and definitions**

4. **Strategic objectives/goals**

   Including reference to agreed international standards and objectives for sustainable forest management.

5. **National policies**

   Policies and strategies that are relevant to, and adopted by, the participant country.
   Including special requirements for developing countries/economies in transition; cross-sectoral coordination; research.

6. **Means of implementation and modalities**

   Including financial arrangements; international and regional cooperation; capacity-building; transfer of environmentally sound technologies; and involvement of major groups and relevant stakeholders.
   Assumes institutional arrangements and governance are covered in the relevant Economic and Social Council resolution.

7. **Process for assessment/monitoring/reporting**

8. **Process for information exchange/cooperation/peer review**

9. **Mechanism to review future effectiveness/renewal of the instrument**

III. Proposal of Brazil

International understanding on the management, conservation and sustainable development of all types of forests

The United Nations Forum on Forests,

Reaffirming the relevance of the forest-related commitments made in Agenda 21, in the Non-Legally Binding Authoritative Statement of Principles for a Global Consensus on the Management, Conservation and Sustainable Development of All Types of Forests (Forest Principles) and the Johannesburg Declaration and Plan of Implementation,

Reaffirming also the importance of achieving the Millennium Development Goals within their time frame and concerned that some countries may not be in a position to do so in view of lack of adequate financial and technical resources,

Reaffirming further the principles of the Rio Declaration on Environment and Development, in particular those relating to the sovereign right of countries to take advantage of their own resources according to their policies on environment and development as well as to the common but differentiated responsibilities of the countries, based on their historical contribution towards the degradation of the global environment,

Reaffirming the decisions of the United Nations Forum on Forests and the proposals for action identified by the Intergovernmental Panel on Forests and the Intergovernmental Forum on Forests, and welcoming ongoing efforts to implement such actions,

Reaffirming also Economic and Social Council resolution 2000/35 of 18 October 2000, which stated that the main objective of the international arrangement on forests is to promote the management, conservation and sustainable development of all types of forests and to strengthen long-term political commitment to that end; that the purpose of such an international arrangement would be to promote the implementation of internationally agreed actions on forests at the national, regional and global levels in order to provide a coherent, transparent and participatory global framework for policy implementation, coordination and development and to carry out principal functions, based on the Rio Declaration on Environment and Development, the Non-Legally Binding Authoritative Statement of Principles for a Global Consensus on the Management, Conservation and Sustainable Development of All Types of Forests (Forest Principles), chapter 11 of Agenda 21 and the proposals for action adopted by the Intergovernmental Panel on Forests and the Intergovernmental Forum on Forests, in a manner consistent with and complementary to existing international legally binding instruments relevant to forests,

Expressing concern about continued deforestation and forest degradation and its adverse impact on the livelihoods of over a billion people (including many of the poorest and most vulnerable), and about the need for more effective implementation of actions to facilitate the management, conservation and sustainable development of all types of forests,

Reaffirming the United Nations Forum on Forests, with the assistance of the Collaborative Partnership on Forests as the key intergovernmental mechanisms to facilitate and coordinate the implementation of sustainable forest management at the national, regional and global levels, and stressing the importance of their appropriate strengthening,

Recognizing that the implementation of policies and measures to promote the management, conservation and sustainable development of all types of forests requires significant technical and institutional capacities and substantive investments,

Noting that sufficient new and additional financial resources have yet to be channelled to support national policies and programmes aimed at the conservation, management and sustainable development of forests,

Convinced that policies and measures adopted at global, regional, subregional and national levels should enhance the capacity of countries to significantly increase the production of forest products from sustainably managed sources,

Aware that States should cooperate to promote a supportive and open international economic system that would lead to economic growth and sustainable development in all countries to better address the problems of environmental degradation and that trade policy measures for environmental purposes should not constitute a means of arbitrary or unjustifiable discrimination or a disguised restriction on international trade,

Reaffirming the special needs and requirements of low forest cover countries and other countries with fragile ecosystems,

1. *Decides* to adopt the following International Understanding on the Management, Conservation and Sustainable Development of All Types of Forests (referred to below as the "Understanding") as a voluntary instrument to enhance international cooperation and to support national, regional and subregional policies and measures, within the International Arrangement on Forests and the mandate of the United Nations Forum on Forests;

2. *Decides also* that the Understanding is based on the Non-Legally Binding Authoritative Statement of Principles for a Global Consensus on the Management, Conservation and Sustainable Development of All Types of Forests (Forest Principles);

3. *Recognizes* in the implementation of the Understanding that:

(a) Each country is responsible for the conservation and sustainable management of its forests and the enforcement of its forest laws, which are essential to achieving sustainable forest management;

(b) International cooperation plays a crucial and catalytic role in reinforcing the efforts of developing countries and countries with economies in transition to improve the management of their forests;

(c) The private sector, forest owners, local and indigenous communities and other stakeholders can contribute to achieving sustainable forest management and should be involved in a transparent and participatory way in decision-making on forests that affects them;

Strategic objectives

4. *Agrees* on the following strategic objectives to be achieved through the implementation of the Understanding:

1. Increase significantly the area of protected and sustainably managed forests and reverse the loss of forest cover around the world;
2. Eradicate poverty in forest areas and improve the quality of life in forest-dependent communities through social and economic policies and measures and sustainable forest management;

3. Reversing the decline in official development assistance allocated to forest-related activities and mobilize significantly increased new and additional financial resources to the implementation of sustainable forest management;
4. Consistently increase the economic value and market share, including for export, of forest products originated from sustainably managed forests and their associated environmental functions;

Policies and measures

5. *Resolves* that the following actions should be developed at global, regional and subregional levels to achieve the above-mentioned strategic objectives:

(a) Initiate or strengthen public-private partnerships with the private sector, civil society organizations and other stakeholders to promote implementation of national forest programmes, criteria and indicators for sustainable forest management, good business practices and improved market transparency;

(b) Promote research and development of forests by means of a network of established centres of excellence in all regions of the world, especially in developing countries;

(c) Promote international cooperation, including South-South cooperation, and the participation of local communities;

(d) Promote long-term political commitments and strengthen existing commitments, which would allow countries to adopt concrete actions in institutional, economic and social fields for the integration of conservation and sustainable forest management within national development policies;

6. *Also resolves* that the following actions should be developed at the national level to achieve the above-mentioned strategic objectives:

(a) Formulate, implement, publish and regularly update national programmes containing measures to support and increase sustainable forest management and combat deforestation;

(b) Establish and make public national goals related to strategic objectives (1) to (4) established in paragraph 4 of the Understanding;

(c) Develop, periodically update and make available to the Forum national reports on actions and instruments adopted to achieve the strategic objectives of the Understanding, using comparable methodologies to be agreed upon by the Forum and taking into account reports required by other multilateral environmental agreements;

(d) Countries should seek, through the respective governing bodies of States members of the Collaborative Partnership on Forests, to ensure that their forest-related programmes are consistent with the priorities and are supportive of the actions adopted to implement the Understanding;

(e) Include forests in national poverty reduction strategies and, as appropriate, in strategies to achieve the Millennium Development Goals and to carry out the actions agreed upon in Agenda 21 and the Johannesburg Plan of Implementation, with a view to mobilizing new and additional financial resources for sustainable forest management;

(f) Integrate conservation and sustainable forest management within national development policies;

Means of implementation

7. *Decides* to develop the following means of implementation:

(a) Secure high-level political commitment and support to provide financial and technical resources to meet the strategic objectives of the present resolution, including by the establishment of a global forest fund, with the aim of providing specific financial resources for achieving the objectives of the Understanding;

(b) Establish a clearing house mechanism to facilitate a better exchange of experiences and good practices and to facilitate access by developing countries to better technology for a sustainable forest management and an increase of in situ value added for forest products;

(c) Promote the transfer of technology to and capacity-building in developing countries to enable them to implement national policies and measures aimed at reversing the loss of forest cover in their territories as well as significantly increase the area of protected and sustainably managed forests;

(d) Invite the Global Environment Facility Council to strengthen its role in implementing sustainable forest management by establishing a new operational programme on forests with sufficient additional funds to be allocated by the current replenishment negotiations without prejudice to other operational programmes;

Institutional modalities

8. *Decides also* that the Proposals for Action adopted by the Intergovernmental Panel on Forests and the Intergovernmental Forum on Forests should be fully taken into account in the development of the actions referred to in paragraph 4 above;

9. *Decides further* that the Forum should meet every two years to assess the implementation of the Understanding and to review national reports, the provision of financial resources and the adequacy of the modalities for transfer of technology and to provide guidance for further action to achieve the objectives established above;

10. *Decides* that regional and subregional meetings should be held at least every two years to discuss practical steps at that level for the implementation of the Understanding; such meetings, which should be conducted by regional or subregional organizations mandated by their member States and acknowledged by the Forum, would be prepared jointly by the designated organizations and the Forum secretariat;

11. *Decides also* that the Forum should continue to encourage and facilitate the participation of stakeholders from all major groups in its work, in an open and transparent way;

12. *Decides further* that the Forum should agree on a multi-year programme of work for 2006-2015 and the strengthening of the secretariat to fulfil its mandate;

13. *Decides* that the Forum should review, in 2015, the progress achieved in international cooperation for the

conservation, management and sustainable development of all types of forests and should consider ways for further strengthening the international arrangement on forests, taking into account the Intergovernmental Panel on Forests/Intergovernmental Forum on Forests proposals for action as well as Economic and Social Council resolution 2000/35.

IV. Proposal of Canada

Possible elements of an international convention on forests

An international convention on forests should build on the many recommendations produced by the international dialogue of the past 15 years and, at a minimum, should:

(a) Establish the overarching objectives, fundamental principles and definitions that would provide a common understanding of sustainable forest management;

(b) Specify the obligations that parties would undertake to implement sustainable forest management, for example:

- Maintain a national forest estate as a percentage of total area
- Complete, review and update forest inventories
- Develop national frameworks of criteria and indicators for sustainable forest management
- Develop and implement national forest programmes
- Integrate traditional forest-related knowledge in forest management
- Safeguard forests, as appropriate, from fire, insects, diseases, pollution and alien species
- Apply management plans
- Complete networks of protected areas
- Strengthen transparent forest concession allocation systems
- Require environmental impact assessments for projects with likely adverse effects
- Ensure the participation of stakeholders in forest policy decisions
- Encourage industry to develop and use voluntary codes going beyond national legislation
- Support the development of certification schemes that reflect "essential" principles
- Promote research, capacity-building, education and public awareness

(c) Promote cooperation among parties and between parties and international organizations (for example, through agreements);

(d) Consider enhanced access to public and private financial resources and the transfer of environmentally sound technology to help developing countries and countries with economies in transition to meet their obligations (likely a new forest fund);

(e) Establish a compliance regime and dispute settlement process;

(f) Create a permanent governance body with the power to monitor, periodically review and recommend approaches to strengthen the effectiveness of the convention and advance its implementation through the establishment of subsidiary bodies and actions such as programmes of work;

(g) Establish a secretariat to provide coordination;

(h) Create a structure to enable periodic monitoring and reporting on global and regional progress in achieving sustainable forest management as well as peer reviews;

(i) Define its relationship to other international legally binding forest-related agreements.

V. Proposal of the European Union

Part A: Strengthening of the International Arrangement on Forests

- Preambular paragraphs, including reaffirmation of Economic and Social Council resolution 2000/35 of 18 October 2000 (reference to the 2012–2013 cycle of the Commission on Sustainable Development)
- Global goals and national commitments
- Text on multi-year programme of work, including prioritization of implementation and emerging issues
- Means of implementation
- Invitation to the secretariat of the United Nations Forum on Forests, with support of the Collaborative Partnership on Forests members, to develop terms of reference for country reports
- Text on the Forum secretariat
- Text on Collaborative Partnership on Forests, including on its joint initiatives (such as continued work on streamlining forest-related reporting) and on monitoring, assessment and reporting on sustainable forest management (reference to criteria and indicators for sustainable forest management)
- Text on working modalities (periodicity, location, regionalization of meetings of the International Arrangement on Forests)
- Text on interim review (2011) and review (2015), including consideration of the establishment of a legally binding instrument on all types of forests at the latest in the context of the review in 2015
- Discontinuation

Part B: Draft international instrument on all types of forests

Preamble

The [subscribing] States,

- Reconfirmation of the Rio Declaration, the Forest Principles and the Intergovernmental Panel on Forests/Intergovernmental Forum on Forests proposals for action
- Recognition of valuable contributions of the Intergovernmental Panel on Forests, the Intergovernmental Forum on Forests, the United Nations Forum on Forests and the Collaborative Partnership on Forests towards building consensus on forest policy and sustainable forest management
- Reconfirmation of the United Nations Conference on Environment and Development, the World Summit on Sustainable Development, the Millennium Development Goals and the 2005 World Summit Outcome

- Underscoring of multiple economic, environmental, social and cultural benefits provided by forests
- Emphasis on contribution of sustainable forest management to sustainable development and to achieving the Millennium Development Goals
- Expression of concern about continued deforestation and forest degradation
- Affirmation that the sustainable management of forests is a common concern of humankind
- Recognition of contribution of regional processes
- Recognition that the shared global goals are mutually supportive and intersect with the seven thematic elements of sustainable forest management
- Desire to enhance and complement existing international arrangements for the sustainable management of forests
- Determination regarding sustainable forest management for the benefit of present and future generations

Have agreed as follows:

I. Purpose

I.1 Purpose of the international instrument on all types of forests is:

- To strengthen the implementation function of Economic and Social Council resolution 2000/35 of 18 October 2000
- To strengthen the long-term commitment to sustainable forest management
- To achieve the global goals

II. Use of terms

II.1 Definition of terms used for the purposes of the international instrument, including:

- States
- Regional economic integration organizations
- Collaborative Partnership on Forests
- Forests

III. Principles

III.1 Principles should include:

- National sovereignty over and responsibility for forests
- Common, but differentiated responsibilities
- Role of international cooperation in supporting national efforts
- Recognition of the importance of forest governance
- Recognition of the role and contribution of the private sector and stakeholders
- Recognition of the importance of partnerships

IV. Global goals and national commitments

IV.1 With a view to the achievement of internationally agreed development goals, including the Millennium Development Goals, [subscribing] States agree to achieve, by 2015, the following shared global goals on forests:

Goal 1

[Agreed ad ref.] Reverse the loss of forest cover worldwide through sustainable forest management, including protection, restoration, afforestation and reforestation, and increase efforts to prevent forest degradation;

Goal 2

[Agreed ad ref.] Enhance forest-based economic, social and environmental benefits and the contribution of forests to the achievement of internationally agreed development goals, including those contained in the Millennium Declaration, in particular with respect to poverty eradication and environmental sustainability, including by improving the livelihoods of forest dependent people;

Goal 3

[Agreed ad ref.] Increase significantly the area of protected forests worldwide and the area of sustainably managed forests and increase the proportion of forest products from sustainably managed forests;

Goal 4

[Agreed ad ref.] Reverse the decline in official development assistance for sustainable forest management and mobilize significantly increased new and additional financial resources from all sources for the implementation of sustainable forest management;

IV.2 [Subscribing] States agree to develop national targets contributing to the achievement of the global goals;

V. National measures

V.1 In order to achieve sustainable forest management and the global goals and to meet the related national commitments, [subscribing] States shall:

(a) Develop, further elaborate, where appropriate, and implement national forest programmes or other forest strategies;

(b) Integrate national forest programmes or other forest strategies into national strategies for sustainable development, national action plans in relation to multilateral environmental agreements and, where appropriate, into poverty reduction strategies;

VI. Strengthening of coordination and international cooperation

VI.1 [Subscribing] States to cooperate, at the regional and global level, with other [subscribing] States, directly or, where appropriate, through competent international organizations, on matters of mutual interest, for sustainable forest management and the achievement of the global goals;

VI.2 [Subscribing] States to promote cooperation and cross-sectoral policy and programme coordination;

VI.3 [Subscribing] States to involve stakeholders in a transparent and participatory manner in forest decision-making;

VII. Monitoring, assessment, reporting, and multilateral consultative process

VII.1 [Subscribing] States to monitor contributions to global goals, the achievement of national targets and the implementation of national forest programmes and other forest strategies and report to the United Nations Forum on Forests;

VII.2 Development of terms of reference for country reports;

VII.3 Establishment of a process for facilitation, peer review and dialogue;

VIII. Institutional modalities

United Nations Forum on Forests/[subscribing] States

VIII.1 The United Nations Forum on Forests to monitor the implementation of the international instrument, including through monitoring of:

- Mobilization of resources
- Activities of the Collaborative Partnership on Forests related to the international instrument
- Cooperation with other forest-related international processes
- Forest law enforcement, governance and trade

VIII.2 To identify forest-related priorities;

VIII.3 To consider and adopt amendments to the international instrument;

VIII.4 To consider and undertake any additional action at the international level that may be required for the achievement of the global goals of the international instrument in the light of experience gained;

Regional cooperation

VIII.5 Work with existing regional bodies related with forests or the Food and Agriculture Organization of the United Nations as Chair of the Collaborative Partnership on Forests, through its Regional Forestry Commissions:

(a) To facilitate and strengthen regional cooperation and close collaboration with relevant regional and subregional organizations and processes and through building regional partnerships;

(b) To be complementary to, and avoid duplication of, existing processes;

(c) To be open to members of the Forum, members of the Collaborative Partnership on Forests, major groups and interested parties;

(d) [Should be held in alternating years to the Forum];

(e) To address issues identified in the multi-year programme of work, including through assessing implementation and progress towards achieving the global goals;

(f) To provide regional input to the Forum;

(g) To build awareness of the work of the Forum and the agreed Intergovernmental Panel on Forests/Intergovernmental Forum on Forests proposals for action;

(h) Ensure participation by the Forum secretariat;

Collaborative Partnership on Forests

VIII.6 Text explaining the relationship between the international instrument and the Collaborative Partnership on Forests [to be informed by the outcomes of the Forum deliberations];

Secretariat

VIII.7 The Forum secretariat shall serve as secretariat of instrument;

VIII.8 Functions of the secretariat;

IX. Means of implementation [to be informed by the outcomes of the deliberations of the Forum]

Financial resources

IX.1 [Subscribing] States:

(a) To strengthen existing forest-related funds hosted by members of the Collaborative Partnership on Forests, including the National Forest Programme Facility, the Programme on Forests and the Bali Partnership Fund, to support national actions to implement sustainable forest management and commit to contribute to them;

(b) To create an effective enabling environment for private sector investment for sustainable forest management;

(c) To develop innovative financial mechanisms for generating revenue or public-private partnerships within context of sustainable forest management;

Incentives measures

IX.2 [Subscribing] State shall, as appropriate, adopt economically and socially sound measures that act as incentives for the conservation and sustainable management of forests;

Research, capacity-building and training and technology transfer

IX.3 [Subscribing] States:

(a) To develop, via the International Union of Forest Research Organizations, the Center for International Forestry Research and the World Agroforestry Centre in collaboration with other members of the Collaborative Partnership on Forests, a joint initiative on science and technology to support the implementation of the international instrument by assessing available information and producing reports on forest-related issues;

(b) To promote, via the Food and Agriculture Organization of the United Nations, in collaboration with members of the Collaborative Partnership on Forests, exchange of experiences and good practice, and a clearing house mechanism to facilitate access by developing countries to better technology for sustainable forest management;

IX.4 [Subscribing] States to promote effective protection, use and related benefit-sharing of traditional knowledge in sustainable forest management;

[X. Subscription

X.1 The international instrument shall be open for subscription by States and regional economic integration organizations through submission of a diplomatic note to the secretariat;

X.2 The secretariat shall serve as an immediate central contact for receiving and announcing the subscription of States or regional economic integration organizations to the international instrument;

X.3 The present international instrument becomes operational […].]

VI. Proposal of the United States of America

Structure and elements for a Voluntary [?] for Sustainable Forest Management (Codex Sylvanus)

The subscribing States/Members of the General Assembly of the United Nations:

1. Preamble

- Emphasize the multiple benefits provided by forests
- Emphasize the contribution of sustainable forest management to sustainable development and the achievement of the Millennium Development Goals
- Recall the World Summit on Sustainable Development, the Forest Principles, the proposals for action of the Intergovernmental Panel on Forests/Intergovernmental Forum on Forests, the establishment of the International Arrangement on Forests
- Welcome the work of the United Nations Forum on Forests and the Collaborative Partnership on Forests
- Recognize the importance of forest governance and public-private partnerships
- Recognize the importance of international cooperation
- Recognize the importance of political commitment at all levels

2. Adoption/endorsement of a Codex Sylvanus

3. Principles

- National sovereignty over forests
- National responsibility for forests
- Role of international cooperation in supporting national efforts
- International obligations
- Contribution of the private sector, communities and other stakeholders
- Importance of cross-sectoral coordination at all levels
- Seven thematic elements of sustainable forest management

4. Global goals or strategic objectives

- Reversing forest cover loss
- Promoting forest benefits through sustainable forest management and legally harvested forest products
- Increasing effectively managed protected forest areas
- Mobilizing financial resources—domestic, foreign, public and private

5. National policies/actions

- Identify policies and measures for country action
- Strengthen public-private partnerships
- Identify/implement measures to improve cross-sectoral coordination
- Support regional cooperation efforts
- Include forests in national poverty reduction and development strategies
- Promote mutually supportive forest-related programmes of the members of the Collaborative Partnership on Forests

6. Cooperation and means of implementation

- Initiate or strengthen public-private partnerships
- Promote research and development and technology transfer
- Promote international cooperation
- Strengthen regional processes
- Catalyse financial resources
- Facilitate international support, especially through the Collaborative Partnership on Forests
- Forest priorities of the members of the Collaborative Partnership on Forests are mutually supportive

7. Report and review

- Report progress on implementation to the United Nations Forum on Forests and the members of the Collaborative Partnership on Forests
- Assess progress/review of effectiveness in 2015

Annex

List of subscribing States

[Mechanism for informing the Secretary-General]

VII. Co-Chairs' draft indicative elements for a non-legally binding instrument

The following is a list of common elements for an indicative list of elements that could be considered in developing a [instrument/code/guidelines/international understanding]:

Context/preamble

- Recognition of global importance of forests
- Economic, social and environmental benefits
- Principles
- Need for political support
- Recognizing regional differences

Strategic objectives/goals

- Same as in resolution

Policies and measures

- Strengthening subregional initiatives

Means of implementation

- Technology transfer
- Funding mechanism
- Capacity-building
- Enhanced international cooperation and assistance
- Involvement of major groups

Institutional modalities

- Review in 2015
- Secretariat of the United Nations Forum on Forests as secretariat for the instrument

Annex

Proposed list of elements of an understanding/instrument

Context/preamble

- Importance of forests and multiple benefits
- Concern over deforestation and forest degradation
- Sustainable forest management for benefit of present and future generations
- Rio Declaration, Agenda 21, Intergovernmental Panel on Forests/Intergovernmental Forum on Forests processes
- Role of forests in sustainable development (World Summit on Sustainable Development)
- Contribution of forests to the Millennium Development Goals (2005 World Summit)

- Economic and Social Council resolution 2000/35
- Need to strengthen the International Arrangement on Forests
- Need for adequate means of implementation
- Special needs (developing countries, including least developed countries, small island developing States, landlocked developing States, as well as countries with economies in transition)
- Need for strong political commitment
- Shared global goals/strategic objectives
- National sovereignty over forests
- National responsibility for forests
- International obligations
- Need to reflect regional nuances and variations
- Need for policies and strategies to be relevant to national circumstances
- Role of international cooperation in supporting national efforts
- Importance of dialogue and cooperation at regional and subregional levels
- Importance of cross-sectoral coordination at all levels
- Importance of forest governance
- Contribution of major groups, for example, the private sector, communities and other stakeholders
- Need to address social, environmental and economic aspects of sustainable forest management, using framework of seven thematic elements

Strategic objectives/goals

- Same as in resolution

Policies and measures

- Identify policy measures for country action through development and implementation of national forestry programme (or equivalent)
- Set national goals
- Integration with other policies (for example, national development plans, poverty reduction strategies)
- Identify/implement measures to improve cross-sectoral coordination
- Strengthen regional and subregional processes
- Strengthen public/private partnerships
- Secure participation of major groups
- Promote mutually supportive forest-related programmes of members of the Collaborative Partnership on Forests

Means of implementation

- Official development assistance for forest-related activities
- Mobilizing finance from private, public and voluntary sources
- Enabling environment for investment
- Existing forest-related funds
- Global forest fund
- Innovative financial mechanisms
- Payment for environmental services
- Transfer of environmentally sustainable technology
- Research and development (including clearing house)
- Support to scientific and technological innovations
- Capacity-building
- Tackling illegal forest-related activities/forest law enforcement
- Better coordination of existing programmes and processes
- International cooperation (including South-South cooperation and triangular cooperation)
- Peer review and monitoring, assessment and reporting

Institutional modalities

- Secretariat of the United Nations Forum on Forests as secretariat for the instrument
- Submit voluntary national reports to the United Nations Forum on Forests on progress in implementation
- Assess effectiveness of instrument in 2015
- Adoption/subscription

International Year of Forests

By **decision 2006/230** of 24 July, the Economic and Social Council, recognizing the need to raise awareness of forest-related issues, recommended that the General Assembly, at its sixty-first (2006) session, proclaim 2011 the International Year of Forests.

GENERAL ASSEMBLY ACTION

On 20 December [meeting 83], the General Assembly, on the recommendation of the Second Committee [A/61/422/Add.1 & Corr.1], adopted **resolution 61/193** without vote [agenda item 53 *(a)*].

International Year of Forests, 2011

The General Assembly,

Reaffirming its commitment to the Non-legally Binding Authoritative Statement of Principles for a Global Consensus on the Management, Conservation and Sustainable Development of All Types of Forests and Agenda 21, adopted at the United Nations Conference on Environment and Development, the United Nations Millennium Declaration, adopted at the Millennium Summit in 2000, the Johannesburg Declaration on Sustainable Development and the Plan of Implementation of the World Summit on Sustainable Development, adopted at the World Summit on Sustainable Development, held in Johannesburg, South Africa, in 2002,

Recalling the Convention on Biological Diversity, the United Nations Framework Convention on Climate Change, the United Nations Convention to Combat Desertification in Those Countries Experiencing Serious Drought and/or Desertification, Particularly in Africa, and other relevant conventions dealing with the complexity of forest issues,

Recognizing that forests and sustainable forest management can contribute significantly to sustainable development, poverty eradication and the achievement of internationally agreed development goals, including the Millennium Development Goals,

Recalling Economic and Social Council decision 2006/230 of 24 July 2006,

Emphasizing the need for sustainable management of all types of forests, including fragile forest ecosystems,

Convinced that concerted efforts should focus on raising awareness at all levels to strengthen the sustainable management, conservation and sustainable development of all types of forests for the benefit of current and future generations,

1. *Decides* to declare 2011 the International Year of Forests;

2. *Requests* the secretariat of the United Nations Forum on Forests of the Department of Economic and Social Affairs of the Secretariat, to serve as the focal point for the implementation of the Year, in collaboration with Governments, the Collaborative Partnership on Forests and international, regional and subregional organizations and processes as well as relevant major groups;

3. *Invites*, in particular, the Food and Agriculture Organization of the United Nations, as the Chair of the Collaborative Partnership on Forests, within its mandate, to support the implementation of the Year;

4. *Calls upon* Governments, relevant regional and international organizations, and major groups to support activities related to the Year, inter alia, through voluntary contributions, and to link their relevant activities to the Year;

5. *Encourages* voluntary partnerships among Member States, international organizations and major groups to facilitate and promote activities related to the Year at the local and national levels, including by creating national committees or designating focal points in their respective countries;

6. *Requests* the Secretary-General to report to the General Assembly at its sixty-fourth session on the state of preparations for the Year.

Sustainable mountain development

Mountain Partnership

The fourteenth session of the Commission on Sustainable Development (New York, 1-12 May) considered an April report prepared by the Mountain Partnership [E/CN.17/2006/12] on its activities and achievements. The Partnership, formerly known as the International Partnership for Sustainable Development in Mountain Regions, was launched as an outcome of the 2002 World Summit on Sustainable Development [YUN 2002, p. 821] and was dedicated to improving the well-being, livelihoods and opportunities of mountain people. The report described progress with regard to organizational development, and coordination and implementation activities. Significant progress was made in certain areas, particularly in defining a functional organizational structure and governance mechanism and in making operational the support structures necessary to promote and facilitate joint action among partners. Coordinating mechanisms had been developed within the membership, including member-designated focal points intended to foster liaison and communication among members in collaborative work. The report also discussed challenges to developing a more effective, action-oriented Partnership, including issues related to the scope of activities and level of involvement by members; the size of the Partnership; types of members; the lack of involvement by the private sector; the balance between political and operational support; and funding. The report also identified a number of lessons learned over the years in developing the Partnership.

Marine ecosystems

Oceans and seas

In response to General Assembly resolution 60/30 [YUN 2005, p. 1436], the seventh meeting of the United Nations Open-ended Informal Consultative Process on Oceans and Law of the Sea (New York, 12-16 June) [A/61/156] focused on ecosystem approaches and oceans. It agreed on elements relating to that issue, including proposals for the implementation of an ecosystem approach, for consideration by the Assembly. The meeting agreed that ecosystem approaches to oceans management should focus on managing human activities in order to maintain and restore ecosystem health to sustain goods and environmental services; provide social and economic benefits for food security; sustain livelihoods in support of international development goals, including those contained in the Millennium Declaration [YUN 2000, p. 49]; and conserve marine biodiversity.

The Assembly took action with regard to the Consultative Process in section XIV of **resolution 61/222** of 20 December (see p. 1566).

Global waters assessment

In March, UNEP issued the final report of the Global International Waters Assessment (GIWA) [UNEP/GCSS.IX/INF/9], which was inaugurated in 2000 [YUN 2000, p. 982] and completed in 2005 [YUN 2005, p. 1158]. GIWA assessed international waters and causes of environmental problems in 66 water regions, focusing on the aquatic environment in transboundary waters. The complex interactions between mankind and aquatic resources were studied within four specific major concerns: freshwater shortage, pollution, overfishing and habitat modification; a fifth, overarching concern—global change—was also considered. GIWA confirmed that pressures from human activities had weakened the ability of aquatic ecosystems to perform essential functions, which compromised human well-being and development. The five concerns were serious worldwide problems that were expected to increase in severity by 2020. The GIWA regional teams determined that transboundary pollution was a top priority concern in 20 of the 66 regions assessed, and it appeared that agricultural run-off and municipal and industrial discharges were the most prevalent pollution sources. The final report discussed the root causes of water-related concerns, including population growth; agricultural development and economic growth; lack of knowledge concerning water-related environmental issues; market failures in the areas of water resources and fisheries; and policy failures. The report proposed options for responding to the concerns, including through the development of international governance frameworks for water allocation and an integrated approach linking water management to land and economic management; improved policies and pricing; and ecosystem-based management.

Assessment of assessments

The Ad Hoc Steering Group for the "assessment of assessments" of the regular process for global reporting and assessment of the state of the marine environment, including socio-economic aspects, established by the General Assembly in resolution 60/30 [YUN 2005, p. 1436], held its first meeting (New York, 7-9 June) [A/61/GRAME/AHSG/1]. The meeting called for a review of the updated survey of regional and global marine assessments to provide feedback to the UNEP World Conservation Monitoring Centre. It recommended that the thematic and geographic scope of the "assessment of assessments" should cover marine and coastal environment assessments. It also decided on the selection of the group of experts for the "assessment of assessments"; and the inclusion of observers at its next meeting. The Ad Hoc Steering Group agreed to a budget of $2.1 million for implementation of the workplan for the "assessment of assessments", and to convene its second meeting three days prior to the eighth (2007) meeting of the United Nations Open-ended Informal Consultative Process on Oceans and Law of the Sea.

The Assembly, in section XII of **resolution 61/222** of 20 December (see p. 1566), took note of the report of the Ad Hoc Steering Group and urged Member States from the African and Asian regional groups to propose the remaining representatives to the Chairmen of those groups.

Global Programme of Action

The second session of the Intergovernmental Review Meeting on the Implementation of the Global Programme of Action (GPA) for the Protection of the Marine Environment from Land-based Activities (Beijing, 16-20 October) [UNEP/GPA/IGR.2/7] adopted the Beijing Declaration on Furthering the Implementation of the Global Programme of Action, by which Governments recommitted themselves to GPA as a flexible and effective tool for the sustainable development of oceans, coasts and islands. Governments also committed themselves to furthering the implementation of GPA from 2007 to 2011 by applying ecosystem approaches; valuing the social and economic costs and benefits of the goods and services provided by coasts and oceans; establishing partnerships at the national, regional and international levels; cooperating at the regional and interregional levels; mainstreaming GPA into national development planning and budgetary mechanisms; and supporting the UNEP GPA Coordination Office. Governments also resolved to take actions at the national, regional and international levels. The UNEP Executive Director was requested to convene the third session of the Intergovernmental Review Meeting in 2011. The Meeting also considered a GPA secretariat note [UNEP/GPA/IGR.2/2] providing an overview of progress made in advancing GPA at the national, regional and international levels from 2002 to 2006, and endorsed the proposed 2007-2011 programme of work of the GPA Coordination Office [UNEP/GPA/IGR.2/4]. A December note by the Executive Director [UNEP/GC/24/INF/18] provided additional information on the planned activities of the Coordination Office during the 2007-2011 period and indicators to assess GPA implementation.

In section IX of **resolution 61/222** of 20 December (see p. 1563), the General Assembly welcomed the outcomes of the second Intergovernmental Review Meeting of GPA and called on States to take all appropriate measures to fulfil the commitments of the international community embodied in the Beijing Declaration.

Coral reefs

UNEP Coral Reef Unit worked with the International Coral Reef Network, in collaboration with the South Asian Cooperative Environment Programme, regional Governments and other partners, to implement a project for the long-term management and conservation of marine and coastal protected areas encompassing warm-water reefs. UNEP also issued a report on coral reefs, entitled "Our Precious Coasts: Marine Pollution, Climate Change and Resilience of Coastal Ecosystems", which highlighted the links between the sustainability of coastal ecosystems and levels of pollution in a changing climate. In October, the Global Cold-Water Database and Geographic Information System (GIS) was launched.

Regional Seas Programme

In a November report [UNEP/GC/24/4], the Executive Director provided information on the UNEP Regional Seas Programme, which focused on strengthening the individual regional seas programmes, particularly through the implementation of the global strategic directions agreed upon at the fifth Global Meeting of the Regional Seas Conventions and Action Plans [YUN 2003, p. 1068] and finalized at the sixth Global Meeting [YUN 2004, p. 1060]. Within that focus, UNEP activities resulted in increased partnership and collaboration, as well as the increased visibility of the regional seas programmes; the launch of the UNEP Global Initiative on Marine Litter during the second session of the Intergovernmental Review Meeting on the Implementation of GPA in October (see above); increased financing for the regional seas programmes; provision of legal advice at the regional level to enhance the effectiveness of regional seas programmes in translating the conventions and protocols into national legislation; continued provision by the UNEP Regional Seas Programme of a platform for promoting synergies and coordinated regional implementation of multilateral environmental agreements and global and regional initiatives; training courses on the management of marine and coastal invasive species; a significant increase in the number of marine protected areas; and continued awareness raising on ecosystem-based management related to the marine and coastal environment.

The eighth Global Meeting of the Regional Seas Conventions and Action Plans (Beijing, 13-14 October) [UNEP(DEC)/RS.8] discussed global strategic directions; delineation of the continental shelf; global and regional cooperation; and other issues.

Caribbean Sea management

In response to General Assembly resolution 59/230 [YUN 2004, p. 1061], the Secretary-General submitted an August report [A/61/268] assessing progress made in promoting an integrated management approach to the Caribbean Sea area in the context of sustainable development. It described activities undertaken by the Association of Caribbean States (ACS), charged with monitoring the management of the Caribbean Sea, the Caribbean Community, the Economic Commission for Latin America and the Caribbean, the Food and Agriculture Organization of the United Nations, the International Monetary Fund, the International Telecommunication Union, UNEP, and UNESCO. The Secretary-General also reported on national activities.

Annexed to the Secretary-General's report was the ACS report. In his conclusions, the Secretary-General noted the establishment by ACS ministers in March of the Follow-up Commission for the Caribbean Sea Initiative as a multidisciplinary, intergovernmental agency with a mandate to replace the Technical Advisory Group on the Caribbean Sea. The Commission held its first meeting in Trinidad and Tobago on 27 July.

GENERAL ASSEMBLY ACTION

On 20 December [meeting 83], the General Assembly, on the recommendation of the Second Committee [A/61/422/Add.2], adopted **resolution 61/197** without vote [agenda item 53 *(b)*].

Towards the sustainable development of the Caribbean Sea for present and future generations

The General Assembly,

Reaffirming the principles and commitments enshrined in the Rio Declaration on Environment and Development, the principles embodied in the Declaration of Barbados, the Programme of Action for the Sustainable Development of Small Island Developing States, the Johannesburg Declaration on Sustainable Development and the Plan of Implementation of the World Summit on Sustainable Development ("Johannesburg Plan of Implementation"), as well as other relevant declarations and international instruments,

Recalling the Declaration and review document adopted by the General Assembly at its twenty-second special session,

Taking into account all other relevant General Assembly resolutions, including resolutions 54/225 of 22 December 1999, 55/203 of 20 December 2000, 57/261 of 20 December 2002 and 59/230 of 22 December 2004,

Taking into account also the Mauritius Strategy for the Further Implementation of the Programme of Action for the Sustainable Development of Small Island Developing States,

Recalling the 2005 World Summit Outcome,

Recalling also the Convention for the Protection and Development of the Marine Environment of the Wider Caribbean Region, signed at Cartagena de Indias, Colombia, on 24 March 1983, and its protocols, which contain the definition of the wider Caribbean region of which the Caribbean Sea is part,

Reaffirming the United Nations Convention on the Law of the Sea, which provides the overall legal framework for ocean activities, and emphasizing its fundamental character, conscious that the problems of ocean space are closely interrelated and need to be considered as a whole through an integrated, interdisciplinary and intersectoral approach,

Emphasizing the importance of national, regional and global action and cooperation in the marine sector as recognized by the United Nations Conference on Environment and Development in chapter 17 of Agenda 21,

Recalling the relevant work done by the International Maritime Organization,

Considering that the Caribbean Sea area includes a large number of States, countries and territories, most of which are developing countries and small island developing States that are ecologically fragile, structurally weak and economically vulnerable and are also affected, inter alia, by their limited capacity, narrow resource base, need for financial resources, high levels of poverty and the resulting social problems and the challenges and opportunities of globalization and trade liberalization,

Recognizing that the Caribbean Sea has a unique biodiversity and highly fragile ecosystem,

Emphasizing that the Caribbean countries have a high degree of vulnerability occasioned by climate change, climate variability and associated phenomena, such as the rise in sea level, the El Niño phenomenon and the increase in the frequency and intensity of natural disasters caused by hurricanes, floods and droughts, and that they are also subject to natural disasters, such as those caused by volcanoes, tsunamis and earthquakes,

Bearing in mind the heavy reliance of most of the Caribbean economies on their coastal areas, as well as on the marine environment in general, to achieve their sustainable development needs and goals,

Acknowledging that the intensive use of the Caribbean Sea for maritime transport, as well as the considerable number and interlocking character of the maritime areas under national jurisdiction where Caribbean countries exercise their rights and duties under international law, present a challenge for the effective management of the resources,

Noting the problem of marine pollution caused, inter alia, by land-based sources and the continuing threat of pollution from ship-generated waste and sewage, as well as from the accidental release of hazardous and noxious substances in the Caribbean Sea area,

Taking note of the relevant resolutions of the General Conference of the International Atomic Energy Agency on safety of transport of radioactive materials,

Mindful of the diversity and dynamic interaction and competition among socio-economic activities for the use of the coastal areas and the marine environment and their resources,

Mindful also of the efforts of the Caribbean countries to address in a more holistic manner the sectoral issues relating to the management of the Caribbean Sea area and, in so doing, to promote an integrated management approach to the Caribbean Sea area in the context of sustainable development, through a regional cooperative effort among Caribbean countries,

Welcoming the continued efforts of the States members of the Association of Caribbean States to develop and implement regional initiatives to promote the sustainable conservation and management of coastal and marine resources, and noting in this regard the commitment by Heads of State and Government of the Association of Caribbean States to further develop their concept of the Caribbean Sea as a special area within the context of sustainable development, as referenced in paragraph 31 of the Mauritius Strategy, and without prejudice to relevant international law,

Cognizant of the importance of the Caribbean Sea to present and future generations and to the heritage and the continuing economic well-being and sustenance of people living in the area, and the urgent need for the countries of the region to take appropriate steps for its preservation and protection, with the support of the international community,

1. *Recognizes* that the unique biodiversity and highly fragile ecosystem of the Caribbean Sea require that Caribbean States and relevant regional and international development partners work together to develop and implement regional initiatives to promote the sustainable conservation and management of coastal and marine resources including, inter alia, the further development of their concept of the designation of the Caribbean Sea as a special area in the context of sustainable development, without prejudice to relevant international law;

2. *Takes note with interest* of the creation by the Association of Caribbean States of the Commission on the Caribbean Sea;

3. *Takes note* of the efforts of the Caribbean States to further develop their concept of the Caribbean Sea as a special area in the context of sustainable development, without prejudice to relevant international law, and invites the international community to recognize such efforts;

4. *Recognizes* the efforts of Caribbean countries to create conditions leading to sustainable development aimed at combating poverty and inequality, and in this regard notes with interest the initiatives of the Association of Caribbean States in the focal areas of sustainable tourism, trade, transport and natural disasters;

5. *Calls upon* the United Nations system and the international community to assist, as appropriate, Caribbean countries and their regional organizations in their efforts to ensure the protection of the Caribbean Sea from degradation as a result of pollution from ships, in particular through the illegal release of oil and other harmful substances, and from illegal dumping or accidental release of hazardous waste, including radioactive materials, nuclear waste and dangerous chemicals, in violation of relevant international rules and standards, as well as pollution from land-based activities;

6. *Invites* the Association to submit a report on its progress in the implementation of the present resolution to the Secretary-General for consideration during the sixty-third session of the General Assembly;

7. *Calls upon* all States to become contracting parties to relevant international agreements to enhance maritime safety and promote the protection of the marine environment of the Caribbean Sea from pollution, damage and degradation from ships and ship-generated waste;

8. *Supports* the efforts of Caribbean countries to implement sustainable fisheries management programmes;

9. *Calls upon* States, taking into consideration the Convention on Biological Diversity, to develop national, regional and international programmes to halt the loss of marine biodiversity in the Caribbean Sea, in particular fragile ecosystems such as coral reefs;

10. *Invites* Member States and intergovernmental organizations within the United Nations system to continue their efforts to assist Caribbean countries in becoming parties to the relevant conventions and protocols concerning the management, protection and sustainable utilization of Caribbean Sea resources and in implementing them effectively;

11. *Calls upon* the international community, the United Nations system and the multilateral financial institutions, and invites the Global Environment Facility, within its mandate, to support actively the national and regional activities of the Caribbean States towards the promotion of the sustainable management of coastal and marine resources;

12. *Urges* the United Nations system and the international community to continue to provide aid and assistance to the countries of the Caribbean region in the implementation of their long-term programmes of disaster prevention, preparedness, mitigation, management, relief and recovery, based on their development priorities, through the integration of relief, rehabilitation and reconstruction into a comprehensive approach to sustainable development;

13. *Calls upon* Member States to improve as a matter of priority their emergency response capabilities and the containment of environmental damage, particularly in the Caribbean Sea, in the event of natural disasters or of an accident or incident relating to maritime navigation;

14. *Requests* the Secretary-General to report to it at its sixty-third session, under the sub-item entitled "Follow-up to and implementation of the Mauritius Strategy for the Further Implementation of the Programme of Action for the Sustainable Development of Small Island Developing States" of the item entitled "Sustainable development", on the implementation of the present resolution, taking into account the views expressed by relevant regional organizations.

Conservation of wildlife

In May, the UNEP Great Apes Survival Project (GRASP) and the secretariat of the Convention on International Trade in Endangered Species (CITES) undertook a joint mission to Indonesia to investigate the smuggling of orangutans and preventive measures put in place by the Indonesian Government. The report on the mission's findings was presented at the fifty-fourth meeting of the CITES Standing Committee (Geneva, 2-6 October), during which Indonesia responded to the issues raised by the mission. Under the auspices of UNEP-GRASP and the CITES secretariat, wildlife law enforcement officers from nine African great ape range States and Indonesia, metting at UNEP headquarters in Nairobi in November formed a network for monitoring and controlling illegal wildlife trade.

Protection against harmful products and waste

Chemical safety

As at 31 December, 111 States and the EC were parties to the 1998 Rotterdam Convention on the Prior Informed Consent (PIC) Procedure for Certain Hazardous Chemicals and Pesticides in International Trade [YUN 1998, p. 997], which entered into force in 2004 [YUN 2004, p. 1063].

The Chemical Review Committee, a subsidiary body of the Conference of the Parties to the Rotterdam Convention, at its second meeting (Geneva, 13-17 February) [UNEP/FAO/RC/CRC.2/20], reviewed the notifications of final regulatory action for nine chemicals; finalized the decision-guidance document on chrysotile asbestos; and responded to requests made by the Conference of the Parties at its second meeting [YUN 2005, p. 1160] for consideration of papers on risk evaluations completed under the auspices of other multilateral environmental agreements and their relevance to candidate chemicals [UNEP/FAO/RC/CRC.2/4] and on trade restrictions under such agreements [UNEP/FAO/RC/CRC.2/5]. The Committee also considered further measures to enhance the efficiency of its intersessional work.

The third meeting of the Conference of the Parties to the Convention (Geneva, 9-13 October) [UNEP/FAO/RC/COP.3/26] adopted the programme of work for the regional and national delivery of technical assistance for 2007-2008; and approved the operational budget of $3,521,430 for 2007 and $3,547,928 for 2008. It requested the Convention secretariat to provide, at the fourth meeting of the Conference, a further study of the advantages and disadvantages of using the euro, Swiss franc or United States dollar as the currency of the Convention accounts and budget. Other decisions dealt with the inclusion of chrysotile asbestos in annex III to the Convention; the draft text of the procedures and mechanisms on compliance with the Convention; the financial mechanism of the Convention; and cooperation and coordination between the Rotterdam Convention, the 1989 Basel Convention on the Control of Transboundary Movements of Hazardous Wastes and their Disposal [YUN 1989, p. 420] and the 2001 Stockholm Convention on Persistent Organic Pollutants [YUN 2001, p. 971]. The Conference of the Parties had before it an October note by the Convention secretariat [UNEP/FAO/RC/COP.3/INF/16] containing a UNEP report on its activities in support of the Convention, including activities related to persistent organic pollutants, mercury, and other heavy metals and chemicals; the Green Customs Initiative, which was aimed at strengthening compliance with and enforcement of multilateral environmental agreements; the Strategic Approach to International Chemicals Management (see below); and capacity-building to assist countries in promoting the sound management of chemicals.

International chemicals management

The first session of the International Conference on Chemicals Management (Dubai, United Arab Emirates, 4-6 February) [SAICM/ICCM.1/7], adopted the Strategic Approach to International Chemicals Management (SAICM), which consisted of the Overarching Policy Strategy, the Global Programme of Action, and the Dubai Declaration on International Chemicals Management.

The Overarching Policy Strategy outlined the scope of the Strategic Approach and provided a statement of needs with regard to chemicals management. The overall objective of SAICM was to achieve the sound management of chemicals throughout their life cycle, so that, by 2020, chemicals would be used and produced in ways that would minimize significant adverse affects on human health and the environment, in line with the Johannesburg Plan of Implementation, adopted by the 2002 World Summit on Sustainable Development [YUN 2002, p. 821]. Other objectives were related to risk reduction; knowledge and information; governance; capacity-building and technical support; and illegal international traffic in toxic, hazardous, banned and severely restricted chemicals. The Overarching Policy and Strategy discussed the financing of SAICM and identified principles and approaches for developing and implementing the Strategic Approach and Global Plan of Action. It also described institutional arrangements for implementing SAICM and monitoring progress towards its objectives. To that end, the International Conference on Chemicals Management would undertake periodic reviews of the Strategic Approach.

The SAICM Global Plan of Action was structured into work areas and associated activities to be undertaken voluntarily by stakeholders in pursuit of the commitments and objectives of the Overarching Policy and Strategy and the Dubai Declaration (see below). It outlined measures to support risk reduction; strengthen knowledge and information on chemicals management, as well as institutions, law and policy with regard to chemicals management; enhance capacity-building; address illegal international traffic of chemicals and hazardous waste; and improve general chemicals management practices. The Global Programme of Action contained a list of possible work areas and associated activities. It also listed possible actors, targets/timeframes, indicators of progress and implementation aspects, but agreement on them was not achieved during the development of SAICM.

In the Dubai Declaration on International Chemicals Management, participants declared, among other things, that the sound management of chemicals was essential to the achievement of sustainable development and expressed their commitment to implement applicable chemicals agreements, strengthen coherence and synergies and address gaps in the framework of international chemical policy. They adopted the Overarching Policy Strategy. They also recommended the use and further development of the Global Programme of Action as a working tool and guidance document for meeting the commitments to chemicals management expressed in the Rio Declaration on Environment and Development [YUN 1992, p. 670] and the Agenda 21 action plan on sustainable development [ibid., p. 672], both adopted by the 1992 United Nations Conference on Environment and Development [ibid., p. 670]; the 2000 Bahia Declaration on Chemical Safety, adopted by the Intergovernmental Forum on Chemical Safety [YUN 2001, p. 969]; the Johannesburg Plan of Implementation; the 2005 World Summit Outcome, adopted by the Assembly in resolution 60/1 [YUN 2005, p. 48]; and the Strategic Approach.

In a separate resolution, the Conference established a Quick Start Programme for the implementation of SAICM, the objective of which would be to support capacity-building and implementation activities in developing countries, least developed countries, small island developing States and countries with economies in transition. The Programme would include a UNEP trust fund and multilateral, bilateral and other forms of cooperation and strategic priorities and institutional arrangements. The Conference also established the Quick Start Programme Executive Board. The SAICM secretariat would facilitate meetings of the Board and the Trust Fund Implementation Committee, and establish a working relationship with the Intergovernmental Forum on Chemical Safety (IFCS) to draw on its expertise. Further Conference resolutions dealt with arrangements for SAICM implementation and other matters.

Governing Council consideration. The UNEP Governing Council, at its ninth special session in February [A/61/25], considered addenda to the 2005 report of the UNEP Executive Director on chemicals management [YUN 2005, p. 1161] containing the

Dubai Declaration on International Chemicals Management and the Overarching Policy Strategy [UNEP/GCSS.IX/6/Add.1], and the executive summary of the Global Plan of Action [UNEP/GCSS.IX/6/Add.2]. It also had before it a background paper [UNEP/GCSS.IX/9/Add.2] for the ministerial-level consultations on chemicals management.

The Council endorsed SAICM as contained in the Dubai Declaration on International Chemicals Management, the Overarching Policy Strategy and the Global Plan of Action, and requested the Executive Director to convene future sessions of the International Conference on Chemicals Management back-to-back with meetings of the governing bodies of relevant intergovernmental organizations, where appropriate [A/61/25 (dec. SS.IX/1)]. The Executive Director would also establish and assume overall administrative responsibility for the SAICM secretariat. The Council authorized the participation of the UNEP secretariat in the SAICM secretariat, in accordance with relevant decisions of the Council in 2005 [YUN 2005, p. 1161]. It also authorized the Executive Director to establish and manage the Quick Start Programme Trust Fund to support initial SAICM implementation. Governments, other intergovernmental organizations and NGOs were invited to provide voluntary extrabudgetary resources in support of the SAICM secretariat. Governments, regional economic integration organizations, intergovernmental organizations and NGOs were invited to contribute resources to support the SAICM implementation activities of UNEP and the Quick Start Programme, and to make contributions to the voluntary trust fund established by UNEP to support implementation. The Executive Director was asked to report to the Council in 2007 on initial activities and planning in support of UNEP SAICM implementation.

IFCS session. The fifth session of the Intergovernmental Forum on Chemical Safety (IFCS) (Budapest, Hungary, 25-29 September) [IFCS/FORUM-V/05w] considered the future role of IFCS as a contributor to SAICM implementation. It requested its secretariat to establish and maintain a close working relationship and cooperation with the SAICM secretariat, and invited the SAICM secretariat to participate in IFCS meetings as appropriate. It also discussed approaches in applying precaution in the domestic chemicals management activities and issues related to the chemical safety of toys. The Forum adopted the Budapest Statement on Mercury, Lead and Cadmium, which, among other things, called on IFCS participants to address the health and environmental impacts of mercury, lead and cadmium.

Lead and cadmium

In response to a 2005 Governing Council decision [YUN 2005, p. 1161], the Executive Director submitted a December note [UNEP/GC/24/INF/16] containing information on the interim reviews of scientific information on lead and cadmium. Subsequent to the 2005 decision, UNEP established the Lead and Cadmium Working Group to assist it in developing reviews of scientific information. The Working Group (Geneva, 18-22 September) prepared summaries of the key findings of the interim reviews, which showed that there were significant risks to human health and the environment arising from the release of lead and cadmium in the environment to warrant international action. The note summarized the main findings on the adverse impacts of lead and cadmium related to transport, use, waste disposal, exposure and toxicity. The Working Group was unable to complete its review of the health effects of lead and cadmium, and delegated that responsibility to WHO. UNEP further developed the interim reviews of scientific information on lead and cadmium based on the recommendations of the Working Group.

The Clearing-House of the Partnership for Clean Fuels and Vehicles (PCFV), hosted by UNEP, was instrumental in achieving a complete phase-out of leaded gasoline in sub-Saharan Africa by January. The Partnership was working on a global campaign to eliminate the use of leaded gasoline worldwide by the end of 2008, and was helping the remaining 25 countries in Eastern Europe, the Middle East and Asia that used leaded gasoline to accomplish that goal.

Mercury

UNEP worked with the secretariat of the 1989 Basel Convention on the Control of Transboundary Movements of Hazardous Wastes and their Disposal to draft guidelines on handling mercury waste. A pilot draft toolkit for the identification and quantification of mercury releases was developed for use by interested countries. UNEP also prepared a draft report summarizing the supply, trade and demand information for mercury, which was circulated among Governments and interested parties for consideration of possible further action on mercury by the UNEP Governing Council in 2007.

Persistent organic pollutants

As at 31 December, 135 States and the EC were parties to the 2001 Stockholm Convention on Persistent Organic Pollutants (POPS) [YUN 2001,

p. 971], which entered into force in 2004 [YUN 2004, p. 1066].

The second meeting of the Conference of the Parties to the Stockholm Convention (Geneva, 1-5 May) [UNEP/POPS/COP.2/30] approved the revised operational budget of $5,608,250 for 2007. It adopted criteria to be applied in the review process for entries in the Register of Specific Exemptions established under article 4 of the Convention; the process for reviewing and updating national implementation plans; terms of reference for regional and subregional centres for capacity-building and transfer of technology under the Convention, and for work on modalities on the needs assessment for parties that were developing countries or countries with economies in transition to implement the provisions of the Convention over the 2006-2010 period; a format for reporting on polychlorinated biphenyls (PCBs); and, on an interim basis, the process for the reporting on the assessment and evaluation of the continued use of dichloro-diphenyl-trichoroethane (DDT).

The Conference agreed to complete the first effectiveness evaluation at its fourth meeting in 2009, implement a global monitoring plan, and establish a provisional ad hoc technical working group to coordinate and oversee its implementation. It also called for improved cooperation and coordination between the 1989 Basel Convention on the Control of Transboundary Movements of Hazardous Wastes and their Disposal, the 1998 Rotterdam Convention on the Prior Informed Consent Procedure for Certain Hazardous Chemicals and Pesticides in International Trade, and the Stockholm Convention. Other decisions dealt with guidelines on best available techniques and provisional guidelines on best environmental practices; the ongoing review and updating of the Standardized Toolkit for Identification and Quantification of Dioxin and Furan Releases; measures to reduce or eliminate releases from wastes; the listing of chemicals in annexes A, B, and/or C of the Convention; non-compliance; official communications with parties to the Convention and observers; the clearing house mechanism for information on POPs; and additional guidance on financial matters.

The second meeting of the Persistent Organic Pollutants Review Committee (Geneva, 6-10 November) [UNEP/POPS/POPRC.2/17] adopted decisions on the approach for considering isomers or groups of isomers of chemicals proposed for listing in annexes A, B and/or C to the Convention; confidentiality arrangements; short-chained chlorinated paraffins; and the chemicals chlordecone, hexabromobiphenyl, lidane, perfluorooctane sulfonate, pentachlorobenzene, commercial pentabromodiphenyl and octabromodiphenyl ether, and alpha and beta hexachlorocyclohexane.

Hazardous wastes

As at 31 December, 168 States and the EC were parties to the 1989 Basel Convention on the Control of Transboundary Movements of Hazardous Wastes and their Disposal [YUN 1989, p. 420], which entered into force in 1992 [YUN 1992, p. 685]. The 1995 amendment to the Convention [YUN 1995, p. 1333], not yet in force, had been ratified, accepted or approved by 63 parties. The number of parties to the 1999 Basel Protocol on Liability and Compensation for Damage Resulting from Transboundary Movements of Hazardous Wastes and their Disposal [YUN 1999, p. 998] stood at seven.

The fifth session of the Open-ended Working Group of the Basel Convention on the Control of Transboundary Movements of Hazardous Wastes and their Disposal (Geneva, 3-7 April) [UNEP/CHW/OEWG/5/5] approved the draft training manual on illegal traffic in hazardous wastes [UNEP/CHW/OEWG/5/2/Add.3]. Other decisions dealt with the role and activities of the Convention regional and coordinating centres in the Strategic Plan for the Implementation of the Basel Convention to 2010, adopted by the Conference of the Parties in 2002 [YUN 2002, p. 1065]; the Basel Convention Partnership Programme; guidelines for the Mobile Phone Partnership Initiative; synergies between the Basel Convention, the 2001 Stockholm Convention on POPs, and the 1998 Rotterdam Convention on the Prior Informed Consent (PIC) Procedure for Certain Hazardous Chemicals and Pesticides in International Trade; the abandonment of ships and the environmentally sound management of ship dismantling; amendments to the lists of wastes contained in annexes VIII and IX of the Convention; the 1999 Basel Protocol [YUN 1999, p. 998]; technical guidelines on POPs; the harmonization of forms for notification and movement documents and related instructions; cooperation with the World Trade Organization (WTO); and administrative and financial matters.

The eighth meeting of the Conference of the Parties to the Basel Convention (27 November–1 December) [UNEP/CHW.8/16 & Corr.1] condemned the dumping of hazardous wastes in Abidjan, Côte d'Ivoire, in August and called on parties to the Convention, countries and other stakeholders to offer technical and financial assistance to that country in support of its emergency plan to deal with the effects of the dumping. It approved the programme budget for the Basel Convention

Trust Fund of $3,975,397 for 2007 and $4,282,677 for 2008, and adopted the workplan of the Basel Convention Partnership Programme for 2007-2008; the work programme of the Open-ended Working Group for 2007-2008; and technical guidelines on POPs as wastes and the environmentally sound management of hazardous wastes. The Conference agreed to participate in the process to improve coordination between the Stockholm, Rotterdam and Basel Conventions, as called for by the second (2006) meeting of the Conference of the Parties to the Stockholm Convention (see p. 1248), including the establishment of an ad hoc joint working group.

Other decisions were related to creating solutions for the environmentally sound management of electrical and electronic wastes; the establishment of a working group to consider setting up a Basel Convention regional centre for south Asia; adoption of the guidance document for the Mobile Phone Partnership Initiative; international cooperation and coordination; cooperation between the Basel Convention and the International Maritime Organization; the dismantling, scrapping, and abandonment of ships, including the draft ship recycling convention to be adopted by the International Maritime Organization; reporting by parties to the Convention; clarification of the procedure for the review or adjustments of the lists of wastes contained in annexes VIII and IX of the Convention; the harmonization of forms for notification and movement documents and related instructions; the working relationship between the Open-ended Working Group and the United Nations Subcommittee of Experts on the Globally Harmonized System of Classification and Labelling of Chemicals; and the separate identification in the World Customs Organization Harmonized Commodity Description and Coding System of certain wastes in annexes VIII and IX of the Convention.

Further decisions dealt with the classification and hazard characterization of wastes; hazardous waste minimization; a draft instruction manual on the prosecution of illegal trafficking in hazardous wastes; the Basel Protocol; national legislation and other measures adopted by the parties to implement the Convention; national definitions of hazardous wastes; bilateral, multilateral or regional arrangements under article 11 of the Convention; the designation of competent authorities and focal points; interpretation of article 17, paragraph 5, of the Convention; and administrative and budgetary matters.

(For information on the human rights aspects of the illicit movement and dumping of toxic and dangerous products and wastes, see p. 909.)

Cleaner production and sustainable consumption patterns

In 2006, UNEP continued its role in the development of the 10-Year Framework of Programmes on Sustainable Consumption and Production (SCP)—the Marrakech Process—agreed to in 2003 [YUN 2003, p. 840]. The 10-Year Framework, launched in May in Ethiopia, was endorsed by the African Ministerial Conference on Environment, the New Partnership for Africa's Development and the African Union. The Asia Pacific Help Desk on SCP was established in Beijing, China. Three new Marrakech Task Forces were launched in 2006, bringing the total to seven. UNEP, supported by the United Kingdom Department for the Environment, Food and Rural Affairs, carried out a two-year project on National Strategies on SCP; the main output of the project would be a manual for national SCP strategies. UNEP continued its project on integrating SCP in poverty reduction strategies by developing a manual, implementing pilot projects in Ghana and Senegal, and strengthening the Marrakech Cooperation Dialogue with development agencies.

Regarding cleaner production, UNEP developed the strategy for the second phase of the Life Cycle Initiative, which promoted tools for evaluating the opportunities, risks and trade-offs associated with products and services over their life cycle to achieve sustainable development. It also conducted a global assessment of the status, challenges and opportunities for National Cleaner Production Centres.

Human settlements

Follow-up to the 1996 UN Conference on Human Settlements (Habitat II) and the 2001 General Assembly special session

In August [A/61/262], the Secretary-General, in response to General Assembly resolution 60/203 [YUN 2005, p. 1166], reported on follow-up to the Assembly's twenty-fifth special session [YUN 2001, p. 973] to review and appraise the implementation of the Habitat Agenda [YUN 1996, p. 994], adopted by the 1996 United Nations Conference on Human Settlements (Habitat II) [ibid., p. 992], and on the strengthening of the United Nations Human

Settlements Programme (UN-Habitat). The report *State of the World's Cities 2006/7: the Millennium Development Goals and Urban Sustainability—30 Years of Shaping the Habitat Agenda* provided concrete evidence that the rapidly growing urban poor were, in many cases, worse off that their rural counterparts in terms of health, nutrition, HIV/AIDS and other diseases. In most rapidly urbanizing countries and regions, the rate of slum formation was almost the same as the rate of urban growth. However, some countries in sub-Saharan Africa, including Burkina Faso, Senegal and the United Republic of Tanzania, had shown growing political support for slum upgrading and prevention. Several low or middle-income countries, including Colombia, El Salvador, Indonesia, Myanmar, the Philippines and Sri Lanka, managed to stem slum formation by anticipating and planning for growing urban populations, expanding economic and employment opportunities, investing in low-cost, affordable housing, and instituting pro-poor reforms and policies.

The report's findings indicated that slum formation was neither inevitable nor acceptable. As a result, UN-Habitat adopted a more comprehensive and results-based approach to mobilizing, guiding and coordinating more effective and cohesive responses to the urbanization of poverty and social exclusion. The objectives of the new strategic approach were to: mainstream urbanization and the urban poverty agenda at the global and national levels; strengthen the capacity of Governments and local authorities to adopt and implement pro-poor, gender-sensitive and environmentally sound slum upgrading and water and sanitation policies and strategies; promote innovative financing mechanisms for pro-poor housing and urban development to help prevent the growth of slums; contribute to more sustainable post-disaster reconstruction; and strengthen management and budget structure to ensure more efficient programme delivery. UN-Habitat assisted cities and national authorities in setting up urban monitoring systems by creating local and national urban observatories that compiled and analysed urban indicators and best practices for reporting on progress towards achieving the target of the MDGs to significantly improve the lives of at least 100 million slum-dwellers by 2020. It produced an updated version of a global urban database, containing information on more than 80 countries and 300 cities. A methodology for the rapid assessment of pro-poor, gender-sensitive policies and legislation was developed and tested in nine pilot countries, and strategic partnerships established to monitor slum formation, urban poverty and deprivation, and assess gender issues in water and sanitation.

UN-Habitat strengthened the coordination of its activities at the country level by appointing Habitat Programme Managers, who worked closely with UNDP offices and UN country teams. A key issue addressed was the fragmented approach of the international community in supporting countries in attaining the internationally agreed development goals. UN-Habitat strengthened its collaboration with multilateral partners to provide technical cooperation and capacity-building services to 30 countries in Africa and the Arab States. In the Asia-Pacific region, UN-Habitat further diversified its portfolio of operational projects on pro-poor human settlements in terms of funding sources, and in Latin America and the Caribbean continued cooperation with other agencies on poor settlement upgrading projects. It took the lead in packaging capacity-building technical assistance with domestic and international finance to support Member States to achieve the MDG target on water and sanitation. The Water for African Cities programme, which helped African countries to manage the growing urban water and sanitation crisis and protect the continent's threatened water resources and aquatic ecosystems, was implemented in 17 cities in 14 countries. UN-Habitat and the African Development Bank signed a memorandum of understanding to facilitate safe water supply and sanitation in African cities and small urban centres through, among other things, grants valued at approximately $217 million over five years. The Water for Asian Cities programme, sponsored by UN-Habitat and the Asian Development Bank, provided pro-poor water and sanitation in China, India, the Lao People's Democratic Republic and Nepal with investments totalling over $280 million. UN-Habitat also began an initiative to attain the MDG target to reduce by half the proportion of people without sustainable access to safe drinking water by 2015 within four to five years in the Lake Victoria transboundary ecosystem. The initiative mobilized investment to support pro-poor water, sanitation, solid-waste management and infrastructure in 15 secondary urban centres and reduce the environmental impact of urbanization in the Lake Victoria basin. UN-Habitat responded to humanitarian and crisis situations by supporting Governments, local authorities and civil society in strengthening their capacity to recover from human-made and natural disasters in the human settlements sector, and to develop prevention and reconstruction programmes.

Contributions to the United Nations Habitat and Human Settlements Foundation increased by 44 per cent, from $32.7 million in 2004 to $47.1 million in 2005. Non-earmarked contributions remained at $10.5 million, while earmarked contributions rose from $22.2 million in 2004 to $36.6 million in 2005. The increasing imbalance between earmarked and non-earmarked contributions continued to pose a major challenge, affecting UN-Habitat's ability to engage in strategic planning and results-based management in a predictable manner.

The Secretary-General concluded that the struggle to provide safe water and basic sanitation and attain the MDGS required a more integrated approach to deal with the growing crisis of rapid and unplanned urbanization, and recognize the importancc of local authorities in planning and mobilizing investments in housing, urban infrastructure and basic services. Well-planned and managed human settlements were critical to reducing the ecological footprint of human activity and promoting the sustainable use of natural resources.

The Secretary-General encouraged Governments to: accord the highest priority to integrating slum upgrading and prevention into national development strategies and poverty reduction strategy papers for attaining the MDGS; and work with Habitat Programme Managers to promote slum upgrading, affordable shelter and housing finance, and sustainable urbanization, and with UN-Habitat to assess and monitor trends in slum formation, urban poverty and urban deprivation as a basis for informing and adopting pro-poor gender-sensitive urban policies and strategies. Governments in a position to do so should increase non-earmarked funding and regular budget resources. Governments, financial institutions and other public and private entities were also encouraged to contribute to the capitalization of the United Nations Habitat and Human Settlements Foundation as an effective means of providing financial and seed-capital support to slum upgrading, slum prevention and pro-poor water and sanitation activities in urban areas.

Coordinated implementation of Habitat Agenda

In response to a 2005 Economic and Social Council decision [YUN 2005, p. 1166], the Secretary-General submitted a May report [E/2006/71] on the coordinated implementation of the Habitat Agenda. The report summarized UN-Habitat activities in the areas of global monitoring and advocacy in support of shelter for all and the achievement of the MDG target on slums [YUN 2000, p. 52]; policy development; the provision of capacity-building and technical advisory services; and mobilizing domestic resources and investment in pro-poor housing and urban development. The report also highlighted the new strategic approach to meeting the goals of the Habitat Agenda (see p. 1249).

The Secretary-General said that, while considerable progress had been made in furthering the coordinated implementation of the Habitat Agenda at the global level, substantial obstacles remained at the national and local levels to address the complex issues of rapid urbanization and urban poverty. Attaining the MDGS in urban areas required a more integrated approach to deal with the growing crisis of rapid and unplanned urbanization in a holistic manner and recognize the role of local authorities in planning and mobilizing investments in urban infrastructure and basic services. Support for efforts to attain the MDGS and sustain the benefits accrued beyond target dates in rapidly urbanizing countries would depend largely on strengthening partnerships among Governments, local authorities and the international community to work with local stakeholders in a concerted manner. The Secretary-General encouraged Governments to mainstream the urban agenda in preparing and implementing comprehensive national development strategies to achieve the commitments of the Habitat Agenda and the MDGS, as called for in the 2005 World Summit Outcome [YUN 2005, p. 48]. He invited them to work with the UN-Habitat integrated and multi-stakeholder approach to implement pro-poor housing, water and sanitation and urban development; strengthen slum prevention and slum improvement; and ensure the effective participation of local authorities, the private sector and civil society. They should designate a single focal point for urban affairs in their interaction with UN country teams.

On 27 July, the Economic and Social Council, by **decision 2006/247**, took note of the Secretary-General's report; decided to transmit it to the General Assembly for consideration at its sixty-first (2006) session; and requested the Secretary-General to submit a report on the coordinated implementation of the Habitat Agenda to the Council in 2007.

In response to the Council's decision, the Secretary-General, by a September note [A/61/363], transmitted his May report to the Assembly.

Special annex to financial regulations. The Secretary-General, in a July bulletin [ST/SGB/2006/8], promulgated a revised edition of the special annex for the United Nations Habitat and Human Settlements Foundation (series 300) to the Financial Rules and Regulations of the United Nations (series 100). The special annex of the 300 series Rules, which entered into force on 1 August, authorized certain exceptions and additions to the 100 series Rules for the Foundation.

GENERAL ASSEMBLY ACTION

On 20 December [meeting 83], the General Assembly, on the recommendation of the Second Committee [A/61/423], adopted **resolution 61/206** without vote [agenda item 54].

Implementation of the outcome of the United Nations Conference on Human Settlements (Habitat II) and strengthening of the United Nations Human Settlements Programme (UN-Habitat)

The General Assembly,

Recalling its resolutions 3327 (XXIX) of 16 December 1974, 32/162 of 19 December 1977, 34/115 of 14 December 1979, 56/205 and 56/206 of 21 December 2001, 57/275 of 20 December 2002, 58/226 and 58/227 of 23 December 2003, 59/239 of 22 December 2004 and 60/203 of 22 December 2005,

Taking note of Economic and Social Council resolutions 2002/38 of 26 July 2002 and 2003/62 of 25 July 2003 and Council decisions 2004/300 of 23 July 2004, 2005/298 of 26 July 2005 and 2006/247 of 27 July 2006,

Recalling the goal contained in the United Nations Millennium Declaration of achieving a significant improvement in the lives of at least 100 million slum-dwellers by 2020 and the goal contained in the Plan of Implementation of the World Summit on Sustainable Development ("Johannesburg Plan of Implementation") to halve, by 2015, the proportion of people who lack access to safe drinking water and sanitation,

Recalling also the Habitat Agenda, the Declaration on Cities and Other Human Settlements in the New Millennium, the Johannesburg Declaration on Sustainable Development, the Johannesburg Plan of Implementation and the Monterrey Consensus of the International Conference on Financing for Development,

Recalling further the 2005 World Summit Outcome,

Recognizing that the overall thrust and strategic vision of the United Nations Human Settlements Programme (UN-Habitat) and its emphasis on the two global campaigns on secure tenure and urban governance are strategic points of entry for the effective implementation of the Habitat Agenda, especially for guiding international cooperation in respect of adequate shelter for all and sustainable human settlements development,

Conscious of the unique opportunity provided by the Cities Without Slums Initiative mentioned in the Millennium Declaration for realizing economies of scale and substantial multiplier effects in helping to attain the other Millennium Development Goals,

Acknowledging the significance of the urban dimension of poverty eradication and the need to integrate water and sanitation issues within a broad-based approach to human settlements,

Noting with appreciation the convening by the Government of Pakistan of the second South Asian Conference on Sanitation, held in Islamabad on 20 and 21 September 2006,

Expressing its appreciation to the Government of Kenya, the African Union and UN-Habitat for hosting the second African Ministerial Conference on Housing and Urban Development and the Africities Summit in Nairobi on 3 and 4 April 2006 and from 18 to 24 September 2006, respectively,

Expressing its appreciation also to the Government of Canada and the city of Vancouver for hosting the third session of the World Urban Forum from 19 to 23 June 2006 and to the Government of China and the city of Nanjing for their willingness to host the fourth session of the World Urban Forum in 2008,

Expressing its appreciation further to the Government of India for its offer to host the first Asia-Pacific Ministerial Conference on Housing and Human Settlements in New Delhi in December 2006,

Expressing its appreciation to the Government of Uruguay for hosting the fifteenth regular Assembly of Ministers and High-level Authorities of the Housing and Urban Development Sector in Latin America and the Caribbean, held from 4 to 6 October 2006 in Montevideo,

Taking note of the report entitled *State of the World's Cities 2006/7: the Millennium Development Goals and Urban Sustainability—30 Years of Shaping the Habitat Agenda*,

Recognizing the need for UN-Habitat to sharpen its focus on all areas within its mandate,

Recognizing also the continued urgent need for increased and predictable financial contributions to the United Nations Habitat and Human Settlements Foundation to ensure timely, effective and concrete global implementation of the Habitat Agenda, the Declaration on Cities and Other Human Settlements in the New Millennium and the relevant internationally agreed development goals, including those contained in the Millennium Declaration and the Johannesburg Declaration and Plan of Implementation,

Noting the efforts by UN-Habitat to strengthen its collaboration with the United Nations Development Programme, the World Bank and other international organizations and its participation in the Executive Committee on Humanitarian Affairs,

Taking note of the report of the Secretary-General on the coordinated implementation of the Habitat Agenda and the report of the Secretary-General on the implementation of the outcome of the United Nations Conference on Human Settlements (Habitat II) and strengthening of the United Nations Human Settlements Programme (UN-Habitat),

Taking note also of the special annex for the United Nations Habitat and Human Settlements Foundation appended by the Secretary-General to the financial regulations and rules of the United Nations,

1. *Requests* the Governing Council of the United Nations Human Settlements Programme (UN-Habitat) to address, in a comprehensive manner, any issues relating to the United Nations Habitat and Human Settle-

ments Foundation at its twenty-first session, bearing in mind the need to effectively mobilize resources for the Foundation;

2. *Encourages* Governments to consider an enhanced approach to achieving the Cities Without Slums Initiative mentioned in the United Nations Millennium Declaration by upgrading existing slums and creating policies and programmes, according to national circumstances, to forestall the growth of future slums, and in this regard invites the international donor community and multilateral and regional development banks to support the efforts of developing countries, inter alia, through increased voluntary financial assistance;

3. *Recognizes* that Governments have the primary responsibility for the sound and effective implementation of the Habitat Agenda, the Declaration on Cities and Other Human Settlements in the New Millennium and the Millennium Declaration, and stresses the need for the international community to fully implement commitments to support Governments of developing countries and countries with economies in transition in their efforts, through the provision of the requisite resources, capacity-building, the transfer of technology on mutually agreed terms and the creation of an international enabling environment;

4. *Calls for* continued financial support to UN-Habitat through increased voluntary contributions to the United Nations Habitat and Human Settlements Foundation, and invites Governments to provide predictable multi-year funding to support programme implementation;

5. *Also calls for* increased, non-earmarked contributions to the Foundation;

6. *Requests* the Secretary-General to keep the resource needs of UN-Habitat under review so as to enhance its effectiveness in supporting national policies, strategies and plans in attaining the poverty eradication, gender equality, water and sanitation and slum upgrading targets of the Millennium Declaration, the Johannesburg Plan of Implementation and the 2005 World Summit Outcome;

7. *Emphasizes* the importance of the Nairobi headquarters location of the United Nations Human Settlements Programme, and requests the Secretary-General to keep the resource needs of UN-Habitat and the United Nations Office at Nairobi under review so as to permit the delivery, in an effective manner, of necessary services to UN-Habitat and the other United Nations organs and organizations in Nairobi;

8. *Welcomes* the ongoing efforts of UN-Habitat to develop a results-based and less fragmented budget structure with a view to securing maximum efficiency, accountability and transparency in programme delivery regardless of funding source;

9. *Invites* the international donor community and financial institutions to contribute generously to the Water and Sanitation Trust Fund, the Slum Upgrading Facility and the technical cooperation trust funds to enable UN-Habitat to assist developing countries to mobilize public investment and private capital for slum upgrading, shelter and basic services;

10. *Acknowledges* contributions of the regional consultative initiatives, including conferences of ministers in the area of human settlements, for implementation of the Habitat Agenda and the attainment of the Millennium Development Goals, and invites the international community to support such efforts;

11. *Calls upon* UN-Habitat to strengthen its regional approach to the coordination and implementation of its normative and operational activities, and invites all countries in a position to do so to support the activities of UN-Habitat in this regard;

12. *Requests* UN-Habitat to intensify coordination in the framework of the United Nations Development Assistance Framework and the common country assessment and to continue to work with the World Bank, regional development banks, other development banks, regional organizations and other relevant partners to field-test innovative policies, practices and pilot projects in order to mobilize resources to increase the supply of affordable credit for slum upgrading and other pro-poor human settlements development in developing countries and countries with economies in transition;

13. *Invites* all Governments to participate actively in the fourth session of the World Urban Forum, and invites donor countries to support the participation of representatives from developing countries, in particular the least developed countries, and countries with economies in transition, including women and youth, in the Forum;

14. *Recognizes* the important role and contribution of UN-Habitat in supporting the efforts of countries affected by natural disasters and complex emergencies to develop prevention, rehabilitation and reconstruction programmes for the transition from relief to development, and in this regard requests UN-Habitat, within its mandate, to continue to work closely with other relevant agencies in the United Nations system, and strongly reiterates its invitation to the Inter-Agency Standing Committee to consider including UN-Habitat in its membership;

15. *Requests* UN-Habitat, through its involvement in the Executive Committee on Humanitarian Affairs and through contacts with relevant United Nations agencies and partners in the field, to promote the early involvement of human settlements experts in the assessment and development of prevention, rehabilitation and reconstruction programmes to support the efforts of developing countries affected by natural disasters and complex humanitarian emergencies;

16. *Requests* the Secretary-General to submit to the General Assembly at its sixty-second session a report on the implementation of the present resolution;

17. *Decides* to include in the provisional agenda of its sixty-second session the item entitled "Implementation of the outcome of the United Nations Conference on Human Settlements (Habitat II) and strengthening of the United Nations Human Settlements Programme (UN-Habitat)".

UN Human Settlements Programme

Governing Council

In accordance with General Assembly resolution 56/206 [YUN 2001, p. 987], the Governing Council of the United Nations Human Settlements Programme (UN-Habitat), which met biennially, did not meet in 2006. The twenty-first session of the Governing Council would take place in 2007.

Committee of Permanent Representatives

The Committee of Permanent Representatives, the intersessional body of the UN-Habitat Governing Council, met four times in 2006 (16 March, 8 June, 28 September and 7 December). The Committee discussed the UN-Habitat workplan for 2006; preparations for and the outcome of the third session of the World Urban Forum (see p. 1255); the UN-Habitat strategic framework for 2008-2009; the proposed Medium-term Strategic and Institutional Plan 2008-2013; the UN-Habitat financial situation; and preparations for the twenty-first (2007) Governing Council session.

UN-Habitat activities

In 2006, UN-Habitat focused its attention on strengthening its capacity and the accelerated implementation of the key components of its work programme in line with the goals of the international community, the UN system and the Governing Council's 2005 resolutions [YUN 2005, p. 1168]. UN-Habitat, in cooperation with youth groups, other UN bodies and external partners, and the Committee of Permanent Representatives, finalized the Action Plan and Strategy for Youth Engagement. The Plan focussed on five key areas of support to youth empowerment: youth participation in UN Habitat organs and forums at the global, national and local levels; youth leadership and entrepreneurship; policies and strategies to strengthen youth participation in local decision making; knowledge sharing and communications; and coordination and partnerships.

Gender mainstreaming strategies and action plans were developed in consultation with gender experts, city authorities and NGOs for the Water for African Cities and Water for Asian Cities programmes. The findings from gender assessments carried out in 17 cities in Africa and four in Asia were integrated into project design, planning and management to ensure the effective contribution of women as change agents. Guidelines for improving gender mainstreaming in disaster management, especially in the areas of governance and land administration, were being prepared.

Collaboration between UN-Habitat and the African Ministerial Conference on Housing and Urban Development intensified during the year. A special ministerial conference was convened jointly with Kenya and South Africa (Nairobi, 3-4 April), under the theme "Achieving the Millennium Development Goals in Africa: strategies for the realization of the World Summit Outcome on Slums". UN-Habitat also participated in the fourth Africities Summit (Nairobi, 18-22 September). The UN-Habitat secretariat convened, in collaboration with India, the Asia-Pacific Ministerial Conference on Human Settlements (New Delhi, India, 13-16 December), the theme of which was "A vision for sustainable urbanization in the Asia-Pacific by 2020". The Conference adopted the Delhi Declaration and an Enhanced Framework of Implementation. A key result of the Conference was the establishment of a standing consultative mechanism on the promotion of sustainable development of housing and urban development in the Asia-Pacific region. UN-Habitat also worked closely with the secretariat of the New Partnership for Africa's Development (NEPAD) in implementing the NEPAD Cities Programme.

In follow-up to a 2005 Governing Council resolution on the sustainable development of Arctic cities [YUN 2005, p. 1169], the UN-Habitat secretariat established working relations with the UNEP/GRID-Arendal centre to map out joint activities between the two programmes. Consultations were held with a wide range of stakeholders, including local authorities in the Far North, academic institutions with programmes dedicated to development issues in the Arctic and civil society organizations representing indigenous peoples in those areas. UN-Habitat incorporated the needs of least developed countries (LDCs) throughout its advocacy and monitoring activities, as well as in its programmes and country-level activities. Technical support was provided to 20 national statistical offices in LDCs for the collection and analysis of key indicators on urbanization, urban poverty and slum formation. Campaigns on urban governance and secure tenure were launched in 14 LDCs and UN-Habitat responded to requests for ad hoc technical assistance in another three countries. UN-Habitat also continued to address the needs of small island developing States (SIDS) in its programmes and projects, and facilitated the financing of their participation in its international meetings.

Host Governments and Habitat Agenda partners promoted the programmes of the Slum Upgrading

Facility in pilot countries, resulting in the recognition of the Facility by domestic banking institutions as a methodology for establishing credit for local slum upgrading projects. Strong links were developed with the World Bank Group through the grant agreement on the Facility with the Cities Alliance, the alignment of projects with the World Bank and regional banks' projects in the pilot countries, and memoranda of understanding for safe drinking water and basic sanitation with the African Development Bank and the Asian Development Bank. The principles of UN-Habitat Global Campaigns on Urban Governance and for Secure Tenure, launched in 2000 [YUN 2000, p. 995], were applied through the Global Land Tools Network, which was officially launched at the third session of the World Urban Forum (see below); the network aimed to develop pro-poor gender and age-responsive land tools to improve access to land. Work continued on mainstreaming rights-based approaches to the provision of basic infrastructure and services in partnership with other UN bodies, particularly through the Cities Alliance partnership between UN-Habitat and the World Bank, a joint study on cultural rights to the city with UNESCO, a joint review of best practices in inclusive public administration with the UN Department of Economic and Social Affairs, and continued involvement with WHO on developing health indicators for cities. The Global Urban Observatory, which monitored global trends and issues in urbanization and urban poverty, continued to promote and include representatives of civil society in its data collection and analysis activities in more than 200 local urban observatories worldwide. In the area of decentralization and the strengthening of local authorities, the UN-Habitat secretariat mobilized the United Nations Advisory Committee of Local Authorities and the Advisory Group of Experts on Decentralization to finalize the guidelines on decentralization and continue work on the compendium of best practices in support of the guidelines.

Report to Permanent Forum on Indigenous Issues. In response to recommendations made by the fourth (2005) session of the Permanent Forum on Indigenous Issues [YUN 2005, p. 881], UN-Habitat issued a March report [E/C.19/2006/6/Add.2] on its activities related to the rights and needs of indigenous peoples. UN-Habitat efforts involved promoting inclusiveness, social integration and the realization of housing rights, including through the implementation of the MDG target on slums, the Global Campaigns on Urban Governance and for Secure Tenure, and the United Nations Housing Rights Programme. Its work on poverty alleviation and the MDGs had the potential to establish direct links with the livelihoods of indigenous peoples, and its activities in disaster mitigation, post-conflict recovery and safety in human settlements were, in most cases, related to housing and living conditions of indigenous peoples. During the International Expert Meeting on the MDGs, Indigenous Participation and Good Governance (New York, 11-13 January), UN-Habitat highlighted the important changes taking place in the lives of indigenous peoples as a result of urbanization and migration processes, and recommended that the capacities of indigenous peoples and their organizations be strengthened in order to facilitate their participation and effectiveness in urban governance.

World Urban Forum. UN-Habitat convened the third session of the World Urban Forum (Vancouver, Canada, 19-23 June) [HSP/GC/21/INF/2] on the theme "Our Future: Sustainable Cities—Turning Ideas into Action". Forum participants called for practical action to balance economic, environmental and social development objectives in the realization of sustainable urbanization. They recognized the need to come to terms with the urban age and meet the financing challenge of slum upgrading and sustainable infrastructure development; stressed the importance of applying new paradigms for sustainable urban development; and showed a willingness to build effective coalitions to address the needs of the urban poor. The fourth session of the Forum would be held in Nanjing, China, in 2008.

Cooperation with UNEP

A December report [HSP/GC/21/2/Add.5], prepared jointly by the Executive Directors of UN-Habitat and UNEP, described cooperation between the two organizations in the areas of assessment, policy development, and implementation of joint initiatives, cooperation in Africa, Latin America and the Caribbean and Asia and the Pacific, the key results of cooperation, and opportunities for future cooperation.

Strategic evaluation

A December report [HSP/GC/21/INF/4] described the external evaluation of the performance and impact of Habitat Programme Mangers, as requested in a 2005 Governing Council resolution [YUN 2005, p. 1171]. The evaluation team found that the Habitat Programme Manager initiative had significantly enhanced the ability of UN-Habitat to fulfil its mandate at the country level through the establishment of a substantive national presence at a comparatively limited cost per country. However, the initial generic terms of reference for Habitat Programme Managers could not adequately define strategic goals in each country concerned. A consolidated programming effort at the country level, including the definition of strategic goals and expected results, would better address national priorities for UN-Habitat and enable its Programme Managers to operate within a clear planning framework. Several constraints and inadequacies impinged on the effectiveness of Habitat Programme Managers, including an inadequate operating budget, insufficient training and unequally distributed responsibility for their support. The evaluation team endorsed the decisions of the Governing Council, reflected in its 2005 resolution on the Habitat Programme Manager initiative [ibid.] and the 2006-2007 UN-Habitat work programme and budget [ibid., p. 1170], that the initiative should be financed primarily through the general purpose Habitat and Human Settlements Foundation resources. Formulas for contributions from global programmes and operational projects needed to be defined more transparently and systematically as part of an organization-wide strategic programming exercise for each country.

The evaluation team concluded that, while meaningful gains had been achieved, it was essential that Habitat Programme Managers were seen as a long-term investment for UN Habitat. It recommended that: the initiative be continued and funded primarily through the Habitat and Human Settlements Foundation general purpose allocations; the identification of additional countries for Habitat Programme Manager deployment be based on the assessed potential for policy change, government commitment and scope for deployment; more systematic and comprehensive training support be given to Habitat Programme Managers; the recommended country programme documents should be the basis for determining the exit strategy of UN-Habitat from countries where results might have failed to materialize; and the memorandum of understanding between UN-Habitat and UNDP be reviewed and extended to facilitate new cooperation and cost sharing agreements with UNDP country offices.

Other matters

Re-election of Executive Director

By **decision 60/421** of 28 June, the General Assembly, on the Secretary-General's proposal [A/60/895], elected Anna Kajumulo Tibaijuka (United Republic of Tanzania) as UN-Habitat Executive Director for a further four-year term of office beginning on 1 September 2006 and ending on 31 August 2010.

OIOS report

The UN Office of Internal Oversight Services (OIOS), in an addendum to its August report [A/61/264(Part I)], recalled its 2000 recommendation that UN-Habitat develop a procedures manual to ensure the establishment of sound financial and budgetary controls for its technical cooperation projects, and noted that progress on the manual had been exceedingly slow. It stressed the importance of providing UN-Habitat field staff with clear guidance and a good understanding of what was expected of them when discharging their roles and responsibilities, which should reduce the risk of financial and budgetary irregularities.

Chapter VIII

Population

In 2006, world population reached 6.6 billion, as compared with 6.5 billion in 2005, and was projected to reach 9 billion by 2050.

UN population activities continued to be guided, in 2006, by the Programme of Action adopted at the 1994 International Conference on Population and Development (ICPD) and the key actions for its further implementation adopted at the twenty-first special session of the General Assembly in 1999. The Commission on Population and Development, the body responsible for monitoring, reviewing and assessing the implementation of the Programme of Action, considered as its special theme "International migration and development". The Population Division continued to analyse and report on world demographic trends and policies and to make its findings available in publications and on the Internet.

The General Assembly, in September, held the first High-level Dialogue on International Migration and Development to discuss the multidimensional aspects of the phenomenon and identify ways to maximize its developmental benefits and minimize its negative impacts. Participants agreed that international migration could be a positive force for development in both countries of origin and destination, provided that it was supported by the right policies. Several meetings were organized in preparation for the Dialogue and to follow up on its conclusions.

The United Nations Population Fund (UNFPA) continued to assist countries in implementing the ICPD agenda and the Millennium Development Goals. In 2006, UNFPA provided assistance to 154 countries and territories, with special emphasis on increasing the availability and quality of reproductive health services, fighting gender discrimination and violence, formulating effective population policies and intensifying HIV prevention.

Follow-up to 1994 Conference on Population and Development

Implementation of Programme of Action

Commission on Population and Development consideration. In follow-up to the recommendations of the 1994 International Conference on Population and Development (ICPD) [YUN 1994, p. 955], the Commission on Population and Development, at its thirty-ninth session (New York, 3-7 April and 10 May) [E/2006/25], considered as its special theme "International migration and development" and discussed its demographic, social and economic aspects (see below). It also discussed follow-up actions to the ICPD recommendations and national experience in international migration and development.

The Commission had before it the Secretary-General's reports on world population monitoring, focusing on international migration and development [E/CN.9/2006/3], and on the monitoring of population programmes, focusing on international migration and development [E/CN.9/2006/4]; an April note from Mexico transmitting the document entitled "Mexico and the migration phenomenon" [E/CN.9/2006/8]; and statements by two non-governmental organizations (NGOs) in consultative status with the Economic and Social Council: the Population Institute [E/CN.9/2006/NGO/2] and Population Action International [E/CN.9/2006/NGO/1].

The first report [E/CN.9/2006/3] reviewed international migration trends; examined the interactions between international migration and population growth, fertility, mortality and health; discussed the economic aspects of international migration; and concluded with an overview of policy responses at the national, regional and international levels.

The report found that between 1990 and 2005, the world had gained 36 million international migrants, just about half of the 68 million registered between 1975 and 1990. The slowing growth rate of international migrants was due to the decline in the number of refugees in Latin America and the Caribbean and the least developed countries (LDCs) between 1990 and 2005. In Central America, successful peace processes had led to their full repatriation. Similarly, large numbers of refugees hosted by LDCs were able to return home as long-standing conflicts were resolved, particularly in Africa. However, those changes produced an increasing concentration of international migrants in the developed world, which hosted 61 per cent (115.4 million) of all international migrants in 2005, with North America seeing major increases between 1990 and

2005 (17 million), followed by Europe (15 million). Migration for family reunification accounted for an important share of such inflows, as a result of the increase in labour and skilled migrations. The need for workers had been driving the rising levels of migration to developed countries, especially under special programmes for the admission of temporary workers, with options to become long-term residents in several countries. In addition, given the low fertility levels in the more developed regions, net migration became the major driving force behind population growth, accounting for three quarters of growth in 2000-2005.

Against the backdrop of growing international migration to developed countries, there was an increasing recognition of the need to manage migration and prevent and combat clandestine inflows. Key international instruments for addressing clandestine migration had been adopted and widely ratified. In 2005, 75 countries had programmes to facilitate the integration of foreigners, up from 52 in 1996. More than three quarters of developed countries had integration policies, compared to less than a quarter of developing countries. With the exception of the European Union (EU), regional economic integration processes had not yet resulted in freedom of movement for workers. Responding to a need for increased dialogue on international migration issues, a number of regional consultative processes had been established, and were proving useful in building understandings and promoting cooperation. At the global level, several initiatives were launched to address the challenges posed by international migration, key among them being the Global Commission on International Migration [YUN 2004, p. 1077], whose report and recommendations were issued in 2005.

The second report [E/CN.9/2006/4] explored the implications of international migration as they related to development, pointing out its global dimensions and central role in the global development agenda. It described the current international migration situation, with a focus on South-North migration, and on the impact on development of the brain drain, brain gain, brain circulation, remittances, the diaspora, and return migration. It highlighted the importance of building and strengthening the capacities of governments and other stakeholders to meet the challenges posed by international migration. The report considered important elements that had potential for policy intervention that could enhance positive development impacts and mutually beneficial solutions for countries of both origin and destination, as well as for the migrants themselves. It also discussed barriers to, and opportunities for, such policy intervention.

Expert Group meeting. On 27 February [E/CN.9/2006/7], Mexico transmitted to the Secretary-General the conclusions of the Expert Group Meeting on International Migration and Development in Latin America and the Caribbean (Mexico City, 30 November–2 December 2005). The meeting focused on the interrelationships between migration and development and the challenges and opportunities arising from migration in the region, with a view to contributing technical information to the debate on migration policies in force throughout the world. Annexed to the letter were the conclusions of the meeting.

Commission action. The Commission, in a resolution [E/2006/25 (res. 2006/2)], took note of the Secretary-General's reports, as well as his report on the flow of financial resources for assisting in the implementation of the ICPD Programme of Action (see p. 1259), and the *Report of the Global Commission On International Migration*. It reaffirmed the responsibility of Governments for safeguarding and protecting the rights of migrants against illegal or violent acts and requested Member States to cooperate in addressing the challenge of undocumented or irregular migration. They should enact domestic legislation and take further measures to combat international trafficking in persons and the smuggling of migrants. The Commission reiterated the need to consider the extent to which the migration of highly skilled persons and those with advanced education impacted the development efforts of developing countries, and acknowledged the need to analyse the impact of certain forms of temporary and return migration. It requested the Secretary-General to continue his work on international migration and development and, in collaboration with other international organizations and UN funds and programmes, assess the progress in achieving the goals and objectives on international migration and development set out in the outcomes of major UN conferences and summits. It looked forward to the General Assembly's High-level Dialogue on International Migration and Development (see p. 1261), to be held during its sixty-first session and recommended that the Economic and Social Council transmit the Commission's report on its thirty-ninth session to the High-level Dialogue.

By decision **2006/233** of 24 July, the Economic and Social Council decided to transmit the Commission's report on its thirty-ninth session to the High-Level Dialogue on International Migration and Development.

Financial resources

In accordance with General Assembly resolutions 49/128 [YUN 1994, p. 963] and 50/124 [YUN 1995, p. 1094], the Secretary-General submitted to the Commission a January report [E/CN.9/2006/5] on the flow of financial resources for assisting in the implementation of the ICPD Programme of Action. The report examined the flow of funds from donors and domestic expenditure for population activities in developing countries for 2004, as well as estimates for 2005 and projections for 2006. It was encouraging that a gradual increase in both international donor assistance and domestic expenditure for population activities, especially in the funding for HIV/AIDS, had ensured the attainment of the 2005 funding targets of the Programme of Action. Donor assistance was estimated at $5.3 billion in 2004, up from $4.7 billion in 2003, and domestic expenditures at almost $14.5 billion in 2004, up from $11 billion the previous year, for a total estimate of $19.8 billion in 2004. The challenge for the international community was mobilizing the required resources to implement the ICPD agenda within the framework of the Millennim Development Goals (MDGs). Estimates for 2005 and projections for 2006 were encouraging. Donor assistance was estimated to have increased to $6.1 billion in 2005 and was projected to increase to almost $6.4 billion in 2006. Resources mobilized by developing countries were estimated to reach $14.9 billion in 2005 and $15.9 billion in 2006. While the largest share of funding was currently going to AIDS-related activities, the increased resources were still not adequately addressing the growing AIDS pandemic.

The Joint United Nations Programme on HIV/AIDS (UNAIDS) estimated that global resources requirements amounted to $15 billion in 2006; $8.4 billion for prevention and $3 billion for treatment and care. Funding for basic reproductive health services increased slightly, while funding for family planning services decreased significantly.

International migration and development

Gender dimensions of international migration

On 25 July [meeting 41], the Economic and Social Council, having considered the summary of the high-level panel discussion on the gender dimensions of international migration submitted by the Chairperson of the Commission on the Status of Women (see p. 1347), adopted **decision 2006/234** [draft: E/2006/27 & Corr.1] without vote [agenda item 14 *(a)*].

High-level panel discussion on the gender dimensions of international migration

At its 38th plenary meeting, on 25 July 2006, the Economic and Social Council decided to transmit to the General Assembly the following summary of the high-level panel discussion on the gender dimensions of international migration submitted by the Chairperson of the Commission on the Status of Women;

1. At its 9th plenary meeting, on 2 March 2006, the Commission on the Status of Women held a high-level panel discussion on the theme "The gender dimensions of international migration". The panellists were Monica Boyd, Canada Research Chair in Sociology, University of Toronto, Canada; Manuel Orozco, Senior Associate, Inter-American Dialogue, United States of America; Ndioro Ndiaye, Deputy Director-General, International Organization for Migration, Geneva; Maruja Milagros B. Asis, Director of Research and Publications, Scalabrini Migration Centre, Philippines; and Irena Omelaniuk, Migration Adviser, World Bank. The panel was moderated by Carmen María Gallardo (El Salvador), Chairperson of the Commission.

2. The high-level panel discussion provided the opportunity for the Commission to examine the multidimensional aspects of international migration from a gender perspective and to provide input to the General Assembly at its High-level Dialogue on International Migration and Development, to be held in New York on 14 and 15 September 2006.

3. Women were active participants in migration within and between countries. Statistics indicated, for example, that the proportion of women among international migrants had reached 51 per cent in more developed regions. Women moved on their own as the principal wage earners or for family reunification purposes. Most women moved voluntarily, but women and girls were also forced to migrate owing to conflict and violence. There is increasing recognition that gender biases existed in the migration process, resulting in women's experiences being different from those of men, including in relation to exit and entry and in countries of destination. Causes and outcomes of migration could be very different for women and for men.

4. The linkages between migration and development were identified as critical. A holistic and comprehensive approach was required to address the multidimensional aspects of international migration. Poverty and lack of access to economic resources were identified as main factors influencing the propensity of women to migrate. Increased socio-economic development, including through investments in the health sector, might lead to disincentives for migration. Increased gender equality within countries of origin might also reduce women's need for and interest in migration, including for economic reasons. Perceptions about the roles of women and men, relationships within households and resource allocations determined the ability of women to make migration decisions autonomously, to contribute to decision-making on migration within the household and to access resources for migration.

5. Sufficient information was not available on the impact of migration of both women and men on the families remaining in the countries of origin. A closer examination of the structural conditions, including underdevelopment and poverty, that led people to migrate and leave their families behind was needed. The importance of national policies in ensuring the welfare of those left behind was noted, and it was recommended that the High-level Dialogue on International Migration and Development give attention to that issue.

6. The empowerment of women in the migration process required the increased participation of women in migration decisions. The empowerment of migrant women should be given specific attention in migration policies and legislation. The need for countries of origin and destination to examine their exit and entry policies to determine the impact on women was noted, as well as the need for greater collaboration between ministries to ensure increased attention to gender equality and the linkages between gender equality, migration and development.

7. It was recognized that the migration of women and men was linked to specific demand for different types of labour. In some countries, the demand for labour in traditionally male-dominated jobs, for example, in construction, led to high levels of male migration. In other countries, the demand for care workers led to increased labour migration of women. Participants noted, however, that the care sector was often a precarious and unprotected sector.

8. Agreements between countries of origin and countries of destination to encourage and facilitate migration were generally economically driven. Gender equality issues were often not given attention in such agreements, which could result in negative impacts on women. The issue of "brain drain" was raised, and it was pointed out that some developing countries had experienced a huge migration of professionals, including women, to developed countries to earn higher incomes.

9. The living and working conditions of both legal and undocumented migrant women workers should be examined further, including to identify their mistreatment and abuse. Violence against women migrants was cited as a critical issue. The issue of racial discrimination, xenophobia and other forms of discrimination were also raised by some participants. Gender-sensitive rights-based approaches to migration should include promotion and protection of the rights of migrant women workers, through, for example, the development of an enabling international environment, the ratification and implementation of international legal instruments, including the labour standards of the International Labour Organization and the harmonization of national legislation. Legal frameworks should meet the needs of both States and migrants. Partnerships with trade unions and training for police and border officials were recommended. The key role of non-governmental organizations in promoting the rights of migrant women was highlighted.

10. In some countries, evidence suggested that men migrants remitted more than women because their earnings were higher. In other cases, however, women tended to remit more because the ratio of migrant women to men was higher. Women tended to be the main receivers of remittances and generally invested in education and health care for their children. Both senders and recipients of remittances faced major constraints in having access to financial institutions. Banks and other financial institutions should improve their services. Further research on gender and remittances was needed.

11. Countries of origin and countries of destination both shared responsibility for the welfare of migrant women. The need for awareness-raising on the contributions of women migrants in countries of destination was highlighted. The contributions, while significant, often remained invisible because of the concentration of female migrant workers in the private sphere. The importance of fostering greater sensitivity to the diversity of cultures among migrants was also raised.

12. Attention was drawn to the need to address the social challenges related to migration in countries of destination and the need to link the social and economic aspects of migration. Migrant women themselves could play a key role in addressing social challenges. The important contribution of diaspora communities in providing support to migrant women, including in relation to integration into countries of destination, was highlighted. Migrant associations and migrant non-governmental organizations could play an important role in addressing the challenges of migration.

13. Trafficking was recognized as a development issue that cut across the Millennium Development Goals, particularly the goals on poverty eradication and gender equality and the empowerment of women. The majority of trafficked women came from low-income, socially deprived circumstances, mostly in developing countries and countries with economies in transition. In countries without comprehensive social security systems, women became vulnerable to trafficking and often ended up in unregulated labour sectors.

14. The forced absence of women through trafficking led to the breakdown of families, the neglect of children and the elderly, and negative impacts on health and education. Trafficking could force children into work, denying them education and reinforcing the illiteracy and poverty cycles that hindered development efforts. It could have a negative impact on public health services, including upon the return of victims of trafficking. It was noted that such impacts of trafficking had been researched inadequately and indicators to measure effectively the impacts on families were lacking.

15. It was recommended that organizations focusing on migration, including the International Organization for Migration, investigate the causes of trafficking and develop comprehensive indicators for cross-country analyses. Models for assessing trafficking flows, identifying early warning signals and assessing the impact of trafficking on countries of origin, including costs to public health systems, were needed. Evaluations of counter-trafficking programmes should include analyses of labour market factors and the role of recruiters. The

need for effective legal measures to address trafficking in women and girls, as well as for cross-border collaboration, including on monitoring and prosecution, was also highlighted.

High-level Dialogue on International Migration and Development

The General Assembly conducted the first High-level Dialogue on International Migration and Development (14-15 September), as decided in Assembly resolution 60/227 [YUN 2005, p. 1176]. The Dialogue included four plenary meetings, which were addressed by high-level officials of 127 Member States, including 47 ministers, as well as by representatives of one observer State and 10 intergovernmental entities and organizations. The Dialogue included four interactive round tables, which discussed the effects of international migration on economic and social development; measures to ensure respect for and protection of the human rights of all migrants, and prevent and combat smuggling of migrants and trafficking in persons; the multidimensional aspects of international migration and development, including remittances; and ways of promoting the building of partnerships and capacity-building and the sharing of best practices at all levels, including bilateral and regional, for the benefit of countries and migrants alike. By a 27 July note [A/61/187], the Assembly President transmitted to the Assembly a summary of 22 key findings of the informal interactive hearings, which underscored the positive impact of international migration and called for better use of the UN human rights machinery to prevent or redress violations of the rights of migrants. The meeting also had before it a report of the Secretary-General on international migration and development [A/60/871], which stressed that international migration constituted an ideal means of promoting the coordinated and concerted improvement of economic conditions in both areas of origin and of destination, based on complementarities between them. The report discussed the various ways in which international migration could contribute to development and presented a comprehensive review of the multidimentional aspects of international migration, including migration trends, its impact on countries of destination and countries of origin, as well as on rights, gender, integration, benefits and protection of migrants, and discussed the international normative framework and modes of intergovernmental cooperation developed to improve the governance of migration.

The Assembly President, in his summary of the deliberations of the High-level Dialogue [A/61/515], reported that participants demonstrated a commitment to examining the relationship and synergies between international migration and development and to identifying ways to maximize the developmental benefits of international migration and reduce its negative impacts. They stressed the global character of migration, underscoring its role as a positive force for development in both countries of origin and countries of destination, if supported by the right policies. There was widespread support for incorporating international migration issues in national development plans, including poverty reduction strategies, and for ensuring that people migrated out of choice rather than necessity, as had often been the case for many who migrated to escape poverty, conflict, human rights violations, poor governance or lack of employment. Concerns were raised regarding the outflow of highly skilled workers from the health and education sectors, since it compromised the delivery of services in countries of origin. Participants urged the implementation of measures to retain highly skilled workers by, among other things, ensuring equitable pay and decent working conditions. The promotion of return, even on a temporary basis, of skilled workers was also recommended.

The relatively high presence of female migrant workers had prompted some countries to re-examine their labour migration regulations to ensure that they were gender sensitive and offered adequate protection for female migrants. For many women, migration entailed risks that were often more serious for them than for men, especially when they were relegated to undesirable low-paying jobs. It was important, therefore, to adopt policies that addressed the particular circumstances and experiences of female migrants and reduced their vulnerability to exploitation and abuse.

Participants also recognized the usefulness of bilateral agreements and cited examples of those addressing labour migration, the portability of pensions, the readmission of nationals, the fight against trafficking in persons and the smuggling of migrants. Regional and bilateral initiatives should, however, be complemented by initiatives at the global level. In that regard, they noted the work of the Global Commission on International Migration, the International Agenda for Migration Management and the annual dialogue on migration policy sponsored by the International Organization for Migration (IOM).

As follow-up to the Dialogue, there was widespread support for the Secretary-General's proposal to create a global forum for discussing international migration and development issues. Participants were of the view that the proposed forum should work closely with the recently established Global Migration Group. Belgium offered to host the first meeting of the Global Forum on Migration and Development in 2007. The Secretary-General undertook to establish a voluntary fund to support the initiatives of the Forum. He also indicated his intention to extend the mandate of his Special Representative on International Migration and Development.

GENERAL ASSEMBLY ACTION

On 20 December [meeting 83], the General Assembly, on the recommendation of the Second (Economic and Financial) Committee [A/61/424/Add.2], adopted **resolution 61/208** without vote [agenda item 55 *(b)*].

International migration and development

The General Assembly,

Recalling its resolutions 49/127 of 19 December 1994, 50/123 of 20 December 1995, 52/189 of 18 December 1997, 54/212 of 22 December 1999, 56/203 of 21 December 2001, 58/208 of 23 December 2003, 59/241 of 22 December 2004 and 60/227 of 23 December 2005 on international migration and development, and 60/206 of 22 December 2005 on the facilitation and reduction of the cost of transfer of migrant remittances,

Recalling also the 2005 World Summit Outcome,

Recalling further its resolution 57/270 B of 23 June 2003 on the integrated and coordinated implementation of and follow-up to the outcomes of the major United Nations conferences and summits in the economic and social fields,

Recalling its resolution 60/265 of 30 June 2006 on the follow-up to the development outcome of the 2005 World Summit, including the Millennium Development Goals and the other internationally agreed development goals,

Reaffirming the Universal Declaration of Human Rights, and recalling the International Convention on the Elimination of All Forms of Racial Discrimination, the Convention on the Elimination of All Forms of Discrimination against Women and the Convention on the Rights of the Child,

Recalling the International Convention on the Protection of the Rights of All Migrant Workers and Members of Their Families,

Recalling also Commission on Population and Development resolution 2006/2 of 10 May 2006,

Acknowledging the important nexus between international migration and development and the need to deal with the challenges and opportunities that migration presents to countries of origin, transit and destination, and recognizing that migration brings benefits as well as challenges to the global community,

Acknowledging also the important contribution provided by migrants and migration to development, as well as the complex interrelationship between migration and development,

Reaffirming the resolve expressed by Heads of State and Government to take measures to ensure respect for and protection of the human rights of migrants, migrant workers and members of their families,

Noting the efforts of Member States, relevant United Nations bodies, organizations, funds and programmes and international and intergovernmental organizations, including the International Organization for Migration, in respect of convening events at the national, regional and international levels with a view to advancing the dialogue on the issue of international migration and development,

Noting with interest the offer of the Government of Belgium to convene a state-led initiative, the Global Forum on Migration and Development, in 2007,

1. *Takes note* of the report of the Secretary-General;

2. *Welcomes* the convening of the High-level Dialogue on International Migration and Development in New York on 14 and 15 September 2006, and the high level and broad participation that provided an opportunity to discuss the multidimensional aspects of international migration and development;

3. *Takes note* of the summary of the High-level Dialogue by the President of the General Assembly;

4. *Welcomes* the heightened awareness achieved by the High-level Dialogue on the issue, and decides to consider, at its sixty-third session, possible options for appropriate follow-up to the High-level Dialogue;

5. *Also welcomes* the ongoing efforts of Governments in the area of regional and interregional cooperation and regional consultative processes, where they exist, on migration, and encourages consideration of development dimensions in such processes, towards facilitating the dialogue and the exchange of information and experiences, fostering coordination at the regional and national levels, building common understanding, promoting cooperation, contributing to capacity-building and strengthening partnerships among countries of origin, transit and destination;

6. *Takes note with interest* of the establishment of the Global Migration Group;

7. *Calls upon* all relevant bodies, agencies, funds and programmes of the United Nations system and other relevant intergovernmental, regional and subregional organizations, within their respective mandates, to continue to address the issue of international migration and development, with a view to integrating migration issues, including a gender perspective and cultural diversity, in a more coherent way within the broader context of the implementation of internationally agreed development goals, including the Millennium Development Goals and respect for human rights;

8. *Recalls* its resolution 55/93 of 4 December 2000, by which it proclaimed 18 December International Day of the Migrant, and invites Member States and intergovernmental and non-governmental organizations to include in the observance of International Day of the Migrant the developmental dimension of international

migration, as highlighted by the High-level Dialogue on International Migration and Development held in New York, by sharing experiences and best practices on, inter alia, how to maximize the benefits of international migration and reduce its negative impacts;

9. *Requests* the Secretary-General to submit a report to the General Assembly at its sixty-third session on the implementation of the present resolution;

10. *Decides* to include in the provisional agenda of its sixty-third session the sub-item entitled "International migration and development".

Preparations for the High-level Dialogue

The Secretary-General, in a May note [A/60/864], provided information on the organization of the High-level Dialogue. Recognizing the importance of the contribution of civil society in its preparatory process, the General Assembly would hold informal interactive hearings on 12 July with representative of NGOs, civil society organizations and the private sector (see below). The Assembly also invited UN agencies, funds and programmes, the regional commissions, as well as IOM, to contribute to the preparations.

Communications. By a 31 August letter [A/61/315], Argentina transmitted a document entitled "A paradigm shift: addressing migration from a human rights perspective", as a contribution to the High-level Dialogue. The document called for a shift from a security and border control approach to a more comprehensive human rights perspective in government policies on migration. It urged Governments to find mechanisms for easy access to legal migration, while frustrating the dealings of unscrupulous traffickers who benefited financially from restrictive migration policies.

On 1 September [A/61/316], the President of the Economic and Social Council transmitted to the High-level Dialogue the Chairperson's summary of the panel discussion on international migration and migrants from a social perspective, held during the forty-second session of the Commission for Social Development [YUN 2004, p. 1092].

Regional meetings on international migration

In preparation for the High-level Dialogue, several regional gatherings and conferences were held to address various aspects of international migration. Those included: the Ministerial Conference of the Least Developed Countries on Migrants' Remittances (Cotonou, Benin, 9-10 February) [A/61/230], which adopted a Ministerial Declaration urging Governments of receiving countries to introduce tax relief for remittances similar to tax incentives provided to investment funds and charitable donations, develop financial products to attract migrant savings and investments, and establish a Migrant Remittances Observatory for LDCs; the ninth ordinary session of the African Union Executive Council (Banjul, the Gambia, 25-29 July) [A/61/345], which adopted the Migration Policy Framework for Africa and the African Common Position on Migration and Development; the Euro-African Ministerial Conference on Migration and Development (Rabat, Morocco, 10-11 July) [A/61/170], which adopted a plan of action and a political declaration (Rabat Declaration) calling for close Euro-African partnership to address issues such as controlling migration flows within the context of combating poverty and promoting sustainable development and co-development; the International Conference on Migration and Development (Brussels, 15-16 March), organized jointly with IOM [A/61/73]; the sixth South American Conference on Migration [A/61/86], which adopted, on 5 May, the Asunción Declaration reaffirming support for the human rights of migrants, especially women and unaccompanied minors; the Special International Conference of Developing Countries with Substantial International Migrant Flows (Lima, Peru, 15-16 May) [A/61/91], which adopted the Lima Declaration, by which the participating countries agreed, among other things, to cooperate in the human rights and fundamental freedoms of all migrants regardless of their immigration status; the Regional Consultation on Migration, Remittances and Development in Latin America and the Caribbean (Santo Domingo, Dominican Republic, 27-28 July) [A/61/343]; the fourteenth meeting of the Specialized Forum on Migration of the meeting of Ministers of the Interior of MERCOSUR and associated States (Fortaleza, Brazil, 22-24 August), which adopted a document entitled "Discussion of the Issue of Migration at the meeting of Ministers of the Interior of MERCOSUR and Associated States" focusing on the protection of the human rights of migrants in the region; and the Helsinki Process Meeting on International Migration (25- 26 July) [A/61/506].

UN Population Fund

2006 activities

Report of Executive Director. In response to decisions 2004/7 and 2004/20 [YUN 2004, p. 1083] of the Executive Board of the United Nations Development

Programme/United Nations Population Fund (UNDP/UNFPA), the UNFPA Executive Director submitted a report [DP/FPA/2007/7 (Part I & Add.1, Part II)], which reviewed the implementation of the goals and outputs of the 2004-2007 multi-year funding framework (MYFF). The report described progress made towards achieving major UNFPA goals identified in the MYFF, including in the programme areas of reproductive health; population dynamics, sustainable development and poverty; and gender equality and the empowerment of women.

UNFPA was increasingly engaged in policy work and in strengthening partnerships with national counterparts. Reproductive health and gender issues were included in national development frameworks, such as sector-wide programmes, poverty-reduction strategies and MDG reports over the 2004-2006 period. UNFPA country offices reported increasing involvement in national processes to incorporate reproductive health and gender issues. The Fund also contributed to building national capacity and ownership to improve the availability of reproductive health commodities, resulting in a significant increase in the number of countries allocating national funds for contraceptive purchases. UNFPA assisted Governments in expanding family planning services, improving overall government and donor support, and made accessible quality reproductive health services. It also helped to develop national guidelines and protocols, designing models for improving and strengthening monitoring and evaluation mechanisms. Its country offices reported progress in building national capacity to collect and use data for monitoring national development plans. In partnership with other agencies, it facilitated the incorporation of population and poverty linkages into the formulation of national development plans and policies. UNFPA played an important role in increasing attention paid to gender-based violence, gender equality and women's empowerment issues.

In terms of UNFPA mandate, several lessons emerged. Significant policy and model-building advances had to be capitalized on to strengthen programmes serving the most marginalized groups. Changes in policies and laws were needed, as well as human resources planning, to improve access to reproductive health services. To address the insufficient support provided to the incorporation of population dynamics, gender equality and HIV prevention into policy and expenditure frameworks, UNFPA planned to access expertise on expenditure frameworks, costing and budgeting and strengthen national capacity for integrating population factors into national planning. It developed a strategic framework on young people and planned to strengthen its leadership in the area of HIV prevention among that group. UNFPA, in partnership with other UN organizations, had become a key partner in humanitarian response, transition and recovery assistance.

The implementation of country and subregional programmes continued as the Fund's core work during 2006. By programme area, the largest share of resources, 60.3 per cent, went to reproductive health activities; 20.7 per cent to population and development strategies; 12.5 per cent to programme coordination and assistance; and 6.5 per cent to gender equality and the empowerment of women. By region, sub-Saharan Africa accounted for 34.1 per cent of programme assistance; Asia and the Pacific, 30.4 per cent; the Arab States and Europe, 13.2 per cent; and Latin America and the Caribbean, 9 per cent. Interregional activities accounted for 13.2 per cent.

As at 1 January, the total number of authorized budget posts numbered 1,031, of which 796 were in the field. Women constituted 44 per cent of professionals, one of the highest percentages among UN agencies and organizations.

The Executive Director reported jointly with the UNDP Administrator [DP/FPA/2007/7 (Part II)] on the recommendations of the Joint Inspection Unit (JIU). The report provided a synopsis of UNDP/UNFPA management responses to key JIU recommendations that were relevant to them. Of the six reports issued by JIU in 2006, four had cross-organization impact, addressing gaps in the internal oversight function and analysing the investigative function of oversight units; reviewing the implementation of headquarters agreements with respect to the provision of premises and other facilities by host countries; providing "lessons learned" from the 2004 Indian Ocean tsunami; and making recommendations on results-based management in the context of UN reform. Of the 29 recommendations issued by JIU in 2004-2005 that were relevant to UNDP and UNFPA, 26 had been implemented or were being pursued, and three were in the process of being implemented.

On 27 January [E/2006/35 (dec. 2006/10)], the UNDP/UNFPA Executive Board took note of the 2005 joint report of the UNDP Administrator and the UNFPA Executive Director to the Economic and Social Council [YUN 2005, p. 962].

On 23 June [(dec. 2006/25)], the Executive Board took note of the guidelines on the Board's working methods [YUN 2005, p. 963], annexed to that decision.

By **decision 2006/236** of 26 July, the Economic and Social Council took note of the annual report of the UNDP/UNFPA Executive Board [DP/2006/15], of the decisions adopted by the Board at the first regular session of 2006 [DP/2006/16] and of the joint report of the UNDP Administrator and the UNFPA Executive Director to the Economic and Social Council.

Reproductive health

In 2006, UNFPA invested 60.3 per cent of its financial resources in reproductive health activities, including maternal mortality, adolescents, gender equality, HIV prevalence, under-5 child mortality and unmet family planning needs. The Fund helped to launch two new vaccines against the human papillomavirus—the virus that causes cervical cancer—and worked with donors, Governments and multilateral organizations to establish how national health programmes could make the vaccine rapidly available to women in the developing world. It also contributed to a policy and programme guide. UNFPA, with key partners, including the World Health Organization (WHO), raised awareness of the critical shortage of midwives in developing countries. In December, it organized a forum on midwifery in Tunisia, at which participants signed the Hammamet Call to Action, which recommended that donors and Governments strengthen midwifery services in the developing world. In partnership with WHO, the United Nations Children's Fund (UNICEF) and the World Bank, it supported the development of national maternal and newborn health strategies to help countries realize the MDG on improving maternal health.

UNFPA worked with more than 50 countries to increase contraceptive prevalence and to prevent, control and treat sexually transmitted infections, including HIV. The number of countries allocating their own funds for contraceptive purchases increased to 66, and 13 UNFPA country offices reported increases in national budgets for contraceptives. The Fund helped more than 60 countries to overcome reproductive health commodity shortages. Canada and European Governments financed the programme and established a trust fund of $63.8 million.

A UNFPA-led Campaign to End Fistula—a rupture in the birth canal during prolonged, obstructed labour—was carried out in 40 countries. Eleven Governments and private-sector supporters donated to the campaign. Pakistan launched its own campaign to end fistula, establishing seven regional centres, with UNFPA support, to provide surgical treatment free of charge. UNFPA also helped to open the first comprehensive fistula centre in Darfur (the Sudan), and launched a major awareness-raising campaign in the United Kingdom.

The Fund continued to focus on youth, supporting youth-friendly centres that helped young people to obtain health information and services. In Pakistan, more than 54,000 young people visited 80 centres supported by UNFPA and the EU; in Mongolia, the centres provided safe places to discuss issues rarely mentioned at home or in public; and in Uzbekistan, vocational training in carpet weaving and computer technology added extra value to the centres. Education and training provided young women with information on adolescent and reproductive health in several countries, including Bolivia; Malawi, where 350 community-based agents received training; and Liberia, where young women affected by civil war participated in HIV prevention and vocational training.

As one of 10 co-sponsors of UNAIDS, UNFPA supported national efforts in more than 200 countries to promote country-level discussions on HIV/AIDS prevention, treatment, care and support. In Latin America and the Caribbean, the Fund sensitized decision-makers and urged the region to strengthen HIV prevention services for women and vulnerable groups. UNFPA was instrumental in getting the General Assembly's High-Level meeting on AIDS, in June (see p. 1410), to endorse the linking of HIV prevention with sexual and reproductive health.

Population, development and poverty

In 2006, UNFPA continued to assist countries in integrating population dynamics into national plans to reduce poverty. With the World Bank, UNFPA developed a country-based framework linking population, reproductive health and gender with poverty. The Fund also focused on tracking and monitoring HIV/AIDS and collecting and using gender-disaggregated data in national policies and programmes.

During the year, UNFPA advocated the orderly flow of international migration to maximize its benefits and minimize its negative consequences. The 2006 edition of *The State of the World Population*, entitled *A Passage to Hope: Women and International Migration*, examined the scope and breadth of female migration, the impact of remittances sent home to support families and communities, and women's disproportionate vulnerability to trafficking, exploitation and abuse.

UNFPA also assisted countries in using data to reduce poverty and enhance efforts to achieve the MDGs. In Bangladesh, 150 government officials learned how to analyse census data, with an emphasis on the use of data specific to age and gender.

Results of the UNFPA-supported May census in Haiti helped to determine resource needs in education and reproductive health services. UNFPA provided technical expertise for Nigeria's first census in 15 years.

In the area of population ageing, a UNFPA project in Thailand assisted about 400 elder caregivers of people with AIDS and their children. As part of that project, UNFPA demonstrated to local administrators and national authorities the value of assisting older people affected by HIV/AIDS. City officials from Bangladesh, China, India, Indonesia, Malaysia, Pakistan, Philippines, Thailand and Viet Nam studied urban policy and ageing at a 12-day workshop in Kobe, Japan. The November event applied UNFPA policy guidelines on ageing to the population issue.

Gender equality and empowerment of women

In 2006, UNFPA developed a comprehensive strategy for including a gender perspective in all its programmes. Ten countries contributed to a UNFPA study on the most effective examples of culturally sensitive programming aimed at reducing violence against women. With the United Nations Development Fund for Women, it developed a training manual and resource pack on gender budgeting to build the capacity of national partners and civil society organizations. The Fund continued to advocate measures to protect women and girls from HIV/AIDS and to push for the linking of HIV and AIDS with reproductive health. UNFPA projects succeeded in incorporating gender equality and reproductive rights into the agendas of indigenous organizations and in local and national public policies. Partnerships with faith-based organizations helped UNFPA to reach some of the most vulnerable communities in the world. A campaign alerting religious leaders and the public to the dangers of early marriage was launched in Afghanistan's Badakhshan province, which had the highest maternal death rate in the world. Imams in Mauritania called on government officials and police to protect rape victims, after UNFPA supported an awareness campaign, established a centre for victims and helped the Government to collect data on sexual violence. To help end violence against women, UNFPA assisted in building Algeria's national capacity to report cases of violence, worked with Morocco's health and justice systems to implement a national strategy against such violence, assisted a legal reform commission in Guatemala and joined an awareness campaign in Romania. In November, UNFPA and Senegal hosted an African film festival devoted to gender-based violence featuring 84 films from 18 countries. To end female genital mutilation, UNFPA offered local communities in Uganda and Kenya safe alternative rituals, helped the cutters to find other sources of income and supported the efforts of women's groups and parliamentarians to promote legislation to protect women and girls.

Country and intercountry programmes

UNFPA project expenditures for country, regional, interregional and headquarters activities in 2006 totalled $245.7 million, compared to $234.3 million in 2005, according to the Executive Director's statistical overview report [DP/FPA/2007/7 (Part I)/Add. 1]. The 2006 figure included $197.7 million for country programmes and $48 million for regional, interregional and headquarters activities. In accordance with the Board's procedure for allocating resources [YUN 1996, p. 989], total expenditures in 2006 for Group A countries amounted to $134.3 million, compared to $127 million in 2005.

Africa. Provisional data for UNFPA expenditures for programmes in sub-Saharan Africa gave a total of $83.9 million in 2006, compared to $78 million in 2005. Most of that amount (52.5 per cent) went to reproductive health and family planning, followed by population and development (24.6 per cent), programme coordination and assistance (15 per cent) and gender equality and women's empowerment (8 per cent).

On 27 January [E/2006/35 (dec. 2006/10)], the UNDP/UNFPA Executive Board approved UNFPA country programmes for Burkina Faso, Cape Verde, Chad, Ghana, Namibia, Swaziland and Uganda. On 23 June [dec. 2006/27], it took note of the draft country programme documents for Ethiopia, Guinea, Mozambique and Sao Tome and Principe, and the one-year extensions of country programmes for the Democratic Republic of the Congo, Lesotho, Malawi, Rwanda and Togo. On 13 September [dec. 2006/37], the Board took note of the draft country programme documents for the Central African Republic, Eritrea, Gabon, the Gambia, Senegal, South Africa, the United Republic of Tanzania, Zambia and Zimbabwe.

Arab States, Europe and Central Asia. Provisional expenditures for UNFPA programmes in the Arab States, Europe and Central Asia totalled $32.5 million, compared to $28.4 million in 2005. Most of that amount (64 per cent) was spent on reproductive health, followed by population and development (18.5 per cent), programme coordination and assistance (11.3 per cent) and gender equality and women's empowerment (6.2 per cent).

On 27 January [dec. 2006/10], the Executive Board approved country programmes for Albania, Georgia, the Occupied Palestinian Territory, Turkey and

Ukraine. On 23 June [dec. 2006/27] it took note of the draft country programme documents for Egypt, the Republic of Moldova, Morocco, the Syrian Arab Republic, Tunisia and Yemen, and the one-year extensions of country programmes for Lebanon and the Sudan; and on 13 September [dec. 2006/37], of the draft country programme document for Algeria.

Asia and the Pacific. Provisional expenditures for UNFPA programmes in Asia and the Pacific amounted to $74.7 million, compared to $75.5 million in 2005. Most of the expenditures (70.9 per cent) went to reproductive health, followed by population and development (17.1 per cent), programme coordination and assistance (7.5 per cent) and gender equality and women's empowerment (4.5 per cent).

On 27 January [dec. 2006/10], the Executive Board approved country programmes for Afghanistan, Bangladesh, Cambodia, China, Indonesia and Viet Nam. On 23 June [dec. 2006/27], it took note of the draft country programme documents for Thailand, the one-year extensions of country programmes for Bhutan, Nepal and Sri Lanka, and the report [DP/FPA/2006/10] on the implementation of the UNFPA special programme of assistance to Myanmar. On 13 September [dec. 2006/37], the Executive Board took note of the draft country programme documents for the Democratic People's Republic of Korea, the Lao People's Democratic Republic and Mongolia, as well as of the draft programme of assistance for Myanmar.

Latin America and the Caribbean. Provisional expenditures for UNFPA programmes in Latin America and the Caribbean totaled $22.1 million in 2006, compared to $21.4 million in 2005. As in other regions, most of the total (44.3 per cent) went to reproductive health, followed by population and development (27.8 per cent), gender equality and women's empowerment (14.8 per cent) and programme coordination and assistance (13.1 per cent).

On 27 January [dec. 2006/10], the Executive Board approved a UNFPA country programme for Peru. On 23 June [dec. 2006/27], it took note of one-year extensions of country programmes for Haiti, Mexico and Nicaragua; and on 13 September [dec. 2006/37], it took note of the draft country programme documents for Brazil, the Dominican Republic, El Salvador, the English- and Dutch-speaking Caribbean countries, Honduras, Panama, Paraguay and Uruguay.

Interregional and headquarters programmes. Provisional expenditures for UNFPA interregional and headquarters programmes totalled $32.5 million in 2006, compared to $31 million in 2005. Most of the total (63.1 per cent) went to reproductive health, followed by programme coordination and assistance (18.5 per cent), population and development (16.6 per cent) and gender equality and women's empowerment (1.8 per cent).

Financial and management questions

Financing

UNFPA income from all sources totalled $605.5 million in 2006, a 7.2 per cent increase over the 2005 figure of $565 million [DP/FPA/2007/15]. It comprised $360.5 million from regular resources and $210 million from other resources. Expenditures totalled $536.6 million, up from $523.3 million in 2005, comprising $443.7 million in programme activities. The largest share went to Sub-Saharan Africa ($120 million), followed by Asia and the Pacific ($103.8 million), the Arab States and Europe ($53 million) and Latin America and the Caribbean ($49 million). The rest ($66.3 million) went to interregional projects and procurement services and the Junior Professional Officers programme ($32.3 million).

The increase in regular resource contribution income ($9.3 million, or 2.7 per cent) was due to increased contributions of $9.2 million from nine major donors. Total income for other resources was $216.2 million, comprising contributions of $210 million and other income, including interest, of $6.2 million.

Donor Governments increased to 180 and multi-year pledges to 74, making 2006 the most successful year financially in UNFPA history. Private endowment contributions stood at $15.4 million.

On 13 September [E/2006/35 (dec. 2006/34)], the Executive Board took note of the annual financial review, 2005 [DP/FPA/2006/13]. It welcomed the increase in UNFPA income level, recognizing that increased, predictable and timely payment of contributions was essential to maintaining liquidity and facilitating programme implementation. It encouraged Member States in a position to do so to increase their funding, giving priority to regular resources, and to make multi-year contributions and announce payment schedules.

Audit reports

The Executive Director submitted to the UNDP/UNFPA Executive Board a report [DP/FPA/2006/1] on follow-up action by UNFPA to implement the recommendations of the UN Board of Auditors for 2002-2003 [YUN 2004, p. 1397].

On 27 January [E/2006/35 (dec. 2006/8)], the Executive Board took note of the actions taken or planned by UNFPA in implementing those recommendations. It requested UNFPA to continue to strengthen management and control systems, including risk-management systems, intensify fraud-prevention and anti-corruption measures and further strengthen systems for reporting and investigating possible fraud or misuse of funds.

In an April report [DP/FPA/2006/4], the Executive Director described the internal audit and oversight activities carried out by UNFPA in 2005. Those included: management audits of 17 offices (12 in Africa, one in Latin America and the Caribbean, two in the Arab States and Europe region and two in the Asia and Pacific region); a review of 211 audit reports covering 2004 activities for projects executed by Governments and NGOs; and contracted audits in six country offices in Asia and the Pacific and seven in the Arab States, Europe and Central Asia region. According to the 26 reports issued in 2005, the level of internal controls and the compliance with financial, administrative and programme requirements were found to be satisfactory in three offices, partially satisfactory in 19 and deficient in four. A total of 1,380 recommendations were issued. The Executive Director requested the Division for Oversight Services to revise the audit programme and, in that regard, appointed an independent five-member oversight committee. The Fund updated its Financial Rules and Regulations and undertook initiatives to strengthen fraud monitoring and control, such as establishing an online whistle-blower hotline and creating a policy for informing staff of UNFPA zero tolerance towards fraud and unethical behaviour.

On 16 June [E/2006/35 (dec. 2006/13)], the Executive Board welcomed the Executive Director's report and the creation of an independent audit and oversight committee; expressed support for continued strengthening of the internal audit and oversight services and requested an assessment of the resources required. It recognized the need to strengthen monitoring systems to address audit findings, and expressed support for the initiatives for promoting a risk-management culture. The Board requested UNFPA to accelerate the development of the enterprise risk management systems, taking into account the costs and benefits of introducing such systems.

Multi-year funding commitments

In May [DP/FPA/2006/3], the Executive Director submitted to the UNDP/UNFPA Executive Board updated estimates of regular and other resources for 2006 and future years in the multi-year funding framework (MYFF). As at 1 March, 98 official pledges had been received, several of which were multi-year pledges.

Total resources in 2005 reached about $523.5 million, the Fund's highest total ever, comprising $365.8 million in regular resources and $157.7 million in co-financing arrangements. Compared to 2004, regular resources increased by $38.1 million, or 11 per cent and income for co-financing arrangements by $26.6 million, or 20.3 per cent. UNFPA increased its donor base to 172 Governments in 2005, from 166 in 2004. Multi-year pledges also increased to 55, compared to 49 in 2004. The Fund was particularly gratified to have received pledges in 2005 from all the countries in sub-Saharan Africa. The substantial increase in the 2005 regular income level was due to larger contributions from 11 major donors, as well as a weakening of the United States dollar vis-à-vis other currencies. The Netherlands, Sweden, Norway, Japan and the United Kingdom were the five largest donors. Seventeen major donors provided about 94 per cent of total regular resources. Income projections for 2006 were set at $341.7 million, due to decreases in the United States dollar equivalent for 2006, using the current UN rate of exchange. It was essential that UNFPA continue to focus its resource mobilization efforts on increasing regular resources. A strong and secure base of regular resources should be supplemented by various combinations of co-financing funding.

On 16 June [E/2006/35 (dec. 2006/12)], the UNDP/UNFPA Executive Board welcomed the substantial increase in the 2005 regular income level, the increase in the 2005 co-financing income and the contributions made by programme countries, which had enabled UNFPA to reach its highest ever number of donors. It recognized that sustaining and improving the UNFPA funding level would require countries able to do so to augment their funding efforts during MYFF 2004-2007.

Evaluation

In an April report [DP/FPA/2006/5], the Executive Director provided an overview of UNFPA 2004-2005 evaluation activities, including efforts to adopt and comply with internationally recognized evaluation criteria and quality standards. During that period, the Fund conducted 497 country-level, 23 regional and 18 global evaluations. Many evaluations resulted in extensive follow-up, and there was consistent support for building a stronger evaluation function within UNFPA.

On 16 June [E/2006/35 (dec. 2006/11)], the Executive Board took note of the periodic report on evaluation, welcomed efforts to adopt and comply with international evaluation criteria and standards and looked forward to reviewing them in 2007.

UNFPA role in emergency situations

In response to Executive Board decision 2000/13 [YUN 2000, p. 1003], UNFPA reported in August on its role in emergency preparedness, humanitarian response and transition and recovery [DP/FPA/2006/14]. The report presented a three-year strategy for ensuring that the key issues in the ICPD Programme of Action Programme were integrated into the emergency preparedness, crisis response and recovery programmes of national entities, civil society, regional institutions and the international humanitarian system. The strategy sought to enhance UNFPA capacity to respond more effectively to issues of gender, reproductive health and data in the context of crisis and recovery. The total cost for implementing the strategy was estimated at $23 million. UNFPA proposed using $8 million from regular resources and to seek co-financing contributions for the remainder. It proposed that the emergency fund be maintained at its level of $3 million, and continue to serve as a source for acute emergency response programming and as a buffer to advance emergency funds against pledges made but not yet honoured. UNFPA also proposed the establishment of a voluntary, open-ended trust fund for reproductive health and gender mainstreaming in relief and recovery.

On 13 September [E/2006/35 (dec. 2006/35)], the Executive Board endorsed the strategy for emergency preparedness, humanitarian response and transition and recovery programmes at national, regional and international levels. It requested UNFPA to provide further information in 2007 on resource needs, funding modalities and staff required to implement the strategy; coordination between UNFPA and other UN entities, including the Inter-Agency Standing Committee; and the strategy's monitoring and evaluation framework. The Executive Board encouraged UNFPA to align the strategy with the medium-term strategic plan, to be approved in 2007. It agreed to maintain the emergency fund at $3 million a year, funded from regular resources; and encouraged contributions to UNFPA to implement the strategy.

Joint UNDP/UNFPA/UNICEF programming

An April report by UNDP, UNFPA and UNICEF [DP/FPA/2006/11] reviewed the implementation experience of joint programming of the three entities since 2004. The three organizations were committed to joint programming and joint programmes, as evidenced by the increase in the number of such programmes. That collaboration had been facilitated by the introduction of the common country programming process and the issuance of the inter-organization guidance note on joint programming, which together set out a framework for joint programmes. For the first time, there were common United Nations Development Group (UNDG) operational tools and programming processes with which to develop and implement joint programmes, resulting in enhanced efficiency, effectiveness and coherence. Many of the limitations to joint programming had been identified and were being addressed in the improvements proposed, which would lead to the mainstreaming of joint programming within the country programming process.

On 23 June [E/2006/35 (dec. 2006/27)], the UNDP/UNFPA Executive Board took note of the report.

Improving the harmonized country programme approval process

An April report by UNDP, UNFPA, UNICEF and the World Food Programme [DP/FPA/2006/12] presented options for improving the harmonized country programme approval process by the respective Executive Boards, including by further simplifying and harmonizing the UNDG programming process and by introducing a consolidated document at the country level.

On 23 June [E/2006/35 (dec. 2006/27)], the Executive Board postponed consideration of that report.

UN Population Award

The 2006 United Nations Population Award was presented to Dr. Halida Hanum Akhter, Director-General, Family Planning Association of Bangladesh, in the individual category, and to Haiti's Fondation pour la santé reproductive et l'éducation familiale (FOSREF) in the institutional category.

The Award was established by General Assembly resolution 36/201 [YUN 1981, p. 792], to be presented annually to individuals or institutions for outstanding contributions to increasing awareness of population problems and to their solutions. In August, the Secretary-General transmitted to the Assembly the report of the UNFPA Executive Director on the Population Award [A/61/273].

Other population activities

Commission on Population and Development

The Commission on Population and Development, at its thirty-ninth session (New York, 3-7 April and

10 May) [E/2006/25] considered as its special theme "International migration and development" (see p. 1257). Documents before the Commission included the report of its Bureau on the intersessional meeting (Banjul, the Gambia, 19-20 December 2005) [E/CN.9/2006/2]; reports of the Secretary-General on: world population monitoring, focusing on international migration and development [E/CN.9/2006/3]; monitoring of population programmes, focusing on international migration and development [E/CN.9/2006/4]; flow of financial resources for assisting in the implementation of the ICPD Programme of Action [E/CN.9/2006/5]; and programme implementation and progress of work in the field of population in 2005 [E/CN.9/2006/6].

The Commission adopted and brought to the Economic and Social Council's attention resolutions on its methods of work [E/2006/25 (res. 2006/1)] (see below) and on international migration and development [res. 2006/2] (see p. 1258). The Commission decided that the special theme for its forty-first (2008) session would be "Population distribution, urbanization, internal migration and development" [dec. 2006/101]. In other action [dec. 2006/102], the Commission took note of the documents it had considered at its thirty-ninth session. At a resumed meeting on 10 May, the Commission recommended to the Council the draft provisional agenda for its fortieth (2007) session.

By **decision 2006/233** of 24 July, the Economic and Social Council took note of the report of the Commission on Population and Development on its thirty-ninth (2006) session and approved the provisional agenda for the Commission's fortieth (2007) session.

In preparation for its fortieth session, the Commission's Bureau held two meetings in 2006 (New York, 3 November and 7 December) [E/CN.9/2007/2].

Improving the Commission's methods of work

The Commission, on 10 May [E/2006/25 (res. 2006/1)], decided to adopt a multi-year programme of work limited to a two-year planning horizon, and to select a special theme for each year based on the ICPD Programme of Action. In considering each annual theme, the Commission would continue to review and assess both its substantive and policy aspects, as well as the progress made in programme implementation in relation to that theme.

The Commission would address at its general debate the challenges to the implementation of the goals, objectives and commitments of the Programme of Action, and the means for accelerating their implementation. The outcomes of the Commission's discussions, including on its special theme, should contain substantive recommendations and key actions for furthering its implementation. The Commission's programme of work would include new and emerging issues, as recommended by Member States. To maintain and enhance the quality and impact of the debates, Member States were invited to include, among their representatives at the Commission's sessions, those with technical expertise in the particular areas of population and development under consideration.

The Commission's Bureau would meet as frequently as necessary in preparation for annual sessions, and facilitate regular and informal briefings on the status of preparations. The Secretary-General was requested to ensure strengthened cooperation and coordination among UN system entities in the technical preparation of future Commission sessions.

UN activities

In a report on programme implementation and progress of work of the UN Population Division in 2006 [E/CN.9/2007/7], the Secretary-General described the Division's major activities relating to the analysis of fertility, mortality and international migration; world population estimates and projections; population policies; population and development interrelationship; and monitoring, coordination and dissemination of population information. Several activities revolved around the September General Assembly's High-level Dialogue (see p. 1261).

The Division's work in fertility and family planning included the preparation of a report entitled *Childlessness: A Global Survey*, which provided a statistical overview of childlessness worldwide, focusing on the past few decades. In the area of fertility, the Division prepared two datasets for electronic publication: the *Database on Fertility 2007*, which contained fertility indicators for 192 countries or areas and the *Database on Marriage 2007*, containing indicators of marital status for 192 countries or areas.

On mortality and health, progress was made in reviewing mortality estimation methods and in proposing methodological improvements to obtain more timely and robust estimates of age-specific mortality and life expectancy for as many countries as possible. The focus was on developing new and more flexible models of mortality patterns by age that could be used to fit the partial information available for countries with deficient data. Work also advanced in compiling data for estimating mortality and documenting their sources and limitations. To facilitate the use of the varied types of data available for the estimation of mortality, a database was developed to store both the data and the metadata describing them. To promote collaboration on those tasks with other institutions, the Division organized an expert group meeting on the theme "Current issues in the estimation of adult mortality" (New York, 26-27 October).

Concerning international migration, the Division issued the *Compendium of Recommendations on International Migration and Development*, containing a compilation of all the principles, guidelines, commitments and recommendations for action adopted by Member States at the various conferences and summits held since 1990, as well as at the population conferences of 1974 and 1984. It also issued the wall chart *International Migration 2006*, with the most recent estimates and information, including the estimated number of international migrants in each country, estimates of net migration, remittances, government views on immigration and emigration policies, and the status of ratification of relevant UN instruments. The Division organized, with the Economic and Social Commission for Western Asia, an expert group meeting on "International migration and development in the Arab region: challenges and opportunities" (Beirut, 15-17 May); in collaboration with Turin's Fondazione Rosselli, the International Symposium on International Migration and Development (Turin, Italy, 28-30 June); and the fifth coordination meeting on international migration (New York, 20-21 November).

With regard to world population projections, the Division issued the third volume, *Analytical Report* of *World Population Prospects: The 2004 Revision*, which analysed the results of the population estimates and projections presented in the previous two volumes. The data covered the 228 countries or areas for the period 1950-2050. The results of the 2005 revision of *World Urbanization Prospects* were issued in both electronic form and in a number of publications. In collaboration with Columbia University and the International Union for the Scientific Study of Population, the Division organized an expert group meeting on "Rethinking the estimation and projection of urban and city populations" (New York, 9 January), which brought together demographers, geographers, urban planners, experts in remote-sensing and geographic information systems, as well as representatives of UN entities.

As to population policies, the Division published the 2005 edition of *World Population Policies*, a recurrent survey of the views and policies of Governments. A panel discussion on "Challenges of world population in the twenty-first century: the changing age structure of population and its consequences for development" (New York, 12 October) highlighted the implications of population ageing becoming a major concern, with Governments considering how best to address the expected increase in health and pension costs associated with growing numbers of older persons. With regard to population and development, the Division published the wall chart *Population Ageing 2006*, which presented data for 228 countries or areas in the world on the absolute and relative numbers of older persons, the proportions of older persons married, living alone and in the labour force classified by sex, the sex ratio of populations aged 60 or over and 80 or over, the potential support ratio, the statutory retirement age for men and women, and the male and female life expectancies at age 60. The Division continued its tradition of organizing a "member-initiated meeting" to present its work at the annual meeting of the Population Association of America. The 30 March event in Los Angeles, California, focused on the major findings of the report "Living Arrangements of Older Persons around the World", which presented a global survey of the patterns and trends in the living arrangements of people aged 60 or over.

On monitoring population trends and policies, the annual world population monitoring report produced for the Commission was devoted to international migration and development. In disseminating population information and data, the Division continued to update and expand its website (www.unpopulation.org), to which a portal on international migration and development (www.unmigration.org) was added. Complementing those websites was the Population Information Network (www.popin.org), which provided a portal to population information and data available throughout the UN system.

Chapter IX

Social policy, crime prevention and human resources development

In 2006, the United Nations continued to promote social, cultural and human resources development, and strengthen its crime prevention and criminal justice programme.

The Commission for Social Development considered as its priority theme the review of the first United Nations Decade for the Eradication of Poverty (1997-2006). It adopted resolutions on the social dimensions of the New Partnership for Africa's Development and on the modalities for the first review and appraisal of the Madrid International Plan of Action on Ageing, 2002. The Commission also reviewed relevant UN plans and programmes of actions pertaining to the situation of social groups.

The Secretary-General reported on the implementation of the Copenhagen Declaration on Social Development and the Programme of Action, adopted at the 1995 World Summit for Social Development, and on further initiatives for social development, adopted by the General Assembly's twenty-fourth (2000) special session.

The Ad Hoc Committee on the Comprehensive and Integral International Convention on the Protection and Promotion of the Rights and Dignity of Persons with Disabilities negotiated and adopted the final draft text of the International Convention on the Rights of Persons with Disabilities, which was welcomed by the Economic and Social Council, and later adopted by the General Assembly.

The Commission on Crime Prevention and Criminal Justice, at its fifteenth session, focused on, among other things, UN standards and norms in crime prevention; action against transnational crime, such as kidnapping and trafficking in persons; strengthening the rule of law and the criminal justice systems in Africa; technical assistance for prison reform in Africa; strengthening basic principles of judicial conduct; international cooperation against corruption; and follow-up to the Eleventh United Nations Congress on Crime Prevention and Criminal Justice.

The Secretary-General reported on the activities undertaken to implement the International Plan of Action for the United Nations Literacy Decade (2003-2012). Concerned about meeting the goals of the Decade, the Assembly appealed to Governments to mobilize enough resources and called for increased investments in education. The Secretary-General also reported on the work of the United Nations Institute for Training and Research, and the development of the academic and professional training programmes of the University for Peace.

Social policy and cultural issues

Social development

Follow-up to the 1995 World Summit and the General Assembly special session

In response to General Assembly resolution 60/130 [YUN 2005, p. 1189], the Secretary-General submitted a June report [A/61/99] on the implementation of the Copenhagen Declaration on Social Development and the Programme of Action, adopted at the 1995 World Summit for Social Development [YUN 1995, p. 1113], and of further initiatives for social development, adopted by the Assembly's twenty-fourth (2000) special session [YUN 2000, p. 1012]. The report provided an overview of the substantive discussions on the review of the United Nations Decade for the Eradication of Poverty (1997-2006), which took place during the forty-fourth session of the Commission for Social Development (New York, 8-17 February) (see p. 1276). It noted that the implementation of commitments made during the Decade had fallen short of expectations and there was evidence of an inverse correlation between promises made at Copenhagen and the results achieved. Although the levels of absolute poverty at the global level had been reduced by the rapid economic expansion of China and India, overall progress in poverty eradication was slow and uneven. In sub-Saharan Africa and Latin America, poverty reduction was stagnant, and in Western Asia, poverty had actually increased. Emerging trends also suggested that progress on some social indicators, such as school enrolment and infant mortality, had slowed down in the past decade. While the Decade for the Eradication of Poverty had been successful in placing poverty eradication at the centre of the international agenda and public opinion, and had increasingly shaped national agendas, there was limited progress, especially in increasing the developing countries' access to international economic opportunities, achieving a system of fair trade, and providing debt relief to heavily indebted countries.

The understanding of poverty had evolved from the early focus on income poverty to a more multidimensional understanding, including its human dimensions and structural causes, reflecting a growing convergence of views on the critical links between the macroeconomic architecture and the social dimensions of poverty and inequality. However, while that understanding had widened, poverty eradication policies had not been substantially transformed, partly because the structural causes of poverty were not being adequately addressed. A global initiative established at the 2005 World Summit [YUN 2005, p. 1188] set out to explore how nations could reduce poverty through reforms that expanded critical access to legal protection and opportunities for all citizens. The High-Level Commission on Legal Empowerment of the Poor would examine how increased access to property and labour rights, legal protection and financial services could provide greater opportunities and empowerment for poor people.

To strengthen social development, including through a people-centred approach, the Secretary-General suggested that it was imperative to balance measures to achieve growth with measures to achieve economic and social equity for there to be an impact on overall poverty levels. In that context, poverty eradication policies should address the root and structural causes of poverty, while incorporating equity and equality measures. Productive employment and decent work should be made an integral part of growth-enhancing and poverty-reduction strategies, with particular attention paid to incorporating employment creation in marcroeconomic policies. Poverty reduction strategies should also adopt an integrated approach to respond to the multidimensional nature of poverty, with priority accorded to measures that fostered social integration, cohesion and access to social services. Initiatives were also required to strengthen capacity-building and participation of the poor in poverty eradication strategies. Efforts should be intensified to help countries achieve social development goals through the provision of resources and to eliminate their debilitating debt burden.

GENERAL ASSEMBLY ACTION

On 19 December [meeting 81], the General Assembly, on the recommendation of the Third (Social, Humanitarian and Cultural) Committee [A/61/437 & Corr.1], adopted **resolution 61/141** without vote [agenda item 60 *(a)*].

Implementation of the outcome of the World Summit for Social Development and of the twenty-fourth special session of the General Assembly

The General Assembly,

Recalling the World Summit for Social Development, held at Copenhagen from 6 to 12 March 1995, and the twenty-fourth special session of the General Assembly entitled "World Summit for Social Development and beyond: achieving social development for all in a globalizing world", held at Geneva from 26 June to 1 July 2000,

Reaffirming that the Copenhagen Declaration on Social Development and the Programme of Action and the further initiatives for social development adopted by the General Assembly at its twenty-fourth special session, as well as a continued global dialogue on social development issues, constitute the basic framework for the promotion of social development for all at the national and international levels,

Recalling the United Nations Millennium Declaration and the development goals contained therein, as well as the commitments made at major United Nations summits, conferences and special sessions, including the commitments made at the 2005 World Summit,

Recalling also its resolution 60/209 of 22 December 2005 on the implementation of the first United Nations Decade for the Eradication of Poverty (1997-2006),

Recalling further its resolution 57/270 B of 23 June 2003 on the integrated and coordinated implementation of and follow-up to the outcomes of the major United Nations conferences and summits in the economic and social fields,

Emphasizing the need to enhance the role of the Commission for Social Development in the follow-up and review of the World Summit for Social Development and the outcome of the twenty-fourth special session of the General Assembly,

1. *Takes note* of the report of the Secretary-General;

2. *Welcomes* the reaffirmation by Governments of their will and commitment to continue implementing the Copenhagen Declaration on Social Development and the Programme of Action, in particular to eradicate poverty, promote full and productive employment and foster social integration to achieve stable, safe and just societies for all;

3. *Recognizes* that the implementation of the Copenhagen commitments and the attainment of the internationally agreed development goals, including the Millennium Development Goals, are mutually reinforcing and that the Copenhagen commitments are crucial to a coherent people-centred approach to development;

4. *Reaffirms* that the Commission for Social Development continues to have the primary responsibility for

the follow-up and review of the World Summit for Social Development and the outcome of the twenty-fourth special session of the General Assembly and that it serves as the main United Nations forum for an intensified global dialogue on social development issues, and calls upon Member States, the relevant specialized agencies, funds and programmes of the United Nations system and civil society to enhance their support for its work;

5. *Recognizes* that the broad concept of social development affirmed by the World Summit for Social Development and the twenty-fourth special session of the General Assembly has been weakened in national and international policymaking and that, while poverty eradication is a central part of development policy and discourse, further attention should be given to the other commitments agreed to at the Summit, in particular those concerning employment and social integration, which have also suffered from a general disconnect between economic and social policymaking;

6. *Acknowledges* that the first United Nations Decade for the Eradication of Poverty (1997-2006), launched after the World Summit for Social Development, has provided the long-term vision for sustained and concerted efforts at the national and international levels to eradicate poverty, and recognizes that the implementation of the commitments made by Governments during the Decade has fallen short of expectations;

7. *Emphasizes* that the major United Nations conferences and summits, including the Millennium Summit and the 2005 World Summit, have reinforced the priority and urgency of poverty eradication within the United Nations development agenda;

8. *Also emphasizes* that poverty eradication policies should attack poverty by addressing its root and structural causes and manifestations, and that equity and the reduction of inequalities need to be incorporated in those policies;

9. *Stresses* that an enabling environment is a critical precondition for achieving equity and social development and that, while economic growth is essential, entrenched inequality and marginalization are an obstacle to the broad-based and sustained growth required for sustainable, inclusive people-centred development, and recognizes the need to balance and ensure complementarity between measures to achieve growth and measures to achieve economic and social equity in order for there to be an impact on overall poverty levels;

10. *Also stresses* that policies and programmes designed to achieve poverty eradication should include specific measures to foster social integration, including by providing marginalized socio-economic sectors and groups with equal access to opportunities and social protection;

11. *Reaffirms* that social integration policies should seek to reduce inequalities, promote access to basic social services, education for all and health care, increase the participation and integration of social groups, particularly youth, older persons and persons with disabilities, and address the challenges posed by globalization and market-driven reforms to social development in order for all people in all countries to benefit from globalization;

12. *Recognizes* the need to promote respect for all human rights and fundamental freedoms in order to address the most pressing social needs of people living in poverty, including through the design and development of appropriate mechanisms to strengthen and consolidate democratic institutions and governance;

13. *Reaffirms* the commitment to the empowerment of women and gender equality and to strengthening policies and programmes that improve, ensure and broaden the full participation of women in all spheres of political, economic, social and cultural life, as equal partners, and to improving their access to all resources needed for the full exercise of all their human rights and fundamental freedoms by removing persistent barriers;

14. *Welcomes* the ministerial declaration, adopted at the high-level segment of the substantive session of 2006 of the Economic and Social Council, on "Creating an environment at the national and international levels conducive to generating full and productive employment and decent work for all, and its impact on sustainable development";

15. *Reaffirms* that there is an urgent need to create an environment at the national and international levels that is conducive to the attainment of full and productive employment and decent work for all as a foundation for sustainable development and that an environment that supports investment, growth and entrepreneurship is essential to the creation of new job opportunities, and also reaffirms that opportunities for men and women to obtain productive work in conditions of freedom, equity, security and human dignity are essential to ensuring the eradication of hunger and poverty, the improvement of economic and social well-being for all, the achievement of sustained economic growth and sustainable development of all nations and a fully inclusive and equitable globalization;

16. *Also reaffirms* the commitment to employment policies that promote full and productive employment and decent work for all under conditions of equity, equality, security and dignity, and further reaffirms that employment creation should be incorporated into macroeconomic policies;

17. *Further reaffirms* the commitments made in respect of "Meeting the special needs of Africa" at the 2005 World Summit, underlines the call of the Economic and Social Council for enhanced coordination within the United Nations system and the ongoing efforts to harmonize the current initiatives on Africa, and requests the Commission for Social Development to continue to give due prominence in its work to the social dimensions of the New Partnership for Africa's Development;

18. *Reaffirms* that each country has the primary responsibility for its own economic and social development and that the role of national policies and development strategies cannot be overemphasized, and underlines the importance of adopting effective measures, including new financial mechanisms, as appropriate, to support the efforts of developing countries to achieve sustained

economic growth, sustainable development, poverty eradication and the strengthening of their democratic systems;

19. *Also reaffirms*, in this context, that international cooperation has an essential role in assisting developing countries, including the least developed countries, in strengthening their human, institutional and technological capacity;

20. *Stresses* that the international community shall enhance its efforts to create an enabling environment for social development and poverty eradication through increasing market access for developing countries, technology transfer on mutually agreed terms, financial aid and a comprehensive solution to the external debt problem;

21. *Acknowledges* that good governance and the rule of law at the national and international levels are essential for sustained economic growth, sustainable development and the eradication of poverty and hunger;

22. *Urges* developed countries that have not yet done so in accordance with their commitments, to make concrete efforts towards meeting the targets of 0.7 per cent of their gross national product for official development assistance to developing countries and 0.15 to 0.2 per cent of their gross national product to least developed countries, and encourages developing countries to build on the progress achieved in ensuring that official development assistance is used effectively to help meet development goals and targets;

23. *Welcomes* the contribution to the mobilization of resources for social development by the initiatives on a voluntary basis taken by groups of Member States based on innovative financing mechanisms, including those that aim to provide further drug access at affordable prices to developing countries on a sustainable and predictable basis, such as the International Drug Purchase Facility, UNITAID, as well as other initiatives, such as the International Finance Facility for Immunisation, and notes the New York Declaration of 20 September 2004, which launched the Action against Hunger and Poverty initiative and called for further attention to raise funds urgently needed to help meet the Millennium Development Goals and to complement and ensure long-term stability and predictability to foreign aid;

24. *Reaffirms* that social development requires the active involvement of all actors in the development process, including civil society organizations, corporations and small businesses, and that partnerships among all relevant actors are increasingly becoming part of national and international cooperation for social development, and also reaffirms that, within countries, partnerships among the Government, civil society and the private sector can contribute effectively to the achievement of social development goals;

25. *Underlines* the responsibility of the private sector, at both the national and the international levels, including small and large companies and transnational corporations, regarding not only the economic and financial but also the development, social, gender and environmental implications of their activities, their obligations towards their workers and their contributions to achieving sustainable development, including social development, and emphasizes the need to take concrete actions on corporate responsibility and accountability, including through the participation of all relevant stakeholders, inter alia, for the prevention or prosecution of corruption;

26. *Invites* the Secretary-General, the Economic and Social Council, the regional commissions, the relevant specialized agencies, funds and programmes of the United Nations system and other intergovernmental forums, within their respective mandates, to continue to integrate into their work programmes and give priority attention to the Copenhagen commitments and the Declaration on the tenth anniversary of the World Summit for Social Development, to continue to be actively involved in their follow-up and to monitor the achievement of those commitments and undertakings;

27. *Decides* to include in the provisional agenda of its sixty-second session the sub-item entitled "Implementation of the outcome of the World Summit for Social Development and of the twenty-fourth special session of the General Assembly", and requests the Secretary-General to submit a report on the question to the Assembly at that session.

Coordination segment of Economic and Social Council

The Economic and Social Council, at the coordination segment of its 2006 substantive session (6-7, 10 and 17 July) [A/61/3], discussed the theme, "Sustained economic growth for social development, including the eradication of poverty and hunger", in accordance with its decision 2005/221 [YUN 2005, p. 1540]. The Council held two panel discussions on the theme, one on the normative and policy dimension, as well as the programme and operational dimension, and the other with the Chairpersons of its functional commissions and other subsidiary bodies. The Council also had before it a report of the Secretary-General on the subject [E/2006/56], which provided an overview of the current trends and lessons learned. It concluded that countries needed to adopt comprehensive, coherent and participatory policy approaches to respond to the needs of each country, and achieve sustained economic growth and social development. Also, an enabling international environment should be created through greater policy coherence, including programme coherence within the UN system. Efforts should be made to bridge the intellectual gap on the dynamic effects of specific economic and social policies through the pursuit of a comprehensive research agenda. The Secretary-General made a number of recommendations emphasizing the principle of national ownership and policy space in the formulation of effective implementation strategies. He also emphasized the need for countries to build capacities for developing such strategies, for the international community to harmonize and align its efforts with national development strategies, and for the United Nations to shift from a sectoral to a more comprehensive approach. He called for major initiatives to better understand the complex linkages between sustained economic growth and social development.

ECONOMIC AND SOCIAL COUNCIL ACTION

On 17 July [meeting 29], the Economic and Social Council adopted **resolution 2006/4** [draft: E/2006/L.14] without vote [agenda item 4].

Sustained economic growth for social development, including the eradication of poverty and hunger

The Economic and Social Council,

Recalling General Assembly resolutions 45/264, 48/162, 50/227 and 57/270 B regarding the role of the United Nations in the economic, social and related fields,

Recalling also its decision 2005/221 of 6 July 2005, in which it decided to consider, during the coordination segment of the substantive session of 2006, the theme "Sustained economic growth for social development, including the eradication of poverty and hunger",

Recognizing that the eradication of hunger and poverty is a fundamental objective that must be at the centre of integral development initiatives and programmes of the United Nations system, including those aimed at the achievement of internationally agreed development goals, including the Millennium Development Goals,

Recalling the outcomes of the major United Nations conferences and summits in the economic, social and related fields, and recognizing the vital role played by these conferences and summits in shaping broad development visions and in identifying commonly agreed objectives,

1. *Urges* the United Nations system to enhance its assistance to developing countries, upon their request, in facilitating the realization of the internationally agreed development goals, including the Millennium Development Goals, and efforts towards the eradication of poverty and hunger through comprehensive and multidimensional approaches;

2. *Requests* the United Nations system to conduct common country assessments and United Nations Development Assistance Framework processes under the leadership of national Governments in such a way as to optimize their harmonization and alignment with national development strategies and priorities as well as efforts to improve the support for national development priorities and policies, and stresses that full national ownership, participation and leadership are required at all stages of those processes;

3. *Recognizes* the need to improve understanding of the complex interlinkages between economic growth and social development, and requests the Secretary-General to encourage the organizations and bodies of the United Nations system, with the involvement of all stakeholders, where relevant, to undertake studies and analytical work at all levels on the social impact of the realization of the internationally agreed development goals, including the Millennium Development Goals;

4. *Invites* the regional commissions, in cooperation with other entities of the United Nations system, regional organizations and other regional processes, where appropriate, to further contribute, within their respective mandates, to the implementation and review of the outcomes of the major United Nations conferences and summits in the economic, social and related fields including, inter alia, sustained economic growth for social development, including the eradication of poverty and hunger;

5. *Requests* the Secretary-General, in his capacity as Chairman of the United Nations System Chief Executives Board for Coordination, to encourage the organizations and bodies of the United Nations system, within their respective mandates, to review their current approaches in the area of economic growth and social development in order to effectively address and facilitate the realization of the internationally agreed development goals, including the Millennium Development Goals; in this regard underlines the need for exchange of experiences and the application, where appropriate, of relevant lessons learned; and in this context, requests that these be brought to the attention of Member States and the relevant governing bodies.

On the same date, the Council, by **decision 2006/220** on the finalization of a multi-year work programme for its coordination segment, took note of the Secretary-General's report on sustained economic growth for social development, including poverty eradication and hunger.

Commission for Social Development

The Commission for Social Development, at its forty-fourth session (New York, 18 February 2005, 8-17 February and 22 March 2006) [E/2006/26], considered the priority theme "Review of the first United Nations Decade for the Eradication of Poverty (1997-2006)". In addition to a general discussion, it also held a panel discussion on the theme and decided to transmit to the coordination segment of the Economic and Social Council the Chairperson's summary of the panel discussions. The Commission adopted a resolution on "Social dimensions of the New Partnership for Africa's Development" (NEPAD) [YUN 2001, p. 900], according to which the Council would recommend that the Commission continue to give prominence to the social dimensions of NEPAD during its forty-fifth (2007) session.

(For further information on NEPAD, see p. 1071.)

In connection with its review of plans and programmes of action pertaining to the situation of social groups, the Commission adopted a resolution on modalities for the first review and appraisal of the Madrid International Plan of Action on Ageing, 2002 [YUN 2002, p. 1194]. It also recommended to the Council for adoption a resolution on a comprehensive and integral international convention to protect and promote the rights and dignity of persons with disabilities and a resolution on promoting youth employment. The Commission considered the further review of its methods of work and recommended that the theme for the 2007/2008 review and policy cycle be "Promoting full employment and decent work for all", taking into account the interrelationship between employment, poverty eradication and social integration. In accordance with General Assembly resolution 60/227 [YUN 2005, p. 1176], the Commission transmitted, through the Council, to the high-level dialogue on international migration and development (see p. 1261), the Chairperson's summary of the panel discussion on "International migration and migrants from a social perspective", held during the forty-second (2004) session of the Commission [YUN 2004, p. 1092].

The Commission also considered a Secretariat note [E/CN.5/2006/5] on the review of its future organization and work methods, submitted in accordance with Assembly resolution 57/270 B [YUN 2003, p. 1468] and Council resolution 2005/11 [YUN 2005, p. 1192].

On 26 July, the Council took note of the Commission's report on its forty-fourth session and approved the provisional agenda and documentation for its forty-fifth (2007) session (**decision 2006/238**).

Future organization and methods of work of the Commission for Social Development

On 26 July [meeting 40], the Economic and Social Council, on the recommendation of the Commission for Social Development [E/2006/26], adopted **resolution 2006/18** without vote [agenda item 14 *(b)*].

Future organization and methods of work of the Commission for Social Development

The Economic and Social Council,

Recalling its resolution 2005/11 of 21 July 2005 on the future organization and methods of work of the Commission for Social Development in which the Council decided that in order for the Commission to fulfil its mandate, beginning with its forty-fifth session, the work of the Commission would be organized in a series of two-year action-oriented implementation cycles on the three core themes of Copenhagen, poverty eradication, full employment and social integration, which would include a review and a policy segment,

Recalling also that in the same resolution the Council also decided that the Commission would continue to review plans and programmes of action pertaining to social groups, including in relation to the priority theme,

Bearing in mind General Assembly resolution 57/270 B of 23 June 2003 on integrated and coordinated implementation of and follow-up to the outcomes of the major United Nations conferences and summits in the economic and social fields, in which the Assembly invited the functional commissions and relevant follow-up mechanisms, as appropriate, to contribute, from their specific perspectives, to the assessment by the Council of the cross-sectoral thematic issues selected for the coordination segment of its substantive session,

Re-emphasizing the importance of an increased exchange of national, regional and international experiences in the cycles of the Commission, focusing on the implementation of the outcomes of the World Summit for Social Development and the twenty-fourth special session of the General Assembly,

1. *Decides* that the outcome of the Commission's review shall be in the form of a chairperson's summary, done in close coordination with other members of the Bureau, and that the policy segment shall have a negotiated outcome with action-oriented strategies;

2. *Also decides* that the theme for the 2007-2008 review and policy cycle will be "Promoting full employment and decent work for all", taking into account its interrelationship with poverty eradication and social integration;

3. *Notes* the usefulness of identifying the themes for the 2009-2010 review and policy cycle during the forty-sixth session;

4. *Decides* to include the item entitled "Emerging issues" in its programme of work;

5. *Invites* the relevant specialized agencies and entities of the United Nations system to contribute to the work of the Commission for Social Development by, inter alia, providing relevant information within their respective mandates;

6. *Stresses* the importance to identify relevant subthemes within the priority theme to focus interventions and discussions, also taking into account cross-cutting issues.

UN Research Institute for Social Development

During 2006, the United Nations Research Institute for Social Development (UNRISD) continued to conduct research on the social dimensions of the development process within a holistic and multidisciplinary framework, focusing on decision-making processes and the social impact of development policies.

A November report of the UNRISD Board [E/CN.5/2007/6] described the Institute's activities in 2005-2006, among which were the conclusion of a research project on social policy in a development context, and the publication of the UNRISD report, *Gender Equality: Striving for Justice in an Unequal World*. A new phase of the research programme was initiated for the period 2005-2009, with a focus on social policy, poverty reduction and equity. Research was organized in six programme areas: social policy and development; democracy, governance and well-being; markets, business and regulation; civil society and social movements; identities, conflict and cohesion; and gender and development. UNRISD issued 99 publications in 2005-2006 and redeveloped its website. Its core funding came from the voluntary contributions of six Governments, while project-specific contributions came from the European Community, Governments, international agencies and foundations.

The Institute's relevance, quality, impact and cost-effectiveness were also evaluated during the year.

Persons with disabilities

Pursuant to Economic and Social Council resolution 2005/9 [YUN 2005, p. 1196], the Secretary-General submitted to the Commission for Social Development the annual report [E/CN.5/2006/4] of the Special Rapporteur on Disability on the monitoring of the implementation of the Standard Rules on the Equalization of Opportunities for Persons with Disabilities, adopted by the General Assembly in resolution 48/96 [YUN 1993, p. 977]. The report contained the preliminary results of the first comprehensive global survey of government actions for the implementation of the Standard Rules.

The Special Rapporteur noted that, despite the commitment demonstrated by Member States for the promotion and protection of the rights and dignity of persons with disabilities, as well as the equalization of opportunities for full participation, most had not matched their political commitment with a financial one.

International convention on the rights of persons with disabilities

In accordance with General Assembly resolution 60/232 [YUN 2005, p. 1200], the Ad Hoc Committee on a Comprehensive and Integral International Convention on the Protection and Promotion of the Rights and Dignity of Persons with Disabilities, established by Assembly resolution 56/168 [YUN 2001, p. 1012], held its seventh (16 January–3 February) [A/AC.265/2006/2] and eighth (14-25 August and 5 December) [A/AC.265/2006/4 & Add.1] sessions in New York. At its eighth session, the Committee adopted the draft text of a convention on the rights of persons with disabilities, including an optional protocol. It established an open-ended drafting group to ensure uniformity of terminology throughout the text and to report on the results to the Committee's resumed eighth session, in order to enable the Committee to forward the finalized text of the Convention to the Assembly. The Committee's final report [A/61/611] was transmitted by the Secretary-General to the Assembly in December.

ECONOMIC AND SOCIAL COUNCIL ACTION

On 26 July [meeting 40], the Economic and Social Council, on the recommendation of the Commission for Social Development [E/2006/26], adopted **resolution 2006/16** without vote [agenda item 14 *(b)*].

Comprehensive and integral international convention on the protection and promotion of the rights and dignity of persons with disabilities

The Economic and Social Council,

Recalling General Assembly resolution 56/168 of 19 December 2001, by which the Assembly established an ad hoc Committee, open to the participation of all Member States and observers of the United Nations, to consider proposals for a comprehensive and integral international convention on the protection and promotion of the rights and dignity of persons with disabilities, based on the holistic approach in the work carried out in the fields of social development, human rights and non-discrimination and taking into account the recommendations of the Commission on Human Rights and the Commission for Social Development,

Recalling also its resolution 2005/10 of 21 July 2005 on a comprehensive and integral international convention on the protection and promotion of the rights and dignity of persons with disabilities,

Recalling further General Assembly resolution 60/232 of 23 December 2005,

Reaffirming the universality, indivisibility, interdependence and interrelatedness of all human rights and fundamental freedoms and the need for their full enjoyment to be guaranteed to persons with disabilities, without discrimination,

Convinced of the contribution that a convention will make in this regard, and welcoming the firm support of the international community for such a convention and the continued engagement in its elaboration,

Recognizing the strong commitment and the positive steps taken by Governments to protect and promote the rights and inherent dignity of persons with disabilities, including through collaboration and cooperation at the regional and international levels, with the aim of strengthening national capacities and supporting national efforts in order to improve the living conditions of persons with disabilities in all regions,

Welcoming the important contributions made so far to the work of the Ad Hoc Committee on a Comprehensive and Integral International Convention on the Protection and Promotion of the Rights and Dignity of Persons with Disabilities by all stakeholders,

1. *Welcomes* the progress achieved by the Ad Hoc Committee on a Comprehensive and Integral International Convention on the Protection and Promotion of the Rights and Dignity of Persons with Disabilities in the negotiation of a draft convention at its seventh session, and invites Member States and observers to continue to participate actively and constructively in the Committee, with the aim of concluding a draft convention and submitting it to the General Assembly, as a matter of priority, for adoption at its sixty-first session;

2. *Requests* the Commission for Social Development to continue to contribute to the process of negotiation of a draft international convention, bearing in mind its area of expertise and the positive impact of a convention in promoting an inclusive approach to social development;

3. *Welcomes* the contributions of the Special Rapporteur on Disability of the Commission for Social Development to the process of elaboration of a draft convention, and requests the Special Rapporteur to contribute further to the work of the Ad Hoc Committee, drawing from her experience in the monitoring of the Standard Rules on the Equalization of Opportunities for Persons with Disabilities;

4. *Requests* the Department of Economic and Social Affairs of the Secretariat and the Office of the United Nations High Commissioner for Human Rights to continue to support the work of the Ad Hoc Committee, and underlines the importance of continuing cooperation and coordination between the two offices in order to provide substantive and technical support to the Committee and to promote public awareness regarding its work, including in collaboration with the Special Rapporteur;

5. *Requests* bodies, organs and entities of the United Nations system to continue to participate, as appropriate, in the Ad Hoc Committee and to contribute to its work;

6. *Invites* non-governmental organizations, national disability and human rights institutions and independent experts with an interest in the matter to continue their active participation in and contributions to the work of the Ad Hoc Committee, and encourages the relevant bodies of the United Nations to continue to promote and support such active participation of civil society, in accordance with General Assembly resolutions 56/510 of 23 July 2002 and 57/229 of 18 December 2002;

7. *Requests* the Secretary-General and the Special Rapporteur to report to the Commission for Social Development at its forty-fifth session on the implementation of the present resolution.

The open-ended drafting group established by the Ad Hoc Committee at its eighth session held nine meetings from 6 September to 17 November. At its resumed eighth session, on 5 December, the Committee recommended for adoption a draft resolution entitled "Convention on the Rights of Persons with Disabilities", which was adopted by the Assembly in **resolution 61/106** (see p. 785).

Cultural development

Children and a culture of peace

Report of UNESCO Director-General. In response to General Assembly resolution 60/3 [YUN 2005, p. 746] on the International Decade for a Culture of Peace and Non-Violence for the Children of the World, 2001-2010, proclaimed in 1998 [YUN 1998, p. 639], and resolution 60/10 [YUN 2005, p. 1203] on the promotion of inter-religious dialogue and cooperation for peace, as well as resolution 60/11 [ibid., p. 1204] on the promotion of religious and cultural understanding, harmony and cooperation, the Secretary-General transmitted a report [A/61/175] of the Director-General of the United Nations Educational, Scientific and Cultural Organization (UNESCO) on a culture of peace. It followed the mid-term global review of the International Decade, prepared by UNESCO [YUN 2005, p. 746].

The report analysed the work undertaken by the UN system, with the participation of other UN entities, Governments and civil society actors, to implement the Programme of Action on a Culture of Peace [YUN 1999, p. 594]. Those activities corresponded to the eight areas of the Programme of Action: foster a culture of peace through education; promote sustainable economic and social development; promote respect for all human rights; ensure equality between women and men; foster democratic participation; advance understanding, tolerance and solidarity; support participatory communication and the free flow of information and knowledge; and promote international peace and security. Also addressed were the role of civil society, and communication and networking arrangements.

The Director-General recommended that Member States ratify the UNESCO legal instruments for the protection of cultural heritage, increase educational efforts to develop curricula, textbooks and activities on cultural and religious tolerance, promote the objectives of the Decade through activities at the local, national and international levels, observe the International Day of Peace on 21 September, ensure access to communication and information technologies for marginalized communities to close the digital divide and ensure the free flow of ideas, and urge the media to support the global campaign for a culture of peace, as well as the dialogue among civilizations, cultures and peoples.

GENERAL ASSEMBLY ACTION

On 4 December [meeting 64], the General Assembly adopted **resolution 61/45** [draft: A/61/L.16 & Add.1] without vote [agenda item 44].

International Decade for a Culture of Peace and Non-Violence for the Children of the World, 2001-2010

The General Assembly,

Bearing in mind the Charter of the United Nations, including the purposes and principles contained therein, and especially the dedication to saving succeeding generations from the scourge of war,

Recalling the Constitution of the United Nations Educational, Scientific and Cultural Organization, which states that, "since wars begin in the minds of men, it is in the minds of men that the defences of peace must be constructed",

Recalling also its previous resolutions on a culture of peace, in particular resolution 52/15 of 20 November 1997 proclaiming 2000 the International Year for the Culture of Peace, resolution 53/25 of 10 November 1998 proclaiming the period 2001-2010 the International Decade for a Culture of Peace and Non-Violence for the Children of the World, and resolutions 56/5 of 5 November 2001, 57/6 of 4 November 2002, 58/11 of 10 November 2003, 59/143 of 15 December 2004 and 60/3 of 20 October 2005,

Reaffirming the Declaration and Programme of Action on a Culture of Peace, recognizing that they serve, inter alia, as the basis for the observance of the Decade, and convinced that the effective and successful observance of the Decade throughout the world will promote a culture of peace and non-violence that benefits humanity, in particular future generations,

Recalling the United Nations Millennium Declaration, which calls for the active promotion of a culture of peace,

Taking note of Commission on Human Rights resolution 2000/66 of 26 April 2000 entitled "Towards a culture of peace",

Taking note also of the report of the Secretary-General on the International Decade for a Culture of Peace and Non-Violence for the Children of the World, including paragraph 28 thereof, which indicates that each of the ten years of the Decade will be marked with a different priority theme related to the Programme of Action,

Noting the relevance of the World Summit on Sustainable Development, held in Johannesburg, South Africa, from 26 August to 4 September 2002, the International Conference on Financing for Development, held in Monterrey, Mexico, from 18 to 22 March 2002, the special session of the General Assembly on children, held in New York from 8 to 10 May 2002, the World Conference against Racism, Racial Discrimination, Xenophobia and Related Intolerance, held in Durban, South Africa, from 31 August to 8 September 2001, and the United Nations Decade for Human Rights Education, 1995-2004, for the International Decade for a Culture of Peace and Non-Violence for the Children of the World, 2001-2010, as well as the need to implement, as appropriate, the relevant decisions agreed upon therein,

Recognizing that all efforts made by the United Nations system in general and the international community at large for peacekeeping, peacebuilding, the prevention of conflicts, disarmament, sustainable development, the promotion of human dignity and human rights, democracy, the rule of law, good governance and gender equality at the national and international levels contribute greatly to the culture of peace,

Noting that its resolution 57/337 of 3 July 2003 on the prevention of armed conflict could contribute to the further promotion of a culture of peace,

Taking into account the "Manifesto 2000" initiative of the United Nations Educational, Scientific and Cultural Organization promoting a culture of peace, which has so far received over seventy-five million signatures of endorsement throughout the world,

Taking note with appreciation of the report of the Director-General of the United Nations Educational, Scientific and Cultural Organization on the implementation of resolution 60/3,

Taking note of the 2005 World Summit Outcome adopted on 16 September 2005 at the High-level Plenary Meeting of the General Assembly,

Welcoming the establishment of the Peacebuilding Commission,

1. *Reiterates* that the objective of the International Decade for a Culture of Peace and Non-Violence for the Children of the World, 2001-2010, is to strengthen further the global movement for a culture of peace following the observance of the International Year for the Culture of Peace in 2000;

2. *Invites* Member States to continue to place greater emphasis on and expand their activities promoting a culture of peace and non-violence, in particular during the Decade, at the national, regional and international levels and to ensure that peace and non-violence are fostered at all levels;

3. *Commends* the United Nations Educational, Scientific and Cultural Organization for recognizing the promotion of a culture of peace as the expression of its fundamental mandate, and encourages it, as the lead agency for the Decade, to strengthen further the activities it has undertaken for promoting a culture of peace, including the dissemination of the Declaration and Programme of Action on a Culture of Peace and related materials in various languages across the world;

4. *Also commends* the relevant United Nations bodies, in particular the United Nations Children's Fund, the United Nations Development Fund for Women and the University for Peace, for their activities in further promoting a culture of peace and non-violence, including the promotion of peace education and activities related to specific areas identified in the Programme of Action,

and encourages them to continue and further strengthen and expand their efforts;

5. *Encourages* the Peacebuilding Commission to promote a culture of peace and non-violence for children in its activities;

6. *Encourages* the appropriate authorities to provide education, in children's schools, that includes lessons in mutual understanding, tolerance, active citizenship, human rights and the promotion of a culture of peace;

7. *Commends* civil society, including non-governmental organizations and young people, for their activities in further promoting a culture of peace and non-violence, including through their campaign to raise awareness on a culture of peace, and notes the progress achieved by more than seven hundred organizations in more than one hundred countries;

8. *Encourages* civil society, including non-governmental organizations, to further strengthen its efforts in furtherance of the objectives of the Decade, inter alia, by adopting its own programme of activities to complement the initiatives of Member States, the organizations of the United Nations system and other international and regional organizations;

9. *Encourages* the involvement of the mass media in education for a culture of peace and non-violence, with particular regard to children and young people, including through the planned expansion of the Culture of Peace News Network as a global network of Internet sites in many languages;

10. *Welcomes* the efforts made by the United Nations Educational, Scientific and Cultural Organization to continue the communication and networking arrangements established during the International Year for providing an instant update of developments related to the observance of the Decade;

11. *Invites* Member States to observe 21 September of each year as the International Day of Peace, as a day of global ceasefire and non-violence, in accordance with resolution 55/282 of 7 September 2001;

12. *Invites* Member States, as well as civil society, including non-governmental organizations, to continue providing information to the Secretary-General on the observance of the Decade and the activities undertaken to promote a culture of peace and non-violence;

13. *Appreciates* the participation of Member States in the day of plenary meetings to review progress made in the implementation of the Declaration and Programme of Action and the observance of the Decade at its mid-point;

14. *Requests* the Secretary-General to explore enhancing mechanisms for the implementation of the Declaration and Programme of Action;

15. *Also requests* the Secretary-General to submit to the General Assembly at its sixty-second session a report on the implementation of the present resolution;

16. *Decides* to include in the provisional agenda of its sixty-second session the item entitled "Culture of peace".

On 22 December, the Assembly decided that the agenda item "Culture of peace" would remain for consideration during its resumed sixty-first (2007) session (**decision 61/552**).

Religious and cultural understanding

On 20 December [meeting 83], the General Assembly adopted **resolution 61/221** [draft: A/61/L.11/Rev.2 & Add.1] without vote [agenda item 44].

Promotion of interreligious and intercultural dialogue, understanding and cooperation for peace

The General Assembly,

Reaffirming the purposes and principles enshrined in the Charter of the United Nations and the Universal Declaration of Human Rights, in particular the right to freedom of thought, conscience and religion,

Recalling its resolutions 56/6 of 9 November 2001, on the Global Agenda for Dialogue among Civilizations, 57/6 of 4 November 2002, concerning the promotion of a culture of peace and non-violence, 57/337 of 3 July 2003, on the prevention of armed conflict, 58/128 of 19 December 2003, on the promotion of religious and cultural understanding, harmony and cooperation, 59/23 of 11 November 2004, on the promotion of interreligious dialogue, 59/143 of 15 December 2004, on the International Decade for a Culture of Peace and Non-Violence for the Children of the World, 2001–2010, and 59/199 of 20 December 2004, on the elimination of all forms of religious intolerance,

Underlining the importance of promoting understanding, tolerance and friendship among human beings in all their diversity of religion, belief, culture and language, and recalling that all States have pledged themselves under the Charter to promote and encourage universal respect for and observance of human rights and fundamental freedoms for all, without distinction as to race, sex, language or religion,

Taking note of the adoption of the 2005 World Summit Outcome in which the Heads of State and Government acknowledged the importance of respect and understanding for religious and cultural diversity, reaffirmed the value of the dialogue on interfaith cooperation and committed themselves to advancing human welfare, freedom and progress everywhere, as well as to encouraging and promoting tolerance, respect, dialogue and cooperation at the local, national, regional and international levels and among different cultures, civilizations and peoples in order to promote international peace and security,

Alarmed that serious instances of intolerance and discrimination on the grounds of religion or belief, including acts of violence, intimidation and coercion motivated by religious intolerance, are on the increase in many parts of the world and threaten the enjoyment of human rights and fundamental freedoms,

Emphasizing the need, at all levels of society and among nations, for strengthening freedom, justice, democracy, tolerance, solidarity, cooperation, pluralism, respect for diversity of culture and religion or belief, dialogue and understanding, which are important elements for peace, and convinced that the guiding principles of democratic society need to be actively promoted by the international community,

Reaffirming that freedom of expression, media pluralism, multilingualism, equal access to art and to scientific and technological knowledge, including in digital form, and the possibility for all cultures to have access to the means of expression and dissemination are the guarantees of cultural diversity, and that in ensuring the free flow of ideas by word and image, care should be exercised that all cultures can express themselves and make themselves known,

Affirming the need for all States to continue international efforts to enhance dialogue and broaden understanding among civilizations, in an effort to prevent the targeting of different religions and cultures, contribute to the peaceful resolution of conflicts and disputes and reduce the potential for animosity, clashes and even violence,

Considering that tolerance for cultural, ethnic, and religious and linguistic diversities, as well as dialogue among and within civilizations, is essential for peace, understanding and friendship among individuals and people of different cultures and nations of the world, while manifestations of cultural prejudice, intolerance and xenophobia towards different cultures and religions may generate hatred and violence among peoples and nations throughout the world,

Recognizing the richness of nomadic civilization and its important contribution to promoting dialogue and interaction among all forms of civilization,

Taking note of the valuable contribution of various initiatives at the national, regional and international levels, such as the Alliance of Civilizations initiative, the Bali Declaration on Building Interfaith Harmony within the International Community, the Congress of Leaders of World and Traditional Religions, the Dialogue among Civilizations and Cultures, Enlightened Moderation, the Informal Meeting of Leaders on Interfaith Dialogue and Cooperation for Peace, the Islam-Christianity Dialogue, the Moscow World Summit of Religious Leaders and the Tripartite Forum on Interfaith Cooperation for Peace, which are all mutually inclusive, reinforcing and interrelated,

Mindful that those initiatives identify areas for practical action in all sectors and levels of society for the promotion of interreligious, intercultural and intercivilizational dialogue, understanding and cooperation,

Recognizing the commitment of all religions to peace,

1. *Affirms* that mutual understanding and interreligious dialogue constitute important dimensions of the dialogue among civilizations and of the culture of peace;

2. *Takes note with appreciation* of the work of the United Nations Educational, Scientific and Cultural Organization on interreligious dialogue in the context of its efforts to promote dialogue among civilizations, cultures and peoples, as well as activities related to a culture of peace, and welcomes its focus on concrete action at the global, regional and subregional levels and its flagship project on the promotion of interfaith dialogue;

3. *Recognizes* that respect for religious and cultural diversity in an increasingly globalizing world contributes to international cooperation, promotes enhanced dialogue among religions, cultures and civilizations and helps to create an environment conducive to the exchange of human experience;

4. *Also recognizes* that, despite intolerance and conflicts that are creating a divide across countries and regions and constitute a growing threat to peaceful relations among nations, all cultures, religions and civilizations share a common set of universal values and can all contribute to the enrichment of humankind;

5. *Reaffirms* the solemn commitment of all States to fulfil their obligations to promote universal respect for, and observance and protection of, all human rights and fundamental freedoms for all in accordance with the Charter of the United Nations, the Universal Declaration of Human Rights and other instruments relating to human rights and international law; the universal nature of these rights and freedoms is beyond question;

6. *Urges* States, in compliance with their international obligations, to take all necessary action to combat incitement to or acts of violence, intimidation and coercion motivated by hatred and intolerance based on culture, religion or belief, which may cause discord and disharmony within and among societies;

7. *Also urges* States to take effective measures to prevent and eliminate discrimination on the grounds of religion or belief in the recognition, exercise and enjoyment of human rights and fundamental freedoms in all fields of civil, economic, political, social and cultural life and to make all efforts to enact or rescind legislation, where necessary, in order to prohibit any such discrimination, and to take all appropriate measures to combat intolerance on the grounds of religion or belief;

8. *Reaffirms* that the promotion and protection of the rights of persons belonging to national or ethnic, religious and linguistic minorities contribute to political and social stability and peace and enrich the cultural diversity and heritage of society as a whole in the States in which such persons live, and urges States to ensure that their political and legal systems reflect the multicultural diversity within their societies and, where necessary, to improve democratic and political institutions, organizations and practices so that they are more fully participatory and avoid the marginalization and exclusion of, and discrimination against, specific sectors of society;

9. *Encourages* Governments to promote, including through education, as well as the development of progressive curricula and textbooks, understanding, tolerance and friendship among human beings in all their diversity of religion, belief, culture and language, which will address the cultural, social, economic, political and religious sources of intolerance, and to apply a gender perspective while doing so, in order to promote understanding, tolerance, peace and friendly relations among nations and all racial and religious groups, recognizing that education at all levels is one of the principal means to build a culture of peace;

10. *Recognizes* the contribution of the media to developing a better understanding among all religions, beliefs, cultures and peoples and to facilitating a dialogue among societies, as well as to creating an environment conducive to the exchange of human experience;

11. *Supports* practical initiatives at the regional and national levels by all parties concerned, including the media representatives themselves, to encourage the media to enhance its capacity in promoting interfaith and intercultural understanding and cooperation for peace, development and human dignity;

12. *Encourages* the promotion of dialogue among the media from all cultures and civilizations, emphasizes that everyone has the right to freedom of expression, and reaffirms that the exercise of this right carries with it special duties and responsibilities and may therefore be subject to certain restrictions, but these shall only be such as are provided by law and necessary for respect of the rights or reputations of others, protection of national security or of public order, or of public health or morals;

13. *Affirms* that the relevant United Nations bodies, including the General Assembly and the Human Rights Council, shall endeavour to undertake coordinated measures to promote universal respect on matters of freedom of religion or belief and cultural diversity and to prevent instances of intolerance, discrimination and incitement of hatred against members of any community or adherents of any religion or belief;

14. *Decides* to convene in 2007 a high-level dialogue on interreligious and intercultural cooperation for the promotion of tolerance, understanding and universal respect on matters of freedom of religion or belief and cultural diversity, in coordination with other similar initiatives in this area;

15. *Decides also* to consider declaring one of the coming years as the Year of Dialogue among Religions and Cultures;

16. *Requests* the Secretary-General to ensure the systematic and organizational follow-up of all interreligious, intercultural and intercivilizational matters within the United Nations system and overall coordination and coherence in its interreligious, intercultural and intercivilizational dialogue and cooperation efforts, inter alia, through the designation of a focal unit in the Secretariat to handle these matters;

17. *Also requests* the Secretary-General to report to the General Assembly at its sixty-second session on the implementation of the present resolution.

Sport for development and peace

In response to General Assembly resolution 60/9 [YUN 2005, p. 1207], the Secretary-General submitted a September report [A/61/373] on "Sport for Development and Peace: the way forward", which described the establishment of the United Nations Action Plan on Sport for Development and Peace, and reviewed the achievements of the International Year of Sport and Physical Education (2005) [YUN 2005, p. 1206], including the activities of Member States, the UN system and other stakeholders to build on the momentum generated by the International Year. The report also described the activities, initiatives and networking carried out in counties worldwide, under the leadership of the Special Adviser to the Secretary-General on Sport for Development and Peace.

The Action Plan presented a framework to enable partners to build on the achievements of the International Year (see below). It was a strategy for better integrating sport into the development agenda; incorporating sport in programmes for health, education, development and peace; utilizing sport as a tool to achieve the Millennium Development Goals (MDGs) [YUN 2000, p. 51] by 2015; and focusing greater attention and resources on Sport for Development and Peace. The three-year Action Plan set out the lines of action, including a number of challenges and proposed actions, as well as other action points aimed at specific sectors and stakeholders to maximize the positive impact of sport.

Among positive results during the International Year were: making sports a stronger partner in development; recognition of sports and physical education as international priorities, and the role they played in public health; unanimous adoption of the International Convention against Doping by the UNESCO General Conference at its thirty-third session [YUN 2005, p. 1570]; increased recognition of the potential of sport to bridge social, religious, ethnic and gender divides; and sport as a mobilizing force to raise resources for relief activities for natural disasters, and for the Year as a springboard for launching new and strengthening existing programmes to achieve international development goals, including the MDGs. The Year also highlighted, among other things, the importance of non-governmental organizations and the private sector in moving forward sport and physical education as tools for the promotion of education, health, development and peace. The Year proved that international sport federations and organizations, such as the International Olympic Committeee, the International Football Federation and the International Paralympic Committee, were increasingly willing to become involved in humanitarian actions. The International Disability in Sport Working Group was formed in January to advance the human rights of persons with disabilities relating to sports. During 2006, UN agencies, funds and programmes carried out a broad range of activities that helped to build on the momentum of the International Year and were increasingly forging partnerships for sports-related activities towards that end.

GENERAL ASSEMBLY ACTION

On 3 November [meeting 48], the General Assembly adopted **resolution 61/10** [draft: A/61/L.12 & Add.1] without vote [agenda item 49].

Sport as a means to promote education, health, development and peace

The General Assembly,

Recalling its resolutions 58/5 of 3 November 2003, 59/10 of 27 October 2004 and 60/9 of 3 November 2005, its decision to proclaim 2005 the International Year for Sport and Physical Education to strengthen sport as a means to promote education, health, development and peace, and its resolution 60/1 of 16 September 2005, in which it underlined that sport could foster development and peace and could contribute to an atmosphere of tolerance and understanding,

Taking note with appreciation of the report of the Secretary-General, which includes the Action Plan that serves as an initial road map for a three-year period to expand and strengthen partnerships, sport for development and peace programmes and projects and advocacy and communications activities,

Acknowledging the major role of the Member States and the United Nations system in promoting human development through sport and physical education, through the country programmes,

Acknowledging also that sport and physical education can present opportunities for solidarity and cooperation in order to promote tolerance, a culture of peace, social and gender equality, adequate responses to the special needs of persons with disabilities, intercultural dialogue, social cohesion and harmony,

Recognizing the need for greater coordination of efforts at the international level to facilitate a more effective fight against doping,

Noting the need to further develop a common framework within the United Nations to promote sport for education, health, development and peace, thereby broadening the mission of the Working Group on Sport for Development and Peace of the United Nations Communications Group to establish a policy and communications platform that will define common strategies, policy and programmes to increase coherence and synergies, while simultaneously raising awareness within the United Nations system and among external partners,

Recalling the "Call to Action", which was adopted on 6 December 2005 in Magglingen, Switzerland, at the culminating conference of the International Year for Sport and Physical Education, to promote sport for development and peace among Governments, the United Nations system and international sports organizations,

Taking note with appreciation of the organization in 2006 of the Global Youth Leadership Summit that highlighted the use of the convening power of sport as an entry point towards the achievement of the Millennium Development Goals by 2015,

1. *Appreciates* the appointment of sports celebrities as spokespersons and Goodwill Ambassadors for the United Nations, representing the positive values of sport;

2. *Encourages* the strengthening of cooperation with the International Olympic Committee, the International Paralympic Committee, sports organizations and other partners of the world of sport;

3. *Invites* Member States, the United Nations system, including the governing bodies of the United Nations agencies, sport-related organizations, the media, civil society and the private sector to collaborate to promote greater awareness and action to foster peace and accelerate the attainment of the Millennium Development Goals through sport-based initiatives and to promote the integration of sport for development and peace in the development agenda, by working along the following points, adapted from the Action Plan included in the report of the Secretary-General:

(a) Further develop a global framework to strengthen a common vision, define priorities and further raise awareness to promote and mainstream sport for development and peace policies that are easily replicable;

(b) Promote and support the integration and mainstreaming of sport for development and peace in development programmes and policies;

(c) Promote innovative funding mechanisms and multi-stakeholder arrangements on all levels, on a voluntary basis, including the engagement of sports organizations, civil society, athletes and the private sector;

(d) Promote common evaluation and monitoring tools, indicators and benchmarks based on commonly agreed standards;

4. *Invites* Member States to initiate sports programmes to promote gender equality and the empowerment of women;

5. *Invites* Governments and international sports organizations to assist developing countries, in particular the least developed countries, in their capacity-building efforts in sport and physical education, by providing national experiences and best practices, as well as financial, technical and logistic resources for the development of sports programmes;

6. *Encourages* Member States to ratify the International Convention Against Doping in Sport;

7. *Encourages* the Secretary-General to maintain the mandate of Special Adviser on Sport for Development and Peace and to provide guidance on the institutional future of sport for development and peace within the United Nations system;

8. *Invites* Member States to provide voluntary contributions to ensure adequate execution of and follow-up to the activities being implemented by the Office of Sport for Development and Peace in Geneva and in New York;

9. *Requests* the Secretary-General to report to the General Assembly at its sixty-second session on the implementation of the present resolution and on progress at the national, regional and international levels to en-

courage policies and best practices related to sport for development and peace, under the item entitled "Sport for peace and development".

Olympic Truce

On 6 February, just prior to the XX Olympic Winter Games, held in Turin, Italy (10-26 February), and the Paralympic Winter Games, also in Turin (10-19 March), the President of the General Assembly made a solemn appeal [A/60/662] to Member States to demonstrate their commitment to global peace by observing the Olympic Truce during the Winter Games, as earlier urged by the Assembly in resolution 60/8 [YUN 2005, p. 1206].

By **decision 60/552** of 6 February, the Assembly took note of the President's solemn appeal in connection with the observance of the Olympic Truce.

Cultural property

Return of cultural property

The Secretary-General, in July [A/61/176], transmitted to the General Assembly the UNESCO Director-General's report covering a three-year period on actions taken by the organization to facilitate the return and restitution of cultural property illicitly removed from its country of origin. In addition to promoting and assisting Member States in the national implementation of relevant international standard-setting instruments, UNESCO adopted a model export certificate for cultural objects, launched the Cultural Heritage Laws Database and took steps to fulfil the recommendations adopted by the Intergovernmental Committee for Promoting the Return of Cultural Property to its Countries of Origin or its Restitution in Case of Illicit Appropriation at its 2003 and 2005 sessions.

Among the recommendations contained in the report were that Member States that had not done so should consider joining relevant international standard-setting conventions; revise and strengthen national legislation to better protect cultural properties by, among other things, establishing State ownership of any cultural property not yet excavated or illicitly excavated; regulate the excavation of archaeological sites; and establish clear sanctions for violations, and effective export and import regimes and controls, as well as national inventory of cultural properties. Member States were encouraged to develop a strong national policy specific to cultural heritage protection, which should include coordination between relevant ministries, training of professionals in the field, cooperation with international and regional agencies, and public awareness campaigns on the need to protect cultural heritage and fight against illicit trafficking. They were also requested to undertake specific practical measures to better protect cultural heritage, such as establishing inventories using Object-ID standards as a minimum level of identification, using export certificates, posting relevant national legislation on the UNESCO Cultural Heritage Law Database, providing specialized training to police and customs agents, reporting all thefts to the International Criminal Police Organization (INTERPOL) and furnishing the appropriate information and photographs. Other measures included encouraging dealers to keep registries of all purchases and sales of cultural objects; monitoring the sale of cultural objects on the Internet; ensuring the broad use of anti-theft and other security measures; and promoting the UNESCO international code of ethics for dealers in cultural property.

GENERAL ASSEMBLY ACTION

On 4 December [meeting 65], the General Assembly adopted **resolution 61/52** [draft: A/61/L.15/Rev.1 & Add.1] without vote [agenda item 43].

Return or restitution of cultural property to the countries of origin

The General Assembly,

Reaffirming the relevant provisions of the Charter of the United Nations,

Recalling its resolutions 3026 A (XXVII) of 18 December 1972, 3148(XXVIII) of 14 December 1973, 3187(XXVIII) of 18 December 1973, 3391(XXX) of 19 November 1975, 31/40 of 30 November 1976, 32/18 of 11 November 1977, 33/50 of 14 December 1978, 34/64 of 29 November 1979, 35/127 and 35/128 of 11 December 1980, 36/64 of 27 November 1981, 38/34 of 25 November 1983, 40/19 of 21 November 1985, 42/7 of 22 October 1987, 44/18 of 6 November 1989, 46/10 of 22 October 1991, 48/15 of 2 November 1993, 50/56 of 11 December 1995, 52/24 of 25 November 1997, 54/190 of 17 December 1999, 56/97 of 14 December 2001 and 58/17 of 3 December 2003,

Recalling also its resolution 56/8 of 21 November 2001, in which it proclaimed 2002 the United Nations Year for Cultural Heritage,

Recalling further the Convention for the Protection of Cultural Property in the Event of Armed Conflict, adopted at The Hague on 14 May 1954, and the two Protocols thereto, adopted in 1954 and 1999,

Recalling the Convention on the Means of Prohibiting and Preventing the Illicit Import, Export and Transfer of Ownership of Cultural Property, adopted on 14 November 1970 by the General Conference of the United Nations Educational, Scientific and Cultural Organization,

Recalling also the Convention concerning the Protection of the World Cultural and Natural Heritage, adopted on 16 November 1972 by the General Conference of the United Nations Educational, Scientific and Cultural Organization,

Recalling further the Convention on Stolen or Illegally Exported Cultural Objects, adopted in Rome on 24 June 1995 by the International Institute for the Unification of Private Law,

Taking note of the adoption of the Convention on the Protection of the Underwater Cultural Heritage by the General Conference of the United Nations Educational, Scientific and Cultural Organization on 2 November 2001,

Noting the adoption of the Convention for the Safeguarding of the Intangible Cultural Heritage by the General Conference of the United Nations Educational, Scientific and Cultural Organization on 17 October 2003 and the Convention on the Protection and Promotion of the Diversity of Cultural Expressions by the General Conference of the United Nations Educational, Scientific and Cultural Organization on 20 October 2005,

Noting also the adoption of the United Nations Convention on Jurisdictional Immunities of States and Their Property on 2 December 2004, as it might apply to cultural property,

Recalling the Medellin Declaration for Cultural Diversity and Tolerance and the Plan of Action on Cultural Cooperation, adopted at the first Meeting of the Ministers of Culture of the Movement of Non-Aligned Countries, held in Medellin, Colombia, on 4 and 5 September 1997,

Noting the adoption of the Universal Declaration on Cultural Diversity and the Action Plan for its implementation, adopted by the General Conference of the United Nations Educational, Scientific and Cultural Organization on 2 November 2001,

Welcoming the report of the Secretary-General submitted in cooperation with the Director-General of the United Nations Educational, Scientific and Cultural Organization,

Aware of the importance attached by some countries of origin to the return of cultural property that is of fundamental spiritual and cultural value to them, so that they may constitute collections representative of their cultural heritage,

Expressing concern about the illicit traffic in cultural property and its damage to the cultural heritage of nations,

Expressing concern also about the loss, destruction, removal, theft, pillage, illicit movement or misappropriation of and any acts of vandalism or damage directed against cultural property, in particular in areas of armed conflict, including territories that are occupied, whether such conflicts are international or internal,

Recalling Security Council resolution 1483(2003), adopted on 22 May 2003, in particular paragraph 7 relating to the restitution of the cultural property of Iraq,

1. *Commends* the United Nations Educational, Scientific and Cultural Organization and the Intergovernmental Committee for Promoting the Return of Cultural Property to its Countries of Origin or its Restitution in Case of Illicit Appropriation on the work they have accomplished, in particular through the promotion of bilateral negotiations, for the return or restitution of cultural property, the preparation of inventories of movable cultural property and the implementation of the Object-ID standard related thereto, as well as for the reduction of illicit traffic in cultural property and the dissemination of information to the public;

2. *Calls upon* all relevant bodies, agencies, funds and programmes of the United Nations system and other relevant intergovernmental organizations to work in coordination with the United Nations Educational, Scientific and Cultural Organization, within their mandates and in cooperation with Member States, in order to continue to address the issue of return or restitution of cultural property to the countries of origin and to provide appropriate support accordingly;

3. *Welcomes* the adoption by the General Conference of the United Nations Educational, Scientific and Cultural Organization on 17 October 2003 of the Declaration concerning the Intentional Destruction of Cultural Heritage;

4. *Reaffirms* the importance of the Convention on the Means of Prohibiting and Preventing the Illicit Import, Export and Transfer of Ownership of Cultural Property, as well as the Convention on Stolen or Illegally Exported Cultural Objects of the International Institute for the Unification of Private Law, and of their implementation, and invites Member States that have not already done so to consider becoming parties to these Conventions;

5. *Recognizes* the importance of the Convention on the Protection of the Underwater Cultural Heritage and the Convention on the Protection and Promotion of the Diversity of Cultural Expressions, notes that these Conventions have still not entered into force, and invites Member States that have not already done so to consider becoming parties to these Conventions;

6. *Also recognizes* the importance of the United Nations Convention on Jurisdictional Immunities of States and Their Property, notes that this Convention has still not entered into force, and invites Member States that have not already done so to consider becoming parties to the Convention;

7. *Reaffirms* the importance of the principles and provisions of the Convention for the Protection of Cultural Property in the Event of Armed Conflict, and of their implementation, and invites Member States that have not already done so to become parties to the Convention;

8. *Also reaffirms* the importance of the Second Protocol to the Convention, adopted at The Hague on 26 March 1999, and of its implementation, and invites all States parties to the Convention that have not already done so to consider becoming parties to the Second Protocol;

9. *Welcomes* the most recent efforts made by the United Nations Educational, Scientific and Cultural Organization for the protection of the cultural heritage of countries in conflict, including the safe return to those countries of cultural property and other items of archaeological, historical, cultural, rare scientific and religious importance that have been illegally removed, and calls

upon the international community to contribute to these efforts;

10. *Urges* Member States to introduce effective national and international measures to prevent and combat illicit trafficking in cultural property, including special training for police, customs and border services;

11. *Invites* Member States, in cooperation with the United Nations Educational, Scientific and Cultural Organization, to continue to draw up systematic inventories of their cultural property, as well as to work towards the creation of a database of their national cultural legislation, in particular in electronic format;

12. *Welcomes* the launch of the Cultural Heritage Laws Database of the United Nations Educational, Scientific and Cultural Organization in 2005, and invites Member States to provide their legislation in electronic format for inclusion in the database, to provide regular updates to the database and to promote it;

13. *Reaffirms* the efforts of the United Nations Educational, Scientific and Cultural Organization to promote the use of identification systems, in particular the application of the Object-ID standard, and to encourage the linking of identification systems and existing databases, including the one developed by Interpol, to allow for the electronic transmission of information in order to reduce illicit trafficking in cultural property, and encourages the United Nations Educational, Scientific and Cultural Organization to make further efforts in this regard in cooperation with Member States, where appropriate;

14. *Recognizes* the revision of the Statutes of the Intergovernmental Committee for Promoting the Return of Cultural Property to its Countries of Origin or its Restitution in Case of Illicit Appropriation to include mediation and conciliation processes, and invites Member States to consider the possibility of using such processes as appropriate;

15. *Welcomes* the development of the model export certificate for cultural objects by the United Nations Educational, Scientific and Cultural Organization and the World Customs Organization as a tool to combat illicit trafficking in cultural property, and invites Member States to consider adopting the model export certificate as their national export certificate, in accordance with domestic law and procedures;

16. *Notes* the decision taken in resolution 45, adopted on 20 October 2005 by the General Conference of the United Nations Educational, Scientific and Cultural Organization at its thirty-third session, that the subject of cultural objects displaced in connection with the Second World War should be the subject of a non-binding standard-setting instrument;

17. *Recognizes* the public awareness and increased mobilization and action in favour of heritage values that was achieved in 2002, the United Nations Year for Cultural Heritage, and calls upon the international community and the United Nations to continue to cooperate with the United Nations Educational, Scientific and Cultural Organization on the basis of that work;

18. *Welcomes* the endorsement of the International Code of Ethics for Dealers in Cultural Property by the General Conference of the United Nations Educational, Scientific and Cultural Organization on 16 November 1999, which was adopted in January 1999 by the Intergovernmental Committee for Promoting the Return of Cultural Property to its Countries of Origin or its Restitution in Case of Illicit Appropriation, and invites those who deal with trade in cultural property and their associations, where they exist, to encourage the implementation of the Code;

19. *Recognizes* the importance of the creation, by the General Conference of the United Nations Educational, Scientific and Cultural Organization, of the International Fund for the Return of Cultural Property to its Countries of Origin or its Restitution in Case of Illicit Appropriation, launched in November 2000, and encourages the United Nations Educational, Scientific and Cultural Organization to continue to promote the Fund and render it operational;

20. *Requests* the Secretary-General to cooperate with the United Nations Educational, Scientific and Cultural Organization in its efforts to bring about the attainment of the objectives of the present resolution;

21. *Also requests* the Secretary-General, in cooperation with the Director-General of the United Nations Educational, Scientific and Cultural Organization, to submit to the General Assembly at its sixty-fourth session a report on the implementation of the present resolution;

22. *Decides* to include in the provisional agenda of its sixty-fourth session the item entitled "Return or restitution of cultural property to the countries of origin".

Protection against trafficking in cultural property

Pursuant to Economic and Social Council resolution 2004/34 [YUN 2004, p. 1106], the Secretary-General submitted a February report [E/CN.15/2006/14] on protection against trafficking in cultural property, which provided an overview and analysis of the replies received from Member States on their efforts to implement the resolution. He noted that the United Nations Office on Drugs and Crime planned to convene, with the cooperation of UNESCO, an expert group meeting to explore and assess the challenges posed and the difficulties encountered in the fight against the trafficking in cultural property.

Crime prevention and criminal justice

Follow-up to Eleventh UN Crime Congress

At its fifteenth session, the Commission on Crime Prevention and Criminal Justice considered the report of the Secretary-General [E/CN.15/2006/7] on the follow-up to the Eleventh United Nations

Congress on Crime Prevention and Criminal Justice [YUN 2005, p. 1208]. The report, submitted pursuant to Economic and Social Council resolution 2005/15 [ibid., p. 1213], contained an analysis of the replies received by the Secretariat from 21 Member States on possible ways of ensuring appropriate follow-up to the Bangkok Declaration, adopted at the Eleventh Congress. It also provided information on action taken by Member States and on proposals of possible future activity by the United Nations Office on Drugs and Crime (UNODC), including recommendations for facilitating consideration of the matter by the Commission.

The Secretary-General suggested that the Commission should consider the proposal made by some Member States to organize after its fifteenth session, in cooperation with UNODC, an intergovernmental expert group meeting to discuss the best way to operationalize the recommendations contained in the Bangkok Declaration. The expert group should identify an appropriate follow-up mechanism, as well as an adequate reporting system, to monitor implementation, so as to facilitate a final review of the follow-up at the twelfth Congress in 2010.

The Commission recommended to the Council for adoption a resolution on the follow-up to the Eleventh United Nations Congress on Crime Prevention and Criminal Justice.

ECONOMIC AND SOCIAL COUNCIL ACTION

On 27 July [meeting 41], the Economic and Social Council, on the recommendation of the Commission on Crime Prevention and Criminal Justice [E/2006/30 & Corr.1], adopted **resolution 2006/26** without vote [agenda item 14 *(c)*].

Follow-up to the Eleventh United Nations Congress on Crime Prevention and Criminal Justice

The Economic and Social Council,

Emphasizing the responsibility assumed by the United Nations in the field of crime prevention and criminal justice in pursuance of Economic and Social Council resolution 155 C(VII) of 13 August 1948 and General Assembly resolution 415(V) of 1 December 1950,

Acknowledging that the United Nations congresses on crime prevention and criminal justice, as major intergovernmental forums, have influenced national policies and practices and promoted international cooperation in that field by facilitating the exchange of views and experience, mobilizing public opinion and recommending policy options at the national, regional and international levels,

Noting General Assembly resolution 56/201 of 21 December 2001 on the triennial policy review of operational activities for development of the United Nations system, and Economic and Social Council resolution 2003/3 of 11 July 2003 on the progress in the implementation of Assembly resolution 56/201, in which the Council recommended that all organizations of the United Nations development system consider lessons learned and their dissemination as a specific required component of their activities; emphasized the importance of evaluation of operational activities of the United Nations system in order to enhance their effectiveness and impact; and called upon the Secretary-General to integrate a stronger focus on lessons learned, results and outcome into future reports,

Recalling General Assembly resolution 57/270 B of 23 June 2003, in which it emphasized that the United Nations system had an important responsibility to assist Governments to stay fully engaged in the follow-up to and implementation of agreements and commitments reached at the major United Nations conferences and summits,

Recalling also General Assembly resolution 59/151 of 20 December 2004, in which it requested the Secretary-General to ensure proper follow-up to the resolution and to report thereon, through the Commission on Crime Prevention and Criminal Justice, to it at its sixtieth session,

Recalling further General Assembly resolution 60/177 of 16 December 2005, in which it endorsed the Bangkok Declaration on Synergies and Responses: Strategic Alliances in Crime Prevention and Criminal Justice, adopted at the high-level segment of the Eleventh United Nations Congress on Crime Prevention and Criminal Justice and approved by the Commission on Crime Prevention and Criminal Justice at its fourteenth session and subsequently by the Economic and Social Council in its resolution 2005/15 of 22 July 2005,

Bearing in mind General Assembly resolution 60/175 of 16 December 2005 on strengthening the United Nations Crime Prevention and Criminal Justice Programme, in particular its technical cooperation capacity, and the role of the United Nations Office on Drugs and Crime in the implementation of the measures outlined in the Bangkok Declaration,

Bearing in mind also the United Nations Millennium Declaration, adopted by the Heads of State and Government at the Millennium Summit of the United Nations on 8 September 2000, in which Heads of State and Government resolved to strengthen respect for the rule of law in international as well as in national affairs, to make the United Nations more effective in maintaining peace and security by giving it the resources and tools it needed for conflict prevention, peaceful resolution of disputes, peacekeeping, post-conflict peacebuilding and reconstruction, to take concerted action against international terrorism and accede as soon as possible to all the relevant international conventions, to redouble their efforts to implement their commitment to counter the world drug problem and to intensify their collective efforts to fight transnational crime in all its dimensions, including trafficking as well as smuggling in human beings and money-laundering,

Bearing in mind further General Assembly resolution 60/1 of 16 September 2005, by which the Assembly adopted the 2005 World Summit Outcome,

Recognizing that capturing lessons learned can be a valuable management tool for future planning and programmes and provide feedback to effect future improvement, and helps develop effective and informed policies,

1. *Takes note* of the report of the Secretary-General;

2. *Reiterates its invitation* to Governments to implement the Bangkok Declaration on Synergies and Responses: Strategic Alliances in Crime Prevention and Criminal Justice and the recommendations adopted by the Eleventh United Nations Congress on Crime Prevention and Criminal Justice in formulating legislation and policy directives and taking all other relevant measures, taking into account the economic, social, legal and cultural specificities of their respective States;

3. *Invites* Member States, in a spirit of common and shared responsibility, as acknowledged in the Bangkok Declaration, to improve international cooperation in the fight against crime and terrorism, at the multilateral, regional and bilateral levels, in areas including extradition and mutual legal assistance within the framework of existing relevant legal instruments;

4. *Requests* the United Nations Office on Drugs and Crime, within available extrabudgetary resources, not excluding the use of existing resources from the regular budget of the Office, to convene an intergovernmental group of experts with equitable geographical representation to discuss the Eleventh Congress and previous congresses in order to accumulate and consider lessons learned from prior congresses with a view to developing a methodology for capturing lessons learned for future congresses, and to submit a report on its work to the Commission on Crime Prevention and Criminal Justice at its sixteenth session for its consideration;

5. *Welcomes* the offer of the Government of Thailand to act as host to the intergovernmental group of experts;

6. *Reiterates its request* to the United Nations Office on Drugs and Crime, within available extrabudgetary resources, not excluding the use of existing resources from the regular budget of the Office, to engage in consultations with the Governments that have offered to host the Twelfth United Nations Congress on Crime Prevention and Criminal Justice, to be held in 2010, and to report thereon to the Commission on Crime Prevention and Criminal Justice at its sixteenth session.

Commission on Crime Prevention and Criminal Justice

The Commission on Crime Prevention and Criminal Justice, at its fifteenth session (Vienna, 27 May 2005 and 24-28 April 2006) [E/2006/30 & Corr.1], recommended, through the Economic and Social Council, two draft resolutions for adoption by the General Assembly, and ten draft resolutions and two draft decisions by the Council. The draft texts related to: the strengthening of the United Nations Crime Prevention and Criminal Justice Programme and the role of the Commission; international cooperation in the prevention, combating and elimination of kidnapping and in providing assistance to victims; UN standards and norms in crime prevention; implementation of the Programme of Action, 2006-2010, on strengthening the rule of law and the criminal justice system in Africa; providing technical assistance for prison reform in Africa and the development of viable alternatives to imprisonment; strengthening basic principles of judicial conduct; international cooperation in the fight against corruption; strengthening the rule of law and the reform of criminal justice institutions; follow-up to the Eleventh United Nations Congress on Crime Prevention and Criminal Justice [YUN 2005, p. 1208]; strengthening international cooperation in preventing and combating trafficking in persons and protecting victims; the International Permanent Observatory on Security Measures during Major Events; and crime prevention and criminal justice responses to violence against women and girls (see p. 1337).

Discussions were held, among other subjects, on maximizing the effectiveness of technical assistance provided to Member States in crime prevention and criminal justice, on the basis of a note submitted by the Secretary-General [E/CN.15/2006/CRP.2]. The Commission also considered strategic management and programme questions and the provisional agenda for its 2007 session.

On 27 July, the Council took note of the Commission's report on its fifteenth session and approved the provisional agenda and documentation for the sixteenth (2007) session, on the understanding that the Commission would examine and finalize the provisional agenda and documentation at its intersessional meetings (**decision 2006/239**). The Council also endorsed the Commission's appointment of a new member to the Board of Trustees of the United Nations Interregional Crime and Justice Research Institute (**decision 2006/240**), whose nomination had been proposed in an April note by the Secretary-General [E/CN.15/2006/18].

Strengthening the role of the Commission

Pursuant to Economic and Social Council resolutions 2003/31 [YUN 2003, p. 1116] and 2003/24 [ibid., p. 1123], the Secretary-General submitted a report on strengthening the role of the Commission on Crime Prevention and Criminal Justice [E/CN.15/2006/16 & Corr.1]. The report described the Commission's establishment and discussed the implementation of its mandates, its relationship with the Conference of the Parties to the United Nations

Convention against Transnational Organized Crime and the Conference of the States Parties to the United Nations Convention against Corruption, the Commission's role in relation to the United Nations Crime Prevention and Criminal Justice Fund and the methods of work of the Commission.

On the revitalization of the Commission, the Secretary-General suggested that the Commission consider the recommendation of the Advisory Committee on Administrative and Budgetary Questions (ACABQ) that further thought be given to establishing a consultative body to assist the UNODC Executive Director with the management of both drug and crime programmes and unifying the two separate governing bodies into one. To make its work more interactive, the Commission should request the Secretariat to include in its agenda examples of good practice and experiences that might trigger discussion and provide new ideas for policy guidance. It should propose ways to strengthen the participation and contribution of the institutes of the UN Crime Prevention and Criminal Justice Programme network to the work of the Commission, and seek more interactive participation and involvement in its work by UN funds and programmes and entities, the Bretton Woods institutions (the World Bank Group and the International Monetary Fund) and civil society. The Commission should also consider its methods of work, including strengthening its intersessional work, re-establishing the practice of multi-year programmes of work and facilitating the timely submission and discussion of draft proposals.

The Commission, at its fifteenth session, recommended that the Economic and Social Council approve for adoption by the General Assembly a draft resolution on strengthening the United Nations Crime Prevention and Criminal Justice Programme and the role of the Commission as its governing body. Under its terms, the Assembly would authorize the Commission to approve the budget of the United Nations Crime Prevention and Criminal Justice Fund, including its administrative and programme support cost budget, and request the Commission to report to the Council in 2007 on its plan for carrying out those administrative and financial functions.

On 27 July [E/2006/SR.41], the Council deferred action on the draft resolution, pending an explanation from the Secretariat on the programme budget implications of the resolution and, in particular, why additional resources were required.

On 28 July, the Council decided to transmit to the Assembly the draft resolution, as contained in chapter I, section A of the Commission's report (**decision 2006/256**). On 28 September [A/C.3/61/L.2], the Secretray-General transmitted the draft text to the Assembly's Third Committee, whose Chairman on 19 October [A/C.5/61/9], noting that the Fifth (Administrative and Budgetary) Committee was the appropriate Main Committee of the Assembly entrusted with the responsibilities of administrative and budgetary matters, transmitted the draft resolution to the Fifth Committee for its consideration. On 6 November [A/C.5/61/10], the Fifth Committee noted that, should the Assembly adopt the draft resolution and provided that a reconvened Commission session was held between 26 and 30 November 2007, net additional resources totalling $95,800 would be required under section 2 of the programme budget for the 2006-2007 biennium. It was envisaged that the net additional requirements would be accommodated within the existing appropriation. Accordingly, no additional appropriation was sought above the level of funding approved in the 2006-2007 programme budget.

On 7 December [A/C.5/61/SR.27], the ACABQ Chairman said that it was anticipated that additional requirements would be accomodated within existing resources and reflected in the second performance report for the 2006-2007 biennium.

On 22 December, the Assembly, in section XI of **resolution 61/252** (see p. 1617), authorized the Commission to approve the budget of the United Nations Crime Prevention and Criminal Justice Fund, including its administrative and programme support cost budget, other than expenditures borne by the regular budget of the United Nations. It also requested ACABQ to submit to the Commission its comments and recommendations on the biennial consolidated budget for UNODC. The Assembly requested the Secretary-General to promulgate financial rules for the Fund and called on the Commission to report to the Assembly at its sixty-second (2007) session, through the Council, on how it planned to carry out its administrative and financial functions.

Follow-up to Vienna Declaration and Programme of Action

The General Assembly, at its sixty-first (2006) session, decided to include in its agenda, under the item "Promotion and protection of human rights", the sub-item on "Comprehensive implementation and follow-up to the Vienna Declaration and Programme of Action", and to allocate it to the Third Committee [A/61/443/Add.4]. The Committee held a discussion on the sub-item on 17 and 18 October, but no action was taken. The Vienna Declaration on Crime and Justice was adopted by the Assembly in December 2000 [YUN 2000, p. 1091], and the Programme of Action at the 1995 World Summit for Social Development [YUN 1995, p. 1113].

On 20 December, the Assembly took note of the report of the Third Committee (**decision 61/530**).

Crime prevention programme

At its fifteenth session, the Commission on Crime Prevention and Criminal Justice considered the UNODC Executive Director's report on "Development, security and justice for all: towards a safer world" [E/CN.7/2006/5-E/CN.15/2006/2], and examined the Office's 2005 strategy to counter the problems of trafficking in human beings, terrorism and money-laundering. It highlighted the UNODC work on peace and security, sustainable development and poverty eradication, the rule of law and good governance, and Africa's special needs. UNODC assisted States in complying with international conventions on international drug control, organized crime, corruption and terrorism, through the provision of legal and technical assistance and law enforcement support in the context of its Global Programme against Trafficking in Human Beings, and its Global Programme against Money Laundering. Special emphasis was placed on HIV/AIDS prevention in the context of drug abuse. In 2005, UNODC strengthened its programme for criminal justice reform and worked at linking global initiatives and projects to become a centre of expertise in the different areas of criminal justice reform. Among its many activities, UNODC advised Governments in enhancing their capacities to administer criminal law, such as in Afghanistan, where the Office provided legal advice to Afghan authorities on drug control law, mutual legal assistance and the organization of courts. UNODC assisted major seaports in eastern and southern Africa to develop the drug interdiction capacity of law enforcement agencies.

The Commission also considered the Secretary-General's report [E/CN.15/2006/3], submitted in response to Economic and Social Council resolution 2004/25 [YUN 2004, p. 1111], on strengthening the rule of law and the reform of criminal justice institutions, including in post-conflict reconstruction. The report contained an analysis of the replies of Member States to the Secretary-General's request for information on the implementation of the resolution, as well as a review of UNODC technical assistance in the rule of law and criminal justice reform. It concentrated on new initiatives relating to the rule of law, in particular in countries emerging from conflict and those with economies in transition, and to activities aimed at reforming the criminal justice systems. It also took into account the added emphasis placed by Member States and the UN system on the rule of law, in particular in the 2005 World Summit Outcome [YUN 2005, p. 48]. The report should be read in conjunction with the Secretary-General's reports on UN standards and norms in crime prevention and criminal justice (see p. 1306), and on combating the spread of HIV/AIDS in criminal justice pre-trial and correctional facilities (see p. 1314).

ECONOMIC AND SOCIAL COUNCIL ACTION

On 27 July [meeting 41], the Economic and Social Council, on the recommendation of the Commission on Crime Prevention and Criminal Justice [E/2006/30 & Corr.1], adopted **resolution 2006/25** without vote [agenda item 14 *(c)*].

Strengthening the rule of law and the reform of criminal justice institutions, including in post-conflict reconstruction

The Economic and Social Council,

Recalling the recommitment made by Heads of State and Government in the 2005 World Summit Outcome,

Recalling also General Assembly resolution 60/159 of 16 December 2005 on human rights in the administration of justice,

Welcoming the emphasis on the rule of law in the Bangkok Declaration on Synergies and Responses: Strategic Alliances in Crime Prevention and Criminal Justice, adopted at the high-level segment of the Eleventh United Nations Congress on Crime Prevention and Criminal Justice, held in Bangkok from 18 to 25 April 2005, in which Member States recognized the importance of upholding the rule of law and good governance and, as appropriate, the importance of further developing restorative justice policies, procedures and programmes, and expressed their commitment to the development and maintenance of fair and efficient criminal justice institutions, including the humane treatment of all those in pre-trial and correctional facilities, in accordance with applicable international standards,

Recognizing the system-wide efforts within the United Nations towards strengthening activities to promote the rule of law, including the establishment of the Peacebuilding Commission, the planned establishment of a rule of law assistance unit and the work of the United Nations Rule of Law Focal Point Network,

Recalling its resolution 2004/25 of 21 July 2004 entitled "The rule of law and development: strengthening the rule of law and the reform of criminal justice institutions, with emphasis on technical assistance, including in post-conflict reconstruction",

Recalling also its resolution 2005/21 of 22 July 2005 on strengthening the technical cooperation capacity of the United Nations Crime Prevention and Criminal Justice Programme in the area of the rule of law and criminal justice reform, in which it recognized that effective criminal justice systems could only be developed based on the rule of law and that the rule of law itself required the protection of effective criminal justice measures,

Recalling further all relevant resolutions of the Commission on Human Rights, including its resolution 2004/43, on human rights in the administration of justice, in particular juvenile justice, in which the Commission stressed the special need for national capacity-building in the field of the administration of justice, in particular to establish and maintain stable societies and the rule of law in post-conflict situations, through reform of the judiciary, the police and the penal system, as well as juvenile justice reform,

Bearing in mind the need to establish and strengthen the rule of law as an essential element of reconstruction efforts, in order to support the emergence of stable social, political and economic structures and to protect human rights in the administration of justice,

Acknowledging that United Nations standards and norms in crime prevention and criminal justice are important tools for establishing fair and effective criminal justice systems enshrined in the rule of law and that their use and application in the provision of technical assistance should be enhanced, as appropriate,

Mindful of the importance of ensuring respect for the rule of law and human rights in the administration of justice, in particular in post-conflict situations, as a crucial contribution to building peace and justice and ending impunity,

Noting with appreciation the work on juvenile justice and the cooperation through the Inter-Agency Coordination Panel on Juvenile Justice to develop common indicators, tools and manuals, to share information and to pool capacities and interests in order to increase the effectiveness of programme implementation, and taking note of the publication entitled "Protecting the rights of children in conflict with the law",

Welcoming the efforts by some Member States to provide assistance to countries in the areas of the rule of law and criminal justice institutions through bilateral or multilateral channels,

1. *Takes note* of the report of the Secretary-General entitled "The rule of law and development: strengthening the rule of law and the reform of criminal justice institutions, including in post-conflict reconstruction";

2. *Notes* the progress made by the United Nations Office on Drugs and Crime in the development of a comprehensive set of assessment tools for criminal justice, in cooperation with the Department of Peacekeeping Operations of the Secretariat and other relevant entities, and encourages the Office, within available extrabudgetary resources, not excluding the use of existing resources from the regular budget of the Office, to continue to develop tools and training manuals on criminal justice reform, where appropriate, in cooperation with others, and to disseminate them widely;

3. *Encourages* the United Nations Office on Drugs and Crime, within available extrabudgetary resources, not excluding the use of existing resources from the regular budget of the Office, while recognizing the importance of avoiding duplication between and ensuring proper coordination with relevant United Nations entities, to further develop its comprehensive programme in strengthening the rule of law and the reform of criminal justice institutions with a continued focus on vulnerable groups, such as women and children, countries with economies in transition and countries in post-conflict situations and the need for capacity-building at the field office level, and to develop innovative approaches and partnerships in that area;

4. *Also encourages* the United Nations Office on Drugs and Crime, within available extrabudgetary resources, not excluding the use of existing resources from the regular budget of the Office, to continue to provide long-term sustainable technical assistance in the area of criminal justice reform to Member States in post-conflict situations, in cooperation with the Department of Peacekeeping Operations and other relevant entities, and to increase synergies between the involved agencies;

5. *Invites* the United Nations Office on Drugs and Crime, within available extrabudgetary resources, not excluding the use of existing resources from the regular budget of the Office, to provide its expertise, where appropriate and upon request, to the Peacebuilding Commission, the rule of law assistance unit, in the ongoing work of the United Nations Rule of Law Focal Point Network and other relevant entities;

6. *Invites* Member States to provide resources to the United Nations Office on Drugs and Crime in order for it to continue to provide assistance, upon request, to Member States in long-term sustainable criminal justice reform and also to make use of technical assistance offered in that area by the Office and other United Nations entities;

7. *Invites* relevant entities of the United Nations system, including the World Bank, as well as organizations such as the Organization for Security and Cooperation in Europe, to increase their cooperation and coordination with the United Nations entities concerned with supporting the rule of law, including the United Nations Office on Drugs and Crime, in order to promote a more integrated approach to the provision of assistance for building capacity in the area of the rule of law and criminal justice reform and to further explore joint projects in that area;

8. *Requests* the Secretary-General to report to the Commission on Crime Prevention and Criminal Justice at its seventeenth session, in 2008, on the implementation of the present resolution.

Strengthening technical cooperation

Pursuant to General Assembly resolution 60/175 [YUN 2005, p. 1220], the Secretary-General submitted a July report [A/61/179] on strengthening the UN Crime Prevention and Criminal Justice Programme, in particular its technical cooperation capacity, which highlighted the crime prevention and criminal justice work of UNODC. The report focused specifically on UNODC activities to assist States in responding more effectively to the challenges posed by transnational crime, corruption and terrorism, and in building their capacity to prevent crime and enhance criminal justice activities. It also dealt with the strengthening of the United Nations Crime Prevention and Criminal Office, including the elaboration of a strategy and the search for more and better information, as well as the mobilization of material support and partnerships. Special attention was given to the revitalization of the Commission on Crime Prevention and Criminal Justice and follow-up to the Eleventh United Nations Congress on Crime Prevention and Criminal Justice [YUN 2005, p. 1208]. The report included a set of recommendations aimed at further strengthening the Criminal Justice Programme.

GENERAL ASSEMBLY ACTION

On 20 December [meeting 82], the General Assembly, on the recommendation of the Third Committee [A/61/444], adopted **resolution 61/181** without vote [agenda item 98].

Strengthening the United Nations Crime Prevention and Criminal Justice Programme, in particular its technical cooperation capacity

The General Assembly,

Recalling its resolution 46/152 of 18 December 1991 on the creation of an effective United Nations crime prevention and criminal justice programme, in which it approved the statement of principles and programme of action annexed thereto, its resolution 60/175 of 16 December 2005 on strengthening the United Nations Crime Prevention and Criminal Justice Programme, in particular its technical cooperation capacity, its resolution 60/1 of 16 September 2005 on the 2005 World Summit Outcome, in particular the sections on terrorism and transnational crime, and its resolutions relating to the urgent need to strengthen international cooperation and technical assistance in promoting and facilitating the ratification and implementation of the United Nations Convention against Transnational Organized Crime and the Protocols thereto, the United Nations Convention against Corruption and the international conventions and protocols against terrorism,

Recognizing the importance of the United Nations Global Counter-Terrorism Strategy, adopted on 8 September 2006, in which Member States resolved to take urgent action to prevent and combat terrorism in all its forms and manifestations, including enhancing cooperation and technical assistance among Member States, United Nations bodies dealing with counter-terrorism, relevant specialized agencies, relevant international, regional and subregional organizations and the donor community, and in particular encouraged the United Nations Office on Drugs and Crime, including its Terrorism Prevention Branch, to enhance, in close consultation with the Counter-Terrorism Committee and its Executive Directorate, its provision of technical assistance to States, upon request, to facilitate the implementation of the international conventions and protocols related to the prevention and suppression of terrorism and relevant United Nations resolutions,

Bearing in mind all relevant Economic and Social Council resolutions, in particular resolutions 2006/19, 2006/20, 2006/21, 2006/22, 2006/23, 2006/24, 2006/25, 2006/26, 2006/27, 2006/28 and 2006/29 of 27 July 2006 and all those relating to the strengthening of international cooperation as well as the technical assistance and advisory services of the United Nations Crime Prevention and Criminal Justice Programme of the United Nations Office on Drugs and Crime in the field of crime prevention and criminal justice, promotion and reinforcement of the rule of law and reform of criminal justice institutions, including with regard to the implementation of technical assistance, in particular in Africa,

Recognizing that action against global crime is a common and shared responsibility, and stressing the need to work collectively to prevent and combat transnational crime,

Recognizing also the need to maintain a balance in the technical cooperation capacity of the United Nations Office on Drugs and Crime between all relevant priorities identified by the General Assembly and the Economic and Social Council,

Recalling the Bangkok Declaration on Synergies and Responses: Strategic Alliances in Crime Prevention and Criminal Justice,

Bearing in mind the efforts for the revitalization of the General Assembly,

1. *Takes note with appreciation* of the report of the Secretary-General on the progress made in the implementation of General Assembly resolution 60/175;

2. *Reaffirms* the importance of the United Nations Crime Prevention and Criminal Justice Programme in promoting effective action to strengthen international cooperation in crime prevention and criminal justice, as well as of the work of the United Nations Office on Drugs and Crime in the fulfilment of its mandate in crime prevention and criminal justice, including providing to Member States, upon request and as a matter of high priority, technical cooperation, advisory services and other forms of assistance, and coordinating with and complementing the work of all relevant and competent United Nations bodies and offices;

3. *Recognizes* the progress made in the implementation of the global programmes addressing trafficking in human beings, including the support and protection of victims, corruption, organized crime, money-laundering and terrorism, and calls upon the Secretary-General to enhance further the effectiveness of these global programmes and to strengthen the focus of the United Na-

tions Office on Drugs and Crime on these global programmes in crime prevention and criminal justice, taking into account also the elements necessary for building national capacity in order to strengthen fair and effective criminal justice systems and the rule of law;

4. *Urges* States and relevant international organizations to develop national and regional strategies, as appropriate, and other necessary measures to complement the work of the United Nations Crime Prevention and Criminal Justice Programme in addressing effectively transnational organized crime, including trafficking in persons and related criminal activities such as kidnapping and the smuggling of migrants, as well as corruption and terrorism;

5. *Reaffirms* the importance of the United Nations Office on Drugs and Crime and its regional offices in building capacity at the local level in the fight against transnational organized crime and drug trafficking, and urges the Office to consider regional vulnerabilities, projects and impact in the fight against transnational organized crime, in particular in developing countries, when deciding to close and allocate offices, with a view to maintaining an effective level of support to national and regional efforts in those areas;

6. *Urges* all States and competent regional economic integration organizations that have not yet done so to consider signing, ratifying or acceding to the United Nations Convention against Transnational Organized Crime (Palermo Convention) and the Protocols thereto, the United Nations Convention against Corruption and the international conventions and protocols related to terrorism, and encourages States parties to continue to provide full support to the Conference of the Parties to the United Nations Convention against Transnational Organized Crime and the Conference of the States Parties to the United Nations Convention against Corruption;

7. *Reiterates its request* to the Secretary-General to provide the United Nations Crime Prevention and Criminal Justice Programme with sufficient resources for the full implementation of its mandates, in conformity with its high priorities, and to provide adequate support to the Commission on Crime Prevention and Criminal Justice;

8. *Invites* all States to increase their support to the operational activities of the United Nations Crime Prevention and Criminal Justice Programme through voluntary contributions to the United Nations Crime Prevention and Criminal Justice Fund or through voluntary contributions in direct support of such activities;

9. *Requests* the Secretary-General to submit a report to the General Assembly at its sixty-second session on the implementation of the mandates of the United Nations Crime Prevention and Criminal Justice Programme, reflecting also emerging policy issues and possible responses, for the purpose of contributing to a comprehensive discussion on the subject.

Crime Prevention and Criminal Justice Programme network

A February report [E/CN.15/2006/5 & Corr.1] of the Secretary-General summarized the activities of the institutions comprising the United Nations Crime Prevention and Criminal Justice Programme network, which included the United Nations Interregional Crime and Justice Research Institute (UNICRI), 13 regional and affiliated institutes, and the International Scientific and Professional Advisory Council.

UN African crime prevention institute

In a July report [A/61/135] submitted in response to resolution 60/176 [YUN 2005, p. 1223], the Secretary-General highlighted the operations of the African Institute for the Prevention of Crime and the Treatment of Offenders (UNAFRI) and discussed funding and support for the Institute, as well as its future and strategies for ensuring its sustainability. The report reviewed the Institute's governance and management, described measures taken to initiate and maintain international cooperation and partnerships with other agencies, and addressed the future of the Institute as a unique regional promoter of socio-economic development through crime prevention initiatives.

For the period from January to June 2006, the total resources of the Institute amounted to $568,247, consisting of assessed contributions from Member States, UN grants and other income received from the rental of Institute premises, and interest on deposits.

The Institute would consolidate partnerships with African governmental crime prevention agencies and authorities, work with influential traditional cultural and religious institutions, and explore possibilities for joint activities with development agencies in the region. It would identify the support needed to strengthen its programmes, including through communication with heads of specialized units and departments, such as the national revenue authorities, and with tax bodies, federations of employers and employees, as well as with human rights institutions.The Institute would continue to develop partnerships with the private sector, academic institutions, the media, civil society and regional organizations.

GENERAL ASSEMBLY ACTION

On 20 December [meeting 82], the General Assembly, on the recommendation of the Third Committee [A/61/444], adopted **resolution 61/182** without vote [agenda item 98].

United Nations African Institute for the Prevention of Crime and the Treatment of Offenders

The General Assembly,

Recalling its resolution 60/176 of 16 December 2005 and all other relevant resolutions,

Taking note of the report of the Secretary-General,

Bearing in mind the urgent need to establish effective crime prevention strategies for Africa, as well as the importance of law enforcement agencies and the judiciary at the regional and subregional levels,

Bearing in mind also the Programme of Action, 2006-2010, endorsed by the Round Table for Africa, held in Abuja on 5 and 6 September 2005,

Noting that the financial situation of the United Nations African Institute for the Prevention of Crime and the Treatment of Offenders has greatly affected its capacity to deliver its services to African Member States in an effective and comprehensive manner,

1. *Commends* the United Nations African Institute for the Prevention of Crime and the Treatment of Offenders for its efforts to promote and coordinate regional technical cooperation activities related to crime prevention and criminal justice systems in Africa;

2. *Commends* the Secretary-General for his efforts to mobilize the financial resources necessary to provide the Institute with the core professional staff required to enable it to function effectively in the fulfilment of its mandated obligations;

3. *Reiterates* the need to strengthen further the capacity of the Institute to support national mechanisms for crime prevention and criminal justice in African countries;

4. *Urges* the States members of the Institute to make every possible effort to meet their obligations to the Institute;

5. *Calls upon* all Member States and non-governmental organizations to continue adopting concrete practical measures to support the Institute in the development of the requisite capacity and to implement its programmes and activities aimed at strengthening crime prevention and criminal justice systems in Africa;

6. *Requests* the Secretary-General to intensify efforts to mobilize all relevant entities of the United Nations system to provide the necessary financial and technical support to the Institute to enable it to fulfil its mandate;

7. *Also requests* the Secretary-General to continue his efforts to mobilize the financial resources necessary to maintain the Institute with the core professional staff required to enable it to function effectively in the fulfilment of its mandated obligations;

8. *Calls upon* the United Nations Crime Prevention and Criminal Justice Programme and the United Nations Office on Drugs and Crime to work closely with the Institute;

9. *Requests* the Secretary-General to enhance the promotion of regional cooperation, coordination and collaboration in the fight against crime, especially in its transnational dimension, which cannot be dealt with adequately by national action alone;

10. *Also requests* the Secretary-General to continue making concrete proposals, including the provision of additional core professional staff, to strengthen the programmes and activities of the Institute and to report to the General Assembly at its sixty-second session on the implementation of the present resolution.

International Permanent Observatory on Security Measures during Major Events

The Commission, at its fifteenth session, adopted a resolution on the International Permanent Observatory (IPO) on Security Measures during Major Events. IPO, launched in 2003 by the United Nations Interregional Crime and Justice Research Institute (UNICRI), in cooperation with the European Police Office (EUROPOL), aimed to improve the capabilities of relevant national agencies to maintain the security of major events, such as the Olympic Games, high-level summits and mass events.

ECONOMIC AND SOCIAL COUNCIL ACTION

On 27 July [meeting 41], the Economic and Social Council, on the recommendation of the Commission on Crime Prevention and Criminal Justice [E/2006/30 & Corr.1], adopted **resolution 2006/28** without vote [agenda item 14 *(c)*].

International Permanent Observatory on Security Measures during Major Events

The Economic and Social Council,

Recognizing the increasing importance of major events, such as large-scale sporting events, including Olympic Games, high-level summits and other mass events such as national and religious festivals,

Recognizing also the principle of freedom of assembly,

Mindful of the fact that, owing to their scale and/or high visibility, major events can be a target for unlawful activities, including terrorism, and can be exploited by organized criminal groups for their illegal activities,

Mindful also that major events offer opportunities for host countries to strengthen their capacity to manage security,

Aware of the need to share information, in full respect of the principle of data protection, on possible threats to the security of major events and to exchange experience and proven practices in addressing such threats,

Welcoming the establishment by the United Nations Interregional Crime and Justice Research Institute of the International Permanent Observatory on Security Measures during Major Events,

Noting with appreciation the work done by the United Nations Interregional Crime and Justice Research Institute in the framework of the Observatory, such as the development of relevant analytical tools and the organization of expert meetings in China, Italy, Norway, Portugal, the Russian Federation, Spain and the United States of America,

1. *Encourages* Member States, in particular those planning major events in the coming years, to strengthen their cooperation, including in the framework of the International Permanent Observatory on Security Measures during Major Events, by sharing knowledge of possible threats to major events and relevant practices related to security during such events;

2. *Invites* the United Nations Interregional Crime and Justice Research Institute, subject to the availability of extrabudgetary resources, to continue and to expand its work on the Observatory, including by providing technical assistance and advisory services on security during major events to Member States upon request;

3. *Invites* Member States to make voluntary and in-kind contributions to the Institute for the continuation and expansion of the activities of the Observatory, and invites the Institute to mobilize funds from the private sector for such activities;

4. *Requests* the Secretary-General to bring the present resolution to the attention of Member States.

Strengthening crime data collection

Pursuant to Economic and Social Council resolution 2005/23 [YUN 2005, p. 1213], the Secretary-General transmitted to the Commission on Crime Prevention and Criminal Justice the report of the meeting of the open-ended expert group on ways of improving crime data collection, reserach and analysis, with a view to enhancing the work of UNODC and other relevant international entities (Vienna, 8-10 February) [E/CN.15/2006/4]. The main goal of the survey was to collect data on the incidence of reported crime and the operations of the criminal justice systems.

The expert group identified and discussed the strengths and weaknesses of data collection systems and suggested strategies to achieve data collection purposes. It recommended that the questionnaire used for the United Nations Survey of Crime Trends and Operations of Criminal Justice Systems be revised and refocused, by reducing its length, identifying the main issues to be covered, improving and clarifying definitions, and collecting data on the context and metadata. Efforts should be made to substantially improve the response rate and establish a more effective procedure for reaching the appropriate provider of information. A core annual version of the questionnaire could be developed, to be supplemented by additional modules. A study to assess the extent to which the data were used by different users, as well as to identify their profile, would be useful in improving the focus of the questionnaire. The United Nations should help to further promote the conduct of victim surveys, especially in developing countries, while qualitative and quantitative measures on organized crime and corruption should also be developed. In the absence of a common definition of organized crime, a dialogue with the Conference of the Parties to the United Nations Convention against Transnational Organized Crime [YUN 2000, p. 1048] should be initiated to develop an understanding about the scope of that concept for data collection purposes. For such purposes and analysis, a dialogue should be initiated also with the Conference of the States Parties to the United Nations Convention against Corruption [YUN 2003, p. 1127]. Integration of data collection and research should be promoted in order to establish estimates, magnitude and trends of crime, assess risks and forecast trends, and monitor trends in criminal justice operations and output. The United Nations should help to build the capacity of countries for the production, collection and analysis of data on crime and criminal justice, and act as a repository of methodologies for data collection, analysis and dissemination (best practices), developing guidelines and promoting the use of the *Manual for the Development of a System of Criminal Justice Statistics*, as well as a repository of information on victim surveys and data collection systems. The United Nations should aim at combining findings based on statistics, victim surveys and relevant data on transnational organized crime and corruption. UNODC, UNICRI and other UN entities, including intergovernmental bodies, should collaborate in order to develop synergies, avoid duplication and identify common areas of concern and objectives.

Transnational organized crime

International convention

Conference of States Parties. By **decision 61/531** of 20 December, the General Assembly took note of the Secretary-General's note [A/61/96], transmitting the reports of the Conference of the State Parties to the United Nations Convention against Transnational Organized Crime [YUN 2000, p. 1050] on its first [YUN 2004, p. 117] and second [YUN 2005, p. 1224] sessions.

Trafficking in persons

In a March report on the United Nations Convention against Transnational Organized Crime and the Protocols thereto [E/CN.15/2006/8], which was submitted to the Commission on Crime Prevention and Criminal Justice at its fifteenth session, the Secretary-General noted that, in 2005, 18 States had ratified the Protocol to Prevent, Suppress and Punish Trafficking in Persons,

Especially Women and Children, supplementing the Convention, adopted by the General Assembly in resolution 55/25, annex II [YUN 2000, p. 1063]. During deliberations, a number of speakers informed the Commission of the action taken by their Governments to prevent and combat trafficking in persons, including the adoption of national strategies, programmes and policies, the establishment of national mechanisms and the development of bilateral and regional frameworks and agreements against trafficking in persons. Several speakers expressed their appreciation for the work of UNODC in promoting the ratification and implementation of the Protocol, and welcomed the publication, in April 2006, of the report entitled *Trafficking in Persons: Global Patterns*.

The Special Rapporteur on the human rights aspects of victims of trafficking in persons, especially women and children, submitted a report on the subject [E/CN.4/2006/62 & Add. 1-3] to the Commission on Human Rights (see PART TWO, Chapter II).

ECONOMIC AND SOCIAL COUNCIL ACTION

On 27 July [meeting 41], the Economic and Social Council, on the recommendation of the Commission on Crime Prevention and Criminal Justice [E/2006/30 & Corr.1], adopted **resolution 2006/27** without vote [agenda item 14 *(c)*].

Strengthening international cooperation in preventing and combating trafficking in persons and protecting victims of such trafficking

The Economic and Social Council,

Recalling the Declaration of Basic Principles of Justice for Victims of Crime and Abuse of Power,

Taking note of guideline 8, Special measures for the protection and support of child victims of trafficking, contained in the report of the United Nations High Commissioner for Human Rights,

Recalling the Convention on the Rights of the Child, and noting the entry into force of the Optional Protocol thereto on the sale of children, child prostitution and child pornography,

Recalling also the International Labour Organization Convention concerning the Prohibition and Immediate Action for the Elimination of the Worst Forms of Child Labour, 1999 (Convention No. 182), which prohibits forced or obligatory labour of all people under the age of 18,

Recalling further paragraphs 4 and 13 of the Bangkok Declaration on Synergies and Responses: Strategic Alliances in Crime Prevention and Criminal Justice, adopted at the high-level segment of the Eleventh United Nations Congress on Crime Prevention and Criminal Justice, held in Bangkok from 18 to 25 April 2005,

Recalling the United Nations Convention against Transnational Organized Crime and, in particular, the Protocol to Prevent, Suppress and Punish Trafficking in Persons, Especially Women and Children, supplementing that Convention,

Recalling also General Assembly resolution 58/137 of 22 December 2003 on strengthening international cooperation in preventing and combating trafficking in persons and protecting victims of such trafficking,

Recalling further the note by the United Nations System Chief Executives Board for Coordination on joint action to curb transnational crime,

Condemning trafficking in persons as an abhorrent form of modern-day slavery and as an act that is contrary to universal human rights,

Decrying the treatment of human beings as commodities to be bartered, bought or sold by traffickers, in particular exploiters,

Deeply concerned at the worldwide occurrence of trafficking in persons for the purpose of exploitation of all kinds by transnational organized criminal groups, many of which are also involved in other forms of illegal activity, including trafficking in firearms, money-laundering, drug trafficking and corruption,

Profoundly alarmed by the fact that trafficking in persons is a growing and profitable trade in most parts of the world, aggravated by, inter alia, poverty, armed conflict, inadequate social and economic conditions and demand in the illicit labour and sex markets,

Expressing dismay at the ability of criminal networks to avoid punishment while preying on the vulnerabilities of their victims,

Noting the distinctions and interlinkages between the two criminal behaviours of trafficking in persons, as set forth in the Protocol to Prevent, Suppress and Punish Trafficking in Persons, Especially Women and Children, supplementing the United Nations Convention against Transnational Organized Crime and of smuggling of migrants, as set forth in the Protocol against the Smuggling of Migrants by Land, Sea and Air, supplementing the United Nations Convention against Transnational Organized Crime,

Convinced of the urgent need for broad and concerted international cooperation among all Member States, especially among related countries of origin, transit and destination, employing a multidisciplinary, balanced and global approach, including adequate technical assistance, in order to prevent and combat trafficking in persons,

Recognizing that broad international cooperation between Member States, especially among related countries of origin, transit and destination, and relevant intergovernmental and non-governmental organizations and other members of civil society, is essential to counter effectively the threat of trafficking in persons,

Convinced that civil society, including non-governmental organizations, can play a role in raising awareness, in reducing existing and future opportunities for victimization in the field of trafficking and in assisting Governments in promoting the protection of victims through comprehensive and non-stigmatizing social and appropriate economic assistance to victims, including in the areas of health, education, housing and employment,

Welcoming efforts of Member States, in particular countries of origin, transit and destination, to raise awareness of the seriousness of the crime of trafficking and of its various forms, as well as of the role of the public in preventing victimization and assisting victims of trafficking,

Bearing in mind the establishment of the Conference of the Parties to the United Nations Convention against Transnational Organized Crime in accordance with article 32 of the Convention, which has now taken up its work in that area,

Noting the thematic discussion on trafficking in human beings, especially women and children, held by the Commission on Crime Prevention and Criminal Justice at its twelfth session, and the panel discussion on human trafficking held by the Human Security Network on 17 October 2005 as a side event during the second session of the Conference of the Parties to the United Nations Convention against Transnational Organized Crime,

1. *Urges* Member States that have not done so to consider taking measures to ratify or accede to the United Nations Convention against Transnational Organized Crime, the Protocol to Prevent, Suppress and Punish Trafficking in Persons, Especially Women and Children, supplementing that Convention, and the Optional Protocol to the Convention on the Rights of the Child on the sale of children, child prostitution and child pornography;

2. *Urges* all Member States:

(a) To criminalize trafficking in persons;

(b) To promote cooperation among law enforcement authorities in combating trafficking in persons;

(c) To ensure the security and control of travel or identity documents;

(d) To establish the offence of trafficking in persons as a predicate offence for money-laundering offences;

3. *Invites* Member States to adopt measures, in accordance with their domestic law, inter alia:

(a) To fight sexual exploitation with a view to abolishing it, by prosecuting and punishing those who engage in that activity, not including the victims of trafficking for the purpose of sexual exploitation;

(b) To raise awareness, especially through training, among criminal justice officials and others, as appropriate, of the needs of victims of trafficking and of the crucial role of victims in detecting and prosecuting that crime by, inter alia:

(i) Investigating all cases reported by victims, preventing further victimization and, in general, treating victims with respect;

(ii) Treating victims and witnesses with sensitivity throughout criminal judicial proceedings, in accordance with articles 24 and 25 of the United Nations Convention against Transnational Organized Crime and article 6, paragraph 2, of the Protocol to Prevent, Suppress and Punish Trafficking in Persons, Especially Women and Children, where applicable;

4. *Also invites* Member States to adopt measures, in accordance with their domestic law, inter alia:

(a) To provide assistance and protection to victims of trafficking in persons, including measures to permit victims of trafficking to remain in their territory temporarily or permanently, as appropriate;

(b) To promote the legislative and other measures necessary to establish a wide range of assistance, including legal, psychological, medical and social assistance to the actual victims of trafficking, subject to the determination of the existence of victimization;

(c) To provide humane treatment for all victims of trafficking, taking into account their age, gender and particular needs, in accordance with article 6, paragraphs 3 and 4, of the Protocol to Prevent, Suppress and Punish Trafficking in Persons, Especially Women and Children, where applicable;

(d) To assist in the reintegration of victims of trafficking into society;

(e) To develop guidelines for the protection of victims of trafficking before, during and after criminal proceedings, as appropriate;

5. *Urges* Member States to employ a comprehensive approach to combating trafficking in persons, incorporating law enforcement efforts and the protection of victims and preventive measures, including measures against activities that derive profit from the exploitation of victims of trafficking and, where appropriate, the confiscation and seizure of the proceeds of trafficking;

6. *Calls upon* Member States to collaborate with a view to preventing trafficking in persons, including for the purpose of sexual exploitation, through:

(a) Improved technical cooperation to strengthen local and national institutions aimed at preventing trafficking in persons, especially women and children, in countries of origin;

(b) Information campaigns on the techniques and methods of traffickers, programmes of education aimed at prospective targets, including those who create the demand, as well as vocational training in social skills and assistance in the reintegration of victims of trafficking into society;

(c) A focus on regions in post-conflict situations and regions of natural disaster, where patterns of human trafficking are increasingly recognized as a serious problem, and the early incorporation of measures to combat trafficking, including the training and establishment of standards of behaviour of military and civilian personnel involved in peacekeeping operations;

(d) Encouraging Member States to participate in regional forums as a means to develop practical strategies to combat trafficking in persons and to protect victims;

7. *Urges* Member States to take measures against trafficking in persons, especially women and children, that are consistent with internationally recognized principles of non-discrimination and that respect the human rights and fundamental freedoms of victims;

8. *Invites* Member States to set up mechanisms for coordination and collaboration between governmental and non-governmental organizations and other members

of civil society, with a view to responding to the immediate needs of victims of trafficking;

9. *Also invites* Member States to allocate appropriate resources for victim services, public awareness campaigns and law enforcement activities directed at eliminating trafficking and exploitation and to foster international cooperation, including adequate technical assistance and capacity-building programmes, to improve the ability of Member States to take effective measures against trafficking in persons;

10. *Encourages* Member States to examine the role of the exploitation of the prostitution of others in encouraging trafficking in persons;

11. *Also encourages* Member States to adopt legislative or other measures to reduce the demand that fosters all forms of trafficking in persons, including by cooperating with non-governmental organizations and civil society and by raising public awareness of how all forms of exploitation degrade their victims and the related risks of trafficking in persons, especially women and children;

12. *Further encourages* Member States to take measures, including raising public awareness, to discourage and reduce, especially among men, the demand that fosters sexual exploitation as well as other forms of human trafficking, in accordance with article 9, paragraph 5, of the Protocol to Prevent, Suppress and Punish Trafficking in Persons, Especially Women and Children, where applicable;

13. *Encourages* Member States to target the link between trafficking in persons for purposes of all forms of exploitation and other types of crime;

14. *Encourages* the United Nations Office on Drugs and Crime to continue its close cooperation and coordination with relevant international and regional organizations, non-governmental organizations and other members of civil society;

15. *Requests* the United Nations Office on Drugs and Crime to continue to promote the ratification of, and to assist, upon request, Member States in the implementation of the Protocol to Prevent, Suppress and Punish Trafficking in Persons, Especially Women and Children, within available extrabudgetary resources, not excluding the use of existing resources from the regular budget of the Office;

16. *Also requests* the United Nations Office on Drugs and Crime to organize a meeting on technical assistance for Member States in order to coordinate, with due regard to the work of the Conference of the Parties to the United Nations Convention against Transnational Organized Crime, the work of agencies and bodies of the United Nations system, as well as other relevant intergovernmental organizations, within available extrabudgetary resources, not excluding the use of existing resources from the regular budget of the Office;

17. *Encourages* Member States to make voluntary contributions to further strengthen and support the United Nations Office on Drugs and Crime and its Global Programme against Trafficking in Human Beings, in particular in the area of technical assistance activities;

18. *Requests* the Secretary-General to report to the Commission on Crime Prevention and Criminal Justice at its seventeenth session on the implementation of the present resolution and thereafter to share its report with the Conference of the Parties to the United Nations Convention against Transnational Organized Crime.

GENERAL ASSEMBLY ACTION

On 20 December [meeting 82], the General Assembly, on the recommendation of the Third Committee [A/61/444], adopted **resolution 61/180** without vote [agenda item 98].

Improving the coordination of efforts against trafficking in persons

The General Assembly,

Recalling its resolutions 55/25 of 15 November 2000, 58/137 of 22 December 2003, 59/166 of 20 December 2004 and other relevant General Assembly resolutions on trafficking in persons and other contemporary forms of slavery,

Recalling also Economic and Social Council resolution 2006/27 of 27 July 2006 on strengthening international cooperation in preventing and combating trafficking in persons and protecting victims of such trafficking, and previous Council resolutions on trafficking in persons that have emerged from the Commission on Crime Prevention and Criminal Justice,

Recalling further the United Nations Convention against Transnational Organized Crime and, in particular, the Protocol to Prevent, Suppress and Punish Trafficking in Persons, Especially Women and Children, supplementing the United Nations Convention against Transnational Organized Crime, the Optional Protocol to the Convention on the Rights of the Child on the sale of children, child prostitution and child pornography and the Supplementary Convention on the Abolition of Slavery, the Slave Trade, and Institutions and Practices Similar to Slavery,

Welcoming the progress achieved by the Conference of the Parties to the United Nations Convention against Transnational Organized Crime in accordance with article 32 of the Convention, and by the Working Group on Contemporary Forms of Slavery in accordance with Economic and Social Council decisions 16(LVI) and 17(LVI) of 17 May 1974 and 1980/127 of 2 May 1980,

Recognizing that contemporary forms of slavery violate human rights and that trafficking in persons impairs the enjoyment of human rights, continues to pose a serious challenge to humanity and requires a concerted international response,

Recognizing also that Member States have an obligation to exercise due diligence to prevent trafficking in persons, to investigate this crime and to ensure that perpetrators do not enjoy impunity,

Recognizing further that Member States have an obligation to provide protection for the victims, and acknowledging the necessity for Member States to adopt, in accordance with their international obligations, measures for prosecuting traffickers, preventing trafficking in persons and protecting and assisting its victims,

Welcoming international cooperation in order to promote and protect the human rights of persons exploited through trafficking and other contemporary forms of slavery and to advocate for their liberation and for economic, educational and other means of support to victims of trafficking and other contemporary forms of slavery,

Welcoming also the efforts of Member States and intergovernmental and non-governmental organizations in preventing and combating trafficking in persons and other contemporary forms of slavery and enhancing the protection of and assistance to victims of trafficking in persons and other contemporary forms of slavery,

Taking note of the reports of the Special Rapporteur on the human rights aspects of the victims of trafficking in persons, especially women and children, and of the Working Group on Contemporary Forms of Slavery on its thirty-first session,

Underlining the need to continue to work towards a comprehensive, coordinated and holistic approach to the problem of trafficking in persons and other contemporary forms of slavery, including devising, enforcing and strengthening effective measures to prosecute traffickers, prevent trafficking in persons and other contemporary forms of slavery and protect their victims,

1. *Recognizes* that broad international cooperation between Member States and relevant intergovernmental and non-governmental organizations is essential for effectively countering the threat of trafficking in persons and other contemporary forms of slavery, and invites them to foster a global partnership against trafficking in persons and other contemporary forms of slavery, with a view to eliminating all contemporary forms of slavery and trafficking in persons and protecting and assisting their victims;

2. *Underlines* the importance of bilateral, subregional and regional partnerships, initiatives and actions, and encourages their development;

3. *Urges* Member States that have not yet done so to consider taking measures to ratify or accede to the United Nations Convention against Transnational Organized Crime and the Protocol to Prevent, Suppress and Punish Trafficking in Persons, Especially Women and Children, supplementing the United Nations Convention against Transnational Organized Crime, and to implement fully all aspects of these instruments;

4. *Also urges* Member States that have not yet done so to consider taking measures to ratify or accede to the Optional Protocol to the Convention on the Rights of the Child on the sale of children, child prostitution and child pornography, the Convention on the Elimination of All Forms of Discrimination against Women, and the Supplementary Convention on the Abolition of Slavery, the Slave Trade, and Institutions and Practices Similar to Slavery, and to implement fully all aspects of these instruments;

5. *Recognizes* the need to arrive at a better understanding of what constitutes demand and how to combat it, decides to strengthen efforts to counter the demand for victims of trafficking in persons, and encourages Member States to consider adopting legislative or other measures, such as educational, social or cultural measures, to discourage and reduce the demand that fosters all forms of exploitation of persons, especially women and children, and that thus promotes trafficking;

6. *Also recognizes* the need to address the factors that make persons, especially women and children, vulnerable to trafficking, including poverty, underdevelopment and lack of equal opportunities, lack of equal access to education and lack of equal access to the labour market, and encourages Member States to adopt measures, including through bilateral or multilateral cooperation, to counter those factors;

7. *Invites* Member States to give necessary guidelines and provide training and adequate resources to law enforcement bodies and other relevant authorities to combat trafficking in persons, to care for the rights and needs of the victims and to consider establishing coordination and cooperation mechanisms at the national and international levels on extradition, mutual legal assistance and sharing police intelligence information, as appropriate, taking into account the information and communication tools offered by Interpol;

8. *Also invites* Member States to improve and promote the collection, compilation and dissemination of statistics and indicators on trafficking in persons, including by strengthening bilateral, regional and international cooperation and coordination;

9. *Further invites* Member States to take all appropriate measures to promote the physical, cognitive and psychological recovery, rehabilitation and social integration of human beings who have become victims of exploitation, violence and abuse as a result of trafficking in persons and other contemporary forms of slavery;

10. *Encourages* Member States to initiate and develop working-level contacts among countries of origin, transit and destination, especially among police, prosecutors and social authorities;

11. *Welcomes* the holding, in Tokyo on 26 and 27 September 2006, of a meeting of United Nations offices, funds and programmes with other international organizations to enhance cooperation on trafficking in persons, as requested by the Economic and Social Council in its resolution 2006/27, and encourages continued collaboration to eliminate gaps and overlaps in the activities of the concerned bodies;

12. *Requests* the Secretary-General to improve upon the fledgling inter-agency coordination group on trafficking in persons in order to enhance cooperation and coordination and facilitate a holistic and comprehensive approach by the international community to the problem of trafficking in persons;

13. *Also requests* the Secretary-General to entrust the Executive Director of the United Nations Office on Drugs and Crime with coordinating the activities of the inter-agency coordination group, which should be based in Vienna, bearing in mind the availability of extrabudgetary resources;

14. *Encourages* the United Nations Office on Drugs and Crime to cooperate with relevant international organizations outside of the United Nations system and to invite such organizations and interested Member States to participate, when appropriate, in the meetings of the inter-agency coordination group and to keep Member States informed of the schedule of the inter-agency coordination group and progress made by the group;

15. *Invites* the inter-agency coordination group, drawing on the comparative advantages of the respective agencies, to promote effective and efficient use of existing resources, using, to the extent possible, mechanisms already in place at the regional and national levels, and to share information, experiences and good practices on anti-trafficking activities of the partner agencies with Governments, international and regional organizations, non-governmental organizations and other relevant bodies;

16. *Invites* Member States to provide voluntary contributions to the United Nations Office on Drugs and Crime in order to facilitate optimum implementation of its coordination functions;

17. *Welcomes* the report of the United Nations Office on Drugs and Crime entitled "Trafficking in persons: global patterns", requests the Office to continue to prepare such periodic reports, subject to the availability of extrabudgetary resources, and invites the inter-agency coordination group to provide information to the Office and contribute to the elaboration of the periodic comprehensive reports, database and website on trafficking in persons, subject to the availability of extrabudgetary resources;

18. *Invites* Member States to consider the advisability of a United Nations strategy or plan of action on preventing trafficking in persons, prosecuting traffickers and protecting and assisting victims of trafficking;

19. *Requests* the Secretary-General to submit to the Conference of the Parties to the United Nations Convention against Transnational Organized Crime and to the General Assembly at its sixty-third session a report on the implementation of the present resolution and the proposals on strengthening the capacities of the United Nations Office on Drugs and Crime for the efficient implementation of its coordination functions.

Strategies for crime prevention

Corruption

UN Convention against Corruption

The Secretary-General, in a February report [E/CN.15/2006/9], highlighted the progress made in the ratification of the United Nations Convention against Corruption, which was adopted by the General Assembly in 2003 in resolution 58/4 [YUN 2003, p. 1127]. Its entry into force on 14 December 2005 led to the establishment of the Conference of States Parties to the Convention, which was scheduled to convene in Amman, Jordan, in December (see below). As at 31 December 2006, there were 140 signatories and 81 parties to the Convention.

ECONOMIC AND SOCIAL COUNCIL ACTION

On 27 July [meeting 41], the Economic and Social Council, on the recommendation of the Commission on Crime Prevention and Criminal Jutice [E/2006/30 & Corr.1], adopted **resolution 2006/24** without vote [agenda item 14 *(c)*].

International cooperation in the fight against corruption

The Economic and Social Council,

Reiterating its deep concern about the impact of corruption on the political, social and economic stability and development of societies,

Convinced that a comprehensive and multidisciplinary approach is required to prevent and combat corruption effectively, and recognizing the need for closer coordination and cooperation among States and other relevant entities in this regard,

Recalling General Assembly resolution 58/4 of 31 October 2003, in which it adopted the United Nations Convention against Corruption, and reaffirming that the Convention constitutes a significant development in international law and an important instrument for effective and multidimensional international cooperation against corruption,

Recalling also that, in the 2005 World Summit Outcome, Heads of State and Government urged all States that had not yet done so to consider becoming parties to the relevant international conventions on organized crime and corruption and, following their entry into force, to implement them effectively, including by incorporating the provisions of those conventions into national legislation and by strengthening criminal justice systems,

Recalling further General Assembly resolution 60/207 of 22 December 2005, on preventing and combating corrupt practices and transfer of assets of illicit origin and returning such assets, in particular to the countries of origin, consistent with the United Nations Convention against Corruption,

Welcoming the Bangkok Declaration on Synergies and Responses: Strategic Alliances in Crime Prevention and Criminal Justice, adopted at the high-level segment of the Eleventh United Nations Congress on Crime Prevention and Criminal Justice, held in Bangkok from 18 to 25 April 2005, in which Member States stated that the proper management of public affairs and public property and the rule of law were essential to the prevention and control of corruption, and recognized that, in order to curb corruption, it was necessary to promote a culture of integrity and accountability in both the public and the private sector,

Welcoming also the Programme of Action, 2006-2010, for Africa, adopted by the Round Table for Africa, held in Abuja on 5 and 6 September 2005, in which the need to prevent and combat corruption in Africa is highlighted,

Recalling its resolution 2005/18 of 22 July 2005, on action against corruption: assistance to States in capacity-building with a view to facilitating the entry into force and subsequent implementation of the United Nations Convention against Corruption,

Noting the regional conventions on corruption and the work already done by regional organizations on this issue,

1. *Takes note with appreciation* of the report of the Secretary-General on the United Nations Convention against Corruption;

2. *Welcomes* the entry into force on 14 December 2005 of the United Nations Convention against Corruption, and urges Member States from all regions of the world and relevant economic integration organizations that have not yet done so to consider ratifying or acceding to the Convention as soon as possible in order to facilitate its effective implementation;

3. *Looks forward* to the first session of the Conference of the States Parties to the United Nations Convention against Corruption, to be held in December 2006, and, taking into account article 63 of the Convention, urges Member States to contribute to the successful outcome of the Conference;

4. *Calls upon* all Member States to hold intensive consultations and make proposals for the preparation of the Conference of the States Parties to the United Nations Convention against Corruption, including by open-ended consultations facilitated by the United Nations Office on Drugs and Crime, within available extrabudgetary resources, not excluding the use of existing resources from the regular budget of the Office, and without prejudice to the mandate and work of the Conference of the States Parties;

5. *Stresses* the value of participation at the Conference of the States Parties to the United Nations Convention against Corruption of experts on specific aspects of the Convention, including representatives of preventive anti-corruption bodies, and encourages Member States to facilitate the participation of such experts at the Conference of the States Parties;

6. *Commends* the United Nations Office on Drugs and Crime for its work in promoting the ratification of the United Nations Convention against Corruption, and looks forward to the finalization and dissemination of the legislative guide designed to facilitate the ratification and subsequent implementation of the Convention;

7. *Requests* the United Nations Office on Drugs and Crime, building on the experience gained in the preparation of the legislative guide and work done by others, including by the members of the International Group for Anti-Corruption Coordination, to continue its collaboration with the United Nations Interregional Crime and Justice Research Institute in its ongoing efforts to prepare a technical guide aimed specifically at supporting practitioners in the implementation of the Convention;

8. *Urges* all Member States, consistent with the United Nations Convention against Corruption, to abide by the principles of proper management of public affairs and public property, fairness, responsibility and equality before the law and the need to safeguard integrity and to foster a culture of transparency, accountability and the rejection of corruption;

9. *Notes with appreciation* the financial support provided by several donors to facilitate capacity-building in the fight against corruption, and encourages Member States to continue to make voluntary contributions to promote the implementation of the United Nations Convention against Corruption, through the United Nations Crime Prevention and Criminal Justice Fund or in direct support of such activities and initiatives;

10. *Requests* the Secretary-General to continue to provide the United Nations Office on Drugs and Crime with the resources necessary to enable it to promote, in an effective manner, the implementation of the United Nations Convention against Corruption and to discharge its functions as the secretariat of the Conference of the States Parties in accordance with its mandate;

11. *Requests* the United Nations Office on Drugs and Crime, within available extrabudgetary resources, not excluding the use of existing resources from the regular budget of the Office, and in particular through its Global Programme against Corruption, to continue to assist States, upon request, with sustainable capacity-building focused on the promotion of the implementation of the United Nations Convention against Corruption;

12. *Welcomes* the efforts made by the United Nations Office on Drugs and Crime to cooperate with others, within its mandate, in the field of preventing and combating corruption, and encourages the Office to increase further such cooperation;

13. *Invites* relevant entities of the United Nations system and international financial institutions and regional and national funding agencies to increase their support to and their interaction with the United Nations Office on Drugs and Crime in order to benefit from synergies and avoid duplication of effort and to ensure that, as appropriate, activities aimed at preventing and combating corruption are considered in their sustainable development agenda and that the expertise of the Office is fully utilized;

14. *Expresses its appreciation* to individuals and groups outside the public sector, such as civil society, non-governmental organizations and community-based organizations, for their active participation in the prevention of, and the fight against, corruption;

15. *Calls for* international cooperation to prevent and combat corrupt practices and the transfer of assets of illicit origin, as well as for asset recovery consistent with the principles of the United Nations Convention against Corruption, in particular its chapter V;

16. *Encourages* Member States to consider utilizing the public awareness materials offered by the United Nations Office on Drugs and Crime and to engage in special activities, including, if appropriate, with relevant sectors of civil society, in particular on International Anti-Corruption Day, on 9 December, in order to focus on the problem of corruption;

17. *Requests* the Secretary-General, if the Conference of the States Parties to the United Nations Conven-

tion against Corruption so decides, to make available to the Commission on Crime Prevention and Criminal Justice, for its information, the reports of the Conference;

18. *Also requests* the Secretary-General to report on the implementation of the present resolution to the Commission on Crime Prevention and Criminal Justice at its sixteenth session and thereafter to share the report with the Conference of the States Parties to the United Nations Convention against Corruption.

Conference of States Parties to the Convention

The first session of the Conference of the States Parties to the United Nations Convention against Corruption was held in Amman, Jordan, from 10 to 14 December 2006 [CAC/COSP/2006/12], adopting eight resolutions and one decision. In resolution 1/1 on the review of implementation, the Conference decided to establish an open-ended intergovernmental expert working group to make recommendations to the Conference at its second session on the appropriate mechanisms for reviewing the Convention's implementation. In resolution 1/2, it decided that a self-assessment checklist should be used as a tool to facilitate the gathering of information on the implementation of the Convention, and requested the Secretary-General to finalize it. In resolution 1/3, it appealed to all States parties to adapt their legislation and regulations, in accordane with article 65 of the Convention, to establish as criminal offences the acts descrided in articles 15 and 16, paragraph 1 of article 17, and articles 23 and 25. In resolutions 1/4 and 1/5, respectively, the Conference established an interim open-ended intergovernmental working groups to advise and assist the Conference in the implementation of its mandates on the return of proceeds of corruption, and on technical assistance. In resolution 1/6, it recommended that a workshop of relevant practitioners and experts be held, bringing together development and legal expertise related to anti-corruption policies, in order to contribute to mutual understanding among experts in the field on issues related to best practices and coordination. In resolution 1/7, the Conference requested UNODC to invite relevant international organizations to participate with States parties in an open-ended dialogue on the issues of privileges and immunities, jurisdiction and the role of international organizations, and to report to the Conference at its second sesssion. In resolution 1/8, it decided to hold during its second session a meeting on best practices in the fight against corruption, and in decision 1/1, it decided that its second session would be held in Indonesia in 2007.

Funds of illicit origin

In response to General Assembly resolution 60/207 [YUN 2005, p. 1229], the Secretary-General submitted, in July, a report [A/61/177] on preventing and combating corrupt practices and the transfer of assets of illicit origin, and their return to the countries of origin, which contained an update on the status of the ratification of the United Nations Convention against Corruption and the preparation for the first session of the Conference of the States Parties to the Convention. The report also reflected on the need for coordination of ongoing anti-corruption initiatives. It provided information on attempts and methodologies used to estimate the scale of corruption and its impact on development and economic growth, summarized efforts to recover assets derived from corruption and suggested how the implementation of chapter V of the Convention on asset recovery could have an impact on the return of those funds.

GENERAL ASSEMBLY ACTION

On 20 December [meeting 83], the General Assembly, on the recommendation of the Second (Economic and Financial) Committee [A/61/424/Add.4], adopted **resolution 61/209** without vote [agenda item 55 *(d)*].

Preventing and combating corrupt practices and transfer of assets of illicit origin and returning such assets, in particular to the countries of origin, consistent with the United Nations Convention against Corruption

The General Assembly,

Recalling its resolutions 54/205 of 22 December 1999, 56/186 of 21 December 2001 and 57/244 of 20 December 2002, and recalling also its resolutions 58/205 of 23 December 2003, 59/242 of 22 December 2004 and 60/207 of 22 December 2005,

Welcoming the entry into force on 14 December 2005 of the United Nations Convention against Corruption,

Welcoming also the convening of the first session of the Conference of the States Parties to the United Nations Convention against Corruption, in Jordan, from 10 to 14 December 2006,

1. *Takes note* of the report of the Secretary-General;

2. *Also takes note* of the generous offer of the Government of Indonesia to host the second session of the Conference of the States Parties to the United Nations Convention against Corruption;

3. *Urges* all Member States and competent regional economic integration organizations, within the limits of their competence, to consider ratifying or acceding to the United Nations Convention against Corruption as a matter of priority, and calls upon all States parties to fully implement the Convention as soon as possible;

4. *Requests* the Secretary-General to submit to the General Assembly at its sixty-second session a report, completed within existing resources, on the implementation of previous resolutions that would elaborate further on the magnitude of corruption at all levels and on any scale, and on the scale of the transfer of assets of illicit origin derived from corruption and the impact of corruption and such transfers on economic growth and sustainable development, taking into account the outcome of, and also transmitting the report on, the first session of the Conference of the States Parties to the Convention;

5. *Decides* to include in the provisional agenda of its sixty-second session, under the item entitled "Globalization and interdependence", the sub-item entitled "Preventing and combating corrupt practices and transfer of assets of illicit origin and returning such assets, in particular to the countries of origin, consistent with the United Nations Convention against Corruption".

Kidnapping

Pursuant to Economic and Social Council resolution 59/154 [YUN 2004, p. 1128], the UNODC Executive Director presented to the Commission on Crime Prevention and Criminal Justice, at its fifteenth session [E/2006/30 & Corr.1], the *Counter-Kidnapping Manual* developed by the Office. The Government of Colombia contributed to the production and funding of the Manual. During Commission deliberations, a number of speakers welcomed the launching of the Manual as a practical tool to assist Member States in combating kidnapping and as a demonstration of effective cooperation between UNODC and Members States. Concern was expressed at the continued growth of kidnapping and the need for international cooperation in countering it; assistance to victims was also stressed.

Following deliberations, the Commission recommended to the Council a draft resolution for adoption by the General Assembly.

ECONOMIC AND SOCIAL COUNCIL ACTION

On 27 July [meeting 41], the Economic and Social Council, on the recommendation of the Commission on Crime Prevention and Criminal Justice [E/2006/30 & Corr.1], adopted **resolution 2006/19** without vote [agenda item 14 *(c)*].

International cooperation in the prevention, combating and elimination of kidnapping and in providing assistance to victims

The Economic and Social Council,

Recommends to the General Assembly the adoption of the following draft resolution:

[For text, see General Assembly resolution 61/179 below.]

GENERAL ASSEMBLY ACTION

On 20 December [meeting 82], the General Assembly, on the recommendation of the Third Committee [A/61/444], adopted **resolution 61/179** without vote [agenda item 98].

International cooperation in the prevention, combating and elimination of kidnapping and in providing assistance to victims

The General Assembly,

Concerned at the increase in the offence of kidnapping in various countries of the world and at the harmful effects of that crime on victims and their families, and determined to support measures to assist and protect them and to promote their recovery,

Reiterating that the kidnapping of persons under any circumstances and for any purpose constitutes a serious crime and a violation of individual freedom that undermines human rights,

Concerned at the growing tendency of organized criminal groups and also of terrorist groups in certain circumstances to resort to kidnapping, especially for the purpose of extortion, as a method of accumulating capital with a view to consolidating their criminal operations and undertaking other illegal activities, regardless of their purposes, such as trafficking in firearms and drugs and money-laundering,

Convinced that any linkage of various illegal activities involving kidnapping poses an additional threat to quality of life and hinders economic and social development,

Convinced also that the United Nations Convention against Transnational Organized Crime provides a legal framework when necessary for international cooperation with a view to preventing, combating and eradicating kidnapping,

Recalling its resolution 59/154 of 20 December 2004 entitled "International cooperation in the prevention, combating and elimination of kidnapping and in providing assistance to victims", in which it requested the United Nations Office on Drugs and Crime, subject to the availability of extrabudgetary resources, to prepare a manual, for use by competent authorities, of proven and promising practices in the fight against kidnapping,

Acknowledging the financial and technical contributions made by Member States to the preparation of the manual,

1. *Vigorously condemns and rejects once again* the offence of kidnapping, under any circumstances and for any purpose;

2. *Notes with satisfaction* the publication of the operational manual against kidnapping prepared pursuant to its resolution 59/154, and expresses its appreciation to the intergovernmental group of experts entrusted with the preparation of the manual;

3. *Encourages* Member States to continue to foster international cooperation, especially extradition, mutual legal assistance, collaboration between law enforcement

authorities and exchange of information, with a view to preventing, combating and eradicating kidnapping;

4. *Calls upon* Member States that have not yet done so, in furtherance of the fight against kidnapping, to strengthen their measures against money-laundering and to engage in international cooperation and mutual legal assistance in, inter alia, the tracing, detection, freezing and confiscation of proceeds of kidnapping;

5. *Calls upon* Member States to take measures intended to provide adequate assistance and protection to victims of kidnapping and their families;

6. *Invites* Member States, once they have considered the operational manual, to consider the possibility of using it in their national efforts to combat kidnapping, and requests the United Nations Office on Drugs and Crime, within available extrabudgetary resources, not excluding the use of existing resources from the regular budget of the Office, to provide to Member States, upon request, technical assistance and advice in implementing the provisions of the manual;

7. *Requests* the Executive Director of the United Nations Office on Drugs and Crime to report to the Commission on Crime Prevention and Criminal Justice at its sixteenth session on the implementation of the present resolution, and thereafter, to share its report with the Conference of the Parties to the United Nations Convention against Transnational Organized Crime.

Terrorism

In February [E/CN.15/2006/12], the Secretary-General submitted to the Commission on Crime Prevention and Criminal Justice, at its fifteenth session, a report on strengthening international cooperation and technical assistance in promoting the implementation of the universal conventions and protocols related to terrorism within the framework of UNODC activities. The report, prepared pursuant to Economic and Social Council resolution 2005/19 [YUN 2005, p. 1232], reviewed the progress made in the delivery of technical assistance by the Terrorism Prevention Branch of the UNODC Division for Treaty Affairs, in the context of the Secretary-General's comprehensive global strategy against terrorism (see p. 65). It also provided information on the status of ratification of the universal conventions and protocols related to terrorism and on voluntary contributions made by countries in support of UNODC in terrorism prevention.

The UNODC Terrorism Prevention Branch continued to provide assistance in requesting countries for the ratification and legislative incorporation of the universal instruments relating to terrorism. It intended to continue to ensure follow-up through focused subregional activities, including the International Convention for the Suppression of Acts of Nuclear Terrorism [YUN 2005, p. 601]. It would also reinforce initiatives in subregions that had lagged behind in the ratification and legislative incorporation processes, and increase assistance to Member States that were late in submitting national reports on the implementation of Security Council resolution 1373(2001) [YUN 2001, p. 61] to the Counter-Terrorism Committee. In view of the increase in the number of universal ratifications and countries reached through regional, subregional and bilateral assistance activities, the work of the Branch would focus increasingly on follow-up activities and capacity-building. In particular, the Branch would devote its attention to assisting States in reinforcing their capacity to prosecute and provide an effective judicial response to terrorist acts, in compliance with the rule of law and with due regard to the mechanisms of international cooperation. It was therefore important for the Commission to provide guidance for the longer-term build-up of the UNODC programme elements addressing counter-terrorism.

In July [A/61/178], the Secretary-General submitted to the General Assembly a related report, prepared pursuant to Economic and Social Council resolution 2005/19, highlighting the technical assistance delivery role of UNODC, particularly as a component of the Secretary-General's recommendations for a global counter-terrorism strategy, which he submitted to the Assembly in April. The report also contained information on UNODC cooperation with relevant committees and expert groups established by relevant Security Council resolutions, as well as with various international, regional and subregional organizations, and an overview of substantive developments, including the deliberations of the fifteenth session of the Commission.

On 20 December, the Assembly, took note of the Secretary-General's report on strengthening international cooperation and technical assistance in promoting the implementation of the universal conventions and protocols related to terrorism within the framework of UNODC activities (**decision 61/531**).

Trafficking in human organs

Pursuant to Economic and Social Council resolution 59/156 [YUN 2004, p. 1127], the Secretary-General submitted to the Commission on Crime Prevention and Criminal Justice a February report on preventing, combating and punishing trafficking in human organs [E/CN.15/2006/10]. The report, based on a summary and initial analysis of Member States' replies to the Secretary-General's request for information on their efforts to implement the resolution, provided an assessment of the extent of trafficking in human organs and tissues, as well as the involvement of organized criminal groups.

The assessment indicated that the extent of the problem remained unclear and the issue had not yet received priority attention. Despite numerous reports from the media and international organizations, the role played by organized crime in the trade in human organs continued to be poorly understood, and the lack of evidence and information on its involvement often impeded the creation of an effective national strategy. It was evident that human organs had become a commodity, being traded in an unfair and inequitable manner across the globe, and there was an organized black market. The clandestine nature of trafficking in organs and the complex combination of the different actors involved required a multifaceted response. To address the problem, specific acts had to be established as criminal offences and appropriate legislation implemented. The absence of internationally agreed definitions and legal standards to provide a framework for cooperation in combating the trafficking in human organs made it more difficult to understand and analyse the problem and its extent, and eventually to take appropriate countermeasures at the national, regional and international levels.

The Secretary-General suggested that States should be encouraged to formulate and implement comprehensive national policies that provided for more severe penalties for organ trafficking. Member States should consider the application of comprehensive legislation that addressed criminalization, prevention and victim protection. The application of international agreements to address the regulation of organ procurement and broker activities should be considered, as well as a voluntary system of organ donation in accordance with the World Health Organization Guiding Principles on Human Organ Transplantation. States should establish oversight and monitoring tools, which were critical to preventing, detecting and countering illicit trading in human organs, in order to ensure the existence and maintenance of hospital safety standards aimed at reducing the risk of disease transmission by organs and tissues used for transplantations. The role of law enforcement agencies in investigating, gathering information and sharing intelligence about possible cases had to be strengthened. Those agencies should acknowledge that the investigation of organ trafficking required a different approach than that of other types of crime, and officers should be trained and equipped accordingly. The awareness of medical and paramedical services concerning such crime should be raised, and awareness-raising campaigns about the risks and possible health consequences of organ donation should be promoted. Moreover, collaboration among law enforcement agencies, financial institutions and health officials should be strengthened. Member States should develop and enhance cooperation with national and international law enforcement agencies, such as Interpol and the European Police Office. Civil society should play the leading role in promoting public discussions, conducting research and monitoring the donation of organs. Member States should consider holding a group of experts meeting to discuss further the extent of the problem of trafficking in human organs and the possible remedies at the national, regional and international levels.

UN standards and guidelines

The Intergovernmental Expert Group Meeting on United Nations standards and norms in crime prevention and criminal justice (Vienna, 20-22 March) [E/CN.15/2006/CRP.1], convened pursuant to Economic and Social Council resolution 2004/28 [YUN 2004, p. 1131], finalized and adopted a draft information-gathering instrument on standards and norms primarily related to crime prevention. The questionnaire was designed as a tool for collecting information to assist in the preparation of the Secretary-General's report, in particular regarding the difficulties encountered in the application of standards and norms in crime prevention, ways in which technical assistance could be provided, and useful practices and emerging challenges. The questionnaire was divided in five sections: governmental structure for crime prevention; streams of crime prevention; implementation issues; international cooperation and networking; and other relevant and concluding questions.

The Secretary-General submitted to the Commission a March report [E/CN.15/2006/13 & Corr.1] on UN standards and norms in crime prevention and criminal justice, in response to Council resolution 2004/28 [YUN 2004, p. 1131]. The report analysed the replies received from Governments on the use and application of the standards and norms related primarily to persons in custody, non-custodial measures, and juvenile and restorative justice.

ECONOMIC AND SOCIAL COUNCIL ACTION

On 27 July [meeting 41], the Economic and Social Council, on the recommendation of the Commission on Crime Prevention and Criminal Justice [E/2006/30 & Corr.1], adopted **resolution 2006/20** without vote [agenda item 14 *(c)*].

United Nations standards and norms in crime prevention

The Economic and Social Council,

Taking note of General Assembly resolution 56/261 of 31 January 2002, entitled "Plans of action for the implementation of the Vienna Declaration on Crime and Justice: Meeting the Challenges of the Twenty-first Century", in particular section VIII of the plans of action, relating to action in the context of crime prevention to implement the relevant commitments undertaken in the Vienna Declaration,

Bearing in mind its resolution 2002/13 of 24 July 2002, in which it accepted the Guidelines for the Prevention of Crime annexed to the resolution, invited Member States to draw upon these Guidelines, as appropriate, in the development or strengthening of their policies in the field of crime prevention and criminal justice, and requested the Secretary-General to report to the Commission on Crime Prevention and Criminal Justice at its fourteenth session on the implementation of the resolution,

Recalling its resolution 2003/26 of 22 July 2003 on the prevention of urban crime, in which it encouraged Member States to draw upon the Guidelines for the Prevention of Crime and to share their experience gained in that regard, including in their inputs to the report of the Secretary-General on the Guidelines, and requested the United Nations Office on Drugs and Crime and the United Nations Human Settlements Programme (UN-Habitat) to assist Member States, upon request, to prepare proposals for the provision of technical assistance in the area of crime prevention in accordance with the Guidelines,

Recalling also its resolution 2004/31 of 21 July 2004 on the prevention of urban crime, in which it welcomed the initiative of the United Nations Office on Drugs and Crime to establish a database of good practices in the area of urban crime prevention, in coordination with the United Nations Human Settlements Programme and the relevant institutes of the United Nations Crime Prevention and Criminal Justice Programme network,

Taking note of its resolution 2005/22 of 22 July 2005 on action to promote effective crime prevention, in which it invited Member States, the United Nations Office on Drugs and Crime and other entities to support a more integrated approach to building capacity in crime prevention and to promote crime prevention cooperation as a contribution to the establishment and strengthening of the rule of law, and requested the United Nations Office on Drugs and Crime to continue to undertake action in relation to gathering information on standards and norms in crime prevention and criminal justice, given its importance as a platform for the exchange of information and successful practices in crime prevention, and to pay due attention to crime prevention with a view to achieving a balanced approach between crime prevention and criminal justice responses,

Recalling its resolution 2003/30 of 22 July 2003 on United Nations standards and norms in crime prevention and criminal justice, in which it decided to group such standards and norms into categories for the purpose of targeted collection of information, in order to better identify the specific needs of Member States with a view to improving technical cooperation, and in which it called upon Member States, in responding to inquiries on the application of such standards and norms, to focus on identifying difficulties that had been encountered in their application, ways in which technical assistance could overcome those difficulties and desirable practices in the prevention and control of crime,

Recalling also its resolution 2004/28 of 21 July 2004 on United Nations standards and norms in crime prevention and criminal justice, in which it requested the Secretary-General to convene a meeting of intergovernmental experts and, in cooperation with the institutes of the United Nations Crime Prevention and Criminal Justice Programme network, to design information-gathering instruments on, inter alia, standards and norms related primarily to crime prevention and victim issues,

Aware that the Bangkok Declaration on Synergies and Responses: Strategic Alliances in Crime Prevention and Criminal Justice, endorsed by the General Assembly in its resolution 60/177 of 16 December 2005, recognized that comprehensive and effective crime prevention strategies can significantly reduce crime and victimization, and urged that such strategies address the root causes and risk factors of crime and victimization and that they be further developed and implemented at the local, national and international levels, taking into account, as appropriate, inter alia, the Guidelines for the Prevention of Crime,

Recalling that concern was expressed in the Bangkok Declaration over the expansion of transnational organized crime and of terrorism,

Calling attention to the report entitled "Crime and Drugs as Impediments to Security and Development in Africa: a Programme of Action 2006-2010", which was endorsed by the Round Table for Africa held in Abuja on 5 and 6 September 2005, hosted by the Government of Nigeria and organized by the United Nations Office on Drugs and Crime, which includes application of the Guidelines for the Prevention of Crime as one potential priority for addressing conventional crime,

Aware of the scope for significant reduction in crime and victimization through knowledge-based approaches, technical and financial assistance and cooperation, and of the contribution that effective crime prevention can make in terms of the safety and security of individuals and their property, as well as to the quality of life in communities around the world,

1. *Notes with appreciation* the work of the Intergovernmental Expert Group Meeting on Crime Prevention, held in Vienna from 20 to 22 March 2006;

2. *Expresses its gratitude* to the Government of Canada for its financial support in the organization of the Intergovernmental Expert Group Meeting and to the European Institute for Crime Prevention and Control, affiliated with the United Nations, as well as the International Centre for the Prevention of Crime, associated with the United Nations, for assisting in the preparation of the information-gathering instrument on United

Nations standards and norms related primarily to crime prevention;

3. *Approves* the information-gathering instrument for United Nations standards and norms related primarily to crime prevention, contained in the annex to the present resolution, for purposes of dissemination;

4. *Requests* the Secretary-General to forward the information-gathering instrument to Member States;

5. *Invites* Member States to reply to the information-gathering instrument and to include any comments or suggestions they may have in relation to the instrument;

6. *Requests* the United Nations Office on Drugs and Crime, within available extrabudgetary resources, not excluding the use of existing resources from the regular budget of the Office, to seek information from relevant intergovernmental and non-governmental organizations, within the mandate of the Commission on Crime Prevention and Criminal Justice, and from the institutes of the United Nations Crime Prevention and Criminal Justice Programme network and other relevant United Nations entities with respect to their capacity to provide technical assistance in relation to areas outlined in the information-gathering instrument;

7. *Invites* Member States and other relevant entities to inform the United Nations Office on Drugs and Crime of existing centres and focal points in the area of crime prevention, if applicable, in order to facilitate networking and cooperation, also keeping in mind the invitation to that end contained in the annex to Economic and Social Council resolution 2003/30;

8. *Requests* the Secretary-General to convene, within available extrabudgetary resources, not excluding the use of existing resources from the regular budget of the United Nations Office on Drugs and Crime, an intergovernmental expert group meeting, based on equitable geographical representation and open to observers, in cooperation with the institutes of the United Nations Crime Prevention and Criminal Justice Programme network, to design an information-gathering instrument in relation to United Nations standards and norms related primarily to victim issues and to study ways and means to promote their use and application, and to report on progress made in that connection to the Commission at its sixteenth session;

9. *Requests* the United Nations Office on Drugs and Crime, when submitting a proposed questionnaire to the Commission on Crime Prevention and Criminal Justice for approval, to provide a report on whether the information being sought could be obtained from existing mechanisms so as to avoid duplication and overlap;

10. *Requests* the Secretary-General to report to the Commission on Crime Prevention and Criminal Justice at its sixteenth session on the use and application of United Nations standards and norms related primarily to crime prevention, in particular as regards the following:

(a) The difficulties encountered in the application of United Nations standards and norms related primarily to crime prevention;

(b) Ways in which technical assistance can be provided to overcome those difficulties;

(c) Useful practices in addressing existing and emerging challenges in this field;

(d) Suggestions from Member States on ways to further improve the existing standards and norms.

Annex

Information-gathering instrument on United Nations standards and norms related primarily to the prevention of crime

Pursuant to Economic and Social Council resolution 2004/28 of 21 July 2004, the following questionnaire is designed as a tool to collect information to assist in the preparation of the report of the Secretary-General, in particular as regards the following:

(a) The difficulties encountered in the application of United Nations standards and norms in crime prevention;

(b) Ways in which technical assistance can be provided; and

(c) Useful practices and emerging challenges.

It is not intended to produce a scorecard of how well States are doing. It addresses the main sections of the Guidelines for the Prevention of Crime (Council resolution 2002/13, annex) and, as the case may be, other relevant instruments.

The Economic and Social Council, in its resolution 2002/13 of 24 July 2002 on action to promote effective crime prevention accepted the Guidelines for the Prevention of Crime, and also requested the Secretary-General to report to the Commission on Crime Prevention and Criminal Justice on the implementation of that resolution. In the Guidelines, crime prevention refers to "strategies and measures that seek to reduce the risk of crimes occurring" by influencing "their multiple causes" (para. 3). It includes social crime prevention (or prevention through social development), local, community or neighbourhood-based crime prevention, situational crime prevention and measures to prevent recidivism. The definition does not include law enforcement and other criminal justice intervention, even though these may have crime prevention aspects. It is cognizant, however, of the need to take account of "the growing internationalization of criminal activities" (para. 4). When referring to the community, it refers in essence to "the involvement of civil society at the local level" (para. 5).

Other instruments relevant to the prevention of crime include:

- Economic and Social Council resolution 1995/9 of 24 July 1995, the annex to which contains the Guidelines for cooperation and technical assistance in the field of urban crime prevention
- General Assembly resolution 51/60 of 12 December 1996, the annex to which contains the United Nations Declaration on Crime and Public Security

The questionnaire is divided into five sections: structuring crime prevention at the government level; crime prevention approaches; implementation issues; international cooperation, networking and technical assistance;

and concluding questions. In developing the questionnaire, related paragraphs have been grouped for simplicity and clarity.

I. Structuring crime prevention at the government level

The following paragraphs of the Guidelines for the Prevention of Crime refer to government responsibility, leadership and structures to organize and deliver effective crime prevention:

2. It is the responsibility of all levels of government [national, regional and local] *to create, maintain and promote a context within which relevant governmental institutions and all segments of civil society, including the corporate sector, can better play their part in preventing crime.*

Government leadership

7. All levels of government should play a leadership role in developing effective and humane crime prevention strategies and in creating and maintaining institutional frameworks for their implementation and review.

Cooperation/partnerships

9. Cooperation/partnerships should be an integral part of effective crime prevention, given the wide-ranging nature of the causes of crime and the skills and responsibilities required to address them. This includes partnerships working across ministries and between authorities, community organizations, non-governmental organizations, the business sector and private citizens.

Government structures

17. Governments should include prevention as a permanent part of their structures and programmes for controlling crime, ensuring that clear responsibilities and goals exist within government for the organization of crime prevention, by, inter alia:

(a) Establishing centres or focal points with expertise and resources;

(b) Establishing a crime prevention plan with clear priorities and targets;

(c) Establishing linkages and coordination between relevant government agencies or departments;

(d) Fostering partnerships with non-governmental organizations, the business, private and professional sectors and the community;

(e) Seeking the active participation of the public in crime prevention by informing it of the need for and means of action and its role.

Training and capacity-building

18. Governments should support the development of crime prevention skills by:

(a) Providing professional development for senior officials in relevant agencies;

(b) Encouraging universities, colleges and other relevant educational agencies to offer basic and advanced courses, including in collaboration with practitioners;

(c) Working with the educational and professional sectors to develop certification and professional qualifications;

(d) Promoting the capacity of communities to develop and respond to their needs.

Supporting partnerships

19. Governments and all segments of civil society should support the principle of partnership, where appropriate, including:

(a) Advancing knowledge of the importance of this principle and the components of successful partnerships, including the need for all of the partners to have clear and transparent roles;

(b) Fostering the formation of partnerships at different levels and across sectors;

(c) Facilitating the efficient operation of partnerships.

1. Have Government bodies in your country taken steps to implement the approach to crime prevention defined in the Guidelines?
   ( ) Yes ( ) No
   If the answer is "Yes", please describe briefly.
2. In your country, have specific crime prevention policies or strategies been adopted?
   (a) At the national level?
   ( ) Yes ( ) No
   If the answer is "Yes", please indicate the title and date of adoption.
   Has this policy or strategy been enshrined in legislation?
   ( ) Yes ( ) No
   If the answer is "Yes", please provide the reference and date of adoption.
   (b) At the regional level?
   ( ) Yes ( ) No
   (c) At the local level?
   ( ) Yes ( ) No
   If the answer to *(b)* and/or *(c)* above is "Yes", please specify.
3. In your country, which Government department, ministry or organization at the national level has the responsibility for leadership in crime prevention? Please specify.
4. In your country, does the organization or framework of crime prevention include:
   (a) A centre or focal point at the national level?
   ( ) Yes ( ) No
   If the answer is "Yes", please cite the name and status of the responsible agency or agencies.
   (b) Centres or focal points at the regional level?
   ( ) Yes ( ) No
   ( ) Not applicable
   (c) Establishing crime prevention plans with clear priorities?
   (i) At the national level?
   ( ) Yes ( ) Yes, in part
   ( ) No
   (ii) At the regional level?
   ( ) Yes ( ) Yes, in part
   ( ) No ( ) Not applicable
   (iii) At the local level?
   ( ) Yes ( ) Yes, in part
   ( ) No

(*d*) Establishing linkages and coordination between relevant government agencies and organizations?
 (i) At the national level?
 ( ) Yes ( ) Yes, in part
 ( ) No
 (ii) At the regional level?
 ( ) Yes ( ) Yes, in part
 ( ) No ( ) Not applicable

(*e*) Fostering partnerships with non-governmental organizations, the business, private and professional sectors and the community?
 (i) At the national level?
 ( ) Yes ( ) Yes, in part
 ( ) No
 (ii) At the regional level?
 ( ) Yes ( ) Yes, in part
 ( ) No ( ) Not applicable
 (iii) At the local level?
 ( ) Yes ( ) Yes, in part
 ( ) No

(*f*) Seeking the active participation of the general public?
 (i) At the national level?
 ( ) Yes ( ) Yes, in part
 ( ) No
 (ii) At the regional level?
 ( ) Yes ( ) Yes, in part
 ( ) No ( ) Not applicable
 (iii) At the local level?
 ( ) Yes ( ) Yes, in part
 ( ) No

(*g*) A specific role for the police and other institutions performing similar roles?
 ( ) Yes ( ) No

If the answer is "Yes", please describe.

5. In your country, do Government bodies support the development of crime prevention skills by:
 (*a*) Providing professional development?
 ( ) Yes ( ) No
 (*b*) Encouraging relevant educational institutions to offer basic and advanced courses?
 ( ) Yes ( ) No
 (*c*) Working to develop certification and professional qualifications?
 ( ) Yes ( ) No
 (*d*) Promoting the capacity of communities to develop and respond to their own needs?
 ( ) Yes ( ) No

II. Crime prevention approaches

Crime prevention as defined in the relevant instruments refers to various approaches generally called social, community-based and situational crime prevention, as well as preventing recidivism.

In respect to social crime prevention, relevant paragraphs of the Guidelines for the Prevention of Crime include:

6. Crime prevention encompasses a wide range of approaches, including those which:

(a) Promote the well-being of people and encourage pro-social behaviour through social, economic, health and educational measures, with a particular emphasis on children and youth, and focus on the risk and protective factors associated with crime and victimization (prevention through social development, or social crime prevention);

Socio-economic development and inclusion

8. Crime prevention considerations should be integrated into all relevant social and economic policies and programmes, including those addressing employment, education, health, housing and urban planning, poverty, social marginalization and exclusion. Particular emphasis should be placed on communities, families, children and youth at risk.

Social development

25. Governments should address the risk factors of crime and victimization by:

(a) Promoting protective factors through comprehensive and non-stigmatizing social and economic development programmes, including health, education, housing and employment;

(b) Promoting activities that redress marginalization and exclusion;

(c) Promoting positive conflict resolution;

(d) Using education and public awareness strategies to foster a culture of lawfulness and tolerance while respecting cultural identities.

6. Is the concept of social crime prevention (as defined in paragraph 6 (*a*) of the Guidelines for the Prevention of Crime) part of your country's crime prevention policy, strategy or programmes?
 ( ) Yes ( ) No

7. Do your country's crime prevention policies, strategies or programmes include a specific focus on:
 (*a*) Children and youth at risk of victimization or offending?
 ( ) Yes ( ) No
 If the answer is "Yes", please specify.
 (*b*) Vulnerable groups?
 ( ) Yes ( ) No
 If the answer is "Yes", please specify.
 (*c*) The different needs of men and women?
 ( ) Yes ( ) No
 If the answer is "Yes", please specify.

8. Are crime prevention considerations integrated into relevant social and economic policies and programmes?
 ( ) Yes ( ) No
 If the answer is "Yes", please specify.

9. In your country, do crime prevention policies, strategies or programmes:
 (*a*) Promote protective factors (e.g. staying in school, positive parenting, job training for youth, etc.)?
 ( ) Yes ( ) No
 If the answer is "Yes", please describe briefly.
 (*b*) Promote activities to redress marginalization or exclusion?
 ( ) Yes ( ) No

If the answer is "Yes", please describe briefly.

(c) Promote positive conflict resolution (e.g. mediation, restorative justice, etc.)?

( ) Yes ( ) No

If the answer is "Yes", please describe briefly.

(d) Use education and public awareness?

( ) Yes ( ) No

If the answer is "Yes", please describe briefly.

(e) Involve the media?

( ) Yes ( ) No

If the answer is "Yes", please describe briefly.

In respect of community or locally based crime prevention, relevant paragraphs of the Guidelines for the Prevention of Crime include:

6. Crime prevention encompasses a wide range of approaches, including those which:

(b) Change the conditions in neighbourhoods that influence offending, victimization and insecurity that results from crime by building on the initiatives, expertise and commitment of community members (locally based crime prevention);

10. Does your country have specific crime prevention policies, strategies or programmes designed to change the conditions that influence offending, victimization and insecurity in neighbourhoods?

( ) Yes ( ) No

If the answer is "Yes", please specify.

11. Does your crime prevention policy or strategy include an integrated approach to address the multiple risk and protective factors in highly vulnerable neighbourhoods or communities?

( ) Yes ( ) No

If the answer is "Yes", please specify.

In respect of situational crime prevention, relevant paragraphs of the Guidelines for the Prevention of Crime include:

6. Crime prevention encompasses a wide range of approaches, including those which:

(c) Prevent the occurrence of crimes by reducing opportunities, increasing risks of being apprehended and minimizing benefits, including through environmental design, and by providing assistance and information to potential and actual victims (situational crime prevention;

Situational prevention

26. Governments and civil society, including, where appropriate, the corporate sector, should support the development of situational crime prevention programmes by, inter alia:

(a) Improved environmental design;

(b) Appropriate methods of surveillance that are sensitive to the right to privacy;

(c) Encouraging the design of consumer goods to make them more resistant to crime;

(d) Target "hardening" without impinging upon the quality of the built environment or limiting free access to public space;

(e) Implementing strategies to prevent repeat victimization.

12. Does your country have specific situational crime prevention policies, strategies or programmes to:

(a) Improve environmental design and management?

( ) Yes ( ) No

If the answer is "Yes", please specify.

(b) Implement appropriate methods of surveillance that are sensitive to privacy?

( ) Yes ( ) No

If the answer is "Yes", please specify.

(c) Promote target hardening without impinging on the quality of the built environment?

( ) Yes ( ) No

If the answer is "Yes", please specify.

(d) Encourage the design of crime-resistant consumer goods?

( ) Yes ( ) No

If the answer is "Yes", please specify.

(e) Implement strategies to prevent repeat victimization?

( ) Yes ( ) No

If the answer is "Yes", please specify.

In respect of the prevention of recidivism, relevant paragraphs of the Guidelines for the Prevention of Crime include:

6. Crime prevention encompasses a wide range of approaches, including those which:

(d) Prevent recidivism by assisting in the social reintegration of offenders and other preventive mechanisms (reintegration programmes). 13. In your country, do you have specific policies, strategies or programmes to prevent recidivism by assisting in the social reintegration of offenders and other preventive mechanisms?

( ) Yes ( ) No

If the answer is "Yes", please specify.

III. Implementation issues

Sustainability and accountability are important principles to ensure the implementation of effective crime prevention programmes and initiatives. The relevant paragraphs of the Guidelines for the Prevention of Crime are:

1. There is clear evidence that well-planned crime prevention strategies not only prevent crime and victimization, but also promote community safety and contribute to the sustainable development of countries. Effective, responsible crime prevention enhances the quality of life of all citizens. It has long-term benefits in terms of reducing the costs associated with the formal criminal justice system, as well as other social costs that result from crime. Crime prevention offers opportunities for a humane and more cost-effective approach to the problems of crime.

Sustainability/accountability

10. Crime prevention requires adequate resources, including funding for structures and activities, in order to be sustained. There should be clear accountability for funding, implementation and evaluation and for the achievement of planned results.

Sustainability

20. Governments and other funding bodies should strive to achieve sustainability of demonstrably effective crime prevention programmes and initiatives through, inter alia:

(a) Reviewing resource allocation to establish and maintain an appropriate balance between crime prevention and the criminal justice and other systems, to be more effective in preventing crime and victimization;

(b) Establishing clear accountability for funding, programming and coordinating crime prevention initiatives;

(c) Encouraging community involvement in sustainability

14. In your country, what measures have been taken to ensure the sustainability of crime prevention policies, strategies and programmes?

Please describe briefly.

15. In your country, have there been systematic attempts to assess the costs of crime and crime control measures, including crime prevention measures?

( ) Yes ( ) No

If the answer is "Yes", please provide the source of funding and an estimate of the total costs.

In implementing crime prevention, elements of a rigorous process have been identified. The relevant paragraphs of the Guidelines for the Prevention of Crime are:

Knowledge base

11. Crime prevention strategies, policies, programmes and actions should be based on a broad, multidisciplinary foundation of knowledge about crime problems, their multiple causes and promising and proven practices.

21. As appropriate, Governments and/or civil society should facilitate knowledge-based crime prevention by, inter alia:

(a) Providing the information necessary for communities to address crime problems;

(b) Supporting the generation of useful and practically applicable knowledge that is scientifically reliable and valid;

(c) Supporting the organization and synthesis of knowledge and identifying and addressing gaps in the knowledge base;

(d) Sharing that knowledge, as appropriate, among, inter alia, researchers, policymakers, educators, practitioners from other relevant sectors and the wider community;

(e) Applying this knowledge in replicating successful interventions, developing new initiatives and anticipating new crime problems and prevention opportunities;

(f) Establishing data systems to help manage crime prevention more cost-effectively, including by conducting regular surveys of victimization and offending;

(g) Promoting the application of those data in order to reduce repeat victimization, persistent offending and areas with a high level of crime.

Planning intervention

22. Those planning interventions should promote a process that includes:

(a) A systematic analysis of crime problems, their causes, risk factors and consequences, in particular at the local level;

(b) A plan that draws on the most appropriate approach and adapts interventions to the specific local problem and context;

(c) An implementation plan to deliver appropriate interventions that are efficient, effective and sustainable;

(d) Mobilizing entities that are able to tackle causes;

(e) Monitoring and evaluation.

Support evaluation

23. Governments, other funding bodies and those involved in programme development and delivery should:

(a) Undertake short- and longer-term evaluation to test rigorously what works, where and why;

(b) Undertake cost-benefit analyses;

(c) Assess the extent to which action results in a reduction in levels of crime and victimization, in the seriousness of crime and in fear of crime;

(d) Systematically assess the outcomes and unintended consequences, both positive and negative, of action, such as a decrease in crime rates or the stigmatization of individuals and/or communities.

16. In your country, is the use of knowledge-based crime prevention strategies, policies or programmes facilitated by:

(a) Supporting the generation and utilization of useful information and data?

( ) Yes ( ) No

If the answer is "Yes", please describe briefly.

(b) Supporting the sharing of useful information and data?

( ) Yes ( ) No

If the answer is "Yes", please describe briefly.

(c) Promoting the application of useful information and data to reduce repeat victimization, persistent offending and high crime areas?

( ) Yes ( ) No

If the answer is "Yes", please describe briefly.

17. In your country, do the crime prevention policies, strategies or programmes promote a planning process that includes:

(a) A systematic analysis of crime problems, their causes and risk factors and consequences, in particular at the local level?

( ) Yes ( ) No

If the answer is "Yes", please describe briefly.

(b) A plan that draws on the most appropriate approaches and adapts interventions to the specific local problems and local context?

( ) Yes ( ) No

If the answer is "Yes", please describe briefly.

(c) An implementation plan to deliver efficient, effective and sustainable interventions?

( ) Yes ( ) No

If the answer is "Yes", please describe briefly.

(d) Mobilizing entities that are able to tackle causes?

( ) Yes ( ) No

If the answer is "Yes", please describe briefly.

(e) Monitoring and evaluation?

( ) Yes ( ) No

If the answer is "Yes", please describe briefly.

18. In your country, do the crime prevention policies, strategies or programmes include:

    (a) Undertaking evaluation to test rigorously what works?

    ( ) Yes ( ) No

    If the answer is "Yes", please describe briefly.

    (b) Undertaking cost-benefit analyses?

    ( ) Yes ( ) No

    If the answer is "Yes", please describe briefly.

    (c) Assessing reduction in crime, victimization and fear of crime?

    ( ) Yes ( ) No

    If the answer is "Yes", please describe briefly.

    (d) Assessing outcomes and unintended consequences?

    ( ) Yes ( ) No

    If the answer is "Yes", please describe briefly.

19. Has an evaluation of components or specific activities of your country's national crime prevention policy or strategy been undertaken?

    ( ) Yes ( ) No

    If the answer is "Yes", please describe briefly.

The Guidelines for the Prevention of Crime recognize the links between local and transnational organized crime and the need to prevent organized crime. The relevant paragraphs of the Guidelines are:

Interdependency

13. National crime prevention diagnoses and strategies should, where appropriate, take account of links between local criminal problems and international organized crime.

Prevention of organized crime

27. Governments and civil society should endeavour to analyse and address the links between transnational organized crime and national and local crime problems by, inter alia:

(a) Reducing existing and future opportunities for organized criminal groups to participate in lawful markets with the proceeds of crime, through appropriate legislative, administrative or other measures;

(b) Developing measures to prevent the misuse by organized criminal groups of tender procedures conducted by public authorities and of subsidies and licences granted by public authorities for commercial activity;

(c) Designing crime prevention strategies, where appropriate, to protect socially marginalized groups, especially women and children, who are vulnerable to the action of organized criminal groups, including trafficking in persons and smuggling of migrants.

Links between transnational and local crime

31. Member States should collaborate to analyse and address the links between transnational organized crime and national and local crime problems.

20. In your country, do crime prevention policies, strategies or programmes assess the potential links between local and national crime problems and transnational organized crime?

    ( ) Yes ( ) No

    If the answer is "Yes", please describe briefly.

21. In your country, do the crime prevention policies, strategies or programmes include:

    (a) Measures to reduce opportunities for organized criminal groups to participate in lawful markets?

    ( ) Yes ( ) No

    If the answer is "Yes", please describe briefly.

    (b) Measures to prevent the misuse of public tender procedures, subsidies and licences?

    ( ) Yes ( ) No

    If the answer is "Yes", please describe briefly.

    (c) Measures to protect socially marginalized groups, especially women and children, who are vulnerable to exploitation by organized criminal groups, including preventing trafficking in persons and the smuggling of migrants?

    ( ) Yes ( ) No

    If the answer is "Yes", please describe briefly.

IV. International cooperation, networking and technical assistance

Member States are encouraged to facilitate international cooperation and develop networks for the exchange of practices and knowledge. The relevant paragraphs of the Guidelines for the Prevention of Crime include:

Technical assistance

29. Member States and relevant international funding organizations should provide financial and technical assistance, including capacity-building and training, to developing countries and countries with economies in transition, communities and other relevant organizations for the implementation of effective crime prevention and community safety strategies at the regional, national and local levels. In that context, special attention should be given to research and action on crime prevention through social development.

Networking

30. Member States should strengthen or establish international, regional and national crime prevention networks with a view to exchanging proven and promising practices, identifying elements of their transferability and making such knowledge available to communities throughout the world.

Prioritizing crime prevention

32. The Centre for International Crime Prevention of the Office for Drug Control and Crime Prevention of the Secretariat, the United Nations Crime Prevention and Criminal Justice Programme network of affiliated and associated institutes and other relevant United Nations entities should include in their priorities crime prevention as set out in these Guidelines, set up a coordination mechanism and establish a roster of experts to undertake needs assessment and to provide technical advice.

Dissemination

33. Relevant United Nations bodies and other organizations should cooperate to produce crime prevention information in as many languages as possible, using both print and electronic media.

22. Does your country participate in international networks for the exchange of information and knowledge on crime prevention policies, strategies or programmes?
( ) Yes ( ) No
If the answer is "Yes", please specify.

23. What are the main obstacles to your country participating in international networking?
Please describe.

24. Please identify guides, toolkits, compendiums or manuals of crime prevention practices from your country that can be shared with other countries.

25. Does your country need technical assistance in any area of crime prevention?
( ) Yes ( ) No

26. Is your country able to provide technical assistance in any area of crime prevention?
( ) Yes ( ) No

If the answer to questions 25 and/or 26 is "Yes", please mark the appropriate box(es) below:	*Need technical assistance*	*Can provide technical assistance*
(*a*) Including prevention as a permanent part of government structures (para. 17)		
(*b*) Government support for the development of crime prevention skills (para. 18)		
(*c*) Government and civil society support of partnerships (para. 19)		
(*d*) Social crime prevention (paras. 6 (*a*), 8 and 25)		
(*e*) Locally based or neighbourhood crime prevention (para. 6 (*b*))		
(*f*) Situational crime prevention (paras. 6 (*c*) and 26)		
(*g*) Prevention of recidivism (para. 6 (*d*))		
(*h*) Sustainability and accountability of crime prevention (paras. 1, 10 and 20)		
(*i*) Knowledge-based crime prevention (paras. 11 and 21)		
(*j*) Planning interventions (para. 22)		
(*k*) Monitoring and evaluation (para. 23)		
(*l*) Assessing the links between local crime problems and transnational organized crime (paras. 13, 27 and 31)		
(*m*) Of the areas identified, is there a priority? If so, please identify		

V. **Concluding questions**

27. What are some of the main lessons your country has derived from national experience in implementing crime prevention policies, strategies and programmes?
Please describe.

28. What are the main challenges in your country for delivering effective crime prevention?
Please describe.

HIV/AIDS in criminal justice

The Secretary-General, in response to Economic and Social Council resolution 2004/35 [YUN 2004, p. 1137], submitted a February report [E/CN.15/2006/15] on combating the spread of HIV/AIDS in criminal justice pre-trial and correctional facilities. The report provided a summary of responses received from 35 States to the Secretariat's request for information on the situation of HIV/AIDS in those facilities, with a view to providing Governments with programmatic and policy guidance responses, and an overview of the Secretariat's own work in the implementation of the resolution. In most of the responding countries, concerted efforts were being taken to ensure that national HIV/AIDS strategies and related legislative frameworks included a specific prison component. Respondents recognized that to limit the spread of the virus, efforts were needed to be made to reduce overcrowding by improving prison conditions and considering alternatives to imprisonment; ensure access to prevention, care and treatment services; guarantee the right to adequate health care and access to qualified medical personnel; provide appropriate training to prison staff; and ensure adequate funding for such efforts.

UNODC continued to expand its programme of technical assistance to respond to HIV/AIDS in prisons by conducting advisory missions, providing opportunities for policy debate, developing training material, holding training seminars and supporting national efforts to implement specific projects. Considering the responses received and the work being undertaken by UNODC, it was recommended that the Commission should consider addressing measures to reduce overcrowding and violence in prisons, such as encouraging Member States to seek alternatives to imprisonment as a way of preventing the further spread of HIV/AIDS among prison populations. That should include a focus on `responding to HIV/AIDS in prisons in the Programme of Action, 2006-2010, endorsed by the Round Table for Africa, held in 2005 (see below).

Strengthening the rule of law and criminal justice system in Africa

The Commission on Crime Prevention and Criminal Justice, at its fifteenth session, discussed the Programme of Action, 2006-2010 on strengthening the rule of law and the criminal justice systems in Africa within the context of the application of UN standards and norms in crime prevention and criminal justice, endorsed by the Round Table for Africa on Crime and Drugs as Impediments to Security and Development in Africa: Strengthening the Rule of Law (Abuja, Nigeria, 5 and 6 September 2005). The Programme of Action was clustered around the rule of law and the reform of the criminal justice systems and the strengthening of their institutions; measures to prevent and counter all serious forms of conventional crime; organized crime, money-laundering, corruption, trafficking and terrorism; measures to prevent drug abuse and HIV/AIDS; the promotion, ratification and implementation of regional and international conventions (against drug trafficking, transnational organized crime, corruption and terrorism); efforts to improve data collection, analysis and dissemination; and the promotion of public awareness and the role of civil society as an overarching theme. All together, six clusters were adopted, each identifying the main objectives, the proposed actions, as well as possible key partners, in the implementation of objectives and actions. The Programme of Action was the strategic and operationally oriented framework for technical cooperation over the next five years directed towards the reduction of crime and drugs as impediments to security and development in Africa.

ECONOMIC AND SOCIAL COUNCIL ACTION

On 27 July [meeting 41], the Economic and Social Council, on the recommendation of the Commission on Crime Prevention and Criminal Justice [E/2006/30 & Corr.1], adopted **resolution 2006/21** without vote [agenda item 14 *(c)*].

Implementation of the Programme of Action, 2006-2010, on strengthening the rule of law and the criminal justice systems in Africa

The Economic and Social Council,

Recalling the United Nations Millennium Declaration, in which Heads of State and Government pledged to support the consolidation of democracy in Africa and to assist Africans in their struggle for lasting peace, poverty eradication and sustainable human development,

Recalling also General Assembly resolution 59/159 of 20 December 2004 on strengthening the United Nations Crime Prevention and Criminal Justice Programme, in particular its technical cooperation capacity,

Recalling further General Assembly resolution 60/1 of 16 September 2005 on the 2005 World Summit Outcome, in particular paragraph 68 on meeting the special needs of Africa,

Recalling its resolution 2004/32 of 21 July 2004 on the implementation of technical assistance projects in Africa by the United Nations Office on Drugs and Crime and decision 2005/248 of 22 July 2005, in which it requested the Office to organize a special event among interested Member States, relevant agencies and institutes providing technical assistance to Africa, as well as those promoting South-South cooperation,

Recalling also General Assembly resolution 60/178 of 16 December 2005, in which the Assembly took note of the comprehensive Programme of Action, 2006-2010, that emanated from the Round Table for Africa held in Abuja on 5 and 6 September 2005, pursuant to Economic and Social Council decision 2005/248,

Recalling further decision EX.CL/Dec.169(VI), adopted by the Executive Council of the African Union at its sixth ordinary session and endorsed by the Assembly of Heads of State and Government at its fourth ordinary session, held in Abuja in January 2005,

Recognizing the important role of the New Partnership for Africa's Development, the African Peer Review Mechanism and its implementation process,

Welcoming the Paris Declaration on Aid Effectiveness: Ownership, Harmonization, Alignment, Results and Mutual Accountability, adopted at the Paris High-level Forum, held from 28 February to 2 March 2005, by the attending ministers of developed and developing countries, together with heads of bilateral and multilateral development institutions,

Welcoming also the adoption by the European Council of the European Union Strategy for Africa: towards a Euro-African pact to accelerate Africa's development,

Taking note of the report of the Secretary-General entitled "In larger freedom: towards development, security and human rights for all",

1. *Welcomes* the publication in June 2005 of the study by the United Nations Office on Drugs and Crime entitled "Crime and Development in Africa";

2. *Welcomes also* the outcome of the Round Table for Africa on Crime and Drugs as Impediments to Security and Development in Africa: Strengthening the Rule of Law, hosted by the Government of Nigeria in Abuja on 5 and 6 September 2005, embodied in the comprehensive Programme of Action, 2006-2010, aimed at strengthening the rule of law and the criminal justice systems in Africa;

3. *Expresses its appreciation* to the Government of Nigeria for hosting the Round Table for Africa, to the Governments of France and the United Kingdom of Great Britain and Northern Ireland and other development partners for their financial and related support for the meeting, as well as to the United Nations Office on Drugs and Crime for organizing the event;

4. *Invites* all African States and regional and subregional institutions to mainstream crime and drug control measures in their national and regional development

strategies, to mobilize all national stakeholders and to make every effort to allocate national resources for the implementation of the Programme of Action;

5. *Invites* the Chairman of the Commission on Crime Prevention and Criminal Justice to notify the Commission of the African Union of the need for its member States to endorse the Programme of Action, to support its implementation and to review regularly the progress made;

6. *Invites* the Commission of the African Union to present the Programme of Action, to the next Summit of Heads of State and Government of the African Union for its endorsement;

7. *Invites* bilateral and multilateral aid agencies and financial institutions to review as appropriate their funding policies for development assistance and to consider including a crime prevention and criminal justice component in such assistance;

8. *Requests* the United Nations Office on Drugs and Crime, within available extrabudgetary resources, not excluding the use of existing resources from the regular budget of the Office, to support the implementation of the Programme of Action, in cooperation with all African States, the African Union and other regional organizations, in particular in the context of the New Partnership for Africa's Development;

9. *Invites* relevant entities of the United Nations system, including the United Nations Development Programme, the World Bank and other international funding agencies, to increase further their interaction with the United Nations Office on Drugs and Crime in supporting the implementation of the Programme of Action, and to integrate crime prevention and drug control measures into their development programmes;

10. *Invites* Member States to make adequate voluntary contributions for the implementation of the Programme of Action;

11. *Requests* the Executive Director of the United Nations Office on Drugs and Crime, within available extrabudgetary resources, not excluding the use of existing resources from the regular budget of the Office, to devote high priority to the implementation of the Programme of Action, 2006-2010, and to present a progress report to the Commission on Crime Prevention and Criminal Justice at its seventeenth session, in 2008.

Technical assistance for prison reform in Africa

The Commission on Crime Prevention and Criminal Justice, at its fifteenth session, discussed providing technical assistance for prison reform in Africa and the development of viable alternatives to imprisonment, within the context of UN standards and norms in crime prevention and criminal justice. The importance of providing prisoners with access to prevention, treatment and care services, and health education, as well as training for prison staff, was emphasized. The control and management of infectious diseases in African correctional facilities was essential in order to protect the health of inmates, staff and ultimately the community.

The Commission also took into consideration the Secretary-General's report on combating the spread of HIV/AIDS in criminal justice pre-trial and correctional facilities (see p. 1314).

ECONOMIC AND SOCIAL COUNCIL ACTION

On 27 July [meeting 41], the Economic and Social Council, on the recommendation of the Commission on Crime Prevention and Criminal Justice [E/2006/30 & Corr.1], adopted **resolution 2006/22** without vote [agenda item 14 *(c)*].

Providing technical assistance for prison reform in Africa and the development of viable alternatives to imprisonment

The Economic and Social Council,

Recalling the Standard Minimum Rules for the Treatment of Prisoners, approved by the Economic and Social Council in its resolutions 663 C (XXIV) of 31 July 1957 and 2076(LXII) of 13 May 1977, the Basic Principles for the Treatment of Prisoners and the United Nations Standard Minimum Rules for Non-custodial Measures (The Tokyo Rules),

Having regard to the regional efforts in the promotion of basic rights of prisoners, as considered by the Pan-African Conference on Penal and Prison Reform in Africa, held in Ouagadougou from 18 to 20 September 2002, and the Latin American Conference on Penal Reform and Alternatives to Imprisonment, held in San José from 6 to 8 November 2002, and pursued by the African Union and the Organization of American States, as well as the Asian Conference on Prison Reform and Alternatives to Imprisonment, held in Dhaka from 12 to 14 December 2002,

Recalling its resolutions 1997/36 of 21 July 1997, on international cooperation for the improvement of prison conditions, in which it took note of the Kampala Declaration on Prison Conditions in Africa, annexed to the resolution; 1998/23 of 28 July 1998, on international cooperation aimed at the reduction of prison overcrowding and the promotion of alternative sentencing, in which it took note of the Kadoma Declaration on Community Service, contained in annex I to that resolution; and 1999/27 of 28 July 1999, on penal reform, in which it took note of the Arusha Declaration on Good Prison Practice, annexed to the resolution,

Recalling also its resolutions 2004/25 of 21 July 2004, on the rule of law and development: strengthening the rule of law and the reform of criminal justice institutions, with emphasis on technical assistance, including in post-conflict reconstruction, and 2005/21 of 22 July 2005, on strengthening the technical cooperation capacity of the United Nations Crime Prevention and Criminal Justice Programme in the area of the rule of law and criminal justice reform,

Recalling in particular its resolution 2004/35 of 21 July 2004, on combating the spread of HIV/AIDS in criminal justice pre-trial and correctional facilities, and deeply concerned at the spread of HIV/AIDS in pre-trial and correctional facilities in Africa and the risks posed to society as a whole, especially in situations of overcrowding in prisons,

Noting the Conference on Legal Aid in Criminal Justice: the Role of Lawyers, Non-Lawyers and Other Service Providers in Africa, in Lilongwe from 22 to 24 November 2004,

Recalling the commitments undertaken by Member States in the Vienna Declaration on Crime and Justice: Meeting the Challenges of the Twenty-first Century to contain the growth and overcrowding of prison populations in pre-trial and correctional facilities by promoting, as appropriate, safe and effective alternatives to incarceration and national and international actions recommended to implement and follow up on the Declaration as contained in the plan of action on prison overcrowding and alternatives to incarceration and in the Bangkok Declaration on Synergies and Responses: Strategic Alliances in Crime Prevention and Criminal Justice to the development and maintenance of fair and efficient criminal justice institutions, including the humane treatment of all those in pre-trial and correctional facilities, in accordance with applicable international standards,

Welcoming the Programme of Action, 2006-2010, on strengthening the rule of law and the criminal justice systems in Africa, adopted by the Round Table for Africa, held in Abuja on 5 and 6 September 2005, in particular the actions on penal reform, alternative and restorative justice, HIV/AIDS in prisons, reduction of the backlog of cases and prison overcrowding and vulnerable groups,

Taking into account the diverse views concerning imprisonment, especially for prisoners serving short sentences, and the cost of imprisonment to society as a whole,

Recognizing the serious problems posed by prison overcrowding and the potential threat to the rights of prisoners in many Member States, in particular in many African States,

Alarmed at the proportion of prisoners detained for long periods of time without being charged or sentenced and without access to legal advice and assistance in many African countries,

Recognizing that providing for effective alternatives to imprisonment in policy and practice is a viable long-term solution to prison overcrowding,

Recognizing also that community-based alternatives can provide for rehabilitation of offenders in a more efficient and cost-effective manner than imprisonment and that examples of good practices in reducing imprisonment can be found at the African level,

Recognizing further the need to enhance HIV/AIDS prevention efforts in pre-trial and correctional facilities in Africa,

Recognizing the particular needs of women and girls in prisons and children detained with their mothers, as well as the needs of persons with mental illness and the physically challenged, and the need for Governments to design specific responses in that regard,

Emphasizing that efforts to ease prison overcrowding require sustained efforts and resources at all levels of the criminal justice system, such as law enforcement institutions, prosecution and legal aid services, judiciary, case and court management and prison management,

Recognizing the impact of the action of civil society organizations in improving prison conditions and in respecting the rights of prisoners,

1. *Notes* the progress made by Member States in meeting the commitments mentioned above and recent efforts to ease prison overcrowding taken by some Member States;

2. *Encourages* Member States implementing criminal justice and prison reforms to promote the participation of civil society organizations in that endeavour and to cooperate with them;

3. *Welcomes* the report of the Secretary-General entitled "The rule of law and development: strengthening the rule of law and the reform of criminal justice institutions, including in post-conflict reconstruction", and the information contained therein with regard to penal reform activities in Member States and in the United Nations Office on Drugs and Crime;

4. *Also welcomes* the report of the Secretary-General on combating the spread of HIV/AIDS in criminal justice pre-trial and correctional facilities;

5. *Notes with appreciation* the designation in the 2005 UNAIDS publication on the division of labour for technical support, of the United Nations Office on Drugs and Crime as the lead agency among the co-sponsors of the Joint United Nations Programme on HIV/AIDS on matters relating to HIV/AIDS in prisons;

6. *Welcomes* the work of the United Nations Office on Drugs and Crime in providing advisory services and technical assistance to Member States in the area of HIV/AIDS in prisons, in particular the development of the toolkit on HIV/AIDS in prison settings, which offers guidance to senior policymakers, prison managers, prison staff and prison health-care workers, and encourages the Office, within available extrabudgetary resources, not excluding the use of existing resources from the regular budget of the Office, to continue its work in that area, in partnership with other members of the Joint United Nations Programme on HIV/AIDS;

7. *Invites* Member States to develop and adopt measures and guidelines, where appropriate and in accordance with national legislation and relevant international instruments, including the international conventions related to drugs, to ensure that the particular challenges of HIV/AIDS in pre-trial and correctional facilities are adequately addressed;

8. *Notes with appreciation* the accomplishments of the United Nations Office on Drugs and Crime in developing tools and manuals on penal reform, in particular the handbooks on alternatives to imprisonment and restorative justice;

9. *Welcomes* the efforts undertaken by the United Nations Office on Drugs and Crime focusing on providing

long-term sustainable technical assistance in the area of penal reform to Member States in post-conflict situations, in particular in Africa, in cooperation with the Department of Peacekeeping Operations of the Secretariat, and the increased synergy between the two entities;

10. *Invites* the United Nations Office on Drugs and Crime, within available extrabudgetary resources, not excluding the use of existing resources from the regular budget of the Office, to develop further tools and training manuals, based on international standards and best practices, in the area of penal reform and alternatives to imprisonment, in particular in the areas of prison management, legal advice and assistance and the special needs in prison of women and children, as well as of persons with mental illness and the physically challenged;

11. *Requests* the United Nations Office on Drugs and Crime, within available extrabudgetary resources, not excluding the use of existing resources from the regular budget of the Office, in cooperation with relevant partners, to continue to provide advisory services and technical assistance to Member States, upon request, in the area of penal reform, including restorative justice, alternatives to imprisonment, HIV/AIDS in prisons and the special needs of women and girls in prisons;

12. *Also requests* the United Nations Office on Drugs and Crime, within available extrabudgetary resources, not excluding the use of existing resources from the regular budget of the Office, to develop a programme of technical assistance for Africa in penal reform and provision of alternatives to imprisonment, building on the commitments made at the Round Table for Africa and in its Programme of Action, 2006-2010;

13. *Invites* Member States, international financial institutions and private donors to provide support to the activities above, through voluntary contributions to the United Nations Crime Prevention and Criminal Justice Fund or through voluntary contributions in direct support of such activities;

14. *Requests* the Secretary-General to submit a report on the implementation of the present resolution to the Commission on Crime Prevention and Criminal Justice at its seventeenth session, in 2008.

Strengthening basic principles of judicial conduct

On 27 July [meeting 41], the Economic and Social Council, on the recommendation of the Commission on Crime Prevention and Criminal Justice [E/2006/30 & Corr.1], adopted **resolution 2006/23** without vote [agenda item 14 *(c)*].

Strengthening basic principles of judicial conduct

The Economic and Social Council,

Recalling the Charter of the United Nations, in which Member States affirm, inter alia, their determination to establish conditions under which justice can be maintained to achieve international cooperation in promoting and encouraging respect for human rights and fundamental freedoms without any discrimination,

Recalling also the Universal Declaration of Human Rights, which enshrines in particular the principles of equality before the law, the presumption of innocence and the right to a fair and public hearing by a competent, independent and impartial tribunal established by law,

Recalling further the International Covenant on Economic, Social and Cultural Rights and the International Covenant on Civil and Political Rights, which both guarantee the exercise of those rights, and recalling that the International Covenant on Civil and Political Rights further guarantees the right to be tried without undue delay,

Recalling the United Nations Convention against Corruption, which, in article 11, obliges States parties, in accordance with the fundamental principles of their legal systems and without prejudice to judicial independence, to take measures to strengthen integrity and to prevent opportunities for corruption among members of the judiciary, including rules with respect to the conduct of members of the judiciary,

Convinced that corruption of members of the judiciary undermines the rule of law and affects public confidence in the judicial system,

Convinced also that the integrity, independence and impartiality of the judiciary are essential prerequisites for the effective protection of human rights and economic development,

Recalling General Assembly resolutions 40/32 of 29 November 1985 and 40/146 of 13 December 1985, in which the Assembly endorsed the Basic Principles on the Independence of the Judiciary, adopted by the Seventh United Nations Congress on the Prevention of Crime and the Treatment of Offenders, held in Milan, Italy, from 26 August to 6 September 1985,

Recalling also the recommendations adopted by the Ninth United Nations Congress on the Prevention of Crime and the Treatment of Offenders, held in Cairo from 29 April to 8 May 1995, concerning the independence and impartiality of the judiciary and the proper functioning of prosecutorial and legal services in the field of criminal justice,

Recalling further that in 2000 the Centre for International Crime Prevention of the Secretariat invited a group of chief justices of the common law tradition to develop a concept of judicial integrity, consistent with the principle of judicial independence, which would have the potential to have a positive impact on the standard of judicial conduct and to raise the level of public confidence in the rule of law,

Recalling the second meeting of the Judicial Group on Strengthening Judicial Integrity, held in 2001 in Bangalore, India, at which the chief justices recognized the need for universally acceptable standards of judicial integrity and drafted the Bangalore Principles of Judicial Conduct,

Recalling also that the Judicial Group on Strengthening Judicial Integrity thereafter conducted extensive consultations with judiciaries of more than eighty countries of all legal traditions, leading to the endorsement of the Bangalore Principles of Judicial Conduct by various judicial forums, including a Round Table Meeting of Chief Justices, held in The Hague on 25 and 26 November 2002, which was attended by senior judges of the civil law tradition as well as judges of the International Court of Justice,

Recalling further Commission on Human Rights resolution 2003/43 of 23 April 2003, on the independence and impartiality of the judiciary, jurors and assessors and the independence of lawyers, in which the Commission took note of the Bangalore Principles of Judicial Conduct and brought those principles to the attention of Member States, relevant United Nations organs and intergovernmental and non-governmental organizations for their consideration,

Recalling Commission on Human Rights resolution 2003/39 of 23 April 2003, on the integrity of the judicial system, in which the Commission emphasized the integrity of the judicial system as an essential prerequisite for the protection of human rights and for ensuring that there was no discrimination in the administration of justice,

1. *Invites* Member States, consistent with their domestic legal systems, to encourage their judiciaries to take into consideration the Bangalore Principles of Judicial Conduct, annexed to the present resolution, when reviewing or developing rules with respect to the professional and ethical conduct of members of the judiciary;

2. *Emphasizes* that the Bangalore Principles of Judicial Conduct represent a further development and are complementary to the Basic Principles on the Independence of the Judiciary, endorsed by the General Assembly in its resolutions 40/32 and 40/146;

3. *Acknowledges* the important work carried out by the Judicial Group on Strengthening Judicial Integrity under the auspices of the United Nations Office on Drugs and Crime, as well as other international and regional judicial forums that contribute to the development and dissemination of standards and measures to strengthen judicial independence, impartiality and integrity;

4. *Requests* the United Nations Office on Drugs and Crime, within available extrabudgetary resources, not excluding the use of existing resources from the regular budget of the Office and in particular through its Global Programme against Corruption, to continue to support the work of the Judicial Group on Strengthening Judicial Integrity;

5. *Expresses its appreciation* to Member States that have made voluntary contributions to the United Nations Office on Drugs and Crime in support of the work of the Judicial Group on Strengthening Judicial Integrity;

6. *Invites* Member States to make voluntary contributions, as appropriate, to the United Nations Crime Prevention and Criminal Justice Fund to support the Judicial Group on Strengthening Judicial Integrity, and to continue to provide, through the Global Programme against Corruption, technical assistance to developing countries and countries with economies in transition, upon request, to strengthen the integrity and capacity of their judiciaries;

7. *Also invites* Member States to submit to the Secretary-General their views regarding the Bangalore Principles of Judicial Conduct and to suggest revisions, as appropriate;

8. *Requests* the United Nations Office on Drugs and Crime, within available extrabudgetary resources, not excluding the use of existing resources from the regular budget of the Office, to convene an open-ended intergovernmental expert group, in cooperation with the Judicial Group on Strengthening Judicial Integrity and other international and regional judicial forums, to develop a technical guide to be used in providing technical assistance aimed at strengthening judicial integrity and capacity, as well as a commentary on the Bangalore Principles of Judicial Conduct, taking into account the views expressed and the revisions suggested by Member States;

9. *Requests* the Secretary-General to report to the Commission on Crime Prevention and Criminal Justice at its sixteenth session on the implementation of the present resolution.

Annex

Bangalore Principles of Judicial Conduct

WHEREAS the Universal Declaration of Human Rights recognizes as fundamental the principle that everyone is entitled in full equality to a fair and public hearing by an independent and impartial tribunal, in the determination of rights and obligations and of any criminal charge,

WHEREAS the International Covenant on Civil and Political Rights guarantees that all persons shall be equal before the courts and that in the determination of any criminal charge or of rights and obligations in a suit at law, everyone shall be entitled, without undue delay, to a fair and public hearing by a competent, independent and impartial tribunal established by law,

WHEREAS the foregoing fundamental principles and rights are also recognized or reflected in regional human rights instruments, in domestic constitutional, statutory and common law, and in judicial conventions and traditions,

WHEREAS the importance of a competent, independent and impartial judiciary to the protection of human rights is given emphasis by the fact that the implementation of all the other rights ultimately depends upon the proper administration of justice,

WHEREAS a competent, independent and impartial judiciary is likewise essential if the courts are to fulfil their role in upholding constitutionalism and the rule of law,

WHEREAS public confidence in the judicial system and in the moral authority and integrity of the judiciary is of the utmost importance in a modern democratic society,

WHEREAS it is essential that judges, individually and collectively, respect and honour judicial office as a public trust and strive to enhance and maintain confidence in the judicial system,

WHEREAS the primary responsibility for the promotion and maintenance of high standards of judicial conduct lies with the judiciary in each country,

AND WHEREAS the Basic Principles on the Independence of the Judiciary are designed to secure and promote the independence of the judiciary and are addressed primarily to States,

THE FOLLOWING PRINCIPLES are intended to establish standards for ethical conduct of judges. They are designed to provide guidance to judges and to afford the judiciary a framework for regulating judicial conduct. They are also intended to assist members of the executive and the legislature, and lawyers and the public in general, to better understand and support the judiciary. These principles presuppose that judges are accountable for their conduct to appropriate institutions established to maintain judicial standards, which are themselves independent and impartial, and are intended to supplement and not to derogate from existing rules of law and conduct that bind the judge.

Value 1
Independence

Principle

Judicial independence is a prerequisite to the rule of law and a fundamental guarantee of a fair trial. A judge shall therefore uphold and exemplify judicial independence in both its individual and institutional aspects.

Application

1.1. A judge shall exercise the judicial function independently on the basis of the judge's assessment of the facts and in accordance with a conscientious understanding of the law, free of any extraneous influences, inducements, pressures, threats or interference, direct or indirect, from any quarter or for any reason.

1.2. A judge shall be independent in relation to society in general and in relation to the particular parties to a dispute that the judge has to adjudicate.

1.3. A judge shall not only be free from inappropriate connections with, and influence by, the executive and legislative branches of government, but must also appear to a reasonable observer to be free therefrom.

1.4. In performing judicial duties, a judge shall be independent of judicial colleagues in respect of decisions that the judge is obliged to make independently.

1.5. A judge shall encourage and uphold safeguards for the discharge of judicial duties in order to maintain and enhance the institutional and operational independence of the judiciary.

1.6. A judge shall exhibit and promote high standards of judicial conduct in order to reinforce public confidence in the judiciary, which is fundamental to the maintenance of judicial independence.

Value 2
Impartiality

Principle

Impartiality is essential to the proper discharge of the judicial office. It applies not only to the decision itself but also to the process by which the decision is made.

Application

2.1. A judge shall perform his or her judicial duties without favour, bias or prejudice.

2.2. A judge shall ensure that his or her conduct, both in and out of court, maintains and enhances the confidence of the public, the legal profession and litigants in the impartiality of the judge and of the judiciary.

2.3. A judge shall, as far as is reasonable, so conduct himself or herself as to minimize the occasions on which it will be necessary for the judge to be disqualified from hearing or deciding cases.

2.4. A judge shall not knowingly, while a proceeding is before, or could come before, the judge, make any comment that might reasonably be expected to affect the outcome of such proceeding or impair the manifest fairness of the process, nor shall the judge make any comment in public or otherwise that might affect the fair trial of any person or issue.

2.5. A judge shall disqualify himself or herself from participating in any proceedings in which the judge is unable to decide the matter impartially or in which it may appear to a reasonable observer that the judge is unable to decide the matter impartially. Such proceedings include, but are not limited to, instances where:

(a) The judge has actual bias or prejudice concerning a party or personal knowledge of disputed evidentiary facts concerning the proceedings;

(b) The judge previously served as a lawyer or was a material witness in the matter in controversy; or

(c) The judge, or a member of the judge's family, has an economic interest in the outcome of the matter in controversy;

provided that disqualification of a judge shall not be required if no other tribunal can be constituted to deal with the case or, because of urgent circumstances, failure to act could lead to a serious miscarriage of justice.

Value 3
Integrity

Principle

Integrity is essential to the proper discharge of the judicial office.

Application

3.1. A judge shall ensure that his or her conduct is above reproach in the view of a reasonable observer.

3.2. The behaviour and conduct of a judge must reaffirm the people's faith in the integrity of the judiciary. Justice must not merely be done but must also be seen to be done.

Value 4
Propriety

Principle

Propriety, and the appearance of propriety, are essential to the performance of all of the activities of a judge.

Application

4.1. A judge shall avoid impropriety and the appearance of impropriety in all of the judge's activities.

4.2. As a subject of constant public scrutiny, a judge must accept personal restrictions that might be viewed as burdensome by the ordinary citizen and should do so freely and willingly. In particular, a judge shall conduct himself or herself in a way that is consistent with the dignity of the judicial office.

4.3. A judge shall, in his or her personal relations with individual members of the legal profession who practise regularly in the judge's court, avoid situations that might reasonably give rise to the suspicion or appearance of favouritism or partiality.

4.4. A judge shall not participate in the determination of a case in which any member of the judge's family represents a litigant or is associated in any manner with the case.

4.5. A judge shall not allow the use of the judge's residence by a member of the legal profession to receive clients or other members of the legal profession.

4.6. A judge, like any other citizen, is entitled to freedom of expression, belief, association and assembly, but, in exercising such rights, a judge shall always conduct himself or herself in such a manner as to preserve the dignity of the judicial office and the impartiality and independence of the judiciary.

4.7. A judge shall inform himself or herself about the judge's personal and fiduciary financial interests and shall make reasonable efforts to be informed about the financial interests of members of the judge's family.

4.8. A judge shall not allow the judge's family, social or other relationships improperly to influence the judge's judicial conduct and judgement as a judge.

4.9. A judge shall not use or lend the prestige of the judicial office to advance the private interests of the judge, a member of the judge's family or of anyone else, nor shall a judge convey or permit others to convey the impression that anyone is in a special position improperly to influence the judge in the performance of judicial duties.

4.10. Confidential information acquired by a judge in the judge's judicial capacity shall not be used or disclosed by the judge for any other purpose not related to the judge's judicial duties.

4.11. Subject to the proper performance of judicial duties, a judge may:

(a) Write, lecture, teach and participate in activities concerning the law, the legal system, the administration of justice or related matters;

(b) Appear at a public hearing before an official body concerned with matters relating to the law, the legal system, the administration of justice or related matters;

(c) Serve as a member of an official body, or other government commission, committee or advisory body, if such membership is not inconsistent with the perceived impartiality and political neutrality of a judge; or

(d) Engage in other activities if such activities do not detract from the dignity of the judicial office or otherwise interfere with the performance of judicial duties.

4.12. A judge shall not practise law while the holder of judicial office.

4.13. A judge may form or join associations of judges or participate in other organizations representing the interests of judges.

4.14. A judge and members of the judge's family shall neither ask for, nor accept, any gift, bequest, loan or favour in relation to anything done or to be done or omitted to be done by the judge in connection with the performance of judicial duties.

4.15. A judge shall not knowingly permit court staff or others subject to the judge's influence, direction or authority to ask for, or accept, any gift, bequest, loan or favour in relation to anything done or to be done or omitted to be done in connection with his or her duties or functions.

4.16. Subject to law and to any legal requirements of public disclosure, a judge may receive a token gift, award or benefit as appropriate to the occasion on which it is made provided that such gift, award or benefit might not reasonably be perceived as intended to influence the judge in the performance of judicial duties or otherwise give rise to an appearance of partiality.

Value 5
Equality

Principle

Ensuring equality of treatment to all before the courts is essential to the due performance of the judicial office.

Application

5.1. A judge shall be aware of, and understand, diversity in society and differences arising from various sources, including but not limited to race, colour, sex, religion, national origin, caste, disability, age, marital status, sexual orientation, social and economic status and other like causes ("irrelevant grounds").

5.2. A judge shall not, in the performance of judicial duties, by words or conduct, manifest bias or prejudice towards any person or group on irrelevant grounds.

5.3. A judge shall carry out judicial duties with appropriate consideration for all persons, such as the parties, witnesses, lawyers, court staff and judicial colleagues, without differentiation on any irrelevant ground, immaterial to the proper performance of such duties.

5.4. A judge shall not knowingly permit court staff or others subject to the judge's influence, direction or control to differentiate between persons concerned, in a matter before the judge, on any irrelevant ground.

5.5. A judge shall require lawyers in proceedings before the court to refrain from manifesting, by words or conduct, bias or prejudice based on irrelevant grounds, except such as are legally relevant to an issue in proceedings and may be the subject of legitimate advocacy.

Value 6
Competence and diligence

Principle

Competence and diligence are prerequisites to the due performance of judicial office.

Application

6.1. The judicial duties of a judge take precedence over all other activities.

6.2. A judge shall devote the judge's professional activity to judicial duties, which include not only the performance of judicial functions and responsibilities in court and the making of decisions, but also other tasks relevant to the judicial office or the court's operations.

6.3. A judge shall take reasonable steps to maintain and enhance the judge's knowledge, skills and personal qualities necessary for the proper performance of judicial duties, taking advantage for that purpose of the training and other facilities that should be made available, under judicial control, to judges.

6.4. A judge shall keep himself or herself informed about relevant developments of international law, including international conventions and other instruments establishing human rights norms.

6.5. A judge shall perform all judicial duties, including the delivery of reserved decisions, efficiently, fairly and with reasonable promptness.

6.6. A judge shall maintain order and decorum in all proceedings before the court and be patient, dignified and courteous in relation to litigants, jurors, witnesses, lawyers and others with whom the judge deals in an official capacity. The judge shall require similar conduct of legal representatives, court staff and others subject to the judge's influence, direction or control.

6.7. A judge shall not engage in conduct incompatible with the diligent discharge of judicial duties.

Implementation

By reason of the nature of judicial office, effective measures shall be adopted by national judiciaries to provide mechanisms to implement these principles if such mechanisms are not already in existence in their jurisdictions.

Definitions

In this statement of principles, unless the context otherwise permits or requires, the following meanings shall be attributed to the words used:

"Court staff" includes the personal staff of the judge, including law clerks;

"Judge" means any person exercising judicial power, however designated;

"Judge's family" includes a judge's spouse, son, daughter, son-in-law, daughter-in-law and any other close relative or person who is a companion or employee of the judge and who lives in the judge's household;

"Judge's spouse" includes a domestic partner of the judge or any other person of either sex in a close personal relationship with the judge.

Other crime prevention and criminal justice issues

Second World Summit of Attorneys General and General Prosecutors, Chief Prosecutors and Ministers of Justice

Pursuant to Economic and Social Council resolution 2004/30 [YUN 2004, p. 1138], the Secretary-General submitted to the Commission on Crime Prevention and Criminal Justice the recommendations adopted by the Second World Summit of Attorneys General and General Prosecutors, Chief Prosecutors and Minsiters of Justice (Doha, Qatar, 14-16 November 2005) [E/CN.15/2006/17]. The recommendations pertained to the requirements of prosecution services to deal with new and sophisticated forms of crime, particularly cybercrime and economic and financial crimes; strategies and practical measures to strengthen the capacity of prosecution services in dealing with transnational organized crime, terrorism and corruption; the role of prosecutors in promoting and strengthening the rule of law; and measures and mechanisms to strengthen international cooperation among prosecution services.

Human resources development

UN research and training institutes

UN Institute for Training and Research

A report [A/61/14] of the Executive Director of the United Nations Institute for Training and Research (UNITAR) described the Institute's activities during the period from 1 January 2004 to 31 December 2005. He reviewed the UNITAR programmes in international affairs, peace and security, which included 33 short-duration training activities in Geneva, Vienna and Nairobi, benefiting over 500 diplomats from 122 Member States; sustainable development and environment, which supported, among other things, 250 country projects involving roughly 4,000 beneficiaries; decentralized cooperation, which aimed to ensure a sustainable environment by enhancing the capacities of local authorities, parliamentarians and local partners to achieve sustainable development; debt and financial management training programme, which provided capacity-building through seminars, workshops and e-learning courses in the legal aspects of debt, financial management and negotiation; information and communication technologies, which included the development of innovative partnerships between UNITAR, the private sector and academic networks; and activities through its four outposted offices in New York, Hiroshima (Japan), Port Harcourt (Nigeria), and Dushanbe (Tajikistan). The report also reviewed UNITAR mandate, training methodologies, partnerships and networks, as well as monitoring and evaluation.

On 20 December, the General Assembly took note of the Executive Director's report and decided to consider, in accordance with its resolution 60/213 [YUN 2005, p. 1243], the harmonization of the submission of the report and the Secretary-General's report to thc Assembly at its sixty-second (2007) session (**decision 61/542**).

United Nations University

The Council of the United Nations University (UNU), at its fifty-second session (Tokyo, Japan, 5-9 December), reviewed UNU activities, approved the academic programme and budget for the 2006-2007 biennium and a fund-raising strategy. It considered a report on the evaluation of the UNU financial assistance programme for students from developing countries, as well as the Rector's response to the recommendations contained in the evaluation report. The Council took note of progress reports on the preparation of strategic options to increase the University's impact in Africa, the status of implementation of the strategic plan for follow-up to the World Summit on Sustainable Development [YUN 2002, p. 821] and the UNU initiative on education for sustainable development.

During 2005, UNU celebrated the thirtieth anniversary of its establishment, in Tokyo, and the twentieth anniversary of the World Institute for Development Economic Research, in Helsinki. Its Institute for New Technologies (UNU-INTECH) and the Maastricht Economic Research Centre on Innovation and Technology (MERIT) completed the formal integration of their academic activities, to form UNU-MERIT in January 2006. The University's Institute for Environment and Human Security (UNU-EHS) implemented cooperative ventures with the International Institute for Geo-Information Science and Earth Observation, in Enschede, the Netherlands. UNU and the University of Namibia agreed to designate the University of Namibia's Marine and Coastal Resources Research Centre as an operating unit of the UNU Institute for Natural Resources in Africa (UNU-INRA). The University began the search for a new Rector to assume the post in September 2006 upon the retirement of Hans van Ginkel.

The Secretary-General provided a comprehensive report [A/61/31] on UNU activities in 2005. In its annual report for 2006, UNU reported that it had signed an agreement with the Malaysian Ministry of Higher Education to establish the International Institute for Global Health (UNU-IIGH) in Kuala Lumpur.

At its fifty-third session, the UNU Council adopted the draft UNU Strategic Directions 2007-2010 and approved the terms of reference for an evaluation on the University. It also approved a panel of names proposed by the Nominating Council for the selection of a successor to the current Rector, Hans van Ginkel, which was transmitted to the Secretary-General and the UNESCO Director-General for final selection in 2007.

GENERAL ASSEMBLY ACTION

On 20 December [meeting 83], the General Assembly, on the recommendation of the Second Committee [A/61/428/Add.1 & Corr.1], adopted **resolution 61/216** without vote [agenda item 59 *(a)*].

United Nations University

The General Assembly,

Recalling its previous resolutions on the United Nations University, including resolution 59/253 of 22 December 2004,

Having considered the report of the Council of the United Nations University,

1. *Takes note* of the continuing efforts of the United Nations University and its research and training centres and programmes to generate and share knowledge to address the pressing global problems of human survival, development and welfare as set out in the Charter of the University, and encourages the University to intensify those efforts;

2. *Expresses its deep gratitude and appreciation* for the dedication and commitment, as well as the accomplishments, of Professor Hans van Ginkel during his tenure as Under-Secretary-General and Rector of the United Nations University, allowing the University to significantly grow and progress as an institution in the past ten years;

3. *Expresses its deep appreciation* to Japan and the other host countries of the University and its research and training centres and programmes, and to public and private entities, for the financial, intellectual and other contributions to enhancing the work of the University;

4. *Encourages* the University to intensify its communication and dialogue with Member States, including in particular its host countries, as well as joint activities with other relevant international organizations and educational networks to increase their awareness and understanding of its work, which is essential for strengthening the relevance and outreach of the University, and in this regard takes note with appreciation of the increased level of communication and cooperation between the Univer-

sity and the Permanent Missions to the United Nations, the Secretariat, non-governmental organizations and civil society entities in New York, and requests that such activities be continued and further strengthened;

5. *Notes with particular appreciation* the University's support of scholars and academic institutions in developing countries and the countries with economies in transition, including in particular young scholars, through its research and capacity and network development activities, highly appreciates the efforts of the University and its research and training centres and programmes in expanding their cooperative networks of institutions, academic associations and individual scholars worldwide and in developing innovative interdisciplinary programmes that produce concrete outcomes, and encourages the University to further expand those efforts;

6. *Welcomes* the diversification of the University's budgetary sources, and encourages the international community to provide voluntary contributions in order to ensure a sound funding base for the activities of the University;

7. *Notes with interest* the signing of the agreement to establish a new research and training centre, the United Nations University-International Institute for Global Health, in Kuala Lumpur, and encourages the University to continue its efforts to expand and strengthen its network of research and training centres and programmes in furtherance of the needs of developing countries;

8. *Requests* the Secretary-General to continue to encourage other bodies of the United Nations system to utilize more fully the capacity of the University for mobilizing a worldwide network of researchers to assist the United Nations, through research and capacity development programmes, in resolving pressing global problems, and to keep Member States informed of the progress;

9. *Requests* the University to make renewed efforts to identify the critical areas where University research is most needed by other United Nations organizations and to carry out research that yields effective outcomes contributing to policymaking in the United Nations system, and encourages the University to disseminate the outcome of its research more widely and to make it available in a readily accessible form;

10. *Takes note with appreciation* of the efforts made by the University to streamline and improve the administrative management at its headquarters in Japan, requests that such reform measures be continued to increase the efficiency and cost-effectiveness of the University's operations, and encourages the renewed efforts of the University to implement its projects in an efficient and cost-effective manner in order to make the best use of the resources placed at the disposal of the University;

11. *Takes note* of the full integration of activities of the United Nations University-Institute for New Technologies with the Maastricht Economic Research Institute on Innovation and Technology of Maastricht University and the subsequent renaming of the Institute as the United Nations University-Maastricht Economic and Social Research and Training Centre on Innovation and Technology;

12. *Takes note*, in particular, of the progress made by the University in forging cooperative links with the Department of Economic and Social Affairs of the Secretariat related to the Water Virtual Learning Centre and with the Department of Political Affairs of the Secretariat in relation to the research of the United Nations University-Programme for Comparative Regional Integration Studies on comparative regional integration;

13. *Takes note with appreciation* of the University's contributions to the World Conference on Disaster Reduction, held in Kobe, Japan, from 18 to 22 January 2005 and to the World Summit on the Information Society, held in Tunis from 16 to 18 November 2005;

14. *Welcomes* the planned external evaluation of the University after its thirtieth year of operation in the framework of its quality assurance procedures, and requests that the evaluation, which is to commence early in 2007, be undertaken to thoroughly review how and to what extent the University and its activities have met the original mission assigned to the University and be used as a means to strengthen the University's capacity development activities and its role as a think tank for the United Nations system;

15. *Decides* that, instead of being submitted in 2008, the report of the Council of the United Nations University and other reports on the work of the University shall be submitted biennially to the Economic and Social Council, rather than to the General Assembly for its consideration, beginning in 2009.

On the same day, the Assembly took note of the report of the Second Committee [A/61/428] on training and research (**decision 61/541**).

University for peace

In response to General Assembly resolution 58/12 [YUN 2003, p. 1162], the Secretary-General, in August [A/61/285], submitted a report on the development and implementation of the academic and professional training programmes of the Costa Rica-based University for Peace in fields related to peace and security. In addition to its eight master's degree programmes at headquarters, the University expanded its activities into different regions of the world, developing networks of partner academic and research institutions. It also developed a sharing knowledge for a peace programme, using information technologies to enable its materials to reach those who could not participate in face-to-face teaching. Although donor support had increased over the years, full implementation of the programmes depended on enhanced and sustained support. The University had demonstrated the capacity to fulfil its mandate by providing capacity-building to large numbers of young people, civil leaders and professionals to gain the knowledge and skills needed for the prevention, management and resolution of conflict. By the end of 2006, the

University would have achieved the targets established by its Council for its five-year revitalization programme.

GENERAL ASSEMBLY ACTION

On 14 December [meeting 79], the General Assembly, on the recommendation of the Fourth (Special Political and Decolonization) Committee [A/61/404], adopted **resolution 61/108** without vote [agenda item 28].

University for Peace

The General Assembly,

Recalling its resolution 58/12 of 10 November 2003, in which it recalled that, in its resolution 34/111 of 14 December 1979, it had approved the idea of establishing the University for Peace as a specialized international centre for higher education, research and the dissemination of knowledge relative to peace and its universal promotion within the United Nations system, and in which it also recalled its resolution 35/55 of 5 December 1980, in which it had approved the establishment of the University, as well as all preceding resolutions on this item,

Noting with appreciation the vigorous actions taken by the Secretary-General, in consultation with the Director-General of the United Nations Educational, Scientific and Cultural Organization and with the encouragement and support of the Government of Costa Rica, to revitalize the University,

Recognizing the significant progress made in the implementation of the five-year revitalization programme, leading to the achievement of the targets established by the Council of the University for Peace, by building high-quality programmes on subjects related to peace and security and extending them to different regions of the world through networks of partner academic and research institutions,

Noting with appreciation that the future development strategy of the University focuses on consolidating the progress already made in developing and conducting innovative academic and training programmes and at the same time strengthening its collaborative arrangement in different regions of the world and promoting the sharing knowledge for peace programme, including distance learning and dissemination of toolkits for teaching, with a view to strengthening education for peace,

Noting with satisfaction the activities directed towards expanding the University's educational and research programmes to Africa, Asia and the Pacific, Central Asia and Latin America and the Caribbean,

Also noting with satisfaction the progress made in the development of teaching programmes at the master's level, short courses, programmes to disseminate course materials and distance education and the establishment of a digital library on peace-related issues,

Noting that the University has placed special emphasis on the areas of conflict prevention, peacekeeping, peacebuilding and the peaceful settlement of disputes, and that it has launched academic and training programmes in the areas of democratic consensus-building and the techniques of peaceful settlement of conflicts,

Noting also that the University has launched a broad programme for building a culture of peace worldwide in the context of the efforts being made by the United Nations and the United Nations Educational, Scientific and Cultural Organization for the development and promotion of a culture of peace,

Noting with appreciation the intensifying collaboration between the University and organizations and agencies of the United Nations system, particularly the United Nations University, the United Nations Educational, Scientific and Cultural Organization, the Department of Political Affairs and the Department for Disarmament Affairs of the Secretariat, the United Nations Development Programme, the United Nations Institute for Training and Research and others,

Considering the importance of promoting education that fosters peaceful coexistence among people, including respect for the life, dignity and integrity of human beings, irrespective of their nationality, race, sex, religion or culture, as well as friendship and solidarity among peoples,

1. *Welcomes* the report of the Secretary-General outlining the progress made in revitalizing the University for Peace, especially in regard to implementation of the five-year programme of expansion and revitalization;

2. *Requests* the Secretary-General, in view of the important work of the University and its potential role in developing new concepts and approaches to security through research, training and dialogue in order to respond effectively to emerging threats to peace, to consider ways to further strengthen cooperation between the United Nations and the University, and invites the University to consider ways to further strengthen its programmes and activities for cooperation with and capacity-building for Member States in the areas of conflict prevention, conflict resolution and peacebuilding;

3. *Also requests* the Secretary-General to continue using the services of the University as part of his conflict-resolution and peacebuilding efforts, in providing training to staff in building their capacities in this area and in the promotion of the Declaration and the Programme of Action on a Culture of Peace;

4. *Encourages* Member States, intergovernmental bodies, non-governmental organizations and interested individuals to contribute to the programmes and core budget of the University to enable it to continue to perform its valuable work;

5. *Invites* Member States to accede to the International Agreement for the Establishment of the University for Peace, thereby demonstrating their support for an educational institution devoted to the promotion of a universal culture of peace;

6. *Decides* to include in the provisional agenda of its sixty-fourth session the item entitled "University for Peace", and requests the Secretary-General to submit to the General Assembly at that session a report on the work of the University.

Education for all

In accordance with General Assembly resolution 59/149 [YUN 2004, p. 1142], the Secretary-General transmitted, in July [A/61/151], a report by the Director-General of the United Nations Educational, Scientific and Cultural Organization (UNESCO) on the implementation of the International Plan of Action for the United Nations Literacy Decade (2003-2012), proclaimed by the Assembly in resolution 56/116 [YUN 2001, p. 1052]. The report, which covered the period 2005-2006, reviewed the global literacy situation based on data provided by the UNESCO Institute for Statistics and the *EFA Global Monitoring Report: Literacy for Life, 2006*. It examined the evolving international context and the relation between the Literacy Decade and other international education and development frameworks. It reported the findings of a questionnaire sent by the UNESCO secretariat in December 2005 and February 2006 to Member States, UN agencies and non-governmental organizations. The report also drew attention to challenges and the way forward, and reviewed reports from some UN system agencies, concluding with consideration of the available tools to assess commitment and progress.

The Director-General recommended that efforts by all Literacy Decade stakeholders should be strengthened. To encourage such actions, Member States should increase their political commitment and financial support to addressing literacy challenges and achieving the Decade's goals, recognizing that the lack of such commitment and support had a negative impact on development as a whole, and more specifically on socio-economic growth and poverty eradication. Member States should make further efforts to enhance partnerships with all Literacy Decade stakeholders. To that end, they should develop and implement integrated education policies and programmes, giving priority to literacy throughout formal and non-formal education. The international community should support those efforts, which should be aligned with other international and country-led initiatives, such as the MDGs. UNESCO should prepare and conduct a mid-Decade review, in collaboration with all Literacy Decade partners during 2007 and 2008, the results of which should be submitted to the Assembly in 2008.

GENERAL ASSEMBLY ACTION

On 19 December [meeting 81], the General Assembly, on the recommendation of the Third (Social, Humanitarian and Cultural) Committee [A/61/437 & Corr.1], adopted **resolution 61/140** without vote [agenda item 60 *(c)*].

United Nations Literacy Decade: education for all

The General Assembly,

Recalling its resolution 56/116 of 19 December 2001, by which it proclaimed the ten-year period beginning on 1 January 2003 the United Nations Literacy Decade, its resolution 57/166 of 18 December 2002, in which it welcomed the International Plan of Action for the United Nations Literacy Decade, and its resolution 59/149 of 20 December 2004,

Recalling also the United Nations Millennium Declaration, in which Member States resolved to ensure that, by 2015, children everywhere, boys and girls alike, will be able to complete a full course of primary schooling and that girls and boys will have equal access to all levels of education, which requires a renewed commitment to promote literacy for all,

Reaffirming the emphasis placed by the 2005 World Summit on the critical role of both formal and informal education in the achievement of poverty eradication and other development goals as envisaged in the Millennium Declaration, in particular basic education and training for eradicating illiteracy, and the need to strive for expanded secondary and higher education as well as vocational education and technical training, especially for girls and women, the creation of human resources and infrastructure capabilities and the empowerment of those living in poverty,

Reaffirming also that a basic education is crucial to nation-building, that literacy for all is at the heart of basic education for all and that creating literate environments and societies is essential for achieving the goals of eradicating poverty, reducing child mortality, curbing population growth, achieving gender equality and ensuring sustainable development, peace and democracy,

Convinced that literacy is crucial to the acquisition by every child, youth and adult of the essential life skills that will enable them to address the challenges that they can face in life and represents an essential step in basic education, which is an indispensable means for effective participation in the societies and economies of the twenty-first century,

Affirming that the realization of the right to education, especially for girls, contributes to the promotion of gender equality and the eradication of poverty,

Welcoming the considerable efforts that have been made to address the objectives of the Decade at various levels,

Noting with deep concern that 771 million adults over the age of 15 lack basic literacy skills worldwide and about 100 million children of primary school age are still not enrolled in primary schools, that the issue of illiteracy may not be sufficiently high on national agendas to generate the kind of political and economic support required to address global illiteracy challenges and that the world is unlikely to meet those challenges if the present trends continue,

Deeply concerned about the persistence of the gender gap in education, which is reflected by the fact that nearly two thirds of the world's adult illiterates are women,

1. *Takes note* of the report of the Director-General of the United Nations Educational, Scientific and Cul-

tural Organization on the implementation of the International Plan of Action for the United Nations Literacy Decade;

2. *Welcomes* the efforts made so far by Member States and the international community in implementing the International Plan of Action;

3. *Appeals* to all Governments to develop reliable literacy data and information and to further reinforce political will, mobilize adequate national resources, develop more inclusive policymaking environments and devise innovative strategies for reaching the poorest and most marginalized groups and for seeking alternative formal and non-formal approaches to learning with a view to achieving the goals of the Decade;

4. *Urges* all Governments to take the lead in coordinating the activities of the Decade at the national level, bringing all relevant national actors together in a sustained dialogue and collaborative action on policy formulation, implementation and evaluation of literacy efforts;

5. *Appeals* to all Governments and professional organizations to strengthen national and professional educational institutions in their countries with a view to expanding their capacity and promoting the quality of education, with particular focus on literacy;

6. *Appeals* to all Governments and to economic and financial organizations and institutions, both national and international, to lend greater financial and material support to the efforts to increase literacy and achieve the goals of Education for All and those of the Decade, through, inter alia, the 20/20 initiative, as appropriate;

7. *Invites* Member States, the specialized agencies and other organizations of the United Nations system, as well as relevant intergovernmental and non-governmental organizations, to intensify their efforts to implement effectively the International Plan of Action and to integrate substantially those efforts in the Education for All process and other initiatives and activities of the United Nations Educational, Scientific and Cultural Organization and within the framework of the internationally agreed development goals, including those contained in the United Nations Millennium Declaration;

8. *Requests* the United Nations Educational, Scientific and Cultural Organization to reinforce its lead role in coordinating and catalysing the activities of the Decade at the regional and international levels, prepare and conduct the mid-Decade review in collaboration with all Decade partners during 2007 and 2008 and submit its results to the General Assembly;

9. *Invites* Member States and the relevant intergovernmental and non-governmental organizations to take an active part in the preparation and organization of high-level regional conferences, scheduled to be held in 2007-2008 in Qatar, Azerbaijan, Mali, Costa Rica and in Asia and the Pacific, aimed at marshalling high political commitment, building an effective partnership among all the stakeholders and mobilizing resources needed for achieving the goals of the Decade and the International Plan of Action;

10. *Requests* all relevant entities of the United Nations system, particularly the United Nations Educational, Scientific and Cultural Organization, in cooperation with national Governments, to take immediate, concrete steps to address the needs of countries with high illiteracy rates and/or with large populations of illiterate adults, with particular regard to women, including through programmes that promote low-cost and effective literacy provisions;

11. *Requests* the Secretary-General, in cooperation with the Director-General of the United Nations Educational, Scientific and Cultural Organization, to seek the views of Member States on the progress achieved in implementing their national programmes and plans of action for the Decade and to submit the next progress report on the implementation of the International Plan of Action to the General Assembly in 2008;

12. *Decides* to include in the provisional agenda of its sixty-third session, under the item entitled "Social development", the sub-item entitled "United Nations Literacy Decade: education for all".

Chapter X

Women

In 2006, United Nations efforts to promote the advancement of the status of women worldwide continued to be directed by the principles and guidelines of the Beijing Declaration and Platform for Action, adopted at the Fourth (1995) World Conference on Women, and the outcome of the General Assembly's twenty-third (2000) special session (Beijing+5), which reviewed progress in their implementation. In July, the Secretary-General transmitted to the General Assembly an in-depth study on all forms of violence against women, which provided recommendations for making measurable progress in preventing and eliminating violence against women. During the year, both the Economic and Social Council and the Assembly adopted resolutions on violence against women. The Assembly also adopted a resolution on trafficking in women and girls. Progress was achieved in gender mainstreaming, with the October endorsement by the UN System Chief Executives Board for Coordination of a draft system-wide policy on gender equality and the empowerment of women. In November, the Secretary-General's High-level Panel on UN System-wide Coherence in the areas of development, humanitarian assistance and the environment submitted its report entitled "Delivering as one", which addressed gender equality and recommended the establishment of a new UN gender architecture, with an Executive Director at the level of Under-Secretary-General to head the new proposed office.

At its fiftieth session in March, the Commission on the Status of Women convened a high-level panel discussion on the gender dimensions of international migration, a summary of which was transmitted to the Assembly for its high-level dialogue on international migration in September. The Commission recommended to the Council for adoption draft resolutions on women and girls in Afghanistan, assistance to Palestinian women, and the future organization and methods of the Commission's work. It also adopted resolutions on women and children taken hostage in armed conflict; women, the girl child and HIV/AIDS; and the advisability of appointing a special rapporteur on laws that discriminate against women. In July, the Economic and Social Council adopted a resolution on the organization and working methods of the Commission.

The United Nations Development Fund for Women continued to focus on the implementation of its multi-year funding framework, which targeted goals in four key areas: feminized poverty, violence against women, the spread of HIV/AIDS and gender equality in democratic governance and in post-conflict countries. Efforts by the United Nations Development Group Task Team on Gender Equality resulted in progress in the areas of performance indicators for country teams and an action learning process to devise UN models for gender equality programmes.

In 2006, the United Nations continued to strengthen and revitalize the International Research and Training Institute for the Advancement of Women (INSTRAW). In May, the Executive Board considered the report of its Subcommittee on the Resource Mobilization Strategy on a proposed fund-raising strategy, which had been submitted by the INSTRAW Director as part of the continuing efforts to strengthen the Institute.

Follow-up to the Fourth World Conference on Women and Beijing+5

During 2006, the Commission on the Status of Women, the Economic and Social Council and the General Assembly considered follow-up to the 1995 Fourth World Conference on Women, particularly the implementation of the Beijing Declaration and Platform for Action [YUN 1995, p. 1170] and the political declaration and further actions and initiatives to implement both instruments, adopted at the twenty-third (2000) special session of the Assembly (Beijing+5) by resolution S/23-2 [YUN 2000, p. 1084]. The Declaration had reaffirmed the commitment of Governments to the goals and objectives of the Fourth World Conference and to the implementation of the 12 critical areas of concern outlined in the Platform for Action: women and poverty; education and training of women; women and health; violence against women; women and armed conflict; women and the economy; women in power and decision-making; institutional mechanisms for the advancement of women; human rights of women; women and the media; women and the environment; and the girl child (see pp. 1333-1354 for action taken regarding the critical areas of concern). The issue of mainstreaming a gender perspective into UN policies and programmes continued to be addressed (see World Summit Outcome below and p. 1350).

World Summit Outcome implementation. In response to mandates in the 2005 World Summit Outcome document [YUN 2005, p. 48] to take further steps in mainstreaming a gender perspective in the Organization's policies and decisions, the Secretary-General, in his report on implementation of the outcome decisions [YUN 2005, p. 77], requested all UN entities to review and strengthen their gender mainstreaming programmes with a view to developing a system-wide policy and strategy on gender mainstreaming with related accountability mechanisms. In June 2006 [E/2006/83], the Secretary-General reported on progress achieved and UN system efforts to develop such an instrument, including consultations through the Inter-Agency Network on Women and Gender Equality (IANWGE) (see p. 1349) and the High-Level Committees on Programme and on Management of the UN System Chief Executives Board for Coordination (CEB). Consequently, a number of broad principles and practical elements were established, which would be further developed and refined through a system-wide survey of UN system capacity on gender mainstreaming and the findings of the High-level Panel on System-wide Coherence (see p. 1352).

The Secretary-General concluded that achieving gender equality and empowerment of women was central to realizing internationally agreed development goals, including the Millennium Development Goals (MDGs) [YUN 2000, p. 51], and to the pursuit of peace, human rights and poverty alleviation. In that context, UN entities had made significant progress in supporting Member States to attain gender equality. He highlighted the role of senior managers in creating an environment that supported gender mainstreaming and said that that element would form part of his compact with senior managers, where their management goals were set. A report on mainstreaming a gender perspective into all UN policies and programmes with a focus on training activities was issued in a separate document (see p. 1350).

On 24 July, the Economic and Social Council took note of the Secretary-General's report (**decision 2006/227**).

Report of Secretary-General. Pursuant to General Assembly resolution 60/140 [YUN 2005, p. 1248], the Secretary-General, in a July report [A/61/174], reviewed steps taken by the Assembly and its Main Committees during its sixtieth (2005) session to promote the achievement of gender equality through the gender mainstreaming strategy, by assessing the extent to which resolutions had taken into account gender perspectives or had made specific recommendations for action. The report also reviewed from a gender perspective the resolutions submitted by the Assembly's Main Committees as well as outcomes of major events, including the 2005 World Summit [YUN 2005, p. 47], the second phase of the World Summit on the Information Society [ibid., p. 933], and the High-Level Meeting on HIV/AIDS (New York, 31 May–2 June) (see p. 1410). It also assessed the extent to which reports and notes of the Secretary-General had supported attention to gender perspectives in the Assembly's deliberations and outcomes.

The Secretary-General concluded that gender perspectives had not been fully incorporated into resolutions adopted by the Assembly's Main Committees and into the outcomes of major events over the past year. Approximately 25 per cent of all resolutions included gender perspectives, and only half of those made gender-specific, action-oriented recommendations. As in previous years, resolutions submitted by the Second (Economic and Social) and Third (Social, Humanitarian and Cultural) Committees, as well as those adopted without reference to a Main Committee, paid greater attention to gender perspectives than other Assembly Committees. Similarly, increased attention was given to gender perspectives in documentation prepared for major events, and in reports submitted to the Second and Third Committees. Some correlation also existed between the inclusion of gender perspectives in reports of the Secretary-General and their integration into Assembly resolutions. The Secretary-General recommended that the Assembly should ensure the integration of gender perspectives in the implementation of and follow-up to major international conferences and summits by its subsidiary bodies, particularly the 2005 World Summit, as well as in the outcomes of the High-Level Dialogue on International Migration and Development (see p. 1261) and the high-level meeting on the midterm comprehensive global review of the implementation of the Programme of Action for the Least Developed Countries for the decade 2001-2010 (see p. 1011). The Assembly should also ensure gender mainstreaming in the preparation and follow-up to the special session on children (see p. 1361); encourage its Committees and subsidiary bodies to pay more attention to gender perspectives by including action-oriented recommendations on gender equality in their resolutions and decisions, and enhance monitoring of gender mainstreaming progress through systematic reviews; ensure that the Peacebuilding Commission and the Human Rights Council include gender perspectives in the development of their work methods and in consideration of the issues on their respective agendas; and request that reports submitted to the Assembly facilitate gender-sensitive policy development, based on qualitative gender analysis, with concrete conclusions and recommendations for further action.

GENERAL ASSEMBLY ACTION

On 19 December [meeting 81], the General Assembly, on the recommendation of the Third Committee [A/61/438], adopted **resolution 61/145** without vote [agenda item 61 *(b)*].

Follow-up to the Fourth World Conference on Women and full implementation of the Beijing Declaration and Platform for Action and the outcome of the twenty-third special session of the General Assembly

The General Assembly,

Recalling its previous resolutions on the question, including resolution 60/140 of 16 December 2005,

Deeply convinced that the Beijing Declaration and Platform for Action and the outcome of the twenty-third special session of the General Assembly entitled "Women 2000: gender equality, development and peace for the twenty-first century" are important contributions to the achievement of gender equality and the empowerment of women, and must be translated into effective action by all States, the United Nations system and other organizations concerned,

Reaffirming the commitments to gender equality and the advancement of women made at the Millennium Summit, the 2005 World Summit and other major United Nations summits, conferences and special sessions, and reaffirming also that their full, effective and accelerated implementation are integral to achieving the internationally agreed development goals, including the Millennium Development Goals,

Welcoming progress made towards achieving gender equality, but stressing that challenges and obstacles remain in the implementation of the Beijing Declaration and Platform for Action and the outcome of the twenty-third special session,

Recognizing that the responsibility for the implementation of the Beijing Declaration and Platform for Action and the outcome of the twenty-third special session rests primarily at the national level and that strengthened efforts are necessary in this respect, and reiterating that enhanced international cooperation is essential for full, effective and accelerated implementation,

Reaffirming that gender mainstreaming is a globally accepted strategy for promoting the empowerment of women and achieving gender equality by transforming structures of inequality, and reaffirming also the commitment to actively promote the mainstreaming of a gender perspective in the design, implementation, monitoring and evaluation of policies and programmes in all political, economic and social spheres, as well as the commitment to strengthen the capabilities of the United Nations system in the area of gender equality,

Bearing in mind the challenges and obstacles to changing discriminatory attitudes and gender stereotypes, and stressing that challenges and obstacles remain in the implementation of international standards and norms to address the inequality between men and women,

Expressing serious concern that the urgent goal of 50/50 gender balance in the United Nations system, especially at senior and policymaking levels, with full respect for the principle of equitable geographical distribution, in conformity with Article 101, paragraph 3, of the Charter of the United Nations, remains unmet, and that the representation of women in the United Nations system has remained almost static, with negligible improvement in some parts of the system, and in some cases has even decreased, as reflected in the report of the Secretary-General on the improvement of the status of women in the United Nations system,

Reaffirming the important role of women in the prevention and resolution of conflicts and in peacebuilding,

Reaffirming also the Declaration of Commitment on HIV/AIDS and the Political Declaration on HIV/AIDS adopted at the High-level Meeting on AIDS, held from 31 May to 2 June 2006, which, inter alia, acknowledged the feminization of the pandemic,

Noting with appreciation the report of the Secretary-General on the United Nations system-wide policy and strategy on gender mainstreaming,

1. *Takes note with appreciation* of the report of the Secretary-General on the measures taken and progress achieved in follow-up to the implementation of the Beijing Declaration and Platform for Action and the outcome of the twenty-third special session of the General Assembly;

2. *Reaffirms* the Beijing Declaration and Platform for Action adopted at the Fourth World Conference on Women, the outcome of the twenty-third special session of the General Assembly, and the declaration adopted on the occasion of the ten-year review and appraisal of the Beijing Declaration and Platform for Action at the forty-ninth session of the Commission on the Status of Women, and also reaffirms its commitment to their full, effective and accelerated implementation;

3. *Recognizes* that the implementation of the Beijing Declaration and Platform for Action and the fulfilment of the obligations under the Convention on the Elimination of All Forms of Discrimination against Women are mutually reinforcing in achieving gender equality and the empowerment of women, and in this regard welcomes the contributions of the Committee on the Elimination of Discrimination against Women to promoting the implementation of the Platform for Action and the outcome of the twenty-third special session, and invites States parties to the Convention to include information on measures taken to enhance implementation at the

national level in their reports to the Committee under article 18 of the Convention;

4. *Calls upon* Governments, the United Nations system and other international and regional organizations, and all sectors of civil society, including non-governmental organizations, as well as all women and men, to fully commit themselves and to intensify their contributions to the implementation of the Beijing Declaration and Platform for Action and the outcome of the twenty-third special session;

5. *Calls upon* States parties to comply fully with their obligations under the Convention on the Elimination of All Forms of Discrimination against Women and the Optional Protocol thereto and to take into consideration the concluding comments as well as the general recommendations of the Committee, urges States parties to consider limiting the extent of any reservations that they lodge to the Convention, to formulate any reservations as precisely and narrowly as possible, and to regularly review such reservations with a view to withdrawing them so as to ensure that no reservation is incompatible with the object and purpose of the Convention, also urges all Member States that have not yet ratified or acceded to the Convention to consider doing so, and calls upon those Member States that have not yet done so to consider signing, ratifying or acceding to the Optional Protocol;

6. *Encourages* all actors, inter alia, Governments, the United Nations system, other international organizations and civil society, to continue to support the work of the Commission on the Status of Women in fulfilling its central role in the follow-up to and review of the implementation of the Beijing Declaration and Platform for Action and the outcome of the twenty-third special session, and, as applicable, to carry out its recommendations, and welcomes, in this regard, the revised programme and methods of work of the Commission adopted at its fiftieth session, which give particular attention to the sharing of experiences, lessons learned and good practices in overcoming challenges to full implementation at the national and international levels as well as to the evaluation of progress in the implementation of priority themes;

7. *Calls upon* Governments, and the relevant funds and programmes, organs and specialized agencies of the United Nations system, within their respective mandates, and invites the international financial institutions and all relevant actors of civil society, including non-governmental organizations, to intensify action to achieve the full and effective implementation of the Beijing Declaration and Platform for Action and the outcome of the twenty-third special session, through, inter alia:

(a) Sustained political will and commitment at the national, regional and international levels to take further action, inter alia, through the mainstreaming of gender perspectives, including through the development and use of gender equality indicators, as applicable, in all policies and programmes and the promotion of full and equal participation and empowerment of women, and enhanced international cooperation;

(b) Promotion and protection of, and respect for, the full enjoyment of all human rights and fundamental freedoms by women and girls, including through the full implementation by States of their obligations under all human rights instruments, especially the Convention on the Elimination of All Forms of Discrimination against Women;

(c) Ensuring full representation and full and equal participation of women in political, social and economic decision-making as an essential condition for gender equality, and the empowerment of women and girls as a critical factor in the eradication of poverty;

(d) Respect for the rule of law, including legislation, and continued efforts to repeal laws and eradicate policies and practices that discriminate against women and girls, and to adopt laws and promote practices that protect their rights;

(e) Strengthening the role of national institutional mechanisms for gender equality and the advancement of women, including through financial and other appropriate assistance, to increase their direct impact on women;

(f) Undertaking socio-economic policies that promote sustainable development and ensure poverty eradication programmes, especially for women and girls, and strengthening the provision of and ensuring equal access to adequate, affordable and accessible public and social services, including education and training at all levels, as well as to all types of permanent and sustainable social protection/social security systems for women throughout their life cycle, and supporting national efforts in this regard;

(g) Taking further steps to ensure that the educational system and the media, to the extent consistent with freedom of expression, support the use of non-stereotypic, balanced and diverse images of women presenting them as key actors of the process of development as well as promoting non-discriminatory roles of women and men in their private and public life;

(h) Incorporating gender perspectives and human rights in health-sector policies and programmes, paying attention to women's specific needs and priorities, ensuring women's right to the highest attainable standards of physical and mental health and their access to affordable and adequate health-care services, including sexual, reproductive and maternal health care and lifesaving obstetric care, in accordance with the Programme of Action of the International Conference on Population and Development, and recognizing that the lack of economic empowerment and independence has increased women's vulnerability to a range of negative consequences, involving the risk of contracting HIV/AIDS, malaria, tuberculosis and other poverty-related diseases;

(i) Eliminating gender inequalities, gender-based abuse and violence; increasing the capacity of women and adolescent girls to protect themselves from the risk of HIV infection, principally through the provision of health care and services, including, inter alia, sexual and reproductive health, and the provision of full access to comprehensive information and education; ensuring that women can exercise their right to have control over, and decide freely and responsibly on, matters related to their sexuality in order to increase their ability to protect

themselves from HIV infection, including their sexual and reproductive health, free of coercion, discrimination and violence; and taking all necessary measures to create an enabling environment for the empowerment of women and to strengthen their economic independence, while, in this context, reiterating the importance of the role of men and boys in achieving gender equality;

(j) Strengthening national health and social infrastructures to reinforce measures to promote women's access to public health and taking action at the national level to address shortages of human resources for health, by, inter alia, developing, financing and implementing policies, within national development strategies, to improve training and management and effectively govern the recruitment, retention and deployment of health workers, including through international cooperation in this area;

(k) Adequate mobilization of resources at the national and international levels, as well as new and additional resources for the developing countries, including the least developed countries and countries with economies in transition, from all available funding mechanisms, including multilateral, bilateral and private sources;

(l) Increased partnerships among Governments, civil society and the private sector;

(m) Encouraging joint responsibility of men and boys with women and girls in the promotion of gender equality, based on the conviction that this is essential to the achievement of the goals of gender equality, development and peace;

(n) Removing structural and legal barriers, as well as eliminating stereotypic attitudes, to gender equality at work, promoting equal pay for equal work, and promoting the recognition of the value of women's unremunerated work, as well as developing and promoting policies that facilitate the reconciliation of employment and family responsibilities;

8. *Reaffirms* that States have an obligation to exercise due diligence to prevent violence against women and girls, provide protection to the victims and investigate, prosecute and punish the perpetrators of violence against women and girls, and that failure to do so violates and impairs or nullifies the enjoyment of their human rights and fundamental freedoms, and calls upon Governments to eliminate violence against women and girls and to elaborate and implement strategies in this regard;

9. *Strongly encourages* Governments to continue to support the role and contribution of civil society, in particular non-governmental organizations and women's organizations, in the implementation of the Beijing Declaration and Platform for Action and the outcome of the twenty-third special session;

10. *Resolves* to intensify the efforts of its Main Committees and subsidiary bodies to fully mainstream a gender perspective in their work, as well as in all United Nations summits, conferences and special sessions and in their follow-up processes;

11. *Requests* that reports of the Secretary-General submitted to the General Assembly and its subsidiary bodies systematically address gender perspectives through qualitative gender analysis and, where available, quantitative data, in particular through concrete conclusions and recommendations for further action on gender equality and the advancement of women, in order to facilitate gender-sensitive policy development;

12. *Urges* Governments and all entities of the United Nations system, including United Nations agencies, funds and programmes, and all relevant actors of civil society, to ensure the integration of gender perspectives in the implementation of and follow-up to all United Nations summits, conferences and special sessions and to give attention to gender perspectives in preparation for such events, including the upcoming special session on children;

13. *Reaffirms its call* to recently established subsidiary bodies, namely, the Peacebuilding Commission and the Human Rights Council, to integrate attention to gender perspectives into their consideration of all issues in their respective agendas, including the development of their methods of work;

14. *Encourages* the Economic and Social Council to continue its efforts to ensure that gender mainstreaming is an integral part of its work and that of its subsidiary bodies, through, inter alia, implementation of its agreed conclusions 1997/2 of 18 July 1997 and its resolution 2004/4 of 7 July 2004;

15. *Welcomes* the ministerial declaration of the high-level segment of the substantive session of 2006 of the Economic and Social Council, which, inter alia, underlined the need for the consistent use of a gender mainstreaming strategy for the creation of an enabling environment for women's participation in development, and calls upon all stakeholders to work to ensure the full incorporation of gender perspectives in the implementation of the declaration;

16. *Requests* all bodies that deal with programme and budgetary matters, including the Committee for Programme and Coordination, to ensure that programmes, plans and budgets visibly mainstream gender perspectives;

17. *Reaffirms* the primary and essential role of the General Assembly and the Economic and Social Council, as well as the central role of the Commission on the Status of Women, in promoting the advancement of women and gender equality;

18. *Also reaffirms* the commitment made at the 2005 World Summit to the full and effective implementation of Security Council resolution 1325 (2000) of 31 October 2000, while noting the sixth anniversary of its adoption and the open debates in the Council on women and peace and security;

19. *Urges* Governments and the United Nations system to take further steps to ensure the integration of a gender perspective and the full and equal participation of women in all efforts to promote peace and security, as well as to increase their role in decision-making at all levels, including through the development of national action plans and strategies;

20. *Calls upon* all parts of the United Nations system to continue to play an active role in ensuring the full,

effective and accelerated implementation of the Beijing Platform for Action and the outcome of the twenty-third special session, through, inter alia, the work of the Office of the Special Adviser on Gender Issues and Advancement of Women and the Division for the Advancement of Women and the maintenance of gender specialists in all entities of the United Nations system, as well as by ensuring that all personnel, especially in the field, receive training and appropriate follow-up, including tools, guidance and support, for accelerated gender mainstreaming, and reaffirms the need to strengthen the capabilities of the United Nations system in the area of gender;

21. *Requests* the Secretary-General to review and redouble his efforts to make progress towards achieving the goal of 50/50 gender balance at all levels in the Secretariat and throughout the United Nations system, with full respect for the principle of equitable geographical distribution, in conformity with Article 101, paragraph 3, of the Charter of the United Nations, considering in particular women from developing and least developed countries, from countries with economies in transition and from unrepresented or largely underrepresented Member States, and to ensure managerial and departmental accountability with respect to gender balance targets, and strongly encourages Member States to identify and regularly submit more women candidates for appointment to positions in the United Nations system, especially at more senior and policymaking levels;

22. *Also requests* the Secretary-General to continue to report annually to the General Assembly, under the item entitled "Advancement of women", as well as to the Commission on the Status of Women and the Economic and Social Council, on the follow-up to and progress made in the implementation of the Beijing Declaration and Platform for Action and the outcome of the twenty-third special session, with an assessment of progress in gender mainstreaming, including information on key achievements, lessons learned and good practices, and recommendations on further measures to enhance implementation.

Critical areas of concern

Violence against women

In compliance with General Assembly resolution 50/166 [YUN 1995, p. 1188], the Secretary-General transmitted a report [A/HRC/4/469-E/CN.6/2007/6] of the United Nations Development Fund for Women (UNIFEM) on its 2006 activities to eliminate violence against women and manage the UN Trust Fund in Support of Actions to Eliminate Violence against Women. Implementation of the 2005-2008 revised strategy for the Trust Fund [YUN 2005, p. 1251] continued, including measures to enhance UN system-wide involvement with the Fund, increase the resources available for end-violence work, and target the critical areas of support for national-level implementation and the intersection of violence against women with cross-cutting issues. In addition to convening global meetings, UNIFEM convened 12 subregional project appraisal committees. While efforts to increase the Trust Fund's resource base yielded significant results totalling $3.5 million during the year, demand for support greatly exceeded available funds, with $190 million in requests. Grant-making focused on supporting the implementation of laws, policies and plans to eliminate violence against women and innovative approaches for addressing the interlinkages between HIV/AIDS and violence against women. In 2006, the Trust Fund, under its eleventh grant-making cycle, provided $2.8 million to 28 initiatives in 20 countries, bringing the total awarded since its inception in 1997 to nearly $13 million in grants to 226 initiatives in more than 100 countries. The Secretary-General stressed the need to increase resources for end-violence work and recommended that States, donors and international organizations significantly increase their support to the Trust Fund.

In-depth study on violence against women

Pursuant to General Assembly resolution 58/185 [YUN 2003, p. 1172], the Secretary-General submitted a July report [A/61/122/Add.1 & Corr.1] containing an in-depth study on all forms of violence against women, which was prepared by the UN Division for the Advancement of Women to highlight the persistence and unacceptability of violence against women worldwide, strengthen the political commitment and joint efforts of stakeholders to prevent and eliminate violence against women, and identify ways to ensure more sustained and effective implementation of State obligations to address such violence and increase State accountability. The study provided an overview of the emergence of violence against women as a public concern and responsibility, discussed the context where such violence occurred and its causes, and reviewed forms and manifestations of violence, as well as its consequences and costs. Data availability, States' responsibilities and promising practices for addressing violence against women were also covered.

The study concluded that violence against women was a widespread and serious problem that affected the lives of countless women and hampered progress towards the achievement of equality, development and peace everwhere. It endangered women's lives, impeded the full development of their capabilities and was a violation of human rights, rooted in historically unequal power relations between men and women and the systemic discrimination against women that pervaded both the public and private spheres. While violence against women was universal and present in every society and culture, it took various forms and was experienced differently, shaped by the intersection of gender with other factors, such as race, ethnicity, class, age, sexual orientation, disability, nationality, legal status, religion and culture. Significant progress had been made over the past two decades in elaborating and agreeing on international standards and norms to address violence against women. States had a duty to prevent violence against women, investigate and prosecute such acts when they occurred, punish perpetrators, and provide remedies and redress to victims. However, those obligations were not being met and there was a significant gap between the international standards on violence against women and the commitment of political capital and resources to implement those standards. A series of recommendations for action at the national level focused on six key areas: securing gender equality and protecting women's human rights; exercising leadership to end violence against women; closing the gaps between international standards and national laws, policies and practices; strengthening the knowledge base on all forms of violence against women to inform policy and strategy development; building and sustaining multisectoral strategies, coordinated nationally and locally; and allocating adequate resources and funding. Recommendations directed at the international level centred on the leadership role of intergovernmental bodies and UN system entities, and on other aspects related to the UN system, such as coordination and institutional support, collection of data and research, as well as operational activities at the country level, including humanitarian assistance and peacekeeping missions.

In July [A/61/122], the Secretary-General transmitted the in-depth study (see above) to the General Assembly for consideration and action, and provided a summary of the mandate, preparatory process, content and recommendations of the study. The inputs and contributions of many actors were reflected in the study, including among others, 129 Member States, 150 States parties to the Convention on the Elimination of All Forms of Discrimination against Women (CEDAW) (see p. 1354), as well as UN system entities, human rights treaty bodies and special procedures, in particular, the Special Rapporteur on violence against women, its causes and consequences, and non-governmental organizations (NGOs) and other civil society actors. Voluntary contributions to support the preparation of the study had been received from eight Member States. The Secretary-General stressed the need for the elimination of violence against women to become a local, national, regional and global priority, and for the effective and accelerated implementation of actions to prevent and respond to such violence. He commended the study and its recommendations, which he said constituted a clear strategy for Member States and the UN system to make measurable progress in preventing and eliminating violence against women.

GENERAL ASSEMBLY ACTION

On 19 December [meeting 81], the General Assembly, on the recommendation of the Third Committee [A/61/438], adopted **resolution 61/143**, without vote [agenda item 61 *(a)*].

Intensification of efforts to eliminate all forms of violence against women

The General Assembly,

Reaffirming the obligation of all States to promote and protect all human rights and fundamental freedoms, and reaffirming also that discrimination on the basis of sex is contrary to the Charter of the United Nations, the Convention on the Elimination of All Forms of Discrimination against Women and other international human rights instruments, and that its elimination is an integral part of efforts towards the elimination of all forms of violence against women,

Reaffirming also the Declaration on the Elimination of Violence against Women, the Beijing Declaration and Platform for Action, the outcome of the twenty-third special session of the General Assembly entitled "Women 2000: gender equality, development and peace for the twenty-first century", and the declaration adopted at the forty-ninth session of the Commission on the Status of Women,

Reaffirming further the international commitments in the field of social development and to gender equality and the advancement of women made at the World Conference on Human Rights, the International Conference on Population and Development, the World Summit for Social Development and the World Conference against Racism, Racial Discrimination, Xenophobia and Related Intolerance, as well as those made in the United Nations Millennium Declaration and at the 2005 World Summit,

Recalling all its previous resolutions on the elimination of violence against women and on the in-depth study on all forms of violence against women, and Security Council resolution 1325(2000) of 31 October 2000 on women and peace and security,

Recalling also Commission on Human Rights resolution 2005/41 of 19 April 2005 on the elimination of violence against women,

Recalling further the inclusion of gender-related crimes and crimes of sexual violence in the Rome Statute of the International Criminal Court,

Recognizing that violence against women is rooted in historically unequal power relations between men and women and that all forms of violence against women seriously violate and impair or nullify the enjoyment by women of all human rights and fundamental freedoms and constitute a major impediment to the ability of women to make use of their capabilities,

Recognizing also that women's poverty and lack of empowerment, as well as their marginalization resulting from their exclusion from social policies and from the benefits of sustainable development, can place them at increased risk of violence,

Recognizing further that violence against women impedes the social and economic development of communities and States, as well as the achievement of the internationally agreed development goals, including the Millennium Development Goals,

Recognizing the serious immediate and long-term implications for health, including sexual and reproductive health, as well as an increased vulnerability to HIV/AIDS, and the negative impact on psychological, social and economic development that violence against women represents for individuals, families, communities and States,

Deeply concerned about the pervasiveness of violence against women and girls in all its forms and manifestations worldwide, and reiterating the need to intensify efforts to prevent and eliminate all forms of violence against women and girls throughout the world,

Taking note of the report of the Secretary-General on the in-depth study on all forms of violence against women, and having considered with interest the recommendations contained therein,

1. *Recognizes* that violence against women and girls persists in every country in the world as a pervasive violation of the enjoyment of human rights and a major impediment to achieving gender equality, development and peace;

2. *Welcomes* the efforts and important contributions at the local, national, regional and international levels to eliminate all forms of violence against women, and takes note with appreciation of the work done by the Committee on the Elimination of Discrimination against Women and the Special Rapporteur on violence against women, its causes and consequences;

3. *Stresses* that "violence against women" means any act of gender-based violence that results in, or is likely to result in, physical, sexual or psychological harm or suffering to women, including threats of such acts, coercion or arbitrary deprivation of liberty, whether occurring in public or in private life;

4. *Strongly condemns* all acts of violence against women and girls, whether these acts are perpetrated by the State, by private persons or by non-State actors, calls for the elimination of all forms of gender-based violence in the family, within the general community and where perpetrated or condoned by the State, and stresses the need to treat all forms of violence against women and girls as a criminal offence, punishable by law;

5. *Stresses* that it is important that States strongly condemn violence against women and refrain from invoking any custom, tradition or religious consideration to avoid their obligations with respect to its elimination as set out in the Declaration on the Elimination of Violence against Women;

6. *Stresses also* that challenges and obstacles remain in the implementation of international standards and norms to address the inequality between men and women and violence against women in particular, and pledges to intensify action to ensure their full and accelerated implementation;

7. *Stresses further* that States have the obligation to promote and protect all human rights and fundamental freedoms of women and girls and must exercise due diligence to prevent, investigate and punish the perpetrators of violence against women and girls and to provide protection to the victims, and that failure to do so violates and impairs or nullifies the enjoyment of their human rights and fundamental freedoms;

8. *Urges* States to take action to eliminate all forms of violence against women by means of a more systematic, comprehensive, multisectoral and sustained approach, adequately supported and facilitated by strong institutional mechanisms and financing, through national action plans, including those supported by international cooperation and, where appropriate, national development plans, including poverty eradication strategies and programme-based and sector-wide approaches, and to this end:

(a) To ensure that all human rights and fundamental freedoms are respected and protected;

(b) To consider ratifying or acceding to all human rights treaties, including, as a particular matter of priority, the Convention on the Elimination of All Forms of Discrimination against Women and the Optional Protocol thereto, limit the extent of any reservations that they lodge and regularly review such reservations with a view to withdrawing them so as to ensure that no reservation is incompatible with the object and purpose of the relevant treaty;

(c) To review and, where appropriate, revise, amend or abolish all laws, regulations, policies, practices and customs that discriminate against women or have a discriminatory impact on women, and ensure that provisions of multiple legal systems, where they exist, comply with international human rights obligations, commitments and principles, including the principle of non-discrimination;

(d) To exercise leadership to end all forms of violence against women and support advocacy in this regard at all levels, including at the local, national, regional and international levels, and by all sectors, especially by political and community leaders, as well as the public and private sectors, the media and civil society;

(e) To empower women, particularly poor women, through, inter alia, social and economic policies that guarantee them full and equal access to all levels of quality education and training and to affordable and adequate public and social services, as well as full and equal rights to own land and other property, and to take further appropriate measures to address the increasing rate of homelessness or inadequate housing for women in order to reduce their vulnerability to violence;

(f) To take positive measures to address structural causes of violence against women and to strengthen prevention efforts that address discriminatory practices and social norms, including with regard to women who need special attention in the development of policies to address violence, such as women belonging to minority groups, including those based on nationality, ethnicity, religion or language, indigenous women, migrant women, stateless women, women living in underdeveloped, rural or remote communities, homeless women, women in institutions or in detention, women with disabilities, elderly women, widows and women who are otherwise discriminated against;

(g) To ensure that diverse strategies that take into account the intersection of gender with other factors are developed in order to eradicate all forms of violence against women;

(h) To exercise due diligence to prevent all acts of violence against women, including by improving the safety of public environments;

(i) To end impunity for violence against women, by prosecuting and punishing all perpetrators, by ensuring that women have equal protection of the law and equal access to justice and by holding up to public scrutiny and eliminating those attitudes that foster, justify or tolerate violence;

(j) To strengthen national health and social infrastructure to reinforce measures to promote women's equal access to public health and address the health consequences of violence against women, including by providing support to victims;

(k) To recognize that gender inequalities and all forms of violence against women and girls increase their vulnerability to HIV/AIDS and ensure that women can exercise their right to have control over, and decide freely and responsibly on, matters related to their sexuality in order to increase their ability to protect themselves from HIV infection, including their sexual and reproductive health, free of coercion, discrimination and violence;

(l) To ensure that men and women and boys and girls have access to education and literacy programmes and are educated on gender equality and human rights, particularly women's rights and their responsibility to respect the rights of others, inter alia, by integrating women's rights into all appropriate curricula and by developing gender-sensitive teaching materials and classroom practices, especially for early childhood education;

(m) To provide training and capacity-building on gender equality and women's rights for, inter alia, health workers, teachers, law enforcement personnel, military personnel, social workers, the judiciary, community leaders and the media;

(n) To promote awareness and information campaigns on women's rights and the responsibility to respect them, including in rural areas, and encourage men and boys to speak out strongly against violence against women;

(o) To protect women and girls in situations of armed conflict, post-conflict settings and refugee and internally displaced persons settings, where women are at greater risk of being targeted for violence and where their ability to seek and receive redress is often restricted, bearing in mind that peace is inextricably linked with equality between women and men and development, that armed and other types of conflicts and terrorism and hostage-taking still persist in many parts of the world and that aggression, foreign occupation and ethnic and other types of conflicts are an ongoing reality affecting women and men in nearly every region, undertake efforts to eliminate impunity for all gender-based violence in situations of armed conflict, bearing in mind relevant General Assembly resolutions and Security Council resolution 1325(2000) on women and peace and security, and adopt, consistent with their obligations under the 1951 Convention relating to the Status of Refugees and the 1967 Protocol thereto, international human rights norms and relevant conclusions of the Executive Committee of the Programme of the United Nations High Commissioner for Refugees and General Assembly resolutions, a gender-sensitive approach to the consideration of claims for the granting of asylum and refugee status;

(p) To integrate a gender perspective into national plans of action and establish or strengthen specific national plans of action on the elimination of violence against women, supported by the necessary human, financial and technical resources, including, where appropriate, time-bound measurable targets, to promote the protection of women against any form of violence, and accelerate the implementation of existing national action plans that are regularly monitored and updated by Governments, taking into account inputs by civil society, in particular women's organizations, networks and other stakeholders;

(q) To allocate adequate resources to promote the empowerment of women and gender equality and to prevent and redress all forms and manifestations of violence against women;

9. *Calls upon* the international community, including the United Nations system and, as appropriate, regional and subregional organizations, to support national efforts to promote the empowerment of women and gender equality in order to enhance national efforts to eliminate violence against women and girls, including, upon request, in the development and implementation of national action plans on the elimination of violence against women and girls, through, inter alia, and taking into account national priorities, official development assistance and other appropriate assistance, such as facilitating the sharing of guidelines, methodologies and best practices;

10. *Urges* States to integrate gender perspectives into the comprehensive national development plans and poverty eradication strategies that address social, structural and macroeconomic issues, and to ensure that such strategies address violence against women and girls, and urges the United Nations funds and programmes and the specialized agencies and invites the Bretton Woods institutions to support national efforts in this regard;

11. *Also urges* States to ensure the systematic collection and analysis of data on violence against women,

including with the involvement of national statistical offices and, where appropriate, in partnership with other actors, taking note of the World Health Organization multi-country study on women's health and domestic violence against women and its recommendation to enhance capacity and establish systems for data collection to monitor violence against women;

12. *Urges* the United Nations bodies, entities, funds and programmes and the specialized agencies, and invites the Bretton Woods institutions, in accordance with their mandates, to support, upon request and within existing resources, the strengthening of national capacities and efforts on the collection, processing and dissemination of data, including data disaggregated by sex, age and other relevant information, for their possible use for legislative, policy and programme development and in the national plans of action against all forms of violence against women;

13. *Notes* the work carried out for the elimination of all forms of violence against women by relevant United Nations bodies, entities, funds and programmes and relevant specialized agencies, including those responsible for the promotion of gender equality and women's rights, and urges them and invites the Bretton Woods institutions:

(a) To enhance the coordination of and intensify their efforts to eliminate all forms of violence against women and girls in a more systematic, comprehensive and sustained way, inter alia, through the Inter-Agency Network on Women and Gender Equality supported by the newly established Task Force on Violence against Women, in close collaboration with relevant civil society, including non-governmental organizations;

(b) To enhance coordination in a more systematic, comprehensive and sustained way of their assistance to States in their efforts to eliminate all forms of violence against women, including in the development or implementation of national action plans and, where appropriate, national development plans, including poverty reduction strategies where they exist, and programme-based and sector-wide approaches and in close collaboration with relevant civil society, including non-governmental organizations;

14. *Calls upon* the Inter-Agency Network on Women and Gender Equality to consider ways and means to enhance the effectiveness of the United Nations Trust Fund in Support of Actions to Eliminate Violence against Women as a system-wide funding mechanism for preventing and redressing all forms of violence against women and girls;

15. *Strongly encourages* States to increase significantly their voluntary financial support for activities related to preventing and eliminating all forms of violence against women, the empowerment of women and gender equality carried out by the specialized agencies and the United Nations funds and programmes, including the United Nations Trust Fund in Support of Actions to Eliminate Violence against Women;

16. *Stresses* that within the United Nations system adequate resources should be assigned to those bodies, specialized agencies, funds and programmes responsible for the promotion of gender equality and women's rights and to efforts throughout the United Nations system to eliminate violence against women and girls;

17. *Invites* the Economic and Social Council and its functional commissions, the Peacebuilding Commission, the Human Rights Council and other relevant United Nations bodies to discuss, by 2008, within their respective mandates, the question of violence against women in all its forms and manifestations, bearing in mind the recommendations contained in the report of the Secretary-General on the in-depth study on all forms of violence against women, and to set priorities for addressing this issue in their future efforts and work programmes and to transmit the outcome of those discussions to the Secretary-General for his annual report to the General Assembly;

18. *Requests* the Statistical Commission to develop and propose, in consultation with the Commission on the Status of Women, and building on the work of the Special Rapporteur on violence against women, its causes and consequences, a set of possible indicators on violence against women in order to assist States in assessing the scope, prevalence and incidence of violence against women;

19. *Requests* the Secretary-General to establish a coordinated database, containing data provided by States, in particular national statistical offices, including, where appropriate, through relevant United Nations entities and other relevant regional intergovernmental organizations, disaggregated by sex, age and other relevant information, on the extent, nature and consequences of all forms of violence against women, and on the impact and effectiveness of policies and programmes for, including best practices in, combating such violence;

20. *Also requests* the Secretary-General to submit an annual report to the General Assembly on the implementation of the present resolution, addressing the question of violence against women, and requests that the report include:

(a) At the sixty-second session of the General Assembly, information provided by the United Nations bodies, funds and programmes and the specialized agencies on their follow-up activities to implement the resolution;

(b) At the sixty-third session of the General Assembly, information provided by States on their follow-up activities to implement the resolution;

21. *Decides* to continue its consideration of the question at its sixty-second session under the item entitled "Advancement of women".

Crime prevention and criminal justice response to violence against women

On 25 April, the Commission on Crime Prevention and Criminal Justice [E/2006/30 & Corr.1] (see p. 1289) convened a thematic discussion on maximizing the effectiveness of technical assistance provided to Member States in crime prevention and criminal justice. In a statement at the opening of the debate, the Special Rapporteur of the Commission on Human Rights on violence against women, its causes and consequences (see p. 888) highlighted the importance of an adequate response to violence against women, at both the international and national level. She indicated that the international legal framework aimed at ending violence against women was being progressively strengthened, particularly with the inclusion of sexual offences in a range of international conventions. Given the mandate of the UN Office on Drugs and Crime in the area of crime prevention and criminal justice, there was scope for greater coordination between her work and that of the Commission on Crime Prevention and Criminal Justice. The Commission recommended a draft resolution to the Economic and Social Council for adoption on crime prevention and criminal justice responses to violence against women and girls.

ECONOMIC AND SOCIAL COUNCIL ACTION

On 27 July [meeting 41], the Economic and Social Council, on the recommendation of the Commission on Crime Prevention and Criminal Justice [E/2006/30 & Corr.1], adopted **resolution 2006/29**, without vote [agenda item 14 *(c)*].

Crime prevention and criminal justice responses to violence against women and girls

The Economic and Social Council,

Recalling that, at the 2005 World Summit held at United Nations Headquarters from 14 to 16 September 2005, Heads of State and Government underscored the importance of eliminating all forms of discrimination and violence against women and girls,

Recalling also the Beijing Declaration and the Platform for Action adopted by the Fourth World Conference on Women, held in Beijing from 4 to 15 September 1995, and, in particular, the determination of Governments to prevent and eliminate all forms of violence against women and girls,

Bearing in mind that, in the Vienna Declaration on Crime and Justice: Meeting the Challenges of the Twenty-first Century, adopted by the Tenth United Nations Congress on the Prevention of Crime and the Treatment of Offenders, held in Vienna from 10 to 17 April 2000, Member States committed themselves to taking into account and addressing, within the United Nations Crime Prevention and Criminal Justice Programme, as well as within national crime prevention and criminal justice strategies, any disparate impact of programmes and policies on women and men,

Recalling that, in the plans of action for the implementation of the Vienna Declaration, specific national and international measures on the special needs of women as criminal justice practitioners, victims, prisoners and offenders were recommended,

Recalling also that the Bangkok Declaration on Synergies and Responses: Strategic Alliances in Crime Prevention and Criminal Justice, adopted at the high-level segment of the Eleventh United Nations Congress on Crime Prevention and Criminal Justice, held in Bangkok from 18 to 25 April 2005, emphasized the importance of promoting the interests of victims of crime, including taking account of their gender,

Reaffirming General Assembly resolution 52/86 of 12 December 1997 on crime prevention and criminal justice measures to eliminate violence against women, in which the Assembly adopted the Model Strategies and Practical Measures on the Elimination of Violence against Women in the Field of Crime Prevention and Criminal Justice, and called upon the Commission on Crime Prevention and Criminal Justice to continue to consider the elimination of violence against women within the training and technical assistance efforts of the United Nations Crime Prevention and Criminal Justice Programme,

Noting Security Council resolution 1325(2000) of 31 October 2000 on women, peace and security, in which the Council recognized the serious impact of armed conflict and resulting violence directed against women in such situations,

Recalling its resolution 1996/12 of 23 July 1996 on the elimination of violence against women, in which it urged Member States to review or monitor legislation and legal principles, procedures, policies and practices relating to criminal matters to determine if they had an adverse or negative impact on women and, if they had such an impact, to modify them in order to ensure that women were treated fairly by the criminal justice system,

Recalling also its resolution 2005/20 of 22 July 2005, in which it adopted the Guidelines on Justice in Matters involving Child Victims and Witnesses of Crime, which contain a gender perspective,

Reaffirming its resolution 2005/21 of 22 July 2005 on strengthening the rule of law and the reform of criminal justice institutions, in which it encouraged the United Nations Office on Drugs and Crime to continue to develop tools and training manuals on criminal justice reform, based on international standards and best practices,

Noting previous and ongoing work of the United Nations Office on Drugs and Crime in the area of violence against women and children,

Noting also the holding of the Workshop on Violence against Women in the Twenty-first Century, organized by the Government of France, the United Nations and the Organization for Security and Cooperation in Europe in Paris on 28 and 29 April 2005,

Recognizing the challenge of developing effective criminal justice initiatives targeting violence against women and girls, in particular in the area of designing appropriate law enforcement responses in developing countries and countries with societies in transition, which would ensure the protection of victims while guaranteeing that perpetrators are effectively prosecuted and held accountable for their acts,

Noting the progress made by the independent expert in preparing the study on violence against children, requested by the General Assembly in its resolution 57/190 of 18 December 2002, which will pay particular attention to the situation of girls, and the contribution of the United Nations Office on Drugs and Crime to that study,

Welcoming the in-depth study on all forms of violence against women requested by the General Assembly in its resolution 58/185 of 22 December 2003 and looking forward to its publication, and also welcoming the contribution of the United Nations Office on Drugs and Crime to that study in the form of the co-sponsoring, with the Division for the Advancement of Women of the Secretariat, of an expert group meeting held in May 2005 on good practices in combating and eliminating violence against women,

Expressing concern at the high levels of violence against women and girls in many societies,

1. *Urges* Member States to consider, to the utmost extent possible, using the Model Strategies and Practical Measures on the Elimination of Violence against Women in the Field of Crime Prevention and Criminal Justice in developing and undertaking strategies and practical measures to eliminate violence against women and in promoting women's equality within the criminal justice system;

2. *Strongly encourages* Member States to promote an active and visible policy for integrating a gender perspective into the development and implementation of policies and programmes in the field of crime prevention and criminal justice in order to assist with the elimination of violence against women and girls;

3. *Requests* the United Nations Office on Drugs and Crime, within available extrabudgetary resources, not excluding the use of existing resources from the regular budget of the Office, and invites the institutes comprising the United Nations Crime Prevention and Criminal Justice Programme Network to consider providing assistance, upon request, to Member States in the area of crime prevention and criminal justice responses to violence against women and girls, in cooperation with other relevant entities of the United Nations system, and to integrate the elimination of violence against women and girls into their training and technical assistance efforts, including their crime prevention activities;

4. *Welcomes* the development by the United Nations Office on Drugs and Crime of a handbook for law enforcement officials on effective responses to violence against women, and encourages the Office, within available extrabudgetary resources, not excluding the use of existing resources from the regular budget of the Office, to continue to develop tools and training manuals on criminal justice reform, with a gender perspective, and targeting the special needs of women in the criminal justice system, including women in prison settings;

5. *Also welcomes* the work already carried out by the United Nations Office on Drugs and Crime in providing assistance to victims of violence, in particular women and children, by setting up one-stop centres and supporting non-governmental organizations active in that area, and invites the Office, within available extrabudgetary resources, not excluding the use of existing resources from the regular budget of the Office, to draw on its experience to expand such activities;

6. *Invites* Member States to provide resources to the United Nations Office on Drugs and Crime to enable it to provide effective assistance to Member States in the area of crime prevention and criminal justice responses to violence against women and girls;

7. *Requests* the Secretary-General to report to the Commission on Crime Prevention and Criminal Justice at its seventeenth session, in 2008, on the implementation of the present resolution.

Women and armed conflict

Women, peace and security

Report of Secretary-General. In response to the Security Council request in presidential statement S/PRST/2005/52 [YUN 2005, p. 1255] to annually review the implementation and integration of the System-wide Action Plan developed in 2005 [ibid.] for the implementation of resolution 1325(2000) [YUN 2000, p. 1113], the Secretary-General submitted a September report on women, peace and security [S/2006/770]. The Action Plan, which covered virtually all major areas of action in the field of women, peace and security, encompassed a total of 269 actions and provided a framework for inter-agency activities during the period 2005-2007. The review focused on implementation of the Plan by UN entities, the assessment of institutional capacities, including monitoring, reporting and accountability procedures, and ways of strengthening implementation of resolution 1325(2000) and mainstreaming a gender perspective in all areas of action of the Plan. Progress achieved, including examples of good practices, was summarized in the report, in addition to gaps and challenges in capacity to implement the Plan and lessons learned. Recommendations for future action were also provided.

The Secretary-General observed that, while gender equality was increasingly recognized as a core issue in the maintenance of international peace and security, the role of women in peace processes continued to be viewed as a side issue rather than a fundamental element in the development of viable democratic institutions and the establishment of sustainable peace. Significant progress had been made in many areas of the Plan, particularly in peacekeeping, peacemaking and peacebuilding, but more could be done by the UN system at all levels, both at Headquarters and in the field. He concluded that the review had confirmed the benefit of the Action Plan and the revisions proposed in the report were essential to make it a more effective tool for strengthened inter-agency coordination, enhanced accountability and ownership, and improved organizational culture supportive of the goals and ideals contained in resolution 1325(2000). In that connection, the Secretary-General recommended that the Action Plan be renewed beyond 2007 and prepared in line with the report's findings and actions.

Communications. On 4 October [S/2006/793], Japan indicated that the Security Council was scheduled to hold a debate on "The roles of women in the consolidation of peace" on 26 October, which would also mark the sixth anniversary of the adoption of resolution 1325(2000). On 23 October [A/61/541-S/2006/848], Sweden forwarded the report of the High-level meeting on "Gender justice in Liberia: the way forward" (Monrovia, 9-10 October), which was organized by the Partners for Gender Justice in Conflict Affected Societies, in cooperation with the Ministry of Gender and Development and the Ministry of Justice of Liberia and discussed priority requirements and assistance needs in the area of justice, particularly gender justice in a post-conflict society.

SECURITY COUNCIL ACTION

On 26 October [meeting 5556], following consultations among Security Council members, the President made statement **S/PRST/2006/42** on behalf of the Council:

> The Security Council reaffirms its commitment to the full and effective implementation of resolution 1325(2000) and recalls the statements by its President of 31 October 2001, 31 October 2002, 28 October 2004 and 27 October 2005, as reiterating that commitment.
>
> The Council recalls the 2005 World Summit Outcome, the Beijing Declaration and Platform for Action, the outcomes of the twenty-third special session of the General Assembly and the declaration of the Commission on the Status of Women at its forty-ninth session on the occasion of the tenth anniversary of the Fourth World Conference on Women.
>
> The Council recognizes the vital roles of and contributions by women in consolidating peace. The Council welcomes the progress made in increasing the participation of women in decision-making in several countries emerging from conflict and requests the Secretary-General to collect and compile good practices and lessons learned and identify remaining gaps and challenges in order to further promote the efficient and effective implementation of resolution 1325(2000).
>
> The Council recognizes that the protection and empowerment of women and support for their networks and initiatives are essential in the consolidation of peace to promote the equal and full participation of women and to improve their human security, and encourages Member States, donors and civil society to provide support in this respect.
>
> The Council recognizes the importance of integrating gender perspectives into institutional reform in post-conflict countries at both the national and the local levels. The Council encourages Member States in post-conflict situations to ensure that gender perspectives are mainstreamed into institutional reform, ensuring that the reforms, in particular of the security sector, justice institutions and restoration of the rule of law, provide for the protection of women's rights and safety. The Council also requests the Secretary-General to ensure that United Nations assistance in this context appropriately addresses the needs and priorities of women in the post-conflict process.
>
> The Council requests the Secretary-General to ensure that disarmament, demobilization and reintegration programmes take specific account of the situation of women ex-combatants and women associated with combatants, as well as their children, and provide for their full access to these programmes.
>
> The Council welcomes the role that the Peacebuilding Commission can play in mainstreaming gender perspectives into the peace consolidation process. In this context, the Council welcomes in particular the Chairman's summaries of the country-specific meetings of the Commission on Sierra Leone and Burundi held on 12 and 13 October 2006.
>
> The Council remains deeply concerned by the pervasiveness of all forms of violence against women in armed conflict, including killing, maiming, grave sexual violence, abductions and trafficking in persons. The Council reiterates its utmost condemnation of such practices and calls upon all parties to armed conflict to ensure full and effective protection of women, and emphasizes the necessity to end the impunity of those responsible for gender-based violence.
>
> The Council reiterates its condemnation, in the strongest terms, of all acts of sexual misconduct by all categories of personnel in United Nations peacekeeping missions. The Council urges the Secretary-General and troop-contributing countries to ensure the full implementation of the recommendations of the Special Committee on Peacekeeping Operations. In this connection, the Council expresses its support for further efforts by the United Nations to fully implement codes of conduct and disciplinary procedures to prevent and respond to sexual exploitation and abuse, and enhance monitoring and enforcement mechanisms based on a zero-tolerance policy.
>
> The Council requests the Secretary-General to include in his reporting to the Council progress in gender mainstreaming throughout United Nations peacekeeping missions as well as on other aspects relating specifically to women and girls. The Council emphasizes the need for the inclusion of gender components in peacekeeping operations. The Council further encourages Member States and the Secretary-General to increase the participation of women in all areas and at all levels of peacekeeping operations, civilian, police and military, where possible.
>
> The Council reiterates its call to Member States to continue to implement resolution 1325(2000), including through the development and implementation of national action plans or other national-level strategies.
>
> The Council recognizes the important contribution of civil society to the implementation of resolution 1325(2000) and encourages Member States to continue to collaborate with civil society, in particular with local women's networks and organizations, in order to strengthen implementation.
>
> The Council looks forward to the report of the High-level Panel on United Nations System-wide Coherence in the Areas of Development, Humanitarian Assistance and the Environment and hopes that this will play a role in ensuring a coordinated United Nations approach to women and peace and security.
>
> The Council welcomes the first follow-up report of the Secretary-General on the United Nations System-wide Action Plan for the implementation of resolution 1325(2000) across the United Nations system. The Council requests the Secretary-General to continue to update, monitor and review the imple-

mentation and integration of the Action Plan and report to the Council as stipulated in the statement by the President of the Council of 27 October 2005.

Women and children taken hostage

Report of Secretary-General. In response to Commission on the Status of Women resolution 48/3 [YUN 2004, p. 1156], the Secretary-General submitted a report [E/CN.6/2006/6] on the release of women and children taken hostage, including those subsequently imprisoned, in armed conflicts, which included information provided by seven Member States, 12 UN system entities and one international organization. It outlined actions taken by Governments in the development of policies and legislation, as well as the provision of humanitarian support to women and children taken hostage. UN entities continued to provide technical assistance and capacity-building to all actors, and focused efforts on providing health services, including reproductive health services, and psychosocial support; preventing and dealing with the consequences of violence, including sexual exploitation; and supporting reintegration processes, particularly in relation to child soldiers. The Secretary-General indicated that the lack of sex-disaggregated data was a constraint that needed to be addressed.

Commission action. In a March resolution [E/2006/27 (res. 50/1)], the Commission reaffirmed that hostage-taking was an illegal act aimed at the destruction of human rights and called for an effective response to such acts, in particular the immediate release of women and children taken hostage in armed conflicts. It requested the Secretary-General to ensure the widest possible dissemination of relevant material, in particular material relating to Security Council resolution 1325(2000), facilitate the immediate release of civilian women and children who had been taken hostage, and report to the Commission at its fifty-second (2008) session on implementation of the resolution.

Women and health

Women, the girl child and HIV/AIDS

In a March resolution on women, the girl child and HIV/AIDS [E/2006/27 & Corr.1 (res. 50/2)], the Commission on the Status of Women stressed that the HIV/AIDS pandemic, with its devastating scale and impact, required urgent action in all fields and at all levels. It called on Governments and the international donor community to integrate a gender perspective into all matters of international assistance and cooperation, and ensure that resources commensurate with the impact of HIV/AIDS on women and girls were made available, in particular funding to national HIV/AIDS programmes to promote and protect the human rights of women and girls in the context of the epidemic. The Commission requested the Joint UN Programme on HIV/AIDS (UNAIDS), other UN agencies responding to the HIV/AIDS pandemic, and the Global Fund to Fight HIV/AIDS, Tuberculosis and Malaria to integrate a gender and human rights perspective throughout their HIV/AIDS-related operations. It also requested the Secretary-General to direct the United Nations Development Programme (UNDP), as lead agency on technical support on gender and human rights within UNAIDS, to develop the HIV-related gender and human rights capacity for all UN staff providing technical assistance to Governments, advance the national response to AIDS, and report on those efforts in 2008.

The girl child

In March [E/2006/27 & Corr.1], the Commission on the Status of Women submitted the draft provisional agenda and documentation for its fifty-first (2007) session to the Economic and Social Council for consideration. On 25 July, by **decision 2006/235**, the Council approved the agenda and documentation, and on the same date, decided that the priority theme in 2007 would be "The elimination of all forms of discrimination and violence against the girl child" (**resolution 2006/9**) (see p. 1356).

Women and human rights

Division for the Advancement of Women and OHCHR activities

On 6 October, the newly established Human Rights Council, by decision 2/102 (see p. 756), requested the Secretary-General and the High Commissioner for Human Rights to continue their activities in accordance with the previous decisions adopted by the Commission on Human Rights, including the update of relevant reports and studies. In December, the Secretary-General transmitted a report [A/HRC/4/68-E/CN.6/2007/5] on implementation of the 2006 joint workplan of the UN Division for the Advancement of Women and the Office of the UN High Commissioner for Human Rights (OHCHR), which also contained the joint workplan for 2007.

Special Rapporteur on laws that discriminate against women

In response to Commission resolution 49/3 [YUN 2005, p. 1259], the Secretary-General submitted a report [E/CN.6/2006/8] on the advisability of the appointment of a special rapporteur on laws that discriminate against women, which presented an overview of international human rights instruments, policy documents and mechanisms aimed at eliminating laws that discriminated against women, as well as the views of 26 Member States and observers, CEDAW and OHCHR. Nine Member States supported the appointment of a special rapporteur, as did OHCHR. The remaining replies included four that supported it, provided there was no duplication of the work of existing mechanisms; eight that did not support it or considered it necessary; one that had no objection; one that said it would be useful; and two that could not comment definitely without a specific proposal or draft mandate for a special rapporteur. Concerns included the ongoing reform discussions on UN human rights machinery; the relationship between a special rapporteur and UN mechanisms; the criteria for selecting a special rapporteur; and the financial implications. The report concluded that, while de jure discrimination persisted in many areas, its elimination would not require significant investment of resources or the longer time periods needed to modify social and cultural patterns of behaviour. Moreover, with the exception of CEDAW, none of the mechanisms had a specific mandate to address laws that discriminated against women. A dedicated mechanism to tackle such laws from a global perspective could provide the necessary momentum for change. The Secretary-General made recommendations on the matter and indicated that the Commission's consideration of its working methods and future multi-year programme constituted a timely opportunity to consider the question of such a mechanism and its mandate.

Commission action. In a March resolution [E/2006/27 (res. 50/3)] on the advisability of the appointment of a special rapporteur on laws that discriminate against women, the Commission invited the Secretary-General to bring his report (see above) to the attention of CEDAW and other relevant treaty bodies, as well as OHCHR, to elicit their views on ways to best complement the work of the existing mechanisms and enhance the Commission's capacity with respect to discriminatory laws. It also decided to consider the issue at its fifty-first (2007) session, bearing in mind the existing mechanisms, with a view to avoiding duplication.

Trafficking in women and girls

In July, the Secretary-General transmitted to the General Assembly an in-depth study [A/61/122/Add.1 & Corr.1] on all forms of violence against women (see p. 1333), which contained information on trafficking in women and girls. The report indicated that trafficking was a form of violence that took place in multiple settings, involving many different actors, including families, local brokers, international criminal networks and immigration authorities. Women and children comprised the majority of human trafficking victims, and were often trafficked for sexual exploitation purposes. According to the UN Office on Drugs and Crime (UNODC) database, there were 127 countries of origin and 137 countries of destination for trafficking in human beings. Although sources suggested that hundreds of thousands of people were trafficked globally every year, few came to the attention of the authorities. Available statistics were unreliable and trafficking legislation was either inadequate or non-existent in many countries. Trafficked women rarely reported their situation to authorities and were unwilling to cooperate with law enforcement officials if identified and rescued due to fear of reprisals, lack of trust in the authorities, rejection by their families, and lack of opportunities in their home countries. Most estimates on trafficking were difficult to compare or verify because the methodology for computing them were rarely given and the coverage of the estimates was often unclear. Several regional and national initiatives had begun to develop comprehensive databases to provide information on international trafficking routes, sources, transit and destination countries, and on the number of trafficked victims and offenders. With regard to laws, 93 States had some legislative provision regarding trafficking in human beings, of which ten had provisions that applied only to children. The report also summarized the obstacles faced by trafficking victims in accessing services, including protection, medical care, legal advice and counselling. The study proposed recommendations for action in a number of key areas.

GENERAL ASSEMBLY ACTION

On 19 December [meeting 81], the General Assembly, on the recommendation of the Third Committee [A/61/438], adopted **resolution 61/144** without vote [agenda item 61 *(a)*].

Trafficking in women and girls

The General Assembly,

Recalling all international conventions that deal specifically with the problem of trafficking in women and girls, such as the Convention on the Elimination of All Forms of Discrimination against Women and the Optional Protocol thereto, the Convention on the Rights of the Child and the Optional Protocol thereto on the sale of children, child prostitution and child pornography, the Convention for the Suppression of the Traffic in Persons and of the Exploitation of the Prostitution of Others, the United Nations Convention against Transnational Organized Crime and the Protocols thereto, in particular the Protocol to Prevent, Suppress and Punish Trafficking in Persons, Especially Women and Children, supplementing the United Nations Convention against Transnational Organized Crime and the Protocol against the Smuggling of Migrants by Land, Sea and Air, supplementing the United Nations Convention against Transnational Organized Crime, as well as previous resolutions of the General Assembly, the Economic and Social Council and the Commission on Human Rights on the issue,

Reaffirming the provisions pertaining to trafficking in women and girls contained in the outcome documents of relevant international conferences and summits, in particular the strategic objective on the issue of trafficking contained in the Beijing Declaration and Platform for Action adopted by the Fourth World Conference on Women,

Reaffirming also the commitment made by world leaders at the Millennium Summit and the 2005 World Summit to devise, enforce and strengthen effective measures to combat and eliminate all forms of trafficking in persons to counter the demand for trafficked victims and to protect the victims,

Recalling the reports of the Special Rapporteur on the sale of children, child prostitution and child pornography, the Special Rapporteur on trafficking in persons, especially women and children, and the Special Rapporteur on violence against women, its causes and consequences, as well as the information that deals with trafficking in women and girls contained in the report of the Secretary-General on the in-depth study on all forms of violence against women,

Recalling also the report of the United Nations Office on Drugs and Crime entitled "Trafficking in Persons: Global Patterns", and the attention paid in it to the situation of trafficked women and girls,

Acknowledging the inclusion of gender-related crimes in the Rome Statute of the International Criminal Court, which entered into force on 1 July 2002,

Bearing in mind that all States have an obligation to exercise due diligence to prevent, investigate and punish perpetrators of trafficking in persons, to rescue victims as well as provide for their protection and that not doing so violates and impairs or nullifies the enjoyment of the human rights and fundamental freedoms of the victims,

Recognizing the need for a stronger gender- and age-sensitive approach in all efforts to fight trafficking and protect its victims, taking into account that women and girls are particularly vulnerable to trafficking for the purposes of sexual exploitation, as well as for forced labour or services,

Recognizing also the need to address the impact of globalization on the particular problem of trafficking in women and children, in particular girls,

Recognizing further the challenges to combating trafficking in women and girls owing to the lack of adequate legislation and implementation of existing legislation, the lack of availability of reliable sex-disaggregated data and statistics, as well as the lack of resources,

Seriously concerned that an increasing number of women and girls from developing countries and from some countries with economies in transition are being trafficked to developed countries, as well as within and between regions and States, and that men and boys are also victims of trafficking, including for sexual exploitation,

Concerned about the use of new information technologies, including the Internet, for purposes of exploitation of the prostitution of others, for trafficking in women as brides, for sex tourism exploiting women and children and for child pornography, paedophilia and any other forms of sexual exploitation of children,

Concerned also about the increasing activities of transnational criminal organizations and others that profit from international trafficking in persons, especially women and children, without regard to dangerous and inhuman conditions and in flagrant violation of domestic laws and international standards,

Recognizing that victims of trafficking are particularly exposed to racism, racial discrimination, xenophobia and related intolerance and that women and girl victims are often subject to multiple forms of discrimination and violence, including on the grounds of their gender, age, ethnicity, culture and religion, as well as their origins, and that these forms of discrimination themselves may fuel trafficking in persons,

Noting that some of the demand for prostitution and forced labour is met by trafficking in persons in some parts of the world,

Acknowledging that women and girl victims of trafficking, on account of their gender, are further disadvantaged and marginalized by a general lack of information or awareness and recognition of their human rights and by the stigmatization often associated with trafficking, as well as by the obstacles they meet in gaining access to information and recourse mechanisms in cases of violation of their rights, and that special measures are required for their protection and to increase their awareness,

Recognizing the importance of bilateral, subregional, regional and international cooperation mechanisms and initiatives, including information exchanges on best practices, of Governments and intergovernmental and non-governmental organizations to address the problem of trafficking in persons, especially women and children,

Recognizing also that global efforts, including international cooperation and technical assistance programmes, to eradicate trafficking in persons, especially women and children, demand the strong political commitment, shared responsibility and active cooperation of all Governments of countries of origin, transit and destination,

Recognizing further that policies and programmes for prevention, rehabilitation, repatriation and reintegration should be developed through a gender- and age-sensitive, comprehensive and multidisciplinary approach, with concern for the security of the victims and respect for the full enjoyment of their human rights and with the involvement of all actors in countries of origin, transit and destination,

Convinced of the need to protect and assist all victims of trafficking, with full respect for the victims' human rights,

1. *Welcomes* the efforts of Governments, United Nations bodies and agencies and intergovernmental and non-governmental organizations to address the particular problem of trafficking in women and girls, and encourages them to continue doing so and to share their knowledge and best practices as widely as possible;

2. *Calls upon* Governments to eliminate the demand for trafficked women and girls for all forms of exploitation;

3. *Also calls upon* Governments to take appropriate measures to address the factors that increase vulnerability to being trafficked, including poverty and gender inequality, as well as other factors that encourage the particular problem of trafficking in women and girls for prostitution and other forms of commercialized sex, forced marriage and forced labour, in order to eliminate such trafficking, including by strengthening existing legislation with a view to providing better protection of the rights of women and girls and to punishing perpetrators, through both criminal and civil measures;

4. *Urges* Governments to devise, enforce and strengthen effective gender- and age-sensitive measures to combat and eliminate all forms of trafficking in women and girls, including for sexual and economic exploitation, as part of a comprehensive anti-trafficking strategy that integrates a human rights perspective and takes into account the situation of trafficked victims, and to draw up, as appropriate, national action plans in this regard;

5. *Also urges* Governments to consider signing and ratifying and States parties to implement relevant United Nations legal instruments, such as the United Nations Convention against Transnational Organized Crime and the Protocols thereto, in particular the Protocol to Prevent, Suppress and Punish Trafficking in Persons, Especially Women and Children, supplementing the United Nations Convention against Transnational Organized Crime, the Convention on the Elimination of All Forms of Discrimination against Women, the Convention on the Rights of the Child, the Optional Protocol to the Convention on the Elimination of All Forms of Discrimination against Women and the Optional Protocol to the Convention on the Rights of the Child on the sale of children, child prostitution and child pornography, as well as the Convention concerning Forced or Compulsory Labour, 1930 (Convention No. 29), the Convention concerning Discrimination in respect of Employment and Occupation, 1958 (Convention No. 111) and the Convention concerning the Prohibition and Immediate Action for the Elimination of the Worst Forms of Child Labour, 1999 (Convention No. 182), of the International Labour Organization;

6. *Encourages* Member States to conclude bilateral, subregional, regional and international agreements, as well as to undertake initiatives, including regional initiatives, to address the problem of trafficking in persons, and to ensure that such agreements and initiatives pay particular attention to the problem of trafficking in women and girls;

7. *Calls upon* all Governments to criminalize all forms of trafficking in persons, recognizing its increasing occurrence for purposes of sexual exploitation and sex tourism, and to condemn and penalize all those offenders involved, including intermediaries, whether local or foreign, through the competent national authorities, either in the country of origin of the offender or in the country in which the abuse occurs, in accordance with due process of law, as well as to penalize persons in authority found guilty of sexually assaulting victims of trafficking in their custody;

8. *Urges* Governments to take all appropriate measures to ensure that victims of trafficking are not penalized for being trafficked and that they do not suffer from revictimization as a result of actions taken by government authorities, and encourages Governments to prevent, within their legal framework and in accordance with national policies, victims of trafficking in persons from being prosecuted for their illegal entry or residence;

9. *Recognizes* the urgent need for broad and concerted cooperation among all relevant actors, including States, intergovernmental organizations and civil society, to counter effectively the threat of trafficking in persons, particularly women and girls;

10. *Invites* Governments to strengthen bilateral, regional and international cooperation aimed at preventing and combating corruption and the laundering of proceeds derived from trafficking, including for purposes of commercialized sexual exploitation;

11. *Also invites* Governments to consider setting up or strengthening a national coordinating mechanism, for example, a national rapporteur or an inter-agency body, with the participation of civil society, including non-governmental organizations, to encourage the exchange of information and to report on data, root causes, factors and trends in violence against women, in particular trafficking;

12. *Encourages* Governments and relevant United Nations bodies, within existing resources, to take appropriate measures to raise public awareness of the issue of trafficking in persons, particularly in women and girls; to discourage, with a view to eliminating, the demand that fosters all forms of exploitation, including sexual exploitation and forced labour; to publicize the laws, regulations and penalties relating to this issue; and to emphasize that trafficking is a serious crime;

13. *Encourages* Governments to take appropriate measures to eliminate sex tourism demand, especially of children, through all possible preventive actions;

14. *Urges* concerned Governments, in cooperation with intergovernmental and non-governmental organizations, to support and allocate resources for programmes to strengthen preventive action, in particular education for women and men, as well as for boys and girls, on gender equality, self-respect and mutual respect, and

campaigns to increase public awareness of the issue at the national and grass-roots levels;

15. *Calls upon* concerned Governments to allocate resources, as appropriate, to provide comprehensive programmes for the physical, psychological and social recovery of victims of trafficking, including through job training, legal assistance, including in a language that they can understand, and health care, including for HIV/AIDS, and by taking measures to cooperate with intergovernmental and non-governmental organizations to provide for the social, medical and psychological care of the victims;

16. *Encourages* Governments, in cooperation with intergovernmental and non-governmental organizations, to undertake or strengthen campaigns aimed at clarifying opportunities, limitations and rights in the event of migration, as well as information on the risks of irregular migration and the ways and means used by traffickers so as to enable women to make informed decisions and to prevent them from becoming victims of trafficking;

17. *Also encourages* Governments to intensify collaboration with non-governmental organizations to develop and implement gender- and age-sensitive programmes for effective counselling, training and reintegration into society of victims of trafficking and programmes that provide shelter and helplines to victims or potential victims;

18. *Calls upon* Governments to take steps to ensure that the treatment of victims of trafficking, as well as all measures taken against trafficking in persons, in particular those that affect the victims of such trafficking, pay particular attention to the needs of women and girls, are applied with full respect for the human rights of those victims and are consistent with internationally recognized principles of non-discrimination, including the prohibition of racial discrimination and the availability of appropriate legal redress, which may include measures that offer victims the possibility of obtaining compensation for damage suffered;

19. *Invites* Governments to take steps to ensure that criminal justice procedures and witness protection programmes are sensitive to the particular situation of trafficked women and girls and that they are supported and assisted, as appropriate, in making complaints to the police or other authorities, without fear, and being available when required by the criminal justice system, and to ensure that during this time they have access to protection and social, medical, financial and legal assistance, as appropriate;

20. *Also invites* Governments to encourage media providers, including Internet service providers, to adopt or strengthen self-regulatory measures to promote the responsible use of media, particularly the Internet, with a view to eliminating the exploitation of women and children, in particular girls, which could foster trafficking;

21. *Invites* the business sector, in particular the tourism and telecommunications industries, including mass media organizations, to cooperate with Governments in eliminating trafficking in women and children, in particular girls, including through the dissemination by the media of information regarding the dangers of trafficking, the rights of trafficked persons and the services available to victims of trafficking;

22. *Stresses* the need for the systematic collection of sex- and age-disaggregated data and comprehensive studies at both the national and the international levels and the development of common methodologies and internationally defined indicators to make it possible to develop relevant and comparable figures, and encourages Governments to enhance information-sharing and data-collection capacity as a way of promoting cooperation to combat the trafficking problem;

23. *Urges* Governments to strengthen national programmes to combat trafficking in persons, especially women and girls, through increased bilateral, regional and international cooperation, taking into account innovative approaches and best practices, and invites Governments, United Nations bodies and organizations, intergovernmental and non-governmental organizations and the private sector to undertake collaborative and joint research and studies on trafficking in women and girls that can serve as a basis for policy formulation or change;

24. *Invites* Governments, with the support of the United Nations, when necessary, and other intergovernmental organizations, taking into account best practices, to formulate training manuals and other informational materials and provide training for law enforcement, judicial and other relevant officers, and medical and support personnel, with a view to sensitizing them to the special needs of women and girl victims;

25. *Urges* Governments to provide or strengthen training for law enforcement, judicial, immigration and other relevant officials in the prevention and combating of trafficking in persons, including the sexual exploitation of women and girls, which should focus on methods used in preventing such trafficking, prosecuting the traffickers and protecting the rights of victims, including protecting the victims from traffickers, to ensure that the training includes human rights and gender- and age-sensitive perspectives, and to encourage cooperation with non-governmental organizations, other relevant organizations and other elements of civil society;

26. *Encourages* Governments, relevant intergovernmental bodies and international organizations to ensure that military, peacekeeping and humanitarian personnel deployed in conflict, post-conflict and other emergency situations are provided training on conduct that does not promote, facilitate or exploit trafficking in women and girls, including for sexual exploitation, and to raise the awareness of such personnel of the potential risks to victims of conflict and other emergency situations, including natural disasters, of being trafficked;

27. *Invites* States parties to the Convention on the Elimination of All Forms of Discrimination against Women, the Convention on the Rights of the Child and the International Covenants on Human Rights to include information and statistics on trafficking in women and girls as part of their national reports to their respective committees and to work towards developing a common methodology and statistics to obtain comparable data;

28. *Requests* the Secretary-General to submit to the General Assembly at its sixty-third session a report that compiles successful interventions and strategies, as well as challenges, in addressing the gender dimensions of the problem of trafficking in persons, that identifies gender-related aspects of anti-trafficking efforts that remain unaddressed or inadequately addressed, and that evaluates the measures taken through appropriate indicators; and invites the Secretary-General to take into account in his report the work of Governments, relevant United Nations agencies and mechanisms and other international organizations.

Women in Afghanistan

In response to Economic and Social Council resolution 2005/8 [YUN 2005, p. 1260], the Secretary-General submitted to the Commission a report [E/CN.6/2006/5] on the situation of women and girls in Afghanistan, which provided an update on their situation, and focused, in particular, on the electoral process; efforts to promote and protect women's rights; and social and economic reconstruction and rehabilitation. It included activities undertaken by the UN system in support of the Government of Afghanistan towards the advancement of women and gender equality. The September 2005 elections to the Wolesi Jirga (Lower House of Parliament), which resulted in women representing 27 per cent in national parliament and 29 per cent in the provincial councils, had significantly increased the participation of Afghan women in public life. Other progress achieved included: increased awareness of gender equality issues within the Government and among the public at large; the reduction of child and maternal mortality; and improved literacy of women and girls, and access to education. In addition, the Government had increasingly addressed matters previously considered private, such as violence against women.

The Secretary-General observed that, despite those gains, Afghan women and girls continued to face formidable security, human rights, social and economic challenges. The security situation and basic human rights conditions remained poor in many parts of the country, especially outside of Kabul. Armed factions, including the remaining Taliban forces, routinely abused women's human rights. Many of the advances made by women in the economic, employment and educational spheres were offset by the effects of widespread poverty. Moreover, continuing discrimination against women in access to education, health care, land, credit and productive means stifled reconstruction and development efforts. The Secretary-General concluded that promoting an inclusive, participatory and gender equal society that responded to the aspirations of all Afghan women and men continued to offer the best prospect for improving the overall security and development situation. Steps taken by the Afghan Government, with support from UN entities, needed to be strengthened. Prompt action on behalf of the Government, civil society and the international community was needed to promote and protect the human rights of women and girls and to end gender-based discrimination. Economic and social assistance programmes needed to build on women's acquired de jure rights, encourage women to participate in public life and new economic activities, and ensure more gender balance in accessing productive resources and labour markets.

The Secretary-General made a number of recommendations for the Afghan Government and the UN system, donor Governments and civil society to further strengthen the status of women and girls in Afghanistan.

ECONOMIC AND SOCIAL COUNCIL ACTION

On 25 July [meeting 38], the Economic and Social Council, on the recommendation of the Commission on the Status of Women [E/2006/27 & Corr.1], adopted **resolution 2006/7** without vote [agenda item 14 *(a)*].

Situation of women and girls in Afghanistan

The Economic and Social Council,

Recalling General Assembly resolutions 60/32 A and B of 30 November 2005, on the situation in Afghanistan and its implications for international peace and security and emergency international assistance for peace, normalcy and reconstruction of war-stricken Afghanistan, in particular the references to the situation of women and girls,

Recalling also Security Council resolutions 1589(2005) of 24 March 2005 and 1659(2006) of 15 February 2006 on the situation in Afghanistan, and resolution 1325(2000) of 31 October 2000 on women and peace and security,

Recalling further its resolution 2005/8 of 21 July 2005 on the situation of women and girls in Afghanistan,

1. *Takes note with appreciation* of the report of the Secretary-General;

2. *Welcomes* the references to the situation of women and girls in General Assembly resolutions 60/32 A and B;

3. *Invites* the Secretary-General to take into account a gender perspective when preparing the reports requested by the General Assembly in its resolutions 60/32 A and B and to include a specific and substantive section focusing on the situation of women and girls in Afghanistan in those reports;

4. *Requests* the Secretary-General to transmit those reports to the Commission on the Status of Women at its fifty-first session.

Palestinian women

In response to Economic and Social Council resolution 2005/43 [YUN 2005, p. 534], the Secretary-General reported [E/CN.6/2006/4] to the Commission on the Status of Women on the situation of and assistance to Palestinian women during the period from October 2004 to September 2005 (see p. 1355).

On 25 July, the Council took action on the situation of and assistance to Palestinian women in **resolution 2006/8** (see p. 546).

Women and poverty

Participation of women in development

On 28 February [E/2006/27 & Corr.1], the Commission on the Status of Women held a panel discussion on the enhanced participation of women in development: an enabling environment for achieving gender equality and the advancement of women, taking into account education, health and work. It had before it the report of the Secretary-General on the topic [E/CN.6/2006/12], which noted that the uneven progress in implementing the international commitments on gender equality and empowerment of women, and the large gap between policy and practice, highlighted the importance of a more coherent, integrated approach to ensuring an enabling environment. The lack of integrated policies and mechanisms to promote gender equality and the empowerment of women into national development policy frameworks and programmes presented a major challenge to the creation of such an environment. Systematic efforts to strengthen the capabilities of women and girls, as measured by health and education status, were required. Other challenges identified included the lack of coherence between national development policies and gender equality policies and strategies; gaps between policy and implementation; underrepresentation of women in decision-making; insufficient protection and promotion of women's human rights; discriminatory socio-cultural practices and attitudes; and persistent violence against women. Progress was further hampered by institutional hindrances, such as the lack of political will and resources, inadequate implementation of gender mainstreaming, insufficient mechanisms for monitoring and accountability, and lack of coordination and strategic partnerships. The report concluded with a series of recommendations for action by Governments, international organizations, including the United Nations, civil society and other relevant stakeholders, with an emphasis on the areas of education, health and work.

By decision 50/101, the Commission took note of the Secretary-General's report. On 16 March, the Commission adopted its agreed conclusions on the enhanced participation of women in development: an enabling environment for achieving gender equality and the advancement of women, taking into account, inter alia, the fields of education, health and work, which it also brought to the attention of the Economic and Social Council.

Gender dimensions of international migration

On 2 March [E/2006/27 & Corr.1], the Commission on the Status of Women held a high-level panel discussion on the gender dimensions of international migration, which examined various aspects of international migration from a gender perspective, such as linkages between migration and development; the impact of migration on families; the empowerment of migrant women; the brain drain; demand for specific types of labour; living and working conditions of women migrant workers, including mistreatment and abuse; human rights of women migrant workers; gender and remittances; and trafficking of women and its impact on development, as well as on families, health and education. The discussion revealed that women were active participants in migration within and between countries, representing 51 per cent of international migrants in more developed regions. While most women moved voluntarily—either as the principal wage earners or for family reunification purposes—forced migration of women and girls occurred due to conflict and violence. Gender biases in the migration process resulted in women's experiences differing from those of men, including with regard to the causes and outcomes of migration.

The meeting observed that a holistic and comprehensive approach was needed to address the multidimensional aspects of international migration. As poverty and the lack of economic resources were identified as the main factors influencing migration, increased socio-economic development and gender equality within countries of origin could lead to disincentives for migration. Attention was drawn to the need to address the social challenges related to migration and to raise awareness on the contributions of women migrants in destination countries. In the area of trafficking, it was recommended that organizations, such as the International Organization for Migration, investigate its causes and develop comprehensive indicators for cross-country analyses. The need for effective legal measures to address trafficking in women and girls, as well as for cross-border collaboration, including on monitoring and prosecution, was also highlighted.

A summary of the high-level panel meeting, submitted by the Commission, was brought to the attention of the Economic and Social Council to provide input to the General Assembly at its High-level Dialogue on International Migration and Development (see p. 1261). On 25 July, by **decision 2006/234**, the Council transmitted the Commission's summary to the Assembly.

(For more information on international migration, see pp. 1259 and 1263.)

Women and the economy

Economic advancement for women

Responding to Commission resolution 49/8 [YUN 2005, p. 1268], the Secretary-General submitted a report [E/CN.6/2006/7] on economic advancement for women, which was based on information provided by Member States in 2004 in response to a questionnaire on the 10-year review and appraisal of implementation of the Beijing Platform for Action, and inputs from Member States to update that information. The report examined issues relating to the status of women in the labour market, including occupational segregation, wage gaps between women and men, economic decision-making, harmonization of work and family responsibilities, and pensions and taxes. It also highlighted women's access to information and communication technologies, rural women's income-generating potential, employment opportunities of migrant women and the importance of gender-sensitive statistics and information for informed decision-making on the economic advancement of women.

The Secretary-General concluded that most countries had made progress in promoting women's economic rights and independence. A wide range of gender-sensitive legislation, policies and programmes had facilitated women's participation in both wage employment and self-employment. However, progress had been slow and uneven. The problems related to women's over-representation in part-time work and in the informal sector needed to be addressed. Further efforts were needed to fully utilize the potential of information and communication technologies for women's economic advancement. In addition, further research and strengthened data-collection efforts were needed to understand the employment situations of and opportunities for rural women and migrant women. To address those issues, as well as others raised in the report, the Secretary-General outlined a series of recommendations that the Commission might wish to encourage Governments to undertake, with the support of the UN system, civil society and other stakeholders. On 10 March, the Commission took note of the report [E/2006/27 (dec.50/101)].

Women in power and decision-making

Equal participation of women and men in decision-making processes

In accordance with the 2002-2006 programme of work of the Commission on the Status of Women [YUN 2001, p. 1084] and in response to General Assembly resolution 58/142 [YUN 2003, p. 1167], the Secretary-General submitted a report [E/CN.6/2006/13] on equal participation of women and men in decision-making processes at all levels, which analysed the current situation of women in decision-making processes, with emphasis on their political participation and leadership at the international, national and local levels. It proposed policy recommendations for achieving that objective, based on the identification of the most promising practices and lessons learned. In that connection, conditions identified for attaining that goal included increasing both the numerical and substantive representation of women in decision-making. The report also highlighted the significant impact that women's participation and leadership in political processes had on promoting gender equality.

The Secretary-General observed that, despite incremental changes over the past decade, women continued to face persistent challenges to their participation in decision-making. Serious obstacles included their underrepresentation in such male-dominated domains as the military, economic policy and foreign affairs; the absence of gender-sensitive enabling environments in parliaments and legislatures; and the persistence of traditional stereotypical attitudes and behaviour. The lack of sex-disaggregated data on women's access to decision-making at all levels of the economy, the judiciary, the media, academia and international affairs, remained a serious constraint to monitoring progress. The Secretary-General made recommendations for increasing the participation of women in decision-making and enhancing the impact of their increased presence in Governments, international actors, including the United Nations, parliaments, political parties, NGOs, the media and other stakeholders, and election management bodies.

Commission action. On 28 February, during its fiftieth session [E/2006/27 & Corr.1], the Commission on the Status of Women held a panel discussion on equal participation of women and men in decision-making processes at all levels and on 10 March, adopted its agreed conclusions on the topic, which it brought to the attention of the Economic and Social Council (see p. 1355).

Institutional mechanisms for the advancement of women

Inter-Agency Network. The United Nations Inter-Agency Network on Women and Gender Equality (IANWGE), at its fifth session (New York, 22-24 February) [IANWGE/2006/REPORT], focused on identifying key elements of a UN system-wide gender mainstreaming policy and strategy. The outcome of the deliberations would serve as input to the joint session of the High-level Committee on Management (HLCM) and the High-Level Committee on Programmes (HLCP) of the UN System Chief Executives Board for Coordination (CEB), and to the substantive (2006) session of the Economic and Social Council in July. The Network noted that UN reform presented both challenges and opportunities to gender mainstreaming and women's empowerment. Concerns were raised that gender equality might be sidelined in the reform process and human and financial resources allocated to gender issues reduced. Nevertheless, strong support was expressed for a system-wide gender strategy with clear benchmarks and timelines and a focus on results that would include the required accountability mechanisms and mainstreaming resource allocations. Participants agreed that the system should include accountability mechanisms; results-based management, monitoring, evaluation and reporting; financial and human resources allocation; capacity-building for all staff; coherence and coordination; and joint programming among entities.

The report also presented the analysis of the preliminary survey on Gender Mainstreaming in Programming, Monitoring, Evaluation and Reporting in Results-based Management Systems by the International Labour Organization (ILO) and the Office of Internal Oversight Services (OIOS), provided an update on the Secretary-General's in-depth study on violence against women (see p. 1333), and highlighted the conclusions of the joint biennial workshop convened by the Network and the Organisation for Economic Co-operation and Development (OECD)/Development Assistance Committee (DAC) Network on Gender Equality on the topic "Aid modalities and the promotion of gender equality" (Nairobi, 30-31 January). In conclusion, it was agreed that the ILO/OIOS preliminary survey would be expanded to collect and analyse responses from the entire UN system and that the Network would establish a new Task Force on violence against women.

Report of Secretary-General. Responding to Commission resolution 49/4 [YUN 2005, p. 1269], the Secretary-General submitted a report [E/CN.6/2006/2] on measures taken and progress achieved in the follow-up to the Fourth World Conference on Women and the General Assembly's twenty-third special session in mainstreaming a gender perspective in the development, implementation and evaluation of national policies and programmes. The report provided an analysis of activities carried out by Governments toward that aim and presented examples of how UN system entities supported gender mainstreaming at the national level.

The Secretary-General concluded that an increasing number of Member States utilized gender mainstreaming and specific interventions to promote gender equality and empowerment of women. Policy frameworks had improved at the national level, with some action plans having time-bound goals and targets, and many countries providing guidance on the implementation of policies on gender mainstreaming. Considerable advances were made in methodologies and tools, and in incorporating gender perspectives into sector policies, strategies and programmes. However, gaps between policy and practice remained. Constraints to full implementation included lack of clear mandates and enforcement of accountability mechanisms; insufficient allocation of gender-mainstreaming resources; lack of practical implementation strategies and skills; and underutilization or non-systematic use of methodologies and tools. Moreover, few countries had reported on successful implementation of accountability mechanism. The need to strengthen efforts to compile and disseminate sex-disaggregated data for use in monitoring and reporting was highlighted, as well as the catalytic role of national mechanisms, such as ministries, gender equality commissions and committees, and parliamentary bodies in supporting gender mainstreaming. The Secretary-General made recommendations to the Commission for encouraging UN entities, civil society and other stakeholders to ensure that action plans included concrete targets, indicators and clearly allocated responsibilities; incorporate gender perspectives in the budget process; institutionalize the use of gender analysis, gender impact assessment and evaluation for all policy areas; strengthen accountability systems in all government bodies; systematically document and disseminate lessons learned and good practices; and develop and strengthen the roles of national mechanisms.

Commission action. On 27 February [E/2006/27 & Corr.1], the Commission on the Status of Women held high-level round tables on the theme "Incorporating gender perspectives into national development strategies, as requested at the 2005 World Summit, for achieving the internationally agreed development goals, including the Millennium Development Goals (MDGs)". On 10 March, the Commission took note of the summary of the meetings [E/CN.6/2006/CRP.7] and, by decision 50/101, took note of the Secretary-General's report (see above).

Further report of Secretary-General. Pursuant to Economic and Social Council resolution 2005/31 [YUN 2005, p. 1270] on mainstreaming a gender perspective into all UN system policies and programmes, the Secretary-General submitted a May report [E/2006/65], which provided an overview of the gender training efforts of UN entities, emphasized the importance of training for capacity-building for gender mainstreaming and identified some of the critical elements for conducting successful training, including institutional context, support structures, systematic monitoring and evaluation and follow-up mechanisms. It highlighted examples of gender-specific training provided within the UN system for managers, field-level staff, gender specialists and focal points, and personnel working in the area of peace and security, as well as the use of the Internet as a tool for building capacity on gender mainstreaming. The UN system response to the increasing demand for technical support and capacity-building on gender mainstreaming at the national level was also covered.

The Secretary-General observed that, although policies and strategies on gender equality were in place in many entities, a large gap remained between policy and practice. Many training programmes had been organized on an ad hoc basis, with little institutional follow-up, an approach that underestimated the knowledge and skills required for effective gender mainstreaming. Noting that considerable effort had been made to develop new approaches and introduce important innovations, he advocated further assessment of such initiatives. Insufficient mechanisms to ensure accountability among staff to utilize the skills acquired in training, limited regular budget resources, and the lack of mechanisms and tools for evaluating its impact were also constraints to the provision of effective gender training and assessment.

The Secretary-General recommended that the Economic and Social Council encourage UN entities to make specific commitments to training in all gender equality policies, strategies and action plans; make gender mainstreaming training mandatory for all staff; integrate gender perspectives in all training courses; develop innovative forms of capacity-building, in addition to formal training; ensure that managers provide the leadership and support required; ensure that offices of human resource management advocate for gender mainstreaming capacity-building and provide resources; develop more effective forms of follow-up to training; strengthen accountability systems for all staff; allocate sufficient resources to ensure mandatory training, follow-up and evaluation and monitoring of training activities; strengthen inter-agency collaboration, including through IANWGE; and strengthen capacity-building activities for national mechanisms for the advancement of women.

On 24 July, by **decision 2006/227**, the Economic and Social Council took note of the Secretary-General's report.

UNDP consideration. In response to United Nations Development Programme/United Nations Population Fund (UNDP/UNFPA) Executive Board decision 2005/27 [YUN 2005, p. 1270], UNDP presented its gender action plan for 2006-2007 [DP/2006/9] and a progress report on implementation of the 2005 gender action plan [DP/2006/8]. It also submitted the findings of an independent evaluation of gender mainstreaming in UNDP [DP/2006/5], as well as the response of UNDP management to the evaluation [DP/2006/7]. The Executive Board endorsed [E/2006/35 (dec. 2006/3)] the 2006-2007 gender action plan and requested UNDP to report in 2007 on progress in implementing it and the commitments in the management response, particularly those concerning clarification of the role and responsibilities of UNDP and the United Nations Development Fund for Women (UNIFEM) (see p. 1359).

ECONOMIC AND SOCIAL COUNCIL ACTION

On 27 July [meeting 41], the Economic and Social Council adopted **resolution 2006/36** [draft: E/2006/L.30] without vote [agenda item 7 *(e)*].

Mainstreaming a gender perspective into all policies and programmes in the United Nations system

The Economic and Social Council,

Reaffirming its agreed conclusions 1997/2 of 18 July 1997 on mainstreaming a gender perspective into all policies and programmes in the United Nations system, and recalling its resolutions 2001/41 of 26 July 2001, 2002/23 of 24 July 2002, 2003/49 of 24 July 2003, 2004/4 of 7 July 2004 and 2005/31 of 26 July 2005,

Reaffirming also the commitment made at the 2005 World Summit to actively promote the mainstreaming of a gender perspective in the design, implementation, monitoring and evaluation of policies and programmes in all political, economic and social spheres and to further undertake to strengthen the capabilities of the United Nations system in the area of gender,

Acknowledging that enhancing women's opportunities, potential and activities requires a dual focus, namely, programmes aimed at meeting the basic needs and the specific needs of women for capacity-building, organizational development and empowerment, together with gender mainstreaming in all programme formulation and implementation activities,

Reaffirming that gender mainstreaming is a globally accepted strategy for promoting gender equality and constitutes a critical strategy in the implementation of the Beijing Platform for Action and the outcome of the twenty-third special session of the General Assembly,

Recognizing that training is critical for increasing the awareness, knowledge, commitment and capacity of staff to mainstream a gender perspective into United Nations policies and programmes and that the provision of effective gender training requires adequate financial and human resources,

Underlining the catalytic role played by the Commission on the Status of Women, as well as the important role played by the Economic and Social Council and the General Assembly, in promoting and monitoring gender mainstreaming within the United Nations system,

1. *Welcomes* the report of the Secretary-General on follow-up to and progress in the implementation of the Beijing Declaration and Platform for Action and the outcome of the twenty-third special session of the General Assembly, especially in regard to mainstreaming a gender perspective in entities of the United Nations system;

2. *Notes with appreciation* the progress and continued efforts made by United Nations entities to address gaps between policy and practice in mainstreaming a gender perspective in their respective fields of work, including through the development of training, methodologies and tools;

3. *Expresses concern* at the large gap remaining between policy and practice, with the result that a gender equality perspective is not yet fully integrated into the work of the United Nations;

4. *Recognizes* that training is critical for increasing the awareness, knowledge, commitment and capacity of staff in respect of mainstreaming a gender perspective into United Nations policies and programmes, and, in this regard, calls upon all entities of the United Nations system, including United Nations agencies, funds and programmes, within the United Nations Staff Development Programme budget and other existing United Nations training budgets, without prejudice to the achievement of other training priorities:

(a) To make specific commitments annually to gender mainstreaming training, including in core competence development, and ensure that all gender equality policies, strategies and action plans include such commitments;

(b) To provide specific ongoing capacity-building, inter alia, through training, for gender specialists and gender focal points, including in the field;

(c) To make gender training mandatory for all staff and personnel and develop specific training for different categories and levels of staff;

(d) To ensure the integration of gender perspectives in relevant training courses, including in induction courses, training on results-based management frameworks and training on the project and programme cycle;

(e) To develop innovative forms of capacity-building, in addition to formal training, including by using information and communication technologies, and systematically assess the effectiveness of new approaches;

(f) To ensure that managers provide the leadership and support required, including by enhancing awareness, commitment and capacity through innovative approaches specifically developed for management levels;

(g) To ensure that, as relevant, offices of human resources management advocate for gender training and the enhancement of pertinent skills for all trainers within the United Nations;

(h) To develop more effective forms of follow-up to training to ensure full utilization of best practices and maximum impact on work programmes;

(i) To strengthen accountability systems for both management and staff, through, inter alia, the inclusion of objectives and results related to gender mainstreaming in personnel workplans and appraisals;

(j) To develop effective means of impact assessment, including the use of indicators for the systematic monitoring and evaluation of training and the performance of trainers;

(k) To create or expand electronic knowledge networks on gender mainstreaming to increase effective support for and follow-up to capacity-building activities;

(l) To strengthen inter-agency collaboration, including through the work of the Inter-Agency Network on Women and Gender Equality, to ensure systematic exchange of resources and tools across the system to promote cross-fertilization of ideas;

(m) To ensure that resident coordinators systematically promote, monitor and report on capacity-building activities related to gender mainstreaming within their country teams;

(n) To strengthen country team collaboration on gender training at the country level, including through sharing methodologies and tools, undertaking joint activities and strengthening the capacity of gender theme groups to support such activities;

5. *Recognizes* the important role that senior management plays in creating an environment that actively supports gender mainstreaming, and strongly encourages it to do so;

6. *Takes note* of the work already undertaken to implement General Assembly resolution 59/164 of 20 December 2004 on the improvement of the status of women

in the United Nations system, and urges continued efforts towards its full implementation;

7. *Encourages* all relevant United Nations entities to maintain their efforts to raise awareness of gender issues within their organizations and across the United Nations system;

8. *Requests* that the Inter-Agency Network on Women and Gender Equality continue to provide practical support to its members in gender mainstreaming, explore possibilities for developing an accessible and consolidated database of trained facilitators at the country and regional levels, in consultation with Member States, and report regularly to the United Nations System Chief Executives Board for Coordination through its High Level Committee on Programmes and its High Level Committee on Management in order to facilitate the incorporation of gender mainstreaming perspectives into their work;

9. *Requests* the Secretary-General to report to the Economic and Social Council at its substantive session of 2007 on the implementation of the present resolution.

System-wide gender policy and strategy. On 27 October [CEB/2006/2], at the second regular session of CEB, the Special Adviser on Gender Issues and the Advancement of Women introduced the draft system-wide gender mainstreaming policy and strategy, which the joint meeting of HLCP and HLCM (Paris, 27 March-1 February) had recommended to the Board for endorsement. The six main elements of the strategy focused on: accountability; results-based management for gender equality; oversight through monitoring, evaluation, audit and reporting; human and financial resources; capacity development; and coherence, coordination and knowledge and information management. She cited accountability, commitment at the highest level, and overall leadership as key ingredients for progress addressed in the policy and strategy. Following their adoption by the Board, she indicated that IANWGE would develop a system-wide action plan to operationalize the strategy. The action plan, which was expected to be ready for consideration at the joint HLCP/HLCM meeting in 2007, would specify actions required to implement the six main elements of the strategy, with time frames and indicators, allocation of responsibilities and accountability mechanisms and resources. CEB endorsed the draft policy and strategy entitled "UN system wide-policy on gender equality and the empowerment of women: focusing on results and impact", which was included as an annex to the report of the session.

Strengthening of UN gender equality architecture

During 2006, United Nations efforts toward strengthening the gender architecture of the Organization continued. In follow-up to the outcome of the Millennium Summit [YUN 2005, p. 48], the Secretary-General submitted a March report [A/60/733 & Corr.1] on mandating and delivering, which contained analyses and recommendations to facilitate the review of UN mandates older than five years originating from the General Assembly and other organs, and provided a framework and the initial tools to undertake that exercise. He stated that gender issues deserved the same consideration as other cross-cutting priorities in the work of the Organization and that there was need for a thorough review of mandates on gender equality. Of particular concern was the large number of reports on the status of women prepared on an annual, biennial or triennial basis, which could be consolidated. He recommended an examination of overlapping mandates for reports on gender, as well as an overall assessment and evaluation of institutional resources on gender equality across the UN system. He also called on the High-level Panel on System-wide Coherence to include in its work an assessment of how gender equality could be better and more fully addressed in the work of the United Nations, particularly in its operational activities (see below).

Report of High-level Panel. By a 20 November note [A/61/583] (see p. 1060), the Secretary-General transmitted the report of the High-level Panel on UN System-wide Coherence in the areas of development, humanitarian assistance and the environment entitled, "Delivering as one", which also addressed the cross-cutting issues of sustainable development, gender equality and human rights. The report presented a set of recommendations for delivering as one and overcoming systemic fragmentation in the Organization. In the section of the report dealing with gender issues, the Secretary-General stated that, within the UN framework, the international community had made strong commitments to the advancement of women over the past six decades and had entrusted the Organization with an important mandate in that area. However, based on input from Governments, civil society representatives, and UN staff at headquarters and at regional and country offices, the Panel indicated that, while the United Nations remained a key actor in supporting countries to achieve gender equality and women's empowerment, there was a strong sense that the UN system's contribution had been incoherent, under-resourced and fragmented. There were inspiring examples of UN initiatives that helped change women's lives, but those were isolated best practices.

The Panel concluded that the United Nations needed to replace its weak structures with a much stronger voice on women's issues to ensure that gender equality and women's empowerment were taken seriously throughout the UN system and that the United Nations worked more effectively with Governments and civil society. The Panel recommended the consolidation of the three existing UN gender institutions—Office of the Special Adviser on Gender Issues and the Advancement of Women (OSAGI), the Division for the Advancement of Women, and UNIFEM—into one enhanced and independent gender entity, headed by an Executive Director with the rank of Under-Secretary-General. The gender entity would have a dual mandate, combining normative, analytical and monitoring functions with policy advisory and targeted programming functions and should be fully funded. The Panel also recommended that gender equality should be a component of all One United Nations country programmes and that commitment to gender equality should remain a mandate of the entire UN system. The report also outlined the mandate, structure and funding of the proposed gender entity.

The Secretary-General indicated that he had decided to move forward on some of the Panel's recommendations, and had started the process to implement the Panel's recommendation on strengthening the UN gender architecture and taken steps to request the establishment of the Under-Secretary-General for Gender Equality and Empowerment of Women post. He added that a detailed proposal to the General Assembly was forthcoming and urged Member States to support it.

Report of Secretary-General. In a November report [A/61/590] on the UN gender architecture, the Secretary-General said that a critical analysis of the UN system-wide capacities for gender equality and gender mainstreaming showed that the existing architecture was too incoherent, under-resourced and fragmented to provide effective support to Member States, particularly at the country level where it was difficult to integrate norms and standards into policy and operational support. Fragmented intergovernmental and national decision-making institutions further exacerbated the situation. In order to address those challenges, a new gender architecture was needed that would enhance the links between norms and standards, and policies and operational work; and would have sufficient status, authority and resources to effectively carry out its mandate.

The proposed institutional arrangements for the new office on gender equality and the advancement of women entailed consolidating OSAGI, the Division for the Advancement of Women and UNIFEM into one entity, to be headed by an Executive Director, who would also serve as the chief adviser to the Secretary-General on gender issues. The office would combine the normative, analytical, monitoring and focused operational mandates and responsibilities of the existing gender architecture and be the catalyst for technical and policy matters, and the authority on gender equality and women's empowerment issues, with the support of high-quality technical and substantive expertise. The Executive Director would report through the Secretary-General to the Economic and Social Council, the Commission on the Status of Women and the General Assembly on its normative and analytical work and to the Executive Board of UNDP/UNFPA on its programmatic work. Functions carried out by OSAGI regarding improvement of the status of women would be transferred to the Office of Human Resources Management. The office would also play an integral role in the UN country teams, as well as the "One Country Programme" arrangements. The office would be funded from a combination of assessed and voluntary contributions.

In his proposal to establish the post of Executive Director at the level of Under-Secretary-General to head the new office, the Secretary-General indicated that the Executive Director would work on the details of the basic structure of the new office and would oversee the development of the new entity in consultation with the relevant intergovernmental bodies and institutions of the UN system. The proposed terms of reference for the Executive Director were annexed to the report. In conclusion, the Secretary-General recommended that the General Assembly endorse the creation of an office on gender equality and advancement of women; approve the establishment of a post of Executive Director at the Under-Secretary-General level; and appropriate additional resources in the amount of $306,500 of the programme budget for the 2006-2007 biennium to cover the estimated resource requirements to establish the new office.

Status of women in the United Nations

In response to General Assembly resolution 59/164 [YUN 2004, p. 1429], the Secretary-General submitted a report [A/61/318] on progress made in the representation of women in the organizations and agencies of the UN system as at 31 December 2004 and in the UN Secretariat from 1 July 2004 to 30 June 2006 (see p. 1700). In addition, OSAGI provided an oral update to the Commission on the Status of Women at its fiftieth (2006) session [E/2006/27 & Corr.1,2] in March.

On 19 December, the General Assembly took note of the Secretary-General's report (**decision 61/525**).

UN machinery

Convention on the elimination of discrimination against women

As at 31 December 2006, 185 States were parties to the 1979 Convention on the Elimination of All Forms of Discrimination against Women, adopted by the General Assembly in resolution 34/180 [YUN 1979, p. 895]. During the year, Brunei Darussalam, Cook Islands, Marshall Islands and Oman acceded to the Convention; while Montenegro succeeded to it. At year's end, 49 States parties had accepted the amendment to article 20, paragraph 1, of the Convention in respect of the meeting time of the Committee on the Elimination of Discrimination against Women, which was adopted by the States parties in 1995 [YUN 1995, p. 1178]. The amendment would enter into force when accepted by a two-thirds majority of States parties.

The Optional Protocol to the Convention, adopted by the Assembly in resolution 54/4 [YUN 1999, p. 1100] and which entered into force in 2000 [YUN 2000, p. 1123], had 83 States parties as at 31 December 2006.

CEDAW

In 2006, the Committee on the Elimination of Discrimination against Women (CEDAW), established in 1982 [YUN 1982, p. 1149] to monitor compliance with the 1979 Convention, held three regular sessions in New York [A/61/38].

At its thirty-fourth session (16 January–3 February), CEDAW reviewed the initial or periodic reports of Australia, Cambodia, Eritrea, Mali, Thailand, The former Yugoslav Republic of Macedonia, Togo and Venezuela on measures taken to implement the Convention. CEDAW considered a Secretariat report on ways of expediting its work [CEDAW/C/2006/I/4 & Add.1] and a report on the status of submission of reports by States parties under article 18 of the Convention, including a list of reports that had been submitted but not considered by the Committee [CEDAW/C/2006/I/2]. Three specialized agencies, the United Nations Educational, Scientific and Cultural Organization (UNESCO), the Food and Agriculture Organization of the United Nations (FAO) and ILO, had submitted reports in accordance with article 21 of the Convention [CEDAW/C/2006/I/3 & Add.1,3,4]. With regard to treaty body reform, the Committee decided that no decision should be taken on the question of a possible transfer of the Committee and its secretariat. Instead, it recommended that further reflection should take place once the details of the reform proposals were available and that the inputs of the Committee should be taken into consideration in the decision-making process [A/61/38 (dec. 34/1)].

At its thirty-fifth session (15 May–2 June), CEDAW reviewed the initial or periodic reports of Bosnia and Herzegovina, Cyprus, Guatemala, Malawi, Malaysia, Romania, Saint Lucia and Turkmenistan. The Committee considered a report on the status of submission of reports by States parties under article 18 of the Convention [CEDAW/C/2006/II/2]. It also considered the report on ways of expediting its work [CEDAW/C/2006/II/4] and the reports of specialized agencies [CEDAW/C/2006/II/3 & Add.3,4] on the implementation of the Convention in areas falling within the scope of their activity. By two decisions, CEDAW adopted working methods of the Committee pertaining to its meetings in parallel chambers [A/61/38 (dec. 35/I)] and a statement entitled, "Towards a harmonized and integrated human rights treaty bodies system", which it also decided to bring to the attention of the fifth Inter-Committee Meeting for discussion and support [A/61/38 (dec. 35/II)]. In respect of issues arising from article 2 of the Optional Protocol, the Committee continued its consideration of matters arising in conjunction with its work and decided to take action at its next session. On the views adopted under article 7, paragraph 3 of the Optional Protocol in 2005 [YUN 2005, p. 1271], CEDAW agreed to request further information from the State party on follow-up steps taken in response to the Committee's recommendations.

At its thirty-sixth session (7-25 August), the Committee met for the first time in parallel chambers, where it reviewed the initial or periodic reports of Cape Verde, Chile, China, Cuba, Czech Republic, the Democratic Republic of the Congo, Denmark, Georgia, Ghana, Jamaica, Mauritius, Mexico, Moldova, the Philippines and Uzbekistan. It also considered reports on: ways of expediting the Committee's work [CEDAW/C/2006/III/4]; the status of reports by States parties under article 18 of the Convention [CEDAW/C/2006/III/2]; and implementation by specialized agencies of the Convention [CEDAW/C/2006/III/3 & Add. 1,3,4]. The Committee concluded that the first experience with parallel chambers had allowed for a more in-depth and careful consideration of the status of implementation of, and compliance with the Convention in the reporting States. It was satisfied with the working methods in the parallel chambers, and confirmed that their flexible use enhanced constructive dialogue. The Committee intended to further build on the experience gained and improve its working methods in parallel chambers at future sessions, including its time management [A/61/38 (dec. 36/I)]. The Committee also reported that the extension of its meeting time in 2006 and 2007 would allow CEDAW to reduce significantly the backlog of reports awaiting consideration and it anticipated that effective and timely implementation of its responsibilities after the 2006-2007 biennium would require extended meeting time in 2008 and beyond. In that connection, the Committee intended to submit a further proposal for extended meeting time to the General Assembly at its sixty-second (2007) session, based on an assessment of existing requirements. The Committee also adopted a statement on the situation of women in the Middle East [A/61/38 (dec. 36/II)].

In other action, the Committee, in respect of issues arising under article 2 of the Optional Protocol, took note of the report of the Working Group on Communications under the Optional Protocol on its eighth session (annexed to the report). It also adopted views under article 7, paragraph 3, of the Optional Protocol in respect of communications 3/2004 and 4/2004 (annexed to the report).

On 19 December, by **decision 61/525**, the General Assembly took note of the report of CEDAW on the work of its thirty-fourth to thirty-sixth sessions.

Commission on the Status of Women

The Commission on the Status of Women, at its fiftieth session (New York, 22 March 2005, 27 February–10 March and 16 March, 2006) [E/2006/27 & Corr.1,2] recommended three draft resolutions to the Economic and Social Council for adoption on the situation of women and girls in Afghanistan (see p. 1346); the situation of and assistance to Palestinian women (see p. 1347); and the future organization and methods of work of the Commission (see p. 1356). It further recommended a draft decision for Council adoption on the report of the Commission's fiftieth (2006) session and the provisional agenda for its fifty-first (2007) session (see below), and brought to the Council's attention the High-level panel discussion on the gender dimensions of international migration (see p. 1261). The Commission also adopted and brought to the Council's attention three resolutions on the release of women and children taken hostage in armed conflicts (see p. 1341); women, the girl child and HIV/AIDS (see p. 1341); and the advisability of the appointment of a special rapporteur on laws that discriminate against women (see p. 888); the Commission's agreed conclusions on enhanced participation of women in development (see p. 1347) and on equal participation of women and men in decision-making processes at all levels (see p. 1348); as well as decisions on the future work of the Working Group on Communications [dec. 50/102] (see below) and on documents before the Commission under agenda item 3, of which it took note [dec. 50/101], among them the UNIFEM report on the elimination of violence against women [E/CN.6/2006/10-E/CN.4/2006/60] and the joint workplan of the Division for the Advancement of Women and OHCHR [E/CN.4/2006/59-E/CN.6/2006/9].

Election of officers. Pursuant to Economic and Social Council resolution 1987/21 [YUN 1987, p. 843] and decision 2002/234 [YUN 2002, p. 1163], the Commission held the first meeting of its fiftieth (2006) session on 22 March 2005 [E/CN.6/2006/1], during which it elected its Chairperson and other Bureau members of the fiftieth (2006) and fifty-first (2007) sessions of the Commission.

By **decision 2006/235** of 25 July, the Council took note of the Commission's report on its fiftieth session and approved the provisional agenda for its fifty-first (2007) session.

Communications. In a letter dated 10 April [E/2006/52], the Commission brought to the attention of the Economic and Social Council the note [E/CN.6/2006/CRP.4] prepared by the Secretariat entitled "Creating an environment at the national and international levels, conductive to generating full and productive employment and decent work for all, and its impact on sustainable development", as action-oriented input to the Council's 2006 high-level segment. The note highlighted recommendations for action to promote women's full employment and access to decent work.

In a letter dated 2 November [E/CN.6/2007/7] to the Commission, the Council detailed the outcome of its 2006 substantive session, including its discussion during the humanitarian affairs segment on gender-based violence (see p. 1053), and attached a list of resolutions adopted by the Council calling for action by the functional commissions.

Future organization and working methods

In response to General Assembly resolution 60/140 [YUN 2005, p. 1248], the Secretary-General submitted a report [E/CN.6/2006/3] on proposals for a multi-year programme of work for the period 2007-2009, which would enhance the working methods of the Commission. The proposals were based on the

Commission's work since 1996, the outcome of the 10-year review and appraisal of the implementation of the Beijing Declaration and Platform for Action [YUN 2005, p. 1247], the 2005 World Summit [ibid.], as well as the experience of other functional commissions of the Economic and Social Council. The Secretary-General proposed that the Commission continue its practice of developing a fixed multi-year programme of substantive themes, which would allow for in-depth reviews of progress in implementation of the critical areas of concern in the Platform for Action, and provide substantive input to intergovernmental processes and their follow-up, such as major UN conferences and summits. One theme per year should be selected, with a sustained focus over two sessions: the first session would be devoted to policy development and the second (two years later) to a review of the implementation of the agreed conclusions adopted after consideration of the theme at the first session. Therefore, in the proposed multi-year (2007-2009) work programme, the Commission would undertake policy development of a substantive theme in 2007 and review its implementation in 2009. The cycle of policy development followed by a review after two years would allow the Commission to enhance its follow-up on the implementation of its agreed conclusions more systematically and effectively.

Substantive themes proposed for 2007-2009 included the elimination of discrimination against the girl child (2007), with a review in 2009; financing for gender equality and empowerment of women (2008), with a review in 2010; and sharing of responsibilities for home and family, including caregiving in the context of HIV/AIDS (2009), with a review in 2011. During 2007 and 2008, the Commission would follow up on implementation of its agreed conclusions adopted in the 2002-2006 multi-year programme of work. It was further proposed that the Bureau of the Commission identify an emerging issue to be considered by the Commission prior to each session.

ECONOMIC AND SOCIAL COUNCIL ACTION

On 25 July [meeting 38], the Economic and Social Council, on the recommendation of the Commission on the Status of Women [E/2006/27 & Corr.1], adopted **resolution 2006/9** without vote [agenda item 14 *(a)*].

Future organization and methods of work of the Commission on the Status of Women

The Economic and Social Council,

Recalling its resolution 2005/48 of 27 July 2005, in which the Council welcomed the progress made in the review of the working methods of several functional commissions and invited those functional commissions and other relevant subsidiary bodies that had not yet done so to continue to examine their methods of work, as mandated by the General Assembly in its resolution 57/270 B of 23 June 2003, in order to better pursue the implementation of the outcomes of the major United Nations conferences and summits, and to submit their reports to the Council in 2006,

Reaffirming the primary responsibility of the Commission on the Status of Women for the follow-up to the Fourth World Conference on Women and the outcome of the twenty-third special session of the General Assembly,

Recognizing that the organization of work of the Commission should contribute to advancing the implementation of the Beijing Declaration and Platform for Action and the outcome of the twenty-third special session of the General Assembly,

Recognizing also that the implementation of the Beijing Declaration and Platform for Action, the outcome of the twenty-third special session of the General Assembly and the fulfilment of the obligations under the Convention on the Elimination of All Forms of Discrimination against Women are mutually reinforcing in achieving gender equality and the empowerment of women,

Reaffirming that gender mainstreaming constitutes a critical strategy in the implementation of the Beijing Declaration and Platform for Action and the outcome of the twenty-third special session of the General Assembly, and underlining the catalytic role of the Commission in promoting gender mainstreaming,

Recognizing the importance of non-governmental organizations, as well as other civil society actors, in advancing the implementation of the Beijing Declaration and Platform for Action and, in this respect, the work of the Commission,

A. Methods of work of the Commission on the Status of Women

1. *Decides* that, from its fifty-first session, the Commission on the Status of Women will consider one priority theme at each session, based on the Beijing Platform for Action and the outcome of the twenty-third special session of the General Assembly;

2. *Also decides* that the Commission will continue to hold, on an annual basis, a general discussion on the follow-up to the Fourth World Conference on Women and to the twenty-third special session of the General Assembly, entitled "Women 2000: gender equality, development and peace for the twenty-first century", and recommends that statements identify goals attained, achievements, gaps and challenges in relation to the implementation of previous commitments made with regard to the priority theme;

3. *Further decides* that the annual interactive high-level round table will focus on experiences, lessons learned and good practices, including results with supporting data, where available, in relation to the implementation of previous commitments made with regard to the priority theme;

4. *Decides* that each year the Commission will discuss ways and means to accelerate the implementation of the previous commitments made with regard to the priority theme through:

(a) An interactive expert panel to identify key policy initiatives in order to accelerate their implementation;

(b) An interactive expert panel on capacity-building for gender mainstreaming in relation to the priority theme, based on an exchange of national and regional experiences, lessons learned and good practices, including results with supporting data, where available, with the participation of technical experts and statisticians;

5. *Also decides* that there will be one outcome to the annual discussions on the priority theme, in the form of agreed conclusions, negotiated by all States, which shall both identify gaps and challenges in the implementation of previous commitments and make action-oriented recommendations for all States, relevant intergovernmental bodies, mechanisms and entities of the United Nations system and other relevant stakeholders, in order to accelerate their implementation, and which would be widely disseminated to the United Nations system, where relevant, and made widely available by all States to the public in their own countries, as appropriate;

6. *Further decides* that each year the Commission will evaluate progress in the implementation of the agreed conclusions on a priority theme from a previous session through an interactive dialogue among all States and observers to identify means to accelerate their implementation, focusing on national and regional activities in support of the implementation of the agreed conclusions, including, where appropriate, supported by reliable statistics, sex-disaggregated data and other quantitative and qualitative information to illustrate monitoring and reporting;

7. *Decides* that the outcome of this evaluation will be in the form of a summary submitted by the Chairperson of the Commission, prepared in consultation with the regional groups, through the members of the Bureau;

8. *Also decides* that the Commission will continue to discuss emerging issues, trends and new approaches to issues affecting the situation of women or equality between women and men that require urgent consideration;

9. *Requests* the Bureau of the Commission, prior to each session, to identify, in consultation with all States, through their regional groups, an emerging issue for consideration by the Commission, taking into account developments at the global and regional levels as well as planned activities within the United Nations, where increased attention to gender perspectives is required;

10. *Decides* that the emerging issue will be addressed by an interactive expert panel focusing on achievements, gaps and challenges through an exchange of national and regional experiences, lessons learned and good practices, including results with supporting data, where available, and that the outcome of this discussion will be in the form of a summary submitted by the Chairperson of the Commission, prepared in consultation with the regional groups, through the members of the Bureau;

11. *Requests* that, from the fifty-first session of the Commission, the Division for the Advancement of Women of the Department of Economic and Social Affairs of the Secretariat will organize a panel event in the margins of each annual session to enable a preliminary discussion on the priority theme of the subsequent session;

12. *Invites* all gender-specific United Nations entities and other relevant United Nations entities, including the Committee on the Elimination of Discrimination against Women, to contribute, where appropriate, to the discussion on the priority theme of the Commission;

13. *Decides*, in view of the traditional importance of non-governmental organizations in the advancement of women, that, in accordance with Economic and Social Council resolutions 1996/6 of 22 July 1996 and 1996/31 of 25 July 1996, such organizations should be encouraged to participate, to the maximum extent possible, in the work of the Commission and in the monitoring and implementation process related to the Fourth World Conference on Women, and requests the Secretary-General to make appropriate arrangements to ensure full utilization of existing channels of communication with non-governmental organizations in order to facilitate broad-based participation and dissemination of information;

14. *Notes with appreciation* the continuation of the annual parliamentary meetings organized by the Inter-Parliamentary Union, as well as the programme of side events held on the occasion of the sessions of the Commission;

15. *Invites* the regional commissions to continue to contribute to the work of the Commission;

16. *Encourages* all States to consider having technical experts and statisticians, including from ministries with expertise relevant to the themes under consideration, as well as representatives of non-governmental organizations and other civil society actors, as appropriate, on their delegations to the Commission;

17. *Requests* the Secretary-General to submit to the Commission, on an annual basis, a report on the priority theme, including proposals for possible indicators, elaborated in cooperation with the Statistical Commission, to measure progress made in implementation, with regard to the priority theme;

18. *Also requests* the Secretary-General to submit to the Commission, on an annual basis, a report on progress made in mainstreaming a gender perspective in the development, implementation and evaluation of national policies and programmes, with a particular focus on the priority theme;

19. *Further requests* the Secretary-General to include in the annual report to the General Assembly on measures taken and progress achieved in the follow-up to the implementation of the Beijing Declaration and Platform for Action and the outcome of the twenty-third special session of the Assembly and the annual report to the Council on the review and appraisal of the system-wide implementation of its agreed conclusions 1997/2 of 18 July 1997 on mainstreaming a gender perspective into all policies and programmes in the United

Nations system, an assessment of the impact of the Commission's input to discussions within the United Nations system;

20. *Welcomes* the continuation of the biennial consideration by the Commission of the proposed programme of work of the Office of the Special Adviser on Gender Issues and Advancement of Women and the Division for the Advancement of Women;

21. *Decides* that the Commission, at its fifty-third session, should review the functioning of its revised methods of work, in the light of the outcome of the discussions on strengthening of the Economic and Social Council, in order to ensure the effective functioning of the Commission;

22. *Also decides* that, at its fifty-third session, the Commission will discuss the possibility of conducting in 2010 a review and appraisal of the Beijing Declaration and Platform for Action and the outcome of the twenty-third special session of the General Assembly;

B. Themes for the period 2007–2009

23. *Further decides* that:

(a) In 2007, the priority theme will be "The elimination of all forms of discrimination and violence against the girl child", and progress will be evaluated in the implementation of the agreed conclusions from the forty-eighth session of the Commission on the role of men and boys in achieving gender equality;

(b) In 2008, the priority theme will be "Financing for gender equality and the empowerment of women", and progress will be evaluated in the implementation of the agreed conclusions from the forty-eighth session of the Commission on women's equal participation in conflict prevention, management and conflict resolution and in post-conflict peacebuilding;

(c) In 2009, the priority theme will be "The equal sharing of responsibilities between women and men, including caregiving in the context of HIV/AIDS", and progress will be evaluated in the implementation of the agreed conclusions from the fiftieth session of the Commission on the equal participation of women and men in decision-making processes at all levels.

Communications on the status of women

Working Group. At a closed meeting in March [E/2006/27 & Corr.1,2] the Commission considered the report of the Working Group on Communications on the Status of Women, established in 1993 [YUN 1993, p. 1050], which considered 18 confidential communications received directly by the Division for the Advancement of Women and 11 by the Office of the United Nations High Commissioner for Human Rights (OHCHR). No non-confidential communications were received. The Group noted that Governments had replied to five of the 18 communications received directly by the Division and to 10 of the 11 transmitted by OHCHR. The Group also noted that a number of communications of a general nature had been submitted, as opposed to communications alleging specific cases of discrimination or injustice against individual women. Several communications had brought to light the issue of harmful traditional practices, including female genital mutilation, and their adverse effects on the sexual and reproductive health of women, including possible HIV/AIDS transmission.

The Group ascertained that communications were most frequently submitted on abuse of power, arbitrary detention and inhumane treatment in detention and lack of due process; sexual violence, including rape and gang rape, committed by law enforcement personnel, private individuals and military personnel; discriminatory legislation against women in the areas of family, health, employment, social benefits, voting rights and the right to own and inherit property; other forms of violence against women, including domestic violence and sexual harassment, forced and early marriage and harmful traditional practices; abduction of women and girls by parties in armed conflict; torture and other cruel, inhuman and degrading treatment; differential application of punishments in law based on sex; the impact of armed conflicts on women and girls and the failure of States to abide by international humanitarian law and international human rights law, and to protect and assist them; and threatening or pressuring of victims of violence by members of security forces to force retraction of complaints or control and suppress potential opposition. The Working Group was concerned about the abuse of power by government officials in conducting arbitrary detention, torture and ill-treatment; violence against women, especially sexual violence, and the apparent lack of commitment by some States to tackle impunity; the failure by some States, in contravention of their human rights obligations, to exercise due diligence to prevent violence against women, adequately investigate such crimes and punish perpetrators; and the continued existence of legislation or practices intended to or with the effect of discriminating against women, despite the international obligations and commitments of States and their constitutional provisions to outlaw such discrimination.

From the replies received, the Working Group noted that some Governments had already adopted or were in the process of adopting new legislation, amending discriminatory legislation, making efforts to harmonize legislation with relevant international standards, removing gender bias in the administration of justice, bringing perpetrators to justice and/or providing remedies to the victims.

In a March decision [E/2006/27 (dec. 50/102)], the Commission decided to postpone until its fifty-second (2008) session further consideration of the Secretary-General's report on the future work of the Working Group [YUN 2004, p. 1170].

UN Development Fund for Women (UNIFEM)

During 2006 [A/62/188], the activities of the United Nations Development Fund for Women (UNIFEM) continued to focus on four key goals: reducing feminized poverty; ending violence against women; halting and reversing the spread of HIV/AIDS; and achieving gender equality in democratic governance and in post-conflict countries, which were defined in its 2004-2007 multi-year funding framework (MYFF), endorsed by the UNDP/UNFPA Executive Board in 2004 [YUN 2004, p. 1172]. The strategic framework also comprised four outcomes: implementation of legislation and policies at the national and regional levels; demonstrated leadership, commitment and accountability for gender equality by mainstream institutions; increased capacity of gender equality advocates; and changes in attitudes and practices to support gender equality.

Over the 2004-2006 period, UNIFEM contributed to strengthening legal and policy frameworks in 89 countries; contributed to reducing feminized poverty through support to efforts in 36 countries and ending violence against women through increased number of laws and policies, registering progress in 35 countries; supported initiatives to bring a gender equality dimension to Millennium Development Goal processes in 42 countries and in four regions; and supported 94 catalytic initiatives related to capacity development of national, regional and global governmental and non-governmental organizations and networks of gender equality advocates. UNIFEM contributed to multi-stakeholder initiatives in 22 countries; identified a total of 75 countries that were engaged in some form of gender-responsive budgeting; worked with national AIDS councils to mainstream gender into the plans and policies of 16 countries and to provide training in gender analysis and women's human rights approaches in 19 countries; supported training for women to enhance their participation in elections in 15 countries; and supported efforts in 50 countries to enhance media coverage of gender equality issues. The UN Development Group Task Team on Gender Equality, chaired by UNIFEM, secured UN Development Group endorsement of a process to finalize country team performance indicators on gender equality programming and the pilot of an action learning process to devise UN models for gender equality programmes. The Task Team also completed its second review of the resident coordinator annual reports.

In 2006, UNIFEM resources totalled $56.3 million, an increase of $6 million over the 2005 figure, of which $25 million was in core resources and $31.3 million in non-core resources. While the rise in non-core resources during 2004-2006 was double or triple the projections, the increase in core resources fell short of MYFF projections and was a concern. During the year, 54 Governments, 15 NGOs and private organizations, five national committees and four UN entities contributed resources.

In August [A/61/292], the Secretary-General transmitted to the General Assembly a report on UNIFEM activities in 2005 [YUN 2005, p. 1276]. On 19 December, the Assembly took note of the report by **decision 61/525**.

UNDP/UNFPA Executive Board action. In January, the UNDP/UNFPA Executive Board [E/2006/35 (dec. 2006/5)] took note of the report commissioned by the UNIFEM Consultative Committee "Organizational assessment: UNIFEM past, present and future" [YUN 2005, p. 1275] and requested the UNDP Administrator to report to the Executive Board on the assessment at the annual 2006 session; ensure that UNIFEM gained access to relevant UN forums and report on progress in 2006; and strengthen collaboration at the programme level between UNDP and UNIFEM.

In June [E/2006/35 (dec. 2006/21)], the Board took note of the UNIFEM report on implementing its multi-year funding framework, 2005 [DP/2006/25] and the Administrator's report on the organizational assessment [DP/2006/26]; and requested the UNDP Administrator and the UNIFEM Executive Director to explore ways to cooperate on strategic planning, funding, programming arrangements and the results framework in the context of the preparation of the 2008-2011 MYFF.

INSTRAW

The report of the Executive Board of the United Nations International Research and Training Institute for the Advancement of Women (INSTRAW) (third session, New York, 18 May) [E/2006/80] provided a review of the implementation of the programme of work during the period November 2005–April 2006; the presentation of the proposed workplan and operational budget for 2007; and the report of its Subcommittee on the Resource Mobilization Strategy on the proposed fund-raising strategy for INSTRAW [INSTRAW/EB/2006/R.2], which was contained in an annex to the report. The Board approved the workplan and operational budget for 2007, recommended that INSTRAW take measures to increase its visibility both within and outside the United Nations and with the general public, and agreed that INSTRAW should seek closer coordination with UN regional commissions. It stressed the need to increase fund-raising efforts in order to guarantee the activities of the Institute and requested the Director to strengthen her efforts in that regard. The Board requested the Director to fully implement the Subcommittee's recommendations on the proposed fund-raising strategy to enhance INSTRAW's visibility and decided to review progress at its 2007 session.

In July, by **decision 2006/250**, the Economic and Social Council took note of the report of the INSTRAW Executive Board.

Commission on the Status of Women. In response to Commission resolution 49/6 [YUN 2005, p. 1278], the Secretary-General transmitted the report [E/CN.6/2006/11] of the INSTRAW Director on strengthening the Institute, which provided information on the implementation of its 2004-2007 programme of work and focused on its three strategic areas: applied research, information gathering and dissemination and capacity-building on gender issues. The report also detailed INSTRAW contribution to the review and appraisal of the Beijing Declaration and Platform for Action through an analysis and identification of future work, and its development of a pioneer initiative to include gender in the analysis of remittances and development, as well as policy recommendations to improve women's economic benefits.

The Director concluded that, as a result of the revitalization process, INSTRAW was better positioned to contribute to women's empowerment, gender equality, mainstreaming gender issues in the MDGs, and gender mainstreaming throughout the UN system. She added that the commitment of sufficient resources by Member States was indispensable to securing the medium- and long-term sustainability for the Institute to comply with its mandate.

On 10 March, the Commission [dec.50/101] took note of the Director's report on INSTRAW.

Chapter XI

Children, youth and ageing persons

In 2006, the sixtieth year of its operation, the United Nations Children's Fund (UNICEF) continued its work to ensure that every child received the best possible start in life; was fully immunized and protected from disease, including HIV/AIDS, and disability; had access to quality primary school education; and was protected from violence, abuse, exploitation and discrimination. In commemoration of UNICEF sixtieth anniversary, the General Assembly adopted a resolution commending the Fund for its work to achieve the Millennium Development Goals and other international development goals in the interest of children. The Assembly also held a plenary meeting devoted to UNICEF history and accomplishments.

Progress was made towards mainstreaming children's priorities into national policy. Of the 190 countries that had adopted "A world fit for children"—the outcome document of the General Assembly's twenty-seventh (2002) special session on children—177 were engaged in follow-up activities incorporating the goals contained in the document into their planning processes by developing plans of action on children's issues or integrating the goals into mainstream national development plans, or both.

UNICEF began the first year of its medium-term 2006-2009 strategic plan, focusing on the priority areas of young child survival and development; basic education and gender equality; HIV/AIDS and children; child protection from violence, exploitation and abuse; and policy advocacy and partnerships for children's rights. UNICEF 2006 income increased by 1 per cent over 2005, with a low but somewhat improved ratio of regular to other resources.

Efforts continued to implement the 1995 World Programme for Youth to the Year 2000 and Beyond. The Economic and Social Council considered the issue of the promotion of youth employment. In a resolution on the subject, the Council urged Governments to consider youth employment as an integral part of overall strategies for development and collective security.

In 2006, UN efforts to implement the 2002 Madrid International Plan of Action on Ageing included plans for its review and appraisal, to commence in 2007, under the theme "Addressing the challenges and opportunities of ageing". In December, the Assembly called upon Governments to take a participatory approach throughout the Plan's implementation process and stressed the need for additional capacity-building at the national level.

Children

Follow-up to 2002 General Assembly special session on children

The fourth report [A/61/270] on follow-up to the General Assembly's twenty-seventh (2002) special session on children [YUN 2002, p. 1168], submitted by the Secretary-General in response to Assembly resolution 59/261 [YUN 2004, p. 779], provided an update on progress achieved in realizing the commitments relating to children and young people set out in the Declaration and Plan of Action contained in the session's final document entitled "A world fit for children", adopted in resolution S-27/2 [YUN 2002, p. 1169]. Those commitments focused particularly on health, education, protection from abuse, exploitation and violence, and combating HIV/AIDS.

The number of countries translating those commitments into concrete actions had risen from that of the previous year, with 177 of them engaged in follow-up activities. A total of 47 countries had completed national action plans on children's issues, 99 had incorporated the document's goals into national development plans, and 90 had targeted them explicitly in sectoral plans. The convergence between the Millennium Development Goals (MDGs) [YUN 2000, p. 51] and those of "A world fit for children" resulted in an increased focus on the health and educational goals of the latter in national plans. At the same time, the issue of child protection continued to be insufficiently addressed. Despite the drafting of new legislation and the undertaking of initiatives regarding violence against children in many countries, public agencies responsible for child protection faced severe resource constraints. As to the impact of the planning goals of "A world fit for children" on national budgets, the link between plan preparation and budgeting processes needed to be strengthened. In a number of industrialized countries, commitment to those goals and the MDGs had led to increased development assistance in education, basic health services and water supply and sanitation. Governments used intergovernmental mechanisms to follow up on the goals of the special session, and civil society alliances and coalitions continued to work at all levels to promote and support them. Progress towards child-related goals was monitored by the majority of countries, and Governments continued to improve their databases, evaluate progress in plan implementation and develop surveillance systems and other monitoring tools, including the establishment of independent watchdogs, such as observers and ombudsmen. The report outlined the progress achieved in promoting healthy lives, providing quality education, protecting against abuse, exploitation and violence, and combating HIV/AIDS.

Despite the advances made, many obstacles remained to the effective implementation of child-related plans, including weak links between plans and budgets in many countries; weak institutional capacity; natural disasters, conflicts, violence and insecurity; the loss of human resources to the AIDS pandemic; inadequate resources to meet the cost of achieving all the goals of "A world fit for children"; and challenges in the generation of data to support programmes for disadvantaged families and children. The participation of civil society in the follow-up process should be extended from plan preparation to implementation and monitoring, and greater provision made for the participation of children and youth in the full cycle of national planning.

Among the ways forward suggested by the Secretary-General were the establishment of high-level national councils for children, assistance in capacity-building of national children's agencies, promotion of child-focused national budgets, strengthening of local government agencies, expediting action towards eliminating the worst forms of child labour by 2016, and facilitating the ongoing involvement of civil society, including children and young people. He noted the positive role played by the Committee on the Rights of the Child (see p. 777), and advised that the Committee's recommendations should take into consideration the experience gained with national plans of action, and the trend in many regions towards increased mainstreaming of children's issues into other planning processes. Use should be made of the Committee's concluding observations on State party reports to maintain government and public mobilization with respect to the goals for children, and the UN system should continue to assist Member States in their follow-up to those observations. Noting that 2007 would mark the mid-decade point of the Assembly's special session, the Secretary-General said that the review to be undertaken by the Assembly should, among other things, mobilize partners to accelerate progress towards the goals of "A world fit for children".

General Assembly action. The General Assembly, in **resolution 61/146** (see p. 777), noting the Secretary-General's reports on progress made towards achieving the commitments set out in the outcome document of its twenty-seventh special session, decided to pay particular attention to the protection of the rights of children living in poverty at the commemorative plenary meeting to be held in 2007 devoted to the follow-up to the outcome of that session. The Assembly, in **resolution 61/45** (see p. 1280), encouraged efforts to promote the objectives of the International Decade for a Culture of Peace and Non-violence for the Children of the World, 2001-2010 (see p. 1279) [YUN 2001, p. 609].

United Nations Children's Fund

In 2006, UNICEF remained committed to achieving the MDGs, and the goals contained in the outcome document "A world fit for children", adopted by the General Assembly in resolution S-27/2 [YUN 2002, p. 1169], at its twenty-seventh (2002) special session on children (see above). The two documents, which complemented each other, formed a strategy—a Millennium agenda—for protecting childhood in the twenty-first century. UNICEF work was also guided by the 1989 Convention on the Rights of the Child, adopted by the Assembly in resolution 44/25 [YUN 1989, p. 560], and its Optional Protocols (see p. 777). Its mission was to defend children's rights, help meet their basic needs, ensure their survival and increase their opportunities to flourish. It was also mandated to rally political will and resources to invest in children's well-being; respond to emergencies to protect children and work with partners to provide a rapid response for those in need; ensure special protection for the most disadvantaged children, such as victims of war, disasters, extreme poverty and all forms of violence and exploitation and those with disabilities. The Fund further aimed to promote equal rights for women and girls and encourage their full participation in developing their communities; and work towards the human development goals adopted by the world community and the peace, justice and social progress enshrined in the United Nations Charter. In line with its 2006-2009 medium-term strategic plan (MTSP) [YUN 2005, p. 1284], UNICEF focused its work, in 2006, on young child survival and development; basic education and gender equality; HIV/AIDS and children; child protection from violence, exploitation and abuse; and policy advocacy and partnerships for children's rights.

UNICEF annual flagship publication, *The State of the World's Children 2006,* highlighted the plight of those children most in need: the poorest, the most vulnerable, the exploited and the abused. As the pledges made in the MDGs and "A world fit for children" remained unfulfilled for such children, the report examined ways to include them in the Millennium agenda. It assessed global efforts to realize the MDGs and demonstrated the marked impact that their achievement would have on the lives of children and future generations. That was illustrated by the fact that the lives of 3.8 million children under the age of five would be saved if the MDGs were met in 2015. The report stated that children denied of their right to a formal identity, and those suffering from child protection abuses or facing early marriage, armed combat and hazardous labour were among those most at risk of exclusion from the Millennium agenda. It cautioned that the focus of the MDGs on national averages put children in marginalized communities at risk of missing out on essential services.

As the world continued to press ahead with policies, programmes and funding to make the vision outlined in the Millennium Declaration [YUN 2000, p. 49] a reality, it should not allow those children, who were excluded and marginalized and often invisible, to be forgotten.

In 2006, UNICEF cooperated with 155 countries, areas and territories: 44 in sub-Saharan Africa; 35 in Latin America and the Caribbean; 35 in Asia; 20 in the Middle East and North Africa; and 21 in Central and Eastern Europe and the Commonwealth of Independent States (CIS).

Total expenditures, including write-offs, amounted to $2,343 million (compared to $2,197 million in 2005), of which 96.5 per cent ($2,261 million) was for programme assistance and support; 3.2 per cent ($76 million) for management and administration; and 0.3 per cent ($7 million) for write-offs. UNICEF operations in 2006 were described in the UNICEF annual report covering the period from 1 January to 31 December 2006; the annual report to the Economic and Social Council [E/2007/6]; and the annual report of the Executive Director on progress and achievements against UNICEF's 2006-2009 MTSP [E/ICEF/2007/9].

In 2006, the UNICEF Executive Board held its first regular session (16-20 and 23 January), its annual session (5-9 June) and its second regular session (6-8 September), all in New York [E/2006/34/Rev.1], during which it adopted 20 decisions.

By **decision 2006/236** of 26 July, the Economic and Social Council took note of the Board's report on the work of its first, second and annual sessions of 2005 [E/2005/34/Rev.1]; the Board's report on the work of its first regular session of 2006 [E/2006/34/Rev.1; and the annual report of the Executive Director covering the year 2005 [E/2006/6].

On 8 September, the Executive Board adopted the programme of work and dates for its 2007 sessions [E/2006/34/Rev.1 (dec. 2006/20)].

Sixtieth anniversary of UNICEF

In 2006, UNICEF observed its sixtieth anniversary as a Fund of the United Nations system. Establishment by the General Assembly in 1946 by resolution 57(I) [YUN 1946, p. 163] as the International Children's Emergency Fund to respond to the millions of refugee and displaced children in the aftermath of the Second World War, it evolved over the years to become a development agency committed to tackling hunger, fighting disease and advocating the rights of children all over the world. UNICEF became a permanent Fund in 1953 by Assembly resolution 802(VIII) [YUN 1953, p. 467] and was renamed the United Nations Children's Fund.

In November, UNICEF issued the publication *1946-2006 Sixty Years for Children*, a historical review commemorating its sixtieth anniversary and tracing the evolution of the international cause of helping children since the Second World War.

GENERAL ASSEMBLY ACTION

On 28 November [meeting 59], the General Assembly, on the recommendation of the Second (Economic and Financial) Committee [A/61/427], adopted **resolution 61/20** without vote [agenda item 58].

Commemoration of the sixtieth anniversary of the operations of the United Nations Children's Fund

The General Assembly,

Recalling its resolutions 57(I) of 11 December 1946, by which it established the International Children's Emergency Fund, 417(V) of 1 December 1950, by which it affirmed the Fund's decision to devote a greater share of its resources to programmes outside Europe, 802(VIII) of 6 October 1953, by which it changed the name of the organization to the United Nations Children's Fund and removed the time limits from its mandate, 1391(XIV) of 20 November 1959, in which it saw aid provided by the Fund as a practical way to carry out the aims proclaimed in the Declaration of the Rights of the Child, and 2057(XX) of 16 December 1965, in which it applauded the award of the Nobel Peace Prize for 1965 to the United Nations Children's Fund,

Recalling also its resolutions 2855(XXVI) of 20 December 1971, in which it commended the Fund for its very substantial and significant achievements during its twenty-five years of operation, and 51/192 of 16 December 1996, in which it recognized the important contribution of the Fund in promoting the survival, development and protection of children during its first fifty years of operation,

Recalling further its resolutions 33/83 of 15 December 1978 on the International Year of the Child, 44/25 of 20 November 1989 on the Convention on the Rights of the Child, 45/217 of 21 December 1990 on the World Summit for Children and S-27/2 of 10 May 2002 in which it adopted the document entitled "A world fit for children", annexed to that resolution,

1. *Congratulates* the United Nations Children's Fund on the occasion of its sixtieth anniversary;

2. *Commends* the United Nations Children's Fund for the substantial assistance it has provided to programme countries in achieving the Millennium Development Goals and other agreed development goals in the interest of children;

3. *Commends* the staff of the United Nations Children's Fund and the National Committees and other partners for their contributions to the substantial achievements of the Fund;

4. *Commends* Member States, civil society organizations and the private sector for the generous financial support of the activities of the United Nations Children's Fund, and invites them to consider increasing their support to the work of the Fund;

5. *Requests* the President of the General Assembly to convene, in December 2006, a special commemorative meeting of the Assembly devoted to the sixtieth anniversary of the operations of the United Nations Children's Fund.

Assembly's commemorative session

In accordance with General Assembly resolution 61/20 (above), on 8 December, the Assembly convened a special commemorative meeting devoted to the sixtieth anniversary of the operations of UNICEF [A/61/PV.70].

The Secretary-General, in his statement to the Assembly, said that over the six decades since its establishment, UNICEF advocacy on behalf of children had changed the international discourse, putting a human face on development. Its campaigns for child survival, girls' education and HIV/AIDS had proved to be models of partnership across agencies. Its emergency responses had saved the lives of millions of children caught up in wars and natural disasters; health programmes had saved millions of others from disease, under-nourishment, illnesses and death; and its education programmes had saved millions from trafficking, sexual exploitation, violence and abuse. Currently, UNICEF work to realize the rights of all children was at the heart of efforts to reach the MDGs. The Secretary-General extended profound thanks to the staff and leadership of UNICEF, as well as the national committees and their Goodwill Ambassadors.

The Executive Director of UNICEF spoke of accomplishments achieved over the previous sixty years, including a decrease in under-five mortality rates in developing countries, from 222 deaths to 87 deaths per 1,000 live births between 1960 and 2004; immunization reaching more than 70 per cent of children worldwide, compared to between 10 and 20 per cent in the 1980s; the eradication of smallpox and the declaration of some 175 countries as polio-free; an estimated 1 billion additional people with access to safe water compared to 1990; and increased numbers of children in school, with gender disparities in enrolment narrowing in most parts of the world. She acknowledged, however, that much remained to be done to advance and protect the rights of children in a world in which 10 million children under the age of five still died every year of largely preventable causes; natural disasters, exploitation, famine and hunger continued to undermine peace and stability; at least one child became HIV-positive every minute; and more than 2 billion people lived on $2 a day or less.

Programme policies

In her annual report to the Economic and Social Council covering 2006 [E/2007/6], the Executive Director described UNICEF actions to implement the MDGs and the outcome document of the 2005 World Summit [YUN 2005, p. 48] by putting more emphasis on partnerships, increasingly integrating its programmes and harmonizing work with other parts of the United Nations. The report also provided information on funding for operational activities and efforts to strengthen national capacity-building; examined financial management, including transaction costs and efficiency; assessed coherence, effectiveness and relevance of operational activities for development; and reported on the evaluation of operational activities and gender mainstreaming. It also discussed follow-up to international conferences and panels, notably the Assembly's special session on children (see p. 1361), and efforts to ensure the visibility of the rights of the girl child through participation in the fiftieth session of the Commission on the Status of Women (see p. 1355). The Executive Director concluded that a culture of continual improvement was being established at UNICEF within the process of

UN reform, leading to more efficient and effective programming and advocacy for children and to the creation of measurable results.

Medium-term strategic plan (2006-2009)

The Executive Director, in a report [E/ICEF/2007/9] describing major initiatives taken and progress and results achieved in 2006, the first year of the medium-term strategic plan (MTSP) 2006-2009, said that UNICEF had strengthened its emphasis on support, through effective partnerships in five focus areas (see p. 1363), as well as the MDGs and the child-related commitments of the Millennium Declaration [YUN 2000, p. 49]. It had also implemented a series of cross-cutting strategies to sharpen the effectiveness of its partnerships and operations, grounded in human rights-based approaches and gender equality, and reflecting UN reform efforts, results-based management, knowledge generation, the more systematic use of evidence, performance monitoring and operational effectiveness.

Innovations in the first year of the new plan period included the introduction of new indicators for assessing progress, results and organizational performance. Most indicators of programmatic effectiveness showed continued improvement during 2006, and the growth in UNICEF income was sustained. Other major initiatives included intensified, integrated approaches to the delivery of high-impact interventions for health and nutrition, closely linked with water, sanitation and hygiene (WASH), child protection and the fight against HIV/AIDS. UNICEF helped to raise awareness through support to the United Nations study on violence against children (see p. 916), and clear improvements were seen in the protective environment for children in many countries.

However, a range of new challenges had become more evident, including weaknesses in the design of sanitation programmes; the ineffectiveness of some interventions in response to the 2004 Indian Ocean tsunami [YUN 2004, p. 952]; and problems of school retention following expanded enrolment. Much remained to be done to increase the use of tested interventions for dramatic improvements in child survival and in strengthening national capacities to deliver and sustain those efforts. UNICEF programme cooperation and procurement services had a critical and strategic role to play in helping countries expand coverage and achieve results. The comprehensive organizational review (see p. 1378) under way was a major effort to diagnose UNICEF strengths and weaknesses and identify strategies to increase effectiveness as a partner in achieving results for children.

Medium-term financial plan (2006-2009)

In September, the Executive Board considered the MTSP: planned financial estimates for the period 2006-2009 [E/ICEF/2006/AB/L.6]. UNICEF recommended that the Board approve the framework of planned financial estimates for 2006-2009, including forecast expenditure of $2,388 million for 2006 and projected expenditure of $2,719 million for 2009; the preparation of programme expenditure submissions to the Board of up to $1,500 million from regular resources in 2007, subject to the availability of resources and the continued validity of those planned financial estimates; and the revised annual transfer of $30 million to the reserve for after-service health insurance for the period 2006-2009.

On 8 September [dec. 2006/15], the Board approved the recommendations.

MTSP support strategies

At its January session, the Board had before it the UNICEF joint health and nutrition strategy for 2006-2015 [E/ICEF/2006/8] and the UNICEF water, sanitation and hygiene strategy for 2006-2015 [E/ICEF/2006/6] for endorsement as the official strategy documents of programmes of support in those areas.

On 19 January [dec. 2006/3 and dec. 2006/4], the Board welcomed both strategies and requested the Executive Director to ensure that UNICEF increased its efforts to further develop national capacities to improve sustainable outcomes as outlined in them; ensure that comments thereon by Board members at its first regular session of 2006 were taken into consideration when implementing programmes of support in the areas of health and nutrition and water, sanitation and hygiene; and monitor the impact of both strategies on health and nutrition and water, sanitation and hygiene through the MTSP assessment process. The Executive Director should ensure that the MTSP review process analysed scientific developments and programming experience in health and nutrition and water, sanitation and hygiene and ensure that its findings were taken into consideration when implementing programmes of support in those areas. She should also include in the strategies an annex outlining how they would contribute to the achievement of the MTSP focus areas and key performance indicators, and update those annexes as necessary following agreement on subsequent MTSPs.

The Board, at its annual (June) session, had before it a report [E/ICEF/2006/17 & Corr.1] on the UNICEF post-crisis transition strategy in support of the MTSP, which outlined how the Fund aimed to contribute to transition strategies in order to produce results for children. UNICEF response to post-crisis transitions was guided by the principles of national ownership, partnerships, capacity development, a bottom-up approach to programming, building back better, gender sensitivity and the participation of children and young people. It would continue to be founded on the Millennium Declaration, the MDGs, and the Convention on the Rights of the Child; based on the operational commitments of the Core Commitments for Children in emergencies [YUN 2003, p. 1205]; and linked to the five MTSP focus areas. The report described actions planned or undertaken to strengthen UNICEF capacity for post-crisis transition in the areas of management and coordination; human and financial resources; monitoring and evaluation; and knowledge management and reporting. It recommended that the Board endorse the UNICEF strategy document for its programmes in post-crisis transition situations.

On 9 June [dec. 2006/6], the Board endorsed the UNICEF transition strategy as the support strategy for MTSP programmes in situations of transition from relief to development.

Medium-term strategic plan (2002-2005)

Under the MTSP for 2002-2005, UNICEF submitted to the Executive Board in January, a report on thematic funding [E/ICEF/2006/9]—contributions made by donors based on existing programmes and which were pooled and allocated to achieve the goals of the respective priority areas outside of regular funding. They supported MTSP goals and objectives and allowed for longer-term planning and sustainability. As at 31 October 2005, the total amount of thematic funding received was $703 million. Between 2003 and 2005, the Government of Norway was the largest contributor to thematic funding, followed by the United States Fund for UNICEF, the Government of Sweden, and the German and United Kingdom Committees for UNICEF. Girls' education and humanitarian response were the largest recipients of thematic funding.

At the annual session in June, the Executive Director submitted a report on results achieved for children in support of the Millennium Summit agenda, through the MTSP (2002-2005) [E/ICEF/2006/11]. The report analysed progress made in the context of MTSP (2002-2005) in the areas of early childhood development; immunization "plus"; girls' education; fighting HIV/AIDS; protection of children from violence, abuse and exploitation; and emergency preparedness and response. It also examined UNICEF commitment to UN reform and partnership initiatives, and highlighted programme management and operational performance; and income, expenditure and resource mobilization.

Evaluation system

In response to a 2004 Executive Board decision [YUN 2004, p. 1180], UNICEF submitted a report on its evaluation function [E/2006/15], which reviewed performance against its 2002-2005 workplan objectives, summarized the evaluations conducted from 2004 to 2005, and identified evaluation challenges in the context of the 2006-2009 MTSP. The report noted that, during the 2002-2005 MTSP period, 1,251 evaluations and 3,106 studies and surveys were conducted in country offices, reflecting an 18 per cent reduction in evaluations and a 26 per cent reduction in studies over the period. From 2004 to 2005, evaluations were conducted in several areas, including HIV/AIDS, community-based child protection initiatives and UNICEF response to humanitarian crises, such as the 2004 Indian Ocean tsunami. A self-assessment carried out by the Evaluation Office, using United Nations Evaluation Group norms and standards, highlighted UNICEF main strengths, among them, intellectual independence; credibility to clients; participatory and human rights-based approaches; and gender-balanced evaluation teams. Its weaknesses included limited availability of human and financial resources; limited evidence that evaluation findings were used; inconsistent distillation of lessons learned; and insufficient opportunities for professional development.

In the context of the 2006-2009 MTSP, evaluation priorities were identified as national capacity-building and strengthened national leadership in country-level evaluations; strengthening evaluation in humanitarian crises; strengthening evaluation within the UN system and with other partners; evaluation related to MTSP focus areas, strategies and operational effectiveness; strengthening UNICEF organizational capacity in evaluation; and heightened management attention to the evaluation function.

On 9 June [dec. 2006/9], the Executive Board called upon UNICEF to conduct evaluations of operations at the country level in close association with Governments, and assist them in developing national evaluation capacities. It should also prepare a comprehensive evaluation policy for consideration by the Executive Board in 2007; focus more on evaluating the results of the MTSP, country programmes and its humanitarian response; and, beginning in 2008, submit a biennial report on the implementation of the evaluation policy at various levels of the organization, including evaluation expenditures and funding sources.

Emergency assistance

In 2006, UNICEF response covered 53 emergencies in a wide range of humanitarian crises, from hostilities in the Middle East and the severe drought in the Horn of Africa to an earthquake in Indonesia and "forgotten emergencies" in the Central African Republic and Haiti. The increased funding ceiling of $75 million for the Emergency Programme Fund (EPF) had a significant positive impact on UNICEF's ability to respond to the acute needs of children and families. In 2006, $44.5 million was released from the Fund to 29 countries and two regional offices. The emergency preparedness and response plans of some 107 country offices were reviewed and, where necessary, updated. Efforts were also intensified to ensure that offices worldwide were prepared to address the threat of avian flu and human influenza. UNICEF worked closely with other UN agencies to ensure a common approach to such threat, focusing primarily on communication for behavioural change, supply pre-positioning and community-based initiatives.

UNICEF provided the lead for emergency response in water and sanitation, education, nutrition, non-food items, emergency shelter and emergency telecommunications in the Democratic Republic of the Congo (DRC), assisting more than 600,000 conflict-affected people with life-saving shelter and household items. It also supported the release and reintegration of almost 10,500 children associated with armed groups and forces, and made substantial efforts to combat sexual violence. In response to severe drought and floods in the Horn of Africa, millions of children were reached through a comprehensive set of interventions, including water treatment and diarrhoea prevention, measles vaccination, vitamin A supplementation and other nutrition initiatives. Despite the dangerous conditions that prevailed in the Sudan's Darfur region, 1.2 million children received polio vaccination and vitamin A supplementation. The number of conflict-affected children enrolled in primary school increased from an estimated 382,800 to 516,500, including 225,000 girls by the end of the year. Nationally, Sudanese children enjoyed increased access to health care in 2006, and the "Go to School" campaign in southern Sudan saw over 850,000 children registered in schools, supported by UNICEF through the delivery of educational materials and the training of teachers. In neighbouring Chad, UNICEF led the coordination of the UN country team's humanitarian actions for internally displaced persons (IDPs), but continued insecurity reduced the international humanitarian presence.

In the Middle East, collaboration with the Lebanese Red Cross at the inception of conflict (see p. 576) was crucial in delivering assistance for displaced children and families in otherwise inaccessible areas. UNICEF supported non-governmental organizations (NGOs) to run mobile primary health care units, immunization outlets and child-friendly spaces and to provide psychosocial support, reaching an estimated 300,000 people. Partnerships with NGOs in the Occupied Palestinian Territory also enabled the provision of key humanitarian assistance.

UNICEF continued to respond to the humanitarian needs of conflict-affected people in Sri Lanka. During the crisis in Timor-Leste, its response in the areas of immunization, nutrition screening and water and sanitation helped to avert the deterioration of the health and nutrition status of over 110,000 children and 70,000 IDPs. In the second year of its response to the 2004 Indian Ocean tsunami, UNICEF shifted its focus towards support for reconstruction, and assisted some 4.8 million children and women in eight countries. By late 2006, it had supported the reconstruction and renovation of over 50 health facilities and delivered medical equipment to nearly 6,100 hospitals and clinics in affected areas. Over 1 million people had access to safe water sources built with UNICEF support, some 1.2 million children received vitamin A supplements, and almost 1 million women and children were provided with insecticide-treated nets (ITNs) to protect against malaria. Nearly 400,000 children benefited from UNICEF-assisted psychosocial support, and through its intervention, tens of thousands of others were able to study at newly constructed or repaired schools, with over 1 million having received educational supplies for the new school year.

Maurice Pate Award

In June, the Executive Board considered a draft decision on the revision of the Maurice Pate Leadership for Children Award [E/ICEF/2006/16], established in 1966 in memory of UNICEF first Executive Director [YUN 1966, p. 385]. While the purpose and selection criteria of the Award remained valid in most respects, developments since the last revision in 2002 [YUN 2002, p. 1184], including the emphasis on partnerships to achieve the MDGs and the increased involvement in global movements and initiatives, suggested that a slight revision was timely. The Award would be a valuable way of acknowledging and commending key leading individuals and organizations in the global partnership for the achievement of the MDGs, most of which had a direct impact on the condition of children. The revision also sought to simplify the selection process to make it more feasible and manageable by changing the periodicity of the Award from yearly to occasional and allowing the option of bestowing the Award symbolically rather than for monetary value.

On 9 June [dec. 2006/12], the Board amended the procedure related to the objectives and criteria, recipients, nominations, selection, and value for the Award. Under the revisions, the Award would not necessarily be of monetary value but might be bestowed as a symbolic appreciation of an individual's or organization's dedication to the cause of children. When of monetary value, the Award would confer no more than $50,000 in any one year, the amount to be met from regular resources.

UNICEF programmes by region

In 2006, UNICEF regional programme expenditure totalled $2,118.6 million, of which $1,099 million (51.9 per cent) went to sub-Saharan Africa (including programme assistance for Djibouti and the Sudan); $650 million (30.7 per cent) to Asia; $147.3 million (7 per cent) to the Middle East and North Africa; $98.8 million (4.7 per cent) to the Americas and the Caribbean; $65.3 million (3.1 per cent) to Central and Eastern Europe and CIS; and $58.3 million (2.8 per cent) to interregional programmes. Programme support costs amounted to an additional $142 million.

Programme expenditures were highest in countries with low income and high, or very high, under-five mortality rates. The 53 lowest income countries—defined as those with a per capita gross national income of $875 or less—which had a total child population in 2005 of 1.2 billion, or 52 per cent of all children worldwide, received 64 per cent of total programme expenditures. An estimated 85 per cent of expenditures for young child survival and development were in 60 countries with high under-five mortality rates and/or large numbers of child deaths.

In September [E/2006/34/Rev.1], the Executive Board had before it summaries of the mid-term reviews and major evaluations of country programmes in Eastern and Southern Africa [E/ICEF/2006/P/L.28], West and Central Africa [E/ICEF/2006/P/L.29], the Americas and the Caribbean [E/ICEF/2006/P/L.30], East Asia and the Pacific [E/ICEF/2006/P/L.31], South Asia [E/ICEF/2006/P/L.32], Central and Eastern Europe and CIS [E/ICEF/2006/P/L.33], and the Middle East and North Africa [E/ICEF/2006/P/L.34]. The reports assessed resources used, constraints faced, adjustments made and results achieved in country programmes. They also examined the rationale for, design of and lessons learned from major evaluations.

(For information regarding the UNICEF country programme approval process, see p. 1377.)

Field visits

The visit of the President of the Executive Board to the Central African Republic (26 February–5 March) [E/ICEF/2006/CRP.8] focused on the implementation of the country programme in relation to the MTSP priorities and the quality of UNICEF coordination and partnership with the Government, UN agencies, donors and civil society. It also provided an important overview of the situation of children's rights in the country and UNICEF contribution to its improvement. The UNICEF programme of cooperation in the country had four main elements: child survival and development, girls' education, HIV/AIDS and child protection. Challenges, such as the prevailing insecurity, insufficient government revenues and destruction of basic social infrastructure, made for a difficult programming environment. While the Government's political will to improve the situation of children was strong, sustained political stabilization and greater international assistance were critical for any lasting developments. Moreover, community mobilization, women's empowerment and participation of young people were key ingredients for community development.

In a joint visit to Indonesia (8-22 March) [E/ICEF/2006/CRP.16], members of the Executive Boards of the United Nations Development Programme (UNDP)/United Nations Population Fund (UNFPA), UNICEF and the World Food Programme (WFP) sought to understand the ways and extent to which the United Nations contributed to the transition from a humanitarian disaster to reconstruction and recovery, following the December 2004 earthquake and tsunami. Board members gained insight into how multilateral agencies worked together at the country level, and paid particular attention to issues relevant to UN reform. They concluded that, although coordination among agencies, funds and programmes was present in Indonesia, the efforts to achieve coordination sometimes outstripped the results. Coordination and collaboration between UN organizations and local authorities was found to be insufficient. The team recommended that UN organizations should set overall standards across the board for the projects they initiated; UN humanitarian agencies should strengthen their collaboration and cooperation, and seek to make humanitarian operations cost-efficient; and relief and rehabilitation agencies should provide training in entrepreneurship to local communities, especially to women, and extend small grants to participants with feasible business plans.

Executive Board members visited Chad (2-8 April) [E/ICEF/2006/CRP.14] to view UNICEF operations in a humanitarian crisis, having received some 232,000 refugees from the Darfur region of the Sudan and the Central African Republic since 2003. The delegation found that, while UNICEF presence had been an advantage in the humanitarian response, it would be difficult for the Fund to continue to support the Government effectively without an improvement in the security situation. Board members were struck by the dedication of the UNICEF staff in Chad, but observed difficulties in recruiting experienced national and international staff, a need for greater support from the regional office, and the inadequate attention paid by the United Nations to the security of staff members of partner NGOs.

During their visit to India (13-21 May) [E/ICEF/2006/CRP.15], members of the Bureau of the UNICEF Executive Board reviewed the progress, challenges and programming for the achievement of the MDGs. They observed that key steps towards polio eradication, salt iodization, vitamin A supplementation, and the provision of water and sanitation facilities had been taken in recent years. Effective models for reducing child mortality in the first month of life, reducing malnutrition and improving children's performance in school had also been developed. As the UN focus in India in the future would be on capacity development, advocacy, monitoring standards and norms and emergency and post-emergency response, UNICEF role in the country would shift towards modelling innovative interventions, knowledge management and analysis, systems-strengthening at the district level, community empowerment and behavioural change. The members concluded that effective intervention strategies would have to include the integrated approach; behaviour-change communication, coupled with well-targeted service delivery; participatory approaches, such as village planning; and effective partnerships with the private sector. They noted that tackling the implementation gap for social development was a critical challenge for reaching the MDGs, and recommended that the UNICEF programming cycle be harmonized with government planning cycles.

UNICEF programmes by sector

In 2006, UNICEF programme expenditures, which were linked to the five organizational priorities established in 2005 under the 2006-2009 MTSP [YUN 2005, p. 1284], totalled $2,118.6 million [E/ICEF/2007/9], an 8 per cent increase over 2005. The largest share of total expenditure, $1,079.6 million (51 per cent), went to young child survival and development; $450.2 million (21.3 per cent) to basic education and gender equality; $233.4 million (11 per cent) to policy advocacy and partnerships for children's rights; $216.6 million (10.2 per cent) to child protection from violence, exploitation and abuse; and $116.3 million (5.5 per cent) to HIV/AIDS and children. Some $22.5 million (1.1 per cent) was expended in other areas. Programme support costs amounted to an additional $142 million.

The estimated shares of the focus areas in total programme assistance for young child survival and development and child protection were very close to projected levels. The overall shares for basic education and gender equality and policy advocacy and partnerships for children's rights were above the projected levels, whereas the share for HIV/AIDS and children was well below the projected level. Some distortions in those estimates were believed to have arisen due to the revision of the expenditure coding system and lack of experience with its use in the first year.

Young child survival and development

In 2006, UNICEF supported national immunization programmes in all countries with high child mortality rates and/or with large numbers of child deaths, and helped to leverage new government funding for immunization. Some 113 countries achieved the target of 90 per cent or greater national coverage of combined diphtheria/pertussis/tetanus vaccine (DTP3). At the subnational level, strategies were developed to improve immunization coverage in low-performing districts through the "reach every district" approach. Measles-related deaths fell by some 60 per cent worldwide between 1999 and 2005. UNICEF helped to spearhead the Measles Initiative, which supported the vaccination of more than 220 million children in 2006, saving the lives of an additional 90,000 to 100,000 young children. During the year, 22 countries conducted tetanus toxoid supplementary immunization activities, which reached some 11.5 million women of child-bearing age for the first dose and another

29 million for the second and/or third. UNICEF worked closely with the World Health Organization (WHO) and other partners to develop innovative service delivery systems to address the issue of the refusal of polio vaccine in some areas. The number of polio-endemic countries was reduced from six to four, as both Egypt and the Niger successfully stopped all endemic virus transmission.

UNICEF assisted national vitamin A supplementation programmes by distributing 641 million capsules to 75 countries and through awareness-raising and support for food fortification, policy development and integration of vitamin supplementation into routine delivery systems. Progress was also made in combating iodine deficiency disorders (IDD), with 71 per cent of households in the developing world consuming adequately iodized salt, and approximately 82 million newborns protected from learning disabilities caused by IDD.

Among its efforts to combat malaria, UNICEF supported capacity development among health workers, as well as communication at the community level. It also procured 25 million insecticide-treated nets (ITNs), the majority of which were distributed as part of integrated child and maternal health programmes, including antenatal care. Some 42 countries were using artemisinin-based combination therapy (ACT) as a first-line treatment, whose high efficacy made it the most cost-effective malaria control strategy. UNICEF procured nearly $15 million worth of ACT during the year, and assisted in the training of health workers and the development of ACT roll-out plans.

Although cotrimoxazole prophylaxis represented a simple, cost-effective intervention for HIV-exposed children, global coverage was lower than that for paediatric anti-retroviral treatment (ART). WHO issued new guidelines in 2006 to facilitate wide-scale implementation of the treatment, while UNICEF worked with national partners on acceleration efforts linked to other child survival interventions.

The Accelerated Child Survival and Development programme supported by UNICEF and other partners in West Africa continued to provide an important model for integrated community-based programmes. Despite the strengths of the programme, such as its community-based approach, emphasis on capacity-building, supervision and monitoring, the enhancement of interventions, and effective advocacy and national policy uptake of ACSD strategies, it suffered from weaknesses that needed to be addressed, such as stock-outs of commodities, and the lack of sustainable funding and motivation of community health workers.

Rapid increases in breastfeeding rates were registered in several countries with community support networks and vigorous media campaigns. Other efforts for improving infant and young child feeding supported by UNICEF included the Baby-Friendly Hospital Initiative and implementation and monitoring of the International Code of Marketing of Breast Milk Substitutes. UNICEF assisted in updating the UN guidelines on HIV and infant and young child feeding on the basis of new evidence. The new Strategic Guidance Note on Newborns, prepared by UNICEF and Save the Children, was used by numerous countries to help design strategies and interventions.

Although the estimated percentage of families reached through good parenting programmes rose from around 28 to 32 per cent between 2005 and 2006, there was still an urgent need to expand such programmes, incorporating locally adapted communication strategies for reaching families and communities. In response to high rates of childhood accidents and injuries in some countries, UNICEF as envisaged under the MTSP, supported a range of interventions, including advocacy and technical support for regulations on child safety, pilot initiatives to prevent injuries and surveillance systems, particularly in China and Viet Nam.

In 2006, UNICEF supported water, sanitation and hygiene (WASH) interventions in 93 countries, including most least developed countries. A global task force was established with a wide range of public and private partners and organizations to advise and engage more closely with UNICEF on WASH-related issues. New comprehensive programmes were established with UNICEF assistance to pursue Millennial targets in priority countries, and ongoing programmes were strengthened elsewhere. UNICEF addressed water quality issues through support for mass testing of wells; mapping and providing alternative safe water supplies; promoting safe storage and treatment of drinking water; and household rainwater harvesting. Direct UNICEF support for reconstruction and emergency response resulted in millions of people gaining access to safe water and sanitation in 2006. In many countries in sub-Saharan Africa, UNICEF supported initiatives to improve national preparedness capacities and responses for the immediate control of any cholera outbreak. Cholera contingency plans were credited with reducing deaths in Angola, the DRC, Ethiopia, the Sudan and other countries. The UNICEF global WASH and nutrition clusters for emergencies became operational, and funding was being sought to place emergency water and sanitation advisers in all regional offices.

In other emergency action, the Fund assisted countries in the meningitis belt to procure pre-positioned vaccine stockpiles to expedite outbreak response. In response to outbreaks, mainly in West and Central Africa, more than 3.5 million children were vaccinated against meningitis and approximately 6 million against yellow fever. Under its Core Commitments for Children in emergencies, revised in 2003 [YUN 2003, p. 1205], UNICEF assisted rapid responses in Africa, Asia and Latin America, supporting emergency water supply, storage and treatment, emergency sanitation and the supply of hygiene kits. Assistance was also provided to countries emerging from crisis, including Sierra Leone and those affected by the 2004 Indian Ocean tsunami.

UNICEF supported therapeutic feeding for children with severe acute malnutrition in over 20 countries and community-based management of severe acute malnutrition as a complement to in-patient therapeutic feeding in priority countries in sub-Saharan Africa.

Basic education and gender equality

Progress continued in many countries towards achieving the education- and gender-related MDGs. Global primary school enrolment increased significantly, with the number of primary-school-aged children not enrolled down to some 77 million, although household surveys revealed that many of those enrolled in school might not be attending regularly, if at all. UNICEF collaborated in an initiative for the abolition of school fees, which produced a major surge in enrolment in those countries where enrolment was lagging, including among children from poor families. Its advocacy and support also helped to extend and focus national programmes for early childhood development, the incorporation of which in national development plans was particularly strong in sub-Saharan Africa and in Latin America and the Caribbean.

UNICEF assisted programmes in all regions to reduce disparities in access to quality basic education, especially data collection and studies, and through support to policy development and advocacy for compulsory free primary education and special measures for girls and marginalized children. Some 91 developing and 34 industrialized countries were on track to achieving gender parity in primary education, although significant intra-country disparities often remained, while only one third of countries had achieved gender parity at the secondary level. Formally recognized United Nations Girls' Education Initiative partnerships existed in 36 countries in 2006, two more than in 2005, and UNICEF was involved in ongoing sector-wide approaches to address gender disparities in access to and quality of education in 23 countries, compared to 15 in 2004.

To improve educational quality and address problems of retention and achievement, some 54 countries adopted quality standards for primary education based on the child-friendly school or similar models, compared to 43 countries in 2005. Secondary school retention was addressed in UNICEF-sponsored studies in Bulgaria, Chile, Mexico and Morocco, which highlighted the negative societal impact of secondary school drop-out rates and suggested new strategies for addressing the problem. In those and other countries, UNICEF supported the development of new evidence-based approaches for lowering drop-out rates.

UNICEF expanded its support for WASH programmes in schools in 85 countries in 2006. Activities included the placement of hygiene education in primary school curricula, the training of teachers, the construction of facilities, the development of child- and girl-friendly designs and promotion of communication for behavioural change through students. Important gains were made in dealing with the impact of emergencies on education. Tens of thousands of students were provided access to safe, child-friendly and gender-segregated school sanitation facilities in countries in transition from emergencies. Strategies and tool kits were developed for restoring schooling to affected populations. UNICEF-supported back-to-school campaigns helped nearly 10 million children in countries affected by conflict or in transition to return to school in 2006, including in Afghanistan, Côte d'Ivoire, the DRC, Iraq, Lebanon, the Sudan and Uganda, as well as in the Occupied Palestinian Territory. UNICEF also acted as the Inter-Agency Standing Committee country cluster lead organization for education in Iraq, Somalia, the Sudan and other countries.

The impact of HIV/AIDS on the education sector continued to be a very significant constraint, particularly in parts of Africa. Development partners, including UNICEF, worked jointly towards a comprehensive response.

HIV/AIDS

In 2006, the Joint United Nations Programme on HIV/AIDS (UNAIDS) reported that many countries had developed national plans of action for children and HIV/AIDS and frameworks for monitoring and evaluating results. Thanks to partnerships in which UNICEF played a significant role, national survey data for 2005 from six of the most affected countries showed a 25 per cent reduction in HIV prevalence among young people aged 15 to 24 years. In 2006, UNICEF focused its support to countries on the "four P" priority areas (prevention of mother-to-child transmission of HIV (PMTCT) plus; paediatric treatment; protection, care and support for children affected by HIV/AIDS; and prevention among adolescents), in line with the goals of the *Unite for Children, Unite against AIDS* campaign [YUN 2005, p. 1290] and the 2006-2009 MTSP. The campaign had evolved and incorporated the decisions taken at the General Assembly's 2006 High-level Meeting on AIDS (see p. 1410) and its commitment towards universal access to prevention, treatment, care and support.

UNICEF supported PMTCT programmes in 91 countries. The number of pregnant women and children with access to anti-retrovirals (ARVs) continued to increase and substantial expansion of PMTCT services was reported in a number of countries in Africa and Asia. Rising numbers of children were receiving treatment as a result of better testing, lower drug prices and simpler formulations, but paediatric care still lagged behind adult care. UNICEF and WHO hosted an expert consultation to define strategies for improving paediatric care, support and treatment in resource-constrained settings. In 2006, UNICEF procured 4.5 million ARV treatment packs, compared to 2.8 million in 2005. The focus in the area of HIV/AIDS-related supplies continued to be placed on widening the availability of improved paediatric ARVs and PMTCT-related products.

UNICEF field reports indicated that, by the end of 2006, HIV/AIDS education had been fully integrated in the secondary curricula by some 62 programme countries and partially by another 40 countries, especially in sub-Saharan Africa and Latin America and the Caribbean. Another key UNICEF focus was ensuring that the legal and operational framework for youth-friendly health services was integrated with existing health-care systems. Particular progress in that regard was registered in Central and Eastern Europe and CIS. In 31 countries, awareness of HIV/AIDS prevention was raised through UNICEF support to media events organized around the *Unite for Children, Unite against AIDS* campaign. UNICEF and partners also used sporting events to transmit messages on HIV/AIDS prevention and safe reproductive health to young people.

UNAIDS programme coordination

At its second regular session in September, the Executive Board considered a July report [E/ICEF/2006/20] on the implementation of the decisions and recommendations of the UNAIDS Programme Coordinating Board at its seventeenth [YUN 2005, p. 1327] and eighteenth (27-28 June, 2006) (see p. 1418) meetings. Key issues addressed in the report included accelerating implementation of the recommendations of the Global Task Team on Improving AIDS Coordination among Multilateral Institutions and International Donors [ibid.]; progress made in intensifying HIV prevention; the UNAIDS unified budget and workplan; and follow-up to the General Assembly's 2006 High-level Meeting on AIDS (see p. 1410).

Child protection from violence, exploitation and abuse

Trends in data availability and analysis on child protection issues were positive in 2006. UNICEF supported national systems for monitoring and reporting in 41 countries during the year, and some 52 UNICEF country offices indicated that they were monitoring and reporting, either fully or partly, violations of children's protection rights. The Fund supported or carried out rapid assessments in several countries, and worked with government and civil society partners to develop an agreed set of child protection indicators in several others. Burundi, Côte d'Ivoire, the DRC, Nepal, Somalia, Sri Lanka and the Sudan established monitoring and reporting mechanisms on child rights violations in compliance with Security Council resolution 1612(2005) [YUN 2005, p. 863]. Despite that progress, widespread absence of agreed indicators at the national level remained a major constraint in measuring results for child protection. During the year, significant data on child protection were included in poverty reduction strategies, national development plans and their equivalents in 24 programme countries, up from 14 in 2005. A further 44 countries included partial data.

The Fund supported efforts against female genital mutilation/cutting (FGM/C) in 18 countries, including advocacy and alliance-building with local and national decision makers, public awareness-raising and the training of health workers and traditional healers. FGM/C decreased in Djibouti, and communities and regions in Benin, Ethiopia and Senegal abandoned the practice. New laws or legislative amendments on violence against women and children were passed in several countries, and national studies, campaigns and strategy development took place to raise awareness of the UN study on violence against children [ibid., p. 860].

Globally, the International Labour Organization (ILO) reported reductions of 11 per cent in child labour and 26 per cent in hazardous child labour in 2002-2006. In India, Mexico and Nicaragua, UNICEF helped to improve national child labour monitoring mechanisms. Over one half of the nearly 60 UNICEF-assisted country programme components for the reduction of child labour were being implemented in collaboration with the ILO International Programme on the Elimination of Child Labour. UNICEF assisted with national surveys on child labour in Guatemala, Myanmar, Nicaragua, Rwanda and other countries, conducted various studies and led training sessions for government officials, civil society organizations and the private sector.

The Fund helped to build the capacities of its partners by conducting training programmes for the protection of children in emergencies in Bangladesh, Ethiopia, Indonesia, Myanmar, Somalia and Venezuela. It contributed to the strengthening of the monitoring of child recruitment and other grave violations of children's rights in the Darfur region of the Sudan. UNICEF assisted in demobilizing and reintegrating thousands of child soldiers and other children affected by war in Afghanistan, Burundi, Colombia, Côte d'Ivoire, the Sudan and other countries. UNICEF-coordinated mine-risk education programmes reached some 80,000 people in Chechnya, Russian Federation, almost 400,000 in the Sudan, 13,000 in Bosnia and Herzegovina and an estimated 1 million in Lebanon. A decline in casualties from landmines and unexploded ordnance was seen in 2006, due in part to the success of mine-risk education programmes.

The Fund helped to improve the protection of imprisoned children through the development of training programmes and materials for prison guards and police forces in Ghana, Haiti, Timor-Leste and Turkey, and promoted greater use of diversion and alternatives to the detention of children. According to available information, some 16 programme countries were using child-friendly and gender-appropriate investigation and court procedures, and some 34 others had taken measures to implement the United Nations Guidelines on Justice in Matters involving Child Victims and Witnesses of Crime [ibid., p. 1236], compared to 22 in 2005. Major constraints were still posed, however, by a lack of proper juvenile justice structures and technical resources and a high turnover of police staff.

In 2006, some 44 programme countries had policies on the provision of alternative care for children, in line with international standards, compared to 36 in 2005. UNICEF worked with national partners on formulating new standards and policies for such care. UNICEF support to tracing systems and reintegration programmes facilitated the reunification of thousands of children separated from their families in Indonesia, Liberia, Sri Lanka and the Sudan.

Policy advocacy and partnerships for children's rights

Renewed efforts by UNICEF to build partnerships to generate dialogue on public policies affecting children, young people and women and to promote child-friendly budgetary and legislative reforms saw significant progress. Successful large-scale staff training on public policy helped to lay the basis for more effective advocacy and partnership-building, particularly at country and regional levels. The formulation of new Common Country Assessments and United Nations Development Assistance Frameworks provided entry points for more systematic analysis and advocacy for addressing the rights and priority needs of children and women. In that regard, collaborative efforts with other UN agencies, the World Bank, civil society, donors and academic institutions intensified.

UNICEF supported multiple indicator cluster surveys in 55 countries to collect data on key indicators on the MDGs, fill knowledge gaps on the situation of children and women and strengthen the evidence base for national planning and advocacy. It promoted and supported the use of *DevInfo*, a database for compiling and presenting child-related data, in 103 countries, including training of government staff, the provision of equipment, assistance in software customization, development of manuals and support for data collection. The Fund helped to develop knowledge management systems to impact children's policies and programmes in Bangladesh, Honduras, India and Mozambique, and a child rights index advocacy tool helped to raise awareness in several Latin American countries. While 94 of 115 UNICEF country offices significantly supported the national reporting process to the Committee on the Rights of the Child, support for such reporting to the Committee on the Elimination of Discrimination against Women (see p. 1354) remained at lower levels.

The Fund also supported a variety of child-friendly budget analyses and advocacy initiatives, which helped to raise awareness of resource allocation shortfalls for child-related goals in several countries. It worked increasingly with Governments and civil society partners to strengthen systems to monitor and analyse national budgets, with systems in place in at least 17 programme countries. UNICEF contributed to increasing knowledge on issues related to children and women through the sponsorship of major thematic studies or analyses in 87 countries in 2005 and 2006.

In an estimated 61 per cent of countries for which field reports were available, national development plans, poverty reduction strategies, transition plans and similar policy instruments addressed key challenges for children, women and gender equality, as compared to 57 per cent in 2005. UNICEF assisted policy processes, such as poverty reduction strategies, in 84 countries during the year, compared with 67 in 2004. UNICEF engagement with sector-wide approaches (SWAps) and multi-donor budget support mechanisms helped to strengthen policies and leverage new resources for child-focused programmes in Ghana, Kenya, Rwanda and Uganda. The Fund supported the development, implementation and/or monitoring of SWAps in 40 countries in 2006, compared to 29 in 2004. It provided Governments with technical support in preparing proposals for global development funds, helping to secure significant funding for child survival and development programmes. Wider access to critical supplies for children and families was also supported by the growing value of UNICEF procurement services.

Progress was steady in promoting the wider participation of children and adolescents in the formulation, implementation and monitoring of policies, programmes and legislation. UNICEF helped support the "Junior 8" Summit (St. Petersburg, Russian Federation, 8-17 July), allowing 64 children to hold discussions and present recommendations directly to the leaders of the Group of Eight (G-8) most industrialized countries. The Fund worked extensively with national, subnational and community media organizations to disseminate information for young people and children, including through youth-led outlets. In Burundi, Guinea-Bissau and Sao Tome and Principe, UNICEF-assisted initiatives helped to facilitate peer-to-peer communication and highlight the opinions of young people. UNICEF also expanded its "sports for development" initiative as a framework for youth participation and for reaching young people with life-skills messages and promoting physical activity and recreation.

Operational and administrative matters

UNICEF finances

In 2006, UNICEF income totalled $2,781 million, an increase of $19 million (1 per cent) over 2005, 18 per cent higher than forecast in the financial plan. Income to regular resources increased by 30 per cent to $1,056 million in 2006, and total contributions to other resources decreased by 12 per cent to $1,725 million, as a result of a 47 per cent reduction in funding for emergencies. UNICEF derived its income primarily from Governments, which contributed $1,614 million (58 per cent), and $799 million (29 per cent) from private sector sources. The balance came from inter-organizational arrangements, with contributions of $178 million (6 per cent), and other sources, with contributions of $190 million (7 per cent).

Budget appropriations

On 17 January [dec. 2006/1], the Executive Board approved a regular resources programme budget for the 2006-2007 biennium in the amount of $25,190,000 and a budget of $25 million for the Emergency Programme Fund (see p. 1375). It authorized the Executive Director to transfer, if necessary, between programme fields an amount not exceeding 10 per cent of the approved budget of the Fund to which the transfer was made. The Board also approved a programme budget ceiling of $302.2 million for other resources for the 2006-2007 biennium, subject to the availability of specific-purpose contributions. Funds in excess of indicated amounts for specific programme areas and regions could be received provided the total amount was within the approved limit.

The Executive Board also considered the biennial support budget for 2006-2007 [E/ICEF/2006/AB/L.1 & Corr.1] and the related report of the Advisory Committee on Administrative and Budgetary Questions (ACABQ) [E/ICEF/2006/AB/L.3 & Corr.1]. On 19 January [dec. 2006/2], it approved gross appropriations of $746,794,000 for programme support and management and administration, to be offset by estimated income of $190,000,000, resulting in estimated net appropriations of $556,794,000, and authorized the Executive Director to redeploy resources between appropriation lines up to 5 per cent of the appropriation to which the resources were deployed. The Board decided to reflect the centrally-shared security costs mandated by the United Nations as a separate line in the UNICEF resource plan and approved $26,204,000 from regular resources to cover such costs. The Board established a separation fund to cover separation and termination liabilities, approved an initial allocation of $10,000,000 from regular resources for the fund and requested UNICEF to ensure that the initiative was in line with the harmonization efforts of UN funds and programmes. It also requested UNICEF, at its 2006 annual session, to include in a report on harmonized country programme approval procedures (see p. 1377), to be elaborated jointly with UNDP and UNFPA, an assessment of possible implications of that procedure for the timing of the approval of the biennial support budget by the Board.

In accordance with its decisions 2004/7 [YUN 2004, p. 1187] and 2005/16 [YUN 2005, p. 1292], the Board approved an interim one-month allocation for January 2008 in the amount of $31,600,000, to be absorbed in the 2008-2009 biennial support budget. Welcoming the continued improvement in results-based budgeting, it urged the Executive Director to give high priority to implementing that process for the 2008-2009 biennium and ensure that UNICEF programme countries received sufficient support to enable them to contribute to the achievement of MTSP objectives and the MDGs.

On 9 June [dec. 2006/10], the Board approved the aggregate indicative budgets for 9 country programmes for 2007, 1 for 2007-2009, 2 for 2007-2010 and 12 for 2007-2011, amounting to the following totals for regular and other resources, respectively, by region: Africa, $180,224,000 and $479,334,000; East Asia and the Pacific, $12,016,000 and $49,200,000; Central and Eastern Europe and CIS, $3,595,000 and $15,250,000; Middle East and North Africa, $72,486,000 and $473,205,000. Based on the recommendation contained in an April report [E/ICEF/2006/P/L.27], the Board also approved $51,603,065 in additional regular resources for 38 country programmes for 2006 and 2007 [dec. 2006/11].

On 8 September, the Board approved [dec. 2006/13] the aggregate indicative budgets for 6 country programmes for 2007, 2 for 2007-2009, 3 for 2007-2010, 16 for 2007-2011, as well as the Gulf Area subregional programme for 2007-2009, amounting to the following totals for regular and other resources, respectively, by region: Africa, $126,094,000 and $326,288,000; the Americas and the Caribbean, $33,527,000 and $152,634,000; Asia, $17,118,000 and $72,340,000; Central and Eastern Europe and CIS, $1,803,000 and $9,800,000; Middle East and North Africa, $0 and $7,500,000. It also approved, on the basis of a July report [E/ICEF/2006/P/L.63], additional other resources for 18 country programmes, totalling $375,850,000 [dec. 2006/14].

Additionally, the Board, on the same date [dec. 2006/16], having considered a proposal for strengthening UNICEF emergency response capacity [E/ICEF/2006/P/L.62], approved an increase in the ceiling of the Emergency Programme Fund from $25 million to $75 million, effective 2006, to be met through existing resources, in order to improve UNICEF's ability to provide an effective, predictable and timely response to the needs of children and women affected by humanitarian emergencies. It encouraged UNICEF to strengthen its internal capacities and coordination with Governments, relevant parts of the UN system and civil society to ensure effective, predictable and timely responses to natural disasters and complex emergencies.

The Board considered a July report [E/ICEF/2006/AB/L.9 & Corr.1] proposing a supplementary budget of $13.4 million to cover the additional costs in the 2006-2007 biennial support budget for strengthening capacities for crisis management and operational continuity in the event of a pandemic crisis, including the establishment and equipping of an alternate data centre outside New York and the establishment of a specialized unit to be known as the Operations Preparedness and Business Continuity Unit, as well as the related ACABQ report [E/ICEF/2006/AB/L.10]. It approved [dec. 2006/17] an immediate supplementary budget in gross and net appropriations of $1 million for additional costs related to stocking necessary medical supplies. It requested UNICEF to resubmit its remaining budget for crisis and business continuity capacity, including for an influenza pandemic or other disasters, to the Board, through ACABQ at its first regular session of 2007, and to make every effort to coordinate and share resources with other UN entities. On 8 September [dec. 2006/14], on the basis of a July report [E/ICEF/2006/P/L.63], the Board approved additional other resources for 18 country programmes, totalling $375,850,000.

Audits

According to its July report [E/ICEF/2006/AB/L.8] on internal audit activities in 2005, the Office of Internal Audit (OIA) completed 40 audits, consisting of 33 country office audits, four headquarters audits, two regional office audits, and one global summary report. In its audit of headquarters divisions, OIA found the Supply Division's management of shipping and handling of UNICEF-procured supplies to be satisfactory, but noted weaknesses in several divisions' management of internal performance information, as well as in some aspects of headquarters and regional offices' coordinated responses to the onset of sudden emergencies. Controls in UNICEF country offices were satisfactory in the areas of office management, basic information and communication technology, and in the implementation of prior audit recommendations. Controls were also generally satisfactory in finance, basic programme management and the provision of supply assistance, although there was scope for improvement. While the profile of country offices' risk-management practices in 2005 improved slightly, programme and operations support from regional offices needed to be enhanced, as well as regional and global monitoring of country office practices in areas of common weakness. In 2006, a revised Audit Committee Charter was promulgated, with enhanced responsibilities, including the review of the UNICEF oversight system, the quality and integrity of its accounting and reporting practices, and the review of the internal and external audit practices.

On 8 September [dec. 2006/18], the Executive Board noted the OIA report and the further strengthening of the UNICEF Audit Committee. It requested OIA to include more analytical content in its reports, identifying common areas of risk and tracking their evolution, analysing the systematic causes of risk and recommending system improvement. The OIA Director should include in his annual audit reports a summary of key and recurrent findings and a table identifying unresolved audit findings by year and prioritization category. The Executive Director should provide separate management responses to key and recurring issues identified in the OIA Director's annual report, including an explanation of findings that had remained unresolved for 18 months or more, and submit that report to the Board along with the annual report of the OIA Director. The Executive Director should work closer with UNDP, UNFPA and other agencies to achieve the highest possible internal auditing standards, harmonize their audit and management reporting, including by standardizing audit terms and definitions and aligning them with internationally recognized norms, assess the resources required, and report on those steps at the Board's 2007 annual session.

Recovery policy

At its June session, the Executive Board considered an April review of UNICEF cost-recovery policy [E/ICEF/2006/AB/L.4], submitted in response to its 2003 decision [YUN 2003, p. 1212] requesting the Executive Director to review the performance of the policy, which was adopted in that year [ibid., p. 1213] as an interim measure. The report found that, although regular and other resources had increased since the adoption of the policy, its complexity, especially its 15 different contribution rates and seven recovery rates, hindered UNICEF ability to be an effective partner, gave the appearance that UNICEF was a difficult organization to work with, and that its recovery rates were higher than those of other UN agencies. It recommended that the Board adopt a base recovery rate of 7 per cent for other resources income, with thematic contributions assessed at 5 per cent; maintain the 5 per cent rate for non-thematic funding raised by the private sector in programme countries; assess a 1 per cent reduction to joint programmes where the Executive Director considered it in the best interests of enhancing the collective interests of UN agencies; and assess a 1 per cent reduction for contributions over $40 million, where the Executive Director was satisfied that economies of scale were met. ACABQ, in its May report [E/ICEF/2006/AB/L.5], recommended approval of the revised recovery policy.

On 9 June [dec. 2006/7], the Board approved the recommendations of the cost-recovery policy review. It requested the Executive Director to keep it regularly informed on the actual costs recovered and the impact of the applied rates on regular and other resources and, in close cooperation with the United Nations Development Group (UNDG), present a status report in 2007 on the progress towards the harmonization on cost recovery, including information on cost-recovery methodologies.

Resource mobilization

UNICEF collaborated with Governments to mobilize regular and other resources. At the seventh pledging event in January, 42 countries committed a total of $257.5 million. By year's end, 104 countries had contributed $466 million in regular resources and $1,148 million in other resources. While Government contributions to regular resources showed a small decline compared to 2005, the increase in regular resources contributions from the private sector and "other income" resulted in overall growth of regular resources income of 30 per cent over 2005. The United States remained the largest donor to regular resources ($126 million), followed by Sweden ($58 million), Norway ($47 million), the Netherlands ($37 million), the United Kingdom ($36 million), Japan ($21 million) and Canada ($12 million). Thematic funding (excluding humanitarian) increased by 40 per cent over 2005 levels, with the largest increase being for child protection. A total of 20 Governments and 34 National Committees provided thematic funding for MTSP focus areas and the humanitarian thematic pool. The private sector mobilized 34 per cent of the overall thematic funds in 2006. The top 10 donors to MTSP thematic funds contributed $154,461,702. Of the sought $1.2 billion for humanitarian interventions 77 per cent were received, compared to 47 per cent for consolidated appeals.

Private Sector Division

Net income from UNICEF Private Sector Division (PSD) activities for the year ended 31

December 2006 totalled $392.6 million for regular resources, $104 million (36 per cent) higher than the $288.6 million raised in 2005 [E/ICEF/2007/AB/L.10]. That total included $337.6 million from private sector fund-raising activities, $56.9 million from the sale of UNICEF cards and gifts, and a positive exchange rate adjustment of $15.3 million, less investment fund expenditures of $17.2 million. An additional $342.3 million of earmarked funds were raised for other resources from private sector fund-raising activities. The net consolidated income for 2006, including both regular and other resources, amounted to $734.9 million, a decrease of $323.3 million (30.5 per cent) compared with the 2005 net consolidated income of $1,058.2 million.

On 19 January [dec. 2006/5], the Executive Board approved budgeted expenditures of $105.3 million for the 2006 PSD work plan [E/ICEF/2006/AB/L.2]. It authorized UNICEF to redeploy resources between the various budget lines up to a maximum of 10 per cent of the amounts approved, and to spend between Executive Board sessions an additional amount up to that caused by currency fluctuations, to implement the 2006 approved workplan. The Board renewed investment funds, with $21.4 million established for 2006; authorized UNICEF to incur expenditures in 2006 related to the cost of goods delivered (production/purchase of raw materials, cards and other products) for 2007, up to $32.7 million; and approved the PSD medium-term plan for 2007-2010.

In September, the Board took note of the PSD financial report and statements for the year ended 31 December 2005 [E/ICEF/2006/AB/L.7].

Country programme approval process

In response to a 2005 Executive Board decision [YUN 2005, p. 1293], UNICEF submitted an April report [E/ICEF/2006/12] on options for improving the harmonized country programme approval process. Annexed to the report were the UNDG process for simplifying and harmonizing the UN programming process and documentation; an outline of the contents of a consolidated document at the country level (the Consolidated United Nations Development Assistance Framework (UNDAF)), intended to reduce transaction costs and redundancies in programme documentation and strengthen the results focus and UN country teams coherence in implementation; and a format for the simplified presentation of organization-specific contributions to the Consolidated UNDAF. Included in the report was a draft decision for adoption by the Board.

At the Board's June session, concern was expressed that the proposals for harmonizing the country programme approval procedure did not take into account the principle that national priorities and strategies in the work of the UN funds and programmes should govern any proposals relating to country programmes. It approved a statement of its President requesting UNICEF, jointly with UNDP and UNFPA, to make further proposals for improving and streamlining the procedure.

At the September session, UNDP, UNFPA and UNICEF submitted a joint report on options to further improve and streamline the harmonized country programme approval process [E/ICEF/2006/CRP.17], which recognized and reaffirmed the principle of national ownership and leadership. It also sought to ensure the continuance of the respective Executive Boards' functions through the process for reviewing and approving multi-year cooperation programmes, mainly by focusing on the consistency and coherence of those programmes with the multi-year framework or strategic plan of the particular agency, fund or programme.

On 8 September [dec. 2006/19], the UNICEF Executive Board decided that, in order to decrease the time frame for the country programme approval process and create more scope for synchronization with the length of national programme cycles, the practice of presenting draft country programme documents for discussion at its annual session would continue. The revised country programme documents would then be posted on the UNICEF website no later than six weeks after the discussion, and a hard copy provided, upon request, to Board members by the secretariat. The country programmes would then be approved by the Board at the second regular session on a no-objection basis without presentation or discussion, unless at least five members gave prior written notification of their wish to bring a particular country programme before the Board. Approval of those country programmes for which revised documents were not posted within the six-week period would be postponed to the Board's first regular session of the following year. It also decided to continue to follow the guidelines regarding length and content adopted in its decision 2002/4 [YUN 2002, p. 1191] for the submission and approval of country programmes. Continued efforts should be made to improve results-based planning and management, and to strengthen the alignment of country programmes with national strategies, as well as with the approved MTSP. UNICEF country programme documents should clearly contribute to and derive from national plans and strategies, as well as the outcomes established in the UNDAF.

Joint programming

At its June session, the Executive Board had before it an April report on the implementation experience of joint programming and joint programmes by UNDP, UNFPA and UNICEF since 2004 [E/ICEF/2006/13], which responded to a 2005 Executive Board request [YUN 2005, p. 1293]. The report reflected on the experience of the joint programmes implemented or developed within the framework of the common country programming process and the inter-organization guidance note on joint programming, taking stock of its benefits and challenges. The report stated that UNDG, and its Executive committee organizations in particular, had promoted joint programmes where they added value, and programming manuals and training had been amended to reflect applicable procedures. The inter-organization joint programmes working group and the joint programmes focal point in the UNDG Office provided advice and support to UN country teams. A key development was the establishment of a joint programmes database on the UNDG website, which, when fully developed, would provide a comprehensive view of collective joint programme activity. The benefits of joint programing included reduced duplication and transaction costs and increased coherence. It also improved the information and knowledge base in countries; increased the coherence of activities for greater effectiveness; helped to maintain a focus on organization mandates and ensure transparency and accountability; enabled marginalized populations to be reached; facilitated a swift response to crises; and allowed additional resources to be leveraged.

However, several challenges remained, including a reduction in the level of collaboration once the UNDAF had been completed; joint programmes that did not merit the transaction costs; limited use of joint programmes in the broader national programmatic context; the perception that joint programmes were UN-centred rather than promoting partnerships with others; and the need to improve monitoring and evaluation. The report recommended that a full evaluation of joint programming be undertaken once there was sufficient experience to draw meaningful results.

An addendum to the report [E/ICEF/2006/13/Add.1] focused on UNICEF experience with joint programming since 2004.

Sector-wide approaches

At its June session, the Executive Board considered a May report on UNICEF engagement in sector-wide approaches (SWAps) [E/ICEF/2006/14]. UNICEF had increased its involvement in SWAps as those instruments became more widely used by countries as a development planning approach. UNICEF contributions included capacity development, technical and policy advice, support to data collection and use, and monitoring and evaluation. It worked closely with other UN agencies to share the challenge of involvement and ensure that the broad viewpoints and international experience of development were made available to national planning authorities. It also set up networking and training opportunities for its staff to help them overcome several knowledge and skills gaps. Within the context of MTSP priorities, UNICEF was uniquely positioned to proactively lead and cultivate effective sector-wide partnerships to leverage resources, assistance and results for children. In the report, it was recommended that UNICEF provide regular updates on the issue as part of the results frameworks included in the annual report of the Executive Director.

On 9 June [dec. 2006/8], the Board approved the recommendation.

JIU reports

In January, the Executive Board considered a secretariat note [E/ICEF/2006/4] on the activities of the Joint Inspection Unit (JIU) of specific relevance to UNICEF. The document provided information on reports prepared between September 2004 and September 2005, action taken by UNICEF, and views held on the issues raised by the inspectors. At its January session, the Board took note of the reports.

Organizational review

In 2006, UNICEF initiated a comprehensive organizational review, which identified critical success factors and the strengths and weaknesses of the Fund in terms of programme and management effectiveness. It assessed UNICEF capacity to carry out its mandate for children against the background of external trends. Conducted by external consultants and supported by a small secretariat, the review drew extensively on other management initiatives, incorporating their findings into its overall diagnosis. While the review confirmed the continuing critical role of UNICEF around the world, it identified the need for change in its approaches to programme development and strategy, technical assistance, resource mobilization and allocation, partnerships, management practices and business processes. Implementation of the recommendations, which emphasized the importance of knowledge, innovation and learning, would require significant changes in UNICEF structure, staffing and systems.

A small unit was established to provide impetus to and monitor the change processes at all levels and in all locations of the organization.

Youth

World Programme of Action for Youth

In 2006, UN policies and programmes on youth continued to focus on efforts to implement the 1995 World Programme of Action for Youth to the Year 2000 and Beyond, adopted by the General Assembly in resolution 50/81 [YUN 1995, p. 1211]. The Programme of Action addressed problems faced by youth worldwide and identified ways to enhance youth participation in national and international policy- and decision-making. The Programme of Action identified 10 priority issues for youth: education, employment, hunger and poverty, health, environment, drug abuse, juvenile delinquency, leisure-time activities, girls and young women, and participation in society and decision-making. In resolution 60/2 [YUN 2005, p. 1294], the General Assembly added five additional issues of concern to young people: globalization, the increased use of information and communication technology, HIV/AIDS, the increased participation of young people in armed conflict, as both victims and perpetrators, and the growing importance of intergenerational relations in an ageing global society. The Division for Social Policy and Development (DSPD) of the United Nations Department of Economic and Social Affairs (DESA) organized several meetings and workshops related to those priorities. It organized a regional expert group meeting (Bangkok, Thailand, 28-30 March), hosted by the Economic and Social Commission for Asia and the Pacific, which addressed development challenges for young people in Asia in preparation for the World Youth Report 2007. DSPD and the Economic Commission for Africa held a capacity-building workshop (Addis Ababa, Ethiopia, 27-29 June) on major youth development challenges in Africa. In collaboration with the Office of the Special Adviser on Africa, DSPD organized an expert group meeting on the participation of youth as partners in peace and development in post-conflict countries (Windhoek, Namibia, 14-16 November).

At the culmination of a series of five regional summits, the United Nations Office of Sport for Development and Peace organized the Global Youth Leadership Summit (New York, 29-31 October). The Summit sought to encourage young leaders from around the world to explore ways in which they could better the future of their communities, regions, and the emerging global society through achievement of the MDGs. The declaration adopted by the Summit called for the empowerment and capacity-building of young leaders, and for a more active representation of youth in the institutions of government, and regional and international organizations and bodies.

The United Nations Educational, Scientific and Cultural Organization, as part of the activities organized for the celebration of its sixtieth anniversary, held a thematic week on youth (Paris, 16-17 August) under the theme "Acting with and for youth".

Youth employment

Report of Secretary-General. In an April report on generating full and productive employment for all [E/2006/55], the Secretary-General stated that, although they made up only 25 per cent of the working-age population, almost half of the world's unemployed were young people. The integration of youth, especially from poor households, into the labour market was relevant for growth prospects, social mobility and cohesion, and the interruption of the intergenerational transmission of poverty, all of which had been taken into account by the MDGs and the United Nations Youth Employment Network [YUN 2001, p. 1100]. The Secretary-General noted the importance of creating policies to stimulate additional employment opportunities for young people, complemented by targeted measures to overcome the specific disadvantages they encountered in entering or remaining in the labour market. Measures should also be taken to create an enabling business environment; inform and assist young people in establishing or joining small enterprises; and help young persons move from the informal to the formal economy. In order to mainstream youth employment into national development strategies, measures to enhance the employability of youth should be a key component of labour-market policies and educational reforms. Countries were invited to consider integrating vocational training approaches into their education systems, at the primary, secondary and tertiary levels.

The Economic and Social Council [A/61/3/Rev.1], in a ministerial declaration adopted at the high-level segment (Geneva, 3-5 July) of its 2006 substantive session, reaffirmed the commitment to developing and implementing strategies to give youth everywhere a real and equal opportunity to find full and productive employment and decent work. It pledged to mainstream youth employment into national development strategies and agendas; develop policies and programmes for enhancing the employability of youth, including through education, training and lifelong learning that met labour-market requirements; and promote access to work through integrated policies that enabled the creation of and facilitated access to new and quality jobs for young people, including through information and training initiatives. The declaration recognized the importance of the Youth Employment Network as a peer exchange, support and review mechanism, and invited Member States, the United Nations and partner organizations to strengthen and expand the Network at the national, regional and international levels.

The Network's Youth Consultative Group developed a methodology to support the participation of youth NGOs in the formulation of national action plans on youth employment. The Group also highlighted the challenges of successful youth employment policy and its implementation at a workshop (Geneva, 29-30 June) organized as part of the Civil Society Forum to the 2006 meeting of the Economic and Social Council. During the year, a Network office was established at the United Nations Office for West Africa in Dakar, Senegal, to facilitate national strategies on youth employment and increase private sector involvement in the creation of employment for youth.

ECONOMIC AND SOCIAL COUNCIL ACTION

On 26 July [meeting 40], the Economic and Social Council, on the recommendation of the Commission for Social Development [draft: E/2006/26], adopted **resolution 2006/15** without vote [agenda item 14 (*b*)].

Promoting youth and employment

The Economic and Social Council,

Reaffirming the resolve of heads of State and Government, as contained in the United Nations Millennium Declaration, to develop and implement strategies that give young people everywhere a real chance to find decent and productive work and, as contained in the 2005 World Summit Outcome, to make the goals of full and productive employment and decent work for all, including women and young people, a central objective of their relevant national and international policies and their national development strategies, including poverty reduction strategies, as part of their efforts to achieve the Millennium Development Goals,

Recalling and reaffirming the commitments relating to youth employment made at the major United Nations conferences and summits since 1990 and their follow-up processes,

Recalling General Assembly resolution 54/120 of 17 December 1999, in which the Assembly took note with appreciation of the Lisbon Declaration on Youth Policies and Programmes adopted at the World Conference of Ministers Responsible for Youth in 1998, which set forth important commitments regarding youth employment, and recalling also Assembly resolutions 56/117 of 19 December 2001 and 57/165 of 18 December 2002,

Recognizing that young people are an asset for sustainable economic growth and social development, and expressing deep concern about the magnitude and disproportionate effect upon youth of unemployment and underemployment throughout the world and its profound implications for the future of our societies,

Recognizing also that Governments have a primary responsibility to educate young people, to encourage them to seek training so as to increase their employability and to create an enabling environment that will promote youth employment,

Recognizing further the need to promote, protect and fully respect the basic rights of young workers as defined by relevant International Labour Organization and other international instruments,

1. *Takes note* of the report of the Secretary-General on the global analysis and evaluation of national action plans on youth employment;

2. *Takes note also* of the report of the Economic Commission for Africa entitled *Economic Report on Africa, 2005: Meeting the Challenges of Unemployment and Poverty in Africa*;

3. *Takes note further* of the relevant provisions on employment of the Declaration of Mar del Plata of 5 November 2005 adopted at the Fourth Summit of the Americas, and the conclusions of the Presidency of the European Council of 23 March 2005, in which it was agreed that the European Youth Pact would be an integrated part of the Lisbon Strategy;

4. *Encourages* the international community to provide technical and capacity-building support to developing countries, as appropriate, in support of national development strategies, including poverty reduction strategy papers, where they exist, mainstreaming youth employment;

5. *Encourages* Governments that have prepared national reviews and action plans on youth employment to move forward to implementation, and also encourages Governments that have not yet prepared their reviews, national action plans or progress reports to do so as soon as possible;

6. *Also encourages* Governments to develop their national action plans through collaboration among governmental bodies, representative youth organizations, employers' and workers' organizations and civil society, to promote partnerships among public authorities, the private sector, educational institutions and civil society and to integrate these action plans into their broader national development programmes, including poverty reduction strategy papers, where they exist, in order to create a methodology to evaluate the plans and strategies

and to prioritize therein the necessary resources for their implementation;

7. *Further encourages* Governments to contribute to the possible development by the appropriate intergovernmental bodies of the United Nations of new policy-oriented indicators to better monitor and evaluate progress in implementing their national action plans, and invites the Youth Employment Network to contribute to that process, taking into account young people, including students and those who are unemployed, underemployed, working in the informal economy or who may have dropped out of the labour market altogether;

8. *Urges* Governments to consider youth employment as integral to their overall strategies for development and collective security, and within that context to give renewed attention to the United Nations Millennium Declaration commitment concerning decent and productive work for young people as key to achieving the Millennium Development Goals;

9. *Renews* the invitation contained in General Assembly resolutions 57/165 of 18 December 2002 and 58/133 of 22 December 2003 to the International Labour Organization, in collaboration with the Secretariat and the World Bank and other relevant specialized agencies, within the framework of the Youth Employment Network, to assist and support, upon request, the efforts of Governments in the elaboration and implementation of national reviews and action plans;

10. *Encourages* Governments to improve the education, training, mobility, vocational integration and social inclusion of young people and, where appropriate, to promote entrepreneurship and facilitate the reconciliation of family life and working life, in order to support the integration of young people into the labour market;

11. *Also encourages* Governments to facilitate interaction among educational institutions and the public and private sectors to prevent unemployment and the low returns on investment in training that result from a skills mismatch, and in that regard calls for technical support from relevant United Nations organizations and the international community for national and regional programmes such as the New Partnership for Africa's Development and other regional economic groups in order to facilitate public-private integration;

12. *Underlines* the fact that non-formal and informal learning are complementary elements to the formal educational process and are useful instruments in facilitating the transition from education to employment;

13. *Invites* new countries and partner organizations to join the Youth Employment Network; encourages the lead countries to strengthen the work of the Network as a peer exchange, support and review mechanism; and, in support of the further development of this mechanism, invites the International Labour Organization, in close cooperation with the World Bank and the Secretariat, within the framework of the Youth Employment Network, to undertake regular updates of the global analysis and evaluation of progress made in the development and implementation of national reviews and action plans on youth employment;

14. *Recommends* that the Youth Consultative Group of the Youth Employment Network be strengthened so that, in addition to its overall advisory role, it can play a more active role at the country level through its constituent youth organizations in supporting the development and implementation of national action plans;

15. *Encourages* Governments to promote the participation of national youth organizations in supporting the development and implementation of their national action plans on youth employment;

16. *Notes with appreciation* the provision by some Member States of expertise and financial resources to support the activities of the Youth Employment Network, and invites all Member States and intergovernmental and non-governmental organizations to contribute to the Network in support of action taken at the country level within the framework of the Network;

17. *Requests* the Secretary-General to include in his comprehensive report on the implementation of the cluster entitled "Youth in the global economy" of the World Programme of Action for Youth to the Year 2000 and Beyond, to be submitted to the General Assembly at its sixty-second session, and to the Economic and Social Council at its substantive session of 2007, through the Commission for Social Development at its forty-fifth session, information on the implementation of the present resolution, including progress achieved by the Youth Employment Network.

Ageing persons

Follow-up to the Second World Assembly on Ageing (2002)

Report of Secretary-General. In response to General Assembly resolution 59/150 [YUN 2004, p. 1193], the Secretary-General submitted to the Commission for Social Development, at its forty-fourth session (New York, 8-17 February and 22 March) [E/2006/26] (see p. 1276), a report [E/CN.5/2006/2] on modalities for the review and appraisal of the Madrid International Plan of Action on Ageing [YUN 2002, p. 1194], adopted by the Second World Assembly on Ageing in 2002 [ibid., p. 1193]. The report reviewed progress in defining the modalities and possible arrangements for the first cycle of the review and appraisal of the Plan of Action at the national, regional and international levels.

The Secretary-General proposed that the Commission request those Member States that had not done so, to establish national mechanisms for the implementation of the Madrid Plan of Action and inform the UN Secretariat accordingly, in order to facilitate international cooperation and exchange of information and good practices. The Secretariat should coordinate efforts in identifying support to Governments to undertake a participatory review and appraisal of the implementation of the Madrid Plan of Action. Regional commissions should identify modalities for conducting the regional review and appraisal and ask interested Governments to offer assistance, including financial contributions, to support national action and the convening of regional review and appraisal activities and events during 2006 and 2007.

The Commission should endorse the proposed calendar for the first cycle of review and appraisal of the Madrid Plan of Action in 2006, 2007 and 2008; request the Secretary-General to submit to its forty-fifth (2007) session a report on major developments in ageing since the Second World Assembly on Ageing; and invite Governments to present information on actions they had taken since then for review, using a bottom-up participatory approach. The concluding event of the global segment of the first cycle of the review and appraisal should include, along with a plenary debate, a series of panel discussions and parallel events related to the theme of the cycle; and all major stakeholders should be invited to participate in the process and contribute to its various activities and events. The Commission should recommend to the Economic and Social Council the integration of ageing into the monitoring, review and appraisal exercises of other major international development initiatives and policy frameworks, including the Millennium Declaration [YUN 2000, p. 49], the Programme of Action of the International Conference on Population and Development [YUN 1994, p. 955], the Copenhagen Declaration on Social Development and the Programme of Action of the World Summit for Social Development [YUN 1995, p. 1113] and the Beijing Platform for Action [ibid., p. 1170], as well as their follow-up processes. It was suggested that the Commission should consider "Adjusting to an ageing world" as its theme for the first review and appraisal cycle.

Commission action. In a February resolution [E/2006/26 (res. 44/1)] on modalities for the first review and appraisal of the Madrid International Plan of Action on Ageing, the Commission, taking note of the Secretary General's report, endorsed as the global theme for the first review and appraisal of the implementation of the Madrid Plan of Action "Addressing the challenges and opportunities of ageing". It approved the report's other recommendations and decided to start the first global cycle of review and appraisal at its forty-fifth (2007) session and to conclude it at its forty-sixth (2008) session. The Commission requested the regional commissions to identify modalities for conducting the regional review and appraisal and invited interested Governments to offer support and assistance, including voluntary financial contributions, to support national action in the context of the regional implementation and the convening of regional review and appraisal activities and events during 2006-2007. It invited all major stakeholders, including civil society, to participate in the process and to contribute to its various activities and events, and requested Member States to identify specific areas for in-depth participatory inquiries, using a bottom-up approach. The Commission requested the Secretary-General to submit to its forty-sixth session a report, which should include the conclusions of the first review and appraisal exercise, along with the identification of current and emerging issues and related policy options.

Report of Secretary-General. In a July report [A/61/167], submitted in response to General Assembly resolution 60/135 [YUN 2005, p. 1298], the Secretary-General highlighted national and international efforts to build capacity for implementation of the Madrid Plan of Action. It outlined achievements of and challenges for Member States in national capacity development, including in the areas of institutional infrastructure; human resources; mobilization of financial resources; research, data collection and analysis; and sound policy process.

The report noted that, due to the lack of resources for technical cooperation in the regional commissions, DESA had drafted a funding proposal to offer training at the regional and subregional levels to assist national focal points on ageing in organizing national reviews and appraisals, and to provide resources for regional review and appraisal conferences. It also prepared a publication to assist Governments in organizing and conducting their review and appraisal exercises entitled *Guidelines for Review and Appraisal of the Madrid International Plan of Action on Ageing: Bottom-up Participatory Approach*. In an effort to build capacity in data collection, the United Nations Statistics Division was active in a number of country-level initiatives to improve data collection and analysis. UNFPA was involved in formulating national plans and programmes on ageing; supporting projects aimed at strengthening government capacity to formulate and implement evidence-based strategic plans and policies on ageing; and training for the development of national capacity on ageing. ILO, the Food and Agriculture Organization of the United Nations and WHO were also active in capacity-building on ageing issues.

The Secretary-General concluded that issues related to ageing and older persons remained relatively low on both national and international development agendas, and as a result, many Member States lacked awareness of the Madrid Plan of Action and its recommendations. He recommended that greater attention be paid to building capacity to reduce poverty among older persons, particularly older women, by mainstreaming ageing issues into poverty reduction strategies and national development frameworks, and encouraging greater consultation with older persons in the course of developing, implementing and monitoring poverty reduction plans. Ageing-related policies should be conducted through inclusive consultations involving government ministries and parliaments, as well as other stakeholders and social partners. Governments and organizations should forge stronger partnerships with civil society groups, including organizations of older persons, academia, research foundations, community-based organizations and the private sector; designate specific institutions, such as agencies, ministries, national committees or advisory councils, to be primarily responsible for handling follow-up of national plans of action on ageing; and with intergovernmental organizations and NGOs, demonstrate commitment and provide additional funding to research and data-collection initiatives on ageing.

GENERAL ASSEMBLY ACTION

On 19 December [meeting 81], the General Assembly, on the recommendation of the Third (Social, Humanitarian and Cultural) Committee [A/61/437 & Corr.1], adopted **resolution 61/142** without vote [agenda item 60 (*d*)].

Follow-up to the Second World Assembly on Ageing

The General Assembly,

Recalling its resolution 57/167 of 18 December 2002, in which it endorsed the Political Declaration and the Madrid International Plan of Action on Ageing, 2002, as well as its resolution 58/134 of 22 December 2003, in which it took note, inter alia, of the road map for the implementation of the Madrid Plan of Action, and its resolutions 59/150 of 20 December 2004 and 60/135 of 16 December 2005,

Recalling also Economic and Social Council resolution 2003/14 of 21 July 2003, in which the Council invited Governments, the United Nations system and civil society to participate in a "bottom-up" approach to the review and appraisal of the Madrid Plan of Action,

Recalling further Commission for Social Development resolution 42/1 of 13 February 2004, in which the Commission decided to undertake the review and appraisal of the Madrid Plan of Action every five years,

Mindful that, in its resolution 44/1 of 17 February 2006, the Commission for Social Development endorsed the calendar and the global theme for the first review and appraisal of the implementation of the Madrid Plan of Action, "Addressing the challenges and opportunities of ageing", and decided to start the first global cycle of review and appraisal in 2007 at its forty-fifth session and to conclude it in 2008 at its forty-sixth session,

Taking note of the report of the Secretary-General,

1. *Encourages* Governments to pay greater attention to building capacity to eradicate poverty among older persons, particularly older women, by mainstreaming ageing issues into poverty eradication strategies and national development plans, and by encouraging greater consultation with older persons in the course of developing, implementing and monitoring poverty eradication plans;

2. *Invites* Governments to conduct their ageing-related policies through inclusive consultations with relevant stakeholders and social development partners, in the interest of creating national policy ownership and consensus-building;

3. *Encourages* the international community to support national efforts to forge stronger partnerships with civil society, including organizations of older persons, academia, research foundations, community-based organizations, including caregivers, and the private sector, in an effort to help to build capacity on ageing issues;

4. *Invites* Governments that have not done so to designate focal points for handling follow-up of national plans of action on ageing;

5. *Calls upon* Governments to promote a bottom-up participatory approach throughout the entire implementation process;

6. *Encourages* the international community to support national efforts to provide funding for research and data-collection initiatives on ageing in order to better understand the challenges and opportunities presented by population ageing and provide policymakers with more accurate and more specific information on gender and ageing;

7. *Stresses* the need for additional capacity-building at the national level in order to promote and facilitate implementation of the Madrid International Plan of Action on Ageing, 2002, and in this connection encourages Governments to support the United Nations Trust Fund for Ageing to enable the Department of Economic and Social Affairs of the Secretariat to provide expanded assistance to countries, upon their request;

8. *Recommends* that ongoing efforts to achieve the internationally agreed development goals, including those contained in the United Nations Millennium Declaration, take into account the situation of older persons;

9. *Takes note* of Commission for Social Development resolution 44/1, in this context invites Member States to undertake an initial identification of actions they have taken since the Second World Assembly on Ageing in 2002 as well as policy recommendations for the further implementation of the Madrid Plan of Action, and encourages regional commissions to iden-

tify modalities for conducting the regional review and appraisal, including best practices, with the aim of presenting this information to the Commission at its forty-fifth session in 2007;

10. *Recommends* to the Economic and Social Council the integration of ageing into the monitoring, review and appraisal exercises of other major international development initiatives and policy frameworks, including the United Nations Millennium Declaration, the Programme of Action of the International Conference on Population and Development, the Copenhagen Declaration on Social Development, the Programme of Action of the World Summit for Social Development and the Beijing Platform for Action and their follow-up processes;

11. *Requests* the Secretary-General to report to the General Assembly at its sixty-second session on the implementation of the present resolution, including information on the commemoration of the five-year review and appraisal of the implementation of the Madrid Plan of Action in 2007.

Chapter XII

Refugees and displaced persons

In 2006, the worldwide declining refugee trend was reversed as some 1.2 million new Iraqi refugees in Jordan, Lebanon and the Syrian Arab Republic were registered. The number of persons of concern to the Office of the United Nations High Commissioner for Refugees (UNHCR) rose to 32.9 million, from 20.8 million in 2005. Of the total, some 9.9 million were refugees, 12.8 million internally displaced persons (IDPs), 5.8 million stateless persons, and 738,000 asylum-seekers. Some 2.6 million returned to their place of origin and the remaining 1 million were forced migrants and others of concern.

During the year, UNHCR achieved success in some areas, but was thwarted by constraints in others. In addition to its core protection and assistance activities to refugees, UNHCR committed itself to shared humanitarian responsibilities under the inter-agency cluster approach, whereby it assumed the global leadership of the protection cluster and co-led the camp coordination and camp management cluster with the International Organization for Migration. Almost all continents witnessed at least some progress towards solutions to forced displacement. A total of 2.6 million refugees and IDPs returned to their homes, including almost 400,000 to Afghanistan and around 1.4 million in Africa. In Latin America, UNHCR supported the local integration of refugees and facilitated their self-reliance in urban and border areas. However, a number of new, renewed, accelerating or entrenched crises produced millions of new refugees and IDPs in Africa, Asia and the Middle East. Ongoing violence in Iraq resulted in massive displacements, both internally and externally to Jordan and the Syrian Arab Republic, while the July/August war that erupted in Lebanon displaced 1 million Lebanese. The political instability and violence in Timor-Leste displaced 150,000 people, the breakdown of the peace process in Sri Lanka resulted in the internal displacement of 200,000 persons and a renewed crisis in the 15-year old conflict in Somalia caused thousands of Somalis to cross the border into Kenya. In the Darfur region of the Sudan, 2 million people were internally displaced by the end of the year, which adversely impacted neighbouring Chad. Rebel uprisings and cross-border raids caused disruptions to operations for 222,000 Sudanese refugees living in camps in the east of the country and increased the number of people displaced inside Chad to 113,000.

Another issue of concern to UNHCR was the complexity of mixed migrations, especially the increasing number of people migrating by boat in the Gulf of Aden, the Caribbean, the Mediterranean, along Africa's Atlantic coast and between Indonesia and Australia. A significant number of refugees were caught up in those flows. UNHCR made efforts to help States address the issue.

Despite an improved refugee protection environment, UNHCR continued to highlight the need for a clear framework for the exercise of the "responsibility to protect", particularly with regard to the situation of IDPs in the Darfur region, and emphasized the importance of preserving the institution of asylum, opposing all forms of refoulement and ensuring respect for international refugee law. In October, the UNHCR Executive Committee adopted conclusions on women and girls at risk and on the identification, prevention and reduction of statelessness and protection of stateless persons, which included mechanisms and standards for addressing the protection issues of those vulnerable groups. Financially, 2006 was a difficult year for UNHCR. Austerity measures were put in place and the resulting cutbacks meant that some projects had to be delayed or suspended. During the year, UNHCR reassessed its mission and implemented structural and management reform. On 1 January, Erika Feller began her duties in the newly-established post of Assistant High Commissioner for Protection.

Office of the United Nations High Commissioner for Refugees

Programme policy

Executive Committee action. At its fifty-seventh session (Geneva, 2-6 October) [A/61/12/Add.1], the Executive Committee of the UNHCR Programme, in a conclusion on women and girls at risk, acknowledged that forcibly displaced women and girls were exposed to particular protection risks related to their gender, such as trafficking. It underlined the importance of identifying and analysing the range of factors that put women and girls at risk; recommended preventive strategies to be adopted by States, UNHCR and other agencies and partners; and provided a non-exhaustive list of recommended individual responses and solutions. The Committee recommended that UNHCR include a more detailed elaboration of those issues in the UNHCR *Handbook on the Protection of Women and Girls*.

In other actions, the Committee adopted a conclusion on identification, prevention and reduction of statelessness and protection of stateless persons, and decisions on institutional and on administrative, financial and programme matters.

In his opening statement to the Committee [A/AC.96/SR.599], the High Commissioner provided an update on the status of the six commitments he had made at the Committee's fifty-sixth (2005) session [YUN 2005, p. 1301]. They concerned: strengthening UNHCR identity as a protection agency; making UNHCR a fully engaged partner in the cluster approach to internal displacement situations; addressing protection concerns in mixed population flows (migrants seeking work and persons in need of protection); placing greater emphasis on the sustainability of returns and the enhanced role of resettlement; re-establishing a quick and flexible emergency response capacity; and reforming the structure and management of UNHCR to make it more flexible, effective and results-oriented. With regard to preserving asylum and rebuilding trust in the asylum systems, the High Commissioner cited Burundi's application of fair and effective asylum procedures for Rwandan refugees. In the area of strengthening protection capacity, the Assistant High Commissioner for Protection would lead the debate across the organization on such critical protection issues as mixed population flows, data protection, facilitation and promotion of voluntary repatriation, sexual and gender-based violence, statelessness, exit strategies, exclusion in a time of terrorism, alliances for protection, resettlement and internal displacement. As to the cluster approach to internal displacement, the High Commissioner stated that it had opened up new opportunities for durable solutions and the lessons learned in the pilot countries where the approach had been applied, such as Uganda, would guide UNHCR in the future. On mixed population flows, he stated that the UNHCR role involved creating an environment where migrants in need of international protection could be detected and assisted. The UNHCR 10-point Plan of Action set out measures that could be incorporated into migration procedures to address asylum and would be piloted in North Africa and Southern Europe. The High Commissioner also highlighted the improvement in UNHCR capacity in resettlement services, its strengthened emergency response abilities and the increased number of staff available for immediate deployment. On the other hand, financial constraints had hampered the establishment of sufficient emergency stockpiles. The High Commissioner expressed concern that the steady rise in fixed costs and financial problems were increasingly affecting core activities. Hence, reform was essential for long-term sustainability. A review had been launched of all UNHCR processes, structures and staffing. In particular, efforts were being made to move field support closer to the point of delivery to maximize its impact and make administrative services more cost-effective.

The High Commissioner described measures taken to address the precarious financial situation, including a zero-growth policy for staff at Headquarters, as a result of which UNHCR was able to avoid disruptive budget cuts in 2006. The Deputy High Commissioner had been involved in efforts to reinvigorate the Council of Business Leaders in order to raise funds from the private sector. The 2007 budget, which was $100 million less than that of 2006, represented a clear shift in policy. It was based on transparency and realistic assumptions about possible funding levels, with items classified as operations representing a higher percentage of global costs than staff and administrative costs.

GENERAL ASSEMBLY ACTION

On 19 December [meeting 81], the General Assembly, on the recommendation of the Third (Social, Humanitarian and Cultural) Committee [A/61/436], adopted **resolution 61/137** without vote [agenda item 41].

Office of the United Nations High Commissioner for Refugees

The General Assembly,

Having considered the report of the United Nations High Commissioner for Refugees on the activities of his Office and the report of the Executive Committee of the Programme of the United Nations High Commissioner for Refugees on the work of its fifty-seventh session and the conclusions and decisions contained therein,

Recalling its previous annual resolutions on the work of the Office of the High Commissioner since its establishment by the General Assembly,

Expressing its appreciation for the leadership shown by the High Commissioner, commending the staff and implementing partners of the Office of the High Commissioner for the competent, courageous and dedicated manner in which they discharge their responsibilities, and underlining its strong condemnation of all forms of violence to which humanitarian personnel and United

Nations and associated personnel are increasingly exposed,

1. *Endorses* the report of the Executive Committee of the Programme of the United Nations High Commissioner for Refugees on the work of its fifty-seventh session;

2. *Welcomes* the important work undertaken by the Office of the United Nations High Commissioner for Refugees and its Executive Committee in the course of the year, and notes in this context the adoption of the conclusion on women and girls at risk and the conclusion on identification, prevention and reduction of statelessness and protection of stateless persons, which are aimed at strengthening the international protection regime, consistent with the Agenda for Protection, and at assisting Governments in meeting their protection responsibilities in today's changing international environment, including by promoting the progressive implementation of mechanisms and standards through relevant national public policies supported by the international community;

3. *Reaffirms* the 1951 Convention relating to the Status of Refugees and the 1967 Protocol thereto as the foundation of the international refugee protection regime, recognizes the importance of their full and effective application by States parties and the values they embody, notes with satisfaction that one hundred and forty-six States are now parties to one instrument or to both, encourages States not parties to consider acceding to those instruments, underlines in particular the importance of full respect for the principle of non-refoulement, and recognizes that a number of States not parties to the international refugee instruments have shown a generous approach to hosting refugees;

4. *Notes* that sixty-two States are now parties to the 1954 Convention relating to the Status of Stateless Persons and that thirty-three States are parties to the 1961 Convention on the Reduction of Statelessness, encourages States that have not done so to give consideration to acceding to these instruments, notes the work of the High Commissioner in regard to identifying stateless persons, preventing and reducing statelessness, and protecting stateless persons, and urges the Office of the High Commissioner to continue to work in this area in accordance with relevant General Assembly resolutions and Executive Committee conclusions;

5. *Takes note* of the current activities of the Office of the High Commissioner related to protection of and assistance to internally displaced persons, including in the context of inter-agency arrangements in this field, emphasizes that such activities should be consistent with relevant General Assembly resolutions and should not undermine the mandate of the Office for refugees and the institution of asylum, and encourages the High Commissioner to continue his dialogue with States on the role of his Office in this regard;

6. *Re-emphasizes* that the protection of refugees is primarily the responsibility of States, whose full and effective cooperation, action and resolve are required to enable the Office of the High Commissioner to fulfil its mandated functions, and strongly emphasizes, in this context, the importance of active international solidarity and burden- and responsibility-sharing;

7. *Emphasizes* that prevention and reduction of statelessness are primarily the responsibility of States, in appropriate cooperation with the international community;

8. *Also emphasizes* that protection of and assistance to internally displaced persons are primarily the responsibility of States, in appropriate cooperation with the international community;

9. *Urges* all States and relevant non-governmental and other organizations, in conjunction with the Office of the High Commissioner, in a spirit of international solidarity and burden- and responsibility-sharing, to cooperate and to mobilize resources with a view to enhancing the capacity of and reducing the heavy burden borne by host countries, in particular those that have received large numbers of refugees and asylum-seekers, and calls upon the Office to continue to play its catalytic role in mobilizing assistance from the international community to address the root causes as well as the economic, environmental and social impact of large-scale refugee populations in developing countries, in particular the least developed countries, and countries with economies in transition;

10. *Strongly condemns* attacks on refugees, asylum-seekers and internally displaced persons as well as acts that pose a threat to their personal security and well-being, and calls upon all concerned States and, where applicable, parties involved in an armed conflict to take all necessary measures to ensure respect for human rights and international humanitarian law;

11. *Deplores* the refoulement and unlawful expulsion of refugees and asylum-seekers, and calls upon all concerned States to ensure respect for the principles of refugee protection and human rights;

12. *Emphasizes* that international protection of refugees is a dynamic and action-oriented function that is at the core of the mandate of the Office of the High Commissioner and that it includes, in cooperation with States and other partners, the promotion and facilitation of, inter alia, the admission, reception and treatment of refugees in accordance with internationally agreed standards and the ensuring of durable, protection-oriented solutions, bearing in mind the particular needs of vulnerable groups and paying special attention to those with specific needs, and notes in this context that the delivery of international protection is a staff-intensive service that requires adequate staff with the appropriate expertise, especially at the field level;

13. *Affirms* the importance of mainstreaming the protection needs of women and children to ensure their participation in the planning and implementation of programmes of the Office of the High Commissioner and State policies and the importance of according priority to addressing the problem of sexual and gender-based violence;

14. *Acknowledges* that forcibly displaced women and girls can be exposed to particular protection problems

related to their gender, their cultural and socio-economic position, and their legal status, that they may be less likely than men and boys to be able to exercise their rights, and that, therefore, specific action in favour of women and girls may be necessary to ensure that they can enjoy protection and assistance on an equal basis with men and boys, and notes the important guidance provided in the Executive Committee conclusion on women and girls at risk to address issues of identification of those individuals and action to be taken in prevention and response;

15. *Strongly reaffirms* the fundamental importance and the purely humanitarian and non-political character of the function of the Office of the High Commissioner of providing international protection to refugees and seeking permanent solutions to refugee problems, and recalls that those solutions include voluntary repatriation and, where appropriate and feasible, local integration and resettlement in a third country, while reaffirming that voluntary repatriation, supported by necessary rehabilitation and development assistance to facilitate sustainable reintegration, remains the preferred solution;

16. *Expresses concern* about the particular difficulties faced by the millions of refugees in protracted situations, and emphasizes the need to redouble international efforts and cooperation to find practical and comprehensive approaches to resolving their plight and to realize durable solutions for them, consistent with relevant General Assembly resolutions and international law;

17. *Recalls* the important role of effective partnerships and coordination in meeting the needs of refugees and in finding durable solutions to their situations, welcomes the efforts under way, in cooperation with countries hosting refugees and countries of origin, including their respective local communities, United Nations agencies and other development actors, to promote a framework for durable solutions, particularly in protracted refugee situations, which includes the "4Rs" approach (repatriation, reintegration, rehabilitation and reconstruction) to sustainable return, and encourages States, in cooperation with United Nations agencies and other development actors, to support, inter alia, through the allocation of funds, the development and implementation of the 4Rs and other programming tools to facilitate the transition from relief to development;

18. *Welcomes* the progress that has been achieved in increasing the number of refugees resettled and the number of States offering opportunities for resettlement, notes that the Multilateral Framework of Understandings on Resettlement sets out the strategic use of resettlement as part of a comprehensive approach to refugee situations aimed at improving access to durable solutions for a greater number of refugees, and invites interested States, the Office of the High Commissioner and other relevant partners to make use of the Multilateral Framework, where appropriate and feasible;

19. *Notes* the progress that is being made by interested States and the Office of the High Commissioner to take forward elements outlined in the Mexico Plan of Action to Strengthen International Protection of Refugees in Latin America, adopted on 16 November 2004, and expresses its support for the efforts to promote its implementation with the cooperation and assistance of the international community, as appropriate, including in the area of resettlement, as well as in supporting host communities that receive large numbers of persons who require international protection;

20. *Also notes* that some progress is being made by interested States and the Office of the High Commissioner within the context of the European-Asian Programme on Forced Displacement and Migration on issues related to asylum and forced displacement, consistent with the mandate of the Office;

21. *Further notes* the importance of States and the Office of the High Commissioner discussing and clarifying the role of the Office in mixed migratory flows, in order to better address protection needs in the context of mixed migratory flows, including by safeguarding access to asylum for those in need of international protection, and notes the readiness of the High Commissioner, consistent with his mandate, to assist States in fulfilling their protection responsibilities in this regard;

22. *Emphasizes* the obligation of all States to accept the return of their nationals, calls upon States to facilitate the return of their nationals who have been determined not to be in need of international protection, and affirms the need for the return of persons to be undertaken in a safe and humane manner and with full respect for their human rights and dignity, irrespective of the status of the persons concerned;

23. *Encourages* the Office of the High Commissioner to continue to improve its management systems and to ensure effective and transparent use of its resources, recognizes that adequate and timely resources are essential for the Office to continue to fulfil the mandate conferred upon it through its statute and by subsequent General Assembly resolutions on refugees and other persons of concern, recalls its resolutions 58/153 of 22 December 2003, 58/270 of 23 December 2003, 59/170 of 20 December 2004 and 60/129 of 16 December 2005 concerning, inter alia, the implementation of paragraph 20 of the statute of the Office, and urges Governments and other donors to respond promptly to annual and supplementary appeals issued by the Office for requirements under its programmes;

24. *Calls upon* the Office of the High Commissioner to widen its donor base, so as to achieve greater burden-sharing by reinforcing cooperation with traditional governmental donors, non-traditional donors and the private sector;

25. *Requests* the High Commissioner to report on his activities to the General Assembly at its sixty-second session.

Strengthening UNHCR

Oral report of UNHCR. In response to General Assembly resolution 58/153 [YUN 2003, p. 1226] on strengthening UNHCR capacity to carry out its mandate, a UNHCR representative provided a 26 July oral report to the Economic and Social Council [E/2006/

SR.40]. Concerning the coordination aspects of its work, the respresentative said that the Office supported efforts to improve global humanitarian response capacity. The inter-agency dialogue carried out within the Inter-Agency Standing Committee (IASC) on improving the collaborative response to internal displacement had led to the "cluster leadership approach" (see p. 1054), a new arrangement aimed at bringing greater predictability, accountability and capacity to emergency management and early recovery, under which UNHCR had the lead role in protection, camp coordination and management and emergency shelter for internally displaced persons (IDPs) in situations of conflict-generated displacement. UNHCR continued to work to combat HIV/AIDS among refugees and other persons of concern and ensure their inclusion within host countries' HIV/AIDS policies and programmes. UNHCR partnerships with non-governmental organizations (NGOs) continued to progress beyond traditional core operative arrangements.

UNHCR worked to build on its partnerships with NGOs. It initiated a review of the sub-project agreement (grants management) process and the levels of UNHCR contributions to NGO headquarters' overhead costs and expatriate salaries. In 2006, the Office channelled some 20 per cent of its annual budget ($247.7 million) through implementing partner agreements with some 645 NGOs, including 489 national NGOs.

With regard to Africa, which accounted for some 30 per cent of the world's refugees (approximately 2.5 million persons) and over 9 million IDPs or returnees, the UNHCR representative provided an update on the status of various UNHCR repatriation operations on the continent where significant progress had been made, including in Burundi, the Democratic Republic of the Congo (DRC), Liberia and southern Sudan, and on resettlement operations in Guinea and the United Republic of Tanzania. In its repatriation and reintegration operations, UNHCR continued to improve the registration and documentation of refugees, to prevent sexual and gender-based violence and to build awareness of the role African Governments could play in supporting conflict prevention. Through both the cluster approach and UNHCR bilateral and multilateral partnerships, progress was achieved in combating malnutrition among refugees and other persons of concern, including refugees in national and regional HIV/AIDS programmes. However, deteriorating security related to conflict-generated displacement, combined with funding constraints, had had a significant impact on UNHCR presence in many situations, notably in the Darfur region of the Sudan where its operations had to be downsized. There was a chronic disparity between growing needs and available resources, including consistent food supplies. UNHCR desperately needed sustained international support in order to continue to deliver minimum standards of protection and assistance to refugees and IDPs in Africa.

Coordination of emergency humanitarian assistance

In 2006 [A/62/12], UNHCR continued to participate in the initiatives to reform the UN system and improve the global humanitarian response capacity, including follow-up to the humanitarian response review [YUN 2005, p. 991] through IASC, implementation of the 2005 World Summit Outcome [ibid., p. 48], and the relevant recommendations of the Secretary-General's High-Level Panel on System-wide Coherence "Delivering as One" (see p. 1060). The Office also worked with the Peacebuilding Commission and the Peacebuilding Support Office, established in 2005 [YUN 2005, p. 93] (see p. 55), as the successful return and reintegration of displaced persons depended on sustainable peace and development. UNHCR participated in other coordination bodies, such as the UN System Chief Executives Board for Coordination (CEB) and its subsidiary bodies, the UN Development Group, the Executive Committee on Peace and Security and the Executive Committee on Humanitarian Affairs (ECHA). Through ECHA, the Office supported efforts to address operational challenges for the humanitarian community, such as in the Chad/Darfur situation.

Bilateral collaboration with a large number of agencies remained a key feature of the implementation of UNHCR mandate. High-level advocacy with the World Food Programme (WFP) yielded positive results in covering serious gaps in funding of food aid for refugees and raising awareness about their nutritional needs, while close cooperation on logistical and supply-related matters continued between the United Nations Children's Fund (UNICEF), WFP and UNHCR. The Food and Agriculture Organization of the United Nations (FAO) and UNHCR collaborated on assessments and the promotion of food security for refugees and others of concern. Together with FAO and the International Labour Organization (ILO), the Office carried out activities in a number of countries and discussed a possible ILO/FAO/UNHCR initiative for recovery in priority post-conflict situations. Close cooperation continued between UNHCR and the Office of the United Nations High Commissioner for Human Rights (OHCHR). In July,

UNHCR and OHCHR signed a memorandum of understanding on the human rights of IDPs to address outstanding policy gaps on the human rights and protection of IDPs.

To ensure that the integrity of asylum was upheld, UNHCR cooperated with the UN Office on Drugs and Crime (UNODC) to ensure that legislation to address security concerns did not curtail the right to seek and obtain asylum. The two Offices also worked with other bodies, such as the Organization for Security and Cooperation in Europe (OSCE), on anti-trafficking legislation that would include measures to protect the victims. With the International Organization for Migration (IOM), UNHCR co-led the inter-agency cluster on camp coordination and management, with IOM taking the lead in natural disaster situations and UNHCR in cases of conflict-generated displacement. Cooperation with the International Committee of the Red Cross (ICRC) on activities in favour of refugees was expanded to IDPs, in tandem with the progressive involvement of UNHCR in situations of internal displacement.

New international humanitarian order

In an August report [A/61/224] (see. p. 1063), the Secretary-General described action taken to develop further the new international humanitarian order agenda. Five key issues that were the cornerstones for contemporary humanitarian action around the world were examined: prevention; access to people in need; the right to humanitarian assistance; local capacity-building; and burden-sharing. The report noted that, although the number of IDPs had become greater than the number of refugees, their needs had not been met satisfactorily outside national efforts.

On 19 December, in **resolution 61/138** (see p. 1063), the General Assembly invited Governments, the UN Office for the Coordination of Humanitarian Affairs (OCHA), relevant UN system entities, intergovernmental organizations and NGOs to reinforce activities and cooperation in order to further develop an agenda for humanitarian action.

Evaluation activities

UNHCR, in a July report [A/AC.96/1029], described evaluation and policy development activities since its previous report [YUN 2005, p. 1304], including the replacement of the former Evaluation and Policy Analysis Unit by the Policy Development and Evaluation Service (PDES), which would assume responsibility for the formulation, development and implementation of the organization's evaluation activities. With the establishment of PDES, a review of UNHCR evaluation policy was initiated. The revised policy would take account of the Norms and Standards for Evaluation adopted by the inter-agency United Nations Evaluation Group and introduce enhanced mechanisms for the implementation of evaluation recommendations, which would be compiled in a newly established database. Steps would also be taken to ensure that there was a clear division of labour between UNHCR evaluation, inspection and audit functions.

Due to the reorganization of the UNHCR evaluation function, the level of evaluation activity was lower than in previous years. Nevertheless, several projects and their corresponding reports were completed, including: case studies of refugee livelihoods; an evaluation of the utilization and management of the UNHCR fleet of light vehicles; a review of the deployment of the Royal Canadian Mounted Police in Guinea; a review of the role of "the Desk" in UNHCR, along with a comparative review of its role in other UN organizations; and an evaluation of the Protection Information Section. Ongoing projects included: the formulation of a new UNHCR policy and implementation guide on refugees and asylum-seekers in urban areas; an evaluation of UNHCR three-year programme for IDPs in Liberia, which entailed the return of some 310,000 IDPs to their place of origin; an evaluation of UNHCR response to the December 2004 tsunami in Indonesia [YUN 2004, p. 952]; and a review of UNHCR role in international migration, which resulted in, among other documents, a 10-Point Plan of Action for Addressing Mixed Migratory Movements. PDES also resumed responsibility for the publication of the research paper series "New Issues in Refugee Research".

Inspections

During 2006 [A/62/12], the UNHCR Inspector General's Office carried out 23 inspections at the country level and one at headquarters, resulting in over 400 recommendations to address: recurring problems, such as the improper use of non-staff personnel; difficulties faced by managers in addressing conflicts; unclear relationships between field offices and functional units at headquarters; the need for standardized protection monitoring guidelines for implementing partners; the uneven use of standards and indicators; and the fact that the level of available resources, rather than the actual needs of beneficiaries, was the main basis for programme planning and implementation. Other activities included 131 investigations resulting in 32 investigation reports sent to the Department for Human Resources Management for disciplinary action. A total of 13 management implication reports were issued, highlighting procedural or management problems and covering a range of topics from asset management to implementation of refugee status determination (RSD) procedures. A report [A/AC.96/1028] on the activities of the Inspector General' Office undertaken since 2005 was transmitted to the UNHCR Executive Committee in July.

The audit service of the UN Office of Internal Oversight Services (OIOS) continued to perform the internal audit function for UNHCR. In 2006, the audit service introduced a more risk-based approach to its planning process by selecting and prioritizing audit assignments based on the level of risk they posed to UNHCR, which ensured that audit resources were focused on higher-risk areas, and determined which programmes and activities should be audited and how often. OIOS conducted 32 audits and issued 197 recommendations to improve accountability mechanisms and control systems, as well as recommendations for the development or clarification of policies and procedures and workflow processes. In July, OIOS submitted to the UNHCR Executive Committee a report on its internal audit of UNHCR for the period 1 July 2005 to 30 June 2006 [A/AC.96/1027].

Enlargement of Executive Committee

On 26 July, the Economic and Social Council, by **decision 2006/237**, took note of requests from Costa Rica [E/2006/3] and Estonia [E/2006/82] for membership in the UNHCR Executive Committee and recommended that the General Assembly take a decision at its sixty-first (2006) session on the question of enlarging the Committee's membership from 70 to 72 States.

GENERAL ASSEMBLY ACTION

On 19 December [meeting 81], the General Assembly, on the recommendation of the Third Committee [A/61/436], adopted **resolution 61/136** without vote [agenda item 41].

Enlargement of the Executive Committee of the Programme of the United Nations High Commissioner for Refugees

The General Assembly,

Taking note of Economic and Social Council decision 2006/237 of 26 July 2006 concerning the enlargement of the Executive Committee of the Programme of the United Nations High Commissioner for Refugees,

Taking note also of the requests regarding the enlargement of the Executive Committee contained in the letter dated 8 March 2006 from the Deputy Permanent Representative of Costa Rica to the United Nations addressed to the Secretary-General and the letter dated 30 May 2006 from the Permanent Representative of Estonia to the United Nations addressed to the Secretary-General,

1. *Decides* to increase the number of members of the Executive Committee of the Programme of the United Nations High Commissioner for Refugees from seventy to seventy-two States;

2. *Requests* the Economic and Social Council to elect the additional members at its resumed organizational session for 2007.

On 29 November [E/2006/92], Benin requested admission in the membership of the UNHCR Executive Committee.

Financial and administrative questions

The UNHCR initial annual programme budget target for 2006 was set at $1,136.8 million by the Executive Committee in 2005 [YUN 2005, p. 1305]. Income for 2006 totalled some $1,228 million, comprising $922.3 million in contributions, transfers and miscellaneous income (including currency exchange gains) towards the annual programme budget and $251.4 million towards supplementary programmes, $16.6 million for the Junior Professional Officer (JPO) programme and $31.5 million from the regular UN budget. Expenditures totalled $1,100.7 million, of which Africa accounted for $490.4 million; Central Asia, South-West Asia, North Africa and the Middle East $170.2 million; Europe $99.3 million; Asia and the Pacific $80.4 million; and the Americas, $33.4 million.

In an October decision [A/61/12/Add.1], the Executive Committee approved the revised annual programme budget for 2006, amounting to $1,136.8 million, including the UN regular budget contribution of $32.9 million, which, with the provisions for JPOs of $10 million and $288 million for supplementary programmes, brought total requirements in 2006 to $1,434.8 million.

The Committee approved $1,032.9 million for the 2007 annual programme budget, which included the UN regular budget contribution, an operational reserve of $89.4 million, or 10 per cent of programme activities, and $50 million for new or additional mandate-related activities. Those provisions, together with $10 million for JPOs, brought total requirements in 2007 to $1,042.9 million. The Committee authorized the High Commissioner, within the total appropriation, to effect adjustments in regional and global programmes and the headquarters budgets, and to create supplementary programmes and issue special appeals when new emergency needs could not be met from the operational reserve.

The Committee requested UNHCR to finalize the criteria for the inclusion or non-inclusion of supplementary programme budgets for refugee or refugee-related programmes in the annual programme budget and to consult on how supplementary programme budgets could be best managed to support UNHCR role as cluster lead in certain internal displacement situations. UNHCR was called upon to keep its administrative expenditure under review in order to reduce it as a proportion of total expenditure.

Accounts

The audited financial statements of voluntary funds administered by UNHCR for the year ending 31 December 2005 [A/61/5/Add.5] showed total expenditures of $1,144.7 million and total available funds of $1,278 million, with a reserve balance of $133.3 million.

The UN Board of Auditors found that, since there was no audit certificate available at UNHCR when the 2005 financial statements were prepared and signed for amounts paid to implementing partners in 2005, which totalled $340 million as at 31 December 2005, UNHCR had no reasonable assurance on the proper use of funds disbursed to those partners. It also found that the financial position of UNHCR had weakened, showing an excess of expenditure over income of $32 million, raising questions about the UNHCR financial position and its ability to sustain such a trend. UNHCR lacked efficient tools for its treasury information and cash forecasting, which limited the efficient management of its Treasury. There was no formalized foreign-exchange risk policy, leaving UNHCR facing global exposure as payments and receipts were not made in the same currencies and during the same period. Completed travels were posted as unliquidated obligations and had not been settled six months after completion, and the amounts in previous-year subprojects covered by audit certificates had increased from 53 per cent in June 2005 to 67 per cent in June 2006. UNHCR had not completed the phase-out of the use of "project staff" by the deadline established in 2001, nor had it devoted sufficient resources to income-generating activities or properly defined or monitored performance indicators for fund-raising activities. UNHCR had signed agreements that were not in compliance with UN rules for staff, suppliers and audit arrangements, and its internal audit service had not devoted all the agreed resources to the audit of UNHCR. As the needs assessment could not be properly conducted for tsunami-related operations, UNHCR could not spend all the resources it had requested, or stored items that it had purchased in excess. The procurement service had little information on procurement conducted by field offices and implementing partners. The Board of Auditors made recommendations to improve financial management and reporting and programme management. It observed that UNHCR had actively responded to most recommendations, although some had not yet been implemented.

UNHCR, in a September report [A/AC.96/1025/Add.1], described measures taken or proposed in response to the Board's recommendations.

The Advisory Committee on Administrative and Budgetary Questions (ACABQ), in September [A/61/350], expressed concern regarding the sustainability of UNHCR expenditures. It noted that the gap between available funds and the approved budget for 2005 had forced UNHCR to impose caps on programme budgets and non-staff administrative costs. Factors contributing to the situation included the fact that contributions received fell short of the increase in the annual programme budget; a good portion of contributions received went to supplementary programmes; and high exchange-rate losses ($36 million in 2005), due to the organization's vulnerability to foreign-currency fluctuations. Hence, UNHCR ended 2005 having to borrow $12.2 million from the Working Capital and Guarantee Fund. ACABQ stressed the importance of ensuring predictability, flexibility and early funding, especially in the context of the upcoming biennial budget cycle and of efforts to expand the base, as 97 per cent of UNHCR resources came in the form of voluntary contributions. It noted that the UNHCR proposed programme budget for 2007 [A/AC.96/1026 & Add.1] included several initiatives to ensure financial stability and welcomed the implementation of centrally managed incentive-based fund-raising at the field level. It also encouraged further efforts to increase private-sector funding.

The Executive Committee, in an October decision [A/61/12/Add.1], requested that it be regularly informed on measures taken to address the recommendations made by the Board of Auditors and ACABQ.

Management and administrative change

In February, UNHCR launched an in-depth process of structural and management change, with the overall aim of streamlining and simplifying organizational processes, reducing administrative costs and enhancing the efficiency of field operations, so as to improve its flexibility and responsiveness to the needs of beneficiaries. The change process involved reviewing and realigning structures and processes, as well as workforce and implementing arrangements, to maximize overall performance. Under the structural part of the reform, a number of UNHCR centralized administrative and support functions were to be outposted to Budapest, Hungary, freeing up resources for beneficiaries. Accrued savings from outposting were expected to total some $10 million per year once the initial investment in the establishment of the new centre was made. The Office also examined ways to improve operational effectiveness by strengthening regional structures, decentralizing a number of operational support functions and strengthening its capacity to undertake situational and solutions planning at the subregional level. Work in the area of processes included clarifying priorities by revising UNHCR Global Strategic Objectives and establishing clear linkages between those objectives and UNHCR planning processes. Procedural guidelines and structures were being developed to support those process-related reforms. Meanwhile, staffing policies and strategies were being aligned with organizational needs, and the deployment of staff between capital cities and field locations and the balance between international and national staff were being reviewed. In November, a Global Staff Survey was carried out to underpin UNHCR reform efforts.

UNHCR continued to develop a management approach that emphasized the achievement of results. It finalized its Results-based Management (RBM) Conceptual Framework and made significant progress in developing RBM *Focus* software to assist its field and headquarters units with results-based planning, managing and reporting. The *Focus* software would be fully integrated with the Management Systems Renewal Project (MSRP) and UNHCR registration software. Progress was also made in information management with the September launch of the first components of MSRP Human Resources. The successful development of Project Profile (refugee registration system), which was closed down at the end of 2006 as planned, resulted in a global roll-out of refugee registration standards and *proGres*, a standardized information technology application. *ProGres* biometric technologies increased efficiency in the registration exercises of several UNHCR operations during the year.

Policy guidelines for consultants. In response to General Assembly resolution 59/270 [YUN 2004, p. 1368], the Secretary-General submitted a July report [A/61/201] on the development and use of comprehensive policy guidelines for the selection and management of consultants in UNHCR. The guidelines, which were implemented in 2005, were developed to ensure transparency and objectivity in the engagement, monitoring and evaluation of consultants, and ensure a geographical balance in the use of qualified consultants. The changes resulting from the new policy included: the introduction of a new type of consultancy, the locally hired international consultant; limiting the duration of consultancy to 24 months within a 36-month period, with a mandatory break after 11 consecutive months; review and approval by the Headquarters Committee on Contracts when expenditure on a contract or related extension reached $100,000 or more; basing a request for consultants on detailed terms of reference; a full medical examination for consultants assigned to or on mission to category B, C, D and E duty stations, and a certificate of good health for category H and A duty stations; and the successful completion of security training prior to travel for consultants on mission or assigned to a duty station with phase I security status or above. Attached to the policy were administrative guidelines outlining the steps to be taken when hiring consultants, the roles and responsibilities of the parties involved in a consultant contract, and the procedures for work and travel. The report described the process for the evaluation and monitoring of consultants and provided statistics on consultants for 2005.

Standing Committee

The UNHCR Standing Committee held three meetings in 2006 (7-9 March [A/AC.96/1022]; 26-28 June [A/AC.96/1032]; and 20-21 September [A/AC.96/1034]). It considered issues relating to UNHCR programme budgets and funding; international protection; regional activities and global programmes; programme/protection policy; coordination; management, financial control, administrative oversight and human resources; governance; and consultations.

In October [A/61/12/Add.1], the Executive Committee requested its Bureau to continue consultations on the nature and value of Executive Committee conclusions on international protection, including a review of the process for their adoption and its effectiveness with regard to contributions by Standing Committee Observers, in order for the Committee to take a decision on the question in 2007; and to resume and finalize, prior to its 2007 session, consultations to investigate options for extending the input from NGOs that were UNHCR implementing or operating partners in the work of the Executive Committee. It requested the Standing Committee to report on its work in 2007. The Executive Committee also approved applications by Governments to participate as observers in Standing Committee meetings and a list of intergovernmental and international organizations to be invited to participate as observers.

Staff safety

At the September meeting of the Standing Committee [A/AC.96/1034], the Director of the UNHCR Division of Operational Services, in an update on staff safety and security management [EC/57/SC/CRP.24], described efforts to implement the recommendations of the UNHCR Security Policy and Policy Implementation Review, as well as new initiatives to strengthen a culture of security and other security-related activities. He said that UNHCR needed to strike a balance between working within the framework established by the UN Department of Safety and Security and effectively serving refugees and other persons of concern. Achievements in 2005-2006 included the provision of more security training for middle and senior-level managers; security training for representatives of implementing partners; and the establishment of measures for minimum operating security standards (MOSS) compliance in all countries with Phase III and above conditions by the end of 2006. During 2006-2007, the Office planned to organize more functional training and enhance links with staff welfare issues and with the Staff Council. The Director confirmed that UNHCR interventions, particularly in situations of internal displacement, were sometimes complicated by the positions and actions taken by States and non-State actors and by the lack of specifically binding legal instruments for IDPs. A component on dealing with IDPs had been included in the Workshop on Emergency Management and steps were being taken to incorporate IDPs into planning tools and training programmes. Delegates expressed regret about the increase of incidents against humanitarian actors and the funding shortfalls that had affected staffing and security.

Refugee protection and assistance

Protection issues

In his annual report covering 2006 [A/62/12], the High Commissioner described challenges facing States and UNHCR in protecting persons of concern, such as armed conflict; targeted violence based on religion, ethnicity, social group or political opinion; refusal of asylum; recruitment by rebel movements of refugees in camps; political turmoil; and eruptions of violence and fighting, which restricted humanitarian access to camps and IDPs. Issues affecting States' efforts to manage migration, especially the identification of persons in need of protection within mixed migratory movements, were of particular concern to UNHCR. In addition to its core protection and assistance activities for refugees, UNHCR committed itself to the framework of shared humanitarian responsibilities under the inter-agency "cluster approach", which resulted in an increasing demand for its services to address the needs of IDPs. UNHCR assumed the global leadership of the protection cluster and co-led the camp coordination and camp management cluster with IOM. By the end of 2006, some 12.8 million IDPs were receiving humanitarian assistance under the cluster approach and other arrangements involving UNHCR.

In the context of protecting people with a well-founded fear of persecution within broader migration movements, UNHCR launched its 10-Point Plan of Action to ensure that measures taken to curb irregular migration movements were consistent with international refugee law. UNHCR also worked to preserve asylum space and put refugee protection on the agenda of the migration debate. To address the increasing number of deaths in journeys across the Mediterranean Sea, the Gulf of Aden and other maritime areas, UNHCR collaborated with IOM in publishing the leaflet "Rescue at Sea: a guide to principles and practice as applied to migrants and refugees", as a reference guide for shipmasters.

In October, the Executive Committee requested UNHCR to intensify action to address statelessness in cooperation with States and relevant UN bodies, in particular, UNICEF and the United Nations Population Fund (UNFPA). In that regard, UNHCR activities were divided into four broad areas: identification, prevention and reduction of statelessness, and protection of stateless persons. Renewed efforts to identify stateless people led to the number of such persons known to UNHCR rising to 5.8 million in 49 countries in 2006.

In a July note on international protection [A/AC.96/1024], the High Commissioner described developments with regard to refugee movements up to May 2006 and outlined protection measures taken within the framework of the Agenda for Protection [YUN 2002, p. 1205], including strengthening implementation of the 1951 Convention relating to the Status of Refugees [YUN 1951, p. 520] and its 1967 Protocol [YUN 1967, p. 477]; protecting refugees within broader migration movements; sharing burdens and responsibilities more equitably and building capacities to receive and protect refugees; addressing security-related concerns more effectively; redoubling the search for durable solutions; and meeting the protection needs of refugee women and children.

The High Commissioner concluded that protection was the primary responsibility of States and UNHCR protection efforts were as effective as States would have them. Outstanding gaps in the protection of persons of concern required greater commitment on the part of all. He stated that the preparation of a comprehensive progress report on implementation of the Agenda for Protection, five years after its endorsement by the Executive Committee, as had been suggested in 2005 [YUN 2005, p. 1309], would be a timely way forward to take stock of gaps, challenges and future directions.

In October [A/61/12/Add.1], the UNHCR Executive Committee adopted conclusions on women and girls at risk and on identification, prevention and reduction of statelessness and protection of stateless persons, calling for measures to protect those vulnerable groups.

International instruments

In 2006, Montenegro succeeded to the 1951 Convention relating to the Status of Refugees [YUN 1951, p. 520] and its 1967 Protocol [YUN 1967, p. 477], bringing the number of parties to each instrument to 144. The number of States parties to one or both instruments totalled 147. Belize, Montenegro, Romania and Rwanda ratified the 1954 Convention relating to the Status of Stateless Persons [YUN 1954, p. 416], bringing the number of States parties to 62. With the accessions of New Zealand, Romania and Rwanda, the number of States Parties to the 1961 Convention on the Reduction of Statelessness [YUN 1961, p. 533] increased to 33.

In December, the legal protection framework was strengthened by the adoption of two new human rights conventions: the Convention on the Rights of Persons with Disabilities (see p. 785) and the International Convention for the Protection of All Persons from Enforced Disappearance (see p. 800), which introduced a new non-refoulement obligation and stipulated that the widespread or systematic practice of enforced disappearance constituted a crime against humanity.

Convention Plus

In 2006, the "Convention Plus" initiative, launched in 2003 [YUN 2003, p. 1229] to improve international protection and strengthen the commitment of States and UNHCR partners to resolving refugee situations, was mainstreamed into UNHCR operations, as announced in 2005 [YUN 2005, p. 1309]. Although, as a result, no meetings of the High Commissioner's Forum took place in 2006, the Forum's Co-Chairs issued a February statement [FORUM/2005/8] on the targeting of development assistance for durable solutions to forced displacement, one of the Convention Plus initiative's strands. The statement summarized the viewpoints of States and other stakeholders in discussions within the Convention Plus framework, including in the Forum. A number of States had recommended that the discussion on targeting development assistance be incorporated in the work of the Executive Committee and its Standing Committee as part of the mainstreaming.

Assistance measures

The global population of concern to UNHCR increased to 32.9 million in 2006, from 20.8 million in 2005. For the first time since 2002, the trend of declining refugee figures was reversed, reaching 9.9 million. That primarily reflected the 1.2 million new Iraqi refugees in Jordan, Lebanon and the Syrian Arab Republic. The number of IDPs receiving UNHCR assistance rose from 6.6 million in 2005 to 12.8 million in 2006, due mainly to the large numbers of new displacements in the Central African Republic, Chad, Colombia, Iraq, Somalia, Sri Lanka and Timor-Leste, the activation of the cluster approach, which resulted in an expansion of activities, and the revision upwards by several countries of their IDP estimates. While the number of stateless persons had more than doubled from 2.4 million in 2005 to 5.8 million in 2006, the figure did not capture the full magnitude of the phenomenon, as a significant number of stateless people had not been systematically identified and statistical data on statelessness was not always available. Moreover, the increased numbers did not necessarily indicate new situations of statelessness, but rather the result of better identification methods. The number of asylum-seekers fell to 738,000 by year's end, some 35,000 fewer than in 2005.

Situations of concern included the constant insecurity in Iraq; the plight of Iraqi Palestinians who had fled targeted violence in Baghdad but were refused entry by neighbouring countries already hosting large numbers of Palestinian refugees; the 200,000 Lebanese who remained internally displaced after the cessation of hostilities in August between Israel and Hizbullah (see p. 574); ethnic violence in eastern Chad, which strained the Government's ability to protect internally displaced Chadians and Sudanese refugees, and restricted humanitarian access to camps and IDPs in surrounding villages; the precarious situation of 2.1 million Sudanese displaced by the violence in Darfur; and armed conflict in Somalia, which led to a continuous outflow of Somalis into Ethiopia, Kenya and Yemen. The displacements of an additional 200,000 persons in Sri Lanka due to the deteriorating security situation in the country, and the 150,000 people in Timor-Leste in and around the capital Dili, as a result of political unrest, were also of concern.

During the year, an estimated 734,000 refugees returned voluntarily to their places of origin, mainly to Afghanistan (387,917), Angola (47,017), Burundi (48,144), the DRC (41,228), Liberia (107,954) and the Sudan (42,258). UNHCR further assisted the return of some 238,000 IDPs in Liberia. The number of resettled people in 2006 (29,500) was 11 per cent lower than in 2005. Admitting countries included: Australia (13,400), Canada (10,700), New Zealand (700), Norway (1,000), Sweden (2,400) and the United States (41,300). The main beneficiaries were refugees from Afghanistan, the DRC, Myanmar, Somalia and the Sudan. Under the "Solidarity Resettlement" chapter of the Mexico Plan of Action [YUN 2004, p. 1210], several States in Latin America emerged as new resettlement countries. Significant numbers of refugees were also granted citizenship by their asylum countries: Armenia (1,200); Belgium (2,500); Kyrgyzstan (600); the Russian Federation (420); Turkmenistan (9,500); and the United States (98,500). Progress was also made on negotiations with several African Governments on local integration opportunities for long-staying refugees who were unlikely to return to their countries of origin.

Refugees and the environment

During the year, UNHCR continued to implement its environmental policy in accordance with the four principles outlined in the 2005 revision [YUN 2005, p. 1310] of its *Environmental Guidelines*: prevention, integration, cost-effectiveness and community participation, which was in line with the Office's broader objective to defend the institution of asylum, as excessive damage to the environment or the depletion of resources could affect host countries' decisions to provide asylum to refugees. UNHCR provided technical guidance to field operations in Africa and Asia, including carrying out environmental assessments and developing community environmental action plans at camp and village levels. The Office raised awareness of environmental issues in Africa and designed educational materials for schools, teachers and ecological clubs to ensure that refugees and returnees were better informed about the management of natural resources. On the occasion of World Environment Day (5 June), the Office, together with the United Nations Environment Programme (UNEP) and the United Nations Educational, Scientific and Cultural Organization (UNESCO), distributed information packages to field offices worldwide. Other initiatives included the application of environmentally-friendly agro-forestry techniques in Ethiopia and the United Republic of Tanzania and the training of some 200 refugees in sustainable small-scale agriculture; the construction of 50 environmentally friendly houses in Rwanda utilizing mud bricks, which reduced the amount of wood used by 70 per cent; and the introduction of biofuel, ethanol and solar cooking techniques in over 1,000 households in Chad, Ethiopia and Nepal. UNHCR introduced environmental assessment, monitoring and evaluation tools in Ethiopia and Uganda.

Refugees and HIV/AIDS

During 2006, in line with its HIV/AIDS Strategic Plan [YUN 2005, p. 1310], UNHCR continued to collaborate with its partners to combat HIV/AIDS among refugees and other persons of concern and ensure that the basic rights of those affected by HIV/AIDS were fully respected. The Office expanded its HIV/AIDS programmes to the Americas, Europe and the Middle East. As designated lead agency for refugees and IDPs within the Joint United Nations Programme on HIV/AIDS (UNAIDS), UNHCR expanded technical support and conducted HIV and IDP assessment missions in Colombia, Eastern Europe and Nepal. In March, the Standing Committee endorsed the recommendations of the Global Task Team on Improving AIDS Coordination among Multilateral Institutions and International Donors and all related decisions of the UNAIDS Programme Coordinating Board [ibid., 2005, p. 1327]. In April, UNHCR released a note on HIV/AIDS and the Protection of Refugees, IDPs and Other Persons of Concern to inform staff and Governments of recognized standards in the field of HIV/AIDS and the protection of people of concern to UNHCR. Together with UNFPA, UNHCR expanded its support to countries in Central and Southern Africa for the provision of post-exposure prophylaxis. Other activities included: the issuance of a UNHCR/UNAIDS policy brief on HIV/AIDS and refugees, focusing on actions required to address the effects of HIV/AIDS on refugees and their surrounding communities; and the conduct of two HIV sentinel and three behavioural surveillance surveys in Africa.

In 2006, UNHCR received funding for HIV/AIDS activities from global, regional and country donors, including additional earmarked contributions and in-kind donations of over $2 million.

Refugee women

In 2006, UNHCR continued to implement its pilot project on age, gender and diversity mainstreaming (AGDM), launched in 2004 [YUN 2004, p. 1205], in order to: develop an accountability framework with a reporting mechanism for senior managers to provide feedback on the completion of agreed actions; foster partnerships on Security Council resolution 1325(2000) [YUN 2000, p. 1113] on women, peace and security; and undertake initiatives for the prevention of and response to sexual and gender-based violence. During the year, the UNHCR ADGM strategy was introduced in 41 country operations across Africa, Asia and Europe, bringing the number of offices applying the strategy to 97. The Office also observed the "16 Days of Activism" campaign to end sexual and gender-based violence.

In March, the Standing Committee considered a paper on women at risk [EC/57/SC/CRP.7], which highlighted the importance of moving away from labelling refugee women as being vulnerable and broadening common understanding of specific risk factors in the legal, social and economic environment that heightened their vulnerability to harm.

In October [A/61/12/Add.1], the Executive Committee adopted a conclusion on women and girls at risk.

Refugee children

In 2006, UNHCR continued to emphasize education, nutrition and protection from violence in addressing the needs of refugee children. In June [A/AC.96/1032], the Standing Committee encouraged UNHCR to enhance its partnership with child protection agencies to build common understanding and develop an implementation strategy for child protection in all operations. To strengthen the prevention of and response to sexual and gender-based violence, UNHCR issued instructions to all country offices to establish standard operating procedures. To prevent malnutrition and improve the nutritional status of refugees and others of concern, UNHCR carried out assessments and analyses; ensured access to adequate food, including infant and young child feeding; and adopted an integrated approach to public health. UNHCR strengthened its partnership with WFP, conducting joint assessment missions and nutritional reviews that led to the development of a joint global nutrition strategy. Austerity measures in 2006 severely affected educational services for refugee children. While pupil-to-teacher ratios increased, the overall quality of education decreased. Although reduced support for refugees' secondary education and vocational training in a number of countries left adolescents more exposed to the risk of abuse and exploitation, some advances were made. UNHCR conducted an in-depth follow-up to the standards and indicators on education to monitor progress and reassess priority countries for technical support. Progress was noted in many countries, while new countries facing educational challenges were identified. Support was provided to a number of priority countries with low enrolment or retention rates of girls.

In June [A/AC.96/1032], the Standing Committee called on Governments and UNHCR humanitarian partners to include all persons of concern to the Office, notably refugee women and children, in future national, regional and international initiatives, such as the Ending Child Hunger and Undernutrition Initiative. In a June decision on the five global priorities for refugee children (sexual exploitation and violence; under-age military recruitment; education; unaccompanied minors; and adolescents) [YUN 1997, p. 1241], the Committee encouraged UNHCR to enhance cooperation with Governments and UN agencies, particularly UNICEF, and civil society, in support of the implementation of the Monitoring and Reporting Mechanism outlined in Security Council resolution 1612(2005) on children and armed conflict [YUN 2005, p. 863].

Regional activities

Africa

In 2006, persons of concern to UNHCR in Africa, excluding North Africa, rose to 11 million, more than double the 4.9 million recorded in 2005 [YUN 2005, p. 1311]. The total comprised some 2.4 million refugees, 6.8 million IDPs, 225,690 asylum-seekers, 1.4 million returned refugees and IDPs, and others of concern.

Report of Secretary-General. In response to General Assembly resolution 60/128 [ibid., p. 1313], the Secretary-General submitted an August report [A/61/301] on assistance to refugees, returnees and displaced persons in Africa, covering 2005 and the first half of 2006. He stated that the consolidation of peace in several African countries had maximized opportunities for the voluntary and safe return of large numbers of refugees and IDPs to their places of origin, notably to Angola, Burundi, the DRC, Liberia and southern Sudan. However, with more than 16 million persons uprooted, Africa remained the continent most affected by forced displacement. The estimated 13 million IDPs represented more than half the global IDP population and, despite a decrease, some 2.6 million refugees remained in

Africa. Meanwhile, volatile situations persisted. The steady deterioration of security in the northern Central African Republic, Chad and the Darfur region of the Sudan triggered the forced displacement of people to safer regions, both internally and to neighbouring countries. Violence in Côte d'Ivoire, the DRC and Somalia continued to drive people from their homes. Efforts to uphold international protection principles continued in cooperation with Governments, NGOs and regional organizations, with a special focus on the plight of IDPs. The report described specific areas of inter-agency cooperation, such as IDPs, protection, durable solutions, delivery of assistance and special needs, cooperation with regional organizations and the coordination of resources, and provided a regional overview of the refugee situation on the continent.

In East Africa and the Horn of Africa, the Sudan, with over 6 million people displaced by conflict, remained at the heart of the international community's attention, particularly the situation in Darfur and its impact on neighbouring Chad. Moreover, severe drought in the region affected an estimated 5.5 million persons and caused additional population movements, including to refugee settlements in Kenya. In Somalia, the emergence of the Islamic Courts Union in Mogadishu in June weakened the position of the Transitional Federal Government and the humanitarian needs of an estimated 350,000 to 400,000 IDPs were not fully met. The 20-year old armed conflict in northern Uganda had displaced some 1.5 million persons from their homes into camp settlements, where their needs were largely unrealized. However, the cluster leadership approach had strengthened humanitarian protection strategies.

In West Africa, significant improvements in the humanitarian situation in the Mano River Union countries (Guinea, Liberia, Sierra Leone) resulted in a decline in the overall number of refugees in the region. However, the socio-economic situation in Sierra Leone, as in most West African countries with extreme poverty and massive youth unemployment, remained a concern. The plight of Côte d'Ivoire's estimated 709,000 IDPs prompted OCHA to ask UNHCR to chair an IDP protection cluster to enhance the operational response to displaced persons. Armed confrontations along Guinea-Bissau's border with Senegal displaced some 12,500 persons, both internally and externally. More than 70,000 Liberian refugees returned under UNHCR auspices, while an estimated 200,000 returned spontaneously. Some 314,000 IDPs were assisted by the Government, the United Nations and NGOs to return to their places of origin.

Although advances were made in the Central Africa and Great Lakes region, security incidents in Burundi, the Central African Republic and the DRC, which led to displacements, illustrated the fragility of the peace. The humanitarian situation in Chad deteriorated due to increased insecurity within the country, as well as in northern Central African Republic and in Darfur (the Sudan). Violence in the DRC continued to create a cycle of displacement, despite developments in the democratic process. In addition to an estimated 1.6 million IDPs, some 1.6 million returnees, mostly women and children, required reintegration assistance.

In Southern Africa, there was a marked decrease in the number of persons of concern to UNHCR. However, a large number of Angolan refugees remained in Zambia, and many of the estimated 700,000 persons who lost their homes or livelihoods in the "clean-up" operation by the Zimbabwe Government in 2005 [YUN 2005, p. 371] continued to be in need of protection and assistance.

The Secretary-General concluded that protracted situations of displacement across the African continent necessitated continued efforts and initiatives to alleviate its humanitarian consequences and address the root causes. Access to persons of concern and adequate security were vital preconditions for successful humanitarian operations. He called for the cooperation of all concerned to ensure unhindered access to displaced persons. Firm action was required by Governments to ensure the civilian character of refugee camps and translate commitments for consolidated peace processes, enhanced good governance and conflict prevention into concrete actions leading to successful resolutions and the prevention of displacement. He stressed the importance of funding predictability to ensure the smooth delivery of assistance and protection to displaced persons. More action and commitment were needed to ensure the sustainability of durable solutions. In addition, the application of the cluster leadership approach, while promising, would need to be evaluated soon to draw lessons learned.

Subregional developments

UNHCR report. According to the UNHCR *Global Report 2006,* UNHCR provided humanitarian assistance to more than 350,000 camp-based refugees in Central Africa and the Great Lakes subregion and facilitated the return of over 90,000 refugees to several States in the area, including Angola (2,600), Burundi (44,000), the DRC (29,000), Rwanda (6,000) and the Sudan (10,600). UNHCR helped Burundi clear the backlog of pending Rwandan asylum requests, with more than 2,700 cases adjudicated, 200 people granted refugee status and 18,700 people, whose claims had been rejected or who had withdrawn their asylum applications, returned to Rwanda with UNHCR assistance. In the DRC and the Central African Republic, UNHCR worked to improve the physical safety and promote the human rights of IDPs. The remaining 132,000 Angolan refugees in the DRC and 9,300 Republic of the Congo refugees in Gabon who were unwilling to return home received UNHCR assistance towards local integration and self-reliance. UNHCR also established standard operating procedures to prevent and respond to sexual and gender-based violence in Burundi, Rwanda, the DRC and the United Republic of Tanzania. Despite progress achieved, natural disasters, such as floods and drought, and ongoing conflicts hampered UNHCR efforts to find durable solutions for displaced persons. Increasing instability in the northern prefectures of the Central African Republic resulted in the internal displacement of 150,000 people and caused an additional 70,000 to seek refuge in Cameroon and Chad. The Office continued to work closely with the African Union (AU) and other regional institutions on issues concerning refugees and IDPs in Africa.

In East Africa and the Horn of Africa, poor security, escalating conflicts, as well as drought and floods, caused major population movements within and from Somalia. Limited humanitarian access to populations of concern in central and southern Somalia aggravated conditions there. UNHCR protected some 34,000 Somali refugees who fled to neighbouring countries when armed conflict broke out between the Transitional Federal Government and the Union of Islamic Courts militias in December. The unresolved border dispute between Eritrea and Ethiopia hindered development and humanitarian activities. Limited absorption capacity was a problem in southern Sudan, slowing down the repatriation of Sudanese refugees from Ethiopia, Kenya and Uganda. UNHCR signed repatriation agreements with Ethiopia, the Sudan and Uganda, which enabled it to assist 5,000 refugees to return to southern Sudan and repatriate 4,600 Sudanese refugees from Ethiopia. The August cessation of hostilities agreement between the Government of Uganda and rebel forces in the north, led to the UNHCR-assisted return of some 300,000 IDPs to their areas of origin. Insecurity hampered UNHCR operations in Chad and the Sudan, as well as the presence of landmines, the long rainy season, poor infrastructure and epidemics of cholera and meningitis. UNHCR developed a strategy to address the protracted situation of mainly camp-based Eritrean refugees in eastern Sudan by enhancing the quality of asylum and providing access to services and opportunities for self-reliance to urban and camp-based refugees. The geographical focus of UNHCR intervention for the voluntary repatriation of southern Sudanese refugees was expanded to the Eastern Equatoria, Jonglei and Upper Nile states. More than 26,000 refugees and 4,000 IDPs were able to return to their places of origin in southern Sudan with UNHCR assistance. In Chad, refugees were registered in 13 of the 15 camps in the southern and eastern part of the country, which strengthened UNCHR ability to deliver protection and assistance. However, insecurity in eastern Chad—a foiled coup attempt in April and a rebel attack on Abéché in November—hampered UNHCR operations and internal displacement continued unabated. By year's end, there were more than 112,000 IDPs in the country. Two new refugee camps were set up in West Darfur to accommodate some 3,000 Chadian refugees who were moved from the Chad-Sudan border. Despite the signing of the Darfur Peace Agreement in May (see p. 274), the security situation in west Darfur worsened. Violent attacks increased, causing further displacement, and humanitarian staff were targeted. Six relief workers were killed during the year. In August, the Security Council, in **resolution 1706(2006)** (see p. 282), strengthened the United Nations Mission in the Sudan to facilitate the voluntary return of refugees and IDPs and requested the Secretary-General to report on the protection of civilians in refugee and IDP camps in Chad.

In West Africa, the relative stability of most countries allowed UNHCR to advance its search for durable solutions. The Office facilitated the return of 43,000 Liberian refugees from neighbouring countries and some 51,000 Liberian IDPs, following which all 35 IDP camps in Liberia were closed. Some 10,000 Nigerian refugees from Cameroon returned home and 2,400 Togolese refugees were repatriated from Benin. UNHCR examined conditions for the local integration of residual groups, particularly Liberians in Guinea, Nigeria and Sierra Leone, and became formally involved with IDPs in Côte d'Ivoire and Liberia as part of the inter-agency response to internal displacement. It continued the implementation of its AGDM strategy in Cameroon, Côte d'Ivoire, Ghana, Mali, Liberia and Senegal. Participatory assessments enabled UNHCR to better address a wide range of protection issues, including sexual exploitation of refugee girls, child labour, discrimination against persons with HIV/AIDS and prostitution of adolescent girls. An average of 74 per cent of refugee children in camps and settlements were enrolled in primary schools and UNHCR helped to provide preventive and curative care for measles, malaria, acute respiratory infections and diarrhea. Despite positive developments, the region witnessed some conflict, which resulted in population displacement. Fighting in the Casamance region of Senegal forced more than 6,000 people to flee to the Gambia, renewed clashes between rebel groups and the army in the northern Central African Republic drove 25,000 refugees into Cameroon, and some 709,000 people remained displaced in Côte d'Ivoire. Meanwhile, mixed migratory flows assumed significant proportions in Mali and Senegal. A major preoccupation for refugees and others of concern in West Africa was the difficult socio-economic situation. Many refugees and returnees had problems settling locally or reintegrating back home without UNHCR support; some 44,000 urban refugees in the subregion were affected by the unfavourable economic conditions.

In Southern Africa, more than 47,000 Angolan refugees returned home in the last phase of the repatriation operation from neighbouring countries; with the return of nearly 400,000 Angolans since 2002, the number of refugees and others of concern to UNHCR in Southern Africa continued to decline. UNHCR worked with Governments to ensure that they had functioning refugee status determination (RSD) and registration systems in line with international standards; notable improvements in the capacity to process asylum claims were achieved. Other key advances included the launching of an RSD initiative in Mozambique to address 4,000 pending asylum claims; the establishment of a unit in Malawi to clear outstanding applications and some 30,000 long-standing asylum claims in South Africa; and a registration exercise in Zimbabwe. A major positive development was the increased willingness of Governments in the region to consider local integration as a durable solution for long-term refugee populations, including Congolese from the DRC in Angola, Angolans in Botswana, Namibia and Zambia, and Somalis and Congolese in South Africa. In the light of the decreasing refugee population in the region and a shift in priorities from repatriation to reintegration, local integration and mixed migratory flows, UNHCR developed a comprehensive plan of action for 2006-2008, which included specific country targets. Uncertainty over the political and security situation in the DRC made it impossible to start organized return movements. Nonetheless, thousands of refugees made their own way back to the country, particularly from Zambia. Mixed flows continued to strain the institution of asylum and Governments were overwhelmed by the number of asylum-seekers. For the same reason, UNHCR faced challenges in ensuring that only those with genuine needs received assistance.

By subregion, UNHCR assisted 3.1 million persons in Central Africa and the Great Lakes region, which received $190 million in agency expenditures. In East Africa and the Horn of Africa, $159.6 million was spent on 6.2 million persons of concern, while some $94.1 million was spent on programmes assisting 1.4 million persons in need in West Africa. In Southern Africa, $46.8 million was spent on 379,120 persons of concern.

Other developments. The AU Executive Council, at its eighth ordinary session (Khartoum, Sudan, 16-21 January), adopted a decision (EX. CL/Dec.240(VIII)) on the situation of refugees, returnees and displaced persons in Africa, in which it called on the international community to increase support to States and populations concerned and requested its Commission to formulate a policy to facilitate the access of refugees and IDPs to education, including at the post-primary level. The AU Ministerial Meeting on Refugees and Displaced Persons was held in Ouagadougou, Burkina Faso, from 1 to 2 June.

GENERAL ASSEMBLY ACTION

On 19 December [meeting 81], the General Assembly, on the recommendation of the Third Committee [A/61/436], adopted **resolution 61/139** without vote [agenda item 41].

Assistance to refugees, returnees and displaced persons in Africa

The General Assembly,

Recalling the Organization of African Unity Convention governing the specific aspects of refugee problems in Africa of 1969 and the African Charter on Human and Peoples' Rights,

Reaffirming that the 1951 Convention relating to the Status of Refugees, together with the 1967 Protocol thereto, as complemented by the Organization of African Unity Convention of 1969, remains the foundation of the international refugee protection regime in Africa,

1. *Takes note* of the reports of the Secretary-General and the United Nations High Commissioner for Refugees;

2. *Notes* the need for African States to address resolutely the root causes of all forms of forced displacement in Africa and to foster peace, stability and prosperity throughout the African continent so as to forestall refugee flows;

3. *Notes with great concern* that, despite all of the efforts made so far by the United Nations, the African Union and others, the situation of refugees and displaced persons in Africa remains precarious, and calls upon States and other parties to armed conflict to observe scrupulously the letter and spirit of international humanita-

rian law, bearing in mind that armed conflict is one of the principal causes of forced displacement in Africa;

4. *Welcomes* decision EX.CL/Dec.284 (IX) on the situation of refugees, returnees and displaced persons in Africa, adopted by the Executive Council of the African Union at its ninth ordinary session, held at Banjul on 28 and 29 June 2006;

5. *Expresses its appreciation* for the leadership shown by the Office of the United Nations High Commissioner for Refugees, and commends the Office for its ongoing efforts, with the support of the international community, to assist African countries of asylum and to respond to the protection and assistance needs of refugees, returnees and displaced persons in Africa;

6. *Recognizes* that, among refugees, returnees and internally displaced persons, women and children are the majority of the population affected by conflict, and in this context notes the conclusion on women and girls at risk adopted by the Executive Committee of the Programme of the United Nations High Commissioner for Refugees at its fifty-seventh session;

7. *Notes* the conclusion on identification, prevention and reduction of statelessness and protection of stateless persons adopted by the Executive Committee at its fifty-seventh session, which is aimed at enhancing the protection of stateless persons as well as the prevention and reduction of statelessness;

8. *Reiterates* the importance of the full and effective implementation of standards and procedures, including the monitoring and reporting mechanism outlined in Security Council resolution 1612(2005) of 26 July 2005, to better address the specific protection needs of refugee children and adolescents and to safeguard rights and, in particular, to ensure adequate attention to unaccompanied and separated children and children affected by armed conflict, including former child soldiers in refugee settings, as well as in the context of voluntary repatriation and reintegration measures;

9. *Recognizes* the importance of early registration and effective registration systems and censuses as a tool of protection and as a means to the quantification and assessment of needs for the provision and distribution of humanitarian assistance and to implement appropriate durable solutions;

10. *Recalls* the conclusion on registration of refugees and asylum-seekers adopted by the Executive Committee at its fifty-second session, notes the many forms of harassment faced by refugees and asylum-seekers who remain without any form of documentation attesting to their status, recalls the responsibility of States to register refugees on their territories, and, as appropriate, the responsibility of the Office of the High Commissioner or mandated international bodies to do so, reiterates in this context the central role which early and effective registration and documentation can play, guided by protection considerations, in enhancing protection and supporting efforts to find durable solutions, and calls upon the Office, as appropriate, to help States to conduct this procedure should they be unable to register refugees on their territory;

11. *Calls upon* the international community, including States and the Office of the High Commissioner and other relevant United Nations organizations, within their respective mandates, to take concrete action to meet the protection and assistance needs of refugees, returnees and displaced persons and to contribute generously to projects and programmes aimed at alleviating their plight and facilitating durable solutions for refugees and displaced persons;

12. *Reaffirms* the importance of timely and adequate assistance and protection for refugees, also reaffirms that assistance and protection are mutually reinforcing and that inadequate material assistance and food shortages undermine protection, notes the importance of a rights- and community-based approach in engaging constructively with individual refugees and their communities to achieve fair and equitable access to food and other forms of material assistance, and expresses concern in regard to situations in which minimum standards of assistance are not met, including those in which adequate needs assessments have yet to be undertaken;

13. *Also reaffirms* that respect by States for their protection responsibilities towards refugees is strengthened by international solidarity involving all members of the international community and that the refugee protection regime is enhanced through committed international cooperation in a spirit of solidarity and burden- and responsibility-sharing among all States;

14. *Further reaffirms* that host States have the primary responsibility to ensure the civilian and humanitarian character of asylum, and calls upon States, in cooperation with international organizations, within their mandates, to take all necessary measures to ensure respect for the principles of refugee protection and, in particular, to ensure that the civilian and humanitarian nature of refugee camps is not compromised by the presence or the activities of armed elements or used for purposes that are incompatible with their civilian character, and encourages the High Commissioner to continue efforts, in consultation with States and other relevant actors, to ensure the civilian and humanitarian character of camps;

15. *Condemns* all acts that pose a threat to the personal security and well-being of refugees and asylum-seekers, such as refoulement, unlawful expulsion and physical attacks, and calls upon States of refuge, in cooperation with international organizations, where appropriate, to take all necessary measures to ensure respect for the principles of refugee protection, including the humane treatment of asylum-seekers;

16. *Deplores* the continuing violence and insecurity which constitute an ongoing threat to the safety and security of staff members of the Office of the High Commissioner and other humanitarian organizations and an obstacle to the effective fulfilment of the mandate of the Office and the ability of its implementing partners and other humanitarian personnel to discharge their respective humanitarian functions, urges States, parties to conflict and all other relevant actors to take all necessary measures to protect activities related to humanitarian assistance, prevent attacks on and kidnapping of national

and international humanitarian workers and ensure the safety and security of the personnel and property of the Office and that of all humanitarian organizations discharging functions mandated by the Office, and calls upon States to investigate fully any crime committed against humanitarian personnel and bring to justice the persons responsible for such crimes;

17. *Calls upon* the Office of the High Commissioner, the African Union, subregional organizations and all African States, in conjunction with agencies of the United Nations system, intergovernmental and non-governmental organizations and the international community, to strengthen and revitalize existing partnerships and forge new ones in support of the international refugee protection system;

18. *Calls upon* the Office of the High Commissioner, the international community and other concerned entities to intensify their support to African Governments through appropriate capacity-building activities, including training of relevant officers, disseminating information about refugee instruments and principles, providing financial, technical and advisory services to accelerate the enactment or amendment and implementation of legislation relating to refugees, strengthening emergency response and enhancing capacities for the coordination of humanitarian activities;

19. *Reaffirms* the right of return and the principle of voluntary repatriation, appeals to countries of origin and countries of asylum to create conditions that are conducive to voluntary repatriation, recognizes that, while voluntary repatriation remains the pre-eminent solution, local integration and third-country resettlement, where appropriate and feasible, are also viable options for dealing with the situation of African refugees who, owing to prevailing circumstances in their respective countries of origin, are unable to return home;

20. *Also reaffirms* that voluntary repatriation should not necessarily be conditioned on the accomplishment of political solutions in the country of origin in order not to impede the exercise of the refugees right to return, recognizes that the voluntary repatriation and reintegration process is normally guided by the conditions in the country of origin, in particular that voluntary repatriation can be accomplished in conditions of safety and dignity, and urges the High Commissioner to promote sustainable return through the development of durable and lasting solutions, particularly in protracted refugee situations;

21. *Calls upon* the international donor community to provide financial and material assistance that allows for the implementation of community-based development programmes that benefit both refugees and host communities, as appropriate, in agreement with host countries and consistent with humanitarian objectives;

22. *Appeals* to the international community to respond positively, in the spirit of solidarity and burden- and responsibility-sharing, to the third-country resettlement needs of African refugees, notes in this regard the importance of using resettlement strategically, as part of situation-specific comprehensive responses to refugee situations, and to this end encourages interested States, the Office of the High Commissioner and other relevant partners to make full use of the Multilateral Framework of Understandings on Resettlement, where appropriate;

23. *Calls upon* the international donor community to provide material and financial assistance for the implementation of programmes intended for the rehabilitation of the environment and infrastructure affected by refugees in countries of asylum;

24. *Urges* the international community, in the spirit of international solidarity and burden-sharing, to continue to fund generously the refugee programmes of the Office of the High Commissioner and, taking into account the substantially increased needs of programmes in Africa, inter alia, as a result of repatriation possibilities, to ensure that Africa receives a fair and equitable share of the resources designated for refugees;

25. *Encourages* the Office of the High Commissioner and interested States to identify protracted refugee situations which might lend themselves to resolution through the development of specific, multilateral, comprehensive and practical approaches to resolving such refugee situations, including improvement of international burden- and responsibility-sharing and realization of durable solutions, within a multilateral context;

26. *Expresses grave concern* at the increasing numbers of internally displaced persons in Africa, calls upon States to take concrete action to pre-empt internal displacement and to meet the protection and assistance needs of internally displaced persons, recalls in this regard the Guiding Principles on Internal Displacement, takes note of the current activities of the Office of the High Commissioner related to protection of and assistance to internally displaced persons, including in the context of inter-agency arrangements in this field, emphasizes that such activities should be consistent with relevant General Assembly resolutions and should not undermine the mandate of the Office and the institution of asylum, and encourages the High Commissioner to continue his dialogue with States on the role of his Office in this regard;

27. *Invites* the Representative of the Secretary-General on the human rights of internally displaced persons to continue his ongoing dialogue with Member States and the intergovernmental and non-governmental organizations concerned, in accordance with his mandate, and to include information thereon in his reports to the Human Rights Council and the General Assembly;

28. *Requests* the Secretary-General to submit a comprehensive report on assistance to refugees, returnees and displaced persons in Africa to the General Assembly at its sixty-second session, taking fully into account the efforts expended by countries of asylum, under the item entitled "Report of the United Nations High Commissioner for Refugees, questions relating to refugees, returnees and displaced persons and humanitarian questions".

The Americas

UNHCR activities in North America and the Caribbean centred on refugee protection, resettlement, RSD procedures and mobilization of support for refugees. During the year, the United States accepted some 41,000 people for resettlement, despite admission difficulties relating to terrorism and national security measures. Waivers of the material support bar to admission to the United States allowed the resettlement of over 2,100 refugees from Myanmar. The United States continued to strengthen its refugee protection capacity, especially through its Asylum Division and Refugee Corps. Almost 11,000 persons were resettled in Canada. Public confidence in the refugee system in Canada was lost due to perceived misuse by undeserving claimants. The Government postponed plans to overhaul the system and informed UNHCR that the statutory provision to establish the Refugee Appeal Division would not be implemented in 2006. As a result, despite its generous policies towards asylum-seekers and refugees, Canada still had no mechanism for appeals based on merits. UNHCR made periodic recommendations to the Government on management and operational issues relating to asylum-seekers, which led to improvements in their treatment and the processing of claims, as well as better coordination between UNHCR and Canada. In the Caribbean, progress was limited by the lack of political priority on asylum issues, limited UNHCR human and financial resources, and the complexity of mixed migratory movements from South to North, mostly by sea. The majority of those migrants were from Cuba, the Dominican Republic and Haiti, but increasing numbers of Africans were also reported. Asylum-seekers and refugees found themselves within those wider migratory movements, and the lack of national refugee legislation and asylum procedure in most Caribbean countries presented a challenge to UNHCR. Nevertheless, the Office carried out RSD in nine Caribbean countries and collaborated with Governments in contingency planning in the event of mass migration or refugee emergencies.

In Central America and Mexico, the refugee population remained constant at some 5,500 people. Durable solutions were found for a number of refugees, including the naturalization of 131 refugees in Belize. In El Salvador, Honduras and Nicaragua, 55 refugees received permanent or temporary residence or were naturalized. In Mexico, the UNHCR programme was affected by political changes following the elections, including frequent management changes within the UNHCR main government counterpart entities. Consequently, a pilot project to receive resettled refugees, the process to establish a new asylum law and the drafting of a new decree regulating the asylum procedure were halted. Lack of employment opportunities was a major obstacle to refugee integration and self-sufficiency. Migratory movements in the region were characterized by a massive flow of undocumented migrants, including persons arriving through human trafficking, mostly from Central America, crossing Mexico and heading for Canada or the United States. Of the 180,000 migrants intercepted at Tapachula, Mexico's principal border crossing with Central America, 86,000 were deported, including some 5,000 unaccompanied minors. As human smuggling and trafficking were widespread, the UNHCR presence in Tapachula was essential to ensure that persons of concern had access to international protection. A mapping exercise on the situation of unaccompanied and separated children in migratory flows was carried out at Mexico's southern border as a first step towards strengthening protection and assistance. A capacity-building pilot project for border and migration officials in Belize, El Salvador, Guatemala, Honduras and Nicaragua was launched to improve access to asylum procedures, strengthen protection monitoring capacities and reinforce networking.

The major issues of concern in northern South America related to the ongoing conflict and worsening humanitarian situation in Colombia, which had led to a steady influx of Colombians into Costa Rica, Ecuador, Panama and Venezuela. More than 11,000 Colombians applied for asylum in neighbouring countries in 2006; however, the majority of displaced Colombians did not seek asylum. The lack of legal status of the estimated 500,000 unregistered Colombians living in border communities and marginal neighbourhoods in the large cities of the region made them vulnerable to deportation and hindered their access to basic human rights, such as education and health care. In line with the Mexico Plan of Action [YUN 2004, p. 1210], UNHCR developed a new strategy for the region that focused on the protection of and assistance for unregistered Colombians. The Borders of Solidarity and Cities of Solidarity pillars of the Mexico Plan of Action were further developed and over 100 projects were implemented to foster a positive environment for local integration and good coordination with local development plans. In follow-up to the Mexico Plan of Action, the first meeting on Resettlement in Solidarity in the Americas (Quito, Ecuador, February) strengthened resettlement as a durable solution. Some 845 Colombian refugees were resettled in countries within or outside the region. Security remained the main concern for the delivery of protection and assistance in the region; violent incidents in border areas were increasingly reported and included death threats and assassination, disappearance or the killing of asylum-seekers.

In most countries in southern South America, poverty, unemployment and underemployment affected large parts of the population. Most of the refugees in the region (8,500), mainly from Latin America with some from Africa, were working in the informal sector and their concerns were usually overshadowed by national priorities. Some 1,900 new asylum-seekers, mostly Colombians, were reported in 2006, compared to 1,400 the previous year. The increased number of applications for asylum was most significant in Bolivia and Chile. UNHCR was unable to provide assistance in line with established minimum standards due to budget caps, creating hardship among refugees and asylum-seekers. However, positive developments included the passage of new refugee laws in Argentina and Uruguay, the reinforcement of national eligibility commissions and the strengthening of national and regional protection networks, most notably in Brazil, which facilitated the local integration of refugees and the provision of timely information on border movements. Brazil also approved a decree granting complementary protection to asylum-seekers who did not meet the refugee definition of the 1951 Convention but were in need of international protection on humanitarian grounds.

Total UNHCR expenditure in the Americas and the Caribbean for the year was $33.4 million for a population of concern of 4.7 million.

Asia and the Pacific and the Arab States

In 2006, UNHCR spent $80.4 million on activities in Asia and the Pacific for a population of concern of 6.2 million. Expenditures for operations in Central Asia, South-West Asia, North Africa and the Middle East amounted to $170.2 million for a population of concern of 7.8 million.

South Asia

In 2006, UNHCR led the collective humanitarian response in Sri Lanka after hostilities between Government forces and the separatist Liberation Tigers of Tamil Eelam resulted in the displacement of 200,000 people, adding to the 300,000 already displaced since the ceasefire agreement in 2002 [YUN 2002, p. 1213]. More than 18,000 refugees sought safety in south India. Meanwhile, all parties to the conflict had hardened their positions and rhetoric, further hampering access by the humanitarian community to the displaced. In addition, the humanitarian space for UN agencies and NGOs came under pressure and 17 staff members of the NGO Action contre la Faim were killed. In Bangladesh and Nepal, national priorities took precedence over issues related to refugees and asylum. In Nepal, the camp population was increasingly concerned about the stalemate in negotiations between Bhutan and Nepal regarding returns to Bhutan. Nepal and UNHCR conducted a census for the more than 100,000 refugees living for some 15 years in seven camps, and the Government approved the resettlement of those with special needs. UNHCR formed a steering group of Governments to sharpen the international focus on refugees from Myanmar in Bangladesh. Consequently, participatory assessments were conducted and registration completed in the camps, capturing previously unregistered persons. In India, a positive shift in relations between UNHCR and the Government improved the outlook for refugee protection, and progress was made towards durable solutions for Hindu and Sikh refugees from Afghanistan. The High Commissioner visited India at the end of the year in an environment of increased openness to UNHCR concerns.

East Asia and the Pacific

During 2006, UNHCR made a concerted effort to find durable solutions, through resettlement, for refugees in Thailand, Malaysia and Hong Kong, China. Of the 23,400 applications for resettlement from refugees in Malaysia and Thailand, some 6,000 refugees were accepted and subsequently departed. Although Thailand experienced political instability arising from a military coup and lacked clear policies on refugees, the interim Prime Minister said that the issue of refugees was among the top three concerns of the Government. Nevertheless, UNHCR and the international community were alarmed by Thailand's hardening attitude towards refugees, particularly those from the Lao People's Democratic Republic, with a number of Laotians of Hmong ethnicity being deported without UNHCR being given access to them. There was also a rise in the number of asylum-seekers in Indonesia and Malaysia, which placed an additional burden on UNHCR resources. Restricted access to detention facilities in Malaysia limited UNHCR monitoring and protection interventions. In Timor-Leste, the displacement of 150,000 people in the capital, Dili, and the surrounding districts, due to political unrest, triggered UNHCR participation in an inter-agency emergency response. In Myanmar, the Government's acceptance of two UN political missions to the country was considered a positive sign. However, restrictions on humanitarian agencies and control over their operations continued. UNHCR strengthened its operation in the south-east of the country along the border of Thailand and focused on providing a legal status to all residents pending the resolution of their citizenship status. In that connection, UNHCR was able to convince the Myanmar Ministry of Immigration to accelerate the issuance of personal documents to more than 200,000 eligible stateless people over 10 years of age. UNHCR consolidated its access to returnees in the central highlands of Viet Nam and the Prime Minister issued a directive in December to begin the process of the naturalization of some 9,500 stateless persons, mostly former Cambodian refugees. There were also promising indications that durable solutions would be found for at least half of the 240 long-staying Afghan and Iraqi nationals living in legal uncertainty in Indonesia.

Central Asia, South-West Asia, North Africa and the Middle East

In South-West Asia, while some 399,000 Afghans returned home during the year, the number repatriated with UNHCR assistance (139,000) was the lowest in five years. The downward trend could be attributed to deteriorating security in some provinces, difficult economic and social conditions, and the fact that many refugees had been in exile for more than 20 years. Notable progress included the compilation of an overall profile of the Afghan presence and displacement in the region; the implementation of reintegration programmes, including the construction of shelters, the digging of water points and completion of income-generation and vocational projects; and the agreement between the Government and the international community, known as the Afghanistan Compact (see p. 363), which outlined key objectives in governance and economic and social development. The registration process in Iran enumerated some 920,000 Afghans living there. A similar exercise was started in Pakistan to account for the estimated 2.1 million Afghans in the country. Through a joint project between UNHCR and the Iranian authorities, registered Afghan refugees would benefit from skills training and access to basic services to improve their prospects for repatriation. In Pakistan, preliminary needs assessments in the health, education, water and sanitation sectors were carried out in 38 districts hosting Afghans. Security was the single most important determinant in finding successful solutions for displacement in and from Afghanistan.

In Central Asia, the search for solutions for Tajiks progressed, with the naturalization of more than 9,300 Tajik refugees in Kyrgyzstan and 9,500 in Turkmenistan. In June, in the light of the improved conditions in Tajikistan and under the terms of the 1951 Convention, refugee status for Tajiks was considered no longer applicable. UNHCR phased out its reintegration programme for returnees and ended its repatriation programme for refugees by year's end. Some 1,500 refugees in Tajikistan, mostly Afghans, were resettled in third countries and the Office developed a project with the Government on local integration of the remaining 1,000 Afghan refugees. The fallout from the 2005 Andijan events in Uzbekistan [YUN 2005, p. 456] continued to affect the overall situation in Central Asia and resulted in the deterioration of the protection environment in the country. The April decision of the Uzbek Government to close down the UNHCR Office was indicative of the changed working environment. The United Nations Development Programme (UNDP) took over UNHCR activities related to finding a solution to the 1,400 Afghan refugees in Uzbekistan; half were referred for group resettlement in the United States. Political instability in Kyrgyzstan persisted in 2006 and had a negative impact on UNHCR activities.

In 2006, UNHCR continued to reinforce its presence in North Africa, thereby expanding protection space in the Libyan Arab Jamahiriya, Mauritania and Morocco. Thousands of asylum-seekers were able to avail themselves of international protection, including RSD. With no early political solution to the conflict in Western Sahara (see p. 329), UNHCR continued to provide basic assistance to the Saharawi refugees in the Tindouf camps in Algeria. The Office also implemented the Confidence-Building Measures project for Western Saharan refugees in the Tindouf camps and the residents of the Western Sahara Territory, which helped to reunite many separated families. In February, torrential downpours in Tindouf damaged schools, health centres and refugee dwellings. Some 60,000 refugees, or 12,000 families, lost their personal belongings. The UNHCR emergency programme met the needs of the affected population. During the year, UNHCR focused on strengthening the institution of asylum in North Africa through the promotion of national refugee legislation and the establishment of national procedures. The member States of the Union of the Arab Maghreb (Algeria, Libyan Arab Jamahiriya, Mauritania, Morocco, Tunisia) witnessed a steep increase in mixed flows of asylum-seekers and economic migrants from sub-Saharan Africa transiting their territories en route to Europe; the Office cooperated with the European Commission (EC) in implementing a mixed asylum-migration project to address the issue. The complex asylum-migration situation in the region posed a great challenge to UNHCR and, as it reinforced protection in the Union of the Arab Mahgreb countries, increased staffing and funding were required.

In the Middle East, massive internal and external displacement of Iraqis continued unabated. By year's end, nearly 4 million Iraqis were displaced, with some 2 million having fled to Egypt, Jordan, Lebanon and the Syrian Arab Republic. While most countries in the Middle East were generous in hosting refugees, tolerance toward Iraqis in neighbouring States declined as their numbers increased and the prospect of a speedy return diminished. UNHCR protected and assisted the most vulnerable among the increasing number of IDPs and non-Iraqi refugees inside Iraq, as well as Iraqis in neighbouring countries. A less visible emergency developed in Yemen, where persons continued to arrive from across the Gulf of Aden. Some 25,000 new arrivals entered Yemen and as no additional support was forthcoming to help the Government increase its absorption capacity, the protection climate in the country was fragile. The situation in Lebanon remained volatile. UNHCR responded to the emergency humanitarian crisis that resulted from a month-long conflict that began in July (see p. 574), displacing up to 1 million people. The Office provided protection and assistance to 150,000 IDPs, refugees and returnees in the country, and to more than 20,000 Lebanese refugees in the Syrian Arab Republic. The cessation of hostilities in August triggered the massive return of IDPs and refugees. In other activities, UNHCR re-established dialogue with Sudanese communities in Egypt after the December 2005 deaths of 28 Sudanese demonstrators demanding more assistance and resettlement, and strengthened its representation in Israel to help the Government receive Sudanese and other asylum-seekers from sub-Saharan Africa.

Europe

In 2005, UNHCR expenditures for activities in Europe totalled $99.3 million for a population of concern of 4.6 million. More than one third of that amount ($38 million) was for the 608,840 persons of concern in South-Eastern Europe.

Western, Central and Eastern Europe

The number of asylum-seekers arriving in Europe in 2006 continued to decline significantly compared to previous years. France remained the leading asylum destination, with some 30,000 claims. In Switzerland, more than 68,100 persons were in the asylum procedure, compared to 71,900 the previous year. The significant drop in applications across Europe could be partially due to more restrictive border control mechanisms established in response to mixed migration flows. In the Mediterranean, on the other hand, Italy, Malta, Spain and, to a lesser extent, Greece, continued to receive irregular arrivals of undocumented migrants by sea, mostly from North and sub-Saharan Africa, some of whom were possibly in need of international protection. The development of the UNHCR Ten-Point Plan of Action for Addressing Mixed Migratory Movements provided a framework for the Office's efforts to address the problem. The Office worked, in particular, with Greece, Italy, Malta and Spain to establish procedures to address the needs of unaccompanied and separated children and build national capacities to counter and prevent sexual and gender-based violence. In Sweden, there was a 39 per cent increase in asylum applications, with over 24,300 applications at the end of the year, representing the largest upsurge amongst all Western European countries. That was due to almost 9,000 asylum applications from Iraqi nationals. The majority of asylum applications to the European Union (EU) came from Iraq (20,000) and the Russian Federation (mainly from Chechnya) (13,000). Other significant asylum-seeker arrivals were registered from Afghanistan, Iran, Serbia (mainly from Kosovo) and Turkey. UNHCR continued to work with the EC, national authorities and NGOs to support the transposition of the main EU asylum directives, especially those linked to asylum procedures and qualifications. An agreement reached between the Italian authorities and UNHCR resulted in the Office establishing a permanent presence in southern Italy. UNHCR also strengthened its relations with the new EU agency, FRONTEX, and worked on common priorities relating to interception and reception. It was particularly concerned about cases of insufficient legal counselling mechanisms for asylum-seekers; inadequate identification, referral and protection mechanisms for those with special needs; and reception and detention conditions. Significant variations in refugee recognition across countries, particularly in respect of Iraqi nationals, were also a growing concern. Additionally, integration was recognized as a considerable challenge in Europe. In view of negative public attitudes with respect to asylum and towards refugees in general, UNHCR sought to raise public awareness and emphasized the need to fight intolerance and xenophobia.

In Central Europe and the Baltic States, the number of asylum-seekers continued to decrease. In 2006, some 11,200 people applied for asylum in Bulgaria, Hungary, Poland, Romania, Slovakia and Slovenia, approximately 2,400 fewer than in 2005. UNHCR continued to observe key areas in which gaps were apparent, including the right of access to national territory and asylum procedures; problems in processing asylum claims (especially the lack of access to legal advice and confinement in detention or transit/border zones); and the quality of decision-making. In line with UNHCR strategic objectives for Europe, the Office facilitated access for asylum-seekers to the territories of European States and to RSD procedures. Hungary, Poland, Slovakia and Slovenia agreed to be the primary providers of protection and assistance to asylum-seekers and refugees, allowing UNHCR to phase out its material assistance and legal and social services and concentrate on strengthening the asylum systems in those and other European countries. UNHCR was concerned that some Governments in the region were giving less priority to the protection of asylum-seekers and refugees, for whom the primary durable solution continued to be local integration. Conversely, refugees continued to face obstacles to integration due to difficulties in learning the national language, finding jobs, acquiring housing and accessing social services. The Office was also concerned about the significant number of people with unclear nationality status. The removal of thousands of citizens of the former Yugoslav republics from the Slovenian population records in 1997 had resulted in a so-called "erased" group of people, who were at risk of becoming stateless. Governments continued to cooperate closely with UNHCR in amending their national asylum legislation. The Office welcomed the accession of Romania to the 1954 Convention relating to the Status of Stateless Persons and the 1961 Convention on the Reduction of Statelessness.

In Eastern Europe, Belarus, Moldova and Ukraine underwent significant political, socio-economic and institutional reforms. In the field of migration and asylum, the reform process resulted in institutional restructuring, but the allocation of government resources in support of the asylum system remained insufficient. The geopolitical situation of the three countries, located along the EU external borders, triggered a complex situation of mixed migration flows from and through their territories. UNHCR continued to provide training, support and technical advice to the Governments to improve their national asylum systems. The Söderköping Cross Border Cooperation Process, focusing on the three countries, as well as on seven neighbouring EU member States, continued to be a forum for the exchange of experience and policy development on migration and asylum issues. Progress in the legislative field in Belarus, Moldova and Ukraine led to a better reflection of international standards on refugee protection in draft national refugee legislation; UNHCR continued to ensure that all amendments were in line with national standards. The unresolved situation in Abkhazia and South Ossetia in Georgia remained a concern, as did the unresolved issue of Nagorny Karabakh in Azerbaijan. Negotiations over Abkhazia and South Ossetia continued despite the tense political climate, but numerous security incidents affected UNHCR programme delivery. Consequently, there were no refugee returns from North Ossetia/Alania in 2006 and only a few IDPs in Georgia requested assistance to return to South Ossetia. With regard to IDPs, UNHCR assisted Georgia in developing a national strategy, and in the Northern Caucasus (Russian Federation), close to 159,000 IDPs benefited from UNHCR protection and shelter activities. The Office also met the protection and assistance needs of 4,000 Chechen refugees in Azerbaijan and Georgia and supported Armenia in carrying out a census of ethnic Armenian refugees from Azerbaijan.

South-Eastern Europe

During the year, UNHCR provided protection and facilitated durable solutions for some 504,000 people in South-Eastern Europe, of whom 120,000 were refugees and 384,000 were IDPs. The decrease from 600,000 in 2005 was accounted for partly by repatriation and returns of refugees and IDPs from Croatia and Bosnia and Herzegovina and partly by the local integration of refugees in Serbia. More than 4,600 refugees repatriated to Croatia, of whom 1,400 were assisted by UNHCR. Close to 4,200 IDPs returned to their homes in Bosnia and Herzegovina, 3,540 with UNHCR assistance, while more than 1,400 refugees repatriated from abroad, with 128 being assisted by the Office. A total of 22 collective centres were closed in Serbia, decreasing the number of refugees and IDPs living in centres from 9,130 to 7,480. The 2005 Sarajevo Declaration [YUN 2005, p. 1320], which resulted from an initiative jointly undertaken by UNHCR, the EC and OSCE, helped to provide political impetus and a platform for cooperation to remove obstacles to durable solutions for refugees who fled the wars in Croatia and Bosnia and Herzegovina in the 1990s. Consequently, some progress was made in de-registering refugees who had found durable solutions in Serbia and Bosnia and Herzegovina and through the Croatian reconstruction and alternative housing care programmes. The positive results, however, did not adequately reflect the problem of the long-term economic sustainability of those who were de-registered, or the fact that there was a high proportion of extremely vulnerable individuals among the remaining refugees and IDPs who continued to rely on UNHCR for protection and assistance. The number of displaced from Kosovo was still high, with 207,000 in Serbia, 16,000 in Montenegro, and 22,000 within Kosovo itself. Hence, repatriation of displaced Kosovar minorities could only take place on a strictly voluntary basis. Therefore, the Office adopted a flexible strategy by continuing to facilitate voluntary returns through "go-and-see" visits and by strengthening the protection regime of IDPs. The main constraints to finding solutions to the Croatian IDP and refugee problem continued to be the issue of tenancy rights, the validation of social rights and the lack of employment opportunities. In Serbia, the fluid political situation held back the adoption of a new asylum law. Meanwhile, the election of a new Government in Albania, the overhaul of the Directorate for Refugees and the appointment of new staff, slowed UNHCR capacity-building efforts in the asylum sector.

Chapter XIII

Health, food and nutrition

In 2006, the United Nations continued to promote human health and food security, coordinate food aid and support research in nutrition.

About 40 million people were living with HIV/AIDS at the end of the year and an estimated 4.3 million became infected with the virus; approximately 2.9 million people lost their lives due to AIDS-related illnesses. *The Human Development Report 2006* noted that HIV/AIDS had driven human development into reverse across a large group of countries and was shaping the demographic structure of many African nations. The Joint United Nations Programme on HIV/AIDS (UNAIDS), which celebrated its tenth anniversary in 2006, continued to coordinate UN activities for AIDS prevention and control, developing an action plan for the UN system that specified 18 "key UNAIDS-deliverables" to effectively help strengthen HIV prevention. The General Assembly adopted a Political Declaration on HIV/AIDS, committing world leaders to address the epidemic through much stronger national and international action, and designated a Voluntary HIV Counselling and Testing Day in 2007.

The World Health Organization (WHO) established the Global Malaria Programme in order to respond cohesively and strongly to the needs of malaria-endemic countries through a new strategic direction. It also launched guidelines for the treatment of malaria. In its 2006 update of activities and progress made in meeting the 2010 goals of the Roll Back Malaria Partnership, WHO reported substantial progress in addressing the disease over the preceding few years. However, it concluded that effective coverage of malaria control interventions was inadequate due largely to funding shortages, lack of technical expertise and weak health systems.

WHO also launched a new global strategy to stop tuberculosis, while the Assembly designated 14 November as an annual World Diabetes Day, beginning in 2007, and proclaimed 2008 as the International Year of Sanitation.

The United Nations Road Safety Collaboration, in preparation for the First United Nations Global Road Safety Week, scheduled for 2007, created formal working groups on fleet safety and infrastructure, and decided to work towards a new Assembly resolution on road safety in 2007.

The World Health Assembly agreed to the immediate voluntary implementation of influenza-related provisions of the revised 2005 International Health Regulations, which laid out the role of countries and WHO in identifying and responding to public health emergencies. WHO also released its strategic plan for addressing the disease.

As few major emergencies occurred in 2006, the World Food Programme (WFP) was able to focus on protracted relief and recovery operations. It responded to the May earthquake in Indonesia; natural disasters in Bolivia, Ecuador, El Salvador and Nicaragua; floods in Nepal; conflicts in Lebanon and Kenya; and the continuing crisis in the Darfur region of western Sudan, which claimed thousands of lives and destroyed many homes and livelihoods. WFP also distributed 4 million metric tons of food to 87.8 million people in 78 countries.

The Food and Agriculture Organization of the United Nations (FAO) continued to implement the Plan of Action adopted at the 1996 World Food Summit for meeting, by 2015, the commitments to halve the number of undernourished people worldwide. In support of an FAO resolution highlighting the importance of natural fibres as a source of income for small farmers in low-income and developing countries, the Assembly declared 2009 the International Year of Natural Fibres.

Health

Follow-up to 2005 World Summit

The General Assembly, in **resolution 60/265** of 30 June on the follow-up to the development outcome of the 2005 World Summit (see p. 986), called upon Member States to achieve universal access to reproductive health by 2015, as set out at the International Conference on Population and Development [YUN 1994, p. 955], integrating that goal in strategies to attain the internationally agreed development goals, including the Millennium Development Goals (MDGs) [YUN 2000, p. 51], aimed at reducing maternal and child mortality, improving maternal health, promoting gender equality, combating HIV/AIDS and eradicating poverty.

AIDS prevention and control

Comprehensive review of implementation of the Declaration of Commitment on HIV/AIDS

General Assembly 2006 High-level Meeting on HIV/AIDS. In accordance with its resolution 60/224 [YUN 2005, p. 1323], the General Assembly, during a high-level meeting (31 May-2 June), undertook a comprehensive review of progress achieved in implementing the 2001 Declaration of Commitment on HIV/AIDS, in accordance with resolution S-26/2, adopted at its twenty-sixth special session [YUN 2001, p. 1126]. The review focused on constraints and opportunities for full implementation, considered recommendations on how the targets set out in the Declaration could be reached, and renewed the political commitment.

The meeting was attended by Heads of State and Government, including representatives of civil society, the private sector, UN agencies, international organizations and persons living with HIV. Organized around five round tables, five panel discussions, an informal interactive hearing with civil society and two parallel sessions (Segments A and B) on the final day, it considered the draft final document [A/60/L.57]. The panel discussions focused on: overcoming stigma and discrimination, and changing the way societies responded to people living with HIV; dealing with health worker shortages and other health and social sectors constraints to universal access to treatment; breaking the cycle of infection for sustainable AIDS responses; ways to end the increased feminization of AIDS; and sustainable and predictable financing for scaled-up AIDS responses.

The meeting also had before it the report of the Secretary-General entitled "Declaration of Commitment on HIV/AIDS: five years later [A/60/736] (see p. 1415), and a note entitled "Scaling up HIV prevention, treatment, care and support [A/60/737] (ibid.).

The Secretary-General, in his statement at the opening session of the high-level meeting on 2 June, said that the presence of so many Governments signalled a real commitment to fighting HIV/AIDS, which, in 25 years, had killed 25 million people and had become the leading cause of death of persons aged 15 to 59, as well as the greatest challenge for current generations. Since the Assembly's 2001 special session, the global response to AIDS had gained strength. In some countries, fewer young people were infected in 2006 than five years earlier, and seven times more people had access to treatment. Still, there were more new infections and HIV/AIDS-related deaths than ever before. Without radical change, near universal access to HIV prevention, treatment, care and support by 2010—the goal set at the 2005 World Summit—would not be achieved, nor would the MDG of halting and beginning to reverse the spread of HIV/AIDS by 2015.

The Secretary-General said that turning the tide against the epidemic required every President, Prime Minister, parliamentarian and politician to decide and declare that "AIDS stops with me". It also required real, positive change that would give more power and confidence to women and girls, and transform relations between women and men at all levels of society, and for everyone to make the fight against AIDS a personal priority until the epidemic was reversed.

Dr. Peter Piot, Executive Director of the Joint United Nations Programme on HIV/AIDS (UNAIDS), said that the 2001 Declaration of Commitment marked a true turning point in the global fight against AIDS. The stakes were higher than ever and to lose momentum or fail would be unforgivable. While much had been achieved, there was still a long road ahead. The meeting had to resolve that fighting AIDS would be as high a priority on the national and global agendas as promoting economic growth and maintaining security. Nothing less would do because AIDS was a long-term development crisis. The meeting also had to resolve to allocate more than $20 billion needed annually, from 2008 onwards; accelerate universal access to HIV prevention, treatment, care and support; rapidly devolve microbicides, better drugs and vaccines, as well as ensure access to them; add a long-term response to the much-needed crisis management approach; and address the epidemic's fundamental drivers, including the low status of women, sexual violence, homophobia and AIDS-related stigma and discrimination. A large coalition had to be organized to realize such an ambitious goal. Mr. Piot expressed hope that the Declaration of Commitment and the draft political declaration would provide a common minimum programme for such an expanding movement against AIDS.

On 2 June, the Assembly adopted, in resolution 60/262, the Political Declaration on HIV/AIDS (see below).

GENERAL ASSEMBLY ACTION

On 2 June [meeting 87], the General Assembly adopted **resolution 60/262** [draft: A/60/L.57] without vote [agenda item 45].

Political Declaration on HIV/AIDS

The General Assembly

Adopts the Political Declaration on HIV/AIDS annexed to the present resolution.

Annex

Political Declaration on HIV/AIDS

1. We, Heads of State and Government and representatives of States and Governments participating in the comprehensive review of the progress achieved in realizing the targets set out in the Declaration of Commitment on HIV/AIDS, held on 31 May and 1 June 2006, and the High-Level Meeting, held on 2 June 2006;

2. Note with alarm that we are facing an unprecedented human catastrophe; that a quarter of a century into the pandemic, AIDS has inflicted immense suffering on countries and communities throughout the world; and that more than 65 million people have been infected with HIV, more than 25 million people have died of AIDS, 15 million children have been orphaned by AIDS and millions more made vulnerable, and 40 million people are currently living with HIV, more than 95 per cent of whom live in developing countries;

3. Recognize that HIV/AIDS constitutes a global emergency and poses one of the most formidable challenges to the development, progress and stability of our respective societies and the world at large, and requires an exceptional and comprehensive global response;

4. Acknowledge that national and international efforts have resulted in important progress since 2001 in the areas of funding, expanding access to HIV prevention, treatment, care and support and in mitigating the impact of AIDS, and in reducing HIV prevalence in a small but growing number of countries, and also acknowledge that many targets contained in the Declaration of Commitment on HIV/AIDS have not yet been met;

5. Commend the Secretariat and the Co-sponsors of the Joint United Nations Programme on HIV/AIDS for their leadership role on HIV/AIDS policy and coordination, and for the support they provide to countries through the Joint Programme;

6. Recognize the contribution of, and the role played by, various donors in combating HIV/AIDS, as well as the fact that one third of resources spent on HIV/AIDS responses in 2005 came from the domestic sources of low- and middle-income countries, and therefore emphasize the importance of enhanced international cooperation and partnership in our responses to HIV/AIDS worldwide;

7. Remain deeply concerned, however, by the overall expansion and feminization of the pandemic and the fact that women now represent 50 per cent of people living with HIV worldwide and nearly 60 per cent of people living with HIV in Africa, and in this regard recognize that gender inequalities and all forms of violence against women and girls increase their vulnerability to HIV/AIDS;

8. Express grave concern that half of all new HIV infections occur among children and young people under the age of 25, and that there is a lack of information, skills and knowledge regarding HIV/AIDS among young people;

9. Remain gravely concerned that 2.3 million children are living with HIV/AIDS today, and recognize that the lack of paediatric drugs in many countries significantly hinders efforts to protect the health of children;

10. Reiterate with profound concern that the pandemic affects every region, that Africa, in particular sub-Saharan Africa, remains the worst-affected region, and that urgent and exceptional action is required at all levels to curb the devastating effects of this pandemic, and recognize the renewed commitment by African Governments and regional institutions to scale up their own HIV/AIDS responses;

11. Reaffirm that the full realization of all human rights and fundamental freedoms for all is an essential element in the global response to the HIV/AIDS pandemic, including in the areas of prevention, treatment, care and support, and recognize that addressing stigma and discrimination is also a critical element in combating the global HIV/AIDS pandemic;

12. Reaffirm also that access to medication in the context of pandemics, such as HIV/AIDS, is one of the fundamental elements to achieve progressively the full realization of the right of everyone to the enjoyment of the highest attainable standard of physical and mental health;

13. Recognize that in many parts of the world, the spread of HIV/AIDS is a cause and consequence of poverty, and that effectively combating HIV/AIDS is essential to the achievement of internationally agreed development goals and objectives, including the Millennium Development Goals;

14. Recognize also that we now have the means to reverse the global pandemic and to avert millions of needless deaths, and that to be effective, we must deliver an intensified, much more urgent and comprehensive response, in partnership with the United Nations system, intergovernmental organizations, people living with HIV and vulnerable groups, medical, scientific and educational institutions, non-governmental organizations, the business sector, including generic and research-based pharmaceutical companies, trade unions, the media, parliamentarians, foundations, community organizations, faith-based organizations and traditional leaders;

15. Recognize further that to mount a comprehensive response, we must overcome any legal, regulatory, trade and other barriers that block access to prevention, treatment, care and support; commit adequate resources; promote and protect all human rights and fundamental freedoms for all; promote gender equality and empowerment of women; promote and protect the rights of the girl child in order to reduce the vulnerability of the girl child to HIV/AIDS; strengthen health systems and support health workers; support greater involvement of people living with HIV; scale up the use of known effective and comprehensive prevention interventions; do everything necessary to ensure access to life-saving drugs and prevention tools; and develop with equal urgency better

tools—drugs, diagnostics and prevention technologies, including vaccines and microbicides—for the future;

16. Convinced that without renewed political will, strong leadership and sustained commitment and concerted efforts on the part of all stakeholders at all levels, including people living with HIV, civil society and vulnerable groups, and without increased resources, the world will not succeed in bringing about the end of the pandemic;

17. Solemnly declare our commitment to address the HIV/AIDS crisis by taking action as follows, taking into account the diverse situations and circumstances in different regions and countries throughout the world;

Therefore, we:

18. Reaffirm our commitment to implement fully the Declaration of Commitment on HIV/AIDS, entitled "Global Crisis—Global Action", adopted by the General Assembly at its twenty-sixth special session, in 2001; and to achieve the internationally agreed development goals and objectives, including the Millennium Development Goals, in particular the goal to halt and begin to reverse the spread of HIV/AIDS, malaria and other major diseases, the agreements dealing with HIV/AIDS reached at all major United Nations conferences and summits, including the 2005 World Summit and its statement on treatment, and the goal of achieving universal access to reproductive health by 2015, as set out at the International Conference on Population and Development;

19. Recognize the importance, and encourage the implementation, of the recommendations of the inclusive, country-driven processes and regional consultations facilitated by the Secretariat and the Co-sponsors of the Joint United Nations Programme on HIV/AIDS for scaling up HIV prevention, treatment, care and support, and strongly recommend that this approach be continued;

20. Commit ourselves to pursuing all necessary efforts to scale up nationally driven, sustainable and comprehensive responses to achieve broad multisectoral coverage for prevention, treatment, care and support, with full and active participation of people living with HIV, vulnerable groups, most affected communities, civil society and the private sector, towards the goal of universal access to comprehensive prevention programmes, treatment, care and support by 2010;

21. Emphasize the need to strengthen policy and programme linkages and coordination between HIV/AIDS, sexual and reproductive health, national development plans and strategies, including poverty eradication strategies, and to address, where appropriate, the impact of HIV/AIDS on national development plans and strategies;

22. Reaffirm that the prevention of HIV infection must be the mainstay of national, regional and international responses to the pandemic, and therefore commit ourselves to intensifying efforts to ensure that a wide range of prevention programmes that take account of local circumstances, ethics and cultural values is available in all countries, particularly the most affected countries, including information, education and communication, in languages most understood by communities and respectful of cultures, aimed at reducing risk-taking behaviours and encouraging responsible sexual behaviour, including abstinence and fidelity; expanded access to essential commodities, including male and female condoms and sterile injecting equipment; harm-reduction efforts related to drug use; expanded access to voluntary and confidential counselling and testing; safe blood supplies; and early and effective treatment of sexually transmitted infections;

23. Reaffirm also that prevention, treatment, care and support for those infected and affected by HIV/AIDS are mutually reinforcing elements of an effective response and must be integrated in a comprehensive approach to combat the pandemic;

24. Commit ourselves to overcoming legal, regulatory or other barriers that block access to effective HIV prevention, treatment, care and support, medicines, commodities and services;

25. Pledge to promote, at the international, regional, national and local levels, access to HIV/AIDS education, information, voluntary counselling and testing and related services, with full protection of confidentiality and informed consent, and to promote a social and legal environment that is supportive of and safe for voluntary disclosure of HIV status;

26. Commit ourselves to addressing the rising rates of HIV infection among young people to ensure an HIV-free future generation through the implementation of comprehensive, evidence-based prevention strategies, responsible sexual behaviour, including the use of condoms, evidence- and skills-based, youth-specific HIV education, mass media interventions and the provision of youth-friendly health services;

27. Commit ourselves also to ensuring that pregnant women have access to antenatal care, information, counselling and other HIV services and to increasing the availability of and access to effective treatment to women living with HIV and infants in order to reduce mother-to-child transmission of HIV, as well as to ensuring effective interventions for women living with HIV, including voluntary and confidential counselling and testing, with informed consent, access to treatment, especially life-long antiretroviral therapy and, where appropriate, breast-milk substitutes and the provision of a continuum of care;

28. Resolve to integrate food and nutritional support, with the goal that all people at all times will have access to sufficient, safe and nutritious food to meet their dietary needs and food preferences, for an active and healthy life, as part of a comprehensive response to HIV/AIDS;

29. Commit ourselves to intensifying efforts to enact, strengthen or enforce, as appropriate, legislation, regulations and other measures to eliminate all forms of discrimination against and to ensure the full enjoyment of all human rights and fundamental freedoms by people living with HIV and members of vulnerable groups, in particular to ensure their access to, inter alia, education, inheritance, employment, health care, social and health services, prevention, support and treatment, information and legal protection, while respecting their

privacy and confidentiality; and developing strategies to combat stigma and social exclusion connected with the epidemic;

30. Pledge to eliminate gender inequalities, gender-based abuse and violence; increase the capacity of women and adolescent girls to protect themselves from the risk of HIV infection, principally through the provision of health care and services, including, inter alia, sexual and reproductive health, and the provision of full access to comprehensive information and education; ensure that women can exercise their right to have control over, and decide freely and responsibly on, matters related to their sexuality in order to increase their ability to protect themselves from HIV infection, including their sexual and reproductive health, free of coercion, discrimination and violence; and take all necessary measures to create an enabling environment for the empowerment of women and strengthen their economic independence; and in this context, reiterate the importance of the role of men and boys in achieving gender equality;

31. Commit ourselves to strengthening legal, policy, administrative and other measures for the promotion and protection of women's full enjoyment of all human rights and the reduction of their vulnerability to HIV/AIDS through the elimination of all forms of discrimination, as well as all types of sexual exploitation of women, girls and boys, including for commercial reasons, and all forms of violence against women and girls, including harmful traditional and customary practices, abuse, rape and other forms of sexual violence, battering and trafficking in women and girls;

32. Commit ourselves also to addressing as a priority the vulnerabilities faced by children affected by and living with HIV; providing support and rehabilitation to these children and their families, women and the elderly, particularly in their role as caregivers; promoting child-oriented HIV/AIDS policies and programmes and increased protection for children orphaned and affected by HIV/AIDS; ensuring access to treatment and intensifying efforts to develop new treatments for children; and building, where needed, and supporting the social security systems that protect them;

33. Emphasize the need for accelerated scale-up of collaborative activities on tuberculosis and HIV, in line with the Global Plan to Stop TB 2006-2015, and for investment in new drugs, diagnostics and vaccines that are appropriate for people with TB-HIV co-infection;

34. Commit ourselves to expanding to the greatest extent possible, supported by international cooperation and partnership, our capacity to deliver comprehensive HIV/AIDS programmes in ways that strengthen existing national health and social systems, including by integrating HIV/AIDS intervention into programmes for primary health care, mother and child health, sexual and reproductive health, tuberculosis, hepatitis C, sexually transmitted infections, nutrition, children affected, orphaned or made vulnerable by HIV/AIDS, as well as formal and informal education;

35. Undertake to reinforce, adopt and implement, where needed, national plans and strategies, supported by international cooperation and partnership, to increase the capacity of human resources for health to meet the urgent need for the training and retention of a broad range of health workers, including community-based health workers; improve training and management and working conditions, including treatment for health workers; and effectively govern the recruitment, retention and deployment of new and existing health workers to mount a more effective HIV/AIDS response;

36. Commit ourselves, invite international financial institutions and the Global Fund to Fight AIDS, Tuberculosis and Malaria, according to its policy framework, and encourage other donors, to provide additional resources to low- and middle- income countries for the strengthening of HIV/AIDS programmes and health systems and for addressing human resources gaps, including the development of alternative and simplified service delivery models and the expansion of the community-level provision of HIV/AIDS prevention, treatment, care and support, as well as other health and social services;

37. Reiterate the need for Governments, United Nations agencies, regional and international organizations and non-governmental organizations involved with the provision and delivery of assistance to countries and regions affected by conflicts, humanitarian emergencies or natural disasters to incorporate HIV/AIDS prevention, care and treatment elements into their plans and programmes;

38. Pledge to provide the highest level of commitment to ensuring that costed, inclusive, sustainable, credible and evidence-based national HIV/AIDS plans are funded and implemented with transparency, accountability and effectiveness, in line with national priorities;

39. Commit ourselves to reducing the global HIV/AIDS resource gap through greater domestic and international funding to enable countries to have access to predictable and sustainable financial resources and ensuring that international funding is aligned with national HIV/AIDS plans and strategies; and in this regard welcome the increased resources that are being made available through bilateral and multilateral initiatives, as well as those that will become available as a result of the establishment of timetables by many developed countries to achieve the targets of 0.7 per cent of gross national product for official development assistance by 2015 and to reach at least 0.5 per cent of gross national product for official development assistance by 2010 as well as, pursuant to the Brussels Programme of Action for the Least Developed Countries for the Decade 2001-2010, 0.15 per cent to 0.20 per cent for the least developed countries no later than 2010, and urge those developed countries that have not yet done so to make concrete efforts in this regard in accordance with their commitments;

40. Recognize that the Joint United Nations Programme on HIV/AIDS has estimated that 20 billion to 23 billion United States dollars per annum is needed by 2010 to support rapidly scaled-up AIDS responses in low- and middle-income countries, and therefore commit ourselves to taking measures to ensure that new and additional re-

sources are made available from donor countries and also from national budgets and other national sources;

41. Commit ourselves to supporting and strengthening existing financial mechanisms, including the Global Fund to Fight AIDS, Tuberculosis and Malaria, as well as relevant United Nations organizations, through the provision of funds in a sustained manner, while continuing to develop innovative sources of financing, as well as pursuing other efforts, aimed at generating additional funds;

42. Commit ourselves also to finding appropriate solutions to overcome barriers in pricing, tariffs and trade agreements, and to making improvements to legislation, regulatory policy, procurement and supply chain management in order to accelerate and intensify access to affordable and quality HIV/AIDS prevention products, diagnostics, medicines and treatment commodities;

43. Reaffirm that the World Trade Organization's Agreement on Trade-Related Aspects of Intellectual Property Rights does not and should not prevent members from taking measures now and in the future to protect public health. Accordingly, while reiterating our commitment to the TRIPS Agreement, reaffirm that the Agreement can and should be interpreted and implemented in a manner supportive of the right to protect public health and, in particular, to promote access to medicines for all including the production of generic antiretroviral drugs and other essential drugs for AIDS-related infections. In this connection, we reaffirm the right to use, to the full, the provisions in the TRIPS Agreement, the Doha Declaration on the TRIPS Agreement and Public Health and the World Trade Organization's General Council decision of 2003 and amendments to Article 31, which provide flexibilities for this purpose;

44. Resolve to assist developing countries to enable them to employ the flexibilities outlined in the TRIPS Agreement, and to strengthen their capacities for this purpose;

45. Commit ourselves to intensifying investment in and efforts towards the research and development of new, safe and affordable HIV/AIDS-related medicines, products and technologies, such as vaccines, female-controlled methods and microbicides, paediatric antiretroviral formulations, including through such mechanisms as Advance Market Commitments, and to encouraging increased investment in HIV/AIDS-related research and development in traditional medicine;

46. Encourage pharmaceutical companies, donors, multilateral organizations and other partners to develop public-private partnerships in support of research and development and technology transfer, and in the comprehensive response to HIV/AIDS;

47. Encourage bilateral, regional and international efforts to promote bulk procurement, price negotiations and licensing to lower prices for HIV prevention products, diagnostics, medicines and treatment commodities, while recognizing that intellectual property protection is important for the development of new medicines and recognizing the concerns about its effects on prices;

48. Recognize the initiative by a group of countries, such as the International Drug Purchase Facility, based on innovative financing mechanisms that aim to provide further drug access at affordable prices to developing countries on a sustainable and predictable basis;

49. Commit ourselves to setting, in 2006, through inclusive, transparent processes, ambitious national targets, including interim targets for 2008 in accordance with the core indicators recommended by the Joint United Nations Programme on HIV/AIDS, that reflect the commitment of the present Declaration and the urgent need to scale up significantly towards the goal of universal access to comprehensive prevention programmes, treatment, care and support by 2010, and to setting up and maintaining sound and rigorous monitoring and evaluation frameworks within their HIV/AIDS strategies;

50. Call upon the Joint United Nations Programme on HIV/AIDS, including its Co-sponsors, to assist national efforts to coordinate the AIDS response, as elaborated in the "Three Ones" principles and in line with the recommendations of the Global Task Team on Improving AIDS Coordination among Multilateral Institutions and International Donors; assist national and regional efforts to monitor and report on efforts to achieve the targets set out above; and strengthen global coordination on HIV/AIDS, including through the thematic sessions of the Programme Coordinating Board;

51. Call upon Governments, national parliaments, donors, regional and subregional organizations, organizations of the United Nations system, the Global Fund to Fight AIDS, Tuberculosis and Malaria, civil society, people living with HIV, vulnerable groups, the private sector, communities most affected by HIV/AIDS and other stakeholders to work closely together to achieve the targets set out above, and to ensure accountability and transparency at all levels through participatory reviews of responses to HIV/AIDS;

52. Request the Secretary-General of the United Nations, with the support of the Joint United Nations Programme on HIV/AIDS, to include in his annual report to the General Assembly on the status of implementation of the Declaration of Commitment on HIV/AIDS, in accordance with General Assembly resolution S-26/2 of 27 June 2001, the progress achieved in realizing the commitments set out in the present Declaration;

53. Decide to undertake comprehensive reviews in 2008 and 2011, within the annual reviews of the General Assembly, of the progress achieved in realizing the Declaration of Commitment on HIV/AIDS, entitled "Global Crisis—Global Action", adopted by the General Assembly at its twenty-sixth special session, and the present Declaration.

After the adotpion of the resolution, the United States representative said that his country understood that the Declaration's reference to the International Conference on Population and Development and the phrase "reproductive health" did not create any rights and could neither be interpreted to constitute support for, nor endorsement or promotion of abortion. He also understood that all references to "responsible sexual behaviour" denoted abstinence and fidelity.

Report of Secretary-General. As requested in Assembly resolution 60/224, the Secretary-General submitted to the high-level meeting his report, "Declaration of Commitment on HIV/AIDS: five years later" [A/60/736]. The report provided an update on progress in the global AIDS response since 2001, identified critical challenges that had to be addressed and made recommendations for strengthening AIDS efforts at the global, regional and country levels.

The Secretary-General observed that the epidemic continued to expand in all regions, although it had begun to stabilize in some African countries. In recent years, the burden of the epidemic had increased, notably on women, who represented half of all people living with HIV and nearly 60 per cent of all infections in Africa. However, since 2001, major progress had been recorded in some key aspects of the global AIDS response, but with inadequate progress on other critical fronts. In general, the strengthened global response, while heartening, was being rapidly outpaced by the epidemic itself. In most countries, a strong foundation existed on which to build an effective AIDS response, with 90 per cent of those reporting having a national strategy, and 85 per cent having a national body to coordinate AIDS efforts. Financial resources had significantly increased, but more funding would be needed to support a response capable of reversing the epidemic. In 2005, some $8.3 billion was spent on AIDS programmes in low- and middle-income countries, reaching the financing target in the Declaration of Commitment. Treatment access had greatly expanded, with 24 countries meeting or exceeding the "3 by 5" target of 50 per cent coverage of those in need of treatment. Some countries had dramatically increased access to HIV prevention programmes. In more than 70 countries, utilization of testing and counselling services quadrupled, and several countries achieved nearly 70 per cent coverage of pregnant women with services to prevent mother-to-child transmission.

However, prevention programmes were failing to reach the populations most at risk and prevention efforts remained notably inadequate for young people, who accounted for half of all new infections. Stigma and discrimination against people living with HIV were key barriers to HIV prevention, treatment and support programmes, with women experiencing the most severe forms. In addition, AIDS response was insufficiently grounded in the promotion, protection and fulfilment of human rights. Legal systems in many countries also failed to provide adequate protection to children affected by HIV/AIDS and to elderly caregivers. Governments, international partners and communities were failing to sufficiently provide care and support for the 15 million children orphaned by AIDS.

The Secretary-General recommended that Governments should lead and take greater accountability for the national response, allocating substantially greater resources themselves, promoting inclusion of all sectors of society and vigorously working to promote HIV awareness and alleviate stigma. In addition to substantially financing AIDS responses in many low-income countries, especially in sub-Saharan Africa, donors should ensure stable funding through long-term financial commitments and permit flexibility in the way funds were spent to reflect evolving priorities.

People living with HIV and other members of civil society, including faith-based organizations, business, labour and the private sector, should be equal partners in the development, implementation and monitoring of the national response.

The UN system should support countries in implementing and expanding effective national responses, be more accountable for its own activities, promote the fulfilment by countries and donors of their pledges and commitments, and better coordinate the diverse multilateral partners, particularly through the establishment of joint country AIDS teams.

UNAIDS assessment. Also in response to Assembly resolution 60/224, the Secretary-General transmitted in March [A/60/737] a note containing the UNAIDS assessment of inclusive, country-driven processes for scaling up HIV prevention, treatment, care and support. The Global Fund to Fight AIDS, Tuberculosis and Malaria [YUN 2002, p. 1217] provided low- and middle-income countries with additional financing. More domestic and international resources had been mobilized, prices of some AIDS medicines greatly reduced, and the "3 by 5" initiative had helped to mobilize a substantial increase in the number of people on antiretroviral treatment. The "Three Ones" principles for the coordination of AIDS responses and the recommendations of the Global Task Team on Improving AIDS Coordination among Multilateral Institutions and International Donors [YUN 2005, p. 1327] improved the efficiency and effectiveness of resource utilization. The Unite for Children, Unite against AIDS campaign [ibid., p. 1290] put children affected by the disease at the centre of the AIDS agenda. Major steps had been taken in recent years, especially in the expansion of treatment.

A renewed emphasis on HIV prevention was critically needed. The internationally agreed UNAIDS policy paper, "Intensifying HIV prevention" [ibid., p. 1327], provided a framework for strengthening evidence-informed HIV prevention within a comprehensive response, including treatment, care and support for those infected with and affected by HIV. However, universal access would depend largely on massive social mobilization to dramatically decrease the number of new HIV infections, along with efforts to increase HIV treatment coverage. The provision of HIV prevention, treatment, care and support to all those in need was an extremely ambitious goal. The concept of universal access implied that everyone should be able to have access to information and services. Scaling up towards universal access should be equitable, accessible, affordable, comprehensive and sustainable.

On the basis of those challenges and the solutions proposed in national, regional and global consultations, UNAIDS identified six major requirements for reaching the common goal. It made specific recommendations for setting and supporting national priorities; ensuring predictable and sustainable financing, including the commissioning of a group of experts to explore options to make domestic and international funding for AIDS more long-term and predictable; strengthening human resources and systems; making commodities affordable; dealing with stigma, discrimination, gender and human rights issues; and setting targets and accountability. Every country should set ambitious AIDS targets to scale up HIV prevention, treatment, care and support; and move as close as possible to the goal of universal access by 2010; and develop action plans to reach, by 2008, at least 50 per cent of their 2010 targets. The UNAIDS secretariat and the World Health Organization (WHO) would provide countries with key indicators and guidelines to help set national targets and measure progress towards universal access. Countries should ensure the accountability of all partners through transparent peer-review mechanisms and regular reporting of country and regional progress, and establish inclusive and transparent national processes for public financial management and expenditure tracking to verify the allocation, use and impact of AIDS funding. Those recommendations would help overcome major obstacles to scaling up integrated AIDS programmes and moving towards universal access.

Preparations for review meeting

On 27 March, by **decision 60/554**, the General Assembly approved the list of civil society representatives [A/60/CRP.2] to participate in the high-level meeting and comprehensive review of the Declaration of Commitment on HIV/AIDS. On 30 May, by **decision 60/557,** it invited, in their capacity as rapporteurs for the panel discussions, Wu Zunyou, National Centre for AIDS/STD Control and Prevention (China); Sigrun Møgedal, HIV/AIDS Ambassador (Norway); Keesha Effs, National Youth Ambassador for Positive Living (Jamaica); Omolou Falobi, Journalists against AIDS (Nigeria); and Raminta Stuikyte, Director of the Central and Eastern European Harm Reduction Network (Lithuania), to present a summary of the discussions at the plenary meeting on 1 June.

Dr. Peter Piot, UNAIDS Executive Director, and Dr. Richard Feachem, Executive Director of the Global Fund to Fight AIDS, Tuberculosis and Malaria, were also invited to make statements at the opening of the plenary meeting on 2 June; Khensani Mavasa, Deputy Chairperson of Treatment Action Campaign (South Africa), and William Harvey Roedy, President, MTV Networks International and Chairman of the Global Media AIDS Initiative (United Kingdom), represented the private sector.

On 1 June, by **decision 60/558**, the Assembly, without setting a precedent, asked that the high-level meeting of 2 June, be conducted in two parallel segments in separate venues with full conference services, and form an integral part of the meeting. The meeting would reconvene in one venue for consideration of the final document and the closing session.

HIV Counselling and Testing Day

On 4 December [meeting 65], the General Assembly adopted **decision 61/512** [draft: A/61/L.40 & Add.1] without vote [agenda item 46].

International Voluntary HIV Counselling and Testing Day

At its 65th plenary meeting on 4 December, the General Assembly, on the proposal of a number of Member States, and recalling its resolution 60/262 of 2 June 2006, including its commitment to scale up efforts towards the goal of universal access to comprehensive prevention programmes, treatment, care and support by 2010, and its pledge to promote, at the international, regional, national and local levels, access to HIV/AIDS education, information, voluntary counselling and testing and related services, with full protection of confidentiality and informed consent, and to promote a social and legal environment that is supportive of and safe for voluntary disclosure of HIV status, decides to call on Member States to designate a Voluntary HIV Counselling and Testing Day in 2007 and to encourage Member States, the Joint United Nations Programme on HIV/AIDS and its co-sponsors, and other relevant international and national organizations to take measures, as appropriate, in accordance with nationally determined action plans and policies, and, as part of scaling up nationally driven, sustainable and comprehensive responses to achieving broad multisectoral coverage for prevention, treatment, care and support, to observe the day on 1 December 2007 or on such other day or days in 2007 as individual Member States may decide.

Bangkok Statement of Commitment

The 2006 International Parliamentarians' Conference on the Implementation of the International Conference on Population and Development's Programme of Action (Bangkok, Thailand, 21-22 November) adopted the Bangkok Statement of Commitment, which addressed the problem of HIV/AIDS. The signatories committed themselves to dedicating at least 10 per cent of national development and development assistance budgets to population and reproductive health programmes, including HIV and AIDS prevention.

Joint UN Programme on HIV/AIDS

UNAIDS, which became fully operational in 1996 [YUN 1996, p. 1121], continued to serve as the main advocate for global action on HIV/AIDS.

Report of Executive Director. The UNAIDS Executive Director, in an annual report to the UNAIDS Programme Coordinating Board (PCB), summarized key UNAIDS activities and achievements, including the major trends in and the impact of the epidemic, support for action in countries, and efforts to strengthen the multilateral response to AIDS. It also made proposals for future direction.

Noting that the PCB meeting was occurring at a historic moment in the AIDS epidemic—25 years after it was first detected—the Executive Director highlighted in his proposed future direction the necessity of mainstreaming work on AIDS into broader development efforts. As there was still no vaccine or cure in sight, full-scale action would have to be sustained over the longer term. Episodic and crisis-management approaches would have to be replaced by a more strategic forward-looking response, and the global funding for HIV programmes significantly increased. National strategies should be converted into costed action plans, with clear goals and milestones, while donors and stakeholders should adhere to the "Three Ones" principles. A renewed emphasis on HIV prevention was needed and the UN system should provide stronger support to countries as they implemented more sustainable responses. UNAIDS priority areas would include improving the coherence and effectiveness of UN efforts, pursuing harmonization and alignment, and increasing technical support, in addition to reducing vulnerability, and maintaining focus on advocacy, resource mobilization, policy advice and partnership for development.

Trends

According to UNAIDS, at the end of 2006, an estimated 39.5 million people were living with HIV, comprising 37.2 million adults and 2.3 million children under the age of 15. An estimated 4.3 million new infections were recorded and approximately 2.9 million people died of AIDS-related illnesses. Some 17.7 million women were living with HIV—almost 50 per cent of all adults with the disease.

The epidemic continued to expand in sub-Saharan Africa, where almost 25 million people had the virus, resulting in a 5.9 per cent prevalence rate. A total of 2.1 million Africans died of AIDS-related illnesses in 2006, almost three quarters of all AIDS deaths worldwide. However, some declines in HIV prevalence were noted in Burkina Faso, Côte d'Ivoire, Ghana, Kenya, Rwanda, the United Republic of Tanzania and Zimbabwe.

In Asia, approximately 8.6 million people were living with HIV and 960,000 new infections were recorded. East Asia experienced the fastest growth in the world, mainly in China. Infection levels were highest in Southeast Asia.

The level of infection in Oceania was still very low, with 81,000 people living with the disease. In the Middle East and North Africa, available data pointed to a 12 per cent increase in infection rates, with an estimated 460,000 people with HIV.

The most striking increases were in Eastern Europe and Central Asia, where approximately 1.7 million people had HIV, including 270,000 newly infected persons. Ukraine had the highest prevalence rate in Europe, but the epidemic was also expanding in the Russian Federation and to a smaller extent in Tajikistan and Uzbekistan.

With 1.7 million people living with HIV and 65,000 AIDS-related deaths in 2006, Latin America's epidemic remained generally stable, particularly in Brazil. The Caribbean, with the second highest prevalence rate in the world, at 1.2 per cent, had 250,000 people living with the disease.

In Western and Central Europe, 740,000 people were living with HIV, while in North America, that number stood at 1.4 million.

The number of people dying from AIDS worldwide grew from 2.2 million in 2001 to 2.9 million in 2006, while the number with advanced HIV infection and in urgent need of treatment rose faster than the number of people starting antiretroviral therapy. Gender inequality continued to drive the feminization of the epidemic, with women comprising 48 per cent of people living with HIV. In general, prevention measures were failing to keep pace with the epidemic's growth. In some countries that had previously reported declines in infection prevalence, including Uganda, the United States and Western Europe, and certain populations in Thailand, the trends had reversed. Global funding levels rose from $300 million in 1996 to $8.9 billion in 2006, which, while impressive, was only about half the amount needed to support AIDS responses in low- and middle-income countries.

UNAIDS activities

In response to the request of the UNAIDS PCB that action plans be developed to implement the recommendations of the Global Task Team on improving coordination among Governments, civil society, multilateral institutions and international donors in the global response to HIV/AIDS [YUN 2005, p. 1327], WHO, in an April report [A/59/8], stated that it had been closely involved in the implementation of the Team's recommendations, taking the lead in several cases. It supported steps to create joint UN teams on AIDS, promoted more effective joint programming in countries and led in setting up the Global Joint Problem-Solving and Implementation Support Team in July 2005, which, by April 2006, had solved acute problems in the implementation of major grants in some countries and provided emergency assistance in nine others and one region. WHO worked closely with UNAIDS and its co-sponsors to establish a more functional division of labour. It was designated as the leader on matters concerning antiretroviral therapy, opportunistic infections, universal precautions, blood and injection safety, counselling and testing, diagnosis and treatment of sexually transmitted diseases, surveillance of HIV and prevention of mother-to-child transmission. WHO, with UNAIDS and its other co-sponsors, prepared a consolidated technical support plan for 2006-2007 to help countries make effective use of large grants from the Global Fund to Fight AIDS, Tuberculosis and Malaria, as well as other sources.

At its meeting in London in May, the Inter-agency Task Team on Children and HIV and AIDS, created by the UNAIDS Committee of Co-sponsoring Organizations in 2001, identified several key activities for follow up. Working groups on different follow-up actions were established, and a steering committee was formed to increase involvement and ownership of Task Team members and ensure continuity. The Task Team's terms of reference were accordingly updated.

PCB, at its eighteenth meeting (Geneva, 27-28 June), requested UNAIDS to strengthen its assistance to national AIDS programmes; elaborate options for strengthening global coordination on AIDS; assist national and regional efforts to monitor and report on activities to achieve national targets, as called for in the Political Declaration on HIV/AIDS; strengthen its engagement with civil society; and develop for the PCB review a 2007-2010 framework for the Joint Programme's support for countries' efforts to implement the Declaration of Commitment on HIV/AIDS and the 2006 Political Declaration. PCB endorsed the 2006-2007 Unified Budget and Workplan Performance Monitoring and Evaluation Framework, and approved the revision of the key results of UNAIDS co-sponsors and the secretariat in the budget and work plan, the planned reprogramming of resources, and $40 million as a supplemental budget line for the provision of technical support to countries. It also endorsed the directions for the future contained in the Executive Director's report (see p. 1417) as a guideline for stronger UNAIDS support.

PCB, at its nineteenth meeting (Lusaka, Zambia, 6-8 December), endorsed the 2007-2010 Strategic Framework for UNAIDS support to countries' efforts to move towards universal access as the principal guide to global, regional and country planning, budgeting, implementation and monitoring of progress towards that goal, and requested the secretariat to provide a mid-term review report in 2008. It established a process for further elaborating the UNAIDS role in strengthening the global coordination of AIDS and in developing PCB into a more relevant and effective policy-making body. PCB requested UNAIDS to strengthen AIDS responses in humanitarian emergencies and security operations through the development of a strategic framework for action with the United Nations Office for the Coordination of Humanitarian Affairs. It also requested that the final report of the Global Task Team's independent assessment be presented to PCB at its June 2007 meeting. The Board reviewed UNAIDS tasks, and endorsed a list of activities proposed for retirement and requested the secretariat to regularly review others for potential retirement.

UNDP/UNFPA/UNICEF/WFP consideration. The Executive Boards of the United Nations Development Programme (UNDP), the United Nations Population Fund (UNFPA), the United Nations Children's Fund (UNICEF) and the World Food Programme (WFP) held a joint session (20-23 January) to consider HIV/AIDS: follow-up to the recommendations of the Global Task Team, including updates on follow-up to the Team's process and links with UN reform efforts, country-level experiences and assessment of progress and challenges in implementing the Team's recommendations [YUN

2005, p. 1327]. Delegations emphasized that commitment and accountability for advancing those recommendations should come from all stakeholders. They underscored that successful implementation depended on the full participation of all key actors to ensure alignment, simplification and harmonization for effective action and results at the country level.

In June, as a follow-up to the seventeenth [YUN 2005, p. 1327] and eighteenth PCB meetings (see p. 1418), the Executive Boards held another meeting to consider a joint report on the implementation of PCB recommendations, which discussed accelerating such implementation, intensifying HIV prevention and the progress made in that regard, the 2006-2007 unified budget and work plan, and follow-up to the 2006 high-level meeting on AIDS.

The meeting stressed the need to strengthen assistance to national AIDS coordination entities by setting aside funds for use in combating the epidemic, even if donor funding were to cease, and underscored the importance of supporting the "Three Ones" principles. All organizations were encouraged to address gender issues within the HIV/AIDS epidemic to provide a stronger basis for responding to the needs of vulnerable groups. The United Nations was encouraged to address the feminization of the epidemic, and the scaling up of strategies to meet the needs of women and girls.

The UNDP/UNFPA Executive Board, at its annual session in June, considered the report of the Evaluation Office [DP/2006/29] on the UNDP role and contribution in the HIV and AIDS response in Southern Africa and Ethiopia. It was recommended that, in the Southern Africa subregion, where AIDS was the most severe in the world, offices in case-study countries should demonstrate a much higher level of urgency in their work on HIV/AIDS. Specific recommendations were made for country offices to clarify the strategic direction, formulate or update UNDP strategies and integrate them into national country strategies and programmes, shift programme focus, strengthen HIV/AIDS capacity and foster a culture of monitoring and evaluation. The Regional Bureau for Africa should assume a new leadership role; the Bureau for Development should review corporate strategy; the Bureau of Management should accelerate implementation of financial management programmes; and the Office of the Associate Administrator should clarify working relationships. The Executive Board should request a report for the 2007 annual session on the implementation of the recommendations.

On 23 June [E/2006/35 (dec. 2006/16)], the Executive Board welcomed the evaluation report and encouraged UNDP to address the recommendations contained therein, in particular the need for capacity-building, national ownership and working closely with other key stakeholders.

International Year of Sanitation

On 20 December [meeting 83], the General Assembly adopted **resolution 61/192** [draft: A/61/422/Add.1 & Corr.1] without vote [agenda item 53].

International Year of Sanitation, 2008

The General Assembly,

Recalling the Rio Declaration on Environment and Development, Agenda 21, the Programme for the Further Implementation of Agenda 21, the Johannesburg Declaration on Sustainable Development and the Plan of Implementation of the World Summit on Sustainable Development ("Johannesburg Plan of Implementation"), as well as the Monterrey Consensus of the International Conference on Financing for Development,

Reaffirming the commitment to implement Agenda 21, the Programme for the Further Implementation of Agenda 21, the Johannesburg Plan of Implementation, including the time-bound goals and targets, and the other internationally agreed development goals, including the Millennium Development Goals,

Recalling the 2005 World Summit Outcome,

Reaffirming the need to assist the efforts of developing countries to prepare integrated water resources management and water efficiency plans as part of their national development strategies and to provide access to safe drinking water and basic sanitation in accordance with the United Nations Millennium Declaration and the Johannesburg Plan of Implementation, including halving by 2015 the proportion of people who are unable to reach or afford safe drinking water and who do not have access to basic sanitation,

Also reaffirming the necessity to take into account sanitation in complementarity with water, in conjunction with the International Decade for Action, "Water for Life", 2005-2015,

Appreciating the ongoing work in the United Nations system and the work of other intergovernmental organizations on sanitation,

Taking note with appreciation of the contribution made by the Advisory Board on Water and Sanitation and its work on the Hashimoto Action Plan, a compendium of water-related actions which relevant actors should consider, as appropriate,

Deeply concerned by the slow and insufficient progress in providing access to basic sanitation services, and conscious of the impact of the lack of sanitation on people's health, poverty reduction and economic and social development, and on the environment, in particular water resources,

Convinced that progress can be achieved through active commitment and action by all States, including at the national and local levels, as well as United Nations agencies, regional and international organizations, civil society organizations and other relevant stakeholders,

1. *Decides* to declare 2008 the International Year of Sanitation;

2. *Requests* the Department of Economic and Social Affairs of the Secretariat to serve as the focal point for the Year and to develop, in a timely manner, relevant proposals on possible activities at all levels, including possible sources of funding;

3. *Calls upon* States, as well as subregional, regional and international organizations and other relevant stakeholders, including the private sector and civil society, to make voluntary contributions;

4. *Encourages* all States, as well as the United Nations system and all other relevant stakeholders, to take advantage of the Year to increase awareness of the importance of sanitation and to promote action at all levels, taking into account, inter alia, the policy recommendations adopted by the Commission on Sustainable Development at its thirteenth session as well as, where appropriate, the relevant recommendations made in the Hashimoto Action Plan;

5. *Requests* the Secretary-General to submit to the General Assembly at its sixty-fourth session a report on the implementation of the present resolution.

World Diabetes Day

On 20 December [meeting 83], the General Assembly adopted **resolution 61/225** [draft: A/61/L.39/Rev.1 & Add.1] without vote [agenda item 113].

World Diabetes Day

The General Assembly,

Recalling the 2005 World Summit Outcome and the United Nations Millennium Declaration, as well as the outcomes of the major United Nations conferences and summits in the economic, social and related fields, in particular the health-related development goals set out therein, and its resolutions 58/3 of 27 October 2003, 60/35 of 30 November 2005 and 60/265 of 30 June 2006,

Recognizing that strengthening public-health and health-care delivery systems is critical to achieving internationally agreed development goals, including the Millennium Development Goals,

Recognizing also that diabetes is a chronic, debilitating and costly disease associated with severe complications, which poses severe risks for families, Member States and the entire world and serious challenges to the achievement of internationally agreed development goals, including the Millennium Development Goals,

Recalling World Health Assembly resolutions WHA42.36 of 19 May 1989 on the prevention and control of diabetes mellitus and WHA57.17 of 22 May 2004 on a global strategy on diet, physical activity and health,

Welcoming the fact that the International Diabetes Federation has been observing 14 November as World Diabetes Day at a global level since 1991, with cosponsorship of the World Health Organization,

Recognizing the urgent need to pursue multilateral efforts to promote and improve human health, and provide access to treatment and health-care education,

1. *Decides* to designate 14 November, the current World Diabetes Day, as a United Nations Day, to be observed every year beginning in 2007;

2. *Invites* all Member States, relevant organizations of the United Nations system and other international organizations, as well as civil society, including nongovernmental organizations and the private sector, to observe World Diabetes Day in an appropriate manner, in order to raise public awareness of diabetes and related complications, as well as its prevention and care, including through education and the mass media;

3. *Encourages* Member States to develop national policies for the prevention, treatment and care of diabetes in line with the sustainable development of their health-care systems, taking into account the internationally agreed development goals, including the Millennium Development Goals;

4. *Requests* the Secretary-General to bring the present resolution to the attention of all Member States and organizations of the United Nations system.

Tobacco

The WHO Framework Convention on Tobacco Control (FCTC), adopted in May 2003 by the World Health Assembly [YUN 2003, p. 1251], with WHO as the interim secretariat, entered into force on 27 February 2005. As at 31 December 2006, 141 States and the European Community were parties to the Convention.

The first session of the Conference of the Parties to the Framework Convention (Geneva, 6-17 February) discussed the recommendations of the Open-ended Intergovernmental Working Group on FCTC. During the session, the Conference of the Parties decided to set up a permanent FCTC secretariat within WHO in Geneva, with an $8 million budget for the first two years of operation, funded through voluntary assessed contributions. It also decided to create working groups to develop protocols on cross-border advertising and illicit trade; develop guidelines to help countries create smoke-free places and effective ways to regulate tobacco products; establish an ad hoc group of experts to study economically viable alternatives to tobacco growing and production; and allow the Conference to assess the countries' progress in implementing FCTC through a pilot reporting questionnaire.

Ad Hoc Inter-Agency Task Force

In May, the Secretary-General submitted to the Economic and Social Council, in accordance with resolution 2004/62 [YUN 2004, p. 1221], a report on progress made by the Ad Hoc Inter-Agency Task Force on Tobacco Control [E/2006/62] in implementing multi-sectoral collaboration on tobacco and health. The report described the social and economic concerns of tobacco use and the specific areas where inter-agency collaboration could be important, including exposure to second-hand smoke, the link between tobacco and poverty, the WHO Framework Convention on Tobacco Control, the development of a protocol to curb illicit trade in tobacco products and the issue of corporate social responsibility of the tobacco industry.

The Secretary-General recommended that the Council call for the implementation of a smoke-free policy at the United Nations, and a ban on sales of tobacco products on its premises. He also recommended that the International Labour Organization and WHO jointly develop a code of practice on smoking in the workplace, and a stronger inter-agency collaboration to help include tobacco control in the national development programmes of countries, particularly the low-income ones.

ECONOMIC AND SOCIAL COUNCIL ACTION

On 27 July [meeting 42], the Economic and Social Council adopted **resolution 2006/42** [draft: E/2006/L.10/Rev.1,2] without vote [agenda item 7*(b)*].

Smoke-free United Nations premises

The Economic and Social Council,

Recalling its resolution 2004/62 of 23 July 2004,

Taking note of the report of the Secretary-General on the Ad Hoc Inter-Agency Task Force on Tobacco Control,

Noting with concern the serious harmful impact of second-hand smoke on the health of non-smokers, which can lead to disease, disability and death,

Acknowledging that second-hand smoke at the workplace is a fully preventable occupational health hazard,

Recalling article 8 of the World Health Organization Framework Convention on Tobacco Control, entitled "Protection from exposure to tobacco smoke", which states, inter alia, that each party shall adopt and implement measures to provide "protection from exposure to tobacco smoke in indoor workplaces, public transport, indoor places and, as appropriate, other public places",

Emphasizing the importance of protecting the well-being of individuals in their working environments,

1. *Recommends* that the General Assembly, at its sixty-first session, consider the implementation of a complete ban on smoking at all United Nations indoor premises, at Headquarters as well as at regional and country offices throughout the United Nations system, and the implementation of a complete ban on sales of tobacco products at all United Nations premises;

2. *Also recommends* that the General Assembly request the Secretary-General to submit a report on the implementation of the present resolution to the Economic and Social Council at its substantive session of 2008;

3. *Decides* to continue its consideration of the agenda item entitled "Tobacco or health" at its substantive session of 2008.

On the same day, the Council requested the Secretary-General to submit at its 2008 substantive session a report on the work of the Inter-Agency Task Force on Tobacco Control (**decision 2006/248**).

Roll Back Malaria initiative

Pursuant to General Assembly resolution 60/221 [YUN 2005, p. 1329], the Secretary-General transmitted an August report [A/61/218 & Corr.1], prepared by WHO on the Decade to Roll Back Malaria in Developing Countries, Particularly in Africa (2001-2010), which was proclaimed in Assembly resolution 55/284 [YUN 2001, p. 1139]. It highlighted the activities undertaken and the progress made since the last report [YUN 2005, p. 1328] in meeting the 2010 malaria goals, in the context of resolution 60/221 and the 2000 Abuja Declaration on Roll Back Malaria in Africa. It provided an evaluation of the Roll Back Malaria Programme for the period 2000-2005 and a vision for malaria control from 2006 onwards; reviewed, among other issues, developments in case-management and prevention and prospects for the elimination of malaria, including issues related to research and development and resource mobilization; addressed the problems associated with malaria in pregnant women and the special challenges of malaria epidemics in complex emergencies; and provided recommendations for the consideration of the Assembly.

Despite international attention and support for malaria control, the availability of new tools, including long-lasting insecticide-treated nets, rapid diagnostic tests and highly effective artemisinin-based combination therapies (ACTs), increased bilateral funding, together with the inception of the Global Fund to Fight AIDS, Tuberculosis and Malaria and the World Bank's increased funding for malaria, the record on malaria control progress over the past five years was mixed. The significant gap between targets and achievements could be attributed to several factors, such as the lack of strong technical leadership from WHO, the Roll Back Malaria Partnership's "loose" governance structure, which introduced inefficiencies in decision-making and ineffective coordination; incorrect technical policies adopted in countries, or correct ones adopted too slowly to save lives; lack of consensus on clear strategies by the Partnership for achieving agreed targets; and ineffective monitoring and evaluation. As a result, many of the funds pledged for malaria control did not become available or were significantly delayed.

In addition, a rapid increase in demand and inadequate attention to supply chain management led to global shortages of key commodities, notably single-source ACTs, or limited-source long-lasting insecticide-treated nets, resulting in the lack of cohesive, coordinated support to malaria-endemic countries. During the past five years, the Partnership had not been successful in implementing the most appropriate policies and strategies and the impact on the ground was negligible in comparison to the investment.

In terms of a vision for malaria control in 2006 and onwards, WHO re-strategized its policies by establishing the Global Malaria Programme to respond cohesively and strongly to the needs of malaria-endemic States. The Programme had already begun to demonstrate the success of that revitalized strategic direction. Broad stakeholder consensus was reached on the three main interventions—diagnosis of malaria cases and treatment with effective medicines, distribution of insecticide-treated nets to achieve full coverage of populations at risk, and indoor residual spraying as a major means of malaria vector control. The Roll Back Malaria Partnership initiated a "change process" to make the secretariat and the Board more responsive to needs, including revising the targets upwards to 80 per cent coverage and looking for ways to make the Partnership more effective. Working within the Roll Back Malaria "change process", WHO delivered more robust strategic and technical leadership on curative and preventive interventions, and worked with partners, such as UNICEF at the country level, to scale up the distribution of insecticide-treated nets, and with the World Bank, to ensure the adoption of appropriate drug policies and increased access to ACT worldwide. In 2006, WHO launched its Guidelines for the Treatment of Malaria.

In terms of funding and resource mobilization, approximately $3 billion annually, including $1.8 billion for Africa, was needed worldwide to effectively roll back malaria. The Global Fund, which was active in 73 countries, as at July, had disbursed a total of $748 million. Recent pledges from major donors had raised expectations that additional funds would be available for malaria. The United States doubled its funding, from $118 million in 2002 to $246 million in 2005. The Malaria Initiative announced a funding increase of more than $1.2 billion over five years for malaria prevention and treatment, and added Malawi, Mozambique, Rwanda and Senegal as focus countries. As at August, only half of the $1.5 billion promised at the 2005 summit of the Group of Eight (G-8) most industrialized countries [YUN 2005, 1328] had been reached. In 2006, the World Bank's total commitments for malaria control in Africa reached $167 million.

In terms of treatment, the shortfall in 2004 and 2005 of ACTs was remedied in 2006. The production capacity of the six major pharmaceutical companies for those therapies was estimated at 130 million treatment courses, exceeding public-sector demand. A sharp increase in production capacity of existing manufacturers and the entry of several new producers eliminated the bottleneck for long-lasting insecticide-treated nets. In the light of the need for malaria medicines to replace those being lost to parasite resistance, the Drugs for Neglected Diseases Initiative and pharmaceutical company partners, as well as the drug company Novartis and the Medicines for Malaria Venture, were developing three new formulations of existing ACT therapies. Research on malaria vaccines advanced further in 2006, with the Special Programme for Research and Training in Tropical Diseases, which was in its most advanced stages of clinical testing (phase III clinical trials).

The Secretary-General urged the General Assembly to call on malaria-endemic countries to apply WHO-recommended policies and strategies to their specific context; ensure adequate levels of skilled health personnel to meet technical and operational needs; respond to their need for stronger health systems and integrated health services delivery; prohibit the marketing of oral artemisinin monotherapies; waive taxes and tariffs for nets, drugs and malaria control products; and strengthen and develop, with WHO support, drug resistance surveillance systems. He also called on international partners to use WHO monitoring and evaluation systems as minimum core indicators; bilateral and multilateral funding partners to become fully knowledgeable about WHO technical policies and strategies; donor agencies and food-importing countries to issue a clear statement outlining their position on the use of dichlorodiphenyltrichloroethane (DDT) for indoor residual spraying; producers of long-lasting insecticide-treated nets to accelerate technology transfer to developing countries; and the international community to fight the counterfeit drug trade in developing countries, reach consensus on appropriate levels and sources for long-lasting insecticide-treated nets and artemisinin-based combination therapies, and increase financial support for the Global Fund.

GENERAL ASSEMBLY ACTION

On 22 December [meeting 84], the General Assembly adopted **resolution 61/228** [draft: A/60/L.50 & Add.1] without vote [agenda item 48].

2001-2010: Decade to Roll Back Malaria in Developing Countries, Particularly in Africa

The General Assembly,

Recalling that the period 2001-2010 has been proclaimed the Decade to Roll Back Malaria in Developing Countries, Particularly in Africa, by the General Assembly, and that combating HIV/AIDS, malaria, tuberculosis and other diseases is included in the internationally agreed development goals, including those contained in the United Nations Millennium Declaration,

Recalling also its resolution 60/221 of 23 December 2005 and all previous resolutions concerning the struggle against malaria in developing countries, particularly in Africa,

Bearing in mind the relevant resolutions of the Economic and Social Council relating to the struggle against malaria and diarrhoeal diseases, in particular resolution 1998/36 of 30 July 1998,

Taking note of the declarations and decisions on health issues adopted by the Organization of African Unity, in particular the declaration and plan of action on the "Roll Back Malaria" initiative adopted at the Extraordinary Summit of Heads of State and Government of the Organization of African Unity, held in Abuja on 24 and 25 April 2000, as well as decision AHG/Dec.155 (XXXVI) concerning the implementation of that declaration and plan of action, adopted by the Assembly of Heads of State and Government of the Organization of African Unity at its thirty-sixth ordinary session, held in Lomé from 10 to 12 July 2000,

Also taking note of the Maputo Declaration on Malaria, HIV/AIDS, Tuberculosis and Other Related Infectious Diseases, adopted by the Assembly of the African Union at its second ordinary session, held in Maputo from 10 to 12 July 2003, and the Abuja call for accelerated action towards universal access to HIV and AIDS, tuberculosis and malaria services in Africa, issued by the Heads of State and Government of the African Union at the special summit of the African Union on HIV and AIDS, tuberculosis and malaria, held in Abuja from 2 to 4 May 2006,

Recognizing the linkages in efforts being made to reach the targets set at the Abuja Summit in 2000 as necessary and important for the attainment of the "Roll Back Malaria" goal and the targets of the Millennium Declaration by 2010 and 2015, respectively,

Also recognizing that malaria-related ill health and deaths throughout the world can be substantially eliminated with political commitment and commensurate resources if the public is educated and sensitized about malaria and appropriate health services are made available, particularly in countries where the disease is endemic,

Emphasizing the importance of implementing the Millennium Declaration, and welcoming in this connection the commitment of Member States to respond to the specific needs of Africa,

Commending the efforts of the World Health Organization, the United Nations Children's Fund and other partners to fight malaria over the years, including the launching of the Roll Back Malaria Partnership in 1998,

Recalling resolution 58.2 adopted by the World Health Assembly on 23 May 2005 urging a broad range of national and international actions to scale up malaria control programmes,

Taking note of the Roll Back Malaria Global Strategic Plan 2005-2015 developed by the Roll Back Malaria Partnership,

1. *Takes note* of the note by the Secretary-General transmitting the report of the World Health Organization, and calls for support for the recommendations contained therein;

2. *Welcomes* the increased funding for malaria interventions and for research and development of preventative and control tools from the international community, through targeted funding from multilateral and bilateral sources and from the private sector;

3. *Calls upon* the international community to continue to support the "Roll Back Malaria" partner organizations, including the World Health Organization, the World Bank and the United Nations Children's Fund, as vital complementary sources of support for the efforts of malaria-endemic countries to combat the disease;

4. *Appeals* to the international community to work towards increased and sustained bilateral and multilateral assistance to combat malaria, including support for the Global Fund to Fight AIDS, Tuberculosis and Malaria, in order to assist States, in particular malaria-endemic countries, to implement sound national plans to control malaria in a sustained and equitable way that, inter alia, contributes to health system development;

5. *Welcomes* the contribution to the mobilization of resources for development by voluntary innovative financing initiatives taken by groups of Member States, and in this regard notes the International Drug Purchase Facility, UNITAID, the International Finance Facility for Immunization and the commitment to launch a pilot project in 2006 within the advance market commitment initiatives;

6. *Urges* malaria-endemic countries to work towards financial sustainability, to increase, to the extent possible, domestic resource allocation to malaria control and to create favourable conditions for working with the private sector in order to improve access to good-quality malaria services;

7. *Calls upon* Member States, in particular malaria-endemic countries, to establish and/or strengthen national policies and operational plans, aspiring to ensure that at least 80 per cent of those at risk of or suffering from malaria may benefit from major preventive and curative

interventions by 2010, in accordance with the technical recommendations of the World Health Organization, so as to ensure a reduction in the burden of malaria by at least 50 per cent by 2010 and 75 per cent by 2015;

8. *Urges* Member States to assess and respond to the needs for integrated human resources at all levels of the health system, in order to achieve the targets of the Abuja Declaration on Roll Back Malaria in Africa and the internationally agreed development goals of the United Nations Millennium Declaration, to take actions, as appropriate, to effectively govern the recruitment, training and retention of skilled health personnel, and to give particular focus to the availability of skilled personnel at all levels to meet technical and operational needs as increased funding for malaria control programmes becomes available;

9. *Calls upon* the international community, inter alia, by helping to meet the financial needs of the Global Fund to Fight AIDS, Tuberculosis and Malaria and through country-led initiatives with adequate international support, to intensify access to affordable, safe and effective antimalarial combination treatments, intermittent preventive treatment in pregnancies, insecticide-treated mosquito nets, including through the free distribution of such nets where appropriate, and insecticides for indoor residual spraying for malaria control, taking into account relevant international rules, standards and guidelines;

10. *Requests* relevant international organizations, in particular the World Health Organization and the United Nations Children's Fund, to assist efforts of national Governments to establish universal protection of young children and pregnant women in malaria-endemic countries, particularly in Africa, with insecticide-treated nets as rapidly as possible, with due regard to ensuring sustainability through full community participation and implementation through the health system;

11. *Encourages* all African countries that have not yet done so to implement the recommendations of the Abuja Summit in 2000 to reduce or waive taxes and tariffs for nets and other products needed for malaria control, both to reduce the price of the products to consumers and to stimulate free trade in those products;

12. *Expresses its concern* about the increase in resistant strains of malaria in several regions of the world, and calls upon Member States, with support from the World Health Organization, to strengthen surveillance systems for drug and insecticide resistance;

13. *Urges* all Member States experiencing resistance to conventional monotherapies to replace them with combination therapies, as recommended by the World Health Organization, and to develop the necessary financial, legislative and regulatory mechanisms in order to introduce artemisinin combination therapies at affordable prices and to prohibit the marketing of oral artemisinin monotherapies, in a timely manner;

14. *Recognizes* the importance of the development of safe and cost-effective vaccines and new medicines to prevent and treat malaria and the need for further and accelerated research, including into safe, effective and high-quality traditional therapies, using rigorous standards, including by providing support to the Special Programme for Research and Training in Tropical Diseases and through effective global partnerships such as the various malaria vaccine initiatives and the Medicines for Malaria Venture, where necessary stimulated by new incentives to secure their development;

15. *Calls upon* the international community, including through existing partnerships, to increase investment in and efforts towards the research and development of new, safe and affordable malaria-related medicines, products and technologies, such as vaccines, rapid diagnostic tests, insecticides and delivery modes, to prevent and treat malaria, especially for at-risk children and pregnant women, in order to enhance effectiveness and delay the onset of resistance;

16. *Reaffirms* the right to use, to the fullest extent, the provisions contained in the World Trade Organization Agreement on Trade-Related Aspects of Intellectual Property Rights (TRIPS Agreement), the Doha Declaration on the TRIPS Agreement and Public Health, the decision of the World Trade Organization's General Council of 30 August 2003 and amendments to article 31 of the Agreement, which provide flexibilities for the protection of public health, and in particular to promote access to medicines for all, including the production, under compulsory licensing, of generic drugs in the prevention and treatment of malaria;

17. *Resolves* to assist developing countries to employ the flexibilities outlined in the TRIPS Agreement in the fight against malaria and to strengthen their capacities for this purpose;

18. *Calls upon* the international community to support ways to expand access to and the affordability of key products, such as vector control measures, including indoor residual spraying, long-lasting insecticide-treated nets and artemisinin-based combination therapy for populations at risk of exposure to resistant strains of falciparum malaria in malaria-endemic countries, particularly in Africa, including the commitment of new funds, innovative mechanisms for the financing and national procurement of artemisinin-based combination therapy, and the scaling up of artemisinin production to meet the increased need;

19. *Applauds* the increased level of public-private partnerships for malaria control and prevention, including the financial and in kind contributions of private sector partners and companies operating in Africa, as well as increased engagement of non-governmental service providers;

20. *Encourages* the producers of long-lasting insecticide-treated nets to accelerate technology transfer to developing countries, and encourages malaria-endemic countries, including with the support of the International Finance Corporation, to explore and pursue possible opportunities to scale up production of long-lasting insecticide-treated nets;

21. *Calls upon* the international community and malaria-endemic countries, in accordance with existing guidelines and recommendations from the World Health Organization and the requirements of the Stockholm

Convention on Persistent Organic Pollutants to increase capacity for the safe, effective and judicious use of indoor residual spraying and other forms of vector control;

22. *Urges* the international community to become fully knowledgeable about World Health Organization technical policies and strategies, including for indoor residual spraying, insecticide-treated nets and case management, intermittent preventive treatment for pregnant women and monitoring of in vivo resistance studies to artemisinin-based combination therapy treatment, so that projects support those policies and strategies;

23. *Requests* the World Health Organization, the United Nations Children's Fund and donor agencies to provide support to those countries which choose to use DDT for indoor residual spraying so as to ensure that it is implemented in accordance with international rules, standards and guidelines, and to provide all possible support to malaria-endemic countries to manage the intervention effectively and prevent the contamination of agricultural products with DDT and other insecticides used for indoor residual spraying;

24. *Calls upon* malaria-endemic countries to encourage regional and intersectoral collaboration, both public and private, at all levels, especially in education, agriculture, economic development and the environment, to advance malaria control objectives;

25. *Calls upon* the international community to support increased interventions, in line with the recommendations of the World Health Organization and the Roll Back Malaria Partnership, in order to ensure their rapid, efficient and effective implementation, to strengthen health systems, to monitor and fight against the trade in counterfeit antimalarial medicines and prevent the distribution and use of them, and to support coordinated efforts, inter alia, by providing technical assistance to improve surveillance, monitoring and evaluation systems and their alignment with national plans and systems so as to better track and report changes in coverage, the need for scaling up recommended interventions and the subsequent reductions in the burden of malaria;

26. *Urges* Member States, the international community and all relevant actors, including the private sector, to promote the coordinated implementation and enhance the quality of malaria-related activities, including via the Roll Back Malaria Partnership, in accordance with national policies and operational plans that are consistent with the technical recommendations of the World Health Organization and recent efforts and initiatives, including the Paris Declaration on Aid Effectiveness;

27. *Requests* the Secretary-General to report to the General Assembly at its sixty-second session on the implementation of the present resolution under the agenda item entitled "2001-2010: Decade to Roll Back Malaria in Developing Countries, Particularly in Africa".

Global public health

On 26 May, the World Health Assembly, at its fifty-ninth session (Geneva, 22–27 May), in response to the emerging human cases of avian influenza, adopted a resolution [WHA59.2] calling for the immediate voluntary implementation of provisions of the revised International Health Regulations, 2005 [YUN 2005, p. 1331], which were considered relevant for the risk posed by avian influenza and a potential pandemic of human influenza. The provisions included rapid and transparent notification, support for countries requesting assistance in investigating and controlling outbreaks and recommendations for control measures.

On 17 March, WHO launched the new "stop TB strategy" to address the challenges facing countries in responding to tuberculosis, and to scale up TB-control activities. The new six-point strategy, which underpinned the Global Campaign to stop TB (2006-2015), was aimed at achieving the related MDG.

WHO Report. The Secretary-General, in response to General Assembly resolution 60/35 [YUN 2005, p. 1332], transmitted a September report [A/61/383] prepared by WHO on enhancing capacity-building in global public health. The report described the current state of key infectious diseases, including human cases of avian influenza, HIV/AIDS, tuberculosis, malaria and major health issues confronting developing countries and economies in transition, as well as frameworks and strategies that could prevent, detect, report, prepare for and respond to disease outbreaks and major epidemics. It stated that the ability of countries to respond to existing and emerging infectious diseases and chronic illnesses depended on robust national public health institutions and their organization and management, available trained health personnel, appropriate drugs and vaccines, and financing. To date, the inadequate supply of health personnel in particular limited those responses.

On the status of public health, the WHO report noted that the threat of a human influenza pandemic remained high and, in addition to the emergence of new pathogens such as H5N1, other well-characterized infectious diseases, including cholera, Marburg, Crimean-Congo, Dengue and Ebola haemorrhagic fevers, meningitis and yellow fever posed very significant threats to human health. HIV/AIDS, tuberculosis and malaria continued to afflict large numbers of people worldwide.

Concerning the revised International Health Regulations 2005, the report said WHO had, in 2006, asked all countries to identify their national focal point for the regulations, assess their capacities to meet the requirements outlined in annex 1 to World Health Assembly resolution 58.3 and secure the necessary resources to implement plans to eliminate gaps. Effective national implementation would require Member States to invest in, manage and improve their epidemiological surveillance and information management systems, laboratories, health preparedness systems and health communication, as well as ensure that core capabilities were in place and functioning by June 2012.

To address those challenges and enhance public health capacity, increased investment in health systems and personnel would be needed to deliver good outcomes and achieve internationally agreed development goals, including the MDGs.

Avian Influenza

In 2006, WHO released its strategic action plan for pandemic influenza, which set out five key action areas: reducing human exposure to the H5N1 virus; strengthening the early warning system; intensifying rapid containment operations; building capacity to cope with a pandemic; and coordinating global scientific research and development.

As at September, almost all countries had established an avian and human influenza preparedness plan. The coordinator of the United Nations response to influenza, David Nabarro, spearheaded the development of the Consolidated Action Plan for Contributions of the UN System, released on 3 July, outlining common objectives, strategic directions and results to be attained by the UN system and its international and regional partners. The Plan responded to Governments' requests for coordinated and sustained international support to implement influenza programmes.

At its 2006 substantive session on 10 July, in Geneva, the Economic and Social Council held a special event on Avian influenza: a global emergency, which addressed international coordination of the global emergency of avian influenza. During the event, in which senior officials of UN programmes and specialized agencies participated, the President of the Council called on all Member States to quickly fulfil the pledges made at the International Pledging Conference on Avian and Human Influenza, held in Beijing in January.

Road Safety

The United Nations Road Safety Collaboration, at its fifth meeting (Geneva, 30–31 October), called for support by Governments to prepare national events for the first United Nations Global Road Safety Week, to be held in 2007, through country offices of WHO, UNICEF, the World Bank, the Global Road Safety Partnership, the International Federation of Red Cross and Red Crescent Societies, and national automobile associations. The meeting also called for the creation of formal working groups on fleet safety and infrastructure and for a new General Assembly resolution on road safety in 2007.

In August, WHO, the Global Road Safety Partnership, the World Bank and the FIA Foundation for the Automobile and Society published a manual for road safety decision-makers and practitioners on how to increase helmet-wearing among users of two-wheeled vehicles.

On 26 January [A/60/658], the Russian Federation transmitted a document on the implementation of Assembly resolutions and the Secretary-General's reports to build capacity in road safety. On 23 April, the European Conference of Ministers of Transport, the World Bank and WHO launched the Road Safety Performance in the Russian Federation Peer Review, which provided an overview of the country's dimensions of the health burden of traffic-related injuries, including an analysis of the main risk factors, strategies and effective interventions to avoid them.

In 2006, the Commission for Global Road Safety published its report "Make Roads Safe: A new priority for sustainable development", which focused attention on the global road traffic injury epidemic, which had claimed the lives of more than 1.2 million people, injured around 50 million annually, and had an impact on every development objective, including delivery of the MDGs. The report included recommendations for addressing the problem, including the holding, in 2008, of a Ministerial Conference on Global Road Safety under UN auspices and the creation of a Global Road Safety Charter.

Food and agriculture

Food aid

World Food Programme

At its 2006 substantive session in July, the Economic and Social Council had before it two reports pertaining to the World Food Programme (WFP): the annual report of the Executive Director for 2005 [E/2006/14], and a report of the Executive Board [E/2006/36] containing the decisions and recommendations of its 2005 sessions. By **decision 2006/236** of 26 July, the Council took note of those reports.

The WFP Executive Board, at its 2006 sessions held in Rome—first regular session (20-23 February), annual session (12-16 June) and second regular session (6-9 November)—decided on organizational and programme matters and approved a number of projects.

WFP activities

The Annual Performance Report (APR) for 2006 [WFP/EB.A/2007/4] measured WFP activities during the year, in line with the performance and results framework laid out in the 2006-2009 strategic plan [YUN 2003, p. 1259] and the 2006-2007 biennial work plan approved in 2005 [YUN 2005, p. 1335].

In 2006, overall global food aid deliveries fell to an estimated 6.7 million tons, compared to 8.2 million tons in 2005. Of that amount, WFP delivered 4 million tons of food to 87.8 million people, down from 96.7 million people the previous year. Of those assisted, 16.4 million benefited from emergency operations, 47.1 million from protracted relief and recovery operations, and 24.3 million were reached by development projects. The figures reflected a year in which there were few major emergencies and WFP attention focused on protracted relief and recovery operations.

The Sudan continued to be one of the largest single-country operations, accounting for one fifth of the Programme's direct operational expenditures, which reached some 6.4 million people; Kenya, the second largest recipient, received $106 million worth of food aid. During the conflict in Lebanon (see p. 574), WFP reached 824,000 displaced persons with food assistance and supported the entire humanitarian community with logistics, security and telecommunications services. Natural disasters in 2006 challenged WFP to meet unforeseen needs in demanding environments. The earthquake in Indonesia in May, the natural disasters of short duration in Bolivia, Ecuador, Nicaragua and El Salvador, as well as floods in Nepal, prompted large-scale responses from WFP, which continued to address the food emergency in Ethiopia.

Children, representing two thirds of beneficiaries, remained the primary focus of WFP assistance. Women and children accounted for 76.4 million of WFP beneficiaries, with 7.2 million internally displaced persons, 1.9 million refugees and 1.2 million returnees.

At the regional level, sub-Saharan Africa received the largest share of WFP assistance, with 66 per cent of direct expenditures, followed by Asia, with 18 per cent, Latin America and the Caribbean, the Middle East and North Africa, 3 per cent each, and Eastern Europe and the Commonwealth of Independent States, 1 per cent.

Administrative and financial matters

Continued progress was made in addressing WFP organizational weaknesses, strengthening procedures and mainstreaming capacity-building initiatives. WFP was able to respond more rapidly and effectively, thanks to additional humanitarian response depots and a record number of donors and diverse partners. It signed an agreement with Islamic Relief Worldwide to improve services for beneficiaries in Muslim countries, which comprised about half of all beneficiaries in 2006. WFP also launched the *World Hunger Series,* which served as a global reference on hunger-related issues. It made substantial progress in improving management performance measurement and risk-management, with the percentage of targets met having increased since 2004. However, the challenge was to ensure that such practices matched the expectations of decision-makers. Although uneven funding affected a number of operations, a study found that advance funding mechanisms were significant in minimizing pipeline breaks and response times. WFP also improved reporting on corporate outcome indicators, providing evidence that its work with Governments, the private sector and individuals contributed to progress in 2006 toward achieving the MDGs.

The WFP Executive Board, in a joint meeting with the Executive Boards of UNDP/UNFPA and UNICEF (New York, 20 and 24 January) [DP/2006/15], discussed, among other subjects, simplification and harmonization, with a special focus on the programming process, and transition from relief to development, focusing on natural disasters. WFP and other Executive Board members of the United Nations Development Group initiated the first pilot joint office in Cape Verde as part of their initiatives on common country programming, common services and premises.

Resources and financing

In 2006, WFP operational expenditures totalled almost $2.7 billion, down from $2.9 billion in 2005. Confirmed contributions reached $2.7 billion, a slight decrease from the 2005 figure of $2.9 billion. The United States was again the largest contributor, providing some $1.1 billion to the Programme. Of the total contributions, $1.09 billion went to protracted relief and recovery operations, $1.04 million to the International Emergency Food Reserve, $248 million to development activities, $203 million to special operations, $31.9 million to the

Immediate Response Account, and $83.7 million to other initiatives.

Food security

Follow-up to the 1996 World Food Summit

At its one hundred and thirty-first session (Rome, 20-25 November) [CL 131/6], the Council of the Food and Agriculture Organization of the United Nations (FAO) considered the FAO report on the State of Food and Agriculture 2006 [CL 131/2] and a report of the FAO Committee on World Food Security (CFS) on assessment of the world food security situation [CFS:2006/2]. The Council also considered a summary of the outcome of the multi-stakeholder special forum held during the Committee's thirty-second session (Rome, 30 October–4 November) to review the implementation of the Plan of Action adopted at the 1996 World Food Summit [YUN 1996, p. 1129], which called on countries to halve the number of undernourished people by 2015.

According to the CFS assessment, as at June, 39 countries, comprising 25 in Africa, 11 in Asia and the Near East, 2 in Latin America and 1 in Europe, faced serious food shortages. Although various factors contributed to the shortages, civil strife and adverse weather were the most common. The report concluded that urgent attention and action were required to tackle the root causes of food insecurity over the long-term in sub-Saharan Africa, where most of the food emergencies occurred. Although detailed analysis was still required to confirm feasibility, the emerging opportunities for biofuel production in the region could potentially help mitigate chronic food insecurity, while development assistance focused on socially and ecologically sustainable biofuel production could meet increasing global alternative fuel demands.

International Year of Natural Fibres

On 25 November 2005, the FAO Conference (Rome, 19-26 November) adopted resolution 3/2005, declaring 2009 the International Year of Natural Fibres. Natural fibres were recognized as an important source of income for small farmers in low-income and developing countries, and also contributed to food security and poverty alleviation. The General Assembly, in resolution 61/189 (see below), joined FAO in the declaration.

GENERAL ASSEMBLY ACTION

On 20 December [meeting 83], the General Assembly, on the recommendation of the Second (Economic and Financial) Committee [A/61/420/Add. 4], adopted **resolution 61/189** without vote [agenda item 51 *(d)*].

International Year of Natural Fibres, 2009

The General Assembly,

Noting resolution 3/2005 of 25 November 2005 of the Conference of the Food and Agriculture Organization of the United Nations,

Noting also that the diverse range of natural fibres produced in many countries provides an important source of income for farmers, and thus can play an important role in contributing to food security and in eradicating poverty and hence in contributing to the achievement of the Millennium Development Goals,

1. *Decides* to proclaim 2009 the International Year of Natural Fibres;
2. *Invites* the Food and Agriculture Organization of the United Nations to facilitate the observance of the International Year of Natural Fibres, in collaboration with Governments, regional and international organizations, non-governmental organizations, the private sector and relevant organizations of the United Nations system, and further invites the Food and Agriculture Organization to keep the General Assembly informed of progress made in this regard;
3. *Calls upon* Governments and relevant regional and international organizations to make voluntary contributions and to lend other forms of support to the Year;
4. *Invites* non-governmental organizations and the private sector to make voluntary contributions to and to support the Year;
5. *Encourages* all Governments, the United Nations system and all other actors to take advantage of the Year in order to increase awareness of the importance of these natural products.

Nutrition

Standing Committee on Nutrition

At its thirty-third session (Geneva, Switzerland, 13-17 March), the United Nations System Standing Committee on Nutrition conducted a symposium entitled "Tackling the Double Burden of Malnutrition: A Global Agenda". The Committee considered reports from the working groups on breastfeeding and complementary feeding; nutrition of school-aged children; nutrition and HIV/AIDS; nutrition in emergencies; nutrition throughout the life cycle; nutrition, ethics and human rights; micronutrients; household food security; and capacity development in food.

On 17 March, participants agreed on a statement entitled "Double Burden of Malnutrition—A common agenda", which called on Governments to promote actions that reduced under- and overnutrition, as well as diet-related chronic diseases, within the context of respecting, protecting and fulfilling the right to adequate food. UN agencies were called upon to accelerate the prevention and mitigation of all forms of malnutrition throughout the life cycle, and to promote and mainstream nutrition programmes at the country level into national development policies. Among the top global priorities were empowering women and protecting their nutrition, human rights and entitlements, including those of their children; focusing on the window of opportunity from pre-conception to around 24 months of age, the critical period of establishing lifelong health; urging schools to be nutrition- and physical activity-friendly; and promoting production and consumption of culturally appropriate foods rich in micronutrients.

The Working Group on Nutrition, Ethics and Human Rights, along with the Working Group on Nutrition Throughout the Life Cycle, issued a statement on the human rights of children and adolescents to adequate food and to be free from obesity and related diseases. The Working Group on Household Food Security, in a statement on avian influenza, recommended that the Standing Committee encourage relevant UN agencies and partners to commit resources to determine the impact of avian influenza on smallholders in developing countries, as well as the ability of government and UN programmes to contain outbreaks.

UNU activities

The United Nations University, through its Food and Nutrition Programme for Human and Social Development (UNU-FNP), assisted developing regions in enhancing individual, organizational and institutional capacities, carried out coordinated global research activities and served as an academic arm for the UN system in areas of food and nutrition that were best addressed in a non-regulatory, non-normative environment.

In April, UNU-FNP and WHO completed a major global nutrition research initiative, culminating in the release of new growth standards for infants and young children that would allow for more accurate malnutrition estimates. Supported by the United States, the next stage was a global inter-agency review of the feasibility of similar international anthropometric standards for school-aged children, which was motivated by the worldwide increase in childhood obesity. Eleven commissioned papers were published in the December issue of the UNU-FNP *Food and Nutrition Bulletin*. UNU-FNP was also leading a global review of potential approaches for harmonization of nutrient-based dietary standards, aimed at resolving differences in setting national and international standards that made it difficult to set public and clinical health objectives, design food policies and ensure that national standards were applied transparently to trade and regulatory activities. Ten of the commissioned papers would be published in March 2007.

During the year, UNU-FNP organized capacity-building initiatives in Africa, Latin America, Asia, the Middle East and Eastern Europe, as well as web-based collaboration in the nutritional sciences, through its African Nutrition Leadership Programme. The UNU Institute for Natural Resources in Africa (INRA) joined with the International Crop Research Institute for the Semi-Arid Tropics and other concerned agricultural research organizations to implement a project on enhancing rainwater and nutrient-use efficiency for improved crop productivity, farm income and rural livelihoods in the Volta Basin. In April, five UNU-Kirin Fellows from Asia completed their 12-month training programme at the National Food Research Institute in Tsukuba, Japan, and five new Fellows began their training.

Chapter XIV

International drug control

In 2006, United Nations efforts to strengthen international cooperation in countering the world drug problem were conducted mainly through the work of the Commission on Narcotic Drugs, the International Narcotic Control Board (INCB) and the United Nations Office on Drugs and Crime (UNODC). Drug control activities throughout the UN system focused, in particular, on carrying out the 1999 Action Plan for the Implementation of the Declaration on the Guiding Principles of Drug Demand Reduction, which served as a guide for Member States in adopting strategies and programmes for reducing illicit drug demand in order to achieve significant results by 2008.

UNODC coordinated the drug control activities of UN organizations and delivered technical assistance and knowledge-based expertise to Member States. As the custodian of international conventions to counter the world drug problem, it assisted States in complying with the provisions of those conventions and supported INCB in monitoring their implementation. Throughout 2006, UNODC enhanced its policy dialogue with financial stakeholders, expanded its partnership network and continued to improve data and analysis made available to States and to strengthen the international drug control system through its global programmes and regional and country projects. The Office increased support for alternative development programmes and initiated activities aimed at mainstreaming efforts to combat illicit crop cultivation, including development-oriented drug control interventions within broader development programmes.

The Commission on Narcotic Drugs—the main UN policy-making body dealing with drug control—recommended a number of draft resolutions to the Economic and Social Council and adopted resolutions on the follow-up to the General Assembly's twentieth (1998) special session on countering the world drug problem, the implementation of international drug control treaties, demand reduction and the prevention of drug abuse, and illicit drug trafficking and supply.

In July, the Council urged Governments to contribute to maintaining a balance between the licit supply of and demand for opiate raw materials for medical and scientific needs and to preventing the proliferation of sources of production of opiate raw materials. It emphasized the importance of mainstreaming alternative development into national and international development strategies and called upon States to adopt policies that promoted international cooperation, including in the area of alternative development, and to share their experience and expertise in the eradication of illicit crops. Noting the increased illicit cultivation of opium poppy in Afghanistan, the Council urged that country to maintain drug control among its highest priorities and to enhance regional cooperation. It welcomed the bilateral and multilateral support provided by the international community and its commitment to the development and reconstruction of Afghanistan. The Council also called upon States to combat the traffic in narcotic drugs and psychotropic substances, in accordance with the Baku Accord on Regional Cooperation against Illicit Drugs and Related Matters: a Vision for the Twenty-first Century. In December, the Assembly adopted a resolution on international cooperation against the world drug problem, which addressed guiding principles; international conventions; implementation of the outcome of the twentieth special session; demand reduction; international cooperation in illicit crop eradication and alternative development; illicit synthetic drugs; judicial cooperation; data collection; countering money-laundering; and the UN drug control machinery.

INCB reviewed the implementation of alternative development programmes, highlighting best practices and models for increasing their effectiveness. It continued to oversee the implementation of the three major international drug control conventions, analyse the drug situation worldwide and draw the attention of Governments to weaknesses in national control and treaty compliance, making suggestions and recommendations for improvements at the national and international levels.

Follow-up to the twentieth special session

Report of Secretary-General. In response to General Assembly resolution 60/178 [YUN 2005, p. 1340], the Secretary-General, in an August report [A/61/221] on international cooperation aimed at combating the world drug problem, provided an overview of the implementation of that resolution, with a focus on transit countries, as well as the mandates contained in the outcome of the Assembly's twentieth special session on countering the world drug problem [YUN 1998, p. 1135]. The report described trends in the world drug markets and reviewed related issues in the 2005 World Summit Outcome [YUN 2005, p. 48]. It also covered follow-up activities by the Commission on Narcotic Drugs; adherence to international conventions on drugs and crime; international cooperation among judicial and law enforcement authorities; countering money-laundering; global trends in illicit manufacture, trafficking and abuse of amphetamine-type stimulants (ATS) and their precursors; and the work of the subsidiary bodies of the Commission. It also considered demand reduction, including drug abuse prevention, treatment and rehabilitation; international cooperation in illicit crop eradication and alternative development; and action by the UN system, including the work of the United Nations Office on Drugs and Crime (UNODC); strengthening cooperation with Member States and relevant agencies and organizations; and broadening the UNODC donor base and increasing voluntary contributions.

The Secretary-General foresaw long-term containment of the world drug problem and encouraging signs for the medium-term. Global opium production had fallen, while cocaine production remained stable. Seizures of both drugs, especially cocaine, reached record levels. Overall, global drug market trends appeared to be moving in the right direction, but Governments needed to intensify their efforts to reduce both supply and demand. He recommended that measures against drugs and crime be included in strategies to achieve sustained economic development, and States, relevant intergovernmental and international financial institutions and development organizations should mainstream drug and crime issues into their programmes. He called upon States that had not done so to become parties to and implement the international drug control conventions. States, the international community, non-governmental organizations (NGOs) and civil society should evaluate progress made in meeting the goals and targets set at the Assembly's twentieth special session. States should also make significant contributions to the Fund of the UNODC drug control programme.

Commission on Narcotic Drugs. On 17 March [E/2006/28 (res. 49/1)], the Commission on Narcotic Drugs underscored the value of a global assessment by Member States of the progress achieved and the difficulties encountered in meeting the goals and targets set by the Assembly's twentieth special session. Following the global assessment, there should be a period of reflection by States, based on the international drug control treaties and taking account of measures that had led to positive outcomes and those aspects requiring greater effort. The Commission called upon UNODC to engage with national and regional experts from all geographical regions, as well as from relevant international organizations in the field of drug control, on the collection and use of complementary drug-related data and expertise to support the assessment. The Executive Director should report to the Commission on the results of those efforts, together with recommendations on the collection and use of data and expertise. The Executive Director was requested to report in 2006 on the implementation of the Commission's resolution.

Also on 17 March [res. 49/2], the Commission acknowledged the contribution made by civil society in curbing drug abuse, particularly with regard to demand reduction, and encouraged States to work with NGOs in developing and implementing demand reduction policies and programmes. It also encouraged civil society and NGOs to raise public awareness regarding the negative consequences of drug abuse, and urged NGOs to reflect on their achievements in addressing the drug problem and to report to their national bodies, in the context of reporting on the goals and targets for 2008. The Commission called upon the Executive Director to work with relevant UN entities, international organizations and NGOs to facilitate participation by NGO representatives in the preparations for the tenth anniversary of the Assembly's twentieth special session.

GENERAL ASSEMBLY ACTION

On 20 December [meeting 82], the General Assembly, on the recommendation of the Third (Social, Humanitarian and Cultural) Committee [A/61/445], adopted **resolution 61/183** without vote [agenda item 99].

International cooperation against the world drug problem

The General Assembly,

Recalling the United Nations Millennium Declaration, the provisions of the 2005 World Summit Outcome addressing the world drug problem, its resolution 60/178 of 16 December 2005 and its other previous resolutions,

Reaffirming the Political Declaration adopted by the General Assembly at its twentieth special session and the importance of meeting the objectives targeted for 2008,

Reaffirming also the joint ministerial statement adopted at the ministerial segment of the forty-sixth session of the Commission on Narcotic Drugs, the Action Plan for the Implementation of the Declaration on the Guiding Principles of Drug Demand Reduction and the Action Plan on International Cooperation on the Eradication of Illicit Drug Crops and on Alternative Development,

Gravely concerned that, despite continued increased efforts by States, relevant organizations, civil society and non-governmental organizations, the drug problem continues to constitute a serious threat to public health and safety and the well-being of humanity, in particular children and young people, and to the national security and sovereignty of States, and that it undermines socio-economic and political stability and sustainable development,

Concerned by the serious challenges and threats posed by the continuing links between illicit drug trafficking and terrorism and other national and transnational criminal activities and transnational criminal networks, inter alia, trafficking in human beings, especially women and children, money-laundering, financing of terrorism, corruption, trafficking in arms and trafficking in chemical precursors, and reaffirming that strong and effective international cooperation is needed to counter these threats,

Bearing in mind that the ten-year assessment of the implementation by Member States of the goals and targets of the twentieth special session of the General Assembly is scheduled for 2008, and looking forward to its outcome,

Taking note with concern of the report of the United Nations Office on Drugs and Crime entitled "Afghanistan Opium Survey 2006", which emphasized that the cultivation and production of and trafficking in narcotic drugs had significantly increased and threatened the security and stability of that country and had negative regional and international implications, taking note of Economic and Social Council resolution 2006/32 of 27 July 2006 entitled "Support for the National Drug Control Strategy of the Government of Afghanistan", welcoming the ongoing efforts of Afghanistan in the fight against narcotics, and calling upon the Government of Afghanistan and the international community to intensify those efforts within the framework of the Afghanistan Compact,

Recognizing that international cooperation in countering drug abuse and illicit production and trafficking has shown that positive results can be achieved through sustained and collective efforts, and expressing its appreciation for the initiatives in this regard,

Bearing in mind the important role that civil society, including non-governmental organizations, plays in combating the drug problem,

Taking note of the thematic debate on alternative development as an important drug control strategy and establishing alternative development as a cross-cutting issue, held by the Commission on Narcotic Drugs at its forty-ninth session,

1. *Reaffirms* that countering the world drug problem is a common and shared responsibility that must be addressed in a multilateral setting, requires an integrated and balanced approach and must be carried out in full conformity with the purposes and principles of the Charter of the United Nations and other provisions of international law, and in particular with full respect for the sovereignty and territorial integrity of States, the principle of non-intervention in the internal affairs of States and all human rights and fundamental freedoms, and on the basis of the principles of equal rights and mutual respect;

2. *Also reaffirms* that there shall be a balanced approach between demand reduction and supply reduction, each reinforcing the other, in an integrated approach to solving the drug problem;

3. *Urges* States that have not done so to consider ratifying or acceding to, and States parties to implement all the provisions of, the Single Convention on Narcotic Drugs of 1961 as amended by the 1972 Protocol, the Convention on Psychotropic Substances of 1971 and the United Nations Convention against Illicit Traffic in Narcotic Drugs and Psychotropic Substances of 1988;

4. *Invites* all States, as a matter of priority, to consider signing, ratifying or acceding to, and States parties to fully implement, the United Nations Convention against Transnational Organized Crime and the Protocols thereto and the United Nations Convention against Corruption, in order to counter comprehensively the transnational criminal activities that are related to illicit drug trafficking;

5. *Urges* all States to promote and implement the outcome of the twentieth special session of the General Assembly, as well as the outcome of the ministerial segment of the forty-sixth session of the Commission on Narcotic Drugs, to implement the Action Plan for the Implementation of the Declaration on the Guiding Principles of Drug Demand Reduction and to strengthen their national efforts to counter the abuse of illicit drugs in their population;

6. *Calls upon* States and other relevant actors to evaluate progress made since 1998 towards meeting, in their respective areas of concern, the goals and targets set at the twentieth special session of the General Assembly;

7. *Calls upon* all States to strengthen their efforts to achieve the goals set for 2008 at the twentieth special session of the General Assembly, by:

(a) Promoting international initiatives to eliminate or reduce significantly the manufacture and marketing of and trafficking in illicit drugs and other illicit psychotropic substances, including synthetic drugs, the diversion of precursors and money-laundering;

(b) Achieving significant and measurable results in the field of demand reduction, including through prevention and treatment strategies and programmes to reduce drug use;

8. *Urges* Member States to fulfil their reporting obligations on the follow-up action to implement the

outcome of the twentieth special session of the General Assembly on the world drug problem and to report fully on all measures agreed upon at the special session;

9. *Encourages* States to consider consulting and working with civil society, including non-governmental organizations, in developing, implementing and evaluating policies and programmes, in particular those related to demand reduction and prevention of drug abuse, and to consider cooperating with civil society, including non-governmental organizations, in alternative development programmes;

10. *Urges* all Member States to implement the Action Plan for the Implementation of the Declaration on the Guiding Principles of Drug Demand Reduction and to strengthen their national efforts to counter the abuse of illicit drugs in their population, in particular among children and young people;

11. *Calls upon* States and organizations with expertise in community capacity-building to provide, as needed, access to treatment, health care and social services for drug users, in particular those living with HIV/AIDS and other blood-borne diseases, and to extend support to States requiring such expertise, consistent with the international drug control treaties;

12. *Urges* States, in order to achieve a significant and measurable reduction of drug abuse by 2008:

(a) To further implement comprehensive demand reduction policies and programmes, including research, covering all the drugs under international control, in order to raise public awareness of the drug problem, paying special attention to prevention and education and providing, especially to young people and others at risk, information on developing life skills, making healthy choices and engaging in drug-free activities;

(b) To further develop and implement comprehensive demand reduction policies, including risk reduction activities, under the supervision of competent health authorities, that are in line with sound medical practice and the international drug control treaties and that reduce the adverse health and social consequences of drug abuse, and to provide a wide range of comprehensive services for the treatment, rehabilitation and social reintegration of drug abusers, with appropriate resources being devoted to such services, since social exclusion constitutes an important risk factor for drug abuse;

(c) To enhance early intervention programmes that dissuade children and young people from using illicit drugs, including, inter alia, polydrug use and the recreational use of substances such as cannabis and synthetic drugs, especially amphetamine-type stimulants, and to encourage the active participation of the younger generation and their families in campaigns against drug abuse;

(d) To consider strengthening and implementing broadly based prevention and treatment programmes and to ensure that such programmes adequately address the gender-specific barriers that limit access for young girls and women, taking into account all attendant circumstances, including social and clinical histories, in the context of education, the family and the community, as appropriate;

13. *Reaffirms* the need for a comprehensive approach to the elimination of illicit narcotic crops in line with the Action Plan on International Cooperation on the Eradication of Illicit Drug Crops and on Alternative Development, adopted at the twentieth special session of the General Assembly;

14. *Invites* States to continue to strengthen their efforts to implement innovative alternative programmes, inter alia, in reforestation, agriculture and small and medium enterprises, and stresses the importance of the United Nations system and the international community's contributing to the economic and social development of the communities that benefit from such programmes;

15. *Calls for* a comprehensive approach integrating alternative development programmes, including, where appropriate, preventive alternative development, into wider economic and social development programmes, with the support of deeper international cooperation and the participation of the private sector, as appropriate;

16. *Invites* States to consider adjusting their drug control strategies, taking into account, inter alia, the results of the annual surveys by the United Nations Office on Drugs and Crime of illicit crop cultivation;

17. *Calls upon* Member States and national and international development organizations to increase their efforts to empower local communities and authorities in project areas and to enhance their participation in the decision-making process in order to increase their ownership of the development measures taken in accordance with national legislation and the sustainability of those measures and to create a law-abiding and prosperous rural society;

18. *Encourages* States to establish or strengthen mechanisms and procedures to ensure strict control of substances used to manufacture illicit drugs, to support international operations aimed at preventing their diversion, including through coordination and cooperation between regulatory and enforcement services involved in precursor control, in cooperation with the International Narcotics Control Board, and to counter smuggling networks effectively, particularly in source and transit countries, by conducting, inter alia, backtracking law enforcement investigations;

19. *Urges* all States and relevant international organizations to cooperate closely with the International Narcotics Control Board, in particular in Project Cohesion and Project Prism, in order to enhance the success of those international initiatives and to initiate, where appropriate, investigations by their law enforcement authorities into seizures and cases involving the diversion or smuggling of precursors and essential equipment, with a view to tracking them back to the source of diversion in order to prevent continuing illicit activity;

20. *Reaffirms* that preventing the diversion of precursors from legitimate commerce to illicit drug manufacture is an essential component of the comprehensive strategy against drug abuse and trafficking, which requires the effective cooperation of exporting, importing and transit States, and calls upon all States to adopt and implement measures to prevent the diversion of precursors to illicit drug manufacture, in cooperation with competent inter-

national and regional bodies, in particular the International Narcotics Control Board, and, if necessary and to the extent possible, with the private sector of each State, in accordance with the objectives targeted for 2008 in the Political Declaration adopted by the General Assembly at its twentieth special session and the resolution on the control of precursors also adopted at the special session;

21. *Emphasizes* the need to ensure that adequate mechanisms are in place, where necessary and to the extent possible, to prevent the diversion of preparations containing substances listed in tables I and II of the United Nations Convention against Illicit Traffic in Narcotic Drugs and Psychotropic Substances of 1988, pertaining to illicit drug manufacture, in particular those containing ephedrine and pseudoephedrine, that could easily be used or recovered by readily applicable means;

22. *Stresses* that international cooperation on domestic precursor policies and practices would assist in complementing existing law enforcement cooperative initiatives, and encourages States to cooperate at the regional level on measures to prevent and control the domestic diversion of precursors, drawing on best practices and sharing experiences;

23. *Invites* Member States to continue to share information on illicit synthetic drugs and other emerging substances of abuse with the United Nations Office on Drugs and Crime and the International Narcotics Control Board;

24. *Calls upon* Member States to strengthen international cooperation among judicial and law enforcement authorities, at all levels, in order to prevent and combat illicit drug trafficking and to share and promote best operational practices in order to interdict illicit drug trafficking, including by establishing and strengthening regional mechanisms, providing technical assistance and establishing effective methods for cooperation, in particular in the areas of air, maritime, port and border control and in the implementation of extradition treaties, while respecting international human rights obligations;

25. *Urges* Member States, consistent with their legal systems, to cooperate with a view to enhancing the effectiveness of law enforcement action in relation to the use of the Internet to combat drug-related crime;

26. *Stresses* that data collection, analysis and evaluation of the results of ongoing national and international policies and programmes aimed at eliminating and reducing demand and supply are essential tools for further developing sound, evidence-based drug control strategies, and therefore encourages Member States to further develop and institutionalize monitoring and evaluation tools and to utilize existing available data, including from drug testing laboratories, research centres and other sources, as appropriate, and to exchange and share information, to the extent possible, at all levels;

27. *Urges* States to strengthen action, in particular international cooperation and technical assistance aimed at preventing and combating the laundering of proceeds derived from drug trafficking and related criminal activities, with the support of the United Nations system, international institutions such as the World Bank and the International Monetary Fund, as well as regional development banks and, where appropriate, the Financial Action Task Force on Money Laundering and similarly styled regional bodies, to develop and strengthen comprehensive international regimes to combat money-laundering and its possible links with organized crime and the financing of terrorism, and to improve information-sharing among financial institutions and agencies in charge of preventing and detecting the laundering of those proceeds;

28. *Calls upon* States to consider including provisions in their national drug control plans for the establishment of national networks to enhance their respective capabilities to prevent, monitor, control and suppress serious offences connected with money-laundering and the financing of terrorism, to counter in general all acts of transnational organized crime and to supplement existing regional and international networks dealing with money-laundering;

29. *Reaffirms its resolve* to continue to strengthen the United Nations machinery for international drug control, in particular the Commission on Narcotic Drugs, the United Nations Office on Drugs and Crime and the International Narcotics Control Board, in order to enable them to fulfil their mandates;

30. *Encourages* the Commission on Narcotic Drugs, as the global coordinating body in international drug control and as the governing body of the drug programme of the United Nations Office on Drugs and Crime, and the International Narcotics Control Board to continue their useful work on the control of precursors and other chemicals used in the illicit manufacture of narcotic drugs and psychotropic substances;

31. *Notes* that the International Narcotics Control Board needs sufficient resources to carry out all its mandates, including those that will enable it to perform effectively its task within the framework of Project Cohesion and Project Prism, and therefore urges Member States to commit themselves in a common effort to assigning adequate and sufficient budgetary resources to the Board, in accordance with Economic and Social Council resolution 1996/20 of 23 July 1996, emphasizes the need to maintain its capacity, inter alia, through the provision of appropriate means by the Secretary-General and adequate technical support by the United Nations Office on Drugs and Crime, and calls for enhanced cooperation and understanding between Member States and the Board to enable it to implement all its mandates under the international drug control conventions;

32. *Reaffirms* the importance of the United Nations Office on Drugs and Crime and its regional offices in building capacity at the local level in the fight against transnational organized crime and drug trafficking, and urges the Office to consider regional vulnerabilities, projects and impact in the fight against drug trafficking, in particular in developing countries, when deciding to close or allocate offices, with a view to maintaining an effective level of support to national and regional efforts in combating the world drug problem;

33. *Welcomes* the work carried out by the United Nations Office on Drugs and Crime in implementing its mandate, and requests the Office to continue:

(*a*) To strengthen a constructive and effective dialogue with Member States and also to ensure continued improvement in management, so as to contribute to enhanced and sustainable programme delivery and further encourage the Executive Director to maximize the effectiveness of the drug programme of the United Nations Office on Drugs and Crime, inter alia, through the full implementation of Commission on Narcotic Drugs resolutions, in particular the recommendations contained therein;

(*b*) To strengthen cooperation with Member States and with United Nations programmes, funds and relevant agencies, as well as relevant regional organizations and agencies and non-governmental organizations, and to provide, upon request, assistance in implementing the outcome of the twentieth special session of the General Assembly;

(*c*) To increase its assistance, within the available voluntary resources, to countries that are deploying efforts to reduce illicit crop cultivation by, in particular, adopting alternative development programmes and incorporating them into wider economic and social development programmes, and to explore new and innovative funding mechanisms;

(*d*) To allocate, while keeping the balance between supply and demand reduction programmes, adequate resources to allow it to fulfil its role in the implementation of the Action Plan for the Implementation of the Declaration on the Guiding Principles of Drug Demand Reduction, and to support countries, upon their request, in further continuing to develop and implement drug demand reduction policies;

(*e*) To take into account the outcome of the twentieth special session of the General Assembly, to include in its report on illicit drug trafficking an updated, objective and comprehensive assessment of worldwide trends in illicit traffic and transit in narcotic drugs and psychotropic substances, including methods and routes used, and to recommend ways and means of improving the capacity of States along those routes to address all aspects of the drug problem;

(*f*) To engage, subject to the availability of extrabudgetary resources, with national and regional experts from all geographical regions, as well as experts from relevant international organizations in the field of drug control, on the collection and use of complementary drug-related data and expertise to support the global assessment by Member States of the implementation of the declarations and measures adopted by the General Assembly at its twentieth special session;

(*g*) To publish the *World Drug Report*, with comprehensive and balanced information about the world drug problem, and to seek additional extrabudgetary resources for its publication in all the official languages;

(*h*) To provide technical assistance, from available voluntary contributions for that purpose, to those States identified by relevant international bodies as the most affected by the transit of drugs, in particular developing countries in need of such assistance and support;

(*i*) To provide assistance to Member States requesting support in establishing or strengthening scientific and forensic capabilities, and to promote the integration of scientific support to national, regional and international drug control frameworks, legislation and practices;

(*j*) To provide legal advisory services to Member States, upon request, in support of their implementation of the international drug control conventions;

(*k*) To share information with Member States on the work carried out towards the assessment of the implementation of the goals and targets of the twentieth special session of the General Assembly;

(*l*) To report annually to the General Assembly on the work of the Office in connection with the areas mentioned in the present paragraph;

34. *Urges* all Governments to provide the fullest possible financial and political support to the United Nations Office on Drugs and Crime by widening its donor base and increasing voluntary contributions, in particular general-purpose contributions, so as to enable it to continue, expand and strengthen its operational and technical cooperation activities, within its mandates, and recommends that a sufficient share of the regular budget of the United Nations be allocated to the Office to enable it to carry out its mandates and to work towards securing assured and predictable funding;

35. *Encourages* the meetings of the Heads of National Drug Law Enforcement Agencies and of the Subcommission on Illicit Drug Traffic and Related Matters in the Near and Middle East of the Commission on Narcotic Drugs to continue to contribute to the strengthening of regional and international cooperation;

36. *Welcomes* the outcome of the Second Ministerial Conference on Drug Trafficking Routes from Afghanistan, organized by the Government of the Russian Federation in cooperation with the United Nations Office on Drugs and Crime and held in Moscow from 26 to 28 June 2006, in continuance of the Paris Pact initiative, and calls upon States to strengthen international and regional cooperation to counter the threat to the international community posed by the illicit production of and trafficking in drugs originating in Afghanistan and continue to take concerted measures within the framework of the Paris Pact;

37. *Calls upon* the relevant United Nations agencies and entities and other international organizations, and invites international financial institutions, including regional development banks, to mainstream drug control issues into their programmes, and calls upon the United Nations Office on Drugs and Crime to maintain its leading role by providing relevant information and technical assistance;

38. *Takes note* of the report of the Secretary-General, and, taking into account the promotion of integrated reporting, requests the Secretary-General to submit to the General Assembly at its sixty-second session a report on the implementation of the present resolution.

Conventions

International efforts to control narcotic drugs were governed by three global conventions: the 1961 Single Convention on Narcotic Drugs [YUN 1961, p. 382], which, with some exceptions of detail, replaced earlier narcotics treaties and was amended by the 1972 Protocol [YUN 1972, p. 397] to strengthen the role of the International Narcotics Control Board (INCB); the 1971 Convention on Psychotropic Substances [YUN 1971, p. 380]; and the 1988 United Nations Convention against Illicit Traffic in Narcotic Drugs and Psychotropic Substances [YUN 1988, p. 690].

As at 31 December 2006, 181 States were parties to the 1961 Convention, as amended by the 1972 Protocol. During 2006, Montenegro acceded to the Convention, in addition to Angola, Bhutan, Cambodia and Nicaragua, which had acceded the previous year.

The number of parties to the 1971 Convention stood at 180 as at 31 December 2006, with the accession of Montenegro.

At year's end, 180 States and the European Community were parties to the 1988 Convention, with Gabon, Montenegro and Vanuatu acceding in 2006.

Commission action. In March [E/2006/28], the Commission on Narcotic Drugs reviewed implementation of the international drug control treaties. It had before it the INCB report covering its 2005 activities [YUN 2005, p. 1348] and the 2005 INCB technical report on the implementation of article 12 of the 1988 Convention entitled "Precursors and Chemicals Frequently Used in the Illicit Manufacture of Narcotic Drugs and Psychotropic Substances" [E/INCB/2005/4].

The Commission acknowledged the importance of a comprehensive approach to alternative development, incorporating aspects of community development, sustainable social and economic development and preventive alternative development. The Commission stressed the importance of prevention at all levels and agreed that civil society played a central role in preventing illicit drug trafficking and abuse. As to the supply of and demand for opiates used for medical purposes, it welcomed the joint activities undertaken by the World Health Organization (WHO) and INCB to facilitate the treatment of pain using opioid analgesics and urged Governments to ensure that opioids were available to patients who required them. It also called upon Governments to ensure that the provisions of the international treaties were implemented, so as to prevent traffickers from taking advantage of any loopholes in national and international control measures. The Commission welcomed INCB efforts in combating the smuggling of drugs by mail and urged Governments to strengthen their national control measures by limiting the number of entry points for parcels and ensuring that regular and thorough searches of mail were conducted for illicit drug consignments. Regarding the 1988 Convention, and in particular the implementation of article 12, the Commission recognized the importance of universal adherence to that Convention and of actions to implement it. The Commission urged Governments that had not done so to ratify the Convention and implement its provisions as soon as possible. It noted that the illicit manufacture of synthetic drugs, in particular amphetamine-type stimulants (ATS), had spread beyond the countries initially affected by their abuse and that all regions were experiencing similar problems. The Commission encouraged Governments to adopt the new electronic system of pre-export notifications, which was a quick and effective means of exchanging information on individual shipments in licit international trade, and stressed the importance of investigating cases of diversion or attempted diversion. It welcomed INCB role in initiating an assessment of Operation Purple and Operation Topaz, resulting in the merger of the two operations into a single activity, called Project Cohesion—a global initiative for assisting countries in addressing the diversion of acetic anhydride and potassium permanganate—which provided for the exchange of real time information, backtracking investigations and regular evaluation of activities.

On 17 March [E/2006/28 (res. 49/3)], the Commission requested Member States to provide INCB with annual estimates of their legitimate requirements for 3,4 methylenedioxyphenyl-2-propanone, pseudoephedrine, ephedrine and phenyl-2-propanone and estimated requirements for imports of preparations containing those substances that could be easily used or recovered by readily applicable means, and to report to INCB on the feasibility and usefulness of preparing, reporting and using those estimates in preventing diversion. It called upon INCB to provide those estimates to States in a manner that ensured that they were used only for drug control purposes; and requested exporting States to verify the legitimacy of each export authorization for those substances and for preparations containing them. Exporting States should continue, under Project Prism, to provide INCB with information on their shipments and on preparations containing them, subject to national legislation and regulations.

States should permit INCB to share with concerned national law enforcement and regulatory authorities shipment information on preparations containing those substances, following the standard operating procedures established under Project Prism and using the online system of pre-export notifications or other mechanisms. Importing States should ensure that the quantities of those substances and preparations containing them were commensurate with their legitimate requirements for manufacture or domestic consumption, using INCB estimates, and carry out backtracking investigations, providing information to INCB and exporting States. The Commission requested the Secretary-General to ensure that INCB precursor programmes were adequately funded, and invited Member States to provide additional support.

Also on 17 March [res. 49/6], the Commission called upon Member States to pay attention to the emerging problem of widespread abuse of and trafficking in ketamine, in particular in East and South-East Asia, and to place it on the list of substances controlled under their national legislation, where the domestic situation so required. It encouraged States to adopt a system of import-export certificates and to share, through bilateral, regional and international channels, relevant information on the licit import and export of ketamine and its abuse and trafficking.

On the same date [res. 49/7], the Commission called upon Member States to continue to collaborate in preventing the diversion of precursors and strengthen cooperation with associations, persons or companies engaged in activities involving precursors; control all safrole-rich oils in the same manner as safrole; and collect information on safrole-rich oils, using form D to provide to INCB information on their licit trade and trafficking. The Commission requested INCB to provide a definition of "safrole-rich oils" for the purpose of controlling such substances in the same manner as safrole under the 1988 Convention. It invited States and relevant international organizations to cooperate with the Board, in particular its Project Prism, to enhance the success of its international initiatives.

INCB action. In its report covering 2006 [Sales No. E.07.XI.11], INCB called upon States that were not party to one or more of the international drug control treaties to accede to them without delay. It reiterated its request to Governments to furnish in a timely manner all statistical reports required under the treaties and to implement fully the system of estimates and export authorizations. The Board also requested Governments to promote the rational use of narcotic drugs for medical purposes and to furnish their own estimates of requirements. It urged countries manufacturing and exporting psychotropic substances to provide annual statistics within the deadline required under the 1971 Convention and to update the assessments of their annual medical and scientific requirements. It also urged all parties, pursuant to article 12 of the 1988 Convention, to monitor the manufacture and distribution of precursor chemicals, and called upon States that had not done so to furnish their estimated requirements for precursors.

ECONOMIC AND SOCIAL COUNCIL ACTION

On 27 July [meeting 41], the Economic and Social Council, on the recommendation of the Commission on Narcotic Drugs [E/2006/28], adopted **resolution 2006/34** without vote [agenda item 14 (*d*)].

The need for a balance between demand for and supply of opiates used to meet medical and scientific needs

The Economic and Social Council,

Recalling its resolution 2005/26 of 22 July 2005 and previous relevant resolutions,

Recognizing that the medical use of narcotic drugs, including opiates, is indispensable for the relief of pain and suffering,

Emphasizing that the need for a balance between the global licit supply of opiates and the legitimate demand for opiates used to meet medical and scientific needs is central to the international strategy and policy of drug control,

Noting the fundamental need for international cooperation with the traditional supplier countries in drug control to ensure universal application of the provisions of the Single Convention on Narcotic Drugs of 1961 and that Convention as amended by the 1972 Protocol,

Reiterating that a balance between consumption and production of opiate raw materials was achieved in the past as a result of efforts made by the two traditional supplier countries, India and Turkey, together with established supplier countries,

Expressing deep concern at the increase in the global production of opiate raw materials and the significant accumulation of stocks over the past few years as a consequence of the operation of market forces, which has the potential to upset the delicate balance between the licit supply of and demand for opiates to meet medical and scientific needs,

Emphasizing the importance of the system of estimates, based on actual consumption and utilization of narcotic drugs, furnished to and confirmed by the International Narcotics Control Board on the extent of cultivation and production of opiate raw materials, in particular in view of the current oversupply,

Recalling the Joint Ministerial Statement adopted during the ministerial segment of the forty-sixth session of the Commission on Narcotic Drugs, in which ministers and other Government representatives called upon States to continue to contribute to the maintenance of a balance between the licit supply of and demand for opiate raw materials used for medical and scientific purposes and to cooperate in preventing the proliferation of sources of production of opiate raw materials,

Considering that opiate raw materials and the opiates derived from them are not just ordinary commodities that can be subjected to the operation of market forces and that, therefore, market economy considerations alone should not determine the extent of cultivation of opium poppy,

Reiterating the importance of the medical use of opiates in pain relief therapy, as advocated by the World Health Organization,

Noting that countries differ significantly in their level of licit demand for narcotic drugs and that in most developing countries the use of narcotic drugs for medical purposes has remained at an extremely low level,

1. *Urges* all Governments to continue to contribute to maintaining a balance between the licit supply of and demand for opiate raw materials used for medical and scientific purposes, supporting traditional and established supplier countries, and to cooperate in preventing the proliferation of sources of production of opiate raw materials;

2. *Urges* Governments of all producer countries to adhere strictly to the provisions of the Single Convention on Narcotic Drugs of 1961 and that Convention as amended by the 1972 Protocol, and to take effective measures to prevent the illicit production or diversion of opiate raw materials to illicit channels, and encourages improvements in practices in the cultivation of opium poppy and production of opiate raw materials;

3. *Urges* Governments of consumer countries to assess their licit needs for opiate raw materials realistically on the basis of actual consumption and utilization of opiate raw materials and the opiates derived therefrom and to communicate those needs to the International Narcotics Control Board in order to ensure effective supply, calls upon Governments of countries producing opium, taking into account the current level of global stocks, to limit the cultivation of opium poppy to the estimates furnished to and confirmed by the Board, in accordance with the requirements of the 1961 Convention, and urges that, in providing estimates of such cultivation, producer countries consider the actual demand requirements of importing countries;

4. *Endorses* the concern expressed by the International Narcotics Control Board in its report for 2005 regarding the advocacy by a non-governmental organization of legalization of opium poppy cultivation in Afghanistan, and urges all Governments to resist such proposals and to continue to strengthen drug control in compliance with their obligations emanating from the international drug control treaties;

5. *Urges* the Governments of all countries where opium poppy has not been cultivated for the licit production of opiate raw materials, in the spirit of collective responsibility, to refrain from engaging in the commercial cultivation of opium poppy, in order to avoid the proliferation of supply sites, and calls upon Governments to enact enabling legislation to prevent and prohibit the proliferation of sites used for the production of opiate raw materials;

6. *Commends* the International Narcotics Control Board for its efforts in monitoring the implementation of the relevant Economic and Social Council resolutions and, in particular:

(a) In urging the Governments concerned to adjust global production of opiate raw materials to a level corresponding to actual licit requirements and to avoid creating imbalances between the licit supply of and demand for opiates caused by the exportation of products manufactured from seized and confiscated drugs;

(b) In inviting the Governments concerned to ensure that opiates imported into their countries for medical and scientific use do not originate in countries that transform seized and confiscated drugs into licit opiates;

(c) In arranging informal meetings, during the sessions of the Commission on Narcotic Drugs, with the main States that import and produce opiate raw materials;

7. *Requests* the International Narcotics Control Board to continue its efforts to monitor the implementation of the relevant Economic and Social Council resolutions in full compliance with the Single Convention on Narcotic Drugs of 1961 and that Convention as amended by the 1972 Protocol;

8. *Requests* the Secretary-General to transmit the text of the present resolution to all Governments for consideration and implementation.

International Narcotics Control Board

The 13-member International Narcotics Control Board held its eighty-fifth (30 January–3 February), eighty-sixth (8-19 May) and eighty-seventh (30 October–16 November) sessions, all in Vienna.

The Board monitored the implementation of the international drug control treaties and maintained a permanent dialogue with Governments. The information received from Governments was used to identify the enforcement of treaty provisions requiring them to limit to medical and scientific purposes the licit manufacture of, trade in and distribution and use of narcotic drugs and psychotropic substances. The Board, which was required to report annually on the drug control situation worldwide, noted weaknesses in national control and treaty compliance and made recommendations for improvements at the national and international levels.

The Board's 2006 report [Sales No. E.07.XI.11] reviewed the availability of internationally controlled drugs in the unregulated market for drugs, where unlicensed or licensed individuals and/or entities traded in drugs that they were not authorized or entitled to deal with, in contravention of the applicable laws, regulations and norms. The Board noted that the variety of internationally controlled substances available on the unregulated market had increased and drug traffickers had turned to innovative ways of diverting and smuggling them. The unregulated market, which exposed patients to risks by providing access to poorly or incorrectly labelled medicines without professional supervision, was driven by such factors as limited access to health-care facilities; the cost of drugs; privacy issues; the lack of public awareness; drug control regulations and their enforcement; and consumer demand for illicit drugs. In some regions, people abused licitly produced prescription medicines in quantities similar to or greater than the quantities of illicitly manufactured heroin, cocaine, amphetamine and opioids. In many countries, the Internet, which allowed easy access to internationally controlled substances, was inadequately regulated at national and international levels. Websites providing consultations with "cyberdoctors", recommending medicinal products and facilitating access to prescribed drugs were a matter of increasing concern. The widespread availability of counterfeit drugs compounded the problems associated with the unregulated market. According to WHO, 25 to 50 per cent of the medicines consumed in developing countries were believed to be counterfeit. The Board recommended that States enforce legislation to ensure that narcotic drugs and psychotropic substances were not illegally manufactured, imported or exported, nor diverted to the unregulated market. In compliance with the 1971 Convention, States should conduct inspections of manufacturers, exporters, importers and distributors, as well as of stocks and records. They should assess their requirements of narcotic drugs and psychotropic substances on a systematic basis to ensure that supplies were sufficient to meet legitimate demand and increase the availability of drugs through legitimate channels and implement the Board's recommendations on Internet trading. States should also address the unregulated market for drugs in national policies and legislation; build the capacity of staff attached to the drug regulatory authority and related agencies; and implement policies and provide a legal framework to combat counterfeit drugs. The Board recommended that WHO undertake studies to better understand the dynamics underlying the unregulated market and develop a guide on best practices. The United Nations Office on Drugs and Crime (UNODC) and WHO should provide technical assistance to States for building capacity and updating drug control laws, and the pharmaceutical industry and relevant associations should notify national and international authorities of consignments diverted to the unregulated market or attempts to manufacture and distribute counterfeit drugs.

As to the diversion and abuse of narcotic drugs containing pharmaceutical products from licit domestic distribution channels, INCB noted that it continued to be underreported, in particular codeine, dextropropoxyphene, fentanyl, hydrocodone, ketobemidone, levomethorphan, methadone, oxycodone and pethidine. The Board urged Governments to develop programmes to prevent the abuse of such drugs and take countermeasures, in cooperation with health-care professionals, to provide feedback on seized pharmaceutical products to regulatory authorities. Concerning psychotropic substances, diversion from licit domestic distribution channels was the main source of supply to illicit markets. The most diverted substances were stimulants, benzodiazepines and the analgesic, buprenorphine. Noting that the abuse of prescription drugs, including pharmaceutical preparations containing controlled substances, continued to be a matter of concern in Canada, the United States and a number of European countries, the Board urged the Governments concerned to develop prevention programmes that targeted their abuse among youth. Noting also the increasing trafficking in and abuse of the sedative-hypnotic, gamma-hydroxybutyric acid (GHB), the Board called on UNODC to include abuse prevention of that medication in its programmes.

With regard to precursors, the Board noted that mechanisms for the rapid verification of their transactions, particularly through the system of pre-export notifications, remained the most effective way of addressing their diversion and trafficking. In March, it launched the Pre-Export Notification Online (PEN Online), a new electronic system for exchanging pre-export notifications. Within the framework of Project Prism and Project Cohesion, which continued to be the key elements of the international precursor control system, the Board assisted national authorities in monitoring shipments of chemicals in international trade and in preventing their diversion into illicit channels. Activities under Project Prism, which focused on precursor chemicals used in the illicit manufacture of ATS, assisted Governments and the Board in identifying new trends, such as the diversion of raw materials from Africa, Central America and West and South Asia, ephedra shipments from East Asia to Canada and Europe, and the smuggling of pharmaceutical preparations into and within Africa, Central and South America and West Asia. The Board was concerned that Africa and West Asia had started to be used by organized criminal networks as transshipment points for consignments of ephedrine and pseudoephedrine destined for the illicit manufacture of methamphetamine. It urged importing countries in those regions to monitor the manufacture, distribution and export of preparations containing them to ensure that the end-users were legitimate and to prevent their accumulation in quantities exceeding the licit requirements. As to the diversion of precursors used in the illicit manufacture of methamphetamine, the Board recommended the adoption of measures, in particular pre-export notifications for pharmaceutical preparations, as well as the estimation of licit requirements for ephedrine and pseudoephedrine and preparations containing them. With regard to Project Cohesion, the Board invited participating Governments to launch activities in precursor chemicals that targeted trafficking in relevant regions, in particular, in the Americas, where authorities should address the trafficking of potassium permanganate. It invited Governments that had not yet done so to join Project Cohesion in order to prevent traffickers from identifying new routes of diversion and avoiding controls. More focused efforts were required in the investigation of cases and the launching of operations to counter trafficking at the subregional level, such as Operation Trans-shipment, carried out in Central Asia to identify and seize consignments of acetic anhydride smuggled into Afghanistan.

As to ensuring the availability of drugs for medical purposes, global stocks of opiate raw materials should normally cover global demand for about one year. However, at the end of 2005, stocks of opiate raw materials rich in morphine were sufficient to cover annual demand for two years. Global demand for opiates continued to increase the demand for opiate raw materials rich in morphine, as well as opiate raw materials rich in thebaine. The Board urged producing countries to maintain production at planned levels to avoid excessive stocks. Producing countries should submit estimates in a timely manner; maintain opium poppy cultivation within the limits of the estimates confirmed by the Board or furnish supplementary estimates; and report the amounts of raw materials produced, as well as the alkaloids contained in them. The Board called upon Governments to maintain a balance between the licit supply of and demand for opiate raw materials, prevent the proliferation of sources of their production, and comply with Council resolution 2006/34 (see p. 1437). Pursuant to Council resolution 2005/26 [YUN 2005, p. 1346] and at the request of India and Turkey, the Board convened an informal consultation on the supply of and demand for opiates for medical and scientific purposes to inform producers and importers of opiate raw materials of developments affecting global production and demand and to discuss policy issues. The Board requested Governments to promote the rational use of narcotic drugs for medical treatment, in accordance with the relevant WHO recommendations.

Illicit sale of pharmaceuticals containing controlled narcotic drugs and psychotropic substances via the Internet and their illicit distribution by mail continued. The Board noted that smuggling by mail was increasingly recognized as a method of drug trafficking and constituted a major problem for law enforcement authorities. In view of the global nature of the use of the mail for that purpose, concerted international action was required, in particular, the establishment of a mechanism for sharing experiences and the exchange of information on specific cases, as well as for standardizing data collected. The substances most commonly traded over the Internet were psychotropic substances, mainly benzodiazepines and stimulants. With regard to narcotic drugs, sales of codeine and dextropropoxyphene were also reported.

The INCB report was supplemented by three technical reports—Narcotic Drugs: Estimated World Requirements for 2007; Statistics for 2005 [E/INCB/2006/2]; Psychotropic Substances: Statistics for 2005; Assessments of Annual Medical and Scientific Requirements for Substances in Schedules II, III and IV of the Convention on Psychotropic Substances of 1971 [E/INCB/2006/3]; and Precursors and Chemicals Frequently Used in the Illicit Manufacture of Narcotic Drugs and Psychotropic Substances: Report of INCB for 2006 on the Implementation of article 12 of the UN Convention against Illicit Traffic in Narcotic Drugs and Psychotropic Substances of 1988 [E/INCB/2006/4].

World drug situation

In its 2006 report [Sales No.E.07.XI.11], INCB presented a regional analysis of world drug abuse trends and control efforts, in order to keep Governments aware of situations that might endanger the objectives of international drug control treaties.

Africa

The cultivation and production of cannabis, the major drug of abuse in Africa, rose, despite intensive eradication efforts in the region. In Morocco, the world's largest producer of cannabis resin, the total area under cultivation decreased by 40 per cent, from 120,500 hectares in 2004 to 72,500 hectares in 2005, and its production declined by 62 per cent (to 1,066 tons) in 2005. The decrease was the result of unfavourable weather conditions combined with a successful eradication campaign. Egypt, Morocco, Nigeria and South Africa remained important sources of cannabis herb and the continent as a whole accounted for almost one third of its global seizures. Overall, seizures of cannabis resin decreased in North Africa, except for Algeria where it increased. Africa's share of global trafficking in cannabis increased, as evidenced by the number of multi-ton seizures during the year. The rise in cannabis production was accompanied by an increase in its abuse. While the abuse of cannabis resin was largely confined to Northern Africa, the abuse of cannabis herb took place throughout the region. Cannabis herb continued to be the most widely smuggled drug within Africa, and was also smuggled out of the region, mainly into Europe.

One particularly worrisome development in Africa was the large-scale trafficking in cocaine. Taking advantage of the weak interdiction capacities, drug traffickers used the region as a transit area for cocaine from South America, through Western, Central and Southern Africa. Both the number of couriers apprehended and the volume of bulk seizures increased significantly. Efforts by African countries to deal with the problem were impeded by a lack of drug control mechanisms and skilled human resources. Cocaine was trafficked along maritime routes leading predominantly to the Gulf of Guinea. The most affected countries were Benin, Cape Verde, Ghana, Guinea-Bissau, Nigeria and Togo, while Ghana served as a major trans-shipment area and logistics base. As a spillover effect, the abuse of cocaine, including crack cocaine, increased in Western Africa. It continued to be seized in South Africa, where its abuse was on the increase.

Heroin from South-East and South-West Asia continued to be smuggled through Africa, intended for Europe and, to a lesser extent, North America. While increased heroin seizures were reported, the total quantity of heroin seized in Africa remained small compared with the global figure. Significant seizures continued to be made at international airports in Ethiopia, Kenya, Mauritius and the United Republic of Tanzania. As a spillover effect, its abuse became a problem in Eastern Africa, as well as in South Africa and in some countries in Western Africa.

Pharmaceutical preparations containing controlled substances were easily obtained on unregulated markets throughout Western, Central and Northern Africa. Those products were usually diverted from domestic distribution channels. The availability and abuse of prescription drugs containing controlled substances became a problem in many African countries, especially preparations containing ephedrine and diazepam (Valium) in Western and Central Africa. Prescription drugs could be obtained without prescription in pharmacies and other retail outlets. While legislation prohibiting such practices was in place in most countries, it was often not adequately implemented and there was a shortage of trained pharmacists and pharmacy inspectors in many countries. The illicit manufacture and abuse of psychotropic substances, notably methaqualone (Mandrax), methamphetamine, methcathinone and methylenedioxymethamphetamine (MDMA) (Ecstasy) were limited to South Africa and some countries in Southern and Eastern Africa. Their abuse was also reported in Egypt. Furthermore, seizures of buprenorphine increased in Mauritius. As most countries did not have the legislation and institutional framework in place to combat trafficking in precursors, such chemicals continued to be diverted through the region. Of particular concern was the diversion of ephedrine and pseudoephedrine.

Khat, a substance not under international control, continued to be cultivated in Eastern Africa, mainly Ethiopia and Kenya and, to a lesser extent, the Comoros, Madagascar and the United Republic of Tanzania. It was commonly chewed as a stimulant in that subregion and parts of the Arabian peninsula.

With regard to regional cooperation, the Board noted the efforts made by the Economic Community of West African States (ECOWAS) to coordinate drug control activities in Western Africa, including its decision, in July, to develop a new regional action plan on drugs and crime. The West African Drug Regulatory Agencies Network, a subregional body of drug regulators aimed at combating counterfeit and fake drugs, was established in Abuja, in March. The WHO Regional Committee for Africa, at its fifty-sixth session (Addis Ababa, Ethiopia, 28 August–1 September), addressed drug regulatory matters, urging Governments that had not done so to accede to the international drug control treaties and stressing the importance of training drug control authorities to establish a sound regulatory system to ensure the availability of controlled substances for medical needs. Joint operations were carried out by drug law enforcement authorities from Cape Verde, Ghana and Senegal. Egypt and the Libyan Arab Jamahiriya signed a memorandum of understanding to strengthen cooperation at their joint border control points.

At the national level, the Libyan Arab Jamahiriya established a new drug control committee, while Kenya stepped up efforts aimed at drug abuse prevention and treatment, and Morocco launched an eradication initiative aimed at making the Province of Taounate free of cannabis by the end of 2006. In October, South Africa approved the national drug control master plan for 2006-2011. The Board called upon the Governments concerned to improve the efficiency and effectiveness of their drug regulatory authorities, with a view to preventing illicit distribution practices or counterfeiting, while facilitating access to medication. INCB sent a mission to Djibouti in January, the Gambia in May, and Malawi in August.

Americas

Central America and the Caribbean

Central America and the Caribbean continued to be used as a major transit and trans-shipment area for cocaine from South America destined for North America and Europe. About 90 per cent of the cocaine entering North America passed through Central America. Moreover, the Caribbean was situated along one of the main cocaine trafficking routes leading to Europe. The Netherlands made 40 per cent of their total seizures in the waters of the Netherlands Antilles, while Jamaica and Martinique continued to play an important role in the trans-shipment of cocaine to the United Kingdom and France, respectively. In El Salvador, authorities seized over three times more illicit drugs during 2000-2005 than during the previous five-year period. Institutional weaknesses and corruption undermined efforts to combat the drug problem.

In spite of being used as major trans-shipment areas, all countries in Central America and the Caribbean, with the exception of El Salvador, experienced relatively low levels of drug abuse. The region was not a main drug-producing area, although some countries, such as Guatemala and Jamaica, were threatened by increasing production. Cannabis was the most commonly abused drug in the region, followed by cocaine hydrochloride and "crack" cocaine. Jamaica was the main illicit producer and exporter of cannabis; its illicit cultivation was done on small plots of land hidden in inaccessible mountainous areas. Saint Vincent and the Grenadines was also an important producer. Illicit trafficking had penetrated the licit economy, making the population dependent on the illicit cultivation of, and trafficking in, cannabis. In Costa Rica, the abuse of drugs, particularly "crack" cocaine, increased; in Guatemala, almost 490 hectares of illicit opium poppy cultivation were eradicated in 2005, an increase of more than 250 per cent, compared with 2004.

Trafficking in precursors of amphetamine-type stimulants (ATS) had also become a problem in the region. The Dominican Republic continued to be a major trans-shipment area for MDMA (Ecstasy) from Europe to the United States.

As part of efforts at regional cooperation, the Inter-American Drug Abuse Control Commission (CICAD) of the Organization of American States (OAS) developed a regional framework for drug control plans and policies, as well as an evaluation system for the region and hemispheric guidelines on school-based prevention programmes aimed at standardizing interventions for preventing abuse in schools. To prevent the smuggling of drugs by land, the United States assisted Central American States in improving their border inspection facilities by establishing mobile inspection and law enforcement teams. Mexico and countries in Central America (San Salvador, El Salvador, September) discussed the creation of a regional centre to fight drug trafficking. During a regional workshop organized by UNODC (Panama City, Panama, March), experts and representatives from Belize, Costa Rica, El Salvador, Guatemala, Honduras, Mexico, Nicaragua and Panama developed a strategy for Central America and the Caribbean based on national studies of the services available for the treatment, rehabilitation and social reintegration of drug-dependent persons in the region.

At the national level, Belize started a cooperative national information exchange system to intercept civilian aircraft and facilitate the detection of trafficking routes and the arrest of traffickers. Costa Rica implemented a national database system for cross-checking sales reported by distributors of controlled substances and pharmacies, as well as prescriptions for medicines distributed in pharmacies. It also enacted the Regulations on Granting and Oversight of Licenses to Handle Psychotropic Substances and Narcotics in the context of the 2005-2007 national drug control plan. Cuba strengthened efforts to counter drug trafficking, while Guatemala restructured the procedures for approval of the production, import and sale of narcotic drugs and psychotropic substances, and Panama strengthened its controls over precursor chemicals.

In August, an INCB mission visited El Salvador and noted a high degree of coordination among drug control agencies, and a good control over the licit movement of narcotic drugs and psychotropic substances. Nevertheless, the availability of controlled substances for medical purposes was very low, and the Board encouraged the Government to ensure their sufficient availability. During a technical visit to Honduras in August, the Board noted that the legal framework for drug control was outdated and inadequate resources and coordination among drug control agencies hampered the Government's efforts to combat trafficking. The Board requested the Government to enact a more comprehensive law in line with international treaties and to address the lack of adequate resources for the Unit for the Regulation of Pharmaceutical Products, the competent authority in charge of the licit movement of drugs.

North America

North America continued to be one of the prime targets of drug traffickers. Substance abuse in the United States remained a matter of concern, particularly the high level of abuse of prescription drugs by adolescents and adults. The gradual increase in the abuse of sedatives, tranquillizers and narcotic drugs other than heroin resulted in prescription drugs becoming the second most abused drugs after cannabis. The spread in their abuse was also related to the increasing use of the World Wide Web as a global drug market. Methamphetamine trafficking and abuse continued to be problems in Canada and the United States. While United States drug law enforcement agencies closed down illicit methamphetamine laboratories, domestic illicit manufacturers were replaced by transnational drug trafficking organizations based in Canada and Mexico. In Canada, domestic illicit manufacturers accounted for the largest share of trafficked methamphetamine.

Cannabis continued to be the most abused and trafficked illicit drug in North America. Illicit cannabis plant cultivation became a thriving illegal industry in Canada where, in addition to outdoor cultivation, more sophisticated indoor crop-growing methods were increasingly used to produce high-potency cannabis (cannabis with a high tetrahydrocannabinol (THC) content). Criminal groups gained control over the production and distribution of high-potency cannabis in Canada and were the principal suppliers to the United States. A large part of cannabis products available in the United States were smuggled by Mexican organizations and criminal groups. Mexican drug trafficking organizations increased the size and sophistication of their cannabis plant cultivation operations in the United States, using new techniques to produce a larger, more potent outdoor crop with a THC content of at least 5 per cent and an increased street value. Such higher-potency cannabis accounted for more than half of the total seized in 2005.

Another major problem in the region was the increasing methamphetamine manufacture, abuse and trafficking, particularly in the United States. Its abuse extended from the western to the eastern states, and was especially problematic in rural areas and small cities. Domestic illicit methamphetamine manufacture, the main source for the United States market, declined as a result of law enforcement pressure and restrictions on the sale and use of pseudoephedrine and ephedrine. However, its reduction in the United States was offset by sharp increases in its large-scale manufacture in Mexico. The prevalence of methamphetamine abuse was relatively low in Canada, but rising among youth. It was manufactured mostly in many small clandestine laboratories operated by individuals in rural areas, but there was an increase in the number of "super laboratories". The level of sophistication of the laboratory setups and the involvement of organized criminal groups in methamphetamine manufacture increased.

The Board was concerned about the increasing abuse in the United States of prescription drugs listed as controlled substances, including painkillers, stimulants, sedatives and tranquillizers. Levels of non-medical use and abuse of pharmaceuticals were higher than that for most illicit drugs, second only to cannabis abuse. Pharmaceuticals commonly abused in the United States included cocaine, codeine, fentanyl, hydrocodone, hydromorphone, methadone, methylphenidate, morphine, oxycodone, the amphetamine group and the benzodiazepine group. In the United States, 11 per cent of persons aged 12 to 17 reported lifetime non-medical use of painkillers. The increase in the amount of prescription drugs abused appeared to be related to an increase in sales of prescription narcotic drugs, depressants and stimulants. Of particular concern were the rise in sales of commonly abused pharmaceuticals, such as hydrocodone and oxycodone, and the increase in the abuse of fentanyl in the United States and, to a lesser extent, in Canada. Fentanyl, a synthetic opioid 80 times as potent as heroin, was diverted by means of pharmacy theft, fraudulent prescriptions and illicit distribution by patients, physicians and pharmacists. However, its illicit manufacture was growing, with over 12 different analogues of fentanyl manufactured clandestinely and identified in seizures in the United States.

Cocaine abuse in the United States was stable. The Board noted that, as traditional maritime routes of cocaine trafficking were disturbed by joint law enforcement operations, traffickers evaded interdiction by moving fishing-vessel operations farther out in the Pacific Ocean, as far as the Galapagos Islands. The cocaine smuggled into the United States was derived from coca produced mainly in Colombia, but also in Bolivia and Peru, with Mexico being used as the principal trans-shipment country. Cocaine abuse increased in Mexico. Its demand in Canada remained strong, and its large-scale illegal importations continued. The most common trans-shipment points for smuggling cocaine into Canada were Antigua and Barbuda, Haiti, Jamaica, Saint Lucia, Saint Martin, Trinidad and Tobago and the United States. It was the third most widely used illicit drug in Canada, after cannabis and hallucinogens (such as lysergic acid diethylamide (LSD) and phencyclidine).

The total amount of heroin seized decreased from 2,773 kg in 2002 to 1,845 kg in 2004. Most of the heroin abused was manufactured in Colombia and Mexico, though opium production in those countries accounted for less than 4 per cent of global production. Colombia remained the main supplier to the United States, accounting for 60 to 70 per cent of the heroin sold. In 2005, the total area of eradicated opium poppy crops increased to 20,464 hectares or 28 per cent over the previous year. In Canada, the volume of heroin seized remained comparatively low, but that of opium increased. Consignments of opium and heroin from Afghanistan, India, Iran and Pakistan were routed through a European country or the United States to Canada. Since 2002, the seizures of heroin originating in South-East Asia had declined and the market share of Latin American heroin had increased. The Board regarded the decrease in heroin abuse among adolescents in the United States as an encouraging sign.

The sharp increase in MDMA (Ecstasy) trafficking in the United States had been halted. The amount seized had also declined. However, in Canada, significant seizures from clandestine laboratories indicated the involvement of larger and more sophisticated operations by organized criminal groups. The total amount of seized MDMA (Ecstasy) increased to record levels. In Canada, MDMA (Ecstasy), methylenedioxyamphetamine (MDA) and gamma-hydroxybutyric acid (GHB) continued to be abused.

As to substances not under international control, the abuse of inhalants was on the rise in the United States, especially among adolescents, making it the third most widely used illicit drugs. The abuse of high doses of dimenhydrinate was reported also. Khat from various countries was smuggled into Canada, mainly via the United Kingdom, where it was not a prohibited substance.

With regard to regional cooperation, all three countries in the region responded to the threat of drug trafficking operations with increased cooperation and mutual support. The close cooperation between Mexico and the United States included major institution-building initiatives, as well as financial and technical support. Mexico initiated Operation Secure Mexico to counter violence among criminal organizations fighting for control over smuggling routes along the border with the United States. In 2005, Mexico and the United States started Operation Border Unity, a bilateral, multi-agency effort to address violence on both sides of the border in the Laredo/Nuevo Laredo area. The involvement of criminal groups in drug trafficking between Canada and the United States was counteracted by close cooperation of the two countries. The Shiprider Agreement concluded between the two countries strengthened law enforcement cooperation by providing transborder law enforcement authority to Canadian officers operating along and across the border. The two countries also cooperated to combat trafficking in the transit zone from South America to North America.

As to national action, the Uniting and Strengthening America by Providing Appropriate Tools Required to Intercept and Obstruct Terrorism (USA PATRIOT) Improvement and Reauthorization Act of 2005, signed in March 2006, contained provisions to combat the illicit manufacture of, and trafficking in, methamphetamine. In addition, individual states in the United States responded to the new challenge posed by methamphetamines by enacting additional state-level legislation on precursor control. Canada moved methamphetamine to a more strictly controlled national schedule, and Mexico introduced a policy limiting the importation of pseudoephedrine and ephedrine to manufacturers only.

South America

The total area under coca bush cultivation in the Andean subregion increased slightly. In Bolivia and Peru, decreases were offset by an increase in Colombia where, despite intensified eradication efforts, coca bush growers moved their operations from one area to another. Cocaine continued to reach the United States and Europe through the main trafficking routes in Central America and the Caribbean, as well as through Africa. With a view to monitoring the total area under coca bush cultivation, field research measuring coca leaf and cocaine yields from coca leaves conducted in

Colombia, in 2006, confirmed that the yields were higher than reported in 2005. In Peru, work to update the methods used to measure coca leaf and cocaine yields started in 2006.

Approximately 18 per cent of global illicit cannabis herb production occurred in South America. Though illicit cultivation of cannabis for sale on the local market continued to be detected in most of the countries of the region, cannabis grown in Paraguay and, to a lesser extent, Colombia, was also smuggled into other countries, both in South America and in other regions. Paraguay remained a major producer, with illicit production spreading to areas previously not affected. The discovery of a new hybrid capable of growing during the winter months was reported.

In 2005, the majority of illicit coca bush cultivation continued to take place in Bolivia, Colombia and Peru. Despite eradication efforts, cultivation in Colombia increased by 6,000 hectares to 86,000 hectares in 2005, and even spread to new areas. The most significant increase occurred in two areas bordering Ecuador and Venezuela. In Peru, the area under cultivation decreased by 4 per cent, to 48,200 hectares between 2004 and 2005 due to alternative development efforts and manual eradication campaigns. In Bolivia, the area under cultivation dropped by 8 per cent, to 25,400 hectares in 2005. In Venezuela, with the use of a satellite monitoring detection system, 80 hectares of coca bush were eradicated at the north-western border with Colombia in November 2005. Maceration pits and coca paste or coca base laboratories continued to be detected in all three coca-producing countries, whereas cocaine laboratories were found mainly in Colombia, where the amount of cocaine hydrochloride seized (168 tons) was almost 50 times higher than the total amount seized in Bolivia and Peru. Some illicit manufacture of cocaine continued to take place in non-traditional illicit manufacturing countries, such as Argentina. Every year, almost 250 tons of cocaine entered the European Union (EU), the second largest market after the United States, transported by sea from Argentina, Brazil, Colombia, Ecuador, Suriname and Venezuela. In Brazil, the volume of cocaine seizures doubled. In Venezuela, they increased by 87 per cent, to 58.4 tons in 2005, and a further 23 tons were seized in the first nine months of 2006. Most of the shipments intercepted were destined for Spain and the United Kingdom. According to UNODC data for 2004-2005, the annual prevalence of cocaine abuse in South America was 0.7 per cent, but was higher in Bolivia and Chile, and increasing in Peru.

In Colombia, the area under illicit opium poppy cultivation dropped by 49 per cent in 2005 to 2,000 hectares as a result of eradication efforts. In Peru, in 2004, it was estimated at 1,500 hectares. More than 92 hectares were eradicated in 2005, and a further 88 hectares during the first eight months of 2006. Heroin seizures were reported in Argentina, Brazil, Chile, Colombia, Ecuador, Guyana, Peru, Uruguay and in Venezuela, which recorded the most significant increase. In South America, the abuse of opiates, in particular heroin, was among the lowest in the world.

Seizures of precursor chemicals, including potassium permanganate and acetic anhydride, were reported in the region. Although the total amount of ATS seized was not significant, the popularity of stimulants increased in some countries, including Argentina and Peru. MDMA (Ecstasy), mainly from the Netherlands, was the most commonly abused synthetic drug in Brazil. Several countries reported a rising trend in the non-therapeutic use of sedatives and tranquillizers. Pharmaceutical preparations containing narcotic drugs and psychotropic substances were often smuggled into the region and sold in non-licensed outlets.

With regard to regional cooperation, CICAD continued to provide its member States with training and technical assistance. The establishment of a network of national drug observatories to ensure that Governments were supplied with high quality information on drug production, trafficking and abuse and related crimes, was one of its priorities. The VIII High-Level Meeting of the Coordination and Cooperation Mechanism on Drugs between the EU and Latin America and the Caribbean was held in Vienna, on 6 and 7 March. Experts from the Americas, the Caribbean and Europe, participating in the Latin American conference on cocaine trafficking via maritime routes (Cartagena de Indias, Colombia, 14-17 February) recommended that the capacity of law enforcement agencies be strengthened through investigative techniques, such as controlled delivery. The first international meeting of drug observatories of Europe, Latin America and the Caribbean was held in Caracas, Venezuela, from 28 to 30 November 2005.

At the national level, a new national drug strategy plan was adopted in Suriname in January 2006. In Bolivia, a Ministerial Regulation adopted in June, allowed coca producers to trade their coca on licit coca markets. The Board urged the Government to ensure that, in addition to strengthening its measures for countering drug trafficking, all provisions of its new drug control legislation, including those relating to the cultivation of coca bush and the use of coca leaf, were in line with international treaties. In October, following Peru's decision on the decentralization of the national coca leaf enterprise, the Board urged the Government to ensure that the measure did not violate the provisions of the 1961 Convention, nor undermined efforts to combat illicit coca bush cultivation and drug trafficking. In Argentina, Chile, Paraguay and Venezuela, new laws on precursors and regulations establishing control mechanisms, defining codes of conduct for precursor traders and providing for the exchange of information, were adopted.

An INCB mission to Argentina, in May, found that laws and regulations on drug control were not in line with international treaties and urged the Government to comply with the provisions of the 1961 Convention concerning the use of coca leaf, and to harmonize laws and jurisdiction between provinces.

Asia

East and South-East Asia

Despite campaigns in East and South-East Asia to eradicate cannabis plants, illicit cultivation continued throughout the region, particularly in South-East Asia. Cannabis plants were illicitly cultivated in Indonesia, the Philippines, Thailand, and the central and southern parts of Myanmar. Illicit production in the Lao People's Democratic Republic took place mainly in the lowlands, in the south and in areas near the Mekong. In Cambodia, there was limited cultivation along its borders and the Mekong. Cannabis continued to be abused in Brunei Darussalam, China, Indonesia, Japan, Malaysia, Myanmar, the Philippines and the Republic of Korea.

Illicit opium poppy cultivation, especially in Myanmar, continued to decrease in the region. In the Lao People's Democratic Republic, all provinces and the former special opium poppy growing zone were declared opium-free. However, limited illicit cultivation continued in several northern provinces. In Viet Nam, the area under cultivation was negligible. Heroin was illicitly manufactured in Myanmar, but remained limited in the Lao People's Democratic Republic, where most of the heroin seized was smuggled through Myanmar. In 2005, China, Thailand and Viet Nam reported large heroin seizures. Heroin continued to be smuggled into Thailand over its northern, north-eastern and eastern borders; 924 kg were seized in 2005, the highest reported volume since 1998. Traffickers also continued to use the country as a transit point for consignments. In 2005, the volume of heroin smuggled into China from the Golden Triangle—the main illicit opium producing area in the region—decreased, while small amounts were seized in Cambodia, Indonesia and Japan. Heroin remained the drug of choice in most countries, such as China (including the Hong Kong and the Macao Special Administrative Regions (SARs)), Indonesia, Malaysia, Myanmar and Viet Nam. In Malaysia, morphine continued to be the drug abused by almost one third of persons undergoing treatment for drug abuse. Since 2004, there had been an increase in cocaine seizures in the Hong Kong SAR of China. In 2005, small amounts of cocaine were seized in Cambodia and Thailand.

Large-scale clandestine laboratories involved in the illicit manufacture of methamphetamine continued to be uncovered in East and South-East Asia. In 2005, significant amounts of ATS were seized in Cambodia, the Lao People's Democratic Republic and Viet Nam. Many of the ATS tablets seized in the Hong Kong SAR of China did not originate in Europe, which was often the case, but in Asia. The volume of methamphetamine seizures increased throughout the region, with China, Indonesia, Malaysia and Thailand reporting an increase in the seizure of tablets. The smuggling of methamphetamine from the Lao People's Democratic Republic into Cambodia increased and continued in Thailand over its north-eastern and eastern borders. A few countries, including Japan and the Philippines, reported a decrease in methamphetamine seized, but the amount smuggled into China increased. MDMA (Ecstasy) continued to be smuggled into Thailand across its border with Malaysia. In 2005, the seizure of MDMA (Ecstasy) tablets in Myanmar increased, and Japan reported the largest volume of seizures since 2001. However, several countries, including China, Indonesia, Malaysia and Thailand, reported a decrease in seizures. In 2005, the amount of diazepam seized in the Philippines increased. Prescription drugs containing controlled psychotropic substances were smuggled from Thailand into Europe and the United States through air parcel services. Precursor chemicals, including acetic anhydride, continued to be smuggled into the Golden Triangle. Seizures of ephedrine in Myanmar increased significantly in 2006. ATS abuse emerged as a fast-growing problem in the Lao People's Democratic Republic, while in Japan, methamphetamine was the drug of choice, accounting for 83.5 per cent of arrests for drug-related offences. It was also the drug of choice in the Philippines, the Republic of Korea and Thailand, was widely abused in Brunei Darussalam, Indonesia, Myanmar and Singapore, and had gained in popularity in Malaysia, where, in 2005, more than twice as many people abused it than in 2004. MDMA (Ecstasy) continued to be abused throughout Japan and was the second most abused drug after ketamine among persons aged 11 to 20 in the Hong Kong SAR of China, where an increase in the abuse of GHB, LSD and nimetazepam (Erimin 5) was also noted. The illicit manufacture of, trafficking in and abuse of substances not under international control were growing in the region, especially in China, the Hong Kong SAR of China, Japan and the Republic of Korea. The illicit manufacture of and trafficking in ketamine continued in 2005, especially in the Hong Kong SAR of China, where it was the main drug of abuse among persons aged 11 to 20, as well as in China, the Macao SAR of China, Malaysia, the Philippines and Singapore.

With regard to regional cooperation, a memorandum of understanding relating to drug control was signed by the Association of Southeast Asian Nations (ASEAN) and the Economic Cooperation Organization, in January. The second Training Course on Precursor and Chemical Control for ASEAN Narcotics Law Enforcement Officers was held in Bangkok, from 16 to 22 May. At the national level, Indonesia's National Narcotics Board launched its 2005-2009 strategy to combat drug abuse and illicit trafficking. The Lao People's Democratic Republic launched a national strategy, calling for a balanced approach to eliminating opium in the country during the period 2006-2009, and the Philippines classified ketamine as a dangerous drug, in efforts to prevent its illicit manufacture.

In January, an INCB mission visited China. The Board, while acknowledging the Government's cooperation in providing pre-export notifications for exports of ephedrine and pseudoephedrine, requested it to do the same for pharmaceutical preparations containing those substances and to monitor their domestic distribution to ensure that no diversion took place. It noted the increasing role played by China in drug control in the region through bilateral and multilateral cooperation. In June, an INCB mission to the Democratic People's Republic of Korea (DPRK) welcomed the adoption of a new national drug control legislation and the establishment of a coordinating committee for drug control. The Board urged DPRK to cooperate with its neighbouring countries to combat the problem of ATS trafficking in the region. An INCB October mission to Myanmar encouraged the Government to continue efforts to eradicate illicit drug production and recommended that it cooperate with neighbouring countries in strengthening law enforcement activities and identifying the sources and trafficking routes of precursor chemicals used for the illicit manufacture of ATS.

South Asia

Despite measures taken by India against the diversion of licitly cultivated opium, some opium and poppy husk continued to be diverted to illicit markets. Crude heroin manufactured from such diverted opium was trafficked and sold in the country or smuggled into other countries. In addition, heroin from South-West Asia continued to be smuggled into India on its way to other countries. The State of Punjab emerged as a new hub for smuggling drugs into India, the traditional hubs being New Delhi and Mumbai. Smuggling between India and Nepal, in particular of cannabis from Nepal into India, continued. The smuggling of heroin into Maldives increased, though it remained at a low level. Drug traffickers used Bangladesh as a trans-shipment point for smuggling drugs into Europe, and Sri Lanka remained an important trans-shipment point for heroin from Afghanistan and India. The abuse of opiates, including illicitly manufactured heroin and low-quality heroin base known as "brown sugar" remained a problem in several countries, including Bangladesh, India, Maldives, Nepal and Sri Lanka. In Maldives, drug abuse reached alarming levels. Preventive measures taken by Bangladesh resulted in a decrease in the abuse of buprenorphine and pethidine, but that had resulted in an increase in heroin abuse. There was a trend in the region among addicts to move rapidly from inhaling to injecting drugs, mainly heroin and buprenorphine, one of the main factors in the spread of HIV/AIDS, particularly in India. South Asia, particularly Bangladesh, India and Nepal, continued to be faced by the long-standing problem of the licit control of pharmaceutical preparations containing controlled substances. Many of those preparations manufactured in India were diverted from domestic distribution routes at all levels of the supply chain and sold without prescription in pharmacies and other retail outlets, resulting in their widespread abuse, including buprenorphine, the main drug of injection in most areas of India, and cough syrups containing a high level of codeine. The latter was also trafficked into Bangladesh and, in some cases, pharmaceuticals were trafficked to Myanmar. The abuse of dextropropoxyphene, a synthetic pain reliever, increased in the north-eastern states of India. ATS were also an increasing problem in several countries, in particular India, where the abuse of MDMA (Ecstasy) and methamphetamine also increased. Ephedrine and pseudoephedrine were smuggled from India into Myanmar for use in the illicit manufacture of methamphetamine.

Though trafficking in and abuse of opiates and pharmaceutical preparations usually commanded the most attention in South Asia, cannabis also posed a problem. In addition to growing wild in a number of countries, including Nepal, it was illicitly cultivated in India and Sri Lanka.

With regard to international cooperation, the South Asian Association for Regional Cooperation (SAARC) (Dhaka, Bangladesh, 11 May) reviewed measures taken against drug trafficking and terrorism. Generally, the countries of South Asia continued to conduct activities against drug abuse and trafficking under the umbrella of the Drug Advisory Programme of the Colombo Plan. At the national level, Maldives finalized its 2006-2010 drug control master plan, while India and UNODC launched a nationwide drug abuse prevention campaign.

West and Central Asia

The drug control situation in Afghanistan worsened, despite efforts by the Government and the international community. In 2006, the total area under illicit opium poppy cultivation increased to a record 165,000 hectares, an increase of 59 per cent over 2005, and the level of production increased by nearly 50 per cent, reaching 6,100 tons of opium. Only six of Afghanistan's 34 provinces were free of illicit cultivation. The Board urged the Government and the international community to take measures to eradicate illicit cultivation and ensure that opium poppy farmers were provided with sustainable, legitimate livelihoods. Illicit opium poppy cultivation in Pakistan also increased, but in several countries in Central Asia, cultivation was on a smaller scale. Large amounts of opiates continued to be seized in West and Central Asia, reflecting the amounts of Afghan opiates smuggled through that area. Seizures of Afghan opiates in Iran increased in 2005, reaching 350 tons. Opium seizures in Pakistan remained at a relatively low level. In Turkey, heroin seizures continued to increase, due to strengthened law enforcement efforts, as well as in Israel, the Syrian Arab Republic and the United Arab Emirates. The smuggling of large quantities of opium poppy from Afghanistan continued to create severe problems in the abuse of opiates in neighbouring countries, in particular Iran and Pakistan. Iran had the world's highest rate of opiate abuse and was also facing increasing heroin abuse by injection. Drug abuse was a growing problem in Afghanistan and among Afghan refugees in neighbouring countries. Abuse also increased in Iraq and Pakistan. In Central Asia, opiate seizures declined by 37 per cent in 2005, but increased by 32 per cent in the first half of 2006, reaching a total of 4.3 tons. Armenia, Azerbaijan and Georgia experienced an increase in trafficking and abuse. Heroin seizures increased in all Central Asian States, except Kazakhstan. The amount of heroin seized in Tajikistan during the first half of 2006 increased by 45 per cent. In Central Asia, drug abuse increased, with heroin replacing cannabis and opium as the main drug of abuse. The number of registered abusers reached 89,000 in 2005, 55,000 of whom were in Kazakhstan. According to official estimates, however, the actual number of abusers was at least five times higher.

Besides opium poppy, cannabis plant was illicitly cultivated in Afghanistan, Lebanon and in the countries of Central Asia, in particular Kyrgyzstan. Cannabis accounted for 72 per cent of all drugs seized in Central Asia. In 2005, about 25.5 tons were seized, 85 per cent of which occurred in Kazakhstan. Cannabis resin was the most commonly abused drug in Afghanistan, with an abuse rate of 2.2 per cent.

The abuse of ATS also spread in various countries, including Iran, Turkey and countries on the Arabian peninsula. In Turkey, there was a significant increase in trafficking in MDMA (Ecstasy) intended for the domestic market, and in Iran, the abuse of synthetic drugs, in particular MDMA (Ecstasy), also increased. The trafficking in and abuse of fenetylline remained a problem in countries on the Arabian peninsula. Jordan was a transit point for fenetylline tablets destined for Saudi Arabia, and Turkey, the trans-shipment point of fenetylline destined for countries on the Arabian peninsula. Trafficking in and abuse of synthetic drugs and psychotropic substances were also reported in the countries of Central Asia. In particular, MDMA (Ecstasy) and amphetamines were increasingly available in Kazakhstan. The abuse of pharmaceutical medications remained a problem in Afghanistan, as a wide range of pharmaceutical preparations containing controlled substances continued to be available without prescription in pharmacies, other retail outlets and roadside stalls.

With regard to regional cooperation, experts met in Dushanbe (Tajikistan) from 10 to 11 April to discuss cross-border cooperation between Afghanistan and its neighbouring countries. The meeting was part of a series of round tables held pursuant to the Paris Pact [YUN 2003, p. 1263] to improve recommendations for law enforcement coordination in countries affected by heroin trafficking from Afghanistan. Central Asian States continued to cooperate in bilateral and multilateral efforts, including through the Central Asian Drug Action

Programme, the EU and the Central Asian Regional Drug Information Network Border Management Programme in Central Asia. In February, the parties to the Memorandum of Understanding on Subregional Drug Control Cooperation (Azerbaijan, Kazakhstan, Kyrgyzstan, the Russian Federation, Tajikistan, Turkmenistan, Uzbekistan) agreed on the legal framework of the Central Asia Regional Information and Coordination Centre and signed a resolution for its establishment in Almaty, Kazakhstan. In July, the North Atlantic Treaty Organization (NATO)-Russia Council initiated a programme to strengthen law enforcement efforts in Central Asia and Afghanistan. Under the programme, training teams from NATO member States and the Russian Federation visited Afghanistan and five Central Asian countries, providing training in counter-narcotics operations to local law enforcement agencies. China and Pakistan agreed, in July, to strengthen further bilateral cooperation against drug trafficking and other forms of cross-border crime. In July, the Board and UNODC launched Operation Trans-shipment, aimed at streamlining measures to prevent the smuggling of acetic anhydride through Central Asia to Afghanistan. Concerned that regional cooperation in drug control in the southern Caucasus remained inadequate, the Board urged countries to participate in related international projects and task forces. At the national level, in August, Afghanistan established the Drug Regulation Committee to regulate the licensing, sale, dispensation, import and export of drugs for licit purposes. A training seminar on the control of licit activities relating to narcotic drugs, psychotropic substances and precursors was organized jointly by UNODC and the Board (Kabul, July). It focused on the provisions of international treaties and the obligations of Afghanistan, with a view to strengthening its capacity to prevent diversion and ensure the availability of those substances for legitimate purposes. Kazakhstan signed, in November 2005, a strategy for combating drug trafficking and for abuse prevention for 2006-2014, and in February 2006, adopted a law amending the national drug control legislation. In April, Turkmenistan approved a national programme on the fight against trafficking for 2006-2010.

In January, an INCB mission visited Yemen, where the lack of a legal framework and financial resources hampered drug control activities. The Board recommended that the authorities, with WHO support, assess the situation and plan adequate control and preventive measures. Concerned about the widespread cultivation and abuse of khat, the Board called upon the authorities to control its cultivation, trade and use, and recommended that campaigns be initiated to raise awareness regarding its addictive nature and negative impact on society.

Afghanistan

The National Drug Control Strategy of Afghanistan [S/2006/106], adopted in January, addressed supply and demand reduction, alternative livelihoods and the strengthening of Government institutions. The Afghan Ministry of Counter Narcotics was the lead agency for its implementation. The Board urged the Government and the international community to ensure that the strategy was implemented properly.

The London Conference on Afghanistan (31 January–1 February), which brought together Afghanistan, the international community and a wide range of stakeholders, resulted in the adoption of the Afghanistan Compact (see p. 363). The Compact, endorsed by the Security Council in its resolution 1659(2006) (ibid.), identified three interdependent areas of activity over a five-year period: security; governance, rule of law and human rights; and economic and social development. A further cross-cutting area was the elimination of the narcotic industry. The aim would be to achieve a sustained and significant reduction in the production and trafficking of narcotics, with a view to complete elimination. Essential elements included improved interdiction, law enforcement and judicial capacity building; enhanced cooperation among Afghanistan, neighbouring countries and the international community on disrupting the drug trade; wider provision of economic alternatives for farmers and labourers in the context of comprehensive rural development; and building national and provincial counter-narcotics institutions. It would enforce policy towards corruption; pursue eradication; reinforce the message that producing or trading opiates was both immoral and a violation of Islamic law; and reduce the demand for their illicit use.

The International Conference on Border Management and Regional Cooperation (Doha, Qatar, 28 February), hosted by Qatar under the auspices of the UN Assistance Mission in Afghanistan, adopted the Doha Declaration on Border Management in Afghanistan: a regional approach, which agreed to promote closer cooperation between countries in the region and to support Afghanistan in its fight against narcotics by strengthening its border control and modernizing its border crossing points, and urged the international community to support the implementation of a border management system and foster regional partnership in security and police cooperation.

On 17 March [E/2006/28 (res. 49/5)], the Commission on Narcotic Drugs supported the proposal of the Russian Federation to convene in Moscow, in June, an international conference on drug routes from Central Asia to Europe in continuation of the Paris Pact [YUN 2003, p. 1263]. It encouraged the conference to take stock of the progress made under the Pact and of existing structures, in order to improve them; invited the parties concerned to take part in the conference; and requested the UNODC Executive Director to facilitate its organization and to report in 2007.

The Second Ministerial Conference on Drug Trafficking Routes from Afghanistan ("Paris 2–Moscow 1") (Moscow, 26-28 June), hosted by the Russian Federation, with the support of UNODC, adopted the Moscow Declaration [A/61/208-S/2006/598], which called for further support to Afghanistan in implementing its National Drug Control Strategy, improvement of regional measures against trafficking in precursor chemicals, a more systematic exchange of information and an extension of the Paris Pact.

INCB, concerned that the drug control situation in Afghanistan had deteriorated, despite the commitment of the Government and the assistance provided by the international community, urged the Government to address the problem and redouble its efforts to remove impediments to the rule of law. It also called upon the international community, particularly donor countries, to assist Afghanistan to achieve the goals of its National Drug Control Strategy.

ECONOMIC AND SOCIAL COUNCIL ACTION

On 27 July [meeting 41], the Economic and Social Council, on the recommendation of the Commission on Narcotic Drugs [E/2006/28], adopted **resolution 2006/32** without vote [agenda item 14 (*d*)].

Support for the National Drug Control Strategy of the Government of Afghanistan

The Economic and Social Council,

Recognizing the scale and complexity of the problem of narcotic drugs and the risk that the cultivation of opium poppy and the production of and trafficking in opium poses to the security, development and governance of Afghanistan, as well as at the regional and international levels,

Noting with appreciation the continued efforts of the Government of Afghanistan and the personal commitment of President Hamid Karzai to foster and implement counter-narcotics measures, including the publication in 2006 of the updated National Drug Control Strategy, which was welcomed by the international community at the Conference on Afghanistan held in London on 31 January and 1 February 2006,

Welcoming the inclusion of counter-narcotics as a cross-cutting theme in the Afghanistan Compact and the Government of Afghanistan's interim National Development Strategy,

Welcoming also the noteworthy progress made in the fight against narcotics in Afghanistan, including the adoption of counter-narcotics legislation, the establishment of a counter-narcotics tribunal, the use of extradition as a tool and the development of the country's counter-narcotics law enforcement and criminal justice capacity, which has resulted in the conviction of over ninety drug traffickers and an increase in drug-related seizures,

Recalling the report of the United Nations Office on Drugs and Crime entitled "Afghanistan Opium Survey 2005", in which it is indicated that, for the first time since 2001, Afghanistan has succeeded in achieving a decrease of 20 per cent in the area under cultivation of opium poppy, from 130,000 hectares to 104,000 hectares,

Welcoming the commitment by Afghanistan and its neighbours to enhanced regional cooperation as expressed in the Doha Declaration on Border Management in Afghanistan of 28 February 2006,

Noting with concern, however, the reported potential for increases in 2006 in the cultivation of opium poppy, in particular in specific provinces of Afghanistan,

Bearing in mind that securing the sustainable elimination of drug crop cultivation and drug trafficking in Afghanistan will take time and that it is a common and shared responsibility to be addressed through international efforts, as recognized by Member States in the Political Declaration adopted by the General Assembly at its twentieth special session,

Recalling General Assembly resolutions 59/161 of 20 December 2004 and 60/179 of 16 December 2005, in which the Assembly requested the international community to support the Government of Afghanistan in its fight against the illicit cultivation of opium poppy and trafficking in narcotic drugs,

Recalling also Security Council resolution 1659 (2006) of 15 February 2006, in which the Council endorsed the Afghanistan Compact and its annexes, welcomed the updated National Drug Control Strategy presented by the Government of Afghanistan at the London Conference, and encouraged additional international support for the four priorities identified in that Strategy, including through contributions to the Counter-Narcotics Trust Fund,

1. *Welcomes* the bilateral and multilateral support being provided to Afghanistan by the international community, including through contributions to the Government of Afghanistan's Counter-Narcotics Trust Fund, through the United Nations Office on Drugs and Crime and through other entities;

2. *Notes with appreciation* the strong commitment of the international community to the development and reconstruction of Afghanistan, as reflected in its endorsement of the Afghanistan Compact during the Confer-

ence on Afghanistan held in London on 31 January and 1 February 2006;

3. *Commends* the National Drug Control Strategy of 2006 of the Government of Afghanistan, including its identification of the following four priority areas of activity:

(a) Disrupting the illicit drug trade by targeting traffickers and their backers;

(b) Strengthening and diversifying legal rural livelihoods;

(c) Reducing the demand for illicit drugs and enhancing the treatment of problem drug users, including support for the action steps on demand reduction identified by Afghanistan and its partners at the Conference on Behavioural Health held in Kabul in May 2005;

(d) Developing state institutions at the central and provincial levels vital to the implementation of the counter-narcotics strategy;

4. *Invites* the international community to provide the necessary support to enable the Government of Afghanistan to implement its National Drug Control Strategy by:

(a) Continued provision of expertise and financial assistance, including through the Counter-Narcotics Trust Fund, in support of the key priorities set out in the National Drug Control Strategy;

(b) Making every effort to control smuggling into Afghanistan of precursors and chemicals used in the manufacture of narcotic drugs;

(c) Enhancing the steps already being taken aimed at a global reduction in illicit drug demand, thereby helping the Government of Afghanistan to fight illicit production of and trafficking in narcotic drugs;

5. *Reiterates* the concern expressed by the International Narcotics Control Board in its report for 2005 regarding the recent advocacy by a non-governmental organization of so-called legal cultivation of opium poppy in Afghanistan;

6. *Urges* the Government of Afghanistan to maintain control of illicit drugs among its highest priorities, as stipulated in article 7 of the Afghan Constitution and in line with the National Drug Control Strategy, with a view to enhancing its efforts to combat illicit cultivation of opium poppy and trafficking in drugs;

7. *Encourages* the Government of Afghanistan and all members of the international community to implement the Afghanistan Compact, which aims at achieving a sustained and significant reduction in the production of and trafficking in narcotics with a view to completely eliminating them, with drug control as a cross-cutting issue;

8. *Invites* the Government of Afghanistan and its neighbours, while appreciating their existing cooperation, to enhance regional cooperation in order to strengthen border control and security belts in the region, with a view to disrupting the smuggling of drugs out of Afghanistan and the smuggling of precursors into Afghanistan, including through participation in the Paris Pact initiative that emerged from the Paris Statement, which was issued at the end of the Conference on Drug Routes from Central Asia to Europe, held in Paris on 21 and 22 May 2003, and in the work of the Central Asian Regional Information and Coordination Centre;

9. *Invites* Member States to provide the necessary resources to the United Nations Office on Drugs and Crime to support the work of the Central Asian Regional Information and Coordination Centre;

10. *Calls upon* the United Nations Office on Drugs and Crime to strengthen its efforts, subject to the availability of extrabudgetary resources, to ensure that multilateral assistance is provided to Afghanistan in full support of its National Drug Control Strategy;

11. *Decides* to continue the consideration of this matter at future sessions.

Europe

Cannabis continued to be the most abused drug in Europe, especially in the Czech Republic, Denmark, France and the United Kingdom, with Spain and Portugal being the main trans-shipment points for consignments from Morocco. Albania remained a major exporter of cannabis herb, smuggled by land through the former Yugoslav Republic of Macedonia (FYROM) and Bulgaria into Turkey, Bosnia and Herzegovina, Croatia, Montenegro, Serbia and Slovenia and then into Western Europe. Illicit cannabis plant cultivation was also reported in Bulgaria and in central, south-eastern and western Poland. While its abuse was associated with cannabis resin, the market for cannabis herb was also significant.

Cocaine trafficking had increased sharply in Europe in 2005, making the region the second largest illicit market for the drug. Traffickers increasingly used routes leading through Portugal and Spain to smuggle cocaine into the region. The authorities in Spain identified three main routes: the north route, leading from the Caribbean to the Azores, Galicia (Spain), Portugal and the coast of the Cantábrico (Spain); the central route, leading from South America to the European coast, from Cape Verde or Madeira and the Canary Islands, the most frequently used sea route; and the African route, leading from South America mainly to Western Africa and the Gulf of Guinea, then to Galicia or northern Portugal, either by air or by sea. Cocaine seizures increased in the region as a whole, particularly in Portugal, where they rose by 125 per cent in 2005. Western and Central Europe accounted for about one quarter of all cocaine abused worldwide. After opiates and cannabis, cocaine was the most common drug of abuse in EU member States, as well as in Iceland, Liechtenstein, Norway and Switzerland. Spain and the United Kingdom had the highest prevalence rate of its abuse.

Most of the heroin found in Europe came from Afghanistan. Seizures of opiates rose by 49 per cent to 29 tons, the highest figure ever recorded. The increase was mainly attributable to a doubling of seizures in South-Eastern Europe, especially in Albania, Croatia, Montenegro, Serbia, FYROM and Turkey. Record seizures were also made in the Russian Federation. Most of the heroin on the illicit market in Europe continued to be smuggled from Turkey along the Balkan route, via Bulgaria, Romania and Hungary. In addition, a southern branch of the Balkan route had developed, through which heroin and other opiates from Turkey were smuggled via Bulgaria and FYROM into Albania, Austria, Germany and Italy. Shipments of opiates from Afghanistan to Iran were smuggled through the Caucasus into Ukraine and then into Romania before reaching Western Europe. The northern route through Central Asia was increasingly used to transport heroin to other major markets, such as the Russian Federation and countries in Eastern Europe. Large seizures were recorded in France, Germany, Italy, the Netherlands, the Russian Federation and the United Kingdom. Clandestine laboratories were detected in Moldova and the Russian Federation. In 2006, the market for illicit drugs in Belarus experienced a shift from heroin to synthetic drugs, as the availability of methadone and ATS on the local markets increased. Methadone replaced heroin as the most commonly abused substance. Since 2003, the number of registered drug abusers in Georgia had increased by 80 per cent. In Sweden, the drug abuse level was about one third of that in Europe as a whole, and HIV related abuse by injection was about one tenth of the European average.

Europe remained one of the main illicit markets for stimulants. The abuse of amphetamine and MDMA (Ecstasy) among young adults increased, the exceptions being Germany and Greece. The illicit manufacture of amphetamine continued to expand throughout Europe, with Bosnia and Herzegovina and Bulgaria, as well as Montenegro and Serbia, used as source countries. Amphetamine was also illicitly manufactured in Estonia and Lithuania. The illicit manufacture of metamphetamine took place mainly in the Czech Republic, Lithuania, Moldova and Slovakia. Many young Europeans were experimenting with hallucinogenic ("magic") mushrooms. Since 2001, six EU member States had tightened controls on those substances in response to their increased use.

With regard to regional cooperation, in July 2005, the second German-French working conference was held in Strasbourg (France) to discuss the treatment of cannabis abusers and crossborder cooperation to prevent cannabis abuse. In October and December 2005, the federal drug control service of the Russian Federation, in cooperation with drug control authorities of member States of the Collective Security Treaty Organization (CSTO), carried out a two-phase operation, Channel 2005, with the participation of the law enforcement authorities of CSTO observer States. From 22 to 29 May 2006, the first phase of operation Channel 2006 was carried out, with the participation of law enforcement authorities of CSTO observer States, as well as Mongolia and the United States.

At the national level, in Bosnia and Herzegovina, a law on the prevention and suppression of the abuse of narcotic drugs entered into force in February. However, the Board regretted that the new legislation did not take into account aspects of the control of psychotropic substances. Denmark took initiatives aimed at reducing the demand for drugs, especially cannabis, among young people, and supported projects to establish services for the treatment for young drug abusers. In France, a national information campaign to boost medical treatment for cannabis and heroin abusers was launched in 2005. Germany continued to implement its Action Plan on Drugs and Addiction, launched in 2003. In Italy, new legislation was adopted in March 2006, making the possession of drugs for personal use virtually illegal. In November, it increased the maximum quantity of cannabis permitted for personal use from 500 mg to 1,000 mg without incurring penal sanctions. In 2005, Latvia approved a programme for the control of narcotic drugs and psychotropic substances for 2005-2008, aimed at reducing abuse, especially among young people, and promoting the rehabilitation of abusers. Also in 2005, Romania adopted the 2005-2012 National Anti-Drug Strategy. In addition, a law on the judicial regime of narcotic drugs and psychotropic substances and plants and pharmaceutical products containing such substances entered into effect in July 2006, providing for enhanced security in the dispensing of prescriptions for controlled pharmaceuticals.

In May, the Board sent a mission to Belarus, which had adopted a new national drug control programme, built up a strong law enforcement system and made efforts to resolve the increasing trafficking in synthetic drugs and precursors. The Board encouraged the Government to strengthen customs and border guard services to prevent the smuggling of drugs, in particular through the Russian Federation. Noting the worsening drug abuse situation, particularly with regard to abuse by injection and heroin addiction, the Board urged the Government to accord higher priority to the treatment and rehabilitation of drug abusers and to increase the resources and efficiency of such treatment services. In May also, a mission of the Board visited Estonia, which was experiencing a shift from the abuse of natural products (such as cannabis) to synthetic drugs, such as amphetamines and MDMA (Ecstasy). Of particular concern was the prevalence of the abuse by injection of heroin, amphetamines and illicitly manufactured fentanyl and 3-methylfentanyl. Also in May, an INCB mission visited Latvia, where drug control policies, national legislation and the institutional framework to carry out those policies were well developed. A council for the coordination of drug control and the prevention of drug addiction was established to ensure the implementation of the national programme for combating drug abuse. However, additional funds were required to implement it, enhance training programmes and improve technical equipment. In October, the Board sent a mission to Luxembourg. Noting with concern that a drug injection room had been in operation since 2005, in violation of international drug treaties, the Board urged the Government to close the facility and implement measures against abuse. The Government should also improve coordination among the ministries and agencies involved in drug control and strengthen efforts to collect information on the drug abuse situation.

Oceania

Cannabis continued to be abused in many countries in the region and remained the drug of choice in Australia, Micronesia, New Zealand, Papua New Guinea, Samoa, Solomon Islands, Tonga and Vanuatu. Micronesia and Papua New Guinea had the highest prevalence of its abuse. The majority of the cannabis abused in Australia was produced locally. In New Zealand, the large-scale cultivation of cannabis plants took place in a number of rural areas, and outdoor cultivation was supplemented by operations using sophisticated indoor hydroponics. Cannabis plants were also illicitly cultivated in Fiji, Papua New Guinea, Samoa and Tonga. There had been reports of illicit drugs being bartered for arms in the coastal cities of Papua New Guinea.

The largest seizures of opium, heroin and cocaine in Oceania were reported in Australia. Large seizures of heroin were also made in Fiji and Vanuatu. The amount of cocaine seized in Australia in 2005 was the lowest since 1999. While cocaine consignments detected at the Australian border decreased during 2004-2005, most of the cocaine entered the country through the postal system.

Organized criminal groups used Oceania as a trans-shipment area for ATS, including methamphetamine and MDMA (Ecstasy). In Australia, ATS were supplied by clandestine laboratories operating within the country, which primarily manufactured methamphetamine. The illicit manufacture of methamphetamine increased in New Zealand, where larger amounts were also seized. Most of the pseudoephedrine used in illicit methamphetamine manufacture was extracted from commercially available pharmaceutical preparations. South East Asian methamphetamine was smuggled through Oceania to Canada and, to a lesser extent, the United States. The police in New Zealand continued to detect attempted diversions of consignments of medicines containing pseudoephedrine from China. The abuse of methamphetamine among young drug abusers increased in Australia.

As to substances not under international control, 10 kilogrammes of gamma-butyrolactone (GBL) were seized in 2005 in New Zealand, where it was becoming increasingly popular. In addition, the abuse of "party pills" containing benzylpiperazine became a growing problem. In Australia, seizures of khat increased.

Regionally, Australia and New Zealand continued to provide capacity-building assistance to other countries in Oceania. The seventeenth administrative meeting of contact points of the Regional Intelligence Liaison Office for Asia and the Pacific was held in Christchurch, New Zealand, in November 2005. Nationally, in December 2005, the New Zealand Customs Service updated the focus of its drug law enforcement strategy, while Australia promoted a campaign to prevent illegal sales of pseudoephedrine, where national legislation to tighten its control went into effect in January.

UN action to combat drug abuse

UN Office on Drugs and Crime

The United Nations Office on Drugs and Crime (UNODC) implemented the Organization's drug and crime programmes in an integrated manner, addressing the interrelated issues of drug control, crime prevention and international terrorism in the context of sustainable development and human security. The drug programme continued to be implemented in accordance with General Assembly resolution 45/179 [YUN 1990, p. 874]. The Office served as the central drug control entity responsible for coordinating all UN drug control activities, and as the repository of technical expertise in international drug control for the UN Secretariat. It acted on behalf of the Secretary-General in fulfilling his responsibilities under the terms of international treaties and resolutions relating to drug control, and provided services to the Assembly, the Economic and Social Council, and committees and conferences dealing with drug control matters.

The UNODC Executive Director described the Office's 2006 activities in a report to the Commission on Narcotic Drugs and to the Commission on Crime Prevention and Criminal Justice [E/CN.7/2007/6-E/CN.15/2007/14]. UNODC supported Member States through technical assistance, legal advice and research in international drug control, and assisted them in implementing the provisions of the three international drug control conventions. It maintained an online library of legislation adopted by States and territories to implement those conventions, as well as a directory of competent national authorities empowered to take action, in accordance with the 1988 Convention against Illicit Traffic in Narcotic Drugs and Psychotropic Substances [YUN 1998, p. 690], in relation to vessels involved in illicit drug trafficking by sea.

With regard to sustainable development and illicit crop monitoring and eradication, the Office's alternative development strategy addressed illicit crop cultivation through poverty reduction. UNODC promoted partnerships between affected States, international financial institutions, development actors and civil society to increase the scope of the assistance reaching poor farmers engaged in illicit cultivation, and assisted States in enhancing institutional capacities and mechanisms to plan, implement, evaluate and monitor alternative development interventions. In Afghanistan, it strengthened the institutional and operational capabilities of the key ministries at the national and provincial levels to ensure the inclusion of counter-narcotic objectives in development strategies and programmes; advocated the consolidation of a central opium-free area to achieve a reduction of opium poppy cultivation by 2010, breaking the North-South axis of trafficking and enhancing the impact of state-building and legitimization efforts; and developed a road map for expanding the provinces free of opium. UNODC alternative development programmes in the three Andean countries placed emphasis on environmental protection, gender equality and participatory approaches. In Colombia, it supported alternative development programmes promoting forest conservation, forest products, coffee, honey and cacao, reaching 8,000 families, and fostered partnerships with the private sector. In Peru, the Office worked with farmers' associations to provide technical assistance. In Bolivia, a new four-year phase of the agroforestry programme started in 2006 and was expected to benefit 4,500 farmer families in the targeted areas. In South-East Asia, UNODC alternative development programmes focused on food security and poverty alleviation. In the Lao People's Democratic Republic, UNODC provided assistance to improve the capacity of communities to address development and drug abuse, in partnership with other UN agencies. In Myanmar, its Wa alternative development project reached 40,000 people, mitigating the impact of opium poppy eradication through community-based activities in basic health care and education, sustainable livelihoods and infrastructure development. In both the Lao People's Democratic Republic and Myanmar, the Office supported projects focusing on environmental conservation and livelihoods. In the framework of its Illicit Crop Monitoring Programme, the Office, together with national agencies, conducted annual surveys in Afghanistan, Bolivia, Colombia, the Lao People's Democratic Republic, Morocco, Myanmar and Peru. In Afghanistan, UNODC strengthened its monitoring activities by conducting annual assessment surveys and monthly opium price monitoring reports, in addition to the annual opium surveys. It also verified the Government's eradication activities. During the year, UNODC published *Sweden's Successful Drug Policy: a Review of the Evidence*; *Coca Cultivation in the Andean Region: a Survey of Bolivia, Colombia and Peru*; *Afghanistan: Opium Survey 2006*; and *Morocco: Cannabis Survey 2005*.

UNODC continued its focus on drug abuse prevention and treatment, particularly among young people, with the aim of reducing demand by 2008. In 2006, the Global Youth Network against Drug Abuse expanded through regional networks, reaching more than 500 groups throughout the world. Other prevention work focused on approaches to preventing amphetamine-type stimulants (ATS) abuse, with training on prevention for policymakers and non-governmental organizations (NGOs). UNODC also assisted States in the development of evidence-based treatment services and, in partnership with the Joint United Nations Programme on HIV/AIDS (UNAIDS), increased the coverage of HIV/AIDS prevention and treatment services for injecting drug abusers. In Kenya, training for abuse prevention and HIV/AIDS among abusers and vulnerable populations continued, and several treatment centres were opened. In South Africa, the Office implemented a drug abuse and HIV/AIDS awareness project in three juvenile prisons. In March, UNODC and Cape

Verde launched an integrated programme addressing illicit trafficking, good governance, and uncivil behaviour.

In data collection and drug abuse epidemiology, the Office improved the coverage and quality of data and analysis available to Member States and, through the Global Assessment Programme on Drug Abuse, assisted over 70 countries in surveys and studies. UNODC was reviewing the strategy of that programme and developing a new approach to respond to emerging priorities.

UNODC also published the World Drug Report 2006 [Sales No. E.06.XI.10], which presented the trends in drug markets, showed the progress made in 2005, and highlighted weak elements in the global drug control system, most notably heroin supply in Afghanistan, cocaine demand in Europe and cannabis supply and demand everywhere.

Administrative and budgetary matters

In March, the Commission on Narcotic Drugs considered a Secretariat note on the preparation of the proposed strategic framework for the 2008-2009 biennium [E/CN.7/2006/9]. Pursuant to the Secretary-General's report entitled "Implementation of decisions from the 2005 World Summit Outcome for action by the Secretary-General" [YUN 2005, p. 77], the preparation of the framework would be initiated by the Secretary-General subsequent to the Assembly's approval of the review of all mandates older than five years, as requested in the 2005 World Summit Outcome [YUN 2005, p. 48]. The strategic framework would be submitted to the Committee for Programme and Coordination in 2006, so that its recommendations might be presented to the Assembly's sixty-first session.

As to the precarious financial state of the general-purpose funds of the UNODC drug programme, the cost-saving and efficiency measures detailed in the UNODC consolidated 2006-2007 budget [YUN 2005, p. 1362] had been implemented. Average annual general-purpose contributions to the drug programme were projected at $11.5 million for 2006. Special-purpose contributions increased to $58 million (1999-2005). The cost recovery proposal made at the Commission's reconvened forty-eighth session [ibid.] would leave a gap between projected general-purpose income and expenditure in 2006, reducing the general-purpose fund balance from $6 million to $4.5 million by the end of the year and leaving insufficient funds to cover costs in the first half of 2007. In order to alleviate the situation of general-purpose funds, local field office costs would have to be recovered. The Commission agreed that the cost factors and formulas for itemized direct cost recovery from projects would be agreed on a project-by-project and donor-by-donor basis, taking into consideration the proportionate infrastructure requirements of the respective field office for each UNODC project and ensuring that it was in line with donors' financial regulations and that recovery did not duplicate charges already subject to recovery as project support costs.

Commission on Narcotic Drugs

The Commission on Narcotic Drugs, at its forty-ninth session (Vienna, 13-17 March) [E/2006/28], recommended five resolutions and two decisions for adoption by the Economic and Social Council. It also adopted eight resolutions, which it brought to the attention of the Council.

Following the closure of its forty-ninth session on 17 March, the Commission opened its fiftieth session to elect the new chairman and other bureau members.

By **decision 2006/241** of 27 July, the Council took note of the Commission's report on its forty-ninth session. It approved the provisional agenda and documentation for the fiftieth (2007) session, on the understanding that intersessional meetings would be held in Vienna, at no additional cost, to finalize the items to be included in the provisional agenda and the documentation requirements for that session.

Drug demand reduction and drug abuse

The Commission on Narcotic Drugs had before it a January report by the Secretariat [E/CN.7/2006/2 & Corr.1], which provided an overview of trends in drug abuse for the period 1998-2004, based on information received from Member States in response to the annual reports questionnaire. Analysis of the responses indicated that there was a general lack of reliable information for North Africa and the Middle East, where the abuse of opioids and cannabis was increasing. However, cocaine abuse decreased and ATS abuse increased in a few countries. In sub-Saharan Africa, heroin and cannabis abuse was a major problem, while ATS and cocaine abuse was low and decreasing. In North America, the prevalence rates for cannabis and cocaine remained high. Heroin and methamphetamine abuse stabilized and MDMA (Ecstasy) continued to decrease. In Latin America and the Caribbean, cannabis abuse was slowly stabilizing, heroin abuse was relatively low and stable, but injecting drug abuse was a cause of concern. ATS abuse was low but increasing. The abuse of cocaine also seemed to be tapering off. In East and South-East Asia, heroin and opium abuse declined, cannabis and ATS consumption continued to increase and cocaine abuse remained low. In Central, South and South-West Asia, heroin and opium abuse had shown a steep increase since 2002, and almost all countries reported an increase in heroin and drug abuse by injection. Cannabis abuse was common and increasing in many countries. Cocaine abuse, which was not significant, remained stable but ATS abuse increased. In Eastern and South-Eastern Europe, cannabis abuse increased, even though it remained relatively low compared with Western and Central Europe. The abuse of heroin and other opioids increased, as well as cocaine, though not a primary substance of abuse. ATS abuse was low but had increased steadily since 1998. In Western and Central Europe, cannabis remained the main drug of abuse. Cocaine abuse increased considerably, while heroin declined as its abuser population was ageing. ATS abuse increased in many countries, although there were signs of stabilization or decline in some countries reporting high prevalence. For Oceania, the decrease in cannabis abuse was the result of the drop in its high prevalence in Australia. Heroin abuse decreased and cocaine and ATS abuse remained stable.

Analysed by substance, cannabis abuse increased in almost all regions and stabilized mainly in countries where the prevalence rate was high. The abuse of heroin and opium declined in some of the regions where they were traditionally abused, but increased in other regions. Cocaine abuse was generally stable, but its decline in North America was offset by its increase in Europe. Overall, ATS abuse showed signs of stabilization and, in some cases, decline.

The report stressed the need to improve the information available to Member States and the Secretariat in order to provide a better picture of the drug abuse situation and of progress made in demand reduction. In that regard, the Commission should reiterate the importance of developing national drug information systems, establishing regional epidemiological networks to ensure the exchange of expertise and good practice and harmonizing data collection methods and techniques to ensure global comparability.

Another January report by the Secretariat [E/CN.7/2006/2/Add.1] provided an overview of the evolution of drug abuse among young people since 1998. It indicated that cannabis remained the illicit drug most abused around the world by young people. Lifetime use increased in many countries but remained stable or decreased in others. Its use was perceived as being "normal" or more socially acceptable in a number of countries, an attitude that could lead to further increases. The abuse of MDMA (Ecstasy) stabilized or decreased in some countries, but was increasing in others. Cocaine abuse decreased in North America but increased in Europe. Heroin abuse, particularly by injection, decreased considerably in industrialized countries, but was increasing in Eastern Europe, Central and South-East Asia. The use of alcohol and tobacco and their relation to illicit drug abuse remained a problem for young people. While the availability of prevention programmes was increasing, their quality and effectiveness needed to be monitored and evaluated, with a view to improving them. Programmes targeting vulnerable and marginalized young people were insufficient, and countries with severe drug problems among youth populations continued to experience difficulties in initiating or sustaining abuse prevention programmes. Treatment services were not sought by or accessible to young people, and stimulant abuse treatment, an area of concern with regard to youth, was underdeveloped.

The report concluded that data on drug abuse among young people needed to be improved and more regions should provide information disaggregated by age and gender. Information on lifetime prevalence should be matched with that on such matters as demand for treatment, other health and social consequences, and the perception of risks and availability of drugs, with a view to developing and implementing prevention and treatment programmes. While most countries were engaged in abuse prevention, those efforts were concentrated in school settings and targeted interventions were not widespread. It was important that countries respond effectively to the identified priorities and needs of young people.

HIV/AIDS and other blood-borne viruses

On 17 March [E/2006/28 (res. 49/4)], the Commission invited Member States, in accordance with their national legislation, to develop demand reduction actions based on studies and research that demonstrated the efficacy and efficiency of drug-related treatment and prevention; adopt drug-related health policies that facilitated drug abuse prevention and access to different types of prevention, treatment and care for drug dependency, drug-related HIV/AIDS, hepatitis and other blood-borne diseases; promote access to health and social care for drug users and their families without discrimination and cooperate with relevant NGOs; and provide access to medications, vaccines and other measures consistent with international treaties and that were effective in reducing the risk of HIV/AIDS, hepatitis and other blood-borne diseases among injecting and other drug users. The Commission endorsed the recommendations of the Global Task Team on Improving AIDS Coordination among Multilateral Institutions and International Donors, as well as related decisions of the UNAIDS Programme Coordinating Board. It requested UNODC, in conformity with the document UNAIDS *Technical Support Division of Labour*, to provide technical assistance to States in developing demand reduction strategies and measures, including HIV/AIDS prevention and care in the context of drug abuse, consistent with international treaties. The UNODC Executive Director was requested to report to the Commission biennially, starting in 2008.

Illicit cultivation, manufacture and trafficking

The Commission considered a January report by the Executive Director on international assistance to States affected by the transit of illicit drugs [E/CN.7/2006/6], prepared in response to Economic and Social Council resolution 2005/27 [YUN 2005, p. 1364]. The UNODC strategic approach included support to transit States to upgrade legislation and judicial procedures; strengthen the technical skills of law enforcement agencies; improve data collection by national agencies to support informed responses to combat illicit drug trafficking and its associated problems; provide equipment to front-line operations; and strengthen cross-border and regional cooperation and assistance to develop self-sustaining training in the best operating practices for law enforcement services. In its review of UNODC initiatives, the report focused on: the global container control programme; the Central Asian regional information and coordination centre; the Paris Pact initiative [YUN 2003, p. 1263]; the Automated Donor Assistance Mechanism; computer-based training; precursor chemical control in South-East Asia; witness protection; and demand reduction.

On 17 March [E/2006/28 (res. 49/8)], the Commission called upon Member States to place emphasis on cooperative arrangements at the operational level to disrupt the manufacture of and trafficking in illicit drugs at their source or as close to it as possible. It urged them to enter into bilateral and multilateral arrangements between and among national law enforcement agencies to ensure the exchange of law enforcement information, the sharing of resources and expertise, including training methodologies, and the conduct of joint investigations targeting international organized criminal groups, and to minimize profiteering from the trade in illicit drugs. It also urged the continued and strengthened commitment of States to multi-jurisdictional law enforcement investigations targeting transnational criminal syndicates involved in the manufacture of and trafficking in illicit drugs.

Secretariat report. A report by the Secretariat [E/CN.7/2007/4] described global trends in illicit drug crop cultivation and production of plant-based drugs during 2004-2006 and regional and global patterns in illicit drug trafficking up to 2005, mainly based on drug seizure data. Information on cultivation and production trends was drawn from UNODC's crop monitoring surveys, and information on seizures was based on the replies by Governments to the annual reports questionnaire relating to illicit supply for the years up to and including 2005, both of which were supplemented by country reports received by UNODC or submitted to the Commission and its subsidiary bodies. According to the report, cannabis continued to be the most widely produced, trafficked and consumed plant-based drug worldwide. In 2004, global interdiction of cannabis herb stood at 6,190 tons and cannabis resin at 1,470 tons. In 2006, illicit opium poppy production in Afghanistan was estimated at 6,100 tons, compared to an estimate of 4,620 tons for 2005. Myanmar accounted for 4.75 per cent of global production, and the Lao People's Democratic Republic, 0.3 per cent, the same figure as in 2005. In 2004, global interdiction of opium stood at 210 tons, and heroin, at 60 tons. In 2005, 340 tons of opium and 57 tons of heroin were intercepted. Morphine interdiction increased between 2004 and 2005, from 39 to 50 tons. In 2005, the area under coca bush cultivation in the three principal coca-producing countries of Bolivia, Colombia and Peru was estimated at 159,600 hectares, and potential cocaine manufacture at 910 tons. Global seizures of cocaine stood at 588 tons, and its total interdiction at 644 tons. Crack cocaine interceptions increased from 0.5 to 3 tons in the 2004-2005 period. The global interdiction of ATS, excluding MDMA (Ecstasy), stood at 20 tons. Rates of interdiction were rising and, in 2005, totalled 29 tons of ATS and 5 tons of MDMA (Ecstasy).

In its recommendations, the report stressed that Governments should support the development of inter-agency and cross-border cooperation in order to extend the effectiveness of controls and strengthen countermeasures against trafficking. National law enforcement training academies should also be supported. States should post drug liaison officers to source countries that posed significant risks from illicit trafficking and encourage law enforcement agencies to establish and maintain communication and cooperation with the counterpart drug law enforcement authorities of Afghanistan, so as to assist them in achieving operational effectiveness. New trafficking challenges should be addressed, such as those posed by the use of the Internet. Governments undertaking eradication programmes should ensure that they were accompanied by a viable commercial alternative. In the face of the growing speed and integration of international trade and transport, Governments should ensure that their front-line law enforcement authorities were prepared and equipped to screen, evaluate and examine sea freight containers, and support agencies in coordinating with counterparts in other ports in and outside their regions. They should also ensure that their domestic legislation exercised effective control over precursor chemicals used in the illicit manufacture of narcotic drugs and ATS, and provide such powers as necessary to investigate, prosecute and penalize those persons engaged in their diversion and manufacture.

Alternative development

In a January report [E/CN.7/2006/7] on strengthening alternative development as an important drug control strategy and a cross-cutting issue, the Executive Director reviewed progress made in implementing Commission resolution 48/9 [YUN 2005, p. 1365] and described UNODC's catalytic role in preventing the re-emergence of illicit crop cultivation; integrating drug control as a cross-cutting issue; supporting a comprehensive approach to wider economic and social development and protecting the environment; creating a balanced approach between law enforcement, interdiction, eradication and alternative development; empowering the community and mainstreaming gender; creating partnerships with the private sector; and strengthening its capacity to provide guidance to Member States and partner institutions.

The report concluded that action in alternative development projects was hampered by a lack of technical and financial resources. The accessibility to alternative development projects should be increased and consideration given to the impact of trade policies and systems of preferences on alternative development products. The use of indicators as measures of the success of alternative development should be re-examined, and indicators gauging progress in social welfare improvement should be used, such as new income-generating opportunities. Although activities addressing development-oriented drug crop control were being considered, alternative development was not adequately mainstreamed because it was not being incorporated into general national development programmes. There was also insufficient focus on land tenure rights and micro-credit mechanisms, and marketing support by some States and development agencies created barriers to sustainable project activities. Private sector participation in marketing and product support was vital for project success. While the need to fuse eradication with development-oriented crop control was recognized, each project should measure the impact of eradication on creating the conditions to dissuade farmers from engaging in illicit crop cultivation.

International organizations, financial institutions, and development agencies and States should provide stable and adequate funding to alternative development programmes and projects. Development-oriented drug control interventions should be included in the national development programmes for concerned States, and alternative development mainstreamed within broader development programmes. The international community was urged to support States in implementing preventive alternative development programmes, and States, international development agencies and financial institutions and donors were encouraged to ensure that proper care was taken in the design of development activities, providing adequate funding for studies and research on the forces behind illicit crop cultivation. Programmes and projects should take into account the principle of land tenure and its importance to rural development, and UNODC should explore regional support mechanisms with the private sector and seek cooperation with other regional organizations.

ECONOMIC AND SOCIAL COUNCIL ACTION

On 27 July [meeting 41], the Economic and Social Council, on the recommendation of the Commission on Narcotic Drugs [E/2006/28], adopted **resolution 2006/33** without vote [agenda item 14 (*d*)].

Strengthening international cooperation for alternative development, including preventive alternative development, with due regard for environmental protection

The Economic and Social Council,

Reaffirming the Joint Ministerial Statement and further measures to implement the action plans emanating from the twentieth special session of the General Assembly, adopted during the ministerial segment of the forty-sixth session of the Commission on Narcotic Drugs, in which States were urged to provide greater access to their markets for products of alternative development programmes, which were necessary for the creation of employment and the eradication of poverty,

Reaffirming also its resolution 2003/37 of 22 July 2003 on strengthening alternative development through trade and socio-environmental preservation, in which it called upon the United Nations International Drug Control Programme and all Member States to continue to cooperate effectively on programmes to promote alternative development, including, where appropriate, preventive alternative development,

Reaffirming further Commission on Narcotic Drugs resolution 45/14 of 15 March 2002, in which the Commission invited Member States to make more comprehensive and determined efforts in the area of financial and technical cooperation aimed at promoting alternative development, including, where appropriate, preventive alternative development,

Bearing in mind Commission on Narcotic Drugs resolution 48/9 of 11 March 2005 and the report of the Executive Director of the United Nations Office on Drugs and Crime on strengthening alternative development as an important drug control strategy and establishing alternative development as a cross-cutting issue,

Recognizing with concern that in some Member States illicit crop cultivation and illicit drug production degrade, among other things, forest areas, areas under environmental protection and areas used for licit crops, causing serious environmental damage,

Taking into account the Millennium Development Goals, the Rio Declaration on Environment and Development and Agenda 21, adopted by the United Nations Conference on Environment and Development in 1992, and the Johannesburg Declaration on Sustainable Development,

Noting with concern that, in lands adjacent to areas used for the cultivation of illicit crops, there is a high risk of displacement of licit crops and their replacement by illicit crops,

Recognizing the importance of achieving a balance between law enforcement, demand reduction, interdiction, eradication and alternative development, including, where appropriate, preventive alternative development,

1. *Emphasizes* the importance of mainstreaming alternative development, including, where appropriate, preventive alternative development, into national and international development strategies as well as into development efforts;

2. *Requests* the United Nations Office on Drugs and Crime, subject to the availability of extrabudgetary resources, and all Member States to continue to cooperate effectively on programmes and projects to promote alternative development, including, where appropriate, preventive alternative development;

3. *Urges* donor Governments, in conformity with the principle of shared responsibility and as a sign of their commitment to fight against illicit drugs in a comprehensive and balanced manner, to increase their cooperation on alternative development matters, including, where appropriate, preventive alternative development, by taking into account environmental protection, sustainable forest management, including agroforestry and reforestation, technical assistance, production infrastructure and the promotion of private investment and the agricultural industry;

4. *Calls upon* Member States, consistent with their national and international obligations, and invites relevant international organizations to consider measures to facilitate access to and positioning in international markets for alternative development products;

5. *Invites* Member States, relevant international organizations, financial institutions, regional development banks, funds for the protection of the environment and non-governmental organizations to support and promote financing for programmes and projects in the context of alternative development, including, where appropriate, preventive alternative development, taking into account that, in areas affected by or vulnerable to illicit crop cultivation and illicit drug production, protecting the environment, preventing its degradation and promoting its sustainable recovery should be considered;

6. *Requests* the United Nations Office on Drugs and Crime, Member States and relevant international organizations to redouble their efforts to obtain new and additional voluntary financial resources, at the bilateral and multilateral levels, in support of programmes and projects related to alternative development, including, where appropriate, preventive alternative development, with due regard for environmental protection;

7. *Requests* the Executive Director of the United Nations Office on Drugs and Crime to report to the Commission on Narcotic Drugs at its fiftieth session on the implementation of the present resolution.

On the same day [meeting 41], the Council, on the recommendation of the Commission [E/2006/28], adopted **resolution 2006/31** without vote [agenda item 14 (*d*)].

Using alternative development programmes to reduce the cultivation of cannabis plants

The Economic and Social Council,

Recalling the provisions of the Single Convention on Narcotic Drugs of 1961, that Convention as amended by the 1972 Protocol, the Convention on Psychotropic Substances of 1971 and the United Nations Convention against Illicit Traffic in Narcotic Drugs and Psychotropic Substances of 1988,

Recalling also the Political Declaration adopted by the General Assembly at its twentieth special session, in which Member States recognized that action against the world drug problem was a common and shared responsibility,

Recalling further General Assembly resolution 59/160 of 20 December 2004 on the control of cultivation of and trafficking in cannabis,

Recalling Commission on Narcotic Drugs resolution 45/8 of 15 March 2002 on the control of cannabis in Africa,

Noting the progress made by the United Nations Office on Drugs and Crime in the implementation of General Assembly resolution 59/160, and looking forward to the forthcoming release of the market survey on cannabis requested by the Assembly in that resolution,

Emphasizing the need for States parties to continue to honour their obligations under the 1961 Convention, that Convention as amended by the 1972 Protocol, the 1971 Convention and the 1988 Convention,

Noting that cannabis is by far the most widely and most frequently abused of the drugs listed in the international drug control treaties,

Concerned that cultivation of cannabis plants and trafficking in and abuse of cannabis are on the increase in Africa, in part as a result of extreme poverty, the absence of any crops offering viable alternatives and the lack of resources for the identification and eradication of cultivation of cannabis plants and for interdiction efforts and in part because of the profitability of such activities and the high demand for cannabis in other regions,

Emphasizing the importance of international cooperation in combating both drug trafficking and drug abuse in a balanced and integrated manner,

Recognizing that alternative development programmes have proved to be a useful tool in efforts to eradicate illicit drug crop cultivation,

Aware of the importance of programmes promoting alternative development, including, where appropriate, preventive alternative development,

Having regard to the successes recorded so far in the reduction of coca bush and opium poppy cultivation through the application of alternative development programmes,

Taking note of the report of the International Narcotics Control Board for 2005, in which the Board regretted the absence of alternative development projects or programmes in Africa, despite the large amount of cannabis produced in the region,

Desiring that the successful application of alternative development programmes in efforts to sustain the reduction of coca bush and opium poppy cultivation be replicated, as appropriate and possible, in efforts to reduce the cultivation of cannabis plants,

1. *Calls upon* Member States to continue to adhere to the international drug control treaties and to adopt policies that promote international cooperation;

2. *Also calls upon* Member States, and requests the United Nations Office on Drugs and Crime, to implement General Assembly resolution 59/160 on the control of cultivation of and trafficking in cannabis;

3. *Urges* Member States, in accordance with the principle of shared responsibility and as part of their commitment to the fight against illicit drugs, to extend cooperation to affected States, especially in Africa, in the area of alternative development, including research into crops offering viable alternatives to cannabis, and technical assistance, with due regard to the environmental degradation caused by the cultivation of cannabis plants;

4. *Calls upon* Member States, and invites organizations with experience and relevant expertise in the eradication of illicit crops and in the design and implementation of alternative development programmes, to share that experience and expertise, upon request, with States seeking to develop and implement eradication and alternative development programmes with a view to reducing the cultivation of cannabis plants, especially in Africa, and requests the United Nations Office on Drugs and Crime to facilitate efforts in that regard;

5. *Urges* Member States in which the large-scale cultivation of cannabis plants is taking place to carry out, as a matter of priority and as appropriate, a comprehensive assessment of the extent of such cultivation and to use that assessment to inform both eradication and alternative development strategies with a view to further reducing the supply of cannabis;

6. *Requests* the United Nations Office on Drugs and Crime, when requested by States reporting the large-scale cultivation of cannabis plants, to conduct a study with development partners, subject to the availability of extrabudgetary resources, on the feasibility of implementing alternative development programmes in those countries;

7. *Urges* Member States implementing alternative development programmes to integrate them into other drug control measures, including demand reduction strategies, at the national and regional levels in such a way as to ensure the sustainability of those programmes;

8. *Requests* the United Nations Office on Drugs and Crime to consider the possibility of developing a global, integrated and balanced strategy for alternative development in consultation with Member States, in coordination with ongoing efforts to establish an overarching strategy, pursuant to paragraphs 9 and 10 of Commission on Narcotic Drugs resolution 48/14 of 8 December 2005;

9. *Requests* the Executive Director of the United Nations Office on Drugs and Crime to report to the Commission on Narcotic Drugs at its fifty-first session on the implementation of the present resolution.

Regional cooperation

In a December report [E/CN.7/2007/5], the Secretariat reviewed action taken by subsidiary bodies of the Commission on Narcotic Drugs in 2006. Following a review of drug trafficking trends and regional and subregional cooperation, each subsidiary body addressed drug law enforcement issues of priority in its region and made recommendations. The forty-first session of the Subcommission on Illicit Drug Traffic and Related Matters in the Near and Middle East (Amman, Jordan, 26-30 June) [UNODC/SUBCOM/2006/5] considered regional trends in trafficking in opiates; and regional cooperation in the exchange of criminal intelligence on drug trafficking. It also identified sound practice in the training of law enforcement officials. The sixteenth meeting of Heads of National Drug Law Enforcement Agencies (HONLEA), Africa (Nairobi, Kenya, 25-29 September) [UNODC/HONLAF/2006/5] considered the growing importance of Africa in international trafficking in cocaine; illicit cultivation of cannabis plant in Africa, trafficking in cannabis and its impact; and the identification and maintaintenance of effective control over the essential precursors scheduled in Tables I and II of the 1988 UN Convention against Illicit Traffic in Narcotic Drugs and Psychotropic Substances. The sixteenth meeting of HONLEA, Latin America and the Caribbean (Buenos Aires, Argentina, 23-27 October) [UNODC/HONLAC/2006/5] examined the response of the region to cocaine manufacture and trafficking; the rising threat of the abuse of ATS; and maritime trafficking in illicit drugs. The thirtieth meeting of HONLEA, Asia and the Pacific (Bangkok, Thailand, 14-17 November) [UNODC/HONLAP/2006/5] considered illicit traffic in and consumption of heroin; witness protection; control of ATS and their precursors; and illicit traffic by sea, confined waters and inland waterways.

Baku Accord on Regional Cooperation

ECONOMIC AND SOCIAL COUNCIL ACTION

On 27 July [meeting 41], the Economic and Social Council, on the recommendation of the Commission on Narcotic Drugs [E/2006/28], adopted **resolution 2006/30** without vote [agenda item 14 (*d*)].

Baku Accord on Regional Cooperation against Illicit Drugs and Related Matters: a Vision for the Twenty-first Century

The Economic and Social Council,

Recalling the Political Declaration adopted by the General Assembly at its twentieth special session, the Action Plan for the Implementation of the Declaration on the Guiding Principles of Drug Demand Reduction and the measures to enhance international cooperation to counter the world drug problem,

Recalling also General Assembly resolutions 53/115 of 9 December 1998, 54/132 of 17 December 1999, 55/65 of 4 December 2000, 56/124 of 19 December 2001 and 57/174 of 18 December 2002, in which the Assembly stressed the importance of the Subcommission on Illicit Drug Traffic and Related Matters in the Near and Middle East of the Commission on Narcotic Drugs, as well as the other subsidiary bodies of the Commission,

Recalling further General Assembly resolutions 53/115, 54/132, 55/65, 56/124, 57/174, 58/141 of 22 December 2003 and 59/163 of 20 December 2004, in which the Assembly encouraged the Subcommission, as well as the other subsidiary bodies of the Commission on Narcotic Drugs, to continue to contribute to the strengthening of regional and international cooperation, taking into account the outcome of the twentieth special session of the Assembly,

Recalling its resolution 1997/39 of 21 July 1997, entitled "Baku Accord on Regional Cooperation against Illicit Cultivation, Production, Trafficking, Distribution and Consumption of Narcotic Drugs and Psychotropic Substances and Their Precursors",

Convinced that the Baku Accord on Regional Cooperation against Illicit Drugs and Related Matters: a Vision for the Twenty-first Century will enhance cooperation against drug trafficking in the Near and Middle East,

1. *Takes note* of the Baku Accord on Regional Cooperation against Illicit Drugs and Related Matters: a Vision for the Twenty-first Century, the text of which is annexed to the present resolution;

2. *Urges* Member States to take appropriate measures to combat the traffic in narcotic drugs and psychotropic substances in accordance with the Baku Accord on Regional Cooperation against Illicit Drugs and Related Matters and the relevant resolutions of the Commission on Narcotic Drugs, the Economic and Social Council and the General Assembly and consistent with their national legislation and the provisions of the international drug control treaties;

3. *Requests* the Secretary-General to inform all Member States, relevant specialized agencies and other entities of the United Nations system and other intergovernmental organizations of the Baku Accord on Regional Cooperation against Illicit Drugs and Related Matters.

ANNEX

Baku Accord on Regional Cooperation against Illicit Drugs and Related Matters: a Vision for the Twenty-first Century

We, the representatives of States members of the Subcommission on Illicit Drug Traffic and Related Matters in the Near and Middle East,

Having gathered at the fortieth session of the Subcommission, held in Baku from 12 to 16 September 2005, to consider the Baku Accord on Regional Cooperation against Illicit Drugs and Related Matters: a Vision for the Twenty-first Century,

Bearing in mind the Political Declaration adopted by the General Assembly at its twentieth special session, the Action Plan for the Implementation of the Declaration on the Guiding Principles of Drug Demand Reduction and the measures to enhance international cooperation to counter the world drug problem,

Recalling Economic and Social Council resolution 1997/39 of 21 July 1997, entitled "Baku Accord on Regional Cooperation against Illicit Cultivation, Production, Trafficking, Distribution and Consumption of Narcotic Drugs and Psychotropic Substances and Their Precursors",

Recalling also Economic and Social Council resolution 2005/24 of 22 July 2005, entitled "Providing support to Afghanistan with a view to ensuring the effective implementation of its Counter-Narcotics Implementation Plan",

Recalling further Economic and Social Council resolution 2005/27 of 22 July 2005, entitled "International assistance to States affected by the transit of illicit drugs",

Bearing in mind the Joint Ministerial Statement and further measures to implement the action plans emanating from the twentieth special session of the General Assembly, adopted during the ministerial segment of the forty-sixth session of the Commission on Narcotic Drugs,

Recalling various other United Nations resolutions and recommendations, including General Assembly resolution 59/161 of 20 December 2004 and the recommendations of the International Narcotics Control Board in its report for 2004, requesting the international community to support the Government of Afghanistan in its fight against the illicit cultivation of opium poppy and trafficking in narcotic drugs,

Taking note of the third biennial report of the Executive Director of the United Nations Office on Drugs and Crime on the implementation of the outcome of the twentieth special session of the General Assembly and other relevant reports submitted to the Commission on Narcotic Drugs at its forty-eighth session, including the report on the world situation with regard to drug trafficking and the report on the world situation with regard to drug abuse,

Deeply concerned about the spread of drug abuse in the Near and Middle East and its effects on youth and on future generations,

Deeply concerned also about the increasing illicit cultivation of narcotic drug crops and illicit production of and trafficking in drugs, which threaten the political, economic and social structure and stability of the region,

Alarmed at the serious and growing threat posed by organized criminal groups involved in drug trafficking, money-laundering and various other forms of organized crime and their potential and, in some cases, actual links with terrorist groups,

Aware that in a number of countries illicit drug production represents a major obstacle to sustainable economic, social and political development,

Taking into account the multifaceted challenges faced by States situated along international trafficking routes and the effects of trafficking in drugs, including related crime and drug abuse, resulting from the transit of illicit drugs through the territory of transit States,

Recognizing the need to take further urgent measures against the illicit cultivation of narcotic drug crops and the illicit production of and trafficking in drugs in regions where drug traffickers and organized criminal groups take advantage of territories affected by conflict, war, foreign occupation or other situations to engage in illicit activities,

Mindful of the essential need to strengthen international, regional and subregional cooperation aimed at enhancing the capacity of States to tackle drug trafficking effectively and to meet the goals and targets for the year 2008 set by the General Assembly at its twentieth special session,

Reiterating the principle of shared responsibility and the need for all States to promote and implement the action necessary to counter the world drug problem in all its aspects,

Convinced that specific action and comprehensive, well-coordinated national plans are the most effective means by which to combat problems involving illicit drugs and related crime,

Have agreed on the following:

Cooperation between drug law enforcement agencies

1. We reaffirm our commitment to promoting coordinated drug control strategies and unified responses to drug trafficking and, in that context, encourage the development, effective implementation and further strengthening of measures for the prevention and suppression of drug trafficking and the reduction of illicit drug demand in transit States, as well as cooperation in areas such as border control, mutual legal assistance, law enforcement, including controlled delivery, and exchange of information between transit States, countries of destination and countries of origin.

2. In promoting a unified response to combating drug trafficking in the region, States members of the Subcommission on Illicit Drug Traffic and Related Matters in the Near and Middle East should promote closer coordination between drug law enforcement agencies of neighbouring States, such as through joint training, through the establishment of effective systems to promote the sharing of operational experience to facilitate the identification and arrest of drug traffickers and the dismantling of criminal groups and through the facilitation of regular meetings of drug law enforcement agencies with their cross-border counterparts.

3. Drug law enforcement agencies in the region should establish specific mechanisms for the regular exchange of information between national drug law enforcement agencies and their counterparts in neighbouring States and beyond on drug trafficking networks active in the region.

4. We emphasize the importance of coordinating law enforcement activities, in particular the exchange of information at the international level, which can benefit greatly by the establishment of coordination centres, such as the Central Asian Regional Information and Coordination Centre of the United Nations Office on Drugs and Crime.

5. Governments should designate national law enforcement authorities to be responsible for dealing with requests for mutual legal assistance, as provided for in article 7 of the United Nations Convention against Illicit Traffic in Narcotic Drugs and Psychotropic Substances of 1988, as well as cooperating closely with other authorities with a view to enhancing the effectiveness of law enforcement action, as provided for in article 9 of that Convention.

6. In order to expand their operational capacities, States members of the Subcommission should consider implementing coordinated operations at border stations, through coordinated mobile patrols and by strengthening joint drug law enforcement efforts at land and sea borders involving neighbouring States.

7. States members of the Subcommission should work towards greater harmonization of their criminal justice systems and national drug control legislation in order to expedite the taking of appropriate measures and other action against drug traffickers and related offenders.

8. States members of the Subcommission should work to support the efforts of the international community to provide the necessary support to the counter-narcotics objectives of the Government of Afghanistan, by continued technical assistance and financial commitment, in particular, to all eight pillars of the Counter-Narcotics Implementation Plan of Afghanistan.

9. The Subcommission should continue to meet on an annual basis in the capital city of one of its member States.

Drug demand reduction

10. States members of the Subcommission should promote awareness, in particular among young people, of the health, social and psychological problems that may result from the abuse of illicit drugs.

11. States members of the Subcommission should consider amending their national legislation, where necessary, to facilitate the treatment and rehabilitation of drug abusers through, for example, the introduction of drug courts, police referral to voluntary treatment programmes and other recognized alternative approaches to treatment.

12. States members of the Subcommission should strengthen their political commitment to implement drug abuse prevention policies and strategies effectively and to continue their drug demand reduction programmes, paying attention to early intervention, rehabilitation and social reintegration of drug users, in order to prevent the transmission of HIV/AIDS and other blood-borne diseases in the context of drug abuse.

13. States members of the Subcommission should continue to incorporate substance abuse prevention, treatment and health care into their national drug control strategies, as well as into their socio-economic development programmes, especially programmes designed to enhance the social and economic empowerment of women, and child welfare, including in relation to preventing and reducing the spread of HIV/AIDS and other blood-borne diseases in the context of drug abuse.

14. States members of the Subcommission are also encouraged to ensure that substance abuse treatment is accessible and affordable to drug abusers living with HIV/AIDS and other blood-borne diseases and to work to eliminate barriers to access for drug abusers in need of HIV/AIDS care and support.

Assistance to transit States

15. We welcome the follow-up of the United Nations Office on Drugs and Crime to the Paris Pact initiative that emerged from the Paris Statement, which was issued at the end of the Conference on Drug Routes from Central Asia to Europe, held in Paris on 21 and 22 May 2003, and encourage the development of similar strategies in other regions for countries affected by the transit of illicit drugs through their territory.

16. International financial institutions and other potential donors are encouraged to provide financial assistance to States affected by the transit of illicit drugs through their territory, including for empowering and building the capacity of locally available human resources, so that those States may intensify their efforts to combat drug trafficking and drug abuse and deal with their consequences.

17. States members of the Subcommission should integrate projects, where appropriate, for illicit drug demand reduction and strengthen treatment and rehabilitation services for drug abusers in the programmes for international assistance to those transit States which are affected by drug abuse as a result of the transit of illicit drugs through their territory, to enable them to deal effectively with the problem.

Control of precursors

18. States members of the Subcommission should cooperate closely with the International Narcotics Control Board to further strengthen international cooperation in the implementation of article 12 of the 1988 Convention, in accordance with the measures to control precursors adopted by the General Assembly at its twentieth special session.

19. States members of the Subcommission should support international operations aimed at preventing diversion of chemical precursors used in the illicit manufacture of cocaine, heroin and amphetamine-type stimulants, in particular Operation Topaz, Operation Purple and Project Prism coordinated by the International Narcotics Control Board, by exchanging information with other States and conducting timely joint law enforcement operations, including the use of controlled deliveries and backtracking investigations into the sources and origins of seizures.

20. States members of the Subcommission are urged to take immediate steps to ensure that the substances listed in Tables I and II of the 1988 Convention are placed under the control of their regulatory authorities.

Money-laundering

21. States members of the Subcommission should strengthen action to prevent and combat money-laundering, including by enhancing international cooperation, adopting legislation that makes money-laundering a criminal and extraditable offence, establishing financial intelligence units to support the effective investigation and prosecution of money-laundering offences and removing any impediments to criminal investigation linked to bank secrecy.

International cooperation in illicit crop eradication and alternative development

22. The international community should be requested to assist and cooperate in the development of illicit crop eradication programmes and to promote alternative development programmes and, in particular, support should be given to Afghanistan in this respect.

United Nations Convention against Transnational Organized Crime and the Protocols thereto and the United Nations Convention against Corruption

23. States members of the Subcommission welcome the entry into force of the United Nations Convention

against Transnational Organized Crime and its Protocol to Prevent, Suppress and Punish Trafficking in Persons, Especially Women and Children, the Protocol against the Smuggling of Migrants by Land, Sea and Air and the Protocol against the Illicit Manufacturing of and Trafficking in Firearms, Their Parts and Components and Ammunition.

24. States members of the Subcommission that have not yet done so should become parties to and implement the organized crime Convention and the Protocols thereto, as well as the universal conventions and protocols related to terrorism, as soon as possible and, where appropriate, request assistance to that end from the United Nations Office on Drugs and Crime, in coordination with other relevant United Nations bodies, such as the Counter-Terrorism Committee.

25. States members of the Subcommission should also consider signing and ratifying the United Nations Convention against Corruption as soon as possible in order to allow its early entry into force and subsequent implementation.

26. States members of the Subcommission and relevant regional economic integration organizations should take all necessary measures to improve international cooperation in criminal matters, especially in the form of extradition and mutual legal assistance, in accordance with the relevant conventions.

Strengthening UN mechanisms

The Commission on Narcotic Drugs had before it a report [E/CN.7/2006/8] by the Executive Director on strengthening UNODC drug programme and the role of the Commission as its governing body, and securing assured and predictable voluntary funding. The report, prepared in response to Commission resolutions 48/2 [YUN 2005, p. 1367] and 48/3 [ibid., p. 1361], reviewed action taken to facilitate dialogue between Member States and the UNODC drug programme; operations and management; and the funding of the UNODC drug programme.

Chapter XV

Statistics

In 2006, the United Nations statistical work programme was conducted mainly through the activities of the Statistical Commission and the United Nations Statistics Division. In March, the Statistical Commission recommended to the Economic and Social Council the adoption of a draft resolution urging donors and the international and regional statistical community to support developing countries and countries with economies in transition in strengthening statistical capacity in support of development; the Council adopted the resolution in July. The Commission also approved its multi-year work programme for 2006-2009.

The Commission reviewed the work of groups of countries and international organizations in various areas of economic, social, demographic and environmental statistics and made specific recommendations and suggestions.

Work of Statistical Commission

The Statistical Commission, in accordance with Economic and Social Council decision 2005/244 [YUN 2005, p. 1368], held its thirty-seventh session in New York from 7 to 10 March [E/2006/24]. Among other actions, the Commission: recommended a draft resolution on strengthening statistical capacity, by which the Council would call upon Member States to strengthen national statistical capacity in order to produce reliable and timely statistics and indicators for monitoring national development policies and strategies, the implementation of commitments and the achievement of all development goals; urge donors and the international and regional statistical communities to support developing countries and countries with economies in transition in strengthening statistical capacity in support of development; and call upon international agencies to improve the coverage, transparency and reporting on all indicators in order to enhance the database on all Millennium Development Goals (MDGs) [YUN 2000, p. 51], including by defining priorities and developing a strategy to improve data for all indicators.

The Commission endorsed the work of the Statistics Division on the revision of the statistical standards and its initiative and strategy for revising recommendations in distributive trade statistics; recommended the establishment of a friends of the chair to prepare a concept paper on the modalities of the integrated approach to economic statistics, including the feasibility of establishing a mechanism for improving coordination among international organizations and work groups engaged in economic statistics; recognized the need for adequate response to Member States' requests for assistance in capacity-building to implement the revision of the 1993 System of National Accounts (SNA) [YUN 1993, p. 1112]; and accepted the proposal by the Intersecretariat Working Group on National Accounts to prepare a programme of implementation by 2008.

The Commission adopted the structures of the International Standard Industrial Classification of All Economic Activities, Revision 4 and the Central Product Classification, Version 2, as the recognized international standards for economic activity and product classifications. It took note of the World Bank's report on the International Comparison Programme [YUN 2005, p. 1369] and supported the Programme's continuation. It agreed with the Programme's Executive Board that an evaluation of the 2005 round of data collection and a plan for the Programme's future be submitted in 2007. The Commission encouraged the UN Committee of Experts on Environmental Economic Accounting to establish a website for facilitating exchanges of best practices and the use of environmental economic accounts. It emphasized the urgent need for harmonizing energy definitions, compiling methodologies and developing international standards in energy statistics. The Commission also emphasized the importance of statistical capacity-building and technical assistance as vehicles for improving gender statistics at the national level. It noted that the Committee for the Coordination of Statistical Activities had recognized the importance of the principles governing international statistical activities in guiding the professional statistical activities of international agencies; agreed that statistical capacity-building was key to improving the availability of data for monitoring the MDGs; and recommended that the terms of reference of the Intersecretariat Working Group on

Health Statistics be redrafted and submitted to the Statistical Commission in 2007 for approval. The Commission also approved its 2006-2009 multi-year programme of work.

On 24 July (**decision 2006/232**), the Council took note of the Commission's report on its thirty-seventh session [E/2006/24], decided that the thirty-eighth session would be held in New York from 27 February to 2 March 2007 and approved the provisional agenda and documentation for that session.

Economic statistics

National accounts

Responding to a 2005 Statistical Commission request [YUN 2005, p. 1369], the Secretary-General submitted the Intersecretariat Working Group on National Accounts (ISWGNA) report [E/CN.3/2006/6] on progress made in updating the 1993 SNA [YUN 1993, p. 1112], including an overview of activities taken, the mechanism of global consultations on recommendations, progress made on the 44 agreed issues and on management of the update process. The Working Group provided information on the implementation of the 1993 SNA work programme, including meetings of the Advisory Expert Group, which reported that the resolution of the 44 agreed issues considered by the Group was proceeding according to schedule. As requested by the Commission, the Advisory Expert Group's recommendations on the issues had been sent to all national statistical offices and central banks for global consultation, and those recommendations and supporting issue papers had also been posted on the 1993 SNA update website. The process of developing and refining recommendations on the issues involved close interaction between the task forces and the Advisory Expert Group, which had either completed or nearly completed consideration of about three quarters of the SNA update issues. With the issues-oriented phase coming to a conclusion, attention was focused on transforming the recommendations into the 1993 SNA, Rev.1. Two further Advisory Expert Group meetings would be held in 2007 to address the overall consistency of recommendations and the integrity of the system as embodied in the draft of the 1993 SNA, Rev.1. The Statistical Commission would be requested to review the full set of recommendations for the SNA update in March 2007 and the final draft in March 2008.

In March [E/2006/24], the Commission commended the progress made in updating the 1993 SNA in the issues-oriented phase of the update process and expressed confidence in the Working Group to maintain the momentum in the drafting and review phases of the update process in 2006 and 2007. It attributed the progress made to the adoption of the project management approach and the extensive use of a transparent interactive website, and recommended that that approach and technology be used in similar statistical projects and programmes. The Commission welcomed the inclusion of a chapter on the measurement of informal sector activities in the revision of the 1993 SNA and took note of the concerns on the treatment of unfunded government pension schemes and the need for continuing consultations on the recommendation of the Advisory Expert Group on that issue. It recommended that the Working Group continue to include the treatment of government social services in its research agenda and recognized the need for adequate response to Member States' requests for assistance in capacity-building for the implementation of the revision of the 1993 SNA. It accepted the Working Group's proposal to prepare an implementation programme by 2008.

Service statistics

The Statistical Commission had before it a report of the Organisation for Economic Cooperation and Development (OECD) on service statistics [E/CN.3/2006/22], which summarized the main developments in service statistics in various expert groups, described progress in the creation of an intersecretariat working group on service statistics and incorporated a report on developments in the future agenda of the Voorburg Group on Service Statistics.

Progress continued on the coordinated revision and updating of the fundamental frameworks that underpinned the production of useful and comparable statistics on services, including: the updated 1993 SNA and the revised *Balance of Payments Manual*, both scheduled to be published in 2008; the International Standard Industry Classification of All Economic Activities; and the Central Product Classification, to be revised in 2007. The Interagency Task Force on Statistics of International Trade in Services agreed to update the *Manual on Statistics of International Trade in Services* by 2009 in order to maintain its usefulness and relevance for countries. A worldwide consultation on updating the Manual would be conducted in 2006. The Statistics Division was developing a worldwide database for trade in services in cooperation with OECD to complement the United Nations Commodity Trade Statistics Database (Comtrade) merchandise trade database. Following the Statistical Commission's 2005 recommendation [YUN 2005, p. 1369] to create an intersecretariat working group on service statistics, OECD invited international organizations to participate in the group. Five organizations had so far indicated their wish to do so and a draft terms of reference had been circulated for consideration by those organizations.

The report noted that the Voorburg Group on Service Statistics, at its September 2005 meeting in Helsinki, confirmed its objective, focus and scope and adopted measures to develop the working agenda for the near future. To advance the development of producer price indices and turnover of services, it was agreed that some changes needed to be introduced to the workplan, its process and the meeting's format. In that context, a task force was established to, among other things, develop a workplan for the next few years with a tangible objective and timetable.

In March [E/2006/24], the Commission took note of the OECD report on service statistics.

The Interagency Task force on Statistics of International Trade in Services (Paris, France, 15 September) [BOPCOM-06/20] considered revisions to the International Monetary Fund (IMF) *Balance of Payments Manual* related to trade in services frameworks, especially draft chapter 9 on the goods and services account. It reviewed responses to worldwide consultations on updating the *Manual on Statistics of International Trade in Services*. The Task Force agreed to complete the review of the responses in 2007 and to prepare a draft annotated outline of the new Manual for discussion. The Task Force also considered knowledge transfer and technical cooperation, and noted the call by the Coordinating Committee of Statistical Agencies for more formal coordination of statistical technical assistance to avoid waste and duplication.

International Comparison Programme

The Statistical Commission had before it the Secretary-General's note transmitting a World Bank report on the International Comparison Programme (ICP) [E/CN.3/2006/8], which provided an overview of the global programme, reviewed the ICP Executive Board actions, discussed preparations for remaining price collection activities and described regional status reports. The report noted that significant progress had been made, with all regions fully engaged in data collection. All had reviewed preliminary data and calculated purchasing power parities at the basic heading level for analysis. The ring product list had been finalized, as had specifications for collecting prices for the equipment, construction, health and government sectors comparisons. All regions expected to meet the requirements for national annual prices for the 2005 reference year. The global programme faced a $1 million funding shortfall to carry out the programme until the end of 2007, half of which was needed in the first part of 2006 to support final data collection for construction, equipment and the Global Ring Comparison Programme. Countries and regional coordinators were raising questions about the ICP's future, especially the potential loss of expertise and experience if there were no plans to continue it. The ICP Executive Board had agreed to continue the Programme beyond the current round with a business model that would spread the work out over time. It directed the ICP Global Office to begin the evaluation process, and regional coordinators to complete their self-evaluations by October. As to the Global Ring Comparison Programme, a ring product list containing 950 consumption items had been developed with input from regional offices and ring countries. While it was possible to find similar products among regions, it was necessary to harmonize the terminology defining the products. The ICP handbook had 14 chapters describing the methodology underpinning the Programme's current ICP round.

In March [E/2006/24], the Commission recommended that, for transparency and data quality, the price and survey data from each region should be reviewed by other regional coordinators, and there should be full consultation with countries on the estimation of purchasing power parities and publication plans, without restrictions on releasing the results. It advised that regional coordinators and the ICP Global Office should be cautious about the level of detail to be published in the preliminary reports. The Commission supported the Programme's continuation so as to utilize the improved capacity in price data compilation and the established infrastructure, and agreed with the Executive Board's recommendation that an evaluation of the 2005 round and a plan on the Programme's future be submitted to the Commission at its 2007 session. It requested that increased efforts be made to expand the Programme's country coverage.

Other economic statistics

Energy statistics

The Statistical Commission considered a report prepared by Statistics Norway [E/CN.3/2006/11] on quality components of oil statistics. Focusing on national oil statistics as the key to the quality of international oil statistics, the report analysed the main quality challenges and made recommendations for improvement, both at the governance and technical levels. The report noted that the economy in most countries was influenced by what happened in the international oil markets. Shortcomings in national and global oil statistics had contributed to market volatility and created enormous challenges for economic policymaking in many countries. Elevating oil statistics to the level of official statistics would help improve their quality. Statistics Norway's recommendations for addressing those problems included: strengthening the role of national statistical offices in the production of good-quality energy statistics; attaining international agreement on a common set of definitions; establishing a broad-based review team to analyse different definitions and suggest a common definition for each product and key concepts so as to prevent double reporting; and failing that, agree on an international reporting standard to be applied when completing questionnaires. It also recommended establishing common international routines for revising data to secure consistency and continuity and analysing statistical differences in reporting; and documenting national production routines for oil statistics. To provide the oil market with information on the likely future development of production in the medium and long run, information on investment in oil and gas exploration and production and remaining resources was needed. The possibility of establishing an internationally approved method for those estimates should be discussed. It was especially important to find ways to further improve the timeliness of data, while reducing the use of preliminary and estimated figures.

The Commission also considered the report of the Oslo Group on Energy Statistics [E/CN.3/2007/20], which described the Group's activities in 2006, including the main findings of its first meeting in February 2006, the establishment and working of its electronic discussion forum, the survey on official energy statistics and issues related to coordination with other groups. The report also included information about items for the draft agenda of the Group's second meeting, to be held in New Delhi in 2007.

In March [E/2006/24] the Commission, recognizing the significance of energy statistics, recommended their development as part of official statistics. It supported the establishment and mandate of the Oslo Group on Energy Statistics and the Intersecretariat Working Group on Energy Statistics and requested proper coordination between them. The Commission also supported the review of UN manuals on energy statistics, which should be based on all relevant methodological work in energy statistics, and emphasized the urgent need for harmonization of energy definitions and compilation methodologies and the development of international standards in energy statistics. It also supported the establishment of a broadly based review team to propose common concepts and definitions, and requested that the UN Statistics Division submit the modalities of that review team to the Statistical Commission's Bureau for approval.

Business surveys and informal sector statistics

The Statistical Commission had before it the report of the Round Table on Business Survey Frames [E/CN.3/2006/23], which outlined the issues discussed at its 2005 meeting (Cardiff, United Kingdom, 16-21 October), including: the role of the business register in the statistical system; quality and coverage; enterprise group recording and measurement; developing new register system and tools; dissemination of register data; implementing classification changes; confidentiality; and the Round Table's future. The meeting established a steering group to, among other things, promote the Round Table's work and seek inputs regarding its future activities, and to prepare a paper reviewing the Round Table's achievements and setting out its scope and goals for future years.

Also before the Commission was the report of the Delhi Group on Informal Sector Statistics [E/CN.3/2006/26], which described the issues discussed at the Group's eighth meeting, summarized its recommendations and outlined the Group's future activities, including identifying, defining and developing a core set of indicators in line with the importance placed on informal employment by the Task Force on Education and Gender Equality of the UN Millennium Project.

In March [E/2006/24], the Commission took note of the reports of the Round Table on Business Survey Frames and the Delhi Group on Informal Sector Statistics.

Environment statistics

The Statistical Commission considered the report of the Intersecretariat Working Group on Environment Statistics [E/CN.3/2006/21] and the Secretary-General's report on environmental accounting [E/CN.3/2006/9]. The Working Group, outlining its activities for 2006-2007, reported that it would focus on continuing methodological and harmonization work in the area of water through the Subgroup on Water Statistics; setting up a new subgroup on land-use and land cover statistics for the discussion of methodological issues; reviewing the draft chapters of the revised UN Statistics Division *Glossary of Environmental Statistics*; and organizing the international work session on land-use and land cover statistics in 2007.

The Secretary-General's report presented the conclusions of the preliminary meeting of the Committee of Experts on Environmental Economic Accounting and reviewed the Committee's long-term objectives, work programme and governance structure. Established by the Statistical Commission in 2005 [YUN 2005, p. 1371], the Committee, at its preliminary meeting (New York, 29-31 August 2005), agreed on its overall objectives, namely: mainstreaming environmental economic accounting and related statistics; elevating the System of Integrated Environmental and Economic Accounting (SEEA) to an international statistical standard; and advancing SEEA implementation at the global level. To achieve those objectives, five components for the Committee's work programme were identified: coordination, promotion of accounts, SEEA implementation, methodological research, and harmonization of data-collection activities with environmental-economic accounting concepts and definitions. Annexed to the report were the Committee's terms of reference.

In March [E/2006/24], the Commission endorsed the long-term objectives, work programme and governance structure of the United Nations Committee of Experts on Environmental Economic Accounting, and encouraged the Committee to establish a website for facilitating exchanges of best practices and use of environmental economic accounts. The Committee should focus on the development and promotion of environmental accounting and refine its working relationship with those groups responsible for the development of environmental, energy and related statistics.

Industrial statistics

The Secretary-General transmitted to the Statistical Commission the report on industrial statistics [E/CN.3/2006/3] of the Director General for Policy Planning (Statistical Standards) of Japan's Ministry of Internal Affairs and Communications which described the situation and practices in international industrial statistics, issues and challenges, international responses to those challenges, and progress made. The report also addressed recommendations to national statistical agencies for developing internationally comparable industrial statistics and to international organizations in the areas of data collection standards, data dissemination standards, training and capacity-building and international coordination. It called on the Statistics Division, international partners and States to revise UN recommendations related to industrial statistics, produce new recommendations or manuals with new methodologies, expand the scope of the recommendations and develop an integrated economic statistics programme. It should also review international standards and recommendations.

In March [E/2006/24], the Commission agreed with the report's recommendations and endorsed the work carried out by the Statistics Division on the revision of statistical standards. It requested the Division to prepare a position paper on the recommendations contained in the report, describing institutional arrangements, deliverables, timetables and consequences of implementing them for submission to the Commission in 2007. The Commission, noting that the integration of industrial statistics with other statistics, such as services statistics, needed to be improved, supported the creation of an integrated economic statistics programme. In that regard, it proposed that a concept paper be prepared for further discussion.

International trade statistics

The Secretary-General transmitted to the Statistical Commission the report of the Task Force on International Merchandise Trade Statistics [E/CN.3/2006/25], which discussed the development by the Task Force of a Manual on Export and Import Price Indices, under the aegis of the IMF, and its endorsement of the provisional draft of the fourth revision of the Standard International Trade Classification, prepared by the Statistics Division. It also described the Task Force's activities since 2003, as well as new issues and related future activities, especially the reconciliation of balance-of-payments and foreign trade statistics, structural business and trade statistics and the review of country compilation and reporting practices.

Also before the Commission was a report of the UN Statistics Division and OECD on the Joint United Nations/OECD System for collection and processing of international merchandise trade statistics [E/CN.3/2006/24]. Developed between 2002 and 2005, the Joint System included: an agreement on arrangements for data collection and data sharing; common data-processing standards; and computer applications for use in data processing and dissemination.

In March [E/2006/24], the Commission took note of both reports.

Distributive trade statistics

The Statistical Commission had before it the Secretary-General's report on distributive trade statistics [E/CN.3/2006/4], which outlined the Statistics Division's strategy for revising international recommendations on distributive trade statistics, its actions in that regard in 2005, and a summary of its 2006-2007 action plan. The report noted that in 2004, the Statistics Division had developed a multi-year strategy for updating international recommendations on distributive trade statistics, including, among other things, establishing an Expert Group on Distributive Trade Statistics to assist the Division in the updating process, preparing a manual on the compilation of distributive trade statistics by 2008, and developing a UN database for storing, processing and disseminating such statistics by 2007 and to report to the Commission in 2011.

In March [E/2006/24], the Commission endorsed the Statistics Division's strategy for revising recommendations in that area of statistics, to be carried out in consultation with national statistical officers so as to fully reflect the specific needs and circumstances of various groups of countries, particularly those with a substantial informal sector. While endorsing the Division's plans for compiling distributive trade statistics worldwide and building a corresponding database, the Commission cautioned that the level of detail requested for international reporting should be commensurate with country needs and capacity to compile, and requested the Division to review international databases in that area of statistics to avoid creating an additional reporting burden on countries and duplication of work. It also advised the Division to develop practical guidance on compilation of distributive trade statistics, including description of good practices, and provide technical assistance as a matter of priority. The Division should submit a progress report to the Commission in 2007 and revised draft recommendations in 2008 for approval.

Integrated economic statistics

The Statistical Commission considered the Secretary-General's report on integrated economic statistics [E/CN.3/2006/5], which proposed the establishment of an integrated programme on economic statistics based on the recommendations of the Expert Group Meeting on Distributive Trade, the Expert Group on Industrial Statistics and the International Workshop on Economic Census. The report discussed the five components of work for the integrated economic statistics programme: promotion of an integrated approach to economic statistics; development of concepts; coordination among various statistical groups operating in the field of economic statistics; implementation of the integrated economic statistics programme in countries; and harmonization of data collection activities.

In March [E/2006/24], the Commission endorsed the concept of an integrated economic statistics approach as the appropriate strategy for the development of national and international economic and financial statistics programmes. The concept should be operationalized by, among other measures, identifying the building blocks, such as business registers, economic censuses, structural and short-term business statistics across economic activities and class sizes; formulating priorities reflecting country and regional policy needs; and developing institutional arrangements to ensure coordination. The Commission also recommended the establishment of a friends of the chair to prepare a concept paper on the modalities of the integrated approach to economic statistics, including a mechanism for improving coordination among international organizations and work groups engaged in economic statistics.

Demographic and social statistics

Population and housing censuses

The Statistical Commission had before it a Secretary-General's report on population and housing censuses [E/CN.3/2006/16], which summarized activities regarding the Statistics Division's role as secretariat of the 2010 World Programme on Population and Housing Censuses; work on the revision of the United Nations *Principles and Recommendations for Population and Housing Censuses* by a UN expert group, specifically the group's 2005 recommendations (New York, 22-26 August); Economic and Social Council resolution 2005/13 [YUN 2005, p. 1372] on the 2010 World Programme; and the coordination of regional activities in preparation for the 2010 round of population and housing censuses.

In March [E/2006/24], the Commission took note of the Secretary-General's report on population and housing censuses.

Health statistics

The Statistical Commission had before it a report of the World Health Organization (WHO) on health statistics [E/CN.3/2006/17], which described progress since the establishment in 2004 [YUN 2004, p. 1259] of an intersecretariat working group on health statistics to develop a coordinated and integrated agenda for the production of health statistics and agree on standard definitions, classifications and methodologies. In response to the Commission's 2005 request [YUN 2005, p. 1372], WHO also provided an update on the release of microdata from the World Health Survey (2002-2003) with appropriate metadata; and summarized ongoing efforts to coordinate the generation of health statistics and to support countries in strengthening their health information systems. The report noted that the membership of the WHO-based Health Metrics Network (HMN), officially launched at the World Health Assembly in May 2005 [ibid., p. 1573], reflected the collaboration's strong focus on bringing together the health and statistics constituencies at global, regional and country levels in order to strengthen the ability of countries to generate, analyse, disseminate and use sound health statistics. The Intersecretariat Working Group on Health Statistics, at its 2005 meeting (Rome, 28 November), finalized its terms of reference and discussed its priorities: vital statistics systems, HMN, health and disability statistics and the update and revision of the International Statistical Classification of Diseases and Health Related Problems.

In March [E/2006/24], the Commission welcomed the HMN initiative and expressed the need for greater data harmonization and enhanced collaboration with national statistical offices. Regarding the Intersecretariat Working Group on Health Statistics, the Commission took note of the special circumstances under which the first meeting had been organized and requested WHO to hold a second meeting with adequate representation of countries and agencies. It recommended that the Group's terms of reference be redrafted and submitted to the Statistical Commission in 2007 for approval and a workplan developed, taking into consideration the Budapest Initiative, a Joint UN Economic Commission for Europe (ECE)/WHO/Eurostat Task Force on Measuring Health Status, established in 2004 [YUN 2004, p. 1259] to develop a common instrument for doing so in multiple dimensions. The work of the Task Force had been referred to as the Budapest Initiative, since its meeting in that city in 2005.

Labour statistics

The Statistical Commission took note of the report of the Paris Group on Labour and Compensation [E/CN.3/2006/18], which summarized the activities of the Group on the measurement of working time during 2004 and 2005. The Paris Group's work on working-time measurement was being undertaken to assist the International Labour Organization in developing a resolution on working time for the 2008 International Conference of Labour Statisticians. Further work on both working-time measurement and on the ageing labour force would be undertaken in the context of the seventh meeting of the Paris Group (Budapest, 15-17 May).

Poverty statistics

The Statistical Commission had before it the report of the Secretary-General on poverty statistics [E/CN.3/2006/19], which described the final stages of the preparation of the *United Nations Handbook on Poverty Statistics*, including a global consultation on country practices on poverty measurement. The draft handbook was the product of a three-year study that sought to enhance the understanding of the ways in which countries measured poverty, thereby identifying strengths and weaknesses in data-collection processes. The draft handbook contained recommendations on good practices, which should help to make national statistics more comparable. Also before the Commission was a report of the Rio Group on Poverty Statistics [E/CN.3/2006/20], which discussed preparations to complete a compendium of good practices on poverty statistics.

In March [E/2006/24], the Commission took note of both reports.

Social statistics

The Statistical Commission had before it the Secretary-General's report on social statistics [E/CN.3/2006/12], which analysed and reviewed the availability of data and assessed progress made in the provision of gender statistics in the past 30 years. It also summarized the findings of *The World's Women 2005: Progress in Statistics*, published by the Statistics Division. Stark disparities were identified in national statistical capacity to report such statistics. *The World's Women 2005: Progress in Statistics* identified three key actions to improve gender statistics and proposed strategies for implementing each action, namely: strengthening national statistical capacity; mainstreaming gender in national statistical systems to encompass all aspects of the production of statistics; and developing of and improving concepts and methods for collecting and analysing gender statistics.

In March [E/2006/24], the Commission endorsed the actions and strategies proposed for improving gender statistics, and emphasized the importance of statistical capacity-building and technical assistance in that regard at the national level. It requested that progress in the national production and reporting of gender statistics should be evaluated, and recommended that such analysis and presentation of national statistical capacity should display official national statistics to better reveal data gaps. It also requested that MDGs indicators take that perspective into consideration. The Commission recognized that, while gender statistics units played an important role in promoting gender statistics in national statistical systems, many other approaches existed to advance gender statistics. It reiterated the importance of developing and improving basic sources of reliable data, and underscored the need to develop concepts and methods for assessing gender differences in poverty and measuring domestic violence and violence against women.

Other statistical activities

International economic and social classifications

The Statistical Commission considered the Secretary-General's report on international economic and social classifications [E/CN.3/2006/7], which described the status of revisions of the International Standard Industrial Classification of All Economic Activities, the Central Product Classification, the International Standard Classification of Occupations, the Standard International Trade Classification and the agricultural classifications.

In March [E/2006/24], the Commission adopted the structures of the International Standard Industrial Classification of All Economic Activities, Revision 4 and the Central Product Classification, Version 2, as the recognized international standards for economic activity and product classifications. Countries should adapt their national classifications so as to be able to report data at least at the two-digit level of the International Standard Classification of All Economic Activities without loss of information. The Commission requested further elaboration on the plan for implementing the International Standard Industrial Classification of All Economic Activities and the Central Product Classification and asked the UN Statistics Division to formulate a plan of work for presentation in 2007. It reaffirmed its confidence in the process for the completion of the International Standard Classification of Occupations, planned for 2008, and welcomed the reassurance that, prior to finalization, it would be brought back to the Commission for consultation and advice. The Commission agreed not to pursue the creation of a correspondence between the Central Product Classification and the UN Standard Product and Services Code and recognized that the potential of the Central Product Classification for satisfying the statistical needs with regard to price statistics of the Ottawa Group on Price Indexes [YUN 2005, p. 1370] needed to be further assessed.

Statistical capacity-building

The Statistical Commission had before it the Secretary-General's report on statistical capacity-building [E/CN.3/2006/27], which provided an overview of the Statistics Division's approach to capacity-building and reported on technical cooperation activities in 2004-2005.

Also before the Commission was the report of the Partnership in Statistics for Development in the Twenty-first Century (PARIS 21) on statistical capacity-building [E/CN.3/2006/28], which outlined the Partnership's efforts in promoting the better use of improved statistics as a central part of the enabling environment for development progress, particularly through support to countries in the design, implementation and monitoring of national strategies for the development of statistics with a focus on low-income countries. The report also described the Partnership's role in the national strategy process and progress in supporting country efforts towards designing, implementing and monitoring national strategies for the development of statistics and directions for future work.

ECONOMIC AND SOCIAL COUNCIL ACTION

On 24 July [meeting 37], the Economic and Social Council, on the recommendation of the Statistical Commission [E/2006/24], adopted **resolution 2006/6** without vote [agenda item 13 (*c*)].

Strengthening statistical capacity

The Economic and Social Council,

Deeply concerned that (*a*) there still exists in many countries a lack of adequate data to (i) assess national trends in the context of monitoring progress towards the realization of all the internationally agreed development goals, including the Millennium Development Goals, and (ii) inform and monitor the implementation of national development policies and strategies, and (*b*) in many countries where data do exist, there is lack of capacity to use them and, in certain cases where country data are available, they are not used to the extent possible,

Affirming that without a coordinated effort to enhance and sustain statistical capability in many developing countries and countries with economies in transition, effective monitoring of progress towards national as well as internationally agreed development goals, including the Millennium Development Goals, is being compromised,

Recognizing the fundamental importance of sustainable national statistical capacity to produce reliable and timely indicators of a country's progress,

Expressing its concern about the validity of the use by international agencies of imputed data, particularly when there is a lack of transparency in their methodology,

Recalling its resolution 2000/27 of 28 July 2000, in which it reaffirmed the importance of national efforts to build statistical capacity in all countries, including through statistical training, and of effective international support in this context for developing countries and countries with economies in transition,

Recalling also its resolution 2005/13 of 22 July 2005, in which it noted the critical importance of the 2010 round of population and housing censuses for meeting data needs for the follow-up activities to the international conferences and summits, including the Millennium Summit,

Stressing that all review and follow-up processes of the major United Nations conferences and summits in the economic, social and related fields must focus on the progress made in the implementation of commitments,

Reiterating the need for continued efforts by the Statistical Commission to further improve the list of indicators on implementation of the outcomes of the major United Nations conferences and summits in the economic, social and related fields, including by means of methodological and technical refinement of the existing indicators,

Reiterating also the need to apply and further develop implementation indicators to evaluate progress towards conference goals to create an enabling environment for development,

1. *Calls upon* Member States to intensify their efforts to strengthen national statistical capacity in order to produce reliable and timely statistics and indicators for the monitoring of:

(a) National development policies and strategies;

(b) The implementation of commitments and the achievement of all development goals at the national, regional and international levels;

2. *Calls upon* the United Nations system, including the Statistics Division of the Department of Economic and Social Affairs of the Secretariat and the regional commissions and international agencies, to support national efforts in building and strengthening national statistical capacity, in particular of developing countries;

3. *Encourages* the strengthening of statistical capacity of the relevant international agencies;

4. *Urges* donor countries and organizations and the international and regional statistical community to support developing countries and countries with economies in transition in strengthening statistical capacity in support of development; they should largely build upon existing national, regional and international initiatives in a coordinated manner and encourage other initiatives to address significant gaps that might emerge;

5. *Calls upon* all international agencies, through the Inter-Agency and Expert Group on Millennium Development Goals Indicators, under the coordination of the Statistics Division and in accordance with the guidance provided by Member States through the Statistical Commission, to improve the coverage, transparency and reporting on all indicators in order to enhance the database on all Millennium Development Goals, including by:

(a) Defining priorities and developing a strategy to improve data for all indicators;

(b) Identifying ways, including through capacity-building where needed, to improve reporting by countries on all Millennium Development Goals;

(c) Avoiding imputation unless specific country data are available for reliable imputations following consultations with concerned countries and through transparent methodologies;

(d) Ensuring that the supporting metadata comply with guidelines developed by an expert panel constituted by the Statistical Commission for that purpose, and in this regard requests the Secretariat to forward recommendations to the Statistical Commission for consideration and adoption;

6. *Requests* the Secretary-General to report on the implementation of the present resolution in the context of the regular report on statistical capacity-building to be presented under the relevant agenda item for discussion by the Statistical Commission at its thirty-eighth session.

Follow-up to UN conferences and summits

The Statistical Commission had before it the Secretary-General's report on development indicators [E/CN.3/2006/14], which described the results of an assessment conducted by the UN Statistics Division of countries' capacity to produce the MDG indicators, and provided an update of the work of the Inter-agency and Expert Group on MDG Indicators in 2005 in the following areas: compilation and analysis of the indicators; review of methodologies related to the agreed indicators; coordination of data collection at the global level; coordination and support to countries in the compilation and analysis of indicators at the national level; and preparation of analysis and reporting on progress towards the MDGs.

Also before the Statistical Commission was the report of the Friends of the Chair on MDG Indicators [E/CN.3/2006/15], which addressed concerns related to the assessment of country capacity to produce indicators for monitoring the follow-up to the United Nations Millennium Summit [YUN 2000, p. 49]. The report outlined the discussion of major concerns, limitations to the database used for the Statistics Division's report, metadata and the way forward. It offered recommendations including: the need for the international community, individual countries and their advisers to better understand the serious shortcomings in the MDG indicators; strong international and national support for the successful implementation of the Marrakesh Action Plan for Statistics [YUN 2004, p. 1261]; and continued support for the Inter-agency and Expert Group initiative, led by the Statistics Division, for improving the availability and quality of metadata supporting the MDG database.

Another report of the Secretary-General on indicators for monitoring the MDGs [E/CN.3/2007/13] described the work in 2006 of the Inter-Agency and Expert Group on MDG Indicators in the following areas: improvement of the coverage, transparency and reporting on all indicators as presented in the database on all MDGs; review of methodologies related to the agreed indicators; coordination of global data collection; and preparation of the yearly analysis and reports on progress towards the MDGs. It noted that the Inter-Agency and Expert Group on MDG indicators met twice in 2006, from 27 to 30 March, in Washington, D.C., and from 13 to 16 November, in Geneva.

In March [E/2006/24], the Commission took note of the recommendations of the Friends of the Chair on MDG Indicators and stressed the importance of addressing those issues in the context of strengthening the statistical capacity-building of Member States, in particular developing countries. It recommended that international agencies turn to data imputation only when country data were not available, and recognized that the mechanisms for reporting data from national to international statistical systems should be improved. It agreed that statistical capacity-building was key to improving the availability of data for monitoring the MDGs and should be extended to regional institutions, and the process of assessing and supporting the building of country capacities should continue. The Commission requested the Inter-Agency and Expert Group on MDG Indicators to take into account the relevant recommendations of the Friends of the Chair to improve further the compilation of all the indicators and the monitoring of all the MDGs and report to the Commission in 2008.

Coordination and integration of statistical programmes

The Statistical Commission considered the Secretary-General's report on principles governing international statistical activities [E/CN.3/2006/13], which presented a set of principles and related good practices for international organizations and described the process that had led to the endorsement of those principles by the chief statisticians of international organizations in the Committee for the Coordination of Statistical Activities (CCSA). Also before the Commission was the Secretary-General's report on CCSA work [E/CN.3/2006/30].

In March [E/2006/24], the Commission, welcoming the principles governing international statistical activities, noted that CCSA had recognized their importance in guiding the professional statistical activities of international agencies and had agreed that they could be used in different ways by agencies depending on their mandate and governance. It requested CCSA to assess the implementation of the principles by organizations and report to the Commission in 2008, include in the preamble to the principles the description of the role of international organizations in the global statistical system, expand the best practices associated with the principles and extend the adoption of the principles to subregional organizations.

The Commission noted the Secretary-General's report on CCSA activities.

In 2006, CCSA held two meetings: the seventh (New York, 6 March) and eighth (Montreal, Canada, 4-5 September) [E/CN.3/2007/24]. Subjects discussed included: international quality assurance frameworks; implementation of the Principles for statistical activities in international organizations; statistical training for the staff of international agencies; implementation plan of the Statistical Data and Metadata Exchange; coordination of technical cooperation activities; and country regional grouping and coding.

Follow-up to Economic and Social Council policy decisions

The Statistical Commission had before it a note by the Commission's Bureau [E/CN.3/2006/2] on follow-up actions taken by the Bureau since the Commission's 2005 session. The note covered actions related to the review of the Commission's working methods [YUN 2005, p.1375], and the approval of various expert group mechanisms, as well as the Commission's agenda.

Also before the Commission were a note by the Secretary-General on policy decisions of the Economic and Social Council adopted in 2005 that were relevant to the Commission's work [E/CN.3/2006/29] and a report on Economic and Social Council policy decisions that were relevant to the Commission's work [E/CN.3/2007/27].

In March [E/2006/24], the Commission took note of both notes.

Programme and institutional questions

The Commission approved its 2006-2009 multi-year programme of work [E/CN.3/2006/31], as orally amended; recommended that the topic for the 2008 programme review be employment statistics; and approved the provisional agenda and documentation for its thirty-eighth (2007) session, to be held in New York from 27 February to 2 March.

PART FOUR

Legal questions

Chapter 1

International Court of Justice

In 2006, the International Court of Justice (ICJ) delivered one Judgment, made five Orders and had 14 contentious cases pending before it. In a 26 October address to the General Assembly, the ICJ President underlined the role and importance of the Court and its contribution to the promotion and development of a unified international legal system. She emphasized that the Court, as the principal judicial organ of the United Nations, served as the Court of all Member States. The ICJ President noted that the sixtieth anniversary of ICJ provided an occasion for the Court to reflect on what it had achieved and areas where it could improve. She observed that, since the inception of ICJ, new courts and tribunals had been established to deal with a variety of international needs and it was gratifying to see that those courts and tribunals had regularly referred to the Judgments of ICJ with respect to questions of international law and procedure, thus acknowledging the authoritative nature of the Court's Judgments.

Judicial work of the Court

During 2006, the Court delivered a Judgment on the merits of the case concerning the *Armed Activities on the Territory of the Congo (New Application: 2002) (Democratic Republic of the Congo v. Rwanda)*.

During the year, the Court was seized of three new cases: *Status vis-à-vis the Host State of a Diplomatic Envoy to the United Nations (Commonwealth of Dominica v. Switzerland); Pulp Mills on the River Uruguay (Argentina v. Uruguay)*; and *Certain Questions of Mutual Assistance in Criminal Matters (Djibouti v. France)*.

It held public hearings in the cases concerning *Application of the Convention on the Prevention and Punishment of the Crime of Genocide (Bosnia and Herzegovina v. Serbia and Montenegro)* [YUN 1993, p. 1138] and *Pulp Mills on the River Uruguay (Argentina v. Uruguay)*.

The Court or its President further made five Orders on the conduct of the proceedings in the cases concerning *Pulp Mills on the River Uruguay (Argentina v. Uruguay)*; *Maritime Delimitation in the Black Sea (Romania v. Ukraine)*; *Certain Questions of Mutual Assistance in Criminal Matters (Djibouti v. France)*; *Status vis-à-vis the Host State of a Diplomatic Envoy to the United Nations (Commonwealth of Dominica v. Switzerland)*; and *Certain Criminal Proceedings in France (Republic of the Congo v. France)*.

During the year, there were no new developments in the cases concerning *Gabcikovo-Nagymaros Project (Hungary/Slovakia)* [YUN 1998, p. 1186]; *Armed Activities on the Territory of the Congo (Democratic Republic of the Congo v. Uganda)* [YUN 1999, p. 1209]; *Maritime Delimitation between Nicaragua and Honduras in the Carribean Sea (Nicaragua v. Honduras)* [ibid., p. 1210]; *Application of the Convention on the Prevention and Punishment of the Crime of Genocide (Croatia v. Serbia and Montenegro)* [ibid.]; *Territorial and Maritime Dispute (Nicaragua v. Colombia)* [YUN 2001, p. 1195]; *Certain Criminal Proceedings in France (Republic of the Congo v. France)* [YUN 2002, p. 1263]; and *Dispute regarding Navigational and Related Rights (Costa Rica v. Nicaragua)* [YUN 2005, p. 1385].

ICJ activities were covered in two reports to the General Assembly, for the periods 1 August 2005 to 31 July 2006 [A/61/4] and 1 August 2006 to 31 July 2007 [A/62/4]. On 26 October 2006, the Assembly took note of the 2005/2006 report (**decision 61/507**).

Application of the Convention on the Prevention and Punishment of the Crime of Genocide (Bosnia and Herzegovina v. Serbia and Montenegro)

Bosnia and Herzegovina instituted proceedings in 1993 [YUN 1993, p. 1138] against Serbia and Montenegro, then known as the Federal Republic of Yugoslavia, for alleged violations of the 1948 Convention on the Prevention and Punishment of the Crime of Genocide, adopted by the General Assembly in resolution 260 A (III) [YUN 1948-49, p. 959]. The Court delivered its Judgment in 1996 [YUN 1996, p. 1179], rejecting the preliminary objections raised by Serbia and Montenegro in 1995 [YUN 1995, p. 1307]. In 1997, Serbia and Montenegro filed a Counter-Memorial that included counterclaims against Bosnia and Herzegovina [YUN 1997, p. 1315]. Bosnia and Herzegovina filed a Reply in 1998 [YUN 1998, p. 1186], and Serbia and Montenegro filed a Rejoinder in 1999 [YUN 1999, p. 1204].

By an Order of 10 September 2001, the President of the Court placed on record the withdrawal by Serbia and Montenegro of the counterclaims submitted in its Counter-Memorial [YUN 2001, p. 1184].

Serbia and Montenegro had submitted to the Court, on 4 May 2001, a document entitled "Initiative to the Court to reconsider *ex officio* Jurisdiction over Yugoslavia". Submissions presented in the document were, firstly, that the Court had no jurisdiction *ratione persona* over Serbia and Montenegro and, secondly, that the Court should suspend proceedings regarding the merits of the case until a decision on the jurisdictional issue had been rendered. In a 12 June 2003 letter, the ICJ Registrar informed the Parties that the Court had decided that it could not effect a suspension of the proceedings in the circumstances of the case [YUN 2003, p. 1302].

Public hearings on the merits of the case were held from 27 February to 9 May 2006. At the conclusion of the hearings, the Parties presented submissions to the Court. Bosnia and Herzegovina requested the Court to adjudge and declare that Serbia and Montenegro, by intentionally destroying in part non-Serb national, ethnic or religious groups within, but not limited to, the territory of Bosnia and Herzegovina, including in particular the Muslim population, through its organs or entities under its control, had violated its obligations under the Convention on the Prevention and Punishment of the Crime of Genocide by: complicity in genocide, and aiding and abetting individuals, groups and entities engaged in acts of genocide; conspiring to commit genocide, inciting to commit genocide; having failed to prevent genocide, punish acts of genocide or any other act prohibited by the Convention, and transfer individuals accused of genocide or any other act prohibited by the Convention to the International Tribunal for the Former Yugoslavia and for not cooperating fully with the Tribunal; and that it had violated the Orders of the Court on provisional measures of 8 April and 13 September 1993 [YUN 1993, p. 1338] by having failed to comply with those measures. Bosnia and Herzegovina further requested the Court to declare that Serbia and Montenegro should immediately take steps to ensure full compliance with the obligations to punish acts of genocide and transfer individuals accused of genocide; redress the consequences of its international wrongful acts and pay for damage caused; and that Bosnia and Herzegovina was entitled to receive, in its own right and as *parens patriae* for its citizens, full compensation for the damages and losses caused. The Court should also determine the nature, form and amount of the compensation, and Serbia and Montenegro would provide specific guarantees and assurances that it would not repeat the wrongful acts.

Serbia and Montenegro requested the Court to adjudge and declare that it had no jurisdiction because Serbia and Montenegro, as the respondent State, had no access to the Court at the relevant moment, or, in the alternative, that the Court had no jurisdiction over Serbia and Montenegro because Serbia and Montenegro never remained or became bound by Article IX of the Convention, and because there was no other ground on which jurisdiction over Serbia and Montenegro could be based. Serbia and Montenegro further requested that, in case the Court determined that jurisdiction existed, the Court should adjudge and declare that the submissions of Bosnia and Herzegovina relating to alleged violations of the obligations under the Convention be rejected as lacking a basis either in law or in fact; that the acts and/or omissions for which Serbia and Montenegro was alleged to be responsible were not attributable to it, as such attribution would necessarily involve breaches of the law applicable in the proceedings; that without prejudice to the foregoing, the relief available to Bosnia and Herzegovina as the applicant State in proceedings, in accordance with the appropriate interpretation of the Convention, was limited to the rendering of a declaratory judgment; and furthermore that any question of legal responsibility for alleged breaches of the Orders for the indication of provisional measures, as stated above, would not fall within the competence of the Court to provide appropriate remedies to an applicant State in the context of contentious proceedings, and accordingly that the request in the submissions of Bosnia and Herzegovina be rejected. The Court was expected to announce its judgment in February 2007.

Ahmadou Sadio Diallo (Guinea v. Democratic Republic of the Congo)

In 1998 [YUN 1998, p. 1190], Guinea instituted proceedings against the Democratic Republic of the Congo (DRC) by an "Application with a view to diplomatic protection", in which it requested the Court to condemn the DRC for the grave breaches of international law perpetrated upon the person of a Guinean national, Ahmadou Sadio Diallo.

According to Guinea, Mr. Diallo, a businessman, who had been a resident of the DRC for 32 years, was "unlawfully imprisoned by the authorities of that State" for two and a half months, "divested from his important investments, companies, bank accounts, movable and immovable properties, then expelled". The expulsion took place on 2 February 1996, as a result of his attempts to recover sums owed to him by the DRC (especially by Gécamines, a State enterprise and mining monopoly) and by oil companies operating in that country (Zaire Shell, Zaire Mobil and Zaire Fina), by virtue of contracts concluded with businesses owned by him, namely Africom-Zaire and Africacontainers-Zaire.

As a basis of the Court's jurisdiction, Guinea invoked its own declaration of acceptance of the compulsory jurisdiction of the Court of 11 November 1998 and a declaration of the DRC of 8 February 1989. On 3 October 2002, within the time limit for the deposit of its Counter-Memorial [YUN 2000, p. 1213], the DRC filed preliminary objections to the Court's jurisdiction and the admissibility of the Application; the proceedings on the merits were accordingly suspended.

By an Order of 7 November 2002, the Court fixed 7 July 2003 as the time limit within which Guinea might present a written statement of its observations and submissions on the preliminary objections raised by the DRC; the written statements was filed within the time limit.

Public hearings on the preliminary objections were held from 27 November to 1 December, 2006, during which the Parties presented final submissions to the Court. The DRC requested the Court to adjudge and declare that the Application of Guinea was inadmissible on the grounds that Guinea had no status to exercise diplomatic protection in the proceedings, since its Application sought essentially to secure reparation for injury suffered on account of the violation of rights of companies which did not possess its nationality, and, in any event, neither the companies in question nor Mr. Diallo had exhausted the effective local remedies available in the DRC.

Guinea requested the Court to reject the preliminary objections raised by the DRC; declare its Application admissible; and fix time limits for further proceedings. A Judgment on the preliminary objections was expected in May 2007.

Armed Activities on the Territory of the Congo (New Application: 2002) (Democratic Republic of the Congo v. Rwanda)

On 28 May 2002 [YUN 2002, p. 1271], the Democratic Republic of the Congo (DRC) filed an Application instituting proceedings against Rwanda in respect of a dispute concerning massive, serious and flagrant violations of human rights and international humanitarian law resulting "from acts of armed aggression perpetrated by Rwanda on the territory of the DRC in flagrant breach of the sovereignty and territorial integrity of the [latter], as guaranteed by the Charters of the United Nations and the Organization of African Unity (OAU)." The DRC requested the Court to adjudge and declare that, by violating human rights, Rwanda had violated and was violating the UN Charter, as well as articles 3 and 4 of the OAU Charter; that it further violated a number of instruments protecting human rights; that, by shooting down a Boeing 727 owned by Congo Airlines on 9 October 1998 in Kindu, thereby causing the deaths of 40 civilians, Rwanda had violated certain conventions regarding international civil aviation; and that, by engaging in killing, slaughter, rape, throat-slitting and crucifying, Rwanda was guilty of genocide against more than 3.5 million Congolese, including the victims of massacres in the city of Kisangani, and had violated the sacred right to life provided for in certain instruments protecting human rights, as well as the 1948 Convention on the Prevention and Punishment of the Crime of Genocide. It further asked the Court to adjudge and declare that all Rwandan armed forces should be withdrawn from Congolese territory and that the DRC was entitled to compensation. In its Application, the DRC, in order to found the jurisdiction of the Court, relied on a number of compromissory clauses in treaties.

Also on 28 May 2002 [YUN 2002, p. 1272], the DRC submitted a request for the indication of provisional measures. Following public hearings on the request, the Court delivered its Order, by which, having found that it had no prima facie jurisdiction, it rejected the request of the DRC. The Court also rejected the submissions by Rwanda seeking the removal of the case from the Court's List.

By an Order of 18 September 2002 [ibid.], the Court decided that the written pleadings would first be addressed to the questions of the jurisdiction of the Court and the admissibility of the Application, and fixed 20 January 2003 as the time limit for the Memorial of Rwanda and 20 May 2003 for the DRC Counter-Memorial. The pleadings were filed within the time limits [YUN 2003, p. 1306].

Public hearings to address the questions of the jurisdiction of the Court and the admissibility of the Application were held from 4 to 8 July 2005. At the conclusion of those hearings, the Parties presented their final submissions to the Court. Rwanda requested the Court to adjudge and declare that it lacked jurisdiction over the claims brought against Rwanda by the DRC, and that such claims were inadmissible. The DRC asked the Court to find that the objections to jurisdiction and admissibility raised by Rwanda were unfounded, and that the Court had jurisdiction to entertain the case on those merits and that the Application of the DRC was admissible as submitted. It further asked the Court to proceed with the case on the merits.

In its Judgment delivered on 3 February 2006, the Court by 15 votes to 2, found that it had no jurisdiction to entertain the Application filed by the DRC.

Appended to the Judgment were: declarations by Judges Kooijmans and Elaraby; separate opinions by Judge Al-Khasawneh and ad hoc Judge Dugard; a joint separate opinion by Judges Higgins, Kooijmans, Elaraby, Owada and Simma; and dissenting opinions by Judge Koroma and Judge ad hoc Mavungu.

Sovereignty over Pedra Branca/Pulau Batu Puteh, Middle Rocks and South Ledge (Malaysia/Singapore)

On 24 July 2003 [YUN 2003, p. 1308], Malaysia and Singapore jointly notified the Court of a Special Agreement, which was signed between them on 6 February 2003 at Putrajaya, Malaysia, and entered into force on 9 May 2003. In article 2 of the Special Agreement, the Parties requested the Court to determine whether sovereignty over Pedra Branca/ Pulau Batu Puteh, Middle Rocks and South Ledge belonged to Malaysia or Singapore. In article 6, the Parties agreed to accept the judgment of the Court as final and binding upon them. The Parties further set out their views on the procedure to be followed.

On 1 September 2003 [ibid., p. 1309], the Court fixed 25 March 2004 and 25 January 2005 as the respective time limits for the filing, by each of the Parties of a Memorial and of a Counter-Memorial. The Memorials were filed within the time limit. On 1 February 2005, the Court fixed 25 November 2005 as the time limit for the filing of a Reply by each of the Parties. The Replies were duly filed within the time limit fixed.

By a joint letter of 23 January 2006, the Parties informed the Court that they had agreed that there was no need for an exchange of Rejoinders in the case. The Court itself subsequently decided that no further pleadings were necessary and that the written proceedings were accordingly closed. The Court set 6 November 2007 as the date for the opening of hearings in the case.

Maritime Delimitation in the Black Sea (Romania v. Ukraine)

On 16 September 2004 [YUN 2004, p. 1271], Romania filed an Application instituting proceedings against Ukraine in respect of a dispute concerning the establishment of a single maritime boundary between the two States in the Black Sea, thereby delimiting the continental shelf and the exclusive economic zones appertaining to them. Romania had requested the Court to draw, in accordance with international law, and specifically the criteria laid down in article 4 of the Additional Agreement to the June 1997 Treaty on Relations of Co-operation and Good Neighbourliness between Romania and Ukraine, a single maritime boundary between the continental shelf and the exclusive economic zone of the two States in the Black Sea.

As a basis for the Court's jurisdiction, Romania invoked article 4 *(h)* of the Additional Agreement, which provided that, if the negotiations should not determine the conclusion of an agreement on the delimitation of the continental shelf and the exclusive economic zones in the Black Sea in a reasonable period of time, no later than two years after their initiation, Romania and Ukraine would agree that the delimitation problem would be solved by ICJ, at their request, provided that the treaty on the regime of the State border between Romania and Ukraine had entered into force. However, should ICJ consider that the delay of the entry into force of the treaty on the border regime was the result of the other Party's fault, it might examine the request concerning the delimitation before the entry into force of the treaty.

Romania contended that the two conditions set out in article 4 *(h)* of the Additional Agreement had been fulfilled, since the negotiations had by far exceeded two years and the Treaty on the Romanian-Ukrainian State Border Régime had entered into force on 27 May 2004.

In its Application, Romania further provided an overview of the applicable law for solving the dispute, citing a number of provisions of the Additional Agreement of 1997, as well as the 1982 United Nations Convention on the Law of the Sea [YUN 1982, p. 181], to which both Ukraine and Romania were parties, together with other relevant instruments binding the two countries.

On 19 November 2004, the Court fixed 19 August 2005 and 19 May 2006, respectively, as the time limits for the filing of a Memorial by Romania and a Counter-Memorial by Ukraine.

By an Order of 30 June 2006, the Court authorized the filing of a Reply by Romania and a Rejoinder by Ukraine and fixed 22 December 2006 and 15 June 2007 as the respective time limits for the filing of those pleadings. Romania filed its Reply within the time limit.

Certain Questions of Mutual Assistance in Criminal Matters (Djibouti v. France)

On 9 January 2006, Djibouti filed an Application instituting proceedings against France regarding the alleged violation by the latter of its international obligations in respect of mutual assistance in criminal matters in the context of the investigation into the death of French Judge Bernard Borrel in Djibouti in 1995.

In its Application, Djibouti explained that the dispute concerned the refusal by the French governmental and judicial authorities to execute an international letter rogatory regarding the transmission to the Djiboutian judicial authorities of the records relating to the investigation in the case against X for the murder of Bernard Borrel. Djibouti maintained that the refusal constituted a violation of France's international obligations under the 1977 Treaty of Friendship and Co-operation signed by the two States and the 1986 Convention on Mutual Assistance in Criminal Matters between France and Djibouti. Djibouti further asserted that, in summoning certain internationally protected nationals of Djibouti, including the Head of State, as *témoins assistés* (legally represented witnesses) in connection with a criminal complaint for subornation of perjury against X in the Borrel case, France had violated its obligation to prevent attacks on the person and on the freedom or dignity of persons enjoying such protection.

In its Application, Djibouti sought to found the jurisdiction of the Court on Article 38, paragraph 5, of the Rules of Court. In accordance with that Article, the Application by Djibouti was transmitted to the French Government.

In a letter dated 25 July 2006, France informed the Court that it consented to the jurisdiction of the Court to entertain the Application filed by Djibouti, pursuant to Article 38, paragraph 5, of its Rules. That consent made it possible to enter the case in the Court's General List on 9 August 2006 and to open the proceedings.

By an Order of 15 November 2006, the Court fixed 15 March 2007 as the time limit for the filing of a Memorial by Djibouti and 13 July 2007 as the time limit for the filing of a Counter-Memorial by France.

Status vis-à-vis the Host State of a Diplomatic Envoy to the United Nations (Commonwealth of Dominica v. Switzerland)

On 26 April 2006, the Commonwealth of Dominica instituted proceedings against Switzerland concerning alleged violations by the latter of the Vienna Convention on Diplomatic Relations [YUN 1961, p. 512], as well of other international instruments and rules, with respect to a diplomatic envoy of Dominica to the United Nations in Geneva.

In its Application, Dominica stated that the diplomat in question, Mr. Roman Lakschin, had been accredited to the United Nations and its specialized agencies and to the World Trade Organization (WTO) since March 1996 as a member of the Permanent Mission of Dominica to the United Nations in Geneva (first as Counsellor, and later as Chargé d'affaires and Deputy Permanent Representative, with the rank of Ambassador). Dominica emphasized that accreditation was "effected to the organisations and not to Switzerland", but that, nevertheless, Switzerland had claimed the right to withdraw the accreditation of the said envoy, stating that he was a businessman and as such would have no right to be a diplomat. Dominica contended that Switzerland could not be allowed to control a small State like Dominica, with a population of merely some 70,000 people, and thus restrict its selection of foreign envoys. It further stated that it had the right to send whichever envoy it considered appropriate to the United Nations in Geneva in its attempt to better its tourism prospects and economy. Dominica maintained that Switzerland had deprived it of "welcome and competent assistance" in establishing and running a Mission in Geneva and thereby impeded its efforts to develop trade and investment.

As basis for the Court's jurisdiction, Dominica invoked the declarations of acceptance of the Court's jurisdiction under Article 36, paragraph 2, of its Statute made by Dominica on 17 March 2006 and by Switzerland on 28 July 1948, as well as Article 1 of the Optional Protocol to the Vienna Convention for the Compulsory Settlement of Disputes [ibid., p. 516], to which both parties had adhered.

By letter of 15 May 2006, the Prime Minister of Dominica informed the Court that his Government did not wish to continue with the proceedings instituted against Switzerland and requested the Court to make an Order "officially recording [their] unconditional discontinuance", directing the removal of the case from the General List. By letter of 24 May, the Swiss Ambassador in The Hague advised the Court that he had duly informed the competent Swiss authorities of the discontinuance.

Accordingly, on 9 June, the Court made an Order in which, after having noted that the Government of the Swiss Confederation had not taken any step in the proceedings in the case, recorded the discontinuance of the proceedings at the request of Dominica and ordered that the case be removed from the General List.

Pulp Mills on the River Uruguay (Argentina v. Uruguay)

On 4 May 2006, Argentina filed an Application instituting proceedings against Uruguay for alleged breaches by Uruguay of obligations incumbent upon it under the Statute of the River Uruguay, a treaty signed between the two States on 26 February 1975 for the purpose of establishing the joint machinery for the optimum and rational utilization of that part of the river which constituted their joint boundary.

In its Application, Argentina charged the Government of Uruguay with having unilaterally authorized the construction of two pulp mills on the River Uruguay without complying with the obligatory prior notification and consultation procedures under the Statute. Argentina claimed that the mills posed a threat to the river and its environment and were likely to impair the quality of the river's waters and cause significant transboundary damage to Argentina.

As basis for the Court's jurisdiction, Argentina cited the first paragraph of Article 60 of the 1975 Statute, which provided that any dispute concerning the interpretation or application of that Statute, which could not be settled by direct negotiations, might be submitted by either party to the Court; Argentina claimed that direct negotiations between the Parties had failed.

Argentina's Application was accompanied by a request for the indication of provisional measures, whereby Argentina asked that Uruguay be ordered to suspend the authorizations for the construction of the mills and all building works, pending a final decision by the Court, and to cooperate with Argentina, with a view to protecting and conserving the aquatic environment of the River Uruguay, as well as to refrain from taking any further unilateral action with respect to construction of the two mills incompatible with the 1975 Statute, and from any other action which might aggravate the dispute or render its settlement more difficult.

On 8 and 9 June, public hearings were held on the request by Argentina for the indication of provisional measures. By an Order of 13 July, the Court, by 14 votes to one, found that the circumstances, as they presented themselves to the Court, were not such as to require the exercise of its power under Article 41 of the Statute to indicate provisional measures.

By an Order of 13 July, the Court fixed 15 January 2007 as the time limit for the filing of a Memorial by Argentina and 20 July 2007 as the time limit for the filing of a Counter-Memorial by Uruguay.

On 29 November 2006, Uruguay submitted a request for the indication of provisional measures on the ground that, from 20 November 2006, organized groups of Argentine citizens had blockaded an international bridge over the Uruguay River, thus causing it considerable economic prejudice and that Argentina had taken no action to end the blockade. Furthermore, Uruguay requested the Court to order Argentina to take "all reasonable and appropriate steps" to prevent or end the interruption of transit between Uruguay and Argentina; refrain from any measure that might aggravate, extend or make more difficult the settlement of the dispute; and abstain from any other measure which might prejudice the rights of Uruguay being considered before the Court.

Public hearings were held on 18 and 19 December on Uruguay's request for the indication of provisional measures. The Court's decision on the request would be delivered in 2007.

Other questions

Rules of the Court

In the ongoing review of its procedures and working methods, the Court took further measures to increase its productivity. The Court amended Practice Direction IX, serving as a reminder that a party wishing to produce new documents after the close of the written proceedings, including during the oral proceedings, had to follow the procedure as set out in Article 56, paragraphs 1 and 2, of the Rules of the Court; and deleted the first sentence in Practice Direction XI. It adopted two new Practice Directions: Practice Direction IX bis, providing the parties with guidance concerning their entitlement under Article 56, paragraph 4, of the Rules of the Court; and Practice Direction IX ter, providing further guidance to the parties concerning preparation of documents for the convenience of judges during oral proceedings.

Sixtieth anniversary of the International Court of Justice

To mark its sixtieth anniversary, ICJ, in cooperation with the United Nations Institute for Training and Research, organized a colloquium at the Peace Palace in The Hague on 10 and 11 April. The colloquium, held under "Chatham House" rules (i.e., the ideas expressed might be cited, but on an unattributed basis), was attended by hundreds of practitioners. It addressed issues of the Court's jurisdiction, rules of procedure and access. The proceedings of the colloquium were expected to be published in early 2007.

GENERAL ASSMEBLY ACTION

On 4 December [meeting 64], the General Assembly, on the recommendation of the Sixth

(Legal) Committee [A/61/455], adopted **resolution 61/37** without vote [agenda item 79].

Commemoration of the sixtieth anniversary of the International Court of Justice

The General Assembly,

Mindful that, in accordance with Article 2, paragraph 3, of the Charter of the United Nations, all Members shall settle their international disputes by peaceful means in such a manner that international peace and security, and justice, are not endangered,

Bearing in mind the Declaration on Principles of International Law concerning Friendly Relations and Cooperation among States in accordance with the Charter of the United Nations and the Manila Declaration on the Peaceful Settlement of International Disputes,

Recognizing the need for universal adherence to and implementation of the rule of law at both the national and international levels,

Recalling that the International Court of Justice is the principal judicial organ of the United Nations, and reaffirming its authority and independence,

Noting that 2006 marks the sixtieth anniversary of the inaugural sitting of the International Court of Justice,

Noting with appreciation the special commemorative event held at The Hague in April 2006 to celebrate the anniversary,

1. *Solemnly commends* the International Court of Justice for the important role that it has played as the principal judicial organ of the United Nations over the past sixty years in adjudicating disputes among States, and recognizes the value of its work;

2. *Expresses its appreciation* to the Court for the measures adopted to operate an increased workload with maximum efficiency;

3. *Stresses* the desirability of finding practical ways and means to strengthen the Court, taking into consideration, in particular, the needs resulting from its workload;

4. *Encourages* States to continue considering recourse to the Court by means available under its Statute, and calls upon States that have not yet done so to consider accepting the jurisdiction of the Court in accordance with its Statute;

5. *Calls upon* States to consider means of strengthening the Court's work, including by supporting the Secretary-General's Trust Fund to Assist States in the Settlement of Disputes through the International Court of Justice on a voluntary basis, in order to enable the Fund to carry on and to strengthen its support to the countries which submit their disputes to the Court;

6. *Stresses* the importance of promoting the work of the International Court of Justice, and urges that efforts be continued through available means to encourage public awareness by the teaching, study and wider dissemination of the activities of the Court in the peaceful settlement of disputes, in view of both its judiciary and advisory functions.

Trust Fund to Assist States in the Settlement of Disputes

In September [A/61/380], the Secretary-General reported on the activities and status of the Trust Fund to Assist States in the Settlement of Disputes through the International Court of Justice since the submission of his 2005 report [YUN 2005, p. 1386]. The Fund, established in 1989 [YUN 1989, p. 818], provided financial assistance to States for financial expenses incurred in connection with a dispute submitted to ICJ by way of a special agreement or the execution of a Judgment resulting from such an agreement.

During the period under review (1 July 2005–30 June 2006), four States contributed to the Fund. As at 30 June 2006, the Fund's balance stood at approximately $2.2 million.

The Fund did not receive any applications for assistance from States during the reporting period.

Noting that, since its inception, the Fund had had a decreasing level of resources, the Secretary-General urged States and other relevant entities to consider making substantial and regular contributions.

Chapter II

International tribunals and court

In 2006, the international tribunals for the former Yugoslavia and Rwanda worked towards completing their mandates, while the International Criminal Court saw the arrest and indictment of its first accused.

The International Tribunal for the Prosecution of Persons Responsible for Serious Violations of International Humanitarian Law Committed in the Territory of the Former Yugoslavia since 1991 (ICTY) made significant progress towards accomplishing its mandate by 2010, by conducting multiple accused trials and implementing a number of reforms. In February, the Security Council amended the ICTY Statute, increasing the number of ad litem (short-term) judges from 9 to 12 and allowing for the appointment of reserve ad litem judges for certain trials of multiple accused. In March, the remodelling of the three ICTY courtrooms was completed, allowing for up to 18 accused to be tried simultaneously. However, a number of factors could affect the Court's ability to meet its completion deadline, most notably the status of trials referred to national courts in the former Yugoslavia and the critical issue of six outstanding fugitives.

During the year, the International Criminal Tribunal for the Prosecution of Persons Responsible for Genocide and Other Serious Violations of International Humanitarian Law Committed in the Territory of Rwanda and Rwandan Citizens Responsible for Genocide and Other Such Violations Committed in the Territory of Neighbouring States between 1 January and 31 December 1994 (ICTR) delivered six judgements and commenced four new trials. The Tribunal was on course to complete all ongoing trials by 2008 and all its work by 2010, depending on progress in current and future cases and on the availability of sufficient resources. In order to ensure continuity and ICTR ability to implement its Completion Strategy, the Council, in June, extended the mandates of 11 permanent judges whose terms of office were due to end in May 2007. In August and October, the Council also extended the terms of 18 ad litem judges.

The International Criminal Court (ICC), in its third year of operation, began its first proceedings against one accused and continued investigations into situations of concern in three countries. Five warrants of arrest were outstanding.

International Tribunal for the Former Yugoslavia

In 2006, the International Tribunal for the Former Yugoslavia (ICTY), established by Security Council resolution 827(1993) [YUN 1993, p. 440], continued to implement its completion strategy [YUN 2002, p. 1275], adopting further reforms to ensure compliance with Council resolutions 1503(2003) [YUN 2003, p. 1330] and 1534(2004) [YUN 2004, p. 1292]. Those resolutions called on the Tribunal to take all possible measures to complete first-instance trials before the end of 2008 and all appeals before the end of 2010. During the year, ICTY amended or modified a number of rules in order to enhance the efficiency of proceedings, based on recommendations made by a working group on speeding up appeals. In February, the Council adopted resolution 1660(2006) (see p. 1490), which amended article 12 and article 13 quater of the ICTY Statute, increasing the number of ad litem (short-term) judges from 9 to 12 and allowing for the assignment of reserve ad litem judges to specific trials of multiple accused. Despite those efforts to implement the completion strategy, ICTY President Fausto Pocar informed the Council on 15 December [S/PV.5594] that all trials of accused persons in custody would only be completed by 2009, and all appellate work could be concluded within two years of the end of the trials. However, a number of factors could influence that timetable, notably the success or otherwise of cases referred to national courts in the former Yugoslavia and the critical issue of the six outstanding indicted fugitives, in particular Radovan Karadzic and Ratko Mladic.

By letters of 31 May [S/2006/353] and 16 November [S/2006/898], the Secretary-General, in response to Council resolution 1534(2004), transmitted assessments by the ICTY President and Prosecutor on progress made towards implementing the completion strategy.

The Tribunal continued to develop the judicial capacity of national authorities in the former Yugoslavia, liaising closely with local judiciaries in the region and participating in efforts to strengthen their capacity to try war crimes cases. It also intensified its outreach efforts, with Tribunal staff participating in seminars and professional symposia and explaining cases in the successor States of the former Yugoslavia. Key materials were distributed in the region, and the Tribunal's website served as a vital conduit for updated information on its work.

In March, Milan Babic and Slobodan Milosevic died in the United Nations Detention Unit (UNDU) in The Hague, Netherlands. It was established that Mr. Milosevic died of natural causes, while Mr. Babic committed suicide. Mr. Babic, who had been sentenced to 13 years in prison for crimes against humanity and violations of the laws or customs of war in 2004 [YUN 2004, p. 1277], was brought back to The Hague to testify in the case against Milan Martic. The Dutch authorities carried out independent inquests in both cases and full internal inquiries into the deaths were launched by ICTY. Both investigations concluded that there was no criminal conduct involved in either case. A consequent independent audit of UNDU by Swedish authorities expressed general satisfaction with the Unit's operation and made a number of recommendations on ways to improve the conditions of detention of detainees and ensure greater clarity of management. Following the termination of the Milosevic proceedings, the ICTY President reorganized the Trial Chambers to fully engage the judges of that Chamber as soon as possible and to allow for the three trials of multi-accused to start much earlier than planned.

The activities of ICTY were covered in two reports to the Council and the General Assembly, for the periods 1 August 2005 to 31 July 2006 [A/61/271-S/2006/666] and 1 August 2006 to 31 July 2007 [A/62/172-S/2007/469]. On 9 October, the Assembly took note of the 2005/2006 report (**decision 61/506**).

The Chambers

The judicial activities of the Tribunal's three Trial Chambers, which ran six trials simultaneously and three trials of multi-accused during the year, and of its Appeals Chamber, included first-instance and appeals proceedings against judgements, interlocutory decisions and State requests for review, proceedings regarding the Tribunal's primacy and contempt cases. ICTY had a total of 28 judges—16 permanent judges, including two judges of the International Criminal Tribunal for Rwanda (ICTR) serving in the Appeals Chamber, and 12 ad litem judges.

New arrests and surrenders

In 2006, no new indictments were issued by the Prosecutor, except for those for contempt of the Tribunal. In September, Domagoj Margetic, former editor of two Croatian weekly magazines, was charged for a second time with contempt of court for publishing information about protected witnesses in the Blaskic case [YUN 2004, p. 1282; YUN 2005, p. 1389]. He entered a plea of not guilty. The trial commenced on 30 November and a judgement was expected in early 2007.

Two accused who had been located and arrested in 2005 [YUN 2005, p. 1388], Milan Lukic and Dragan Zelenovic, were handed over to the Tribunal on 21 February and 10 June, respectively. Both cases, which concerned offences allegedly committee in Bosnia and Herzegovina, were before the Referral Bench. Mr. Lukic was indicted in 1998 for the killing of Muslim men, women and children in Visegrad and Mr. Zelenovic was indicted for torture and rape in Foca.

Ongoing cases and trials

The trial for contempt of Ivica Marijacic, a journalist and editor-in-chief of a Zagreb-based weekly publication, and Markica Rebic, former head of the Security Information Service of the Republic of Croatia [YUN 2005, p. 1389], took place from 17 to 19 January. On 10 March, the Trial Chamber found both accused guilty of disclosing information in a Croatian newspaper about a protected Tribunal witness in the Tihomir Blaskic case [YUN 2004, p. 1282], in violation of a closed session order. The Trial Chamber sentenced each of them to a fine of €15,000. Both accused filed a notice of appeal against the judgement on 20 March. On 5 April, Mr. Rebic filed a motion asking for a suspension of the payment of the fines until the Appeals Chamber had rendered its judgement in the case. The request was granted by the Appeals Chamber on 7 April, with the decision applying equally to the co-respondent. In its 27 September judgement, the Appeals Chamber dismissed all appeals and affirmed the sentence imposed by the Trial Chamber.

On 23 February, in the case of Mitar Rasevic and Savo Todovic [YUN 2003, p. 1312; YUN 2004, p. 1277], who were, respectively, commander of the guards at the Kazneno Popravni Dom detention facility in Foca and deputy commander of the prison staff, the Appeals Chamber quashed the 2005 Referral Bench decision to transfer Mr. Todovic's case to Bosnia and Herzegovina and returned the matter to the Referral Bench for further consideration. It suspended the execution of the Referral Bench's ruling with respect to Mr. Rasevic until a decision on the form of the indictment and a confirmation of the operative indictment were issued. The prosecution submitted a modified indictment on 7 April and both accused were jointly charged with persecutions, murder, torture, imprisonment, and enslavement, committed against Bosnian Muslims and other imprisoned non-Serbs between April 1992 and October 1994. On 31 May, the Referral Bench reordered the referral to Bosnia and Herzegovina. On 4 September, dismissing Mr. Todovic's appeal, the Appeals Chamber affirmed the decision of the Referral Bench to refer the case to Bosnia and Herzegovina. On 3 October, both accused were transferred to Sarajevo.

In the case of Miroslav Kvocka and Others [YUN 2001, p. 1201], the defence of Mlado Radic, a policeman who was sentenced to 20 years in prison in 2005 [YUN 2005, p. 1389], submitted a request for review on 27 February. On 31 October, the Appeals Chamber dismissed the request in its entirety. In the case against Zoran Zigic [YUN 2001, p. 1201], the accused was transferred to Austria on 8 June to serve his 25-year prison sentence. On 26 June, the motion Mr. Zigic had filed requesting that the Appeals Chamber reconsider its 2005 appeal judgement [YUN 2005, p. 1389] and either order a retrial or acquit him of all convictions, except for those where he admitted his criminal responsibility, was denied.

In the appeal of Momir Nikolic, the Appeals Chamber delivered its judgement on 8 March. Mr. Nikolic, an assistant chief of Security and Intelligence in the Bosnian Serb Army, had pleaded guilty to persecuting Bosnian Muslim civilians in Srebrenica in 1995 and was sentenced to 27 years' imprisonment in 2003 [YUN 2003, p. 1313]. He appealed his sentence in 2004 [YUN 2004, p. 1281], arguing that the Trial Chamber made errors in determining it. The Appeals Chamber reduced the sentence to 20 years' imprisonment, having accepted three of the twelve grounds for appeal: the Trial Chamber had wrongly considered Mr. Nikolic's role twice when determining the sentence; the Trial Chamber relied significantly upon an incorrect translation of remarks made by Mr. Nikolic's defence counsel during his closing argument; and the Trial Chamber erred when assessing Mr. Nikolic's cooperation with the prosecution, and thus attached insufficient weight to that mitigating circumstance.

In the case against Ramush Haradinaj, a former senior commander of the Kosovo Liberation Army (KLA), who surrendered to the Tribunal in 2005 [YUN 2005, p. 1388], the Appeals Chamber, on 10 March, denied the prosecution's motion to set aside the Trial Chamber's 2005 decision granting Mr. Haradinaj provisional release, and instead amended that decision. The Trial Chamber had ordered the accused to obtain agreement from the United Nations Interim Administration Mission in Kosovo (UNMIK) before appearing in public or engaging in public political activities. The Appeals Chamber added five conditions allowing the prosecution to be better informed of UNMIK decisions and asked for the decisions to contain a reasoned explanation of why an appearance had been granted. Mr. Haradinaj was jointly indicted in 2005 with Idriz Balaj and Lahi Brahimaj, former members of the KLA, on 37 counts of crimes against humanity and violations of the laws or customs of war. On 26 April, the prosecution filed an amended indictment and the Trial Chamber confirmed it as the operative indictment in the case on 25 October, ruling that the changes would not cause prejudice to the accused or delay the proceedings unduly. The prosecution submitted a revised second amended indictment on 10 November. The trial was still pending at the end of the year.

Following a trial that lasted from 2 December 2003 [YUN 2003, p. 1314] to 14 July 2005 [YUN 2005, p. 1390], the Trial Chamber, by a 15 March judgement, found Enver Hadzihasanovic and Amir Kubura guilty for having failed to take necessary and reasonable measures to prevent or punish crimes committed by their subordinates; the accused were high-level commanders in the Army of Bosnia and Herzegovina. Mr. Hadzihasanovic was sentenced to five years in prison and Mr. Kubura to two and a half years. Both accused filed notices of appeal in April.

In the appeal of Milomir Stakic, the former president of the Prijedor Municipal Assembly, the Appeals Chamber rendered its judgement on 22 March. In 2003, Mr. Stakic was found guilty of participating in the murder, extermination and persecutions of non-Serbs in Prijedor in 1992, and was sentenced to life imprisonment, the maximum penalty [YUN 2003, p. 1313; YUN 2004, p. 1279]. In its judgement, the Appeals Chamber affirmed the Trial Chamber's conviction of Mr. Stakic and also agreed with its decision to acquit Mr. Stakic of genocide and complicity in genocide. The Appeals Chamber also found that the Trial Chamber incorrectly failed to convict him for deporting and forcibly transferring elsewhere the non-Serb population, and addressed, on its own initiative, how to legally define his responsibility for the crimes he had committed. The Appeals Chamber found that Mr. Stakic participated in a joint criminal enterprise, the purpose of which was to commit crimes against the Bosnian Muslim and Bosnian Croat populations of Prijedor; it also stated that the Trial Chamber had committed errors in determining his sentence, and reduced Mr. Stakic's sentence to 40 years in prison.

In the case of Fatmir Limaj, Haradin Bala and Isak Musliu, who were arrested in 2003 [YUN 2003, p. 311], the prosecution and Mr. Bala's defence filed notices of appeal on 30 December 2005 against the Trial Chamber's November 2005 sentencing of Mr. Bala to 13 years in prison for participating in the murder of prisoners and other crimes in Kosovo [YUN 2005, p. 1391]. On 29 March, the prosecution filed a motion of appeal against the acquittals, by the same judgement, of Messrs. Limaj and Musliu. The appeals were pending at year's end.

Pavle Strugar, a former commander in the Yugoslav People's Army, sentenced by the Trial Chamber in 2005 to eight years' imprisonment [YUN 2005, p. 1389] for having failed to prevent attacks against civilians and the destruction of property in Dubrovnik in 1991 [YUN 2003, p. 1314; YUN 2004, p. 1279], returned to UNDU on 5 April, having received medical treatment in Montenegro; his provisional release for a period no longer than four months was ordered by the Appeals Chamber in late 2005. On 15 September 2006, both the prosecution and the defence withdrew their appeals against the Trial Chamber's judgement, on the basis of "the exceptional humanitarian circumstances pertaining to Pavle Strugar, in particular his advanced age, poor state of health and general condition". On 20 September, the Appeals Chamber declared proceedings closed in the case. Thus, Mr. Strugar's sentence became definitive.

On 5 April, in the case against Milan Milutinovic, Nikola Sainovic, Dragoljub Ojdanic, Nebojsa Pavkovic, Vladimir Lazarevic and Sreten Lukic, the prosecution submitted the second amended joinder indictment following the defence challenge against a 2005 amended indictment [YUN 2005, p 1390]. On 17 May, the pre-trial judge ordered the prosecution to correct some typographical errors in the third amended joinder indictment (filed on 12 May), and to sever Vlastimir Dordevic, who was still at large, from the other accused in order that the trial could commence as scheduled. On 26 June, the Trial Chamber granted the severance and accepted the redacted third amended joinder indictment as the operative indictment against the six accused (Vlastimir Dordevic was assigned a new case number). The operative indictment alleged that the accused participated in a joint criminal enterprise, the purpose of which was, among other things, the modification of the ethnic balance in Kosovo to ensure continued Serbian control over the province. They were indicted for crimes against humanity and for violations of the laws or customs of war. The accused, all of whom had been provisionally released, returned to UNDU on 4 July. The trial commenced on 10 July.

In the case against Jovica Stanisic, former head of the State Security Service (DB) of the Ministry of Internal Affairs of the Republic of Serbia, and Franko Simatovic, commander of the DB Special Operations Unit [YUN 2003, p. 1311], the Trial Chamber, on 12 April, ordered the prosecution to make some linguistic corrections and clarify certain sections of the second amended indictment from 2004 [YUN 2004, p. 1279]. On 31 May, the Trial Chamber ordered that the revised second amended indictment, filed by the prosecution on 15 May, be the operative indictment in the case. It charged Mr. Stanisic and Mr. Simatovic with four counts of crimes against humanity and one count of violation of the laws or customs of war.

On 12 April, the Tribunal's Referral Bench referred to Bosnia and Herzegovina the case of Pasko Ljubicic, the former commander of the Fourth Military Police Battalion of the Croatian Defence Council [YUN 2001, p. 200; YUN 2002, p. 1279; YUN 2003, p. 1313; YUN 2004, p. 1282; YUN 2005, p. 1391]. On 25 April, Mr. Ljubicic filed an appeal brief. The Appeals Chamber affirmed the referral decision on 4 July and, on 22 September, the accused was transferred to Sarajevo.

Also on 12 April, the Trial Chamber found Vladimir Kovacevic unfit to enter a plea or stand trial; criminal proceedings against him could be reinstated should it be determined at a future date that he was again fit. Mr. Kovacevic, who was charged in 2001 with six counts of violations of the laws or customs of war [YUN 2001, p. 1200], was transferred to ICTY in 2003 [YUN 2003, p. 1312]. On 17 November 2006, the Tribunal's Referral Bench referred the case to the Republic of Serbia for the ongoing monitoring of Mr. Kovacevic's health and resumption of proceedings should he become fit for trial. On 1 December, the defence for Mr. Kovacevic filed a notice of appeal against the decision of the referral.

On 26 April, the trial began of six high-level leaders of the Bosnian Croat wartime entity of Herzeg-Bosna—Jadranko Prlic, Bruno Stojic, Slobodan Praljak, Milivoj Petkovic, Valentin Coric and Berislav Pusic. The six, who surrendered in April 2004 [YUN 2004, p. 276], pleaded not guilty to nine counts of grave breaches of the Geneva Conventions, nine counts of violations of the laws or customs of war and eight counts of crimes against humanity, all committed against Serbs and Muslims in the Croatian-held part of northern Bosnia in 1992 and 1993. They were granted provisional release on 17 August.

The Appeals Chamber, on 3 May, upheld the conviction and sentences of the accused Bosnian Croat commanders, Mladen Naletilic and Vinko Martinovic, who were sentenced in 2003 to 20 and 18 years' imprisonment, respectively, for grave breaches of the Geneva Conventions, violations of the laws or customs of war and crimes against humanity [YUN 2003, p 1312], and for their involvement in the ethnic cleansing of Bosnian Muslim civilians in the Mostar area of Bosnia and Herzegovina between April 1993 and January 1994. Both the prosecution and the defence had appealed the Trial Chamber's 2003 judgement. In its judgement, the Appeals Chamber dismissed most of the grounds for appeal raised by both sides. It also set aside, in part, some of the convictions entered by the Trial Chamber against the accused. However, taking into account the particular circumstances of the case, the form and degree of the participation of the accused in the crimes affirmed on appeal, as well as the seriousness of the crimes, the Appeals Chamber confirmed the sentences.

In the case of Milorad Trbic, initially charged jointly with Popovic and Others [YUN 2005, p. 1390] with one count of murder as a crime against humanity, the prosecution filed a 4 May motion for referral to the authorities of Bosnia and Herzegovina. On 16 June, the prosecution filed a motion seeking to sever Mr. Trbic's case from Popovic and Others. On 26 June, the Trial Chamber ordered his case to be severed and the prosecution was ordered to file two new versions of the second consolidated amended indictment. The new indictment charged Mr. Trbic, on the basis of his individual criminal responsibility, with genocide and conspiracy to commit genocide, extermination, murder, persecutions and forcible transfer (crimes against humanity), and violations of the laws or customs of war. The referral motion was pending at year's end.

Blagoje Simic's motion for temporary provisional release to attend memorial services for his mother in Bosnia and Herzegovina was granted by the Appeals Chamber on 5 May. He was provisionally released from 10 to 25 May. In 2003, Mr. Simic was found guilty of a crime against humanity for persecutions he committed against Bosnian Muslim and Bosnian Croat civilians when he was the highest-ranking civilian official in the Bosanski Samac municipality. He was sentenced to 17 years' imprisonment [YUN 2003, p. 1315]. Both the prosecution and defence appealed the judgement in 2003. On 28 November 2006, the Appeals Chamber rendered its final judgement on the appeal of the accused and reduced his sentence to 15 years' imprisonment. The Appeals Chamber found that Mr. Simic was not informed that he was being accused of participating in a joint criminal enterprise until the prosecution had finished presenting its case, which rendered the trial unfair. It also reversed his conviction for persecution through cruel and inhumane treatment in the form of torture and beating. However, the Appeals Chamber upheld his conviction for aiding and abetting persecution against non-Serb civilians.

By an 8 May decision of the Trial Chamber, Ivica Rajic, a former Commander of the Second Operational Group of the Croatian Defence Council, was sentenced to 12 years in prison. In 2005, Mr. Rajic had pleaded guilty to four counts of willful killing, inhumane treatment, extensive destruction and the appropriation of property in the area of Stupni Do in central Bosnia in 1993 [YUN 2005, p. 1391]. At year's end, Mr. Rajic was awaiting transfer to the country where he would serve his sentence.

In the case against Zeljko Mejakic, Momcilo Gruban, Dusan Fustar and Dusko Knezevic, jointly charged in 2002 [YUN 2002, p. 1279] with crimes against humanity and violations of the laws or customs of war, the Appeals Chamber upheld the Referral Bench's 2005 decision to refer the case to Bosnia and Herzegovina for trial [YUN 2005, p. 391]. On 9 May, the four accused were transferred to the State Court of Bosnia and Herzegovina; their trial commenced on 20 December.

On 31 May, in the case of Popovic and Others, following various motions alleging defects in the form of the consolidated amended indictment, the Trial Chamber ordered the prosecution to file an amended indictment. The second consolidated amended indictment was filed on 14 June. On 20 June, the Trial Chamber ordered Radivoje Miletic and Milan Gvero, who had been provisionally released, to return to UNDU by 4 July. The Popovic and Others trial commenced on 14 July. The operative indictment jointly charged Vujadin Popovic, Ljubisa Beara, Drago Nikolic, Ljubomir Borovcanin and Vinko Pandurevic with genocide, conspiracy to commit genocide, extermination, murder, persecutions, forcible transfer and deportation, committed during the period from July to November 1995; it also charged Radivoje Miletic and Milan Gvero with crimes against humanity and a violation of the laws or customs of war. All the charges related to the mass murder and ethnic cleansing of Bosnian Muslims in Srebrenica after the fall of the former UN safe haven to Bosnian Serb forces in July 1995.

Dario Kordic, one of the leading political figures in the Bosnian Croat community during the war, was transferred to Austria, on 8 June, to serve the

25-year prison term handed down by the Tribunal in 2001 [YUN 2001, p. 1200] and affirmed by the Appeals Chamber in 2004 [YUN 2004, p. 1280].

On 20 June, the prosecution completed its case-in-chief against Milan Martic. The trial, for crimes against humanity and violations of the laws or customs of war, had begun in December 2005 [YUN 2005, p. 1392]. On 3 July, the Trial Chamber stated that there was no basis on which it could enter a judgement of acquittal. The defence began presenting its case on 11 July and concluded it on 16 November.

In the case of Dragan Nikolic, commander of the Bosnian Serb-run Susica detention camp, the accused was transferred to Italy on 21 June to serve his 20-year prison sentence [YUN 2003, p. 1314]. Mr. Nikolic's sentence was reduced from 23 years by the Appeals Chamber in 2005 [YUN 2005, p. 389].

The Trial Chamber, in a 30 June judgement, found Naser Oric, a former senior commander of Bosnian Muslim forces in and around Srebrenica, guilty of having failed to take necessary and reasonable measures to prevent the commission of crimes by his subordinates in 1992 and 1993. Mr. Oric was sentenced to two years in prison and was entitled to credit for time spent in custody since 2003 [YUN 2003, p. 1311]; the judges therefore ordered that he be released as soon as the necessary practical arrangements were made. He was officially released on 1 July. On 31 July, both the defence and the prosecution filed notices of appeal against the trial judgement. On 16 October, the defence filed its appeal brief and, on 18 October, the prosecution filed the latest version of its appeal brief; both appeals were pending at year's end.

The contempt proceedings against Josip Jovic, which had initially been due to begin on 3 July, were re-scheduled for 11 July due to the non-attendance in court of the accused. Mr. Jovic, a former editor-in-chief of a Croatian daily newspaper, was indicted for contempt of the Tribunal in the Tihomir Blaskic case for disclosing information in direct violation of a court order and was provisionally released [YUN 2005, p. 1388]. On 30 August, he was convicted of contempt and sentenced to pay a fine of €20,000. On 14 September, Mr. Jovic filed a notice of appeal against the judgement. The appeal was pending at the end of the year.

On 14 July, the Trial Chamber decided to join two cases involving Ante Gotovina [ibid.] and Ivan Cermak/Mladen Markac [YUN 2004, p. 1276] in one indictment and accepted the proposed amendments to the indictment. The three accused were charged with persecutions, deportation, inhumane acts, plunder of public or private property, wanton destruction of cities, towns or villages, murder and cruel treatment, all allegedly committed against Serbs in 1995, during, and in the aftermath of a Croatian military offensive. At that time, Mr. Gotovina and Mr. Cermak were senior military commanders on the ground, while Mr. Markac was the commander of the Croatian Special Police. All three accused appealed the Trial Chamber's decision. On 25 October, the Appeals Chamber confirmed the Trial Chamber's decision, making the joinder indictment the operative indictment in the case. On 5 December, all the defendants pleaded not guilty to the charges in the amended indictment.

In the case against Momcilo Krajisnik, a member of the Bosnian Serb leadership during the war, who was charged in 2000 [YUN 2000, p. 1221] with eight counts of genocide, crimes against humanity and violations of the laws or customs of war in Bosnia and Herzegovina in 1991 and 1992, the Trial Chamber, in a 27 September judgement, sentenced him to 27 years' imprisonment. He was convicted of persecutions, extermination, murder, deportation and forced transfer of non-Serb civilians, but was acquitted of genocide, complicity in genocide and one count of murder as a violation of the laws or customs of war. The Trial Chamber also established the existence of a joint criminal enterprise, involving Radovan Karadzic and other Bosnian Serb leaders, intended to "ethnically recompose the territories targeted by the Bosnian-Serb leadership by drastically reducing the proportion of Bosnian Muslims and Bosnian Croats through expulsion". On 26 October, the prosecution filed its notice of appeal, asking for the sentence to be raised to life imprisonment, and its appeal brief on 27 November. The appeal was pending at the end of the year.

Miodrag Jokic was transferred to Denmark on 5 October to serve his seven-year prison sentence. Mr. Jokic, a former commander in the Yugoslav navy, who pleaded guilty to crimes committed during the 1991 attack on Dubrovnik, was sentenced by the Trial Chamber in 2004 [YUN 2004, p. 1280]. In 2005, the Appeals Chamber upheld the sentence.

On 23 November, the Appeals Chamber rejected the review of Tihomir Blaskic's case requested by the prosecution in 2005. In 2004, the Appeals Chamber had reduced Mr. Blaskic's sentence from 45 to 9 years' imprisonment [YUN 2004, p. 1282]. The Appeals Chamber found in its judgement that the prosecution's request for review did not contain "new facts" in accordance with the Rules of Procedure and Evidence, but rather additional evidence in relation to facts considered earlier in the case. It concluded that a review of the appeals judgement was not warranted, thereby putting an end to the case.

The trial of Vojislav Seselj, charged with 14 counts alleging crimes against humanity and violations of the laws or customs of war in the territory of Croatia, in large parts of Bosnia and Herzegovina and in Vojvodina (Serbia) from 1991 until 1993 [YUN 2003, p. 311; YUN 2004, p. 1277], commenced on 27 November in his absence. Mr. Seselj had been on a hunger strike since 10 November and refused to appear in court. In the light of that situation, the Trial Chamber issued a 27 November decision terminating his self-representation status and once more assigned counsel to conduct his defence. On 1 December, given the medical situation of the accused, the Trial Chamber ordered an adjournment of the trial until further notice. On 7 December, Mr. Seselj filed an appeal against the decision on imposed counsel and, on 8 December, the Appeals Chamber issued its decision to nullify the opening of the proceeding and ordered that the trial restart when Mr. Seselj was able to fully represent himself. Before the trial began, the Trial Chamber invited the prosecution to reduce the scope of the indictment against Mr. Seselj. Having considered the prosecution's proposals in that regard, the Trial Chamber rendered an 8 November decision reducing the indictment by five counts and ruled inadmissible evidence in respect of crimes allegedly committed in five municipalities, thus reducing the indictment by approximately one-third.

On 30 November, the Appeals Chamber handed down its judgement in the case of Stanislav Galic, a former Bosnian Serb Army commander who was found guilty by the Trial Chamber in 2003 [YUN 2003, p. 1315] and sentenced to 20 years in prison. In its judgement, the Appeals Chamber allowed the appeal by the prosecution on the length of the sentence, quashed the sentence imposed by the Trial Chamber and instead sentenced Mr. Galic to life imprisonment. That was the first time the maximum penalty had been rendered by the Tribunal's Appeals Chamber. The Appeals Chamber also dismissed all 19 grounds of appeal by Mr. Galic, who was awaiting transfer to the country where he would serve his sentence.

With regard to Mile Mrksic, Miroslav Radic and Veselin Sljivancanin, who were indicted in 1997 [YUN 1997, p. 1322] for alleged involvement in the execution of some 200 Croatians and non-Serb persons removed from Vukovar hospital in 1991, the prosecution concluded its case on 23 June and the defence made its case from 30 August until 8 December. The trial had begun in October 2005 [YUN 2005, p. 1391].

Judges of the Court

Ad litem judges

In January, the ICTY President proposed that the Security Council amend the statute of the Tribunal so that the Secretary-General, at the request of the President, could authorize the appointment of reserve judges from among the current pool of ad litem judges elected in accordance with article 13 ter of the statute, to be present at each stage of the proceedings and ready to step in should one of the original judges not be able to finish the case, thus preventing disruption to the proceedings or a retrial. The pool of ad litem judges should be increased from 9 to 12. Under the Rules of Procedure and Evidence, if two of the original judges assigned to a case were not able to be present during the entire proceedings, the trial had to start again from the beginning.

SECURITY COUNCIL ACTION

On 28 February [meeting 5382], the Security Council unanimously adopted **resolution 1660(2006)**. The draft [S/2006/130] was prepared in consultations among Council members.

The Security Council,

Reaffirming its resolutions 827(1993) of 25 May 1993, 1166(1998) of 13 May 1998, 1329(2000) of 30 November 2000, 1411(2002) of 17 May 2002, 1431(2002) of 14 August 2002, 1481(2003) of 19 May 2003, 1503(2003) of 28 August 2003, 1534(2004) of 26 March 2004 and 1597(2005) of 20 April 2005,

Having considered the proposal made by the President of the International Tribunal for the Prosecution of Persons Responsible for Serious Violations of International Humanitarian Law Committed in the Territory of the Former Yugoslavia since 1991 that the Secretary-General, at the request of the President, appoint reserve judges from among the ad litem judges elected in accordance with article 13 ter of the statute of the Tribunal to be present at each stage of a trial to which they have been appointed and to replace a judge if that judge is unable to continue sitting,

Convinced of the advisability of allowing the Secretary-General to appoint reserve judges to specific trials at the International Tribunal for the Former Yugoslavia when so requested by the President of the Tribunal,

Acting under Chapter VII of the Charter of the United Nations,

1. *Decides* to amend article 12 and article 13 quater of the statute of the International Tribunal for the Former Yugoslavia and to replace those articles with the provisions set out in the annex to the present resolution;
2. *Decides also* to remain seized of the matter.

Annex

Article 12
Composition of the Chambers

1. The Chambers shall be composed of sixteen permanent independent judges, no two of whom may be nationals of the same State, and a maximum at any one time of twelve ad litem independent judges appointed in accordance with article 13 ter, paragraph 2, of the statute, no two of whom may be nationals of the same State.
2. Three permanent judges and a maximum at any one time of nine ad litem judges shall be members of each Trial Chamber. Each Trial Chamber to which ad litem judges are assigned may be divided into sections of three judges each, composed of both permanent and ad litem judges, except in the circumstances specified in paragraph 5 below. A section of a Trial Chamber shall have the same powers and responsibilities as a Trial Chamber under the statute and shall render judgement in accordance with the same rules.
3. Seven of the permanent judges shall be members of the Appeals Chamber. The Appeals Chamber shall, for each appeal, be composed of five of its members.
4. A person who for the purposes of membership of the Chambers of the International Tribunal could be regarded as a national of more than one State shall be deemed to be a national of the State in which that person ordinarily exercises civil and political rights.
5. The Secretary-General may, at the request of the President of the International Tribunal appoint, from among the ad litem judges elected in accordance with article 13 ter, reserve judges to be present at each stage of a trial to which they have been appointed and to replace a judge if that judge is unable to continue sitting.
6. Without prejudice to paragraph 2 above, in the event that exceptional circumstances require for a permanent judge in a section of a Trial Chamber to be replaced resulting in a section solely comprised of ad litem judges, that section may continue to hear the case, notwithstanding that its composition no longer includes a permanent judge.

Article 13 quater
Status of ad litem judges

1. During the period in which they are appointed to serve in the International Tribunal, ad litem judges shall:

(a) Benefit from the same terms and conditions of service mutatis mutandis as the permanent judges of the International Tribunal;

(b) Enjoy, subject to paragraph 2 below, the same powers as the permanent judges of the International Tribunal;

(c) Enjoy the privileges and immunities, exemptions and facilities of a judge of the International Tribunal;

(d) Enjoy the power to adjudicate in pretrial proceedings in cases other than those that they have been appointed to try.

2. During the period in which they are appointed to serve in the International Tribunal, ad litem judges shall not:

(a) Be eligible for election as, or to vote in the election of, the President of the Tribunal or the Presiding Judge of a Trial Chamber pursuant to article 14 of the statute;

(b) Have power:

(i) To adopt rules of procedure and evidence pursuant to article 15 of the statute. They shall, however, be consulted before the adoption of those rules;

(ii) To review an indictment pursuant to article 19 of the statute;

(iii) To consult with the President in relation to the assignment of judges pursuant to article 14 of the statute or in relation to a pardon or commutation of sentence pursuant to article 28 of the statute.

3. Notwithstanding, paragraphs 1 and 2 above, an ad litem judge who is serving as a reserve judge shall, during such time as he or she so serves:

(a) Benefit from the same terms and conditions of service mutatis mutandis as the permanent judges of the International Tribunal;

(b) Enjoy the privileges and immunities, exemptions and facilities of a judge of the International Tribunal;

(c) Enjoy the power to adjudicate in pretrial proceedings in cases other than those that they have been appointed to and for that purpose to enjoy subject to paragraph 2 above, the same powers as permanent judges.

4. In the event that a reserve judge replaces a judge who is unable to continue sitting, he or she will, as of that time, benefit from the provisions of paragraph 1 above.

General Assembly action. In a May report [A/60/844], the Secretary-General informed the General Assembly that, in the light of the Security Council's decision to increase the number of ICTY ad litem judges from 9 to 12 (above), estimated additional requirements in connection with the appointment of up to three reserve judges for the 2006-2007 biennium would amount to $896,600. The Advisory Committee on Administrative and Budgetary Questions (ACABQ), in a May report [A/60/854], submitted its comments on the revised estimates.

On 30 June, the Assembly requested the Secretary-General to report on any additional requirements arising from the appointment of the three reserve judges in the context of the second performance report for the biennium 2006-2007 (**decision 60/560**).

Extension of terms of office

In identical letters of 27 March [A/60/741-S/2006/199], the Secretary-General transmitted to the General Assembly and Security Council Presidents a request from the ICTY President that Judge Joaquin Martin Canivell (Spain) be allowed to continue to sit in the Krajisnik case [YUN 2000, p. 1221] beyond the end of April and see the case through to its completion, despite the fact that the cumulative period of his service in ICTY would then attain and exceed three years. The Secretary-General stated that the request directly related to the Tribunal's ability to implement its completion strategy [YUN 2002, p. 1275].

SECURITY COUNCIL ACTION

On 10 April [meeting 5407], the Security Council unanimously adopted **resolution 1668(2006)**. The draft [S/2006/223] was prepared in consultations among Council members.

The Security Council,

Recalling its resolution 1581(2005) of 18 January 2005,

Taking note of the letter dated 27 March 2006 from the Secretary-General to the President of the Security Council,

1. *Decides*, in response to the request of the Secretary-General, to confirm that Judge Joaquín Canivell can continue to sit in the *Krajišnik* case beyond April 2006 and see the case through to its completion, notwithstanding the fact that the cumulative period of his service in the International Tribunal for the Prosecution of Persons Responsible for Serious Violations of International Humanitarian Law Committed in the Territory of the Former Yugoslavia since 1991 would then attain and exceed three years;
2. *Decides also* to remain seized of the matter.

The Council President transmitted the text of the resolution to the General Assembly President by a 10 April letter [A/60/746-S/2006/231]. The Assembly, by **decision 60/402 B** of 13 April, endorsed the Secretary-General's recommendation.

Office of the Prosecutor

In 2006, no new indictments (except for contempt of court) were issued. The Prosecutor focused her efforts on bringing the remaining accused at large to the Tribunal and, in that regard, on obtaining the full cooperation of relevant countries, which resulted in several arrests and better production of documents. The Office continued to assist in furthering the reform of the judicial systems of the countries of the former Yugoslavia, to transfer cases to national courts and cooperate with the national prosecutorial authorities on non-referred war crimes cases. Of the seven motions for referral on which ICTY was working during the year, three (involving seven accused) were granted on appeal and transferred to Bosnia and Herzegovina. Decisions on the other four motions (involving five accused) were pending at the end of the year.

The cooperation of the Government of Croatia remained swift and satisfactory and that of the Federation of Bosnia and Herzegovina also continued to be satisfactory. However, cooperation by Serbia and Montenegro was not complete, consistent or expeditious and no progress was made on any of the six remaining fugitives, all of whom had connections to Serbia. The cooperation of Republika Sprska (Bosnia and Herzegovina) was not fully sufficient either. Some significant archival collections had become available to the Office, but some other archives were still missing. The new Republika Sprska government confirmed its commitment to full cooperation and positive efforts were made to target the fugitives' support networks, even if no arrests were actually made by the police. Despite a number of promises, the Serbian authorities failed to arrest Ratko Mladic, a priority target. However, the positive efforts of the President of the National Council for Cooperation resulted in waivers for interviews and access to documents. In May, staff of the Office of the Prosecutor received approval from the State for access to its archives.

In Kosovo, the Office relied on the support and assistance of the Kosovo Force (KFOR) and UNMIK. Of particular concern were continuing problems related to the protection of witnesses in the case against Haradinaj and Others [YUN 2005, p. 1388] and the lack of full cooperation by UNMIK. The independence of Montenegro in June had no immediate negative effects on cooperation.

The Registry

The Registry continued to provide administrative services and judicial support to the Chambers, the Office of the Prosecutor and the defence. It also managed UNDU, the Victims and Witnesses Section, the legal aid office and the interpretation and translation service. The Registry facilitated the implementation of the Tribunal's completion strategy, including the action plan to relocate protected witnesses and their families. In addition to providing legal advice on a vast spectrum of judicial and administrative issues, the Registry facilitated liaison with the UN Office of Legal Affairs, assisted in the transfer of accused, either to serve their sentences or to be tried by domestic criminal courts in the former Yugoslavia, and furthered cooperation with those courts in the context of the transfer of cases. In March, the Registrar and the Ambassador of the Czech Republic signed an agreement for the loan of prison staff to the Tribunal.

In order to accommodate multiple-accused trials, an important part of the completion strategy, the

Registry remodelled each of the Tribunal's three courtrooms. The efficient completion of trials continued to be facilitated by the use of the e-Court system during proceedings cont. The Registry also implemented a procedure to allow the secure use of computers by detainees, providing them with specially configured Registry-owned computers.

The Tribunal continued to develop and improve its outreach programme. In November, it launched an UNDU video on its website to show scenes from within the facility. The Web Unit of the Media/Web/Outreach Office continued to develop the Tribunal's extensive website in English, French and Bosnian/Croatian/Serbian and to provide information in Albanian and Macedonian. The Section also maintained the Internet broadcast of courtroom proceedings in English, French and Bosnian/Croatian/Serbian and, in cases relevant to Kosovo, in Albanian. As of November, the Communication Section began to publish a twice-monthly bilingual newsletter (ICTY Digest/TPIY en bref).

Financing

2006-2007 biennium

The first performance report of ICTY for the 2006-2007 biennium [A/61/585], submitted in response to General Assembly resolution 60/243 [YUN 2005, p. 1396], reflected a requirement of additional appropriations of $18.8 million, net of staff assessment, over the amount apportioned in resolution 60/243. The Assembly was requested to revise the appropriation for 2006-2007 in the amount of $326,573,900 gross ($297,146,300 net) to the ICTY Special Account.

In December [A/61/633], ACABQ recommended approval of the revised appropriation for the 2006-2007 biennium.

GENERAL ASSEMBLY ACTION

On 22 December [meeting 84], the General Assembly, on the recommendation of the Fifth (Administrative and Budgetary) Committee [A/61/656], adopted **resolution 61/242** without vote [agenda item 130].

Financing of the International Tribunal for the Prosecution of Persons Responsible for Serious Violations of International Humanitarian Law Committed in the Territory of the Former Yugoslavia since 1991

The General Assembly,

Having considered the reports of the Secretary-General, namely, his first performance report for the biennium 2006-2007 on the International Tribunal for the Prosecution of Persons Responsible for Serious Violations of International Humanitarian Law Committed in the Territory of the Former Yugoslavia since 1991 and his report on financial and any other implications resulting from the introduction of a staff retention bonus at the International Criminal Tribunal for Rwanda and the International Tribunal for the Former Yugoslavia,

Having also considered the report of the Board of Auditors on the International Tribunal for the Former Yugoslavia and the recommendations contained therein,

Having further considered the related reports of the Advisory Committee on Administrative and Budgetary Questions,

Recalling its resolution 47/235 of 14 September 1993 on the financing of the International Tribunal for the Former Yugoslavia and its subsequent resolutions thereon, the latest of which were resolutions 60/242 and 60/243 of 23 December 2005,

1. *Takes note* of the first performance report of the Secretary-General for the biennium 2006-2007 on the International Tribunal for the Prosecution of Persons Responsible for Serious Violations of International Humanitarian Law Committed in the Territory of the Former Yugoslavia since 1991 and his report on financial and any other implications resulting from the introduction of a staff retention bonus at the International Criminal Tribunal for Rwanda and the International Tribunal for the Former Yugoslavia;

2. *Endorses* the conclusions and recommendations contained in the reports of the Advisory Committee on Administrative and Budgetary Questions;

3. *Emphasizes* the importance of implementing the recommendations of the Board of Auditors, and requests the Secretary-General to report on progress in the implementation of the recommendations of the Board in the context of the proposed budget of the International Tribunal for the Former Yugoslavia for the biennium 2008-2009;

4. *Also emphasizes* the importance of the timely submission of the performance reports on the International Tribunal for the Former Yugoslavia and the related reports of the Advisory Committee on Administrative and Budgetary Questions in order to facilitate the proper consideration thereof by the General Assembly;

5. *Decides* on a revised appropriation to the Special Account for the International Tribunal for the Prosecution of Persons Responsible for Serious Violations of International Humanitarian Law Committed in the Territory of the Former Yugoslavia since 1991 of a total amount of 326,573,900 United States dollars gross (297,146,300 dollars net) for the biennium 2006-2007;

6. *Decides also*, for the year 2007, to apportion among Member States, in accordance with the scale of assessments applicable to the regular budget of the United Nations for the year, the amount of 86,940,250 dollars gross (78,995,675 dollars net), including 10,718,300 dollars gross (9,418,200 dollars net), being the increase in assessments;

7. *Decides further*, for the year 2007, to apportion among Member States, in accordance with the rates of assessment applicable to peacekeeping operations for the year, the amount of 86,940,250 dollars gross (78,995,675 dollars net), including 10,718,300 dollars gross (9,418,200 dollars net), being the increase in assessments;

8. *Decides* that, in accordance with the provisions of its resolution 973 (X) of 15 December 1955, there shall be set off against the apportionment among Member States, as provided for in paragraphs 6 and 7 above, their respective share in the Tax Equalization Fund in the amount of 15,889,150 dollars, including 2,600,200 dollars, being the increase in the estimated staff assessment income approved for the International Tribunal for the Former Yugoslavia for the biennium 2006-2007.

Annex

Financing for the biennium 2006-2007 of the International Tribunal for the Prosecution of Persons Responsible for Serious Violations of International Humanitarian Law Committed in the Territory of the Former Yugoslavia since 1991

	Gross	*Net*
	(United States dollars)	
Initial appropriation for the biennium 2006–2007 (see resolution 60/243)	305 137 300	278 559 400
Add: Proposed changes for the biennium 2006–2007 (see A/61/585)	21 436 600	18 836 400
Less: Estimated income for the biennium 2006–2007	(249 500)	(249 500)
Proposed revised appropriation for the biennium 2006–2007	**326 324 400**	**297 146 300**
Assessment for 2006	(152 443 900)	(139 154 950)
Balance to be assessed for 2007	173 880 500	157 991 350
Including:		
Contributions assessed on Member States in accordance with the scale of assessments applicable to the regular budget of the United Nations for 2007	86 940 250	78 995 675
Contributions assessed on Member States in accordance with the rates of assessment applicable to the peacekeeping operations of the United Nations for 2007	86 940 250	78 995 675

On 22 December, the Assembly deferred consideration of the agenda item on financing of the ICTY to its resumed sixty-first (2007) session (**decision 61/552**).

International Tribunal for Rwanda

In 2006, the International Criminal Tribunal for Rwanda (ICTR), established by Security Council resolution 955(1994) [YUN 1994, p. 299] and based in Arusha, United Republic of Tanzania, delivered six trial judgements. No new indictments were issued by the Prosecutor during the year.

In letters of 29 May [S/2006/358] and 30 November [S/2006/951], submitted in response to Security Council resolutions 1503(2003) [YUN 2003, p. 1330] and 1534(2004) [YUN 2004, p. 1292], the ICTR President, Erik Mose, provided information on the Tribunal's completion strategy. In his November letter, he stated that judgements had been delivered in the first instance in respect of 31 persons. Two cases were at the judgement-writing stage and trials involving 25 accused were in progress. Of 11 detainees awaiting trial, the Prosecutor would request the transfer of a maximum of 5 to national jurisdictions. A further 18 indicted persons were still at large. The Prosecutor intended to request the transfer of at least 12 of them to national jurisdictions for trial. The President estimated that, by the end of 2008, ICTR could complete trials and judgements in the range of 65 to 70 persons.

On 8 September [S/2006/769], Rwanda informed the Security Council that a number of individuals on the Tribunal's staff, including some on defence teams, were alleged genocide suspects in the 1994 genocide in the country. Rwanda considered it unfortunate that the Tribunal was seen to be failing to distance itself from genocide suspects. A suspect named by Rwanda, Callixte Gakwaya, a defence counsel, was arrested by Tanzanian officials on 1 September and released on 5 September. Following the arrest, the ICTR Registrar requested clarification for the arrest, stating that the Tribunal had not received any prior notice of the intention to arrest. On 18 September, Mr. Gakwaya resigned from his position as lead counsel, stating that the allegations made against him had hindered him from fully representing his client.

The activities of ICTR were covered in two reports to the Council and the General Assembly, for the periods 1 July 2005 to 30 June 2006 [A/61/265-S/2006/658] and 1 July 2006 to 30 June 2007 [A/62/284-S/2007/502]. On 9 October, the Assembly took note of the 2005/2006 report (**decision 61/505**).

The Chambers

Ongoing trials

On 26 January, Mikaeli Muhimana, who was found guilty of genocide and crimes against humanity in 2005 [YUN 2005, p. 1398] and sentenced to life imprisonment, filed his appeal upon receiving the French translation of the trial judgement. A decision by the Appeal Chamber was expected in May 2007.

In the joint trial against André Ntagerura, Emmanuel Bagambiki and Samuel Imanishimwe, referred to as the "Cyangugu" case [YUN 1999, p. 1222], the Appeals Chamber, on 6 and 7 February, heard submissions on the merits of the prosecution's appeal and the appeal of Mr. Imanishimwe, a former officer in the Rwandan Armed Forces. On 8 February, the Appeals Chamber rejected the prosecution's appeal against the acquittals of Mr. Ntagerura, former Minister of Transport and Communications in the Interim Government, and Mr. Bagambiki, former Prefect of Cyangugu.

The trial of André Rwamakuba, Minister of Primary and Secondary Education in the 1994 Interim Government [YUN 2005, p. 1398], concluded on 9 February. On 20 September, he was acquitted of all charges against him (genocide, or alternatively, complicity in genocide, and crimes against humanity for acts allegedly committed between 6 and 30 April 1994 in Gikomero commune and at Butare University Hospital). After assessing the evidence as a whole, the Trial Chamber found the prosecution witnesses not credible or reliable. It concluded that the prosecution failed to prove beyond a reasonable doubt the allegations against Mr. Rwamakuba. The Chamber also found that Mr. Rwamakuba's right to legal assistance had been violated as a result of the Registrar's failure to appoint Duty Counsel during the initial months of his detention at the United Nations Detention Facility. It therefore ordered an appropriate remedy; the decision on the remedy was pending appeal.

In the appeal by Sylvestre Gacumbitsi against his 2004 conviction for genocide and crimes against humanity [YUN 2004, p. 1287], the Appeals Chamber heard the submissions on the merits of the appeals of the prosecution and Mr. Gacumbitsi on 8 and 9 February. On 7 July, the Appeals Chamber allowed, in part, the prosecution's appeal and entered a sentence of imprisonment for the remainder of Mr. Gacumbitsi's life. Mr. Gacumbitsi, a bourgmestre in April 1994, had earlier been sentenced to 30 years' imprisonment.

In the case against Joseph Serugendo, who was arrested and indicted in 2005 [YUN 2005, p. 1397], the prosecution and the accused filed a joint plea agreement on 16 February, in which Mr. Serugendo pleaded guilty to direct and public incitement to commit genocide and persecution for his role in Radio-Télévision Libre des Milles Collines (RTLM) radio broadcasts in 1994. Mr. Serugendo was sentenced, on 2 June, to six years in prison, his terminal illness and poor prognosis having been taken into account as a significant mitigating factor. Mr. Serugendo died on 22 August.

On 13 April, Georges Rutaganda, the Second Vice-President of the Interahamwe in Rwanda in 1994, who was handed a life sentence in 1999 [YUN 1999, p. 1221], sought reconsideration and review of the appeal judgement in his case. He alleged several errors in the assessment of the evidence against him and other perceived procedural irregularities, and referred to several alleged new facts that, he contended, undermined his conviction or mitigated his sentence. On 8 December, the Appeals Chamber dismissed the case, determining that it had no jurisdiction to reconsider a final judgement and that Mr. Rutaganda had not identified any new facts in his case that would have resulted in a miscarriage of justice necessitating review.

Paul Bisengimana, the former bourgmestre of Gikoro commune, was convicted by the Trial Chamber on 13 April of aiding and abetting extermination as a crime against humanity. Mr. Bisengimana, who was arrested in 2001, pleaded not guilty in 2002 [YUN 2002, p. 1285] and then pleaded guilty in 2005 [YUN 2005, p. 1399], was sentenced to 15 years' imprisonment, a higher sentence than the range proposed by the parties, in view of the official position of the accused and the large number of persons killed as a result of his crimes.

On 8 May, the defence closed its case against Tharcisse Muvunyi, the former colonel and commander of the École sous-officiers, whose trial had commenced in 2004. Closing arguments took place on 22 and 23 June. On 12 September, the Trial Chamber convicted Mr. Muvunyi of genocide, direct and public incitement to commit genocide and crimes against humanity. He was sentenced to 25 years in prison. Mr. Muvunyi filed his notice of appeal on 12 October, and the prosecution filed its notice of appeal on 17 October.

The case against Michel Bagaragaza was subject to a motion for transfer to Norway in February. The ICTR President had assigned the matter to a specially constituted bench pursuant to rule 11 bis of the Rules of Procedure and Evidence. On 19 May, the Chamber denied the motion on the grounds that Norway lacked jurisdiction over the crime of genocide as pleaded in the indictment. On 1 June, the Prosecutor appealed the decision and filed an appeal brief on 23 June. On 30 August, the Appeals Chamber dismissed the prosecution's appeal and noted that Norway's jurisdiction over Mr. Bagaragaza's crimes would be exercised pursuant to legislative provisions addressed to the prosecution of ordinary crimes; it held that the Tribunal could refer cases only to States with a capacity to charge and convict for those international crimes listed in the Tribunal's statute. On 30 November, the Trial Chamber granted the prosecution leave to amend the indictment to add an additional war crimes count. Mr. Bagaragaza was a member of the Prefectural committee of the political party that established and controlled the Interahamwe militia in Gisenyi Prefecture and an honorary president of the Interahamwe militia in Kabuga, in Kigali-rural Prefecture.

In the case of Aloys Simba, a retired lieutenant colonel found guilty of genocide and crimes against humanity and sentenced to 25 years' imprisonment in 2005 [YUN 2005, p. 1399], an appeal was lodged on 22 June, following an extension of the deadline for filing. The prosecution had filed its appeal of the judgement on 12 January. The Appeals Chamber was scheduled to hear the submissions on the merits of the appeals of both parties in May 2007.

In the joint trial against Pauline Nyiramasuhuko, Arsène Shalom Ntahobali, Sylvain Nsabimana, Alphonse Nteziryayo, Joseph Kanyabashi and Elie Ndayambaje, referred to as the "Butare" case, which began in 2001 [YUN 2001, p. 1208], the Ntahobali case closed on 26 June, except for one witness who was scheduled to testify at a later date. The defence case for Mr. Nsabimana, former Prefect of the Butare prefecture, commenced on 27 June and closed on 11 November; he was the third accused to present his defence in the case. The defence in the case of Mr. Nteziryayo, former Prefect of Butare, started on 2 December.

In the trial of Protais Zigiranyirazo, the prosecution closed its case on 28 June. Mr. Zigiranyirazo, who was arrested in 2001 [YUN 2001, p. 1207] and charged with extermination or murder as a crime against humanity, had been a member of the Akazu, the inner circle of the late President of Rwanda, Juvénal Habyarimana. On 30 October, the Appeals Chamber granted Mr. Zigiranyirazo's appeal of a Trial Chamber decision, which decided to hear a witness in person in the Netherlands while the accused followed the proceedings by video-link. The Appeals Chamber held that the Trial Chamber erred in law in finding that the accused's right to be present at his trial during the testimony of an apparently key witness against him could be met by video-link and excluded the testimony of the witness. On 30 November, the prosecution closed its case for a second time and the defence was expected to finish its case in late 2007.

On 6 July, the Appeals Chamber heard the submissions on the merits of the appeal of Emmanuel Ndindabahizi, Minister of Finance of the 1994 Interim Government. Mr. Ndindabahizi was convicted in 2004 of genocide and crimes against humanity and sentenced to life in prison [YUN 2004, p. 288]. A decision was expected in January 2007.

The joint trial of Edouard Karemera, Mathieu Ngirumpatse and Joseph Nzirorera concluded its third session on 10 July. The fourth trial session commenced on 26 October and concluded on 13 December. The trial had originally started in 2003 [YUN 2003, p. 1321] and was referred to as the "Government I" case [YUN 1999, pp. 1222 & 1223]. On 12 April, in a decision on jurisdictional appeals relating to the "Government I" case, the Appeals Chamber upheld the Tribunal's jurisdiction to impose a third-category joint criminal enterprise liability on an accused for crimes committed by fellow participants in a joint criminal enterprise of a vast scope. The question of whether third-category joint criminal enterprise liability could be imposed for complicity in genocide, which had been raised in an earlier defence motion, was sent back to the Trial Chamber for decision. On 28 April, the Appeals Chamber dismissed Mr. Nzirorera's interlocutory appeal, finding that the Trial Chamber had not abused its discretion in continuing the proceedings and in relying on the prosecution's representations that the material sought was either not in its possession or not exculpatory. In a 16 June decision, the Trial Chamber was found to have erred in failing to take judicial notice of the existence of widespread and systematic attacks in Rwanda against a civilian population based on Tutsi ethnic identification, the fact that some Rwandan citizens killed or caused serious bodily or mental harm to persons perceived to be Tutsi, and that as a result of those attacks, large numbers of Tutsis were killed. The Appeals Chamber also considered that the Trial Chamber had erred by not taking judicial notice of the fact that an armed conflict of a non-international character had existed in Rwanda at the relevant time and that genocide was committed against the Tutsi ethnic group. On 1 December, the Appeals Chamber dismissed the requests of the three accused to reconsider its "Decision on Prosecutor's Interlocutory Appeal of Decision on Judicial Notice" of 16 June, in which it had ordered the Trial Chamber to take judicial notice of three facts, including that between 6 April and 17 July 1994 there was a genocide in Rwanda against the Tutsi ethnic group. The Appeals Chamber held that the appellants failed to demonstrate a clear error of reasoning in the decision or that reconsideration of the decision was necessary to prevent an injustice. In an additional decision related to the "Government I" case, the

Appeals Chamber found on 30 June that the electronic database created by the Prosecutor for storage and retrieval of documents, allowing the defence to perform its own searches for exculpatory material, had not relieved the prosecution of its obligation to disclose all exculpatory material in its possession.

In the case against Casimir Bizimungu, Justin Mugenzi, Jérôme Bicamumpaka and Prosper Mugiraneza, referred to as the "Government II" case [YUN 1999, pp. 1222 & 1223], the defence for Mr. Mugenzi, Minister of Trade and Industry in April 1994, completed the presentation of its case on 29 August; the defence for Mr. Bizimungu, Minister for Health in the Interim Government, commenced the presentation of his case on 30 August.

On 12 September, Jean Mpambara, the former bourgmestre of Rukara commune, was acquitted of all charges against him. Mr. Mpambara was arrested in 2001 [YUN 2001, p. 1207] and was charged with genocide and extermination for his alleged involvement in attacks at three locations in his commune by aiding and abetting and participating in a joint criminal enterprise. The Chamber found that the evidence had not proven beyond a reasonable doubt that he instigated or positively assisted the attackers; in fact, it found significant evidence suggesting that Mr. Mpambara had made efforts to prevent violence and that his resources were limited.

The trial of Simon Bikindi, a well-known composer and singer of popular music, started on 18 September. The prosecution was expected to close its case in February 2007; it alleged that the accused participated in the anti-Tutsi campaign in Rwanda in 1994 both through his musical compositions and speeches he made at public gatherings. Following the withdrawal of the lead counsel for the accused by the Registrar, a new lead counsel was appointed and the defence case was scheduled to commence in September 2007. Mr. Bikindi was arrested in The Netherlands in 2001 and was transferred to the Tribunal in 2002. [YUN 2002, p. 1285]

In the joint trial of four former high-ranking Rwandan military officers (Théoneste Bagosora, Gratien Kabiligi, Aloys Ntabakuze, Anatole Nsengiyumva), known as the "Military I" case, the Appeals Chamber, on 18 September, allowed, in part, Mr. Ntabakuze's appeal of a Trial Chamber decision on his request to exclude certain evidence as outside the scope of the indictment. The Appeals Chamber found that the Trial Chamber had not erred in its articulation of the principles concerning defects in the indictment and clarified the approach for deciding whether an objection based on a defect in the indictment should be considered timely. The Appeals Chamber instructed the Trial Chamber to consider whether the extent of the defects in the indictment had materially prejudiced the accused's right to a fair trial by hindering the preparation of a proper defence. On 25 September, the Appeals Chamber granted the appeals of Messrs. Kabiligi and Nsengiyumva against a Trial Chamber decision that denied their request for the disclosure of certain documents related to anticipated defence witnesses that were in the prosecution's possession. The Trial Chamber was ordered to reconsider the defence request for the documents. On 4 October, the Appeals Chamber rejected the request of Mr. Ntabakuze to reconsider its "Decision on Prosecutor's Interlocutory Appeal of Decision on Judicial Notice" rendered in the Karemera and Others case. The Appeals Chamber found that Mr. Ntabakuze had no standing to seek reconsideration of a decision rendered in another case. It held that, as a general principle, only a party to a decision could request reconsideration thereof.

The trial against Siméon Nchamihigo, a former Deputy Prosecutor in Cyangugu prefecture, commenced on 25 September. At the time of his arrest in 2001, Mr. Nchamihigo was working at ICTR, under an alias, as an investigator for the defence in the Samuel Imanishimwe case [YUN 2001, p. 1207]. In an amended indictment filed on 11 December, the prosecution charged Mr. Nchamihigo with four counts of genocide and crimes against humanity.

The trial of Emmanuel Rukundo, former military chaplain in the Rwandan Armed Forces, commenced on 15 November. Mr. Rukundo, charged with three counts of genocide and crimes against humanity [ibid.], was arrested in Switzerland in 2001 and transferred to the UN Detention Facility.

The trial of François Karera began on 9 January and concluded on 24 November. A judgement was expected in 2007. Mr. Karera, former Prefect of Kigali-rural prefecture, was arrested in Kenya and transferred to ICTR in 2001. He pleaded not guilty to charges of genocide or complicity in genocide and crimes against humanity [ibid., p. 1208].

In the joint trial of four former senior military officers (Augustin Ndindiliyimana, Augustin Bizimungu, François-Xavier Nzuwonemeye, Innocent Sagahutu), the prosecution closed its case on 7 December. All four accused were arrested in 2000 [YUN 2000, p. 1225] in a case consolidated as the "Military II" case.

On 13 December, the Trial Chamber found Athanase Seromba, a Roman Catholic priest of Nyange Parish in the Kivumu commune, guilty of genocide and extermination as a crime against humanity and sentenced him to 15 years' imprisonment. Both parties filed a notice of appeal against the judgement. In a decision related to the Seromba case, the Appeals Chamber, on 22 May, found that the Tribunal's statute and rules did not provide for an interlocutory appeal to the Appeals Chamber of a decision taken by the Bureau on questions of impartiality of judges.

Joseph Nzabirinda, a former employee of Ngoma commune in Butare working as "encadreur" of youths, pleaded guilty on 14 December to aiding and abetting murder, a crime against humanity. The Chamber accepted his plea and the accused was expected to be sentenced in February 2007.

Judges of the Court

Permanent Judges

On 3 May, the Secretary-General, in identical letters to the General Assembly and Security Council Presidents [A/60/878-S/2006/349], transmitted a letter from the ICTR President, recalling that the terms of office of 11 permanent judges of the Tribunal were to end in May 2007, and that a number of multi-accused trials under way were likely to continue beyond that date. If certain judges were not re-elected, some cases would have to start from the beginning with new judges. In order to ensure continuity and the ability of ICTR to implement its completion strategy, the Secretary-General requested that the terms of the 11 permanent judges be extended until 31 December 2008.

SECURITY COUNCIL ACTION

On 13 June [meeting 5455], the Security Council unanimously adopted **resolution 1684(2006)**. The draft [S/2006/372] was prepared in consultations among Council members.

The Security Council,

Recalling its resolutions 955(1994) of 8 November 1994, 1165(1998) of 30 April 1998, 1329(2000) of 30 November 2000, 1411(2002) of 17 May 2002, 1431(2002) of 14 August 2002, 1449(2002) of 13 December 2002, 1503(2003) of 28 August 2003 and 1534(2004) of 26 March 2004,

Recalling also that on 31 January 2003, the General Assembly, by its decision 57/414 A and in accordance with article 12 bis, paragraph 1 *(b)*, of the statute of the International Criminal Tribunal for Rwanda, as amended, elected from a list of candidates approved in resolution 1449(2002) the following eleven judges to a four-year term of office at the Tribunal, beginning on 25 May 2003 and ending on 24 May 2007: Mr. Mansoor Ahmed (Pakistan), Mr. Sergei Alekseevich Egorov (Russian Federation), Mr. Asoka de Zoysa Gunawardana (Sri Lanka), Mr. Mehmet Güney (Turkey), Mr. Erik Møse (Norway), Ms. Arlette Ramaroson (Madagascar), Mr. Jai Ram Reddy (Fiji), Mr. William Hussein Sekule (United Republic of Tanzania), Ms. Andrésia Vaz (Senegal), Ms. Inés Mónica Weinberg de Roca (Argentina) and Mr. Lloyd George Williams (Saint Kitts and Nevis),

Recalling further that when Judge Mansoor Ahmed resigned, the Secretary-General, after consultations with the Security Council and the General Assembly and in accordance with article 12 bis, paragraph 2, of the statute of the Tribunal, appointed Ms. Khalida Rachid Khan (Pakistan), effective from 7 July 2003, for the remainder of Judge Ahmed's term of office,

Recalling that when Judge Lloyd George Williams resigned, the Secretary-General, after consultations with the Council and the Assembly and in accordance with article 12 bis, paragraph 2, of the statute of the Tribunal, appointed Sir Charles Michael Dennis Byron (Saint Kitts and Nevis), effective from 8 April 2004, for the remainder of Judge Williams' term of office,

Recalling also that when Judge Asoka de Zoysa Gunawardana resigned, the Secretary-General, after consultations with the Council and the Assembly and in accordance with article 12 bis, paragraph 2, of the statute of the Tribunal, appointed Mr. Asoka de Silva (Sri Lanka), effective from 2 August 2004, for the remainder of Judge Gunawardana's term of office,

Taking note of the letter dated 3 May 2006 from the Secretary-General to the President of the Security Council,

1. *Decides*, in response to the request of the Secretary-General and notwithstanding the provisions of article 12 bis of the statute of the International Criminal Tribunal for Rwanda, to extend until 31 December 2008 the term of office at the Tribunal of the following permanent judges of the Tribunal:

Sir Charles Michael Dennis Byron (Saint Kitts and Nevis)
Mr. Asoka de Silva (Sri Lanka)
Mr. Sergei Alekseevich Egorov (Russian Federation)
Mr. Mehmet Güney (Turkey)
Ms. Khalida Rachid Khan (Pakistan)
Mr. Erik Møse (Norway)
Ms. Arlette Ramaroson (Madagascar)
Mr. Jai Ram Reddy (Fiji)
Mr. William Hussein Sekule (United Republic of Tanzania)
Ms. Andrésia Vaz (Senegal)
Ms. Inés Mónica Weinberg de Roca (Argentina)

2. *Requests* States to continue to make every effort to ensure that their nationals who serve as permanent judges of the Tribunal remain available to serve in their positions until 31 December 2008.

General Assembly action. On 13 June [A/60/906-S/2006/437], the Security Council President transmitted to the General Assembly President the text of the above resolution. The Assembly, by **decision 60/422 A** of 28 June, endorsed the recommendations contained in the Secretary-General's 3 May letter (see above).

Ad litem judges

In identical letters of 25 August [A/60/989-S/2006/688], the Secretary-General forwarded to the General Assembly and Security Council Presidents a request from the ICTR President for the term of office of Judge Solomy Balungi Bossa (Uganda) (an ad litem judge whose term was due to expire on 24 June 2007) to be extended beyond the three-year limit. The Secretary-General explained that Judge Bossa was involved in the Butare case, a complex multi-accused trial involving six accused, which was expected to continue into 2007. The extension of her term of office until the completion of that trial would ensure the steady progress of that process and simultaneously help to meet the target dates of the completion strategy.

SECURITY COUNCIL ACTION

On 29 August [meeting 5518], the Security Council unanimously adopted **resolution 1705(2006)**. The draft [S/2006/690] was prepared in consultations among Council members.

The Security Council,

Taking note of the letter dated 25 August 2006 from the Secretary-General to the President of the Security Council,

Decides that, notwithstanding article 12 ter of the statute of the International Criminal Tribunal for Rwanda, and notwithstanding the fact that Judge Solomy Balungi Bossa's elected term as an ad litem judge of the Tribunal will, in accordance with article 12 ter of the statute of the Tribunal, end on 24 June 2007, she shall be authorized, effective 28 August 2006, to continue to serve as a judge in the *Butare* case until its completion.

General Assembly action. On 29 August [A/60/992], the Security Council President transmitted to the General Assembly President the text of the above resolution. The Assembly, by **decision 60/422 B** of the same day, endorsed the recommendations contained in the Secretary-General's 25 August letter (see above).

The Secretary-General, in identical letters of 2 October [A/61/509-S/2006/799], transmitted to the General Assembly and Security Council Presidents a letter from the ICTR President requesting that the terms of office of 18 ad litem judges, which were to expire in June 2007, be extended until 31 December 2008. The extension would allow continuity in the trials in which the judges were involved and help to meet the deadline for the ICTR completion strategy. Otherwise, elections would have to take place at the end of 2006 or in early 2007.

SECURITY COUNCIL ACTION

On 13 October [meeting 5550], the Security Council unanimously adopted **resolution 1717(2006)**. The draft [S/2006/803] was prepared in consultations among Council members.

The Security Council,

Recalling its resolutions 955(1994) of 8 November 1994, 1165(1998) of 30 April 1998, 1329(2000) of 30 November 2000, 1411(2002) of 17 May 2002, 1431(2002) of 14 August 2002, 1449(2002) of 13 December 2002, 1503(2003) of 28 August 2003 and 1534(2004) of 26 March 2004,

Recalling also that on 25 June 2003 the General Assembly, by its decision 57/414 C and in accordance with article 12 ter, paragraph 1 *(d)*, of the statute of the International Criminal Tribunal for Rwanda, elected from a list of candidates approved by the Security Council the following eighteen ad litem judges to a four-year term of office beginning on 25 June 2003 and ending on 24 June 2007: Mr. Aydin Sefa Akay (Turkey), Ms. Florence Rita Arrey (Cameroon), Ms. Solomy Balungi Bossa (Uganda), Mr. Robert Fremr (Czech Republic), Ms. Taghreed Hikmat (Jordan), Ms. Karin Hökborg (Sweden), Mr. Vagn Joensen (Denmark), Mr. Gberdao Gustave Kam (Burkina Faso), Tan Sri Dato' Hj. Mohd. Azmi Dato' Hj. Kamaruddin (Malaysia), Ms. Flavia Lattanzi (Italy), Mr. Kenneth Machin (United Kingdom of Great Britain and Northern Ireland), Mr. Joseph Edward Chiondo Masanche (United Republic of Tanzania), Mr. Lee Gacuiga Muthoga (Kenya), Mr. Seon Ki Park (Republic of Korea), Mr. Mparany Mamy Richard Rajohnson (Madagascar), Mr. Emile Francis Short (Ghana), Mr. Albertus Henricus Joannes Swart (Netherlands), and Ms. Aura E. Guerra de Villalaz (Panama),

Recalling further that the Council, by its resolution 1684(2006) of 13 June 2006, extended the terms of eleven permanent judges serving at the Tribunal until 31 December 2008,

Recalling that the Council, by its resolution 1705(2006) of 29 August 2006, decided, notwithstanding the provisions of article 12 ter of the statute of the Tribunal, and notwithstanding the fact that Judge Bossa's elected term as an ad litem judge of the Tribunal will end on 24 June 2007, to authorize her, effective 28 August 2006, to continue to serve as a judge in the *Butare* case until its completion,

Taking note of the letter dated 2 October 2006 from the Secretary-General to the President of the Security Council,

1. *Decides*, in response to the request of the Secretary-General and notwithstanding the provisions of article 12 ter of the statute of the International Criminal Tribunal for Rwanda, to extend until 31 December 2008 the term of office of the following ad litem judges of the Tribunal who were elected on 25 June 2003:

Mr. Aydin Sefa Akay (Turkey)
Ms. Florence Rita Arrey (Cameroon)
Ms. Solomy Balungi Bossa (Uganda)
Mr. Robert Fremr (Czech Republic)
Ms. Taghreed Hikmat (Jordan)
Ms. Karin Hökborg (Sweden)
Mr. Vagn Joensen (Denmark)
Mr. Gberdao Gustave Kam (Burkina Faso)

Tan Sri Dato' Hj. Mohd. Azmi Dato' Hj. Kamaruddin (Malaysia)
Ms. Flavia Lattanzi (Italy)
Mr. Kenneth Machin (United Kingdom)
Mr. Joseph Edward Chiondo Masanche (United Republic of Tanzania)
Mr. Lee Gacuiga Muthoga (Kenya)
Mr. Seon Ki Park (Republic of Korea)
Mr. Mparany Mamy Richard Rajohnson (Madagascar)
Mr. Emile Francis Short (Ghana)
Mr. Albertus Henricus Joannes Swart (Netherlands)
Ms. Aura E. Guerra de Villalaz (Panama)

2. *Decides also*, in response to the request of the Secretary-General, to allow ad litem Judges Arrey, Bossa, Hikmat, Hökborg, Kam, Lattanzi, Muthoga, Park and Short to serve in the Tribunal beyond the cumulative period of service provided for under article 12 ter of the statute and until 31 December 2008;

3. *Requests* States to continue to make every effort to ensure that their nationals who were elected as ad litem judges of the Tribunal remain available to serve until 31 December 2008;

4. *Decides* to remain seized of the matter.

General Assembly action. On 13 October [A/61/548], the Security Council President transmitted to the General Assembly President the text of the above resolution. The Assembly, by **decision 61/403** of 2 November, endorsed the recommendations contained in the Secretary-General's 2 October letter (see p. 1499).

Office of the Prosecutor

The Prosecutor continued to implement the completion strategy, in consultation with the President of the Tribunal. Further efforts were made to identify States willing to try Tribunal indictees that were referred to them. In May, the first transfer request, brought by the Prosecutor under rule 11 bis, was denied by the Trial Chamber; the Prosecutor appealed that decision. During the year, various actions were taken to improve the prosecution's information and evidence management capacity and implementation of prosecutorial best practices. In that regard, staff training and continuing education remained a priority in the pursuit of the completion strategy. In March, the Prosecutor convened a strategic planning workshop to assess how effectively the Office of the Prosecutor had implemented the completion strategy, while identifying areas for improvement in performance.

The Registry

The Registry continued to support the judicial process by servicing the Tribunal's other organs and the defence and by seeking support from States, international organizations and other stakeholders in the conduct of proceedings. During the year, it maintained high-level diplomatic contacts and drafted a number of agreements with States or international organizations to ensure their continued cooperation with ICTR. Outreach activities were stepped up, especially through judicial visits to the Tribunal and capacity-building training for members of the Rwandan judiciary and universities. ICTR also planned an attachment programme of Rwandan judicial officials to the Office of the Prosecutor and the Registry, to enable them to get first-hand experience in international humanitarian law. The attachment programme would also help Rwandan legal practitioners to acquire the experience necessary for handling cases that could be transferred to Rwanda as part of the ICTR completion strategy. Diplomatic efforts continued, in order to relocate some acquitted persons who remained under ICTR protection; in December, those efforts led to the successful relocation of one such person. The Press and Public Affairs Unit increased its monitoring and internal circulation of Tribunal-related media reports, updated information brochures and posters and continued to improve the Tribunal's website.

Financing

2006-2007 biennium

In response to General Assembly resolution 60/241 [YUN 2005, p. 1400], the Secretary-General submitted the first performance report of ICTR for the 2006-2007 biennium [A/61/586]. The report requested an additional appropriation of $7.9 million, net of staff assessment, over the initial amount appropriated in resolution 60/241. The increased requirement reflected changes with respect to exchange rates resulting from the weakening of the United States dollar vis-à-vis the euro and inflation ($4,432,100) and standard salary costs ($2,937,200). The Assembly was requested to approve a revised appropriation for 2006-2007 in the amount of $277,127,700 gross ($254,757,400 net) for the Special Account for ICTR.

In a 14 December report [A/61/633], ACABQ recommended approval of the revised appropriation for the 2006-2007 biennium, as recommended by the Secretary-General.

GENERAL ASSEMBLY ACTION

On 22 December [meeting 84], the General Assembly, on the recommendation of the Fifth

Committee [A/61/655], adopted **resolution 61/241** without vote [agenda item 129].

Financing of the International Criminal Tribunal for the Prosecution of Persons Responsible for Genocide and Other Serious Violations of International Humanitarian Law Committed in the Territory of Rwanda and Rwandan Citizens Responsible for Genocide and Other Such Violations Committed in the Territory of Neighbouring States between 1 January and 31 December 1994

The General Assembly,

Having considered the reports of the Secretary-General, namely, his first performance report for the biennium 2006-2007 on the International Criminal Tribunal for the Prosecution of Persons Responsible for Genocide and Other Serious Violations of International Humanitarian Law Committed in the Territory of Rwanda and Rwandan Citizens Responsible for Genocide and Other Such Violations Committed in the Territory of Neighbouring States between 1 January and 31 December 1994 and his report on financial and any other implications resulting from the introduction of a staff retention bonus at the International Criminal Tribunal for Rwanda and the International Tribunal for the Former Yugoslavia,

Having also considered the report of the Board of Auditors on the International Criminal Tribunal for Rwanda and the recommendations contained therein,

Having further considered the related reports of the Advisory Committee on Administrative and Budgetary Questions,

Recalling its resolution 49/251 of 20 July 1995 on the financing of the International Criminal Tribunal for Rwanda and its subsequent resolutions thereon, the latest of which were resolutions 60/240 and 60/241 of 23 December 2005,

1. *Takes note* of the first performance report of the Secretary-General for the biennium 2006-2007 on the International Criminal Tribunal for the Prosecution of Persons Responsible for Genocide and Other Serious Violations of International Humanitarian Law Committed in the Territory of Rwanda and Rwandan Citizens Responsible for Genocide and Other Such Violations Committed in the Territory of Neighbouring States between 1 January and 31 December 1994 and his report on the financial and any other implications resulting from the introduction of a staff retention bonus at the International Criminal Tribunal for Rwanda and the International Tribunal for the Former Yugoslavia;

2. *Endorses* the conclusions and recommendations contained in the reports of the Advisory Committee on Administrative and Budgetary Questions;

3. *Emphasizes* the importance of implementing the recommendations of the Board of Auditors, and requests the Secretary-General to report on progress in the implementation of the recommendations of the Board in the context of the proposed budget of the International Criminal Tribunal for Rwanda for the biennium 2008-2009;

4. *Also emphasizes* the importance of the timely submission of the performance reports on the International Criminal Tribunal for Rwanda and the related reports of the Advisory Committee on Administrative and Budgetary Questions in order to facilitate the proper consideration thereof by the General Assembly;

5. *Recalls* paragraph 9 of its resolution 60/241, and requests the Secretary-General to report thereon in the context of the proposed budget of the International Criminal Tribunal for Rwanda for the biennium 2008-2009;

6. *Decides* on a revised appropriation to the Special Account for the International Criminal Tribunal for the Prosecution of Persons Responsible for Genocide and Other Serious Violations of International Humanitarian Law Committed in the Territory of Rwanda and Rwandan Citizens Responsible for Genocide and Other Such Violations Committed in the Territory of Neighbouring States between 1 January and 31 December 1994 of a total amount of 277,127,700 United States dollars gross (254,757,400 dollars net) for the biennium 2006-2007;

7. *Also decides*, for the year 2007, to apportion among Member States, in accordance with the scale of assessments applicable to the regular budget of the United Nations for the year, the amount of 71,124,250 dollars gross (65,656,200 dollars net), including 3,684,650 dollars gross (3,933,700 dollars net), being the increase in assessments;

8. *Further decides*, for the year 2007, to apportion among Member States, in accordance with the rates of assessment applicable to peacekeeping operations for the year, the amount of 71,124,250 dollars gross (65,656,200 dollars net), including 3,684,650 dollars gross (3,933,700 dollars net), being the increase in assessments;

9. *Decides* that, in accordance with the provisions of its resolution 973(X) of 15 December 1955, there shall be set off against the apportionment among Member States, as provided for in paragraphs 7 and 8 above, their respective share in the Tax Equalization Fund in the amount of 10,936,100 dollars, including 498,100 dollars, being the decrease in the estimated staff assessment income approved for the International Criminal Tribunal for Rwanda for the biennium 2006-2007.

Annex

Financing for the biennium 2006-2007 of the International Criminal Tribunal for the Prosecution of Persons Responsible for Genocide and Other Serious Violations of International Humanitarian Law Committed in the Territory of Rwanda and Rwandan Citizens Responsible for Genocide and Other Such Violations Committed in the Territory of Neighbouring States between 1 January and 31 December 1994

	Gross	*Net*
	(United States dollars)	
Initial appropriation for the biennium 2006–2007 (see resolution 60/241)	269 758 400	246 890 000
Add: Proposed changes for the biennium 2006–2007 (see A/61/586)	7 369 300	7 867 400

Proposed revised appropriation for the biennium 2006–2007	**277 127 700**	**254 757 400**
Assessment for 2006	134 879 200	123 445 000
Balance to be assessed for 2007	142 248 500	131 312 400
Including:		
Contributions assessed on Member States in accordance with the scale of assessments applicable to the regular budget of the United Nations for 2007	71 124 250	65 656 200
Contributions assessed on Member States in accordance with the rates of assessment applicable to the peacekeeping operations of the United Nations for 2007	71 124 250	65 656 200

On 22 December, the Assembly deferred consideration of the agenda item on financing of ICTR to its resumed sixty-first (2007) session (**decision 61/552**).

Functioning of the Tribunals

Staff retention

In response to General Assembly resolutions 60/241 [YUN 2005, p. 1400] and 60/243 [ibid., p. 1396], the Secretary-General submitted an October report [A/61/522] on financial and other implications resulting from the proposed introduction of a staff retention bonus for ICTR and ICTY. In a 2005 report [ibid., p. 1401], the Secretary-General had proposed that, as the Tribunals moved closer to the completion of their mandates and staff departures increased, a retention bonus should be introduced for staff in order to avoid disrupting the normal operations of the Tribunals and to ensure the timely completion of their mandates. He estimated that payments of such a bonus would total $11.2 million for ICTR and $12.1 million for ICTY.

In a November report [A/61/591], ACABQ noted the improvement in turnover rates achieved through the implementation of numerous measures under the authority of the Secretary-General, such as extending the length of contracts of all staff in the Tribunals from one to two years. However, while recognizing merit in the requirement to retain necessary staff to ensure the continued smooth functioning of the Tribunals until the completion of their mandates, ACABQ stated that the Secretary-General's proposal for a retention bonus was too broad and could lead to the creation of a new entitlement, which could be used as a precedent and have implications for the common system as a whole. It recommended that the Assembly request the Secretary-General to further explore ways to apply the Staff Regulations and Rules to achieve the desired objective. He should also submit a comprehensive proposal on any additional measures that might be required within the time frame of the completion strategy in the context of the 2008-2009 budget submissions for the tribunals.

By **decision 61/552** of 22 December, the Assembly deferred consideration of the item on financing of ICTR and ICTY to its resumed sixty-first (2007) session.

Implementation of completion strategies

ICTY

In response to Security Council resolutions 1503(2003) [YUN 2003, p. 1330] and 1534(2004) [YUN 2004, p. 1292], the ICTY President submitted reports in May [S/2006/353] and November [S/2006/898] that assessed progress made in implementing the ICTY completion strategy.

In his May report, the President described the activities of two working groups—the Working Group on Speeding up Trials and the Working Group on Speeding up Appeals. He stated that the measures taken by the judges to amend the Rules of Procedure and Evidence in order to expedite the appeals process had had a substantial impact on the swift and fair disposal of interlocutory appeals and appeals from judgement by the Appeals Chamber. However, the Rules concerning appeals remained under the close scrutiny of the judges and further innovative ways of expediting the appeals process without sacrificing due process were constantly being sought.

The Working Group on Speeding up Trials made specific recommendations on ways to enhance the efficiency of proceedings by making greater use of the existing Rules. The issuance of the Working Group's final report, in February, led to an open dialogue between the judges, which culminated in an informal plenary of judges in April and the adoption of specific proposals. Those proposals were implemented by the judges and their enforcement had a fundamental impact on the way trials were conducted. To accommodate the trials of multiple accused, ICTY had all three of its courtrooms remodelled. The new arrangement allowed up to 18 accused to be tried simultaneously and permitted simultaneous interpretation in four languages. New holding cells were created to accommodate the appropriate number of accused persons for each of the courtrooms.

In accordance with the recommendations of the Working Group on Pre-Trial Proceedings, pre-trial judges played a much more active role in preparing cases for trial and ensuring that cases were trial-ready. The use of the e-Court system in the Tribunal's proceedings had also been a factor in the efficient completion of trials, resulting in significant savings in court time.

In November, the ICTY President confirmed that, despite the Tribunal's best efforts, trials would run into 2009. ICTY had seen decisive results in appeal and trial efficiency. However, six fugitives remained at large, including Radovan Karadzic and Ratko Mladic, both of whom were indicted in 1995 [YUN 1995, p. 1314]. If those two fugitives were not arrested immediately, the 2009 date for the completion of all trials was doubtful.

ICTR

In response to Security Council resolutions 1503(2003) [YUN 2003, p. 1330] and 1534(2004) [YUN 2004, p. 1292], the ICTR President submitted reports in June [S/2006/358] and December [S/2006/951] that assessed progress made in implementing the ICTR completion strategy.

The reports reviewed recent judgements and trials in progress; cases for transfer to national jurisdictions for trial; the actual number of persons brought to trial; and progress on the tracking of fugitives. Although Council resolution 1503(2003) anticipated that the work of ICTR and ICTY should be completed by 2010, the report noted that it was difficult to indicate a completion strategy for the ICTR Appeals Chamber, as it was linked to the ICTY completion strategy. Recalling that most judgements rendered had been appealed, the ICTR President anticipated that the Appeals Chamber's already heavy workload would continue to increase as the workload of the Trial Chambers decreased and the focus shifted to appeals. He stated that the number of judges at the Appeals Chamber would need to be augmented for there to be any reasonable prospects of completing all appeals by 2010.

The cases involving 25 accused whose trials were in progress would be completed from 2007 onwards. Trials of the remaining 12 indictees (six detained and six at large) would commence as soon as Trial Chamber and court room availability permitted. It was estimated that by the end of 2008 ICTR would have completed trials involving 65 to 70 persons.

International Criminal Court

In 2006, the International Criminal Court (ICC), established by the Rome Statute [YUN 1998, p. 1209] as a permanent institution with jurisdiction over persons accused of the most serious crimes of international concern (genocide, crimes against humanity, war crimes and the crime of aggression), carried out investigations in the Democratic Republic of the Congo (DRC), the Sudan (Darfur) and Uganda. Reports covering ICC activities during the year were submitted to the General Assembly [A/61/217; A/62/314]. On 26 January, the Assembly of States Parties to the Rome Statute re-elected five ICC judges whose terms had expired, as well as a new judge, to serve nine-year, non-renewable terms. The judges began their terms of office on 11 March. Also on 11 March, the 18 ICC judges re-elected Judge Philippe Kirsch as President of the Court, Judge Akua Kuenyehia as First Vice-President and Judge René Blattmann as Second Vice-President, all to three-year terms. As at 31 December, 104 States had ratified the Rome Statute and 139 had signed it.

A major development was the arrest and surrender to the Court in March of its first accused, Thomas Lubanga Dyilo (DRC) (see p. 1506). Although warrants of arrest were issued in 2005 for five members of the Lord's Resistance Army (LRA) (Uganda), none of them had been arrested. As ICC did not have its own police, it relied on the cooperation of States and international organizations to carry out arrests.

In 2006, the Court adopted the first version of its strategic plan, which provided a framework for the Court's activities over the next 10 years, with emphasis on the objectives for the immediate three years. The plan set out how the Court would proceed to realize the aims of the Rome Statute, set a clear direction for its future, ensure continuous coordination of its activities, demonstrate its transparency and further strengthen its relationships with States parties and other actors. The plan identified three strategic goals for fulfilling the ICC mission: ensure the quality of justice; become a well-recognized and adequately supported institution; and serve as a model for public administration. Thirty strategic objectives detailed the steps to reach those goals.

During the year, the Prosecutor received more than 96 communications relating to situations that fell within the jurisdiction of the Court. In addition to the situations under investigation, the Prosecutor was monitoring five other situations around the world, including in the Central African Republic and Côte d'Ivoire.

GENERAL ASSEMBLY ACTION

On 20 November [meeting 56], the General Assembly adopted **resolution 61/15** [draft: A/61/L.21 & Add.1] without vote [agenda item 74].

Report of the International Criminal Court

The General Assembly,

Recalling its resolution 60/29 of 23 November 2005 and all its previous relevant resolutions,

Recalling also that the Rome Statute of the International Criminal Court reaffirms the purposes and principles of the Charter of the United Nations,

Emphasizing that justice, especially transitional justice in conflict and post-conflict societies, is a fundamental building block of sustainable peace,

Noting with satisfaction the fact that the International Criminal Court is fully operational and has achieved considerable progress in its analyses, investigations and judicial proceedings in various situations and cases which were referred to it by States parties to the Rome Statute and by the Security Council, in accordance with the Rome Statute,

Recalling that effective cooperation and assistance by States, the United Nations and other international and regional organizations remain essential for the International Criminal Court to carry out its activities,

Welcoming the continuous support given by civil society to the International Criminal Court,

Expressing its appreciation to the Secretary-General for providing effective and efficient assistance to the International Criminal Court in accordance with the Relationship Agreement between the United Nations and the International Criminal Court ("Relationship Agreement"),

Acknowledging the Relationship Agreement as approved by the General Assembly in its resolution 58/318 of 13 September 2004, including paragraph 3 of the resolution with respect to the payment in full of expenses accruing to the United Nations as a result of the implementation of the Relationship Agreement, which provides a framework for continued cooperation between the Court and the United Nations, which could include the facilitation by the United Nations of the Court's field activities, and encouraging the conclusion of supplementary arrangements and agreements, as necessary,

Recognizing the role of the International Criminal Court in a multilateral system that aims to end impunity, establish the rule of law, promote and encourage respect for human rights and achieve sustainable peace, in accordance with international law and the purposes and principles of the Charter,

Expressing its appreciation to the International Criminal Court for providing assistance to the Special Court for Sierra Leone and for granting a leave of absence to its Deputy Prosecutor for Investigations to enable him to work for the International Independent Investigation Commission,

Reiterating the historic significance of the adoption of the Rome Statute,

1. *Welcomes* the report of the International Criminal Court for 2005-2006;

2. *Welcomes* the States that have become parties to the Rome Statute of the International Criminal Court in the past year, and calls upon all States from all regions of the world that are not yet parties to the Rome Statute to consider ratifying or acceding to it without delay;

3. *Calls upon* all States that have not yet done so to consider becoming parties to the Agreement on the Privileges and Immunities of the International Criminal Court;

4. *Encourages* States parties to the Rome Statute that have not yet done so to adopt national legislation to implement obligations emanating from the Rome Statute and to cooperate with the International Criminal Court in the exercise of its functions, and recalls the provision of technical assistance by States parties in this respect;

5. *Welcomes* the effective cooperation and assistance provided to the International Criminal Court by States, the United Nations and other international and regional organizations, and calls upon them to continue providing such cooperation and assistance in the future;

6. *Encourages* States to contribute to the Trust Fund established for the benefit of victims of crimes within the jurisdiction of the International Criminal Court, and of the families of such victims, as well as to the Trust Fund for the participation of least developed countries, and acknowledges with appreciation contributions made to both trust funds so far;

7. *Emphasizes* the importance of the full implementation of the Relationship Agreement, which forms a framework for close cooperation between the two organizations and for consultation on matters of mutual interest pursuant to the provisions of that Agreement and in conformity with the respective provisions of the Charter of the United Nations and the Rome Statute, as well as the need for comprehensive information from the Secretary-General with respect to steps taken in the implementation of the Agreement;

8. *Notes* the establishment and operationalization of the International Criminal Court liaison office to United Nations Headquarters, and encourages the Secretary-General to work closely with that office;

9. *Welcomes* the report of the Secretary-General on the work of the Organization, in which reference is made to the important role of the International Criminal Court in advancing the cause of justice and the rule of law;

10. *Recalls* that, by virtue of article 12, paragraph 3, of the Rome Statute, a State which is not a party to the Statute may, by declaration lodged with the Registrar of the International Criminal Court, accept the exercise of jurisdiction by the Court with respect to specific crimes that are mentioned in paragraph 2 of that article;

11. *Notes* the work of the Special Working Group on the Crime of Aggression, which is open to all States on an equal footing, and encourages all States to consider

participating actively in the Working Group with a view to elaborating proposals for a provision on the crime of aggression;

12. *Looks forward* to the fifth session of the Assembly of States Parties to the Rome Statute of the International Criminal Court, to be held in The Hague from 23 November to 1 December 2006, as well as the resumed fifth session to be held in New York from 29 to 31 January 2007, and encourages the widest possible participation of States in these proceedings;

13. *Takes note* of the decision of the Assembly of States Parties to the Rome Statute at its fourth session, while recalling that according to article 112, paragraph 6, of the Rome Statute, the Assembly of States Parties shall meet at the seat of the International Criminal Court or at United Nations Headquarters, to hold its sixth session in New York in 2007, and requests the Secretary-General to provide the necessary services and facilities in accordance with the Relationship Agreement and resolution 58/318;

14. *Invites* the International Criminal Court to submit, in accordance with article 6 of the Relationship Agreement, a report on its activities for 2006-2007, for consideration by the General Assembly at its sixty-second session.

Assembly of States Parties

The Assembly of States Parties to the Rome Statute of the International Criminal Court, at its fifth session (The Hague, 23 November–1 December) [ICC-ASP/5/32 & Corr.1], adopted four resolutions.

In 2006, the Assembly adopted a plan of action for achieving universality and full implementation of the Rome Statute. The plan set out how the Assembly and its States Parties would each continue to contribute to achieving universality in the coming years.

With regard to permanent premises for the Court, the Assembly requested ICC to focus on the option of constructing purpose-built premises on the Alexander Kazerne site, with a view to allowing the Assembly to take an informed decision at its 2007 session. ICC should prepare: a detailed functional brief that would include user and safety requirements reflecting scalability in terms of staffing levels; cost estimates for the project, in consultation with the host State (The Netherlands); a provisional timetable and a summary of planning and permit issues; and a planning strategy for the site, also in consultation with the host State. The Assembly requested the host State, in consultation with the Assembly's Bureau and ICC, to propose the modalities for an international architectural concept competition. ICC was asked to establish and staff a project management structure in line with the programme budget for 2007.

In a resolution on the Court's strategic planning process, the Assembly considered the Strategic Plan submitted by ICC [ICC-ASP/5/6] and invited it to further develop the dialogue on the Plan already initiated with the Bureau. That dialogue should focus on the concrete implementation of the plan and include cross-cutting issues, such as location of the Court's activities, position of victims, outreach and communication activities and the relationship between the Strategic Plan and the budget. ICC was invited to submit an update of the Strategic Plan to the Assembly's 2007 session.

In connection with strengthening the ICC and the Assembly of States Parties, the Assembly adopted a resolution that addressed: the Rome Statute and other agreements; institution-building; cooperation with regard to the implementation of the Rome Statute; and institutional matters regarding the Assembly of States Parties. The Assembly approved the draft headquarters agreement between ICC and the host State, which was annexed to the resolution. It welcomed the conclusion of the Cooperation Agreement between ICC and the European Union (EU) and looked forward to the early conclusion of cooperation agreements with the African Union; other regional organizations were invited to consider concluding such agreements with the Court. The Assembly also welcomed the establishment of an ICC New York Liaison Office, which was due to become operational in January 2007. Also annexed to the resolution was the plan of action of the Assembly for achieving universality and full implementation of the Rome Statute and nine recommendations on the arrears of contributions of States Parties.

As to financing, the Assembly approved the programme budget for 2007, with appropriations totalling €88,871,800. It also approved the staffing table for the Court and established the Working Capital Fund for 2007 in the amount of €7,405,983.

The Chambers

The judicial activities of the Court were conducted by the Chambers, which consisted of 18 judges, organized in three divisions: the Appeals Division, the Trial Division and the Pre-Trial Division. The Presidency constituted three Pre-Trial Chambers: Pre-Trial Chamber I–the DRC, and Darfur (the Sudan); Pre-Trial Chamber II–Uganda; and Pre-Trial Chamber III–Central African Republic. On 10 February, Pre-Trial Chamber I issued a warrant of arrest (unsealed on 17 March) against Thomas Lubanga Dyilo (see below). On 13 July, the Appeals Chamber issued its first decision on the merits of an appeal of the Pre-Trial Chamber on jurisdiction and admissibility, dismissing the Prosecutor's application for extraordinary review of a decision by Pre-Trial Chamber I. In the underlying decision, Pre-Trial Chamber I had denied the Prosecutor leave to appeal its decision granting the applications of six victims to participate in proceedings.

Office of the Prosecutor

New arrests and surrenders

On 17 March, Thomas Lubanga Dyilo, the alleged leader of the Union des patriotes congolais pour la reconciliation et la paix and commander-in-chief of its military wing, the Forces patriotiques pour la Liberation du Congo, was arrested and surrendered to the Court in The Hague. Mr. Lubanga was accused of the war crimes of enlisting, conscripting and using children under the age of 15 to participate actively in hostilities. On 20 March, Pre-Trial Chamber I held a hearing to ensure that Mr. Lubanga was informed of the charges against him and of his rights under the Rome Statute. Subsequently, numerous hearings were held in relation to a host of pre-trial issues litigated for the first time before the Court. Mr. Lubanga was indicted on 28 August. A hearing to confirm the charges took place from 9 to 28 November; Pre-Trial Chamber I was expected to confirm charges of war crimes against Mr. Lubanga in early 2007. In addition to the prosecution and the defence, four victims participated in the hearing through their legal representatives, marking the first time in the history of an international criminal court or a tribunal that victims participated in proceedings in their own right, without being called as witnesses. The legal representatives presented their observations at the opening and closing sessions and attended the court sessions throughout the hearing.

Investigations

The Office of the Prosecutor continued investigations into three situations: the DRC and Uganda—which were referred to the Court by the States Parties themselves—and Darfur, the Sudan, referred to the Court by the Security Council. The Office was also collecting information on five other situations of concern, including in the Central African Republic, following the referral by that State party, and in Côte d'Ivoire, a non-State party which had filed a declaration accepting the jurisdiction of the Court.

Its investigations in the situation in Uganda involved allegations of large-scale abductions, killings, torture and sexual violence. The majority of alleged abductees were children. The Office of the Prosecutor continued to conduct field missions to carry out investigative work in Uganda and assess the security of witnesses. It conducted 16 missions to interview witnesses and others and collect documents and materials in preparation for the confirmation of the charges in five outstanding arrest warrants for alleged members of the Lord's Resistance Army (LRA) [YUN 2005, p 1404], accused of crimes against humanity and war crimes. On 1 June, at the request of the Court's Prosecutor, Interpol (the International Criminal Police Organization) issued "red notices" alerting its member countries of the arrest warrants. By the end of the year, more than 12 months after ICC had issued its first warrants of arrest in Uganda, the five accused remained at large. In addition to numerous missions to Uganda, the Office of the Prosecutor visited the DRC and the Sudan in connection with the Uganda investigation and established contact with other authorities to build support for arrest efforts. Cooperation with the Government of Uganda was critical for the success of the Office's investigative efforts.

The investigation of the situation in the DRC involved allegations of thousands of deaths by mass murder and summary execution since 2002, as well as large-scale patterns of rape, torture and use of child soldiers. Numerous armed groups active in the DRC were allegedly involved in those crimes. The Office of the Prosecutor conducted 45 investigation missions to six countries to gather evidence and witness testimony in relation to the situation in the DRC; the investigation led to the issuance of an arrest warrant and the subsequent arrest and surrender of Thomas Lubanga Dyilo (see above). The Office of the Prosecutor opened a second case in the DRC investigation and continued to analyse the possibility of opening a third case.

In the Darfur region of the Sudan, the Office of the Prosecutor investigated allegations of the killing of thousands of civilians and widespread destruction and looting of villages, leading to the displacement of approximately 1.9 million civilians, as well as allegations of a pervasive pattern of rape and sexual violence and persistent targeting and intimidation of humanitarian personnel. The ongoing conflict had prevented the Office from investigating on the ground in Darfur as the necessary security conditions did not exist to ensure the protection of victims, witnesses or staff members. It therefore focused its investigative activities outside Darfur, especially in Chad, where many victims and witnesses had fled. Since the Security Council's referral of the case to ICC by resolution 1593(2005) [ibid., p. 324], the Office had conducted more than 50 missions to 15 countries, screened more than 500 potential witnesses and collected and reviewed more than 8,800 documents. On 14 June, the Prosecutor submitted his third report on the Sudan to a closed meeting of the Security Council [S/PV. 5460] (see p. 291). He stated that, given the scale of the alleged crimes in Darfur and the complexities associated with the identification of the individuals bearing the greatest responsibility for the crimes, the Office anticipated the investigation and prosecution of a sequence of cases, rather than a single case dealing with the situation in Darfur as a whole. The Prosecutor also emphasized that the full cooperation of the Government of the Sudan and other parties to the conflict was vital and that the cooperation of organizations with a significant presence there would continue to be essential. In accordance with Council resolution 1593(2005), the Prosecutor reported on 14 December to a closed meeting of the Council [meeting 5589] on the status of the investigation into the situation in Darfur (see p. 292).

The Registry

The ICC Registry provided judicial and administrative support to all organs of the Court and carried out its specific responsibilities concerning victims, witnesses, defence and outreach. It continued efforts to develop understanding and awareness of ICC and its activities by strengthening the Court's public information capacity for outreach services in countries where the Court was active.

The Registry also provided security, administrative and logistical support to the investigations, including through field offices in the DRC, Uganda, and Chad (in relation to the investigation in Darfur). Together, the Office of the Prosecutor and the Registry developed measures to ensure the safety of victims, witnesses and others at risk due to the Court's investigations in all three situations. It also tailored situation-specific outreach strategies for each situation, which included bilateral meetings, workshops, seminars and training activities, and saw the distribution of some 500 copies of basic legal texts to representatives of legal communities and related facilities in both Uganda and the DRC.

In 2006, the Court increased its outreach activities in northern Uganda and held informative meetings with over 120 local non-governmental organizations, 150 cultural leaders, 60 local government representatives and 50 religious leaders from across that region, and with journalists and legal associations, such as the Uganda Human Rights Commission; it also disseminated information through local radio programmes, newspapers and other printed materials.

In the DRC, the Court used radio and television to provide general information about its activities and about the case against Thomas Lubanga Dyilo. Through partnerships with local radio stations in remote areas, the Court increased its ability to reach out to local populations affected by the situation under investigation. In order to ensure effective participation of victims in proceedings before the Court, the Office of Public Counsel for Victims was established.

International cooperation

In 2006, ICC substantially developed its framework for institutional cooperation with the United Nations and with States, regional organizations and other actors. It took steps to further facilitate information-sharing and operational cooperation with the United Nations by establishing an office in New York.

On 29 March, ICC signed an agreement with the International Committee of the Red Cross (ICRC), governing visits by ICRC to persons deprived of liberty pursuant to the jurisdiction of the Court. On 28 and 29 June, ICRC made its first visit to the Court's Detention Centre.

On 10 April, the Court concluded a cooperation agreement with the EU covering such issues as the sharing of classified information, the testimony of EU personnel, the waiver of privileges and immunities, cooperation with the Prosecutor, the provision of facilities and services, including support in the field, attendance at EU meetings and cooperation on training for judges, prosecutors, officials and counsel.

The President of the Special Court for Sierra Leone and ICC concluded a Memorandum of Understanding related to the trial of the former President of Liberia, Charles Taylor, at the ICC seat in The Hague. On 16 June, the Security Council adopted **resolution 1688(2006)** (see p. 242) in relation to the trial being held in the Netherlands.

Chapter III

International legal questions

In 2006, the International Law Commission (ILC) continued to examine topics relating to the progressive development and codification of international law. It adopted the Guiding Principles applicable to unilateral declarations of States capable of creating legal obligations, which the General Assembly commended for dissemination. It also completed the second reading of draft articles on diplomatic protection, the first reading of draft articles on the law of transboundary aquifers and the second reading of draft principles on international liability in case of loss for transboundary harm arising out of hazardous activities. The Assembly, in December, took note of the draft principles and commended them to the attention of Governments.

United Nations bodies dealing with international terrorism continued their work to combat the phenomenon. The Ad Hoc Committee established by the Assembly continued to elaborate a draft comprehensive convention on international terrorism. In August, the Secretary-General reported on measures taken by 22 States, five UN system entities and six intergovernmental organizations to implement the 1994 General Assembly Declaration on Measures to Eliminate International Terrorism. In December, the Assembly condemned all acts, methods and practices of terrorism as criminal and unjustifiable and called on States to adopt further measures to prevent terrorism.

At its thirty-ninth session, the United Nations Commission on International Trade Law (UNCITRAL) finalized and adopted revised articles on the form of the arbitration agreement and interim measures of the UNCITRAL Model Law on International Commercial Arbitration. It also finalized and adopted recommendations regarding the interpretation of two articles of the 1958 Convention on the Recognition and Enforcement of Foreign Arbitral Awards. In addition, UNCITRAL approved the recommendations of a draft legislative guide on secured transactions, designed to facilitate secured financing, thus promoting access to low-cost credit and enhancing national and international trade.

The Special Committee on the Charter of the United Nations and on the Strengthening of the Role of the Organization continued to consider, among other subjects, proposals relating to the maintenance of international peace and security, with a view to strengthening the Organization, and the implementation of Charter provisions on assistance to third States affected by the application of sanctions under Chapter VII.

The Committee on Relations with the Host Country addressed a number of issues raised by permanent missions to the United Nations, including transportation and parking issues, acceleration of immigration and customs procedures, delays in issuing visas and travel regulations.

Legal aspects of international political relations

International Law Commission

The 34-member International Law Commission (ILC) held its fifty-eighth session in Geneva in two parts (1 May–9 June; 3 July–11 August) [A/61/10]. During the second part, the International Law Seminar held its forty-second session, which was attended by 25 participants, mostly from developing countries. They observed ILC meetings, attended specially arranged lectures and participated in working groups on specific topics.

ILC, assisted by working groups and a Drafting Committee, considered the seventh report of the Special Rapporteur on diplomatic protection, completed the second reading of the topic and recommended to the General Assembly the elaboration of a convention on the basis of the 19 draft articles on diplomatic protection. It also considered eight draft principles on the legal regime for allocating loss in case of transboundary harm arising out of hazardous activities and recommended that the General Assembly endorse the draft principles by a resolution. On the topic of shared natural resources, the Commission adopted 19 draft articles on the law of transboundary aquifers, together with commentaries, and transmitted them to Governments for comments and observations. Concerning responsibility of international organizations, the Commission adopted 14 draft articles, together with commentaries, dealing with circumstances precluding wrongfulness, and the responsibility of a State in connection with the act of an international organization.

On the topic of reservations to treaties, the Commission referred to the Drafting Committee 16 draft guidelines dealing with the definition of the object and purpose of the treaty and the determination of the validity of reservations. ILC also adopted five draft guidelines dealing with the validity of reservations, together with commentaries.

With regard to the unilateral acts of States, the Commission adopted 10 Guiding Principles, together with commentaries, relating to unilateral declarations of States capable of creating legal obligations and commended the Principles to the attention of the Assembly.

The Commission also considered the second report of the Special Rapporteur on the effects of armed conflicts on treaties, the preliminary report of the Special Rapporteur on the obligation to extradite or prosecute (*aut dedere aut judicare*) and the second report by the Special Rapporteur on the expulsion of aliens. Regarding the fragmentation of international law: difficulties arising from the diversification and expansion of international law, ILC considered the report of the study group, which considered the issue, took note of its conclusions, and commended them to the attention of the Assembly. (See below for expanded treatment of these topics.)

It decided to hold its fifty-ninth session from 7 May to 8 June and from 9 July to 10 August 2007.

GENERAL ASSEMBLY ACTION

On 4 December [meeting 64], the General Assembly, on the recommendation of the Sixth (Legal) Committee [A/61/454], adopted **resolution 61/34** without vote [agenda item 78].

Report of the International Law Commission on the work of its fifty-eighth session

The General Assembly,

Having considered the report of the International Law Commission on the work of its fifty-eighth session,

Emphasizing the importance of furthering the codification and progressive development of international law as a means of implementing the purposes and principles set forth in the Charter of the United Nations and in the Declaration on Principles of International Law concerning Friendly Relations and Cooperation among States in accordance with the Charter of the United Nations,

Recognizing the desirability of referring legal and drafting questions to the Sixth Committee, including topics that might be submitted to the International Law Commission for closer examination, and of enabling the Sixth Committee and the Commission to enhance further their contribution to the progressive development of international law and its codification,

Recalling the need to keep under review those topics of international law which, given their new or renewed interest for the international community, may be suitable for the progressive development and codification of international law and therefore may be included in the future programme of work of the International Law Commission,

Welcoming the holding of the International Law Seminar, and noting with appreciation the voluntary contributions made to the United Nations Trust Fund for the International Law Seminar,

Stressing the usefulness of focusing and structuring the debate on the report of the International Law Commission in the Sixth Committee in such a manner that conditions are provided for concentrated attention to each of the main topics dealt with in the report and for discussions on specific topics,

Wishing to enhance further, in the context of the revitalization of the debate on the report of the International Law Commission, the interaction between the Sixth Committee as a body of governmental representatives and the Commission as a body of independent legal experts, with a view to improving the dialogue between the two bodies,

Welcoming initiatives to hold interactive debates, panel discussions and question time in the Sixth Committee, as envisaged in resolution 58/316 of 1 July 2004 on further measures for the revitalization of the work of the General Assembly,

1. *Takes note* of the report of the International Law Commission on the work of its fifty-eighth session, and recommends that the Commission continue its work on the topics in its current programme, taking into account the comments and observations of Governments, whether submitted in writing or expressed orally in debates in the General Assembly;

2. *Expresses its appreciation* to the International Law Commission for the work accomplished at its fifty-eighth session, in particular for the following accomplishments:

(*a*) The completion of the second reading of the draft articles on diplomatic protection;

(*b*) The completion of the second reading of the draft principles on the allocation of loss in the case of transboundary harm arising out of hazardous activities under the topic "International liability for injurious consequences arising out of acts not prohibited by international law (International liability in case of loss for transboundary harm arising out of hazardous activities)";

(*c*) The completion of the first reading of the draft articles on the law of transboundary aquifers under the topic "Shared natural resources";

(*d*) The completion of the work on "Unilateral acts of States" by the adoption of the Guiding Principles applicable to unilateral declarations of States capable of creating legal obligations;

(*e*) The completion by its Study Group of the report and the conclusions on the topic "Fragmentation of international law: difficulties arising from diversification and expansion of international law";

3. *Takes note* of the Guiding Principles applicable to unilateral declarations of States capable of creating legal obligations under the topic "Unilateral acts of States", contained in paragraph 176 of the report of the International Law Commission and commends their dissemination;

4. *Also takes note* of the forty-two conclusions of the Commission's Study Group on the topic "Fragmentation of international law: difficulties arising from diversification and expansion of international law", contained in paragraph 251 of the report of the International Law Commission, together with the analytical study on which they were based;

5. *Draws the attention* of Governments to the importance for the International Law Commission of having their views on the various aspects involved in the topics on the agenda of the Commission identified in chapter III of its report, including in particular on the draft articles and commentaries on the law of transboundary aquifers;

6. *Invites* Governments to provide to the International Law Commission, as requested in chapter III of its report, information on legislation and practice regarding the topic "The obligation to extradite or prosecute (*aut dedere aut judicare*)";

7. *Takes note* of the decision of the International Law Commission to include five topics in its long-term programme of work;

8. *Invites* the International Law Commission to continue taking measures to enhance its efficiency and productivity and to consider making proposals to that end;

9. *Encourages* the International Law Commission to continue taking cost-saving measures at its future sessions without prejudice to the efficiency of its work;

10. *Takes note* of paragraph 270 of the report of the International Law Commission, and decides that the next session of the Commission shall be held at the United Nations Office at Geneva from 7 May to 8 June and from 9 July to 10 August 2007;

11. *Welcomes* the enhanced dialogue between the International Law Commission and the Sixth Committee at the sixty-first session of the General Assembly, stresses the desirability of further enhancing the dialogue between the two bodies, and in this context encourages, inter alia, the continued practice of informal consultations in the form of discussions between the members of the Sixth Committee and the members of the Commission attending the sixty-second session of the Assembly;

12. *Encourages* delegations, during the debate on the report of the International Law Commission, to adhere as far as possible to the structured work programme agreed to by the Sixth Committee and to consider presenting concise and focused statements;

13. *Encourages* Member States to consider being represented at the level of legal adviser during the first week in which the report of the International Law Commission is discussed in the Sixth Committee (International Law Week) to enable high-level discussions on issues of international law;

14. *Requests* the International Law Commission to continue to pay special attention to indicating in its annual report, for each topic, any specific issues on which expressions of views by Governments, either in the Sixth Committee or in written form, would be of particular interest in providing effective guidance for the Commission in its further work;

15. *Takes note* of paragraphs 271 to 274 of the report of the International Law Commission with regard to cooperation with other bodies, and encourages the Commission to continue the implementation of article 16, paragraph (*e*), and article 26, paragraphs 1 and 2, of its statute in order to further strengthen cooperation between the Commission and other bodies concerned with international law, having in mind the usefulness of such cooperation;

16. *Notes* that the International Law Commission, in accordance with article 25, paragraph 1, of its statute, envisages a meeting during its fifty-ninth session with United Nations experts in the field of human rights, including representatives from human rights treaty bodies, in order to hold a discussion on issues relating to human rights treaties;

17. *Also notes* that consulting with national organizations and individual experts concerned with international law may assist Governments in considering whether to make comments and observations on drafts submitted by the International Law Commission and in formulating their comments and observations;

18. *Reaffirms* its previous decisions concerning the indispensable role of the Codification Division of the Office of Legal Affairs of the Secretariat in providing assistance to the International Law Commission;

19. *Approves* the conclusions reached by the International Law Commission in paragraphs 262 to 267 of its report, and reaffirms its previous decisions concerning the documentation and summary records of the Commission;

20. *Notes with appreciation* the expansion of the website of the International Law Commission to include all its documentation, and welcomes the continuous efforts of the Codification Division to maintain and improve the website;

21. *Expresses the hope* that the International Law Seminar will continue to be held in connection with the sessions of the International Law Commission and that an increasing number of participants, in particular from developing countries, will be given the opportunity to attend the Seminar, and appeals to States to continue to make urgently needed voluntary contributions to the United Nations Trust Fund for the International Law Seminar;

22. *Requests* the Secretary-General to provide the International Law Seminar with adequate services, including interpretation, as required, and encourages him to continue considering ways to improve the structure and content of the Seminar;

23. *Also requests* the Secretary-General to forward to the International Law Commission, for its attention, the records of the debate on the report of the Commission at the sixty-first session of the General Assembly, together with such written statements as delegations may circulate in conjunction with their oral statements, and to prepare and distribute a topical summary of the debate, following established practice;

24. *Requests* the Secretariat to circulate to States, as soon as possible after the conclusion of the session of the International Law Commission, chapter II of its report containing a summary of the work of that session, chapter III containing the specific issues on which the views of Governments would be of particular interest to the Commission and the draft articles adopted on either first or second reading by the Commission;

25. *Recommends* that the debate on the report of the International Law Commission at the sixty-second session of the General Assembly commence on 29 October 2007.

International liability

Under the topic international liability for injurious consequences arising out of acts not prohibited by international law (international liability in case of loss from transboundary harm arising out of hazardous activities), the Commission considered the third report by Special Rapporteur Pemmaraju Sreenivasa Rao (India) [A/CN.4/566] on the legal regime for the allocation of loss in case of transboundary harm arising out of hazardous activities, along with the comments and observations received from Governments [A/CN.4/562/Add.1]. The Commission also considered the report of the Drafting Committee. It adopted on second reading the text of the preamble and a set of eight draft principles with commentaries thereto, recommended that the General Assembly endorse the draft by a resolution, and urged States to implement them.

GENERAL ASSEMBLY ACTION

On 4 December [meeting 64], the General Assembly, on the recommendation of the Sixth Committee [A/61/454], adopted **resolution 61/36** without vote [agenda item 78].

Allocation of loss in the case of transboundary harm arising out of hazardous activities

The General Assembly,

Recalling that the International Law Commission at its fifty-third session completed the draft articles on prevention of transboundary harm from hazardous activities and recommended to the General Assembly the elaboration of a convention on the basis of the draft articles,

Recalling also its resolution 56/82 of 12 December 2001,

Having considered chapter V of the report of the Commission on the work of its fifty-eighth session, which contains the draft principles on the allocation of loss in the case of transboundary harm arising out of hazardous activities,

Noting that the Commission decided to recommend to the General Assembly that it endorse the draft principles by a resolution and urge States to take national and international action to implement them,

Emphasizing the continuing importance of the codification and progressive development of international law, as referred to in Article 13, paragraph 1 (*a*), of the Charter of the United Nations,

Noting that the questions of prevention of transboundary harm from hazardous activities and allocation of loss in the case of such harm are of major importance in the relations of States,

Taking into account views and comments expressed in the Sixth Committee on chapter V of the report of the Commission on international liability in case of loss from transboundary harm arising out of hazardous activities of the report of the Commission at its fifty-eighth session,

1. *Expresses its appreciation* to the International Law Commission for its continuing contribution to the codification and progressive development of international law;

2. *Takes note* of the principles on the allocation of loss in the case of transboundary harm arising out of hazardous activities, presented by the Commission, the text of which is annexed to the present resolution, and commends them to the attention of Governments;

3. *Decides* to include in the provisional agenda of its sixty-second session an item entitled "Consideration of prevention of transboundary harm from hazardous activities and allocation of loss in the case of such harm".

Annex

Principles on the allocation of loss in the case of transboundary harm arising out of hazardous activities

The General Assembly,

Reaffirming Principles 13 and 16 of the Rio Declaration on Environment and Development,

Recalling the draft articles on the Prevention of Transboundary Harm from Hazardous Activities,

Aware that incidents involving hazardous activities may occur despite compliance by the relevant State with its obligations concerning prevention of transboundary harm from hazardous activities,

Noting that as a result of such incidents other States and/or their nationals may suffer harm and serious loss,

Emphasizing that appropriate and effective measures should be in place to ensure that those natural and legal persons, including States, that incur harm and loss as a result of such incidents are able to obtain prompt and adequate compensation,

Concerned that prompt and effective response measures should be taken to minimize the harm and loss which may result from such incidents,

Noting that States are responsible for infringements of their obligations of prevention under international law,

Recalling the significance of existing international agreements covering specific categories of hazardous activities and stressing the importance of the conclusion of further such agreements,

Desiring to contribute to the development of international law in this field,

...

Principle 1
Scope of application

The present draft principles apply to transboundary damage caused by hazardous activities not prohibited by international law.

Principle 2
Use of terms

For the purposes of the present draft principles:

(a) "damage" means significant damage caused to persons, property or the environment; and includes:

(i) loss of life or personal injury;

(ii) loss of, or damage to, property, including property which forms part of the cultural heritage;

(iii) loss or damage by impairment of the environment;

(iv) the costs of reasonable measures of reinstatement of the property, or environment, including natural resources;

(v) the costs of reasonable response measures;

(b) "environment" includes natural resources, both abiotic and biotic, such as air, water, soil, fauna and flora and the interaction between the same factors, and the characteristic aspects of the landscape;

(c) "hazardous activity" means an activity which involves a risk of causing significant harm;

(d) "State of origin" means the State in the territory or otherwise under the jurisdiction or control of which the hazardous activity is carried out;

(e) "transboundary damage" means damage caused to persons, property or the environment in the territory or in other places under the jurisdiction or control of a State other than the State of origin;

(f) "victim" means any natural or legal person or State that suffers damage;

(g) "operator" means any person in command or control of the activity at the time the incident causing transboundary damage occurs.

Principle 3
Purposes

The purposes of the present draft principles are:

(*a*) to ensure prompt and adequate compensation to victims of transboundary damage; and

(*b*) to preserve and protect the environment in the event of transboundary damage, especially with respect to mitigation of damage to the environment and its restoration or reinstatement.

Principle 4
Prompt and adequate compensation

1. Each State should take all necessary measures to ensure that prompt and adequate compensation is available for victims of transboundary damage caused by hazardous activities located within its territory or otherwise under its jurisdiction or control.

2. These measures should include the imposition of liability on the operator or, where appropriate, other person or entity. Such liability should not require proof of fault. Any conditions, limitations or exceptions to such liability shall be consistent with draft principle 3.

3. These measures should also include the requirement on the operator or, where appropriate, other person or entity, to establish and maintain financial security such as insurance, bonds or other financial guarantees to cover claims of compensation.

4. In appropriate cases, these measures should include the requirement for the establishment of industry-wide funds at the national level.

5. In the event that the measures under the preceding paragraphs are insufficient to provide adequate compensation, the State of origin should also ensure that additional financial resources are made available.

Principle 5
Response measures

Upon the occurrence of an incident involving a hazardous activity which results or is likely to result in transboundary damage:

(a) the State of origin shall promptly notify all States affected or likely to be affected of the incident and the possible effects of the transboundary damage;

(b) the State of origin, with the appropriate involvement of the operator, shall ensure that appropriate response measures are taken and should, for this purpose, rely upon the best available scientific data and technology;

(c) the State of origin, as appropriate, should also consult with and seek the cooperation of all States affected or likely to be affected to mitigate the effects of transboundary damage and if possible eliminate them;

(d) the States affected or likely to be affected by the transboundary damage shall take all feasible measures to mitigate and if possible to eliminate the effects of such damage;

(e) the States concerned should, where appropriate, seek the assistance of competent international organizations and other States on mutually acceptable terms and conditions.

Principle 6
International and domestic remedies

1. States shall provide their domestic judicial and administrative bodies with the necessary jurisdiction and competence and ensure that these bodies have prompt, adequate and effective remedies available in the event of transboundary damage caused by hazardous activities located within their territory or otherwise under their jurisdiction or control.

2. Victims of transboundary damage should have access to remedies in the State of origin that are no less prompt, adequate and effective than those available to victims that suffer damage, from the same incident, within the territory of that State.

3. Paragraphs 1 and 2 are without prejudice to the right of the victims to seek remedies other than those available in the State of origin.

4. States may provide for recourse to international claims settlement procedures that are expeditious and involve minimal expenses.

5. States should guarantee appropriate access to information relevant for the pursuance of remedies, including claims for compensation.

Principle 7
Development of specific international regimes

1. Where, in respect of particular categories of hazardous activities, specific global, regional or bilateral agreements would provide effective arrangements concerning compensation, response measures and international and domestic remedies, all efforts should be made to conclude such specific agreements.

2. Such agreements should, as appropriate, include arrangements for industry and/or State funds to provide supplementary compensation in the event that the financial resources of the operator, including financial security measures, are insufficient to cover the damage suffered as a result of an incident. Any such funds may be designed to supplement or replace national industry-based funds.

Principle 8
Implementation

1. Each State should adopt the necessary legislative, regulatory and administrative measures to implement the present draft principles.

2. The present draft principles and the measures adopted to implement them shall be applied without any discrimination such as that based on nationality, domicile or residence.

3. States should cooperate with each other to implement the present draft principles.

Shared natural resources

The Commission reconvened the Working Group on shared natural resources, chaired by Enrique Candioti (Argentina). The Group completed the review and revision of the 19 draft articles on transboundary groundwaters submitted by the Special Rapporteur in 2005 [YUN 2005, p. 1409]. The Commission considered the report of the Group and referred the draft articles to the Drafting Committee. On 9 June, the Commission considered the report of the Drafting Committee and adopted on first reading the 19 draft articles on the law of transboundary aquifers, as well as commentaries thereto. On 2 August, the Commission decided to transmit the draft articles, through the Secretary-General, to Governments for comments and observations, which should be submitted to the Secretary-General by 1 January 2008.

Responsibility of international organizations

ILC considered the fourth report on responsibility of international organizations [A/CN.4/564 & Add. 1, 2] by Special Rapporteur Giorgio Gaja (Italy), as well as written comments received from Governments and international organizations [A/CN.4/568]. The report contained 13 draft articles: eight corresponding to those contained in Chapter V of the articles on responsibility of States for international wrongful acts, under the heading "Circumstances precluding wrongfulness; and five on the responsibility of a State in connection with the wrongful act of an international organization. The eight articles (17 to 24) related to circumstances precluding wrongfulness, consent, self-defence, countermeasures, force majeure, distress, necessity, compliance with peremptory norms and consequences of invoking a circumstance precluding wrongfulness. The five draft articles (25 to 29) covered aid or assistance by a State in the commission of an internationally wrongful act by an international organization, direction and control exercised by a State over the commission of an internationally wrongful act by an international organization, coercion of an international organization by a State, use by a State that was a member of an international organization of the separate personality of that organization and responsibility of a State that was a member of an international organization for the internationally wrongful act of that organization.

The Commission considered the report and referred those draft articles to the Drafting Committee, whose report on the articles and commentaries thereto it adopted.

Unilateral acts of States

ILC considered the ninth report on unilateral acts of States [A/CN.4/569 & Add.1] by Special Rapporteur Víctor Rodríguez Cedeño (Venezuela), which presented draft guiding principles, together with a description and analysis of those principles. The first part of the report related to the causes of invalidity and termination of unilateral acts, and the second, to the definition, capacity of a State to formulate a unilateral act, competence to formulate unilateral acts on behalf of the State, subsequent confirmation of an act formulated by a person without authorization, the basis for the binding nature of the unilateral acts and the interpretation of such acts.

On 5 July, the Commission reconstituted the Working Group on the subject, with Alain Pellet (France) as its chair, and requested it to prepare conclusions and principles on the topic. The

Commission observed that it was important for States to be in a position to judge with reasonable certainty whether and to what extent their unilateral conduct might legally bind them internationally, as the concept of a unilateral act was not uniform. On the one hand, certain unilateral acts were formulated in the framework and on the basis of an express authorization under international law, whereas others were formulated by States in exercise of their freedom to act on the international plane. In accordance with the Commission's previous decisions, only the latter had been examined by the Commission and its Special Rapporteur. In the second case, there existed a wide spectrum of conduct designated as "unilateral acts" and the differences among legal cultures partly accounted for the misunderstandings to which the topic had given rise. For some, the concept of a juridical act necessarily implied an express manifestation of a will to be bound on the part of the author State, whereas, for others, any unilateral conduct by the State producing international legal effects could be categorized as a unilateral act.

The Rapporteur said that the result of the work needed not be final. The Commission could take up the topic again and perhaps cast it in the form of a work of codification and progressive development. The set of non-binding guiding principles might be useful to States in their international legal relations.

On 4 August, the Commission considered the Working Group's report and adopted 10 Guiding Principles, together with commentaries applicable to unilateral declarations of States capable of creating legal obligations, which it commended to the attention of the General Assembly.

Expulsion of aliens

ILC had before it the second report of Special Rapporteur Maurice Kamto (Cameroon) [A/CN.4/573] on the expulsion of aliens, containing two draft articles on the scope of the topic and definitions on alien, expulsion, territory, frontier and expulsion, and constituent elements of expulsion. It also had before it a study [A/CN.4/565] prepared by the Secretariat, as requested by the Commission in 2005 [YUN 2005, p. 1410]. The study provided a comprehensive analysis of possible issues requiring consideration, offered an analytical summary of legal materials contained in treaty law, international jurisprudence, other international documents, national legislation and national jurisprudence, and surveyed material adopted at the international, regional and national levels. The scope of the topic raised a number of issues, such as whether the Commission should consider special rules that might apply to specific categories of aliens; similar measures that might be taken by States to compel the departure of aliens; the expulsion of aliens in time of armed conflict; and the collective and mass expulsion of aliens.

The Commission decided to consider the Special Rapporteur's report at its 2007 session.

Extradition

ILC had before it the preliminary report of Special Rapporteur Zdzislaw Galicki on the obligation to extradite or prosecute (*aut dedere aut judicare*) [A/CN.4/571]. The report contained observations on the substance of the topic, highlighting the most important points for further consideration, and included a preliminary plan of action for future work. A key question for the Commission's consideration was whether the obligation derived exclusively from the relevant treaty or whether it also reflected a general obligation under customary international law, at least in respect to specific international offences. Although there was no consensus on the doctrine, there was growing support for the concept of an international legal obligation. It was suggested that an analysis of the link between the principle of universal jurisdiction in criminal matters and the principle of *aut dedere aut judicare* should be undertaken. The Special Rapporteur stated his intention to formulate draft rules concerning the concept, structure and operation of the obligation, undertake a thorough analysis of the practice of States, and compile a complete list of relevant treaty provisions reflecting the obligation. The Special Rapporteur recalled that, while the obligation was traditionally formulated as an alternative, there was the possibility of a "triple alternative", which contemplated the exercise of a jurisdictional competence by an international criminal court. He proposed that the Commission ask Member States for information concerning their practice.

The Commission welcomed the preliminary report, including the proposed plan of action. The Special Rapporteur supported the general consensus during the debate in the Commission that the scope of the topic be limited. He agreed that the focus of the exercise should be on the elaboration of secondary rules and that both international and national judicial decisions should be considered.

Fragmentation of international law

ILC considered the report [A/CN.4/L.682 & Corr. 1] of the study group on fragmentation of international law: difficulties arising from the diversification and expansion of international law. The report and its draft conclusions were prepared on the basis of an analytical study finalized by the study group Chairman, which summarized and analysed the phenomenon, taking account of studies prepared by various members of the study group. An addendum to the report [A/CN.4/L.682/Add.1] incorporated the draft conclusions of the work done by the group between 2002 and 2005, as well as additional draft conclusions.

The Commission took note of the study group's 42 conclusions, which it commended to the attention of the General Assembly. It also requested that the analytical study be made available on its web site and be published in its *Yearbook*.

Effects of armed conflicts on treaties

In July, ILC considered the second report of Special Rapporteur Ian Brownlie (United Kingdom) on the effects of armed conflicts on treaties [A/CN.4/570], which contained the first seven draft articles. The report focused on: consideration of specific elements of the debate in the Commission and the substantial points made by various Governments in the debate in the Sixth Committee at the General Assembly's sixtieth (2005) session; and implementation of the first report [YUN 2005, p. 1410] by asking the Commission to consider the first seven draft articles, with a view to referring them to the Drafting Committee or to a working group. He noted that there was general support for his view that the topic was generally part of the law of treaties and not on the use of force. The Special Rapporteur was of the view that, given the nature of the debate in the Commission and the substantial difference of opinion on important aspects of the subject, it would be premature to send the matter to a working group. Accordingly, a third report should be prepared, which could, together with the first two reports, form the basis for consideration by such a group in the future.

International State relations and international law

Jurisdictional immunities of States and their property

The General Assembly, by resolution 59/38 [YUN 2004, p. 1304], adopted the Convention on Jurisdictional Immunities of States and Their Property. The Convention was opened for signature from 17 January 2005 until 17 January 2007 at UN Headquarters in New York. As at 31 December 2006, the Convention had 24 signatories and three States parties.

International terrorism

Convention on international terrorism

Ad Hoc Committee. In accordance with General Assembly resolution 60/43 [YUN 2005, p. 1417], the Ad Hoc Committee established by Assembly resolution 51/210 [YUN 1996, p. 1208] held its tenth session (New York, 27 February–3 March) to continue, within the framework of a working group of the Sixth Committee, the elaboration of a draft comprehensive convention on international terrorism, including consideration of outstanding issues.

The Ad Hoc Committee held informal contacts regarding the draft comprehensive convention and informal consultations on whether to convene a high-level conference under UN auspices to formulate a joint international response to terrorism in all its forms. Delegations agreed on the importance of preserving the integrity of the bulk of the text on which there seemed to be substantial agreement. Discussions were held on various aspects of the draft convention, including the possible development of fresh proposals to narrow the gap between the various viewpoints and the refinement of the language of some of the proposals that had been submitted for discussion. While suggestions were made on some elements of the draft convention, no concrete proposals were submitted in respect of draft article 18 dealing with the scope and application of such a convention. A written proposal was submitted by Argentina to amend the premabular paragraph, which, it was suggested, should also emphasize that the utilization of Interpol mechanisms and expertise would facilitate the efforts of States in the prevention and suppression of acts of international terrorism.

Regarding the convening of a high-level conference, Egypt renewed its proposal for such a conference to the Secretary-General [A/60/329] and submitted a working paper for discussion [A/C.660/2, annex]. Some delegations supported the proposal, noting that the convening of the conference would facilitate finding a solution to outstanding issues on the draft convention. Other delegations felt that the conference should be convened only after the completion of the convention, and the work on the draft convention should not be hindered by the discussion on the conference. Egypt said that the conference and the conclusion of the draft convention were not mutually exclusive, as the conference would address broader issues than the convention.

As a way forward, Egypt remained open to alternative approaches, including the convening of a high-level meeting of the General Assembly during its sixty-second (2007) session and any proposals that might be submitted regarding a work plan of the conference.

On 3 March, the Ad Hoc Committee adopted its report [A/61/37], to which were annexed the Chairman's informal summary of the general discussions and amendments and proposals submitted to the Committee in connection with the elaboration of a draft comprehensive convention on international terrorism—namely, a proposal by Argentina regarding a preambular paragraph on the right of peoples to self-determination.

Measures to eliminate international terrorism

In accordance with General Assembly resolution 50/53 [YUN 1995, p. 1330], the Secretary-General, in August, issued his annual report [A/61/210] on measures taken by 22 States, five UN system entities and six intergovernmental organizations to implement the 1994 Declaration on Measures to Eliminate International Terrorism, approved by Assembly resolution 49/60 [YUN 1994, p. 1293] and Security Council resolution 1269(1999) [YUN 1999, p. 1240]. It listed 30 international instruments pertaining to terrorism, indicating the status of State participation in each, and provided information on workshops and training courses on combating terrorism by two UN bodies. Two later addenda to the report [A/61/210/Add.1, 2] summarized information submitted by five other countries.

GENERAL ASSEMBLY ACTION

On 4 December [meeting 64], the General Assembly, on the recommendation of the Sixth Committee [A/61/457], adopted **resolution 61/40** without vote [agenda item 100].

Measures to eliminate international terrorism

The General Assembly,

Guided by the purposes and principles of the Charter of the United Nations,

Reaffirming the United Nations Global Counter-Terrorism Strategy in all its aspects adopted on 8 September 2006, enhancing the overall framework for the efforts of the international community to effectively counter the scourge of terrorism in all its forms and manifestations,

Recalling the Declaration on the Occasion of the Fiftieth Anniversary of the United Nations,

Recalling also the United Nations Millennium Declaration,

Recalling further the 2005 World Summit Outcome, and reaffirming in particular the section on terrorism,

Recalling the Declaration on Measures to Eliminate International Terrorism, contained in the annex to General Assembly resolution 49/60 of 9 December 1994, and the Declaration to Supplement the 1994 Declaration on Measures to Eliminate International Terrorism, contained in the annex to resolution 51/210 of 17 December 1996,

Recalling also all General Assembly resolutions on measures to eliminate international terrorism, and Security Council resolutions on threats to international peace and security caused by terrorist acts,

Convinced of the importance of the consideration of measures to eliminate international terrorism by the General Assembly as the universal organ having competence to do so,

Deeply disturbed by the persistence of terrorist acts, which have been carried out worldwide,

Reaffirming its strong condemnation of the heinous acts of terrorism that have caused enormous loss of human life, destruction and damage, including those which prompted the adoption of General Assembly resolution 56/1 of 12 September 2001, as well as Security Council resolutions 1368(2001) of 12 September 2001, 1373(2001) of 28 September 2001 and 1377(2001) of 12 November 2001, and those that have occurred since the adoption of the latter resolution,

Recalling the strong condemnation of the atrocious and deliberate attack against the headquarters of the United Nations Assistance Mission for Iraq in Baghdad on 19 August 2003 in General Assembly resolution 57/338 of 15 September 2003 and Security Council resolution 1502(2003) of 26 August 2003,

Affirming that States must ensure that any measure taken to combat terrorism complies with all their obligations under international law and adopt such measures in accordance with international law, in particular international human rights, refugee and humanitarian law,

Stressing the need to strengthen further international cooperation among States and among international organizations and agencies, regional organizations and arrangements and the United Nations in order to prevent, combat and eliminate terrorism in all its forms and manifestations, wherever and by whomsoever committed, in accordance with the principles of the Charter, international law and the relevant international conventions,

Noting the role of the Security Council Committee established pursuant to resolution 1373(2001) concerning counter-terrorism in monitoring the implementation of that resolution, including the taking of the necessary financial, legal and technical measures by States and the ratification or acceptance of the relevant international conventions and protocols,

Mindful of the need to enhance the role of the United Nations and the relevant specialized agencies in combating international terrorism, and of the proposals of the Secretary-General to enhance the role of the Organization in this respect,

Mindful also of the essential need to strengthen international, regional and subregional cooperation aimed at enhancing the national capacity of States to prevent and suppress effectively international terrorism in all its forms and manifestations,

Reiterating its call upon States to review urgently the scope of the existing international legal provisions on the prevention, repression and elimination of terrorism in all its forms and manifestations, with the aim of ensuring that there is a comprehensive legal framework covering all aspects of the matter,

Emphasizing that tolerance and dialogue among civilizations, and enhancing interfaith and intercultural understanding, are among the most important elements in promoting cooperation and success in combating terrorism, and welcoming the various initiatives to this end,

Reaffirming that no terrorist act can be justified in any circumstances,

Recalling Security Council resolution 1624(2005) of 14 September 2005, and bearing in mind that States must ensure that any measure taken to combat terrorism complies with their obligations under international law, in particular international human rights, refugee and humanitarian law,

Taking note of the recent developments and initiatives at the international, regional and subregional levels to prevent and suppress international terrorism, including those of, inter alia, the African Union, the ASEAN Regional Forum, the Asia-Pacific Economic Cooperation, the Association of Southeast Asian Nations, the Bali Counter-Terrorism Process, the Central American Integration System, the Collective Security Treaty Organization, the Common Market for Eastern and Southern Africa, the Cooperation Council for the Arab States of the Gulf, the Council of Europe, the Economic Community of West African States, the Euro-Mediterranean Partnership, the European Free Trade Association, the European Union, the Group of Eight, the Intergovernmental Authority on Development, the International Maritime Organization, the International Civil Aviation Organization, the League of Arab States, the Movement of Non-Aligned Countries, the North Atlantic Treaty Organization, the Organization for Economic Cooperation and Development, the Organization for Security and Cooperation in Europe, the Organization of American States, the Organization of the Islamic Conference, the Pacific Islands Forum, the Shanghai Cooperation Organization, the Southern African Development Community and the World Customs Organization,

Noting regional efforts to prevent, combat and eliminate terrorism in all its forms and manifestations, wherever and by whomsoever committed, including through the elaboration of and adherence to regional conventions,

Recalling its decision in resolutions 54/110 of 9 December 1999, 55/158 of 12 December 2000, 56/88 of 12 December 2001, 57/27 of 19 November 2002, 58/81 of 9 December 2003, 59/46 of 2 December 2004 and 60/43 of 8 December 2005 that the Ad Hoc Committee established by General Assembly resolution 51/210 of 17 December 1996 should address, and keep on its agenda, the question of convening a high-level conference under the auspices of the United Nations to formulate a joint organized response of the international community to terrorism in all its forms and manifestations,

Recalling also the Final Document of the Fourteenth Conference of Heads of State or Government of Non-Aligned Countries, adopted in Havana on 16 September 2006, which reiterated the collective position of the Movement of Non-Aligned Countries on terrorism and reaffirmed its previous initiative calling for an international summit conference under the auspices of the United Nations to formulate a joint organized response of the international community to terrorism in all its forms and manifestations, as well as other relevant initiatives,

Aware of its resolutions 57/219 of 18 December 2002, 58/187 of 22 December 2003, 59/191 of 20 December 2004 and 60/158 of 16 December 2005,

Having examined the report of the Secretary-General, the report of the Ad Hoc Committee established by resolution 51/210 and the oral report presented by the Chairman of the Working Group established by the Sixth Committee during the sixty-first session of the General Assembly,

1. *Strongly condemns* all acts, methods and practices of terrorism in all its forms and manifestations as criminal and unjustifiable, wherever and by whomsoever committed;

2. *Calls upon* all Member States, the United Nations and other appropriate international, regional and subregional organizations to implement the United Nations Global Counter-Terrorism Strategy in all its aspects at the international, regional, subregional and national levels without delay, including through mobilizing resources and expertise;

3. *Recalls* the pivotal role of the General Assembly in following up the implementation and updating of the Strategy, and in this regard also recalls its invitation to the Secretary-General to contribute to the future deliberations of the General Assembly, and requests the Secretary-General when doing so to provide information on relevant activities within the Secretariat to ensure overall coordination and coherence in the counter-terrorism efforts of the United Nations system;

4. *Reiterates* that criminal acts intended or calculated to provoke a state of terror in the general public, a group of persons or particular persons for political purposes are in any circumstances unjustifiable, whatever the considerations of a political, philosophical, ideological, racial, ethnic, religious or other nature that may be invoked to justify them;

5. *Reiterates its call upon* all States to adopt further measures in accordance with the Charter of the United Nations and the relevant provisions of international law, including international standards of human rights, to prevent terrorism and to strengthen international cooperation in combating terrorism and, to that end, to consider in particular the implementation of the measures set out in paragraphs 3(*a*) to (*f*) of resolution 51/210;

6. *Also reiterates its call upon* all States, with the aim of enhancing the efficient implementation of relevant legal instruments, to intensify, as and where appropriate, the exchange of information on facts related to terrorism and,

in so doing, to avoid the dissemination of inaccurate or unverified information;

7. *Reiterates its call upon* States to refrain from financing, encouraging, providing training for or otherwise supporting terrorist activities;

8. *Urges* States to ensure that their nationals or other persons and entities within their territory that wilfully provide or collect funds for the benefit of persons or entities who commit, or attempt to commit, facilitate or participate in the commission of terrorist acts are punished by penalties consistent with the grave nature of such acts;

9. *Reminds* States of their obligations under relevant international conventions and protocols and Security Council resolutions, including Security Council resolution 1373(2001), to ensure that perpetrators of terrorist acts are brought to justice;

10. *Reaffirms* that international cooperation as well as actions by States to combat terrorism should be conducted in conformity with the principles of the Charter, international law and relevant international conventions;

11. *Recalls* the adoption of the International Convention for the Suppression of Acts of Nuclear Terrorism, the Amendment to the Convention on the Physical Protection of Nuclear Material, the Protocol of 2005 to the Convention for the Suppression of Unlawful Acts against the Safety of Maritime Navigation and the Protocol of 2005 to the Protocol for the Suppression of Unlawful Acts against the Safety of Fixed Platforms Located on the Continental Shelf, and urges all States to consider, as a matter of priority, becoming parties to these instruments;

12. *Urges* all States that have not yet done so to consider, as a matter of priority, and in accordance with Security Council resolution 1373(2001), and Council resolution 1566(2004) of 8 October 2004, becoming parties to the relevant conventions and protocols as referred to in paragraph 6 of General Assembly resolution 51/210, as well as the International Convention for the Suppression of Terrorist Bombings, the International Convention for the Suppression of the Financing of Terrorism, the International Convention for the Suppression of Acts of Nuclear Terrorism, and the Amendment to the Convention on the Physical Protection of Nuclear Material, and calls upon all States to enact, as appropriate, the domestic legislation necessary to implement the provisions of those conventions and protocols, to ensure that the jurisdiction of their courts enables them to bring to trial the perpetrators of terrorist acts, and to cooperate with and provide support and assistance to other States and relevant international and regional organizations to that end;

13. *Urges* States to cooperate with the Secretary-General and with one another, as well as with interested intergovernmental organizations, with a view to ensuring, where appropriate within existing mandates, that technical and other expert advice is provided to those States requiring and requesting assistance in becoming parties to and implementing the conventions and protocols referred to in paragraph 12 above;

14. *Notes with appreciation and satisfaction* that, consistent with the call contained in paragraphs 9 and 10 of resolution 60/43, a number of States became parties to the relevant conventions and protocols referred to therein, thereby realizing the objective of wider acceptance and implementation of those conventions;

15. *Reaffirms* the Declaration on Measures to Eliminate International Terrorism and the Declaration to Supplement the 1994 Declaration on Measures to Eliminate International Terrorism, and calls upon all States to implement them;

16. *Calls upon* all States to cooperate to prevent and suppress terrorist acts;

17. *Urges* all States and the Secretary-General, in their efforts to prevent international terrorism, to make the best use of the existing institutions of the United Nations;

18. *Requests* the Terrorism Prevention Branch of the United Nations Office on Drugs and Crime in Vienna to continue its efforts to enhance, through its mandate, the capabilities of the United Nations in the prevention of terrorism, and recognizes, in the context of the United Nations Global Counter-Terrorism Strategy and Security Council resolution 1373(2001), its role in assisting States in becoming parties to and implementing the relevant international conventions and protocols relating to terrorism, including the most recent among them, and in strengthening international cooperation mechanisms in criminal matters related to terrorism, including through national capacity-building;

19. *Welcomes* the publication by the Secretariat of the second edition of *International Instruments related to the Prevention and Suppression of International Terrorism*, prepared by the Codification Division of the Office of Legal Affairs of the Secretariat pursuant to paragraph 10 (*a*) of the Declaration on Measures to Eliminate International Terrorism, in English and French, and considers it useful to examine the possibility of having future editions issued in all official languages;

20. *Invites* regional intergovernmental organizations to submit to the Secretary-General information on the measures they have adopted at the regional level to eliminate international terrorism, as well as on intergovernmental meetings held by those organizations;

21. *Notes* the progress attained in the elaboration of the draft comprehensive convention on international terrorism during the meetings of the Ad Hoc Committee established by General Assembly resolution 51/210 of 17 December 1996 and the Working Group established by the Sixth Committee during the sixty-first session of the General Assembly, and welcomes continuing efforts to that end;

22. *Decides* that the Ad Hoc Committee shall, on an expedited basis, continue to elaborate the draft comprehensive convention on international terrorism, and shall continue to discuss the item included in its agenda by General Assembly resolution 54/110 concerning the question of convening a high-level conference under the auspices of the United Nations;

23. *Decides also* that the Ad Hoc Committee shall meet on 5, 6 and 15 February 2007 in order to fulfil the mandate referred to in paragraph 22 above;

24. *Requests* the Secretary-General to continue to provide the Ad Hoc Committee with the necessary facilities for the performance of its work;

25. *Requests* the Ad Hoc Committee to report to the General Assembly at its sixty-first session in the event of the completion of the draft comprehensive convention on international terrorism;

26. *Also requests* the Ad Hoc Committee to report to the General Assembly at its sixty-second session on progress made in the implementation of its mandate;

27. *Decides* to include in the provisional agenda of its sixty-second session the item entitled "Measures to eliminate international terrorism".

On 22 December (**decision 61/552**) the General Assembly decided that the item on measures to eliminate international terrorism would remain for consideration during its resumed sixty-first (2007) session.

Additional Protocols I and II to the 1949 Geneva Conventions

In response to General Assembly resolution 59/36 [YUN 2004, p. 1313], the Secretary-General submitted an August report [A/61/222] on the status of the two 1977 Protocols Additional to the Geneva Conventions of 12 August 1949 relating to the protection of victims of armed conflicts [YUN 1977, p. 706], as well as on measures taken to strengthen the existing body of international humanitarian law with respect to, among other things, its dissemination and implementation at the national level, based on information received from 25 States and the International Committee of the Red Cross (ICRC). Annexed to the report was a list of 166 States parties to one or both Protocols, as at 20 July 2006. Two later addenda [A/61/222/Add.1,2] summarized information received from four States and ICRC.

GENERAL ASSEMBLY ACTION

On 4 December [meeting 64], the General Assembly, on the recommendation of the Sixth Committee [A/61/451], adopted **resolution 61/30** without vote [agenda item 75].

Status of the Protocols Additional to the Geneva Conventions of 1949 and relating to the protection of victims of armed conflicts

The General Assembly,

Recalling its resolutions 32/44 of 8 December 1977, 34/51 of 23 November 1979, 37/116 of 16 December 1982, 39/77 of 13 December 1984, 41/72 of 3 December 1986, 43/161 of 9 December 1988, 45/38 of 28 November 1990, 47/30 of 25 November 1992, 49/48 of 9 December 1994, 51/155 of 16 December 1996, 53/96 of 8 December 1998, 55/148 of 12 December 2000, 57/14 of 19 November 2002 and 59/36 of 2 December 2004,

Having considered the report of the Secretary-General,

Thanking Member States and the International Committee of the Red Cross for their contribution to the report of the Secretary-General,

Reaffirming the continuing value of established humanitarian rules relating to armed conflicts and the need to respect and ensure respect for those rules in all circumstances within the scope of the relevant international instruments, pending the earliest possible termination of such conflicts,

Stressing the possibility of making use of the International Humanitarian Fact-Finding Commission in relation to an armed conflict, pursuant to article 90 of Protocol I to the Geneva Conventions of 1949,

Stressing also the possibility for the International Humanitarian Fact-Finding Commission to facilitate, through its good offices, the restoration of an attitude of respect for the Geneva Conventions and Protocol I,

Stressing further the need to consolidate the existing body of international humanitarian law through its universal acceptance and the need for wide dissemination and full implementation of such law at the national level, and expressing concern about all violations of the Geneva Conventions and the Additional Protocols,

Noting with satisfaction the increasing number of national commissions and other bodies involved in advising authorities at the national level on the implementation, dissemination and development of international humanitarian law,

Noting with appreciation the meetings of representatives of those bodies organized by the International Committee of the Red Cross to facilitate the sharing of concrete experience and the exchange of views on their roles and on the challenges they face,

Mindful of the role of the International Committee of the Red Cross in offering protection to the victims of armed conflicts,

Noting with appreciation the continuing efforts of the International Committee of the Red Cross to promote and disseminate knowledge of international humanitarian law, in particular the Geneva Conventions and the Additional Protocols,

Recalling that the Twenty-eighth International Conference of the Red Cross and Red Crescent stressed the need to reinforce the implementation of and respect for international humanitarian law,

Welcoming the entry into force of the Protocol on Explosive Remnants of War to the Convention on Prohibitions or Restrictions on the Use of Certain Conventional Weapons Which May be Deemed to Be Excessively Injurious or to Have Indiscriminate Effects (Protocol V),

Noting the adoption, on 8 December 2005, of the Protocol additional to the Geneva Conventions of 12 August 1949, and relating to the Adoption of an Additional Distinctive Emblem (Protocol III),

Welcoming the significant debate generated by the recent publication of the study on Customary International Humanitarian Law by the International Committee of the Red Cross, and looking forward to further constructive discussion on the subject,

Calling upon Member States to disseminate knowledge of international humanitarian law as widely as possible, and calling upon all parties to armed conflict to apply international humanitarian law,

Recalling the entry into force, on 9 March 2004, of the second Protocol to the 1954 Hague Convention, and appreciating the ratifications received so far,

Acknowledging the fact that the Rome Statute of the International Criminal Court, which entered into force on 1 July 2002, includes the most serious crimes of international concern under international humanitarian law, and that the Statute, while recalling that it is the duty of every State to exercise its criminal jurisdiction over those responsible for such crimes, shows the determination of the international community to put an end to impunity for the perpetrators of such crimes and thus to contribute to their prevention,

Acknowledging also the usefulness of discussing in the General Assembly the status of instruments of international humanitarian law relevant to the protection of victims of armed conflicts,

1. *Welcomes* the universal acceptance of the Geneva Conventions of 1949, and notes the trend towards a similarly wide acceptance of the two Additional Protocols of 1977;

2. *Calls upon* all States parties to the Geneva Conventions that have not yet done so to consider becoming parties to the Additional Protocols at the earliest possible date;

3. *Calls upon* all States that are already parties to Protocol I, or those States not parties, on becoming parties to Protocol I, to make the declaration provided for under article 90 of that Protocol and to consider making use, where appropriate, of the services of the International Humanitarian Fact-Finding Commission in accordance with the provisions of article 90 of Protocol I;

4. *Calls upon* all States that have not yet done so to consider becoming parties to the Convention for the Protection of Cultural Property in the Event of Armed Conflict and the two Protocols thereto, and to other relevant treaties on international humanitarian law relating to the protection of victims of armed conflict;

5. *Calls upon* all States parties to the Protocols Additional to the Geneva Conventions to ensure their wide dissemination and full implementation;

6. *Notes with appreciation* the Declaration and Agenda for Humanitarian Action adopted by the Twenty-eighth International Conference of the Red Cross and Red Crescent, which noted that all States must take national measures to implement international humanitarian law, including training of the armed forces and making this law known among the general public, as well as the adoption of legislation to punish war crimes in accordance with their international obligations;

7. *Affirms* the necessity of making the implementation of international humanitarian law more effective;

8. *Welcomes* the advisory service activities of the International Committee of the Red Cross in supporting efforts made by Member States to take legislative and administrative action to implement international humanitarian law and in promoting the exchange of information on those efforts between Governments;

9. *Also welcomes* the increasing number of national commissions or committees for the implementation of international humanitarian law and for promoting the incorporation of treaties on international humanitarian law into national law and disseminating the rules of international humanitarian law;

10. *Calls upon* States to consider becoming parties to the Optional Protocol to the Convention on the Rights of the Child on the involvement of children in armed conflict;

11. *Requests* the Secretary-General to submit to the General Assembly at its sixty-third session a report on the status of the Additional Protocols relating to the protection of victims of armed conflicts, as well as on measures taken to strengthen the existing body of international humanitarian law, inter alia, with respect to its dissemination and full implementation at the national level, based on information received from Member States and the International Committee of the Red Cross;

12. *Decides* to include in the provisional agenda of its sixty-third session the item entitled "Status of the Protocols Additional to the Geneva Conventions of 1949 and relating to the protection of victims of armed conflicts".

Privileges and Immunities

In accordance with articles 35 and 36 of the 1947 Convention on the Privileges and Immunities of the Specialized Agencies of the United Nations, adopted by General Assembly resolution 179 (II) [YUN 1947-1948, p. 190], the Secretary-General, by a June note [E/2006/70], transmitted the request of the World Tourism Organization (UNWTO) that the Economic and Social Council note resolution 489 (XVI) of the UNWTO General Assembly accepting that the Convention be applied to itself, and the draft annex outlining the privileges and immunities of UNWTO.

On 27 July (**decision 2006/245**) and 15 December (**decision 2006/263**), respectively, the Council deferred consideration of the draft annex until its 2006 resumed substantive session, and to its organizational session for 2007.

Diplomatic relations

Protection of diplomatic and consular missions and representatives

As at 31 December, the States parties to the following conventions relating to the protection of diplomatic and consular relations numbered: 185 States parties to the 1961 Vienna Convention on Diplomatic Relations [YUN 1961, p. 512], 51 parties to the Optional Protocol concerning the acquisition of nationality [ibid., p. 516] and 65 parties to the Optional Protocol concerning the compulsory settlement of disputes [ibid.].

The 1963 Vienna Convention on Consular Relations [YUN 1963, p. 510] had 171 parties, the Optional Protocol concerning acquisition of nationality [ibid., p. 512] had 38, while the Optional Protocol concerning the compulsory settlement of disputes [ibid.] had 45, after the United States withdrew from that Protocol in March 2005.

Parties to the 1973 Convention on the Prevention and Punishment of Crimes against Internationally Protected Persons, including Diplomatic Agents [YUN 1973, p. 775], numbered 164.

Report of Secretary-General. In a July report [A/61/119], with later addenda [A/61/119/Add.1, 2], the Secretary-General summarized information received from 24 States and the Holy See, pursuant to General Assembly resolution 59/37 [YUN 2004, p. 1318] on instances of serious violations of the protection, security and safety of diplomatic and consular missions and representatives.

GENERAL ASSEMBLY ACTION

On 4 December [meeting 64], the General Assembly, on the recommendation of the Sixth Committee [A/61/452], adopted **resolution 61/31** without vote [agenda item 76].

Consideration of effective measures to enhance the protection, security and safety of diplomatic and consular missions and representatives

The General Assembly,

Having considered the report of the Secretary-General,

Conscious of the need to develop and strengthen friendly relations and cooperation among States,

Convinced that respect for the principles and rules of international law governing diplomatic and consular relations is a basic prerequisite for the normal conduct of relations among States and for the fulfilment of the purposes and principles of the Charter of the United Nations,

Alarmed by the recent acts of violence against diplomatic and consular representatives, as well as against representatives of international intergovernmental organizations and officials of such organizations, which have endangered or taken innocent lives and seriously impeded the normal work of such representatives and officials,

Expressing sympathy for the victims of such illegal acts,

Concerned at the failure to respect the inviolability of diplomatic and consular missions and representatives,

Recalling that, without prejudice to their privileges and immunities, it is the duty of all persons enjoying such privileges and immunities to respect the laws and regulations of the receiving State,

Recalling also that diplomatic and consular premises must not be used in any manner incompatible with the functions of diplomatic and consular missions,

Emphasizing the duty of States to take all appropriate measures as required by international law, including measures of a preventive nature, and to bring offenders to justice,

Welcoming measures already taken by States to this end in conformity with their international obligations,

Convinced that the role of the United Nations, which includes the reporting procedures established pursuant to General Assembly resolution 35/168 of 15 December 1980 and further elaborated in subsequent Assembly resolutions, is important in promoting efforts to enhance the protection, security and safety of diplomatic and consular missions and representatives,

1. *Takes note* of the report of the Secretary-General;

2. *Strongly condemns* acts of violence against diplomatic and consular missions and representatives, as well as against missions and representatives of international intergovernmental organizations and officials of such organizations, and emphasizes that such acts can never be justified;

3. *Urges* States to strictly observe, implement and enforce the applicable principles and rules of international law governing diplomatic and consular relations, including during a period of armed conflict, and, in particular, to ensure, in conformity with their international obligations, the protection, security and safety of the missions, representatives and officials mentioned in paragraph 2 above officially present in territories under their jurisdiction, including practical measures to prohibit in their territories illegal activities of persons, groups and organizations that encourage, instigate, organize or engage in the perpetration of acts against the security and safety of such missions, representatives and officials;

4. *Also urges* States to take all appropriate measures at the national and international levels to prevent any acts of violence against the missions, representatives and officials mentioned in paragraph 2 above, including during a period of armed conflict, and to ensure, with the participation of the United Nations where appropriate, that such acts are fully investigated with a view to bringing offenders to justice;

5. *Recommends* that States cooperate closely through, inter alia, contacts between the diplomatic and consular missions and the receiving State with regard to practical measures designed to enhance the protection, security and safety of diplomatic and consular missions and representatives and with regard to the exchange of information on the circumstances of all serious violations thereof;

6. *Urges* States to take all appropriate measures, in accordance with international law, at the national and international levels, to prevent any abuse of diplomatic or consular privileges and immunities, in particular serious abuses, including those involving acts of violence;

7. *Recommends* that States cooperate closely with the State in whose territory abuses of diplomatic and consular privileges and immunities may have occurred, including by exchanging information and providing assistance to its juridical authorities in order to bring offenders to justice;

8. *Calls upon* States that have not yet done so to consider becoming parties to the instruments relevant to the protection, security and safety of diplomatic and consular missions and representatives;

9. *Calls upon* States, in cases where a dispute arises in connection with a violation of their international obligations concerning the protection of the missions or the security of the representatives and officials mentioned in paragraph 2 above, to make use of the means available for peaceful settlement of disputes, including the good offices of the Secretary-General, and requests the Secretary-General, when he deems it appropriate, to offer his good offices to the States directly concerned;

10. *Requests*:

(*a*) All States to report to the Secretary-General as promptly as possible serious violations of the protection, security and safety of diplomatic and consular missions and representatives as well as missions and representatives with diplomatic status to international intergovernmental organizations;

(*b*) The State in which the violation took place—and, to the extent possible, the State where the alleged offender is present—to report to the Secretary-General as promptly as possible on measures taken to bring the offender to justice and eventually to communicate, in accordance with its laws, the final outcome of the proceedings against the offender, and to report on measures adopted with a view to preventing a repetition of such violations;

(*c*) The States so reporting to consider using or taking into account the guidelines prepared by the Secretary-General;

11. *Requests* the Secretary-General:

(*a*) To send, without delay, a circular note to all States reminding them of the request contained in paragraph 10 above;

(*b*) To circulate to all States, upon receipt, the reports received by him pursuant to paragraph 10 above, unless the reporting State requests otherwise;

(*c*) To draw the attention, when appropriate, of the States directly concerned to the reporting procedures provided for in paragraph 10 above, when a serious violation has been reported pursuant to subparagraph 10 (*a*) above;

(*d*) To address reminders to States where such violations have occurred if reports pursuant to subparagraph 10 (*a*) above or follow-up reports pursuant to subparagraph 10 (*b*) above have not been made within a reasonable period of time;

12. *Also requests* the Secretary-General to invite States, in the circular note referred to in paragraph 11 (*a*) above, to inform him of their views with respect to any measures needed or already taken to enhance the protection, security and safety of diplomatic and consular missions and representatives as well as missions and representatives with diplomatic status to international intergovernmental organizations;

13. *Further requests* the Secretary-General to submit to the General Assembly at its sixty-third session a report containing:

(*a*) Information on the state of ratification of, and accessions to, the instruments referred to in paragraph 8 above;

(*b*) A summary of the reports received and views expressed pursuant to paragraphs 10 and 12 above;

14. *Invites* the Secretary-General to include in his report to the General Assembly any views he may wish to express on the matters referred to in paragraph 13 above;

15. *Decides* to include in the provisional agenda of its sixty-third session the item entitled "Consideration of effective measures to enhance the protection, security and safety of diplomatic and consular missions and representatives".

ILC consideration. ILC, at its fifty-eighth session [A/61/10], had before it the seventh report of Special Rapporteur Christopher John R. Dugard (South Africa) on diplomatic protection [A/CN.4/567] containing proposals for the consideration of draft articles 1 to 19 on diplomatic protection on second reading, as well as a proposal for an additional draft article in the light of the comments and observations received from Governments. The Commission also had before it comments and observations from Governments [A/CN.4/561 & Add. 1, 2; A/CN.4/575]. The Commission instructed the Drafting Committee to commence the second drafting of the draft articles, taking into account the comments provided by Governments and the debate in the plenary. On 30 May, the Commission considered the Drafting Committee's report and adopted the entire set of draft articles on second reading. In August, the Commission adopted the commentaries on the draft articles and submitted them to the General Assembly, with the recommendation to elaborate a convention on the basis of those articles.

GENERAL ASSEMBLY ACTION

On 4 December [meeting 64], the General Assembly, on the recommendation of the Sixth Committee [A/61/454], adopted **resolution 61/35** without vote [agenda item 78].

Diplomatic protection

The General Assembly,

Having considered chapter IV of the report of the International Law Commission on the work of its fifty-eighth session, which contains the draft articles on diplomatic protection,

Noting that the Commission decided to recommend to the General Assembly the elaboration of a convention on the basis of the draft articles on diplomatic protection,

Emphasizing the continuing importance of the codification and progressive development of international law, as referred to in Article 13, paragraph 1 (*a*), of the Charter of the United Nations,

Noting that the subject of diplomatic protection is of major importance in the relations of States,

Taking into account views and comments expressed in the Sixth Committee on chapter IV on diplomatic protection of the report of the Commission,

1. *Expresses its appreciation* to the International Law Commission for its continuing contribution to the codification and progressive development of international law;

2. *Takes note* of the draft articles on diplomatic protection, presented by the Commission, and invites Governments to submit comments concerning the recommendation by the Commission to elaborate a convention on the basis of these articles;

3. *Decides* to include in the provisional agenda of its sixty-second session an item entitled "Diplomatic protection".

Treaties and agreements

Reservation to treaties

ILC, at its fifty-eighth session [A/61/10], considered the second part of the tenth report of Special Rapporteur Alain Pellet (France) [YUN 2005, p. 1422] on validity of reservations and the concept of the object and purpose of the treaty, and a note [A/CN.4/572 & Corr.1] relating to draft guideline 3.1.5 on the definition of the object and purpose of the treaty. He also presented a new version of the guideline, including two alternative texts.

The Commission provisionally adopted, together with commentaries thereto, draft guidelines 3.1 (permissible reservations), 3.1.1 (reservations expressly prohibited by the treaty), 3.1.2 (definition of specified reservations), 3.1.3 (permissibility of reservations not prohibited by the treaty) and 3.1.4 (permissibility of specified reservations). In addition, the Commission reconsidered, in the light of new terminology, two previously adopted draft guidelines dealing with the scope of definitions and the procedure in case of manifestly invalid reservations.

The Special Rapporteur submitted his eleventh report [A/CN.4/574] devoted to procedural questions, which the Commission decided to consider in 2007.

Treaties involving international organizations

The 1986 Vienna Convention on the Law of Treaties between States and International Organizations or between International Organizations [YUN 1986, p. 1006], which had not yet entered into force, had 40 States parties as at 31 December 2006.

Registration and publication of treaties by the United Nations

During 2006, 1,626 treaties were received and 2,284 subsequent actions were registered or filed and recorded by the Secretariat. In addition, 1,458 treaty actions (signatures, ratifications, acceptances, approvals, accessions, and other formalities) were undertaken and deposited with the Secretary-General, in his capacity as depositary of multilateral treaties. Twelve issues of the *Monthly Statement of Treaties and International Agreements* were published.

In addition, 60 volumes of the *UN Treaty Series* (UNTS) were published, incorporating the texts of treaties registered or filed and recorded and related subsequent actions in the original languages, with translations into English and French where necessary, reflecting the registration period September 2003 through February 2005. The United Nations Treaty Collection on the Internet (UNTC), which contained published UNTS volumes up to 2005, the *League of Nations Treaty Series,* the *Treaty Handbook, Multilateral Treaties Deposited with the Secretary-General,* the *Summary of Practice of the Secretary-General as Depositary of Multilateral Treaties,* the Treaty Event Booklets, information on training and a range of materials on treaty law and practice, received an average of over 2 million hits and over 400,000 page views per month in 2006.

The Treaty Event "Focus 2006: Crossing Borders" (New York, 13-15 September) resulted in 86 treaty actions undertaken by 46 States with respect to 40 treaties deposited with the Secretary-General. Those treaties related to refugees and stateless persons, migrant workers and human rights, human security and trafficking in persons and firearms, sustainable development, disarmament, health and other areas.

Advice and capacity-building in treaty law and practice

Advice and assistance on treaty law and practice, in particular on final clauses, were provided to Member States, specialized agencies, regional commissions, other UN bodies and other entities. Five seminars on treaty law and practice were conducted at UN Headquarters for legal advisers from Member States and other officials. Four training courses were held at UN Headquarters and one in Monrovia, Liberia, hosted by the Liberian Ministry for Foreign Affairs and attended by 130 participants from major Ministries.

Multilateral treaties

The UN *Treaty Series* and the regularly updated status of multilateral treaties deposited with the Secretary-General were available on the Internet at the UN Treaty Collection website.

New multilateral treaties concluded under UN auspices

The following new treaties, concluded under UN auspices, were deposited with the Secretary-General during 2006:

International Tropical Timber Agreement, adopted in Geneva on 27 January 2006

Convention on the Rights of Persons with Disabilities, adopted in New York on 13 December 2006

Optional Protocol to the Convention on the Rights of Persons with Disabilities, adopted in New York on 13 December 2006

International Convention for the Protection of All Persons from Enforced Disappearance, adopted in New York on 20 December 2006

Intergovernmental Agreement on the Trans-Asian Railway Network, adopted in Jakarta, Indonesia, on 12 April 2006

Regulations No. 121 and No. 122 to the Agreement concerning the Adoption of Uniform Technical Prescriptions for Wheeled Vehicles, Equipment and Parts, which can be fitted and/or be used on Wheeled Vehicles and the Conditions for Reciprocal Recognition of Approvals Granted on the Basis of These Prescriptions, adopted in Geneva on 18 January 2006

Multilateral treaties deposited with the Secretary-General

At the end of 2006, the Secretary-General performed depositary functions for 534 multilateral treaties. During the year, 101 signatures were affixed to treaties for which he performed depositary functions and approximately 1,300 instruments of ratification, accession, acceptance and approval were deposited.

The following multilateral treaties, among others, deposited with the Secretary-General, came into force in 2006:

Optional Protocol to the Convention against Torture and Other Cruel, Inhuman or Degrading Treatment or Punishment, adopted in New York on 18 December 2002

Regulations No. 121 and No. 122 to the Agreement concerning the Adoption of Uniform Technical Prescriptions for Wheeled Vehicles, Equipment and Parts, which can be fitted and/or be used on Wheeled Vehicles and the Conditions for Reciprocal Recognition of Approvals Granted on the Basis of These Prescriptions, adopted in Geneva on 18 January 2006

Memorandum of Understanding on Maritime Transport Cooperation in the Arab Mashreq, adopted in Damascus, Syria, on 9 May 2005

Protocol on Explosive Remnants of War to the Convention on the Use of Certain Conventional Weapons which may be deemed to be Excessively Injurious or to have Indiscriminate Effects (Protocol V), adopted in Geneva on 28 November 2003

Information for 2006 regarding all multilateral treaties deposited with the Secretary-General was contained in *Multilateral Treaties Deposited with the Secretary-General: Status as at 31 December 2006*, vols. I & II [ST/LEG/SER.E/25].

Other international legal questions

Rule of law at national and international levels

Communication. On 11 May [A/61/142], Liechtenstein and Mexico requested the inclusion in the provisional agenda of the General Assembly's sixty-first session of an item entitled "The rule of law at the national and international levels". In an explanatory memorandum, the two countries recalled the political support expressed at the 2005 World Summit [YUN 2005, p. 47] for strengthening the rule of law worldwide, especially the need for universal adherence to and implementation of the rule of law at national and international levels, complemented by concrete commitments aimed at its strengthening. While the United Nations had in recent years greatly improved its tools for strengthening the rule of law at the national level, in particular in post-conflict situations, it still lacked the appropriate tools to promote the rule of law in a coherent manner, especially with regard to its international dimension. It had paid much attention to the development and codification of international law in a number of areas, but those efforts were not within a coherent global framework. The General Assembly should therefore consider the issue in a comprehensive and coherent manner, as it was uniquely positioned to fill that gap and promote universal adherence to the concept of the rule of law.

Sixth Committee consideration. On 13 September [A/61/456], the Assembly decided to include the item in its agenda and allocate it to the Sixth Committee, which considered it on 16 and 17 October and on 6 and 16 November. The Committee Chairman, on 16 November, introduced a draft resolution [A/C.6/61/L.18] that was adopted, as orally revised.

GENERAL ASSEMBLY ACTION

On 4 December [meeting 64], the General Assembly, on the recommendation of the Sixth Committee [A/61/456], adopted **resolution 61/39** without vote [agenda item 80].

The rule of law at the national and international levels

The General Assembly,

Reaffirming its commitment to the purposes and principles of the Charter of the United Nations and international law, which are indispensable foundations of a more peaceful, prosperous and just world, and reiterating its determination to foster strict respect for them and to establish a just and lasting peace all over the world,

Reaffirming also that human rights, the rule of law and democracy are interlinked and mutually reinforcing and that they belong to the universal and indivisible core values and principles of the United Nations,

Reaffirming further the need for universal adherence to and implementation of the rule of law at both the national and international levels and its solemn commitment to an international order based on the rule of law and international law, which together with the principles of justice, is essential for peaceful coexistence and cooperation among States,

Convinced that the advancement of the rule of law at the national and international levels is essential for the realization of sustained economic growth, sustainable development, the eradication of poverty and hunger and the protection of all human rights and fundamental freedoms, and acknowledging that collective security depends on effective cooperation, in accordance with the Charter and international law, against transnational threats,

Reaffirming the duty of all States to refrain in their international relations from the threat or use of force in any manner inconsistent with the purposes and principles of the United Nations and to settle their international disputes by peaceful means in such a manner that international peace and security, and justice, are not endangered, and calling upon States that have not yet done so to consider accepting the jurisdiction of the International Court of Justice in accordance with its Statute,

Convinced that the promotion of and respect for the rule of law at the national and international levels, as well as justice and good governance, should guide the activities of the United Nations and of its Member States,

1. *Requests* the Secretary-General to seek the views of Member States on matters pertaining to the issues addressed in the present resolution and to submit a report thereon at its sixty-second session;

2. *Also requests* the Secretary-General to prepare an inventory of the current activities of the various organs, bodies, offices, departments, funds and programmes within the United Nations system devoted to the promotion of the rule of law at the national and international levels for submission at its sixty-third session, and to submit an interim report thereon to the General Assembly for its consideration at its sixty-second session;

3. *Further requests* the Secretary-General, after having sought the views of Member States, to prepare and submit, at its sixty-third session, a report identifying ways and means for strengthening and coordinating the activities listed in the inventory to be prepared pursuant to paragraph 2 above, with special regard to the effectiveness of assistance that may be requested by States in building capacity for the promotion of the rule of law at the national and international levels;

4. *Urges* the Secretary-General, as a matter of priority, to submit the report on the establishment of a rule of law assistance unit within the Secretariat, in conformity with paragraph 134 (*e*) of the 2005 World Summit Outcome;

5. *Decides* to include in the provisional agenda of its sixty-second session the item entitled "The rule of law at the national and international levels", and recommends that, as from the sixty-second session and after consultations among Member States, the Sixth Committee annually choose one or two sub-topics to facilitate a focused discussion for the subsequent session, without prejudice to the consideration of the item as a whole.

International economic law

In 2006, legal aspects of international economic law continued to be considered by the United Nations Commission on International Trade Law (UNCITRAL) and by the Sixth Committee of the General Assembly.

International trade law

At its thirty-ninth session (New York, 19 June–7 July), UNCITRAL finalized and adopted revised articles of the UNCITRAL Model Law on International Commercial Arbitration, annexed to the report of its thirty-ninth session, and the recommendation regarding the interpretation of articles II, paragraph 2, and VII, paragraph 1, of the 1958 Convention on the Recognition and Enforcement of Foreign Arbitral Awards [YUN 1958, p. 390], also annexed to its report.

It continued its work on public procurement, arbitration, transport law, electronic commerce, insolvency law and security interests. It also reviewed the implementation of the 1958 New York Convention on the Recognition and Enforcement of Foreign Arbitral Awards (the New York Convention), the work on the collection and dissemination of case law on UNCITRAL texts (CLOUT), and training and technical assistance activities.

The report of the session [A/61/17] described actions taken on those topics. (For details, see below.)

GENERAL ASSEMBLY ACTION

On 4 December [meeting 64], the General Assembly, on the recommendation of the Sixth Committee [A/61/453], adopted **resolution 61/32** without vote [agenda item 77].

Report of the United Nations Commission on International Trade Law on the work of its thirty-ninth session

The General Assembly,

Recalling its resolution 2205 (XXI) of 17 December 1966, by which it established the United Nations Commission on International Trade Law with a mandate to further the progressive harmonization and unification of the law of international trade and in that respect to bear in mind the interests of all peoples, in particular those of developing countries, in the extensive development of international trade,

Reaffirming its belief that the progressive modernization and harmonization of international trade law, in reducing or removing legal obstacles to the flow of international trade, especially those affecting the developing countries, would contribute significantly to universal economic cooperation among all States on a basis of equality, equity and common interest and to the elimination of discrimination in international trade and, thereby, to the well-being of all peoples,

Having considered the report of the Commission on the work of its thirty-ninth session,

Reiterating its concern that activities undertaken by other bodies in the field of international trade law without adequate coordination with the Commission might lead to undesirable duplication of efforts and would not be in keeping with the aim of promoting efficiency, consistency and coherence in the unification and harmonization of international trade law,

Reaffirming the mandate of the Commission, as the core legal body within the United Nations system in the field of international trade law, to coordinate legal activities in this field, in particular to avoid duplication of efforts, including among organizations formulating rules of international trade, and to promote efficiency, consistency and coherence in the modernization and harmonization of international trade law, and to continue, through its secretariat, to maintain close cooperation with other international organs and organizations, including regional organizations, active in the field of international trade law,

1. *Takes note with appreciation* of the report of the United Nations Commission on International Trade Law on the work of its thirty-ninth session;

2. *Commends* the Commission for the finalization and adoption of revised articles of the Model Law on International Commercial Arbitration of the United Nations Commission on International Trade Law on the form of the arbitration agreement and interim measures, and of the recommendation regarding the interpretation of article II, paragraph 2, and article VII, paragraph 1, of the Convention on the Recognition and Enforcement of Foreign Arbitral Awards, done at New York, 10 June 1958;

3. *Also commends* the Commission for the approval of the substance of the recommendations of the draft legislative guide on secured transactions, which has been designed to facilitate secured financing, thus promoting increased access to low-cost credit and enhancing national and international trade;

4. *Welcomes* the progress made by the Commission in its work on a revision of its Model Law on Procurement of Goods, Construction and Services, and on a draft instrument on transport law, and endorses the decision of the Commission to take up new topics in the areas of arbitration and insolvency law;

5. *Endorses* the efforts and initiatives of the Commission, as the core legal body within the United Nations system in the field of international trade law, aimed at increasing coordination of and cooperation on legal activities of international and regional organizations active in the field of international trade law, as well as promoting the rule of law at the national and international levels in this field, and in this regard appeals to relevant international and regional organizations to coordinate their legal activities with those of the Commission, to avoid duplication of efforts and to promote efficiency, consistency and coherence in the modernization and harmonization of international trade law;

6. *Reaffirms* the importance, in particular for developing countries, of the work of the Commission concerned with technical assistance and cooperation in the field of international trade law reform and development, and in this connection:

(a) Welcomes the initiatives of the Commission towards expanding, through its secretariat, its technical assistance and cooperation programme;

(b) Expresses its appreciation to the Commission for carrying out technical assistance and cooperation activities in Belarus, Benin (for the United Nations Conference on Trade and Development/World Trade Organization International Trade Centre seminar), Colombia, Egypt, the Republic of Korea, Singapore, Slovakia and Switzerland (for the United Nations Conference on Trade and Development/World Trade Organization International Trade Centre symposium on multilateral trade treaties and developing countries) and for providing assistance with legislative drafting in the field of international trade law to China, Georgia, Greece, Malaysia, Peru, Rwanda (through the joint project with the International Law Institute), Serbia, Slovenia and The former Yugoslav Republic of Macedonia, and to the Commonwealth Telecommunications Organisation;

(*c*) Expresses its appreciation to the Governments whose contributions enabled the technical assistance and cooperation activities to take place, and appeals to Governments, the relevant bodies of the United Nations system, organizations, institutions and individuals to make voluntary contributions to the United Nations Commission on International Trade Law Trust Fund for Symposia and, where appropriate, to the financing of special projects, and otherwise to assist the secretariat of the Commission in carrying out technical assistance activities, in particular in developing countries;

(*d*) Reiterates its appeal to the United Nations Development Programme and other bodies responsible for development assistance, such as the World Bank and regional development banks, as well as to Governments in their bilateral aid programmes, to support the technical assistance programme of the Commission and to cooperate and coordinate their activities with those of the Commission, in the light of the relevance and importance of the work and programmes of the Commission to the implementation of the United Nations development agenda, including the achievement of the Millennium Development Goals;

7. *Takes note with regret* that, since the thirty-sixth session of the Commission, no contributions have been made to the trust fund established to provide travel assistance to developing countries that are members of the Commission, at their request and in consultation with the Secretary-General, stresses the need for contributions to the trust fund in order to increase expert representation from developing countries at sessions of the Commission and its working groups, necessary to build local expertise and capacities in the field of international trade law in those countries to facilitate the development of international trade and the promotion of foreign investment, and reiterates its appeal to Governments, the relevant bodies of the United Nations system, organizations, institutions and individuals to make voluntary contributions to the trust fund;

8. *Decides*, in order to ensure full participation by all Member States in the sessions of the Commission and its working groups, to continue, in the competent Main Committee during the sixty-first session of the General Assembly, its consideration of granting travel assistance to the least developed countries that are members of the Commission, at their request and in consultation with the Secretary-General;

9. *Recalls* that the responsibility for the work of the Commission lies with the meetings of the Commission and its intergovernmental working groups, and stresses in this regard that information should be provided regarding meetings of experts, which bring an essential contribution to the work of the Commission;

10. *Recalls* its resolutions on partnerships between the United Nations and non-State actors, in particular the private sector, and in this regard encourages the Commission to further explore different approaches to the use of partnerships with non-State actors in the implementation of its mandate, in particular in the area of technical assistance, in accordance with the applicable principles and guidelines and in cooperation and coordination with other relevant offices of the Secretariat, including the Global Compact Office;

11. *Reiterates its request* to the Secretary-General, in conformity with the General Assembly resolutions on documentation-related matters, which, in particular, emphasize that any reduction in the length of documents should not adversely affect either the quality of the presentation or the substance of the documents, to bear in mind the particular characteristics of the mandate and work of the Commission in implementing page limits with respect to the documentation of the Commission;

12. *Requests* the Secretary-General to continue providing summary records of the meetings of the Commission relating to the formulation of normative texts;

13. *Recalls* its resolution approving the establishment of the *Yearbook of the United Nations Commission on International Trade Law*, with the aim of making the work of the Commission more widely known and readily available, expresses its concern regarding the timeliness of the publication of the *Yearbook*, and requests the Secretary-General to explore options to facilitate the timely publication of the *Yearbook*;

14. *Stresses* the importance of bringing into effect the conventions emanating from the work of the Commission for the global unification and harmonization of international trade law, and to this end urges States that have not yet done so to consider signing, ratifying or acceding to those conventions;

15. *Welcomes* the preparation of digests of case law relating to the texts of the Commission, such as a digest of case law relating to the United Nations Convention on Contracts for the International Sale of Goods and a digest of case law relating to the Model Law on International Commercial Arbitration of the United Nations Commission on International Trade Law, with the aim of assisting in dissemination of information on those texts and promoting their use, enactment and uniform interpretation;

16. *Welcomes also* the decision of the Commission to hold, in the context of its fortieth session in 2007, a congress on international trade law in Vienna, with a view to reviewing the results of the past work of the Commission as well as related work of other organizations active in the field of international trade law, assessing current work programmes and considering topics and areas for future work, and acknowledges the importance of holding such a congress for the coordination and promotion of activities aimed at the modernization and harmonization of international trade law;

17. *Recalls* its resolutions affirming the importance of high-quality, user-friendly and cost-effective United Nations websites and the need for their multilingual development, maintenance and enrichment, commends the restructured website of the Commission in the six official languages of the United Nations, and welcomes the continuous efforts of the Commission to maintain and improve its website in accordance with the applicable guidelines.

Procurement

UNCITRAL [A/61/17] took note of the reports of Working Group I (Procurement) on its eighth (Vienna, 7-11 November 2005) [A/CN.9/590] and ninth (New York, 24-28 April 2006) [A/CN.9/595] sessions relating to the revision of the UNCITRAL Model Law on Procurement of Goods, Constructions and Services, in response to the Commission's 2004 request [YUN 2004, p. 1356]. UNCITRAL was informed that, at those sessions, the Group had continued to consider topics related to the use of electronic communications and technologies in the procurement process. At its ninth session, the Group came to preliminary agreement on draft revisions of the Model Law and the Guide on the use of electronic communications and technology, including electronic reverse auctions. It decided to address the remaining aspects of electronic reverse auctions and the investigation of abnormally low tenders, as well as the topics of framework agreements and suppliers' lists.

Commending the Group for the progress made, UNCITRAL recommended that the Group, in considering the topics of coordination and cooperation, take into account conflict of interest issues, and consider whether any specific provisions addressing those issues were warranted.

International commercial arbitration

UNCITRAL [A/61/17] considered the revised version of the draft legislative provisions on interim measures and the form of arbitration agreement adopted by Working Group II (Arbitration and Conciliation) at its forty-fourth session (New York, 23–27 January) [A/CN.9/592]. On 7 July, UNCITRAL adopted the revised articles of the UNCITRAL Model Law on International Commercial Arbitration, as annexed to its report, and recommended that States give favourable consideration to the revised articles when enacting or revising their laws, in view of the desirability of uniformity of the law of dispute settlement procedures and the specific needs of international commercial arbitration practice.

With respect to future work, UNCITRAL agreed that the Working Group should give priority to the revision of the UNCITRAL Arbitration Rules, and consideration of the arbitrability of intra-corporate disputes and the implications of electronic communications.

Implementation of the 1958 New York Convention

UNCITRAL [A/61/17] considered the revised version of a draft declaration regarding the interpretation of articles II (2) and VII (1) of the 1958 New York Convention [YUN 1958, p. 390], adopted by Working Group II (Arbitration and Conciliation) at its forty-fourth session (New York, 23-27 January) [A/CN.9/592]. On 7 July, UNCITRAL agreed that the most appropriate form of such a document was that of a recommendation, instead of a declaration, which could be misrepresented as to its nature. Accordingly, it adopted a recommendation regarding the interpretation of those articles, as annexed to its report, which it felt would promote the uniform interpretation and application of the Convention.

GENERAL ASSEMBLY ACTION

On 4 December [meeting 64], the General Assembly, on the recommendation of the Sixth Committee [A/61/453], adopted **resolution 61/33** without vote [agenda item 77].

Revised articles of the Model Law on International Commercial Arbitration of the United Nations Commission on International Trade Law, and the recommendation regarding the interpretation of article II, paragraph 2, and article VII, paragraph 1, of the Convention on the Recognition and Enforcement of Foreign Arbitral Awards, done at New York, 10 June 1958

The General Assembly,

Recognizing the value of arbitration as a method of settling disputes arising in the context of international commercial relations,

Recalling its resolution 40/72 of 11 December 1985 regarding the Model Law on International Commercial Arbitration,

Recognizing the need for provisions in the Model Law to conform to current practices in international trade and modern means of contracting with regard to the form of the arbitration agreement and the granting of interim measures,

Believing that revised articles of the Model Law on the form of the arbitration agreement and interim measures reflecting those current practices will significantly enhance the operation of the Model Law,

Noting that the preparation of the revised articles of the Model Law on the form of the arbitration agreement and interim measures was the subject of due deliberation and extensive consultations with Governments and interested circles and would contribute significantly to the establishment of a harmonized legal framework for a fair and efficient settlement of international commercial disputes,

Believing that, in connection with the modernization of articles of the Model Law, the promotion of a uniform interpretation and application of the Convention on the Recognition and Enforcement of Foreign Arbitral Awards, done at New York, 10 June 1958, is particularly timely,

1. *Expresses its appreciation* to the United Nations Commission on International Trade Law for formulating and adopting the revised articles of its Model Law on International Commercial Arbitration on the form of the arbitration agreement and interim measures, the text of which is contained in annex I to the report of the United Nations Commission on International Trade Law on the work of its thirty-ninth session, and recommends that all States give favourable consideration to the enactment of the revised articles of the Model Law, or the revised Model Law on International Commercial Arbitration of the United Nations Commission on International Trade Law, when they enact or revise their laws, in view of the desirability of uniformity of the law of arbitral procedures and the specific needs of international commercial arbitration practice;

2. *Also expresses its appreciation* to the United Nations Commission on International Trade Law for formulating and adopting the recommendation regarding the interpretation of article II, paragraph 2, and article VII, paragraph 1, of the Convention on the Recognition and Enforcement of Foreign Arbitral Awards, done at New York, 10 June 1958, the text of which is contained in annex II to the report of the United Nations Commission on International Trade Law on the work of its thirty-ninth session;

3. *Requests* the Secretary-General to make all efforts to ensure that the revised articles of the Model Law and the recommendation become generally known and available.

Transport law

UNCITRAL [A/61/17] considered the reports of Working Group III (Transport Law) on its sixteenth (Vienna, 28 November–9 December 2005) [A/CN.9/591 & Corr.1] and seventeenth (New York, 3-13 April 2006) [A/CN.9/594] sessions describing its continuing work on a draft instrument on the carriage of goods wholly or partly by sea. UNCITRAL was informed that the Working Group had proceeded with its second reading of the draft convention and had made good progress regarding a number of difficult issues, including jurisdiction, arbitration obligations of the shipper, delivery of goods, especially the period of responsibility of the carrier, the right of control, delivery to the consignee, scope of application and freedom of contract, and transport documents and electronic transport records. The Working Group also considered the transfer of rights and the issue of whether any of the substantive topics currently included in the draft convention should be deferred for consideration in a possible future instrument. The Working Group planned to complete its second reading of the draft at the end of 2006 and the final reading at the end of 2007, with a view to presenting the draft convention for finalization by UNCITRAL in 2008. While agreeing that 2008 would be a desirable goal for completing the project, UNCITRAL was of the view that at the current stage it was not desirable to establish a firm deadline.

Electronic commerce

In 2005 [YUN 2005, p. 1464], UNCITRAL considered undertaking work in the area of electronic commerce and requested the Secretariat to prepare a study, with proposals on the form and nature of a comprehensive reference document, which UNCITRAL might consider preparing to assist legislators and policymakers around the world. In a note [A/CN.9/604], the Secretariat identified possible components of such a document: authentication and cross-border recognition of electronic signatures; liability and standards of conduct for information-services providers; electronic invoicing and legal issues related to supply chains; transfer of rights in tangible goods and other rights through electronic communications; unfair competition and deceptive trade practices; and privacy and data protection. Other issues identified for possible inclusion were: protection of intellectual property rights, unsolicited electronic communications (spam) and cyber crime.

Given the variety of issues involved, it was agreed that Member States might need more time to consider the desirability and scope of future legislative work on those issues, and the Commission should postpone a decision on the topics to be covered until 2007. The Commission therefore requested the Secretariat to prepare a document dealing specifically with issues related to authentication and cross-border recognition of electronic signatures for review at its 2007 session.

Insolvency law

After considering proposals by the Secretariat [A/CN.9/596] for possible future work on insolvency law, especially the treatment of corporate groups, cross-border insolvency protocols in transnational cases, post-commencement financing in international reorganization, directors' and officers' responsibilities and liabilities and commercial fraud and insolvency, UNCITRAL [A/61/17] agreed that Working Group V (Insolvency Law) should consider, in 2006, the treatment of corporate groups in insolvency, including post-commencement finance, with a view to making recommendations. Initial work to promote practical experience on negotiating and using cross-border protocols in transnational insolvency cases should be developed informally in consultation with judges and insolvency practitioners, with a view to submitting a preliminary progress report to UNCITRAL in 2007.

Commercial fraud

UNCITRAL considered a Secretariat note [A/CN.9/600], which reported on ongoing and possible future work in commercial fraud. It heard a progress report by the Secretariat on materials listing common features in typical fraudulent schemes and took note of the suggested format for the preparation of such features set out in the Secretariat note.

The Commission concluded that its secretariat should, in conjunction with experts and other interested organizations, identify common features of fraudulent schemes, and present interim or final materials for its future consideration. The secretariat should continue to cooperate with the United Nations Office on Drugs and Crime in its study on fraud, the criminal misuse and falsification of identity and related crimes and keep the Commission informed on progress made.

Security interests

UNCITRAL [A/61/17] had before it the reports of its Working Group VI (Security Interests) at its ninth (New York, 30 January–3 February) [A/CN.9/593] and tenth (New York, 1-5 May) [A/CN.9/603] sessions on progress in the preparation of a legislative guide on secured transactions. UNCITRAL expressed satisfaction with the progress achieved by the Working Group in developing the draft guide and noted that the views and suggestions made would be taken into account in the next version of the guide. It referred the issue of terminology of the draft guide to the Working Group.

UNCITRAL approved the substance of the Working Group's recommendations on: key objectives and scope of application; basic approaches to security; creation of the security right; effectiveness of the security right against third parties and registration; priority of the security right over the rights of competing claimants; pre-default rights and obligations of the parties; rights and obligations of third-party obligors; default and enforcement; insolvency; acquisition financing devices; conflict of laws; and transitional arrangements.

The Working Group was expected to hold one session in Vienna in December and another in New York in February 2007 and submit the draft guide for approval at UNCITRAL next session in 2007.

As to future work, UNCITRAL requested the Secretariat to prepare a note on intellectual property financing and organize a colloquium on the topic.

Case law on UNCITRAL texts

UNCITRAL [A/61/17] noted the continuing work under the system for the collection and dissemination of case law on UNCITRAL texts (CLOUT), consisting of the preparation of case abstracts and research aids and analytical tools, such as thesauri and indices, and the compilation of full texts of decisions. A total of 54 issues of CLOUT had been prepared for publication dealing with 604 cases.

It was widely agreed that CLOUT continued to be an important aspect of UNCITRAL technical assistance activities, and that its broad dissemination promoted the uniform interpretation and application of UNCITRAL texts. UNCITRAL expressed its appreciation to national correspondents for their work in selecting decisions and preparing case abstracts. It noted that the digest of case law on the United Nations Sales Convention, published in 2004 [YUN 2004, p. 1356], was being reviewed and edited, and that the first draft of a digest of case law relating to the Arbitration Model Law was being finalized for publication.

Training and technical assistance

UNCITRAL [A/61/17] had before it a note by the Secretariat [A/CN.9/599] describing technical assistance activities undertaken since 2005 and the direction of future activities. Among the activities reported were 59 briefing missions, seminars and conferences to familiarize participants with UNCITRAL texts and their use; law reform assessments to assist Governments, legislative organs and other authorities in reviewing legislation and assessing their need for law reform in the commercial field; assistance in drafting national legislation to implement UNCITRAL texts; advice and assistance to international organizations, professional associations, organizations of attorneys, chambers of commerce and arbitration centres on the use of UNCITRAL texts; and group training activities to facilitate the implementation and interpretation by judiciaries and legal practitioners of commercial legislation based on UNCITRAL texts.

UNCITRAL reiterated its appeal to States, international organizations and other entities to contribute to its trust fund for symposia, so as to help the Secretariat meet the increasing requests for training, and to its trust fund established to provide travel assistance to developing countries that were UNCITRAL members.

Future work

Following its 2005 decision [YUN 2005, p. 1464] to hold an UNCITRAL Congress on Uniform Commercial Law in the Twenty-first Century, UNCITRAL considered the proposed programme outline and agreed that the Congress would not formulate conclusions or recommendations. UNCITRAL would however draw inspiration from views expressed at the Congress. It also agreed that the duration of formal deliberations at its 2007 session should be shortened to a maximum of two weeks, and that the Congress, which should commence after the completion of the session, should not exceed four days.

It agreed to a Secretariat proposal that the Unidroit Principles of International Commercial Contracts be circulated to States, with a view to its possible endorsement by the Commission in 2007.

International organizations and international law

Strengthening the role of the United Nations

Special Committee on United Nations Charter

In accordance with General Assembly resolution 60/20 [YUN 2004, p. 1448], the Special Committee on the Charter of the United Nations and on the Strengthening of the Role of the Organization, at its sixty-first session (New York, 3-13 April) [A/61/33], continued to consider proposals relating to: the maintenance of international peace and security; the peaceful settlement of disputes between States; proposals concerning the Trusteeship Council; the improvement of the Committee's working methods; and the status of the publications: *Repertory of Practice of United Nations Organs* and *Repertoire of the Practice of the Security Council.*

With regard to the first item, the Committee discussed a revised working paper submitted by Belarus and the Russian Federation, which recommended that an advisory opinion be requested from the International Court of Justice (ICJ) as to the legal consequences of the resort to the use of force by States without prior Security Council authorization, except in case of self-defence. Some delegations expressed support for the proposal, as it would strengthen the Charter principle of the non-use of force or threat of force. Concern was expressed over attempts to justify the unilateral use of force without Council authorization, which was seen as a violation of the Charter. The question was raised, however, as to whether the current wording of the proposal, in view of recent developments, took sufficient account of the many variables that the Court would have to consider when forming an opinion. The Committee also discussed a revised Libyan Arab Jamahiriya proposal on strengthening the UN role in the maintenance of international peace and security and a Russian Federation working paper on fundamentals of the legal basis for UN peacekeeping operations in the context of Chapter VI of the Charter.

After discussing a working paper on strengthening the role of the Organization and enhancing its effectiveness, submitted by Cuba at its 1997 session, the Committee recognized the value of considering measures within the United Nations, with a view to ensuring the revitalization of the General Assembly, in order to effectively and efficiently exercise the functions assigned to it under the Charter.

During the exchange of views on the peaceful settlement of disputes, delegations expressed support for the use of existing mechanisms at early stages to peacefully settle disputes, as well as the Charter principle of free choice of means. Strong support was also expressed for ICJ as the principal judicial organ of the United Nations. The promotion of a culture of prevention and the strengthening of the UN conflict prevention capacity, including the role of the Secretary-General, were emphasized. On a proposal by Egypt, the Working Group of the Whole recommended by consensus to the Committee the draft resolution entitled "Commemoration of the sixtieth anniversary of the International Court of Justice" for adoption by the General Assembly (see p. 1483).

On the future of the Trusteeship Council, references were made to the 2005 World Summit Outcome in General Assembly resolution 60/1 [YUN 2005, p. 48], in which the Assembly recommended that, considering that the Trusteeship Council "no longer meets and has no remaining functions", Chapter XIII of the Charter and references to the Council in Chapter XII be deleted. While support was expressed for such a deletion, the point was also made that amendments to the Charter should be considered in the overall context of the reform of the Organization.

The Committee recommended that the Assembly commend the Secretary-General for the progress made in the preparation of studies of the *Repertory of Practice of United Nations Organs*, including the increased use of UN interns and the wider cooperation with academic institutions, as well as the progress made towards updating the *Repertoire of the Practice of the Security Council.* The Committee called again for voluntary contributions to the trust funds for updating the *Repertoire* and for eliminating the backlog in the *Repertory*, as well as for sponsoring, at no cost to the United Nations, associate experts to assist in updating the two publications.

The Committee adopted a working paper submitted by Japan and other co-sponsors in 2005 [YUN 2005, p. 1447] on improving the Committee's working methods and increasing its efficiency. The working paper encouraged delegations submitting new proposals to do so as far in advance as possible and to ensure that they did not duplicate the work being done by other bodies. Delegations should request the Committee to conduct a preliminary exchange of views on a proposal's usefulness, assess its priority in comparison with other proposals, or consider postponing its consideration. Delegations should also look into the usefulness of further discussing the proposal, taking into account the likelihood of reaching a consensus. For its part, the Special Committee should ensure that meetings accorded priority to the consideration of those areas on which general agreement was possible and reviewed ways of improving the procedure for the adoption of its report.

Concerning the identification of new subjects, Guyana, on behalf of the Rio Group, suggested the addition of two items to the Special Committee's agenda: "Review of the rules of procedures of the General Assembly" and "Consideration of the legal aspects of the reform of the United Nations". Guyana indicated that it would provide further details on those proposals.

Report of Secretary-General. In response to General Assembly resolution 60/23 [YUN 2005, p. 1447], the Secretary-General submitted a July report [A/61/153] outlining progress made in updating the *Repertory of Practice of United Nations Organs* and the *Repertoire of the Practice of the Security Council.* With respect to the *Repertory*, the Secretary-General remarked that the Assembly might wish to note the progress made in the preparation of *Repertory* studies and their posting on the Internet in English, French and Spanish; and consider the Special Committee's recommendations (see above). With regard to the *Repertoire*, the Secretary-General concluded that the Assembly might wish to note the progress made towards its updating, and the desirability of continuing to make it available on the Internet; call for voluntary contributions to the trust fund for updating the *Repertorie*; note the contributions made by Japan, Nigeria, Qatar, the Republic of Korea, the Russian Federation, Turkey and the United Kingdom, as well as the support of Germany and Italy for associate experts; and encourage other States to consider providing such assistance.

GENERAL ASSEMBLY ACTION

On 4 December [meeting 64], the General Assembly, on the recommendation of the Sixth Committee [A/61/455], adopted **resolution 61/38** without vote [agenda item 79].

Report of the Special Committee on the Charter of the United Nations and on the Strengthening of the Role of the Organization

The General Assembly,

Recalling its resolution 3499 (XXX) of 15 December 1975, by which it established the Special Committee on the Charter of the United Nations and on the Strengthening of the Role of the Organization, and its relevant resolutions adopted at subsequent sessions,

Recalling also its resolution 47/233 of 17 August 1993 on the revitalization of the work of the General Assembly,

Recalling further its resolution 47/62 of 11 December 1992 on the question of equitable representation on and increase in the membership of the Security Council,

Taking note of the report of the Open-ended Working Group on the Question of Equitable Representation on and Increase in the Membership of the Security Council and Other Matters related to the Security Council,

Recalling the elements relevant to the work of the Special Committee contained in its resolution 47/120 B of 20 September 1993,

Recalling also its resolution 51/241 of 31 July 1997 on the strengthening of the United Nations system and its resolution 51/242 of 15 September 1997, entitled "Supplement to an Agenda for Peace", by which it adopted the texts on coordination and the question of sanctions imposed by the United Nations, which are annexed to that resolution,

Concerned about the special economic problems confronting certain States arising from the carrying out of preventive or enforcement measures taken by the Security Council against other States, and taking into account the obligation of Members of the United Nations under Article 49 of the Charter of the United Nations to join in affording mutual assistance in carrying out the measures decided upon by the Council,

Recalling the right of third States confronted with special economic problems of that nature to consult the Security Council with regard to a solution of those problems, in accordance with Article 50 of the Charter,

Recalling also that the International Court of Justice is the principal judicial organ of the United Nations, and reaffirming its authority and independence,

Noting the adoption of the revised working papers on the working methods of the Special Committee,

Taking note of the report of the Secretary-General on the *Repertory of Practice of United Nations Organs* and the *Repertoire of the Practice of the Security Council*,

Taking note also of paragraphs 106 to 110, 176 and 177 of the 2005 World Summit Outcome,

Mindful of the decision of the Special Committee, in which it expressed its readiness to engage, as appropriate, in the implementation of any decisions that may be taken at the High-level Plenary Meeting of the sixtieth session of the General Assembly in September 2005 that concern the Charter and any amendments thereto,

Recalling the provisions of its resolutions 50/51 of 11 December 1995, 51/208 of 17 December 1996, 52/162 of 15 December 1997, 53/107 of 8 December 1998, 54/107 of 9 December 1999, 55/157 of 12 December 2000, 56/87 of 12 December 2001, 57/25 of 19 November 2002, 58/80 of 9 December 2003 and 59/45 of 2 December 2004,

Recalling also its resolution 60/23 of 23 November 2005,

Having considered the report of the Special Committee on the work of its session held in 2006,

Noting with appreciation the work done by the Special Committee to encourage States to focus on the need to prevent and to settle peacefully their disputes which are likely to endanger the maintenance of international peace and security,

1. *Takes note* of the report of the Special Committee on the Charter of the United Nations and on the Strengthening of the Role of the Organization;

2. *Decides* that the Special Committee shall hold its next session from 7 to 14 and 16 February 2007;

3. *Notes with appreciation* the adoption, as a decision, of the working methods of the Special Committee, contained in paragraph 72 of its 2006 report;

4. *Requests* the Special Committee, at its session in 2007, in accordance with paragraph 5 of General Assembly resolution 50/52 of 11 December 1995:

(a) To continue its consideration of all proposals concerning the question of the maintenance of international peace and security in all its aspects in order to strengthen the role of the United Nations, and, in this context, to consider other proposals relating to the maintenance of international peace and security already submitted or which may be submitted to the Special Committee at its session in 2007;

(b) To continue to consider, on a priority basis and in an appropriate substantive manner and framework, the question of the implementation of the provisions of the Charter of the United Nations related to assistance to third States affected by the application of sanctions under Chapter VII of the Charter based on all of the related reports of the Secretary-General and the proposals submitted on the question;

(c) To keep on its agenda the question of the peaceful settlement of disputes between States;

(d) To consider, as appropriate, any proposal referred to it by the General Assembly in the implementation of the decisions of the High-level Plenary Meeting of the sixtieth session of the Assembly in September 2005 that concern the Charter and any amendments thereto;

(e) To continue to consider, on a priority basis, ways and means of improving its working methods and enhancing its efficiency with a view to identifying widely acceptable measures for future implementation;

5. *Invites* the Special Committee at its session in 2007 to continue to identify new subjects for consideration in its future work with a view to contributing to the revitalization of the work of the United Nations;

6. *Notes* the readiness of the Special Committee to provide, within its mandate, such assistance as may be sought at the request of other subsidiary bodies of the General Assembly in relation to any issues before them;

7. *Requests* the Special Committee to submit a report on its work to the General Assembly at its sixty-second session;

8. *Recognizes* the important role of the International Court of Justice, the principal judicial organ of the United Nations, in adjudicating disputes among States and the value of its work, as well as the importance of having recourse to the Court in the peaceful settlement of disputes, and requests the Secretary-General to distribute, in due course, the advisory opinions requested by the principal organs of the United Nations as official documents of the United Nations;

9. *Commends* the Secretary-General for the progress made in the preparation of studies of the *Repertory of Practice of United Nations Organs*, including the increased use of the internship programme of the United Nations and the wider cooperation with academic institutions for this purpose, as well as the progress made towards updating the *Repertoire of the Practice of the Security Council*;

10. *Calls upon* the Secretary-General to continue his efforts towards updating the two publications;

11. *Reiterates* the responsibility of the Secretary-General for the quality of the *Repertory of Practice of United Nations Organs* and the *Repertoire of the Practice of the Security Council* and, in particular, with regard to the *Repertoire of the Practice of the Security Council*, requests the Secretary-General to continue to follow the modalities outlined in paragraphs 102 to 106 of his report of 18 September 1952;

12. *Recognizes* the desirability of making available electronically the *Repertory of Practice of United Nations Organs* and the *Repertoire of the Practice of the Security Council* in all their respective language versions;

13. *Reiterates its call* for voluntary contributions to the trust fund for the updating of the *Repertoire of the Practice of the Security Council*, as well as the trust fund for the elimination of the backlog in the *Repertory of Practice of United Nations Organs*, and the sponsoring, on a voluntary basis, and at no cost to the United Nations, of associate experts to assist in the updating of the two publications;

14. *Requests* the Secretary-General to submit a report on both the *Repertory of Practice of United Nations Organs* and the *Repertoire of the Practice of the Security Council* to the General Assembly at its sixty-second session;

15. *Also requests* the Secretary-General to submit to the Special Committee for its consideration the information referred to in paragraph 12 of his report on implementation of the provisions of the Charter of the United Nations related to assistance to third States affected by the application of sanctions, on modalities, technical procedures and guidelines on coordination of technical assistance available to third States affected by the implementation of sanctions, as well as a possible methodology for assessing the adverse consequences actually incurred by third States, in the report mentioned in paragraph 16 below;

16. *Further requests* the Secretary-General to submit a report on the implementation of the provisions of the Charter of the United Nations related to assistance to third States affected by the application of sanctions to the General Assembly at its sixty-second session, under the item entitled "Report of the Special Committee on the Charter of the United Nations and on the Strengthening of the Role of the Organization";

17. *Decides* to include in the provisional agenda of its sixty-second session the item entitled "Report of the Special Committee on the Charter of the United Nations and on the Strengthening of the Role of the Organization".

Also on the same date, the Assembly adopted **resolution 61/37** (see p. 1483) on the commemoration of the sixtieth anniversary of the International Court of Justice.

The Security Council, in presidential statement **S/PRST/2006/28** (see p. 46), reaffirmed its commitment to the Charter and international law and to actively supporting the peaceful settlement of disputes.

Charter provisions relating to sanctions

Special Committee consideration. During the Special Committee's [A/61/33] consideration of the implementation of the Charter provisions related to assistance to third States affected by sanctions, support was expressed for continuing consideration of the issue within the Committee and through a working group of the Sixth Committee. The view was expressed that attention should be paid to discussions of the subject in other UN forums, such as the Security Council's informal working group on general issues of sanctions and the Analytical Support and Sanctions Monitoring Team. Some delegations called attention to the negative consequences of sanctions on civilian populations and third States and stressed the importance of minimizing them. Other delegations pointed out that assistance to third States affected by sanctions would contribute to the effectiveness of the sanctions regime. A view was expressed that the Security Council's primary responsibility in applying sanctions was accompanied by a parallel responsibility towards affected third States. Concerning possible measures, a view was expressed in favour of devising a system to assess the impact of preventive or enforcement measures on third States and of exploring ways to assist those States, including through financial arrangements and economic assistance. Some delegations felt that sanctions had been effectively applied against States, entities and groups threatening international peace and security, and remained an important tool to maintain peace and security without resorting to force. Sanctions should be carefully targeted in support of clear objectives, and their implementation should balance effectiveness with care to minimize harm to populations and third States.

The Committee discussed the revised working paper by the Russian Federation on "Declaration on the basic conditions and standard criteria for the introduction and implementation of sanctions and other coercive measures". Many delegations supported the adoption of the revised working paper by the Committee and favoured the format of a General Assembly declaration. However, other delegations did not support the working paper on the grounds that the Special Committee should not duplicate the work of other UN organs. The Russian Federation said that it would hold further consultations aimed at reaching a consensus. The Committee also addressed the Libyan Arab Jamahiriya revised working paper on the strengthening of certain principles concerning the impact and application of sanctions.

Report of Secretary-General. In response to General Assembly resolution 60/23 [YUN 2005, p. 1447], the Secretary-General submitted an August report [A/61/304] highlighting measures taken to further improve the procedures and working methods of the Security Council and its sanctions committees relating to assistance to third States affected by the application of sanctions. It also reviewed developments concerning the activities of the Assembly and the Economic and Social Council in the area of assistance to such States, and the Secretariat's arrangements relating to such assistance.

Improving the effectiveness of UN sanctions

Report of Working Group. In December, the Security Council President transmitted to the Council the report [S/2006/997] submitted by the Chairman of the informal working group of the Security Council on general issues of sanctions. The report recommended best practices with respect to sanctions design, implementation, evaluation and follow-up, sanctions committee working methods, monitoring and enforcement, and methodological standards and reporting format for expert groups.

The working group had been established in 2000 [YUN 2000, p. 1270] to develop general recommendations on how to improve the effectiveness of UN sanctions. Extending the group's mandate for one year in 2005 [YUN 2005, p. 1449], the Council tasked it with addressing several other issues, including the assessment of the unintended impact of sanctions and ways to assist affected untargeted States; the enforcement of targeted sanctions, especially asset freezes or travel bans targeting individuals or entities; and de-listing procedures in relation to targeted sanctions.

In January [S/2006/66], the Council's President announced the Council's agreement that Adamantios Th. Vassilakis (Greece) would serve as the working group Chairman until 31 December 2006.

During the year, the Council adopted several recommendations aimed at improving the effectiveness of its sanctions (see below).

Communication. On 14 June [A/60/887-S/2006/331], Germany, Sweden and Switzerland transmitted to the Presidents of the General Assembly and the Security Council a white paper prepared by the Watson Institute Targeted Sanctions Project of Brown University entitled "Strengthening targeted sanctions through fair and clear procedures". The paper, which was commissioned by those Governments, was intended to analyse current practices and recommend proposals for strengthening UN target sanctions procedures. The paper noted that recent challenges before various courts had raised important questions regarding targeted sanctions imposed under Chapter VII of the Charter. While no national court had invalidated those measures, the legal challenges could potentially affect the efficacy of targeted sanctions. Beyond procedural improvements, there was a need for some form of review mechanism to which individuals and entities might appeal decisions regarding their designation or listing for such sanctions. Mechanisms proposed included a review mechanism under the authority of the Council, such as a monitoring team, Ombudsman or Panel of Experts; an independent arbitral panel to consider delisting proposals; or judicial review of delisting decisions.

SECURITY COUNCIL ACTION

On 21 December [meeting 5605], the Security Council unanimously adopted **resolution 1732(2006)**. The draft [S/2006/1004] was prepared in consultations among Council members.

The Security Council,

Welcomes the report of the Informal Working Group on General Issues of Sanctions, established pursuant to paragraph 3 of the note by the President of the Security Council dated 17 April 2000.

Decides that the Working Group has fulfilled its mandate as contained in the note by the President of the Security Council dated 29 December 2005, to develop general recommendations on how to improve the effectiveness of United Nations sanctions;

Takes note with interest of the best practices and methods contained in the report of the Working Group, and requests its subsidiary bodies to take note as well.

Other sanctions measures

The Security Council, in presidential statement **S/PRST/2006/28** of 22 June (see p. 46), considered sanctions an important tool in the maintenance and restoration of peace and security and resolved to ensure that they were carefully targeted in support of clear objectives and were implemented in ways that balanced effectiveness against possible adverse consequences.

On 8 August [meeting 5507], the Security Council unanimously adopted **resolution 1699(2006)**. The draft [S/2006/616] was submitted by Argentina, Denmark, France, Japan, Slovakia, the United Kingdom and the United States.

The Security Council,

Recalling its resolution 1617(2005) requesting increased cooperation between the International Criminal Police Organization (Interpol) and the Committee established pursuant to resolution 1267(1999) (the "1267 Committee"),

Recalling also the cooperation agreement of 8 July 1997 between the United Nations and Interpol, and the exchange of letters of 8 December 2005 and 5 January 2006 supplementing the agreement,

Welcoming the constructive role that Interpol has played to help the 1267 Committee fulfil its mandate, inter alia, through the creation of the Interpol-United Nations Security Council Special Notices,

Noting that such cooperation with Interpol could also benefit the other sanctions committees established by the Security Council (the "Committees"), further noting that each committee might come up with its own conclusion in this regard,

Stressing that Security Council sanctions measures are often implemented under national law, including criminal law where applicable, and that enhanced cooperation between the United Nations and Interpol would enhance States' enforcement of those laws,

Emphasizing the obligations placed upon all Member States to implement, in full, the mandatory measures adopted by the Security Council,

1. *Requests* the Secretary-General to take the necessary steps to increase cooperation between the United Nations and Interpol in order to provide the Committees with better tools, to fulfil their mandates more effectively, and to give Member States better optional tools to implement those measures adopted by the Security Council and monitored by the Committees, as well as similar measures that may be adopted by the Security Council in the future, particularly the freezing of assets, travel bans, and arms embargoes;

2. *Encourages* Member States to use the tools offered by Interpol, particularly the I-24/7 global police communications system, to reinforce the implementation of such measures and similar measures that may be adopted by the Security Council in the future;

3. *Decides* to remain seized of the matter.

On 19 December [meeting 5599], the Security Council unanimously adopted **resolution 1730(2006)**. The draft [S/2006/996] was submitted by Argentina, Denmark, France, Greece, Japan, Peru, the Russian Federation, Slovakia, the United Kingdom and the United States.

The Security Council,

Recalling the statement of its President of 22 June 2006,

Emphasizing that sanctions are an important tool in the maintenance and restoration of international peace and security,

Further emphasizing the obligations placed upon all Member States to implement, in full, the mandatory measures adopted by the Security Council,

Continuing in its resolve to ensure that sanctions are carefully targeted in support of clear objectives and implemented in ways that balance effectiveness against possible adverse consequences,

Committed to ensuring that fair and clear procedures exist for placing individuals and entities on sanctions lists and for removing them, as well as for granting humanitarian exemptions,

1. *Adopts* the de-listing procedure set forth in the annex to the present resolution and requests the Secretary-General to establish within the Secretariat (Security Council Subsidiary Organs Branch), a focal point to receive de-listing requests and to perform the tasks described in the attached annex;

2. *Directs* the sanctions committees established by the Security Council, including those established pursuant to resolution 751(1992), 918(1994), 1132(1997), 1267(1999), 1518(2003), 1521(2005), 1533(2004), 1572(2004), 1591(2005), 1636(2005), and 1718(2006), to revise their guidelines accordingly;

3. *Decides* to remain seized of the matter.

Annex
De-listing procedure

The Security Council requests the Secretary-General to establish, within the Secretariat (Security Council Subsidiary Organs Branch), a focal point to receive de-listing requests. Petitioners seeking to submit a request for de-listing can do so either through the focal point process outlined below or through their State of residence or citizenship.

The focal point will perform the following tasks:

1. Receive de-listing requests from a petitioner (individual(s), groups, undertakings, and/or entities on the Sanctions Committee's lists).

2. Verify if the request is new or is a repeated request.

3. If it is a repeated request and if it does not contain any additional information, return it to the petitioner.

4. Acknowledge receipt of the request to the petitioner and inform the petitioner on the general procedure for processing that request.

5. Forward the request, for their information and possible comments to the designating government(s) and to the government(s) of citizenship and residence. Those governments are encouraged to consult with the designating government(s) before recommending de-listing. To this end, they may approach the focal point, which, if the designating state(s) so agree(s), will put them in contact with the designating state(s).

6. *(a)* If, after these consultations, any of these governments recommend de-listing, that government will forward its recommendation, either through the focal point or directly to the Chairman of the Sanctions Committee, accompanied by that government's explanation. The Chairman will then place the de-listing request on the Committee's agenda.

(b) If any of the governments, which were consulted on the de-listing request under paragraph 5 above oppose the request, the focal point will so inform the Committee and provide copies of the de-listing request. Any member of the Committee, which possesses information in support of the de-listing request, is encouraged to share such information with the governments that reviewed the de-listing request under paragraph 5 above.

(c) If, after a reasonable time (3 months), none of the governments which reviewed the de-listing request under paragraph 5 above comment, or indicate that they are working on the de-listing request to the Committee and require an additional definite period of time, the focal point will so notify all members of the Committee and provide copies of the de-listing request. Any member of the Committee may, after consultation with the designating government(s), recommend de-listing by forwarding the request to the Chairman of the Sanctions Committee, accompanied by an explanation. (Only one member of the Committee needs to recommend de-listing in order to place the issue on the Committee's agenda.) If after one month, no Committee member recommends de-listing, then it shall be deemed rejected and the Chairman of the Committee shall inform the focal point accordingly.

7. The focal point shall convey all communications, which it receives from Member States, to the Committee for its information.

8. Inform the petitioner:

(a) Of the decision of the Sanctions Committee to grant the de-listing petition; or

(b) That the process of consideration of the de-listing request within the Committee has been completed and that the petitioner remains on the list of the Committee.

Cooperation with Asian-African Legal Consultative Organization

Pursuant to General Assembly resolution 59/3 [YUN 2004, p. 1349], the Secretary-General, in his report on cooperation between the United Nations and regional and other organizations [A/61/256/Add.1], provided information on cooperation between the United Nations and the Asian-African Legal Consultative Organization (AALCO) from June 2004 to May 2006. In line with the cooperative framework agreed upon by the two organizations, both routinely consulted and exchanged information and documentation on matters of common interest in the area of international law, including the law of the sea, international trade law, international environmental law, human rights law, refugee law, humanitarian law and peaceful settlement of disputes. AALCO continued to orient its work programme in order to accord priority to matters of concern to the United Nations and to initiate action aimed at strengthening its role.

The report provided details on AALCO representation at UN meetings and conferences and UN representation at AALCO sessions; measures taken by AALCO to further the work of the General Assembly's Sixth Committee, to monitor progress in the work of the United Nations Commission on International Trade Law and to promote the ratification and implementation of the 1982 United Nations Convention on the Law of the Sea [YUN 1982, p. 181]; and AALCO ongoing study of refugee law and work, in close cooperation with the Office of the United Nations High Commissioner for Refugees. Also described were activities relating to issues on AALCO agenda, including environment and sustainable development; extraterritorial application of national legislation; deportation of Palestinians and other Israeli practices; cooperation against trafficking in women and children; legal protection of migrant workers; international terrorism; recent developments related to the work of the International Criminal Court; and elaboration of an international legal instrument against corruption. The report also covered the activities of the AALCO Centre for Research and Training and its annual publications.

In its statement before the Assembly on 20 October [meeting 39], India, as AALCO President for the year, encouraged the organization to expand its activities, citing in particular, the promotion of teaching and expertise in advising on international law issues; the offering of fellowships to Asian and African students for higher studies in international law; and the publication of books devoted to international law.

GENERAL ASSEMBLY ACTION

On 20 October [meeting 39], the General Assembly adopted **resolution 61/5** [draft: A/61/L.5 & Add.1] without vote [agenda item 108(b)].

Cooperation between the United Nations and the Asian-African Legal Consultative Organization

The General Assembly,

Recalling its resolutions 36/38 of 18 November 1981, 37/8 of 29 October 1982, 38/37 of 5 December 1983, 39/47 of 10 December 1984, 40/60 of 9 December 1985, 41/5 of 17 October 1986, 43/1 of 17 October 1988, 45/4 of 16 October 1990, 47/6 of 21 October 1992, 49/8 of 25 October 1994, 51/11 of 4 November 1996, 53/14 of 29 October 1998, 55/4 of 25 October 2000, 57/36 of 21 November 2002 and 59/3 of 22 October 2004,

Having considered the report of the Secretary-General on cooperation between the United Nations and the Asian-African Legal Consultative Organization,

Having heard the statement made by the Secretary-General of the Asian-African Legal Consultative Organization on the steps taken by the Consultative Organization to ensure continuing, close and effective cooperation between the two organizations,

Acknowledging in particular the close interaction between the Consultative Organization and the Sixth Committee,

1. *Takes note with appreciation* of the report of the Secretary-General;

2. *Recognizes* the continuing efforts of the Asian-African Legal Consultative Organization towards strengthening the role and function of the United Nations and its various organs in enhancing the rule of law and wider adherence to related international instruments;

3. *Notes with satisfaction* the commendable progress achieved towards enhancing cooperation between the United Nations, its agencies, other international organizations and the Consultative Organization;

4. *Notes with appreciation* the work of the Consultative Organization aimed at strengthening the efforts of the United Nations in respect of issues such as combating corruption, international terrorism and trafficking in women and children, as well as human rights issues;

5. *Also notes with appreciation* the initiative and efforts the Consultative Organization has undertaken to promote the objectives and principles set out in the United Nations Millennium Declaration, including wider acceptance of treaties deposited with the Secretary-General;

6. *Recommends* that, with a view to promoting close interaction between the Consultative Organization and the Sixth Committee, the consideration of the sub-item entitled "Cooperation between the United Nations and the Asian-African Legal Consultative Organization" should be scheduled to coincide with the deliberations of the Committee on the work of the International Law Commission;

7. *Requests* the Secretary-General to submit to the General Assembly at its sixty-third session a report on cooperation between the United Nations and the Consultative Organization;

8. *Decides* to include in the provisional agenda of its sixty-third session the sub-item entitled "Cooperation between the United Nations and the Asian-African Legal Consultative Organization".

Host country relations

At five meetings held in New York (18 January, 17 May, 2 August, 29 September and 30 October), the Committee on Relations with the Host

Country considered the following aspects of relations between the UN diplomatic community and the United States, the host country: transportation, including use of motor vehicles, parking and related matters; acceleration of immigration and customs procedures; entry visas issued by the host country; host country travel regulations; and the question of privileges and immunities.

The recommendations and conclusions on those items, approved by the Committee at its October meeting, were incorporated in its report [A/61/26]. The Committee expressed appreciation for the host country's efforts to maintain appropriate conditions for delegations and permanent missions accredited to the United Nations and anticipated that all issues raised at its meetings would be duly settled in a spirit of cooperation and in accordance with international law. Stressing the importance of the observance of privileges and immunities, the Committee emphasized the need to solve, through negotiations, problems that might arise in that regard for the normal functioning of accredited delegations and missions. It urged the host country to continue to take appropriate action, such as the training of police, security, customs and border control officers, with a view to maintaining respect for diplomatic privileges and immunities. In case of violations, the Committee urged the host country to ensure that such cases were properly investigated and remedied, in accordance with applicable law. Considering that the security of missions and the safety of their personnel were indispensable for their effective functioning, the Committee appreciated the host country's efforts to that end and anticipated that all measures to prevent any interference with the missions' functioning would continue to be taken.

Noting the problems experienced by some missions in connection with the implementation of the Parking Programme for Diplomatic Vehicles, in force since 2002 [YUN 2002, p. 1338], the Committee decided to conduct another review of the Programme's implementation during the General Assembly's sixty-first session and proceed in line with its outcome. The Committee noted the host country's comments on efforts made to improve the implementation of the Programme, as well as participation of the representatives of the City of New York in its meetings.

The Committee requested the host country to continue to bring to the attention of New York City officials reports about other problems experienced by permanent missions or their staff, in order to improve the conditions for their functioning and to promote compliance with international norms concerning diplomatic privileges and immunities. It anticipated that the host country would enhance its efforts to ensure the issuance, in a timely manner, of entry visas to representatives of Member States, pursuant to the Headquarters Agreement, to travel to New York on official UN business, and noted that a number of delegations had requested shortening the time frame applied by the host country for issuance of entry visas since the current time frame posed difficulties for the full-fledged participation of Member States in UN meetings.

Concerning travel regulations issued by the host country with regard to personnel of certain missions and staff members of the Secretariat of certain nationalities, the Committee noted the removal of some travel restrictions during the past year and urged the host country to remove all restrictions.

The Committee stressed the importance of permanent missions, their personnel and Secretariat personnel meeting their financial obligations. Finally, the Committee reiterated its appreciation to the representative of the United States Mission in charge of host country affairs and to the Host Country Affairs Section of the United States Mission to the United Nations, as well as to those local entities, in particular the New York City Commission for the United Nations, Consular Corps and Protocol, that contributed to its efforts to help accommodate the needs, interests and requirements of the diplomatic community and to promote mutual understanding between the diplomatic community and the people of the City of New York.

Communications. Letters were submitted to the Committee by Cuba [A/AC.154/367, A/AC.154/368] concerning the denial of the requests of its officials to travel to New York, and from Venezuela [A/61/474] protesting action taken by the United States Immigration Service.

GENERAL ASSEMBLY ACTION

On 4 December [meeting 64], the General Assembly, on the recommendation of the Sixth Committee [A/61/461], adopted **resolution 61/41** without vote [agenda item 148].

Report of the Committee on Relations with the Host Country

The General Assembly,

Having considered the report of the Committee on Relations with the Host Country,

Recalling Article 105 of the Charter of the United Nations, the Convention on the Privileges and Immunities of the United Nations, the Agreement between the United Nations and the United States of America regarding the Headquarters of the United Nations and the responsibilities of the host country,

Recalling also that, in accordance with paragraph 7 of General Assembly resolution 2819 (XXVI) of 15 December 1971, the Committee should consider, and advise the host country on, issues arising in connection with the implementation of the Agreement between the United Nations and the United States of America regarding the Headquarters of the United Nations,

Recognizing that effective measures should continue to be taken by the competent authorities of the host country, in particular to prevent any acts violating the security of missions and the safety of their personnel,

1. *Endorses* the recommendations and conclusions of the Committee on Relations with the Host Country contained in paragraph 86 of its report;

2. *Considers* that the maintenance of appropriate conditions for the normal work of the delegations and the missions accredited to the United Nations and the observance of their privileges and immunities, which is an issue of great importance, are in the interest of the United Nations and all Member States, and requests the host country to continue to solve, through negotiations, problems that might arise and to take all measures necessary to prevent any interference with the functioning of missions; and urges the host country to continue to take appropriate action, such as training of police, security, customs and border control officers, with a view to maintaining respect for diplomatic privileges and immunities and if violations occur to ensure that such cases are properly investigated and remedied, in accordance with applicable law;

3. *Notes* the problems experienced by some permanent missions in connection with the implementation of the Parking Programme for Diplomatic Vehicles and shall remain seized of the matter, with a view to continuing to maintain the proper implementation of the Parking Programme in a manner that is fair, non-discriminatory, effective and therefore consistent with international law, and also notes the decision of the Committee to conduct another review of the implementation of the Programme during the sixty-first session of the General Assembly and, subject to its outcome, will proceed accordingly;

4. *Requests* the host country to consider removing the remaining travel restrictions, notes that during the reporting period some travel restrictions previously imposed by the host country on staff of certain missions and staff members of the Secretariat of certain nationalities were removed, and, in this regard, notes the positions of affected States as reflected in the report of the Committee, of the Secretary-General and of the host country;

5. *Notes* that the Committee anticipates that the host country will enhance its efforts to ensure the issuance, in a timely manner, of entry visas to representatives of Member States, pursuant to article IV, section 11, of the Agreement between the United Nations and the United States of America regarding the Headquarters of the United Nations to travel to New York on United Nations business; and notes that the Committee anticipates that the host country will enhance efforts to facilitate participation, including visa issuance, of representatives of Member States in other United Nations meetings as appropriate;

6. *Notes also* that a number of delegations have requested shortening the time frame applied by the host country for issuance of entry visas to representatives of Member States, since this time frame poses difficulties for the full-fledged participation of Member States in United Nations meetings;

7. *Expresses its appreciation* for the efforts made by the host country, and hopes that the issues raised at the meetings of the Committee will continue to be resolved in a spirit of cooperation and in accordance with international law;

8. *Affirms* the importance of the Committee being in a position to fulfil its mandate and meet on short notice to deal with urgent and important matters concerning the relations between the United Nations and the host country, and in that connection requests the Secretariat and the Committee on Conferences to accord priority to requests from the Committee on Relations with the Host Country for conference-servicing facilities for meetings of that Committee that must be held while the General Assembly and its Main Committees are meeting, without prejudice to the requirements of those bodies and on an "as available" basis;

9. *Requests* the Secretary-General to remain actively engaged in all aspects of the relations of the United Nations with the host country;

10. *Requests* the Committee to continue its work in conformity with General Assembly resolution 2819 (XXVI);

11. *Decides* to include in the provisional agenda of its sixty-second session the item entitled "Report of the Committee on Relations with the Host Country".

Chapter IV

Law of the sea

The United Nations continued in 2006 to promote universal acceptance of the 1982 United Nations Convention on the Law of the Sea and its two implementing Agreements on the conservation and management of straddling fish stocks and highly migratory fish stocks and to facilitate the work of the International Tribunal for the Law of the Sea.

The three institutions created by the Convention–the International Seabed Authority, the International Tribunal for the Law of the Sea and the Commission on the Limits of the Continental Shelf–held sessions during the year. A ceremony to mark the tenth anniversary of the International Tribunal was held on 29 September at the seat of the Tribunal in Hamburg, Germany.

In May, a review conference in New York assessed the Agreement on the conservation and management of straddling and highly migratory fish stocks, four years after it had entered into force, and made recommendations to strengthen its implementation.

UN Convention on the Law of the Sea

Signatures and ratifications

In 2006, Belarus, Montenegro and Niue ratified or acceded to the United Nations Convention on the Law of the Sea (UNCLOS), bringing the number of parties to 152. The Convention, which was adopted by the Third United Nations Conference on the Law of the Sea in 1982 [YUN 1982, p. 178], entered into force on 16 November 1994 [YUN 1994, p. 1301].

Meeting of States Parties

The sixteenth Meeting of States Parties to the Convention (New York, 19-23 June) [SPLOS/148] discussed the 2005 activities of the International Tribunal for the Law of the Sea [YUN 2005, p. 1434] and took action on a number of Tribunal-related financial and administrative issues, including approving the 2007-2008 budget, amounting to €17.2 million, and the establishment of a staff pension committee. Also discussed were the 2005 activities of the International Seabed Authority (see p. 1554) and the Commission on the Limits of the Continental Shelf (see p. 1555), as well as the Secretary-General's report under article 319 of the Convention on his role as depositary.

Agreement relating to the Implementation of Part XI of the Convention

During 2006, the number of parties to the 1994 Agreement relating to the Implementation of Part XI of the Convention (governing exploitation of seabed resources beyond national jurisdiction), adopted by the General Assembly in resolution 48/263 [YUN 1994, p. 1301], reached 126. The Agreement, which entered into force on 28 July 1996 [YUN 1996, p. 1215], was to be interpreted and applied together with the Convention as a single instrument, and in the event of any inconsistency between the Agreement and Part XI of the Convention, the provisions of the Agreement would prevail. Any ratification of or accession to the Convention after 28 July 1994 represented consent to be bound by the Agreement. Parties to the Convention prior to the Agreement's adoption had to deposit a separate instrument of ratification of or accession to the Agreement.

Agreement relating to conservation and management of straddling fish stocks and highly migratory fish stocks

As at 31 December, the number of parties to the Agreement for the Implementation of the Provisions of the United Nations Convention on the Law of the Sea of 10 December 1982 relating to the Conservation and Management of Straddling Fish Stocks and Highly Migratory Fish Stocks [YUN 1995, p. 1334] reached 63. Referred to as the Fish Stocks Agreement, it entered into force on 11 December 2001 [YUN 2001, p. 1232].

Report of Secretary-General. In response to General Assembly resolution 60/31 [YUN 2005, p. 1425], the Secretary-General submitted a July report [A/61/154] on actions taken by States and regional fisheries management organizations (RFMOs) and arrangements to give effect to paragraphs 66 to 69 of Assembly resolution 59/25 [YUN 2004, p. 1322] on sustainable fisheries, regarding the impact of fishing on vulnerable marine ecosystems. The report described some of the most vulnerable marine ecosystems, fishing practices that, in specific circumstances, could be harmful, and the types of damage that could be caused, either directly or indirectly, by such practices. It also outlined actions taken by States, either by themselves or through RFMOs, to address destructive fishing practices, as well as such actions taken by RFMOs, including to expand their competence. FAO had established a regional fisheries body, the South West Indian Ocean Fisheries Commission [YUN 2004, p. 1487] in the southwestern Indian Ocean, to promote the sustainable development and utilization of fishery resources in areas under the national jurisdiction of the States in the region, as well as to encourage regional cooperation to that effect. In addition, a new regional agreement, the South Indian Ocean Fisheries Agreement, was adopted on 7 July, with the mandate to conserve and manage non-tuna resources in areas beyond the national jurisdiction of coastal States in the southern Indian Ocean.

The report concluded that States and RFMOs had adopted a wide range of measures to address the impact of destructive fishing practices on vulnerable marine ecosystems both in areas under their jurisdiction and beyond, such as the management of fishing capacity, prohibition of certain fishing practices, restrictions on gear types and their use in certain areas, measures to address by-catch and to improve control by flag States over their vessels fishing on the high seas, as well as improve monitoring, control and surveillance, compliance and enforcement, the establishment of marine protected areas, and more extensive use of scientific advice. However, it was difficult to assess the extent to which such measures were being effectively implemented. Efforts to protect fishery habitats on the high seas were lacking and fisheries that targeted newly discovered resources or those serving a new market opportunity proceeded unregulated. Many fisheries were not managed until they were overexploited and clearly depleted. Although the precautionary and ecosystem approaches had received wide recognition and were being incorporated into fisheries management policies in an increasing number of cases, there were still critical needs for habitat mapping in the deep sea, improved understanding of the impact of various types of fishing activities and greater knowledge of ecosystem processes and functions. Moreover, beyond the visual, short-term impacts on biodiversity, there was uncertainty on the long-term detrimental impacts of trawling on vulnerable marine ecosystems, and further research was urgently needed.

Review Conference

The Review Conference on the Agreement for the Implementation of the Provisions of the United Nations Convention on the Law of the Sea of 10 December 1982 relating to the Conservation and Management of Straddling Fish Stocks and Highly Migratory Fish Stocks was held in New York, from 22 to 26 May [A/CONF.210/2006/15]. Convened in accordance with article 36 of the Agreement [YUN 1995, p. 1334] and General Assembly resolution 59/25 [YUN 2004, p. 1322], the Conference assessed the effectiveness of the Agreement in securing the conservation and management of such fish stocks by reviewing and assessing the adequacy of its provisions and, if necessary, proposing means for strengthening their substance and methods of implementation to better address problems in the conservation and management of those stocks. The Conference had before it the Secretary-General's report submitted in accordance with Assembly resolution 59/25 [A/CONF.210/2006/1 & Corr.1], a Secretariat paper on elements for assessing the adequacy and effectiveness of the Agreement [A/CONF.210/2006/5], and a Secretariat note transmitting the financial report on the status of the Assistance Fund under Part VII of the Agreement [A/CONF.210/2006/2]. Also submitted to the Conference were notes verbales by Iceland on information measures it had adopted to implement the Agreement [A/CONF.210/2006/7] and updated information on the performance of the North-East Atlantic Fisheries Commission [A/CONF.210/2006/8]; Namibia, on progress in implementing the Agreement [A/CONF.210/2006/9]; Canada, on the post-Agreement overview of RFMOs regulation of straddling fish stocks and highly migratory fish stocks [A/CONF.210/2006/10]; and Argentina, Chile, Colombia, Cuba, Ecuador, El Salvador, Guatemala, Mexico and Peru, transmitting the Declaration of the Latin American and Caribbean countries ahead of the Review Conference [A/CONF.210/2006/12]. The Conference, chaired by David Balton (United States), adopted its report [A/CONF.210/2006/15], which contained the "Outcome of the Review Conference". Participants agreed to suspend the Conference and to reconvene at a date not later than 2011. They also agreed that further review of the effectiveness and implementation of the Agreement was necessary, and in that regard, decided to continue the informal consultations of States parties through the resumption of the Review Conference. The Secretary-General was requested to convene those consultations.

Outcome of Review Conference. The Review Conference affirmed that UNCLOS and the Straddling Fish Stocks and Highly Migratory Fish

Stocks Agreement provided the legal framework for conservation and management of such fish stocks. While acknowledging that fish stocks were a significant food source and livelihood for large parts of the world's population, the Conference expressed concern over the significant adverse impacts of overfishing on the state of fish stocks and the ecological integrity of the world's oceans.

The Conference's recommendations covered conservation and management of fish stocks; mechanisms for international cooperation and non-members; monitoring, control and surveillance, as well as compliance and enforcement; and developing States and non-parties to the Agreement. They also addressed the question of further review.

The Conference recommended that States, individually and collectively through RFMOs, should strengthen their commitment to adopt and fully implement conservation and management measures for fish stocks, including those that were unregulated; improve cooperation between flag States whose vessels fished on the high seas; establish regional fisheries management organizations or arrangements for the conservation and management of straddling and migratory fish stocks; commit to reducing urgently the capacity of the world's fishing fleet to levels commensurate with the sustainability of fish stocks; and eliminate subsidies that contributed to illegal, unregulated and unreported fishing, overfishing and overcapacity. States should also provide catch and effort data, and fishery-related information, and develop where they did not exist processes to strengthen data collection and reporting by RFMOs members.

The Conference underscored that international cooperation was necessary for the effective and long-term conservation and management of fish stocks and to modernize and strengthen RFMOs to ensure robust and systematic approaches in international fisheries governance. States should continue to strengthen the mandates of RFMOs to implement the Agreement and address participatory rights, including through the development of transparent criteria for allocating fishing opportunities.

States should also provide incentives to encourage non-members to join RFMOs, while improving their transparency by providing for the participation of intergovernmental and non-governmental organizations. In addition, States should examine and clarify the role of the "genuine link" in relation to the duty of flag States to exercise effective control over fishing vessels flying their flag.

The Conference agreed that effective compliance and enforcement of agreed conservation and management measures, supported by effective monitoring, control and surveillance, were critical to achieving the long-term conservation and sustainable use of the fish stocks under consideration.

As for monitoring, control, surveillance, compliance and enforcement, the Conference recommended that States strengthen effective control over vessels flying their flags and ensure that such vessels complied with RFMOs conservation and management measures. They should adopt stringent measures to regulate trans-shipment and develop a legally binding instrument on minimum standards for port State measures.

States should ensure that only fish taken in accordance with applicable conservation and management measures reached their markets; prohibit supply and refuelling vessels flying their flag from engaging in operations listed as engaging in illegal, unregulated and unreported fishing activities; ensure that vessels fishing on the high seas carried vessel-monitoring systems; and recognize that the development of alternative mechanisms for compliance and enforcement could facilitate accession to the Agreement by some States.

The Conference affirmed that increasing adherence to the Agreement was vital to promoting its full implementation. It recognized the need to provide assistance to developing States in data collection; scientific research; monitoring, control and surveillance; human resource development and information sharing; as well as technical training and assistance. It recommended that States urgently contribute to the assistance fund or other mechanisms to assist developing States in the conservation and management of straddling and highly migratory fish stocks.

Report of Secretary-General. To assist the conference, and pursuant to General Assembly resolution 59/25 [YUN 2004, p. 1322], the Secretary-General submitted a January report [A/CONF.210/2006/1], prepared in cooperation with the Food and Agriculture Organization of the United Nations (FAO), which provided an overview of the status of the fish stocks under consideration, the status of discrete high seas fish stocks and the possible impact that fishing the stocks concerned might have on other marine species. It reviewed the implementation of the Agreement by subregional and regional agreements or arrangements, as well as national legislation relating to its implementation. The report further examined the extent to which States parties, individually and through RFMOs and other multilateral mechanisms, took into account the special requirements of developing States in relation to the implementation of the Agreement and provided assistance to those States. Finally, the report examined issues that had prevented some States from becoming parties to the Agreement.

The report concluded that, while most of the straddling fish stocks were generally well studied, knowledge about some of them and many highly migratory fish stocks was uncertain, and information about discrete high seas fish stocks and associated species was limited. More scientific research was therefore needed to ascertain the status of those stocks and provide a basis for adopting conservation and management measures. Information provided by States and RFMOs indicated that substantive work had been undertaken to implement the Agreement. However, implementation was an ongoing process and much remained to be done.

GENERAL ASSEMBLY ACTION

On 8 December [meeting 71], the General Assembly adopted **resolution 61/105** [draft: A/61/L.38 & Add.1] without vote [agenda item 71 *(b)*].

Sustainable fisheries, including through the 1995 Agreement for the Implementation of the Provisions of the United Nations Convention on the Law of the Sea of 10 December 1982 relating to the Conservation and Management of Straddling Fish Stocks and Highly Migratory Fish Stocks, and related instruments

The General Assembly,

Reaffirming its resolutions 46/215 of 20 December 1991, 49/116 and 49/118 of 19 December 1994, 50/25 of 5 December 1995 and 57/142 of 12 December 2002, as well as other resolutions on large-scale pelagic drift-net fishing, unauthorized fishing in zones of national jurisdiction and on the high seas, fisheries by-catch and discards, and other developments, its resolutions 56/13 of 28 November 2001 and 57/143 of 12 December 2002 on the Agreement for the Implementation of the Provisions of the United Nations Convention on the Law of the Sea of 10 December 1982 relating to the Conservation and Management of Straddling Fish Stocks and Highly Migratory Fish Stocks ("the Agreement"), and its resolutions 58/14 of 24 November 2003, 59/25 of 17 November 2004 and 60/31 of 29 November 2005 on sustainable fisheries, including through the Agreement and related instruments,

Recalling the relevant provisions of the United Nations Convention on the Law of the Sea ("the Convention"), and bearing in mind the relationship between the Convention and the Agreement,

Recognizing that, in accordance with the Convention, the Agreement sets forth provisions concerning the conservation and management of straddling fish stocks and highly migratory fish stocks, including provisions on compliance and enforcement by the flag State and subregional and regional cooperation in enforcement, binding dispute settlement and the rights and obligations of States in authorizing the use of vessels flying their flags for fishing on the high seas, and specific provisions to address the requirements of developing States in relation to the conservation and management of straddling fish stocks and highly migratory fish stocks and the development of fisheries for such stocks,

Welcoming the fact that a growing number of States, and entities referred to in the Convention and in article 1, paragraph 2 *(b)*, of the Agreement, as well as regional and subregional fisheries management organizations and arrangements, have taken measures, as appropriate, towards the implementation of the provisions of the Agreement,

Welcoming also the work of the Food and Agriculture Organization of the United Nations and its Committee on Fisheries and the 2005 Rome Declaration on Illegal, Unreported and Unregulated Fishing, adopted by the Ministerial Meeting on Fisheries of the Food and Agriculture Organization of the United Nations on 12 March 2005, which calls for effective implementation of the various instruments already developed to ensure responsible fisheries, and recognizing that the Code of Conduct for Responsible Fisheries of the Food and Agriculture Organization of the United Nations ("the Code") and its associated international plans of action set out principles and global standards of behaviour for responsible practices for conservation of fisheries resources and the management and development of fisheries,

Noting with concern that effective management of marine capture fisheries has been made difficult in some areas by unreliable information and data caused by unreported and misreported fish catch and fishing effort and this lack of accurate data contributes to overfishing in some areas, and therefore welcoming the adoption of the Strategy for Improving Information on Status and Trends of Capture Fisheries and the development of the Fishery Resources Monitoring System (FIRMS) initiative by the Food and Agriculture Organization of the United Nations to improve knowledge and understanding of fishery status and trends,

Recognizing the significant contribution of sustainable fisheries to food security, income and wealth for present and future generations,

Recognizing also the urgent need for action at all levels to ensure the long-term sustainable use and management of fisheries resources through the wide application of the precautionary approach,

Deploring the fact that fish stocks, including straddling fish stocks and highly migratory fish stocks, in many parts of the world are overfished or subject to sparsely regulated and heavy fishing efforts, as a result of, inter alia, illegal, unreported and unregulated fishing, inadequate flag State control and enforcement, including monitoring, control and surveillance measures, inadequate regulatory measures, harmful fisheries subsidies and overcapacity,

Particularly concerned that illegal, unreported and unregulated fishing constitutes a serious threat to fish stocks and marine habitats and ecosystems, to the detriment of sustainable fisheries as well as the food security and the economies of many States, particularly developing States,

Recognizing the duty provided in the Convention, the Agreement to Promote Compliance with International Conservation and Management Measures by Fishing Vessels on the High Seas ("the Compliance Agreement"), the Agreement and the Code for flag States to exercise effective control over fishing vessels flying their flag, and vessels flying their flag which provide support to fishing vessels, to ensure that the activities of such fishing and support vessels do not undermine the effectiveness of conservation and management measures taken in accordance with international law and adopted at the national, subregional, regional or global levels,

Noting the obligation of all States, pursuant to the provisions of the Convention, to cooperate in the conservation and management of living marine resources, and recognizing the importance of coordination and cooperation at the global, regional, subregional as well as national levels in the areas, inter alia, of data collection, information-sharing, capacity-building and training for the conservation, management and sustainable development of marine living resources,

Noting with appreciation the report of the Review Conference on the Agreement ("the Review Conference"), held in New York from 22 to 26 May 2006, and welcoming the adoption of the recommendations therein, which assessed the effectiveness of the Agreement in securing the conservation and management of straddling and highly migratory fish stocks by reviewing and assessing the adequacy of its provisions and proposed means of strengthening the substance and methods of implementation of those provisions in order better to address any continuing problems in the conservation and management of those stocks, and also noting that the Conference agreed that there is a compelling need for all States and subregional and regional fisheries management organizations and arrangements to ensure the conservation and sustainable use of straddling and highly migratory fish stocks,

Noting with satisfaction that the Review Conference agreed to continue the informal consultations of States parties to the Agreement and to keep the Agreement under review through the resumption of the Conference at a date not later than 2011, to be agreed at a future informal consultation of States parties to the Agreement,

Calling attention to the need for more work to develop port State measures and schemes, and the critical need for cooperation with developing States to build their capacity in this regard,

Concerned that marine pollution from all sources, including vessels and, in particular, land-based sources, constitutes a serious threat to human health and safety, endangers fish stocks, marine biodiversity and marine habitats and has significant costs to local and national economies,

Recognizing that marine debris is a global transboundary pollution problem and that, due to the many different types and sources of marine debris, different approaches to their prevention and removal are necessary,

Noting that the contribution of sustainable aquaculture to global fish supplies continues to respond to opportunities in developing countries to enhance local food security and poverty alleviation and, together with efforts of other aquaculture producing countries, will make a significant contribution to meeting future demands in fish consumption, bearing in mind article 9 of the Code,

Calling attention to the circumstances affecting fisheries in many developing States, in particular African States and small island developing States, and recognizing the urgent need for capacity-building, including the transfer of marine technology and in particular fisheries-related technology, to enhance the ability of such States to meet their obligations and exercise their rights under international instruments, in order to realize the benefits from fisheries resources,

Recognizing the need for appropriate measures to minimize waste, discards, loss of fishing gear and other factors, which adversely affect fish stocks,

Recognizing also the importance of applying ecosystem approaches to oceans management and the need to integrate such approaches into fisheries conservation and management, and in this regard welcoming the report of the seventh meeting of the United Nations Open-ended Informal Consultative Process on Oceans and the Law of the Sea, held in New York from 12 to 16 June 2006,

Recognizing further the economic and cultural importance of sharks in many countries, the biological importance of sharks in the marine ecosystem, the vulnerability of certain shark species to overexploitation, some of which are threatened with extinction, and the need for measures to promote the long-term sustainability of shark populations and fisheries, and the relevance of the International Plan of Action for the Conservation and Management of Sharks, adopted by the Food and Agriculture Organization of the United Nations in 1999, in providing development guidance of such measures,

Reaffirming its support for the initiative of the Food and Agriculture Organization of the United Nations and relevant regional and subregional fisheries management organizations and arrangements on the conservation and management of sharks, while noting with concern that only a small number of countries have implemented the International Plan of Action for the Conservation and Management of Sharks,

Taking note with appreciation of the report of the Secretary-General on the impacts of fishing on vulnerable marine ecosystems: actions taken by States and regional fisheries management organizations and arrangements to give effect to paragraphs 66 to 69 of General Assembly resolution 59/25 on sustainable fisheries, regarding the impacts of fishing on vulnerable marine ecosystems, in particular its useful role in gathering and disseminating information on this issue,

Expressing concern that the practice of large-scale pelagic drift-net fishing remains a threat to marine living resources, although the incidence of this practice has continued to be low in most regions of the world's oceans and seas,

Emphasizing that efforts should be made to ensure that the implementation of resolution 46/215 in some parts of the world does not result in the transfer to other parts of the world of drift nets that contravene the resolution,

Expressing concern over reports of continued losses of seabirds, particularly albatrosses and petrels, as well as other marine species, including sharks, fin-fish species and marine turtles, as a result of incidental mortality in fishing operations, particularly longline fishing, and other activities, while recognizing considerable efforts to reduce by-catch in longline fishing by States and through various regional fisheries management organizations and arrangements,

I

Achieving sustainable fisheries

1. *Reaffirms* the importance it attaches to the long-term conservation, management and sustainable use of the marine living resources of the world's oceans and seas and the obligations of States to cooperate to this end, in accordance with international law, as reflected in the relevant provisions of the Convention, in particular the provisions on cooperation set out in Part V and Part VII, section 2, of the Convention, and where applicable, the Agreement;

2. *Encourages* States to give due priority to the implementation of the Plan of Implementation of the World Summit on Sustainable Development ("Johannesburg Plan of Implementation"), in relation to achieving sustainable fisheries;

3. *Emphasizes* the obligations of flag States to discharge their responsibilities, in accordance with the Convention and the Agreement, to ensure compliance by vessels flying their flag with the conservation and management measures adopted and in force with respect to fisheries resources on the high seas;

4. *Calls upon* all States that have not done so, in order to achieve the goal of universal participation, to become parties to the Convention, which sets out the legal framework within which all activities in the oceans and seas must be carried out, taking into account the relationship between the Convention and the Agreement;

5. *Calls upon* all States, directly or through regional fisheries management organizations and arrangements, to apply widely, in accordance with international law and the Code, the precautionary approach and an ecosystem approach to the conservation, management and exploitation of fish stocks, including straddling fish stocks, highly migratory fish stocks and discrete high seas fish stocks, and also calls upon States parties to the Agreement to implement fully the provisions of article 6 of the Agreement as a matter of priority;

6. *Encourages* States to increase their reliance on scientific advice in developing, adopting and implementing conservation and management measures, and to increase their efforts to promote science for conservation and management measures that apply, in accordance with international law, the precautionary approach and an ecosystem approach to fisheries management, enhancing understanding of ecosystem approaches, in order to ensure the long-term conservation and sustainable use of marine living resources, and in this regard encourages the implementation of the international Strategy for Improving Information on Status and Trends of Capture Fisheries of the Food and Agriculture Organization of the United Nations as a framework for the improvement and understanding of fishery status and trends;

7. *Also encourages* States to apply the precautionary approach and an ecosystem approach in adopting and implementing conservation and management measures addressing, inter alia, by-catch, pollution, overfishing, and protecting habitats of specific concern, taking into account existing guidelines developed by the Food and Agriculture Organization of the United Nations;

8. *Calls upon* States and regional fisheries management organizations and arrangements to collect and, where appropriate, report to the Food and Agriculture Organization of the United Nations required catch and effort data, and fishery-related information, in a complete, accurate and timely way, including for straddling fish stocks and highly migratory fish stocks within and beyond areas under national jurisdiction, discrete high seas fish stocks, and by-catch and discards; and where they do not exist, to establish processes to strengthen data collection and reporting by members of regional fisheries management organizations and arrangements, including through regular reviews of member compliance with such obligations, and when such obligations are not met, require the member concerned to rectify the problem, including through the preparation of plans of action with timelines;

9. *Invites* States and regional fisheries management organizations and arrangements to cooperate with the Food and Agriculture Organization of the United Nations in the implementation and further development of the Fishery Resources Monitoring System (FIRMS) initiative;

10. *Urges* States, including those working through subregional or regional fisheries management organizations and arrangements, to implement fully the International Plan of Action for the Conservation and Management of Sharks, notably through the collection of scientific data regarding shark catches and the adoption of conservation and management measures, particularly where shark catches from directed and non-directed fisheries have a significant impact on vulnerable or threatened shark stocks, in order to ensure the conservation and management of sharks and their long-term sustainable use, including by banning directed shark fisheries conducted solely for the purpose of harvesting shark fins and by taking measures for other fisheries to minimize waste and discards from shark catches, and to encourage the full use of dead sharks;

11. *Urges* States to eliminate barriers to trade in fish and fisheries products which are not consistent with their rights and obligations under the World Trade Organization agreements, taking into account the importance of the trade in fish and fisheries products, particularly for developing countries;

12. *Urges* States and relevant international and national organizations to provide for participation of small-scale fishery stakeholders in related policy development and fisheries management strategies in order to achieve long-term sustainability for such fisheries, consistent with the duty to ensure the proper conservation and management of fisheries resources;

II

Implementation of the 1995 Agreement for the Implementation of the Provisions of the United Nations Convention on the Law of the Sea of 10 December 1982 relating to the Conservation and Management of Straddling Fish Stocks and Highly Migratory Fish Stocks

13. *Calls upon* all States, and entities referred to in the Convention and in article 1, paragraph 2 (*b*), of the Agreement, that have not done so to ratify or accede to the Agreement and in the interim to consider applying it provisionally;

14. *Calls upon* States parties to the Agreement to harmonize, as a matter of priority, their national legislation with the provisions of the Agreement, and to ensure that the provisions of the Agreement are effectively implemented into regional fisheries management organizations and arrangements of which they are a member;

15. *Emphasizes* the importance of those provisions of the Agreement relating to bilateral, regional and subregional cooperation in enforcement, and urges continued efforts in this regard;

16. *Calls upon* all States to ensure that their vessels comply with the conservation and management measures that have been adopted by regional and subregional fisheries management organizations and arrangements in accordance with relevant provisions of the Convention and of the Agreement;

17. *Urges* States parties to the Agreement, in accordance with article 21, paragraph 4, thereof to inform, either directly or through the relevant regional or subregional fisheries management organization or arrangement, all States whose vessels fish on the high seas in the same region or subregion of the form of identification issued by those States parties to officials duly authorized to carry out boarding and inspection functions in accordance with articles 21 and 22 of the Agreement;

18. *Also urges* States parties to the Agreement, in accordance with article 21, paragraph 4, to designate an appropriate authority to receive notifications pursuant to article 21 and to give due publicity to such designation through the relevant subregional or regional fisheries management organization or arrangement;

19. *Calls upon* States individually and, as appropriate, through regional and subregional fisheries management organizations and arrangements with competence over discrete high seas fish stocks, to adopt the necessary measures to ensure the long-term conservation, management and sustainable use of such stocks in accordance with the Convention and consistent with the general principles set forth in the Agreement;

20. *Invites* States and international financial institutions and organizations of the United Nations system to provide assistance according to Part VII of the Agreement, including, if appropriate, the development of special financial mechanisms or instruments to assist developing States, in particular the least developed among them and small island developing States, to enable them to develop their national capacity to exploit fishery resources, including developing their domestically flagged fishing fleet, value-added processing and the expansion of their economic base in the fishing industry, consistent with the duty to ensure the proper conservation and management of fisheries resources;

21. *Invites* States to assist developing States in enhancing their participation in regional fisheries management organizations or arrangements, including through facilitating access to fisheries for straddling fish stocks and highly migratory fish stocks, in accordance with article 25, paragraph 1 (*b*), of the Agreement, taking into account the need to ensure that such access benefits the developing States concerned and their nationals;

22. *Notes with satisfaction* that the Assistance Fund under Part VII of the Agreement has begun to operate and consider applications for assistance by developing States parties to the Agreement, and encourages States, intergovernmental organizations, international financial institutions, national institutions and non-governmental organizations, as well as natural and juridical persons, to make voluntary financial contributions to the Assistance Fund;

23. *Requests* that the Food and Agriculture Organization of the United Nations and the Division for Ocean Affairs and the Law of the Sea of the Office of Legal Affairs of the Secretariat further publicize the availability of assistance through the Assistance Fund, and solicit views from developing States parties to the Agreement regarding the application and award procedures of the Fund, and consider changes where necessary to improve the process;

24. *Encourages* States, individually and, as appropriate, through regional and subregional fisheries management organizations and arrangements, to implement the recommendations of the Review Conference;

25. *Recalls* paragraph 6 of resolution 56/13, and requests the Secretary-General to convene in 2007, in accordance with past practice, a sixth round of informal consultations of States parties to the Agreement, for the purposes and objectives of considering the national, regional, subregional and global implementation of the Agreement, as well as considering initial preparatory steps for the resumption of the Review Conference convened by the Secretary-General pursuant to article 36 of the Agreement, and making any appropriate recommendation to the General Assembly;

26. *Requests* the Secretary-General to invite States, and entities referred to in the Convention and in article 1, paragraph 2 (*b*), of the Agreement, not party to the Agreement, as well as the United Nations Development Programme, the Food and Agriculture Organization of the United Nations and other specialized agencies, the

Commission on Sustainable Development, the World Bank, the Global Environment Facility and other relevant international financial institutions, subregional and regional fisheries management organizations and arrangements, other fisheries bodies, other relevant intergovernmental bodies and relevant non-governmental organizations, in accordance with past practice, to attend the sixth round of informal consultations of States parties to the Agreement as observers;

27. *Requests* the Food and Agriculture Organization of the United Nations to initiate arrangements with States for the collection and dissemination of data on fishing in the high seas by vessels flying their flag at the subregional and regional levels where none exist;

28. *Also requests* the Food and Agriculture Organization of the United Nations to revise its global fisheries statistics database to provide information on straddling fish stocks, highly migratory fish stocks and discrete high seas fish stocks on the basis of where the catch is taken;

III

Related fisheries instruments

29. *Emphasizes* the importance of the effective implementation of the provisions of the Compliance Agreement, and urges continued efforts in this regard;

30. *Calls upon* all States and other entities referred to in article X, paragraph 1, of the Compliance Agreement that have not yet become parties to that Agreement to do so as a matter of priority and, in the interim, to consider applying it provisionally;

31. *Urges* States and subregional and regional fisheries management organizations and arrangements to implement and promote the application of the Code within their areas of competence;

32. *Urges* States to develop and implement, as a matter of priority, national and, as appropriate, regional plans of action to put into effect the international plans of action of the Food and Agriculture Organization of the United Nations;

IV

Illegal, unreported and unregulated fishing

33. *Emphasizes once again its serious concern* that illegal, unreported and unregulated fishing remains one of the greatest threats to marine ecosystems and continues to have serious and major implications for the conservation and management of ocean resources, and renews its call upon States to comply fully with all existing obligations and to combat such fishing and urgently to take all necessary steps to implement the International Plan of Action to Prevent, Deter and Eliminate Illegal, Unreported and Unregulated Fishing of the Food and Agriculture Organization of the United Nations;

34. *Urges* States to exercise effective control over their nationals, including beneficial owners, and vessels flying their flag in order to prevent and deter them from engaging in or supporting illegal, unreported and unregulated fishing activities, and to facilitate mutual assistance to ensure that such actions can be investigated and proper sanctions imposed;

35. *Also urges* States to take effective measures, at the national, regional and global levels, to deter the activities, including illegal, unreported and unregulated fishing, of any vessel which undermines conservation and management measures that have been adopted by regional and subregional fisheries management organizations and arrangements in accordance with international law;

36. *Calls upon* States not to permit vessels flying their flag to engage in fishing on the high seas or in areas under the national jurisdiction of other States, unless duly authorized by the authorities of the States concerned and in accordance with the conditions set out in the authorization, and to take specific measures, including deterring the reflagging of vessels by their nationals, in accordance with the relevant provisions of the Convention, the Agreement and the Compliance Agreement, to control fishing operations by vessels flying their flag;

37. *Reaffirms* the need to strengthen, where necessary, the international legal framework for intergovernmental cooperation, in particular at the subregional and regional levels, in the management of fish stocks and in combating illegal, unreported and unregulated fishing, in a manner consistent with international law, and for States and entities referred to in the Convention and in article 1, paragraph 2 (*b*), of the Agreement to collaborate in efforts to address these types of fishing activities, including, inter alia, the development and implementation of vessel monitoring systems and the listing of vessels in order to prevent illegal, unreported and unregulated fishing activities and, where appropriate and consistent with international law, trade monitoring schemes, including to collect global catch data, through subregional and regional fisheries management organizations and arrangements;

38. *Calls upon* States to take all measures consistent with international law necessary to prevent, deter and eliminate illegal, unreported and unregulated fishing activities, such as developing measures consistent with national law to prohibit vessels flying their flag from supporting vessels engaging in illegal, unreported and unregulated fishing activities, including those listed by regional fisheries management organizations or arrangements;

39. *Also calls upon* States to take all necessary measures consistent with international law, without prejudice to reasons of force majeure or distress, including the prohibition of vessels from accessing their ports followed by a report to the flag State concerned, when there is clear evidence that they are or have been engaged in or have supported illegal, unreported and unregulated fishing, or when they refuse to give information either on the origin of the catch or on the authorization under which the catch has been made;

40. *Urges* further international action to eliminate illegal, unreported and unregulated fishing by vessels flying "flags of convenience" as well as to require that a "genuine link" be established between States and fishing vessels flying their flags, and calls upon States to implement the 2005 Rome Declaration on Illegal, Unreported and Unregulated Fishing as a matter of priority;

41. *Urges* States individually and collectively through regional fisheries management organizations and arrangements to cooperate to clarify the role of the "genuine link" in relation to the duty of States to exercise effective control over fishing vessels flying their flag and to develop appropriate processes to assess performance of States with respect to implementing the obligations regarding fishing vessels flying their flag set out in relevant international instruments;

42. *Recognizes* the need for enhanced port State controls to combat illegal, unreported and unregulated fishing, and urges States to cooperate, in particular at the regional level and through subregional and regional fisheries management organizations and arrangements, to adopt all necessary port measures, consistent with international law taking into account article 23 of the Agreement, particularly those identified in the Model Scheme on Port State Measures to Combat Illegal, Unreported, and Unregulated Fishing, adopted by the Food and Agriculture Organization of the United Nations in 2005, and to promote the development and application of minimum standards at the regional level;

43. *Encourages* States to initiate, as soon as possible, a process within the Food and Agriculture Organization of the United Nations to develop, as appropriate, a legally binding instrument on minimum standards for port State measures, building on the Model Scheme on Port State Measures to Combat Illegal, Unreported, and Unregulated Fishing and the International Plan of Action to Prevent, Deter and Eliminate Illegal, Unreported and Unregulated Fishing;

44. *Encourages* States, with respect to vessels flying their flag, and port States, to make every effort to share data on landings and catch quotas, and in this regard encourages regional fisheries management organizations or arrangements to consider developing open databases containing such data for the purpose of enhancing the effectiveness of fisheries management;

45. *Calls upon* States to take all necessary measures to ensure that vessels flying their flag do not engage in trans-shipment of fish caught by fishing vessels engaged in illegal, unreported and unregulated fishing;

46. *Urges* States, individually and through regional fisheries management organizations and arrangements, to adopt and implement internationally agreed market-related measures in accordance with international law, including principles, rights and obligations established in World Trade Organization agreements, as called for in the International Plan of Action to Prevent, Deter and Eliminate Illegal, Unreported and Unregulated Fishing;

V

Monitoring, control and surveillance and compliance and enforcement

47. *Calls upon* States in accordance with international law to strengthen implementation of or, where they do not exist, adopt comprehensive monitoring, control and surveillance measures and compliance and enforcement schemes individually and within those regional fisheries management organizations or arrangements in which they participate in order to provide an appropriate framework for promoting compliance with agreed conservation and management measures, and further urges enhanced coordination among all relevant States and regional fisheries management organizations and arrangements in these efforts;

48. *Encourages* further work by competent international organizations, including the Food and Agriculture Organization of the United Nations and subregional and regional fisheries management organizations and arrangements, to develop guidelines on flag State control of fishing vessels;

49. *Urges* States, individually and through relevant regional fisheries management organizations and arrangements, to establish mandatory vessel monitoring, control and surveillance systems, in particular to require that vessel monitoring systems be carried by all vessels fishing on the high seas as soon as practicable, and in the case of large-scale fishing vessels no later than December 2008, and share information on fisheries enforcement matters;

50. *Calls upon* States, individually and through regional fisheries management organizations or arrangements, to strengthen or establish, consistent with national and international law, positive or negative lists of vessels fishing within the areas covered by relevant regional fisheries management organizations and arrangements in order to verify compliance with conservation and management measures and identify products from illegal, unreported and unregulated catches, and encourages improved coordination among all parties and regional fisheries management organizations and arrangements in sharing and using this information, taking into account the forms of cooperation with developing States as set out in article 25 of the Agreement;

51. *Requests* States and relevant international bodies to develop, in accordance with international law, more effective measures to trace fish and fishery products to enable importing States to identify fish or fishery products caught in a manner that undermines international conservation and management measures agreed in accordance with international law, taking into account the special requirements of developing States and the forms of cooperation with developing States as set out in article 25 of the Agreement, and at the same time to recognize the importance of market access, in accordance with provisions 11.2.4, 11.2.5 and 11.2.6 of the Code, for fish and fishery products caught in a manner that is in conformity with such international measures;

52. *Encourages* States to establish and undertake cooperative surveillance and enforcement activities in accordance with international law to strengthen and enhance efforts to ensure compliance with conservation and management measures, and prevent and deter illegal, unreported and unregulated fishing;

53. *Urges* States, individually and through regional fisheries management organizations or arrangements, to develop and adopt effective measures to regulate trans-shipment, in particular at-sea trans-shipment, in order

to, inter alia, monitor compliance, collect and verify fisheries data, and to prevent and suppress illegal, unregulated and unreported fishing activities in accordance with international law; and, in parallel, encourage and support the Food and Agriculture Organization of the United Nations in studying the current practices of transshipment as it relates to fishing operations for straddling fish stocks and highly migratory fish stocks and produce a set of guidelines for this purpose;

54. *Encourages* States to join and actively participate in the existing voluntary International Monitoring, Control and Surveillance Network for Fisheries-Related Activities and to consider supporting, when appropriate, transformation of the Monitoring, Control and Surveillance Network in accordance with international law into an international unit with dedicated resources to further assist Network members, taking into account the forms of cooperation with developing States as set out in article 25 of the Agreement;

55. *Notes with satisfaction* the completion of the first Global Fisheries Enforcement Training Conference, held in Kuala Lumpur from 18 to 22 July 2005 and hosted by the Government of Malaysia in cooperation with the Monitoring, Control and Surveillance Network and the Fish Code programme of the Food and Agriculture Organization of the United Nations, and encourages widespread participation in the upcoming Second Global Fisheries Enforcement Training Conference, to be held in Trondheim, Norway, in August 2008 and sponsored by the Norwegian Directorate of Fisheries in conjunction with the Network;

56. *Encourages* States to cooperate in the development of a comprehensive global record within the Food and Agriculture Organization of the United Nations of fishing vessels, including refrigerated transport vessels and supply vessels, that incorporates available information on beneficial ownership, subject to confidentiality requirements in accordance with national law, as called for in the 2005 Rome Declaration on Illegal, Unreported and Unregulated Fishing;

VI

Fishing overcapacity

57. *Calls upon* States to commit to urgently reducing the capacity of the world's fishing fleets to levels commensurate with the sustainability of fish stocks, through the establishment of target levels and plans or other appropriate mechanisms for ongoing capacity assessment, while avoiding the transfer of fishing capacity to other fisheries or areas in a manner that undermines the sustainable management of fish stocks, including, inter alia, those areas where fish stocks are overexploited or in a depleted condition, and recognizing in this context the legitimate rights of developing States to develop their fisheries for straddling fish stocks and highly migratory fish stocks consistent with article 25 of the Agreement, article 5 of the Code, and paragraph 10 of the International Plan of Action for the Management of Fishing Capacity;

58. *Urges* States to eliminate subsidies that contribute to illegal, unreported and unregulated fishing and to fishing overcapacity, while completing the efforts undertaken at the World Trade Organization in accordance with the Doha Declaration to clarify and improve its disciplines on fisheries subsidies, taking into account the importance of this sector, including small-scale and artisanal fisheries and aquaculture, to developing countries;

VII

Large-scale pelagic drift-net fishing

59. *Reaffirms* the importance it attaches to continued compliance with its resolution 46/215 and other subsequent resolutions on large-scale pelagic drift-net fishing, and urges States and entities referred to in the Convention and in article 1, paragraph 2 (*b*), of the Agreement to enforce fully the measures recommended in those resolutions;

VIII

Fisheries by-catch and discards

60. *Urges* States, regional and subregional fisheries management organizations and arrangements and other relevant international organizations that have not done so to take action to reduce or eliminate by-catch, catch by lost or abandoned gear, fish discards and post-harvest losses, including juvenile fish, consistent with international law and relevant international instruments, including the Code, and in particular to consider measures including, as appropriate, technical measures related to fish size, mesh size or gear, discards, closed seasons and areas and zones reserved for selected fisheries, particularly artisanal fisheries, the establishment of mechanisms for communicating information on areas of high concentration of juvenile fish, taking into account the importance of ensuring confidentiality of such information, and support for studies and research that will reduce or eliminate by-catch of juvenile fish;

61. *Encourages* States and entities referred to in the Convention and in article 1, paragraph 2 (*b*), of the Agreement to give due consideration to participation, as appropriate, in regional and subregional instruments and organizations with mandates to conserve non-target species taken incidentally in fishing operations;

62. *Requests* States and regional fisheries management organizations and arrangements to urgently implement, as appropriate, the measures recommended in the Guidelines to Reduce Sea Turtle Mortality in Fishing Operations and the International Plan of Action for Reducing Incidental Catch of Seabirds in Longline Fisheries of the Food and Agriculture Organization of the United Nations in order to prevent the decline of sea turtles and seabird populations by reducing by-catch and increasing post-release survival in their fisheries, including through research and development of gear and bait alternatives, promoting the use of available by-catch mitigation technology, and promotion and strengthening of data-collection programmes to obtain standardized information to develop reliable estimates of the by-catch of these species;

IX

Subregional and regional cooperation

63. *Urges* coastal States and States fishing on the high seas, in accordance with the Convention and the Agreement, to pursue cooperation in relation to straddling fish stocks and highly migratory fish stocks, either directly or through appropriate subregional or regional fisheries management organizations or arrangements, to ensure the effective conservation and management of such stocks;

64. *Urges* States fishing for straddling fish stocks and highly migratory fish stocks on the high seas, and relevant coastal States, where a subregional or regional fisheries management organization or arrangement has the competence to establish conservation and management measures for such stocks, to give effect to their duty to cooperate by becoming members of such an organization or participants in such an arrangement, or by agreeing to apply the conservation and management measures established by such an organization or arrangement, or to otherwise ensure that no vessel flying their flag be authorized to access the fisheries resources to which regional fisheries management organizations and arrangements or conservation and management measures established by such organizations or arrangements apply;

65. *Invites*, in this regard, subregional and regional fisheries management organizations and arrangements to ensure that all States having a real interest in the fisheries concerned may become members of such organizations or participants in such arrangements, in accordance with the Convention and the Agreement;

66. *Encourages* relevant coastal States and States fishing on the high seas for a straddling fish stock or a highly migratory fish stock, where there is no subregional or regional fisheries management organization or arrangement to establish conservation and management measures for such stocks, to cooperate to establish such an organization or enter into another appropriate arrangement to ensure the conservation and management of such stocks, and to participate in the work of the organization or arrangement;

67. *Welcomes* the adoption of conservation measures by the South-East Atlantic Fisheries Organization at its third annual meeting, held in Windhoek on 4 October 2006, including an interim prohibition of fishing activities in ten marine areas with prominent seamounts, and urges all signatory States and other States whose vessels fish within the area of the Convention on the Conservation and Management of Fishery Resources in the South-East Atlantic Ocean for fishery resources covered by that Convention to become parties to that Convention as a matter of priority and, in the interim, to ensure that vessels flying their flags fully comply with the measures adopted;

68. *Also welcomes* the adoption of the South Indian Ocean Fisheries Agreement in Rome on 7 July 2006, encourages signatory States and States having a real interest to become parties to that Agreement, and urges those States to agree on and implement interim measures to ensure the conservation and management of the fisheries resources and their marine ecosystems and habitats in the area to which that Agreement applies until such time as that Agreement enters into force;

69. *Further welcomes* the initiation and progress of negotiations to establish regional and subregional fisheries management organizations or arrangements in several fisheries, in particular in the South Pacific and North-West Pacific, encourages States having a real interest to participate in such negotiations, urges participants to expedite those negotiations and to apply provisions of the Convention and the Agreement to their work, and further urges participants to agree on and implement interim conservation and management measures until such regional and subregional fisheries management organizations or arrangements are established;

70. *Urges* further efforts by regional fisheries management organizations and arrangements, as a matter of priority, in accordance with international law, to strengthen and modernize their mandates and the measures adopted by such organizations or arrangements, to implement modern approaches to fisheries management as reflected in the Agreement and other relevant international instruments relying on the best scientific information available and application of the precautionary approach, and incorporating an ecosystem approach to fisheries management and biodiversity considerations, where these aspects are lacking, to ensure that they effectively contribute to long-term conservation and management and sustainable use of marine living resources;

71. *Urges* States to strengthen and enhance cooperation among existing and developing regional fisheries management organizations and arrangements in which they participate, including increased communication and further coordination of measures, and in this regard encourages wide participation in the joint tuna regional fisheries management organization and arrangement meeting that will be hosted by the Government of Japan in 2007, and encourages members of other existing regional fisheries management organizations or arrangements and participants in establishing new regional fisheries management organizations or arrangements to hold similar consultations;

72. *Urges* regional fisheries management organizations and arrangements to improve transparency and to ensure that their decision-making processes are fair and transparent, rely on best scientific information available, incorporate the precautionary approach and ecosystem approaches, address participatory rights, including through, inter alia, the development of transparent criteria for allocating fishing opportunities which reflects, where appropriate, the relevant provisions of the Agreement, taking due account, inter alia, of the status of the relevant stocks and the respective interests in the fishery, and strengthen integration, coordination and cooperation with other relevant fisheries organizations, regional seas arrangements and other relevant international organizations;

73. *Urges* States, through their participation in regional fisheries management organizations and arrangements, to undertake, on an urgent basis, performance

reviews of those regional fisheries management organizations and arrangements, initiated either by the organization or arrangement itself or with external partners, including in cooperation with the Food and Agriculture Organization of the United Nations, using transparent criteria based on the provisions of the Agreement and other relevant instruments, including the best practices of regional fisheries management organizations or arrangements; and further encourages that such performance reviews include some element of independent evaluation and that the results be made publicly available, noting that the North East Atlantic Fisheries Commission has completed a performance review;

74. *Also urges* States to cooperate to develop best practice guidelines for regional fisheries management organizations and arrangements and to apply, to the extent possible, those guidelines to organizations and arrangements in which they participate;

75. *Encourages* the development of regional guidelines for States to use in establishing sanctions, for non-compliance by vessels flying their flag and by their nationals, to be applied in accordance with national law, that are adequate in severity for effectively securing compliance, deterring further violations and depriving offenders of the benefits deriving from their illegal activities, as well as in evaluating their systems of sanctions to ensure that they are effective in securing compliance and deterring violations;

X

Responsible fisheries in the marine ecosystem

76. *Encourages* States to apply by 2010 the ecosystem approach, notes the Reykjavik Declaration on Responsible Fisheries in the Marine Ecosystem and decision VII/11 and other relevant decisions of the Conference of the Parties to the Convention on Biological Diversity, notes the work of the Food and Agriculture Organization of the United Nations related to guidelines for the implementation of the ecosystem approach to fisheries management, and also notes the importance to this approach of relevant provisions of the Agreement and the Code;

77. *Also encourages* States, individually or through regional fisheries management organizations and arrangements and other relevant international organizations, to work to ensure that fisheries and other ecosystem data collection is performed in a coordinated and integrated manner, facilitating incorporation into global observation initiatives, where appropriate;

78. *Further encourages* States to increase scientific research in accordance with international law on the marine ecosystem;

79. *Calls upon* States, the Food and Agriculture Organization of the United Nations and other specialized agencies of the United Nations, subregional and regional fisheries management organizations and arrangements, where appropriate, and other appropriate intergovernmental bodies, to cooperate in achieving sustainable aquaculture, including through information exchange, developing equivalent standards on such issues as aquatic animal health and human health and safety concerns, assessing the potential positive and negative impacts of aquaculture, including socio-economics, on the marine and coastal environment, including biodiversity, and adopting relevant methods and techniques to minimize and mitigate adverse effects;

80. *Calls upon* States to take action immediately, individually and through regional fisheries management organizations and arrangements, and consistent with the precautionary approach and ecosystem approaches, to sustainably manage fish stocks and protect vulnerable marine ecosystems, including seamounts, hydrothermal vents and cold water corals, from destructive fishing practices, recognizing the immense importance and value of deep sea ecosystems and the biodiversity they contain;

81. *Reaffirms* the importance it attaches to paragraphs 66 to 69 of its resolution 59/25 concerning the impacts of fishing on vulnerable marine ecosystems;

82. *Welcomes* the important progress made by States and regional fisheries management organizations or arrangements with the competence to regulate bottom fisheries to give effect to paragraphs 66 to 69 of its resolution 59/25 to address the impacts of fishing on vulnerable marine ecosystems, including through initiating negotiations to establish new regional fisheries management organizations or arrangements, but on the basis of the review called for in paragraph 71 of that resolution, recognizes that additional actions are urgently needed;

83. *Calls upon* regional fisheries management organizations or arrangements with the competence to regulate bottom fisheries to adopt and implement measures, in accordance with the precautionary approach, ecosystem approaches and international law, for their respective regulatory areas as a matter of priority, but not later than 31 December 2008:

(a) To assess, on the basis of the best available scientific information, whether individual bottom fishing activities would have significant adverse impacts on vulnerable marine ecosystems, and to ensure that if it is assessed that these activities would have significant adverse impacts, they are managed to prevent such impacts, or not authorized to proceed;

(b) To identify vulnerable marine ecosystems and determine whether bottom fishing activities would cause significant adverse impacts to such ecosystems and the long-term sustainability of deep sea fish stocks, inter alia, by improving scientific research and data collection and sharing, and through new and exploratory fisheries;

(c) In respect of areas where vulnerable marine ecosystems, including seamounts, hydrothermal vents and cold water corals, are known to occur or are likely to occur based on the best available scientific information, to close such areas to bottom fishing and ensure that such activities do not proceed unless conservation and management measures have been established to prevent significant adverse impacts on vulnerable marine ecosystems;

(d) To require members of the regional fisheries management organizations or arrangements to require vessels flying their flag to cease bottom fishing activities in areas where, in the course of fishing operations, vulnerable marine ecosystems are encountered, and to

report the encounter so that appropriate measures can be adopted in respect of the relevant site;

84. *Also calls upon* regional fisheries management organizations or arrangements with the competence to regulate bottom fisheries to make the measures adopted pursuant to paragraph 83 of the present resolution publicly available;

85. *Calls upon* those States participating in negotiations to establish a regional fisheries management organization or arrangement competent to regulate bottom fisheries to expedite such negotiations and, by no later than 31 December 2007, to adopt and implement interim measures consistent with paragraph 83 of the present resolution and make these measures publicly available;

86. *Calls upon* flag States to either adopt and implement measures in accordance with paragraph 83 of the present resolution, mutatis mutandis, or cease to authorize fishing vessels flying their flag to conduct bottom fisheries in areas beyond national jurisdiction where there is no regional fisheries management organization or arrangement with the competence to regulate such fisheries or interim measures in accordance with paragraph 85 of the present resolution, until measures are taken in accordance with paragraph 83 or 85 of the present resolution;

87. *Further calls upon* States to make publicly available through the Food and Agriculture Organization of the United Nations a list of those vessels flying their flag authorized to conduct bottom fisheries in areas beyond national jurisdiction, and the measures they have adopted pursuant to paragraph 86 of the present resolution;

88. *Emphasizes* the critical role played by the Food and Agriculture Organization of the United Nations in providing expert technical advice, in assisting with international fisheries policy development and management standards, and in collection and dissemination of information on fisheries-related issues, including the protection of vulnerable marine ecosystems from the impacts of fishing;

89. *Commends* the Food and Agriculture Organization of the United Nations for its work on the management of deep sea fisheries in the high seas, including the expert consultation held from 21 to 23 November 2006 in Bangkok, and further invites the Food and Agriculture Organization of the United Nations to establish at its next Committee on Fisheries meeting a time frame of relevant work with respect to the management of deep sea fisheries in the high seas, including enhancing data collection and dissemination, promoting information exchange and increased knowledge on deep sea fishing activities, such as through convening a meeting of States engaged in such fisheries, developing standards and criteria for use by States and regional fisheries management organizations or arrangements in identifying vulnerable marine ecosystems and the impacts of fishing on such ecosystems, and establishing standards for the management of deep sea fisheries, such as through the development of an international plan of action;

90. *Invites* the Food and Agriculture Organization of the United Nations to consider creating a global database of information on vulnerable marine ecosystems in areas beyond national jurisdiction to assist States in assessing any impacts of bottom fisheries on vulnerable marine ecosystems, and invites States and regional fisheries management organizations or arrangements to submit information to any such database on all vulnerable marine ecosystems identified in accordance with paragraph 83 of the present resolution;

91. *Requests* the Secretary-General, in cooperation with the Food and Agriculture Organization of the United Nations, to include in his report concerning fisheries to the General Assembly at its sixty-fourth session a section on the actions taken by States and regional fisheries management organizations and arrangements in response to paragraphs 83 to 90 of the present resolution, and decides to conduct a further review of such actions at that session in 2009, with a view to further recommendations, where necessary;

92. *Encourages* accelerated progress to establish criteria on the objectives and management of marine protected areas for fisheries purposes, and in this regard welcomes the proposed work of the Food and Agriculture Organization of the United Nations to develop technical guidelines in accordance with the Convention on the design, implementation and testing of marine protected areas for such purposes, and urges coordination and cooperation among all relevant international organizations and bodies;

93. *Notes* that the Second Intergovernmental Review Meeting of the Global Programme of Action for the Protection of the Marine Environment from Land-based Activities was held from 16 to 20 October 2006 in Beijing, and urges all States to implement the Global Programme of Action and to accelerate activity to safeguard the marine ecosystem, including fish stocks, against pollution and physical degradation;

94. *Reaffirms* the importance it attaches to paragraphs 77 to 81 of its resolution 60/31 concerning the issue of lost, abandoned, or discarded fishing gear and related marine debris and the adverse impacts such debris and derelict fishing gear have on, inter alia, fish stocks, habitats and other marine species, and urges accelerated progress by States and regional fisheries management organizations and arrangements in implementing those paragraphs of the resolution;

95. *Further encourages* the Committee on Fisheries of the Food and Agriculture Organization of the United Nations to consider the issue of derelict fishing gear and related marine debris at its next meeting in 2007, and in particular the implementation of relevant provisions of the Code;

XI

Capacity-building

96. *Reiterates* the crucial importance of cooperation by States directly or, as appropriate, through the relevant regional and subregional organizations, and by other international organizations, including the Food and Agriculture Organization of the United Nations through its FishCode programme, including through financial and/or technical assistance, in accordance with

the Agreement, the Compliance Agreement, the Code, the International Plan of Action to Prevent, Deter and Eliminate Illegal, Unreported and Unregulated Fishing, the International Plan of Action for the Conservation and Management of Sharks, the International Plan of Action for the Management of Fishing Capacity, the International Plan of Action for Reducing Incidental Catch of Seabirds in Longline Fisheries, and the Guidelines to Reduce Sea Turtle Mortality in Fishing Operations of the Food and Agriculture Organization of the United Nations, to increase the capacity of developing States to achieve the goals and implement the actions called for in the present resolution;

97. *Welcomes* the work of the Food and Agriculture Organization of the United Nations in developing guidance on the strategies and measures required for the creation of an enabling environment for small-scale fisheries, including the development of a code of conduct and guidelines for enhancing the contribution of small-scale fisheries to poverty alleviation and food security that include adequate provisions with regard to financial measures and capacity-building, including transfer of technology, and encourages studies for creating possible alternative livelihoods for coastal communities;

98. *Encourages* increased capacity-building and technical assistance by States, international financial institutions and relevant intergovernmental organizations and bodies for fishers, in particular small-scale fishers, in developing countries, and in particular small island developing States, consistent with environmental sustainability;

99. *Encourages* the international community to enhance the opportunities for sustainable development in developing countries, in particular the least developed countries, small island developing States and coastal African States, by encouraging greater participation of those States in authorized fisheries activities being undertaken within areas under their national jurisdiction, in accordance with the Convention, by distant-water fishing nations in order to achieve better economic returns for developing countries from their fisheries resources within areas under their national jurisdiction and an enhanced role in regional fisheries management, as well as by enhancing the ability of developing countries to develop their own fisheries, as well as to participate in high seas fisheries, including access to such fisheries, in conformity with international law, in particular the Convention and the Agreement;

100. *Requests* distant-water fishing nations, when negotiating access agreements and arrangements with developing coastal States, to do so on an equitable and sustainable basis, including by giving greater attention to fish processing, including fish processing facilities, within the national jurisdiction of the developing coastal State to assist the realization of the benefits from the development of fisheries resources, and also including, inter alia, the transfer of technology and assistance for monitoring, control and surveillance and compliance and enforcement within areas under the national jurisdiction of the developing coastal State providing fisheries access, taking into account the forms of cooperation set out in article 25 of the Agreement;

101. *Encourages* States individually and through regional fisheries management organizations and arrangements to provide greater assistance and to promote coherence in such assistance for developing States in designing, establishing and implementing relevant agreements, instruments and tools for the conservation and sustainable management of fish stocks, including in designing and strengthening their domestic regulatory fisheries policies and those of regional fisheries management organizations or arrangements in their regions, and the enhancement of research and scientific capabilities through existing funds, such as the Assistance Fund under Part VII of the Agreement, bilateral assistance, regional fisheries management organizations and arrangements assistance funds, the FishCode programme, the World Bank's global programme on fisheries and the Global Environment Facility;

102. *Calls upon* States to promote, through continuing dialogue and the assistance and cooperation provided in accordance with articles 24 to 26 of the Agreement, further ratification of or accession to the Agreement by seeking to address, inter alia, the issue of lack of capacity and resources that might stand in the way of developing States becoming parties;

XII

Cooperation within the United Nations system

103. *Requests* the relevant parts of the United Nations system, international financial institutions and donor agencies to support increased enforcement and compliance capabilities for regional fisheries management organizations and their member States;

104. *Invites* the Food and Agriculture Organization of the United Nations to continue its cooperative arrangements with United Nations agencies on the implementation of the international plans of action and to report to the Secretary-General, for inclusion in his annual report on sustainable fisheries, on priorities for cooperation and coordination in this work;

105. *Invites* the Division for Ocean Affairs and the Law of the Sea, the Food and Agriculture Organization of the United Nations and other relevant bodies of the United Nations system to consult and cooperate in the preparation of questionnaires designed to collect information on sustainable fisheries, in order to avoid duplication;

XIII

Sixty-second session of the General Assembly

106. *Requests* the Secretary-General to bring the present resolution to the attention of all members of the international community, relevant intergovernmental organizations, the organizations and bodies of the United Nations system, regional and subregional fisheries management organizations and relevant non-governmental organizations, and to invite them to provide the Secretary-General with information relevant to the implementation of the present resolution;

107. *Also requests* the Secretary-General to submit to the General Assembly at its sixty-second session a report on "Sustainable fisheries, including through the 1995 Agreement for the Implementation of the Provisions of the United Nations Convention on the Law of the Sea of 10 December 1982 relating to the Conservation and Management of Straddling Fish Stocks and Highly Migratory Fish Stocks, and related instruments", taking into account information provided by States, relevant specialized agencies, in particular the Food and Agriculture Organization of the United Nations, and other appropriate organs, organizations and programmes of the United Nations system, regional and subregional organizations and arrangements for the conservation and management of straddling fish stocks and highly migratory fish stocks, as well as other relevant intergovernmental bodies and non-governmental organizations, and consisting, inter alia, of elements provided in relevant paragraphs in the present resolution;

108. *Decides* to include in the provisional agenda of its sixty-second session, under the item entitled "Oceans and the law of the sea", the sub-item entitled "Sustainable fisheries, including through the 1995 Agreement for the Implementation of the Provisions of the United Nations Convention on the Law of the Sea of 10 December 1982 relating to the Conservation and Management of Straddling Fish Stocks and Highly Migratory Fish Stocks, and related instruments".

Institutions created by the Convention

International Seabed Authority

Through the International Seabed Authority, established by UNCLOS and the 1994 Implementation Agreement [YUN 1994, p. 1301], States organized and conducted exploration of the resources of the seabed and ocean floor and subsoil beyond the limits of national jurisdiction. In 2006, the Authority, which had 152 members as at 31 December, held its twelfth session (Kingston, Jamaica, 7-18 August) [ISBA/12/A/13]. Its subsidiary bodies, namely, the Assembly, the Council, the Legal and Technical Commission and the Finance Committee, also met during the session.

The Assembly considered the annual report of the Authority's Secretary-General [ISBA/12/A/2 & Corr.1], which reviewed the Authority's work since the eleventh session and outlined the future work programme of the secretariat. The Secretary-General observed that, for the seven former registered pioneer investors, 2006 marked the end of the first five-year programme of work since contracts for exploring for polymetallic nodules in the seabed were issued in 2001. That development provided an opportunity for the contractors to submit a comprehensive account of their operations and the results achieved during the period, as well as a review of their expenditure. The Authority continued to develop the Central Data Repository, with the establishment of a bibliographic database in 2006. The Authority would continue to implement its work programme (2005-2007), with emphasis on its supervisory functions relating to exploration contracts, the development of an appropriate regulatory framework for the future development of the mineral resources of the international seabed Area and the promotion and encouragement of marine scientific research in the Area, among others.

The Assembly elected 17 States to the 36-member Council, who would serve a four-year term beginning 1 January 2007. It considered the report of the Finance Committee [ISBA/12/A/7-ISBA/12/C/9] and approved the 2007-2008 budget of the Authority in the amount of $11,782,400. It also approved the establishment of a special account, the Endowment Fund for Marine Scientific Research in the Area, whose rules and procedures would be prepared for the consideration of the Council at its next session.

The Council resumed its consideration of the draft regulations for prospecting and exploring polymetallic sulphides and cobalt-rich ferromanganese crusts in the Area. It decided that the draft should be revised, and that two separate regulations—one dealing with polymetallic sulphides and the other dealing with cobalt-rich ferromanganese crusts—should be drafted. Priority was to be given to the drafting of the regulations on polymetallic sulphides, to be presented to the Council at its next session.

The Legal and Technical Commission reported to the Council on its work during the twelfth session [ISBA/12/C/8], in which it discussed the fifth set of annual reports of the seven contractors; an update on progress in the geological model on polymetallic nodule deposits in the Clarion-Clipperton fracture zone (north-east Pacific); a report on a workshop on cobalt-rich crusts and the diversity and distribution patterns of seamount fauna; a proposal to establish a mineral resource/reserve classification system for the international seabed area; environmental issues within the Commission's mandate; and a report on a workshop on mining of cobalt-rich ferromanganese crusts and polymetallic sulphides—technical and economic considerations.

The Council elected 25 new members of the Commission for a four-year term of office beginning 1 January 2007, increasing the size of the Commission from 15 to 25 members, without prejudice for future elections.

International Tribunal for the Law of the Sea

The International Tribunal for the Law of the Sea held its twenty-first (6-17 March) and twenty-second (18-29 September) sessions, both in Hamburg, Germany [SPLOS/152]. It considered draft guidelines regarding the posting of a bond or other financial security with the Tribunal in prompt release proceedings, as well as questions regarding its competence in maritime delimitation cases. On 19 September, the Tribunal re-elected Philippe Gautier (Belgium) as Registrar for a five-year term. A series of events were held to celebrate the tenth anniversary of the Tribunal.

The case pending before the Tribunal was *Conservation and Sustainable Exploitation of Swordfish Stocks in the South-Eastern Pacific Ocean (Chile/European Community)*.

Commission on the Limits of the Continental Shelf

In 2006, the Commission on the Limits of the Continental Shelf, established in 1997 [YUN 1997, p. 1362], held its seventeenth (20 March–21 April) [CLCS/50] and eighteenth (21 August–15 September) [CLCS/52] sessions, both in New York.

At its seventeenth session, the Commission continued the examination of the submissions made by Australia, Brazil and Ireland for the establishment of the outer limits of the continental shelf where it extended beyond 200 nautical miles from the baselines from which the breadth of the territorial sea was measured. The subcommissions that had been established at previous sessions to examine those submissions reported on the work that they had carried out intersessionaly and continued the examination of those submissions. The Commission also discussed the issue of the projected workload associated with the submissions expected in the coming years.

At its eighteenth session, the Commission began the examination of the submission made by New Zealand and the joint submission made by France, Ireland, Spain and the United Kingdom. For both submissions, the Commission decided to proceed by way of subcommissions. The Commission also continued the examination of the submissions made by Australia, Brazil and Ireland. The subcommissions that had been established to examine those submissions reported on the work that had been carried out intersessionaly. The subcommission established for consideration of the submission made by Ireland completed its work at the session and presented its recommendations. The Commission decided to defer further consideration of those recommendations to its nineteenth session, in order to allow all Commission members to study them in more detail.

On 27 November, Norway made its submission to the Commission.

Other developments related to the Convention

Report of Secretary-General. In response to General Assembly resolution 60/30 [YUN 2005, p. 1436], the Secretary-General submitted a March report, with a later addendum, on oceans and the law of the sea [A/61/63 & Add.1], describing the status of UNCLOS and its two implementing agreements and discussing developments regarding international shipping, safety and security of navigation, people at sea, protection of the marine environment, conservation of marine living resources and the Indian Ocean tsunami. The report also provided information on the settlement of disputes and inter-agency coordination and cooperation.

Although a wide range of actions were taken to address issues related to ocean affairs and the law of the sea, much more remained to be done to translate the objectives of UNCLOS and other instruments into concrete action. The report highlighted three areas requiring attention: the deposit of charts or of lists of geographical coordinates of points; ecosystem approaches and oceans; and maritime security and safety. In the light of developments with regard to various uses of the sea and its resources, the deposit of charts or of lists of geographical coordinates of points with the UN Secretary-General had become an increasingly important tool for providing adequate information to the international community and users of the seas regarding the outer limits of maritime zones of coastal States, the lines of maritime boundaries delimitation, as well as baselines. The deposit—an international act required by UNCLOS—was also in the best interests of coastal States. Making available information on the outer limits of maritime zones, delimitations and baselines helped to safeguard the rights of coastal States in the zones under their national jurisdiction and facilitated the exercise of such jurisdiction. Coastal States parties should therefore proceed accordingly.

The application of ecosystem approaches to ocean management was important for achieving sustainable development. They built on the concept of integrated ocean management, which involved comprehensive planning and regulation of human activities aimed at minimizing user conflicts, while ensuring longer-term sustainability. Adopting and implementing an ecosystem approach should therefore be an evolutionary step, and emphasis should be placed on ways to facilitate its implementation. Regional cooperation was essential because ecosystems did not respect maritime boundaries. As the scientific understanding of ocean ecosystems was still limited, further research was needed, as well as the application of the precautionary approach in the face of uncertainty.

In the context of fisheries management, the ecosystem approach should reflect concern about the long-term effects of fishery management on marine ecosystems by restricting the environmental impacts of fishing to acceptable levels, including by reducing by-catch and incidental mortality of non-target species. Stronger capacity-building was crucial to the effective management of resources and protection of the marine environment by developing countries, in particular small island developing States.

Another important area of cooperation was maritime security and safety. As challenges to maritime security were global, wide-ranging and connected, cooperation on all threats to security was crucial. Cooperation should address threats to maritime security through bilateral and multilateral instruments and mechanisms aimed at monitoring, preventing and responding to such threats.

Oceans and the law of the sea had become increasingly important for the international community, and an enhanced focus on the oceans was essential to achieve sustainable development. The conservation and sustainable use of ocean resources were vital for the future of humanity. Scientific research had increased the understanding of marine ecosystems and the human activities affecting them, and while States were discussing the need to manage the oceans in a more systematic and integrated way, a cross-sectoral approach was necessary at the national, regional and global level, together with increased international cooperation and coordination.

Communications. By a July note [A/61/160], the Secretary-General transmitted to the General Assembly, the report of the Ad Hoc Consultative Meeting of senior representatives of international organizations (London, 7-8 July 2005), convened by the International Maritime Organization (IMO) on the role of the "genuine link" in relation to the duty of flag States to exercise their control over ships flying their flag, including fishing vessels. The Assembly had invited IMO to study the topic by resolutions 58/240 [YUN 2003, p. 1355] and 58/14 [ibid., p. 1347].

By a March letter [A/61/65], the Ad Hoc Open-ended Informal Working Group to study issues relating to the conservation and sustainable use of marine biological diversity beyond areas of national jurisdiction, established by Assembly resolution 59/24 [YUN 2004, p. 1333], transmitted to the Assembly the report on its meeting (New York, 13-17 February), which called for more effective implementation of UNCLOS and associated instruments. It observed that sectoral activities affecting biological diversity beyond areas of national jurisdiction should be better managed and destructive fishing practices, identified as one of the major threats, should be urgently addressed. Illegal, unreported and unregulated fishing remained a major impediment to conservation and sustainable use of marine biological diversity, and should be addressed by tackling issues such as flag State responsibilities, port measures, compliance and enforcement. Governance gaps in areas beyond national jurisdiction should be examined and the legal status of marine biological diversity, including genetic resources beyond national jurisdiction, elaborated. Areas for further study included the extent and nature of marine biological diversity and anthropogenic impacts beyond national jurisdiction; the development of management options; improved understanding of the economic and socio-economic aspects of conservation; and related legal and institutional issues.

The International Labour Conference of the International Labour Organization (ILO), on 23 February, adopted the consolidated Maritime Labour Convention, which consolidated and updated more than 60 maritime labour instruments.

IMO and ILO adopted Guidelines on Fair Treatment of Seafarers in the Event of a Maritime Accident. The Guidelines were adopted by the IMO Legal Committee on 27 April and by the ILO Governing Body on 12 June.

IMO, on 19 May, adopted amendments to the 1974 International Convention for the Safety of Life at Sea [YUN 1974, p. 1030], introducing long-range identification and tracking systems.

The 1996 Protocol to the 1972 Convention on the Prevention of Marine Pollution by Dumping of Wastes and Other Matter [YUN 1996, p. 1431] came into force on 24 March; the 2000 Protocol on Preparedness, Response and Cooperation to Pollution Incidents by Hazardous and Noxious Substances [YUN 2000, p. 1438] came into force on 14 June.

The Oceans and Coastal Areas Network (UN-Oceans), the inter-secretariat mechanism for the coordination of United Nations activities related to oceans and coastal areas established by the Assembly in resolution 58/240 [YUN 2003, p. 1355], held its fourth meeting on 9 June in New York.

Marine environment: Global Marine Assessment

The first meeting [A/61/GRAME/AHSG/1] of the Ad Hoc Steering Group for the "assessment of assessments" of the regular process for global reporting and assessment of the state of the marine environment, including socio-economic aspects, was held in New York from 7 to 9 June. The meeting was convened pursuant to General Assembly resolution 60/30 [YUN 2005, p. 1436], by which the Assembly established the Ad Hoc Steering Group and invited the United Nations Environment Programme (UNEP) and the Intergovernmental Oceanographic Commission (IOC) of the United Nations Educational, Scientific and Cultural Organization (UNESCO) to jointly lead the process of, amongst other things, producing a report on the results of the "assessment of assessments" for the Assembly.

The Group undertook an in-depth review of the updated survey of regional and global marine assessments by UNEP-World Conservation Monitoring Centre, features of the "assessment of assessments", technical elements that might be considered by a group of experts and a budget and resources mobilization strategy for the "assessment of assessments". It adopted decisions on the scope, key questions, process, budget, implementation plan and time-schedule for the "assessment of assessments", which, as stipulated by the Assembly, was to be completed within two years of its launch. It also adopted a tentative two-year work plan and recommended national profile and selection criteria for the group of experts.

United Nations Open-ended Informal Consultative Process

In response to General Assembly resolution 60/30 [YUN 2005, p. 1436], the seventh meeting of the United Nations Open-ended Informal Consultative Process on Oceans and the Law of the Sea (New York, 12-16 June) [A/61/156] focused its discussions on ecosystem approaches and oceans. It also addressed cooperation and coordination of ocean issues and recommended topics for further consideration, including the social aspects of oceans and the law of the sea, maritime security and State flag responsibility, and climate change and oceans.

GENERAL ASSEMBLY ACTION

On 20 December [meeting 83], the General Assembly adopted **resolution 61/222** [draft: A/61/L.30 & Add.1] by recorded vote (157-1-3) [agenda item 71 *(a)*].

Oceans and the law of the sea

The General Assembly,

Recalling its resolutions 49/28 of 6 December 1994, 52/26 of 26 November 1997, 54/33 of 24 November 1999, 57/141 of 12 December 2002, 58/240 of 23 December 2003, 59/24 of 17 November 2004, 60/30 of 29 November 2005 and other relevant resolutions concerning the United Nations Convention on the Law of the Sea ("the Convention"),

Having considered the report of the Secretary-General, the addendum thereto, the report of the Ad Hoc Open-ended Informal Working Group to study issues relating to the conservation and sustainable use of marine biological diversity beyond areas of national jurisdiction and also the reports on the work of the United Nations Open-ended Informal Consultative Process on Oceans and the Law of the Sea ("the Consultative Process") at its seventh meeting and on the sixteenth Meeting of States Parties to the Convention,

Emphasizing the pre-eminent contribution provided by the Convention to the strengthening of peace, security, cooperation and friendly relations among all nations in conformity with the principles of justice and equal rights and to the promotion of the economic and social advancement of all peoples of the world, in accordance with the purposes and principles of the United Nations as set forth in the Charter of the United Nations, as well as for the sustainable development of the oceans and seas,

Emphasizing also the universal and unified character of the Convention, and reaffirming that the Convention sets out the legal framework within which all activities in the oceans and seas must be carried out and is of strategic importance as the basis for national, regional and global action and cooperation in the marine sector, and that its integrity needs to be maintained, as recognized also by the United Nations Conference on Environment and Development in chapter 17 of Agenda 21,

Recognizing the important contribution of sustainable development and management of the resources and uses of the oceans and seas to the achievement of international development goals, including those contained in the United Nations Millennium Declaration,

Conscious that the problems of ocean space are closely interrelated and need to be considered as a whole through an integrated, interdisciplinary and intersectoral approach, and reaffirming the need to improve cooperation and coordination at the national, regional and global levels, in accordance with the Convention, to support and supplement the efforts of each State in promoting the implementation and observance of the Convention, and the integrated management and sustainable development of the oceans and seas,

Reiterating the essential need for cooperation, including through capacity-building and transfer of marine technology, to ensure that all States, especially developing countries, in particular the least developed countries and small island developing States, as well as coastal African States, are able both to implement the Convention and to benefit from the sustainable development of the oceans and seas, as well as to participate fully in global and regional forums and processes dealing with oceans and law of the sea issues,

Emphasizing the need to strengthen the ability of competent international organizations to contribute, at the global, regional, subregional and bilateral levels, through cooperation programmes with Governments, to the development of national capacity in marine science and the sustainable management of the oceans and their resources,

Recalling that marine science is important for eradicating poverty, contributing to food security, conserving the world's marine environment and resources, helping to understand, predict and respond to natural events and promoting the sustainable development of the oceans and seas, by improving knowledge, through sustained research efforts and the evaluation of monitoring results, and applying such knowledge to management and decision-making,

Recalling also its decision, in resolutions 57/141 and 58/240, to establish a regular process under the United Nations for global reporting and assessment of the state of the marine environment, including socio-economic aspects, both current and foreseeable, building on existing regional assessments, as recommended by the World Summit on Sustainable Development, and noting the need for cooperation among all States to this end,

Reiterating its concern at the adverse impacts on the marine environment and biodiversity, in particular on vulnerable marine ecosystems, including corals, of human activities, such as overutilization of living marine resources, the use of destructive practices, physical impacts by ships, the introduction of alien invasive species and marine pollution from all sources, including from land-based sources and vessels, in particular through the illegal discharge of oil and other harmful substances, the loss or release of fishing gear and the dumping of hazardous waste such as radioactive materials, nuclear waste and dangerous chemicals,

Expressing its concern over the projected adverse effects of anthropogenic and natural climate change and ocean acidification on the marine environment and marine biodiversity,

Recognizing that there is a need for a more integrated approach and to further study and promote measures for enhanced cooperation and coordination relating to the conservation and sustainable use of marine biodiversity in areas beyond national jurisdiction,

Recognizing also that the realization of the benefits of the Convention could be enhanced by international cooperation, technical assistance and advanced scientific knowledge, as well as by funding and capacity-building,

Recognizing further that hydrographic surveys and nautical charting are critical to the safety of navigation and life at sea, environmental protection, including the protection of vulnerable marine ecosystems, and the economics of the global shipping industry, and recognizing in this regard that the move towards electronic charting not only provides significantly increased benefits for safe navigation and management of ship movement, but also provides data and information that can be used for sustainable fisheries activities and other sectoral uses of the marine environment, the delimitation of maritime boundaries and environmental protection,

Noting with concern the continuing problem of transnational organized crime and threats to maritime safety and security, including piracy, armed robbery at sea, smuggling and terrorist acts against shipping, offshore installations and other maritime interests, and noting the deplorable loss of life and adverse impact on international trade, energy security and the global economy resulting from such activities,

Reaffirming the importance of the work of the Commission on the Limits of the Continental Shelf ("the Commission") for coastal States and the international community as a whole,

Noting the important role of the Commission in assisting States parties in the implementation of Part VI of the Convention, through the examination of information submitted by coastal States regarding the outer limits of the continental shelf beyond 200 nautical miles,

Recognizing the importance and the contribution of the work over the past seven years of the Consultative Process established by resolution 54/33 to facilitate the annual review of developments in ocean affairs by the General Assembly and extended by resolutions 57/141 and 60/30,

Noting the responsibilities of the Secretary-General under the Convention and related resolutions of the General Assembly, in particular resolutions 49/28, 52/26 and 54/33, and in this context the increase in activities of the Division for Ocean Affairs and the Law of the Sea of the Office of Legal Affairs of the Secretariat ("the Division"), in particular in view of the growing number of requests to the Division for additional outputs and servicing of meetings, the increasing capacity-building activities and assistance to the Commission, and the role of the Division in interagency coordination and cooperation,

Emphasizing that underwater archaeological, cultural and historical heritage, including shipwrecks and watercrafts, holds essential information on the history of humankind and that such heritage is a resource that needs to be protected and preserved,

Reaffirming the importance of the work of the International Seabed Authority ("the Authority") in accordance with the Convention and the Agreement relating to the Implementation of Part XI of the United Nations Convention on the Law of the Sea of 10 December 1982 ("the Agreement"),

I

Implementation of the Convention and related agreements and instruments

1. *Reaffirms* its resolutions 49/28, 52/26, 54/33, 57/141, 58/240, 59/24, 60/30 and other relevant resolutions concerning the Convention;

2. *Also reaffirms* the unified character of the Convention and the vital importance of preserving its integrity;

3. *Calls upon* all States that have not done so, in order to achieve the goal of universal participation, to become parties to the Convention and the Agreement;

4. *Calls upon* all States that have not done so, in order to achieve the goal of universal participation, to become parties to the Agreement for the Implementation of the Provisions of the United Nations Convention on the Law of the Sea of 10 December 1982 relating to the Conservation and Management of Straddling Fish Stocks and Highly Migratory Fish Stocks ("the Fish Stocks Agreement");

5. *Calls upon* States to harmonize, as a matter of priority, their national legislation with the provisions of the Convention and, where applicable, relevant agreements and instruments, to ensure the consistent application of those provisions and to ensure also that any declarations or statements that they have made or make when signing, ratifying or acceding to the Convention do not purport to exclude or to modify the legal effect of the provisions of the Convention in their application to the State concerned and to withdraw any such declarations or statements;

6. *Calls upon* States parties to the Convention to deposit with the Secretary-General charts or lists of geographical coordinates, as provided for in the Convention;

7. *Urges* all States to cooperate, directly or through competent international bodies, in taking measures to protect and preserve objects of an archaeological and historical nature found at sea, in conformity with the Convention, and calls upon States to work together on such diverse challenges and opportunities as the appropriate relationship between salvage law and scientific management and conservation of underwater cultural heritage, increasing technological abilities to discover and reach underwater sites, looting and growing underwater tourism;

8. *Notes* the effort made by the United Nations Educational, Scientific and Cultural Organization with respect to the preservation of underwater cultural heritage, and notes in particular the rules annexed to the 2001 Convention on the Protection of the Underwater Cultural Heritage that address the relationship between salvage law and scientific principles of management, conservation and protection of underwater cultural heritage among parties, their nationals and vessels flying their flag;

II

Capacity-building

9. *Calls upon* donor agencies and international financial institutions to keep their programmes systematically under review to ensure the availability in all States, particularly in developing States, of the economic, legal, navigational, scientific and technical skills necessary for the full implementation of the Convention and the objectives of the present resolution, as well as the sustainable development of the oceans and seas nationally, regionally and globally, and in so doing to bear in mind the interests and needs of landlocked developing States;

10. *Encourages* intensified efforts to build capacity for developing countries, in particular for the least developed countries and small island developing States, as well as coastal African States, to improve hydrographic services and the production of nautical charts, including electronic charts, as well as the mobilization of resources and building of capacity with support from international financial institutions and the donor community;

11. *Calls upon* States and international financial institutions, including through bilateral, regional and global cooperation programmes and technical partnerships, to continue to strengthen capacity-building activities, in particular in developing countries, in the field of marine scientific research by, inter alia, training personnel to develop and enhance relevant expertise, providing the necessary equipment, facilities and vessels and transferring environmentally sound technologies;

12. *Recognizes* the need to build the capacity of developing States to raise awareness of, and support implementation of, improved waste management practices, noting the particular vulnerability of small island developing States to the impact of marine pollution from land-based sources and marine debris;

13. *Also recognizes* the importance of assisting developing States, in particular the least developed countries and small island developing States, as well as coastal African States, in implementing the Convention, and urges States, intergovernmental organizations and agencies, national institutions, non-governmental organizations and international financial institutions, as well as natural and juridical persons, to make voluntary financial or other contributions to the trust funds, as referred to in resolution 57/141, established for this purpose;

14. *Encourages* States to use the Criteria and Guidelines on the Transfer of Marine Technology, adopted by the Assembly of the Intergovernmental Oceanographic Commission of the United Nations Educational, Scientific and Cultural Organization, and recalls the important role of the secretariat of the International Oceanographic Commission in the implementation and promotion of those Criteria and Guidelines;

15. *Also encourages* States to assist developing States, and especially the least developed countries and small island developing States, as well as coastal African States, at the bilateral and, where appropriate, multilateral level, in the preparation of submissions to the Commission regarding the establishment of the outer limits of the continental shelf beyond 200 nautical miles, including the assessment of the nature and extent of the continental shelf of a coastal State through a desktop study, and the delineation of the outer limits of its continental shelf;

16. *Notes with appreciation* the successful conduct by the Division of regional training courses, most recently in Accra from 5 to 9 December 2005 and in Buenos Aires from 8 to 12 May 2006, the purpose of which was to train technical staff of coastal developing States in the delineation of the outer limits of the continental shelf beyond 200 nautical miles and in the preparation of submissions to the Commission, and requests the Secretary-General, in cooperation with States and relevant international or-

ganizations and institutions, to continue making such training courses available;

17. *Also notes with appreciation* the first regional workshop of the International Tribunal for the Law of the Sea ("the Tribunal"), held in Dakar from 31 October to 2 November 2006 on the role of the Tribunal in the settlement of disputes relating to the law of the sea in West Africa;

18. *Invites* Member States and others in a position to do so to support the capacity-building activities of the Division, including, in particular, the training activities to assist developing States in the preparation of their submissions to the Commission, and invites Member States and others in a position to do so to contribute to the trust fund established by the Secretary-General for the Office of Legal Affairs of the Secretariat to support the promotion of international law;

19. *Recognizes* the importance of the Hamilton Shirley Amerasinghe Memorial Fellowship on the Law of the Sea, advises the Secretary-General to continue to finance the Fellowship from resources made available through an appropriate Office of Legal Affairs trust fund, and urges Member States and others in a position to do so to contribute to the further development of the Fellowship;

20. *Takes note with satisfaction* of the ongoing implementation of the United Nations and the Nippon Foundation Fellowship Programme, focusing on human resources development for developing coastal States parties and non-parties to the Convention in the field of ocean affairs and the law of the sea or related disciplines;

III

Meeting of States Parties

21. *Welcomes* the report of the sixteenth Meeting of States Parties to the Convention;

22. *Requests* the Secretary-General to convene the seventeenth Meeting of States Parties to the Convention in New York on 14 and from 18 to 22 June 2007, bearing in mind that the current term of office of the members of the Commission expires on 15 June 2007, and to provide the services required;

23. *Calls upon* States parties to transmit to the Secretariat the credentials of representatives attending the Meeting as far in advance as is practicable, and no later than 13 June 2007;

IV

Peaceful settlement of disputes

24. *Notes with satisfaction* the continued and significant contribution of the Tribunal to the settlement of disputes by peaceful means in accordance with Part XV of the Convention, and underlines the important role and authority of the Tribunal concerning the interpretation or application of the Convention and the Agreement;

25. *Equally pays tribute* to the important and longstanding role of the International Court of Justice with regard to the peaceful settlement of disputes concerning the law of the sea;

26. *Notes* that States parties to an international agreement related to the purposes of the Convention may submit to, inter alia, the Tribunal or the International Court of Justice any dispute concerning the interpretation or application of that agreement submitted in accordance with that agreement, and notes also the possibility, provided for in the statutes of the Tribunal and the Court, to submit disputes to a chamber;

27. *Encourages* States parties to the Convention that have not yet done so to consider making a written declaration choosing from the means set out in article 287 of the Convention for the settlement of disputes concerning the interpretation or application of the Convention and the Agreement, bearing in mind the comprehensive character of the dispute settlement mechanism provided for in Part XV of the Convention;

V

The Area

28. *Notes* the progress of the discussions on issues relating to the regulations for prospecting and exploration for polymetallic sulphides and cobalt-rich ferromanganese crusts in the Area, and reiterates the importance of the ongoing elaboration by the Authority, pursuant to article 145 of the Convention, of rules, regulations and procedures to ensure the effective protection of the marine environment, the protection and conservation of the natural resources of the Area and the prevention of damage to its flora and fauna from harmful effects that may arise from activities in the Area;

29. *Takes note with satisfaction* of the contract signed on 19 July 2006 between Germany and the Authority regarding the exploration of polymetallic nodules in an area in the Pacific Ocean;

30. *Notes* the importance of the responsibilities entrusted to the Authority by articles 143 and 145 of the Convention, which refer to marine scientific research and protection of the marine environment respectively;

VI

Effective functioning of the Authority and the Tribunal

31. *Appeals* to all States parties to the Convention to pay their assessed contributions to the Authority and to the Tribunal in full and on time, and also appeals to States parties in arrears with their contributions to fulfil their obligations without delay;

32. *Urges* all States parties to the Convention to attend the sessions of the Authority, and calls upon the Authority to continue to pursue all options, including the issue of dates, in order to improve attendance in Kingston and to ensure global participation;

33. *Calls upon* States that have not done so to consider ratifying or acceding to the Agreement on the Privileges and Immunities of the Tribunal and to the Protocol on the Privileges and Immunities of the Authority;

34. *Emphasizes* the importance of the Tribunal's rules and staff regulations promoting the recruitment of a geographically representative staff in the Professional

and higher categories, and calls for wider dissemination of vacancy announcements to achieve that goal;

VII

The continental shelf and the work of the Commission

35. *Encourages* States parties to the Convention that are in a position to do so to make every effort to submit information to the Commission regarding the establishment of the outer limits of the continental shelf beyond 200 nautical miles, in conformity with article 76 of the Convention and article 4 of annex II to the Convention, taking into account the decision of the eleventh Meeting of States Parties to the Convention;

36. *Notes with satisfaction* the progress in the work of the Commission, that it is giving current consideration to five submissions that have been made regarding the establishment of the outer limits of the continental shelf beyond 200 nautical miles and that a number of States have advised of their intention to make submissions in the near future;

37. *Notes* that the anticipated heavy workload of the Commission, owing to an increasing number of submissions, places additional demands on its members and the Division, and in that regard emphasizes the need to ensure that the Commission can perform its functions effectively and maintain its high level of quality and expertise;

38. *Emphasizes* the need to maintain, to the extent possible given the term of office of the members of the Commission, continuity in the composition of subcommissions throughout the consideration of a submission;

39. *Takes note* of the decision of the sixteenth Meeting of States Parties to the Convention to address, as a matter of priority, issues related to the workload of the Commission and funding for its members attending the sessions of the Commission and the meetings of the subcommissions;

40. *Calls upon* States whose experts are serving on the Commission to do their utmost to ensure the full participation of those experts in the work of the Commission, including the meetings of subcommissions, in accordance with the Convention;

41. *Endorses* the call by the Meeting of States Parties to the Convention to strengthen the Division, serving as the secretariat of the Commission, for the purpose of enhancing its technical support for the Commission;

42. *Urges* the Secretary-General to continue to take all necessary actions to ensure that the Commission can fulfil the functions entrusted to it under the Convention;

43. *Encourages* States to make additional contributions to the voluntary trust fund established by resolution 55/7 of 30 October 2000 for the purpose of facilitating the preparation of submissions to the Commission for developing States, in particular the least developed countries and small island developing States, and compliance with article 76 of the Convention;

44. *Expresses its concern* regarding the resources available in the voluntary trust fund established by resolution 55/7 for the purpose of defraying the cost of participation of the members of the Commission from developing States in the meetings of the Commission, and urges States to make additional contributions to the trust fund;

45. *Approves* the convening by the Secretary-General of the nineteenth and twentieth sessions of the Commission in New York from 5 March to 13 April 2007 and from 20 August to 7 September 2007, respectively, on the understanding that the following periods will be used for the technical examination of submissions at the Geographic Information System laboratories and other technical facilities of the Division: 5 to 23 March 2007; 9 to 13 April 2007; 20 to 24 August 2007; and 4 to 7 September 2007;

46. *Expresses its firm conviction* about the importance of the work of the Commission, carried out in accordance with the Convention, including with respect to the participation of the coastal State in relevant proceedings concerning its submission;

47. *Notes with satisfaction* the amendments to rule 52 of and annex III to the rules of procedure of the Commission, and recognizes the continued need for active interaction between submitting States and the Commission;

48. *Encourages* States to continue exchanging views in order to increase understanding of issues, including expenditures involved, arising from the application of article 76 of the Convention, thus facilitating preparation of submissions by States, in particular developing States, to the Commission;

49. *Requests* the Secretary-General, in cooperation with the Member States, to continue supporting and organizing workshops or symposiums on scientific and technical aspects of the establishment of the outer limits of the continental shelf beyond 200 nautical miles, taking into account the deadline for submissions, and welcomes initiatives of States in coordination with the United Nations, such as the international symposium held in Tokyo on 6 and 7 March 2006;

VIII

Maritime safety and security and flag State implementation

50. *Encourages* States to ratify or accede to international agreements addressing the safety and security of navigation and to adopt the necessary measures consistent with the Convention, aimed at implementing and enforcing the rules contained in those agreements;

51. *Welcomes* the adoption of the consolidated Maritime Labour Convention, 2006, by the International Labour Conference on 23 February 2006, and encourages States to become parties to that Convention;

52. *Also welcomes* the adoption and continuing review by the International Maritime Organization and the International Labour Organization of Guidelines on Fair Treatment of Seafarers in the Event of a Maritime Accident, and encourages States to implement the Guidelines;

53. *Calls upon* States to consider becoming members of the International Hydrographic Organization, and urges all States to work with that Organization to increase the coverage of hydrographic information on a global basis to enhance capacity-building and technical assistance and to promote safe navigation, especially in areas used for international navigation, ports and where there are vulnerable or protected marine areas;

54. *Encourages* States to draw up plans and to establish procedures to implement the Guidelines on Places of Refuge for Ships in Need of Assistance;

55. *Notes* the progress in the implementation of the Action Plan for the Safety of Transport of Radioactive Material, approved by the Board of Governors of the International Atomic Energy Agency in March 2004, and encourages States concerned to continue their efforts in the implementation of all areas of the Action Plan;

56. *Also notes* that cessation of the transport of radioactive materials through the regions of small island developing States is an ultimate desired goal of small island developing States and some other countries, and recognizes the right of freedom of navigation in accordance with international law; that States should maintain dialogue and consultation, in particular under the aegis of the International Atomic Energy Agency and the International Maritime Organization, with the aim of improved mutual understanding, confidence-building and enhanced communication in relation to the safe maritime transport of radioactive materials; that States involved in the transport of such materials are urged to continue to engage in dialogue with small island developing States and other States to address their concerns; and that these concerns include the further development and strengthening, within the appropriate forums, of international regulatory regimes to enhance safety, disclosure, liability, security and compensation in relation to such transport;

57. *Encourages* States to cooperate to address threats to maritime safety and security, including piracy, armed robbery at sea, smuggling and terrorist acts against shipping, offshore installations and other maritime interests, through bilateral and multilateral instruments and mechanisms aimed at monitoring, preventing and responding to such threats;

58. *Urges* all States, in cooperation with the International Maritime Organization, to combat piracy and armed robbery at sea by adopting measures, including those relating to assistance with capacity-building through training of seafarers, port staff and enforcement personnel in the prevention, reporting and investigation of incidents, bringing the alleged perpetrators to justice, in accordance with international law, and by adopting national legislation, as well as providing enforcement vessels and equipment and guarding against fraudulent ship registration;

59. *Calls upon* States to become parties to the Convention for the Suppression of Unlawful Acts against the Safety of Maritime Navigation and the Protocol for the Suppression of Unlawful Acts against the Safety of Fixed Platforms Located on the Continental Shelf, invites States to consider becoming parties to the 2005 Protocols amending those instruments, and also urges States parties to take appropriate measures to ensure the effective implementation of those instruments, through the adoption of legislation, where appropriate;

60. *Also calls upon* States to effectively implement the International Ship and Port Facility Security Code and related amendments to the International Convention for the Safety of Life at Sea, and to work with the International Maritime Organization to promote safe and secure shipping while ensuring freedom of navigation;

61. *Takes note* of the adoption by the International Maritime Organization of amendments to the International Convention for the Safety of Life at Sea introducing the long-range identification and tracking of ships system;

62. *Notes* the work of the International Maritime Organization with regard to the preparation of the wreck removal convention for the prompt and effective removal of wrecks which may pose a hazard to navigation or the marine environment;

63. *Requests* States to take appropriate measures with regard to ships flying their flag or of their registry to address hazards that may be caused by wrecks and drifting or sunken cargo to navigation or the marine environment;

64. *Urges* all States, in cooperation with the International Maritime Organization, to improve the protection of offshore installations by adopting measures related to the prevention, reporting and investigation of acts of violence against installations, in accordance with international law, and by implementing such measures through national legislation to ensure proper and adequate enforcement;

65. *Calls upon* States to ensure freedom of navigation and the rights of transit passage and innocent passage in accordance with international law, in particular the Convention;

66. *Welcomes* the work of the International Maritime Organization relating to the protection of shipping lanes of strategic importance and significance, and in particular in enhancing safety, security and environmental protection in straits used for international navigation, and calls upon the International Maritime Organization, States bordering straits and user States to continue their cooperation efforts to keep such straits safe and open to international navigation at all times, consistent with international law, in particular the Convention;

67. *Calls upon* user States and States bordering straits for international navigation to cooperate by agreement on matters relating to navigational safety, including safety aids for navigation, and the prevention, reduction and control of pollution from ships;

68. *Welcomes* the progress in regional cooperation, including the Jakarta and Kuala Lumpur Statements on Enhancement of Safety, Security and Environmental Protection in the Straits of Malacca and Singapore, adopted on 8 September 2005 and 20 September 2006, respectively, the progress made in establishing a cooperative mechanism on safety of navigation and

environmental protection to promote dialogue and facilitate close cooperation between the littoral States, user States, shipping industry and other stakeholders and in implementing the Marine Electronic Highway Demonstration Project for the Straits of Malacca and Singapore, and the entry into force of the Regional Cooperation Agreement on Combating Piracy and Armed Robbery against Ships in Asia on 4 September 2006, by which the Information Sharing Centre was launched and established in Singapore in November 2006, and calls upon States to give immediate attention to adopting, concluding and implementing cooperation agreements at the regional level;

69. *Calls upon* States that have not yet done so to become parties to the Protocol against the Smuggling of Migrants by Land, Sea and Air, supplementing the United Nations Convention against Transnational Organized Crime and the Protocol to Prevent, Suppress and Punish Trafficking in Persons, Especially Women and Children, supplementing the United Nations Convention against Transnational Organized Crime, and to take appropriate measures to ensure their effective implementation;

70. *Calls upon* States to ensure that masters on ships flying their flag take the steps required by relevant instruments to provide assistance to persons in distress at sea, and urges States to cooperate and to take all necessary measures to ensure the effective implementation of the amendments to the International Convention on Maritime Search and Rescue and to the International Convention for the Safety of Life at Sea relating to the delivery of persons rescued at sea to a place of safety, as well as of the associated Guidelines on the Treatment of Persons Rescued at Sea;

71. *Urges* flag States without an effective maritime administration and appropriate legal frameworks to establish or enhance the necessary infrastructure, legislative and enforcement capabilities to ensure effective compliance with, and implementation and enforcement of, their responsibilities under international law and, until such action is taken, to consider declining the granting of the right to fly their flag to new vessels, suspending their registry or not opening a registry, and calls upon flag and port States to take all measures consistent with international law necessary to prevent the operation of substandard vessels;

72. *Welcomes* the adoption by the International Maritime Organization of the resolutions on the establishment of the Voluntary International Maritime Organization Member State Audit Scheme, the Code for the implementation of mandatory International Maritime Organization instruments and the future development of the Voluntary Audit Scheme, and encourages all flag States to volunteer to be audited;

73. *Takes note* of the report of the Ad Hoc Consultative Meeting of senior representatives of international organizations on the "genuine link" held by the International Maritime Organization in July 2005 in response to the invitation extended to the Organization and other relevant competent international organizations in resolutions 58/14 of 24 November 2003 and 58/240 to examine and clarify the role of the "genuine link" in relation to the duty of flag States to exercise effective control over ships flying their flag, including fishing vessels, and the potential consequences of non-compliance with duties and obligations of flag States described in relevant international instruments;

IX

Marine environment and marine resources

74. *Emphasizes once again* the importance of the implementation of Part XII of the Convention in order to protect and preserve the marine environment and its living marine resources against pollution and physical degradation, and calls upon all States to cooperate and take measures consistent with the Convention, directly or through competent international organizations, for the protection and preservation of the marine environment;

75. *Encourages* States to ratify or accede to international agreements addressing the protection and preservation of the marine environment and its living marine resources against the introduction of harmful aquatic organisms and pathogens and marine pollution from all sources, and other forms of physical degradation, as well as agreements that provide for compensation for damage resulting from marine pollution, and to adopt the necessary measures consistent with the Convention aimed at implementing and enforcing the rules contained in those agreements;

76. *Welcomes* the entry into force on 24 March 2006 of the 1996 Protocol to the Convention on the Prevention of Marine Pollution by Dumping of Wastes and Other Matter, 1972, and on 14 June 2007 of the Protocol on Preparedness, Response and Cooperation to Pollution Incidents by Hazardous and Noxious Substances, 2000, and encourages States that have not done so to become parties to those Protocols;

77. *Encourages* States, in accordance with the Convention and other relevant instruments, either bilaterally or regionally, to jointly develop and promote contingency plans for responding to pollution incidents, as well as other incidents that are likely to have significant adverse effects on the marine environment and biodiversity;

78. *Welcomes* the activities of the United Nations Environment Programme relating to marine debris carried out in cooperation with relevant United Nations bodies and organizations, and encourages States to further develop partnerships with industry and civil society to raise awareness of the extent of the impact of marine debris on the health and productivity of the marine environment and consequent economic loss;

79. *Urges* States to integrate the issue of marine debris into national strategies dealing with waste management in the coastal zone, ports and maritime industries, including recycling, reuse, reduction and disposal, and to encourage the development of appropriate economic

incentives to address this issue, including the development of cost recovery systems that provide an incentive to use port reception facilities and discourage ships from discharging marine debris at sea, and encourages States to cooperate regionally and subregionally to develop and implement joint prevention and recovery programmes for marine debris;

80. *Welcomes* the decision of the International Maritime Organization to review annex V to the International Convention for the Prevention of Pollution from Ships, 1973, as modified by the Protocol of 1978 relating thereto, to assess its effectiveness in addressing sea-based sources of marine debris, and encourages all relevant organizations and bodies to assist in that process;

81. *Encourages* States that have not done so to become parties to the Protocol of 1997 (Annex VI-Regulations for the Prevention of Air Pollution from Ships) to the International Convention for the Prevention of Pollution from Ships, 1973, as modified by the Protocol of 1978 relating thereto, and furthermore to ratify or accede to the International Convention on the Control of Harmful Anti-Fouling Systems on Ships, 2001, as well as the International Convention for the Control and Management of Ships' Ballast Water and Sediments, 2004, thereby facilitating their early entry into force;

82. *Notes* the ongoing work of the International Maritime Organization in accordance with its resolution on International Maritime Organization policies and practices related to the reduction of greenhouse gas emissions from ships and the work plan to identify and develop the mechanisms needed to achieve the limitation or reduction of CO_2 emissions from international shipping agreed by the Marine Environment Protection Committee of the International Maritime Organization at its fifty-fifth session from 9 to 13 October 2006, and welcomes ongoing efforts of that Organization in that regard;

83. *Notes with appreciation* the efforts of the International Maritime Organization in developing and approving an action plan to address the inadequacy of port waste reception facilities, and urges States to cooperate in correcting the shortfall in such facilities in accordance with the action plan;

84. *Welcomes* the outcomes of the Second Intergovernmental Review Meeting of the Global Programme of Action for the Protection of the Marine Environment from Land-based Activities, convened in Beijing from 16 to 20 October 2006, and calls upon States to take all appropriate measures to fulfil the commitments of the international community embodied in the Beijing Declaration on Furthering the Implementation of the Global Programme of Action;

85. *Also welcomes* the continued work of States, the United Nations Environment Programme and regional organizations in the implementation of the Global Programme of Action, and encourages increased emphasis on the link between freshwater, the coastal zone and marine resources in the implementation of international development goals, including those contained in the United Nations Millennium Declaration and of the time-bound targets in the Plan of Implementation of the World Summit on Sustainable Development ("Johannesburg Plan of Implementation"), in particular the target on sanitation, and the Monterrey Consensus of the International Conference on Financing for Development;

86. *Invites* States, in particular those States with advanced technology and marine capabilities, to explore prospects for improving cooperation with, and assistance to, developing States, in particular least developed countries and small island developing States, as well as coastal African States, with a view to better integrating into national policies and programmes sustainable and effective development in the marine sector;

87. *Encourages* the competent international organizations, the United Nations Development Programme, the World Bank and other funding agencies to consider expanding their programmes within their respective fields of competence for assistance to developing countries and to coordinate their efforts, including in the allocation and application of Global Environment Facility funding;

88. *Requests* the Secretary-General to prepare a study, in cooperation with and based on information provided by States and competent international organizations and global and regional funding agencies, on the assistance available to and measures that may be taken by developing States, in particular the least developed States and small island developing States, as well as coastal African States, to realize the benefits of sustainable and effective development of marine resources and uses of the oceans within the limits of national jurisdiction, and further requests the Secretary-General to present the study to the General Assembly at its sixty-third session and to report to the Assembly at its sixty-second session on progress in the preparation of the study;

X

Marine biodiversity

89. *Reaffirms its role* relating to the conservation and sustainable use of marine biological diversity beyond areas of national jurisdiction, notes the work of States and relevant complementary intergovernmental organizations and bodies on those issues, including the Convention on Biological Diversity and the Food and Agriculture Organization of the United Nations, and invites them to contribute to its consideration of these issues within the areas of their respective competence;

90. *Welcomes* the meeting of the Ad Hoc Open-ended Informal Working Group, established by paragraph 73 of resolution 59/24 to study issues relating to the conservation and sustainable use of marine biological diversity beyond areas of national jurisdiction, held in New York from 13 to 17 February 2006, and takes note of the possible options, approaches and timely follow-up process discussed by the Working Group;

91. *Takes note* of the report of the Working Group, and requests the Secretary-General to convene, in accordance with paragraph 73 of resolution 59/24, and with full conference services, a meeting of the Working Group in 2008, to consider:

(a) The environmental impacts of anthropogenic activities on marine biological diversity beyond areas of national jurisdiction;

(b) Coordination and cooperation among States as well as relevant intergovernmental organizations and bodies for the conservation and management of marine biological diversity beyond areas of national jurisdiction;

(c) The role of area-based management tools;

(d) Genetic resources beyond areas of national jurisdiction;

(e) Whether there is a governance or regulatory gap, and if so, how it should be addressed;

92. *Requests* the Secretary-General to report on the issues referred to in paragraph 91 above in the context of his report on oceans and the law of the sea to the General Assembly at its sixty-second session, in order to assist the Working Group in preparing its agenda, in consultation with all relevant international bodies, and to arrange for support for the performance of its work to be provided by the Division;

93. *Encourages* States to include relevant experts in their delegations attending the meeting of the Working Group;

94. *Recognizes* the importance of making the outcomes of the Working Group widely available;

95. *Notes* the work under the Jakarta Mandate on Marine and Coastal Biological Diversity and the Convention on Biological Diversity elaborated programme of work on marine and coastal biological diversity, as well as the relevant decisions adopted at the eighth meeting of the Conference of the Parties to the Convention on Biological Diversity, held in Curitiba, Brazil, from 20 to 31 March 2006;

96. *Reaffirms* the need for States and competent international organizations to urgently consider ways to integrate and improve, based on the best available scientific information and in accordance with the Convention and related agreements and instruments, the management of risks to the marine biodiversity of seamounts, cold water corals, hydrothermal vents and certain other underwater features;

97. *Also reaffirms* the need for States to continue their efforts to develop and facilitate the use of diverse approaches and tools for conserving and managing vulnerable marine ecosystems, including the possible establishment of marine protected areas, consistent with international law and based on the best scientific information available, and the development of representative networks of any such marine protected areas by 2012;

98. *Notes* the work of States, relevant intergovernmental organizations and bodies, including the Convention on Biological Diversity, in the assessment of scientific information on, and compilation of ecological criteria for the identification of, marine areas that require protection, in light of the objective of the World Summit on Sustainable Development to develop and facilitate the use of diverse approaches and tools such as the establishment of marine protected areas consistent with international law and based on scientific information, including representative networks by 2012;

99. *Also notes* the report of the Scientific Experts' Workshop on Criteria for Identifying Ecologically or Biologically Significant Areas beyond National Jurisdiction, held in Ottawa from 6 to 8 December 2005, and encourages experts to participate in follow-up workshops;

100. *Further notes* the Millennium Ecosystem Assessment synthesis reports and the urgent need to protect the marine biodiversity expressed therein;

101. *Calls upon* States and international organizations to urgently take action to address, in accordance with international law, destructive practices that have adverse impacts on marine biodiversity and ecosystems, including seamounts, hydrothermal vents and cold water corals;

102. *Reiterates its support* for the International Coral Reef Initiative, takes note of the International Coral Reef Initiative General Meetings, held in Koror from 31 October to 2 November 2005, and in Cozumel, Mexico, on 22 and 23 October 2006, supports the work under the Jakarta Mandate on Marine and Coastal Biological Diversity and the elaborated programme of work on marine and coastal biological diversity related to coral reefs, and notes the progress that the International Coral Reef Initiative and other relevant bodies have made to incorporate cold water coral ecosystems into their programmes and activities and to promote the conservation and sustainable use of all coral reef resources;

103. *Expresses its concern* that coral bleaching has become more frequent and severe throughout tropical seas over the last two decades, and highlights the need for improved monitoring to predict and identify bleaching events to support and strengthen action during such events and improve strategies to support the natural resilience of reefs;

104. *Welcomes* the publication of the *Status of Coral Reefs in Tsunami Affected Countries: 2005* by the Global Coral Reef Monitoring Network;

105. *Encourages* States to cooperate, directly or through competent international bodies, in exchanging information in the event of accidents involving vessels on coral reefs and in promoting the development of economic assessment techniques for both restoration and non-use values of coral reef systems;

106. *Emphasizes* the need to mainstream sustainable coral reef management and integrated watershed management into national development strategies, as well as into the activities of relevant United Nations agencies and programmes, international financial institutions and the donor community;

107. *Encourages* further studies and consideration of the impacts of ocean noise on marine living resources, and requests the Division to compile the peer-reviewed scientific studies it receives from Member States and to make them available on its website;

XI

Marine science

108. *Calls upon* States, individually or in collaboration with each other or with relevant international or-

ganizations and bodies, to improve understanding and knowledge of the oceans and the deep sea, including, in particular, the extent and vulnerability of deep sea biodiversity and ecosystems, by increasing their marine scientific research activities in accordance with the Convention;

109. *Notes* the contribution of the Census of Marine Life to marine biodiversity research, and encourages participation in the initiative;

110. *Takes note with appreciation* of the work of the Advisory Body of Experts on the Law of the Sea of the Intergovernmental Oceanographic Commission on the development of procedures for the implementation of Parts XIII and XIV of the Convention and on the development of a consensual text on the legal framework for the collection of oceanographic data within the context of the Convention;

111. *Stresses* the importance of increasing the scientific understanding of the oceans/atmosphere interface, including through participation in ocean observing programmes and geographic information systems, such as the Global Ocean Observing System, a programme of the Intergovernmental Oceanographic Commission, particularly considering their role in monitoring climate variability and in the establishment of tsunami warning systems;

112. *Recognizes* the significant progress made by the Intergovernmental Oceanographic Commission and Member States towards the establishment of regional tsunami warning and mitigation systems, welcomes the continued collaboration of the World Meteorological Organization and other United Nations and intergovernmental organizations in this effort, and encourages Member States to establish and sustain their national warning and mitigation systems, within a global, ocean-related multi-hazard approach, as necessary, to reduce loss of life and damage to national economies and strengthen the resilience of coastal communities to natural disasters;

XII

Regular process for global reporting and assessment of the state of the marine environment, including socio-economic aspects

113. *Recalls* that the Ad Hoc Steering Group was established by resolution 60/30;

114. *Takes note* of the report of the first meeting of the Ad Hoc Steering Group for the "assessment of assessments" launched as a preparatory stage towards the establishment of the regular process for global reporting and assessment of the state of the marine environment, including socio-economic aspects, held in New York from 7 to 9 June 2006, and urges Member States from the African and Asian regional groups to propose the remaining representatives to the Chairmen of their regional groups so that the appointment to the Ad Hoc Steering Group of those representatives can be made by the President of the General Assembly without further delay;

115. *Urges* the Ad Hoc Steering Group to complete the "assessment of assessments" within two years, as provided for in resolution 60/30;

116. *Welcomes with appreciation* the support of the United Nations Environment Programme and the Intergovernmental Oceanographic Commission for the "assessment of assessments" in providing secretariat services to the Ad Hoc Steering Group and establishing the group of experts, as approved by the Ad Hoc Steering Group;

117. *Invites* Member States, the Global Environment Facility and other interested parties to contribute financially to the "assessment of assessments", taking into account the workplan and budget approved by the Ad Hoc Steering Group, in order to complete the "assessment of assessments" within the specified period;

XIII

Regional cooperation

118. *Notes* that there have been a number of initiatives at the regional level, in various regions, to further the implementation of the Convention, takes note in that context of the Caribbean-focused Assistance Fund, which is intended to facilitate, mainly through technical assistance, the voluntary undertaking of maritime delimitation negotiations between Caribbean States, takes note once again of the Fund for Peace: Peaceful Settlement of Territorial Disputes, established by the General Assembly of the Organization of American States in 2000 as a primary mechanism, given its broader regional scope, for the prevention and resolution of pending territorial, land border and maritime boundary disputes, and calls upon States and others in a position to do so to contribute to these funds;

XIV

Open-ended informal consultative process on oceans and the law of the sea

119. *Welcomes* the report on the work of the Consultative Process at its seventh meeting, and invites States to consider the agreed consensual elements relating to ecosystem approaches and oceans, as suggested by the Consultative Process, as set out in part A of the report, in particular the proposed elements of an ecosystem approach, means to achieve implementation of an ecosystem approach and requirements for improved application of an ecosystem approach and also:

(a) Notes that continued environmental degradation in many parts of the world and increasing competing demands require an urgent response and the setting of priorities for management interventions aimed at conserving ecosystem integrity;

(b) Notes that ecosystem approaches to ocean management should be focused on managing human activities in order to maintain and, where needed, restore ecosystem health to sustain goods and environmental services, provide social and economic benefits for food security, sustain livelihoods in support of international development goals, including those contained in the Millennium Declaration, and conserve marine biodiversity;

(c) Recalls that States should be guided in the application of ecosystem approaches by a number of existing instruments, in particular the Convention, which sets out the legal framework for all activities in the oceans and seas, and its implementing Agreements, as well as other commitments, such as those contained in the Convention on Biological Diversity and the World Summit on Sustainable Development call for the application of an ecosystem approach by 2010;

(d) Encourages States to cooperate and coordinate their efforts and take, individually or jointly, as appropriate, all measures, in conformity with international law, including the Convention and other applicable instruments, to address impacts on marine ecosystems in areas within and beyond national jurisdiction, taking into account the integrity of the ecosystems concerned;

120. *Requests* the Secretary-General to convene the eighth meeting of the Consultative Process, in New York, from 25 to 29 June 2007, to provide it with the necessary facilities for the performance of its work and to arrange for support to be provided by the Division, in cooperation with other relevant parts of the Secretariat, as appropriate;

121. *Recalls* the need to strengthen and improve the efficiency of the Consultative Process, and encourages States, intergovernmental organizations and programmes to provide guidance to the co-chairpersons to this effect, particularly before and during the preparatory meeting for the Consultative Process;

122. *Expresses its concern* regarding the insufficient resources available in the voluntary trust fund established by resolution 55/7 for the purpose of assisting developing countries, in particular least developed countries, small island developing States and landlocked developing States, in attending the meetings of the Consultative Process by covering the costs of travel and daily subsistence allowance, and urges States to make additional contributions to the trust fund;

123. *Decides* that, in its deliberations on the report of the Secretary-General on oceans and the law of the sea at its forthcoming meetings in 2007 and 2008, the Consultative Process will focus its discussions on the topics "Marine genetic resources" in 2007 and "Maritime security and safety" in 2008;

XV

Coordination and cooperation

124. *Encourages* States to work closely with and through international organizations, funds and programmes, as well as the specialized agencies of the United Nations system and relevant international conventions, to identify emerging areas of focus for improved coordination and cooperation and how best to address these issues;

125. *Requests* the Secretary-General to bring the present resolution to the attention of heads of intergovernmental organizations, the specialized agencies, funds and programmes of the United Nations engaged in activities relating to ocean affairs and the law of the sea, as well as funding institutions, and underlines the importance of their constructive and timely input for the report of the Secretary-General on oceans and the law of the sea and of their participation in relevant meetings and processes;

126. *Welcomes* the work done by the secretariats of relevant United Nations specialized agencies, programmes, funds and bodies and the secretariats of related organizations and conventions to enhance inter-agency coordination and cooperation on ocean issues, including through UN-Oceans, the inter-agency coordination mechanism on ocean and coastal issues within the United Nations system;

127. *Encourages* continued updates to Member States by UN-Oceans regarding its priorities and initiatives, in particular with respect to the proposed participation in UN-Oceans;

XVI

Activities of the Division for Ocean Affairs and the Law of the Sea

128. *Expresses its appreciation* to the Secretary-General for the annual comprehensive report on oceans and the law of the sea, prepared by the Division, as well as for the other activities of the Division, which reflect the high standard of assistance provided to Member States by the Division;

129. *Requests* the Secretary-General to continue to carry out the responsibilities and functions entrusted to him in the Convention and by the related resolutions of the General Assembly, including resolutions 49/28 and 52/26, and to ensure the allocation of appropriate resources to the Division for the performance of its activities under the approved budget for the Organization;

XVII

Sixty-second session of the General Assembly

130. *Requests* the Secretary-General to prepare a comprehensive report, in its current comprehensive format and in accordance with established practice, for the consideration of the General Assembly at its sixty-second session, on developments and issues relating to ocean affairs and the law of the sea, including the implementation of the present resolution, in accordance with resolutions 49/28, 52/26 and 54/33, and to make the report available at least six weeks in advance of the meeting of the Consultative Process;

131. *Emphasizes* the critical role of the annual comprehensive report of the Secretary-General, which integrates information on developments relating to the implementation of the Convention and the work of the Organization, its specialized agencies and other institutions in the field of ocean affairs and the law of the sea at the global and regional levels, and as a result constitutes the basis for the annual consideration and review of developments relating to ocean affairs and the law of the sea by the General Assembly as the global institution having the competence to undertake such a review;

132. *Notes* that the report referred to in paragraph 130 above will also be presented to States parties pursuant to article 319 of the Convention regarding issues

of a general nature that have arisen with respect to the Convention;

133. *Also notes* the desire to further improve the efficiency of, and effective participation of delegations in, the informal consultations concerning the annual General Assembly resolution on oceans and the law of the sea and the resolution on sustainable fisheries, and decides to limit the period of the informal consultations on both resolutions to a maximum of four weeks in total and to ensure that the consultations are scheduled in such a way as to avoid overlap with the period during which the Sixth Committee is meeting and that the Division has sufficient time to produce the report referred to in paragraph 130 above;

134. *Decides* to include in the provisional agenda of its sixty-second session the item entitled "Oceans and the law of the sea".

RECORDED VOTE ON RESOLUTION 61/222:

In favour: Afghanistan, Albania, Algeria, Andorra, Angola, Antigua and Barbuda, Argentina, Armenia, Australia, Austria, Bahamas, Bahrain, Bangladesh, Belarus, Belgium, Belize, Benin, Bhutan, Bolivia, Botswana, Brazil, Brunei Darussalam, Bulgaria, Burkina Faso, Burundi, Canada, Cape Verde, Central African Republic, Chile, China, Comoros, Congo, Costa Rica, Côte d'Ivoire, Croatia, Cuba, Cyprus, Czech Republic, Denmark, Djibouti, Dominica, Dominican Republic, Ecuador, Egypt, Eritrea, Estonia, Fiji, Finland, France, Gambia, Georgia, Germany, Ghana, Greece, Grenada, Guatemala, Guinea, Guinea-Bissau, Guyana, Haiti, Honduras, Hungary, Iceland, India, Indonesia, Iran, Ireland, Israel, Italy, Jamaica, Japan, Kenya, Kuwait, Latvia, Lebanon, Lesotho, Liberia, Liechtenstein, Lithuania, Luxembourg, Madagascar, Malawi, Malaysia, Maldives, Mali, Malta, Marshall Islands, Mauritania, Mauritius, Mexico, Micronesia, Moldova, Monaco, Mongolia, Morocco, Mozambique, Myanmar, Namibia, Nauru, Nepal, Netherlands, New Zealand, Nicaragua, Niger, Nigeria, Norway, Oman, Pakistan, Palau, Panama, Papua New Guinea, Paraguay, Peru, Philippines, Poland, Portugal, Qatar, Republic of Korea, Romania, Russian Federation, Saint Lucia, Saint Vincent and the Grenadines, Samoa, San Marino, Sao Tome and Principe, Saudi Arabia, Senegal, Serbia, Sierra Leone, Singapore, Slovakia, Slovenia, Solomon Islands, South Africa, Spain, Sri Lanka, Sudan, Suriname, Swaziland, Sweden, Switzerland, Thailand, The former Yugoslav Republic of Macedonia, Timor-Leste, Togo, Tonga, Trinidad and Tobago, Tunisia, Ukraine, United Arab Emirates, United Kingdom, United States, Uruguay, Viet Nam, Yemen, Zambia, Zimbabwe.

Against: Turkey.

Abstaining: Colombia, Libyan Arab Jamahiriya, Venezuela.

Division for Ocean Affairs and the Law of the Sea

During 2006, the Division for Ocean Affairs and the Law of the Sea of the Office of Legal Affairs continued to fulfil its role as the substantive unit of the UN Secretariat responsible for reviewing and monitoring all developments concerning to the law of the sea and ocean affairs, as well as for the implementation of UNCLOS and related General Assembly resolutions.

The Division, in cooperation with intergovernmental bodies and host Governments, continued its capacity-building efforts through the organization of training courses. It also held its fourth regional workshop (Argentina, 8-12 May).

The Secretariat had upgraded the technical facilities, as well as the conference room of the Division, which was fitted with state-of-the-art equipment, allowing it to be used as a Geographic Information System (GIS) Laboratory, especially for the technical examination of submissions on the establishment of the outer limits of the continental shelf.

The twenty-first Hamilton Shirley Amerasinghe Fellowship, established in 1981 [YUN 1981, p. 139], was awarded to Viet Nguyen Hong of Viet Nam.

OIOS report. In March [E/AC.51/2006/5], the Office of Internal Oversight Services (OIOS) transmitted to the Committee for Programme and Coordination (CPC) a report on the triennial review of the implementation of the Committee's recommendations at its forty-third session on the in-depth evaluation of the programme on the law of the sea and ocean affairs [YUN 2003, p. 1362]. The review described the extent to which those recommendations were implemented, the implementation of the Division for Ocean Affairs and Law of the Sea integrated programme on ocean affairs and the law of the sea, coordination with and technical assistance to the General Assembly and other relevant intergovernmental bodies, and the annual review of implementation by the Assembly.

CPC, at its forty-sixth session (14 August–8 September) [A/61/16 & Corr.1], concluded that the Division had implemented all of the recommendations made by the Committee at its forty-third session.

PART FIVE

Institutional, administrative and budgetary questions

Chapter I

UN restructuring and institutional matters

In 2006, the Secretary-General presented further reform proposals aimed at significantly re-orienting the management and operation of the Organization in the execution of its mandates. In a report entitled "Investing in the United Nations: for a stronger Organization worldwide", the Secretary-General proposed further measures to enable future Secretaries-General to carry out their managerial responsibilities effectively and to make better use of the Organization's managerial and human resources. He also created a High-level Panel on United Nations System-wide Coherence to help find ways to effect a more coherent and effective response to the needs of Member States. In its report entitled "Delivering as one", the Panel proposed a framework for a unified and coherent UN structure at the country level, with appropriate governance, funding and management arrangements in the areas of development, humanitarian assistance and the environment, as well as a number of cross-cutting issues, such as gender equality and human rights. The Secretary-General also presented a report on the review, requested by the 2005 World Summit, of UN mandates, which addressed key challenges in the mandate generation cycle and made recommendations in relation to each of the Organization's programme priorities.

The Ad Hoc Working Group on the Revitalization of the Work of the General Assembly continued to identify ways to further enhance the Assembly's role, authority, effectiveness and efficiency. The Open-ended Working Group on the Question of Equitable Representation on and Increase in the Membership of the Security Council considered ways to advance progress on Security Council reform. The Assembly also adopted a number of decisions for strengthening the Economic and Social Council.

The Assembly continued its focus on administrative and institutional matters. It resumed its sixtieth session and opened its sixty-first session on 12 September; it also resumed its tenth emergency special session. Two high-level plenary meetings were convened, one on international migration and development (14-15 September) and one on the midterm review of the Implementation of the Programme of Action for the Least Developed Countries for the Decade 2001-2010 (18-19 September). The Assembly admitted Montenegro to membership in the United Nations, bringing the total membership to 192, and granted observer status to the Organization of the Petroleum Exporting Countries Fund for International Development, the Indian Ocean Commission and the Association of Southeast Asian Nations.

The Security Council held 272 formal meetings to deal with regional conflicts, peacekeeping operations and other issues related to the maintenance of peace and security. The Assembly again took up the issue of expanding the Council's membership.

In addition to its organizational and substantive sessions, the Economic and Social Council held a special high-level meeting with the Bretton Woods institutions (the World Bank Group and the International Monetary Fund), the World Trade Organization and the United Nations Conference on Trade and Development.

Restructuring issues

Programme of reform

Implementation of World Summit Outcome

The General Assembly, in the 2005 World Summit Outcome [YUN 2005, p. 48], had requested the Secretary-General to take a number of actions for strengthening the United Nations in the context of the Secretariat's management reform, including an external evaluation of auditing and oversight as part of the comprehensive review of governance arrangements, and to submit proposals for the creation of an oversight advisory committee. In his report on the establishment of an ethics office [ibid., p. 1476], the Secretary-General set out the proposed terms of reference for the comprehensive review of governance and oversight arrangements. Consistent with those terms of reference, he established the independent Steering Committee for the Comprehensive Review of Governance and Oversight within the United Nations and its Funds, Programmes and Specialized Agencies, led by Mervyn E. King (South Africa). The review was to: establish governance and oversight best practices in the private and public sectors; compare UN entities' best practices and point out significant gaps; make recommendations for improvement based on an examination of a sample of five entities; and provide an in-depth review and recommendations for strengthening and improving the Office of Internal Oversight Services (OIOS).

In a July report [A/60/883], with later addenda [A/60/883/Add.1,2], the Secretary-General transmitted to the Assembly the Committee's report in five volumes: Executive summary and project scope, background and context (Volume I); Governance and oversight principles and practices (Volume II); Governance: current UN practices, gap analysis and recommendations (Volume III); Oversight: current UN practices, gap analysis and recommendations (Volume IV); and Review of OIOS (Volume V) (see p. 1651). The report provided an opportunity for the Assembly to renew the system of governance and oversight and recommended improvements for the Organization's management and governance structures.

In terms of governance, the Steering Committee stated that, while much had been done to improve budgetary practices, further effort was required to institutionalize results-based management; improve the use of information to make more effective decisions; steer efforts towards clearly defined goals; focus on results to make better policy decisions; and design better strategies within an overall accountability framework.

The Steering Committee recommended strengthening results-based management in the areas of budgets and reporting, the overall accountability of Secretariat executive management, the term limits and qualifications of expert committees and the independence of their members, and the procedures of the Assembly's Fifth (Administrative and Budgetary) Committee. It also recommended improving the coordination of decisions on programmes and resource allocation, strengthening the effectiveness, transparency and independence of all committees, and establishing disclosure, ethics and whistle-blower policies.

The proposal to strengthen the accountability of executive management was considered a priority. Management structures should be enhanced through the creation of a management committee, supported by a secretariat.

On oversight, the Steering Committee recommended implementing a risk management framework; assigning responsibility for internal controls and reporting on their effectiveness to the executive management; implementing the General Assembly decision to establish an Independent Audit Advisory Committee (IAAC); discontinuing the Joint Inspection Unit (JIU); setting new standards for oversight of inter-agency programmes; setting up an audit committee for the International Civil Aviation Organization (ICAO); enhancing the operational independence of the internal audit function within the Office of the United Nations High Commissioner for Refugees (UNHCR), the United Nations Development Programme (UNDP) and the United Nations Children's Fund (UNICEF); and clarifying responsibilities of the UNHCR oversight committees with joint responsibilities for internal audit, investigations and evaluations. (See p. 1648 for more information on oversight.)

The review also found that UN governing bodies were often too large and their decision-making processes complex; decision-making on strategic objectives and resource allocation was sometimes disconnected; and there was need for greater executive management accountability for supporting governance and oversight processes. In terms of the committee structure of governing bodies, the review noted that the use of independent experts by those bodies was growing but limited, and the mandates and functions of some committees overlapped. In addition, there was insufficient transparency in nominations and appointments to those committees and to executive management, and no consistent formal process of evaluation of governing bodies or their committees' performance. The system of declaration and disclosure of personal financial interests for officials was not yet in place in all entities and, while they all shared the International Civil Service Commission's code of conduct, its implementation was not common.

The review recommended a United Nations Code of Governance, founded on external best practices adapted to UN circumstances, for consideration and adoption by UN entities. The proposed Code would cover six themes: strategy, mission, planning and the governing body; governing body and committee structures; human resources management; transparency and disclosure; ethical environment; and audit, risk and compliance.

Other recommendations on governance included strengthening results-based management in budgets and reporting, the overall accountability of executive management of the Secretariat, the term limits and qualifications of expert committees and the independence of their members, and the procedures of the Advisory Committee on Administrative and Budgetary Questions (ACABQ). The report also contained 23 recommendations regarding OIOS and others that fell within the authority of intergovernmental organs.

In presenting the report, the Secretary-General indicated that terms of reference would be prepared with a view to seeking expert advice for reviewing and developing proposals to improve results-based management, as well as for an in-depth review of the Secretariat's accountability framework and for the establishment of an enterprise-wide risk management system. The comments of JIU on the review were contained in an August report [A/60/1004]. JIU agreed with the OIOS assessment that several of the Committee's recommendations would weaken oversight in the United Nations.

ACABQ, in its comments and recommendations [A/61/605], said that the report was not well organized and was repetitive. The quality was uneven and in some cases lacked empirical data to support its conclusions. It identified five issues for early decisions: strengthening the results-based approach; accountability; putting IAAC into effect; enhancing the operational independence of OIOS; and strengthening the internal control framework and related application of risk management Organization-wide. ACABQ agreed that a study to improve results-based management should be undertaken and recommended the use of expertise from within the Organization for that purpose, as well as a study on enhancing the accountability framework, which should include proposals for specific sanctions to be applied in the case of non-performance. It recommended that the Assembly take note of the recommendation on the establishment of disclosure, ethics and whistle-blower policies.

On 18 December [A/C.5/61/17], the Secretary-General indicated that the activities outlined in draft resolution [A/C.5/61/L.15] would give rise to an additional estimated requirement of $1,316,200 gross ($1,206,300 net) for the 2006-2007 biennium.

By **decision 61/550** of 22 December, the Assembly noted that, should it adopt the draft resolution entitled "Comprehensive review of governance and oversight within the United Nations and its funds, programmes and specialized agencies", resource requirements for the activities requested would amount to $1,316,200 gross ($1,206,300 net) for the 2006-2007 biennium, to be accommodated to the extent possible from within existing appropriations. Any additional requirements would be reported in the context of the second performance report for the 2006-2007 biennium.

GENERAL ASSEMBLY ACTION

On 22 December [meeting 84], the General Assembly, on the recommendation of the Fifth (Administrative and Budgetary) Committee [A/61/658], adopted **resolution 61/245** without vote [agenda items 47, 113, 116, 117, 122, 123, 132 & 149].

Comprehensive review of governance and oversight within the United Nations and its funds, programmes and specialized agencies

The General Assembly,

Having considered the report of the Secretary-General on the comprehensive review of governance and oversight within the United Nations and its funds, programmes and specialized agencies and the related report of the Advisory Committee on Administrative and Budgetary Questions, the report of the Joint Inspection Unit on oversight lacunae in the United Nations system and the note by the Secretary-General transmitting his comments and those of the United Nations System Chief Executives Board for Coordination thereon, the comments of the Joint Inspection Unit on the report of the Steering Committee on the Comprehensive Review of Governance and Oversight within the United Nations and Its Funds, Programmes and Specialized Agencies, the report of the Secretary-General on accountability and the related report of the Advisory Committee, the report of the Secretary-General on accountability measures, the report of the Secretary-General on updated terms of reference for the Independent Audit Advisory Committee and the interim report of the Advisory Committee on Administrative and Budgetary Questions thereon, and the report of the Office of Internal Oversight Services on proposals for strengthening the Office,

1. *Takes note* of the report of the Secretary-General on the comprehensive review of governance and oversight within the United Nations and its funds, programmes and specialized agencies, the report of the Joint Inspection Unit on oversight lacunae in the United Nations system and the note by the Secretary-General transmitting his comments and those of the United Nations System Chief Executives Board for Coordination thereon, the comments of the Joint Inspection Unit on the report of the Steering Committee on the Comprehensive Review of Governance and Oversight within the United Nations and Its Funds, Programmes and Specialized Agencies, the report of the Secretary-General on accountability and the related report of the Advisory Committee on Administrative and Budgetary Questions, the report of the Secretary-General on accountability measures, the report of the Secretary-General on updated terms of reference for the Independent Audit Advisory Committee and the interim report of the Advisory Committee on Administrative and Budgetary Questions thereon;

2. *Endorses* the conclusions and recommendations of the Advisory Committee on Administrative and Budgetary Questions on the comprehensive review of governance and oversight within the United Nations and its funds, programmes and specialized agencies;

3. *Requests* the Secretary-General to submit to the General Assembly for consideration at the first part of its resumed sixty-first session reports on the following:

(a) Revised terms of reference for the Independent Audit Advisory Committee;

(b) Strengthening of the Office of Internal Oversight Services;

4. *Also requests* the Secretary-General to submit to the General Assembly for consideration at the second part of its resumed sixty-first session if possible, but no later than by the end of its sixty-first session, reports on the following:

(a) Enterprise risk management and internal control framework;

(b) Results-based management;

(c) Accountability framework.

Mandate review

In March [A/60/733 & Corr.1], the Secretary-General submitted a report entitled "Mandating and delivering: analysis and recommendations to facilitate the review of mandates", in response to a request of the 2005 World Summit [YUN 2005, p. 47] for a review of all mandates older than five years. The Secretariat compiled an electronic inventory of mandates originating from the resolutions of the Assembly, the Economic and Social Council and the Security Council that were older than five years, and the resolutions from which they derived. The Secretary-General noted that the mandate-generation cycle through which mandates were adopted, funded and implemented, and then considered for continuation, change or elimination, had to be re-examined. The system had not sufficiently allowed an intergovernmental organ to analyse the effectiveness of its mandate and how it contributed to the overall priorities of the Organization, as a basis for subsequent decision-making. That critical gap created problems that were common to issue areas, departments and entities throughout the Organization, including burdensome reporting requirements; an overlap between and within UN organs, which adopted mandates on the same issues; an unwieldy and duplicative implementation architecture; and a gap between mandates and resources.

More strategic interaction through better reporting on the state of mandates would unburden the Secretariat and help Member States to ascertain whether their mandates were effectively implemented, and contributed to the Organization's overall goals and priorities. A more transparent system would allow them, when considering the adoption or renewal of mandates, to make informed decisions. To make such a system effective, reporting should be improved and consolidated to provide timely, concise and clear information in a way that met the needs of Member States and did not overburden the Secretariat. Member States should provide strategic direction and objectives when adopting resolutions and, for fuller accountability, the Secretary-General should determine which entity or department was the most competent to lead implementation efforts. To ensure that information provided met the true demand for knowledge about the work of the United Nations, a set of core policy reports on each of the Organization's priority areas could be prepared to provide a full picture of all the activities in each thematic area. When a draft resolution was being considered, the Secretariat could provide, in addition to estimates of budget implications, information about the proposed mandates contained in the resolution, including information on the status of implementation, and evaluation of the effectiveness of previous mandates that addressed the same issue; an explanation of how the proposed mandate would complement or supplement existing structures, conferences, reports and activities; and indications of how the mandate might serve the overall goals of the Organization.

The Secretary-General also addressed the way those problems played out in the Organization's programme priorities and in relation to UN research and training institutes. In the area of the maintenance of peace and security, he noted that the increasing complexity of conflicts and the interconnectedness of security and development issues had led to overlaps between various UN organs. He recommended less frequent reporting on situations that were no longer crisis-driven, and the consolidation of reports of different organs on the same issue. To ensure effective and timely responses, mandated requirements should be matched with adequate resources. Regarding sustained growth and development, the Economic and Social Council should better review, guide and monitor the work of its subsidiary machinery. Given the peculiarities of each issue area, Member States could review mandates, using the analytical framework, and the support of the various networks created in the context of the Executive Committee on Economic and Social Affairs. Reporting requirements should be streamlined to better serve the follow-up to the Millennium Declaration. As to the Assembly's 2002 resolution on UN support for the New Partnership for Africa's Development (NEPAD) [YUN 2002, p. 907], the Secretary-General suggested a review of all pre-NEPAD mandates in order to streamline them and ensure full support to the priorities identified by the African Union.

General Assembly resolution 60/251 (see p. 757) establishing the Human Rights Council, which called for a streamlining of the various mandates, offered an opportunity to improve reporting requirements in that area. Concerning humanitarian assistance, the scale and magnitude of the latest emergencies and disasters demonstrated the need for a timely and coordinated response. While some overlap in mandates among implementing entities existed, the main concern was the fragmented manner in which the principal organs often approached humanitarian assistance, with the potential for implementation gaps. In the area of justice and international law, mandates had expanded greatly in scope and intricacy, stretching the capacity of the Office of Legal Affairs to respond effectively and efficiently. Providing information to Member States in that area in a more efficient manner would better serve UN goals and priorities. In the field of disarmament, the Secretary-General suggested the adoption of fewer resolutions of a general nature. Unnecessary overlaps and duplications had to be identified in the fields of drug control, transnational crime prevention and combating international terrorism so that resources could be shifted to work in the field. In addition, Member States should explore further the idea of one commission to deal with both drugs and crime issues, as well as ways to better coordinate the actions of the three counter-terrorism subsidiary bodies of the Security Council. Overlapping mandates for reports on gender could be examined and assessment and evaluation of the institutional resources across the system strengthened. Better coordination, an accountability system and a common policy among research and training institutes would streamline decision-making and ensure relevance of research to policy. Consolidating those institutes into one UN educational research and training system would make it possible to articulate a unifying vision and an overarching set of strategic directions.

The Secretary-General recommended that Member States divide their review of mandates into two phases: one examining mandates in those areas where problems had been clearly identified and a solution could be reached in a relatively short time; and the other considering groups of mandates which required new processes and guidelines for reaching agreement over a longer period of time.

Ad hoc committee on mandate review

On 31 May [S/2006/354], the Security Council President informed the Secretary-General that the Council had agreed to establish an ad hoc committee to review Security Council mandates and to follow up on the recommendations contained in the Secretary-General's report on the subject (see above), to be chaired by Slovakia and the United States.

By **decision 61/546** of 22 December, the General Assembly, noting the progress made on mandate review, decided to continue the review process during its resumed sixty-first (2007) session.

Strengthening of UN System

In March [A/60/692 & Corr.1], the Secretary-General submitted to the General Assembly a report entitled "Investing in the United Nations: for a stronger Organization worldwide", which set out his latest reform proposals for strengthening the operation and management of the Secretariat to better serve the needs of the United Nations.

The Secretary-General explained that, although the United Nations was vastly different from when it was created in 1945, its normative work remained important and substantive. Its operations had expanded in a wide range of fields, the most notable being a fourfold increase in peacekeeping, with several new missions, a $5 billion budget and 80,000 peacekeepers in the field. In short, the United Nations was no longer a conference-servicing Organization located in a few headquarters locations, but had become highly diverse, working worldwide to improve the lives of people in need. Such a radically expanded range of activities called for a radical overhaul of the Secretariat—its rules, structure, systems and culture. Previous reform efforts, while generating significant improvements, had addressed the symptoms rather than the causes of the Organization's weaknesses, and failed to adequately address new needs and requirements. Responding to the request made by Member States at the 2005 World Summit [YUN 2005, p. 47], the proposed measures were to enable future Secretaries-General to carry out their managerial responsibilities effectively, and the Organization as a whole to make better use of its managerial and human resources. The measures would give Member States the tools to provide strategic direction and hold the Secretariat fully accountable for its performance. To achieve that goal, the reviews of oversight systems and internal justice needed to be combined with reforms in six other broad areas: people, leadership, information and communication technology, services delivery, budget and finance, and governance. A dedicated change management office should be created, with clear terms of reference and time limits, to work with heads of departments and other key Secretariat leaders to plan and coordinate the implementation of the reforms. The process had to be underpinned by a carefully constructed staff buyout programme to reinvigorate the UN workforce.

To ensure that the Organization hired the best people, the Assembly should modify the requirements for recruiting, promoting and placing UN staff; authorize the Secretary-General to move staff according to organizational need; broaden mobility requirements and approve a simplified contract system; invest more in staff development and training; and align benefits for UN staff in the field with those of UN funds and programmes. To improve the Secretariat's ability to manage large and complex operations, the role of the Deputy Secretary-General should be redefined, to include formal authority and accountability for the management and overall direction of the Secretariat's functions; the 25 departments and entities reporting directly to the Secretary-General should be reorganized to reduce the reporting span; and a new leadership development plan developed, covering recruitment, training and career development, to build middle and senior management capacity. To equip the Organization with up-to-date information and communication technologies, the post of Chief Information Technology Officer should be created. There should also be a system-wide commitment to developing a fully integrated global UN information and communication technology management support system, subject to the results of a feasibility study. To ensure that the Organization got the best value for money spent on services, the Secretary-General recommended reviewing guidance on alternative service delivery and agreeing to the preparation of cost/benefit analyses in certain administrative areas. At the same time, transparent and efficient financial and budgetary management could be achieved by shortening the cycle for review and adoption of the Organization's programme budget, giving greater budgetary discretion to the Secretary-General in consolidating peacekeeping accounts for separate field operations, improving the system of financial management, including delegation of financial authority with clear controls, and increasing performance monitoring and evaluation. To improve the Secretariat's accountability to Member States, improved reporting mechanisms to intergovernmental bodies were needed, as well as improved interaction with the Secretariat on management issues. The creation of change management capacity and process should be supported to ensure that change was resolute and sustained.

ACABQ, in a March report [A/60/735 & Corr.1], drew attention to the need to define the meaning of accountability in the UN context and set out the parameters of its application and the instruments for its enforcement. ACABQ recommended that the Secretary-General be requested to prepare a detailed report that would bring together interrelated issues, while reflecting the unique nature of the United Nations and its central role. ACABQ was informed that, if requested, the Secretariat could submit such a report by May. A report on human resources, however, was already scheduled to be submitted in September, and could be considered separately by the Assembly at the main part of its sixty-first (2006) session. The report should include all areas covered by the current report of the Secretary-General and incorporate all additional reports (with the exception of the report on human resources management issues mentioned above). For each proposal, the detailed report should include: an indication of any previous related proposals and how they developed into their current form, with concise references to relevant Assembly resolutions and decisions and ACABQ recommendations; an assessment of the impact of previous and ongoing reforms as they related to current proposals; specific cost and administrative implications (including changes to regulations, rules and procedures), with detailed analysis and justification; an explanation of how accountability would be defined and enforced; the projected impact on the enhancement of the effectiveness of the work of the Organization, as well as the return on investment; and projected time lines for implementation. ACABQ also provided observations on the Secretary-General's individual proposals.

GENERAL ASSEMBLY ACTION

On 8 May [meeting 79], the General Assembly, on the recommendation of the Fifth Committee [A/60/831], adopted **resolution 60/260** by recorded vote (121-50-2) [agenda items 46, 118, 120, 122, 124, 128, 129, 136].

Investing in the United Nations: for a stronger Organization worldwide

The General Assembly,

Recalling its resolution 60/1 of 16 September 2005,

Reaffirming its determination to strengthen further the role, capacity, effectiveness and efficiency of the United Nations, and thus improve its performance, in order to realize the full potential of the Organization, in accordance with the purposes and principles of the Charter of the United Nations, and to respond more effectively to the needs of Member States and existing and new global challenges facing the United Nations in the twenty-first century,

Recalling its resolutions 41/213 of 19 December 1986, 42/211 of 21 December 1987, 49/233 A of 23 December 1994, 57/300 of 20 December 2002 and 58/269 of 23 December 2003,

Recalling also its resolutions 55/258 of 14 June 2001, 57/305 and 57/307 of 15 April 2003, 58/296 of 18 June 2004, 59/266 of 23 December 2004, 59/283 of 13 April 2005 and 60/238 of 23 December 2005, as well as its other relevant resolutions and decisions on human resources management and administration of justice,

Recalling further its resolutions 54/14 of 29 October 1999, 54/256 of 7 April 2000, 55/232 of 23 December 2000, 55/247 of 12 April 2001, 57/279 of 20 December 2002, 58/276 and 58/277 of 23 December 2003 and 59/288 and 59/289 of 13 April 2005, as well as its other relevant resolutions on procurement and outsourcing practices,

Recalling its resolutions 52/12 B of 19 December 1997, 52/220 of 22 December 1997, 55/231 of 23 December 2000, 57/304 of 15 April 2003, 58/268 of 23 December 2003, 59/275 of 23 December 2004, 59/296 of 22 June 2005, 60/237 of 23 December 2005 and 60/254, 60/257 and 60/259 of 8 May 2006,

Recalling also Article 2, paragraph 1, and Articles 17, 18, 97 and 100 of the Charter,

Reaffirming the rules of procedure of the General Assembly,

Recalling the Regulations and Rules Governing Programme Planning, the Programme Aspects of the Budget, the Monitoring of Implementation and the Methods of Evaluation and the Financial Regulations and Rules of the United Nations,

Stressing the intergovernmental, multilateral and international character of the United Nations,

Reaffirming the role of the General Assembly and its relevant intergovernmental and expert bodies, within their respective mandates, in planning, programming, budgeting, monitoring and evaluation,

Stressing the need for Member States to participate in the budget preparation process, from its early stages and throughout the process,

Recognizing the ongoing efforts to reform human resources management, the system of administration of justice, the budgetary and planning processes and the procurement system of the United Nations, in accordance with the provisions of the relevant General Assembly resolutions and decisions,

Having considered the report of the Secretary-General entitled "Investing in the United Nations: for a stronger Organization worldwide" and the related report of the Advisory Committee on Administrative and Budgetary Questions,

1. *Welcomes* the commitment of the Secretary-General to strengthening the United Nations;

2. *Takes note* of the report of the Secretary-General;

3. *Also takes note* of the report of the Advisory Committee on Administrative and Budgetary Questions;

4. *Reaffirms* its oversight role and the role of the Fifth Committee in administrative and budgetary matters;

5. *Also reaffirms* its primary role in the consideration of and action taken on reports submitted to it;

6. *Stresses* that setting the priorities of the United Nations is the prerogative of the Member States, as reflected in legislative decisions;

7. *Reaffirms* its role in carrying out a thorough analysis and approval of human and financial resources and policies, with a view to ensuring full, effective and efficient implementation of all mandated programmes and activities and the implementation of policies in this regard;

I

Accountability

1. *Stresses* the importance of strengthened accountability in the Organization and of ensuring greater accountability of the Secretary-General to Member States, inter alia, for the effective and efficient implementation of legislative mandates and the use of human and financial resources;

2. *Requests* the Secretary-General, in the context of the reports requested in the present resolution and the proposals contained therein, to specifically define accountability as well as clear accountability mechanisms, including to the General Assembly, and to propose clear parameters for its application and the instruments for its rigorous enforcement, without exception, at all levels;

3. *Emphasizes* the need for strengthening oversight in the Organization, and looks forward to considering and taking action on the report on the strengthening of the Office of Internal Oversight Services and the terms of reference requested in section XIII, paragraph 4, of its resolution 60/248 of 23 December 2005;

II

Proposals 1 to 4 and 7

1. *Recalls* its requests for reports, as contained in the relevant paragraphs of its resolutions 59/266 and 60/238;

2. *Requests* the Secretary-General to submit to the General Assembly at its sixty-first session, in addition to the reports and assessments requested in its resolutions 59/266, 59/296 and 60/238, a report, including details regarding proposals 1 to 4 and 7 contained in the report of the Secretary-General, focusing on the following elements:

(a) Information on all relevant previous reform proposals as agreed by the General Assembly, including concise references to previous relevant resolutions and decisions of the Assembly, as well as an outline of the measures taken to implement them;

(b) An assessment of the impact of previous and ongoing reforms as they relate to the proposals;

(c) Specific costs and administrative implications, including required changes to the regulations, rules and procedures, with detailed analysis and justification;

(d) Detailed explanation and concrete examples of how it is envisaged that the proposals will enhance the effectiveness of the work of the Organization and address current deficiencies;

(e) Proposals to effectively increase the representation of developing countries in the Secretariat, in particular at senior levels, with due regard to the principle of equitable geographical distribution of posts;

(f) Proposals on how gender targets can be strictly enforced;

(g) An assessment of the impact of the proposals on the role and authority of the centralized human resources function;

3. *Reaffirms* that the staff of the United Nations is an invaluable asset of the Organization, and requests the Secretary-General, in the context of the reports requested in the present resolution, to provide information on the consultations undertaken with the staff representatives, in accordance with article VIII of the Staff Regulations, to develop the proposals on personnel policies;

III

Proposals 5 and 6

1. *Recalls* the role of the Secretary-General as the chief administrative officer of the Organization, in accordance with the provisions of Article 97 of the Charter of the United Nations;

2. *Reaffirms* paragraphs 1 and 2 of its resolution 52/12 B;

3. *Recalls* its resolutions 52/12 B and 52/220, by which it decided to establish the post of Deputy Secretary-General as an integral part of the Office of the Secretary-General, without prejudice to the mandate of the Secretary-General as provided by the Charter, and noted that the Secretary-General would appoint the Deputy Secretary-General following consultations with Member States;

4. *Also recalls* that in its resolution 52/12 B, the General Assembly identified functions of the post of Deputy Secretary-General and the duration of the term of office, and decides that the functions of the post should be in accordance with that resolution and should not diminish the role or responsibilities of the Secretary-General as the chief administrative officer of the Organization, including in management policies and overall operational matters;

5. *Recognizes* that the delegation of authority on the part of the Secretary-General should be in order to facilitate the better management of the Organization, but stresses that the overall responsibility for management of the Organization rests with the Secretary-General as the chief administrative officer;

6. *Reaffirms* its role with regard to the structure of the Secretariat, and stresses that proposals that amend the overall departmental structure, as well as the format of the programme budget and the biennial programme plan are subject to the review and approval of the General Assembly;

7. *Emphasizes* that proposal 6 would be developed in the light of paragraph 13 of the report of the Advisory Committee on Administrative and Budgetary Questions;

IV

Proposals 8 to 12, 17 and 18

1. *Requests* the Secretary-General to submit a detailed report, bearing in mind the unique intergovernmental nature and international character of the United Nations and the provisions of previous resolutions, including paragraph 15 of its resolution 60/237, to the General Assembly on proposals 8 to 10, 17 and 18 contained in his report, which would respond to the following elements:

(a) Information on all relevant previous reform proposals as agreed by the General Assembly, including concise references to previous relevant resolutions and decisions of the Assembly, as well as an outline of the measures taken to implement them;

(b) An assessment of the impact of previous and ongoing reforms as they relate to the proposals;

(c) Specific costs and administrative implications, including required changes to the regulations, rules and procedures, with detailed analysis and justification;

(d) Detailed explanation and concrete examples of how it is envisaged that the proposals will enhance the effectiveness of the work of the Organization and address current deficiencies;

(e) A clear definition of the terminologies and rationale for the proposals;

(f) An assessment of previous investments in information and communication technology, as well as lessons learned and expected time frames for introducing the proposed system and arrangements for the continuation of the present system during the transitional period;

(g) Proposals on how to increase public access to United Nations information materials and important documents, including in languages other than the six official languages;

2. *Notes* that the short-term study of Department for General Assembly and Conference Management documentation outsourcing options was conducted by the Secretariat without a General Assembly mandate, and reaffirms, in this context, paragraph 27 of its resolution 53/208 B of 18 December 1998 and its resolution 55/232;

3. *Takes note* of proposal 12, requests the Secretary-General to provide additional information in this regard, and decides to revert to the issue of undertaking a detailed cost-benefit analysis of relocation, outsourcing and telecommuting opportunities on the following selected administrative services at its sixty-first session:

(a) Internal printing and publishing processes;

(b) Medical insurance plan administration;

(c) Information technology support services;

(d) Payables, receivables and payroll processes;

(e) Staff benefits administration;

4. *Recalls* paragraphs 9 to 15 of its resolution 60/257, paragraph 8 of its resolution 60/259 and paragraphs 4 to 7 of its resolution 60/254, and requests the Secretary-General, in the report referred to in paragraph 1 of the present section, to include information on how to ensure the implementation of the provisions of the abovementioned resolutions when proposing measures to improve the performance evaluation and reporting of the Secretariat, as stated in proposal 18;

5. *Requests* the Secretary-General to submit a detailed proposal on strengthening the monitoring and evaluation tools in the Secretariat, taking into account recent experience in results-based budgeting;

V

Proposals 14 and 15

Requests the Secretary-General to submit a detailed report, bearing in mind the unique intergovernmental nature and international character of the United Nations, to the General Assembly on proposals 14 and 15 contained in his report, which would respond to the following elements:

(a) Information on all relevant previous reform proposals as agreed by the General Assembly, including concise references to previous relevant resolutions and decisions of the Assembly, as well as an outline of the measures taken to implement them;

(b) An assessment of the impact of previous and ongoing reforms as they relate to the proposals;

(c) Specific costs and administrative implications, including required changes to the regulations, rules and procedures, with detailed analysis and justification;

(d) Detailed explanation and concrete examples of how it is envisaged that the proposals will enhance the effectiveness of the work of the Organization and to address current deficiencies;

(e) Clear definition of the terminologies and rationale for the proposals;

(f) Proposals on how to increase the use of open source software in the Secretariat;

(g) Proposals to effectively increase procurement opportunities and participation of vendors from developing countries;

(h) An assessment of the effectiveness of the internal controls of the United Nations organizations referred to in proposal 14, as well as an assessment of how these internal controls differ from those of the United Nations Procurement Service;

VI

Proposal 16

1. *Recalls* paragraph 11 of its resolution 60/246 of 23 December 2005, in which it recognized the need for limited discretion in budgetary implementation for the Secretary-General, within defined parameters to be agreed by the General Assembly, with clear accountability mechanisms to the Assembly for its use;

2. *Recognizes* that the proposals contained in proposal 16 do not respond to the request of the General Assembly, as contained in paragraph 11 of its resolution 60/246, and requests the Secretary-General to submit proposals to the Assembly at the second part of its resumed sixtieth session in full conformity with paragraph 11 of resolution 60/246;

3. *Stresses* that the General Assembly will review the planning and budgetary reform experiment at its sixty-second session with a view to making a final decision thereon, in accordance with its resolutions 58/269 and 60/257;

4. *Reaffirms* the provisions of section I of its resolution 49/233 A;

VII

Proposal 19

1. *Emphasizes* the importance of providing the information necessary to enable Member States to make well-informed decisions;

2. *Recalls* paragraph 20 of its resolution 57/300, paragraph 6 of the annex to resolution 58/316 of 1 July 2004 and paragraph 16 of its resolution 59/313 of 12 September 2005, and requests the Secretary-General to implement measures in accordance with the above-mentioned paragraphs with a view to consolidating reports on related subjects;

3. *Reaffirms* that all reports pertaining to administrative and budgetary matters are subject to the consideration of the Fifth Committee as the appropriate Main Committee of the General Assembly entrusted with responsibilities for those matters;

VIII

Proposals 20 and 21

1. *Reaffirms* that the Fifth Committee is the appropriate Main Committee of the General Assembly entrusted with responsibilities for administrative and budgetary matters;

2. *Also reaffirms* the role of the Committee for Programme and Coordination as the main subsidiary organ of the General Assembly and the Economic and Social Council for planning, programming and coordination;

3. *Further reaffirms* that no changes to the budget methodology, to established budgetary procedures and practices or to the financial regulations may be implemented without prior review and approval by the General Assembly, in accordance with established budgetary procedures;

4. *Recalls* paragraph 162 of its resolution 60/1, whereby the General Assembly called upon the Secretary-General to make proposals to the Assembly for its consideration on the conditions and measures necessary for him to carry out his managerial responsibilities effectively, and stresses that proposals 20 and 21 do not bear any relation to the requests of the Assembly as outlined in resolution 60/1 or in any other legislative mandate adopted by the Assembly;

5. *Also recalls*, in this context, section II of its resolution 41/213, and reaffirms that the decision-making process is governed by the provisions of the Charter of the United Nations, in particular Article 18, and the rules of procedure of the General Assembly;

IX

Proposals 22 and 23

1. *Takes note* of the idea of a dedicated capacity within the Secretariat with the aim of facilitating the management reform efforts within the Secretariat by the Secretary-General, and requests the Secretary-General to take into account existing capacity and expertise already available in the Secretariat in formulating future proposals in this regard;

2. *Stresses* that the implementation of reform measures approved by the General Assembly is the responsi-

bility of the Secretary-General as the chief administrative officer of the Organization and should be undertaken in full transparency with the entire membership of the Organization through established reporting lines to the Assembly;

3. *Recalls* paragraph 163 *(c)* of its resolution 60/1, and requests the Secretary-General to present a detailed and justified proposal in line with the provisions and intent of paragraph 163 *(c)*.

RECORDED VOTE FOR RESOLUTION 60/260:

In favour: Algeria, Angola, Antigua and Barbuda, Argentina, Bahamas, Bahrain, Bangladesh, Barbados, Belarus, Belize, Benin, Bhutan, Bolivia, Botswana, Brazil, Brunei Darussalam, Burkina Faso, Cambodia, Cameroon, Cape Verde, Central African Republic, Chad, Chile, China, Colombia, Comoros, Congo, Costa Rica, Côte d'Ivoire, Cuba, Democratic People's Republic of Korea, Democratic Republic of the Congo, Djibouti, Dominica, Ecuador, Egypt, El Salvador, Equatorial Guinea, Eritrea, Fiji, Gabon, Gambia, Ghana, Grenada, Guatemala, Guinea, Guinea-Bissau, Guyana, Haiti, Honduras, India, Indonesia, Iran, Iraq, Jamaica, Jordan, Kenya, Kuwait, Lao People's Democratic Republic, Lebanon, Lesotho, Liberia, Libyan Arab Jamahiriya, Madagascar, Malawi, Malaysia, Maldives, Mali, Mauritania, Mauritius, Mexico, Mongolia, Morocco, Mozambique, Myanmar, Namibia, Nepal, Nicaragua, Niger, Nigeria, Oman, Pakistan, Panama, Papua New Guinea, Paraguay, Peru, Philippines, Qatar, Russian Federation, Rwanda, Saint Kitts and Nevis, Saint Lucia, Saint Vincent and the Grenadines, Samoa, Saudi Arabia, Senegal, Seychelles, Sierra Leone, Singapore, Solomon Islands, Somalia, South Africa, Sri Lanka, Sudan, Suriname, Swaziland, Syrian Arab Republic, Thailand, Timor-Leste, Togo, Trinidad and Tobago, Tunisia, United Arab Emirates, United Republic of Tanzania, Uruguay, Uzbekistan, Venezuela, Viet Nam, Yemen, Zambia, Zimbabwe.

Against: Albania, Andorra, Australia, Austria, Belgium, Bosnia and Herzegovina, Bulgaria, Canada, Croatia, Cyprus, Czech Republic, Denmark, Estonia, Finland, France, Georgia, Germany, Greece, Hungary, Iceland, Ireland, Israel, Italy, Japan, Latvia, Liechtenstein, Lithuania, Luxembourg, Malta, Monaco, Netherlands, New Zealand, Palau, Poland, Portugal, Republic of Korea, Republic of Moldova, Romania, San Marino, Serbia and Montenegro, Slovakia, Slovenia, Spain, Sweden, Switzerland, The former Yugoslav Republic of Macedonia, Turkey, Ukraine, United Kingdom, United States.

Abstaining: Norway, Uganda.

Implementation of Assembly resolution 60/260

Report of Secretary-General. Pursuant to General Assembly resolution 60/260 (see above), the Secretary-General, in May [A/60/846], submitted a detailed report addressing the interrelated proposals outlined in his March report (see p. 1575), as well as four addenda on: investing in information and communication technology [A/60/846/Add.1] (see p. 1664); budget implementation [A/60/846/Add.2] and financial management practices [A/60/846/Add.3] (see p. 1610); improving reporting mechanisms, including access to UN documentation [A/60/846/Add.4] (see p. 1643); procurement reform [A/60/846/Add.5] (see p. 1644); accountability [A/60/846/Add.6] (see p. 1688); and updated terms of reference for the Independent Audit Advisory Committee [A/60/846/Add.7] (see p. 1610). Separate reports on human resources issues and on the framework for a one-time staff buyout were to be submitted to the Assembly at its sixty-first (2006) session. The Secretary-General said that he was proceeding with a major new leadership development plan covering recruitment, training and career development to build middle and senior management capacity. Upon completion of the cost-benefit analysis of relocation, outsourcing and telecommuting opportunities for administrative service delivery, separate reports would be submitted to the Assembly for consideration in 2007. Investigations and a comprehensive review of procurement services were ongoing. Upon completion of that work, a separate report would be submitted, which would include measures to improve and tighten procedures for the procurement of goods and services. In the area of monitoring and evaluation, the Secretary-General proposed to revert to the Assembly at its sixty-first session, drawing on the recommendations of the review of governance and oversight systems to be completed in June. With respect to trust fund matters, administrative instructions were under preparation and were expected to be finalized later in the year. Consultations with programme managers continued on revised rules and procedures for ensuring adequate financial control, improving the administration and management of voluntary contributions, including the provision of support costs for the management of those contributions, and simplifying and standardizing procedures. In the area of change management, the Secretary-General said that it would be premature to request additional resources and any further requirements would be met within available capacity and expertise in the Secretariat. He indicated that the overall impact of the proposals would require additional requirements of $6,381,300 for the 2006-2007 biennium.

The comments of ACABQ on the Secretary-General's detailed report were contained in a June report to the Assembly [A/60/870].

GENERAL ASSEMBLY ACTION

On 7 July [meeting 93], the General Assembly, on the recommendation of the Fifth Committee [A/60/831/Add.1], adopted **resolution 60/283** without vote [agenda items 46, 118, 120, 122, 124, 128, 129, 136].

Investing in the United Nations for a stronger Organization worldwide: detailed report

The General Assembly,

Recalling its resolutions 41/213 of 19 December 1986, 60/1 of 16 September 2005 and 60/260 of 8 May 2006,

Reaffirming the role of the General Assembly and its relevant intergovernmental and expert bodies, within their respective mandates, in planning, programming, budgeting, monitoring and evaluation,

Stressing the need for Member States to participate in the budget preparation process, from its early stages and throughout the process,

Having considered the report of the Secretary-General entitled "Investing in the United Nations: for a stronger Organization worldwide: detailed report" and the related report of the Advisory Committee on Administrative and Budgetary Questions,

1. *Renews its appeal* to Member States to demonstrate their commitment to the United Nations by, inter alia, meeting their financial obligations on time, in full and without conditions, in accordance with the Charter of the United Nations and the Financial Regulations and Rules of the United Nations;

2. *Endorses* the conclusions and recommendations of the Advisory Committee on Administrative and Budgetary Questions contained in its report, subject to the provisions of the present resolution;

I

Oversight and accountability

1. *Requests* the Secretary-General to ensure the full operationalization of the Ethics Office, including through the expeditious filling of vacancies;

2. *Emphasizes* the need for strengthening oversight in the Organization, and stresses the importance of strengthened accountability in the Organization and of ensuring greater accountability of the Secretary-General to Member States, inter alia, for the effective and efficient implementation of legislative mandates and the use of human and financial resources;

3. *Looks forward* to considering the results of the independent external evaluation of the audit and oversight system of the United Nations, as well as other relevant reports in this regard, and to taking action on proposals contained therein on, inter alia, ensuring the full operational independence of the Office of Internal Oversight Services and strengthening the evaluation capacity of the Office at the programme and subprogramme levels, as well as any budget requirements;

4. *Recalls* section XIII, paragraph 4, of its resolution 60/248 of 23 December 2005, whereby it established the Independent Audit Advisory Committee, and looks forward to considering and taking action on its proposed terms of reference with a view to operationalizing it;

II

Information and communication technology

1. *Decides* to establish the post of Chief Information Technology Officer at the level of Assistant Secretary-General in the Executive Office of the Secretary-General;

2. *Requests* the Secretary-General to rejustify the level and resource requirements for the post of Chief Information Technology Officer in the Executive Office of the Secretary-General, in the context of the proposed programme budget for the biennium 2008-2009 to be considered at its sixty-second session, taking fully into account the existing staffing structure and resources dedicated to information and communication technology functions in the Organization;

3. *Also requests* the Secretary-General to provide to the General Assembly, at its resumed sixty-first session, detailed information on the structure and staffing requirements of the envisaged information and communication technology structure, as well as the lines of responsibility, the functions of the proposed structure and its relationship with other information and communication technology units in the Secretariat, offices away from Headquarters, regional commissions, peacekeeping operations, special political missions and other field offices;

4. *Decides* to replace the Integrated Management Information System with a next-generation enterprise resource planning system or other comparable system;

5. *Requests* the Secretary-General to submit to the General Assembly, at its resumed sixty-first session, the comprehensive report referred to in paragraphs 17 and 18 of his report, and to respond to relevant General Assembly resolutions, including on the following matters:

(a) Substantive improvements to the information and communication technology systems that may be required, including the systems at offices away from Headquarters, the regional commissions and peacekeeping operations;

(b) A detailed implementation plan, including on the user needs, scope, timetable, strategy and detailed resource requirements and information technology needs arising from the adoption of the International Public Sector Accounting Standards;

(c) The expected contribution of the information and communication technology system to enhancing the effective and transparent use of the resources of the Organization;

(d) Any revisions to the existing information and communication technology strategy that may be required, bearing in mind requests previously made by the General Assembly in its consideration of the 2002 information and communication technology strategy, including its resolutions 56/239 of 24 December 2001 and 57/304 of 15 April 2003;

(e) Projected resource requirements over the life cycle of the project;

(f) A detailed explanation and concrete examples of how it is envisaged that the proposals will enhance the effectiveness of the work of the Organization and address current deficiencies;

(g) A clear definition of the terminologies and rationale for the proposals;

(h) An assessment of previous investments in information and communication technology, as well as lessons learned and expected time frames for introducing the proposed system and arrangements for the continuation of the current system during the transitional period;

6. *Decides* to revert to the consideration of the report of the Joint Inspection Unit on policies of United Nations system organizations towards the use of open-

source software in the secretariats at its resumed sixty-first session;

III
Limited budgetary discretion

1. *Recalls* its resolution 59/275 of 23 December 2004, in which it set the priorities for the Organization for the biennium 2006-2007;

2. *Reaffirms* the role and prerogative of Member States in setting the priorities of the Organization, as reflected in legislative decisions;

3. *Reaffirms* its role in carrying out a thorough analysis and approval of human and financial resources and policies with a view to ensuring full, effective and efficient implementation of all mandated programmes and activities and the implementation of policies in this regard;

4. *Emphasizes again* that the resources proposed by the Secretary-General should be commensurate with all mandated programmes and activities in order to ensure their full, efficient and effective implementation;

5. *Recalls* paragraph 11 of its resolution 60/246 of 23 December 2005, whereby it recognized the need for limited discretion in budgetary implementation for the Secretary-General, within defined parameters to be agreed by the General Assembly along with clear accountability mechanisms to the Assembly for its use;

6. *Decides* to authorize the Secretary-General, on an experimental basis, a limited discretion for budgetary implementation for the bienniums 2006-2007 and 2008-2009, to enter into commitments up to 20 million United States dollars in each biennium for positions and non-post requirements for the purpose of meeting the evolving needs of the Organization in attaining its mandated programmes and activities;

7. *Also decides* to authorize the Secretary-General to utilize the Working Capital Fund to finance the implementation of the authorization referred to in paragraph 6 above, which shall be offset by savings identified and attained, including through the efficient use and assignment of resources, during the course of each biennium within the authorized appropriation level, as reported in the performance reports;

8. *Decides* that the authorization referred to in paragraph 6 above shall be implemented in accordance with the following principles:

(*a*) The experiment shall not be utilized for unforeseen and extraordinary expenses that are authorized in respect of the maintenance of peace and security;

(*b*) The experiment shall not imply any changes in the human resources management policies of the Organization;

(*c*) The proposed programme budget shall remain the principal instrument in which the Secretary-General sets out the resources and staffing requirements of the Organization, including the requirements for all reform proposals as agreed by Member States;

(*d*) The experiment shall in no way prevent the Secretary-General from requesting additional posts during the course of the experiment;

(*e*) The experiment shall not be implemented in pursuance of General Assembly resolutions calling for the implementation of decisions "within existing resources";

(*f*) The experiment shall not imply any changes to the provisions guiding the use of the contingency fund;

(*g*) The utilization of authorization shall be exercised with the prior concurrence of the Advisory Committee on Administrative and Budgetary Questions when the total amount utilized exceeds 6 million dollars per biennium;

(*h*) The experiment shall not alter the priorities of the Organization as agreed by the General Assembly;

(*i*) The utilization of the funds provided for under the experiment shall be subject to the Financial Regulations and Rules of the United Nations;

9. *Requests* the Secretary-General to report to the General Assembly, through the Advisory Committee, in the context of the performance reports, on the utilization of all commitments made within the context of the experiment, together with the circumstances relating thereto, as well as the impact on programme delivery and the ability to meet the evolving needs of the Organization;

10. *Decides* to review the experiment at its sixty-fourth session with a view to taking a final decision on its continuation, and requests the Secretary-General to submit a comprehensive report on the implementation of the experiment for its consideration, including the following aspects:

(*a*) The utilization of the experiment during the course of the two bienniums;

(*b*) Implications, if any, for the human resources management policies and the Financial Regulations and Rules;

(*c*) The impact on programme delivery, as well as on the priorities of the Organization as set by Member States;

(*d*) The criteria used by the Secretary-General to define the evolving needs of the Organization;

11. *Recalls* paragraph 14 of its resolution 58/270 of 23 December 2003 and paragraph 7 of its resolution 60/246, decides that the experiment will not be extended beyond the current biennium, and requests the Secretary-General to report to the General Assembly at its sixty-second session on the results of the experiment as well as lessons learned that can be applied to the experiment referred to in paragraph 6 above;

12. *Requests* the Secretary-General to expeditiously implement paragraph 8 of its resolution 60/246 and to report thereon in the context of the first performance report on the programme budget for the biennium 2006-2007;

13. *Recalls its request* to the Secretary-General to specifically define accountability as well as clear accountability mechanisms, including to the General Assembly, and to propose clear parameters for their application and the instruments for their rigorous enforcement, without exception, at all levels;

14. *Recognizes* that it will consider the related report of the Secretary-General referred to in paragraph 13

above at its sixty-first session with a view to taking decisions to strengthen accountability in the Organization;

IV

Financial management practices

International Public Sector Accounting Standards

1. *Decides* to approve the adoption by the United Nations of the International Public Sector Accounting Standards;

2. *Approves* the resources requested to permit the Secretary-General to begin implementation of the Standards, bearing in mind paragraph 42 of the report of the Advisory Committee on Administrative and Budgetary Questions;

Working Capital Fund

3. *Recalls* its resolution 60/250 of 23 December 2005;

4. *Resolves* that the Working Capital Fund for the biennium 2006-2007 shall be increased to 150 million dollars effective from 1 January 2007;

5. *Also resolves* that Member States shall make advances to the Working Capital Fund in accordance with the scale of assessments to be adopted by the General Assembly for contributions to the regular budget for the year 2007;

6. *Further resolves* that there shall be set off against these advances:

(a) The surplus balance of the programme budget for the biennium 2004-2005;

(b) Cash advances paid by Member States to the Working Capital Fund for the biennium 2006-2007 in accordance with General Assembly resolution 60/250;

V

Improving reporting mechanisms: public access to United Nations documentation

Comprehensive annual report

1. *Emphasizes* the importance of providing the information necessary to enable Member States to make well-informed decisions;

2. *Reaffirms* that all reports pertaining to administrative and budgetary matters are subject to the consideration of the Fifth Committee as the appropriate Main Committee of the General Assembly entrusted with responsibilities for those matters;

3. *Takes note* of the intention of the Secretary-General to prepare a single comprehensive annual report containing both financial and programme information, with the aim of enhancing the transparency of the Organization and the accountability of the Secretariat to Member States;

4. *Emphasizes* that the report would be developed in the context of paragraphs 68 and 69 of the report of the Advisory Committee on Administrative and Budgetary Questions, bearing in mind paragraph 2 above;

5. *Also emphasizes* that the report would be complementary in nature and would not replace the report of the Secretary-General on the work of the Organization required under Article 98 of the Charter of the United Nations, nor reports that are subject to the consideration of the Fifth Committee;

Public access

6. *Notes* the proposal of the Secretary-General on the policy for access to United Nations documentation by Member States and the public and also the observations of the Advisory Committee thereon, and requests the Secretary-General to submit to the General Assembly at its sixty-first session, for consideration and action, a comprehensive report containing detailed parameters of the above proposal, including information on resource requirements, financing mechanisms and the possibility of a fee structure, and also addressing the implementation of the existing mandates governing the issue of facilitating the access of Member States and the public to United Nations documentation and information materials, as contained in relevant resolutions of the General Assembly;

VI

Procurement

Authorizes the Secretary-General to enter into commitments of up to 706,600 dollars to strengthen the United Nations procurement system, including by enhancing internal controls and developing business seminar programmes for vendors in developing countries, pending consideration of and action on the report of the Secretary-General on procurement reform by the General Assembly at its sixty-first session;

VII

Future consideration of management reform

1. *Decides* to defer consideration of the following proposals contained in the addendum on financial management practices to the above-mentioned detailed report of the Secretary-General as follows:

(a) Consolidation of peacekeeping accounts and increases in the Peacekeeping Reserve Fund and commitment authority for peacekeeping operations (paragraphs 112 *(b)* to *(l)*)— until the second part of its resumed sixty-first session;

(b) Establishment of a reserve fund (paragraphs 112 *(p)* and *(q)*) —within the context of the programme budget for the biennium 2008-2009;

2. *Looks forward* to considering at its sixty-first session proposals on:

(a) Governance, oversight and accountability;

(b) Human resources management;

(c) Procurement;

(d) Administration of justice;

3. *Reaffirms* its intention to continue the consideration of measures to fulfil the commitments made by Heads of State and Government in the 2005 World Summit Outcome to strengthen the United Nations by ensuring the efficient and effective functioning of the Organization and a culture of accountability, transparency and integrity in the Secretariat;

4. *Pledges* to provide the United Nations with adequate resources, on a timely basis, to enable the Or-

ganization to implement its mandates and achieve its objectives, having regard to the priorities agreed by the General Assembly and the need to respect budget discipline;

VIII

Appropriation

1. *Approves* an additional appropriation of 4,433,100 dollars in the programme budget for the biennium 2006-2007, broken down as follows:

Section	*Amount (United States dollars)*
1. Overall policymaking, direction and coordination	145 600
28A. Office of the Under-Secretary-General for Management	1 860 000
28B. Office of Programme Planning, Budget and Accounts	1 428 900
28D. Office of Central Support Services	574 600
30. Jointly financed administrative activities	424 000
Total	**4 433 100**

2. *Also approves* an additional appropriation in the amount of 127,300 dollars under section 35, Staff assessment, to be offset by an equivalent amount under income section 1, Income from staff assessment.

On the same day, the General Assembly deferred until its sixty-first (2006) session consideration of the item on United Nations reform: measures and proposals (**decision 60/551 C**).

On 11 September, the Assembly also deferred consideration of the item on strengthening of the United Nation system and included it in the draft agenda of its sixty-first (2006) session (**decision 60/565**).

Reports of Secretary-General. Pursuant to Assembly resolutions 60/260 (see p. 1576) and 60/283 (see above), the Secretary-General submitted an August report [A/61/255] on the new human resources framework outlined in his March report on investing in the United Nations (see p. 1575). In particular, the report provided detailed proposals on staffing and recruitment; an integrated approach to mobility; enhanced career development; streamlined contractual arrangements and harmonized conditions of service; strengthened leadership; and staff buyout. An addendum to the report on reforming the field service category: investing in meeting the human resources requirements of United Nations peace operations in the twenty-first century was also submitted [A/61/255/Add.1 & Corr.1] (see p. 1689).

By a September note [A/61/434], the Secretary-General, in response to paragraph V of resolution 60/283, submitted the *United Nations Secretariat First Consolidated Report 2005* [Sales No. E.06.I.35] on financial and programme information. The report was a prototype for review and consideration by Member States and contained consolidated information already available elsewhere.

By **decision 61/552** of 22 December, the Assembly deferred until its resumed sixty-first (2007) session consideration of the items on United Nations reform: measures and proposals, and on strengthening of the UN system.

High-level Panel on United Nations System-wide Coherence

In December [A/61/583], the Secretary-General transmitted to the General Assembly the report of the High-level Panel on United Nations System-wide Coherence in the Areas of Development, Humanitarian Assistance and the Environment, which he had appointed in February in response to the call by Heads of State and Government at the 2005 World Summit [YUN 2005, p. 47] for stronger system-wide coherence across the UN system and strengthened management and coordination of UN operational activities.

The Panel, co-chaired by Prime Ministers Shaukat Aziz (Pakistan), Luísa Dias Diogo (Mozambique) and Jens Stoltenberg (Norway), brought together 15 eminent persons, whose experience and authority were a measure of the importance the Secretary-General attached to the Panel's work.

The aim of the study was to make recommendations on a process of revitalization that would maximize available resources for UN system relief and development programmes, while minimizing overhead and administrative costs; make proposals for improving management, coordination and effectiveness at the country level; and identify a short, medium and longer-term vision and benchmarks in the form of an implementation plan.

The report, entitled "Delivering as one", made the case for further reform and presented in-depth analyses in the areas of development: delivering as one at the country level; humanitarian assistance and the transition from relief to development: strengthening the capacity to respond; environment: building a global consensus and capacity for action; and cross-cutting issues: sustainable development, gender equality and human rights. It also looked at governance and management, particularly the consolidation of some functions, while strengthening others; funding the UN system for results; and reforming UN system business practices: building institutions of public trust. The Panel benefited from regional and country-level consultations, thematic consultations, consultative meetings with intergovernmental forums, bilateral meetings, and meetings with UN system organizations, as well as from several papers that were commissioned. It also benefited from the deliberations of inter-agency bodies, including the United Nations System Chief Executives Board for Coordination (CEB) [E/2006/66] and its High-level Committees on Programmes [CEB/2006/7] and Management.

The Panel found that the Organization's work in development and the environment was often fragmented and weak, with inefficient and ineffective governance contributing to policy incoherence, duplication and operational ineffectiveness. Cooperation among organizations was hindered by competition for funding, "mission creep" and outdated business practices. The Panel's recommendations were based on five strategic directions: ensuring coherence and consolidation of UN activities; establishing appropriate governance, managerial and funding mechanisms; overhauling business practices to focus on outcome; ensuring significant further opportunities for consolidation and effective delivery of "One United Nations" through an in-depth review; and undertaking carefully planned implementation. It made specific recommendations on development (see p. 992), humanitarian assistance (see p. 1060), environment (see p. 1210), and gender (see p. 1352). In terms of coordination with other multilateral agencies, the Panel recommended that the Secretary-General, the President of the World Bank and the Executive Director of the International Monetary Fund should conclude formal agreements on their respective roles and relations at the global and country levels.

In his note transmitting the report, Secretary-General Kofi Annan said that he was also transmitting the report to his successor, Ban Ki-moon, to enable him to formulate specific proposals on how the Panel's recommendations should be taken forward. The Secretary-General suggested that informal dialogue on the Panel's report should be initiated to build common understanding of its objectives, contents and proposals. In addition to the General Assembly, the Economic and Social Council and its commissions, and the governing bodies of UN system organizations should be involved, as well as regional and other groupings. The consultations and dialogue could culminate in a formal plenary meeting of the Assembly in 2007, to be followed by preparation of a resolution for the Assembly's consideration. There would also be extensive UN inter-agency discussions on the Panel's recommendations.

The Secretary-General said that he had decided to move forward on some of the recommendations, since many of them built on reforms and initiatives already being carried out by UN agencies, funds and programmes. In particular, he had initiated the establishment of the five pilot One Country Programmes. He also planned to move forward in the area of business practices, for there was a need to modernize and achieve full compatibility on processes for resource planning, human resources, common services and evaluation, as they were important drivers of coherence in the UN system. He was taking steps to implement the recommendation on the functioning of CEB, and to request the establishment of the post of Under-Secretary-General for Gender Equality and Empowerment of Women. Taken as a whole, the Panel's recommendations could change the way the United Nations operated at Headquarters and in each region and country, deliver a better focus on performance, efficiency, accountability and results, and enhance the role and voice of developing countries. They would strengthen the role of the Organization at the heart of the multilateral system.

Substantial change was also required in governance, management and funding arrangements to realize the vision of a more effective and coherent United Nations. The Panel proposed measures to enable the Organization to deliver as one on global development challenges, and in particular, to make the "One United Nations" at the country level a reality for developing countries. At the intergovernmental level, the Panel recommended the establishment of a Global Leaders Forum of the Economic and Social Council to provide high-level strategic guidance on sustainable development policy and global public goods, as well as the creation of a Sustainable Development Board to provide operational oversight and supervision of the "One United Nations" at the country level. At the regional level, the Panel called for the establishment of regional hubs to support UN country teams and clarification of the roles of the regional commissions. At the organizational level, CEB should improve its decision-making role on reform and drive managerial reform. The Development Policy and Operations Group should be the central coordinating mechanism for UN work on development at the country level. The Group, which would bring policy and operational roles together, would be chaired by a Development Coordinator (the UNDP Administrator), and comprise major UN development organizations. A clear firewall and accountability framework should be established between repositioned UNDP support to the resident coordinator system and its reduced operations role. A Development Finance and Performance Unit should support the Development Policy and Operations Group in providing information and analysis on UN system funding, expenditures and results. The Panel recommended that the Secretary-General establish an independent task force to build on the foundation of its work on the functioning of the UN system at the country, regional and global levels. The task force would clearly delineate the roles of the United Nations and its funds, programmes and specialized agencies to ensure complementarity of mandates and eliminate duplicated functions, and make concrete recommendations for consolidating or merging UN entities where necessary. Such a process had the potential to lead to significant annual savings of up to 20 per cent, which should be redirected to supporting the "One United Nations" at the country level. The task force would review the assessed funding required by UN specialized agencies to address the imbalance between assessed and voluntary resources dedicated to the implementation of normative mandates, and determine whether the policy of zero real growth would allow UN agencies to deliver on global mandates. It would also review the functioning and continuing relevance of regional structures in addressing regional needs.

Institutional matters

Intergovermental machinery

Revitalization of the work of the General Assembly

Report of Secretary-General. In August, at its resumed sixtieth session, the General Assembly had before it a report of the Secretary-General on the revitalization of the General Assembly [A/60/971]. The report, submitted in accordance with Assembly resolution 58/316 [YUN 2004, p. 1374], outlined the draft programme of work of the plenary and the Main Committees of the Assembly for its sixty-first (2006) session. An addendum to the report [A/60/971/Add.1] contained the status of the documentation for that session as at 24 August 2006.

Ad Hoc Working Group. The Assembly also had before it the report of the Ad Hoc Working Group on the Revitalization of the General Assembly [A/60/999], established by resolution 59/313 [YUN 2005, p. 1478] to identify ways to further enhance the Assembly's role, authority, effectiveness and efficiency by reviewing the Assembly's agenda and working methods and by building on relevant resolutions. The Working Group reviewed the Assembly's role and authority, its role in the selection of the Secretary-General, and its working methods. It submitted to the Assembly a draft resolution for adoption (see below).

GENERAL ASSEMBLY ACTION

On 8 September [meeting 99], the General Assembly, on the basis of the report of the Ad Hoc Working Group on the Revitalization of the General Assembly, adopted **resolution 60/286** without vote [agenda item 116].

Revitalization of the General Assembly

The General Assembly,

Reaffirming the central position of the General Assembly as the chief deliberative, policymaking and representative organ of the United Nations, as well as the role of the Assembly in the process of standard-setting and the codification of international law,

Reaffirming also the authority of the General Assembly and the strengthening of its role on global matters of concern to the international community, as set out in the Charter of the United Nations, and reaffirming its central role in the reform process,

Recognizing that the General Assembly is the universal and representative forum comprising all Members of the United Nations,

Stressing the need fully to respect and maintain the balance between the principal organs of the United Nations within their respective purviews and mandates in accordance with the Charter,

Reaffirming that the plenary meetings of the General Assembly should constitute a forum for high-level policy statements, as well as for the consideration, inter alia, of agenda items of special importance or urgency,

Underlining the importance of providing adequate resources for the implementation of mandated programmes and activities,

Reaffirming its authority in the consideration of all budgetary issues, as stipulated in the Charter,

Reaffirming also its previous resolutions relating to the revitalization of its work, in particular resolutions 58/126 of 19 December 2003, 58/316 of 1 July 2004 and 59/313 of 12 September 2005,

Recalling its resolution 51/241 of 31 July 1997,

Noting with appreciation the report of the Ad Hoc Working Group on the Revitalization of the General Assembly established by Assembly resolution 59/313,

Decides to adopt the text contained in the annex to the present resolution.

Annex

The General Assembly,

Cluster I. Role and authority of the General Assembly

In the context of further strengthening the role and authority of the General Assembly as set out in the Charter of the United Nations,

1. *Reaffirms* the role and the authority of the General Assembly, including on questions relating to international peace and security, as stipulated in Articles 10 to 14 and 35 of the Charter of the United Nations, where appropriate using the procedures set forth in rules 7 to 10 of the rules of procedure of the General Assembly, which enable swift and urgent action by the Assembly, bearing in mind that the Security Council has primary responsibility for the maintenance of international peace and security in accordance with Article 24 of the Charter;

2. *Urges* the Presidents of the General Assembly, the Security Council and the Economic and Social Council to meet periodically to ensure increased cooperation and coordination of their work programmes in accordance with their respective responsibilities under the Charter; the President of the Assembly shall inform Member States about the outcome of those meetings on a regular basis;

3. *Encourages* the holding of thematic interactive debates on current issues of critical importance to the international community in the General Assembly, and *invites* the President of the Assembly to propose themes for such interactive debates, in consultation with Member States;

4. *Invites* the Security Council to further its initiatives to improve the quality of its annual report to the General Assembly, mandated by Article 24, paragraph 3, of the Charter, in order to provide the Assembly with a substantive and analytical report;

5. In carrying out the assessment of the debate on the annual report of the Security Council called for in paragraph 12 of the annex to resolution 51/241 of 31 July 1997, the President shall inform the General Assembly of his decision regarding the need for further consideration of the report of the Council, including in respect of the convening of informal consultations, on the need for, and content of, any action by the Assembly based on the debate, as well as on any matters to be brought to the attention of the Council;

6. *Invites* the Security Council to update the General Assembly on a regular basis on the steps it has taken or is contemplating with respect to improving its reporting to the Assembly;

7. *Also invites* the Security Council to submit periodically, in accordance with Articles 15 and 24 of the Charter, special subject-oriented reports to the General Assembly for its consideration on issues of current international concern;

8. *Invites* the Economic and Social Council to continue to prepare its report to the General Assembly in accordance with Assembly resolution 50/227 of 24 May 1996, striving to make it more concise and action-oriented by highlighting the critical areas requiring action by the Assembly and, as appropriate, by making specific recommendations for consideration by the Member States;

9. *Requests* the President of the General Assembly, at the end of his/her tenure, to provide an informal, short report on best practices and lessons learned to his/her successor;

10. *Takes note* of paragraph 3 (*b*) of its resolution 59/313 of 12 September 2005, and *also takes note* of paragraph 9 of its resolution 60/246 of 23 December 2005, by which two additional positions at management and senior levels were made available to the Office of the President of the General Assembly, within the programme budget for the biennium 2006-2007, as part of the effort to strengthen the Office of the President;

11. *Requests* the Secretary-General to continue to make the necessary arrangements for the provision of transitional office accommodation and other support to the President-elect of the General Assembly, in accordance with resolution 58/126 of 19 December 2003;

12. *Encourages* enhanced interaction, as and where appropriate, with civil society, including non-governmental organizations, in particular those from developing countries, on relevant issues, while fully respecting the intergovernmental nature of the General Assembly and in conformity with the relevant rules of procedure;

13. *Also encourages*, where appropriate, continued cooperation between the General Assembly and national and regional parliaments, particularly through the Inter-Parliamentary Union;

14. *Requests* the Department of Public Information of the Secretariat, in cooperation with countries concerned and with the relevant organizations and bodies of the United Nations system, to continue to take appropriate measures to enhance world public awareness of the work of the General Assembly;

15. *Urges* the Secretariat to continue its endeavours to raise the visibility of the General Assembly and, to that end, *requests* the rearrangement of items in the *Journal of the United Nations* so that listings of plenary meetings and other major events of the General Assembly may appear alongside those of the meetings of the Security Council;

16. *Encourages* the Presidents of the General Assembly to increase their public visibility, including through enhanced contacts with representatives of the media and civil society, thus promoting the activities of the Assembly, and *encourages* the Secretary-General to continue the practice of providing to the Office of the President of the Assembly a Spokesperson for the President of the Assembly and an assistant to the Spokesperson;

Cluster II. Selection of the Secretary-General

17. *Recalls* Article 97 of the Charter, as well as the provisions of General Assembly resolutions 11(I) of 24 January 1946 and 51/241, as relevant to the role of the Assembly in appointing the Secretary-General, upon the recommendation of the Security Council;

18. *Emphasizes*, bearing in mind the provisions of Article 97 of the Charter, the need for the process of selection of the Secretary-General to be inclusive of all Member States and made more transparent and that, in the course of the identification and appointment of the best candidate for the post of Secretary-General, due regard should be given to regional rotation and gender equality, and *invites* the Security Council to regularly

update the General Assembly on the steps it has taken in this regard;

19. *Encourages*, without prejudice to the role of the principal organs as enshrined in Article 97 of the Charter, the President of the General Assembly to consult with Member States to identify potential candidates endorsed by a Member State and, upon informing all Member States of the results, to forward those results to the Security Council;

20. *Also encourages* formal presentation of candidatures for the position of Secretary-General in a manner that allows sufficient time for interaction with Member States, and requests candidates to present their views to all States members of the General Assembly;

21. *Recalls* paragraph 61 of its resolution 51/241, in which it is stated that, in order to ensure a smooth and efficient transition, the Secretary-General should be appointed as early as possible, preferably no later than one month before the date on which the term of the incumbent expires;

22. *Emphasizes* the importance of candidates for the post of Secretary-General possessing and displaying, inter alia, commitment to the purposes and principles of the Charter of the United Nations, extensive leadership, and administrative and diplomatic experience;

Cluster III. Working methods

23. *Reaffirms* the sovereign right of Member States to submit proposals in the context of the rules of procedure of the General Assembly, and encourages Member States to submit draft resolutions in a more concise, focused and action-oriented form;

24. *Requests* the Secretary-General to issue the rules of procedure of the General Assembly in a consolidated version in all official languages, in print and online, and requests the Office of Legal Affairs of the Secretariat to make precedents and past practice available in the public domain with respect to rules and practices of the intergovernmental bodies of the Organization;

25. *Requests* the Main Committees to continue their efforts to further rationalize their agendas and to improve their working methods, and invites the Bureaux of the Main Committees to enhance their cooperation, in conformity with the rules of procedure;

26. *Decides*, in that respect, to give due consideration to those recommendations of the Main Committees regarding the improvement of their working methods and the allocation of agenda items which require the approval of the General Assembly for their implementation;

27. *Reiterates* its call for the effective implementation of rule 42 of the rules of procedure of the General Assembly;

28. *Requests* an update on its recommendation, in paragraph 15 of its resolution 59/313, regarding consideration of the use of optical scanners as a means of expediting the counting of votes cast through secret ballots during elections, taking due account of the security requirements in this regard and the credibility, reliability and confidentiality of such means, and requests the Secretary-General to report on the modalities thereof to the General Assembly;

29. *Requests* the Secretary-General to implement further the measures set out in paragraph 20 of resolution 57/300 of 20 December 2002 on the consolidation of reports and in paragraph 6 of the annex to resolution 58/316 of 1 July 2004 on documentation;

30. *Recalls* paragraph 19 of its resolution 59/313, and requests the Secretary-General to submit a status report with a factual chart to the General Assembly at its sixty-first session on the implementation of all resolutions regarding the revitalization of its work, including resolutions 58/126, 58/316 and 59/313, and the present resolution;

31. *Decides* to invite the President of the sixty-first session of the General Assembly to convene consultations among Member States to decide on the establishment of an ad hoc working group on the revitalization of the Assembly, open to all Member States: to identify ways to further enhance the role, authority, effectiveness and efficiency of the Assembly, inter alia, by building on relevant Assembly resolutions and reviewing the agenda and working methods of the Assembly; and to submit a report to the Assembly at its sixty-first session.

Report of Secretary-General. In October [A/61/483], pursuant to General Assembly resolutions 58/316 [YUN 2004, p. 1374], 59/313 [YUN 2005, p. 1478] and 60/286 (see above), the Secretary-General submitted a report on the revitalization of the General Assembly. The report provided an overview of the status of implementation of resolutions adopted by the Assembly at its fifty-eighth (2003) and fifty-ninth (2004) sessions. In terms of both structure and content, it paralleled closely the areas and issues examined by the Ad Hoc Working Group on the Revitalization of the General Assembly (see above). The report analysed a number of issues, including how to enhance the Assembly's authority and role and improve its working methods, the Assembly's agenda, the work of the General Committee, the role of the Assembly President, the Assembly's documentation and the work of the Open-ended Ad Hoc Working Group.

In November, the General Assembly considered the report of the Fourth (Special Political and Decolonization) Committee [A/61/416] on the revitalization of the work of the General Assembly. The Committee Chairman drew the attention of the Committee to a paper, annexed to the report, regarding the approximate dates for the consideration of the items by the Fourth Committee at the Assembly's sixty-second (2007) session.

On 14 December, the Assembly took note of the report of the Fourth Committee (**decision 61/523**).

On 22 December, the Assembly decided that the item on the revitalization of the work of the General Assembly would remain for consideration during its resumed sixty-first (2007) session (**decision 61/552**).

Review of Security Council membership and related matters

The Open-ended Working Group on the Question of Equitable Representation on and Increase in the Membership of the Security Council and Other Matters related to the Security Council submitted a report on its work during three formal meetings held on 20 April and 8 September [A/60/47]. The Vice-Chairpersons of the Working Group also conducted informal consultations with various delegations. At its first and second sessions (20 April), the Working Group, among other things, was briefed on the informal consultations, exchanged views on issues, such as the enlargement of the Council and its working methods, and heard concluding remarks by a Vice-Chairperson, which were annexed to the report. In informal consultations carried out during the Assembly's intersessional period, it was suggested that, during the plenary of the Assembly's sixty-first session, the Working Group should discuss the relationship between its work and the process of implementation of the 2005 World Summit Outcome [YUN 2005, p. 48]. In that context, the Working Group could also consider its mandate and functions. At its third session (8 September), the Working Group adopted its report to the Assembly, which included a draft decision for adoption by the Assembly.

By **decision 60/568** of 11 September, the Assembly took note of the Working Group's report and urged it to continue to exert efforts during the Assembly's sixty-first (2006) session, aimed at achieving progress on all the issues relevant to the question of equitable representation on and increase in the membership of the Security Council and other matters related to the Council. It decided that the question should be considered during the Assembly's sixty-first session, and that the Working Group should continue its work, taking into account progress achieved during the forty-eighth (1993) to sixtieth (2005) sessions of the Assembly and drawing on the experience of the sixtieth session, as well as the views expressed during the sixty-first session, taking into account paragraph 15 of the report (see above), and the discussion on the implementation of the 2005 World Summit Outcome. It further decided that the Working Group should submit a report to the Assembly before the end of its sixty-first session, including any agreed recommendations.

On 22 December, the General Assembly decided that the item on equitable representation on and increase in the membership of the Security Council and related matters would remain for consideration during its resumed sixty-first (2007) session (**decision 61/552**).

Revitalization of the United Nations in the economic, social and related fields

On 20 November [meeting 56], the General Assembly adopted **resolution 61/16** [draft: A/61/L.24] without vote [agenda items 47 and 113].

Strengthening of the Economic and Social Council

The General Assembly,

Recalling the 2005 World Summit Outcome,

Recalling also its resolutions 45/264 of 13 May 1991, 50/227 of 24 May 1996, 52/12 B of 19 December 1997, 57/270 B of 23 June 2003, 59/250 of 22 December 2004 and 60/265 of 30 June 2006,

Recalling further its resolution 60/180 of 20 December 2005 and Security Council resolution 1645(2005) of 20 December 2005,

Reaffirming the role that the Charter of the United Nations and the General Assembly have vested in the Economic and Social Council, and recognizing the need for a more effective Council as a principal body for coordination, policy review, policy dialogue and recommendations on issues of economic and social development, as well as for implementation of the international development goals agreed at the major United Nations conferences and summits, including the Millennium Development Goals,

Reaffirming also the commitments to and emphasizing the need to fully implement the global partnership for development set out in the United Nations Millennium Declaration, the Monterrey Consensus of the International Conference on Financing for Development and the Plan of Implementation of the World Summit on Sustainable Development ("Johannesburg Plan of Implementation") and to enhance the momentum generated by the 2005 World Summit in order to operationalize and implement, at all levels, the commitments set out in the outcomes of the major United Nations conferences and summits, including the 2005 World Summit, in the economic, social and related fields,

Reiterating that the Economic and Social Council should continue to strengthen its role as the central mechanism for system-wide coordination and thus promote the integrated and coordinated implementation of and follow-up to the outcomes of the major United Nations conferences in the economic, social and related fields, in accordance with the Charter and relevant General Assembly resolutions, in particular resolutions 50/227 and 57/270 B,

Resolving to accelerate the implementation of the measures and mechanisms defined in its resolution 57/270 B on integrated and coordinated implementation of and follow-up to the outcomes of the major United

Nations conferences and summits in the economic and social fields,

Welcoming Economic and Social Council decision 2006/206 of 10 February 2006, entitled "Adapting the work of the Economic and Social Council",

Recalling that the Economic and Social Council should increase its role in overseeing system-wide coordination and the balanced integration of economic, social and environmental aspects of United Nations policies and programmes aimed at promoting sustainable development, and reaffirming that the Commission on Sustainable Development should continue to be the high-level commission on sustainable development within the United Nations system and serve as a forum for consideration of issues related to integration of the three dimensions of sustainable development,

In pursuance of paragraphs 155 and 156 of the 2005 World Summit Outcome,

1. *Decides* to maintain the current segment structure of the substantive session of the Economic and Social Council;

2. *Also decides* that the Economic and Social Council should continue to promote global dialogue, inter alia, through strengthening existing arrangements, including:

(a) The special high-level meeting with the Bretton Woods institutions, the World Trade Organization and the United Nations Conference on Trade and Development;

(b) An annual high-level policy dialogue with international financial and trade institutions held in the framework of a strengthened high-level segment of the annual substantive session of the Council;

(c) A thematic discussion on a theme from economic, social and related fields to be decided by the Council and informed by a report of the Secretary-General;

3. *Further decides* that the biennial high-level Development Cooperation Forum will be held within the framework of the high-level segment of the Economic and Social Council, while stressing the need to preserve the distinct identity of the Forum so as to facilitate high-level participation, with a view to enhancing the implementation of international development cooperation issues affecting the realization of the internationally agreed development goals, including the Millennium Development Goals, and to promote dialogue to find effective ways to support it;

4. *Decides* that the biennial Development Cooperation Forum will be held in alternate years in the framework of the high-level segment of the Economic and Social Council and that it should:

(a) Review trends and progress in international development cooperation and give policy guidance and recommendations to promote more effective international development cooperation;

(b) Identify gaps and obstacles with a view to making recommendations on practical measures and policy options to enhance coherence and effectiveness and to promote development cooperation for the realization of the internationally agreed development goals, including the Millennium Development Goals;

(c) Provide a platform for Member States to exchange lessons learned and share experiences in formulating, supporting and implementing national development strategies;

(d) In accordance with the rules of procedure, be open to participation by all stakeholders, including the organizations of the United Nations, the international financial and trade institutions, the regional organizations, civil society and private sector representatives;

5. *Requests* the Economic and Social Council to consider launching the Development Cooperation Forum during the high-level segment of its substantive session of 2007 and thereafter meeting in New York, starting in 2008;

6. *Decides* that the Economic and Social Council should undertake a regular and periodic review and assessment of international economic and development policies and their impact on development;

7. *Requests* the Secretary-General to prepare an analytical background report for consideration by the Development Cooperation Forum;

8. *Decides* that the Economic and Social Council should hold annual ministerial-level substantive reviews as part of its high-level segment, and also decides that such reviews should be conducted by means of a cross-sectoral approach focusing on thematic issues common to the outcomes of the major United Nations conferences and summits in the economic, social and related fields, including the Millennium Development Goals and other internationally agreed development goals, review progress made in the implementation of the outcomes of those conferences and summits and their follow-up processes and assess its impact on the achievement of the goals and targets of the conferences and summits, and in this regard:

(a) Recommends that such reviews provide an opportunity for countries to make voluntary national presentations;

(b) Requests the Council to urge the functional commissions and other relevant subsidiary bodies and follow-up mechanisms, as appropriate, to contribute, in accordance with their mandates and taking into account their specificity, to the assessment;

(c) Recommends that the Council establish a multi-year programme of work for the ministerial-level substantive reviews;

(d) Invites the organizations of the United Nations system, including the Bretton Woods institutions and the World Trade Organization, to contribute within their respective mandates to the consideration by the Council;

9. *Requests* the Economic and Social Council to urge the United Nations regional commissions, in collaboration with other regional and subregional organizations and processes, as appropriate, to contribute, within their mandates, to the review of progress made in the implementation of and follow-up to the outcomes of the major United Nations conferences and summits in the economic, social and related fields and to provide input

to the discussions of the Council in accordance with its rules of procedure;

10. *Requests* the Secretary-General, when submitting his reports for the high-level segment, to include a concise, analytical section providing an assessment of progress, identifying gaps and obstacles in implementation and making recommendations to overcome those gaps and obstacles for consideration by Member States;

11. *Decides* that the outcome of the high-level segment should be one ministerial declaration;

12. *Also decides* that the Economic and Social Council should support and complement international efforts aimed at addressing humanitarian emergencies, including natural disasters, in order to promote an improved, coordinated response by the United Nations;

13. *Stresses* the importance of the humanitarian affairs segment of the Economic and Social Council in strengthening the coordination and effectiveness of United Nations humanitarian assistance;

14. *Emphasizes* that in addition to the humanitarian affairs segment, the Economic and Social Council should convene ad hoc meetings, in accordance with its rules of procedure, on specific humanitarian emergencies on the request of the affected Member State and following a recommendation of the Bureau, and that such ad hoc meetings should raise awareness and promote the engagement of all stakeholders in support of international relief efforts aimed at addressing those emergencies;

15. *Reaffirms* the role of the Economic and Social Council in providing overall coordination and guidance for operational development programmes and funds on a system-wide basis, including objectives, priorities and strategies in the implementation of the policies formulated by the General Assembly, as well as in concentrating on cross-cutting and coordination issues related to operational activities, in accordance with relevant Assembly resolutions;

16. *Also reaffirms* the importance of the triennial comprehensive policy review of operational activities, through which the General Assembly establishes key system-wide policy orientations for the development cooperation and country-level modalities of the United Nations system;

17. *Recalls* the role of the Economic and Social Council in providing coordination and guidance to the United Nations system to ensure that those policy orientations are implemented on a system-wide basis in accordance with General Assembly resolutions 48/162 of 20 December 1993, 50/227 and 57/270 B;

18. *Expresses concern* that insufficient provision of conference services and substantive support to the meetings of the Economic and Social Council has at times impeded its ability to fulfil its mandate despite its status as a Charter body, and in this regard decides to ensure provision of full and substantive support and conference services to the Council for all meetings necessary to enable it to fulfil its strengthened mandate;

19. *Recognizes* that the Economic and Social Council, as a Charter body, is entitled to convene meetings as and when needed, with full substantive support and conference services, and in this regard decides that the Council, beginning with its 2007 session, is entitled to convene additional meetings, of up to two weeks, in order to facilitate the fulfilment of its newly assigned responsibilities for organizing the annual ministerial reviews and the Development Cooperation Forum, as well as to hold ad hoc meetings, in order to effectively fulfil its mandate under the Charter;

20. *Recalls* its resolution 60/180 on the Peacebuilding Commission that addresses the special needs of countries emerging from conflict towards recovery, reintegration and reconstruction and assists them in laying the foundation for sustainable development, and in this regard reaffirms the importance of interaction between the Economic and Social Council and the Commission;

21. *Underlines* the experience of the Economic and Social Council in the area of post-conflict peacebuilding and the success of its ad hoc advisory groups on countries emerging from conflict, and invites the Peacebuilding Commission to benefit from it;

22. *Reiterates* that the agenda of the Peacebuilding Commission will be based on, inter alia, requests for advice from the Economic and Social Council with the consent of a concerned Member State in exceptional circumstances on the verge of lapsing or relapsing into conflict and of which the Security Council is not seized in accordance with Article 12 of the Charter;

23. *Reiterates its request* to the Peacebuilding Commission to make the outcomes of its discussions, recommendations and other reports available as United Nations documents to, inter alia, the Economic and Social Council;

24. *Decides* to review the implementation of the present resolution at its sixty-fifth session.

Follow-up to General Assembly resolution 61/16

On 15 December [meeting 48], the Economic and Social Council adopted **decision 2006/274** [draft: E/2006/L.40] without vote [agenda item 1].

Follow-up to the implementation of General Assembly resolution 61/16 on the strengthening of the Economic and Social Council

At its 48th plenary meeting, on 15 December 2006, the Economic and Social Council decided:

(a) To defer consideration of the focus of its 2007 thematic discussion and the theme for its 2007 annual ministerial review to the first meeting of its organizational session for 2007;

(b) To devote consideration of the theme "The role of the United Nations system in promoting full and productive employment and decent work for all" at the coordination segment of its substantive session of 2007;

(c) To approve the contributions of relevant subsidiary bodies of the Economic and Social Council, including functional and regional commissions, and the organizations of the United Nations system to the annual ministerial-level substantive review and the Development Cooperation Forum as follows:

(i) Decided, in accordance with paragraph 8, on annual ministerial-level substantive reviews, of General Assembly resolution 61/16 of 20 November 2006:

a. To urge its functional commissions and other relevant subsidiary bodies and follow-up mechanisms, as appropriate, to contribute, in accordance with their mandates and taking into account their specificity, to the assessment;

b. To invite the organizations of the United Nations system, including the Bretton Woods institutions and the World Trade Organization, to contribute within their respective mandates to the consideration by the Council;

(ii) Also decided, in accordance with paragraph 9 of General Assembly resolution 61/16, to urge the regional commissions, in collaboration with other regional and subregional organizations and processes, as appropriate, to contribute, within their mandates, to the review of progress made in the implementation of and follow-up to the outcomes of the major United Nations conferences and summits in the economic, social and related fields and to provide input to the discussions of the Economic and Social Council in accordance with its rules of procedure;

(iii) Further decided that this decision should apply to the first annual ministerial-level substantive review and the Development Cooperation Forum to be held in 2007, without prejudice to the future modalities of interaction between the Economic and Social Council and its subsidiary bodies beyond the substantive session of 2007 of the Council.

Institutional machinery

Admission of new member: Montenegro

On 22 June [meeting 5473], the Security Council considered the application of the Republic of Montenegro for United Nations membership [A/60/890-S/2006/409], following a 21 May referendum, in which Montenegro voted to separate from Serbia (see p. 472).

The Council, acting on the recommendation of the Committee on the Admission of New Members [S/2006/425], adopted **resolution 1691(2006)** without vote.

The Security Council,

Having examined the application of the Republic of Montenegro for admission to the United Nations,

Recommends to the General Assembly that the Republic of Montenegro be admitted to membership in the United Nations.

Following adoption of the resolution, the Council President made statement **S/PRST/2006/27** on behalf of the Council:

The Security Council has decided to recommend to the General Assembly that the Republic of Montenegro be admitted as a Member of the United Nations. On behalf of the members of the Council, I wish to extend my congratulations to the Republic of Montenegro on this historic occasion.

The Council notes with great satisfaction the Republic of Montenegro's solemn commitment to uphold the purposes and principles of the Charter of the United Nations and to fulfil all the obligations contained therein.

We look forward to the Republic of Montenegro joining us as a Member of the United Nations and to working closely with its representatives.

GENERAL ASSEMBLY ACTION

On 28 June [meeting 91], the General Assembly adopted **resolution 60/264** [draft: A/60/L.58 & Add.1] without vote [agenda item 114].

Admission of the Republic of Montenegro to membership in the United Nations

The General Assembly,

Having received the recommendation of the Security Council of 22 June 2006 that the Republic of Montenegro should be admitted to membership in the United Nations,

Having considered the application for membership of the Republic of Montenegro,

Decides to admit the Republic of Montenegro to membership in the United Nations.

On 22 December, the Assembly decided that the item on the admission of the new members would remain for consideration during its resumed sixty-first (2007) session (**decision 61/552**).

General Assembly

The General Assembly held its resumed sixtieth session and the major part of its sixty-first session. The sixtieth session was resumed in plenary meetings on 6 February; 7, 15, 16, 27 and 30 March; 13 and 28 April; 2, 8, 9, 16, 30 and 31 May; 1, 2, 6, 8, 28 and 30 June; 7, 20 and 21 July; 29 August; and 7, 8 and 11 September. The sixty-first session opened on 12 September and continued until its suspension on 22 December.

The Assembly held a High-level Dialogue on International Migration and Development (14-15 September) (see p. 1261), and High-level meetings on the Midterm Comprehensive Global Review of the Implementation of the Programme of Action for the Least Developed Countries for the Decade 2001-2010 (18-19 September) (see p. 1014) and on HIV/AIDS (2 to 3 June) (see p. 1410). The Assembly also resumed its tenth emergency special session (17 November and 15 December) to discuss "Illegal Israeli actions in Occupied East Jerusalem and the rest of the Occupied Palestinian Territory" (see p. 521). Other key meetings included one to appoint the United Nations Secretary-General, Ban Ki-moon (Republic of Korea) (13 October) (see p. 1676), and an informal thematic debate on the theme of "Partnerships towards achieving the Millennium Development Goals: Taking stock, moving forward" (27 November). A special commemorative meeting devoted to the sixtieth anniversary of the operations of the United Nations Children's Fund (UNICEF) was held on 8 December (see p. 1363).

Organization of Assembly sessions

2006 sessions

By **decision 61/501** of 12 September, the General Assembly authorized a number of bodies to meet in New York during the main part of its sixty-first (2006) session. By **decision 61/502** of 13 September, the Assembly adopted a number of provisions concerning the organization of the sixty-first (2006) session [A/61/250 & Add. 1-4].

Credentials

The Credentials Committee, at its meeting on 14 December [A/61/648], had before it a memorandum by the Secretary-General, which indicated that, to date, 131 Member States had submitted the formal credentials of their representatives. Information concerning the representatives of 46 other Member States had been also communicated.

The Committee adopted a resolution accepting the credentials received and recommended a draft resolution to the General Assembly for adoption.

On 22 December, the Assembly, by **resolution 61/227**, approved the Committee's report.

Agenda

During its resumed sixtieth (2006) session, the General Assembly, by **decision 60/503 B**, decided on those items to be considered directly in plenary, and those on which consideration would be reopened. The Assembly, by decisions of 8 May (**decision 60/551 B**), 7 July (**decision 60/551 C**) and 11 September (**decisions 60/564, 60/565, 60/566,** and **60/567**) also decided on those items to be deferred to its sixty-first (2006) session.

On 28 April, the Assembly decided to invite the Administrator of UNDP and Coordinator of International Cooperation on Chernobyl and the Executive Director of UNICEF to make statements at the special commemorative meeting held on the same day, in observance of the twentieth anniversary of the Chernobyl catastrophe (**decision 60/502 B**).

At its sixty-first (2006) session, the Assembly, by **decision 61/503** of 13 September, adopted, on the recommendation of the General Committee [A/61/250 & Add. 1,2,3], the agenda [A/61//251] and the allocation of agenda items [A/61/252 & Corr.2], including those to be deferred and included in the provisional agenda of its sixty-second (2007) session. By that same decision it decided to consider in the Third (Social, Humanitarian and Cultural) Committee, the item on the report of the Human Rights Council to the Assembly, including those that dealt with the development of international law in the field of human rights. The Assembly also decided to consider, in plenary, the annual report of the Council on its activities for the year, and that the arrangement would in no way be a reinterpretation of resolution 60/251 (see p. 757) and would be reviewed before the beginning of its sixty-second session.

(Lists of the Assembly's agendas and the allocation of items are to be found in APPENDIX IV.)

By its **decision 61/552** of 22 December, the Assembly decided to retain 74 items on the agenda of its resumed sixty-first (2007) session. On the same date, the Assembly, on the recommendation of the Fifth Committee [A/61/667], deferred until the resumed sixty-first session the item on the report of the activities of the Office of Internal Oversight Services (**decision 61/551 A**), and the item on the scale of assessments for the apportionment of the expenses of the United Nations until the sixty-second (2007) session (**decision 61/551 B**). On 6 December, the Assembly, by a recorded vote of 128 to 3, with 44 abstentions, included in the provisional agenda of its sixty-second session the item "United Nations conference to identify ways of eliminating nuclear dangers in the context of nuclear disarmament" (**decision 61/515**).

Resolutions and decisions of the General Assembly

By **decision 61/508** of 16 November, the Assembly deferred consideration of the agenda item "Implementation of the resolutions of the United Nations" and included it in the provisional agenda of its sixty-second (2007) session.

First, Second, Third and Sixth Committees

The General Assembly, on 4 December, noted that the Sixth Committee had adopted its provisional programme of work for the sixty-second (2007) session (**decision 61/509**). On 6 December, the Assembly approved the work programme and timetable of the First (Disarmament and

International Security) Committee for 2007 (**decision 61/516**). On 20 December, it approved the programmes of work of the Third (**decision 61/532**) and Second Committees (**decision 61/544**) for the sixty-second (2007) session.

Security Council

The Security Council held 272 formal meetings in 2006, adopted 87 resolutions and issued 59 presidential statements. It considered 34 agenda items (see APPENDIX IV). In a September note [A/61/371], the Secretary-General, in accordance with Article 12, paragraph 2 of the Charter of the United Nations and with the consent of the Council, notified the General Assembly of 60 matters related to the maintenance of international peace and security that the Council had discussed since his previous annual notification [YUN 2005, p. 1539]. The Secretary-General also listed 80 matters that the Council had not discussed since then. The Assembly, on 11 December, took note of the Secretary-General's note (**decision 61/518**).

On 12 December, the Assembly took note of the Council's report for the period 1 August 2005 to 31 July 2006 [A/61/2 & Corr.1] (**decision 61/519**).

Membership

The General Assembly continued to examine the question of expanding the Security Council's membership. It considered the report of the Open-ended Working Group on the Equitable Representation on and Increase in the Membership of the Security Council and Other Matters related to the Security Council [A/60/47]. The Assembly took action with regard to the report in decision **61/552** of 22 December.

Economic and Social Council

The Economic and Social Council held its organizational session for 2006 on 17 January, 7 and 10 February, 14 and 22 March and 8 May; a resumed organizational session on 10 and 12 May; and a special high-level meeting with the Bretton Woods institutions (the World Bank Group and the International Monetary Fund), the World Trade Organization (WTO) and the United Nations Conference on Trade and Development (UNCTAD) on 24 April, all in New York. It held its substantive session from 3 to 28 July, in Geneva, and resumed substantive session on 11 October, 30 November and 15 December, all in New York. The work of the Council in 2006 was covered in its report to the General Assembly [A/61/3/Rev.1].

On 17 January and 22 March, the Council elected its Bureau (a President and four Vice-Presidents) for 2006 and adopted the agenda of the organizational session [E/2006/2 & Add.1 & Add.1/Corr.1].

On 10 February, the Council decided that, as soon as possible after the Assembly's adoption of its draft resolution in pursuance of paragraphs 155 and 156 of the 2005 World Summit Outcome [YUN 2005, p. 48], the President of the Council should convene consultations to adapt its organization of work, agenda and methods of work, so as to begin implementation in 2007 (**decision 2006/206**). On the same date, the Council approved the provisional agenda and documentation for its 2006 substantive session (**decision 2006/208**), and decided on the working arrangements for that session (**decision 2006/210**). It also decided that the letter of the Director-General of the International Labour Organization (ILO) of 30 June 2005 addressed to the Secretary-General [E/2006/11] should be placed under agenda item 14 (*b*) "social development" of the provisional agenda of the 2006 substantive session (**decision 2006/207**). On 3 July, the Council adopted the agenda [E/2006/100] and approved the proposed programme of work of that session [E/2006/L.4]. At the same meeting, it approved the requests for hearings from non-governmental organizations (NGOs) [E/2006/78] (**decision 2006/218**).

The General Assembly, by **decision 61/552** of 22 December, decided that the Council's report would remain for consideration during its resumed sixty-first (2007) session.

Sessions and segments

During 2006, the Economic and Social Council adopted 49 resolutions and 77 decisions. By **decision 2006/210**, the Council decided that its high-level segment would be held from 3 to 5 July; the coordination segment from 6 to 10 July; the operational activities segment from 11 to 13 July; the humanitarian affairs segment from 14 to 19 July; the general segment from 19 to 27 July; and to conclude its work on 27 and 28 July. It also decided that the dialogue with the executive secretaries of the regional commissions would be held on 6 July. On 7 February, the Council decided that the special high-level meeting with the Bretton Woods institutions, WTO and UNCTAD would be held in New York on 24 April (**decision 2006/202**).

On 17 July, the Council deferred until a resumed session the finalization of the multi-year work programme for the coordination segment and took note of the Secretary-General's report on sustained economic growth for social development, including poverty eradication and hunger (see p. 994) (**decision 2006/220**).

2006 and 2007 sessions

On 10 February (**decision 2006/211**), the Council decided that the theme for the item on regional cooperation at its 2006 substantive session would be "The regional dimension of creating an environment conducive to generating full and productive employment, and decent work for all, and its impact on sustainable development". On 14 March (**decision 2006/214**), the Council decided that the theme of the humanitarian affairs segment of its 2006 substantive session would be "Strengthening of the coordination of United Nations humanitarian assistance: implementing improved humanitarian response at all levels, including strengthening capacity, with particular attention to recent humanitarian emergencies, including severe natural disasters". On 22 March, the Council decided that the work of the operational activities segment of its 2006 substantive session should be devoted to examining the operational activities of the UN system in order to evaluate the implementation of General Assembly resolution 59/250 of 22 December 2004 [YUN 2004, p. 868], with a view to ensuring its full implementation, including through a comprehensive review of trends and perspectives in funding for development cooperation, and in that context decided to apply General Assembly decision 60/547 of 22 December 2005 [YUN 2005, p. 958] (**decision 2006/215**).

Work programme

On 10 February, the Council took note of the list of questions for inclusion in the programme of work of the Council for 2007 [E/2006/1 & Corr.1] (**decision 2006/209**).

Coordination, monitoring and cooperation

Institutional mechanisms

CEB activities

According to its annual overview report for 2006-2007 [E/2007/69], the United Nations System Chief Executives Board for Coordination (CEB) addressed a number of emerging and important programme issues with system-wide implications, including international migration and development, the midterm review of the Brussels Programme of Action for Least Developed Countries, and the cross-cutting issue of employment and decent work. Other topics were addressed from the perspective of developing common understanding and coherent responses to emerging issues on the international agenda, including aid-for-trade, system-wide coherence and "One United Nations" at the country level. CEB continued its consideration of management issues, with the support of its High-level Committee on Programmes (HLCP) and High-level Committee on Management (HLCM), focusing on management harmonization and reform. A number of new issues were on the Committee's agenda, including the harmonization of UN system business practices, the confidentiality of internal audit reports, and the United Nations security management system. Renewed attention was given to enhancing the effectiveness of CEB in addressing the major strategic challenges facing the UN system, in order to respond more effectively to major global issues, ensure that all the analytical and operational capacities available in the system were brought to bear on meeting those challenges, and maximize the system's responsiveness to the requirements of Member States and the international community. In that regard, the Secretary-General had requested the Directors-General of ILO and WTO to lead a review of the functioning of CEB.

CEB held two regular sessions in 2006: the first in Madrid (7 April) [CEB/2006/1] and the second in New York (27 October) [CEB/2006/2 & Corr.1]. Its principal subsidiary bodies met as follows: HLCM, eleventh (Villiers-le-Mahieu, France, 27-28 February) [CEB/2006/3] and twelfth (Rome, 30 September–1 October) [CEB/2006/5] sessions; HLCP, eleventh (Paris, 27 February–1 March) [CEB/2006/4] and twelfth (Rome, 29-30 September) [CEB/2006/7] sessions, with an intersessional meeting (Geneva, 6 July) [CEB/2006/6], held in conjunction with the substantive session of the Economic and Social Council.

CEB report

The Committee for Programme and Coordination (CPC) [A/61/16 & Corr.1] considered the CEB annual overview report for 2005/2006 [YUN 2005, p. 1540]. CPC recommended that the Assembly request CEB to continue to monitor the effective collaboration of system-wide efforts against hunger and poverty; express regret that the international response to reducing undernutrition had generally been insufficient and that the share of agricultural official development assistance during the past decade had sharply declined; request the Secretary-General to address that situation; and request CEB to report on the main difficulties encountered by organizations of the system in addressing malnutrition and hunger. CPC also highlighted the high priority that CEB continued to attach to ensuring the effectiveness and coordination of UN system support for Africa and the New Partnership for Africa's Development (NEPAD), and requested CEB to ensure that support for NEPAD remained a priority for the UN system. It encouraged CEB member organizations to further align their priorities with those of NEPAD and to scale up their efforts to support it.

On 24 July, the Economic and Social Council took note of the CEB annual overview report for 2005/2006 (**decision 2006/227**).

Programme coordination

CPC held an organizational meeting on 21 June and its forty-sixth session from 14 August to 8 September, all in New York [A/61/16 & Corr.1].

CPC dealt with questions related to the programme performance of the United Nations for the 2004-2005 biennium and the proposed 2008-2009 strategic framework. It considered the United Nations Office of Internal Oversight Services (OIOS) reports on strengthening the role of evaluation and the application of evaluation findings on programme design, delivery and policy directives; thematic evaluation of knowledge management networks in the pursuit of the goals of the Millennium Declaration; usefulness of the pilot thematic evaluation; in-depth evaluation of political affairs; and triennial review of the in-depth evaluation of the programme on the law of the sea and ocean affairs. In addition, CPC considered the Secretary-General's report on UN system support for NEPAD, as well as an agenda item on improving its working methods and procedures within the framework of its mandate. (See p. 1635 for more information on the work of CPC.)

On 11 October, the Economic and Social Council took note of the CPC report (**decision 2006/257**).

Other coordination matters

Follow-up to international conferences

In response to Economic and Social Council resolution 2005/48 [YUN 2005, p. 1541], the Secretary-General submitted, in June [A/61/90-E/2006/84], an updated report on the role of the Council in the integrated and coordinated implementation of the outcomes of and follow-up to major United Nations conferences and summits.

The report contained recommendations on: strengthening the role of the Council; the role of the functional commissions; the role of the regional commissions; the role of the Committee for Policy Development; and strengthening implementation at the inter-agency and country levels. It also reviewed the division of labour between the General Assembly (Second and Third Committees), the Council and the functional commissions, as well as the role of partnerships. It noted that at the 2005 World Summit [YUN 2005, p. 47] Member States had resolved to adopt, by 2006, comprehensive national strategies to meet the internationally agreed development goals and assigned new functions to the Economic and Social Council, notably the annual ministerial reviews and the biennial development cooperation forums. Those two new functions provided the Council and its subsidiary bodies with an opportunity to further strengthen the integrated and coordinated follow-up to the major UN conferences and summits, placing the Council at the centre of the global effort to monitor and advance implementation.

ECONOMIC AND SOCIAL COUNCIL ACTION

On 28 July [meeting 43], the Economic and Social Council adopted **resolution 2006/44** [draft: E/2006/L.35] without vote [agenda items 6, 8, 13 and 14].

Role of the Economic and Social Council in the integrated and coordinated implementation of the follow-ups to major United Nations conferences and summits, in the light of General Assembly resolutions 50/227, 52/12 B and 57/270 B.

The Economic and Social Council,

Recalling its agreed conclusions 1995/1 of 28 July 1995 and 2002/1 of 26 July 2002 and its relevant resolutions on the integrated and coordinated implementation of and follow-up to the outcomes of the major United Nations conferences and summits,

Recalling also the internationally agreed development goals, including the Millennium Development Goals, and the outcomes of the major United Nations conferences and summits and the reviews of their implementation in the economic, social and related fields, including the Millennium Summit and 2005 World Summit,

Recalling further General Assembly resolutions 50/227 of 24 May 1996, 52/12 B of 19 December 1997, 57/270 B of 23 June 2003 and 60/265 of 30 June 2006,

Bearing in mind the ongoing process of reform of the United Nations,

1. *Takes note* of the report of the Secretary-General, and underlines the need for the Secretariat to implement the decisions of the Council regarding reports in response to the Council's decisions and resolutions;

2. *Decides* to continue to promote the integrated and coordinated implementation of and follow-up to the out-

comes of the major United Nations conferences and summits, bearing in mind the need to respect the thematic unity of each of the conferences and the interlinkages between them;

3. *Welcomes* the progress made in their review of their working methods by several functional commissions and subsidiary bodies of the Economic and Social Council during their 2006 sessions, and in this regard invites those functional commissions and other relevant subsidiary bodies that have not yet done so to continue to examine their methods of work, as mandated by the General Assembly in its resolution 57/270 B, in order to better pursue the implementation of the outcomes of the major United Nations conferences and summits, and to submit their reports to the Council with the aim of concluding the review of their working methods by 2007;

4. *Decides* to replace the individual joint bureaux meetings with one meeting of the chairs of the functional commissions and the Economic and Social Council to be held in the beginning of each calendar year, making use of teleconferencing whenever possible;

5. *Notes* the progress made in 2006 to enhance cooperation between the functional commissions and the regional commissions, and invites the functional commissions that have not yet done so to work towards strengthening their cooperation with the regional commissions, as well as relevant funds and programmes of the United Nations and the specialized agencies;

6. *Invites* the regional commissions, in cooperation with regional organizations and other regional processes, as appropriate, to further contribute within their respective mandates to the implementation and reviews of the outcomes of the major United Nations conferences and summits in the economic, social and related fields;

7. *Decides* to further strengthen its linkages with the regional commissions, including through the contribution of the commissions to the preparation of reports on reviews of implementation;

8. *Underscores* that the functional commissions, when mandated, should continue to have the primary responsibility for the review and assessment of progress made in implementing the outcomes of the United Nations conferences and summits in the economic, social and related fields;

9. *Reiterates its request* to the Secretary-General, in his capacity as Chairman of the United Nations System Chief Executives Board for Coordination, to continue to include in the annual overview report of the Chief Executives Board, information on the mainstreaming, integration and coordination of development activities at the Secretariat level, and, in this regard, decides to strengthen the consideration of the report of the Chief Executives Board;

10. *Decides* to continue to take necessary steps towards the effective implementation of the provisions of General Assembly resolutions 50/227, 52/12 B and 57/270 B that are relevant to the work of the Economic and Social Council and its subsidiary system;

11. *Also decides* to take further steps to enable the Council to perform its crucial coordination responsibility effectively, and requests the Secretary-General to submit proposals, in particular for making the documentation more user-friendly;

12. *Requests* the Secretary-General to submit a report on the role of the Economic and Social Council in the integrated and coordinated implementation of the outcomes of and follow-up to major United Nations conferences and summits, in the light of General Assembly resolutions 50/227, 52/12 B, 57/270 B and 60/265, which should also adequately reflect the work of the functional commissions in 2007, including actions taken to follow up on the present resolution, for consideration by the Council at its substantive session of 2007.

On 22 December, the General Assembly decided that the item on integrated and coordinated implementation of and follow-up to the outcomes of the major UN conferences and summits in the economic, social and related fields would remain for consideration during its resumed sixty-first (2007) session (**decision 61/552**).

UN and other organizations

Cooperation with organizations

In response to General Assembly resolution 58/316 [YUN 2004, p.1374], the Secretary-General submitted an August consolidated report [A/61/256] on cooperation between the United Nations and regional and other organizations, including the African Union (see p. 339); the Association of Southeast Asian Nations (see p. 1170); the Caribbean Community (see p. 359); the Community of Portuguese-speaking Countries (see p. 1598); the Council of Europe (see p. 496); the Economic Community of Central African States (see p. 1155); the League of Arab States (see p. 1598); the Organization of the Islamic Conference (see p. 1600); the Organization of American States (see p. 360); the International Organization of la Francophonie (see p. 1602); the Pacific Islands Forum (see p. 1167); the Southern African Development Community (see p. 1153); the Black Sea Economic Cooperation Organization (see p. 1186); the Economic Cooperation Organization (see p. 1166); the Inter-Parliamentary Union (see p. 1604); the Organization for the Prohibition of Chemical Weapons (see p. 655); and the Preparatory Commission for the Comprehensive Nuclear-Test-Ban Treaty Organization (see p. 630).

In a later addendum [A/61/256/Add.1], the Secretary-General submitted a report on cooperation between the United Nations and the Latin American Economic System (see p. 1195) and the

Asian-African Legal Consultative Organization (see p. 1537).

Community of Portuguese-speaking Countries

In response to General Assembly resolution 59/21 [YUN 2004, p. 1458], the Secretary-General, in his August consolidated report [A/61/256], provided information on cooperation between the United Nations and the Community of Portuguese-speaking Countries (CPLP). In order to fully implement the resolution, a formal cooperation agreement between CPLP and the United Nations was being considered. The Executive Secretary of CPLP participated in two high-level meetings between the United Nations and regional and other intergovernmental organizations, highlighting CPLP's contribution to peacekeeping and international development, particularly its work with the United Nations Peacebuilding Support Office in Guinea-Bissau. CPLP established joint priorities with the United Nations Educational, Scientific and Cultural Organization (UNESCO) and, in that context, celebrated Portuguese Language Day on 5 May. In March, CPLP signed a technical cooperation project with the Food and Agriculture Organization of the United Nations (FAO), aimed at elaborating a regional capacity-building programme on territorial property, land management and legal aspects targeted at CPLP member States. Cooperation with UNCTAD included technical training programmes on ports and the negotiation of international investment agreements. Regarding cooperation with the International Labour Organization (ILO), the CPLP Executive Secretariat and the Portuguese Government co-organized a conference on the fight against the exploitation of child labour in CPLP countries, in April.

GENERAL ASSEMBLY ACTION

On 20 December [meeting 83], the General Assembly adopted **resolution 61/223** [draft: A/61/L.43 & Add.1] without vote [agenda item 108 *(f)*].

Cooperation between the United Nations and the Community of Portuguese-speaking Countries

The General Assembly,

Recalling its resolution 54/10 of 26 October 1999, by which it granted observer status to the Community of Portuguese-speaking Countries and considered it mutually advantageous to provide for cooperation between the United Nations and the Community of Portuguese-speaking Countries, and its resolution 59/21 of 8 November 2004, in which it invited the Secretary-General of the United Nations to undertake consultations with the Executive Secretary of the Community of Portuguese-speaking Countries, and requested the specialized agencies and other bodies and programmes of the United Nations system to cooperate to that end with the Secretary-General and the Executive Secretary,

Recalling also the Articles of the Charter of the United Nations that encourage activities through regional cooperation for the promotion of the purposes and principles of the United Nations,

Considering that the activities of the Community of Portuguese-speaking Countries complement and support the work of the United Nations,

Welcoming the participation of the Community of Portuguese-speaking Countries in the seventh high-level meeting between the United Nations and regional and other intergovernmental organizations, held in New York on 22 September 2006,

Recalling the celebration by the United Nations Educational, Scientific and Cultural Organization, for the first time, of the Portuguese language day on 5 May 2006,

1. *Notes with appreciation* the progress achieved in cooperation between the Community of Portuguese-speaking Countries and the specialized agencies and other bodies and programmes of the United Nations system, in particular the United Nations Conference on Trade and Development, the International Labour Organization, the Food and Agriculture Organization of the United Nations and the United Nations Educational, Scientific and Cultural Organization;

2. *Welcomes* the signature of the agreement between the United Nations High Commissioner for Human Rights and the Community of Portuguese-speaking Countries on 9 November 2006 regarding consultation, exchange of information and technical cooperation on their respective activities in the field of human rights;

3. *Invites* the Secretary-General of the United Nations to continue to undertake consultations with the Executive Secretary of the Community of Portuguese-speaking Countries with a view to promoting cooperation between the secretariats of the two bodies, in particular by encouraging meetings that enable their representatives to consult one another on projects, measures and procedures that will facilitate and expand their mutual cooperation and coordination;

4. *Invites* the Secretary-General and the Executive Secretary to start consultations with a view to considering the establishment of a formal cooperation agreement;

5. *Requests* the Secretary-General to submit a report on the implementation of the present resolution to the General Assembly at its sixty-third session;

6. *Decides* to include in the provisional agenda of its sixty-third session the sub-item entitled "Cooperation between the United Nations and the Community of Portuguese-speaking Countries".

League of Arab States

In response to General Assembly resolution 59/9 [YUN 2004, p. 1454], the Secretary-General, in his August consolidated report [A/61/256], provided information on cooperation between the United

Nations and the League of Arab States (LAS) (see p. 1200).

GENERAL ASSEMBLY ACTION

On 13 November [meeting 52], the General Assembly adopted **resolution 61/14** [draft: A/61/L.17 & Add.1], without vote [agenda item 108 *(m)*].

Cooperation between the United Nations and the League of Arab States

The General Assembly,

Recalling its previous resolutions on cooperation between the United Nations and the League of Arab States,

Having considered the report of the Secretary-General on cooperation between the United Nations and regional and other organizations,

Recalling article 3 of the Pact of the League of Arab States, which entrusts the Council of the League with the function of determining the means whereby the League will collaborate with the international organizations which may be created in the future to guarantee peace and security and organize economic and social relations,

Noting the desire of both organizations to consolidate, develop and enhance further the ties existing between them in the political, economic, social, humanitarian, cultural, technical and administrative fields,

Taking into account the report of the Secretary-General entitled "An Agenda for Peace", in particular section VII concerning cooperation with regional arrangements and organizations, and the "Supplement to an Agenda for Peace",

Convinced of the need for more efficient and coordinated utilization of available economic and financial resources in order to promote the common objectives of the two organizations,

Recognizing the need for the further strengthening of cooperation between the United Nations system and the League of Arab States and its specialized organizations for the realization of the common goals and objectives of the two organizations,

1. *Takes note with satisfaction* of the report of the Secretary-General;

2. *Commends* the continued efforts of the League of Arab States to promote multilateral cooperation among Arab States, and requests the United Nations system to continue to lend its support;

3. *Expresses its appreciation* to the Secretary-General for the follow-up action taken by him to implement the proposals adopted at the meetings between representatives of the Secretariat of the United Nations and other organizations of the United Nations system and the General Secretariat of the League of Arab States and its specialized organizations, including the sectoral meeting in 2005 on the theme "Achieving and financing the Millennium Development Goals and sustainable development in the Arab region" and the general meeting on cooperation held in 2006;

4. *Requests* the Secretariat of the United Nations and the General Secretariat of the League of Arab States, within their respective fields of competence, to intensify further their cooperation for the realization of the purposes and principles embodied in the Charter of the United Nations, the strengthening of international peace and security, economic and social development, disarmament, decolonization, self-determination and the eradication of all forms of racism and racial discrimination;

5. *Requests* the Secretary-General to continue his efforts to strengthen cooperation and coordination between the United Nations and other organizations and agencies of the United Nations system and the League of Arab States and its specialized organizations in order to enhance their capacity to serve the mutual interests and objectives of the two organizations in the political, economic, social, humanitarian, cultural and administrative fields;

6. *Calls upon* the specialized agencies and other organizations and programmes of the United Nations system:

(a) To continue to cooperate with the Secretary-General and among themselves, as well as with the League of Arab States and its specialized organizations, in the follow-up of multilateral proposals aimed at strengthening and expanding cooperation in all fields between the United Nations system and the League of Arab States and its specialized organizations;

(b) To strengthen the capacity of the League of Arab States and of its institutions and specialized organizations to benefit from globalization and information technology and to meet the development challenges of the new millennium;

(c) To step up cooperation and coordination with the specialized organizations of the League of Arab States in the organization of seminars and training courses and in the preparation of studies;

(d) To maintain and increase contacts and improve the mechanism of consultation with the counterpart programmes, organizations and agencies concerned regarding projects and programmes in order to facilitate their implementation;

(e) To participate whenever possible with organizations and institutions of the League of Arab States in the execution and implementation of development projects in the Arab region;

(f) To inform the Secretary-General of the progress made in their cooperation with the League of Arab States and its specialized organizations and, in particular, of the follow-up action taken on the multilateral and bilateral proposals adopted at the previous meetings between the two organizations;

7. *Also calls upon* the specialized agencies and other organizations and programmes of the United Nations system to increase their cooperation with the League of Arab States and its specialized organizations in the priority sectors of energy, rural development, desertification and green belts, training and vocational education, technology, environment, information and documentation, trade and finance, water resources, development of the

agricultural sector, empowerment of women, transport, communications and information, promotion of the role of the private sector and capacity-building;

8. *Requests* the Secretary-General of the United Nations, in cooperation with the Secretary-General of the League of Arab States, to encourage periodic consultation between representatives of the Secretariat of the United Nations and of the General Secretariat of the League of Arab States in order to review and strengthen coordination mechanisms with a view to accelerating implementation of, and follow-up action on, the multilateral projects, proposals and recommendations adopted at the meetings between the two organizations;

9. *Recommends* that the United Nations and all organizations of the United Nations system make the greatest possible use of Arab institutions and technical expertise in projects undertaken in the Arab region;

10. *Reaffirms* that, in order to enhance cooperation and for the purpose of the review and appraisal of progress, a general meeting between representatives of the United Nations system and the League of Arab States should be held once every two years and that joint inter-agency sectoral meetings should also be convened on a biennial basis to address priority areas of major importance to the development of Arab States, on the basis of agreement between the United Nations system and the League of Arab States and its specialized organizations;

11. *Also reaffirms* the importance of holding the sectoral meeting between the United Nations and the League of Arab States and its specialized organizations during 2007 and also of holding the general meeting on cooperation between representatives of the secretariats of the organizations of the United Nations system and the General Secretariat of the League of Arab States and its specialized organizations during 2008;

12. *Requests* the Secretary-General to submit to the General Assembly at its sixty-third session a report on the implementation of the present resolution;

13. *Decides* to include in the provisional agenda of its sixty-third session the sub-item entitled "Cooperation between the United Nations and the League of Arab States".

Organization of the Islamic Conference

In response to resolution 59/8 [YUN 2004, p.1453], the Secretary-General, in his August consolidated report [A/61/256], provided information on cooperation between the United Nations and the Organization of the Islamic Conference (OIC). A memorandum of understanding on technical cooperation in human rights between the Office of the High Commissioner for Human Rights (OHCHR) and OIC was signed at the general meeting on cooperation between the representatives of the UN system and OIC and its specialized institutions (Rabat, Morocco, 11-13 July). A joint statement was issued in Doha, Qatar, on 25 February, by the UN Secretary-General and his counterparts in OIC and LAS, together with representatives of Qatar, Spain and Turkey, appealing for restraint and calm after the controversial publication in a Danish newspaper of caricatures of the Prophet Mohammed. The statement contained a commitment to formulate a joint strategy and agreed measures to overcome the crisis, prevent its recurrence and promote tolerance and mutual respect between all religions and communities throughout the world. In May, the United Nations and OIC worked together to help alleviate famine in Kenya, Somalia and Ethiopia. Furthermore, continued OIC funding of reconstruction projects in parts of Afghanistan, Bosnia and Herzegovina and Sierra Leone strengthened the work of the United Nations in those countries.

GENERAL ASSEMBLY ACTION

On 4 December [meeting 65], the General Assembly adopted **resolution 61/49** [draft: A/61/L.26 & Add.1] without vote [agenda item 108 (*q*)].

Cooperation between the United Nations and the Organization of the Islamic Conference

The General Assembly,

Recalling its resolutions 37/4 of 22 October 1982, 38/4 of 28 October 1983, 39/7 of 8 November 1984, 40/4 of 25 October 1985, 41/3 of 16 October 1986, 42/4 of 15 October 1987, 43/2 of 17 October 1988, 44/8 of 18 October 1989, 45/9 of 25 October 1990, 46/13 of 28 October 1991, 47/18 of 23 November 1992, 48/24 of 24 November 1993, 49/15 of 15 November 1994, 50/17 of 20 November 1995, 51/18 of 14 November 1996, 52/4 of 22 October 1997, 53/16 of 29 October 1998, 54/7 of 25 October 1999, 55/9 of 30 October 2000, 56/47 of 7 December 2001, 57/42 of 21 November 2002 and 59/8 of 22 October 2004,

Recalling also its resolution 3369 (XXX) of 10 October 1975, by which it decided to invite the Organization of the Islamic Conference to participate in the sessions and the work of the General Assembly and of its subsidiary organs in the capacity of observer,

Welcoming the efforts of the Secretary-General of the Organization of the Islamic Conference in strengthening the role of the Organization in conflict prevention, confidence-building, peacekeeping, conflict resolution and post-conflict rehabilitation in member States as well as in conflict situations involving Muslim communities,

Noting the adoption by the third extraordinary session of the Islamic Summit Conference, held in Mecca, Saudi Arabia, on 7 and 8 December 2005, of the Ten-Year Programme of Action,

Having considered the report of the Secretary-General on cooperation between the United Nations and regional and other organizations,

Taking into account the desire of the two organizations to continue to cooperate closely in the political, economic, social, humanitarian, cultural and scientific fields and in their common search for solutions to global problems, such as questions relating to international peace and security, disarmament, self-determination, the promotion of a culture of peace through dialogue and cooperation, decolonization, fundamental human rights and economic and social development,

Recalling the Articles of the Charter of the United Nations that encourage activities through regional cooperation for the promotion of the purposes and principles of the United Nations,

Noting the strengthening of cooperation between the United Nations, its funds and programmes and the specialized agencies and the Organization of the Islamic Conference, its subsidiary organs and its specialized and affiliated institutions,

Noting also the encouraging progress made in the ten priority areas of cooperation between the two organizations and their respective agencies and institutions, as well as in the identification of other areas of cooperation between them,

Convinced that the strengthening of cooperation between the United Nations and other organizations of the United Nations system and the Organization of the Islamic Conference and its organs and institutions contributes to the promotion of the purposes and principles of the United Nations,

Welcoming the results of the general meeting of the organizations and agencies of the United Nations system and the Organization of the Islamic Conference and its subsidiary organs and specialized and affiliated institutions, held in Rabat from 11 to 13 July 2006, and the fact that these meetings are now being held every two years, with the next one scheduled for 2008, and also welcoming the memorandum of understanding on technical cooperation in the field of human rights between the Office of the United Nations High Commissioner for Human Rights and the Organization of the Islamic Conference signed at the Rabat meeting,

Welcoming also the issuance of a joint statement in Doha on 25 February 2006 by the Secretaries-General of the United Nations, the Organization of the Islamic Conference and the League of Arab States, together with the representatives of Qatar, Spain and Turkey, in the context of the Alliance of Civilizations, committing themselves to formulate a joint strategy to promote tolerance and mutual respect,

Welcoming further the close and multifaceted cooperation between the organizations and specialized institutions of the United Nations and the Organization of the Islamic Conference with a view to strengthening the capacities of the two organizations in addressing challenges to development and social progress,

Noting with appreciation the determination of the two organizations to strengthen further the existing cooperation by developing specific proposals in the designated priority areas of cooperation, as well as in the political field,

1. *Takes note with satisfaction* of the report of the Secretary-General;

2. *Urges* the United Nations system to cooperate with the Organization of the Islamic Conference in areas of mutual interest, as appropriate;

3. *Notes with satisfaction* the active participation of the Organization of the Islamic Conference in the work of the United Nations towards the realization of the purposes and principles embodied in the Charter of the United Nations;

4. *Requests* the United Nations and the Organization of the Islamic Conference to continue to cooperate in their common search for solutions to global problems, such as questions relating to international peace and security, disarmament, self-determination, promotion of a culture of peace through dialogue and cooperation, decolonization, human rights and fundamental freedoms, terrorism, emergency relief and rehabilitation, social and economic development and technical cooperation;

5. *Welcomes* the efforts of the United Nations and the Organization of the Islamic Conference to continue to strengthen cooperation between the two organizations in areas of common concern and to review and explore innovative ways and means of enhancing the mechanisms of such cooperation;

6. *Welcomes with appreciation* the continuing cooperation between the United Nations and the Organization of the Islamic Conference in the fields of peacemaking, preventive diplomacy, peacekeeping and peacebuilding, and notes the close cooperation between the two organizations in reconstruction and development in Afghanistan, Bosnia and Herzegovina and Sierra Leone;

7. *Welcomes* the efforts of the secretariats of the two organizations to strengthen information exchange, coordination and cooperation between them in areas of mutual interest in the political field and to develop practical modalities of such cooperation;

8. *Also welcomes* the periodic high-level meetings between the Secretary-General of the United Nations and the Secretary-General of the Organization of the Islamic Conference, as well as between senior secretariat officials of the two organizations, and encourages their participation in important meetings of the two organizations;

9. *Encourages* the specialized agencies and other organizations of the United Nations system to continue to expand their cooperation with the subsidiary organs and specialized and affiliated institutions of the Organization of the Islamic Conference, in particular by negotiating cooperation agreements, and through necessary contacts and meetings of the respective focal points for cooperation in priority areas of interest to the United Nations and the Organization of the Islamic Conference;

10. *Urges* the United Nations and other organizations of the United Nations system, especially the lead agencies, to provide increased technical and other forms of assistance to the Organization of the Islamic Conference and its subsidiary organs and specialized and affiliated institutions in order to enhance cooperation;

11. *Expresses its appreciation* to the Secretary-General for his continued efforts to strengthen cooperation and coordination between the United Nations and other organizations of the United Nations system and the Organization of the Islamic Conference and its subsidiary organs and specialized and affiliated institutions to serve the mutual interests of the two organizations in the

political, economic, social, cultural, humanitarian and scientific fields;

12. *Requests* the Secretary-General to report to the General Assembly at its sixty-third session on the state of cooperation between the United Nations and the Organization of the Islamic Conference;

13. *Decides* to include in the provisional agenda of its sixty-third session the sub-item entitled "Cooperation between the United Nations and the Organization of the Islamic Conference".

International Organization of la Francophonie

In response to resolution 59/22 [YUN 2004, p. 1456], the Secretary-General, in his August consolidated report [A/61/256], detailed cooperation between the United Nations and the International Organization of la Francophonie (OIF). Several joint meetings were held in New York aimed at increasing the contribution of francophone countries to UN peacekeeping operations. A joint working group of the Department of Peacekeeping Operations (DPKO) and the missions of francophone countries was created in March to initiate a dialogue between DPKO and OIF, with a view to improving participation by OIF member States and observers in issues related to peacekeeping operations and promoting the use of the French language in those operations in francophone communities. In that regard, OIF experts (May-June) participated in a DPKO pilot project in Dakar, Senegal, and Yaoundé, Cameroon for the training and recruitment of police officers for peacekeeping operations. With regard to crisis and conflict prevention, and warning capacities, OIF took part in the sixth high-level meeting between the United Nations and regional organizations held in New York on 25 and 26 July, 2005, which established a standing committee to act as a link between high-level plenary meetings. The standing committee held its first meeting on 23 and 24 February 2006 in New York. A francophone ministerial conference on conflict prevention and human security was held in May 2006 in Saint Boniface, Canada, in keeping with the recommendation of the General Assembly to discuss in detail the concept of human security. OIF also strengthened cooperation with the United Nations in the field of electoral observation and assistance, and collaborated with the United Nations on various electoral timetables in French-speaking areas.

GENERAL ASSEMBLY ACTION

On 20 October [meeting 39], the General Assembly adopted **resolution 61/7** [draft: A/61/L.7 & Add.1] without vote [agenda item 108 (*j*)].

Cooperation between the United Nations and the International Organization of la Fracophonie

The General Assembly,

Recalling its resolutions 33/18 of 10 November 1978, 50/3 of 16 October 1995, 52/2 of 17 October 1997, 54/25 of 15 November 1999, 56/45 of 7 December 2001, 57/43 of 21 November 2002 and 59/22 of 8 November 2004, as well as its decision 53/453 of 18 December 1998,

Considering that the International Organization of la Francophonie brings together a considerable number of States Members of the United Nations, among which it promotes multilateral cooperation in areas of interest to the United Nations,

Bearing in mind the Articles of the Charter of the United Nations which encourage the promotion of the purposes and principles of the United Nations through regional cooperation,

Bearing in mind also that, according to the Charter of la Francophonie adopted on 23 November 2005 at the Ministerial Conference of la Francophonie, held in Antananarivo, the objectives of the International Organization of la Francophonie are to assist in the establishment and development of democracy, the prevention, management and settlement of conflicts and support for the rule of law and for human rights, the intensification of dialogue between cultures and civilizations, the establishment of closer ties among peoples through mutual knowledge and strengthening of their solidarity through multilateral cooperation activities with a view to promoting the growth of their economies, and the promotion of education and training,

Welcoming the steps taken by the International Organization of la Francophonie to strengthen its ties with the organizations of the United Nations system and with international and regional organizations with a view to attaining its objectives,

Noting with satisfaction the commitment to multilateral cooperation for sustainable development, in particular through education and information technologies, for the purpose of meeting the Millennium Development Goals, undertaken by the Heads of State and Government of countries using French as a common language, at their eleventh summit, held in Bucharest on 28 and 29 September 2006, and their determination to extend the scope of francophone collaboration and cooperation in order to narrow the digital divide, fight poverty and contribute to the emergence of a more equitable form of globalization that will bring progress, peace, democracy and human rights, in full respect for cultural and linguistic diversity, in the interests of the most vulnerable populations and the development of all countries,

Having considered the report of the Secretary-General on the implementation of resolution 59/22,

Noting with satisfaction the substantial progress achieved in cooperation between the United Nations, the specialized agencies and other United Nations bodies and programmes and the International Organization of la Francophonie,

Convinced that strengthening cooperation between the United Nations and the International Organization of la Francophonie serves the purposes and principles of the United Nations,

Noting the desire of the two organizations to consolidate, develop and strengthen the ties that exist between them in the political, economic, social and cultural fields,

1. *Takes note with satisfaction* of the report of the Secretary-General, and welcomes the increasingly close and productive cooperation between the United Nations and the International Organization of la Francophonie;

2. *Notes with satisfaction* that the International Organization of la Francophonie participates actively in the work of the United Nations, to which it makes a valuable contribution;

3. *Notes with great satisfaction* the initiatives taken by the International Organization of la Francophonie in the areas of conflict prevention, the promotion of peace and support for democracy, the rule of law and human rights, in accordance with the commitments reaffirmed at the Ministerial Conference of la Francophonie on Conflict Prevention and Human Security, held on 13 and 14 May 2006 in Saint Boniface, Canada, and commends it on the genuine contribution it makes, in cooperation with the United Nations, in Haiti, the Comoros, Côte d'Ivoire, Burundi, the Democratic Republic of the Congo and the Central African Republic;

4. *Welcomes* the initiation of cooperation between the United Nations and the International Organization of la Francophonie, with the participation of other regional and subregional organizations, as well as non-governmental organizations, in the fields of early warning and conflict prevention, and encourages the pursuit of this initiative with a view to formulating practical recommendations to facilitate the establishment of relevant operational mechanisms, where necessary;

5. *Expresses its gratitude* to the International Organization of la Francophonie for the steps it has taken in recent years to promote cultural and linguistic diversity and dialogue between cultures and civilizations;

6. *Expresses its appreciation* to the Secretary-General of the United Nations and the Secretary-General of the International Organization of la Francophonie for their sustained efforts to strengthen cooperation and coordination between the two organizations, thereby serving their mutual interests in the political, economic, social and cultural fields;

7. *Welcomes* the initiation of cooperation between the International Organization of la Francophonie and the Department of Peacekeeping Operations of the Secretariat with a view to increasing the number of French-speaking personnel in United Nations peacekeeping operations;

8. *Also welcomes* the fact that the eleventh summit of la Francophonie was devoted to the use of new technologies in the service of education, and calls upon the specialized agencies and the funds and programmes of the United Nations system to enhance their cooperation with the International Organization of la Francophonie in the area of sustainable development;

9. *Further welcomes* the involvement of the countries that use French as a common language, particularly through the International Organization of la Francophonie, in the preparation for, conduct of and follow-up to international conferences organized under United Nations auspices;

10. *Commends* the high-level meetings held periodically between the United Nations Secretariat and the Secretariat of the International Organization of la Francophonie, and advocates the participation of those Secretariats in major meetings of the two organizations;

11. *Expresses its appreciation* to the Secretary-General for including the International Organization of la Francophonie in the periodic meetings he holds with heads of regional organizations, and invites him to continue doing so, taking into account the role played by the International Organization of la Francophonie in conflict prevention and support for democracy and the rule of law;

12. *Notes with satisfaction* the continued collaboration between the United Nations and the International Organization of la Francophonie in the area of electoral monitoring and assistance, and advocates the strengthening of cooperation between the two organizations in that area;

13. *Requests* the Secretary-General of the United Nations, acting in cooperation with the Secretary-General of the International Organization of la Francophonie, to encourage the holding of periodic meetings between representatives of the United Nations Secretariat and representatives of the Secretariat of the International Organization of la Francophonie in order to promote the exchange of information, coordination of activities and identification of new areas of cooperation;

14. *Welcomes* the participation of the International Organization of la Francophonie in the Peacebuilding Commission's work on Burundi, and strongly encourages the International Organization of la Francophonie and the Peacebuilding Commission to continue to cooperate actively;

15. *Invites* the Secretary-General of the United Nations to take the necessary steps, in consultation with the Secretary-General of the International Organization of la Francophonie, to continue to promote cooperation between the two organizations;

16. *Invites* the specialized agencies and the funds and programmes of the United Nations system, as well as the regional commissions, including the Economic Commission for Africa, to collaborate to this end with the Secretary-General of the International Organization of la Francophonie by identifying new synergies in favour of development, in particular in the areas of poverty elimination, energy, sustainable development, education, training and the development of new information technologies;

17. *Requests* the Secretary-General to submit to the General Assembly at its sixty-third session a report on the implementation of the present resolution;

18. *Decides* to include in the provisional agenda of its sixty-third session the sub-item entitled "Coopera-

tion between the United Nations and the International Organization of la Francophonie".

Inter-Parliamentary Union

Pursuant to General Assembly resolution 59/19 [YUN 2004, p. 1456], the Secretary-General, in his August consolidated report [A/61/256], detailed the growing cooperation between the United Nations and the Inter-Parliamentary Union (IPU) in bringing a parliamentary dimension to the work of the United Nations, including in the areas of peace and security, economic and social development, humanitarian affairs and crisis management, international law and human rights, democracy and gender issues. The report also addressed the institutional efforts aimed at strengthening the partnership between the United Nations and IPU. The Secretary-General invited IPU to work closely with the United Nations in devising a permanent mechanism for consultation and coordination, with a view to building greater coherence in the work of the two organizations and maximizing parliamentary support for the work of the United Nations. The Secretary-General invited the Economic and Social Council to consider involving IPU in the implementation of the new functions devolved to it by the 2005 World Summit, namely the annual ministerial-level substantive reviews of progress in conference implementation and the biennial high-level Development Cooperation Forum.

GENERAL ASSEMBLY ACTION

On 20 October [meeting 39], the General Assembly adopted **resolution 61/6** [draft: A/61/L.6 & Add.1], as orally revised, without vote [agenda item 108 (*k*)].

Cooperation between the United Nations and the Inter-Parliamentary Union

The General Assembly,

Having considered the report of the Secretary-General of 16 August 2006, which takes stock of the broad and substantive cooperation between the United Nations and the Inter-Parliamentary Union over the past two years,

Taking note of the resolutions adopted by the Inter-Parliamentary Union and circulated in the General Assembly and the many activities undertaken by the organization in support of the United Nations,

Welcoming the annual parliamentary hearings at the United Nations as a regular feature of the programme of events held at United Nations Headquarters on the occasion of the sessions of the General Assembly, as well as other specialized parliamentary meetings organized by the Inter-Parliamentary Union in cooperation with the United Nations in the context of major United Nations conferences and events,

Taking into consideration the Cooperation Agreement between the United Nations and the Inter-Parliamentary Union of 1996, which laid the foundation for cooperation between the two organizations,

Recalling the United Nations Millennium Declaration and the 2005 World Summit Outcome, in which Heads of State and Government resolved to strengthen further cooperation between the United Nations and national parliaments through their world organization, the Inter-Parliamentary Union, in all fields of work of the United Nations and for the effective implementation of United Nations reform,

Also recalling its resolution 57/32 of 19 November 2002, in which the Inter-Parliamentary Union was invited to participate in the work of the General Assembly in the capacity of observer, as well as resolutions 57/47 of 21 November 2002 and 59/19 of 8 November 2004,

Taking note of the recommendations contained in the report of the Panel of Eminent Persons on United Nations-Civil Society Relations in regard to engaging parliamentarians more systematically in the work of the United Nations,

1. *Welcomes* the efforts made by the Inter-Parliamentary Union to provide for a greater parliamentary contribution and enhanced support to the United Nations;

2. *Takes note* of the conclusions of the second World Conference of Speakers of Parliament, held at United Nations Headquarters from 7 to 9 September 2005 in conjunction with the 2005 World Summit;

3. *Encourages* the United Nations and the Inter-Parliamentary Union to continue to cooperate closely in various fields, in particular peace and security, economic and social development, international law, human rights, and democracy and gender issues, bearing in mind the significant benefits of cooperation between the two organizations, to which the report of the Secretary-General attests;

4. *Encourages* the Inter-Parliamentary Union to strengthen further its contribution to the work of the General Assembly, including its revitalization, as envisaged in resolution 60/286 of 8 September 2006, and in relation to the newly established bodies such as the Human Rights Council and the Peacebuilding Commission;

5. *Also encourages* the Inter-Parliamentary Union to play an active role in support of the Economic and Social Council, particularly in the implementation of the new functions devolved to the Council by the 2005 World Summit;

6. *Welcomes* the partnership agreement concluded recently between the United Nations Democracy Fund and the Inter-Parliamentary Union, and looks forward to growing cooperation in the realm of democracy and good governance;

7. *Calls for* the further development of the annual parliamentary hearing at the United Nations and other specialized parliamentary meetings in the context of major United Nations meetings as joint United Nations-Inter-Parliamentary Union events;

8. *Also calls for* closer involvement, as appropriate, of the Inter-Parliamentary Union in the elaboration of

system-wide strategies for consideration by the United Nations system and the United Nations System Chief Executives Board for Coordination, with a view to ensuring greater and more coherent support by parliaments to the work of the United Nations;

9. *Decides* to include in the provisional agenda of its sixty-third session the sub-item entitled "Cooperation between the United Nations and the Inter-Parliamentary Union".

Participation in UN work

Observer status

Procedure for requests for observer status

On 8 September [A/61/232], Liechtenstein requested the inclusion in the agenda of the General Assembly's sixty-first session of an additional item entitled "Requests for observer status in the General Assembly". An explanatory memorandum annexed to the request noted that the General Committee of the sixty-first session had before it, once again, requests for the inclusion of agenda items related to the granting of observer status in the Assembly. According to Liechtenstein, the practice of including a specific agenda item for every single organization requesting observer status in the Assembly seemed unnecessarily burdensome and bureaucratic. In the spirit of revitalization of the General Assembly and its working methods, it would be simpler if the Sixth Committee could deal with the merits of such requests directly, without the need to involve the General Committee in every single request. In that regard, Liechtenstein submitted a request to include a generic item on the matter in the Assembly's agenda and to allocate it to the Sixth Committee.

On 22 December, the General Assembly (**decision 61/552**) decided that the item on requests for observer status in the General Assembly would remain for consideration during its resumed sixty-first (2007) session.

OPEC Fund for International Development

On 11 May [A/61/141], Saudi Arabia requested the inclusion in the agenda of the General Assembly's sixty-first session of an item on observer status for the Organization of Petroleum Exporting Countries (OPEC) Fund for International Development. An explanatory memorandum annexed to the request stated that the Fund was established in 1976 by OPEC to consolidate its financial assistance to developing countries. Observer status at the United Nations would enhance further cooperation between the Organization and the Fund and facilitate the Fund's work as an intergovernmental development organization.

GENERAL ASSEMBLY ACTION

On 4 December [meeting 64], the General Assembly, on the recommendation of the Sixth (Legal) Committee [A/61/462], adopted **resolution 61/42** without vote [agenda item 153].

Observer status for the OPEC Fund for International Development in the General Assembly

The General Assembly,

Wishing to promote cooperation between the United Nations and the OPEC Fund for International Development,

1. *Decides* to invite the OPEC Fund for International Development to participate in the sessions and the work of the General Assembly in the capacity of observer;

2. *Requests* the Secretary-General to take the necessary action to implement the present resolution.

Indian Ocean Commission

On 14 September [A/61/487], Mauritius requested the inclusion in the agenda of the General Assembly's sixty-first session of an item on observer status for the Indian Ocean Commission (IOC) in the Assembly. An explanatory memorandum stated that the Commission, which was created in 1984, initially brought together Madagascar, Mauritius and the Seychelles. In 1986, the Comoros and France, acting on behalf of its department of Réunion, joined. The Commission's activities aimed at providing a regional platform for cooperation, thus contributing to the improvement of the quality of life of its population through the promotion of interests of member States based on their specificities. Most of the programmes undertaken by IOC were focused on the reduction of poverty and the promotion of sustainable development.

GENERAL ASSEMBLY ACTION

On 4 December [meeting 64], the General Assembly, on the recommendation of the Sixth Committee [A/61/462], adopted **resolution 61/43** without vote [agenda item 153].

Observer status for the Indian Ocean Commission

The General Assembly,

Wishing to promote cooperation between the United Nations and the Indian Ocean Commission,

1. *Decides* to invite the Indian Ocean Commission to participate in the sessions and the work of the General Assembly in the capacity of observer;

2. *Requests* the Secretary-General to take the necessary action to implement the present resolution.

Association of Southeast Asian Nations

On 9 October [A/61/510], the Philippines requested the inclusion in the agenda of the General Assembly's sixty-first session of an item on observer status for the Association of Southeast Asian Nations (ASEAN) in the Assembly. An explanatory memorandum annexed to the request stated that the aims and purposes of the Association were to accelerate economic growth, social progress and cultural development in the region, in addition to promoting regional peace and stability. The Association's participation as an observer would further enhance cooperation between ASEAN and the United Nations (see p. 1170), particularly in support of ASEAN community-building efforts, as well as broaden and deepen its interactions with countries and regional and international organizations.

GENERAL ASSEMBLY ACTION

On 4 December [meeting 64], the General Assembly, on the recommendation of the Sixth Committee [A/61/462], adopted **resolution 61/44** without vote [agenda item 153].

Observer status for the Association of Southeast Asian Nations in the General Assembly

The General Assembly,

Wishing to promote cooperation between the United Nations and the Association of Southeast Asian Nations,

1. *Decides* to invite the Association of Southeast Asian Nations to participate in the sessions and the work of the General Assembly in the capacity of observer;
2. *Requests* the Secretary-General to take the necessary action to implement the present resolution.

Collaborative Intergovernmental Scientific Research Institute

On 21 July [A/61/191 & Add.1], Iraq requested the inclusion in the agenda of the General Assembly's sixty-first session of an item on observer status for the Collaborative Intergovernmental Scientific Research Institute in the Assembly.

On 5 October [A/61/503], Iraq withdrew its request.

Islamic Development Bank Group

On 15 December [A/61/646], Saudi Arabia requested the inclusion in the agenda of the General Assembly's sixty-first session of an item on observer status for the Islamic Development Bank Group (ISDB) in the Assembly. An explanatory memorandum stated that ISDB was a multilateral development bank with a mandate to promote economic development and social progress in its 56 member countries, with a cumulative commitment of $44.7 billion covering some 5,200 operations. ISDB was engaged in international development and worked closely with a number of UN agencies and programmes. Furthermore, the establishment of the ISDB poverty alleviation fund provided an opportunity to further cement the partnership for development between the United Nations and ISDB.

Intergovernmental organizations

On 7 February, the Economic and Social Council approved the request of the Inter-American Institute for Cooperation on Agriculture to participate as an observer in the Council's work (**decision 2006/204**).

On 12 May, the Council included in the agenda of its 2006 substantive session the applications for observer status of the Convention on Wetlands [E/2006/21] and the South Centre [E/2006/68] (**decision 2006/216**).

On 27 July, the Council decided to grant observer status to the Intergovernmental Forum on Mining, Minerals, Metals and Sustainable Development [E/2006/76], and the South Centre. It also decided to defer consideration of the application of the Ramsar Convention [E/2006/21] and the International Emergency Management Organization (IEMO) [E/2006/87] until its resumed substantive session (**decision 2006/244**). On 15 December, the Council deferred until its 2007 organizational session the application of observer status of IEMO (**decision 2006/264**).

Non-governmental organizations

Committee on NGOs

The Committee on Non-Governmental Organizations (NGOs) held its 2006 regular session (19-27 January) [E/2006/32 (Part I)] and its resumed 2006 session (10-19 May) [E/2006/32 (Part II)], both in New York. In January, the Committee considered 144 applications for consultative status with the Economic and Social Council, including those deferred from its 1999 to 2005 sessions. It recommended 97 applications for consultative status, deferred consideration of 39 applications, recommended not to grant consultative status to three organizations, and closed consideration of two other applications. The Committee also had before it three requests for reclassification of consultative status, of which it recommended two. It reviewed 52 quadrennial reports and heard seven NGO representatives.

The Committee recommended six draft decisions for action by the Council, including a decision to withdraw special consultative status of an NGO (see below). The Chairperson made a statement on the reinstatement of the status of the organization Indian Movement "Tupaj Amaru".

The Committee reviewed its working methods relating to the implementation of Economic and Social Council resolution 1996/31 [YUN 1996, p. 1360], including the process of accreditation of representatives of NGOs, and Council decision 1995/304 [YUN 1995, p. 1445]. It also considered implementation of Council decision 2001/295 [YUN 2001, p. 1377] relating to requests by those NGOs referred to in Council decision 1993/220 [YUN 1993, p. 668] to expand participation in other fields of the Council's work. The Committee postponed consideration of the item on the general voluntary trust fund in support of the United Nations NGO Informal Regional Network (UN-NGO-IRENE) to its resumed session (see below) in order to cover one year of reporting of the UN Secretariat's NGO Section on its outreach programme.

On 24 January, the Committee decided to recommend special consultative status to the BADIL Resource Centre for Palestinian Residency and Refugee Rights. Germany, France and the United States disassociated themselves from the consensus. On the same date, following a proposal by Cuba, the Committee, by a roll call vote of 9 to 4, with 4 abstentions, decided not to recommend granting status to People in Need, an NGO based in the Czech Republic. A proposal by the United States to suspend the debate on the issue was rejected by a roll-call vote of 5 to 8, with 4 abstentions. On 21 July, the Council, by a roll-call vote of 25 to 18, with 6 abstentions, decided not to grant consultative status to People in Need (**decision 2006/223**).

In other action, following a proposal by Iran, the Committee, by a roll call vote of 10 to 5, with 3 abstentions, decided not to recommend granting consultative status to the International Lesbian and Gay Association. A proposal by Germany to adjourn debate on the matter was rejected by a roll-call vote of 5 to 10, with 3 abstentions. On 21 July, the Council, by a roll-call vote of 22 to 19, with 9 abstentions, decided not to grant consultative status to the International Lesbian and Gay Association (**decision 2006/222**).

The Committee also examined the application of the Danish Association for Gays and Lesbians. A proposal by Germany to adjourn debate was rejected by a roll-call vote of 5 to 10 with 3 abstentions. Following another roll-call vote of 10 to 5, with 3 abstentions, the Committee recommended not granting status to the organization. On 11 December, the Council, following a roll-call vote of 23 to 16, with 11 abstentions, decided to grant special consultative status to the Danish National Association for Gays and Lesbians (**decision 2006/259**).

Under its consideration of special reports, the Committee recommended the withdrawal of the consultative status of the Islamic African Relief Agency. The Council adopted the Committee's draft decision on 21 July (**decision 2006/224**).

At its resumed session, in May, the Committee considered 96 applications for consultative status, including applications deferred from previous sessions. It recommended 55 applications for consultative status, deferred 37 organizations for further consideration and closed its consideration of two others. It recommended one request for reclassification, reviewed 33 quadrennial reports and heard seven representatives of NGOs.

The Committee recommended five draft decisions for action by the Council. It also reviewed its working methods relating to the implementation of Council resolution 1996/31, including the process of accreditation of representatives of NGOs, and decision 1995/304. It considered implementation of Council decision 2001/295 relating to requests by those NGOs referred to in Council decision 1993/220 to expand participation in other fields of the Council's work. It also considered the general voluntary trust fund in support of UN-NGO-IRENE. In addition, the Committee considered the strengthening of the NGO Section of the Department of Economic and Social Affairs. It took note of the fact that the one year suspension of the NGO "A Women's Voice International" would end on 21 July.

Following a proposal by Iran, the Committee, by a roll-call vote of 9 to 7, with two abstentions, recommended a draft decision not to grant consultative status to the Lesbian and Gay Federation in Germany. That action followed a roll-call vote of 11 to 7, with one abstention, by which the Committee rejected a motion by Germany to adjourn the debate on the issue. On 11 December, the Council decided to grant special consultative status to the Lesbian and Gay Federation in Germany by a roll-call vote of 24 to 16, with 10 abstentions (**decision 2006/261**).

On a proposal by Iran, the Committee decided, by a roll-call vote of 9 to 7, with two abstentions, to recommend not granting consultative status to the International Lesbian and Gay Association–Europe. A proposal by Germany to adjourn the debate on the matter was rejected by a roll-call vote of 11 to 7, with one abstention. On 11 December, the Council decided to grant consultative status to the International Lesbian and Gay Association–Europe by a roll-call vote of 23 to 17, with 10 abstentions (**decision 2006/260**).

On 21 July, the Council granted consultative status to 89 organizations and placed 7 others on its roster; reclassified one organization from special to general consultative status, and one organization from roster to special consultative status. It also decided not to reclassify one organization; referred back to the Committee the NGO "Geneva Call" for further consideration; and noted that the Committee had taken note of 42 quadrennial reports and closed consideration of requests made by two NGOs for consultative status (**decision 2006/221**).

Also on 21 July, the Council granted consultative status to 55 organizations and placed 3 others on the roster; reclassified one organization from roster to special consultative status and noted that the Committee had taken note of 27 quadrennial reports and closed consideration of requests for consultative status made by two NGOs (**decision 2006/225**). On the same day, the Council decided that the Committee's 2007 regular session would be held from 22 January to 2 February, and its resumed session from 14 to 18 May, and approved the provisional agenda and documentation for the session (**decision 2006/226**).

On 28 July, the Council deferred until its resumed substantive session consideration of draft decisions I, III and IV, contained in the first part of the Committee's report of January 2006, and draft decisions II, III and V, contained in the second part of the Committee's report of May 2006 (**decision 2006/252**).

On 11 December, the Council took note of the Committee's reports on its regular and resumed 2006 sessions (**decision 2006/262**).

Proclamation of international years

On 20 December [meeting 83], the General Assembly, on the recommendation of the Second Committee [A/61/432], adopted **resolution 61/185** without vote [agenda item 42].

Proclamation of international years

The General Assembly,

Recalling its resolution 53/199 of 15 December 1998 on the proclamation of international years and Economic and Social Council resolution 1980/67 of 25 July 1980 on international years and anniversaries and the guidelines contained in the annex thereto, adopted by the General Assembly in its decision 35/424 of 5 December 1980,

1. Requests the Secretary-General to draw the attention of the specialized agencies and organizations of the United Nations system to the guidelines for future international years contained in the annex to Economic and Social Council resolution 1980/67, and to make those guidelines available;

2. *Stresses* the need to take into account and apply the criteria and procedures contained in the guidelines in considering future proposals for international years.

Chapter II

United Nations financing and programming

The financial situation of the United Nations showed some improvement in 2006, although it remained fragile. Following the June assessment by the UN Controller that the Organization would run out of cash by mid-July, and at the request of the Secretary-General, the General Assembly lifted the $950 million spending cap and authorized expenditure of up to $3.8 billion of appropriated funds to avoid a budget crisis. By the end of the year, assessments issued had fallen by $73 million and were lower under all categories, except for the capital master plan. Unpaid assessments reached $361 million, compared to $333 million in 2005, cash resources for peacekeeping activities totalled over $1.7 billion and the debt owed to Member States stood at $1 billion.

In December, the Assembly adopted revised budget appropriations for the 2006-2007 biennium of $4,173,895,900, an increase of $343,979,700 over the revised appropriation of $3,829,916,200 approved in June and July. It invited the Secretary-General to prepare his proposed 2008-2009 programme budget on the basis of a preliminary estimate of $4,194,726,800.

As part of his continuing reform efforts, the Secretary-General, in his report on investing in the United Nations for a stronger Organization, elaborated on further proposals for improving budget implementation and financial management practices.

The Committee on Contributions considered the methodology for calculating future scales of assessments for the contributions of Member States to the regular budget and for the apportionment of costs of UN peacekeeping operations, the assessment of new and non-member States and multi-year payments plans. In December, the Assembly adopted the scale of assessments for 2007-2009.

The Assembly also examined the proposed strategic framework for 2008-2009 and endorsed the proposed biennial programme plan for that period.

Financial situation

Although the financial situation of the United Nations showed some improvement in 2006, it remained fragile. In November [A/61/556], the Secretary-General reported that unpaid assessed contributions were heavily concentrated among a few Member States and the final outcome for 2006 would depend in large measure on payments made by those States in the final quarter of the year. As at 31 October, aggregate assessments were $5.5 billion (compared to $5.4 billion at 7 October 2005). That amount included increased assessments of $109 million for the capital master plan (CMP), compared to $18 million in 2005. Cash availability under the regular budget at the beginning of the year stood at $123 million; as at 31 October, that amount totaled $68 million, with another $322 million in related reserve accounts.

As at 31 October, unpaid assessments for the regular budget, peacekeeping and the two international tribunals totaled $3.2 billion, which included: $2.5 billion for peacekeeping (compared to $2.1 billion at 7 October 2005); $661 million for the regular budget ($78 million less than in 2005) and $55 million for the tribunals ($18 million less than in 2005). It was forecast that the Organization would owe Member States $1,039 million for troop and equipment costs as at 31 December 2006, due to the full deployment of troops to missions in Côte d'Ivoire and the Sudan, the deployment of additional troops to the mission in the Democratic Republic of the Congo; the expansion of the United Nations Interim Force in Lebanon; and the establishment of the mission in Timor-Leste. Member States that had paid their regular budget assessments in full as at 31 October numbered 122 (four less than at 7 October 2005).

In his end-of-year review of the financial situation [A/61/556/Add.1], the Secretary-General noted that the performance of the four main indicators of the Organization's financial health was generally positive, but not uniformly so: assessments issued during 2006 had fallen by some $73 million; unpaid assessments to the regular budget had increased to $361 million from $333 million at 31 December 2005; cash balances were higher for the regular budget and CMP, as well as for peacekeeping operations, which totalled over $1.7 billion; and the debt owed to Member States was $1 billion. The position of the international tribunals deteriorated, as amounts outstanding increased to $51 million, from $25 million in 2005. The number of Member States paying their regular budget assessments in full was 139, one fewer than in 2005.

On 11 September, the General Assembly deferred consideration of the agenda item on improving the financial situation of the United Nations and included it in the draft agenda of its sixty-first (2006) session (**decision 60/566**). On 22 December, the Assembly again deferred consideration of the item to its resumed sixty-first (2007) session (**decision 61/552**).

UN budget

Reform of budget process and financial management

The Secretary-General, in his March report [A/60/692] entitled "Investing in the United Nations: for a stronger Organization worldwide" (see p. 1575), proposed broad reform measures in a number of areas, including measures for improving UN financial management practices. He said that the Organization suffered from a highly detailed, cumbersome and insufficiently strategic budgeting process, with more than 150 separate trust funds and 37 distinct peacekeeping accounts, each with its own support cost arrangements. The financial management process was manual and highly fragmented, and not enough authority was delegated. He proposed shortening the budget cycle; consolidating budget appropriations from the current 35 sections into 13 parts; having his authority expanded to redeploy posts and to use savings from vacant posts; consolidating peacekeeping accounts and streamlining trust fund management; increasing the level of the Working Capital Fund and re-engineering the Organization's financial process to allow significant delegation of authority; linking the budget planning process to results and management performance; and introducing new principles to guide interaction between the Secretariat and the General Assembly on management and budget issues. The Secretary-General also indicated that he would seek to have the Organization adopt the International Public Sector Accounting Standards (IPSAS).

The Assembly, in **resolution 60/260** of 8 May (see p. 1576) requested further detailed reporting on the Secretary-General's proposals. In May [A/60 846], the Secretary-General provided that report, with several addenda, including on budget implementation [A/60/846/Add.2]; financial management practices [A/60/846/Add. 3]; proposals for budget and financial reporting contained in his overall report on improving reporting mechanisms, including public access to UN documentation [A/60/846/Add.4]; and updated terms of reference for the Independent Audit Advisory Committee [A/60/846/Add.7].

In his report on financial management practices, the Secretary-General recommended that the Assembly approve the adoption of IPSAS by 2010 and the amount of $2 million for its implementation; consolidate the various peacekeeping accounts retroactively as of 1 July 2007 (see p. 96), as well as individual resolutions on their financing and the various assessments into two bi-annual assessments, starting with the 2007-2008 financial period; approve the de-linking of assessments for peacekeeping operations from the duration of their mandates; apply to the consolidated accounts the practice of utilizing unencumbered balances, interest income and other income to provide the first element of financing for the subsequent financial period; consolidate individual performance reports into one single report; return to Member States credits available in the accounts of closed missions with cash surpluses; and settle outstanding liabilities in the accounts of those missions having cash deficits.

The Assembly should authorize the Secretary-General, with the concurrence of the Advisory Committee on Administrative and Budgetary Questions (ACABQ), to enter into commitments not to exceed the current authorized level of the Peacekeeping Reserve Fund of $150 million; increase the delegation of commitment authority to ACABQ to that level (see p. 97) and amend financial regulations 4.6 and 4.8 accordingly; and authorize an increase in the Working Capital Fund from $100 million to $250 million. It should also decide on the retention of temporary budgetary surpluses and on the application of future distribution of surpluses; establish a fund to accommodate unanticipated expenditures arising from exchange-rate fluctuations and inflation; meet the Organization's unfunded liabilities arising from the after-service health-insurance scheme or increase the Working Capital Fund; establish a reserve fund for adjustments resulting from currency fluctuations, inflation in non-staff costs and statutory cost increases for staff; decide on the charging of interest on Member States' arrears of assessed contributions, as well as for the peacekeeping accounts and the tribunals; and appropriate $2,009,700 under the 2006-2007 programme budget.

Reporting mechanisms. In his report on improving reporting mechanisms, including public access to UN documentation [A/60/846/Add.4], the

Secretary-General proposed that financial and programme information be contained in a single, comprehensive annual report; the over 40 reports on management and finance be consolidated into six reports; and a new UN policy on public access to documentation be established, which would be implemented in two phases. Estimated funding requirements for both phases totalled $6.8 million, with $1.8 million of that amount to be charged under the 2006-2007 biennium for the first phase.

Report of ACABQ. ACABQ recommended the adoption of IPSAS and approval of the requested resources to begin its implementation. With regard to transfers of appropriations between budget sections, the Committee requested the Secretary-General to resubmit his proposal to provide more clarity and detail on various aspects, including an effective system of accountability and justification of the scope and level of the authority requested. ACABQ concluded that providing one annual report to serve the needs of both the general public and the Assembly would be too technical for the former and too general for the latter. Therefore, it requested the Secretary-General to develop a comprehensive financial and programme report for the Assembly. The Committee also decided that action on the proposals relating to adjustments to the staffing table, an increase of the level of the Working Capital Fund, the utilization of budget surpluses, the charging of interest on the arrears of Member States and the consolidation of peacekeeping accounts should await decision by the Assembly.

On 7 July, by **resolution 60/283** (see p. 1580), the General Assembly authorized, on an experimental basis, a limited discretion to the Secretary-General for budgetary implementation for the 2006-2007 and 2008-2009 bienniums, to enter into commitments of up to $20 million in each biennium for positions and non-post requirements and to utilize the Working Capital Fund to finance the implementation of that authorization. He should report in the performance reports to the Assembly on the utilization of all commitments made in the context of the experiment, and provide a comprehensive report on its implementation at its sixty-fourth (2009) session, at which time the Assembly would review and take a final decision on the continuation of the experiment. The Assembly also approved the adoption of IPSAS and the resources requested for its implementation; an increase in the level of the Working Capital Fund for the 2006-2007 biennium to $150 million, effective 1 January 2007; and additional appropriations of some $4.6 million in the 2006-2007 programme budget.

Budget for 2006-2007

Request for expenditure authorization

The General Assembly, in resolution 60/247 A [YUN 2005, p. 1491], had authorized the Secretary-General, as an exceptional measure, to enter into expenditure of a first tranche (limited to $950 million) of the $3,798,912,500 appropriated for the 2006-2007 programme budget, and decided that it would respond to his request for expenditure of the remaining funds. The Secretary-General, in view of the level of authorized expenditure and related charges against the provisions, requested, in June [A/60/889], authorization to enter into expenditure above the $950 million and up to the $3,798,912,500 appropriated by the Assembly.

Report of ACABQ. In June [A/60/7/Add.40], ACABQ, in considering the Secretary-General's report (above), noted that a total $879.8 million would have been expended by the end of June, and that the Secretary-General would reach the limit of his spending authority before the end of July. It therefore recommended that the Assembly take the foregoing into account when considering further action.

On 30 June, the Assembly authorized expenditure of the remaining funds (**decision 60/561**).

Revised appropriations

In the first performance report on the 2006-2007 programme budget [A/61/593], the Secretary-General identified adjustments to the level of appropriations as a result of variations in the rates of inflation and exchange, unforeseen and extraordinary items, as well as additional mandates approved by the General Assembly and the Security Council.

The adjustments yielded revised requirements of $3,911.2 million, an increase of $81.2 million more than the revised appropriation level of $3,830 million approved by resolutions 60/281 (see p. 1621) and 60/283 (see p. 1580), and an increase in income of $28.9 million, resulting in a revised income estimate of $463.7 million. Consequently, the revised net requirements for the 2006-2007 biennium amounted to $3,447.4 million, an increase of $52.4 million over the appropriations approved in Assembly resolutions 60/247 A and B [YUN 2005, p. 1491], 60/281 and 60/283.

In a November addendum [A/61/593/Add.1], the Secretary-General presented details on the utilization of the $11.2 million subvention for the Special Court for Sierra Leone, appropriated under Assembly resolution 60/245 [YUN 2005, p. 1483] and indicated that the estimated unspent balance of $2,401,327 of the appropriation for the 2004-2005 biennium would be surrendered under the programme budget as at 31 December 2006.

ACABQ, in December [A/61/635], recommended that the Assembly approve the revised estimates submitted by the Secretary-General, subject to such adjustments resulting from its consideration of matters currently before it, including estimates related to special political missions (see p. 1618) and the consolidated statement of revised estimates and programme budget implications.

GENERAL ASSEMBLY ACTION

On 22 December [meeting 84], the General Assembly, on the recommendation of the Fifth (Administrative and Budgetary) Committee [A/61/592/Add.2], adopted **resolutions 61/253 A-C** without vote [agenda item 117].

Programme budget for the biennium 2006-2007

A

REVISED BUDGET APPROPRIATIONS FOR THE BIENNIUM 2006-2007

The General Assembly

Resolves that, for the biennium 2006-2007, the amount of 3,829,916,200 United States dollars appropriated by it in its resolutions 60/247 A of 23 December 2005, 60/281 of 30 June 2006, and 60/283 of 7 July 2006 shall be adjusted by 343,979,700 dollars, as follows:

Section		*Amount approved in resolutions 60/247 A, 60/281 and 60/283*	*Increase (decrease)*	*Revised appropriation*
			(United States dollars)	
	Part I. *Overall policymaking, direction and coordination*			
1.	Overall policymaking, direction and coordination	74 959 100	2 044 600	77 003 700
2.	General Assembly and Economic and Social Council affairs and conference management	586 776 200	15 736 300	602 512 500
	Total, part I	**661 735 300**	**17 780 900**	**679 516 200**
	Part II. *Political affairs*			
3.	Political affairs	451 092 600	235 778 400	686 871 000
4.	Disarmament	20 381 100	90 400	20 471 500
5.	Peacekeeping operations	94 091 000	2 579 600	96 670 600
6.	Peaceful uses of outer space	5 906 800	268 900	6 175 700
	Total, part II	**571 471 500**	**238 717 300**	**810 188 800**
	Part III. *International justice and law*			
7.	International Court of Justice	34 956 900	1 828 100	36 785 000
8.	Legal affairs	42 289 400	(136 400)	42 153 000
	Total, part III	**77 246 300**	**1 691 700**	**78 938 000**
	Part IV. *International cooperation for development*			
9.	Economic and social affairs	157 930 900	(456 800)	157 474 100
10.	Least developed countries, landlocked developing countries and small island developing States	5 056 800	(4 100)	5 052 700
11.	United Nations support for the New Partnership for Africa's Development	10 791 900	11 200	108 03 100
12.	Trade and development	111 091 600	6 061 300	117 152 900
13.	International Trade Centre UNCTAD/WTO	25 915 800	985 700	26 901 500
14.	Environment	11 977 100	309 500	12 286 600
15.	Human settlements	17 864 500	424 900	18 289 400
16.	International drug control, crime prevention and criminal justice	31 527 800	1 310 600	32 838 400
	Total, part IV	**372 156 400**	**8 642 300**	**380 798 700**
	Part V. *Regional cooperation for development*			
17.	Economic and social development in Africa	106 011 400	1 392 800	107 404 200
18.	Economic and social development in Asia and the Pacific	71 858 100	2 806 700	74 664 800
19.	Economic development in Europe	54 176 700	2 933 300	57 110 000
20.	Economic and social development in Latin America and the Caribbean	94 630 400	2 549 700	97 180 100
21.	Economic and social development in Western Asia	53 416 900	2 907 700	56 324 600
22.	Regular programme of technical cooperation	45 622 000	1 259 400	46 881 400
	Total, part V	**425 715 500**	**13 849 600**	**439 565 100**
	Part VI. *Human rights and humanitarian affairs*			
23.	Human rights	83 088 400	4 920 700	88 009 100
24.	Protection of and assistance to refugees	64 645 200	2 386 000	67 031 200
25.	Palestine refugees	35 184 800	1 546 500	36 731 300
26.	Humanitarian assistance	26 140 500	425 500	26 566 000
	Total, part VI	**209 058 900**	**9 278 700**	**218 337 600**

Section		Amount approved in resolutions 60/247 A, 60/281 and 60/283	Increase (decrease)	Revised appropriation
		(United States dollars)		
Part VII. *Public information*				
27. Public information		177 302 500	1 549 300	178 851 800
	Total, part VII	**177 302 500**	**1 549 300**	**178 851 800**
Part VIII. *Common support services*				
28. Management and support services		515 239 300	12 738 900	527 978 200
	Total, part VIII	**515 239 300**	**12 738 900**	**527 978 200**
Part IX. *Internal oversight*				
29. Internal oversight		31 330 100	215 100	31 545 200
	Total, part IX	**31 330 100**	**215 100**	**31 545 200**
Part X. *Jointly financed administrative activities and special expenses*				
30. Jointly financed administrative activities		11 602 800	(3 803 600)	7 799 200
31. Special expenses		92 798 000	680 900	93 478 900
	Total, part X	**104 400 800**	**(3 122 700)**	**101 278 100**
Part XI. *Capital expenditures*				
32. Construction, alteration, improvement and major maintenance		74 841 300	3 690 700	78 532 000
	Total, part XI	**74 841 300**	**3 690 700**	**78 532 000**
Part XII. *Safety and security*				
33. Safety and security		190 131 400	5 406 400	195 537 800
	Total, part XII	**190 131 400**	**5 406 400**	**195 537 800**
Part XIII. *Development Account*				
34. Development Account		13 954 100	2 526 800	16 480 900
	Total, part XIII	**13 954 100**	**2 526 800**	**16 480 900**
Part XIV. *Staff assessment*				
35. Staff assessment		405 332 800	31 014 700	436 347 500
	Total, part XIV	**405 332 800**	**31 014 700**	**436 347 500**
	Grand total	**3 829 916 200**	**343 979 700**	**4 173 895 900**

B

REVISED INCOME ESTIMATES FOR THE BIENNIUM 2006-2007

The General Assembly

Resolves that, for the biennium 2006-2007, the estimates of income of 434,860,100 United States dollars approved by it in its resolutions 60/247 B of 23 December 2005, 60/281 of 30 June 2006, and 60/283 of 7 July 2006 shall be increased by 51,509,800 dollars, as follows:

Income section	Amount approved in resolutions 60/247 B, 60/281 and 60/283	Increase (decrease)	Revised estimate
	(United States dollars)		
1. Income from staff assessment	409 239 700	31 547 800	440 787 500
Total, income section 1	**409 239 700**	**31547 800**	**440 787 500**
2. General income	20 867 000	20 774 400	41 641 400
3. Services to the public	4 753 400	(812 400)	3 941 000
Total, income sections 2 and 3	**25 620 400**	**19 962 000**	**45 582 400**
Grand total	**434 860 100**	**51 509 800**	**486 369 900**

C

FINANCING OF THE APPROPRIATIONS FOR THE YEAR 2007

The General Assembly

Resolves that, for the year 2007:

1. Budget appropriations totalling 2,274,439,650 United States dollars, and consisting of 1,899,456,250 dollars, being half of the appropriation initially approved for the biennium 2006-2007 in its resolution 60/247 A of 23 December 2005, 26,443,300 dollars, being the additional appropriation approved for the biennium in its resolution 60/281 of 30 June 2006, 4,560,400 dollars, being the additional appropriation approved for the biennium in its resolution 60/283 of 7 July 2006, and 343,979,700 dollars, being the increase approved in resolution A above, shall be financed in accordance with regulations 3.1 and 3.2 of the Financial Regulations and Rules of the United Nations, as follows:

(*a*) 32,772,200 dollars, consisting of:

(i) 12,810,200 dollars, being half of the estimated income other than staff assessment approved for the biennium in its resolution 60/247 B of 23 December 2005;

(ii) 19,962,000 dollars, being the increase in income other than staff assessment approved for the biennium in resolution B above;

(*b*) 2,241,667,450 dollars, being the assessment on Member States in accordance with its resolution 61/237 of 22 December 2006;

2. There shall be set off against the assessment on Member States, in accordance with the provisions of General Assembly resolution 973 (X) of 15 December 1955, their respective share in the Tax Equalization Fund in the total amount of 240,912,700 dollars, consisting of:

(a) 200,867,400 dollars, being half of the estimated staff assessment income approved by the Assembly in its resolution 60/247 B;

(b) 7,377,600 dollars, being the estimated increase in income from staff assessment approved by the Assembly in its resolution 60/281;

(c) 127,300 dollars, being the estimated increase in income from staff assessment approved by the Assembly in its resolution 60/283;

(d) 31,547,800 dollars, being the estimated increase in income from staff assessment approved by the Assembly in resolution B above;

(e) 992,600 dollars, being the increase in income from staff assessment for the biennium 2004-2005 compared with the revised estimates approved by the Assembly in its resolution 60/245 B of 23 December 2005.

Questions relating to the 2006-2007 programme budget

The Fifth Committee considered a number of questions related to the 2006-2007 programme budget, among them revised estimates resulting from resolutions and decisions by the Economic and Social Council and by the Human Rights Council in 2006, estimates in respect of special political missions, good offices and other political initiatives authorized by the General Assembly and/or the Security Council, the first performance report on the programme budget for the 2006-2007 biennium, the contingency fund, and the comprehensive review of governance and oversight within the United Nations and its funds, programmes and specialized agencies.

Other subjects covered concerned the construction of additional conference facilities at the Vienna International Centre (see p. 1672) and office facilities at the Economic Commission for Africa in Addis Ababa (see p. 1672), the contingent liability reserve for the UN Postal Administration (see p. 1622), identification of additional resources for the Development Account (see p. 1044), the International Civil Service Commission (see p. 1678), the UN Joint Staff Pension Board (see p. 1703), strengthening the UN Crime Prevention and Criminal Justice Programme and the role of the Commission on Crime Prevention and Justice as its governing body (see p. 1287), and the UN Fund for International Partnerships (see p. 1046).

GENERAL ASSEMBLY ACTION

On 22 December [meeting 84], the General Assembly, on the recommendation of the Fifth Committee [A/61/592/Add.2], adopted **resolution 61/252** without vote [agenda item 117].

Questions relating to the programme budget for the biennium 2006-2007

The General Assembly,

I

Construction of additional conference facilities at the Vienna International Centre

Having considered the report of the Secretary-General and the related report of the Advisory Committee on Administrative and Budgetary Questions,

1. *Takes note with appreciation* of the efforts by the Government of Austria, as host country, to construct conference facilities at the Vienna International Centre;

2. *Takes note* of the report of the Secretary-General, and endorses the related observations and recommendations of the Advisory Committee on Administrative and Budgetary Questions contained in its report;

II

Construction of additional office facilities at the Economic Commission for Africa in Addis Ababa

Having considered the report of the Secretary-General and the related report of the Advisory Committee on Administrative and Budgetary Questions,

1. *Takes note with appreciation* of the efforts of the Government of Ethiopia, as host country, in facilitating the construction of additional office facilities at the Economic Commission for Africa in Addis Ababa;

2. *Takes note* of the report of the Secretary-General, and endorses the related observations and recommendations of the Advisory Committee on Administrative and Budgetary Questions contained in its report;

III

Contingent liability reserve for the United Nations Postal Administration

Having considered the report of the Secretary-General on a contingent liability reserve for the United Nations Postal Administration and the related report of the Advisory Committee on Administrative and Budgetary Questions,

1. *Takes note* of the report of the Secretary-General and the related report of the Advisory Committee on Administrative and Budgetary Questions;

2. *Requests* the Secretary-General to submit, at the second part of its resumed sixty-first session, a comprehensive report setting out:

(a) Options for reducing the risk posed to the United Nations Postal Administration by the use of its services for commercial and bulk mail;

(b) Options other than the establishment of the contingent liability reserve for the United Nations Postal Administration;

(c) The status of the negotiations between the United Nations Postal Administration and postal authorities where the United Nations Postal Administration operates;

(d) Further elaboration of the proposals contained in the report of the Secretary-General;

IV

Identification of additional resources for the Development Account

Recalling its resolutions 52/12 B of 19 December 1997, 52/220 and 52/221 A of 22 December 1997, 52/235 of 26 June 1998, 53/220 A of 7 April 1999, 53/220 B of 8 June 1999, 54/15 of 29 October 1999, 56/237 of 24 December 2001 and 60/246 of 23 December 2005,

Reaffirming its resolution 56/237, whereby it requested the Secretary-General to intensify efforts to enhance efficiency measures that might result in sustainable savings, with a view to augmenting the Development Account, in accordance with the provisions of General Assembly resolution 54/15,

Noting with concern that since the establishment of the Development Account in 1997, no savings from possible reductions in administration and other overhead costs have been identified for transfer to the Development Account, notwithstanding the decisions of the General Assembly, including its resolution 52/12 B,

Having considered the report of the Secretary-General on the identification of additional resources for the Development Account and the related report of the Advisory Committee on Administrative and Budgetary Questions,

1. *Takes note* of the report of the Secretary-General;

2. *Also takes note* of the report of the Advisory Committee on Administrative and Budgetary Questions;

3. *Recalls* paragraph 14 of its resolution 60/246, and regrets that the Secretary-General has not been able to provide recommendations to the General Assembly on how additional resources in the region of 5 million United States dollars could be added to the Development Account;

4. *Requests* the Secretary-General to submit to it at its sixty-second session a comprehensive report setting out recommendations on how additional resources, without using surpluses, could be identified for transfer to the Development Account, including:

(*a*) A review of the modalities and rationale for the funding of the Development Account as contained in the report of the Secretary-General on the Account submitted to the General Assembly at its fifty-second session and subsequent reports of the Secretary-General and resolutions of the Assembly, in the light of experience;

(*b*) A definition of procedures to identify efficiency or other gains, including but not limited to any potential savings that might be identified by Member States for transfer to the Development Account in the context of intergovernmental processes, as well as their practical measures of implementation;

5. *Decides* to appropriate under section 34, Development Account, of the programme budget for the biennium 2006-2007 the amount of 2.5 million dollars as an immediate exceptional measure towards addressing the lack of transfer of resources to the Account since its inception;

6. *Requests* the Secretary-General to provide recommendations to the General Assembly on identifying a further 2.5 million dollars in the context of his report to be submitted in accordance with paragraph 4 (*b*) above;

7. *Also requests* the Secretary-General to prepare an assessment of the impact of the Development Account in terms of its aims and purposes and to report thereon to the General Assembly at its sixty-second session;

V

Revised estimates resulting from resolutions and decisions adopted by the Human Rights Council at its first, resumed second, and third sessions and its first, second and third special sessions in 2006

Takes note of the reports of the Secretary-General on the revised estimates resulting from resolutions and decisions adopted by the Human Rights Council at its first, resumed second, and third sessions and its first, second and third special sessions in 2006, and endorses the related oral report of the Advisory Committee on Administrative and Budgetary Questions;

VI

Administrative and financial implications of decisions and recommendations contained in reports of the International Civil Service Commission for 2005 and 2006

Recalling its resolution 61/239 of 22 December 2006, entitled "United Nations common system: report of the International Civil Service Commission",

Takes note of the statement submitted by the Secretary-General on the administrative and financial implications of the decisions and recommendations contained in the reports of the International Civil Service Commission for 2005 and 2006 and the related report of the Advisory Committee on Administrative and Budgetary Questions;

VII

Estimates in respect of special political missions, good offices and other political initiatives authorized by the General Assembly and/or the Security Council

Recalling its resolutions 60/247 A and 60/248 of 23 December 2005, 60/255 of 8 May 2006 and 60/281 of 30 June 2006,

Having considered the reports of the Secretary-General on the estimates in respect of special political missions, good offices and other political initiatives authorized by the General Assembly and/or the Security Council and the report of the Office of Internal Oversight Services on the audit of the management of special political missions by the Department of Political Affairs of the Secretariat, as well as the report of the Advisory Committee on Administrative and Budgetary Questions,

1. *Takes note* of the reports of the Secretary-General;

2. *Endorses* the conclusions and recommendations of the Advisory Committee on Administrative and Budgetary Questions, subject to the provisions of the present resolution;

3. *Takes note with appreciation* of the report of the Office of Internal Oversight Services, and decides to

revert to the consideration of this report during its consideration of the proposed programme budget for the biennium 2008-2009;

4. *Notes with appreciation* the efforts made to include information on actual and potential synergies and complementarities for each individual mission, and requests the Secretary-General to continue to develop and improve the presentation of information in this regard;

5. *Underlines* the continued importance of the Secretary-General's ensuring, when appointing his Special Representatives and Envoys, the highest standards of integrity, competency, impartiality and professionalism;

6. *Recalls* that in paragraph 9 of its resolution 55/231 of 23 December 2000, it requested the Secretary-General to ensure that, in presenting the programme budget, expected accomplishments and, where possible, indicators of achievement were included to measure achievements in the implementation of the programmes of the Organization and not those of individual Member States;

7. *Notes* the concerns expressed by Member States and requests the Secretary-General to review the logical frameworks for all special political missions in order to ensure that their programmatic aspects and resource requirements are consistent with mandates of the General Assembly and the Security Council, and to report thereon to the Assembly no later than the early part of the second part of its resumed sixty-first session;

8. *Requests* the Secretary-General to submit his future budget proposals in full compliance with its resolution 55/231;

9. *Approves* a charge of 326,500,000 dollars for the budgets of special political missions for the year 2007;

10. *Takes note* of the estimated unencumbered balance of 95,883,600 dollars;

11. *Decides* to appropriate, after taking into account the estimated unencumbered balance of 95,883,600 dollars, under the procedures provided for in paragraph 11 of annex I to resolution 41/213 of 19 December 1986, an amount of 230,616,400 dollars under section 3, Political affairs, of the programme budget for the biennium 2006-2007;

12. *Also decides* to appropriate an amount of 22,383,900 dollars under section 35, Staff assessment, to be offset by a corresponding amount under income section 1, Income from staff assessment, of the programme budget for the biennium 2006-2007;

VIII

First performance report on the programme budget for the biennium 2006-2007

Having considered the first performance report of the Secretary-General on the programme budget for the biennium 2006-2007 and the related report of the Advisory Committee on Administrative and Budgetary Questions,

Recalling its resolutions 60/247 A and B of 23 December 2005, 60/281 of 30 June 2006 and 60/283 of 7 July 2006,

1. *Reaffirms* the budgetary process as approved in its resolution 41/213 and as reaffirmed in subsequent resolutions;

2. *Takes note* of the first performance report of the Secretary-General on the programme budget for the biennium 2006-2007 and the addendum on the utilization of the subvention for the Special Court for Sierra Leone and endorses the observations and recommendations of the Advisory Committee on Administrative and Budgetary Questions contained in its report;

3. *Recalls* paragraph 14 of its resolution 58/270 of 23 December 2003 and section III, paragraph 12, of its resolution 60/283 and, noting with concern that within the context of the fifty posts experiment, no available posts were provided for the new post requests referred to in paragraphs IV.2, IV.28 and IV.29 of the first report of the Advisory Committee on Administrative and Budgetary Questions on the proposed programme budget for the biennium 2006-2007, reiterates once again its request to the Secretary-General to expeditiously implement paragraph 8 of its resolution 60/246 of 23 December 2005 and to report thereon in the context of the second performance report on the programme budget for the biennium 2006-2007;

4. *Also recalls* section III, paragraph 6, of its resolution 60/283, and requests the Secretary-General to implement its provisions and to report thereon in the context of the second performance report on the programme budget for the biennium 2006-2007;

5. *Emphasizes* that the performance report should be submitted in a timely manner in order to allow Member States to analyse it and to facilitate budget preparation;

6. *Approves* a net increase of 81,246,800 dollars in the appropriation approved for the biennium 2006-2007 and a net increase of 28,857,800 dollars in the estimates of income for the biennium, to be apportioned among expenditure and income sections as indicated in the report of the Secretary-General;

IX

Revised estimates resulting from resolutions and decisions adopted by the Economic and Social Council at its substantive session of 2006

Takes note of the report of the Secretary-General on the revised estimates resulting from resolutions and decisions adopted by the Economic and Social Council at its substantive session of 2006 and endorses the related report of the Advisory Committee on Administrative and Budgetary Questions;

X

Administrative and financial implications arising from the report of the United Nations Joint Staff Pension Board

Having considered the report of the Secretary-General on the administrative and financial implications arising from the report of the United Nations Joint Staff Pension Board and the related oral report of the Advisory Committee on Administrative and Budgetary Questions,

1. *Takes note* of the report of the Secretary-General on the administrative and financial implications arising from the report of the United Nations Joint Staff Pension Board;

2. *Requests* the Secretary-General to report on any additional requirements arising from the recommendations of the Board in the context of the second performance report on the programme budget for the biennium 2006-2007;

XI

Strengthening the United Nations Crime Prevention and Criminal Justice Programme and the role of the Commission on Crime Prevention and Criminal Justice as its governing body

Recalling its resolution 46/152 of 18 December 1991, in which it approved the statement of principles and programme of action of the United Nations Crime Prevention and Criminal Justice Programme, according to which the United Nations Trust Fund for Social Defence was renamed the United Nations Crime Prevention and Criminal Justice Fund and became an integral part of the Programme,

Recalling also its resolution 55/25 of 15 November 2000, in which it decided that, until the Conference of the Parties to the United Nations Convention against Transnational Organized Crime decided otherwise, the account referred to in article 30 of the Convention would be operated within the United Nations Crime Prevention and Criminal Justice Fund,

Recalling further its resolution 58/4 of 31 October 2003, in which it decided that, until the Conference of the States Parties to the United Nations Convention against Corruption decided otherwise, the account referred to in article 62 of the Convention would be operated within the United Nations Crime Prevention and Criminal Justice Fund,

Taking note of the Secretary-General's bulletin on the organization of the United Nations Office on Drugs and Crime, by which the Secretary-General decided that the Office would be established to implement the Organization's drug programme and crime programme in an integrated manner and that the Executive Director would be responsible for all the activities of the Office, as well as its administration,

Considering that, starting from the biennium 2004-2005, a consolidated budget for the United Nations Office on Drugs and Crime has been prepared, including budgets for its drug and crime programmes,

Considering also that the Commission on Crime Prevention and Criminal Justice, in accordance with the procedures established by the General Assembly in its resolution 41/213 and relevant subsequent resolutions, already provides its views and guidance on the proposed biennial programme plan and on the crime programme, which forms the basis for the formulation of the proposed programme budget for the following biennium and whose narrative part is subsequently considered by the Commission,

Noting the delegation of authority for the management of the United Nations Crime Prevention and Criminal Justice Fund from the Secretary-General to the Director-General of the United Nations Office at Vienna,

Considering that it would be opportune to grant the Commission on Crime Prevention and Criminal Justice the same powers with respect to the United Nations Crime Prevention and Criminal Justice Fund as the Commission on Narcotic Drugs has with respect to the Fund of the United Nations International Drug Control Programme,

Having considered the letter dated 19 October 2006 from the Chairman of the Third Committee addressed to the Chairman of the Fifth Committee transmitting a draft resolution entitled "Strengthening the United Nations Crime Prevention and Criminal Justice Programme and the role of the Commission on Crime Prevention and Criminal Justice as its governing body", the relevant note by the Secretary-General, and the related oral report of the Advisory Committee on Administrative and Budgetary Questions,

1. *Authorizes* the Commission on Crime Prevention and Criminal Justice, as the principal United Nations policymaking body on crime prevention and criminal justice issues, to approve, on the basis of the proposals of the Executive Director of the United Nations Office on Drugs and Crime, bearing in mind the comments and recommendations of the Advisory Committee on Administrative and Budgetary Questions, the budget of the United Nations Crime Prevention and Criminal Justice Fund, including its administrative and programme support costs budget, other than expenditures borne by the regular budget of the United Nations, without prejudice to the powers of the Conference of the Parties to the United Nations Convention against Transnational Organized Crime, as provided for in that Convention, and to the powers of the Conference of the States Parties to the United Nations Convention against Corruption, as provided for in that Convention;

2. *Requests* the Advisory Committee on Administrative and Budgetary Questions to submit its comments and recommendations on the biennial consolidated budget for the United Nations Office on Drugs and Crime to the Commission on Crime Prevention and Criminal Justice;

3. *Requests* the Commission on Crime Prevention and Criminal Justice to report to the General Assembly at its sixty-second session, through the Economic and Social Council, on the ways in which it plans to carry out the administrative and financial functions;

4. *Requests* the Secretary-General to promulgate financial rules for the United Nations Crime Prevention and Criminal Justice Fund, in accordance with the Financial Regulations and Rules of the United Nations, it being understood that the references in the said financial rules to the role and functions of the Commission on Crime Prevention and Criminal Justice shall be consistent with the role of the Commission given in paragraph 1 above;

5. *Decides* that, notwithstanding regulations 6.1 and 6.5 of the Financial Regulations of the United Nations, the Executive Director of the United Nations Office on Drugs and Crime shall maintain the accounts of the Fund and shall be responsible for submitting the said accounts and related financial statements, no later than 31 March following the end of the financial period, to the Board of Auditors and for submitting financial reports to the Commission on Crime Prevention and Criminal Justice and to the General Assembly;

XII

Contingency fund

Notes that a balance of 637,300 dollars remains in the contingency fund.

On 22 December, the Assembly decided that the item on the programme budget for the 2006-2007 biennium would remain for consideration during its resumed sixty-first (2007) session (**decision 61/552**).

Contingency fund

The contingency fund, established by General Assembly resolution 41/213 [YUN 1986, p. 1024], accommodated additional expenditures relating to each biennium that derived from legislative mandates not provided for in the proposed programme budget or from revised estimates. Guidelines for its use were annexed to Assembly resolution 42/211 [YUN 1987, p. 1098].

Revised estimates in respect of matters of which the Security Council was seized

In January, the Secretary-General submitted an addendum [A/60/585/Add.1] to his 2005 report [YUN 2005, p. 1496], which contained the mission-by-mission substantive and financial information for 26 special political missions, including total estimated requirements of $280,803,200 net ($297,498,900 gross) for the 2006-2007 biennium. By resolution 60/248 [ibid., p. 1494], the General Assembly had approved charges of $100 million against the provision for special political missions under section 3, Political affairs, of the 2006-2007 programme budget. Consequently, additional requirements of the 26 missions to be charged against the provision amounted to $180,803,200. In February [A/60/585/Add.2], additional estimated requirements for three special political missions [YUN 2005, p. 1496] were submitted, totalling $22,548,400 net ($25,002,800 gross).

In March [A/60/7/Add.37], ACABQ noted that estimated requirements for the 29 special political missions amounted to $303,351,600 for the period 1 January to 31 December 2006. The Committee recommended against the establishment of three new posts and that resources for travel ($324,700), experts and consultants ($244,500) be reduced. It therefore recommended approval of total resources amounting to $302,469,500.

GENERAL ASSEMBLY ACTION

On 8 May [meeting 79], the General Assembly, on the recommendation of the Fifth Committee [A/60/608/Add.1], adopted **resolution 60/255** without vote [agenda item 124].

Special subjects relating to the programme budget for the biennium 2006-2007

The General Assembly,

I

Estimates in respect of special political missions, good offices and other political initiatives authorized by the General Assembly and/or the Security Council

Having considered the report of the Secretary-General on the estimates in respect of special political missions, good offices and other political initiatives authorized by the General Assembly and/or the Security Council, as well as the related report of the Advisory Committee on Administrative and Budgetary Questions,

Recalling its resolution 60/248 of 23 December 2005, by which it approved a charge of 100 million United States dollars for the twenty-six special political missions dealt with in the report of the Secretary-General against the provision for special political missions in the programme budget for the biennium 2006-2007,

Noting the importance of enhancing the efficiency and effectiveness of political missions of the United Nations,

Recognizing the need to identify and achieve greater complementarities and synergies, where possible, among the various special political missions and good offices of United Nations entities,

1. *Takes note* of the report of the Secretary-General;
2. *Endorses* the conclusions and recommendations of the Advisory Committee on Administrative and Budgetary Questions, subject to the provisions of the present resolution;
3. *Requests* the Secretary-General to reflect the improvements proposed in paragraphs 11 and 12 of the report of the Advisory Committee on Administrative and Budgetary Questions in the presentation of the budgets for special political missions for 2007;
4. *Recalls* paragraph 7 of section VII of its resolution 59/276 of 23 December 2004, and requests the Secretary-General to ensure that future budget proposals for special political missions are presented at an early date in order to facilitate proper consideration by the General Assembly;
5. *Welcomes* the efforts of the Secretary-General to utilize the existing expertise of staff within the United

Nations system, including experts from regions where special political missions are located;

6. *Encourages* the Secretary-General to ensure the deployment of staff with relevant knowledge and experience to special political missions and good offices of the United Nations and to include information on progress made in future budget proposals;

7. *Notes with appreciation* efforts made to include information on actual and potential synergies and complementarities for each individual mission, and requests the Secretary-General to continue to develop and improve the presentation of information in this regard;

8. *Requests* the Secretary-General to identify means to achieve greater complementarities and synergies among the various special political missions and good offices of United Nations entities, including, where possible, through greater sharing of human resources and logistical arrangements, particularly where mandates are similar or interconnected, while being cognizant of their respective mandates;

9. *Recalls* that in paragraph 9 of its resolution 55/231 of 23 December 2000, it requested the Secretary-General to ensure that, in presenting the programme budget, expected accomplishments and, where possible, indicators of achievement are included to measure achievements in the implementation of the programmes of the Organization and not those of individual Member States;

10. *Requests* the Secretary-General to submit his future budget proposals in full compliance with its resolution 55/231;

11. *Notes* the lack of information analysing the growth and decrease in resources proposed as well as the variances between appropriations and expenditures in the report of the Secretary-General;

12. *Also notes* the variance between the vacancy rates used in formulating budgets and the actual vacancy situation, in particular in medium-sized to large missions;

13. *Requests* the Secretary-General to formulate and present future budgets of special political missions on the basis of an analysis of actual expenditure patterns, including the latest vacancy situation and variances between appropriations and expenditures, for the purpose of achieving more realistic budgeting;

14. *Also requests* the Secretary-General to entrust to the Office of Internal Oversight Services a management review as outlined in paragraph 16 of the report of the Advisory Committee and to submit it to the General Assembly at the main part of its sixty-first session;

15. *Reiterates* that experts and consultants for all special political missions, good offices and other political initiatives should be used in full compliance with the existing rules and the relevant resolutions of the General Assembly and in cases where the required expertise is not available within the United Nations system;

16. *Requests* the Secretary-General, in this connection, to provide full justification in future budget submissions when requesting resources for experts and consultants;

17. *Notes* the observation of the Advisory Committee in paragraph 52 *(c)* of its report regarding the two positions funded from general temporary assistance, and requests the Secretary-General to include specific information on their status in the budget submission for 2007;

18. *Takes note* of paragraph 29 of the report of the Advisory Committee, and decides to establish a position for a Political Affairs Officer at the P-4 level within the Office of the Personal Representative of the Secretary-General for Lebanon;

19. *Approves* an additional charge of 202,469,500 dollars against the provision for special political missions already approved under section 3, Political affairs, of the programme budget for the biennium 2006-2007;

II

2005 World Summit Outcome: Peacebuilding Support Office; revised estimates to the programme budget for the biennium 2006-2007

Having considered the report of the Secretary-General on the Peacebuilding Support Office and the related revised estimates to the programme budget for the biennium 2006-2007, as well as the related report of the Advisory Committee on Administrative and Budgetary Questions,

1. *Takes note* of the report of the Secretary-General;

2. *Also takes note* of the report of the Advisory Committee on Administrative and Budgetary Questions;

3. *Decides* to authorize the Secretary-General to utilize an amount of up to 1,571,300 dollars from the approved initial provision for special political missions under section 3, Political affairs, of the programme budget for the biennium 2006-2007, to operationalize a peacebuilding support office;

4. *Stresses* that the authorization from the provision for special political missions referred to in paragraph 3 above is a provisional and exceptional measure, decides that the Peacebuilding Support Office shall be financed from the programme budget, and requests the Secretary-General to include a provision for the Peacebuilding Support Office in the appropriate section of the programme budget, commencing with the proposed programme budget for the biennium 2008-2009, to ensure sustainable and reliable long-term financing of the Office;

5. *Decides* to revert to the issues regarding level, staffing and functions of the Peacebuilding Support Office as contained in the report of the Secretary-General in the context of its consideration of the proposed programme budget for the biennium 2008-2009 and in the light of decisions, if any, that may result from the consideration by the General Assembly of the report of the Secretary-General to be submitted in accordance with paragraph 25 of its resolution 60/180 of 20 December 2005;

6. *Requests* the Secretary-General to ensure that the Peacebuilding Support Office has the necessary gender competence to support the Peacebuilding Commission in implementing its mandate to integrate a gender perspective into all of its work, taking into account, inter alia, Security Council resolution 1325(2000) of 31 October

2000 and drawing on the appropriate expertise in the United Nations system;

7. *Also requests* the Secretary-General to ensure the efficient use of the resources approved in the provision for special political missions for the biennium 2006-2007, taking into account the provisions of paragraph 23 of its resolution 60/180;

III

Liabilities and proposed funding for after-service health insurance benefits

Recalling its resolution 58/249 A of 23 December 2003,

Having considered the report of the Secretary-General on liabilities and proposed funding for after-service health insurance benefits and the related report of the Advisory Committee on Administrative and Budgetary Questions,

1. *Takes note* of the report of the Secretary-General and the related report of the Advisory Committee on Administrative and Budgetary Questions;

2. *Also takes note* of the background information on the after-service health insurance programme provided in paragraphs 6 to 9 of the report of the Secretary-General, and requests further explanation of the programme;

3. *Recognizes* the end-of-service accrued benefit liabilities reported by the Secretary-General in his report, and requests the Secretary-General to take the necessary steps to disclose those liabilities in the United Nations financial statements;

4. *Requests* the Secretary-General to submit to the General Assembly at its sixty-first session a report that addresses the issues raised in paragraph 2 above, as well as the issues raised by the Advisory Committee on Administrative and Budgetary Questions in its report, and that provides updated information on the status of liabilities, clarifications with regard to the assumptions used to determine liabilities and alternative strategies to fund the liabilities;

IV

Harmonization of the conditions of travel

Noting with appreciation the report of the Joint Inspection Unit on harmonization of the conditions of travel throughout the United Nations system and the note by the Secretary-General transmitting his comments and those of the United Nations System Chief Executives Board for Coordination thereon,

1. *Decides* to revert to the consideration of the report of the Joint Inspection Unit, the note by the Secretary-General and any relevant contributions by the International Civil Service Commission at its sixty-first session, together with the question "Standards of accommodation for air travel";

2. *Requests* the Secretary-General to initiate, within the framework of the United Nations System Chief Executives Board for Coordination, a review of the standards of travel and entitlements for staff members, members of organs and subsidiary organs of the United Nations and organizations of the United Nations system, with a view to adopting a common policy at the United Nations system level;

3. *Also requests* the Secretary-General to submit the results of the review to the General Assembly at the first part of its resumed sixty-first session.

The Secretary-General, in May [A/60/585/Add.3], submitted proposed resource requirements for the period from 1 April to 31 December 2006 for the United Nations Assistance Mission in Afghanistan (UNAMA), estimated at $54,890,600 net ($59,835,200 gross). Part of that requirement would be met from the unencumbered balance remaining at the end of its mandate period in March 2006, totalling $2,780,900.

ACABQ observed [A/60/7/Add.39] that the logical framework of the Secretary-General's report could be further refined and made recommendations to be taken into account for the presentation of the 2007 budget. The Committee recommended against the establishment of a position at the D-1 level, the reclassification of two P-5 posts to the D-1 level and the reclassification of a P-3 post to the P-5 level, recommending instead that the post be upgraded to the P-4 level. Consequently, ACABQ recommended that the Assembly approve a budget of $54,744,100 net ($59,647,600 gross) for UNAMA for the period 1 April to 31 December 2006; approve charges of $51,908,500 against the unallocated balance for special political missions and appropriate $54,700 under section 3, Political affairs, of the 2006-2007 programme budget; and $4,903,500 under section 35, Staff assessment.

In June [A/60/585/Add.4], the Secretary-General submitted proposed resource requirements of $17,189,000 net ($19,175,100 gross) for the period from 16 June to 31 December 2006 for the International Independent Investigation Commission (IIIC) in Lebanon (see p. 596), and requirements of $5,253,500 net ($5,776,200 gross) for a technical roll-over of the mandate of the United Nations Office in Timor-Leste (UNOTIL) for the period from 21 June to 31 August 2006. Estimated requirements for the two missions for the respective periods amounted to $22,442,500 net ($24,951,300 gross). After taking into account unencumbered balances totalling $3,262,500 against the appropriations for the Commission ($3,006,200) and UNOTIL ($256,300), net additional requirements totalled $19,180,000 net ($21,688,800 gross).

ACABQ recommended [A/60/7/Add.41] against the addition of four Field Service positions to replace services previously provided by the United Nations Interim Force in Lebanon for IIIC. It therefore recommended that the Assembly approve the budgets for IIIC in the amount of $17,020,000 net

($18,971,400 gross) and for UNOTIL in the amount of $5,253,500 net ($5,776,200 gross); and appropriate $19,011,000 for IIIC and UNOTIL under section 3, Political affairs.

GENERAL ASSEMBLY ACTION

On 30 June [meeting 92], the General Assembly, on the recommendation of the Fifth Committee [A/60/608/Add.4], adopted **resolution 60/281** without vote [agenda item 124].

Estimates in respect of special political missions, good offices and other political initiatives authorized by the General Assembly and/or the Security Council

The General Assembly,

Having considered the reports of the Secretary-General on the estimates in respect of special political missions, good offices and other political initiatives authorized by the General Assembly and/or the Security Council, as well as the related reports of the Advisory Committee on Administrative and Budgetary Questions,

1. *Takes note* of the reports of the Secretary-General;

2. *Endorses* the conclusions and recommendations of the Advisory Committee on Administrative and Budgetary Questions contained in its reports;

3. *Reaffirms* the relevant provisions of section I of its resolution 60/255 of 8 May 2006, and requests the Secretary-General to ensure their full implementation;

4. *Approves* the budgets of 59,647,600 United States dollars gross (54,744,100 dollars net) for the United Nations Assistance Mission in Afghanistan for the period from 1 April to 31 December 2006, 18,971,400 dollars gross (17,020,000 dollars net) for the International Independent Investigation Commission for the period from 16 June to 31 December 2006 and 5,776,200 dollars gross (5,253,500 dollars net) for the United Nations Office in Timor-Leste for the period from 21 June to 31 August 2006;

5. *Takes note* of the unencumbered balances in the amounts already appropriated for the three missions totalling 6,043,400 dollars;

6. *Decides* to approve a charge of 51,908,500 dollars, corresponding to the unassigned balance against the provision for special political missions, appropriated under section 3, Political affairs, of the programme budget for the biennium 2006-2007;

7. *Also decides* to appropriate, under the procedure provided for in paragraph 11 of annex I to its resolution 41/213 of 19 December 1986, an amount of 19,065,700 dollars under section 3, Political affairs, of the programme budget for the biennium 2006-2007 and an amount of 7,377,600 dollars under section 35, Staff assessment, the latter to be offset by a corresponding amount under income section 1, Income from staff assessment.

In December [A/61/525 & Corr. 1], the Secretary-General submitted proposed additional requirements for the period until 31 December 2007 for 27 political missions authorized by the Security Council and/or the General Assembly estimated at $268,987,600 net ($294,005,100 gross), after taking account of the estimated unencumbered balances for those missions at the end of 2006, totalling $95,883,600. Details of the proposed resource requirements ($364,871,200) for 2007 were contained in five addenda [A/61/525/Add.1-5 & Add.3/Corr.1] to his report.

ACABQ [A/61/640 & Corr.1] drew attention to the pattern of expenditures for special political missions for the current period, particularly that of the United Nations Assistance Mission in Iraq, which continued to have large unencumbered balances. The Committee, therefore, recommended a 10 per cent overall reduction ($36,487,120) in the resource requirements of $364,871,200 proposed in the Secretary-General's report (above) and that the Assembly appropriate $232,500,480 under section 3, Political Affairs for those missions.

Revised estimates resulting from Economic and Social Council action

In a September report [A/61/370 & Corr.1], the Secretary-General submitted expenditure requirements resulting from resolutions and decisions adopted by the Economic and Social Council at its 2006 substantive session, relating to activities of the Ad Hoc Advisory Group on Haiti, follow-up to the World Summit on the Information Society, the Commission on Science and Technology for Development and the United Nations Forum on Forests. Those requirements were estimated at $257,500, which could be absorbed within the resources provided for the 2006-2007 biennium.

In October [A/61/498], ACABQ stated that it had no objection to the Secretary-General's proposed expenditure requirements and noted that, should actual requirements exceed the absorptive capacity of the relevant sections of the budget, additional provisions would be reported in the second performance report for the 2006-2007 biennium.

Unforeseen and extraordinary expenses

Under the terms of General Assembly resolution 60/249 [YUN 2005, p. 1498], the Secretary-General was authorized, with the prior concurrence of ACABQ, to enter into commitments to meet unforeseen and extraordinary expenses arising either during or subsequent to the 2006-2007 biennium, without reverting to the Assembly for approval.

In his first performance report on the 2006-2007 programme budget [A/61/593], the Secretary-General informed the Assembly that he had entered into commitments in the amount of $4,966,400, of which $4,376,400 was for activities relating to the maintenance of peace and security and $590,000 for commitments certified by the President of the International Court of Justice.

Working Capital Fund

On 7 July, by **resolution 60/283** (see p. 1580), the General Assembly resolved that the Working Capital Fund for the 2006-2007 biennium [YUN 2005, p. 1497] would be increased from $100 million to $150 million, effective 1 January 2007, and that Member States would make advances to the Fund in accordance with the scale of assessments for contributions to the regular budget for 2007. The Fund was to be used to finance appropriations pending the receipt of assessed contributions; pay for unforeseen and extraordinary expenses, miscellaneous self-liquidating purchases and advance insurance premiums; and enable the Tax Equalization Fund to meet commitments pending the accumulation of credits.

In December [ST/ADM/SER.B/701], the Secretariat issued an assessment of Member States' additional advances to the Fund for the 2006-2007 biennium and contributions to the 2007 regular budget, together with an assessment of the new Member State's (Montenegro) advance to the Fund for the 2006-2007 biennium and contribution to the 2006 regular budget.

Reserve for United Nations Postal Administration

In August [A/61/295], the Secretary-General reported that over the past 20 years, the United Nations Postal Administration (UNPA) [YUN 1950, p. 172], in accordance with the agreements in force with the postal services where it operated (United States, Switzerland and Austria), had paid on average 12.2 per cent of its $249.2 million income for that period, representing $1.5 million annually, to reimburse the respective postal services for mailing charges for UN stamps. However, the other 87.8 per cent could constitute a contingent liability in view of the theoretical possibility that the remaining stamps sold could be presented for mailing at any time and UNPA would be required to accept such mail and reimburse the national postal services for the agreed costs. Therefore, he recommended the establishment of a $3.3 million reserve for contingent liabilities, which should be financed from UNPA net income.

ACABQ [A/61/480] concurred with the Secretary-General's proposal and recommended the establishment of a contingent liability reserve for UNPA. To reach the $3.3 million target ceiling level, UNPA should further streamline its operations for greater efficiency.

Programme budget outline for 2008-2009

Report of Secretary-General. In November [A/61/576], the Secretary-General presented the proposed programme budget outline for the 2008-2009 biennium, describing the preliminary estimate of resources, priorities, real growth compared with the previous budget and the size of the contingency fund as a percentage of the overall level of resources. The preliminary estimate for the 2008-2009 biennium, expressed in 2006-2007 prices, amounted to $4,138.5 million. Recosted for inflation, but not for exchange rates, the total requirements for 2008-2009 would amount to $4,373.5 million, reflecting the priorities proposed in the strategic framework for that biennium (see p. 1635).

The preliminary estimate ($3,480.5 million), before the inclusion of special political missions, represented an increase of $14.4 million, or 0.4 per cent, compared with the 2006-2007 biennium. Taking account of the full inclusion of provisions for those missions, the total preliminary estimate of $4,138.5 million represented an increase of $299 million, or 7.8 per cent, compared with the 2006-2007 biennium.

The Secretary-General also recommended that for the 2008-2009 biennium, the contingency fund should be adjusted upwards by 0.6 per cent, from the current level of 0.75 per cent to 1.35 per cent, or $55.9 million.

Report of ACABQ. In December [A/61/615], ACABQ pointed out that, as the level of the contingency fund was set as a percentage of the overall level of resources, the amount of the fund increased with the size of the budget. Experience had shown that the level of the fund had almost never been exceeded, but exceptional circumstances had prevailed in the 2006-2007 biennium due to activities related to the implementation of the 2005 World Summit Outcome [YUN 2005, p. 48]. Moreover, by **resolution 60/283** (see p. 1580), the Assembly had authorized the Secretary-General budgetary discretion to enter into commitments up to $20 million for the 2006-2007 and 2008-2009 bienniums to meet the evolving needs of the Organization. The Committee therefore recommended that the level of the fund remain at 0.75 per cent, or $31 million.

With regard to the preliminary estimate of $4,138.5 million for the 2008-2009 budget outline, ACABQ had been informed that using the adjustments consequential to the first performance report for the 2006-2007 biennium (see p. 1611), the estimate would increase to $4,219.7 million. In addition, the overall level of estimated requirements would depend on decisions by the General Assembly on revised estimates and programme budget implications, which were in various stages of preparation or consideration. It therefore recommended that the Assembly adopt a preliminary estimate of $4,219.7 million for 2008-2009 at revised 2006-2007 rates.

GENERAL ASSEMBLY ACTION

On 22 December [meeting 84], the General Assembly, on the recommendation of the Fifth Committee [A/61/667], adopted **resolution 61/254** without vote [agenda item 116].

Proposed programme budget outline for the biennium 2008-2009

The General Assembly,

Reaffirming its resolution 41/213 of 19 December 1986, in which it requested the Secretary-General to submit in off-budget years an outline of the proposed programme budget for the following biennium,

Reaffirming also section VI of its resolution 45/248 B of 21 December 1990,

Reaffirming further rule 153 of its rules of procedure,

Recalling its resolution 58/269 of 23 December 2003,

Having considered the report of the Secretary-General on the proposed programme budget outline for the biennium 2008-2009 and the recommendations contained in the related report of the Advisory Committee on Administrative and Budgetary Questions,

1. *Reaffirms* that the Fifth Committee is the appropriate Main Committee of the General Assembly entrusted with responsibilities for administrative and budgetary matters;

2. *Endorses* the observations and recommendations contained in the report of the Advisory Committee on Administrative and Budgetary Questions;

3. *Reaffirms* that the proposed programme budget outline shall contain an indication of the following:

(a) A preliminary estimate of resources needed to accommodate the proposed programme of activities during the biennium;

(b) Priorities, reflecting general trends of a broad sectoral nature;

(c) Real growth, positive or negative, compared with the previous budget;

(d) Size of the contingency fund expressed as a percentage of the overall level of resources;

4. *Also reaffirms* that the budget outline should provide a greater level of predictability of resources required for the following biennium and promote greater involvement of Member States in the budgetary process, thereby facilitating the broadest possible agreement on the programme budget;

5. *Further reaffirms* that the budget proposals of the Secretary-General should reflect resource levels commensurate with mandates for their full, efficient and effective implementation;

6. *Notes* that the budget outline is a preliminary estimate of resources;

7. *Invites* the Secretary-General to prepare his proposed programme budget for the biennium 2008-2009 on the basis of a preliminary estimate of 4,194,726,800 United States dollars at revised 2006-2007 rates;

8. *Decides* that the proposed programme budget for the biennium 2008-2009 shall contain provisions for recosting on the basis of the existing methodology;

9. *Decides also* that the priorities for the biennium 2008-2009 shall be the following:

(a) Maintenance of international peace and security;

(b) Promotion of sustained economic growth and sustainable development, in accordance with the relevant resolutions of the General Assembly and recent United Nations conferences;

(c) Development of Africa;

(d) Promotion of human rights;

(e) Effective coordination of humanitarian assistance efforts;

(f) Promotion of justice and international law;

(g) Disarmament;

(h) Drug control, crime prevention and combating international terrorism in all its forms and manifestations;

10. *Requests* the Secretary-General, in view of his preliminary indicative estimates contained in the proposed budget outline, to reflect the priorities outlined in paragraph 9 above when presenting the proposed programme budget for the biennium 2008-2009;

11. *Decides* that the contingency fund shall be set at the level of 0.75 per cent of the preliminary estimate, namely at 31,460,500 dollars, that this amount shall be in addition to the overall level of the preliminary estimate and that it shall be used in accordance with the procedures for the use and operation of the contingency fund;

12. *Requests* the Secretary-General to review the experience of the utilization of the contingency fund and to report thereon to the General Assembly at its sixty-second session;

13. *Takes note* of the observation of the Advisory Committee on Administrative and Budgetary Questions in paragraph 9 of its report on the experiment for a limited discretion for budgetary implementation;

14. *Recalls* section III of its resolution 60/283 of 7 July 2006, and stresses that the experiment for a limited discretion for budgetary implementation shall not imply any changes to the provisions guiding the use of the contingency fund.

Contributions

According to the Secretary-General's report on improving the financial situation of the United Nations [A/61/556/Add.1], unpaid assessed contributions to the UN budget at the end of 2006 totalled $361 million (compared to $333 million in 2005); outstanding peacekeeping arrears totalled over $1,800 million (compared to $2,900 million in 2005); and total unpaid assessments to the international tribunals increased to $51 million (compared to $25 million in 2005).

The number of Member States paying their regular budget assessment in full was 139 (compared to 140 at the end of 2005).

Assessments

The Committee on Contributions, at its sixty-sixth session (New York, 5-30 June) [A/61/11 & Corr.1], considered issues related to the payment of assessments, including the methodology for preparing the scale of assessments for the period 2007-2009, multi-year payment plans and the application of Article 19 of the Charter. The Committee decided to hold its sixty-seventh (2007) session from 11 to 27 June 2007. The General Assembly took action on the Committee's recommendations in October and December (see below).

Application of Article 19

Committee on Contributions. The Committee on Contributions [A/61/11 & Corr.1] reviewed requests from eight Member States for exemption under Article 19 of the UN Charter, whereby a Member would lose its vote in the General Assembly if the amount of its arrears should equal or exceed the amount of contributions due from it for the preceding two full years. The Committee duly noted the Members' written and oral representations and evaluated them against their payment records and economic and political circumstances.

Determining that the failure of the Central African Republic, the Comoros, Georgia, Guinea-Bissau, Liberia, the Niger, Somalia and Tajikistan to pay the full minimum amount of arrears necessary to avoid the application of Article 19 was due to conditions beyond their control, and recalling the Article's provision that a Member might be permitted to vote if the Assembly was satisfied that its failure to do so was due to such conditions, the Committee recommended that they be allowed to vote until the end of the sixty-first session of the Assembly. The Committee urged the Central African Republic, which had made no payments since 1998, to begin to make some payments so as to reduce, or at least avoid a further increase in, its unpaid assessed contributions, and to submit the multi-year payment plan that it had earlier announced. The Committee, noting the information provided concerning the situation of the Comoros, recalled that the country's payment in 2005 had slightly reduced its arrears. It also noted that country's commitment to submitting a multi-year payment plan for paying those arrears. It welcomed Liberia's submission of a payment plan covering 2006 and noted the receipt of a first payment of $50,000. The Committee recalled that the Niger had also submitted and was adhering to a multi-year payment plan. It noted Tajikistan's continuing payments under its multi-year payment plan. With regard to that country's request that its arrears for peacekeeping activities that had accrued before 2000 be written off, the Committee reiterated its earlier conclusion that the request went beyond its competence as a technical advisory body [YUN 2005, p. 1499]. The Committee noted that four of the Member States requesting exemption under Article 19 had presented multi-year payment plans for paying their arrears, and encouraged all Member States requesting an exemption, if they were in a position to do so, to consider presenting such a plan.

At the end of the Committee's session on 30 June, nine Member States—the Central African Republic, the Comoros, Georgia, Guinea-Bissau, Liberia, the Niger, Sao Tome and Principe, Somalia and Tajikistan—were in arrears in the payment of their assessed contributions under the terms of Article 19 but had been permitted to vote in the Assembly until the end of the sixtieth session, pursuant to General Assembly resolution 60/237 [YUN 2005, p. 1501]. The Committee noted that Ethiopia and Pakistan, availing themselves of the opportunity afforded by Assembly resolution 55/5 B [YUN 2000, p. 1311], had paid the equivalent of $1,053,808.09 in non-United States dollar currencies.

Report of Secretary-General. During the year, the Secretary-General reported to the Assembly on payments made by certain Member States to reduce their level of arrears below that specified in Article 19, so that they could vote in the Assembly. As at 12 January [A/60/650], 20 Member States were below the gross amount assessed for the preceding two full years (2004-2005). That number was reduced to nine by 8 September [A/61/310] and remained at that number through 16 November [A/ES-10/368].

Communication. On 4 October [A/C.5/61/3], Sao Tome and Principe requested an exemption under Article 19. Despite the efforts made, the country had not been able to pay its assessed contributions owing to economic constraints, but had demonstrated its commitment to meeting its financial obligation through the multi-year payment plan submitted in 2002, including the first instalment, which had already been made.

GENERAL ASSEMBLY ACTION

On 12 October [meeting 28], the General Assembly, on the recommendation of the Fifth Committee [A/61/512], adopted **resolution 61/2** without vote [agenda item 122].

Scale of assessments for the apportionment of the expenses of the United Nations: requests under Article 19 of the Charter

The General Assembly,

Having considered chapter V of the report of the Committee on Contributions on its sixty-sixth session,

Reaffirming the obligation of Member States under Article 17 of the Charter of the United Nations to bear the expenses of the Organization as apportioned by the General Assembly,

1. *Reaffirms* its role in accordance with the provisions of Article 19 of the Charter of the United Nations and the advisory role of the Committee on Contributions in accordance with rule 160 of the rules of procedure of the General Assembly;

2. *Also reaffirms* its resolution 54/237 C of 23 December 1999;

3. *Requests* the Secretary-General to continue to bring to the attention of Member States the deadline specified in resolution 54/237 C, including through an early announcement in the *Journal of the United Nations* and through direct communication;

4. *Urges* all Member States requesting exemption under Article 19 of the Charter to submit as much information as possible in support of their requests and to consider submitting such information in advance of the deadline specified in resolution 54/237 C so as to enable the collation of any additional detailed information that may be necessary;

5. *Agrees* that the failure of the Central African Republic, the Comoros, Georgia, Guinea-Bissau, Liberia, the Niger, Somalia and Tajikistan to pay the full minimum amount necessary to avoid the application of Article 19 of the Charter was due to conditions beyond their control;

6. *Decides* that the Central African Republic, the Comoros, Georgia, Guinea-Bissau, Liberia, the Niger, Somalia and Tajikistan should be permitted to vote in the General Assembly until the end of its sixty-first session;

7. *Takes note* of the information provided by the Chargé d'affaires a.i. of the Permanent Mission of Sao Tome and Principe to the United Nations with regard to a request for exemption under Article 19 of the Charter;

8. *Invites* the Government of Sao Tome and Principe to submit appropriate information to the Committee on Contributions if similar circumstances prevail in the future;

9. *Agrees* that the failure of Sao Tome and Principe to pay the full minimum amount necessary to avoid the application of Article 19 of the Charter was due to conditions beyond its control;

10. *Decides* that Sao Tome and Principe should be permitted to vote in the General Assembly until the end of its sixty-first session.

Multi-year payment plans

Report of Secretary-General. Pursuant to General Assembly resolutions 57/4 B [YUN 2002, p. 1385] and 60/237 [YUN 2005, p. 1500], the Secretary-General submitted a March report [A/61/68] on multi-year payment plans, which provided information on the payment plans/schedules submitted by Georgia, Iraq, the Niger, the Republic of Moldova, Sao Tome and Principe and Tajikistan, and on the status of their implementation as at 31 December 2005. Under the plans, each year a Member State would pay for the current year's assessments and a part of its arrears, so as to eliminate the arrears within six years. However, some of the plans had durations of between 8 and 11 years. In 2005, the Republic of Moldova and Iraq exceeded payments included in their respective payment plans, and Georgia and the Niger had payments and credits applied to the assessed contributions, which exceeded the amounts foreseen in their payment plans. During the period 2000-2005, Tajikistan significantly exceeded the payments foreseen in its schedule, while Sao Tome and Principe fell short of its schedule. The Secretary-General recommended that the Assembly encourage Member States with significant arrears to consider submitting a multi-year payment plan.

Committee on Contributions. The Committee [A/61/11 & Corr.1] concluded that the system of multi-year payment plans had a positive impact in encouraging Member States to reduce their unpaid assessed contributions and demonstrate their commitment to meeting their financial obligations to the United Nations. The Committee took note of the submission of a multi-year payment plan by Liberia, including its initial payment under the plan; the completion of payments by Iraq under its plan; as well as the full payments made by Georgia and the Niger.

Other matters related to payment of assessed contributions

Scale of assessments

The General Assembly also considered the recommendations of the Committee on Contributions on the methodology for future scales of assessments, multi-year payment plans and the assessment of new Member and non-member States, in addition to the issue of the outstanding assessed contributions of the former Yugoslavia [YUN 2003, p. 1428] and the scale of assessments for peacekeeping operations (see sections below).

GENERAL ASSEMBLY ACTION

On 22 December [meeting 84], the General Assembly, on the recommendation of the Fifth Committee [A/61/512/Add.1], adopted **resolution 61/237** without vote [agenda item 122].

Scale of assessments for the apportionment of the expenses of the United Nations

The General Assembly,

Recalling its previous resolutions and decisions on the scale of assessments for the apportionment of the expenses of the United Nations, including its resolutions 43/223 B of 21 December 1988, 46/221 B of 20 December 1991, 55/5 B, C and D of 23 December 2000, 57/4 B of 20 December 2002 and 58/1 B of 23 December 2003,

Recalling in particular its resolution 55/5 B, in which it decided to fix the elements of the scale of assessments for two successive scale periods until 2006, subject to the provisions of its resolution 55/5 C,

Recalling paragraphs 5 and 6 of its resolution 58/1 B,

Noting that the application of the current methodology has led to substantial increases in the rate of assessment of some Member States, including developing countries,

Having considered the report of the Committee on Contributions,

1. *Affirms* that the determination of the scale of assessments for the apportionment of the expenses of the United Nations shall remain the prerogative of the General Assembly;

2. *Reaffirms* the obligation of all Member States to bear the expenses of the United Nations, as apportioned by the General Assembly, in conformity with Article 17, paragraph 2, of the Charter of the United Nations;

3. *Also reaffirms* the fundamental principle that the expenses of the Organization shall be apportioned broadly according to capacity to pay;

4. *Further reaffirms* that the Committee on Contributions as a technical body is required to prepare the scale of assessments strictly on the basis of reliable, verifiable and comparable data;

5. *Decides* that the scale of assessments for the period 2007-2009 shall be based on the following elements and criteria:

(*a*) Estimates of gross national income;

(*b*) Average statistical base periods of three and six years;

(*c*) Conversion rates based on market exchange rates, except where that would cause excessive fluctuations and distortions in the income of some Member States, when price-adjusted rates of exchange or other appropriate conversion rates should be employed, taking due account of its resolution 46/221 B;

(*d*) The debt-burden approach employed in the scale of assessments for the period 2004-2006;

(*e*) A low per capita income adjustment of 80 per cent, with a threshold per capita income limit of the average per capita gross national income of all Member States for the statistical base periods;

(*f*) A minimum assessment rate of 0.001 per cent;

(*g*) A maximum assessment rate for the least developed countries of 0.01 per cent;

(*h*) A maximum assessment rate of 22 per cent;

6. *Resolves* that the scale of assessments for the contributions of Member States to the regular budget of the United Nations for 2007, 2008 and 2009 shall be as follows:

Member State	*Percentage*
Afghanistan	0.001
Albania	0.006
Algeria	0.085
Andorra	0.008
Angola	0.003
Antigua and Barbuda	0.002
Argentina	0.325
Armenia	0.002
Australia	1.787
Austria	0.887
Azerbaijan	0.005
Bahamas	0.016
Bahrain	0.033
Bangladesh	0.010
Barbados	0.009
Belarus	0.020
Belgium	1.102
Belize	0.001
Benin	0.001
Bhutan	0.001
Bolivia	0.006
Bosnia and Herzegovina	0.006
Botswana	0.014
Brazil	0.876
Brunei Darussalam	0.026
Bulgaria	0.020
Burkina Faso	0.002
Burundi	0.001
Cambodia	0.001
Cameroon	0.009
Canada	2.977
Cape Verde	0.001
Central African Republic	0.001
Chad	0.001
Chile	0.161
China	2.667
Colombia	0.105
Comoros	0.001
Congo	0.001
Costa Rica	0.032
Côte d'Ivoire	0.009
Croatia	0.050
Cuba	0.054
Cyprus	0.044
Czech Republic	0.281
Democratic People's Republic of Korea	0.007

Member State	*Percentage*
Democratic Republic of the Congo	0.003
Denmark	0.739
Djibouti	0.001
Dominica	0.001
Dominican Republic	0.024
Ecuador	0.021
Egypt	0.088
El Salvador	0.020
Equatorial Guinea	0.002
Eritrea	0.001
Estonia	0.016
Ethiopia	0.003
Fiji	0.003
Finland	0.564
France	6.301
Gabon	0.008
Gambia	0.001
Georgia	0.003
Germany	8.577
Ghana	0.004
Greece	0.596
Grenada	0.001
Guatemala	0.032
Guinea	0.001
Guinea-Bissau	0.001
Guyana	0.001
Haiti	0.002
Honduras	0.005
Hungary	0.244
Iceland	0.037
India	0.450
Indonesia	0.161
Iran	0.180
Iraq	0.015
Ireland	0.445
Israel	0.419
Italy	5.079
Jamaica	0.010
Japan	16.624
Jordan	0.012
Kazakhstan	0.029
Kenya	0.010
Kiribati	0.001
Kuwait	0.182
Kyrgyzstan	0.001
Lao People's Democratic Republic	0.001
Latvia	0.018
Lebanon	0.034
Lesotho	0.001
Liberia	0.001
Libyan Arab Jamahiriya	0.062
Liechtenstein	0.010
Lithuania	0.031
Luxembourg	0.085
Madagascar	0.002
Malawi	0.001
Malaysia	0.190
Maldives	0.001
Mali	0.001
Malta	0.017
Marshall Islands	0.001
Mauritania	0.001
Mauritius	0.011
Mexico	2.257
Micronesia	0.001

Member State	*Percentage*
Moldova	0.001
Monaco	0.003
Mongolia	0.001
Montenegro	0.001
Morocco	0.042
Mozambique	0.001
Myanmar	0.005
Namibia	0.006
Nauru	0.001
Nepal	0.003
Netherlands	1.873
New Zealand	0.256
Nicaragua	0.002
Niger	0.001
Nigeria	0.048
Norway	0.782
Oman	0.073
Pakistan	0.059
Palau	0.001
Panama	0.023
Papua New Guinea	0.002
Paraguay	0.005
Peru	0.078
Philippines	0.078
Poland	0.501
Portugal	0.527
Qatar	0.085
Republic of Korea	2.173
Romania	0.070
Russian Federation	1.200
Rwanda	0.001
Saint Kitts and Nevis	0.001
Saint Lucia	0.001
Saint Vincent and the Grenadines	0.001
Samoa	0.001
San Marino	0.003
Sao Tome and Principe	0.001
Saudi Arabia	0.748
Senegal	0.004
Serbia	0.021
Seychelles	0.002
Sierra Leone	0.001
Singapore	0.347
Slovakia	0.063
Slovenia	0.096
Solomon Islands	0.001
Somalia	0.001
South Africa	0.290
Spain	2.968
Sri Lanka	0.016
Sudan	0.010
Suriname	0.001
Swaziland	0.002
Sweden	1.071
Switzerland	1.216
Syrian Arab Republic	0.016
Tajikistan	0.001
Thailand	0.186
The former Yugoslav Republic of Macedonia	0.005
Timor-Leste	0.001
Togo	0.001
Tonga	0.001
Trinidad and Tobago	0.027
Tunisia	0.031
Turkey	0.381

Member State	Percentage
Turkmenistan	0.006
Tuvalu	0.001
Uganda	0.003
Ukraine	0.045
United Arab Emirates	0.302
United Kingdom	6.642
United Republic of Tanzania	0.006
United States	22.000
Uruguay	0.027
Uzbekistan	0.008
Vanuatu	0.001
Venezuela	0.200
Viet Nam	0.024
Yemen	0.007
Zambia	0.001
Zimbabwe	0.008
Total	**100.00**

7. *Requests* the Committee on Contributions, in accordance with its mandate and the rules of procedure of the General Assembly, to review the elements of the methodology of the scale of assessments in order to reflect the capacity of Member States to pay and to report thereon to the Assembly by the main part of its sixty-third session;

8. *Resolves* that:

(a) Notwithstanding the terms of financial regulation 3.9, the Secretary-General shall be empowered to accept, at his discretion and after consultation with the Chairman of the Committee on Contributions, a portion of the contributions of Member States for the calendar years 2007, 2008 and 2009 in currencies other than the United States dollar;

(b) In accordance with financial regulation 3.8, the Holy See, which is not a member of the United Nations but which participates in certain of its activities, shall be called upon to contribute towards the expenses of the Organization for 2007, 2008 and 2009 on the basis of a notional assessment rate of 0.001 per cent, which represents the basis for the calculation of the flat annual fees to be charged to the Holy See in accordance with its resolution 44/197 B of 21 December 1989;

9. *Endorses* the recommendations of the Committee on Contributions contained in paragraph 132 of its report;

10. *Decides* that the rate of assessment for Montenegro, admitted to membership in the United Nations on 28 June 2006, shall be 0.001 per cent for 2006;

11. *Also decides* that Montenegro shall contribute at the rate of one twelfth of this percentage for each full month of membership in 2006;

12. *Further decides* that the contributions of Montenegro for 2006 shall be applied to the same basis of assessment as for other Member States, except that, in the case of appropriations or apportionments approved by the General Assembly for the financing of peacekeeping operations, the contributions of Montenegro, as determined by the level of contributions for peacekeeping operations to which it is assigned in 2006, pursuant to the provisions of Assembly resolution 55/235 of 23 December 2000, shall be calculated in proportion to the calendar year;

13. *Decides* that the assessments of Montenegro for 2006 shall be deducted from those of the former Serbia and Montenegro for that year;

14. *Also decides* that, in accordance with financial regulation 3.7, the advance of Montenegro to the Working Capital Fund shall be calculated by the application of its rate of assessment for 2006 to the authorized level of the Fund and should be added to the Fund, pending its incorporation in a 100 per cent scale for the Fund for 2006-2007, pursuant to the related provisions of General Assembly resolution 60/283 of 7 July 2006,

15. *Notes* that, pursuant to its resolution 47/217 of 23 December 1992, the assessment of Montenegro for the Peacekeeping Reserve Fund will be calculated by the application of its first rate of assessment for peacekeeping operations to the authorized level of the Fund;

16. *Takes note* of the report of the Secretary-General on multi-year payment plans and of the related conclusions and recommendations of the Committee on Contributions;

17. *Reaffirms* paragraph 1 of its resolution 57/4 B;

18. *Urges* all Member States to pay their assessed contributions in full, on time and without imposing conditions;

19. *Encourages* Member States in arrears with their assessed contributions to the United Nations to consider submitting multi-year payment plans.

Also on 22 December, the Assembly decided that the item on the scale of assessments for the apportionment of the expenses of the United Nations would remain for consideration during its resumed sixty-first (2007) session (**decision 61/552**).

Apportionment of costs of UN peacekeeping operations

In a July report with a later addendum [A/61/139 & Corr.1 & A/61/139/Add.1], the Secretary-General described the implementation of resolution 55/235 [YUN 2000, p. 102], by which the Assembly had adopted a new system of adjustments of the scale of assessments for the regular budget to be used in fixing rates of assessment applicable to Member States for peacekeeping operations, and resolution 55/236 [ibid., p. 104] establishing the criteria for voluntary movements within that system. Annexed to the report were: the list of peacekeeping levels, based on average per capita gross national income (GNI) of Member States and other factors (annex I); and a table showing the initial levels and voluntary movements for 2006, the initial composition of levels and assumed voluntary movements for 2007-2009 and relevant transitional periods, and the respective percentage of rates of assessment for the regular budget payable by each Member State for peacekeeping operations during 2007-2009 (annex II).

Also annexed were the effective rates of assessment for 1 January 2007 to 31 December 2009, based on the application of the methodology used in preparing the scale of assessments for 2004-2006 to GNI data for 1999-2004. The updated composition of levels, reflected in annex II, would be used, together with the 2007-2009 scale of assessments, to establish each Member State's peacekeeping assessments during the Assembly's consideration of the question at its sixty-first (2006) session.

Based on national income and population data available at the UN Statistics Division, the Committee on Contributions [A/61/11 & Corr.1] recommended that the rate of assessment of Montenegro in 2006 should be 0.001 per cent, and that both Serbia and Montenegro be assigned to level I in 2006.

In March, the Philippines, which had voluntarily contributed to peacekeeping operations at a rate higher than required, requested that it be allowed to return to level I of the peacekeeping scale in view of the significant increase in the peacekeeping budget over the last three years and the economic situation that made it difficult for the country to meet its financial obligations to the United Nations. In keeping with the fundamental principle of capacity to pay, the change of the Philippines from level H to level I was reflected in the updated composition of levels (annex II).

GENERAL ASSEMBLY ACTION

On 22 December [meeting 84], the General Assembly, on the recommendation of the Fifth Committee [A/61/665], adopted **resolution 61/243** without vote [agenda item 131]

Scale of assessments for the apportionment of the expenses of United Nations peacekeeping operations

The General Assembly,

Recalling its resolutions 55/235 and 55/236 of 23 December 2000 and 58/256 of 23 December 2003,

Recalling also its request to the Secretary-General in paragraph 15 of resolution 55/235 to update the composition of the levels of contribution of Member States for peacekeeping operations described in the resolution on a triennial basis, in conjunction with the regular budget scale of assessment reviews, in accordance with the criteria established in the resolution, and to report thereon to the General Assembly,

Recalling further its request to the Secretary-General in paragraph 3 of resolution 58/256 to report to it at its sixty-first session on the updating of the composition of levels of contribution for peacekeeping operations for the period from 2007 to 2009, in accordance with the provisions of resolution 55/235,

Recalling its decision, in paragraph 16 of resolution 55/235, to review the structure of levels of contribution for peacekeeping operations after nine years,

Having considered the report of the Secretary-General on the implementation of resolutions 55/235 and 55/236,

1. *Takes note* of the report of the Secretary-General;
2. *Endorses* the updated composition of levels to be applied in adjusting regular budget scale rates to establish Member States' rates of assessment for peacekeeping operations for the period from 2007 to 2009;
3. *Decides* that Montenegro and Serbia should both be assigned to level I for 2006;
4. *Also decides* to review the structure of levels of contribution for peacekeeping operations at its sixty-fourth session;
5. *Requests* the Secretary-General to report to the General Assembly at its sixty-fourth session on the updating of the composition of levels of contribution for peacekeeping operations for the period from 2010 to 2012 in the light of the decision of the Assembly to review the structure of levels.

Also on 22 December, by **decision 61/552**, the Assembly decided that the item on the scale of assessments for the apportionment of the expenses of UN peacekeeping operations would remain for consideration during its resumed sixty-first (2007) session.

Scale methodology

Committee on Contributions. Pursuant to General Assembly resolution 58/1 B [YUN 2003, p. 1424], the Committee on Contributions [A/61/11 & Corr.1] continued to review the different elements of the methodology for preparing future scales of assessments, focusing on elements relating to income measure; conversion rates; the base period; debt-burden adjustment; low per capita income adjustment; minimum (floor) and maximum (ceiling) assessment rates; and other possible elements for the scale methodology. It decided to review the scale of assessments for the period 2007-2009.

With regard to income measure, the Committee recommended that the scale of assessments for 2007-2009 should be based on the most current, comprehensive and comparable data available for GNI. In that context, data up to 2004 would be used in preparing the next scale. The Committee considered the purchasing power parity (PPP) and the World Bank Atlas methods as conversion rates. It noted that the Atlas method, which was based on a three-year moving average and incorporated some price adjustment, smoothed exchange rate fluctuations to a degree, but did not address problems such as the situation of countries whose exchange rate was fixed for many years. Regarding PPP, for which a survey was under way for 147 countries, some members felt that it could be a useful approach to measuring capacity to pay, as the cost of living in different countries using market exchange rates (MERs) was different. Other members expressed concern that PPP did not measure capacity to pay in United States dollars, as it included goods and services that were not tradable internationally. Concern was also expressed about the variable quality of the data, given that PPP was not available for many countries. Consequently, the Committee recommended the use of conversion rates on MERs, and price-adjusted rates of exchange or other appropriate conversion rates in instances where it would cause excessive fluctuations and distortions in the income of some Member States. The question of the level of the threshold figures of plus 50 per cent or minus 33 per cent in changes in per capita GNI in United States dollars and MER valuation index figures of 1.2 and 0.8 would be considered at future sessions of the Committee. The Committee also decided to consider questions related to debt-burden adjustment, the base period, low per capita income and automatic annual recalculation of the scale at future sessions, on the basis of any guidance from the General Assembly.

Following its review of which MERs should be replaced, the Committee decided that a better basis for recommendations would be to focus attention on countries whose MER valuation index (MVI) reflected overvaluation or undervaluation of over 50 per cent, while basing the adjustment on the MVI figure of 1.2 to 0.8. The Committee adjusted the conversion rates of Afghanistan, Angola, Turkmenistan and Zimbabwe; used UN operational rates of exchange for Myanmar and the Syrian Arab Republic and official rates for the Democratic People's Republic of Korea; and applied MERs for Argentina.

To assess the impact of the inclusion of new GNI data in calculations for the 2007-2009 scale, including the decisions on data and conversion rates but excluding the effects of any methodological changes, the Committee considered the application of the new data to the methodology used in preparing the scale of assessments. On the basis of those results and the application of the current methodology, the Committee identified 21 Member States whose rates of assessment for 2007-2009 would increase or decrease by more than 50 per cent, compared to the rates recommended by the Committee on Contributions for 2004-2006. The Committee did not consider that any of them necessitated any further adjustments.

Communications. On 22 May [A/60/859], Japan transmitted to the Committee on Contributions a proposal for the preparation of the scale of assessments for the 2007-2009 period. Mexico had also submitted proposals on 28 April and 3 May.

The Committee took note of the representations.

Assessment of new Member State and non-member State

The Committee on Contributions [A/61/11 & Corr.1] also considered the assessments for one new Member State (Montenegro), which was admitted to UN membership on 28 June 2006 (see p. 472) and one non-member State (the Holy See). The Committee recommended that Montenegro be assessed at the rate of 0.001 per cent for 2006, that it should pay six-twelfths of that rate for 2006, based on its date of admission; and that those assessments should be deducted from those of the former Serbia and Montenegro. The Committee also recommended continuation of the simplified methodology for assessing non-member States, endorsed by the Assembly in resolution 58/1 [YUN 2003, p. 1424] and that the flat annual fee percentage of the Holy See should remain fixed at 50 per cent. The Committee also recommended that the notional rate of assessment for the Holy See for the 2007-2009 period should be fixed at 0.001 per cent.

Outstanding assessed contributions

On 2 November [A/C.5/61/11], Slovenia, on behalf of the successor States of the Socialist Federal Republic of Yugoslavia, presented a proposal for the final resolution of the issue of the unpaid assessed contributions of the former Yugoslavia [YUN 2003, p. 1428]. The proposal established the unpaid assessed amount at $784,545. Each successor State would remit the equitable portion of that amount in accordance with the 2001 Agreement on Succession Issues [YUN 2001, p. 323]. Any sum that could be considered outstanding that exceeded that amount should be reversed in the books and records of the United Nations.

On 22 December, by **decision 61/551 B**, the General Assembly deferred until its sixty-second (2007) session consideration of the Secretary-General's report on unpaid assessed contributions [YUN 2005, p. 1502] and his note on outstanding assessed contributions of the former Yugoslavia [YUN 2003, p. 1428], his letter dated 27 December 2001 to the Assembly President [YUN 2001, p. 1325], as well as the letter from Slovenia (see above).

Accounts and auditing

The General Assembly, at its resumed sixtieth (2006) session, considered the report of the Board of Auditors on UN peacekeeping operations for the period 1 July 2004 to 30 June 2005 [A/60/5, vol. II & Corr.1], together with the Secretary-General's report on the implementation of the Board's recommendations [A/60/691] and ACABQ related comments and recommendations [A/60/784].

On 30 June, the Assembly, in **resolution 60/234 B**, endorsed the Board's report (see p. 98).

Board of Auditors report. The Chairman of the Board of Auditors transmitted to the Secretary-General the financial reports and audited financial statements for the biennium ended 31 December 2005 on the United Nations [A/61/5, vol. I] and on the following 13 entities: the International Trade Centre UNCTAD/WTO [A/61/5, vol. III], the United Nations University [A/61/5, vol. IV], the United Nations Development Programme (UNDP) [A/61/5/Add.1], the United Nations Children's Fund [A/61/5/Add.2], the United Nations Relief and Works Agency for Palestine Refugees in the Near East [A/61/5/Add.3], the United Nations Institute for Training and Research [A/61/5/Add.4], the voluntary funds administered by the United Nations High Commissioner for Refugees [A/61/5/Add.5], the Fund of the United Nations Environment Programme (UNEP) [A/61/5/Add.6], the United Nations Population Fund (UNFPA) [A/61/5/Add.7], the United Nations Human Settlements Programme [A/61/5/Add.8], the Fund of the United Nations International Drug Control Programme [A/61/5/Add.9], the International Criminal Tribunal for the Prosecution of Persons Responsible for Genocide and Other Serious Violations of International Humanitarian Law Committed in the Territory of Rwanda and Rwandan Citizens Responsible for Genocide and Other Such Violations Committed in the Territory of Neighbouring States between 1 January and 31 December 1994 [A/61/5/Add.11 & Corr.1] and the International Tribunal for the Prosecution of Persons Responsible for Serious Violations of International Humanitarian Law Committed in the Territory of the Former Yugoslavia since 1991 [A/61/5/Add.12 & Corr.1]. The Board submitted its report on the financial statements of the United Nations Joint Staff Pension Fund for the biennium ended 31 December 2005, which was incorporated into the report of the UN Joint Staff Pension Board [A/61/9].

Introducing the reports in the Fifth Committee [A/C.5/61/SR.4], the Chairman of the Board drew attention to improvements in their presentation, including the identification in the annex of each report of the financial period in which the Board's recommendations had initially been made, in order to reflect the ageing of those recommendations which had not been fully implemented, and the introduction of an executive summary, providing a snapshot of the financial and operational condition of a particular organization. He stated that the report of the UN Office for Project Services [A/61/5/Add.10], which had postponed submission of its financial statements to the Board until 30 November 2006, was not included in the 15 reports before the Committee, and that the report on the capital master plan project would be introduced at a later date.

According to the Chairman, the Board had issued an unqualified opinion on the financial statements of each of the organizations audited during the 2004-2005 biennium. Regarding UNDP, it was concerned that the Programme had not analysed the audit qualifications regarding modified audit opinions relating to material amounts, which auditors of national projects had put in since 2004; bank accounts had not been reconciled on a monthly basis, which could have resulted in fraud and errors going undetected; and controls for the new enterprise resource planning system (ATLAS) introduced during the biennium were deficient in several respects. With regard to UNFPA, a number of modified opinions were issued in the independent audit reports for national projects. At UNEP, the figures for non-expendable property in the financial statements differed from the inventory report, where property was shown at market value instead of acquisition cost.

On management deficiencies and the fraudulent use of resources, the Board would submit a concise summary of its principal findings and conclusions for the biennium (see below). Concerning non-expendable property, the Board noted the inclusion in a number of inventory reports of various items which could not be traced or accounted for; the lack of a physical count, resulting in the exclusion of items; and inconsistency in the valuation of items. On liabilities for end-of-service and post-retirement benefits, only about $200 million of the actuarial valuations for after-service health insurance had been funded at the time of the audit, out of an estimated combined liability of over $3 billion. The Chairman pointed out that the impact of those two factors on implementation of the International Public Sector Accounting Standards (IPSAS) should not be underestimated.

By a July note [A/61/182], the Secretary-General transmitted to the Assembly a concise summary of the Board's principal findings, conclusions and recommendations, classified by audit area. According to the note, nine of the 15 audited organizations had reported cases of fraud and presumptive fraud for the financial period that ended 31 December 2005. The administrations had informed the Board that they had taken action against the perpetrators, in addition to strengthening controls to prevent recurrences. The Board noted that some country offices had not submitted information on fraud and presumptive fraud to their headquarters. Although an ethics office had been established and financial disclosure statements introduced, fraud prevention was still under consideration by the United Nations and a common approach had yet to be defined.

In August, the Secretary-General submitted reports on measures taken to implement the Board's recommendations on the accounts of the United Nations for the biennium ended 31 December 2005 [A/61/214], and on the financial statements of the UN funds and programmes for that period [A/61/214/Add.1]. The related comments and observations of ACABQ were contained in its September report [A/61/350].

GENERAL ASSEMBLY ACTION

On 22 December [meeting 84], the General Assembly, on the recommendation of the Fifth Committee [A/61/631], adopted **resolution 61/233 A** without vote [agenda item 115].

Financial reports and audited financial statements, and reports of the Board of Auditors

The General Assembly,

Reaffirming its resolutions 50/222 of 11 April 1996, 51/218 E of 17 June 1997, 52/212 B of 31 March 1998, 53/204 of 18 December 1998, 53/221, section VIII, of 7 April 1999, 54/13 B of 23 December 1999, 55/220 A of 23 December 2000, 55/220 B and C of 12 April and 14 June 2001, 57/278 A of 20 December 2002 and 60/234 A of 23 December 2005 and 60/234 B of 30 June 2006,

Having considered, for the period ended 31 December 2005, the financial reports and audited financial statements and the reports and audit opinions of the Board of Auditors on the United Nations, the International Trade Centre UNCTAD/WTO, the United Nations University, the United Nations Development Programme, the United Nations Children's Fund, the United Nations Relief and Works Agency for Palestine Refugees in the Near East, the United Nations Institute for Training and Research, the voluntary funds administered by the United Nations High Commissioner for Refugees, the Fund of the United Nations Environment Programme, the United Nations Population Fund, the United Nations Human Settlements Programme, the Fund of the United Nations International Drug Control Programme, the International Criminal Tribunal for the Prosecution of Persons Responsible for Genocide and Other Serious Violations of International Humanitarian Law Committed in the Territory of Rwanda and Rwandan Citizens Responsible for Genocide and Other Such Violations Committed in the Territory of Neighbouring States between 1 January and 31 December 1994 and the International Tribunal for the Prosecution of Persons Responsible for Serious Violations of International Humanitarian Law Committed in the Territory of the Former Yugoslavia since 1991, the concise summary of principal findings and conclusions contained in the reports prepared by the Board of Auditors, the reports of the Secretary-General on the implementation of the recommendations of the Board of Auditors on the accounts of the United Nations as well as on the implementation of its recommendations on the financial statements of the funds and programmes of the United Nations for the financial period ended 31 December 2005, and the report of the Advisory Committee on Administrative and Budgetary Questions,

1. *Accepts* the financial reports and audited financial statements and the reports and audit opinions of the Board of Auditors for the above-mentioned organizations;

2. *Approves* the recommendations and conclusions contained in the reports of the Board of Auditors;

3. *Endorses* the observations and recommendations contained in the report of the Advisory Committee on Administrative and Budgetary Questions;

4. *Recalls* the relevant provisions of the Financial Regulations and Rules of the United Nations;

5. *Notes* that the opinion expressed in paragraph 28 of the report of the Advisory Committee on Administrative and Budgetary Questions does not constitute another request by the Advisory Committee for certain specific examinations;

6. *Emphasizes* that the Board of Auditors shall be completely independent and solely responsible for the conduct of the audit;

7. *Decides* to consider further the reports of the Board of Auditors on the International Criminal Tribunal for Rwanda and the International Tribunal for the Former Yugoslavia under the respective agenda items relating to the Tribunals;

8. *Expresses concern* that the United Nations Office for Project Services was unable to submit its financial statements to the Board of Auditors and thereby prevented the Board from expressing an opinion on the financial statements, and requests the Office to ensure that this situation is not repeated in future;

9. *Notes* that the report of the Board of Auditors on the financial statements of the United Nations Office for Project Services will be submitted to the General Assembly at the first part of its resumed sixty-first session;

10. *Commends* the Board of Auditors for the superior quality of its reports, in particular with respect to its comments on the management of resources and improving the presentation of financial statements;

11. *Recalls* section VI, paragraph 12, of its resolution 57/292 of 20 December 2002 and paragraph 1 of its resolution 58/267 A of 23 December 2003;

12. *Encourages* the Secretary-General to take into account the relevant experience of the funds and programmes of the United Nations in the process of replacing the Integrated Management Information System with a next-generation enterprise resource planning system or other comparable system, with a view to properly assessing and taking into account the risks and challenges involved in implementing and maintaining such a system;

13. *Recalls* section II, paragraph 5, of its resolution 60/283 of 7 July 2006, and requests the Secretary-General to include information on the measures taken to ensure that the United Nations benefits from the experience gained by its funds and programmes in the implementation of a next-generation enterprise resource planning system or other comparable system, as well as proposals to address any potential problem areas;

14. *Welcomes* the information contained in the report of the Board of Auditors and its focus on the implementation of the International Public Sector Accounting Standards in the United Nations system, and emphasizes the importance of appropriate audit coverage on this issue in its future reports;

15. *Requests* the Secretary-General to include, in his report to be submitted to it at the first part of its resumed sixty-first session, information on its decision on the accounting task force and its interaction with other entities that will be affected by the implementation of the International Public Sector Accounting Standards, as well as the status of implementation and outstanding requirements;

16. *Takes note* of the reports of the Secretary-General on the implementation of the recommendations of the Board of Auditors on the accounts of the United Nations as well as on the implementation of its recommendations on the financial statements of the funds and programmes of the United Nations for the financial period ended 31 December 2005;

17. *Reiterates its request* to the Secretary-General and the executive heads of the funds and programmes of the United Nations to ensure full implementation of the recommendations of the Board of Auditors and the related recommendations of the Advisory Committee on Administrative and Budgetary Questions in a prompt and timely manner and to hold programme managers accountable for non-implementation of the recommendations;

18. *Requests* the Secretary-General to provide in his reports on the implementation of the recommendations of the Board of Auditors on the accounts of the United Nations as well as on the financial statements of its funds and programmes a full explanation for the delays in the implementation of the recommendations of the Board, in particular those recommendations not yet fully implemented which are two or more years old;

19. *Also requests* the Secretary-General to indicate in future reports an expected time frame for the implementation of the recommendations of the Board of Auditors, as well as the priorities for their implementation and the office holders to be held accountable;

20. *Emphasizes* that the forthcoming change of management should not hinder the implementation of the recommendations of the Board of Auditors;

21. *Requests* the Secretary-General, in accordance with paragraph 6 of its resolution 59/264 A of 23 December 2004, to take the necessary measures to make certain that the editing and translation of the reports of the Board of Auditors are completed in a manner that would ensure that they are submitted to the General Assembly in accordance with the six-week rule and thereby enable Member States to have adequate time to consider the large volume of reports prior to the sixty-third session of the Assembly.

Also on 22 December, the Assembly decided that the item on the financial reports and audited financial statements and the reports of the Board of Auditors would remain for consideration during its resumed sixty-first (2007) session (**decision 61/552**).

On the same date, by **resolution 61/245** (see p. 1573), the Assembly requested the Secretary-General to submit revised terms of reference for the establishment of the Independent Audit Advisory Committee, as decided in resolution 60/248 [YUN 2005, p. 1694].

Review of UN administrative and financial functioning

Pursuant to decision 60/551 [YUN 2005, p. 1503], the Fifth Committee resumed its deliberation on the review of the efficiency of the administrative and financial functioning of the United Nations, which included its previous review of the Secretary-General's reports on efforts by the Department of Management to improve its practices [ibid., p. 1470] and on measures to strengthen accountability at the United Nations [ibid., p. 1513], and the related ACABQ report [ibid., p. 1514]; and the establishment of an Ethics Office [ibid., p. 1476]. The Committee also had before it the Secretary-General's note on strengthening the investigation functions in the United Nations [A/60/674] (see p. 1651).

GENERAL ASSEMBLY ACTION

On 8 May [meeting 79], the General Assembly, on the recommendation of the Fifth Committee [A/60/609/Add.1], adopted **resolution 60/254** without vote [agenda item 122].

Review of the efficiency of the administrative and financial functioning of the United Nations

The General Assembly,

Recalling its resolutions 41/213 of 19 December 1986, 54/236 of 23 December 1999 and 59/264 A, 59/272 and 59/275 of 23 December 2004,

Recalling also the importance of accountability and transparency to the Organization,

Having considered the reports of the Secretary-General and the related report of the Advisory Committee on Administrative and Budgetary Questions,

Measures to strengthen the accountability framework

1. *Takes note* of the report of the Secretary-General on measures to strengthen accountability at the United Nations;

2. *Also takes note* of the additional elements that are intended to strengthen the accountability framework, which would seem to be somewhat fragmented;

3. *Requests* the Secretary-General to further strengthen the current framework by establishing and ensuring an effective system of accountability that clearly defines the lines of authority and responsibility, as well as the respective roles of the individual elements of the framework, and efforts aimed at improving coordination between them in order to avoid duplication;

Monitoring and evaluation/performance measures

4. *Stresses* the importance of ensuring that programme managers objectively evaluate programme performance and, in this context, that the Office of Internal Oversight Services should validate self-evaluation and reporting on programme performance by managers;

5. *Requests* the Secretary-General to ensure that programme managers understand and respect the monitoring and evaluation functions performed by the oversight bodies;

6. *Notes* that the electronic performance appraisal system is the formal tool employed by the Secretariat in managing staff performance and that it represents an enhancement of the performance appraisal system;

7. *Decides* that staff performance assessment should be further enhanced in order to strengthen performance management to ensure the accountable implementation of legislative mandates, and in this regard calls upon the Secretary-General to improve performance management measures, including:

(a) A system that recognizes competence as an integral element of performance management and eventual career advancement;

(b) A comprehensive range of measures to address underperformance as well as incentives to encourage outstanding performance;

(c) Establishing direct links between performance and career advancement;

Governance review

8. *Recalls* its resolutions 57/278 A of 20 December 2002 and 59/264 A, and notes that there will be a separate report on the independent external evaluation of the auditing and oversight system of the United Nations, including the specialized agencies, as well as one on a comprehensive governance review;

9. *Notes* that the focus of the comprehensive governance review should be, inter alia, to clarify the roles and responsibilities of management with respect to supporting Member States, and emphasizes the intergovernmental nature of the Organization and its international character;

Oversight bodies

10. *Reaffirms* the importance of respecting the independent nature of the internal and external oversight structures of the United Nations, and recognizes that they are key governance partners;

11. *Recalls* its resolution 59/272 and, bearing in mind paragraph 4 of the report of the Advisory Committee on Administrative and Budgetary Questions, decides to revert to the issue of the terms of reference and title of the high-level follow-up mechanism in the context of its consideration of the report on the independent external evaluation of the auditing and oversight system of the United Nations, including the specialized agencies;

12. *Stresses* the importance of ensuring the full implementation of the recommendations of the oversight bodies, and requests the Secretary-General to ensure that managers are held accountable for the delay or non-implementation of oversight recommendations;

Fraud and corruption

13. *Recalls* its resolution 59/264 A and the recommendations of the Board of Auditors concerning fraud and corruption, and requests the Secretary-General to report to the General Assembly on measures taken to implement the recommendations;

Procurement

14. *Also recalls* its resolutions 57/279 of 20 December 2002 and 59/288 of 13 April 2005, and requests the Secretary-General to continue efforts to make the procurement policies and practices of the United Nations system more transparent, efficient and effective;

Enhancing transparency

15. *Notes* the steps taken by the Secretary-General to institute greater transparency in the appointment of some senior-level positions, including through continued consideration of the applicants put forward by Member States at the request of the Secretary-General;

Ethics Office

16. *Welcomes* the establishment of the Ethics Office, and notes the Secretary-General's bulletin thereon, and in this respect:

(a) Urges the Secretary-General to finalize a system-wide code of ethics for all United Nations personnel, including personnel of the funds and programmes, at an early date;

(b) Requests the Secretary-General to administer and monitor more extensive disclosure of financial and other interests by United Nations officials in accordance with the amended Staff Regulations and to ensure enhanced protection for those who reveal wrongdoing within the Organization;

(c) Endorses the main responsibilities of the Ethics Office as outlined by the Secretary-General in his report and as established by the Secretary-General's bulletin;

(d) Emphasizes that the administration of policy by the Ethics Office for protection of staff against retaliation

when reporting misconduct should be carried out in close cooperation with the Office of Internal Oversight Services and the Office of Human Resources Management;

(e) Also emphasizes that training programmes to cover the range of ethics issues should be designed by the Ethics Office in coordination with the Office of Human Resources Management;

(f) Recognizes the need for incrementally requiring all pertinent staff, in particular those in high-risk areas, to provide relevant financial disclosure, and requests the Secretary-General to report thereon to the General Assembly at its sixty-first session in the context of his report on the activities of the Ethics Office;

(g) Requests the Secretary-General to present a comprehensive review to the General Assembly at the main part of its sixty-second session, as recommended by the Advisory Committee on Administrative and Budgetary Questions in its report, which should include, inter alia, his views on the possible establishment of a group of internationally representative experts to provide periodic, independent assessments of the Ethics Office for the consideration of the Assembly;

(h) Also requests the Secretary-General, in the context of the comprehensive review referred to above, to report on staff perception of the impact of the Ethics Office on improving ethics and integrity in the Organization;

(i) Further requests the Secretary-General to report on the activities of the Ethics Office and the implementation of ethics policies, in the context of his annual report, for the consideration and decision of the General Assembly, as appropriate, under the agenda item relating to human resources management;

Management practices

17. *Takes note* of the report of the Secretary-General on the contribution made by the Department of Management to the improvement of management practices and the time-bound plan for the reduction of duplication, complexity and bureaucracy in the United Nations administrative processes and procedures;

Reporting requirement

18. *Endorses* the recommendations of the Advisory Committee on Administrative and Budgetary Questions as contained in paragraph 12 of its report, and requests the Secretary-General to report thereon to the General Assembly under the relevant agenda items, as well as on an overview of the status of implementation of the provisions of the present resolution, as appropriate.

On 22 December, the Assembly decided that the item on the review of the efficiency of the administrative and financial functioning of the United Nations would remain for consideration during its resumed sixty-first (2007) session (**decision 61/552**).

Administrative and budgetary coordination

CEB report. By a July note [A/61/203 & Corr.1,2], the Secretary-General transmitted to the General Assembly the United Nations System Chief Executives Board (CEB) for Coordination statistical report on the budgetary and financial situation of the organizations of the UN system, which included information on regular resources, extrabudgetary resources, total expenditure, assessed contributions and working capital funds. The Assembly took note of the report on 22 December (**decision 61/548**).

Also on 22 December, the Assembly decided that the item on the administrative and budgetary coordination of the United Nations with the specialized agencies and the International Atomic Energy Agency would remain for consideration during its resumed sixty-first (2007) session (**decision 61/552**).

Programme planning

Strategic framework for 2008-2009

In July, the Secretary-General submitted the proposed strategic framework for 2008-2009 [A/61/6 (Part one) & (Prog.1-27)], as a translation of legislative mandates into programmes and subprogrammes, which constituted the principal policy directive of the United Nations and served as the basis for programme planning, budgeting, monitoring and evaluation. The framework comprised two parts: the plan outline (Part one) and the biennial programme plan (Part two), covering 27 programmes. The priorities for the 2008-2009 biennium, proposed for reaffirmation by the Assembly, included: maintenance of international peace and security; promotion of sustained economic growth and development; development of Africa; promotion of human rights; coordination of humanitarian assistance; promotion of justice and international law; disarmament; and drug control, crime prevention and combating international terrorism. The security and safety coordination subprogramme and the regional field coordination and support subprogramme were combined into a new programme, Safety and security (programme 27).

The Committee for Programme and Coordination (CPC) [A/61/16 & Corr.1], having examined the Secretary-General's proposed 2008-2009 strategic framework, recommended that the Assembly approve the priorities for the 2008-2009 biennium contained in the plan outline in Part one and the programme narrative of 26 of the 27 programmes, with certain modifications. The Assembly should request the Secretary-General to revise the plan outline to ensure that it accurately captured the Organization's longer-term objectives, based on mandates approved by Member States, and that the Assembly allocate, for review and action, subprogramme 1 of programme 7, Economic and social affairs, to the Second (Economic and Financial) Committee and programme 19, Human rights, to the Third (Social, Humanitarian and Cultural) Committee.

On 4, 6 and 14 December, the General Assembly took note, respectively, of the reports of the Sixth (Legal) [A/61/459] (**decision 61/510**), First (Disarmament and International Security) [A/61/403] (**decision 61/517**) and Fourth (Special Political and Decolonization) Committees [A/61/417] (**decision 61/524**).

On 20 December, the Assembly, on the recommendation of the Third Committee [A/61/447], approved programme 19, Human rights (**decision 61/533**), and on the recommendation of the Second Committee [A/61/431], approved subprogramme 1, Economic and Social Council support and coordination, of programme 7, Economic and social affairs (**decision 61/545**), of the proposed strategic framework for 2008-2009.

GENERAL ASSEMBLY ACTION

On 22 December [meeting 84], the General Assembly, on the recommendation of the Fifth Committee [A/61/653], adopted **resolution 61/235** without vote [agenda item 118].

Programme planning

The General Assembly,

Recalling its resolutions 37/234 of 21 December 1982, 38/227 A of 20 December 1983, 41/213 of 19 December 1986, 55/234 of 23 December 2000, 56/253 of 24 December 2001, 57/282 of 20 December 2002, 58/268 and 58/269 of 23 December 2003, 59/275 of 23 December 2004 and 60/257 of 8 May 2006,

Recalling also the terms of reference of the Committee for Programme and Coordination, as outlined in the annex to Economic and Social Council resolution 2008 (LX) of 14 May 1976,

Having considered the report of the Committee for Programme and Coordination on the work of its forty-sixth session, the proposed strategic framework for the period 2008-2009: part one: plan outline and part two: biennial programme plan, the proposed revisions to the biennial programme plan and priorities for the period 2006-2007, the report of the Secretary-General on the programme performance of the United Nations for the biennium 2004-2005 and the report of the Office of Internal Oversight Services on strengthening the role of evaluation and the application of evaluation findings in programme design, delivery and policy directives,

1. *Re-emphasizes* the role of the plenary and the Main Committees of the General Assembly in reviewing and taking action on the appropriate recommendations of the Committee for Programme and Coordination relevant to their work, in accordance with regulation 4.10 of the Regulations and Rules Governing Programme Planning, the Programme Aspects of the Budget, the Monitoring of Implementation and the Methods of Evaluation;

2. *Requests* the General Committee to take fully into account resolutions 56/253, 57/282, 59/275 and 60/257 in the allocation of agenda items to the Main Committees;

Proposed strategic framework for the period 2008-2009

3. *Endorses* the conclusions and recommendations of the Committee for Programme and Coordination on the proposed biennial programme plan for the period 2008-2009 contained in the report of the Committee on the work of its forty-sixth session, subject to the provisions of the present resolution and the additional modifications contained in the annex hereto;

4. *Decides* not to take a decision on the content of part one: plan outline of the proposed strategic framework for the period 2008-2009;

5. *Decides* that the priorities for the period 2008-2009 shall be the following:

(a) Maintenance of international peace and security;

(b) Promotion of sustained economic growth and sustainable development in accordance with the relevant resolutions of the General Assembly and recent United Nations conferences;

(c) Development of Africa;

(d) Promotion of human rights;

(e) Effective coordination of humanitarian assistance efforts;

(f) Promotion of justice and international law;

(g) Disarmament;

(h) Drug control, crime prevention and combating international terrorism in all its forms and manifestations;

6. *Stresses* that setting the priorities of the United Nations is the prerogative of the Member States, as reflected in legislative mandates;

7. *Also stresses* the need for Member States to participate fully in the budget preparation process, from its early stages and throughout the process;

8. *Requests* the Secretary-General to prepare the proposed programme budget for the biennium 2008-2009 on the basis of the above priorities and the biennial programme plan as adopted in the present resolution;

Programme performance report

9. *Takes note* of the report of the Secretary-General on the programme performance of the United Nations for the biennium 2004-2005;

10. *Endorses* the conclusions and recommendations of the Committee for Programme and Coordination regarding the report of the Secretary-General, contained in chapter II, section A, of its report;

11. *Stresses* that, while future reports on programme performance will be more aligned with the objectives,

expected accomplishments and indicators of achievement, information on the outputs shall continue to be provided in the reports;

12. *Recognizes* the role of the Committee for Programme and Coordination in monitoring and evaluation, and encourages the Committee, in reviewing performance and evaluation reports, to provide, inter alia, action-oriented recommendations aimed at enhancing the effectiveness and impact of the activities of the Organization;

13. *Requests* the Secretary-General to ensure that future programme performance reports provide more detailed information on the reasons for the less-than-full implementation of programmed outputs or the postponement or termination thereof;

Evaluation

14. *Endorses* the conclusions and recommendations of the Committee for Programme and Coordination on evaluation, contained in chapter II, section C, of its report;

15. *Recalls* paragraphs 9 and 10 of its resolution 60/257, and encourages intergovernmental bodies to make use of the findings set out in the programme performance reports of the Secretary-General and evaluation reports in planning and policymaking;

16. *Also recalls* paragraphs 14 and 15 of its resolution 60/257, and requests the Secretary-General to report thereon to the General Assembly at its sixty-second session;

17. *Requests* the Secretary-General to submit proposals to the General Assembly at its sixty-second session to improve the links between monitoring, evaluation, programme planning and budgeting;

Coordination questions

18. *Endorses* the conclusions and recommendations of the Committee for Programme and Coordination on the annual overview report of the United Nations System Chief Executives Board for Coordination for 2005-2006, contained in chapter III, section A, of its report, and on the New Partnership for Africa's Development and the report of the Joint Inspection Unit, contained in chapter III, section B;

19. *Invites* the Economic and Social Council to utilize the relevant conclusions and recommendations of the Committee for Programme and Coordination when considering related reports of the Chief Executives Board;

Improving the working methods and procedures of the Committee for Programme and Coordination within the framework of its mandate

20. *Recalls* its resolutions 58/269, 59/275 and 60/257;

21. *Recognizes* the efforts of the Committee for Programme and Coordination during its forty-sixth session to improve its working methods and procedures;

22. *Invites* the Committee for Programme and Coordination, at its forty-seventh session, within the framework of its mandate, to continue its consideration of the agenda item on improving the working methods and procedures of the Committee for Programme and Coordination within the framework of its mandate.

Annex

Additional modifications to the proposed biennial programme plan for the period 2008-2009

Programme 10
Trade and development

Subprogramme 2
Investment, enterprise and technology

Expected accomplishment *(c)* should read as follows: "Improved opportunities for enterprises in developing countries and countries with economies in transition to enhance their competitiveness through deepened linkages between domestic and foreign firms and better understanding of emerging issues in accounting and reporting standards, corporate responsibility, transparency and good corporate practices".

Indicator of achievement *(c)* should read as follows: "Increased percentage of countries indicating that policy advice and technical assistance provided by the United Nations Conference on Trade and Development (UNCTAD) were useful in the design of policies aimed at enhancing the competitiveness of their enterprises".

Strategy

Paragraph 10.9 should read as follows: "This subprogramme is implemented under the responsibility of the Division on Investment, Technology and Enterprise Development. To achieve the objective of the subprogramme, the Division will aim to improve the understanding of issues and policy choices in international investment, enterprise development and technology transfer and will continue to strengthen its role as the major source of comprehensive information and analysis of international investment. It will focus on the development dimension of international investment and technology flows, the interface of global processes and national policymaking and the integration of investment, technology and enterprise-development policies. The Division will also aim to strengthen the capacity of developing countries, in particular the least developed countries, at their request, to formulate and implement integrated policies and to participate in discussions relating to international investment, to support efforts by developing countries to build productive capacities and to respond to technological and scientific changes through science and technology reviews and to promote the transfer of technology and innovation."

Subprogramme 3
International trade

Indicator of achievement *(c)* should read as follows: "Increased number of countries in which improvements have been achieved in integrating commodity production, processing and trade into development in line with UNCTAD research and analyses, and policy deliberations and technical assistance".

Programme 24
Management and support services

Overall orientation

Paragraph 24.3 should read as follows: "The programme is oriented principally towards fully meeting management reform measures, including those approved by the General Assembly, with the support of a communication strategy that ensures that Member States, managers and staff are fully informed of and engaged in the efforts to ensure a more effective and results-oriented Organization."

A. Headquarters

Subprogramme 1

Management services, administration of justice and services to the Fifth Committee of the General Assembly and to the Committee for Programme and Coordination

(a) Management services

Add a new expected accomplishment as follows:

"*(c)* Improved business processes".

Add new indicators of achievement as follows:

"*(c)* (i) An improvement in the timeliness of business processes (reduction in the number of months, weeks or days required)"

"(ii) Amount of efficiency gains resulting from business process improvements".

Subprogramme 3

Human resources management

(a) Operational services

The objective of the Organization should read as follows: "to support the sound management of human resources in the Organization and, with respect to staffing, to pay due regard to the principle of equitable geographical distribution in accordance with Article 101, paragraph 3, of the Charter of the United Nations".

Under indicator of achievement *(a)* (ii), add a new indicator as follows:

"(iii) Increased number of nationals from unrepresented and underrepresented Member States, in particular developing countries, in the Secretariat"

Paragraph 24.18 should read as follows: "The Management Performance Board now monitors the manner in which senior managers exercise all aspects of the authority that has been delegated to them, including their performance in achieving the objectives contained in human resources action plans. Under the current staff selection system, the head of department/office, having been delegated the authority to select staff, is responsible for the progress made towards achieving the targets for geography and gender balance, which will be presented under executive direction and management, and detailed in that context in the programme budget."

Also on 22 December, the Assembly decided that the item on programme planning would remain for consideration during its resumed sixty-first (2007) session (**decision 61/552**).

Programme plan and priorities for 2006-2007

In July [A/61/125], proposed revisions to biennial programme plans and priorities for 2006-2007 were submitted for programmes 7 (Economic and social affairs), 11 (Environment), 14 (Economic and social development in Africa) and 16 (Economic development in Europe).

CPC recommended that the Assembly approve the proposed revisions to the four programmes [A/61/16 & Corr.1].

Programme performance

In an April report [A/61/64] on the programme performance of the United Nations for the 2004-2005 biennium, the Secretary-General provided an overview of key results achieved, delivery of outputs and resource utilization, and proposals for strengthening results-based management, monitoring and reporting. Under the 2004-2005 programme budget, a total of 33,130 outputs were due for implementation, including 28,406 programmed outputs, 643 carried over from the previous biennium, 2,374 added by legislative bodies and 1,707 by the Secretariat. Of the total, 30,028 were implemented, 537 were postponed to the next biennium and 2,565 were terminated. The implementation rate for mandated outputs was 90 per cent, compared to 84 per cent in 2002-2003, while the total implementation rate was 91 per cent, compared to 85 per cent in the previous biennium. Those percentages represented the highest implementation rate achieved by the Secretariat, as a result of more realistic planning and effective use of resources. Of the 30 budget sections, 25 achieved the total implementation rate of 90 per cent or higher and four had rates between 80 and 89 per cent. The most important factor affecting implementation rates was the number of outputs terminated, with the Department for Disarmament Affairs having the largest absolute and relative number of terminations, totalling 1,026, which accounted for 47 per cent of its programmed outputs and 40 per cent of all Secretariat terminations. Implementation utilized 503,226 work-months.

The Secretary-General said that one of the major challenges to progress was the future of the Integrated Monitoring and Documentation Information System (IMDIS) used for programme performance monitoring and reporting. During the reporting period, technical support to IMDIS was scaled down, plans for an advanced version were put on hold and consultations on establishing IMDIS as a Secretariat-wide common service were inconclusive. Moreover, despite the progress achieved, there was still a long way to go before programme performance monitoring would be an effective management tool. The use of IMDIS and the performance data contained in it for managerial assessments and decision-making was still an exception rather than a rule.

Another concern was the unrealistic expectations regarding programme performance reporting on the part of decision makers at different levels, which hinged on the desire to express the performance of a programme through a limited number of highly aggregated indexes, numbers or graphs presented in a simple, straightforward manner conducive to prompt analyses and conclusions. Such an approach was not feasible for application in the realm of highly diverse and multifaceted UN activities. Hence, there was a need for significant strengthening of organizational capacity at all levels, along with investment in the financial viability and development of IMDIS as the backbone tool for programme performance monitoring and reporting.

CPC consideration. CPC [A/61/16 & Corr.1] noted the improved format of the programme performance report, namely, the inclusion in each section of a brief description of challenges, obstacles and unmet goals, as it had requested in 2004 [YUN 2004, p. 1405]. It recommended that the Assembly request the Secretary-General to continue to develop that information, particularly for unmet goals, so as to improve consistency and standardize the presentation of information across all programmes; ensure that, in addition to quantitative parameters, more importance would be given in future reports to the qualitative assessment of programme implementation, and that all programme managers and their staff improved their performance in utilizing programme performance data in decision-making.

Evaluation and programme planning

In April, pursuant to General Assembly decision 60/551 [YUN 2005, p. 1504], the Fifth Committee resumed consideration of the CPC report on the work of its forty-fifth session [ibid., p. 1503], the OIOS report on strengthening and monitoring of programme performance and evaluation [ibid., p. 1504], and the letter from the Assembly President transmitting the recommendations of the Second Committee on the evaluation of linkages between headquarters and field activities and on the in-depth evaluation of the UN Human Settlements Programme [ibid.].

GENERAL ASSEMBLY ACTION

On 8 May [meeting 79], the General Assembly, on the recommendation of the Fifth Committee [A/60/747], adopted **resolution 60/257** without vote [agenda item 125].

Programme planning

The General Assembly,

Recalling its resolutions 37/234 of 21 December 1982, 38/227 A of 20 December 1983, 41/213 of 19 December 1986, 55/234 of 23 December 2000, 56/253 of 24 December 2001, 57/282 of 20 December 2002, 58/268 and 58/269 of 23 December 2003 and 59/275 of 23 December 2004,

Recalling also the terms of reference of the Committee for Programme and Coordination as outlined in the annex to Economic and Social Council resolution 2008 (LX) of 14 May 1976,

Having considered the report of the Committee for Programme and Coordination on the work of its forty-fifth session and the report of the Office of Internal Oversight Services on proposals on the strengthening and monitoring of programme performance and evaluation,

Having received the letter from the President of the General Assembly transmitting the recommendations of the Second Committee concerning the evaluation of linkages between headquarters and field activities: a review of best practices for poverty eradication in the framework of the United Nations Millennium Declaration and concerning the in-depth evaluation of the United Nations Human Settlements Programme,

1. *Reaffirms* the role of the Committee for Programme and Coordination as the main subsidiary organ of the General Assembly and the Economic and Social Council for planning, programming and coordination;

2. *Endorses* the conclusions and recommendations of the Committee for Programme and Coordination as contained in paragraphs 36 to 39, 135 to 139, 151 to 158, 165, 175 to 178, 186, 201 to 212, 227 to 237 and 248 of its report and the recommendations of the Second Committee concerning the evaluation of linkages between headquarters and field activities: a review of best practices for poverty eradication in the framework of the United Nations Millennium Declaration and concerning the in-depth evaluation of the United Nations Human Settlements Programme;

3. *Re-emphasizes* the role of the plenary and the Main Committees in reviewing and taking action on the appropriate recommendations of the Committee for Programme and Coordination relevant to their work, in accordance with regulation 4.10 of the Regulations and Rules Governing Programme Planning, the Programme Aspects of the Budget, the Monitoring of Implementation and the Methods of Evaluation;

4. *Requests* the General Committee to take fully into account resolutions 56/253, 57/282 and 59/275 in the allocation of agenda items to the Main Committees;

Programme questions

5. *Stresses* that setting the priorities of the United Nations is the prerogative of the Member States, as reflected in legislative mandates;

6. *Also stresses* the need for Member States to participate fully in the budget preparation process, from its early stages and throughout the process;

7. *Recalls* paragraph 3 of its resolution 60/246 of 23 December 2005, and invites the Committee for Programme and Coordination at its forty-seventh session, in the light of its recommendations in paragraphs 118 to 120 and 122 of its report, to provide further comments on the various aspects of the review process referred to in paragraphs 12 and 13 of General Assembly resolution 58/269 to facilitate the decision of the Assembly at its sixty-second session;

8. *Requests* the Secretary-General, as an exceptional measure and without prejudice to the provisions of General Assembly resolutions 41/213, 42/211 of 21 December 1987 and 58/269 or to the future scheduling of the sessions of the Committee for Programme and Coordination, and taking into account paragraph 4 of its resolution 60/246, to reschedule the forty-sixth session of the Committee to September 2006 at the latest in order to consider the proposed strategic framework for the period 2008-2009 and other items on the Committee's provisional agenda;

Evaluation

9. *Takes note* of the report of the Office of Internal Oversight Services, and encourages intergovernmental bodies to make use of the findings in the programme performance report of the Secretary-General and evaluation reports in planning and policymaking;

10. *Requests* the Secretary-General to report to the General Assembly, as appropriate, on the measures taken to promote the strengthening of monitoring and evaluation in the Organization, as per the proposals contained in the annex to the report of the Office of Internal Oversight Services;

11. *Concurs* with the findings contained in paragraphs 16 and 17 of the report of the Office of Internal Oversight Services, and requests the Secretary-General to report to the General Assembly in the context of the overall information technology strategy on measures and resources needed to strengthen the use of information technology as a management and monitoring tool;

12. *Notes with concern* that the report of the Office of Internal Oversight Services was not submitted to the General Assembly through the Committee for Programme and Coordination;

13. *Welcomes* the enhanced coordination between the Joint Inspection Unit and the Office of Internal Oversight Services as reflected in the report of the Office, and encourages such coordination in the future;

14. *Requests* the Secretary-General to entrust the Office of Internal Oversight Services with reporting to the General Assembly at its sixty-first session on ongoing efforts and measures taken to strengthen its in-depth and thematic evaluation function, as well as to respond to ad hoc evaluation requests by programme managers to ensure that intergovernmental bodies are provided with high-quality professional and objective reports on the performance of programmes and activities;

15. *Also requests* the Secretary-General to report to the General Assembly at its sixty-second session on the measures taken to strengthen self-evaluation by programme managers and to ensure more extensive and uniform use of self-evaluation at the programme and subprogramme levels, as well as to develop and implement common professional standards and methodologies for self-evaluation throughout the United Nations system, in consultation with the United Nations System Chief Executives Board for Coordination;

Other conclusions and recommendations of the Committee for Programme and Coordination

16. *Welcomes* the high priority that the United Nations System Chief Executives Board for Coordination continues to attach to ensuring effective and coordinated United Nations system support for Africa's development and the implementation of the priorities and programmes of the New Partnership for Africa's Development;

17. *Requests* the Secretary-General, with reference to the conclusions and recommendations of the Committee for Programme and Coordination in paragraphs 227 to 237 of its report, to submit the recommended report to the General Assembly at its sixty-first session on further efforts made to ensure that support for the New Partnership for Africa's Development remains a priority of the United Nations system and that organizations represented on the United Nations System Chief Executives Board for Coordination increase their efforts in support of the New Partnership;

18. *Also requests* the Secretary-General to continue to enhance and monitor the effective coordination of system-wide efforts against hunger and poverty;

19. *Recalls* its resolutions 58/269 and 59/275, as well as discussions held at the forty-fifth session of the Committee for Programme and Coordination, and, in this regard, notes with concern that no conclusions or recommendations were agreed to on improving the working methods and procedures of the Committee for Programme and Coordination during its forty-fifth session, and emphasizes the need for the Committee, within the framework of its mandate, to improve its working methods and procedures without having a negative impact on the effective consideration of other agenda items, in particular the proposed strategic framework for the period 2008-2009, as matters of priority, during its forty-sixth session;

20. *Recognizes* the importance of ensuring the highest level of expertise that is most appropriate for the Committee for Programme and Coordination, and, in this regard, invites the Committee to consider at its forty-sixth session how best to achieve this objective.

OIOS report. In May [A/61/83 & Corr.1], the Secretary-General transmitted to the General Assembly, through CPC, the OIOS report presenting an overview for 2004-2005 of the Secretariat's evaluation capacity and the application of evaluation findings on programme design and delivery and policy directives. It examined progress achieved during the reporting period, including the 214 evaluations that were conducted, compared to 134 evaluations reported during the previous biennium. However, as the programmes responding to those surveys were not identical, it was not possible to discern a trend from the information. The report provided information on planned evaluation activity for 2006-2007 and an assessment of the quality of the evaluation reports. While overall, more than half the sample reports received high quality ratings, the ratings for "soundness of methodology" were not as high, raising questions about methodological rigour, and the usability and potential impact of 75 per cent of the sample evaluation reports that received an average rating.

The report concluded that the lack of clarity in the definition of evaluation responsibilities, the low number of entities dedicated to evaluation within the Secretariat, the limited number of evaluation staff and the lack of precise and credible resource allocations for programme level self-evaluation compromised the overall evaluation capacity in the Secretariat. The OIOS central evaluation capacity was inadequate and unable to fully meet its mandate, and the majority of the 14 Secretariat units that supported self-evaluation were responsible for other activities as well.

To strengthen evaluation practice and capacity, OIOS would conduct a Secretariat-wide needs assessment to identify specific evaluation needs, functions, and resources and capacity required at the programme and subprogramme levels, and issue guidelines for clarifying regulations and rules pertaining to evaluation. In addition, the OIOS programme budget for 2008-2009 would reflect requirements for rigorous and regular central evaluation of performance and outcomes of Secretariat programmes and activities. The report also presented topics for future evaluations, including in-depth evaluations for 2007-2009 for consideration by CPC, as well as the following thematic evaluations proposed by OIOS: UN coordinating bodies; gender mainstreaming; protocols and practices in lessons learned; and coordination and collaboration between the Department of Economic and Social Affairs and the regional commissions.

CPC consideration. CPC [A/61/16 & Corr.1] selected the following topics for in-depth evaluation: "Department of Management, Office of Human Resources Management" in 2008, and "UN support for the least developed countries, landlocked developing countries, small island developing States and Africa," in 2009. It also selected for thematic evaluation, the themes "Lessons learned: protocols and practices" for 2008 and "UN coordinating bodies" for 2009.

OIOS reports to CPC. The Secretary-General transmitted to CPC the OIOS evaluation reports on thematic evaluation of: knowledge management networks in pursuit of the goals of the UN Millennium Declaration [YUN 2000, p. 49] [E/AC.51/2006/2]; usefulness of the pilot thematic evaluation [E/AC.51/2006/3]; in-depth evaluation of political affairs [E/AC.51/2005/4] and the comments of the Secretary-General thereon [E/AC.51/2006/4/Add.1]; and the triennial review of the in-depth evaluation of the programme on the law of the sea and ocean affairs [E/AC.51/2006/5].

CPC comments and recommendations on those reports were contained in the report on its 2006 session [A/61/16 & Corr.1].

By **decision 2006/257** of 11 October, the Economic and Social Council took note of the CPC report on its forty-sixth session.

Chapter III

Administrative and staff matters

In 2006, the General Assembly continued to review the administrative functioning of the Organization and matters related to UN staff, including new reform proposals recommended by the outgoing Secretary-General. Those proposals, contained in a report entitled "Investing in the United Nations: for a stronger Organization worldwide", outlined reform measures dealing with, among others, leadership, service delivery, information and communication technology (ICT), governance and staff issues. The Secretary-General elaborated on those proposals in subsequent detailed reports. The General Assembly took action on them in resolutions of 8 May and 7 July. Regarding ICT, the Assembly established the post of Chief Information Technology Officer at the level of Assistant Secretary-General and decided to replace the Integrated Management Information System with a next-generation enterprise resource planning system. The Assembly also took action on the recommendations of the Steering Committee on the Comprehensive Review of Governance and Oversight within the United Nations and its Funds, Programmes and Specialized Agencies for improving UN oversight practices, including those of the Office of Internal Oversight Services (OIOS).

The Committee on Conferences examined requests for changes to the approved calendar of conferences for 2006 and 2007. The Department of General Assembly and Conference Management launched an information technology global initiative to identify a strategy that would lead to a standardized approach to decision-making and real-time access to data. In July, the Assembly approved the strategy for a phased approach to the capital master plan for the refurbishment of the UN Headquarters complex in New York. In December, it approved the plan, to be carried out from 2006 to 2014. It also approved a renovation of the Secretary-General's residence in New York.

The Assembly requested the Secretary-General to further develop and implement a strengthened and unified security management system for the United Nations.

In December, the Assembly appointed Ban Ki-moon of the Republic of Korea as Secretary-General of the United Nations, effective 1 January 2007, to succeed the outgoing Secretary-General, Kofi Annan.

During the year, the Assembly, through the International Civil Service Commission, continued to review the conditions of service of staff of the UN common system and adopted the Commission's recommendations relating to mobility and hardship allowance; education grant; conditions of service of staff in the Professional and higher categories, and of internationally-recruited staff in non-family duty stations; the base/floor salary scale; the Senior Management Network; and the level of children's and secondary dependant's allowance. The Assembly took note of the Commission's decisions on the framework for contractual arrangements, and requested the Commission to consider the effectiveness of measures to promote recruitment and retention, especially in difficult duty stations, and to report thereon in 2007. Other Commission recommendations addressed by the Assembly related to gender balance, the level of hazard pay, identification of the highest paid national civil service, and the common scale of staff assessment.

The outgoing Secretary-General's latest reform proposal (see above) also addressed human resources management. In his report entitled "Investing in People", the Secretary-General outlined proposals for streamlining contractual arrangements and conditions of service. Other proposals addressed the recruitment system, staff mobility, career development, building leadership and the staff buyout scheme.

The Secretary-General also reported on: the conditions of service and compensation of members of the International Court of Justice, judges of the International Tribunals; safety and security of UN personnel; strengthening accountability at the United Nations; the Management Performance Board; the United Nations Ethics Office; staff composition; the status of women in common system organizations; gratis personnel; the employment of retirees; consultants and individual contractors; a common payroll for UN system organizations; multilingualism; protection from sexual exploitation and abuse; the United Nations Joint Staff Pension Fund; travel and related matters; the review of the UN system administration of justice, including the management review of the Appeals process; the Office of the Ombudsman; and criminal behaviour and disciplinary action.

During the year, the Redesign Panel on the United Nations system of administration of justice, appointed by the Secretary-General to review and redesign the Organization's system of administration of justice, found the current system outmoded, dysfunctional and ineffective and recommended that it be replaced.

Administrative matters

Managerial reform and oversight

Management reform

The Secretary-General, in his March report entitled "Investing in the United Nations: for a stronger Organization worldwide" [A/60/692 & Corr.1], outlined measures for improving leadership, service delivery, information and communication technology (ICT), and governance (see below).

In the area of leadership, the Secretary-General said that the top management structure of the Secretariat was not well equipped to manage large, complex operations, and that too many people were reporting directly to him. To address those issues, he proposed to redefine the role of the Deputy Secretary-General and delegate to that person formal authority and accountability for the management and overall direction of Secretariat functions. The 25 departments and other entities reporting directly to the Secretary-General should be reorganized to significantly reduce the reporting span. A new leadership development plan covering recruitment, training and career development was needed to build middle and senior management capacity.

Despite improvements to the UN ICT infrastructure, the system remained fragmented, outdated and underfunded compared to similar large and complex organizations. The lack of an integrated system to store, search and retrieve information held back progress in other areas. The Secretary-General proposed the creation of the post of Chief Information Technology Officer at the level of Assistant Secretary-General to oversee the creation and implementation of an effective information management strategy. A sustained effort to align ICT priorities with Secretariat performance efforts should begin immediately. The Secretary-General also proposed the replacement of the Integrated Management Information System (IMIS), the Galaxy staff recruitment system and other ICT management support systems with a fully integrated global system, to be introduced by 2009. (For further information on the Secretary-General's ICT proposals, see p. 1664.)

Regarding service delivery, the Secretary-General proposed that the General Assembly modify its guidance on the issue to allow the Secretariat to consider all alternative options, including relocation and outsourcing. Systematic cost-benefit analyses of the potential for applying such options for select administrative services should be completed within 12 months. Measures would be implemented also to improve and tighten procurement procedures (see p. 1664).

As to governance, the Secretary-General said that the budget and its decision-making process often lacked clarity and transparency, and the interaction between the Secretariat and the General Assembly Committees was, at times, dysfunctional. He proposed improving Secretariat reporting mechanisms, including through the development of a single, comprehensive annual report. The 30 reports on management should be consolidated into six reports. New principles to guide the interaction between the Secretariat and the Assembly on management and budgetary issues should be introduced to make it more focused, strategic and results-oriented, and the Assembly should consider ways to reform its interaction with the Secretariat on those issues.

In a March report [A/60/735 & Corr. 1], the Advisory Committee on Administrative and Budgetary Questions (ACABQ) provided its observations and recommendations on the Secretary-General's reform proposals.

The Assembly took action with regard to those proposals and the related ACABQ report in **resolution 60/260** of 8 May (see p. 1576).

In response to resolution 60/260, the Secretary-General submitted, in May, a detailed report on investing in the United Nations [A/60/846], with addenda on specific proposals put forth in his March report. In the addendum on improving reporting mechanisms, including public access to UN documentation [A/60/846/Add.4], the Secretary-General requested the Assembly to note his intention to submit a single, comprehensive annual report to the Assembly on both financial and programme issues. The Assembly was also asked to welcome the Secretary-General's efforts to consolidate reports on related subjects and endorse that consolidation; take note of the policy on public access to UN documentation; and appropriate a total of $1,820,900 under the programme budget for the 2006-2007 biennium for the implementation of those proposals.

Other May addenda to the detailed report dealt with investing in ICT [A/60/846/Add.1] (see p. 1664), budget implementation [A/60/846/Add.2] and financial management practices [A/60/846/Add.3] (see p. 1610).

In June [A/60/870], ACABQ recommended that the Secretary-General develop a comprehensive financial and programme report to complement the Secretary-General's report on the work of the Organization. ACABQ welcomed efforts to consolidate reports and noted that the bulk of those reports were dependent on an Assembly decision on consolidating the financial performance reports and budgets of peacekeeping operations (see p. 1583). It also welcomed efforts to elaborate a policy for public access to UN documentation. In implementing that policy, the possibility of a fee structure and financing mechanisms should be explored and measures taken to ensure multilingualism.

In **resolution 60/283** of 7 July (see p. 1580), the Assembly took action with regard to the Secretary-General's detailed report on investing in the United Nations for a stronger Organization worldwide, the addenda to the report and the related ACABQ report.

Procurement

The Secretary-General, in his March report on investing in the United Nations [A/60/692 & Corr. 1], said that UN procurement rules and regulations were too complex and cumbersome for the quick action often required by field missions, and the limited steps taken to deal with the problem had not been accompanied by sufficient support and controls to prevent mismanagement and abuse. To address those problems, he proposed that ongoing investigations into procurement problems be concluded quickly, and swift action be taken against any UN staff members found to have acted inappropriately. The Secretary-General also proposed that an ongoing comprehensive review of procurement rules, regulations and policies be continued, and a more comprehensive report, including more detailed corrective actions, be issued by June.

In response to resolution 60/260, the Secretary-General issued a June addendum on procurement reform [A/60/846/Add.5 & Corr.1] to his detailed report on investing in the United Nations. He said that, due to an unprecedented surge in peacekeeping operations, the value of procurement had increased from $1.1 billion to $1.8 billion over the two previous years, placing severe pressure on the Procurement Service and its staff in peacekeeping missions. The Secretary-General presented strategic procurement reform actions focusing on strengthening internal control measures, optimizing acquisition management and reducing costs, and developing strategic procurement management. The Secretariat intended to complete action within 18 months, subject to resource availability.

The Secretariat, having reviewed the findings and recommendations of the report of an external consultant on internal controls in procurement and the Office of Internal Oversight Services (OIOS) report on the comprehensive management audit of the Department of Peacekeeping Operations (DPKO) [A/60/717] (see p. 105), had taken swift action to strengthen internal controls. However, with the current and anticipated workload, the allocated resources were not sufficient to meet the medium- to long-term requirements. The Secretary-General recommended that the Assembly, under the support account for peacekeeping operations for the period from 1 July 2006 to 30 June 2007, approve resources for post and non-post costs in the Procurement Service, the Office of Mission Support/DPKO, the Office of the Under-Secretary-General for Management and the General Legal Division/Office of Legal Affairs. He also recommended, under the 2006-2007 programme budget, the reclassification of the D-1 post of Chief of Procurement to the D-2 level.

In its related report [A/60/904], ACABQ welcomed the measures taken to separate procurement duties and processes, avoid conflict of interest and increase transparency. It recognized the importance of training for procurement staff, and requested that information on the required professional qualifications for procurement staff, including certification, be provided in the upcoming report on human resources management reform. While ACABQ recognized the merit of using business seminars to increase awareness among vendors in developing countries and countries with economies in transition, it encouraged the Secretariat to explore additional ways to promote procurement from such countries. ACABQ recommended that the Assembly approve the resources requested by the Secretary-General, totalling $5,151,100.

Procurement Task Force

In December [A/61/603], the Secretary-General reported on the terms of reference, outputs and status of the OIOS Procurement Task Force, established in January to investigate the Procurement Service and resolve critical questions related to procurement activities. Planned Task Force outputs included a strategic plan that would provide a list of priority cases to the Under-Secretary-General for Internal Oversight Services; monthly interim reports to the

Under-Secretary-General updating each of those cases; additional interim reports on significant developments in individual cases; a draft final case report; and a corruption assessment report. The Task Force became fully operational in mid-2006 and focused on matters related to staff members placed on administrative leave with pay. The Task Force had several significant complex matters in its inventory of cases, including more than 20 cases that justified continued examination. The work of the Task Force was expected to be concluded on 31 December 2007, with any residual cases to be handled by the OIOS Investigation Division.

GENERAL ASSEMBLY ACTION

On 22 December [meeting 84], the General Assembly, on the recommendation of the Fifth (Administrative and Budgetary) Committee [A/61/658], adopted **resolution 61/246** without vote [agenda items 47, 113, 116, 117, 122, 123, 132 and 149].

Procurement reform

The General Assembly,

Recalling its resolutions 54/14 of 29 October 1999, 55/247 of 12 April 2001, 57/279 of 20 December 2002, 58/276 and 58/277 of 23 December 2003, 59/288 and 59/289 of 13 April 2005, 60/1 of 16 September 2005, 60/260 of 8 May 2006, 60/266 of 30 June 2006 and 60/283 of 7 July 2006,

Having considered the addendum to the detailed report of the Secretary-General on investing in the United Nations for a stronger Organization worldwide entitled “Procurement reform”, the report of the Joint Inspection Unit on procurement practices within the United Nations system and the note by the Secretary-General transmitting his comments and those of the United Nations System Chief Executives Board for Coordination thereon and the related report of the Advisory Committee on Administrative and Budgetary Questions,

1. *Takes note* of the report of the Secretary-General, the report of the Joint Inspection Unit on procurement practices within the United Nations system and the note by the Secretary-General transmitting his comments and those of the United Nations System Chief Executives Board for Coordination thereon;

2. *Endorses* the conclusions and recommendations contained in the report of the Advisory Committee on Administrative and Budgetary Questions, subject to the provisions of the present resolution;

3. *Stresses* the importance of strengthened accountability in the Organization and of ensuring greater accountability of the Secretary-General to Member States, inter alia, for the effective and efficient implementation of legislative mandates on procurement and the related use of financial and human resources, as well as the provision of necessary information on procurement-related matters to enable Member States to make well-informed decisions;

4. *Recognizes* that procurement reform is an ongoing process and should focus, inter alia, on ensuring the efficiency, transparency and cost-effectiveness of United Nations procurement as well as strengthened internal controls, greater accountability to Member States and full implementation of General Assembly resolutions on procurement reform;

5. *Recalls* its resolutions on procurement reform, and notes that the report of the Secretary-General focused mainly on strengthening of internal controls and optimization of acquisition and procurement management, with emphasis on urgent internal control issues, and that other procurement reform measures will be presented in forthcoming reports;

6. *Reiterates its request* to the Secretary-General to submit proposals to effectively increase procurement opportunities for and the participation of vendors from developing countries;

7. *Requests* the Secretary-General to submit to the General Assembly at its sixty-second session a comprehensive report on all aspects of procurement reform, including the outstanding reports referred to in paragraph 4 of the report of the Advisory Committee on Administrative and Budgetary Questions, as well as measures taken to implement its resolutions on procurement reform and the status of implementation of recommendations of the oversight bodies;

Staff

8. *Also requests* the Secretary-General to ensure that all staff in the Secretariat involved in procurement activities, including at the senior levels, file financial disclosure statements annually;

9. *Regrets* that the Secretary-General has not submitted proposals related to the issue of conflict of interest requested by the General Assembly in section V, paragraph 9, of its resolution 60/266 at the main part of its sixty-first session, and requests him to do so no later than at the second part of its resumed sixty-first session;

10. *Stresses* the importance of developing and implementing an ethics and integrity programme for the procurement staff, and requests the Secretary-General to complete and issue ethics guidelines no later than June 2007 for all staff involved in the procurement process;

11. *Welcomes* the initiatives of the Secretary-General in undertaking training programmes for United Nations procurement staff, including in the field, and requests the Secretary-General to evaluate their impact and monitor their implementation and to submit proposals on making any further improvements necessary in the training of staff in procurement processes;

Internal controls

12. *Requests* the Secretary-General to further enhance transparency in the procurement decision-making process through, inter alia, the establishment of an independent bid protest system outside of the reporting hierarchy of the Procurement Division of the Department of Management of the Secretariat in order to furnish vendors participating in tenders with a means of disputing procurement-related decisions;

13. *Also requests* the Secretary-General to report to the General Assembly on the specific modalities of the bid protest system and related procedures, including possible legal and financial implications;

14. *Further requests* the Secretary-General to include information, as appropriate, on the bid protest system on the website of the Procurement Division;

15. *Notes* the promotion by the Procurement Division of the voluntary principles of the corporate social responsibility initiative, the Global Compact, within the United Nations procurement framework, and requests the Secretary-General, as appropriate, to report to the General Assembly for further consideration;

16. *Notes with appreciation* that the Supplier Code of Conduct has been promulgated and posted on the website of the Procurement Division with a view to achieving the goal of safeguarding the integrity of the United Nations in procurement activities;

17. *Requests* the Secretary-General to continue to simplify and streamline the vendor registration process, to share responsibilities among the various United Nations organizations and to take into account the different circumstances and varying levels of Internet access in countries and to report to the General Assembly at its sixty-second session, in the context of the comprehensive report, on the results achieved;

Governance

18. *Notes with concern* the possible weaknesses in the control environment with regard to procurement activities owing, inter alia, to the splitting of responsibilities between the Department of Management and the Department of Peacekeeping Operations of the Secretariat, as referred to in paragraph 14 of the report of the Advisory Committee on Administrative and Budgetary Questions;

19. *Requests* the Secretary-General to submit to it at the second part of its resumed sixty-first session a comprehensive report on the following elements:

(a) The management arrangements for procurement, including clear lines of accountability and delegation of authority;

(b) The findings of the working group established to examine ways in which the organizational structure could be changed to better align responsibility with authority and to improve the overall control environment for procurement for peacekeeping operations;

(c) The respective responsibilities of the Department of Management and the Department of Peacekeeping Operations;

(d) Streamlined procurement procedures for peacekeeping operations in the field, including specific information on mechanisms for strengthened monitoring, oversight and accountability;

(e) The functioning of the Headquarters Contracts Committee and the local committees on contracts;

Procurement opportunities for vendors from developing countries and countries with economies in transition

20. *Also requests* the Secretary-General to explore additional ways to improve procurement opportunities for vendors from developing countries and countries with economies in transition both at Headquarters and in the field and to report thereon to the General Assembly at the second part of its resumed sixty-first session;

21. *Recalls* section VII, paragraph 2, of its resolution 60/266, and requests the Secretary-General to ensure that information on procurement opportunities at Headquarters and in peacekeeping operations is made available to business communities in developing countries and countries with economies in transition, through, inter alia, continued cooperation between the Department of Public Information and the Procurement Division of the Department of Management, utilizing the United Nations information centres and offices;

22. *Recognizes* the efforts by the Procurement Division to increase the number of business seminars in developing countries, and requests the Secretary-General, in his capacity as Chairman of the United Nations System Chief Executives Board for Coordination, to encourage the organizations of the United Nations system to facilitate, in cooperation with Member States, the organization of business seminars in developing countries and countries with economies in transition;

23. *Requests* the Secretary-General to invite the Inter-Agency Procurement Working Group to continue to study ways and means and recommend concrete proposals to diversify the sourcing of goods and services, in particular from developing countries and countries with economies in transition;

24. *Also requests* the Secretary-General to encourage the organizations of the United Nations system, consistent with their respective mandates, to take further steps to increase procurement opportunities for vendors from developing countries and countries with economies in transition;

Procurement management

25. *Recalls* that the General Assembly has not yet taken a decision on the lead agency concept, and reiterates its request to the Secretary-General to include in his report an assessment of the internal controls of the United Nations organizations and how they differ from those of the Procurement Division;

26. *Recognizes* that the lead agency concept is being developed and that extensive consultations are under way within the United Nations system, and requests the Secretary-General to report to the General Assembly for consideration at its sixty-second session on proposals for the lead agency concept and the status of consultations, including on clear lines of accountability, the applicability of resolutions and decisions of the Assembly, the impact on efforts to improve the diversification of the origin of vendors, possible efficiency gains and cost savings and distribution of resources within the United Nations system, enabling proposed designated buyers to manage larger procurement activities;

27. *Requests* the Secretary-General to continue to encourage all the organizations of the United Nations system, consistent with their respective mandates, to further improve their procurement practices, inter alia, by participating in the United Nations Global Marketplace

with a view to creating one common United Nations global procurement website;

28. *Stresses* the need to ensure transparency in procurement throughout the United Nations system, and requests the Secretary-General to ensure that the United Nations Global Marketplace website is fully accessible to Member States no later than 1 June 2007;

29. *Requests* the Secretary-General to ensure that the United Nations Global Marketplace website, inter alia, features lists of companies that register through the Global Marketplace as vendors of United Nations system entities, as well as statistics on contract awards, acquisition plans and procurement notices;

30. *Encourages* the Secretary-General to extend participation and improve the level of collaboration, coordination and information-sharing among the organizations of the United Nations system with respect to procurement activities in order to achieve economies of scale and eliminate duplication of work;

31. *Notes* the activities of the Inter-Agency Procurement Working Group and of the Common Services Procurement Working Group on enhancing the transparency and increasing the harmonization of procurement practices, and requests the Secretary-General, in consultation with the executive heads of the United Nations funds and programmes, to continue work in this regard;

32. *Recalls* section A, paragraph 10, of its resolution 59/288, and, noting paragraphs 65 and 66 of the report of the Secretary-General requests the Secretary-General to report comprehensively to the General Assembly at its sixty-second session on the principle of best value for money and its implementation in United Nations procurement, including, inter alia, its possible effect on the diversification of vendors and suppliers and on efforts to improve procurement for vendors from developing countries and countries with economies in transition;

33. *Requests* the Secretary-General to continue to develop clear guidelines for the implementation of the best value for money methodology in United Nations procurement and to report thereon to the General Assembly at its sixty-second session;

Other issues

34. *Also requests* the Secretary-General to implement measures to reduce the timeline associated with the payment of invoices;

35. *Further requests* the Secretary-General to ensure that a monthly update of contract award statistics is posted on the website of the Procurement Division;

36. *Requests* the Secretary-General to continue to improve the website of the Procurement Division and make it more user-friendly;

37. *Also requests* the Secretary-General to report to the General Assembly, in the context of the comprehensive report, on the implementation of the provisions of the present resolution;

Resources

38. *Decides* to approve the conversion of twenty positions funded under general temporary assistance to established posts under the support account for peacekeeping operations for the period ending 30 June 2007, as follows:

(a) Procurement Division, Department of Management: eleven posts (one P-5, three P-4, four P-3, one General Service (Principal level) and two General Service (Other level));

(b) Office of Mission Support, Department of Peacekeeping Operations: two posts (one P-5 and one P-4);

(c) Headquarters Committee on Contracts, Department of Management: three posts (one D-1, one P-4 and one General Service (Other level));

(d) General Legal Division, Office of Legal Affairs: four posts (two P-5, one P-4 and one General Service (Other level));

39. *Also decides* to approve the conversion of the six positions (one D-1, four P-4 and one P-3) for the Procurement Division funded under general temporary assistance to established posts and an amount of 706,500 United States dollars, representing the balance of the resource requirements for the six posts under the support account for peacekeeping operations for the period ending 30 June 2007;

40. *Further decides* that three of the posts established above (one P-4, one P-3 and one General Service (Other level)) will be designated to the Vendor Registration and Management Team with a view to, inter alia, promoting the diversification of the origin of vendors among all Member States, including developing countries and countries with economies in transition, simplifying vendor registration, managing the vendor database and liaising with vendors;

41. *Approves* the resource requirements of 1,050,000 dollars proposed in the report of the Secretary-General for the Procurement Division under the support account for peacekeeping operations for the rest of the fiscal year ending 30 June 2007, as follows:

(a) 200,000 dollars for consultants to review industry practices and procurement models in specific industries relevant to United Nations requirements;

(b) 800,000 dollars for training of both Headquarters and peacekeeping mission procurement staff (640,000 dollars for consultants to organize training, 150,000 dollars for travel of staff for procurement training and 10,000 dollars for training-related supplies and materials);

(c) 50,000 dollars for travel in relation to business seminars;

42. *Also approves* the reclassification of the Chief of Procurement post from the D-1 to the D-2 level;

43. *Requests* the Secretary-General to comprehensively review the post and non-post requirements of the Procurement Division, taking into account General Assembly resolutions on procurement reform, including the present one, and to submit proposals based on identified requirements in the context of the budget for the support account for the period from 1 July 2007 to 30 June 2008 and the proposed programme budget for the biennium 2008-2009.

Oversight

Report of JIU. In May [A/60/860], the Secretary-General transmitted a report of the Joint Inspection Unit (JIU) on oversight lacunae in the UN system, which examined the oversight role of Member States, the oversight structure, including the deficiencies in both internal and external oversight and in coordination. The Inspectors found that the system of external (United Nations Board of Auditors, ACABQ, the Committee for Programme and Coordination and the International Civil Service Commission (ICSC)) and internal (the Office of Internal Oversight Services (OIOS)) oversight was not intrinsically deficient in terms of either design or mandates. Moreover, effective mechanisms had been put in place to ensure synergies and avoid duplication. However, some issues remained to be addressed, particularly the level and type of resources provided, working practices and the independence of those bodies. Member States were encouraged to take stock of the oversight system as a whole, identify problems and opportunities and act in a coordinated manner to address them.

The Inspectors recommended, among other measures, that the legislative bodies of each UN system organization should establish an independent external oversight board; ACABQ, JIU, and ICSC should be subject to a peer review every five years; the budget proposals of the external oversight bodies should not be reviewed by entities which were the object of their oversight, but by ACABQ or the external board concerned; audit, inspection and evaluation functions should be consolidated in a single unit, and other internal oversight functions positioned elsewhere in the various secretariats; those organizations that managed biennial resources of at least $250 million should have an internal oversight body, while those managing less than that amount should seek oversight services from any competent UN system organization; each organization should establish an ethics function and a post of ethics officer, and implement mandatory integrity and ethics training; executive heads should establish confidential financial disclosure requirements for all elected officials, staff at the D-1 level and above and other senior managers and procurement officials, and enforce the annual filing of disclosure statements; and the respective oversight boards should establish an effective mechanism for system-wide coordination and cooperation among external and internal oversight bodies.

The Secretary-General and the United Nations System Chief Executives Board for Coordination (CEB), in their comments on the JIU report, transmitted in May [A/60/860/Add.1], said in that JIU placed too much emphasis on its own suggested standards, without a clear description of how those standards were developed or what prior best practice analysis supported them. They expressed concern as to how a uniform standard would function in the UN system, with its diverse range of structures and mandates. However, they generally welcomed the recommendations, some of which were already being implemented, and sought clarification on others.

Report of Steering Committee on Governance and Oversight. The report of the Steering Committee on the Comprehensive Review of Governance and Oversight within the United Nations and its Funds, Programmes and Specialized Agencies, transmitted by the Secretary-General in August [A/60/883], examined governance and oversight principles and practices, UN oversight practices, gap analysis and recommendations and reviewed OIOS (see p. 1651) [A/60/883/Add.2].

The Steering Committee found that the practice of establishing audit committees was not widespread throughout the UN system and their effectiveness varied widely in those organizations that had established them. There were also differences in the level of authority with regard to reporting, budgeting and selection or dismissal of the head of internal audit, as well as variations between UN entities in the degree of internal audit independence. Clear executive responsibility for risk management and internal controls was lacking and the oversight of inter-agency programmes was frequently ineffective. The Steering Committee recommended implementation of a systematic enterprise risk management framework; assigning responsibility for internal controls and reporting on their effectiveness to executive management; implementing the General Assembly decision to establish an independent audit advisory committee [YUN 2005, p. 1496]; the setting up of audit committees at the International Civil Aviation Organization, UNHCR, the United Nations Development Programme and the United Nations Children's Fund and clarification of the responsibilities of the UNHCR Oversight Committee responsible for internal audit, investigations and evaluation. The Committee also recommended the discontinuation of JIU and the setting of new standards for oversight of inter-agency programmes.

JIU [A/60/1004] (see p. 1653) and OIOS [A/60/901] (see p. 1651) submitted their comments on the Steering Committee's report.

ACABQ comments and observations on the report of the Steering Committee were submitted in its December report [A/61/605]. It recommended that the General Assembly request the Secretary-General to make proposals on how to address the issue of new oversight standards for inter-agency programmes, and noted the absence of concrete proposals for improving coordination and cooperation among UN system oversight bodies. It also made recommendations concerning the establishment of an Independent Audit Advisory Committee and OIOS.

The General Assembly, in **resolution 61/245** of 22 December (see p. 1573), endorsed the recommendations of ACABQ on the report of the Steering Committee.

Internal oversight

On 8 May [meeting 79], the General Assembly, having considered the OIOS annual report for the period from 1 July 2004 to 30 June 2005 [YUN 2005, p. 1473], and on the recommendation of the Fifth Committee [A/60/604/Add.1], adopted **resolution 60/259** without vote [agenda item 132].

Report of the Secretary-General on the activities of the Office of Internal Oversight Services

The General Assembly,

Recalling its resolutions 48/218 B of 29 July 1994, 54/244 of 23 December 1999 and 59/272 of 23 December 2004,

Recalling also its resolutions 56/246 of 24 December 2001, 58/101 B of 9 December 2003 and 59/270 of 23 December 2004,

Having considered the annual report of the Office of Internal Oversight Services for the period from 1 July 2004 to 30 June 2005,

1. *Reaffirms* its primary role in the consideration of and action taken on reports submitted to it;

2. *Also reaffirms* its oversight role and the role of the Fifth Committee in administrative and budgetary matters;

3. *Further reaffirms* the independence and the separate and distinct roles of the internal and external oversight mechanisms;

4. *Looks forward* to the results of the independent external evaluation of the audit and oversight system of the United Nations, and stresses that the evaluation should include proposals on:

(a) Ensuring the full operational independence of the Office of Internal Oversight Services;

(b) Strengthening the evaluation capacity of the Office at the programme and subprogramme levels;

(c) Ensuring adequate funding arrangements for timely reimbursement by funds and programmes for services of the Office;

5. *Notes with concern* the description of the mission of the Office of Internal Oversight Services, as outlined in paragraph 1 of its annual report, and in this regard reiterates that, in accordance with paragraph 5 of General Assembly resolution 59/270, the mission of the Office should be in full conformity with its mandate, as approved by the Assembly in its resolution 48/218 B;

6. *Notes with appreciation* the work of the Office of Internal Oversight Services;

7. *Takes note* of the annual report of the Office of Internal Oversight Services;

8. *Stresses* the importance of full implementation of legislative decisions, and requests the Secretary-General to ensure that programme managers provide information to the Office of Internal Oversight Services to be reflected in the programme performance report on the rate of implementation of legislative mandates and decisions and, where applicable, in cases where full implementation has not been achieved, the reasons therefor;

9. *Requests* the Secretary-General to ensure that all relevant resolutions, in particular cross-cutting resolutions, are brought to the attention of relevant managers, and further requests that the Office of Internal Oversight Services also take those resolutions into account in the conduct of its activities;

10. *Also requests* the Secretary-General to ensure that all relevant resolutions pertaining to the work of the Office of Internal Oversight Services are brought to the attention of the relevant managers;

11. *Notes* that not all programme managers have reported the results of investigations to the Office of Internal Oversight Services, as required in paragraph 11 of its resolution 59/287 of 13 April 2005, and requests the Secretary-General to ensure that programme managers comply with this requirement as a measure of accountability;

12. *Requests* the Secretary-General to entrust the Office of Internal Oversight Services to submit a report on the use of the best-value concept in the evaluation and awarding of procurement contracts in order to identify any possible misuse;

13. *Recalls* its request, as contained in section IV, paragraph 4, of its resolution 59/296 of 22 June 2005, notes with concern paragraph 25 of the annual report of the Office of Internal Oversight Services concerning the management of fuel in peacekeeping missions, and welcomes the intention of the Office to report to the General Assembly on the oversight of fuel management in peacekeeping missions;

14. *Welcomes* the comprehensive tsunami risk assessments undertaken by the Office of Internal Oversight Services jointly with United Nations funds and programmes and the specialized agencies, and requests the Secretary-General to ensure that United Nations funds and programmes and the specialized agencies cooperate with the Office in the preparation of a consolidated report on audits and investigative reviews undertaken of the tsunami relief operation and to entrust the Office to report thereon to the General Assembly at its sixty-first session;

15. *Also welcomes* the intention of the Office of Internal Oversight Services to conduct a risk assessment of the activities of the United Nations Joint Staff Pension Fund, and invites the United Nations Joint Staff Pension Board to request the Office, in this context, to conduct an audit of the quality, efficiency and effectiveness of services provided to beneficiaries;

16. *Notes with concern* the numerous allegations of fraud and irregularities in the United Nations Interim Administration Mission in Kosovo, and requests the Office of Internal Oversight Services to submit to the General Assembly at its resumed sixtieth session an overview report on its investigations and follow-up;

17. *Decides* to modify the title of the relevant agenda item to read "Report on the activities of the Office of Internal Oversight Services" in accordance with paragraph 3 of its resolution 59/272.

OIOS activities. In August, the Secretary-General transmitted the twelfth annual OIOS report [A/61/264 (Part I)] covering its activities from 1 July 2005 to 30 June 2006, except for the results of OIOS peacekeeping oversight activities, which would be reported separately. An addendum to the report [A/61/264 (Part I)/Add.1] provided an overall assessment of the implementation of OIOS recommendations and an analysis of those not fully implemented. During the period, OIOS issued 234 oversight reports, including 18 to the General Assembly. In addition to the report on its activities, OIOS issued, in 2006, reports on: the audit of standard costs applied to headquarters overheads [A/60/682]; the global review of discipline in field missions led by DPKO [A/60/713]; the comprehensive management audit of DPKO [A/60/717]; the inspection of the programme and administrative management of the Economic and Social Commission for Western Asia [A/61/61]; programme performance of the United Nations for the 2004-2005 biennium [A/61/64]; strengthening the role of evaluation and the application of evaluation findings on programme design, delivery and policy directives [A/61/83 & Corr.1]; the thematic evaluation of knowledge management networks in pursuit of the goals of the Millennium Declaration [E/AC.51/2006/2]; the usefulness of a 2005 pilot thematic evaluation [YUN 2005, p. 1473] of linkages between headquarters and field staff [E/AC.51/2006/3]; an in-depth evaluation of the Department of Political Affairs [E/AC.51/2006/4]; the investigation conducted by the Investigation Task Force into fraud and corruption at Pristina Airport [A/60/720 & Corr.1]; and the triennial review of the implementation of recommendations made by the Committee for Programme and Coordination (CPC) at its forty-third session on the in-depth evaluation of the programme on the law of the sea and ocean affairs [E/AC.51/2006/5].

OIOS issued 1,919 recommendations to improve internal controls, accountability mechanisms and organizational efficiency and effectiveness; of those recommendations, 932 (49 per cent) were classified as critical. The overall implementation rate for all recommendations declined to 47 per cent, from 50 per cent in the previous period. OIOS said that the decline might be partially explained by the 26 per cent increase in the number of critical recommendations issued in the 2005-2006 period. As at 30 June, the implementation of 11 recommendations issued in 2002-2003 (including four critical), 12 recommendations issued in 2003-2004 (including five critical) and 56 recommendations issued in 2004-2005 (including 18 critical) had not yet started. OIOS identified a total of $49.2 million in cost savings; actual savings and recoveries amounted to $14.2 million.

The report described oversight results in five high-risk areas: staff health, security and safety; programme management; ICT; the capital master plan; and integrity violations. OIOS continued audits of security procedures at various duty stations and initiated a quick-impact audit of the Organization's preparedness for the avian influenza pandemic. Programme planning and management activities included performance monitoring and reporting, inspections and evaluations. ICT issues addressed by the Office included those related to information technology governance, strategic planning access security, and contingency and business continuity planning. OIOS provided continuous audit coverage of the capital master plan project for the refurbishment of the Secretariat complex in New York (see p. 1666). It investigated violations of UN regulations, rules and administrative issuances, as well as allegations of fraud, corruption and sexual misconduct. In January, OIOS established the Procurement Task Force to address weaknesses in internal control and potential fraud in UN procurement activities (see p. 1645).

Some of the more than 60 UN entities for which OIOS provided oversight services required extensive and continuous OIOS coverage due to their high financial exposure and/or their complexity. The report provided a synopsis of work in five such entities: the Department of Management; the Office for the Coordination of Humanitarian Affairs; the Office of the United Nations High Commissioner for Refugees; the United Nations Joint Staff Pension Fund; and the United Nations Compensation Commission.

By a September note [A/61/264 (Part I)/Add.2], the Secretary-General submitted his comments on Part I of the OIOS annual report.

By **decisions 61/551** and **61/552** of 22 December, the General Assembly decided to consider the OIOS annual report at its resumed sixty-first (2007) session.

Strengthening OIOS

The Secretary-General transmitted the report of the Steering Committee on the Comprehensive Review of Governance and Oversight within the United Nations and its Funds, Programmes and Specialized Agencies (see p. 1572) on the review of OIOS [A/60/883/Add.2].

The Steering Committee found that OIOS did not function effectively due to the mixed roles of internal and external oversight. Significant change was needed therefore to strengthen its structure, operation and reporting within the broader UN oversight framework. The Committee recommended, among other measures, that the responsibilities and management of OIOS should be redefined and its management should acknowledge responsibility for setting risk tolerance, implementing controls and managing risks. OIOS should transfer evaluations and management consulting activities to line management; focus on internal auditing; transfer investigations to the UN Office of Legal Affairs; and separate activities related to security from forensic accounting. The Assembly should define those UN organizations for which OIOS was responsible, and there should be no barrier to OIOS access to people or documents in the performance of its work. The OIOS budget should be based on a risk assessment and a strategy for the Office, and the term limit for the head of OIOS should be revisited. OIOS should report administratively to the Secretary-General or Deputy Secretary-General, and functionally to the Independent Audit Advisory Committee. The Steering Committee also recommended measures to strengthen OIOS working practices and improve the reporting process.

OIOS, having considered the report of the Steering Committee, issued a July report [A/60/901] containing proposals for strengthening the Office, which involved institutional changes to support its independence and creation of a proper oversight structure to facilitate professionalism and draw on the synergies of the different disciplines in the oversight function. Under the proposals, internal audit functions would be consolidated into one division headed by a director based in New York, and inspection and evaluation functions would be organized as a separate division. Inspection would be reinforced with regard to its approach, methodology and staffing; the evaluation function would be similarly strengthened. OIOS would continue its monitoring function, but the responsibility for the preparation of the biennial reports of the Secretary-General on programme performance should be transferred to the Department of Management. OIOS would be responsible for assessing the methodology, integrity and discipline of programme performance reporting. The internal management consulting function would be transferred to an appropriate office within the Secretariat. The Office would be restructured by redeploying authorized posts and using the funding allocated for general temporary assistance in lieu of established posts. OIOS proposed additional non-post resources for implementing its risk assessment framework, eliminating the backlog of investigations and enhancing information technology tools and staff training. It also proposed changes to its funding arrangements that would secure its financial independence and the use of risk assessments as a basis for determining the level of resources for internal audit, inspections and evaluations. OIOS strongly disagreed with the recommendation that the Investigations Division should be a part of the Office of Legal Affairs, as that measure would weaken oversight.

In December [A/61/605], ACABQ commented on the report of the Steering Committee, including the review of OIOS, and the OIOS report on strengthening the Office.

The Secretary-General, in a December report [A/61/610], provided revised estimates to the approved 2006-2007 budget, taking into account the proposals made by OIOS in its report. He requested the Assembly to approve an additional appropriation of $1,308,800.

Strengthening investigation functions

In response to resolution 59/287 [YUN 2005, p. 1474], the Secretary-General, in February [A/60/674], reported on progress made in the implementation of measures to strengthen the investigation functions in the United Nations. A full report would be submitted to the sixty-first (2006) session of the General Assembly.

External oversight

Joint Inspection Unit

At its resumed sixtieth session, the General Assembly had before it the annual report of the Joint Inspection Unit (JIU) for 2004 [YUN 2004, p.1372]; a January note by the Assembly President on procedures for the appointment of JIU inspectors [A/60/659]; and a February note by the Unit Chairperson on the JIU work programme for 2006 [A/C.5/60/CRP.1].

In an April note [A/61/109], the Secretary-General indicated that it would be necessary for the Assembly to appoint five persons to fill the JIU vacancies that would arise on 31 December 2007.

GENERAL ASSEMBLY ACTION

On 8 May [meeting 79], the General Assembly, on the recommendation of the Fifth Committee [A/60/748], adopted **resolution 60/258** without vote [agenda item 130].

Joint Inspection Unit

The General Assembly,

I

Reaffirming its previous resolutions on the Joint Inspection Unit, in particular resolutions 31/192 of 22 December 1976, 50/233 of 7 June 1996, 54/16 of 29 October 1999, 55/230 of 23 December 2000, 56/245 of 24 December 2001, 57/284 A and B of 20 December 2002, 58/286 of 8 April 2004 and 59/267 of 23 December 2004,

Having considered the report of the Joint Inspection Unit for 2004 and its programme of work for 2005 and the note by the Chairperson of the Unit on the programme of work of the Unit for 2006,

Noting the ongoing internal reform process of the Joint Inspection Unit aimed at further improving its effectiveness,

1. *Notes* the thematic reports mentioned in the programme of work of the Joint Inspection Unit for 2005, and in this regard reaffirms paragraph 4 of its resolution 50/233;

2. *Reaffirms* the unique role of the Unit as the only system-wide external oversight body;

3. *Welcomes* the efforts made by the Unit to improve the quality of the reports issued in 2004 and also the improvements made in the implementation of its reform process, as indicated in paragraphs 1 to 5 of its report;

4. *Takes note with appreciation* of the single consolidated format of the report of the Unit on its activities for 2004 and its programme of work for 2005;

5. *Notes* paragraphs 28 and 29 of the report of the Unit for 2004, and urges all host countries to facilitate prompt access for inspectors to all offices of participating organizations;

6. *Takes note* of the programme of work for 2006, and requests the Unit to continue to submit an advance version of its programme of work to the General Assembly at the first part of its resumed sessions;

7. *Requests* the Unit to continue to enhance dialogue with participating organizations and thereby to strengthen the follow-up of the implementation of its recommendations, in particular on managing for results;

8. *Reaffirms* the importance of effective coordination, in the implementation of their respective mandates, between the Unit, the Board of Auditors and the Office of Internal Oversight Services, in order to maximize the use of resources and share experiences, knowledge, best practices and lessons learned;

9. *Requests* the Unit to include in future annual reports more information on the impact of full implementation of recommendations, including any cost savings, productivity and efficiency gains achieved;

II

Having considered the note by the President of the General Assembly on the procedures for the appointment of inspectors of the Joint Inspection Unit,

Decides to revert to the consideration of this subject at its sixty-first session.

JIU activities. In its annual report to the General Assembly [A/62/34], JIU gave an overview of its activities in 2006, during which it issued reports on: evaluation of results-based budgeting in peacekeeping operations [JIU/REP/2006/1]; oversight lacunae in the UN system [JIU/REP/2006/2]; follow-up to the management review of the Office of the United Nations High Commissioner for Human Rights [JIU/REP/2006/3]; a second review of the implementation of headquarters agreements concluded by UN system organizations: provision of headquarters premises and other facilities by host countries [JIU/REP/2006/4]; a United Nations humanitarian assistance programme for disaster response and reduction: lessons learned from the Indian Ocean tsunami disaster [JIU/REP/2006/5]; results-based management in the United Nations in the context of the reform process [JIU/REP/2006/6]; and staff mobility in the United Nations [JIU/REP/2006/7]. It also issued a note on Goodwill Ambassadors in the UN system [JIU/NOTE/2006/1].

JIU strengthened its follow-up system by disclosing the intended impact of each of its recommendations in the text of its reports, based on agreed categories and definitions of such impacts. Each report contained an overview table on action to be taken by participating organizations, indicating the relevance of each recommendation to the organization in question. In October, JIU requested all 24 participating organizations to provide updated information on the status of the implementation of recommendations contained in reports issued by the Unit in 2004 and 2005; it received information from 20 organizations. At the end of 2006, 30 per cent of the recommendations issued in 2004 and 2005 were accepted, with some 45 per cent still under consideration. Overall acceptance rates for recommendations contained in single-agency reports reached 72 per cent, with 20 per cent still under consideration. The report indicated that 22 per cent of accepted/approved system-wide or multi-agency recommendations were implemented, and 32 per cent were in progress. In 13 per cent of cases implementation had not yet begun, and no information had been received on the remaining 33 per cent.

During 2006, six management assessments of participating organizations were completed, bringing the total number of completed assessments to 20. It was envisaged that remaining assessments would be completed in 2007.

The annual report also contained the JIU work programme for 2007.

In August [A/60/1004], JIU commented on the report of the Steering Committee on the Comprehensive Review of Governance and Oversight within the United Nations, its Funds, Programmes and Specialized Agencies, which, among other things, had recommended that the Unit be discontinued. JIU re-emphasized that oversight was ultimately the function of Member States and underlined its unique position as the only system-wide external oversight body.

The General Assembly expressed continued support for JIU and its reform efforts in resolution 61/238 of 22 December (see below).

Appointment of JIU members. In September [A/60/659], the General Assembly President submitted a note on procedures for the appointment of JIU inspectors, which he had been asked to review in resolution 59/267 [YUN 2004, 1372], with a view to enhancing the application of article 3, paragraph 2, of the JIU statute. He proposed a simplified procedure, similar to that followed by other governmental bodies.

By **decision 61/552** of 22 December, the Assembly decided that the agenda items on the Unit and on the appointment of its members would remain for consideration during its resumed sixty-first (2007) session.

GENERAL ASSEMBLY ACTION

On 22 December [meeting 84], the General Assembly, on the recommendation of the Fifth Committee [A/61/654], adopted **resolution 61/238** without vote [agenda item 124].

Joint Inspection Unit

The General Assembly,

I

Reaffirming its previous resolutions on the Joint Inspection Unit, in particular resolutions 31/192 of 22 December 1976, 50/233 of 7 June 1996, 54/16 of 29 October 1999, 55/230 of 23 December 2000, 56/245 of 24 December 2001, 57/284 A and B of 20 December 2002, 58/286 of 8 April 2004, 59/267 of 23 December 2004 and 60/258 of 8 May 2006,

Having considered the report of the Unit on its activities for 2005 and its programme of work for 2006,

Noting the ongoing internal reform process of the Unit aimed at further improving its effectiveness,

1. *Takes note with appreciation* of the report of the Joint Inspection Unit for 2005 and its programme of work for 2006;
2. *Welcomes* the ongoing efforts made by the Unit to improve the implementation of its reform process, as indicated in paragraphs 1 to 6 of its report;
3. *Reaffirms* section I, paragraph 6, of its resolution 60/258, and requests the Unit to continue to submit an advance version of its programme of work to the General Assembly at the first part of its resumed sessions;
4. *Welcomes* the increasing focus of the programme of work of the Unit on issues of system-wide relevance, and urges the Unit, as the only system-wide external oversight body, to continue to focus its work and reports, whenever possible, on issues of system-wide interest, value and relevance to the efficient and effective functioning of all organizations to which the Unit provides services;
5. *Encourages* the Unit to increase its efforts to help to improve the efficiency and effectiveness of the respective secretariats in achieving the legislative mandates and to ensure that the mission objectives established for the organizations are carried out in the most economical manner and that optimum use is made of resources available for carrying out those activities;
6. *Welcomes* the information presented in paragraphs 27 to 30 of the report of the Unit, bearing in mind that the methodology is still at the early stage of implementation, and requests that future reports, to the extent possible, also include information on estimated savings, actual savings achieved, acceptance rate of recommendations and implementation status by impact category, particularly regarding system-wide or multi-agency recommendations;
7. *Looks forward* to receiving an analysis of the eight categories of impact as described in paragraphs 29 to 31 of the report, as applied to the actual impact of its recommendations;
8. *Notes* the ongoing efforts of the Unit to improve its working methods, and invites the Unit to undergo external peer reviews as necessary;

II

Having considered the note by the President of the General Assembly on the procedures for the appointment of inspectors of the Joint Inspection Unit,

Bearing in mind paragraphs 8 and 9 of General Assembly resolution 59/267 and article 3, paragraph 2, of the statute of the Unit,

1. *Takes note* of the note by the President of the General Assembly on the procedures for the appointment of inspectors of the Joint Inspection Unit;
2. *Confirms* the existing procedure for the appointment of the inspectors in accordance with article 3 of the statute of the Unit;
3. *Decides* that, beginning on 1 January 2008, the President of the General Assembly, when drawing up a list of countries that will be requested to propose candidates, in accordance with article 3, paragraph 1, of the statute of the Unit, will invite Member States to submit the names of the countries and their respective candidates simultaneously, on the understanding that the can-

didates submitted are the candidates that the respective Member States intend to propose, to the extent possible, for appointment by the General Assembly, in accordance with article 3, paragraph 2, of the statute;

4. *Invites* the President of the General Assembly to submit to the Assembly, for consideration at its sixty-fourth session, a report on the effective application of the above-mentioned selection procedures in enhancing efficiency in implementing article 3, paragraph 2, of the statute.

Oil-for-food programme

The oil-for-food programme, established by Security Council resolution 986(1995) [YUN 1995, p. 475] authorizing the sale of Iraqi petroleum and petroleum products as a temporary measure to finance humanitarian assistance, thereby alleviating the adverse consequences of the sanctions regime imposed by the Council, was phased out on 21 November 2003 [YUN 2003, p. 362]. In April 2004, the Secretary-General established the Independent Inquiry Committee (IIC) to investigate the administration and management of the programme, including allegations of fraud and corruption [YUN 2004, p. 364]. IIC, headed by Paul A. Volcker (United States), issued its reports and recommendations in 2005 [YUN 2005, p. 1476]. In December 2005, the Secretary-General decided to maintain the Committee's operation until the end of March 2006 [ibid., p. 436] through a follow-up entity known as the Office of the Independent Inquiry Committee. On 24 March 2006, the Secretary-General extended the Office until 31 December (see p. 409). From 1 January 2007, the Office would be administered by the UN Department of Management for a two-year interim period, which could be extended by the Secretary-General.

In a December bulletin [ST/SGB/2006/16], the Secretary-General promulgated a procedure for the management, preservation and storage of, and access to, the documents, records and other materials that came into the possession of, or were generated by IIC during its operation. During the two-year period, IIC documents would remain unsealed to enable the United Nations to respond to requests for information and assistance by Member States. Documents could be made available to Member States on written request to the Secretary-General. The Office would determine which documents were responsive to the request and make a recommendation to the Secretary-General on their disclosure. Restricted documents under seal would only be released under conditions stipulated in the bulletin. At the conclusion of the interim period, the Office would transfer custody of all IIC documents to the UN Archives and Records Management Section, which would put them in permanent storage in the archives of the United Nations. Restricted documents would remain under seal for 50 years; there would be no declassification of such documents.

By **decision 61/552** of 22 December, the Assembly decided that the follow-up to the recommendations on administrative management and internal oversight of IIC into the oil-for-food programme would remain for consideration during its resumed sixty-first (2007) session.

Other administrative matters

Conference management

Committee on Conferences

At its resumed sixtieth (2006) session, the General Assembly had before it the report of the Committee on Conferences for 2005 [YUN 2005, p. 1545]. It also considered the Secretary-General's 2005 reports on the reform of the UN Department for General Assembly and Conference Management (DGACM) [ibid., p. 1546], and on the pattern of conferences and the related ACABQ report [ibid., p. 1547].

GENERAL ASSEMBLY ACTION

On 8 May [meeting 79], the General Assembly, on the recommendation of the Fifth Committee [A/60/601/Add.1], adopted **resolution 60/236 B** without vote [agenda item 127].

Pattern of conferences

B

The General Assembly,

Recalling its relevant resolutions, including resolutions 40/243 of 18 December 1985, 41/213 of 19 December 1986, 43/222 A to E of 21 December 1988, 51/211 A to E of 18 December 1996, 52/214 of 22 December 1997, 53/208 A to E of 18 December 1998, 54/248 of 23 December 1999, 55/222 of 23 December 2000, 56/242 of 24 December 2001, 56/254 D of 27 March 2002, 56/262 of 15 February 2002, 56/287 of 27 June 2002, 57/283 A of 20 December 2002, 57/283 B of 15 April 2003, 58/250 of 23 December 2003, 59/265 of 23 December 2004 and 60/236 A of 23 December 2005,

Reaffirming its resolution 42/207 C of 11 December 1987, in which it requested the Secretary-General to ensure the equal treatment of the official languages of the United Nations,

Having considered the report of the Committee on Conferences for 2005, the relevant reports of the Secretary-General and the report of the Advisory Committee on Administrative and Budgetary Questions,

Reaffirming the provisions relevant to conference services of its resolutions on multilingualism,

I

Takes note of the report of the Committee on Conferences for 2005;

II

A. Utilization of conference-servicing resources

1. *Reaffirms* the practice that, in the use of conference rooms, priority must be given to the meetings of Member States;

2. *Requests* the Secretary-General, when preparing budget proposals for conference services, to ensure that the level of resources proposed for temporary assistance is commensurate with the full demand of services, estimated on the basis of current experience;

3. *Notes with satisfaction* that the overall utilization factor at the four main duty stations increased to 83 per cent in 2004 from 77 per cent in 2003, exceeding the benchmark for the first time since 2000;

4. *Recognizes* the importance of the meetings of regional and other major groupings of Member States for the smooth functioning of the sessions of intergovernmental bodies, and requests the Secretary-General to ensure that, as far as possible, all requests for conference services for the meetings of regional and other major groupings of Member States are met;

5. *Notes with concern* the continued decrease in the percentage of meetings held by regional and other major groupings of Member States that were provided with interpretation services, at the four main duty stations, from 98 per cent during the period from May 2001 to April 2002, to 92 per cent during the period from May 2002 to April 2003, to 90 per cent during the period from May 2003 to April 2004, to 85 per cent during the period from May 2004 to April 2005, despite the fact that the number of meetings requesting the provision of interpretation noticeably decreased, by 15 per cent, during the period from May 2004 to April 2005;

6. *Recalls* that meetings held by regional and other major groupings of Member States are provided with interpretation services on an ad hoc basis, in accordance with established practice;

7. *Once again urges* intergovernmental bodies to spare no effort at the planning stage to take into account the meetings of regional and other major groupings of Member States, to make provision for such meetings in their programmes of work and to notify conference services, well in advance, of any cancellations so that unutilized conference-servicing resources may, to the extent possible, be reassigned to meetings of regional and other major groupings of Member States;

8. *Notes* that improvements in the utilization factor might entail a reduction in the availability of conference services for meetings of regional groups, and requests the Secretary-General to explore innovative ways to address this problem and to report to the General Assembly through the Committee on Conferences;

9. *Welcomes* the steps taken by those bodies that have adjusted their programmes of work in order to achieve the optimum utilization of conference-servicing resources, and requests the Committee on Conferences to continue consultations with the secretariats and bureaux of bodies that underutilize their conference-servicing resources, in line with what was requested by paragraph 2 of section II.A of its resolution 59/265;

10. *Recalls* its several resolutions, including resolution 59/265, section II.A, paragraph 8, reaffirms that, in conformity with the headquarters rule, all meetings of Nairobi-based United Nations bodies shall take place in Nairobi, except as otherwise authorized by the General Assembly or the Committee on Conferences acting on its behalf, and requests the Secretary-General to report on the subject to the Assembly at its sixty-first session through the Committee on Conferences;

11. *Strongly discourages* any invitation to host meetings that would violate the headquarters rule at the United Nations Office at Nairobi and at other United Nations centres with low utilization levels;

12. *Welcomes* the efforts undertaken so far to increase utilization of the conference facilities at the Economic Commission for Africa, in particular the introduction by the Commission of an integrated system for the management of its conferences and the conducting of a fact-finding mission to identify best practices at similar conference centres within the United Nations system;

13. *Requests* the Secretary-General to continue his efforts to ensure that the conference centre at the Economic Commission for Africa establishes and develops linkages with other centres and bodies and to report thereon to the General Assembly at its sixty-first session through the Committee on Conferences;

14. *Notes* that the strict implementation of the headquarters minimum operating security standards has compelled the Economic Commission for Africa to restrict the utilization of its conference centre to organizations of the United Nations family, foreign representatives accredited to Addis Ababa, the African Union, recognized international non-governmental organizations and the Government of Ethiopia;

15. *Invites* the Secretary-General to explore means to increase the utilization of the conference centre of the Economic Commission for Africa, bearing in mind the headquarters minimum operating security standards, and to report thereon to the General Assembly at its sixty-first session, through the Committee on Conferences;

B. Reform of the Department for General Assembly and Conference Management

1. *Reaffirms* that the Fifth Committee is the appropriate Main Committee of the General Assembly entrusted with responsibilities for administrative and budgetary matters;

2. *Also reaffirms* that the major goals of the reform of the Department for General Assembly and Conference Management of the Secretariat are to provide high-quality documents in a timely manner in all official languages, as well as high-quality conference services to Member States at all duty stations, and to achieve those aims as efficiently and cost-effectively as possible, in ac-

cordance with the relevant resolutions of the General Assembly;

3. *Notes* the ongoing efforts towards the attainment of integrated global management, recognizes the upgrading of the information technology capacity at the United Nations Office at Nairobi, which is essential for the successful achievement of integrated global management, and requests the Secretary-General to keep the General Assembly apprised of progress made in this regard;

4. *Also notes* the initial measures taken so far by the Department to seek the evaluation by Member States of the quality of the conference services provided to them as a key performance indicator of the Department, including through language-specific informational meetings twice a year, and requests the Secretary-General to ensure that such measures provide equal opportunities to Member States to present their evaluation in the six official languages of the United Nations and are in full compliance with relevant resolutions of the General Assembly;

5. *Welcomes* the progress achieved in the implementation of the Electronic Meetings Planning and Resource Allocation System (e-Meets) and the electronic documentation management concept (e-Doc);

6. *Notes* the ongoing efforts towards the establishment of the integrated global management system, and requests the Secretary-General to report to the General Assembly at its sixty-first session on the outcome of the work of the task forces through the Committee on Conferences;

7. *Takes note* of the conclusions of the departmental task force on workload standards, and requests the Secretary-General, while reviewing the issue of workload standards, which date from 1976, and performance measurement tools in the context of the introduction of applicable information technologies, to take fully into account the unique nature of the functions of the language services of the Department;

8. *Requests* the Secretary-General to further explore the issue of offering information technology-related training (including keyboarding) and building basic information technology skills requirements into vacancy announcements;

9. *Recalls* section II.B, paragraph 10, of its resolution 59/265, and in this regard looks forward to the submission of the proposal referred to in that paragraph;

10. *Reaffirms* section II.B, paragraph 10, of its resolution 57/283 B, and in that context stresses the importance of maintaining the official records editing function, as well as the importance of retaining the concordance principle in order to ensure equally valid texts of resolutions in all six official languages;

III

Documentation and publication-related matters

1. *Emphasizes* the paramount importance of the equality of the six official languages of the United Nations;

2. *Notes with concern* the continued high level of late submissions of documentation by author departments, which, in turn, negatively impact the functioning of intergovernmental bodies, and requests the Secretary-General to report to the General Assembly, at its sixty-first session, through the Committee on Conferences, on impediments, if any, to achieving full compliance with the ten-week and six-week rules for the issuance of pre-session documents, including, where appropriate, proposed measures to address such impediments;

3. *Reiterates its request* to the Secretary-General to ensure that the rules concerning the simultaneous distribution of documents in all official languages are followed with respect to both the distribution of printed copies and the posting of parliamentary documentation on the Official Document System and the United Nations website, in keeping with section III, paragraph 5, of its resolution 55/222;

4. *Notes with concern* the non-compliance with rule 59 of the rules of procedure of the General Assembly, and requests the Secretary-General to ensure the communication of resolutions adopted by the Assembly to Member States within fifteen days of the closure of the session;

5. *Reaffirms* its decision in section III, paragraph 9, of its resolution 59/265, that the issuance of documents on planning, budgetary and administrative matters requiring urgent consideration by the General Assembly shall be accorded priority;

6. *Welcomes* the efforts of the interdepartmental task force on documentation in addressing the problem of late issuance of documentation, and requests the Secretary-General to develop a clear accountability mechanism within the Secretariat for the submission, processing and issuance of documentation and to submit a detailed report thereon to the Committee on Conferences for its further consideration and analysis, in order to provide concrete recommendations to the General Assembly at its sixty-first session;

7. *Reiterates its request* to the Secretary-General to direct all departments of the Secretariat to include the following elements in their reports:

(a) Summary of the report;

(b) Consolidated conclusions, recommendations and other proposed actions;

(c) Relevant background information;

8. *Encourages* intergovernmental and expert bodies to include the above-mentioned elements, where appropriate, in their reports to the General Assembly;

9. *Requests* that all documents submitted to legislative organs by the Secretariat, intergovernmental and expert bodies for consideration and action have conclusions and recommendations in bold print;

10. *Requests* the Secretary-General to continue to take steps to improve the quality and accuracy of meeting records in all six official languages through full reliance in the preparation and translation of those records on sound recordings and written texts of statements as they were delivered in the original languages;

11. *Notes* some improvement in the issuance of verbatim and summary records, while recognizing that delay in their issuance still exists;

12. *Requests* the Secretary-General to continue to take appropriate measures to ameliorate the delay in the issuance of verbatim and summary records, with a view to issuing them in a timely manner;

13. *Recalls* section II.B, paragraph 14, of its resolution 59/265, and reiterates its request to the Secretary-General to further elaborate on all options, including those set out in paragraphs 59 to 63 of his report on the reform of the Department for General Assembly and Conference Management, in accordance with legislative mandates, and to report on their practical and financial implications to the General Assembly at its sixty-first session through the Committee on Conferences;

14. *Recalls* section II.B, paragraph 13, of its resolution 59/265, and takes note of paragraphs 57 to 59 of the report of the Secretary-General, and decides to revert to this issue in the context of its consideration of the report referred to in the paragraph above;

IV

Translation and interpretation-related matters

1. *Requests* the Secretary-General to ensure the highest quality of interpretation and translation services in all official languages;

2. *Reiterates its request* to the Secretary-General to make sure that terminology used in translation and interpretation services reflects the latest linguistic norms and terminology of the official languages in order to ensure the highest quality;

3. *Requests* the Secretary-General to continue to improve the accuracy of translation of documents into the official languages, giving particular significance to the quality of translation;

4. *Reiterates its request* to the Secretary-General, when recruiting temporary assistance in the language services, to ensure that all language services are given equal treatment and are provided with equally favourable working conditions and resources, with a view to achieving maximum quality of their services, with full respect for the specificities of the six official languages and taking into account their respective workloads;

5. *Also reiterates its request* to the Secretary-General to address the question of the appropriate level of self-revision that is consistent with quality in all official languages and to report thereon to the General Assembly at its sixty-first session;

6. *Notes with concern* the disparities in interpretation and translation vacancy rates between the United Nations Office at Nairobi and other duty stations;

7. *Expresses deep concern* at the high vacancy rates in the interpretation and translation services at the United Nations Office at Nairobi, especially the chronic difficulty in staffing the Arabic Interpretation Unit, and requests the Secretary-General to address this through, inter alia, assistance from Member States in advertising and facilitating the conduct of competitive examinations to fill these language vacancies;

8. *Requests* the Secretary-General to address the problem of succession planning in order to fill emerging vacancies in language services in a timely manner through outreach to eligible applicants;

9. *Reiterates its request* that the Secretary-General continue efforts to explore the use of new technologies, such as computer-assisted translation, remote and off-site translation and speech recognition, in the six official languages, in order to further enhance the quality and productivity of conference services, and to keep the General Assembly informed of the introduction of any other new technology;

V

Information technology

1. *Notes with appreciation* the progress achieved across duty stations in integrating information technology into meetings management and documentation-processing systems and the global approach to sharing standards, good practices and technological achievements among conference services at all duty stations;

2. *Requests* the Secretary-General to ensure the compatibility of technologies used in all duty stations and to ensure that they are user-friendly in all official languages;

3. *Also requests* the Secretary-General to complete the task of uploading all important older United Nations documents onto the United Nations website in all six official languages on a priority basis, so that these archives are also available to Member States through that medium;

4. *Welcomes* the strengthening of the Information Technology Unit at the United Nations Office at Nairobi, and requests the Secretary-General to continue to address the issue of maintaining parity among duty stations in terms of information technology capacity.

2006 Committee session. The Committee on Conferences held an organizational meeting on 11 May and its substantive session from 11 to 15 September [A/61/32]. It examined requests for changes to the approved calendar of conferences for 2006 and 2007 [A/AC.172/2006/2] and reviewed the draft revised calendar of conferences and meetings for 2007 [A/61/129/Add.1], reflecting the changes for the second year of the biennium since the adoption of the biennial calendar. The Committee recommended a draft resolution for adoption by the Assembly.

The Committee also considered meetings management and improved utilization of conference-servicing resources and facilities; the impact of the capital master plan on meetings held at Headquarters; integrated global management of conference services; and matters related to documentation, publication, translation and interpretation. (The Committee's deliberations and recommendations on those matters are detailed in the sections below.)

The Committee recommended that the Assembly authorize nine of its subsidiary organs, listed in letters from the Committee Chairman of 6 September [A/61/320] and 19 October [A/61/320/Add.1] to meet in New York during the main part of the Assembly's sixty-first (2006) session. The Assembly, by **decision 61/501** of 12 September and 26 October, authorized those organs to meet as recommended.

The Committee approved requests from several bodies for changes to the approved calendar for 2006.

Use of conference services

The Secretary-General, in July [A/61/129], submitted a comprehensive report on issues related to the pattern of conferences, including the integrated global management of conference services, meetings management, document management, and matters related to translation and interpretation (see sections below).

The report also provided information on the utilization of conference servicing resources and facilities. The overall utilization factor in 2005 at the four duty stations—Geneva, Nairobi, New York and Vienna—was 85 per cent, 2 percentage points higher than in 2004.

The Committee on Conferences, in September [A/61/32], welcomed the increase in overall utilization and stressed that, while it was worthwhile to ensure the best use of conference-servicing resources, the needs of the intergovernmental bodies should not be overlooked.

In October [A/61/499], ACABQ stated that a precise identification of what constituted time lost for conference servicing was important for proper calculation of the utilization factor and a detailed explanation should be provided of all factors contributing to the loss of time for conference servicing.

Use of regional conference facilities

Nairobi and Addis Ababa

At the United Nations Office in Nairobi (UNON), including the United Nations Environment Programme and the United Nations Human Settlements Programme, the utilization factor remained high at 96.2 per cent in 2005 and 100 per cent as at 31 May 2006. During the 2004-2005 biennium, the utilization rate for UNON interpreters increased by 40 per cent, as compared with the 2002-2003 biennium. The utilization rate at the Economic Commission for Africa (ECA) (Addis Ababa, Ethiopia) was reduced due to the cancellation of a number of events in 2005. ECA continued to explore innovative ways to further develop its clientele and operations.

In September [A/61/32], the Committee on Conferences was informed that UNON had met all requests by regional groups for meetings with interpretation. However, problems in filling vacant interpretation posts, particularly Arabic posts, continued. The use of the conference centre at ECA, which had a strong information technology team and a well-established printing and publishing facility, had improved considerably since 2005.

In October [A/61/499], ACABQ was informed that, despite various efforts to fill vacant language posts at UNON, the vacancy rate for Arabic interpretation stood at 50 per cent as at August. The Committee reiterated its recommendation that DGACM intensify efforts to improve the vacancy situation in conference services at UNON, including consideration of all possible approaches.

Integrated global management

In his July report on the pattern of conferences [A/61/129], the Secretary-General said that further progress had been made under the DGACM project on integrated global management of conference services. Common approaches to administrative policies, practices and procedures were identified and harmonized/standardized across the four duty stations. At the Seventh Coordination Meeting of Conference Managers (Vienna, June), the four duty stations agreed to pursue proactive document management in order to implement fully General Assembly mandates on the timely issuance of documentation and their control and limitation. They also agreed on standardized formulas to estimate translation, interpretation and editing capacity. The coordination of terminology would be achieved through the establishment of a central terminology database and a terminology coordination board. The duty stations would encourage the use of computer-assisted translation and increase the percentage of documents translated with such technology.

DGACM launched an information technology initiative to identify an information technology strategy that would lead to a global, standardized approach to support decision-making and real-time global access to data, satisfy client needs and align more effectively with the information technology standards and strategies of the Secretariat. As a first step, an information Technology Governance Board was established under the Assistant Secretary-General for General Assembly and Conference Management. The Board, comprised of senior managers and information technology professionals from all duty stations, would provide guidance on an information technology strategy, avoid duplication of information technology development efforts and standardize business processes and technological architecture and applications. Three project teams were established to: set up a centrally-hosted reporting database; further integrate, re-engineer and migrate the meetings management system to an updated, standard, open platform; and conduct a technical evaluation of internal and enterprise document systems.

The Committee on Conferences [A/61/32] welcomed the progress made on integrated global management of conference services and looked forward to receiving information on the work of the task forces established under the DGACM project.

In October [A/61/499], ACABQ encouraged further efforts aimed at enhancing the coordinated approach to conference servicing, while emphasizing the need for quality and consistency in all official languages.

Interpretation for regional and other groupings

In July [A/61/129], the Secretary-General reported that the number of meetings requested by regional and other major groupings of Member States for the January-December 2005 period and held without interpretation increased by 34 per cent, compared with the corresponding period in 2004. Meetings provided with interpretation services also increased from 85 per cent during the previous period to 87 per cent. However, interpretation services continued to be provided to such groupings on an "as available" basis, and depended largely on the cancellation of other meetings. In response to General Assembly resolution 60/236 B of 8 May (see p. 1654), the Secretary-General identified two options to address the problem. The first would allocate interpretation services on a weekly basis for meetings of bodies with an entitlement to meet "as required", offering those services to regional groups when entitled bodies did not require them. The second would earmark specific resources to enhance the predictability for servicing meetings of regional and other major groupings. The first option would not require additional budgetary appropriations, but could not guarantee additional services for regional groups. The second option would guarantee such services, since dedicated resources would be allocated.

The Committee on Conferences [A/61/32] expressed concern that, although the percentage of meetings of regional and other major groups was higher than in 2004, it was below the level attained in previous reporting periods. It welcomed the suggestions contained in the report, but requested clarification as to whether the first option would require additional resources. A Secretariat representative explained that no additional budgetary resources were required under the first option.

Documentation

The Secretary-General, in his July report on the pattern of conferences [A/61/129], said that, after years of strict enforcement, the timeliness of submission of documentation had improved steadily but more could be done. Since delays were often caused by factors beyond the Secretariat's control, the General Assembly might wish to encourage Member States to make their submissions before the deadlines, and allow DGACM to give priority to minimizing very late issuances, especially in cases where overwhelming workload, insufficient processing capacity and late submissions combined to make the issuance of documents six weeks before meetings impracticable.

In September [A/61/32], the Committee on Conferences stressed that much more needed to be done to improve distribution of documents in accordance with the six-week rule, although it was acknowledged that failure to comply with the rule was sometimes due to factors beyond DGACM control. The Committee also stressed the importance of simultaneous distribution of documents in the official UN languages and requested greater vigilance in ensuring that documents were posted on the UN website in all six languages.

In October [A/61/499], ACABQ said that the timely submission of documents should be included in the proposed programme budget as a performance indicator for author departments. It requested that an analysis of the UN printing capacity be included in future conference servicing and document management reports.

Translation and interpretation matters

In July [A/61/129], Secretary-General reported that efforts to enhance the quality of language services and staff training and replenish the ranks of the language services would be a DGACM priority. The Secretariat would participate in outreach activities targeting universities that trained language professionals, in order to make them aware of the staffing needs of international organizations and to help them develop curricula to ensure that graduates could function effectively in those organizations.

In September [A/61/32], the Committee on Conferences expressed concern about the shortage of qualified language staff that could result from the demographic changes in language services, combined with the decline in the number of applicants for UN language examinations, and stressed the need for a plan to deal with the problem.

In October [A/61/499], ACABQ said that it saw merit in the Secretariat's intention to participate in outreach activities targeting universities that trained language professionals. At the same time, the United Nations should try to expedite the replacement of retired language staff, expand the recruitment base of linguists and enhance staff training programmes.

Workload standards

The Secretary-General, in his July report on the pattern of conferences [A/61/129], said that the review of workload standards for specific categories of conference servicing staff, conducted by a DGACM task force in 2004 [YUN 2004, p. 1467] and 2005 [YUN 2005, p. 1549], led to the conclusion that such standards were crude, one-dimensional measures of performance, focusing only on the quantity of output at the individual level. There was a clear need to supplement the standards with more meaningful and multidimensional measures of performance, including timeliness of delivery and quality of services. Responding to the request made by the General Assembly in resolution 58/250 [YUN 2003, p. 1486] that DGACM develop a comprehensive methodology for performance measurement and management from a full-system perspective, the Department proposed to report to the Assembly on a regular basis, beginning in 2007, on additional indicators on timeliness, quality, financial performance and client satisfaction. The proposed "balanced scorecard" approach would shift emphasis to full-system performance and allow more timely and targeted action to address detected weaknesses.

In October [A/61/499], ACABQ said that it remained concerned that the Secretary-General had not yet implemented the Assembly's request with regard to the development of quantitative methods and indicators to assess productivity, efficiency and cost-effectiveness, and welcomed the Secretary-General's intention to report, beginning in 2007, on additional performance indicators.

Impact of CMP on conference services

In August [A/61/300], the Secretary-General reported on the impact of the capital master plan for the refurbishment of the United Nations Headquarters complex on meetings held at Headquarters during implementation, which was expected to take place from 2008 to 2013. The report provided a review of the proposal [YUN 2005, p. 1555] to build a temporary conference facility, or swing space, on the North Lawn of the complex to accommodate part of the meeting space requirements. Construction of the swing space was expected to start in July 2007 and finish in June 2008. Headquarters activities would be largely retained during the renovation and core activities would not be affected if planned ahead and scheduled carefully. However, there would not be sufficient conference facilities to accommodate non-core activities. Parallel consultations and events involving large numbers of participants should be avoided, reduced or held off-site.

The Secretary-General recommended that the Assembly inform calendar bodies to take into consideration the limitations and inflexibility of the conference facilities during the renovation period when planning their meetings; instruct all meeting organizers to consult closely with DGACM to allow maximum predictability in coordinating Headquarters activities and construction work; note that all meetings, with the exception of those of the Security Council, the Assembly and the high-level segment of the Economic and Social Council, should be held strictly within regular meeting hours on working days to ensure that nights and weekends were available for construction work, thus reducing inconvenience and additional costs. The Secretariat should report periodically on the impact of CMP on meetings held at Headquarters during its implementation.

GENERAL ASSEMBLY ACTION

On 22 December [meeting 84], the General Assembly, on the recommendation of the Fifth Committee [A/61/597], adopted **resolution 61/236** without vote [agenda item 121].

Pattern of conferences

The General Assembly,

Recalling its relevant resolutions, including resolutions 40/243 of 18 December 1985, 41/213 of 19 December 1986, 43/222 A to E of 21 December 1988, 51/211 A to E of 18 December 1996, 52/214 of 22 December 1997, 53/208 A to E of 18 December 1998, 54/248 of 23 December 1999, 55/222 of 23 December 2000, 56/242 of 24 December 2001, 56/254 D of 27 March 2002, 56/262 of 15 February 2002, 56/287 of 27 June 2002, 57/283 A of 20 December 2002, 57/283 B of 15 April 2003, 58/250 of 23 December 2003, 59/265 of 23 December 2004, 60/236 A of 23 December 2005 and 60/236 B of 8 May 2006,

Reaffirming its resolution 42/207 C of 11 December 1987, in which it requested the Secretary-General to ensure the equal treatment of the official languages of the United Nations,

Having considered the report of the Committee on Conferences for 2006 and the relevant reports of the Secretary-General,

Having also considered the report of the Advisory Committee on Administrative and Budgetary Questions,

Reaffirming the provisions relevant to conference services of its resolutions on multilingualism,

I

Calendar of conferences and meetings

1. *Welcomes* the report of the Committee on Conferences for 2006;

2. *Approves* the draft revised calendar of conferences and meetings of the United Nations for 2007, as submitted by the Committee on Conferences, taking into account the observations of the Committee and subject to the provisions of the present resolution;

3. *Authorizes* the Committee on Conferences to make any adjustments to the calendar of conferences and meetings for 2007 that may become necessary as a result of actions and decisions taken by the General Assembly at its sixty-first session;

4. *Notes with satisfaction* that the Secretariat has taken into account the arrangements referred to in General Assembly resolutions 53/208 A, 54/248, 55/222, 56/242, 57/283 B, 58/250, 59/265 and 60/236 A concerning Orthodox Good Friday and the official holidays of Eid al-Fitr and Eid al-Adha, and requests all intergovernmental bodies to observe those decisions when planning their meetings;

5. *Requests* the Secretary-General to ensure that any modification to the calendar of conferences and meetings is implemented strictly in accordance with the mandate of the Committee on Conferences and other relevant resolutions of the General Assembly;

II

A. Utilization of conference-servicing resources

1. *Reaffirms* the practice that, in the use of conference rooms, priority must be given to the meetings of Member States;

2. *Notes with satisfaction* that the overall utilization factor at the four main duty stations increased to 85 per cent in 2005 from 83 per cent in 2004;

3. *Welcomes* the steps taken by those bodies that have adjusted their programmes of work in order to achieve the optimum utilization of conference-servicing resources, and requests the Committee on Conferences to continue consultations with the secretariats and bureaux of bodies that underutilize their conference-servicing resources;

4. *Recognizes* the importance of meetings of regional and other major groupings of Member States for the smooth functioning of the sessions of intergovernmental bodies, and requests the Secretary-General to ensure that, as far as possible, all requests for conference services for the meetings of regional and other major groupings of Member States are met;

5. *Notes with concern* the difficulties experienced by Member States owing to the lack of conference services for some meetings of regional and other major groupings of Member States;

6. *Also notes with concern* that, although the percentage of meetings held by regional and other major groupings of Member States that were provided with interpretation services in the four main duty stations in 2005 increased to 87 per cent, as compared with 85 per cent in 2004, the figure is still below the 98 per cent provided with services from May 2001 to April 2002, 92 per cent from May 2002 to April 2003 and 90 per cent from May 2003 to April 2004;

7. *Recalls* that meetings held by regional and other major groupings of Member States have so far been provided with interpretation services on an ad hoc basis, in accordance with established practice, and requests the Secretary-General to continue to explore innovative ways to address this problem and to report to the General Assembly through the Committee on Conferences;

8. *Once again urges* intergovernmental bodies to spare no effort at the planning stage to take into account the meetings of regional and other major groupings of Member States, to make provision for such meetings in their programmes of work and to notify conference services, well in advance, of any cancellations so that unutilized conference-servicing resources may, to the extent possible, be reassigned to meetings of regional and other major groupings of Member States;

9. *Notes with satisfaction* that, in accordance with several General Assembly resolutions, including resolution 60/236 B, section II.A, paragraph 10, in conformity with the headquarters rule, all meetings of Nairobi-based United Nations bodies took place in Nairobi in 2005, but reiterates the need for vigilance in this respect, and requests the Secretary-General to report thereon to the Assembly at its sixty-second session through the Committee on Conferences;

10. *Welcomes* the fact that international and local corporations and academic institutions are being allowed to host events at the conference centre of the Economic Commission for Africa after screening, on a case-by-case basis, by the United Nations Security and Safety Service to ensure compliance with the headquarters minimum operating security standards, which is likely to contribute to increasing the utilization of the centre;

11. *Also welcomes* the efforts undertaken to increase utilization of the conference facilities at the Economic Commission for Africa and to align the methodology used to compile utilization statistics with that of Conference Services at the four main duty stations, including building on the cooperative agreement the Commission established with the Division of Conference Services at the United Nations Office at Nairobi;

12. *Requests* the Secretary-General to continue efforts to ensure that the Economic Commission for Africa strengthens linkages with other centres and bodies;

13. *Also requests* the Secretary-General to continue to explore means to increase the utilization of the conference centre of the Economic Commission for Africa, bearing in mind the headquarters minimum operating security standards, and to report thereon to the General

Assembly at its sixty-second session through the Committee on Conferences;

B. Impact of the capital master plan (strategy IV (phased approach)) on meetings held at Headquarters during its implementation

1. *Takes note* of the report of the Secretary-General on the impact of the capital master plan on meetings to be held at Headquarters during its implementation;

2. *Requests* bodies having their meetings listed in the calendar of conferences and meetings, when planning their meetings, especially major or high-level conferences, summits and special meetings, organs created under the Charter of the United Nations, their subsidiary bodies and other intergovernmental organizations and treaty bodies that normally meet at Headquarters to take into consideration the limitations and inflexibility of the entire conference facilities at Headquarters throughout the renovation period;

3. *Notes in particular* that there will be noise during the construction, which will be carried out in the evenings and at weekends;

4. *Requests* all meeting requesters and organizers to liaise closely with the Department for General Assembly and Conference Management of the Secretariat on all matters related to the scheduling of meetings to allow maximum predictability in coordinating activities at Headquarters during the construction period;

5. *Requests* the Committee on Conferences to keep the matter under constant review, and requests the Secretary-General to report regularly to the Committee on matters pertaining to the calendar of conferences and meetings of the United Nations during the construction period;

6. *Requests* the Secretary-General to ensure that implementation of the capital master plan will not compromise the quality of conference services provided to Member States and the equal treatment of the language services, which should be provided with equally favourable working conditions and resources, with a view to receiving maximum quality of services;

III

Integrated global management

1. *Notes with appreciation* the progress achieved across duty stations in integrating information technology into meetings management and documentation-processing systems and the global approach to sharing standards, good practices and technological achievements among conference services at all duty stations;

2. *Welcomes* the establishment of a regular budget technology post at the United Nations Office at Nairobi and other efforts there to share best practices, which are essential for the successful achievement of integrated global management;

3. *Reaffirms* that the major goals of the reform of the Department for General Assembly and Conference Management are to provide high-quality documents in a timely manner in all official languages, as well as high-quality conference services to Member States at all duty stations, and to achieve those aims as efficiently and cost-effectively as possible, in accordance with the relevant resolutions of the General Assembly;

4. *Requests* the Secretary-General to ensure the compatibility of technologies used in all duty stations and to ensure that they are user-friendly in all official languages;

5. *Also requests* the Secretary-General to complete the task of uploading all important older United Nations documents onto the United Nations website in all six official languages on a priority basis, so that these archives are also available to Member States through that medium;

6. *Recalls* section II.B, paragraph 4, of its resolution 60/236 B, in which it requested the Secretary-General to ensure that measures taken by the Department for General Assembly and Conference Management to seek the evaluation by Member States of the quality of the conference services provided to them as a key performance indicator of the Department provide equal opportunities to Member States to present their evaluation in the six official languages of the United Nations and are in full compliance with relevant resolutions of the General Assembly, and requests the Secretary-General to report to the Assembly, through the Committee on Conferences, on progress made in this regard;

7. *Also recalls* section II.B, paragraph 6, of its resolution 60/236 B, and requests the Secretary-General to report to the General Assembly at its sixty-second session, through the Committee on Conferences, on both the results of the work of the task forces and the outcome of the ongoing consultations among duty stations on a follow-up to the recommendations of the task forces;

8. *Requests* the Secretary-General to keep the General Assembly apprised of progress made in integrated global management;

IV

Documentation and publication-related matters

1. *Emphasizes* the paramount importance of the equality of the six official languages of the United Nations;

2. *Reaffirms* that the Fifth Committee is the appropriate Main Committee of the General Assembly entrusted with responsibilities for administrative and budgetary matters;

3. *Stresses* that matters related to conference management, including documentation, fall within the purview of the Fifth Committee;

4. *Notes with concern* the continued high level of late submissions of documentation by author departments, which, in turn, have a negative impact on the functioning of intergovernmental bodies, and requests the Secretary-General to report to the General Assembly, at its sixty-second session, through the Committee on Conferences, on impediments, if any, to achieving full compliance with the ten-week and six-week rules for the issuance of pre-session documents, including, where appropriate, proposed measures to address such impediments;

5. *Welcomes* the new accountability mechanism set up in the Secretariat for the submission, processing and issuance of documentation, and requests the Secretary-

General to report thereon to the Committee on Conferences for its further consideration and analysis, in order to provide concrete recommendations to the General Assembly at its sixty-second session;

6. *Reiterates its request* to the Secretary-General to ensure that the rules concerning the simultaneous distribution of documents in all official languages are followed with respect to both the distribution of printed copies and the posting of parliamentary documentation on the Official Document System and the United Nations website, in keeping with section III, paragraph 5, of its resolution 55/222;

7. *Reaffirms* its decision in section III, paragraph 9, of its resolution 59/265, that the issuance of documents on planning, budgetary and administrative matters requiring urgent consideration by the General Assembly shall be accorded priority;

8. *Reiterates its request* to the Secretary-General to direct all departments of the Secretariat to include the following elements in their reports:

(a) Summary of the report;

(b) Consolidated conclusions, recommendations and other proposed actions;

(c) Relevant background information;

9. *Encourages* intergovernmental and expert bodies to include the above-mentioned elements, where appropriate, in their reports to the General Assembly;

10. *Reiterates its request* that all documents submitted to legislative organs by the Secretariat, intergovernmental and expert bodies for consideration and action have conclusions and recommendations in bold print;

11. *Requests* the Secretary-General to continue to take steps to improve the quality and accuracy of meeting records in all six official languages through full reliance in the preparation and translation of those records on sound recordings and written texts of statements as they were delivered in the original languages;

12. *Notes* the efforts of the Secretariat to clear the backlog in the issuance of summary records, while noting with concern that some delays in issuance still occur;

13. *Also notes* the options enumerated in paragraphs 76 to 80 of the report of the Secretary-General;

V

Translation and interpretation-related matters

1. *Requests* the Secretary-General to continue his efforts to ensure the highest quality of interpretation and translation services in all official languages;

2. *Reiterates its request* to the Secretary-General to make sure that terminology used in translation and interpretation services reflects the latest linguistic norms and terminology of the official languages in order to ensure the highest quality;

3. *Also reiterates its request* to the Secretary-General, when recruiting temporary assistance in the language services, to ensure that all language services are given equal treatment and are provided with equally favourable working conditions and resources, with a view to achieving maximum quality of their services, with full respect for the specificities of each of the six official languages and taking into account their respective workloads;

4. *Requests* the Secretary-General to continue to improve the accuracy of translation of documents into the official languages, giving particular significance to the quality of translation;

5. *Also requests* the Secretary-General to continue to seek evaluation by Member States of the quality of the conference services provided to them, including through the language-specific informational meetings held twice a year, and to ensure that such measures provide equal opportunities to Member States to present their evaluation in the six official languages of the United Nations and are in full compliance with relevant resolutions of the General Assembly;

6. *Notes* the efforts made so far to improve the rates of self-revision, and requests the Secretary-General to continue to address the question of the appropriate level of self-revision that is consistent with quality in all official languages and to report thereon to the General Assembly at its sixty-second session;

7. *Also notes* the proposal on workload standards to develop a comprehensive methodology for performance measurement and management from a full-system perspective, and requests the Secretary-General to report to the General Assembly periodically, starting at its sixty-second session, on the specific indicators proposed under the headings of timeliness, quality, financial performance and organizational learning and growth;

8. *Expresses continued concern* at the high vacancy rate in the interpretation and translation services at the United Nations Office at Nairobi, especially the chronic difficulty in staffing the Arabic Interpretation Unit, and requests the Secretary-General to address this as a matter of priority through, inter alia, assistance from Member States in advertising and facilitating the conduct of competitive examinations to fill these language vacancies;

9. *Notes with concern* the high reliance on freelance interpretation at the United Nations Office at Vienna, and requests the Secretary-General to report on any inconsistency in quality of interpretation services related thereto, including at other duty stations, and on measures to address that issue, if needed, to the General Assembly at its sixty-second session through the Committee on Conferences;

10. *Requests* the Secretary-General to provide at all duty stations the adequate staff and grade level with a view to ensuring appropriate quality control for external translations;

11. *Notes* the Secretary-General's plans to address the issue of succession planning by enhancing internal and external training programmes, developing staff exchange programmes between organizations and participating in outreach activities to institutions that train language staff for international organizations;

12. *Requests* the Secretary-General to hold competitive examinations for the recruitment of language staff sufficiently in advance so as to fill current and future vacancies in language services in a timely manner, bearing in mind the persistent situation at the United Nations

Office at Nairobi, and to inform the General Assembly at its sixty-second session of efforts in this regard.

On the same date, the Assembly decided that the agenda item on the pattern of conferences would remain for consideration during its resumed sixty-first (2007) session (**decision 61/552**).

UN Information systems

Information and communication technology

In response to General Assembly resolution 60/260 of 8 May (see p. 1576), the Secretary-General, in May, submitted a detailed report on investing in the United Nations [A/60/846], with an addendum on investing in information and communication technology (ICT) [A/60/846/Add.1]. The Secretary-General requested the Assembly to approve the establishment of the post of Chief Information Technology Officer to oversee the creation and implementation of an effective information management strategy for the Secretariat and replace the Integrated Management Information System (IMIS) with a next-generation enterprise resource planning system to ensure a high level of transparency and accountability with respect to global resource management. The Assembly was also asked to appropriate $2,550,700 under the 2006-2007 programme budget for implementation of the ICT-related proposals. The Secretary-General would submit a comprehensive report outlining the scope, timetable, strategy and detailed resource requirements for replacing IMIS no later than 2009.

In June [A/60/870], ACABQ recommended the creation of the post of Chief Information Technology Officer at the Assistant Secretary-General level through redeployment. Regarding the proposals for replacing IMIS, ACABQ would make its recommendation on the basis of the detailed report and costing plan to be submitted by the Secretary-General. It recommended acceptance of the request for $2,215,200 in additional resources to carry out the ICT cost study and implementation plan.

The Assembly, in section II of **resolution 60/283** of 7 July (see p. 1581), established the post of Chief Information Technology Officer at the level of Assistant Secretary-General in the Executive Office of the Secretary-General, decided to replace IMIS with a next-generation enterprise resource planning system or other comparable system, and took other action on the Secretary-General's ICT proposals and the related ACABQ recommendations.

International cooperation in informatics

In response to Economic and Social Council resolution 2005/12 [YUN 2005, p. 1551], the Secretary-General submitted a May report [E/2006/79] on international cooperation in the field of informatics. The continuing cooperation between the Secretariat and the Ad Hoc Open-ended Working Group on Informatics resulted in practical technology enhancements that facilitated the work of Member States, observers, and non-governmental organizations (NGOs).The Secretariat and the Working Group shared responsibility for creating and maintaining web pages and document updates. Wi-Fi technology, which allowed wireless Internet access, was deployed throughout the public areas and conference rooms at Headquarters, and electronic panels displaying official meeting information were installed at meeting room entrances. Member States submitted more than 1,500 online requests for bilateral meetings using the e-Meets system. The Secretariat and the Working Group were working on a prototype QuickPlace website called CandiWeb to support the process of elections to UN organs. The Secretariat continued to provide electronic mail and website services to permanent missions and maintained the computer servers that supported Mission services.

ECONOMIC AND SOCIAL COUNCIL ACTION

On 27 July [meeting 41], the Economic and Social Council adopted **resolution 2006/35** [draft: E/2006/L.22] without vote [agenda item 7 (c)].

The need to harmonize and improve United Nations informatics systems for optimal utilization and accessibility by all States

The Economic and Social Council,

Welcoming the report of the Secretary-General on international cooperation in the field of informatics and the initiatives of the Ad Hoc Open-ended Working Group on Informatics,

Recognizing the interest of Member States in taking full advantage of information and communication technologies for the acceleration of economic and social development,

Recalling its previous resolutions on the need to harmonize and improve United Nations information systems for optimal utilization and access by all States, with due regard to all official languages,

Welcoming the intensification of efforts by the Information Technology Services Division of the Department of Management of the Secretariat to provide interconnectivity and unhindered Internet access to all Permanent and Observer Missions at the United Nations,

1. *Reiterates once again* the high priority that it attaches to easy, economical, uncomplicated and unhindered access for States Members and Observers of the United Nations, as well as non-governmental organizations accredited to the United Nations, to the computerized databases and information systems and services of the United Nations, provided that the unhindered access of non-governmental

organizations to such databases, systems and services will not prejudice the access of Member States nor impose an additional financial burden for their use;

2. *Requests* the President of the Economic and Social Council to convene the Ad Hoc Open-ended Working Group on Informatics for one more year to enable it to carry out, from within existing resources, the due fulfilment of the provisions of the Council resolutions on this item, to facilitate the successful implementation of the initiatives being taken by the Secretary-General with regard to the use of information technology and to continue the implementation of measures required to achieve its objectives, and, in this regard, requests the Working Group to continue its efforts to act as a bridge between the evolving needs of Member States and the actions of the Secretariat;

3. *Expresses its appreciation* to the Information Technology Services Division for the continuing cooperation it is extending to the Working Group in the endeavour to further improve the information technology services available to all Permanent and Observer Missions at the United Nations and, in particular, for its continuing work in the implementation of wireless Internet (WiFi) in United Nations Headquarters conference rooms and public areas;

4. *Requests* the Secretary-General to extend full cooperation to the Working Group and to give priority to implementing its recommendations;

5. *Also requests* the Secretary-General to report to the Economic and Social Council at its substantive session of 2007 on action taken to follow up on the present resolution, including the findings of the Working Group and an assessment of its work and mandate.

Open source software policy

Use of open source software

By a 3 February note [A/60/665], the Secretary-General transmitted to the General Assembly the 2005 JIU report on the policies of UN system organizations for the use of open source software in the secretariats of those organizations. JIU recommended, among other measures, that the Assembly affirm two principles on the adoption of a software policy by UN system organizations, namely, that all Member States and other stakeholders should have the right to access public information made available in electronic format by the organizations without the obligation to acquire a particular type of software (Principle 1); and that organizations should seek to foster the interoperability of their ICT systems by requiring the use of open standards and open file formats, and ensure that the encoding of data guaranteed the permanence of electronic public records and was not tied to a particular software provider (Principle 2). It also proposed the establishment of a system-wide United Nations Interoperability Framework (UNIF) and a data repository of mature open source software solutions.

On the same date [A/60/665/Add.1], the Secretary-General transmitted his comments and those of CEB on the JIU report. CEB members broadly acknowledged the usefulness of open source software and the opportunities it presented. However, CEB noted that the report addressed issues outside the scope of a study of open source software and did not devote sufficient attention to the issues surrounding the implementation of such software. Further in-depth analysis would be required to properly develop a system-wide direction on the topic.

In section II of **resolution 60/283** of 7 July (see p. 1582), the Assembly decided to revert to consideration of the JIU report.

Use of open source software for development

By a June note [A/61/94], the Secretary-General transmitted to the General Assembly the 2005 JIU report on the policies of UN system organizations towards the use of open source software for development. JIU recommended that the Assembly invite Member States to emphasize the role of ICT in achieving the Millennium Development Goals (MDGs) [YUN 2000, p. 51]; call upon the Secretary-General and other executive heads to support Member States opting to use open-source software to achieve the MDGs; and encourage Member States to adopt pro-poor policies to foster digital inclusion. The Assembly should also call on the donor community to include or maintain in official development assistance programmes adequate funding for open-source software-based poverty-reduction projects, and request the Secretary-General to consider steps that CEB could take to allow UN system organizations to serve as catalysts for multi-stakeholder partnerships involving open source software role players.

On 27 September [A/61/94/Add.1], the Secretary-General transmitted his comments and those of CEB on the JIU report. In general, CEB concurred with the recommendations put forth in the report, but noted that the report did not provide a comprehensive analysis of the benefits and drawbacks of free and open source software use.

UN premises and property

Capital master plan

Implementation of CMP

At its resumed sixtieth (2006) session, the General Assembly had before it the Secretary-General's third annual (2005) progress report on the implementation of the capital master plan (CMP) for the refurbishment of the United Nations Headquarters complex [YUN 2005, p. 1555] and the related ACABQ report [ibid., p. 1556].

GENERAL ASSEMBLY ACTION

On 8 May [meeting 79], the General Assembly, on the recommendation of the Fifth Committee [A/60/608/Add.2], adopted **resolution 60/256** without vote [agenda item 124].

Capital master plan

The General Assembly,

Recalling its resolutions 54/249 of 23 December 1999, 55/238 of 23 December 2000, 56/234 and 56/236 of 24 December 2001 and 56/286 of 27 June 2002, section II of its resolution 57/292 of 20 December 2002, its resolution 59/295 of 22 June 2005, section II of its resolution 60/248 of 23 December 2005 and its decision 58/566 of 8 April 2004,

1. *Takes note* of the third annual progress report of the Secretary-General on the implementation of the capital master plan and the related report of the Advisory Committee on Administrative and Budgetary Questions;
2. *Decides* to appropriate an amount of 23.5 million United States dollars for financing the design and pre-construction phases of the capital master plan, including swing space requirements;
3. *Also decides* that the appropriation of 23.5 million dollars shall be financed in accordance with regulation 3.1 of the Financial Regulations and Rules of the United Nations through assessment on Member States in 2006 on the basis of the regular budget scale of assessments in effect for the year;
4. *Authorizes* the Secretary-General to enter into commitments of up to 77 million dollars for the biennium 2006-2007 to provide for the construction, fit-out and related requirements of a conference swing space building on the North Lawn and for the leasing, design, pre-construction services, fit-out and related requirements of library and office swing space for the capital master plan;
5. *Also authorizes* the Secretary-General to enter into the lease commitments necessary for the implementation of the capital master plan;
6. *Reaffirms* paragraph 28 of its resolution 57/292, and calls upon the Secretary-General to explore the possibility of private donor funding for the capital master plan;
7. *Recalls* paragraph 12 of the report of the Advisory Committee, and requests the Secretary-General to present a more detailed business analysis on the possibility of constructing a new permanent building on the North Lawn by the second part of its resumed sixtieth session;
8. *Decides* to revert, as a matter of priority, to the consideration of the reports on the capital master plan during the second part of its resumed sixtieth session.

By **decision 60/551 C** of 7 June, the Assembly deferred until its sixty-first (2006) session consideration of the reports of the Board of Auditors on CMP for the years ended 31 December 2003 [YUN 2004, p. 1474] and 31 December 2004 [YUN 2005, p. 1554]; OIOS reports on CMP for the periods from August 2003 through July 2004 [YUN 2004, p. 1474] and from August 2004 to July 2005 [YUN 2005, p. 1554]; the 2004 ACABQ report on CMP [YUN 2004, p. 1475]; and the Secretary-General's 2004 reports on plans for three additional conference rooms at Headquarters and solutions for allowing natural light into them [ibid., p. 1469]; and on options for ensuring sufficient parking space at Headquarters [ibid., p. 1473].

Report of Secretary-General. In response to resolution 60/256 (above), the Secretary-General, in June [A/60/874], presented a business analysis on the possibility of constructing a new permanent building on the North Lawn of the Headquarters complex, prepared with the assistance of an outside consultant and the consulting firm retained by the CMP project as the programme manager. The consultants were requested to estimate the costs of construction, based on estimated occupancy in 2015 and 2023, which was the expiry date of the long-term lease agreements between the United Nations and the United Nations Development Corporation (UNDC) for the UNDC-1 and UNDC-2 buildings. The consultants were to identify savings in terms of rent that would not have to be paid for the UNDC buildings or other commercially leased office space occupied by the UN system.

Regarding the first scenario, the total projected cost of constructing a permanent building on the North Lawn for occupancy in 2015 was $626.8 million, with avoided lease cost for the 2015-2023 period projected at $255 million. Under the option for occupancy in 2023, the cost of the project would amount to $939 million, with average annual avoided lease cost for the 2023-2037 period projected at $67 million.

The analysis of the potential benefits of a proposed permanent building on the North Lawn indicated that there would be commercial advantages for the United Nations derived from constructing and owning a building, as compared to long-term leasing. However, the analysis did not take into account other factors, including security, architectural, and host city and community issues. Any decision by the General Assembly to proceed with a comprehensive feasibility study of the proposal should be made independently of the decision on the CMP strategy.

The Secretary-General recommended that the matter be considered independently of the renovation of the Headquarters buildings, given the urgency of that renovation. He also recommended that the Assembly decide to continue with CMP for the Headquarters buildings and approve the phased approach (strategy IV) recommended in 2005 [YUN 2005, p. 1555].

ACABQ report. In its June report on the business analysis [A/60/7/Add.38], ACABQ said that the feasibility study was not merited, as it would lead to unwarranted costs and detract from the focus required for the renovation project. It recommended that the Assembly approve the Secretary-General's recommendations.

GENERAL ASSEMBLY ACTION

On 30 June [meeting 92], the General Assembly, on the recommendation of the Fifth Committee [A/60/608/Add.6], adopted **resolution 60/282** without vote [agenda item 124].

Capital master plan

The General Assembly,

Recalling its resolutions 54/249 of 23 December 1999, 55/238 of 23 December 2000, 56/234 and 56/236 of 24 December 2001, 56/286 of 27 June 2002, section II of its resolution 57/292 of 20 December 2002, its resolution 59/295 of 22 June 2005, section II of its resolution 60/248 of 23 December 2005, its resolution 60/256 of 8 May 2006 and its decision 58/566 of 8 April 2004,

Having considered the second and third annual progress reports of the Secretary-General on the implementation of the capital master plan, the reports of the Secretary-General on viable options for ensuring sufficient parking space at United Nations Headquarters, on plans for three additional conference rooms and viable solutions for allowing natural light into the rooms, on cooperation with the City and State of New York related to the capital master plan, on the status of possible funding arrangements for the capital master plan, on a business analysis of the possibility of constructing a new permanent building on the North Lawn, the note by the Secretary-General transmitting the report of the Board of Auditors on the capital master plan for the biennium ended 31 December 2003, the report of the Board of Auditors for the year ended 31 December 2004, the reports of the Office of Internal Oversight Services on the capital master plan for the period from August 2003 through July 2004 and the period from August 2004 through July 2005 and the related written reports of the Advisory Committee on Administrative and Budgetary Questions, as well as the oral report of the Chairman of the Advisory Committee on Administrative and Budgetary Questions,

1. *Reiterates its serious concern* about the hazards, risks and deficiencies of the current conditions of the United Nations Headquarters Building, which endanger the safety, health and well-being of staff, visitors, tourists and delegations, including high-level delegations;

2. *Takes note* of the second and third annual progress reports of the Secretary-General on the implementation of the capital master plan, the reports of the Secretary-General on cooperation with the City and State of New York related to the capital master plan, on the status of possible funding arrangements for the capital master plan and on the business analysis of the possibility of constructing a new permanent building on the North Lawn;

3. *Decides* to revert, at the main part of its sixty-first session, to the consideration of the reports of the Secretary-General on viable options for ensuring sufficient parking space at United Nations Headquarters and on plans for three additional conference rooms and viable solutions for allowing natural light into the rooms, the note by the Secretary-General transmitting the report of the Board of Auditors on the capital master plan for the biennium ended 31 December 2003, the report of the Board of Auditors for the year ended 31 December 2004 and the reports of the Office of Internal Oversight Services on the capital master plan for the period from August 2003 through July 2004 and the period from August 2004 through July 2005;

4. *Notes* the benefits, including economic ones, accruing to host countries from the presence of the United Nations, and the costs incurred;

5. *Stresses* the special role of the host country Government with regard to support for United Nations Headquarters in New York;

6. *Recalls* the current practices of host Governments with regard to support for United Nations headquarters and United Nations bodies located in their territories;

7. *Requests* the Secretary-General to ensure that no action is taken that would preclude any decision that the General Assembly might take on the construction of a new permanent building on the North Lawn at some future date;

8. *Approves*, effective 1 July 2006, the recommended strategy for the implementation of the capital master plan, strategy IV (phased approach), contained in the third annual progress report of the Secretary-General, including the phasing, swing space and cost, and decides to review the updated projected costs at the main part of its sixty-first session;

9. *Requests* the Secretary-General to submit proposals to the General Assembly at its sixty-first session, through the Committee on Conferences, on the possible adjustment of meeting schedules, including a change in venue of meetings for the United Nations intergovernmental organs that normally meet at Headquarters for the period of the implementation of the capital master plan;

10. *Stresses* the need for a long-term strategy for office accommodation at Headquarters;

11. *Requests* that a comprehensive study on the feasibility of the proposed construction of a building on the North Lawn, including a number of other factors that have not been included in the business analysis contained in the report of the Secretary-General, on security, architectural, and host city and community issues, be included in the context of the proposed programme budget for the biennium 2008-2009;

12. *Requests* the Secretary-General, considering the need to continue to explore ways to increase procurement opportunities for vendors from developing countries and countries with economies in transition, to take the provisions of its resolutions 54/14 of 29 October 1999, 55/247 of 12 April 2001 and 59/288 of 13 April 2005 on procurement reform fully into consideration in the implementation of the capital master plan;

13. *Notes* that the Office of the Capital Master Plan will provide resources to the Office of Internal Oversight Services in order to ensure an appropriate construction audit for the capital master plan, and requests the Secretary-General to report on the findings thereon in the context of the relevant reports, including the annual report of the Office of Internal Oversight Services throughout the phases of the project;

14. *Requests* the Secretary-General to ensure that procurement processes related to the capital master plan are conducted in a transparent manner and in full compliance with relevant General Assembly resolutions;

15. *Welcomes* the establishment of the capital master plan website;

16. *Requests* the Secretary-General ensure that financial disclosure statements are filed by staff involved with the capital master plan in accordance with relevant General Assembly resolutions;

17. *Recognizes* that the cash payment option, based on a one-time assessment or multi-year special assessments, would be the simplest and the most cost-effective approach for meeting the cost of the capital master plan;

18. *Decides* to revert, at the main part of its sixty-first session, to the issue of the funding plan for the capital master plan, including the credit facilities or instruments referred to in paragraph 35 of the third annual progress report of the Secretary-General on the implementation of the capital master plan as well as the feasibility of a one-time upfront payment option, and in this context requests the Secretary-General to propose, inter alia, to the General Assembly, also at the main part of its sixty-first session, a mechanism that would ensure that Member States that pay their assessed contributions for the capital master plan in full and on time will not bear any financial liabilities and/or other obligations derived from the possible utilization of those credit facilities or instruments;

19. *Also decides* to convert the existing commitment authority of 77 million United States dollars into an appropriation, with assessment on Member States in 2006 on the basis of the regular budget scale of assessments in effect for the year;

20. *Requests* the Secretary-General to report to the General Assembly at its sixty-first session on the implementation of the provisions of the present resolution, in his fourth annual progress report on the implementation of the capital master plan.

Review of CMP

Report of Board of Auditors. The report of the Board of Auditors [A/61/5 (Vol.V)] on the CMP for the year ended 31 December 2005, as well as related UN financial statements were submitted to the General Assembly in July. The Board reviewed the financial and programme management operations of the CMP project, as well as the actions taken by CMP to implement the two recommendations it had made in its previous report [YUN 2005, p. 1554]. It found that both recommendations had been partially implemented, but that the implementation of the project had been delayed owing to the unavailability of the swing space building (UNDC-5) envisioned in the original approach, and because the Assembly had yet to consider the option for project strategy, scope and budget, and the funding plan for implementation. It was concerned about the cost implications of the delay. Some of the amendments to contracts for the design development phase contained ambiguous clauses, such as the covenant clause, which did not state the maximum amount that the United Nations was obligated to pay, and others that did not conform to the United Nations Procurement Manual, since the name of the contracting parties and the dates the amendments should take effect were not indicated. Submission of deliverables for design development was behind schedule, as well as the provision of minutes of meetings conducted with the CMP team. Weekly meetings were changed to bi-weekly meetings and some were cancelled for no apparent reason, heightening the Board's concern that issues regarding the progress of work, compliance with schedules and architectural and engineering designs might not be addressed immediately.

The Board recommended that the Administration urge the General Assembly to decide on the renovation strategy and the financing scheme for CMP implementation; ensure that amendments to contracts were in line with the United Nations Procurement Manual; strengthen the monitoring of submission of deliverables; review the propriety of the decision by the United Nations to reduce the frequency of meetings with the programme management firm; and assess the impact of the cancellation of some meetings.

OIOS report. In its August report [A/61/264 (Part I) & Add.1], OIOS said that it had provided continuous audit coverage of the CMP project through direct interaction with all departments and offices involved and its findings and recommendations were communicated for corrective action where appropriate. OIOS continued to follow up on those issues and was finalizing a report to CMP management summarizing its findings

Reports of Secretary-General. In September [A/61/264 Part I)/Add.2], the Secretary-General, in his comments on the August OIOS report, said that, based on the advice of outside counsel engaged to advise the United Nations on the preconstruction phase service agreement and related issues and intensive consultations and meetings among relevant offices, it was determined that some OIOS recommendations regarding the agreement would not be in the interest of the Organization.

In response to Assembly resolution 57/292 [YUN 2002, p. 1375], the Secretary-General, in October [A/61/549], submitted his fourth annual progress report on CMP. The report discussed the status of design and preconstruction work; the project schedule; the strategy for providing swing space; the projected implementation cost; financing options; the status of appropriations and expenditures; the Secretary-General's efforts to create a CMP advisory board; and issues related to procurement and financial disclosure. The total projected costs for implementation had increased from $1,587.8 million to $1,646.3 million, as at August 2006. In addition, it was recommended that options for additional security, redundancy and contingency, estimated at $230.4 million, be added to the base project.

The Secretary-General recommended that the Assembly approve the plan, including the recommended scope options, to be completed during the period from 2006 to 2014, at a total revised budget not to exceed $1,876.7 million, exclusive of any credit facility charges. The Assembly should approve CMP funding based on either a one-time cash assessment, multi-year cash assessments, or a mix of the two, and the establishment of a letter of credit facility. The Assembly should appropriate $45 million to establish a working capital reserve under the CMP account, to be financed through an assessment on Member States in 2007, based on the regular budget scale of assessment in effect for that year. It should also appropriate another $42 million for the design and construction phases and decide that CMP assessments should be considered due and payable in full within 30 days of the date on which the assessment notices were issued. Charges resulting from any drawdown from a credit facility should be apportioned among Member States that had not paid their CMP assessments on time and in full.

ACABQ report. In November [A/61/595], ACABQ recommended approval of the revised CMP budget of $1,876.6 million and appropriation of $42 million for 2007.

GENERAL ASSEMBLY ACTION

On 22 December [meeting 84], the General Assembly, on the recommendation of the Fifth Committee [A/61/592/Add.1], adopted **resolution 61/251** without vote [agenda item 117].

Capital master plan

The General Assembly,

Recalling its resolutions 54/249 of 23 December 1999, 55/238 of 23 December 2000, 56/234 and 56/236 of 24 December 2001 and 56/286 of 27 June 2002, section II of its resolution 57/292 of 20 December 2002, its resolution 59/295 of 22 June 2005, section II of its resolution 60/248 of 23 December 2005, its resolutions 60/256 of 8 May 2006 and 60/282 of 30 June 2006 and section II.B of its resolution 61/236 of 22 December 2006 and its decision 58/566 of 8 April 2004,

Having considered the fourth annual progress report of the Secretary-General on the implementation of the capital master plan, the related reports of the Advisory Committee on Administrative and Budgetary Questions, the reports of the Secretary-General on the viable options for ensuring sufficient parking space at United Nations Headquarters and the plans for three additional conference rooms and viable solutions for allowing natural light into the rooms, the reports of the Office of Internal Oversight Services on the United Nations capital master plan for the periods from August 2003 through July 2004 and from August 2004 to July 2005, the report of the Office of Internal Oversight Services on its activities for the period from 1 July 2005 to 30 June 2006 and the comments of the Secretary-General thereon and the reports of the Board of Auditors on the capital master plan for the biennium ended 31 December 2003 and for the years ended 31 December 2004 and 31 December 2005,

Reaffirming that the costs of the capital master plan are expenses of the Organization to be borne by Member States in accordance with Article 17, paragraph 2, of the Charter of the United Nations,

1. *Reiterates its serious concern* at the hazards, risks and deficiencies of the current condition of the United Nations Headquarters Building, which endanger the safety, health and well-being of staff, delegations, visitors and tourists;

2. *Stresses* the special role of the host country Government with regard to support for United Nations Headquarters in New York;

3. *Recalls* the current practices of host Governments with regard to support for United Nations headquarters and United Nations bodies located in their territories;

4. *Takes note* of the fourth annual progress report of the Secretary-General on the implementation of the capital master plan, the related reports of the Advisory Committee on Administrative and Budgetary Questions, the reports of the Secretary-General on the viable options for ensuring sufficient parking space at United Nations Headquarters and the plans for three additional conference rooms and viable solutions for allowing natural light into the rooms, the reports of the Office of Internal Oversight Services on the United Nations capital master plan for the periods from August 2003 through July 2004 and from August 2004 to July 2005, the report of the Office of Internal Oversight Services on its activities for the period from 1 July 2005 to 30 June 2006 and the comments of the Secretary-General thereon and the

reports of the Board of Auditors on the capital master plan for the biennium ended 31 December 2003 and for the years ended 31 December 2004 and 31 December 2005;

5. *Also takes note* of the conclusions and recommendations contained in the reports of the Advisory Committee on Administrative and Budgetary Questions;

6. *Reaffirms* section VI of its resolution 55/222 of 23 December 2000;

7. *Also reaffirms* paragraph 6 of its resolution 60/256, and calls upon the Secretary-General to explore the possibility of private donor funding for the capital master plan and to continue efforts to secure financial resources from the public and private sectors for upgrading facilities and equipment, including the participation of private companies in infrastructural improvements where such participation has no financial implications for the Organization;

8. *Recalls* that the acceptance of any donation should conform to the international and intergovernmental character of the Organization and should be in full compliance with the Financial Regulations and Rules of the United Nations;

9. *Stresses* the need for establishing sufficient cash flow for the purpose of the capital master plan, based on a practical and predictable assessment plan;

10. *Decides* to approve the capital master plan, including the recommended scope options, to be completed from 2006 to 2014, at a total revised project budget not to exceed 1,876.7 million United States dollars (exclusive of any credit facility fees);

11. *Notes* that forward pricing escalation is already included in the approved budget contained in the fourth annual progress report of the Secretary-General, and requests the Secretary-General to make every effort to avoid budget increases through sound project management practices and to ensure that the capital master plan is completed within the approved budget and the envisaged time schedule;

12. *Requests* the Secretary-General to submit to the General Assembly for its consideration possible options on how to remain within the approved budget of 1,876.7 million dollars in the unlikely event that it becomes evident that the costs will exceed the approved budget;

13. *Decides* that in the unlikely event of cost escalations beyond the approved budget of 1,876.7 million dollars, all Member States will be subject to a further assessment to meet the revised financial requirements as approved by the General Assembly;

14. *Approves* the funding of the capital master plan, based on a mix of one-time and equal multi-year assessments;

15. *Decides* that under the mixed assessment option of one-time and multiyear assessment, all assessments will be based on the regular budget scale of assessments applicable for 2007;

16. *Also decides* that, notwithstanding financial regulation 3.4, assessments for the capital master plan shall be issued on the same day of the first working week of January and shall be considered due and payable in full within one hundred and twenty days of that date;

17. *Agrees*, in this context, that in 2007 Member States will be allowed a period of sixty days, beginning on 5 January, within the period of one hundred and twenty days referred to in paragraph 16 above, to select the option of one-time or multi-year payment of their assessment on a fixed scale, as referred to in paragraph 15 above;

18. *Decides*, on an exceptional and ad hoc basis, unless notified otherwise by a Member State within sixty days of the issuance of the notification by the Secretary-General, to place Member States on the multi-year assessment plan for the full period of the capital master plan;

19. *Also decides* that once a Member State selects the option of one-time payment, that selection shall be irrevocable, unless otherwise notified to the Secretary-General by the end of the period of one hundred and twenty days referred to in paragraph 16 above;

20. *Further decides* to apportion, on the same day of the first working week of January for the period from 2007 to 2011, the amounts applicable, based on each Member State's assessment option of either a one-time payment, based on its share of 1,716.7 million dollars, or equal multi-year payments over five years, in accordance with the regular budget rates of assessment applicable for 2007 for all assessments for the capital master plan, using the scale of assessments for the period 2007-2009;

21. *Decides* to appropriate 42 million dollars for 2007 for the design and pre-construction phases of the capital master plan, including swing-space requirements;

22. *Approves* the establishment of a working capital reserve of 45 million dollars under the capital master plan account, to be operated under the terms of financial regulations 3.5, 4.2 and 4.3;

23. *Resolves* that Member States shall make advances to the working capital reserve in accordance with the regular budget rates of assessment applicable for 2007 in the scale of assessments for the period 2007-2009;

24. *Approves* the establishment of a letter of credit facility as outlined in paragraphs 35 to 38 of the fourth annual progress report of the Secretary-General, pursuant to a bidding process conducted in accordance with the Financial Regulations and Rules of the United Nations;

25. *Stresses* that any drawdown on the letter of credit should be a last resort and solely for the purpose of funding the capital master plan;

26. *Requests* the Secretary-General, in this regard, to ensure that the best possible terms and conditions that preserve the interests of the Organization are negotiated with the construction manager in respect of the internationally syndicated letter of credit;

27. *Also requests* the Secretary-General to enter into consultations with the host country Government regarding the possibility of facilitating the establishment of the letter of credit without the imposition of fees or charges to the United Nations;

28. *Further requests* the Secretary-General to report to the General Assembly on the results of the negotia-

tions and consultations and the status of the establishment of the letter of credit, in the context of his annual report on the capital master plan;

29. *Notes* that the establishment of the letter of credit could incur a fee of between 0.05 and 0.5 per cent of the value of the credit facility at the start of each year, and agrees that Member States will be assessed their share of the fees at the beginning of each calendar year on the basis of the regular budget scale of assessments for 2007;

30. *Approves* any necessary drawdown on the letter of credit, and requests the Secretary-General to advise Member States, as a matter of urgency, if a drawdown on the letter of credit is likely, preferably ninety days in advance;

31. *Recalls* paragraph 18 of its resolution 60/282, and decides that, notwithstanding financial regulation 3.1, any charges arising from a drawdown on the letter of credit would not be a charge on Member States that have paid in full their capital master plan assessments for the applicable period within the one hundred and twenty days of the issuance of the letters of assessment;

32. *Authorizes* the Secretary-General to apportion annually those charges arising from a drawdown on the letter of credit among Member States that did not pay their assessed contributions to the capital master plan in full, within the period of one hundred and twenty days specified in paragraph 16 above, based on a monthly calculation using the total charges levied during each month and the prorated share of each Member State concerned of the average total assessed contributions that are outstanding for the capital master plan during that month;

33. *Requests* the Secretary-General to report to the General Assembly annually on the financial aspects of the capital master plan, in particular on any outstanding contributions and on the amount of the charges specified in paragraph 32 above and the apportionment among Member States;

34. *Reaffirms* that the charges to be apportioned in accordance with the provisions of paragraph 32 above are expenses of the Organization to be borne by Member States in accordance with Article 17, paragraph 2, of the Charter of the United Nations;

35. *Stresses* the importance of oversight with respect to the implementation of the capital master plan, and requests the Board of Auditors and all other relevant oversight bodies to continue to report to the General Assembly annually on the capital master plan;

36. *Requests* the Secretary-General to ensure that amendments to contracts are in line with the *United Nations Procurement Manual*, and emphasizes that contracts should stipulate that the United Nations will not be responsible for any delays, damage or loss on the part of the contractor;

37. *Reiterates its request* to the Secretary-General to continue to explore ways to increase procurement opportunities for vendors from developing countries and countries with economies in transition and to take the provisions of its resolutions 54/14 of 29 October 1999, 55/247 of 12 April 2001, 57/279 of 20 December 2002, 59/288 of 13 April 2005 and 60/1 of 16 September 2005 on procurement reform fully into consideration in the implementation of the capital master plan;

38. *Also reiterates its request* to the Secretary-General to ensure that procurement processes are conducted in a transparent manner and in full compliance with relevant General Assembly resolutions;

39. *Emphasizes* to the Secretary-General the importance of effectively managing the multiple staff relocations under the approved phasing plan in order to keep the project on schedule;

40. *Urges* the Secretary-General to expedite the process of setting up the advisory board, reflecting wide geographical representation, so that it can begin its work as soon as possible, as provided for in section II of General Assembly resolution 57/292;

41. *Requests* the Secretary-General to ensure that works of art, masterpieces and other gifts are appropriately handled during all the stages of the renovation work and that all associated costs are foreseen;

42. *Also requests* the Secretary-General to cooperate with those Member States that wish to take care of their gifts of works of art, masterpieces and other items during the renovation period;

43. *Decides* that, owing to the unique and exceptional circumstances arising from the capital master plan, the decisions set out in the present resolution shall under no circumstances constitute a precedent or imply any changes to the Financial Regulations and Rules of the United Nations.

Additional office/conference facilities

Addis Ababa. In response to General Assembly resolution 56/270 [YUN 2002, p. 1459], the Secretary-General, in July [A/61/158], submitted his annual report on construction of additional office facilities at the Economic Commission for Africa (ECA) in Addis Ababa. The title deed to additional land allocated by Ethiopia to ECA for the project was signed and an addendum to the host country agreement reflecting the allocation was cleared by the UN Office of Legal Affairs and submitted to Ethiopia for approval. At the same time, action was taken to coordinate with local authorities on the design and construction of an alternative public access road. The project schedule was updated following the Assembly's endorsement of the expansion of the original project to include the construction of two additional floors, which were to be completed simultaneously with the originally approved four floors. The total estimated cost of the project remained unchanged at $11,383,300.

ACABQ provided its comments on the Secretary-General's report in September [A/61/362].

The Assembly, in section II of **resolution 61/252** of 22 December (see p. 1614), took note of the Secretary-General's report and endorsed the ACABQ observations and recommendations. It also noted

Ethiopia's efforts in facilitating the construction of additional office facilities.

Geneva. In a June report [A/60/899], the Secretary-General proposed arrangements and related resource requirements for office accommodation for the Office of the United Nations High Commissioner for Human Rights (OHCHR) in Geneva. The expanded office accommodation would give rise to a total additional requirement of $10,451,400, of which $4,975,900, net of staff assessment, would be financed under the 2006-2007 programme budget. The Secretary-General recommended that the Assembly appropriate that additional amount and note the intention of the host Government (Switzerland) to contribute $1,540,300 towards the total requirement.

ACABQ, in a related June report [A/60/7/Add.42], recognized the immediate needs of OHCHR for additional office space and recommended acceptance of the Secretary-General's proposals.

On 30 June, the Assembly, by **decision 60/562**, authorized the Secretary-General to enter into commitments of up to $4,975,900 to meet resource requirements. It welcomed the intention of the host Government to contribute financial resources towards meeting the initial rental obligations until full occupancy was achieved, as well as the cost of exterior perimeter security protection for compliance with Headquarters Minimum Operating Security Standards.

Vienna. Pursuant to section VI of General Assembly resolution 59/276 [YUN 2004, p. 1384], the Secretary-General, in July [A/61/166], reported on the construction of additional conference facilities at the Vienna International Conference Centre, providing an update on cost-sharing arrangements between the United Nations and the three other organizations located at the Centre: the International Atomic Energy Agency, the Preparatory Commission for the Comprehensive Nuclear-Test-Ban Treaty Organization, and the United Nations Industrial Development Organization (UNIDO).

The agreement with Austria to provide a new conference facility set a ceiling for the project at €52.5 million, of which the United Nations and the three other organizations would collectively contribute €2.5 million, payable in the 2008-2009 biennium. An agreement on cost sharing had been reached with those organizations. The United Nations share of the costs amounted to €100,000, which would be payable in 2008 and presented to the Assembly in the context of the proposed programme budget for 2008-2009. Maintenance and operation costs would be shared using the current cost-sharing principle, based on actual usage. The related financial requirements would be dealt with, along with other common support costs, in the 2008-2009 proposed programme budget.

In September [A/61/361], ACABQ noted that the new conference facility would serve as a swing space from 2008 to 2010, while asbestos was being removed from the conference building. The Committee was informed that costs related to asbestos removal were not included as part of the total project cost, as the removal was already being undertaken by the host country Government. ACABQ would welcome updates on the asbestos removal in future reports of the Secretary-General.

The Assembly, in section I of **resolution 61/252** of 22 December, took note of the Secretary-General's report and endorsed ACABQ related observations and recommendations. It also noted the efforts of the host country to construct conference facilities at the Vienna International Centre.

Renovation of residence of Secretary-General

In September [A/61/377], the Secretary-General submitted a report on the proposed renovation to the residence of the Secretary-General in the context of revised estimates for the 2007-2007 programme budget. The residence, a neo-Georgian attached townhouse providing 14,000 square feet of space, was built in 1921 and acquired by the United Nations through a donation in 1972. The Secretary-General proposed a major structural renovation, requiring additional resources estimated at $4,490,400 under the 2006-2007 programme budget.

In October [A/61/523], ACABQ said that the proposal should have been submitted as part of the proposed budget for 2006-2007, rather than as revised estimates in the middle of the biennium, and suggested that the full amount of the estimated cost be absorbed within the appropriations already approved. As the Headquarters Agreement between the United Nations and the United States did not include the Secretary-General's residence, the Secretariat should make every effort to provide for the inclusion of a proposed clause dealing with the residence in the fourth supplement to the Agreement.

ACABQ recommended that the Assembly approve the proposed renovation and authorize the Secretary-General to enter into commitments up to $4,490,400 under the 2006-2007 budget.

GENERAL ASSEMBLY ACTION

On 28 November [meeting 59], the General Assembly, on the recommendation of the Fifth

Committee [A/61/592], adopted **resolution 61/21** without vote [agenda item 117].

Renovation of the residence of the Secretary-General

The General Assembly,

Having considered the report of the Secretary-General entitled "Renovation of the residence of the Secretary-General: revised estimates to the programme budget for the biennium 2006-2007" and the related report of the Advisory Committee on Administrative and Budgetary Questions,

1. *Takes note* of the report of the Secretary-General;
2. *Endorses* the observations and recommendations of the Advisory Committee on Administrative and Budgetary Questions contained in its report;
3. *Regrets* that the proposal to renovate the residence of the Secretary-General was not submitted as part of the proposed programme budget for the biennium 2006-2007;
4. *Approves* the renovation of the residence of the Secretary-General;
5. *Authorizes* the Secretary-General to enter into commitments up to an amount of 4,490,400 United States dollars under the programme budget for the biennium 2006-2007, comprising 202,500 dollars under section 1, Overall policymaking, direction and coordination, and 4,287,900 dollars under section 32, Construction, alteration, improvement and major maintenance, and to report on expenditures in the context of the second performance report for the biennium 2006-2007;
6. *Requests* the Secretary-General to ensure, to the extent possible, that activities approved under section 32 of the programme budget for the biennium 2006-2007 are completed within the envisaged time schedule;
7. *Also requests* the Secretary-General to ensure that procurement processes related to the project are conducted in a transparent manner and in full compliance with its relevant resolutions on procurement reform;
8. *Further requests* the Secretary-General to ensure that targeted mitigation measures are put in place pursuant to established minimum operating security standards;
9. *Requests* the Secretary-General to expedite the action referred to in paragraph 2 of the report of the Advisory Committee.

Security issues

Strengthened and unified security management system

The General Assembly, by **decision 60/551 B** of 8 May, deferred consideration of the 2005 OIOS report on the utilization and management of funds approved by the Assembly for strengthening the security and safety of UN premises [YUN 2005, p. 1556] and the note by the Secretary-General transmitting his comments thereon [ibid., p. 1557].

The Secretary-General submitted, in October [A/61/531], a report on a strengthened and unified security management system for the United Nations, which provided information on progress achieved in establishing such a system at Headquarters and in the field. The report identified areas in which additional work was needed to ensure that the Department of Safety and Security was in a position to manage requirements and respond to unforeseen emergencies. The Department worked to support and enable the effective conduct of UN activities by ensuring a coherent, effective and timely response to all security-related threats and other emergencies; risk mitigation, through the establishment of a coordinated security threat and risk assessment mechanism; and the cost-effective provision and employment of security personnel. It was also working to develop and monitor compliance with security policies, standards and operational procedures across the UN system.

The *Field Security Handbook* and a number of specialized security directives were updated and produced in the six official UN languages and several expanded training initiatives were implemented. Software improvements were made to provide reliable and secure communications and business continuity in the field. Eighty-four per cent of the Department's 1,830 posts had been filled worldwide.

Experience had revealed practical problems with implementing cost-sharing arrangements for the safety and security of UN system staff. The World Bank disagreed with the cost-sharing formula and was withholding its $11 million contribution. The other agencies, funds and programmes had no additional funds to absorb potential shortfalls.

The Secretary-General concluded that the Department had made significant achievements over the previous 18 months and major remaining challenges should be addressed through systematic action. He recommended that the Assembly approve the reclassification of the Department's D-2-level post of Deputy to the Under-Secretary-General to the Assistant Secretary-General-level; approve the maintenance and continuation of the D-2 position of Director of Headquarters Security and Safety Service; authorize the conversion of 134 temporary posts to established posts in the Security and Safety Services; and endorse the establishment of a United Nations crisis management capability and revert to the ongoing requirements in the context of the proposed programme budget for the 2008-2009 biennium.

The Assembly, in resolution 61/133 of 14 December (see p. 1684), took note of the Secretary-

General's report and requested him to further develop and implement the unified security management system. The UN system and Member States were asked to take all appropriate measures to achieve that goal, both at the headquarters and in the field.

An August report [A/61/223] submitted by the Secretary-General summarized the actions taken by the CEB High-Level Committee on Management (HLCM) to improve the operational administration of cost-sharing arrangements and outlined the revised modalities agreed on by the organizations participating in those arrangements. In February 2005, the Committee convened a technical meeting to discuss the budget requirements subject to cost-sharing and options for future cost-sharing arrangements. A consensus emerged that a new minimum level of participation to field-level security budgets subject to cost-sharing would be appropriate, owing to the significant increase of such budgets. In April 2005, the Committee agreed that field-related security costs should be apportioned on the basis of the actual percentage of an organization's staff based in the field with a minimum amount of $75,000 per biennium.

Discussions continued with the World Bank on the cost-sharing formula. Consultations among organizations participating in the cost-sharing arrangements were also under way, addressing not only the cost-sharing modalities but the strategic direction of the security management system and the scope of operational requirements for field-related activities.

Further CEB consideration. The CEB High-level Committee on Management, at its twelfth regular session (Rome, 30 September–1 October) [CEB/2006/5] established a technical working group to consider options for reprioritizing the activities of the Department of Safety and Security and corresponding funding mechanisms in order to best meet the objectives of the Department's strategic framework for 2008-2009 within the 2006-2007 cost-shared budget ceiling; and develop an effective surge capacity, should resources become available.

ACABQ report. In December [A/61/642], ACABQ said that the reclassification of the D-2 post should be considered in the context of the proposed programme budget for the 2008-2009 biennium. It had no objection to the proposed continuation for the D-2 position of Director and recommended approval of the proposed conversion of the 134 temporary posts to established posts in the Security and Safety Service.

ACABQ said that it supported and encouraged HLCM to expeditiously resolve the issue of the World Bank's participation in the cost-sharing arrangements for safety and security. It reiterated its view that the Secretariat and UN organizations, funds and programmes shared a common responsibility for the security and safety of their staff and it was in their interest to provide adequate and assured funding for security.

Standardized access control

In response to General Assembly resolution 59/294 [YUN 2005, p. 1488], the Secretary-General submitted, in February [A/60/695], an interim report on standardized access control, outlining the proposed scope, concept and revised course of action for standardized access control at all main UN locations. The improvements would bring all main duty stations to a baseline security level with regard to control of access to UN premises, except for the Secretariat complex in New York, whose security requirements were being implemented as part of the capital master plan for the renovation of the Headquarters complex.

During 2005, the Department of Safety and Security undertook a comprehensive assessment of the security posture at each of the eight main Secretariat locations and at the International Tribunal for the Former Yugoslavia (ICTY) and the International Criminal Tribunal for Rwanda (ICTR). It proposed that the various sets of minimum operating security standards in use be consolidated by the Department into a single set of operational instructions, while adding flexibility by setting out mandatory, as well as advisory, requirements. The essential features for standardized access control were perimeter fencing and intrusion detection, personnel and vehicle barriers at access points, a reliable pass and identification card system, an operational command and control centre and closed-circuit television coverage at main points. A number of specific additional requirements were also identified, including enhanced or additional vehicle barriers, upgraded perimeter coverage, reinforced security command posts and the introduction or extension of internal zoning.

The Secretary-General proposed a two-phased approach for implementing the standardized global access control system. In the first phase, security shortcomings and gaps at all main locations would be rectified. The related estimated requirements of $23,683,000 would be met through the temporary reprioritization of construction and maintenance projects approved for the current biennium. The Secretariat would prepare a detailed plan for implementing the second phase of the project to be submitted to the Assembly at the main part of its sixty-first session.

ACABQ, in a related report [A/60/7/Add.35], stated that it had no objection to the proposed two-phase approach and it intended to submit comprehensive recommendations on access control when the Secretary-General submitted the project proposals to the Assembly. As to meeting the estimated requirements for the first phase by temporarily setting new priorities in the current biennium budget, ACABQ noted that the Secretary-General would have to request such resources separately.

By **decision 60/551 B** of 8 May, the Assembly deferred until its sixty-first (2006) session consideration of the Secretary-General's 2005 report on the strengthened and unified UN security management system [YUN 2005, p. 1558], his February 2006 report on standardized access control and the related ACABQ reports.

In a November report [A/61/566], the Secretary-General elaborated further on standardized access control measures and proposed additional improvements. In the project's first phase, all main duty stations would be brought into compliance with the headquarters minimum operating security standards for perimeter protection and electronic access control. The second phase would achieve full compliance with those standards by providing a full package of protection measures beyond the perimeter and into the multiple internal layers of protection. Access control devices would include closed-circuit television, optical portals, revolving doors, door alarms, intrusion detection, emergency intercoms and panic alarms. All devices would be fully integrated into the central monitoring control centres. The Secretary-General requested the Assembly to approve the course of action described in the report and authorize him to enter into commitments of $23,683,000 under the 2006-2007 programme budget and the budgets for ICTY and ICTR, to be reported in the context of the respective second performance reports.

In December [A/61/642], ACABQ said that it had no objection to the Secretary-General's proposals.

Information and communication technology security, business continuity and disaster recovery

In response to section XI of General Assembly resolution 59/276 [YUN 2004, p. 1387], the Secretariat submitted a February note [A/60/677] on ICT security, business continuity and disaster recovery. To address the Assembly's request for a detailed proposal on that matter, the Secretariat initiated a comprehensive review of the issues associated with the establishment of the global business continuity and disaster recovery capability, including risk assessment and a business impact analysis survey. The infrastructure, systems and applications and other critical business instruments for each duty station were reviewed and verified. The operational framework requirements for the project were based on the ability of the principal organs to conduct crucial meetings and maintain ICT services; ensure the continuity of key financial transactions; and sustain communications with the staff and the permanent missions to the United Nations. The study indicated that the objectives could be met by building on the Secretariat's ICT infrastructure. Further analysis of possible "value-engineering" alternatives would be required to identify potential cost-saving measures. The Secretary-General proposed to submit to the Assembly at its sixty-first (2006) session his comprehensive report on the project, including the results of the full scope of work involved in the cost-benefit analysis and identification of possible cost-saving approaches. The finalization of the project, its timetable and cost estimates would be undertaken largely from within the resources approved for the current biennium for the UN Office of Central Support Services. The capacity of the Office would be supplemented by independent external specialized expertise, at an estimated cost of $250,000, which would be accommodated within the resources approved for the 2006-2007 biennium.

In a related report [A/60/7/Add.33], ACABQ urged the Secretariat to seek out lessons learned on ICT security, business continuity and disaster recovery from inside and outside the UN system. It expected that the comprehensive report proposed by the Secretary-General would be submitted no later than September 2007, taking into account the capital master plan.

The Assembly, by **decision 60/551 B** of 8 May, deferred until its sixty-first (2006) session consideration of the Secretariat note.

In an August note [A/61/290], the Secretary-General recommended that the preparation of a technical study, with detailed costing and a timetable, be re-examined and coordinated with proposals under preparation for the resumed sixty-first (2007) Assembly session, when a comprehensive proposal on investing in ICT would be submitted. The replacement of IMIS, as proposed in the Secretary-General's report on investing in the United Nations (see p. 1643) represented an opportunity to integrate business continuity and disaster recovery capability into prospective mission-critical systems, including enterprise resource planning. A dedicated examination of approaches and efforts to study costing alternatives, including potential consolidations, outsourcing, offshoring and financial considerations would continue concurrently with the preparation of the comprehensive report, thereby reflecting a cohesive strategy.

In September [A/61/478], ACABQ commented on the Secretary-General's note.

Staff matters

Appointment of Secretary-General

Mr. Ban Ki-moon of the Republic of Korea was appointed Secretary-General of the United Nations on 13 October for a five-year term beginning on 1 January 2007. He was to succeed Kofi Annan of Ghana, who completed his second five-year term on 31 December.

Mr. Ban, at the time of his appointment, was Minister for Foreign Affairs and Trade of the Republic of Korea. His previous assignments included Foreign Policy Advisor to the President (2003); Chef de Cabinet to the President of the fifty-sixth session of the General Assembly (2001-2002); Vice-Minister (2000); National Security Advisor to the President of the Republic of Korea (1996-2000); Deputy Minister for Policy Planning and International Organizations (1995-1996); Deputy Ambassador to the United States (1993-1994); and Director-General of American Affairs at the Ministry for Foreign Affairs and Trade (1990-1992). Other diplomatic postings were in Vienna, New York and New Delhi.

The Republic of Korea, in a 13 July letter [A/61/155-S/2006/524 & Corr. 1] to the Security Council and the General Assembly nominating Mr. Ban, noted that his vision for the world was rooted in the extraordinary experience of his country, where the United Nations and the international community had been instrumental in maintaining peace and security and promoting democratization and rapid economic development. He had worked hard to put that vision into practice, bringing about greater reconciliation and cooperation on the Korean Peninsula through diplomatic efforts. He had also nurtured longstanding ties with the United Nations, contributing to its work throughout his career, and was eminently qualified to provide able leadership in pursuit of the Organization's reforms.

Nominations

The candidates nominated by their Governments for the post of Secretary-General were: Ashraf Ghani (Afghanistan), Shashi Tharoor (India), Prince Zeid Ra'ad Zeid Al-Hussein (Jordan), Ban Ki-Moon (Republic of Korea), Vaira Vīķe-Freiberga (Latvia), Jayantha Dhanapala (Sri Lanka) and Surakiart Sathirathai (Thailand) [S/2006/369, A/61/128-S/2006/480, S/2006/492, S/2006/708, S/2006/744, S/2006/751].

Following informal Security Council ballots to consider those nominations on 24 July, 14 September, 28 September and 2 October, the nominees of the Republic of Korea, India and Thailand emerged as the top three candidates. India withdrew its nominee on 5 October [A/61/496], followed by Thailand the next day [A/61/497].

SECURITY COUNCIL ACTION

At a meeting held in private on 9 October [meeting 5547], the Security Council adopted by acclamation **resolution 1715(2006)**.

The Security Council,

Having considered the question of the recommendation for the appointment of the Secretary-General of the United Nations,

Recommends to the General Assembly that Mr. Ban Ki-moon be appointed Secretary-General of the United Nations for a term of office from 1 January 2007 to 31 December 2011.

GENERAL ASSEMBLY ACTION

On 13 October [meeting 31], the General Assembly adopted **resolution 61/3** [draft: A/61/L.3] without vote [agenda item 104].

Appointment of the Secretary-General of the United Nations

The General Assembly,

Having considered the recommendation contained in Security Council resolution 1715(2006) of 9 October 2006,

Appoints Mr. Ban Ki-moon Secretary-General of the United Nations for a term of office beginning on 1 January 2007 and ending on 31 December 2011.

Tributes to Kofi Annan

SECURITY COUNCIL ACTION

On 22 December [meeting 5607], the Security Council adopted by acclamation **resolution 1733(2006)**. The draft [S/2006/1011] was prepared in consultations among Council members.

The Security Council,

Recognizing the central role that Secretary-General Kofi Annan has played in guiding the Organization in the discharge of his responsibilities under the Charter of the United Nations,

Further recognizing his sustained efforts towards finding just and lasting solutions to various disputes and conflicts around the globe,

Commending the reforms that he has initiated and the many proposals that he has made on the restructuring and strengthening of the role and functioning of the United Nations system,

1. *Acknowledges* the contribution of Secretary-General Kofi Annan to international peace, security and development, his exceptional efforts to solve international problems in economic, social and cultural fields, as well as his endeavours to meet humanitarian needs and to promote and encourage respect for human rights and fundamental freedoms for all;

2. *Expresses its deep appreciation* to Secretary-General Kofi Annan for his dedication to the purposes and principles enshrined in the Charter and to the development of friendly relations among nations.

GENERAL ASSEMBLY ACTION

On 14 December [meeting 78], the General Assembly adopted **resolution 61/107** [draft: A/61/L.48/Rev.1] without vote [agenda item 104].

Tribute to Mr. Kofi Annan, Secretary-General of the United Nations

The General Assembly,

Welcoming Security Council resolution 1715(2006) of 9 October 2006,

Recalling its resolution 61/3 of 13 October 2006 by which it appointed the Secretary-General,

Acknowledging with deep gratitude the indefatigable efforts and dedicated service provided to the Organization during the past ten years by Secretary-General Kofi Annan,

Recognizing the high professional and personal qualities he brought to the performance of his duties and responsibilities,

Placing on special record his many bold initiatives—political, diplomatic and organizational—and his important achievements, in particular with respect to the Millennium Development Goals, peace and security issues, environmental issues and United Nations reform,

1. *Pays warm tribute* to Secretary-General Kofi Annan for his exceptional contribution to international peace and security, as well as his outstanding efforts to strengthen the United Nations system and to promote and protect human rights and fundamental freedoms for all, in the interest of a better world;

2. *Expresses its deep gratitude* to Secretary-General Kofi Annan for having undertaken reforms and advanced numerous proposals with a view to enhancing the Organization's capacity to meet the major challenges of our time.

Conditions of service

International Civil Service Commission

The International Civil Service Commission (ICSC), a 15–member body established in 1974 by General Assembly resolution 3357 (XXIX) [YUN 1975, p. 875], continued in 2006 to regulate and coordinate the conditions of service and the salaries and allowances of the UN common system. ICSC held its sixty-second (Vienna, Austria, 13-31 March) and sixty-third (New York, 10-28 July) sessions [A/61/30 & Add.1], at which it adopted recommendations and decisions relating to organizational matters and the conditions of service applicable to Professional and General Service categories of staff and for locally recruited staff.

On 8 May, the Assembly deferred to its sixty-first (2006) session consideration of the item on the United Nations common system (**decision 60/551 B**).

In a 25 September statement [A/61/381], the Secretary-General estimated the administrative and financial implications of ICSC decisions and recommendations for the 2006-2007 programme budget at $9,562,100, net of staff assessment, which would be taken into consideration in the first performance report for the 2006-2007 biennium.

On 2 October [A/61/484], ACABQ stated that it had no objection to the Secretary-General's statement.

The Assembly, in **resolution 61/252** (section VI) of 22 December (see p. 1615), took note of the Secretary-General's statement and the related ACABQ report.

GENERAL ASSEMBLY ACTION

On 22 December [meeting 84], the General Assembly, on the recommendation of the Fifth Committee [A/61/663], adopted **resolution 61/239** without vote [agenda item 125].

United Nations common system: report of the International Civil Service Commission

The General Assembly,

Recalling its resolutions 44/198 of 21 December 1989, 51/216 of 18 December 1996, 52/216 of 22 December 1997, 53/209 of 18 December 1998, 55/223 of 23 December 2000, 56/244 of 24 December 2001, 57/285 of 20 December 2002, 58/251 of 23 December 2003, 59/268 of 23 December 2004 and 60/248 of 23 December 2005,

Having considered the reports of the International Civil Service Commission for the years 2004, 2005 and 2006, the note by the Secretariat transmitting the report of the Panel on the Strengthening of the International Civil Service and the note by the Secretary-General on the findings and recommendations of the Panel,

Having also considered the notes by the Secretary-General on the Senior Management Network and the mobility and hardship allowance,

Reaffirming its commitment to a single, unified United Nations common system as the cornerstone for the regulation and coordination of the conditions of service of the United Nations common system,

Convinced that the common system constitutes the best instrument through which to secure staff with the highest standards of efficiency, competence and integrity for the international civil service, as stipulated in the Charter of the United Nations,

Reaffirming the statute of the Commission and the central role of the Commission and the General Assembly in the regulation and coordination of the conditions of service of the United Nations common system,

1. *Takes note* of the reports of the International Civil Service Commission for 2005 and 2006;

2. *Invites* the Secretary-General, in his capacity as Chairman of the United Nations System Chief Executives Board for Coordination, to urge the heads of the organizations of the United Nations common system to fully support the work of the Commission, including by providing the latter with relevant information in a timely manner for studies that it conducts under its statutory responsibilities for the common system;

I

Conditions of service applicable to both categories of staff

A. Review of the pay and benefits system

Recalling section I.E, paragraph 1, of its resolution 44/198, section VI of its resolution 51/216, section I.C of its resolution 55/223, section II.A, paragraph 7, of its resolution 57/285, section I.C of its resolution 59/268 and section XVII of its resolution 60/248,

A1
Pilot study of broad-banding/pay-for-performance

1. *Takes note* of the decisions of the Commission contained in paragraph 42 of its 2005 report and paragraph 43 of its 2006 report;

2. *Notes with concern* that a project manager has yet to be selected in accordance with the terms of reference of the pilot project as outlined in paragraph 86 (*a*) of the 2003 report of the Commission and of which note was taken by the General Assembly in section I.A, paragraph 2, of its resolution 58/251;

3. *Requests* the Commission to ensure the dedicated project leadership required for the successful completion of the pilot study;

A2
Spouse benefits

Takes note of the decision of the Commission contained in paragraph 63 of its 2005 report;

A3
Mobility and hardship allowance

1. *Commends* the Working Group for developing the proposed changes in the mobility and hardship scheme;

2. *Approves* the definitions of hardship and mobility as outlined in paragraphs 76 and 77 of the 2005 report of the Commission;

3. *Also approves* the proposed arrangements for mobility, hardship, non-removal and assignment grants as set out in annex II to the 2005 report of the Commission;

4. *Decides* to implement the new system with effect from 1 January 2007;

A4
Education grant: review of the methodology for determining the level of the grant

1. *Takes note* of the decision of the Commission contained in paragraph 110 of its 2005 report;

2. *Approves*, with effect from the school year in progress on 1 January 2007, the recommendation of the Commission in paragraph 63 of its 2006 report modifying the eligibility period for the education grant;

A5
Education grant: review of the level

Approves, with effect from the school year in progress on 1 January 2007, the recommendations of the Commission contained in paragraph 62 of its 2006 report and annex II thereto;

B. Contractual arrangements

Recalling section I.A, paragraph 4, of its resolution 57/285, section IX of its resolution 59/266 of 23 December 2004 and section I.B of its resolution 59/268,

1. *Notes* the decisions of the Commission contained in paragraph 129 of its 2005 report;

2. *Notes with appreciation* the work of the Commission on the framework for contractual arrangements contained in annex IV to its 2005 report;

C. Hazard pay: review of the level

Recalling sections I.D of its resolutions 57/285, 58/251, and 59/268,

Notes the decisions of the Commission contained in paragraph 147 of its 2005 report and annex III thereto for implementation as of 1 January 2007;

D. Entitlements of internationally recruited staff serving in non-family duty stations

Recalling section X, paragraphs 5 and 6, of its resolution 59/266,

Decides to revert to consideration of the entitlements of internationally recruited staff serving in non-family duty stations at the second part of its resumed sixty-first session following receipt of the report of the Commission on this issue;

E. Other

Requests the Commission to consider the effectiveness and impact of measures designed to promote recruitment and retention, especially in difficult duty stations, and to report thereon to it at its sixty-third session;

II

Conditions of service of staff in the Professional and higher categories

A. Evolution of the margin

Recalling section I.B of its resolution 51/216 and the standing mandate from the General Assembly, in which the Commission is requested to continue its review of the relationship between the net remuneration of the United Nations staff in the Professional and higher categories in New York and that of the comparator civil service (the United States federal civil service) employees in comparable positions in Washington, D.C. (referred to as "the margin"),

1. *Notes* that the margin between net remuneration of the United Nations staff in grades P-1 to D-2 in New York and that of officials in comparable positions in the United States federal civil service in Washington, D.C., for the period 1 January to 31 December 2006, is 114.3;

2. *Reaffirms* that the range of 110 to 120 for the margin between the net remuneration of officials in the Professional and higher categories of the United Nations in New York and the officials in comparable positions in the comparator civil service should continue to apply, on the understanding that the margin would be maintained at a level around the desirable midpoint of 115 over a period of time;

B. Base/floor salary scale

Recalling its resolution 44/198, by which it established a floor net salary level for staff in the Professional and higher categories by reference to the corresponding base net salary levels of officials in comparable positions serving at the base city of the comparator civil service (the United States federal civil service),

Approves, with effect from 1 January 2007, as recommended by the Commission in paragraph 94 (*a*) of its 2006 report, the revised base/floor scale of gross and net salaries for staff in the Professional and higher categories contained in annex IV to the report;

C. Senior Management Network

1. *Takes note* of the note by the Secretary-General on the Senior Management Network;

2. *Endorses* the decision of the Commission contained in paragraph 211 of its 2006 report;

3. *Requests* the Commission to continue to monitor the project regarding the improvement of management capacity and performance among senior staff by the United Nations System Chief Executives Board for Coordination and to advise and make recommendations to the General Assembly as appropriate;

D. Gender balance

1. *Takes note* of the findings of the Commission contained in its 2006 report;

2. *Notes with disappointment* the insufficient progress made with regard to the representation of women in the organizations of the United Nations common system, and in particular their significant under-representation at senior levels;

3. *Notes with concern* the findings of the Commission in paragraph 108 of its 2006 report;

4. *Urges* the Commission to continue to make recommendations on practical steps that should be taken to improve the representation of women in the organizations of the United Nations common system;

E. Children's and secondary dependants' allowances: review of the level

Approves the revised amounts of children's and secondary dependants' allowances as outlined in paragraph 126 of the 2006 report of the Commission and annex V thereto;

F. Identification of the highest paid national civil service

Takes note of the decision of the Commission to conclude its current total compensation study and to retain the current comparator;

G. Common scale of staff assessment

Takes note of the decisions of the Commission in paragraph 70 of its 2006 report;

III

Strengthening of the international civil service

Reaffirming that the staff of the United Nations is an invaluable asset of the Organization, and commending its contribution to furthering the purposes and principles of the United Nations,

1. *Emphasizes* that the capacity of the Commission as a source of technical expertise and policy advice should be further strengthened;

2. *Stresses* that the work of the Commission shall be given the importance and attention it deserves by the governing bodies of the organizations of the common system;

3. *Decides* to institute a limit of two full terms for the positions of Chair and Vice-Chair of the Commission;

4. *Also decides* that the provision of paragraph 3 directly above shall apply to Chairs and Vice-Chairs of the Commission appointed after 1 January 2008;

5. *Encourages* Member States to achieve a greater gender balance in the selection of members for the Commission;

6. *Urges* Member States when proposing candidates for membership in the Commission to take into account the qualifications and experience outlined in article 3 of its statute;

7. *Stresses* the importance of ensuring that candidates have managerial, leadership or executive experience, which should include knowledge of at least one of the following fields:

(*a*) Human resources management principles and practices;

(*b*) Organizational design and change management concepts and practices;

(*c*) Leadership and strategic planning concepts and practices;

(*d*) International and global issues: political, social and economic;

8. *Encourages* the Commission to continue to consider its working methods in consultation, where appropriate, with representatives of the staff and the organizations of the common system.

Also on 22 December, the Assembly decided that the item on the United Nations common system would remain for consideration during its resumed sixty-first (2007) session (**decision 61/552**).

Functioning of ICSC

Strengthening of ICSC

In 2006, the General Assembly, in continuing efforts to strengthen ICSC, encouraged the Commission to continue to consider its working methods, in consultation with representatives of the staff and organizations of the common system. The Assembly decided to limit to two full terms the positions of Chair and Vice Chair of the Commission appointed after 1 January 2008. It urged Member States to take into account the requisite qualifications and experience when proposing candidates, particularly regarding managerial, leadership and executive experience.

Remuneration issues

In keeping with General Assembly resolutions 47/216 [YUN 1992, p. 1055] and 55/223 [YUN 2000, p. 1331], ICSC reviewed the relationship between the net remuneration of UN staff in the Professional and higher categories (grades P-1 to D-2) in New York and that of the current comparator, the United States federal civil service employees in comparable positions in Washington, D.C. (referred to as the margin). In its 2006 report to the Assembly [A/61/30 & Add.1], ICSC noted that a net remuneration margin of 114 was forecast for 2006, based on grade equivalences between the United Nations and United States officials in comparable positions, as shown in annex III to its report. The Commission drew the Assembly's attention to the fact that the margin had not reached the desirable midpoint since 1997 and that its average level for the past five years stood at 111.3.

ICSC further noted that, in view of the movement of the federal civil service salaries in the United States since 1 January 2005, a 4.57 per cent adjustment was required in January 2007 for the UN common system's scale, in order to maintain the base/floor scale in line with the comparator's General Schedule base scale. ICSC recommended that the base/floor salary scale for the Professional and higher categories be increased by 4.57 per cent through the standard consolidation procedures of reducing post adjustment multiplier points and increasing base salary, on a no loss/no gain basis, effective 1 January 2007. The proposed adjustment would result in annual financial implications of $808,800 for the scale of separation payments. ICSC also recommended the concurrent introduction of the new arrangements for the mobility and hardship scheme, which it had proposed in 2005 [YUN 2005, p. 1510]. It did not envisage any financial implications as it had recommended that the scheme be de-linked from the base/floor salary scale.

Statement by Secretary-General. The Secretary-General, in his September report [A/61/381] on the administrative and financial implications of ISCS decisions for the 2006-2007 programme budget, noted that the amount of $808,800 in programme budget implications arising from the 4.75 percentage adjustment of the base/floor salary scale related only to the scale of separation payments and that for 2007, the financial implication was estimated at $355,600.

ACABQ report. In October [A/61/484], ACABQ, in its comments and recommendations on the Secretary-General's statement, noted the financial implications for 2007.

On 22 December, the General Assembly, in section II of **resolution 61/239** (see p. 1677), approved, effective 1 January 2007, the revised base/floor scale of gross and net salaries for staff in the Professional and higher categories, as recommended by ICSC and contained in annex IV of its report [A/61/30].

Post adjustment

ICSC reviewed the operation of the post adjustment system, designed to measure cost-of-living movements through periodic place-to-place surveys at all duty stations. In that regard, ICSC considered the report of its Advisory Committee on Post Adjustment Questions, which, at its twenty-eighth session in February, examined the results of the 2005 survey [YUN 2005, p. 1507], involving eight duty stations (Geneva, London, Madrid, Montreal, Paris, Rome, Vienna, Washington D.C.). ICSC found that the estimated financial implications for implementing the survey results, effective 1 April 2006, totalled approximately $19 million yearly, which could vary significantly, depending on the exchange rate movement of the United States dollar. In line with the recommendations of the Advisory Committee, ICSC, at its sixty-second session [A/61/30], approved the 2005 survey results, noting that it should be taken into account when determining the respective post adjustment classification of those duty stations as from 1 April. It requested the Committee to advise it on the validity of using the cost-of-living differential between New York and Washington D.C., established for purposes of post adjustment in the margin calculations. It decided to maintain the item on the agenda of its next session.

The Secretary-General, in a September report [A/61/381], estimated the financial implications of the ICSC decision regarding post adjustment at $3,096,000 for the 2006-2007 biennium.

Noblemaire principle

ICSC reviewed total compensation comparisons under the Noblemaire principle, intended to determine the highest paid civil service. Of the four countries (Belgium, Germany, Singapore, Switzerland) considered during the first phase of the review in 2005 [YUN 2005, p. 1507], ICSC had chosen the Belgian civil service for further study, as none of the others could replace the current comparator, the United States. Based on its study conducted between March and July 2006, ICSC noted that the current comparator had significantly higher salary levels, while the Belgian civil service had more favourable provisions for leave/holidays/work hours and a more costly pension plan. Health benefits between them were assumed to be approximately equal. ICSC observed, however, that the study took into account only compensation and not the design of human resources management systems. Furthermore, the Belgian civil service was making significant strides towards reform, aspects of which would be difficult to reflect in the UN common system, which was moving in a different direction with its own reform efforts. In the light of the results of the study, the Commission determined that it was unlikely that the Belgian civil service could supplant the current comparator. It decided, therefore, to conclude its current Noblemaire study, noting that the current comparator would be retained. Following a further consideration of data relating to the remuneration levels of the World Bank and the Organization for Economic Cooperation and Development (OECD), which it had included in the 2005 Noblemaire study as a reference check [ibid], ICSC decided to report to the General Assembly that those organizations were approximately 29 per cent ahead of the UN common system.

Common staff assessment scale

Consistent with its biennial update of the common scale of staff assessment, ICSC examined tax changes at the eight headquarters duty stations concerned and found that taxes had increased or decreased minimally since the last update [YUN 2004, p. 1412]. Taking into account such minimal changes over the years, it reported that the current common scale of staff assessment continued to apply and that it would review the scale in five years' time or at the next comprehensive review of pensionable remuneration, whichever was first.

The Assembly, in section II G of **resolution 61/239** (see p. 1677), took note of the ICSC decision.

Other remuneration issues

Conditions of service and compensation for non-Secretariat officials

Judges of ICJ and international tribunals

Reports of Secretary-General. In response to General Assembly resolution 59/282 [YUN 2005, p. 1486], the Secretary-General submitted a September report [A/61/554], which reviewed the conditions of service and compensation of members of the International Court of Justice (ICJ), judges of the International Tribunal for the Former Yugoslavia (ICTY) and the International Criminal Tribunal for Rwanda (ICTR), and ad litem judges of both Tribunals. The review was conducted against the backdrop of the Assembly's upward revision of the annual salaries of members of ICJ and the judges and ad litem judges of the Tribunals from $160,000 to $170,080, with effect from 1 January 2005. The Secretary-General noted that, under the applicable floor/ceiling mechanism, the revised salary in euros was equivalent to a floor amount of €14,559 per month, or €174,706 per annum and a currency ceiling of €15,722 per month. While that mechanism provided some protection against the weakening/strengthening of the United States dollar vis-à-vis the euro, it did not allow for proper adjustment as a result of fluctuations of the dollar against the euro. As such, Member States might wish to introduce a mechanism similar to the one pertaining to the salaries of staff in the Professional and higher categories, namely, a net base salary with a corresponding post adjustment amount per index point that was equal to 1 per cent of the net base salary at each level and step of the salary scale. Thus, based on a post adjustment multiplier of 50.2 as at September 2006 for judges serving in The Hague, and of 38.6 for those serving in the United Republic of Tanzania, the Secretary-General recommended an annual remuneration (base salary plus post adjustment) of $255,460 for those serving in The Hague and $235,731 for their counterparts in Arusha. The Secretary-General also proposed that the annual base salaries of members of ICJ and the judges and ad litem judges of the Tribunals be further increased to $177,900 as from 1 January 2007, in order to reflect the 4.57 per cent increase in the base/floor salary scale recommended by ICSC (see p. 1680). With a corresponding increase in post adjustment, that would set the total salary of judges serving in the Netherlands at $225,464, and those serving in the United Republic of Tanzania at $225,716. The annual base salary of the judges as a whole should be adjusted by the same percentage and at the same time as any future revisions of the base scale applicable to staff in the Professional and higher categories.

The Secretary-General also recommended an increase in the special allowance of the ICJ President and the Vice-President when acting as President, and increases in education grant for ICJ members and judges of the Tribunals, additional pension payments in respect of former judges and widows of ICJ members and judges of both Tribunals, and a revision of travel and subsistence regulations to reflect UN practice and the establishment of an instrument to protect pensions payment. He estimated the programme budget implications of his recommendations at $2,186,500 for the 2006-2007 biennium.

Report of ACABQ. On 6 December [A/61/612 & Corr.1], ACABQ, having considered the Secretary-General's report (see above), noted that his proposal to increase the remuneration levels of the judges and ad litem judges of ICTY and ICTR by 14.9 per cent and 38.6 per cent, respectively, using the current net remuneration as the base salary, unduly inflated the remuneration calculated under a post adjustment system, as the current net remuneration already included a cost-of-living component. ACABQ recommended the elaboration of alternative methods for adjusting remuneration according to market exchange rates and movement of the local cost-of-living index, with a view towards protecting the level of the remuneration as requested by the Assembly. It determined nonetheless that the new proposals should be presented to the Assembly at its sixty-second (2007) session.

ACABQ agreed with the proposed revision of the travel and subsistence regulations applicable to ICJ members and the recommendations regarding the protection of pensions. However, it recommended against the proposed increase in the level of the special allowance for the ICJ President and Vice-President, and decided retirement and pension benefits for members of the Court and judges of the Tribunals should be decided by the Assembly.

Dependency allowances

During its biennial review of dependency allowances for the Professional and higher categories [A/61/30], ICSC was informed that the methodology of adjusting the levels of dependency allowances did not reflect fully and accurately overall trends in national tax and social security child-related relief, which it was supposed to gauge. The application of the methodology would, however, require an overall negative adjustment of the dependent child allowance because the final adjustment percentage reflected only relative changes in national child benefit levels over time, without any reference to the absolute levels of those benefits. ICSC proposed that staff who became eligible to receive dependency allowances on or after 1 January 2007 be paid, per annum, children's allowance in the amount of $1,780, disabled child allowance of $3,560 and secondary dependant's allowance of $637. At duty stations where dependency allowances were expressed in local currency, the revised amounts payable as children's and secondary dependant's allowances would be as shown in table 1 of annex V of the ICSC 2006 report [A/61/30]. Staff who were eligible to receive the dependency allowances would continue to receive a children's allowance of $1,936, disabled child allowance of $3,872, and secondary dependant's allowance of $693. At duty stations where the dependency allowances were expressed in local currency, the current amounts of the allowances would continue to be paid, as indicated in table 2 of annex V of the ICSC 2006 report. ICSC also decided to review the methodology for determining dependency allowances at its next session and requested its secretariat to develop proposals aimed at simplifying and improving the fairness of the system.

The Assembly, in section II of **resolution 61/239** of 22 December (see p. 1677), approved ICSC revised amounts of children's and secondary dependants' allowances.

Education grant

Based on the revised methodology endorsed by the General Assembly in resolution 52/216 [YUN 1997, p. 1454], ICSC reviewed the operation of the education grant, based on a related study by the Human Resources Network, which analysed 13,053 claims for the academic year 2004-2005 in the 17 individual countries/currency areas in which the grant was applied. ICSC recommended that, as from 1 January 2007, maximum admissible expenses and maximum education grant for six zones (Denmark, Ireland, Italy, Sweden, the United States, the US dollar area beyond the United States) be adjusted, as indicated in table 1 of annex II to the Commission's 2006 report [A/61/30]. The maximum amount of admissible expenses and the maximum grant should remain at the current level for Austria, Belgium, Finland, France, Germany, Japan, the Netherlands, Spain,

Switzerland and the United Kingdom. The separate zone of Norway should be discontinued and the education claims for that country included in the US dollar area outside the United States. Also, a separate maximum admissible expense level equal to that applicable to the United States should be established for the six English Curriculum schools in France. The amount of the special education grant for each disabled child should be equal to 100 per cent of the revised amounts of the maximum allowable expenses for the regular grant, while special measures would be maintained for China, Indonesia and the Russian Federation. The foregoing measures would apply as from the school year in progress by 1 January 2007. The Commission also recommended that the eligibility period for the education grant should continue up to the end of the school year in which a child completed four years of post-secondary education, even if a degree had been attained after three years. Students would continue to be subject to the age limit of 25 years.

In a September statement [A/61/381], the Secretary-General estimated the annual financial implication of ICSC recommendations regarding the education grant at $2,200,000 and $830,500 for the 2006-2007 programme budget.

The General Assembly, in section I of **resolution 61/239** of 22 December (see p. 1677), approved, with effect from the school year in progress by 1 January 2007, ICSC recommendations relating to the education grant.

Hazard pay

The Commission, in 2005 [YUN 2005, p. 1510], had revised the level of hazard pay—payment for employment under conditions where war or hostilities prevailed or where medical staff was exposed to life-threatening diseases, and the evacuation of families and non-essential staff had taken place, from $1,000 to $1,300 for internationally recruited staff.

The Secretary-General, in a September report [A/61/381], estimated the financial implications of the revision at $3,322,800 for the 2006-2007 programme budget, based on the Secretariat's most recent statistics, which highlighted a significant expansion of personnel deployed in high-risk areas, involving up to 923 posts in special political missions.

Review of methodologies for surveys of best prevailing conditions of employment

On the basis of the 1997 revised methodology for surveys of best prevailing conditions of employment at Headquarters and non-Headquarters duty stations [YUN 1997, p. 1453], ICSC conducted a survey of best prevailing conditions of service for General Service staff in Rome, with a reference date of November 2005. The Commission also undertook a similar survey for the General Service and other locally recruited categories in New York, also with a reference date of November 2005. Both surveys resulted in new salary scales, reproduced in annexes VI and VII of the 2006 report of ICSC [A/61/30], which were recommended to Rome-based and New York-based common system organizations. ICSC also recommended lowering dependency allowance rates, which would be applicable only to the dependents of staff recruited after the revision of that benefit. It envisaged that the reduction would result in estimated savings of $45,000 per annum for the common system.

In September [A/61/381], the Secretary-General estimated the annual financial implications of the results of those surveys at $3,590,000. For the UN programme budget, the financial implications were estimated at $1,957,200, which would be taken into account in adjusting the inflation provisions in the budget within the context of the first performance report for the 2006-2007 biennium.

Staff safety and security

Report of Secretary-General. In response to General Assembly resolution 60/123 [YUN 2005, p. 1523], the Secretary-General, in September [A/61/463], updated information on threats to the safety and security of UN personnel between 1 July 2005 and 30 June 2006 and described progress in efforts to improve the situation. He noted that staff security remained unassured, particularly in Afghanistan, Eritrea, Ethiopia, Israel, Somalia and the Sudan. Some countries continued to detain UN personnel and to refuse the Organization's right of protection, in violation of agreed conventions. Personnel serving in field operations globally continued to face such threats as hostage-taking, physical assault, robbery, harassment and detention. During the reporting period, 15 UN civilian staff members lost their lives, compared to 11 in the previous reporting period, and 19 uniformed peacekeepers were killed in the line of duty. Overall, there were 215 violent incidents, including five cases of rape, nine sexual assaults, 93 armed robberies of significant UN assets, and kidnappings in the Democratic Republic of the Congo, Haiti and Somalia. The number of those arrested, under detention or missing, and regarding whom the Organization had been unable to exercise its right to protection, increased to 26, from 23 cases in

2005. Attacks on humanitarian convoys increased, resulting in 15 cases of injury or death, compared to nine in the previous reporting period. Such incidents undermined the operational efficiency and effectiveness of the United Nations, degraded the personal safety and well-being of staff, and compromised the security of field installations. Other international, non-governmental and intergovernmental organizations also lost many of their staff as a result of malicious acts.

The Secretary-General described measures taken by the Organization, mostly through the Department of Safety and Security, to strengthen staff safety.

In his conclusions and recommendations, the Secretary-General maintained that the primary responsibility for the safety and security of staff remained with host Governments. Despite the strong commitment of several Member States in that regard, he continued to be dismayed by the ongoing difficulties encountered in a few countries to obtain permission to import security-related communications equipment, the unwillingness of some host Governments to provide timely information on the arrest or detention of locally recruited UN personnel and the fact that only few countries had fully investigated attacks against staff or held the perpetrators accountable under international law. The Secretary-General appealed to those countries that had imposed restrictions on the Organization's importation of relevant equipment to lift them promptly and urged Member States as a whole to work with the Department of Safety and Security in fulfilling their Charter obligations to ensure the safety of United Nations and humanitarian personnel.

GENERAL ASSEMBLY ACTION

On 14 December [meeting 79], the General Assembly adopted **resolution 61/133** [draft: A/61/L.45 & Add.1] without vote [agenda item 69].

Safety and security of humanitarian personnel and protection of United Nations personnel

The General Assembly,

Reaffirming its resolution 46/182 of 19 December 1991 on strengthening of the coordination of humanitarian emergency assistance of the United Nations,

Recalling all relevant resolutions on safety and security of humanitarian personnel and protection of United Nations personnel, including its resolution 60/123 of 15 December 2005, as well as Security Council resolution 1502(2003) of 26 August 2003 and relevant statements by the President of the Council,

Recalling also all Security Council resolutions and presidential statements and reports of the Secretary-General to the Council on the protection of civilians in armed conflict,

Recalling further all relevant provisions of international law, including international humanitarian law and human rights law, as well as all relevant treaties,

Reaffirming the need to promote and ensure respect for the principles and rules of international law, including international humanitarian law,

Recalling that primary responsibility under international law for the security and protection of humanitarian personnel and United Nations and associated personnel lies with the Government hosting a United Nations operation conducted under the Charter of the United Nations or its agreements with relevant organizations,

Urging all parties involved in armed conflicts, in compliance with international humanitarian law, in particular their obligations under the Geneva Conventions of 12 August 1949 and the obligations applicable to them under the Additional Protocols thereto, of 8 June 1977, to ensure the security and protection of all humanitarian personnel and United Nations and associated personnel,

Welcoming the fact that the number of States parties to the Convention on the Safety of United Nations and Associated Personnel, which entered into force on 15 January 1999, has continued to rise, the number now having reached eighty-one, and mindful of the need to promote universality of the Convention,

Deeply concerned by the dangers and security risks faced by humanitarian personnel and United Nations and associated personnel at the field level, as they operate in increasingly complex contexts, as well as the continuous erosion, in many cases, of respect for the principles and rules of international law, in particular international humanitarian law,

Commending the courage and commitment of those who take part in humanitarian operations, often at great personal risk, especially locally recruited staff,

Expressing profound regret at the deaths of and violent acts against international and national humanitarian personnel and United Nations and associated personnel involved in the provision of humanitarian assistance, and strongly deploring the rising toll of casualties among such personnel in complex humanitarian emergencies, in particular in armed conflicts and in post-conflict situations,

Strongly condemning acts of murder and other forms of violence, rape and sexual assault and all forms of violence committed in particular against women and children, and intimidation, armed robbery, abduction, hostage-taking, kidnapping, harassment and illegal arrest and detention to which those participating in humanitarian operations are increasingly exposed, as well as attacks on humanitarian convoys and acts of destruction and looting of property,

Expressing deep concern that the occurrence of attacks and threats against humanitarian personnel and United Nations and associated personnel is a factor that increasingly restricts the provision of assistance and protection to populations in need,

Affirming the need for States to ensure that perpetrators of attacks committed on their territory against humanitarian personnel and United Nations and associated personnel do not operate with impunity, and that the perpetrators of such acts are brought to justice as provided for by national law and obligations under international law,

Recalling the inclusion of attacks intentionally directed against personnel involved in a humanitarian assistance or peacekeeping mission in accordance with the Charter as a war crime in the Rome Statute of the International Criminal Court, and noting the role that the Court could play in appropriate cases in bringing to justice those responsible for serious violations of international humanitarian law,

Reaffirming the need to ensure adequate levels of safety and security for United Nations personnel and associated humanitarian personnel, which constitutes an underlying duty of the Organization, and mindful of the need to promote and enhance the security consciousness within the organizational culture of the United Nations and a culture of accountability at all levels,

1. *Welcomes* the report of the Secretary-General;

2. *Urges* all States to take the necessary measures to ensure the full and effective implementation of the relevant principles and rules of international law, including international humanitarian law, human rights law and refugee law related to the safety and security of humanitarian personnel and United Nations personnel;

3. *Strongly urges* all States to take the necessary measures to ensure the safety and security of humanitarian personnel and United Nations and associated personnel and to respect and ensure respect for the inviolability of United Nations premises, which are essential to the continuation and successful implementation of United Nations operations;

4. *Calls upon* all Governments and parties in complex humanitarian emergencies, in particular in armed conflicts and in post-conflict situations, in countries in which humanitarian personnel are operating, in conformity with the relevant provisions of international law and national laws, to cooperate fully with the United Nations and other humanitarian agencies and organizations and to ensure the safe and unhindered access of humanitarian personnel and delivery of supplies and equipment in order to allow those personnel to perform efficiently their task of assisting the affected civilian population, including refugees and internally displaced persons;

5. *Calls upon* all States to consider becoming parties to and to respect fully their obligations under the relevant international instruments;

6. *Also calls upon* all States to consider becoming parties to the Rome Statute of the International Criminal Court;

7. *Takes note with appreciation* of the adoption of the Optional Protocol to the Convention on the Safety of United Nations and Associated Personnel, which expands the scope of legal protection under the Convention, and calls upon all States to consider signing and ratifying the Optional Protocol as soon as possible so as to ensure its rapid entry into force, and urges States parties to put in place appropriate national legislation, as necessary, to enable its effective implementation;

8. *Expresses deep concern* that, over the past decade, threats and attacks against the safety and security of humanitarian personnel and United Nations and associated personnel have escalated dramatically and that perpetrators of acts of violence seemingly operate with impunity;

9. *Strongly condemns* all threats and acts of violence against humanitarian personnel and United Nations and associated personnel, reaffirms the need to hold accountable those responsible for such acts, strongly urges all States to take stronger action to ensure that any such acts committed on their territory are investigated fully and to ensure that the perpetrators of such acts are brought to justice in accordance with international law and national law, and urges States to end impunity for such acts;

10. *Calls upon* all States to provide adequate and prompt information in the event of the arrest or detention of humanitarian personnel or United Nations and associated personnel, so as to afford them the necessary medical assistance and to allow independent medical teams to visit and examine the health of those detained, and urges them to take the necessary measures to ensure the speedy release of those who have been arrested or detained in violation of the relevant conventions referred to in the present resolution and applicable international humanitarian law;

11. *Calls upon* all other parties involved in armed conflicts to refrain from abducting humanitarian personnel or United Nations and associated personnel or detaining them in violation of the relevant conventions referred to in the present resolution and applicable international humanitarian law, and speedily to release, without harm or requirement of concession, any abductee or detainee;

12. *Requests* the Secretary-General to take the necessary measures to ensure full respect for the human rights, privileges and immunities of United Nations and other personnel carrying out activities in fulfilment of the mandate of a United Nations operation, and also requests the Secretary-General to seek the inclusion, in negotiations of headquarters and other mission agreements concerning United Nations and associated personnel, of the applicable conditions contained in the Convention on the Privileges and Immunities of the United Nations, the Convention on the Privileges and Immunities of the Specialized Agencies and the Convention on the Safety of United Nations and Associated Personnel;

13. *Recommends* that the Secretary-General continue to seek the inclusion of, and that host countries include, key provisions of the Convention on the Safety of United Nations and Associated Personnel, among others, those regarding the prevention of attacks against members of the operation, the establishment of such attacks as crimes punishable by law and the prosecution or extradition of offenders, in future as well as, if necessary, in existing status-of-forces, status-of-mission, host country agreements and other related agreements negotiated between the United Nations and those countries, mindful of the

importance of the timely conclusion of such agreements, and encourages further efforts in this regard;

14. *Reaffirms* the obligation of all humanitarian personnel and United Nations and associated personnel to observe and respect the national laws of the country in which they are operating, in accordance with international law and the Charter of the United Nations;

15. *Stresses* the importance of ensuring that humanitarian personnel and United Nations and associated personnel remain sensitive to national and local customs and traditions in their countries of assignment and communicate clearly their purpose and objectives to local populations;

16. *Welcomes* ongoing efforts to promote and enhance the security consciousness within the organizational culture of the United Nations system, and requests the Secretary-General to continue to take the necessary measures in this regard, including by further developing and implementing a unified security management system, as well as by disseminating and ensuring the implementation of the security procedures and regulations and by ensuring accountability at all levels, and also welcomes the creation and the work of the Department of Safety and Security of the Secretariat;

17. *Emphasizes* the importance of paying special attention to the safety and security of United Nations and associated personnel engaged in United Nations peacekeeping and peacebuilding operations;

18. *Also emphasizes* the need to pay particular attention to the safety and security of locally recruited humanitarian personnel, who are particularly vulnerable to attacks and who account for the majority of casualties, and calls upon humanitarian organizations to ensure that their staff are adequately informed about and trained in their respective organization's relevant security measures, plans and initiatives, which should be in line with applicable national law and international law;

19. *Requests* the Secretary-General to continue to take the necessary measures to ensure that United Nations and other personnel carrying out activities in fulfilment of the mandate of a United Nations operation are properly informed about and operate in conformity with the minimum operating security standards and relevant codes of conduct and are properly informed about the conditions under which they are called upon to operate and the standards that they are required to meet, including those contained in relevant national and international law, and that adequate training in security, human rights law and international humanitarian law is provided so as to enhance their security and effectiveness in accomplishing their functions, and reaffirms the necessity for all other humanitarian organizations to provide their personnel with similar support;

20. *Welcomes* the ongoing efforts of the Secretary-General and stresses the need to ensure that all United Nations staff members receive adequate security training, including training to enhance cultural awareness, prior to their deployment to the field, as well as the need to attach a high priority to stress management training and related counselling services for United Nations staff throughout the system;

21. *Takes note* of the report of the Secretary-General on a strengthened and unified security management system for the United Nations;

22. *Emphasizes* the importance of information on the range and scope of security incidents involving humanitarian personnel and United Nations and associated personnel, including attacks against them, to clarify their operating environment;

23. *Welcomes* the ongoing efforts of the Secretary-General to further enhance the security management system of the United Nations, and in this regard invites the United Nations and, as appropriate, other humanitarian organizations, working closely with host States, to further strengthen the analysis of threats to their safety and security in order to manage security risks by facilitating informed decisions on the maintenance of an effective presence in the field, inter alia, to fulfil their humanitarian mandate;

24. *Stresses* that the effective functioning at the country level of security operations requires a unified capacity for policy, standards, coordination, communication, compliance and threat and risk assessment, and notes the benefits thereof to United Nations and associated personnel, including those achieved by the Department of Safety and Security since its establishment;

25. *Recognizes* the need to continue efforts to achieve a strengthened and unified security management system for the United Nations, both at the headquarters and the field levels, and requests the United Nations system, as well as Member States, to take all appropriate measures to that end;

26. *Requests* the Secretary-General, inter alia, through the Inter-Agency Security Management Network, to continue to promote increased cooperation and collaboration among United Nations departments, organizations, funds and programmes and affiliated international organizations, including between their headquarters and field offices, in the planning and implementation of measures aimed at improving staff security, training and awareness, and calls upon all relevant United Nations departments, organizations, funds and programmes and affiliated international organizations to support those efforts;

27. *Recognizes* the steps taken by the Secretary-General thus far, as well as the need for continued efforts to enhance coordination and cooperation, both at the headquarters and the field levels, between the United Nations and other humanitarian and non-governmental organizations on matters relating to the safety and security of humanitarian personnel and United Nations and associated personnel, with a view to addressing mutual security concerns in the field, and encourages collaborative initiatives to address security training needs;

28. *Underlines* the need to allocate adequate and predictable resources to the safety and security of United Nations personnel, including through the consolidated appeals process, and encourages all States to contribute to the Trust Fund for Security of Staff Members of

the United Nations System, inter alia, with a view to reinforcing the efforts of the United Nations Department of Safety and Security for the safety and security of personnel working in emergency and humanitarian operations;

29. *Recalls* the essential role of telecommunication resources in facilitating the safety of humanitarian personnel and United Nations and associated personnel, calls upon States to consider acceding to or ratifying the Tampere Convention on the Provision of Telecommunication Resources for Disaster Mitigation and Relief Operations of 18 June 1998, which entered into force on 8 January 2005, and urges them to facilitate and expedite, consistent with their national laws and international obligations applicable to them, the use of communications equipment in such operations, inter alia, through limiting and, whenever possible, expeditiously lifting the restrictions placed on the use of communications equipment by United Nations and associated personnel;

30. *Requests* the Secretary-General to submit to the General Assembly at its sixty-second session a comprehensive and updated report on the safety and security of humanitarian personnel and protection of United Nations personnel and on the implementation of the present resolution.

Other staff matters

Managerial efficiency and accountability

Senior Management Network

In accordance with General Assembly resolution 59/268 [YUN 2004, p. 1408], ICSC, at its sixty-second session [A/61/30], considered the status of the Senior Management Network (formerly Senior Management Service), the Organization's instrument for building managerial capacity throughout the common system, in order to improve performance. It had before it a progress report on the subject submitted by the Human Resources Network of CEB [CEB/2006/HLCM/12]. The report, which underlined the relevance of the Senior Management Network, in the light of the reform efforts in many common system organizations, noted that a leadership development programme remained its core. However, further work was needed to develop the broader aspects beyond a leadership programme. ICSC observed that the information provided in the report afforded some clarity on the development and direction of the Senior Management Network, as well as the opportunity to raise concerns and identify challenges in its implementation. It decided to request similar updates at regular intervals.

On 22 December, the Assembly, in section II of **resolution 61/239** (see p. 1677), endorsed the ICSC decision and requested it to continue monitoring the project.

Strengthening accountability

In response to General Assembly resolution 60/260 (see p. 1576), the Secretary-General submitted a June report [A/60/846/Add.6] on accountability, which highlighted the need for a definition of accountability, clarified the elements of an effective accountability system and described the situation regarding United Nations accountability mechanisms for results, the management of financial and human resources and procurement.

The Secretary-General proposed two working definitions of accountability: institutional accountability and personal accountability, with the former pertaining to the responsibility of the Secretary-General to explain and justify to the Assembly and other intergovernmental bodies, the performance of the Organization in using resources to achieve results. Personal accountability related to the duty of an individual staff member to exercise defined responsibilities appropriately and explain and justify the results achieved and the manner in which the authority had been exercised. The Secretary-General observed that accountability should be viewed, not only from the perspective of possible malfeasance, but also of competencies for programme performance. Insufficient attention had been given to holding the UN Secretariat or intergovernmental bodies accountable for the achievement of results. While accountability measures had been established for the management of programmes and financial and human resources over the past 10 years their implementation had not been comprehensive. There was limited understanding of the consequences of underperformance, poor performance or non-performance and no sanctions were in place for the non-achievement of results. Moreover, the oversight of performance within the Secretariat was an assignment undertaken by staff appointed to sit on boards, panels and committees, in addition to their regular functions. Consequently, such oversight functions were given low priority. A transparent and effective accountability system required the continuing promotion of a management culture that encouraged improved performance, higher levels of productivity and better quality of work, as well as ethical behaviour and compliance with the standards of conduct in the international civil service.

The Secretary-General recommended that the Assembly endorse his proposed definitions of accountability and note that the UN accountability framework had been strengthened through the implementation of various mechanisms in 2005 and 2006. Further enhancements could be anticipated in the light of recommendations expected from the review of UN governance and oversight and of the internal justice system.

ACABQ, in a June report [A/60/909], stated that forthcoming reports on accountability should link performance to both incentives and disincentives and place greater emphasis on the practical application of an accountability framework. In that connection, particular attention should be paid to the accountability of senior managers. In addition, results-based budgeting and management required further development, as existing instruments for informing Member States about performance were weak. ACABQ recommended that the Assembly take note of enhancements to the accountability framework, such as the establishment of the Independent Audit Advisory Committee, the Management Performance Board and the Oversight Committee. However, it pointed out that only the Management Performance Board had been constituted. It also recommended that the Assembly request the Secretary-General to further develop the definition of accountability.

In October [A/61/546], the Secretary-General submitted a further report summarizing measures undertaken to strengthen accountability, including specific reforms arising from decisions made at the 2005 World Summit [YUN 2005, p. 47], and other ongoing reform measures.

The Assembly, in **resolution 61/245** of 22 December (see p. 1573), took note of the reports of the Secretary-General and ACABQ relating to accountability and requested the Secretary-General to submit a report on the accountability framework by the end of its resumed sixty-first (2007) session.

Personnel policies

Human resources management

On 8 May, the General Assembly decided to defer to its sixty-first (2006) session consideration of the agenda item on human resources management (**decision 60/551 B**).

For its deliberations on the item at that session, the Assembly had before it reports and notes of the Secretary-General, consideration of which had been deferred from previous sessions, on: availability in local labour markets of the skills for which international recruitment for the General Service category took place; [YUN 2004, p. 1430; YUN 2005, p. 1518]; gratis personnel provided by Governments and other entities [ibid., p. 1517]; comprehensive assessment of the system of geographical distribution and assessment of the issues relating to possible changes in the number of posts subject to the system [ibid.]; the JIU report on the review of the Headquarters agreements concluded by UN system organizations: human resources issues affecting staff [YUN 2004, p. 1433]; comments of the Secretary-General and those of the CEB on the JIU report [YUN 2005, p. 1522]; composition of the Secretariat [ibid., p. 1516]; and list of staff of the Secretariat [ibid., p. 1514].

In addition, the Assembly had before it the Secretary-General's reports on special measures for protection from sexual exploitation and abuse [A/60/861]; comprehensive policy guidelines for consultants in the Office of the United Nations High Commissioner for Refugees (UNHCR) [A/61/201]; human resources management reform [A/61/228 & Corr.1]; investing in people [A/61/255]; reforming the Field Service category of staff in UN peace operations [A/61/255/Add.1 & Corr.1]; composition of the Secretariat [A/61/257 & Corr.1]; use of gratis personnel [A/61/257/Add.1 & Corr.1]; employment of retired staff [A/61/257/Add.2]; use of consultants and individual contractors [A/61/257/Add.3]; activities of the Ethics Office [A/61/274]; and activities of the Management Performance Board [A/61/319].

Reform initiatives

In response to General Assembly resolutions 59/266 [YUN 2004, p.1418] and 60/238 [YUN 2005, p. 1515], the Secretary-General submitted an August report [A/61/228 & Corr. 1], which provided an overview of actions taken to advance reform initiatives contained in his 1997 [YUN 1997, p. 1389], 2002 [YUN 2002, p.1352] and 2005 [YUN 2005, p. 67] reports and described some of the challenges facing the Organization's reform process. The report noted that significant progress had been made in bringing about the change envisioned in the integrated reform programme. Major achievements included the establishment of a system of human resources planning that provided the Organization with workforce profiles and trends at Secretariat and departmental levels; the streamlining of policies and rules in a new electronic human resources handbook; the introduction of a new staff selection system for speeding up the selection process and improving efficiency and transparency; the establishment of the policy of organizational mobility in order to develop a more versatile, multi-skilled and experienced international civil service; the development of competencies and core values aimed at promoting shared values and common standards throughout the Secretariat; the introduction of a policy of continuous learning; and the establishment of an enhanced performance appraisal system, which promoted feedback and communication between staff and supervisors. In that process, OHRM role had expanded, from its traditional functions of staff administration and the custodian of regulations and rules to one that was proactive and strategic, as it served as a change agent, introducing and sharing new ideas and good practices on human resources management.

The next steps would be to address the remaining challenges, including further aligning human resources management policies and practices with operational needs and worldwide standards of good practice, and having the resources and tools necessary to implement and manage change. The report outlined the goals of the reform process, further elaborated on the achievements made and detailed future activities and proposals. It underlined the need to further develop the Organization's human resource planning system to enable it carry out a strategic global workforce planning, based on a systematic analyses of supply and demand requirements and the elaboration of solutions to address the gaps between the current workforce and future needs. That need underpinned a new set of reform measures set out in a separate report of the Secretary-General advocating investment in people (see below).

The Secretary-General also examined, as requested in Assembly resolution 60/238 [ibid., p.1515], the policy requirement for UN staff to renounce permanent resident status in a country outside the country of their nationality, highlighting the concerns behind that policy in terms of the need for geographical distribution, and the financial implications. The Secretary-General determined that the circumstances recommending that policy were no longer compelling, and invited the Assembly to reconsider it, taking into account the individual hardship that might result from its continuing application, the changes in the Organization's needs and the profile of its staff.

Investing in people

Pursuant to General Assembly resolutions 60/260 (see p. 1576) and 60/283 (see p. 1580), the Secretary-General, in an August report [A/61/255] entitled "Investing in people", provided details on the new human resources management reform proposals and framework contained in his March report on investing in the United Nations (see p. 1643). In making the case for new reforms, the Secretary-General reviewed previous human resource management reform initiatives, particularly those contained in his 1997 [YUN 1997, p. 1389] and 2000 [YUN 2000, p.1337] reports, highlighting the major progress made. However, the human resources management framework, which was designed for a stable, largely Headquarter-based environment, had been only partially adapted to accommodate more dynamic field-based operations. The Organization's increasingly complex mandates required a new skill profile to respond in an integrated way to needs in areas as diverse as humanitarian assistance, peacekeeping, human rights, electoral assistance, counter-terrorism and drugs and crime. Issues of concern underpinning the need for further human resources reform included the existence of several different contractual arrangements with different benefits and conditions of service for staff members currently serving at the Secretariat; complex, outmoded and fragmented systems and processes hampering the Organization's ability to respond to changing requirements; multiple, restrictive and often contradictory legislative mandates that limited the Secretary-General's ability and authority to effectively manage the Organization; a slow and reactive approach to recruitment, which undermined the Organization's ability to recruit staff to respond promptly to requirements as they arose; limited staff mobility, undercutting the Organization's ability to function with flexibility, responsiveness and effectiveness; insufficient investment in developing and managing talent; and the selection of managers based primarily on substantive expertise or political acumen rather than the requisite expertise for managing people, resources and change.

The Secretary-General outlined proposals to improve human resources management in six core areas—recruitment, staff mobility, career development, contractual arrangements and conditions of service, building leadership and management capacity, and staff buyout. To strengthen the recruitment system, the Secretary-General proposed that the Assembly reduce the advertising time for vacancy announcements from 60 to 30 days for specific vacancies; eliminate eligibility requirements to increase promotion opportunities for General Service staff; and authorize the continuing use of the special roster for pre-screened candidates to P-4 and P-5 posts, in order to improve the geographical representation of unrepresented and underrepresented Member States. In addition, the Secretary-General advocated more extensive outreach in the recruitment process, based on strategic workforce planning; the establishment of a dedicated recruitment service to support managers in staff selection; expedited recruitment processes for surge needs; a revision of examinations and job profiles to match current needs; and strict compliance with geographical and gender targets.

For a more integrated approach to staff mobility, the Secretary-General proposed that the Assembly eliminate the restrictions on staff on assignment to UN peace missions, except missions in a start-up phase or other exceptional circumstances, and review host country agreements and the issuance of work permits in order to support the employment of spouses of UN staff. He should be authorized to move staff to wherever they were needed, enforce strictly post-occupancy limits, designate most international professional posts as rotational, integrate Headquarters and field operations into an Organization-wide mobility programme, expand training and improve work-life conditions and ensure greater opportunity for General Service staff mobility.

To nurture talent and foster career development, the Secretary-General proposed doubling the biennial training budget. Related proposals included a systematic development of entry level Professionals and mandatory requirements for advancement to successive levels of responsibility, development of career models, and mandatory induction and training requirements for managers.

Concerning contractual arrangements, the Secretary-General recommended that the Assembly introduce, among other measures, one UN staff contract, under one set of Staff Rules, with three types of appointment status (temporary, fixed-term and continuing) and conditions of service equivalent to those under the 100 series type of appointment, and replace permanent contracts with continuing appointments, for which staff could be considered if they had completed five years of continuous service.

To build and strengthen the cadre of senior and middle managers, the Secretary-General proposed strengthening leadership recruitment and enhancing management training and development.

The Secretary-General proposed a two-phase staff buyout programme, comprising an initial and voluntary phase, followed by a targeted buyout aligned with the Organization's managerial and strategic priorities. Towards that end, he asked the Assembly to appropriate $12,750,000 to cover the costs of the voluntary phase and to revert to the issue of the targeted phase at its sixty-second (2007) session. Other proposals addressed measures to strengthen accountability among staff and to enhance OHRM information technology resources.

Under each of the core themes underpinning the proposed reform measures, the Secretary-General highlighted expected impact, required changes to staff rules and regulations, specific accountability measures and a timeline for implementation, as well as resource implications. The proposals were to be implemented over a three-year period (2007-2009). The financial implications for 2007 were estimated at $79,432,700 ($36,215,200 under the regular budget, $42,424,500 under the support account for peacekeeping operations and $793,000 from extrabudgetary funding). The resource requirements also included provision for 11 temporary posts for the new OHRM recruitment and staffing center, which would facilitate the implementation of the measures for improving recruitment.

ACABQ report. In its October report [A/61/537], ACABQ acknowledged that the Secretary-General's report (see above) contained innovative ideas, and although some of them required further development, their general thrust and direction were welcome. It also welcomed his intention to ensure that OHRM played a more proactive role in managing human resources, as well as the emphasis on strategic workforce planning. Nonetheless, the Committee did not fully endorse all the proposals, a number of which it cautioned would be affected by major reports to be issued later, including that of ICSC and the Redesign Panel on the UN internal justice system (see p. 1708). Accordingly, ACABQ advised that action on related proposals await the issuance of those reports, which would also afford an opportunity to obtain the input of the new Secretary-General. The views of ICSC needed to be taken into account in determining action to be taken on the proposals on staff contracts and the related harmonization of the conditions of service.

On the issues of accountability and responsibilities, the Committee encouraged the urgent establishment of a system of incentives and sanctions as an integral part of the personnel management system, but was not convinced that adequate thought had been given to the administrative and planning work required for the successful management of the proposed continuation of the special roster for pre-screened candidates. ACABQ also recommended the utilization of existing resources rather than the suggested appropriation and commitment authority for the establishment of a recruitment and staff centre under OHRM to facilitate the implementation of recommended recruitment and staffing measures. Although it supported in principle the promotion of staff mobility, ACABQ was concerned about the financial, administrative and management implications of the mandatory managed reassignment mobility programme. It requested the Secretary-General to report to the Assembly in 2007 on the implementation of the first phase of the managed mobility programme, along with productivity and financial projections for the remaining phases and an assessment of the relevant administrative and management issues.

Observing the financial implications of the suggestion to eliminate restrictions on staff on assignment to UN missions, ACABQ recommended against approval of the proposal to grant the Secretary-General commitment authority for the establishment of more resources, as peacekeeping was not currently involved in the mobility programme. Concerning the recommendation for doubling training resources, ACABQ asked that information be provided in the context of the 2008-2009 programme budget on staff development policy and strategy, outlining priorities, the results and timetables envisaged for the various initiatives proposed, the balance between centrally provided programmes and support for staff members to use other learning vehicles, as well as the means for assessing effectiveness and impact. Pending consideration of that programme budget, ACABQ recommended that the Assembly defer a decision on the matter. In the interim, it approved additional training resources of $3 million under the 2006-2007 programme budget, as against the Secretary-General's proposal to appropriate $10 million. Addressing the staff buyout programme, ACABQ stressed that the mechanism should not be used to address non-performance or underperformance, as provision for action in those cases existed in the staff regulations. It therefore recommended against approval of the resources requested for the voluntary phase of the programme and encouraged the Secretary-General to make proposals for the targeted phase.

Human resources requirements of peace operations

Pursuant to General Assembly resolution 58/257 [YUN 2003, p. 98] regarding the JIU recommendations on reforming the field service category of United Nations peace operations, the Secretary-General submitted an August report [A/61/255/Add.1 & Corr.1] entitled "Reforming the field service category: investing in meeting the human resources requirements of United Nations peace operations in the twenty-first century". Building on work begun by the UN Department of Peacekeeping Operations (DPKO), based on the recommendations of the Panel on United Nations Peace Operations [YUN 2000, p. 83], the Secretary-General examined the baseline human resources requirements of current and future peace operations and analysed issues relating to the management of career civilian staff in those missions.

He concluded that, while peacekeeping had evolved to become a core activity of the Secretariat, the role and composition of field service staff had not kept pace with the dramatic changes to the role and mandates of peace operations. The baseline requirements for expert and experienced staff to serve in those operations had not been met by the human resources strategies developed and applied since the mid-1990s. Despite active programmes that had yielded some 2,000 recruitments yearly in the past two years, high turnover rates and persistently high vacancy rates demonstrated the failure to recruit and retain sufficient numbers of staff with the requisite experience and expertise, thus placing the Organization at operational, managerial and financial risk. As such, investing in building an integrated, versatile, mobile, experienced and expert workforce capable of working both at Headquarters and in the field was indispensable to meeting the complex mandates entrusted to the Organization. The Secretary-General proposed the creation of a standing capacity of 2,500 established positions in key occupational support groups and asked the Assembly to approve that number of career civilian posts, funded against the approved budgets of peacekeeping operations and special political missions.

Report of ACABQ. In October [A/61/537], ACABQ noted that it was up to the General Assembly to decide whether the proposed framework of 2,500 career civilian positions in UN peace operations was a necessary and desirable capacity. It queried the basis for determining that number of posts. While ACABQ saw merit in the proposal, it held that a number of elements needed to be worked out and/or clarified. A more complete analysis was required before a determination could be made. A comprehensive analysis of the financial implications also needed to be carried out.

GENERAL ASSEMBLY ACTION

On 22 December [meeting 84], the General Assembly, on the recommendation of the Fifth Committee [A/61/659], adopted **resolution 61/244** without vote [agenda items 47, 113, 116, 117, 122, 123, 132, 147 & 149].

Human resources management

The General Assembly,

Recalling Articles 8, 97, 100 and 101 of the Charter of the United Nations,

Recalling also its resolutions 49/222 A and B of 23 December 1994 and 20 July 1995, 51/226 of 3 April 1997, 52/219 of 22 December 1997, 52/252 of 8 September 1998, 53/221 of 7 April 1999, 55/258 of 14 June 2001,

57/305 of 15 April 2003, 58/296 of 18 June 2004, 59/266 of 23 December 2004, 60/1 of 16 September 2005 and 60/260 of 8 ay 2006, as well as its other relevant resolutions and decisions,

Having considered the relevant reports on human resources management questions submitted to the General Assembly for its consideration and the related report of the Advisory Committee on Administrative and Budgetary Questions,

Reaffirming that the staff of the United Nations is an invaluable asset of the Organization, and commending its contribution to furthering the purposes and principles of the United Nations,

Paying tribute to the memory of all staff members who have lost their lives in the service of the Organization,

I

Human resources management reform

1. *Expresses concern* over the fact that staff representatives from New York did not participate in the consultation process, stresses the importance of a meaningful dialogue on human resources management issues between staff and management, and calls upon both parties to intensify efforts to overcome differences and to resume the consultative process;

2. *Notes* the Secretary-General's proposals on the new human resources framework, and emphasizes that it shall be based on clear ethical standards, simplicity, clarity and transparency, recruitment based on the highest standards of efficiency, integrity and professionalism, career development, compliance with geographical distribution and gender balance mandates, accountability of managers and staff, and operational needs at Headquarters and in the field;

3. *Emphasizes* the importance of the participation of staff representatives in the work of the central review bodies, and reiterates its request to the Secretary-General and its invitation to staff representatives to engage in the consultative process;

4. *Notes* that minimizing the occurrence of high rates of job turnover in Professional categories in the United Nations is essential to its smooth functioning;

5. *Requests* the Secretary-General to report to it in the context of the biennial human resources management report on the yearly rate of turnover in Professional categories, classified by grade level, in the United Nations Secretariat and in field missions;

II

Recruitment and staffing

1. *Reiterates* that the Secretary-General has to ensure that the highest standards of efficiency, competence and integrity serve as the paramount consideration in the employment of staff, with due regard to the principle of equitable geographical distribution, in accordance with Article 101, paragraph 3, of the Charter of the United Nations;

2. *Also reiterates* section V, paragraph 2, of its resolution 53/221, which states that recruitment, appointment and promotion of staff shall be made without distinction as to race, sex or religion, in accordance with the principles of the Charter and the provisions of the Staff Regulations and Rules of the United Nations;

3. *Requests* the Secretary-General to report on measures being used to verify the application of the highest standards of efficiency, competence and integrity as the paramount consideration in the employment of staff, with due regard to the recruitment of staff on as wide a geographical basis as possible, in accordance with the provisions of Article 101, paragraph 3, of the Charter, and to report thereon to the General Assembly at its sixty-third session;

4. *Also requests* the Secretary-General to ensure the proper functioning and membership of the central review bodies in order to ensure their effective role in the staff selection system and, to that end, to develop an induction and training programme for the members, and to report to it thereon at the second part of its resumed sixty-first session;

5. *Further requests* the Secretary-General to undertake a review of the staff selection system with a particular emphasis on enhancing the performance of the United Nations Secretariat, which would include a survey of opinions of managers relating, inter alia, to the possibilities offered by that system to choose the best-qualified candidate for the job and to improve geographical representation and gender balance, and to report thereon to it at its sixty-third session, in the context of his regular human resources report;

6. *Reaffirms* the provisions of regulation 4.4 of the Staff Regulations and Rules of the United Nations, and decides to retain the criterion of geographical status in the staff selection system as one of the key elements to ensure geographical balance at each level for posts subject to geographical distribution;

7. *Recognizes* the importance of speeding up the recruitment and staffing process, in accordance with Article 101, paragraph 3, of the Charter, which will ensure that staff are diverse, multi-skilled and versatile;

8. *Requests* the Secretary-General, in cooperation with Member States, to explore ways to further increase awareness of job opportunities in the United Nations system, including through more extensive outreach, the Department of Public Information of the Secretariat, the United Nations information centres and United Nations country offices, with a view to achieving more balanced geographical and gender representation in the Organization;

9. *Recognizes* that pre-screened rosters can considerably expedite the recruitment process in the United Nations;

10. *Requests* the Secretary-General to promote the full utilization of existing rosters for recruitment and to further elaborate the use of pre-screened rosters, based on the organizational needs identified through strategic workforce planning, taking into account the need for transparency, support for the provisions of Article 101 of the Charter and administrative and resource implications, as well as geographical and gender mandates, and

to report to it thereon at the second part of its resumed sixty-first session;

11. *Notes* the intention of the Secretary-General to establish a recruitment and staffing centre to support managers in the selection of staff and to enhance the consistency of recruitment across the Secretariat, and invites the Secretary-General to submit proposals in the context of the proposed programme budget for the biennium 2008-2009;

12. *Requests* the Secretary-General to ensure that use of the envisaged expedited recruitment process is confined to surge needs, with established procedures for recruitment being waived only in exceptional cases, and also requests the Secretary-General to report to it on the use of this mechanism, including the criteria for defining such exceptions, in the context of its consideration of human resources management;

13. *Reiterates its request* to the Secretary-General to continue his efforts to reduce the period required to fill vacancies by addressing the factors contributing to delays in the process of selection, recruitment and placement and to report to it thereon at the second part of its resumed sixty-first session;

14. *Decides* to maintain the limitations established by the General Assembly for the assignment of General Service staff to field missions;

15. *Requests* the Secretary-General to continue in future years the innovation set out in his report on the composition of the Secretariat to provide information on all staff under contract with the Secretariat, thus providing a more comprehensive picture of staff by nationality, category and gender;

16. *Reaffirms* the need to respect the equality of each of the two working languages of the Secretariat, also reaffirms the use of additional working languages in specific duty stations as mandated, and in this regard requests the Secretary-General to ensure that vacancy announcements specify the need for either of the working languages of the Secretariat unless the functions of the post require a specific working language;

17. *Acknowledges* that the interaction of the United Nations with the local population in the field is essential and that language skills constitute an important element of the selection and training processes, and therefore affirms that good command of the official language(s) spoken in the country of residence should be taken into account as an additional asset during those processes;

III

National competitive examinations

1. *Reaffirms* that national competitive examinations are the source of recruitment for P-2 posts subject to geographical distribution in order to reduce non-representation and underrepresentation of Member States in the Secretariat, and in this connection requests the Secretary-General to fully use this opportunity and, in particular, to accelerate the recruitment of candidates who have passed national competitive examinations;

2. *Notes with concern* that a large number of candidates who have passed national competitive examinations remain on the roster for years;

3. *Requests* the Secretary-General to ensure the expeditious placement of successful candidates from national competitive examinations;

4. *Welcomes* the enhanced efforts of the Secretary-General to centrally manage the placement of successful candidates from national competitive examinations, and requests the Secretary-General to report on the outcome of those efforts to it at its sixty-third session;

IV

Mobility

1. *Reaffirms* section VIII of its resolution 59/266;

2. *Stresses* that the purpose of enhancing mobility is to improve the effectiveness of the Organization and to foster the skills and capacity of staff;

3. *Notes* the current work of the Secretary-General on mobility policies, and encourages him to continue to make progress in this field in accordance with relevant General Assembly resolutions;

4. *Reaffirms* that the implementation of mobility policies, while recognizing their anticipated positive effects, may also give rise to problems and challenges that should be addressed;

5. *Requests* the Secretary-General, in this regard, to report to it at the main part of its sixty-second session on clear indicators, benchmarks, number of staff, timelines and criteria for the implementation of mobility policies, taking into account the needs of the Organization and ways to protect the rights of staff in the context of the system of administration of justice;

6. *Also requests* the Secretary-General to report to it at its sixty-third session on the implemented phases of the mobility policy, along with projections for the envisaged remaining phases and an assessment of the relevant administrative and management issues;

7. *Further requests* the Secretary-General to provide an analysis of the managed mobility programme, including information on financial implications and on its usefulness in improving organizational efficiency and addressing, inter alia, high vacancy rates, and to report to it thereon at its sixty-third session;

8. *Decides*, in the light of the experience of managed mobility, to review the enforcement of post-occupancy limits at its sixty-third session;

9. *Also decides* to approve the establishment of three new temporary positions—two P-4 and one General Service—to provide support for the work of the Secretary-General in this area;

10. *Further decides* to approve an additional appropriation under the regular budget in the amount of 331,000 United States dollars;

11. *Decides* to approve an additional appropriation in the amount of 35,400 dollars under section 35, Staff assessment, to be offset by an equivalent amount of income under income section 1, Income from staff assessment, of the programme budget for the biennium 2006-2007;

12. *Notes* that the Secretary-General will submit a request for resources in the context of the support account budget for 2007-2008;

13. *Requests* the Secretary-General to continue to consult with staff, including staff representatives, in the development of mobility policies;

14. *Requests* the International Civil Service Commission, within its mandate, to continue to keep under review the question of mobility in the United Nations common system, including its implications for career development, and to make recommendations to the General Assembly, as appropriate, in the context of its annual reports;

15. *Requests* the Secretary-General to take the steps necessary to ensure that mobility is not used as an instrument of coercion against staff and to ensure that appropriate monitoring and accountability measures are in place;

16. *Also requests* the Secretary-General to report to it at its sixty-third session on specific measures taken to facilitate mobility between the United Nations Secretariat and the United Nations funds, programmes and specialized agencies, and on results achieved;

17. *Further requests* the Secretary-General to continue to consider the use of incentives with a view to encouraging staff to move to duty stations with chronically high vacancy rates;

18. *Acknowledges* that mobility needs to be supported through greater efforts to improve conditions of life and work at the various duty stations;

19. *Invites* host countries, as appropriate, to review their policies for granting work permits to spouses of United Nations staff;

20. *Invites* the Secretary-General to continue to explore ways of assisting spouses to find employment opportunities, in consultation with host Governments where necessary, including by taking measures to expedite the issuance of work permits;

21. *Requests* the Secretary-General to continue to provide career counseling and job-search assistance; to explore telecommuting options for spouses; to give spouses priority consideration for consulting opportunities, where appropriate; to give priority to the relocation of spouses within the managed mobility programme, subject to the availability of suitable posts and satisfactory performance; and to support the creation of inter-agency spouse support networks at all duty stations;

22. *Welcomes* the intention of the Secretary-General to provide staff with more specific training opportunities, with a view to preparing staff for diverse responsibilities, working in different departments, offices, duty stations or peacekeeping missions and moving across occupational groups;

V

Career development and support

1. *Encourages* the Secretary-General to enhance career progress within the Secretariat by facilitating career development;

2. *Emphasizes* the importance of defining the target and strategy of training and career development;

3. *Requests* the Secretary-General to report to it at its sixty-third session on staff development policy and the priority of staff development, taking into account the impact of the retirement of many senior staff in the near future;

4. *Notes* that training is important for the staff and the Organization, also notes, recalling section II, paragraph 57, of its resolution 57/305, that the Secretariat should fully use existing resources, and decides to appropriate an additional 3 million dollars specifically devoted to leadership and management development, information technology training, upgrading of substantive skills and expansion of languages and communication;

5. *Decides* to revert to the subject of appropriation for training resources in the context of the proposed programme budget for the biennium 2008-2009;

6. *Requests* the Secretary-General to allocate the resources for training on the basis of needs and in an equitable manner, throughout the Secretariat, including for duty stations and regional commissions, and in this context stresses that equal training opportunities should be available for all staff, in accordance with their functions and categories;

7. *Also requests* the Secretary-General to ensure that programme managers prepare calendars of training of staff working under their supervision on a periodic basis;

8. *Stresses* that workshops, seminars and training courses should take advantage of the diverse sources of training opportunities available throughout the regions of the world;

VI

Contractual arrangements

1. *Notes* that the existing system of contractual arrangements does not fully comply with the proposed International Civil Service Commission framework;

2. *Requests* the International Civil Service Commission to consider the proposals of the Secretary-General, in particular the proposal to introduce one United Nations staff contract under one set of staff rules, and to report to it thereon at the second part of its resumed sixty-first session;

3. *Stresses* the need for rationalization of the current United Nations system of contractual arrangements, which lacks transparency and is complex to administer;

4. *Requests* the Secretary-General to address the conclusions and recommendations contained in paragraphs 49 to 56 of the report of the Advisory Committee on Administrative and Budgetary Questions;

5. *Also requests* the Secretary-General to present a detailed road map on the implementation of the proposed contractual arrangements, including on eligibility criteria, at the second part of its resumed sixty-first session;

6. *Decides* to continue to suspend until 30 June 2007 the application of the four-year limit for appointments of limited duration under the 300 series of the Staff Rules in peacekeeping operations;

7. *Authorizes* the Secretary-General, bearing in mind paragraph 6 above, to reappoint under the 100 series of

the Staff Rules those mission staff whose service under 300–series contracts has reached the four-year limit by 30 June 2007, provided that their functions have been reviewed and found necessary and their performance has been confirmed as fully satisfactory, and requests the Secretary-General to report to it thereon at the second part of its resumed sixty-first session;

VII

Harmonization of conditions of service

1. *Recalls* section X, paragraph 5, of its resolution 59/266, in which it requested the International Civil Service Commission to present to it an analysis of the desirability and feasibility of harmonizing conditions of service in the field;

2. *Notes* that the International Civil Service Commission has established a working group to review conditions of service of internationally recruited staff serving in non-family duty stations, and requests the Commission to submit a report thereon to it at the second part of its resumed sixty-first session;

3. *Requests* the Secretary-General in his capacity as Chairman of the United Nations System Chief Executives Board for Coordination to invite the executive heads to support the work of the International Civil Service Commission by ensuring full and timely compliance with the requests of the Commission for information;

4. *Takes note* of the proposals of the Secretary-General on harmonization of conditions of service for non-family duty stations, and decides to revert to the issue at the second part of its resumed sixty-first session, following issuance of the report of the International Civil Service Commission;

5. *Requests* the Secretary-General to submit a comprehensive report to it on the issue, including possible financial implications, if any, at the second part of its resumed sixty-first session;

VIII

Reform of the field service

Notes the proposal of the Secretary-General to provide for peacekeeping staffing on an ongoing basis and to enhance professionalism and the ability of the United Nations to respond quickly to peacekeeping needs by designating a cadre of continuing civilian positions from within existing capacity, and requests him to submit to it at the second part of its resumed sixty-first session proposals for the operation of the proposed cadre, taking into account the views and observations of the Advisory Committee on Administrative and Budgetary Questions in paragraphs 70 to 77 of its report;

IX

Building leadership and management capacity

1. *Encourages* a more rigorous and systematic approach to selection at the Under-Secretary-General, Assistant Secretary-General and Director levels, in order to incorporate skilful leadership and management, with due regard to geographical representation and gender balance in the selection of candidates for those positions;

2. *Requests* the Secretary-General to report to it at its sixty-third session on the findings and outcomes of this rigorous and systematic approach, as well as on concrete measures to recruit and appoint nationals from unrepresented and underrepresented States, in particular developing countries, including at such senior levels as Under-Secretary-General and Assistant Secretary-General;

3. *Emphasizes* that training should not only improve the managerial skills of senior officers but should also serve to update and complement their substantive knowledge on various United Nations core mandates;

X

Measures to improve equitable geographical distribution

1. *Notes* the progress made since 1994 in reducing the number of countries that are unrepresented and underrepresented;

2. *Also notes* that the number of unrepresented and underrepresented Member States has increased since 2002;

3. *Welcomes* the continuing efforts of the Secretary-General to improve the situation of unrepresented and underrepresented Member States and of those in danger of becoming underrepresented under the system of desirable ranges;

4. *Notes with concern* that the total number of staff from underrepresented Member States and their proportion to the total number of staff in posts subject to geographical distribution decreased in the period between 2002 and 2006, as reflected in the report of the Secretary-General on the composition of the Secretariat;

5. *Welcomes* the analysis of the level of underrepresentation in the report of the Secretary-General on the composition of the Secretariat;

6. *Regrets* the current insufficient accountability of heads of departments in achieving equitable geographical distribution in the Secretariat;

7. *Requests* the Secretary-General to continue his ongoing efforts to attain equitable geographical distribution in the Secretariat and to ensure as wide a geographical distribution of staff as possible in all departments and offices of the Secretariat;

8. *Also requests* the Secretary-General to post information regarding the human resources action plans on the United Nations website and to report to it thereon in the context of the Management Performance Board report;

9. *Recalls* section II, paragraph 38, of its resolution 57/305 and section IV, paragraph 5, of its resolution 59/266, takes note of the information contained in table 5 of the report of the Secretary-General, and expresses concern over the decline in the number of nationals from developing countries at the senior and policymaking levels, as well as the imbalance in different departments of the Secretariat;

10. *Notes* that the system of geographic ranges was designed to apply to countries rather than to regions or groups;

11. *Requests* the Secretary-General to ensure, through the Management Performance Board, the moni-

toring of the implementation of human resources action plans, including the principle of equitable geographical distribution in the Secretariat at all levels as set out in relevant General Assembly resolutions, and the verification of the effective application of measures of transparency and accountability, including in the selection, recruitment and placement processes;

12. *Reiterates its request* to the Secretary-General to intensify his efforts to increase recruitment from unrepresented and underrepresented Member States and to undertake outreach efforts designed to prevent countries from falling under those categories, urges the Secretary-General, to the extent possible, to take the necessary steps to reduce the number of unrepresented and underrepresented Member States in the Secretariat by 20 per cent by 2008 and by 30 per cent by 2010, compared to the level in 2006, and requests the Secretary-General to report to it thereon on a regular basis beginning with its sixty-third session, as appropriate;

13. *Recalls* section IV, paragraph 9, of its resolution 59/266, decides to continue the fast-track roster for an additional two-year period, and requests the Secretary-General to report to it at its sixty-third session on the effectiveness of the roster;

14. *Requests* the Secretary-General to take all necessary measures to ensure, at the senior and policymaking levels of the Secretariat, equitable representation of Member States, especially those with inadequate representation at those levels, and to continue to include relevant information thereon in all future reports on the composition of the Secretariat;

15. *Regrets* that the Secretary-General has not succeeded in complying with the provisions of its resolutions 41/206 B of 11 December 1986, 53/221, 55/258, 57/305 and 59/266, in which it declared that no post should be considered the exclusive preserve of any Member State or group of States, including at the highest levels, reiterates its request that the Secretary-General ensure that, as a general rule, no national of a Member State succeeds a national of that State in a senior post and that there is no monopoly on senior posts by nationals of any State or group of States, and requests the Secretary-General to report to it at its sixty-third session thereon;

16. *Takes note* of the report of the Secretary General on a comprehensive assessment of the system of geographical distribution and assessment of the issues relating to possible changes in the number of posts subject to that system;

17. *Reiterates its requests* to the Secretary-General to present proposals to effectively increase the representation of developing countries in the Secretariat, and decides to revert to this issue at its sixty-third session;

18. *Reaffirms* that the system of desirable ranges is the mechanism for recruitment of staff in posts subject to geographical distribution, in accordance with Article 101, paragraph 3, of the Charter of the United Nations;

19. *Considers* that encouragement of recruitment from unrepresented and underrepresented Member States shall not disallow other qualified candidates from competing;

20. *Affirms* that measures on meeting organizational mandates, accountability targets and indicators of achievement, with respect to geographical distribution of staff, contained in human resources action plans and recruitment procedures, including selection decisions, shall fully correspond to the provisions contained in Article 101, paragraph 3, of the Charter as well as in relevant General Assembly mandates;

21. *Requests* the Secretary-General to review the designation of posts in the radio and website management sections of the Department of Public Information to consider whether they should be treated as language posts and to report thereon to the General Assembly at its sixty-second session for its consideration, including on the possible human resources, administrative and financial implications;

XI

Gender representation

1. *Reaffirms* the goal of 50/50 gender distribution in all categories of posts within the United Nations system, especially at the senior and policymaking levels, with full respect for the principle of equitable geographical distribution, in conformity with Article 101 of the Charter, and regrets that progress towards attaining this goal has been slow;

2. *Expresses concern* at the continuing low proportion of women in the Secretariat, in particular the low proportion among them of women from developing countries, especially at the senior levels, and stresses that the continuing lack of representation or underrepresentation of women from certain countries, in particular from developing countries, should be taken into account and that those women should be accorded equal opportunities in the recruitment process, in full conformity with relevant resolutions;

3. *Notes with concern* that, in posts subject to the system of desirable ranges, only 25 women from developing countries were recruited between 1 July 2005 and 30 June 2006 among the 83 women appointed during that period;

4. *Requests* the Secretary-General to increase his efforts to attain and monitor the goal of gender parity in the Secretariat, in particular at senior levels, and in this context to ensure that women, especially those from developing countries and countries with economies in transition, are appropriately represented within the Secretariat, and to report thereon to the General Assembly at its sixty-third session;

5. *Also requests* the Secretary-General, in the context of attaining this goal, to develop and implement recruitment targets, time frames for meeting those targets and accountability measures;

6. *Further requests* the Secretary-General to clarify the role of departmental focal points, including in the context of the staff selection system, and their participation in the development and monitoring of the departmental human resource action plans;

7. *Encourages* Member States to support the efforts of the Secretary-General by identifying more women can-

didates and encouraging them to apply for appointment to positions in the Secretariat and by creating awareness among their nationals, in particular women, of vacancies in the Secretariat;

XII

Accountability

1. *Takes note* of the report of the Secretary-General on the activities of the Ethics Office;

2. *Also takes note* of the report of the Secretary-General on the Management Performance Board;

3. *Reiterates* the importance of strengthened accountability in the Organization and of ensuring greater accountability of the Secretary-General to Member States, inter alia, for the effective and efficient implementation of legislative mandates and the use of human and financial resources;

4. *Requests* the Secretary-General to strengthen his efforts to achieve greater transparency at all levels;

5. *Recognizes* the role of the Office of Human Resources Management in supporting the Secretary-General in holding programme managers accountable, and requests the continuing strengthening of that role;

6. *Requests* the Secretary-General to present proposals for enforcing the implementation of human resources policies and action plan objectives and to report to it thereon at its sixty-third session;

7. *Also requests* the Secretary-General to submit to it for consideration at its sixty-third session a proposal for the use of incentives and sanctions as an integral part of the personnel management system, bearing in mind the relevant work of the International Civil Service Commission;

8. *Welcomes* the establishment of the Management Performance Board to strengthen the accountability framework of senior managers so as to ensure that they are properly undertaking the responsibilities that have been entrusted to them, including their performance in achieving the objectives contained in human resources action plans;

9. *Stresses* that a fair, transparent and effective administration of justice system is an essential feature of proper accountability;

10. *Requests* the Secretary-General to improve accountability and responsibility in the reform of human resources management as well as the monitoring and control mechanisms and procedures and to report to it at its sixty-third session on action taken in this regard;

XIII

Human resources information technology

1. *Notes* the proposals of the Secretary-General on investing in information and communication technology;

2. *Endorses* paragraph 68 of the report of the Advisory Committee on Administrative and Budgetary Questions, and requests the Secretary-General to ensure that the new information technology infrastructure is compatible with the new system approved in section II of General Assembly resolution 60/283 of 7 July 2006;

3. *Notes* the efforts made by the Secretary-General to make the human resources information technology system available in both working languages of the Secretariat, and invites the Secretary-General to continue those efforts;

4. *Requests* the Secretary-General to report to it at its sixty-third session on the implementation of the human resources information technology system;

XIV

Staff buyout

Takes note of paragraph 64 of the report of the Advisory Committee on Administrative and Budgetary Questions, and decides not to pursue the proposal of the Secretary-General on the staff buyout;

XV

Consultants and individual contractors

1. *Reaffirms* section XI of its resolution 59/266;

2. *Takes note* of the report of the Secretary-General on consultants and individual contractors;

3. *Endorses* the recommendations of the Advisory Committee on Administrative and Budgetary Questions contained in paragraphs 88 to 90 of its report;

4. *Takes note* of the report of the Secretary-General on comprehensive policy guidelines for consultants in the Office of the United Nations High Commissioner for Refugees;

XVI

Employment of retired former staff

1. *Notes with concern* the continuous trend of hiring staff retirees for extended periods of time;

2. *Endorses* paragraph 84 of the report of the Advisory Committee on Administrative and Budgetary Questions;

XVII

Other matters

1. *Reiterates its request* to the Secretary-General, contained in its resolution 60/238 of 23 December 2005, to report to it at its sixty-first session on the implementation of the regulations governing the status, basic rights and duties of officials other than Secretariat officials and experts on mission;

2. *Requests* the Secretary-General to present to it at the first part of its resumed sixty-first session, in consultation with the Office of the United Nations High Commissioner for Human Rights, proposals to address the imbalance in the geographical distribution of the staff in that Office;

3. *Decides* to revert to this issue at the first part of its resumed sixty-first session.

Also on 22 December, the Assembly decided that the item on human resources management would remain for consideration during its resumed sixty-first (2007) session (**decision 61/552**).

Management Performance Board

In response to General Assembly resolution 60/238 [YUN 2005, p.1515], the Secretary-General submitted a September report [A/61/319] covering the activities of the Management Performance Board, established in 2005 to replace the Accountability Panel [ibid., p. 1513], in order to strengthen the accountability framework of senior managers. The Board met in July to review the results achieved by programme managers, against the targets contained in human resources action plans for 2005, and assess the 2006 senior management compacts, an accord between the Secretary-General and senior managers designed to further improve accountability and foster a culture of transparency. The Board examined departmental performance for the first half of the 2005-2006 planning cycle, measuring 25 departments and offices against predefined targets and indicators in nine areas of human resources management and reflecting mostly legislative mandates. It found that several departments experienced difficulty in achieving gender balance targets, especially at the senior level, while others had trouble in meeting geographic targets. Poor performance in that regard suggested insufficient awareness among heads of department that achieving equitable geographical distribution in the Secretariat was part of their responsibility. On the Board's advice, the summary of their performance and reminders were transmitted to those managers who were not meeting their obligations, including warnings that consistent non-achievement could result in the loss of their delegated authority for recruitment and placement decisions. In December, the Board approved a revised framework for the senior management compacts, bringing together a comprehensive set of indicators covering programmatic and managerial objectives for which departmental heads would be held accountable.

The report concluded that the Board's activities in its first year represented a significant step forward towards holding programme managers accountable for their performance in achieving programme objectives. The assessments to be carried out in 2007 would allow the new Secretary-General to examine the performance of the senior management team and identify systematic weaknesses that needed to be addressed.

Ethics Office

The General Assembly, in **resolution 60/254** of 8 May (see p. 1633), welcomed the establishment of the Ethics office and endorsed its main responsibilities as outlined by the Secretary-General in 2005 [YUN 2005, p. 1477]. It urged him to finalize a system-wide code of ethics for all UN personnel, administer and monitor more extensive disclosure of financial and other interests by UN officials, ensure enhanced protection for those who revealed wrongdoing and report on the activities of the Office at its sixty-first (2006) session.

In response to that request, the Secretary-General submitted an August report [A/61/274] on the activities of the Ethics Office from 1 January to 31 July 2006. The Office focused on developing and setting standards of conduct and facilitating annual training on ethical issues, in collaboration with OHRM; working with OIOS to devise a change management plan for raising staff awareness and ensuring compliance with UN standards of conduct and values; providing confidential advice and guidance to both individuals and groups; administering the Organization's financial disclosure programme; and ensuring the protection of staff against retaliation for reporting misconduct. Overall, the Office responded to 153 staff requests for its services, 41 per cent of which involved ethics advice, with 29 per cent relating to protection against retaliation for reporting misconduct. The Office also coordinated the expanded annual financial disclosure exercise, which covered more than 1,800 staff and generated hundreds of inquiries about filing instructions.

Staff composition

In an August annual report on the United Nations Secretariat's staff composition [A/61/257 & Corr.1], the Secretary-General updated information on the demographic characteristics of the staff and on the system of desirable ranges for geographical distribution. The data reviewed the global population of Secretariat staff, staff with contracts of one year or more, staff appointed under the 100 series of staff rules and those in posts subject to geographical distribution. As distinct from previous reports, which only considered contracts of one year or more, the current report, covering the period from 1 July 2005 to 30 June 2006, included information on all staff with valid contracts irrespective of the funding source, type of engagement, duration of contract, level or duty station.

The report noted that the global number of Secretariat staff as at 30 June 2006 totalled 30,548. Of that number, up to 25,543 (83.6 per cent) held contracts of one year or more. Some 9,355 (30.6 per cent) staff were in the Professional and higher categories and 21,193 (69.4 per cent) in the General Service and related categories. Staff in field missions administered by DPKO numbered 15,839 (52 per cent). Up to 19,451 of the global Secretariat staff

(63.7 per cent) were men, while women accounted for 11,097 (36.3 per cent). More than 61.9 per cent of all staff came from 20 Member States, each of which had over 400 nationals. Overall, 18 Member States were unrepresented, compared with 17 in 2005, while 11 were underrepresented and 21 over-represented, as against nine and 20, respectively, the previous year. Appointments to posts subject to geographical distribution totalled 219.

The report also provided information on the demographic profile of Secretariat staff, including the breakdown of staff by department or office, gender, age, and length of service, and movements of staff, covering recruitment, promotion, transfer, separation, turnover and forecasts of anticipated retirements between 2004 and 2008. In addition, the report analysed the implementation status of the human resources action planning system and the level of underrepresentation in the composition of the Secretariat during the reporting period.

Status of women

ICSC consideration. ICSC [A/61/30] considered a progress report submitted by its secretariat on the representation of women by region and on common system organizations' gender plans. The report included staffing data on composition, recruitment, promotion and separation by gender and level, as well on staff distribution by gender. Based on its findings, ICSC expressed disappointment at the insufficient progress made in the representation of women in the Professional and higher categories, particularly at the senior level, where women continued to be significantly underrepresented. It urged organizations that had not done so to designate a senior-level focal point for gender issues to provide leadership in formulating plans and strategies for achieving gender balance, including responsive workforce and succession planning to cater for retirements. Common system organizations were also urged to set realistic gender goals and review them annually to assess progress; hold managers accountable, through their annual performance appraisal, for achieving established gender goals; and focus on strategies for retaining women at mid-level professional grades. ICSC also decided to continue to monitor gender balance every two years and requested its secretariat to submit a report on the issue for consideration in 2008.

Report of Secretary-General. In response to General Assembly resolution 59/164 [YUN 2004, p. 1429], the Secretary-General submitted a September report [A/61/318] on progress made in improving the representation of women in UN system organizations and agencies between 31 December 2003 and 31 December 2004, and in the UN Secretariat from 1 July 2004 to 30 June 2006. He observed that, in both the UN system and the Secretariat, the representation of women in the Professional and higher categories was either static or had experienced a negligible improvement, and in some cases, it even decreased. In UN system organizations, the proportion of women in the Professional and higher categories increased from 36.3 per cent to 36.9 per cent. At the senior policy-making levels (D-1 and above), the cumulative representation of women rose from 21.7 per cent in 2003 to 23.7 per cent in 2004. Across the board, however, gender balance in UN system organizations was only achieved at the P-1 and P-2 levels.

In the UN Secretariat, the percentage of women in the Professional category (P-5 and below) barely moved up from 38.3 per cent to 38.6 per cent (2,226 out of 5,761). That was attributable largely to an increase of 1.8 per cent at the P-4 level. Comparatively, the P-5, P-3 and P-2 levels witnessed declines of 0.3 per cent, 0.5 per cent and 1.8 per cent, respectively. At the senior positions of D-1 and above, the proportion of women (145 out of 573) actually fell by 3.7 per cent, with the largest drop of 6.9 per cent occurring at the D-1 level, where women held 93 positions out of 367. A similar decrease was recorded at the Under-Secretary-General level, where the proportion of women (6 out of 39) fell from 16.7 per cent to 15.4 percent. On the positive side, increases of 4.1 per cent and 2.8 per cent, respectively, were registered at the Assistant Secretary-General and D-2 levels. For the professional and higher categories combined, the overall proportion of women (2,371 out of 6,334) increased negligibly from 37.3 percent as at 30 June 2004, to 37.4 per cent by 30 June 2006. In the field service officer category, women constituted 25.1 per cent (573 out of 2,283) as at 30 June 2006, compared with 23.4 per cent in 2004, while in the General Service and related category, women continued to constitute the majority of staff, accounting for 60.6 per cent (3,852 out of 6,348), compared to 62 per cent in 2004.

The report identified the factors responsible for the slow advancement of women in the UN system. Also highlighted were recent activities undertaken to achieve gender balance in the Secretariat, focusing on the staff selection system, human resources action plans and work/life policies, as well as the role of the Office of the Special Adviser on Gender Issues and the Advancement of Women.

The Secretary-General concluded that the lack of progress required a re-thinking of policies. The staffing system was neither proactive nor sufficiently targeted, and relied heavily on web-based vacancy announcements. The objective of introducing work/life policies to attract and retain quality staff, especially women, was yet to have a positive impact on the managerial culture. Where policies were in place, they needed to be better and more rigorously implemented and monitored, including through the insertion of a gender-sensitive variable into the performance appraisal of managers, and where they did not exist, they should be promulgated.

Gratis personnel

Pursuant to General Assembly resolution 57/281 B [YUN 2003, 1448], the Secretary-General submitted his biennial report [A/61/257/Add.1 & Corr.1] on the use of gratis personnel between 1 January 2004 and 31 December 2005. The number of type I gratis personnel (associate experts, technical cooperation experts on non-reimbursable loan and interns) decreased from 1,395 in 2004 to 1,332 in 2005. A total of 109 nationalities were represented, compared to 112 in 2004. Women constituted 61 per cent and 70 per cent in 2004 and 2005, respectively, while interns continued to represent the majority for both years. The number of associate experts decreased by 13 per cent in 2005, compared to 2004, while the number of technical cooperation experts on non-reimbursable loan doubled in 2005.

A total of 85 type II gratis personnel (provided by Governments or other entities) representing 33 nationalities were employed in 2005, which was a significant drop from 2004 figures. The average duration of service for type II gratis personnel increased from 1.8 months to 4.3 months yearly, a 59 per cent rise. Female representation in that category of personnel rose markedly from 26 per cent in 2004 to 41 per cent in 2005.

Employment of retirees

In response to General Assembly resolutions 57/305 [YUN 2003, p. 1440] and 59/266 [YUN 2004, p. 1418], the Secretary-General submitted an August report [A/61/257/Add.2] on the employment of retired staff in the UN Secretariat during the 2004-2005 biennium. Some 491 UN retirees, representing 74 nationalities, were employed, which reflected reductions of 12.8 per cent and 16.9 per cent in the number hired and in national representation, respectively. The four departments/offices accounting for most of the retirees engaged included the Department for General Assembly and Conference Management, which hired 41.2 per cent of the total; the United Nations Office at Geneva (17.4 per cent); the United Nations Office at Vienna (9.6 per cent) and field missions administered by DPKO (8.5 per cent). Retired staff were used mainly in three groups of functions: language services, particularly revisers and interpreters (59 per cent of all engagements); administrative functions (24.2 per cent); and political, economic, social, environmental, humanitarian, advisory and technical assistance functions (11 per cent). Other functions accounted for 5 per cent. The total expenditure on retirees in the 2004-2005 biennium amounted to $33.5 million, of which language services and administrative functions accounted for $20.8 million and $6.5 million, respectively. The report also provided information regarding the employment of former staff 60 years or older who had opted for a withdrawal settlement and were re-employed for six months or more, those rehired in decision-making positions and for an accrued service period exceeding two years, as well as staff extensions beyond the mandatory age of separation.

The report concluded that retired staff possessed the requisite specialized skills and institutional knowledge that enabled them to perform immediately and fully without a learning curve. In many instances, the use of retirees was considered to be the most cost effective way to support operational needs, particularly in peacekeeping and humanitarian field operations, and their use did not hamper long-term recruitment plans.

Consultants and individual contractors

In response to General Assembly resolutions 57/305 [YUN 2003, p. 1440] and 59/266 [YUN 2004, p. 1418], the Secretary-General, in August, submitted a biennial report [A/61/257/Add.3] on the use of consultants and individual contractors within the Secretariat and the regional Commissions during the 2004-2005 biennium. The report indicated that, in 2004, 1,833 consultants and 544 individual contractors were engaged for 2,061 and 748 contracts, respectively, while in 2005, the number rose to 2,152 consultants and 772 individual contractors for 2,455 and 1,122 contracts, respectively. Those figures represented a 35 per cent drop compared to the numbers registered for 2002-2003 biennium. The total expenditure for consultants, which amounted to $19.7 million in 2004 and $22.9 million 2005, reflected a reduction of $40.3 million as compared to 2002-2003. For individual contractors, the total expenditure of $3.3 million and $6.7 million in 2004 and 2005, respectively, corresponded to a reduction of $11.7 million (53.8 per cent) compared with the previous biennium. For both cycles, consultants were used mainly for programme implementation and advisory services, while individual contractors were mostly engaged for lectures, training courses and the preparation of meetings, in addition to programme implementation. The main United Nations entities hiring consultants and individual contractors included the Economic Commission for Latin America and the Caribbean, the United Nations Department of Economic and Social Affairs, the United Nations Conference on Trade and Development, the United Nations Office at Geneva, the United Nations Environment Programme, the Economic Commission for Africa, the Economic and Social Commission for Asia and the Pacific and the Office of the United Nations High Commissioner for Human Rights.

The Secretary-General also reported [A/61/201] on the implementation of comprehensive policy guidelines for consultants at the Office of the United Nations High Commissioner for Refugees (see p. 1303).

Common payroll

The Secretary-General, in an April report [A/60/582/Add.1], transmitted his comments and those of CEB on the 2005 JIU report on a common payroll for UN system organizations [YUN 2005, p.1520], in which it had advocated the consolidation of the payroll processing function across all the organizations, with potential saving up to $100 million over 10 years. CEB believed that, while such savings might be possible through the consolidation of administrative systems, it would be necessary to address many issues not thoroughly explored in the JIU report, which did not provide adequate financial analysis, thereby making its case for a common payroll unclear. One major obstacle to moving towards a common enterprise resource planning software stemmed from the fact that many organizations had already invested heavily in existing systems and were unlikely to consider alternatives until the costs of those investments were fully amortized. Numerous organizations also felt that, as a precondition for any system consolidation, the more difficult problem of the complicated manner in which human resources and payroll rules had evolved across the system would have to be resolved. Despite their misgivings about the analysis contained in the JIU report, particularly regarding the idea of moving towards a common payroll, common system organizations generally supported the overall recommendations.

The Secretary-General and CEB recommended that the General Assembly endorse the development of a common payroll system as the first step towards a common system-wide enterprise resource planning, and request the Secretary-General to seek the commitment of UN system organizations by setting up a governance structure to speed up, coordinate and oversee the development and implementation of a common payroll system and a common enterprise resource planning system. He should invite CEB to establish lead organizations or common service entities that could provide payroll services to agencies with old and antiquated systems; harmonize, simplify and standardize the application across the common system of staff rules and regulations relating to payroll and allowances; and report thereon to the Assembly at its sixty-second (2007) session.

Multilingualism

Pursuant to General Assembly resolution 59/309 [YUN 2005, p. 1521], the Secretary-General submitted a September report [A/61/317] on the status of multilingualism in the Secretariat, which reviewed the Organization's working and official languages, the place of multilingualism in UN communications, focusing on the role of the Coordinator for multilingualism, issues relating to internal and external communications and the related question of human resources. The Secretary-General observed that multilingualism had been approached by most Departments in a pragmatic way, focusing on ensuring the greatest efficiency and professional quality of work. Nonetheless, the greatest obstacle to multilingualism in outputs was the shortage of resources, for while consistent funding was available for translating parliamentary documents into the six official languages, the same was not true for publications. The maintenance of websites in various languages ought to be largely accomplished within existing resources, and Departments should prepare their sites in the official languages selectively, both with regard to the materials and the languages covered. The report advocated other measures, including the establishment of a network of focal points for multilingualism; the establishment of partnerships with external institutions and bodies; the adoption of a pragmatic approach to internal communications; the development of a common language base in DPKO to facilitate and accelerate communications and avoid the complication of potentially difficult procedures; the introduction of a proactive policy for planning replacements in relation to staff retirements; safeguarding institutional memory through the establishment of a programme/system for sharing and pooling staff members' knowledge prior to their retirement; and implementing a proactive human resources policy to enable the immediate replacement of departing staff.

By **decision 61/552** of 22 December, the Assembly decided that the item on multilingualism would remain for consideration during its resumed sixty-first (2007) session.

Protection from sexual exploitation and abuse

Report of Secretary-General. Pursuant to General Assembly resolution 57/306 [YUN 2003, p. 1237], the Secretary-General submitted a May report on special measures for protection from sexual exploitation and abuse [A/60/861]. Between January and December 2005, information on allegations was received from 41 UN entities. The number of alleged cases totalled 373, compared with 121 in 2004, and possibly reflected greater awareness and use of reporting mechanisms. Thirty-three allegations were reported by all UN entities other than DPKO, 14 of which related to the distribution of pornography through e-mail, while seven involved sex with minors. None related to sexual assault or rape. The majority of all allegations (340) were from DPKO (see p. 80).

Progress was made in implementing baseline measures to discourage the occurrence of sexual exploitation and abuse and to facilitate response to and reporting on such incidents. In that regard, all UN entities were to uphold specific minimum standards set out in the Secretary-General's bulletin on sexual exploitation and abuse [YUN 2004, p.107]. All UN entities had taken steps to comply with those standards, and OHRM continued to monitor compliance with them. The Organization had also established a joint Task Force on Protection from Sexual Exploitation and Abuse, chaired by DPKO and the United Nations Office for the Coordination of Humanitarian Affairs, which developed mechanisms for accountability, including clear guidance and support to managers for dealing with the problem. Despite the progress made, preventive measures needed to be strengthened. The Secretariat anticipated that increased public awareness about the availability of such measures might lead to increased reports of allegations. By strengthening community outreach and reporting mechanisms, it hoped to gain a better understanding of the extent of the problem and improve its own vigilance and response. It remained committed to changing the organizational culture that permitted such acts and urged Member States to assist the Organization by adopting policies to ensure the application of the Secretary-General's zero-tolerance policy to all troop contingents.

UN Joint Staff Pension Fund

As at 31 December 2006, the United Nations Joint Staff Pension Fund (UNJSPF) had 98,433 active participants as compared to 93,683 at the end of 2005 [YUN 2005, p. 1527]; the number of periodic payments in awards increased from 55,140 to 56,718. The breakdown of those awards was 18,732 retirement benefits; 12,772 early retirement benefits; 6,687 deferred retirement benefits; 9,265 widows' and widowers' benefits; 1,057 disability benefits; 8,158 child benefits; and 47 secondary dependants' benefits. During the year, 6,047 lump-sum withdrawal and other settlements were paid.

The Fund was administered by the 33-member United Nations Joint Staff Pension Board (UNJSPB), which held its fifty-third session (Nairobi, Kenya, 13-21 July) [A/61/9] to consider actuarial matters, including the twenty-eighth actuarial valuation of the Fund as at 31 December 2005; the management of the Fund's investments and reports on the investment strategy, policies, practices and performance for the biennium ending on 31 March 2006; the final report of the Working Group established to review the size and composition of the Board and its Standing Committee; revised budget estimates for the 2006-2007 biennium; and the Board's 2002 recommendations relating to the benefit provisions of the Fund. The Board also examined and approved financial statements and schedules for the 2004-2005 biennium and considered the report of the Board of Auditors on the accounts and operations of the Fund. In addition, the Board considered the proposed transfer agreement between the Fund and the World Bank Group and with Coordinated Organizations; applications for membership in the Fund by the International Organization for Migration (IOM) and the International Commission for the Conservation of Atlantic Tunas; as well as membership in its subsidiary bodies.

ACABQ report. ACABQ, in October [A/61/545], having considered the UNJSPB report (see above), agreed with the Board's recommendation that the current contribution rate of 23.7 per cent should be retained. The Committee recommended that significant changes in the Fund's investment policy be deferred, pending the provision of clear and convincing information on the interaction between the indexation of the Fund's North American stock portfolio, financial risks and asset allocation; the consideration of serious internal investment management issues; a comprehensive asset-liability management study; and the filling of all vacant Professional posts in the Investment Management Service. ACABQ also recommended General Assembly approval of the Board's recommendations that, as from 1 April

2007, the current reduction in the consumer price index adjustment be reduced from 1 per cent to 0.5 per cent, and that a 0.5 per cent increase be applied during the next adjustment to benefits in payment to retirees and beneficiaries who had already had the 1 per cent reduction applied to their benefits. In addition, ACABQ agreed with the Board's decision to eliminate, as from 1 April, the limitation on the right to restoration for existing and future contributing participants based on the length of prior service. The Committee also recommended Assembly approval of the Board's revised budget estimates for the Fund's operation for the 2006-2007 biennium, covering additional resources of $493,800 for the Fund's administrative costs relating to general temporary assistance, travel and external audit expenses, and the reclassification of several posts, as well as the amount of $964,200 relating to investment costs. ACABQ also concurred with the Board's recommendation that, effective 1 January 2007, IOM be admitted as a new member. It also recommended approval of the revised transfer agreement between the Fund and the World Bank, and the new transfer agreement it had with six other organizations, with effect from 1 January 2007.

Report of Secretary-General. In a November report [A/61/577], the Secretary-General noted that approval by the General Assembly of the recommendations of the Board and those of ACABQ would result in additional requirements for the United Nations of an estimated amount of $111,500. The cost to the regular budget for the 2006-2007 biennium would amount to $69,400, while a balance of $42,100 would be reimbursed to the Organization by the United Nations Development Programme, the United Nations Population Fund and the United Nations Children's Fund.

The General Assembly, in section X of **resolution 61/252** of 22 December (see p. 1616), took note of the Secretary-General's report and requested him to report on any additional requirements arising from the Board's recommendations in the context of the second performance report on the programme budget for the 2006-2007 biennium.

GENERAL ASSEMBLY ACTION

On 22 December [meeting 84], the General Assembly, on the recommendation of the Fifth Committee [A/61/664], adopted **resolution 61/240** without vote [agenda item 126].

United Nations pension system

The General Assembly,

Recalling its resolutions 55/224 of 23 December 2000, 57/286 of 20 December 2002 and 59/269 of 23 December 2004 and section III of its resolution 60/248 of 23 December 2005,

Having considered the report of the United Nations Joint Staff Pension Board on its fifty-third session to the General Assembly and to the member organizations of the United Nations Joint Staff Pension Fund, the report of the Secretary-General on the investments of the Fund and the related report of the Advisory Committee on Administrative and Budgetary Questions,

I

Actuarial matters

Recalling its resolutions 57/286, section I, and 59/269, section I,

Having considered the results of the valuation of the United Nations Joint Staff Pension Fund, which revealed a fifth consecutive actuarial surplus as at 31 December 2005, and the observations thereon by the consulting actuary of the Fund, the Committee of Actuaries and the United Nations Joint Staff Pension Board,

1. *Takes note* of the results of the actuarial valuation of the United Nations Joint Staff Pension Fund, which went from an actuarial surplus of 0.36 per cent of pensionable remuneration as at 31 December 1997 to an actuarial surplus of 4.25 per cent of pensionable remuneration as at 31 December 1999, to an actuarial surplus of 2.92 per cent of pensionable remuneration as at 31 December 2001, to an actuarial surplus of 1.14 per cent of pensionable remuneration as at 31 December 2003 and to an actuarial surplus of 1.29 per cent of pensionable remuneration as at 31 December 2005 and, in particular, of the opinions provided by the consulting actuary and the Committee of Actuaries, as reproduced in annexes VII and VIII, respectively, to the report of the United Nations Joint Staff Pension Board;

2. *Notes* that the Committee of Actuaries expressed the view that, based on the continuation of the surplus, a portion of the surplus disclosed in 2005 could be made available at the present time to improve benefits, but that prudence would dictate that most of the surplus should be retained;

3. *Recalls* that the Assembly had already approved in 2002, in principle, the change in the benefit provisions of the Regulations of the Fund that would eliminate the limitation on the right to restoration based on the length of prior service;

4. *Approves* the change in the benefit provisions of the Regulations of the Fund, as set out in annex XVII to the report of the Board, to eliminate the limitation on the right to restoration for existing and future participants based on the length of prior contributory service;

5. *Takes note* of the decision of the Board to amend the rules of procedure of the Fund to provide for the appointment of ad hoc members to the Committee of Actuaries as well as to the Investments Committee;

6. *Concurs*, in accordance with article 13 of the Regulations of the Fund and with a view to securing continuity of pension rights, with the following:

(a) The revised Agreement on the transfer of pension rights of participants in the United Nations Joint Staff

Pension Fund and of participants in the World Bank Group Staff Retirement Plan, as approved by the Board and set out in section A of annex IX to the report of the Board, which will take effect from 1 January 2007;

(b) The new Agreement on the transfer of pension rights of participants in the United Nations Joint Staff Pension Fund and of participants in the Coordinated Organizations, as set out in section B of annex IX to the report of the Board, which will take effect from 1 January 2007;

7. *Decides*, upon the affirmative recommendation of the Board, that the International Organization for Migration shall be admitted as a new member organization of the Fund, effective 1 January 2007;

II

Pension adjustment system

Recalling its resolutions 57/286, section II, and 59/269, section II,

Having considered the reviews carried out by the consulting actuary, the Committee of Actuaries and the United Nations Joint Staff Pension Board, as set out in the report of the Board, of various aspects of the pension adjustment system,

1. *Takes note* of the recommendation of the United Nations Joint Staff Pension Board that as from 1 April 2007, the current reduction in the first consumer price index adjustments due under the pension adjustment system of the United Nations Joint Staff Pension Fund to benefits in award should be lowered from 1.0 per cent to 0.5 per cent and that a 0.5 per cent increase should be applied on the occasion of the next adjustment to benefits being paid to existing retirees and beneficiaries who have already had the 1.0 per cent reduction applied to their benefits;

2. *Approves*, accordingly, with effect from 1 April 2007, the changes in the pension adjustment system, as set out in annex XVIII to the report of the Board;

3. *Recalls* its decision in section II of its resolution 59/269 to invite the Board to provide information on the special situation of pensioners living in countries having undergone dollarization and on possible proposals to attenuate the adverse consequences arising therefrom, and notes that the Board did not agree on a recommendation to attenuate the adverse consequences of pensioners living in countries having undergone dollarization;

4. *Takes into account* that the Board reached consensus on the fact that dollarization has had adverse effects on the purchasing power of some retirees and beneficiaries living in Ecuador, and requested the Secretary/Chief Executive Officer to visit the Fund's retirees living there;

5. *Invites* the Board to present in 2007 a viable ad hoc measure to adequately attenuate the adverse consequences arising from dollarization in Ecuador after consulting with the Committee of Actuaries;

III

Financial statements of the United Nations Joint Staff Pension Fund and report of the Board of Auditors

Having considered the financial statements of the United Nations Joint Staff Pension Fund for the biennium ended 31 December 2005, the audit opinion and report of the Board of Auditors thereon, the information provided on the internal audits of the Fund and the observations of the United Nations Joint Staff Pension Board,

Notes that the report of the Board of Auditors on the accounts of the United Nations Joint Staff Pension Fund for the biennium ended 31 December 2005 indicated that the financial statements were in compliance with accepted standard accounting principles and that the transactions of the Pension Fund were, in all significant respects, in accordance with the Financial Regulations and legislative authority;

IV

Administrative arrangements and revised budget of the United Nations Joint Staff Pension Fund

Recalling section IV of its resolution 57/286, section X of its resolution 58/272 of 23 December 2003, section IV of its resolution 59/269 and section III of its resolution 60/248 concerning the administrative arrangements and expenses of the United Nations Joint Staff Pension Fund,

Having considered chapter VII of the report of the United Nations Joint Staff Pension Board on the administrative arrangements of the Fund,

1. *Takes note* of the information set out in paragraphs 132 and 133 of the report of the United Nations Joint Staff Pension Board on the revised budget estimates for the biennium 2006-2007;

2. *Approves* the increase in total additional resources for the biennium 2006-2007 from 108,262,500 United States dollars to 110,665,500 dollars for the following:

(a) Reclassification of two information technology posts in the Fund secretariat;

(b) Travel expenses related to the newly established Audit Committee;

(c) Enhancement of the Investment Management Service through the addition of five new posts, indexed management costs, including the costs of transition management services, and consultant costs;

(d) Enhancement of the external audit functions of the Fund and expansion of the Fund's internal audit coverage;

(e) Administrative costs to implement the approved modifications in the benefit provisions;

3. *Notes* that the Board requested the Fund to continue its efforts to consolidate the information technology services of the secretariat of the Fund and those of the Investment Management Service;

4. *Also notes* that the Board agreed that its expenses would continue to be shared and charged to the member organizations of the Fund under the current methodology until 1 January 2008, at which time all Board

expenses would be included in the Fund's budget and charged as administrative expenses;

V

Survivors' benefits

Recalling its resolutions 55/224, section V, 57/286, section V, and 59/269, section VI,

1. *Notes* that the Board requested the Secretary/Chief Executive Officer to present to the Board in 2007 a comprehensive study on the benefit provisions related to family members of the United Nations Joint Staff Pension Fund participants and retirees;

2. *Also notes* that the Board agreed that the Fund would record, for the purposes of eventually determining entitlements to pension benefits under articles 34 and 35 of the Regulations of the Fund, the personal status of a participant as recognized and reported to the Fund by the participant's employing organization;

VI

Size and composition of the United Nations Joint Staff Pension Board and its Standing Committee

Stressing the importance of fair representation of participating organizations in the United Nations Joint Staff Pension Board and its Standing Committee,

1. *Takes note* of the information set out in the report of the United Nations Joint Staff Pension Board on the review of the size and composition of the Board and its Standing Committee, in particular the decision of the Board not to recommend any change in its size and composition;

2. *Notes,* in this regard, that the Board recognized that its decision to retain its current size, and its composition and allocation of seats did not fully respond to General Assembly resolution 57/286 regarding the size and composition of the Board to achieve fairer representation;

3. *Also notes* that the Board agreed to review its size and composition after it had had adequate time to assess the results of its other decisions under this item, which focused primarily on improving efficiency;

4. *Notes with satisfaction* the recommendations adopted by the Board with a view to improving the efficiency of its work and its intention to consider a policy paper in 2007 on membership and attendance at meetings of the Board and its Standing Committee;

5. *Takes note* of the decision of the Board to amend the rules of procedure of the Fund in order to make formal provision for the additional alternate representative of the General Assembly to attend the meetings of the Standing Committee, as approved provisionally by the Board in 2004;

6. *Also takes note* of the decision of the Board that the costs related to two retiree representatives attending the sessions of the Board and one retiree representative attending the sessions of the Standing Committee would be shared as an expense of the Board on a provisional basis until its session in 2008, at which time the Board would consider means for duly electing the representatives for the retirees;

7. *Notes* that the Board also decided to revert to annual sessions as from 2007 with the aim of completing its work within five working days; the focus of the Board during the odd-numbered years will be on the budget of the Fund;

VII

Other matters

1. *Takes note* of the decision of the Board to establish an Audit Committee to provide an enhanced communications channel for the internal auditors, the external auditors and the Pension Board, with the consequent revision in the rules of procedure of the Fund and, in this regard, endorses the recommendation of the Advisory Committee on Administrative and Budgetary Questions that the Audit Committee be composed of members with relevant expertise in accounting, financial management, including risk management, and audit;

2. *Notes* that the Board endorsed the Fund's enterprise-wide risk management policy;

3. *Takes note* of the observations of the Board, as set out in its report, on the review and conclusions reached by the International Civil Service Commission on the changes in average tax rates at the headquarters duty stations, which formed the basis for the development of the current common scale of staff assessment for pensionable remuneration;

4. *Notes* that the Board considered a detailed report of the medical consultant covering the period from 1 January 2004 to 31 December 2005;

5. *Also notes* that the Board intends to review the current provisions for special adjustments for small pensions and the current arrangements regarding the periodicity of cost-of-living adjustments at its sessions in 2007 and 2008, respectively;

6. *Requests* the Pension Board to consider, during its review of small pensions, the negative impact of administrative expenses, transaction fees or bank commissions regarding the benefits in order to remedy such impact and to report to it thereon at its sixty-third session as part of the review by the Board, and invites the Board to explore the possibility of further diversifying banking transactions;

7. *Notes* that the Board intends to keep the possible provision for the purchase of additional years of contributory service under periodic review;

8. *Also notes* that the Board decided to maintain both the current system for establishing benefits in respect of locally recruited staff in the Professional category and the methodology currently used in the determination of final average remuneration for staff in the General Service category; both issues will continue to be monitored by the Fund secretariat;

9. *Takes note* of the other matters dealt with in the report of the Board;

10. *Calls upon* the Investment Management Service to expeditiously implement the recommendations of the Board of Auditors with regard to the determination of

the level of tolerance for risk, improvement in internal review of performance and the trade order management system;

11. *Requests* that all vacant Professional posts, including the five new posts in the Investment Management Service endorsed by the present resolution, be expeditiously filled;

VIII

Investments of the United Nations Joint Staff Pension Fund

1. *Takes note* of the report of the Secretary-General on the investments of the United Nations Joint Staff Pension Fund and the observations of the United Nations Joint Staff Pension Board, as set out in its report;

2. *Notes* the increase in the market value of the assets of the Fund and the positive returns achieved during the biennium and, in particular, the 4.3 per cent annualized real rate of return over the 46-year period ending on 31 March 2006;

3. *Stresses* the need for a comprehensive asset-liability management study, including assessment of financial risks and recommendations on asset allocation, and a study of the Fund's governance, with special regard to the relationship between the Fund secretariat and the Investment Management Service, the results thereof to be provided to the Board for consideration;

4. *Notes* that the Board endorsed the intention of the representative of the Secretary-General for the investments of the fund to manage the North American equities portfolio in the passive mode using the current benchmark indices;

5. *Requests* the Secretary-General to fully adhere to the Financial Rules and Regulations of the United Nations and General Assembly resolutions on procurement when procuring services for the passive management and report to the Board thereon at its next session;

6. *Notes* that the Board encouraged the Investment Management Service of the Fund to adhere to the principles of the Global Compact to the extent possible without compromising the four established investment criteria of safety, profitability, liquidity and convertibility, and urged the Investment Management Service to continue its efforts to collect tax refunds from several Member States;

IX

Diversification

Recalling its resolutions 36/119 A to C of 10 December 1981 and 59/269,

1. *Takes note with concern* of the modest increases in investments of the United Nations Joint Staff Pension Fund in developing countries, and requests the Secretary-General to report to the General Assembly at its sixty-third session on further steps and efforts undertaken to increase, to the maximum extent possible, investments in developing countries;

2. *Reaffirms* the policy of diversification of the investments of the Fund across geographical areas, wherever this serves the interests of the participants and beneficiaries of the Fund, in accordance with the four criteria of safety, profitability, liquidity and convertibility.

Also on 22 December, the Assembly decided that the item on the United Nations pension system would remain for consideration during its sixty-first (2007) session (**decision 61/552**).

Pension fund investment

The market value of UNJSPF assets as at 31 December was $36.7 billion, an increase of $5,169 million over the previous year. The Fund had a one-year annualized rate of return of 15.9 per cent compared to 16.0 per cent for the benchmark. After adjustment for a 2.6 per cent rise in the consumer price index, the Fund's real rate of return was 13 per cent. Over periods of three and five years, however, it had a total return of 12.3 per cent and 11.4 per cent, while the benchmark had returns of 10.2 per cent and 9.9 per cent, respectively. As at 31 December 2006, the Fund's investment assets were distributed in equities (62.4 per cent), bonds (29.7 per cent), real-estate related instruments (4.3 per cent) and short-term investments (3.6 per cent).

In October [A/C.5/61/2], the Secretary-General described the economic and investment conditions prevailing in the reporting period ended 31 March 2006 and provided statistical information on the Fund's investment returns and diversification, including development-related investments.

Travel-related matters

Report of Secretary-General. In July, the Secretary-General submitted his biennial report on standards of accommodation for air travel [A/61/188 & Corr.1], listing exceptions to those standards from 1 July 2004 to 30 June 2006 and comparative statistics for the two-year period ended 30 June 2004.

ACABQ report. On 21 December [A/61/661], ACABQ recommended that the General Assembly request an audit by OIOS of all categories of exceptions authorized within the framework of standards of accommodation for air travel. The Committee asked the Assembly to consider a revision of the policy on first class travel. Upon enquiry, ACABQ was informed that a review was being conducted of the standards of travel and the related entitlements of staff members, members of United Nations organs and subsidiary organs and of common system organizations, as requested by the Assembly in resolution 60/255 (see p. 1620), with a view to adopting a common UN system policy for the Assembly's consideration at its resumed sixty-first (2007) session.

Administration of justice

The General Assembly, by **decision 60/551 B** of 8 May, deferred to its sixty-first (2006) session consideration of the Secretary-General's reports on the activities of the Ombudsman [YUN 2005, p. 1534], the administration of justice in the Secretariat: outcome of the work of the Joint Appeals Board during 2003 and 2004; and statistics on the disposition of cases and the work of the Panel of Counsel [ibid., p. 1533], the practice of the Secretary-General in disciplinary matters and cases of criminal behaviour, 1 January 2004–30 June 2005 [ibid., 1534], the administration of justice in the Secretariat [ibid., p. 1533], as well as the letter dated 14 October 2005 from the President of the General Assembly addressed to the Chairman of the Fifth Committee [A/C.5/60/10] and the ACABQ report on the administration of justice in the Secretariat [A/60/7/Add.1].

At that session, the Assembly had before it reports of the Secretary-General on the administration of justice in the Secretariat: implementation of resolution 59/283 [A/61/342] (see below); activities of the Ombudsman [A/61/524] (see p. 1709); outcome of the work of the Joint Appeals Board and statistics on the disposition of cases and the work of the Panel of Counsel [A/61/71] (see below); and on the practice in disciplinary matters and possible criminal behaviour [A/61/206] (see p. 1709). It also had before it the report of the Redesign Panel on the United Nations system of administration of justice [A/61/205] (see below).

By **decision 61/552** of 22 December, the Assembly decided that the item on administration of justice at the United Nations would remain for consideration at its resumed sixty-first (2007) session.

Joint Appeals Board

In response to General Assembly resolution 55/258 [YUN 2001, p. 1337], the Secretary-General submitted an April report [A/ 61/71] on the outcome of the work of the Joint Appeals Board (JAB) in New York, Geneva, Vienna and Nairobi for 2005. The report also provided information on the disposition of cases and on the work of the Panel of Counsel. The Secretary-General observed that 144 appeals and suspension-of-action cases were filed with JAB in those duty stations in 2005, as compared to 84 the previous year. Of that number, JAB disposed of 131 cases, compared to 143 in 2004. Regarding disciplinary cases, which were accorded priority, 41 such cases were referred to the Joint Disciplinary Committee, of which 19 were considered, compared to 11 the previous year. The Secretary-General accepted fully or partially 116 (or 92 per cent) of unanimous JAB decisions, compared to 73 (or 87 per cent) in 2004, and rejected 22 (17 per cent), compared to 10 (12 per cent) in 2004.

Follow-up to resolution 59/283

In September [A/61/342], the Secretary-General reported on efforts to implement the decisions and requests contained in General Assembly resolution 59/283 [YUN 2005, p. 1529] and the related recommendations of OIOS on the management review of the United Nations appeals process [YUN 2004, p. 1442], with a view to improving the administration of justice in the Organization. The report focused on general guidelines, formal and informal justice mechanisms and the review of the internal justice system. Cross-cutting issues included mandatory time limits for the appeals process, the appearance of a conflict of interest in formulating decisions on appeals; the training of all staff involved in the justice system; increasing staff participation in JAB (jury system); and the financial liability of managers. The report outlined progress made with respect to each of those issues and the challenges remaining, especially the approach for eliminating the appearance of a conflict of interest in making decisions on appeals. The recommendation of the Assembly and OIOS that the responsibility for such decisions be transferred from the Department of Management to the Secretary-General's Office could not be implemented because it was determined that the current composition, structure and work exigencies of the Secretary-General's Office would make it impossible for it to undertake that task. As such, there was no alternative but for the Under-Secretary-General for Management to continue approve or reject JAB recommendations regarding appeals. On the issue of formal mechanisms of administration of justice, the report detailed measures being taken to improve the various components of that mechanism, including the Panel of Counsel, the Administrative Law Unit and JAB. Among other initiatives were the approval of additional resources for the Panel of Counsel and its growing capacity to undertake outreach activities; the amendment of the staff rules to ensure that those wishing to appeal an administrative decision followed the appropriate procedure; amendments to JAB rules of procedure and the provision of additional resources to its four secretariats to strengthening their capacity to clear the backlog of cases; the efforts of those secretariats to enhance their electronic tracking systems to improve the accessibility of information for the regular monitoring of trends in the appeal process; and provisions for annual meetings of JAB members in New York and their counterparts on the Joint Disciplinary

Committee. The report also highlighted measures designed to implement OIOS and Assembly recommendations for strengthening the United Nations Administrative Tribunal. The Secretary-General informed the Assembly that the measures taken to strengthen the system might be subject to further change resulting from any Assembly decisions regarding the report of the Redesign Panel (see below).

Redesign Panel

Pursuant to General Assembly resolution 59/283 [YUN 2005, p. 1529], the Secretary-General established a Redesign Panel on the United Nations system of administration of justice, comprising independent experts, to review and possibly redesign that system. The Panel, which submitted its report in July [A/61/205], examined the idea of a unified justice system and its scope and jurisdiction, the situation in offices away from Headquarters; the Organization's system of informal justice; the role of the Ombudsman and how it might be strengthened; and the legal basis of the formal justice system. It also considered issues relating to legal representation.

After extensive consultations with UN system staff and managers and with numerous other stakeholders within and beyond the Organization, the Panel concluded that the UN system of administration of justice was outmoded, dysfunctional and ineffective, lacked independence and entailed enormous financial and other costs to the Organization. The Panel pointed out that a new and redesigned system would be far more effective than any attempt to improve the current one. Furthermore, effective reform of the United Nations could not be achieved without an efficient and well resourced internal justice system that would safeguard the rights of staff members and ensure the accountability of mangers and staff alike.

The Panel recommended the establishment of a completely new system of administration of justice, which should be professional, independent, decentralized and fully consistent with international human rights standards, which could reduce conflicts through more effective informal dispute resolution and ensure the expeditious disposal of cases in the formal justice system. The new structure would be a two-tiered system of formal justice comprising a first instance decentralized Tribunal—the United Nations Dispute Tribunal—composed of professional judges with the power to make binding decisions. The Tribunal would replace advisory bodies, including JAB and the Joint Disciplinary Committees, but not the rebuttal panels and Classification Appeals and Review Committees. The United Nations Administrative Tribunal should be renamed the United Nations Appeals Tribunal and its structure amended to include a new appellate jurisdiction. The Office of the Ombudsman should be strengthened and decentralized, with a merger of the Ombudsmen Offices in the Secretariat and those of UN funds and programmes. The Panels on Discrimination and Other Grievances should be abolished, with their informal functions transferred to the new Office of the Ombudsman, and their other functions reassigned to the formal justice system. The Panel recommended the establishment, effective 1 January 2008, of the proposed system, and the early establishment of an Office of Administration of Justice.

On 4 December, the General Assembly took note of the decision of the Sixth (Legal) Committee to hold a resumed session in March 2007 to consider the legal aspects of the Redesign Panel's report (**decision 61/511**).

Office of Ombudsman

Pursuant to General Assembly resolution 59/283 [YUN 2005, p. 1529], the Secretary-General submitted an October report [A/61/524] on the activities of the Ombudsman, covering the period from 1 September 2005 to 31 August 2006. Since its inception in 2002 [YUN 2002, p. 30], nearly 2,000 staff members had sought the assistance of the Office, and over the reporting period, its activities had expanded, including through increased recourse to mediation and a better understanding of its role by both management and staff. Some 50 new cases were opened monthly, while the total number of new cases during the reporting period stood at 611, of which 316 were closed. The Office expanded its outreach to peacekeeping missions; the percentage of cases initiated by staff in those missions increased from 23 per cent in 2002 to 44 per cent of the total number of cases opened between January and August 2006. The most important issues raised by staff related to promotion or career considerations (24 per cent of all cases, followed by interpersonal issues (23 per cent), conditions of service (11 per cent), standard of conduct-related issues (10 per cent) and entitlement cases (9 per cent). Compared to other UN staff, field mission staff had more issues relating to separation/termination (17 per cent) and entitlements (14 per cent). In 48 per cent of all cases opened, the assistance provided by the Office of the Ombudsman involved helping staff to explore options and solutions to work-related problems. Direct action by the Ombudsman to resolve problems was undertaken in 37 per cent of the cases, while referral to other offices and direct mediation were provided in 8 per cent and 1 per cent of the cases, respectively.

Criminal behaviour and disciplinary action

In response to General Assembly resolution 59/287 [YUN 2005, p. 1475], the Secretary-General transmitted a July report [A/61/206] on disciplinary matters and cases of criminal behaviour, covering the period from 1 July 2005 to 30 June 2006. The report provided information on the disciplinary and/or legal action taken in cases of established misconduct and/or criminal behaviour. It reviewed the administrative machinery in disciplinary matters and summarized cases for which a disciplinary measure was imposed by the Secretary-General, which mostly related to abuse of authority/harassment; fraud/misrepresentation; theft/misappropriation; and sexual exploitation and abuse. Some 42 cases were completed, resulting in 10 summary dismissals, two disciplinary measures after waiver of referral to the Joint Disciplinary Committee, five disciplinary measures after a Joint Disciplinary Committee review and 10 administrative measures. In 15 cases, no disciplinary or administrative action was taken.

The General Assembly, by **resolution 61/29** of 4 December (see p. 109) on criminal accountability of UN officials and experts on mission, established an Ad Hoc Committee to consider the report [A/60/980] of the Group of Legal Experts on ensuring the accountability of UN staff and experts on mission with respect to criminal acts committed in peacekeeping operations.

UN Administrative Tribunal

In its annual note to the General Assembly [A/INF/61/6], the seven-member United Nations Administrative Tribunal (UNAT) reported, through the Secretary-General, that it had delivered 35 judgements in 2006, relating to cases brought by staff against the Secretary-General or the executive heads of other UN bodies concerning disputes involving terms of appointment and other issues. The Tribunal met in New York on 21 November and held two panel sessions (Geneva, 26 June–28 July; New York, 23 October–22 November).

Appendices

Appendix I

Roster of the United Nations

There were 192 Member States as at 31 December 2006.

MEMBER	DATE OF ADMISSION
Afghanistan	19 Nov. 1946
Albania	14 Dec. 1955
Algeria	8 Oct. 1962
Andorra	28July 1993
Angola	1 Dec. 1976
Antigua and Barbuda	11 Nov. 1981
Argentina	24 Oct. 1945
Armenia	2 Mar. 1992
Australia	1 Nov. 1945
Austria	14 Dec. 1955
Azerbaijan	2 Mar. 1992
Bahamas	18 Sep. 1973
Bahrain	21 Sep. 1971
Bangladesh	17 Sep. 1974
Barbados	9Dec. 1966
Belarus	24 Oct. 1945
Belgium	27 Dec. 1945
Belize	25 Sep. 1981
Benin	20 Sep. 1960
Bhutan	21 Sep. 1971
Bolivia	14 Nov. 1945
Bosnia and Herzegovina	22 May 1992
Botswana	17 Oct. 1966
Brazil	24 Oct. 1945
Brunei Darussalam	21 Sep. 1984
Bulgaria	14 Dec. 1955
Burkina Faso	20 Sep. 1960
Burundi	18 Sep. 1962
Cambodia	14 Dec. 1955
Cameroon	20 Sep. 1960
Canada	9 Nov. 1945
Cape Verde	16 Sep. 1975
Central African Republic	20 Sep. 1960
Chad	20 Sep. 1960
Chile	24 Oct. 1945
China	24 Oct. 1945
Colombia	5 Nov. 1945
Comoros	12 Nov. 1975
Congo	20 Sep. 1960
Costa Rica	2 Nov. 1945
Côte d'Ivoire	20 Sep. 1960
Croatia	22 May 1992
Cuba	24 Oct. 1945
Cyprus	20 Sep. 1960
Czech Republic[1]	19 Jan. 1993
Democratic People's Republic of Korea	17 Sep. 1991
Democratic Republic of the Congo	20 Sep. 1960
Denmark	24 Oct. 1945
Djibouti	20 Sep. 1977
Dominica	18 Dec. 1978
Dominican Republic	24 Oct. 1945
Ecuador	21 Dec. 1945
Egypt[2]	24 Oct. 1945
El Salvador	24 Oct. 1945
Equatorial Guinea	12 Nov. 1968
Eritrea	28 May 1993
Estonia	17 Sep. 1991
Ethiopia	13 Nov. 1945
Fiji	13 Oct. 1970
Finland	14 Dec. 1955
France	24 Oct. 1945
Gabon	20 Sep. 1960
Gambia	21 Sep. 1965
Georgia	31 July 1992
Germany[3]	18 Sep. 1973
Ghana	8 Mar. 1957
Greece	25 Oct. 1945
Grenada	17 Sep. 1974
Guatemala	21 Nov. 1945
Guinea	12 Dec. 1958
Guinea-Bissau	17 Sep. 1974
Guyana	20 Sep. 1966
Haiti	24 Oct. 1945
Honduras	17 Dec. 1945
Hungary	14 Dec. 1955
Iceland	19 Nov. 1946
India	30 Oct. 1945
Indonesia[4]	28 Sep. 1950
Iran (Islamic Republic of)	24 Oct. 1945
Iraq	21 Dec. 1945
Ireland	14 Dec. 1955
Israel	11 May 1949
Italy	14 Dec. 1955
Jamaica	18 Sep. 1962
Japan	18 Dec. 1956
Jordan	14 Dec. 1955
Kazakhstan	2 Mar. 1992
Kenya	16 Dec. 1963
Kiribati	14 Sep. 1999
Kuwait	14 May 1963
Kyrgyzstan	2 Mar. 1992
Lao People's Democratic Republic	14 Dec. 1955
Latvia	17 Sep. 1991
Lebanon	24 Oct. 1945
Lesotho	17 Oct. 1966
Liberia	2 Nov. 1945
Libyan Arab Jamahiriya	14 Dec. 1955
Liechtenstein	18 Sep. 1990
Lithuania	17 Sep. 1991
Luxembourg	24 Oct. 1945
Madagascar	20 Sep. 1960
Malawi	1 Dec. 1964
Malaysia[5]	17 Sep. 1957
Maldives	21 Sep. 1965
Mali	28 Sep. 1960
Malta	1 Dec. 1964
Marshall Islands	17 Sep. 1991
Mauritania	27 Oct. 1961
Mauritius	24 Apr. 1968
Mexico	7 Nov. 1945
Micronesia (Federated States of)	17 Sep. 1991
Monaco	28 May 1993
Mongolia	27 Oct. 1961
Montenegro	28 Jun. 2006[9]
Morocco	12 Nov. 1956
Mozambique	16 Sep. 1975
Myanmar	19 Apr. 1948
Namibia	23 Apr. 1990
Nauru	14 Sep. 1999
Nepal	14 Dec. 1955
Netherlands	10 Dec. 1945
New Zealand	24 Oct. 1945
Nicaragua	24 Oct. 1945
Niger	20 Sep. 1960
Nigeria	7 Oct. 1960
Norway	27 Nov. 1945
Oman	7 Oct. 1971
Pakistan	30 Sep. 1947
Palau	15 Dec. 1994
Panama	13 Nov. 1945
Papua New Guinea	10 Oct. 1975
Paraguay	24 Oct. 1945
Peru	31 Oct. 1945
Philippines	24 Oct. 1945
Poland	24 Oct. 1945
Portugal	14 Dec. 1955
Qatar	21 Sep. 1971
Republic of Korea	17 Sep. 1991
Republic of Moldova	2 Mar. 1992
Romania	14 Dec. 1955
Russian Federation[6]	24 Oct. 1945
Rwanda	18 Sep. 1962
Saint Kitts and Nevis	23 Sep. 1983
Saint Lucia	18 Sep. 1979
Saint Vincent and the Grenadines	16 Sep. 1980
Samoa	15 Dec. 1976
San Marino	2 Mar. 1992
Sao Tome and Principe	16 Sep. 1975
Saudi Arabia	24 Oct. 1945
Senegal	28 Sep. 1960
Serbia	1 Nov. 2000
Seychelles	21 Sep. 1976
Sierra Leone	27 Sep. 1961
Singapore[5]	21 Sep. 1965
Slovakia[1]	19 Jan. 1993
Slovenia	22 May 1992
Solomon Islands	19 Sep. 1978
Somalia	20 Sep. 1960
South Africa	7 Nov. 1945
Spain	14 Dec. 1955

MEMBER	DATE OF ADMISSION	MEMBER	DATE OF ADMISSION	MEMBER	DATE OF ADMISSION
Sri Lanka	14 Dec. 1955	Tonga	14 Sep. 1999	United Republic of Tanzania[7]	14 Dec. 1961
Sudan	12 Nov. 1956	Trinidad and Tobago	18 Sep. 1962	United States of America	24 Oct. 1945
Suriname	4 Dec. 1975	Tunisia	12 Nov. 1956	Uruguay	18 Dec. 1945
Swaziland	24 Sep. 1968	Turkey	24 Oct. 1945	Uzbekistan	2 Mar. 1992
Sweden	19 Nov. 1946	Turkmenistan	2 Mar. 1992	Vanuatu	15 Sep. 1981
Switzerland	10 Sep. 2002	Tuvalu	5 Sep. 2000	Venezuela (Bolivarian Republic of)	15 Nov. 1945
Syrian Arab Republic[2]	24 Oct. 1945	Uganda	25 Oct. 1962	Viet Nam	20 Sep. 1977
Tajikistan	2 Mar. 1992	Ukraine	24 Oct. 1945	Yemen[8]	30 Sep. 1947
Thailand	16 Dec. 1946	United Arab Emirates	9 Dec. 1971	Zambia	1 Dec. 1964
The former Yugoslav Republic of Macedonia	8 Apr. 1993	United Kingdom of Great Britain and Northern Ireland	24 Oct. 1945	Zimbabwe	25 Aug. 1980
Timor-Leste	27 Sep. 2002				
Togo	20 Sep. 1960				

[1]Czechoslovakia, which was an original Member of the United Nations from 24 October 1945, split up on 1 January 1993 and was succeeded by the Czech Republic and Slovakia.

[2]Egypt and Syria, both of which became Members of the United Nations on 24 October 1945, joined together—following a plebiscite held in those countries on 21 February 1958—to form the United Arab Republic. On 13 October 1961, Syria, having resumed its status as an independent State, also resumed its separate membership in the United Nations; it changed its name to the Syrian Arab Republic on 14 September 1971. The United Arab Republic continued as a Member of the United Nations and reverted to the name of Egypt on 2 September 1971.

[3]Through accession of the German Democratic Republic to the Federal Republic of Germany on 3 October 1990, the two German States (both of which became United Nations Members on 18 September 1973) united to form one sovereign State. As from that date, the Federal Republic of Germany has acted in the United Nations under the designation Germany.

[4]On 20 January 1965, Indonesia informed the Secretary-General that it had decided to withdraw from the United Nations. By a telegram of 19 September 1966, it notified the Secretary-General of its decision to resume participation in the activities of the United Nations. On 28 September 1966, the General Assembly took note of that decision and the President invited the representatives of Indonesia to take their seats in the Assembly.

[5]On 16 September 1963, Sabah (North Borneo), Sarawak and Singapore joined with the Federation of Malaya (which became a United Nations Member on 17 September 1957) to form Malaysia. On 9 August 1965, Singapore became an independent State and on 21 September 1965 it became a Member of the United Nations.

[6]The Union of Soviet Socialist Republics was an original Member of the United Nations from 24 October 1945. On 24 December 1991, the President of the Russian Federation informed the Secretary-General that the membership of the USSR in all United Nations organs was being continued by the Russian Federation.

[7]Tanganyika was admitted to the United Nations on 14 December 1961, and Zanzibar, on 16 December 1963. Following ratification, on 26 April 1964, of the Articles of Union between Tanganyika and Zanzibar, the two States became represented as a single Member: the United Republic of Tanganyika and Zanzibar; it changed its name to the United Republic of Tanzania on 1 November 1964.

[8]Yemen was admitted to the United Nations on 30 September 1947 and Democratic Yemen on 14 December 1967. On 22 May 1990, the two countries merged and have since been represented as one Member.

[9]Montenegro became a Member of the United Nations on 28 June 2006. It had declared itself independent from Serbia following a 21 May 2006 referendum.

Appendix II

Charter of the United Nations and Statute of the International Court of Justice

Charter of the United Nations

NOTE: The Charter of the United Nations was signed on 26 June 1945, in San Francisco, at the conclusion of the United Nations Conference on International Organization, and came into force on 24 October 1945. The Statute of the International Court of Justice is an integral part of the Charter.

Amendments to Articles 23, 27 and 61 of the Charter were adopted by the General Assembly on 17 December 1963 and came into force on 31 August 1965. A further amendment to Article 61 was adopted by the General Assembly on 20 December 1971 and came into force on 24 September 1973. An amendment to Article 109, adopted by the General Assembly on 20 December 1965, came into force on 12 June 1968.

The amendment to Article 23 enlarges the membership of the Security Council from 11 to 15. The amended Article 27 provides that decisions of the Security Council on procedural matters shall be made by an affirmative vote of nine members (formerly seven) and on all other matters by an affirmative vote of nine members (formerly seven), including the concurring votes of the five permanent members of the Security Council.

The amendment to Article 61, which entered into force on 31 August 1965, enlarged the membership of the Economic and Social Council from 18 to 27. The subsequent amendment to that Article, which entered into force on 24 September 1973, further increased the membership of the Council from 27 to 54.

The amendment to Article 109, which relates to the first paragraph of that Article, provides that a General Conference of Member States for the purpose of reviewing the Charter may be held at a date and place to be fixed by a two-thirds vote of the members of the General Assembly and by a vote of any nine members (formerly seven) of the Security Council. Paragraph 3 of Article 109, which deals with the consideration of a possible review conference during the tenth regular session of the General Assembly, has been retained in its original form in its reference to a "vote of any seven members of the Security Council", the paragraph having been acted upon in 1955 by the General Assembly, at its tenth regular session, and by the Security Council.

WE THE PEOPLES
OF THE UNITED NATIONS
DETERMINED

to save succeeding generations from the scourge of war, which twice in our lifetime has brought untold sorrow to mankind, and

to reaffirm faith in fundamental human rights, in the dignity and worth of the human person, in the equal rights of men and women and of nations large and small, and

to establish conditions under which justice and respect for the obligations arising from treaties and other sources of international law can be maintained, and

to promote social progress and better standards of life in larger freedom,

AND FOR THESE ENDS

to practice tolerance and live together in peace with one another as good neighbours, and

to unite our strength to maintain international peace and security, and

to ensure, by the acceptance of principles and the institution of methods, that armed force shall not be used, save in the common interest, and

to employ international machinery for the promotion of the economic and social advancement of all peoples,

HAVE RESOLVED TO
COMBINE OUR EFFORTS TO
ACCOMPLISH THESE AIMS

Accordingly, our respective Governments, through representatives assembled in the city of San Francisco, who have exhibited their full powers found to be in good and due form, have agreed to the present Charter of the United Nations and do hereby establish an international organization to be known as the United Nations.

Chapter I
PURPOSES AND PRINCIPLES

Article 1

The Purposes of the United Nations are:

1. To maintain international peace and security, and to that end: to take effective collective measures for the prevention and removal of threats to the peace, and for the suppression of acts of aggression or other breaches of the peace, and to bring about by peaceful means, and in conformity with the principles of justice and international law, adjustment or settlement of international disputes or situations which might lead to a breach of the peace;

2. To develop friendly relations among nations based on respect for the principle of equal rights and self-determination of peoples, and to take other appropriate measures to strengthen universal peace;

3. To achieve international co-operation in solving international problems of an economic, social, cultural or humanitarian character, and in promoting and encouraging respect for human rights and for fundamental freedoms for all without distinction as to race, sex, language or religion; and

4. To be a centre for harmonizing the actions of nations in the attainment of these common ends.

Article 2

The Organization and its Members, in pursuit of the Purposes stated in Article 1, shall act in accordance with the following Principles:

1. The Organization is based on the principle of the sovereign equality of all its Members.

2. All Members, in order to ensure to all of them the rights and benefits resulting from membership, shall fulfil in good faith the obligations assumed by them in accordance with the present Charter.

3. All Members shall settle their international disputes by peaceful means in such a manner that international peace and security, and justice, are not endangered.

4. All Members shall refrain in their international relations from the threat or use of force against the territorial integrity or political independence of any state, or in any other manner inconsistent with the Purposes of the United Nations.

5. All Members shall give the United Nations every assistance in any action it takes in accordance with the present Charter, and shall refrain from giving assistance to any state against which the United Nations is taking preventive or enforcement action.

6. The Organization shall ensure that states which are not Members of the United Nations act in accordance with these Principles so far as may be necessary for the maintenance of international peace and security.

7. Nothing contained in the present Charter shall authorize the United Nations to intervene in matters which are essentially within the domestic jurisdiction of any state or shall require the Members to submit such matters to settlement under the present Charter; but this principle shall not prejudice the application of enforcement measures under Chapter VII.

Chapter II
MEMBERSHIP

Article 3

The original Members of the United Nations shall be the states which, having participated in the United Nations Conference on International Organization at San Francisco or having previously signed the Declaration by United Nations of 1 January 1942, sign the present Charter and ratify it in accordance with Article 110.

Article 4

1. Membership in the United Nations is open to all other peace-loving states which accept the obligations contained in the present Charter and, in the judgment of the Organization, are able and willing to carry out these obligations.

2. The admission of any such state to membership in the United Nations will be effected by a decision of the General Assembly upon the recommendation of the Security Council.

Article 5

A Member of the United Nations against which preventive or enforcement action has been taken by the Security Council may be suspended from the exercise of the rights and privileges of membership by the General Assembly upon the recommendation of the Security Council. The exercise of these rights and privileges may be restored by the Security Council.

Article 6

A Member of the United Nations which has persistently violated the Principles contained in the present Charter may be expelled from the Organization by the General Assembly upon the recommendation of the Security Council.

Chapter III
ORGANS

Article 7

1. There are established as the principal organs of the United Nations: a General Assembly, a Security Council, an Economic and Social Council, a Trusteeship Council, an International Court of Justice, and a Secretariat.

2. Such subsidiary organs as may be found necessary may be established in accordance with the present Charter.

Article 8

The United Nations shall place no restrictions on the eligibility of men and women to participate in any capacity and under conditions of equality in its principal and subsidiary organs.

Chapter IV
THE GENERAL ASSEMBLY

Composition

Article 9

1. The General Assembly shall consist of all the Members of the United Nations.

2. Each Member shall have not more than five representatives in the General Assembly.

Functions and Powers

Article 10

The General Assembly may discuss any questions or any matters within the scope of the present Charter or relating to the powers and functions of any organs provided for in the present Charter, and, except as provided in Article 12, may make recommendations to the Members of the United Nations or to the Security Council or both on any such questions or matters.

Article 11

1. The General Assembly may consider the general principles of co-operation in the maintenance of international peace and security, including the principles governing disarmament and the regulation of armaments, and may make recommendations with regard to such principles to the Members or to the Security Council or to both.

2. The General Assembly may discuss any questions relating to the maintenance of international peace and security brought before it by any Member of the United Nations, or by the Security Council, or by a state which is not a Member of the United Nations in accordance with Article 35, paragraph 2, and, except as provided in Article 12, may make recommendations with regard to any such questions to the state or states concerned or to the Security Council or to both. Any such question on which action is necessary shall be referred to the Security Council by the General Assembly either before or after discussion.

3. The General Assembly may call the attention of the Security Council to situations which are likely to endanger international peace and security.

4. The powers of the General Assembly set forth in this Article shall not limit the general scope of Article 10.

Article 12

1. While the Security Council is exercising in respect of any dispute or situation the functions assigned to it in the present Charter, the General Assembly shall not make any recommendation with regard to that dispute or situation unless the Security Council so requests.

2. The Secretary-General, with the consent of the Security Council, shall notify the General Assembly at each session of any matters relative to the maintenance of international peace and security which are being dealt with by the Security Council and shall similarly notify the General Assembly, or the Members of the United Nations if the General Assembly is not in session, immediately the Security Council ceases to deal with such matters.

Article 13

1. The General Assembly shall initiate studies and make recommendations for the purpose of:

a. promoting international co-operation in the political field and encouraging the progressive development of international law and its codification;
b. promoting international co-operation in the economic, social, cultural, educational and health fields, and assisting in the realization of human rights and fundamental freedoms for all without distinction as to race, sex, language or religion.

2. The further responsibilities, functions and powers of the General Assembly with respect to matters mentioned in paragraph 1 (*b*) above are set forth in Chapters IX and X.

Article 14

Subject to the provisions of Article 12, the General Assembly may recommend measures for the peaceful adjustment of any situation, regardless of origin, which it deems likely to impair the general welfare or friendly relations among nations, including situations resulting from a violation of the provisions of the present Charter setting forth the Purposes and Principles of the United Nations.

Article 15

1. The General Assembly shall receive and consider annual and special reports from the Security Council; these reports shall include an account of the measures that the Security Council has decided upon or taken to maintain international peace and security.
2. The General Assembly shall receive and consider reports from the other organs of the United Nations.

Article 16

The General Assembly shall perform such functions with respect to the international trusteeship system as are assigned to it under Chapters XII and XIII, including the approval of the trusteeship agreements for areas not designated as strategic.

Article 17

1. The General Assembly shall consider and approve the budget of the Organization.
2. The expenses of the Organization shall be borne by the Members as apportioned by the General Assembly.
3. The General Assembly shall consider and approve any financial and budgetary arrangements with specialized agencies referred to in Article 57 and shall examine the administrative budgets of such specialized agencies with a view to making recommendations to the agencies concerned.

Voting

Article 18

1. Each member of the General Assembly shall have one vote.
2. Decisions of the General Assembly on important questions shall be made by a two-thirds majority of the members present and voting. These questions shall include: recommendations with respect to the maintenance of international peace and security, the election of the non permanent members of the Security Council, the election of the members of the Economic and Social Council, the election of members of the Trusteeship Council in accordance with paragraph 1 (*c*) of Article 86, the admission of new Members to the United Nations, the suspension of the rights and privileges of membership, the expulsion of Members, questions relating to the operation of the trusteeship system, and budgetary questions.
3. Decisions on other questions, including the determination of additional categories of questions to be decided by a two-thirds majority, shall be made by a majority of the members present and voting.

Article 19

A Member of the United Nations which is in arrears in the payment of its financial contributions to the Organization shall have no vote in the General Assembly if the amount of its arrears equals or exceeds the amount of the contributions due from it for the preceding two full years. The General Assembly may, nevertheless, permit such a Member to vote if it is satisfied that the failure to pay is due to conditions beyond the control of the Member.

Procedure

Article 20

The General Assembly shall meet in regular annual sessions and in such special sessions as occasion may require. Special sessions shall be convoked by the Secretary-General at the request of the Security Council or of a majority of the Members of the United Nations.

Article 21

The General Assembly shall adopt its own rules of procedure. It shall elect its President for each session.

Article 22

The General Assembly may establish such subsidiary organs as it deems necessary for the performance of its functions.

Chapter V
THE SECURITY COUNCIL

Composition

Article 23[1]

1. The Security Council shall consist of fifteen Members of the United Nations. The Republic of China, France, the Union of Soviet Socialist Republics, the United Kingdom of Great Britain and Northern Ireland and the United States of America shall be permanent members of the Security Council. The General Assembly shall elect ten other Members of the United Nations to be non-permanent members of the Security Council, due regard being specially paid, in the first instance to the contribution of Members of the United Nations to the maintenance of international peace and security and to the other purposes of the Organization, and also to equitable geographical distribution.
2. The non-permanent members of the Security Council shall be elected for a term of two years. In the first election of the non-permanent members after the increase of the membership of the Security Council from eleven to fifteen, two of the four additional members shall be chosen for a term of one year. A retiring member shall not be eligible for immediate re-election.
3. Each member of the Security Council shall have one representative.

Functions and Powers

Article 24

1. In order to ensure prompt and effective action by the United Nations, its Members confer on the Security Council primary responsibility for the maintenance of international peace and security, and agree that in carrying out its duties under this responsibility the Security Council acts on their behalf.
2. In discharging these duties the Security Council shall act in accordance with the Purposes and Principles of the United Nations. The specific powers granted to the Security Council for the discharge of these duties are laid down in Chapters VI, VII, VIII and XII.
3. The Security Council shall submit annual and, when necessary, special reports to the General Assembly for its consideration.

Article 25

The Members of the United Nations agree to accept and carry out the decisions of the Security Council in accordance with the present Charter.

Article 26

In order to promote the establishment and maintenance of international peace and security with the least diversion for armaments of the world's human and economic resources, the Security Council shall be responsible for formulating, with the assistance of the Military Staff Committee referred to in Article

47, plans to be submitted to the Members of the United Nations for the establishment of a system for the regulation of armaments.

Voting

Article 27[2]

1. Each member of the Security Council shall have one vote.

2. Decisions of the Security Council on procedural matters shall be made by an affirmative vote of nine members.

3. Decisions of the Security Council on all other matters shall be made by an affirmative vote of nine members including the concurring votes of the permanent members; provided that, in decisions under Chapter VI, and under paragraph 3 of Article 52, a party to a dispute shall abstain from voting.

Procedure

Article 28

1. The Security Council shall be so organized as to be able to function continuously. Each member of the Security Council shall for this purpose be represented at all times at the seat of the Organization.

2. The Security Council shall hold periodic meetings at which each of its members may, if it so desires, be represented by a member of the government or by some other specially designated representative.

3. The Security Council may hold meetings at such places other than the seat of the Organization as in its judgment will best facilitate its work.

Article 29

The Security Council may establish such subsidiary organs as it deems necessary for the performance of its functions.

Article 30

The Security Council shall adopt its own rules of procedure, including the method of selecting its President.

Article 31

Any Member of the United Nations which is not a member of the Security Council may participate, without vote, in the discussion of any question brought before the Security Council whenever the latter considers that the interests of that Member are specially affected.

Article 32

Any Member of the United Nations which is not a member of the Security Council or any state which is not a Member of the United Nations, if it is a party to a dispute under consideration by the Security Council, shall be invited to participate, without vote, in the discussion relating to the dispute. The Security Council shall lay down such conditions as it deems just for the participation of a state which is not a Member of the United Nations.

Chapter VI
PACIFIC SETTLEMENT OF DISPUTES

Article 33

1. The parties to any dispute, the continuance of which is likely to endanger the maintenance of international peace and security, shall, first of all, seek a solution by negotiation, enquiry, mediation, conciliation, arbitration, judicial settlement, resort to regional agencies or arrangements, or other peaceful means of their own choice.

2. The Security Council shall, when it deems necessary, call upon the parties to settle their dispute by such means.

Article 34

The Security Council may investigate any dispute, or any situation which might lead to international friction or give rise to a dispute, in order to determine whether the continuance of the dispute or situation is likely to endanger the maintenance of international peace and security.

Article 35

1. Any Member of the United Nations may bring any dispute, or any situation of the nature referred to in Article 34, to the attention of the Security Council or of the General Assembly.

2. A state which is not a Member of the United Nations may bring to the attention of the Security Council or of the General Assembly any dispute to which it is a party if it accepts in advance, for the purposes of the dispute, the obligations of pacific settlement provided in the present Charter.

3. The proceedings of the General Assembly in respect of matters brought to its attention under this Article will be subject to the provisions of Articles 11 and 12.

Article 36

1. The Security Council may, at any stage of a dispute of the nature referred to in Article 33 or of a situation of like nature, recommend appropriate procedures or methods of adjustment.

2. The Security Council should take into consideration any procedures for the settlement of the dispute which have already been adopted by the parties.

3. In making recommendations under this Article the Security Council should also take into consideration that legal disputes should as a general rule be referred by the parties to the International Court of Justice in accordance with the provisions of the Statute of the Court.

Article 37

1. Should the parties to a dispute of the nature referred to in Article 33 fail to settle it by the means indicated in that Article, they shall refer it to the Security Council.

2. If the Security Council deems that the continuance of the dispute is in fact likely to endanger the maintenance of international peace and security, it shall decide whether to take action under Article 36 or to recommend such terms of settlement as it may consider appropriate.

Article 38

Without prejudice to the provisions of Articles 33 to 37, the Security Council may, if all the parties to any dispute so request, make recommendations to the parties with a view to a pacific settlement of the dispute.

Chapter VII
ACTION WITH RESPECT TO THREATS TO THE PEACE, BREACHES OF THE PEACE, AND ACTS OF AGGRESSION

Article 39

The Security Council shall determine the existence of any threat to the peace, breach of the peace, or act of aggression and shall make recommendations, or decide what measures shall be taken in accordance with Articles 41 and 42, to maintain or restore international peace and security.

Article 40

In order to prevent an aggravation of the situation, the Security Council may, before making the recommendations or deciding upon the measures provided for in Article 39, call upon the parties concerned to comply with such provisional measures as it deems necessary or desirable. Such provisional measures shall be without prejudice to the rights, claims or position of the parties concerned. The Security Council shall duly take account of failure to comply with such provisional measures.

Article 41

The Security Council may decide what measures not involving the use of armed force are to be employed to give effect to its decisions, and it may call upon the Members of the United Nations to apply such measures. These may include complete or partial interruption of economic relations and of rail, sea, air, postal, telegraphic, radio and other means of communication, and the severance of diplomatic relations.

Article 42

Should the Security Council consider that measures provided for in Article 41 would be inadequate or have proved to be inadequate, it may take such action by air, sea or land forces as may be necessary to maintain or restore international peace and security. Such action may include demonstrations, blockade, and other operations by air, sea, or land forces of Members of the United Nations.

Article 43

1. All Members of the United Nations, in order to contribute to the maintenance of international peace and security, undertake to make available to the Security Council, on its call and in accordance with a special agreement or agreements, armed forces, assistance and facilities, including rights of passage, necessary for the purpose of maintaining international peace and security.

2. Such agreement or agreements shall govern the numbers and types of forces, their degree of readiness and general location, and the nature of the facilities and assistance to be provided.

3. The agreement or agreements shall be negotiated as soon as possible on the initiative of the Security Council. They shall be concluded between the Security Council and Members or between the Security Council and groups of Members and shall be subject to ratification by the signatory states in accordance with their respective constitutional processes.

Article 44

When the Security Council has decided to use force it shall, before calling upon a Member not represented on it to provide armed forces in fulfilment of the obligations assumed under Article 43, invite that Member, if the Member so desires, to participate in the decisions of the Security Council concerning the employment of contingents of that Member's armed forces.

Article 45

In order to enable the United Nations to take urgent military measures, Members shall hold immediately available national air-force contingents for combined international enforcement action. The strength and degree of readiness of these contingents and plans for their combined action shall be determined, within the limits laid down in the special agreement or agreements referred to in Article 43, by the Security Council with the assistance of the Military Staff Committee.

Article 46

Plans for the application of armed force shall be made by the Security Council with the assistance of the Military Staff Committee.

Article 47

1. There shall be established a Military Staff Committee to advise and assist the Security Council on all questions relating to the Security Council's military requirements for the maintenance of international peace and security, the employment and command of forces placed at its disposal, the regulation of armaments, and possible disarmament.

2. The Military Staff Committee shall consist of the Chiefs of Staff of the permanent members of the Security Council or their representatives. Any Member of the United Nations not permanently represented on the Committee shall be invited by the Committee to be associated with it when the efficient discharge of the Committee's responsibilities requires the participation of that Member in its work.

3. The Military Staff Committee shall be responsible under the Security Council for the strategic direction of any armed forces placed at the disposal of the Security Council. Questions relating to the command of such forces shall be worked out subsequently.

4. The Military Staff Committee, with the authorization of the Security Council and after consultation with appropriate regional agencies, may establish regional sub-committees.

Article 48

1. The action required to carry out the decisions of the Security Council for the maintenance of international peace and security shall be taken by all the Members of the United Nations or by some of them, as the Security Council may determine.

2. Such decisions shall be carried out by the Members of the United Nations directly and through their action in the appropriate international agencies of which they are members.

Article 49

The Members of the United Nations shall join in affording mutual assistance in carrying out the measures decided upon by the Security Council.

Article 50

If preventive or enforcement measures against any state are taken by the Security Council, any other state, whether a Member of the United Nations or not, which finds itself confronted with special economic problems arising from the carrying out of those measures shall have the right to consult the Security Council with regard to a solution of those problems.

Article 51

Nothing in the present Charter shall impair the inherent right of individual or collective self-defence if an armed attack occurs against a Member of the United Nations, until the Security Council has taken measures necessary to maintain international peace and security. Measures taken by Members in the exercise of this right of self-defence shall be immediately reported to the Security Council and shall not in any way affect the authority and responsibility of the Security Council under the present Charter to take at any time such action as it deems necessary in order to maintain or restore international peace and security.

Chapter VIII
REGIONAL ARRANGEMENTS

Article 52

1. Nothing in the present Charter precludes the existence of regional arrangements or agencies for dealing with such matters relating to the maintenance of international peace and security as are appropriate for regional action, provided that such arrangements or agencies and their activities are consistent with the Purposes and Principles of the United Nations.

2. The Members of the United Nations entering into such arrangements or constituting such agencies shall make every effort to achieve pacific settlement of local disputes through such regional arrangements or by such regional agencies before referring them to the Security Council.

3. The Security Council shall encourage the development of pacific settlement of local disputes through such regional arrangements or by such regional agencies either on the initiative of the states concerned or by reference from the Security Council.

4. This Article in no way impairs the application of Articles 34 and 35.

Article 53

1. The Security Council shall, where appropriate, utilize such regional arrangements or agencies for enforcement action under its authority. But no enforcement action shall be taken under regional arrangements or by regional agencies without

the authorization of the Security Council, with the exception of measures against any enemy state, as defined in paragraph 2 of this Article, provided for pursuant to Article 107 or in regional arrangements directed against renewal of aggressive policy on the part of any such state, until such time as the Organization may, on request of the Governments concerned, be charged with the responsibility for preventing further aggression by such a state.

2. The term enemy state as used in paragraph 1 of this Article applies to any state which during the Second World War has been an enemy of any signatory of the present Charter.

Article 54

The Security Council shall at all times be kept fully informed of activities undertaken or in contemplation under regional arrangements or by regional agencies for the maintenance of international peace and security.

Chapter IX
INTERNATIONAL ECONOMIC AND SOCIAL CO-OPERATION

Article 55

With a view to the creation of conditions of stability and well-being which are necessary for peaceful and friendly relations among nations based on respect for the principle of equal rights and self-determination of peoples, the United Nations shall promote:

a. higher standards of living, full employment, and conditions of economic and social progress and development;
b. solutions of international economic, social, health, and related problems; and international cultural and educational co-operation; and
c. universal respect for, and observance of, human rights and fundamental freedoms for all without distinction as to race, sex, language, or religion.

Article 56

All Members pledge themselves to take joint and separate action in co-operation with the Organization for the achievement of the purposes set forth in Article 55.

Article 57

1. The various specialized agencies, established by intergovernmental agreement and having wide international responsibilities, as defined in their basic instruments, in economic, social, cultural, educational, health, and related fields, shall be brought into relationship with the United Nations in accordance with the provisions of Article 63.

2. Such agencies thus brought into relationship with the United Nations are hereinafter referred to as specialized agencies.

Article 58

The Organization shall make recommendations for the coordination of the policies and activities of the specialized agencies.

Article 59

The Organization shall, where appropriate, initiate negotiations among the states concerned for the creation of any new specialized agencies required for the accomplishment of the purposes set forth in Article 55.

Article 60

Responsibility for the discharge of the functions of the Organization set forth in this Chapter shall be vested in the General Assembly and, under the authority of the General Assembly, in the Economic and Social Council, which shall have for this purpose the powers set forth in Chapter X.

Chapter X
THE ECONOMIC AND SOCIAL COUNCIL

Composition

Article 61[3]

1. The Economic and Social Council shall consist of fifty four Members of the United Nations elected by the General Assembly.

2. Subject to the provisions of paragraph 3, eighteen members of the Economic and Social Council shall be elected each year for a term of three years. A retiring member shall be eligible for immediate re-election.

3. At the first election after the increase in the membership of the Economic and Social Council from twenty-seven to fifty-four members, in addition to the members elected in place of the nine members whose term of office expires at the end of that year, twenty-seven additional members shall be elected. Of these twenty-seven additional members, the term of office of nine members so elected shall expire at the end of one year, and of nine other members at the end of two years, in accordance with arrangements made by the General Assembly.

4. Each member of the Economic and Social Council shall have one representative.

Functions and Powers

Article 62

1. The Economic and Social Council may make or initiate studies and reports with respect to international economic, social, cultural, educational, health, and related matters and may make recommendations with respect to any such matters to the General Assembly, to the Members of the United Nations, and to the specialized agencies concerned.

2. It may make recommendations for the purpose of promoting respect for, and observance of, human rights and fundamental freedoms for all.

3. It may prepare draft conventions for submission to the General Assembly, with respect to matters falling within its competence.

4. It may call, in accordance with the rules prescribed by the United Nations, international conferences on matters falling within its competence.

Article 63

1. The Economic and Social Council may enter into agreements with any of the agencies referred to in Article 57, defining the terms on which the agency concerned shall be brought into relationship with the United Nations. Such agreements shall be subject to approval by the General Assembly.

2. It may co-ordinate the activities of the specialized agencies through consultation with and recommendations to such agencies and through recommendations to the General Assembly and to the Members of the United Nations.

Article 64

1. The Economic and Social Council may take appropriate steps to obtain regular reports from the specialized agencies. It may make arrangements with the Members of the United Nations and with the specialized agencies to obtain reports on the steps taken to give effect to its own recommendations and to recommendations on matters falling within its competence made by the General Assembly.

2. It may communicate its observations on these reports to the General Assembly.

Article 65

The Economic and Social Council may furnish information to the Security Council and shall assist the Security Council upon its request.

Article 66

1. The Economic and Social Council shall perform such functions as fall within its competence in connexion with the carrying out of the recommendations of the General Assembly.

2. It may, with the approval of the General Assembly, perform services at the request of Members of the United Nations and at the request of specialized agencies.

3. It shall perform such other functions as are specified elsewhere in the present Charter or as may be assigned to it by the General Assembly.

Voting

Article 67

1. Each member of the Economic and Social Council shall have one vote.

2. Decisions of the Economic and Social Council shall be made by a majority of the members present and voting.

Procedure

Article 68

The Economic and Social Council shall set up commissions in economic and social fields and for the promotion of human rights, and such other commissions as may be required for the performance of its functions.

Article 69

The Economic and Social Council shall invite any Member of the United Nations to participate, without vote, in its deliberations on any matter of particular concern to that Member.

Article 70

The Economic and Social Council may make arrangements for representatives of the specialized agencies to participate, without vote, in its deliberations and in those of the commissions established by it, and for its representatives to participate in the deliberations of the specialized agencies.

Article 71

The Economic and Social Council may make suitable arrangements for consultation with non-governmental organizations which are concerned with matters within its competence.

Such arrangements may be made with international organizations and, where appropriate, with national organizations after consultation with the Member of the United Nations concerned.

Article 72

1. The Economic and Social Council shall adopt its own rules of procedure, including the method of selecting its President.

2. The Economic and Social Council shall meet as required in accordance with its rules, which shall include provision for the convening of meetings on the request of a majority of its members.

Chapter XI
DECLARATION REGARDING NON-SELF-GOVERNING TERRITORIES

Article 73

Members of the United Nations which have or assume responsibilities for the administration of territories whose peoples have not yet attained a full measure of self-government recognize the principle that the interests of the inhabitants of these territories are paramount, and accept as a sacred trust the obligation to promote to the utmost, within the system of international peace and security established by the present Charter, the well-being of the inhabitants of these territories and, to this end:

a. to ensure, with due respect for the culture of the peoples concerned, their political, economic, social, and educational advancement, their just treatment, and their protection against abuses;
b. to develop self-government, to take due account of the political aspirations of the peoples, and to assist them in the progressive development of their free political institutions, according to the particular circumstances of each territory and its peoples and their varying stages of advancement;
c. to further international peace and security;
d. to promote constructive measures of development, to encourage research, and to co-operate with one another and, when and where appropriate, with specialized international bodies with a view to the practical achievement of the social, economic, and scientific purposes set forth in this Article; and
e. to transmit regularly to the Secretary-General for information purposes, subject to such limitation as security and constitutional considerations may require, statistical and other information of a technical nature relating to economic, social, and educational conditions in the territories for which they are respectively responsible other than those territories to which Chapters XII and XIII apply.

Article 74

Members of the United Nations also agree that their policy in respect of the territories to which this Chapter applies, no less than in respect of their metropolitan areas, must be based on the general principle of good-neighbourliness, due account being taken of the interests and well-being of the rest of the world, in social, economic, and commercial matters.

Chapter XII
INTERNATIONAL TRUSTEESHIP SYSTEM

Article 75

The United Nations shall establish under its authority an international trusteeship system for the administration and supervision of such territories as may be placed there under by subsequent individual agreements. These territories are hereinafter referred to as trust territories.

Article 76

The basic objectives of the trusteeship system, in accordance with the Purposes of the United Nations laid down in Article 1 of the present Charter, shall be:

a. to further international peace and security;
b. to promote the political, economic, social, and educational advancement of the inhabitants of the trust territories, and their progressive development towards self government or independence as may be appropriate to the particular circumstances of each territory and its peoples and the freely expressed wishes of the peoples concerned, and as may be provided by the terms of each trusteeship agreement;
c. to encourage respect for human rights and for fundamental freedoms for all without distinction as to race, sex, language, or religion, and to encourage recognition of the interdependence of the peoples of the world; and
d. to ensure equal treatment in social, economic, and commercial matters for all Members of the United Nations and their nationals, and also equal treatment for the latter in the administration of justice, without prejudice to the attainment of the foregoing objectives and subject to the provisions of Article 80.

Article 77

1. The trusteeship system shall apply to such territories in the following categories as may be placed there under by means of trusteeship agreements:

a. territories now held under mandate;
b. territories which may be detached from enemy states as a result of the Second World War; and
c. territories voluntarily placed under the system by states responsible for their administration.

2. It will be a matter for subsequent agreement as to which territories in the foregoing categories will be brought under the trusteeship system and upon what terms.

Article 78

The trusteeship system shall not apply to territories which have become Members of the United Nations, relationship among which shall be based on respect for the principle of sovereign equality.

Article 79

The terms of trusteeship for each territory to be placed under the trusteeship system, including any alteration or amendment, shall be agreed upon by the states directly concerned, including the mandatory power in the case of territories held under mandate by a Member of the United Nations, and shall be approved as provided for in Articles 83 and 85.

Article 80

1. Except as may be agreed upon in individual trusteeship agreements, made under Articles 77, 79 and 81, placing each territory under the trusteeship system, and until such agreements have been concluded, nothing in this Chapter shall be construed in or of itself to alter in any manner the rights whatsoever of any states or any peoples or the terms of existing international instruments to which Members of the United Nations may respectively be parties.

2. Paragraph 1 of this Article shall not be interpreted as giving grounds for delay or postponement of the negotiation and conclusion of agreements for placing mandated and other territories under the trusteeship system as provided for in Article 77.

Article 81

The trusteeship agreement shall in each case include the terms under which the trust territory will be administered and designate the authority which will exercise the administration of the trust territory. Such authority, hereinafter called the administering authority, may be one or more states or the Organization itself.

Article 82

There may be designated, in any trusteeship agreement, a strategic area or areas which may include part or all of the trust territory to which the agreement applies, without prejudice to any special agreement or agreements made under Article 43.

Article 83

1. All functions of the United Nations relating to strategic areas, including the approval of the terms of the trusteeship agreements and of their alteration or amendment, shall be exercised by the Security Council.

2. The basic objectives set forth in Article 76 shall be applicable to the people of each strategic area.

3. The Security Council shall, subject to the provisions of the trusteeship agreements and without prejudice to security considerations, avail itself of the assistance of the Trusteeship Council to perform those functions of the United Nations under the trusteeship system relating to political, economic, social, and educational matters in the strategic areas.

Article 84

It shall be the duty of the administering authority to ensure that the trust territory shall play its part in the maintenance of international peace and security. To this end the administering authority may make use of volunteer forces, facilities, and assistance from the trust territory in carrying out the obligations towards the Security Council undertaken in this regard by the administering authority, as well as for local defence and the maintenance of law and order within the trust territory.

Article 85

1. The functions of the United Nations with regard to trusteeship agreements for all areas not designated as strategic, including the approval of the terms of the trusteeship agreements and of their alteration or amendment, shall be exercised by the General Assembly.

2. The Trusteeship Council, operating under the authority of the General Assembly, shall assist the General Assembly in carrying out these functions.

Chapter XIII
THE TRUSTEESHIP COUNCIL

Composition

Article 86

1. The Trusteeship Council shall consist of the following Members of the United Nations:
a. those Members administering trust territories;
b. such of those Members mentioned by name in Article 23 as are not administering trust territories; and
c. as many other Members elected for three-year terms by the General Assembly as may be necessary to ensure that the total number of members of the Trusteeship Council is equally divided between those Members of the United Nations which administer trust territories and those which do not.

2. Each member of the Trusteeship Council shall designate one specially qualified person to represent it therein.

Functions and Powers

Article 87

The General Assembly and, under its authority, the Trusteeship Council, in carrying out their functions, may:
a. consider reports submitted by the administering authority;
b. accept petitions and examine them in consultation with the administering authority;
c. provide for periodic visits to the respective trust territories at times agreed upon with the administering authority; and
d. take these and other actions in conformity with the terms of the trusteeship agreements.

Article 88

The Trusteeship Council shall formulate a questionnaire on the political, economic, social, and educational advancement of the inhabitants of each trust territory, and the administering authority for each trust territory within the competence of the General Assembly shall make an annual report to the General Assembly upon the basis of such questionnaire.

Voting

Article 89

1. Each member of the Trusteeship Council shall have one vote.

2. Decisions of the Trusteeship Council shall be made by a majority of the members present and voting.

Procedure

Article 90

1. The Trusteeship Council shall adopt its own rules of procedure, including the method of selecting its President.

2. The Trusteeship Council shall meet as required in accordance with its rules, which shall include provision for the convening of meetings on the request of a majority of its members.

Article 91

The Trusteeship Council shall, when appropriate, avail itself of the assistance of the Economic and Social Council and of the specialized agencies in regard to matters with which they are respectively concerned.

Chapter XIV
THE INTERNATIONAL COURT OF JUSTICE

Article 92

The International Court of Justice shall be the principal judicial organ of the United Nations. It shall function in accordance with the annexed Statute, which is based upon the Statute of the Permanent Court of International Justice and forms an integral part of the present Charter.

Article 93

1. All Members of the United Nations are ipso facto parties to the Statute of the International Court of Justice.

2. A state which is not a Member of the United Nations may become a party to the Statute of the International Court of Justice on conditions to be determined in each case by the General Assembly upon the recommendation of the Security Council.

Article 94

1. Each Member of the United Nations undertakes to comply with the decision of the International Court of Justice in any case to which it is a party.

2. If any party to a case fails to perform the obligations incumbent upon it under a judgment rendered by the Court, the other party may have recourse to the Security Council, which may, if it deems necessary, make recommendations or decide upon measures to be taken to give effect to the judgment.

Article 95

Nothing in the present Charter shall prevent Members of the United Nations from entrusting the solution of their differences to other tribunals by virtue of agreements already in existence or which may be concluded in the future.

Article 96

1. The General Assembly or the Security Council may request the International Court of Justice to give an advisory opinion on any legal question.

2. Other organs of the United Nations and specialized agencies, which may at any time be so authorized by the General Assembly, may also request advisory opinions of the Court on legal questions arising within the scope of their activities.

Chapter XV
THE SECRETARIAT

Article 97

The Secretariat shall comprise a Secretary-General and such staff as the Organization may require. The Secretary-General shall be appointed by the General Assembly upon the recommendation of the Security Council. He shall be the chief administrative officer of the Organization.

Article 98

The Secretary-General shall act in that capacity in all meetings of the General Assembly, of the Security Council, of the Economic and Social Council, and of the Trusteeship Council, and shall perform such other functions as are entrusted to him by these organs. The Secretary-General shall make an annual report to the General Assembly on the work of the Organization.

Article 99

The Secretary-General may bring to the attention of the Security Council any matter which in his opinion may threaten the maintenance of international peace and security.

Article 100

1. In the performance of their duties the Secretary-General and the staff shall not seek or receive instructions from any government or from any other authority external to the Organization. They shall refrain from any action which might reflect on their position as international officials responsible only to the Organization.

2. Each Member of the United Nations undertakes to respect the exclusively international character of the responsibilities of the Secretary-General and the staff and not to seek to influence them in the discharge of their responsibilities.

Article 101

1. The staff shall be appointed by the Secretary-General under regulations established by the General Assembly.

2. Appropriate staffs shall be permanently assigned to the Economic and Social Council, the Trusteeship Council, and, as required, to other organs of the United Nations. These staffs shall form a part of the Secretariat.

3. The paramount consideration in the employment of the staff and in the determination of the conditions of service shall be the necessity of securing the highest standards of efficiency, competence, and integrity. Due regard shall be paid to the importance of recruiting the staff on as wide a geographical basis as possible.

Chapter XVI
MISCELLANEOUS PROVISIONS

Article 102

1. Every treaty and every international agreement entered into by any Member of the United Nations after the present Charter comes into force shall as soon as possible be registered with the Secretariat and published by it.

2. No party to any such treaty or international agreement which has not been registered in accordance with the provisions of paragraph 1 of this Article may invoke that treaty or agreement before any organ of the United Nations.

Article 103

In the event of a conflict between the obligations of the Members of the United Nations under the present Charter and their obligations under any other international agreement, their obligations under the present Charter shall prevail.

Article 104

The Organization shall enjoy in the territory of each of its Members such legal capacity as may be necessary for the exercise of its functions and the fulfilment of its purposes.

Article 105

1. The Organization shall enjoy in the territory of each of its Members such privileges and immunities as are necessary for the fulfilment of its purposes.

2. Representatives of the Members of the United Nations and officials of the Organization shall similarly enjoy such privileges and immunities as are necessary for the independent exercise of their functions in connexion with the Organization.

3. The General Assembly may make recommendations with a view to determining the details of the application of paragraphs 1 and 2 of this Article or may propose conventions to the Members of the United Nations for this purpose.

Chapter XVII
TRANSITIONAL SECURITY ARRANGEMENTS

Article 106

Pending the coming into force of such special agreements referred to in Article 43 as in the opinion of the Security Council enable it to begin the exercise of its responsibilities under Article 42, the parties to the Four-Nation Declaration, signed at Moscow, 30 October 1943, and France, shall, in accordance with the provisions of paragraph 5 of that Declaration, consult with one another and as occasion requires with other Members of the United Nations with a view to such joint action on behalf of the Organization as may be necessary for the purpose of maintaining international peace and security.

Article 107

Nothing in the present Charter shall invalidate or preclude action, in relation to any state which during the Second World War has been an enemy of any signatory to the present Charter, taken or authorized as a result of that war by the Governments having responsibility for such action.

Chapter XVIII
AMENDMENTS

Article 108

Amendments to the present Charter shall come into force for all Members of the United Nations when they have been adopted by a vote of two thirds of the members of the General Assembly and ratified in accordance with their respective constitutional processes by two thirds of the Members of the United Nations, including all the permanent members of the Security Council.

Article 109[4]

1. A General Conference of the Members of the United Nations for the purpose of reviewing the present Charter may be held at a date and place to be fixed by a two-thirds vote of the members of the General Assembly and by a vote of any nine members of the Security Council. Each Member of the United Nations shall have one vote in the conference.

2. Any alteration of the present Charter recommended by a two-thirds vote of the conference shall take effect when ratified in accordance with their respective constitutional processes by two thirds of the Members of the United Nations including all the permanent members of the Security Council.

3. If such a conference has not been held before the tenth annual session of the General Assembly following the coming into force of the present Charter, the proposal to call such a conference shall be placed on the agenda of that session of the General Assembly, and the conference shall be held if so decided by a majority vote of the members of the General Assembly and by a vote of any seven members of the Security Council.

Chapter XIX
RATIFICATION AND SIGNATURE

Article 110

1. The present Charter shall be ratified by the signatory states in accordance with their respective constitutional processes.

2. The ratifications shall be deposited with the Government of the United States of America, which shall notify all the signatory states of each deposit as well as the Secretary-General of the Organization when he has been appointed.

3. The present Charter shall come into force upon the deposit of ratifications by the Republic of China, France, the Union of Soviet Socialist Republics, the United Kingdom of Great Britain and Northern Ireland and the United States of America, and by a majority of the other signatory states. A protocol of the ratifications deposited shall thereupon be drawn up by the Government of the United States of America which shall communicate copies thereof to all the signatory states.

4. The states signatory to the present Charter which ratify it after it has come into force will become original Members of the United Nations on the date of the deposit of their respective ratifications.

Article 111

The present Charter, of which the Chinese, French, Russian, English, and Spanish texts are equally authentic, shall remain deposited in the archives of the Government of the United States of America. Duly certified copies thereof shall be transmitted by that Government to the Governments of the other signatory states.

IN FAITH WHEREOF the representatives of the Governments of the United Nations have signed the present Charter.

DONE at the city of San Francisco the twenty-sixth day of June, one thousand nine hundred and forty-five.

---

[1] Amended text of Article 23, which came into force on 31 August 1965.
(The text of Article 23 before it was amended read as follows:

1. The Security Council shall consist of eleven Members of the United Nations. The Republic of China, France, the Union of Soviet Socialist Republics, the United Kingdom of Great Britain and Northern Ireland and the United States of America shall be permanent members of the Security Council. The General Assembly shall elect six other Members of the United Nations to be non-permanent members of the Security Council, due regard being specially paid in the first instance to the contributions of Members of the United Nations to the maintenance of international peace and security and to the other purposes of the Organization, and also to equitable geographical distribution.

2. The non-permanent members of the Security Council shall be elected for a term of two years. In the first election of the non-permanent members, however, three shall be chosen for a term of one year. A retiring member shall not be eligible for immediate re-election.

3. Each member of the Security Council shall have one representative.)

[2] Amended text of Article 27, which came into force on 31 August 1965.
(The text of Article 27 before it was amended read as follows:

1. Each member of the Security Council shall have one vote.
2. Decisions of the Security Council on procedural matters shall be made by an affirmative vote of seven members.
3. Decisions of the Security Council on all other matters shall be made by an affirmative vote of seven members including the concurring votes of the permanent members; provided that, in decisions under Chapter VI, and under paragraph 3 of Article 52, a party to a dispute shall abstain from voting.)

[3] Amended text of Article 61, which came into force on 24 September 1973.
(The text of Article 61 as previously amended on 31 August 1965 read as follows:

1. The Economic and Social Council shall consist of twenty-seven Members of the United Nations elected by the General Assembly.

2. Subject to the provisions of paragraph 3, nine members of the Economic and Social Council shall be elected each year for a term of three years. A retiring member shall be eligible for immediate re-election.

3. At the first election after the increase in the membership of the Economic and Social Council from eighteen to twenty-seven members, in addition to the members elected in place of the six members whose term of office expires at the end of that year, nine additional members shall be elected. Of these nine additional members, the term of office of three members so elected shall expire at the end of one year, and of three other members at the end of two years, in accordance with arrangements made by the General Assembly.

4. Each member of the Economic and Social Council shall have one representative.)

[4] Amended text of Article 109, which came into force on 12 June 1968.

(The text of Article 109 before it was amended read as follows:
1. A General Conference of the Members of the United Nations for the purpose of reviewing the present Charter may be held at a date and place to be fixed by a two-thirds vote of the members of the General Assembly and by a vote of any seven members of the Security Council. Each Member of the United Nations shall have one vote in the conference.
2. Any alteration of the present Charter recommended by a two-thirds vote of the conference shall take effect when ratified in accordance with their respective constitutional processes by two thirds of the Members of the United Nations including all the permanent members of the Security Council.
3. If such a conference has not been held before the tenth annual session of the General Assembly following the coming into force of the present Charter, the proposal to call such a conference shall be placed on the agenda of that session of the General Assembly, and the conference shall be held if so decided by a majority vote of the members of the General Assembly and by a vote of any seven members of the Security Council.)

Statute of the International Court of Justice

Article 1

The International Court of Justice established by the Charter of the United Nations as the principal judicial organ of the United Nations shall be constituted and shall function in accordance with the provisions of the present Statute.

Chapter I
ORGANIZATION OF THE COURT

Article 2

The Court shall be composed of a body of independent judges, elected regardless of their nationality from among persons of high moral character, who possess the qualifications required in their respective countries for appointment to the highest judicial offices, or are juris consults of recognized competence in international law.

Article 3

1. The Court shall consist of fifteen members, no two of whom may be nationals of the same state.

2. A person who for the purposes of membership in the Court could be regarded as a national of more than one state shall be deemed to be a national of the one in which he ordinarily exercises civil and political rights.

Article 4

1. The members of the Court shall be elected by the General Assembly and by the Security Council from a list of persons nominated by the national groups in the Permanent Court of Arbitration, in accordance with the following provisions.

2. In the case of Members of the United Nations not represented in the Permanent Court of Arbitration, candidates shall be nominated by national groups appointed for this purpose by their governments under the same conditions as those prescribed for members of the Permanent Court of Arbitration by Article 44 of the Convention of The Hague of 1907 for the pacific settlement of international disputes.

3. The conditions under which a state which is a party to the present Statute but is not a Member of the United Nations may participate in electing the members of the Court shall, in the absence of a special agreement, be laid down by the General Assembly upon recommendation of the Security Council.

Article 5

1. At least three months before the date of the election, the Secretary-General of the United Nations shall address a written request to the members of the Permanent Court of Arbitration belonging to the states which are parties to the present Statute, and to the members of the national groups appointed under Article 4, paragraph 2, inviting them to undertake, within a given time, by national groups, the nomination of persons in a position to accept the duties of a member of the Court.

2. No group may nominate more than four persons, not more than two of whom shall be of their own nationality. In no case may the number of candidates nominated by a group be more than double the number of seats to be filled.

Article 6

Before making these nominations, each national group is recommended to consult its highest court of justice, its legal faculties and schools of law, and its national academies and national sections of international academies devoted to the study of law.

Article 7

1. The Secretary-General shall prepare a list in alphabetical order of all the persons thus nominated. Save as provided in Article 12, paragraph 2, these shall be the only persons eligible.

2. The Secretary-General shall submit this list to the General Assembly and to the Security Council.

Article 8

The General Assembly and the Security Council shall proceed independently of one another to elect the members of the Court.

Article 9

At every election, the electors shall bear in mind not only that the persons to be elected should individually possess the qualifications required, but also that in the body as a whole the representation of the main forms of civilization and of the principal legal systems of the world should be assured.

Article 10

1. Those candidates who obtain an absolute majority of votes in the General Assembly and in the Security Council shall be considered as elected.

2. Any vote of the Security Council, whether for the election of judges or for the appointment of members of the conference envisaged in Article 12, shall be taken without any distinction between permanent and non-permanent members of the Security Council.

3. In the event of more than one national of the same state obtaining an absolute majority of the votes both of the General Assembly and of the Security Council, the eldest of these only shall be considered as elected.

Article 11

If, after the first meeting held for the purpose of the election, one or more seats remain to be filled, a second and, if necessary, a third meeting shall take place.

Article 12

1. If, after the third meeting, one or more seats still remain unfilled, a joint conference consisting of six members, three appointed by the General Assembly and three by the Security Council, may be formed at any time at the request of either the General Assembly or the Security Council, for the purpose of choosing by the vote of an absolute majority one name for each seat still vacant, to submit to the General Assembly and the Security Council for their respective acceptance.

2. If the joint conference is unanimously agreed upon any person who fulfils the required conditions, he may be included in its list, even though he was not included in the list of nominations referred to in Article 7.

3. If the joint conference is satisfied that it will not be successful in procuring an election, those members of the Court who have already been elected shall, within a period to be fixed by the Security Council, proceed to fill the vacant seats by selection from among those candidates who have obtained votes either in the General Assembly or in the Security Council.

4. In the event of an equality of votes among the judges, the eldest judge shall have a casting vote.

Article 13

1. The members of the Court shall be elected for nine years and may be re-elected; provided, however, that of the judges elected at the first election, the terms of five judges shall expire at the end of three years and the terms of five more judges shall expire at the end of six years.

2. The judges whose terms are to expire at the end of the above-mentioned initial periods of three and six years shall be chosen by lot to be drawn by the Secretary-General immediately after the first election has been completed.

3. The members of the Court shall continue to discharge their duties until their places have been filled. Though replaced, they shall finish any cases which they may have begun.

4. In the case of the resignation of a member of the Court, the resignation shall be addressed to the President of the Court for transmission to the Secretary-General. This last notification makes the place vacant.

Article 14

Vacancies shall be filled by the same method as that laid down for the first election, subject to the following provision: the Secretary-General shall, within one month of the occurrence of the vacancy, proceed to issue the invitations provided for in Article 5, and the date of the election shall be fixed by the Security Council.

Article 15

A member of the Court elected to replace a member whose term of office has not expired shall hold office for the remainder of his predecessor's term.

Article 16

1. No member of the Court may exercise any political or administrative function, or engage in any other occupation of a professional nature.

2. Any doubt on this point shall be settled by the decision of the Court.

Article 17

1. No member of the Court may act as agent, counsel, or advocate in any case.

2. No member may participate in the decision of any case in which he has previously taken part as agent, counsel, or advocate for one of the parties, or as a member of a national or international court, or of a commission of enquiry, or in any other capacity.

3. Any doubt on this point shall be settled by the decision of the Court.

Article 18

1. No member of the Court can be dismissed unless, in the unanimous opinion of the other members, he has ceased to fulfil the required conditions.

2. Formal notification thereof shall be made to the Secretary-General by the Registrar.

3. This notification makes the place vacant.

Article 19

The members of the Court, when engaged on the business of the Court, shall enjoy diplomatic privileges and immunities.

Article 20

Every member of the Court shall, before taking up his duties, make a solemn declaration in open court that he will exercise his powers impartially and conscientiously.

Article 21

1. The Court shall elect its President and Vice-President for three years; they may be re-elected.

2. The Court shall appoint its Registrar and may provide for the appointment of such other officers as may be necessary.

Article 22

1. The seat of the Court shall be established at The Hague. This, however, shall not prevent the Court from sitting and exercising its functions elsewhere whenever the Court considers it desirable.

2. The President and the Registrar shall reside at the seat of the Court.

Article 23

1. The Court shall remain permanently in session, except during the judicial vacations, the dates and duration of which shall be fixed by the Court.

2. Members of the Court are entitled to periodic leave, the dates and duration of which shall be fixed by the Court, having in mind the distance between The Hague and the home of each judge.

3. Members of the Court shall be bound, unless they are on leave or prevented from attending by illness or other serious reasons duly explained to the President, to hold themselves permanently at the disposal of the Court.

Article 24

1. If, for some special reason, a member of the Court considers that he should not take part in the decision of a particular case, he shall so inform the President.

2. If the President considers that for some special reason one of the members of the Court should not sit in a particular case, he shall give him notice accordingly.

3. If in any such case the member of the Court and the President disagree, the matter shall be settled by the decision of the Court.

Article 25

1. The full Court shall sit except when it is expressly provided otherwise in the present Statute.

2. Subject to the condition that the number of judges available to constitute the Court is not thereby reduced below eleven, the Rules of the Court may provide for allowing one or more judges, according to circumstances and in rotation, to be dispensed from sitting.

3. A quorum of nine judges shall suffice to constitute the Court.

Article 26

1. The Court may from time to time form one or more chambers, composed of three or more judges as the Court may determine, for dealing with particular categories of cases; for example, labour cases and cases relating to transit and communications.

2. The Court may at any time form a chamber for dealing with a particular case. The number of judges to constitute such a chamber shall be determined by the Court with the approval of the parties.

3. Cases shall be heard and determined by the chambers provided for in this Article if the parties so request.

Article 27

A judgment given by any of the chambers provided for in Articles 26 and 29 shall be considered as rendered by the Court.

Article 28

The chambers provided for in Articles 26 and 29 may, with the consent of the parties, sit and exercise their functions elsewhere than at The Hague.

Article 29

With a view to the speedy dispatch of business, the Court shall form annually a chamber composed of five judges which, at the request of the parties, may hear and determine cases by summary procedure. In addition, two judges shall be selected for the purpose of replacing judges who find it impossible to sit.

Article 30

1. The Court shall frame rules for carrying out its functions. In particular, it shall lay down rules of procedure.

2. The Rules of the Court may provide for assessors to sit with the Court or with any of its chambers, without the right to vote.

Article 31

1. Judges of the nationality of each of the parties shall retain their right to sit in the case before the Court.

2. If the Court includes upon the Bench a judge of the nationality of one of the parties, any other party may choose a person to sit as judge. Such person shall be chosen preferably from among those persons who have been nominated as candidates as provided in Articles 4 and 5.

3. If the Court includes upon the Bench no judge of the nationality of the parties, each of these parties may proceed to choose a judge as provided in paragraph 2 of this Article.

4. The provisions of this Article shall apply to the case of Articles 26 and 29. In such cases, the President shall request one or, if necessary, two of the members of the Court forming the chamber to give place to the members of the Court of the nationality of the parties concerned, and, failing such, or if they are unable to be present, to the judges specially chosen by the parties.

5. Should there be several parties in the same interest, they shall, for the purpose of the preceding provisions, be reckoned as one party only. Any doubt upon this point shall be settled by the decision of the Court.

6. Judges chosen as laid down in paragraphs 2, 3 and 4 of this Article shall fulfil the conditions required by Articles 2, 17 (paragraph 2), 20, and 24 of the present Statute. They shall take part in the decision on terms of complete equality with their colleagues.

Article 32

1. Each member of the Court shall receive an annual salary.

2. The President shall receive a special annual allowance.

3. The Vice-President shall receive a special allowance for every day on which he acts as President.

4. The judges chosen under Article 31, other than members of the Court, shall receive compensation for each day on which they exercise their functions.

5. These salaries, allowances, and compensation shall be fixed by the General Assembly. They may not be decreased during the term of office.

6. The salary of the Registrar shall be fixed by the General Assembly on the proposal of the Court.

7. Regulations made by the General Assembly shall fix the conditions under which retirement pensions may be given to members of the Court and to the Registrar, and the conditions under which members of the Court and the Registrar shall have their travelling expenses refunded.

8. The above salaries, allowances, and compensation shall be free of all taxation.

Article 33

The expenses of the Court shall be borne by the United Nations in such a manner as shall be decided by the General Assembly.

Chapter II
COMPETENCE OF THE COURT

Article 34

1. Only states may be parties in cases before the Court.

2. The Court, subject to and in conformity with its Rules, may request of public international organizations information relevant to cases before it, and shall receive such information presented by such organizations on their own initiative.

3. Whenever the construction of the constituent instrument of a public international organization or of an international convention adopted there under is in question in a case before the Court, the Registrar shall so notify the public international organization concerned and shall communicate to it copies of all the written proceedings.

Article 35

1. The Court shall be open to the states parties to the present Statute.

2. The conditions under which the Court shall be open to other states shall, subject to the special provisions contained in treaties in force, be laid down by the Security Council, but in no case shall such conditions place the parties in a position of inequality before the Court.

3. When a state which is not a Member of the United Nations is a party to a case, the Court shall fix the amount which that party is to contribute towards the expenses of the Court. This provision shall not apply if such state is bearing a share of the expenses of the Court.

Article 36

1. The jurisdiction of the Court comprises all cases which the parties refer to it and all matters specially provided for in the Charter of the United Nations or in treaties and conventions in force.

2. The states parties to the present Statute may at any time declare that they recognize as compulsory ipso facto and without special agreement, in relation to any other state accepting the same obligation, the jurisdiction of the Court in all legal disputes concerning:

a. the interpretation of a treaty;
b. any question of international law;
c. the existence of any fact which, if established, would constitute a breach of an international obligation;
d. the nature or extent of the reparation to be made for the breach of an international obligation.

3. The declarations referred to above may be made unconditionally or on condition of reciprocity on the part of several or certain states, or for a certain time.

4. Such declarations shall be deposited with the Secretary-General of the United Nations, who shall transmit copies thereof to the parties to the Statute and to the Registrar of the Court.

5. Declarations made under Article 36 of the Statute of the Permanent Court of International Justice and which are still in force shall be deemed, as between the parties to the present Statute, to be acceptances of the compulsory jurisdiction of the International Court of Justice for the period which they still have to run and in accordance with their terms.

6. In the event of a dispute as to whether the Court has jurisdiction, the matter shall be settled by the decision of the Court.

Article 37

Whenever a treaty or convention in force provides for reference of a matter to a tribunal to have been instituted by the League of Nations, or to the Permanent Court of International Justice, the matter shall, as between the parties to the present Statute, be referred to the International Court of Justice.

Article 38

1. The Court, whose function is to decide in accordance with international law such disputes as are submitted to it, shall apply:
   a. international conventions, whether general or particular, establishing rules expressly recognized by the contesting states;
   b. international custom, as evidence of a general practice accepted as law;
   c. the general principles of law recognized by civilized nations;
   d. subject to the provisions of Article 59, judicial decisions and the teachings of the most highly qualified publicists of the various nations, as subsidiary means for the determination of rules of law.
2. This provision shall not prejudice the power of the Court to decide a case ex aequo et bono, if the parties agree thereto.

Chapter III
PROCEDURE

Article 39

1. The official languages of the Court shall be French and English. If the parties agree that the case shall be conducted in French, the judgment shall be delivered in French. If the parties agree that the case shall be conducted in English, the judgment shall be delivered in English.
2. In the absence of an agreement as to which language shall be employed, each party may, in the pleadings, use the language which it prefers; the decision of the Court shall be given in French and English. In this case the Court shall at the same time determine which of the two texts shall be considered as authoritative.
3. The Court shall, at the request of any party, authorize a language other than French or English to be used by that party.

Article 40

1. Cases are brought before the Court, as the case may be, either by the notification of the special agreement or by a written application addressed to the Registrar. In either case the subject of the dispute and the parties shall be indicated.
2. The Registrar shall forthwith communicate the application to all concerned.
3. He shall also notify the Members of the United Nations through the Secretary-General, and also any other states entitled to appear before the Court.

Article 41

1. The Court shall have the power to indicate, if it considers that circumstances so require, any provisional measures which ought to be taken top reserve the respective rights of either party.
2. Pending the final decision, notice of the measures suggested shall forthwith be given to the parties and to the Security Council.

Article 42

1. The parties shall be represented by agents.
2. They may have the assistance of counsel or advocates before the Court.
3. The agents, counsel, and advocates of parties before the Court shall enjoy the privileges and immunities necessary to the independent exercise of their duties.

Article 43

1. The procedure shall consist of two parts: written and oral.
2. The written proceedings shall consist of the communication to the Court and to the parties of memorials, counter memorials and, if necessary, replies; also all papers and documents in support.
3. These communications shall be made through the Registrar, in the order and within the time fixed by the Court.
4. A certified copy of every document produced by one party shall be communicated to the other party.
5. The oral proceedings shall consist of the hearing by the Court of witnesses, experts, agents, counsel, and advocates.

Article 44

1. For the service of all notices upon persons other than the agents, counsel, and advocates, the Court shall apply direct to the government of the state upon whose territory the notice has to be served.
2. The same provision shall apply whenever steps are to be taken to procure evidence on the spot.

Article 45

The hearing shall be under the control of the President or, if he is unable to preside, of the Vice-President; if neither is able to preside, the senior judge present shall preside.

Article 46

The hearing in Court shall be public, unless the Court shall decide otherwise, or unless the parties demand that the public be not admitted.

Article 47

1. Minutes shall be made at each hearing and signed by the Registrar and the President.
2. These minutes alone shall be authentic.

Article 48

The Court shall make orders for the conduct of the case, shall decide the form and time in which each party must conclude its arguments, and make all arrangements connected with the taking of evidence.

Article 49

The Court may, even before the hearing begins, call upon the agents to produce any document or to supply any explanations. Formal note shall be taken of any refusal.

Article 50

The Court may, at any time, entrust any individual, body, bureau, commission, or other organization that it may select, with the task of carrying out an enquiry or giving an expert opinion.

Article 51

During the hearing any relevant questions are to be put to the witnesses and experts under the conditions laid down by the Court in the rules of procedure referred to in Article 30.

Article 52

After the Court has received the proofs and evidence within the time specified for the purpose, it may refuse to accept any further oral or written evidence that one party may desire to present unless the other side consents.

Article 53

1. Whenever one of the parties does not appear before the Court, or fails to defend its case, the other party may call upon the Court to decide in favour of its claim.
2. The Court must, before doing so, satisfy itself, not only that it has jurisdiction in accordance with Articles 36 and 37, but also that the claim is well founded in fact and law.

Article 54

1. When, subject to the control of the Court, the agents, counsel, and advocates have completed their presentation of the case, the President shall declare the hearing closed.

2. The Court shall withdraw to consider the judgment.

3. The deliberations of the Court shall take place in private and remain secret.

Article 55

1. All questions shall be decided by a majority of the judges present.

2 In the event of an equality of votes, the President or the judge who acts in his place shall have a casting vote.

Article 56

1. The judgment shall state the reasons on which it is based.

2. It shall contain the names of the judges who have taken part in the decision.

Article 57

If the judgment does not represent in whole or in part the unanimous opinion of the judges, any judge shall be entitled to deliver a separate opinion.

Article 58

The judgment shall be signed by the President and by the Registrar. It shall be read in open court, due notice having been given to the agents.

Article 59

The decision of the Court has no binding force except between the parties and in respect of that particular case.

Article 60

The judgment is final and without appeal. In the event of dispute as to the meaning or scope of the judgment, the Court shall construe it upon the request of any party.

Article 61

1. An application for revision of a judgment may be made only when it is based upon the discovery of some fact of such a nature as to be a decisive factor, which fact was, when the judgment was given, unknown to the Court and also the party claiming revision, always provided that such ignorance was not due to negligence.

2. The proceedings for revision shall be opened by a judgment of the Court expressly recording the existence of the new fact, recognizing that it has such a character as to lay the case open to revision, and declaring the application admissible on this ground.

3. The Court may require previous compliance with the terms of the judgment before it admits proceedings in revision.

4. The application for revision must be made at latest within six months of the discovery of the new fact.

5. No application for revision may be made after the lapse of ten years from the date of the judgment.

Article 62

1. Should a state consider that it has an interest of a legal nature which may be affected by the decision in the case, it may submit a request to the Court to be permitted to intervene.

2. It shall be for the Court to decide upon this request.

Article 63

1. Whenever the construction of a convention to which states other than those concerned in the case are parties is in question, the Registrar shall notify all such states forthwith.

2. Every state so notified has the right to intervene in the proceedings; but if it uses this right, the construction given by the judgment will be equally binding upon it.

Article 64

Unless otherwise decided by the Court, each party shall bear its own costs.

Chapter IV
ADVISORY OPINIONS

Article 65

1. The Court may give an advisory opinion on any legal question at the request of whatever body may be authorized by or in accordance with the Charter of the United Nations to make such a request.

2. Questions upon which the advisory opinion of the Court is asked shall be laid before the Court by means of a written request containing an exact statement of the question upon which an opinion is required, and accompanied by all documents likely to throw light upon the question.

Article 66

1. The Registrar shall forthwith give notice of the request for an advisory opinion to all states entitled to appear before the Court.

2. The Registrar shall also, by means of a special and direct communication, notify any state entitled to appear before the Court or international organization considered by the Court, or, should it not be sitting, by the President, as likely to be able to furnish information on the question, that the Court will be prepared to receive, within a time limit to be fixed by the President, written statements, or to hear, at a public sitting to be held for the purpose, oral statements relating to the question.

3. Should any such state entitled to appear before the Court have failed to receive the special communication referred to in paragraph 2 of this Article, such state may express a desire to submit a written statement or to be heard; and the Court will decide.

4. States and organizations having presented written or oral statements or both shall be permitted to comment on the statements made by other states or organizations in the form, to the extent, and within the time limits which the Court, or, should it not be sitting, the President, shall decide in each particular case. Accordingly, the Registrar shall in due time communicate any such written statements to states and organizations having submitted similar statements.

Article 67

The Court shall deliver its advisory opinions in open court, notice having been given to the Secretary-General and to the representatives of Members of the United Nations, of other states and of international organizations immediately concerned.

Article 68

In the exercise of its advisory functions the Court shall further be guided by the provisions of the present Statute which apply in contentious cases to the extent to which it recognizes them to be applicable.

Chapter V
AMENDMENT

Article 69

Amendments to the present Statute shall be effected by the same procedure as is provided by the Charter of the United Nations for amendments to that Charter, subject however to any provisions which the General Assembly upon recommendation of the Security Council may adopt concerning the participation of states which are parties to the present Statute but are not Members of the United Nations.

Article 70

The Court shall have power to propose such amendments to the present Statute as it may deem necessary, through written communications to the Secretary-General, for consideration in conformity with the provisions of Article 69.

Appendix III

Structure of the United Nations

General Assembly

The General Assembly is composed of all the Members of the United Nations

SESSIONS

Resumed sixtieth session: 24 December 2005–11 September 2006.
Resumed tenth emergency special session: 17 November, 15 December 2006 (suspended).
Sixty-first session: 12 September–22 December 2006 (suspended).

OFFICERS

Resumed sixtieth and tenth emergency special sessions.
President: Jan Eliasson (Sweden).
*Vice-Presidents:*Angola, Armenia, Brazil, Central African Republic, China, France, Guinea-Bissau, India, Iran, Israel, Kenya, Malaysia, Mali, Myanmar, Pakistan, Paraguay, Russian Federation, Tunisia, United Kingdom, United States, Venezuela.

Sixty-first session
President: Sheikha Haya Rashed Al Khalifa (Bahrain).[1]
Vice-Presidents:[2] Bhutan, Cameroon, Chile, China, Colombia, Croatia, France, Guinea, Haiti, Indonesia, Kuwait, Libyan Arab Jamahiriya, Liechtenstein, Netherlands, Nigeria, Philippines, Russian Federation, Uganda, United Kingdom, United States, Zimbabwe.

The Assembly has four types of committees: (1) Main Committees; (2) procedural committees; (3) standing committees; (4) subsidiary and ad hoc bodies. In addition, it convenes conferences to deal with specific subjects.

Main Committees

Six Main Committees have been established as follows:

Disarmament and International Security Committee (First Committee)
Special Political and Decolonization Committee (Fourth Committee)
Economic and Financial Committee (Second Committee)
Social, Humanitarian and Cultural Committee (Third Committee)
Administrative and Budgetary Committee (Fifth Committee)
Legal Committee (Sixth Committee)

The General Assembly may constitute other committees, on which all Members of the United Nations have the right to be represented.

OFFICERS OF THE MAIN COMMITTEES

Resumed sixtieth session

Fourth Committee[3]

Chairman: Yashar Aliyev (Azerbaijan).
Vice-Chairpersons: Subhas Gujadhur (Mauritius), Amparo Anguiano Rodriguez (Mexico), Alexander Gerts (Netherlands).
Rapporteur: Muhammed Shahrul Nizzam Umar (Brunei Darussalam).

Fifth Committee[3]

Chairman: John W. Ashe.
Vice-Chairpersons: Dariusz Mańczyk (Poland), Muhammad A. Muhith (Bangladesh), Eric Franck Saizonou (Benin).
Rapporteur: Katja Pehrman (Finland).

Sixth Committee[3]

Chairman: Juan Antonio Yañez-Barnuevo (Spain).
Vice-Chairpersons: Mahmoud Hmoud (Jordan), Mahmoud Samy (Egypt), Grzegorz Zyman (Poland).
Rapporteur: Shermain Jeremy (Antigua and Barbuda).

Sixty-first session[4]

First Committee

Chairman: Mona Juul (Norway).
Vice-Chairmen: Andy Rachmianto (Indonesia), Boštjan Malovrh (Slovenia), Federico Perazza (Uruguay).
Rapporteur: Abdelhamid Gharbi (Tunisia).

Fourth Committee

Chairman: Madhu Raman Acharya (Nepal).
Vice-Chairmen: Mahieddine Djeffal (Algeria), Monica Bolanos-Perez (Guatemala), Urban Andersson (Sweden).
Rapporteur: Rana Salayeva (Azerbaijan).

Second Committee

Chairman: Tiina Intelmann (Estonia).
Vice-Chairpersons: Benedicto Fonseca Filho (Brazil), Prayono Atiyanto (Indonesia), Aboubacar Sadikh Barry (Senegal).
Rapporteur: Vanessa Gomes (Portugal).

Third Committee

Chairman: Hamid al Bayati (Iraq).
Vice-Chairmen: Jorge Ballesteros (Costa Rica), Lamin Faati (Gambia), Sergei A. Rachkov (Belarus).
Rapporteur: Elena Molaroni (San Marino).

Fifth Committee

Chairman: Youcef Yousfi (Algeria).
Vice-Chairmen: Ilgar Mammadov (Republic of Azerbaijan), Alexios Mitsopoulos (Greece), Tirtha Raj Wagle (Nepal).
Rapporteur: Diego Simancas (Mexico).

Sixth Committee

Chairman: Juan Manuel Gómez Robledo (Mexico).
Vice-Chairmen: Ganeson Sivagurunathan (Malaysia), Theodor Cosmin Onisii (Romania), Stefan Barriga (Liechtenstein).
Rapporteur: Mamadou Moustapha Loum (Senegal).

Procedural committees

General Committee

The General Committee consists of the President of the General Assembly, as Chairman, the 21 Vice-Presidents and the Chairmen of the six Main Committees.

Credentials Committee

The Credentials Committee consists of nine members appointed by the General Assembly on the proposal of the President.

Resumed sixtieth session

Cameroon, China, Panama, Portugal, Saint Lucia, Samoa, Sierra Leone, the Russian Federation and the United States.

Sixty-first session

China, Guyana, Kenya, Madagascar, Monaco, Peru, Russian Federation, Tonga and the United States.

Decision: GA 61/401

Standing committees

The two standing committees consist of experts appointed in their individual capacity for three-year terms.

Advisory Committee on Administrative and Budgetary Questions (ACABQ)

To serve until 31 December 2007: Jerry Kramer (Canada); Jorge Flores Callejas (Honduras); Jun Yamazaki (Japan); Ronald Elkhuizen (Netherlands); Rajat Saha (India); Sun Minqin (China).

To serve until 31 December 2008: Guillermo Kendall (Argentina); Igor V. Khalevinsky (Russian Federation); Susan M. McLurg (United States of America); Tommo Monthe (Cameroon); Christina Vasak France).

To serve until 31 December 2009: Andrzej T Abraszewski, *Chairman* (Poland); Collen V. Kelapile (Botswana); Stafford Neil (Jamaica); Mohammad Mustafa Tal (Jordan); Nonye Udo (Nigeria).

On 16 November 2006 (dec 61/405), the General Assembly appointed the following for a three-year term beginning on 1 January 2007 to fill the vacancies occurring on 31 December 2006: Andrzej T. Abraszewski (Poland); Collen V. Kelapile (Botswana); Stafford Neil (Jamaica); Mohammad Mustafa Tal (Jordan); Nonye Udo (Nigeria).

Committee on Contributions

To serve until 31 December 2007: Eduardo Manuel da Fonseca Fernandes Ramos (Portugal); Gordon Eckersley (Australia); Paul Ekorong Á. Dong (Cameroon); Bernardo Greiver (Uruguay); Hassan Mohammed Hassan (Nigeria); Eduardo Iglesias (Argentina)

To serve until 31 December 2008: Sujata Ghorai (Germany); Vyacheslav A. Logutov (Russian Federation); Richard Moon (United Kingdom of Great Britain and Northern Ireland); Hae-yun Park (Republic of Korea); Henrique da Silveira Sardinha Pinto (Brazil); Wu Gang (China)

To serve until 31 December 2009: Kenshiro Akimoto (Japan); Meshal Al-Mansour (Kuwait); Petru Dumitriu (Romania); Ihor V. Humenny (Ukraine); Gobona Susan Mapitse (Botswana); Lisa P. Spratt (United States)

On 16 March 2006 (dec. 60/411 B) the General Assembly appointed Gordon Eckersley for a 17-month term beginning on 16 March and ending on 31 December, as a result of the resignation of David Dutton.

On 16 November 2006 (dec. 61/406), the General Assembly appointed the following for a three-year term beginning on 1 January 2007 to fill the vacancies occurring on 31 December 2006: Kenshiro Akimoto (Japan), Meshal Al-Mansour (Kuwait), Petru Dumitriu (Romania), Ihor V Humenny (Ukraine), Gobona Susan Mapitse (Botswana), Lisa P Spratt (United States).

Subsidiary and ad hoc bodies

The following is a list of subsidiary and ad hoc bodies functioning in 2006, including the number of members, dates of meetings/sessions in 2006, document numbers of reports (which generally provide specific information on membership), and relevant decision numbers pertaining to elections.

Ad Hoc Committee on a Comprehensive and Integral International Convention on Protection and Promotion of the Rights and Dignity of Persons with Disabilities

Sessions: Seventh and eighth, New York, 16 January–3 February and 14-25 August

Chairman: Don MacKay (New Zealand)

Membership: Open to all Member States and observers of the United Nations

Reports: A/AC265/2006/2, A/AC265/2006/4, A/60/266

Ad Hoc Committee established by General Assembly resolution 51/210 of 17 December 1996

Session: Tenth, New York, 27 February–3 March

Chairman: Rohan Perera (Sri Lanka)

Membership: Open to all States Members of the United Nations or members of the specialized agencies or of IAEA

Report: A/61/37

Ad Hoc Committee on the Indian Ocean

Meeting: Did not meet in 2006

Membership: 43

Board of Auditors

Sessions: Special session, Manila, 6 December

Chairman: Guillermo N. Carague (Philippines)

Membership: 3

Committee on Conferences

Sessions: New York, 11 May (organizational), 11-15 September (substantive)

Chairman: Nonye Udo (Nigeria)

Membership: 21

Report: A/61/32

Decision: GA 61/412

Committee on the Exercise of the Inalienable Rights of the Palestinian People

Meetings: Throughout the year

Chairman: Paul Badji (Senegal)

Membership: 22

Report: A/61/35

Committee on Information

Session: Twenty-eighth, New York, 24 April–5 May

Chairman: Mihnea Ioan Motoc (Romania)

Membership: 110

Report: A/61/21

Decision: GA 61/413, 61/521

Committee on the Peaceful Uses of Outer Space

Session: Forty-ninth, Vienna, 7-16 June

Chairman: Gérard Brachet (France)

Membership: 67

Report: A/61/20

Committee for Programme and Coordination (CPC)

Session: Forty-sixth, New York, 21 June (organizational), 14 August–8 September (substantive)

Chairman: Norma Elaine Taylor Roberts (Jamaica)

Membership: 32

Report: A/61/16

Decisions: ESC 2006/201 A, B, C, D; GA 60/405 B, 61/410

Committee on Relations with the Host Country

Meetings: New York, 18 January, 17 May, 2 August, 29 September, 28 October

Chairman: Andreas D Mavroyiannis (Cyprus)

Membership: 19 (including the United States as host country)

Report: A/61/26

Committee for the United Nations Population Award

Meetings: New York, 7 March, 10-12 May
Chairman: Judith Mbula Bahemuka (Kenya)
Membership: 10 (plus 5 honorary members, the Secretary-General and the UNFPA Executive Director)
Report: A/61/273
Decision: ESC 2006/201 E

Disarmament Commission

Sessions: New York, 28 March (organizational), 10-28 April (substantive)
Chairman: Joon Oh (Republic of Korea)
Membership: All UN Members
Report: A/61/42

Human Rights Council

Sessions: Geneva, first, 19-30 June; second (18 September–6 October and 27-29 November; third (29 November–3 December; first special, 5-6 July; second, 11 August; third (15 November; fourth (12-13 December)
President: Luis Alfonso de Alba (Mexico)
Membership: 47
Report: A/61/53, A/62/53

International Civil Service Commission (ICSC)

Sessions: Sixty-second, Vienna, 13-31 March; sixty-third, New York, 10-28 July
Chairman: Mohsen Bel Hadj Amor (Tunisia)
Membership: 15
Report: A/61/30
Decision: 61/409

ADVISORY COMMITTEE ON POST ADJUSTMENT QUESTIONS

Session: Twenty-eighth, New York, 30 January–6 February
Chairman: Eugeniusz Wyzner (Poland)
Membership: 6

International Law Commission

Session: Fifty-eighth, Geneva, 1 May–9 June and 3 July–11 August
Chairman: Djamchid Momtaz (Iran)
Membership: 34
Report: A/61/10
Decision: GA 61/411

Investments Committee

Chairman: William J McDonough (United States)
Membership: 9
Decision: GA 61/407

Joint Advisory Group on the International Trade Centre UNCTAD/WTO

Session: Thirty-ninth, Geneva, 24-28 April
Chairman: Mary Whelan (Ireland)
Membership: Open to all States members of UNCTAD and all members of WTO
Report: ITC/AG(XXXIX)/206

Joint Inspection Unit (JIU)

Chairman: Deborah Wynes (United States)
Membership: 11
Report: A/62/34
Decision: GA 60/258

Office of the United Nations High Commissioner for Refugees (UNHCR)

EXECUTIVE COMMITTEE OF THE HIGH COMMISSIONER'S PROGRAMME

Session: Fifty-seventh, Geneva, 2-6 October
Chairman: Ichiro Fujisaki (Japan)
Membership: 70
Report: A/61/12/Add.1
Decision: ESC 2006/237 & 2006/201 B; GA 61/136

High Commissioner: Antônio Manuel de Oliveira Guterres

Panel of External Auditors

Session: Forty-seventh, Manila, 4 December
Chairman: Guillermo N. Caraque (Philippines)
Membership: Members of the UN Board of Auditors and the appointed external auditors of the specialized agencies and IAEA

Special Committee on the Charter of the United Nations and on the Strengthening of the Role of the Organization

Meetings: New York, 3-13 April
Chairman: Eduardo J. Sevilla Somoza (Nicaragua)
Membership: Open to all States Members of the United Nations
Report: A/61/33

Special Committee to Investigate Israeli Practices Affecting the Human Rights of the Palestinian People and Other Arabs of the Occupied Territories

Meetings: Geneva, 16-23 March, 31 July–2 August
Chairperson: Prasad Kariyawasam (Sri Lanka)
Membership: 3
Report: A/61/500

Special Committee on Peacekeeping Operations

Meetings: New York, 27 February–17 March,
Chairperson: Aminu Bashir Wali (Nigeria)
Membership: 124
Report: A/60/19

Special Committee on the Situation with regard to the Implementation of the Declaration on the Granting of Independence to Colonial Countries and Peoples

Session: New York, 23 February, 29 March and 27 April (first part); 5, 6, 7, 9, 12, 13, 15, 16, 22, 30 June (second part)
Chairman: Julian Robert Hunte (Saint Lucia)
Membership: 27
Report: A/61/23

United Nations Administrative Tribunal

Sessions: Geneva, 26 June–28 July; New York, 23 October–22 November
President: Spyridon Flogaitis (Greece)
Membership: 7
Report: A/INF/61/6
Decision: GA 61/408

United Nations Capital Development Fund (UNCDF)

EXECUTIVE BOARD

The UNDP/UNFPA Executive Board acts as the Executive Board of the Fund.

Sessions: 20-27 January, first regular session, New York; 11-15 September, second regular annual session, New York; 12-23 June, annual session, Geneva
President: Valeriy Kuchinsky (Ukraine)
Report: DP/2006/16

United Nations Commission on International Trade Law (UNCITRAL)

Session: Thirty-ninth, New York, 19 June–7 July
Chairman: Stephen Karangizi (Uganda)
Membership: 60
Report: A/61/17

United Nations Conciliation Commission for Palestine

Membership: 3
Report: A/61/172

United Nations Conference on Trade and Development (UNCTAD)

Session: Did not meet in 2006
Membership: Open to all States Members of the United Nations or members of the specialized agencies or of IAEA

Secretary-General of UNCTAD: Supachai Panitchpakdi (Thailand)

TRADE AND DEVELOPMENT BOARD

Sessions: Thirty-eighth executive, 20 April; thirty-ninth executive, 30 June; twenty-third special, 3-10 October; fifty-third, 27 September–2 October and 10 October; all in Geneva
President: Ransford A. Smith (Jamaica) (thirty-eighth and thirty-ninth executive sessions); Gyan Chandra Acharya (Nepal) (twenty-third special session); Mohamed Saleck Ould Mohamed Lemine (Mauritania) (fifty-third session)
Membership: Open to all States members of UNCTAD
Report: A/61/15

SUBSIDIARY ORGANS OF THE TRADE AND DEVELOPMENT BOARD

COMMISSION ON ENTERPRISE, BUSINESS FACILITATION AND DEVELOPMENT

Session: Tenth, Geneva, 21-24 February
Chairperson: Iouri Afanassiev (Russian Federation)
Membership: Open to all States members of UNCTAD
Report: TD/B/COM3/76

COMMISSION ON INVESTMENT, TECHNOLOGY AND RELATED FINANCIAL ISSUES

Session: Tenth, Geneva, 6-10 March
President: Ian De Jong (Netherlands)
Membership: Open to all States members of UNCTAD
Report: TD/B/COM2/71

Intergovernmental Group of Experts on Competition Law and Policy
Session: Seventh, Geneva, 31 October–2 November
President: Cecilia Escolan (El Salvador)
Membership: Open to all States members of UNCTAD
Report: TD/B/COM2/CLP/57

Intergovernmental Working Group of Experts on International Standards of Accounting and Reporting
Session: Twenty-third, Geneva, 10-12 October
Chairperson: Aziz Dieye (Senegal)
Membership: 34
Report: TD/B/COM.2/ISAR/32
Decisions: ESC 2006/201 C & E

COMMISSION ON TRADE IN GOODS AND SERVICES, AND COMMODITIES

Session: Tenth, Geneva, 6-10 February
Chairperson: Love Mtesa (Zambia)
Membership: Open to all States members of UNCTAD
Report: TD/B/COM.1/80

WORKING PARTY ON THE MEDIUM-TERM PLAN AND THE PROGRAMME BUDGET

Sessions: Forty-sixth, Geneva, 28-29 June 2006; forty-seventh, Geneva, 11-15 September
Chairperson: Carlos-Alberto Chocano (Peru) (forty-sixth session), Naïm Akibou (Benin) (forty-seventh session
Membership: Open to all States members of UNCTAD
Reports: TD/B/WP/191, TD/B/WP/186/Corr1, TD/B/WP/187, TD/B/WP/188

United Nations Development Fund for Women (UNIFEM)

CONSULTATIVE COMMITTEE

Session: Forty-sixth, New York, 14-15 February
Chairperson: Prince Zeid Ra'ad Zeid Al-Hussein
Membership: 6
Report: A/62/188
Decision: GA 61/414

Executive Director of UNIFEM: Noeleen Heyzer

United Nations Environment Programme (UNEP)

GOVERNING COUNCIL

Session: Ninth special, Dubai, United Arab Emirates,
President: Rachmat Witoelar (Indonesia)
Membership: 58
Report: A/61/25

Executive Director of UNEP: Achim Steiner[5]

United Nations Human Settlements Programme (UN-Habitat)

GOVERNING COUNCIL

Session: Did not meet in 2006
Membership: 58 (ESC dec. 2006/201 C & E)

Executive Director of UN-Habitat: Anna Kajumulo Tibaijuka[6]

United Nations Institute for Disarmament Research (UNIDIR)

BOARD OF TRUSTEES

Sessions: Forty-sixth, New York, 8-10 February; forty-seventh, Geneva, 21-23 June
Chairman: Joy Ogwu (Nigeria)
Membership: 19, plus 1 ex-officio member (Director of UNIDIR)
Report: A/61/180

Director of UNIDIR: Patricia Lewis

United Nations Institute for Training and Research (UNITAR)

BOARD OF TRUSTEES

Session: Forty-fourth, Geneva, 25-27 April
Chairman: Omar Hilale (Morocco)
Membership: 21, plus 4 ex-officio members
Report: A/61/14

Executive Director of UNITAR: Marcel A. Boisard

United Nations Joint Staff Pension Board

Session: Fifty-third, Nairobi, 13-21 July
Chairman: Vladimir Yossifov (Russia)
Membership: 33
Report: A/61/9

Executive Director: Bernard Cochemé

United Nations Relief and Works Agency for Palestine Refugees in the Near East (UNRWA)

ADVISORY COMMISSION OF UNRWA

Meeting: Amman, Jordan, 27-28 September
Chairperson: Frans Makken (Netherlands)
Membership: 24
Report: A/61/13
Decision: GA 61/114

WORKING GROUP ON THE FINANCING OF UNRWA

Meetings: New York, 1, 12-13 September
Chairman: Baki Ilkin (Turkey)
Membership: 9
Report: A/61/347

Commissioner-General of UNRWA: Karen Koning AbuZayd
Deputy Commissioner-General: Filippo Grandi

United Nations Scientific Committee on the Effects of Atomic Radiation

Session: Fifty-fourth, Vienna, 29 May–2 June
Chairman: Peter Burns (Australia)
Membership: 21
Report: A/61/46
Decision: GA 61/109

United Nations University (UNU)

COUNCIL OF THE UNITED NATIONS UNIVERSITY

Session: Fifty-third, Tokyo, Japan, 6-10 November
Chairperson: Peter H Katjavivi (Namibia)
Membership: 24 (plus 3 ex-officio members and the UNU Rector)

Rector of the University: Hans J. A. van Ginkel

United Nations Voluntary Fund for Indigenous Populations

BOARD OF TRUSTEES

Session: Nineteenth, Geneva, 13-17 February
Chairperson: Nadir Bekirov (Ukraine)
Membership: 5
Reports: E/CN.4/Sub.2/AC.4/2006/5, A/61/376

United Nations Voluntary Fund for Victims of Torture

BOARD OF TRUSTEES

Session: Twenty-fifth, Geneva, 5-11 April
Chairman: Krassimir Kanev (Bulgaria)
Membership: 5
Report: A/61/226

United Nations Voluntary Trust Fund on Contemporary Forms of Slavery

BOARD OF TRUSTEES

Session: Eleventh, Geneva, 30 January–3 February
Chairperson: Cheikh Saad-Bouh Kamara (Mauritania)
Membership: 5
Report: E/CN.4/2006/76

Security Council

The Security Council consists of 15 Member States of the United Nations, in accordance with the provisions of Article 23 of the United Nations Charter as amended in 1965.

MEMBERS

Permanent members: China, France, Russian Federation, United Kingdom, United States

Non-permanent members: Argentina, Congo, Denmark, Ghana, Greece, Japan, Peru, Qatar, Slovakia, United Republic of Tanzania

On 16 October and 7 November 2006 (dec. 61/402), the General Assembly elected Belgium, Indonesia, Italy, Panama and South Africa for a two-year term beginning on 1 January 2007, to replace Argentina, Denmark, Greece, Japan and the United Republic of Tanzania whose terms of office were to expire on 31 December 2006.

PRESIDENT

The presidency of the Council rotates monthly, according to the English alphabetical listing of its Member States. The following served as President during 2006:

Month	*Member*	*Representative*
January	Argentina	César Mayoral
February	China	Wang Guangya
March	Congo	Basile Ikouebe
April	Denmark	Ellen Margrethe Løj
May	France	Jean-Marc de La Sablière
June	Ghana	Nana Effah-Apenteng
July	Greece	Adamantios Vassilakis
August	Japan	Kenzo Oshima
September	Peru	Jorge Voto-Bernales
October	Qatar	Nassir Abdulaziz Al-Nasser
November	United Republic of Tanzania	Augustine P. Mahiga
December	United States	John Bolton

Military Staff Committee

The Military Staff Committee consists of the chiefs of staff of the permanent members of the Security Council or their representatives. It meets fortnightly.

Standing committees

Each of the three standing committees of the Security Council is composed of representatives of all Council members:

Committee of Experts (to examine the provisional rules of procedure of the Council and any other matters entrusted to it by the Council)
Committee on the Admission of New Members
Committee on Council Meetings Away from Headquarters

Subsidiary bodies

Counter-Terrorism Committee (CTC)

Session: Did not meet in 2006
Chairman: Ellen Margrethe Løj (Denmark)
Membership: 15

United Nations Compensation Commission

GOVERNING COUNCIL

Sessions: Geneva, fifty-ninth, 7-9 March; sixtieth, 27- 29 June; sixty-first, 31 October–3 November
Chairman: Tassos Kriekoukis (Greece)
Membership: 15

United Nations Monitoring, Verification and Inspection Commission (UNMOVIC)

Acting Executive Chairman: Dimitri Perricos (Greece)
Reports: S/2006/133, S/2006/342, S/2006/701, S/2006/912

1540 Committee

Chairman: Peter Burian (Slovakia)
Membership: 129
Report: S/2006/257

Peacebuilding Commission

ORGANIZATIONAL COMMITTEE

Sessions: 23 June, 13 July, 9 October, 7 December, 12 December
Chairman: Ismael Gaspar Martins (Angola)
Membership: 31
Report: A/62/137
Decision: 60/417; ESC dec, 2006/201 E

Sanctions Committee

Chairman: César Mayoral (Argentina)
Reports: S/2006/154, S/2006/750

International Criminal Tribunal for the former Yugoslavia (ICTY)

President: Judge Fausto Pocar (Italy)

International Criminal Tribunal for Rwanda (ICTR)

President: Judge Erik Møse (Norway)

Peacekeeping operations

United Nations Truce Supervision Organization (UNTSO)

Chief of Staff: Brigadier-General Clive William Lilley

United Nations Military Observer Group in India and Pakistan (UNMOGIP)

Chief Military Observer: Major-General Dragutin Repinc

United Nations Peacekeeping Force in Cyprus (UNFICYP)

Special Representative of the Secretary-General and Head of Mission: Michael Møller
Force Commander: Major-General Rafael Barni

United Nations Disengagement Observer Force (UNDOF)

Force Commander: Major-General Bala Nanda Sharma

United Nations Interim Force in Lebanon (UNIFIL)

Personal Representative of the Secretary-General for Southern Lebanon: Geir O Pedersen
Force Commander: Major-General Alain Pellegrini

United Nations Mission for the Referendum in Western Sahara (MINURSO)

Special Representative of the Secretary-General and Head of Mission: Francesco Bastagli
Force Commander: Brigadier-General Kurt Mosgaard

United Nations Observer Mission in Georgia (UNOMIG)

Special Representative of the Secretary-General and Head of Mission: Heidi Tagliavini (until 31 July), Jean Arnault (from 1 August)
Deputy Special Representative of the Secretary-General : Ivo Petrov
Chief Military Observer: Major-General Niaz Muhammad Khan Khattak

United Nations Interim Administration Mission in Kosovo (UNMIK)

Special Representative of the Secretary-General and Head of Mission: Søren Jessen-Petersen (until July), Joachim Rücker (from September)
Principal Deputy Special Representative: Steven Schook
Deputy Special Representative for Reconstruction: Paul Acda
Deputy Special Representative for Institutional Building: Werner Wnendt

United Nations Integrated Office in Sierra Leone (UNIOSIL)

Executive Representative for the United Nations Integrated Office in Sierra Leone : Victor da Silva Ângelo
Force Commander: Major-General Sajjad Akram

United Nations Organization Mission in the Democratic Republic of the Congo (MONUC)

Special Representative of the Secretary-General and Chief of Mission: William Lacy Swing
Deputy Special Representative: Haile Menkerios
Force Commander: Lieutenant-General Babacar Gaye

United Nations Mission in Ethiopia and Eritrea (UNMEE)

Special Representative of the Secretary-General: Azouz Ennifar
Deputy Special Representative: Lebohang K. Moleko
Force Commander: Major-General Mohammed Taisir Masadeh

United Nations Integrated Mission in Timor-Leste (UNMIT)[8]

Special Representative of the Secretary-General and Head of Mission: Sukehiro Hasegawa (until September), Atul Khare (from November)
Deputy Special Representative for Governance Support, Development and Humanitarian Coordination: Finn Reske-Nielsen
Deputy Special Representative for Security Sector Support and Rule of Law: Eric Tan Huck Gim
Police Commissioner: Rodolfo Asel Tor

United Nations Mission in Liberia (UNMIL)

Special Representative of the Secretary-General and Head of Mission: Alan Claude Doss
Deputy Special Representative: Luiz Carlos da Costa
Force Commander: Lieutenant-General Joseph Olorungbon Owonibi

United Nations Operation in Côte d'Ivoire (UNOCI)

Special Representative of the Secretary-General and Head of Mission: Pierre Schori
Principal Deputy Special Representative: Abou Moussa
Force Commander: Major-General Abdoulaye Fall (until April), Major-General Fernand Marcel Amoussou (from 12 September)

United Nations Operation in Burundi (ONUB)[9]

Special Representative of the Secretary-General and Chief of Mission (Acting): Nureldin Satti
Deputy Special Representative: Youssef Mahmoud
Force Commander: Major-General Derrick Mbuyiselo Mgwebi

United Nations Stabilization Mission in Haiti (MINUSTAH)

Special Representative of the Secretary-General and Head of Mission: Edmond Mulet
Principal Deputy Special Representatives: Lawrence G. Rossin (until October), Luiz Carlos da Costa (from 10 November)
Force Commander: Lieutenant-General José Elito Siqueira Carvalho

United Nations Mission in the Sudan (UNMIS)

Special Representative of the Secretary-General and Head of Mission: Jan Pronk
Deputy Special Representative: Taye-Brook Zerihoun
Force Commander: Major-General Fazle Elahi Akbar

Political, peacebuilding and other missions

United Nations Political Office for Somalia (UNPOS)

Representative of the Secretary-General and Head of UNPOS: François Lonseny Fall

Office of the Special Representative of the Secretary-General for the Great Lakes Region

Special Representative: Ibrahima Fall

United Nations Peace-building Support Office in Guinea-Bissau (UNOGBIS)

Representative of the Secretary-General and Head of UNOGBIS: Shola Omoregie

Office of the United Nations Special Coordinator for the Middle East (UNSCO)

Special Coordinator for the Middle East Peace Process and Personal Representative of the Secretary-General to the Palestine Liberation Organization and the Palestinian Authority: Alvaro de Soto

United Nations Peace-building Office in the Central African Republic (BONUCA)

Representative of the Secretary-General and Head of BONUCA: General Lamine Cissé

United Nations Tajikistan Office of Peace-building (UNTOP)

Representative of the Secretary-General: Vladimir Sotirov

Office of the Special Representative of the Secretary-General for West Africa (UNOWA)

Special Representative of the Secretary-General: Ahmedou Ould-Abdallah

United Nations Assistance Mission in Afghanistan (UNAMA)

Special Representative of the Secretary-General and Head of UNAMA: Tom Koenigs

United Nations Assistance Mission for Iraq (UNAMI)

Special Representative of the Secretary-General for Iraq: Ashraf Jehangir Qazi

United Nations Office in Timor-Leste (UNOTIL) [10]

Special Representative of the Secretary-General and Head of Mission: Sukehiro Hasegawa

Economic and Social Council

The Economic and Social Council consists of 54 Member States of the United Nations, elected by the General Assembly, each for a three-year term, in accordance with the provisions of Article 61 of the United Nations Charter as amended in 1965 and 1973.

MEMBERS

To serve until 31 December 2006: Armenia, Bangladesh, Belgium, Belize, Canada, Colombia, Indonesia, Italy, Mauritius, Namibia, Nigeria, Panama, Poland, Republic of Korea, Spain, Tunisia, Turkey, United Arab Emirates, United Republic of Tanzania, United States.

To serve until 31 December 2007: Albania, Australia, Brazil, Chad, China, Costa Rica, Democratic Republic of the Congo, Denmark, Guinea, Iceland, India, Lithuania, Mexico, Pakistan, Russian Federation, South Africa, Thailand, United Kingdom.

To serve until 31 December 2008: Angola, Austria, Benin, Cuba, Czech Republic, France, Germany, Guinea-Bissau, Guyana, Haiti, Japan, Madagascar, Mauritania, Paraguay, Saudi Arabia, Sri Lanka.

On 2 November 2006 (dec. 61/404), the General Assembly elected the following for a three-year term beginning on 1 January 2007 to fill the vacancies occurring on 31 December 2006: Armenia, Bangladesh, Belgium, Belize, Canada, Colombia, Indonesia, Italy, Mauritius, Namibia, Nigeria, Panama, Poland, the Republic of Korea, Tunisia, United Arab Emirates, United Republic of Tanzania, United States.

SESSIONS

Organizational session for 2006: New York, 17 January, 7 and 10 February, 14 and 22 March and 8 May.

Resumed organizational session for 2006: New York, 10 and 12 May

Special high-level meeting with the Bretton Woods institutions, the World Trade Organization and UNCTAD: New York, 24 April.

Substantive session of 2006: Geneva, 3-28 July.

Resumed organizational session for 2006: New York, 11 October, 30 November and 11 and 15 December.

OFFICERS

President: Ali Hachani (Tunisia).

Vice-Presidents: Leo Mérorès (Haiti), Hjálmar W. Hannesson (Iceland), Gediminas Šerkšnys (Lithuania), Prasad Kariyawasam (Sri Lanka).

Subsidiary and other related organs

SUBSIDIARY ORGANS

The Economic and Social Council may, at each session, set up committees or working groups, of the whole or of limited membership, and refer to them any item on the agenda for study and report.

Other subsidiary organs reporting to the Council consist of functional commissions, regional commissions, standing committees, expert bodies and ad hoc bodies.

The inter-agency United Nations System Chief Executives Board for Coordination also reports to the Council.

Functional commissions

Commission on Crime Prevention and Criminal Justice

Session: Fifteenth, New York, 27 May 2005 and 24-28 April
Chairman: Gabriele de Ceglie (Italy)
Membership: 40
Report: E/2006/30
Decision: ESC 2006/201 B

Commission on Human Rights

Session: Sixty-second and final, Geneva, 13-27 March
Chairperson: Manuel Rodríguez-Cuadros (Peru)
Membership: 53
Report: E/2006/23

SUBCOMMISSION ON THE PROMOTION AND PROTECTION OF HUMAN RIGHTS

Session: Fifty-eighth, Geneva, 7-25 August
Chairperson: Marc Bossuyt (Belgium)
Membership: 26
Report: A/HRC/2/2

Commission on Narcotic Drugs

Session: Forty-ninth, 8 December 2005 and 13-17 March
Chairperson: Györgyi Martin Zanathy (Hungary)
Membership: 48
Report: E/2006/28
Decision: ESC 2006/201 A, B & E

Commission on Population and Development

Session: Thirty-ninth, New York, 14 April 2005, 3-7 April and 10 May
Chairman: Crispin Grey-Johnson (Gambia)
Membership: 45
Report: E/2006/25
Decision: ESC 2006/201 B and E

Commission on Science and Technology for Development

Session: Ninth, Geneva, 15-19 May
Chairman: Pedro Sebastião Teta (Angola)
Membership: 33
Report: E/2006/31
Decision: ESC 2006/201 A, B & E

Commission for Social Development

Session: Forty-fourth, New York, 18 February 2005, 8-17 February and 22 March
Chairperson: Ernesto Araníbar Quiroga (Bolivia)
Membership: 46
Report: E/2006/26
Decision: ESC 2006/201 B & C

Commission on the Status of Women

Session: Fiftieth, 22 March 2005, 27 February–10 March and 16 March 2006
Chairperson: Carmen María Gallardo (El Salvador)
Membership: 45

Report: E/2006/27
Decision: ESC 2006/201 B

Commission on Sustainable Development

Session: Fourteenth, New York, 22 April 2005 and 1-12 May
Chairperson: Aleksi Aleksishvili (Georgia)
Membership: 53
Report: E/2006/29
Decision: ESC 2006/201 B & C

Statistical Commission

Session: Thirty-seventh, New York, 7-10 March
Chairman: Gilberto Calvillo Vives (Mexico)
Membership: 24
Report: E/2006/24

United Nations Forum on Forests

Session: Sixth, New York, 27 May 2005, 13-24 February
Chairman: Judith Mbula Bahemuka (Kenya)
Membership: Open to all States Members of the United Nations and members of the specialized agencies
Report: E/2006/42

Regional commissions

Economic Commission for Africa (ECA)

Session: Thirty-ninth session of the Commission/Conference of African Ministers of Finance, Planning and Economic Development, Ouagadougou, Burkina Faso, 10-15 May
Chairman: Ngozi Okonjo-Iweala (Nigeria)
Membership: 53
Decision: ESC 2006/205 C

Economic Commission for Europe (ECE)

Session: Sixty-first, Geneva, 21-23 February
Chairman: François Roux (Belgium)
Membership: 55
Report: E/2006/37

Economic Commission for Latin America and the Caribbean (ECLAC)

Session: Thirty-first, Montevideo, Uruguay, 20-24 March
Chairperson: Uruguay
Membership: 40 members, 2 associate members
Report: LC/G2318

Economic and Social Commission for Asia and the Pacific (ESCAP)

Session: Sixty-second, Jakarta, Indonesia, 6-12 April
Chairperson: N. Hassan Wirajuda (Indonesia)
Membership: 49 members, 3 associate members
Report: E/2006/39, E/ESCAP/1390

Economic and Social Commission for Western Asia (ESCWA)

Session: Twenty-fourth, Beirut, Lebanon, 8-11 May
Chairman: Ahmad Ibrahim Hikmi (Saudi Arabia)
Membership: 14
Report: E/2006/41

Standing committees

Committee on Non-Governmental Organizations

Session: New York, 19-27 January
Chairperson: Beatriz Patti Londoño (Colombia)
Membership: 19
Report: E/2006/32 (Part I)
Decision: ESC 2006/201 B

Committee for Programme and Coordination (CPC)

Sessions: Forty-sixth, New York, 21 June (organizational), 14 August–6 September (substantive)
Chairman: Norma Elaine Taylor Roberts (Jamaica)
Membership: 33
Report: A/61/16
Decisions: ESC 2006/201 A, B, C, D; GA 60/405 B, 61/410

Expert bodies

Committee of Experts on International Cooperation in Tax Matters

Session: Second, Geneva, 30 October–3 November
Chairman: Noureddine Bensouda (Morocco)
Membership: 22
Report: E/2006/45
Decision: ESC 2006/201 B & E

Committee for Development Policy

Session: Eighth, New York, 20-24 March
Chairperson: Suchitra Punyaratabandhu (Thailand)
Membership: 22
Report: E/2006/33
Decision: ESC 2006/201 B & D

Committee on Economic, Social and Cultural Rights

Sessions: Thirty-sixth and thirty-seventh, Geneva, 1-19 May; 6-24 November
Chairperson: Virginia Bonoan-Dandan (Philippines)
Membership: 18
Report: E/2006/22
Decision: ESC 2006/201 B, D & E

Committee of Experts on Public Administration

Session: Fifth, New York, 27-31 March
Chairperson: Jocelyne Bourgon (Canada)
Membership: 24
Report: E/2006/44
Decision: ESC 2006/203

Committee of Experts on the Transport of Dangerous Goods and on the Globally Harmonized System of Classification and Labelling of Chemicals

Session: Third, Geneva, 14 December
Chairperson: S Benassai (Italy)
Membership: 20
Reports: E/2007/53, ST/SG/AC.10/34

International Narcotics Control Board

Sessions: Vienna, eighty-fifth, 30 January–3 February; eighty-sixth, 8-19 May; eighty-seventh, 30 October–16 November
Membership: 13 (ESC dec. 2006/201 B)

Permanent Forum on Indigenous Issues

Session: Fifth, New York, 15-26 May
Chairperson: Victoria Tauli-Corpuz (Philippines)
Membership: 16
Report: E/2006/43

United Nations Group of Experts on Geographical Names

Session: Twenty-third, Vienna, Austria, 28 March–4 April
Chairperson: Helen Kerfoot (Canada)
Membership: Representatives of the 22 geographical/linguistic divisions of the Group of Experts
Report: E/2006/57

Ad hoc body

United Nations System Chief Executives Board for Coordination

Sessions: Madrid, first regular session, 7 April; New York, second regular session, 27 October
Chairman: The Secretary-General
Membership: Organizations of the UN system
Reports: CEB/2006/1, CEB/2006/2

Other related bodies

International Research and Training Institute for the Advancement of Women (INSTRAW)

EXECUTIVE BOARD

Session: Third, New York, 18 May
President: Juan Antonio Yáñez-Barnuevo (Spain)
Membership: 10 plus 5 ex-officio members
Report: E/2006/80, INSTRAW/EB/2006/R2
Decision: ESC 2006/201 B, C & E

Director of INSTRAW: Carmen Moreno

Joint United Nations Programme on Human Immunodeficiency Virus/Acquired Immunodeficiency Syndrome (UNAIDS)

PROGRAMME COORDINATING BOARD

Meetings: Eighteenth, Geneva, 27-28 June; nineteenth, Lusaka, 6-8 December
Chair: Gunilla Carlsson (Sweden)
Membership: 22
Reports: UNAIDS/PCB(18)/0618, UNAIDS/PCB(19)/0619
Decisions: ESC 2006/201 A & B

Executive Director of UNAIDS: Peter Piot

United Nations Children's Fund (UNICEF)

EXECUTIVE BOARD

Sessions: New York, first regular, 16-20 and 23 January; second regular, 6-8 September; annual, 5-9 June
President: Andrei Dapkiunas (Belarus)
Membership: 36
Report: E/2006/34/Rev1
Decision: ESC 2006/201 B

Executive Director of UNICEF: Ann M. Veneman

United Nations Development Programme (UNDP)/ United Nations Population Fund (UNFPA)

EXECUTIVE BOARD

Sessions: First and second regular, New York, 20-27 January, 11-15 September; annual, Geneva, 12-23 June
President: Valery P. Kuchinsky (Ukraine)
Membership: 36
Report: E/2006/35
Decision: ESC 2006/201 B & E

Administrator of UNDP: Kemal Dervis
Associate Administrator: Ad Melkert
Executive Director of UNFPA: Thoraya Ahmed Obaid

United Nations Research Institute for Social Development (UNRISD)

BOARD

Session: Forty-fourth, Geneva, 3-4 April
Chairperson: Lourdes Arizpe (Mexico)
Membership: 11

Director of UNRISD: Thandika Mkandawire

United Nations Interregional Crime and Justice Research Institute (UNICRI)

Session: Fifth, New York, 15-26 May
Board of Trustees
Membership: 4 ex-officio, 7 elected (ESC dec. 2006/240)
Director of UNICRI: Sandro Calvani (Italy)

World Food Programme (WFP)

EXECUTIVE BOARD

Sessions: First regular, 20-23 February; annual, 12-16 June; second regular, 6-9 November (all in Rome)
President: Mirza Qamar Beg (Pakistan)
Membership: 36
Report: E/2007/36
Decisions: ESC 2006/201 B

Executive Director of WFP: James T. Morris

Trusteeship Council

The Trusteeship Council suspended operation on 1 November 1994, with the indepndence of Palau, the last remaining trust territory. The General Assembly, in resolution 60/1 of 16 September 2005, considering that the Council no longer met, and had no remaining functions, decided to delete Chapter XIII of the UN Charter and references to the Council in Chapter XII.

International Court of Justice

Judges of the Court

The International Court of Justice consists of 15 Judges elected for nine-year terms by the General Assembly and the Security Council

The following were the Judges of the Court serving in 2006, listed in the order of precedence:

Judge	*Country of nationality*	*End of term*
Rosalyn Higgins, *President*	United Kingdom	2009
Awn Shawkat Al-Khasawneh, *Vice-President*	Jordan	2009
Raymond Ranjeva	Madagascar	2009
Shi Jiuyong	China	2012
Abdul G. Koroma	Sierra Leone	2012
Gonzalo Parra-Aranguren	Venezuela	2009
Thomas Buergenthal	United States	2006
Hisashi Owada	Japan	2012
Bruno Simma	Germany	2012
Peter Tomka	Slovakia	2012
Ronny Abraham	France	2009
Kenneth Keith	New Zealand	2009
Bernardo Sepúlveda Amor	Mexico	2012
Mohamed Bennouna	Morocco	2009
Leonid Skotnikov	Russian Federation	2009

Registrar: Philippe Couvreur
Deputy Registrar: Jean-Jacques Arnaldez

Chamber of Summary Procedure

Members: Rosalyn Higgins (ex officio), Awn Shawkat Al-Khasawneh (ex officio), Gonzalo Parra-Aranguren, Thomas Buergenthal, Leonid Skotnikov

Substitute members: Abdul G Koroma, Ronny Abraham

Parties to the Court's Statute

All Members of the United Nations are ipso facto parties to the Statute of the International Court of Justice.

States accepting the compulsory jurisdiction of the Court

Declarations made by the following States, a number with reservations, accepting the Court's compulsory jurisdiction (or made under the Statute of the Permanent Court of International Justice and deemed to be an acceptance of the jurisdiction of the International Court) were in force at the end of 2006:

Australia, Austria, Barbados, Belgium, Botswana, Bulgaria, Cambodia, Cameroon, Canada, Dominica, Costa Rica, Côte d'Ivoire, Cyprus, Democratic Republic of the Congo, Denmark, Djibouti, Dominican Republic, Egypt, Estonia, Finland, Gambia, Georgia, Greece, Guinea, Guinea-Bissau, Haiti, Honduras, Hungary, India, Japan, Kenya, Lesotho, Liberia, Liechtenstein, Luxembourg, Madagascar, Malawi, Malta, Mauritius, Mexico, Nauru, Netherlands, New Zealand, Nicaragua, Nigeria, Norway, Pakistan, Panama, Paraguay, Peru, Philippines, Poland, Portugal, Senegal, Serbia and Montenegro, Slovakia, Somalia, Spain, Sudan, Suriname, Swaziland, Sweden, Switzerland, Togo, Uganda, United Kingdom, Uruguay.

United Nations organs and specialized and related agencies authorized to request advisory opinions from the Court

Authorized by the United Nations Charter to request opinions on any legal question: General Assembly, Security Council

Authorized by the General Assembly in accordance with the Charter to request opinions on legal questions arising within the scope of their activities: Economic and Social Council, Trusteeship Council, Interim Committee of the General Assembly, ILO, FAO, UNESCO, ICAO, WHO, World Bank, IFC, IDA, IMF, ITU, WMO, IMO, WIPO, IFAD, UNIDO, IAEA

Committees of the Court

BUDGETARY AND ADMINISTRATIVE COMMITTEE

Members: Rosalyn Higgins (ex officio), Awn Shawkat Al-Khasawneh (ex officio), Raymond Ranjeva, Thomas Buergenthal, Hisashi Owada, Peter Tomka

LIBRARY COMMITTEE

Members: Thomas Buergenthal (Chair), Bruno Simma, Peter Tomka, Kenneth Keith, Mohamed Bennouna

RULES COMMITTEE

Members: Hisashi Owada (Chair), Bruno Simma, Ronny Abraham, Kenneth Keith, Bernardo Sepúlveda Amor, Mohamed Bennouna

Report: A/61/4

Other United Nations-related bodies

The following bodies are not subsidiary to any principal organ of the United Nations but were established by an international treaty instrument or arrangement sponsored by the United Nations and are thus related to the Organization and its work. These bodies, often referred to as "treaty organs", are serviced by the United Nations Secretariat and may be financed in part or wholly from the Organization's regular budget, as authorized by the General Assembly, to which most of them report annually.

Committee on the Elimination of Discrimination against Women (CEDAW)

Sessions: Thirty-fourth, thirty-fifth, thirty-sixth, New York, 16 January–3 February; 15 May–2 June; 7-25 August

Chairperson: Rosario Manalo (Philippines)

Membership: 23

Report: A/61/38

Committee on the Elimination of Racial Discrimination (CERD)

Sessions: Sixty-eighth and sixty-ninth, Geneva, 20 February–10 March and 31 July–8 August

Chairperson: Régis de Gouttes (France)

Membership: 18

Report: A/61/18

Committee on the Protection of the Rights of All Migrant Workers and Members of Their Families

Sessions: Third and fourth, Geneva, 12-16 December and 24-28 April

Chairperson: Prasad Kariyawasam (Sri Lanka)

Membership: 10

Report: A/61/48

Committee on the Rights of the Child

Sessions: Forty-first, Geneva, 9-27 January; forty-second, Geneva, 15 May (Chamber A) and 24 May (Chamber B)

Chairpersons: Jakob Egbert Doek (Netherlands) (Chamber A) and Moushira Khattab (Egypt) (Chamber B)

Membership: 10

Reports: CRC/C/SR.1121, CRC/C/SR.1145

Committee against Torture

Sessions: Thirty-fifth and thirty-sixth, Geneva, 14-25 November 2005 and 1-19 May

Chairperson: Andreas Mavrommatis (Cyprus)

Membership: 10

Reports: A/61/44

Conference on Disarmament

Meetings: Geneva, 23 January–31 March, 15 May–30 June, 31 July–15 September

President: Poland, Republic of Korea, Romania, Russian Federation, Senegal and Slovakia (successively)

Membership: 65

Report: A/61/27

Human Rights Committee

Sessions: eighty-sixth and eighty-seventh, New York, 13-31 March and 10-28 July

Chairperson: Christine Chanet (France)

Membership: 18

Reports: A/61/40 (Vol I)

International Narcotics Control Board (INCB)

Sessions: eighty-fifth, eighty-sixth and eighty-seventh, New York, 30 January–3 February, 8-19 May, 30 October–16 November

President: Philip Onagewele Emafo (Nigeria)

Membership: 13

Report: E/INCB/2006/1

Principal members of the United Nations Secretariat

(as at 31 December 2006)

Secretariat

The Secretary-General: Kofi A. Annan
Deputy Secretary-General: Mark Malloch Brown

Executive Office of the Secretary-General

Under-Secretary-General, Chef de Cabinet: Alicia Bárcena Ibarra (from June)
Under-Secretary-General, Special Adviser to the Secretary-General: Vijay Nambiar
Assistant Secretary-General, Deputy Chef de Cabinet: Alicia Bárcena Ibarra (until June)
Assistant Secretary-General for Policy Planning: Robert Orr

Office of Internal Oversight Services

Under-Secretary-General: Inga-Britt Ahlenius

Office of Legal Affairs

Under-Secretary-General, Legal Counsel: Nicolas Michel
Assistant Secretary-General: Ralph Zacklin (until April 30); Larry D Johnson (from 1 May)

Department of Political Affairs

Under-Secretary-General: Ibrahim Gambari
Assistant Secretary-General, Executive Director, Counter-Terrorism Committee: Javier Rupérez
Assistant Secretary-General: Angela Kane

Department for Disarmament Affairs

Under-Secretary-General: Nobuyasu Abe

Department of Peacekeeping Operations

Under-Secretary-General: Jean-Marie Guéhenno
Assistant Secretaries-General: Hédi Annabi, Jane Holl Lute

Office for the Coordination of Humanitarian Affairs

Under-Secretary-General for Humanitarian Affairs, Emergency Relief Coordinator: Jan Egeland
Assistant Secretary-General, Deputy Emergency Relief Coordinator: Eva Margareta Wahlstrom

Department of Economic and Social Affairs

Under-Secretary-General: José Antonio Ocampo
Assistant Secretary-General, Special Adviser on Gender Issues and Advancement of Women: Rachel Mayanja
Assistant Secretary-General: Patrizio M Civili

Department for General Assembly and Conference Management

Under-Secretary-General: Jian Chen
Assistant Secretary-General: Yohannes Mengesha

Department of Public Information

Under-Secretary-General for Communications and Public Information: Shashi Tharoor

Department of Management

Under-Secretary-General: Christopher Bancroft Burnham

OFFICE OF PROGRAMME PLANNING, BUDGET AND ACCOUNTS
Assistant Secretary-General, Controller: Warren Sach

OFFICE OF HUMAN RESOURCES MANAGEMENT
Assistant Secretary-General: Jan Beagle

OFFICE OF CENTRAL SUPPORT SERVICES
Assistant Secretary-General: Andrew Toh

CAPITAL MASTER PLAN PROJECT
Assistant Secretary-General, Executive Director: Louis Frederick Reuter IV

Office of the United Nations Ombudsman

Assistant Secretary-General, Ombudsman: Patricia M. Durrant

Economic Commission for Africa

Under-Secretary-General, Executive Secretary: Abdoulie Janneh

Economic Commission for Europe

Under-Secretary-General, Executive Secretary: Marek Belka

Economic Commission for Latin America and the Caribbean

Under-Secretary-General, Executive Secretary: José Luis Machinea

Economic and Social Commission for Asia and the Pacific

Under-Secretary-General, Executive Secretary: Kim Hak-Su

Economic and Social Commission for Western Asia

Under-Secretary-General, Executive Secretary: Mervat Tallawy

United Nations Office at Geneva

Under-Secretary-General, Director-General of the United Nations Office at Geneva: Sergei Ordzhonikidze

Office of the United Nations High Commissioner for Human Rights

Under-Secretary-General, High Commissioner: Louise Arbour
Assistant Secretary-General, Deputy High Commissioner: Mehr Khan Williams

United Nations Office at Vienna

Under-Secretary-General, Director-General of the United Nations Office at Vienna and Executive Director of the United Nations Office on Drugs and Crime: Antonio Maria Costa

International Court of Justice Registry

Assistant Secretary-General, Registrar: Philippe Couvreur

Secretariats of subsidiary organs, special representatives and other related bodies

International Trade Centre UNCTAD/WTO

Executive Director: J. Denis Bélisle

Office of the High Representative for the Least Developed Countries, Landlocked Developing Countries and Small Island Developing States

Under-Secretary-General, High Representative: Anwarul Karim Chowdhury

Office of the Special Adviser to the Secretary-General on Africa

Under-Secretary-General, Special Adviser: Legwaila Joseph Legwaila

Office of the Special Adviser to the Secretary-General for Special Assignments in Africa

Under-Secretary-General, Special Adviser: Ibrahim Gambari

Office of the Special Envoy of the Secretary-General for Myanmar

Under-Secretary-General, Special Envoy: Razali Ismail

Office of the Special Representative of the Secretary-General for Children and Armed Conflict

Under-Secretary-General, Special Representative: Radhika Coomaraswamy

Office of the Special Representative of the Secretary-General for the Great Lakes Region

Assistant Secretary-General, Special Representative: Ibrahima Fall

Office of the Special Representative of the Secretary-General for West Africa

Under-Secretary-General, Special Representative: Ahmedou Ould-Abdallah

Office of the United Nations High Commissioner for Refugees

Under-Secretary-General, High Commissioner: António Manuel de Oliveira Guterres

Office of the United Nations Special Coordinator for the Middle East

Under-Secretary-General, Special Coordinator for the Middle East Peace Process and Personal Representative of the Secretary-General to the Palestine Liberation Organization and the Palestinian Authority: Alvaro de Soto

Special Adviser to the Secretary-General on Latin American Issues

Under-Secretary-General, Special Adviser: Diego Cordovez

Special Envoy of the Secretary-General for the Commonwealth of Independent States

Under-Secretary-General, Special Envoy: vacant

Special Envoy of the Secretary-General for the Humanitarian Crisis in the Horn of Africa

Under-Secretary-General, Special Envoy: Kjell Magne Bondevik

Special Representative of the Secretary-General for the Sudan

Under-Secretary-General, Special Representative: Johannes Pronk

Assistant Secretary-General, Principal Deputy Special Representtive: Tayé-Brook Zerihoun

United Nations Assistance Mission in Afghanistan

Under-Secretary-General, Special Representative of the Secretary-General: Tom Koenigs

United Nations Assistance Mission for Iraq

Under-Secretary-General, Special Representative of the Secretary-General for Iraq: Ashraf Jehangir Qazi

United Nations Children's Fund

Under-Secretary-General, Executive Director: Ann M. Veneman

Assistant Secretaries-General, Deputy Executive Directors: Kul C Gautam, Rima Salah

United Nations Compensation Commission

Assistant Secretary-General, Executive Secretary: Tassos Kriekoukis

United Nations Conference on Trade and Development

Assistant Secretary-General, Officer-in-Charge: Supachai Panitchpakdi

United Nations Development Programme

Administrator: Kemal Dervis

Under-Secretary-General, Associate Administrator: Ad Melkert

Assistant Administrator and Director, Bureau for Crisis Prevention and Recovery: Kathleen Cravero

Assistant Administrator and Director, Bureau of Management: Akiko Yuge

Assistant Administrator and Director, Bureau for Development Policy: Shoji Nishimoto

Assistant Administrator and Regional Director, UNDP Africa: Gilbert Fossoun Houngbo

Assistant Administrator and Regional Director, UNDP Arab States: Amat Al Aleem Ali Alsoswa

Assistant Administrator and Regional Director, UNDP Asia and the Pacific: Hafiz A. Pasha

Assistant Administrator and Regional Director, UNDP Europe and the Commonwealth of Independent States: Kalman Mizsei

Assistant Administrator and Regional Director, UNDP Latin America and the Caribbean: Rebeca Grynspan

United Nations Disengagement Observer Force

Assistant Secretary-General, Force Commander: Major-General Bala Nanda Sharma

United Nations Environment Programme

Under-Secretary-General, Executive Director: Klaus Töpfer (until March); Achim Steiner (from June)

Assistant Secretary-General, Deputy Executive Director: Shafqat S. Kakakhel

Assistant Secretary-General, Executive Secretary: Yvo de Boer

United Nations Human Settlements Programme (UN-Habitat)

Under-Secretary-General, Executive Director: Anna Kajumulo Tibaijuka

United Nations Institute for Training and Research

Assistant Secretary-General, Executive Director: Marcel A. Boisard

United Nations Interim Administration Mission in Kosovo

Under-Secretary-General, Special Representative of the Secretary-General and Head of Mission: Søren Jessen-Petersen

Assistant Secretary-General, Principal Deputy Special Representative: Steven Schook

Assistant Secretary-General, Deputy Special Representative: Werner Wnendt (from April)

United Nations Interim Force in Lebanon

Assistant Secretary-General, Personal Representative of the Secretary-General for Southern Lebanon: Geir O. Pedersen

Assistant Secretary-General, Force Commander: Major-General Alain Pellegrini

United Nations Joint Staff Pension Fund

Assistant Secretary-General, Chief Executive Officer: Bernard G. Cochemé

United Nations Military Observer Group in India and Pakistan

Chief Military Observer: Major-General Guido Palmieri, Major-General Dragutin Repinc

United Nations Mission in Ethiopia and Eritrea

Under-Secretary-General, Special Representative of the Secretary-General: Azouz Ennifar

Assistant Secretary-General, Deputy Special Representative: Lebohang K. Moleko

Force Commander: Major-General Taisir Masadeh

United Nations Mission in Liberia

Under-Secretary-General, Special Representative of the Secretary-General and Head of Mission: Alan Claude Doss

Assistant Secretary-General, Deputy Special Representative: Luiz Carlos da Costa

Assistant Secretary-General, Force Commander: Lieutenant-General Joseph Olorungbon Owonibi

United Nations Mission for the Referendum in Western Sahara

Under-Secretary-General, Special Representative of the Secretary-General and Chief of Mission: Francesco Bastagli

Force Commander: Brigadier-General Kurt Mosgaard

United Nations Integrated Office in Sierra Leone

Under-Secretary-General, Special Representative of the Secretary-General and Chief of Mission: Victor da Silva Ângelo

Assistant Secretary-General, Force Commander: Major-General Sajjad Akram

United Nations Integrated Mission in Timor-Leste (UNMIT)

Special Representative of the Secretary-General and Head of Mission: Sukehiro Hasegawa (until September), Atul Khare (from November)
Deputy Special Representative for Governance Support, Development and Humanitarian Coordination: Finn Reske-Nielsen
Deputy Special Representative for Security Sector Support and Rule of Law: Eric Tan Huck Gim
Police Commissioner: Rodolfo Asel Tor

United Nations Monitoring, Verification and Inspection Commission

Assistant Secretary-General, Acting Executive Chairman: Demetrius Perricos

United Nations Observer Mission in Georgia (UNOMIG)

Special Representative of the Secretary-General and Head of Mission: Heidi Tagliavini (until 31 July), Jean Arnault (from 1 August)
Deputy Special Representative of the Secretary-General: Ivo Petrov
Chief Military Observer: Major-General Niaz Muhammad Khan Khattak

United Nations Office for Project Services

Assistant Secretary-General, Executive Director: Jan Mattsson

United Nations Operation in Burundi (ONUB)

Special Representative of the Secretary-General and Chief of Mission (Acting): Nureldin Satti
Deputy Special Representative: Youssef Mahmoud
Force Commander: Major-General Derrick Mbuyiselo Mgwebi

United Nations Operation in Côte d'Ivoire (UNOCI)

Special Representative of the Secretary-General and Head of Mission: Pierre Schori
Principal Deputy Special Representative: Abou Moussa
Force Commander: Major-General Abdoulaye Fall (until April), Major-General Fernand Marcel Amoussou (from 12 September)

United Nations Organization Mission in the Democratic Republic of the Congo (MONUC)

Special Representative of the Secretary-General and Chief of Mission: William Lacy Swing
Deputy Special Representative: Haile Menkerios
Force Commander: Lieutenant-General Babacar Gaye

United Nations Peace-building Office in the Central African Republic

Representative of the Secretary-General and Head of Office: General Lamine Cissé

United Nations Peace-building Support Office in Guinea-Bissau

Representative of the Secretary-General and Head of Office: Shola Omoregie

United Nations Peacekeeping Force in Cyprus (UNFICYP)

Special Representative of the Secretary-General and Head of Mission: Michael Møller
Force Commander: Major-General Rafael José Barni

United Nations Political Office for Somalia

Representative of the Secretary-General and Head of Office: François Lonseny Fall

United Nations Population Fund

Under-Secretary-General, Executive Director: Thoraya Ahmed Obaid

United Nations Relief and Works Agency for Palestine Refugees in the Near East

Under-Secretary-General, Commissioner-General: Karen Koning AbuZayd
Assistant Secretary-General, Deputy Commissioner-General: Filippo Grandi

United Nations Stabilization Mission in Haiti

Under-Secretary-General, Special Representative of the Secretary-General: Edmond Mulet
Assistant Secretary-General, Principal Deputy Special Representative: Lawrence G. Rossin (until October), Luiz Carlos da Costa (from 10 November)
Assistant Secretary-General, Deputy Special Representatives: Adama Guindo (until November), Joel Boutroue (from December)
Force Commander: Lieutenant-General José Elito Siqueira Carvalho

United Nations Tajikistan Office of Peacebuilding

Assistant Secretary-General, Representative of the Secretary-General: Vladimir Sotirov

United Nations Truce Supervision Organization

Assistant Secretary-General, Chief of Staff: Brigadier-General Clive William Lilley

United Nations University

Under-Secretary-General, Rector: Hans J. A. van Ginkel
Director, World Institute for Development Economics Research: Anthony F. Shorrocks

On 31 December 2006, the total number of staff of the United Nations Secretariat with continuous service or expected service of a year or more was 30,548. Of these, 7,573 were in the Professional and higher categories, 1,163 were experts (200-series Project Personnel staff) and 17,562 were in the General Service and related categories.

[1] Elected on 8 June 2006 (dec. 60/418).
[2] Elected on 8 June 2006 (dec. 60/420).
[3] The Main Committees that met during the resumed session.
[4] Chairmen elected by the Committees; announced by the Assembly President on 8 June (dec. 60/419 A, B)
[5] Elected by the General Assembly on 16 March for a period of four years from 15 June 2006 and ending on 14 June 2010 (dec. 60/409 B).
[6] Elected by the General Assembly for a period of five years from 1 September 2006 and ending on 31 August 2010 (dec. 60/421).
[7] Established on 1 January 2006.
[8] Established in August 2006.
[9] Mission completed on 31 December 2006.
[10] Mission completed in 2006.

Appendix IV

Agendas of United Nations principal organs in 2006

This appendix lists the items on the agendas of the General Assembly, the Security Council and the Economic and Social Council during 2006. For the Assembly, the column headed "Allocation" indicates the assignment of each item to plenary meetings or committees.

Agenda item titles have been shortened by omitting mention of reports, if any, following the subject of the item. Where the subject matter of an item is not apparent from its title, the subject is identified in square brackets; this is not part of the title.

General Assembly

Agenda items remaining for consideration at the resumed sixtieth session 6 February–11 September 2006

Item No.	*Title*	*Allocation*
2.	Minute of silent prayer or meditation.	Plenary
4.	Election of the President of the General Assembly.	Plenary
6.	Election of the Vice-Presidents of the General Assembly.	Plenary
7.	Organization work, adoption of the agenda and allocation of items.	Plenary
10.	Support by the United Nations system of the efforts of Governments to promote and consolidate new or restored democracies.	Plenary
12.	Prevention of armed conflict.	Plenary
19.	Question of Cyprus.	Plenary
20.	Armed aggression against the Democratic Republic of the Congo.	Plenary
21.	Question of the Falkland Islands (Malvinas).	Plenary
22.	The situation of democracy and human rights in Haiti.	Plenary
23.	Armed Israeli aggression against the Iraqi nuclear installations and its grave consequences for the established international system concerning the peaceful uses of nuclear energy, the non-proliferation of nuclear weapons and international peace and security.	Plenary
24.	Consequences of the Iraqi occupation of and aggression against Kuwait.	Plenary
25.	Declaration of the Assembly of Heads of State and Government of the Organization of African Unity on the aerial and naval military attack against the Socialist People's Libyan Arab Jamahiriya by the present United States administration in April 1986.	Plenary
32.	Comprehensive review of the whole question of peacekeeping operations in all their aspects.	4th
40.	The situation in the occupied territories of Azerbaijan.	Plenary
45.	Follow-up to the outcome of the twenty-sixth special session: implementation of the Declaration of Commitment on HIV/AIDS.	Plenary
46.	Integrated and coordinated implementation of and follow-up to the outcomes of the major United Nations conferences and summits in the economic, social and related fields.	Plenary
48.	Sport for peace and development:	
	(*a*) Building a peaceful and better world through sport and the Olympic ideal:	
	Solemn appeal made by the President of the General Assembly in connection with the observance of the Olympic Truce.	Plenary
49.	Information and communication technologies for development.	Plenary
71.	Human rights questions	
	(*b*) Human rights questions, including alternative approaches for improving the effective enjoyment of human rights and fundamental freedoms.	Plenary
73.	Strengthening of the coordination of humanitarian and disaster relief assistance of the United Nations, including special economic assistance:	
	(*c*) Strengthening of international cooperation and coordination of efforts to study, mitigate and minimize the consequences of the Chernobyl disaster: special commemorative meeting in observance of the twentieth anniversary of the Chernobyl catastrophe.	Plenary
112.	Elections to fill vacancies in subsidiary organs and other elections:	
	(*a*) Election of twenty members of the Committee for Programme and Coordination;	Plenary

Item No.	*Title*	*Allocation*
	(c) Election of the Executive Director of the United Nations Environment Programme;	Plenary
	(d) Election of the Executive Director of the United Nations Human Settlement Programme;	Plenary
	(f) Election of seven members of the Organizational Committee of the Peacebuilding Commission:	Plenary
113.	Appointments to fill vacancies in subsidiary organs and other appointments:	
	(b) Appointment of members of the Committee on Contributions.	Plenary
114.	Admission of new Members to the United Nations.	Plenary
116.	Revitalization of the work of the General Assembly.	Plenary, 1st, 2nd, 3rd, 4th, 5th, 6th
117.	Question of equitable representation on and increase in the membership of the Security Council and related matters.	Plenary
118.	United Nations reform: measures and proposals.	5th
119.	Strengthening of the United Nations system.	Plenary
120.	Follow-up to the outcome of the Millennium Summit.	Plenary
121.	Financial reports and audited financial statements, and reports of the Board of Auditors.	5th
122.	Review of the efficiency of the administrative and financial functioning of the United Nations.	5th
124.	Proposed programme budget for biennium 2006-2007.	5th
125.	Programme planning.	5th
126.	Improving the financial situation of the United Nations.	5th
127.	Pattern of conferences.	5th
128.	Scale of assessments for the apportionment of the expenses of the United Nations.	5th
129.	Human resources management.	5th
130.	Joint Inspection Unit.	5th
131.	United Nations common system.	5th
132.	Report of the Secretary-General on the activities of the Office of Internal Oversight Services.	5th
135.	Financing of the International Tribunal for the Prosecution of Persons Responsible for Serious Violations of International Humanitarian Law Committed in the Territory of the Former Yugoslavia since 1991.	5th
136.	Administrative and budgetary aspects of the financing of the United Nations peacekeeping operations.	5th
137.	Financing of the United Nations Operation in Burundi.	5th
138.	Financing of the United Nations Operation in Cote d'Ivoire.	5th
139.	Financing of the United Nations Peacekeeping Force in Cyprus.	5th
140.	Financing of the United Nations Organization Mission in the Democratic Republic of the Congo.	5th
141.	Financing of the United Nations Mission in East Timor.	5th
142.	Financing of the United Nations Mission of Support in East Timor.	5th
143.	Financing of the United Nations Mission in Ethiopia and Eritrea.	5th
144.	Financing of the United Nations Observer Mission in Georgia.	5th
145.	Financing of the United Nations Stabilization Mission in Haiti.	5th
146.	Financing of the activities arising from Security Council resolution 687 (1991):	
	(a) United Nations Iraq-Kuwait Observation Mission.	5th
147.	Financing of the United Nations Interim Administration Mission in Kosovo.	5th
148.	Financing of the United Nations Mission in Liberia.	5th
149.	Financing of the United Nations peacekeeping forces in the Middle East:	
	(a) United Nations Disengagement Observer Force;	5th
	(b) United Nations Interim Force in Lebanon.	5th
150.	Financing of the United Nations Mission in Sierra Leone.	5th
151.	Financing of the United Nations Mission in the Sudan.	5th
152.	Financing of the United Nations Mission for the Referendum in Western Sahara.	5th
154.	Cooperation between the United Nations and the Organization for Security and Cooperation in Europe.	Plenary
157.	Election of judges of the International Tribunal for the Prosecution of Persons Responsible for Serious Violations of International Humanitarian Law Committed in the Territory of the Former Yugoslavia since 1991.	Plenary
160.	Follow-up to the recommendations on administrative and internal oversight of the Independent Inquiry Committee into the United Nations Oil-for-Food Programme.	Plenary
161.	Extension of the term of the permanent judges of the International Criminal Tribunal for the Prosecution of Persons Responsible for Genocide and other Serious Violations of International Humanitarian Law Committed in the Territory of Rwanda and Rwandan Citizens Responsible for Genocide and Other Such Violations Committed in the Territory of Neighbouring States between 1 January and 31 December 1994.	Plenary

Agenda of the sixty-first session first part, 12 September-22 December 2006

A. Maintenance of international peace and security

Item No.	*Title*	*Allocation*
9.	Report of the Security Council.	Plenary
10.	The role of diamonds in fuelling conflict.	Plenary
11.	Prevention of armed conflict.	Plenary
12.	The situation in Central America: progress in fashioning a region of peace, freedom, democracy and development.	Plenary
13.	The situation in the Middle East.	Plenary
14.	Question of Palestine.	Plenary
15.	Zone of peace and cooperation of the South Atlantic.	Plenary
16.	The situation in Afghanistan.	Plenary
17.	The situation in the occupied territories of Azerbaijan.	Plenary
18.	Necessity of ending the economic, commercial and financial embargo imposed by the United States of America against Cuba	Plenary
19.	Question of Cyprus.	Plenary
20.	Armed aggression against the Democratic Republic of the Congo.	Plenary
21.	Question of the Falkland Islands (Malvinas).	Plenary
22.	The situation of democracy and human rights in Haiti.	Plenary
23.	Armed Israeli aggression against the Iraqi nuclear installations and its grave consequences for the established international system concerning the peaceful uses of nuclear energy, the non-proliferation of nuclear weapons and international peace and security.	Plenary
24.	Consequences of the Iraqi occupation of and aggression against Kuwait.	Plenary
25.	Declaration of the Assembly of Heads of State and Government of the Organization of African Unity on the aerial and naval military attack against the Socialist People's Libyan Arab Jamahiriya by the present United States Administration in April 1986.	Plenary
26.	Report of the Peacebuilding Commission.	Plenary
27.	Protracted conflicts in the GUAM area and their implications for international peace, security and development.	Plenary
28.	University for Peace.	4th
29.	Effects of atomic radiation.	4th
30.	International cooperation in the peaceful uses of outer space.	4th
31.	United Nations Relief and Works Agency for Palestine Refugees in the Near East.	4th
32.	Report of the Special Committee to Investigate Israeli Practices Affecting the Human Rights of the Palestinian People and Other Arabs of the Occupied Territories.	4th
33.	Comprehensive review of the whole question of peacekeeping operations in all their aspects.	4th
34.	Questions relating to information.	4th
35.	Information from Non-Self-Governing Territories transmitted under Article 73 e of the Charter of the United Nations.	4th
36.	Economic and other activities which affect the interests of the peoples of the Non-Self-Governing Territories.	4th
37.	Implementation of the Declaration on the Granting of Independence to Colonial Countries and Peoples by the specialized agencies and the international institutions associated with the United Nations.	4th
38.	Offers by Member States of study and training facilities for inhabitants of Non-Self-Governing Territories.	4th
39.	Implementation of the Declaration on the Granting of Independence to Colonial Countries and Peoples.	4th
40.	Permanent sovereignty of the Palestinian people in the Occupied Palestinian Territory, including East Jerusalem, and of the Arab population in the occupied Syrian Golan over their natural resources.	2nd
41.	Report of the United Nations High Commissioner for Refugees, questions relating to refugees, returnees and displaced persons and humanitarian questions.	3rd

B. Promotion of sustained economic growth and sustainable development in accordance with the relevant resolutions of the General Assembly and recent United Nations conferences

42.	Report of the Economic and Social Council.	Plenary
43.	Return or restitution of cultural property to the countries of origin.	Plenary
44.	Culture of peace.	Plenary

Item No.	Title	Allocation
45.	The role of the United Nations in promoting a new global human order.	Plenary
46.	Follow-up to the outcome of the twenty-sixth special session: implementation of the Declaration of Commitment on HIV/AIDS.	Plenary
47.	Integrated and coordinated implementation of and follow-up to the outcomes of the major United Nations conferences and summits in the economic, social and related fields.	Plenary
48.	2001-2010: Decade to Roll Back Malaria in Developing Countries, Particularly in Africa.	Plenary
49.	Sport for peace and development.	Plenary
50.	Information and communication technologies for development.	Plenary, 2nd
51.	Macroeconomic policy questions:	
	(a) International trade and development;	2nd
	(b) International financial system and development;	2nd
	(c) External debt crisis and development;	2nd
	(d) Commodities.	2nd
52.	Follow-up to and implementation of the outcome of the International Conference on Financing for Development.	Plenary, 2nd
53.	Sustainable development:	
	(a) Implementation of Agenda 21, the Programme for the Further Implementation of Agenda 21 and the outcomes of the World Summit on Sustainable Development;	2nd
	(b) Follow-up to and implementation of the Mauritius Strategy for the Further Implementation of the Programme of Action for the Sustainable Development of Small Island Developing States;	2nd
	(c) International Strategy for Disaster Reduction;	2nd
	(d) Protection of global climate for present and future generations of mankind;	2nd
	(e) Implementation of the United Nations Convention to Combat Desertification in Those Countries Experiencing Serious Drought and/or Desertification, Particularly in Africa;	2nd
	(f) Convention on Biological Diversity;	2nd
	(g) Report of the Governing Council of the United Nations Environment Programme on its ninth special session.	2nd
54.	Implementation of the outcome of the United Nations Conference on Human Settlements (Habitat II) and strengthening of the United Nations Human Settlements Programme (UN-Habitat).	2nd
55.	Globalization and interdependence:	
	(a) Globalization and interdependence;	2nd
	(b) International migration and development;	2nd
	(c) Culture and development;	2nd
	(d) Preventing and combating corrupt practices and transfer of assets of illicit origin and returning such assets, in particular to the countries of origin, consistent with the United Nations Convention against Corruption;	2nd
	(e) Integration of the economies in transition into the world economy.	2nd
56.	Groups of countries in special situations:	
	(a) Third United Nations Conference on the Least Developed Countries;	2nd
	(b) Specific actions related to the particular needs and problems of landlocked developing countries: outcome of the International Ministerial Conference of Landlocked and Transit Developing Countries and Donor Countries and International Financial and Development Institutions on Transit Transport Cooperation.	2nd
57.	Eradication of poverty and other development issues:	
	(a) Implementation of the first United Nations Decade for the Eradication of Poverty 1997-2006;	2nd
	(b) Industrial development cooperation.	2nd
58.	Operational activities for development: operational activities for development of the United Nations system.	2nd
59.	Training and research:	
	(a) United Nations University;	2nd
	(b) United Nations Institute for Training and Research.	2nd
60.	Social development:	
	(a) Implementation of the outcome of the World Summit for Social Development and of the twenty-fourth special session of the General Assembly;	3rd
	(b) Social development, including questions relating to the world social situation and to youth, ageing, disabled persons and the family;	3rd
	(c) United Nations Literacy Decade: education for all;	3rd
	(d) Follow-up to the International Year of Older Persons: Second World Assembly on Ageing.	3rd

Item No.	Title	Allocation
61.	Advancement of women:	
	(a) Advancement of women;	3rd
	(b) Implementation of the outcome of the Fourth World Conference on Women and of the twenty-third special session of the General Assembly.	3rd
C.	**Development of Africa**	
62.	New Partnership for Africa's Development: progress in implementation and international support:	
	(a) New Partnership for Africa's Development: progress in implementation and international support;	Plenary
	(b) Causes of conflict and the promotion of durable peace and sustainable development in Africa.	Plenary
D.	**Promotion of human rights**	
63.	Promotion and protection of the rights of children:	
	(a) Promotion and protection of the rights of children;	3rd
	(b) Follow-up to the outcome of the special session on children.	3rd
64.	Indigenous issues:	
	(a) Indigenous issues;	3rd
	(b) Second International Decade of the World's Indigenous People.	3rd
65.	Elimination of racism and racial discrimination:	
	(a) Elimination of racism and racial discrimination;	3rd
	(b) Comprehensive implementation of and follow-up to the Durban Declaration and Programme of Action.	3rd
66.	Right of peoples to self-determination.	3rd
67.	Promotion and protection of human rights:	
	(a) Implementation of human rights instruments;	3rd
	(b) Human rights questions, including alternative approaches for improving the effective enjoyment of human rights and fundamental freedoms;	3rd
	(c) Human rights situations and reports of special rapporteurs and representatives;	3rd
	(d) Comprehensive implementation of and follow-up to the Vienna Declaration and Programme of Action.	3rd
68.	Report of the Human Rights Council.	3rd
E.	**Effective coordination of humanitarian assistance efforts**	
69.	Strengthening of the coordination of humanitarian and disaster relief assistance of the United Nations, including special economic assistance:	
	(a) Strengthening of the coordination of emergency humanitarian assistance of the United Nations;	Plenary
	(b) Special economic assistance to individual countries or regions;	2nd
	(c) Participation of volunteers, "White Helmets", in the activities of the United Nations in the field of humanitarian relief, rehabilitation and technical cooperation for development;	2nd
	(d) Assistance to the Palestinian people.	Plenary
F.	**Promotion of justice and international law**	
70.	Report of the International Court of Justice.	Plenary
71.	Oceans and the law of the sea:	
	(a) Oceans and the law of the sea;	Plenary
	(b) Sustainable fisheries, including through the 1995 Agreement for the Implementation of the Provisions of the United Nations Convention on the Law of the Sea of 10 December 1982 relating to the Conservation and Management of Straddling Fish Stocks and Highly Migratory Fish Stocks, and related instruments.	Plenary
72.	Report of the International Criminal Tribunal for the Prosecution of Persons Responsible for Genocide and Other Serious Violations of International Humanitarian Law Committed in the Territory of Rwanda and Rwandan Citizens Responsible for Genocide and Other Such Violations Committed in the Territory of Neighbouring States between 1 January and 31 December 1994.	Plenary
73.	Report of the International Tribunal for the Prosecution of Persons Responsible for Serious Violations of International Humanitarian Law Committed in the Territory of the Former Yugoslavia since 1991.	Plenary
74.	Report of the International Criminal Court.	Plenary
75.	Status of the Protocols Additional to the Geneva Conventions of 1949 and relating to the protection of victims of armed conflicts.	6th

Item No.	*Title*	*Allocation*
76.	Consideration of effective measures to enhance the protection, security and safety of diplomatic and consular missions and representatives.	6th
77.	Report of the United Nations Commission on International Trade Law on the work of its thirty-ninth session.	6th
78.	Report of the International Law Commission on the work of its fifty-eighth session.	6th
79.	Report of the Special Committee on the Charter of the United Nations and on the Strengthening of the Role of the Organization.	6th
80.	The rule of law at the national and international levels.	1st

G. Disarmament

81.	Report of the International Atomic Energy Agency.	Plenary
82.	Reduction of military budgets.	1st
83.	Maintenance of international security — good-neighbourliness, stability and development in South-Eastern Europe.	1st
84.	Verification in all its aspects, including the role of the United Nations in the field of verification.	1st
85.	Developments in the field of information and telecommunications in the context of international security.	1st
86.	Role of science and technology in the context of international security and disarmament.	st
87.	Establishment of a nuclear-weapon-free zone in the region of the Middle East.	1st
88.	Conclusion of effective international arrangements to assure non-nuclear-weapon States against the use or threat of use of nuclear weapons.	1st
89.	Prevention of an arms race in outer space.	1st
90.	General and complete disarmament:	
	(a) Notification of nuclear tests;	1st
	(b) Missiles;	1st
	(c) Measures to uphold the authority of the 1925 Geneva Protocol;	1st
	(d) Mongolia's international security and nuclear-weapon-free status;	1st
	(e) Consolidation of peace through practical disarmament measures;	1st
	(f) Disarmament and non-proliferation education;	1st
	(g) Towards a nuclear-weapon-free world: accelerating the implementation of nuclear disarmament commitments;	1st
	(h) Nuclear-weapon-free southern hemisphere and adjacent areas;	1st
	(i) Promotion of multilateralism in the area of disarmament and non-proliferation;	1st
	(j) Observance of environmental norms in the drafting and implementation of agreements on disarmament and arms control;	1st
	(k) Relationship between disarmament and development;	1st
	(l) The Hague Code of Conduct against Ballistic Missile Proliferation;	1st
	(m) Regional disarmament;	1st
	(n) Confidence-building measures in the regional and subregional context;	1st
	(o) Transparency and confidence-building measures in outer space activities;	1st
	(p) Implementation of the Convention on the Prohibition of the Development, Production, Stockpiling and Use of Chemical Weapons and on Their Destruction;	1st
	(q) Nuclear disarmament;	1st
	(r) Assistance to States for curbing the illicit traffic in small arms and light weapons and collecting them;	1st
	(s) Problems arising from the accumulation of conventional ammunition stockpiles in surplus;	1st
	(t) Conventional arms control at the regional and subregional levels;	1st
	(u) Follow-up to the advisory opinion of the International Court of Justice on the Legality of the Threat or Use of Nuclear Weapons;	1st
	(v) Measures to prevent terrorists from acquiring weapons of mass destruction;	1st
	(w) Reducing nuclear danger;	1st
	(x) Implementation of the Convention on the Prohibition of the Use, Stockpiling, Production and Transfer of Anti-personnel Mines and on Their Destruction;	1st
	(y) The illicit trade in small arms and light weapons in all its aspects;	1st
	(z) Information on confidence-building measures in the field of conventional arms;	1st
	(aa) Transparency in armaments;	1st
	(bb) Establishment of a nuclear-weapon-free zone in Central Asia;	1st
	(cc) United Nations conference to identify ways of eliminating nuclear dangers in the context of nuclear disarmament;	1st
	(dd) Convening of the fourth special session of the General Assembly devoted to disarmament.	1st

Item No.		*Title*	*Allocation*
91.		Review and implementation of the Concluding Document of the Twelfth Special Session of the General Assembly:	
	(a)	United Nations disarmament fellowship, training and advisory services;	1st
	(b)	United Nations Disarmament Information Programme;	1st
	(c)	United Nations regional centres for peace and disarmament;	1st
	(d)	United Nations Regional Centre for Peace, Disarmament and Development in Latin America and the Caribbean;	1st
	(e)	United Nations Regional Centre for Peace and Disarmament in Asia and the Pacific;	1st
	(f)	United Nations Regional Centre for Peace and Disarmament in Africa;	st
	(g)	Regional confidence-building measures: activities of the United Nations Standing Advisory Committee on Security Questions in Central Africa;	1st
	(h)	Convention on the Prohibition of the Use of Nuclear Weapons.	1st
92.		Review of the implementation of the recommendations and decisions adopted by the General Assembly at its tenth special session:	
	(a)	Advisory Board on Disarmament Matters;	1st
	(b)	United Nations Institute for Disarmament Research;	1st
	(c)	Report of the Conference on Disarmament;	1st
	(d	Report of the Disarmament Commission.	1st
93.		The risk of nuclear proliferation in the Middle East.	1st
94.		Convention on Prohibitions or Restrictions on the Use of Certain Conventional Weapons Which May Be Deemed to Be Excessively Injurious or to Have Indiscriminate Effects.	1st
95.		Strengthening of security and cooperation in the Mediterranean region.	1st
96.		Comprehensive Nuclear-Test-Ban Treaty.	1st
97.		Convention on the Prohibition of the Development, Production and Stockpiling of Bacteriological (Biological) and Toxin Weapons and on Their Destruction.	1st
H.		**Drug control, crime prevention and combating international terrorism in all its forms and manifestations**	
98.		Crime prevention and criminal justice.	3rd
99.		International drug control.	3rd
100.		Measures to eliminate international terrorism.	6th
I.		**Organizational, administrative and other matters**	
1.		Opening of the session by the President of the General Assembly.	Plenary
2.		Minute of silent prayer or meditation.	Plenary
3.		Credentials of representatives to the sixty-first session of the General Assembly:	
	(a)	Appointment of the members of the Credentials Committee	Plenary
	(b)	Report of the Credentials Committee	Plenary
4.		Election of the President of the General Assembly.	Plenary
5.		Election of the officers of the Main Committees.	1st, 4th, 2nd, 3rd, 5th, 6th
6.		Election of the Vice-Presidents of the General Assembly.	Plenary
7.		Organization of work, adoption of the agenda and allocation of items: reports of the General Committee.	Plenary
8.		General debate.	Plenary
101.		Notification by the Secretary-General under Article 12, paragraph 2, of the Charter of the United Nations.	Plenary
102.		Report of the Secretary-General on the work of the Organization.	Plenary
103.		Elections to fill vacancies in principal organs:	
	(a)	Election of five non-permanent members of the Security Council;	Plenary
	(b)	Election of eighteen members of the Economic and Social Council.	Plenary
104.		Appointment of the Secretary-General of the United Nations.	Plenary
105.		Elections to fill vacancies in subsidiary organs and other elections:	
	(a)	Election of seven members of the Committee for Programme and Coordination;	Plenary
	(b)	Election of thirty members of the United Nations Commission on International Trade Law;	Plenary
	(c)	Election of the members of the International Law Commission;	Plenary
	(d)	Election of two members of the Organizational Committee of the Peacebuilding Commission;	Plenary
	(e)	Election of fourteen members of the Human Rights Council.	Plenary
106.		Appointments to fill vacancies in subsidiary organs and other appointments:	

Item No.		*Title*	*Allocation*
	(a)	Appointment of members of the Advisory Committee on Administrative and Budgetary Questions;	5th
	(b)	Appointment of members of the Committee on Contributions;	5th
	(c)	Confirmation of the appointment of members of the Investments Committee;	5th
	(d)	Appointment of members of the United Nations Administrative Tribunal;	5th
	(e)	Appointment of members of the International Civil Service Commission:	
		i Appointment of members of the Commission;	5th
		ii Designation of the Chairman and the Vice-Chairman of the Commission;	5th
	(f)	Appointment of members of the Committee on Conferences;	Plenary
	(g)	Appointment of the members of the Consultative Committee of the United Nations Development Fund for Women;	Plenary
	(h	Appointment of members of the Joint Inspection Unit.	Plenary
107.		Admission of new Members to the United Nations.	Plenary
108.		Cooperation between the United Nations and regional and other organizations:	
	(a)	Cooperation between the United Nations and the African Union;	Plenary
	(b	Cooperation between the United Nations and the Asian-African Legal Consultative Organization;	Plenary
	(c)	Cooperation between the United Nations and the Association of Southeast Asian Nations;	Plenary
	(d)	Cooperation between the United Nations and the Black Sea Economic Cooperation Organization;	Plenary
	(e)	Cooperation between the United Nations and the Caribbean Community;	Plenary
	(f)	Cooperation between the United Nations and the Community of Portuguese-speaking Countries;	Plenary
	(g)	Cooperation between the United Nations and the Council of Europe;	Plenary
	(h)	Cooperation between the United Nations and the Economic Community of Central African States;	Plenary
	(i)	Cooperation between the United Nations and the Economic Cooperation Organization;	Plenary
	(j)	Cooperation between the United Nations and the International Organization of la Francophonie;	Plenary
	(k)	Cooperation between the United Nations and the Inter-Parliamentary Union;	Plenary
	(l)	Cooperation between the United Nations and the Latin American Economic System;	Plenary
	(m)	Cooperation between the United Nations and the League of Arab States;	Plenary
	(n)	Cooperation between the United Nations and the Organization for the Prohibition of Chemical Weapons;	Plenary
	(o)	Cooperation between the United Nations and the Organization for Security and Cooperation in Europe;	Plenary
	(p)	Cooperation between the United Nations and the Organization of American States;	Plenary
	(q)	Cooperation between the United Nations and the Organization of the Islamic Conference;	Plenary
	(r)	Cooperation between the United Nations and the Pacific Islands Forum;	Plenary
	(s)	Cooperation between the United Nations and the Preparatory Commission for the Comprehensive Nuclear-Test-Ban Treaty Organization;	Plenary
	(t)	Cooperation between the United Nations and the Southern African Development Community.	Plenary
109.		Implementation of the resolutions of the United Nations.	Plenary
110.		Revitalization of the work of the General Assembly.	1st, 4th, 2nd, 3rd, 5th, 6th
111.		Question of equitable representation on and increase in the membership of the Security Council and related matters.	Plenary
112.		Strengthening of the United Nations system.	Plenary
113.		Follow-up to the outcome of the Millennium Summit.	Plenary
114.		Multilingualism.	Plenary
115.		Financial reports and audited financial statements, and reports of the Board of Auditors:	
	(a)	United Nations;	5th
	(b)	United Nations Development Programme;	5th
	(c)	United Nations Children's Fund;	5th
	(d)	United Nations Relief and Works Agency for Palestine Refugees in the Near East;	5th
	(e)	United Nations Institute for Training and Research;	5th
	(f)	Voluntary funds administered by the United Nations High Commissioner for Refugees;	5th
	(g)	Fund of the United Nations Environment Programme;	5th
	(h)	United Nations Population Fund;	5th
	(i)	United Nations Human Settlements Programme;	5th
	(j)	Fund of the United Nations International Drug Control Programme;	5th
	(k)	United Nations Office for Project Services;	5th

Item No.	*Title*	*Allocation*
	(l) International Tribunal for the Prosecution of Persons Responsible for Serious Violations of International Humanitarian Law Committed in the Territory of the Former Yugoslavia since 1991;	5th
	(m) International Criminal Tribunal for the Prosecution of Persons Responsible for Genocide and Other Serious Violations of International Humanitarian Law Committed in the Territory of Rwanda and Rwandan Citizens Responsible for Genocide and Other Such Violations Committed in the Territory of Neighbouring States between 1 January and 31 December 1994;	5th
	(n) Capital master plan.	5th
116.	Review of the efficiency of the administrative and financial functioning of the United Nations.	5th
117.	Programme budget for the biennium 2006-2007.	5th
118.	Programme planning.	5th
119.	Improving the financial situation of the United Nations.	5th
120.	Administrative and budgetary coordination of the United Nations with the specialized agencies and the International Atomic Energy Agency.	5th
121.	Pattern of conferences.	5th
122.	Scale of assessments for the apportionment of the expenses of the United Nations.	5th
123.	Human resources management.	5th
124.	Joint Inspection Unit.	5th
125.	United Nations common system.	5th
126.	United Nations pension system.	5th
127.	Report on the activities of the Office of Internal Oversight Services.	5th
128.	Administration of justice at the United Nations.	5th
129.	Financing of the International Criminal Tribunal for the Prosecution of Persons Responsible for Genocide and Other Serious Violations of International Humanitarian Law Committed in the Territory of Rwanda and Rwandan Citizens Responsible for Genocide and Other Such Violations Committed in the Territory of Neighbouring States between 1 January and 31 December 1994.	5th
130.	Financing of the International Tribunal for the Prosecution of Persons Responsible for Serious Violations of International Humanitarian Law Committed in the Territory of the Former Yugoslavia since 1991.	5th
131.	Scale of assessments for the apportionment of the expenses of United Nations peacekeeping operations.	5th
132.	Administrative and budgetary aspects of the financing of the United Nations peacekeeping operations.	5th
133.	Financing of the United Nations Operation in Burundi.	5th
134.	Financing of the United Nations Operation in Côte d'Ivoire.	5th
135.	Financing of the United Nations Peacekeeping Force in Cyprus.	5th
136.	Financing of the United Nations Organization Mission in the Democratic Republic of the Congo.	5th
137.	Financing of the United Nations Mission in East Timor.	5th
138.	Financing of the United Nations Mission of Support in East Timor.	5th
139.	Financing of the United Nations Mission in Ethiopia and Eritrea.	5th
140.	Financing of the United Nations Observer Mission in Georgia.	5th
141.	Financing of the United Nations Stabilization Mission in Haiti.	5th
142.	Financing of the United Nations Interim Administration Mission in Kosovo.	5th
143.	Financing of the United Nations Mission in Liberia.	5th
144.	Financing of the United Nations peacekeeping forces in the Middle East:	
	(a) United Nations Disengagement Observer Force;	5th
	(b) United Nations Interim Force in Lebanon.	5th
145.	Financing of the United Nations Mission in Sierra Leone.	5th
146.	Financing of the United Nations Mission in the Sudan.	5th
147.	Financing of the United Nations Mission for the Referendum in Western Sahara.	5th
148.	Report of the Committee on Relations with the Host Country.	5th
149.	United Nations reform: measures and proposals.	5th
150.	International Year of Reconciliation, 2009.	Plenary
151.	Financing of the United Nations Integrated Mission in Timor-Leste.	5th
152.	Report of the Secretary-General on the Peacebuilding Fund.	Plenary
153.	Requests for observer status in the General Assembly.	6th
154.	Follow-up to the recommendations on administrative management and internal oversight of the Independent Inquiry Committee into the United Nations Oil-for-Food Programme.	Plenary
155.	Commemoration of the two-hundredth anniversary of the abolition of the trans-Atlantic slave trade.	Plenary

Item No.	Title	Allocation
156.	Extension of the terms of the ad litem judges of the International Criminal Tribunal for the Prosecution of Persons Responsible for Genocide and Other Serious Violations of International Humanitarian Law Committed in the Territory of Rwanda and Rwandan Citizens Responsible for Genocide and Other Such Violations Committed in the Territory of Neighbouring States between 1 January and 31 December 1994.	Plenary
157.	Support by the United Nations system of the efforts of Governments to promote and consolidate new or restored democracies.	Plenary

Agenda item considered at the resumed tenth emergency special session
17 November, 15 December 2006

Item No.	Title
5.	Illegal Israeli actions in Occupied East Jerusalem and the rest of the Occupied Palestinian Territory

Security Council

Agenda items considered during 2006

Item No.	Title
1.	The situation in Afghanistan.
2.	Peace and security in Africa.
3.	The role of the Security Council in the prevention of armed conflicts.
4.	The situation in Burundi.
5.	The situation in the Central African Republic.
6.	Relations between Chad and Sudan.
7.	Children and armed conflict.
8.	Protection of civilians in armed conflict.
9.	Political conditions in Cote d'Ivoire.
10.	The situation in Cyprus.
11.	Relations between the Democratic Republic of the Congo and Uganda.
12.	The situation in the Democratic Republic of the Congo.
13.	Disarmament matters.
14.	Relations between Eritrea and Ethiopia
15.	The situation in the former Yugoslavia.
16.	The situation in Georgia.
17.	Peace and security in the Great Lakes region of Africa.
18.	Political conditions in Haiti.
19.	Election of members of the International Court of Justice.
20.	International peace and security.
21.	International Tribunal for the Prosecution of Persons Responsible for Serious Violations of International Humanitarian Law Committed in the Territory of the Former Yugoslavia since 1991.
22.	International Criminal Tribunal for the Prosecution of Persons Responsible for Genocide and Other Serious Violations of International Humanitarian Law Committed in the Territory of Rwanda and Rwandan Citizens Responsible for Genocide and Other Such Violations Committed in the Territory of Neighbouring States between 1 January and 31 December 1994.
23.	The situation in Iraq.
24.	The situation in Liberia.
25.	The situation in the Middle East.
26.	Political conditions in Myanmar.
27.	Political conditions in Nepal.
28.	Matters concerning the non-proliferation of nuclear weapons.
29.	Building peace.
30.	United Nations peacekeeping operations.
31.	Matters concerning refugees.

Item No.	*Title*
32.	Cooperation between the United Nations and regional organizations.
33.	The situation of human rights in Rwanda.
34.	Sanctions.
35.	Implementation of sanctions by Member States.
36.	Political conditions in Sierra Leone.
37.	Small arms.
38.	The Somalia situation.
39.	Political conditions in the Sudan.
40.	International terrorism.
41.	The situation in Timor-Leste.
42.	Membership in the United Nations.
43.	Secretary-General of the United Nations
44.	Annual report of the Security Council to the General Assembly.
45.	The question of Western Sahara.
46.	Women and armed conflicts.

Economic and Social Council

Agenda of the organizational and resumed organizational sessions for 2006

17 January, 7 and 10 February, 14 and 22 March, 8 May, 10 and 12 May

Item No.	*Title*
1.	Election of the Bureau.
2.	Adoption of the agenda and other organizational matters.
3.	Basic programme of work of the Council.
4.	Elections, nominations, confirmations and appointments.

Agenda of the substantive and resumed substantive sessions of 2006

3-28 July, 11 October, 30 November, 15 December

Item No. *Title*

1. Adoption of the agenda and other organizational matters.

   High-level segment

2. Creating an environment at the national and international levels conducive to generating full and productive employment and decent work for all, and its impact on sustainable development.

   Operational activities of the United Nations for international development cooperation segment

3. Operational activities of the United Nations for international development cooperation:
   - *(a)* Follow-up to policy recommendations of the General Assembly and the Council;
   - *(b)* Reports of the Executive Boards of the United Nations Development Programme/United Nations Population Fund, the United Nations Children's Fund and the World Food Programme.

   Coordination segment

4. Sustained economic growth for social development, including the eradication of poverty and hunger.

   Humanitarian affairs segment

5. Special economic, humanitarian and disaster relief assistance.

   General segment

6. Implementation of and follow-up to major United Nations conferences and summits:
   - *(a)* Follow-up to the International Conference on Financing for Development;
   - *(b)* Review and coordination of the implementation of the Programme of Action for the Least Developed Countries for the Decade 2001-2010.

Item No.	Title
7.	Coordination, programme and other questions:
	(a) Reports of coordination bodies;
	(b) Proposed strategic framework for the biennium 2008-2009;
	(c) International cooperation in the field of informatics;
	(d) Long-term programme of support for Haiti;
	(e) Mainstreaming a gender perspective into all policies and programmes in the United Nations system;
	(f) Information and Communication Technologies Task Force;
	(g) Ad hoc advisory groups on African countries emerging from conflict;
	(h) Tobacco or health.
8.	Implementation of General Assembly resolutions 50/227, 52/12 B and 57/270 B.
9.	Implementation of the Declaration on the Granting of Independence to Colonial Countries and Peoples by the specialized agencies and the international institutions associated with the United Nations.
10.	Regional cooperation.
11.	Economic and social repercussions of the Israeli occupation on the living conditions of the Palestinian people in the occupied Palestinian territory, including Jerusalem, and the Arab population in the occupied Syrian Golan.
12.	Non-governmental organizations.
13.	Economic and environmental questions:
	(a) Sustainable development;
	(b) Science and technology for development;
	(c) Statistics;
	(d) Human settlements;
	(e) Environment;
	(f) Population and development;
	(g) Public administration and development;
	(h) International cooperation in tax matters;
	(i) United Nations Forum on Forests;
	(j) Assistance to third States affected by the application of sanctions;
	(k) Cartography;
	(l) Women and development.
14.	Social and human rights questions:
	(a) Advancement of women;
	(b) Social development;
	(c) Crime prevention and criminal justice;
	(d) Narcotic drugs;
	(e) United Nations High Commissioner for Refugees;
	(f) Comprehensive implementation of and follow-up to the Durban Declaration and Programme of Action;
	(g) Human rights;
	(h) Permanent Forum on Indigenous Issues.

Appendix V

United Nations information centres and services

(as at January 2009)

ACCRA. United Nations Information Centre
Gamel Abdul Nassar/Liberia Roads
(P.O. Box GP 2339)
Accra, Ghana

Serving: Ghana, Sierra Leone

ALGIERS. United Nations Information Centre
Algerian Business Center, El Mohamadia, 16035
(Boîte postale 444, Hydra-Alger)
Algiers, Algeria

Serving: Algeria

ANKARA. United Nations Information Centre
Birlik Mahallesi, 2 Cadde No. 11
06610 Cankaya
Ankara, Turkey

Serving: Turkey

ANTANANARIVO. United Nations Information Centre
22 rue Rainitovo, Antasahavola
(Boîte postale 1348)
Antananarivo, Madagascar

Serving: : Madagascar

ASUNCION. United Nations Information Centre
Avda. Mariscal López esq. Saraví
Edificio Naciones Unidas
(Casilla de Correo 1107)
Asunción, Paraguay

Serving: Paraguay

BANGKOK. United Nations Information Service, Economic and Social Commission for Asia and the Pacific
United Nations Building
Rajdamnern Nok Avenue
Bangkok 10200, Thailand

Serving: Cambodia, Lao People's Democratic Republic, Malaysia, Singapore, Thailand, Viet Nam, ESCAP

BEIRUT. United Nations Information Centre/ United Nations Information Service, Economic and Social Commission for Western Asia
UN House
Riad El-Solh Square
(P.O. Box 11-8575-4656)
Beirut, Lebanon

Serving: Jordan, Kuwait, Lebanon, Syrian Arab Republic, ESCWA

BOGOTA. United Nations Information Centre
Calle 100 No. 8A-55, Piso 10
Edificio World Trade Center - Torre "C"
(Apartado Aéreo 058964)
Bogotá 2, Colombia

Serving: Colombia, Ecuador, Venezuela

BRAZZAVILLE. United Nations Information Centre
Avenue Foch, Case ortf 15
(Boîte postale 13210)
Brazzaville, Congo

Serving: Congo

BRUSSELS. Regional United Nations Information Centre
Résidence Palace
rue de la Loi/Wetstraat 155
Quartier Rubens, Block C2
1040 Brussels, Belgium

Serving: Belgium, Cyprus, Denmark, Finland, France, Germany, Greece, Holy See, Iceland, Ireland, Italy, Luxembourg, Malta, Monaco Netherlands, Norway, Portugal, San Marino, Spain, Sweden, United Kingdom, European Union

BUCHAREST. United Nations Information Centre
48 A Primaverii Blvd.
Bucharest 011975 1, Romania

Serving: Romania

BUENOS AIRES. United Nations Information Centre
Junín 1940, 1er piso
1113 Buenos Aires, Argentina

Serving: Argentina, Uruguay

BUJUMBURA. United Nations Information Centre
117 Avenue de la Révolution
(Boîte postale 2160)
Bujumbura, Burundi

Serving: Burundi

CAIRO. United Nations Information Centre
1 Osiris Street, Garden City
(P.O. Box 262)
Cairo, Egypt

Serving: Egypt, Saudi Arabia

CANBERRA. United Nations Information Centre
Level 1 Barton, 7 National Circuit
(P.O. Box 5366, Kingston, ACT 2604)
Canberra ACT 2600
Australia

Serving: Australia, Fiji, Kiribati, Nauru, New Zealand, Samoa, Tonga, Tuvalu, Vanuatu

COLOMBO. United Nations Information Centre
202/204 Bauddhaloka Mawatha
(P.O. Box 1505, Colombo)
Colombo 7, Sri Lanka

Serving: Sri Lanka

DAKAR. United Nations Information Centre
Immeuble Soumex, Mamelles-Almadies
(Boîte postale 154)
Dakar, Senegal

Serving: Cape Verde, Côte d'Ivoire, Gambia, Guinea, Guinea-Bissau, Mauritania, Senegal

DAR ES SALAAM. United Nations Information Centre
Kings Way/Mafinga Street
Plot 134-140, Kinondoni
(P.O. Box 9224)
Dar es Salaam, United Republic of Tanzania

Serving: United Republic of Tanzania

DHAKA. United Nations Information Centre
IDB Bhaban (8th floor)
Sher-e-Bangla Nagar
(G.P.O. Box 3658, Dhaka-1000)
Dhaka-1207, Bangladesh

Serving: Bangladesh

GENEVA. United Nations Information Service, United Nations Office at Geneva
Palais des Nations
1211 Geneva 10, Switzerland

Serving: Switzerland

HARARE. United Nations Information Centre
Sanders House (2nd floor)
Cnr. First Street/Jason Moyo Avenue
(P.O. Box 4408)
Harare, Zimbabwe

Serving: Zimbabwe

ISLAMABAD. United Nations Information Centre
House No. 26, Street 88 G-6/3
(P.O. Box 1107)
Islamabad, Pakistan

Serving: Pakistan

JAKARTA.United Nations Information Centre
Gedung Surya (14th floor)
Jl. M. H. Thamrin Kavling 9
Jakarta 10350, Indonesia

Serving: Indonesia

KATHMANDU. United Nations Information Centre
Harihar Bhavan, Lalitpur
(P.O. Box 107, UN House)
Kathmandu, Nepal

Serving: Nepal

KHARTOUM. United Nations Information Centre
United Nations Compound
Gamma'a Avenue
(P.O. Box 1992)
Khartoum, Sudan

Serving: Somalia, Sudan

LAGOS. United Nations Information Centre
17 Alfred Rewane (ex Kingsway) Road, Ikoyi
(P.O. Box 1068)
Lagos, Nigeria

Serving: Nigeria

LA PAZ. United Nations Information Centre
Calle 14 esq. S. Bustamante
Edificio Metrobol II, Calacoto
(Apartado Postal 9072)
La Paz, Bolivia

Serving: Bolivia

LIMA. United Nations Information Centre
Lord Cochrane 130
San Isidro (L-27)
(P.O. Box 14-0199)
Lima, Peru

Serving: Peru

LOME. United Nations Information Centre
468 Angle Rue Atime
Avenue de la Libération
(Boîte postale 911)
Lomé, Togo

Serving: Benin, Togo

LUSAKA. United Nations Information Centre
Revenue House (ground floor)
Cairo Road (Northend)
(P.O. Box 32905, Lusaka 10101)
Lusaka, Zambia

Serving: Botswana, Malawi, Swaziland, Zambia

MANAMA. United Nations Information Centre
United Nations House
Bldg. 69, Road 1901
(P.O. Box 26004, Manama)
Manama 319, Bahrain

Serving: Bahrain, Qatar, United Arab Emirates

MANILA. United Nations Information Centre
Jaka II Building, 5th floor
150 Legaspi Street, Legaspi Village
(P.O. Box 7285 ADC (DAPO), Pasay City)
Makati City
Metro Manila, Philippines

Serving: Papua New Guinea, Philippines, Solomon Islands

MASERU. United Nations Information Centre
United Nations Road
UN House
(P.O. Box 301, Maseru 100)
Maseru, Lesotho

Serving: Lesotho

MEXICO CITY. United Nations Information Centre
Presidente Masaryk 29-2do piso
Col. Chaputelpec Morales
11570 México D.F., Mexico

Serving: Cuba, Dominican Republic, Mexico

MOSCOW. United Nations Information Centre
4/16 Glazovsky Pereulok
Moscow 119002, Russian Federation

Serving: Russian Federation

NAIROBI. United Nations Information Centre
United Nations Office
Gigiri
(P.O. Box 30552)
Nairobi, Kenya

Serving: Kenya, Seychelles, Uganda

NEW DELHI. United Nations Information Centre
55 Lodi Estate
New Delhi 110 003, India

Serving: Bhutan, India

OUAGADOUGOU. United Nations Information Centre
14 Avenue de la Grande Chancellerie
Secteur no. 4
(Boîte postale 135)
Ouagadougou 01, Burkina Faso

Serving: Burkina Faso, Chad, Mali, Niger

PANAMA CITY. United Nations Information Centre
UN House Bldg. 154
Ciudad del Saber, Clayton
(P.O. Box 0819-01082)
Panama City, Panama

Serving: Panama

PORT OF SPAIN. United Nations Information Centre
2nd floor, Bretton Hall
16 Victoria Avenue
(P.O. Box 130)
Port of Spain, Trinidad and Tobago, W.I.

Serving: Antigua and Barbuda, Aruba, Bahamas, Barbados, Belize, Dominica, Grenada, Guyana, Jamaica, Netherlands Antilles, Saint Kitts and Nevis, Saint Lucia, Saint Vincent and the Grenadines, Suriname, Trinidad and Tobago

PRAGUE. United Nations Information Centre
nam. Kinskych 6
15000 Prague 5, Czech Republic

Serving: Czech Republic

PRETORIA. United Nations Information Centre
Metro Park Building
351 Schoeman Street
(P.O. Box 12677)
Pretoria, South Africa

Serving: South Africa

RABAT. United Nations Information Centre
6 Angle avenue Tarik Ibnou Ziyad et Ruet Roudana
(Boîte postale 601, Casier ONU, Rabat-Chellah)
Rabat, Morocco

Serving: Morocco

RIO DE JANEIRO. United Nations Information Centre
Palácio Itamaraty
Av. Marechal Floriano 196
20080-002 Rio de Janeiro RJ, Brazil

Serving: Brazil

SANA'A. United Nations Information Centre
Street 5, off Al-Bonyia Street
Handlal Zone, beside Handhal Mosque
(P.O. Box 237)
Sana'a, Yemen

Serving: Yemen

SANTIAGO. United Nations Information Service, Economic Commission for Latin America and the Caribbean
Edificio Naciones Unidas
Avenida Dag Hammarskjöld 3477, Vitacura
(Casilla 179-D)
Santiago, Chile

Serving: Chile, ECLAC

TEHRAN. United Nations Information Centre
No. 39, Shahrzad Blvd.
(P.O. Box 15875-4557, Tehran)
Darous, Iran

Serving: Iran

TOKYO. United Nations Information Centre
UNU Building (8th floor)
53-70 Jingumae 5-chome, Shibuya-Ku
Tokyo 150-0001, Japan

Serving: Japan

TRIPOLI. United Nations Information Centre
Khair Aldeen Baybers Street
Hay El-Andalous
(P.O. Box 286)
Tripoli, Libyan Arab Jamahiriya

Serving: Libyan Arab Jamahiriya

TUNIS. United Nations Information Centre
61 Boulevard Bab-Benath
(Boîte postale 863)
Tunis, Tunisia

Serving: Tunisia

VIENNA. United Nations Information Service, United Nations Office at Vienna
Vienna International Centre
Wagramer Strasse 5
(P.O. Box 500, A-1400 Vienna)
A-1220 Vienna, Austria

Serving: Austria, Hungary, Slovakia, Slovenia

WARSAW. United Nations Information Centre
A. Niepodleglosci 186
(UN Centre P.O. Box 1, 02-514 Warsaw 12)
00-608 Warszawa, Poland

Serving: Poland

WASHINGTON, D.C. United Nations Information Centre
1775 K Street, N.W., Suite 400
Washington, D.C. 20006, United States

Serving: United States

WINDHOEK. United Nations Information Centre
372 Paratus Building
Independence Avenue
(Private Bag 13351)
Windhoek, Namibia

Serving: Namibia

YANGON. United Nations Information Centre
6 Natmauk Road, Tamwe Township
(P.O. Box 230)
Yangon, Myanmar

Serving: Myanmar

YAOUNDE. United Nations Information Centre
Immeuble Tchinda, Rue 2044, derrière camp SIC TSINGA
(Boîte postale 836)
Yaoundé, Cameroon

Serving: Cameroon, Central African Republic, Gabon

For more information on UNICs, access the Internet: http: //www.un.org/aroundworld/unics

Appendix VI

Intergovernmental organizations

HEADQUARTERS

International Atomic Energy Agency (IAEA)
P.O. Box 100
Wagramerstrasse 5
A-1400 Vienna, Austria
Telephone: (43) (1) 2600-0
Fax: (43) (1) 2600-7
Internet: www.iaea.org
E-mail: official.mail@iaea.org

NEW YORK LIAISON OFFICE

IAEA Office at the United Nations
1 United Nations Plaza, Room 1155
New York, NY 10017, United States
Telephone: (1) (212) 963-6010/6011
Fax: (1) (917) 367-4046
E-mail: iaeany@un.org

Director-General: Mohamed El Baradei
Membership: 143
Conference: Fiftieth, Vienna, 19-21 September, IAEA General Conference Special Event
Report: Annual Report 2006

HEADQUARTERS

International Labour Organization (ILO)
4, route des Morillons
CH-1211 Geneva 22, Switzerland
Telephone: (41) (22) 799-6111
Fax: (41) (22) 798-8685
Internet: www.ilo.org
E-mail: ilo@ilo.org

LIAISON OFFICE

International Labour Organization
Liaison Office with the United Nations
220 East 42nd Street, suite 3101
New York, NY 10017, United States
Telephone: (1) (212)697-0150
Fax: (1) (212) 697-0150
E-mail: newyork@ilo.org

Director-General: Juan Somavia
Membership: 175
Session: Ninety-fifth, Geneva, 31 May–16 June
Report: Report of the Chairperson of the Governing Body to the Conference for the year 2005-2006

HEADQUARTERS

Food and Agriculture Organization (FAO)
Telephone: (39) (06) 57051
Fax: (39) (06) 5705-3152
Internet: www.fao.org
E-mail: fao-ho@fao.org

NEW YORK LIAISON OFFICE

Food and Agriculture Organization Liaison Office with the United Nations
1 United Nations Plaza, Room 1125
New York, NY 10017, United States
Telephone: (1) (212) 963-6036
Fax: (1) (212) 963-5425
E-mail: fao-lony@fao.org

Director-General: Jacques Diouf
Membership: 191
Session: FAO Council, one hundred and thirty-first, Rome, 20-25 November
Report: The State of Food and Agriculture 2006

FAO also maintained liaison offices in Brussels, Geneva, Washington, D.C., and Yokohama, Japan; regional offices in Accra, Ghana; Bangkok, Thailand; Cairo, Egypt; and Santiago, Chile; and subregional offices in Apia, Samoa; Bridgetown, Barbados; Budapest, Hungary; Harare, Zimbabwe; and Tunis, Tunisia.

HEADQUARTERS

United Nations Educational, Scientific and Cultural Organization (UNESCO)
UNESCO House
7, Place de Fontenoy
75352 Paris 07 sp, France
Telephone: (33) (1) 45-68-10-00
Fax: (33) (1) 45-67-16-90
Internet: www.unesco.org

NEW YORK LIAISON OFFICE

2 United Nations Plaza, Room 900
New York, NY 10017, United States
Telephone: (1) (212) 963-5995
Fax: (1) (212) 963-8014
E-mail: newyork@unesco.org

Director-General: Koïchiro Matsuura
Membership: 191
Session: Did not meet in 2006
Report: EFA Global Monitoring Report 2007–Strong Foundations

HEADQUARTERS

World Health Organization (WHO)
20, Avenue Appia
CH-1211 Geneva 27, Switzerland
Telephone: +41 (22) 791-21-11
Fax: +41 (22) 791-31-11
Internet: http://www.who.int
E-mail: info@who.int

NEW YORK LIAISON OFFICE

WHO Office at the United Nations
2 United Nations Plaza, DC-2, Rooms 0956 to 0976
New York, N.Y. 10017, U.S.A.
Telephone: +1 (212) 963-43-88
Fax: +1 (212) 963-85-65

Director-General: Lee Jong-wook (until May 2006)
Acting Director-General: Anders Nordström (from 23 May 2006 until 3 January 2007, following the untimely death of Lee Jong-wook on 22 May 2006)
Membership: 193
Report: The World Health Report 2006-Working Together for Health

WHO is a decentralized organization, with regional offices in Brazzaville, Congo; Cairo, Egypt; Copenhagen, Denmark; Manila, Philippines; New Delhi, India; and Washington, D.C., U.S.A.

HEADQUARTERS
World Bank (IBRD and IDA)
1818 H Street, NW
Washington, D. C. 20433, United States
Telephone: (1) (202) 473-1000
Fax: (1) (202) 477-6391
Internet: www.worldbank.org
E-mail: feedback@worldbank.org

NEW YORK LIAISON OFFICE
The World Bank Mission to the United Nations
1 Dag Hammarskjöld Plaza
885 Second Avenue, 26th floor
New York, NY 10017, United States
Telephone: (1) (212) 355-5112
Fax: (1) (212) 355-4523

Director-General: Paul Wolfowitz
Membership: IBRD: 185; IDA: 166
Meeting: Singapore, September 19-20
Report: The World Bank Annual Report 2006 (which covers the period from July 1, 2005, to June 30, 2006)
Report: The World Bank Annual Report 2007 (which covers the period from July 1, 2006, to June 30, 2007)

The World Bank also maintained offices in Brussels, Belgium; Frankfurt, Germany; Geneva; London; Paris; Sydney, Australia; and Tokyo, Japan.

HEADQUARTERS
International Finance Corporation (IFC)
2121 Pennsylvania Avenue, NW
Washington, DC 20433, United States
Telephone: (1) (202) 473-3800
Fax: (1) (202) 974-4384
Internet: http://www.ifc.org
E-mail: webmaster@ifc.org

NEW YORK LIAISON OFFICE
International Finance Corporation
c/o The World Bank, Office of the Special Representative to the UN
1 Dag Hammarskjöld Plaza
885 Second Avenue, 26th floor
New York, NY 10017, United States
Telephone: (1) (212) 355-5112
Fax: (1) (212) 355-5523

Executive Vice President & CEO: Lars H. Thunell
Membership: 179 member countries
Meeting: Singapore, September 19-20
Report: Increasing Impact: The Year in Review 2006

HEADQUARTERS
International Monetary Fund (IMF)
700 19th Street, NW
Washington, DC 20431, United States
Telephone: (1) (202) 623-7000
Fax: (1) (202) 623-4661
Internet: www.imf.org
E-mail: publicaffairs@imf.org

IMF OFFICE, UNITED NATIONS, NEW YORK
International Monetary Fund
885 Second Avenue, 26th floor
New York, NY 10017, United States
Telephone: (1) (212) 893-1700
Fax: (1) (212) 893-1715

Managing Director: Rodrigo de Rato y Figaredo
First Deputy Managing Director: Anne O. Krueger
Deputy Managing Directors: Agustín Carstens, Takatoshi Kato
Membership: 185
Session: Singapore, September 19-20
Reports: World Economic Outlook—Globalization and Inflation, April; World Economic Outlook—Financial Systems and Economic Cycles, September

IMF also maintained offices in Geneva, Paris and Tokyo.

HEADQUARTERS
International Civil Aviation Organization (ICAO)
999 University Street
Montreal, Quebec, Canada H3C 5H7
Telephone: (1) (514) 954-8219
Fax: (1) (514) 954-6077
Internet: www.icao.int
E-mail: icaohq@icao.int

Secretary-General: Taïeb Chérif
Membership: 189
Session: Did not meet in 2006
Report: 2006 Annual Report of the Council

ICAO maintained regional offices in Bangkok, Thailand; Cairo, Egypt; Dakar, Senegal; Lima, Peru; Mexico, D.F.; Nairobi, Kenya; and Paris.

HEADQUARTERS
Universal Postal Union (UPU)
Weltpoststrasse 4
3015 Berne, Switzerland
Telephone: (41) (31) 350 31 10
Fax: (41) (31) 350 31 10
Internet: www.upu.int
E-mail: info@upu.int

Director-General: Edouard Dayan
Membership: 191

HEADQUARTERS
International Telecommunication Union (ITU)
Place des Nations
CH-1211, Geneva 20, Switzerland
Telephone: (41) (22) 730-5111
Fax: (41) (22) 733-7256
Internet: www.itu.int
E-mail: itumail@itu.int

Secretary-General: Yoshio Utsumi
Membership: 191
Sessions: Final meeting of the 2006 session of the ITU Council, Antalya, 4 November; Council Extraordinary Session, Antalya, 24 November
Report: World Information Society Report 2006

HEADQUARTERS
World Meteorological Organization (WMO)
7 bis, avenue de la Paix
(Case postale No. 2300)
CH-1211 Geneva 2, Switzerland
Telephone: (41) 22-730-8111
Fax: (41) (22) 730-8181
Internet: www.wmo.ch
E-mail: wmo@wmo.int

NEW YORK LIAISON OFFICE
World Meteorological Organization Liaison Office at the United Nations
866 United Nations Plaza, Room A-302
New York, NY 10017, United States
Telephone: (1) (212) 963-9444
Fax: (1) (917) 367-9868
E-mail: zbatjargal@wmo.int

Director-General: Alexander Bedritsky
Secretary-General: Michel Jarraud
Membership: 187
Session: WMO Executive Council–58th session, 20-30 June
Report: Global Atmosphere Watch (GAW) 2006

HEADQUARTERS
International Maritime Organization (IMO)
4 Albert Embankment
London SE1 7SR, United Kingdom
Telephone: (44) (207) 735-7611
Fax: (44) (207) 587-3210
Internet: www.imo.org
E-mail: info@imo.org

Director-General: Efthimios E. Mitropoulos
Membership: 167
Session: Ninety-seventh, 6-10 November

HEADQUARTERS
World Intellectual Property Organization (WIPO)
34, Chemin des Colombettes (P.O. Box 18)
CH-1211 Geneva 20, Switzerland
Telephone: (41) (22) 338-9111
Fax: (41) (22) 733-5428
Internet: www.wipo.int
E-mail: wipo-mail@wipo.int

WIPO OFFICE AT THE UNITED NATIONS
2 United Nations Plaza, Suite 2525
New York, NY 10017, United States
Telephone: (1) (212) 963-6813
Fax: (1) (212) 963-4801
E-mail: wipo@un.org

Director-General: Kamil Idris
Membership: 183
Meeting: 2006 WIPO Assemblies, Geneva, 25 September

HEADQUARTERS
International Fund for Agricultural Development (IFAD)
Via del Serafico, 107
00142 Rome, Italy
Telephone: (39) (06) 54591
Fax: (39) (06) 5043463
Internet: www.ifad.org
E-mail: ifad@ifad.org

IFAD LIAISON OFFICE
2 United Nations Plaza, Room 1128-29
New York, NY 10017, United States
Telephone: (1) (212) 963-0546
Fax: (1) (212) 963-2787

President: Lennart Båge
Membership: 164
Session: Twenty-ninth session, Rome, 15-16 February
Report: Annual Report 2006*:* Enabling the rural poor to overcome poverty

IFAD also maintained offices in Eschbom, Germany, and Washington, D.C.

HEADQUARTERS
United Nations Industrial Development Organization (UNIDO)
Vienna International Centre
P.O. Box 300
A-1400 Vienna, Austria
Telephone: (43) (1) 26026
Fax: (43) (1) 269-26-69
Internet: http://www.unido.org
E-mail: unido@unido@org

UNIDO OFFICE AT GENEVA
Palais des Nations
Le Bocage 1, Room 79
Avenue de la Paix 8-14
CH-1211 Geneva 10, Switzerland
Telephone: (41) (22) 917-1434
Fax: (41) (22) 917-0059
E-mail: office.geneva@unido.org

UNIDO OFFICE IN NEW YORK
1 United Nations Plaza, Room DC1-1118
New York, NY 10017, United States
Telephone: (1) (212) 963-6890
Fax: (1) (212) 963-7904
E-mail: office.newyork@unido.org

Director-General: Kandeh K. Yumkella
Membership: 172
Session: Thirty-first, Vienna, 6-7 June; Thirty-second, Vienna, 29 November–1 December; Fortieth anniversary, Vienna, 28 November
Report: Annual Report 2006

HEADQUARTERS
World Trade Organization (WTO)
Centre William Rappard
154, rue de Lausanne
CH-1211 Geneva 21, Switzerland

Telephone: (41) (22) 739-5111
Fax: (41) (22) 731-4206
Internet: www.wto.org
E-mail: enquiries@wto.org

Director-General: Pascal Lamy
Membership: 151
Session: Did not meet in 2006
Report: World Trade Report: Exploring the links between subsidies, trade and the WTO

HEADQUARTERS
World Tourism Organization (UNWTO)
Capitán Haya, 42
28020 Madrid, Spain
Telephone: (34) (91) 567-8100
Fax: (34) (91) 571-3733
Internet: www.world-tourism.org
E-mail: omt@world-tourism.org

Secretary-General: Francesco Frangialli
Membership: 150
Session: Did not meet in 2006
Report: Tourism Highlights 2007 Edition (a concise overview of international tourism in the world based on the results for the year 2006)

The UNWTO secretariat maintained a regional support office for Asia and the Pacific, in Osaka, Japan.

Indexes

USING THE SUBJECT INDEX

To assist the researcher in reading and searching the *Yearbook* index, three typefaces have been employed.

ALL BOLD CAPITAL LETTERS are used for major subject entries, including chapter topics (e.g., **DEVELOPMENT, DISARMAMENT**), as well as country names (e.g., **TAJIKISTAN**), region names (e.g., **AFRICA**) and principal UN organs (e.g., **GENERAL ASSEMBLY**).

CAPITAL LETTERS are used to highlight major sub-topics (e.g., POVERTY), territories (e.g., MONTSERRAT), subregions (e.g., CENTRAL AMERICA) and official names of specialized agencies (e.g., UNIVERSAL POSTAL UNION) and regional commissions (e.g., ECONOMIC COMMISSION FOR EUROPE).

Regular body text is used for single entries and cross-reference entries, e.g., armed conflict, mercenaries, terrorism.

1—An asterisk (*) next to a page number indicates the presence of a text (reproduced in full) of General Assembly, Security Council or Economic and Social Council resolutions and decisions, or Security Council presidential statements.

2—Entries, which are heavily cross-referenced, appear under key substantive words, as well as under the first word of official titles.

3—United Nations bodies are listed under major subject entries and alphabetically.

Subject index

Abkhazia, *see* Georgia
Aden Declaration (2006, Somalia), 255, *301-304
Advisory Committee on Administrative and Budgetary Questions (ACABQ), 1572-73, 1575
ECA subregional offices, 1152
UN budget, 1610-11, 1622-23
UNDP financing, 1045
UN Joint Staff Pension Fund, *1703-1707
UN management reform, 1643
UN personnel policies, *1691-98
UN remuneration issues, 1682
UN security issues, 1674
AFGHANISTAN, *362-89
Afghanistan Compact (2006), *362-76, 379
Al-Qaida, *365-67, 375, *381-89
arms embargo, 382-84
Bonn Agreement (2001), *362-67, 379, 1069
Consolidation of Peace in Afghanistan, Second Conference on (2006, Tokyo), 367
drug control, 378, *1449-51
humanitarian situation, 1069-70
human rights, 379, 948, *1346-47
International Security Assistance Force (ISAF), 361-62, 375, *380-81
London Conference, 362-63, 375, 1069
National Action Plan on Peace, Reconciliation and Justice (2005), 362
and Pakistan, 369, 375
sanctions, *381-89
security situation, 363-65, *369-74,
security sector reform, 377
SC Mission, 374-76
Taliban, 363, *365-67, *368-76, 379, *381-89
UNAMA, 64-65, 86, 361-62, *364-67, 378-80, 948
women and girls, *1346
AFRICA, *112-340
Ad Hoc Working Group on Conflict Prevention and Resolution in, 114
African Union, *see* African Union
aid to, 1126
Algeria, 330-35
Angola, 115, *1079-81
(Beijing) Summit of the Forum on China-Africa Cooperation, (2006) Declaration of the, 114-15
Burundi, 54-55, 57, 78, 86, 88, 120, *130-31, *148-62, 938, 1064-65, *1082-85
Cameroon, 173, 252-54
Central Africa and Great Lakes Region, 114-15, *120-72, *684-87, 811, *814-15, 1064
Special Representative of the Secretary-General for the Great Lakes Region, Office of the, 64, *125-26
Central African Republic, 64, 120, *162-68, 255, 1063-64
Chad, 120, *162-68, 255, 258, 261, 269, 271-72, 279, 289, 291, *297-301, 1064
children in, 922
conflict, countries emerging from, *1082-86
Congo, Republic of the, 1064, 1477
Côte d'Ivoire, *50-54, 78, 86, 88, 115, 172-73, *176-211, 1067-68
Decade to Roll Back Malaria in Developing Countries, Particularly in Africa (2001-2010), *1421-25
diamonds, *see* conflict prevention; *subheading:* conflict diamonds
disarmament, *see* disarmament; *subheading* regional and other approaches
Djibouti, 1477, 1480-81
Democratic Republic of the Congo (DRC), 51, 54, 61, 78, 86, 88, 114-15, *120-24, *127-48, 857, 938-39, 1065, 1478-80
drug situation in, 1440-42
ECA, *see* Economic Commission for Africa
economic recovery and development, *1071-86
economic and social activities, regional, *1146-55
Eritrea, 86, 88, 115, 255-56, *315-29
Ethiopia, 86, 88, 115, 255-56, *315-29, 1105
Great Lakes region, *see* Central Africa and Great Lakes Region
Guinea, 173, 254, 1068, 1478-79
Guinea-Bissau, 64, 173, 244-51, 1068, 1082-83, *1085-86
Horn of Africa, *254-329, 684, 1105
humanitarian assistance, *see* humanitarian assistance; *subheading*: Africa
human rights, *see* human rights
Kenya, 1066, 1105-1106
Liberia, 50, 54, 78, 86, 88, 115, 172-73, *211-30, 939-40, 1068, *1081-82
Mauritania, 334
Morocco, *329-36
Mozambique, 1082
New Partnership for Africa's Development (NEPAD), *see* New Partnership for Africa's Development
Nigeria, 173, 252-54
North Africa, *329-39, *see also* country names
nuclear-weapon-free zone, 644
Office of the Special Adviser on Africa (OSSA), 114, 116
promotion of peace in, *114-19
refugees, *1397-1402
rule of law, strengthening the, *1315-16
Rwanda, *121-24, 131, 141, 171-72, 857, 1477, 1479-80
Senegal, 246
Sierra Leone, 55, 57, 64-65, 78, 115, 173, *230-44, 940-41
Somalia, 64, 115, 255, *301-15, 941, 1066
Sudan, 54-55, 78, 86, 88, 114-16, *254-301, 941-43, 1066-67, 1367
Uganda, 114-16, *120-24, 131-32, 141-43, *168-71, 943-44, 1065-66, 1477
UN African Institute for the Prevention of Crime and the Treatment of Offenders, *1294-95
West Africa, *see* West Africa
Western Sahara, 86-87, 115, *329-39, 717
Zimbabwe, 1068-69
see also country names; African Union; Economic Commission for Africa; Economic Community of Central African States; Economic Community of West African States; Southern Africa Development Community
African Union (AU)
African Peer Review Mechanism, 1074
AU/IGAD peace support mission in Somalia, *309-10
Convention on Preventing and Combating Corruption, 219
Extraordinary Summit on Employment and Poverty Alleviation in Africa and Plan of Action (Ouagadougou, 2004), 1147
Migration Policy Framework and Common African Position on International Migration, 1147

UN, cooperation with, 62, 340, 1597
AGEING PERSONS, *1381-84
Macao Plan of Action on Ageing for Asia and the Pacific (2007), 1164
World Assembly on Ageing, Second (2002)
follow-up to, *1381-84
Madrid International Plan of Action on (2002), 1191, 1277, *1381-84
AIDS, *see* HIV/AIDS
ALGERIA
and Western Sahara, 330-32, 334-35
Algiers Agreements (Ethiopia-Eritrea, 2000), *315-24, 326
Al-Qaida, *365-67, 375, 866
sanctions against, *381-89
AMERICAS, *341-60
Colombia, 944-45, 1477
Costa Rica, 1477
Cuba, 341-42, *357-59, 945-46
drug situation in, 1442-46
El Salvador, 1055, 1104
Ecuador, 863
Guatemala, 341, 946-47, 1055, 1104
Haiti, 54-55, 61, 78, 86, 88, *342-57, 947-48, *1086-88, 1193
Honduras, 864, 869, 1477
Nicaragua, 341, 864, 1477
refugees, 1402-1404
see also country names; Caribbean; Central America; Economic Commission for Latin America and the Caribbean; Latin America and the Caribbean; Organization of American States
ANGOLA, 115, *1079-81
arbitrary detention, 862-66
Guantánamo Bay, 865-66
ARGENTINA
Falkland Islands (Malvinas), 713
ICJ case, 1477, 1481-82
armed conflict
children in, 158, 292, 451, *918-22
law during, 857
sexual exploitation during, 913
women in, *1339-41
ARMENIA
Azerbaijan, conflict with, 453, *484-86
Minsk Group of OSCE, 484-85
Nagorny Karabakh region, 452
arms embargoes
Afghanistan, 382-84
Bosnia and Herzegovina, 456
Côte d'Ivoire, 176, 203
DPRK, 641
DRC, 120, *140-45
Lebanon, 588
Liberia, 226
Rwanda (non-governmental forces), 171-72
Somalia, 302, *311-15
Arusha Agreement on Peace and Reconciliation (Burundi, 2000), 157
ASEAN, *see* Association of South-East Asian Nations
Asian-African Legal Consultative Organization (AALCO), *1536-37, 1598
ASIA AND THE PACIFIC, *361-452
Afghanistan, 61, 64-65, 86, *361-89, 948, 1069-70, *1346-47, *1449-51
Association of South-East Asian Nations (ASEAN), 61, 647, 688-89, 812, *1170, 1597
Cambodia, 447-48, 868, 948-49
confidence building measures in, Second Summit (Almaty, 2006), 452, 691
Democratic People's Republic of Korea (DPRK), 64, 361-62, *441-47, 609, 641, 689, *949-52
disarmament, *see* disarmament; *subheading* regional and other approaches
drug situation, *1446-51, 1453
economic and social activities, regional, *1155-70
Asian and Pacific Conference on Population and Poverty, (Fifth), 1064
Fiji, 447
human rights, *948-61, *1346-47
India, *72, 86-87, 448, 842
Indian Ocean tsunami, *see* disaster relief
Indonesia, 836-37, 1006
Iran, 361, *432-41, 451-52, 609, 641, 689, 830, 874, *952-54
Iraq, 64-65, *71-72, 86, 361, *389-412, 867-68
Jakarta Declaration on MDGs in, 1155, 1157, 1159
Kyrgyzstan, 937
Macao Plan of Action on Ageing for (2007), 1164
Ministerial Conference on Space Applications for Sustainable Development in, Third (2007), 1159, 1162
Myanmar, 448-49, *954-58
and natural disasters, 1165
Nepal, 362, *449-51, 958-60, 1070
nuclear-weapon-free zones, *644-47, 649
Pakistan, 86-87, 448, 1055, 1106-1107
Philippines, *1088, 1106
Programme of Technical Assistance for, 1158
Republic of Korea, 64, *442-43, 689, 836
Shanghai Cooperation Organization (SCO), 688
Shanghai Declaration, 1163
Sri Lanka, 72, 960, 1071
Tajikistan, 64-65, 451, 1107
Timor-Leste, 64-65, 78, 86, 89, 361, *413-31, 960
Turkmenistan, 960
Uzbekistan, 866, 960-61
see also country names; Economic and Social Commission for Asia and the Pacific; Economic and Social Commission for Western Asia
Association of South-East Asian Nations (ASEAN), 61, 647, 688-89, 812, *1170, 1597
AZERBAIJAN
Armenia, conflict with, 453, *484-86
Minsk Group of OSCE, 484-85
Nagorny Karabakh, 452

bacteriological (biological) weapons, *650-53
Convention (1972), 610, *650-52
Review Conference (Sixth), 650-51
(Geneva Protocol) for the Prohibition of the Use in War of Asphyxiating, Poisonous or Other Gases, and of Bacteriological Methods of Warfare (1925), *652-53
BELARUS
Chernobyl aftermath, conference on, 751, 1107
human rights, *961-63
bin Laden, Osama, 381
BINUB, *see* United Nations Integrated Office in Burundi
bioethics, 912
biotechnology
Convention on Biological Diversity (1992), 1216, 1219, *1223-25
Cartagena Protocol on Biosafety (2000), 1223
International Year of Biodiversity (2010), 1223, *1225
Black Sea Economic Cooperation Organization, *1186-87, 1597

Bonn Agreement, *see* Afghanistan
BONUCA, *see* United Nations Peace-building Office in the Central African Republic
BOSNIA AND HERZEGOVINA, *453-62
elections, 454-55
European Partnership with, 454
European Union Force (EUFOR), 86-87, 454, 461-62
European Union Police Mission in (EUPM), 454, 461-62
EU Stabilization and Association Process, 453-55
General Framework Agreement for Peace in (1995 Peace Agreement), *453-60, 462
civil affairs, 454-55
Mission Implementation Plan (MIP), 454
Peace Implementation Council (PIC), 453
ICJ case, 1477-78
ICTY, 455-56, *1484-94
NATO Partnership for Peace, 454, 458
police restructuring, 455, 457, 462
Republika Srpska, 454-56, 457
BRAZIL
extralegal executions, 869
leprosy victims, 842
Bretton Woods Institutions, *see* International Monetary Fund; World Bank
BURUNDI, 54-55, 57, 120, 131, *148-62
Agreement on Principles towards Lasting Peace, Security and Stability in Burundi (Dar-es-Salaam), 148, 151
Arusha Agreement on Peace and Reconciliation (2000), 157
BINUB, 148, *152-55, 158, 1065
children in armed conflict, 158
Comprehensive Ceasefire Agreement, 148, *153-57
humanitarian situation, 150, 1064-65
human rights, *149-51, 156, 938
ONUB, 54, 78, 86, 88, 120, *130-31, 148, *150-62
political developments, *148-58
security situation, *149-50

CAMBODIA
Agreement concerning Prosecution under Cambodian Law of Crimes Committed during the Period of Democratic Kampuchea (1975-1979), 447-48, 868
human rights, 948-49
CAMEROON
Cameroon-Nigeria Mixed Commission, 173, 252-54
and Nigeria (ICJ case), 173, 252
CARIBBEAN
Caribbean Community (CARICOM), 341-42, 353, *359-60, 1597
Caribbean Sea management, *1243-45
Cuba, 341-42, *357-59, 945-46
Haiti, 54-55, 61, 78, 86, 88, *342-57, 947-48, *1086-88, 1193
see also country names; Economic Commission for Latin America and the Caribbean; Latin America and the Caribbean
CARICOM, *see* Caribbean, *subheading* Caribbean Community
CARTOGRAPHY
geographical names standardization of, 1205
UN Group of Experts on Geographical Names, 1205
UN Regional Cartographic Conference for Asia and the Pacific, Eighteenth (2009), 1204; Seventeenth (Bangkok, 2006), 1204
CEB, *see* United Nations System Chief Executives Board for Coordination
CEDAW, *see* Elimination of Discrimination Against Women, Committee on
CEMAC, *see* Central African Economic and Monetary Community
CENTRAL AFRICA AND GREAT LAKES REGION,
Council for Peace and Security in Central Africa (2000), 685
humanitarian situation, 1064
International Conference on Peace, Security, Democracy and Development in the Great Lakes Region, First (2004, Dar es Salaam), 121, 124; Second (2006, Nairobi), 120-21, *124-26
Lusaka Ceasefire Agreement (1999), 122
Nairobi Protocol for the Prevention, Control and Reduction of Small Arms and Light Weapons in the Great Lakes Region and the Horn of Africa, 684
Pact on Security, Stability and Development in the Great Lakes Region, 121, 124-25
Special Representative of the Secretary-General for the Great Lakes Region, 64, *125-26
UN Standing Advisory Committee on Security Questions in Central Africa, 126, *685-87
UN Subregional Centre for Human Rights and Democracy in Central Africa, 811, *814-15
see also country names
Central African Economic and Monetary Community (CEMAC), 162
CENTRAL AFRICAN REPUBLIC, 120, *162-68
BONUCA, 64, 162, *165-66
and Chad, 120, *162-68
and Darfur region of Sudan, 120, 162-64, 255
humanitarian assistance, 163, 1063-64
human rights, 163
political and security developments, *162-66
CENTRAL AMERICA, 341-42, 1193-94
Guatemala, 341, 946-47, 1055, 1104
Nicaragua, 341, 864, 1477
see also country names; Economic Commission for Latin America and the Caribbean; Latin America and the Caribbean
Central Emergency Response Fund (CERF), 1054, 1060-61
CHAD, 120
and the Central African Republic, 120, *162-68
humanitarian assistance, 167, 1064
N'Djamena Agreement (2006), 164, 167
and the Sudan, 255, 258, 261, 269, 271-72, 279, 289, 291, *297-301
Tripoli Agreement (Chad/Sudan), 120, 163, 167, 269, 297, 300
CHEMICALS
chemicals management, international conference on (Dubai, 2006), 1217
Dubai Declaration, 1246-47
Convention on the Control of Transboundary Movements of Hazardous Wastes and their Disposal (Basel, 1989), 1245, 1247-49
harmful products and waste, protection against, 1245-49
cadmium, 1247
hazardous wastes, 1248-49
lead, 1247
mercury, 1247
persistent organic pollutants (POPs), 1247-1248
Stockholm Convention on, 1216, 1245
Intergovernmental Forum on Chemical Safety, (Budapest, 2006), 1247
Rotterdam Convention on the Prior Informed Consent (PIC) Procedure for Certain Hazardous Chemicals and Pesticides in International Trade (1998), 1245, 1248
see also pollution
chemical weapons

Convention (1993), 407, 650, *653-54, 691, 713
Organization for the Prohibition of Chemical Weapons (OPCW), *654-55
CHILDREN, *1361-79
abduction of, in Africa, 922
and armed conflict, 158, 292, 451, *918-22
Working Group of the Security Council on, *920-22
ILO International Programme on the Elimination of, 1373
education and gender equality, 1371
exploitation of, 1372-73
GA special session (2002)
Declaration and Plan of Action, 1361-62
the girl child, 1341, *1346, 1355, 1364
HIV/AIDS, 1362-65, 1370-72, 1418
International Decade for a Culture of Peace and Non-Violence for the Children of the World (2001-2010), *1279-81, 1362
labour, 917, 1362, 1373
protection measures, 1372-733
refugees, 1397
rights of, 916-22, 1373-74
Committee on the Rights of the Child, 768, 777, 918, 1362, 1373
Convention on the Rights of the Child (1989)
and Optional Protocols (2000), 768, *777-84, 917-18, 1362, 1366
sale of children, child prostitution and child pornography, 917-18
The State of the World's Children 2006, 1363
survival and development, 1369-71
violence against, 1362, 1372-73
see also country names; United Nations Children's Fund; youth
CHINA
(Beijing) Summit of the Forum on China-Africa Cooperation, Declaration of the, 114-15
torture and cruel treatment, 875
CIVIL AND POLITICAL RIGHTS, *820-85
disappearance of persons, *800-808, *861-62, 872-74
extralegal executions, *868-72
freedom of expression, 878-79
Holocaust remembrance, 874
International Covenant on Civil and Political Rights (1966), 756, 832, 844, 857, 865-66, 880-81
and Optional Protocols (1966, 1989), 768, 771
justice, administration of, *855-85
arbitrary detention, 862-66
capital punishment, 868
impunity, 866
judicial system, independence of, 867-68
international personnel in peace support operations, 856
military tribunals, 856
rule of law, 857
the truth, right to, 866-67
racism and racial discrimination, *see* racism and racial discrimination
self-determination, right to, 329, 331-32, *851-53
mercenaries impeding, *853-55
torture and cruel treatment, *see* torture and cruel treatment
see also human rights
climate change
Intergovernmental Authority on Development Climate Prediction and Applications Centre (Nairobi), 1099
Intergovernmental Panel on, 1097, 1228
UN Framework Convention on (1992), 1097, 1216, *1219-22, 1228
Kyoto Protocol (1997), 1163, 1220
see also environment; pollution; World Meteorological Organization
Collective Security Treaty Organization, 61
COLOMBIA
human rights, 944-45
ICJ case, 1477
commodities, *see* trade
Commonwealth of Independent States (CIS)
Abkhaz-Georgian conflict, *see* Georgia
Community of Portuguese-speaking Countries, *1597-98
Comprehensive Ceasefire Agreement (Burundi), 148, *153-57
Comprehensive and Integral International Convention on the Protection and Promotion of the Rights and Dignity of Persons with Disabilities, Ad Hoc Committee on, *785-800, 925, *1278-79, 1395
Comprehensive Nuclear-Test-Ban Treaty (CTBT) (1996), 616, *628-32, 691
Preparatory Commission, 628, *630-31, 1597
Comprehensive Peace Agreement (Liberia, 2003) (Accra), 172, 211-13
Comprehensive Peace Agreement (Nepal, 2006), 362, *450-51
Comprehensive Peace Agreement (Sudan, 2005), 170, *256-65, 941-43, 1066
conference, *see main part of name*
conflict prevention, *48-53
Ad Hoc Working Group on Conflict Prevention and Resolution in Africa, 114
conflict diamonds, *50-53
Kimberley Process, *50-53, 206, 213, 218, 220
CONGO, REPUBLIC OF THE
humanitarian situation, 1064
ICJ case, 1477
Conservation and Management of Straddling Fish Stocks and Highly Migratory Fish Stocks, Agreement on the, *1540-54
conventional weapons, *see* disarmament
Convention on the Abolition of Slavery, the Slave Trade and Institutions and Practices Similar to Slavery, Supplementary (1956),
Convention on Biological Diversity (1992), 1216, 1219, *1223-25
Cartagena Protocol on Biosafety (2000), 1223
Convention on the Control of Transboundary Movements of Hazardous Wastes and their Disposal (Basel, 1989), 1245, 1247-49
Convention on the Elimination of All Forms of Discrimination against Women (1979), 768, 777, *1334-37, 1342, 1354-55
Convention on International Interests in Mobile Equipment (2001), 750
Convention on International Trade in Endangered Species of Wild Fauna and Flora, 1214, 1245
Convention on Jurisdictional Immunities of States and Their Property (2004), 1515
Convention on Long-Range Transboundary Air Pollution (1979), 1222-23
Convention on Preventing and Combating Corruption (AU), 219
Convention on the Prevention of Marine Pollution by Dumping of Wastes and Other Matter (1972)
Protocols (1996 and 2000), 1556
Convention on the Prevention and Punishment of the Crime of Genocide (1948), 784-85, 1477-79
Convention on the Prevention and Punishment of Crimes against Internationally Protected Persons, including Diplomatic Agents (1973), *1520-22

Convention on the Privileges and Immunities of the United Nations (1946), 815
Convention on the Prohibition of the Development, Production and Stockpiling of Bacteriological (Biological) and Toxin Weapons and on Their Destruction (1972), 610, *650-52
Review Conference (sixth), 650-51
Convention on the Prohibition of the Development, Production, Stockpiling and Use of Chemical Weapons and on Their Destruction (1993), 407, 650, *653-54, 691, 713
Convention on Prohibitions or Restrictions on the Use of Certain Conventional Weapons Which May Be Deemed to Be Excessively Injurious or to Have Indiscriminate Effects (1980), *663-65
Convention on the Prohibition of the Use of Nuclear Weapons, *631-32
Convention on the Prohibition of the Use, Stockpiling, Production and Transfer of Anti-personnel Mines and on Their Destruction (1997), *670-72, 691
Convention on Psychotropic Substances (1971), 1436, 1439
Convention on the Recognition and Enforcement of Foreign Arbitral Awards, New York (1958), 1525, *1528-29
Convention on the Reduction of Statelessness (1961), 1395
Convention on the Registration of Objects Launched into Outer Space (1974), 750
Convention on the Rights of the Child (1989)
and Optional Protocols (2000), 768, *777-84, 917-18, 1362, 1366
Convention relating to the Status of Refugees (1951) and Protocol (1967), 1394-95
Convention relating to the Status of Stateless Persons (1954), 1395
Convention against Torture and Other Cruel, Inhuman or Degrading Treatment or Punishment (1984) and Optional Protocol (2002), 768, 776, 865, *876-78, 881
Cooperative Threat Reduction Umbrella Agreement (1992), 610, 620
Coordination of Humanitarian Affairs, Office for the (OCHA), 270-271, 516, 1024, 1057, 1094, 1100
the cluster approach, 1054, 1057, 1065
Cluster Appeal for Improving Humanitarian Response Capacity, 1057
Humanitarian Reform Support Unit, 1057
see also humanitarian assistance
COSTA RICA
ICJ case, 1477
CÔTE D'IVOIRE, 115, *176-211
conflict diamonds, *50-53, 205
elections, 177, 182-85, 189, 191-92, 202
humanitarian situation, 181, *183-85, 1067-68
human rights, 179, *186-87
International Working Group (AU), *179-83, *185-90, *193-94, *202-203
and Liberia, 185, 212
political situation, 183, 187
Pretoria Agreement (2005), 172, 176, 185
sanctions, *203-207
security situation, *181-82, 184-85, 187
toxic waste crisis, 194
UN Group of Experts, 50, *204-207
UNOCI, 54, 78, 86, 88, 172, *176-79, *181-86, *188-90, 193, *196-202, 204, *207-11
Yamoussoukro meeting of Ivorian leaders and benchmarks, *182-84, *189-95
Counter-Terrorism Committee (CTC), *73-77, 636, 879, 1305
Executive Directorate (CTED), *75-77
CPC, *see* Programme and Coordination, Committee for
CRIME PREVENTION AND CRIMINAL JUSTICE, *1287-1322
Africa
prison reform, *1316-18
Round Table for Africa on Crime and Drugs as Impediments to Security and Development in Africa: Strengthening the Rule of Law, *1315-16
UN African Institute for the Prevention of Crime and the Treatment of Offenders, *1294-95
basic principles of judicial conduct, *1318-22
Commission on, 1287, 1289-91, 1293, 1296, *1304-1305, 1315-16, 1318, 1337-38, 1454
corruption, 217, 899
Convention on Preventing and Combating Corruption (AU), 219
UN Convention against, 1290, *1301-1304
crime data collection, 1296
human organs trafficking, 1305-1306
human trafficking
Global Programme against Trafficking in Human Beings, 1291
Trafficking in Persons: Global Patterns, 1297
UN Convention against Transnational Organized Crime, 1289-90
Optional Protocol to Prevent, Suppress and Punish Trafficking in Persons, especially Women and Children, 915, *1296-1301
International Criminal Police Organization (Interpol), 382-83
Interpol Weapons Electronic Tracing System, 657
International Permanent Observatory on Security Measures during Major Events, 1289, *1295-96
kidnapping, *1304-1305
Counter-Kidnapping Manual, 1304
terrorism *see* terrorism
transnational organized crime
UN Convention against (2007), 1289-90 and Protocols, 915, *1296-1301
UN Congress on Crime Prevention and Criminal Justice, Eleventh (2005) (Bangkok), *1287-89, 1293
Bangkok Declaration, 1288
UN Crime Prevention and Criminal Justice Fund, 1290
UN Crime Prevention and Criminal Justice Programme, *1290-94
UN Interregional Crime and Justice Research Institute, 1289, 1294
UNODC, *see* United Nations Office on Drugs and Crime
UN standards and norms in, *1306-14
Vienna Declaration on Crime and Justice, 1290-91
CROATIA
ICJ case, 1477
CUBA
human rights, 945-46
United States embargo against, 341-42, *357-59, 945-46
cultural development, *1279-87
cultural property, return of, *1285-87
protection against trafficking in, 1287
peace, culture of
religious and cultural understanding, *1281-83
sport for development and peace, *1283-85
International Year of Sport and Physical Education (2005), 1283
Olympic truce (2006), 1285
UN Action Plan on Sport for Development and Peace, 1283
UN Office of Sport for Development and Peace, 1379
Culture of Peace and Non-Violence for the Children of the World (2001-2010), International Decade for, *1279-81, 1362

CYPRUS, 454, *487-94
Comprehensive Settlement of the Cyprus Problem, 487-88
human rights, 963-64
"Turkish Republic of Northern Cyprus," 487-88
UNFICYP, 86-87, 454, *487-94

Dar es Salaam Declaration (Great Lakes Region, 2004), 121, 124
Darfur, *see* Sudan
debt
developing countries, *1130-33
Heavily Indebted Poor Countries (HIPC) Initiative, 1057-58, 1072, *1130-33
Multilateral Debt Relief Initiative, 986, 1072, 1074, 1130, 1147
Declaration on the Elimination of All Forms of Intolerance and of Discrimination Based on Religion or Belief (1981), 843-44
Declaration on the Granting of Independence to Colonial Countries and Peoples (1960), 695, *699-702
Declaration on Measures to Eliminate International Terrorism (1994), *1516-19
Declaration on the Protection of All Persons from Enforced Disappearance (1992), 873-74
Declaration on the Rights of Persons Belonging to National or Ethnic, Religious and Linguistic Minorities (1992), 839, 841
Declaration on the Right and Responsibility of Individuals, Groups and Organs of Society to Promote and Protect Universally Recognized Human Rights and Fundamental Freedoms (1998), 766
DECOLONIZATION, *699-726
Declaration on the Granting of Independence to Colonial Countries and Peoples (1960), 695, *699-702
Special Committee on, 699
International Decade for the Eradication of Colonialism, Second (2001-2010), 695, *699-702
deforestation, *1228-41
International Year of Forests (2011), 1228, *1240-41
UN Forum on Forests, *1228-40
democracy
democratic and equitable international order, *890-92
International Conference of New or Restored Democracies, Sixth (2006, Doha), 695, *697-99; Seventh (2009), 697
Doha Declaration, 697
support for, *696-99
UN Democracy Fund (UNDEF), 49, 697-98, 818, 1046
UNDP programme, 1033
DEMOCRATIC PEOPLE'S REPUBLIC OF KOREA, *441-47
armistice agreement (1953), 64
arms embargo, 641
human rights, *949-52
missile programme, 362, *441-43, 628
nuclear programme, 361, *442-47, 449-50, 609, 641, 689, 1202
Pyongyang Declaration (2002), 442
sanctions, 442, *444-47
DEMOCRATIC REPUBLIC OF THE CONGO, 114-15, *120-24, *127-48
arms embargo, 120, *140-45
elections, 128, *132-36, *138-39
EUFOR R.D. Congo, *128-30, 135
Global and All-Inclusive Agreement on the Transition in the DRC (2002), *127
Group of Experts, *141-45
humanitarian situation, 115, 1065
human rights, 132, 938-39
ICC case, 127, 132, 1503
ICJ case, 857, 1477-80
MONUC, 54, 78, 86, 88, 115, 120-21, 127, *130-40, *145-48, 169-70
political developments, *127-30
International Committee of Eminent Persons, *134-35
SC mission, 132-33
and Uganda, 169
Department of, *see under main part of name*
desertification
UN Convention to Combat Desertification in those Countries Experiencing Serious Drought and/or Desertification, particularly in Africa (1994), 902, 1216, 1219, *1225-27
DEVELOPING COUNTRIES
debt problems, *1130-33
Decade to Roll Back Malaria in Developing Countries, Particularly in Africa (2001-2010), *1421-25
economic and technical cooperation among, 1050
Expert Meeting on Capacity Building in the Area of Foreign Direct Investment: Data Compilation and Policy Formulation in Developing Countries, 1136-37
Expert Meeting on Enabling Small Commodity Producers and Processors in Developing Countries to Reach Global Market, 1117
Expert meeting on the Participation of Developing Countries in New and Dynamic Sectors of World Trade: Review of the Energy Sector, 1117
Expert Meeting on Positive Corporate Contributions to the Economic and Social Development of Host Developing Countries, 1136-37
LDCs, *see* least developed countries
South-South cooperation, 1050, 1079
UN Manual for the Negotiation of Bilateral Tax Treaties between Developed and Developing Countries, 1140
DEVELOPMENT, *975-1022
Africa
information for development, 1149
New Partnership for Africa's Development (NEPAD), *see* New Partnership for Africa's Development
women, integration of in development, 1151
Americas
Haiti, 354
Commission on Population and, 1257-58
cultural, *see* cultural development
Development Policy, Committee for, *1007-1008, 1010-11
and disarmament, *674-76
Doha Development Round, *1111-15, 1121, 1189
Expert Group Meeting on International Migration and Development in Latin America and the Caribbean, 1258
financing for, *1133-36
Global Microcredit Summit (2006), *996-97
High-level Panel on UN System-wide Coherence, 818, 992, 1060, 1210, 1227, 1329, 1352, 1389
human development, 1006-1007
Human Development Report 2006, 1006-1007, 1032, 1204
human resources development, *1322-27
International Conference on Financing for (Monterrey Consensus) (2002), 976, 1127, *1134-36
International Conference on Population and Development (ICPD) (1994), 1382, 1409
Programme of Action, 1060, 1191, 1257-59
Conference on Implementation (Bangkok, 2006), 1417-18
International Development Association, 1130
international economic cooperation, *976-81
industrial development, *979-81
and international financial system, *1128-30
and international migration, 1164

High-level Dialogue on International Migration and Development, 1164, *1261-63, 1329
and international trade, *1113-15
International Year of Microcredit (2005), *996-97
Latin America and the Caribbean, 1190-92
LDCs, *see* least developed countries
operational activities for, *1023-52
United Nations Pledging Conference for Development Activities (2006), 1030
population and poverty, 1164, 1265-66
and public administration, *1007-1009
right to, *885-90
science and technology, *997-1004
social, *see* social development
Trade and Development Report, 2006, 1004, 1111, 1118
UN Conference on Environment and Development (1992) (UNCED)
Agenda 21, *981-85, 1202, 1246
UNDAF, *see* United Nations Development Assistance Framework
UNDG, *see* United Nations Development Group
UNDP, *see* United Nations Development Programme
United Nations Comprehensive Human Rights Guidelines on Development-based Displacement (1997), 906
UN role in promoting development in the context of globalization and interdependence, *977-79
and women, 1347
see also country names; economic cooperation, international; sustainable development
diamonds, *see* conflict prevention; *subheading* conflict diamonds
diplomatic relations, *1520-22
Convention on the Prevention and Punishment of Crimes against Internationally Protected Persons, including Diplomatic Agents (1973), *1520-22
Vienna Convention on Consular Relations (1963), 1520
Vienna Convention on Diplomatic Relations (1961), 1520
DISABILITIES, PERSONS WITH, 924-25, *1278-79
Ad Hoc Committee on a Comprehensive and Integral International Convention on the Protection and Promotion of the Rights and Dignity of Persons with Disabilities, *785-800, 925, *1278-79, 1395
Committee on the Rights of Persons with Disabilities, 785
Convention on the Rights of Persons with Disabilities, 785-800*
disappearance of persons, *800-808, *861-62, 872-74
Declaration on the Protection of All Persons from Enforced Disappearance (1992), 873-74
International Convention on the Protection of All Persons from Enforced Disappearance (2006), *800-808, 874, 1395
DISARMAMENT, *609-94
arms limitation and disarmament agreements
environment, effect on, *676-77
multilateral, 615-16
bacteriological (biological) weapons, 610, *650-52
chemical weapons
Convention (1993), 407, 650, *653-54, 691, 713
Organization for the Prohibition of (OPCW), *654-55
Conference on, 609, *613-19, 638, 667, 672
conventional weapons, *655-72, *663-65
anti-personnel mines, Convention (1997), *670-72, 691
towards an arms trade treaty, *655-56
excessively injurious, Convention (1980), 610, *663-65
practical disarmament, *665-67
small arms
Group of Interested States in Practical Disarmament Measures, 657
illicit trade, *659-63
Antigua Declaration, 692
United Nations Conference on the Illicit Trade in Small Arms and Light Weapons in All Its Aspects (2001)
Programme of Action, 60-61, 609, 657-59, 689, 691
Interpol Weapons Electronic Tracing System, 657
transparency
in armaments, *667-70
of military expenditures, 669-70
UN register of, 610, 667-68, 677
verification, 670
Cooperative Threat Reduction Agreement (1992), 610
and development, *674-76
Disarmament Commission, 609, *612-14, 619, 666
Disarmament Decade (Fourth) (2010-2019), 609, *609-11
and human rights, 676
missiles, *627-28
DPRK, 362, *441-43, 628
Hague Code of Conduct, 627
Missile Technology Control Regime, 627
multilateral agreements, 615-16
non-proliferation, *635-39
nuclear disarmament, *616-33
bilateral agreements and unilateral measures, *619-27
Comprehensive Nuclear-Test-Ban Treaty (CTBT) (1996), 616, *628-32, 691
Preparatory Commission for CTBT organization, 628, *630-31, 1597
Cooperative Threat Reduction Umbrella Agreement (1992), 620
DPRK, 361, *442-47, 449-50, 609, 689
fissile material, 617
IAEA safeguards, 616, 620
Non-Proliferation of Nuclear Weapons, Treaty on the (NPT) (1968), 361, *432-35, 616, 633
Review Conference (2005), 616; (2010), *633-34
nuclear-weapon-free zones, 609, 644-50
security assurances, *617-19
Strategic Offensive Reductions Treaty (SORT) (Moscow Treaty) (2002), 610, 620
nuclear weapons,
ICJ advisory opinion, 617, *632-33
Convention on the Prohibition of, *631-32
outer space arms race, prevention, *672-74
radioactive waste, 643
Reduction and Limitation of Strategic Offensive Arms, Treaty on the (START I) (1991), 610, 619-20
regional and other approaches, *681-94
Africa, *684-88
African Nuclear-Weapon-Free Zone Treaty (Treaty of Pelindaba, 1996), 644, 687
ECOWAS Convention on Small Arms and Light Weapons, Their Ammunition and Other Related Materials, 176, 684-85
Nairobi Protocol for the Prevention, Control and Reduction of Small Arms and Light Weapons in the Great Lakes Region and the Horn of Africa, 684
Programme for Coordination and Assistance for Security and Development (PCASED), 685
SADC Protocol on the Control of Firearms, Ammunition and Other Related Materials, 685

Standing Advisory Committee on Security Questions in Central Africa, 126, *685-87
UN Regional Centre for Peace and Disarmament in Africa, *687-88
Asia and the Pacific, *688-90
Conference on Interaction and Confidence Building Measures in Asia, Second Summit (Almaty, 2006), 452, 691
South-East Asia Nuclear-Weapon-Free Zone Treaty (Bangkok Treaty, 1995), 646, 689
South Pacific Nuclear-Free Zone Treaty (1985) (Treaty of Rarotonga), 649
Treaty on a Nuclear-Weapon-Free Zone in Central Asia, 644
UN Regional Centre for Peace and Disarmament in Asia and the Pacific, *689-90
UN-Republic of Korea Joint Conference on Disarmament and Non-proliferation (Jeju) (2006), 689
Europe and the Mediterranean, 690-92
Regional Arms Control Verification and Implementation Assistance Centre, 691
South-Eastern and Eastern Europe Clearinghouse for the Control of Small Arms and Light Weapons, 691
Stability Pact for South-Eastern Europe, 691
Treaty on Conventional Armed Forces in Europe (1990), 691
Vienna Declaration, 692
Latin America and the Caribbean, *692-94
Agency for the Prohibition of Nuclear Weapons in Latin America and the Caribbean (OPANAL), 647, 692
Antigua Declaration, 692
Treaty for the Prohibition of Nuclear Weapons in Latin America and the Caribbean (Treat of Tlatelolco), 647
UN Regional Centre for Peace, Disarmament and Development in, 687, *692-94
Vienna Declaration, 692
Southern hemisphere and adjacent areas, *649-50
science and technology, role of, *740-41
studies, information and training, *677-81
Advisory Board on Disarmament Matters, 617
disarmament studies programme, *677-78
UN disarmament fellowship, training and advisory services, *680-81
UN Disarmament Information Programme, *678-80
Voluntary Trust Fund, 679
UN Institute for Disarmament Research (UNIDIR), 613, 617, 676, 680
UN Conference on Disarmament Issues (Yokohama) (2006), 689
UNMOVIC, 407-409, 609
UN role, *610-16
weapons of mass destruction
Commission, 609, 616, 636
new types of, 636
non-proliferation of, *634-37
and terrorism, *636-37
see also terrorism
Disarmament Affairs, UN Department of (DDA), 610, 659, 665, 668-70, 678-79, 692, 735
Disarmament Commission, 609, *612-14, 619, 666
DISASTER RELIEF, *1089-1107, 1165
Central Emergency Response Fund (CERF), 1054, 1060-61
Central Register of Disaster Management Capacities, 1090
El Salvador, 1104
Ethiopia, 1105
FAO, 1094
Global Facility for Disaster Reduction and Recovery, 1093
Global Platform for Disaster Risk Reduction, 1094
Guatemala, 1104
Guidelines on the Use of Military and Civil Defence Assets in Disaster Relief (Oslo Guidelines, 1994), 1090
Humanitarian Early Warning Service, 1090
In-Country Self Assessment Tool for Natural Disaster Response Preparedness, 1093
Indian Ocean tsunami, *1100-1104, 1214, 1555
Global Consortium for Tsunami Recovery (2006), 1100
Intergovernmental Coordination Group for the Indian Ocean Tsunami Warning and Mitigation System, 1100
Multi-Donor Voluntary Trust Fund on Tsunami Early Warning Arrangements in the Indian Ocean and Southeast Asia, 1165
Tsunami Recovery Impact Assessment Land Monitoring System, 1100
Indonesia, 1106
International Charter on Space and Major Disasters, 747
International Conference on Early Warning, Third (Bonn, 2006), 1093
International Decade for Natural Disaster Reduction (1990-2000), 1093
International Satellite System for Search and Rescue, 747
International Strategy for Disaster Reduction (ISDR), *1093-97, 1214
Kenya, 1105-1106
Pakistan, 1055, 1106-1107
Philippines, 1106
Somalia, 1106
Tajikistan, 1107
Tampere Convention on the Provision of Telecommunication Resources for Disaster Mitigation and Relief Operations, 1090
UN inter-agency Disaster Management Training Programme, 1093
UN Platform for Space-based Information for Disaster Management and Emergency Response, 745, *748-50
UN Trust Fund for Disaster Reduction, 1094
World Conference on Disaster Reduction (Hyogo, Japan) (2005), 747
Hyogo Declaration and the Hyogo Framework for Action 2005-2015, 1093-94, 1214
displaced persons
internally displaced persons, 477, 922-24, 1067, 1079
Guiding Principles on Internal Displacement (1998), 922-24
see also, refugees, United Nations High Commissioner for Refugees, Office of the
DJIBOUTI
ICJ case, 1477, 1480-81
Doha Declaration, *see* democracy
DOMINICA
ICJ case, 1477, 1481
DRUG ABUSE AND CONTROL, *1430-64
Commission on Narcotic Drugs, 1431-37, *1454-64
Convention on Psychotropic Substances (1971), 1436, 1439
drug demand reduction and drug abuse, 1455-57
Global Assessment Programme on Drug Abuse, 1455
Global Youth Network against Drug Abuse, 1454
illicit cultivation and manufacture, 1457-58
international cooperation, *1431-35
alternative development for, *1458-60
International Narcotics Control Board, *1436-40
Project Cohesion, 1436, 1439-40
Project Prism, *1436-39
regional cooperation, 1460-61

Baku Accord on Regional Cooperation against Illicit Drugs and Related Matters: a Vision for the Twenty-first Century, *1461-64
Single Convention on Narcotic Drugs (1961)
Protocol (1972), 1436
trafficking
UN Convention against Illicit Traffic in Narcotic Drugs and Psychotropic Substances (1988), 1436, 1454, 1461
UN mechanisms, strengthening of, 1464
UNODC, *see* United Nations Office on Drugs and Crime
world drug situation, 1440-53

EAST TIMOR *see* Timor-Leste
ECO, *see* Economic Cooperation Organization
ECONOMIC COMMISSION FOR AFRICA (ECA), *1146-53
activities in 2006, *1148-53
promoting trade and regional integration, 1150-51
subregional offices, 1151-53
ECONOMIC COMMISSION FOR EUROPE (ECE), *1171-87
activities, 1172-75
Ministerial Declaration on Social and Economic Challenges in Distressed Urban Areas in the ECE Region, 1174-75
operational activities, 1175
reform, *1175-87
ECONOMIC COMMISSION FOR LATIN AMERICA AND THE CARIBBEAN (ECLAC), *1187-95
activities, 1188-94
Statistical Yearbook for Latin America and the Caribbean, 1192
subregional activities, 1193-94
technical cooperation, 1192
Economic Survey of Latin America and the Caribbean, 1188
Preliminary Overview of the Economies of Latin America and the Caribbean, 1188
programme and organizational questions, 1194
UN, cooperation with, 1195
Economic Community of Central African States (ECCAS), 126, 811, 1155, 1597
Economic Community of West African States (ECOWAS), 61, 172-73, 177, 195-96, 211, 244, 811, 1149
Convention on Small Arms and Light Weapons, Their Ammunition and Other Related Materials, 176, 684-85
Cross-Border Initiatives Programme, 176
ECONOMIC COOPERATION, INTERNATIONAL, *975-1022
coercive economic measures, *897-99
international economic relations, *976-1004
see also development
Economic Cooperation Organization, *1166-67, 1597
Economic and Social Affairs, Executive Committee of (ECESA), 1024
Economic and Social Affairs, UN Department of (DESA)
Division for Social Policy and Development, 1379
Millennium Development Goals Report 2006, 986
technical cooperation projects, 1045-46
ECONOMIC AND SOCIAL COMMISSION FOR ASIA AND THE PACIFIC (ESCAP), *1155-70
activities, 736, 1157-66
programme and organizational questions, 1165
Programme of Technical Assistance for Asia and the Pacific, 1158
social development, 1163-65
ECONOMIC AND SOCIAL COMMISSION FOR WESTERN ASIA (ESCWA), 1195-1200
activities, 1196-99
Annual Review of Development in Globalization and Regional Integration in the Arab Countries, 2006, 1196
Damascus Declaration on the Realization of the MDGs, 1196
LAS, cooperation with, 1200
programme and organizational questions, 1199-1200
see also Western Asia; *specific country*
ECONOMIC AND SOCIAL COUNCIL
High-level meeting with Bretton Woods institutions, WTO and UNCTAD, 1133-34
humanitarian affairs segment, *1053-57
international conferences and summits, follow-up to, *1596-97
operational activities segment, 1023-24
sessions and segments, 1594-95
strengthening, *1589-92
ECONOMIC, SOCIAL AND CULTURAL RIGHTS, *885-936
International Covenant on, (1966), 756, 768, 772
see also human rights
economic and social trends, 1004-1007, *1145-1200
Africa, *1147-55
Americas, 1188
Asia and the Pacific, 1155-70, 1195-96
economies in transition, *1020-22
Europe and the Mediterranean, 1171-72
Latin America and the Caribbean, 1188
Western Asia, 1195-96
Trade and Development Report, 2006, 1004, 1111, 1118
World Economic Situation and Prospects 2007, 1005, 1110, 1121, 1125, 1131, 1171
World Economic and Social Survey, 2006, 1006, 1125
see also statistics
ecosystems
Ecosystems and Human Well-being, 1228
Living Beyond Our Means: Natural Assets and Human Well-being, 1228
marine, *1241-45
Caribbean Sea management, *1243-45
coral reefs, 1242-43
International Coral Reef Network, 1242
Global Meeting of Regional Seas Conventions and Action Plans, Eighth (2006), 1159
Global Programme of Action for the Protection of the Marine Environment from Land-based Activities (Beijing), 1242
global waters assessment, 1241-42
oceans and seas, 1241, 1243
Millennium Ecosystem Assessment, 1228
terrestrial, *1228-41
deforestation, *see* deforestation
sustainable mountain development, 1241
wildlife conservation, 1245
see also environment
ECUADOR, 863
EDUCATION
education for all
EFA Global Monitoring Report: Literacy for Life, 2006, 1326
girls, 908
right to, 908-909
UN Literacy Decade (2003-2012), 1164, *1326-27
EGYPT
terrorism, *71
Elimination of Discrimination against Women, Committee on the (CEDAW), 768, 907, 1218, 1342, 1354-55, 1373
El Niño, *1098-99
EL SALVADOR
disaster relief, 1104

humanitarian assistance, 1055
ENERGY
and the environment, 1213
Expert meeting on the Participation of Developing Countries in New and Dynamic Sectors of World Trade: Review of the Energy Sector, 1117
Global Forum on Sustainable Energy, Fifth (Vienna), 985
International Partnership on a Hydrogen Economy, 1213
and natural resources, *1201-1204
nuclear, *1202-1203
ENVIRONMENT, 1033, *1206-49
activities, *1227-49
arms limitation and disarmament agreements, effect of on, *676-77
atmosphere, 1228
and energy, 1213
Environmental Guidelines, 1396
Environmental Management Group, 1208-1209
Environment Watch Strategy Vision 2020, 1211
Europe and the Mediterranean, 1174
Ministerial Conference "Environment for Europe," Sixth (Belgrade, 2007), 1174
Global Environment Facility, 1216, 1228
Global Forum for Sport and the Environment (Lausanne, 2006), 1217
Global Ministerial Environment Forum, Seventh (Dubai, 2006), *1132-34
harmful products and waste, protection against, 1245-49
International environmental governance, 1208
marine, 1557
Rotterdam Convention on the Prior Informed Consent (PIC) Procedure for Certain Hazardous Chemicals and Pesticides in International Trade (1998), 1245, 1248
and scientific concerns, 909-10
and sustainable development, 1212-14
and tourism, 1213-14
toxic waste, 194, 909-10
and trade, 1214
UN Conference on Environment and Development (1992) (UNCED)
Agenda 21
Programme for the Further Implementation of, *981-85, 1202, 1246
UNEP, *see* United Nations Environment Programme
UN Framework Convention on Climate Change (UNFCCC) (1992), 1097, 1216, *1219-22, 1228
Kyoto Protocol (1997), 1163, 1220
Vienna Convention on the Protection of the Ozone Layer (1985), 1222
Montreal Protocol on Substances that Deplete the Ozone Layer (1987), 1222
see also climate change; ecology; marine resources; pollution; sustainable development; World Meteorological Organization
ERITREA, 115, *315-29
Algiers Agreements (Ethiopia-Eritrea, 2000), *315-24, 326
Boundary Commission, 255-56, *315-24
and Sudan, 260
UNMEE, 86, 88, 256, *315-23, *325-29
ETHIOPIA
Algiers Agreements (Ethiopia-Eritrea, 2000), *315-24, 326
Boundary Commission, 255-56, *315-24
disaster relief, 1105
and Somalia, 308
UNMEE, 86, 88, 256, *315-23, *325-29
European Union (EU)
EUFOR (Bosnia and Herzegovina), 86-87, 454, 461-62; (R.D. Congo), *128-30, 135
European Partnership Action Plan (Kosovo Province of Serbia and Montenegro), 453, 465-66, 468
European Partnership with Bosnia and Herzegovina, 455
EU Police Mission in Bosnia and Herzegovina (EUPM), 454, 461-62
EU Stabilization and Association Process (Bosnia and Herzegovina), 453
EUROPE AND THE MEDITERRANEAN, *453-98
Armenia, 453, *484-86
Azerbaijan, *484-86
Belarus, *961-63, 1107
Bosnia and Herzegovina, 86-87, *453-62, 1477-78
Council of Europe, 61, *497-98, 812, 1597
Croatia, 1477
Cyprus, 86-87, 454, *487-94, 963-64
drug situation, 1451-53
economic and social activities, *1171-87
Economic Survey of Europe, 2005, 1171
France, 239, *715-17, 1477, 1480-81
Georgia, 86-87, 453, *473-84
Hungary, 840, 1477
Montenegro, 1088, *see also subheading* Serbia and Montenegro
Organization for Democracy and Economic Development (GUAM), 487
OSCE, *see* Organization for Security and Cooperation in Europe
Republic of Moldova, 453-54, 486-87
Romania, 1477, 1480
Russian Federation, 832, 1071
security and cooperation in the Mediterranean, *494-95
Serbia and Montenegro, 61, 86-87, 453, *462-73, 1477-78
Slovakia, 1477
South-Eastern Europe, stability and development in, *495-97
Ukraine, 1477, 1480
see also country names; Economic Commission for Europe; European Union
extralegal executions, *868-72

FALKLAND ISLANDS (MALVINAS), 713
FIJI, 447
FINANCE, INTERNATIONAL
financial policy, *1125-33
financial flows, 1126
financial system, *1127-30
and development, *1128-30
International Conference on Financing for Development (Monterrey Consensus) (2002), 976, 1127
follow-up, *1134-36
International Monetary and Financial Committee, 1127
investment, technology and related financial issues, *1136-41
Expert Meeting on Capacity Building in the Area of Foreign Direct Investment: Data Compilation and Policy Formulation in Developing Countries, 1136-37
international standards of accounting and reporting, 1136-37, 1139
taxation, *1139-41
see also International Monetary Fund; World Bank
financing of UN missions
BONUCA, 166
MINURSO, *337-39

MINUSTAH, *355-57
MONUC, *146-48
ONUB, *158-62
UNAMA, 379-80
UNAMET, 431
UNAMI, 402
UNAMSIL, *240-41
UNDOF, *607-608
UNFICYP, *492-94, 593
UNIFIL, *591-96
UNIKOM, *411-12
UNIOSIL, 240
UNMEE, *326-29
UNMIK, *470-72
UNMIL, *221-23
UNMIS, *266-68
UNMISET, *428-30
UNMIT, *430-31
UNOCI, *207-11
UNOGBIS, 251
UNOMIG, *483-84
UNOTIL, 430
UNOWA, 176
UNPOS, 311
UNRWA, 563
FOOD
FAO, *see* Food and Agricultural Organization of the United Nations
food aid, 1426-28
food security, 1428
International Year of Natural Fibers (2009), *1428
nutrition, 1428-29
right to, *902-905
WFP, *see* World Food Programme
World Food Summit (1996), 1428
FOOD AND AGRICULTURE ORGANIZATION OF THE UNITED NATIONS (FAO), 378, 1598
FORMER YUGOSLAVIA
International Tribunal for the (ICTY) *see* International Tribunals
FRANCE
ICJ case, 1477, 1480-81
and Mauritius, 239
New Caledonia, *715-17

Gaza Strip, *see* Middle East
General Agreement on Trade in Services (GATS), 1117
GENERAL ASSEMBLY
Agenda, 1593
Credentials, 1593
Emergency special session (Palestine), *521-24, 528
resolutions and decisions, 1593-94
revitalization, *1586-89
2005 World Summit, follow-up, *986-92, 1208, 1210, 1409
General Framework Agreement for Peace in Bosnia and Herzegovina (1995 Peace Agreement), *454-60, 462
Geneva Convention, Fourth (1949), *542-44
genocide
Convention on the Prevention and Punishment of the Crime of Genocide (1948), 784-85, 1477-79
Rwanda, 172
The Rwanda Genocide and the United Nations, 172
GEORGIA, *473-84
Abkhazia, 453, *473-83
Agreement on a Ceasefire and Separation of Forces (1994, Moscow Agreement), 453, 474, *478-79, 481-82
Basic Principles for the Distribution of Competences between Tbilisi and Sukhumi (2001), 453, 473
CIS peacekeeping force, 453, *474-79
Group of Friends of the Secretary-General on, *474-77
humanitarian situation, 482-83
human rights, 479, 482-83
UNOMIG, 86-87, 453, *474-84
GIBRALTAR, 695, 713-15
Global and All-Inclusive Agreement on the Transition in the DRC (2002), *127
Global Assessment Programme on Drug Abuse, 1455
Global Forum on Migration and Development, 1262
Global Forum on Reinventing Government, Seventh (Vienna, 2007), 1008
Global Forum on Sustainable Energy, Fifth (Vienna), 985
Global International Water Assessment, 1241-42
globalization, *893-94
Commission on Globalization and Systemic Issues, 1142
and human rights, 821, *893-94
and interdependence, 1118
UN role in promoting development in the context of globalization and interdependence, *977-79
Global Microcredit Summit (2006), *996-97
Global Programme against Trafficking in Human Beings, 1291
Global Science Corps, 1050
GUATEMALA
disappearance of persons, 873
disaster relief, 1104
humanitarian assistance, 1055
human rights, 946-47
MINUGUA, 341
GUINEA, 254
humanitarian situation, 1068
ICJ case, 1478-79
and Sierra Leone, 232, 235
GUINEA-BISSAU, 244-51
elections, 173, 249
humanitarian situation, 1068
political and security developments, 244, 245-46, 248-49
and Senegal, 246
UNOGBIS, 64, 173, 244-45, 247-51, 1598

HAITI, *342-57
Advisory Group on, 353
economic assistance, *1086-88
elections, 61, *342-48
humanitarian situation, 354
human rights, 354, 947-48
judicial system, 349
MINUSTAH, 54-55, 78, 86, 88, *342-57, 1193
security situation, 343, 347-48
HEALTH, *1409-29
AIDS, *see* HIV/AIDS
avian influenza, 1426
International Pledging Conference on Avian and Human Influenza (Beijing, 2006), 1426
Global Fund to Fight AIDS, Tuberculosis and Malaria, 1341, 1415, 1421
global public health, 1425-26
harmful products and waste, protection against, 1245-49
HIV/AIDS, *see* HIV/AIDS
malaria
Decade to Roll Back Malaria in Developing Countries, Particularly in Africa (2001-2010), *1421-25
Global Fund to Fight AIDS, Tuberculosis and Malaria, 1341, 1415, 1421

physical and mental health, right to, 910-12
road safety, 1426
UN Global Road Safety Week (2007), 1173
*1419-20
tobacco, *1420-21
tuberculosis
Global Campaign to Stop TB (2006-2015), 1425
Global Fund to Fight AIDS, Tuberculosis and Malaria, 1341, 1415, 1421
water and sanitation services, 911-12
International Year of Sanitation (2008),
WHO, *see* World Health Organization
World Diabetes Day, *1420
HIV/AIDS, 1033-35
children, 1362-65, 1370-72, 1418
Counselling and Testing Day, *1416-17
Declaration of Commitment on (2001), *1410-16, 1418
Global Fund to Fight AIDS, Tuberculosis and Malaria, 1341, 1415, 1421
Global Task Team on Improving AIDS Coordination among Multilateral Institutions and International Donors, 1396, 1415, 1418, 1457
High-Level Meeting, 1329
prevention and control, *1410-19
and refugees, 1396
Strategic Plan (UNHCR), 1396
UNAIDS *see* Joint United Nations Programme on HIV/AIDS
United Nations Integrated Framework on HIV/AIDS, 1082
Holocaust remembrance, 874
HONDURAS
arbitrary detention, 864
extralegal executions, 869
ICJ case, 1477
HORN OF AFRICA, *254-329
disaster relief, 1105
Nairobi Protocol for the Prevention, Control and Reduction of Small Arms and Light Weapons in the Great Lakes Region and the Horn of Africa, 684
see also country names
Human Development Report 2006, 1006-1007, 1032, 1204
HUMANITARIAN ASSISTANCE
Africa
Burundi, 150, 1064-65
Central African Republic, 1063-64
Chad, 167, 1064
Congo, 1064
Côte d'Ivoire, 1067-68
DRC, 115, 1065
Great Lakes Region, 1064
Guinea, 1068
Guinea-Bissau, 1068
Kenya, 1066
Liberia, 1068, *1081-82
Sierra Leone, 230, 241
Somalia, 302, 308, 941, 1066
Sudan, 943, 1066-67
Uganda, 1065-66
West Africa, 1067
Zimbabwe, 1068-69
Americas
El Salvador, 1055
Guatemala, 1055
Haiti, 354
Asia and the Pacific
Afghanistan, 1069-70
Iraq, 399
Myanmar, 448
Nepal, 1070
Pakistan, 1055
Sri Lanka, 1071
Timor-Leste, 420-21
consolidated appeals, 1054, 1061, 1063-71, 1105
coordination of, *1053-61, 1389-90
Europe and the Mediterranean
Georgia, 482-83
Russian Federation, 1071
Executive Committee on Humanitarian Affairs (ECHA), 1389
Middle East
Lebanon, 574, 576-79, 587, 1070
Palestine, 1070-71
new international humanitarian order, *1063
see also Coordination of Humanitarian Affairs, Office for the
HUMAN RESOURCES
development, *1322-27
Management, Office of Human Resources (OHRM), 108, 1353, 1390
UN Institute for Training and Research (UNITAR), 1322-23
University of Peace (Costa Rica), *1324-25
UN University, *1323-24
HUMAN RIGHTS
Africa
Burundi, *148-51, 156, 913, 938
Central African Republic, 163
Côte d'Ivoire, 179, *186-87
DRC, 132, 913-14, 938-39
Liberia, 213, 220, 914-15, 939-40
Sierra Leone, 915-16, 940-41
Somalia, 916
Sudan, 916-918, 941-43
Uganda, 918, 943-44
Americas
Colombia, 919-20, 944-45
Cuba, 920-21, 945-46
Guatemala, 921-22, 946-47
Haiti, 354, 922-23, 947-48
arbitrary detention, 862-66
Asia and the Pacific
Afghanistan, 379, 923, 948, *1346-47
Cambodia, 923-24, 948-49
DPRK, 924, *925-27, *949-52
Iran, *927-29, *952-54
Iraq, 396, 399
Kyrgyzstan, 937
Myanmar, 448-49, *929-33, *954-58
Nepal, 450, 933-35, 958-60
Sri Lanka, 935, 960
Tajikistan, 451
Timor-Leste, 414, 427, 935, 960
Turkmenistan, 935, 960
Uzbekistan, 935, 960-61
bioethics, 887
children, rights of, *95-97, 892-94
Convention on (1989), *777
civil and political rights, *see* civil and political rights
Commission on, 755-56, 762, 839, 918, 924, 937, 1338
Subcommission on the Promotion and Protection of Human Rights, 762, 842, 855-57, 886, 937
Committee on, 768-69, 851, 857
corruption, 899
Council, 49, 734, *756-63, 810, 822, 824, 833, 835, 841-42, 844-46, 853, 856, 866-67, 869, 883, 886, 1574
Declaration on the Rights and Responsibility of Individuals, Groups and Organs of Society to Promote and Protect

Universally Recognized Human Rights and Fundamental Freedoms (1998), 766
democratic and equitable international order, *890-92
development, right to, *885-89
Digest of Jurisprudence of the United Nations and Regional Organizations on the Protection of Human Rights while Countering Terrorism, 881
disappearance of persons, *800-808, *861-62, 872-74
Protection of All Persons from Enforced Disappearance, Declaration on (1992), 873-74; International Convention on (2006), *800-808, 874, 1395
and disarmament, 676
economic, social and cultural rights, 768, 772, 885-936
International Covenant on (1966), 772
education in, 809
World Programme on Human Rights Education, 815
education, right to, 908-909
International Conference on the Right to Basic Education as a Fundamental Human Right and the Legal Framework for its Financing (Jakarta, 2005), 909
elderly, rights of the, 922
environmental and scientific concerns, 909-10
Europe and the Mediterranean
Belarus, *961-63
Cyprus, 963-64
Georgia, 479, 482-83
and extreme poverty, *899-902
food, right to, *902-905
general aspects, 937-38
and globalization, 821, *893-94
and good governance, 767-68
instruments
children rights on, 768, *777-84, 917-18, 1362, 1366
civil and political rights (1966), 756, 768, 771, 832, 844, 857, 865-66, 880-81
discrimination against women (1979), 768, 777, *1334-37, 1342, 1354-55
economic, social and cultural rights (1966), 756, 768, 772
genocide (1948), 784-85, 1477-79
migrant workers and their families (1990), 768, 784, *835-39
persons with disabilities, *785-800, 925, *1278-79, 1395
protection from enforced disappearance, *800-808, 873-74, 1385
racial discrimination (1965), 768, *773-76, 821-22
torture and other cruel, inhuman or degrading punishment (1984), 768, 776, 865, *876-78, 881
International Conference of National Human Rights Institutions (Santa Cruz, Bolivia, 2006), 810
International cooperation in the field of, *815-18
International Coordinating Committee (ICC) of National Human Rights Institutions, 809-10
intolerance, forms of, *839-52
anti-terrorism measures that violate rights, 840
cultural prejudice, 839
leprosy victims, 842
minorities, discrimination against, 839-43
religious intolerance, *843-51
work and descent, discrimination based on, 842-43
justice, administration of, *855-85, 862-66
Middle East
Lebanon, *964-67
UN Human Rights and Documentation Centre for South West Asia and the Arab region, 815
promotion of, *755-818
protection, *819-935
racism and racial discrimination, *820-39
treaties, reservations to, 770-71
Universal Declaration of (1948), 756, 809, 844, 946
Universal Periodic Review (UPR), 761, 768
women and girls, *see* women
World Conference on (1993)
follow up, 808-809
Vienna Declaration and Programme of Action, 768
HUMAN SETTLEMENTS
Europe and the Mediterranean, 1174-75
Latin America and the Caribbean, 1190
State of the World's Cities 2006/7: the Millennium Development Goals and Urban Sustainability—30 Years of Shaping the Habitat Agenda, 1250
UN Conference on Human Settlements (Habitat II) (1996), *1249-53
UN Habitat and Human Settlements Foundation, 1250-52
UN Human Settlements Programme (UN-Habitat), 1130, *1249-56
OIOS review, 1256
UNEP, cooperation with, 1217, 1255
World Urban Forum, 1174, 1190, 1255
HUNGARY
ICJ case, 1477
minorities, discrimination against, 840

IAMB, *see* International Advisory and Monitoring Board
IASC, *see* Inter-Agency Standing Committee
ICAO, *see* International Civil Aviation Organization
ILO, *see* International Labour Organization
IMF, *see* International Monetary Fund
Independent Audit Advisory Committee (IAAC), 1572
INDIA
and Pakistan
Jammu and Kashmir, 448
UNMOGIP, 86-87, 448
terrorism, *72
INDIGENOUS PEOPLE, *925-36
International Decade of the World's Indigenous People (1995-2004), First, 931; (2004-2013), Second, 933, 935
UN Voluntary Fund for the, 935
natural resources, permanent sovereignty over, 936
Permanent Forum on Indigenous Issues, 935-36
rights of (draft declaration), *925-31
Working Group on Indigenous Populations, 933-35
INDONESIA
disaster relief, 1106
migrants, 836-37
INFORMATION AND COMMUNICATION
Digital Solidarity Fund, 1146
disaster relief
Tampere Convention on the Provision of Telecommunication Resources for Disaster Mitigation and Relief Operations, 1090
International Computer Centre, 1004
international security, *738-40
role of science and technology, *740-41
Internet-based Poverty Reduction Strategy Knowledge Network, 1148
Internet Governance Forum (2006), 1001, 1003
Plan of Action for the Information Society in Latin America and the Caribbean, 1189
technologies, *999-1004
Global Alliance for ICT and Development, 1001, 1004
Global Telecommunication System, 1165
network, 1004
Technologies Task Force, 999, 1003-1004

UN Committee on Information, 726
UN public information, *726-38
Department of Public Information (DPI), 726, 734-38
UN Communications Group, 738
UN Information Centres (UNICs), 736-38, 967
UN website, 735, 738
library services, 735-36
World Information Society Day, 1000
World Summit on the Information Society, 879, 977, *998-1004, 1145-46, 1159, 1162, 1329
Geneva Declaration of Principles and Plan of Action, *999-1000
Tunis Commitment and Tunis Agenda, *999-1000, 1004, 1198
INSTRAW, *see* International Research and Training Institute for the Advancement of Women
intellectual property rights
Trade-related Aspects of Intellectual property Rights (TRIPS) Agreement on (1994), 1111, 1147
Inter-Agency Standing Committee (IASC)
humanitarian assistance coordination, 1389-90
humanitarian reform agenda, *1057-60
Intergovernmental Authority on Development (IGAD)
Somalia, *309-10
internally displaced persons, *see* displaced persons
Internal Oversight Services, UN Office of (OIOS)
DPA audit, 63
ECA, subregional offices, 1151-52
gender mainstreaming, 1349
programme coordination, 1596
statistics (Western Asia), 1198
UN-Habitat, 1256
UNHCR, 1391
UN oversight, *1648-51
UN programme performance evaluation, 1640-41
U N Voluntary Fund for Victims of Torture, 876
International Advisory and Monitoring Board for Iraq (IAMB), 406-407
INTERNATIONAL ATOMIC ENERGY AGENCY (IAEA)
activities, 640, *1202-1203
counter-terrorism, 77, 636
DPRK, 641, 1202
International Project on Innovative Nuclear Reactors and Fuel Cycles, 640
Iran, *432-41, 641
Iraq, 409
Middle East, *642-43
nuclear disarmament, *639-43
safeguards, 616, 620, *640-43
Model Additional Protocol to Safeguards Agreement, 639-41
International Charter on Space and Major Disasters, 747
INTERNATIONAL CIVIL AVIATION ORGANIZATION (ICAO), 750, 1572
International Civil Service Commission, *1677-80
International Commission of Inquiry for Darfur, 943
International Committee of the Red Cross (ICRC), 576, 664, 857, 1507
International Conference on Early Warning, Third (Bonn, 2006), 1093
International Conference on Financing for Development (Monterrey Consensus) (2002), 976, 1127, *1134-36
International Conference of New or Restored Democracies, Sixth (Doha) (2006), 697, *697-99; Seventh (2009), 697
International Conference on Peace, Security, Democracy and Development in the Great Lakes Region, First (2004, Dar es Salaam), 121, 124; Second (2006, Nairobi), 120-21, *124-26
International Conference on Population and Development (ICPD) (1994), 1382, 1409
Programme of Action, 1060, 1191, 1257-59
Conference on Implementation (Bangkok, 2006), 1417-18
International Convention on the Elimination of All Forms of Racial Discrimination (1965), 768, *773-76, 821-22
International Convention on the Protection of All Persons from Enforced Disappearance (2006), *800-808, 874, 1395
International Convention on the Protection of the Rights of All Migrant Workers and Members of Their Families (1990), 768, 784, *835-39
International Convention against the Recruitment, Use, Financing and Training of Mercenaries (1989), 853
International Convention for the Safety of Life at Sea (1974), 1249
International Convention for the Suppression of Acts of Nuclear Terrorism, 1305
INTERNATIONAL COURT OF JUSTICE (ICJ), *1477-83
Ahmadou Sadio Diallo (Guinea v. DRC), 1478-79
Armed Activities (DRC v. Rwanda), 857, 1477, 1479-80
Armed Activities (DRC v. Uganda), 1477
Criminal Proceedings in France (Republic of the Congo v. France), 1477
Gabcikovo-Nagymaros Project (Hungary/Slovakia), 1477
Genocide (Bosnia and Herzegovina v. Serbia and Montenegro), 1477-78
Genocide (Croatia v. Serbia and Montenegro), 1477
Israeli security barrier, 500, 527, 857
Land and Maritime Boundary (Cameroon/Nigeria), 173, 252
Maritime Delimitation in the Black Sea (Romania v. Ukraine), 1477, 1480
Maritime Delimitation in the Caribbean Sea (Nicaragua v. Honduras), 1477
Morocco's Claim Over Western Sahara, 330
Mutual Assistance in Criminal Matters (Djibouti v. France), 1477, 1480-81
Navigational and Related Rights (Costa Rica v. Nicaragua), 1477
Pulp Mills on the River Uruguay (Argentina v. Uruguay), 1477, 1481-82
rules of the Court, 1482
Sixtieth Anniversary, *1482-83, 1531
Sovereignty over Various Territories (Malaysia/ Singapore), 1480
Status of Diplomatic Envoy (Dominica v. Switzerland), 1477, 1481
Territorial and Maritime Dispute (Nicaragua v. Colombia), 1477
Trust Fund to Assist States in the Settlement of Disputes, 1483
International Covenant on Civil and Political Rights (1966), 756, 832, 844, 857, 865-66, 880-81
and Optional Protocols (1966), 768, 771
International Covenant on Economic, Social and Cultural Rights (1966), 756, 768, 772
International Criminal Court (ICC), 801-802, *1503-1507
Chambers, 1505-1507
Prosecutor, Office of the, 1506-1507
investigations, 1506-1507
new arrests and surrenders, 1506
Registry, 1507
DRC, 127, 132, 1503
Rome Statute (1998), 1503
Assembly of States Parties to, 1505
Sudan, 291-92, 1503
Uganda, 1503
International Criminal Police Organization (Interpol), 382-83

International Decade for the Eradication of Colonialism, Second (2001-2010), 695, *699-702
International Decade for Natural Disaster Reduction (1990-2000), 1093
International Decade of the World's Indigenous People (1995-2004), First, 931; (2004-2013), Second, 933, 935
Voluntary Fund for, 935
International Global Navigation Satellite System, 745
INTERNATIONAL LABOUR ORGANIZATION (ILO), 1214, 1598
ageing issues, 1382
child labour, 917
International Programme on the Elimination of, 1373
Maritime Labour Convention, 1556
INTERNATIONAL LAW
Commission (ILC), *1508-15
aliens, expulsion of, 1514
armed conflict, effect of on treaties, 1515
extradition, 1514
international law, fragmentation of, 1514-15
international organizations, responsibility of, 1513
liability for transboundary harm resulting from hazardous activities, *1511-13
shared natural resources, 1513
unilateral acts of States, 1513-14
economic law, *1525-30
international State relations and, *1515-20
Convention on Jurisdictional Immunities of States and their property, 1515
international terrorism, *1515-19
Declaration on Measures to Eliminate International Terrorism (1994), *1516-19
rule of law at national and international levels, 1524-25
trade law, *1525-30
see also treaties and agreements; United Nations Commission on International Trade Law (UNCITRAL)
INTERNATIONAL MARITIME ORGANIZATION (IMO), 1249, 1556
International Convention for the Safety of Life at Sea (1974), 1249
International Ministerial Conference of Landlocked and Transit Developing Countries and Donor Countries and International Financial and Development Institutions on Transit Transport Cooperation (2003), *1018-20
Almaty Declaration and Programme of Action, 1018, 1159, 1161
INTERNATIONAL MONETARY FUND (IMF), 1594
IMF/World Bank Development Committee, 1127-28, 1130
Multilateral Debt Relief Initiative, 986, 1072, 1074, 1130, 1147
International Narcotics Control Board, *1436-40
International Organization of la Francophonie, 1597, *1602-1604
International Organization for Migration (IOM), 261, 1261, 1347, 1390
INTERNATIONAL PEACE AND SECURITY, *45-111, 884-85
Executive Committee on Peace and Security, 1389
information and communications in the context of security, *738-40
peacekeeping operations, *77-111
peacemaking and peacebuilding, 53-64
Peacebuilding Commission, *55-57
Peacebuilding Fund, 57-58
political and peacebuilding missions, 64-65
promotion of, *45-65
rule of law and maintenance of, *45-48, 47-48
Task Force for the Development of Comprehensive Rule of Law Strategies for Peace Operations, 47
science and technology, role of, *740-41
threats to, *65-77
see also terrorism
International Pledging Conference on Avian and Human Influenza (Beijing, 2006), 1426
International Police Task Force (IPTF), 462
International Research and Training Institute for the Advancement of Women (INSTRAW), 1359
International Satellite System for Search and Rescue, 747
International Seabed Authority, 1554
International Security Assistance Force (Afghanistan), 361-62, 375, *380-81
International Strategy for Disaster Reduction (ISDR), *1093-97, 1214
INTERNATIONAL TELECOMMUNICATION UNION (ITU), 750, 999, 1004
INTERNATIONAL TRIBUNALS, *1484-1503
for the Former Yugoslavia (ICTY), 455-56, *1484-94
Chambers, *1485-92
Judges of the Court, *1490-92, 1502
new arrests and surrenders, 1485
ongoing cases and trials, 1485-90
financing, *1493-94
functioning, 1502-1503
completion strategies, implementation of
ICTR, 1503
ICTY, 1502-1503
for the Law of the Sea, 1555
for Rwanda (ICTR), *1494-1502
Chambers, 1494-1500
judges of the Court, *1498-1500
ongoing trials, 1494-98
financing, *1500-1502
International Weapons of Mass Destruction Commission, 609, 616, 636
International Year of Biodiversity (2010), 1223, *1225
International Year of Forests (2011), 1228, *1240-41
International Year of Microcredit (2005), *996-97
International Year of Reconciliation (2009), *53-54
International Year of Sanitation (2008), *1419-20
International Year of Sport and Physical Education (2005), 1283
Inter-Parliamentary Union, 1597, *1604-1605
IRAN, 361, *432-41
human rights, *952-54
nuclear programme, *432-41, 609, 641, 689, 1203
and United Arab Emirates, 451-52
IRAQ, 361, *389-409
Baghdad Peace Initiative, 400
elections, *389-91
humanitarian situation, 399
human rights, 396, 399
International Advisory and Monitoring Board for Iraq (IAMB), 406-407
International Compact with Iraq, 391-92, 401
Iraq Special Tribunal, 867-68
and Kuwait, 361, *409-12
Multinational Force (MNF), 394-95, 397, *400-406
National Reconciliation Plan, 392-93, 397, 399-402
oil-for-food programme, 409-10, 1654
POWs, Kuwaiti property and missing persons, 410-11
trial and sentencing of, Saddam Hussein, 393-94, 868
Special Tribunal, 867-68
UNAMI, 64-65, 86, 361, 389, *394-402
UNIKOM, *411-12
UN Compensation Commission and Fund, 412
UNMOVIC, 407-409, 609

ISAF, *see* International Security Assistance Force
Islamic Educational, Scientific and Cultural Organization (ISESCO), 811
ISRAEL
Armistice Agreement with Lebanon (1949), 579
diplomatic missions, transfer of, 531
East Jerusalem, *531-32
elections, *501-505
post-election situation, 507-10
escalation of violence, 498, 566-67, 572, *574-90
human rights, *964-67, 967-71
peace process, *498-547
Quartet, 498-502, 505, 507-10, 517-19, *525-28
road map (June 2003), 504, 525, 548
security barrier, 498, 503, 509, *529-31, 533, 548, 551
ICJ case, 500, 527, 857
territories occupied by, *see also* Palestine
economic and social situation, *532-36
Golan Heights, *603-605, 970
Israeli settlements, 500, 508-509, 515-16, *544-45, 551
Special Committee on Israeli Practices, 499, *536-42, 603, 967
UNDOF, 499, 526, 565, 603, *605-608
UNIFIL, 498-99, *565-69, 574, *576-78, *582-96, 965
UNTSO, 499, 565-66
see also Middle East; Palestine

JAMAICA
extralegal executions, 869
Jammu and Kashmir, 447-48
Joint Appeals Board, 1708
Joint Inspection Unit (JIU), 1378, 1572, *1652-54
Joint United Nations Programme on HIV/AIDS (UNAIDS), 1073, 1341, 1371-72, 1396, 1410, 1416, 1417-19, 1454-55
JORDAN
torture and cruel treatment, 875
justice, administration of, *855-85, 862-66
independence of the judicial system, 867-68
international personnel in peace support operations, 856
military tribunals, 856
rule of law, 857
Vienna Declaration on Crime and Justice, 1290-91

Kashmir (and Jammu), 447-48
KENYA
disaster relief, 1105-1106
humanitarian situation, 1066
KOSOVO, *see* Serbia
KUWAIT
and Iraq, 361, *409-12
POWs, property and missing persons, 410-11
UN Compensation Commission and Fund, 412
UNIKOM, *411-12
KYRGYZSTAN
human rights, 937

labour
child labour, 917
ILO, 1373
landlocked developing countries, *1018-20, 1159-60
International Ministerial Conference of Landlocked and Transit Developing Countries and Donor Countries and International Financial and Development Institutions on Transit Transport Cooperation (2003), *1018-20
Almaty Declaration and Programme of Action, 1018, 1159, 1161
Special Body on Least Developed and Landlocked Developing Countries, 1159
LATIN AMERICA AND THE CARIBBEAN
CARICOM, 341-42, 353, *359-60, 1597
Colombia, 944-45, 1477
Costa Rica, 1477
Cuba, 341-42, *357-59, 945-46
disarmament, *see* disarmament; *subheading* regional and other approaches
economic and social activities, regional, 1189-93
Statistical Yearbook for Latin America and the Caribbean, 1192
economic and social activities, subregional
Caribbean, 1193
Mexico and Central America, 1193-94
El Salvador, 1055, 1104
Ecuador, 863
Expert Group Meeting on International Migration and Development in Latin America and the Caribbean, 1258
Guatemala, 341, 946-47, 1055, 1104
Haiti, 54-55, 61, 78, 86, 88, *342-57, 947-48, *1086-88, 1193
Nicaragua, 341, 863, 1477
nuclear-weapon-free zone, 647
see also Americas; Caribbean; Central America; *country names*; Economic Commission for Latin America and the Caribbean
LAW OF THE SEA, *1540-68
Commission on the Limits of the Continental Shelf, 1555
Division for Ocean Affairs and the, 1568
International Seabed Authority, 1554
International Tribunal for the, 1555
UN Convention on the (UNCLOS) (1982), *1540-68
Conservation and Management of Straddling Fish Stocks and Highly Migratory Fish Stocks, Agreement on the, *1540-54
UN Open-ended Informal Consultative Process on Oceans and Law of the Sea, 1241, *1557-68
League of Arab States (LAS), 61, 504, 1200, *1597-1600
least developed countries (LDCs), *1010-16
Bangkok Programme of Action (2006) for LDCs for the Decade (2001-2010), 1159, 1195, 1199
Brussels Declaration (2001) and the Programme of Action for LDCs for the Decade (2001-2010), 1115, 1142, 1147-48, 1159
Cotonu Ministerial Declaration and Strategy for the Further Implementation of, 1014
Midterm Comprehensive Global Review, *1014-16, 1110, 1115
Least Developed Countries Report 2006, 1012
list of, 1010-11
UN Conference on LDCs, Third (2001), 1010
see also landlocked developing countries; small island developing states
LEBANON, *566-603
Armistice Agreement with Israel (1949), 579
arms embargo, 588
assassination of Industry Minister Pierre Gemayel, 596
assassination of Prime Minister Hariri, 498-99, 569-70, *596-603
UN International Independent Investigation Commission (UNIIIC), 498-99, 556, *596-603
Commission of Inquiry on Lebanon, 965
Hizbullah, 498, 566-67, 572, *574-90
humanitarian situation, 574, 576-79, 587, 1070
human rights, *964-67

Office of the Personal Representative of the Secretary-General for, 65
oil spillage on Lebanese coast, *1215-16
peacekeeping operations, *566-603
Seven-Point-Plan, 579-81
and Syria, 570-72
UNIFIL, 498-99, *565-69, 574, *576-78, *582-96, 965

LIBERIA, 115, 172-73, *211-30
anti-corruption campaign, 217
arms embargo, 226
arrest of, Former President Charles Taylor, 211-12, *214-15, 217, 224, 233, *241-44
conflict diamonds, 50, 213, 218, 220, 227
humanitarian assistance, 1068, *1081-82
human rights, 213, 220, 939-40
reform efforts, 214, 216-18, 220
political developments, 215
sanctions, 211, 220, *223-30
Panel of Experts, 211, *224-30
security situation, 212, 215, 217, 219, 221
UNMIL, 54, 78, 86, 88, 172-73, 176, 178, 202, *211-25

LIBYAN ARAB JAMAHARIYA
U.S. military attack (1986), 339

Limits of the Continental Shelf, Commission on the, 1555

Madrid Accords (1975) (Spain/Morocco/Mauritania), 330

MALAYSIA
ICJ case, 1480

MALVINAS (FALKLAND ISLANDS), 713

marine resources
ecosystems, *1241-45
see also ecosystems; oceans and seas; pollution

MARITIME ISSUES
Convention on the Prevention of Marine Pollution by Dumping of Wastes and Other Matter (1972)
Protocols (1996 and 2000), 1556
International Convention for the Safety of Life at Sea (1974), 1249
law of the sea, *1540-68
Review of Maritime Transport 2006, 1141
transport, 1141
see also International Maritime Organization

MAURITANIA, 334

MAURITIUS
and France, 239
and United Kingdom, 239

mercenaries, *853-55
International Convention against the Recruitment, Use, Financing and Training of Mercenaries (1989), 853

MEXICO, 1193-94

MIDDLE EAST, *498-608
Madrid conference (1991), 526
nuclear proliferation, *642-43
nuclear-weapon-free zone, *647-49
Office of the Personal Representative of the Secretary-General for Lebanon, 65
peace process, *498-547
Quartet, 498-502, 505, 507-10, 517-19, *525-28
road map (June 2003), 504, 525, 548
UNDOF, 499, 526, 565, 603, *605-608
UNIFIL, 498-99, *565-69, 574, *576-78, *582-96, 965
UNSCO, 64
UNTSO, 499, 565-66
see also country names; Palestine

migrant workers and their families, 768, 784, *835-39
International Convention on the Protection of the Rights of All Migrant Workers and Members of Their Families (1990), 768, 784, *835-39

migration
Global Commission on International Migration, 1258, 1261
Global Forum on Migration and Development, 1262
international, and development, *1258-63
gender dimension, *1259-61, 1265, 1347-48
High-level Dialogue on International Migration and Development, 1164, 1258, *1261-63, 1329
International Organization for Migration (IOM), 261, 1261, 1347, 1390
see also movement, freedom of

MILLENNIUM SUMMIT (2000)
Millennium Development Goals (MDGs), 49, 885, 976, *986-92, 1060, 1110, 1145, 1158, 1201-1202, 1329, 1350, 1361, 1365, 1409
Damascus Declaration on the Realization of the MDGs, 1196
Jakarta Declaration on MDGs in Asia and the Pacific: the Way Forward 2015, 1155, 1157, 1159
Millennium Development Goals Report 2006, 986

minorities, discrimination against, 839-43

MINUGUA, *see* United Nations Verification Mission in Guatemala

MINURSO, *see* United Nations Mission for the Referendum in Western Sahara

MINUSTAH, *see* United Nations Stabilization Mission in Haiti

missing persons, *see* disappearance of persons

MONGOLIA
nuclear-weapon-free zone, *645-46

MONTENEGRO (formerly Serbia and Montenegro)
admission to UN membership, *1592
economic assistance, 1088
independence referendum, 472
see also Serbia and Montenegro

Monterrey Consensus, *see* International Conference on Financing for Development (2002)

MONUC, *see* United Nations Organization Mission in the Democratic Republic of the Congo

MOROCCO
and Western Sahara, *329-36

MOZAMBIQUE, 1082

MYANMAR
humanitarian situation, 448
human rights, 448-49, *954-58
national reconciliation and democratization, 448

NATURAL RESOURCES
and energy, *1201-1204
indigenous peoples' permanent sovereignty over, 936
Latin America and the Caribbean, 1192
shared, 1513
water, 1203-1204

N'Djamena Agreement (2006) (Chad/Sudan), 164, 167

N'Djamena Humanitarian Ceasefire Agreement (2004) (Sudan), 86, 88, 268-69, 271-72, 291, 293

NEPAL, 362, *449-51
Comprehensive Peace Agreement (2006), 362, *450-51
humanitarian situation, 1070
human rights, 450, 958-60

NEW CALEDONIA, *715-17

New Partnership for Africa's Development (NEPAD), 114, 116, *1071-79, 1148-49, 1212, 1574
Advisory Panel for International Support for, 116
international support, *1075-77
social dimension of, *1077-79, 1276

NEW ZEALAND
Tokelau, 695, 699, *717-19
NICARAGUA, 341, 864
ICJ case, 1477
NIGERIA
and Cameroon (ICJ case), 173, 252
Cameroon-Nigeria Mixed Commission, 173, 252-54
non-governmental organizations (NGOs)
Committee on, 1606-1608
Non-Proliferation of Nuclear Weapons, Treaty on the (NPT) (1968), 361, *432-35, 616, 633
Review Conference (2005), 616; (2010), *633-34
Non-Self-Governing Territories (NSGTs)
economic activities affecting, *707-709
Falkland Islands (Malvinas), 713
Gibraltar, 713-15
information, dissemination of, *709-11
Island Territories, *719-26
American Samoa, *719-22
Anguilla, *719-22
Bermuda, *719-23
British Virgin Islands, *719-21, *723
Cayman Islands, *719-21, *723
Guam, *719-21, *723-24
Montserrat, *719-21, *724
Pitcairn, *719-21, *724-25
Saint Helena, *719-21, *725
Turks and Caicos Islands, *719-21, *725
United States Virgin Islands, *719-21, *725-26
New Caledonia, *715-17
Puerto Rico, 712-13
Tokelau, *717-19
Western Sahara, 717
see also decolonization
NORTH AFRICA, *329-39
see also country names
North Atlantic Treaty Organization (NATO)
Afghanistan, 361-62, 375, 380
Bosnia and Herzegovina, 453-54, 456, 458
Kosovo (Serbia and Montenegro), 463, 465, 472, 1492
Nouméa Accord, (New Caledonia, 1998), *715-17
nuclear energy, *1202-1203
Chernobyl accident, 751, 1107
see also International Atomic Energy Agency

oceans and seas, 1241, 1243, 1556-57
ecology, 1241
Intergovernmental Oceanographic Commission, 1100, 1557
Oceans and Coastal Areas Network (UN-Oceans), 1556
Regional Seas Programme, 1243
see also law of the sea; marine resources; maritime issues
OCHA, *see* Coordination of Humanitarian Affairs, Office for the
office of, *see under main part of name*
OHCHR, *see* United Nations High Commissioner for Human Rights, Office of the
oil
Iraq, oil-for-food programme, 1654
Independent Inquiry Committee, 409-10
United Nations Iraq Account (UNIA), 410
Ombudsman, Office of, 1709-10
ONUB, *see* United Nations Operation in Burundi
Organisation for Economic Cooperation and Development (OECD), 687, 1141, 1172, 1349, 1466
Organization of American States (OAS), 61, 343, 713
UN, cooperation with, 360, 1597
Organization of the Islamic Conference (OIC), 61, 811, 1597, *1600-1602
Organization for the Prohibition of Chemical Weapons (OPCW), *654-55
UN cooperation with, *655, 1597
Organization for Security and Cooperation in Europe (OSCE), 61, 484, 691, 1390
UN cooperation with, 498
OUTER SPACE
arms race in, prevention, *672-74
Committee on the Peaceful Uses of, 695, 741-51
Legal Subcommittee, 750-51
Scientific and Technical Subcommittee, *746-50
Convention on the Registration of Objects Launched into (1974), 750
International Charter on Space and Major Disasters, 747
International Global Navigation Satellite System, 745
International Satellite System for Search and Rescue, 747
Outer Space Affairs, UN Office for, 747-48
UN Conference on the Exploration and Peaceful Uses of Outer Space, Third (UNISPACE-III) (1999), 695, 741, 745-46
UN Platform for Space-based Information for Disaster Management and Emergency Response, 745, *748-50
UN Programme on Space Applications, 747

Pacific Islands Forum, *1167-70, 1597
PAKISTAN
and Afghanistan, 369, 375
earthquake, 1055, 1106-1107
and India
Jammu and Kashmir, 448
UNMOGIP, 86-87, 448
PALESTINE
Agreement on Movement and Access, Agreed Principles for the Rafah Crossing, 505, 507, 519, 524
assistance to Palestinians, *554-57
Committee on the Exercise of the Inalienable Rights of the Palestinian People, 499, 531, *547-52, 967
UN International Conference of Civil Society in Support of the Palestinian People (Geneva) (2006), 551
UN International Meeting in Support of Israeli-Palestinian Peace (Vienna) (2006), 551
displaced persons, *563-65
East Jerusalem, *531-32
economic and social situation, 517, *532-36
elections, *501-505
post-election situation, 507-10
escalation of violence, 503, 510-14, 516, 518-20, 522, 524, 526, 551, 575, 577
General Assembly emergency session, *521-24, 528
Geneva Convention, Fourth (1949), *542-44
humanitarian situation, 500, 508, 513-16, 551, 555, 1070-71
International Day of Solidarity with the Palestinian People, 547
Israeli security barrier, 498, 503, 509, *529-31, 533, 548, 551
ICJ case, 500, 527, 857
Israeli settlements in, 500, 508-509, 515-16, *544-45, 551
peace process, *498-547
Quartet, 498-502, 505, 507-10, 517-19, *525-28
road map (June 2003), 504, 525, 548
political situation, 519
refugees, *see* subheading: UNRWA
self-determination, right to, *852-53
Special Committee on Israeli Practices, 499, *536-42, 603, 967
UN Conciliation Commission for Palestine, 558
UNRWA, 499, 533, 554, *557-64, 967-68

UNTSO, 499, 565-66
women, *545-47, 1347
see also Israel; Middle East
PEACEBUILDING
Commission, 49, *55-59, 63, 818
Fund, *57-58, 1060
International Year of Reconciliation (2009), *53-54
missions and offices
in Africa
Central African Republic, 64, 162, *165-66
Guinea-Bissau, 64
Office of the Special Representative of the Secretary-General for West Africa, 65
Office of the Special Representative of the Secretary-General for the Great Lakes Region, 64, *125-26
Sierra Leone, 64-65, 78, 173, 231-35, 239-40
Somalia, 64, 301, 311
in Asia and the Pacific
Afghanistan, 64-65, 86, 361-62, *364-67, 378-80, 948
Iraq, 64-65, 86, 361, 389, *394-402
Tajikistan, 64-65, 451
in Middle East
Office of the Personal Representative of the Secretary-General for Lebanon, 65
Special Coordinator, 64
post-conflict, *53-55
Support Office, 55, 58-59, 63, 82
PEACEKEEPING OPERATIONS, *77-111
in Africa, 61
Burundi, 54, 78, 86, 88, 120, *130-31, 148, *150-52
Côte d'Ivoire, 54, 78, 86, 88, 172, *176-79, *181-86, *188-90, 193, *196-202, 204, *207-11
Eritrea, 86, 88, 256, *315-23, *325-29
Ethiopia, 86, 88, 256, *315-23, *325-29
Liberia, 54, 78, 86, 88, 172-73, 176, 178, 202, *211-25
Sierra Leone, 64-65, 78, 173, 231-35, 239-40
Sudan, 54-55, 78, 86, 88, 166-67, 169-70, 254, 257, *259-60, *262-71, 280-81, 290, 810
Western Sahara, 86-87, 329, *332-39
in Americas
Haiti, 54-55, 78, 86, 88, *342-57
in Asia and the Pacific
India-Pakistan, 86-87, 448
Timor-Leste, 64-65, 78, 86, 89, 361, *413-18, 428, 430
complex operations, strategies for, 82-83
comprehensive review, *85-86
cooperation with regional organizations, 84
in Europe and the Mediterranean
Cyprus, 86-87, 454, *487-94
Georgia, 86-87, 453, *474-84
Kosovo (Serbia), 86-87, 453, *462-72, 906, 1486, 1492
financial and administrative aspects, *89-111
UN Logistics Base in Brindisi (UNLB), *102-104
general aspects, *77-85
in Middle East, 565-608
Israel-Syrian Arab Republic, 499, 526, 565, 603, *605-608
Lebanon, 498-99, *565-69, 574, *576-78, *582-96, 965
Palestine, 499, 565-66
roster of 2006 operations, 86-89
Rule-of-law tools for post-conflict States, 856
safety and security, 83-84, *578
sexual exploitation and abuse in, *77-81, 146
Secretary-General's Special Adviser on, 77-79, 85, 107
Special Committee on, 55, *77-86, 119
women, participation of in all aspects and levels, 84-85
see also country names
Peacekeeping Operations, Department of (UN), 77, *79-82, 104-106, 108, 119, 163, 204, 211-12, 475, 735
Permanent Forum on Indigenous Issues, 935-36
PHILIPPINES
disaster relief, 1106
economic assistance, *1088
Political Affairs, Department of (UN), 60, 63, 237, 248, 700, 709
pollution
Convention on the Control of Transboundary Movements of Hazardous Wastes and their Disposal (Basel, 1989), 1245, 1247-49
Convention on Long-Range Transboundary Air Pollution (1979), 1222-23
Convention on the Prevention of Marine Pollution by Dumping of Wastes and Other Matter (1972)
Protocols (1996 and 2000), 1556
harmful products and waste, protection against, 1245-49
radioactive waste, 643
Rotterdam Convention on the Prior Informed Consent (PIC) Procedure for Certain Hazardous Chemicals and Pesticides in International Trade (1998), 1245, 1248
Stockholm Convention on Persistent Organic Pollutants (POPs), 1216, 1245
toxic waste, 194, 909-10
see also climate change; environment
POPULATION
Commission on Population and Development, 1257-58, 1269-70
International Conference on Population and Development (1994), 1382, 1409
Programme of Action, 1060, 1191, 1257-59
Conference on Implementation (Bangkok, 2006), 1417-18
international migration and development, *1258-63
and poverty, 1164, 1265-66
Asian and Pacific Conference on Population and Poverty, Fifth, 1064
UN Population Division
UN Population Fund (UNFPA), *see* United Nations Population Fund
World Programme on Population and Housing Censuses (2010), 1470
POVERTY
eradication of, *992-97, *1275-76
International Day for the (17 October), 992-93
UN Decade for the (1997-2006), 896, *992-95, 1272-73
Extraordinary Summit on Employment and Poverty Alleviation in Africa and Plan of Action (Ouagadougou, 2004), 1147
extreme poverty and human rights, *899-902
Global Microcredit Summit (2006), *996-97
High-level Commission on Legal Empowerment of the Poor, 1271
International Year of Microcredit (2005), *996-97
Pretoria Agreement (Côte d'Ivoire), 172, 176, 185
Programme and Coordination, Committee for (CPC), 995-96, 1072-73, 1595-96, 1641
public administration, *1007-1009
Public Information, Department of (UN), *see* information and communication

racism and racial discrimination, *820-39
commemoration of the abolition of the transatlantic slave trade, *828-30
Committee on the Elimination of Racial Discrimination (CERD), 768-69, 773, 821-24

contemporary forms, 830, 832, 874
and globalization, 820-21
International Convention on the Elimination of All Forms of Racial Discrimination (1965), 768, *773-76, 821-22
Working Group on people of African descent, 824
World Conference against Racism, Racial Discrimination, Xenophobia and Related Intolerance (2001), 773, *820-28
Durban Declaration and Programme of Action (DDPA), *820-28, 846
see also human rights
radiation
atomic, effects of, *751-52
Chernobyl accident, 751
radioactive waste, 643
UN Scientific Committee on the Effects of Atomic Radiation, 751
REFUGEES, *1385-1408
Agenda for Protection, 1394-95
assistance measures, 1395-97
Convention on the Reduction of Statelessness (1961), 1395
Convention relating to the Status of (1951) and Protocol (1967), 1394-95
Convention relating to the Status of Stateless Persons (1954), 1395
and the environment, 1396
and HIV/AIDS, 1396
regional activities, *1397-1408
see also displaced persons; United Nations High Commissioner for Refugees, Office of the
REGIONAL, ECONOMIC AND SOCIAL ACTIVITIES, *1145-1200
regional cooperation, 1145-46
see also economic and social trends; *specific regional commissions; specific regions*
religious intolerance, *843-51
REPUBLIC OF KOREA
armistice agreement (1953), 64
nuclear weapon-free peninsula, *442-43, 689
UN-Republic of Korea Joint Conference on Disarmament and Non-proliferation (Jeju) (2006), 689
REPUBLIC OF MOLDOVA, 485-86
Transnistrian independence referendum, 485
Rio Declaration on Environment and Development (1992), 1246
ROMANIA
ICJ case, 1477, 1480
Rotterdam Convention on the Prior Informed Consent (PIC) Procedure for Certain Hazardous Chemicals and Pesticides in International Trade (1998), 1245, 1248
RWANDA, *121-24, 131, 141, 171-72
arms embargo, 171-72
genocide, 172
ICJ case, 857, 1477, 1479-80
International Criminal Tribunal for (ICTR), *see* International Tribunals

Safety and Security, UN Department of (DSS), 83, 1394, 1673-75
sanctions
Afghanistan, *381-89
assistance to third States affected by, 1089
Charter provisions, *1534-36
Côte d'Ivoire, *203-207
DPRK, 442, *444-47
Iran, *436-41
Liberia, 211, 220, *223-30
Sierra Leone, 244
Sudan, *292-97
SCIENCE AND TECHNOLOGY FOR DEVELOPMENT, *997-1004
Commission on, 997-99, *1001-1003
Ministers of Science and Technology of the Group of 77 and China meeting, 977
peace and security, role in, *740-41
Strategic Plan for Technology Support and Capacity-building (Bali), 1208-12
UNCTAD Science and Technology for Development Network, 998
SCO, *see* Shanghai Cooperation Organization
SECRETARIAT, UN
Department of Public Information, *see* information and communication
Disarmament Affairs, Department for, 610, 659, 665, 668-70, 678-79, 692, 735
General Assembly and Conference Management, Department of, 1654, 1658, 1660
Legal Affairs, Office of, 1492, 1575
Division for Ocean Affairs and the Law of the Sea, 1568
UN Legal Counsel, 46
Management, Department of, 738
Palestinian Rights, Division for, *552-53
Peacekeeping Operations, Department of, 105-108
Political Affairs, Department of, 63
premises and property, 1665-73
Secretary General Report on work of the Organization, 3-41
SECURITY COUNCIL
agenda, 1594
Counter-Terrorism Committee, *see* terrorism
membership, 1589, 1594
missions to
Afghanistan, 374-76
DRC, 132-33
Repertoire of the Practice of the Security Council, *1531-34
see also specific topics
SENEGAL
and Guinea-Bissau, 246
SERBIA (formerly Serbia and Montenegro), *see* Serbia and Montenegro
SERBIA AND MONTENEGRO, *461-72
ICJ case, 1477-78
Kosovo province, 61, 458
Constitutional Framework for Provisional Self-Government (2001), 453, 462-66, 468
European Partnership Action Plan, 453, 465-66, 468
Kosovo Force (KFOR) (NATO), 463, 465, 472, 1492
Kosovo Standards Implementation Plan (2004), 453, 465, 468-70
UNMIK, 86-87, 453, *462-72, 906, 1486, 1492
Shanghai Cooperation Organization (SCO), 688
Shanghai Declaration, 1163
SIERRA LEONE, 55, 57, 115, *230-44
elections, 173, 230, 235-37
and Guinea, 232, 235
humanitarian situation, 230, 241
human rights, 940-41
political developments, 231
security, 230-31, 233-35
Special Court for, *241-44
UNAMSIL, 230-32, *240-41
UNIOSIL, 64-65, 78, 173, 231-35, 239-40
SINGAPORE
ICJ case, 1480
Single Convention on Narcotic Drugs (1961)

Protocol (1972), 1436
slavery and related issues, 912-13
UN Voluntary Trust Fund on Contemporary Forms of Slavery, 912-13
SLOVAKIA
ICJ case, 1477
small arms trafficking, *659-63
Antigua Declaration, 692
International Instrument to Enable States to Identify and Trace, in a Timely and Reliable Manner, Illicit Small Arms and Light Weapons, 656-57, 659
UN Conference on the Illicit Trade in Small Arms and Light Weapons in All Its Aspects (2001), Programme of Action, 60-61, 609, 657-59, 689, 691
UN Register of Conventional Arms, 610, 667-68, 677
small island developing states
Global Conference on Sustainable Development of Small Island Developing States (1994)
Barbados Programme of Action, 1016
Mauritius Strategy, 985, *1016-18, 1160, 1193, 1201-1202, 1212
Special Body on Pacific Island Developing Countries (Jakarta, 2006), 1160
SOCIAL DEVELOPMENT
Commission for, 993-94, *1276-77, *1381-84
UN Research Institute for Social Development (UNRISD), 1277-78
World Summit for (1995), 994, 1164, *1272-75
Copenhagen Declaration on Social Development and the Programme of Action, 1272, 1382
Social Forum (2006), 895-96
SOMALIA, 115, 255, *301-15
Aden Declaration (2006), 255, *301-304
arms embargo, 302, *311-15
humanitarian situation, 302, 308, 941, 1066
human rights, 305, 941
Intergovernmental Authority on Development (IGAD), *309-10
International Contact Group on Somalia, 307, 311
Mogadishu violence, 304-305
national reconciliation process, *302-11
peace efforts, 307-309
piracy, 302
Union of Islamic Courts, *305-11, 313
UNPOS, 64, 301, 311
SOUTHERN AFRICA, *see specific countries*
Southern African Development Community (SADC), 811
UN, cooperation with, *1153-55, 1597
SOUTH GEORGIA, 713
SOUTH SANDWICH ISLANDS, 713
SPAIN
Gibraltar, 713-15
SRI LANKA
humanitarian situation, 1071
human rights, 960
terrorism, 72
STATISTICS, *1465-74
Committee for the Coordination of Statistical Activities, 1465
demographic and social, 1470-72
health, 1470-71
labour, 1471
population and housing censuses, 1470
World Programme on (2010), 1470
poverty, 1471
economic, 1466-70
business surveys and informal sector statistics, 1468
distributive trade, 1469-70
energy, 1467-68
environment, 1465, 1468-69
industrial, 1469
International Comparison Programme (ICP), 1465, 1467
international trade, 1469
national accounts
System of National Accounts (1993), 1465-66
service statistics, 1466-67
Central Product Classification, 1466
Manual on Statistics of International Trade in Services, 1466-67
UN Commodity Trade Statistics Database, 1466
UN Statistical Commission, 1175, *1465-74
Status of Women, Commission on the, 913, 1328, 1341-42, 1347-53, *1355-58, 1360, 1364
Stockholm Convention on Persistent Organic Pollutants (POPs), 1216, 1245
Strategic Offensive Reductions Treaty (SORT) (Moscow Treaty) (2002), 610, 620
SUDAN, *254-301
Abuja peace process, 268, *270-71, 276
and Chad, 255, 258, 261, 269, 271-72, 279, 289, 291, *297-301
Comprehensive Peace Agreement (2005), 170, *256-65, 941-43, 1066
Darfur, 114-16, 254-55, *257-62, *268-92, 1066-67, 1367
and Central African Republic, 120, 162-64, 255
humanitarian situation, 1066-67, 1367
human rights, 276, 941-43
internally displaced persons, 272, 275, 286, 288
International Commission of Inquiry for, 943
Janjaweed, 279, 281, 287, 289, 292, 296
N'Djamena Agreement (2006), 164, 167
N'Djamena Humanitarian Ceasefire Agreement (2004), 86, 88, 268-69, 271-72, 291, 293
Peace Agreement (2006), *274-78
Eastern Sudanese Peace Agreement, 257, 264
and Eritrea, 260
ICC case, 291-92, 1503
sanctions, *292-97
Tripoli Agreement (Chad/Sudan), 167, 269, 297, 300
and Uganda, 169
UN/AU peacekeeping mission, 116, *279-91
UNMIS, 88, *259-60, *262-71, 280-81, 290
SUSTAINABLE DEVELOPMENT, *981-92
Commission on (CSD), 745-46, *982-86, 1022, 1201-1202, and environment, 1212-14
Global Conference on Sustainable Development of Small Island Developing States (1994)
Barbados Programme of Action
Mauritius Strategy, 985, *1016-18, 1160, 1193, 1201-1202
mountains, 1241
Mountain Partnership, 985-86
rural development, 997
World Summit on (2002), 747, 1022, 1206, 1323
Johannesburg Declaration and Plan of Implementation, *981-85, 1163, 1201-1202, 1206, 1246
SWITZERLAND
ICJ case, 1477, 1481
racism and racial discrimination, 831
SYRIAN ARAB REPUBLIC, *603-608
Golan Heights, *603-605
investigation into assassination of Lebanese Premier Rafik Hariri, 597, 599-600, *see also* Lebanon
and Lebanon, 570-72
UNDOF, 499, 526, 565, 603, *605-608

TAJIKISTAN
humanitarian assistance, 1107
human rights, 451
UNMOT, 451
UNTOP, 64-65, 451
Taliban, 363, *365-67, *368-76, 375-76, 379, *381-89
terrorism, *879-83
anti-terrorism measures and human rights, 840, *882-83
Digest of Jurisprudence of the United Nations and Regional Organizations on the Protection of Human rights while Countering Terrorism, 881
international, *65-77, *1515-19
measures to eliminate, *72-77
Counter-Terrorism Committee (CTC), *73-77, 636, 879, 1305
Executive Directorate (CTED), *75-77
Counter-Terrorism Implementation Task Force, 66
Declaration on Counter-Terrorism, 636
Declaration on Measures to Eliminate International Terrorism (1994), *1516-19
Global Initiative to Combat Nuclear Terrorism, 610, 620
IAEA, 77, 636
Terrorism Prevention Watch (UNDOC), 1305
UN Global Counter-Terrorism Strategy, *65-71, 609, 636
2006 incidents
Afghanistan, 367
Egypt, *71
India, *72
Iraq, *71-72, 391, 400
Israel, 499, 506-507, 512, 518
Sri Lanka, 72
and weapons of mass destruction, *636-37
International Convention for the Suppression of Acts of Nuclear Terrorism, 1305
Thematic Trust Fund for Crisis Prevention and Recovery, 1060
TIMOR-LESTE, *413-31
assessment mission, 422
elections, 413-14, 416, 419
human rights, 414, 427, 960
Independent Special Commission of Inquiry for, 425-26, 427
political situation, *419-21
security, *419-22, 425
UNAMET, 428, 431
UNMISET, 86, *428-30
UNMIT, 64, 78, 86, 89, 361, 413, *422-31
UNOTIL, 64-65, 361, *413-18, 428, 430
TOKELAU, 695, 699, *717-19
torture and cruel treatment, 768, 776, *874-78
Committee against, 768, 776
Convention against Torture and Other Cruel, Inhuman or Degrading Treatment or Punishment (1984) and Optional Protocol (2002), 768, 776, 865, *876-78, 881
UN Voluntary Fund for Victims of Torture, 876
tobacco, 420-21
tourism
Asia and the Pacific, 1161-62
Plan of Action for Sustainable Tourism Development in Asia and the Pacific, 1161
and the environment, 1213-14
High-level Intergovernmental Meeting on Sustainable Tourism Development (2006), 1161
TRADE
commodities, *1121-25
Common Fund for, 1124-25
Expert Meeting on Enabling Small Commodity Producers and Processors in Developing Countries to Reach Global Market, 1117
International Task Force on Commodities, 1121
timber
UN Conference for the Negotiation of a Successor Agreement to the International Tropical Timber Agreement, 1124
and the environment, 1214
General Agreement on Trade in Services (GATS), 1117
international trade, *1110-25
Commission on Enterprise, Business Facilitation and Development, 1119-21
subsidiary bodies, meetings of, 1120-21
Commission on Trade in Goods and Services, and Commodities, 1115-16
Convention on International Trade in Endangered Species of Wild Fauna and Flora, 1214, 1245
and development, *1113-15
interdependence and global economic issues, 1118
International Trade Centre (ITC), 1118-19
law, *1525-30
multilateral trading system, *1111-15
Rotterdam Convention on the Prior Informed Consent (PIC) Procedure for Certain Hazardous Chemicals and Pesticides in International Trade (1998), 1245, 1248
trade policy, 1115-18
trade promotion and facilitation, 1118
transnational corporations, 896-97
United Nations Commission on International Trade Law (UNCITRAL), *see* United Nations Commission on International Trade Law
and regional integration in Africa, 1150-51
Subsidies and Countervailing Measures, Agreement on, 1111
Trade and Development Report, 2006, 1004, 1111, 1118
Trade-related Aspects of Intellectual Property Rights, Agreement on, 1111, 1147
Trade-related Investment Measures, Agreement on, 1111, 1147
UN Conference on Trade and Development (UNCTAD), *see* United Nations Conference on Trade and Development
TRANSPORT
Africa, 1150-51
Asia and the Pacific, 1161-62
Convention on International Customs Transit Procedures for the Carriage of Goods by Rail under Cover of Senior Management Groups Consignment Notes, 1173
dangerous goods, 1141
Globally Harmonized System of Classification and Labelling of Chemicals, 1141
Model Regulations, 1141
Europe and the Mediterranean, 1173
maritime, 1141
Ministerial Conference on Transport (Busan, Republic of Korea, 2006), 1159, 1161
Busan Declaration on Transport Development in Asia and the Pacific, 1161
Western Asia, 1197-98
treaties and agreements
international organizations, 1523
multilateral, 615-16, 1523-24
registration and publication by UN, 1523
reservations, 770-71, 1523
Vienna Convention on the Law of Treaties between States and International Organizations or between International Organizations (1986), 1523

see also main part of name
Tripoli Agreement (Chad/Sudan), 120, 163, 167, 269, 297, 300
TUNISIA, 879
TURKEY, 864-65
TURKMENISTAN
human rights, 960
TURKS AND CAICOS ISLANDS, 712

UGANDA, 116, *120-24, 131-32, 141-43, *168-71
Agreement on Cessation of Hostilities, 120, 170
disarmament, demobilization and reintegration (DDR), 170
and DRC, 169
hostilities, 168-71
humanitarian situation, 114-15, 168, 170, 1065-66
human rights, 943-44
ICC, 1503, 1505-1506
ICJ, 1477
and Sudan, 169
UKRAINE
ICJ case, 1477, 1480
UNAMA, *see* United Nations Assistance Mission in Afghanistan
UNAMET, *see* United Nations Mission in East Timor
UNAMI, *see* United Nations Assistance Mission for Iraq
UNAMSIL, *see* United Nations Mission in Sierra Leone
UNCDF, *see* United Nations Capital Development Fund
UNCITRAL, *see* United Nations Commission on International Trade Law
UNCTAD, *see* United Nations Conference on Trade and Development
UNDAF, *see* United Nations Development Assistance Framework
UNDEF, *see* United Nations Democracy Fund
UNDG, *see* United Nations Development Group
UNDOF, *see* United Nations Disengagement Observer Force
UNDP, *see* United Nations Development Programme
UNESCO, *see* United Nations Educational, Scientific and Cultural Organization
UNFICYP, *see* United Nations Peacekeeping Force in Cyprus
UNFIP, *see* United Nations Fund for International Partnerships
UNFPA, *see* United Nations Population Fund
UNHCR, *see* United Nations High Commissioner for Refugees
UNICEF, *see* United Nations Children's Fund
UNIDIR, *see* United Nations Institute for Disarmament Research
UNIFEM, *see* United Nations Development Fund for Women
UNIFIL, *see* United Nations Interim Force in Lebanon
UNIIIC, *see* United Nations International Independent Investigation Commission
UNIKOM, *see* United Nations Iraq-Kuwait Observation Mission
UNIOSIL, *see* United Nations Integrated Office in Sierra Leone
UNITED ARAB EMIRATES
and Iran, 451-52
UNITED KINGDOM
Falkland Islands (Malvinas), 713
Gibraltar, 713-15
and Mauritius, 239
UNITED NATIONS
accounts and auditing, *1631-35
budgets
2006-2007, *1611-22
2008-2009, *1622-23
reform and financial management, 1610-11
Charter
sanctions provisions, *1534-36
Special Committee on the Charter of the United Nations and on the Strengthening of the Role of the Organization, *1531-36
contributions, assessed, *1624-30
Article 19, application of, *1624-25
peacekeeping operations, *1628-29
financial situation, 1609-10
host country, relations with, *1537-39
immunity
Convention on the Privileges and Immunities of the United Nations and of Specialized Agencies (1947), 815
institutional and administrative matters
Committee on Conferences, *1654-64
cooperation with other organizations
ASEAN, *1170, 1597
Asian-African Legal Consultative Organization (AALCO), *1536-37, 1598
AU, 62, 340, 1597
Black Sea Economic Cooperation Organization, *1186-87, 1597
CARICOM, *359-60, 1597
Community of Portuguese-speaking Countries, *1597-98
Council of Europe, *497-98, 1597
ECCAS, 1155, 1597
ECLAC, 1195
ECO, *1166-67, 1597
International Organization of la Francophonie, 1597, *1602-1604
Inter-Parliamentary Union, 1597, *1604-1605
LAS, *1597-1600
OAS, 360, 1597
Organization of the Islamic Conference (OIC), 1597, *1600-1602
OPCW, *655, 1597
OSCE, 498
Pacific Islands Forum, *1167-70, 1597
Preparatory Commission for the Comprehensive Nuclear-Test-Ban Treaty (CTBT) (1996), 628, *630-31, 1597
SADC, *1153-55, 1597
coordination and monitoring
UN System Chief Executives Board for Coordination (CEB), *see* United Nations System Chief Executives Board for Coordination
information systems
informatics, international cooperation in, *1664-66
new member, admission of, *1592
non-governmental organizations, 1606-1608
observer status, *1605-1606
premises and properties, 1421, *1666-73
staff
accountability, 1688-89
conditions of service, *1677-84
International Civil Service Commission, *1677-80
remuneration issues, 1680-84
justice, administration of, 1707-10
multilingualism, 1702
Office of Human Resources Management (OHRM), 108, 1353, 1390
personnel policies, *1689-1702
ethics office, 1699
gratis personnel, 1700-1701
human resources management, *1692-98
women, status of, 1353-54, 1699-1700
safety and security, *578, 1060-61, *1684-87

Secretary-General, appointment of, *1676-77
Senior Management Network, 1687-88
sexual exploitation and abuse, 1702-1703
UN Joint Staff Pension Fund, *1703-1707
programme planning, *1635-41
programme performance, *1638-41
programme plan and priorities 2006-2007, 1638
strategic framework 2008-2009, *1635-38
restructuring issues
oversight, *1648-54
Comprehensive Review of Governance and Oversight within the United Nations and its Funds, Programmes and Specialized Agencies, *1571-74
programme of reform, *1571-86
strengthening UN System, *1575-86
High-level Panel on UN System-wide Coherence, 1584-86
Security Council, *see* Security Council
Repertory of Practice of United Nations Organs, *1531-34
United Nations Action Plan on Sport for Development and Peace, 1283
United Nations Administrative Tribunal, 1710
United Nations African Institute for the Prevention of Crime and the Treatment of Offenders, *1294-95
United Nations Capital Development Fund (UNCDF), 1031, 1040, 1050-52
United Nations Children's Fund (UNICEF), 986, 992, 1024, 1418
emergency assistance, 1367
humanitarian assistance, 1389
Maurice Pate Award, 1367-68
operational and administrative matters, 1374-79
programmes, 1368-74
refugees, 1394
reproductive health, 1265
sixtieth anniversary, *1363-64
see also children; youth
United Nations Commission on International Trade Law (UNCITRAL), *1525-30
arbitration, 1525, *1528-29
Convention on the Recognition and enforcement of Foreign Arbitral Awards, New York (1958), 1525, *1528-29
case law on texts, 1530
commercial fraud, 1529-30
Congress on Uniform Commercial Law in the Twenty-first Century, 1530
electronic commerce, 1529
insolvency law, 1529
procurement, 1527-28
security interests, 1530
training and technical assistance, 1530
transport, 1529
Unidroit Principles of International Commercial Contracts, 1530
United Nations Communications Group, 738
United Nations Conciliation Commission for Palestine, 558
United Nations Conference on Disarmament Issues (Yokohama) (2006), 689
United Nations Conference on Environment and Development (1992) (UNCED)
Agenda 21, *981-85, 1202, 1246
United Nations Conference on the Exploration and Peaceful Uses of Outer Space, Third (UNISPACE-III) (1999), 695, 741, 745-46
United Nations Conference on Human Settlements (Habitat II) (1996), *1249-53
United Nations Conference on the Standardization of Geographical Names, Ninth (2007), 1205
United Nations Conference on Trade and Development (UNCTAD), 1141
Commission on Investment, Technology and Related Financial Issues, 1136-37
subsidiary bodies, 1137-38
institutional and organizational questions, 1141-44
technical cooperation, 1143-44
international trade, *1110-25
Trade and Development Board (TDB), 1012, 1109-10, 1126, 1141
trade and the environment, 1214
UNCTAD XI (2004)
follow-up, 1109-10
mid-term review, 1109-10, 1141-42
São Paulo Consensus (Brazil), 1109-10
United Nations Congress on Crime Prevention and Criminal Justice, Eleventh (2005) (Bangkok), *1287-89, 1293
Bangkok Declaration, 1288
United Nations Convention to Combat Desertification in those Countries Experiencing Serious Drought and/or Desertification, particularly in Africa (1994), 902, 1216, 1219, *1225-27
United Nations Convention against Corruption, 1290, *1301-1304
United Nations Convention against Illicit Traffic in Narcotic Drugs and Psychotropic Substances (1988), 1436, 1454, 1461
United Nations Convention on the Law of the Sea (UNCLOS) (1982), *1540-68
United Nations Convention against Transnational Organized Crime and the Protocols Thereto, 915, 1289-90, *1296-1301
United Nations Crime Prevention and Criminal Justice Fund, 1290
United Nations Crime Prevention and Criminal Justice Programme, *1290-94
United Nations Decade for the Eradication of Poverty (1997-2006), 896, *992-95, 1272-73
United Nations Democracy Fund (UNDEF), 49, 697-98, 818, 1046
United Nations Development Assistance Framework (UNDAF), 1000, 1011, 1024, 1089, 1373, 1377
United Nations Development Fund for Women (UNIFEM), 913, 1031, 1040, 1266, 1333, 1350, 1359
United Nations Development Group (UNDG), 392, 395, 1000, 1024-25, 1036, 1210, 1378, 1389
United Nations Development Programme (UNDP), 1030-44
Audit and Performance Review, office of, 1049
Executive Board (UNDP/UNFPA), 1006-1007, 1024, 1031-32, 1204, 1263, 1350
financing, 1040-41
Human Development Report, 1006-1007, 1032, 1204
multi-year funding framework (MYFF), 1031, 1038, 1040
operational activities, 1032-35
programme planning and management, 1035-40
programme results, 1033-35
technical cooperation through, 1030-44
Thematic Trust Fund for Crisis Prevention and Recovery, 1060
United Nations Disengagement Observer Force (UNDOF), 499, 526, 565, 603, *605-608
United Nations Division for the Advancement of Women, 915, 1333, 1341, 1358
UNITED NATIONS EDUCATIONAL, SCIENTIFIC AND CULTURAL ORGANIZATION (UNESCO)
children and a culture of peace, *1279-81

cultural development, 1279
human rights education, 809
information and communication technologies, 999
Intergovernmental Oceanographic Commission, 1100, 1557
International Oceanographic Commission, 1165
International Plan of Action for the United Nations Literacy Decade (2003-2012), 1164, *1326-27
United Nations Emergency Relief Coordinator, 1057
United Nations Environment Programme (UNEP), *1206-19
activities, 1211-12
administrative and budgetary matters, 1218-19
Atmospheric Brown Cloud project, 1212
civil society, participation of
Tunza strategy (2003-2008), 1216-17
coordination and cooperation, *1214-17
Global Compact National Networks (Barcelona), 1214
Environmental Management Group, 1208-1209
Environment Watch Strategy Vision 2020, 1211
Global Environment Outlook
Yearbook 2006, 1218
Global Ministerial Environment Forum, Seventh (Dubai, 2006), *1132-34
Regional Seas Programme, 1243
10-Year Framework of Programmes on Sustainable Consumption and Production (Marrakech, 2006), 1249
UN-Habitat, cooperation with, 1217, 1255
water policy and strategy, 1212
World Conservation Monitoring Centre, 1242, 1557
see also environment
United Nations Forum on Forests, *1228-40
United Nations Framework Convention on Climate Change (1992), 1097, 1216, *1219-22, 1228
Kyoto Protocol (1997), 1163, 1220
United Nations Fund for International Partnerships (UNFIP), 1046
United Nations Global Compact (2000), 1090
United Nations Global Counter-Terrorism Strategy, 65-71
United Nations Habitat and Human Settlements Foundation, 1250-52
United Nations High Commissioner for Human Rights, Office of the (OHCHR), *762-66, 769-70, *821-28, 833, 1389
country engagements, strengthening, 937-38
see also human rights
United Nations High Commissioner for Refugees, Office of the (UNHCR), *1385-94
emergency humanitarian assistance, coordination of, 1389-90
evaluation activities, 1390
Executive Committee, enlargement of, *1391
financial and administrative questions, 1391-94
Global Strategic Objectives, 1393
staff safety, 1394
strengthening, 1303, 1388-89
see also refugees
United Nations Human Settlements Programme (UN-Habitat), *see* Human Settlements
United Nations Institute for Disarmament Research (UNIDIR), 613, 617, 676, 680
United Nations Institute for Training and Research (UNITAR), 1322-23
United Nations Integrated Mission in Timor-Leste (UNMIT), 64, 78, 86, 89, 361, 413, *422-31
United Nations Integrated Office in Burundi (BINUB), 148, *152-55, 158, 1065
United Nations Integrated Office in Sierra Leone (UNIOSIL), 64-65, 78, 173, 231-35, 239-40
United Nations Integrated Peace Consolidation Assistance Framework, 157
United Nations Inter-Agency Network on Women and Gender Equality, 1329, *1349-52
United Nations Interim Administration Mission in Kosovo (UNMIK), 86-87, 453, *462-72, 906, 1486, 1492
United Nations Interim Force in Lebanon (UNIFIL), 498-99, *565-69, 574, *576-78, *582-96, 965
United Nations International Independent Investigation Commission (UNIIIC) (Lebanon), 498-99, 556, *596-603
United Nations Interregional Crime and Justice Research Institute, 1289, 1294
United Nations Iraq-Kuwait Observation Mission (UNIKOM), 411-12
United Nations Joint Staff Pension Fund, *1703-1707
United Nations Logistics Base in Brindisi (UNLB), *102-104
United Nations Military Observer Group in India and Pakistan (UNMOGIP), 86-87, 448
United Nations Mission in East Timor (UNAMET), 428, 431
United Nations Mission in Ethiopia and Eritrea (UNMEE), 86, 88, 256, *315-23, *325-29
United Nations Mission in Liberia (UNMIL), 54, 78, 86, 88, 172-173, 176, 178, 202, *211-25
United Nations Mission of Observers in Tajikistan (UNMOT), 451
United Nations Mission for the Referendum in Western Sahara (MINURSO), 86-87, 329, *332-39
United Nations Mission in Sierra Leone (UNAMSIL), 230-32, *240-41
United Nations Mission in the Sudan (UNMIS), 54-55, 78, 86, 88, 166-67, 169-70, 254, 257, *259-60, *262-71, 280-81, 290, 810
United Nations Mission of Support in East Timor (UNMISET), 86, *428-30
United Nations Monitoring, Verification and Inspection Commission (UNMOVIC), 407-409, 609
United Nations Observer Mission in Georgia (UNOMIG), 86-87, 453, *474-84
United Nations Office on Drugs and Crime (UNODC), 369, 378, 1288, 1291, 1390, *1431-35, 1439, 1453-55, 1458, 1464
World Drug Report 2006, 1455
United Nations Office for Project Services (UNOPS), 1046-49
United Nations Office in Timor-Leste (UNOTIL), 64-65, 361, *413-18, 428, 430
United Nations Open-ended Informal Consultative Process on Oceans and Law of the Sea, 1241, *1557-68
United Nations Operation in Burundi (ONUB), 54, 78, 86, 88, 120, *130-31, 148, *150-62
United Nations Operation in Côte d'Ivoire (UNOCI), 86, 88, 172, *176-79, *181-86, *188-90, 193, *196-202, 204, *207-11
United Nations Organization Mission in the Democratic Republic of the Congo (MONUC), 54, 78, 86, 88, 115, 120-21, 127, *130-40, *145-48, 169-70
United Nations Peacebuilding Office in the Central African Republic (BONUCA), 64, 162, *165-66
United Nations Peacebuilding Support Office in Guinea-Bissau (UNOGBIS), 64, 173, 244-45, 247-51, 1598
United Nations Peacekeeping Force in Cyprus (UNFICYP), 86-87, 454, *487-94
United Nations Pledging Conference for Development Activities (2006), 1030
United Nations Political Office for Somalia (UNPOS), 64, 301, 311
United Nations Population Fund (UNFPA), 992, 1263-69, 1378
country and intercountry programmes, 1266-67
emergency situations, role in, 1269
Executive Board (UNDP/UNFPA), *see* United Nations Development Programme

financing, 1267-68
reproductive health, 1265
UN Population Award, 1269
United Nations Programme on Space Applications, 747
United Nations Register of Conventional Arms, 610, 667-68, 677
United Nations Relief and Works Agency for Palestine Refugees in the Near East (UNRWA), 554, *557-64, 570, 967-68
United Nations Research Institute for Social Development (UNRISD), 1277-78
United Nations Scientific Committee on the Effects of Atomic Radiation, 751
United Nations Stabilization Mission in Haiti (MINUSTAH), 54-55, 78, 86, 88, *342-57, 1193
United Nations Standing Advisory Committee on Security Questions in Central Africa, 126, *685-87
United Nations Statistical Commission, 1175, *1465-74
United Nations System Chief Executives Board for Coordination (CEB), 100, 1000, 1072-73, 1075, 1389, 1595-96
High-level Committee on Management (HLCM), 1004, 1329, 1349, 1595, 1674
High-level Committee on Programmes (HLCP), 983, 1004, 1329, 1349, 1595
United Nations Tajikistan Office of Peacebuilding (UNTOP), 64-65, 451
United Nations Truce Supervision Organization (UNTSO), 499, 565-66
United Nations Trust Fund for Disaster Reduction, 1094
United Nations University (UNU), *1323-24
United Nations Verification Mission in Guatemala (MINUGUA), 341
United Nations Voluntary Fund for the Second International Decade of the World's Indigenous People, 935
United Nations Voluntary Fund for Victims of Torture, 876
United Nations Voluntary Trust Fund on Contemporary Forms of Slavery, 912-13
United Nations Volunteers (UNV), 1031, 1040, 1049-50, 1094
UNITED STATES
and Cuba, 341-42, *357-59, 945-46
as host country, relations with UN, *1537-39
and Libyan Arab Jamahiriya, 339
Universal Declaration of Human Rights (1948), 756, 809, 844
University of Peace (Costa Rica), *1324-25
UNLB, *see* United Nations Logistics Base in Brindisi
UNMEE, *see* United Nations Mission in Ethiopia and Eritrea
UNMIK, *see* United Nations Interim Administration Mission in Kosovo
UNMIL, *see* United Nations Mission in Liberia
UNMIS, *see* United Nations Mission in the Sudan
UNMIT, *see* United Nations Integrated Mission in Timor-Leste
UNMOGIP, *see* United Nations Military Observer Group in India and Pakistan
UNMOT, *see* United Nations Mission of Observers in Tajikistan
UNMOVIC, *see* United Nations Monitoring, Verification and Inspection Commission
UNOCI, *see* United Nations Operation in Côte d'Ivoire
UNOGBIS, *see* United Nations peacebuilding Support Office in Guinea-Bissau
UNOMIG, *see* United Nations Observer Mission in Georgia
UNOPS, *see* United Nations Office for Project Services
UNOTIL, *see* United Nations Office in Timor-Leste
UNOWA, *see* United Nations Office for West Africa
UNPOS, *see* United Nations Political Office in Somalia
UNRWA, *see* United Nations Relief and Works Agency for Palestine Refugees in the Near East
UNTOP, *see* United Nations Tajikistan Office of peacebuilding
UNTSO, *see* United Nations Truce Supervision Organization
UNV, *see* UN Volunteers
URUGUAY
ICJ case, 1477, 1481-82
UZBEKISTAN
human rights, 960-61

Vienna Convention on Consular Relations (1963)
Optional Protocols, 1520
Vienna Convention on Diplomatic Relations (1961)
Optional Protocols, 1520
Vienna Convention on the Law of Treaties between States and International Organizations or between International Organizations (1986), 1523
Vienna Convention on the Protection of the Ozone Layer (1985), 1222
Montreal Protocol on Substances that Deplete the Ozone Layer, 1222
Vienna Declaration (disarmament), 692
Vienna Declaration on Crime and Justice, 1290-91
Vienna Declaration and Programme of Action (human rights), 768
Voluntary Fund for Technical Cooperation in the Field of Human Rights, 818

water, 1203-1204
Global International Waters Assessment, 1241-42
International Decade for Action: Water for Life, (2005-2015), 1163
right to water and sanitation services, 911-12
International Year of Sanitation (2008), *1419-20
UN World Water Assessment Programme, 1204
Water Action and Networking Database, 1204
water policy and strategy (UNEP), 1212
World Water Forum (Fourth) (Mexico City, 2006), 1163, 1192, 1203
weather
WMO, *see* World Meteorological Organization
see also climate change; environment
WEST AFRICA, 114, *172-254, 687
Special Representative for West Africa, Office of the, 65
UNOWA, 65, 172, 175-76
see also country names; Economic Community of West African States
WESTERN ASIA, 1196-99
economic development and cooperation, 1196-97
economic trends, 1195-96
social development, 1198-99
see also Economic and Social Commission for Western Asia; *specific countries*
WESTERN SAHARA, 115, *329-39, 717
and Algeria, 330-32, 334-35
Baker Plan (2003), 332
Framework Agreement on the Status of Western Sahara (2001), *329-36
Houston Accords, 332
Madrid Accords (1975) (Spain/Morocco/Mauritania), 330
MINURSO, 86-87, 329, *332-39
and Morocco, *329-36
Peace Plan for Self-determination of the People of Western Sahara (2003), 329, 331-32
refugees, 332
United Nations Settlement Plan (1991), 331
WOMEN
in Africa, 1151
in Asia and the Pacific

Afghanistan, *1346
in armed conflict, *1339-41
System-wide Action Plan (2005), 1339-40
Commission on the Status of, 913, 1328, 1341-42, 1347-53, *1355-58, 1360, 1364
Committee on the Elimination of Discrimination against Women (CEDAW), 768, 907, 1218, 1342, 1354-55, 1373
Convention on the Elimination of All Forms of Discrimination against Women (1979), 768, 777, *1334-37, 1342, 1354-55
and development, 1347
economic advancement, 1348
the girl child, 1341, *1346, 1355, 1364
health, 1341, 1358
High-level Panel on UN System-wide Coherence
gender mainstreaming, 1329, 1349, 1352, 1354
human rights, 915, 1266, 1278, *1341-47
institutional mechanisms for the advancement of, *1349-52
International Research and Training Institute for the Advancement of Women (INSTRAW), 1359-60
in Latin America and the Caribbean, 354-55, 1191-92
in Middle East, *545-47, 1347
and poverty, 1347-48
power and decision-making, 1348-49
status, communications on, 1358-59
trafficking in women and girls, 854, 915, *1296-1301, *1342-46
UN Development Fund for Women, *see* United Nations Development Fund for Women
UN Division for the Advancement of Women, 915, 1333, 1341, 1358
UN gender equality architecture, 1352-54
UN Inter-Agency Network on Women and Gender Equality, 1329, *1349-52
UN Office of the Special Adviser on Gender Issues and the Advancement of Women, 1352-53
UN staff, status of, 1353-54, 1699-1700
UN System-wide Action Plan on women, peace and security, 49
violence against, 913-15, *1333-39
in Western Asia, 1199
World Conference on Women, Fourth (1995)
follow-up to, 1165, *1328-33, 1348, 1360
World Assembly on Ageing, Second (2002)
Madrid International Plan of Action on Ageing (2002), 1190-91, 1277
WORLD BANK, 1594
African countries affected by conflict, 117
Catalytic Growth Fund, 1072
Joint IMF/World Bank Development Committee, 1127-28, 1130
World Conference on Disaster Reduction (Hyogo, Japan) (2005), 747
Hyogo Declaration and the Hyogo Framework for Action 2005-2015, 1093-94, 1214
World Conference on Human Rights (1993), 768, 808-809
World Conference against Racism, Racial Discrimination, Xenophobia and Related Intolerance (2001), 773, *820-28
Durban Declaration and Programme of Action (DDPA), *820-28, 846
World Conference on Women, Fourth (1995), 1165, *1328-33, 1348, 1360
World Economic Situation and Prospects 2007, 1005, 1110, 1121, 1125, 1131, 1171
World Economic and Social Survey, 2006, 1006, 1125
World Food Programme (WFP), 246, 332, 378, 992, 1024, 1094, 1190, 1380, 1418, 1426-28
ECLAC/WFP, 1190
see also food
World Food Summit (1996), 1428
WORLD HEALTH ORGANIZATION (WHO), 413, 986, 1073, 1214, 1415, 1418
AIDS, *see* HIV/AIDS
children, 917, 1370
drug control, 1436, 1439
Framework Convention on Tobacco Control, 1420
global public health, 1425-26
malaria, *1421-25
reproductive health, 1265
statistics, 1470-71
World Intellectual Property Organization (WIPO), 1760
WORLD METEOROLOGICAL ORGANIZATION (WMO), 1093, 1165
World Programme of Action for Youth to the Year 2000 and Beyond (1995), 1379
World Programme for Human Rights Education, 809, 815
World Summit of Attorneys General and General Prosecutors, Chief Prosecutors and Ministers of Justice, 1322
World Summit on the Information Society, 879, 977, *998-1004, 1145-46, 1159, 1162, 1329
Tunis Commitment and Tunis Agenda, *999-1000, 1004, 1198
World Summit for Social Development (1995), 994, 1164, *1272-75
Copenhagen Declaration on Social Development and the Programme of Action, 1272, 1382
World Summit on Sustainable Development (2002), 747, 1022, 1163, 1201-1202, 1206, 1241, 1246, 1323
WORLD TOURISM ORGANIZATION (UNWTO), 1101, 1161, 1213
WORLD TRADE ORGANIZATION (WTO), 1594
Doha Development Round, 986, 1156
suspension of, *1111-15, 1121, 1189
Ministerial Conference, Sixth (2005), Hong Kong, 1111
World Urban Forum, 1174, 1190, 1255
World Water Forum, Fourth (Mexico City, 2006), 1163, 1192, 1203

YOUTH, *1379-81
employment, *1379-81
Global Youth Leadership Summit (New York, 2006), 1379
Global Youth Network against Drug Abuse, 1454
World Programme of Action for Youth to the Year 2000 and Beyond (1995), 1194-95, 1379
World Youth Report 2007, 1379

ZIMBABWE, 1068-69

Index of resolutions and decisions

Resolution/decision numbers in italics indicate that the text is summarized rather than reprinted in full. (For dates of sessions, refer to Appendix III.)

General Assembly

Sixtieth session

Resolution No.	*Page*
60/17 Res. B	207
60/18 Res. B	355
60/121 Res. B	146
60/122 Res. B	266
60/234 Res. B	98
60/236 Res. B	1654
60/251	757
60/252	999
60/253	696
60/254	1633
60/255	1618
60/256	1666
60/257	1639
60/258	1652
60/259	1649
60/260	1576
60/261	56
60/262	1410
60/263	85
60/264	1592
60/265	986
60/266	89
60/267	102
60/268	94
60/269	158
60/270	491
60/271	428
60/272	326
60/273	482
60/274	411
60/275	470
60/276	221
60/277	607
60/278	591
60/279	240
60/280	337
60/281	1621
60/282	1667
60/283	1580
60/284	50
60/285	484
60/286	1586
60/287	58
60/288	66
60/289	80

Decision No.	*Page*
60/402 Dec. B	1492
60/405 Dec. B	1731
60/409 Dec. B	1219, 1742
60/411 Dec. B	1731
60/416	759
60/417	1734
60/418	1742
60/419 Dec. A	1742
60/419 Dec. B	1742
60/420	1742
60/421	1256, 1742
60/422 Dec. A	1498
60/422 Dec. B	1499
60/502 Dec. B	1593
60/503 Dec. B	1593
60/551 Dec. B	84, 1593, 1673, 1675, 1677, 1688, 1707
60/551 Dec. C	92, 100, 107, 108, 472, 1584, 1593, 1666
60/552	1285
60/553	447
60/554	1416
60/555	759
60/556	1014
60/557	1416
60/558	1416
60/559	611
60/560	1491
60/561	1611
60/562	1672
60/563	109
60/564	484, 1593
60/565	1584, 1593
60/566	1593, 1610
60/567	1593
60/568	1589

Sixty-first session

Resolution No.	*Page*
61/1	1015
61/2	1625
61/3	1676
61/4	1186
61/5	1537
61/6	1604
61/7	1602
61/8	1203
61/9	160
61/10	1284
61/11	358
61/12	1166
61/13	496
61/14	1599
61/15	1504
61/16	1589
61/17	53
61/18	370
61/19	829
61/20	1363
61/21	1673
61/22	551
61/23	552
61/24	553
61/25	548
61/26	532
61/27	604
61/28	51
61/29	109
61/30	1519
61/31	1521
61/32	1525
61/33	1528
61/34	1509
61/35	1522
61/36	1511
61/37	1483
61/38	1532
61/39	1524
61/40	1516
61/41	1538
61/42	1605
61/43	1605
61/44	1606
61/45	1280
61/46	1170
61/47	630
61/48	1168
61/49	1600
61/50	359
61/51	1153
61/52	1285
61/53	495
61/54	739
61/55	740
61/56	648
61/57	618
61/58	672
61/59	627
61/60	611
61/61	652
61/62	638
61/63	676
61/64	675
61/65	620
61/66	659
61/67	610
61/68	653
61/69	649
61/70	634
61/71	660
61/72	662
61/73	678
61/74	621
61/75	674
61/76	666
61/77	668
61/78	623
61/79	662
61/80	682
61/81	682
61/82	683
61/83	632
61/84	671
61/85	625
61/86	637
61/87	646
61/88	645
61/89	655
61/90	684
61/91	681
61/92	693
61/93	688
61/94	690
61/95	679
61/96	685
61/97	631
61/98	613
61/99	615
61/100	664
61/101	493
61/102	651
61/103	642
61/104	629
61/105	1543
61/106	785
61/107	1677
61/108	1325
61/109	751
61/110	748
61/111	741
61/112	560
61/113	563
61/114	561
61/115	564
61/116	541
61/117	543
61/118	544
61/119	538
61/120	605
61/121 Res. A	727
61/121 Res. B	727
61/122	710

GENERAL ASSEMBLY
61st SESSION *(cont.)*

Resolution No.	Page
61/123	707
61/124	711
61/125	335
61/126	715
61/127	717
61/128 Res. A	719
61/128 Res. B	722
61/129	709
61/130	700
61/131	1091
61/132	1101
61/133	1684
61/134	1058
61/135	555
61/136	1391
61/137	1386
61/138	1063
61/139	1400
61/140	1326
61/141	1273
61/142	1383
61/143	1334
61/144	1342
61/145	1330
61/146	777
61/147	833
61/148	774
61/149	824
61/150	851
61/151	853
61/152	852
61/153	876
61/154	966
61/155	861
61/156	893
61/157	900
61/158	814
61/159	764
61/160	890
61/161	849
61/162	838
61/163	903
61/164	846
61/165	837
61/166	817
61/167	812
61/168	816
61/169	886
61/170	897
61/171	882
61/172	883
61/173	870
61/174	950
61/175	962
61/176	952
61/177	800
61/178	925
61/179	1304
61/180	1299
61/181	1293
61/182	1295
61/183	1431
61/184	535

Resolution No.	*Page*
61/185	1608
61/186	1113
61/187	1128
61/188	1131
61/189	1428
61/190	1122
61/191	1135
61/192	1419
61/193	1240
61/194	1215
61/195	983
61/196	1017
61/197	1243
61/198	1094
61/199	1099
61/200	1097
61/201	1220
61/202	1226
61/203	1225
61/204	1223
61/205	1207
61/206	1252
61/207	977
61/208	1262
61/209	1303
61/210	1021
61/211	1012
61/212	1019
61/213	994
61/214	996
61/215	980
61/216	1323
61/217	1088
61/218	1081
61/219	1080
61/220	1062
61/221	1281
61/222	1557
61/223	1598
61/224	655
61/225	1420
61/226	698
61/227	1593
61/228	1423
61/229	1075
61/230	117
61/231	705
61/232	956
61/233 Res. A	1632
61/234	1152
61/235	1636
61/236	1660
61/237	1626
61/238	1653
61/239	1677
61/240	1703
61/241	1501
61/242	1493
61/243	1629
61/244	1691
61/245	1573
61/246	1645
61/247 Res. A	209

Resolution No.	*Page*
61/248 Res. A	327
61/249	430
61/250 Res. A	594
61/251	1669
61/252	1614
61/253 Res. A	1612
61/253 Res. B	1613
61/253 Res. C	1613
61/254	1623

Decision No.	*Page*
61/401	1731
61/402	1734
61/403	1500
61/404	1736
61/405	1731
61/406	1731
61/407	1732
61/408	1732
61/409	1732
61/410	1737
61/411	1732
61/412	1731
61/413	726, 1731
61/414	1733
61/501	1593, 1658
61/502	1593
61/503	1593
61/504	3
61/505	1494
61/506	1485
61/507	1477
61/508	1593
61/509	1593
61/510	1636
61/511	1708
61/512	1416
61/513	670
61/514	670
61/515	626, 1593
61/516	1594
61/517	1636
61/518	1594
61/519	1594
61/520	86
61/521	726
61/522	714
61/523	1588
61/524	1636
61/525	1354, 1355, 1359
61/526	777
61/527	933, 935
61/528	851
61/529	764, 767, 769, 771, 776, 784, 815, 845, 846, 861, 868, 874, 876, 880, 885, 895, 897, 900, 911, 938, 939, 942, 955, 960, 961, 969
61/530	809, 1291
61/531	809, 1296, 1305
61/532	1594
61/533	1636
61/534	1004
61/535	976
61/536	985
61/537	979
61/538	979
61/539	1010
61/540	995
61/541	1324
61/542	1323
61/543	1059
61/544	1594
61/545	1636
61/546	1575
61/547	760
61/548	1635
61/549	1046
61/550	1573
61/551 Dec. A	1200, 1593
61/551 Dec. B	1593, 1630, 1650
61/552	50, 56, 58, 86, 92, 140, 148, 161, 211, 223, 241,268, 329, 339, 340, 341, 357, 360, 412, 429, 431, 471, 483, 485, 486, 491, 493, 497, 542, 550, 596, 612, 699, 713, 714, 760, 830, 948, 1007, 1136, 1155, 1195, 1281, 1494, 1502, 1519, 1584, 1589, 1592, 1593, 1594, 1597, 1605, 1610, 1618, 1628, 1629, 1633, 1635, 1638, 1650, 1653, 1654, 1664, 1680, 1697, 1702, 1706, 1707, 1708

Tenth emergency special session

Resolution No.	*Page*
ES-10/16	522
ES-10/17	529

Security Council

Resolution No.	*Page*
1652(2006)	178
1653(2006)	122
1654(2006)	141
1655(2006)	567
1656(2006)	473
1657(2006)	181
1658(2006)	344
1659(2006)	363

SECURITY COUNCIL
(cont.)

Resolution No.	Page
1660(2006)	1490
1661(2006)	317
1662(2006)	365
1663(2006)	259
1664(2006)	601
1665(2006)	294
1666(2006)	474
1667(2006)	214
1668(2006)	1492
1669(2006)	130
1670(2006)	318
1671(2006)	128
1672(2006)	295
1673(2006)	635
1674(2006)	858
1675(2006)	332
1676(2006)	312
1677(2006)	416
1678(2006)	318
1679(2006)	277
1680(2006)	571
1681(2006)	320
1682(2006)	188
1683(2006)	224
1684(2006)	1498
1685(2006)	606
1686(2006)	598
1687(2006)	488
1688(2006)	242
1689(2006)	226
1690(2006)	419
1691(2006)	1592
1692(2006)	152
1693(2006)	133
1694(2006)	216
1695(2006)	441
1696(2006)	433
1697(2006)	578
1698(2006)	143
1699(2006)	1535
1700(2006)	398
1701(2006)	583
1702(2006)	350
1703(2006)	421
1704(2006)	422
1705(2006)	1499
1706(2006)	282
1707(2006)	381
1708(2006)	205
1709(2006)	263
1710(2006)	322
1711(2006)	137
1712(2006)	218
1713(2006)	295
1714(2006)	263
1715(2006)	1676
1716(2006)	477
1717(2006)	1499
1718(2006)	444
1719(2006)	153
1720(2006)	335
1721(2006)	197
1722(2006)	457
1723(2006)	403
1724(2006)	313
1725(2006)	308
1726(2006)	202
1727(2006)	205
1728(2006)	490
1729(2006)	606
1730(2006)	1535
1731(2006)	228
1732(2006)	1535
1733(2006)	1676
1734(2006)	238
1735(2006)	384
1736(2006)	140
1737(2006)	436
1738(2006)	860

Economic and Social Council

Organizational session, 2006

Resolution No.	Page
2006/1	1007
2006/2	755

Decision No.	Page
2006/201	
Dec. A	1736, 1737, 1738
2006/202	1594
2006/203	57, 108
2006/204	1606
2006/205	1146
2006/206	1594
2006/207	1594
2006/208	1594
2006/209	1595
2006/210	1023, 1594
2006/211	1145, 1595
2006/212	997
2006/213	1139
2006/214	1053, 1595
2006/215	1023, 1595

Resumed organizational session, 2006

Resolution No.	Page
2006/3	57

Decision No	Page
2006/201	
Dec. B	1732, 1736, 1737, 1738
2006/216	1066
2006/217	1053

Substantive session, 2006

Resolution No.	Page
2006/4	1276
2006/5	1055
2006/6	1472
2006/7	1346
2006/8	546
2006/9	1356
2006/10	1087
2006/11	1086
2006/12	1084
2006/13	1083
2006/14	1025
2006/15	1380
2006/16	1278
2006/17	1077
2006/18	1277
2006/19	1304
2006/20	1307
2006/21	1315
2006/22	1316
2006/23	1318
2006/24	1301
2006/25	1291
2006/26	1288
2006/27	1297
2006/28	1295
2006/29	1338
2006/30	1461
2006/31	1459
2006/32	1450
2006/33	1458
2006/34	1437
2006/35	1664
2006/36	1350
2006/37	702
2006/38	1176
2006/39	1194
2006/40	1194
2006/41	1011
2006/42	1421
2006/43	533
2006/44	1596
2006/45	1134
2006/46	1001
2006/47	1009
2006/48	1139
2006/49	1229

Decision No.	Page
2006/201	
Dec. C	1733, 1736, 1737, 1738
2006/218	1594
2006/219	1006
2006/220	994, 1276, 1595
2006/221	1608
2006/222	1607
2006/223	1607
2006/224	1607
2006/225	1608
2006/226	1608
2006/227	1329, 1350, 1596
2006/228	986
2006/229	1205
2006/230	1240
2006/231	1228
2006/232	1466
2006/233	1258, 1270
2006/234	1259, 1348
2006/235	1341, 1355
2006/236	1031, 1264, 1363, 1426
2006/237	1391, 1732
2006/238	1277
2006/239	1289
2006/240	1289
2006/241	1455
2006/242	777
2006/243	936
2006/244	1606
2006/245	1520
2006/246	1146
2006/247	1251
2006/248	1421
2006/249	534
2006/250	756, 763, 772, 1360
2006/251	1004
2006/252	1608
2006/253	1003
2006/254	998
2006/255	1228
2006/256	1290

Resumed substantive session, 2006

Decision No.	Page
2006/201	
Dec. D	1737
2006/201	
Dec. E	1732, 1733, 1734, 1736, 1737, 1738
2006/257	1596, 1641
2006/258	777
2006/259	1607
2006/260	1608
2006/261	1607
2006/262	1608
2006/263	1520
2006/264	1606
2006/265	1008, 1011
2006/266	1008, 1011
2006/267	998
2006/268	998
2006/269	936, 1223
2006/270	936
2006/271	936
2006/272	936
2006/273	936
2006/274	1591

Index of 2006 Security Council presidential statements

Number	Subject	Date	Page
S/PRST/2006/1	The question concerning Haiti	6 January	342
S/PRST/2006/2	The situation in Côte d'Ivoire	19 January	180
S/PRST/2006/3	The situation in the Middle East	23 January	569
S/PRST/2006/4	The situation concerning the Democratic Republic of the Congo	25 January	127
S/PRST/2006/5	Reports of the Secretary-General on the Sudan	3 February	269
S/PRST/2006/6	The situation in the Middle East, including the Palestinian question	3 February	501
S/PRST/2006/7	The question concerning Haiti	9 February	345
S/PRST/2006/8	The question concerning Iraq	14 February	390
S/PRST/2006/9	The situation in Côte d'Ivoire	23 February	182
S/PRST/2006/10	The situation between Eritrea and Ethiopia	24 February	316
S/PRST/2006/11	The situation in Somalia	15 March	303
S/PRST/2006/12	The situation in Burundi	23 March	150
S/PRST/2006/13	The question concerning Haiti	27 March	347
S/PRST/2006/14	The situation in Côte d'Ivoire	29 March	183
S/PRST/2006/15	Non-proliferation	29 March	432
S/PRST/2006/16	Reports of the Secretary-General on the Sudan	11 April	272
S/PRST/2006/17	Reports of the Secretary-General on the Sudan	25 April	273
S/PRST/2006/18	Threats to international peace and security caused by terrorist acts	25 April	71
S/PRST/2006/19	The situation in Chad and the Sudan	25 April	297
S/PRST/2006/20	The situation in Côte d'Ivoire	27 April	186
S/PRST/2006/21	Reports of the Secretary-General on the Sudan	9 May	276
S/PRST/2006/22	The question concerning Haiti	15 May	347
S/PRST/2006/23	The situation in Côte d'Ivoire	24 May	187
S/PRST/2006/24	The situation concerning Iraq	24 May	391
S/PRST/2006/25	The situation in Timor-Leste	25 May	417
S/PRST/2006/26	The situation in the Middle East	13 June	607
S/PRST/2006/27	Admission of New Members	22 June	1592
S/PRST/2006/28	Strengthening international law: rule of law and maintenance of international peace and security	22 June	46
S/PRST/2006/29	Threats to international peace and security caused by terrorist acts	29 June	71
S/PRST/2006/30	Threats to international peace and security caused by terrorist acts	12 July	72
S/PRST/2006/31	The situation in Somalia	13 July	306
S/PRST/2006/32	The situation in Côte d'Ivoire	19 July	190
S/PRST/2006/33	Children and armed conflict	24 July	920
S/PRST/2006/34	The situation in the Middle East	27 July	578
S/PRST/2006/35	The situation in the Middle East	30 July	580
S/PRST/2006/36	The situation concerning the Democratic Republic of the Congo	3 August	134
S/PRST/2006/37	The situation in Côte d'Ivoire	7 August	193
S/PRST/2006/38	Peace consolidation in West Africa	9 August	174
S/PRST/2006/39	Cooperation between the United Nations and regional organizations in maintaining international peace and security	20 September	61
S/PRST/2006/40	The situation concerning the Democratic Republic of the Congo	22 September	136
S/PRST/2006/41	Letter dated 4 July 2006 from the Permanent Representative of Japan to the United Nations addressed to the President of the Security Council	6 October	443
S/PRST/2006/42	Women and peace and security	26 October	1340

Number	Subject	Date	Page
S/PRST/2006/43	The situation in the Middle East	30 October	573
S/PRST/2006/44	The situation concerning the Democratic Republic of the Congo	7 November	138
S/PRST/2006/45	The situation in the Great Lakes region	16 November	170
S/PRST/2006/46	The situation in the Middle East	21 November	596
S/PRST/2006/47	The situation in the Central African Republic	22 November	165
S/PRST/2006/48	Children and armed conflict	28 November	921
S/PRST/2006/49	Letter dated 22 November 2006 from the Secretary-General addressed to the President of the Security Council	1 December	450
S/PRST/2006/50	The situation concerning the Democratic Republic of the Congo	6 December	139
S/PRST/2006/51	The situation in the Middle East	12 December	528
S/PRST/2006/52	The situation in the Middle East	12 December	589
S/PRST/2006/53	The situation in Chad and the Sudan	15 December	299
S/PRST/2006/54	The situation in the Middle East	15 December	607
S/PRST/2006/55	Reports of the Secretary-General on the Sudan	19 December	291
S/PRST/2006/56	Threats to international peace and security caused by terrorist acts	20 December	76
S/PRST/2006/57	The situation in the Great Lakes region	20 December	125
S/PRST/2006/58	The situation in Côte d'Ivoire	21 December	203
S/PRST/2006/59	The situation in Somalia	22 December	310

How to obtain volumes of the Yearbook

Recent volumes of the Yearbook may be obtained in many bookstores throughout the world, as well as from United Nations Publications, Room DC2-853, United Nations, New York, N.Y. 10017, e-mail (publications@un.org); or from United Nations Publications, Palais des Nations, CH-1211 Geneva 10, Switzerland, e-mail (unpubli@unog.ch).

Yearbook of the United Nations, 2005
Vol. 59. Sales No. E.0.7.I.1 $175.

Yearbook of the United Nations, 2004
Vol. 58. Sales No. E.0.6.I.1 $175.

Yearbook of the United Nations, 2003
Vol. 57. Sales No. E.05.I.1 $150.

Yearbook of the United Nations, 2002
Vol. 56. Sales No. E.04.I.1 $150.

Yearbook of the United Nations, 2001
Vol. 55. Sales No. E.03.I.1 $150.

Yearbook of the United Nations, 2000
Vol. 54. Sales No. E.02.I.1 $150.

Yearbook of the United Nations, 1999
Vol. 53. Sales No. E.01.I.4 $150.

Yearbook of the United Nations, 1998
Vol. 52. Sales No. E.01.I.1 $150.

Yearbook of the United Nations, 1997
Vol. 51. Sales No. E.00.I.1 $150.

Yearbook of the United Nations, 1996
Vol. 50. Sales No. E.97.I.1 $150.

Yearbook of the United Nations, 1995
Vol. 49. Sales No. E.96.I.1 $150.

Yearbook of the United Nations, 1994
Vol. 48. Sales No. E.95.I.1 $150.

Yearbook of the United Nations, 1993
Vol. 47. Sales No. E.94.I.1 $150.

Yearbook of the United Nations, 1992
Vol. 46. Sales No. E.93.I.1 $150.

Yearbook of the United Nations, 1991
Vol. 45. Sales No. E.92.I.1 $115.

Yearbook of the United Nations, 1990
Vol. 44. Sales No. E.98.I.16 $150.

Yearbook of the United Nations, 1989
Vol. 43. Sales No. E.97.I.11 $150.

Yearbook of the United Nations, 1988
Vol. 42. Sales No. E.93.I.100 $150.

Yearbook of the United Nations

Sales No. E.08.I.1 H $175

All editions of the Yearbook, from the 1946-47 edition to the 2006 edition are available online at:

unyearbook.un.org

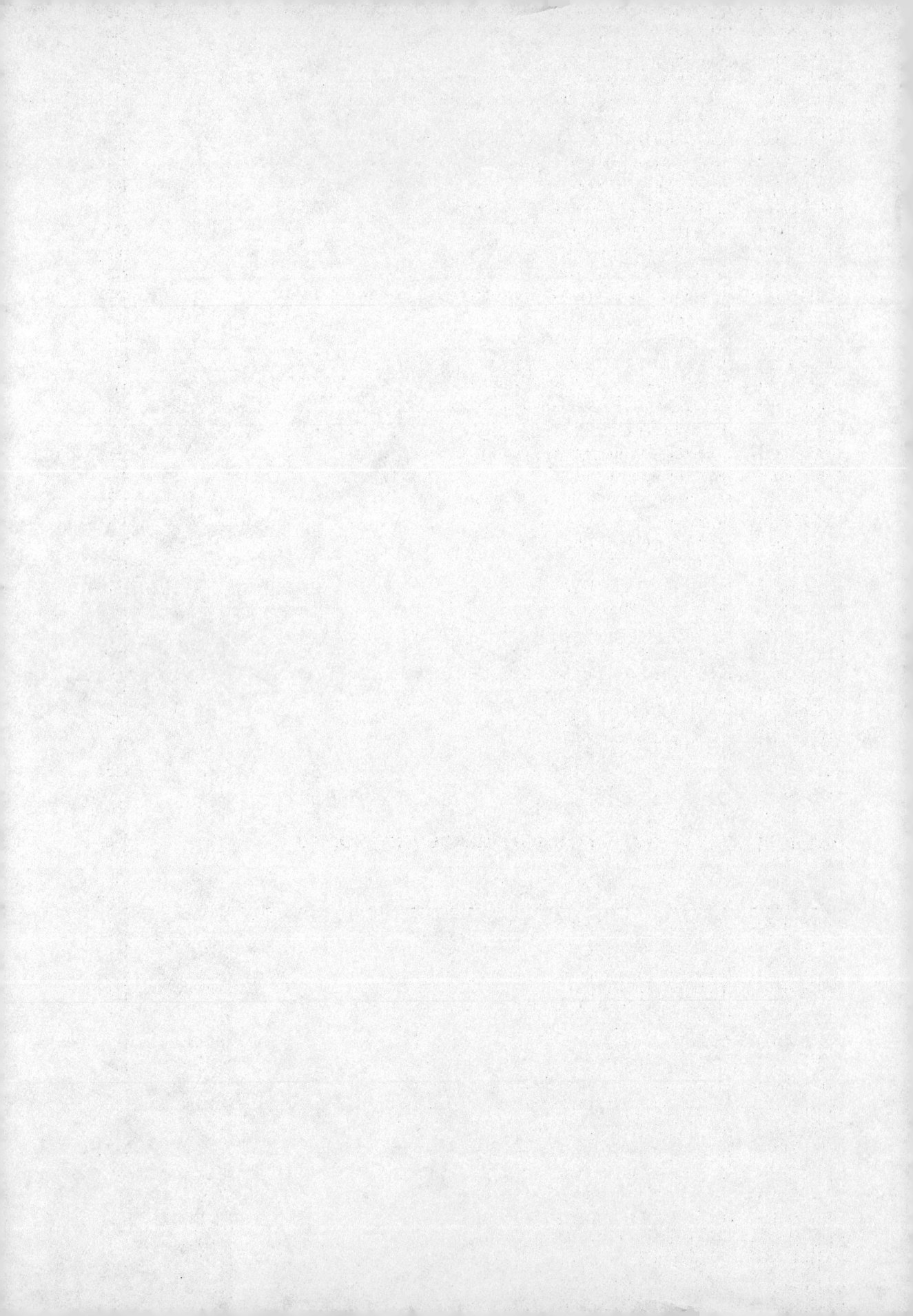